Stanley Gibbo
SIMPLIFIED CATALOGUE

Stamps of the World

2006 Edition

IN COLOUR

An illustrated and priced five-volume guide to the postage stamps of the whole world, excluding changes of paper, perforation, shade and watermark

VOLUME 5

COUNTRIES S–Z

STANLEY GIBBONS LTD
London and Ringwood

By Appointment to
Her Majesty the Queen
Stanley Gibbons Limited
London
Philatelists

71st Edition

Published in Great Britain by
Stanley Gibbons Ltd
Publications Editorial, Sales Offices and Distribution Centre
Parkside, Christchurch Road,
Ringwood, Hampshire BH24 3SH
Telephone 01425 472363

ISBN: 085259-608-1

Published as Stanley Gibbons Simplified Stamp Catalogue from 1934 to 1970, renamed Stamps of the World in 1971, and produced in two (1982-88), three (1989-2001), four (2002-2005) or five (from 2006) volumes as Stanley Gibbons Simplified Catalogue of Stamps of the World.
This volume published October 2005

S.G. Item No. 2884 (06)

Printed in Great Britain by CPI Bath Press, Somerset

Stanley Gibbons
SIMPLIFIED CATALOGUE
Stamps of the **World**

This popular catalogue is a straightforward listing of the stamps that have been issued everywhere in the world since the very first–Great Britain's famous Penny Black in 1840.

This edition, in which both the text and the illustrations have been captured electronically, is arranged completely alphabetically in a five-volume format. Volume 1 (Countries A–C), Volume 2 (Countries D–H), Volume 3 (Countries I–M), Volume 4 (Countries N–R) and Volume 5 (Countries S-Z).

Readers are reminded that the Catalogue Supplements, published in each issue of **Gibbons Stamp Monthly**, can be used to update the listings in **Stamps of the World** as well as our 22-part standard catalogue. To make the supplement even more useful the Type numbers given to the illustrations are the same in the Stamps of the World as in the standard catalogues. The first Catalogue Supplement to this Volume appeared in the September 2005 issue of **Gibbons Stamp Monthly**.

Gibbons Stamp Monthly can be obtained through newsagents or on postal subscription from Stanley Gibbons Publications, Parkside, Christchurch Road, Ringwood, Hants BH24 3SH.

The catalogue has many important features:

- The vast majority of illustrations are now in full colour to aid stamp identification.
- All Commonwealth and all Europe and Asia miniature sheets are now included.
- As an indication of current values virtually every stamp is priced. Thousands of alterations have been made since the last edition.
- By being set out on a simplified basis that excludes changes of paper, perforation, shade, watermark, gum or printer's and date imprints it is particularly easy to use. (For its exact scope see "Information for users" pages following.)
- The thousands of colour illustrations and helpful descriptions of stamp designs make it of maximum appeal to collectors with thematic interests.
- Its catalogue numbers are the world-recognised Stanley Gibbons numbers throughout.
- Helpful introductory notes for the collector are included, backed by much historical, geographical and currency information.
- A very detailed index gives instant location of countries in this volume, and a cross-reference to those included in the other volumes.

Over 2,100 stamps and miniature sheets and 640 new illustrations have been added to the listings in this volume.

The listings in this edition are based on the standard catalogues: Part 1, Commonwealth & British Empire Stamps 1840–1952, Part 2 (Austria & Hungary) (6th edition), Part 3 (Balkans) (4th edition), Part 4 (Benelux) (5th edition), Part 5 (Czechoslovakia & Poland) (6th edition), Part 6 (France) (5th edition), Part 7 (Germany) (6th edition), Part 8 (Italy & Switzerland) (6th edition), Part 9 (Portugal & Spain) (5th edition), Part 10 (Russia) (5th edition), Part 11 (Scandinavia) (5th edition), Part 12 (Africa since Independence A-E) (2nd edition), Part 13 (Africa since Independence F-M) (1st edition), Part 14 (Africa since Independence N-Z) (1st edition), Part 15 (Central America) (2nd edition), Part 16 (Central Asia) (3rd edition), Part 17 (China) (6th edition), Part 18 (Japan & Korea) (4th edition), Part 19 (Middle East) (6th edition), Part 20 (South America) (3rd edition), Part 21 (South-East Asia) (4th edition) and Part 22 (United States) (5th edition).

This edition includes major repricing for some Europe countries in addition to the changes for Germany Part 7, Portugal and Spain Part 9 and Middle East Part 19.

Acknowledgements

A wide-ranging revision of prices for European countries has been undertaken for this edition with the intention that the catalogue should be more accurate to reflect the market for foreign issues.

Many dealers in both Great Britain and overseas have participated in this scheme by supplying copies of their retail price lists on which the research has been based.

We would like to acknowledge the assistance of the following for this edition:

ALMAZ CO
of Brooklyn, U.S.A.

AMATEUR COLLECTOR LTD, THE
of London, England

AVION THEMATICS
of Nottingham, England

J BAREFOOT LTD
of York, England

Sir CHARLES BLOMEFIELD
of Chipping Camden, England

T. BRAY
of Shipley, West Yorks, England

CENTRAL PHILATELIQUE
of Brussels, Belgium

EUROPEAN & FOREIGN STAMPS
of Pontypridd, Wales

FILATELIA LLACH SL
of Barcelona, Spain

FILATELIA RIVA RENO
of Bologna, Italy

FILATELIA TORI
of Barcelona, Spain

FORMOSA STAMP COMPANY, THE
of Koahsiung, Taiwan

HOLMGREN STAMPS
of Bollnas, Sweden

INDIGO
of Orewa, New Zealand

ALEC JACQUES
of Selby, England

M. JANKOWSKI
of Warsaw, Poland

D.J.M. KERR
of Earlston, England

LEO BARESCH LTD
of Hassocks, England

LORIEN STAMPS
of Chesterfield, England

MANDARIN TRADING CO
of Alhambra, U.S.A.

MICHAEL ROGERS INC
of Winter Park, U.S.A.

NORAYR AGOPIAN
of Lymassol, Cyprus

PHIL-INDEX
of Eastbourne, England

PHILTRADE A/S
of Copenhagen, Denmark

PITTERI SA
of Chiasso, Switzerland

KEVIN RIGLER
of Shifnal, England

ROLF GUMMESSON AB
of Stockholm, Sweden

R. D. TOLSON
of Undercliffe, England

R. SCHNEIDER
of Belleville, U.S.A.

ROBSTINE STAMPS
of Hampshire, England

ROWAN S BAKER
of London, England

REX WHITE
of Winchester, England

Where foreign countries have been repriced this year in Stamps of the World and where there is no up-to-date specialised foreign volume in a country these will be the new Stanley Gibbons prices.

It is hoped that this improved pricing scheme will be extended to other foreign countries and thematic issues as information is consolidated.

Information for users

Aim

The aim of this catalogue is to provide a straightforward illustrated and priced guide to the postage stamps of the whole world to help you to enjoy the greatest hobby of the present day.

Arrangement

The catalogue lists countries in alphabetical order and there is a complete index at the end of each volume. For ease of reference country names are also printed at the head of each page.

Within each country, postage stamps are listed first. They are followed by separate sections for such other categories as postage due stamps, parcel post stamps, express stamps, official stamps, etc.

All catalogue lists are set out according to dates of issue of the stamps, starting from the earliest and working through to the most recent.

Scope of the Catalogue

The *Simplified Catalogue of Stamps of the World* contains listings of postage stamps only. Apart from the ordinary definitive, commemorative and air-mail stamps of each country – which appear first in each list – there are sections for the following where appropriate:

- postage due stamps
- parcel post stamps
- official stamps
- express and special delivery stamps
- charity and compulsory tax stamps
- newspaper and journal stamps
- printed matter stamps
- registration stamps
- acknowledgement of receipt stamps
- late fee and too late stamps
- military post stamps
- recorded message stamps
- personal delivery stamps

We receive numerous enquiries from collectors about other items which do not fall within the categories set out above and which consequently do not appear in the catalogue lists. It may be helpful, therefore, to summarise the other kinds of stamp that exist but which we deliberately exclude from this postage stamp catalogue.

We do *not* list the following:

Fiscal or revenue stamps: stamps used solely in collecting taxes or fees for non-postal purposes. Examples would be stamps which pay a tax on a receipt, represent the stamp duty on a contract or frank a customs document. Common inscriptions found include: Documentary, Proprietary, Inter. Revenue, Contract Note.

Local stamps: postage stamps whose validity and use are limited in area, say to a single town or city, though in some cases they provided, with official sanction, services in parts of countries not covered by the respective government.

Local carriage labels and Private local issues: many labels exist ostensibly to cover the cost of ferrying mail from one of Great Britain's offshore islands to the nearest mainland post office. They are not recognised as valid for national or international mail. Examples: Calf of Man, Davaar, Herm, Lundy, Pabay, Stroma. Items from some other places have only the status of tourist souvenir labels.

Telegraph stamps: stamps intended solely for the prepayment of telegraphic communication.

Bogus or "phantom" stamps: labels from mythical places or non-existent administrations. Examples in the classical period were Sedang, Counani, Clipperton Island and in modern times Thomond and Monte Bello Islands. Numerous labels have also appeared since the War from dissident groups as propaganda for their claims and without authority from the home governments. Common examples are labels for "Free Albania", "Free Rumania" and "Free Croatia" and numerous issues for Nagaland, Indonesia and the South Moluccas ("Republik Maluku Selatan").

Railway letter fee stamps: special stamps issued by railway companies for the conveyance of letters by rail. Example: Talyllyn Railway. Similar services are now offered by some bus companies and the labels they issue likewise do not qualify for inclusion in the catalogue.

Perfins ("perforated initials"): numerous postage stamps may be found with initial letters or designs punctured through them by tiny holes. These are applied by private and public concerns as a precaution against theft and do not qualify for separate mention.

Information for users

Labels: innumerable items exist resembling stamps but – as they do not prepay postage – they are classified as labels. The commonest categories are:

- propaganda and publicity labels: designed to further a cause or campaign;
- exhibition labels: particularly souvenirs from philatelic events;
- testing labels: stamp-size labels used in testing stamp-vending machines;
- Post Office training school stamps: British stamps overprinted with two thick vertical bars or SCHOOL SPECIMEN are produced by the Post Office for training purposes;
- seals and stickers: numerous charities produce stamp-like labels, particularly at Christmas and Easter, as a means of raising funds and these have no postal validity.

Cut-outs: items of postal stationery, such as envelopes, cards and wrappers, often have stamps impressed or imprinted on them. They may usually be cut out and affixed to envelopes, etc., for postal use if desired, but such items are not listed in this catalogue.

Collectors wanting further information about exact definitions are referred to *Philatelic Terms Illustrated,* published by Stanley Gibbons and containing many illustrations in colour.

There is also a priced listing of the postal fiscals of Great Britain in our *Commonwealth & British Empire Stamps 1840–1952* Catalogue and in Volume 1 of the *Great Britain Specialised* Catalogue (5th and later editions).

Catalogue Numbers

Stanley Gibbons catalogue numbers are recognised universally and any individual stamp can be identified by quoting the catalogue number (the one at the left of the column) prefixed by the name of the country and the letters "S.G.". Do not confuse the catalogue number with the type numbers which refer to illustrations.

Prices

Prices in the left-hand column are for unused stamps and those in the right-hand column for used. Prices are given in pence and pounds:

100 pence (p) 1 pound (£1).

Prices are shown as follows:

10 means 10p (10 pence);
1.50 means £1.50 (1 pound and 50 pence);
For £100 and above, prices are in whole pounds.

Our prices are for stamps in fine condition, and in issues where condition varies we may ask more for the superb and less for the sub-standard.

The minimum catalogue price quoted is 10p. For individual stamps prices between 10p and 45p are provided as a guide for catalogue users. The lowest price charged for individual stamps purchased from Stanley Gibbons is £1.00.

The prices quoted are generally for the cheapest variety of stamps but it is worth noting that differences of watermark, perforation, or other details, outside the scope of this catalogue, may often increase the value of the stamp.

Prices quoted for mint issues are for single examples. Those in se-tenant pairs, strips, blocks or sheets may be worth more.

Where prices are not given in either column it is either because the stamps are not known to exist in that particular condition, or, more usually, because there is no reliable information as to value.

All prices are subject to change without prior notice and we give no guarantee to supply all stamps priced. Prices quoted for albums, publications, etc. advertised in this catalogue are also subject to change without prior notice.

Due to different production methods it is sometimes possible for new editions of Parts 2 to 22 to appear showing revised prices which are not included in that year's *Stamps of the World.*

Unused Stamps

In the case of stamps from *Great Britain* and the *Commonwealth,* prices for unused stamps of Queen Victoria to King George V are for lightly hinged examples; unused prices of King Edward VIII to Queen Elizabeth II issues are for unmounted mint. The prices of unused Foreign stamps are for lightly hinged examples for those issued before 1946, thereafter for examples unmounted mint.

Used Stamps

Prices for used stamps generally refer to fine postally used examples, though for certain issues they are for cancelled-to-order.

Information for users

Guarantee

All stamps supplied by us are guaranteed originals in the following terms:

If not as described, and returned by the purchaser, we undertake to refund the price paid to us in the original transaction. If any stamp is certified as genuine by the Expert Committee of the Royal Philatelic Society, London, or by B.P.A. Expertising Ltd., the purchaser shall not be entitled to make any claim against us for any error, omission or mistake in such certificate.

Consumers' statutory rights are not affected by the above guarantee.

Currency

At the beginning of each country brief details give the currencies in which the values of the stamps are expressed. The dates, where given, are those of the earliest stamp issues in the particular currency. Where the currency is obvious, e.g. where the colony has the same currency as the mother country, no details are given.

Illustrations

Illustrations of any surcharges and overprints which are shown and not described are actual size; stamp illustrations are reduced to $\frac{3}{4}$ linear, *unless otherwise stated.*

"Key-Types"

A number of standard designs occur so frequently in the stamps of the French, German, Portuguese and Spanish colonies that it would be a waste of space to repeat them. Instead these are all illustrated on page xiv together with the descriptive names and letters by which they are referred to in the lists.

Type Numbers

These are the bold figures found below each illustration. References to "Type **6**", for example, in the lists of a country should therefore be understood to refer to the illustration below which the number **"6"** appears. These type numbers are also given in the second column of figures alongside each list of stamps, thus indicating clearly the design of each stamp. In the case of Key-Types – see above – letters take the place of the type numbers.

Where an issue comprises stamps of similar design, represented in this catalogue by one illustration, the corresponding type numbers should be taken as indicating this general design.

Where there are blanks in the type number column it means that the type of the corresponding stamps is that shown by the last number above in the type column of the same issue.

A dash (–) in the type column means that no illustration of the stamp is shown.

Where type numbers refer to stamps of another country, e.g. where stamps of one country are overprinted for use in another, this is always made clear in the text.

Stamp Designs

Brief descriptions of the subjects of the stamp designs are given either below or beside the illustrations, at the foot of the list of the issue concerned, or in the actual lists. Where a particular subject, e.g. the portrait of a well-known monarch, recurs frequently the description is not repeated, nor are obvious designs described.

Generally, the unillustrated designs are in the same shape and size as the one illustrated, except where otherwise indicated.

Surcharges and Overprints

Surcharges and overprints are usually described in the headings to the issues concerned. Where the actual wording of a surcharge or overprint is given it is shown in bold type.

Some stamps are described as being "Surcharged in words", e.g. **TWO CENTS**, and others "Surcharged in figures and words", e.g. **20 CENTS**, although of course many surcharges are in foreign languages and combinations of words and figures are numerous. There are often bars, etc., obliterating old values or inscriptions but in general these are only mentioned where it is necessary to avoid confusion.

No attention is paid in this catalogue to colours of overprints and surcharges so that stamps with the same overprints in different colours are not listed separately.

Numbers in brackets after the descriptions of overprinted or surcharged stamps are the catalogue numbers of the unoverprinted stamps.

Note – the words "inscribed" or "inscription" always refer to wording incorporated in the design of a stamp and not surcharges or overprints.

Coloured Papers

Where stamps are printed on coloured paper the description is given as e.g. "4 c. black on blue" – a stamp printed in black on blue paper. No attention is paid in this catalogue to difference in the texture of paper, e.g. laid, wove.

Information for users

Watermarks

Stamps having different watermarks, but otherwise the same, are not listed separately. No reference is therefore made to watermarks in this volume.

Stamp Colours

Colour names are only required for the identification of stamps, therefore they have been made as simple as possible. Thus "scarlet", "vermilion", "carmine" are all usually called red. Qualifying colour names have been introduced only where necessary for the sake of clearness.

Where stamps are printed in two or more colours the central portion of the design is in the first colour given, unless otherwise stated.

Perforations

All stamps are perforated unless otherwise stated. No distinction is made between the various gauges of perforation but early stamp issues which exist both imperforate and perforated are usually listed separately.

Where a heading states "Imperf. or perf". or "Perf. or rouletted" this does not necessarily mean that all values of the issue are found in both conditions.

Dates of Issue

The date given at the head of each issue is that of the appearance of the earliest stamp in the series. As stamps of the same design or issue are usually grouped together a list of King George VI stamps, for example, headed "1938" may include stamps issued from 1938 to the end of the reign.

Se-tenant Pairs

Many modern issues are printed in sheets containing different designs or face values. Such pairs, blocks, strips or sheets are described as being "se-tenant" and they are outside the scope of this catalogue, although reference to them may occur in instances where they form a composite design.

Miniature Sheets

As an increasing number of stamps are now only found in miniature sheets, Stamps of the World will, in future, list these items. This edition lists all Commonwealth, European and Asian countries' miniature sheets, plus those of all other countries which have appeared in the catalogue supplement during the past three years. Earlier miniature sheets of non-Commonwealth countries will be listed in future editions.

"Appendix" Countries

We regret that, since 1968, it has been necessary to establish an Appendix (at the end of each country as appropriate) to which numerous stamps have had to be consigned. Several countries imagine that by issuing huge quantities of unnecessary stamps they will have a ready source of income from stamp collectors – and particularly from the less-experienced ones. Stanley Gibbons refuse to encourage this exploitation of the hobby and we do not stock the stamps concerned.

Two kinds of stamp are therefore given the briefest of mentions in the Appendix, purely for the sake of record. Administrations issuing stamps greatly in excess of true postal needs have the offending issues placed there. Likewise it contains stamps which have not fulfilled all the normal conditions for full catalogue listing.

These conditions are that the stamps must be issued by a legitimate postal authority, recognised by the government concerned, and are adhesives, valid for proper postal use in the class of service for which they are inscribed. Stamps, with the exception of such categories as postage dues and officials, must be available to the general public at face value with no artificial restrictions being imposed on their distribution.

The publishers of this catalogue have observed, with concern, the proliferation of 'artificial' stamp-issuing territories. On several occasions this has resulted in separately inscribed issues for various component parts of otherwise united states or territories.

Stanley Gibbons Publications have decided that where such circumstances occur, they will not, in the future, list these items in the SG catalogue without first satisfying themselves that the stamps represent a genuine political, historical or postal division within the country concerned. Any such issues which do not fulfil this stipulation will be recorded in the Catalogue Appendix only.

Stamps in the Appendix are kept under review in the light of any newly acquired information about them. If we are satisfied that a stamp qualifies for proper listing in the body of the catalogue it is moved there.

Information for users

"Undesirable Issues"

The rules governing many competitive exhibitions are set by the Federation Internationale de Philatelie and stipulate a downgrading of marks for stamps classed as "undesirable issues".

This catalogue can be taken as a guide to status. All stamps in the main listings and Addenda are acceptable. Stamps in the Appendix should not be entered for competition as these are the "undesirable issues".

Particular care is advised with Aden Protectorate States, Ajman, Bhutan, Chad, Fujeira, Khor Fakkan, Manama, Ras al Khaima, Sharjah, Umm al Qiwain and Yemen. Totally bogus stamps exist (as explained in Appendix notes) and these are to be avoided also for competition. As distinct from "undesirable stamps" certain categories are not covered in this catalogue purely by reason of its scope (see page viii). Consult the particular competition rules to see if such are admissable even though not listed by us.

Where to Look for More Detailed Listings

The present work deliberately omits details of paper, perforation, shade and watermark. But as you become more absorbed in stamp collecting and wish to get greater enjoyment from the hobby you may well want to study these matters.

All the information you require about any particular postage stamp will be found in the main Stanley Gibbons Catalogues.

Commonwealth countries before 1952 are covered by the Commonwealth & British Empire Stamps 1840–1952 published annually.

For foreign countries you can easily find which catalogue to consult by looking at the country headings in the present book.

To the right of each country name are code letters specifying which volume of our main catalogues contains that country's listing.

The code letters are as follows:

Pt. 2   Part 2
Pt. 3   Part 3 etc.

(See page xiii for complete list of Parts.)

So, for example, if you want to know more about Chinese stamps than is contained in the *Simplified Catalogue of Stamps of the World* the reference to

CHINA   Pt. 17

guides you to the Gibbons Part 17 *(China)* Catalogue listing for the details you require.

New editions of Parts 2 to 22 appear at irregular intervals.

Correspondence

Whilst we welcome information and suggestions we must ask correspondents to include the cost of postage for the return of any stamps submitted plus registration where appropriate. Letters should be addressed to The Catalogue Editor at Ringwood.

Where information is solicited purely for the benefit of the enquirer we regret we cannot undertake to reply.

Identification of Stamps

We regret we do not give opinions as to the genuineness of stamps, nor do we identify stamps or number them by our Catalogue.

Users of this catalogue are referred to our companion booklet entitled *Stamp Collecting – How to Identify Stamps.* It explains how to look up stamps in this catalogue, contains a full checklist of stamp inscriptions and gives help in dealing with unfamiliar scripts.

Stanley Gibbons would like to complement your collection

At Stanley Gibbons we offer a range of services which are designed to complement your collection.

Our modern stamp shop, the largest in Europe, together with our rare stamp department has one of the most comprehensive stocks of Great Britain in the world, so whether you are a beginner or an experienced philatelist you are certain to find something to suit your special requirements.

Alternatively, through our Mail Order services you can control the growth of your collection from the comfort of your own home. Our Postal Sales Department regularly sends out mailings of Special Offers. We can also help with your wants list—so why not ask us for those elusive items?

Why not take advantage of the many services we have to offer? Visit our premises in the Strand or, for more information, write to the appropriate address on page x.

The Stanley Gibbons Group Addresses

Stanley Gibbons Limited,
Stanley Gibbons Auctions

339 Strand, London WC2R 0LX
Telephone 020 7836 8444, Fax 020 7836 7342,
E-mail: enquiries@stanleygibbons.co.uk
Website: www.stanleygibbons.com for all departments.

Auction Room and Specialist Stamp Departments. Open Monday–Friday 9.30 a.m. to 5 p.m.

Shop. Open Monday–Friday 9 a.m. to 5.30 p.m. and Saturday 9.30 a.m. to 5.30 p.m.

Fraser's Autographs, photographs, letters, documents

399 Strand, London WC2R 0LX
Autographs, photographs, letters and documents

Telephone 020 7836 8444, Fax 020 7836 7342,
E-mail: info@frasersautographs.co.uk
Website: www.frasersautographs.com

Monday–Friday 9 a.m. to 5.30 p.m. and Saturday 10 a.m. to 4 p.m.

Stanley Gibbons Publications

Parkside, Christchurch Road, Ringwood, Hants BH24 3SH.
Telephone 01425 472363 (24 hour answer phone service), Fax 01425 470247,
E-mail: info@stanleygibbons.co.uk
Website: www.stanleygibbons.com

Publications Mail Order. FREEPHONE 0800 611622
Monday–Friday 8.30 a.m. to 5 p.m.

Stanley Gibbons Publications Overseas Representation

Stanley Gibbons Publications are represented overseas by the following sole distributors (*), distributors (**) or licensees (***).

Australia
Lighthouse Philatelic (Aust.) Pty. Ltd.*
Locked Bag 5900 Botany DC, New South Wales, 2019 Australia.

Stanley Gibbons (Australia) Pty. Ltd.***
Level 6, 36 Clarence Street, Sydney, New South Wales 2000, Australia.

Belgium and Luxembourg**
Davo c/o Philac, Rue du Midi 48, Bruxelles, 1000 Belgium.

Canada*
Lighthouse Publications (Canada) Ltd., 255 Duke Street, Montreal Quebec, Canada H3C 2M2.

Denmark**
Samlerforum/Davo, Ostergade 3, DK 7470 Karup, Denmark.

Finland**
Davo c/o Kapylan Merkkikky Pohjolankatu 1 00610 Helsinki, Finland.

France*
Davo France (Casteilla), 10, Rue Leon Foucault, 78184 St. Quentin Yvelines Cesex, France.

Hong Kong**
Po-on Stamp Service, GPO Box 2498, Hong Kong.

Israel**
Capital Stamps, P.O. Box 3769, Jerusalem 91036, Israel.

Italy*
Ernesto Marini Srl, Via Struppa 300, I-16165, Genova GE, Italy.

Japan**
Japan Philatelic Co. Ltd., P.O. Box 2, Suginami-Minami, Tokyo, Japan.

Netherlands*
Davo Publications, P.O. Box 411, 7400 AK Deventer, Netherlands.

New Zealand***
Mowbray Collectables.
P.O. Box 80, Wellington, New Zealand.

Norway**
Davo Norge A/S, P.O. Box 738 Sentrum, N-0105, Oslo, Norway.

Singapore**
Stamp Inc Collectibles Pte Ltd., 10 Ubi Cresent, #01-43 Ubi Tech Park, Singapore 408564.

Sweden*
Chr Winther Soerensen AB, Box 43, S-310 Knaered, Sweden.

Abbreviations

Anniv.	denotes	Anniversary
Assn.	,,	Association
Bis.	,,	Bistre
Bl.	,,	Blue
Bldg.	,,	Building
Blk.	,,	Black
Br.	,,	British or Bridge
Brn.	,,	Brown
B.W.I.	,,	British West Indies
C.A.R.I.F.T.A.	,,	Caribbean Free Trade Area
Cent.	,,	Centenary
Chest.	,,	Chestnut
Choc.	,,	Chocolate
Clar.	,,	Claret
Coll.	,,	College
Commem.	,,	Commemoration
Conf.	,,	Conference
Diag.	,,	Diagonally
E.C.A.F.E.	,,	Economic Commission for Asia and Far East
Emer.	,,	Emerald
E.P.T. Conference	,,	European Postal and Telecommunications Conference
Exn.		Exhibition
F.A.O.	,,	Food and Agriculture Organization
Fig.	,,	Figure
G.A.T.T.	,,	General Agreement on Tariffs and Trade
G.B.	,,	Great Britain
Gen.	,,	General
Govt.	,,	Government
Grn.	,,	Green
Horiz.	,,	Horizontal
H.Q.	,,	Headquarters
Imperf.	,,	Imperforate
Inaug.	,,	Inauguration
Ind.	,,	Indigo
Inscr.	,,	Inscribed or inscription
Int.	,,	International
I.A.T.A.	,,	International Air Transport Association
I.C.A.O.	,,	International Civil Aviation Organization
I.C.Y.	,,	International Co-operation Year
I.G.Y.	,,	International Geophysical Year
I.L.O.	,,	International Labour Office (or later, Organization)
I.M.C.O.	,,	Inter-Governmental Maritime Consultative Organization
I.T.U.	,,	International Telecommunication Union
Is.	,,	Islands
Lav.	,,	Lavender
Mar.	,,	Maroon
mm.	,,	Millimetres
Mult.	,,	Multicoloured
Mve.	denotes	Mauve
Nat.	,,	National
N.A.T.O.	,,	North Atlantic Treaty Organization
O.D.E.C.A.	,,	Organization of Central American States
Ol.	,,	Olive
Optd.	,,	Overprinted
Orge. or oran.	,,	Orange
P.A.T.A.	,,	Pacific Area Travel Association
Perf.	,,	Perforated
Post.	,,	Postage
Pres.	,,	President
P.U.	,,	Postal Union
Pur.	,,	Purple
R.	,,	River
R.S.A.	,,	Republic of South Africa
Roul.	,,	Rouletted
Sep.	,,	Sepia
S.E.A.T.O.	,,	South East Asia Treaty Organization
Surch.	,,	Surcharged
T.	,,	Type
T.U.C.	,,	Trades Union Congress
Turq.	,,	Turquoise
Ultram.	,,	Ultramarine
U.N.E.S.C.O.	,,	United Nations Educational, Scientific Cultural Organization
U.N.I.C.E.F.	,,	United Nations Children's Fund
U.N.O.	,,	United Nations Organization
U.N.R.W.A.	,,	United Nations Relief and Works Agency for Palestine Refugees in the Near East
U.N.T.E.A.	,,	United Nations Temporary Executive Authority
U.N.R.R.A.	,,	United Nations Relief and Rehabilitation Administration
U.P.U.	,,	Universal Postal Union
Verm.	,,	Vermilion
Vert.	,,	Vertical
Vio.	,,	Violet
W.F.T.U.	,,	World Federation of Trade Unions
W.H.O.	,,	World Health Organization
Yell.	,,	Yellow

Arabic Numerals

As in the case of European figures, the details of the Arabic numerals vary in different stamp designs, but they should be readily recognised with the aid of this illustration:

٠	١	٢	٣	٤
0	1	2	3	4
٥	٦	٧	٨	٩
5	6	7	8	9

Stanley Gibbons Stamp Catalogue
Complete List of Parts

1 Commonwealth & British Empire Stamps 1840–1952 (Annual)

Foreign Countries

2 Austria & Hungary (6th edition, 2002)
Austria · U.N. (Vienna) · Hungary

3 Balkans (4th edition, 1998)
Albania · Bosnia & Herzegovina · Bulgaria · Croatia · Greece & Islands · Macedonia · Rumania · Slovenia · Yugoslavia

4 Benelux (5th edition, 2003)
Belgium & Colonies · Luxembourg · Netherlands & Colonies

5 Czechoslovakia & Poland (6th edition, 2002)
Czechoslovakia · Czech Republic · Slovakia · Poland

6 France (5th edition, 2001)
France · Colonies · Post Offices · Andorra · Monaco

7 Germany (6th edition, 2002)
Germany · States · Colonies · Post Offices

8 Italy & Switzerland (6th edition, 2003)
Italy & Colonies · Liechtenstein · San Marino · Switzerland · U.N. (Geneva) · Vatican City

9 Portugal & Spain (5th edition, 2004)
Andorra · Portugal & Colonies · Spain & Colonies

10 Russia (5th edition, 1999)
Russia · Armenia · Azerbaijan · Belarus · Estonia · Georgia · Kazakhstan · Kyrgyzstan · Latvia · Lithuania · Moldova · Tajikistan · Turkmenistan · Ukraine · Uzbekistan · Mongolia

11 Scandinavia (5th edition, 2001)
Aland Islands · Denmark · Faroe Islands · Finland · Greenland · Iceland · Norway · Sweden

12 Africa since Independence A-E (2nd edition, 1983)
Algeria · Angola · Benin · Burundi · Cameroun · Cape Verdi · Central African Republic · Chad · Comoro Islands · Congo · Djibouti · Equatorial Guinea · Ethiopia

13 Africa since Independence F-M (1st edition, 1981)
Gabon · Guinea · Guinea-Bissau · Ivory Coast · Liberia · Libya · Malagasy Republic · Mali · Mauritania · Morocco · Mozambique

14 Africa since Independence N-Z (1st edition, 1981)
Niger Republic · Rwanda · St. Thomas & Prince · Senegal · Somalia · Sudan · Togo · Tunisia · Upper Volta · Zaire

15 Central America (2nd edition, 1984)
Costa Rica · Cuba · Dominican Republic · El Salvador · Guatemala · Haiti · Honduras · Mexico · Nicaragua · Panama

16 Central Asia (3rd edition, 1992)
Afghanistan · Iran · Turkey

17 China (6th edition,1998)
China · Taiwan · Tibet · Foreign P.O.s · Hong Kong · Macao

18 Japan & Korea (4th edition, 1997)
Japan · Korean Empire · South Korea · North Korea

19 Middle East (6th edition, 2005)
Bahrain · Egypt · Iraq · Israel · Jordan · Kuwait · Lebanon · Oman · Qatar · Saudi Arabia · Syria · U.A.E. · Yemen

20 South America (3rd edition, 1989)
Argentina · Bolivia · Brazil · Chile · Colombia · Ecuador · Paraguay · Peru · Surinam · Uruguay · Venezuela

21 South-East Asia (4th edition, 2004)
Bhutan · Burma · Indonesia · Kampuchea · Laos · Nepal · Philippines · Thailand · Vietnam

22 United States (5th edition, 2000)
U.S. & Possessions · Marshall Islands · Micronesia · Palau · U.N. (New York, Geneva, Vienna)

Thematic Catalogues

Stanley Gibbons Catalogues for use with **Stamps of the World.**
Collect Aircraft on Stamps (out of print)
Collect Birds on Stamps (5th edition, 2003)
Collect Chess on Stamps (2nd edition, 1999)
Collect Fish on Stamps (1st edition, 1999)
Collect Fungi on Stamps (2nd edition, 1997)
Collect Motor Vehicles on Stamps (1st edition, 2004)
Collect Railways on Stamps (3rd edition, 1999)
Collect Shells on Stamps (1st edition, 1995)
Collect Ships on Stamps (3rd edition, 2001)

Key-Types

(see note on page vii)

French Group

A. "Blanc."

B. "Mouchon."

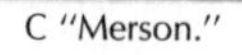
C "Merson."

D. "Tablet."

E.

F.

G.

H.

"International Colonial Exhibition."

I. "Faidherbe."

J. "Palms."

K. "Balay."

L. "Natives."

M. "Figure."

German Group

N. "Yacht."

O. "Yacht."

Spanish Group

X. "Alfonso XII."

Y. "Baby."

Z. "Curly Head"

Portuguese Group

P. "Crown."

Q. "Embossed."

R. "Figures."

S. "Carlos."

T. "Manoel."

U. "Ceres."

V. "Newspaper."

W. "Due."

STANLEY GIBBONS SIMPLIFIED CATALOGUE OF STAMPS OF THE WORLD—VOLUME 5 COUNTRIES S–Z

SAAR Pt. 7

A German territory South-east of Luxembourg. Occupied by France under League of Nations control from 1920 to 1935. Following a plebiscite, Saar returned to Germany in 1935 from when German stamps were used until the French occupation in 1945, after which Nos. F1/13 of Germany followed by Nos. 203 etc of Saar were used. The territory was autonomous under French protection until it again returned to Germany at the end of 1956 following a national referendum. Issues from 1957 were authorised by the German Federal Republic pending the adoption of German currency on 6 July 1959, after which West German stamps were used.

1920–May 1921. 100 pfennig = 1 mark.
May 1921–March 1935. 100 centimes = 1 franc.
1935–47. 100 pfennig = 1 reichsmark.
1947. 100 pfennig = 1 Saarmark.
November 1947–July 1959. 100 centimes = 1 franc.
From 1959. 100 pfennig = 1 Deutsche mark.

LEAGUE OF NATIONS COMMISSION

1920. German stamps inscr "DEUTSCHES REICH" optd **Sarre** and bar.
1 **24** 2pf. grey . . . 1·10 4·25
2 c 2½pf. grey . . . 1·90 6·00
3 **10** 3pf. brown . . . 85 2·40
4 c 5pf. green . . . 45 2·20
5 **24** 7½pf. orange . . . 45 2·20
6 **10** 10pf. red . . . 45 2·20
7 **24** 15pf. violet . . . 45 2·20
8 **10** 20pf. blue . . . 45 2·20
9 25pf. black & red on yellow . . . 10·00 22·00
10 30pf. black & orange on buff . . . 19·00 34·00
11 **24** 35pf. brown . . . 45 2·20
12 **10** 40pf. black and red . . . 45 2·20
13 50pf. black & pur on cream . . . 45 2·20
14 60pf. purple . . . 45 2·20
15 75pf. black and green . . . 45 2·20
16 80pf. black and red on red . . . £225 £275
17ab **12** 1m. red . . . 23·00 32·00

1920. Bavarian stamps optd **Sarre** or **SARRE** (Nos. 30/1) and bars.
18 **15** 5pf. green . . . 65 2·20
19 10pf. red . . . 65 2·20
19a 15pf. red . . . 1·00 1·90
21 20pf. blue . . . 65 2·20
22 25pf. grey . . . 10·00 17·00
23 30pf. orange . . . 7·00 11·50
24 40pf. green . . . 11·00 17·00
25 50pf. brown . . . 1·30 2·50
26 60pf. green . . . 3·50 10·00
27 **16** 1m. brown . . . 17·00 30·00
28 2m. violet . . . 60·00 £140
29 3m. red . . . £110 £180
30 – 5m. blue (No. 192) . . . £700 £850
31 – 10m. green (No. 193) . . . £130 £275

1920. German stamps inscr "DEUTSCHES REICH" optd **SAARGEBIET**.
32 **10** 5pf. green . . . 25 55
33 5pf. brown . . . 45 55
34 10pf. red . . . 25 55
35 10pf. orange . . . 30 45
36 **24** 15pf. violet . . . 25 55
37 **10** 20pf. blue . . . 25 55
38 20pf. green . . . 45 55
39 30pf. black & orange on buff . . . 25 55
40 30pf. blue . . . 65 85
41 40pf. black and red . . . 25 55
42 40pf. red . . . 1·00 85
43 50pf. black & purple on buff . . . 25 55
44 60pf. purple . . . 60 55
45 75pf. black and green . . . 65 55
46 **12** 1m.25 green . . . 1·50 1·50
47 1m.50 brown . . . 1·50 1·50
48 **13** 2m.50 purple . . . 3·50 16·00
49 **10** 4m. red and black . . . 9·00 22·00

1920. No. 45 of Saar surch **20** and No. 102 of Germany surch **SAARGEBIET**, arms and value.
50 **10** 20 on 75pf. black and green 35 1·30
51 **24** 5m. on 15pf. purple . . . 4·25 19·00
52 10m. on 15pf. purple . . . 6·50 22·00

9 Miner

11 Colliery Shafthead

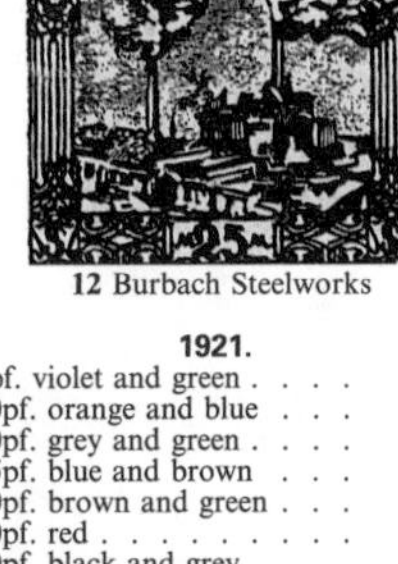
12 Burbach Steelworks

1921.
53 – 5pf. violet and green . . . 45 45
54 **9** 10pf. orange and blue . . . 30 50
55 – 20pf. grey and green . . . 30 1·10
56 – 25pf. blue and brown . . . 35 1·10
57 – 30pf. brown and green . . . 35 85
58 – 40pf. red . . . 35 50
59 – 50pf. black and grey . . . 85 3·75
60 – 60pf. brown and red . . . 1·70 3·75
61 – 80pf. blue . . . 65 1·30
62 – 1m. black and red . . . 70 1·70
63 **11** 1m.25 green and brown . . . 1·10 2·20
64 – 2m. black and orange . . . 2·50 4·00
65 – 3m. sepia and brown . . . 3·50 10·50
66 – 5m. violet and yellow . . . 10·00 26·00
67 – 10m. brown and green . . . 13·00 27·00
68 **12** 25m. blue, black and red . . . 34·00 85·00

DESIGNS—As Type **11**. HORIZ: 5pf. Mill above Mettlach; 20pf. Pit head at Reden; 25pf. River traffic, Saarbrucken; 30pf. River Saar at Mettlach; 40pf. Slag-heap, Volklingen; 50pf. Signal gantry, Saarbrucken; 80pf. "Old Bridge", Saarbrucken; 1m. Wire-rope Railway; 2m. Town Hall, Saarbrucken; 3m. Pottery, Mettlach; 5m. St. Ludwig's Church; 10m. Chief Magistrate's and Saar Commissioner's Offices. VERT: 60pf. Gothic Chapel, Mettlach.

See also Nos. 84/97.

1921. Nos. 55/68 surch in French currency.
70 3c. on 20pf. grey and green . . . 35 65
71 5c. on 25pf. blue and brown . . . 35 45
72 10c. on 30pf. brown and green . . . 35 45
73 15c. on 40pf. red . . . 45 45
74 20c. on 50pf. black and grey . . . 35 45
75 25c. on 60pf. brown and red . . . 50 45
76 30c. on 80pf. blue . . . 1·70 1·10
77 40c. on 1m. black and red . . . 2·40 65
78 50c. on 1m.25 green & brown . . . 3·75 1·10
79 75c. on 2m. black and orange . . . 3·50 1·50
80 1f. on 3m. black and brown . . . 3·75 2·50
81 2f. on 5m. violet and yellow . . . 12·50 6·50
82 3f. on 10m. brown and green . . . 15·00 28·00
83 5f. on 25m. blue, black and red . . . 22·00 41·00

1922. Larger designs (except 5f.) and value in French currency.
84 3c. green (as No. 62) . . . 35 65
85 5c. black & orange (as No. 54) . . . 35 20
86 10c. green (as No. 61) . . . 35 20
87 15c. brown (as No. 62) . . . 85 20
98 15c. orange (as No. 62) . . . 2·50 50
88 20c. blue & yellow (as No. 64) . . . 10·50 20
100 25c. red and yellow (as No. 64) . . . 2·50 35
90 30c. red and yellow (as No. 58) . . . 2·20 2·40
91 40c. brown & yell (as No. 65) 85 20
92 50c. blue & yellow (as No. 56) . . . 85 20
93 75c. green & yellow (as No. 65) . . . 8·50 19·00
94 1f. brown (as No. 66) . . . 2·50 85
95 2f. violet (as No. 63) . . . 4·00 3·25
96 3f. green & orange (as No. 60) . . . 17·00 7·25
97 5f. brown & choc (as No. 68) 19·00 55·00

14 Madonna of Blieskastel

15 Army Medical Service

1925.
102 **14** 45c. purple . . . 3·00 4·00
103 10f. brown (31 × 36 mm) 16·00 26·00

1926. Welfare Fund.
104 **15** 20c.+20c. green . . . 8·50 22·00
105 – 40c.+40c. brown . . . 8·50 22·00
106 – 50c.+50c. orange . . . 8·50 19·00
107 – 1f.50+1f.50 blue . . . 22·00 60·00

DESIGNS: 40c. Hospital work (nurse and patient); 50c. Child welfare (children at a spring); 1f.50, Maternity nursing service.

18 Tholey Abbey

1926.
108 – 10c. brown . . . 65 20
109 – 15c. green . . . 65 1·10
110 – 20c. brown . . . 65 20
111 **18** 25c. blue . . . 65 35
112 – 30c. green . . . 65 20
113 – 40c. brown . . . 65 20
114 **18** 50c. red . . . 65 20
114a – 60c. orange . . . 3·25 40
115 – 75c. purple . . . 65 20
116 – 80c. orange . . . 2·75 11·00
116a – 90c. red . . . 8·00 16·00
117 – 1f. violet . . . 2·75 45
118 – 1f.50 blue . . . 4·75 45
119 – 2f. red . . . 5·50 45
120 – 3f. green . . . 12·00 1·30
121 – 5f. brown . . . 13·00 8·25

DESIGNS—VERT: 10, 30c. Fountain, St. Johann, Saarbrucken. HORIZ: 15, 75c. Saar Valley near Gudingen; 20, 40, 90c. View from Saarlouis fortifications; 60, 80c., 1f. Colliery shafthead; 1f.50, 2, 3, 5f. Burbach Steelworks.

1927. Welfare Fund. Optd **1927–28**.
122 **15** 20c.+20c. green . . . 7·75 14·50
123 40c.+40c. brown . . . 6·50 18·00
124 50c.+50c. orange . . . 5·50 11·00
125 1f.50+1f.50 blue . . . 10·00 34·00

19 Breguet 14 Biplane over Saarbrucken

20 "The Blind Beggar" by Dyckmanns

1928. Air.
126 **19** 50c. red . . . 2·50 2·40
127 1f. violet . . . 2·75 2·75

1928. Christmas Charity.
128 **20** 40c.(+40c.) brown . . . 11·50 80·00
129 50c.(+50c.) purple . . . 11·50 80·00
130 1f.(+1f.) violet . . . 11·50 80·00
131 – 1f.50(+1f.50) blue . . . 11·50 80·00
132 – 2f.(+2f.) red . . . 15·00 £120
133 – 3f.(+3f.) green . . . 15·00 £160
134 – 10f.(+10f.) brown . . . £400 £4250

DESIGNS: 1f.50, 2, 3f. "Almsgiving" by Schiestl; 10f. "Charity" by Raphael (picture in circle).

1929. Christmas Charity. Paintings. As T **20**.
135 40c.(+15c.) green . . . 1·90 6·50
136 50c.(+20c.) red . . . 4·75 11·00
137 1f.(+50c.) purple . . . 4·75 12·00
138 1f.50(+75c.) blue . . . 4·75 12·00
139 2f.(+1f.) red . . . 4·75 12·00
140 3f.(+2f.) green . . . 8·50 28·00
141 10f.(+8f.) brown . . . 47·00 £160

DESIGNS: 40c. to 1f. "Orphaned" by H. Kaulbach; 1f.50, 2, 3f. "St. Ottilia" by M. Feuerstein; 10f. "The Little Madonna" by Ferruzzio.

1930. Nos. 114 and 116 surch.
141a **18** 40c. on 50c. red . . . 1·30 1·50
142 – 60c. on 80c. orange . . . 1·70 2·40

1931. Christmas Charity (1930 issue). Paintings. As T **20**.
143 40c.(+15c.) brown . . . 8·50 28·00
144 60c.(+20c.) orange . . . 8·50 28·00
145 1f.(+50c.) red . . . 8·50 55·00
146 1f.50(+75c.) blue . . . 13·00 55·00
147 2f.(+1f.) brown . . . 13·00 55·00
148 3f.(+2f.) green . . . 22·00 55·00
149 10f.(+10f.) brown . . . £110 £325

DESIGNS: 40, 60c., 1f.50, "The Safetyman" (miner and lamp) by F. Zolnhofer; 1, 2, 3f. "The Good Samaritan" by J. Heinemann; 10f. "At the Window" by F. G. Waldmuller.

1931. Christmas Charity. Paintings. As T **20**.
150 40c.(+15c.) brown . . . 13·00 43·00
151 60c.(+20c.) red . . . 13·00 43·00
152 1f.(+50c.) purple . . . 15·00 65·00
153 1f.50(+75c.) blue . . . 19·00 65·00
154 2f.(+1f.) red . . . 26·00 65·00
155 3f.(+2f.) green . . . 32·00 £120
156 5f.(+5f.) brown . . . £110 £375

DESIGNS: 40c. to 1f. "St. Martin" by F. Boehle; 1f.50, 2f. "Charity" by Ridgeway-Knight; 5f. "The Widow's Mite" by Dubufe.

29 Focke Wulf A-17 Mowe over Saarbrucken Airport

30 Kirkel Castle Ruins

1932. Air.
157 **29** 60c. red . . . 6·50 5·25
158 5f. brown . . . 43·00 £100

1932. Christmas Charity.
159 **30** 40c.(+15c.) brown . . . 11·00 28·00
160 – 60c.(+20c.) red . . . 11·00 28·00
161 – 1f.(+50c.) purple . . . 15·00 47·00
162 – 1f.50(+75c.) blue . . . 22·00 55·00
163 – 2f.(+1f.) red . . . 22·00 65·00
164 – 3f.(+2f.) green . . . 65·00 £200
165 – 5f.(+5f.) brown . . . £130 £325

DESIGNS—VERT: 60c. Blieskastel Church; 1f. Ottweiler Church; 1f.50, St. Michael's Church, Saarbrucken; 2f. Cathedral and fountain, St. Wendel; 3f. St. John's Church, Saarbrucken. HORIZ: 5f. Kerpen Castle, Illingen.

32 Scene of the Disaster

33 "Love"

1933. Neunkirchen Explosion Disaster.
166 **32** 60c.(+60c.) orange . . . 15·00 26·00
167 3f.(+3f.) green . . . 43·00 85·00
168 5f.(+5f.) brown . . . 43·00 85·00

1934. Christmas Charity.
169 **33** 40c.(+15c.) brown . . . 5·50 19·00
170 – 60c.(+20c.) red . . . 5·50 19·00
171 – 1f.(+50c.) mauve . . . 8·50 22·00
172 – 1f.50(+75c.) blue . . . 15·00 41·00
173 – 2f.(+1f.) red . . . 13·00 41·00
174 – 3f.(+2f.) green . . . 15·00 41·00
175 – 5f.(+5f.) brown . . . 34·00 95·00

DESIGNS: 60c. "Solicitude". 1f. "Peace". 1f.50, "Consolation". 2f. "Welfare". 3f. "Truth". 5f. Countess Elizabeth von Nassau.

Nos. 169/74 show statues by C. L. Pozzi in church of St. Louis, Saarbrucken.

1934. Saar Plebiscite. Optd **VOLKSABSTIMMUNG 1935**. (a) Postage. On Nos. 108/15, 116a/21 and 103.
176 – 10c. brown . . . 45 65
177 – 15c. green . . . 45 65
178 – 20c. brown . . . 65 1·30
179 **18** 25c. blue . . . 65 1·30
180 – 30c. green . . . 45 50
181 – 40c. brown . . . 45 85
182 **18** 50c. red . . . 75 1·30
183 – 60c. orange . . . 45 65
184 – 75c. purple . . . 75 1·50
185 – 90c. red . . . 75 1·50
186 – 1f. violet . . . 85 1·60
187 – 1f.50 blue . . . 1·30 3·50
188 – 2f. red . . . 1·90 4·75
189 – 3f. green . . . 3·50 8·25
190 – 5f. brown . . . 19·00 34·00
191 **14** 10f. brown . . . 24·00 65·00

(b) Air. On Nos. 126/7 and 157/8.
192 **19** 50c. red . . . 4·50 8·25
193 **29** 60c. red . . . 3·50 3·00
194 **19** 1r. violet . . . 6·00 10·50
195 **29** 5f. brown . . . 7·25 14·00

1934. Christmas Charity. Nos. 169/75 optd **VOLKSABSTIMMUNG 1935**.
196 **33** 40c.(+15c.) brown . . . 4·00 19·00
197 – 60c.(+20c.) red . . . 4·00 19·00
198 – 1f.(+50c.) mauve . . . 11·00 32·00
199 – 1f.50(+75c.) blue . . . 8·50 32·00
200 – 2f.(+1f.) red . . . 11·00 47·00
201 – 3f.(+2f.) green . . . 10·00 41·00
202 – 5f.(+5f.) brown . . . 17·00 43·00

FRENCH OCCUPATION

36 Coal-miner

37 Loop of the Saar

1947. Inscr "SAAR".
203 **36** 2pf. grey 20 20
204 3pf. orange 20 50
205 6pf. green 20 25
206 8pf. red 20 35
207 10pf. mauve 20 25
208 12pf. green 20 35
209 – 15pf. brown . . . . 20 4·75
210 – 16pf. blue 20 35
211 – 20pf. red 20 35
212 – 24pf. brown 20 35
213 – 25pf. mauve . . . . 50 24·00
214 – 30pf. green 20 85
215 – 40pf. brown 20 85
216 – 45pf. red . . . . 60 22·00
217 – 50pf. violet . . . . 50 24·00
218 – 60pf. violet . . . . 50 24·00
219 – 75pf. blue 20 45
220 – 80pf. orange 20 45
221 – 84pf. brown 20 45
222 **37** 1m. green 20 55
DESIGNS—As T **36**: 15pf. to 24pf. Steel workers; 25pf. to 50pf. Sugar beet harvesters; 60pf. to 80pf. Mettlach Abbey. As T **37**—VERT: 84pf. Marshal Ney.

1947. As last surch in French currency.
223B **36** 10c. on 2pf. grey 20 65
224B 60c. on 3pf. orange . . . 20 1·30
225B 1f. on 10pf. mauve 20 65
226B 2f. on 12pf. green . . . . 35 1·70
227B – 3f. on 15pf. brown . . . 20 1·70
228B – 4f. on 16pf. blue . . . . 20 9·50
229B – 5f. on 20pf. red . . . . 20 1·30
230B – 6f. on 24pf. brown . . . 20 85
231B – 9f. on 30pf. green . . . . 45 13·50
232B – 10f. on 50pf. violet . . . 45 26·00
233B – 14f. on 60pf. violet . . . 55 15·00
234B – 20f. on 84pf. brown . . . 95 15·00
235B **37** 50f. on 1m. green . . . . 1·30 34·00

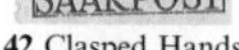
42 Clasped Hands

43 Builders

44 Saar Valley

1948. Inscr "SAARPOST".
236 **42** 10c. red (postage) . . . . 85 2·20
237 60c. blue . . . . 85 2·20
238 1f. black 25 20
239 – 2f. red 45 20
240 – 3f. brown 45 20
241 – 4f. red 45 20
242 – 5f. violet 45 20
243 – 6f. red 85 20
244 – 9f. blue . . . . 5·50 45
245 – 10f. blue . . . . 3·00 50
246 – 14f. purple . . . . 4·25 1·30
247 **43** 20f. red . . . . 8·50 1·30
248 – 50f. blue . . . . 17·00 2·75

249 **44** 25f. red (air) . . . . 6·00 4·00
250 50f. blue . . . . 3·25 2·20
251 200f. red . . . . 30·00 37·00
DESIGNS—As Type **42**: 2, 3f. Man's head;. 4, 5f. Woman's head; 6, 9f. Miner's head. As Type **43**: 10f. Blast furnace chimney; 14f. Foundry; 50f. Facade of Mettlach Abbey.

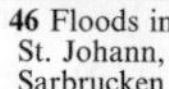
46 Floods in St. Johann, Sarbrucken

47 Map of Saarland

1948. Flood Disaster Relief Fund. Flood Scenes.
252 – 5f.+5f. green (postage) . . 4·25 39·00
253 **46** 6f.+4f. purple . . . . . . 4·25 34·00
254 – 12f.+8f. red . . . . 6·00 47·00
255 – 18f.+12f. blue . . . . . . 7·25 55·00
256 – 25f.+25f. brown (air) . . . 32·00 £275
MS255a 147 × 104 mm. Nos. 252/5. Imperf £475 £1900
MS256a 90 × 60 mm. No. 256 . . £375 £1500
DESIGNS—VERT: 18f. Flooded street, Saarbrucken. HORIZ: 5f. Flooded industrial area; 12f. Landtag building, Saarbrucken; 25f. Floods at Ensdorf, Saarlouis.

1948. 1st Anniv of Constitution.
257 **47** 10f. red . . . . 1·90 2·75
258 25f. blue . . . . 3·00 8·50

48 Hikers and Ludweiler Hostel

1949. Youth Hostels Fund.
259 **48** 8f.+5f. brown . . . . . . 2·75 £130
260 – 10f.+7f. green . . . . . . 3·50 £130
DESIGN: 10f. Hikers and Weisskirchen hostel.

49 Chemical Research

50 Mare and Foal

1949. Saar University.
261 **49** 15f. red . . . . 7·25 35

1949. Horse Day.
262 **50** 15f.+5f. red . . . . 14·00 34·00
263 – 25f.+15f. blue . . . . . . 19·00 41·00
DESIGN: 25f. Two horses in steeple-chase.

51 Symbolic of Typography

52 Labourer and Foundry

1949.
264 – 10c. purple . . . . 25 2·20
265 – 60c. black . . . . 25 1·00
266 – 1f. red . . . . 1·30 20
267 – 3f. brown . . . . 10·00 45
268 – 5f. violet . . . . 2·40 20
269 – 6f. green . . . . 12·50 35
270 – 8f. green 85 35
271 **51** 10f. orange . . . . 6·00 20
272 – 12f. green . . . . 17·00 20
273 – 15f. red . . . . 8·25 20
274 – 18f. mauve . . . . 3·25 5·75
275 **52** 20f. grey . . . . 2·20 25
276 – 25f. blue . . . . 25·00 25
277 – 30f. red . . . . 17·00 50
278 – 45f. purple . . . . 5·50 50
279 – 60f. green . . . . 8·50 2·20
280 – 100f. brown . . . . 12·50 2·75
DESIGNS—As Type **51**: 10c. Building trade; 60c. Beethoven; 1f. and 3f. Heavy industries; 5f. Slag heap; 6f. and 15f. Colliery; 8f. Posthorn and telephone; 12f. and 18f. Pottery. As Type **52**—VERT: 25f. Blast furnace worker; 60f. Landsweiler; 100f. Wiebelskirchen. HORIZ: 30f. St. Arnual; 45f. "Giant's Boot", Rentrisch.

53 Detail from "Moses Striking the Rock" (Murillo)

54 A. Kolping

1949. National Relief Fund.
281 **53** 8f.+2f. blue . . . . 8·50 47·00
282 – 12f.+3f. green . . . . . . 11·00 55·00
283 – 15f.+5f. purple . . . . . . 17·00 90·00
284 – 25f.+10f. blue . . . . . . 24·00 £140
285 – 50f.+20f. purple . . . . . 41·00 £250
DESIGNS: 12f. "Our Lord healing the Paralytic" (Murillo); 15f. "The Sick Child" (Metsu); 25f. "St. Thomas of Villanueva" (Murillo); 50f. "Madonna of Blieskastel".

1950. Honouring Adolf Kolping (miners' padre).
286 **54** 15f.+5f. red . . . . 28·00 80·00

55 P. Wust

1950. 10th Death Anniv of Peter Wust (philosopher).
287 **55** 15f. red . . . . 15·00 7·00

56 Mail Coach

1950. Stamp Day.
288 **56** 15f.+5f. brown and red . . 65·00 £120

57 "Food for the Hungry"

58 St. Peter

1950. Red Cross Fund.
289 **57** 25f.+10f. lake and red . . 26·00 65·00

1950. Holy Year.
290 **58** 12f. green . . . . 4·25 10·00
291 15f. red . . . . 5·50 10·00
292 25f. blue . . . . 9·50 22·00

59 Town Hall, Ottweiler

61

1950. 400th Anniv of Ottweiler.
293 **59** 10f. brown . . . . 4·25 8·50

1950. Saar's Admission to Council of Europe.
294 **61** 25f. blue (postage) . . . . 43·00 14·00
295 – 200f. red (air) £170 £250
DESIGN: 200f. As T **61** but with dove in flight over book.

62 St. Lutwinus enters Monastery

1950. National Relief Fund. Inscr "VOLKSHILFE".
296 **62** 8f.+2f. brown . . . . . . 7·00 39·00
297 – 12f.+3f. green . . . . . . 7·00 39·00
298 – 15f.+5f. brown . . . . . . 8·25 60·00
299 – 25f.+10f. blue . . . . . . 13·00 85·00
300 – 50f.+20f. purple . . . . . 19·00 95·00
DESIGNS: 12f. Lutwinus builds Mettlach Abbey; 15f. Lutwinus as Abbot; 25f. Bishop Lutwinus confirming children at Rheims; 50f. Lutwinus helping needy.

63 Orphans

65 Allegory

64 Mail-carriers, 1760

1951. Red Cross Fund.
301 **63** 25f.+10f. green and red . . 19·00 60·00

1951. Stamp Day.
302 **64** 15f. purple . . . . 7·75 20·00

1951. Trade Fair.
303 **65** 15f. green . . . . 3·00 5·50

66 Flowers and Building

67 Calvin and Luther

1951. Horticultural Show, Bexbach.
304 **66** 15f. green . . . . 2·75 1·70

1951. 375th Anniv of Reformation in Saar.
305 **67** 15f.+5f. brown . . . . . . 1·70 6·50

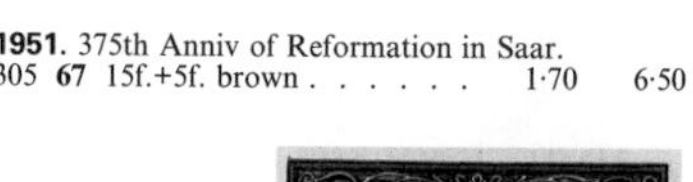

68 "The Good Mother" (Lepicie)

69 Mounted Postman

1951. National Relief Fund. Inscr "VOLKSHILFE 1951".
306 **68** 12f.+3f. green . . . . . . 6·50 19·00
307 – 15f.+5f. violet . . . . . . 6·50 19·00
308 – 18f.+7f. red . . . . 7·25 19·00
309 – 30f.+10f. blue . . . . . . 12·50 37·00
310 – 50f.+20f. brown . . . . . 25·00 75·00
PAINTINGS: 18f. "Outside the Theatre" (Kampf); 18f. "Sisters of Charity" (Browne); 30f. "The Good Samaritan" (Bassano); 50f. "St. Martin and the Poor" (Van Dyck).

1952. Stamp Day.
311 **69** 30f.+10f. blue . . . . . . 10·00 30·00

70 Athlete bearing Olympic Flame

71 Globe and Emblem

1952. 15th Olympic Games, Helsinki. Inscr "OLYMPISCHE SPIELE 1952".
312 **70** 15f.+5f. green . . . . . . 7·00 12·50
313 – 30f.+5f. blue . . . . . . 7·00 14·50
DESIGN: 30f. Hand, laurels and globe.

1952. Saar Fair.
314 **71** 15f. red . . . . 2·50 1·60

72 Red Cross and Refugees

73 G.P.O., Saarbrucken

1952. Red Cross Week.
315 **72** 15f. red . . . . 3·50 1·60

1952. (A) Without inscr in or below design. (B) With inscr.
316 – 1f. green (B) 20 20
317 – 2f. violet 20 20
318 – 3f. red 20 20
319 **73** 5f. green (A) . . . . . . 6·25 20
320 5f. green (B) 20 20
321 – 6f. purple 35 20
322 – 10f. brown 50 20
323 **73** 12f. green (B) 65 20
324 – 15f. brown (A) . . . . . . 8·50 20
325 – 15f. brown (B) . . . . . . 4·25 20
326 – 15f. red (B) 25 20
327 – 18f. purple . . . . 3·50 5·50
329 – 30f. blue . . . . 1·10 1·10
334 – 500f. red . . . . 19·00 65·00
DESIGNS—HORIZ: 1, 15f. (3) Colliery shafthead; 2, 10f. Ludwigs High School, Saarbrucken; 3, 18f. Gersweiler Bridge; 6f. Mettlach Bridge; 30f. University Library, Saarbrucken. VERT: 500f. St. Ludwig's Church, Saarbrucken.

74 "Count Stroganov as a Boy" (Greuze)

75 Fair Symbol

1952. National Relief Fund. Paintings inscr "VOLKSHILFE 1952".
335 **74** 15f.+5f. brown . . . . . . 4·25 11·50
336 – 18f.+7f. red . . . . . . 5·25 16·00
337 – 30f.+10f. blue . . . . . . 6·50 19·00
PORTRAITS: 18f. "The Holy Shepherd" (Murillo); 30f. "Portrait of a Boy" (Kraus).

1953. Saar Fair.
338 **75** 15f. blue . . . . 2·50 1·70

76 Postilions

77 Henri Dunant

1953. Stamp Day.
339 **76** 15f. blue . . . . 3·75 13·00

1953. Red Cross Week and 125th Anniv of Birth of Dunant (founder).
340 **77** 15f.+5f. brown and red . . 2·20 7·00

78 "Painter's Young Son" (Rubens)

79 St. Benedict blessing St. Maurus

1953. National Relief Fund. Paintings inscr "VOLKSHILFE 1953".
341 – 15f.+5f. violet . . . . . . 1·90 6·00
342 – 18f.+7f. red . . . . 2·20 6·50
343 **78** 30f.+10f. green . . . . . 5·25 11·00
DESIGNS—VERT: 15f. "Clarice Strozzi" (Titian). HORIZ: 18f. "Painter's Children" (Rubens).

1953. Tholey Abbey Fund.
344 **79** 30f.+10f. black . . . . . 2·20 8·25

80 Saar Fair

82 Red Cross and Child

81 Postal Motor Coach

1954. Saar Fair.
345 **80** 15f. green . . . . 2·20 1·10

1954. Stamp Day.
346 **81** 15f. red . . . . 4·00 11·00

1954. Red Cross Week.
347 **82** 15f.+5f. brown . . . . . . 2·20 6·50

83 Madonna and Child (Holbein)

1954. Marian Year.
348 **83** 5f. red . . . . 1·10 2·20
349 – 10f. green . . . . 1·30 2·75
350 – 15f. blue . . . . 1·70 4·25
DESIGNS: 10f. "Sistine Madonna" (Raphael); 15f. "Madonna and Child with Pear" (Durer).

84 "Street Urchin with a Melon" (Murillo)

85 Cyclist and Flag

1954. National Relief Fund. Paintings inscr "VOLKSHILFE 1954".
351 **84** 5f.+3f. red . . . . 85 1·30
352 – 10f.+5f. green . . . . . . 85 1·50
353 – 15f.+7f. violet . . . . . . 1·10 2·40
DESIGNS: 10f. "Maria de Medici" (A. Bronzino); 15f. "Baron Emil von Maucler" (J. F. Dietrich).

1955. World Cross-Country Cycle Race.
354 **85** 15f. blue, red and black . . 35 70

86 Rotary Emblem and Industrial Plant

1955. 50th Anniv of Rotary International.
355 **86** 15f. brown 35 70

87 Exhibitors' Flags

88 Nurse and Baby

1955. Saar Fair.
356 **87** 15f. multicoloured 35 70

1955. Red Cross Week.
357 **88** 15f.+5f. black and red . . 40 1·10

89 Postman

91 "Mother" (Durer)

1955. Stamp Day.
358 **89** 15f. purple . . . . 70 1·60

1955. Referendum. Optd **VOLKSBEFRAGUNG 1955.**
359 15f. red (No. 326) 25 45
360 18f. purple (No. 327) 35 55
361 30f. blue (No. 329) 55 85

1955. National Relief Fund. Durer paintings inscr as in T **91**.
362 **91** 5f.+3f. green 50 85
363 – 10f.+5f. green . . . . . . 85 1·50
364 – 15f.+7f. bistre . . . . . . 1·10 1·90
PAINTINGS: 10f. "The Praying Hands"; 15f. "The Old Man from Antwerp".

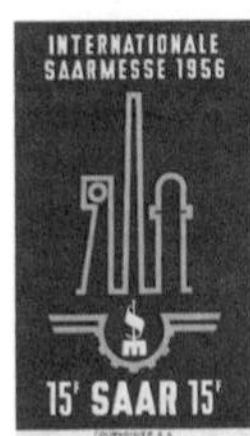

92

93 Radio Tower

1956. Saar Fair.
365 **92** 15f. green and red 25 75

1956. Stamp Day.
366 **93** 15f. green and turquoise 30 70

94 Casualty Station

95

1956. Red Cross Week.
367 **94** 15f.+5f. brown 30 75

1956. Olympic Games.
368 **95** 12f.+3f. blue and green . . 45 80
369 15f.+5f. brown & purple 45 80

96 Winterberg Memorial

97 "Portrait of Lucrezia Crivelli" (da Vinci)

1956. Winterberg Memorial Reconstruction Fund.
370 **96** 5f.+2f. green 20 25
371 12f.+3f. purple 25 55
372 15f.+5f. brown 25 60

1956. National Relief Fund. Inscr as in T **97**.
373 **97** 5f.+3f. blue 15 25
374 – 10f.+5f. red 20 55
375 – 15f.+7f. green 35 95
PAINTINGS: 10f. "Saskia" (Rembrandt); 15f. "Lady Playing Spinet" (Floris).

RETURN TO GERMANY

98 Arms of the Saar

99 President Heuse

1957. Return of the Saar to Germany.
376 **98** 15f. blue and red 15 25

1957. (a) Without "F" after figure of value.
377 **99** 1f. green 15 15
378 2f. violet 15 15
379 3f. brown 15 15
380 4f. mauve 30 70
381 5f. green 15 15
382 6f. red 15 45
383 10f. grey 15 30
384 12f. orange 15 15
385 15f. green 15 15
386 18f. red . . . . 70 1·90
387 25f. lilac 45 75
388 30f. purple 35 70
389 45f. green . . . . 1·00 2·50
390 50f. brown . . . . 1·00 1·10
391 60f. red . . . . 1·60 3·00
392 70f. orange . . . . 2·50 4·50
393 80f. green . . . . 85 2·50
394 90f. grey . . . . 2·50 5·50
395 100f. red (24 × 29½ mm) . . 2·20 7·00
396 200f. lilac (24 × 29½ mm) 5·50 20·00

(b) With "F" after figure of value.
406 **99** 1f. grey 15 15
407 3f. blue 15 15
408 5f. green 15 15
409 6f. brown 15 40
410 10f. violet 15 20
411 12f. orange 15 15
412 15f. green 35 15
413 18f. grey . . . . 1·70 4·50
414 20f. green . . . . 1·00 2·50
415 25f. brown 45 35
416 30f. mauve 85 35
417 35f. brown . . . . 1·90 3·00
418 45f. green . . . . 1·70 3·50
419 50f. brown . . . . 85 1·60
420 70f. green . . . . 4·25 4·75
421 80f. blue . . . . 2·10 4·50
422 90f. red . . . . 5·25 5·50
423 100f. orange (24 × 29½ mm) 4·00 6·50
424 200f. green (24 × 29½ mm) 8·00 20·00
425 300f. blue (24 × 29½ mm) 8·50 24·00

100 Iron Foundry

101 Arms of Merzig and St. Pierre Church

1957. Saar Fair.
397 **100** 15f. red and black 10 25

1957. Centenary of Merzig.
398 **101** 15f. blue 10 25

101a "Europa" Tree

101b Young Miner

1957. Europa.
399 **101a** 20f. orange and yellow 35 85
400 35f. violet and pink . . . 70 1·00

1957. Humanitarian Relief Fund.
401 **101b** 6f.+4f. black & brown 10 15
402 – 12f.+6f. black & green 15 20
403 – 15f.+7f. black and red 30 40
404 – 30f.+10f. black & blue 35 60
DESIGNS: 12f. Miner drilling at coalface; 15f. Miner with coal-cutting machine; 30f. Operator at mine lift-shaft.

101c Carrier Pigeons

101d Max and Moritz (cartoon characters)

1957. International Correspondence Week.
405 **101c** 15f. black and red . . . 15 25

1958. 150th Death Anniv of Wilhelm Busch (writer and illustrator).
426 **101d** 12f. green and black . . 15 20
427 – 15f. red and black . . . 20 35
DESIGN: 15f. Wilhelm Busch.

101e "Prevent Forest Fires"

101g "The Fox who stole the Goose"

101f Diesel and First Oil Engine

1958. Forest Fires Prevention Campaign.
428 **101e** 15f. black and red . . . 15 25

1958. Birth Centenary of Rudolf Diesel (engineer).
429 **101f** 12f. green 10 25

1958. Berlin Students' Fund.
430 **101g** 12f.+6f. red, black and green 15 20
431 – 15f.+7f. brown, green and red 15 35
DESIGN: 15f. "A Hunter from the Palatinate".

102 Saarbrucken Town Hall and Fair Emblem

103 Homburg

1958. Saar Fair.
432 **102** 15f. purple 10 25

1958. 400th Anniv of Homburg.
433 **103** 15f. green 10 25

103a Emblem

103b Schulze-Delitzsch

1958. 150th Anniv of German Gymnastics.
434 **103a** 12f. black, green and grey 10 25

1958. 150th Birth of Schulze-Delitzsch (pioneer of German Co-operative Movement).
435 **103b** 12f. green 10 25

103c "Europa"

103d Friedrich Raiffeisen (philanthropist)

1958. Europa.
436 **103c** 12f. blue and green . . . 50 85
437 – 30f. red and blue . . . . 70 1·40

1958. Humanitarian Relief and Welfare Funds.
438 **103d** 6f.+4f. brn, lt brn & chest 15 15
439 – 12f.+6f. red, yell & grn 15 30
440 – 15f.+7f. blue, grn & red 35 40
441 – 30f.+10f. yellow, grn & bl 40 60
DESIGNS—Inscr "WOHLFAHRTSMARKE": 12f. Dairymaid; 15f. Vine-dresser 30f. Farm labourer.

103e Fugger

104 Hands holding Crates

1959. 500th Birth Anniv of Jakob Fugger (merchant prince).
442 **103e** 15f. black and red . . . 10 25

1959. Saar Fair.
443 **104** 15f. red 10 25

105 Saarbrucken

105a Humboldt

1959. 50th Anniv of Greater Saarbrucken.
444 **105** 15f. blue 10 25

1959. Death Centenary of Alexander von Humboldt (naturalist).
445 **105a** 15f. blue 10 25

OFFICIAL STAMPS

1922. Nos. 84 to 94 optd **DIENSTMARKE**.

O 98	3c. green	2·40	31·00
O 99	5c. black and orange	75	30
O100	10c. green	1·00	30
O101	15c. brown	1·00	30
O109	15c. orange	4·75	40
O102	20c. blue and yellow	1·00	30
O111	25c. red and yellow	4·75	40
O104	30c. red and yellow	1·20	30
O105	40c. brown and yellow	1·60	30
O106	50c. blue and yellow	1·60	30
O112	75c. green and yellow	12·50	2·20
O108a	1f. brown	27·00	2·20

1927. Nos. 108/15, 117 and 119 optd **DIENSTMARKE**.

O128	10c. brown	5·50	2·10
O129	15c. green	5·50	5·75
O130	20c. brown	5·50	1·40
O131	25c. blue	7·50	5·50
O122	30c. green	5·50	45
O133	40c. brown	6·50	30
O134	50c. red	10·50	30
O135	60c. orange	3·75	30
O136	75c. purple	6·25	70
O137	1f. violet	8·50	35
O138	2f. red	8·50	35

O 51 Arms

1949.

O264	O 51	10c. red	40	17·00
O265		30c. black	30	20·00
O266		1f. green	30	50
O267		2f. red	1·40	1·40
O268		5f. blue	1·90	50
O269		10f. black	75	50
O270		12f. mauve	6·50	11·00
O271		15f. blue	70	50
O272		20f. green	1·70	1·40
O273		30f. mauve	1·20	4·50
O274		50f. purple	1·20	3·75
O275		100f. brown	60·00	£350

SABAH Pt. 1

Formerly North Borneo, now part of Malaysia.

100 cents = 1 Malaysian dollar.

1964. Nos. 391/406 of North Borneo optd **SABAH**.

408	1c. green and red	10	10
409	4c. olive and orange	15	50
410	5c. sepia and violet	30	10
411	6c. black and turquoise	80	10
412	10c. green and red	1·25	10
413	12c. brown and myrtle	20	10
414	20c. turquoise and blue	3·50	10
415	25c. black and red	75	90
416	30c. sepia and olive	30	10
417	35c. slate and brown	30	20
418	50c. green and bistre	30	10
419	75c. blue and purple	3·25	65
420	$1 brown and green	6·50	65
421	$2 brown and slate	13·00	2·00
422	$5 green and purple	13·00	12·00
423	$10 red and blue	13·00	27·00

138 "Vanda hookeriana"

1965. As No. 115/21 of Kedah, but with Arms of Sabah inset as T **138**.

424	138	1c. multicoloured	10	1·25
425	–	2c. multicoloured	10	1·50
426	–	5c. multicoloured	10	10
427	–	6c. multicoloured	30	1·50
428	–	10c. multicoloured	30	10
429	–	15c. multicoloured	2·00	10
430	–	20c. multicoloured	2·75	75

The higher values used in Sabah were Nos. 20/7 of Malaysia.

139 "Hebomoia glaucippe"

1971. Butterflies. As Nos. 124/30 of Kedah, but with Sabah Arms inset as T **139**.

432	–	1c. multicoloured	65	2·50
433	–	2c. multicoloured	75	2·50
434	–	5c. multicoloured	80	50
435	–	6c. multicoloured	1·00	2·00
436	139	10c. multicoloured	80	15
437	–	15c. multicoloured	1·00	10
438	–	20c. multicoloured	1·10	1·25

The higher values in use with this issue were Nos. 64/71 of Malaysia.

140 "Hibiscus rosa-sinensis"

141 Coffee

1979. As Nos. 135/41 of Kedah, but with Arms of Sabah as T **140**.

445	1c. "Rafflesia hasseltii"	10	1·60
446	2c. "Pterocarpus indicus"	10	1·60
447	5c. "Lagerstroemia speciosa"	15	50
448	10c. "Durio zibethinus"	30	10
449	15c. Type **140**	50	10
450	20c. "Rhododendron scortechinii"	30	10
451	25c. "Etlingera elatior" (inscr "Phaeomeria speciosa")	65	20

The higher values in use with this issue were Nos. 190/7 of Malaysia.

1986. As Nos. 152/8 of Kedah but with Arms of Sabah as in T **141**.

459	1c. Type **141**	10	10
460	2c. Coconuts	10	10
461	5c. Cocoa	10	10
462	10c. Black pepper	10	10
463	15c. Rubber	10	10
464	20c. Oil palm	10	10
465	30c. Rice	10	15

ST. CHRISTOPHER Pt. 1

One of the Leeward Is. Stamps superseded in 1890 by Leeward Islands general issue.

12 pence = 1 shilling.

1

1870.

11	1	½d. green	1·75	1·75
6		1d. mauve	65·00	7·00
13		1d. red	1·50	2·25
14		2½d. brown	£180	60·00
16		2½d. blue	2·00	1·50
8		4d. blue	£200	15·00
18		4d. grey	1·50	1·00
9		6d. green	55·00	5·00
19		6d. olive	85·00	£375
20		1s. mauve	90·00	65·00

1885. Surch in words.

23	1	½d. on half of 1d. red	25·00	40·00
26		1d. on ½d. green	38·00	45·00
28		1d. on 2½d. blue	65·00	65·00
24		1d. on 6d. green	20·00	30·00
22		4d. on 6d. green	65·00	50·00

1886. Surch in figures.
25 **1** 4d. on 6d. green . . . . . . 48·00 90·00

ST. HELENA Pt. 1

An island in the South Atlantic Ocean, west of Africa.

1856. 12 pence = 1 shilling;
20 shillings = 1 pound.
1971. 100 pence = 1 pound.

1

11

The early stamps of St. Helena, other than the 6d., were formed by printing the 6d., in various colours and surcharging it with new values in words or (in case of the 2½d.) in figures.

1856. Imperf.

3	1	1d. on 6d. red	£110	£160
5		4d. on 6d. red	£500	£250
1		6d. blue	£500	£180

1861. Perf.

36	1	½d. on 6d. green	2·25	2·50
37		1d. on 6d. red	4·25	3·50
39		2d. on 6d. yellow	2·25	7·00
40		2½d. on 6d. blue	2·75	5·50
42		3d. on 6d. purple	4·75	4·75
14		4d. on 6d. red	90·00	50·00
43c		4d. on 6d. brown	24·00	16·00
25		6d. blue	£350	50·00
44		6d. grey	20·00	4·75
30		1s. on 6d. green	20·00	12·00
20		5s. on 6d. yellow	50·00	60·00

1890.

46	11	½d. green	2·75	6·00
47		1d. red	15·00	1·75
48		1½d. brown and green	4·50	7·50
49		2d. yellow	5·00	12·00
50		2½d. blue	13·00	12·00
51		5d. violet	11·00	29·00
52		10d. brown	23·00	60·00

12

13 Government House

14 The Wharf

1902. Inscr "POSTAGE POSTAGE".

53	12	½d. green	1·50	2·50
54		1d. red	7·00	70

1903.

55	13	½d. brown and green	2·00	3·25
56	14	1d. black and red	1·50	35
57	13	2d. black and green	6·50	1·25
58	14	8d. black and brown	22·00	32·00
59	13	1s. brown and orange	23·00	40·00
60	14	2s. black and violet	48·00	85·00

1908. Inscr "POSTAGE & REVENUE".

64	12	2½d. blue	1·50	1·50
66a		4d. black and red on yellow	3·00	18·00
67a		6d. purple	4·75	14·00
71		10s. green and red on green	£190	£250

1912. As T **13/14** but with medallion of King George V.

72	13	½d. black and green	2·25	10·00
73	14	1d. black and red	4·75	1·75
89		1d. green	1·75	29·00
74		1½d. black and orange	3·50	6·00
90		1½d. red	10·00	29·00
75	13	2d. black and grey	4·50	1·75
76	14	2½d. black and blue	3·50	5·50
77	13	3d. black & purple on yellow	3·50	5·00
91		3d. blue	19·00	60·00
78	14	8d. black and purple	7·00	50·00
79	13	1s. black on green	9·00	35·00
80	14	2s. black and blue on blue	40·00	80·00
81		3s. black and violet	55·00	£130

18

22 Badge of St. Helena

1912. Inscr "POSTAGE & REVENUE".

83	18	4d. black and red on yellow	12·00	25·00
84		6d. purple	4·00	5·00

1913. Inscr "POSTAGE POSTAGE".

85	18	4d. black and red on yellow	8·00	2·75
86		6d. purple	14·00	28·00

1916. Surch **WAR TAX ONE PENNY**.
87 1d.+1d. black and red (No. 73) . . . . 1·75 3·25

1919. Surch **WAR TAX 1d.**
88 1d.+1d. black and red (No. 73) . . . . 1·50 4·50

1922.

97 **22** ½d. grey and black . . . . 2·25 2·25
98 1d. grey and green . . . . 2·50 1·60
99 1½d. red . . . . 2·75 13·00
100 2d. grey and brown . . . 3·75 2·00
101 3d. blue . . . . 2·00 4·00
92 4d. grey and black on yellow . . . . 11·00 6·00
103 5d. green and red on green 3·00 5·50
104 6d. grey and purple . . . . 4·50 8·00
105 8d. grey and violet . . . . 3·75 7·00
106 1s. grey and brown . . . . 6·50 9·00
107 1s.6d. grey & green on grn 15·00 45·00
108 2s. purple and blue on blue 17·00 42·00
109 2s.6d. grey & red on yellow 14·00 60·00
110 5s. grey and green on yellow . . . . 38·00 75·00
111 7s.6d. grey and orange . . 80·00 £120
112 10s. grey and green £110 £170
113 15s. grey and purple on blue £850 £1500
96 £1 grey and purple on red £400 £450

23 Lot and Lot's Wife

1934. Centenary of British Colonization.
114 **23** ½d. black and purple . . . 1·00 80
115 – 1d. black and green . . . 65 85
116 – 1½d. black and red . . . . 2·50 3·25
117 – 2d. black and orange . . . 2·25 1·25
118 – 3d. black and blue . . . . 1·40 4·50
119 – 6d. black and blue . . . . 3·25 3·00
120 – 1s. black and brown . . . 6·50 18·00
121 – 2s.6d. black and red . . . 35·00 48·00
122 – 5s. black and brown . . . 75·00 80·00
123 – 10s. black and purple . . . £225 £250
DESIGNS—HORIZ: 1d. The "Plantation"; 1½d. Map of St. Helena; 2d. Quay, Jamestown; 3d. James Valley; 6d. Jamestown; 1s. Munden's Promontory; 5s. High Knoll; 10s. Badge of St. Helena. VERT: 2s.6d. St. Helena.

32a Windsor Castle

1935. Silver Jubilee.
124 **32a** 1½d. blue and red . . . . 1·00 5·50
125 2d. blue and grey . . . . 1·50 90
126 6d. green and blue . . . . 7·00 3·25
127 1s. grey and purple . . . 13·00 15·00

32b King George VI and Queen Elizabeth

1937. Coronation.
128 **32b** 1d. green 40 75
129 2d. orange 55 45
130 3d. blue 80 50

33 Badge of St. Helena

1938.

131 **33** ½d. violet 10 65
132 1d. green . . . . 9·00 2·25
132a 1d. orange 20 30
149 1d. black and green . . . 1·00 1·50
133 1½d. red 20 40
150 1½d. black and red . . . 1·00 1·50
134 2d. orange 20 15
151 2d. black and red . . . . 1·00 1·50
135 3d. blue . . . . 80·00 18·00
135a 3d. grey 30 30
135b 4d. blue . . . . 2·00 80
136 6d. blue . . . . 2·00 1·25
136a 8d. green . . . . 3·25 90
137 1s. brown . . . . 1·00 30
138 2s.6d. purple . . . . . . 17·00 6·50
139 5s. brown . . . . 18·00 12·00
140 10s. purple . . . . 18·00 18·00

33a Houses of Parliament, London

1946. Victory.
141 **33a** 2d. orange 30 40
142 4d. blue 30 30

33b King George VI and Queen Elizabeth

33c King George VI and Queen Elizabeth

1948. Silver Wedding.
143 **33b** 3d. black 30 30
144 **33c** 10s. blue . . . . 25·00 30·00

33d Hermes, Globe and Forms of Transport

33e Hemispheres, Jet-powered Vickers Viking Airliner and Steamer

33f Hermes and Globe

33g U.P.U. Monument

1949. U.P.U.
145 **33d** 3d. red . . . . 25 1·00
146 **33e** 4d. blue . . . . 3·00 1·40
147 **33f** 6d. green . . . . 45 1·75
148 **33g** 1s. black . . . . 35 1·10

33h Queen Elizabeth II

34 Badge of St. Helena

1953. Coronation.
152 **33h** 3d. black and lilac . . . . 1·00 1·50

1953.

153 **34** ½d. black and green . . . 30 30
154 – 1d. black and green . . . 15 20
155 – 1½d. black and purple . . . 3·00 1·50
156 – 2d. black and red 50 30
157 – 2½d. black and red 40 30
158 – 3d. black and brown . . . 3·25 30
159 – 4d. black and blue . . . . 40 1·00
160 – 6d. black and violet . . . 40 30
161 – 7d. black and grey . . . . 65 1·75
162 – 1s. black and red 40 70
163 – 2s.6d. black and violet . . 11·00 5·50
164 – 5s. black and sepia . . . . 14·00 8·00
165 – 10s. black and yellow . . . 32·00 13·00
DESIGNS—HORIZ: 1d. Flax plantation; 2d. Lace-making; 2½d. Drying flax; 3d. St. Helena sand plover; 4d. Flagstaff and The Barn (hills); 6d. Donkeys carrying flax; 7d. Map; 1s. The Castle; 2s.6d. Cutting flax; 5s. Jamestown; 10s. Longwood House. VERT: 1½d. Heart-shaped Waterfall.

45 Stamp of 1856

47 East Indiaman "London" off James Bay

1956. Cent of First St. Helena Postage Stamp.
166 **45** 3d. blue and red 10 10
167 4d. blue and brown 10 20
168 6d. blue and purple 15 25

1959. Tercentenary of Settlement.
169 – 3d. black and red 10 15
170 **47** 6d. green and blue 40 75
171 – 1s. black and orange . . . 40 75
DESIGNS—HORIZ: 3d. Arms of East India Company; 1s. Commemoration Stone.

1961. Tristan Relief Fund. Nos. 46 and 49/51 of Tristan da Cunha surch **ST. HELENA Tristan Relief** and premium.
172 2½c.+3d. black and red . . . £1000 £450
173 5c.+6d. black and blue . . . £1100 £475
174 7½c.+9d. black and red . . . £1600 £600
175 10c.+1s. black and brown . . £1800 £700

50 St. Helena Butterflyfish

63 Queen Elizabeth II with Prince Andrew (after Cecil Beaton)

1961.

176 **50** 1d. multicoloured 40 20
177 – 1½d. multicoloured 50 20
178 – 2d. red and grey 15 20
179 – 3d. multicoloured 70 20
180 – 4½d. multicoloured 60 60
181 – 6d. red, sepia and olive . . 5·50 70
182 – 7d. brown, black and violet 35 70
183 – 10d. purple and blue . . . 35 70
184 – 1s. yellow, green and brown . . . . 55 1·25
185 – 1s.6d. grey and blue . . . 11·00 4·75
186 – 2s.6d. red, yellow & turq 2·50 2·50
187 – 5s. yellow, brown and green . . . . 13·00 4·25
188 – 10s. red, black and blue . . 13·00 10·00
189 **63** £1 brown and blue . . . . 12·00 14·00
DESIGNS—VERT (as Type **50**): 1½d. Yellow canary; 3d. Queen Elizabeth II; 4½d. Red-wood flower; 6d. Madagascar red fody; 1s. Gum-wood flower; 1s.6d. White tern; 5s. Night-blooming Cereus. HORIZ (as T **50**): 2d. Brittle starfish; 7d. Trumpetfish; 10d. Feather starfish; 2s.6d. Orange starfish; 10s. Deep-water bullseye.

63a Protein Foods

1963. Freedom from Hunger.
190 **63a** 1s.6d. blue 75 40

63b Red Cross Emblem

1963. Centenary of Red Cross.
191 **63b** 3d. red and black 30 25
192 1s.6d. red and blue . . . 70 1·50

1965. First Local Post. Optd **FIRST LOCAL POST 4th JANUARY 1965.**
193 **50** 1d. multicoloured 10 25
194 – 3d. multicoloured (No. 179) 10 25
195 – 6d. red, sepia and olive (No. 181) 40 30
196 – 1s.6d. grey & blue (No. 185) 60 35

64a I.T.U. Emblem

1965. Centenary of I.T.U.
197 **64a** 3d. blue and brown . . . 25 25
198 6d. purple and green . . . 35 25

64b I.C.Y. Emblem

1965. Centenary of I.C.Y.
199 **64b** 1d. purple and turquoise 30 15
200 6d. green and lavender . . 30 15

64c Sir Winston Churchill and St. Paul's Cathedral in Wartime

1966. Churchill Commemoration.
201 **64c** 1d. blue 15 20
202 3d. green 25 20
203 6d. brown 40 25
204 1s.6d. violet 45 75

64d Footballer's Legs, Ball and Jules Rimet Cup

1966. World Cup Football Championship.
205 **64d** 3d. multicoloured 50 35
206 6d. multicoloured 75 35

64e W.H.O. Emblem

1966. Inauguration of W.H.O. Headquarters, Geneva.
207 **64e** 3d. black, green and blue 75 20
208 1s.6d. black, purple & ochre . . . . 2·25 1·00

64f "Education"

64g "Science"

64h "Culture"

1966. 20th Anniv of UNESCO.
209 **64f** 3d. multicoloured 75 20
210 **64g** 6d. yellow, violet and olive . . . . 1·25 50
211 **64h** 1s.6d. black, purple & orge . . . . 2·00 1·75

65 Badge of St. Helena

1967. New Constitution.
212 **65** 1s. multicoloured 10 10
213 2s.6d. multicoloured . . . 20 20

66 Fire of London

1967. 300th Anniv of Arrival of Settlers after Great Fire of London.
214 **66** 1d. red and black 15 10
215 – 3d. blue and black 20 10
216 – 6d. violet and black . . . 20 15
217 – 1s.6d. green and black . . 20 20
DESIGNS: 3d. East Indiaman "Charles"; 6d. Settlers landing at Jamestown; 1s.6d. Settlers clearing scrub.

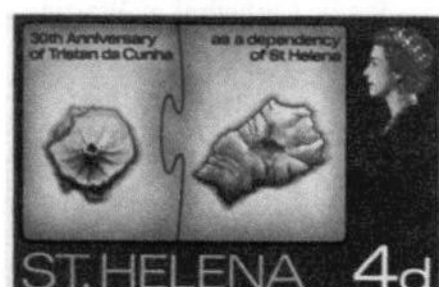

70 Interlocking Maps of Tristan and St. Helena

1968. 30th Anniv of Tristan da Cunha as a Dependency of St. Helena.
218 **70** 4d. purple and brown . . . 10 10
219 – 8d. olive and brown . . . 10 30
220 **70** 1s.9d. blue and brown . . 10 40
221 – 2s.3d. blue and brown . . 15 40
DESIGNS: 8d. and 2s.3d. Interlocking maps of Tristan and St. Helena (different).

72 Queen Elizabeth and Sir Hudson Lowe

1968. 150th Anniv of Abolition of Slavery in St. Helena.
222 **72** 3d. multicoloured 10 15
223 9d. multicoloured 10 20
224 – 1s.6d. multicoloured . . . 15 30
225 – 2s.6d. multicoloured . . . 25 45
DESIGN: Nos. 224 and 225, Queen Elizabeth and Sir George Bingham.

74 Blue Gum Eucalyptus and Road Construction

1968. Multicoloured.
226 ½d. Type **74** 10 10
227 1d. Electricity development 10 10
228 1½d. Dental unit 15 10
229 2d. Pest control 15 10
230 3d. Flats in Jamestown . . . 30 10
231 4d. Livestock improvement 20 10
232 6d. Schools broadcasting . . 50 10
233 8d. Country Cottages 30 10
234 10d. New school buildings . . 30 10
235 1s. Reafforestation 30 10
236 1s.6d. Heavy lift crane . . . 70 2·75
237 2s.6d. Lady Field Children's Home . . . . 70 3·25
238 5s. Agricultural training . . . 70 3·50
239 10s. New General Hospital 2·00 4·00
240 £1 Lifeboat "John Dutton" 6·00 15·00
PLANTS SHOWN: ½, 4d., 1s.6d. Blue gum eucalyptus; 1d., 6d., 2s.6d. Cabbage-tree; 1½d., 8d., 5s. St. Helena redwood; 2, 10d., 10s. Scrubweed; 3d., 1s., £1 Tree-fern.

89 Brig "Perseverance"

1969. Mail Communications. Multicoloured.
241 4d. Type **89** 20 20
242 8d. "Phoebe" (screw steamer) 25 40
243 1s.9d. "Llandovery Castle" (liner) 25 60
244 2s.3d. "Good Hope Castle" (cargo liner) 25 75

93 W.O. and Drummer of the 53rd Foot, 1815

1969. Military Uniforms. Multicoloured.
245 6d. Type **93** 15 25
246 8d. Officer and Surgeon, 20th Foot, 1816 . . . . 15 25
247 1s.8d. Drum Major, 66th Foot, 1816, and Royal Artillery Officer, 1920 . . . 20 45
248 2s.6d. Private, 91st Foot, and 2nd Corporal, Royal Sappers and Miners, 1832 20 55

97 Dickens, Mr. Pickwick and Job Trotter ("Pickwick Papers")

1970. Death Cent of Charles Dickens. Mult.
249 4d. Type **97** 40 15
250 8d. Mr. Bumble and Oliver ("Oliver Twist") 50 15
251 1s.6d. Sairey Gamp and Mark Tapley ("Martin Chuzzlewit") 60 20
252 2s.6d. Jo and Mr. Turveydrop ("Bleak House") 70 25
All designs include a portrait of Dickens as Type **97**.

98 "Kiss of Life"

1970. Centenary of British Red Cross.
253 **98** 6d. bistre, red and black 15 15
254 – 9d. green, red and black 15 20
255 – 1s.9d. grey, red and black 20 30
256 – 2s.3d. lilac, red and black 20 45
DESIGNS: 9d. Nurse with girl in wheelchair; 1s.9d. Nurse bandaging child's knee; 2s.3d. Red Cross emblem.

99 Officer's Shako Plate (20th Foot)

1970. Military Equipment (1st issue). Mult.
257 4d. Type **99** 20 20
258 9d. Officer's breast plate (66th Foot) 25 30
259 1s.3d. Officer's Full Dress shako (91st Foot) 25 40
260 2s.11d. Ensign's shako (53rd Foot) 30 60
See also Nos. 281/4, 285/8 and 291/4.

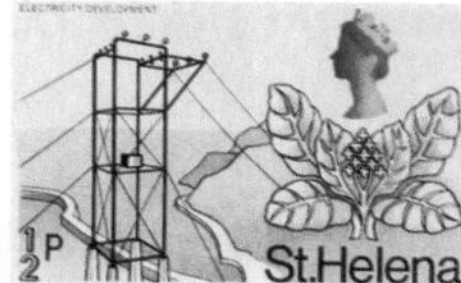

100 Electricity Development

1971. Decimal Currency. Designs as Nos. 227/40, inscr as T **100**.
261 ½p. multicoloured 10 10
262 1p. multicoloured 10 10
263 1½p. multicoloured 10 10
264 2p. multicoloured . . . . . 1·75 1·00
265 2½p. multicoloured 10 10
266 3½p. multicoloured 30 10
267 4½p. multicoloured 10 10
268 5p. multicoloured 10 10
269 7½p. multicoloured 40 35
270 10p. multicoloured 30 35
271 12½p. muticoloured 30 50
272 25p. multicoloured . . . . . 60 1·25
273 50p. multicoloured . . . . . 1·00 2·00
274 £1 multicoloured . . . . . . 20·00 15·00

101 St. Helena holding the "True Cross"

102 Napoleon (after painting by J. L. David) and Tomb on St. Helena

1971. Easter.
275 **101** 2p. multicoloured 10 10
276 5p. multicoloured 10 15
277 7½p. multicoloured . . . 15 20
278 12½p. multicoloured . . . 20 25

1971. 150th Death Anniv of Napoleon. Mult.
279 2p. Type **102** 20 50
280 34p. "Napoleon at St. Helena" (H. Delaroche) 45 1·00

1971. Military Equipment (2nd issue). As T **99**. Multicoloured.
281 1½p. Artillery Private's hanger 20 30
282 4p. Baker rifle and socket bayonet 25 60
283 6p. Infantry Officer's sword 25 80
284 22½p. Baker rifle and sword bayonet . . . . 40 1·25

1972. Military Equipment (3rd issue). As T **99**. Multicoloured.
285 2p. multicoloured 15 20
286 5p. lilac, blue and black . . . 15 40
287 7½p. multicoloured 20 50
288 12½p. sepia, brown and black 30 60
DESIGNS: 2p. Royal Sappers and Miners breast-plate, post 1823; 5p. Infantry sergeant's spontoon, c. 1830; 7½p. Royal Artillery officer's breast-plate, c. 1830; 12½p. English military pistol, c. 1800.

103 St. Helena Sand Plover and White Tern

1972. Royal Silver Wedding.
289 **103** 2p. green 20 40
290 16p. brown 30 85

1973. Military Equipment (4th issue). As T **99**. Multicoloured.
291 2p. Other Rank's shako, 53rd Foot, 1815 . . . . 25 55
292 5p. Band and Drums sword, 1830 . . . . 30 1·00
293 7½p. Royal Sappers and Miners Officer's hat, 1830 40 1·25
294 12½p. General's sword, 1831 45 1·50

103a Princess Anne and Captain Mark Phillips

1973. Royal Wedding. Multicoloured, background colours given.
295 **103a** 2p. blue 15 10
296 18p. green 25 20

104 "Westminster" and "Claudine" beached, 1849

1973. Tercentenary of East India Company Charter. Multicoloured.
297 1½p. Type **104** 30 55
298 4p. "True Brition", 1790 . . 40 80
299 6p. "General Goddard" in action, 1795 . . . . 40 80
300 22½p. "Kent" burning in the Bay of Biscay, 1825 . . . 85 2·25

105 U.P.U. Emblem and Ships

1974. Centenary of U.P.U. Multicoloured.
301 5p. Type **105** 20 25
302 25p. U.P.U. emblem and letters 40 55
MS303 89 × 84 mm. Nos. 301/2 75 1·50

106 Churchill in Sailor Suit and Blenheim Palace

1974. Birth Cent of Sir Winston Churchill.
304 **106** 5p. multicoloured 20 20
305 – 25p. black, pink and purple 30 60
MS306 108 × 93 mm. Nos. 304/5 75 2·00
DESIGN: 25p. Churchill and River Thames.

107 Capt. Cook and H.M.S. "Resolution"

108 "Mellissia begonifolia" (tree)

1975. Bicentenary of Capt. Cook's Return to St. Helena. Multicoloured.
307 5p. Type **107** 30 20
308 25p. Capt. Cook and Jamestown 40 40

1975. Centenary of Publication of "St. Helena" by J. C. Melliss. Multicoloured.
310 2p. Type **108** 15 30
311 5p. "Mellissius adumbratus" (beetle) 15 35
312 12p. St. Helena sand plover (bird) (horiz) 50 80
313 25p. Melliss's scorpionfish (horiz) . . . . 50 1·00

109 £1 Note

1976. First Issue of Currency Notes. Mult.
314 8p. Type **109** 30 30
315 33p. £5 Note 60 80

110 1d. Stamp of 1863

1976. Festival of Stamps, London.
316 **110** 5p. brown, black and pink 15 15
317 – 8p. black, green & lt green 20 30
318 – 25p. multicoloured . . . 35 45
DESIGNS—VERT: 8p. 1d. stamp of 1922. HORIZ: 25p. Mail carrier "Good Hope Castle".

111 "High Knoll, 1806" (Capt. Barnett)

1976. Aquatints and Lithographs of St. Helena. Multicoloured.
319B 1p. Type **111** 30 75
320A 3p. "The Friar Rock, 1815" (G. Bellasis) . . . . . . 40 1·25
321A 5p. "The Column Lot, 1815" (G. Bellasis) . . . 30 1·25
322A 6p. "Sandy Bay Valley, 1809" (H. Salt) . . . . . 30 1·25
323A 8p. "Scene from Castle Terrace, 1815" (G. Bellasis) . . . . . . 40 1·25
324A 9p. "The Briars, 1815" . . 40 1·25
325A 10p. "Plantation House, 1821" (J. Wathen) . . . 50 60
326A 15p. "Longwood House, 1821" (J. Wathen) . . . 45 55
327A 18p. "St. Paul's Church" (V. Brooks) . . . . . . 45 1·50
328A 26p. "St. James's Valley, 1815" (Capt. Hastings) 45 1·50
329A 40p. "St. Matthew's Church, 1860" (V. Brooks) . . . . . . 70 1·75
330A £1 "St. Helena, 1815" (G. Bellasis) . . . . . . 1·25 3·75
331B £2 "Sugar Loaf Hill, 1821" (J. Wathen) . . . . . . 2·00 5·00
Nos. 330A and 331B are larger, 47 × 34 mm.
The 1 and 10p. and the £2 come with or without date imprint.

112 Duke of Edinburgh paying Homage

1977. Silver Jubilee. Multicoloured.
332 8p. Royal Visit, 1947 . . . . 10 20
333 15p. Queen's sceptre with dove 20 25
334 26p. Type **112** 30 35

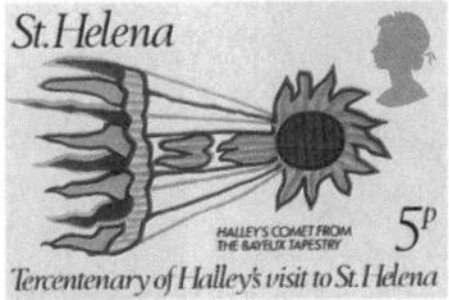

113 Halley's Comet (from Bayeux Tapestry)

1977. Tercentenary of Halley's Visit. Mult.
335 5p. Type **113** 35 25
336 8p. Late 17th-century sextant 50 25
337 27p. Halley and Halley's Mount, St. Helena . . . . 1·00 60

114 Sea Lion

1978. 25th Anniv of Coronation.
338 – 25p. agate, red and silver 30 50
339 – 25p. multicoloured . . . 30 50
340 **114** 25p. agate, red and silver 30 50
DESIGNS: No. 338, Black Dragon of Ulster; No. 339, Queen Elizabeth II.

115 Period Engraving of St. Helena

1978. Wreck of the "Witte Leeuw". Multicoloured.
341 3p. Type **115** 15 15
342 5p. Chinese porcelain 15 20
343 8p. Bronze cannon 15 30
344 9p. Chinese porcelain (different) 15 35
345 15p. Pewter mug and ceramic flasks 20 55
346 20p. Dutch East Indiaman 30 70

116 H.M.S. "Discovery" **117** Sir Rowland Hill

1979. Bicentenary of Captain Cook's Voyages, 1768–79. Multicoloured.
347 3p. Type **116** 15 15
348 8p. Cook's portable observatory 15 25
349 12p. "Pharnaceum acidum" (sketch by Joseph Banks) 20 35
350 25p. Flaxman/Wedgwood medallion of Capt. Cook 30 90

1979. Death Centenary of Sir Rowland Hill.
351 **117** 5p. multicoloured 10 15
352 – 8p. multicoloured 15 20
353 – 20p. multicoloured . . . 30 40
354 – 32p. black, magenta & mve 40 55
DESIGNS—HORIZ: 8p. 1965 1d. First Local Post stamp; 20p. 1863 1d. on 6d. surcharged stamp; 32p. 1902 1d. stamp.

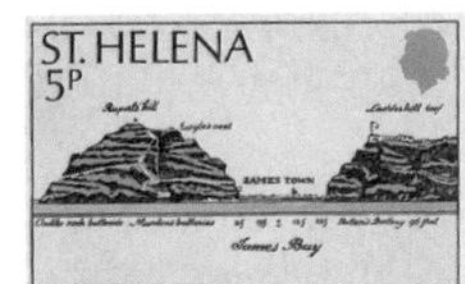

118 R. F. Seal's Chart of 1823 showing the Elevation of the Coastline

1979. 150th Anniv of Inclined Plane.
355 **118** 5p. black, grey and stone 15 15
356 – 8p. black, grey and stone 15 20
357 – 50p. multicoloured . . . 60 75
DESIGNS—HORIZ: 8p. The Inclined Plane in 1829; VERT: 50p. The Inclined Plane in 1979.

119 Napoleon's Tomb, 1848

1980. Centenary of Empress Eugenie's Visit.
358 **119** 5p. brown, pink and gold 10 20
359 – 8p. brown, stone and gold 15 25
360 – 62p. brown, flesh and gold 65 80
MS361 180 × 110 mm. Nos. 358/60 80 1·10
DESIGNS: 8p. Landing at St. Helena; 62p. The Empress at Napoleon's Tomb.

120 East Indiaman

1980. "London 1980" Int Stamp Exhibition. Mult.
362 5p. Type **120** 10 15
363 8p. "Dolphin" postal stone 10 15
364 47p. Postal stone outside Castle entrance, Jamestown 50 60
MS365 111 × 120 mm. Nos. 362/4 60 80

121 Queen Elizabeth the Queen Mother in 1974

1980. 80th Birthday of the Queen Mother.
366 **121** 24p. multicoloured . . . 35 50

122 The Briars, 1815

1980. 175th Anniv of Wellington's Visit. Multicoloured.
367 9p. Type **122** 15 15
368 30p. "Wellington" (Goya) (vert) 45 45

123 Redwood

1981. Endemic Plants. Multicoloured.
369 5p. Type **123** 15 20
370 8p. Old father live forever . . 15 20
371 15p. Gumwood 20 25
372 27p. Black cabbage 35 45

124 Detail from Reinel Portolan Chart, c. 1530

1981. Early Maps.
373 **124** 5p. multicoloured 15 15
374 – 8p. black, red and grey 15 20
375 – 20p. multicoloured . . . 30 35
376 – 30p. multicoloured . . . 35 50
MS377 114 × 83 mm. 24p. black and grey 40 65
DESIGNS: 8p. John Thornton's Map of St. Helena, c. 1700; 20p. Map of St. Helena, 1815; 24p. Part of Gastaldi's map of Africa, 16th-century; 30p. Map of St. Helena, 1817.

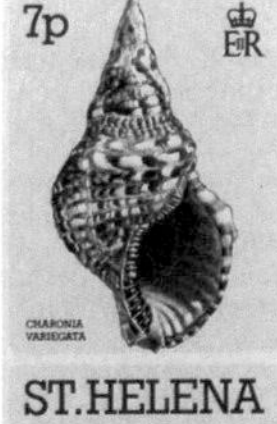

125 Prince Charles as Royal Navy Commander **126** Atlantic Trumpet Triton

1981. Royal Wedding. Multicoloured.
378 14p. Wedding bouquet from St. Helena 15 20
379 29p. Type **125** 25 30
380 32p. Prince Charles and Lady Diana Spencer 30 35

1981. Sea Shells. Multicoloured.
381 7p. Type **126** 15 20
382 10p. St. Helena cowrie . . . 15 20
383 25p. Common purple janthina 30 40
384 53p. Rude pen shell . . . . 50 1·00

127 Traffic Duty

1981. 25th Anniv of Duke of Edinburgh Award Scheme. Multicoloured.
385 7p. Type **127** 15 10
386 11p. Signposting 15 15
387 25p. Animal care 30 30
388 50p. Duke of Edinburgh, in Guard's uniform, on horseback 50 60

128 "Sympetrum dilatatum" (dragonfly)

1981. Insects (1st series). Multicoloured.
389 7p. Type **128** 20 20
390 10p. "Aplothorax burchelli" (beetle) 20 20
391 25p. "Ampulex compressa" (wasp) 35 35
392 32p. "Labidura herculeana" (earwig) 35 35
See also Nos. 411/14.

129 Charles Darwin

1982. 150th Anniv of Charles Darwin's Voyage. Multicoloured.
393 7p. Type **129** 20 20
394 14p. Flagstaff Hill and Darwin's hammer 25 35
395 25p. Common pheasant ("Ring-necked Pheasant") and Chukar partridge . . . 50 70
396 29p. H.M.S. "Beagle" off St. Helena 60 80

130 Prince and Princess of Wales at Balmoral, Autumn, 1981 **132** Lord Baden-Powell

1982. 21st Birthday of Princess of Wales. Multicoloured.
397 7p. St. Helena coat of arms 10 15
398 11p. Type **130** 25 15
399 29p. Bride on Palace balcony 30 35
400 55p. Formal portrait 70 60

1982. Commonwealth Games, Brisbane. Nos. 326 and 328 optd **1st PARTICIPATION COMMONWEALTH GAMES 1982.**
401 15p. "Longwood House, 1821" (J. Wathen) 25 25
402 26p. "St. James's Valley, 1815" (Capt. Hastings) . . 45 45

1982. 75th Anniv of Boy Scout Movement.
403 **132** 3p. brown, grey and yellow 15 15
404 – 11p. brown, grey and green 20 25
405 – 29p. brown, grey & orange 30 60
406 – 59p. brown, grey and green . . . . 60 1·25

DESIGNS—HORIZ: 11p. Boy Scout (drawing by Lord Baden-Powell); 59p. Camping at Thompsons Wood. VERT: 29p. Canon Walcott.

133 King and Queen Rocks

134 "Trametes versicolor" ("Coriolus versicolor")

1982. Views of St. Helena by Roland Svensson. Multicoloured.
407 7p. Type **133** 15 20
408 11p. "Turk's Cap" 15 25
409 29p. Coastline from Jamestown (horiz) 35 65
410 59p. "Mundens Point" (horiz) 60 1·40

1983. Insects (2nd series). As T **128**. Mult.
411 11p. "Acherontia atropos" (hawk moth) 15 30
412 15p. "Helenasaldula aberrans" (shore-bug) . . . 15 35
413 29p. "Anchastus compositarum" (click beetle) 25 55
414 59p. "Lamprochrus cossonoides" (weevil) . . . 55 1·25

1983. Fungi. Multicoloured.
415 11p. Type **134** 20 25
416 15p. "Pluteus brunneisucus" 20 40
417 29p. "Polyporus induratus" (horiz) 30 60
418 59p. "Coprinus angulatus" 55 1·25

135 Java Sparrow

136 Birth of St. Helena

1983. Birds. Multicoloured.
419 7p. Type **135** 30 20
420 15p. Madagascar red fody . . 45 35
421 33p. Common waxbill . . . 80 70
422 59p. Yellow canary . . . . . 1·50 1·40

1983. Christmas. Life of St. Helena (1st series). Multicoloured.
423 10p. Type **136** 20 35
424 15p. St. Helena being taken to convent 20 35
See also Nos. 450/3 and 468/71.

137 1934 Centenary ½d. Stamp

139 "St. Helena" (schooner)

138 Prince Andrew and H.M.S. "Invincible" (aircraft carrier)

1984. 150th Anniv of St. Helena as a British Colony. Multicoloured.
425 1p. Type **137** 10 20
426 3p. 1934 1d. stamp 10 20
427 6p. 1934 1½d. stamp 10 30
428 7p. 1934 2d. stamp 15 30
429 11p. 1934 3d. stamp 20 40
430 15p. 1934 6d. stamp 25 45
431 29p. 1934 1s. stamp 40 95
432 33p. 1934 5s. stamp . . . . 45 1·25
433 59p. 1934 10s. stamp . . . . 65 2·00
434 £1 1934 2s.6d. stamp . . . . 1·00 3·25
435 £2 St. Helena Coat of Arms 1·75 5·00

1984. Visit of Prince Andrew. Multicoloured.
436 11p. Type **138** 25 25
437 60p. Prince Andrew and H.M.S. "Herald" (survey ship) . . . . 75 1·40

1984. 250th Anniv of "Lloyd's List" (newspaper). Multicoloured.
438 10p. Type **139** 20 20
439 18p. Solomons Facade (local agent) 25 35
440 25p. Lloyd's Coffee House, London 30 55
441 50p. "Papanui" (freighter) . . 75 1·00

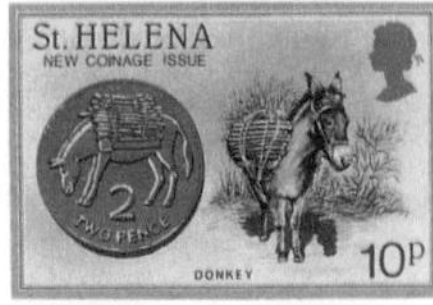

140 Twopenny Coin and Donkey

1984. New Coinage. Multicoloured.
442 10p. Type **140** 20 35
443 15p. Five pence coin and St. Helena sand plover . . 20 45
444 29p. Penny coin and yellow-finned tuna 30 75
445 50p. Ten pence coin and arum lily . . . . 40 1·25

141 Mrs. Rebecca Fuller (former Corps Secretary)

142 Queen Elizabeth the Queen Mother aged Two

1984. Centenary of Salvation Army on St. Helena. Multicoloured.
446 7p. Type **141** 15 35
447 11p. Meals-on-wheels service (horiz) 15 45
448 25p. Salvation Army Citadel, Jamestown (horiz) 20 80
449 60p. Salvation Army band at Jamestown Clock Tower 55 2·00

1984. Christmas. Life of St. Helena (2nd series). As T **136**. Multicoloured.
450 6p. St. Helena visits prisoners 15 20
451 10p. Betrothal of St. Helena 20 30
452 15p. Marriage of St. Helena to Constantius 25 40
453 33p. Birth of Constantine . . 50 70

1985. Life and Times of Queen Elizabeth the Queen Mother. Multicoloured.
454 11p. Type **142** 20 25
455 15p. At Ascot with the Queen 20 35
456 29p. Attending Gala Ballet at Covent Garden 40 65
457 55p. With Prince Henry at his christening . . . . 60 1·00
MS458 91 × 73 mm. 70p. The Queen Mother with Ford "V8 Pilot" 1·75 1·60

143 Axillary Cardinalfish

144 John J. Audubon

1985. Marine Life. Multicoloured.
459 7p. Type **143** 15 25
460 11p. Chub mackerel 15 30
461 15p. Skipjack tuna 20 40
462 33p. Yellow-finned tuna . . . 35 75
463 50p. Stump . . . . 50 1·25

1985. Birth Bicentenary of John J. Audubon (ornithologist).
464 **144** 11p. black and brown . . 15 25
465 – 15p. multicoloured . . . 30 35
466 – 25p. multicoloured . . . 40 55
467 – 60p. multicoloured . . . 65 1·40
DESIGN—HORIZ (from original Audubon paintings): 15p. Moorhen ("Common Gallinule); 25p. White-tailed tropic bird; 68p. Common noddy.

1985. Christmas. Life of St. Helena (3rd series). As T **136**. Multicoloured.
468 7p. St. Helena jouneys to the Holy Land 20 25
469 10p. Zambres slays the bull 20 30
470 15p. The bull restored to life: conversion of St. Helena 25 40
471 60p. Resurrection of the corpse: the True Cross identified . . . . 75 1·50

145 Church Provident Society for Women Banner

1986. Friendly Societies' Banners. Mult.
472 10p. Type **145** 15 25
473 11p. Working Men's Christian Association . . . 15 25
474 25p. Church Benefit Society for Children 25 55
475 29p. Mechanics and Friendly Benefit Society 25 65
476 33p. Ancient Order of Foresters 30 70

145a Princess Elizabeth making 21st Birthday Broadcast, South Africa, 1947

146 Plaque at Site of Halley's Observatory on St. Helena

1986. 60th Birthday of Queen Elizabeth II. Mult.
477 10p. Type **145a** 15 20
478 15p. Silver Jubilee photograph, 1977 . . . . 25 30
479 20p. Princess Elizabeth on board H.M.S. "Vanguard", 1947 . . . . 30 35
480 50p. In the U.S.A., 1976 . . 45 1·00
481 65p. At Crown Agents Head Office, London, 1983 . . . 50 1·10

1986. Appearance of Halley's Comet. Multicoloured.
482 9p. Type **146** 25 35
483 12p. Edmond Halley 30 35
484 20p. Halley's planisphere of the southern stars 55 70
485 65p. "Unity" on passage to St. Helena, 1676 . . . . . 1·75 2·50

146a Prince Andrew and Miss Sarah Ferguson

1986. Royal Wedding. Multicoloured.
486 10p. Type **146a** 20 25
487 40p. Prince Andrew with Governor J. Massingham on St. Helena 80 85

147 James Ross and H.M.S. "Erebus"

1986. Explorers.
488 **147** 1p. brown and pink . . . 30 1·50
489 – 3p. deep blue and blue . . 30 1·50
490 – 5p. deep green and green 30 1·50
491 – 9p. brown and red . . . 40 1·50
492 – 10p. deep brown and brown . . . . 40 1·50
493 – 12p. green and light green 40 1·50
494 – 15p. brown and pink . . . 50 1·50
495 – 20p. blue and light blue 55 1·50
496 – 25p. sepia and pink . . . 55 1·50
497 – 40p. deep green and green 60 1·75
498 – 60p. deep brown and brown . . . . 70 2·00
499 – £1 deep blue and blue . . 1·00 3·00
500 – £2 deep lilac and lilac . . 1·50 5·00
DESIGNS: 3p. Robert FitzRoy and H.M.S. "Beagle"; 5p. Adam Johann von Krusenstern and "Nadezhda"; 9p. William Bligh and H.M.S. "Resolution"; 10p. Otto von Kotzebue and "Rurik"; 12p. Philip Carteret and H.M.S. "Swallow"; 15p. Thomas Cavendish and "Desire"; 20p. Louis-Antoine de Bougainville and "La Boudeuse"; 25p. Fyedor Petrovich Litke and "Senyavin"; 40p. Louis Isidore Duperrey and "La Coquille"; 60p. John Byron and H.M.S. "Dolphin"; £1 James Cook and H.M.S. "Endeavour"; £2 Jules Dumont d'Urville and "L'Astrolabe".

148 Prince Edward and H.M.S. "Repulse" (battle cruiser), 1925

1987. Royal Visits to St. Helena. Multicoloured.
501 9p. Type **148** 85 70
502 13p. King George VI and H.M.S. "Vanguard" (battleship), 1947 . . . . . 1·25 1·00
503 38p. Prince Philip and Royal Yacht "Britannia", 1957 2·25 2·75
504 45p. Prince Andrew and H.M.S. "Herald" (survey ship), 1984 . . . . 2·25 3·00

149 St. Helena Tea Plant

1987. Rare Plants (1st series). Multicoloured.
505 9p. Type **149** 65 60
506 13p. Baby's toes 80 80
507 38p. Salad plant . . . . . . 1·50 2·25
508 45p. Scrubwood . . . . . . 1·75 2·50
See also Nos. 531/4.

150 Lesser Rorqual

1987. Marine Mammals. Multicoloured.
509 9p. Type **150** . . . . 1·25 75
510 13p. Risso's dolphin . . . . 1·25 1·00
511 45p. Sperm whale . . . . . 3·00 3·25
512 60p. Euphrosyne dolphin . . 3·25 3·75
MS513 102 × 72 mm. 75p. Humpback whale (48 × 31 mm) 6·50 7·00

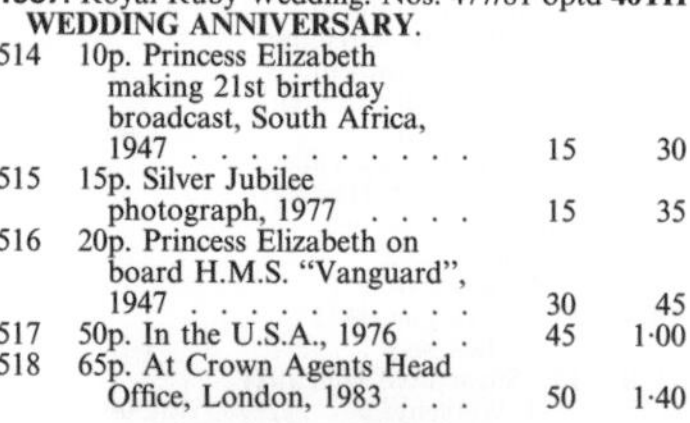

1987. Royal Ruby Wedding. Nos. 477/81 optd **40TH WEDDING ANNIVERSARY**.
514 10p. Princess Elizabeth making 21st birthday broadcast, South Africa, 1947 . . . . 15 30
515 15p. Silver Jubilee photograph, 1977 . . . . 15 35
516 20p. Princess Elizabeth on board H.M.S. "Vanguard", 1947 . . . . 30 45
517 50p. In the U.S.A., 1976 . . 45 1·00
518 65p. At Crown Agents Head Office, London, 1983 . . . 50 1·40

151 "Defence" and Dampier's Signature. 1691

1988. Bicentenary of Australian Settlement. Ships and Signatures. Multicoloured.
519 9p. Type **151** . . . . 1·50 90
520 13p. H.M.S. "Resolution" (Cook), 1775 . . . . . . 2·00 2·00
521 45p. H.M.S. "Providence" (Bligh), 1792 . . . . . . 3·25 4·00
522 60p. H.M.S. "Beagle" (Darwin), 1836 . . . . . . 4·25 5·50

152 "The Holy Virgin with the Child"

152a Lloyds Underwriting Room, 1886

1988. Christmas. Religious Paintings. Mult.
523 5p. Type **152** 10 30
524 20p. "Madonna" 40 50

525 38p. "The Holy Family with St. John" . . . . 75 1·50
526 60p. "The Holy Virgin with the Child" . . . . 1·25 2·00

1988. 300th Anniv of Lloyd's of London.
527 **152a** 9p. deep brown and brown 25 30
528 – 20p. multicoloured . . . 1·25 60
529 – 45p. multicoloured . . . 1·75 1·40
530 – 60p. multicoloured . . . 2·00 1·60
DESIGNS—VERT: 60p. "Spangereid" (full-rigged ship) on fire, St. Helena, 1920. HORIZ: 20p. "Edinburgh Castle" (liner); 45p. "Bosun Bird" (freighter).

153 Ebony

154 Private, 53rd Foot

1989. Rare Plants (2nd series). Multicoloured.
531 9p. Type **153** 40 40
532 20p. St. Helena lobelia . . . 70 70
533 45p. Large bellflower . . . . 1·40 2·00
534 60p. She cabbage tree . . . . 1·60 2·50

1989. Military Uniforms of 1815. Multicoloured.
535 9p. Type **154** 65 90
536 13p. Officer, 53rd Foot . . . 75 1·00
537 20p. Royal Marine . . . . . 85 1·10
538 45p. Officer, 66th Foot . . . 1·40 1·90
539 60p. Private, 66th Foot . . . 1·60 2·25

1989. "Philexfrance 89" International Stamp Exhibition, Paris. Nos. 535/9 optd **PHILEXFRANCE 89** and emblem.
540 9p. Type **154** . . . . 80 1·10
541 13p. Officer, 53rd Foot . . . 90 1·25
542 20p. Royal Marine . . . . . 1·10 1·40
543 45p. Officer, 66th Foot . . . 1·50 2·00
544 60p. Private, 66th Foot . . . 1·60 2·25

156 Agricultural Studies

1989. New Prince Andrew Central School. Mult.
545 13p. Type **156** 60 55
546 20p. Geography lesson . . . 1·00 1·00
547 25p. Walkway and classroom block . . . . 1·10 1·10
548 60p. Aerial view of School 2·50 3·50

157 "The Madonna with the Pear" (Durer)

159 Sheep

158 Chevrolet "6" 30 cwt Lorry, 1930

1989. Christmas. Religious Paintings. Multicoloured.
549 10p. Type **157** 60 50
550 20p. "The Holy Family under the Appletree" (Rubens) 85 90
551 45p. "The Virgin in the Meadow" (Raphael) . . . 2·00 2·50
552 60p. "The Holy Family with St. John" (Raphael) . . . 2·50 3·50

1989. Early Vehicles. Multicoloured.
553 9p. Type **158** 85 80
554 20p. Austin "Seven", 1929 . . 1·50 1·50
555 45p. Morris "Cowley" 11.9h.p., 1929 . . . . . . 2·25 2·75
556 60p. Sunbeam 25h.p., 1932 2·75 3·75
MS557 93 × 74 mm. £1 Ford "Model A Fordor" . . . . 7·00 8·00

1990. Farm Animals. Multicoloured.
558 9p. Type **159** 50 65
559 13p. Pigs 60 80
560 45p. Cow and calf . . . . . 1·50 2·50
561 60p. Geese . . . . 2·00 3·50

160 1840 Twopence Blue

1990. "Stamp World London 90" International Stamp Exhibition, London.
562 **160** 13p. black and blue . . . 50 50
563 – 20p. multicoloured . . . 75 85
564 – 38p. multicoloured . . . 1·25 2·00
565 – 45p. multicoloured . . . 1·60 2·25
DESIGNS: 20p. 1840 Penny Black and 19th-century St. Helena postmark; 38p. Delivering mail to sub-post office; 45p. Mail van and Post Office, Jamestown.

161 Satellite Dish

161a Lady Elizabeth Bowes-Lyon, April, 1923

1990. Modern Telecommunications Links. Mult.
566 20p. Type **161** . . . . 75 1·10
567 20p. Digital telephone exchange . . . . 75 1·10
568 20p. Public card phone . . . 75 1·10
569 20p. Facsimile machine . . . 75 1·10

1990. 90th Birthday of Queen Elizabeth the Queen Mother.
570 **161a** 25p. multicoloured . . . 1·00 75
571 – £1 black and brown . . 2·75 3·75
DESIGN—29 × 37 mm: £1 Queen Elizabeth visiting communal kitchen, 1940.

162 "Dane" (mail ship), 1857

1990. Maiden Voyage of "St. Helena II". Multicoloured.
572 13p. Type **162** . . . . 1·25 85
573 20p. "St. Helena I" off-loading at St. Helena . . . 1·60 1·40
574 38p. Launch of "St. Helena II" . . . . 2·25 2·75
575 45p. The Duke of York launching "St. Helena II" 2·75 3·50
MS576 100 × 100 mm. £1 "St. Helena II" and outline map of St. Helena . . . . 8·50 9·00

163 Baptist Chapel, Sandy Bay

1990. Christmas. Local Churches. Multicoloured.
577 10p. Type **163** 30 30
578 13p. St. Martin in the Hills Church 35 35
579 20p. St. Helena and the Cross Church 55 65
580 38p. St. James Church . . . 1·00 2·00
581 45p. St. Paul's Cathedral . . 1·25 2·00

164 "Funeral Cortege, Jamestown Wharf" (detail V. Adam)

1990. 150th Anniv of Removal of Napoleon's Body.
582 **164** 13p. black, brown & green . . . . 1·00 80
583 – 20p. black, brown and blue . . . . 1·50 1·50
584 – 38p. black, brown & mauve . . . . 2·25 2·75
585 – 45p. multicoloured . . . 2·50 3·50
DESIGNS: 20p. "Coffin being conveyed to the 'Belle Poule' " (detail, V. Adam); 38p. "Transfer of the Coffin to the 'Normandie', Cherbourg" (detail, V. Adam); 45p. "Napoleon's Tomb, St. Helena" (T. Sutherland).

165 Officer, Leicestershire Regiment

165a Queen Elizabeth II

1991. Military Uniforms of 1897. Multicoloured.
586 13p. Type **165** . . . . 1·00 1·00
587 15p. Officer, York & Lancaster Regiment . . . 1·10 1·10
588 20p. Colour-sergeant, Leicestershire Regiment . . 1·40 1·40
589 38p. Bandsman, York and Lancaster Regiment . . . 2·25 2·75
590 45p. Lance-corporal, York and Lancaster Regiment 2·75 3·25

1991. 65th Birthday of Queen Elizabeth II and 70th Birthday of Prince Philip. Multicoloured.
591 25p. Type **165a** . . . . . . 80 1·25
592 25p. Prince Philip in naval uniform . . . . 80 1·25

166 "Madonna and Child" (T. Vecellio)

1991. Christmas. Religious Paintings. Multicoloured.
593 10p. Type **166** 70 55
594 13p. "The Holy Family" (A. Mengs) 80 65
595 20p. "Madonna and Child" (W. Dyce) . . . . 1·25 1·00
596 38p. "The Two Trinities" (B. Murillo) . . . . 2·00 2·50
597 45p. "The Virgin and Child" (G. Bellini) . . . . . . 2·25 3·00

167 Matchless (346cc) Motorcycle, 1947

1991. "Phila Nippon '91" International Stamp Exn, Tokyo. Motorcycles. Multicoloured.
598 13p. Type **167** . . . . 1·00 80
599 20p. Triumph "Tiger 100" (500cc), 1950 . . . . . . 1·50 1·10
600 38p. Honda "CD" (175cc), 1967 . . . . 2·25 2·75
601 45p. Yamaha "DTE 400", 1976 . . . . 2·50 3·00
MS602 72 × 49 mm. 65p. Suzuki "RM" (250cc), 1984 . . . . . 7·50 9·00

168 "Eye of the Wind" (cadet brig) and Compass Rose

1992. 500th Anniv of Discovery of America by Columbus and Re-enactment Voyages. Multicoloured.
603 15p. Type **168** . . . . 1·25 90
604 25p. "Soren Larsen" (cadet brigantine) and map of Re-enactment Voyages . . . . 1·75 1·75
605 35p. "Santa Maria", "Nina" and "Pinta" . . . . 2·25 2·75
606 50p. Columbus and "Santa Maria" . . . . 2·50 3·50

168a Prince Andrew Central School

1992. 40th Anniv of Queen Elizabeth II's Accession. Multicoloured.
607 11p. Type **168a** 40 40
608 15p. Plantation House . . . 55 55
609 25p. Jamestown 85 95
610 35p. Three portraits of Queen Elizabeth . . . . 1·10 1·50
611 50p. Queen Elizabeth II . . . 1·40 1·90

169 H.M.S. "Ledbury" (minesweeper)

1992. 10th Anniv of Liberation of Falkland Islands. Ships. Multicoloured.
612 13p. Type **169** 80 80
613 20p. H.M.S. "Brecon" (minesweeper) . . . . . . 1·10 1·10
614 38p. "St. Helena I" (mail ship) off South Georgia . . 1·75 2·25
615 45p. Launch collecting first mail drop, 1982 . . . . . 2·25 3·00
MS616 116 × 116 mm. 13p.+3p. Type **169**; 20p.+4p. As No. 613; 38p.+8p. As No. 614; 45p.+9p. As No. 615 . . . . 5·50 5·50
The premium on No. **MS**616 were for the S.S.A.F.A.

170 Shepherds and Angel Gabriel

1992. Christmas. Children's Nativity Plays. Multicoloured.
617 13p. Type **170** . . . . 1·00 85
618 15p. Shepherds and Three Kings . . . . 1·10 95
619 20p. Mary and Joseph . . . 1·25 1·00
620 45p. Nativity scene . . . . . 2·50 3·75

171 Disc Jockey, Radio St. Helena (25th anniv)

172 Moses in the Bulrush

1992. Local Anniversaries. Multicoloured.
621 13p. Type **171** 75 70
622 20p. Scout parade (75th anniv of Scouting on St. Helena) . . . . 1·25 1·10
623 38p. H.M.S. "Providence" (sloop) and breadfruit (bicent of Capt. Bligh's visit) . . . . 2·25 3·00
624 45p. Governor Brooke and Plantation House (bicent) 2·25 3·00

1993. Flowers (1st series). Multicoloured.
625 9p. Type **172** 85 75
626 13p. Periwinkle . . . . . . 1·10 90
627 20p. Everlasting flower . . . 1·40 1·25
628 38p. Cigar plant . . . . . . 2·50 3·25
629 45p. "Lobelia erinus" . . . . 2·50 3·25
See also Nos. 676/80.

173 Adult St. Helena Sand Plover and Eggs

1993. Endangered Species. St. Helena Sand Plover ("Wirebird"). Multicoloured.
630 3p. Type **173** 60 60
631 5p. Male attending brooding female 60 60
632 12p. Adult with downy young 1·25 1·25
633 25p. Two birds in immature plumage . . . . 1·40 1·40
634 40p. Adult in flight . . . . . 1·50 1·75
635 60p. Young bird on rocks . . 1·75 2·50
Nos. 634/5 are without the W.W.F. emblem.

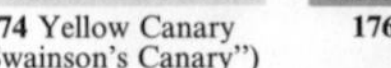
174 Yellow Canary ("Swainson's Canary")

176 Arum Lily

175 Football and Teddy Bear

1993. Birds. Multicoloured.
636 1p. Type **174** 30 80
637 3p. Rock partridge 40 80
638 11p. Feral rock pigeon . . . 55 70
639 12p. Common waxbill . . . 55 70
640 15p. Common mynah 60 75
641 18p. Java sparrow 65 75
642 25p. Red-billed tropic bird (horiz) 80 90
643 35p. Madeiran storm petrel (horiz) . . . . 1·10 1·25
644 75p. Madagascar red fody . . 2·00 3·00
645 £1 White tern ("Common fairy tern") (horiz) . . . . 2·25 3·25
646 £2 Giant petrel (horiz) . . . 4·25 6·50
647 £5 St. Helena sand plover ("Wirebird") . . . . . . 10·00 12·00

1993. Christmas. Toys. Multicoloured.
648 12p. Type **175** 75 70
649 15p. Yacht and doll 80 75
650 18p. Palette and rocking horse 85 80
651 25p. Model airplane and kite 1·25 1·50
652 60p. Guitar and roller skates 2·25 3·50

1994. Flowers and Children's Art. Multicoloured.
653 12p. Type **176** 40 65
654 12p. "Arum Lily" (Delphia Mittens) 40 65
655 25p. Ebony . . . . 75 1·00
656 25p. "Ebony" (Jason Rogers) 75 1·00
657 35p. Shell ginger . . . . . . 95 1·10
658 35p. "Shell Ginger" (Jeremy Moyce) . . . . 95 1·10

177 Abyssinian Guinea Pig

1994. "Hong Kong '94" International Stamp Exhibition. Pets. Multicoloured.
659 12p. Type **177** 70 70
660 25p. Common tabby cat . . 1·40 1·40
661 53p. Plain white and black rabbits . . . . 2·25 3·00
662 60p. Golden labrador . . . . 2·50 3·25

178 Springer's Blenny

1994. Fishes. Multicoloured.
663 12p. Type **178** 75 75
664 25p. St. Helena damselfish . . 1·50 1·50
665 53p. Melliss's scorpionfish . . 2·25 3·25
666 60p. St. Helena wrasse . . . 2·75 3·50

179 "Lampides boeticus"

1994. Butterflies. Multicoloured.
667 12p. Type **179** 75 75
668 25p. "Cynthia cardui" . . . 1·50 1·50
669 53p. "Hypolimnas bolina" . . 2·25 2·75
670 60p. "Danaus chrysippus" . . 2·75 3·25

180 "Silent Night!"

1994. Christmas. Carols. Multicoloured.
671 12p. Type **180** 55 45
672 15p. "While Shepherds watched their Flocks by Night" 60 50
673 25p. "Away in a Manger" . . 1·00 90
674 38p. "We Three Kings" . . . 1·50 2·25
675 60p. "Angels from the Realms of Glory" . . . . 2·25 3·75

1994. Flowers (2nd series). As T **172**. Multicoloured.
676 12p. Honeysuckle 35 35
677 15p. Gobblegheer 40 40
678 25p. African lily 70 80
679 38p. Prince of Wales feathers 1·00 1·60
680 60p. St. Johns lily . . . . . 1·75 3·25

181 Fire Engine

1995. Emergency Services. Multicoloured.
681 12p. Type **181** . . . . 1·25 75
682 25p. Lifeboat . . . . 1·40 90
683 53p. Police car . . . . 2·75 3·00
684 60p. Ambulance . . . . . . 3·00 3·50

182 Site Clearance

1995. Construction of Harpers Valley Earth Dam. Multicoloured.
685 25p. Type **182** . . . . 80 1·10
686 25p. Earthworks in progress 80 1·10
687 25p. Laying outlet pipes . . . 80 1·10
688 25p. Revetment block protection . . . . 80 1·10
689 25p. Completed dam . . . . 80 1·10
Nos. 685/9 were printed together, se-tenant, forming a composite design.

182a "Lady Denison Pender" (cable ship)

1995. 50th Anniv of End of Second World War. As T **161** of Ascension. Multicoloured.
690 5p. Type **182a** . . . . 80 1·10
691 5p. H.M.S. "Dragon" (cruiser) . . . . 80 1·10
692 12p. R.F.A. "Darkdale" (tanker) . . . . 1·25 1·50
693 12p. H.M.S. "Hermes" (aircraft carrier, launched 1919) . . . . 1·25 1·50
694 25p. Men of St. Helena Rifles 1·75 2·00
695 25p. Governor Major W. J. Bain Gray taking salute . . 1·75 2·00
696 53p. 6-inch coastal gun, Ladder Hill . . . . 2·00 2·50
697 53p. Flags signalling "VICTORY" . . . . . . 2·00 2·50
MS698 75 × 85 mm. £1 Reverse of 1939–45 War Medal (vert) . . 2·50 2·75
The two designs for each value were printed together, se-tenant, forming composite designs.

183 Blushing Snail

1995. Endemic Invertebrates. Multicoloured.
699 12p. Type **183** 80 80
700 25p. Golden sail spider . . . 1·50 1·50
701 53p. Spiky yellow woodlouse 2·25 3·25
702 60p. St. Helena shore crab 2·50 3·50
MS703 85 × 83 mm. £1 Giant earwig 4·50 6·00

184 Epidendrum ibaguense

1995. "Singapore '95" International Stamp Exhibition. Orchids. Sheet, 122 × 74 mm, containing T **184** and similar vert design. Multicoloured.
MS704 50p. Type **184**; 50p. "Vanda Miss Joaquim" . . . . 5·00 6·00

185 "Santa Claus outside Market" (Jason Alex Rogers)

1995. Christmas. Children's Paintings. Multicoloured.
705 12p. Type **185** 35 35
706 15p. "Santa Claus and band" (Che David Yon) 45 45
707 25p. "Santa Claus outside Community Centre" (Leon Williams) 70 75
708 38p. "Santa Claus in decorated street" (Stacey McDaniel) . . . . 1·00 1·40
709 60p. "Make a better World" (Kissha Karla Kacy Thomas) . . . . 1·75 3·50

186 "Walmer Castle", 1915

1996. Union Castle Mail Ships (1st series). Multicoloured.
710 12p. Type **186** 60 40
711 25p. "Llangibby Castle", 1934 . . . . 90 75
712 53p. "Stirling Castle", 1940 1·60 2·25
713 60p. "Pendennis Castle", 1965 . . . . 1·75 2·50
See also Nos. 757/60.

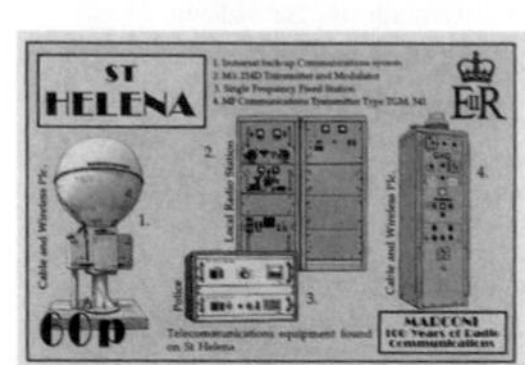

187 Early Telecommunications Equipment

1996. Centenary of Radio. Multicoloured.
714 60p. Type **187** . . . . 1·50 2·00
715 £1 Guglielmo Marconi and "Elettra" (yacht) . . . . . 2·50 3·50

1996. 70th Birthday of Queen Elizabeth II. As T **55** of Tokelau, each incorporating a different photograph of the Queen. Multicoloured.
716 15p. Jamestown 50 40
717 25p. Prince Andrew School 75 65
718 53p. Castle entrance . . . . 1·50 2·25
719 60p. Plantation House . . . 1·75 2·50
MS720 64 × 86 mm. £1.50 Queen Elizabeth II . . . . 3·25 4·50

188 Helicopter Mail to H.M.S. "Protector" (ice patrol ship), 1964

1996. "CAPEX '96" International Stamp Exhibition, Toronto. Mail Transport. Mult.
721 12p. Type **188** 50 45
722 25p. Postman on motor scooter, 1965 . . . . . . 75 65
723 53p. Loading mail plane, Wideawake Airfield, Ascension Island . . . . . 1·40 2·00
724 60p. "St. Helena II" (mail ship) unloading at St. Helena . . . . 1·50 2·25
MS725 98 × 73 mm. £1 L.M.S. No. 5624 "St. Helena" locomotive (43 × 27 mm) . . . . 2·75 3·75

189 "Mr. Porteous's House"

1996. Napoleonic Sites. Multicoloured.
726 12p. Type **189** 50 45
727 25p. "The Briars' Pavilion" 75 65
728 53p. "Longwood House" . . 1·50 2·25
729 60p. "Napoleon's Tomb" . . 1·75 2·50

190 Frangipani and Sandy Bay from Diana's Peak

191 Black Cabbage Tree

1996. Christmas. Flowers and Views. Multicoloured.
730 12p. Type **190** 40 40
731 15p. Bougainvillaea and Upper Jamestown from Sampsons's Battery 50 50
732 25p. Jacaranda and Jacob's Ladder 75 75
733 £1 Pink periwinkle and Lot's Wife Ponds . . . . 2·75 5·00

1997. Endemic Plants from Diana's Peak National Park. Multicoloured.
734 25p. Type **191** . . . . 1·25 1·40
735 25p. Whitewood . . . . . . 1·25 1·40
736 25p. Tree fern . . . . 1·25 1·40
737 25p. Dwarf jellico . . . . . 1·25 1·40
738 25p. Lobelia . . . . 1·25 1·40
739 25p. Dogwood . . . . 1·25 1·40
Nos. 734/9 were printed together, se-tenant, with the backgrounds forming a composite design.

1997. "HONG KONG '97" International Stamp Exhibition. Sheet 130 × 90 mm, containing design as No. 644.
MS740 75p. Madagascar red fody 1·75 2·25

192 Joao da Nova's Lookout sighting St. Helena, 1502

192a Royal Family's Visit, 1947

1997. 500th Anniv of the Discovery of St. Helena (1st issue). Multicoloured.
741 20p. Type **192** . . . . 1·00 80
742 25p. Don Fernando Lopez (first inhabitant) and cockerel, 1515 . . . . . . 1·10 80
743 30p. Thomas Cavendish and "Desire", 1588 . . . . . . 1·25 1·00
744 80p. "Royal Merchant" (English galleon), 1591 . . 2·50 3·50
See also Nos. 762/5, 786/9, 810/13, 828/31 and 857/60.

1997. Return of Hong Kong to China. Sheet 130 × 90 mm, containing design as No. 647, but changed face value and imprint date. W w **14** (sideways). P 14½ × 14.
MS745 75p. St. Helena Sand Plover ("Wirebird") . . . . 1·75 2·25

1997. Golden Wedding of Queen Elizabeth and Prince Philip. Multicoloured.
746 10p. Type **192a** 75 85
747 10p. Wedding photograph of Princess Elizabeth and Prince Philip 75 85
748 15p. Princess Elizabeth and Prince Philip, 1947 . . . . 90 1·10
749 15p. Presenting bouquets, Royal Visit, 1947 . . . . . 90 1·10
750 50p. Prince Philip on Royal Visit, 1957 . . . . 1·75 2·25
751 50p. Wedding party on balcony, 1947 . . . . 1·75 2·25
MS752 111 × 70 mm. £1.50, Queen Elizabeth and Prince Philip in landau (horiz) . . . . 6·00 7·00

193 Flower Arrangement

1997. Christmas. 25th Anniv of the Duke of Edinburgh's Award in St. Helena. Multicoloured.
753 15p. Type **193** 50 35
754 20p. Calligraphy 60 45
755 40p. Camping . . . . 1·25 1·40
756 75p. Table laid for Christmas dinner . . . . 2·25 3·50

1998. Union Castle Mail Ships (2nd series). As T **186**. Multicoloured.
757 20p. "Avondale Castle", 1900 1·40 85
758 25p. "Dunnottar Castle", 1936 . . . . 1·50 85
759 30p. "Llandovery Castle", 1943 . . . . 1·60 1·10
760 80p. "Good Hope Castle", 1977 . . . . 3·00 4·25

194 Wearing green and white Hat, 1983

1998. Diana, Princess of Wales Commemoration. Sheet 145 × 70 mm containing vert designs as T **194**.
MS761 30p. Wearing white jacket; 30p. Wearing green jacket, 1996; 30p. In evening dress, 1991 (sold at £1.20 + 20p. charity premium) 2·75 3·25

1998. 500th Anniv of the Discovery of St. Helena (2nd issue). As T **192**. Multicoloured.
762 20p. Settlers planting crops, 1659 . . . . 80 70
763 25p. Dutch invasion, 1672 . . 1·00 70
764 30p. Recapture by the English, 1673 . . . . . . 1·25 1·00
765 80p. Royal Charter of 1673 2·50 3·50

195 "Desire" (Cavendish), 1588

1998. Maritime Heritage. Multicoloured.
766 10p. Type **195** . . . . 90 1·00
767 15p. "Witte Leeuw" (Dutch East Indiaman), 1602 . . . 1·40 1·25
768 20p. H.M.S. "Swallow" and H.M.S. "Dolphin" (Carteret), 1751 . . . . . 1·50 1·00
769 25p. H.M.S. "Endeavour" (Cook), 1771 . . . . . . 1·75 1·00
770 30p. H.M.S. "Providence" (sloop), 1792 . . . . . . 1·50 1·00
771 35p. "St. Helena" (East India Company schooner), 1815 1·75 1·40
772 40p. H.M.S. "Northumberland" (ship of the line), 1815 . . . . . . 1·75 1·40
773 50p. "Rurik" (Von Kotzebue), 1815 . . . . . 2·00 2·00
774 75p. H.M.S. "Erebus" (Ross), 1826 . . . . 2·75 3·00
775 80p. "Keying" (junk), 1847 2·75 3·00
776 £2 "La Belle Poule" (French frigate), 1840 . . . . . . 4·50 6·00
777 £5 H.M.S "Rattlesnake" (screw corvette), 1861 . . . 11·00 13·00
No. 771 is inscribed "H.M.S." in error.

196 Metal Lanterns

1998. Christmas. Island Crafts. Multicoloured.
778 15p. Type **196** 50 40
779 20p. Wood-turned bowls . . 60 50
780 30p. Inlaid woodwork on jewellery box 85 80
781 85p. Hessian and seedwork bag and hat . . . . 2·25 3·50

197 H.M.S. "Endeavour" (Cook), 1771

1999. "Australia '99" World Stamp Exhibition, Melbourne. Sheet 120 × 80 mm.
MS782 **197** £1.50, multicoloured 5·00 5·50

197a Photographs of Prince Edward and Miss Sophie Rhys-Jones

1999. Royal Wedding. Multicoloured.
783 30p. Type **197a** 60 65
784 £1.30 Engagement photograph . . . . 2·50 3·25

1999. 500th Anniv of the Discovery of St. Helena (3rd issue). As T **192** but horiz. Multicoloured.
786 20p. Jamestown fortifications 1·10 75
787 25p. Roadway up Ladder Hill, 1718 . . . . 1·25 80
788 30p. Governor Skottowe with Captain Cook at St. James Church, 1775 . . . . . . 2·75 1·50
789 80p. Presentation of sword of honour to Governor Brooke, 1799 . . . . . . 3·00 4·00

199 King and Queen visiting Jamestown

1999. "Queen Elizabeth the Queen Mother's Century". Multicoloured.
790 15p. Type **199** 70 55
791 25p. Viewing bomb damage, Buckingham Palace, 1940 85 65
792 30p. With Prince Andrew, 1997 . . . . 1·00 85
793 80p. Presenting colour to R.A.F. Central Flying School, and with Red Arrows . . . . 2·25 3·25
MS794 145 × 70 mm. £1.50, Queen Elizabeth, 1937, and Royal Family on balcony after Coronation 4·00 4·50

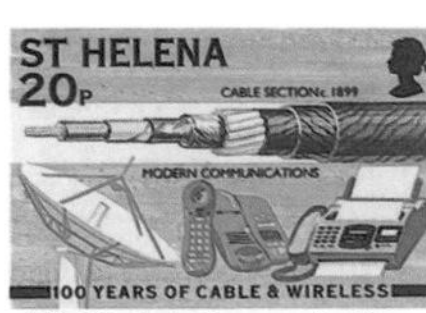

200 Modern Communications Equipment and Section of 1899 Cable

1999. Centenary of Cable & Wireless Communications plc on St. Helena.
795 **200** 20p. multicoloured . . . 85 85
796 – 25p. black, brown and bistre . . . . 1·10 90
797 – 30p. black, brown and bistre . . . . 1·25 1·10
798 – 80p. multicoloured . . . 2·00 3·00
DESIGNS: 25p. "Seine" (cable ship); 30p. "Anglia" (cable ship); 80p. Cable & Wireless Headquarters, The Briars.

201 "Victoria" (cruise liner) at St. Helena

1999. Union Castle Line Centenary Voyage. Sheet 88 × 72 mm.
MS799 **201** £2 multicoloured . . 10·00 11·00

202 King Edward VI

2000. "Stamp Show 2000" International Stamp Exhibition, London. Kings and Queens of England. Multicoloured.
800 30p. Type **202** . . . . . . 1·40 1·40
801 30p. King James I . . . . . 1·40 1·40
802 30p. King William III and Queen Mary II . . . . . 1·40 1·40
803 30p. King George II . . . . 1·40 1·40
804 30p. Queen Victoria . . . . 1·40 1·40
805 30p. King George VI . . . . 1·40 1·40

203 Distillation Plant at Ruperts

2000. Centenary of Second Boer War (1st issue). Multicoloured.
806 15p. Type **203** 65 60
807 25p. Camp at Broadbottom 80 70
808 30p. Committee of Boer prisoners 90 80
809 80p. General Cronje and family at Kent Cottage . . 2·25 3·00

2000. 500th Anniv of the Discovery of St. Helena (4th issue). As T **192**, but horiz. Multicoloured.
810 20p. East India Company flag with crest and Union Jack with colony badge . . 80 70
811 25p. Sir Hudson Lowe and Sir George Bingham with broken chains (abolition of slavery, 1832) 80 70
812 30p. Napoleon, British warship and funeral cortege 1·00 80
813 80p. Chief Dinizulu in exile, 1890 . . . . 2·00 3·00

204 Princess Margaret

2000. Royal Birthdays. Sheet, 145 × 75 mm, containing T **204** and similar multicoloured designs.
MS814 25p. Type **204**; 25p. Prince William; 25p. Duke of York; 25p. Princess Royal; 50p. Queen Mother (42 × 56 mm) . . . . . 18·00 18·00

205 *Beauty and the Beast*

2000. Christmas. Pantomimes. Multicoloured.
815 20p. Type **205** 70 80
816 20p. *Puss in Boots* 70 80
817 20p. *Little Red Riding Hood* 70 80
818 20p. *Jack and the Beanstalk* 70 80
819 20p. *Snow White and the Seven Dwarfs* 70 80

206 Chinese White Dolphin

2001. "HONG KONG 2001" Stamp Exhibition. Sheet 150 × 90 mm, containing T **206** and similar horiz design showing dolphins. Multicoloured.
MS820 30p. Type **206**; 40p. Striped dolphin . . . . 4·50 5·00

207 First St. Helena Postage Stamp

2001. Death Centenary of Queen Victoria. Mult.
821 10p. Type **207** 30 25
822 15p. H.M.S. *Beagle* off St. Helena, 1836 . . . . . 60 45
823 20p. Jamestown Square (horiz) 60 50
824 25p. Queen Victoria with Prince Albert and children (horiz) 70 70
825 30p. Diamond Jubilee procession (horiz) 80 80
826 50p. Lewis Carroll and characters from *Alice in Wonderland* . . . . 1·25 1·50
MS827 105 × 80 mm. £1.50, Sacks of St. Helena coffee at Great Exhibition . . . . 3·75 4·50

2001. 500th Anniv of the Discovery of St. Helena (5th series). As T **192**, but horiz. Multicoloured.
828 20p. Men of St. Helena Rifles 1·25 85
829 25p. Prince Andrew School and Jamestown Community Centre . . . . 1·00 85
830 30p. Flax industry . . . . . 1·10 1·00
831 80p. *St. Helena II* (mail ship) 3·25 3·75

208 H.M.S. *Dunedin* (light cruiser)

2001. Royal Navy Ships of Second World War. Multicoloured.
832 15p. Type **208** 65 65
833 20p. H.M.S. *Repulse* (battle cruiser) 70 70
834 25p. H.M.S. *Nelson* (battleship) 80 80
835 30p. H.M.S. *Exmoor* (destroyer) 90 90
836 40p. H.M.S. *Eagle* (aircraft carrier, launched 1918) . . 1·10 1·25
837 50p. H.M.S. *Milford* (sloop) 1·40 1·75

209 Tammy Wynette and "It came upon the Midnight Clear"

2001. Christmas. Carols. Each showing carol title and Tammy Wynette ("First Lady of Country Music"). Multicoloured.
838 10p. Type **209** 45 45
839 15p. "Joy to the World" . . 55 55
840 20p. "Away in a Manger" . . 65 65
841 30p. "Silent Night" 75 85
MS842 65 × 99 mm. £1.50 Tammy Wynette (vert) . . . . 3·75 4·50

210 Napoleon as a Young Man

2001. 180th Death Anniv of Napoleon Bonaparte. Multicoloured.
843 20p. Type **210** 70 70
844 25p. Napoleon at military school 80 80
845 30p. Napoleon dancing . . . 90 90
846 80p. Napoleon with children 2·25 2·75

211 Princess Elizabeth and Princess Margaret as Girl Guides

2002. Golden Jubilee.
847 **211** 20p. agate, red and gold . . . 85 75
848 – 25p. multicoloured . . . 90 85
849 – 30p. brown, red and gold 1·00 95
850 – 80p. multicoloured . . . 2·75 3·00
MS851 162 × 95 mm. Nos. 847/50 and 50p. multicoloured . . . . 7·00 7·00
DESIGNS—HORIZ: 25p. Queen Elizabeth in evening dress, 1967; 30p. Queen Elizabeth with Prince Charles and Princess Anne, 1952; 80p. Queen Elizabeth on Remembrance Sunday, Durban, 1999. VERT (38 × 51 mm)— 50p. Queen Elizabeth after Annigoni.

Designs as Nos. 847/50 in No. **MS**851 omit the gold frame around each stamp and the "Golden Jubilee 1952-2002" inscription.

212 Young St. Helena Sand Plover

2002. St. Helena Sand Plover ("Wirebird"). Multicoloured.
852 10p. Type **212** 55 65
853 15p. Chick running (vert) . . 70 80
854 30p. Adult bird in flight . . . 1·00 90
855 80p. Chick . . . . 2·25 2·75
MS856 175 × 80 mm. 25p. Adult bird (vert) and Nos. 852/5 . . . . . 5·00 5·50

213 Sir William Doveton (Council member) and Jamestown Harbour

2002. 500th Anniv of the Discovery of St. Helena (6th issue). Local Celebrities. All showing Jamestown Harbour. Multicoloured.
857 20p. Type **213** 70 70
858 25p. Canon Lawrence Walcott 80 80
859 30p. Governor Hudson Janisch 90 90
860 80p. Dr. Wilberforce Arnold 2·25 2·75

214 H.M.S. *Hermes* (aircraft carrier)

2002. Royal Navy Ships from the Falklands War. Multicoloured.
861 15p. Type **214** 60 60
862 20p. H.M.S. *Leeds Castle* (patrol vessel) 70 70
863 25p. H.M.S. *Intrepid* (assault ship) 80 80
864 30p. H.M.S. *Glasgow* (destroyer) 90 90
865 40p. St. Helena I supplying H.M.S. *Brecon* and H.M.S. *Ledbury* (minesweepers) . . 1·10 1·25
866 50p. H.M.S. *Courageous* (submarine) . . . . 1·40 1·60

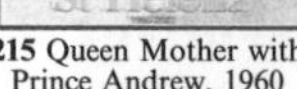

215 Queen Mother with Prince Andrew, 1960 **217** The Princess Royal in Blues and Royals' Uniform

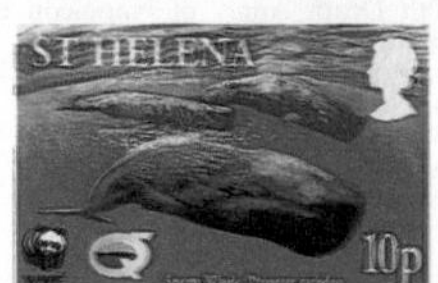

216 Sperm Whale Pod Underwater

2002. Queen Elizabeth the Queen Mother Commemoration.
867 **215** 20p. brown, gold and purple 70 70
868 – 25p. multicoloured . . . 80 80
869 – 30p. brown, gold and purple 90 90
870 – 50p. multicoloured . . . 1·40 1·60
MS871 145 × 70 mm. 35p. black and gold; £1 multicoloured . . . . 3·50 4·00

DESIGNS: 25p. Queen Mother at Cheltenham Races; 30p. Lady Elizabeth Bowes-Lyon, 1923; 35p. Queen Elizabeth, 1945; 50p. Queen Mother at St. Patrick's Day Parade, 1984; £1 Queen Mother at Sandown Races, 1998. Designs in No. **MS**871 omit the "1900–2002" inscription and the coloured frame.

2002. Endangered Species. Sperm Whale. Multicoloured.
872 10p. Type **216** 40 40
873 15p. Sperm whale on surface 55 55
874 20p. Two sperm whales underwater 60 60
875 30p. Tail fin of sperm whale 75 75

2002. Visit of the Princess Royal to St. Helena. Sheet 62 × 72 mm.
MS876 **217** £2 multicoloured . . 6·00 6·50

218 Plantation House and Arms

2003. Tourism. Multicoloured.
877 25p. Type **218** 75 80
878 25p. *St. Helena II* (mail ship) in Jamestown harbour . . 75 80
879 25p. *QE2* (cruise liner) off St. Helena 75 80
880 25p. Napoleon's Tomb and Briars Pavilion 75 80
881 25p. Ebony Flower and Diana's Peak 75 80
882 25p. St. Helena sand plover ("Wirebird") and Napoleon's House 75 80
883 25p. Broadway House 75 80
884 25p. St. Helena Golf Course 75 80
885 25p. Yacht and dolphins . . 75 80
886 25p. Sport fishing 75 80
887 25p. Diving 75 80
888 25p. St. Helena Museum . . 75 80

219 Queen Elizabeth II in Coronation Robes (photograph by Cecil Beaton)

2003. 50th Anniv of Coronation. Multicoloured.
889 30p. Type **219** 90 90
890 50p. Queen and Duke of Edinburgh in Coronation Coach . . . . 1·50 1·75
MS891 95 × 115 mm. 30p. As Type **219**; 50p. As No. 890 . . 2·40 2·75

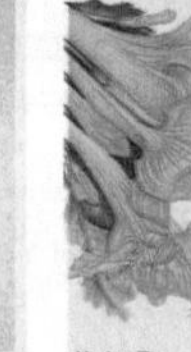

220 Queen Elizabeth II **221** *Leonotis nepetifolia*

2003.
892 **220** £2.50 multicoloured . . . 5·00 5·00

2003. Wild Flowers. Multicoloured.
893 10p. Type **221** 20 25
894 15p. *Buddleia madagascariensis* 30 35
895 20p. *Datura suaveolens* . . . 40 45
896 25p. *Fuchsia boliviana* . . . 50 55
897 30p. *Commelina diffusa* . . . 60 65
898 40p. *Solanum mauritianum* 80 85
899 50p. *Tecoma stans* . . . . . 1·00 1·10
900 75p. *Kalanchoe pinnata* . . . 1·50 1·60
901 80p. *Hedychium chrysoleucum* . . . . 1·60 1·75
902 £1 *Canna indica* . . . . . . 2·00 2·10
903 £2 *Alpinia nutans* . . . . . 4·00 4·25
904 £5 *Lantana camara* . . . . 10·00 10·50

222 Westland WG-13 Lynx Helicopter

2003. Centenary of Powered Flight. Multicoloured.
905 10p. Type **222** 40 35
906 15p. Douglas C-124 Globemaster 55 45
907 20p. British Aerospace Nimrod AEW Mk 3 . . . 60 50
908 25p. Lockheed C-130 Hercules 60 55
909 30p. Lockheed L-1011 TriStar 90 90
910 50p. *Wright Flyer* . . . . . 1·25 1·50
MS911 115 × 65 mm. £1.80 Supermarine *Walrus* . . . . . 5·00 5·50

223 Large Magellanic Cloud

2003. Christmas. The Southern Sky. Multicoloured.
912 10p. Type **223** 30 30
913 15p. Small Magellanic cloud 40 40
914 20p. Omega Centauri globular cluster 50 50
915 25p. Eta Carinae nebula ("ETA CARRNAE") . . . 60 65
916 30p. Southern Cross constellation 65 75

224 Christiaan Barnard (heart transplant pioneer) **226** St. Matthew

225 Freesia

2004. Medical Pioneers. Multicoloured.
917 10p. Type **224** 30 30
918 25p. Marie Curie (developer of X-radiography) 65 60
919 30p. Louis Pasteur (bacteriologist) 75 75
920 50p. Sir Alexander Fleming (discoverer of penicillin) . . 1·25 1·40

2004. Bicentenary of Royal Horticultural Society. Multicoloured.
921 10p. Type **225** 30 30
922 15p. Bottle Brush 40 40
923 30p. Ebony 75 80
924 50p. Olive . . . . 1·10 1·25
MS925 111 × 111 mm. £1 Maurandya . . . . 2·50 2·75

2004. Christmas. Stained Glass Windows. Multicoloured.
926 10p. Type **226** 35 30
927 15p. St. John 55 40
928 20p. St. Peter 70 60
929 30p. St. James . . . . 1·00 1·00
930 50p. St. Paul . . . . 1·75 2·25

227 SS *Umtata*

2004. Merchant Ships. Multicoloured.
931 20p. Type **227** 70 60
932 30p. SS *Umzinto* . . . . . . 1·00 90
933 50p. SS *Umtali* . . . . . . 1·50 1·60
934 80p. SS *Umbilo* . . . . . . 2·00 2·40

228 The Friar

2005. Rock Formations. Multicoloured.
935 35p. Type **228** . . . . 1·10 1·25
936 40p. Sugar Loaf . . . . . . 1·25 1·40
937 50p. The Turk's Cap . . . . 1·50 1·75
938 £1 Lot's Wife . . . . 2·50 2·75

POSTAGE DUE STAMPS

D 1 Outline Map of St. Helena

1986.
D1 **D 1** 1p. deep brown and brown 10 30
D2 2p. brown and orange . . 10 30
D3 5p. brown and red . . . 15 30
D4 7p. black and violet . . . 20 30
D5 10p. black and blue . . . 25 30
D6 25p. black and green . . 65 70

ST. KITTS Pt. 1

On 23 June 1980 separate postal administrations were formed for St. Kitts and for Nevis, although both islands remained part of the State of St. Kitts-Nevis.

100 cents = 1 West Indian dollar.

1980. As Nos. 394/406 of St. Kitts-Nevis optd **St Kitts**.
29B 5c. multicoloured 10 10
30B 10c. multicoloured 10 10
31A 12c. multicoloured 35 80
32B 15c. multicoloured 10 10
33B 25c. multicoloured 10 10
34B 30c. multicoloured 10 10
35B 40c. multicoloured 10 15
36A 45c. multicoloured 50 15
37A 50c. multicoloured 10 15
38A 55c. multicoloured 15 15
39A $1 multicoloured 10 25
40A $5 multicoloured . . . . . 30 1·00
41A $10 multicoloured . . . . . 35 1·75

9 H.M.S. "Vanguard", 1762

1980. Ships. Multicoloured.
42 4c. Type **9** 10 10
43 10c. H.M.S. "Boreas", 1787 10 10
44 30c. H.M.S. "Druid", 1827 . . 15 10
45 55c. H.M.S. "Winchester", 1831 . . . . 15 15
46 $1.50 Harrison Line "Philosopher", 1857 . . . . 30 35
47 $2 Harrison Line "Contractor", 1930 . . . . 35 45

10 Queen Elizabeth the Queen Mother at Royal Variety Performance, 1978

1980. 80th Birthday of The Queen Mother.
48 **10** $2 multicoloured 25 60

11 The Three Wise Men

1980. Christmas. Multicoloured.
49 5c. Type **11** 10 10
50 15c. The Shepherds 10 10
51 30c. Bethlehem 10 10
52 $4 Nativity scene 50 60

12 Purple-throated Carib **13** Bananaquit

1981. Birds. Multicoloured.
53A 1c. Magnificent frigate bird 15 20
54A 4c. Wied's crested flycatcher 25 20

55A 5c. Type **12** 25 20
56A 6c. Burrowing owl 35 30
57A 8c. Caribbean martin ("Purple Martin") 30 30
58A 10c. Yellow-crowned night heron 25 20
59A 15c. Type **13** 25 20
60A 20c. Scaly-breasted thrasher 30 20
61A 25c. Grey kingbird 30 20
62A 30c. Green-throated carib . . 30 20
63A 40c. Ruddy turnstone . . . 35 30
64A 45c. Black-faced grassquit . . 35 30
65A 50c. Cattle egret 40 30
66A 55c. Brown pelican 40 30
67A $1 Lesser Antillean bullfinch 60 60
68A $2.50 Zenaida dove . . . . 1·25 2·25
69A $5 American kestrel ("Sparrow Hawk") . . . 2·25 3·50
70A $10 Antillean crested hummingbird . . . . . . 4·50 6·00

The 1c. to 10c. are vertical as Type **12**. The remainder are horizontal as Type **13**.

14 Battalion Company Sergeant 3rd Regt of Foot ("The Buffs"), c. 1801

1981. Military Uniforms. Multicoloured.
71 5c. Type **14** 10 10
72 30c. Battalion Company Officer, 45th Regt of Foot, 1796–97 . . . . 15 10
73 55c. Battalion Company Officer, 9th Regt of Foot, 1790 . . . . 15 10
74 $2.50 Grenadier, 38th Regt of Foot, 1751 . . . . 45 35

14a "Saudadoes"

14b Prince Charles and Lady Diana Spencer (½-size illustration)

1981. Royal Wedding. Royal Yachts. Mult.
75 55c. Type **14a** 10 10
82 55c. Type **14b** 15 30
77 $2.50 "Royal George" 25 30
78 $2.50 As No.76 . . . . 70 70
79 $4 "Britannia" 35 50
80 $4 As No. 76 . . . . 75 1·00
MS81 120 × 109 mm. $5 No. 76 1·00 1·00

15 Miriam Pickard (first Guide Commissioner)

16 Stained-glass Windows

1981. 50th Anniv of St. Kitts Girl Guide Movement. Multicoloured.
84 5c. Type **15** 10 10
85 30c. Lady Baden-Powell's visit, 1964 . . . . 15 10
86 55c. Visit of Princess Alice, 1960 . . . . 25 10
87 $2 Thinking Day parade, 1980's 45 35

1981. Christmas.
88 **16** 5c. multicoloured 10 10
89 – 30c. multicoloured 10 10
90 – 55c. multicoloured 15 10
91 – $3 multicoloured 50 50
DESIGNS: 30c. to $3, Various designs showing stained-glass windows.

17 Admiral Samuel Hood

1982. Bicentenary of Brimstone Hill Siege.
92 **17** 15c. multicoloured 10 10
93 – 55c. multicoloured 20 10
MS94 96 × 71 mm.–$5 black, orange and brown . . . . 1·10 1·10
DESIGNS: 55c. Marquis De Bouille; $5 Battle scene.

18 Alexandra, Princess of Wales, 1863

20 Naturalist Badge

1982. 21st Birthday of Princess of Wales. Multicoloured.
95 15c. Type **18** 10 10
96 55c. Coat of arms of Alexandra of Denmark . . 15 15
97 $6 Diana, Princess of Wales 55 80

1982. Birth of Prince William of Wales. Nos. 95/7 optd **ROYAL BABY**.
98 15c. Type **18** 10 10
99 55c. Coat of Arms of Alexandra of Denmark . . 15 15
100 $6 Diana, Princess of Wales 55 80

1982. 75th Anniv of Boy Scout Movement. Multicoloured.
101 5c. Type **20** 10 10
102 55c. Rescuer badge 30 15
103 $2 First Aid badge 80 90

21 Santa with Christmas Tree and Gifts

1982. Christmas. Children's Paintings. Multicoloured.
104 5c. Type **21** 10 10
105 55c. The Inn 15 10
106 $1.10 Three Kings 20 15
107 $3 Annunciation 40 40

22 Cruise Ship "Stella Oceanis" at Basseterre

1983. Commonwealth Day. Multicoloured.
108 55c. Type **22** 15 10
109 $2 "Queen Elizabeth 2" at Basseterre 35 40

1983. Military Uniforms (2nd series). As T **14**. Multicoloured.
110 15c. Light Company Private, 15th Regt. of Foot, c. 1814 20 10
111 30c. Battalion Company Officer, 15th Regt. of Foot, c. 1780 . . . . . 30 15
112 55c. Light Company Officer, 5th Regt. of Foot, c. 1822 30 20
113 $2.50 Battalion Company Officer, 11th Regt. of Foot, c. 1804 . . . . . 60 1·60

23 Sir William Smith (founder)

25 Montgolfier Balloon, 1783

1983. Centenary of Boys' Brigade. Multicoloured.
114 10c. Type **23** 25 10
115 45c. B.B. members on steps of Sandy Point Methodist Church 30 10
116 50c. Brigade drummers . . . 30 10
117 $3 Boys' Brigade badge . . . 70 2·25

1983. Nos. 55, 59/63 and 66/70 optd **INDEPENDENCE 1983**.
118A 5c. Type **12** 15 10
119B 15c. Type **13** 30 10
120B 20c. Scaly-breasted thrasher 35 10
121B 25c. Grey kingbird 40 10
122B 30c. Green-throated carib 45 15
123B 40c. Turnstone 50 20
124B 55c. Brown pelican 55 30
125B $1 Lesser Antillean bullfinch . . . . 1·00 50
126B $2.50 Zenaida dove . . . . 1·75 1·75
127A $5 American kestrel . . . . 2·50 2·75
128B $10 Antillean crested hummingbird . . . . . 4·00 5·50

1983. Bicentenary of Manned Flight. Multicoloured.
129 10c. Type **25** 10 10
130 45c. Sikorsky "Russkiy Vityaz" biplane (horiz) . . 15 10
131 50c. Lockhead Tristar 500 (horiz) 15 15
132 $2.50 Bell XS-1 (horiz) 70 90
MS133 108 × 145 mm. Nos. 129/32 1·00 1·25

26 Star over West Indian Town

1983. Christmas. Multicoloured.
134 15c. Type **26** 10 10
135 30c. Shepherds watching Star 10 10
136 55c. Mary and Joseph . . . 10 10
137 $2.50 The Nativity 30 40
MS138 130 × 130 mm. Nos. 134/7 50 1·10

27 Parrot in Tree

1984. Batik Designs (1st series).
139 **27** 45c. multicoloured 10 10
140 – 50c. multicoloured 10 10
141 – $1.50 blue, yellow and purple 35 70
142 – $3 multicoloured . . . . . 55 1·75
DESIGNS: 50c. Man under coconut tree; $1.50, Women with fruit; $3 Butterflies.
See also Nos. 169/72.

28 Cushion Star

1984. Marine Life. Multicoloured.
143 5c. Type **28** 30 30
144 10c. Rough file shell 35 30
145 15c. Red-lined cleaning shrimp 35 15
146 20c. Bristleworm 35 15
147 25c. Flamingo tongue 40 15
148 30c. Christmas tree worm . . 40 20
149 40c. Pink-tipped anemone . . 55 25
150 50c. Smallmouth grunt . . . 55 30
151 60c. Glass-eyed snapper . . . 1·25 75
152 75c. Reef squirrelfish 90 70
153 $1 Sea fans and flamefish (vert) . . . . 1·00 60
154 $2.50 Reef butterflyfish (vert) 2·25 3·50
205 $5 Black-barred soldierfish (vert) . . . . 6·00 10·00
156 $10 Cocoa damselfish (vert) 7·50 14·00
The 10c., 60c., $5 and $10 come with or without imprint date.

29 Agriculture

1984. 25th Anniv of The 4-H Organisation. Multicoloured.
157 30c. Type **29** 15 10
158 55c. Animal husbandry . . . 20 15
159 $1.10 The 4-H Pledge 35 60
160 $3 On parade . . . . 65 1·25

30 Construction of Royal St. Kitts Hotel

1984. 1st Anniv of Independence of St. Kitts-Nevis. Multicoloured.
161 15c. Type **30** 15 10
162 30c. Independence celebrations 20 15
163 $1.10 National Anthem and aerial view (vert) 40 60
164 $3 "Dawn of a New Day" (vert) . . . . 1·00 1·40

31 Opening Presents

1984. Christmas. Multicoloured.
165 15c. Type **31** 15 10
166 60c. Singing carols 45 35
167 $1 Nativity play 75 60
168 $2 Leaving church on Christmas Day . . . . . . 1·40 1·10

1985. Batik Designs (2nd series). Horiz designs as T **27**.
169 15c. black, green and light green 15 10
170 40c. black, blue and light blue 30 15
171 60c. black, orange and red 45 25
172 $3 black, brown and light brown . . . . 1·25 2·25
DESIGNS: 15c. Country bus; 40c. Donkey cart; 60c. Rum shop and man on bicycle; $3 "Polynesia" (cruise schooner).

32 Container Ship "Tropic Jade"

1985. Ships. Multicoloured.
173 40c. Type **32** . . . . 1·00 30
174 $1.20 "Atlantic Clipper" (schooner) . . . . 2·00 1·50
175 $2 "Mandalay" (schooner) 2·25 2·50
176 $2 "Cunard Countess" (liner) 2·25 2·50

33 James Derrick Cardin (leading Freemason)

34 Map of St. Kitts

1985. 150th Anniv of Mount Olive S. C. Masonic Lodge. Multicoloured.
177 15c. Type **33** 65 30
178 75c. Banner of Mount Olive Lodge . . . . 1·40 1·25
179 $1.20 Masonic symbols (horiz) . . . . 1·40 3·00
180 $3 Lodge Charter, 1835 . . . 1·75 5·00

1985. Christmas. 400th Anniv of Sir Francis Drake's Visit. Multicoloured.
181 10c. Type **34** 30 15
182 40c. "Golden Hind" 60 35
183 60c. Sir Francis Drake . . . 60 50
184 $3 Drake's heraldic shield . . 75 3·50

35 Queen Elizabeth and Prince Philip on St. Kitts

38 Adult Green Monkey with Young

36 Family on Smallholding

1986. 60th Birthday of Queen Elizabeth. Multicoloured.
185 10c. Type **35** 15 10
186 20c. Queen Elizabeth on St. Kitts 25 15
187 40c. At Trooping the Colour 50 30
188 $3 In Sweden . . . . 2·00 3·00

1986. Royal Wedding. As T **146a** of St. Helena. Multicoloured.
189 15c. Prince Andrew and Miss Sarah Ferguson 15 10
190 $2.50 Prince Andrew . . . . 1·00 2·00

1986. Agriculture Exhibition. Multicoloured.
191 15c. Type **36** 20 10
192 $1.20 Hands holding people, computers and crops . . . 1·25 1·60

1986. 40th Anniv of U.N. Week. Nos. 185/8 optd **40th ANNIVERSARY U.N. WEEK 19-26 OCT.**
207 10c. Type **35** 15 15
208 20c. Queen Elizabeth on St. Kitts 25 20
209 40c. At Trooping the Colour 30 30
210 $3 In Sweden . . . . 1·00 3·25

1986. Endangered Species. Green Monkeys on St. Kitts. Multicoloured.
211 15c. Type **38** . . . . 3·00 50
212 20c. Adult on ground . . . . 3·25 50
213 60c. Young monkey in tree 6·50 2·50
214 $1 Adult grooming young monkey . . . . 6·50 4·50

39 Frederic Bartholdi (sculptor)

40 Officer, 9th Regt. (East Norfolk), 1792

1986. Centenary of Statue of Liberty. Multicoloured.
215 40c. Type **39** 30 30
216 60c. Torch (1876) and head (1878) on exhibition (horiz) 40 60
217 $1.50 "Isere" (French warship) carrying statue (horiz) . . . . 1·00 1·75
218 $3 Statue of Liberty, Paris 1884 . . . . 1·25 3·00
MS219 70 × 85 mm. $3.50 Head of Statue of Liberty . . . . 2·25 3·50

1987. Military Uniforms (3rd series). Multicoloured.
220 15c. Type **40** 40 30
221 15c. Officer, Regt de Neustrie, 1779 . . . . . . 40 30
222 40c. Sergeant, 3rd Regt of Foot ("The Buffs"), 1801 65 45
223 40c. Officer, French Artillery, 1812 . . . . 65 45
224 $2 Light Company Private, 5th Regt, 1778 . . . . . 1·25 3·00
225 $2 Grenadier of the Line, 1796 . . . . 1·25 3·00
MS226 121 × 145 mm. Nos. 220/5 6·75 8·00

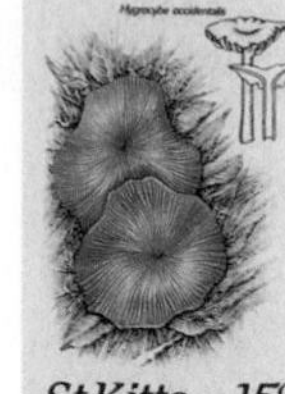

41 Sugar Cane Warehouse

43 "Hygrocybe occidentalis"

42 B.W.I.A. L-1011 TriStar 500

1987. Sugar Cane Industry. Multicoloured (colour of panel behind "ST. KITTS" given).
227 **41** 15c. yellow 20 30
228 – 15c. brown 20 30
229 – 15c. lilac 20 30
230 – 15c. blue 20 30
231 – 15c. turquoise 20 30
232 – 75c. light green 25 85
233 – 75c. lilac 25 85
234 – 75c. deep green 25 85
235 – 75c. yellow 25 85
236 – 75c. turquoise 25 85
DESIGNS: Nos. 227/31, Sugar cane factory; Nos. 232/6, Loading sugar train.
Nos. 227/31 and 232/6 were each printed together, se-tenant, forming composite designs.

1987. Aircraft visiting St. Kitts. Multicoloured.
237 40c. Type **42** 75 30
238 60c. L.I.A.T. Hawker Siddeley Super 748 . . . . 95 60
239 $1.20 W.I.A. De Havilland DHC-6 Twin Otter . . . . 1·50 2·75
240 $3 American Eagle Aerospatiale/Aeritalia ATR-42 . . . . 2·75 4·75

1987. Fungi. Multicoloured.
241 15c. Type **43** 80 20
242 40c. "Marasmius haematocephalus" . . . . 1·25 40
243 $1.20 "Psilocybe cubensis" 2·75 2·75
244 $2 "Hygrocybe acutoconica" 3·50 3·50
245 $3 "Boletellus cubensis" . . . 4·00 4·50

44 Carnival Clown

45 Ixora

1987. Christmas. Different clowns.
246 **44** 15c. multicoloured 25 15
247 – 40c. multicoloured 55 30
248 – $1 multicoloured . . . . . 1·25 1·40
249 – $3 multicoloured . . . . . 2·50 4·00
See also Nos. 266/9.

1988. Flowers. Multicoloured.
250 15c. Type **45** 30 15
251 40c. Shrimp plant 55 30
252 $1 Poinsettia . . . . 1·00 1·40
253 $3 Honolulu rose . . . . . 2·50 4·00

46 Fort Thomas Hotel

47 Ball, Wicket and Leeward Islands Cricket Association Emblem

1988. Tourism (1st series). Hotels. Multicoloured.
254 60c. Type **46** 70 70
255 60c. Fairview Inn 70 70
256 60c. Frigate Bay Beach Hotel 70 70
257 60c. Ocean Terrace Inn . . . 70 70
258 $3 The Golden Lemon . . . 2·25 2·75
259 $3 Royal St. Kitts Casino and Jack Tar Village . . . 2·25 2·75
260 $3 Rawlins Plantation Hotel and Restaurant . . . . 2·25 2·75
See also Nos. 270/5.

1988. 75th Anniv of Leeward Islands Cricket Tournament. Multicoloured.
261 40c. Type **47** . . . . 2·00 30
262 $3 Cricket match at Warner Park . . . . 4·25 4·50

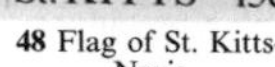

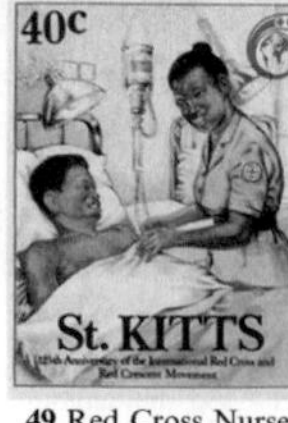

48 Flag of St. Kitts-Nevis

49 Red Cross Nurse with Hospital Patient

1988. 5th Anniv of Independence. Multicoloured.
263 15c. Type **48** 75 20
264 60c. Arms of St. Kitts . . . 1·00 80
MS265 61 × 53 mm. $5 Princess Margaret presenting Constitutional Instrument to Prime Minister Kennedy Simmonds, 1983 . . . . 4·00 4·25

1988. Christmas. As T **44** showing carnival masqueraders.
266 15c. multicoloured 10 10
267 40c. multicoloured 20 25
268 80c. multicoloured 40 55
269 $3 multicoloured . . . . . . 1·25 2·50

1989. Tourism (2nd series). Colonial Architecture. As T **46**. Multicoloured.
270 20c. Georgian house 20 15
271 20c. Colonial-style house . . 20 15
272 $1 Romney Manor 50 80
273 $1 Lavington Great House 50 80
274 $2 Government House . . . 70 1·60
275 $2 Treasury Building . . . . 70 1·60
For a redrawn version of No. 275 in a miniature sheet, see No. **MS**400.

1989. 125th Anniv of International Red Cross.
276 **49** 40c. multicoloured 30 30
277 – $1 multicoloured 65 75
278 – $3 red and black . . . . . 1·75 2·75
DESIGNS: $1 Loading patient into ambulance; $3 125th anniversary logo.

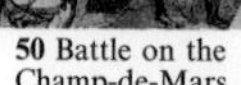

50 Battle on the Champ-de-Mars

50a Lunar Rover on Moon

1989. "Philexfrance 89" International Stamp Exhibition, Paris. Sheet 115 × 99 mm.
MS279 **50** $5 multicoloured . . . 3·25 3·75

1989. 20th Anniv of First Manned Landing on Moon. Multicoloured.
280 10c. Type **50a** 10 10
281 20c. Crew of "Apollo 13" (30 × 30 mm) 10 10
282 $1 "Apollo 13" emblem (30 × 30 mm) 45 65
283 $2 "Apollo 13" splashdown, South Pacific . . . . . . 95 1·50
MS284 100 × 83 mm. $3 Aldrin leaving "Apollo 11" lunar module 3·50 4·00

51 Outline Map of St. Kitts

52 "Santa Mariagallante" passing St. Kitts, 1493

1989.
285 **51** 10c. mauve and black . . . 20 20
286 15c. red and black 25 10
287 20c. orange and black . . . 25 10
288 40c. yellow and black . . . 40 20
289 60c. blue and black 60 50
290 $1 green and black . . . . 90 1·25

1989. 500th Anniv (1992) of Discovery of America by Columbus (1st issue). Multicoloured.
291 15c. Type **52** . . . . 1·75 30
292 80c. Arms of Columbus and map of fourth voyage, 1502–04 . . . . 3·00 1·75
293 $1 Navigation instruments c. 1500 . . . . 3·00 1·75
294 $5 Columbus and map of second voyage, 1493–96 . . 8·50 11·00
See also Nos. 359/60.

53 Poinciana Tree

1989. "World Stamp Expo '89" International Stamp Exhibition, Washington. Multicoloured.
295 15c. Type **53** 40 10
296 40c. Fort George Citadel, Brimstone Hill 80 30
297 $1 Private, Light Company, 5th Foot, 1778 . . . . . . 2·25 1·40
298 $3 St. George's Anglican Church . . . . 3·00 5·00

54 "Junonia evarete"

1990. Butterflies. Multicoloured.
299 15c. Type **54** . . . . 1·00 40
300 40c. "Anartia jatrophae" . . 1·75 40
301 60c. "Heliconius charitonia" 1·75 80
302 $3 "Biblis hyperia" . . . . . 3·75 5·50

1990. "Expo '90" International Garden and Greenery Exhibition, Osaka. Nos. 299/302 optd **EXPO 90** and logo.
303 15c. Type **54** . . . . 1·25 50
304 40c. "Anartia jatrophae" . . 2·00 50
305 60c. "Heliconius charitonia" 2·00 85
306 $3 "Biblis hyperia" . . . . . 4·25 6·00

56 Brimstone Hill

1990. 300th Anniv of English Bombardment of Brimstone Hill. Multicoloured.
307 15c. Type **56** 30 20
308 40c. Restored Brimstone Hill fortifications 50 30
309 60c. 17th-century English marine and Fort Charles under attack . . . . 70 1·10
310 $3 English sailors firing cannon . . . . 2·50 3·50
The 309 exists se-tenant, as a horizontal pair, with No. 310. Each pair shows a composite design.

57 Supermarine Spitfire Mk Vb "St. Kitts Nevis I" 71 Squadron

1990. 50th Anniv of Battle of Britain. Sheet 103 × 76 mm. containing T **57** and similar horiz design. Multicoloured.
MS311 $3 Type **57**; $3 Supermarine Spitfire Mk Vb "St. Kitts Nevis II" 345 Squadron . . . . . . 11·00 11·00

58 "Romney" (freighter)

1990. Ships. Multicoloured.
312 10c. Type **58** 60 20
313 15c. "Baralt" (freighter) . . . 75 20
314 20c. "Wear" (mail steamer) 75 20
315 25c. "Sunmount" (freighter) 75 20
316 40c. "Inanda" (cargo liner) 1·00 25
317 50c. "Alcoa Partner" (freighter) . . . . 1·00 30
318 60c. "Dominica" (freighter) 1·10 30
319 80c. "C.G.M Provence" (container ship) . . . . . 1·25 40
320 $1 "Director" (freighter) . . . 1·25 70
321 $1.20 Barque . . . . 1·75 1·75
322 $2 "Chignecto" (packet steamer) . . . . 2·50 2·50
323 $3 "Berbice" (mail steamer) 2·75 3·50
324 $5 "Vamos" (freighter) . . . 4·00 5·00
325 $10 "Federal Maple" (freighter) . . . . 6·50 8·50

59 Single Fork Game

1990. Christmas. Traditional Games. Multicoloured.
326 10c. Type **59** 15 10
327 15c. Boulder breaking . . . 15 10
328 40c. Double fork 30 30
329 $3 The run up . . . . 1·75 3·50

60 White Periwinkle

1991. Flowers. Multicoloured.
330 10c. Type **60** 70 20
331 40c. Pink oleander . . . . . 1·25 30
332 60c. Pink periwinkle (vert) . . 1·75 70
333 $2 White oleander (vert) . . 3·00 4·25

61 Census Logo

1991. National Census.
334 **61** 15c. multicoloured 30 15
335 $2.40 multicoloured . . . 2·50 3·25
The $2.40 differs from Type **61** by showing "ST. KITTS" in a curved panel.

1991. 65th Birthday of Queen Elizabeth II and 70th Birthday of Prince Philip. As T **165a** of St. Helena. Multicoloured.
336 $1.20 Prince Philip . . . . . 75 1·00
337 $1.80 Queen holding bouquet of flowers . . . . 1·00 1·10

62 Nassau Grouper

1991. Fishes. Multicoloured.
338 10c. Type **62** 50 20
339 60c. Hogfish . . . . 1·25 50
340 $1 Red hind . . . . 2·00 1·50
341 $3 Porkfish . . . . 3·50 5·00

63 School of Continuing Studies, St. Kitts and Chancellor Sir Shridath Ramphal

1991. 40th Anniv of University of West Indies. Multicoloured.
342 15c. Type **63** 40 15
343 50c. Administration Building, Barbados 70 40
344 $1 Engineering Building, Trinidad and Tobago . . . 1·25 1·25
345 $3 Mona Campus, Jamaica and Sir Shridath Ramphal 3·00 4·50

64 Whipping The Bull

1991. Christmas. "The Bull" (Carnival play). Multicoloured.
346 10c. Type **64** 40 10
347 15c. Death of The Bull . . . 40 10
348 60c. Cast of characters and musicians . . . . 1·25 60
349 $3 The Bull in procession . . 3·00 4·50

1992. 40th Anniv of Queen Elizabeth II's Accession. As T **168a** of St. Helena. Multicoloured.
350 10c. St. Kitts coastline . . . 40 10
351 40c. Warner Park Pavilion 2·00 50
352 60c. Brimstone Hill 75 40
353 $1 Three portraits of Queen Elizabeth . . . . 1·00 1·00
354 $3 Queen Elizabeth II . . . 1·90 2·75

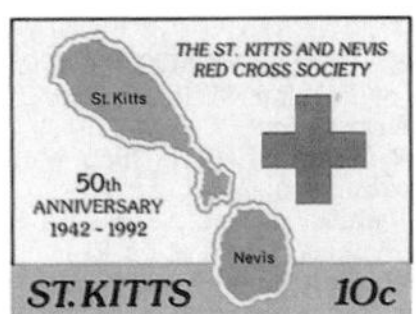

65 Map of St. Kitts-Nevis

1992. 50th Anniv of St. Kitts-Nevis Red Cross Society. Multicoloured.
355 10c. Type **65** . . . . 1·25 45
356 20c. St. Kitts-Nevis flag . . . 2·00 45
357 50c. Red Cross House, St. Kitts . . . . 1·50 80
358 $2.40 Henri Dunant . . . . 3·25 5·00

66 Columbus meeting Amerindians

1992. Organization of East Caribbean States. 500th Anniv of Discovery of America by Columbus (2nd issue). Multicoloured.
359 $1 Type **66** . . . . 1·50 1·00
360 $2 Ships approaching island 3·25 3·75

67 Fountain, Independence Square **68** Joseph and Mary travelling to Bethlehem

1992. Local Monuments. Multicoloured.
361 25c. Type **67** 25 20
362 50c. Berkeley Memorial Drinking Fountain 35 35
363 80c. Sir Thomas Warner's Tomb 55 65
364 $2 War Memorial . . . . . 1·10 2·00

1992. Christmas. Multicoloured.
365 20c. Type **68** 30 20
366 25c. Shepherds and star . . . 30 20
367 80c. Wise Men with gifts . . 65 55
368 $3 Mary, Joseph and Holy Child . . . . 1·75 3·25

68a Short Singapore III

1993. 75th Anniv of Royal Air Force. Aircraft. Multicoloured.
369 25c. Type **68a** 85 20
370 50c. Bristol Beaufort Mk II 1·40 30
371 80c. Westland Whirlwind Series 3 H.A.R. 10 helicopter . . . . 3·00 1·50
372 $1.60 English Electric Canberra . . . . 3·00 3·50
MS373 110 × 78 mm. $2 Handley Page 0/400; $2 Fairey Long Range monoplane; $2 Vickers Wellesley; $2 Sepecat Jaguar G.R.1 . . . 11·00 11·00

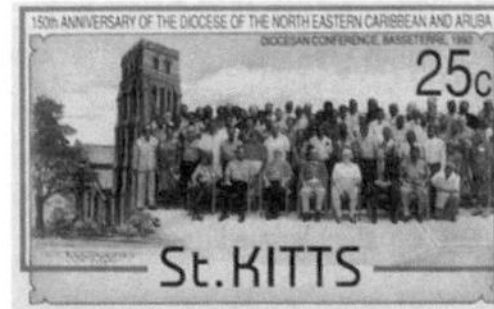

69 Members of Diocesan Conference, Basseterre, 1992

1993. 150th Anniv of Anglican Diocese of North-eastern Caribbean and Aruba. Multicoloured.
374 25c. Type **69** 15 10
375 50c. Cathedral of St. John the Divine (vert) 40 35
376 80c. Coat of arms and motto 70 85
377 $2 The Right Revd. Daniel Davis (first bishop) (vert) 1·50 2·75

70 1953 Coronation 2c. Stamp and Ampulla

1993. 40th Anniv of Coronation. Multicoloured.
378 10c. Type **70** 40 20
379 25c. 1977 Silver Jubilee $1.50 stamp and anointing spoon 50 20
380 80c. 1977 Silver Jubilee 55c. stamp and tassels . . . . 1·00 1·25
381 $2 1978 25th anniv of Coronation stamps and sceptre . . . . 2·00 3·50

71 Flags of Girls Brigade and St. Kitts-Nevis

1993. Centenary of Girls Brigade. Multicoloured.
382 80c. Type **71** . . . . 2·50 1·00
383 $3 Girls Brigade badge and coat of arms . . . . 4·00 4·50

72 Aspects of St. Kitts on Flag

1993. 10th Anniv of Independence. Multicoloured.
384 20c. Type **72** . . . . 1·00 15
385 80c. Coat of arms and Independence anniversary logo . . . . 1·25 80
386 $3 Coat of arms and map . . 4·25 4·50

73 "Hibiscus sabdariffa"

1993. Christmas. Flowers. Multicoloured.
387 25c. Type **73** 25 10
388 50c. "Euphorbia pulcherrima" 60 45
389 $1.60 "Euphorbia leucocephala" . . . . . . 1·75 2·50

74 Mesosaurus **75** Sir Shridath Ramphal

1994. Prehistoric Aquatic Reptiles. Multicoloured.
390 $1.20 Type **74** . . . . 1·40 1·75
391 $1.20 Placodus . . . . 1·40 1·75
392 $1.20 Liopleurodon . . . . . 1·40 1·75
393 $1.20 Hydrotherosaurus . . . 1·40 1·75
394 $1.20 Caretta . . . . 1·40 1·75
Nos. 390/4 were printed together, se-tenant, with the background forming a composite design.

1994. "Hong Kong '94" International Stamp Exhibition. Nos. 390/4 optd **HONG KONG '94** and emblem.
395 $1.20 Type **74** . . . . 1·90 2·25
396 $1.20 Placodus . . . . 1·90 2·25
397 $1.20 Liopleurodon . . . . . 1·90 2·25
398 $1.20 Hydrotherosaurus . . . 1·90 2·25
399 $1.20 Caretta . . . . 1·90 2·25

1994. First Recipients of Order of the Caribbean Community. Multicoloured.
401 10c. Type **75** 30 50
402 10c. Star of Order 20 30
403 10c. Derek Walcott 30 50
404 10c. William Demas 30 50
405 $1 Type **75** . . . . 1·25 1·40
406 $1 As No. 402 . . . . 1·00 1·00
407 $1 As No. 403 . . . . 1·25 1·40
408 $1 As No. 404 . . . . 1·25 1·40

76 Family singing Carols

1994. Christmas. Int Year of the Family. Mult.
409 25c. Type **76** 15 10
410 25c. Family unwrapping Christmas presents 15 10
411 80c. Preparing for Christmas carnival 60 60
412 $2.50 Nativity . . . . 1·90 3·00

77 Green Turtle swimming

1995. Endangered Species. Green Turtle. Multicoloured.
427 10c. Type **77** 40 50
428 40c. Turtle crawling up beach 55 60
429 50c. Burying eggs 60 60
430 $1 Young heading for sea . . 75 1·00

78 St. Christopher 1d. Stamps of 1870

1995. 125th Anniv of St. Kitts Postage Stamps. Each including the St. Christopher 1870 1d. Multicoloured.
431 25c. Type **78** 15 15
432 80c. St. Kitts-Nevis 1935 Silver Jubilee 1d. 45 50
433 $2.50 St. Kitts-Nevis 1946 Victory 1d. . . . . 1·75 2·25
434 $3 St. Christopher Nevis Anguilla 1953 Coronation 2c. . . . . 2·00 2·50

1995. 50th Anniv of End of Second World War. As T **182a** of St. Helena. Multicoloured.
435 20c. Caribbean Regiment patrol, North Africa . . . 15 15
436 50c. Grumman TBF Avengers (bombers) . . . 35 35
437 $2 Supermarine Spitfire MK Vb (fighter) . . . . 1·25 1·50
438 $8 U. S. Navy destroyer escort . . . . 5·00 6·50
MS439 75 × 85 mm. $3 Reverse of 1939–45 War Medal (vert) . . 1·75 2·00

79 Telecommunication Links between Islands

1995. 10th Anniv of SKANTEL (telecommunications company). Multicoloured.
440 10c. Type **79** 25 10
441 25c. Payphone and computer link 30 15
442 $2 Telecommunications tower and dish aerial . . . . . . 2·25 2·50
443 $3 Silhouette of dish aerial at sunset . . . . 2·50 3·50

80 Water Treatment Works

1995. 50th Anniv of United Nations. Multicoloured.
444 40c. Type **80** 35 25
445 50c. Beach 55 30
446 $1.60 Dust cart . . . . . . 1·75 2·25
447 $2.50 Forest . . . . 2·75 3·75

81 F.A.O. Emblem and Vegetables

1995. 50th Anniv of F.A.O. Multicoloured.
448 25c. Type **81** 20 10
449 50c. Glazed carrots and West Indian peas with rice . . . 35 30
450 80c. Tania and cassava plants 50 60
451 $1.50 Waterfall, Green Hill Mountain . . . . 2·25 2·75

82 Flame Helmet

84 Athlete and National Flag

83 L.M.S. No. 45614 Steam Locomotive "Leeward Islands" in Green Livery

1996. Sea Shells. Multicoloured.
452 $1.50 Type **82** . . . . 95 1·10
453 $1.50 Triton's trumpet . . . 95 1·10
454 $1.50 King helmet . . . . . 95 1·10
455 $1.50 True tulip . . . . . . 95 1·10
456 $1.50 Queen conch . . . . . 95 1·10

1996. "CAPEX '96" International Stamp Exhibition, Toronto.
457 10c. Type **83** 50 30
MS458 110 × 80 mm. $10 L.M.S. No. 5614 "Leeward Islands" steam locomotive in red livery (48 × 31½ mm) . . . . 7·50 7·50

1996. Centennial Olympic Games, Atlanta. Multicoloured.
459 10c. Type **84** 15 15
460 25c. High jumper and U.S.A. flag 20 20
461 80c. Athlete and Olympic flag 50 55
462 $3 Poster for 1896 Olympic Games, Athens . . . . . . 1·75 2·50
MS463 70 × 64 mm. $6 Olympic torch . . . . 3·25 3·50

85 Volunteer Rifleman, 1896

86 "Holy Virgin and Child" (A. Colin)

1996. Centenary of Defence Force. Multicoloured.
464 10c. Type **85** 15 15
465 50c. Mounted infantryman, 1911 . . . . 35 35
466 $2 Drummer, 1940–60 . . . 1·25 1·75
467 $2.50 Ceremonial uniform, 1996 . . . . 1·40 2·00

1996. Christmas. Religious Paintings. Multicoloured.
468 15c. Type **86** 20 10
469 25c. "Holy Family" (after Rubens) 25 10
470 50c. "Madonna with the Goldfinch" (Krause after Raphael) 45 35
471 80c. "Madonna on Throne with Angels" (17th-cent Spanish) . . . . 75 1·00

1997. "HONG KONG '97" International Stamp Exhibition. Sheet 130 × 90 mm, containing No. 323.
MS472 $3 "Berbice" (mail steamer) 1·60 2·00

87 Princess Parrotfish

1997. Fishes. Multicoloured.
473 $1 Type **87** 80 80
474 $1 Yellow-bellied hamlet . . 80 80
475 $1 Coney 80 80
476 $1 Fin-spot wrasse 80 80
477 $1 Doctor fish 80 80
478 $1 Squirrelfish 80 80
479 $1 Queen angelfish 80 80
480 $1 Spanish hogfish 80 80
481 $1 Red hind 80 80
482 $1 Red grouper 80 80
483 $1 Yellow-tailed snapper . . 80 80
484 $1 Mutton hamlet 80 80

1997. Golden Wedding of Queen Elizabeth and Prince Philip. As T **192a** of St. Helena. Multicoloured.
485 10c. Queen Elizabeth in evening dress . . . . 70 1·00
486 10c. Prince Philip and Duke of Kent at Trooping the Colour . . . . 70 1·00
487 25c. Queen Elizabeth in phaeton at Trooping the Colour . . . . 90 1·10
488 25c. Prince Philip in naval uniform . . . . 90 1·10
489 $3 Queen Elizabeth and Prince Philip . . . . . . 2·50 2·75
490 $3 Peter Phillips on horseback . . . . 2·50 2·75
MS491 110 × 70 mm. $6 Queen Elizabeth and Prince Philip in landau (horiz). . . . . 5·50 6·50

Nos. 485/6, 487/8 and 489/90 respectively were printed together, se-tenant, with the backgrounds forming composite designs.

88 C. A. Paul Southwell (first Chief Minister)

1997. National Heroes Day. Multicoloured.
492 25c. Type **88** 15 25
493 25c. Sir Joseph France (trade union leader) 15 25
494 25c. Robert Bradshaw (first Prime Minister) 15 25
495 $3 Sir Joseph France, Robert Bradshaw and C. A. Paul Southwell (horiz) . . . . . 1·75 2·50

89 Wesley Methodist Church

1997. Christmas. Churches. Multicoloured.
496 10c. Type **89** 10 10
497 10c. Zion Moravian Church 10 10
498 $1.50 St. George's Anglican Church (vert) . . . . . . 1·00 1·00
499 $15 Co-Cathedral of the Immaculate Conception (vert) . . . . 8·50 11·00

90 Common Long-tail Skipper

1997. Butterflies. Multicoloured.
500 10c. Type **90** 10 10
501 15c. White peacock 10 10
502 25c. Caribbean buckeye . . . 10 15
503 30c. The red rim 10 15
504 40c. Cassius blue 15 20
505 50c. The flambeau 20 25
506 60c. Lucas's blue 25 30
507 90c. Cloudless sulphur . . . 35 40
508 $1 The monarch 40 45
509 $1.20 Fiery skipper 50 55
510 $1.60 The zebra 65 70
511 $3 Southern dagger tail . . . 1·20 1·30
512 $5 Polydamus swallowtail . . 2·00 2·10
513 $10 Tropical chequered skipper . . . . 4·00 4·25

1998. Diana, Princess of Wales Commemoration. As T **62a** of Tokelau. Multicoloured.
514 30c. Wearing hat 30 30
MS515 145 × 70 mm. $1.60, As 30c.; $1.60, Wearing red jacket; $1.60, Wearing white jacket; $1.60, Carrying bouquets. (sold at $6.40 + 90c. charity premium) . . . 3·00 3·50

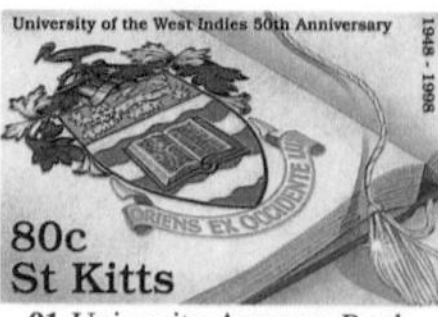

91 University Arms on Book

1998. 50th Anniv of University of West Indies. Multicoloured.
516 80c. Type **91** 45 40
517 $2 University arms and mortar-board . . . . . . 95 1·40

92 Santa at Carnival

1998. Christmas. Multicoloured.
518 80c. Type **92** 45 40
519 $1.20 Santa with two carnival dancers . . . . 65 1·00

93 Launching Rowing Boat

94a Lift-off

94 Caribbean Martin

1999. 125th Anniv of Universal Postal Union. Multicoloured.
520 30c. Type **93** 25 20
521 90c. Pictorial map of St. Kitts 50 60

1999. Birds of the Eastern Caribbean. Multicoloured.
522 80c. Type **94** 55 60
523 80c. Spotted sandpiper . . . 55 60
524 80c. Sooty tern 55 60
525 80c. Red-tailed hawk 55 60
526 80c. Brown trembler 55 60
527 80c. Belted kingfisher 55 60
528 80c. Black-billed whistling duck 55 60
529 80c. Yellow warbler 55 60
530 80c. Blue-headed hummingbird 55 60
531 80c. Antillean Euphonia . . 55 60
532 80c. Fulvous whistling duck 55 60
533 80c. Mangrove cuckoo . . . 55 60
534 80c. Carib grackle 55 60
535 80c. Caribbean elaenia . . . 55 60
536 80c. Scaly-breasted ground dove 55 60
537 80c. Forest thrush 55 60

1999. 30th Anniv of First Manned Landing on Moon. Multicoloured.
538 80c. Type **94a** 60 40
539 90c. In Moon orbit 70 65
540 $1 Buzz Aldrin on Moon's surface 80 85
541 $1.20 Heat shields burning during re-entry . . . . . . 90 1·25
MS542 90 × 80 mm. $10 Earth as seen from Moon (circular, 40 mm diam) . . . . 4·75 5·00

95 Local Quartet

1999. Christmas. Musicians. Multicoloured.
543 10c. Type **95** 20 10
544 30c. Trio 30 20
545 80c. Sextet 60 40
546 $2 Quartet in green jerseys 1·10 2·00

96 "Rockets, Saturn and Earth" (A. Taylor)

1999. New Millennium. Children's Paintings. Multicoloured.
547 10c. Type **96** 25 15
548 30c. "Y2K, computer and Earth weeping" (T. Liburd) 35 25
549 50c. "Alien destroying computer" (D. Moses) . . 40 35
550 $1 "Technology past, present and future" (P. Liburd) . . 70 1·25

97 Carnival Celebrations

2000. "Carifesta VII" Arts Festival. Multicoloured.
551 30c. Type **97** 30 20
552 90c. Carifesta logo 75 65
553 $1.20 Stylized dancer with streamer (vert) . . . . . . 1·00 1·40

98 Steam Locomotive No. 133, U.S. Military Railroad, 1864

2001. Railways in the American Civil War. Multicoloured (except for Nos. **MS**578a and c).
554 $1.20 Type **98** 50 55
555 $1.20 Locomotive *Quigley*, Louisville and Nashville Railroad, 1860 . . . . . . 50 55
556 $1.20 Locomotive *Colonel Holobird*, New Orleans, Opelousas and Great Western Railroad, 1865 . . 50 55
557 $1.20 Locomotive No. 150, U.S. Military Railroad, 1864 . . . . 50 55
558 $1.20 Locomotive *Doctor Thompson*, Atlanta and West Point Railroad, 1860 50 55
559 $1.20 Locomotive No. 156, U.S. Military Railroad, 1856 . . . . 50 55
560 $1.20 Locomotive *Governor Nye*, U.S. Military Railroad, 1863 . . . . . 50 55
561 $1.20 Locomotive No. 31, Illinois Central Railroad, 1856 . . . . 50 55
562 $1.20 Locomotive *C.A. Henry*, Memphis, Clarksville and Louisville Line, 1863 . . . . 50 55
563 $1.20 Locomotive No. 152, Illinois Central Railroad, 1856 . . . . 50 55
564 $1.20 Locomotive No. 116, U.S. Military Railroad, 1863 . . . . 50 55
565 $1.20 Locomotive *Job Terry* (shown as No. 111 of the Wilmington and Weldon Railroad, 1890) 50 55
566 $1.60 Locomotive *Dover*, U.S. Military Railroad, 1856 . . . . 65 70
567 $1.60 Locomotive *Scout*, Richmond to Gordonsville Line, 1861 . . . . 65 70
568 $1.60 Baltimore & Ohio Railroad Locomotive, 1861 65 70
569 $1.60 Locomotive *John. M. Forbes*, Philadelphia, Wilmington and Baltimore Railroad, 1861 . . . . . . 65 70
570 $1.60 Locomotive *Edward Kidder*, Wilmington and Weldon Railroad, 1866 . . 65 70
571 $1.60 Locomotive *William W. Wright*, U.S. Military Railroad, 1863 . . . . . . 65 70

572 $1.60 Locomotive No. 83, Illinois Central Railroad, 1856 . . . . 65 70
573 $1.60 Locomotive *The General*, Western and Atlantic Railroad, 1855 . . 65 70
574 $1.60 Locomotive No. 38, Louisville and Nashville Railroad, 1860 . . . . . . 65 70
575 $1.60 Locomotive *Texas*, Western and Atlantic Railroad, 1856 . . . . . . 65 70
576 $1.60 Locomotive No. 162, U.S. Military Railroad, 1864 . . . . 65 70
577 $1.60 Locomotive *Christopher Adams Jr.*, Memphis and Littlerock Line, 1853 . . . 65 70
MS578 Four sheets, each 99 × 78 mm. (a) $5 Brigadier-general Herman Haupt (Federal railway chief) (brown and black) (vert). (b) $5 General George B. McClellan (vert). (c) $5 General Ulysses S. Grant (brown, grey and black) (vert). (d) $5 General Robert E. Lee (vert). Set of 4 sheets . . . . 8·00 8·25

No. 577 is inscribed "Chritopher" in error.

99 Bananaquit

100 Symbolic Family and House

2001. Caribbean Flora and Fauna. Multicoloured.
579 $1.20 Type **99** 50 55
580 $1.20 Anthurium (face value in white) 50 55
581 $1.20 Common dolphin . . . 50 55
582 $1.20 Horse mushroom . . . 50 55
583 $1.20 Green anole 50 55
584 $1.20 Monarch butterfly . . 50 55
585 $1.20 Heliconia 50 55
586 $1.20 Anthurium (black face value) 50 55
587 $1.20 *Oncidium splendidum* 50 55
588 $1.20 Trumpet creeper . . . 50 55
589 $1.20 Bird of paradise . . . 50 55
590 $1.20 Hibiscus 50 55
591 $1.60 Beaugregory 65 70
592 $1.60 Banded butterflyfish . . 65 70
593 $1.60 Cherubfish 65 70
594 $1.60 Rock beauty 65 70
595 $1.60 Red snapper 65 70
596 $1.60 Leatherback turtle . . 65 70
597 $1.60 Figure-of-eight butterfly 65 70
598 $1.60 Banded king shoemaker 65 70
599 $1.60 Orange theope 65 70
600 $1.60 Grecian shoemaker . . 65 70
601 $1.60 Clorinde 65 70
602 $1.60 Small lace-wing 65 70
603 $1.60 Laughing gull 65 70
604 $1.60 Sooty tern 65 70
605 $1.60 Red-billed tropic bird ("White-tailed Tropicbird") 65 70
606 $1.60 Painted bunting 65 70
607 $1.60 Belted kingfisher . . . 65 70
608 $1.60 Yellow-bellied sapsucker 65 70
MS609 Five sheets, each 82 × 112 mm. (a) $5 Iguana (horiz). (b) $5 *Leochilus carinatus* (orchid). (c) $5 Redband parrotfish (horiz). (d) $5 Common morpho (butterfly) (horiz). (e) $5 Ruby-throated hummingbird (horiz). Set of 5 sheets . . . . 10·00 10·50

No. 608 is inscribed "Yello-bellied" in error.

2001. Population and Housing Census. Multicoloured.
610 30c. Type **100** 10 15
611 $3 People with Census symbol . . . . 1·20 1·30

101 Coronation of Queen Victoria

2001. Death Centenary of Queen Victoria. Multicoloured (except No. **MS**616).
612 $2 Type **101** 80 85
613 $2 Wedding of Queen Victoria and Prince Albert 80 85
614 $2 Royal Family with Crimean War veterans . . 80 85
615 $2 Queen Victoria with Prince Albert 80 85
MS616 88 × 113 mm. $5 Queen Victoria as Empress of India. (43 × 52 mm) (black) . . . . . 2·00 2·10

102 Mao Tse-tung, 1926

2001. 25th Death Anniv of Mao Tse-tung (Chinese leader). Multicoloured.
617 $2 Type **102** 80 85
618 $2 Mao Tse-tung, 1945 (face value at top left) 80 85
619 $2 Mao Tse-tung, 1945 (face value at bottom left) 80 85
MS620 160 × 142 mm. $3 Mao Tse-tung in blue jacket . . . . . . 1·20 1·30

103 "On the Coast at Trouville" (Monet)

2001. 75th Death Anniv of Claude-Oscar Monet (French painter). Multicoloured.
621 $2 Type **103** 80 85
622 $2 "Vetheuil in Summer" . . 80 85
623 $2 "Yellow Iris near Giverny" 80 85
624 $2 "Coastguard's Cottage at Varengeville" 80 85
MS625 137 × 111 mm. $5 "Poplars on Banks of Epte" (vert) . . . 2·00 2·10

104 Queen Elizabeth carrying Bouquet

105 French Dragoons from *Sicilian Vespers* (opera)

2001. 75th Birthday of Queen Elizabeth II. Multicoloured.
626 $2 Type **104** 80 85
627 $2 Wearing cream floral hat 80 85
628 $2 Wearing blue coat and hat 80 85
629 $2 Queen in beige hat and dress 80 85
MS630 80 × 109 mm. $5 Queen Elizabeth riding . . . . 2·00 2·10

2001. Death Centenary of Giuseppe Verdi (Italian composer). Designs showing *Sicilian* (opera). Multicoloured.
631 $2 Type **105** 80 85
632 $2 French dragoons, drinking round table 80 85
633 $2 Original costume design 80 85
634 $2 Inhabitants of Palermo . . 80 85
MS635 80 × 108 mm. $5 Montserrat Caballe as Elena . . . . . . 2·00 2·10

Nos. 631/2 are inscribed "FREWNCH" and **MS**635 "MOUNTSERRAT", all in error.

106 "Hatsufunedayu as a Tatebina" (Shigenobu)

2001. "Philanippon 01" International Stamp Exhibition, Tokyo. Japanese Woodcuts. Multicoloured.
636 50c. Type **106** 20 25
637 80c. "Samurai Kodenji as Tsuyu No Mae" (Kiyonobu I) 30 35
638 $1 "Nakamura Senya as Tokonatsu" (Kiyomasu I) 40 45
639 $1.60 "Sunida River" (Shunsho) 65 70
640 $2 "Kuemon Yoba the Wrestler" (Shune I) 80 85
641 $3 "Two actors" (Kiyonobu I/Tori I) . . . . 1·20 1·30
MS642 78 × 78 mm. $5 "Actors with swords" (Shune I) . . . . . . 2·00 2·10

107 Submarine "A1", 1902

2001. Centenary of Royal Navy Submarine Service. Multicoloured.
643 $1.50 Type **107** 60 65
644 $1.50 H.M.S. *Dreadnought* (battleship), 1906 . . . . . 60 65
645 $1.50 H.M.S. *Amethyst* (cruiser), 1903 . . . . . . 60 65
646 $1.50 H.M.S. *Barham* (battleship), 1914 . . . . . 60 65
647 $1.50 H.M.S. *Exeter* (cruiser), 1929 . . . . 60 65
648 $1.50 H.M.S. *Eagle* (aircraft carrier), 1918 . . . . . . 60 65
MS649 129 × 90 mm. $5 H.M.S. *Dreadnought* (nuclear submarine), 1960 (43 × 57 mm) . . . . . . 2·00 2·10

Nos. 644 and **MS**649 are inscribed "DREADNAUGHT" and No. 646 "BARNHAM", both in error.

108 *Maxillaria cucullata* (orchid)

109 Christmas Tree and Angel

2001. . Caribbean Flora and Fauna. Multicoloured.
650 $1.20 Type **108** 50 55
651 $1.20 *Cattleya dowiana* . . . 50 55
652 $1.20 *Rossioglossum grande* 50 55
653 $1.20 *Aspasia epidendroides* 50 55
654 $1.20 *Lycaste skinneri* . . . 50 55
655 $1.20 *Cattleya percivaliana* 50 55
656 $1.20 Brown trembler ("Trembler") 50 55
657 $1.20 Red-billed tropicbird 50 55
658 $1.20 Red-footed booby . . . 50 55
659 $1.20 Red-legged thrush . . . 50 55
660 $1.20 Painted bunting 50 55
661 $1.20 Bananaquit 50 55
662 $1.60 Killer whale (horiz) . . 65 70
663 $1.60 Cuvier's beaked whale (horiz) 65 70
664 $1.60 Humpback whale (horiz) 65 70
665 $1.60 Sperm whale (horiz) . . 65 70
666 $1.60 Blue whale (horiz) . . 65 70
667 $1.60 Whale shark (horiz) . . 65 70
668 $1.60 *Pholiota spectabilis* . . 65 70
669 $1.60 *Flammula penetrans* . . 65 70
670 $1.60 *Ungulina marginata* . . 65 70
671 $1.60 *Collybia iocephala* . . 65 70
672 $1.60 *Amanita muscaria* . . 65 70
673 $1.60 *Coprinus comatus* . . . 65 70
674 $1.60 Orange-barred sulphur 65 70
675 $1.60 Giant swallowtail . . . 65 70
676 $1.60 Orange theope butterfly 65 70
677 $1.60 Blue night butterfly . . 65 70
678 $1.60 Grecian shoemaker . . 65 70
679 $1.60 Cramer's mesene . . . 65 70
MS680 Five sheets, each 99 × 69 mm (No. **MS**680c) or 69 × 99 mm (others). (a) $5 *Psychilis atropurpurea* (orchid). (b) $5 Ruby-throated hummingbird. (c) $5 Sei Whale (*horiz*). (d) $5 *Lepiota procera* (*fungus*). (e) $5 Figure-of-eight butterfly. Set of 5 sheets . . . . 10·00 10·50

No. 672 is inscribed "Aminita" and No. 673 "Corinus", both in error.

2001. Christmas and Carnival. Multicoloured.
681 10c. Type **109** 10 10
682 30c. Fireworks 10 15
683 80c. Christmas wreath . . . 30 35
684 $2 Steel drums 80 85

110 Coronation Coach

2002. Golden Jubilee (2nd issue). Multicoloured.
685 $2 Type **110** 80 85
686 $2 Prince Philip after polo . . 80 85
687 $2 Queen Elizabeth and the Queen Mother in evening dress 80 85
688 $2 Queen Elizabeth in evening dress 80 85
MS689 76 × 108 mm. $5 Queen Elizabeth presenting Prince Philip with polo trophy . . . . . . 2·00 2·10

111 Downhill Ski-ing

2002. Winter Olympic Games, Salt Lake City. Multicoloured.
690 $3 Type **111** . . . . 1·20 1·30
691 $3 Cross country ski-ing . . 1·20 1·30
MS692 82 × 102 mm. Nos. 690/1 2·40 2·50

112 Xiong Nu Tribesman and Dog

113 World Cup Poster, Spain, 1982

2002. Chinese New Year ("Year of the Horse"). "Wen-Gi's Return to Han" (Chang Yu). Multicoloured.
693 $1.60 Type **112** 65 70
694 $1.60 Group of Xiong Nu tribesmen 65 70
695 $1.60 Wen-Gi (Chinese noblewoman) 65 70
696 $1.60 Standard bearer . . . 65 70

2002. World Cup Football Championship, Japan and Korea (2002). Multicoloured.
697 $1.65 Type **113** 65 70
698 $1.65 Just Fontaine, (France) 65 70
699 $1.65 American footballer . . 65 70
700 $1.65 Swedish footballer . . 65 70
701 $6 Daegu Stadium, Korea (56 × 42 mm) . . . . . . 2·40 2·50
MS702 51 × 3 mm. $6 Roger Milla (Cameroun), Italy, 1990 . . . 2·40 2·50

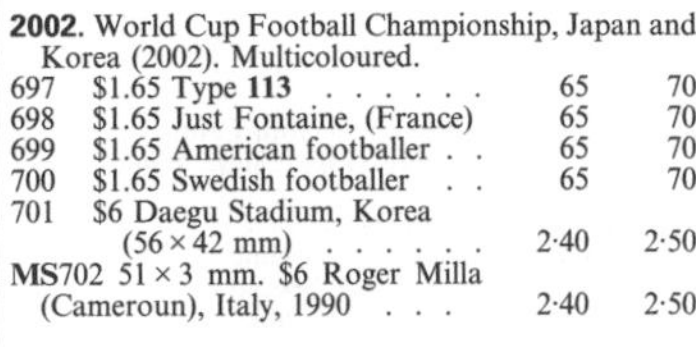

114 Policeman's Cap, Fireman's Helmet with U.S. and St. Kitts Flags

2002. "United We Stand". Support for Victims of 11 September 2001 Terrorist Attacks.
703 **114** 80c. multicoloured 30 35

115 Sakura-jima Volcano, Kyushu, Japan

2002. International Year of Mountains. Multicoloured.
704 $2 Type **115** 80 85
705 $2 Mount Assiniboine, Alberta, Canada 80 85
706 $2 Mount Asgard, Baffin Island, Canada 80 85
707 $2 Bugaboo Spire, British Columbia, Canada 80 85
MS708 75 × 57 mm. $6 Mount Owen, Wyoming, U.S.A. . . . 2·40 2·50

116 Scout saluting

2002. 20th World Scout Jamboree, Thailand. Multicoloured.

709 $2 Type **116** 80 85

710 $2 Silver Award 2 badge 80 85

711 $2 Illinois Scout badge 80 85

712 $2 Scout with ceremonial sword 80 85

MS713 78 × 84 mm. $6 Environmental Merit badge (vert) 2·40 2·50

117 Amerigo Vespucci

2002. 500th Anniv of Amerigo Vespucci's Third Voyage. Multicoloured.

714 $3 Type **117** 1·20 1·30

715 $3 Map of the World by Waldseemüller, 1507 1·20 1·30

716 $3 Vespucci with globe 1·20 1·30

MS717 55 × 76 mm. $6 Vespucci as an old man (vert) 2·40 2·50

118 Kim Collins running

119 Charles Lindbergh

2002. Kim Collins (Commonwealth Games gold medallist) Commemoration. Multicoloured.

718 30c. Type **118** 10 15

719 90c. Collins with World Championship bronze medal 35 40

2002. Famous People of the 20th Century. (a) 75th Anniv of First Solo Transatlantic Flight. Sheet 130 × 145 mm.

MS720 $1.50 Type **119** (black, violet and red); $1.50 Lindbergh holding propellor of Ryan NYP Special *Spirit of St. Louis* (maroon, violet and red); $1.50 Lindbergh (brown, violet and red); $1.50 Lindbergh and *Spirit of St. Louis* (maroon and red); $1.50 Lindbergh wearing flying helmet (purple, violet and red); $1.50 Lindbergh (claret, violet and red) 3·75 4·00

(b) Life and Times of President John F. Kennedy. Two sheets, each 132 × 145 mm. Multicoloured.

MS721 $2 John Kennedy in Solomon Islands, 1942; $2 Torpedo boat commander, 1942; Naval ensign, 1941; Receiving medal for gallantry, 1944 1·60 1·70

MS722 $2 President Kennedy forming Peace Corps; $2 Promoting Space Programme; $2 With Civil Rights leaders; $2 Signing Nuclear Disarmament Treaty with Soviet Union 3·25 3·50

(c) 5th Death Anniv of Diana, Princess of Wales. Two sheets, each 132 × 145 mm. Multicoloured.

MS723 $2 Princess Diana wearing jacket with mauve edged collar; $2 Wearing dress with frilled neckline; $2 Wearing pink dress; $2 Wearing mauve dress 3·25 3·50

MS724 $2 Wearing protective vest; $2 Wearing turquoise jacket; $2 Wearing yellow blouse; $2 Wearing red dress 3·25 3·50

(d) Queen Elizabeth the Queen Mother Commemoration. Sheet 200 × 143 mm, containing two of each design. Multicoloured.

MS725 $2 × 2 Duchess of York; $2 × 2 Queen Mother 3·25 3·50

120 Sour Sop

121 Ram

2002. Christmas. Island Fruits. Multicoloured.

726 10c. Type **120** 10 10

727 80c. Passion fruit 30 35

728 $1 Sugar apple 40 45

729 $2 Custard apple 80 85

2003. Chinese New Year ("Year of the Ram"). Multicoloured.

MS730 110 × 122 mm. $1 × 2 Type **121**; $1 × 2 Brown and white ram with spiral horns; $1 × 2 Brown ram with long horns 2·40 2·50

122 Pelican and Emblem

2003. 30th Anniv of CARICOM.

731 **122** 30c. multicoloured 10 15

123 Queen Victoria Bear

2003. Centenary of the Teddy Bear. Multicoloured.

MS732 135 × 156 mm. $2 Type **123**; $2 Teddy Roosevelt bear; $2 George Washington bear; $2 General Patton bear 3·25 3·50

MS733 90 × 113 mm. $5 Buffalo Bill bear 2·00 2·25

124 Queen Elizabeth II

125 Prince William as Toddler

2003. 50th Anniv of Coronation. Multicoloured.

MS734 156 × 94 mm. $3 Type **124**; $3 Queen wearing tiara and pink sash; $3 Wearing tiara and blue sash 3·75 4·00

MS735 106 × 76 mm. $6 Wearing tiara and blue robes 2·40 2·50

2003. 21st Birthday of Prince William. Multicoloured.

MS736 156 × 86 mm. $3 Type **125**; $3 As schoolboy; $3 As adult 3·75 4·00

MS737 106 × 76 mm. $5 As young boy, waving from carriage 2·00 2·10

126 Voisin LA5

2003. Centenary of Powered Flight. Multicoloured.

MS738 185 × 106 mm. $2 Type **126**; $2 Gotha G.V.; $2 Polikarpov I-16; $2 Bell YFM-1 3·25 3·50

MS739 106 × 76 mm. $5 Bristol Type 142 Blenheim Mk I 2·00 2·10

127 Miguel Indurain (1991–95)

128 "Child with Wooden Horse (Claude)"

2003. Centenary of Tour de France. Designs showing past winners. Multicoloured.

MS740 166 × 106 mm. $2 Type **127**; $2 Miguel Indurain (1995); $2 Bjarne Riis (1996); $2 Jan Ullrich (1997) 3·25 3·50

MS741 105 × 75 mm. $5 Miguel Indurain (1991–5) 2·00 2·10

2003. 30th Death Anniv of Pablo Picasso (artist). Multicoloured.

MS742 178 × 103 mm. $1.60 Type **128**; $1.60 "Child with a Ball (Claude)"; $1.60 "The Butterfly Catcher"; $1.60 "Boy with a Lobster"; $1.60 "Baby wearing Polka-Dot Dress"; $1.60 "El Bobo" (after Murillo) 4·00 4·25

MS743 68 × 86 mm. $5 Woman with baby (63 × 80 mm). Imperf 2·00 2·10

129 Scout and Seaman with Globe (1937)

131 "A Family Group" (detail)

130 "Tokiwa Gozen with her Son in the Snow" (Shunkyokusai Hokumei)

2003. 25th Death Anniv of Norman Rockwell (artist). T **129** and similar vert designs showing illustrations from scout calendars. Multicoloured.

MS744 131 × 180 mm. $2 Type **129**; $2 Scouts hiking (1937); $2 Boy and dog at window (1968); $2 Scout and statue (1932) 3·25 3·50

MS745 60 × 83 mm. $5 Scout with cub scout (1950) 2·00 2·10

2003. Japanese Art. Multicoloured.

746 90c. Type **130** 35 40

747 $1 "Courtesan and Asahina" (attrib. Eshosai Choki) 40 45

748 $1.50 "Parody of Sugawara no Michizane seated on an Ox" (Utagawa Toyokuni) 60 65

749 $3 "Visiting a Flower Garden" (detail) (Utagawa Kunisada) 1·20 1·30

MS750 147 × 147 mm. $2 "Akugenta Yoshihira" holding crossbow; $2 Holding painting; $2 As woman, with hand outstretched; $2 Holding sword 3·25 3·50

MS751 86 × 115 mm. $6 "The Courtesan Katachino under a Cherry Tree" (Utagawa Toyoharu) 2·40 2·50

No. **MS**750 shows a set of four prints of "Akugenta Yoshihira" by Utagawa Kunisada.

2003. Rembrandt (artist) Commemoration. Multicoloured.

752 50c. Type **131** 20 25

753 $1 "Portrait of Cornelis Claesz Anslo and Aeltje Gerritsdr Schouten" (horiz) 40 45

754 $1.60 "Portrait of a Young Woman" 65 70

755 $3 "Man in Military Costume" 1·20 1·30

MS756 181 × 172 mm. $2 "An Old Woman Reading"; $2 "Hendrickje Stoffels"; $2 "Rembrandt's Mother"; $2 "Saskia" 3·25 3·50

MS757 152 × 112 mm. $5 "Judas returning the Thirty Pieces of Silver" 2·00 2·10

132 "White Gibbon" (Giuseppe Castiglione)

133 Jiri Guth Jarkovsky

2004. Chinese New Year ("Year of the Monkey").

MS758 156 × 141 mm. **132** $1.60 × 4 multicoloured 2·50 2·75

MS759 158 × 92 mm. **132** $3 multicoloured (30 × 37 mm) 1·20 1·30

2004. Olympic Games, Athens. Multicoloured.

760 50c. Type **133** 20 25

761 90c. Olympic poster, Munich (1972) 35 40

762 $1 Medal and Eiffel Tower, Paris (1900) 40 45

763 $3 Wrestling (Greek bronze statue) (horiz) 1·20 1·30

134 12th SP Panzer Division and Map

2004. 60th Anniv of D-Day Landings.

MS764 Two sheets. (a) 178 × 106 mm. $2 × 4 multicoloured; purple; maroon; purple and deep purple. (b) 100 × 68 mm. $5 multicoloured Set of 2 sheets 5·00 5·25

DESIGNS: **MS**764 (a) $2 × 4 Type **134**; German heavy tank; Soldier aiming weapon; Soldiers and tank. (b) $5 Allied cemetery, Normandy.

135 Pope John Paul II

136 Berti Vogts

2004. 25th Anniv of the Pontificate of Pope John Paul II. Multicoloured.

MS765 147 × 105 mm. $2 × 4 Type **135**; Walking in gardens; Standing with hands crossed; Holding Pastoral Staff 3·25 3·50

2004. European Football Championship 2004, Portugal. Commemoration of Match between Germany and Czech Republic (1996). Multicoloured.

MS766 Two sheets (a) 147 × 86 mm. $2 × 4 Type **136**; Patrik Berger; Oliver Bierhoff; Empire Stadium. (b) 97 × 86 mm. $5 German team (1996) (51 × 48 mm) Set of 2 sheets 5·00 5·25

OFFICIAL STAMPS

1980. Nos. 32/41 optd **OFFICIAL**.

O 1A 15c. multicoloured 10 10

O 2A 25c. multicoloured 10 10

O 3A 30c. multicoloured 10 10

O 4A 40c. multicoloured 10 15

O 5A 45c. multicoloured 15 15

O 6A 50c. multicoloured 15 15

O 7A 55c. multicoloured 15 15

O 8A $1 multicoloured 25 25

O 9A $5 multicoloured 80 1·50

O10A $10 multicoloured 1·00 2·50

1981. Nos. 59/70 optd **OFFICIAL**.

O11 15c. Bananaquit 20 10

O12 20c. Scaly-breasted thrasher 20 10

O13 25c. Grey kingbird 25 10

O14 30c. Green-throated carib 25 10

O15 40c. Turnstone 35 15

O16 45c. Black-faced grassquit 40 20

O17 50c. Cattle egret 40 20

O18 55c. Brown pelican 50 25

O19 $1 Lesser Antillean bullfinch 75 45

O20 $2.50 Zenaida dove 1·60 1·00

O21 $5 American kestrel 2·75 2·00

O22 $10 Antillean crested hummingbird 5·00 4·25

1983. Nos. 75/80 optd **OFFICIAL** or surch also.

O23 45c. on $2.50 "Royal George" 15 15

O24 45c. on $2.50 Prince Charles and Lady Diana Spencer 25 25

O25 55c. "Saudadoes" 15 15
O26 55c. Prince Charles and Lady Diana Spencer . . . 30 30
O27 $1.10 on $4 "Britannia" . . 30 40
O28 $1.10 on $4 Prince Charles and Lady Diana Spencer 60 70

1984. Nos. 145/56 optd **OFFICIAL**.
O29 15c. Red-lined cleaning shrimp . . . . 70 1·25
O30 20c. Bristleworm . . . . . 80 1·50
O31 25c. Flamingo tongue . . . 80 1·50
O32 30c. Christmas tree worm . . 90 1·50
O33 40c. Pink-tipped anemone . . 1·00 1·50
O34 50c. Small-mouthed grunt . . 1·00 1·50
O35 60c. Glass-eyed snapper . . 1·25 2·00
O36 75c. Reef squirrelfish . . . . 1·50 2·50
O37 $1 Sea fans and flamefish (vert) . . . . 2·00 2·50
O38 $2.50 Reef butterflyfish (vert) 3·75 6·00
O39 $5 Black-barred soldierfish (vert) . . . . 5·50 3·00
O40 $10 Cocoa damselfish (vert) 8·50 6·00

ST. KITTS-NEVIS Pt. 1

Islands of the Leeward Is., Br. W. Indies. The general issues for Leeward Is, were in concurrent use until 1 July 1956. From 1952 the stamps are inscribed "St. Christopher, Nevis and Anguilla". Achieved Associated Statehood on 27 February 1967. St. Kitts and Nevis had separate postal administrations from 23 June 1980.

1903. 12 pence = 1 shilling;
20 shillings = 1 pound.
1951. 100 cents = 1 West Indian dollar.

1 Christopher Columbus
2 Medicinal Spring

1903.
1 1 ½d. purple and green . . . 1·75 70
12 ½d. green . . . . 1·00 60
13 2 1d. grey and red . . . . . 1·75 25
14a 1d. red 70 20
3 1 2d. purple and brown . . . 2·50 11·00
16 2½d. black and blue . . . 14·00 3·25
17 2½d. blue . . . . 2·50 50
18a 2 3d. green and orange . . . 2·75 2·75
19ab 1 6d. black and purple . . . 6·00 25·00
7 1s. green and orange . . . 6·50 11·00
8 2s. green and black . . . . 12·00 20·00
9 2s.6d. black and violet . . 18·00 42·00
10 2 5s. purple and green . . . 55·00 55·00

1916. Optd **WAR TAX**.
22 1 ½d. green . . . . 1·00 50

1918. Optd **WAR STAMP**.
23 1 1½d. orange 80 80

4
5

1920.
37a 4 ½d. green . . . . 1·50 80
38 5 1d. red 65 15
39 1d. violet . . . . 4·00 90
26 4 1½d. yellow . . . . 1·25 1·75
40 1½d. red . . . . 2·50 2·75
40a 1½d. brown . . . . 1·00 30
41 5 2d. grey 50 60
44 4 2½d. blue . . . . 1·50 1·75
43 2½d. brown . . . . 2·25 9·00
45a 5 3d. purple on yellow . . . 75 4·50
45 3d. blue . . . . 1·00 4·25
46aw 4 6d. purple and mauve . . 4·00 6·00
31 5 1s. black on green . . . . 3·50 4·00
47 4 2s. purple and blue on blue . . . . 8·00 23·00
33 5 2s.6d. black and red on blue . . . . 5·00 32·00
34 4 5s. green and red on yellow . . . . 5·00 40·00
35 5 10s. green and red on green . . . . 12·00 48·00
36 4 £1 purple and black on red £225 £300

6 Old Road Bay and Mount Misery

1923. Tercentenary Commemoration.
48 6 ½d. black and green . . . . 2·25 7·00
49 1d. black and violet . . . . 4·50 1·50
50 1½d. black and red . . . . . 4·50 10·00
51 2d. black and grey . . . . . 3·75 1·50
52 2½d. black and brown . . . . 6·00 32·00
53 3d. black and blue . . . . . 3·75 15·00
54 6d. black and purple . . . . 9·50 32·00
55 1s. black and green . . . . . 14·00 32·00
56 2s. black and blue on blue . . 42·00 60·00
57 2s.6d. black and red on blue 48·00 75·00
59 5s. black and red on yellow 75·00 £170
58 10s. black and red on green £275 £400
60 £1 black and purple on red £700 £1400

1935. Silver Jubilee. As T **32a** of St. Helena.
61 1d. blue and red . . . . . . 1·00 70
62 1½d. blue and grey 75 75
63 2½d. brown and blue . . . . 1·00 80
64 1s. grey and purple . . . . . 5·50 15·00

1937. Coronation. As T **32b** of St. Helena.
65 1d. red 30 20
66 1½d. brown 40 10
67 2½d. blue 60 80
Nos. 61/7 are inscribed "ST. CHRISTOPHER AND NEVIS".

7 King George VI
8 King George VI and Medicinal Spring

10 King George VI and Anguilla Island

1938.
68a 7 ½d. green 10 10
69a 1d. red . . . . 1·50 50
70 1½d. orange 20 30
71b 8 2d. red and grey . . . . 1·25 1·25
72a 7 2½d. blue 70 30
73g 8 3d. purple and red . . . 6·00 6·00
74c – 6d. green and purple . . 5·00 1·50
75b 8 1s. black and green . . . 4·00 85
76ab 2s.6d. black and red . . . 12·00 3·75
77b – 5s. green and red . . . 24·00 12·00
77e 10 10s. black and blue . . . 13·00 19·00
77f £1 black and brown . . . 13·00 23·00
The 6d. and 5s. are as Type **8**, but with the Christopher Columbus device as in Type **4**.

1946. Victory. As T **33a** of St. Helena.
78 1½d. orange 10 10
79 3d. red 10 10

1949. Silver Wedding. As T **33b/c** of St. Helena.
80 2½d. blue 10 50
81 5s. red . . . . 6·50 3·00

1949. U.P.U. As T **33d/g** of St. Helena.
82 2½d. blue 15 20
83 3d. red . . . . 1·50 1·25
84 6d. mauve 20 50
85 1s. green 20 30

1950. Tercentenary of British Settlement in Anguilla. Optd **ANGUILLA TERCENTENARY 1650–1950.**
86 7 1d. red 10 20
87 1½d. orange 10 35
88 2½d. blue 15 20
89 8 3d. purple and red 15 60
90 – 6d. green and purple (No. 74d) 15 20
91 8 1s. black and green 60 25

10a Arms of University
10b Princess Alice

1951. Inauguration of B.W.I. University College.
92 10a 3c. black and orange . . . 30 15
93 10b 12c. green and mauve . . . 30 1·25

ST. CHRISTOPHER, NEVIS AND ANGUILLA

13 Bath House and Spa

1952.
94 13 1c. green and ochre . . . . 15 1·25
95 – 2c. green . . . . 1·00 1·00
96 – 3c. red and violet . . . . 30 1·25
97 – 4c. red 20 20
98 – 5c. blue and grey 30 10
99 – 6c. blue 30 15
100 – 12c. blue and brown . . . 1·25 10
101 – 24c. black and red 30 10
102 – 48c. olive and brown . . . 2·25 2·50
103 – 60c. ochre and green . . . 2·00 3·00
104 – $1.20 green and blue . . . 7·00 2·75
105 – $4.80 green and red . . . 13·00 18·00
DESIGNS—HORIZ: 2c. Warner Park; 4c. Brimstone Hill; 5c. Nevis from the sea, North; 6c. Pinney's Beach, Nevis; 24c. Old Road Bay; 48c. Sea Island cotton, Nevis; 60c. The Treasury; $1.20, Salt pond, Anguilla; $4.80, Sugar factory. VERT: 3c. Map of the islands; 12c. Sir Thomas Warner's tomb.

1953. Coronation. As T **33h** of St. Helena.
106 2c. black and green 30 15

1954. As 1952 but with portrait of Queen Elizabeth II.
106a ½c. olive (as $1.20) 30 10
107 1c. green and ochre 20 10
108 2c. green 50 10
109 3c. red and violet 65 10
110 4c. red 15 10
111 5c. blue and grey 15 10
112 6c. blue 50 10
112b 8c. black . . . . 3·00 10
113 12c. blue and brown 15 10
114 24c. black and red 15 10
115 48c. olive and brown . . . 60 60
116 60c. ochre and green . . . 5·50 4·50
117 $1.20 green and blue . . . 18·00 2·25
117b $2.40 black and orange . . . 10·00 11·00
118 $4.80 green and red . . . . 13·00 11·00
DESIGNS (new values)—VERT: 8c. Sombrero Lighthouse. HORIZ: $2.40, Map of Anguilla and Dependencies.

27 Alexander Hamilton and View of Nevis

1956. Birth Bicent of Alexander Hamilton.
119 27 24c. green and blue 30 15

27a Federation Map

1958. British Caribbean Federation.
120 27a 3c. green 60 15
121 6c. blue . . . . 90 2·50
122 12c. red . . . . 1·00 35

28 1d. Stamp of 1861

1961. Centenary of Nevis Stamp.
123 28 2c. red and green 15 20
124 8c. red and blue 20 10
125 12c. lilac and red 30 15
126 24c. green and orange . . . 35 15
The 8c., 12c. and 24c. show the original 4d., 6d. and 1s. stamps of Nevis respectively.

1963. Cent of Red Cross. As T **63b** of St. Helena.
127 3c. red and black 10 10
128 12c. red and blue 20 40

33 Loading Sugar Cane, St. Kitts

1963. Multicoloured.
129 ½c. New Lighthouse, Sombrero 10 10
130 1c. Type **33** 10 10
131 2c. Pall Mall Square, Basseterre 10 10
132 3c. Gateway, Brimstone Hill Fort, St. Kitts 10 10
133 4c. Nelson's Spring, Nevis . . 10 10
134 5c. Grammar School, St. Kitts . . . . 2·25 10
135 6c. Crater, Mt. Misery, St. Kitts 10 10
136 10c. Hibiscus 15 10
137 15c. Sea Island cotton, Nevis 55 10
138 20c. Boat-building, Anguilla 20 10
139 25c. White-crowned pigeon 2·00 10
140 50c. St. George's Church Tower, Basseterre 40 25
141 60c. Alexander Hamilton . . 1·00 30
142 $1 Map of St. Kitts-Nevis . . 2·50 40
143 $2.50 Map of Anguilla . . . 2·50 2·50
144 $5 Arms of St. Christopher, Nevis and Anguilla . . . . 5·50 4·00
The ½, 2, 3, 15, 25, 60c., $1 and $5 are vert, the rest horiz.

1964. Arts Festival. Optd **ARTS FESTIVAL ST KITTS 1964.**
145 3c. multicoloured (No. 132) 10 15
146 25c. multicoloured (No. 139) 20 15

1965. Cent of I.T.U. As T **64a** of St. Helena.
147 2c. bistre and red 10 10
148 50c. blue and olive 40 50

1965. I.C.Y. As T **64b** of St. Helena.
149 2c. purple and green 10 20
150 25c. green and violet 20 10

1966. Churchill Commemoration. As T **64c** of St. Helena.
151 ½c. blue . . . . 10 2·00
152 3c. green 30 10
153 15c. brown 70 20
154 25c. violet 75 20

48a Queen Elizabeth and Duke of Edinburgh

1966. Royal Visit.
155 48a 3c. black and blue 25 30
156 25c. black and mauve . . 55 30

1966. World Cup Football Championship. As T **64d** of St. Helena.
157 6c. multicoloured 40 20
158 25c. multicoloured 60 10

49 Festival Emblem

1966. Arts Festival.
159 49 3c. multicoloured 10 10
160 25c. multicoloured 20 10

1968. Inauguration of W.H.O. Headquarters, Geneva. As T **64e** of St. Helena.
161 3c. black, green and blue . . 10 10
162 40c. black, purple and brown 30 20

1966. 20th Anniv of UNESCO. As T **64f/h** of St. Helena.
163 3c. multicoloured 10 10
164 6c. yellow, violet and olive 10 10
165 40c. black, purple and orange 30 35

50 Government Headquarters, Basseterre

1967. Statehood. Multicoloured.
182 3c. Type **50** 10 10
183 10c. National flag 10 10
184 25c. Coat of arms 15 15

53 John Wesley and Cross

1967. West Indies Methodist Conference.
185 53 3c. black, red and violet . . 10 10
186 – 25c. black, turquoise & blue 15 10
187 – 40c. black, yellow & orange 15 15
DESIGNS: 25c. Charles Wesley and cross; 40c. Thomas Coke and cross.

56 Handley Page Dart Herald over "Jamaica Producer" (freighter)

1968. Caribbean Free Trade Area.
188 **56** 25c. multicoloured 40 10
189 50c. multicoloured 40 20

57 Dr. Martin Luther King

58 "Mystical Nativity" (Botticelli)

1968. Martin Luther King Commemoration.
190 **57** 50c. multicoloured 15 10

1968. Christmas.
191 **58** 12c. multicoloured 10 10
192 – 25c. multicoloured 10 10
193 **58** 40c. multicoloured 15 10
194 – 50c. multicoloured 15 10
DESIGN: 25c., 50c. "The Adoration of the Magi" (Rubens).

60 Tarpon Snook

1968. Fishes.
195 **60** 6c. multicoloured 10 10
196 – 12c. black, green and blue 15 10
197 – 40c. multicoloured 25 10
198 – 50c. multicoloured 30 15
FISHES: 12c. Needlefish; 40c. Horse-eyed jack; 50c. Black-finned snapper.

64 The Warner Badge and Islands

1969. Sir Thomas Warner Commem. Multicoloured.
199 20c. Type **64** 10 10
200 25c. Sir Thomas Warner's tomb 10 10
201 40c. Charles I's Commission 15 15

67 "The Adoration of the Kings" (Mostaert)

73 Portuguese Caravels (16th-cent)

1969. Christmas. Multicoloured.
202 10c. Type **67** 10 10
203 25c. As 10c. 10 10
204 40c. "The Adoration of the Kings" (Geertgen) 10 10
205 50c. As 40c. 10 10

1970. Multicoloured. (except ½c.).
206 ½c. Pirates and treasure at Frigate Bay (black, orange and green) 10 10
207 1c. English two-decker warship, 1650 . . . . . 30 10
208 2c. Naval flags of colonizing nations 15 10
209 3c. Rapier hilt (17th-century) 15 10
210 4c. Type **73** 20 10
211 5c. Sir Henry Morgan and fireships, 1669 . . . . . 30 10
212 6c. L'Ollonois and pirate carrack (16th-century) . . 30 10
213 10c. 17th-century smugglers' ship 30 10
214a 15c. "Piece of Eight" . . . 1·75 10
215 20c. Cannon (17th-century) 35 10
216 25c. Humphrey Cole's astrolabe, 1574 . . . . . 40 10
217 50c. Flintlock pistol (17th-cent) 85 80
218 60c. Dutch flute (17th-cent) 1·50 70
219 $1 Capt. Bartholomew Roberts and his crew's death warrant . . . . . 1·50 75
220 $2.50 Railing piece (gun) (16th-century) . . . . . 1·25 3·25
221 $5 Drake, Hawkins and sea battle . . . . 1·50 4·50
280 $10 The Apprehension of Blackbeard (Edward Teach) . . . . 20·00 13·00
The ½c. to 3c., 15c., 25c., 60c. and $1 are vert designs.

85 Graveyard Scene ("Great Expectations")

1970. Death Cent of Charles Dickens.
222 **85** 4c. brown, gold and green 10 35
223 – 20c. brown, gold and purple 10 20
224 – 25c. brown, gold and green 10 20
225 – 40c. brown, gold and blue 15 35
DESIGNS—HORIZ: 20c. Miss Havisham and Pip ("Great Expectations"). VERT: 25c. Dickens' birthplace; 40c. Charles Dickens.

86 Local Steel Band

1970. Festival of Arts. Multicoloured.
226 20c. Type **86** 10 10
227 25c. Local string band . . . 10 10
228 40c. Scene from "A Midsummer Night's Dream" 15 15

87 1d. Stamp of 1870 and Post Office, 1970

1970. Stamp Centenary.
229 **87** ½c. green and red 10 10
230 – 20c. purple, green and red 10 10
231 – 25c. purple, green and red 10 10
232 – 50c. red, green and black 30 45
DESIGNS: 20c., 25c., 1d. and 6d. stamps of 1870; 50c.6d. stamp of 1870 and early postmark.

88 "Adoration of the Shepherds" (Frans van Floris)

1970. Christmas. Multicoloured.
233 3c. Type **88** 10 10
234 20c. "The Holy Family" (Van Dyck) 10 10
235 25c. As 20c. 10 10
236 40c. Type **88** 15 50

89 Monkey Fiddle

1971. Flowers. Multicoloured.
237 ½c. Type **89** 10 20
238 20c. Tropical mountain violet 15 10
239 30c. Trailing morning glory 15 15
240 50c. Fringed epidendrum . . 30 1·00

90 Royal Poinciana

1971. Philippe de Poincy Commem. Mult.
241 20c. Type **90** 10 10
242 30c. Chateau de Poincy . . . 10 10
243 50c. De Poincy's badge (vert) 20 15

91 The East Yorks

1971. Siege of Brimstone Hill, 1782. Multicoloured.
244 ½c. Type **91** 10 10
245 20c. Royal Artillery 20 10
246 30c. French infantry 30 10
247 50c. The Royal Scots 40 20

92 "Crucifixion" (Massys)

1972. Easter.
248 **92** 4c. multicoloured 10 10
249 20c. multicoloured 10 20
250 30c. multicoloured 10 25
251 40c. multicoloured 10 25

93 "Virgin and Child" (Borgognone)

1972. Christmas. Multicoloured.
252 3c. Type **93** 10 10
253 20c. "Adoration of the Kings" (J. Bassano) (horiz) 15 10
254 25c. "Adoration of the Shepherds" (Domenichino) 15 10
255 40c. "Virgin and Child" (Fiorenzo di Lorenzo) . . 20 10

1972. Royal Silver Wedding. As T **103** of St. Helena, but with brown pelicans in background.
256 20c. red 35 20
257 25c. blue 35 20

95 Landing on St. Christopher, 1623

1973. 300th Anniv of Sir Thomas Warner's Landing on St. Christopher. Multicoloured.
258 4c. Type **95** 15 10
259 25c. Growing tobacco . . . 15 10
260 40c. Building fort at Old Road 20 10
261 $2.50 "Concepcion" . . . . 80 1·10

96 "The Last Supper" (Titian)

100 "Madonna and Child" (Murillo)

99 Harbour Scene and 2d. Stamp of 1903

1973. Easter. Paintings of "The Last Supper" by the artists listed. Multicoloured.
262 4c. Type **96** 10 10
263 25c. Ascribed to Roberti . . 10 10
264 $2.50 Juan de Juanes (horiz) 70 60

1973. Royal Visit. Nos. 258/61 optd **VISIT OF H. R. H. THE PRINCE OF WALES 1973.**
265 **95** 4c. multicoloured 10 15
266 – 25c. multicoloured 10 15
267 – 40c. multicoloured 15 15
268 – $2.50 multicoloured . . . 45 50

1973. 70th Anniv of First St. Kitts-Nevis Stamps. Multicoloured.
285 4c. Type **99** 10 10
286 25c. Sugar-mill and 1d. stamp of 1903 . . . . 15 10
287 40c. Unloading boat and ½d. stamp of 1903 . . . . . 35 10
288 $2.50 Rock-carvings and 3d. stamp of 1903 . . . . . . 1·00 1·00
MS289 144 × 95 mm. Nos. 285/8 1·50 4·50

1973. Royal Wedding. As T **103a** of St. Helena. Multicoloured, background colours given.
290 25c. green 15 10
291 40c. brown 15 10

1973. Christmas. Paintings of "The Holy Family" by the artists listed. Multicoloured.
292 4c. Type **100** 10 10
293 40c. Mengs 15 10
294 60c. Sassoferrato 20 15
295 $1 Filippino Lippi (horiz) . . 25 30

101 "Christ carrying the Cross" (S. del Piombo)

103 Hands reaching for Globe

102 University Centre, St. Kitts

1974. Easter. Multicoloured.
296 4c. Type **101** 10 10
297 25c. "The Crucifixion" (Goya) 15 10
298 40c. "Trinity" (Ribera) . . . 15 10
299 $2.50 "The Deposition" (Fra Bartolomeo) (horiz) . . 1·00 75

1974. 25th Anniv of University of West Indies. Multicoloured.
300 10c. Type **102** 10 10
301 $1 As Type **102** but showing different buildings 20 25
MS302 99 × 95 mm. Nos. 300/1 35 65

1974. Family Planning.
303 **103** 4c. brown, blue and black 10 10
304 – 25c. multicoloured 10 10
305 – 40c. multicoloured 10 10
306 – $2.50 multicoloured . . . 35 55
DESIGNS—HORIZ: 25c. Instruction by nurse; $2.50, Emblem and globe on scales. VERT: 40c. Family group.

104 Churchill as Army Lieutenant

106 "The Last Supper" (Dore)

105 Aeroplane and Map

1974. Birth Centenary of Sir Winston Churchill. Multicoloured.
307 4c. Type **104** 10 10
308 25c. Churchill as Prime Minister 15 10
309 40c. Churchill as Knight of the Garter 15 10
310 60c. Churchill's statue, London 25 15
MS311 99 × 148 mm. Nos. 307/10 75 1·25

1974. Opening of Golden Rock Airport, St. Kitts. Sheets 98 × 148 mm.
MS312 **105** 40c. multicoloured 20 40
MS313 45c. multicoloured . . . 20 40

1975. Easter. Paintings by Dore. Multicoloured.
314 4c. Type **106** 10 10
315 25c. "Christ Mocked" . . . 10 10
316 40c. "Jesus falling beneath the Cross" 10 10
317 $1 "The Erection of the Cross" 25 30

107 E.C.C.A. H.Q. Buildings, Basseterre

1975. Opening of East Caribbean Currency Authority's Headquarters.
318 **107** 12c. multicoloured 10 10
319 – 25c. multicoloured 10 10
320 – 40c. red, silver and grey 15 10
321 – 45c. multicoloured 15 15
DESIGNS: 25c. Specimen one-dollar banknote; 40c. Half-dollar of 1801 and current 4-dollar coin; 45c. Coins of 1801 and 1960.

108 Evangeline Booth (Salvation Army General)

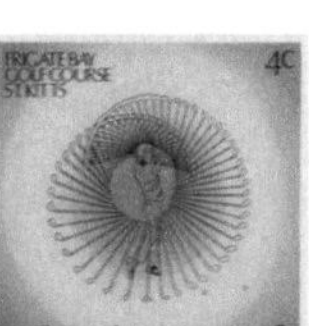

109 Golfer

1975. International Women's Year. Multicoloured.
338 4c. Type **108** 30 10
339 25c. Sylvia Pankhurst 35 10
340 40c. Marie Curie . . . . . . 2·25 80
341 $2.50 Lady Annie Allen (teacher and guider) . . . 1·50 4·25

1975. Opening of Frigate Bay Golf Course.
342 **109** 4c. black and red 70 10
343 25c. black and yellow . . 1·00 10
344 40c. black and green . . . 1·25 20
345 $1 black and blue . . . . 1·75 2·25

110 "St. Paul" (Pier Francesco Sacchi)

111 "Crucifixion" (detail)

1975. Christmas. Religious Paintings. Multicoloured.
346 25c. Type **110** 25 10
347 40c. "St. James" (Bonifazio di Pitati) 30 10
348 45c. "St. John the Baptist" (Mola) 30 10
349 $1 "St. Mary" (Raphael) . . 80 1·75

1976. Easter. Stained Glass Window. Multicoloured.
350 4c. Type **111** 10 20
351 4c. Type **111** 10 20
352 4c. Type **111** 10 20
353 25c. "Last Supper" 35 10
354 40c. "Last Supper" (different) 40 10
355 $1 "Baptism of Christ" . . . 70 70
Nos. 350/2 were printed together, se-tenant, forming a composite design, No. 350 being the left-hand stamp.
Nos. 353/5 are size 27 × 35 mm.

1976. West Indian Victory in World Cricket Cup. As Nos. 559/60 of Barbados.
356 12c. Map of the Caribbean 60 20
357 40c. Prudential Cup . . . . 1·40 50
MS358 95 × 80 mm. Nos. 356/7 4·25 3·75

112 Crispus Attucks and the Boston Massacre

1976. Bicentenary of American Revolution. Mult.
359 20c. Type **112** 15 10
360 40c. Alexander Hamilton and Battle of Yorktown 20 10
361 45c. Jefferson and Declaration of Independence 20 10
362 $1 Washington and the Crossing of the Delaware 45 85

113 "The Nativity" (Sforza Book of Hours)

114 Royal Visit, 1966

1976. Christmas. Multicoloured.
363 20c. Type **113** 10 10
364 40c. "Virgin and Child with St. John" (Pintoricchio) . . 15 10
365 45c. "Our Lady of Good Children" (Ford Maddox-Brown) 15 10
366 $1 "Little Hands Outstretched to Bless" (Margaret Tarrant) 35 50

1977. Silver Jubilee. Multicoloured.
367 50c. Type **114** 10 10
368 55c. The Sceptre 10 10
369 $1.50 Bishops paying homage 25 50

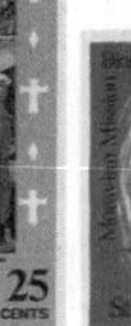

115 "Christ on the Cross" (Niccolo di Liberatore)

116 Estridge Mission

1977. Easter. Paintings from National Gallery, London. Multicoloured.
370 25c. Type **115** 10 10
371 30c. "The Resurrection" (imitator of Mantegna) . . 10 10
372 50c. "The Resurrection" (Ugolino da Siena) (horiz) 15 10
373 $1 "Christ Rising from the Tomb" (Gaudenzio Ferrari) 25 30

1977. Bicentenary of Moravian Mission.
374 **116** 4c. black, green and blue 10 10
375 – 20c. black, mauve & violet 10 10
376 – 40c. black, yellow & orge 15 15
DESIGNS: 20c. Mission symbol; 40c. Basseterre Mission.

117 Laboratory Instruments

118 "Nativity" (West Window)

1977. 75th Anniv of Pan-American Health Organization.
377 **117** 3c. multicoloured 20 10
378 – 12c. multicoloured 35 30
379 – 20c. multicoloured 40 10
380 – $1 brown, orange and black . . . . 1·00 1·40
DESIGNS: 12c. Fat cells, blood cells and nerve cells; 20c. "Community participation in health"; $1 Inoculation.

1977. Christmas. Stained-glass windows from Chartres Cathedral. Multicoloured.
381 4c. Type **118** 10 10
382 6c. "Three Magi" (west window) 10 10
383 40c. "La Belle Verriere" . . . 35 10
384 $1 "Virgin and Child" (Rose window) 75 45

119 Savanna Monkey with Vervet

120 Falcon of Edward III

1978. The Savanna Monkey.
385 **119** 4c. brown, red and black 10 10
386 – 5c. multicoloured 10 10
387 **119** 55c. brown, green & black 30 10
388 – $1.50 multicoloured 75 60
DESIGN: 5c., $1.50, Savanna monkeys on branch.

1978. 25th Anniv of Coronation.
389 **120** $1 brown and red 15 20
390 – $1 multicoloured 15 20
391 – $1 brown and red 15 20
DESIGNS: No. 390, Queen Elizabeth II; No. 391, Brown pelican.

121 Tomatoes

1978. Multicoloured.
392 1c. Type **121** 10 20
393 2c. Defence Force band . . . 10 20
394 5c. Radio and T.V. station 10 10
395 10c. Technical college 10 10
396 12c. T.V. assembly plant . . 10 75
397 15c. Sugar canoe harvesting 15 20
398 25c. Crafthouse (craft centre) 15 10
399 30c. "Europa" (liner) . . . . 1·50 1·50
400 40c. Lobster and sea crab . . 30 10
401 45c. Royal St. Kitts Hotel and golf course . . . . . 2·75 1·25
402 50c. Pinney's Beach, Nevis 30 10
403 55c. New runway at Golden Rock . . . . 1·25 10
404 $1 Cotton picking 35 30
405 $5 Brewery . . . . 75 1·25
406 $10 Pineapples and peanuts 1·00 1·75

122 Investiture

123 Wise Man with Gift of Gold

1978. 50th Anniv of Boy Scout Movement on St. Kitts and Nevis. Multicoloured.
407 5c. Type **122** 10 30
408 10c. Map reading 10 30
409 25c. Pitching tent 20 30
410 40c. Cooking 35 45
411 50c. First aid 40 55
412 55c. Rev. W. A. Beckett (founder of scouting in St. Kitts) 45 55

1978. Christmas. Multicoloured.
413 5c. Type **123** 10 10
414 15c. Wise Man with gift of Frankincense 10 10
415 30c. Wise Man with gift of Myrrh 10 10
416 $2.25 Wise Man paying homage to the Infant Jesus 35 50

124 "Canna coccinea"

126 "The Woodman's Daughter"

125 St. Christopher 1870 1d. Stamp and Sir Rowland Hill

1979. Local Flowers (1st series). Multicoloured.
417 5c. Type **124** 10 10
418 30c. "Heliconia bihai" . . . 25 20
419 55c. "Ruellia tuberosa" . . . 30 30
420 $1.50 "Gesneria ventricosa" 50 1·60
See also Nos. 430/3.

1979. Death Centenary of Sir Rowland Hill. Multicoloured.
421 5c. Type **125** 10 10
422 15c. 1970 Stamp Centenary 50c. commemorative . . . 10 10
423 50c. Great Britain 1841 2d. blue 30 35
424 $2.50 St. Kitts-Nevis 1923 300th Anniv of Colony £1 commemorative . . . . . 70 1·10

1979. Christmas. International Year of the Child. Paintings by Sir John Millais. Multicoloured.
425 5c. Type **126** 10 10
426 25c. "Cherry Ripe" 25 25
427 30c. "The Rescue" 25 25
428 55c. "Bubbles" 30 30

1980. Local Flowers (2nd series). As T **124**. Multicoloured.
430 4c. "Clerodendrum aculeatum" 30 10
431 55c. "Inga laurina" 30 20
432 $1.50 "Epidendrum difforme" 1·40 1·75
433 $2 "Salvia serotina" . . . . 60 2·00

127 Nevis Lagoon

1980. "London 1980" International Stamp Exhibition. Multicoloured.
434 5c. Type **127** 15 10
435 30c. Fig Tree Church (vert) 25 10
436 55c. Nisbet Plantation . . . 45 25
437 $3 "Nelson" (Fuger) (vert) 1·75 1·60
MS438 107 × 77 mm. 75c. Detail of "Nelson Falling" (D. Dighton) 1·40 75

OFFICIAL STAMPS

1980. Nos. 396, 398 and 400/6 optd OFFICIAL.
O1 12c. multicoloured . . . . . 80 1·25
O2 25c. multicoloured 15 20
O3 40c. multicoloured 40 50
O4 45c. multicoloured . . . . . 2·00 2·00
O5 50c. multicoloured 30 40
O6 55c. multicoloured . . . . . 1·25 50
O7 $1 multicoloured . . . . . 70 2·25
O8 $5 multicoloured . . . . . 80 2·50
O9 $10 multicoloured . . . . . 1·50 3·50

ST. LUCIA Pt. 1

One of the Windward Islands, British West Indies. Achieved Associated Statehood on 1 March 1967.

1860. 12 pence = 1 shilling;
20 shillings = 1 pound.
1949. 100 cents = 1 West Indian dollar.

1

HALFPENNY
(3)

1860. No value on stamps.
5ax **1** (1d.) red . . . . 70·00 85·00
11a (1d.) black . . . . 20·00 11·00
7 (4d.) blue £120 £130
16 (4d.) yellow . . . . £100 20·00
8 (6d.) green £170 £170
17a (6d.) violet . . . . £100 19·00
18a (1s.) orange . . . . £140 16·00

1881. With value added by surch as T **3**.
25 **1** ½d. green . . . . 20·00 28·00
26 1d. black . . . . 28·00 10·00
24 2½d. red . . . . 32·00 23·00
27 4d. yellow . . . . £300 19·00
28 6d. violet . . . . 29·00 28·00
29 1s. orange £275 £170

5

9

1882.
43 **5** ½d. green . . . . 2·25 1·00
32 1d. red . . . . 38·00 10·00
46 2½d. blue . . . . 4·50 1·00
48 4d. brown . . . . 2·75 2·25
35 6d. lilac £250 £200
36 1s. brown £375 £150

1886.
44 **5** 1d. mauve . . . . 3·50 30
45 2d. blue and orange . . . . 3·25 1·00
47 3d. mauve and green . . . . 4·50 5·50
41 6d. mauve and blue . . . . 4·00 9·50
50 1s. mauve and red . . . . 6·00 5·00
51 5s. mauve and orange . . . . 50·00 £130
52 10s. mauve and black . . . . 90·00 £140

1891. Surch in words.
56 **5** ½d. on 3d. mauve and green 75·00 23·00
55 1d. on 4d. brown . . . . . 4·75 3·50

1891. Surch **½d.**
54 **5** ½d. on half 6d. (No. 41) . . . 23·00 3·25

1902.
58 **9** ½d. purple and green . . . . 2·75 1·50
65 ½d. green . . . . 1·75 1·00
66a 1d. purple and red . . . . 4·00 1·25
67 1d. red . . . . 4·25 30
68a 2½d. purple and blue . . . . 11·00 4·50
69 2½d. blue . . . . 3·75 1·75
70 3d. purple and yellow . . . 6·00 3·00
71 3d. purple on yellow . . . 2·75 12·00
72 6d. purple and violet . . . 15·00 19·00
73 6d. purple . . . . 55·00 70·00
62 1s. green and black . . . . 10·00 28·00
75 1s. black on green . . . . 4·75 8·00
76 5s. green and red . . . . 70·00 £170
77 5s. green and red on yellow 60·00 70·00

11 The Pitons

12

13

14

1902. 400th Anniv of Discovery by Columbus.
63 **11** 2d. green and brown . . . . 9·00 1·75

1912.
78 **12** ½d. green 70 50
79 1d. red . . . . 1·90 10
93 1d. brown . . . . 1·40 15
94 **14** 1½d. red . . . . 75 2·50
95 **13** 2d. grey 75 15
81a **12** 2½d. blue . . . . 2·50 2·75
97 2½d. orange . . . . . . 11·00 50·00
82 3d. purple on yellow . . . 1·25 2·25
99a 3d. blue . . . . 2·50 11·00
83a **14** 4d. black and red on yellow . . . . 70 1·50
102 **12** 6d. purple . . . . 2·00 4·75
85 1s. black on green . . . . 3·25 5·00
103 1s. brown . . . . 2·25 3·25
104 **13** 2s.6d. black & red on blue 18·00 27·00
88 **12** 5s. green and red on yellow . . . . 24·00 75·00

1916. No. 79 optd **WAR TAX** in two lines.
89 **12** 1d. red . . . . 10·00 10·00

1916. No. 79 optd **WAR TAX** in one line.
90 **12** 1d. red . . . . 1·25 30

1935. Silver Jubilee. As T **32a** of St. Helena.
109 ½d. black and green . . . . 20 1·00
110 2d. blue and grey . . . . . 50 1·00
111 2½d. brown and blue . . . . 1·00 1·25
112 1s. grey and purple . . . . . 7·50 9·00

19 Port Castries

1936. King George V.
113 **19** ½d. black and green . . . 30 50
114 – 1d. black and brown . . . 40 10
115 – 1½d. black and red . . . 55 30
116 **19** 2d. black and grey . . . 50 20
117 – 2½d. black and blue . . . 50 15
118 – 3d. black and green . . . 1·25 70
119 **19** 4d. black and brown . . . 50 1·00
120 – 6d. black and orange . . . 1·00 1·00
121 – 1s. black and blue . . . 1·25 2·50
122 – 2s.6d. black and blue . . . 9·00 14·00
123 – 5s. black and violet . . . 10·00 20·00
124 – 10s. black and red . . . . 50·00 70·00
DESIGNS—HORIZ: 1d., 2½d., 6d. Columbus Square, Castries (inscr "Colombus Square" in error); 1s. Fort Rodney, Pigeon Island; 5s. Government House; 10s. Badge of Colony. VERT: 1½d, 3d. Ventine Falls; 2s.6d. Inniskilling Monument.

1937. Coronation. As T **32b** of St. Helena.
125 1d. violet 30 35
126 1½d. red 55 20
127 2½d. blue . . . . 55 1·25

26 King George VI

27 Columbus Square

1938. King George VI.
128a **26** ½d. green 10 10
129a 1d. violet 10 15
129c 1d. red 10 10
130a 1½d. red . . . . 1·25 1·00
131a 2d. grey 10 10
132a 2½d. blue 10 10
132b 2½d. violet . . . . . . 1·00 10
133a 3d. orange 10 10
133b 3½d. blue 80 15
134a **27** 6d. red . . . . 2·75 35
134c **26** 8d. brown . . . . 3·50 30
135 – 1s. brown 55 30
136 – 2s. blue and purple . . . 3·50 1·25
136a **26** 3s. purple . . . . 8·00 1·75
137 – 5s. black and mauve . . . 14·00 8·00
138 – 10s. black on yellow . . . 8·00 9·00
141 **26** £1 sepia . . . . 11·00 8·00
DESIGNS—As Type **27**: 1s. Government House; 2s. The Pitons; 5s. "Lady Hawkins" loading bananas. VERT: 10s. Device of St. Lucia as Type **33**.

1946. Victory. As T **33a** of St. Helena.
142 1d. violet 10 10
143 3½d. blue 10 10

1948. Silver Wedding. As T **33b/c** of St. Helena.
144 1d. red 15 10
145 £1 purple . . . . 16·00 35·00

33 Device of St. Lucia

34 Phoenix rising from Burning Buildings

1949. New Currency.
146 **26** 1c. green 25 10
147 2c. mauve . . . . 1·00 10
148 3c. red . . . . 1·00 1·75
149 4c. grey 75 10
150 5c. violet . . . . 1·00 10
151 6c. orange . . . . 75 2·50
152 7c. blue . . . . 3·00 2·50
153 12c. red . . . . 5·50 2·75
154 16c. brown . . . . 3·50 50
155 **33** 24c. blue 50 10
156 48c. olive . . . . 1·50 1·25
157 $1.20 purple . . . . 2·25 8·00
158 $2.40 green . . . . 3·25 17·00
159 $4.80 red . . . . 9·00 18·00

1949. U.P.U. As T **33d/g** of St. Helena.
160 5c. violet 15 60
161 6c. orange . . . . 1·60 2·00
162 12c. mauve 20 20
163 24c. green 30 20

1951. Inauguration of B.W.I. University College. As T **10a/b** of St. Kitts-Nevis.
164 3c. black and red 45 50
165 12c. black and red 65 50

1951. Reconstruction of Castries.
166 **34** 12c. red and blue . . . . 25 1·00

1951. New Constitution. Optd **NEW CONSTITUTION 1951.**
167 **26** 2c. mauve 15 80
168 4c. grey 15 60
169 5c. violet 15 80
170 12c. red 70 60

1953. Coronation. As T **33h** of St. Helena.
171 3c. black and red 70 10

1953. As 1949 but portrait of Queen Elizabeth II facing left and new Royal Cypher.
172 **26** 1c. green 10 10
173 2c. purple 10 10
174 3c. red 10 10
175 4c. grey 10 10
176 5c. violet 10 10
177 6c. orange 15 30
178 8c. red 30 10
179 10c. blue 10 10
180 15c. brown 30 10
181 **33** 25c. blue 30 10
182 50c. olive . . . . 4·50 1·25
183 $1 green . . . . 4·00 3·50
184 $2.50 red . . . . 5·00 6·00

1958. British Caribbean Federation. As T **27a** of St. Kitts-Nevis.
185 3c. green 40 20
186 6c. blue . . . . 65 1·75
187 12c. red 90 80

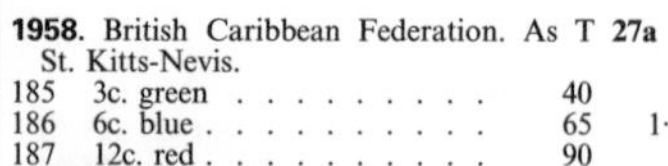

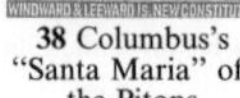
38 Columbus's "Santa Maria" off the Pitons

39 Stamp of 1860

1960. New Constitution for the Windward and Leeward Islands.
188 **38** 8c. red 30 45
189 10c. orange 30 45
190 25c. blue 50 50

1960. Stamp Centenary.
191 **39** 5c. red and blue 15 10
192 16c. blue and green 25 60
193 25c. green and red 25 15

1963. Freedom from Hunger. As T **63a** of St. Helena.
194 25c. green 30 10

1963. Cent of Red Cross. As T **63b** of St. Helena.
195 4c. red and black 20 50
196 25c. red and blue . . . . . 50 1·75

40 Queen Elizabeth II (after A. C. Davidson-Houston)

41 Queen Elizabeth II (after A. C. Davidson-Houston)

42 Fishing Boats

1964.
197 **40** 1c. red 10 10
198 2c. violet 30 70
199 4c. green . . . . 1·00 30
200 5c. blue 30 10
201 6c. brown . . . . 1·00 1·50
202 **41** 8c. multicoloured 10 10
203 10c. multicoloured . . . . 1·00 10
204 **42** 12c. multicoloured . . . . 50 1·25
205 – 15c. multicoloured 20 10
206 – 25c. multicoloured 20 10
207 – 35c. blue and buff . . . . 2·75 10
208 – 50c. multicoloured . . . . 2·25 10
209 – $1 multicoloured . . . . . 1·25 2·00
210 – $2.50 multicoloured . . . 2·25 2·00
HORIZ (as Type **42**): 15c. Pigeon Island; 25c. Reduit Beach; 35c. Castries Harbour; 50c. The Pitons. VERT (as Type **42**): $1 Vigie Beach. (As Type **41**): $2.50, Head and shoulders portrait of Queen Elizabeth II.
The 35c. and 50c. show a royal Cypher in place of the portrait.

45a Shakespeare and Memorial Theatre, Stratford-upon-Avon

1964. 400th Birth Anniv of Shakespeare.
211 **45a** 10c. green 30 10

1965. Centenary of I.T.U. As T **64a** of St. Helena.
212 2c. mauve and purple 10 10
213 50c. lilac and green 70 90

1965. I.C.Y. As T **64b** of St. Helena.
214 1c. purple and green 10 10
215 25c. green and violet 20 20

1966. Churchill Commemoration. As T **64c** of St. Helena.
216 4c. blue 10 10
217 6c. green . . . . 25 1·40
218 25c. brown 35 15
219 35c. violet 40 20

1966. Royal Visit. As T **48a** of St. Kitts-Nevis.
220 4c. black and blue 25 25
221 25c. black and mauve 75 75

1966. World Cup Football Championship. As T **64d** of St. Helena.
222 4c. multicoloured 25 10
223 25c. multicoloured 75 30

1966. Inauguration of W.H.O. Headquarters, Geneva. As T **64e** of St. Helena.
224 4c. black, green and blue . . 15 30
225 25c. black, purple and brown 45 40

1966. 20th Anniv of U.N.E.S.C.O. As T **64f/h** of St. Helena.
226 4c. multicoloured 15 10
227 12c. yellow, violet and olive 25 65
228 25c. black, purple and orange 50 35

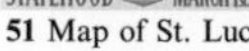
51 Map of St. Lucia

52 "Madonna and Child with the Infant Baptist" (Raphael)

1967. Statehood. Nos. 198, 202/9 and 257 optd **STATEHOOD 1st MARCH 1967.**
229 **40** 2c. violet (postage) 20 15
230 5c. blue 10 10

231 6c. brown 10 10
232 **41** 8c. multicoloured 20 10
233 10c. multicoloured 25 10
234 **42** 12c. multicoloured 20 10
235 – 15c. multicoloured 60 50
236 – 25c. multicoloured 30 50
237 – 35c. blue and buff 50 35
238 – 50c. multicoloured 50 55
239 – $1 multicoloured 50 55

240 **51** 15c. blue (air) 10 10

1967. Christmas.
241 **52** 4c. multicoloured 10 10
242 25c. multicoloured 30 10

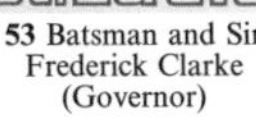

53 Batsman and Sir Frederick Clarke (Governor)

54 "The Crucified Christ with the Virgin Mary, Saints and the Angels" (Raphael)

1968. M.C.C.'s West Indies Tour.
243 **53** 10c. multicoloured 20 30
244 35c. multicoloured 45 55

1968. Easter Commemoration.
245 **54** 10c. multicoloured 10 10
246 – 15c. multicoloured 10 10
247 **54** 25c. multicoloured 15 10
248 – 35c. multicoloured 15 10
DESIGN: 15, 35c. "Noli me tangere" (detail by Titian).

56 Dr. Martin Luther King

57 "Virgin and Child in Glory" (Murillo)

1968. Martin Luther King Commemoration.
250 **56** 25c. blue, black and flesh 15 15
251 35c. blue, black and flesh 15 15

1968. Christmas.
252 **57** 5c. multicoloured 10 10
253 – 10c. multicoloured 10 10
254 **57** 25c. multicoloured 15 10
255 – 35c. multicoloured 15 10
DESIGN: 10, 35c. "Madonna with Child" (Murillo).

59 Purple-throated Carib

1969. Birds. Multicoloured.
256 10c. Type **59** 40 35
257 15c. St. Lucia amazon . . . 60 40
258 25c. Type **59** 70 45
259 35c. As 15c. 85 50

61 "Head of Christ Crowned with Thorns" (Reni)

1969. Easter. Multicoloured.
260 10c. Type **61** 10 10
261 15c. "Resurrection of Christ" (Sodoma) 10 10
262 25c. Type **61** 15 15
263 35c. As the 15c. 15 15

63 Map showing CARIFTA Countries

1969. 1st Anniv of CARIFTA.
264 **63** 5c. multicoloured 10 15
265 10c. multicoloured 10 15
266 – 25c. multicoloured 15 15
267 – 35c. multicoloured 15 15
DESIGN: 25, 35c. Handclasp and names of CARIFTA countries.

65 Emperor Napoleon and Empress Josephine

1969. Birth Bicent of Napoleon Bonaparte.
268 **65** 15c. multicoloured 10 10
269 25c. multicoloured 10 10
270 35c. multicoloured 10 10
271 50c. multicoloured 15 55

66 "Virgin and Child" (P. Delaroche)

69 "The Sealing of the Tomb" (Hogarth)

68 House of Assembly

1969. Christmas. Paintings. Multicoloured, background colours given.
272 **66** 5c. gold and purple 10 10
273 – 10c. gold and blue 10 10
274 **66** 25c. gold and red 20 10
275 – 35c. gold and green 20 10
DESIGN: 10c., 35c. "Holy Family" (Rubens).

1970. Multicoloured.
276 1c. Type **68** 10 10
277 2c. Roman Catholic Cathedral 15 10
278 4c. The Boulevard, Castries 1·00 10
279 5c. Castries Harbour . . . 1·50 10
280 6c. Sulphur springs 15 10
281 10c. Vigie Airport . . . . . 1·75 10
282 12c. Reduit Beach 20 10
283 15c. Pigeon Island 30 10
284 25c. The Pitons and yacht 80 10
285 35c. Marigot Bay 40 10
286 50c. Diamond Waterfall . . 70 80
287 $1 Flag of St. Lucia 40 70
288 £2.50 St. Lucia coat of arms 55 1·75
289 $5 Queen Elizabeth II . . . 1·00 4·00
289a $10 Map of St. Lucia . . . 3·00 9·00
Nos. 286/9a are vert.

1970. Easter. Multicoloured.
290 25c. Type **69** 15 20
291 35c. "The Three Marys at the Tomb" (Hogarth) 15 20
292 $1 "The Ascension" (Hogarth) 30 40
The $1 is larger 39 × 54 mm.
Nos. 290/2 were issued in a triptych, with the $1 value 10 mm higher than the other values.

72 Charles Dickens and Dickensian Characters

1970. Death Cent of Charles Dickens.
293 **72** 1c. multicoloured 10 10
294 25c. multicoloured 20 10
295 35c. multicoloured 25 10
296 50c. multicoloured . . . . 35 1·25

73 Nurse and Emblem

1970. Cent of British Red Cross. Multicoloured.
297 10c. Type **73** 15 15
298 15c. Flags of Great Britain, Red Cross and St. Lucia 25 25
299 25c. Type **73** 35 40
300 35c. As 15c. 40 40

74 "Madonna with the Lilies" (Luca della Robbia)

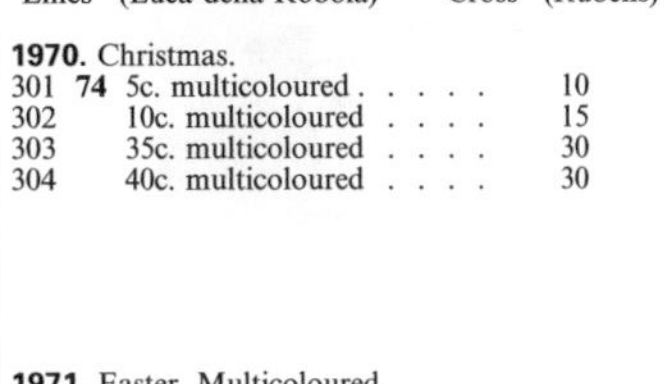

75 "Christ on the Cross" (Rubens)

1970. Christmas.
301 **74** 5c. multicoloured 10 10
302 10c. multicoloured 15 10
303 35c. multicoloured 30 10
304 40c. multicoloured 30 30

1971. Easter. Multicoloured.
305 10c. Type **75** 10 10
306 15c. "Descent from the Cross" (Rubens) 15 10
307 35c. Type **75** 30 10
308 40c. As 15c. 30 40

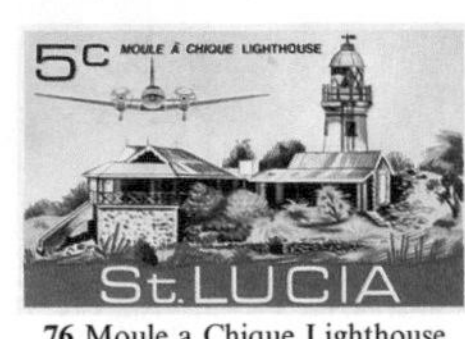

76 Moule a Chique Lighthouse

1971. Opening of Beane Field Airport. Mult.
309 5c. Type **76** 50 15
310 25c. Boeing 727-200 landing at Beane Field 50 15

77 Morne Fortune

78 Morne Fortune, Modern View

1971. Old and New Views of St. Lucia. Multicoloured.
311 5c. Type **77** 10 20
312 5c. Type **78** 10 20
313 10c. Castries City (old view) 10 20
314 10c. Castries City (modern view) 10 20
315 25c. Pigeon Island (old view) 15 30
316 25c. Pigeon Island (modern view) 15 30
317 50c. Old view from grounds of Government House . . 25 75
318 50c. Modern view from grounds of Government House 25 75
The old views are taken from paintings by J. H. Caddy.

79 "Virgin and Child with two Angels" (Verrocchio)

81 "The Dead Christ Mourned" (Carracci)

80 "St. Lucia" (Dolci School) and Coat of Arms

1971. Christmas. Multicoloured.
319 5c. Type **79** 10 10
320 10c. "Virgin and Child, St. John the Baptist and an Angel" (Morando) 10 10
321 35c. "Madonna and Child" (Battista) 15 10
322 40c. Type **79** 20 25

1971. National Day.
323 **80** 5c. multicoloured 10 10
324 10c. multicoloured 15 10
325 25c. multicoloured 25 10
326 50c. multicoloured 45 40

1972. Easter. Multicoloured.
327 10c. Type **81** 10 10
328 25c. "Angels weeping over the dead Christ" (Guercino) 20 10
329 35c. Type **81** 30 10
330 50c. As 25c. 40 40

82 Science Block and Teachers' College

1972. Morne Educational Complex. Mult.
331 5c. Type **82** 10 10
332 15c. University Centre . . . 10 10
333 25c. Secondary School . . . 10 10
334 35c. Technical College . . . 15 10

83 Steamship Stamp and Map

1972. Centenary of First Postal Service by St. Lucia Steam Conveyance Co. Ltd.
335 **83** 5c. multicoloured 15 10
336 – 10c. blue, mauve and black 20 10
337 – 35c. red, blue and black . . 45 10
338 – 50c. multicoloured . . . . 75 1·00
DESIGNS: 10c. Steamship stamp and Castries Harbour; 35c. Steamship stamp and Soufriere; 50c. Steamship stamps.

84 "The Holy Family" (Sebastiano Ricci)

1972. Christmas.
339 **84** 5c. multicoloured 10 10
340 10c. multicoloured 10 10
341 35c. multicoloured 20 10
342 40c. multicoloured 25 15

1972. Royal Silver Wedding. As T **103** of St. Helena, but with Arms and St. Lucia Amazon.
343 **83** 15c. red 40 20
344 35c. green 40 20

86 Week-day Headdress **87** Coat of Arms

1973. Local Headdresses. Multicoloured.

345	5c. Type **86**	10	10
346	10c. Formal style	10	10
347	25c. Unmarried girl's style	15	10
348	50c. Ceremonial style	25	85

1973.

349A	**87** 5c. green	10	75
350A	10c. blue	15	75
953	10c. green	75	75
351A	25c. brown	15	75

88 H.M.S. "St. Lucia", 1830

1973. Historic Ships. Multicoloured.

352	15c. Type **88**	20	10
353	35c. H.M.S. "Prince of Wales", 1765	30	10
354	50c. "Oliph Blossom", 1605	40	75
355	$1 H.M.S. "Rose", 1757	70	1·00
MS356	122 × 74 mm. Nos. 352/5	1·00	2·75

89 Plantation and Flower

1973. Banana Industry. Multicoloured.

357	5c. Type **89**	10	10
358	15c. Aerial spraying	15	10
359	35c. Boxing plant	20	10
360	50c. Loading a boat	50	40

90 "The Virgin with Child" (Maratta) **92** 3-Escalins Coins, 1798

91 "The Betrayal"

1973. Christmas. Multicoloured.

361	5c. Type **90**	10	10
362	15c. "Madonna in the Meadow" (Raphael)	10	10
363	35c. "The Holy Family" (Bronzino)	20	10
364	50c. "Madonna of the Pear" (Durer)	30	35

1973. Royal Wedding. As T **103a** of St. Helena. Multicoloured, background colours given.

365	40c. green	10	10
366	50c. lilac	10	10

1974. Easter. Paintings by Ugolino da Siena. Multicoloured.

369	5c. Type **91**	10	10
370	35c. "The Way to Calvary"	15	10
371	80c. "The Deposition"	15	15
372	$1 "The Resurrection"	20	25
MS373	180 × 140 mm. Nos. 369/72	1·00	2·00

1974. Coins of Old St. Lucia. Multicoloured.

374	15c. Type **92**	15	10
375	35c. 6-esculins coins, 1798	15	10
376	40c. 2-livres 5-sols coins, 1813	20	10
377	$1 6-livres 15-sols coins, 1813	35	65
MS378	151 × 115 mm. Nos. 374/7	1·00	2·75

93 Baron de Laborie **94** "Virgin and Child" (Andrea del Verrocchio)

1974. Past Governors of St. Lucia. Mult.

379	5c. Type **93**	10	10
380	35c. Sir John Moore	10	10
381	80c. Sir Dudley Hill	15	10
382	$1 Sir Frederick Clarke	25	35
MS383	153 × 117 mm. Nos. 379/82	50	2·00

1974. Christmas. Multicoloured.

384	5c. Type **94**	10	10
385	35c. "Virgin and Child" (Andrea della Robbia)	10	10
386	80c. "Madonna and Child" (Luca della Robbia)	15	15
387	$1 "Virgin and Child" (Rossellino)	20	25
MS388	92 × 140 mm. Nos. 384/7	70	2·00

95 Churchill and Montgomery

1974. Birth Centenary of Sir Winston Churchill.

389	5c. Type **95**	10	10
390	$1 Churchill and Truman	30	35

96 "Christ on the Cross" (School of Van der Weyden) **97** "Nativity" (French Book of Hours)

1975. Easter. Multicoloured.

391	5c. Type **96**	10	10
392	35c. "Noli me tangere" (Romano)	10	10
393	80c. "Calvary" (Gallego)	20	20
394	$1 "Noli me tangere" (Correggio)	30	35

1975. Christmas. Multicoloured.

399	5c. Type **97**	10	10
400	10c. "King" (stained glass window)	10	30
401	10c. "Virgin and Child" (stained glass window)	10	30
402	10c. "King and Cattle" (stained glass window)	10	30
403	40c. "Nativity" (Hastings Book of Hours)	30	10
404	$1 "Virgin and Child with Saints" (Borgognone)	70	90
MS405	105 × 109 mm. Nos. 399 and 403/4	75	1·00

Nos. 400/2 were printed together, se-tenant, forming a composite design of the Epiphany.

98 America Schooner "Hanna"

1975. Bicent of American Revolution. Ships. Mult.

406	½c. Type **98**	10	10
407	1c. "Prince of Orange" (British sailing packet)	10	10
408	2c. H.M.S. "Edward" (sloop)	10	10
409	5c. "Millern" (British merchantman)	20	10
410	15c. "Surprise" (American lugger)	30	10
411	35c. H.M.S. "Serapis" (frigate)	35	10
412	50c. "Randolph" (American frigate)	40	1·00
413	$1 "Alliance" (American frigate)	45	2·50
MS414	142 × 116 mm. Nos. 410/13	3·00	4·50

99 Laughing Gull **100** H.M.S. "Ceres"

99a Caribbean Map

1976. Birds. Multicoloured.

415	1c. Type **99**	30	1·75
416	2c. Little blue heron	30	1·75
417	4c. Belted kingfisher	35	1·25
418	5c. St. Lucia amazon ("St Lucia Parrot")	1·75	1·25
419	6c. St. Lucia oriole	1·25	1·75
420	8c. Grey trembler ("Trembler")	1·50	2·50
421	10c. American kestrel ("Sparrow Hawk")	1·25	35
422	12c. Red-billed tropic bird	2·00	2·50
423	15c. Moorhen ("Common Gallinule")	1·25	15
424a	25c. Common noddy ("Brown Noddy")	1·00	30
425	35c. Sooty tern	3·25	1·25
426	50c. Osprey	7·00	3·50
427	$1 White-breasted trembler ("White-breasted Thrasher")	4·00	3·50
428	$2.50 St. Lucia black finch	7·00	6·50
429	$5 Red-necked pigeon ("Ramier")	7·50	4·50
430a	$10 Caribbean elaenia	2·25	7·50

1976. West Indies Victory in World Cricket Cup. Multicoloured.

431	50c. Type **99a**	1·00	1·00
432	$1 Prudential Cup	1·00	2·50
MS433	92 × 79 mm. Nos. 431/2	3·50	4·50

1976. Royal Navy Crests. Multicoloured.

434	10c. Type **100**	35	10
435	20c. H.M.S. "Pelican"	60	10
436	40c. H.M.S. "Ganges"	85	10
437	$2 H.M.S. "Ariadne"	2·00	2·25

101 "Madonna and Child" (Murillo) **103** Scouts from Tapion School

102 Queen Elizabeth II

1976. Christmas. Multicoloured.

438	10c. Type **101**	10	10
439	20c. "Madonna and Child with Angels" (Costa)	10	10
440	50c. "Madonna and Child Enthroned" (Isenbrandt)	15	10
441	$2 "Madonna and Child with St. John" (Murillo)	50	65
MS442	105 × 93 mm. $2.50 As Type **101**	1·00	1·25

1977. Silver Jubilee.

443	**102** 10c. multicoloured	10	10
444	20c. multicoloured	10	10
445	40c. multicoloured	10	15
446	$2 multicoloured	40	90
MS447	128 × 95 mm. **102** $2.50 multicoloured	45	1·00

1977. Caribbean Boy Scout Jamboree. Multicoloured.

448	½c. Type **103**	10	10
449	1c. Sea scouts	10	10
450	2c. Scout from Micoud	10	10
451	10c. Two scouts from Tapion School	20	10
452	20c. Venture scout	20	10
453	50c. Scout from Gros Islet	35	45
454	$1 Sea scouts in motor boat	50	1·00
MS455	75 × 85 mm. $2.50 As $1	1·10	3·00

104 "Nativity" (Giotto) **105** "Susan Lunden"

1977. Christmas. Multicoloured.

456	½c. Type **104**	10	10
457	1c. "Perugia triptych" (Fra Angelico)	10	10
458	2c. "Virgin and Child" (El Greco)	10	10
459	20c. "Madonna of the Rosary" (Caravaggio)	15	10
460	50c. "Adoration of the Magi" (Velazquez)	20	10
461	$1 "Madonna of Carmel" (Tiepolo)	30	35
462	$2.50 "Adoration of the Magi" (Tiepolo)	45	80

1977. 400th Birth Anniv of Rubens. Mult.

463	10c. Type **105**	10	10
464	35c. "The Rape of the Sabine Women" (detail)	15	10
465	50c. "Ludovicus Nonnius"	30	10
466	$2.50 "Minerva protects Pax from Mars" (detail)	85	90
MS467	145 × 120 mm. Nos. 463/6	1·25	2·25

106 Yeoman of the Guard and Life Guard

1978. 25th Anniv of Coronation. Mult.

468	15c. Type **106**	10	10
469	20c. Groom and postillion	10	10
470	50c. Footman and coachman	10	10
471	$3 State trumpeter and herald	35	90
MS472	114 × 88 mm. $5 Master of the Horse and Gentleman-at-Arms	60	90

107 Queen Angelfish

1978. Fish. Multicoloured.

473	10c. Type **107**	40	10
474	20c. Four-eyed butterflyfish	60	10
475	50c. French angelfish	90	30
476	$2 Yellow-tailed damselfish	1·10	2·00
MS477	155 × 89 mm. $2.50 Rock beauty	2·25	1·90

108 French Grenadier and Map of the Battle

1978. Bicent of Battle of Cul-de-Sac. Mult.

478	10c. Type **108**	50	10
479	30c. British Grenadier officer and Map of St. Lucia (Bellin), 1762	75	10
480	50c. Coastline from Gros Islet to Cul-de-Sac and British Fleet opposing French landings	95	15
481	$2.50 General James Grant, 1798, and Light Infantrymen of 46th Regiment	1·75	2·00

109 The Annunciation

1978. Christmas. Multicoloured.
482 30c. Type **109** 10 10
483 50c. Type **109** 15 10
484 55c. The Nativity 15 10
485 80c. As 55c. 20 20

110 Hewanorra International Air Terminal

1979. Independence. Multicoloured.
486 10c. Type **110** 10 10
487 30c. New coat of arms . . . 10 10
488 50c. Government House and Sir Allen Lewis (first Governor-General) 15 10
489 $2 French, St. Lucia and Union flags on map of St. Lucia 30 45
MS490 127 × 80 mm. Nos. 486/9 50 1·00

111 Popes Paul VI and John Paul I

1979. Pope Paul VI Commemoration. Mult.
491 10c. Type **111** 10 10
492 30c. Pres. Sadat of Egypt with Pope Paul 20 10
493 50c. Pope Paul with Secretary-General U Thant 35 10
494 55c. Pope Paul and Prince Minister Golda Meir of Israel 40 25
495 $2 Martin Luther King received in audience by Pope Paul . . . . 1·00 70

112 Dairy Farming

1979. Agricultural Diversification. Mult.
496 10c. Type **112** 10 10
497 35c. Fruit and vegetables . . 10 10
498 50c. Water conservation . . . 20 10
499 $3 Copra industry . . . . . 75 1·10

113 Lindbergh and Sikorsky S-38A Flying Boat

1979. 50th Anniv of Lindbergh's Inaugural Airmail Flight via St. Lucia.
500 **113** 10c. black, red and orange 50 10
501 – 30c. multicoloured 60 10
502 – 50c. multicoloured 60 10
503 – $2 multicoloured 80 85
DESIGNS: 30c. Sikorsky S-38A flying boat and route map; 50c. Arrival at La Toc, September, 1929; $2 Letters on first flight.

114 "A Prince of Saxony" (Cranach the Elder)

115 Notice of Introduction of Penny Post

1979. International Year of the Child. Famous Paintings. Multicoloured.
504 10c. Type **114** 10 10
505 50c. "The Infanta Margarita" (Velazquez) 15 10
506 $2 "Girl playing Badminton" (Chardin) 45 40
507 $2.50 "Mary and Francis Wilcox" (Stock) 45 45
MS508 113 × 94 mm. $5 "Two Children" (Picasso) . . . . . 1·10 1·25

1979. Death Cent of Sir Rowland Hill. Mult.
509 10c. Type **115** 10 10
510 50c. Wyon essay 15 10
511 $2 First St. Lucia stamp . . 25 50
512 $2.50 G.B. 1840 Penny Black 35 60
MS513 111 × 85 mm. $5 Sir Rowland Hill 70 90

116 "Madonna and Child" (Bernardino Fungai)

118 Mickey Mouse astride Rocket

117 St. Lucia Steam Conveyance Co. Ltd. Cover, 1873

1979. Christmas. International Year of the Child. Paintings of the "Madonna and Child" by artists named. Multicoloured.
514 10c. Type **116** 10 10
515 50c. Carlo Dolci 20 10
516 $2 Titian 50 50
517 $2.50 Giovanni Bellini . . . 60 50
MS518 94 × 120 mm. Nos. 514/17 1·25 1·20

1980. "London 1980" Int Stamp Exhibition. Mult.
519 10c. Type **117** 10 10
520 30c. S.S. "Assistance" 1d. postmark, 1879 . . . . . 10 10
521 50c. Postage due handstamp, 1929 . . . . 15 10
522 $2 Crowned-circle Paid stamp, 1844 . . . . 40 55
MS523 86 × 76 mm. Nos. 519/22 65 90

1980. 10th Anniv (1979) of Moon Landing. Disney characters in Space Scenes. Multicoloured.
524 ½c. Type **118** 10 10
525 1c. Donald Duck being towed by rocket (horiz) 10 10
526 2c. Minnie Mouse on Moon 10 10
527 3c. Goofy hitching lift to Mars 10 10
528 4c. Goofy and Moondog (horiz) 10 10
529 5c. Pluto burying bone on Moon (horiz) 10 10
530 10c. Donald Duck and love-sick Martian (horiz) . . . 10 10
531 $2 Donald Duck paddling spaceship (horiz) . . . . . 1·60 1·00
532 $2.50 Mickey Mouse driving moonbuggy (horiz) . . . 1·60 1·10
MS533 102 × 127 mm. $5 Goofy leaping from space-ship on to Moon . . . . 3·25 2·75

119 Queen Elizabeth the Queen Mother

1980. 80th Birthday of The Queen Mother.
534 **119** 10c. multicoloured 15 10
535 $2.50 multicoloured . . . 35 1·00
MS536 85 × 65 mm. **119** $3 multicoloured . . . . 60 1·50

120 Hawker Siddeley H.S.748

1980. Transport. Multicoloured.
537 5c. Type **120** 30 30
538 10c. Douglas DC-10-30 airliner 65 30
539 15c. Local bus 35 40
540 20c. "Geestcrest" (freighter) 35 40
541 25c. Britten Norman Islander aircraft 65 30
542 30c. "Charles" (pilot boat) 40 50
543 50c. Boeing 727-200 airliner 1·00 60
544 75c. "Cunard Countess" (liner) . . . . 65 1·25
545 $1 Lockheed TriStar 500 airliner . . . . 85 1·40
546 $2 "Booker Vulcan" (cargo liner) . . . . 1·25 2·00
547 $5 Boeing 707-420 airliner . . 5·00 6·00
548 $10 "Queen Elizabeth 2" (liner) . . . . 5·00 8·00

121 Shot-putting

1980. Olympic Games, Moscow. Mult.
549 10c. Type **121** 10 10
550 50c. Swimming 20 10
551 $2 Gymnastics 80 50
552 $2.50 Weightlifting 90 60
MS553 108 × 83 mm. $5 Athletes with Olympic torch . . . . . 1·50 1·40

122 Coastal Landscape within Cogwheel

123 Sir Arthur Lewis

1980. 75th Anniv of Rotary International. Different coastal landscapes within cogwheel.
554 **122** 10c. multicoloured 10 10
555 – 50c. multicoloured 15 10
556 – $2 black, red and yellow 40 40
557 – $2.50 multicoloured . . . 50 55
MS558 108 × 106 mm. $5 multicoloured . . . . 1·25 1·75

1980. Nobel Prize Winners. Multicoloured.
559 10c. Type **123** 10 10
560 50c. Martin Luther King Jnr 20 15
561 $2 Ralph Bunche 50 60
562 $2.50 Albert Schweitzer . . . 70 80
MS563 115 × 91 mm. $5 Albert Einstein . . . . 2·25 2·00

1980. Hurricane Relief. Nos. 538/9 and 542 surch **$1.50 1980 HURRICANE RELIEF**.
564 $1.50 on 15c. multicoloured 30 40
565 $1.50 on 20c. multicoloured 30 40
566 $1.50 on 50c. multicoloured 30 40

125 "The Nativity" (Giovanni Battista)

126 Brazilian Agouti

1980. Christmas. Paintings. Multicoloured.
567 10c. Type **125** 10 10
568 30c. "Adoration of the Kings" (Pieter the Elder) 10 10
569 $2 "Adoration of the Shepherds" (ascribed to Murillo) 40 60
MS570 102 × 88 mm. $1 × 3, Angel with people of St. Lucia (composite design) (each 30 × 75 mm) 80 90

1981. Wildlife. Multicoloured.
571 10c. Type **126** 15 10
572 50c. St. Lucia amazon ("St. Lucia Parrot") . . . 1·00 20
573 $2 Purple-throated carib . . 1·75 80
574 $2.50 Fiddler crab . . . . . 1·25 1·00
MS575 103 × 87 mm. $5 "Danaus plexippus" (butterfly) . . . . . 2·40 2·50

127 Prince Charles at Balmoral

128 Lady Diana Spencer

1981. Royal Wedding. Multicoloured.
576 25c. Prince Charles and Lady Diana Spencer 10 10
577 50c. Clarence House 10 10
578 $4 Type **127** 40 55
MS579 96 × 82 mm. $5 Class Coach and coachman 50 50

1981. Royal Wedding. Mult. Self-adhesive.
580 50c. Type **128** 25 45
581 $2 Prince Charles 30 60
582 $5 Prince Charles and Lady Diana Spencer . . . . . . 1·50 1·75

129 "The Cock"

130 "Industry"

1981. Birth Bicentenary of Picasso. Mult.
583 30c. Type **129** 25 10
584 50c. "Man with an Ice-cream" 35 10
585 55c. "Woman dressing her Hair" 35 10
586 $3 "Seated Woman" 95 85
MS587 128 × 102 mm. $5 "Night Fishing at Antibes" . . . . . 1·75 1·75

1981. 25th Anniv of Duke of Edinburgh Award Scheme. Multicoloured.
588 10c. Type **130** 10 10
589 35c. "Community service" . . 15 10
590 50c. "Physical recreation" . . 15 10
591 $2.50 Duke of Edinburgh speaking at Caribbean Conference, 1975 . . . . . 45 70

131 Louis Braille

1981. International Year for Disabled People. Famous Disabled People. Multicoloured.
592 10c. Type **131** 20 10
593 50c. Sarah Bernhardt 20 10
594 $2 Joseph Pulitzer 70 70
595 $2.50 Henri de Toulouse-Lautree . . . . 1·00 85
MS596 115 × 90 mm. $5 Franklin Delano Roosevelt . . . . . . 1·00 1·25

132 "Portrait of Fanny Travis Cochran" (Cecilia Beaux)

133 "Adoration of the Magi" (Sfoza)

1981. Decade for Women. Paintings. Mult.
597 10c. Type **132** 10 10
598 50c. "Women with Dove" (Marie Laurencin) 25 10
599 $2 "Portrait of a Young Pupil of David" (Aimee Duvivier) 75 70
600 $2.50 "Self-portrait" (Rosalba Carriera) 90 85
MS601 104 × 78 mm. "Self-portrait" (Elizabeth Vigee-le-Brun) . . . 1·00 1·25

1981. Christmas. Paintings. Multicoloured.
602 10c. Type **133** 10 10
603 30c. "The Adoration of the Kings" (Orcanga) 20 10
604 $1.50 "The Adoration of the Kings" (Gerard) 45 50
605 $2.50 "The Adoration of the Kings" (Foppa) 75 85

134 1860 1d. Stamp

1981. 1st Anniv of U.P.U. Membership. Mult.

606 10c. Type **134** 20 10
607 30c. 1969 First Anniversary of Caribbean Free Trade Area 25c. commemorative 40 10
608 50c. 1979 Independence $2 commemorative 45 50
609 $2 U.P.U. emblem with U.P.U. and St. Lucia flags 95 2·25
MS610 128 × 109 mm. $5 U.P.U. Headquarters, Berne and G.P.O. Building, Castries . . . . . . 1·00 1·50

135 Scene from Football Match

1982. World Cup Football Championship, Spain.

611 **135** 10c. multicoloured 60 10
612 – 50c. multicoloured . . . . 1·25 15
613 – $2 multicoloured . . . . 1·75 90
614 – $2.50 multicoloured . . . 2·00 1·00
MS615 104 × 84 mm.–$5 multicoloured . . . . 2·50 2·25

DESIGNS: 50c. to $5, Scenes from different matches.

136 Pigeon Island National Park

1982. Bicent of Battle of the Saints. Mult.

616 10c. Type **136** 25 15
617 35c. Battle scene 80 15
618 50c. Rodney (English admiral) and De Grasse (French admiral) . . . . . 1·10 65
619 $2.50 Map of the Saints, Martinique and St. Lucia 3·25 4·50
MS620 125 × 75 mm. Nos. 616/19 6·00 7·00

137 Map-reading

138 Leeds Castle

1982. 75th Anniv of Boy Scout Movement. Multicoloured.

621 10c. Type **137** 10 10
622 50c. First Aid practice . . . 30 15
623 $1.50 Camping 75 80
624 $2.50 Campfire singsong . . 1·25 1·50

1982. 21st Birthday of Princess of Wales. Mult.

625 50c. Type **138** 30 20
626 $2 Princess Diana boarding aircraft . . . . 2·25 75
627 $4 Wedding . . . . 2·25 1·40
MS628 102 × 75 mm. $5 Princess of Wales . . . . 4·00 2·00

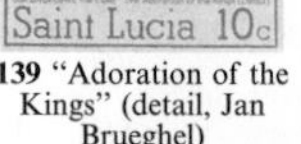

139 "Adoration of the Kings" (detail, Jan Brueghel)

141 Crown Agents Headquarters, Millbank, London

140 The Pitons

1982. Christmas. Multicoloured.

629 10c. Type **139** 10 10
630 30c. "Nativity" (Lorenzo Costa) 15 10
631 50c. "Virgin and Child" (Fra Filippo Lippi) 25 15
632 80c. "Adoration of the Shepherds" (Nicolas Poussin) 40 55

1983. Commonwealth Day. Multicoloured.

633 10c. Type **140** 10 10
634 30c. Tourist beach 15 10
635 50c. Banana harvesting . . . 20 15
636 $2 Flag of St. Lucia . . . . 1·25 1·00

1983. 150th Anniv of Crown Agents. Mult.

637 10c. Type **141** 10 10
638 15c. Road construction . . . 10 10
639 50c. Road network map . . . 20 25
640 $2 First St. Lucia stamp . . 60 1·25

142 Communications at Sea

1983. World Communications Year. Mult.

641 10c. Type **142** 15 10
642 50c. Communications in the air 40 15
643 $1.50 T.V. transmission via satellite 90 75
644 $2.50 Computer communications . . . . . 1·40 1·25
MS645 107 × 88 mm. $5 Weather satellite . . . . 1·50 1·75

143 Long-jawed Squirrelfish

1983. Coral Reef Fishes. Multicoloured.

646 10c. Type **143** 10 10
647 50c. Banded butterflyfish . . 20 15
648 $1.50 Black-barred soldierfish 60 1·50
649 $2.50 Yellow-tailed snapper 80 2·00
MS650 122 × 97 mm. $5 Red hind 2·50 3·25

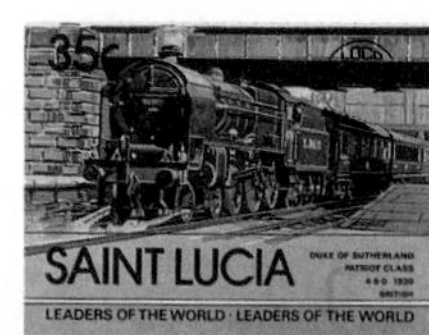

144 "Duke of Sutherland" (1930)

1983. Leaders of the World. Railway Locomotives (1st series).

651 **144** 35c. multicoloured 15 20
652 – 35c. multicoloured 15 20
653 – 35c. multicoloured 15 20
654 – 35c. multicoloured 15 20
655 – 50c. multicoloured 20 30
656 – 50c. multicoloured 20 30
657 – 50c. multicoloured 20 30
658 – 50c. multicoloured 20 30
659 – $1 multicoloured 25 50
660 – $1 multicoloured 25 50
661 – $1 multicoloured 25 50
662 – $1 multicoloured 25 50
663 – $2 multicoloured 30 70
664 – $2 multicoloured 30 70
665 – $2 multicoloured 30 70
666 – $2 multicoloured 30 70

DESIGNS—(The first in each pair shows technical drawings and the second the locomotive at work): Nos. 651/2, "Duke of Sutherland", Great Britain (1930); 653/4, "City of Glasgow", Great Britain (1940); 655/6, "Lord Nelson", Great Britain (1926); 657/8, "Leeds United", Great Britain (1928); 659/60, "Bodmin", Great Britain (1945); 661/2, "Eton", Great Britain (1930); 663/4, "Flying Scotsman", Great Britain (1923); 665/6, "Rocket", Great Britain (1829).

See also Nos. 715/26, 761/76, 824/31 and 858/73.

145 "The Niccolini-Cowper Madonna"

146 George III

1983. Christmas. 500th Birth Anniv of Raphael. Multicoloured.

667 10c. Type **145** 10 10
668 30c. "The Holy Family with a Palm Tree" 15 10
669 50c. "The Sistine Madonna" 20 30
670 $5 "The Alba Madonna" . . 70 3·25

1984. Leaders of the World. British Monarchs. Multicoloured.

671 5c. Battle of Waterloo . . . 10 15
672 5c. Type **146** 10 15
673 10c. George III at Kew . . . 10 15
674 10c. Kew Palace 10 15
675 35c. Coat of Arms of Elizabeth I 10 20
676 35c. Elizabeth I 10 20
677 60c. Coat of Arms of George III 20 35
678 60c. George III (different) . . 20 35
679 $1 Elizabeth I at Hatfield . . 20 40
680 $1 Hatfield Palace 20 40
681 $2.50 Spanish Armada . . . 30 60
682 $2.50 Elizabeth I (different) 30 60

147 Clarke & Co's Drug Store

1984. Historic Buildings. Multicoloured.

683 10c. Type **147** 10 10
684 45c. Colonial architecture (horiz) 30 25
685 65c. Colonial "chattel" house (horiz) 45 35
686 $2.50 Treasury after 1906 earthquake (horiz) . . . . 1·75 1·60

148 Logwood

1984. Forestry Resources. Multicoloured.

699 10c. Type **148** 15 10
700 45c. Calabash 40 30
701 65c. Gommier (vert) 45 55
702 $2.50 Raintree . . . . 65 2·75

149 Bugatti Type "57SC Atlantic Coupe"

1984. Leaders of the World. Automobiles (1st series). The first in each pair showing technical drawings and the second paintings.

703 **149** 5c. black, lilac and yellow 10 10
704 – 5c. multicoloured 10 10
705 – 10c. black, blue and red 10 10
706 – 10c. multicoloured 10 10
707 – $1 black, green and brown 15 25
708 – $1 multicoloured 15 25
709 – $2.50 black, pink and blue 30 40
710 – $2.50 multicoloured . . . 30 40

DESIGNS: Nos. 703/4, Bugatti Type "57SC Atlantic Coupe"; 705/6, Chevrolet "Bel Air Convertible"; 707/8, Alfa Romeo "1750 GS (Zagato)"; 709/10, Duesenberg "SJ Roadster".

See also Nos. 745/60, 789/96 and 902/13.

150 Pygmy Gecko

1984. Endangered Wildlife. Multicoloured.

711 10c. Type **150** 20 10
712 45c. Maria Island ground lizard 35 50
713 65c. Green iguana 40 85
714 $2.50 Couresse snake . . . . 45 3·50

1984. Leaders of the World. Railway Locomotives (2nd series). As T **144**, the first in each pair showing technical drawings and the second the locomotive at work.

715 1c. multicoloured 10 10
716 1c. multicoloured 10 10
717 15c. multicoloured 10 15
718 15c. multicoloured 10 15
719 50c. multicoloured 15 15
720 50c. multicoloured 15 15
721 75c. multicoloured 15 20
722 75c. multicoloured 15 20
723 $1 multicoloured 20 25
724 $1 multicoloured 20 25
725 $2 multicoloured 25 35
726 $2 multicoloured 25 35

DESIGNS: Nos. 715/16, "Taw", Great Britain (1897); 717/18, Class Be 6/8 "Crocodile" electric locomotive, Switzerland (1920); 719/20, "The Countess", Great Britain (1903); 721/2, Class GE 6/6 electric locomotive, Switzerland (1921); 723/4, Class P8, Germany (1906); 725/6, "Adler", Germany (1835).

151 Men's Volleyball

152 Glass of Wine and Flowers

1984. Leaders of the World. Olympic Games, Los Angeles. Multicoloured.

727 5c. Type **151** 10 10
728 5c. Women's volleyball . . . 10 10
729 10c. Women's hurdles 10 10
730 10c. Men's hurdles 10 10
731 65c. Show jumping 15 20
732 65c. Dressage 15 20
733 $2.50 Women's gymnastics 40 50
734 $2.50 Men's gymnastics . . . 40 50

1984. Christmas. Multicoloured.

735 10c. Type **152** 10 10
736 35c. Priest and decorated altar 10 10
737 65c. Nativity scene 15 25
738 $3 Holy Family . . . . . . 50 1·50
MS739 147 × 77 mm. Nos. 735/8 1·60 4·50

153 Slaves preparing Manioc

154 Girl Guide Badge in Shield and Crest of St. Lucia

1984. 150th Anniv of Abolition of Slavery. Each black and brown.

740 10c. Type **153** 10 10
741 35c. Sifting and cooking cassava flour 10 10
742 55c. Cooking pot, and preparing tobacco 10 20
743 $5 Stripping tobacco leaves for twist tobacco . . . . . 90 2·50
MS744 154 × 110 mm. As Nos. 740/3, but without dates and side inscription and with the face values in different positions . . 1·50 4·50

1984. Leaders of the World. Automobiles (2nd series). As T **149**, the first in each pair showing technical drawings and the second paintings.

745 10c. black, green and brown 10 10
746 10c. multicoloured 10 10
747 30c. black, blue and green . . 15 15
748 30c. multicoloured 15 15
749 55c. black, yellow and brown 15 30
750 55c. multicoloured 15 30
751 65c. black, grey and lilac . . 15 35
752 65c. multicoloured 15 35
753 75c. black, brown and red . . 15 35
754 75c. multicoloured 15 35
755 $1 black, brown and blue . . 15 40
756 $1 multicoloured 15 40
757 $2 black, green and red . . . 20 50
758 $2 multicoloured 20 50
759 $3 black, brown and red . . 25 60
760 $3 multicoloured 25 60

DESIGNS: Nos. 745/6, Panhard and Levassor; 747/8, N.S.U. "RO-80" Saloon; 749/50, Abarth "Bialbero"; 751/2, TVR "Vixen 2500M"; 753/4, Ford "Mustang" Convertible; 755/6, Ford "Model T"; 757/8, Aston Martin "DB3S"; 759/60, Chrysler "Imperial CG Dual Cowl" Phaeton.

1985. Leaders of the World. Railway Locomotives (3rd series). As T **144**, the first in each pair showing technical drawings and the second the locomotive at work.

761 5c. multicoloured 10 20
762 5c. multicoloured 10 20
763 15c. multicoloured 10 20
764 15c. multicoloured 10 20
765 35c. multicoloured 15 20
766 35c. multicoloured 15 20
767 60c. multicoloured 15 25
768 60c. multicoloured 15 25
769 75c. multicoloured 15 30
770 75c. multicoloured 15 30
771 $1 multicoloured 15 30
772 $1 multicoloured 15 30
773 $2 multicoloured 25 45
774 $2 multicoloured 25 45
775 $2.50 multicoloured 30 55
776 $2.50 multicoloured 30 55

DESIGNS: Nos. 761/2, Class C53, Japan (1928); 763/4, Class L No. 39, India (1885); 765/6, Class B18¼, Australia (1926); 767/8, "Owain Glyndwr", Great Britain (1923); 769/70, "Lion", Great Britain (1838); 771/2, LNWR locomotive, Great Britain (1873); 773/4, Class Q6 No. 2238, Great Britain (1921); 775/6, Class H No. 106, Great Britain (1920).

1985. 75th Anniv of Girl Guide Movement and 60th Anniv of Guiding in St. Lucia.
777 **154** 10c. multicoloured 50 10
778 35c. multicoloured . . . . 1·50 15
779 65c. multicoloured . . . . 2·00 75
780 $3 multicoloured . . . . 4·25 7·50

155 "Clossiana selene"

156 Grenadier, 70th Regiment, c. 1775

1985. Leaders of the World. Butterflies. Mult.
781 15c. Type **155** 10 10
782 15c. "Inachis io" 10 10
783 40c. "Philaethria dido" . . . 10 15
784 40c. "Callicore sorana" . . . 10 15
785 60c. "Kallima inachus" . . . 15 15
786 60c. "Hypanartia paullus" . . 15 15
787 $2.25 "Morpho helena" . . . 25 50
788 $2.25 "Ornithoptera meridionalis" 25 50

1985. Leaders of the World. Automobiles (3rd series). As T **149**, the first in each pair showing technical drawings and the second paintings.
789 15c. black, blue and red . . . 10 10
790 15c. multicoloured 10 10
791 50c. black, orange and red 15 20
792 50c. multicoloured 15 20
793 $1 black, green and orange 15 20
794 $1 multicoloured 15 20
795 $1.50 black, green and brown 20 35
796 $1.50 multicoloured 20 35
DESIGNS: 789/90, Hudson "Eight" (1940); 791/2, KdF (1937); 793/4, Kissel "Goldbug" (1925); 795/6, Ferrari "246 GTS" (1973).

1985. Military Uniforms. Multicoloured.
928 5c. Type **156** 20 30
798 10c. Officer, Grenadier Company, 14th Regiment, 1780 . . . . 25 15
930 15c. Private, Battalion Company, 2nd West India Regiment, 1803 . . . . . 35 35
799 20c. Officer, Battalion Company, 46th Regiment, 1781 . . . . 40 30
800 25c. Officer, Royal Artillery, c. 1782 . . . . . 40 15
801 30c. Officer, Royal Engineers, 1782 . . . . 60 30
802 35c. Officer, Battalion Company, 54th Regiment, 1782 . . . . 50 20
935 45c. Private, Grenadier Company, 14th Regiment, 1782 . . . . 50 50
936 50c. Gunner, Royal Artillery, 1796 . . . . 60 60
937 60c. Officer, Battalion Company, 5th Regiment, 1778 . . . . 70 70
805 65c. Private, Battalion Company, 85th Regiment, c. 1796 . . . . 70 55
806 75c. Private, Battalion Company, 76th Regiment, c. 1796 . . . . 75 80
940 80c. Officer, Battalion Company, 27th Regiment, c. 1780 . . . . 90 90
807 90c. Private, Battalion Company, 81st Regiment, c. 1796 . . . . 85 90
808 $1 Sergeant, 74th (Highland) Regiment, 1796 . . . . . 90 90
943 $2.50 Private, Light Company, 93rd Regiment, 1803 . . . . 3·00 4·50
944 $5 Private, Battalion Company, 1st West India Regiment, 1803 . . . . . 3·75 9·00
811 $15 Officer, Royal Artillery, 1850 . . . . 8·00 18·00
946 $20 Private, Grenadier Company, 46th Regiment, 1778 . . . . 18·00 25·00

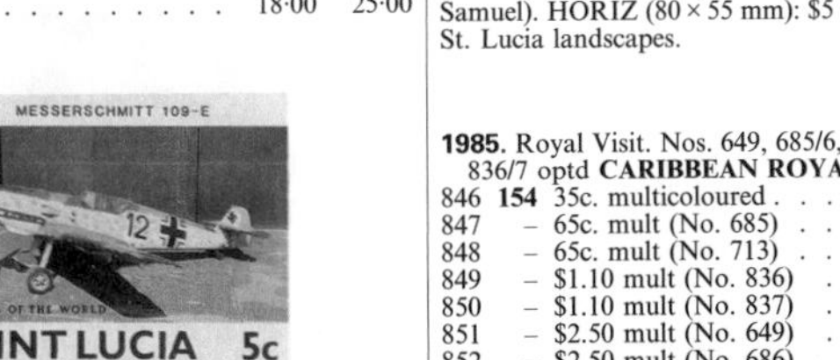

157 Messerschmitt Bf 109E

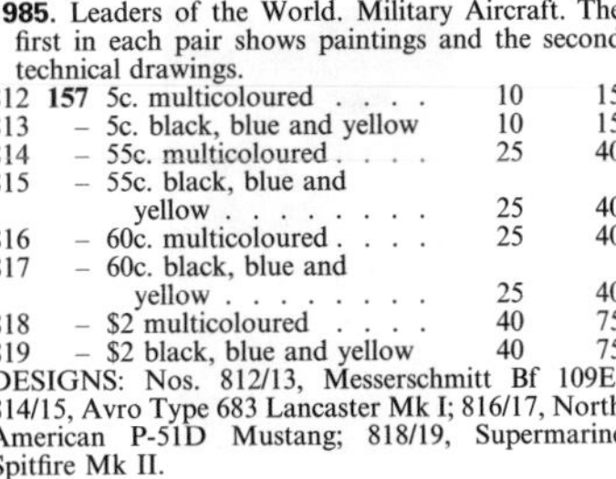

1985. Leaders of the World. Military Aircraft. The first in each pair shows paintings and the second technical drawings.
812 **157** 5c. multicoloured 10 15
813 – 5c. black, blue and yellow 10 15
814 – 55c. multicoloured 25 40
815 – 55c. black, blue and yellow 25 40
816 – 60c. multicoloured 25 40
817 – 60c. black, blue and yellow 25 40
818 – $2 multicoloured 40 75
819 – $2 black, blue and yellow 40 75
DESIGNS: Nos. 812/13, Messerschmitt Bf 109E; 814/15, Avro Type 683 Lancaster Mk I; 816/17, North American P-51D Mustang; 818/19, Supermarine Spitfire Mk II.

158 Magnificent Frigate Birds ("Frigate Bird"), Frigate Island Bird Sanctuary

1985. Nature Reserves. Multicoloured.
820 10c. Type **158** 35 20
821 35c. Mangrove cuckoo, Scorpion Island, Savannes Bay 65 45
822 65c. Lesser yellowlegs ("Yellow Sandpiper"), Maria Island Reserve . . . 75 85
823 $3 Audubon's shearwaters, Lapins Island Reserve . . 1·00 5·00

1985. Leaders of the World Railway Locomotives (4th series). As T **144**. The first in each pair shows technical drawings and the second the locomotive at work.
824 10c. multicoloured 10 10
825 10c. multicoloured 10 10
826 30c. multicoloured 15 15
827 30c. multicoloured 15 15
828 75c. multicoloured 20 25
829 75c. multicoloured 20 25
830 $2.50 multicoloured 40 70
831 $2.50 multicoloured 40 70
DESIGNS: Nos. 824/5, Tank locomotive No. 28, Great Britain (1897); 826/7, Class M No. 1621, Great Britain (1893); 828/9, Class "Dunalastair", Great Britain (1896); 830/1, "Big Bertha" type No. 2290, Great Britain (1919).

159 Queen Elizabeth the Queen Mother

160 "Youth playing Banjo" (Wayne Whitfield)

1985. Leaders of the World. Life and Times of Queen Elizabeth the Queen Mother. Various portraits.
832 **159** 40c. multicoloured 10 20
833 – 40c. multicoloured 10 20
834 – 75c. multicoloured 15 25
835 – 75c. multicoloured 15 25
836 – $1.10 multicoloured . . . 15 35
837 – $1.10 multicoloured . . . 15 35
838 – $1.75 multicoloured . . . 20 55
839 – $1.75 multicoloured . . . 20 55
MS840 84 × 114 mm – $2 multicoloured; $2 multicoloured 60 1·40
Each value was issued in pairs showing a floral pattern across the bottom of the portraits which stops short of the left-hand edge on the first stamp and of the right-hand edge on the second.

1985. International Youth Year. Paintings by Young St. Lucians.
841 **160** 10c. black, blue and mauve 20 10
842 – 45c. multicoloured 60 25
843 – 75c. multicoloured 60 50
844 – $3.50 multicoloured . . . 1·40 3·00
MS845 123 × 86 mm. – $5 multicoloured . . . . 1·25 3·50
DESIGNS—VERT (as T **160**): 45c. "Motor-cyclist" (Mark Maragh); 75c. "Boy and Girl at Pitons" (Bartholomew Eugene); $3.50, "Abstract" (Lyndon Samuel). HORIZ (80 × 55 mm): $5 Young people and St. Lucia landscapes.

1985. Royal Visit. Nos. 649, 685/6, 702, 713, 778 and 836/7 optd **CARIBBEAN ROYAL VISIT 1985**.
846 **154** 35c. multicoloured . . . . 5·50 3·00
847 – 65c. mult (No. 685) . . . 1·00 2·75
848 – 65c. mult (No. 713) . . . 5·00 3·75
849 – $1.10 mult (No. 836) . . 5·00 8·00
850 – $1.10 mult (No. 837) . . 5·00 8·00
851 – $2.50 mult (No. 649) . . 7·00 8·00
852 – $2.50 mult (No. 686) . . 1·00 3·50
853 – $2.50 mult (No. 702) . . 1·00 3·50

161 "Papa Jab"

162 Campfire Cooking Utensils

1985. Christmas. Masqueraders. Mult.
854 10c. Type **161** 30 10
855 45c. "Paille Bananne" . . . 40 30
856 65c. "Cheval Bois" . . . . . 40 1·50
MS857 70 × 83 mm. $4 "Madonna and Child" (Dunstan St. Omer) 1·00 1·90

1986. Leaders of the World. Railway Locomotives (5th series). As T **144**. The first in each pair shows technical drawings and the second the locomotive at work.
858 5c. multicoloured 10 15
859 5c. multicoloured 10 15
860 15c. multicoloured 15 15
861 15c. multicoloured 15 15
862 30c. multicoloured 20 30
863 30c. multicoloured 20 30
864 60c. multicoloured 25 40
865 60c. multicoloured 25 40
866 75c. multicoloured 30 50
867 75c. multicoloured 30 50
868 $1 multicoloured 35 60
869 $1 multicoloured 35 60
870 $2.25 multicoloured 45 80
871 $2.25 multicoloured 45 80
872 $3 multicoloured 45 80
873 $3 multicoloured 45 80
DESIGNS: Nos. 858/9, Cog locomotive "Tip Top", U.S.A. (1983); 860/1, Electric locomotive "Stephenson", Great Britain (1975); 862/3, Class D No. 737, Great Britain (1901); 864/5, No. 13 Class electric locomotive, Great Britain (1922); 866/7, Electric locomotive "Electra", Great Britain (1954); 868/9, "City of Newcastle", Great Britain (1922); 870/1, Von Kruckenburg propeller-driven railcar, Germany (1930); 872/3, No. 860, Japan (1893).

1986. 75th Annivs of Girl Guide Movement and Boy Scouts of America. Two sheets, each 85 × 113 mm, containing vert designs as T **162**. Multicoloured.
MS874 $4 Type **162**: $4 Scout salute 2·50 4·00
MS875 $6 Wickerwork: $6 Lady Baden-Powell . . . . 2·75 4·25
The two stamps in each sheet were printed together, se-tenant, forming a composite design.
Nos. **MS**874/5 exist with plain or decorative margins.
Overprints on these miniature sheets commemorating "Capex '87" International Stamp Exhibition, Toronto, were not authorised by the St. Lucia administration.

162a Queen Elizabeth II

1986. 60th Birthday of Queen Elizabeth II (1st issue). Multicoloured.
876 5c. Type **162a** 10 10
877 $1 Princess Elizabeth 15 30
878 $3.50 Queen Elizabeth II (different) . . . . 40 1·10
879 $6 In Canberrra, 1982 (vert) 55 1·60
MS880 85 × 115 mm. $8 Queen Elizabeth II (different) . . . . 3·25 6·00

163 Queen Elizabeth and Marian Home

1986. 60th Birthday of Queen Elizabeth II (2nd issue). Multicoloured.
881 10c. Type **163** 40 15
882 45c. Queen addressing rally, Mindoo Phillip Park, 1985 75 35
883 50c. Queen opening Leon Hess Comprehensive School, 1985 . . . . . . 85 50
884 $5 Queen Elizabeth and Government House, Castries . . . . 3·00 5·00
MS885 121 × 85 mm. $7 Queen Elizabeth and Royal Yacht "Britannia", Castries . . . . . 4·75 7·50

164 Pope John Paul II kissing Ground, Castries Airport

1986. Visit of Pope John Paul II. Multicoloured.
886 55c. Type **164** . . . . 1·10 80
887 60c. Pope and St. Joseph's Convent . . . . 1·10 90
888 80c. Pope and Castries Catholic Cathedral (vert) 1·60 2·00
MS889 85 × 123 mm. $6 Pope John Paul II (vert) . . . . 8·00 9·00

164a Miss Sarah Ferguson

1986. Royal Wedding (1st issue). Multicoloured.
890 80c. Type **164a** 65 85
891 80c. Prince Andrew 65 85
892 $2 Prince Andrew and Miss Sarah Ferguson (horiz) . . 90 2·00
893 $2 Prince Andrew with Mrs. Nancy Reagan (horiz) . . 90 2·00
See also Nos. 897/901.

165 Peace Corps Teacher with Students

1986. 25th Anniv of United States Peace Corps. Multicoloured.
894 80c. Type **165** 30 40
895 $2 President John Kennedy (vert) . . . . 90 1·75
896 $3.50 Peace Corps emblem between arms of St. Lucia and U.S.A. . . . . 1·25 3·00

166 Prince Andrew in Carriage

1986. Royal Wedding (2nd issue). Mult.
897 50c. Type **166** 40 30
898 80c. Miss Sarah Ferguson in coach 50 50
899 $1 Duke and Duchess of York at altar 55 60
900 $3 Duke and Duchess of York in carriage . . . . 1·00 2·75
MS901 115 × 85 mm. $7 Duke and Duchess of York on Palace balcony after wedding (horiz) 3·75 6·50

1986. Automobiles (4th series). As T **149**, the first in each pair showing technical drawings and the second paintings.
902 20c. multicoloured 15 15
903 20c. multicoloured 15 15
904 50c. multicoloured 15 20
905 50c. multicoloured 15 20
906 60c. multicoloured 15 20
907 60c. multicoloured 15 20
908 $1 multicoloured 15 20
909 $1 multicoloured 15 20
910 $1.50 multicoloured 20 20
911 $1.50 multicoloured 20 20
912 $3 multicoloured 30 45
913 $3 multicoloured 30 45
DESIGNS: Nos. 902/3, AMC "AMX" (1969); 904/5, Russo-Baltique (1912); 906/7, Lincoln "K.B" (1932); 908/9, Rolls-Royce "Phantom II Continental" (1933); 910/11, Buick "Century" (1939); 912/13, Chrysler "300 C" (1957).

167 Chak-Chak Band

1986. Tourism (1st series). Multicoloured.
914 15c. Type **167** 15 10
915 45c. Folk dancing 25 15
916 80c. Steel band 40 55
917 $5 Limbo dancing . . . . . 1·00 3·00
MS918 157 × 109 mm. $10 Fire-eating . . . . 3·75 8·50
See also Nos. 988/92.

168 St. Ann Catholic Church, Mon Repos

1986. Christmas. Multicoloured.
919 10c. Type **168** 15 10
920 40c. St. Joseph the Worker Catholic Church, Gros Islet 30 15
921 80c. Holy Trinity Anglican Church, Castries 45 60
922 $4 Our Lady of the Assumption Catholic Church, Soufriere (vert) . . 90 3·25
MS923 120 × 101 mm. $7 St. Lucy Catholic Church, Micoud . . . 2·50 6·50

169 Outline Map of St. Lucia

170 Statue of Liberty and Flags of France and U.S.A.

1987.
924B **169** 5c. black and brown 20 20
925A 10c. black and green 20 20
926A 45c. black and orange 50 50
927B 50c. black and blue . . 50 50
927cA $1 black and red . . . 75 75

1987. Cent of Statue of Liberty (1986). Mult.
947 15c. Type **170** 50 10
948 80c. Statue and "Mauretania I" (liner) . . . . 1·25 55
949 $1 Statue and Concorde . . . 2·50 1·25
950 $5 Statue and flying boat at sunset . . . . 2·75 5·00
MS951 107 × 88 mm. $6 Statue and Manhattan at night . . . . . 3·00 4·50

171 First Cadastral Survey Map and Surveying Instruments, 1775

172 Ambulance and Nurse, 1987

1987. New Cadastral Survey of St. Lucia. Multicoloured.
955 15c. Type **171** 60 15
956 60c. Map and surveying instruments, 1814 . . . . 1·25 85
957 $1 Map and surveying instruments, 1888 . . . . 1·50 1·50
958 $2.50 Cadastral survey map and surveying instruments, 1987 . . . . 2·75 4·25

1987. Cent of Victoria Hospital, Castries. Mult.
959 **172** $1 multicoloured . . . . 2·25 2·75
960 – $1 blue . . . . 2·25 2·75
961 – $2 multicoloured . . . . 2·75 3·25
962 – $2 blue . . . . 2·75 3·25
MS963 86 × 68 mm. – $4.50 multicoloured . . . . 6·50 8·00
DESIGNS: No. 960, Nurse and carrying hammock, 1913; 961, $2 Victoria Hospital, 1987; 962, Victoria Hospital 1887; $4.50, Hospital gates, 1987.

173 "The Holy Family"

174 St. Lucia Amazon perched on Branch

1987. Christmas. Paintings. Multicoloured.
964 15c. Type **173** 30 10
965 50c. "Adoration of the Shepherds" 60 30
966 60c. "Adoration of the Magi" 60 80
967 90c. "Madonna and Child" 85 2·25
MS968 82 × 67 mm. $6 Type **173** 3·50 6·50

1987. St. Lucia Amazon. Multicoloured.
969 15c. Type **174** . . . . 2·00 40
970 35c. Pair in flight . . . . . . 3·00 55
971 50c. Perched on branch (rear view) . . . . 4·00 2·25
972 $1 Emerging from tree . . . 5·50 5·00

175 Carib Clay Zemi

1988. Amerindian Artifacts. Multicoloured.
973 25c. Type **175** 15 10
974 30c. Troumassee cylinder . . 20 15
975 80c. Three pointer stone . . 45 45
976 $3.50 Dauphine petroglyph 1·75 3·50

176 East Caribbean Currency

1988. 50th Anniv of St. Lucia Co-operative Bank. Multicoloured.
977 10c. Type **176** 20 10
978 45c. Castries branch 55 35
979 60c. As 45c. 75 95
980 80c. Vieux Fort branch . . . 1·25 1·60

177 Rural Telephone Exchange

1988. 50th Anniv of Cable and Wireless (West Indies) Ltd. Multicoloured.
981 15c. Type **177** 15 15
982 25c. Early and modern telephones 15 15
983 80c. St. Lucia Teleport dish aerial 40 45
984 $2.50 Map showing Eastern Caribbean Microwave System . . . . 2·75 2·75

178 Stained Glass Window

1988. Cent of Methodist Church in St. Lucia. Mult.
985 15c. Type **178** 10 10
986 80c. Church interior 40 45
987 $3.50 Methodist Church, Castries . . . . 1·50 2·25

179 Garnished Lobsters

1988. Tourism (2nd series). Designs showing local delicacies. Multicoloured.
988 10c. Type **179** 55 75
989 30c. Cocktail and tourists at buffet 65 85
990 80c. Fresh fruits and roasted breadfruit . . . . 1·10 1·40
991 $2.50 Barbecued red snappers (fish) . . . . 2·25 2·50
MS992 80 × 104 mm. $5.50 Fruit stall, Castries market . . . . . 2·25 3·25
Nos. 988/91 were printed together, se-tenant, forming a composite design of tourists at beach barbecue.

1988. 300th Anniv of Lloyd's of London. As T **152a** of St. Helena.
1004 10c. black, lilac and brown 45 15
1005 60c. multicoloured . . . . . 1·25 75
1006 80c. multicoloured . . . . . 1·60 1·25
1007 $2.50 multicoloured . . . . 3·00 4·50
DESIGNS—VERT: 10c. San Francisco earthquake; $2.50, Castries fire, 1948. HORIZ: 60c. Castries Harbour; 80c. "Lady Nelson" (hospital ship), 1942.

180 Snow on the Mountain

181 Princess Alexandra presenting Constitution

1988. Christmas. Flowers. Multicoloured.
1008 15c. Type **180** 30 10
1009 45c. Christmas candle . . . 55 50
1010 60c. Balisier 70 90
1011 80c. Poinsettia . . . . . . 1·00 1·60
MS1012 79 × 75 mm. $5.50 Christmas flower arrangement 2·00 3·50

1989. 10th Anniv of Independence. Mult.
1013 15c. Type **181** 40 15
1014 80c. Geothermal well . . . 1·10 60
1015 $1 Sir Arthur Lewis Community College . . . 70 60
1016 $2.50 Pointe Seraphine shopping centre . . . . . 1·25 2·25
MS1017 47 × 62 mm. $5 Man with national flag . . . . 2·25 3·25

182 "Gerronema citrinum"

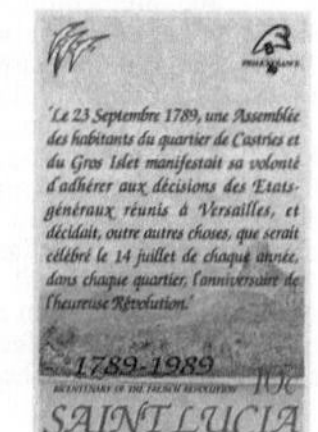

183 Local Revolutionary Declaration, 1789, and View of St. Lucia

1989. Fungi. Multicoloured.
1022 15c. Type **182** . . . . . . 1·25 30
1023 25c. "Lepiota spiculata" . . 1·50 30
1024 50c. "Calocybe cyanocephala" . . . . . . 2·50 1·10
1025 $5 "Russula puiggarii" . . . 7·00 9·50

1989. Bicentenary of the French Revolution. Designs include the "PHILEXFRANCE". International Stamp Exhibition logo. Mult.
1026 10c. Type **183** 40 15
1027 60c. Hoisting Revolutionary flag, Morne Fortune, 1791 (horiz) . . . . 2·25 80
1028 $1 Declaration of Rights of Man and view of St. Lucia . . . . 2·25 1·50
1029 $3.50 Arrival of Capt. La Crosse, Gros Islet, 1792 (horiz) . . . . 8·00 8·50

184 Red Cross Headquarters, St. Lucia

1989. 125th Anniv of Int Red Cross. Mult.
1030 50c. Type **184** . . . . . . 1·25 1·25
1031 80c. Red Cross seminar, Castries, 1987 . . . . . 1·75 2·00
1032 $1 Red Cross ambulance . . 2·00 2·25

185 Christmas Lantern

186 Gwi Gwi

1989. Christmas.
1033 **185** 10c. multicoloured . . . 25 10
1034 – 50c. multicoloured . . . 65 40
1035 – 90c. multicoloured . . . 1·00 1·25
1036 – $1 multicoloured . . . . 1·25 1·25
DESIGNS: 50c. to $1 various decorative "building" lanterns.

1990. Endangered Trees. Multicoloured.
1081 10c. Chinna 10 30
1082 15c. Latanier 15 20
1039 20c. Type **186** . . . . . . 1·00 1·00
1084 25c. L'encens 20 20
1085 50c. Bois lele 30 30
1042 80c. Bois d'amande . . . . 1·00 40
1043 95c. Mahot piman grand bois . . . . 1·25 1·00
1044 $1 Balata . . . . 1·25 75
1045 $1.50 Pencil cedar . . . . 2·50 2·50
1046 $2.50 Bois cendre . . . . . 3·75 4·00
1047 $5 Lowye cannelle . . . . . 5·50 6·50
1048 $25 Chalantier grand bois 15·00 19·00

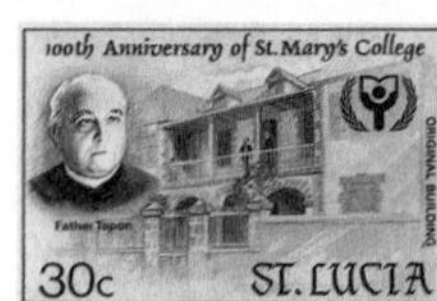

187 Father Tapon and Original College Building

1990. International Literacy Year. Centenary of St. Mary's College, Castries. Multicoloured.
1049 30c. Type **187** 15 15
1050 45c. Brother M. C. Collins and St. Mary's College . . 25 25
1051 75c. Literacy class 45 55
1052 $2 Children approaching "door to knowledge" . . 1·50 2·25

1990. 90th Birthday of Queen Elizabeth the Queen Mother. As T **117a** of Pitcairn Islands.
1053 50c. multicoloured . . . . . 1·00 35
1054 $5 black and blue . . . . . 3·75 4·75
DESIGNS—(21 × 36 mm): 50c. Crowning of Queen Consort, 1937. (29 × 37 mm): $5 Queen Elizabeth arriving at New Theatre, London 1949.

1990. "EXPO 90" International Garden and Greenery Exhibition, Osaka. No. 1047 optd **EXPO '90** and emblem.
1055 $5 Lowye cannelle . . . . . 2·75 3·50

189 "Adoration of the Magi" (Rubens)

191 "Battus polydamas"

190 "Vistafjord" (liner)

1990. Christmas. Religious Paintings. Mult.
1056 10c. Type **189** 50 20
1057 30c. "Adoration of the Shepherds" (Murillo) . . 1·25 20

1058 80c. "Adoration of the Magi" (Rubens) (different) . . . . 1·75 75
1059 $5 "Adoration of the Shepherds" (Philippe de Champaigne) . . . . . . 6·50 8·50

1991. Cruise Ships. Multicoloured.
1060 50c. Type **190** . . . . . . 1·50 40
1061 80c. "Windstar" (schooner) 2·00 1·10
1062 $1 "Unicorn" (brig) . . . . 2·25 1·50
1063 $2.50 Game-fishing launch 4·75 7·50
MS1064 82×65 mm. $5 Ships in Castries Harbour . . . . . . 11·00 11·00

1991. Butterflies. Multicoloured.
1065 60c. Type **191** . . . . . . 2·00 65
1066 80c. "Strymon simaethis" 2·25 1·10
1067 $1 "Mestra cana" . . . . 2·75 1·25
1068 $2.50 "Allosmaitia piplea" 5·50 7·50

192 Mural, Jacmel Church

1991. Christmas. Paintings by Duncan St. Omer. Multicoloured.
1069 10c. Type **192** 30 10
1070 15c. "Red Madonna" (vert) 40 10
1071 80c. Mural, Monchy Church 1·50 70
1072 $5 "Blue Madonna" (vert) 4·50 6·50

193 Yacht and Map

1991. Atlantic Rally for Cruising Yachts. Multicoloured.
1073 60c. Type **193** . . . . . . 1·50 1·50
1074 80c. Yachts off St. Lucia . . 1·75 1·75

1992. Organization of East Caribbean States. 500th Anniv of Discovery of America by Columbus. As T **66** of St. Kitts. Multicoloured.
1075 $1 Columbus meeting Amerindians . . . . . . 2·00 1·75
1076 $2 Ships approaching island 2·75 3·25

194 Amerindian Village

1992. Discovery of St. Lucia. Multicoloured.
1077 15c. Type **194** 40 20
1078 40c. Ships of Juan de la Cosa and islands, 1499 . . 1·50 50
1079 50c. Columbus sailing between Martinique and St. Lucia, 1502 . . . . . 1·60 70
1080 $5 Legendary shipwreck of Gimie . . . . 6·00 8·00

195 "Virgin and Child" (Delaroche)
196 "Death" and Gravestone

1992. Christmas. Religious Paintings. Mult.
1092 10c. Type **195** 50 20
1093 15c. "The Holy Family" (Rubens) 50 20
1094 60c. "Virgin and Child" (Luini) . . . . 2·00 1·75
1095 80c. "Virgin and Child" (Sassoferrato) . . . . . . 2·00 2·00

1993. Anti-drugs Campaign.
1096 **196** $5 multicoloured . . . . 6·00 6·50

197 "Gros Piton from Delcer, Choiseul" (Dunstan St. Omer)

1993. Carib Art. Multicoloured.
1097 20c. Type **197** 20 10
1098 75c. "Reduit Bay" (Derek Walcott) 75 75
1099 $5 "Woman and Child at River" (Nancy Cole Auguste) . . . . 4·25 6·50

198 "The Madonna of the Rosary" (Murillo)

1993. Christmas. Religious Paintings. Mult.
1100 15c. Type **198** 20 10
1101 60c. "The Madonna and Child" (Van Dyck) . . . 65 60
1102 95c. "The Annunciation" (Champaigne) . . . . . 1·10 1·50

199 The Pitons
200 "Euphorbia pulcherrima"

1994. Bicentenary of the Abolition of Slavery in St. Lucia.
1103 **199** 20c. multicoloured . . . 65 45
MS1104 115×75 mm. $5 multicoloured . . . . 4·50 6·00

1994. Christmas. Flowers. Multicoloured.
1105 20c. Type **200** 15 10
1106 75c. "Heliconia rostrata" . . 55 50
1107 95c. "Alpinia purpurata" . . 75 75
1108 $5.50 "Anthurium andreanum" . . . . . . 3·75 6·50
See also Nos. 1122/5 and 1156/9.

201 18th-century Map of St. Lucia

1995. Bicentenary of Battle of Rabot. Multicoloured.
1109 20c. Type **201** 25 15
1110 75c. Insurgent slaves 60 55
1111 95c. 9th Foot (Royal Norfolk Regiment) attacking . . . . 1·10 1·40
MS1112 150×100 mm. $5.50 Plan of battle . . . . 3·25 4·00

1995. 50th Anniv of End of Second World War. As T **182a** of St. Helena. Multicoloured.
1113 20c. St. Lucian members of the A.T.S. 40 15
1114 75c. German U-boat off St. Lucia . . . . 1·25 80
1115 95c. Bren gun-carriers of the Caribbean Regiment, North Africa . . . . . . 1·50 1·25
1116 $1.10 Supermarine Spitfire Mk V "St. Lucia" . . . . 1·75 2·00
MS1117 75×85 mm. $5.50 Reverse of 1939–45 War Medal (vert) 2·75 3·50

201a Sud Aviation SE 330 Puma Helicopter, Cambodia, 1991–93

1995. 50th Anniv of United Nations. Multicoloured.
1118 10c. Type **201a** 15 10
1119 65c. Renault lorry, Bosnia, 1995 . . . . 50 50
1120 $1.35 Transall C-160 aircraft, Cambodia, 1991–93 . . . . 95 1·40
1121 $5 Douglas DC-3 aircraft, Korea, 1950–54 . . . . . 3·75 5·50

1995. Christmas. Flowers. As T **200**, each including Madonna and Child. Multicoloured.
1122 15c. "Eranthemum nervosum" 15 10
1123 70c. Bougainvillea 45 45
1124 $1.10 "Allamanda cathartica" 70 90
1125 $3 "Rosa sinensis" . . . . 1·75 3·50

202 Calypso King
203 Dry River Bed

1996. Carnival. Multicoloured.
1126 20c. Type **202** 70 10
1127 65c. Carnival dancers . . . 1·50 55
1128 95c. King of the Band float 2·00 85
1129 $3 Carnival Queen . . . . 3·50 6·00

1996. Inaug of New Irrigation Project. Mult.
1130 20c. Type **203** 10 10
1131 65c. People bathing in stream 40 45
1132 $5 New dam . . . . 3·00 4·75

204 Produce Market

1996. Tourism. Multicoloured.
1133 65c. Type **204** 45 45
1134 75c. Horse-riding on beach 55 55
1135 95c. Bride and groom . . . 70 75
1136 $5 Jazz band . . . . 2·75 4·50

205 Athlete of 1896

1996. Centenary of Modern Olympic Games. Multicoloured.
1137 15c. Type **205** 25 50
1138 15c. Athlete of 1996 . . . . 25 50
1139 75c. Catamaran and dinghy 1·00 1·40
1140 75c. Sailing dinghies . . . . 1·00 1·40
Nos. 1137/8 and 1139/40 respectively were printed together, se-tenant, forming composite designs.

206 Spanish Royal Standard, 1502, and Caravel

1996. Flags and Ships. Multicoloured.
1141 10c. Type **206** 10 10
1142 15c. Skull and crossbones, 1550, and pirate carrack 10 10
1143 20c. Dutch royal standard, 1650, and galleon 10 15
1144 25c. Union Jack, 1739, and ship of the line 10 15
1145 40c. French royal standard, 1750, and ship of the line 15 20
1146 50c. Martinique and St. Lucia flag, 1766, and French brig 20 25
1147 55c. White Ensign, 1782, and frigate squadron . . 20 25
1148 65c. Red Ensign, 1782, and frigates in action . . . 25 30
1149 75c. Blue Ensign, 1782, and brig 30 35
1150 95c. The Tricolour, 1792, and French frigate . . . 40 45
1151 $1 Union Jack, 1801, and West Indies Grand Fleet 40 45
1152 $2.50 Confederate States of America flag, 1861, and cruiser . . . . 1·00 1·10
1153 $5 Canadian flag, 1915–19, and "V" or "W" class destroyer . . . . 2·00 2·10
1154 $10 United States flag, 1942–48, and "Fletcher" class destroyer . . . . . 4·00 4·25
1155 $25 Flag of St. Lucia and "Royal Princess" (cruise liner) . . . . 10·00 10·50
The design of the $5 value is incorrect. There were no "V" or "W" class destroyers in the Canadian Navy where ships up to 1965 flew the White Ensign.

1996. Christmas. Flowers. As T **200**, each including Madonna and Child. Multicoloured.
1156 20c. "Cordia sebestena" . . 15 10
1157 75c. "Cryptostegia grandiflora" 50 50
1158 95c. "Hibiscus elatus" . . . 65 65
1159 $5 "Caularthron bicornutum" . . . . . . 4·00 5·50

1997. Golden Wedding of Queen Elizabeth and Prince Philip. As T **192a** of St. Helena. Multicoloured.
1160 75c. Queen Elizabeth at Warwick, 1996 . . . . . 1·00 1·25
1161 75c. Prince Philip with carriage horses . . . . . 1·00 1·25
1162 95c. Prince Philip . . . . . 1·00 1·25
1163 95c. Queen in phaeton at Trooping the Colour . . 1·00 1·25
1164 $1 Queen Elizabeth and Prince Philip at Sandringham, 1982 . . . 1·00 1·25
1165 $1 Princess Anne show jumping . . . . 1·00 1·25
MS1166 110×70 mm. $5 Queen Elizabeth and Prince Philip in landau (horiz) . . . . 3·25 4·00
Nos. 1160/1, 1162/3 and 1164/5 respectively were printed together, se-tenant, with the backgrounds forming composite designs.

207 "St. George" capsized, 1935

1997. Marine Disasters. Multicoloured.
1167 20c. Type **207** 85 20
1168 55c. Wreck of "Belle of Bath" (freighter) . . . . 1·40 30
1169 $1 "Ethelgonda" (freighter) aground on rocks, 1897 2·25 1·25
1170 $2.50 Hurricane, 1817 . . . 3·00 4·50

208 Attack on Praslin

1997. Bicentenary of the Brigands' War. Mult.
1171 20c. Type **208** 50 10
1172 55c. British troops at Battle of Dennery 70 30
1173 70c. Discussing peace agreement 75 75
1174 $3 Members of 1st West India Regiment . . . . . 2·50 4·00

209 "Roseau Church" (detail, Dunstan St. Omer)

1997. Christmas. Paintings by Dunstan St. Omer. Multicoloured.
1175 20c. Type **209** 20 10
1176 60c. Altarpiece, Regional Seminary, Trinidad . . . 45 35
1177 95c. "Our Lady of the Presentation", Trinidad 60 60
1178 $5 "The Four Days of Creation" . . . . 2·75 4·75

210 Diana, Princess of Wales
212 St. Lucia Oriole

211 Signatories to CARICOM Treaty, 1973

1998. Diana, Princess of Wales Commemoration.
1179 **210** $1 multicoloured 60 65

1998. 25th Anniv of CARICOM. Multicoloured.
1180 20c. Type **211** 15 10
1181 75c. Flags of CARICOM and St. Lucia 85 75

1998. Wild Life (1st series). Birds. Multicoloured.
1197 70c. Type **212** 80 55
1198 75c. Lesser antillean pewee . . 80 60
1199 95c. Bridled quail dove . . 1·00 85
1200 $1.10 Semper's warbler . . 1·75 1·75
See also Nos. 1212/15.

213 "Siproeta stelenes" and Chain

1998. 50th Anniv of Universal Declaration of Human Rights. Butterflies. Multicoloured.
1201 20c. Type **213** 85 20
1202 65c. "Pseudolycaena marsyas" and chain . . . 1·40 50
1203 70c. "Heliconius melpomene" and rope . . 1·40 50
1204 $5 "Phoebis philea" and chain . . . . 4·00 5·50

214 "Tabebuia serratifolia"

1998. Christmas. Flowers. Multicoloured.
1205 20c. Type **214** 20 10
1206 50c. "Hibiscus sabdariffa" 45 30
1207 95c. "Euphorbia leucocephala" 65 45
1208 $2.50 "Calliandra slaneae" 1·40 2·50

215 "The Black Prometheus" (wall painting)

1998. 50th Anniv of University of West Indies. Multicoloured.
1209 15c. Type **215** 15 10
1210 75c. Sir Arthur Lewis College, St. Lucia 50 40
1211 $5 University arms and the Pitons, St. Lucia . . . . 2·75 4·00

216 St. Lucia Tree Lizard

1999. Wildlife (2nd series). Reptiles. Multicoloured.
1212 20c. Type **216** 25 10
1213 75c. Boa constrictor . . . 70 45
1214 95c. Leatherback turtle . . . 75 50
1215 $5 St. Lucia whiptail . . . 2·75 4·00

217 "Tees" (mail steamer), 1893

1999. 125th Anniv of Universal Postal Union. Multicoloured.
1216 20c. Type **217** 50 20
1217 65c. Sikorsky S.38 (flying boat), 1929 . . . . 90 45
1218 95c. "Lady Drake" (cargo liner), 1930 . . . . 1·00 55
1219 $3 DC10 airliner, 1999 . . . 2·25 3·00
MS1220 100 × 84 mm. $5 Heinrich von Stephan (founder of U.P.U.) (30 × 37 mm) . . . . 2·50 3·50

218 The Nativity

1999. Christmas. New Millennium. Multicoloured.
1221 20c. Type **218** 20 10
1222 $1 Cathedral of the Immaculate Conception 80 1·00

219 Original Badge of the Colony

2000. 21st Anniv of Independence. Multicoloured.
1223 20c. Type **219** 15 10
1224 75c. Colonial badge, 1939 50 50
1225 95c. Coat of Arms as Associated State, 1967 . . 65 75
1226 $1 Coat of Arms on Independence, 1979 . . . 80 85

220 Sugar Factory, Vieux-Fort

2000. History of St. Lucia. Multicoloured.
1227 20c. Type **220** 20 15
1228 65c. Coaling ship, Port Castries 75 45
1229 $1 Fort Rodney, Pigeon Island 85 65
1230 $5 Ruins of military hospital, Pigeon Island . . 3·00 4·25

221 The Old Market, Castries

2000. 150th Anniv of Castries Municipality. Mult.
1231 20c. Type **221** 20 15
1232 75c. Central Library 65 45
1233 95c. Harbour . . . . 1·00 70
1234 $5 Henry H. Breen (first municipality mayor, 1851) and Joseph Desir (first city mayor, 1967) . . . . 2·75 4·00

222 Brownies and Badge

2000. 75th Anniv of Girl Guides in St. Lucia. Multicoloured.
1235 70c. Type **222** 65 40
1236 $1 Girl Guides parade . . . 90 70
1237 $2.50 Brownies in camp and Guides with flag . . . . 2·00 2·75

223 Holy Trinity Church, Castries

2000. Christmas. Churches. Multicoloured.
1238 20c. Type **223** 30 15
1239 50c. St. Paul's Church, Vieux-Fort 50 30
1240 95c. Christ Church, Soufriere 80 55
1241 $2.50 Grace Church, River D'Oree . . . . 2·00 2·75

224 St. Lucia Black Finch

2001. Endangered Species. Birds of St. Lucia. Multicoloured.
1242 20c. Type **224** 60 50
1243 20c. White-breasted trembler ("White-breasted Thrasher") 60 50
1244 95c. St. Lucia oriole . . . . 90 1·10
1245 95c. Forest thrush . . . . . 90 1·10

225 Open-air Jazz Concert

2001. 10th Anniv of Jazz Festival. Multicoloured.
1246 20c. Type **225** 30 15
1247 $1 Jazz concert on the beach 1·00 75
1248 $5 Jazz band . . . . 4·00 4·50

226 Union Jack, Pitons and Frigate (Arrival of Civil Administrator, 1801)

227 Three-panel Stained Glass Window

2001. Bicentenary of Civil Administration. Multicoloured.
1249 20c. Type **226** 30 20
1250 65c. Napoleon, Tricolor and Conseil Superior, 1802 . . 55 40
1251 $1.10 King George III, Union Jack and British fleet (introduction of Privy Council, 1803) . . . 85 75
1252 $3 King George IV and island map (Treaty of Paris, 1814) . . . . . . 2·00 2·50

2001. Christmas. Multicoloured.
1253 20c. Type **227** 25 15
1254 95c. Circular stained glass window 90 55
1255 $2.50 Arched stained glass window . . . . 2·00 2·50

2002. Golden Jubilee. As T **211** of St. Helena.
1256 25c. brown, blue and gold 30 20
1257 65c. multicoloured 65 65
1258 75c. brown, blue and gold 75 80
1259 95c. multicoloured 85 90
MS1260 162 × 95 mm. Nos. 1256/9 and $5 multicoloured . . . . . 4·75 5·50
DESIGNS—HORIZ: 25c. Princess Elizabeth in June 1927; 65c. Queen Elizabeth wearing striped turban; 75c. Princess Elizabeth in 1947; 95c. Queen Elizabeth arriving at St. Paul's Cathedral, 1996. VERT: (38 × 51 mm)—$5 Queen Elizabeth after Annigoni.
Designs as Nos. 1256/9 in No. **MS**1260 omit the gold frame around each stamp and the "Golden Jubilee 1952–2002" inscription.

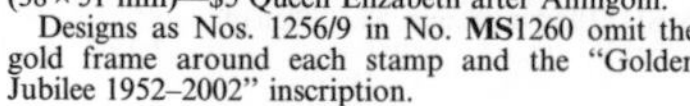

228 H.M.S. *St. Lucia* (brig), 1803

2002. Royal Navy Ships. Multicoloured.
1261 15c. Type **228** 40 25
1262 75c. H.M.S. *Thetis* (frigate), 1781 . . . . 90 60
1263 $1 H.M.S. *Berwick* (cruiser), 1903 . . . . 1·00 1·00
1264 $5 H.M.S. *Victory* (Nelson), 1805 . . . . 3·00 3·50

2002. Queen Elizabeth the Queen Mother Commemoration. As T **215** of St. Helena.
1265 50c. brown, gold and purple 45 45
1266 65c. multicoloured 55 55
1267 95c. brown, gold and purple 75 75
1268 $1 multicoloured 85 90
MS1269 145 × 70 mm. $2 black and gold; $2 multicoloured . . . . 4·00 4·25
DESIGNS: 50c. Duchess of York with Princess Elizabeth, 1926; 65c. Queen Mother at St. Peter's Church Thurso, 1992; 95c. Queen Elizabeth at Church Army services club London, 1943; $1 Queen Mother at Sandown Races, 1999; $2 (black and gold) Duchess of York, 1920s; $2 (multicoloured) Queen Mother at unveiling of S.O.E. Memorial, 1996. Designs in No. **MS**1269 omit the "1900–2002" inscription and the coloured frame.

229 Derek Walcott

2002. 10th Anniv of Award of Nobel Literature Prize to Derek Walcott. Multicoloured.
1270 20c. Type **229** 30 20
1271 65c. Father Christmas with children (horiz) 60 50
1272 70c. Dancers 70 50
1273 $5 Outboard motor boat (cover illustration from *Omeros*) (horiz) . . . . . 3·00 3·50

230 William and Catherine Booth

2002. Centenary of Salvation Army on St. Lucia. Multicoloured.
1274 20c. Type **230** 35 20
1275 $1 Early St. Lucia Salvation Army parade . . . . . . 1·00 1·00
1276 $2.50 Salvation Army shield symbol and crest . . . . 1·75 2·00

231 "The Adoration of the Shepherds" (Bernardino da Asola)

2003. Christmas. Religious Paintings from The National Gallery, London. Multicoloured.
1277 20c. Type **231** 25 10
1278 50c. "The Adoration of the Kings" (Girolamo da Treviso) (vert) 50 30
1279 75c. "The Adoration of the Kings" (Vincenzo Foppa) (vert) 65 40
1280 $5 "The Adoration of the Shepherds" (Le Nain brothers) . . . . 3·50 3·75

2003. 50th Anniv of Coronation. As T **219** of St. Helena. Multicoloured.
1281 20c. Queen Elizabeth II wearing Imperial State Crown 10 15
1282 75c. Coronation Coach passing Buckingham Palace gate 30 35
MS1283 95 × 115 mm. $2.50 As 75 c.; $2.50 As 20 c. . . . . . . 2·00 2·10

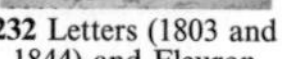

232 Letters (1803 and 1844) and Fleuron

233 St. Lucia Amazon Date Stamp, 1822

2003. Bicentenary of Continuous Mail Service. Multicoloured.
1284 20c. Type **232** 10 15
1285 25c. Stamps of 1860 . . . . 10 15
1286 65c. *Hewanorra* (steam packet), 1920 and map . . 25 30
1287 75c. Post Offices of 1900 and 2003 . . . . 30 35

2003. Coil stamps. Multicoloured.
1288 10c. Type **233** 10 10
1289 25c. The Pitons, St. Lucia 10 15

234 Sikorsky S-38 (flying boat)

2003. Centenary of Powered Flight. Multicoloured.
1290 20c. Type **234** 10 15
1291 70c. Consolidated PBY-5A Catalina (amphibian) . . 30 35
1292 $1 Lockheed Lodestar . . . 40 45
1293 $5 Supermarine Spitfire Mk V *St Lucia* . . . . . 2·00 2·10

235 Sorrel Flowers and Ginger Root

2003. Christmas. Multicoloured.
1294 20c. Type **235** 10 15
1295 75c. Sorrel drink and ginger ale 30 35
1296 95c. Masqueraders 40 45
1297 $1 People making Christmas lanterns 40 45

236 Raising St. Lucia Flag

2004. 25th Anniv of Independence. Multicoloured.
1298 20c. Type **236** 10 15
1299 95c. Sailing ship, aircraft, cargo ship and bananas 40 45
1300 $1.10 Anniversary emblem (horiz) 45 50
1301 $5 Cruise ships, Castries harbour (horiz) . . . . . 2·00 2·10

237 Antillean Crested Hummingbird

2004. Birds of the Caribbean. Multicoloured.
1302 $1 Type **237** 40 45
1303 $1 Lesser Antillian pewee ("Saint Lucia Pewee") . . 40 45
1304 $1 Purple-throated carib . . 40 45
1305 $1 Grey trembler 40 45
1306 $1 Rufous-throated solitaire 40 45
1307 $1 Adelaide's warbler ("Saint Lucia Warbler") 40 45
1308 $1 Antillean euphonia . . . 40 45
1309 $1 Semper's warbler 40 45
Nos. 1302/9 were printed together with the backgrounds forming composite designs.

238 Sailing

2004. Tourism. Multicoloured.
1310 45c. Type **238** 15 20
1311 65c. Horse-riding 25 30
1312 70c. Scuba diving 25 30
1313 $1.10 Walking near waterfall 45 50

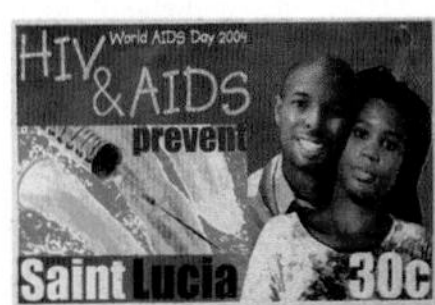

239 Hypodermic Needle and Couple ("Prevent")

2004. World AIDS Awareness Day. Multicoloured.
1314 30c. Type **239** 10 15
1315 30c. Two children ("Educate us") and woman 10 15

240 "The Adoration of the Kings" (Dosso)

2004. Christmas. Religious Paintings. Multicoloured.
1316 30c. Type **240** 10 15
1317 75c. "The Adoration of the Shepherds" (Poussin) (vert) 30 35
1318 95c. "The Adoration of the Kings" (Joos) (vert) . . . 35 40
1319 $1 "The Adoration of the Shepherds" (Fabritius) . . 40 45

241 Convent Schoolgirls

2005. 150th Anniv of St. Joseph's Convent. Multicoloured.
1320 30c. Type **241** 10 15
1321 95c. St. Joseph's Convent 35 40
1322 $2.50 Street scene . . . . . 1·00 1·10

OFFICIAL STAMPS

1983. Nos. 537/48 optd **OFFICIAL**.
O 1 5c. Type **120** 20 20
O 2 10c. Douglas DC-10-30 . . . 30 20
O 3 15c. Local bus 40 30
O 4 20c. "Geestcrest" (freighter) 50 30
O 5 25c. Britten Norman Islander aircraft 60 30
O 6 30c. "Charles" (pilot boat) 70 30
O 7 50c. Boeing 727-200 . . . . 90 40
O 8 75c. "Cunard Countess" (liner) . . . . 1·10 60
O 9 $1 Lockheed TriStar 500 . . 1·50 85
O10 $2 "Booklet Vulcan" (cargo liner) . . . . 2·00 2·00
O11 $5 Boeing 707-420 airliner 3·50 3·75
O12 $10 "Queen Elizabeth 2" (liner) . . . . 6·50 7·50

1985. Nos. 797/811 optd **OFFICIAL**.
O13 5c. Type **156** . . . . 60 1·00
O14 10c. Officer, Grenadier Company, 14th Regiment, 1780 . . . . 60 1·00
O15 20c. Officer, Battalion Company, 46th Regiment, 1781 . . . . 70 80
O16 25c. Officer, Royal Artillery, c. 1782 . . . . 70 80
O17 30c. Officer, Royal Engineers, 1782 . . . . . 80 90
O18 35c. Officer, Battalion Company, 54th Regiment, 1782 . . . . 90 90
O19 45c. Private, Grenadier Company, 14th Regiment, 1782 . . . . 1·00 90
O20 50c. Gunner, Royal Artillery, 1796 . . . . 1·00 90
O21 65c. Private, Battalion Company, 85th Regiment, c. 1796 . . . . 1·25 1·50
O22 75c. Private, Battalion Company, 76th Regiment, 1796 . . . . 1·25 2·00
O23 90c. Private, Battalion Company, 81st Regiment, c. 1796 . . . . 1·50 2·00
O24 $1 Sergeant 74th (Highland) Regiment, 1796 . . . . . 1·75 2·00
O25 $2.50 Private, Light Company, 93rd Regiment, 1803 . . . . 2·75 4·00
O26 $5 Private, Battalion Company, 1st West India Regiment, 1803 . . . . . 4·00 4·00
O27 $15 Officer, Royal Artillery, 1850 . . . . 9·00 9·00

1990. Nos. 1081/2, 1039/40, 1085 and 1042/48 optd **OFFICIAL**.
O28 10c. Chinna 30 70
O29 15c. Latanier 30 70
O30 20c. Type **186** 40 50
O31 25c. L'encens 40 50
O32 50c. Bois lele 50 60
O33 80c. Bois d'amande 60 65
O34 95c. Mahot piman grand bois . . . . 1·00 1·25
O35 $1 Balata . . . . 1·00 1·00
O36 $1.50 Pencil cedar . . . . . 1·50 1·75
O37 $2.50 Bois cendre . . . . . 2·75 3·50
O38 $5 Lowye cannelle . . . . 4·75 5·50
O39 $25 Chalantier grand bois 13·00 16·00

POSTAGE DUE STAMPS

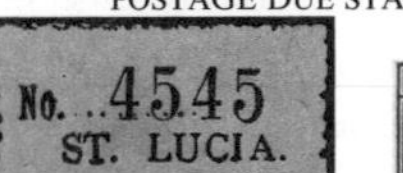
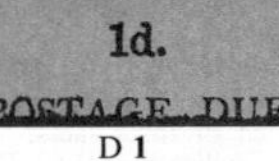

D 1

D 2

1930.
D1 D **1** 1d. black on blue . . . . 4·75 15·00
D2 2d. black on yellow . . . 12·00 40·00

1933.
D3 D **2** 1d. black . . . . 4·75 6·00
D4 2d. black . . . . 19·00 8·00
D5 4d. black . . . . 5·50 42·00
D6 8d. black . . . . 5·50 50·00

D 3

D 4 St. Lucia Coat of Arms

1949.
D 7a D **3** 2c. black . . . . 10 8·50
D 8a 4c. black . . . . 50 11·00
D 9 8c. black . . . . 3·25 25·00
D10a 16c. black . . . . . . 4·50 50·00

1981.
D13 D **4** 5c. purple 10 65
D17 5c. red 10 25
D18 15c. green 10 25
D19 25c. orange 10 25
D20 $1 blue . . . . 45 1·00

STE. MARIE DE MADAGASCAR Pt. 6

An island off the east coast of Madagascar. From 1898 used the stamps of Madagascar and Dependencies.

100 centimes = 1 franc.

1894. "Tablet" key-type inscr "STE MARIE DE MADAGASCAR" in red (1, 5, 15, 25, 75c., 1f.) or blue (others).
1 D 1c. black on blue . . . . 65 1·75
2 2c. brown on buff . . . . . 2·00 1·90
3 4c. brown on grey . . . . . 3·50 4·00
4 5c. green on green . . . . . 6·25 12·50
5 10c. black on lilac . . . . . 10·00 11·50
6 15c. blue . . . . 25·00 32·00
7 20c. red on green . . . . . 9·75 9·50
8 25c. black on pink . . . . . 6·50 4·25
9 30c. brown on drab . . . . 10·50 14·00
10 40c. red on yellow . . . . . 13·00 7·75
11 50c. red on pink . . . . . . 40·00 42·00
12 75c. brown on orange . . . 55·00 29·00
13 1f. green . . . . 40·00 32·00

ST. PIERRE ET MIQUELON Pt. 6

A group of French islands off the S. coast of Newfoundland. The group became an Overseas Department of France on 1 July 1976. The stamps of France were used in the islands from 1 April 1978 until 3 February 1986. Separate issues for the group were reintroduced in 1986.

1885. 100 centimes = 1 franc.
2002. 100 cents = 1 euro.

1885. Stamps of French Colonies surch **S P M** and value in figures only.
1 J 5 on 2c. brown on buff . . . £5000 £1900
4 5 on 4c. brown on grey . . £325 £225
8 05 on 20c. red on green . . 30·00 30·00
9 H 05 on 35c. black on yellow £110 90·00
5 05 on 40c. red on yellow . . 95·00 35·00
10 05 on 75c. red £250 £180
11 05 on 1f. green . . . . . . 26·00 13·50
6 10 on 40c. red on yellow . . 23·00 17·00
7 15 on 40c. red on yellow . . 18·00 21·00
3 25 on 1f. green £2250 £1400
The surcharge on No.1 is always inverted.

1891. French Colonies "Commerce" type surch **15c. S P M.**
15 J 15c. on 30c. brown on drab 42·00 28·00
16 15c. on 35c. black on orange £550 £375
17 15c. on 40c. red on yellow . . 90·00 70·00

1891. Stamps of French Colonies "Commerce" type, optd **ST PIERRE M-on**.
23 J 1c. black on blue . . . . . 10·00 11·00
24 2c. brown on buff . . . . . 10·00 12·00
25 4c. brown on grey . . . . . 14·50 12·50
26 5c. green on green . . . . . 16·00 10·50
22 10c. black on lilac . . . . . 20·00 20·00
28 15c. blue on blue . . . . . 26·00 16·00
29 20c. red on green . . . . . 75·00 65·00
30 25c. black on pink . . . . . 27·00 9·50
31 30c. brown on drab . . . . £110 90·00
32 35c. black on orange £375 £275
33 40c. red on yellow . . . . . 75·00 60·00

34 75c. red on pink . . . . . . £110 90·00
35 1f. green . . . . 75·00 65·00

1891. Stamps of French Colonies, "Commerce" type, surch **ST-PIERRE M-on** and new value in figures and words (**cent.**) above and below opt.
36 J 1c. on 5c. green and green . . 5·00 8·50
37 1c. on 10c. black on lilac . . 10·00 11·00
38 1c. on 25c. black on pink . . 4·75 7·75
39 2c. on 10c. black on lilac . . 6·00 6·75
40 2c. on 15c. blue on blue . . 8·00 6·75
41 2c. on 25c. black on pink . . 7·00 5·25
42 4c. on 20c. red on green . . 6·25 5·75
43 4c. on 25c. black on pink . . 4·75 9·25
44 4c. on 30c. brown on drab . . 19·00 15·00
45 4c. on 40c. red on yellow . . 35·00 16·00

1892. Nos. 26 and 30 surch with figure only on top of opt.
49 J 1c. on 5c. green on green . . 6·75 11·50
46 1 on 25c. black on pink . . . 4·75 6·00
50 2 on 5c. green on green . . . 7·50 13·00
47 2 on 25c. black on pink . . . 3·50 7·00
51 4 on 5c. green on green . . . 7·75 10·00
48 4 on 25c. black on pink . . . 3·00 6·25

1892. Postage Due stamps of French Colonies optd **T ST-PIERRE M-on P**.
52 U 10c. black . . . . 38·00 38·00
53 20c. black . . . . 25·00 23·00
54 30c. black . . . . 23·00 24·00
55 40c. black . . . . 25·00 25·00
56 60c. black £110 £100
57 1f. brown £120 £120
58 2f. brown £200 £200
59 5f. brown £325 £325

1892. "Tablet" key-type inscr "ST PIERRE ET MIQUELON".
60 D 1c. black and red on blue . . 55 1·00
61 2c. brown and blue on buff 1·00 2·00
62 4c. brown and blue on grey 1·00 1·75
63 5c. green and red . . . . . 2·25 2·25
64 10c. black and blue on lilac 5·75 4·25
74 10c. red and blue . . . . . 3·00 2·50
65 15c. blue and red . . . . . 12·00 4·25
75 15c. grey and red . . . . . 50·00 45·00
66 20c. red and blue on green 20·00 17·00
67 25c. black and red on pink 9·75 2·50
76 25c. blue and red . . . . . 10·00 16·00
68 30c. brown and blue on drab 8·00 6·75
77 35c. black and red on yellow 5·25 8·00
69 40c. red and blue on yellow 5·75 7·00
70 50c. red and blue on pink 38·00 29·00
78 50c. brown and red on blue 20·00 32·00
71 75c. brown and red on orange . . . . 18·00 24·00
72 1f. green and red . . . . . 24·00 18·00

17 Fisherman

18 Glaucous Gull

19 Fishing Brigantine

1909.
79 **17** 1c. brown and red 20 25
80 2c. blue and brown 20 35
81 4c. brown and violet . . . 20 4·50
82 5c. olive and green . . . . 1·40 75
109 5c. black and blue . . . . 30 2·25
83 10c. red and pink . . . . 1·50 1·40
110 10c. olive and green . . . 50 2·75
111 10c. mauve and bistre . . . 1·00 2·00
84 15c. red and purple . . . . 1·00 2·75
85 20c. purple and brown . . . 90 3·00
86 **18** 25c. blue and deep blue . . 3·50 2·10
112 25c. green and brown . . . 1·50 1·75
87 30c. brown and orange . . 2·25 2·10
113 30c. red and carmine . . . 1·25 1·75
114 30c. blue and red . . . . 3·75 2·50
115 30c. green and olive . . . 1·25 1·90
88 35c. brown and green . . . 1·60 1·90
89 40c. green and brown . . . 3·00 2·50
90 45c. green and violet . . . 75 2·00
91 50c. green and brown . . . 2·25 1·50
116 50c. light blue and blue . . 1·25 1·60
117 50c. mauve and bistre . . . 1·50 1·50
118 60c. red and blue . . . . 1·00 2·10
119 65c. brown and mauve . . 2·10 1·90
92 75c. green and brown . . . 1·50 1·90
120 90c. red and scarlet . . . 29·00 32·00
93 **19** 1f. blue and green . . . . 4·00 4·00
121 1f.10 red and green . . . . 3·75 5·00
122 1f.50 blue and ultramarine 10·50 16·00
94 2f. brown and violet . . . 4·50 4·50
123 3f. mauve on pink . . . . 10·50 16·00
95 5f. green and brown . . . 10·00 10·00

1912. "Tablet" issue surch in figures.

96	D	05 on 2c. brown and blue on buff	2·75	4·25
97		05 on 4c. brown and blue on grey	40	2·25
98		05 on 15c. blue and red	70	3·00
99		05 on 20c. red and blue on green	30	2·75
100		05 on 25c. black and red on pink	40	2·75
101		05 on 30c. brown and blue on drab	45	2·75
102		05 on 35c. black and red on yellow	70	3·25
103		10 on 40c. red and blue on yellow	1·10	2·50
104		10 on 50c. red and blue	1·00	3·00
105		10 on 75c. brown and red on orange	2·50	4·00
106		10 on 1f. green and red	2·50	4·50

1915. Red Cross. Surch **5c** and red cross.

107	17	10c.+5c. red and pink	50	3·00
108		15c.+5c. red and purple	1·90	3·25

1924. Surch with new value.

124	17	25c. on 15c. red and purple	95	2·50
125	19	25c. on 2f. brown & violet	1·00	2·75
126		25c. on 5f. green & brown	75	2·75
127	18	65 on 45c. green and violet	2·10	2·25
128		85 on 75c. green and brown	2·00	2·25
129		90c. on 75c. red and scarlet	2·40	3·00
130	19	1f.25 on 1f. ultramarine and blue	2·00	4·00
131		1f.50 on 1f. blue and light blue	3·50	5·00
132		3f. on 5f. mauve and brown	3·25	4·50
133		10f. on 5f. green and red	9·00	19·00
134		20f. on 5f. red and violet	16·00	26·00

1931. International Colonial Exhibition, Paris, key-types inscr "ST PIERRE ET MIQUELON".

135	E	40c. green and black	3·50	4·00
136	F	50c. mauve and black	4·00	4·50
137	G	90c. red and black	3·50	4·75
138	H	1f.50 blue and black	4·00	4·50

27 Map of St. Pierre et Miquelon

28 Galantry Lighthouse

29 "Jacques Coeur" (trawler)

1932.

139	27	1c. blue and purple	15	2·50
140	28	2c. green and black	25	2·00
141	29	4c. brown and red	35	2·25
142		5c. brown and mauve	70	2·50
143	28	10c. black and purple	35	2·75
144		15c. mauve and blue	55	3·25
145	27	20c. red and black	55	3·25
146		25c. green and mauve	2·75	2·50
147	29	30c. green and olive	2·75	3·25
148		40c. brown and blue	2·75	3·25
149	28	45c. green and red	2·75	3·00
150		50c. green and brown	2·50	1·40
151	29	65c. red and brown	3·25	3·50
152	27	75c. red and green	3·00	3·25
153		90c. scarlet and red	3·00	3·50
154	29	1f. scarlet and red	2·50	3·00
155	27	1f.25 red and blue	3·25	3·50
156		1f.50 blue and deep blue	3·25	3·50
157	29	1f.75 brown and black	3·75	3·75
158		2f. green and black	9·75	13·00
159	28	3f. brown and green	15·00	17·00
160		5f. brown and red	25·00	29·00
161	29	10f. mauve and green	48·00	65·00
162	27	20f. green and red	40·00	70·00

1934. 400th Anniv of Cartier's Discovery of Canada. Optd **JACQUES CARTIER 1534 - 1934**.

163	28	50c. green and brown	4·25	4·25
164	27	75c. red and green	4·50	4·50
165		1f.50 blue and deep blue	5·50	5·50
166	29	1f.75 brown and black	6·25	6·50
167	28	5f. brown and red	35·00	35·00

32 Commerce

38 Pierre and Marie Curie

1937. International Exhibition, Paris.

168	32	20c. violet	90	4·00
169	–	30c. green	70	4·00
170	–	40c. red	70	4·00
171	–	50c. brown and blue	60	2·75
172	–	90c. red	80	2·75
173	–	1f.50 blue	80	2·75
MS173a		120×100 mm. 3f. blue. Imperf	10·50	40·00

DESIGNS—VERT: 50c. Agriculture. HORIZ: 30c. Sailing ships; 40c. Women of three races; 90c., 3f. France extends Torch of Civilization; 1f.50, Diane de Poitiers.

1938. International Anti-cancer Fund.

174	38	1f.75+50c. blue	8·75	20·00

39 Dog Team

1938.

175	39	2c. green	20	2·75
176		3c. brown	20	2·50
177		4c. purple	45	2·50
178		5c. red	20	2·50
179		10c. brown	20	2·75
180		15c. purple	25	2·50
181		20c. violet	25	2·50
182		25c. blue	1·60	4·00
183	–	30c. purple	25	2·50
184	–	35c. green	70	2·75
185	–	40c. blue	15	2·75
186	–	45c. green	45	2·75
187	–	50c. red	25	2·75
188	–	55c. blue	3·25	4·25
189	–	60c. violet	40	2·75
190	–	65c. brown	3·50	6·00
191	–	70c. orange	1·00	2·75
192	–	80c. violet	2·25	3·00
193	–	90c. blue	2·00	2·75
194	–	1f. red	9·50	13·00
195	–	1f. olive	1·25	2·75
196	–	1f.25 red	2·00	3·75
197	–	1f.40 brown	2·00	3·00
198	–	1r.50 green	60	3·00
199	–	1r.60 purple	1·75	3·00
200	–	1r.75 blue	1·50	3·00
201	–	2r. purple	1·10	2·75
202	–	2f.25 blue	1·50	3·00
203	–	2f.50 orange	1·25	3·25
204	–	3f. brown	50	2·75
205	–	5f. red	65	3·25
206	–	10f. blue	1·00	3·50
207	–	20f. olive	1·75	3·75

DESIGNS: 30 to 70c. St. Pierre harbour; 80c. to 1f.75, Pointe aux Canons lighthouse (wrongly inscr "PHARE DE LA TORTUE"); 2 to 20f. Soldiers' Cove, Langlade.

41

1939. New York World's Fair.

208	41	1f.25 red	1·25	3·50
209		2f.25 blue	2·25	3·50

42 Storming the Bastille

1939. 150th Anniv of French Revolution.

210	42	45c.+25c. green & black	6·50	13·50
211		70c.+30c. brown and black	6·00	13·50
212		90c.+35c. orange and black	7·75	13·50
213		1f.25+1f. red and black	7·75	13·50
214		2f.25+2f. blue and black	7·75	13·50

1941. Free French Plebiscite. Stamps of 1938 optd **Noel 1941 FRANCE LIBRE F.N.F.L.** or surch also.

215	39	10c. brown	60·00	60·00
216		20c. violet	60·00	60·00
217		25c. blue	60·00	60·00
218	–	40c. blue	60·00	60·00
219	–	45c. green	60·00	60·00
220	–	65c. brown	65·00	65·00
221	–	70c. orange	65·00	65·00
222	–	80c. violet	65·00	65·00
223	–	90c. blue	65·00	65·00
224	–	1f. green	65·00	65·00
225	–	1f.25 red	65·00	65·00
226	–	1f.40 brown	65·00	65·00
227	–	1f.60 purple	75·00	75·00
228	–	1f.75 blue	75·00	75·00
229	–	2f. purple	75·00	75·00
230	–	2f.25 blue	75·00	75·00
231	–	2f.50 orange	75·00	75·00
232	–	3f. brown	75·00	75·00
233	39	10f. on 10c. brown	£120	£120
234	–	20f. on 90c. blue	£120	£120

"F.N.F.L." = Forces Navales Francaises Libres (Free French Naval Forces).

1941. Various stamps overprinted **FRANCE LIBRE F. N. F. L.** or surch also. (a) Nos. 111 and 114.

245	17	10c. mauve and bistre	£900	£900
246	18	30c. blue and lake	£1300	£1300
		(b) On stamps of 1932.		
247	28	2c. green and black	£180	£200
248	29	4c. brown and red	50·00	55·00
249		5c. brown and mauve	£750	£750
250		40c. brown and blue	14·50	15·00
251	28	45c. green and red	£140	£150
252		50c. green and brown	13·00	13·50
253	29	65c. red and brown	38·00	40·00
254		1f. red and brown	£300	£300
255		1f.75 brown and black	10·00	15·00
256		2f. green and black	16·00	17·00
257	28	5f. brown and red	£275	£275
258	29	5f. on 1f.75 brown & blk	10·50	18·00
		(c) On stamps of 1938.		
259	39	2c. green	£375	£375
260		3c. brown	£120	£120
261		4c. purple	£100	£110
262		5c. red	£750	£750
263		10c. brown	11·50	12·50
264		15c. purple	£1250	£1250
265		20c. violet	£160	£170
266		20c. on 10c. brown	12·50	13·50
267		25c. blue	8·75	18·00
268		30c. on 10c. brown	7·50	9·00
269	–	35c. green	£650	£650
270	–	40c. blue	18·00	20·00
271	–	45c. green	19·00	22·00
272	–	55c. blue	£8000	£8000
273	–	60c. violet	£500	£500
274	–	60c. on 90c. blue	12·50	10·50
275	–	65c. brown	24·00	34·00
276	–	70c. orange	42·00	44·00
277	–	80c. violet	£375	£375
278	–	90c. blue	22·00	32·00
279	–	1f. green	26·00	32·00
280	–	1f.25 red	21·00	25·00
281	–	1f.40 brown	16·00	21·00
282	–	1f.50 green	£700	£700
283	–	1f.50 on 90c. blue	18·00	16·00
284	–	1f.60 purple	20·00	28·00
285	–	2f. purple	60·00	70·00
286	–	2f.25 blue	13·50	25·00
287	–	2f.50 orange	19·00	35·00
288	7	2f.50 on 10c. brown	20·00	20·00
289	–	3f. brown	£9000	£9000
290	–	5f. red	£1900	£1900
291	7	10f. on 10c. brown	50·00	65·00
292	–	20f. olive	£700	£700
293	–	20f. on 90c. blue	65·00	70·00
		(d) On Nos. 208/9.		
294		1f.25 red	11·00	19·00
295		2f.25 blue	10·00	15·00
296		2f.50 on 1f.25 red	15·00	28·00
297		3f. on 2f.25 blue	20·00	28·00

1942. Stamps of 1932 overprinted **FRANCE LIBRE F. N. F. L.** or surch also.

304	27	20c. red and black	£300	£300
305		75c. red and green	20·00	28·00
306		1f.25 red and blue	15·00	20·00
307		1f.50 blue and deep blue	£375	£375
308		10f. on 1f.25 red and blue	38·00	45·00
309		20f. on 75c. red and green	50·00	60·00

1942. Social Welfare Fund. Nos. 279 and 287 further surch **OEUVRES SOCIALES**, cross and premium.

320		1f.+50c. green	55·00	55·00
321		2f.50+1f. orange	55·00	55·00

47 Fishing Schooner

48 Airliner

1942. (a) Postage.

322	47	5c. blue	20	2·75
323		10c. pink	15	2·50
324		25c. green	15	2·50
325		30c. black	15	2·25
326		40c. blue	15	2·50
327		60c. purple	30	1·60
328		1f. violet	60	2·50
329		1f.50 red	80	2·50
330		2f. brown	60	2·50
331		2f.50 blue	1·00	1·90
332		4f. orange	60	2·75
333		5f. purple	60	2·75
334		10f. blue	1·00	3·00
335		20f. green	1·25	3·50
		(b) Air.		
336	48	1f. orange	55	2·75
337		1f.50 red	90	2·50
338		5f. purple	55	2·75
339		10f. black	1·00	3·25
340		25f. blue	1·50	3·00
341		50f. green	70	3·50
342		100f. red	1·00	4·00

49

1944. Mutual Aid and Red Cross Funds.

343	49	5f.+20f. blue	85	3·50

50 Felix Eboue

1945. Eboue.

344	50	2f. black	55	30
345		25f. green	1·00	3·50

1945. Surch.

346	47	50c. on 5c. blue	25	2·50
347		70c. on 5c. blue	40	3·00
348		80c. on 5c. blue	60	3·00
349		1f.20 on 5c. blue	45	3·00
350		2f.40 on 25c. green	55	3·00
351		3f. on 25c. green	70	3·00
352		4f.50 on 25c. green	1·00	3·75
353		15f. on 2f.50 blue	75	3·75

52 "Victory"

1946. Air. Victory.

354	52	8f. red	35	3·50

53 Legionaries by Lake Chad

1946. Air. From Chad to the Rhine.

355	53	5f. red	80	3·50
356		10f. lilac	80	3·50
357		15f. black	85	3·75
358		20f. violet	1·10	3·75
359		25f. brown	1·25	4·75
360		50f. black	1·60	4·75

54 Soldiers' Cove, Langlade

55 Allegory of Fishing

56 Douglas DC-4 and Wrecked Fishing Schooner

1947.

361	54	10c. brown (postage)	15	1·75
362		30c. violet	15	2·50
363		40c. purple	15	2·50
364		50c. blue	15	2·25
365	55	60c. red	15	2·50
366		80c. blue	20	2·75
367		1f. green	35	2·00
368	–	1f.20 green	25	3·00
369	–	1f.50 black	35	60
370	–	2f. red	55	45
371	–	3f. violet	1·10	1·50
372	–	3f.60 red	1·75	1·60
373	–	4f. purple	2·25	95
374	–	5f. yellow	1·25	55
375	–	6f. blue	1·40	2·75
376	–	8f. sepia	3·00	1·60

377 – 10f. green . . . . 2·25 1·75
378 – 15f. green . . . . 2·25 1·75
379 – 17f. blue . . . . 3·75 2·25
380 – 20f. red . . . . 1·75 1·25
381 – 25f. blue . . . . 2·25 3·25
382 – 50f. green and red (air) . . 5·50 6·25
383 **56** 100f. green . . . . 10·00 9·50
384 – 200f. blue and red . . . . 12·50 11·00

DESIGNS—As Type **55**: 1f.20 to 2f. Cross and fishermen; 3f. to 4f. Weighing Atlantic cod; 5, 6, 10f. Trawler "Colonel Pleven"; 8, 17f. Red fox; 15, 20, 25f. Windswept mountain landscape. As Type **56**: 50f. Airplane and fishing village; 200f. Airplane and snow-bound fishing schooner.

58 People of Five Races, Aircraft and Globe

1949. Air. 75th Anniv of U.P.U.
395 **58** 25f. multicoloured . . . . 5·75 19·00

59 Doctor and Patient **60**

1950. Colonial Welfare Fund.
396 **59** 10f.+2f. red and brown . . 2·25 8·75

1952. Centenary of Military Medal.
397 **60** 8f. blue, yellow and green 4·00 8·00

61 Normandy Landings, 1944

1954. Air. 10th Anniv of Liberation.
398 **61** 15f. red and brown . . . . 6·75 6·00

62 Refrigeration Plant

63 Codfish

64 Dog and Coastal Scene

1955.
399 **62** 30c. blue & dp bl (postage) 25 2·25
400 **63** 40c. brown and blue . . . 15 2·75
401 **62** 50c. brown, grey and black 20 1·75
402 **63** 1f. brown and green . . . 25 3·00
403 2f. indigo and blue . . . . 25 3·00
404 **62** 3f. purple . . . . 35 1·75
405 – 4f. purple, red and lake . . 1·60 3·00
406 – 10f. brown, blue & turq . . 1·75 2·00
407 – 20f. multicoloured . . . . 2·25 2·75
408 – 25f. brown, green and blue 2·50 5·50
409 **62** 40f. turquoise . . . . . . 85 4·50
410 **64** 50f. multicoloured (air) . . 30·00 27·00
411 – 100f. black and grey . . . 14·50 17·00
412 – 500f. indigo and blue . . . 55·00 35·00

DESIGNS—As Type **62/3**: 4, 10f. Pointe aux Canons Lighthouse and fishing dinghies; 20f. Ice hockey players; 25f. American minks. As Type **64**: 100f. Sud Aviation Caravelle airliner over St. Pierre and Miquelon; 500f. Douglas DC-3 over St. Pierre port.

65 Trawler "Galantry" **67** "Picea"

66 "Human Rights"

1956. Economic and Social Development Fund.
413 **65** 15f. sepia and brown . . . 1·25 1·25

1958. 10th Anniv of Declaration of Human Rights.
414 **66** 20f. brown and blue . . . 85 1·60

1959.
415 **67** 5f. multicoloured . . . . . 75 3·50

68 Flaming Torches

1959. Air. Adoption of Constitution.
416 **68** 200f. green, lake and violet 8·00 16·00

69 "Cypripedium acaule"

1962. Flowers.
417 **69** 25f. purple, orange and green (postage) . . . . 4·25 1·75
418 – 50f. red and green . . . . 5·50 5·75
419 – 100f. orange, red and green (air) . . . . 8·00 6·25

DESIGNS—VERT: 50f. "Calopogon pulchellus". HORIZ—48 × 27 mm: 100f. "Sarracenia purpurae".

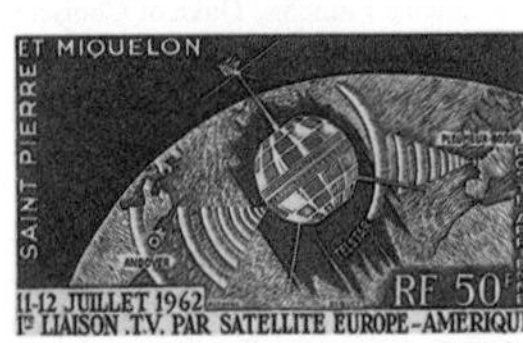

70 Submarine "Surcouf" and Map

1962. Air. 20th Anniv of Adherence to Free French Government.
420 **70** 500f. black, blue and red 90·00 £110

71 "Telstar" Satellite and part of Globe

1962. Air. 1st Transatlantic TV Satellite Link.
421 **71** 50f. brown, green and sepia 4·00 5·75

72 Eiders **73** Dr. A. Calmette

1963. Birds.
422 **72** 50c. bistre, black and blue 75 55
423 – 1f. brown, mauve and blue 1·10 1·10
424 – 2f. brown, black and blue 1·40 1·25
425 – 6f. bistre, blue and turquoise . . . . 4·25 1·50

DESIGNS: 1f. Rock ptarmigan; 2f. Semi-palmated plovers; 6f. Blue-winged teal.

1963. Birth Centenary of Dr. Albert Calmette (bacteriologist).
426 **73** 30f. brown and blue . . . 6·25 5·25

74 Landing of Governor from "Garonne"

1963. Air. Bicentenary of Arrival of First Governor (Dangeac) in St. Pierre and Miquelon.
427 **74** 200f. blue, green and brown . . . . 11·00 14·50

75 Centenary Emblem **76** Globe and Scales of Justice

1963. Red Cross Centenary.
428 **75** 25f. red, grey and blue . . 5·00 6·00

1963. 15th Anniv of Declaration of Human Rights.
429 **76** 20f. orange, purple and blue . . . . 5·75 4·25

77 "Philately"

1964. "PHILATEC 1964" International Stamp Exhibition, Paris.
430 **77** 60f. blue, green and purple 9·75 11·00

78 Common Rabbits

1964. Fauna.
431 **78** 3f. chocolate, brown & grn 2·75 2·75
432 – 4f. sepia, blue and green 3·75 3·00
433 – 5f. brown, sepia and blue 4·00 3·50
434 – 34f. brown, green and blue 7·75 6·25

ANIMALS: 4f. Red fox; 5f. Roe deer; 34f. Charolais bull.

79 Potez 842 Airliner and Map

1964. Air. 1st St. Pierre–New York Airmail Flight.
435 **79** 100f. brown and blue . . . 9·25 9·50

80 Syncom Communications Satellite, Telegraph Poles and Morse Key

1965. Centenary of I.T.U.
436 **80** 40f. blue, brown and purple . . . . 16·00 10·00

81 Rocket "Diamant"

1966. Air. Launching of First French Satellite.
437 **81** 25f. brown, blue and red 9·25 6·25
438 30f. brown, blue and red 9·25 6·25

82 Satellite "D1"

1966. Air. Launching of Satellite "D1".
439 **82** 48f. blue, green and lake 5·25 6·75

83 "Revanche" and Settlers

1966. Air. 150th Anniv of Return of Islands to France.
440 **83** 100f. multicoloured . . . . 8·25 7·50

84 "Journal Officiel" and Old and New Printing Presses

1966. Air. Centenary of "Journal Officiel" Printing Works.
441 **84** 60f. plum, lake and blue 9·75 7·25

85 Map and Fishing Dinghies

1967. Air. Pres. De Gaulle's Visit.
442 **85** 25f. brown, blue and red 29·00 14·00
443 – 100f. blue, turquoise & pur 45·00 35·00

DESIGN: 100f. Maps and cruiser "Richelieu".

86 Trawler and Harbour Plan

1967. Opening of St. Pierre's New Harbour.
444 **86** 48f. brown, blue and red 9·00 4·25

87 Map and Control Tower

1967. Opening of St. Pierre Airport.
445 **87** 30f. multicoloured . . . . 4·00 3·00

88 T.V. Receiver, Aerial and Map

1967. Inauguration of Television Service.
446 **88** 40f. red, green and olive 8·50 4·75

89 Speed Skating

1968. Air. Winter Olympic Games, Grenoble. Multicoloured.
447 50f. Type **89** . . . . 9·75 6·25
448 60f. Ice-hockey goalkeeper . . 10·50 8·00

90 Bouquet, Sun and W.H.O. Emblem **92** Human Rights Emblem

91 J. D. Cassini (discoverer of group), Compasses and Chart

1968. 20th Anniv of W.H.O.
449 **90** 10f. red, yellow and blue 7·25 5·00

1968. Famous Visitors to St. Pierre and Miquelon (1st series).
450 **91** 4f. brown, yellow and lake 4·50 4·00
451 – 6f. multicoloured . . . . . 6·00 4·50
452 – 15f. multicoloured . . . . 6·50 5·00
453 – 25f. multicoloured . . . . 10·50 7·50
CELEBRITIES: 6f. Rene de Chateaubriand and warship; 15f. Prince de Joinville, "Belle Poule" (sail frigate) and "Cassard" (survey ship); 25f. Admiral Gauchet and flagship "Provence" (Ile aux Chiens expedition).

1968. Human Rights Year.
454 **92** 20f. red, blue and yellow 10·00 7·25

93 War Memorial, St. Pierre

1968. Air. 50th Anniv of Armistice.
455 **93** 500f. multicoloured . . . . 26·00 25·00

94 Concorde in Flight

1969. Air. 1st Flight of Concorde.
456 **94** 34f. brown and olive . . . 29·00 18·00

95 Mountain Stream, Langlade

1969. Tourism.
457 **95** 5f. brn, bl & grn (postage) 4·75 4·25
458 – 15f. brown, green and blue 5·00 5·00
459 – 50f. purple, olive & bl (air) 14·50 9·00
460 – 100f. brown, indigo & blue 26·00 14·00
DESIGNS: 15f. River bank, Debon, Langlade; 50f. Wild horses, Miquelon; 100f. Gathering wood, Miquelon. The 50f. and 100f. are larger 48 × 27 mm.

96 Treasury

1969. Public Buildings and Monuments.
461 **96** 10f. black, red and blue . . 3·25 3·25
462 – 25f. red, ultramarine & blue . . . . 5·00 4·25
463 – 30f. brown, green and blue 5·75 6·25
464 – 60f. black, red and blue . . 11·50 10·00
DESIGNS: 25f. Maritime Fisheries Scientific and Technical Institute; 30f. Unknown Sailor's Monument; 60f. St. Christopher's College.

97 "L'Estoile" and Granville, 1690

1969. Maritime Links with France.
465 **97** 34f. lake, green and emerald (postage) . . . 13·00 5·50
466 – 40f. green, red and bistre 16·00 6·25
467 – 48f. multicoloured . . . . 19·00 9·75
468 – 200f. black, lake and green (air) . . . . 40·00 20·00
DESIGNS—As Type **97**: 40f. "La Jolie" and St. Jean de Luz, 1750; 48f. "La Juste" and La Rochelle, 1860; 48 × 27 mm. 200f. "L'Esperance" and St. Malo, 1600.

98 Pierre Loti, Sailing Ship and Book Titles

1969. Air. Pierre Loti (explorer and writer) Commemoration.
469 **98** 300f. multicoloured . . . . 55·00 35·00

99 Ringed Seals

1969. Marine Animals.
470 **99** 1f. brown, purple and lake 5·75 4·00
471 – 3f. blue, green and red . . 6·00 4·00
472 – 4f. green, brown and red 6·00 4·00
473 – 6f. violet, green and red . . 6·25 4·00
DESIGNS: 3f. Sperm whales; 4f. Long-finned pilot whale; 6f. Common dolphins.

100 I.L.O. Building, Geneva

1969. 30th Anniv of International Labour Organization.
474 **100** 20f. brown, slate and salmon . . . . 9·25 5·00

101 New U.P.U. Building, Berne

1970. New U.P.U. Headquarters Building, Berne.
475 **101** 25f. brown, blue and red 8·25 5·00
476 34f. slate, brown & purple 15·00 10·00

102 Rocket and Japanese Women **104** "Rubus chamaemorus"

103 Rowing Fours

1970. Air. World Fair "EXPO 70", Osaka, Japan.
477 **102** 34f. brown, lake and blue 14·50 10·00
478 – 85f. blue, red and orange 26·00 20·00
DESIGN—HORIZ: 85f. "Mountain Landscape" (Y. Taikan) and Expo "star".

1970. World Rowing Championships, St. Catherine, Canada.
479 **103** 20f. brown, blue & lt blue 8·75 6·75

1970. Fruit Plants.
480 **104** 3f. green, purple & brown 2·75 2·50
481 – 4f. yellow, red and green 2·75 2·50
482 – 5f. red, green and violet 3·00 3·00
483 – 6f. violet, green and purple . . . . 4·25 2·50
PLANTS: 4f. "Fragaria vesca"; 5f. "Rubus idaeus"; 6f. "Vaccinium myrtillus".

105 Ewe and Lamb

1970. Livestock Breeding.
484 **105** 15f. brown, purple & green . . . . 6·75 5·00
485 – 30f. brown, grey and green . . . . 8·00 5·00
486 – 34f. brown, purple & green . . . . 12·50 9·00
487 – 48f. purple, brown & blue 11·50 7·00
DESIGNS: 30f. Animal quarantine station; 34f. Charolais bull; 48f. Refrigeration plant and "Narrando" (trawler).

106 Etienne Francois, Duke of Choiseul, and Warships

1970. Air. Celebrities of St. Pierre and Miquelon.
488 **106** 25f. brown, blue & purple 8·50 4·75
489 – 50f. brown, purple & green . . . . 16·00 11·50
490 – 60f. brown, green & purple . . . . 19·00 11·00
DESIGNS: 50f. Jacques Cartier and "Grande Hermine"; 60f. Sebastien Le Gonard de Sourdeval and 17th-century French galleons.

107 "St. Francis of Assisi", 1900

1971. Fisheries' Protection Vessels.
491 **107** 30f. red, blue and turquoise . . . . . . 30·00 15·00
492 – 35f. brown, green and blue . . . . 30·00 12·00
493 – 40f. brown, blue and green . . . . 30·00 12·50
494 – 80f. black, green and blue 30·00 22·00
DESIGNS: 35f. "St. Jehanne", 1920; 40f. "L'Aventure", 1950; 80f. "Commandant Bourdais", 1970.

108 "Aconite"

1971. 30th Anniv of Allegiance to Free French Movement. British Corvettes on loan to Free French.
495 **108** 22f. black, green and blue 18·00 14·50
496 – 25f. brown, turquoise & bl . . . . 19·00 14·50
497 – 50f. black, turquoise & blue . . . . 35·00 29·00
DESIGNS: 25f. "Alyssum"; 50f. "Mimosa".

109 Ship's Bell **110** De Gaulle in Uniform (June 1940)

1971. St. Pierre Museum. Multicoloured.
498 20f. Type **109** . . . . 9·00 6·25
499 45f. Navigational instruments and charts (horiz) . . . . 14·00 5·75

1971. 1st Death Anniv of De Gaulle.
500 **110** 35f. black and red . . . . 11·50 8·50
501 45f. black and red . . . . 17·00 14·00

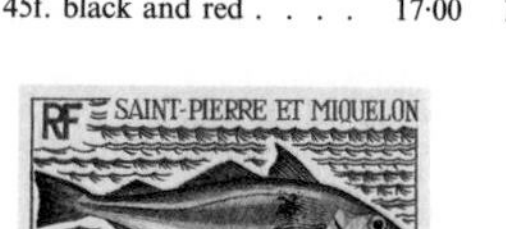

111 Haddock

1972. Ocean Fish.
502 **111** 2f. indigo, red and blue 4·75 4·00
503 – 3f. brown and green . . . 5·00 4·00
504 – 5f. red and blue . . . . . 6·50 4·25
505 – 10f. green and emerald . . 4·00 8·00
DESIGNS: 3f. American plaice; 5f. Deepwater redfish; 10c. Atlantic cod.

112 De Gaulle and Servicemen

1972. Air. General De Gaulle Commemoration.
506 **112** 100f. brown, green & pur 30·00 14·50

113 Long-tailed Ducks **116** Swimming Pool

114 Montcalm and Warships

1973. Currency Revaluation.
507 **113** 6c. brown, purple and blue (postage) . . . . 1·50 1·50
508 – 10c. black, red and blue 1·90 1·50
509 – 20c. bistre, ultram & bl 2·40 2·10
510 **113** 40c. brown, green & violet 4·25 2·25
511 – 70c. black, red and green 6·75 3·00
512 – 90c. bistre, blue and purple . . . . 5·00 6·50
513 **114** 1f.60 violet, indigo and blue (air) . . . . 9·00 4·75
514 – 2f. purple, green and violet . . . . 9·25 4·25
515 – 4f. green, mauve & brown 18·00 10·00

DESIGNS—As Type **113**: 10, 70c. Atlantic puffins; 20, 90c. Snowy owls. As Type **114**: HORIZ: 4f. La Salle, map and warships. VERT: 2f. Frontenac and various scenes.

1973. Inauguration of St. Pierre Cultural Centre.
521 **116** 60c. brown, blue and red 6·00 4·25
522 – 1f. purple, orange and blue . . . . 6·75 4·25
DESIGN: 1f. Centre building.

117 Transall C-160 in Flight

1973. Air.
523 **117** 10f. multicoloured . . . . 50·00 35·00

118 Met Balloon and Weather Ship

1974. World Meteorological Day.
524 **118** 1f.60 blue, green and red 12·50 8·75

119 Northern Gannet with Letter

1974. Centenary of Universal Postal Union.
525 **119** 70c. ultramarine, bl & red 4·75 2·00
526 90c. blue, red and lake . . 6·75 4·25

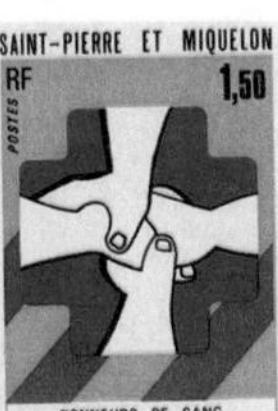

120 Clasped Hands on Red Cross

1974. Campaign for Blood Donors.
527 **120** 1f.50 multicoloured . . . 14·00 8·00

121 Arms and Map of Islands

1974. Air.
528 **121** 2f. multicoloured . . . . 16·00 8·00

122 Banknotes in "Fish" Money-box

123 Copernicus and Famous Scientists

1974. Centenary of St. Pierre Savings Bank.
529 **122** 50c. brown, blue and black . . . . 7·00 4·50

1974. Air. 500th Birth Anniv (1973) of Nicholas Copernicus (astronomer).
530 **123** 4f. violet, red and blue . . 20·00 11·00

124 St. Pierre Church and Caspian Tern, Black-legged Kittiwake and Great Auk

1974. Island Churches.
531 **124** 6c. black, brown and green . . . . 3·00 1·50
532 – 10c. indigo, blue & brown 4·50 2·75
533 – 20c. multicoloured . . . . 6·75 4·00
DESIGNS: 10c. Miquelon Church and fishes; 20c. Our Lady of the Seamen Church and fishermen.

125 Red Admiral

127 "Pottery" (Potter's wheel and products)

126 Cod and St. Pierre et Miquelon Stamp of 1909

1975. Butterflies. Multicoloured.
534 1f. Type **125** . . . . 9·00 4·00
535 1f.20 Orange tiger . . . . . 10·50 6·00

1975. Air. "Arphila 75" International Stamp Exhibition, Paris.
536 **126** 4f. red, indigo and blue 23·00 12·50

1975. Artisan Handicrafts.
537 **127** 50c. purple, brown & green . . . . 6·75 3·50
538 – 60c. blue and yellow . . . 6·25 3·50
DESIGN: 60c. "Sculpture" (wood carving of Virgin and Child).

128 Pointe-Plate Lighthouse and Sea-birds

1975. Lighthouses.
539 **128** 6c. black, violet and green 3·25 1·50
540 – 10c. purple, green and slate . . . . 3·75 2·10
541 – 20c. brown, indigo & blue 6·75 5·00
DESIGNS: 10c. Galantry lighthouse, Atlantic puffin and pintail; 20c. Cap Blanc lighthouse and blue whale.

129 Judo

1975. Air. "Pre-Olympic Year". Olympic Games, Montreal (1976).
542 **129** 1f.90 blue, red and violet 11·00 6·25

130 Concorde in Flight

1976. Air. Concorde's 1st Commercial Flight.
543 **130** 10f. indigo, blue and red 34·00 19·00

131 President Pompidou

1976. President Pompidou Commemoration.
544 **131** 1f.10 grey and purple . . 9·00 6·25

132 Alexander Graham Bell and Early Telephone

1976. Air. Telephone Centenary.
545 **132** 5f. blue, orange and red 10·50 7·00

133 Washington and Lafayette

1976. Bicentenary of American Revolution.
546 **133** 1f. multicoloured . . . . 6·25 4·50

134 Basketball

1976. Olympic Games, Montreal.
547 **134** 70c. agate, blue and brown . . . . 5·25 4·75
548 – 2f.50 turquoise, green and emerald . . . . 16·00 9·00
DESIGN—HORIZ: 2f.50, Swimming.

135 Vigie Dam

1976.
549 **135** 2f.20 brown, blue & turq 9·50 7·00

136 "Croix de Lorraine"

1976. Stern Trawlers. Multicoloured.
550 1f.20 Type **136** . . . . 9·00 6·25
551 1f.50 "Geolette" . . . . . . 16·00 9·50

1986. Nos. 2444 etc of France optd **ST-PIERRE ET MIQUELON**.
552 **916** 5c. green . . . . 25 1·40
553 10c. red . . . . 15 1·10
554 20c. green . . . . 15 1·10
555 30c. red . . . . 15 1·10
556 40c. brown . . . . 15 1·10
557 50c. mauve . . . . 15 1·10
558 1f. green . . . . 25 1·10
559 1f.80 green . . . . 45 1·25
560 2f. green . . . . 50 1·25
561 2f.20 red . . . . 70 1·25
562 2f. brown . . . . 80 1·75
563 3f.20 blue . . . . 90 1·75
564 4f. red . . . . 1·00 1·90
565 5f. blue . . . . 1·25 1·90
566 10f. violet . . . . 2·75 3·25

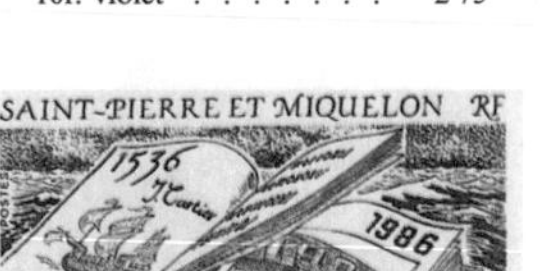

138 Open Book

1986. 450th Anniv of Discovery of Islands by Jacques Cartier and 1st Anniv of New Constitution.
567 **138** 2f.20 brown, deep brown and green . . . . . . 1·25 1·75

139 Statue and Harbour

1986. Centenary of Statue of Liberty.
568 **139** 2f.50 blue and red . . . . 1·50 1·75

141 Atlantic Cod and Detection Equipment

142 "Nativity" (stained glass window, L. Balmet)

1986. Fishing.
578 **141** 1f. red . . . . 40 1·25
579 1f.10 orange . . . . . . 35 1·25
580 1f.30 red . . . . 40 1·25
581 1f.40 blue . . . . 55 1·25
582 1f.40 red . . . . 1·40 1·25
583 1f.50 blue . . . . 50 1·25
584 1f.60 green . . . . 60 1·25
585 1f.70 green . . . . 1·50 1·25

1986. Christmas.
586 **142** 2f.20 multicoloured . . . 1·40 80

143 Buff Cap ("Hygrophorus pratensis")

1987.
587 **143** 2f.50 brown and ochre . . 2·00 1·75
See also Nos. 598, 609 and 645.

144 Dunan and Hospital

1987. Dr. Francois Dunan Commemoration.
588 **144** 2f.20 black, brown and blue . . . . 1·50 1·50

145 Ocean-racing Yachts

1987. Transatlantic Yacht Race (Lorient–St. Pierre et Miquelon–Lorient).
589 **145** 5f. brown, dp blue & blue 3·00 2·00

146 Maps

1987. Visit of President Francois Mitterand.
590 **146** 2f.20 multicoloured . . . 1·90 1·75

147 Schooner on Slipway and Share Certificate

1987. Centenary of Marine Slipway.
591 **147** 2f.50 brown and light brown . . . . 2·25 1·75

148 Hawker Siddeley H.S. 748 (St. Pierre–Montreal first flight, 1987)

1987. Air. Airplanes named "Ville de St. Pierre".
592 **148** 5f. blue, green & turquoise . . . . 3·00 2·00
593 – 10f. dp blue, blue & orge 6·00 3·25
DESIGN: 10f. Flying boat "Ville de Saint-Pierre" (first flight, 1939).

149 "La Normande" (trawler)

1987.
594 **149** 3f. multicoloured . . . . 3·00 2·50

150 "St. Christopher carrying Christ Child" (stained glass window by L. Balmet) and Scout Emblem

1987. Christmas. 50th Anniv of Scouting.
595 **150** 2f.20 multicoloured . . . 1·75 1·75

151 Horses and Ducks

1987. Natural Heritage. Le Grand Barachois. Each orange, green and brown.
596 3f. Type **151** . . . . 2·25 1·40
597 3f. Canada geese, gulls and seals . . . . 2·25 1·40
Nos. 596/7 were printed together, se-tenant, with intervening half stamp size label, each strip forming a composite design.

1988. Fungi. As T **143**.
598 2f.50 black, orange and brown . . . . 1·50 1·50
DESIGN: "Russula paludosa".

152 Ice Hockey Goalkeeper

1988. Winter Olympic Games, Calgary.
599 **152** 5f. blue and red . . . . . 2·50 2·25

153 Thomas and Camera

1988. Birth Centenary of Dr. Louis Thomas (photographer).
600 **153** 2f.20 brown, deep brown and blue . . . . 1·50 1·40

154 Airship "Hindenburg"

1988. Air. Aircraft. Each black, blue and purple.
601 5f. Type **154** . . . . 3·00 2·00
602 10f. Douglas DC-3 . . . . . 6·00 3·25

1988. "Philexfrance 89" International Stamp Exhibition, Paris. No. 2821 of France optd **ST-PIERRE ET MIQUELON**.
603 **1073** 2f.20 red, black and blue 2·25 1·75

156 "Nellie J. Banks" and Crates

1988. 50th Anniv of End of Prohibition and Last Liquor Smuggling Run from St. Pierre to Canada.
604 **156** 2f.50 ultramarine, brn & bl . . . . 2·25 1·75

157 "Le Marmouset" (stern trawler)

1988.
605 **157** 3f. multicoloured . . . . 2·00 1·75

158 Ross Cove

1988. Natural Heritage. Each brown, deep blue and blue.
606 2f.20 Type **158** . . . . . . 1·00 75
607 13f.70 Cap Perce . . . . . . 5·50 2·50

159 Stained Glass Window

161 "Liberty" (Roger Druet)

160 Judo

1988. Christmas.
608 **159** 2f.20 multicoloured . . . 1·25 1·40

1989. Fungi. As T **143**.
609 2f.50 brown and red . . . . 1·50 1·25
DESIGN: 2f.50, "Tricholoma virgatum".

1989. 25th Anniv of Judo in St. Pierre.
610 **160** 5f. black, green and orange . . . . 2·50 2·00

1989. Bicentenary of French Revolution and Declaration of Rights of Man. Multicoloured.
611 2f.20 Type **161** . . . . 1·60 1·50
612 2f.20 "Equality" . . . . . . 1·60 1·50
613 2f.20 "Fraternity" . . . . . 1·60 1·50

162 Piper Aztec

1989. Air.
614 **162** 20f. brown, light brown and blue . . . . 7·25 3·75

163 Tower of Bastille and Phrygian Cap on Tree

1989. "Philexfrance '89" International Stamp Exhibition, Paris (2nd issue) and Bicentenary of French Revolution (2nd issue). Sheet 150 × 140 mm containing T **163** and similar vert designs, each ultramarine, scarlet and black.
MS615 5f. Type **163**; 5f. Two towers of Bastille and brigantine; 5f. Raising tree of liberty; 5f. People cheering . . . . 11·00 11·00

164 Fisherman in Boat

1989. Natural Heritage. Ile aux Marins. Each brown, blue and green.
616 2f.20 Type **164** . . . . 1·75 1·50
617 13f.70 Boy flying kite from boat . . . . 7·00 5·00

165 "Le Malabar" (ocean-going tug)

1989.
618 **165** 3f. multicoloured . . . . 1·75 1·50

166 Georges Landry and Emblem

1989. Centenary of Islands' Bank.
619 **166** 2f.20 blue and brown . . 1·50 1·25

167 "Christmas" (Magali Olano)

1989. Christmas.
620 **167** 2f.20 multicoloured . . . 1·40 1·25

1990. Stamps of France optd **ST-PIERRE ET MIQUELON**.
621 **1118** 10c. brown . . . . . . 65 1·00
622 20c. green . . . . 65 1·00
623 50c. violet . . . . 65 1·00
624 1f. orange . . . . 75 1·00
625 2f. green . . . . 1·00 1·10
626 2f. blue . . . . 80 1·10
627 2f.10 green . . . . . . 95 1·10
628 2f.20 green . . . . . . 1·25 1·25
629 2f.30 red . . . . 1·00 1·25
630 2f.40 green . . . . . . 1·40 1·25
631 2f.50 red . . . . 1·40 1·25
632 2f.70 green 90 20
633 3f.20 blue . . . . 1·25 1·25
634 3f.40 blue . . . . 1·60 1·25
635 3f.50 green . . . . . . 1·75 1·40
636 3f.80 mauve . . . . . . 1·40 1·40
637 3f.80 blue . . . . 1·40 75
638 4f. mauve . . . . 1·75 1·40
639 4f.20 mauve . . . . . . 1·75 1·40
640 4f.40 blue . . . . 1·75 1·40
641 4f.50 mauve . . . . . . 1·75 1·40
642 5f. blue . . . . 1·90 1·50
643 10f. violet . . . . 2·75 2·25
The 2f.50 exists both perforated (ordinary gum) and imperforate (self-adhesive).

1990. Fungi. As T **143**.
645 2f.50 brown, black and orange . . . . 1·75 1·40
DESIGN: 2f.50, Hedgehog fungus ("Hydnum repandum").

168 "Pou du Ciel" and Gull

1990. Air.
646 **168** 5f. green, blue and brown 2·00 1·75

169 De Gaulle and Soldiers

1990. 50th Anniv of De Gaulle's Call to Resist.
647 **169** 2f.30 purple, red and blue 1·60 1·25
For design as T **169** but inscr "1890–1970", see No. 653.

170 Runner and Map

1990. Miquelon 25 km Race.
648 **170** 5f. black, blue and brown 2·00 1·40

171 Moose, Micmac Canoe and Woman

1990.
649 **171** 2f.50 orange, brown & bl 1·60 1·25

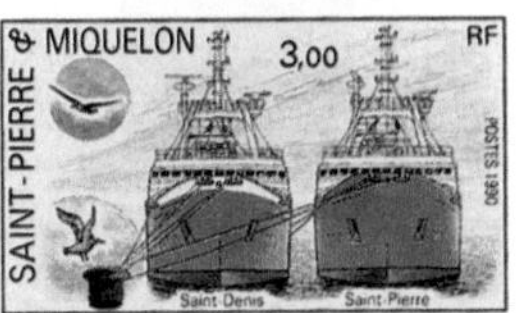

172 "Saint-Denis" and "Saint-Pierre" at Moorings

1990. Trawlers.
650 **172** 3f. multicoloured . . . . 1·75 1·50

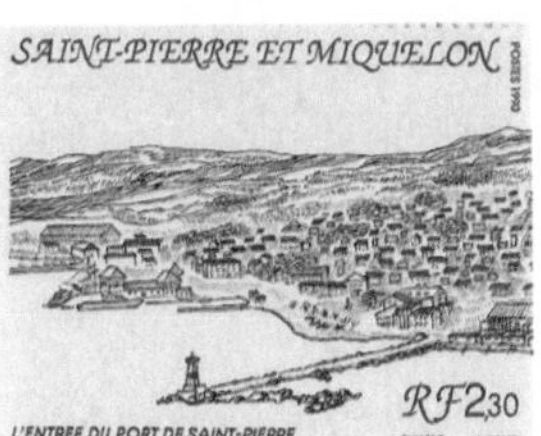

173 Entrance to Saint-Pierre Port

1990. St.-Pierre. Each brown, green and blue.
651 2f.30 Type **173** . . . . 1·60 1·25
652 14f.50 Interpeche fish factory 5·50 3·25
Nos. 651/2 were issued together, se-tenant, with intervening label, forming a composite design of part of St.-Pierre coastline.

1990. Birth Centenary of Charles de Gaulle (French statesman). As T **169** but inscr "1890–1970". Each purple, red and blue.
653 1f.70 Type **169** . . . . 1·40 1·25
654 2f.30 De Gaulle and trawler 1·60 1·25

174 Christmas Scene (Cindy Lechevallier)

1990. Christmas.
655 **174** 2f.30 multicoloured . . . 1·50 1·25

175 Short-tailed Swallowtail on "Heracleum maximum"

1991.
656 **175** 2f.50 multicoloured . . . 1·60 1·25

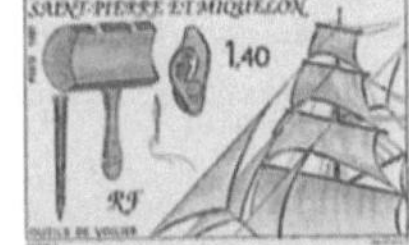

176 Sail-makers' Tools and Sails

1991.
657 **176** 1f.40 green and yellow . . 1·25 1·10
658 1f.70 red and yellow . . . 1·40 1·25

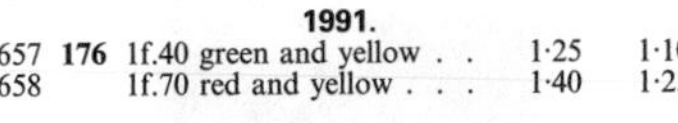

177 Ile aux Marins

1991. Old Views.
659 **177** 1f.70 blue . . . . 1·25 1·25
660 – 1f.70 blue . . . . 1·25 1·25
661 – 1f.70 blue . . . . 1·25 1·25
662 – 1f.70 blue . . . . 1·25 1·25
663 **177** 2f.50 red . . . . 1·50 1·25
664 – 2f.50 red . . . . 1·50 1·25
665 – 2f.50 red . . . . 1·50 1·25
666 – 2f.50 red . . . . 1·50 1·25
DESIGNS: Nos. 660, 664, Langlade; 661, 665, Miquelon; 662, 666, Saint-Pierre.

178 Piper Tomahawk

1991. Air.
667 **178** 10f. blue, turquoise & brown . . . . 3·75 2·50

179 Musicians

1991. Centenary of Lyre Music Society.
668 **179** 2f.50 red, brown & orange 1·60 1·25

180 Oars

1991. St. Pierre–Newfoundland Crossing by Rowing Boat.
669 **180** 2f.50 multicoloured . . . 1·60 1·25

181 Pelota Players

1991. Basque Sports.
670 **181** 5f. green and red . . . . 2·25 1·50

182 Fishermen

1991. Natural Heritage. Multicoloured.
671 2f.50 Type **182** . . . . 1·60 1·25
672 14f.50 Canada geese and shore . . . . 5·50 3·50
Nos. 671/2 were issued together, se-tenant, forming a composite design of Savoyard.

183 "Cryos" (stern trawler)

1991.
673 **183** 3f. multicoloured . . . . 1·75 1·50

184 Free French Central Bank 100f. Note

1991. 50th Anniv of Central Economic Co-operation Bank.
674 **184** 2f.50 multicoloured . . . 1·60 1·25

185 Naval Forces and Cross of Lorraine

1991. Christmas. 50th Anniv of Adherence to Free French Government.
675 **185** 2f.50 multicoloured . . . 1·60 1·25

186 Muselier and Harbour

1992. 110th Birth Anniv of Admiral E. Muselier (commander of 1941 Free French landing force).
676 **186** 2f.50 multicoloured . . . 1·25 1·00

187 Ice Skating

1992. Winter Olympic Games, Albertville.
677 **187** 5f. blue, ultramarine & mve . . . . 1·50 1·40

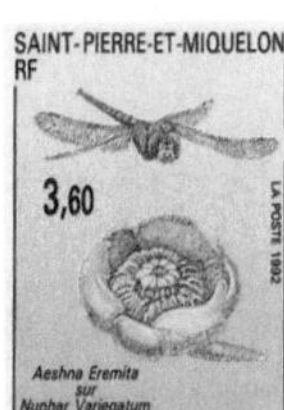

188 "Aeshna eremita" and "Nuphar variegatum"

1992.
678 **188** 3f.60 multicoloured . . . 1·40 1·25

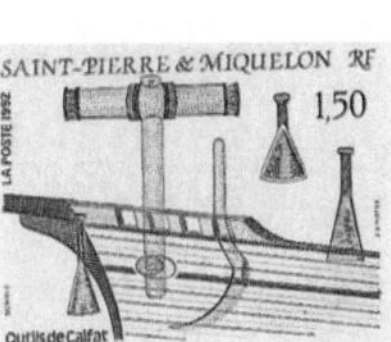

189 Boat-building Tools and Stern of Ship

1992.
679 **189** 1f.50 brown and blue . . 1·10 1·00
680 1f.80 blue and azure . . . 1·25 1·10

190 Model Airplane and Remote Control

1992.
681 **190** 20f. red, orange and brown . . . . 5·25 3·50

191 Ile aux Marins Lighthouse

1992. Lighthouses. Multicoloured.
682 2f.50 Type **191** . . . . 1·25 1·00
683 2f.50 Galantry . . . . 1·25 1·00
684 2f.50 Old Rouge Feu lighthouse, St. Pierre . . . 1·25 1·00
685 2f.50 Pointe-Plate . . . . . 1·25 1·00

192 Cones and Common Flicker

1992. Natural Heritage. Dolisie Valley, Langlade. Multicoloured.
686 2f.50 Type **192** . . . . 1·25 75
687 15f.10 Valley and berries . . 4·00 2·75

193 Columbus and Map on Sails

1992. 500th Anniv of Discovery of America by Columbus.
688 **193** 5f.10 multicoloured . . . 1·75 1·60

194 Baron de l'Esperance, Map and Settlers

1992. 230th Anniv (1993) of Resettlement by French of Miquelon.
689 **194** 2f.50 brown, blue and red 1·10 1·00

195 Nativity

1992. Christmas.
690 **195** 2f.50 multicoloured . . . 1·10 1·00

196 Birot and Free French Corvette

1993. 50th Death Anniv (1992) of Commander R. Birot.
691 **196** 2f.50 multicoloured . . . 1·25 1·10

197 Divers and Wreck of "L'Hortense"

1993. Deep Sea Diving.
692 **197** 5f. multicoloured . . . . 1·90 1·40

198 Longhorn Beetle on "Cichorium intybus"

199 Cutting up Cod

1993.
693 **198** 3f.60 multicoloured . . . 1·40 1·25

1993.
694 **199** 1f.50 multicoloured . . . 90 95
695 1f.80 multicoloured . . . 90 95

200 Greater Shearwater

1993. Air. Migratory Birds. Multicoloured.
696 5f. Type **200** . . . . 2·00 1·40
697 10f. American golden plover 3·25 2·10

201 Fleet of Ships

1993. Bicentenary of Settlement of Madeleine Islands.
698 **201** 5f.10 blue, green & brown 1·50 1·40

1993. No. 3121 of France optd **ST-PIERRE ET MIQUELON.**
699 **1118** (–) red . . . . 1·10 1·10

202 Short-spined Seascorpion

1993. Fishes. Multicoloured.
700 2f.80 Type **202** . . . . 1·10 60
701 2f.80 Fishermen and capelin ("Le Capelan") . . . . . 1·10 60
702 2f.80 Ray ("Le Raie") . . . 1·10 60
703 2f.80 Atlantic halibut ("Le Fletan") . . . . 1·10 60

203 Pine Cones, Otter and Left Bank

1993. Natural Heritage. Sylvain Hills. Multicoloured.
704 2f.80 Type **203** . . . . 1·25 60
705 16f. Otter on all fours, pine cones and right bank . . . 5·00 3·00
Nos. 704/5 were issued together, se-tenant, with intervening ½ stamp-size label, forming a composite design of an otter pool.

204 Prefect's Residence

1993.
707 **204** 3f.70 blue, yellow & brn 1·40 70

205 Father Christmas waving to Child

1993. Christmas.
708 **205** 2f.80 multicoloured . . . 1·25 60

206 Blaison and "Surcouf" (Free French submarine)

1994. 50th Death Anniv (1992) of Commander Louis Blaison.
709 **206** 2f.80 multicoloured . . . 1·75 70

207 Player lining up Shot

1994. 1st French Overseas Territories Petanque Championship.
710 **207** 5f.10 multicoloured . . . 1·90 1·25

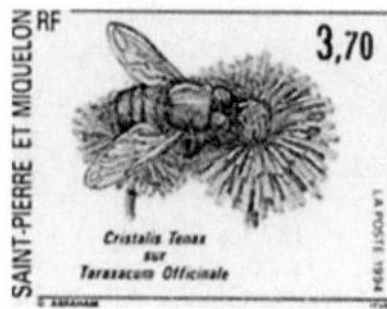

208 "Cristalis tenax" on Dandelion

1994.
711 **208** 3f.70 multicoloured . . . 1·40 90

209 Drying Atlantic Cod

1994.
712 **209** 1f.50 black and green . . 60 40
713 1f.80 multicoloured . . . 80 50

210 Ballot Box and Women outside Town Hall

1994. 50th Anniv of Women's Suffrage.
714 **210** 2f.80 multicoloured . . . 1·00 95

211 "Saint-Pierre" (sail hospital ship)

1994. Centenary of Society of Sea Works.
715 **211** 2f.80 multicoloured . . . 1·10 45

212 "Miquelon" (trawler)

1994. Ships. Multicoloured.
716 2f.80 Type **212** . . . . 1·40 1·40
717 2f.80 "Ile de St. Pierre" (trawler) . . . . 1·40 1·40
718 3f.70 "St. Georges XII" (pleasure cruiser) . . . . . 1·50 1·50
719 3f.70 "St. Eugene IV" (pleasure cruiser) . . . . . 1·50 1·50

213 Poolside

1994. Natural Heritage. Miranda Pool. Mult.
720 2f.80 Type **213** . . . . 1·40 60
721 16f. Pool . . . . 5·25 3·50
Nos. 720/1 were issued together se-tenant with intervening ½ stamp-size label, forming a composite design.

214 Parochial School

1994.
722 **214** 3f.70 black, blue and red 1·40 80

215 Envelope, Magnifying Glass and Tweezers holding "Stamp"

1994. 1st European Stamp Salon, Flower Gardens, Paris.
723 **215** 3f.70 blue, green and yellow . . . . 1·40 90

216 House and Christmas Tree

1994. Christmas.
724 **216** 2f.80 multicoloured . . . 1·10 60

217 Pasteur

1995. Death Centenary of Louis Pasteur (chemist).
725 **217** 2f.80 multicoloured . . . 1·25 60

218 Sports Pictograms

219 "Dicranum scoparium" and "Cladonia cristatella"

1995. Triathlon.
726 **218** 5f.10 multicoloured . . . 1·75 1·00

1995.
727 **219** 3f.70 multicoloured . . . 1·40 70

220 Cooper at Work

1995.
728 **220** 1f.50 multicoloured . . . 60 40
729 1f.80 multicoloured . . . 70 50

221 Arctic Terns

1995. Air. Migratory Birds.
730 **221** 10f. multicoloured . . . . 3·00 1·75

222 Crab

1995. Crustaceans and Molluscs. Multicoloured.
731 2f.80 Winkle . . . . 1·10 60
732 2f.80 Type **222** . . . . 1·10 60
733 2f.80 Scallop . . . . 1·10 60
734 2f.80 Lobster . . . . 1·10 60

223 Geologists working at Cliff Face

1995. Geological Research. Multicoloured.
735 2f.80 Type **223** . . . . 1·25 60
736 16f. Geological map of Langlade . . . . 5·00 3·00

224 Sister Cesarine **225** Building

1995. 150th Birth Anniv of Sister Cesarine.
737 **224** 1f.80 multicoloured . . . 70 50

1995. Francoforum.
738 **225** 3f.70 grey, blue and red 1·40 80

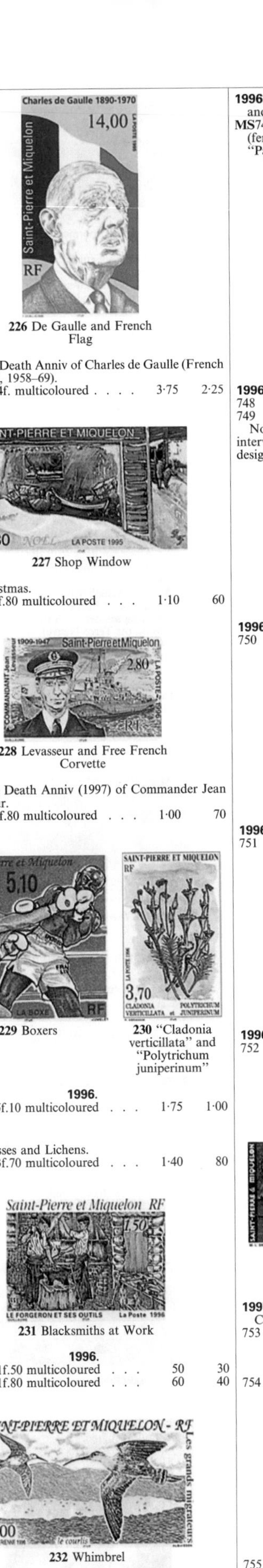

226 De Gaulle and French Flag

1995. 25th Death Anniv of Charles de Gaulle (French President, 1958–69).
739 **226** 14f. multicoloured . . . . 3·75 2·25

227 Shop Window

1995. Christmas.
740 **227** 2f.80 multicoloured . . . 1·10 60

228 Levasseur and Free French Corvette

1996. 50th Death Anniv (1997) of Commander Jean Levasseur.
741 **228** 2f.80 multicoloured . . . 1·00 70

229 Boxers

230 "Cladonia verticillata" and "Polytrichum juniperinum"

1996.
742 **229** 5f.10 multicoloured . . . 1·75 1·00

1996. Mosses and Lichens.
743 **230** 3f.70 multicoloured . . . 1·40 80

231 Blacksmiths at Work

1996.
744 **231** 1f.50 multicoloured . . . 50 30
745 1f.80 multicoloured . . . 60 40

232 Whimbrel

1996. Air. Migratory Birds.
746 **232** 15f. multicoloured . . . . 4·00 2·25

233 "Rader II" (pilot boat)

1996. Ships. Sheet 143 × 100 mm. containing T **233** and similar horiz designs. Multicoloured.
MS747 3f. Type **233**; 3f. "Lanelape" (ferry); 3f. "Pinta" (ferry); 3f. "Pascal-Annie" (trawler) . . . 3·50 2·25

234 The Cape

1996. Miquelon. Multicoloured.
748 3f. Type **234** 90 60
749 15f.50 The village . . . . . 4·00 2·50
Nos. 748/9 were issued together, se-tenant, with intervening ½ stamp-size label, forming a composite design.

235 Customs House

1996. Centenary of Customs House, St. Pierre.
750 **235** 3f.80 blue and black . . . 1·25 60

236 1947 Postage Due Design

1996. 50th Paris Autumn Stamp Show.
751 **236** 1f. multicoloured 40 30

237 Crib in St. Pierre Cathedral

1996. Christmas.
752 **237** 3f. multicoloured . . . . 1·10 50

238 Colmay

239 Common Cormorant and "Sedum rosea"

1997. 32nd Death Anniv of Commandant Constant Colmay.
753 **238** 3f. multicoloured . . . . 1·00 60

1997.
754 **239** 3f.80 multicoloured . . . 90 60

240 Salting House

1997.
755 **240** 1f.70 multicoloured . . . 35 25

241 "Doris" (rowing boat) and Construction Plan

1997.
756 **241** 2f. multicoloured 50 40

242 Player, Ball and Net

1997. Volleyball.
757 **242** 5f.20 multicoloured . . . 50 40

243 Peregrine Falcon

1997. Air. Migratory Birds.
758 **243** 5f. multicoloured . . . . 1·40 70

244 Statue of Liberty, "L'Oiseau Blanc" and Eiffel Tower

1997. Air. 70th Anniv of Disappearance of Charles Nungesser and Francois Coli (aviators) on attempted Non-stop Flight between Paris and New York.
759 **244** 14f. black, blue and brown . . . . 3·50 2·25

245 Atlantic Salmon

1997. Fishes. Multicoloured.
760 3f. Type **245** . . . . 1·00 60
761 3f. Lumpsucker ("Poule d'Eau") . . . . 1·00 60
762 3f. Atlantic mackerel ("Maquereau") . . . . . 1·00 60
763 3f. Porbeagle ("Requin Marache") . . . . 1·00 60

1997. No. 3407 of France (no value expressed) optd **ST-PIERRE ET MIQUELON**. Ordinary gum or self-adhesive.
764 **1313** (3f.) red 70 30

1997. Nos. 3415 etc. of France optd **ST-PIERRE ET MIQUELON**.
765 **1313** 10c. brown 10 10
766 20c. green 10 10
767 50c. violet 10 10
768 1f. orange 20 15
769 2f. blue 40 25
770 2f.70 green 55 35
773 3f.50 green 70 45
775 3f.80 blue 75 45
776 4f.20 red 90 55
778 4f.40 blue 90 55
779 4f.50 mauve 95 60
780 5f. blue . . . . 1·10 70
781 6f.70 green . . . . . . 1·40 85
782 10f. violet . . . . 2·00 60

246 Cap aux Basques

1997. Multicoloured.
785 3f. Type **246** 70 50
786 15f.50 Diamant . . . . . . 3·50 2·25
Nos. 785/6 were issued together, se-tenant, with intervening ½ stamp-size label, forming a composite design.

247 Post Office

1997. Public Buildings.
787 **247** 3f.80 multicoloured . . . 90 60

248 Nativity

1997. Christmas.
788 **248** 3f. multicoloured 70 50

249 Savary and Building

1998. 10th Death Anniv of Alain Savary (Governor).
789 **249** 3f. multicoloured 70 50

250 Curling

1998. Winter Olympic Games, Nagano, Japan.
790 **250** 5f.20 red, blue and scarlet 1·40 80

251 Irises and Horses

1998.
791 **251** 3f.80 multicoloured . . . 90 60

252 Lifting Blocks of Ice

1998. Work on the Ice. Multicoloured.
792 1f.70 Type **252** 50 40
793 2f. Cutting out blocks of ice 50 40

253 Head of American Bald Eagle

1998.
794 **253** 10f. multicoloured . . . . 2·25 1·75

1998. "Philexfrance 99" International Stamp Exhibition, Paris. No. 3460 of France optd **ST-PIERRE ET MIQUELON**.
795 **1334** 3f. red and blue 70 50

254 Yellow House

1998. Local Houses. Multicoloured.
796 3f. Type **254** 60 35
797 3f. Pink house 60 35
798 3f. White house 60 35
799 3f. Grey house 60 35

255 Map of Gulf of St. Lawrence

1998. France in North America.
800 **255** 3f. multicoloured 60 35

256 Pointe Plate

1998. Natural Heritage. Multicoloured.
801 3f. Type **256** 60 35
802 15f.50 Cap Bleu . . . . . . 3·25 1·90

Nos. 801/2 were issued together, se-tenant, with intervening ¾ stamp-size label, forming a composite design.

257 Map of the Americas and Map of France on Football

1998. France, World Cup Football Champion.
803 **257** 3f. multicoloured 65 35

258 War Memorial

1998.
804 **258** 3f.80 purple, red and blue 80 45

259 Santa Claus delivering Presents

1998. Christmas.
805 **259** 3f. multicoloured 65 35

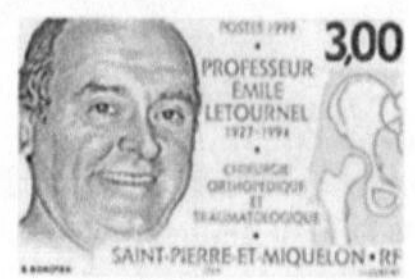

260 Letournel

1999. 5th Death Anniv of Emile Letournel (orthopaedic surgeon).
806 **260** 3f. olive, green and brown 65 35

261 Ile-aux-marins Shore

1999.
807 **261** 5f.20 multicoloured . . . 1·40 80

262 *Rubus chamaemorus*

1999.
808 **262** 3f.80 multicoloured . . . 80 45

1999. Nos. 3553 of France optd **ST-PIERRE ET MIQUELON**. Ordinary or self-adhesive gum.
809 **1376** 3f. red and blue 65 35

No. 809 is denominated in both French francs and euros.

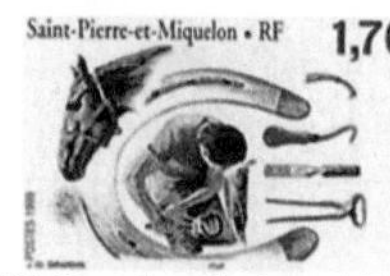

263 Horseshoe, Farrier and Tools

1999. The Farrier. Multicoloured.
811 1f.70 Type **263** 50 40
812 2f. Farrier at work 50 40

264 Northern Pintail

1999. Air. Migratory Birds.
813 **264** 20f. multicoloured . . . . 5·50 3·50

265 France 1849 20c. St. Pierre et Miquelon 1885 5c. on 2c. and 1909 1c. Stamps

1999. "Philexfrance 99" International Stamp Exhibition, Paris (2nd issue). 150th Anniv of First French Postage Stamp. Sheet 132 × 159 mm containing T **265** and similar vert designs. Multicoloured.
MS814 3f. Type **265**; 3f. St. Pierre Miquelon 1932 40c. and 1941 1f.25 stamps; 3f. St.Pierre et Miquelon 1957 50f. and 1967 100f. stamps; 3f. St. Pierre et Miquelon 1986 2f.20 and 1999 3f. stamps . . . 2·50 1·50

266 "Bearn" (steam tug)

1999. Ships. Sheet 143 × 100m containing T **266** and similar horiz designs. Multicoloured.
MS815 3f. Type **266** ; 3f. "Pro-Patria" (mail ship); 3f. "Eminie" (deep sea fishing boat); 3f. "Colombier" (coastal patrol vessel) . . . . 2·50 1·50

267 Cars and Quayside

1999. Place du General de Gaulle. Multicoloured.
816 3f. Type **267** 65 35
817 15f.50 Boats . . . . 3·25 1·90

268 Maps of St. Pierre et Miquelon and France

270 House and Snowman (Best Wishes)

269 Interior

1999. Visit of President Jacques Chirac of France.
818 **268** 3f. multicoloured 65 35

1999. Museum and Archives.
819 **269** 5f.40 mauve . . . . . . 1·50 85

1999. Greetings Stamp.
820 **270** 3f. multicoloured 65 35

271 "Bonjour l'An 2000"

2000. New Millennium.
821 **271** 3f. multicoloured 65 35

272 Humpback Whale

2000. Whales.
822 **272** 3f. black and blue 65 35
823 – 5f.70 black and green . . 1·60 90

DESIGN: 5f.70, Fin whale.

273 "Les Graves"

2000. Art.
824 **273** 5f.20 multicoloured . . . 1·40 80

274 *Vaccinium vitis-idaea*

2000.
825 **274** 3f.80 multicoloured . . . 80 45

275 Wood on Dog-sled

2000. The Collection of Wood.
826 **275** 1f.70 blue and black . . . 50 40
827 2f. brown and black . . . 50 40

276 Fishermen, 1904

2000. The Twentieth Century, 1900–1950 (1st issue). Multicoloured.
828 3f. Type **276** (abandonment of fishing and drying rights on French shore) 65 35
829 3f. Women carrying dried cod, 1905 . . . . 65 35
830 3f. Conscripts leaving New York for Le Havre, 1915 65 35
831 3f. Assault on Souain Hill, 1915 . . . . 65 35
832 3f. People on pack ice and icebound ships (isolation of St. Pierre during exceptional weather), 1923 65 35
833 3f. Unloading contraband during American prohibition era, 1925 . . . 65 35
834 3f. St. Pierre et Miquelon Pavilion at International Colonial Exhibition, Paris, 1931 . . . . 65 35
835 3f. Procession flying French and American flags (end of prohibition in America), 1933 . . . . 65 35
836 3f. Admiral Muselier of Free French Naval Forces inspecting seamen (loss of *Mimosa* off Terre-Neuve), 1942 . . . . 65 35
837 3f. Army vehicles crossing the Rhine, 1945 . . . . . . 65 35

See also Nos. 842/51.

Nos. 818, 820/4, 826/7 and 838 and subsequent St. Pierre et Miquelon issues are denominated both in francs and in euros. As no cash for the latter is in circulation, the catalogue continues to use the franc value.

277 *L'Inger* (wrecked galleon)

2000.
838 **277** 5f.40 green . . . . 1·50 85

278 Houses behind Boat Sheds

2000. Salt Works. Multicoloured.
839 3f. Type **278** 65 35
840 15f.10 Church behind boat sheds . . . . 3·00 1·25

279 Angels, Village and "2000"

2000. Christmas.
841 **279** 3f. multicoloured 65 35

280 Frozen Fish Factory, 1951

2000. The Twentieth Century, 1950–2000 (2nd issue). Multicoloured.
842 2f. Type **280** 50 40
843 2f. *Ravenel* (loss of trawler and crew, 1960) 50 40
844 2f. General de Gaulle meeting ex-servicemen during visit to St. Pierre, 1967 . . . . 50 40
845 2f. First television images (inauguration of local station), 1967 . . . . . . 50 40

846 2f. Construction of new port, 1970 50 40

847 2f. Construction of new college, 1977 50 40

848 2f. View over islands (change of status to Collective Territoriale and resumption of stamp issues, 1986) 50 40

849 2f. Eric Tarbarly's racing yacht (Tarbarly's stop-off in St. Pierre during Round the World Yacht Race, 1987) 50 40

850 2f. Oil rig and map (exploitation of off-shore oil services, 1992) 50 40

851 2f. Runway extension, White Point Airport, 1999 50 40

281 Rough-legged Buzzard

2000. Air.

852 **281** 5f. multicoloured 1·25 75

282 "2001"

2000. New Millennium.

853 **282** 3f. multicoloured 65 35

283 Killer Whale

2001. Whales.

854 **283** 3f. black and blue 65 35

855 – 5f.70 black and green 1·60 90

DESIGN: 5f.70, Long-finned pilot whale.

284 "Reflections"

2001.

856 **284** 5f.20 multicoloured 1·40 80

285 Apple

2001.

857 **285** 3f.80 multicoloured 80 85

286 "Hay gathering"

2001.

858 **286** 1f.70 multicoloured 50 40

859 2f. multicoloured 50 40

287 Great Blue Heron

2001. Air.

860 **287** 15f. multicoloured 3·00 1·25

288 Lake in Autumn

289 Porch (Maison Jugan)

2001. Seasons (1st series). Multicoloured.

861 3f. Type **288** 55 45

862 3f. Lake in winter 55 45

See also Nos.871/2.

2001. Porches. Multicoloured.

863 3f. Type **289** 55 45

864 3f. Marie de L'ile-aux-Marins 55 45

865 3f. Maison Voge 55 45

866 3f. Maison Guillou 55 45

290 Trees, Houses and River

2001. Landscapes. Multicoloured.

867 10f. Type **290** 1·90 1·50

868 10f. Cliff-top houses and church 1·90 1·50

291 Airport

2001. Saint-Pierre Pointe Blanche Airport.

869 **291** 5f. multicoloured 95 75

292 *Marie-Therese*

2001. Wreck of *Marie-Therese* off Pointe-du Diamant.

870 **292** 5f.40 green 1·00 80

2001. Seasons (2nd series). As T **288**. Multicoloured.

871 3f. Lake in spring 55 45

872 3f. Lake in summer 55 45

293 Commander Jacques Pepin Lehalleur and *Alysse* (corvette)

2001.

873 **293** 3f. multicoloured 55 45

294 Father Christmas

2001. Christmas.

874 **294** 3f. multicoloured 55 45

New Currency 100 = 1 euro

2002. Nos. 3770/82 and 3784/90 of France optd **ST-PIERRE ET MIQUELON**. (a) With face value. Ordinary gum.

875 **1318** 1c. yellow 10 10

876 2c. brown 10 10

877 5c. green 10 10

878 10c. violet 15 10

879 20c. orange 30 25

880 41c. green 55 45

881 50c. blue 70 55

882 53c. green 75 60

883 58c. blue 80 50

883a 58c. green 75 60

884 64c. orange 90 70

885 67c. blue 95 65

886 69c. mauve 1·00 80

887 70c. green 90 70

888 90c. blue 1·20 95

889 €1 turquoise 1·40 1·10

890 €1.02 green 1·40 1·10

891 €1.11 purple 1·50 1·20

892 €1.90 purple 2·50 2·00

893 €2 violet 2·75 2·25

(b) (i) No value expressed.

894 (41c.) green 55 45

(ii) Self-adhesive gum.

895 (46c.) red 60 50

295 Magnifying Glass, Birds and Map

2002. "The Archipelago and the Euro".

908 **295** €1 multicoloured 1·40 1·40

296 Common Seal (*Phoca vitulina*)

2002. Seals (1st series).

909 **296** 46c. black and brown 65 65

910 – 87c. black and brown 1·25 1·25

DESIGN: 87c. Grey seal (*Halichoerus grypus*).

See also Nos. 926/7.

297 "La Pomme de Pre"

2002.

911 **297** 58c. multicoloured 80 80

298 Laranaga Farm

2002.

912 **298** 79c. green 1·10 1·10

299 Mending Nets

2002.

913 **299** 26c. orange 35 35

914 30c. blue 40 40

300 Atlantic Puffin

2002.

915 **300** €2.50 multicoloured 3·50 3·50

301 West Point

2002.

916 75c. multicoloured 1·00 1·00

302 "Le Tiaude de Morue" (cod dish)

2002. Traditional Dishes.

917 50c. multicoloured 70 70

2002. No. 3752 of France (no value expressed) optd **ST-PIERRE ET MIQUELON**.

918 **1318** (41c.) red 55 45

303 Arctic Hare (*Lepus timidus*)

2002.

921 **303** 46c. multicoloured 65 65

304 *Le Troutpool*

2002. Wreck of *Le Troutpool* off Pointe-du Diamant.

922 **304** 84c. green 1·25 1·25

305 Grand Colombier Island and Sea Bird

2002. L'Anse a Henry Cove.

923 **305** €2 blue, black and yellow 2·75 2·75

924 – €2 blue and black 2·75 2·75

DESIGN: No. 924, Saint Pierre Island Nos. 923/4 were issued together, se-tenant, forming a composite design.

306 Yacht with Christmas Tree on Sail

2002. Christmas.

925 **306** 46c. multicoloured 65 65

307 Harp Seal (*Phoca groenlandica*)

2003. Seals (2nd series).
926 **307** 46c. black and blue . . . 60 60
927 – 87c. black and blue . . . 1·10 1·10
DESIGNS: Type **307**; 87c. Hooded seal (*Cystophora cristata*)

308 Francois Maurer

2003. 3rd Death Anniv of Monseigner Francois Maurer (bishop of St. Pierre et Miquelon).
928 **308** 46c. multicoloured 60 60

309 Capandeguy Farm

2003.
929 **309** 79c. brown . . . . 1·00 1·00

310 "Les Bleuets" (Marie-Laure Drillet)

2003.
930 **310** 75c. multicoloured . . . . 1·00 1·00

311 "Le Poulieur" (the pulley man)

2003.
931 **311** 30c. blue 40 40

312 Maison Patrice, Maison Jezequel and Maison Jugan (houses)

2003. International Traditional Architecture Congress. Traditional architecture. Multicoloured.
932 €2 Type **312** . . . . 2·60 2·60
933 €2 Notre-Dame des Marins and Maison Borotra . . . 2·60 2·60
Nos. 932/3 were issued together, se-tenant, forming a composite design.

313 Northern Gannet

2003. Air.
934 **313** €2.50 multicoloured . . 3·25 3·25

314 Player

2003. Centenary of Associations Sportives de Saint-Pierre et Miquelon (ASSP).
935 **314** 50c. multicoloured 65 65

315 White-tailed Deer (*Odocoileus virginianus*)

2003.
936 **315** 50c. multicoloured 65 65

316 Strawberries

2003. Langdale Strawberry Jam.
937 **316** 50c. multicoloured 65 65

317 Lions Club Emblem

2003. 50th Anniv of Lions Club (charitable organization).
938 **317** 50c. multicoloured 65 65

318 *L' Afrique*

2003. Shipwrecks (1st series). *L'Afrique* (1920).
939 **318** 90c. black . . . . 1·20 1·20
See also No. 953.

319 Snow-covered Trees and Icicles

2003. Christmas.
940 **319** 50c. multicoloured 65 65

320 Joseph Lehuenen

321 Anse a Rodrigue

2004. Joseph Lehuenen (politician and historian) Commemoration.
941 **320** 50c. brown 65 65

2004.
942 **321** 75c. multicoloured . . . . 1·00 1·00

322 Atlantic White-sided Dolphin (*Lagenorhynchus acutus*)

2004. Dolphins.
943 **322** 50c. purple and black . . 65 65
944 – €1.08 brown and black 1·40 1·40
DESIGN: €1.08 Harbour porpoise (*Phocoena phocoena*).

323 Ollivier Farm

2004.
945 **323** 90c. orange . . . . 1·20 1·20

324 "Back from Fishing"

2004.
946 **324** 30c. multicoloured 40 40

325 Pro Patria Postal Ship and Sail Ships

2003. St. Pierre et Miquelon Port (circa 1928).
947 €2 black, violet and magenta 2·75 2·75
948 €2 black, violet and blue . . 2·75 2·75
DESIGNS: €2 × 2 Type **325**; Sail ships and prow of schooner.
Nos. 947/8 were issued together, se-tenant, forming a composite design.

326 326 Canada Geese

2004. Air. Migrant Birds.
949 **326** €2.50 multicoloured . . 3·25 3·25

327 Map

2004. 500th Anniv of Mi'kmaq (aboriginal Indians) Village.
950 **327** 50c. multicoloured 65 65

328 Fox

2004.
951 **328** 50c. multicoloured 65 65

329 "Bread, Butter and Poor Cod"

2004.
952 **329** 90c. multicoloured . . . . 1·20 1·20

330 Ribs of Ship

2004. Shipwrecks (2nd series). *Fulwood* (1828).
953 **330** 90c. lilac . . . . 1·20 1·20

331 *Le Cap Blanc*

2004. Transport Ships. Multicoloured.
MS954 170 × 115 mm. 50c. × 4, Type **331**; *Le Lisbet-C*; *Le Shamrock*; *L Aldona* . . . . . 2·75 2·75

PARCEL POST STAMPS

1901. Optd **COLIS POSTAUX**.
P79 D 10c. black on lilac . . . . 90·00 90·00

1901. Optd **Colis Postaux**.
P80 D 10c. red . . . . 13·50 20·00

1917. Nos. 83 and 85 optd **Colis Postaux**.
P109 **17** 10c. red and pink . . . 95 4·25
P110 20c. purple and brown 60 3·25

1941. Free French Plebiscite. No. P110 optd **FRANCE LIBRE F. N. F. L.**
P303 **17** 20c. purple and brown . . £700 £700

POSTAGE DUE STAMPS

1892. Postage Due stamps of French Colonies optd **ST-PIERRE M-on.**
D60 U 5c. black . . . . 60·00 65·00
D61 10c. black . . . . 17·00 14·50
D62 15c. black . . . . 13·00 16·00
D63 20c. black . . . . 14·50 14·00
D64 30c. black . . . . 20·00 20·00
D65 40c. black . . . . 11·00 13·50
D66 60c. black . . . . 65·00 65·00
D67 1f. brown £120 £120
D68 2f. brown £120 £120

1925. Postage Due type of France optd **SAINT-PIERRE-ET-MIQUELON** or surch also **centimes à percevoir** and value in figures.
D135 D **11** 5c. blue . . . . . . 15 2·25
D136 10c. brown . . . . . 20 2·25
D137 20c. olive . . . . . 45 2·50
D138 25c. red . . . . . . 65 2·50
D139 30c. red . . . . . . 55 2·75
D140 45c. green . . . . . 85 2·75
D141 50c. red . . . . . . 1·50 4·00
D142 60c. on 50c. brown . . 1·40 4·00
D143 1f. red . . . . . . 1·40 2·50
D144 2f. on 1f. red . . . . 2·00 5·25
D145 3f. mauve . . . . . . 7·25 14·00

D **30** Newfoundland Dog

D **40** Atlantic Cod

1932.
D163 D **30** 5c. black and blue . . 75 3·25
D164 10c. black and green 2·00 3·25
D165 20c. black and red . . 3·25 3·75
D166 25c. black and purple 3·25 3·75
D167 30c. black and orange 4·00 4·50
D168 45c. black and blue . . 4·75 5·50
D169 50c. black and green 8·25 9·50
D170 60c. black and red . . 8·50 13·00
D171 1f. black and brown 25·00 30·00
D172 2f. black and purple 28·00 32·00
D173 3f. black and brown 35·00 35·00

1938.
D208 D **40** 5c. black . . . . . . 25 2·50
D209 10c. purple . . . . . 15 3·00
D210 15c. green . . . . . 25 3·00
D211 20c. blue . . . . . . 25 3·00
D212 30c. red . . . . . . 45 3·00
D213 50c. green . . . . . 90 3·00
D214 60c. blue . . . . . . 1·25 3·00
D215 1f. red . . . . 1·40 3·00
D216 2f. brown . . . . . . 1·75 2·75
D217 3f. violet . . . . . . 2·75 4·75

1941. Free French Plebiscite. Nos. D208/17 optd **NOEL 1941 F N F L.**
D235 D **40** 5c. black . . . . . . 23·00 25·00
D236 10c. purple . . . . . 25·00 25·00
D237 15c. green . . . . . 25·00 25·00
D238 20c. blue . . . . . . 25·00 25·00
D239 30c. red . . . . . . 25·00 25·00
D240 50c. green . . . . . 48·00 48·00
D241 60c. blue £100 £100

D242 1f. red £110 £110
D243 2f. brown £110 £110
D244 3f. violet £120 £120

1941. Postage Due stamps of 1932 optd **FRANCE LIBRE F. N. F. L.** or surch also.
D298 D 30 25c. black and purple £225 £225
D299 30c. black and orange £225 £225
D300 50c. black and green £750 £750
D301 2f. black and purple 48·00 48·00
D302 3f. on 2f. black & pur 25·00 25·00

1941. Free French Plebiscite. Nos. D208/17 optd **FRANCE LIBRE F. N. F. L.**
D310 D 40 5c. black 50·00 50·00
D311 10c. purple 8·75 14·00
D312 15c. green 8·75 14·00
D313 20c. blue 8·50 14·00
D314 30c. red 13·00 14·00
D315 50c. green 8·50 14·00
D316 60c. blue 9·50 18·00
D317 1f. red 26·00 27·00
D318 2f. brown 11·00 27·00
D319 3f. violet £425 £425

D 57 Arms and Galleon

D 115 Newfoundland Dog and Shipwreck Scene

1947.
D385 D 57 10c. orange 15 2·25
D386 30c. blue 15 1·00
D387 50c. green 25 1·00
D388 1f. red 30 3·00
D389 2f. green 1·40 3·00
D390 3f. violet 1·75 3·25
D391 4f. brown 1·75 3·25
D392 5f. green 1·90 3·25
D393 10f. black 2·25 3·50
D394 20f. red 2·50 3·75

1973.
D516 D 115 2c. black and brown 2·40 2·25
D517 10c. black and violet 2·75 2·50
D518 20c. black and green 3·00 3·00
D519 30c. black and red 4·00 4·00
D520 1f. black and blue 9·50 9·75

1986. Nos. D2493/2502 of France optd **ST-PIERRE ET MIQUELON.**
D569 10c. brown and black 1·10 1·10
D570 20c. black 1·10 1·10
D571 30c. red, brown and black 1·10 1·10
D572 40c. blue, brown and black 1·10 1·10
D573 50c. red and black 1·10 1·10
D574 1f. black 1·25 1·25
D575 2f. yellow and black 1·50 1·50
D576 3f. black and red 1·90 1·90
D577 4f. brown and black 2·25 2·25
D578 5f. brown, red and black 2·50 2·50

ST. THOMAS AND PRINCE IS.

Pt. 9; Pt. 14

Two islands in the Gulf of Guinea off the west coast of Africa. A colony and then an Overseas Province of Portugal until 1975, when it became an independent republic.

1870. 1000 reis = 1 milreis.
1913. 100 centavos = 1 escudo.
1977. 100 cents = 1 dobra.

1870. "Crown" key-type inscr "S. THOME E PRINCIPE".
17 P 5r. black 2·50 1·70
18 10r. orange 18·00 9·50
29 10r. green 8·00 4·75
20 20r. bistre 3·75 2·40
30 20r. red 4·00 2·75
21 25r. red 2·10 1·20
31 25r. lilac 3·25 2·00
22 40r. blue 5·75 4·25
32 40r. yellow 5·75 4·75
25 50r. green 18·00 13·50
33a 50r. blue 1·10 60
26 100r. lilac 9·50 5·00
15 200r. orange 11·50 9·50
16 300r. brown 11·50 9·50

1887. "Embossed" key-type inscr "S. THOME E PRINCIPE".
38 Q 5r. black 4·75 3·75
42 10r. green 8·00 2·75
43 20r. red 9·00 3·00
44 25r. mauve 5·25 5·00
45 40r. brown 5·25 3·00
46 50r. blue 6·50 2·75
47 100r. brown 5·25 2·75
48 200r. lilac 18·00 10·00
49 300r. orange 19·00 10·00

1889. Stamps of 1887 surch. No gum.
50 Q 5r. on 10r. green 39·00 31·00
51 5r. on 20r. red 39·00 31·00
52 50r. on 40r. brown £140 £120

1895. "Figures" key-type inscr "S. THOME E PRINCIPE".
60 R 5r. yellow 1·00 95
61 10r. mauve 1·30 80
53 15r. brown 1·90 1·20
54 20r. lilac 1·90 1·30
62 25r. green 1·90 80
63 50r. blue 1·90 80
55 75r. pink 5·25 3·75
64 80r. green 11·00 9·50
56 100r. brown on buff 5·00 3·75
57 150r. red on pink 6·50 4·75
58 200r. blue on blue 9·00 7·25
59 300r. blue on brown 10·00 8·50

1898. "King Carlos" key-type inscr "S. THOME E PRINCIPE". Name and value in red (500r.) or black (others).
66 S 2½r. grey 25 20
67 5r. red 40 20
68 10r. green 40 25
69 15r. brown 1·20 1·00
113 15r. green 1·30 80
70 20r. lilac 80 45
71 25r. green 45 30
114 25r. red 1·30 60
72 50r. blue 70 40
115 50r. brown 5·25 3·25
116 65r. blue 10·00 6·00
73 75r. pink 12·00 6·75
117 75r. purple 2·75 1·20
74 80r. mauve 6·00 5·75
75 100r. blue on blue 2·10 1·90
118 115r. brown on pink 9·25 6·75
119 130r. brown on yellow 9·25 6·75
76 150r. brown on yellow 2·40 1·70
77 200r. purple on pink 4·75 3·25
78 300r. blue on pink 6·75 3·50
120 400r. blue on cream 13·00 7·50
79 500r. black on blue 7·25 5·25
80 700r. mauve on yellow 14·50 11·00

1902. Surch with new value.
121 S 50r. on 65r. blue 4·00 2·40
85 R 65r. on 5r. yellow 4·50 3·00
86 65r. on 10r. mauve 4·50 3·00
87 65r. on 15r. brown 4·50 3·00
81 Q 65r. on 20r. red 9·00 4·00
88 R 65r. on 20r. lilac 4·50 3·00
83 Q 65r. on 25r. mauve 5·75 3·75
84 65r. on 100r. brown 5·75 3·75
90 115r. on 10r. green 5·75 3·75
92 R 115r. on 25r. green 5·75 3·75
89 P 115r. on 50r. green 11·50 3·75
93 R 115r. on 150r. red on pink 4·50 3·00
94 115r. on 200r. blue on blue 4·50 3·00
91 Q 115r. on 300r. orange 5·75 3·75
95 130r. on 5r. black 5·75 3·75
98 R 130r. on 75r. pink 4·50 3·00
99 130r. on 100r. brn on buff 4·50 3·00
97 Q 130r. on 200r. lilac 7·25 3·75
100 R 130r. on 300r. blue on brown 4·50 3·00
108 V 400r. on 2½r. brown 1·30 1·20
101 P 400r. on 10r. yellow 55·00 40·00
102 Q 400r. on 40r. brown 10·00 7·25
103 400r. on 50r. blue 4·50 3·00
105 R 400r. on 50r. blue 1·30 1·20
107 400r. on 80r. green 2·50 2·00

1903. Stamps of 1898 optd **PROVISORIO**.
109 S 15r. brown 2·30 1·00
110 25r. green 2·30 1·00
111 50r. blue 2·50 1·00
112 75r. pink 5·75 4·25

1911. Stamps of 1898 optd **REPUBLICA**.
122 S 2½r. grey 25 20
123 5r. orange 30 25
124 10r. green 30 25
125 15r. green 30 25
126 20r. lilac 30 25
127 25r. red 30 25
128 50r. brown 30 25
129 75r. purple 30 25
130 100r. blue on blue 30 25
131 115r. brown on pink 70 50
132 130r. brown on yellow 1·40 85
267 200r. purple on pink 2·10 1·20
134 400r. blue on cream 75 45
268 500r. black on blue 1·40 1·20
136 700r. mauve on yellow 1·90 80

1912. "King Manoel" key type inscr "S. THOME E PRINCIPE" and optd **REPUBLICA**.
137 T 2½r. lilac 30 25
138 5r. black 30 25
139 10r. green 30 25
140 20r. red 1·20 70
141 25r. brown 70 45
142 50r. blue 70 45
143 75r. brown 70 45
144 100r. brown on green 1·20 60
145 200r. green on orange 1·80 1·90
146 300r. black on blue 2·75 1·20

1913. Nos. 109 and 111/2 optd **REPUBLICA**.
159 S 15r. brown 85 85
243 50r. blue 85 60
272 75r. pink 8·75 5·75

1913. Stamps of 1902 optd **REPUBLICA**.
244 S 50r. on 65r. blue 85 60
245 Q 115r. on 10r. green 2·50 1·50
246 R 115r. on 25r. green 80 40
164 P 115r. on 50r. green £180 £140
247 R 115r. on 150r. red on pink 80 40
248 115r. on 200r. blue on blue 80 40
249 Q 115r. on 300r. orange 2·50 1·80
250 130r. on 5r. black 5·50 3·00
251 R 130r. on 75r. pink 80 40
252 130r. on 100r. brn on buff 1·40 1·30
253 Q 130r. on 200r. lilac 1·70 1·20
254 R 130r. on 300r. blue on brown 1·30 75
197 V 400r. on 2½r. brown 2·75 2·40
198 Q 400r. on 50r. blue 75·00 60·00
200 R 400r. on 50r. blue 2·75 2·40
202 400r. on 80r. green 3·00 2·00

1913. Surch **REPUBLICA S. TOME E PRINCIPE** and new value on "Vasco da Gama" stamps of

(a) Portuguese Colonies.
203 ¼c. on 2½r. green 1·20 80
204 ½c. on 5r. red 1·20 80
205 1c. on 10r. purple 1·20 80
206 2½c. on 25r. green 1·20 80
207 5c. on 50r. blue 1·20 80
208 7½c. on 75r. brown 2·20 2·00
209 10c. on 100r. brown 1·20 80
210 15c. on 150r. brown 1·40 95

(b) Macao.
211 ¼c. on ½c. green 1·70 1·10
212 ½c. on 1a. red 1·70 1·10
213 1c. on 2a. purple 1·70 1·10
214 2½c. on 4a. green 1·70 1·10
215 5c. on 8a. blue 1·80 1·50
216 7½c. on 12a. brown 3·25 2·40
217 10c. on 16a. brown 1·80 1·30
218 15c. on 24a. brown 1·80 1·30

(c) Portuguese Timor.
219 ¼c. on ½a. green 1·70 1·10
220 ½c. on 1a. red 1·70 1·10
221 1c. on 2a. purple 1·70 1·10
222 2½c. on 4a. green 1·70 1·10
223 5c. on 8a. blue 1·80 1·60
224 7½c. on 12a. brown 3·25 2·40
225 10c. on 16a. brown 1·80 1·30
226 15c. on 24a. brown 1·80 1·30

1914. "Ceres" key-type inscr "S. TOME E PRINCIPE" Name and value in black.
276 U ¼c. green 40 35
281 ½c. black 25 20
282 1c. green 25 20
283 1½c. brown 1·60 1·50
284 2c. red 25 20
285 2c. grey 25 20
286 2½c. violet 25 20
287 3c. orange 25 20
288 4c. purple 25 20
289 4½c. grey 25 20
290 5c. blue 40 35
291 6c. mauve 25 20
292 7c. blue 25 20
293 7½c. brown 40 30
294 8c. grey 40 30
295 10c. brown 40 30
296 12c. green 50 40
297 15c. pink 50 35
298 20c. green 50 35
299 24c. blue 1·00 80
300 25c. brown 1·00 80
239 30c. brown on green 2·20 1·10
301 30c. green 80 50
240 40c. brown on pink 2·20 1·10
302 40c. turquoise 80 50
241 50c. orange on orange 5·25 3·50
303 50c. mauve 80 60
304 60c. blue 80 50
305 60c. pink 1·70 80
306 80c. red 1·80 60
242 1e. green on blue 5·25 2·75
307 1e. pink 2·50 1·30
308 1e. blue 1·50 95
309 2e. purple 2·75 1·40
310 5e. brown 16·00 4·25
311 10e. pink 26·00 9·50
312 20e. green 80·00 £346

1919. No. 109 surch **REPUBLICA** and new value.
255 S 2½r. on 15r. brown 85 60

1919. No. 122 surch with new value.
256 S ½c. on 2½r. grey 4·25 3·25
257 1c. on 2½r. grey 3·00 1·80
258 2½c. on 2½r. grey 1·20 80

1919. "Ceres" key-types of St. Thomas and Prince Islands surch.
259 U ½c. on ¼c. green 2·50 2·00
260 2c. on ¼c. green 2·50 2·00
261 2½c. on ¼c. green 8·75 6·25

1919. "Ceres" key-type of St. Thomas and Prince Islands surch **$04 Centavos** and with old value blocked out.
262 U 4c. on 2½c. violet 1·20 80

1923. Stamps of 1913 (optd REPUBLICA) surch **DEZ CENTAVOS** and bars.
313 R 10c. on 115r. on 25r. green 16·00 4·25
314 10c. on 115r. on 150r. red on pink 26·00 9·50
316 10c. on 115r. on 200r. blue on blue 60 45
317 10c. on 130r. on 75r. pink 60 45
318 10c. on 130r. on 100r. brown on buff 60 45
319 10c. on 130r. on 300r. blue on brown 60 45

1925. Stamps of 1902 surch **Republica 40 C.** and bars over original surcharge.
321 V 40c. on 400r. on 2½r. brown 1·20 55
322 R 40c. on 400r. on 80r. green 1·20 55

1931. Nos. 307 and 309 surch.
323 U 70c. on 1e. pink 2·40 1·20
324 1e.40 on 2e. purple 3·00 1·50

32 Ceres

1934.
325 32 1c. brown 15 10
326 5c. brown 25 20
327 10c. mauve 25 20
328 15c. black 25 20
329 20c. grey 25 20
330 30c. green 25 20
331 40c. red 25 20
332 45c. turquoise 50 45
333 50c. brown 40 35
334 60c. green 60 25
335 70c. brown 60 35
336 80c. green 60 35
337 85c. red 3·00 1·20
338 1e. purple 90 45
339 1e.40 blue 2·40 1·20
340 2e. mauve 2·40 1·20
341 5e. green 5·75 3·75
342 10e. brown 16·00 8·25
343 20e. orange 65·00 35·00

1938. As T **54** and **56** of Macao, but inscr "S. TOME".
344 54 1c. green (postage) 20 20
345 5c. brown 20 20
346 10c. red 20 20
347 15c. purple 20 20
348 20c. grey 20 20
349 – 30c. purple 20 20
350 – 35c. green 40 25
351 – 40c. brown 40 25
352 – 50c. mauve 40 25
353 – 60c. black 40 25
354 – 70c. violet 40 25
355 – 80c. orange 40 25
356 – 1e. red 80 50
357 – 1e.75 blue 1·40 70
358 – 2e. red 18·00 5·25
359 – 5e. green 18·00 5·75
360 – 10e. blue 21·00 6·25
361 – 20e. brown 36·00 2·50
362 56 10c. red (air) £100 70·00
363 20c. violet 48·00 34·00
364 50c. orange 2·30 2·20
365 1e. blue 7·50 2·20
366 2e. red 6·00 4·00
367 3e. green 7·50 5·25
368 5e. brown 12·50 10·00
369 9e. red 13·50 10·00
370 10e. mauve 13·50 10·00

DESIGNS: 30 to 50c. Mousinho de Albuquerque; 60c. to 1e. Dam; 1e.75 to 5e. Prince Henry the Navigator; 10, 20e. Afonso de Albuquerque.

See also Nos. 374/400.

37 Portuguese Colonial Column

41 Cola Nuts

1938. President's Colonial Tour.
371 37 80c. green 2·40 1·30
372 1e.75 blue 8·00 4·25
373 20e. brown 48·00 25·00

1939. As Nos. 344/70 but inscr "S. TOME e PRINCIPE".
374 54 1c. green (postage) 20 20
375 5c. brown 20 20
376 10c. red 20 20
377 15c. purple 20 20
378 20c. grey 20 20
379 – 30c. purple 20 20
380 – 35c. green 20 20
381 – 40c. brown 30 20
382 – 50c. mauve 30 25
383 – 60c. black 60 35
384 – 70c. violet 70 35
385 – 80c. orange 70 35
386 – 1e. red 80 50
387 – 1e.75 blue 1·40 70
388 – 2e. red 2·40 1·20
389 – 5e. green 5·25 3·00
390 – 10e. blue 14·50 5·25
391 – 20e. brown 19·00 6·25
392 56 10c. red (air) 45 35
393 20c. violet 45 35
394 50c. orange 45 35
395 1e. blue 45 35
396 2e. red 1·00 60
397 3e. green 1·40 85
398 5e. brown 4·00 2·20
399 9e. red 7·75 4·25
400 10e. mauve 8·00 5·50

1948. Fruits.
401 41 5c. black and yellow 50 20
402 – 10c. black and orange 70 45
403 – 30c. slate and grey 3·50 1·90
404 – 50c. brown and yellow 4·00 3·00
405 – 1e. red and pink 4·50 3·00
406 – 1e.75 blue and grey 8·00 5·25
407 – 2e. black and green 7·25 3·00
408 – 5e. brown and mauve 24·00 11·00
409 – 10e. black and mauve 25·00 11·50
410 – 20e. black and grey 49·00 37·00
MS410a 149 × 136 mm. Nos. 401/10 (sold at 42e.50) £140

DESIGNS: 10c. Bread-fruit; 30c. Custard-apple; 50c. Cocoa beans; 1e. Coffee; 1e.75, Dendem; 2e. Abacate; 5e. Pineapple; 10e. Mango; 20e. Coconuts.

42 Our Lady of Fatima **43** Letter and Globe

1948. Honouring the Statue of Our Lady of Fatima.
411 **42** 50c. violet . . . . 5·75 4·75

1949. 75th Anniv of U.P.U.
412 **43** 3e.50 black . . . . 6·75 4·75

44 Bells and Dove **45** Our Lady of Fatima

1950. Holy Year.
413 **44** 2e.50 blue . . . . 2·50 1·60
414 4e. orange . . . . 5·00 3·75

1951. Termination of Holy Year.
415 **45** 4e. indigo and blue . . . . 2·50 1·50

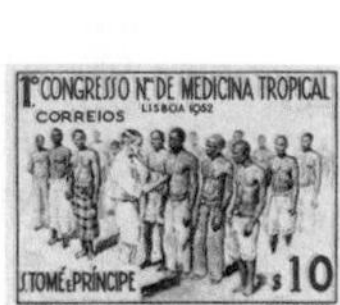

46 Doctor examining Patients **48** J. de Santarem

1952. 1st Tropical Medicine Congress, Lisbon.
416 **46** 10c. blue and brown . . . 30 25

1952. Portuguese Navigators. Multicoloured.
417 10c. Type **48** 10 10
418 30c. P. Escobar 10 10
419 50c. F. de Po 15 10
420 1e. A. Esteves 80 10
421 2e. L. Goncalves 50 15
422 3e.50 M. Fernandes 50 15

49 Cloisters of Monastery **50** Portuguese Stamp of 1853 and Arms of Portuguese Overseas Province

1953. Missionary Art Exhibition.
423 **49** 10c. brown and green . . . 10 10
424 50c. brown and orange . . 65 50
425 3e. indigo and blue . . . . 1·40 1·20

1953. Centenary of First Portuguese Postage Stamps.
426 **50** 50c. multicoloured 75 60

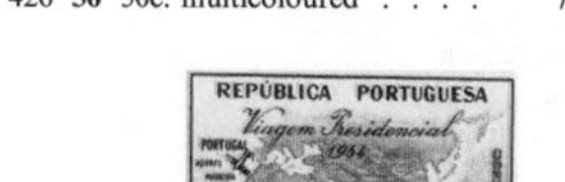

51 Route of President's Tour

1954. Presidential Visit.
427 **51** 15c. multicoloured 10 10
428 5e. multicoloured . . . . . 1·10 75

52 Father M. de Nobrega and View of Sao Paulo

1954. 4th Centenary of Sao Paulo.
429 **52** 2e.50 multicoloured 55 30

53 Exhibition Emblem, Globe and Arms

1958. Brussels International Exhibition.
430 **53** 2e.50 multicoloured 70 45

54 "Cassia occidentalis"

1958. 6th International Congress of Tropical Medicine.
431 **54** 5e. multicoloured . . . . . 2·50 1·60

55 Points of Compass **56** "Religion"

1960. 500th Death Anniv of Prince Henry the Navigator.
432 **55** 10e. multicoloured . . . . 1·10 55

1960. 10th Anniv of African Technical Co-operation Commission.
433 **56** 1e.50 multicoloured 50 30

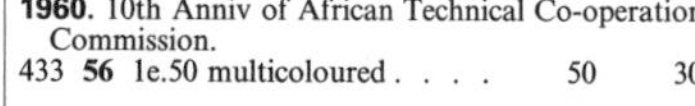

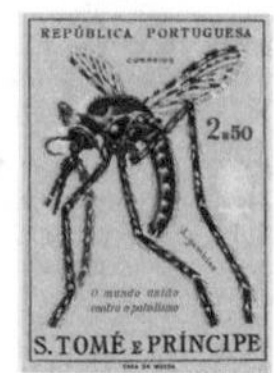

57 Fishing **58** "Anopheles gambiae"

1962. Sports. Multicoloured.
434 50c. Type **57** 10 10
435 1e. Gymnastics 60 15
436 1e.50 Handball 65 25
437 2e. Sailing 70 25
438 2e.50 Running . . . . 1·00 80
439 20e. Skin-diving . . . . . . 3·00 1·20

1962. Malaria Eradication.
440 **58** 2e.50 multicoloured . . . . 1·00 70

59 Map of Africa and Boeing 707 and Lockheed L.1049G Super Constellation Airliners **60** F. de Oliveira Chamico

1963. 10th Anniv of Transportes Aereos Portugueses (airline).
441 **59** 1e.50 multicoloured 65 30

1964. Centenary of National Overseas Bank.
442 **60** 2e.50 multicoloured 70 55

61 I.T.U. Emblem and St. Gabriel **62** Infantry Officer, 1788

1965. Centenary of I.T.U.
443 **61** 2e.50 multicoloured . . . . 1·50 75

1965. Portuguese Military Uniforms. Multicoloured.
444 20c. Type **62** 20 15
445 35c. Infantry sergeant, 1788 20 15
446 40c. Infantry corporal, 1788 20 15
447 1e. Infantryman, 1788 . . . 1·40 55
448 2e.50 Artillery officer, 1806 1·40 60
449 5e. Light infantryman, 1811 2·20 1·40
450 7e.50 Infantry sapper, 1833 3·50 1·80
451 10e. Lancers officer, 1834 . . 4·25 7·25

65 Arts and Crafts School and Anti-Tuberculosis Clinic

1966. 40th Anniv of National Revolution.
452 **65** 4c. multicoloured 65 35

66 C. Rodrigues and Steam Corvette "Vasco da Gama"

1967. Cent of Military Naval Association. Mult.
453 1e.50 Type **66** 75 45
454 2e.50 A. Kopke, microscope and "Glossina palpalis" (insect) . . . . 1·10 70

67 Apparition appearing to Children and Valinhos Monument **68** Medal of the Jeronimos Monastery

1967. 50th Anniv of Fatima Apparitions.
455 **67** 2e.50 multicoloured 25 20

1968. 500th Birth Anniv of Pedro Cabral (explorer).
456 **68** 1e.50 multicoloured 65 40

69 Island Route-map and Monument **70** Da Gama's Fleet and Fireship

1969. Birth Centenary of Admiral Gago Coutinho.
457 **69** 2e. multicoloured 40 25

1969. 500th Birth Anniv of Vasco da Gama (explorer).
458 **70** 2e.50 multicoloured 25 20

71 L. A. Rebello da Silva **72** Manoel Gate, Guarda See

1969. Cent of Overseas Administrative Reforms.
459 **71** 2e.50 multicoloured 20 10

1969. 500th Birth Anniv of King Manoel I.
460 **72** 4e. mulicoloured 40 20

73 Pero Escobar and Joao de Santarem **74** President A. Tomas

1969. 500th Anniv of Discovery of St. Thomas and Prince Islands.
461 **73** 2e.50 multicoloured 25 20

1970. Presidential Visit.
462 **74** 2e.50 multicoloured 40 20

75 Marshal Carmona **76** Stamps on Coffee Plant

1970. Birth Centenary of Marshal Carmona.
463 **75** 5e. multicoloured 25 15

1970. Stamp Centenary. Multicoloured.
464 1e. Type **76** 15 10
465 1e.50 Head Post Office, St. Thomas (horiz) 45 10
466 2e.50 Se Cathedral, St. Thomas 60 30

77 "Descent from the Cross" and Caravel at St. Thomas

1972. 400th Anniv of Camoens' "The Lusiads" (epic poem).
467 **77** 20e. multicoloured . . . . 1·50 20

78 Running and Throwing the Javelin

1972. Olympic Games, Munich.
468 **78** 1e.50 multicoloured 20 15

79 Fairey IIID Seaplane "Lusitania" and Cruiser "Gladiolus" off Rock of San Pedro

1972. 50th Anniv of 1st Flight, Lisbon–Rio de Janeiro.
469 **79** 2e.50 multicoloured 35 20

80 W.M.O. Emblem

1973. Cent of World Meteorological Organization.
470 **80** 5e. multicoloured 55 45

81 Flags of Portugal and St. Thomas and Prince Islands

1975. Independence.

No.	Type	Description	Unused	Used
471	**81**	3e. multicoloured	10	10
472		10e. multicoloured	55	20
473		20e. multicoloured	1·00	55
474		50e. multicoloured	2·50	1·60

82 National Flag

1975. Independence Proclamation.

No.	Type	Description	Unused	Used
475	**82**	1e.50 multicoloured	10	10
476		4e. multicoloured	20	15
477		7e.50 multicoloured	45	35
478		20e. multicoloured	1·00	60
479		50e. multicoloured	2·75	1·60

83 Diagram and Hand

1976. National Reconstruction Fund.

No.	Type	Description	Unused	Used
480	**83**	1e. multicoloured	10	10
481		1e.50 multicoloured	10	10
482		2e. multicoloured	20	10

1976. Optd **Rep. Democr. 12-7-75.**

No.	Type	Description	Unused	Used
483	**48**	10c. Joao de Santarem		
484	**62**	20c. Infantry officer, 1788		
485	–	30c. Pedro Escobar (No. 418)		
486	–	35c. Infantry sergeant, 1788		
487	–	40c. Infantry corporal, 1788		
488	–	50c. Fernao de Po (No. 419)		
489	–	1e. Alvaro Esteves (No. 420)		
490	–	2e.50 Rebello da Silva (No. 459)		
491	**73**	2e.50 Escobar and Santarem		
492	–	3e.50 Martim Fernandes (No. 422)		
493	–	4e. Manoel Gate (No. 460)		
494	–	5e. W.M.O. emblem (No. 470)		
495	–	7e.50 Infantry sapper, 1833 (No. 450)		
496	–	10e. Compass rose (No. 432)		
		Set of 14	4·50	3·25

85 President Pinto da Costa and National Flag

1976. 1st Anniv of Independence.

No.	Type	Description	Unused	Used
497		2e. Type **85**	20	10
498		3e.50 Proclamation of Independence, 12 July 1975	20	10
499		4e.50 As 3e.50	45	20
500		12e.50 Type **85**	90	45

1977. 2nd Anniv of Independence. No. 439 optd **Rep. Democr. 12-7-77.**

No.	Type	Description	Unused	Used
501		20e. multicoloured	80	80

CHARITY TAX STAMPS

The notes under this heading in Portugal also apply here.

1925. Marquis de Pombal Commemoration. As stamps of Portugal, but additionally inscr "S. TOME E PRINCIPE".

No.	Type	Description	Unused	Used
C323	C **73**	15c. black and orange	50	30
C324	–	15c. black and orange	50	30
C325	C **75**	15c. black and orange	50	30

1946. Fiscal stamps as in Type C **1** of Portuguese Colonies surch **Assistencia** and new value.

No.	Type	Description	Unused	Used
C401		50c. on 1e. green	15·00	
C402		50c. on 4e. red	20·00	
C403		1e. on 4e. red	20·00	
C404		1e. on 5e. red	20·00	
C407		1e. on 6e. green	4·25	
C408		1e. on 7e. green	4·25	
C409		1e. on 10e. red	20·00	
C410		1e.50 on 7e. green	15·00	
C411		1e.50 on 8e. green	18·00	
C412		2e.50 on 7e. green	18·00	
C413		2e.50 on 9e. green	18·00	
C414		2e.50 on 10e. green	15·00	

40 Arms

1948. Value in black.

No.	Type	Description	Unused	Used
C415	**40**	50c. green	80	70
C416		1e. pink	2·00	1·50
C417		1e. green	95	70
C418		1e.50 brown	2·40	1·90

1965. (a) Surch **um escudo 1$00** and two heavy bars.

No.	Type	Description	Unused	Used
C452	**40**	1e. on 5e. yellow	1·20	85

(b) Surch **Um escudo.**

No.	Type	Description	Unused	Used
C453	**40**	1e. on 1e. green	1·60	1·50

(c) As No. C 417 but inscr "UM ESCUDO" at foot, surch **1$00.**

No.	Type	Description	Unused	Used
C454	**40**	1e. on 1e. green	1·20	1·10

(d) Previous surch "Cinco escudos" obliterated and further surch **Um escudo 1$00.**

No.	Type	Description	Unused	Used
C455	**40**	1e. on 5e. yellow	2·75	2·20

NEWSPAPER STAMPS

1982. Surch **2½ RS.** No gum.

No.	Type	Description	Unused	Used
N53	Q	2½r. on 5r. black	46·00	39·00
N54		2½r. on 10r. green	60·00	55·00
N55		2½r. on 20r. red	95·00	75·00

1893. "Newspaper" key-type inscr "S. THOME E PRINCIPE".

No.	Type	Description	Unused	Used
N59	V	2½r. brown	80	75

1899. No. N59 optd **PROVISORIO.**

No.	Type	Description	Unused	Used
N81	V	2½r. brown	43·00	20·00

POSTAGE DUE STAMPS

D 14

1904. "Due" key-type inscr "S. THOME E PRINCIPE". Name and value in black.

No.	Type	Description	Unused	Used
D121	W	5r. green	70	60
D122		10r. grey	95	80
D123		20r. brown	95	80
D124		30r. orange	95	80
D125		50r. brown	1·70	1·20
D126		60r. brown	2·40	1·60
D127		100r. mauve	4·00	2·50
D128		130r. blue	4·00	2·50
D129		200r. red	4·25	3·00
D130		500r. lilac	7·75	6·00

1911. As last optd **REPUBLICA.**

No.	Type	Description	Unused	Used
D137	W	5r. green	25	25
D138		10r. grey	25	25
D139		20r. brown	25	25
D140		30r. orange	25	25
D141		50r. brown	35	30
D142		60r. brown	95	70
D143		100r. mauve	95	70
D144		130r. blue	95	70
D145		200r. red	80	70
D146		500r. lilac	2·10	1·40

1921. "Due" key-type inscr "S. TOME E PRINCIPE". Currency changed.

No.	Type	Description	Unused	Used
D313	W	½c. green	4·25	3·25
D314		1c. grey	6·00	3·25
D315		2c. brown	60	45
D316		3c. orange	4·25	3·25
D317		5c. brown	4·25	3·75
D318		6c. brown	4·25	3·75
D319		10c. mauve	4·25	3·75
D320		13c. blue	8·50	7·75
D321a		20c. red	10·00	9·25
D322a		50c. lilac	10·00	9·25

1925. Nos. C323/5 optd **MULTA.**

No.	Type	Description	Unused	Used
D323	C **73**	30c. black and orange	50	30
D324	–	30c. black and orange	50	30
D325	C **75**	30c. black and orange	50	30

1925. Numerals in red, name in black.

No.	Type	Description	Unused	Used
D417	D **14**	10c. brown and yellow	20	15
D418		30c. brown and blue	20	15
D419		50c. blue and pink	20	15
D420		1e. blue and olive	20	20
D421		2e. green and orange	25	25
D422		5e. brown and lilac	45	30

APPENDIX

The following stamps have either been issued in excess of postal needs or have not been available to the public in reasonable quantities at face value. Such stamps may later be given full listing if there is evidence of regular postal use.

1977.

400th Birth Anniv of Rubens. 1, 5, 10, 15, 20, 50e.

150th Death Anniv of Beethoven. 20, 30, 50e.

Centenary of U.P.U. Surch on Navigators and Military Uniforms issues of Portuguese administration. 1e. on 10c., 3e. on 30c., 3e.50 on 3e.50, 5e. on 50c., 10e. on 10c., 15e. on 3e.50, 20e. on 30e. on 30c., 35e. on 35c., 40e. on 40c.

Christmas. 5, 10, 25, 50, 70d.

60th Anniv of Russian Revolution. 15, 30, 40, 50d.

1st Death Anniv of Mao Tse-tung. 50d.

1978.

Nobel Peace Prizes to International Organizations. Surch on Navigators and Military Uniforms issues of Portuguese administration. 3d. on 30c., 5d. on 50c., 10d. on 10c., 15d. on 3e.50, 20d. on 20c., 35d. on 35c.

3rd Anniv of Independence. 5d. × 3.

3rd Anniv of Admission to United Nations. Surch on Military Uniform issue. 40d. on 40c.

International Stamp Exhibition, Essen. 10d. × 5.

Centenary of U.P.U. 5d. × 4, 15d. × 4.

1st Anniv of New Currency. 5d. × 5, 8d. × 5.

World Cup Football Championship, Argentina. 3d. × 4, 25d. × 3.

1979.

World Cup Winners. Optd on 1978 World Cup issues. 3d. × 4, 25d. × 3.

Butterflies. 50c., 10d., 11d. × 4.

Flowers. 1d., 8d. × 4, 25d.

Telecommunications Day and 50th Anniv of C.C.I.R. 1, 11, 14, 17d.

International Year of the Child. 1, 7, 14, 17d.

450th Death Anniv of Durer. 50c. × 2, 1, 7, 8, 25d.

History of Aviation. 50c., 1, 5, 7, 8, 17d.

History of Navigation. 50c., 1, 3, 5, 8, 25d.

Birds. Postage 50c. × 2, 1, 7, 8d.; Air 100d.

1980.

Fishes. Postage 50c., 1, 5, 7, 8d.; Air 50d.

Balloons. 50c., 1, 3, 7, 8, 25d.

Airships. 50c., 1, 3, 7, 8, 17d.

Olympic Games. 50c., 11d. × 4.

Death Centenary of Sir Rowland Hill. 50c., 1, 8, 20d.

10th Anniv of First Manned Moon Landing. 50c., 1, 14, 17d.

1981.

Olympic Games, Moscow. Optd on 1977 Mao Tse-tung issue. 50d.

ST. VINCENT Pt. 1

One of the Windward Islands, British West Indies.

1861. 12 pence = 1 shilling;
20 shillings = 1 pound.
1949. 100 cents = 1 West Indian dollar.

7

1

3

1861.

No.	Type	Description	Unused	Used
36	**7**	½d. orange	7·00	4·25
47		½d. green	1·00	60
48b	**1**	1d. red	1·60	85
18		1d. black	50·00	9·00
29		1d. green	£140	4·25
39		1d. drab	50·00	2·25
61		2½d. blue	4·50	1·75
6		4d. blue	£275	£110
56		4d. yellow	1·60	8·50
51		4d. brown	65·00	75
62		5d. sepia	5·50	22·00
4		6d. green	55·00	18·00
57		6d. purple	2·25	14·00
11		1s. grey	£250	£120
13		1s. blue	£350	90·00
14		1s. brown	£475	£160
45		1s. red	£120	60·00
58		1s. orange	5·50	11·00
53	**3**	5s. lake	27·00	50·00

1880. Surch in figures.

No.	Type	Description	Unused	Used
33	**1**	½d. on half 6d. green	£160	£160
28		1d. on half 6d. green	£475	£350

1881. Surch in words.

No.	Type	Description	Unused	Used
34	**1**	1d. on 6d. green	£450	£325
63		3d. on 1d. mauve	5·00	17·00
60a		5d. on 6d. lake	1·00	1·75

1881. Surch in figures.

No.	Type	Description	Unused	Used
54	**1**	2½d. on 4d. brown	80·00	£110
35		4d. on 1s. orange	£1500	£800

1882. Surch in figures and words.

No.	Type	Description	Unused	Used
40	**1**	2½d. on 1d. red	17·00	1·00
55a		2½d. on 1d. blue	1·50	35
59		5d. on 4d. brown	20·00	32·00

1885. No. 40 further surch **1d** and bars.

No.	Type	Description	Unused	Used
46	**1**	1d. on 2½d. on 1d. lake	22·00	17·00

13

17 Seal of the Colony

1899.

No.	Type	Description	Unused	Used
67	**13**	½d. mauve and green	2·75	2·50
68		1d. mauve and red	4·50	1·25
69		2½d. mauve and blue	4·00	2·00
70		3d. mauve and green	4·00	13·00
71		4d. mauve and orange	4·00	17·00
72		5d. mauve and black	7·00	13·00
73		6d. mauve and brown	13·00	35·00
74		1s. green and red	13·00	48·00
75		5s. green and blue	75·00	£140

1902. As T **13**, but portait of King Edward VII.

No.	Type	Description	Unused	Used
85a		½d. purple and green	1·25	1·25
77		1d. purple and red	4·25	30
78		2d. purple and black	2·75	2·50
79		2½d. purple and blue	5·00	3·50
80		3d. purple and green	5·00	3·50
81		6d. purple and brown	11·00	30·00
90a		1s. green and red	11·00	55·00
83		2s. green and violet	25·00	55·00
91		2s. purple and blue on blue	23·00	42·00
84		5s. green and red	70·00	£120
92		5s. green and red on yellow	17·00	50·00
93		£1 purple and black on red	£275	£325

1907.

No.	Type	Description	Unused	Used
94	**17**	½d. green	3·25	2·25
95		1d. red	3·50	15
96		2d. orange	1·50	6·50
97		2½d. blue	28·00	8·50
98		3d. violet	8·00	15·00

18 Seal of the Colony

19

1909.

No.	Type	Description	Unused	Used
102	**18**	½d. green	1·50	60
99		1d. red	1·25	30
104		2d. grey	4·00	8·50
105		2½d. blue	8·00	3·50
106		3d. purple on yellow	2·50	7·50
107		6d. purple	10·00	5·00
101		1s. black on green	4·25	8·50
139		2s. blue and purple	7·50	13·00
140		5s. red and green	18·00	32·00
141		£1 mauve and black	90·00	£130

1913.

No.	Type	Description	Unused	Used
108	**19**	½d. green	75	20
109		1d. red	80	75
132b		1½d. brown	3·25	15
133		2d. grey	2·50	80
111		2½d. blue	50	75
135		3d. purple on yellow	1·00	1·50
134		3d. blue	1·00	6·00
113		4d. red on yellow	80	2·00
136		5d. green	1·00	6·50
137		6d. purple	1·50	3·50
116		1s. black on green	1·50	3·75
138a		1s. brown	3·25	17·00

1915. Surch **ONE PENNY.**

No.	Type	Description	Unused	Used
121	**19**	1d. on 1s. black on green	7·50	27·00

1916. Optd **WAR STAMP.** in two lines.

No.	Type	Description	Unused	Used
122	**19**	1d. red	7·00	9·50

1916. Optd **WAR STAMP.** in one line.

No.	Type	Description	Unused	Used
126	**19**	1d. red	30	80

1935. Silver Jubilee. As T **32a** of St. Helena.

No.	Type	Description	Unused	Used
142		1d. blue and red	40	2·75
143		1½d. blue and grey	1·00	3·50
144		2½d. brown and blue	1·90	3·50
145		1s. grey and purple	2·00	3·50

1937. Coronation. As T **32b** of St. Helena.
146 1d. violet . . . . 35 1·25
147 1½d. red . . . . 40 1·25
148 2½d. blue . . . . 45 2·25

25 **26** Young's Island and Fort Duvernette

1938.
149 **25** ½d. blue and green . . . 20 10
150 **26** 1d. blue and brown . . . 20 10
151 – 1½d. green and red . . . 20 10
152 **25** 2d. green and black . . . 40 35
153 – 2½d. black and green . . 20 40
153a – 2½d. green and brown . . 40 20
154 **25** 3d. orange and purple . . 20 10
154a – 3½d. blue and green . . . 40 2·50
155 **25** 6d. black and lake . . . 1·00 40
156 – 1s. purple and green . . . 1·00 80
157 **25** 2s. blue and purple . . . 6·00 75
157a 2s.6d. brown and blue . . 1·25 3·50
158 5s. red and green . . . . 10·00 2·50
158a 10s. violet and brown . . 4·00 9·00
159 £1 purple and black . . . 17·00 15·00
DESIGNS—HORIZ: 1½d. Kingstown and Fort Charlotte; 2½d. (No. 153), 3½d. Bathing beach at Villa; 2½d. (No. 153a), 1s. Victoria Park, Kingstown.

1946. Victory. As T **33a** of St. Helena.
160 1½d. red 10 10
161 3½d. blue 10 10

1948. Silver Wedding. As T **33b/c** of St Helena.
162 1½d. red 10 10
163 £1 mauve . . . . 16·00 19·00

1949. As 1938 issue, but values in cents and dollars.
164 **25** 1c. blue and green . . . . 20 1·75
164a 1c. green and black . . . 30 2·50
165 **26** 2c. blue and brown . . . 15 50
166 – 3c. green and red . . . . 50 1·00
166a **25** 3c. orange and purple . . 30 2·50
167 4c. green and black . . . 35 20
167a 4c. blue and green . . . 30 20
168 – 5c. green and brown . . . 15 10
169 **25** 6c. orange and purple . . 50 1·25
169a – 6c. green and red . . . 30 2·25
170 – 7c. black and blue . . . . 5·50 1·50
170a – 10c. black and turquoise 50 20
171 **25** 12c. black and lake . . . 35 15
172 – 24c. purple and green . . 35 55
173 **25** 48c. blue and purple . . . 2·75 2·75
174 60c. brown and blue . . . 2·00 4·00
175 $1.20 red and green . . . 4·25 4·25
176 $2.40 violet and brown . . 6·00 10·00
177 $4.80 purple and black . . 12·00 20·00
DESIGNS—HORIZ: 3c. (No. 166), 6c. (No. 169a) Kingstown and Fort Charlotte; 5, 24c. Victoria Park, Kingstown; 7, 10c. Bathing beach at Villa.

1949. U.P.U. As T **33d/g** of St. Helena.
178 5c. blue 20 20
179 6c. purple . . . . 1·25 2·25
180 12c. mauve . . . . 20 2·25
181 24c. green . . . . 20 1·00

1951. Inauguration of B.W.I. University College. As T **10a/b** of St. Kitts-Nevis.
182 **18** 3c. green and red 65 50
183 **19** 12c. black and purple . . . 30 1·75

1951. New Constitution. Optd **NEW CONSTITUTION 1951.**
184 – 3c. green and red (No. 166) 20 1·75
185 **25** 4c. green and black 20 60
186 – 5c. green & brn (No. 168) 20 60
187 **25** 12c. black and lake . . . . 1·25 1·25

1953. Coronation. As T **33h** of St. Helena.
188 4c. black and green 30 20

30 31

1955.
189 **30** 1c. orange 10 10
190 2c. blue 10 10
191 3c. grey 30 10
192 4c. brown 20 10
215 5c. red 15 10
216 10c. lilac 15 10
195 15c. blue 65 30
218 20c. green 45 10
197 25c. sepia 50 10
198 **31** 50c. brown . . . . 5·00 1·75
199 $1 green . . . . 8·00 1·00
200 $2.50 blue . . . . 8·00 8·00

1958. British Caribbean Federation. As T **27a** of St. Kitts-Nevis.
201 3c. green 30 20
202 6c. blue . . . . 35 1·25
203 12c. red 45 50

1963. Freedom from Hunger. As T **63a** of St. Helena.
204 8c. violet 60 50

1963. Cent of Red Cross. As T **63b** of St. Helena.
205 4c. red and black 15 20
206 8c. red and blue 35 50

32 Scout Badge and Proficiency Badges **33** Tropical Fruits

1964. 50th Anniv of St. Vincent Boy Scouts Association.
221 **32** 1c. green and brown . . . 10 10
222 4c. blue and purple 10 10
223 20c. yellow and violet . . . 30 10
224 50c. red and green 45 70

1965. Bicentenary of Botanic Gardens. Mult.
225 1c. Type **33** 10 10
226 4c. Breadfruit and H.M.S. "Providence" (sloop), 1793 10 10
227 25c. Doric Temple and pond (vert) 15 10
228 40c. Talipot palm and Doric Temple (vert) . . . . . . 30 1·25

1965. Cent of I.T.U. As T **64a** of St. Helena.
229 4c. blue and green 15 10
230 48c. ochre and orange . . . 35 45

37 Boat-building, Bequia

1965. Multicoloured.
231 1c. Type **37** (inscr "BEOUIA") 10 85
231a 1c. Type **37** (inscr "BEQUIA") 65 40
232 2c. Friendship Beach, Bequia 10 10
233 3c. Terminal Building, Arnos Vale Airport . . . 60 10
261 4c. Woman with bananas 30 30
235 5c. Crater Lake 15 10
236 6c. Carib stone 15 40
237 8c. Arrowroot 30 10
238 10c. Owia Salt Pond 30 10
239 12c. Deep water wharf . . . 70 10
240 20c. Sea island cotton . . . 30 10
241 25c. Map of St. Vincent and islands 35 10
242 50c. Breadfruit 50 30
243 $1 Baleine Falls . . . . . 3·00 30
244 $2.50 St. Vincent amazon 18·00 8·00
245 $5 Arms of St. Vincent . . 3·00 10·00
Nos. 261, 236/7 and 240/5 are vert.

1966. Churchill Commem. As T **64b** of St. Helena.
246 1c. blue 10 10
247 4c. green 20 10
248 20c. brown 35 30
249 40c. violet . . . . 55 1·00

1966. Royal Visit. As T **48a** of St. Kitts-Nevis.
250 4c. black, green and blue . . 50 20
251 25c. black and mauve . . . . 1·00 80

1966. Inauguration of W.H.O. Headquarters, Geneva. As T **64e** of St. Helena.
252 4c. black, green and blue . . 25 10
253 25c. black, purple and ochre 50 80

1966. 20th Anniv of UNESCO. As T **64f/h** of St. Helena.
254 4c. multicoloured 30 10
255 8c. yellow, violet and olive 55 10
256 25c. black, purple and orange 1·25 60

38 Coastal View of Mount Coke Area

1967. Autonomous Methodist Church. Mult.
257 2c. Type **38** 10 10
258 8c. Kingstown Methodist Church 10 10
259 25c. First licence to perform marriages 25 10
260 35c. Conference Arms . . . 25 10

39 Meteorological Institute

1968. World Meteorological Day.
262 **39** 4c. multicoloured 10 10
263 25c. multicoloured 10 10
264 35c. multicoloured 15 15

40 Dr. Martin Luther King and Cotton Pickers

1968. Dr. Martin Luther King Commem.
265 **40** 5c. multicoloured 10 10
266 25c. multicoloured 10 10
267 35c. multicoloured 15 15

41 Speaker addressing Demonstrators

1968. Human Rights Year.
268 **41** 3c. multicoloured 10 10
269 – 35c. blue 20 10
DESIGN—VERT: 35c. Scales of Justice and Human Rights emblem.

43 Male Masquerader

1969. St. Vincent Carnival.
270 **43** 1c. multicoloured 10 10
271 – 5c. red and brown 10 10
272 – 8c. multicoloured 10 10
273 – 25c. multicoloured 15 20
DESIGNS—VERT: 5c. Steel bandsman; 25c. Queen of Bands. HORIZ: 8c. Carnival revellers.

1969. Methodist Conference. Nos. 241, 257/8 and 260 optd **METHODIST CONFERENCE MAY 1969.**
274 **38** 2c. multicoloured 10 15
275 – 8c. multicoloured 15 25
276 – 25c. multicoloured 15 25
277 – 35c. multicoloured . . . . 75 2·00

48 "Strength in Unity"

1969. 1st Anniv of C.A.R.I.F.T.A.
278 **48** 2c. black, buff and red . . 10 10
279 – 5c. multicoloured 10 10
280 **48** 8c. black, buff and green 10 10
281 – 25c. multicoloured 35 15
DESIGN—VERT: 5, 25c. Map.

50 Flag of St. Vincent

1969. Statehood.
282 **50** 4c. multicoloured 10 10
283 – 10c. multicoloured 10 10
284 – 50c. grey, black and orange 35 20
DESIGNS: 10c. Battle scene with insets of Petroglyph and Carib Chief Chatoyer; 50c. Carib House with maces and scales.

51 Green-backed Heron ("Green Heron")

1970. Multicoloured.
285 ½c. House wren . . . . . . 10 1·25
286a 1c. Type **51** . . . . 30 1·50
287 2c. Lesser Antillean bullfinches ("Bullfinches") 15 40
288 3c. St. Vincent amazon ("St. Vincent Parrot") . . 15 30
289 4c. Rufous-throated solitaire ("Soufriere Bird") 20 30
364 5c. Red-necked pigeon ("Ramier") 30 20
291 6c. Bananaquits 30 40
292 8c. Purple-throated Carib ("Hummingbird") 40 30
293 10c. Mangrove cuckoo . . . 30 10
294 12c. Common black hawk ("Black Hawk") 40 10
295 20c. Bare-eyed thrush . . . 40 15
296 25c. Lesser Antillean tanager ("Prince") 50 20
297 50c. Blue hooded euphonia 2·00 75
298 $1 Barn owl . . . . 5·00 2·00
299 $2.50 Yellow-bellied elaenia ("Crested Elaenia") . . . 3·25 5·50
300 $5 Ruddy quail dove . . . 3·50 6·50
Nos. 285, 289, 364, 293/4 and 298/9 are vert.

52 De Havilland D.H.C.6 Twin Otter 100

1970. 20th Anniv of Regular Air Services. Multicoloured.
301 5c. Type **52** 10 10
302 8c. Grumman Goose 15 10
303 10c. Hawker Siddeley H.S.748 . . . . 20 10
304 25c. Douglas DC-3 . . . . . 65 30

53 "Children's Nursery"

1970. Centenary of British Red Cross. Mult.
305 3c. Type **53** 10 10
306 5c. "First Aid" 15 10
307 12c. "Voluntary Aid Detachment" . . . . . . 35 1·00
308 25c. "Blood Transfusion" . . 55 50

54 "Angel and the Two Marys at the Tomb" (stained-glass window)

1970. 150th Anniv of St. George's Cathedral, Kingstown. Multicoloured.
309 ½c. Type **54** 10 10
310 5c. St. George's Cathedral (horiz) 10 10
311 25c. Tower, St. George's Cathedral 10 10
312 35c. Interior, St. George's Cathedral (horiz) 15 10
313 50c. Type **54** 20 30

55 "The Adoration of the Shepherds" (Le Nain)

1970. Christmas. Multicoloured.
314 8c. "The Virgin and Child" (Bellini) (vert) 10 10
315 25c. Type **55** 10 10
316 35c. As 8c. 10 10
317 50c. Type **55** 15 20

56 New Post Office and 6d. Stamp of 1861

1971. 110th Anniv of First St. Vincent Stamps. Multicoloured.

318	2c. Type **56**	10	10
319	4c. 1d. stamp of 1861 and new Post Office	10	10
320	25c. Type **56**	10	10
321	$1 As 4c.	35	45

57 Trust Seal and Wildlife

1971. St. Vincent's National Trust. Mult.

322	12c. Type **57**	40	1·10
323	30c. Old cannon, Fort Charlotte	20	25
324	40c. Type **57**	50	40
325	45c. As 30c.	30	1·25

58 "Madonna appearing to St. Anthony" (Tiepolo)

59 Careening

1971. Christmas. Multicoloured.

326	5c. Type **58**	10	10
327	10c. "The Holy Family on the Flight into Egypt" (detail, Pietro da Cortona)	10	10
328	25c. Type **58**	10	10
329	$1 As 10c.	40	35

1971. The Grenadines of St. Vincent. Multicoloured.

330	1c. Type **59**	10	10
331	5c. Seine fishermen	10	10
332	6c. Map of the Grenadines	10	10
333	15c. Type **59**	20	10
334	20c. As 5c.	20	10
335	50c. As 6c.	65	1·00
MS336	177 × 140 mm. Nos. 330/5	6·00	9·50

60 Private, Grenadier Company, 32nd Foot (1764)

61 Breadnut Fruit

1972. Military Uniforms.

337	**60** 12c. multicoloured	50	30
338	– 30c. multicoloured	55	50
339	– 50c. multicoloured	60	1·25

DESIGNS: 30c. Officer, Battalion Company, 31st Foot (1772); 50c. Private, Grenadier Company, 6th Foot (1772).

1972. Fruit. Multicoloured.

340	3c. Type **61**	10	40
341	5c. Pawpaw	10	20
342	12c. Plumrose or roseapple	15	50
343	25c. Mango	35	70

62 Candlestick Cassia

1972. Flowers. Multicoloured.

344	1c. Type **62**	10	10
345	30c. Lobster claw	10	10
346	40c. White trumpet	15	15
347	$1 Soufriere tree	35	1·25

63 Sir Charles Brisbane and Coat of Arms

1972. Birth Bicentenary of Sir Charles Brisbane.

348	**63** 20c. brown, gold and red	15	10
349	– 30c. yellow, mauve & black	35	10
350	– $1 multicoloured	60	70
MS351	171 × 111 mm. Nos. 348/50 (sold at $2)	4·00	6·50

DESIGNS: 30c. H.M.S. "Arethusa", 1807; $1 H.M.S. "Blake", 1808.

1972. Royal Silver Wedding. As T **52** of Ascension, but with Arrowroot and Breadfruit in background.

352	30c. brown	10	10
353	$1 green	20	20

65 Sighting of St. Vincent

1973. 475th Anniv of Columbus's Third Voyage to the West Indies. Multicoloured.

354	5c. Type **65**	20	30
355	12c. Caribs watching Columbus's fleet	25	50
356	30c. Christopher Columbus	40	70
357	50c. "Santa Maria"	70	2·25

66 "The Last Supper" (French stained-glass window)

1973. Easter.

358	**66** 15c. multicoloured	10	10
359	– 60c. multicoloured	20	20
360	– $1 multicoloured	20	20

Nos. 358/60 are in the form of a triptych and make a composite design depicting "The Last Supper".

67 William Wilberforce and Poster

1973. 140th Death Anniv of William Wilberforce. Multicoloured.

369	30c. Type **67**	15	10
370	40c. Slaves cutting cane	20	15
371	50c. Wilberforce and medallion	20	15

68 P.P.F. Symbol

71 "The Descent from the Cross" (Sansovino)

69 Administration Block, Mona

1973. 21st Anniv of International Planned Parenthood Federation. Multicoloured.

372	12c. Type **68**	10	10
373	40c. "IPPF" and symbol	20	20

1973. Royal Wedding. As T **103a** of St. Helena. Multicoloured, background colours given.

374	50c. blue	15	10
375	70c. green	15	10

1973. 25th Anniv of West Indies University. Multicoloured.

376	5c. Type **69**	10	10
377	10c. University Centre, Kingstown	10	10
378	30c. Aerial view, Mona University	15	10
379	$1 University coat of arms (vert)	35	60

1973. Nos. 297, 292 and 298 surch.

380	30c. on 50c. multicoloured	1·25	1·00
381	40c. on 8c. multicoloured	1·25	1·00
382	$10 on $1 multicoloured	4·00	8·50

1974. Easter. Multicoloured.

383	5c. Type **71**	10	10
384	30c. "The Deposition" (English, 14th-century)	10	10
385	40c. "Pieta" (Fernandez)	10	10
386	$1 "The Resurrection" (French, 16th-century)	20	25

72 "Istra"

1974. Cruise Ships. Multicoloured.

387	15c. Type **72**	15	10
388	20c. "Oceanic"	20	10
389	30c. "Aleksandr Pushkin"	20	10
390	$1 "Europa"	35	1·25
MS391	134 × 83 mm. Nos. 387/90	1·00	3·00

73 U.P.U. Emblem

1974. Centenary of U.P.U. Multicoloured.

392	5c. Type **73**	10	10
393	12c. Globe within posthorn	10	10
394	60c. Map of St. Vincent and hand-cancelling	20	10
395	90c. Map of the World	25	30

74 Royal Tern

1974. Multicoloured.

396	30c. Type **74**	2·00	90
397	40c. Brown pelican	2·00	90
398	$10 Magnificent frigate bird ("Frigatebird")	7·50	7·00

75 Scout Badge and Emblems

76 Sir Winston Churchill

1974. Diamond Jubilee of Scout Movement in St. Vincent.

399	**75** 10c. multicoloured	10	10
400	25c. multicoloured	20	10
401	45c. multicoloured	20	15
402	$1 multicoloured	35	1·40

1974. Birth Centenary of Sir Winston Churchill. Multicoloured.

403	25c. Type **76**	10	10
404	35c. Churchill in military uniform	15	10
405	45c. Churchill in naval uniform	15	10
406	$1 Churchill in air force uniform	20	50

77 The Shepherds

1974. Christmas.

407	**77** 3c. blue and black	10	10
408	– 3c. blue and black	10	10
409	– 3c. blue and black	10	10
410	– 3c. blue and black	10	10
411	**77** 8c. green and black	10	10
412	– 35c. pink and black	10	10
413	– 45c. brown and black	10	10
414	– $1 mauve and black	20	50

DESIGNS: Nos. 408, 411, Mary and crib; Nos. 409, 413, Joseph, ox and ass; Nos. 410, 414, The Magi.

78 Faces

1975. Kingstown Carnival. Mult.

415	1c. Type **78**	10	10
416	15c. Pineapple women	15	15
417	25c. King of the Bands	15	15
418	35c. Carnival dancers	15	15
419	45c. Queen of the Bands	15	20
420	$1.25 "African Splendour"	25	55
MS421	146 × 128 mm. Nos. 415/20	1·00	3·00

79 French Angelfish

1975. Marine Life. Multicoloured.

422	1c. Type **79**	15	80
423	2c. Spot-finned butterflyfish	15	1·00
424	3c. Yellow jack	15	55
425	4c. Spanish mackerel	20	10
426	5c. French grunt	20	45
427	6c. Spotted goatfish	20	1·00
428	8c. Ballyhoo	20	2·75
429	10c. Sperm whale	50	10
430	12c. Humpback whale	50	2·50
431	15c. Scribbled cowfish	1·25	2·50
432	15c. Skipjack tuna	3·50	2·50
433	20c. Queen angelfish	30	10
434	25c. Princess parrotfish	30	20
435	35c. Red hind	65	2·75
436	45c. Atlantic flyingfish	80	1·25
437	50c. Porkfish	50	3·00
438	70c. Yellow-finned tuna	6·50	3·25
439	90c. Pompano	6·50	70
440	$1 Queen triggerfish	50	20
441a	$2.50 Sailfish	75	1·25
442	$5 Dolphin (fish)	3·25	2·50
443	$10 Blue marlin	2·00	7·50

80 Cutting Bananas

1975. Banana Industry. Multicoloured.

447 25c. Type **80** 10 10
448 35c. Packaging Station, La Croix 10 10
449 45c. Cleaning and boxing . . 15 10
450 70c. Shipping bananas aboard "Geestide" (freighter) 35 30

81 Snorkel Diving

1975. Tourism. Multicoloured.

451 15c. Type **81** 40 15
452 20c. Aquaduct Golf Course 1·50 1·50
453 35c. Steel band at Mariner's Inn 45 15
454 45c. Sunbathing at Young Island 45 15
455 $1.25 Yachting marina . . . 1·40 3·00

82 George Washington, John Adams, Thomas Jefferson and James Madison

1975. Bicentenary of American Revolution.

456 **82** ½c. black and mauve . . . 10 20
457 – 1c. black and green 10 20
458 – 1½c. black and mauve . . . 10 20
459 – 5c. black and green 10 10
460 – 10c. black and blue 10 10
461 – 25c. black and yellow . . . 10 10
462 – 35c. black and blue 10 10
463 – 45c. black and red 10 10
464 – $1 black and orange . . . 20 40
465 – $2 black and green 30 85
MS466 179 × 156 mm. Nos. 456/65 1·00 1·50

PRESIDENTS: 1c. Monroe, Quincy Adams, Jackson, van Buren; 1½c. W. Harrison, Tyler, Polk, Taylor; 5c. Fillmore, Pierce, Buchanan, Lincoln; 10c. Andrew Johnson, Grant, Hayes, Garfield; 25c. Arthur, Cleveland, B. Harrison, McKinley; 35c. Theodore Roosevelt, Taft, Wilson, Harding; 45c. Coolidge, Hoover, Franklin Roosevelt, Truman; $1 Eisenhower, Kennedy, Lyndon Johnson, Nixon; $2 Pres. Ford and White House.

83/4 "Shepherds"

1975. Christmas.

467A – 3c. black and mauve . . 10 25
468A – 3c. black and mauve . . 10 25
469A – 3c. black and mauve . . 10 25
470A – 3c. black and mauve . . 10 25
471A – 8c. black and blue . . . 10 25
472A – 8c. black and blue . . . 10 25
473A – 35c. black and yellow . . 15 20
474A – 35c. black and yellow . . 15 20
475A **83** 45c. black and green . . 15 20
476A **84** 45c. black and green . . 15 20
477A – $1 black and purple . . . 30 80
478A – $1 black and purple . . . 30 80

DESIGNS: No. 467, "Star of Bethlehem"; No. 468, "Holy Trinity"; No. 469, As Type **83**; No. 470, "Three Kings"; Nos. 471/2, As No. 467; Nos. 473/4, As No. 468; Nos. 475/6, Types **83/4**; Nos. 477/8, As No. 470. The two designs of each value (Nos. 471/8) differ in that the longest side is at the foot or at the top as shown in Types **83/4**.

85 Carnival Dancers

1976. Kingstown Carnival. Mult.

479 1c. Type **85** 10 10
480 2c. Humpty-Dumpty people 10 10
481 5c. Smiling faces 10 10
482 35c. Dragon worshippers . . 15 10
483 45c. Carnival tableaux . . . 20 10
484 $1.25 Bumble-bee dancers . . 30 50

1976. Nos. 424 and 437 surch.

485 70c. on 3c. Horse-eyed jack 55 1·00
486 90c. on 50c. Porkfish . . . . 55 1·25

87 Blue-headed Hummingbird and Yellow Hibiscus

1976. Hummingbirds and Hibiscuses. Mult.

487 5c. Type **87** 30 15
488 10c. Antillean crested hummingbird ("Crested Hummingbird") and pink hibiscus 35 15
489 35c. Purple-throated carib and white hibiscus 45 10
490 45c. Blue-headed hummingbird and red hibiscus 45 10
491 $1.25 Green-throated carib and peach hibiscus . . . . 1·40 4·00

1976. West Indian Victory in World Cricket Cup. As Nos. 431/2 of St. Lucia.

492 15c. Map of the Caribbean 60 25
493 45c. Prudential Cup . . . . 80 1·00

88 St. Mary Church, Kingstown

1976. Christmas. Multicoloured.

494 35c. Type **88** 15 10
495 45c. Anglican Church, Georgetown 15 10
496 50c. Methodist Church, Georgetown 20 10
497 $1.25 St. George's Cathedral, Kingstown 40 60

89 Barrancoid Pot-stand

1977. National Trust. Multicoloured.

498 5c. Type **89** 10 10
499 45c. National Museum . . . 15 10
500 70c. Carib sculpture 20 20
501 $1 Ciboney petroglyph . . . 30 50

90 William I, William II, Henry I and Stephen

1977. Silver Jubilee. Multicoloured.

502 ½c. Type **90** 10 30
503 1c. Henry II, Richard I, John, Henry III 10 30
504 1½c. Edward I, Edward II, Edward III, Richard II . . 10 30
505 2c. Henry IV, Henry V, Henry VI, Edward IV . . 10 30
506 5c. Edward V, Richard III, Henry VII, Henry VIII . . 10 10
507 10c. Edward VI, Lady Jane Grey, Mary I, Elizabeth I 10 10
508 25c. James I, Charles I, Charles II, James II . . . 10 10
509 35c. William III, Mary II, Anne, George I 10 10
510 45c. George II, George III, George IV 10 10
511 75c. William IV, Victoria, Edward VII 15 25
512 $1 George V, Edward VIII, George VI 20 40
513 $2 Elizabeth II leaving Westminster Abbey 30 60
MS514 170 × 146 mm. Nos. 502/13 1·00 2·00

91 Grant of Arms

1977. Centenary of Windward Islands Diocese. Multicoloured.

527 15c. Type **91** 10 10
528 35c. Bishop Berkeley and mitres 10 10
529 45c. Map and arms of diocese 10 10
530 $1.25 St. George's Cathedral and Bishop Woodroffe . . 30 55

1977. Kingstown Carnival. Nos. 426, 429, 432/3 and 440 optd **CARNIVAL 1977 JUNE 25TH - JULY 5TH.**

531 5c. French grunt 10 10
532 10c. Sperm whale 10 10
533 15c. Skipjack tuna 10 10
534 20c. Queen angelfish 10 10
535 $1 Queen triggerfish 40 50

93 Guide and Emblem

95 Map of St. Vincent

1977. 50th Anniv of St. Vincent Girl Guides. Multicoloured.

536 5c. Type **93** 10 10
537 15c. Early uniform, ranger, guide and brownie 10 10
538 20c. Early uniform and guide 10 10
539 $2 Lady Baden-Powell . . . 40 75

1977. Royal Visit. No. 513 optd **CARIBBEAN VISIT 1977.**

540 $2 Queen Elizabeth leaving Westminster Abbey 30 30

1977. Surch as in T **95**.

541 **95** 20c. light blue and blue . . 15 15
542 40c. light orange and orange 25 20
543 40c. pink and mauve . . . 20 15

Nos. 541/3 were originally printed without face values.

96 Opening Verse and Scene

1977. Christmas. Scenes and Verses from the carol "While Shepherds Watched their Flocks by Night". Multicoloured.

544 5c. Type **96** 10 10
545 10c. Angel consoling shepherds 10 10
546 15c. View of Bethlehem . . . 10 10
547 25c. Nativity scene 10 10
548 50c. Throng of angels 10 10
549 $1.25 Praising God 30 65
MS550 150 × 170 mm. Nos. 544/9 1·00 1·75

97 "Cynthia cardui" and "Bougainvillea glabra var alba"

99 "Co-operation in Education Leads to Mutual Understanding and Respect"

98 Rotary International Emblem and Motto

1978. Butterflies and Bougainvilleas. Multicoloured.

551 5c. Type **97** 15 10
552 25c. "Dione juno" and "Golden Glow" 15 10
553 40c. "Anartia amathea" and "Mrs McLean" 20 10
554 50c. "Hypolimnas misippus" and "Cyphen" 25 10
555 $1.25 "Pseudolycaena marsyas" and "Thomasii" 50 80

1978. 25th Anniv of Coronation. As Nos. 422/5 of Montserrat. Multicoloured.

556 40c. Westminster Abbey . . . 10 10
557 50c. Gloucester Cathedral . . 10 10
558 $1.25 Durham Cathedral . . 15 15
559 $2.50 Exeter Cathedral . . . 15 25
MS560 130 × 102 mm. Nos. 556/9 40 1·00

1978. International Service Clubs. Emblems and Mottoes. Multicoloured.

561 40c. Type **98** 15 10
562 50c. Lions International . . . 15 10
563 $1 Jaycees 35 50

1978. 10th Anniv of Project School to School (St. Vincent–Canada school twinning project). Mult.

564 40c. Type **99** 10 10
565 $2 "Co-operation in Education Leads to the Elimination of Racial Intolerance" (horiz) . . . 40 50

100 Arnos Vale Airport

1978. 75th Anniv of Powered Flight. Mult.

566 10c. Type **100** 10 10
567 40c. Wilbur Wright landing Wright Flyer I 15 10
568 50c. Orville Wright in Wright Flyer III 15 10
569 $1.25 Orville Wright and Wright Flyer I airborne . . 45 80

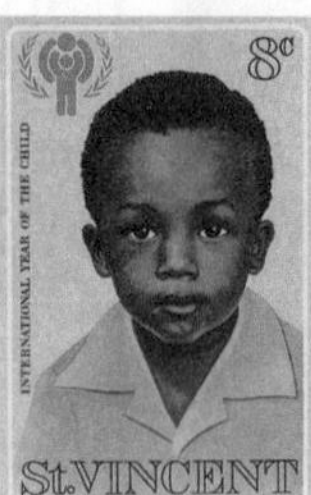

101 Young Child

1979. International Year of the Child.

570 **101** 8c. black, gold and green 10 10
571 – 20c. black, gold and lilac 10 10
572 – 50c. black, gold and blue 15 10
573 – $2 black, gold and flesh 50 50

DESIGNS: 20, 50c., $2 Different portraits of young children.

1979. Soufriere Eruption Relief Fund. As T **95** but surch **SOUFRIERE RELIEF FUND 1979** and premium.

574 **95** 10c.+5c. blue and lilac . . 10 15
575 50c.+25c. brown and buff 20 20
576 $1+50c. brown and grey 25 30
577 $2+$1 green and light green 40 50

103 Sir Rowland Hill

1979. Death Cent of Sir Rowland Hill. Mult.
578 40c. Type **103** 15 10
579 50c. Penny Black and Two Penny Blue stamps 15 15
580 $3 1861 1d. and 6d. stamps 40 1·10
MS581 170 × 123 mm. Nos. 578/80, 594/5 and 599 . . . . 1·40 2·50

104 First and Latest Buccament Postmarks and Map of St. Vincent

1979. Post Office of St. Vincent. Early and modern postmarks. Multicoloured.
582 1c. Type **104** 10 10
583 2c. Sion Hill 10 10
584 3c. Cumberland 10 50
585 4c. Questelles 10 30
586 5c. Layou 10 10
587 6c. New Ground 10 10
588 8c. Mesopotamia 10 10
589 10c. Troumaca 10 10
590 12c. Arnos Vale 10 30
591 15c. Stubbs 10 30
592 20c. Orange Hill 10 30
593 25c. Calliaqua 10 10
594 40c. Edinboro 10 20
595 50c. Colonarie 10 25
596 80c. Biabou 15 35
597 $1 Chateaubelair 20 50
598 $2 Head P.O. Kingstown . . 30 80
599 $3 Barrouallie . . . . 35 1·25
600 $5 Georgetown . . . . . . 50 2·00
601 $10 Kingstown . . . . . . 1·00 4·00

1979. Opening of St. Vincent and the Grenadines Air Service. Optd **ST VINCENT AND THE GRENADINES AIR SERVICE 1979**.
602 10c. Type **100** 10 10

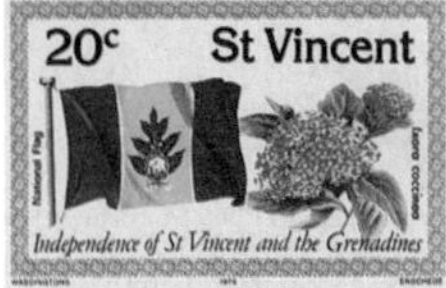

106 National Flag and "Ixora occinea" (flower)

1979. Independence. Multicoloured.
603 20c. Type **106** 15 10
604 50c. House of Assembly and "Ixora stricta" (flower) . . 20 10
605 80c. Prime Minister R. Milton Cato and "Ixora williamsii" (flower) 25 20

1979. Independence. Nos. 422, 425/30, 432, 437/41 and 443 optd **INDEPENDENCE 1979**.
606 1c. Type **79** 10 10
607 4c. Spanish mackerel 10 10
608 5c. French grunt 10 10
609 6c. Spotted goatfish 10 10
610 8c. Ballyhoo 10 10
611 10c. Sperm whale 15 15
612 12c. Humpback whale 15 15
613 15c. Skipjack tuna 10 15
614 25c. Princess parrotfish . . . 10 20
615 50c. Porkfish 15 35
616 70c. Yellow-finned tuna . . . 20 45
617 90c. Pompano 20 50
618 $1 Queen triggerfish 20 50
619 $2.50 Sailfish . . . . 35 1·00
620 $10 Blue marlin . . . . . . 1·10 4·25

108 Virgin and Child

1979. Christmas. Scenes and quotations from "Silent Night" (carol). Multicoloured.
621 10c. Type **108** 10 10
622 20c. Jesus sleeping 10 10
623 25c. Shepherds 10 10
624 40c. Angel 10 10
625 50c. Angels holding Jesus . . 10 10
626 $2 Nativity 40 45
MS627 151 × 170 mm. Nos. 621/6 70 1·25

109 "Polistes cinctus" (wasp) and Oleander

1979. Flowers and Insects. Different varieties of oleander. Multicoloured.
628 5c. Type **109** 10 10
629 10c. "Pyrophorus noctiluca" (click beetle) 10 10
630 25c. "Stagmomantis limbata" (mantid) 10 10
631 50c. "Psiloptera lampetis" (beetle) 10 10
632 $2 "Diaprepies abbreviatus" (weevil) 30 30

1980. Centenary of St. Vincent "Arms" Stamps. Sheet 116 × 72 mm containing designs as T **31**.
MS633 116 × 72 mm. 50c. brown; $1 green; $2.50 blue 50 75

110 Queen Elizabeth II

1980. "London 1980" International Stamp Exhibition. Multicoloured.
634 80c. Type **110** 15 20
635 $1 Great Britain 1954 3d. and St. Vincent 1954 5c. definitives 20 30
636 $2 Unadopted postage stamp design of 1971 . . . . . . 35 60
MS637 165 × 115 mm. Nos. 596/8 and 634/8 . . . . 75 1·50

111 Steel Band

1980. Kingstown Carnival. Multicoloured.
638 20c. Type **111** 15 65
639 20c. Steel band (different) . . 15 65

112 Football

114 Brazilian Agouti

1980. "Sport for All". Multicoloured.
640 10c. Type **112** 10 10
641 60c. Cycling 30 15
642 80c. Basketball 40 40
643 $2.50 Boxing . . . . 40 1·25

1980. Hurricane Relief. Nos. 640/3 surch **HURRICANE RELIEF 50c**.
644 **112** 10c.+50c. multicoloured 15 20
645 – 60c.+50c. multicoloured 40 45
646 – 80c.+50c. multicoloured 45 50
647 – $2.50+50c. mult 40 85

1980. Wildlife. Multicoloured.
648 25c. Type **114** 10 10
649 50c. Giant toad 15 10
650 $2 Small Indian mongoose 40 55

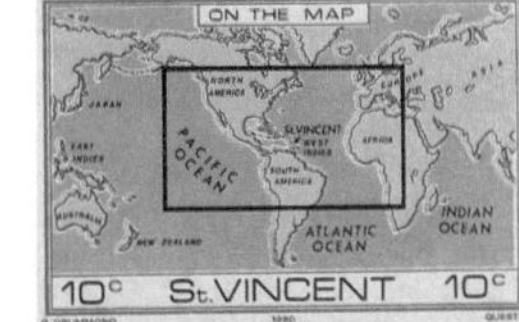

115 Map of World showing St. Vincent

1980. St. Vincent "On the Map". Maps showing St. Vincent. Multicoloured.
651 10c. Type **115** 10 10
652 50c. Western hemisphere . . 25 10
653 $1 Central America 40 15
654 $2 St. Vincent 60 30
MS655 143 × 95 mm. No. 654 . . 70 75

116 "Ville de Paris" (French ship of the line), 1782

1981. Sailing Ships. Multicoloured.
656 50c. Type **116** 25 15
657 60c. H.M.S. "Ramillies" (ship of the line), 1782 . . . . 25 25
658 $1.50 H.M.S. "Providence" (sloop), 1793 . . . . . . 40 70
659 $2 "Dee" (paddle-steamer packet) 50 80

117 Arrowroot Cultivation

1981. Agriculture. Multicoloured.
660 25c. Type **117** 10 20
661 25c. Arrowroot processing . . 10 20
662 50c. Banana cultivation . . . 10 30
663 50c. Banana export packaging station 10 30
664 60c. Coconut plantation . . . 15 35
665 60c. Copra drying frames . . 15 35
666 $1 Cocoa cultivation 15 50
667 $1 Cocoa beans and sun drying frames 15 50

1981. Royal Wedding. Royal Yachts. As T **14a/b** of St. Kitts. Multicoloured.
668 60c. "Isabella" 15 15
669 60c. Prince Charles and Lady Diana Spencer 30 30
670 $2.50 "Alberta" (tender) . . 30 30
671 $2.50 As No. 669 . . . . . 70 70
672 $4 "Britannia" 35 40
673 $4 As No. 669 . . . . 1·00 1·25
MS674 120 × 109 mm. $5 As No. 669 75 75

118/19 Kingstown General Post Office (½-size illustration)

1981. U.P.U. Membership.
677 **118** $2 multicoloured 40 90
678 **119** $2 multicoloured 40 90
Nos. 677/8 were printed together, se-tenant, forming the composite design illustrated.

120 St. Vincent Flag with Flags of other U.N. Member Nations

1981. 1st Anniv of U.N. Membership. Mult.
679 $1.50 Type **120** 25 25
680 $2.50 Prime Minister Robert Milton Cato 35 50
Nos. 679/80 are inscribed "ST. VINCENT and the GRENADINES".

121 Silhouettes of Figures at Old Testament Reading and Bible Extract

1981. Christmas. Designs showing silhouettes of figures. Multicoloured.
681 50c. Type **121** 25 10
682 60c. Madonna and angel . . 30 10
683 $1 Madonna and Bible extract 45 25
684 $2 Joseph and Mary travelling to Bethlehem . . 65 50
MS685 129 × 127 mm. Nos. 681/4 1·00 1·40

122 Sugar Boilers

1982. 1st Anniv of Re-introduction of Sugar Industry. Multicoloured.
686 50c. Type **122** 20 15
687 60c. Sugar drying plant . . . 20 20
688 $1.50 Sugar mill machinery 40 75
689 $2 Crane loading sugar cane 50 1·00

123 Butterfly Float

1982. Carnival 1982 Multicoloured.
690 50c. Type **123** 20 15
691 60c. Angel dancer (vert) . . . 20 15
692 $1.50 Winged dancer (vert) 50 80
693 $2 Eagle float . . . . 70 1·50

124 Augusta of Saxe-Gotha, Princess of Wales, 1736

125 Scout Emblem

1982. 21st Birthday of Princess of Wales. Multicoloured.
694 50c. Type **124** 15 20
695 60c. Coat of arms of Augusta of Saxe-Gotha 15 25
696 $6 Diana, Princess of Wales 1·10 1·25

1982. 75th Anniv of Boy Scout Movement. Multicoloured.
697 $1.50 Type **125** . . . . . . 70 1·00
698 $2.50 75th anniversary emblem . . . . 90 1·50

1982. Birth of Prince William of Wales. Nos. 694/6 optd **ROYAL BABY**.
699 50c. Type **124** 10 20
700 60c. Coat of arms of Augusta of Saxe-Gotha 10 25
701 $6 Diana, Princess of Wales 60 1·50

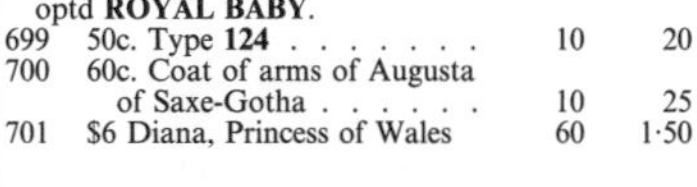

126 De Havilland Gipsy Moth, 1932

1982. 50th Anniv of Airmail Service. Mult.
702 50c. Type **126** 55 30
703 60c. Grumman Goose, 1952 65 40
704 $1.50 Hawker Siddeley H.S.748, 1968 . . . . . . 1·00 1·50
705 $2 Britten Norman "long nose" Trislander, 1982 . . 1·10 2·00

127 "Geestport" (freighter)

1982. Ships. Multicoloured.
706 45c. Type **127** 40 25
707 60c. "Stella Oceanis" (liner) 50 40
708 $1.50 "Victoria" (liner) . . . 80 1·50
709 $2 "Queen Elizabeth 2" (liner) . . . . 1·00 2·00

128 "Pseudocorynactis caribbeorum"

1983. Marine Life. Multicoloured.
710 50c. Type **128** 65 25
711 60c. "Actinoporus elegans" (vert) 75 40
712 $1.50 "Arachnanthus nocturnus" (vert) 1·40 2·25
713 $2 Reid's seahorse (vert) 1·60 2·50

129 Satellite View of St. Vincent

1983. Commonwealth Day. Multicoloured.
714 45c. Type **129** 15 20
715 60c. Flag of St. Vincent 20 25
716 $1.50 Prime Minister R. Milton Cato 30 65
717 $2 Harvesting bananas 45 90
Nos. 714/17 are inscribed "St. Vincent and The Grenadines".

1983. No. 681 surch **45c.**
718 **121** 45c. on 50c. Mult 40 30

131 Symbolic Handshake **132** William A. Smith (founder)

1983. 10th Anniv of Treaty of Chaguaramas. Multicoloured.
719 45c. Type **131** 15 20
720 60c. Commerce emblem 20 30
721 $1.50 Caribbean map 50 1·40
722 $2 Flags of member countries and map of St. Vincent 75 1·60

1983. Centenary of Boys' Brigade. Mult.
723 45c. Type **132** 20 25
724 60c. On parade 25 35
725 $1.50 Craftwork 55 1·50
726 $2 Community service 70 1·60

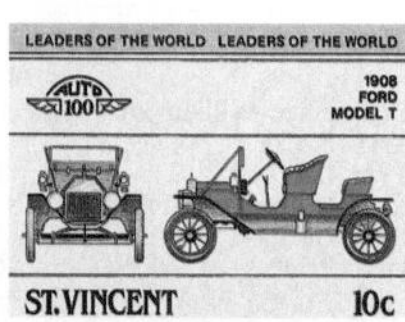

133 Ford "Model T" (1908)

1983. Leaders of the World. Automobiles (1st series).
727 **133** 10c. multicoloured 10 10
728 – 10c. multicoloured 10 10
729 – 60c. multicoloured 10 15
730 – 60c. multicoloured 10 15
731 – $1.50 multicoloured 15 20
732 – $1.50 multicoloured 15 20
733 – $1.50 multicoloured 15 20
734 – $1.50 multicoloured 15 20
735 – $2 multicoloured 15 20
736 – $2 multicoloured 15 20
737 – $2 multicoloured 15 20
738 – $2 multicoloured 15 20
DESIGNS: (the first in each pair shows technical drawings and the second paintings of the cars). Nos. 727/8, Ford "Model T" (1908); 729/30, Supercharged Cord "812" (1937); 731/2, Citroen "Open Tourer" (1937); 733/4, Mercedes Benz "300SL Gull-Wing" (1954); 735/6, Rolls-Royce "Phantom I" (1925); 737/8, Ferrari "Boxer 512BB" (1967).
See also Nos. 820/9, 862/7, 884/91 and 952/63.

134 Appearance of the Nativity Star

1983. Christmas. Multicoloured.
739 10c. Type **134** 10 10
740 50c. Message of the Angel 20 10
741 $1.50 The Heavenly Host 40 75
742 $2.40 Worshipping Jesus 55 1·25
MS743 130 × 130 mm. Nos. 739/42 1·25 1·75

135 "King Henry VIII"

1983. Leaders of the World. Railway Locomotives (1st series). First in each pair shows technical drawings and the second the locomotive at work.
744 **135** 10c. multicoloured 10 10
745 – 10c. multicoloured 10 10
746 – 10c. multicoloured 10 10
747 – 10c. multicoloured 10 10
748 – 25c. multicoloured 10 10
749 – 25c. multicoloured 10 10
750 – 50c. multicoloured 15 20
751 – 50c. multicoloured 15 20
752 – 60c. multicoloured 15 20
753 – 60c. multicoloured 15 20
754 – 75c. multicoloured 15 25
755 – 75c. multicoloured 15 25
756 – $2.50 multicoloured 20 35
757 – $2.50 multicoloured 20 35
758 – $3 multicoloured 25 50
759 – $3 multicoloured 25 50
DESIGNS: Nos. 744/5, "King Henry VIII", Great Britain (1927); 746/7, Diesel locomotive "Royal Scots Greys", Great Britain (1961); 748/9, "Hagley Hall", Great Britain (1928); 750/1, "Sir Lancelot", Great Britain (1925 (dated 1926 in error)); 752/3, Class B12, Great Britain (1912); 754/5, Deeley "Compound type", Great Britain (1902); 756/7, "Cheshire", Great Britain (1927); 758/9, Bulleid "Austerity" Class QI, Great Britain (1942).
See also Nos. 792/807, 834/41, 872/83, 893/904 and 1001/8.

136 Fort Duvernette

1984. Fort Duvernette. Multicoloured.
760 35c. Type **136** 20 30
761 45c. Soldiers on fortifications 25 30
762 $1 Cannon facing bay 40 60
763 $3 Map of St. Vincent and mortar 1·25 1·75

137 White Frangipani

1984. Flowering Trees and Shrubs. Mult.
764 5c. Type **137** 20 10
765 10c. Genip 25 10
766 15c. Immortelle 30 10
767 20c. Pink poui 30 10
768 25c. Buttercup 30 10
769 35c. Sandbox 45 10
770 45c. Locust 45 10
771 60c. Colville's glory 50 30
772 75c. Lignum vitae 50 45
773 $1 Golden shower 50 1·00
774 $5 Angelin 1·25 6·50
775 $10 Roucou 1·75 11·00

138 Trench Warfare, First World War

1984. Leaders of the World. British Monarchs. Multicoloured.
776 1c. Type **138** 10 10
777 1c. George V and trenches 10 10
778 5c. Battle of Bannockburn 10 10
779 5c. Edward II and battle 10 10
780 60c. George V 15 20
781 60c. York Cottage, Sandringham 15 20
782 75c. Edward II 15 20
783 75c. Berkeley Castle 15 20
784 $1 Coat of arms of Edward II 15 25
785 $1 Edward II (different) 15 25
786 $4 Coat of arms of George V 35 60
787 $4 George V and Battle of Jutland 35 60
Nos. 776/7, 778/9, 780/1, 782/3, 784/5 and 786/7 were printed together, se-tenant, each pair forming a composite design.

139 Musical Fantasy Costume

1984. Carnival 1984. Costumes. Multicoloured.
788 35c. Type **139** 15 15
789 45c. African princess 15 20
790 $1 Market woman 35 40
791 $3 Carib hieroglyph 80 1·75

1984. Leaders of the World. Railway Locomotives (2nd series). As T **135**, the first in each pair shows technical drawings and the second the locomotive at work.
792 1c. multicoloured 10 10
793 1c. multicoloured 10 10
794 2c. multicoloured 10 10
795 2c. multicoloured 10 10
796 3c. multicoloured 10 10
797 3c. multicoloured 10 10
798 50c. multicoloured 20 30
799 50c. multicoloured 20 30
800 75c. multicoloured 20 35
801 75c. multicoloured 20 35
802 $1 multicoloured 20 35
803 $1 multicoloured 20 35
804 $2 multicoloured 25 40
805 $2 multicoloured 25 40
806 $3 multicoloured 25 50
807 $3 multicoloured 25 50
DESIGNS: Nos. 792/3, Class 141-R Liberation, France (1945); 794/5, Diesel locomotive "Dreadnought", Great Britain (1967); 796/7, No. 242A1, France (1946); 798/9, Class "Dean Goods", Great Britain (1883); 800/1, Hetton Colliery No. 1, Great Britain (1822); 802/3, "Pen-y-Darren", Great Britain (1804); 804/5, "Novelty", Great Britain (1829); 806/7, Class 44, Germany (1925).

140 Slaves tilling Field

1984. 150th Anniv of Emancipation of Slaves on St. Vincent. Multicoloured.
808 35c. Type **140** 15 20
809 45c. Sugar-cane harvesting 15 25
810 $1 Cutting sugar-cane 30 70
811 $3 William Wilberforce and African slave caravan 1·00 2·75

141 Weightlifting **142** Grenadier, 70th Regt of Foot, 1773

1984. Leaders of the World. Olympic Games, Los Angeles. Multicoloured.
812 1c. Judo 10 10
813 1c. Type **141** 10 10
814 3c. Pursuit cycling 10 10
815 3c. Cycle road-racing 10 10
816 60c. Women's backstroke swimming 15 15
817 60c. Men's butterfly swimming 15 15
818 $3 Sprint start 40 55
819 $3 Finish of long distance race 40 55

1984. Leaders of the World. Automobiles (2nd series). As T **133**, the first in each pair shows technical drawings and the second paintings.
820 5c. black, drab and green 10 10
821 5c. multicoloured 10 10
822 20c. black, pink and blue 10 10
823 20c. multicoloured 10 10
824 55c. black, green and brown 10 20
825 55c. multicoloured 10 20
826 $1.50 black, light turquoise and turquoise 20 30
827 $1.50 multicoloured 20 30
828 $2.50 black, turquoise and lilac 25 35
829 $2.50 multicoloured 25 35
DESIGNS: Nos. 820/1, Austin-Healey "Sprite" (1958); 822/3, Maserati "Ghibli Coupe" (1971); 824/5, Pontiac "GTO" (1964); 826/7, Jaguar "D-Type" (1957); 828/9, Ferrari "365 GTB4 Daytona" (1970).

1984. Military Uniforms. Multicoloured.
830 45c. Type **142** 50 30
831 60c. Grenadier, 6th Regt of Foot, 1775 60 35
832 $1.50 Grenadier, 3rd Regt of Foot, 1768 80 1·10
833 $2 Battalion Company Officer, 14th Regt of Foot, 1780 90 1·60

1984. Leaders of the World. Railway Locomotives (3rd series). As T **135**, the first in each pair shows technical drawings and the second the locomotive at work.
834 5c. multicoloured 10 10
835 5c. multicoloured 10 10
836 40c. multicoloured 15 15
837 40c. multicoloured 15 15
838 75c. multicoloured 15 20
839 75c. multicoloured 15 20
840 $2.50 multicoloured 50 65
841 $2.50 multicoloured 50 65
DESIGNS: Nos. 834/5, 20th Class, Rhodesia (1954); 836/7, "Southern Maid", Great Britain (1928); 838/9, "Prince of Wales", Great Britain (1911); 840/1, Class 05, Germany (1935).

143 N. S. Taylor **144** Eye Lash Orchid

1985. Leaders of the World. Cricketers. The first in each pair shows a head portrait and the second the cricketer in action.
842 **143** 5c. multicoloured 10 10
843 – 5c. multicoloured 10 10
844 – 35c. multicoloured 30 20
845 – 35c. multicoloured 30 20
846 – 50c. multicoloured 30 30
847 – 50c. multicoloured 30 30
848 – $3 multicoloured 50 1·25
849 – $3 multicoloured 50 1·25
DESIGNS: Nos. 842/3, N. S. Taylor; 844/5, T. W. Graveney; 846/7, R. G. D. Willis; 848/9, S. D. Fletcher.

1985. Orchids. Multicoloured.
850 35c. Type **144** 20 30
851 45c. "Ionopsis utricularioides" 20 30
852 $1 "Epidendrum secundum" 30 65
853 $3 "Oncidium altissimum" 40 2·00

145 Brown Pelican **146** Pepper

1985. Leaders of the World. Birth Bicentenary of John J. Audubon (ornithologist). Multicoloured.
854 15c. Type **145** 10 10
855 15c. Green-backed heron ("Green Heron") 10 10
856 40c. Pileated woodpecker 15 20
857 40c. Common flicker 15 20
858 60c. Painted bunting 15 30
859 60c. White-winged crossbill 15 30
860 $2.25 Red-shouldered hawk 30 90
861 $2.25 Common caracara ("Crested Caracara") 30 90

1985. Leaders of the World. Automobiles (3rd series). As T **133**, the first in each pair shows technical drawings and the second paintings.
862 1c. black, yellow and green 10 10
863 1c. multicoloured 10 10
864 55c. black, blue and grey 15 25
865 55c. multicoloured 15 25
866 $2 black, yellow and purple 30 70
867 $2 multicoloured 30 70
DESIGNS: Nos. 862/3, Lancia "Aprilia", (1937); 864/5, Pontiac "Firebird Trans Am", (1973); 866/7, Cunningham "C-5R", (1953).

1985. Herbs and Spices. Multicoloured.
868 25c. Type **146** 15 10
869 35c. Sweet marjoram 15 15
870 $1 Nutmeg 25 65
871 $3 Ginger 60 2·50

1985. Leaders of the World. Railway Locomotives (4th series). As T **135**, the first in each pair shows technical drawings and the second the locomotive at work.
872 1c. multicoloured 10 10
873 1c. multicoloured 10 10
874 10c. multicoloured 10 10
875 10c. multicoloured 10 10
876 40c. multicoloured 15 30
877 40c. multicoloured 15 30
878 60c. multicoloured 15 30
879 60c. multicoloured 15 30
880 $1 multicoloured 25 40
881 $1 multicoloured 25 40
882 $2.50 multicoloured 40 60
883 $2.50 multicoloured 40 60
DESIGNS: Nos. 872/3, "Glen Douglas", Great Britain (1913); 874/5, "Fenchurch", Great Britain (1872); 876/7, No. 1 Stirling "single", Great Britain (1870); 878/9, No. 158A, Great Britain (1866); 880/1, Jones Goods locomotive No. 103, Great Britain (1893); 882/3, "The Great Bear", Great Britain (1908).

1985. Leaders of the World. Automobiles (4th series). As T **133**, the first in each pair shows technical drawings and the second paintings.

884 25c. black, grey and red . . . 10 10
885 25c. multicoloured 10 10
886 60c. black, pink and orange 15 20
887 60c. multicoloured 15 20
888 $1 black, blue and violet . . 15 25
889 $1 multicoloured 15 25
890 $1.50 black, blue and red . . 20 30
891 $1.50 multicoloured 20 30
MS892 180 × 121 mm. $4 × 2 As Nos. 890/1; $5 × 2 As Nos. 888/9 1·75 4·50

DESIGNS: Nos. 884/5, Essex "Coach" (1922); 886/7, Nash "Rambler" (1950); 888/9, Ferrari "Tipo 156" (1961); 890/1, Eagle-Weslake "Type 58" (1967).

1985. Leaders of the World. Railway Locomotives (5th series). As T **135**, the first in each pair shows technical drawings and the second the locomotive at work.

893 **151** 5c. multicoloured 10 10
894 – 5c. multicoloured 10 10
895 – 30c. multicoloured 15 20
896 – 30c. multicoloured 15 20
897 – 60c. multicoloured 20 30
898 – 60c. multicoloured 20 30
899 – 75c. multicoloured 20 30
900 – 75c. multicoloured 20 30
901 – $1 multicoloured 25 40
902 – $1 multicoloured 25 40
903 – $2.50 multicoloured . . . 30 60
904 – $2.50 multicoloured . . . 30 60

DESIGNS: Nos. 893/4, "Loch", Isle of Man (1874); 895/6, Class 47XX, Great Britain (1919); 897/8, Class 121, France (1876); 899/900, Class 24, Germany (1927); 901/2, Tank locomotive No. 1008, Great Britain (1889); 903/4, Class PS-4, U.S.A. (1926).

147 Bamboo Flute

1985. Traditional Musical Instruments. Mult.

905 25c. Type **147** 10 15
906 35c. Quatro (four-stringed guitar) 10 25
907 $1 Ba-ha (bamboo pipe) (vert) 25 55
908 $2 Goat-skin drum (vert) . . 35 1·10
MS909 141 × 100 mm. Nos. 905/8 1·60 1·40

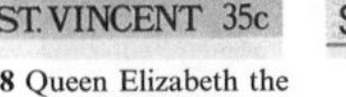

148 Queen Elizabeth the Queen Mother **149** Elvis Presley

1985. Leaders of the World. Life and Times of Queen Elizabeth the Queen Mother. Various portraits.

910 **148** 35c. multicoloured 10 25
911 – 35c. multicoloured 10 25
912 – 85c. multicoloured 10 30
913 – 85c. multicoloured 10 30
914 – $1.20 multicoloured . . . 15 35
915 – $1.20 multicoloured . . . 15 35
916 – $1.60 multicoloured . . . 15 35
917 – $1.60 multicoloured . . . 15 35
MS918 85 × 114 mm. $2.10 multicoloured; $2.10 multicoloured . . . . 50 1·50

Each value issued in pairs showing a floral pattern across the bottom of the portraits which stops short of the left-hand edge on the first stamp and of the right-hand edge on the second.

1985. Leaders of the World. Elvis Presley (entertainer). Various portraits. Multicoloured, background colours given.

919 **149** 10c. multicoloured 15 15
920 – 10c. multicoloured (blue) 15 15
921 – 60c. multicoloured (brown) 20 35
922 – 60c. multicoloured (grey) 20 35
923 – $1 multicoloured (brown) 20 55
924 – $1 multicoloured (blue) 20 55
925 – $5 mult (light blue) . . . 40 1·75
926 – $5 multicoloured (blue) 40 1·75
MS927 Four sheets each 145 × 107 mm. (a) 30c. As Nos. 919/20 each × 2. (b) 50c. As Nos. 921/2 each × 2. (c) $1.50 As Nos. 923/4 each × 2. (d) $4.50 As Nos. 925/6 each × 2. Set of 4 sheets . . . . 21·00 20·00

150 Silos and Conveyor Belt

1985. St. Vincent Flour Milling Industry. Multicoloured.

928 20c. Type **150** 10 15
929 30c. Roller mills 10 20
930 75c. Administration building 20 35
931 $3 Bran finishers . . . . . . 50 1·40

1985. Royal Visit. Nos. 672/3, 697/8, 711, 724 and 912/13 optd **CARIBBEAN ROYAL VISIT 1985** or surch also.

932 – 60c. multicoloured (711) 1·50 2·00
933 – 60c. multicoloured (724) 1·75 2·25
934 – 85c. multicoloured (912) 4·50 6·50
935 – 85c. multicoloured (913) 4·50 6·50
936 **125** $1.50 multicoloured . . . 1·60 3·25
937 – $1.60 on $4 mult (672) . . 1·00 2·50
938 – $1.60 on $4 mult (673) . . 11·00 17·00
939 – $2.50 multicoloured (698) 1·75 4·00

No. 938 shows a new face value only.

151 Michael Jackson **152** "The Serenaders" (Kim de Freitas)

1985. Leaders of the World. Michael Jackson (entertainer). Various portraits. Multicoloured.

940 **151** 60c. multicoloured 15 30
941 – 60c. multicoloured 15 30
942 – $1 multicoloured 15 45
943 – $1 multicoloured 15 45
944 – $2 multicoloured 20 80
945 – $2 multicoloured 20 80
946 – $5 multicoloured . . . . 30 1·50
947 – $5 multicoloured . . . . 30 1·50
MS948 Four sheets, each 144 × 109 mm. (a) 45c. As Nos. 940/1 each × 2. (b) 90c. As Nos. 942/3 each × 2. (c) $1.50 As Nos. 944/5 each × 2. (d) $4 As Nos. 946/7 each × 2. Set of 4 sheets . . . . 3·25 7·50

Each value issued in pairs, the left-hand design showing the face value at top left (as on Type **151**) and the right-hand design at top right.

1985. Christmas. Children's Paintings. Mult.

949 25c. Type **152** 10 15
950 75c. "Poinsettia" (Jackie Douglas) 20 40
951 $2.50 "Jesus our Master" (Bernadette Payne) . . . . 55 2·00

153 "Santa Maria" **154** Guide Salute and Handclasp

1986. 500th Anniv (1992) of Discovery of America by Columbus (1st issue). Multicoloured.

952 60c. Type **153** 50 65
953 60c. Christopher Columbus 50 65
954 $1.50 Columbus at Spanish Court . . . . 70 1·40
955 $1.50 King Ferdinand and Queen Isabella of Spain . . 70 1·40
956 $2.75 "Santa Maria" and fruits . . . . 1·00 2·25
957 $2.75 Maize and fruits . . . 1·00 2·25
MS958 95 × 85 mm. $6 Christopher Columbus (different) . . . . 2·50 6·00

See also Nos. 1125/31, 1305/24, 1639/57, 1677/85, 1895/1901 and 1981/2.

1986. Leaders of the World. Automobiles (5th series). As T **133**, the first in each pair shows technical drawings and the second paintings.

959 30c. black, blue and orange 10 15
960 30c. multicoloured 10 15
961 45c. black, grey and blue . . 10 15
962 45c. multicoloured 10 15
963 60c. black, blue and red . . . 15 20
964 60c. multicoloured 15 20
965 90c. black, yellow and blue 15 25
966 90c. multicoloured 15 25
967 $1.50 black, lilac and mauve 20 40
968 $1.50 multicoloured 20 40
969 $2.50 black, blue and light blue 20 50
970 $2.50 multicoloured 20 50

DESIGNS: Nos. 959/60, Cadillac "Type 53" (1916); 961/2, Triumph "Dolomite" (1939); 963/4, Panther "J-72" (1972); 965/6, Ferrari "275 GTB/4" (1967); 967/8, Packard "Caribbean" (1953); 969/70, Bugatti "Type 41 Royale" (1931).

1986. 75th Annivs of Girl Guide Movement and Boy Scouts of America. Two sheets, each 85 × 113 mm, containing vert designs as T **154**. Multicoloured.

MS971 $5 Type **154**; $5 Palette and paintbrushes . . . . 2·00 5·00
MS972 $6 Cross-tied logs; $6 Lord Baden-Powell . . . . 2·00 6·00

The two stamps in each sheet were printed together, *se-tenant*, in horizontal pairs, each forming a composite design.

Nos. **MS**971/2 exist with plain or decorative margins.

Overprints on these miniature sheets commemorating "Capex '87" International Stamp Exhibition, Toronto, were not authorised by the St. Vincent administration.

155 Halley's Comet

1986. Appearance of Halley's Comet. Multicoloured.

973 45c. Type **155** 40 30
974 60c. Edmond Halley 40 30
975 75c. Newton's telescope and astronomers 50 55
976 $3 Amateur astronomer on St. Vincent . . . . 70 2·75
MS977 155 × 104 mm. Nos. 973/6 2·00 4·50

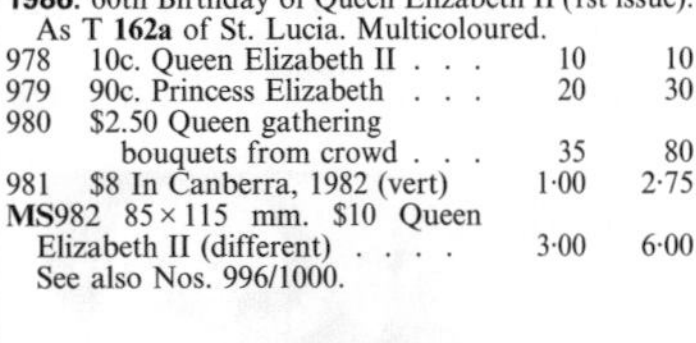

1986. 60th Birthday of Queen Elizabeth II (1st issue). As T **162a** of St. Lucia. Multicoloured.

978 10c. Queen Elizabeth II . . . 10 10
979 90c. Princess Elizabeth . . . 20 30
980 $2.50 Queen gathering bouquets from crowd . . . 35 80
981 $8 In Canberra, 1982 (vert) 1·00 2·75
MS982 85 × 115 mm. $10 Queen Elizabeth II (different) . . . . 3·00 6·00

See also Nos. 996/1000.

156 Mexican Player

1986. World Cup Football Championship, Mexico. Multicoloured.

983 1c. Football and world map (horiz) 10 10
984 2c. Type **156** 10 10
985 5c. Mexican player (different) 10 10
986 5c. Hungary v Scotland . . . 10 10
987 10c. Spain v Scotland 10 10
988 30c. England v U.S.S.R. (horiz) 20 20
989 45c. Spain v France 30 30
990 75c. Mexican team (56 × 36 mm) 45 45
991 $1 England v Italy 45 65
992 $2 Scottish team (56 × 36 mm) . . . . . . 60 1·50
993 $4 Spanish team (56 × 36 mm) . . . . . . 1·00 2·75
994 $5 English team (56 × 36 mm) 1·00 3·25
MS995 Six sheets, each 84 × 114 mm. (a) $1.50 As Type **156**. (b) $1.50 As No. 993.(c) $2.25 As No. 992. (d) $2.50 As No. 990. (e) $3 As No. 989. (f) $5.50 As No. 994. Set of 6 sheets . . . . 7·50 11·00

157 Queen Elizabeth at Victoria Park, Kingstown

1986. 60th Birthday of Queen Elizabeth II (2nd issue). Scenes from 1985 Royal Visit. Multicoloured.

996 45c. Type **157** 50 30
997 60c. Queen and Prime Minister James Mitchell, Bequia 65 55
998 75c. Queen, Prince Philip and Mr. Mitchell, Port Elizabeth, Bequia 75 65
999 $2.50 Queen, Prince Philip and Mr. Mitchell watching Independence Day parade, Victoria Park . . . . . . 1·50 2·50
MS1000 121 × 85 mm. $3 Queen at Victoria Park . . . . 3·50 4·50

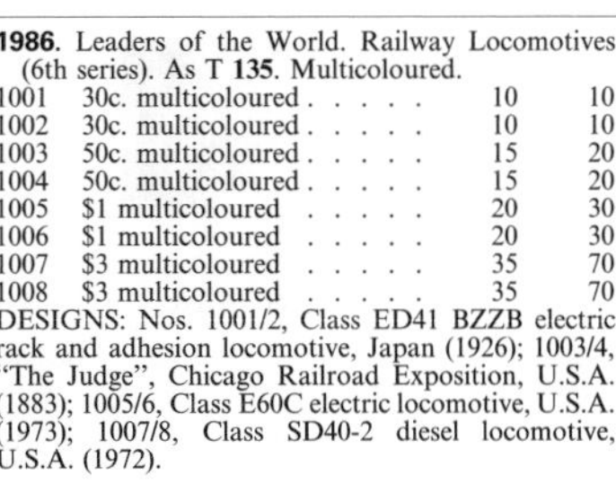

1986. Leaders of the World. Railway Locomotives (6th series). As T **135**. Multicoloured.

1001 30c. multicoloured 10 10
1002 30c. multicoloured 10 10
1003 50c. multicoloured 15 20
1004 50c. multicoloured 15 20
1005 $1 multicoloured 20 30
1006 $1 multicoloured 20 30
1007 $3 multicoloured 35 70
1008 $3 multicoloured 35 70

DESIGNS: Nos. 1001/2, Class ED41 BZZB electric rack and adhesion locomotive, Japan (1926); 1003/4, "The Judge", Chicago Railroad Exposition, U.S.A. (1883); 1005/6, Class E60C electric locomotive, U.S.A. (1973); 1007/8, Class SD40-2 diesel locomotive, U.S.A. (1972).

1986. Royal Wedding (1st issue). As T **164a** of St. Lucia. Multicoloured.

1009 60c. Profile of Prince Andrew 20 25
1010 60c. Miss Sarah Ferguson 20 25
1011 $2 Prince Andrew with Mrs. Nancy Reagan (horiz) . . 45 75
1012 $2 Prince Andrew in naval uniform (horiz) 45 75
MS1013 115 × 85 mm. $10 Duke and Duchess of York in carriage after wedding (horiz) . . . . 2·50 4·50

See also Nos. 1022/5.

158 "Acrocomia aculeata" **159** Cadet Force Emblem and Cadets of 1936 and 1986

1986. Timber Resources of St. Vincent. Mult.

1014 10c. Type **158** 40 20
1015 60c. "Pithecellobium saman" 1·25 80
1016 75c. White cedar . . . . . 1·60 95
1017 $3 "Andira inermis" . . . . 3·50 4·50

1986. 50th Anniv of St. Vincent Cadet Force (45c., $2) and 75th Anniv of St. Vincent Girls' High School (others). Multicoloured.

1018 45c. Type **159** 40 30
1019 60c. Grimble Building, Girls' High School (horiz) . . . 45 40
1020 $1.50 High School pupils (horiz) . . . . 1·00 1·75
1021 $2 Cadets on parade (horiz) 1·50 2·25

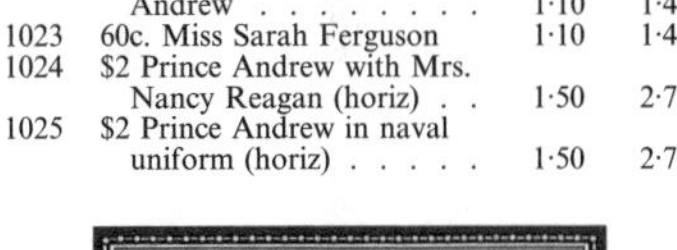

1986. Royal Wedding (2nd issue). Nos. 1009/12 optd **Congratulations to T.R.H. The Duke & Duchess of York.**

1022 60c. Profile of Prince Andrew . . . . 1·10 1·40
1023 60c. Miss Sarah Ferguson 1·10 1·40
1024 $2 Prince Andrew with Mrs. Nancy Reagan (horiz) . . 1·50 2·75
1025 $2 Prince Andrew in naval uniform (horiz) . . . . . 1·50 2·75

160 King Arthur

1986. The Legend of King Arthur. Multicoloured.

1026 30c. Type **160** 40 40
1027 45c. Merlin taking baby Arthur 50 50
1028 60c. Arthur pulling sword from stone 60 60
1029 75c. Camelot 70 70
1030 $1 Arthur receiving Excalibur from the Lady of the Lake 80 80
1031 $1.50 Knights at the Round Table . . . . 1·00 1·50
1032 $2 The Holy Grail . . . . 1·25 1·75
1033 $5 Sir Lancelot jousting . . 2·00 3·00

161 Statue of Liberty Floodlit **163** Baby on Scales

162 Fishing for Tri Tri

1986. Centenary of Statue of Liberty. Designs showing aspects of the Statue.
1034 **161** 15c. multicoloured . . . 10 10
1035 – 25c. multicoloured . . . 10 15
1036 – 40c. multicoloured . . . 15 25
1037 – 55c. multicoloured . . . 20 30
1038 – 75c. multicoloured . . . 25 45
1039 – 90c. multicoloured . . . 25 60
1040 – $1.75 multicoloured . . 35 1·10
1041 – $2 multicoloured . . . . 35 1·25
1042 – $2.50 multicoloured . . 40 1·60
1043 – $3 multicoloured . . . . 40 1·75
MS1044 Three sheets, each 85 × 115 mm. $3.50; $4; $5. Set of 3 sheets . . . . 2·25 7·50

1986. Freshwater Fishing. Multicoloured.
1045 75c. Type **162** 25 55
1046 75c. Plumier's goby ("Tri Tri") 25 55
1047 $1.50 Crayfishing 35 80
1048 $1.50 Crayfish 35 80

1987. Child Health Campaign. Multicoloured.
1049 10c. Type **163** 10 10
1050 50c. Oral rehydration therapy 45 55
1051 75c. Breast feeding 55 90
1052 $1 Nurse giving injection . . 60 1·25

1987. World Population Control. Nos. 1049/52 optd **WORLD POPULATION 5 BILLION 11TH JULY 1987**.
1053 10c. Type **163** 10 10
1054 50c. Oral rehydration therapy 40 55
1055 75c. Breast feeding 50 90
1056 $1 Nurse giving injection . . 55 1·25

165 Hanna Mandlikova

1987. International Lawn Tennis Players. Mult.
1057 40c. Type **165** 20 25
1058 60c. Yannick Noah 20 35
1059 80c. Ivan Lendl 20 50
1060 $1 Chris Evert 20 50
1061 $1.25 Steffi Graf 20 60
1062 $1.50 John McEnroe 20 65
1063 $1.75 Martina Navratilova with Wimbledon trophy . . 20 75
1064 $2 Boris Becker with Wimbledon trophy . . . 30 85
MS1065 115 × 85 mm. $2.25 As No. 1063; $2.25 As No. 1064 1·40 3·50

166 Miss Prima Donna, Queen of the Bands, 1986

1987. 10th Anniv of Carnival. Multicoloured.
1066 20c. Type **166** 10 15
1067 45c. Donna Young, Miss Carnival, 1985 . . . . . 15 15
1068 55c. Miss St. Vincent and the Grenadines, 1986 . . 15 15
1069 $3.70 "Spirit of Hope" costume, 1986 . . . . . 50 1·60
The 45c. value is inscribed "Miss Carival" in error.

1987. 10th Death Anniv of Elvis Presley (entertainer). Nos. 919/26 optd **THE KING OF ROCK AND ROLL LIVES FOREVER AUGUST 16TH 1977–1987**.
1070 **149** 10c. multicoloured . . . 10 20
1071 – 10c. multicoloured (blue) 10 20
1072 – 60c. mult (brown) . . . 20 35
1073 – 60c. multicoloured (grey) 20 35
1074 – $1 multicoloured (brown) 20 60
1075 – $1 multicoloured (blue) 20 60
1076 – $5 mult (light blue) . . . 60 2·25
1077 – $5 multicoloured (blue) 60 2·25
MS1078 Four sheets, each 145 × 107 mm. (a) 30c. As Nos. 1070/1 each × 2. (b) 50c. As Nos. 1072/3 each × 2. (c) $1.50, As Nos. 1074/5 each × 2. (d) $4.50, As Nos. 1076/7 each × 2 . . . 7·50 10·00

168 Queen Victoria, 1841

1987. Royal Ruby Wedding and 150th Anniv of Queen Victoria's Accession. Multicoloured.
1079 15c. Type **168** 10 10
1080 75c. Queen Elizabeth and Prince Andrew, 1960 . . 20 35
1081 $1 Coronation, 1953 . . . . 20 40
1082 $2.50 Duke of Edinburgh, 1948 . . . . 50 1·50
1083 $5 Queen Elizabeth II, c. 1980 . . . 1·50 2·25
MS1084 85 × 115 mm. $6 Princess Elizabeth with Prince Charles at his Christening, 1948 . . . . . 1·75 4·50

169 Karl Benz and Benz Three-wheeler (1886)

1987. Century of Motoring. Multicoloured.
1085 $1 Type **169** 40 60
1086 $2 Enzo Ferrari and Ferrari "Dino 206SP" (1966) . . 50 1·10
1087 $4 Charles Rolls and Sir Henry Royce and Rolls-Royce "Silver Ghost" (1907) . . . . 65 1·50
1088 $5 Henry Ford and Ford "Model T" (1908) . . . . 65 1·75
MS1089 Four sheets, each 144 × 75 mm. (a) $3 As Type **169**. (b) $5 As No. 1086. (c) $6 As No. 1087. (d) $8 As No. 1088. Set of 4 sheets . . . . 7·50 15·00

170 Everton Football Team

1987. English Football Teams. Mult.
1090 $2 Type **170** . . . . 1·25 1·25
1091 $2 Manchester United . . . 1·25 1·25
1092 $2 Tottenham Hotspur . . . 1·25 1·25
1093 $2 Arsenal . . . . 1·25 1·25
1094 $2 Liverpool . . . . 1·25 1·25
1095 $2 Derby County . . . . . 1·25 1·25
1096 $2 Portsmouth . . . . . . 1·25 1·25
1097 $2 Leeds United . . . . . 1·25 1·25

171 Five Cent Coins **172** Charles Dickens

1987. East Caribbean Currency. Mult.
1098 5c. Type **171** 20 10
1099 6c. Two cent coins 20 10
1100 10c. Ten cent coins 20 10
1101 12c. Two and ten cent coins 30 10
1102 15c. Five cent coins 30 10
1103 20c. Ten cent coins 35 10
1104 25c. Twenty-five cent coins 40 15
1105 30c. Five and twenty-five cent coins 40 15
1106 35c. Twenty-five and ten cent coins 40 20
1107 45c. Twenty-five and two ten cent coins 50 30
1108 50c. Fifty cent coins . . . 50 30
1109 65c. Fifty, ten and five cent coins 60 45
1110 75c. Fifty and twenty-five cent coins 60 50
1111 $1 One dollar note (horiz) 75 65
1112 $2 Two one dollar notes (horiz) . . . . 1·25 1·75
1113 $3 Three one dollar notes (horiz) . . . . 1·25 2·50
1114 $5 Five dollar note (horiz) 2·25 5·00
1115 $10 Ten dollar note (horiz) 2·75 8·00
1115s $20 Twenty dollar note (horiz) . . . . 11·00 16·00

1987. Christmas. 175th Birth Anniv of Charles Dickens. Multicoloured.
1116 6c. Type **172** 40 70
1117 6c. "Mr. Fezziwig's Ball" 40 70
1118 25c. Type **172** 45 70
1119 25c. "Scrooge's Third Visitor" 45 70
1120 50c. Type **172** 50 90
1121 50c. "The Cratchits' Christmas" 50 90
1122 75c. Type **172** . . . . . . 50 1·25
1123 75c. "A Christmas Carol" 50 1·25
MS1124 141 × 101 mm. $5 Teacher reading to class . . . . 1·75 4·50
Nos. 1116/17, 1118/19, 1120/1 and 1122/3 were printed together, se-tenant, each pair forming a composite design showing an open book. The first design in each pair shows Type **172** and the second a scene from "A Christmas Carol".

173 "Santa Maria"

1988. 500th Anniv (1992) of Discovery of America by Columbus (2nd issue). Multicoloured.
1125 15c. Type **173** 30 20
1126 75c. "Nina" and "Pinta" . . 40 60
1127 $1 Compass and hourglass 40 60
1128 $1.50 Claiming the New World for Spain . . . . 45 1·40
1129 $3 Arawak village . . . . . 60 2·00
1130 $4 Blue and yellow macaw, Cuban tody, pineapple and maize . . . . 80 2·25
MS1131 114 × 86 mm. $5 Columbus, Arms and "Santa Maria" . . . 2·50 3·00

174 Brown Pelican **175** Windsurfing

1988.
1132 **174** 45c. multicoloured . . . 30 30

1988. Tourism. Multicoloured.
1133 10c. Type **175** 10 10
1134 45c. Scuba diving 20 25
1135 65c. Aerial view of Young Island (horiz) 30 60
1136 $5 Cruising yacht (horiz) . . 2·10 3·50
MS1136a 115 × 85 mm. $10 Two windsurfers off St. Vincent (60 × 40 mm) . . . . 2·75 6·00

176 "Nuestra Senora del Rosario" (Spanish galleon) and Spanish Knight's Cross

1988. 400th Anniv of Spanish Armada. Mult.
1137 15c. Type **176** 25 10
1138 75c. "Ark Royal" (galleon) and English Armada medal 45 40
1139 $1.50 English fleet and Drake's dial 60 85
1140 $2 Dismasted Spanish galleon and 16th-century shot . . . . 65 1·00
1141 $3.50 Attack of English fireships at Calais and 16th-century grenade . . 80 2·00
1142 $5 "Revenge" (English galleon) and Drake's Drum . . . . 90 2·25
MS1143 123 × 92 mm. $8 Sighting the Armada . . . . 2·00 4·50

177 D. K. Lillee **179** Babe Ruth

178 Athletics

1988. Cricketers of 1988 International Season. Multicoloured.
1144 15c. Type **177** 50 30
1145 50c. G. A. Gooch 70 50
1146 75c. R. N. Kapil Dev . . . 90 70
1147 $1 S. M. Gavaskar . . . . 1·00 85
1148 $1.50 M. W. Gatting . . . 1·25 1·50
1149 $2.50 Imran Khan . . . . 1·25 2·00
1150 $3 I. T. Botham . . . . . 1·25 2·25
1151 $4 I. V. A. Richards . . . . 1·25 2·50
MS1152 130 × 80 mm. $2 As $4. $3.50, As $3 . . . . 2·50 5·50

1988. Olympic Games, Seoul. Multicoloured.
1153 10c. Type **178** 10 10
1154 50c. Long jumping (vert) . . 20 25
1155 $1 Triple jumping 40 50
1156 $5 Boxing (vert) . . . . . 2·10 2·75
MS1157 85 × 63 mm. $10 Olympic flame . . . . 4·75 6·50

1988. Famous Baseball Players (1st series).
1158 **179** $2 multicoloured . . . . 1·40 1·40
See also Nos. 1264/75, 1407, 1408/88, 2152/4, 2155/6, 2426 and 3004/12.

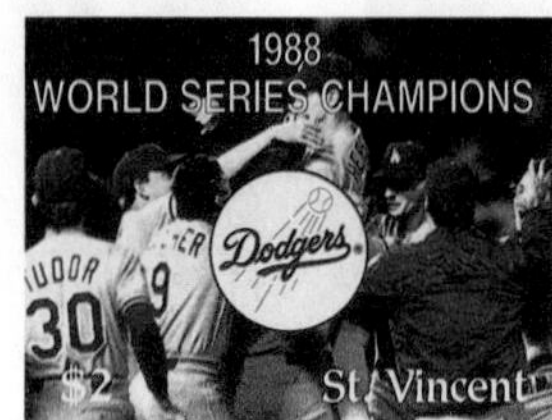

180 Los Angeles Dodgers (National League Champions)

1988. 1988 Baseball World Series. Sheet 115 × 85 mm containing T **180** and similar horiz design. Multicoloured.
MS1159 $2 Type **180**; $2 Team logos of Dodgers and Oakland Athletics 2·00 2·25

180a Minnie Mouse in Railway Van Loaded with Candy

1988. Christmas. "Mickey's Christmas Train". Multicoloured.
1160 1c. Type **180a** 10 10
1161 2c. Mordie and Ferdie in wagon with toys 10 10
1162 3c. Chip n' Dale in wagon with Christmas trees . . . 10 10
1163 4c. Donald Duck's nephews riding with reindeer . . . 10 10
1164 5c. Donald and Daisy Duck in restaurant car 10 10
1165 10c. Grandma Duck, Uncle Scrooge McDuck, Goofy and Clarabelle carol singing in carriage 10 10
1166 $5 Mickey Mouse driving locomotive . . . . 3·25 3·50
1167 $6 Father Christmas in guard's van . . . . 4·00 4·50
MS1168 Two sheets, each 127 × 102 mm. (a) $5 Mickey Mouse and nephews at railway station. (b) $5 Mickey and Minnie Mouse on carousel. Set of 2 sheets 7·00 8·00

181 Mickey Mouse as Snake Charmer

1989. "India-89" International Stamp Exhibition, New Delhi. Multicoloured.
1169 1c. Type **181** 10 10
1170 2c. Goofy with chowsingha antelope 10 10
1171 3c. Mickey and Minnie Mouse with common peafowl 10 10
1172 5c. Goofy with Briolette Diamond and Mickey Mouse pushing mine truck 10 10
1173 10c. Clarabelle with Orloff Diamond 10 10
1174 25c. Mickey Mouse as tourist and Regent Diamond, Louvre, Paris 20 15
1175 $4 Minnie and Mickey Mouse with Kohinoor Diamond 3·50 4·00
1176 $5 Mickey Mouse and Goofy with Indian rhinoceros 3·50 4·00
MS1177 Two sheets, each 127×102 mm. (a) $6 Mickey Mouse riding Indian elephant. (b) $6 Mickey Mouse as postman delivering Hope Diamond to Smithsonian Museum, U.S.A. (vert). Set of 2 sheets 8·50 10·00

182 Harry James

1989. Jazz Musicians. Multicoloured.
1178 10c. Type **182** 40 20
1179 15c. Sidney Bechet 50 20
1180 25c. Benny Goodman 60 20
1181 35c. Django Reinhardt 65 20
1182 50c. Lester Young 80 35
1183 90c. Gene Krupa 95 85
1184 $3 Louis Armstrong 3·00 3·00
1185 $4 Duke Ellington 3·00 3·25
MS1186 Two sheets, each 107×92 mm. (a) $5 Charlie Parker. (b) $5 Billie Holiday. Set of 2 sheets 7·50 8·00

183 Birds in Flight

1989. Wildlife Conservation. Noah's Ark. Multicoloured.
1187 40c. Type **183** 30 30
1188 40c. Rainbow (left side) 30 30
1189 40c. Noah's Ark on mountain 30 30
1190 40c. Rainbow (right side) 30 30
1191 40c. Birds in flight (different) 30 30
1192 40c. Cow elephant 30 30
1193 40c. Bull elephant 30 30
1194 40c. Top of eucalyptus tree 30 30
1195 40c. Kangaroos 30 30
1196 40c. Hummingbird 30 30
1197 40c. Lions 30 30
1198 40c. White-tailed deer 30 30
1199 40c. Koala in fork of tree 30 30
1200 40c. Koala on branch 30 30
1201 40c. Hummingbird approaching flower 30 30
1202 40c. Keel-billed toucan and flower 30 30
1203 40c. Keel-billed toucan facing right 30 30
1204 40c. Camels 30 30
1205 40c. Giraffes 30 30
1206 40c. Mountain sheep 30 30
1207 40c. Ladybirds on leaf 30 30
1208 40c. Swallowtail butterfly 30 30
1209 40c. Swallowtail butterfly behind leaves 30 30
1210 40c. Pythons 30 30
1211 40c. Dragonflies 30 30
Nos. 1187/1211 were printed together, se-tenant, forming a composite design showing Noah's Ark and animals released after the Flood.

183a "Baptism of Christ" (detail)

1989. Easter. 500th Birth Anniv of Titian (artist). Multicoloured.
1212 5c. Type **183a** 10 20
1213 30c. "Temptation of Christ" 25 15
1214 45c. "Ecce Homo" 40 25
1215 65c. "Noli Me Tangere" (fragment) 55 55
1216 75c. "Christ carrying the Cross" (detail) 60 65
1217 $1 "Christ crowned with Thorns" (detail) 70 75
1218 $4 "Lamentation over Christ" (detail) 2·75 3·50
1219 $5 "The Entombment" (detail) 3·25 4·00
MS1220 (a) 98×111 mm. $6 "Piet" (detail). (b) 114×95 mm. $6 "The Deposition" (detail). Set of 2 sheets 7·00 8·00

184 "Ile de France"

1989. Ocean Liners. Multicoloured.
1221 10c. Type **184** 1·00 40
1222 40c. "Liberte" 1·75 30
1223 50c. "Mauretania I" (launched 1906) 1·75 50
1224 75c. "France" 2·25 1·25
1225 $1 "Aquitania" 2·25 1·25
1226 $2 "United States" 3·00 3·00
1227 $3 "Olympic" 3·50 3·75
1228 $4 "Queen Elizabeth" 3·50 4·00
MS1229 Two sheets, each 141×108 mm. (a) $6 "Queen Mary" (85×28 mm). (b) $6 "Queen Elizabeth 2" (85×28 mm). Set of 2 sheets 9·00 11·00

185 Space Shuttle deploying West German Satellite, 1983

186 "Mercury 9" Capsule and Astronaut L. Gordon Cooper

1989. International Co-operation in Space. Mult.
1230 40c. Type **185** 80 20
1231 60c. Vladimir Remek (Czech cosmonaut) and "Soyuz 28", 1978 1·10 50
1232 $1 Projected "Hermes" space plane and "Columbus" Space Station 1·50 1·00
1233 $4 Ulf Merbold (West German astronaut), 1983 and proposed European Spacelab 3·50 4·75
MS1234 93×67 mm. $5 Meeting in space of "Apollo/Soyuz" mission crews, 1975 3·00 4·00

1989. 25th Anniv of Launching of "Telstar II" Communications Satellite (1988). Each showing satellite and T.V. screen. Multicoloured.
1235 15c. Type **186** 20 15
1236 35c. Martin Luther King addressing crowd, 1963 30 20
1237 50c. Speed skater, Winter Olympic Games, Innsbruck, 1964 45 50
1238 $3 Pope John XXIII blessing crowd 1·75 2·75
MS1239 107×77 mm. $5 Launch of "Telstar II", 1963 2·75 3·50

187 Head of St. Vincent Amazon

1989. Wildlife Conservation. St. Vincent Amazon ("St. Vincent Parrot"). Multicoloured.
1240 10c. Type **187** 70 30
1241 20c. St. Vincent amazon in flight 1·25 45
1242 40c. Feeding (vert) 2·00 65
1243 70c. At entrance to nest (vert) 2·75 3·25

188 Blue-hooded Euphonia ("Misletoe Bird")

1989. Birds of St. Vincent. Multicoloured.
1244 25c. Type **188** 45 20
1245 75c. Common black hawk ("Crab Hawk") 1·00 65
1246 $2 Mangrove cuckoo ("Coucou") 1·75 2·00
1247 $3 Hooded tanager ("Prince Bird") 2·00 3·00
MS1248 Two sheets. (a) 75×105 mm. $5 Rufous-throated solitaire ("Soufriere Bird") (vert). (b) 105×75 mm. $5 Purple-throated carib ("Doctor Bird"). Set of 2 sheets 5·50 7·00

188a "Autumn Flowers in Front of the Full Moon" (Hiroshige)

1989. Japanese Arts. Multicoloured.
1249 10c. Type **188a** 30 20
1250 40c. "Hibiscus" (Hiroshige) 45 25
1251 50c. "Iris" (Hiroshige) 50 30
1252 75c. "Morning Glories" (Hiroshige) 70 50
1253 $1 "Dancing Swallows" (Hiroshige) 2·00 85
1254 $2 "Sparrow and Bamboo" (Hiroshige) 2·75 2·25
1255 $3 "Yellow Bird and Cotton Rose" (Hiroshige) 2·75 2·75
1256 $4 "Judos Chrysanthemums in a Deep Ravine in China" (Hiroshige) 2·75 3·00
MS1257 Two sheets, each 102×76 mm. (a) $6 "Rural Cottages in Spring" (Sotatsu). (b) $6 "The Six Immortal Poets portrayed as Cats" (Kuniyoshi) (vert). Set of 2 sheets 7·00 8·50

189 Schooner

1989. "Philexfrance 89" International Stamp Exhibition, Paris and Bicentenary of French Revolution. 18th-century French Naval Vessels. Multicoloured.
1258 30c. Type **189** 70 30
1259 55c. Corvette 90 50
1260 75c. Frigate 1·25 1·10
1261 $1 Ship of the line 1·50 1·40
1262 $3 "Ville de Paris" (ship of the line) 4·00 6·00
MS1263 76×108 mm. $6 Map of St. Vincent in 18th century (vert) 3·50 4·50

190 Johnny Bench **191** Dante Bichette, 1989

1989. Famous Baseball Players (2nd series). Multicoloured.
1264 $2 Type **190** 1·10 1·00
1265 $2 Red Schoendienst 1·10 1·00
1266 $2 Carl Yastrzemski 1·10 1·00
1267 $2 Ty Cobb 1·10 1·00
1268 $2 Willie Mays 1·10 1·00
1269 $2 Stan Musial 1·10 1·00
1270 $2 Ernie Banks 1·10 1·00
1271 $2 Lou Gehrig 1·10 1·00
1272 $2 Jackie Robinson 1·10 1·00
1273 $2 Bob Feller 1·10 1·00
1274 $2 Ted Williams 1·10 1·00
1275 $2 Al Kaline 1·10 1·00

1989. Major League Baseball Rookies. Mult.
1276 60c. Type **191** 50 50
1277 60c. Carl Yastrzemski, 1961 50 50
1278 60c. Randy Johnson, 1989 50 50
1279 60c. Jerome Walton, 1989 50 50
1280 60c. Ramon Martinez, 1989 50 50
1281 60c. Ken Hill, 1989 50 50
1282 60c. Tom McCarthy, 1989 50 50
1283 60c. Gaylord Perry, 1963 50 50
1284 60c. John Smoltz, 1989 50 50
1285 60c. Bob Milacki, 1989 50 50
1286 60c. Babe Ruth, 1915 50 50
1287 60c. Jim Abbott, 1989 50 50
1288 60c. Gary Sheffield, 1989 50 50
1289 60c. Gregg Jeffries, 1989 50 50
1290 60c. Kevin Brown, 1989 50 50
1291 60c. Cris Carpenter, 1989 50 50
1292 60c. Johnny Bench, 1968 50 50
1293 60c. Ken Griffey Jr. 1989 50 50

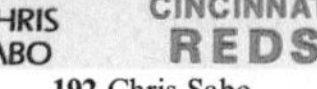

192 Chris Sabo

194 St. Vincent Amazon

193 All-Star Game Line-up (½-size illustration)

1989. Major League Baseball Award Winners. Multicoloured.
1294 60c. Type **192** 50 50
1295 60c. Walt Weiss 50 50
1296 60c. Willie Mays 50 50
1297 60c. Kirk Gibson 50 50
1298 60c. Ted Williams 50 50
1299 60c. Jose Canseco 50 50
1300 60c. Gaylord Perry 50 50
1301 60c. Orel Hershiser 50 50
1302 60c. Frank Viola 50 50

1989. American League v National League All-Star Game, 1989. Sheet 115×81 mm. Imperf.
MS1303 **193** $5 multicoloured 2·40 2·75

1989.
1304 **194** 55c. multicoloured 1·00 35

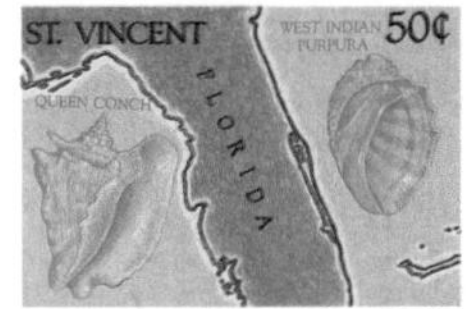

195 Queen or Pink Conch and Wide-mouthed Purpura Shells

1989. 500th Anniv (1992) of Discovery of America by Columbus (3rd issue).
1305 **195** 50c. multicoloured 45 50
1306 – 50c. multicoloured 45 50
1307 – 50c. ultramarine, blk & bl 45 50
1308 – 50c. ultramarine, blk & bl 45 50
1309 – 50c. multicoloured 45 50
1310 – 50c. multicoloured 45 50
1311 – 50c. multicoloured 45 50
1312 – 50c. black and blue 45 50
1313 – 50c. multicoloured 45 50
1314 – 50c. multicoloured 45 50
1315 – 50c. multicoloured 45 50
1316 – 50c. multicoloured 45 50
1317 – 50c. multicoloured 45 50
1318 – 50c. multicoloured 45 50
1319 – 50c. multicoloured 45 50
1320 – 50c. multicoloured 45 50
1321 – 50c. multicoloured 45 50
1322 – 50c. multicoloured 45 50
1323 – 50c. multicoloured 45 50
1324 – 50c. multicoloured 45 50

DESIGNS: No. 1306, Caribbean reef fishes; 1307, Sperm whale; 1308, Fleet of Columbus; 1309, Sharksucker (fish); 1310, Columbus planting flag; 1311, Navigational instruments; 1312, Sea monster; 1313, Kemp's ridley turtle; 1314, Magnificent frigate bird; 1315, Caribbean manatee; 1316, Caribbean monk seal; 1317, Mayan chief, dugout canoe and caravel; 1318, Blue-footed boobies ("Masked Boobies"); 1319, Venezuelan pile village; 1320, Atlantic wing oyster and lion's-paw scallop; 1321, Great hammerhead and short-finned mako; 1322, Brown pelican and hyacinth macaw ("Hyacinthine Macaw"); 1323, Venezuelan bowmen; 1324, Capuchin and squirrel monkeys.

Nos. 1305/24 were printed together, se-tenant, forming a composite design of a map of the Caribbean showing the voyages of Columbus.

196 Command Module "Columbia" returning to Earth

1989. 20th Anniv of First Manned Landing on Moon. Multicoloured.

1325 35c. Type **196** 90 30
1326 75c. Lunar module "Eagle" landing . . . . 1·75 80
1327 $1 "Apollo 11" launch . . . 1·75 80
1328 $2 Buzz Aldrin on Moon . . 2·50 2·50
1329 $2 Lunar module "Eagle" 2·50 2·50
1330 $2 Earth rise from the Moon . . . . 2·50 2·50
1331 $2 Neil Armstrong . . . . 2·50 2·50
1332 $3 "Eagle" and "Columbia" in Moon orbit . . . . . 2·75 2·75
MS1333 Two sheets, each 108 × 79 mm. (a) $3 Command Module "Columbia". $3 Lunar Module "Eagle". (b) $6 Neil Armstrong stepping on to Moon (vert). Set of 2 sheets . . . . . 9·50 12·00

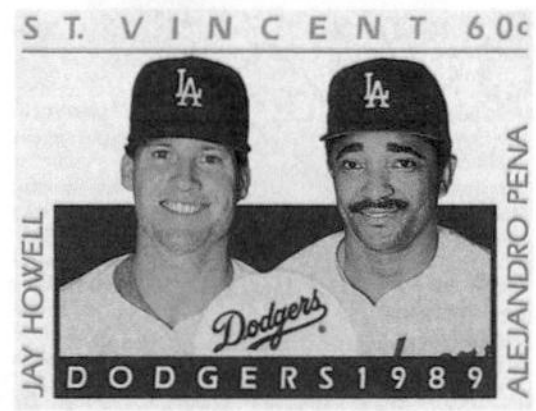

197 Jay Howell and Alejandro Pena

1989. Centenary of the Los Angeles Dodgers (1st issue). Baseball Players. Multicoloured.

1334 60c. Type **197** 45 45
1335 60c. Mike Davis and Kirk Gibson 45 45
1336 60c. Fernando Valenzuela and John Shelby 45 45
1337 60c. Jeff Hamilton and Franklin Stubbs 45 45
1338 60c. Aerial view of Dodger Stadium (no inscription) 45 45
1339 60c. Ray Searage and John Tudor 45 45
1340 60c. Mike Sharperson and Mickey Hatcher 45 45
1341 60c. Coaching staff 45 45
1342 60c. John Wetteland and Ramon Martinez 45 45
1343 60c. Tim Belcher and Tim Crews 45 45
1344 60c. Orel Hershiser and Mike Morgan 45 45
1345 60c. Mike Scioscia and Rick Dempsey 45 45
1346 60c. Dave Anderson and Alfredo Griffin 45 45
1347 60c. Dodgers' emblem . . . 45 45
1348 60c. Kal Daniels and Mike Marshall 45 45
1349 60c. Eddie Murray and Willie Randolph 45 45
1350 60c. Tom Lasorda and Jose Gonzalez 45 45
1351 60c. Lenny Harris, Chris Gwynn and Billy Bean . . 45 45

See also Nos. 1541/58.

198 "Eurema venusta"

1989. Butterflies. Multicoloured.

1352 6c. Type **198** 25 15
1353 10c. "Historis odius" . . . 30 15
1354 15c. "Cynthia virginiensis" 40 15
1355 75c. "Leptotes cassius" . . 80 65
1356 $1 "Battus polydamas" . . 90 75
1357 $2 "Astraptes talus" . . . . 2·00 2·25
1358 $3 "Danaus gilippus" . . . 2·50 2·75
1359 $5 "Myscelia antholia" . . . 3·50 4·00
MS1360 Two sheets, each 76 × 103 mm. (a) $6 "Danaus plexippus" (vert). (b) $6 "Eurema daira" (vert). Set of 2 sheets . . . . 8·00 9·00

199 Young Footballers

1989. World Cup Football Championship, Italy (1990) (1st issue). Multicoloured.

1361 10c. Type **199** 35 20
1362 55c. Youth football teams 70 30
1363 $1 St. Vincent team in training . . . . 1·25 90
1364 $5 National team with trophies . . . . 3·00 4·50
MS1365 Two sheets, each 103 × 73mm. (a) $6 Youth team. (b) $6 National team. Set of 2 sheets . . . . 12·00 11·00

See also Nos. 1559/63.

200 St. Vincent Amazon ("St. Vincent Parrott")

1989. Wildlife. Multicoloured.

1366 65c. Type **200** 75 65
1367 75c. Whistling warbler . . . 90 75
1368 $5 Black snake . . . . . . 4·00 6·00
MS1369 97 × 70 mm. $6 Volcano plant (vert) . . . . 4·50 6·50

1989. California Earthquake Relief Fund. Nos. 1276/302 surch **+10c CALIF. EARTHQUAKE RELIEF**.

1370 60c.+10c. Type **191** 60 70
1371 60c.+10c. Carl Yastrzemski 60 70
1372 60c.+10c. Randy Johnson 60 70
1373 60c.+10c. Jerome Walton . . 60 70
1374 60c.+10c. Ramon Martinez 60 70
1375 60c.+10c. Ken Hill 60 70
1376 60c.+10c. Tom McCarthy 60 70
1377 60c.+10c. Gaylord Perry . . 60 70
1378 60c.+10c. John Smoltz . . 60 70
1379 60c.+10c. Bob Milacki . . . 60 70
1380 60c.+10c. Babe Ruth . . . 60 70
1381 60c.+10c. Jim Abbott . . . 60 70
1382 60c.+10c. Gary Sheffield . . 60 70
1383 60c.+10c. Gregg Jeffries . . 60 70
1384 60c.+10c. Kevin Brown . . 60 70
1385 60c.+10c. Cris Carpenter . . 60 70
1386 60c.+10c. Johnny Bench . . 60 70
1387 60c.+10c. Ken Griffey Jr . . 60 70
1388 60c.+10c. Type **192** 60 70
1389 60c.+10c. Walt Weiss . . . 60 70
1390 60c.+10c. Willie Mays . . . 60 70
1391 60c.+10c. Kirk Gibson . . . 60 70
1392 60c.+10c. Ted Williams . . 60 70
1393 60c.+10c. Jose Canseco . . 60 70
1394 60c.+10c. Gaylord Perry . . 60 70
1395 60c.+10c. Orel Hershiser . . 60 70
1396 60c.+10c. Frank Viola . . . 60 70

201a Mickey Mouse and Minnie Mouse by Seagull Monument, Utah

1989. "World Stamp Expo '89" International Stamp Exhibition, Washington (1st issue). Walt Disney cartoon characters and U.S. monuments. Multicoloured.

1397 1c. Type **201a** 10 10
1398 2c. Mickey Mouse and Goofy at Lincoln Memorial 10 10
1399 3c. Mickey and Minnie Mouse at Crazy Horse Memorial, South Dakota 10 10
1400 4c. Mickey Mouse saluting "Uncle Sam" Wilson statue, New York 10 10
1401 5c. Goofy and Mickey Mouse at Benjamin Franklin Memorial, Philadelphia 10 10
1402 10c. Goofy and Mickey Mouse at George Washington statue, New York 10 10
1403 $3 Mickey Mouse at John F. Kennedy's birthplace, Massachusetts . . . . . . 3·50 4·00
1404 $6 Mickey and Minnie Mouse at Mount Vernon, Virginia . . . . 5·50 6·00
MS1405 Two sheets, each 127 × 100 mm. (a) $5 Mickey and Minnie Mouse over Mount Rushmore, South Dakota. (b) $5 Mickey Mouse and Donald Duck at Stone Mountain, Georgia. Set of 2 sheets . . . . 9·00 10·00

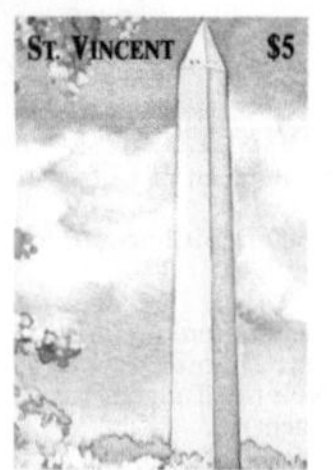

201b Washington Monument

1989. "World Stamp Expo '89" International Stamp Exhibition, Washington (2nd issue). Sheet 61 × 78 mm.

MS1406 **201b** $5 multicoloured 2·10 2·50

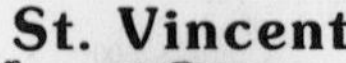

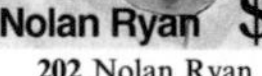

202 Nolan Ryan

204 Arms and 1979 Independence 50c. Stamp

203 Early Wynn

1989. Famous Baseball Players (3rd series).

1407 **202** $2 multicoloured . . . . 85 1·00

1989. Famous Baseball Players (4th series). As T **203**.

1408/88 30c. × 81 multicoloured Set of 81 . . . . 16·00 18·00

1989. 10th Anniv of Independence.

1489 **204** 65c. multicoloured . . . 1·00 70
MS1490 57 × 77 mm. $10 multicoloured . . . . 5·00 6·50

204a Holy Family (detail, "The Adoration of the Magi") (Botticelli)

205 Boy Scout, 1989

1989. Christmas. Paintings by Botticelli and Da Vinci. Multicoloured.

1491 10c. Type **204a** 15 10
1492 25c. Crowd (detail, "The Adoration of the Magi") (Botticelli) 25 15
1493 30c. "The Madonna of the Magnificat" (detail) (Botticelli) 25 15
1494 40c. "The Virgin and Child with St. Anne and St. John the Baptist" (detail) (Da Vinci) 30 20
1495 55c. Angel (detail, "The Annunciation") (Da Vinci) 40 30
1496 75c. Virgin Mary (detail, "The Annunciation") (Da Vinci) 50 50
1497 $5 "Madonna of the Carnation" (detail) (Da Vinci) . . . . 3·00 4·25
1498 $6 "The Annunciation" (detail) (Botticelli) . . . . 3·50 4·75
MS1499 Two sheets, each 70 × 94 mm. (a) $5 "The Virgin of the Rocks" (detail) (Da Vinci). (b) $5 Holy Family (detail, "The Adoration of the Magi") (Botticelli). Set of 2 sheets . . 5·50 6·50

1989. 75th Anniv of Boy Scout and 60th Anniv of Girl Guide Movements in St. Vincent. Mult.

1500 35c. Type **205** 55 50
1501 35c. Guide, ranger and brownie 55 50
1502 55c. Boy scout in original uniform 75 50
1503 55c. Mrs. Jackson (founder of St. Vincent Girl Guides) 75 50
1504 $2 Scouts' 75th Anniv logo 2·00 3·25
1505 $2 Mrs. Russell (Girl Guide leader, 1989) . . . . . . 2·00 3·25
MS1506 Two sheets, each 105 × 75 mm. (a) $5 Scout in canoe. (b) Scout and Guide with flagpoles (horiz). Set of 2 sheets 9·00 10·00

206 Man and Blind Girl

207 Two Pence Blue

206a Scuttling of "Admiral Graf Spee" (German pocket battleship), 1939

1990. 25th Anniv (1989) of Lions Club of St. Vincent. Multicoloured.

1507 10c. Type **206** 40 20
1508 65c. Handing out school books (horiz) 70 50
1509 75c. Teacher explaining diabetes (horiz) 80 60
1510 $2 Blood sugar testing machine (horiz) . . . . . 1·75 2·00
1511 $4 Distributing book on drugs (horiz) . . . . . . 2·75 4·00

1990. 50th Anniv of Second World War. Mult.

1512 5c. Type **206a** 35 35
1513 10c. General de Gaulle and French resistance, 1940 35 30
1514 15c. British tank, North Africa, 1940 . . . . . . 40 30
1515 25c. U.S.S. "Reuben James" (destroyer) in periscope sight, 1941 . . . . 50 30
1516 30c. General MacArthur and map of S.W. Pacific, 1942 . . . . 55 35
1517 40c. American parachute drop on Corregidor, 1945 60 40
1518 55c. H.M.S. "King George V" (battleship) engaging "Bismarck" (German battleship), 1941 70 55
1519 75c. American battleships entering Tokyo Bay, 1945 80 70
1520 $5 Hoisting the Soviet flag on the Reichstag, Berlin, 1945 . . . . 3·25 4·00
1521 $6 American aircraft carriers, Battle of Philippines Sea, 1944 . . 3·75 4·25
MS1522 100 × 70 mm. $6 Japanese Mitsubishi A6M Zero-Sen fighter, Battle of Java Sea, 1942 . . . 3·75 4·25

1990. 150th Anniv of the Penny Black.

1523 **207** $2 black, green and mauve . . . . 1·25 1·50
1524 – $4 black and mauve . . 2·50 3·25
MS1525 130 × 99 mm. – $6 black, red and yellow . . . . 4·00 4·75

DESIGN: $4, $6 Penny Black.

207a Scrooge McDuck as 18th-century Admiral

1990. "Stamp World London '90" International Stamp Exhibition. British Uniforms. Walt Disney cartoon characters. Multicoloured.

1526 5c. Type **207a** 20 15
1527 10c. Huey as Light Infantry bugler, 1854 . . . . . . 25 15
1528 15c. Minnie Mouse as Irish Guards drummer, 1900 35 20
1529 25c. Goofy as Seaforth Highlanders lance-corporal, 1944 . . . . 45 30
1530 $1 Mickey Mouse as 58th Regiment ensign, 1879 . . 1·25 1·00
1531 $2 Donald Duck as Royal Engineers officer, 1813 . . 1·90 2·00
1532 $4 Mickey Mouse as Duke of Edinburgh's Royal Regiment drum major . . 3·00 3·50
1533 $5 Goofy as Cameronians sergeant piper, 1918 . . . 3·00 3·50
MS1534 Two sheets, each 120 × 100 mm. (a) $6 Goofy as officer in King's Lifeguard of Foot, 1643. (b) $6 Mickey Mouse as Grenadier Guards drummer (vert). Set of 2 sheets . . . . . 7·00 8·00

1990. Nolan Ryan—Sixth No-hitter. No. 1407 optd **Sixth No-Hitter 11 June 90 Oakland Athletics.**

1535 **202** $2 multicoloured . . . . 1·00 1·25

208a Queen Elizabeth signing Visitor's Book

210 Maradona, Argentina

1990. 90th Birthday of Queen Elizabeth the Queen Mother.

1536 **208a** $2 black, green and mauve . . . . 1·50 1·75
1537 – $2 black, green and mauve . . . . 1·50 1·75
1538 – $2 black, green and mauve . . . . 1·50 1·75
MS1539 – 90 × 75 mm. $6 multicoloured . . . . 3·50 4·50

DESIGNS: No. 1537, **MS**1539, Queen Elizabeth in evening dress; 1538, Queen Elizabeth the Queen Mother in Coronation robes, 1953.

1990. Nolan Ryan—300th Win. No. 1407 optd **300th Win Milwaukee Brewers July 31, 1990.**

1540 **202** $2 multicoloured . . . . 1·00 1·25

1990. Cent of Los Angeles Dodgers (2nd issue). Baseball Players. As T **197**. Multicoloured.

1541 60c. Mickey Hatcher and Jay Howell 45 50
1542 60c. Juan Samuel and Mike Scioscia 45 50
1543 60c. Lenny Harris and Mike Hartley 45 50
1544 60c. Ramon Martinez and Mike Morgan 45 50
1545 60c. Aerial view of Dodger Stadium (inscr "DODGER STADIUM") 45 50
1546 60c. Stan Javier and Don Aase 45 50
1547 60c. Ray Searage and Mike Sharperson 45 50
1548 60c. Tim Belcher and Pat Perry 45 50
1549 60c. Dave Walsh, Jose Vizcaino, Jim Neidlinger, Jose Offerman and Carlos Hernandez 45 50
1550 60c. Hubie Brooks and Orel Hershiser 45 50
1551 60c. Tom Lasorda and Tim Crews 45 50
1552 60c. Fernando Valenzuela and Eddie Murray . . . 45 50
1553 60c. Kal Daniels and Jose Gonzalez 45 50
1554 60c. Dodgers emblem . . . 45 50
1555 60c. Chris Gwynn and Jeff Hamilton 45 50
1556 60c. Kirk Gibson and Rick Dempsey 45 50
1557 60c. Jim Gott and Alfredo Griffin 45 50
1558 60c. Ron Perranoski, Bill Russell, Joe Ferguson, Joe Amalfitano, Mark Cresse, Ben Hines and Manny Mota 45 50

1990. World Cup Football Championship, Italy (2nd issue). Multicoloured.

1559 10c. Type **210** 40 15
1560 75c. Valderrama, Colombia 85 75
1561 $1 Francescoli, Uruguay . . 1·10 95
1562 $5 Ceulemans, Belgium . . 4·25 5·50
MS1563 Two sheets, each 101 × 85 mm. (a) $6 Klinsmann, West Germany. (b) $6 Careca, Brazil. Set of 2 sheets . . . . 7·50 8·50

1990. 95th Anniv of Rotary International. Nos. 1230/8 optd with Rotary emblem.

1564 10c. Type **186** 30 20
1565 40c. "Liberte" 50 40
1566 50c. "Mauretania I" (launched 1906) 55 45
1567 75c. "France" 80 70
1568 $1 "Aquitania" 90 90
1569 $2 "United States" . . . . 1·60 1·90
1570 $3 "Olympic" . . . . . . 2·00 2·75
1571 $4 "Queen Elizabeth" . . . 2·25 3·00
MS1572 Two sheets, each 141 × 108 mm. (a) $6 "Queen Mary" (85 × 28 mm). (b) $6 "Queen Elizabeth 2" (85 × 28 mm). Set of 2 sheets 8·00 10·00

1990. Olympic Medal Winners, Seoul. Nos. 1153/6 optd.

1573 10c. Type **178** (optd **JOE DELOACH U.S.A. STEVE LEWIS U.S.A. PAUL ERANG KENYA**) 20 20
1574 50c. Long jumping (optd **CARL LEWIS U.S.A.**) . . 60 60
1575 $1 Triple jumping (optd **HRISTO MARKOV BULGARIA**) 90 90
1576 $5 Boxing (optd **HENRY MASKE E. GERMANY**) 3·25 4·00
MS1577 85 × 63 mm. $10 Olympic flame (optd **FINAL MEDAL STANDINGS**) . . . . 6·50 7·50

213 "Dendrophylax funalis" and "Dimerandra emarginata"

214 "Miraculous Draught of Fishes" (detail, Rubens)

1990. "EXPO 90" International Garden and Greenery Exposition, Osaka. Orchids. Mult.

1578 10c. Type **213** 35 20
1579 15c. "Epidendrum elongatum" 40 25
1580 45c. "Comparettia falcata" 60 30
1581 60c. "Brassia maculata" . . 75 60
1582 $1 "Encyclia cochleata" and "Encyclia cordigera" . . 90 80
1583 $2 "Cyrtopodium punctatum" . . . . . . 1·50 1·90
1584 $4 "Cattleya labiata" . . . 2·50 3·50
1585 $5 "Bletia purpurea" . . . 2·75 3·50
MS1586 Two sheets, each 108 × 78 mm. (a) $6 "Vanilla planifolia Jackson". (b) $6 "Ionopsis utricularioides". Set of 2 sheets . . . . 7·50 8·50

1990. Christmas. 350th Death Anniv of Rubens. Multicoloured.

1587 10c. Type **214** 25 20
1588 45c. "Crowning of Holy Katherine" (detail) . . . 45 25
1589 50c. "St. Ives of Treguier" (detail) 50 30
1590 65c. "Allegory of Eternity" (detail) 65 45
1591 $1 "St. Bavo receives Monastic Habit of Ghent" (detail) 90 80
1592 $2 "Crowning of Holy Katherine" (different detail) . . . . 1·50 1·75
1593 $4 "St. Bavo receives Monastic Habit of Ghent" (different detail) 2·75 3·50
1594 $5 "Communion of St. Francis" (detail) . . . 3·00 3·50
MS1595 Four sheets. (a) 70 × 100 mm. $6 "Allegory of Eternity" (different detail). (b) 70 × 100 mm. $6 As 50c. (c) 100 × 70 mm. $6 As Type **214** (horiz). (d) 100 × 70 mm. $6 "St. Bavo receives Monastic Habit of Ghent" (different detail) (horiz). Set of 4 sheets . . . . 12·50 13·00

215 Geoffrey Chaucer

1990. International Literacy Year (1st issue). Chaucer's "Canterbury Tales". Mult.

1596 40c. Type **215** 45 45
1597 40c. "When April with his showers" 45 45
1598 40c. "When Zephyr also has ..." 45 45
1599 40c. "And many little birds ..." 45 45
1600 40c. "And palmers to go seeking out ..." 45 45
1601 40c. Quill in ink well and open book 45 45
1602 40c. Green bird in tree . . . 45 45
1603 40c. Brown bird in tree and franklin's head 45 45
1604 40c. Purple bird in tree and banner 45 45
1605 40c. Canterbury 45 45
1606 40c. Knight's head 45 45
1607 40c. Black bird in tree and squire's head 45 45
1608 40c. Friar 45 45
1609 40c. Franklin 45 45
1610 40c. Prioress and monk holding banner 45 45
1611 40c. Summoner, Oxford clerk and parson 45 45
1612 40c. Sergeant-at-Law and knight on horseback . . . 45 45
1613 40c. Squire 45 45
1614 40c. "In fellowship ..." . . . 45 45
1615 40c. Cockerel and horse's legs 45 45
1616 40c. Hens 45 45
1617 40c. Hen and rabbit 45 45
1618 40c. Horses' legs and butterfly 45 45
1619 40c. "And briefly, when the sun ..." 45 45

Nos. 1596/1619 were printed together, se-tenant, forming a composite design.

See also Nos. 1777/88 and 1790/1801.

215a Self-portrait, 1889

1990. Death Centenary of Vincent van Gogh (artist). Multicoloured.

1620 1c. Type **215a** 45 55
1621 5c. Self-portrait, 1886 . . . 45 55
1622 10c. Self-portrait with hat and pipe, 1888 . . . . . 45 55
1623 15c. Self-portrait at easel, 1888 . . . . 45 55
1624 20c. Self-portrait, 1887 . . . 1·00 1·25
1625 45c. Self-portrait, 1889 (different) . . . . 1·25 1·25
1626 $5 Self-portrait with pipe, 1889 . . . . 3·00 4·00
1627 $6 Self-portrait wearing straw hat, 1887 . . . . . 3·00 4·00

215b "The Photographer"

1990. Hummel Figurines. Multicoloured.

1628 10c. Type **215b** 30 15
1629 15c. "Ladder and Rope" . . 40 15
1630 40c. "Druggist" 60 30
1631 60c. "Hello" 75 45
1632 $1 "Boots" . . . . 1·00 80
1633 $2 "The Artist" . . . . . . 1·40 1·75
1634 $4 "Waiter" . . . . 2·50 3·25
1635 $5 "The Postman" . . . . 2·75 3·25
MS1636 Two sheets, each 94 × 121 mm. (a) Nos. 1628, 1631/2 and 1635. (b) Nos. 1629/30 and 1633/4. Set of 2 sheets . . 10·00 11·00

216 American Football Game

1991. 25th Anniv of Super Bowl American Football Championship (1st issue). T **216** and similar vert designs. Multicoloured.

MS1637 Twenty-five sheets, each 127 × 101 mm, containing 50c. × 2 as horiz pairs forming composite designs of game scenes or 50c. × 3 (final sheet) showing Vince Lombardi Trophy and helmets of participating teams. Set of 25 sheets . . . . 15·00

217 Programme Cover of XXV Super Bowl (1/3-size illustration)

1991. 25th Anniv of Super Bowl American Football Championships (2nd issue). T **217** and similar multicoloured designs, each showing a different programme cover illustration. Imperf.

MS1638 Twenty-five sheets, 125 × 99 mm or 99 × 125 mm, each with a face value of $2. Set of 25 sheets . . . . 29·00

218 U.S.A. 1893 1c. Columbus Stamp

1991. 500th Anniv (1992) of Discovery of America by Columbus (4th issue). Designs showing U.S.A. 1893 Columbian Exposition, Chicago, stamps (Nos. 1639/54) or ships (others). Multicoloured.

1639 1c. Type **218** 50 60
1640 2c. Columbus 2c. 50 60
1641 3c. Columbus 3c. 50 60
1642 4c. Columbus 4c. 50 60
1643 5c. Columbus 5c. 50 60
1644 6c. Columbus 6c. 50 60
1645 8c. Columbus 8c. 50 60
1646 10c. Columbus 10c. 50 60
1647 15c. Columbus 15c. 50 60
1648 30c. Columbus 30c. 60 70
1649 50c. Columbus 50c. 70 80
1650 $1 Columbus $1 . . . . . 75 85
1651 $2 Columbus $2 . . . . . 1·00 1·10
1652 $3 Columbus $3 . . . . . 1·40 1·50
1653 $4 Columbus $4 . . . . . 2·00 2·10
1654 $5 Columbus $5 . . . . . 2·40 2·50
1655 $10 "Santa Maria", scarlet macaw and tropical flower 5·00 5·50
1656 $10 Logo, "Santa Maria" and Amerindian hut . . . 5·00 5·50
MS1657 Two sheets, each 98 × 72 mm. (a) $6 Sailors on ship's fo'c'sle. (b) $6 Ship's figurehead. Set of 2 sheets . . 8·00 9·00

219 Pebbles and Hoppy boxing

1991. Sports. Characters from the "Flintstones" cartoons. Multicoloured.

1658 10c. Type **219** 30 10
1659 15c. Fred Flintstone and Dino playing football . . 45 15
1660 45c. Fred losing rowing race to Barney Rubble 65 30
1661 55c. Betty Rubble, Wilma Flintstone and Pebbles in dressage competition . . . 80 50
1662 $1 Fred playing basketball 1·25 1·00
1663 $2 Bamm Bamm wrestling Barney with Fred as referee . . . . 1·75 1·50
1664 $4 Fred and Barney playing tennis . . . . 2·75 2·75
1665 $5 Fred, Barney and Dino cycling . . . . 2·75 2·75
MS1666 Two sheets, each 117 × 95 mm. (a) $6 Fred at the plate in baseball game. (b) $6 Fred running to homeplate. Set of 2 sheets . . . . 7·50 8·00

220 Board Meeting

1991. "The Jetsons" (cartoon film). Mult.
1667 5c. Type **220** 15 10
1668 20c. Jetsons with Dog 30 15
1669 45c. Judy and Apollo Blue 50 25
1670 50c. Cosmo Spacely and George Jetson 50 35
1671 60c. George and Elroy catching cogs (horiz) 70 50
1672 $1 Judy, Apollo, Elroy and Teddy in cavern (horiz) 1·00 1·00
1673 $2 Drill destroying the cavern (horiz) 1·50 1·50
1674 $4 Jetsons celebrating with the Grungees 2·75 2·75
1675 $5 The Jetsons returning home 2·75 2·75
MS1676 Two sheets, each 114 × 76mm. (a) $6 The Jetsons in spacecraft (horiz). (b) $6 The Jetsons in control room (horiz). Set of 2 sheets 7·00 8·00

220a "Sanger 2" (projected space shuttle)

1991. 500th Anniv (1992) of Discovery of America by Columbus, (5th issue). History of Exploration. Multicoloured.
1677 5c. Type **220a** 15 15
1678 10c. "Magellan" satellite, 1990 15 15
1679 25c. "Buran" space shuttle 25 25
1680 75c. Projected "Freedom" space station 65 65
1681 $1 Projected Mars mission space craft 80 80
1682 $2 "Hubble" telescope, 1990 1·60 1·75
1683 $4 Projected Mars mission "sailship" 2·50 2·75
1684 $5 Projected "Craf" satellite 2·50 2·75
MS1685 Two sheets, each 105 × 71 mm. (a) $6 Bow of caravel (vert). (b) $6 Caravel under full sail. Set of 2 sheets 7·00 8·00

220b Queen and Prince Philip in Spain, 1988

1991. 65th Birthday of Queen Elizabeth II. Multicoloured.
1686 5c. Type **220b** 15 15
1687 60c. Queen and Prince Philip in landau 60 45
1688 $2 Queen at Caen Hill Waterway, 1990 1·75 1·75
1689 $4 Queen at Badminton, 1983 3·00 3·25
MS1690 68 × 91 mm. $5 Queen Elizabeth II in 1988 and Prince Philip in 1989 4·00 4·25

1991. 10th Wedding Anniv of the Prince and Princess of Wales. As T **220b**. Multicoloured.
1691 20c. Prince and Princess in hard hats, 1987 75 20
1692 25c. Portraits of Prince and Princess and sons 75 20
1693 $1 Prince Henry and Prince William, both in 1988 1·25 90
1694 $5 Princess Diana in France and Prince Charles in 1987 6·00 4·75
MS1695 68 × 90 mm. $5 Princes Harry and William in Majorca, and Princess Diana presenting polo trophy to Prince Charles 5·00 4·25

221 Class D51 Steam Locomotive

1991. "Phila Nippon '91" International Stamp Exhibition, Tokyo. Japanese Trains. Mult.
1696 75c. Type **221** 65 65
1697 75c. Class 9600 steam locomotive 65 65
1698 75c. Goods wagons and chrysanthemum emblem 65 65
1699 75c. Passenger coach 65 65
1700 75c. Decorated Class C57 steam locomotive 65 65
1701 75c. Oil tanker wagon 65 65
1702 75c. Class C53 steam locomotive 65 65
1703 75c. First Japanese steam locomotive 65 65
1704 75c. Class C11 steam locomotive 65 65
1705 $1 Class 181 electric unit 65 65
1706 $1 Class EH10 electric locomotive 65 65
1707 $1 Passenger coaches and Special Express symbol 65 65
1708 $1 Class 1 electric tramcar, Sendai City 65 65
1709 $1 Class 485 electric unit 65 65
1710 $1 Street-cleaning tram, Sendai City 65 65
1711 $1 "Hikari" express train 65 65
1712 $1 Class ED11 electric locomotive 65 65
1713 $1 Class EF66 electric locomotive 65 65
MS1714 Four sheets, each 108 × 77 mm. (a) $6 Class C55 steam locomotive (vert). P13 × 13½. (b) $6 Series 400 electric train. (c) $6 Class C62 steam locomotive (vert). (d) $6 "Super Hitachi" electric train. Set of 4 sheets 15·00 16·00

222 Marcello Mastroianni (actor)

1991. Italian Entertainers. Multicoloured.
1715 $1 Type **222** 70 70
1716 $1 Sophia Loren (actress) 70 70
1717 $1 Mario Lanza (singer) 70 70
1718 $1 Federico Fellini (director) 70 70
1719 $1 Arturo Toscanini (conductor) 70 70
1720 $1 Anna Magnani (actress) 70 70
1721 $1 Giancarlo Giannini (actor) 70 70
1722 $1 Gina Lollobrigida (actress) 70 70
1723 $1 Enrico Caruso (operatic tenor) 70 70
MS1724 117 × 80 mm. $6 Luciano Pavarotti (operatic tenor) (horiz) 5·50 6·00

223 Madonna

1991. Madonna (American singer). Mult.
1725 $1 Type **223** 95 95
1726 $1 In strapless dress 95 95
1727 $1 Wearing necklaces, looking right 95 95
1728 $1 In green dress 95 95
1729 $1 Wearing necklaces, looking to front 95 95
1730 $1 With wrist bangles 95 95
1731 $1 With hand to face 95 95
1732 $1 In purple dress 95 95
1733 $1 With microphone 95 95
MS1734 79 × 118 mm. $6 Madonna (25 × 40 mm) 6·50 7·00

224 John Lennon

1991. John Lennon (British musician). Mult.
1735 $1+2c. Type **224** 90 90
1736 $1+2c. With Beatle hair cut 90 90
1737 $1+2c. In cap 90 90
1738 $1+2c. In red polka-dot shirt 90 90
1739 $1+2c. In green polo-neck jumper and jacket 90 90
1740 $1+2c. In glasses and magenta jacket 90 90
1741 $1+2c. With long hair and glasses 90 90
1742 $1+2c. In black jumper 90 90
1743 $1+2c. In polo-neck jumper 90 90

225 Free French Resistance Fighters, 1944

1991. Anniversaries and Events. Multicoloured.
1744 10c. Type **225** 30 25
1745 45c. De Gaulle with Churchill, 1944 1·00 55
1746 50c. Protestor with banner 45 45
1747 65c. Tales around the camp fire (vert) 70 50
1748 75c. Liberation of Paris, 1944 70 60
1749 75c. Building Berlin Wall 70 60
1750 90c. German flag and protestors' shadows 1·00 80
1751 $1 Presidents Bush and Gorbachev shaking hands 80 80
1752 $1 "Marriage of Figaro" 2·50 1·50
1753 $1.50 British trenches and Mafeking Siege 3d. stamp 1·75 2·00
1754 $1.50 Class P-36 steam locomotive, Trans-Siberian Railway 1·75 2·00
1755 $1.50 Map of Switzerland and woman in traditional costume 1·75 2·00
1756 $1.65 Lilienthal's signature and "Flugzeug Nr. 13 Doppeldecker" 2·00 2·25
1757 $2 Street fighting, Kiev 2·50 2·75
1758 $2 Gottfried Leibniz (mathematician) 2·50 2·75
1759 $3 "The Clemency of Titus" 3·75 3·75
1760 $3.50 Angelfish and scout diver 2·50 2·75
MS1761 Four sheets. (a) 101 × 72 mm. $4 Arms of Berlin. (b) 77 × 116 mm. $4 Mozart and signature (vert). (c) 77 × 116 mm. $5 President De Gaulle (vert). (d) 117 × 89 mm. $5 Scout badge and Jamboree emblem. Set of 4 sheets 13·00 15·00

ANNIVERSARIES AND EVENTS: Nos. 1744/5, 1748, **MS**1761c, Birth centenary of Charles de Gaulle (French statesman); Nos. 1746, 1749/51, **MS**1761a, Bicentenary of Brandenburg Gate, Berlin; Nos. 1747, 1753, 1760, **MS**1761d, 50th death anniv of Lord Baden-Powell and World Scout Jamboree, Korea; Nos. 1752, 1759, **MS**1761b, Death bicentenary of Mozart; No. 1754, Centenary of Trans-Siberian Railway; No. 1755, 700th anniv of Swiss Confederation; No. 1756, Centenary of Otto Lilienthal's gliding experiments; No. 1757, 50th anniv of capture of Kiev; No. 1758, 750th anniv of Hanover.

226 Myrvyn Bennion

1991. 50th Anniv of Japanese Attack on Pearl Harbor. Recipients of Congressional Medal of Honor. Multicoloured.
1762 $1 Type **226** 70 70
1763 $1 George Cannon 70 70
1764 $1 John Finn 70 70
1765 $1 Francis Flaherty 70 70
1766 $1 Samuel Fuqua 70 70
1767 $1 Edwin Hill 70 70
1768 $1 Herbert Jones 70 70
1769 $1 Isaac Kidd 70 70
1770 $1 Jackson Pharris 70 70
1771 $1 Thomas Reeves 70 70
1772 $1 Donald Ross 70 70
1773 $1 Robert Scott 70 70
1774 $1 Franklin van Valkenburgh 70 70
1775 $1 James Ward 70 70
1776 $1 Cassin Young 70 70

226a Mickey Mouse, Goofy and Pluto as Pauper Pals

1991. International Literacy Year (1990) (2nd issue). Scenes from Disney cartoon films. Multicoloured. (a) "The Prince and The Pauper".
1777 5c. Type **226a** 30 25
1778 10c. Mickey as the bored prince 30 25
1779 15c. Donald Duck as the valet 35 30
1780 25c. Mickey as the prince and the pauper 40 30
1781 60c. Exchanging clothes 80 55
1782 75c. Prince and pauper with suit of armour 90 65
1783 80c. Throwing food from the battlements 1·00 70
1784 $1 Pete as Captain of the Guard 1·25 85
1785 $2 Mickey and Donald in the dungeon 2·00 1·75
1786 $3 Mickey and Donald at dungeon window 2·50 2·25
1787 $4 Goofy rescuing Mickey and Donald 3·00 3·00
1788 $5 Crowning the real prince 3·00 3·00
MS1789 Four sheets, each 127 × 101 mm. (a) $6 Crowning the wrong prince. (b) $6 Pete holding Mickey. (c) $6 The pauper on the throne. (d) $6 Mickey telling troops to seize the guard. Set of 4 sheets 14·00 15·00

(b) "The Rescuers Down Under".
1790 5c. Miss Bianca 30 25
1791 10c. Bernard 30 25
1792 15c. Matre d'Francoise 35 30
1793 25c. Wilbur the Albatross 40 25
1794 60c. Jake the Kangaroo Mouse 80 55
1795 75c. Bernard, Bianca and Jake in the outback 90 65
1796 80c. Bianca and Bernard to the rescue 1·00 70
1797 $1 Marahute the Eagle 1·25 85
1798 $2 Cody and Marahute with eggs 2·00 1·75
1799 $3 McLeach and his pet, Joanna the Goanna 2·50 2·50
1800 $4 Frank the Frill-necked Lizard 3·00 3·00
1801 $5 Red Kangaroo, Krebbs Koala and Polly Platypus 3·00 3·25
MS1802 Four sheets, each 127 × 102 mm. (a) $6 The Rescuers. (b) $6 Ethiopian and Japanese mice delegates. (c) $6 Wilbur carrying Bianca and Bernard. (d) $6 Wilbur in pain. Set of 4 sheets 14·00 15·00

227 Hans-Dietrich Genscher and "Winged Victory" Statue

1991. European History. Multicoloured.
1803 $1 Type **227** 1·75 1·50
1804 $1 Destruction of Berlin Wall 1·75 1·50
1805 $1 Churchill, De Gaulle and Appeal to the French, 1940 1·75 1·50
1806 $1 Eisenhower, De Gaulle and D-Day, 1944 1·75 1·50
1807 $1 Brandenburg Gate, Berlin (bicentenary) 1·75 1·50
1808 $1 Chancellor Helmut Kohl and meeting of Berlin mayors, 1989 1·75 1·50
1809 $1 De Gaulle with Chancellor Adenauer 1·75 1·50
1810 $1 Pres. Kennedy's visit to Europe, 1961, Washington and Lafayette 1·75 1·50
MS1811 106 × 88 mm. $6 Casablanca Conference, 1942, and demolition of Berlin Wall (24½ × 39 mm) 4·75 6·00

1991. Famous Golfers. As T **227**. Mult.
1812 $1 Gary Player 1·75 1·25
1813 $1 Nick Faldo 1·75 1·25
1814 $1 Severiano Ballesteros 1·75 1·25
1815 $1 Ben Hogan 1·75 1·25
1816 $1 Jack Nicklaus 1·75 1·25
1817 $1 Greg Norman 1·75 1·25
1818 $1 Jose-Maria Olazabal 1·75 1·25
1819 $1 Bobby Jones 1·75 1·25

1991. Famous Entertainers. As T **277**. Mult.
1820 $2 Michael Jackson . . . . 1·75 1·75
1821 $2 Madonna . . . . 1·75 1·75
1822 $2 Elvis Presley . . . . . . 1·75 1·75
1823 $2 David Bowie . . . . . . 1·75 1·75
1824 $2 Prince . . . . 1·75 1·75
1825 $2 Frank Sinatra . . . . . 1·75 1·75
1826 $2 George Michael . . . . 1·75 1·75
1827 $2 Mick Jagger . . . . . . 1·75 1·75
MS1828 Two sheets, each 110 × 82 mm. (a) $6 Madonna (29 × 43 mm). (b) $6 Elvis Presley (29 × 43 mm). Set of 2 sheets 10·00 10·00

1991. Famous Chess Masters. As T **227**. Mult.
1829 $1 Francoise Philidor . . . 1·25 1·00
1830 $1 Karl Anderssen . . . . 1·25 1·00
1831 $1 Wilhelm Steinitz . . . . 1·25 1·00
1832 $1 Alexandrovich Alekhine 1·25 1·00
1833 $1 Boris Spassky . . . . . 1·25 1·00
1834 $1 Robert Fischer . . . . . 1·25 1·00
1835 $1 Anatoly Karpov . . . . 1·25 1·00
1836 $1 Garry Kasparov . . . . 1·25 1·00

1991. Nobel Prize Winners. As T **227**. Mult.
1837 $1 Albert Einstein (mathematical physicist) 1·40 1·00
1838 $1 Wilhelm Rontgen (physicist) . . . . 1·40 1·00
1839 $1 William Shockley (chemist) . . . . 1·40 1·00
1840 $1 Charles Townes (physicist) . . . . 1·40 1·00
1841 $1 Lev Landau (physicist) 1·40 1·00
1842 $1 Guglielmo Marconi (applied physicist) . . . . 1·40 1·00
1843 $1 Willard Libby (chemist) 1·40 1·00
1844 $1 Ernest Lawrence (nuclear physicist) . . . . 1·40 1·00

228 Walt Disney Characters decorating Christmas Tree, 1982

1991. Christmas. Walt Disney Christmas Cards. Multicoloured.
1845 10c. Type **228** 15 15
1846 45c. Mickey and Moose, 1980 . . . . 40 30
1847 55c. Mickey, Pluto and Donald carrying bauble, 1970 . . . . 50 40
1848 75c. Duckling and egg shell, 1943 . . . . 70 70
1849 $1.50 Walt Disney characters decorating globe, 1941 . . . . . . 1·25 1·50
1850 $2 The Lady and the Tramp by Christmas tree, 1986 1·50 1·75
1851 $4 Walt Disney characters carol singing, 1977 . . . 2·75 3·25
1852 $5 Mickey in fairy-tale castle, 1965 . . . . . . 2·75 3·50
MS1853 Two sheets. (a) 102 × 128 mm. $6 Characters in balloon basket, 1966. (b) 128 × 102 mm. $6 Characters in national costumes, 1966. Set of 2 sheets . . . . 9·00 9·50

229 Kings Hill

1992. Preserving the Environment. Mult.
1854 10c. Type **229** 20 20
1855 55c. Planting sapling 50 45
1856 75c. Doric Temple, Botanic Gardens 60 65
1857 $2 18th-century map of Kings Hill . . . . 1·40 2·00

229a Kingstown from the Cliffs

1992. 40th Anniv of Queen Elizabeth II's Accession. Multicoloured.
1858 10c. Type **229a** 20 15
1859 20c. Deep water wharf, Kingstown 35 15
1860 $1 Residential suburb, Kingstown 60 60
1861 $5 Kingstown from the interior . . . . 2·75 3·25
MS1862 Two sheets, each 75 × 92 mm. (a) $6 Deep water wharf (different). (b) $6 Beach. Set of 2 sheets . . . . 9·00 9·50

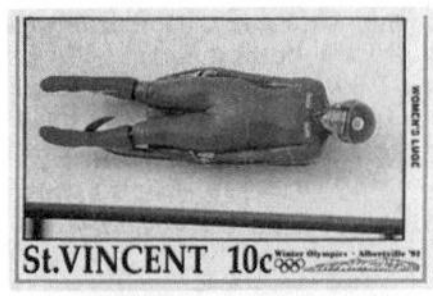

230 Women's Luge

1992. Winter Olympic Games, Albertville (1st issue). Multicoloured.
1863 10c. Type **230** 15 15
1864 15c. Women's figure skating (vert) 20 20
1865 25c. Two-man bobsleigh . . 25 25
1866 30c. Mogul skiing (vert) . . 30 30
1867 45c. Nordic combination . . 40 40
1868 55c. Ski jumping 55 55
1869 75c. Men's giant slalom . . 65 65
1870 $1.50 Women's slalom (vert) 1·10 1·10
1871 $5 Ice hockey . . . . 3·25 3·75
1872 $8 Biathlon (vert) . . . . . 4·25 5·00
MS1873 Two sheets, each 100 × 70 mm. (a) $6 Women's speed skating (vert). (b) $6 Men's downhill skiing (vert). Set of 2 sheets . . . . 9·50 11·00
See also Nos. 1966/80.

231 Women's Synchronized Swimming

1992. Olympic Games, Barcelona. Multicoloured.
1874 10c. Type **231** 20 20
1875 15c. Men's high jump (vert) 20 20
1876 25c. Men's small-bore rifle shooting 30 20
1877 30c. Men's 200 m (vert) . . 30 20
1878 45c. Men's judo (vert) . . . 35 25
1879 55c. Men's 200 m freestyle swimming 40 30
1880 75c. Men's javelin (vert) . . 50 50
1881 $1.50 Men's 4000 m pursuit cycling (vert) . . . . . . 3·75 2·00
1882 $5 Boxing . . . . 2·75 3·75
1883 $8 Women's basketball (vert) . . . . 9·50 9·50
MS1884 Two sheets, each 100 × 70 mm. (a) $15 Sailboarding (vert). (b) $15 Men's singles tennis (vert). Set of 2 sheets . . . . . 18·00 18·00

231a The Wolf as General of Spanish Moors

1992. International Stamp Exhibitions. Walt Disney cartoon characters. Multicoloured. (a) "Granada '92", Spain. The Three Pigs in Spanish Uniforms.
1885 15c. Type **231a** 20 10
1886 40c. Pig as captain of infantry 40 25
1887 $2 Pig as halberdier . . . . 1·25 1·50
1888 $4 Pig as nobleman . . . . 2·25 3·00
MS1889 128 × 102 mm. $6 Nobleman at castle window . . 3·00 3·75

(b) "World Columbian Stamp Expo '92", Chicago Landmarks.
1890 10c. Mickey Mouse and Goofy looking at Picasso sculpture (horiz) 20 15
1891 50c. Mickey and Donald Duck admiring Robie House (horiz) 45 35
1892 $1 Calder sculpture in Sears Tower (horiz) 80 60
1893 $5 Goofy in Buckingham Memorial Fountain (horiz) . . . . 2·50 3·00
MS1894 128 × 102 mm. $6 Mickey painting Minnie . . . . 3·00 3·75

232 "Nina"

1992. 500th Anniv of Discovery of America by Columbus (6th issue). "World Columbian Stamp Expo '92", Chicago. Multicoloured.
1895 5c. Type **232** 40 40
1896 10c. "Pinta" 40 30
1897 45c. "Santa Maria" 75 50
1898 55c. Fleet leaving Palos, 1492 . . . . 75 55
1899 $4 Christopher Columbus (vert) . . . . 3·00 3·50
1900 $5 Arms of Columbus (vert) 3·00 3·50
MS1901 Two sheets, each 115 × 86 mm. (a) $6 "Santa Maria" sighting land ($42\frac{1}{2}$ × 57 mm). (b) $6 Route of voyage ($42\frac{1}{2}$ × 57 mm). Set of 2 sheets . . . . 8·50 10·00

233 Elvis looking Pensive

1992. 15th Death Anniv of Elvis Presley (1st issue). Multicoloured.
1902 $1 Type **233** . . . . 1·25 1·00
1903 $1 Wearing black and yellow striped shirt . . . 1·25 1·00
1904 $1 Singing into microphone 1·25 1·00
1905 $1 Wearing wide-brimmed hat . . . . 1·25 1·00
1906 $1 With microphone in right hand . . . . 1·25 1·00
1907 $1 In Army uniform . . . . 1·25 1·00
1908 $1 Wearing pink shirt . . . 1·25 1·00
1909 $1 In yellow shirt . . . . . 1·25 1·00
1910 $1 In jacket and bow tie . . 1·25 1·00
MS1911 76 × 107 mm. $6 In blue shirt ($28\frac{1}{2}$ × $42\frac{1}{2}$ mm) . . . . . 8·00 8·00
See also Nos. 2029/37, 2038/46 and 2047/9.

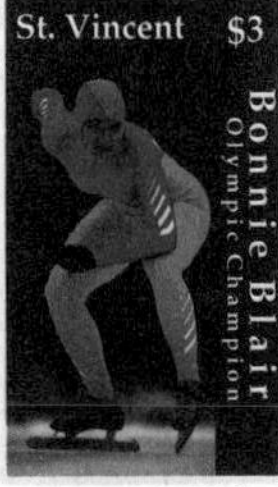

234 Bonnie Blair

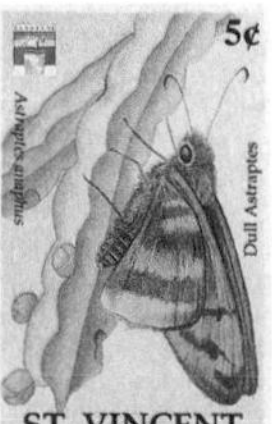

235 "Astraptes anaphus"

1992. Bonnie Blair's Victories in 500 m Speed Skating at Calgary and Albertville Olympic Games. Multicoloured.
1912 $3 Type **234** . . . . 2·25 2·50
MS1913 185 × 127 mm. $2 Turning corner (horiz); $2 With skates in arms (43 × 51 mm); $2 On straight (horiz) . . . . 4·50 4·75

1992. "Genova '92" International Thematic Stamp Exhibition (1st issue). Butterflies. Multicoloured.
1914 5c. Type **235** 30 40
1915 10c. "Anartia jatrophae" (horiz) 30 20
1916 35c. "Danaus eresimus" . . 55 40
1917 45c. "Battus polydamus" . . 60 45
1918 55c. "Junonia evarete" (horiz) 70 50
1919 65c. "Urbanus proteus" . . 80 60
1920 75c. "Pyrgus oileus" (horiz) 90 65
1921 $1 "Biblis hyperia" . . . . 1·00 75
1922 $2 "Eurema daira" . . . . 1·50 1·50
1923 $3 "Leptotes cassius" (horiz) 1·75 2·00
1924 $4 "Ephyriades brunnea" (horiz) . . . . 2·25 2·50
1925 $5 "Victorina stelenes" . . . 2·50 2·75
MS1926 Three sheets, each 98 × 72 mm. (a) $6 Phoebis sennae. (b) $6 Heliconius charitonius (horiz). (c) $6 Dryas julia (horiz). Set of 3 sheets . . . . 12·00 13·00
See also Nos. 1940/52.

236 "Collybia subpruinosa"

237 Rufous-breasted Hermit

1992. Fungi. Multicoloured.
1927 10c. Type **236** 30 20
1928 15c. "Gerronema citrinum" 40 20
1929 20c. "Amanita antillana" . . 45 30
1930 45c. "Dermoloma atrobrunneum" 60 35
1931 50c. "Inopilus maculosus" 70 40
1932 65c. "Pulveroboletus brachyspermus" 80 55
1933 75c. "Mycena violacella" . . 90 60
1934 $1 "Xerocomus brasiliensis" 1·00 70
1935 $2 "Amanita ingrata" . . . 1·50 1·75
1936 $3 "Leptonia caeruleocapitata" . . . . 1·75 2·25
1937 $4 "Limacella myochroa" 2·25 2·75
1938 $5 "Inopilus magnificus" . . 2·50 2·75
MS1939 Three sheets, each 101 × 68 mm. (a) $6 "Limacella guttata". (b) $6 "Amanita agglutinata". (c) $6 "Trogia buccinalis". Set of 3 sheets . . 11·00 12·00
No. 1936 is inscribed "Leptonia caeruleocaptata" in error.

1992. "Genova '92" International Thematic Stamp Exhibition (2nd issue). Hummingbirds. Multicoloured.
1940 5c. Type **237** 30 40
1941 15c. Hispaniolan emerald . . 35 20
1942 45c. Green-throated carib 60 35
1943 55c. Jamaican mango . . . 70 45
1944 65c. Vervain hummingbird 80 60
1945 75c. Purple-throated carib 90 70
1946 90c. Green mango 90 75
1947 $1 Bee hummingbird . . . 1·00 80
1948 $2 Cuban emerald . . . . . 1·75 1·75
1949 $3 Puerto Rican emerald . . 1·90 2·00
1950 $4 Antillean mango . . . . 2·40 2·75
1951 $5 Streamertail . . . . . . 2·75 2·75
MS1952 Three sheets, each 98 × 67 mm. (a) $6 Bahama woodstar. (b) $6 Antillean crested hummingbird. (c) $6 Blue-headed hummingbird. Set of 3 sheets 14·00 14·00

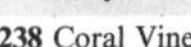
238 Coral Vine

239 Kristi Yamaguchi (U.S.A.) (figure skating)

1992. Medicinal Plants. Multicoloured.
1953 75c. Type **238** 70 85
1954 75c. Cocoplum 70 85
1955 75c. Angel's trumpet 70 85
1956 75c. Lime 70 85
1957 75c. White ginger 70 85
1958 75c. Pussley 70 85
1959 75c. Sea grape 70 85
1960 75c. Indian mulberry . . . 70 85
1961 75c. Plantain 70 85
1962 75c. Lignum vitae 70 85
1963 75c. Periwinkle 70 85
1964 75c. Guava 70 85
MS1965 Three sheets, each 98 × 69 mm. (a) $6 Wild sage. (b) $6 Clover tree. (c) $6 Aloe. Set of 3 sheets . . . . 10·50 11·00

1992. Winter Olympic Games, Albertville (2nd issue). Gold Medal Winners. Multicoloured.
1966 $1 Type **239** . . . . 80 1·00
1967 $1 Pernilla Wiberg (Sweden) (giant slalom skiing) . . . 80 1·00
1968 $1 Lyubov Yegorova (C.I.S.) (10 km cross-country skiing) . . . . . 80 1·00
1969 $1 Josef Polig (Italy) (combined alpine skiing) 80 1·00
1970 $1 Fin Christian-Jagge (Norway) (slalom skiing) 80 1·00
1971 $1 Kerrin Lee-Gartner (Canada) (downhill skiing) 80 1·00
1972 $1 Steffania Belmondo (Italy) (30 km cross-country skiing) . . . . . 80 1·00
1973 $1 Alberto Tomba (Italy) (giant slalom skiing) . . . 80 1·00
1974 $1 Fabrice Guy (France) (nordic combined skiing) 80 1·00
1975 $1 Patrick Ortlieb (Austria) (downhill skiing) . . . . 80 1·00
1976 $1 Vegard Ulvang (Norway) (nordic cross-country skiing) . . . . 80 1·00
1977 $1 Edgar Grospiron (France) (freestyle mogul skiing) . . . . 80 1·00

1978 $1 Andre Aamodt (Norway) (super giant slalom skiing) 80 1·00
1979 $1 Viktor Petrenko (C.I.S.) (figure skating) . . . . . 80 1·00
MS1980 Two sheets. (a) 108 × 78 mm. $6 Kristi Yamaguchi (U.S.A.) (figure skating) (different). (b) 111 × 81 mm. $6 Alberto Tomba (Italy) (giant slalom skiing) (different). Set of 2 sheets . . . . 8·50 9·50

No. 1968 is inscribed "LYUBOV EGOROVA" in error.

1992. 500th Anniv of Discovery of America by Columbus (7th issue). Organization of East Caribbean States. As Nos. 1670/1 of Antigua. Multicoloured.

1981 $1 Columbus meeting Amerindians . . . . . . 1·00 75
1982 $2 Ships approaching island 2·00 2·50

240 "Pinocchio"

1992. Opening of Euro-Disney Resort, Paris. Multicoloured.

1983 $1 Type **240** . . . . 1·40 1·10
1984 $1 "Alice in Wonderland" 1·40 1·10
1985 $1 "Bambi" . . . . 1·40 1·10
1986 $1 "Cinderella" . . . . . . 1·40 1·10
1987 $1 "Snow White and the Seven Dwarfs" . . . . . 1·40 1·10
1988 $1 "Peter Pan" . . . . . . 1·40 1·10
MS1989 187 × 101 mm. $5 Mickey Mouse (56 × 76 mm) . . . . . 4·50 5·00

240a Jacob K. Javits Convention Centre

1992. Postage Stamp Mega Event, New York. Sheet 100 × 70 mm.

MS1990 **240a** $6 multicoloured 4·50 5·50

No. **MS**1990 is inscribed "Jaritts" in error.

241 Spanish Galleon and Paddle-steamer

1992. First use of Adhesive Stamps on Trans-Atlantic Mail, 1840, Commemoration. Sheet 100 × 70 mm.

MS1991 **241** $6 multicoloured . . 6·00 7·00

241a "Hospitality refused to the Virgin Mary and Joseph (detail) (Metsys)

1992. Christmas. Religious Paintings. Multicoloured.

1992 10c. Type **241a** 20 20
1993 40c. "The Nativity" (detail) (Durer) 40 30
1994 45c. "The Nativity" (Geertgen Tot Sint Jans) 40 30
1995 50c. "The Nativity" (Jacopo Tintoretto) 50 35
1996 55c. "The Nativity" (detail) (Follower of Calcar) . . . 50 35
1997 65c. "The Nativity" (Workshop of Fra Angelico) 60 50
1998 75c. "The Nativity" (Master of the Louvre Nativity) 65 50
1999 $1 "The Nativity" (detail) (Lippi) 80 75
2000 $2 "The Nativity" (Petrus Christus) . . . . 1·50 1·50
2001 $3 "The Nativity" (detail) (Edward Burne-Jones) . . 2·00 2·50
2002 $4 "The Nativity" (detail) (Giotto) . . . . 2·50 3·00
2003 $5 "Birth of Christ" (detail) (Domenico Ghirlandaio) 2·75 3·25
MS2004 Three sheets, each 72 × 99 mm. (a) $6 "Birth of Christ" (detail) (Gerard Horenbout). (b) $6 "The Nativity" (detail) (Botticelli). (c) $6 "The Nativity" (detail) (Jean Fouquet). Set of 3 sheets . . . . 12·00 13·00

242 Gaston

1992. Walt Disney's "Beauty and the Beast" (cartoon film). Multicoloured.

2005 2c. Type **242** 30 60
2006 3c. Belle and her father, Maurice 30 60
2007 5c. Lumiere, Mrs. Potts and Cogsworth 35 60
2008 10c. Philippe 35 60
2009 15c. Beast and Lumiere . . 45 60
2010 20c. Lumiere and Feather Duster 45 60
2011 60c. Belle and Gaston . . . 70 75
2012 60c. Maurice 70 75
2013 60c. The Beast 70 75
2014 60c. Mrs. Potts 70 75
2015 60c. Belle and enchanted vase 70 75
2016 60c. Belle discovers enchanted rose 70 75
2017 60c. Belle with wounded Beast 70 75
2018 60c. Belle 70 75
2019 60c. Household objects alarmed 70 75
2020 60c. Belle and Chip (vert) 70 75
2021 60c. Lumiere (vert) 70 75
2022 60c. Cogsworth (vert) . . . 70 75
2023 60c. Armoire (vert) 70 75
2024 60c. Belle and Beast (vert) 70 75
2025 60c. Feather Duster (vert) 70 75
2026 60c. Footstool (vert) 70 75
2027 60c. Belle sitting on stone (vert) 70 75
MS2028 Five sheets. (a) 127 × 103 mm. $6 Lumiere (vert). (b) 127 × 103 mm. $6 Belle reading book (vert). (c) 127 × 103 mm. $6 The Beast (vert). (d) 127 × 103 mm. $6 Belle dancing (vert). (e) 103 × 127 mm. $6 Lumiere, Chip and Mrs. Potts. Set of 5 sheets . . . . 18·00 19·00

1992. 15th Death Anniv of Elvis Presley (2nd issue). Nos. 1902/10 optd **15th Anniversary**.

2029 $1 Elvis looking pensive . . 1·50 1·00
2030 $1 Wearing black and yellow striped shirt . . . 1·50 1·00
2031 $1 Singing into microphone 1·50 1·00
2032 $1 Wearing wide-brimmed hat . . . . 1·50 1·00
2033 $1 With microphone in right hand . . . . 1·50 1·00
2034 $1 In Army uniform . . . . 1·50 1·00
2035 $1 Wearing pink shirt . . . 1·50 1·00
2036 $1 In yellow shirt . . . . . 1·50 1·00
2037 $1 In jacket and bow tie . . 1·50 1·00

1992. 15th Death Anniv of Elvis Presley (3rd issue). Nos. 1820/7 optd **15th Anniversary Elvis Presley's Death August 16, 1977.**

2038 $2 Michael Jackson . . . . 2·50 1·90
2039 $2 Madonna . . . . 2·50 1·90
2040 $2 Elvis Presley . . . . . . 2·50 1·90
2041 $2 David Bowie . . . . . . 2·50 1·90
2042 $2 Prince . . . . 2·50 1·90
2043 $2 Frank Sinatra . . . . . 2·50 1·90
2044 $2 George Michael . . . . 2·50 1·90
2045 $2 Mick Jagger . . . . . . 2·50 1·90
MS2046 110 × 82 mm. $6 Elvis Presley (29 × 43 mm) . . . . . 11·00 8·00

1992. 15th Death Anniv of Elvis Presley (4th issue). As Nos. 1666/8 of Dominica. Mult.

2047 $1 Elvis Presley . . . . . . 1·75 1·75
2048 $1 Elvis with guitar . . . . 1·75 1·75
2049 $1 Elvis with microphone 1·75 1·75

245 Fifer Pig building House of Straw

1992. Walt Disney Cartoon Films. As T **245**.

2050/2138 60c. × 89 multicoloured. . . . Set of 89 . . . . 24·00 28·00
MS2139 Twenty sheets, each 128 × 103 mm or 103 × 128 mm. $6 × 20 multicoloured. Set of 20 sheets . . . . 70·00 75·00

Nos. 2050/2138 were printed as ten se-tenant sheetlets, each of nine different designs except for that for "Darkwing Duck" which contains eight vertical designs (Nos. 2131/8). The other nine sheetlets depict scenes from "The Three Little Pigs", "Thru the Mirror", "Clock Cleaners", "Orphans Benefit", "The Art of Skiing", "Symphony Hour", "How to Play Football", "The Small One" and "Chip N' Dale Rescue Rangers".

No. **MS**2139 contains two sheets for each film, one sheet for "The Three Little Pigs" being in a vert format. The Stamp designs for "The Three Little Pigs" (horiz sheet), "How to Play Football" (one), "Chip N'Dale Rescue Rangers" (both) and "Darkwing Duck" (both) are vert.

For Nos. 2050/8 and **MS**2139a/b ("The Three Little Pigs") with different face values see Nos. 2852/61.

246 Scottie Pippen

1992. Olympic Gold Medal Winners, Barcelona. Members of U.S.A. basketball team. Multicoloured.

2140 $2 Type **246** . . . . 1·50 1·25
2141 $2 Earvin "Magic" Johnson 1·50 1·25
2142 $2 Larry Bird . . . . 1·50 1·25
2143 $2 Christian Laettner . . . 1·50 1·25
2144 $2 Karl Malone . . . . . . 1·50 1·25
2145 $2 David Robinson . . . . 1·50 1·25
2146 $2 Michael Jordan . . . . 1·50 1·25
2147 $2 Charles Barkley . . . . 1·50 1·25
2148 $2 John Stockton . . . . . 1·50 1·25
2149 $2 Chris Mullin . . . . . . 1·50 1·25
2150 $2 Clyde Drexler . . . . . 1·50 1·25
2151 $2 Patrick Ewing . . . . . 1·50 1·25

247 Tom Seaver

248 Don Mattingly

1992. Famous Baseball Players (5th issue). Multicoloured.

2152 $2 Type **247** . . . . 1·40 1·60
2153 $2 Roberto Clemente . . . 1·40 1·60
2154 $2 Hank Aaron . . . . . . 1·40 1·60

1992. Famous Baseball Players (6th issue). Multicoloured.

2155 $5 Type **248** . . . . 3·00 3·75
2156 $5 Howard Johnson . . . . 3·00 3·75

249 Earth and U.N. Emblem

1992. Anniversaries and Events. Mult.

2157 10c. Type **249** 40 20
2158 45c. Airship LZ-11"Viktoria Luise" over Kiel Regatta, 1912 (vert) . . . . 1·25 35
2159 75c. Adenauer and German flag . . . . 1·25 50
2160 75c. Trophy and Bill Koch (skipper) of "America III", 1992 . . . . 75 50
2161 $1 Konrad Adenauer . . . 75 60
2162 $1 Snow leopard and emblem . . . . 1·75 60
2163 $1.50 Caribbean manatee . . 2·00 2·00
2164 $2 Humpback whale . . . . 4·50 2·50
2165 $3 Adenauer and Pres. Kennedy, 1962 . . . . . 1·60 2·25
2166 $3 Doctor checking patient's eye . . . . 3·00 3·00
2167 $4 "Discovery" space shuttle (vert) . . . . 4·25 5·00
2168 $4 Adenauer and Pope John XXIII, 1960 . . . . . 5·50 5·00
2169 $5 Schumacher and racing car . . . . 4·50 5·00
2170 $6 Zeppelin LZ-1 over Lake Constance, 1900 . . . . 5·00 5·50
MS2171 Five sheets. (a) 70 × 100 mm. $6 Cabin of airship LZ-127 "Graf Zeppelin". (b) 70 × 100 mm. $6 Douglas DC-6 airplane from Berlin Airlift. (c) 100 × 70 mm. $6 Konrad Adenauer making speech. (d) 70 × 100 mm. $6 Woolly spider monkey. (e) 119 × 89 mm. $6 Schumacher winning race. Set of 5 sheets . . . . 18·00 19·00

ANNIVERSARIES AND EVENTS: Nos. 2157, 2167, International Space Year; Nos. 2158, 2170, **MS**2171a, 75th death anniv of Count Ferdinand von Zeppelin; Nos. 2159, 2161, 2165, 2168, **MS**2171b/c, 25th death anniv of Konrad Adenauer (German statesman); No. 2160, Americas Cup Yachting Championship; Nos. 2162/4, **MS**2171d, Earth Summit '92, Rio; No. 2166, 75th anniv of International Association of Lions Clubs; No. 2169, **MS**2171e, Michael Schumacher's Victory in 1992 Belgium Grand Prix.

249a Care Bear and American White Pelican

1992. Ecology. Multicoloured.

2172 75c. Type **249a** . . . . . . 1·00 70
MS2173 101 × 72 mm. $2 Care Bear in hot air balloon (horiz) . . . 1·40 2·00

250 Farmer, Fisherman and Emblem

1993. International Conference on Nutrition, Rome.

2174 **250** 65c. multicoloured . . . 1·25 85

251 Coastal Village

1993. "Uniting the Windward Islands". Mult.

2175 10c. Type **251** 55 20
2176 40c. Children from different islands . . . . 1·10 60
2177 45c. Children and palm tree 1·10 60

252 Fisherman holding Catch

1993. Fishing. Multicoloured.

2178 5c. Type **252** 15 15
2179 10c. Fish market 15 15
2180 50c. Fishermen landing catch 60 60
2181 $5 Fishing with nets . . . . 3·00 4·25

253 Brown Pelican

254a "The Woman with Gambling Mania"

254 Sergeant Major

1993. Migratory Birds. Multicoloured.

2182 10c. Type **253** 85 50
2183 25c. Red-necked grebe (horiz) . . . . 1·25 40
2184 45c. Belted kingfisher (horiz) 1·50 40
2185 55c. Yellow-bellied sapsucker . . . . 1·60 40
2186 $1 Great blue heron . . . . 2·00 85
2187 $2 Common black hawk ("Crab Hawk") (horiz) . . 2·75 2·00

2188 $4 Yellow warbler . . . . . 3·25 3·75
2189 $5 Northern oriole (horiz) 3·25 3·75
MS2190 Two sheets, each 100×70 mm. (a) $6 Blue-winged teal (horiz). (b) $6 White ibis (horiz). Set of 2 sheets . . . . 10·00 11·00

1993. Fishes. Multicoloured.
2191 5c. Type **254** 50 50
2192 10c. Rainbow parrotfish . . 55 30
2193 55c. Hogfish 80 30
2194 75c. Porkfish . . . . 1·00 60
2195 $1 Spot-finned butterflyfish 1·10 75
2196 $2 Buffalo trunkfish . . . . 1·75 1·75
2197 $4 Queen triggerfish . . . . 2·50 3·25
2198 $5 Queen angelfish . . . . 2·50 3·25
MS2199 Two sheets, each 100×70 mm. (a) $6 Bigeye (vert). (b) $6 Small-mouthed grunt (vert). Set of 2 sheets . . . . 7·00 7·50

1993. Bicentenary of the Louvre, Paris. As T **254a**.
2200/39 $1×40 multicoloured . . Set of 40 . . . . 21·00 23·00
MS2240 Three sheets, either 70×100 mm or 100×70 mm. $6 ×3 multicoloured. P 14½. Set of 3 sheets . . . . 13·00 15·00
Nos. 2200/39 were printed as five se-tenant sheetlets showing paintings by Gericault, Ingres, Le Sueur and Poussin, Poussin, and Boucher, Brueghel, Dumont, Gainsborough, Goya and Van Eyck.
The three sheets of No. **MS**2240 depict paintings by Chassériau (52×85 mm), Delacroix and Ingres (both 85×52 mm).

255 Hexagonal Muricop

1993. Shells. Multicoloured.
2241 10c. Type **255** 30 30
2242 15c. Caribbean vase 30 30
2243 30c. Measled cowrie 40 30
2244 45c. Dyson's keyhole limpet 50 25
2245 50c. Atlantic hairy triton . . 50 40
2246 65c. Orange-banded marginella 60 45
2247 75c. Bleeding tooth 70 50
2248 $1 Queen or pink conch . . 80 65
2249 $2 Hawk-wing conch . . . 1·25 1·40
2250 $3 Musice volute . . . . . 1·75 2·25
2251 $4 Alphabet cone . . . . . 2·25 2·75
2252 $5 Antillean or incomparable cone . . . 2·25 2·75
MS2253 Three sheets, each 103×76 mm. (a) $6 Wide-mouthed purpura ("Purpura patula") (horiz). (b) $6 Netted olive ("Oliva reticularis") (horiz). (c) $6 Flame auger ("Terebra taurina") (horiz). Set of 3 sheets 14·00 15·00

256 Ishihara holding Tennis Racket

257 "Erynnyis ello"

1993. 7th Death Anniv of Yujiro Ishihara (Japanese actor).
2254 **256** 55c. black, grey and blue 1·10 1·00
2255 – 55c. black, grey and blue 1·10 1·00
2256 – 55c. black, grey and blue 1·10 1·00
2257 – 55c. multicoloured . . . 1·10 1·00
2258 – 55c. multicoloured . . . 1·10 1·00
2259 – $1 multicoloured . . . . 1·10 1·00
2260 – $1 multicoloured . . . . 1·10 1·00
2261 – $1 multicoloured . . . . 1·10 1·00
2262 – $1 multicoloured . . . 1·10 1·00
MS2263 Four sheets, each 180×140 mm. (a) 55c., $1, $2 ×2 multicoloured. (b) 55c. black, grey and gold; $1 multicoloured; $2 black, grey and gold; $2 multicoloured. (c) 55c., $2, $4, multicoloured. (d) 55c., $4 ×2 multicoloured. Set of 4 sheets 20·00 21·00
DESIGNS—VERT (as T **256**)—No. 2255, Ishihara holding camera; No. 2256, In striped shirt; No. 2257, Holding drink and cigarette; No. 2258, On board yacht; No. 2259, In naval uniform; No. 2260, In jacket and tie; No. 2261, Wearing sunglasses; No. 2262, Wearing pink shirt; No. **MS**2263b, 55c. As No. 2255, $1 In formal suit, $2 In white jacket, $2 With guitar. (28×37 mm)—No. **MS**2263a, 55c. As No. 2259, $1 Laughing, $2 In striped shirt, $2 As No. 2258. HORIZ: (56×37 mm)—No. **MS**2263c, 55c. In yellow shirt with actress; No. **MS**2263d, 55c. With cigarette, $4 As No. 2262, $4 As 2261.

256a Queen Elizabeth II at Coronation (photograph by Cecil Beaton)

1993. 40th Anniv of Coronation.
2264 **256a** 45c. multicoloured . . . 65 75
2265 – 65c. multicoloured . . . 75 85
2266 – $2 green and black . . 1·40 1·60
2267 – $4 multicoloured . . . 1·90 2·00
MS2268 – 70×100 mm. $6 multicoloured . . . . 5·00 5·50
DESIGNS: 65c. Queen Elizabeth opening Parliament; $2 Queen Elizabeth during Coronation; $4 Queen Elizabeth with corgi. (28½×42½)—$6 "Queen Elizabeth as a Young Girl" (detail).

1993. Moths. Multicoloured.
2269 10c. Type **257** 20 20
2270 50c. "Aellopos tantalus" . . 55 30
2271 65c. "Erynnyis alope" . . . 60 40
2272 75c. "Manduca rustica" . . 70 50
2273 $1 "Xylophanes pluto" . . 80 65
2274 $2 "Hyles lineata" . . . . 1·50 1·75
2275 $4 "Pseudosphinx tetrio" . . 2·50 3·00
2276 $5 "Protambulyx strigilis" 2·50 3·00
MS2277 Two sheets, each 100×70 mm. (a) $6 "Utetheisa ornatrix". (b) $6 "Xylophanes tersa". Set of 2 sheets . . . . 7·50 8·50

258 Early Astronomical Quadrant

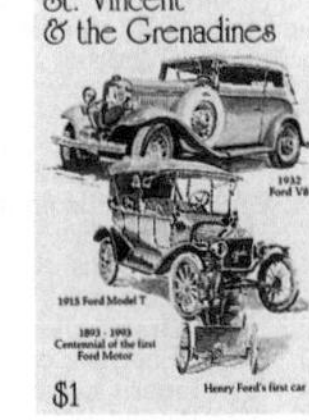

260 First Ford Car, Model "T" and "V8"

259 Supermarine Spitfire

1993. Anniversaries and Events. Red and black (Nos. 2281, 2293) or multicoloured (others).
2278 45c. Type **258** 40 25
2279 45c. "Massacre in Korea" (Picasso) (horiz) 40 25
2280 45c. Marc Girardelli (Luxembourg) (giant slalom) (horiz) 40 25
2281 45c. Willy Brandt and Pres. Nixon, 1971 (horiz) . . . 40 25
2282 45c. Count Johannes and Countess Gloria of Thurn and Taxis 40 25
2283 65c. Count and Countess of Thurn and Taxis with children (horiz) 60 40
2284 65c. Masako Owada and engagement photographs (horiz) 60 40
2285 $1 "Family of Saltimbanques" (Picasso) (horiz) 60 50
2286 $1 Princess Stephanie of Monaco 60 60
2287 $1 "Deux Tetes" (left detail) (S. Witkiewicz) 80 80
2288 $2 Countess Gloria of Thurn and Taxis . . . . 1·25 1·25
2289 $3 "Deux Tetes" (right detail) (S. Witkiewicz) . . 1·50 2·00
2290 $4 Launch of American space shuttle . . . . . . 2·25 2·75
2291 $4 "La Joie de Vivre" (Picasso) (horiz) . . . . . 2·25 2·75
2292 $5 Paul Accola (Switzerland) (downhill skiing) (horiz) 2·75 3·25
2293 $5 Willy Brandt and Robert F. Kennedy, 1967 (horiz) 2·75 3·25
2294 $5 Prince Naruhito in traditional dress and engagement photographs (horiz) . . . . 2·75 3·25
2295 $5 Pres. Clinton with school children (horiz) . . . . . 2·75 3·25
2296 $6 Bogusz Church, Gozlin (horiz) . . . . 3·00 3·50
MS2297 Seven sheets. (a) 110×76 mm. $5 Copernicus. (b) 110×76 mm. $6 "Woman eating a Melon and Boy writing" (detail) (Picasso). (c) 110×76 mm. $6 Thommy Moe (U.S.A.) (downhill skiing). (d) 110×76 mm. $6 Willy Brandt at signing of Common Declaration, 1973 (horiz). (e) 110×76 mm). $6 Masako Owada. (f) 76×110 mm. $6 "Dancing" (detail) (Wladyslaw Roguski). (g) 76×110 mm. $6 Pres. Clinton wearing stetson. Set of 7 sheets 24·00 25·00
ANNIVERSARIES AND EVENTS: Nos. 2278, 2290, **MS**2297a, 450th death anniv of Copernicus (astronomer); Nos. 2279, 2285, 2291, **MS**2297b, 20th death anniv of Picasso (artist); Nos. 2280, 2292, **MS**2297c, Winter Olympic Games '94, Lillehammer; Nos. 2281, 2293, **MS**2297d, 80th birth anniv of Willy Brandt (German politician); Nos. 2282/3, 2288, 500th anniv (1990) of Thurn and Taxis postal service; Nos. 2284, 2294, **MS**2297e, Marriage of Crown Prince Naruhito of Japan; No. 2286, Marriage of Princess Stephanie of Monaco; Nos. 2287, 2289, 2296, **MS**2297f, "Polska '93" International Stamp Exhibition, Poznan; No. 2295, **MS**2297g, Inauguration of U.S. President William Clinton.

1993. Aviation Anniversaries. Multicoloured.
2298 50c. Type **259** 75 30
2299 $1 Eckener and airship "Graf Zeppelin" over Egypt, 1931 . . . . . . 1·25 90
2300 $1 Blanchard and Pres. Washington with balloon, 1793 . . . . 1·25 90
2301 $2 De Havilland Mosquito Mk VI . . . . 1·90 2·00
2302 $2 Eckener and "Graf Zeppelin" over New York, 1928 . . . . 1·90 2·00
2303 $3 Eckener and "Graf Zeppelin" over Tokyo, 1929 . . . . 2·75 3·00
2304 $4 Blanchard's balloon ascending from Walnut St. Prison, Philadelphia 3·00 3·25
MS2305 Three sheets, each 100×70 mm. (a) $6 Hawker Hurricane Mk I. (b) $6 Dr. Hugo Eckener (vert). (c) $6 Blanchard's balloon (vert). Set of 3 sheets 10·50 11·00
ANNIVERSARIES: Nos. 2298, 2301, **MS**2305a, 75th anniv of Royal Air Force; Nos. 2299, 2302/3, **MS**2305b, 125th birth anniv of Hugo Eckener (airship commander); Nos. 2300, 2304, **MS**2305c, Bicentenary of first airmail flight.
No. 2303 is inscr "Toyko" in error.

1993. Centenaries of Henry Ford's First Petrol Engine (Nos. 2306, 2309) and Karl Benz's First Four-wheeled car (others). Multicoloured.
2306 $1 Type **260** 90 60
2307 $2 Benz racing car, 1908, "Stuttgart" and "540K" 1·75 1·75
2308 $3 Benz car, 1894, "Tourenwagen" and "Blitzen Benz" . . . . 2·25 2·75
2309 $4 Ford "Runabout", 1903, Model "T" Tourer and saloon, 1935 . . . . . . 2·50 3·00
MS2310 Two sheets, each 100×70 mm. (a) $6 Henry Ford. (b) $6 Karl Benz. Set of 2 sheets 9·00 10·00

261 Pope John Paul II and Denver Skyline

1993. Papal Visit to Denver, Colorado, U.S.A.
2311 $1 Type **261** 80 60
MS2312 100×70 mm. $6 Pope and clock tower . . . . 4·25 4·75

262 Corvette of 1953

1993. 40th Anniv of Corvette Range of Cars. Multicoloured.
2313 $1 Type **262** . . . . 80 1·00
2314 $1 1993 model . . . . . . 80 1·00
2315 $1 1958 model . . . . . . 80 1·00
2316 $1 1960 model . . . . . . 80 1·00
2317 $1 "40" and symbolic chequered flag emblem . . 80 1·00
2318 $1 1961 model . . . . . . 80 1·00
2319 $1 1963 model . . . . . . 80 1·00
2320 $1 1968 model . . . . . . 80 1·00
2321 $1 1973 model . . . . . . 80 1·00
2322 $1 1975 model . . . . . . 80 1·00
2323 $1 1982 model . . . . . . 80 1·00
2324 $1 1984 model . . . . . . 80 1·00

263 Gedung Shrine, 1920

1993. Asian International Stamp Exhibitions. Multicoloured. As T **263**. (a) "Indopex '93", Surabaya, Indonesia. Horiz designs.
2325/54 5, 10, 20, 45, 55, 75c., $1 ×2, $1.50 ×18, $2, $4, $5 ×2. Set of 30 . . . 23·00 25·00
MS2355 Three sheets. (a) 105×135 mm. $6 Relief of Sudamala epic, Mt. Lawu. (b) 105×135 mm. $6 Plaque from Banyumas, Java. (c) 135×105 mm. $6 Panel from Ramayana reliefs (vert). Set of 3 sheets . . . . 11·00 13·00
Nos. 2325/32 and 2351/4 show Indonesian scenes, Nos. 2333/50 masks (Nos. 2333/8) or paintings (Nos. 2339/50).

(b) "Taipei '93", Taiwan. Horiz designs.
2356/85 5, 10, 20, 45, 55, 75c., $1×2, $1.50×18, $2, $4, $5×2 Set of 30 . . 23·00 25·00
MS2386 Three sheets, each 135×105 mm. (a) $6 Two Stone Guardians, Longmen Caves, Henan. (b) $6 Stone guardian, Longmen Caves, Henan (vert). (c) $6 Giant Buddha, Yungung Caves (vert). Set of 3 sheets . . . . . 11·00 13·00
Nos. 2356/63 and 2382/5 show Chinese scenes, Nos. 2364/81 kites. (Nos. 2364/9) or paintings (Nos. 2370/81).

(c) "Bangkok '93", Thailand. Vert (5, 55c., $2, $4) or horiz (others).
2387/2416 5, 10, 20, 45, 55, 75c., $1×2, $1.50×18, $2, $4, $5×2 Set of 30 23·00 25·00
MS2417 Three sheets, each 105×135 mm. (a) $6 Masked dancer. (b) $6 Standing Buddha, Hua Hin (vert). (c) $6 Carved roof boss, Dusit Mahaprasad (vert). Set of 3 sheets . . . . 11·00 13·00
Nos. 2387/4 and 2413/16 show Thai scenes, Nos. 2395/2412 murals from Buddhaisawan Chapel (Nos. 2395/2400), paintings (Nos. 2401/6) or sculptures (Nos. 2407/12).

264 Players from St. Vincent and Mexico

1993. Qualifying Rounds for World Cup Football Championship, U.S.A. Multicoloured.
2418 5c. Type **264** 15 20
2419 10c. Honduras match . . . 15 15
2420 65c. Costa Rica match . . . 55 35
2421 $5 St. Vincent goalkeeper 3·25 4·75

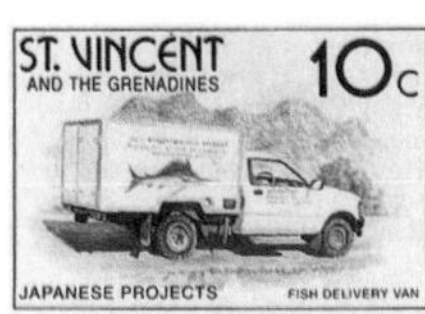

265 Fish Delivery Van

1993. Japanese Aid for Fishing Industry. Multicoloured.
2422 10c. Type **265** 20 10
2423 50c. Fish aggregation device (vert) 45 30
2424 75c. Game fishing launch . . 60 50
2425 $5 Fish market . . . . . . 3·25 4·75

1993. Famous Baseball Players (7th issue). As T **247**. Multicoloured.
2426 $2 Reggie Jackson . . . . . 1·10 1·25

265a "Adoration of the Magi" (detail) (Durer)

1993. Christmas. Religious Paintings. Black, yellow and red (Nos. 2427/9, 2434) or multicoloured (others).

2427 10c. Type **265a** 20 10
2428 35c. "Adoration of the Magi" (different detail) (Durer) 40 20
2429 40c. "Adoration of the Magi" (different detail) (Durer) 45 25
2430 50c. "Holy Family with Saint Francis" (detail) (Rubens) 55 30
2431 55c. "Adoration of the Shepherds" (detail) (Rubens) 55 30
2432 65c. "Adoration of the Shepherds" (different detail) (Rubens) 65 40
2433 $1 "Holy Family" (Rubens) 90 90
2434 $5 "Adoration of the Magi" (different detail) (Durer) 2·50 4·50
MS2435 Two sheets, each 103 × 127 mm. (a) $6 "Adoration of the Magi" (different detail) (Dürer) (horiz). (b) $6 "Holy Family with Sts. Elizabeth and John" (detail) (Rubens). Set of 2 sheets . . . . 8·00 9·00

267 Barbra Streisand

1993. Barbra Streisand's Grand Garden Concert.

2436 **267** $2 multicoloured . . . . 1·40 1·40

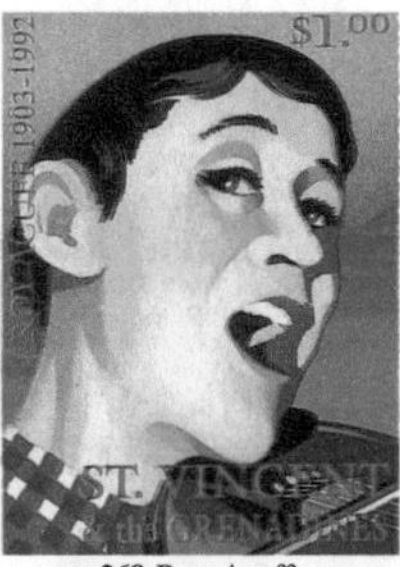

268 Roy Acuff

1994. Legends of Country Music. Multicoloured.

2437 $1 Type **268** 65 75
2438 $1 Patsy Cline in pink shirt 65 75
2439 $1 Jim Reeves in dinner jacket 65 75
2440 $1 Hank Williams in brown jacket 65 75
2441 $1 Hank Williams in purple jacket 65 75
2442 $1 Roy Acuff with microphone 65 75
2443 $1 Patsy Cline wearing white scarf 65 75
2444 $1 Jim Reeves with microphone 65 75
2445 $1 Jim Reeves in orange jacket 65 75
2446 $1 Patsy Cline with microphone 65 75
2447 $1 Hank Williams in grey jacket 65 75
2448 $1 Roy Acuff in grey jacket 65 75

269 Mobile Library

1994. Centenary of Library Service. Multicoloured.

2449 5c. Type **269** 10 20
2450 10c. Old Public Library building 10 10
2451 $1 Family reading 65 85
2452 $1 Line of books joining youth and old man . . . 65 85

270 Woman planting Breadfruit

1994. Bicent of Introduction of Breadfruit. Mult.

2453 10c. Type **270** 15 10
2454 45c. Captain Bligh with breadfruit plant 75 30
2455 65c. Slice of breadfruit . . . 50 40
2456 $5 Breadfruit growing on branch . . . . 3·25 4·75

271 Family Picnic

1994. Int Year of the Family (1st issue). Mult.

2457 10c. Type **271** 15 20
2458 50c. Family in church . . . 40 30
2459 65c. Working in the garden 50 35
2460 75c. Jogging 55 55
2461 $1 Family group (vert) . . . 70 70
2462 $2 On the beach . . . . . . 1·40 2·25

See also No. 2836.

271a Hong Kong 1992 $2.30 Olympic Games stamp and "Hong Kong Harbour in 19th Century"

1994. "Hong Kong '94" International Stamp Exhibition (1st issue). Multicoloured.

2463 40c. Type **271a** 35 50
2464 40c. St. Vincent 1991 $3.50 Scouts Jamboree stamp and "Hong Kong Harbour in 19th Century" 35 50

Nos. 2463/4 were printed together, se-tenant, forming the complete painting.

See also Nos. 2465/94 and 2495/500.

271b Bowl with Bamboo and Sparrows

1994. "Hong Kong '94" International Stamp Exhibition (2nd issue). As T **271b**. Multicoloured.

2465/94 40c. × 12, 45c. × 12, 50c. × 6 Set of 30 . . . 7·50 8·50

Nos. 2465/94 were printed as five se-tenant sheetlets, each of six different designs, depicting Ching porcelain (40c.), dragon boat races (40c.), seed-stitch purses (45c.), junks (45c.) and Qing ceramic figures (vert designs) (50c.).

272 Bird on a Flowering Spray Plate, Qianlong

1994. "Hong Kong '94" International Stamp Exhibition (3rd issue). Multicoloured.

2495 50c. Type **272** 75 75
2496 50c. Large decorated dish, Kangxi 75 75
2497 50c. Cocks on rocky ground plate, Yongzheng 75 75
2498 50c. Green decorated dish, Yuan 75 75
2499 50c. Porcelain pug dog . . . 75 75
2500 50c. Dish decorated with Dutch ship, Qianlong . . 75 75
MS2501 Two sheets, each 126 × 95 mm. (a) $2 Dr. Sun Yat-sen. (b) $2 Chiang Kai-shek. Set of 2 sheets . . . . 3·00 3·50

No. 2497 is incorrectly inscribed "Cocks on a Rocky Groung".

273 Blue Flasher

1994. Butterflies. Multicoloured.

2502 50c. Type **273** 60 55
2503 50c. Tiger swallowtail . . . 60 55
2504 50c. Lustrous copper 60 55
2505 50c. Tailed copper 60 55
2506 50c. Blue copper 60 55
2507 50c. Ruddy copper 60 55
2508 50c. Viceroy 60 55
2509 50c. California sister 60 55
2510 50c. Mourning cloak . . . 60 55
2511 50c. Red passion-flower . . 60 55
2512 50c. Small flambeau 60 55
2513 50c. Blue wave 60 55
2514 50c. Chiricahua metalmark 60 55
2515 50c. Monarch 60 55
2516 50c. Anise swallowtail . . . 60 55
2517 50c. Buckeye 60 55

274 Antonio Cabrini

275 "Epidendrum ibaguense"

1994. Juventus Football Club (Italy) Commemoration. Past and present players. Multicoloured.

2518 $1 Type **274** . . . . 1·00 90
2519 $1 Michel Platini and Roberto Baggio . . . . . 1·00 90
2520 $1 Roberto Bettega . . . . . 1·00 90
2521 $1 Gaetano Scirea . . . . . 1·00 90
2522 $1 Jurgen Kohler . . . . . . 1·00 90
2523 $1 Marco Tardelli . . . . . 1·00 90
2524 $1 Paolo Rossi . . . . . . 1·00 90
2525 $1 Giuseppe Furino . . . . 1·00 90
2526 $1 Dino Zoff . . . . 1·00 90
2527 $1 Franco Causio . . . . . 1·00 90
2528 $1 Claudio Gentile . . . . . 1·00 90
MS2529 100 × 70 mm. $6 U.E.F.A. Cup, Cup Winners Cup and European Cup trophies (all won by Juventus) (horiz) . . . . . 4·25 5·00

1994. Orchids. Multicoloured.

2530 10c. Type **275** 50 30
2531 25c. "Ionopsis utricularioides" 60 30
2532 50c. "Brassavola cucullata" 75 50
2533 65c. "Enclyclia cochleata" 90 60
2534 $1 "Liparis nervosa" . . . 1·00 75
2535 $2 "Vanilla phaeantha" . . 1·60 1·75
2536 $4 "Elleanthus cephalotus" 2·50 3·25
2537 $5 "Isochilus linearis" . . . 2·50 3·25
MS2538 Two sheets, each 100 × 70 mm. (a) $6 "Rodriguezia lanceolata". (b) $6 "Eulophia alta". Set of 2 sheets . . . . . 8·00 9·00

276 Dimorphodon

1994. Prehistoric Animals (1st series). Multicoloured.

2539 75c. Type **276** 60 65
2540 75c. Camarasaurus 60 65
2541 75c. Spinosaurus 60 65
2542 75c. Allosaurus 60 65
2543 75c. Rhamphorhynchus . . 60 65
2544 75c. Pteranodon and body of Allosaurus 60 65
2545 75c. Eudimorphodon . . . 60 65
2546 75c. Ornithomimus 60 65
2547 75c. Protoavis 60 65
2548 75c. Pteranodon 60 65
2549 75c. Quetzalcoatlus 60 65
2550 75c. Lesothosaurus 60 65
2551 75c. Heterodontosaurus . . 60 65
2552 75c. Archaeopteryx 60 65
2553 75c. Cearadactylus 60 65
2554 75c. Anchisaurus 60 65

Nos. 2539/46 and 2547/54 respectively were printed together, se-tenant, forming composite designs.

See also Nos. 2556/604.

277 Triceratops

1994. "Hong Kong '94" International Stamp Exhibition (4th issue). Prehistoric Animals. Sheet 206 × 121 mm, containing T **277** and similar multicoloured designs.

MS2555 $1.50, Type **277**; $1.50, Tyrannosaurus rex (vert); $1.50, Diplodocus; $1.50, Stegosaurus (vert) . . . . 4·75 5·00

278 Albertosaurus

1994. Prehistoric Animals (2nd series). As T **278**. Multicoloured.

2556/2603 75c. × 48. Set of 48 . . 20·00 23·00
MS2604 Four sheets, each 115 × 86 mm. (a) $6 Tyrannosaurus rex. (b) $6 Triceratops. (c) $6 Pteranodon and Diplodocus carnegii. (d) $6 Styracosaurus (vert). Set of 4 sheets . . . . 14·00 15·00

Nos. 2556/2603 were printed together, se-tenant, as four sheetlets of 12 with Nos. 2556/79 being horizontal and Nos. 2580/2603 vertical. The species depicted are Albertosaurus, Chasmosaurus, Brachiosaurus, Coelophysis, Deinonychus, Anatosaurus, Iguanodon, Baryonyx, Steneosaurus, Nanotyrannus, Camptosaurus, Camarasaurus, Hesperonis, Mesosaurus, Plesiosaurus Dolichorhynchops, Squalicorax, Tylosaurus, Plesiosoar, Stenopterygius Ichthyosaurus, Steneosaurus, Eurhinosaurus Longirostris, Cryptocleidus Oxoniensis, Caturus, Protostega, Dimorphodon, Pterodactylus, Rhamphorhynchus, Pteranodon, Gallimimus, Stegosaurus, Acanthopholis, Trachodon, Thecodonts, Ankylosaurus, Compsognathus, Protoceratops, Quetzalcoatlus, Diplodocus, Spinosaurus, Apatosaurus, Ornitholestes, Lesothosaurus, Trachodon, Protoavis, Oviraptor, Coelophysis, Ornitholestes and Archaeopteryx.

279 Mickey Mouse as Pilot

1994. 65th Anniv (1993) of Mickey Mouse. Walt Disney cartoon characters. Multicoloured.

2605 5c. Type **279** 30 30
2606 10c. Mickey in Foreign Legion 30 30
2607 15c. Mickey as frontiersman 40 40
2608 20c. Mickey, Goofy and Donald Duck 40 40
2609 35c. Horace Horsecollar and Clarabelle Cow 50 50
2610 50c. Minnie Mouse, Frankie and Figuro 60 60
2611 75c. Donald and Pluto . . . 70 70
2612 80c. Mickey holding balloons 75 75
2613 85c. Daisy Duck and Minnie 75 75
2614 95c. Minnie 80 80
2615 $1 Mickey in red trousers 80 80
2616 $1.50 Mickey raising hat . . 1·40 1·40
2617 $2 Mickey with hands in pockets . . . . 1·60 1·60
2618 $3 Mickey and Minnie . . . 2·50 2·50
2619 $4 Mickey with birthday cake . . . . 2·75 2·75
2620 $5 Mickey as Uncle Sam . . 2·75 2·75
MS2621 Four sheets. (a) 102 × 127 mm. $6 Pluto looking at portrait of Mickey. (b) 127 × 102 mm. $6 Mickey and camera (horiz). (c) 127 × 102 mm. $6 Minnie disco dancing (horiz). P 14 × 13½. (d) 127 × 102 mm. $6 Donald with Mickey's baby photo (horiz). Set of 4 sheets . . . . 18·00 18·00

280 Argentine Team

1994. World Cup Football Championship, U.S.A. Competing teams. Multicoloured.

2622 50c. Type **280** 45 45
2623 50c. Belgium 45 45
2624 50c. Bolivia 45 45
2625 50c. Brazil 45 45
2626 50c. Bulgaria 45 45
2627 50c. Cameroun 45 45

2628 50c. Colombia 45 45
2629 50c. Germany 45 45
2630 50c. Greece 45 45
2631 50c. Netherlands 45 45
2632 50c. Republic of Ireland 45 45
2633 50c. Italy 45 45
2634 50c. Mexico 45 45
2635 50c. Morocco 45 45
2636 50c. Nigeria 45 45
2637 50c. Norway 45 45
2638 50c. Rumania 45 45
2639 50c. Russia 45 45
2640 50c. Saudi Arabia 45 45
2641 50c. South Korea 45 45
2642 50c. Spain 45 45
2643 50c. Sweden 45 45
2644 50c. Switzerland 45 45
2645 50c. U.S.A. 45 45

281 Marilyn Monroe

1994. Marilyn Monroe (American film star) Commemoration. Different portraits. Multicoloured.
2646 $1 Type **281** 75 75
2647 $1 Asleep 75 75
2648 $1 With long hair style and pendulum earrings 75 75
2649 $1 Wearing striped sweater 75 75
2650 $1 With gloved hand to face 75 75
2651 $1 With bare hand to face 75 75
2652 $1 In black and white dress 75 75
2653 $1 In sequined evening dress 75 75
2654 $1 With short hair and no earrings 75 75

282 Capt. Jean-Luc Picard

1994. "Star Trek – The Next Generation" (T.V. series). Multicoloured.
2655 $2 Type **282** 1·25 1·25
2656 $2 Commander William Riker 1·25 1·25
2657 $2 Lt.-Commander Data 1·25 1·25
2658 $2 Lt. Worf 1·25 1·25
2659 $2 Crew members 1·25 1·25
2660 $2 Dr. Beverley Crusher 1·25 1·25
2661 $2 Lt. Worf and Lt. Tasha Yar 1·25 1·25
2662 $2 Q wearing hat 1·25 1·25
2663 $2 Counsellor Deanna Troi 1·25 1·25
MS2664 83 × 101 mm. $10 As No. 2659 (59 × 40 mm) 6·50 7·00

283 Shigetatsu Matsunaga (Yokohama Marinos)

284 Jef United Team

1994. Japanese Professional Football League. (a) As T **283** showing individual players and league emblem. Multicoloured.
2665/76 55c. × 8, $1.50 × 4. Set of 12 8·50 9·00
DESIGNS: 55c. Masami Ihara (Yokohama Marinos); Shunzoh Ohno (Kashima Antlers); Luiz Carlos Pereira (Verdy Kawasaki); Tetsuji Hashiratani (Verdy Kawasaki); Carlos Alberto Souza dos Santos (Kashima Antlers); Yasuto Honda (Kashima Antlers); Kazuyoshi Miura (Verdy Kawasaki); $1.50, League emblem; Takumi Horiike (Shimizu S-Pulse); Rui Ramos (Verdy Kawasaki); Ramon Angel Diaz (Yokohama Marinos).

(b) As T **284** showing teams.
2677/88 55c. × 8, $1.50 × 4. Set of 12 13·00 13·00
DESIGNS: 55c. Verdy Yomiuri; Yokohama Marinos; A. S. Flugels; Bellmare; Shimizu S-Pulse; Jubilo Iwata; Panasonic Gamba Osaka; $1.50, Kashima Antlers; Red Diamonds; Nagoya Grampus Eight; Sanfrecce Hiroshima.

(c) As T **284** showing players and teams.
2689/94 55c. × 3, $1.50 × 2, $3 A. S. Flugels 5·00 5·00
2695/700 55c. × 3, $1.50 × 2, $3 Bellmare 5·00 5·00
2701/6 55c. × 3, $1.50 × 2, $3 Panasonic Gamba Osaka 5·00 5·00
2707/12 55c. × 3, $1.50 × 2, $3 Jef United 5·00 5·00
2713/18 55c. × 3, $1.50 × 2, $3 Jubilo Iwata 5·00 5·00
2719/24 55c. × 3, $1.50 × 2, $3 Kashima Antlers 5·00 5·00
2725/30 55c. × 3, $1.50 × 2, $3 Nagoya Grampus Eight 5·00 5·00
2731/36 55c. × 3, $1.50 × 2, $3 Sanfrecce Hiroshima 5·00 5·00
2737/42 55c. × 3, $1.50 × 2, $3 Shimizu S-Pulse 5·00 5·00
2743/48 55c. × 3, $1.50 × 2, $3 Red Diamonds 5·00 5·00
2749/54 55c. × 3, $1.50 × 2, $3 Verdy Kawasaki 5·00 5·00
2755/60 55c. × 3, $1.50 × 2, $3 Yokohama Marinos 5·00 5·00
Prices quoted are for se-tenant sheetlets of six stamps.

284a Fred Whipple and Halley's Comet

1994. 25th Anniv of First Manned Moon Landing. Multicoloured.
2761 $1 Type **284a** 80 80
2762 $1 Robert Gilruth and "Gemini 12" 80 80
2763 $1 George Mueller and space walk from "Gemini 4" 80 80
2764 $1 Charles Berry and Johnsville Centrifuge 80 80
2765 $1 Christopher Kraft and "Apollo 4" 80 80
2766 $1 James van Allen and "Explorer 1" 80 80
2767 $1 Robert Goddard and Goddard liquid-fuel rocket 80 80
2768 $1 James Webb and "Spirit of 76" flight 80 80
2769 $1 Rocco Patrone and "Apollo 8" 80 80
2770 $1 Walter Dornberger and German rocket 80 80
2771 $1 Alexander Lippisch and Messerschmitt ME 163B Komet (airplane) 80 80
2772 $1 Kurt Debus and "A4b" rocket 80 80
2773 $1 Hermann Oberth and projected spaceship 80 80
2774 $1 Hanna Reitsch and "Reichenberg" flying bomb 80 80
2775 $1 Ernst Stuhlinger and "Explorer 1" 80 80
2776 $1 Werner von Braun and rocket-powered Heinkel He 112 80 80
2777 $1 Arthur Rudolph and rocket motor 80 80
2778 $1 Willy Ley and rocket airplane 80 80
MS2779 Two sheets, each 131 × 109 mm. (a) $6 Eberhardt Rees and German rocket (50 × 37 mm). (b) $6 Hogler Toftoy (50 × 37 mm) 8·00 9·00

284b Supply Convoy

1994. 50th Anniv of D-Day. Multicoloured.
2780 40c. Type **284b** 75 25
2781 $5 Unloading beached supply ship 3·00 3·75
MS2782 106 × 76 mm. $6 Liberty ship 3·25 3·75

285 Yorkshire Terrier Bitch

285a Peter Fennel (Germany) (20 km walk, 1972)

1994. Chinese New Year ("Year of the Dog"). Multicoloured.
2783 10c. Type **285** 60 35
2784 25c. Yorkshire terrier dog 65 30
2785 50c. Golden retriever 75 70
2786 50c. Pomeranian 75 70
2787 50c. English springer spaniel 75 70
2788 50c. Bearded collie 75 70
2789 50c. Irish wolfhound 75 70
2790 50c. Pekingese 75 70
2791 50c. Irish setter 75 70
2792 50c. Old English sheepdog 75 70
2793 50c. Basset hound 75 70
2794 50c. Cavalier King Charles spaniel 75 70
2795 50c. Kleiner Munsterlander 75 70
2796 50c. Shetland sheepdog 75 70
2797 50c. Dachshund 75 70
2798 65c. Bernese mountain dog 1·00 65
2799 $1 Vorstehhund 1·50 80
2800 $2 Tibetan terrier 2·25 1·75
2801 $4 West Highland terrier 3·25 3·25
2802 $5 Shih tzu 3·50 3·50
MS2803 Two sheets, each 100 × 100 mm. (a) $6 Afghan hound with puppy. (b) $6 German shepherd. Set of 2 sheets 6·50 7·00

1994. Centenary of International Olympic Committee. Gold Medal Winners.
2804 45c. Type **285a** 60 25
2805 50c. Kijung Son (Japan) (marathon), 1936 (vert) 65 30
2806 75c. Jesse Owens (U.S.A.) (100 and 200 m), 1936 (vert) 90 80
2807 $1 Greg Louganis (U.S.A.) (diving), 1984 and 1988 (vert) 1·00 1·10

286 Mark Ramprakash (England) and Wisden Trophy

1994. Centenary of First English Cricket Tour to the West Indies (1995). Multicoloured.
2809 10c. Type **286** 45 20
2810 30c. Phil Simmonds (West Indies) and Wisden Trophy 65 25
2811 $2 Garfield Sobers (West Indies) (vert) 1·75 2·00
MS2812 76 × 96 mm. $3 First English touring team, 1895 (black and brown) 2·25 2·75

286a Oryon Waterfall

288 Sir Shridath Ramphal and Map of Guyana

287 St. Vincent Family

1994. "Philakorea '94" International Stamp Exhibition, Seoul. Multicoloured.
2813 10c. Type **286a** 30 30
2814 45c. Indoor sports stadium, Pyongyang (horiz) 40 25
2815 50c. Illuminated character with house at bottom right 40 50
2816 50c. Illuminated character with red dots in centre 40 50
2817 50c. Illuminated character with animal at right 40 50
2818 50c. Illuminated character with flowers at bottom right 40 50
2819 50c. Illuminated character with dragon at left 40 50
2820 50c. Illuminated character with house at top 40 50
2821 50c. Illuminated character with dragon at top 40 50
2822 50c. Illuminated character with sun at top 40 50
2823 50c. Fish and character 40 50
2824 50c. Two pheasants and character 40 50
2825 50c. Plant and cabinet 40 50
2826 50c. Vases and cabinet 40 50
2827 50c. Books on decorated cabinet 40 50
2828 50c. Pheasant, decorated cabinet and vase 40 50
2829 50c. Pheasant and lamp on table 40 50
2830 50c. Cabinet, vase and table 40 50
2831 65c. Pombong, Chonhwadae 50 60
2832 75c. Uisangdae, Naksansa 55 60
2833 $1 Buddha of the Sokkuram Grotto, Kyangju (horiz) 60 70
2834 $2 Moksogwon (horiz) 1·10 1·40
MS2835 Two sheets. (a) 70 × 100 mm. $4 Chongdong Mirukbul (vert). (b) 100 × 70 mm. Tiger hunting scene (embroidery). Set of 2 sheets 4·25 4·75
Nos. 2825/6 and 2830 are inscr "Bookshlef" in error.

1994. International Year of the Family (2nd issue).
2836 **287** 75c. multicoloured 65 65

1994. First Recipients of Order of the Caribbean Community. Multicoloured.
2837 $1 Type **288** 70 50
2838 $2 Derek Walcott and map of St. Lucia 2·25 2·00
2839 $5 William Demas and map of Trinidad (horiz) 3·25 4·75
No. 2838 is inscribed "Wilcott" in error.

289 Twin-engined Airliner, Bequia Airport

1994. 50th Anniv of I.C.A.O. Multicoloured.
2840 10c. Type **289** 40 40
2841 65c. Union Island Airport 80 60
2842 75c. L.I.A.T. 8-100 at E. T. Joshua Airport 85 70
2843 $1 Aircraft and logo 1·00 1·25
2844 $1 Britten Norman Islander at J. F. Mitchell Airport, Bequia 1·00 1·25

290 "The Annunciation"

1994. Christmas. Religious Paintings from Jean de Berry's "Book of Hours". Multicoloured.
2845 10c. Type **290** 25 20
2846 45c. "The Visitation" 60 25
2847 50c. "The Nativity" 65 30
2848 65c. "The Purification of the Virgin" (detail) 80 40
2849 75c. "Presentation of Jesus in the Temple" 90 45
2850 $5 "Flight into Egypt" 4·00 5·50
MS2851 110 × 126 mm. $6 "Adoration of the Magi" (detail) 4·50 5·50
No. 2847 is inscribed "The Annunciation" in error.

1995. Chinese New Year ("Year of the Pig") (1st issue). Designs as Nos. 2050/8, but with different face values and with Year of the Pig logo.
2852 30c. Type **245** 60 50
2853 30c. Fiddler Pig building house of sticks 60 50
2854 30c. Practical Pig building house of bricks 60 50

2855 30c. The Big Bad Wolf 60 50
2856 30c. Wolf scaring Fiddler and Fifer Pig 60 50
2857 30c. Wolf blowing down straw house 60 50
2858 30c. Wolf in sheep costume 60 50
2859 30c. Wolf blowing down stick house 60 50
2860 30c. Wolf attempting to blow down brick house 60 50
MS2861 Two sheets. (a) 103 × 128 mm. $3 Original sketch of Practical Pig building house of brick. (b) 128 × 103 mm. $3 Practical Pig playing piano (vert). Set of 2 sheets 5·50 5·50
See also Nos. 2900/3.

291 Mealy Amazon Parrot

1995. Parrots. Multicoloured.
2862 $1 Type **291** 1·10 90
2863 $1 Nanday conure 1·10 90
2864 $1 Black-headed caique 1·10 90
2865 $1 Scarlet macaw 1·10 90
2866 $1 Red-masked conure 1·10 90
2867 $1 Blue-headed parrot 1·10 90
2868 $1 Hyacinth macaw 1·10 90
2869 $1 Sun conure 1·10 90
2870 $1 Blue and yellow macaw 1·10 90
MS2871 104 × 76 mm. $5 White-eared conure (vert) 4·00 4·50
Nos. 2862/70 were printed together, se-tenant, forming a composite design.

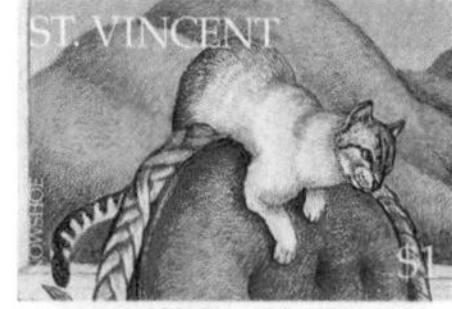

292 Snowshoe

1995. Cats. Multicoloured.
2872 $1 Type **292** 1·10 90
2873 $1 Abyssinian 1·10 90
2874 $1 Ocicat 1·10 90
2875 $1 Tiffany 1·10 90
2876 $1 Russian blue 1·10 90
2877 $1 Siamese 1·10 90
2878 $1 Bi-colour 1·10 90
2879 $1 Malayan 1·10 90
2880 $1 Manx 1·10 90
MS2881 104 × 76 mm. $6 Birman (vert) 4·75 5·50
Nos. 2872/80 were printed together, se-tenant, forming a composite design.

293 Blue-faced Booby ("Masked Booby")

1995. Birds. Multicoloured.
2882 75c. Type **293** 70 60
2883 75c. Pair of blue-faced boobies 70 60
2884 75c. Blue-faced booby preening 70 60
2885 75c. Blue-faced booby stretching 70 60
2886 75c. Great egrets 70 60
2887 75c. Roseate spoonbills 70 60
2888 75c. Ring-billed gull 70 60
2889 75c. Ruddy quail dove 70 60
2890 75c. Royal terns 70 60
2891 75c. Killdeer plover ("Killdeer") 70 60
2892 75c. Osprey 70 60
2893 75c. Magnificent frigate bird 70 60
2894 75c. Blue-faced boobies ("Masked Booby") 70 60
2895 75c. Green-backed heron 70 60
2896 75c. Double-crested cormorants ("Cormorant") 70 60
2897 75c. Brown pelican 70 60
MS2898 Two sheets, each 100 × 69 mm. (a) $5 Greater flamingo ("Flamingo") (vert). (b) $6 American Purple gallinule ("Purple Gallinule") (vert). Set of 2 sheets 9·00 10·00
Nos. 2886/97 were printed together, se-tenant, forming a composite design.

294 Churchill, Roosevelt and Stalin at Yalta Conference

1995. 50th Anniv of V.E. Day.
2899 **294** $1 multicoloured 1·25 1·00

295 Pig

296 National Flag and Globe

1995. Chinese New Year ("Year of the Pig") (2nd issue). Multicoloured, central panel in colours indicated.
2900 75c. Type **295** (green) 55 65
2901 75c. Pig (brown) 55 65
2902 75c. Pig (red) 55 65
MS2903 71 × 101 mm. $2 Two pigs (horiz) 1·25 1·50

1995. 18th World Scout Jamboree, Netherlands. Multicoloured.
2904 $1 Type **296** 70 50
2905 $4 Lord Baden-Powell 2·25 2·75
2906 $5 Handshake 2·50 3·00
MS2907 Two sheets, each 81 × 112 mm. (a) $6 Scout greeting. (b) $6 Scout salute. Set of 2 sheets 7·00 8·50

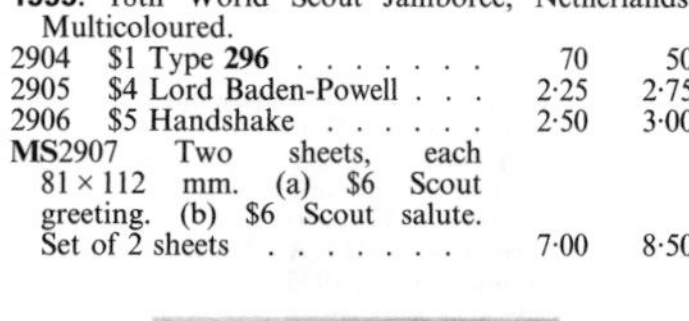

296a Tank of U.S. First Army

1995. 50th Anniv of End of Second World War in Europe. Multicoloured.
2908 $2 Type **296a** 1·25 1·25
2909 $2 V2 rocket 1·25 1·25
2910 $2 Consolidated B-24 Liberator bombers 1·25 1·25
2911 $2 French troops advancing to Strasbourg 1·25 1·25
2912 $2 Gloster G.41 Meteor fighter 1·25 1·25
2913 $2 Berlin on fire 1·25 1·25
2914 $2 Soviet tanks in Berlin 1·25 1·25
2915 $2 "Chicago Daily Tribune" headline 1·25 1·25
MS2916 107 × 77 mm. $6 Sortie markings on aircraft (57 × 42½) 3·50 4·00
No. 2909 is inscribed "Y2" in error.

297 Globe and Peace Dove

298 Women preparing Food

1995. 50th Anniv of United Nations. Multicoloured.
2917 $2 Type **297** 1·10 1·40
2918 $2 Liberty 1·10 1·40
2919 $2 U.N. Building, New York, and peace dove 1·10 1·40
MS2920 71 × 107 mm. $6 Asian child 2·75 3·50
Nos. 2917/19 were printed together, se-tenant, forming a composite design.
No. **MS**2920 is inscribed "1945–1955" in error.

1995. 50th Anniv of F.A.O. Multicoloured.
2921 $2 Type **298** 1·10 1·40
2922 $2 Woman mixing food 1·10 1·40
2923 $2 Harvesting grain 1·10 1·40
MS2924 76 × 106 mm. 76 × 106 mm. $6 Baby and logo 2·75 3·50
Nos. 2921/3 were printed together, se-tenant, forming a composite design.
No. **MS**2924 is inscribed "1945–1955" in error.

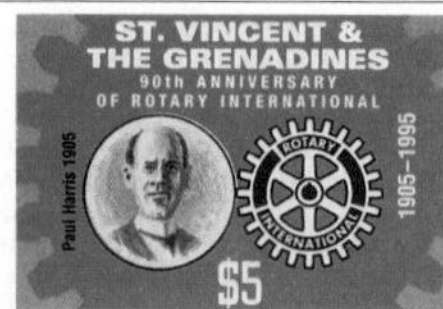

299 Paul Harris (founder) and Logo

1995. 90th Anniv of Rotary International.
2925 **299** $5 multicoloured 2·50 3·25
MS2926 113 × 79 mm. $6 National flag and logo 2·75 3·50

299a Queen Elizabeth the Queen Mother (pastel drawing)

1995. 95th Birthday of Queen Elizabeth the Queen Mother.
2927 **299a** $1.50 brown, light brown and black 2·00 1·50
2928 – $1.50 multicoloured 2·00 1·50
2929 – $1.50 multicoloured 2·00 1·50
2930 – $1.50 multicoloured 2·00 1·50
MS2931 102 × 127 mm. $6 multicoloured 4·75 4·75
DESIGNS: No. 2928, Wearing blue hat; 2929, At desk (oil painting); 2930, Wearing mauve dress; No. **MS**2931, wearing yellow dress.

1995. 50th Anniv of End of Second World War in the Pacific. As T **296a**. Multicoloured.
2932 $2 Douglas Devastator torpedo bomber 1·25 1·25
2933 $2 Doolittle's North American B-25 Mitchell "Ruptured Duck" 1·25 1·25
2934 $2 Curtiss SB2C Helldiver bomber 1·25 1·25
2935 $2 U.S.S. "Yorktown" (aircraft carrier) 1·25 1·25
2936 $2 U.S.S. "Wasp" (aircraft carrier) 1·25 1·25
2937 $2 U.S.S. "Lexington" (aircraft carrier) sinking 1·25 1·25
MS2938 107 × 77 mm. $6 American aircraft carriers 3·75 4·50

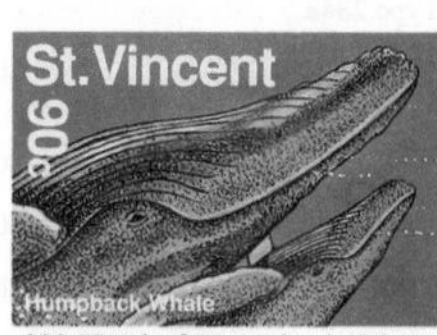

300 Head of Humpback Whale

1995. Marine Life. Multicoloured.
2939 90c. Type **300** 70 70
2940 90c. Green turtles 70 70
2941 90c. Bottlenose dolphin 70 70
2942 90c. Monk seals 70 70
2943 90c. Krill 70 70
2944 90c. Blue sharks 70 70
2945 90c. Porkfish 70 70
2946 90c. Reef butterflyfish 70 70
2947 90c. Shipwreck 70 70
2948 $1 Beaugregory (fish) (horiz) 70 70
2949 $1 Grey angelfish (horiz) 70 70
2950 $1 Yellow-tailed damselfish (horiz) 70 70
2951 $1 Four-eyed butterflyfish (horiz) 70 70
MS2952 Two sheets, each 100 × 70 mm. (a) $6 Sea anemones. (b) $6 "Physalia physalis" (jellyfish). Set of 2 sheets 7·00 7·50
Nos. 2939/47 were printed together, se-tenant, forming a composite design.

301 Symbolic Disabled Athlete

1995. Paralympic Games '95, Connecticut.
2953 **301** $1 yellow, blue and black 1·00 1·00

302 Ingrid Kristiansen

1995. World Athletic Championships, Gothenburg. Norwegian Athletes. Multicoloured.
2954 $1 Type **302** 70 70
2955 $1 Trine Hattestad 70 70
2956 $1 Grete Waitz 70 70
2957 $1 Vebjorn Rodal 70 70
2958 $1 Geir Moen 70 70
2959 $1 Steinar Hoen (horiz) 70 70

303 Nolan Ryan in Blue Jersey

1995. Retirement of Nolan Ryan (baseball player) (1993). Multicoloured.
2960 $1 Type **303** 80 80
2961 $1 With glove 80 80
2962 $1 In white jersey 80 80
2963 $1 Making pitch from left 80 80
2964 $1 Texas Rangers "All Star Game" emblem 80 80
2965 $1 Making pitch from right 80 80
2966 $1 Bleeding from blow to mouth 80 80
2967 $1 Preparing to pitch 80 80
2968 $1 Waving cap 80 80
2969 $1 Wearing "NY" cap 80 80
2970 $1 Wearing stetson with dog 80 80
2971 $1 Wearing "T" cap 80 80
2972 $1 Throwing American football 80 80
2973 $1 Nolan Ryan Foundation emblem 80 80
2974 $1 With son 80 80
2975 $1 Laughing 80 80
2976 $1 With family 80 80
2977 $1 Wearing "H" cap 80 80
MS2978 146 × 101 mm. $6 After final game for Texas Rangers 3·00 3·50

304 Breast and Bowl of Baby Food

1995. "Baby Friendly" Campaign. Multicoloured.
2979 15c. Type **304** 40 15
2980 20c. Hands squeezing milk into bowl (vert) 40 15
2981 90c. Breast-feeding (vert) 1·00 45
2982 $5 Breast-feeding emblem (vert) 3·50 4·50

305 Aerial View of Leeward Coastal Road

1995. 25th Anniv of Caribbean Development Bank. Multicoloured.
2983 10c. Type **305** 25 25
2984 15c. Feeder roads project 30 25
2985 25c. "Anthurium andraeanum" (flower) 30 25
2986 50c. Coconut palm tree (vert) 35 35
2987 65c. Fairhall Housing Scheme 45 45

306 "The God of Fire" (woodcut) (Shunichi Kadowaki)

307 Jean Shiley (U.S.A.) (high jump)

1995. Japanese Art.
2988 **306** $1.40 multicoloured . . 1·00 1·25

1995. Olympic Games, Atlanta (1996) (1st issue). Multicoloured.
2989 $1 Type **307** 75 75
2990 $1 Ruth Fuchs (Germany) (javelin) 75 75
2991 $1 Alessandro Andrei (Italy) (shot put) 75 75
2992 $1 Dorando Pietri (Italy) (marathon) 75 75
2993 $1 Heide Rosendahl (Germany) (long jump) 75 75
2994 $1 Mitsuoki Watanabe (Japan) (gymnastics) . . . 75 75
2995 $1 Yasuhiro Yamashita (Japan) (judo) 75 75
2996 $1 Dick Fosbury (U.S.A.) (high jump) 75 75
2997 $2 Long jumper and dove 1·10 1·10
2998 $2 Hurdler and deer . . . . 1·10 1·10
2999 $2 Sprinter and cheetah . . 1·10 1·10
3000 $2 Marathon runner and tiger . . . . 1·10 1·10
3001 $2 Gymnast and dove . . . 1·10 1·10
3002 $2 Rower and blue-winged teal . . . . 1·10 1·10
MS3003 Two sheets. (a) 70 × 100 mm. $5 Magic Johnson (U.S.A.) (basketball). (b) 106 × 76 mm. $5 Swimmers hand (horiz). Set of 2 sheets . . . . 7·50 7·50
See also Nos. 3357/3400.

308 Frank Thomas

1995. Famous Baseball Players (8th series). Multicoloured.
3004 $1 Type **308** 60 60
3005 $1 Cal Ripken Jnr wearing "8" jersey and helmet . . 60 60
3006 $1 Ken Griffey Jnr wearing "S" cap 60 60
3007 $1 Ken Griffey Jnr wearing turquoise-blue jersey . . . 60 60
3008 $1 Frank Thomas in "Sox" cap with bat on shoulder 60 60
3009 $1 Cal Ripken Jnr with ball and glove 60 60
3010 $1 Cal Ripkin Jnr wearing Orioles cap 60 60
3011 $1 Ken Griffey Jnr wearing "Seattle" jersey and helmet 60 60
3012 $1 Frank Thomas wearing "Chicago 35" jersey . . . 60 60

309 John Lennon

1995. Centenary of Cinema. Entertainers. Mult.
3013/21 $1 × 9 John Lennon (as T **309**) . . . . . .
3022/30 $1 × 9 Elvis Presley . . .
3031/6 $1 × 6 Elvis Presley . . .
3037/45 $1 × 9 Marilyn Monroe (with stairway in centre of sheetlet) . . . . . .
3046/54 $1 × 9 Marilyn Monroe (with superimposed full length portrait) . . . .
3055/63 $1 × 9 Marilyn Monroe (design with hand raised in centre of top row) . . . .
3013/63 Set of 51 . . . . 28·00 30·00
MS3064 Four sheets. (a) 110 × 80 mm. $6 John Lennon. (b) 80 × 110 mm. $6 Elvis Presley. (c) 80 × 110 mm. $6 Marilyn Monroe wearing red jacket. (d) 70 × 100 mm. $6 Marilyn Monroe in black slip. Set of 4 sheets . . 14·00 14·00

310 Heinrich Boll (1972 Literature)

1995. Centenary of Nobel Prize Trust Fund. Multicoloured.
3065/3112 $1 × 48. Set of 48 . . 32·00 35·00
MS3113 Four sheets, each 74 × 104 mm. (a) $6 Adolf Windaus (1928 Chemistry). (b) $6 Hideki Yukawa (1949 Physics). (c) $6 Bertha von Suttner (1905 Peace). (d) $6 Karl Landsteiner (1930 Medicine). Set of 4 sheets 14·00 14·00
DESIGNS: No. 3065, Type **310**; 3066, Walther Bothe (1954 Physics); 3067, Richard Kuhn (1938 Chemistry); 3068, Hermann Hesse (1946 Literature); 3069, Knut Hamsun (1920 Literature); 3070, Konrad Lorenz (1973 Medicine); 3071, Thomas Mann (1929 Literature); 3072, Fridtjof Nansen (1922 Peace); 3073, Fritz Pregl (1923 Chemistry); 3074, Christian Lange (1921 Peace); 3075, Otto Loewi (1936 Medicine); 3076, Erwin Schrodinger (1933 Physics); 3077, Giosue Carducci (1906 Literature); 3078, Wladyslaw Reymont (1924 Literature); 3079, Ivan Bunin (1933 Literature); 3080, Pavel Cherenkov (1958 Physics); 3081, Ivan Pavlov (1904 Medicine); 3082, Pyotr Kapitza (1978 Physics); 3083, Lev Landau (1962 Physics); 3084, Daniel Bovet (1957 Medicine); 3085, Henryk Sienkiewicz (1905 Literature); 3086, Aleksandr Prokhorov (1964 Physics); 3087, Julius von Jauregg (1927 Medicine); 3088, Grazia Deledda (1926 Literature); 3089, Bjornstjerne Bjornson (1903 Literature); 3090, Frank Kellogg (1929 Peace); 3091, Gustav Hertz (1925 Physics); 3092, Har Khorana (1968 Medicine); 3093, Kenichi Fukui (1981 Chemistry); 3094, Henry Kissinger (1973 Peace); 3095, Martin Luther King Jr. (1964 Peace); 3096, Odd Hassel (1969 Chemistry); 3097, Polykarp Kusch (1955 Physics); 3098, Ragnar Frisch (1969 Economics); 3099, Willis Lamb Jr. (1955 Physics); 3100, Sigrid Undset (1928 Literature); 3101, Robert Barany (1914 Medicine); 3102, Ernest Walton (1951 Physics); 3103, Alfred Fried (1911 Peace); 3104, James Franck (1925 Physics); 3105, Werner Forssmann (1956 Medicine); 3106, Yasunari Kawabata (1968 Literature); 3107, Wolfgang Pauli (1945 Physics); 3108, Jean-Paul Sartre (1964 Literature); 3109, Aleksandr Solzhenitsyn (1970 Literature); 3110, Hermann Staudinger (1953 Chemistry); 3111, Igor Tamm (1958 Physics); 3112, Samuel Beckett (1969 Literature).

311 ET4-03 Electric Train, Germany

1995. History of Transport. Modern passenger trains (Nos. 3114/19) or classic cars (Nos. 3120/5). Multicoloured.
3114 $1.50 Type **311** . . . . . . 1·25 1·10
3115 $1.50 TGV express train, France . . . . 1·25 1·10
3116 $1.50 Class 87 electric locomotive, Great Britain 1·25 1·10
3117 $1.50 Class "Beijing" diesel locomotive, China . . . . 1·25 1·10
3118 $1.50 Amtrak turbotrain, U.S.A. . . . . 1·25 1·10
3119 $1.50 Class RC4 electric train, Sweden . . . . . . 1·25 1·10
3120 $1.50 Duesenberg Model "J", 1931 . . . . 1·25 1·10
3121 $1.50 Sleeve-valve Minerva, 1913 . . . . 1·25 1·10
3122 $1.50 Delage "D.8. SS", 1933 . . . . 1·25 1·10
3123 $1.50 Bugatti "Royale Coupe De Ville", 1931–32 1·25 1·10
3124 $1.50 Rolls Royce "Phantom I Landauette", 1926 . . . . 1·25 1·10
3125 $1.50 Mercedes Benz "S236/120/180PS", 1927 1·25 1·10
MS3126 Two sheets, each 105 × 75 mm. (a) $5 Hispano-Suiza Type "H6B" sports car, 1924 (85 × 28½ mm). (b) $6 Eurostar train, Great Britain and France (85 × 28½ mm). Set of 2 sheets 8·00 9·00
Nos. 3120/5 also include the "Singapore '95" International Stamp Exhibition logo.

312 Grey Wolf

1995. Centenary (1992) of Sierra Club (environmental protection society). Multicoloured.
3127 $1 Type **312** 85 75
3128 $1 Grey wolf cub 85 75
3129 $1 Head of grey wolf . . . 85 75
3130 $1 Hawaiian goose 85 75
3131 $1 Pair of Hawaiian geese 85 75
3132 $1 Head of jaguar 85 75
3133 $1 Liontail macaque 85 75
3134 $1 Sand cat kitten 85 75
3135 $1 Three sand cat kittens . . 85 75
3136 $1 Orang-utan in tree (horiz) 85 75
3137 $1 Orang-utan on ground (horiz) 85 75
3138 $1 Young orang-utan (horiz) 85 75
3139 $1 Jaguar lying down (horiz) 85 75
3140 $1 Head of jaguar (horiz) 85 75
3141 $1 Pair of sand cats (horiz) 85 75
3142 $1 Hawaiian goose (horiz) 85 75
3143 $1 Three liontail macaques (horiz) 85 75
3144 $1 Head of liontail macaque (horiz) 85 75
Nos. 3136/8 are inscribed "Orangutang" in error.

313 River Nile, Egypt

1995. Natural Landmarks. Multicoloured.
3145 $1.10 Type **313** . . . . . . 1·00 85
3146 $1.10 River Yangtze, China 1·00 85
3147 $1.10 Niagara Falls, U.S.A.–Canada border . . . . . 1·00 85
3148 $1.10 Victoria Falls, Zambia–Zimbabwe border 1·00 85
3149 $1.10 Grand Canyon, U.S.A. . . . . 1·00 85
3150 $1.10 Sahara Desert, Algeria 1·00 85
3151 $1.10 Mt. Kilimanjaro, Tanzania . . . . 1·00 85
3152 $1.10 River Amazon, Brazil 1·00 85
MS3153 106 × 76 mm. $6 Haleakala Crater, Hawaii . . . . 4·50 4·75

314 Lionel Santa Handcar

1995. Christmas. Antique Disney Toys. Mult.
3154 1c. Type **314** 10 10
3155 2c. Mickey Mouse "choo-choo" 10 10
3156 3c. Minnie Mouse pram . . 10 10
3157 5c. Mickey Mouse acrobats pull-toy 15 10
3158 10c. Mickey and Pluto clockwork cart 20 10
3159 25c. Mickey Mouse motorcycle 55 10
3160 $3 Lionel Mickey Mouse handcar . . . . 3·50 3·75
3161 $5 Casey Jr. Disneyland train . . . . 5·50 6·00
MS3162 Two sheets. (a) 127 × 100 mm. $6 Lionel streamlined locomotive and Mickey Mouse wagon. (b) 100 × 127 mm. $6 "Silver Link" locomotive and Mickey the Stoker tender. Set of 2 sheets . . . . 9·00 10·00

315 Symbolic Rat

316 Spock giving Vulcan Salute

1996. Chinese New Year ("Year of the Rat").
3163 **315** 75c. black, mauve and green 50 60
3164 – 75c. black, red and green 50 60
3165 – 75c. black, purple and green 50 60
MS3166 100 × 50 mm. $1 Type **315**; $1 As No. 3164; $1 As No. 3165 1·50 1·60
MS3167 71 × 102 mm. $2 black, red and green . . . . 1·25 1·50
DESIGNS: Nos. 3164/5, Different rats.

1996. 30th Anniv of "Star Trek" Television Series. Multicoloured.
3168 $1 Type **316** 60 55
3169 $1 Capt. Kirk and Spock dressed as gangsters . . . 60 55
3170 $1 Kirk in front of computer 60 55
3171 $1 Kirk with Tribbles . . . 60 55
3172 $1 Kirk, Spock and Lt. Uhura in front of Time Portal 60 55
3173 $1 Uhura and Lt. Sulu . . . 60 55
3174 $1 Romulan commander and crew 60 55
3175 $1 City and planet 60 55
3176 $1 Khan 60 55
3177 $1 Spock with phaser . . . 60 55
3178 $1 Capt. Kirk 60 55
3179 $1 Lt. Uhura 60 55
3180 $1 Lt. Sulu 60 55
3181 $1 Starship U.S.S. "Enterprise" 60 55
3182 $1 Dr. McCoy 60 55
3183 $1 Chief Engineer Scott . . 60 55
3184 $1 Kirk, Spock and McCoy 60 55
3185 $1 Chekov 60 55
MS3186 152 × 107 mm. $6 Spock and Uhura . . . . 3·25 3·50

317 Goofy the Stamp Dealer

1996. Occupations (1st series). Walt Disney Cartoon Characters at Work. Multicoloured.
3187/95 10c. × 9 (Type **317**; Supermarket assistant; Car salesman; Florist; Fast food assistant; Street vendor; Gift shop assistant; Hobby shop assistant; Baker) . .
3196/3204 50c. × 9 (Delivery man; Truck driver; Aircraft flight crew; Train crew; Bus driver; Tour guide; Cycle messenger; Tram conductor; Air traffic controller) . . . . .
3205/13 75c. × 9 (Postal inspector; Traffic policeman; Private detectives; Highway Patrolman; Justice of the Peace; Security guard; Judge and lawyer; Sheriff; Court stenographer) . . . .
3214/22 90c. × 9 (Basketball player; Referee; Athletic coach; Ice skater; Golfer and caddy; Sports commentator; Tennis players; Football coach; Racing car driver) . . . .
3223/31 95c. × 9 (Paleontologist; Archaeologist; Inventor; Astronaut; Chemist; Engineer; Computer expert; Astronomer; Zoologist) . . . . .
3232/9 $1.10 × 8 (Classroom teacher; Nursery school teacher; Music teacher; Electronic teacher; School psychologist; School principal; Professor; Graduate (all vert))
3240/8 $1.20 × 9 (Ship builders; Fisherman; Pearl diver; Underwater photographer; Bait and tackle shop owner; Swim suit models; Marine life painter; Life guard; Lighthouse keeper)
3187/3248 Set of 62 . . . . 38·00 38·00
MS3249 Seven sheets, each 127 × 102 mm. (a) $6 Ice cream seller. (b) $6 Tug boat captain (vert). (c) $6 Members of Jury (vert). (d) $6 Cheerleaders (vert). (e) $6 Oceanographer. (f) $6 Librarian (vert). (g) $6 Deep sea diver (vert). Set of 7 sheets . . 30·00 32·00
See also Nos. 3510/56.

317a "Moses striking Rock" (Abraham Bloemaert)

1996. 125th Anniv of Metropolitan Museum of Art, New York. Multicoloured.

3250/7 75c. × 8 (Type **317a**; "The Last Communion" (Botticelli); "The Musicians" (Caravaggio); "Francesco Sassetti and Son" (Ghirlandaio); "Pepito Costa y Bunells" (Goya); "Saint Andrew" (Martini); "The Nativity" (The Dutch School); "Christ Blessing" (Solario)) . .

3258/66 90c. × 9 ("Madame Cezanne"; "Still Life with Apples and Pears"; "Man in a Straw Hat"; "Still Life with a Ginger Jar"; "Madame Cezanne in a Red Dress"; "Still Life with Crockery"; "Dominique Aubert"; "Still Life with Flowers"; "The Card Players" (all by Cezanne)) . . . . . .

3267/75 $1 × 9 ("Bullfight" (Goya); "Portrait of a Man" (Hals); "Mother and Son" (Sully); "Portrait of a Young Man" (Memling); "Matilde Stoughton de Jaudenes" (Stuart); "Josef de Jaudenes y Nebot" (Stuart); "Mont Sainte-Victoire" (Cezanne); "Gardanne" (Cezanne); "Empress Eugenie" (Winterhalter)) . . . .

3276/84 $1.10 × 9 ("The Dissolute Household" (Steen); "Gerard de Lairesse" (Rembrandt); "Juan de Pareja" (Velazquez); "Curiosity" (Ter Borch); "The Companions of Rinaldo" (Poussin); "Don Gaspar de Guzman" (Velazquez); "Merry Company on a Terrace" (Steen); "Pilate washing Hands" (Rembrandt); "Portrait of a Man" (Van Dyck))

3250/84 Set of 35 . . . . 17·00 19·00

MS3285 Four sheets, each 95 × 70 mm. (a) $6 "Hagar in the Wilderness" (Corot) (81 × 53 mm). (b) $6 "Two Young Peasant Women" (Pissarro) (81 × 53 mm). (c) $6 "Young Ladies from the Village" (Courbet) (81 × 53 mm). (d) $6 "Allegory of the Planets and Continents" (Tiepolo) (81 × 53 mm). Set of 4 sheets 13·00 15·00

318 Alien Band

319 Yoda

1996. "Star Wars" (film trilogy). Multicoloured. (a) As T **318**.

3286 35c. Type **318** . . . . . . 1·00 90
3287 35c. Darth Vader in battle 1·00 90
3288 35c. Fighter ship . . . . . 1·00 90
3289 35c. Space craft orbiting planet . . . . 1·00 90
3290 35c. Space craft and shuttle 1·00 90
3291 35c. Luke Skywalker on space bike . . . . 1·00 90

(b) As T **319**. Self-adhesive.

3292 $1 Darth Vader . . . . . . 1·90 1·75
3293 $1 Type **319** . . . . 1·90 1·75
3294 $1 Storm trooper . . . . . 1·90 1·75
MS3295 148 × 71 mm. $2 × 3 Designs as Nos. 3292/4 but triangular, 65 × 36½ mm. . . . 4·75 5·00

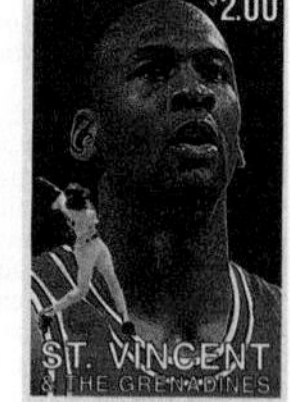

320 "Anteos menippe" **321** Michael Jordan (basketball player)

1996. Butterflies. Multicoloured.

3296 70c. Type **320** 50 40
3297 90c. "Papilio lycophron" . . 60 60
3298 90c. "Prepona buckleyana" 60 60
3299 90c. "Parides agavus" . . . 60 60
3300 90c. "Papilio cacicus" . . . 60 60
3301 90c. "Euryades duponchelli" 60 60
3302 90c. "Diaethria dymena" . . 60 60
3303 90c. "Orimba jansoni" . . . 60 60
3304 90c. "Polystichtis siaka" . . 60 60
3305 90c. "Papilio machaonides" 60 60
3306 $1 "Eunica alcmena" . . . 70 70
3307 $1.10 "Doxocopa lavinia" 80 80
3308 $2 "Tithorea tarricina" . . 1·40 1·60
MS3309 Two sheets, each 75 × 104 mm. (a) $5 "Adelpha albia". (b) $6 "Themone pais". Set of 2 sheets . . . . 6·50 7·50

Nos. 3297/3305 were printed together, se-tenant, the backgrounds forming a composite design.

1996. Sports Legends. (a) As T **321**. Multicoloured. Perf.

3310 $2 Type **321** . . . . 1·25 1·40
3311 $2 Joe Montana (American footballer) . . . . 1·25 1·40

(b) Size 69 × 103 mm. Imperf.

3312 $6 Michael Jordan . . . . 5·00 6·00
3313 $10 Joe Montana . . . . . 7·00 8·50

322 The Monkey King

1996. "CHINA '96" 9th Asian International Stamp Exhibition (1st issue). Chinese Animated Films – "Uproar in Heaven" (Nos. 3314/18) and "Nezha conquers the Dragon King" (Nos. 3319/23). Multicoloured.

3314 15c. Type **322** 20 25
3315 15c. Monkey King flying towards illuminated pole 20 25
3316 15c. Monkey King and flying horses 20 25
3317 15c. Monkey King picking fruit 20 25
3318 15c. Monkey King drinking from flask 20 25
3319 15c. Nezha waking up . . . 20 25
3320 15c. Nezha swimming with fish 20 25
3321 15c. Nezha on back of sea serpent 20 25
3322 15c. Nezha with sword . . . 20 25
3323 15c. Nezha in battle 20 25
MS3324 Two sheets, each 85 × 105 mm. (a) 75c. Monkey King (vert). (b) 75 c. Nezha (vert). Set of 2 sheets . . . . 1·40 1·60

323 Chongqing Dazu Buddha

1996. "CHINA '96" 9th Asian International Stamp Exhibition (2nd issue). Sheet 115 × 80 mm.

MS3325 **323** $2 multicoloured . . 1·40 1·60

323a Queen Elizabeth II

1996. 70th Birthday of Queen Elizabeth II. Showing different photographs. Multicoloured.

3326 $2 Type **323a** . . . . 1·50 1·50
3327 $2 Wearing Garter robes . . 1·50 1·50
3328 $2 Wearing pink hat and coat . . . . 1·50 1·50
MS3329 125 × 103 mm. $6 On Buckingham Palace balcony (horiz) . . . . 4·25 4·50

324 West Indian Boy

1996. 50th Anniv of UNICEF. Multicoloured.

3330 $1 Type **324** 60 55
3331 $1.10 European girl 70 65
3332 $2 South-east Asian girl . . 1·25 1·40
MS3333 104 × 74 mm. $5 Arab boy 2·50 3·00

325 Menorah and The Knesset

1996. 3000th Anniv of Jerusalem. Multicoloured.

3334 $1 Type **325** 70 55
3335 $1.10 The Montefiore Windmill 80 70
3336 $2 Shrine of the Book . . . 1·40 1·60
MS3337 104 × 74 mm. $5 Old City, Jerusalem . . . . 2·75 3·00

The captions on Nos. 3334 and 3336 were transposed in error.

326 Walter Winchell

1996. Centenary of Radio. Entertainers. Mult.

3338 90c. Type **326** 55 50
3339 $1 Fred Allen 60 55
3340 $1.10 Hedda Hopper . . . 70 65
3341 $2 Eve Arden . . . . 1·25 1·40
MS3342 72 × 102 mm. $6 Major Bowes . . . . 3·00 3·50

327 Bananaquit **328** Maurice King (St. Vincent) (weightlifting), Pan American Games, 1959

1996. Birds. Multicoloured.

3343 60c. Type **327** 60 45
3344 $1 Rufous-throated solitare 75 80
3345 $1 Caribbean martin (horiz) 75 80
3346 $1 Broad-winged hawk (horiz) 75 80
3347 $1 White-tailed tropic bird (horiz) 75 80
3348 $1 Black-winged stilt (horiz) 75 80
3349 $1 Bridled tern (horiz) . . . 75 80
3350 $1 Antillean euphonia (horiz) 75 80
3351 $1 Ruddy turnstone (horiz) 75 80
3352 $1 Green-throated carib (horiz) 75 80
3353 $1 Yellow-crowned night heron (horiz) 75 80
3354 $1.10 Lesser Antillean tanager 80 85
3355 $2 Purple-throated carib . . 1·40 1·60
MS3356 Two sheets, each 89 × 92 mm. (a) $5 Red-billed whistling duck. (b) $6 St. Vincent amazon. Set of 2 sheets . . . . 7·00 8·00

Nos. 3345/53 were printed together, se-tenant, with the backgrounds forming a composite design.

1996. Olympic Games, Atlanta (2nd issue). Multicoloured.

3357 20c. Type **328** 30 30
3358 70c. Eswort Coombs (St. Vincent) (400 m sprint, World University Student Games) 50 40
3359 90c. Pamenos Ballantyne (St. Vincent) (O.E.C.S. road-running) and Benedict Ballantyne (St. Vincent) (Guinness Half-marathon, 1994) . . 60 60
3360 90c. Ancient Greek runners, Olympia (horiz) 60 60
3361 $1 London landmarks (horiz) 60 60
3362 $1 Women's archery (Korea), 1988, 1992 . . . 60 60
3363 $1 Gymnastics (Japan),1960–76 . . . . . 60 60
3364 $1 Basketball (U.S.A.), 1936, 1948–68, 1976, 1984 and 1992 . . . . 60 60
3365 $1 Soccer (Spain), 1992 . . 60 60
3366 $1 Water polo (Hungary), 1956 . . . . 60 60
3367 $1 Baseball (Cuba), 1992 . . 60 60
3368 $1 Kayak (Germany), 1980 60 60
3369 $1 Fencing (France), 1980 60 60
3370 $1 Cycling (Germany), 1908, 1964, 1972–76 and 1992 60 60
3371 $1 Vitaly Shcherbo (Russia) (gymnastics), 1992 . . . . 60 60
3372 $1 Fu Mingxia (China) (diving), 1992 . . . . . . 60 60
3373 $1 Wilma Rudolph (U.S.A.) (track and field), 1960 . . 60 60
3374 $1 Rafer Johnson (U.S.A.) (decathlon), 1960 . . . . 60 60
3375 $1 Teofilo Stevenson (Cuba) (boxing), 1972–80 . . . . 60 60
3376 $1 Babe Didrikson (U.S.A.) (track and field), 1932 . . 60 60
3377 $1 Kyoko Iwasaki (Japan) (swimming), 1992 . . . . 60 60
3378 $1 Yoo Namkyu (Korea) (table tennis), 1988 . . . 60 60
3379 $1 Michael Gross (Germany) (swimming), 1984–88 . . . . 60 60
3380 $1 Yasuhiro Yamashita (Japan) (judo), 1984 (horiz) 60 60
3381 $1 Peter Rono (Kenya) (1500m race), 1988 (horiz) 60 60
3382 $1 Aleksandr Kourlovitch (Russia) (weightlifting), 1988 (horiz) 60 60
3383 $1 Juha Tiainen (Finland) (hammer throw), 1984 (horiz) 60 60
3384 $1 Sergei Bubka (Russia) (pole vault), 1988 (horiz) 60 60
3385 $1 Q. F. Newall (Great Britain) (archery), 1908 (horiz) 60 60
3386 $1 Nadia Comaneci (Rumania) (gymnastics), 1976 (horiz) 60 60
3387 $1 Carl Lewis (U.S.A.) (long jump), 1988 (horiz) . . . 60 60
3388 $1 Bob Mathias (U.S.A.) (decathlon), 1948 (horiz) 60 60
3389 $1 Chuhei Nambu (Japan) (triple jump), 1932 (horiz) 60 60
3390 $1 Duncan McNaughton (Canada) (high jump), 1932 (horiz) 60 60
3391 $1 Jack Kelly (U.S.A.) (single sculls), 1920 (horiz) 60 60
3392 $1 Jackie Joyner-Kersee (U.S.A.) (heptathlon), 1988 (horiz) 60 60
3393 $1 Tyrell Biggs (U.S.A.) (super heavyweight boxing), 1984 (horiz) . . 60 60
3394 $1 Larisa Latynina (Russia) (gymnastics), 1964 (horiz) 60 60
3395 $1 Bob Garrett (U.S.A.) (discus), 1896 (horiz) . . . 60 60
3396 $1 Paavo Nurmi (Finland) (5000m), 1924 (horiz) . . 60 60
3397 $1 Eric Lemming (Sweden) (javelin), 1908 (horiz) . . 60 60
3398 $1.10 Rodney Jack (St. Vincent) (1995 Caribbean Nations Football Cup) 70 70
3399 $1.10 Dorando Pietri (Italy) (marathon), 1908 . . . . 70 70
3400 $2 Yachting (horiz) . . . . 1·25 1·50
MS3401 Four sheets. (a) 74 × 104 mm. $5 Olympic flag (horiz). (b) 74 × 104 mm. $5 Carl Lewis (U.S.A.) (relay). (c) 104 × 74 mm. $5 Hannes Kolehmainen (Finland) (marathon), 1920 (horiz). (d) 104 × 74 mm. $5 Alexander Ditiatin (Russia) (gymnastics), 1980 (horiz). Set of 4 sheets . . 11·00 12·00

No. 3371 is inscribed "GYMNASTIECS" in error.

329 Notre Dame Cathedral, Paris

1996. "The Hunchback of Notre Dame". Scenes from the Disney cartoon film. Multicoloured.
3402/7 10c. × 6 (Type **329**; People watching puppet show; Judge Frollo on black horse; Quasimodo and his parents captured; Gargoyles; Quasimodo) . . . . .
3408/16 30c. × 9 (Captain Phoebus meets Esmeralda; Captain Phoebus and Judge Frollo; Esmeralda dancing; Esmeralda and candidates for King of Fools; Quasimodo wearing crown; Quasimodo pelted; Quasimodo carrying Esmeralda; Phoebus on black horse; Quasimodo, Esmeralda and a wounded Phoebus (all horiz)) . . . . . .
3417/25 $1 × 9 (Quasimodo chained to bell tower; Three gargoyles and Quasimodo; Quasimodo pulling down pillars; Quasimodo rescuing Esmeralda; Phoebus leading citizens; Quasimodo throwing wood; Quasimodo weeping over Esmeralda; Quasimodo and Frollo fighting; Quasimodo and Esmeralda on ledge (all horiz)) . . . . . .
3426/33 $1 × 8 (Quasimodo; Phoebus; Laverne and Hugo; Clopin; Frollo; Esmeralda; Victor; Djali) . . . .
3402/33 Set of 32 . . . . . . 17·00 19·00
MS3434 Five sheets. (a) 124 × 102 mm. $6 Quasimodo, Phoebus and Esmerelda (horiz). (b) 124 × 102 mm. $6 Esmerelda. (c) 124 × 102 mm. $6 Quasimodo cheering. (d) 104 × 126 mm. $6 Esmerelda and Quasimodo (horiz). (e) 104 × 126 mm. $6 Esmerelda and Phoebus (horiz). Set of 5 sheets . . . . 24·00 26·00
No. 3416 is inscribed "wonded phoebus" in error.

330 French Angelfish

1996. Fishes. Multicoloured.

3435	70c. Type **330**	50	40
3436	90c. Red-spotted hawkfish	60	50
3437	$1 Barred hamlet	60	60
3438	$1 Flamefish	60	60
3439	$1 Caribbean long-nosed butterflyfish	60	60
3440	$1 Royal gramma ("Fairy Basslet")	60	60
3441	$1 Red-tailed parrotfish . .	60	60
3442	$1 Black-barred soldierfish	60	60
3443	$1 Three-spotted damselfish	60	60
3444	$1 Candy basslet	60	60
3445	$1 Spot-finned hogfish . . .	60	60
3446	$1 Jackknife fish	60	60
3447	$1 Surgeon fish	60	60
3448	$1 Muttonfish	60	60
3449	$1 Seahorse	60	60
3450	$1 Comber fish	60	60
3451	$1 Angel shark	60	60
3452	$1 Moray eel	60	60
3453	$1 Bicolour parrotfish . . .	60	60
3454	$1 "Tritonium nodiferum" (sea snail)	60	60
3455	$1.10 Balloonfish ("Spiny Puffer")	70	70
3456	$2 Grey triggerfish	1·25	1·50

MS3457 Two sheets, each 106 × 76 mm. (a) $5 Queen Triggerfish. (b) $6 Blue Marlin. Set of 2 sheets . . . . 6·00 7·00
Nos. 3446/54 were printed together, se-tenant, with the backgrounds forming a composite design.
No. 3445 is inscribed "HOFGFISH" in error.

331 "Beloperone guttata"

1996. Flowers. Multicoloured.

3458	70c. Type **331**	50	40
3459	90c. "Datura candida" . . .	60	60
3460	90c. "Amherstia nobilis" . .	60	60
3461	90c. "Ipomoea acuminata"	60	60
3462	90c. "Bougainvillea glabra"	60	60
3463	90c. "Cassia alata"	60	60
3464	90c. "Cordia sebestena" . .	60	60
3465	90c. "Opuntia dilenii" . . .	60	60
3466	90c. "Cryptostegia grandiflora"	60	60
3467	90c. "Rodriguezia lanceolata"	60	60
3468	$1 "Epidendrum elongatum"	70	60
3469	$1.10 "Petrea volubilis" . .	70	70
3470	$2 "Oncidium altissimum"	1·50	1·60

MS3471 Two sheets, each 78 × 64 mm. (a) $5 "Hibiscus rosa-sinensis". (b) $5 "Acalypha hispida". Set of 2 sheets . . . 5·50 6·50
Nos. 3459/67 were printed together, se-tenant, with the backgrounds forming a composite design.

332 "Doric", 1923

1996. Passenger Ships. Multicoloured.

3472	$1.10 Type **332**	80	80
3473	$1.10 "Nerissa", 1926 . . .	80	80
3474	$1.10 "Howick Hall", 1910	80	80
3475	$1.10 "Jervis Bay", 1922 . .	80	80
3476	$1.10 "Vauban", 1912 . . .	80	80
3477	$1.10 "Orinoco", 1928 . . .	80	80
3478	$1.10 "Lady Rodney", 1929	80	80
3479	$1.10 "Empress of Russia", 1913	80	80
3480	$1.10 "Providence", 1914 . .	80	80
3481	$1.10 "Reina Victori-Eugenia", 1913	80	80
3482	$1.10 "Balmoral Castle", 1910	80	80
3483	$1.10 "Tivives", 1911 . . .	80	80

MS3484 Two sheets, each 106 × 76 mm. (a) $6 "Aquitania", 1914. (b) $6 "Imperator", 1913. Set of 2 sheets . . . . 6·50 7·50

333 Elvis Presley

334 Sandy Koufax (baseball player)

1996. Elvis Presley (singer) Commemoration. Different portraits. Multicoloured.

3485	$2 Type **333**	1·10	1·10
3486	$2 Wearing checked shirt with guitar	1·10	1·10
3487	$2 Playing piano	1·10	1·10
3488	$2 Wearing black jacket and playing guitar	1·10	1·10
3489	$2 Wearing white shirt and black tie	1·10	1·10
3490	$2 Singing into studio microphone	1·10	1·10

1996. Sports Legends. Sandy Koufax. Multicoloured.

3491	$2 Type **334**	1·00	1·10
3492	$2 Pitching ball	1·00	1·10
3493	$2 Preparing to pitch with arm raised	1·00	1·10
3494	$6 Sandy Koufax (69 × 103 mm)	3·00	3·50

335 Richard Petty's 1990 Pontiac

1996. Richard Petty (stock car driver) Commemoration. Multicoloured.

3495	$2 Type **335**	1·10	1·25
3496	$2 Richard Petty	1·10	1·25
3497	$2 1972 Plymouth	1·10	1·25
3498	$2 1974 Dodge	1·10	1·25

MS3499 Two sheets. (a) 104 × 74 mm. $5 1970 Plymouth "Superbird" (84 × 28 mm). (b) 64 × 48 mm. $6 1996 25th Anniversary STP Pontiac. Set of 2 sheets . . . . 6·00 7·00

336 D.S. Cozier (founder) and Cadet Force Emblem

1996. 60th Anniv of St. Vincent Army Cadet Force. Multicoloured.

3500	70c. Type **336**	45	45
3501	90c. Emblem and first cadets with Cozier	55	55

337 "Virgin and Child" (detail, Memling)

1996. Christmas. Religious Paintings. Multicoloured.

3502	70c. Type **337**	60	40
3503	90c. "St. Anthony" (detail, Memling)	65	50
3504	$1 "Madonna and Child" (detail, D. Bouts)	75	55
3505	$1.10 "Virgin and Child" (detail, Lorenzo Lotto) . .	80	65
3506	$2 "St. Roch" (detail, Lotto)	1·60	1·75
3507	$5 "St. Sebastian" (detail, Lotto)	3·25	4·25

MS3508 Two sheets, each 106 × 76 mm. (a) $5 "Virgin and Child with St. Roch and St. Sebastian" (Lotto). (b) $5 "Virgin and Child with St. Anthony and Donor" (Memling). Set of 2 sheets . . 6·50 7·50

338 Sylvester Stallone in "Rocky IV"

339 Symbolic Ox

1996. 20th Anniv of "Rocky" (film). Sheet 143 × 182 mm.
MS3509 **338** $2 × 3 multicoloured 3·00 3·50
No. **MS**3509 was printed with an enlarged illustrated left-hand margin.

1996. Occupations (2nd series). Multicoloured. As Nos. 3196/3248, but all with face value of 10c.

3510/17	10c. × 8 As Nos. 3196/9 and 3201/4		
3518/25	10c. × 8 As Nos. 3205/8 and 3210/13		
3526/33	10c. × 8 As Nos. 3214/17 and 3519/22		
3534/41	10c. × 8 As Nos. 3523/6 and 3528/31		
3542/8	10c. × 7 As Nos. 3232/4 and 3236/9 (all vert) . .		
3549/56	10c. × 8 As Nos. 3240/3 and 3245/8		
3510/56	Set of 47	8·00	9·00

1997. Chinese New Year ("Year of the Ox").

3557	**339** 75c. black, orange andpink	50	55
3558	– 75c. black, green and lilac	50	55
3559	– 75c. black, pink and red	50	55

MS3560 97 × 48 mm. Nos. 3557/9 1·25 1·50
MS3561 71 × 101 mm. $2 black, orange and yellow . . . . . . 1·25 1·50
DESIGNS: Nos. 3558/9, **MS**3561, Different oxen.

340 Lieut. Tuvok

341 Mickey Mantle

1997. "Star Trek Voyager" (television series). Multicoloured.

3562	$2 Type **340**	1·10	1·10
3563	$2 Kes	1·10	1·10
3564	$2 Tom Paris	1·10	1·10
3565	$2 The Doctor	1·10	1·10
3566	$2 Captain Katherine Janeway	1·10	1·10
3567	$2 B'Elanna Torres	1·10	1·10
3568	$2 Neelix	1·10	1·10
3569	$2 Harry Kim	1·10	1·10
3570	$2 First Officer Chakotay	1·10	1·10

MS3571 88 × 120 mm. $6 Crew of the "Star Trek Voyager" (28 × 45 mm) . . . . 3·50 3·75

1997. Sports Legends. Mickey Mantle (baseball player). Multicoloured. Perf ($2) or imperf. ($6).

3572	$2 Type **341**	1·00	1·10
3573	$6 Mickey Mantle (67 × 100 mm)	3·00	3·50

342 Hong Kong Waterfront

1997. "Hong Kong '97" International Stamp Exhibition. Designs showing the Hong Kong waterfront by day (Nos. 3574/8) or night (Nos. 3579/83). Multicoloured.

3574	90c. Type **342**	60	60
3575	90c. Two ferries in foreground	60	60
3576	90c. Construction site on waterfront	60	60
3577	90c. One launch	60	60
3578	90c. Hong Kong Bank and yellow building in centre	60	60
3579	90c. Large building with spire on right	60	60
3580	90c. Electronic billboards including HITACHI . . .	60	60
3581	90c. Mansions on hillside at right	60	60
3582	90c. Toshiba and NEC billboards in centre . . .	60	60
3583	90c. Hong Kong bank building under Union Jack	60	60

MS3584 Three sheets, each 127 × 85 mm. (a) $2 Boy and girl at Full Moon Festival; $2 Couple on bridge; $2 Two girls with lanterns. (b) $2 Incense candles; $2 Buddhist monk at Polin Monastery; $2 Orchids. (c) $2 Wanchai Market; $2 Chinese couple in street; $2 Man choosing fruit. (all designs 34 × 25 mm). Set of 3 sheets . . . . 9·50 11·00
Nos. 3574/83 were printed together, se-tenant, forming two composite designs.

342a Lord Howe Island, Australia

1997. 50th Anniv of UNESCO. Multicoloured.

3585	70c. Type **342a**	50	40
3586	90c. Uluru-kata Tjuta National Park, Australia	60	50
3587	$1 Cave paintings, Kakadu National Park, Australia	65	55
3588	$1.10 Te Wahipounamu National Park, New Zealand	70	75
3589	$1.10 Castle, Himeji-jo, Japan	70	75
3590	$1.10 Temple, lake and gardens, Kyoto, Japan . .	70	75
3591	$1.10 Walkway, Kyoto, Japan	70	75
3592	$1.10 Buddha, Temple of Ninna, Japan	70	75

3593 $1.10 View from castle, Himeji-jo, Japan 70 75
3594 $1.10 Forest, Shirakami-sanchi, Japan 70 75
3595 $1.10 Forest and mountains, Yakushima, Japan . . . 70 75
3596 $1.10 Forest, Yakushima,Japan 70 75
3597 $1.10 City of San Gimignano, Italy 70 75
3598 $1.10 Cathedral of Santa Maria Asunta, Pisa, Italy 70 75
3599 $1.10 Cathedral of Santa Maria Fiore, Florence, Italy 70 75
3600 $1.10 Archaeological site, Valley of the Boyne, Ireland 70 75
3601 $1.10 Church of St. Savin-sur-Gartempe, France . . 70 75
3602 $1.10 Regency mansion, Bath, England 70 75
3603 $1.10 Rooftop view of Bath, England 70 75
3604 $1.10 Street in Bath, England 70 75
3605 $1.10 Monastery of Rossanou, Meteora, Greece 70 75
3606 $1.10 Ceiling painting, Mount Athos, Greece . . 70 75
3607 $1.10 Monastery Osios Varlaam, Meteora, Greece 70 75
3608 $1.10 Ruins, Athens, Greece 70 75
3609 $1.10 Carvings, Acropolis Museum, Athens, Greece 70 75
3610 $1.10 Painted cloisters, Mount Athos, Greece . . 70 75
3611 $1.10 The port of Zovgraphov Monastery, Greece 70 75
3612 $1.10 Painting above door, Mount Athos, Greece . . 70 75
3613 $1.50 Palace, Wudang Mountains, China (horiz) 85 90
3614 $1.50 Caves, Mogao, China (horiz) 85 90
3615 $1.50 House, Taklamakan Desert, China (horiz) . . 85 90
3616 $1.50 Section going through forest, Great Wall, China (horiz) 85 90
3617 $1.50 Section going through desert, Great Wall, China (horiz) 85 90
3618 $1.50 House and church, Quedlinburg, Germany (horiz) 85 90
3619 $1.50 Decorated house fronts, Quedlinburg (horiz) 85 90
3620 $1.50 Decorative house windows, Quedlinburg, Germany (horiz) 85 90
3621 $1.50 House front, Quedlinburg, Germany (horiz) 85 90
3622 $1.50 Church spires, Quedlinburg (horiz) . . . 85 90
3623 $1.50 Valley of the Ingenios, Cuba (horiz) 85 90
3624 $1.50 City of Zacatecas, Mexico (horiz) 85 90
3625 $1.50 Lima, Peru (horiz) . . 85 90
3626 $1.50 Monastic ruins, Paraguay (horiz) 85 90
3627 $1.50 Mayan ruins, Copan, Honduras (horiz) 85 90
3628 $2 Tongariro National Park, New Zealand (horiz) . . . 1·25 1·40
3629 $5 Tongariro National Park, New Zealand . . . . . . 2·75 3·25
MS3630 Seven sheets, each 127 × 102 mm. (a) $5 Great Wall, China (horiz). (b) $5 Venice, Italy (horiz). (c) $5 Dunbuang Oasis, China (horiz). (d) $5 Wall, Quedlinburg, Germany (horiz). (e) $5 Meteora Monastery, Greece (horiz). (f) $5 Himeji-jo, Japan (horiz). (g) $5 Dome of the Rock, Jerusalem (horiz). Set of 7 sheets 17·00 18·00

343 Microwave Radio Relay Tower, Dorsetshire Hill

1997. 125th Anniv of Telecommunications in St. Vincent. Multicoloured (except 70c.).
3631 5c. Type **343** 10 20
3632 10c. Cable and Wireless headquarters, Kingstown 15 20
3633 20c. Microwave relay tower (vert) 20 25
3634 35c. Cable and Wireless complex, Arnos Vale . . 30 35
3635 50c. Cable and Wireless tower, Mount St. Andrew 40 40
3636 70c. "Docia" (cable ship), 1872 (black and violet) . . 80 50
3637 90c. Eastern telecommunications network map, 1872 . . . . 90 65
3638 $1.10 World telegraph map, 1876 . . . . 1·00 85

344 Smooth-billed Ani

346 Frank Robinson

345 Mandarin Duck

1997. Birds of the World. Multicoloured.
3639 60c. Type **344** 50 40
3640 70c. Belted kingfisher . . . 50 40
3641 90c. Blackburnian warbler 60 50
3642 $1 Blue grosbeak 65 65
3643 $1 Bananaquit 65 65
3644 $1 Cedar waxwing 65 65
3645 $1 Ovenbird 65 65
3646 $1 Hooded warbler 65 65
3647 $1 Common flicker ("Flicker") 65 65
3648 $1.10 Blue tit 70 70
3649 $2 Chaffinch . . . . 1·25 1·40
3650 $2 Song thrush . . . . . . 1·25 1·40
3651 $2 European robin . . . . 1·25 1·40
3652 $2 Blackbird . . . . 1·25 1·40
3653 $2 Great spotted woodpecker . . . . 1·25 1·40
3654 $2 Winter wren ("Wren") 1·25 1·40
3655 $2 River kingfisher ("Kingfisher") . . . . . 1·25 1·40
3656 $5 Ruddy turnstone . . . . 2·75 3·25
MS3657 Two sheets, each 101 × 75 mm. (a) $5 St. Vincent amazon. (b) $5 Tawny owl. Set of 2 sheets . . . . 6·00 6·50
Nos. 3642/7 and 3650/5 respectively were printed together, se-tenant, with the backgrounds forming composite designs.

1997. Sea Birds. Multicoloured.
3658 70c. Type **345** 50 40
3659 90c. Green-backed heron ("Green Heron") 60 50
3660 $1 Ringed teal 65 55
3661 $1.10 Blue-footed booby and chick 70 70
3662 $1.10 Crested auklet (vert) 70 70
3663 $1.10 Whiskered auklet (vert) 70 70
3664 $1.10 Pigeon guillemot (vert) 70 70
3665 $1.10 Adelie penguins (vert) 70 70
3666 $1.10 Rockhopper penguin (vert) 70 70
3667 $1.10 Emperor penguin and chick (vert) 70 70
3668 $2 Comb-crested jacana ("Australian Jacana") (vert) . . . . 1·25 1·40
3669 $5 Reddish egret (vert) . . . 2·75 3·25
MS3670 Two sheets, each 101 × 75 mm. (a) $5 Greater flamingo ("Flamingo"). (b) $5 Snowy egret. Set of 2 sheets . . 6·00 6·50
Nos. 3662/7 were printed together, se-tenant, with the backgrounds forming a composite design.

1997. Baseball Legends. Multicoloured. Imperf ($6) or perf (others). Self-adhesive (No. **MS**3688).
3671 $1 Type **346** 50 55
3672 $1 Satchel Paige 50 55
3673 $1 Billy Williams 50 55
3674 $1 Reggie Jackson 50 55
3675 $1 Roberto Clemente . . . 50 55
3676 $1 Ernie Banks 50 55
3677 $1 Hank Aaron 50 55
3678 $1 Roy Campanella 50 55
3679 $1 Willie McCovey 50 55
3680 $1 Monte Irvin 50 55
3681 $1 Willie Stargell 50 55
3682 $1 Rod Carew 50 55
3683 $1 Ferguson Jenkins 50 55
3684 $1 Bob Gibson 50 55
3685 $1 Lou Brock 50 55
3686 $1 Joe Morgan 50 55
3687 $6 Jackie Robinson (67 × 101 mm) . . . . . 3·00 3·50
MS3688 133 × 67 mm. $1 × 8 Jackie Robinson (32 × 46 mm) . . . . 1·50 1·60

346a Girl sewing ("Curly-Locks")

1997. 300th Anniv of Mother Goose Nursey Rhymes. Sheet, 102 × 72 mm.
MS3689 **346a** $5 multicoloured 3·00 3·25

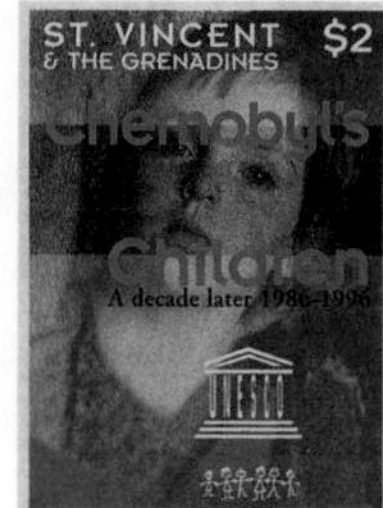

347 Child's Face and UNESCO Emblem

1997. 10th Anniv of Chernobyl Nuclear Disaster. Multicoloured.
3690 $2 Type **347** . . . . 1·00 1·25
3691 $2 As Type **347** but inscribed "CHABAD'S CHILDREN OF CHERNOBYL" at foot 1·00 1·25

347a Paul Harris and Thai Children Receiving Blankets

1997. 50th Death Anniv of Paul Harris (founder of Rotary International).
3692 **347a** $2 multicoloured . . . 1·00 1·25
MS3693 78 × 108 mm. $5 Luis Vincente Giay (International President) with President Carter of the United States . . . . . . 2·50 3·00

347b Queen Elizabeth II

1997. Golden Wedding of Queen Elizabeth and Prince Philip. Multicoloured.
3694 $1.10 Type **347b** . . . . . 90 1·00
3695 $1.10 Royal coat of arms 90 1·00
3696 $1.10 Queen Elizabeth and Prince Philip . . . . . . 90 1·00
3697 $1.10 Queen Elizabeth and Prince Philip on royal visit . . . . 90 1·00
3698 $1.10 Buckingham Palace 90 1·00
3699 $1.10 Prince Philip in naval uniform . . . . 90 1·00
MS3700 100 × 70 mm. $5 Queen Elizabeth on Coronation day 3·25 3·50

347c Bicycle Postman, India, 1800s

1997. "Pacific '97" International Stamp Exhibition, San Francisco. Death Centenary of Heinrich von Stephan (founder of the U.P.U.).
3701 **347c** $2 violet and black . . 1·00 1·25
3702 – $2 brown and black . . 1·00 1·25
3703 – $2 blue and black . . . 1·00 1·25
MS3704 82 × 118 mm. $5 brown 2·75 3·25
DESIGNS: No. 3702, Von Stephan and Mercury; 3703, Ox-drawn postal cart, Indochina; **MS**3704, Von Stephan and post rider, Indochina.

347d "Furukawa River, Hiroo"

1997. Birth Bicentenary of Hiroshige (Japanese painter). "One Hundred Famous Views of Edo". Multicoloured.
3705 $1.50 Type **347d** . . . . . 1·00 1·10
3706 $1.50 "Chiyogaike Pond, Meguro" . . . . 1·00 1·10
3707 $1.50 "New Fuji, Meguro" 1·00 1·10
3708 $1.50 "Moon-viewing Point" 1·00 1·10
3709 $1.50 "Ushimachi, Takanawa" . . . . . . 1·00 1·10
3710 $1.50 "Original Fuji, Meguro" . . . . 1·00 1·10
MS3711 Two sheets, each 102 × 127 mm. (a) $5 "Gotenyama, Shinagawa". (b) $5 "Shinagawa Susaki". Set of 2 sheets . . . . 6·00 6·50

348 Couple with Dog

349 Deng Xiaoping

1997. 175th Anniv of Brothers Grimm's Third Collection of Fairy Tales. "Old Sultan" (Nos. 3712/14) and "The Cobbler and the Elves" (Nos. 3715/17). Multicoloured.
3712 $2 Type **348** . . . . 1·10 1·10
3713 $2 Sheepdog on hillside . . 1·10 1·10
3714 $2 Wolf and sheepdog . . . 1·10 1·10
3715 $2 The cobbler . . . . . . 1·10 1·10
3716 $2 The elves . . . . 1·10 1·10
3717 $2 Cobbler with elf . . . . 1·10 1·10
MS3718 Two sheets. (a) 124 × 96 mm. $5 Couple and baby with Old Sultan. (b) 96 × 124 mm. $5 Elf. Set of 2 sheets . . . . 5·50 6·50

1997. Deng Xiaoping (Chinese statesman) Commemoration.
3719 **349** $2 brown . . . . 1·00 1·10
3720 – $2 brown . . . . 1·00 1·10
3721 – $2 brown . . . . 1·00 1·10
3722 – $2 brown . . . . 1·00 1·10
3723 – $2 blue and light blue . . 1·00 1·10
3724 – $2 blue and light blue . . 1·00 1·10
3725 – $2 blue and light blue . . 1·00 1·10
3726 – $2 blue and light blue . . 1·00 1·10
3727 – $2 black . . . . 1·00 1·10
3728 – $2 black . . . . 1·00 1·10
3729 – $2 black . . . . 1·00 1·10
3730 – $2 black . . . . 1·00 1·10
MS3731 76 × 106 mm. $5 multicoloured . . . . 2·50 3·00
DESIGNS: No. 3720, Looking left; 3721, In military uniform; 3722, Full face; 3723, Looking right; 3724, Smiling; 3725, With head tilted to right; 3726, Looking down; 3727, Looking right; 3728, Looking left; 3729, Full face; 3730, Facing left and smiling; **MS**3731 Deng Xiaoping and Xhue Lin.

350 Alphonso Theodore Roberts

1997. Inaugural Cricket Test Match at Arnos Vale. Multicoloured.
3732 90c. Type **350** . . . . . . 1·00 50
3733 $5 Arnos Vale cricket ground (horiz) . . . . . 3·25 3·50

351 "Cinemax" Mardi Gras Band

1997. 20th Anniv of Vincy Mas Carnival. Multicoloured.
3734 10c. Type **351** 15 20
3735 20c. Queen of the Bands "Jacintha Ballantyne" . . 20 20
3736 50c. Queen of the Bands "Out of the Frying Pan and into the Fire" (vert) 40 40
3737 70c. King of the Bands "Conquistodore" 50 40
3738 90c. Starlift Steel Orchestra 60 50
3739 $2 Frankie McIntosh (musical arranger) (vert) 1·25 1·50

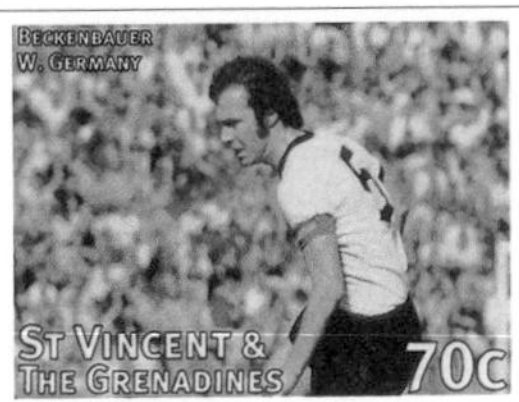

351a Beckenbauer, West Germany

1997. World Cup Football Championship, France (1998). As T **351a**.
3740 70c. multicoloured . . . 50 40
3741 90c. brown 60 50
3742 $1 multicoloured 70 60
3743/50 $1 × 8 (black; multicoloured; black; black; black; black; multicoloured; black)
3751/8 $1 × 8 (each multicoloured) . . . .
3759/66 $1 × 8 (multicoloured; black; multicoloured; black; black; multicoloured; black; multicoloured) . . . .
3767/74 $1 × 8 (blue; multicoloured; blue; multicoloured; multicoloured; blue; multicoloured; blue) . .
3775 $1.10 brown 75 70
3776 $2 multicoloured . . . . 1·25 1·40
3777 $10 black . . . . 6·00 7·00
3740/77 Set of 38 . . . . 27·00 29·00
MS3778 Four sheets, each 102 × 127 mm. (a) $5 multicoloured. (b) $5 multicoloured. (c) $5 black. (d) $5 black. Set of 4 sheets . . . . . 12·00 13·00
DESIGNS—HORIZ: No. 3741, Moore, England; 3742, Lato, Poland; 3759, Argentine and West German players, 1986; 3760 and 3769, English and West German players, 1966; 3761, Goalmouth melee, 1986; 3762, Italian and West German players, 1982; 3763 and 3770, English player heading ball, 1966; 3764, Argentine player with ball, 1978; 3765, Argentine player chasing ball, 1978; 3766, Dutch player with ball; 3767, Wembley Stadium, England, 1966; 3768, West German player with ball; 3771, English player in air heading ball; 3772, German player tackling English player; 3773, Celebrating English team; 3774, Celebrating German player; 3775, Pele, Brazil; 3776, Maier, West Germany; 3777, Eusebio, Portugal; **MS**3778d, Paulao, Angola. VERT: No. 3743, Argentine player kicking ball; 3744, Argentine player holding trophy; 3745, Goalmouth melee; 3746, Dutch player; 3747, Celebrating Argentine player; 3748, Argentine tackling Dutch player; 3749, Argentine and two Dutch players; 3750, Players attempting to head ball; 3751, Bergkamp, Netherlands; 3752, Seaman, England; 3753, Schmeichel, Denmark; 3754, Ince, England; 3755, Futre, Portugal; 3756, Ravanelli, Italy; 3757, Keane, Republic of Ireland; 3758, Gascoigne, England; **MS**3778a, Salvatori Schillaci, Italy; **MS**3778b, Ally McCoist, Scotland; **MS**3778c, Mario Kempes, Argentina.

352 Hand above Globe of Flowers

353 "Rhyncholaelia digbyana"

1997. 10th Anniv of the Signing of the Montreal Protocol on Substances that Deplete the Ozone Layer.
3779 **352** 90c. multicoloured . . . 75 65

1997. Orchids of the World. Multicoloured.
3780 90c. Type **353** 65 50
3781 $1 "Laeliocattleya" "Chitchat Tangerine" . . 70 70
3782 $1 "Eulophia speciosa" . . 70 70
3783 $1 "Aerangis rhodosticta" 70 70
3784 $1 "Angraecum infundibularea" 70 70
3785 $1 "Calanthe sylvatica" . . 70 70
3786 $1 "Phalaenopsis mariae" 70 70
3787 $1 "Paphiopedilum insigne" 70 70
3788 $1 "Dendrobium nobile" . . 70 70
3789 $1 "Aerangis kotschyana" 70 70
3790 $1 "Cyrtorchis chailluana" 70 70
3791 $1.10 "Doritis pulcherrima" 75 75
3792 $2 "Phalaenopsis" "Barbara Moler" . . . . 1·40 1·60
MS3793 Two sheets, each 106 × 81 mm. (a) $5 "Sanguine broughtonia" (50 × 37 mm). (b) $5 "Brassavola nodosa" "Lady of the Night" (50 × 37 mm). Set of 2 sheets . . . . 6·00 6·50

354 Snow Leopard

1997. Sierra Club Conservation. Multicoloured.
3794/3802 20c. × 9 (Type **354**; Polar bear; Plants, Isle Royale National Park; Waterway, Isle Royale National Park; Denali National Park at night; Denali National Park; Plants, Joshua Tree National Park; Mountains, Joshua Tree National Park; Rock, Joshua Tree National Park) . . .
3803/11 40c. × 9 (Mountain gorilla showing teeth; Mountain gorilla; Young mountain gorilla; Snow leopard; Young snow leopard; Polar bear; Polar bear cub; Denali National Park; Isle Royale National Park (all vert)) . . . .
3812/20 50c. × 9 (Sifaka with young; Sifaka on branch; Head of sifaka; Peregrine falcon; Peregrine falcon with stretched wings; Galapagos tortoise; Waterfall, African rainforest; Tree, African rainforest; China's Yellow Mountains (all vert)) . . . . .
3821/9 60c. × 9 (Head of red panda; Red panda on branch; Red panda on ground; Peregrine falcon with chicks; Head of Galapagos tortoise; Galapagos tortoise on grass; African rainforest; Tops of trees, China's Yellow Mountains; Gorge, China's Yellow Mountains) . . . .
3830/8 70c. × 9 (Mountain lion; Siberian tiger; Head of Siberian tiger; Red wolf; Black bear; Lake, Wolong National Reserve; Belize rainforest; Base of tree, Belize rainforest; Mountains, Wolong National Reserve) . .
3839/47 90c. × 9 (Siberian tiger; Head of mountain lion; Mountain lion cubs; Black bear on branch; Head of black bear; Red wolf; Head of red wolf; Belize rainforest; Wolong National Reserve (all vert)) . .
3848/56 $1 × 9 (Indri hanging from tree; Indri face on; Indri holding onto tree; Gopher tortoise inside shell; Gopher tortoise on ground; Black-footed ferret facing forward; Head of black-footed ferret; Haleakala National Park; Grand Teton National Park (all vert)) . . . .
3857/65 $1.10 × 9 (Black-footed ferret; Gopher tortoise; River, Grand Teton National Park; Hillside, Grand Teton National Park; River, Haleakala National Park; Plants, Haleakala National Park; Misty view of Madagascar rainforest; Trees, Madagascar rainforest; Cleared forest, Madagascar rainforest) . . . . .
3794/3865 Set of 72 . . . . 28·00 29·00
MS3866 Three sheets, each 110 × 80 mm. $5 Lake, Olympic National Park. (b) $5 Hillside, Olympic National Park (vert). (c) $5 Snow-covered Mountains, Olympic National Park (vert) Set of 3 sheets . . . . 7·50 8·00

355 Raised Stern of "Titanic"

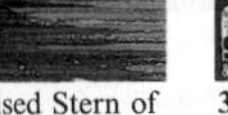

356 "Morrison Hotel" Album Cover, February 1970

1997. 85th Anniv of the Sinking of the "Titanic" (liner). Multicoloured.
3867 $1 Type **355** . . . . 1·25 1·25
3868 $1 Lifeboat rowing away . . 1·25 1·25
3869 $1 One funnel and lifeboat being lowered into water 1·25 1·25
3870 $1 Two funnels . . . . . . 1·25 1·25
3871 $1 One funnel in water and lifeboat rowing away . . 1·25 1·25
Nos. 3867/71 were printed together, se-tenant, forming a composite design.

1997. 30th Anniv of The Doors (rock group) and Rock and Roll Hall of Fame, Cleveland. Multicoloured.
3872 90c. Type **356** 75 50
3873 95c. "Waiting for the Sun" album cover, April 1968 75 65
3874 $1 Rock and Roll Hall of Fame and Museum, Cleveland, Ohio 80 65
3875 $1 "L.A. Women" album cover, April 1971 . . . . 80 65
3876 $1.10 "The Soft Parade" album cover, July 1969 80 65
3877 $1.20 "Strange Days" album cover, October 1967 . . . 85 70
3878 $1.50 Rock and Roll Hall of Fame guitar logo . . . . 1·10 1·25
3879 $1.50 "The Doors" album cover, January 1967 . . . 1·10 1·25

357 Joe "King" Oliver

1997. New Orleans School of Jazz Commemoration. Multicoloured.
3880 $1 Type **357** 75 75
3881 $1 Louis Armstrong 75 75
3882 $1 Sidney Bechet 75 75
3883 $1 Nick Larocca 75 75
3884 $1 Louis Prima 75 75
3885 $1 "Buddy" Charles Bolden 75 75

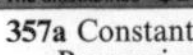

357a Constantin Brancusi

358 Diana, Princess of Wales

1997. Millennium Series. Famous People of the Twentieth Century. (a) Sculptors.
3886 $1.10 Type **357a** 75 75
3887 $1.10 "The New Born" (Brancusi) (56 × 42 mm) 75 75
3888 $1.10 "Four Elements" (Calder) (56 × 42 mm) . . 75 75
3889 $1.10 Alexander Calder . . 75 75
3890 $1.10 Isamu Noguchi . . . 75 75
3891 $1.10 "Dodge Fountain" (Noguchi) (56 × 42 mm) 75 75
3892 $1.10 "The Shuttlecock" (Oldenburg) (56 × 42 mm) 75 75
3893 $1.10 Claes Oldenburg . . . 75 75

(b) Opera Singers.
3894 $1.10 Lily Pons 85 75
3895 $1.10 Lily Pons in Donizetti's "Lucia di Lammermoor" (56 × 42 mm) 85 75
3896 $1.10 Maria Callas in Bellini's "I Puritani" (56 × 42 mm) 85 75
3897 $1.10 Maria Callas 85 75
3898 $1.10 Beverly Sills 85 75
3899 $1.10 Beverly Sills in Donizetti's "La Fille du Regiment" (56 × 42 mm) 85 75
3900 $1.10 Jessye Norman in Schoenberg's "Erwartung" (56 × 42 mm) 85 75
3901 $1.10 Jessye Norman . . . 85 75
3902 $1.10 Enrico Caruso 85 75
3903 $1.10 Enrico Caruso in Verdi's "Rigoletto" (56 × 42 mm) 85 75
3904 $1.10 Mario Lanza in "The Seven Hills of Rome" (56 × 42 mm) 85 75
3905 $1.10 Mario Lanza 85 75
3906 $1.10 Luciano Pavarotti . . 85 75
3907 $1.10 Luciano Pavarotti in Donizetti's "L'Elisir d'Amore" (56 × 42 mm) 85 75
3908 $1.10 Placido Domingo in Puccini's "Tosca" (56 × 42 mm) 85 75
3909 $1.10 Placido Domingo . . 85 75

1997. Diana, Princess of Wales Commemoration. Multicoloured.
3910 $2 Type **358** . . . . 1·10 1·10
3911 $2 Wearing pearl-drop earrings . . . . 1·10 1·10
3912 $2 Wearing black jacket . . 1·10 1·10
3913 $2 Wearing blue jacket and pearl earrings . . . . . . 1·10 1·10
3914 $2 Wearing tiara . . . . . 1·10 1·10
3915 $2 In black evening dress . . 1·10 1·10
3916 $2 Wearing blue jacket . . . 1·10 1·10
3917 $2 Wearing beige blouse . . 1·10 1·10
MS3918 Two sheets, each 100 × 70 mm. (a) $6 Wearing light blue jacket. (b) $6 Wearing white blouse. Set of 2 sheets . . . . 6·50 7·00

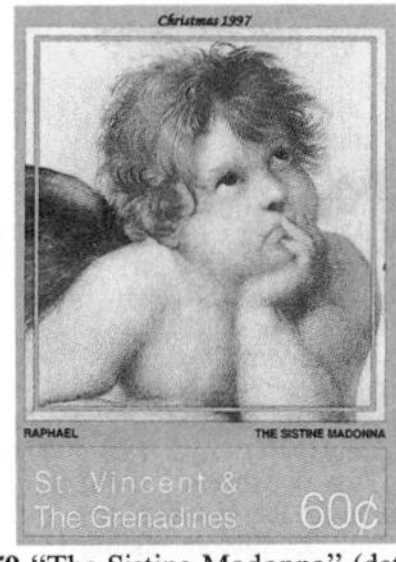

359 "The Sistine Madonna" (detail, Raphael)

1997. Christmas. Paintings and Sculptures. Multicoloured.
3919 60c. Type **359** 45 35
3920 70c. "Angel" (Edward Burne-Jones) 50 40
3921 90c. "Cupid" (sculpture, Etienne-Maurice Flaconet) 60 50
3922 $1 "Saint Michael" (sculpture, Hubert Gerhard) 70 55
3923 $1.10 "Apollo and the Hoare" (Giambattista Tiepolo) 75 65
3924 $2 "Madonna in a Garland of Flowers" (detail, Rubens and Brueghel the Elder) . . . . 1·25 1·50
MS3925 Two sheets, each 106 × 95 mm. (a) $5 "Madonna in a Garland of Flowers" (different detail, Rubens and Brueghel the Elder). (b) $5 "The Sacrifice of Isaac" (Giambattista Tiepolo) (detail) (horiz). Set of 2 sheets 6·00 6·50

360 Symbolic Tiger

361 Children and School Savings Bank

1998. Chinese New Year ("Year of the Tiger").
3926 **360** $1 black, grey and brown 60 65
3927 – $1 black, silver and brown 60 65
3928 – $1 black, lilac and pink 60 65
MS3929 71 × 101 mm. $2 black, lilac and orange . . . . 1·25 1·40
DESIGNS: Nos. 3927/9, Different tigers.

1998. Economic Development. Multicoloured.
3930 20c. Type **361** 20 15
3931 90c. Agricultural workers and Credit Union Office (vert) 55 40
3932 $1.10 Freighter at quay . . 65 70

362 Ice Hockey

1998. Winter Olympic Games, Nagano. Mult.
3933 70c. Type **362** 50 40
3934 $1.10 Bobsleigh 70 70
3935 $1.10 Bjorn Daehlie (Norway) (Gold medal, Nordic skiing, 1994) . . . 70 70

3936 $1.10 Gillis Grafstrom (Sweden) (Gold medal, figure skating, 1924, 1928) 70 70
3937 $1.10 Sonja Henie (Norway) (Gold medal, figure skating, 1928, 1932) . . . 70 70
3938 $1.10 Ingemar Stenmark (Sweden) (Gold medal, slalom and giant slalom, 1980) 70 70
3939 $1.10 Christan Jagge (Norway) (Gold medal, slalom, 1992) 70 70
3940 $1.10 Tomas Gustafson (Sweden) (Gold medal, 5000m speed skating, 1992) 70 70
3941 $1.10 Johann Olav Koss (Norway) (Gold medal, 1500m speed skating, 1992, 1994) 70 70
3942 $1.10 Thomas Wassberg (Sweden) (Gold medal, 50km cross country skiing, 1984) 70 70
3943 $1.50 Downhill (red suit) (vert) 90 90
3944 $1.50 Two-man bobsleigh (vert) 90 90
3945 $1.50 Ski jump (red suit) (vert) 90 90
3946 $1.50 Downhill (red and white suit) (vert) 90 90
3947 $1.50 Luge (vert) 90 90
3948 $1.50 Biathlon (vert) 90 90
3949 $1.50 Downhill (yellow and red suit) (vert) 90 90
3950 $1.50 Figure skating (vert) 90 90
3951 $1.50 Ski jump (green suit)(vert) 90 90
3952 $1.50 Speed skating (vert) 90 90
3953 $1.50 Four-man bobsleigh (vert) 90 90
3954 $1.50 Cross-country skiing (vert) 90 90
3955 $2 Pairs figure skating . . . 1·25 1·40
3956 $2 Aerials (vert) . . . . . . 1·25 1·40
MS3957 Two sheets. (a) 110 × 80 mm. $5 Ice Hockey. (b) 80 × 100 mm. $5 Slalom skiing (vert). Set of 2 sheets . . . . . 6·50 7·00

Nos. 3943/8 and 3949/54 respectively were printed together, se-tenant, with the backgrounds forming composite designs.

363 Rock-iguana (Anegada)

1998. Endangered Species of the Caribbean. Multicoloured.
3958 50c. Type **363** 40 25
3959 70c. "Papilio homerus" (butterfly) (Jamaica) . . . 55 35
3960 90c. Blossom-bat (Cuba) . . 55 40
3961 $1 Haitian solenodon (Dominican Republic) . . 60 50
3962 $1.10 Hawksbill turtle (Grenada) 60 65
3963 $1.10 Roseate spoonbill . . 60 65
3964 $1.10 Golden swallow . . . 60 65
3965 $1.10 Short-snouted spinner dolphin 60 65
3966 $1.10 Queen or pink conch ("Strombus gigas") . . . 60 65
3967 $1.10 American manatee . . 60 65
3968 $1.10 Loggerhead turtle . . 60 65
3969 $1.10 Magnificent frigate bird 60 65
3970 $1.10 Humpback whale . . 60 65
3971 $1.10 "Marpesia petreus" (butterfly) 60 65
3972 $1.10 St. Lucia whiptail . . 60 65
3973 $1.10 St. Lucia oriole . . . 60 65
3974 $1.10 Green turtle 60 65
3975 $2 Black-billed whistling duck (Barbuda) . . . . . 1·25 1·40
MS3976 Two sheets, each 102 × 90 mm. (a) $5 St. Vincent amazon ("St. Vincent Parrot"). (b) $5 Antiguan Racer (snake). Set of 2 sheets . . . . 5·50 6·00

Nos. 3963/8 and 3969/74 respectively were printed together, se-tenant, forming composite background designs.

364 "Gymnopilus spectabilis" and "Atildes halesus" (butterfly)

1998. Fungi. Multicoloured.
3977 10c. Type **364** 20 20
3978 20c. "Entoloma lividium" 40 25
3979 70c. "Pholiota flammans" 55 35
3980 90c. "Panaeolus semiovatus" 60 40
3981 $1 "Stropharia rugosoannulata" 60 65
3982 $1 "Amanita caesarea" . . . 60 65
3983 $1 "Amanita muscaria" . . 60 65
3984 $1 "Amanita ovoidea" . . . 60 65
3985 $1 "Amanita phalloides" . . 60 65
3986 $1 "Amanitopsis inaurata" 60 65
3987 $1 "Amanitopsis vaginata" 60 65
3988 $1 "Psalliota campestris" . . 60 65
3989 $1 "Psalliota arvensis" . . . 60 65
3990 $1 "Coprinus comatus" . . 60 65
3991 $1.10 "Tricholoma sulphureum" 60 65
3992 $1.10 "Coprinus picaceus" 60 65
3993 $1.10 "Stropharia umbonatescens" 60 65
3994 $1.10 "Hebeloma crustuliniforme" 60 65
3995 $1.10 "Cortinarius collinitus" 60 65
3996 $1.10 "Cortinarius violaceus" 60 65
3997 $1.10 "Cortinarius armillatus" 60 65
3998 $1.10 "Tricholoma aurantium" 60 65
3999 $1.10 "Russula virescens" 60 65
4000 $1.10 "Clitocybe infundibuliformis" 60 65
MS4001 Two sheets. (a) 70 × 100 mm. $6 "Hygrocybe conica". (b) 100 × 70 mm. $6 "Amanita caesarea". Set of 2 sheets . . . . 6·50 7·00

365 "Amarynthis meneria meneria"

1998. Butterflies. Multicoloured.
4002 20c. Type **365** 40 25
4003 50c. "Papilio polyxenes" . . 50 30
4004 70c. "Emesis fatima fatima" (vert) 55 35
4005 $1 "Anartia amathea" . . . 60 65
4006 $1 "Heliconius erato" (vert) 60 65
4007 $1 "Danaus plexippus" (vert) 60 65
4008 $1 "Papilio phorcas" (vert) 60 65
4009 $1 "Morpho peleides" (vert) 60 65
4010 $1 "Pandoriana pandora" (vert) 60 65
4011 $1 "Basilarchia astyanax" (vert) 60 65
4012 $1 "Vanessa cardui" (vert) 60 65
4013 $1 "Colobura dirce" (vert) 60 65
4014 $1 "Heraclides cresphontes" (vert) 60 65
MS4015 Two sheets, each 100 × 70 mm. (a) $6 "Colias eurytheme". (b) $6 "Everes comyntas". Set of 2 sheets . . 6·50 7·00

Nos. 4006/14 were printed together, se-tenant, with the backgrounds forming a composite design.

366 Pluto waking Mickey

1998. 70th Birthday of Disney's Mickey Mouse (1st issue). Multicoloured.
4016 2c. Type **366** 10 10
4017 3c. Mickey and Pluto on morning run 10 10
4018 4c. Singing in the bath . . . 10 10
4019 5c. Breakfast time 15 10
4020 10c. Mickey going to school 20 10
4021 65c. Mickey playing basketball 90 50
4022 $1.10 Mickey as drum major (vert) . . . . 1·10 1·10
4023 $1.10 Mickey with hat and cane (vert) . . . . . . 1·10 1·10
4024 $1.10 Mickey in bow tie and tails (vert) . . . . . . 1·10 1·10
4025 $1.10 Mickey the magician (vert) . . . . 1·10 1·10
4026 $1.10 Mickey as circus musician (vert) . . . . . 1·10 1·10
4027 $1.10 Mickey as cowboy (vert) . . . . 1·10 1·10
4028 $3 Mickey in soup kitchen 2·50 2·50
4029 $4 Mickey and Minnie in restaurant . . . . 2·75 2·75
4030 $5 Mickey and Pluto praying . . . . 2·75 2·75
MS4031 Four sheets, each 127 × 104 mm. (a) $5 Mickey reading paper (vert). (b) $6 Using computer (vert). (c) $6 Dancing at piano (vert). (d) $6 Blowing trumpet. Set of 4 sheets . . . . 12·00 13·00

See also Nos. 4179/96.

367 Winnie the Pooh in Window

1998. Stories of Winnie the Pooh. Multicoloured.
4032 $1 Type **367** 85 85
4033 $1 Eeyore, Kanga and Roo 85 85
4034 $1 Winnie the Pooh with balloon 85 85
4035 $1 Pooh stuck in Rabbit's burrow 85 85
4036 $1 Christopher Robin pulling Pooh 85 85
4037 $1 Piglet sweeping leaves . . 85 85
4038 $1 Pooh asleep 85 85
4039 $1 Eeyore 85 85
4040 $1 Pooh and Tigger 85 85
MS4041 127 × 102 mm. $6 Tigger, Pooh and Piglet . . . . 4·75 5·50

368 Australian Terrier

371 Guianan Cock of the Rock ("Cock-of-the-rock")

370 L.M.S. No. 5596 "Bahamas"

1998. Dogs of the World. Multicoloured.
4042 70c. Type **368** 50 35
4043 90c. Bullmastiff 60 45
4044 $1.10 Pomeranian 60 65
4045 $1.10 Beagle (horiz) 60 65
4046 $1.10 German shepherd and cockerel (horiz) 60 65
4047 $1.10 Pointer (horiz) 60 65
4048 $1.10 Vizsla (horiz) 60 65
4049 $1.10 Bulldog (horiz) . . . 60 65
4050 $1.10 Shetland sheepdogs (horiz) 60 65
4051 $1.10 Tyrolean hunting dog (horiz) 60 65
4052 $1.10 King Charles spaniel (horiz) 60 65
4053 $1.10 Fox terriers (horiz) . . 60 65
4054 $1.10 Bernese mountain dog (horiz) 60 65
4055 $1.10 Papillon (horiz) . . . 60 65
4056 $1.10 German shepherd (horiz) 60 65
4057 $2 Dandie dinmont terrier 1·25 1·40
MS4058 Two sheets, each 106 × 76 mm. (a) $6 Scottish Terrier and bush. (b) $6 Scottish Terrier lying down. Set of 2 sheets 6·50 7·00

Nos. 4045/50 and 4051/6 respectively were printed together, se-tenant, with the backgrounds forming composite designs.

The captions on Nos. 4052 and 4055 are transposed in error.

1998. "Israel 98" International Stamp Exhibition, Tel-Aviv. Nos. 3334/6 optd **98** in emblem.
4059 $1 Type **325** 60 45
4060 $1.10 The Montefiore Windmill 65 60
4061 $2 Shrine of the Book . . . 1·25 1·40
MS4062 104 × 74 mm. $5 Old City, Jerusalem . . . . 3·25 3·50

1998. Railway Steam Locomotives of the World. Multicoloured.
4063 10c. Type **370** 20 20
4064 20c. Ex.Mza 1400 . . . . . 40 20
4065 50c. "Mallard" 60 35
4066 70c. Tank locomotive "Monarch" 60 40
4067 90c. "Big Chief" 60 40
4068 $1.10 L.M.S. No. 6228 "Duchess of Rutland" . . 65 70
4069 $1.10 Holmes J36 . . . . . 65 70
4070 $1.10 "Patentee" 65 70
4071 $1.10 "Kingfisher" 65 70
4072 $1.10 No. 23 "St Pierre" . . 65 70
4073 $1.10 South African Railways Class 19c . . . 65 70
4074 $1.10 South African Railways Class 6J 65 70
4075 $1.10 No. 92220 "Evening Star" 65 70
4076 $1.10 No. 1 . . . . 65 70
4077 $1.10 "The Hadrian Flyer" 65 70
4078 $1.10 Class "Highland Jones Goods" No. 103 . . . . . 65 70
4079 $1.10 No. 34023 "Blackmore Vale" 65 70
4080 $1.10 S.E.C.R. No. 27 . . . 65 70
4081 $1.10 Class "Brighton Terrier" "Stepney" . . . 65 70
4082 $1.10 R.E.N.F.E. No. 2184 65 70
4083 $1.10 Southern Railway No. 24 "Calbourne" . . . 65 70
4084 $1.10 "Clun Castle" 65 70
MS4085 Two sheets, each 101 × 70 mm. (a) $5 "Caledonia". (b) $5 No. 6000 "King George V". Set of 2 sheets . . . . 5·50 6·00

The identification of the locomotive on No. 4084 has been reported as incorrect.

1998. Birds of the World. Multicoloured.
4086 50c. Type **371** 45 30
4087 60c. Resplendant quetzal ("Quetzal") 55 40
4088 70c. American wood stork ("Wood Stork") 55 40
4089 90c. St. Vincent amazon (species inscr at right) . . 60 65
4090 90c. Keel-billed toucan ("Toucan") (horiz) . . . 60 65
4091 90c. Racquet-tailed motmot 60 65
4092 90c. Red-billed quelea . . . 60 65
4093 90c. Major Mitchell's cockatoo ("Leadbeater's Cockatoo") 60 65
4094 90c. Green-winged macaw ("Scarlet Macaw") . . . 60 65
4095 90c. Bare-throated bellbird 60 65
4096 90c. Tucaman amazon . . . 60 65
4097 90c. White-winged tanager ("Black-lored Red Tanager") 60 65
4098 90c. Tucuman amazon ("Fig parrot") 60 65
4099 90c. St. Vincent amazon (species inscr at top) . . . 60 65
4100 90c. Peach-faced love birds 60 65
4101 90c. Blue-fronted amazon 60 65
4102 90c. Yellow-billed amazon 60 65
4103 $1 Greater bird of paradise (horiz) 65 65
4104 $1.10 Sun-bittern (horiz) . . 65 65
4105 $2 Green honeycreeper (horiz) . . . . 1·10 1·25
MS4106 Two sheets, each 98 × 62 mm. (a) $5 Hyacinth macaw. (b) $5 Blue-headed hummingbird. Set of 2 sheets 5·50 6·00

Nos. 4091/4102 were printed together, se-tenant, with the backgrounds forming a composite design.

372 White Whale

1998. International Year of the Ocean. Multicoloured.
4107 70c. Type **372** 45 35
4108 90c. Atlantic manta 55 40
4109 $1 Harlequin wrasse and brown pelican (vert) . . . 60 65
4110 $1 Blue surgeonfish (vert) 60 65
4111 $1 Spotted trunkfish and sailing ship (vert) 60 65
4112 $1 Regal angelfish (vert) . . 60 65
4113 $1 Porcupine fish (vert) . . 60 65
4114 $1 Clownfish (vert) 60 65
4115 $1 Lion fish (vert) 60 65
4116 $1 Moray eel (vert) 60 65
4117 $1 French angelfish (vert) 60 65
4118 $1 Lemonpeel angelfish, flying fish and herring gulls (vert) 60 65
4119 $1 Narwhal (vert) 60 65
4120 $1 Panther grouper, atlantic puffin and house (vert) . . 60 65
4121 $1 Fur seal and jellyfish (vert) 60 65
4122 $1 Spiny boxfish (vert) . . . 60 65
4123 $1 Loggerhead turtle (vert) 60 65
4124 $1 Opah (vert) 60 65
4125 $1 Clown triggerfish (vert) 60 65
4126 $1 Bighead searobin (vert) 60 65
4127 $1.10 Forceps butterflyfish, moorish idol and copperband butterflyfish 60 65
4128 $2 Octopus . . . . 1·10 1·25
MS4129 Two sheets, each 98 × 73 mm. (a) $5 Seahorse (vert). (b) $5 Australian Seadragon (vert). Set of 2 sheets . . . . 5·50 6·00

Nos. 4109/17 and 4118/26 respectively were printed together, se-tenant, with the backgrounds forming composite designs.

No. 4109 is inscribed "Harlequin Warasse" in error.

372a Flags of St. Vincent and CARICOM

1998. 25th Anniv of Caribbean Community.
4130 **372a** $1 multicoloured . . . 60 60

372b Stylized "50"

1998. 50th Anniv of Organization of American States.
4131 **372b** $1 violet, green and black 60 60

373 "Landscape"

1998. 25th Death Anniv of Pablo Picasso (painter). Multicoloured.
4132 $1.10 Type **373** 60 50
4133 $2 "The Death of the Female Torero" . . . . . 1·10 1·25
4134 $2 "The Kiss" . . . . . . 1·10 1·25
MS4135 102 × 127 mm. $5 "Flute Player" (vert) . . . . 3·25 3·50

373a 365 GTS

1998. Birth Centenary of Enzo Ferrari (car manufacturer). Multicoloured.
4136 $2 Type **373a** . . . . 1·40 1·50
4137 $2 Testarossa . . . . 1·40 1·50
4138 $2 365 GT4 B B . . . . . 1·40 1·50
MS4139 104 × 70 mm. $6 Dino 206 GT (91 × 34 mm) . . . . . . 3·50 4·00

373b Presentation of Silver Buffalo award to John Glenn (U.S. astronaut)

1998. 19th World Scout Jamboree, Chile.
4140 **373b** $2 lilac, violet and black . . . . 1·10 1·25
4141 – $2 brown, violet and black . . . . 1·10 1·25
4142 – $2 brown, violet and black . . . . 1·10 1·25
MS4143 70 × 100 mm. $5 blue, brown and black . . . . . . 3·25 3·50
DESIGNS—HORIZ: No. 4141, Herb Shriner learning knot-tying, 1960; 4142, Breaking camp, 1940s. VERT: No. **MS**4143, Lord Baden-Powell in court dress.

373c Mahatma Gandhi

374 H. Daisley (64 years of service)

373d AEW 1 (Airborne Early Warning)

1998. 50th Death Anniv of Mahatma Gandhi.
4144 **373c** $1 multicoloured . . . 65 60
MS4145 107 × 76 mm. $5 brown, purple and black . . . . . . 4·50 3·75
DESIGN—HORIZ: $5 Gandhi at conference table.

1998. 80th Anniv of Royal Air Force. Multicoloured.
4146 $2 Type **373d** . . . . 1·25 1·25
4147 $2 Eurofighter EF-2000 . . 1·25 1·25
4148 $2 Sepecat Jaguar GR1A . . 1·25 1·25
4149 $2 BAe Hawk T1A trainer 1·25 1·25
4150 $2 Two Sepecat Jaguar GR1s . . . . 1·25 1·25
4151 $2 Panavia Tornado F3 . . 1·25 1·25
4152 $2 Three BAe Harrier GR7s 1·25 1·25
4153 $2 Panavia Tornado F3 IDV . . . . 1·25 1·25
MS4154 Four sheets, each 90 × 70 mm. (a) $6 Bristol F2B fighter and Falcon (bird). (b) $6 Bristol F2B fighter and Golden Eagle (bird). (c) $6 Mosquito and Eurofighter EF-2000. (d) $6 Vulcan B2 and Eurofighter EF-2000 Set of 4 sheets . . . 13·00 14·00

1998. 1st Death Anniv of Diana, Princess of Wales. As T **317a** of Sierra Leone. Multicoloured.
4155 $1.10 Diana, Princess of Wales 65 65

1998. 150th Anniv of Local Court of Ancient Order of Foresters. Multicoloured (except 70c.).
4156 10c. Type **374** 15 15
4157 20c. R. Jack (17 years of service) 20 15
4158 50c. Ancient Order of Foresters' arms 35 30
4159 70c. Bow and arrow symbol (green and black) 45 45
4160 90c. Court's headquarters 55 55

375 Bi-colour Longhair

376 Flautist

1998. Christmas. Cats. Multicoloured.
4161 20c. Type **375** 20 15
4162 50c. Korat 35 25
4163 60c. Seal-point Siamese . . 45 40
4164 70c. Red self longhair . . . 50 50
4165 90c. Black longhair 55 55
4166 $1.10 Red tabby exotic shorthair 65 70
MS4167 Two sheets, each 75 × 66 mm. (a) $5 Seal-point Colourpoint. (b) $5 Tortoiseshell Shorthair. Set of 2 sheets . . . 5·50 6·00

1998. 900th Birth Anniv of St. Hildegard von Bingen (German mystic). Multicoloured.
4168 $1.10 Type **376** 65 70
4169 $1.10 St. Hildegard and abbey 65 70
4170 $1.10 Viola player 65 70
4171 $1.10 Pope Eugenius 65 70
4172 $1.10 Town of Bingen . . . 65 70
4173 $1.10 St. Hildegard 65 70
MS4174 85 × 110 mm. $5 St. Hildegard . . . . 3·25 3·50

377 Rabbit facing Right

379 Hollywood Hogan

378 Mickey Mouse

1999. Chinese New Year ("Year of the Rabbit"). Designs showing stylized rabbits. Multicoloured (except No. **MS**4178).
4175 $1 Type **377** 60 65
4176 $1 Rabbit facing front . . . 60 65
4177 $1 Rabbit facing left . . . 60 65
MS4178 70 × 100 mm. $2 As No. 4176 (black, lilac and pink) 1·25 1·40

1999. 70th Birthday of Mickey Mouse (2nd issue). Walt Disney characters playing Winter sports. Multicoloured.
4179 $1.10 Type **378** 85 85
4180 $1.10 Goofy on skis wearing goggles 85 85
4181 $1.10 Donald Duck skiing in yellow sweatshirt . . . 85 85
4182 $1.10 Goofy and Mickey in red bobsleigh 85 85
4183 $1.10 Goofy on skis in yellow 85 85
4184 $1.10 Minnie on skis with yellow bow 85 85
4185 $1.10 Daisy Duck on skis wearing purple bow . . . 85 85
4186 $1.10 Mickey on skis wearing goggles 85 85
4187 $1.10 Goofy and Mickey in green bobsleigh 85 85
4188 $1.10 Goofy on skis in blue 85 85
4189 $1.10 Minnie snowboarding 85 85
4190 $1.10 Donald on skis in blue sweatshirt 85 85
4191 $1.10 Minnie skiing with blue and purple bow . . . 85 85
4192 $1.10 Mickey snowboarding 85 85
4193 $1.10 Goofy on skis in blue and purple vest 85 85
4194 $1.10 Donald skiing in blue and purple sweatshirt . . 85 85
4195 $1.10 Mickey snowboarding in yellow hat and goggles 85 85
4196 $1.10 Daisy skiing in blue and purple 85 85
MS4197 Three sheets. (a) 102 × 127 mm. $5 Mickey Mouse. (b) 127 × 102 mm. $5 Minnie Mouse. (c) 127 × 102 mm. $5 Goofy (horiz). Set of 3 sheets 10·00 10·00

1999. World Championship Wrestling. Mult.
4198 70c. Type **379** 40 40
4199 70c. Sting 40 40
4200 70c. Bret Hart 40 40
4201 70c. Giant 40 40
4202 70c. Kevin Nash 40 40
4203 70c. Randy Savage 40 40
4204 70c. Diamond Dallas . . . 40 40
4205 70c. Goldberg 40 40

380 Plateosaurus

1999. "Australia '99" World Stamp Exhibition, Melbourne. Prehistoric Animals. Mult.
4206 70c. Type **380** 45 50
4207 70c. Struthiomimus 45 50
4208 70c. Indricotherium 45 50
4209 70c. Giant moa 45 50
4210 70c. Deinonychus 45 50
4211 70c. Sabre tooth tiger . . . 45 50
4212 70c. Dawn horse 45 50
4213 70c. Peittacosaurus 45 50
4214 70c. Giant ground sloth . . 45 50
4215 70c. Woolly rhinoceros . . . 45 50
4216 70c. Mosasaur 45 50
4217 70c. Mastodon 45 50
4218 70c. Syndyoceras 45 50
4219 90c. Euoplacephalus 50 55
4220 90c. Rhamphorhynchus . . 50 55
4221 90c. Pteranodon 50 55
4222 90c. Archaeopteriyx 50 55
4223 90c. Dimetrodon 35 40
4224 90c. Stegasaurus 50 55
4225 90c. Parasaurolophus . . . 50 55
4226 90c. Iguanadon 50 55
4227 90c. Triceratops 50 55
4228 90c. Tyrannosaurus 50 55
4229 90c. Ichthyosaurus 50 55
4230 90c. Plesiosaurus 50 55
4231 90c. Hesperornis 50 55
4232 $1.10 Pachycephalosaurus . . 65 65
4233 $1.40 Dilophosaurus 75 80
MS4234 Two sheets, each 107 × 77 mm. (a) $5 Diplodocus. (b) $5 Woolly Mammoth (vert). Set of 2 sheets . . . . 6·00 6·50

381 African Elephant and Acacia Tree

1999. Fauna and Flora. Multicoloured.
4235 10c. Type **381** 30 25
4236 20c. Green turtle and coconut palm seedling . . 40 25
4237 25c. White ibis and mangrove tree 50 25
4238 50c. Tiger swallowtail and ironweed 50 30
4239 70c. Eastern box turtle and Jack-in-the-Pulpit (plant) (vert) 50 55
4240 70c. Basilisk lizard and strangler fig (vert) 50 55
4241 70c. Scarlet macaw ("Macaw") and kapok trees (vert) 50 55
4242 70c. Howler monkey and cecropia tree (vert) . . . 50 55
4243 70c. Keel-billed toucan ("Toucan") and cecropia tree (vert) 50 55
4244 70c. Poison-arrow frog and bromiliad (vert) 50 55

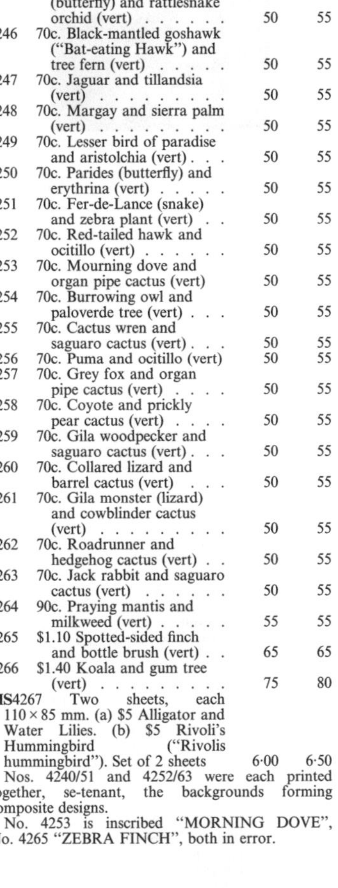
4245 70c. "Heliconius phyllis" (butterfly) and rattlesnake orchid (vert) 50 55
4246 70c. Black-mantled goshawk ("Bat-eating Hawk") and tree fern (vert) 50 55
4247 70c. Jaguar and tillandsia (vert) 50 55
4248 70c. Margay and sierra palm (vert) 50 55
4249 70c. Lesser bird of paradise and aristolchia (vert). . . 50 55
4250 70c. Parides (butterfly) and erythrina (vert) 50 55
4251 70c. Fer-de-Lance (snake) and zebra plant (vert) . . 50 55
4252 70c. Red-tailed hawk and ocitillo (vert) 50 55
4253 70c. Mourning dove and organ pipe cactus (vert) 50 55
4254 70c. Burrowing owl and paloverde tree (vert) . . . 50 55
4255 70c. Cactus wren and saguaro cactus (vert) . . . 50 55
4256 70c. Puma and ocitillo (vert) 50 55
4257 70c. Grey fox and organ pipe cactus (vert) 50 55
4258 70c. Coyote and prickly pear cactus (vert) 50 55
4259 70c. Gila woodpecker and saguaro cactus (vert) . . . 50 55
4260 70c. Collared lizard and barrel cactus (vert) . . . 50 55
4261 70c. Gila monster (lizard) and cowblinder cactus (vert) 50 55
4262 70c. Roadrunner and hedgehog cactus (vert) . . 50 55
4263 70c. Jack rabbit and saguaro cactus (vert) 50 55
4264 90c. Praying mantis and milkweed (vert) 55 55
4265 $1.10 Spotted-sided finch and bottle brush (vert) . . 65 65
4266 $1.40 Koala and gum tree (vert) 75 80
MS4267 Two sheets, each 110 × 85 mm. (a) $5 Alligator and Water Lilies. (b) $5 Rivoli's Hummingbird ("Rivolis hummingbird"). Set of 2 sheets 6·00 6·50
Nos. 4240/51 and 4252/63 were each printed together, se-tenant, the backgrounds forming composite designs.
No. 4253 is inscribed "MORNING DOVE", No. 4265 "ZEBRA FINCH", both in error.

382 Lilenthal's Glider, 1894

1999. Aircraft. Multicoloured.
4268 60c. Montgolfier Balloon, 1783 (vert) 45 30
4269 70c. Type **382** 45 35
4270 90c. "Zeppelin" (airship) . . 50 40
4271 $1 Wilbur Wright and "Flyer", 1903 . . . . . . 60 45
4272 $1.10 M-130 Clipper 60 65
4273 $1.10 DC-3, 1937 . . . . . 60 65
4274 $1.10 Staggerwing Beech CVR FT C-17L 60 65
4275 $1.10 Hughes H-1 Racer . . 60 65
4276 $1.10 Gee Bee Model R-1, 1932 . . . . 60 65
4277 $1.10 Lockheed 8 Sirius Tingmissartoq seaplane 60 65
4278 $1.10 Fokker T-2, 1923 . . 60 65
4279 $1.10 Curtiss CW-16E seaplane 60 65
4280 $1.10 Dayton Wright DH-4 Bomber 60 65
4281 $1.10 Sopwith Camel . . . 60 65
4282 $1.10 Sopwith Dove 60 65
4283 $1.10 Jeannin Stahl Taube 60 65
4284 $1.10 Fokker DR-1 triplane 60 65
4285 $1.10 Albatross Diva . . . 60 65
4286 $1.10 Sopwith Pup 60 65
4287 $1.10 SPAD XIII Smith IV 60 65
MS4288 Two sheets, each 110 × 85 mm. (a) $5 Lebauldy-Juillot airship No. 1 "La Jaune", 1903. (b) $5 Bleriot XI crossing Channel, 1914. Set of 2 sheets 5·50 6·00
Nos. 4272/9 and 4280/7 were each issued, se-tenant, with the backgrounds forming composite designs.
No. **MS**4288a is inscribed "LE BANDY AIRSHIP" in error.

383 NSYNC

385 Prince Edward

384 Galileo Galilei (astronomer, 1609)

1999. NSYNC (pop group) Commemoration.

4289	**383**	$1 multicoloured	60	60

1999. Space Exploration. Multicoloured.

4290	20c. Type **384**	20	15
4291	50c. Konstantin Tsiolkovsky (aeronautical engineer, 1903)	40	25
4292	70c. Robert Goddard (rocket scientist, 1926)	45	35
4293	90c. Sir Isaac Newton (physicist, 1668) (vert)	50	40
4294/302	$1 × 9 ("Explorer" rocket, 1958; "Lunokhod Explorer", 1970; "Viking Lander", 1975; A - 1 (SL-3) rocket, 1959; Edward White (astronaut), 1965; "Salyut 1" space station, 1971; Ancient observatory; "Freedom 7" rocket, 1961; "Ariane" rocket, 1980s (all vert))	4·50	
4303/11	$1 × 9 ("Luna 3", 1959; "Soyuz 11", 1971; "MIR" space station, 1986; "Sputnik 1", 1957; "Apollo 4", 1967; Bruce McCandles (astronaut), 1984; Sir William Herschel's telescope, 1781; John Glenn (astronaut), 1962; Space shuttle "Columbia", 1981	4·50	
4312/20	$1 × 9 (Yuri Gagarin (cosmonaut), 1961; "Lunar Rover", 1971; "Mariner 10", 1974–5; Laika (first dog in space), 1957; Edwin Aldrin on Moon, 1969; "Skylab" space station, 1973; German "V-2" rocket, 1942; "Gemini 4" rocket, 1965; Hubble telescope, 1990; (all vert))	4·50	
MS4321	Two sheets, each 85 × 110 mm. (a) $5 Space Shuttle "Atlantis" docking with "MIR". (b) $5 Saturn 5 rocket, 1969 (vert). Set of 2 sheets	5·50	6·00

Nos. 4294/302, 4303/11 and 4312/20 were each printed together, se-tenant, with the backgrounds forming composite designs.

No. 4297 is inscribed "1957-R7 Rocket", No. 4303 "LUNA 9", No. 4312 "1962" and No. 4316 "NEIL ARMSTRONG" all in error.

1999. Royal Wedding. Multicoloured.

4322	$3 Type **385**	1·75	1·75
4323	$3 Miss Sophie Rhys-Jones and Prince Edward	1·75	1·75
4324	$3 Miss Sophie Rhys-Jones	1·75	1·75
MS4325	78 × 108 mm. $6 Prince Edward and Miss Sophie Rhys-Jones (horiz)	3·25	3·50

385a Steam Locomotive and Power Station

1999. "iBRA '99" International Stamp Exhibition, Nuremberg.

4326	**385a**	$1 multicoloured	60	60

No. 4326 is inscribed "THE KRAUSS-MAFFEI V-200 DIESEL LOCOMOTIVE: GERMANY 1852" in error.

385b "Admiring the Irises at Yatsuhashi"

1999. 150th Death Anniv of Katsushika Hokusai (Japanese artist). Multicoloured.

4327	$1.10 Type **385b**	60	65
4328	$1.10 "Sea Life" (turtle facing top left)	60	65
4329	$1.10 "Admiring the Irises at Yatsuhashi" (different)	60	65
4330	$1.10 "Pilgrims bathing in Roben Waterfall"	60	65
4331	$1.10 "Sea Life" (turtle facing top right)	60	65
4332	$1.10 "Farmers crossing a Suspension Bridge"	60	65
4333	$1.10 "Landscape with a Hundred Bridges" (mountains)	60	65
4334	$1.10 "Sea Life" (turtle facing bottom left)	60	65
4335	$1.10 "Landscape with a Hundred Bridges" (Japanese inscr at top)	60	65
4336	$1.10 "A View of Aoigaoka Waterfall in Edo"	60	65
4337	$1.10 "Sea Life" (crab)	60	65
4338	$1.10 "Women on the Beach at Enoshima"	60	65
MS4339	Two sheets, each 71 × 102 mm. (a) $5 "In the Horse-washing Waterfall". (b) $5 "Fisherman at Kajikazawa". Set of 2 sheets	5·50	6·00

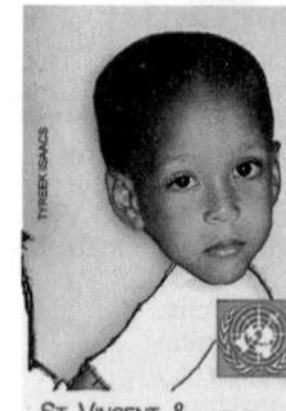

385c Tyreek Isaacs

1999. 10th Anniv of United Nations Rights of the Child Convention. Multicoloured.

4340	90c. Type **385c**	50	50
4341	90c. Fredique Isaacs	50	50
4342	90c. Jerome Burke III	50	50
4343	90c. Kellisha Roberts	50	50
4344	$3 Girl with ribbons in hair	1·75	1·75
4345	$3 Girl in straw hat	1·75	1·75
4346	$3 Girl with kitten	1·75	1·75
MS4347	110 × 80 mm. $5 Japanese child	3·00	3·25

385d Pacific Steam Locomotive for "Fleche d'Or"

1999. "PhilexFrance '99" International Stamp Exhibition, Paris. Railway Locomotives. Two sheets, each 106 × 81 mm containing horiz designs as T **385d**. Multicoloured.

MS4348	(a) $6 Type **385d**. (b) $6 Quadrt electric high-speed locomotive, 1940. Set of 2 sheets	7·00	7·50

385e Faust, Helena and Euphonon

1999. 250th Birth Anniv of Johann von Goethe (German writer).

4349	**385e**	$3 grey and black	1·60	1·75
4350	–	$3 blue, purple and black	1·60	1·75
4351	–	$3 blue and black	1·60	1·75
4352	–	$3 mauve and black	1·60	1·75
4353	–	$3 cinnamon and black	1·60	1·75
MS4354		Two sheets, each 78 × 108 mm. (a) $5 brown and black. (b) $5 brown, deep brown and black. Set of 2 sheets	5·50	6·00

DESIGNS—HORIZ: No. 4350, Von Goethe and Von Schiller; 4351, Mephistopheles leading the Lemures to Faust; 4352, Faust dying; 4353, Faust's spirit being carried by angels. VERT: No. **MS**4354a, Von Goethe; **MS**4354b, Immortal soul of Faust.

386 I. M. Pei

387 Henry Alphaeus Robertson

1999. Year of the Elder Person. Multicoloured.

4355	70c. Type **386**	45	50
4356	70c. Billy Graham	45	50
4357	70c. Barbara Cartland	45	50
4358	70c. Mike Wallace	45	50
4359	70c. Jeanne Moreau	45	50
4360	70c. B. B. King	45	50
4361	70c. Elie Wiesel	45	50
4362	70c. Arthur Miller	45	50
4363	70c. Colin Powell	45	50
4364	70c. Jack Palance	45	50
4365	70c. Neil Simon	45	50
4366	70c. Eartha Kitt	45	50
MS4367	115 × 134 mm. $1.10 Thomas Saunders; $1.10 Mother Sarah Baptiste; $1.10 Sir Sydney Gun-Munro; $1.10 Dr. Earle Kirby	2·40	2·50

1999. World Teachers' Day. Multicoloured.

4368	$2 Type **387**	1·10	1·25
4369	$2 Yvonne Francis-Gibson	1·10	1·25
4370	$2 Edna Peters	1·10	1·25
4371	$2 Christopher Wilberforce Prescod	1·10	1·25

387a Lady Elizabeth Bowes-Lyon, 1909

388 "The Resurrection" (Durer)

1999. "Queen Elizabeth the Queen Mother's Century".

4372	**387a**	$2 black and gold	1·25	1·25
4373	–	$2 black and gold	1·25	1·25
4374	–	$2 multicoloured	1·25	1·25
4375	–	$2 multicoloured	1·25	1·25
MS4376		153 × 156 mm. $6 multicoloured	3·25	3·50

DESIGNS: No. 4373, King George VI and Queen Elizabeth with Princess Elizabeth, 1930; 4374, Queen Mother at Badminton, 1977; 4375, Queen Mother waving, 1983. 37 × 50 mm: No. **MS**4376, Queen Mother wearing yellow dress, 1987.

No. **MS**4376 shows the Royal Arms embossed in gold.

1999. Christmas. Religious Paintings. Multicoloured.

4377	20c. Type **388**	20	15
4378	50c. "Christ in Limbo" (Durer)	35	25
4379	70c. "Christ falling on the Way to Calvary" (Raphael)	45	35
4380	90c. "St. Ildefonso with the Madonna and Child" (Rubens)	50	40
4381	$5 "The Crucifixion" (Raphael)	3·00	3·25
MS4382	76 × 106 mm. $6 "The Sistine Madonna" (Raphael)	3·50	3·75

No. 4378 is inscribed "Christ in Llmbo" in error.

389 Mail Coach, 1800

1999. 125th Anniv of Universal Postal Union. Multicoloured.

4383	$3 Type **389**	1·75	1·75
4384	$3 Sea plane leaving liner	1·75	1·75
4385	$3 Concorde	1·75	1·75

390 "Making It Up" (Elizabeth Murray)

1999. New Millennium. Sculpture of the Twentieth Century. Multicoloured.

4386	60c. Type **390**	35	40
4387	60c. "The Brass Family" (Alexander Calder)	35	40
4388	60c. "Tent" (Charles William Moss)	35	40
4389	60c. "Dolphin Fountain" (Gaston Lachaise)	35	40
4390	60c. "Soft Toilet" (Claes Oldenbury)	35	40
4391	60c. "Nature Study, Velvet Eyes" (Louise Bourgeois)	35	40
4392	60c. "Woman with Dog" (Duane Hanson)	35	40
4393	60c. "Bird in Space" (Brancusi)	35	40
4394	60c. "Lectern Sentinel" (David Smith)	35	40
4395	60c. "Untitled" (Dan Flavin)	35	40
4396	60c. "Unique forms of continue in space" (Boccioni)	35	40
4397	60c. "Walk, Don't Walk" (George Segal)	35	40
4398	60c. "Untitled Box No. 3" (Lucas Samaras)	35	40
4399	60c. "Bicycle Wheel" (Marcel Duchamp)	35	40
4400	60c. "Humpty Dumpty" (Isamu Noguchi)	35	40
4401	60c. "Untitled" (Donald Judd) (59 × 39 mm)	35	40
4402	60c. "Dawn's Wedding Chapel II" (Louise Nevelson)	35	40

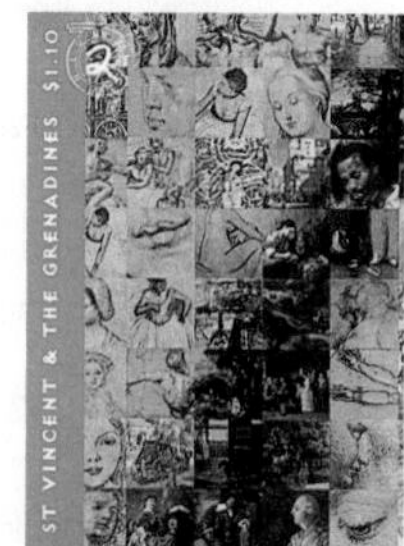

390a Portraits forming Forehead

1999. Faces of the Millennium: "Mona Lisa" (Leonardo da Vinci). Showing collage of miniature details of paintings. Multicoloured.

4403	$1.10 Type **390a**	65	65
4404	$1.10 Forehead (face value at right)	65	65
4405	$1.10 Side of face (face value at left)	65	65
4406	$1.10 Side of face (face value at right)	65	65
4407	$1.10 Cheek (face value at left)	65	65
4408	$1.10 Cheek (face value at right)	65	65
4409	$1.10 Hair (face value at left)	65	65
4410	$1.10 Hair and shoulder (face value at right)	65	65

Nos. 4403/10 were printed together, se-tenant, in sheetlets of 8 with the stamps arranged in two vertical columns separated by a gutter also containing miniature portraits. When viewed as a whole, the sheetlet forms the "Mona Lisa".

391 Clyde Tombaugh and Pluto

392 Dragon

1999. New Millennium. 80th Anniv of Discovery of the Planet Pluto by Clyde Tombaugh.

4411	**391**	60c. multicoloured	50	50

No. 4411 shows a white frame. The design also occurs as No. 4469 with a multicoloured frame and different perforation.

1999. Faces of the Millennium: Diana, Princess of Wales. As T **329a** of Sierra Leone, showing collage of miniature flower photographs. Mult.

4412	$1 Flowers forming top of head (face value at left)	60	65
4413	$1 Top of head (face value at right)	60	65
4414	$1 Ear (face value at left)	60	65

4415 $1 Eye and temple (face value at right) 60 65
4416 $1 Cheek (face value at left) 60 65
4417 $1 Cheek (face value at right) 60 65
4418 $1 Blue background (face value at left) 60 65
4419 $1 Chin (face value at right) 60 65

Nos. 4412/19 were printed together, se-tenant, in sheetlets of 8 with the stamps arranged in two vertical columns separated by a gutter also containing miniature photographs. When viewed as a whole, the sheetlet forms a portrait of Diana, Princess of Wales.

2000. Chinese New Year ("Year of the Dragon"). Multicoloured.

4420 $2 Type **392** (blue and lilac background) 1·10 1·25
4421 $2 Dragon (cinnamon and brown background) 1·10 1·25
4422 $2 Dragon (orange and cerise background) 1·10 1·25
MS4423 70 × 101 mm. $4 Dragon 2·00 2·50

393 Stoplight Parrotfish

2000. Tropical Fish. Multicoloured.

4424 10c. Type **393** 15 15
4425 20c. Spot-finned hogfish 20 15
4426 70c. Beaugregory 45 35
4427 90c. Porkfish 50 40
4428 $1 Barred hamlet 60 45
4429 $1.10 Porcupinefish 65 70
4430 $1.10 Blue tang 65 70
4431 $1.10 Blue-headed wrasse 65 70
4432 $1.10 Queen angelfish (juvenile) 65 70
4433 $1.10 Lined seahorse 65 70
4434 $1.10 Small-mouthed grunt 65 70
4435 $1.10 French angelfish 65 70
4436 $1.10 Smooth trunkfish 65 70
4437 $1.10 Sargassum triggerfish 65 70
4438 $1.10 Indigo hamlet 65 70
4439 $1.10 Yellow-headed jawfish 65 70
4440 $1.10 Peppermint basslet 65 70
4441 $1.40 Queen triggerfish 75 80
MS4442 Two sheets, each 183 × 80 mm. (a) $5 Four-eyed Butterflyfish. (b) $5 Cherub ("Pygmy") Angelfish. Set of 2 sheets 5·50 6·00

Nos. 4429/34 and 4435/40 were each printed together, se-tenant, with the backgrounds forming composite designs.

No. 4438 is inscribed "Indigo Halmet" in error.

394 High Hat

394a Mahatma Gandhi and Supporters, 1930

2000. Marine Life. Multicoloured.

4443 50c. Type **394** 35 40
4444 50c. Sergeant major 35 40
4445 50c. Hawksbill turtle 35 40
4446 50c. Horse-eyed jacks 35 40
4447 50c. Horse-eyed jacks and middle of humpback whale 35 40
4448 50c. Head of humpback whale and horse-eyed jacks 35 40
4449 50c. Black-capped basslet ("Gramma") 35 40
4450 50c. Common dolphins 35 40
4451 50c. French grunts and flipper of humpback whale 35 40
4452 50c. Great barracuda 35 40
4453 50c. Bottle-nosed dolphins 35 40
4454 50c. Reid's seahorse 35 40
4455 50c. French grunt and southern stingray 35 40
4456 50c. French grunts 35 40
4457 50c. Indigo hamlet 35 40
4458 50c. Basking shark 35 40
4459 50c. Nassau grouper 35 40
4460 50c. Nurse shark and jackknife-fish ("Ribbonfish") 35 40
4461 50c. Southern stingray 35 40
4462 50c. Blue shark and southern stingray 35 40
4463 50c. Spanish hogfish 35 40
4464 90c. Spotfin hogfish 50 45
4465 $1 Royal gramma 60 55
4466 $2 Queen angelfish 1·10 1·25
MS4467 Two sheets, each 106 × 76 mm. (a) $5 Rock Beauty. (b) $5 Banded Butterflyfish. Set of 2 sheets 5·50 6·00

Nos. 4444/63 were printed together, se-tenant, with the backgrounds forming a composite design.

2000. New Millennium. People and Events of Twentieth Century (1930–39). Multicoloured.

4468 60c. Type **394a** 45 50
4469 60c. As Type **391**, but with multicoloured frame 45 50
4470 60c. Empire State Building, New York (opened 1931) 45 50
4471 60c. Declaration of Republic, Spain, 1931 45 50
4472 60c. Pres. Franklin D. Roosevelt ("New Deal" inaugurated, 1933) 45 50
4473 60c. Reichstag on fire, 1933 45 50
4474 60c. Mao Tse-tung (Communist Revolution in China, 1934) 45 50
4475 60c. General Franco (Spanish Civil War, 1936) 45 50
4476 60c. King Edward VIII and Abdication document, 1936 45 50
4477 60c. Diego Rivera (Mexican muralist) (50th birthday, 1936) 45 50
4478 60c. Golden Gate Bridge, San Francisco (opened 1937) 45 50
4479 60c. Atomic cloud (first atomic reaction, 1939) 45 50
4480 60c. Troops and newspaper vendor (start of Second World War, 1939) 45 50
4481 60c. New York World's Fair emblem, 1939 45 50
4482 60c. New Dalai Lama chosen in Tibet, 1939 45 50
4483 60c. Explosion of *Hindenburg* (airship), 1937 (59 × 39 mm) 45 50
4484 60c. Igor Sikorsky and VS-300, first successful helicopter, 1939 45 50

No. 4468 is inscribed "Gahndi" in error.

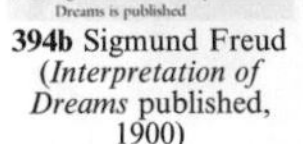

394b Sigmund Freud (*Interpretation of Dreams* published, 1900)

394c "Robert Rich, Earl of Warwick"

2000. New Millennium. People and Events of Twentieth Century (1900–50). Multicoloured.

4485 20c. Type **394b** 25 30
4486 20c. Guglielmo Marconi (first long distance wireless transmission, 1901) 25 30
4487 20c. Orville and Wilbur Wright (construction of Wright *Flyer III* powered aircraft, 1903) 25 30
4488 20c. Albert Einstein (Theory of Relativity, 1905) 25 30
4489 20c. Henry Ford and Model T, 1908 25 30
4490 20c. Alfred Wegener (German meteorologist) (Theory of Continental Drift, 1912) 25 30
4491 20c. Lord Kitchener on recruiting poster (beginning of First World War, 1914) 25 30
4492 20c. Lenin (Russian Revolution, 1917) 25 30
4493 20c. James Joyce (*Ulysses*, published 1922) 25 30
4494 20c. Alexander Fleming (Scottish bacteriologist) (discovery of Penicillin, 1928) 25 30
4495 20c. Edwin Hubble (Hubble's Law on expansion of Universe, 1929) 25 30
4496 20c. Mao Tse-tung and map of Long March, 1934 25 30
4497 20c. Alan Turing (English mathematician) (Theory of digital computing, 1937) 25 30
4498 20c. Berlin researchers (discovery of frission, 1938) 25 30
4499 20c. German Troops and headline (start of Second World War, 1939) 25 30
4500 20c. Churchill, Roosevelt and Stalin (Yalta Conference, 1945) 25 30
4501 20c. Gandhi and Nehru (Independence of India, 1947) 25 30
4502 20c. William Shockley (U.S. physicist) (development of miniature transistor, 1947) 25 30

2000. 400th Birth Anniv of Sir Anthony van Dyck. Multicoloured.

4503 $1 Type **394c** 60 65
4504 $1 "James Stuart, Duke of Lennox and Richmond" 60 65
4505 $1 "Sir John Suckling" 60 65
4506 $1 "Sir Robert Shirley" 60 65
4507 $1 "Teresia, Lady Shirley" 60 65
4508 $1 "Thomas Wentworth, Earl of Strafford" (with dog) 60 65
4509 $1 "Thomas Wentworth, Earl of Strafford" 60 65
4510 $1 "Lady Anne Carr, Countess of Bedford" 60 65
4511 $1 "Portrait of a Member of the Charles Family" 60 65
4512 $1 "Thomas Howard, Earl of Arundel" 60 65
4513 $1 "Diana Cecil, Countess of Oxford" 60 65
4514 $1 "The Violincellist" 60 65
4515 $1 "The Apostle Peter" 60 65
4516 $1 "St. Matthew" 60 65
4517 $1 "St. James the Greater" 60 65
4518 $1 "St. Bartholomew" 60 65
4519 $1 "The Apostle Thomas" 60 65
4520 $1 "The Apostle Jude (Thaddeus)" 60 65
4521 $1 "The Vision of St. Anthony" 60 65
4522 $1 "The Mystic Marriage of St. Catherine" 60 65
4523 $1 "The Vision of the Blessed Herman Joseph" 60 65
4524 $1 "Madonna and Child enthroned with Sts. Rosalie, Peter and Paul" 60 65
4525 $1 "St. Rosalie interceding for the Plague stricken of Palermo" 60 65
4526 $1 "Francesco Orero in Adoration of the Crucifixion" 60 65
MS4527 Three sheets. (a) 102 × 127 mm. $5 "William Fielding, Earl of Denbigh". (b) 127 × 102 mm. $5 "The Mystic Marriage of St. Catherine". (c) 102 × 127 mm. $5 "St. Augustine in Ecstasy" (horiz). Set of 3 sheets 7·50 8·00

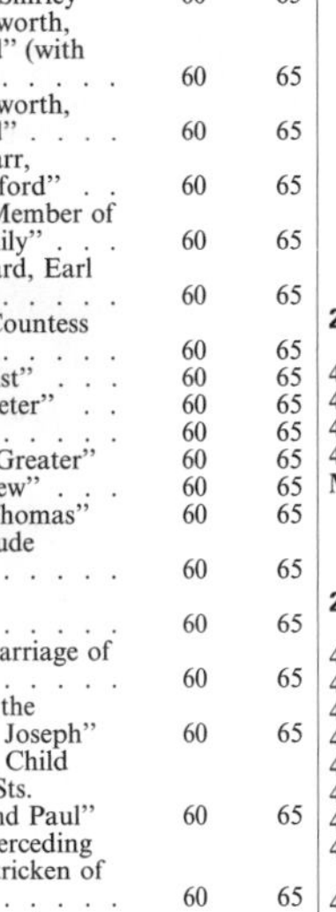

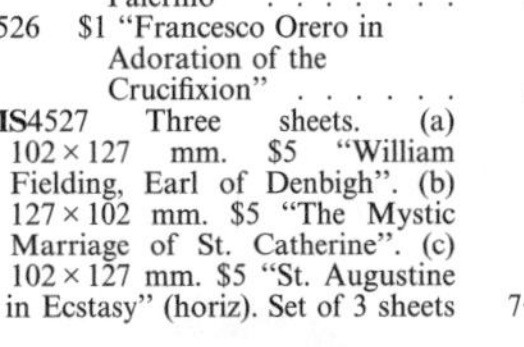

395 *Brassavola nodosa*

2000. "The Stamp Show 2000" International Stamp Exhibition, London. Orchids of the Caribbean. Mult.

4528 70c. Type **395** 45 35
4529 90c. *Bletia purpurea* 50 40
4530 $1.40 *Brassavola cucullata* 80 75
4531 $1.50 *Brassavola cordata* (vert) 85 90
4532 $1.50 *Brassia caudata* (vert) 85 90
4533 $1.50 *Broughotnia sanguinea* (vert) 85 90
4534 $1.50 *Comparettia falcata* (vert) 85 90
4535 $1.50 *Clowesia rosea* (vert) 85 90
4536 $1.50 *Caularthron bicornutum* (vert) 85 90
4537 $1.50 *Cyrtopodium punctatum* (vert) 85 90
4538 $1.50 *Dendrophylax funalis* (vert) 85 90
4539 $1.50 *Dichaea hystricina* (vert) 85 90
4540 $1.50 *Cyrtopodium andersonii* (vert) 85 90
4541 $1.50 *Epidendrum secundum* (vert) 85 90
4542 $1.50 *Dimerandra emarginata* (vert) 85 90
4543 $1.50 *Oncidium urophyllum* (vert) 85 90
4544 $1.50 *Oeceoclades maculata* (vert) 85 90
4545 $1.50 *Vanilla planifolia* (vert) 85 90
4546 $1.50 *Isolhilus linearis* (vert) 85 90
4547 $1.50 *Ionopsis utricularioides* (vert) 85 90
4548 $1.50 *Nidema boothii* (vert) 85 90
MS4549 Two sheets, each 123 × 100 mm. (a) $5 *Edidendrum altissimum* (vert). (b) $5 *Neocogniauxia hexaptera* (vert). Set of 2 sheets 5·50 6·00

Nos. 4531/6, 4537/42 and 4543/8 were each printed together, se-tenant, with the backgrounds forming maps of the Caribbean.

395a In Grey Check Suit

395c *Pane, Amore e Fantasia*, 1954

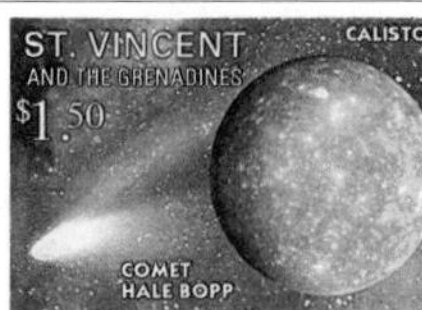

395b Hale Bopp Comet passing Calisto

2000. 18th Birthday of Prince William. Multicoloured.

4550 $1.40 Type **395a** 85 90
4551 $1.40 Wearing scarf 85 90
4552 $1.40 In blue suit 85 90
4553 $1.40 Wearing blue jumper 85 90
MS4554 100 × 80 mm. $5 Wearing Eton uniform (37 × 50 mm) 3·25 3·50

2000. "EXPO 2000" International Stamp Exhibition, Anaheim, U.S.A. Spacecraft. Multicoloured.

4555 $1.50 Type **395b** 85 90
4556 $1.50 "Galileo" spacecraft 85 90
4557 $1.50 "Ulysse" spacecraft 85 90
4558 $1.50 "Pioneer 11" 85 90
4559 $1.50 "Voyager 1" 85 90
4560 $1.50 "Pioneer 10" 85 90
4561 $1.50 "Cassini" spacecraft 85 90
4562 $1.50 "Pioneer 11" approaching Saturn 85 90
4563 $1.50 "Voyager 1" and Ariel 85 90
4564 $1.50 "Huygens" spacecraft 85 90
4565 $1.50 "Deep Space 4 Champollion" 85 90
4566 $1.50 "Voyager 2" 85 90
4567 $1.50 "Voyager 2" passing Umbriel 85 90
4568 $1.50 "Pluto Project" 85 90
4569 $1.50 "Voyager 1" approaching Pluto 85 90
4570 $1.50 Oort Cloud (part of asteroid belt) 85 90
4571 $1.50 "Pluto Kuiper Express" spacecraft 85 90
4572 $1.50 "Voyager 2" above Neptune 85 90
MS4573 Two sheets, each 105 × 75 mm. (a) $5 "Pluto Project" spacecraft. (b) $5 "Stardust" spacecraft approaching Wild 2 Comet. Set of 2 sheets 5·50 6·00

Nos. 4555/60, 4561/6 and 4567/72 were each printed together, se-tenant, with the backgrounds forming composite designs.

2000. 50th Anniv of Berlin Film Festival. Mult.

4574 $1.40 Type **395c** 80 85
4575 $1.40 Lord Olivier in *Richard III*, 1956 80 85
4576 $1.40 *Smultronstallet*, 1958 80 85
4577 $1.40 Sidney Poitier in *The Defiant Ones*, 1958 80 85
4578 $1.40 *The Living Desert*, 1954 80 85
4579 $1.40 *A Bout de Souffle*, 1960 80 85
MS4580 95 × 103 mm. $5 Jean-Luc Godard (director), 1960 3·25 3·50

395d George Stephenson and *Locomotion No. 1*, 1825

2000. 175th Anniv of Stockton and Darlington Line (first public railway). Multicoloured.

4581 $3 As Type **395d** 1·90 1·90
4582 $3 Camden and Amboy Railroad locomotive *John Bull*, 1831 1·90 1·90

No. 4582 is inscribed "Camoen" in error.

396 Albert Einstein

2000. Election of Albert Einstein (mathematical physicist) as *Time Magazine* "Man of the Century". Multicoloured.

4583 $2 Type **396** 1·10 1·25
4584 $2 Two portraits, one with hands clasped 1·10 1·25
4585 $2 Two portraits, one standing by painting 1·10 1·25

396a LZ-6 *Delag*, 1909

2000. Centenary of First Zeppelin Flight.
4586 **396a** $3 blue, black and mauve . . . . 1·75 1·75
4587 – $3 blue, black and mauve . . . . 1·75 1·75
4588 – $3 green, black and mauve . . . . 1·75 1·75
MS4589 116 × 76 mm. $5 green, black and mauve . . . . . . 3·25 3·50
DESIGNS: No. 4587, LZ-127 *Graf Zeppelin*, 1928; 4588, LZ-129 *Hindenburg*, 1936. 50 × 38 mm: No. **MS**4589, LZ-9 ZII (*Ersatz*), 1911.
No. 4588 is inscribed "(129) Hindenberg" in error.

396b Mildred Didrikson (javelin), 1932

2000. Olympic Games, Sydney. Multicoloured.
4590 $2 Type **396b** . . . . 1·25 1·25
4591 $2 Man on vaulting horse 1·25 1·25
4592 $2 Olympic Stadium, Barcelona (1992) and Spanish flag . . . . . . 1·25 1·25
4593 $2 Ancient Greek horse racing . . . . 1·25 1·25

396c Ian Allen

396d Member of The Chantels (value at left and hair clear of perforations)

2000. West Indies Cricket Tour and 100th Test Match at Lord's.
4594 **396c** 10c. multicoloured . . . 20 20
4595 – 20c. black and yellow 35 20
4596 – $1.10 multicoloured . . 70 70
4597 – $1.40 multicoloured . . 90 1·00
MS4598 121 × 114 mm. $5 multicoloured . . . . 3·25 3·50
DESIGNS—VERT: 20c. T. Michael Findlay; $1.10, Winston Davis; $1.40, Nixon McLean. HORIZ: $5 Lord's Cricket Ground.

2000. Girl Pop Groups. Multicoloured.
4599 $1.40 Type **396d** 75 80
4600 $1.40 Member of The Chantels (value at right on background) 75 80
4601 $1.40 Member of The Chantels (value at right on neck) 75 80
4602 $1.40 Member of The Chantels (value at left and hair over perforations) . . 75 80
4603 $1.40 Member of The Chantels (value at left on background) 75 80
4604 $1.40 Member of The Marvelettes (value on background) 75 80
4605 $1.40 Member of The Marvelettes (with curl on forehead) 75 80
4606 $1.40 Member of The Marvelettes (with gap in teeth) 75 80
4607 $1.40 Member of The Marvelettes (with long hair) 75 80
4608 $1.40 Member of The Marvelettes (looking to left) 75 80

397 Mario Andretti in Racing Car

2000. Election of Mario Andretti as "Driver of the Century".
4609 **397** $1.10 brown and red . . 60 65
4610 – $1.10 multicoloured . . 60 65
4611 – $1.10 multicoloured . . 60 65
4612 – $1.10 brown and red . . 60 65
4613 – $1.10 brown and red . . 60 65
4614 – $1.10 multicoloured . . 60 65
4615 – $1.10 multicoloured . . 60 65
4616 – $1.10 brown and red . . 60 65
MS4617 155 × 114 mm. $5 black and red . . . . 3·00 3·20
DESIGNS: No. 4610, In white overalls; 4611, With hands together; 4612, During race; 4613, Standing by saloon car; 4614, With "abc" trophy; 4615, In red overalls; 4616, Watching race; **MS**4617, Holding trophy.

398 Clarinet-player

2000. The Art of Jazz. Multicoloured.
4618 $1.40 Type **398** 75 80
4619 $1.40 Pianist 75 80
4620 $1.40 Trumpeter 75 80
4621 $1.40 Guitarist 75 80
4622 $1.40 Bass-player 75 80
4623 $1.40 Saxophonist 75 80

399 Michael Palin

2000. 30th Anniv of Monty Python. Multicoloured.
4624 $1.40 Type **399** 75 80
4625 $1.40 Eric Idle 75 80
4626 $1.40 John Cleese 75 80
4627 $1.40 Graham Chapman . . 75 80
4628 $1.40 Terry Gilliam 75 80
4629 $1.40 Terry Jones 75 80

400 Barbara Taylor Bradford

2000. Great Writers of the 20th Century: Barbara Taylor Bradford. Sheet 128 × 88 mm.
MS4630 **400** $5 multicoloured . . 3·00 3·25

401 Betty Boop in "Jack and Jill"

2000. Betty Boop (cartoon character). Illustrating nursery rhymes. Multicoloured.
4631 $1 Type **401** 60 65
4632 $1 "Three Blind Mice" . . 60 65
4633 $1 "Wee Willie Winky" . . 60 65
4634 $1 "Hey Diddle Diddle" . . 60 65
4635 $1 "Mother Goose" 60 65
4636 $1 "Little Miss Muffet" . . 60 65
4637 $1 "Three Little Kittens" . . 60 65
4638 $1 "Rub-a-Dub-Dub" . . . 60 65
4639 $1 "Little Jack Horner" . . 60 65
MS4640 Two sheets, each 133 × 91 mm. (a) $5 "Little Bo Peep". (b) $5 "Old Woman that lived in a Shoe". Set of 2 sheets 5·50 6·00

402 David Copperfield

2000. David Copperfield (conjurer) Commemoration. Each incorporating a similar portrait. Mult.
4641 $1.40 Type **402** 75 80
4642 $1.40 David Copperfield levitating (dressed in black) 75 80
4643 $1.40 As No. 4642, but faint figure in brown 75 80
4644 $1.40 As No. 4642, but figure replaced by two large bubbles 75 80

403 Goblet or Monkey

2000. Local Utensils. Multicoloured.
4645 20c. Type **403** 20 15
4646 50c. Goose (iron) 35 25
4647 70c. Boley and calabash (vert) 45 35
4648 $1 Three flat irons 60 65

404 Pink Ginger Lily

405 Queen Elizabeth the Queen Mother

2000. Flowers. Multicoloured.
4649 90c. Type **404** 55 60
4650 90c. *Thumbergia grandiflora* 55 60
4651 90c. Red ginger lily 55 60
4652 90c. Madagascar jasmine . . 55 60
4653 90c. Cluster palm 55 60
4654 90c. Red torch lily 55 60
4655 90c. *Salvia splendens* . . . 55 60
4656 90c. Balsamapple 55 60
4657 90c. Rostrata 55 60
MS4658 Two sheets. (a) 65 × 82 mm. $5 Red Flamingo (b) 82 × 65 mm. $5 Balsamapple (horiz). Set of 2 sheets . . . . 5·50 6·00
Nos. 4649, 4651 and 4654 are all inscribed "Lilly" in error.

2000. Queen Elizabeth the Queen Mother's 100th Birthday.
4659 **405** $1.40 multicoloured . . 1·00 1·00

2000. Faces of the Millennium: Queen Elizabeth the Queen Mother. As T **329a** of Sierra Leone, showing collage of flower photographs. Multicoloured.
4660 $1 Top of head (face value at left) 65 65
4661 $1 Top of head (face value at right) 65 65
4662 $1 Eye and temple (face value at left) 65 65
4663 $1 Temple (face value at right) 65 65
4664 $1 Cheek (face value at left) 65 65
4665 $1 Cheek (face value at right) 65 65
4666 $1 Chin (face value at left) 65 65
4667 $1 Neck (face value at right) 65 65
Nos. 4660/7 were printed together, se-tenant, in sheetlets of 8 with the stamps arranged in two vertical columns separated by a gutter also containing miniature photographs. When viewed as a whole, the sheetlet forms a portrait of the Queen Mother.

406 Ida Cox

2000. New Millennium. "The Birth of The Blues". Showing singers and musicians. Multicoloured.
4668 $1.40 Type **406** 75 80
4669 $1.40 Lonnie Johnson . . . 75 80
4670 $1.40 Muddy Waters . . . 75 80
4671 $1.40 T-Bone Walker . . . 75 80
4672 $1.40 Howlin' Wolf 75 80
4673 $1.40 Sister Rosetta Thorpe 75 80
4674 $1.40 Bessie Smith 75 80
4675 $1.40 Willie Dixon 75 80
4676 $1.40 Gertrude "Ma" Rainey 75 80
4677 $1.40 W. C. Handy 75 80
4678 $1.40 Leadbelly 75 80
4679 $1.40 Big Bill Broonzy . . . 75 80
MS4680 Two sheets, each 80 × 120 mm. (a) $5 Billie Holiday. (b) $5 Robert Johnson. Set of 2 sheets . . . . 5·50 6·00

407 U.S.S. *Shaw* exploding, Pearl Harbor, 1941

2000. Wars of the Twentieth Century. Multicoloured.
4681 $1 Type **407** 60 60
4682 $1 American B-24 Liberators bombing Ploesti oil fields, 1943 . . 60 60
4683 $1 Soviet T-34 tank, Germany, 1945 . . . . . 60 60
4684 $1 U.S.S. *New Jersey* (battleship) off North Korea, 1951 . . . . . . 60 60
4685 $1 American F-86 Sabre fighter over North Korea, 1951 . . . . 60 60
4686 $1 U.S.S. *Enterprise* (aircraft carrier) off Indo-China . . 60 60
4687 $1 American B-52 bomber over Vietnam, 1972 . . . 60 60
4688 $1 American armoured personnel carrier, Tay Ninh, 1967 . . . . 60 60
4689 $1 Two Israeli F-4 Phantoms, 1967 . . . . . 60 60
4690 $1 Abandoned Egyptian T-72 tanks, 1967 . . . . 60 60
4691 $1 SAM 6 rocket launchers, Cairo, 1973 . . . . . . 60 60
4692 $1 Israeli M-48 tanks in desert, 1973 . . . . . . 60 60
4693 $1 H.M.S. *Invincible* (aircraft carrier) on way to Falkland Islands, 1982 60 60
4694 $1 British Harriers and H.M.S. *Hermes* (aircraft carrier), Falkland Islands, 1982 . . . . 60 60
4695 $1 Iraqi SS-1 Scud-B mobile missile launcher, 1990 . . 60 60
4696 $1 American M1-A1 Abrams tanks, advancing, Gulf War, 1990 . . . . . 60 60
MS4697 Two sheets. (a) 85 × 110 mm. $5 Nucleur bomb test, Pershing II missile and B-52 bomber (55 × 40 mm). (b) 106 × 81 mm. $5 Israeli F-4 fighter-bomber, 1973. Set of 2 sheets . . . . 6·00 6·50
No. 4683 is inscribed "SOVIETIC", 4693 "H.M.S. HERMES" and 4696 "NOTHWARD", all in error.

408 Leopold Anthony

410 Blue and Yellow Macaw ("Blue and Gold Macaw")

409 Government House

2000. Local Musicians.
4698 **408** $1.40 multicoloured . . 75 80
4699 – $1.40 black and buff . . 75 80
4700 – $1.40 multicoloured . . 75 80
4701 – $1.40 multicoloured . . 75 80
DESIGNS: No. 4699, "Shake" Kean (trumpeter); 4700, Olsen V. Peters (cornet-player); 4701, Patrick E. Prescod (pianist).

2000. 21st Anniv of Independence. Multicoloured.
4702 10c. Type **409** 15 10
4703 15c. House of Assembly in session 15 10

4704 50c. House of Assembly building 35 25
4705 $2 Government Financial Complex . . . . 1·25 1·40

2000. Birds. Multicoloured.
4706 50c. Type **410** 40 25
4707 90c. English fallow budgerigar 55 40
4708 $1 Superb parrot ("Barraband Parakeet") 60 45
4709 $2 Dominant pied blue . . 1·10 1·25
4710 $2 Canary ("Stafford Canary") . . . . 1·10 1·25
4711 $2 Masked lovebird . . . . 1·10 1·25
4712 $2 Canary ("Parisian Full Canary") . . . . 1·10 1·25
4713 $2 Scarlet macaw . . . . . 1·10 1·25
4714 $2 Blue-fronted amazon . . 1·10 1·25
4715 $2 Buffon's macaw . . . . 1·10 1·25
4716 $2 Canada goose (horiz) . . 1·10 1·25
4717 $2 Mandarin duck (horiz) . 1·10 1·25
4718 $2 Gouldian finch (horiz) . 1·10 1·25
4719 $2 English short-faced tumbler . . . . 1·10 1·25
4720 $2 Diamond dove . . . . . 1·10 1·25
4721 $2 Norwich cropper . . . . 1·10 1·25
MS4722 Two sheets, each 96 × 67 mm. (a) $5 Budgerigar (horiz). (b) $5 Common Peafowl (horiz). Set of 2 sheets . . . . 5·50 6·00

No. 4707 is inscribed "Budgerigan", 4708 "Pazakeet", 4711 "Macked", 4713 "Searlet" and 4721 "Nozwich", all in error. There are also many mistakes in the Latin species names shown on the stamps.

411 Rebecca wearing Checked Coat in Shop

2000. Shirley Temple in *Rebecca of Sunnybrook Farm*. Showing scenes from the film. Multicoloured.
4723 90c. Type **411** 50 55
4724 90c. Rebecca with parents 50 55
4725 90c. Rebecca being reprimanded 50 55
4726 90c. Rebecca singing with mother at piano 50 55
4727 90c. Rebecca with man by fence 50 55
4728 90c. Tea time 50 55
4729 $1.10 Rebecca in check coat with microphone (vert) . . 60 65
4730 $1.10 Rebecca in straw hat with chick (vert) 60 65
4731 $1.10 Rebecca in black and white dress with microphone (vert) 60 65
4732 $1.10 Rebecca in red dress with woman (vert) 60 65
MS4733 106 × 76 mm. $1.10 Rebecca dancing with Bill "Bojangles" Robinson (vert) 65 75

412 Angel praying

2000. Christmas. Multicoloured.
4734 20c. Type **412** 20 15
4735 70c. Heads of two angels looking down 45 35
4736 90c. Heads of two angels, one looking down 50 40
4737 $5 Angel in red with arms folded . . . . 3·25 3·50
MS4738 110 × 121 mm. $5 Angel's head . . . . 3·25 3·50

413 Two Supermarine Spitfires

414 Symbolic Snake on Background of Chinese Characters

2000. 60th Anniv of the Battle of Britain. Multicoloured (except No. 4742).
4739 90c. Type **413** 55 55
4740 90c. Supermarine Spitfire over countryside 55 55
4741 90c. Dornier DO217 on fire 55 55
4742 90c. Two Gloster Gladiators (black, violet and grey) . . 55 55
4743 90c. Two Hawker Hurricanes attacking German fighters 55 55
4744 90c. Junkers JU87-Stuka (face value at bottom left) 55 55
4745 90c. Two Supermarine Spitfires (different) . . . 55 55
4746 90c. Junkers JU88 on fire 55 55
4747 90c. Junkers JU87-Stuka (face value at bottom right) 55 55
4748 90c. Westland Lysander and Gloster Gladiator 55 55
4749 90c. Messerschmitt BF109 55 55
4750 90c. Heinkel HE111 under attack 55 55
4751 90c. Hawker Hurricanes from below 55 55
4752 90c. Bristol Blenheim . . . 55 55
4753 90c. Two Supermarine Spitfires over fields . . . 55 55
4754 90c. Messerschmitt BF110 55 55
MS4755 Two sheets, each 79 × 59 mm. (a) $5 Supermarine Spitfire (42 × 27½ mm). (b) $5 Hawker Hurricane (42 × 27½ mm). Set of 2 sheets . . . . 5·50 6·00

2001. Chinese New Year ("Year of the Snake").
4756 **414** $1 purple, blue and black 60 65
4757 – $1 purple, mauve and black 60 65
4758 – $1 purple, green and black 60 65
MS4759 64 × 93 mm. $2 purple, red and black . . . . 1·10 1·25
DESIGNS: Nos. 4757/8 showing different snakes.

415 "Diana the Huntress" (women hunters and dog) (Rubens)

2001. "EspaNa 2000" International Stamp Exhibition, Madrid. Rubens Paintings from the Prado Museum. Multicoloured.
4760 10c. Type **415** 15 15
4761 90c. "Adoration of the Magi" 50 40
4762 $1 "Diana the Huntress" (Diana with dogs) 60 45
4763 $2 "Prometheus carrying Fire" . . . . 1·10 1·25
4764 $2 "Vulcan forging Jupiter's Thunderbolt" . . . . . . 1·10 1·25
4765 $2 "Saturn devouring one of his Sons" . . . . 1·10 1·25
4766 $2 "Polyphemus" . . . . . 1·10 1·25
4767 $2 "St. Matthias" . . . . . 1·10 1·25
4768 $2 "Death of Seneca" . . . 1·10 1·25
4769 $2 "Maria de Medici, Queen of France" . . . . 1·10 1·25
4770 $2 "Achilles discovered by Ulysses" . . . . 1·10 1·25
4771 $2 "Heraclitus, the Mournful Philosopher" (full length) . . . . . . 1·10 1·25
4772 $2 "Heraclitus, the Mournful Philosopher" (head and shoulders) . . 1·10 1·25
4773 $2 "Anne of Austria, Queen of France" (head and shoulders) . . . . 1·10 1·25
4774 $2 "Anne of Austria, Queen of France" (full length) 1·10 1·25
MS4775 Two sheets. (a) 95 × 150 mm. $5 "Holy Family with St. Anne". (b) 130 × 119 mm. $5 "Judgement of Solomon". Set of 2 sheets . . . . 5·50 6·00

416 "The Concert" (Hendrick ter Brugghen)

2001. Bicentenary of the Rijksmuseum, Amsterdam. Paintings. Multicoloured.
4776 $1.40 Type **416** 75 80
4777 $1.40 "Vertumnus and Pomona" (Paulus Moreleese) 75 80
4778 $1.40 "Elegant Couples courting" (couple standing) (Willem Buytewech) 75 80
4779 $1.40 "Sick Woman" (Jan Steen) 75 80
4780 $1.40 "Elegant Couples courting" (couple seated) (Buytewech) 75 80
4781 $1.40 "Don Ramon Satue" (Goya) 75 80
4782 $1.40 "Spendthrift" (Thomas Asselijn) 75 80
4783 $1.40 "Art Gallery of Jan Gildemeester Jansz" (Adriaan de Lelie) 75 80
4784 $1.40 "Raampoortje, Amsterdam" (Wouter van Troostwijk) 75 80
4785 $1.40 "Winter Landscape" (Barend Koekkoek) . . . 75 80
4786 $1.40 "The Procuress" (elderly woman) (Dirck van Baburen) 75 80
4787 $1.40 "The Procuress" (couple) (Van Baburen) 75 80
4788 $1.40 "Music Party" (Rembrandt) 75 80
4789 $1.40 "Rutger Schimmelpenninck and Family" (Pierre Paul Prud'hon) 75 80
4790 $1.40 "Anna accused by Tobit of stealing a Kid" Rembrandt) 75 80
4791 $1.40 "Syndics of the Amsterdam Goldsmiths' Guild" (Thomas de Keyser) 75 80
4792 $1.40 "Portrait of a Lady" (De Keyser) 75 80
4793 $1.40 "Marriage Portrait of Issac Massa and Beatrix van der Laen" (Hals) . . 75 80
MS4794 Three sheets. (a) 119 × 82 mm. $5 "Donkey riding on the Beach" (Isaac Israels). (b) 119 × 82 mm. $5 "Landscape with Stone Bridge" (Rembrandt) (horiz). (c) 102 × 108 mm. $5 "Still Life of Peacocks" (Rembrandt) (horiz). Set of 3 sheets . . . . 7·50 8·00

417 "Kadabra No. 64"

2001. "Pokemon" (children's cartoon series). Multicoloured.
4795 90c. Type **417** 50 55
4796 90c. "Spearow No. 21" . . 50 55
4797 90c. "Kakuna No. 14" . . . 50 55
4798 90c. "Koffing No. 109" . . 50 55
4799 90c. "Tentacruel No. 73" . . 50 55
4800 90c. "Cloyster No. 91" . . 50 55
MS4801 74 × 115 mm. $3 "Meowth No. 52" . . . . 1·75 1·90

418 Barred Owl

2001. "Hong Kong 2001" Stamp Exhibition. Birds of Prey. Multicoloured.
4802 10c. Type **418** 25 20
4803 90c. Lammergeier 55 55
4804 90c. Common caracara ("Crested Caracara") . . 55 55
4805 90c. Tengmalm's owl ("Boreal Owl") 55 55
4806 90c. Harpy eagle 55 55
4807 90c. Bay owl ("Oriental Bay Owl") 55 55
4808 90c. Hawk owl 55 55
4809 90c. Laughing falcon . . . 55 55
4810 $1 Californian condor . . . 65 65
4811 $1.10 Bateleur 70 70
4812 $1.10 Northern hobby ("Hobby") 70 70
4813 $1.10 Osprey 70 70
4814 $1.10 Northern goshawk ("Goshawk") 70 70
4815 $1.10 African fish eagle . . 70 70
4816 $1.10 Egyptian vulture . . 70 70
4817 $2 Mississippi kite . . . . . 1·25 1·25
MS4818 Two sheets, each 72 × 100 mm. (a) $5 Great grey owl. (b) $5 American kestrel. Set of 2 sheets . . . . 6·00 6·50

Nos. 4804/9 and 4811/16 were each printed together, se-tenant, the backgrounds forming a composite design.

419 Northern Eagle Owl ("Eagle Owl")

420 Woman on Beach

2001. Owls. Multicoloured.
4819 10c. Type **419** 20 20
4820 20c. Barn owl 35 20
4821 50c. Great grey owl 50 35
4822 70c. Long-eared owl 55 35
4823 90c. Tawny owl 60 40
4824 $1 Hawk owl 65 50
4825 $1.40 Ural owl (horiz) . . . 80 85
4826 $1.40 Tengmalm's owl (horiz) 80 85
4827 $1.40 African marsh owl ("Marsh Owl") (horiz) . . 80 85
4828 $1.40 Brown fish owl (horiz) 80 85
4829 $1.40 Little owl (horiz) . . . 80 85
4830 $1.40 Short-eared owl (horiz) 80 85
MS4831 Two sheets. (a) 85 × 109 mm. $5 Hume's Owl. (b) 109 × 85 mm. $5 Snowy Owl. Set of 2 sheets . . . . 6·00 6·50

Nos. 4825/30 were printed together, se-tenant, the backgrounds forming a composite design.

Nos. 4819 and 4823 are inscribed "EAGEL" or "TWANY", both in error.

2001. United Nations Women's Human Rights Campaign. Multicoloured.
4832 90c. Type **420** 50 40
4833 $1 "Caribbean Woman II" 60 60

421 *Amanita fulva*

2001. Fungi. Multicoloured.
4834 20c. Type **421** 20 15
4835 90c. *Hygrophorus speciosus* 50 40
4836 $1.10 *Amanita phalloides* . . 65 50
4837 $1.40 *Amanita muscari* . . 75 80
4838 $1.40 *Boletus zelleri* 75 80
4839 $1.40 *Coprinus picaceus* . . 75 80
4840 $1.40 *Stropharia aeruginosa* 75 80
4841 $1.40 *Lepistra nuda* 75 80
4842 $1.40 *Hygrophorus conicus* 75 80
4843 $1.40 *Lactarius deliciosus* 75 80
4844 $1.40 *Hygrophorus psittacinus* 75 80
4845 $1.40 *Tricholomopsis rutilans* 75 80
4846 $1.40 *Hygrophorus coccineus* 75 80
4847 $1.40 *Collybia iocephala* . . 75 80
4848 $1.40 *Gyromitra esculenta* 75 80
4849 $1.40 *Lactarius peckii* . . . 75 80
4850 $1.40 *Lactarius rufus* . . . 75 80
4851 $1.40 *Cortinarius elatior* . . 75 80
4852 $1.40 *Boletus luridus* . . . 75 80
4853 $1.40 *Russula cyanoxantha* 75 80
4854 $1.40 *Craterellus cornucopioides* 75 80
4855 $2 *Cantharellus cibarius* . . 1·25 1·40
MS4856 Three sheets. (a) 96 × 70 mm. $5 *Cyathus olla*. (b) 70 × 96 mm. $5 *Lycoperdon pyriforme* (horiz). (c) 70 × 96 mm. $5 *Pleurotus ostreatus* (horiz). Set of 3 sheets . . . . 7·50 8·00

422 *Ancyluris formosissima*

2001. Butterflies and Moths of the World. Multicoloured.
4857 20c. Type **422** 25 15
4858 50c. *Callicore cynosura* . . 40 25
4859 70c. *Nessaea obrinus* . . . 50 35
4860 $1 *Euphaedra neophron* . . 65 70
4861 $1 *Milionia grandis* 65 70
4862 $1 *Marpesia petreus* 65 70
4863 $1 *Bocotus bacotus* 65 70
4864 $1 *Arctia vilica* 65 70
4865 $1 *Arctia flavia* 65 70
4866 $1 *Baorisa hiroglyphica* . . 65 70
4867 $1 *Euplagia quadripuntaria* 65 70
4868 $1 *Calisthenia salvinii* . . . 65 70
4869 $1 *Persiama vaninka* . . . 65 70
4870 $1 *Metamorpha stelenes* . . 65 70
4871 $1 *Diaethria aurelia* 65 70
4872 $1 *Perisama conplandi* . . . 65 70

4873 $1 *Mesene phareus* 65 70
4874 $1 *Callisthenia salvinii* . . . 65 70
4875 $1 *arpella districta* 65 70
4876 $2 *Eunica alcmena* . . . . 1·25 1·40
MS4877 Two sheets, each 85 × 110 mm. (a) $5 *Thecla coronata*. (b) $5 *Anaxita drucei*. Set of 2 sheets . . . . 6·00 6·50

Nos. 4857, 4860 and 4867 are inscribed "ANCYCLURIS", "HEOPHRON", "QUADRIPUNTAMA" or "THECKA", all in error.

423 *Tithorea harmonia*

2001. Butterflies of the Caribbean. Multicoloured.
4878 10c. Type **423** 20 20
4879 20c. *Callicore maimuna* . . 25 20
4880 50c. *Colobura dirce* 40 30
4881 90c. *Danaus plexippus* . . . 60 65
4882 90c. *Theope eudocia* 60 65
4883 90c. *Cepheuptychia cephus* 60 65
4884 90c. *Actinote pellenea* . . . 60 65
4885 90c. *Catonephele numilia* . . 60 65
4886 90c. *Anteos clorinde* 60 65
4887 90c. *Phoebis philea* 60 65
4888 90c. *Eumaeus atala* 60 65
4889 90c. *Papilio cresphontes* . . . 60 65
4890 90c. *Prepona meander* . . . 60 65
4891 90c. *Anartia iatrophae* . . . 60 65
4892 90c. *Mesene phareus* . . . 60 65
4893 90c. *Battus polydamas* . . . 60 65
4894 $1 *Doxocopa cherubima* . . 65 65
4895 $2 *Menander menander* . . 1·25 1·40
MS4896 Two sheets, each 68 × 98 mm. (a) $5 *Eueides heliconius*. (b) $5 *Morpho peleides* (vert). Set of 2 sheets . . . . . 6·00 6·50

Nos. 4885 and 4894 are inscribed "numili" or "cherubina", both in error.

424 *Eunica alcmena*

2001. Butterflies and Moths of the Rainforest. Multicoloured.
4897 10c. Type **424** 20 20
4898 70c. *Euphaedra medon* . . . 50 35
4899 90c. *Prepona praeneste* . . 60 65
4990 90c. *Cepora aspasia* 60 65
4901 90c. *Morpho aega* 60 65
4902 90c. *Mazuca amoeva* 60 65
4903 90c. *Amphicallia bellatrix* 60 65
4904 90c. *Helicopsis cupido* . . . 60 65
4905 90c. *Cithaerias esmeralda* 60 65
4906 $1 *Euphaedra neophron* . . 65 65
4907 $1.10 *Asterope rosa* 65 70
4908 $1.10 *Marpesia petreus* . . 65 70
4909 $1.10 *Dismorphia amphione* 65 70
4910 $1.10 *Euphaedra eleus* . . . 65 70
4911 $1.10 *Prepona deiphile* . . . 65 70
4912 $1.10 *Phoebis avellaneda* . . 65 70
MS4913 Two sheets. (a) 100 × 70 mm. $5 *Heliconius sapho*. (b) 70 × 100 mm. $5 *Utethesia ornatrix*. Set of 2 sheets . . . 6·00 6·50

Nos. 4897 and 4911 are inscribed "alamena" or "Phoebus", both in error.

425 Princess Victoria in Blue Dress

2001. Death Centenary of Queen Victoria. Multicoloured.
4914 $1.10 Type **425** 65 70
4915 $1.10 Queen Victoria wearing jewelled hair band 65 70
4916 $1.10 Queen Victoria wearing floral hair wreath 65 70
4917 $1.10 Queen Victoria wearing crown 65 70
4918 $1.10 Queen Victoria wearing pearls and black hair band 65 70
4919 $1.10 Queen Victoria in white veil and blue sash 65 70
MS4920 96 × 120 mm. $5 Queen Victoria in white cap (39 × 51 mm) 3·00 3·25

426 Mao Tse-tung in 1924

2001. 25th Death Anniv of Mao Tse-tung (Chinese leader). Multicoloured.
4921 $2 Type **426** . . . . 1·10 1·25
4922 $2 Mao in 1938 . . . . . . 1·10 1·25
4923 $2 Mao in 1945 . . . . . . 1·10 1·25
MS4924 146 × 139 mm. $5 Mao in grey suit . . . . 2·75 3·25

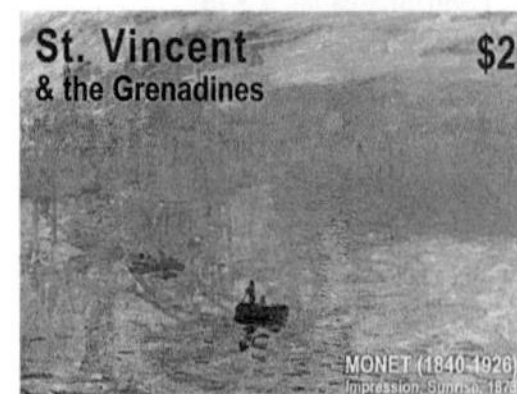

427 "Impression, Sunrise", 1873

2001. 75th Death Anniv of Claude-Oscar Monet (French painter). Multicoloured.
4925 $2 Type **427** . . . . 1·10 1·25
4926 $2 "Hay Stacks, End of Summer", 1891 . . . . 1·10 1·25
4927 $2 "Regatta at Argenteuil", 1872 . . . . 1·10 1·25
4928 $2 "Venice at Dusk", 1908 1·10 1·25
MS4929 137 × 110 mm. $5 "Parisians enjoying the Parc Monceau", 1878 (vert) . . . . 3·00 3·25

428 Princess Elizabeth **429** Queen Elizabeth II

2001. 75th Birthday of Queen Elizabeth II. Multicoloured.
4930 $1.10 Type **428** 70 70
4931 $1.10 Queen Elizabeth in grey suit 70 70
4932 $1.10 Queen Elizabeth in blue dress 70 70
4933 $1.10 Queen Elizabeth in tiara 70 70
4934 $1.10 Queen Elizabeth in blue hat and coat 70 70
4935 $1.10 Queen Elizabeth in green hat and coat . . . 70 70
MS4936 86 × 121 mm. $5 Queen Elizabeth in Guards Uniform (38 × 50 mm) . . . . 3·25 3·50

2001. Golden Jubilee (1st issue).
4937 **429** $1 multicoloured 70 70

See also Nos. 5111/15.

No. 4937 was printed in sheetlets of 8, containing two vertical rows of four, separated by a large illustrated central gutter. Both the stamp and the illustration on the central gutter are made up of a collage of miniature flower photographs.

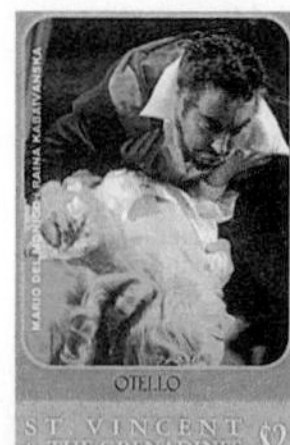

430 Mario del Monaco and Raina Kabaivanska as Othello and Desdemona

2001. Death Centenary of Giuseppe Verde (Italian composer). Multicoloured.
4938 $2 Type **430** . . . . 1·25 1·25
4939 $2 Iago's costume from *Othello*, 1898 . . . . . . 1·25 1·25
4940 $2 Othello's costume, 1898 1·25 1·25
4941 $2 Anna Tomowa-Sintow, as Desdemona . . . . . 1·25 1·25
MS4942 78 × 110 mm. $5 Nicolai Ghiaurov as King Philip in *Don Carlos* (opera) . . . . 3·25 3·50

Nos. 4938 and 4939 are inscribed "MONICO" or "LAGO", both in error.

431 "Countess de Toulouse-Lautrec"

2001. Death Centenary of Henri de Toulouse-Lautrec (French painter). Multicoloured.
4943 $3 Type **431** . . . . 1·75 1·90
4944 $3 "Carmen" . . . . 1·75 1·90
4945 $3 "Madame Lily Grenier" 1·75 1·90
MS4946 66 × 85 mm. $5 "Jane Avril" . . . . 3·00 3·25

432 "Courtesan Sumimoto" (Isoda Koryusai)

2001. "Philanippon '01" International Stamp Exhibition, Tokyo. Japanese Paintings. Multicoloured.
4947 10c. Type **432** 15 15
4948 15c. "Oiran at Shinto Shrine" (Kiyonaga) . . . 15 15
4949 20c. "Cockerel" (horiz) . . 20 20
4950 20c. "Two Girls on a Veranda" (Kiyonaga) . . 20 20
4951 50c. "On Banks of the Sumida" (Kiyonaga) . . . 35 25
4952 70c. "Three Ducks" (horiz) 45 35
4953 90c. "Flock of Ducks in Flight" (horiz) 50 40
4954 $1 "Three Pigeons" (horiz) 60 45
4955 $1.10 "Guineafowl" (horiz) 65 50
4956 $1.40 "Girl on River Bank" (Harunobu) 70 75
4957 $1.40 "Horseman guided by Peasant Girl" (Harunobu) 70 75
4958 $1.40 "Komachi praying for Rain" (Harunobu) . . . 70 75
4959 $1.40 "Washing Clothes in the Stream" (Harunobu) 70 75
4960 $1.40 "Girls by Lespedeza Bush in Moonlight" (Harunobu) 70 75
4961 $1.40 "Warming Sake with Maple Leaves" (Harunobu) 70 75
4962 $1.40 "Young Samurai on Horseback" (Harunobu) 70 75
4963 $1.40 "Ide no Tamagawa" (Harunobu) 70 75
4964 $1.40 "Otani Oniji II as Edohei" (Sharaku) . . . 70 75
4965 $1.40 "Iwai Hanshiro IV" (Sharaku) 70 75
4966 $1.40 "Segawa Kikunojo III" (Sharaku) 70 75
4967 $1.40 "Ichikawa Komazo II as Shiga Daishichi" (Sharaku) 70 75
4968 $1.40 "Toriwagi, Geisha of Kanaya, writing" (Eishi) 70 75
4969 $1.40 "Courtesan preparing for Doll Festival" (Eishi) 70 75
4970 $1.40 "Two Court Ladies in a Garden" (Eishi) . . . 70 75
4971 $1.40 "Lady with a Lute" (Eishi) 70 75
4972 $2 "Wading birds" (horiz) 1·10 1·25
MS4973 Five sheets, each 110 × 77 mm. (a) $5 "Gathering Lotus Flowers" (Harunobu). (b) $5 "Boy spying on Lovers" (Harunobu). (c) $5 "Peasants ferried across the Sumida" (Hokkei). (d) $5 "Shadows on the Shoji" (Kikugawa Eizan). (e) $5 "Tayu Komurasaki and Hanamurasaki of the Kado Tamaya" (Kitao Masanobu). Set of 5 sheets . . . . 13·00 14·00

Nos. 4949, 4952/5 and 4972 are all details from "A Variety of Birds" by Nishiyama Hoen.

433 Dale Earnhardt Jr (son)

2001. Dale Earnhardt (stock car racing driver) Commemoration. Multicoloured.
4974 $2 Type **433** . . . . 1·25 1·40
4975 $2 Father and son with Winston Trophy . . . . 1·25 1·40
4976 $2 Dale Earnhardt in black and white overalls . . . . 1·25 1·40
4977 $2 Earnhardt with racing trophy . . . . 1·25 1·40
4978 $2 Congratulating son . . . 1·25 1·40
4979 $2 Dale Earnhardt Jr holding trophy aloft . . . 1·25 1·40

434 Crown Prince Haakon and Mette-Marit Tjessem Høiby

2001. Wedding of Crown Prince Haakon of Norway and Mette-Marit Tjessem Høiby.
4980 **434** $5 multicoloured . . . . 3·00 3·25

435 Mammoth

2001. Prehistoric Animals. Multicoloured.
4981 10c. Type **435** 15 15
4982 20c. Pinacosaurus 20 20
4983 90c. Oviraptor 55 60
4984 90c. Head of Saltasaurus . . 55 60
4985 90c. Head of Apatosaurus 55 60
4986 90c. Head of Brachiosaurus 55 60
4987 90c. Troodon with body of Saltasaurus 55 60
4988 90c. Deinonychus with bodies of Apatosaurus and Brachiosaurus . . . 55 60
4989 90c. Segnosaurus 55 60
4990 90c. Iguanodon 55 60
4991 90c. Hypacrosaurus 55 60
4992 90c. Ceratosaurus 55 60
4993 90c. Hypsilophodon 55 60
4994 90c. Herrerasaurus 55 60
4995 90c. Velociraptor 55 60
4996 $1 Centrosaurus 60 60
4997 $1.40 Protoceratops 75 80
4998 $1.40 Pteranodon 75 80
4999 $1.40 Archaeopteryx 75 80
5000 $1.40 Eudimorphodon . . . 75 80
5001 $1.40 Shonisaurus 75 80
5002 $1.40 Elasmosaurus 75 80
5003 $1.40 Kronosaurus 75 80
5004 $1.40 Allosaurus 75 80
5005 $1.40 Dilophosaurus 75 80
5006 $1.40 Lambeosaurus 75 80
5007 $1.40 Coelophysis 75 80
5008 $1.40 Ornitholestes 75 80
5009 $1.40 Eustreptospondylus 75 80
5010 $2 Bactrosaurus . . . . . . 1·25 1·40
MS5011 Four sheets. (a) 105 × 78 mm. $5 Stegosaurus (50 × 38 mm). (b) 78 × 105 mm. $5 Parasaurolophus (38 × 50 mm). (c) 78 × 105 mm. $5 Tyrannosaurus (38 × 50 mm). (d) 78 × 105 mm. $5 Triceratops (50 × 38 mm). Set of 4 sheets . . . . 12·00 13·00

Nos. 4984/9, 4990/5, 4998/5003 and 5004/9 were each printed together, se-tenant, with the backgrounds forming composite designs.

436 Hong Myung-Bo and South Korean Flag

2001. World Cup Football Championship, Japan and Korea (2002). Multicoloured.
5012 $1.40 Type **436** 75 80
5013 $1.40 Hidetoshi Nakata and Japanese flag 75 80
5014 $1.40 Ronaldo and Brazilian flag 75 80
5015 $1.40 Paolo Maldini and Italian flag 75 80

No.	Description	Mint	Used
5016	$1.40 Peter Schmeichel and Danish flag	75	80
5017	$1.40 Raul Blanco and Spanish flag	75	80
5018	$1.40 Kim Bong Soo and South Korean Flag	75	80
5019	$1.40 Masami Ihara and Japanese flag	75	80
5020	$1.40 Marcel Desailly and French flag	75	80
5021	$1.40 David Beckham and English flag	75	80
5022	$1.40 Carlos Valderrama and Colombian flag	75	80
5023	$1.40 George Popescu and Rumanian flag	75	80
MS5024	Two sheets, each 98 × 70 mm. (a) $5 International Stadium, Yokohama, Japan (64 × 32 mm). (b) $5 World Cup Stadium, Seoul, South Korea (64 × 32 mm). Set of 2 sheets	5·50	6·00

No. 5015 is inscribed "Paola" in error.

437 John F. Kennedy at Democratic Convention, 1956

438 Princess Diana on Remembrance Day

2001. John F. Kennedy (American President) Commemoration. Multicoloured (except Nos. 5029, **MS**5037a).

No.	Description	Mint	Used
5025	$1.40 Type **437**	70	80
5026	$1.40 Campaigning in New York, 1959	70	80
5027	$1.40 In rocking chair in the White House, 1960	70	80
5028	$1.40 With Robert Kennedy (brother)	70	80
5029	$1.40 Announcing Cuban Blockade, 1962 (black & red)	70	80
5030	$1.40 John Kennedy Jr (son) at father's funeral, 1963	70	80
5031	$1.40 With son, John Jr	70	80
5032	$1.40 With Jacqueline	70	80
5033	$1.40 With daughter, Caroline	70	80
5034	$1.40 With family, 1963	70	80
5035	$1.40 Sailing with wife	70	80
5036	$1.40 President and Mrs. Kennedy in evening dress	70	80
MS5037	Two sheets, each 121 × 88 mm. (a) $5 President John F. Kennedy (violet and black). (b) $5 With children at Hyannis Port. Set of 2 sheets	5·50	6·00

2001. 40th Birth Anniv of Diana, Princess of Wales. Multicoloured.

No.	Description	Mint	Used
5038	$1.40 Type **438**	75	80
5039	$1.40 Princess Diana in pink dress	75	80
5040	$1.40 On wedding day	75	80
MS5041	72 × 95 mm. $5 Princess Diana in evening dress	3·25	3·50

439 Japanese Aircraft bombing Pearl Harbor

2001. 60th Anniv of Japanese Attack on Pearl Harbor. Multicoloured.

No.	Description	Mint	Used
5042	$1.40 Type **439**	75	80
5043	$1.40 Japanese pilot wearing hachimaki (headband)	75	80
5044	$1.40 Emperor Hirohito of Japan	75	80
5045	$1.40 Admiral Yamamoto	75	80
5046	$1.40 Japanese planes over *Akagi* (aircraft carrier)	75	80
5047	$1.40 Japanese "Kate" torpedo bomber	75	80
5048	$1.40 Japanese fighters over Ewa Marine base, Hawaii	75	80
5049	$1.40 Dorie Miller engaging Japanese planes	75	80
5050	$1.40 Japanese aircraft attacking U.S.S. *Nevada* (battleship)	75	80
5051	$1.40 Sinking of U.S.S. *Oklahoma* (battleship)	75	80
5052	$1.40 Japanese plane taking off from Akagi	75	80
5053	$1.40 American casualty on stretcher	75	80
MS5054	Two sheets. (a) $5 Wheeler Field under attack. (b) $5 Dorie Miller receiving Navy Cross from Admiral Nimitz, 1942 (vert). Set of 2 sheets	5·50	6·00

440 *Rhodogastria crokeri*

2001. Butterflies and Moths. Multicoloured.

No.	Description	Mint	Used
5055	70c. Type **440**	45	35
5056	90c. *Gnammia virgo*	50	40
5057	$1 *Zeuzera pyrina*	60	45
5058	$1.40 *Anthela ocellata*	75	80
5059	$1.40 *Euproctis hemicyclia*	75	80
5060	$1.40 *Epicoma melanostica*	75	80
5061	$1.40 *Erateina staudingeri*	75	80
5062	$1.40 *Pseudoips fagana*	75	80
5063	$1.40 *Estigmene acrea*	75	80
5064	$1.40 *Phalera bucephala*	75	80
5065	$1.40 *Deilephila elpenor*	75	80
5066	$1.40 *Protambulyx strigilis*	75	80
5067	$1.40 *Cizara ardeniae*	75	80
5068	$1.40 *Oenochroma vinaria*	75	80
5069	$1.40 *Oenosandra boisduvalii*	75	80
5070	$2 *Campylotes desgodinsi*	1·25	1·40
MS5071	Two sheets, each 96 × 70 mm. (a) $5 *Lymantria dispar*. (b) $5 *Rothschildia orizaba* (Silkworm). Set of 2 sheets	5·50	6·00

Nos. 5058/63 and 5064/9 were each printed together, se-tenant, with the backgrounds forming composite designs.

Nos. 5066 and 5068 are inscribed "strigus" or "vinerea", both in error.

441 Bumble Bee

442 "Madonna and Child" (Francesco Guardi)

2001. Island Fauna. Multicoloured.

No.	Description	Mint	Used
5072	$1.40 Type **441**	75	80
5073	$1.40 Green darner dragonfly	75	80
5074	$1.40 Small lacewing butterfly	75	80
5075	$1.40 Black widow spider	75	80
5076	$1.40 Praying mantis	75	80
5077	$1.40 Firefly	75	80
5078	$1.40 Caspian tern (horiz)	75	80
5079	$1.40 White-tailed tropicbird (horiz)	75	80
5080	$1.40 Black-necked stilt (horiz)	75	80
5081	$1.40 Black-bellied plover (horiz)	75	80
5082	$1.40 Black-winged stilt (horiz)	75	80
5083	$1.40 Ruddy turnstone (horiz)	75	80
MS5084	Two sheets. (a) 65 × 96 mm. $5 Blue Night Butterfly (horiz). (b) 107 × 77 mm. $5 Brown Pelican. Set of 2 sheets	5·50	6·00

Nos. 5072/7 (insects) and 5078/83 (shore birds) were each printed together, se-tenant, with the backgrounds forming composite designs.

2001. Christmas. Religious Paintings. Multicoloured.

No.	Description	Mint	Used
5085	10c. Type **442**	15	15
5086	20c. "Immaculate Conception" (Giambattista Tiepolo)	20	15
5087	70c. "Adoration of the Magi" (Tiepolo)	45	35
5088	90c. "The Virgin" (Tintoretto)	50	40
5089	$1.10 "Annunciation" (Veronese)	65	60
5090	$1.40 "Madonna della Quaglia" (Pisanello)	75	80
MS5091	76 × 136 mm. $5 "Madonna and Child" (Tiepolo)	3·00	3·25

443 Bo Le in the Mountains

2001. Chinese New Year ("Year of the Horse"). Legend of Bo Le. Multicoloured.

No.	Description	Mint	Used
5092	$1.10 Type **443**	65	70
5093	$1.10 Horse and cart	65	70
5094	$1.10 Bo Le accosting cart driver	65	70
5095	$1.10 Horse drinking	65	70
5096	$1.10 Bo Le covering horse with cloak	65	70
5097	$1.10 Horse rearing	65	70

444 Cal Ripken Jr. batting

2001. Retirement of Cal Ripken Jr. (American baseball player). Multicoloured.

No.	Description	Mint	Used
5098	$2 Cal Ripken Jr. greeting spectators (73 × 61 mm)	1·00	1·25
5099	$2 Type **444**	1·00	1·25
5100	$2 Cal Ripken Jr. running	1·00	1·25
5101	$2 Wearing white Orioles shirt, bareheaded	1·00	1·25
5102	$2 Wearing orange shirt and black helmet	1·00	1·25
5103	$2 Holding trophy	1·00	1·25
5104	$2 Cal Ripken Jr. acknowledging applause	1·00	1·25
MS5105	196 × 240 mm. $6 Cal Ripken Jr. (40 × 60 mm)	3·00	3·50

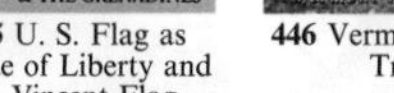

445 U. S. Flag as Statue of Liberty and St. Vincent Flag

446 Vermont Nature Trails

2001. "United We Stand". Support for Victims of 11 September 2001 Terrorist Attacks.

No.	Description	Mint	Used
5106	**445** $2 multicoloured	1·25	1·40

2001. Tourism. Multicoloured.

No.	Description	Mint	Used
5107	20c. Type **446**	20	15
5108	70c. Tamarind Beach Hotel, Kanouan (horiz)	45	35
5109	90c. The Tobago Cays (horiz)	50	40
5110	$1.10 Trinity Falls	65	65

2002. Golden Jubilee (2nd issue). As T **110** of St. Kitts. Multicoloured.

No.	Description	Mint	Used
5111	$2 Queen Elizabeth with Duke of Edinburgh, on aircraft steps	1·25	1·25
5112	$2 Queen Elizabeth with Princess Margaret	1·25	1·25
5113	$2 Queen Elizabeth wearing pearls and blue dress	1·25	1·25
5114	$2 Princess Elizabeth on her wedding day	1·25	1·25
MS5115	76 × 108 mm. $5 Queen Elizabeth wearing orange coat	3·25	3·50

447 Pan American Health Organization Centenary Logo

2002. Centenary of Pan American Health Organization. Multicoloured.

No.	Description	Mint	Used
5116	20c. Type **447**	20	15
5117	70c. Dr. Gideon Cordice	45	35
5118	90c. Dr. Arthur Cecil Cyrus	50	40
5119	$1.10 PAHO Headquarters, Barbados (horiz)	65	65

448 Girls from "Section of the Bands"

2002. 25th Anniv of Vincy Mas Carnival. Multicoloured.

No.	Description	Mint	Used
5120	10c. Type **448**	15	15
5121	20c. Michael Ollivierre from "Cocktail" (horiz)	20	15
5122	70c. Tyson Constantine, from "Snake in the Grass"	45	35
5123	90c. Bridgette Creese from "Joy-C"	50	40
5124	$1.10 Shanelle McKenzie, from "Heatwave" (horiz)	65	60
5125	$1.40 Sion Hill Steel Orchestra (horiz)	75	80

2002. International Year of Mountains. As T **115** of St. Kitts, but vert. Multicoloured.

No.	Description	Mint	Used
5126	$1.40 Mount Ararat, Turkey	75	80
5127	$1.40 Mount Ama Dablam, Nepal	75	80
5128	$1.40 Mount Cook, New Zealand	75	80
5129	$1.40 Mount Kilimanjaro, Tanzania	75	80
5130	$1.40 Mount Kenya, Kenya	75	80
5131	$1.40 Giant's Castle, South Africa	75	80
MS5132	100 × 120 mm. $5 Mount Aconcagua, Argentina	3·00	3·25

Nos. 5131 and **MS**5132 are inscribed "AMERICA" or "ACONCAG", both in error.

2002. Winter Olympic Games, Salt Lake City. As T **111** of St. Kitts. Multicoloured.

No.	Description	Mint	Used
5133	$3 Rifle shooting (biathlon)	1·75	1·90
5134	$3 Slalom skiing	1·75	1·90
MS5135	84 × 115 mm. Nos. 5133/4	3·50	3·75

449 Malachite Butterfly

450 Former Slaves celebrating Freedom

2002. U.N. Year of Eco Tourism. Multicoloured.

No.	Description	Mint	Used
5136	$2 Type **449**	1·25	1·40
5137	$2 Manatee	1·25	1·40
5138	$2 Fallow deer	1·25	1·40
5139	$2 Castor bean plant	1·25	1·40
MS5140	75 × 90 mm. $6 Diver and windsurfer	3·25	3·50

2002. 20th World Scout Jamboree, Thailand. As T **116** of St. Kitts. Multicoloured.

No.	Description	Mint	Used
5141	$5 Scout blowing Kudu horn	2·75	3·00
5142	$5 Scouts rolling up bedding	2·75	3·00
5143	$5 Lord Baden-Powell and Dan Beard (early Scout leaders)	2·75	3·00
MS5144	85 × 118 mm. $5 Scout's head (vert)	2·75	3·00

2002. Emancipation Day (1834) Commemoration. Each black and yellow.

No.	Description	Mint	Used
5145	$2 Type **450**	1·10	1·25
5146	$2 Lt. Governor, 1834	1·10	1·25
5147	$2 Freedom Celebrations	1·10	1·25
5148	$2 Britannia with former slaves	1·10	1·25

451 Elvis Presley

2002. 25th Death Anniv of Elvis Presley. Multicoloured.

No.	Description	Mint	Used
5149	$1 Type **451**	60	45
5150	$1.25 Elvis Presley playing guitar	75	75
5151	$1.25 In Army uniform	75	75
5152	$1.25 Wearing checked jacket	75	75
5153	$1.25 In striped shirt	75	75
5154	$1.25 Wearing striped T shirt	75	75
5155	$1.25 Elvis Presley laughing	75	75

452 World Trade Centre Buildings, New York

2002. 1st Anniv of Terrorist Attacks on U.S.A. Sheet, 141 × 98 mm.
MS5156 **452** $6 multicoloured . . 3·00 3·25

453 Teddy Bear in Red Kimono

2002. Centenary of the Teddy Bear. Multicoloured.
5157 $2 Type **453** . . . . 1·10 1·25
5158 $2 White teddy bear in bridal dress . . . . 1·10 1·25
5159 $2 Teddy bear in traditional Japanese costume with black cap . . . . 1·10 1·25
5160 $2 Teddy bear in black and orange outfit . . . . . . 1·10 1·25
5161 $2 Mother bear with baby bear . . . . 1·10 1·25
5162 $2 Teddy bear in red kimono with flowers on head . . . . 1·10 1·25
5163 $2 Two teddy bears . . . . 1·10 1·25
5164 $2 Two teddy bears with bees . . . . 1·10 1·25
5165 $2 Teddy bear seated on rock . . . . 1·10 1·25
5166 $2 Cowboy teddy (35 × 48 mm) . . . . . . 1·10 1·25
5167 $2 Fisherman teddy (35 × 48 mm) . . . . . . 1·10 1·25
5168 $2 Camper teddy (35 × 48 mm) . . . . . . 1·10 1·25
5169 $2 Hiker teddy (35 × 48 mm) 1·10 1·25
MS5170 Two sheets, each 75 × 57 mm. (a) $5 Teddy bears designed by Tomoko Suenaga (horiz). (b) $5 Teddy bears designed by Terumi Yoshikawa (horiz). Set of 2 sheets . . . . 5·50 6·00

Nos. 5157/61 (Japanese bears), 5162/5 (Japanese bears) and 5166/9 (outdoor bears). The backgrounds of Nos. 5166/9 form a composite design.

454 Waterloo Medal and Charge of the Scots Greys

2002. British War Medals. Nine sheets containing vert designs as T **454**. Multicoloured.
MS5171 Nine sheets. (a) 165 × 100 mm. $5 Type **454**. (b) 165 × 100 mm. $5 Zulu War medal with 1879 clasp and Rorke's Drift. (c) 165 × 100m. $5 South Africa War medal with clasps for defence of Ladysmith and Orange Free State, and British infantry under fire. (d) $5 1914–15 Star and British troops in trench. (e) $5 1916 medal and British troops advancing during Battle of the Somme. (f) $5 Victory medal, 1919. (g) $5 Atlantic Star with aircrew clasp, and convoy. (h) $5 1939–45 Star with Battle of Britain clasp, and squadron scramble. (i) $5 Africa Star with 8th Army clasp, and desert. Set of 9 sheets 23·00 25·00

No. **MS**5171(f) is inscribed "The Victoria Medal" in error.

455 Dimples and Grandfather

2002. Shirley Temple in *Dimples*. Scenes from the film. Multicoloured .
5172 $1.40 Type **455** 75 80
5173 $1.40 Dimples singing for dinner guests 75 80
5174 $1.40 Dimples in black and white dress with grandfather 75 80
5175 $1.40 Singing in minstrel show 75 80
5176 $1.40 Grandfather covering Dimples with blanket . . 75 80
5177 $1.40 Dimples taking tea with rich widow 75 80
5178 $2 Conducting street band (vert) . . . . 1·10 1·25
5179 $2 Dimples in bonnet and Grandfather in top hat (vert) . . . . 1·10 1·25
5180 $2 Dimples adjusting cravat (vert) . . . . 1·10 1·25
5181 $2 Dimples with rich widow (vert) . . . . 1·10 1·25
MS5182 105 × 75 mm. $5 Tap-dancing in minstrel show (vert) 2·75 3·00

456 Ji Sung Park (South Korea) and Dietmar Hamann (Germany)

457 Queen Elizabeth the Queen Mother in Floral Hat

2002. World Cup Football Championship, Japan and Korea. Multicoloured.
5183 $1.40 Type **456** 75 80
5184 $1.40 Miroslav Klose (Germany) and Tae Young Kim (South Korea) 75 80
5185 $1.40 Chong Gug Song (South Korea) and Christoph Metzelder (Germany) 75 80
5186 $1.40 Tae Young Kim (South Korea) and Gerald Asamoah (Germany) . . 75 80
5187 $1.40 Torsten Frings (Germany) and Ji Sung Park (South Korea) . . . 75 80
5188 $1.40 Oliver Neuville (Germany) and Tae Young Kim (South Korea) 75 80
5189 $1.40 Kleberson (Brazil) and Emre Belozoglu (Turkey) 75 80
5190 $1.40 Cafu (Brazil) 75 80
5191 $1.40 Roberto Carlos (Brazil) 75 80
5192 $1.40 Yildiray Basturk (Turkey) 75 80
5193 $1.40 Tugay Kerimoglu (Turkey) and Rivaldo (Brazil) 75 80
5194 $1.40 Bulent (Turkey) . . . 75 80
MS5195 Four sheets, each 82 × 82 mm. (a) $3 Michael Ballack (Germany); $3 Oliver Kahn (Germany). (b) $3 Tae Young Kim (South Korea); $3 Du Ri Cha (South Korea). (c) $3 Ronaldo (Brazil); $3 Cafu (Brazil). (d) $3 Bulent (Turkey); $3 Yildiray Basturk (Turkey). Set of 4 sheets 12·00 13·00

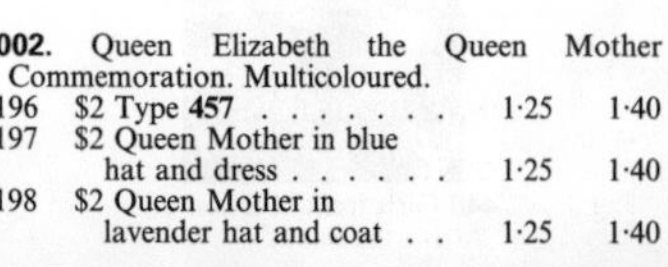

2002. Queen Elizabeth the Queen Mother Commemoration. Multicoloured.
5196 $2 Type **457** . . . . 1·25 1·40
5197 $2 Queen Mother in blue hat and dress . . . . . . 1·25 1·40
5198 $2 Queen Mother in lavender hat and coat . . 1·25 1·40

458 "Greek Madonna" (Giovanni Bellini)

2002. Christmas. Religious Paintings. Multicoloured.
5199 20c. Type **458** 20 15
5200 90c. "Kneeling Agostino Barbarigo" (Bellini) . . . 50 40
5201 $1.10 "Presentation of Jesus in the Temple" (Perugino) 65 50
5202 $1.40 "Madonna and Child with Infant St. John" (Perugino) 75 75
5203 $1.50 "San Giobbe Altarpiece" (Bellini) . . . 80 90
MS5204 105 × 78 mm. $5 "Madonna and Child with Sts John the Baptist and Sebastian" (horiz) 3·00 3·25

No. 5202 is inscribed "MADDONA" in error.

459 Space Rocket in From the Earth to the Moon (Jules Verne)

2002. Famous Science Fiction Authors. Three sheets, each 150 × 108 mm, containing vert designs as T **459**. Multicoloured.
MS5205 Three sheets. (a) $5 Type **459**. (b) $5 Book cover for *The Time Machine* (H. G. Wells). (c) $5 Book cover for *The War of the Worlds* (H. G. Wells). Set of 3 sheets . . . . 7·50 8·00

460 Magnifying Glass and Globe

2002. 50th Anniv of International Federation of Stamp Dealers' Associations.
5206 **460** $2 multicoloured . . . . 1·25 1·40

461 Kid

2003. Chinese New Year ("Year of the Goat (Ram)"). Multicoloured.
5207 $1 Type **461** 60 65
5208 $1 Goat with chicken . . . 60 65
5209 $1 Nanny-goat feeding kid 60 65
5210 $1 Porcelain figure of rider on goat 60 65
5211 $1 Brown and white goat on heathland 60 65
5212 $1 Black and white goat in wood 60 65

462 Westminster Abbey

2003. 50th Anniv of Coronation. Multicoloured.
5213 $2 Type **462** . . . . 1·10 1·25
5214 $2 Queen Elizabeth II in Coronation Coach leaving Buckingham Palace . . . 1·10 1·25
5215 $2 Coronation Coach in procession . . . . 1·10 1·25
5216 $2 Queen and Duke of Edinburgh in Coronation Coach . . . . 1·10 1·25
5217 $2 Queen arriving at Westminster Abbey . . . 1·10 1·25
5218 $2 In procession along nave of Westminster Abbey . . 1·10 1·25
5219 $2 Queen in Chair of State 1·10 1·25
MS5220 96 × 66 mm. $5 Queen wearing Imperial State Crown and Coronation robes (37 × 50 mm) 3·00 3·25

463 *Columbia* Crew

2003. *Columbia* Space Shuttle Commemoration. Three sheets, each 177 × 113 mm, containing T **463** and similar horiz designs. Multicoloured.
MS5221 $2 Type **463**; $2 *Columbia* Space Shuttle on launchpad; $2 *Columbia* in flight; $2 Astronaut David Brown inside *Columbia* 4·00 4·50
MS5222 $2 Type **463**; $2 Mission Commander Rick Husband inside *Columbia*; $2 *Columbia* on runway; $2 *Columbia* in orbit and satellite . . . . 4·00 4·50
MS5223 $2 Type **463**; $2 Pilot William McCool in cockpit; $2 William McCool; $2 *Columbia* in orbit over Earth . . . . 4·00 4·50

464 Embroidery Teddy Bear

2003. Centenary of the Teddy Bear. Embroidered Fabric Teddy Bears. Self-adhesive. Imperf.
5224 **464** $15 ochre, brown and black . . . . 7·50 8·00
MS5225 125 × 158 mm. No. 5224 × 4 26·00 29·00

465 "Composition avec Femme aux cheveux mi-longs"

2003. 30th Death Anniv of Pablo Picasso (artist).Multicoloured (except $1).
5226 60c. Type **465** 35 30
5227 70c. "La Soeur de l'Artiste" (vert) 45 35
5228 90c. "Maternite" (vert) . . . 50 40
5229 $1 "Tete d'Homme" (vert) 60 45
5230 $1.10 "Deux Enfants assis (Claude et Paloma)" (vert) 65 65
5231 $1.40 "Femme a la Collerette bleue" (vert) . . 75 80
MS5232 203 × 165 mm. $2 "Corrida"; $2 "Composition a la Mandoline"; $2 "Le Peintre et son Modele"; $2 "Femme couchee sous la Lampe" . . . . . . 4·00 4·50
MS5233 (a) 82 × 105 mm. $5 "Femme espagnole sur fond orange". Imperf. (b) 102 × 81 mm. $5 "Femme etendue". Imperf 5·50 6·00

466 "Portrait of Jacques de Gheyn III"

2003. Paintings by Rembrandt. Multicoloured.
5234 $1 Type **466** 60 45
5235 $1.10 "Young Man in a Black Beret" 65 50
5236 $1.40 "Hendrickje Stoffels" 75 70
5237 $2 "The Polish Rider" (horiz) . . . . 1·25 1·40
MS5238 185 × 175 mm. $2 "Belthazzar sees the Writing on the Wall" (detail); $2 "Portrait of a Young Man (Titus?)"; $2 "Jacob blessing the Sons of Joseph" (detail); $2 "King Uzziah stricken with Leprosy" . . . . 4·00 4·50
MS5239 158 × 115 mm. $5 "The Stoning of St. Stephen" . . . 2·75 3·25

467 "A Gathering of Sorcerers on the Tokaido Road" (detail) (Utagawa Kunisada)

2003. Japanese Art. Ghosts and Demons. Multicoloured.
5240 70c. Type **467** 45 30
5241 $1.10 "Kiyohime and the Moon" (Yoshu Chikanobu) 65 50
5242 $1.40 "A Gathering of Sorcerers on the Tokaido Road" (different detail) (Utagawa Kunisada) . . . 75 70
5243 $3 "A Gathering of Sorcerers on the Tokaido Road" (different detail) (Utagawa Kunisada) . . . 1·75 1·90
MS5244 148 × 148 mm. $2 "Snake Mountain" (Utagawa Kuniyoshi); $2 "Sadanobu and Oni" (Tsukioka Yoshitoshi); $2 "Shoki" (Tsukioka Yoshitoshi); $2 "The Nightly Weeping Rock" (Utagawa Kuniyoshi) . . . . 4·00 4·50
MS5245 117 × 85 mm. $5 "The Ghosts of Matahachi and Kikuno" (detail) (Utagawa Kumsada) . . . . 2·75 3·25

468 Prince William as Teenager

469 Lady Diana Spencer as Young Girl

2003. 21st Birthday of Prince William of Wales. Multicoloured.
MS5246 148 × 78 mm. $3 Type **468**; $3 Prince William in black and yellow polo shirt; $3 Wearing blue t-shirt . . . . 5·00 5·50
MS5247 98 × 68 mm. $5 Prince William as teenager (different) 3·00 3·25

2003. 5th Death Anniv of Diana, Princess of Wales. Two sheets, each 132 × 146 mm, containing vert designs as T **469**. Multicoloured.
MS5248 $2 Type **469**; $2 Princess Diana with Prince Charles on their wedding day; $2 With Prince William and baby Prince Harry; $2 Wearing mauve jacket . . . 4·00 4·50
MS5249 $2 Princess Diana wearing tiara and yellow dress; $2 Wearing white dress; $2 Wearing mauve cardigan; $2 Wearing mauve dress 4·00 4·50

470 Antonin Magne (1931)

471 Linny

2003. Centenary of Tour de France Cycle Race. Multicoloured.
MS5250 157 × 97 mm. $2 Type **470**; $2 Andre Leducq (1932); $2 Georges Speicher (1933); $2 Antonin Magne (1934) . . . . 4·00 4·50
MS5251 157 × 97 mm. $2 Romain Maes (1935); $2 Silvere Maes (1936); $2 Roger Lapebie (1937); $2 Gino Bartali (1938) . . . . 4·00 4·50
MS5252 157 × 97 mm. $2 Silvere Maes (1939); $2 Jean Lazarides (1946) (additionally inscr "FIVE DAY RACE"); $2 Jean Robic (1947); $2 Gino Bartali (1948) 4·00 4·50
MS5253 Three sheets, each 106 × 78 mm. (a) $5 Antonin Magne (1931, 1934). (b) $5 Fausto Coppi (1949). (c) $5 Ferdinand Kubler (1950) Set of 3 sheets 7·50 8·00

2003. Centenary of Circus Clowns. Multicoloured.
MS5254 116 × 199 mm. $2 Type **471**; $2 Bruce Feiler; $2 Segey Provirin; $2 Weezle . . . . 4·00 4·50
MS5255 145 × 218 mm. $2 Mermaids (acrobats); $2 Robert Wolf (sword swallower); $2 Elbrus Pilev's Group (horsewoman); $2 Stinky (gymnast) . . . . 4·00 4·50
No. **MS**5254 is cut in the shape of a clown on a bicycle and No. **MS**5255 in the shape of a circus elephant.

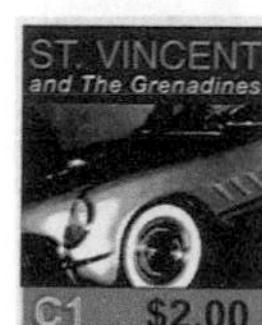

472 C1 Corvette

2003. 50th Anniv of General Motors Chevrolet Corvette. Multicoloured.
MS5256 163 × 202 mm. $2 Type **472**; $2 C2 Corvette; $2 C3 Corvette; $2 C4 Corvette; $2 C5 Corvette 4·75 5·50
MS5257 163 × 202 mm. $3 Corvette (1953); $3 Corvette (2003) (both 50 × 38 mm) . . . . 3·25 3·75

473 Cadillac Eldorado (1953)

2003. Centenary of General Motors Cadillac. Multicoloured.
MS5258 110 × 150 mm. $2 Type **473**; $2 Cadillac Eldorado (2002); $2 Cadillac Eldorado (1967); $2 Cadillac Series 62 (1962) . . . 4·00 4·50
MS5259 102 × 75 mm. $5 Cadillac LaSalle (1927) . . . . 3·00 3·25

2003. Centenary of Powered Flight. As T **126** of St. Kitts. Multicoloured.
MS5260 176 × 96 mm. $2 Handley Page Heyford; $2 Heinkel He 111B; $2 Gloster Gauntlet; $2 Curtiss BF2C-1 . . . . 4·00 4·50
MS5261 176 × 96 mm. $2 Mitsubishi A6M Reisen; $2 Dewoitine D520; $2 Messerschmitt Bf 109E; $2 Republic P-47 Thunderbolt . . 4·00 4·50
MS5262 Two sheets, each 106 × 75 mm. (a) $5 Fairy Flycatcher. (b) $5 Bristol Type 142 Blenheim IV Set of 2 sheets . . 5·50 6·00

474 Owia Salt Pond

475 Musicians

2003. International Year of Freshwater. Multicoloured.
MS5263 150 × 88 mm. $3 Type **474**; $3 The Soufriere; $3 Falls of Baleine . . . . 5·00 5·50
MS5264 100 × 70 mm. $5 Trinity Falls . . . . 3·00 3·25

2003. Centenary of Salvation Army in St. Vincent. Multicoloured.
5265 70c. Type **475** 45 35
5266 90c. District Temple 50 40
5267 $1 Christmas Kettle Appeal Fund 60 55
5268 $1.10 Salvation Army Headquarters (horiz) . . . 65 70

476 General Richard Meyers and Fighter Planes

2003. Operation Iraqi Freedom. Multicoloured.
MS5269 184 × 129 mm. $1 Type **476**; $1 Lt. General David McKiernan, troops and helicopter; $1 Lt. General Michael Moseley and bomber; $1 Vice Admiral Timothy Keating and warships; $1 Lt. General Jay Garner (retired) and troops; $1 General Tommy Franks and troops; $1 Lt. General Earl Hailston and marines in desert; $1 General John Jumper and fighter plane . . . . 4·25 4·75
MS5270 135 × 135 mm. $1.50 Private Jessica Lynch and rescuers; $1.50 General Tommy Franks and troops; $1.50 Troops and Spectre Gunship; $1.50 Stryker Vehicle; $1.50 USS *Constellation* (aircraft carrier); $1.50 USS *Kitty Hawk* (aircraft carrier) . . . . 4·75 5·50

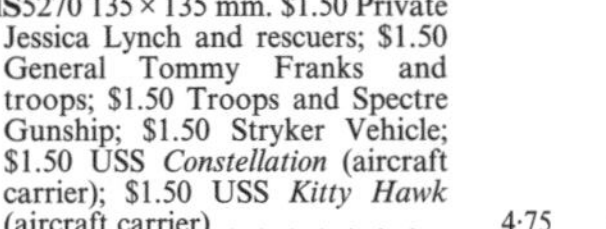

477 Jean Grey

2003. *X2: X-Men United* (film based on Marvel comic characters). Multicoloured.
MS5271 124 × 165 mm. $2 Type **477**; $2 Storm; $2 Wolverine; $2 Cyclops . . . . 4·00 4·50
MS5272 124 × 165 mm. $2 Magneto; $2 Mystique; $2 Stryker; $2 Lady Deathstroke . . . . 4·00 4·50
MS5273 124 × 165 mm. $2 Nightcrawler; $2 Professor X; $2 Iceman; $2 Rogue . . . . . . 4·00 4·50

478 The Hulk

2003. *The Hulk* (film based on Marvel comic characters). Multicoloured.
MS5274 124 × 165 mm. $2 Type **478**; $2 The Hulk (head and shoulders, inscr "HULK" at right); $2 The Hulk (head and shoulders, inscr "HULK" at left); $2 As Type **477** (inscr "HULK" at right) . . . 4·00 4·50
MS5275 124 × 165 mm. $2 The Hulk in wreckage; $2 Crouching in rubble; $2 With fists raised; $2 Punching rubble . . . . 4·00 4·50
No. **MS**5274 depicts scenes from *The Hulk* film and **MS**5275 depicts the Marvel comic character.

479 Spider-man

2003. *Spider-Man 2* (film based on Marvel comic characters). Multicoloured.
MS5276 124 × 165 mm. $2 Type **479**; $2 With arm raised, brandishing weapon; $2 Suspended from building; $2 Clinging to building 4·00 4·50

480 Father Christmas and Beach (Andrew Gonsalves)

2003. Christmas. Childrens Paintings. Multicoloured.
5277 70c. Type **480** 45 35
5278 90c. Father Christmas on raft pulled by dolphin (Georgia Gravel) 50 40
5279 $1.10 Father Christmas on beach (Adam Gravel) (vert) 65 50

481 *Lutjanus kasmira*

482 Chihuahua

2003. Marine Life of the Caribbean. Multicoloured.
5280 70c. Type **481** 45 35
5281 90c. *Chaetadon collare* . . . 50 40
5282 $1.10 *Istiophorus platypterus* 65 55
5283 $2 *Pomacanthus paru* (inscr "Pomacanthidae") . . . . 1·25 1·40
MS5284 118 × 106 mm. $2 *Equetus lanceolatus*; $2 *Hypoplectrus gutavariusi*; $2 *Pomacentridae*; $2 *Cichlidae* . . . . 4·00 4·50
MS5285 67 × 96 mm. $5 Dolphins 2·75 3·00

2003. Dogs and Cats. Multicoloured.
5286 10c. Type **482** 15 15
5287 20c. Bulldog 20 15
5288 50c. British shorthair cat . . 35 25
5289 60c. Weimaraner (dog) . . . 45 30
5290 $1 Burmese cat 60 45
5291 $1.40 American shorthair cat 75 60
5292 $3 Havana brown cat . . . 1·75 1·90
5293 $5 Dalmatian . . . . 3·00 3·25
MS5294 119 × 109 mm. $2 Dachshund; $2 Collie; $2 Springer spaniel; $2 Hamilton hound . . 4·00 4·50
MS5295 119 × 109 mm. $2 Osicat; $2 Manx; $2 Somali; $2 Angora 4·00 4·50
MS5296 Two sheets, each 66 × 96 mm. (a) $5 Golden retriever. (b) $5 Abyssinian cat. Set of 2 sheets . . . . 5·50 6·00

483 *Laelia lobata*

485 Marilyn Monroe (1st issue)

484 Daspletosaurus

2003. Orchids of the Caribbean. Multicoloured.

5297 40c. Type **483** 30 20
5298 90c. *Miltoniopsis phalaenopsis* 50 40
5299 $1 *Phalaenopsis violacea* . . 60 45
5300 $3 *Trichopilia fragrans* . . 1·75 1·90
MS5301 116 × 109 mm. $2 *Masdevallia uniflora*; $2 *Laelia flava*; $2 *Barkeria lindleyana*; $2 *Laelia tenebrosa* . . . . . . 4·00 4·50
MS5302 66 × 96 mm. $5 *Cattleya lawrenceana* . . . . 2·75 3·00

2003. Prehistoric Animals. Multicoloured.

MS5303 178 × 118 mm. $2 Type **484**; $2 Utahraptor; $2 Scutellosaurus; $2 Scelidosaurus . . . . 4·00 4·50
MS5304 178 × 118 mm. $2 Syntarsus; $2 Velociraptor; $2 Mononikus; $2 Massospondylus 4·00 4·50
MS5305 Two sheets, each 98 × 68 mm. (a) $5 Giganotosaurus (vert). (b) $5 Pterodactylus (vert) Set of 2 sheets 5·50 6·00

2003. 50th Anniv of *Playboy* Magazine. T **485** and similar vert designs showing *Playboy* magazine covers.

MS5306 240 × 152 mm. $1.50 Type **485** (black, grey and brown); $1.50 Playboy bunny logo; $1.50 Man with bunny's head: $1.50 Playboy model; $1.50 Woman licking stamp; $1.50 Fiftieth anniversary issue (January 2004) (black, ochre and rose) . . . . 4·75 5·50

486 Monkey

2004. Chinese New Year ("Year of the Monkey").

MS5307 75 × 93 mm. **486** $1.40 × 4 black, brown and cream . . . 2·20 2·30
MS5308 70 × 100 mm. **486** $3 black, brown and pink . . . . 1·20 1·30

487 "Apricot Blossoms"

2004. Hong Kong 2004 International Stamp Exhibition. Paintings by Ma Yuan.Multicoloured.

MS5309 123 × 118 mm. $2 Type **487**; $2 "Peach Blossoms"; $2 "Watching the Deer by a Pine Shaded Stream"; $2 "Drinking in the Moonlight" . . . . 3·25 3·50
MS5310 120 × 80 mm. $5 "On a Mountain Path in Spring". Imperf 2·00 2·10

488 Concorde SST and Map showing Anchorage, Alaska

2004. Last Flight of Concorde (2003). Multicoloured.

MS5311 131 × 90 mm. $3 Type **488**; $3 Concorde SST and map showing Los Angeles; $3 Concorde SST . . . . 3·50 3·75

OFFICIAL STAMPS

1982. Nos. 668/73 optd **OFFICIAL**.

O1 60c. "Isabella" 15 15
O2 60c. Prince Charles and Lady Diana Spencer 40 50
O3 $2.50 "Alberta" (tender) . . . 15 25
O4 $2.50 Prince Charles and Lady Diana Spencer . . . 55 70
O5 $4 "Britannia" 25 30
O6 $4 Prince Charles and Lady Diana Spencer 80 90

SAMOA Pt. 1; Pt. 7

Islands in the W. Pacific administered jointly from 1889–99 by Gt. Britain, Germany and the U.S.A. In 1899 the eastern islands were assigned to the U.S.A. and the western to Germany. The latter were occupied by British forces in 1914 and were taken over by New Zealand, under mandate, in 1920. W. Samoa was under United Nations trusteeship until it became independent on 1 January 1962.

1877. 12 pence = 1 shilling;
20 shillings = 1 pound.
1967. 100 sene or cents = 1 tale or dollar.

INDEPENDENT KINGDOM

1

2 Palm Trees

3 King Malietoa Laupepa

8
SAMOA POST
FIVE 5 PENCE

1877.

15 **1** 1d. blue . . . . 24·00
16 3d. red . . . . 48·00
17 6d. violet . . . . 40·00
20 9d. brown . . . . 60·00 £350
7b 1s. yellow . . . . 80·00 £150
18 2s. brown £150
19 5s. green £400

The majority of the stamps of T **1** found in old collections are worthless reprints. A 2d. stamp exists but was never issued.

1886.

57a **2** ½d. brown . . . . 2·25 1·75
88 ½d. green . . . . 1·75 2·25
58a 1d. green . . . . 7·50 1·75
89 1d. brown . . . . 2·50 2·25
59c 2d. orange . . . . 5·00 8·00
60 **3** 2½d. red . . . . 2·75 10·00
81 2½d. black . . . . 1·50 3·00
61 **2** 4d. blue . . . . 15·00 7·50
72a **8** 5d. red . . . . 3·25 15·00
62 **2** 6d. lake . . . . 10·00 3·00
63 1s. red . . . . 10·00 3·75
64b 2s.6d. violet . . . . 4·75 9·50

1893. Surch **FIVE PENCE** and bar.

65 **2** 5d. on 4d. blue . . . . . . 70·00 45·00

1893. Surch **5d** and bar.

70 **2** 5d. on 4d. blue . . . . . . 29·00 32·00

1893. Surch **Surcharged** and value in figures.

75 **2** 1½d. on 2d. orange . . . . . 3·00 7·00
84 2½d. on 1d. green . . . . . 75 3·00
85 2½d. on 1s. red . . . . 7·50 13·00
87 2½d. on 2s.6d. violet . . . . 8·50 18·00

1895. Surch **R 3d.**

76 **2** 3d. on 2d. orange . . . . . 8·00 10·00

1899. Optd **PROVISIONAL GOVT.**

90 **2** ½d. green . . . . 1·75 3·50
91 1d. brown . . . . 2·50 9·00
92 2d. orange . . . . 2·50 7·50
93 4d. blue . . . . 70 15·00
94a **8** 5d. red . . . . 2·75 9·00
95 **2** 6d. lake . . . . 1·50 8·50
96 1s. red . . . . 1·50 28·00
97 2s.6d. violet . . . . 4·75 21·00

GERMAN COLONY

100 pfennig = 1 mark.

1900. Stamps of Germany optd **Samoa**.

G1 **8** 3pf. brown . . . . 8·75 13·50
G2 5pf. green . . . . 13·00 18·00
G3 **9** 10pf. red . . . . 8·75 18·00
G4 20pf. blue . . . . 18·00 29·00
G5 25pf. orange . . . . 40·00 85·00
G6 50pf. brown . . . . 40·00 70·00

1901. "Yacht" key-type inscr "SAMOA".

G 7 N 3pf. brown . . . . 1·10 1·10
G 8 5pf. green . . . . 1·10 1·10
G 9 10pf. red . . . . 1·10 1·10
G10 20pf. blue . . . . 1·10 2·20
G11 25pf. black & red on yell 1·30 13·50
G12 30pf. black & orge on buff 1·30 11·00
G13 40pf. black and red . . . 1·30 11·00
G14 50pf. black & pur on buff 1·30 13·50
G15 80pf. black & red on pink 2·75 31·00
G16 O 1m. red . . . . 3·50 65·00
G17 2m. blue . . . . 4·50 £100
G18 3m. black . . . . 7·50 £160
G19 5m. red and black £160 £550

NEW ZEALAND DEPENDENCY
(under Mandate from League of Nations and United Nations).

1914. "Yacht" key-types as German Cameroons, but inscr "SAMOA", surch **G.R.I.** and value in British currency.

101 N ½d. on 3pf. brown . . . . 38·00 9·50
102 ½d. on 5pf. green . . . . . 50·00 14·00
103 1d. on 10pf. red . . . . . 95·00 40·00
104 2½d. on 20pf. blue . . . . 42·00 10·00
105 3d. on 25pf. black and red on yellow . . . . 55·00 40·00
106 4d. on 30pf. black and orange on buff . . . . . £110 60·00
107 5d. on 40pf. black and red £110 70·00
108 6d. on 50pf. black and purple on buff . . . . . 60·00 35·00
109 9d. on 80pf. black and red on rose £200 £100
110 O 1s. on 1m. red £3250 £3500
112 2s. on 2m. blue £3000 £2750
113 3s. on 3m. black £1400 £1200
114 5s. on 5m. red and black £1100 £1000

1914. Stamps of New Zealand (King Edward VII) optd **SAMOA**.

115 **51** ½d. green . . . . 1·00 30
116 **50** 1d. red . . . . 1·00 10
117 **51** 2d. mauve . . . . 1·00 1·00
118 **26** 2½d. blue (B) . . . . . . 1·75 1·75
119 **51** 6d. red . . . . 1·75 1·75
121 1s. orange . . . . 5·50 19·00

1914. Large stamps of New Zealand (Queen Victoria) optd **SAMOA**.

127 F **4** 2s. blue . . . . 5·50 5·50
123 2s.6d. brown . . . . 5·50 9·00
129 3s. violet . . . . 16·00 50·00
124 5s. green . . . . 12·00 11·00
125 10s. brown . . . . 27·00 28·00
126 £1 red . . . . 65·00 45·00

1916. Stamps of New Zealand (King George V) optd **SAMOA.**

134 **62** ½d. green . . . . 60 1·25
135 1½d. grey 50 25
136 1½d. brown 30 50
137 2d. yellow . . . . 1·50 20
139 2½d. blue 60 50
140a 3d. brown . . . . 50 1·00
141a 6d. red . . . . 1·50 1·25
142 1s. orange . . . . 2·00 1·50

1920. Stamps of New Zealand (Victory issue. Nos. 453/8) optd **SAMOA.**

143 **64** ½d. green . . . . 3·75 10·00
144 **65** 1d. red . . . . 2·75 10·00
145 – 1½d. orange . . . . 1·50 9·00
146 – 3d. brown . . . . 8·00 9·00
147 – 6d. violet . . . . 4·50 7·00
148 – 1s. orange . . . . 13·00 11·00

16 Native Hut

1921.

153 **16** ½d. green . . . . 4·50 1·75
150 1d. lake . . . . 3·50 40
151 1½d. brown . . . . 1·00 14·00
152 2d. yellow . . . . 2·25 2·00
157 2½d. blue . . . . 1·75 8·00
158 3d. sepia . . . . 1·75 4·50
159 4d. violet . . . . 1·75 3·50
160 5d. blue . . . . 1·75 7·00
161 6d. red . . . . 1·75 6·00
162 8d. brown . . . . 1·75 11·00
163 9d. olive . . . . 2·00 29·00
164 1s. orange . . . . 1·75 25·00

1926. Stamps of New Zealand (King George V) optd **SAMOA.**

167 **71** 2s. blue . . . . 5·00 18·00
168 3s. mauve . . . . 18·00 45·00

1932. Stamps of New Zealand (Arms type) optd **SAMOA.**

171 F **6** 2s.6d. brown . . . . . . 16·00 48·00
172 5s. green . . . . 26·00 50·00
173 10s. red . . . . 45·00 £100
174 £1 pink . . . . 70·00 £140
175 £2 violet £750
176 £5 blue £2000

1935. Silver Jubilee. Stamps of 1921 optd **SILVER JUBILEE OF KING GEORGE V 1910-1935.**

177 **16** 1d. lake 30 30
178 2½d. blue 60 65
179 6d. red . . . . 2·75 2·50

18 Samoan Girl

19 Apla

1935.

180 **18** ½d. green 10 35
181 **19** 1d. black and red 10 10
182 – 2d. black and orange . . . 3·50 3·25
183 – 2½d. black and blue . . . 10 10
184 – 4d. grey and brown . . . 70 15
205 – 5d. brown and blue . . . . 1·50 50
185 – 6d. mauve 50 10
186 – 1s. violet and brown . . . 30 10
187 – 2s. green and purple . . . 80 50
188 – 3s. blue and orange . . . . 1·50 3·50

DESIGNS—HORIZ: 2d. River scene; 4d. Samoan canoe and house; 5d. Apia post office; 6d. R. L. Stevenson's home, "Vailima"; 1s. Stevenson's tomb. VERT: 2½d. Samoan chief and wife; 2s. Lake Lanuto'o; 3s. Falefa Falls.

1935. Stamps of New Zealand (Arms types) optd **WESTERN SAMOA.**

207w F **6** 2s.6d. brown . . . . . 9·00 12·00
208 5s. green . . . . 15·00 16·00
209 10s. red . . . . 20·00 17·00
234 £1 pink . . . . 16·00 48·00
211 30s. brown £180 £300
235 £2 violet . . . . 85·00 £150
213 £3 green £225 £375
194 £5 blue £225 £450

28 Coastal Scene

31 Robert Louis Stevenson

1939. 25th Anniv of New Zealand Control.

195 **28** 1d. olive and red . . . . . 1·00 25
196 – 1½d. blue and brown . . . 1·50 75
197 – 2½d. brown and blue . . . 1·25 75
198 **31** 7d. violet and green . . . 8·00 4·00

DESIGNS—HORIZ: 1½d. Map of Western Samoa; 2½d. Samoan dancing party.

32 Samoan Chief

1940. Surch.

199 **32** 3d. on 1½d. brown 75 10

1946. Peace stamps of New Zealand optd **WESTERN SAMOA.**

215 **132** 1d. green 40 15
216 – 2d. purple (No. 670) . . . 40 15
217 – 6d. brown and orange (No. 674) 40 15
218 **139** 8d. black and red 40 15

35 Making Siapo Cloth

36 Native Houses and Flags

1952.

219 **35** ½d. red and brown . . . . 10 1·75
220 **36** 1d. olive and green 10 20
221 – 2d. red 10 10
222 – 3d. blue and indigo 40 10
223 – 5d. brown and green . . . 6·00 70
224 – 6d. blue and mauve . . . 75 10
225 – 8d. red 30 30
226 – 1s. sepia and blue 15 10
227 – 2s. brown . . . . 1·00 25
228 – 3s. brown and olive . . . 2·00 2·00

DESIGNS—VERT (as Type **35**): 2d. Seal of Samoa; 5d. Tooth-billed pigeon. (As Type **36**): 3s. Samoan chieftainess. HORIZ (as Type **35**): 1s. Thatching native hut. (As Type **36**): 3d. Malifa Falls, wrongly inscr on stamp "Aleisa Falls"; 6d. Bonito fishing canoe; 8d. Cacao harvesting; 2s. Preparing copra.

1953. Coronation. As T **1a** of Tokelau Islands.

229 **1a** 2d. brown . . . . 1·00 15
230 – 6d. grey . . . . 1·00 35

DESIGN: 6d. Westminster Abbey.

48 Map of Samoa, and the Mace

1958. Inaug of Samoan Parliament. Inscr "FONO FOU 1958".
236 – 4d. red (As T **36**) 10 20
237 – 6d. violet (As No. 221) . . 10 20
238 **48** 1s. blue 65 40

INDEPENDENT STATE

49 Samoan Fine Mat

1962. Independence.
239 **49** 1d. brown and red 10 10
240 – 2d. multicoloured 10 10
241 – 3d. brown, green and blue 10 10
242 – 4d. multicoloured 15 20
243 – 6d. yellow and blue 80 20
261 – 8d. turquoise, green and blue 30 10
245 – 1s. brown and green . . . 20 10
246 – 1s.3d. green and blue . . . 1·00 45
247 – 2s.6d. red and blue . . . . 2·25 1·75
248 – 5s. multicoloured . . . . . 2·50 2·25
DESIGNS—HORIZ: 2d. Samoa College; 3d. Public library; 4d. Fono house; 6d. Map of Samoa; 8d. Airport; 1s.3d. "Vailima"; 2s.6d. Samoan flag; 5s. Samoan Seal. VERT: 1s. Samoan orator.

59 Seal and Joint Heads of State

1963. 1st Anniv of Independence.
249 **59** 1d. sepia and green 10 10
250 4d. sepia and blue 10 10
251 8d. sepia and pink 10 10
252 2s. sepia and orange . . . 20 15

60 Signing the Treaty

1964. 2nd Anniv of New Zealand–Samoa Treaty of Friendship.
253 **60** 1d. multicoloured 10 10
254 8d. multicoloured 10 10
255 2s. multicoloured 20 10
256 3s. multicoloured 20 30

62 Red-tailed Tropic Bird

1965. Air.
263 **62** 8d. black, orange and blue 50 10
264 – 2s. black and blue 75 20
DESIGN: 2s. Flyingfish.

64 Aerial View of Deep Sea Wharf

1966. Opening of First Deep Sea Wharf, Apia. Mult.
265 1d. Type **64** 10 10
266 8d. Aerial view of wharf and bay 15 10
267 2s. As 8d. 25 25
268 3s. Type **64** 30 35

66 W.H.O. Building

1966. Inaug of W.H.O. Headquarters, Geneva.
269 **66** 3d. ochre, blue and slate 35 10
270 – 4d. multicoloured . . . 40 15
271 **66** 6d. lilac, green and olive 45 20
272 – 1s. multicoloured 80 25
DESIGN: 4d. and 1s. W.H.O. Building on flag.

1966. Hurricane Relief Fund. No. 244 surch **HURRICANE RELIEF 6d.**
273 8d.+6d. turquoise, green & bl 10 10

69 Hon. Tuatagaloa L. S. (Minister of Justice)

1967. 5th Anniv of Independence.
274 **69** 3d. sepia and violet 10 10
275 – 8d. sepia and blue 10 10
276 – 2s. sepia and olive 10 10
277 – 3s. sepia and mauve . . . 15 15
DESIGNS: 8d. Hon. F. C. F. Nelson (Minister of Works, Marine and Civil Aviation); 2s. Hon. To'omata T. L. (Minister of Lands); 3s. Hon. Fa'alava'au G. (Minister of Post Office, Radio and Broadcasting).

73 Samoan Fales (houses), 1890

1967. Centenary of Mulinu'u as Seat of Government. Multicoloured.
278 8d. Type **73** 15 10
279 1s. Fono (Parliament) House, 1967 . . . . 15 10

75 Carunculated Honeyeater ("Wattled Honey-eater")

1967. Decimal Currency. Birds. Multicoloured.
280 1s. Type **75** 10 10
281 2s. Pacific pigeon 10 10
282 3s. Samoan starling 10 10
283 5s. White-vented flycatcher ("Samoan Broadbill") . . 10 10
284 7s. Red-headed parrot finch 10 10
285 10s. Purple swamphen . . . 15 10
286 20s. Barn owl . . . . . . 1·25 40
287 25s. Tooth-billed pigeon . . 50 15
288 50s. Island thrush 50 30
289 $1 Samoan fantail . . . . . 75 1·75
289a $2 Black-breasted honeyeater ("Mao") . . . 2·50 6·00
289b $4 Savaii-white eye ("Samoan White-eye") . . 32·00 25·00
Nos. 289a/b are larger, 43 × 28 mm.

85 Nurse and Child

1967. South Pacific Health Service. Mult.
290 3s. Type **85** 15 15
291 7s. Leprosarium 20 15
292 20s. Mobile X-ray unit . . . 35 30
293 25s. Apia Hospital 40 35

89 Thomas Trood

1968. 6th Anniv of Independence. Multicoloured.
294 2s. Type **89** 10 10
295 7s. Dr. Wilhelm Solf 10 10
296 20s. J. C. Williams 10 10
297 25s. Fritz Marquardt 15 10

93 Cocoa

1968. Agricultural Development.
298 **93** 3s. brown, green and black 10 10
299 – 5s. green, yellow and brown 10 10
300 – 10s. red, brown and yellow 10 10
301 – 20s. bistre, yellow and olive 15 15
DESIGNS: 5s. Breadfruit; 10s. Copra; 20s. Bananas.

97 Women weaving Mats

1968. 21st Anniv of South Pacific Commission. Multicoloured.
302 7s. Type **97** 10 10
303 20s. Palm trees and bay . . . 15 10
304 25s. Sheltered cove 15 15

1968. 40th Anniv of Kingsford-Smith's Trans-Pacific Flight. No. 285 surch **1928-1968 KINGSFORD-SMITH TRANSPACIFIC FLIGHT 20 SENE.**
305 20s. on 10s. multicoloured . . 10 10

101 Bougainville's Route

1968. Bicent of Bougainville's Visit to Samoa.
306 **101** 3s. blue and black 10 20
307 – 7s. ochre and black . . . 15 20
308 – 20s. multicoloured 45 30
309 – 25s. multicoloured 60 40
DESIGNS: 7s. Louis de Bougainville; 20s. Bougainvillea flower; 25s. Ships "La Boudeuse" and "L'Etoile".

105 Globe and Human Rights Emblem

1968. Human Rights Year.
310 **105** 7s. blue, brown and gold 10 10
311 20s. orange, green and gold 10 15
312 25s. violet, green and gold 15 15

106 Dr. Martin Luther King **107** Polynesian Version of Madonna and Child

1968. Martin Luther King.
313 **106** 7s. black and green . . . 15 10
314 20s. black and purple . . 15 10

1968. Christmas.
315 **107** 1s. multicoloured 10 10
316 3s. multicoloured 10 10
317 20s. multicoloured 10 10
318 30s. multicoloured 15 15

108 Frangipani "Plumeria acuminata"

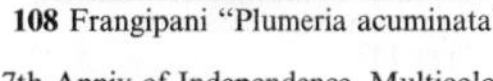
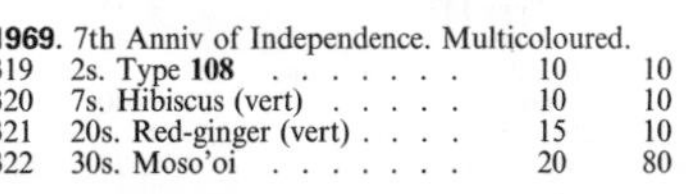

1969. 7th Anniv of Independence. Multicoloured.
319 2s. Type **108** 10 10
320 7s. Hibiscus (vert) 10 10
321 20s. Red-ginger (vert) 15 10
322 30s. Moso'oi 20 80

109 R. L. Stevenson and "Treasure Island"

1969. 75th Death Anniv of Robert Louis Stevenson. Multicoloured.
323 3s. Type **109** 10 10
324 7s. R. L. Stevenson and "Kidnapped" 15 10
325 20s. R. L. Stevenson and "Dr. Jekyll and Mr. Hyde" 15 50
326 22s. R. L. Stevenson and "Weir of Hermiston" . . . 15 50

110 Weightlifting **114** "Virgin with Child" (Murillo)

113 U.S. Astronaut on the Moon and the Splashdown near Samoan Islands

1969. 3rd South Pacific Games, Port Moresby.
327 **110** 3s. black and green . . . 10 10
328 – 20s. black and blue . . . 10 10
329 – 22s. black and orange . . 15 15
DESIGNS: 20s. Yachting; 22s. Boxing.

1969. First Man on the Moon.
330 **113** 7s. multicoloured 15 15
331 20s. multicoloured 15 15

1969. Christmas. Multicoloured.
332 1s. Type **114** 10 10
333 3s. "The Holy Family" (El Greco) 10 10
334 20s. "The Nativity" (El Greco) 20 10
335 30s. "The Adoration of the Magi" (detail) (Velazquez) 25 15
MS336 116 × 126 mm. Nos. 332/5 75 1·25

115 Seventh Day Adventists Sanatorium, Apia

1970. 8th Anniv of Independence.
337 **115** 2s. brown, slate and black 10 10
338 – 7s. violet, buff and black 10 10
339 – 20s. rose, lilac and black 15 10
340 – 22s. green, buff and black 15 15
DESIGNS—HORIZ: 7s. Rev. Father Violette and Roman Catholic Cathedral, Apia; 22s. John Williams, 1797–1839, and London Missionary Society Church, Sapapali'i. VERT: 20s. Mormon Church of Latter Day Saints, Tuasivi-on-Safotulafai.

119 Wreck of "Adler" (German steam gunboat)

1970. Great Apia Hurricane of 1889. Mult.
341 5s. Type **119** 30 10
342 7s. U.S.S. "Nipsic" (steam sloop) 30 10
343 10s. H.M.S. "Calliope" (steam corvette) 30 25
344 20s. Apia after the hurricane 50 75

120 Sir Gordon Taylor's Short S.25 Sandringham 7 Flying Boat "Frigate Bird III"

1970. Air. Multicoloured.

345 3s. Type **120** 45 10
346 7s. Polynesian Airlines Douglas DC-3 55 10
347 20s. Pan-American Airways Sikorsky S-42A flying boat "Samoan Clipper" 75 60
348 30s. Air Samoa Britten Norman Islander 75 1·75

121 Kendal's Chronometer and Cook's Sextant

122 "Peace for the World" (F. B. Eccles)

1970. Cook's Exploration of the Pacific.

349 **121** 1s. red, silver and black 15 15
350 – 2s. multicoloured 15 15
351 – 10s. black, blue and gold 35 25
352 – 30s. multicoloured 1·00 80

DESIGN—VERT: 2s. Cook's statue, Whitby; 10s. Cook's head. HORIZ (83 × 25 mm): 30s. Cook, H.M.S. "Endeavour" and island.

1970. Christmas. Multicoloured.

353 2s. Type **122** 10 10
354 3s. "The Holy Family" (W. E. Jahnke) 10 10
355 20s. "Mother and Child" (F. B. Eccles) 15 10
356 30s. "Prince of Peace" (Meleane Fe'ao) 20 15
MS357 111 × 158 mm. Nos. 353/6 60 1·25

123 Pope Paul VI

124 Native and Tree

1970. Visit of Pope Paul to Samoa.

358 **123** 8s. black and blue 15 15
359 20s. black and red 35 15

1971. Timber Industry. Multicoloured.

360 3s. Type **124** 10 10
361 8s. Bulldozer in clearing 15 10
362 20s. Log in sawmill 30 10
363 22s. Floating logs and harbour 30 15

The 8s. and 20s. are horiz.

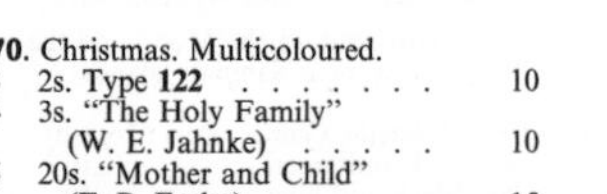

125 Fautasi (large canoe) in Apia Harbour and first stamps of Samoa and U.S.A. (½-size illustration. Actual size 84 × 26 mm)

1971. "Interpex" Stamp Exhibition, New York. Sheet 138 × 80 mm.

MS364 **125** 70s. multicoloured 85 1·40

126 Siva Dance

1971. Tourism. Multicoloured.

365 5s. Type **126** 30 10
366 7s. Samoan cricket 1·25 60
367 8s. Hideaway Hotel 75 35
368 10s. Aggie Grey and her hotel 75 60

127 "Queen Salamasina"

128 "The Virgin and Child" (Bellini)

1971. Myths and Legends of Old Samoa (1st series). Multicoloured.

369 3s. Type **127** 10 10
370 8s. "Lu and his Sacred Hens" 15 10
371 10s. "God Tagaloa fishes Samoa from the sea" 20 10
372 22s. "Mount Vaea and the Pool of Tears" 35 40

1971. Christmas.

373 **128** 2s. multicoloured 10 10
374 3s. multicoloured 10 10
375 – 20s. multicoloured 30 10
376 – 30s. multicoloured 40 20

DESIGN: 20, 30s. "The Virgin and Child with St. Anne and John the Baptist" (Leonardo da Vinci).

129 Map and Scales of Justice

1972. 1st South Pacific Judicial Conference.

377 **129** 10s. multicoloured 15 15

130 Asau Wharf, Savaii

1972. 10th Anniv of Independence. Mult.

378 1s. Type **130** 10 10
379 8s. Parliament Building 10 10
380 10s. Mothers' Centre 10 10
381 22s. "Vailima" Residence and rulers 20 25

131 Flags of Member Countries

132 Expedition Ships

1972. 25th Anniv of South Pacific Commission. Multicoloured.

382 3s. Type **131** 10 15
383 7s. Flag and Afoafouvale Misimoa (Secretary-General) 10 15
384 8s. H.Q. building, Noumea (horiz) 15 15
385 10s. Flags and area map (horiz) 15 15

1972. 250th Anniv of Sighting of Western Samoa by Jacob Roggeveen. Multicoloured.

386 2s. Type **132** 15 10
387 8s. Ships in storm (horiz) 40 10
388 10s. Ships passing island (horiz) 40 10
389 30s. Route of voyage (85 × 25 mm) 1·25 1·50

133 Bull Conch and Reef Heron

1972. Multicoloured.

390 1s. Type **133** 30 30
391 2s. "Oryctes rhinoceros" (beetle) 30 30
392 3s. Skipjack tuna 30 1·00
393 4s. Painted crab 30 30
394 5s. Melon butterflyfish 35 30
395 7s. "Danaus hamata" (butterfly) 2·00 1·00
396 10s. Trumpet triton 2·50 1·00
397 20s. "Chrysochroa abdominalis" (beetle) 1·25 30
398 50s. Spiny lobster 2·00 2·75
399 $1 "Gnathothlibus erotus" (moth) (29 × 45 mm) 8·00 4·50
399a $2 Green turtle (29 × 45 mm) 5·50 2·75
399b $4 Black marlin (29 × 45 mm) 3·00 7·00
399c $5 Green tree lizard (29 × 45 mm) 3·00 10·00

134 "The Ascension"

135 Erecting a Tent

1972. Christmas. Stained-glass windows. Mult.

400 1s. Type **134** 10 10
401 4s. "The Blessed Virgin, and Infant Christ" 10 10
402 10s. "St. Andrew blessing Samoan canoe" 10 10
403 30s. "The Good Shepherd" 40 30
MS404 70 × 159 mm. Nos. 400/3 90 1·25

1973. Boy Scout Movement. Multicoloured.

405 2s. Saluting the flag 10 10
406 3s. First-aid 10 10
407 8s. Type **135** 25 10
408 20s. Samoan action-song 60 85

136 Hawker Siddeley H.S.748

1973. Air. Multicoloured.

409 8s. Type **136** 45 15
410 10s. Hawker Siddeley H.S.748 in flight 55 15
411 12s. Hawker Siddeley H.S.748 on runway 60 35
412 22s. B.A.C. One Eleven 85 60

137 Apia General Hospital

138 Mother and Child, and Map

1973. 25th Anniv of W.H.O. Multicoloured.

413 2s. Type **137** 10 10
414 8s. Baby clinic 15 10
415 20s. Filariasis research 30 20
416 22s. Family welfare 30 30

1973. Christmas. Multicoloured.

417 3s. Type **138** 10 10
418 4s. Mother and child, and village 10 10
419 10s. Mother and child, and beach 10 10
420 30s. Samoan stable 55 50
MS421 144 × 103 mm. Nos. 417/20 65 75

139 Boxing

1973. Commonwealth Games, Christchurch. Mult.

422 8s. Type **139** 10 10
423 10s. Weightlifting 10 10
424 20s. Bowls 20 10
425 30s. Athletics stadium 35 45

1974. Myths and Legends of Old Samoa (2nd series). As T **127**. Multicoloured.

426 2s. Tigilau and sacred dove 10 10
427 8s. Pili, his sons and fishing net 10 10
428 20s. Sina and the origin of the coconut 30 10
429 30s. The warrior, Nafanua 45 55

140 Mail-van at Faleolo Airport

1974. Centenary of U.P.U. Multicoloured.

430 8s. Type **140** 35 10
431 20s. "Mariposa" (cargo liner) at Apia wharf 50 15
432 22s. Early post office, Apia and letter 50 25
433 50s. William Willis and "Age Unlimited" (sailing raft) (87 × 29 mm) 95 1·25
MS434 140 × 82 mm. No. 433 70 1·75

141 "Holy Family" (Sebastiano)

1974. Christmas. Multicoloured.

435 3s. Type **141** 10 10
436 4s. "Virgin and Child with Saints" (Lotto) 10 10
437 10s. "Madonna and Child with St. John" (Titian) 20 10
438 30s. "Adoration of the Shepherds" (Rubens) 55 45
MS439 128 × 87 mm. Nos. 435/8 80 1·40

142 Winged Passion Flower

1975. Tropical Flowers. Multicoloured.

440 8s. Type **142** 10 10
441 20s. Gardenia (vert) 20 15
442 22s. "Barringtonia samoensis" (vert) 20 15
443 30s. Malay apple 25 60

143 "Joyita" (inter-island coaster) loading at Apia

1975. "Interpex 1975" Stamp Exhibition, New York, and "Joyita" Mystery. Multicoloured.

444 1s. Type **143** 10 10
445 8s. "Joyita" sails for Tokelau Islands 15 10
446 20s. Taking to rafts 20 25
447 25s. "Joyita" abandoned 25 30
448 50s. Discovery of "Joyita" north of Fiji 50 1·25
MS449 150 × 100 mm. Nos. 444/8. Imperf 1·50 3·50

144 "Pate" Drum

145 "Mother and Child" (Meleane Fe'ao)

1975. Musical Instruments. Multicoloured.
450 8s. Type **144** 10 10
451 20s. "Lali" drum 20 10
452 22s. "Logo" drum 20 10
453 30s. "Pu" shell horn 35 30

1975. Christmas. Multicoloured.
454 3s. Type **145** 10 10
455 4s. "The Saviour" (Polataia Tuigamala) 10 10
456 10s. "A Star is Born" (Iosua To'afa) 10 10
457 30s. "Madonna and Child" (Ernesto Coter) 30 45
MS458 101 × 134 mm. Nos. 454/7 60 1·25

146 "The Boston Massacre, 1770" (Paul Revere)

1976. Bicent of American Revolution. Mult.
459 7s. Type **146** 20 10
460 8s. "The Declaration of Independence" (John Trumbull) 20 10
461 20s. "The Ship that Sank in Victory, 1779" (J. L. G. Ferris) 30 10
462 22s. "Pitt addressing the Commons, 1782" (R. A. Hickel) 30 10
463 50s. "Battle of Princeton" (William Mercer) . . . . . 60 1·00
MS464 160 × 125 mm. Nos. 459/63 4·00 8·00

147 Mullet Fishing

1976. Fishing. Multicoloured.
465 10s. Type **147** 10 10
466 12s. Fish traps 15 10
467 22s. Samoan fisherman . . . 30 10
468 50s. Net fishing 85 80

148 Paul Revere's Ride

1976. "Interphil" Stamp Exhibition. Sheet 120 × 80 mm.
MS469 **148** $1 gold, black and green 1·00 1·00

149 Boxing

1976. Olympic Games, Montreal. Multicoloured.
470 10s. Type **149** 10 10
471 12s. Wrestling 10 10
472 22s. Javelin 15 10
473 50s. Weightlifting 45 50

150 Mary and Joseph going to Bethlehem

1976. Christmas. Multicoloured.
474 3s. Type **150** 10 10
475 5s. The Shepherds 10 10
476 22s. The Holy Family 15 10
477 50s. The Magi 55 65
MS478 124 × 115 mm. Nos. 474/7 80 1·75

151 Queen Elizabeth and View of Apia

1977. Silver Jubilee and Royal Visit. Mult.
479 12s. Type **151** 10 10
480 26s. Presentation of Spurs of Chivalry 15 20
481 32s. Queen and Royal Yacht "Britannia" 65 25
482 50s. Queen leaving Abbey . . 20 60

152 Map of Flight Route

1977. 50th Anniv of Lindbergh's Transatlantic Flight. Multicoloured.
483 22s. Type **152** 25 10
484 24s. In flight 35 15
485 26s. Landing 35 15
486 50s. Col. Lindbergh 80 75
MS487 194 × 93 mm. Nos. 483/6 2·40 2·75
Designs show the "Spirit of St. Louis".

153 3d. Express Stamp and First Mail Notice

1977. Stamp Centenary.
488 **153** 12s. yellow, red and brown 20 10
489 – 13s. multicoloured 20 30
490 – 26s. multicoloured 30 30
491 – 50s. multicoloured . . . . 60 1·60
DESIGNS: 13s. Early cover and 6d. Express; 26s. Apia P.O. and 1d. Express; 50s. Schooner "Energy" (1877) and 6d. Express.

154 Apia Automatic Telephone Exchange

1977. Telecommunications Project. Mult.
492 12s. Type **154** 15 10
493 13s. Mulinuu radio terminal 15 10
494 26s. Old and new telephones 30 20
495 50s. Global communication 50 70

155 "Samoan Nativity" (P. Feata)

1977. Christmas. Multicoloured.
496 4s. Type **155** 10 10
497 6s. "The Offering" (E. Saofaiga) 10 10
498 25s. "Madonna and Child" (F. Tupou) 20 10
499 50s. "Emmanuel" (M. Sapa'u) 35 40
MS500 117 × 159 mm. Nos. 496/9 55 85

156 Polynesian Airlines Boeing 737

1978. Aviation Progress. Multicoloured.
501 12s. Type **156** 15 10
502 24s. Wright brothers' Flyer I 30 20
503 26s. Kingsford Smith's Fokker F.V11a/3m "Southern Cross" 30 20
504 50s. Concorde 75 85
MS505 150 × 120 mm. Nos. 501/4 1·75 2·75

157 Hatchery, Aleipata

1978. Hawksbill Turtle Conservation Project. Mult.
506 24s. Type **157** . . . . 1·75 30
507 $1 Hawksbill turtle . . . . . 4·25 1·60

158 Pacific Pigeon

160 Captain Cook

159 Flags of Western Samoa and Canada with Canadian National Tower

1978. 25th Anniv of Coronation.
508 – 26s. black, brown & mauve 20 30
509 – 26s. multicoloured 20 30
510 **158** 26s. black, brown & mve 20 30
DESIGNS: No. 508, King's Lion; 509, Queen Elizabeth II.

1978. "Capex '78" International Stamp Exhibition, Toronto. Sheet 119 × 79 mm.
MS511 **159** $1 blue, red and black 75 1·40

1978. 250th Birth Anniv of Captain Cook. Mult.
512 12s. Type **160** 25 15
513 24s. Cook's Cottage, Gt. Ayton, Yorkshire 25 20
514 26s. Old drawbridge over the river Esk, Whitby 25 30
515 50s. H.M.S. "Resolution" . . 80 1·40

161 Thick-edged Cowrie

162 "Madonna on the Crescent"

1978. Shells. Multicoloured.
516 1s. Type **161** 15 10
517 2s. Controversial Isabelle cowrie 15 10
518 3s. Money cowrie 20 10
519 4s. Eroded cowrie 20 10
520 6s. Honey cowrie 20 75
521 7s. Asellus or banded cowrie 20 10
522 10s. Globular or globe cowrie 20 10
523 11s. Mole cowrie 20 10
524 12s. Children's cowrie . . . 20 10
525 13s. Flag cone 20 10
526 14s. Soldier cone 20 10
527 24s. Textile or cloth-of-gold cone 25 10
528 26s. Lettered cone 25 10
529 50s. Tesselate or tiled cone 30 15
530 $1 Black marble cone . . . 45 60
530a $2 Marlin-spike auger . . . 60 70
530b $3 Scorpion conch . . . . 75 1·25
530c $5 Common or major harp 1·50 2·25
Nos. 530a/c are larger, 36 × 26 mm.

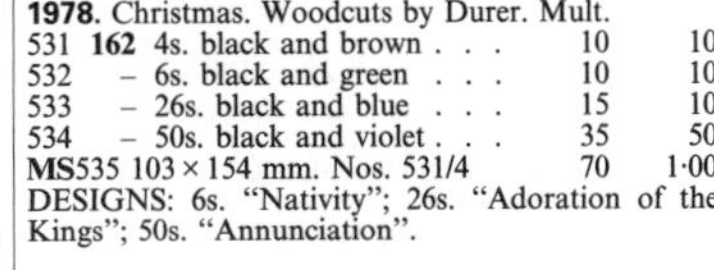

1978. Christmas. Woodcuts by Durer. Mult.
531 **162** 4s. black and brown . . . 10 10
532 – 6s. black and green . . . 10 10
533 – 26s. black and blue . . . 15 10
534 – 50s. black and violet . . . 35 50
MS535 103 × 154 mm. Nos. 531/4 70 1·00
DESIGNS: 6s. "Nativity"; 26s. "Adoration of the Kings"; 50s. "Annunciation".

163 Boy with Coconuts

1979. International Year of the Child. Mult.
536 12s. Type **163** 15 10
537 24s. White Sunday 20 15
538 25s. Children at pump . . . 20 15
539 50s. Girl with ukulele 60 80

164 "Charles W. Morgan"

1979. Sailing Ships (1st series). Whaling Ships. Multicoloured.
540 12s. Type **164** 20 10
541 14s. "Lagoda" 20 10
542 24s. "James T. Arnold" . . . 25 20
543 50s. "Splendid" 45 85
See also Nos. 561/4 and 584/7.

165 Launch of "Apollo 11"

166 Sir Rowland Hill (statue) and Penny Black

1979. 10th Anniv of Moon Landing.
544 **165** 12s. brown and red . . . 20 10
545 – 14s. multicoloured 20 10
546 – 24s. multicoloured 20 15
547 – 26s. multicoloured 20 15
548 – 50s. multicoloured 35 55
549 – $1 multicoloured . . . . 70 1·50
MS550 90 × 130 mm. No. 549 . . 75 1·75
DESIGNS—HORIZ: 14s. Lunar module and astronaut on Moon; 26s. Astronaut on Moon; $1 Command module after splashdown. VERT: 24s. View of Earth from Moon; 50s. Lunar and Command modules in Space.
No. **MS**550 is inscribed "Spashdown" in error.

1979. Death Cent of Sir Rowland Hill. Mult.
551 12s. Type **166** 15 10
552 24s. Two-penny Blue with "Maltese Cross" postmark 15 15
553 26s. Sir Rowland Hill and Penny Black 15 15
554 $1 Two-penny Blue and Sir Rowland Hill 45 75
MS555 128 × 95 mm. Nos. 551/4 80 1·60

167 Anglican Church, Apia

1979. Christmas. Churches.
556 **167** 4s. black and blue 10 10
557 – 6s. black and yellow . . . 10 10
558 – 26s. black and brown . . 15 10
559 – 50s. black and lilac . . . 30 30
MS560 150 × 124 mm. Nos. 556/9 60 1·25
DESIGNS: 6s. Congregational Christian, Leulumoega; 26s. Methodist, Piula; 50s. Protestant, Apia.

1980. Sailing Ships (2nd series). Whaling Ships. As T **164**. Multicoloured.
561 12s. "William Hamilton" . . 25 10
562 14s. "California" 25 10
563 24s. "Liverpool II" 25 15
564 50s. "Two Brothers" 35 75

168 "Equipment for a Hospital"

1980. Anniversaries. Multicoloured.
565 12s. Type **168** 60 10
566 13s. John Williams, dove with olive twig and commemorative inscription 45 1·10
567 14s. Dr. Wilhelm Solf (instigator), flag and commemorative inscription 1·00 15
568 24s. Cairn Monument . . . 1·00 30
569 26s. Williams Memorial, Savai'i 70 30
570 50s. Paul P. Harris (founder) 1·25 2·50
COMMEMORATIONS: 12, 50s. 75th anniv of Rotary International; 13, 26s. 150th anniv of John Williams (missionary) arrival in Samoa; 14, 24s. 80th anniv of raising of German flag.

169 Samoan Village Scene (½-size illustration)

1980. "London 1980" International Stamp Exhibition. Sheet 140 × 81 mm.
MS571 **169** $1 multicoloured . . 60 1·00

170 Queen Elizabeth the Queen Mother in 1970

1980. 80th Birthday of The Queen Mother.
572 **170** 50s. multicoloured 30 30

171 1964 2nd Anniversary of New Zealand–Samoa Treaty of Friendship 2s. Commemorative and "Zeapex '80" Emblem (⅔-size illustration)

1980. "Zeapex '80" International Stamp Exhibition, Auckland. Sheet 130 × 80 mm.
MS573 **171** $1 multicoloured . . 60 1·00

172 Afiamalu Satellite Earth Station

1980. Afiamalu Satellite Earth Station. Mult.
574 12s. Type **172** 15 10
575 14s. Satellite station (different) 20 10
576 24s. Satellite station and map of Savai'i and Upolu . . 30 15
577 50s. Satellite and globe . . . 60 75

173 Afiamalu Satellite Earth Station 24s. Commemorative Stamp and "Sydpex 80" Emblem (⅔-size illustration)

1980. "Sydpex 80" International Stamp Exhibition, Sydney. Sheet 130 × 80 mm. Imperf.
MS578 **173** $2 multicoloured . . 1·00 1·00

174 "The Saviour" (J. Poynton)

176 Hotel Tusitala

175 President Franklin D. Roosevelt and Hyde Park (family home)

1980. Christmas. Paintings. Multicoloured.
579 8s. Type **174** 10 10
580 14s. "Madonna and Child" (Lealofi F. Siaopo) 10 10
581 27s. "Nativity" (Pasila Feata) 15 10
582 50s. "Yuletide" (R. P. Aiono) 25 40
MS583 90 × 105 mm. Nos. 579/82 1·00 1·50

1981. Sailing Ships (3rd series). As T **164**. Mult.
584 12s. "Ocean" (whaling ship) 30 15
585 18s. "Horatio" (whaling ship) 40 20
586 27s. H.M.S. "Calliope" (screw corvette) 55 25
587 32s. H.M.S. "Calypso" (screw corvette) 60 50

1981. Int Year for Disabled Persons. President Franklin D. Roosevelt Commem. Multicoloured.
588 12s. Type **175** 15 10
589 18s. Roosevelt's inauguration, 4 March 1933 . . . . . . 15 10
590 27s. Franklin and Eleanor Roosevelt 20 15
591 32s. Roosevelt's Lend-lease Bill (Atlantic convoy, 1941) 25 20
592 38s. Roosevelt the philatelist 25 25
593 $1 Campobello House (summer home) 50 90

1981. Tourism. Multicoloured.
594 12s. Type **176** 15 10
595 18s. Apia Harbour 25 15
596 27s. Aggie Greys' Hotel . . . 25 20
597 32s. Preparation for Ceremonial Kava 30 30
598 54s. Piula water pool 55 55

177 Wedding Bouquet from Samoa

178 Tattooing Instruments

1981. Royal Wedding. Multicoloured.
599 18s. Type **177** 15 10
600 32s. Prince Charles as Colonel-in-Chief, Gordon Highlanders 20 10
601 $1 Prince Charles and Lady Diana Spencer 30 50

1981. Tattooing. Multicoloured.
602 12s. Type **178** 30 20
603 18s. First stage of tattooing 35 25
604 27s. Progessive stage 35 30
605 $1 Completed tattoo 60 70

179 Black Marlin

180 "Thespesia populnea"

1981. "Philatokyo '81" International Stamp Exhibition, Tokyo. Sheet 130 × 80 mm.
MS606 **179** $2 multicoloured . . 1·00 1·00

1981. Christmas. Flowers. Multicoloured.
607 11s. Type **180** 15 10
608 15s. Copper leaf 15 15
609 23s. "Allamanda cathartica" 20 25
610 $1 Mango . . . . 60 1·00
MS611 86 × 120 mm. Nos. 607/10 1·10 2·25

181 George Washington's Pistol

1982. 250th Birth Anniv of George Washington.
612 **181** 23s. black, brown & stone 25 30
613 – 25s. black, brown & stone 25 30
614 – 34s. black, brown & stone 30 40
MS615 104 × 103 mm. $1 Washington taking Oath of Office as President . . . . 70 1·00
DESIGNS: 25s. Mount Vernon (Washington's home); 34s. George Washington.

182 "Forum Samoa" (container ship)

184 Boxing

183 Scouts map-reading and "75"

1982. 20th Anniv of Independence. Mult.
616 18s. Type **182** . . . . 1·00 20
617 23s. "Air services" . . . . . 1·25 30
618 25s. N.P.F. (National Provident Fund) Building, Apia 50 30
619 $1 "Telecommunications" . . 1·50 1·00

1982. 75th Anniv of Boy Scout Movement. Mult.
620 5s. Type **183** 10 10
621 38s. Scout salute and "75" 40 40
622 44s. Scout crossing river by rope and "75" 50 50
623 $1 "Tower" of Scouts and "75" . . . . 1·00 1·00
MS624 93 × 81 mm. $1 As No. 623 but with portrait of Lord Baden-Powell replacing emblem (47 × 35 mm) . . . . 1·25 1·25

1982. Commonwealth Games, Brisbane. Mult.
625 23s. Type **184** 20 20
626 23s. Hurdling 20 20
627 34s. Weightlifting 25 30
628 $1 Bowling . . . . 75 1·50

185 "Mary and Joseph" (Emma Dunlop)

1982. Christmas. Children's Pictures. Mult.
629 11s. Type **185** 15 10
630 15s. "Mary, Joseph and Baby Jesus" (Marie Tofaeono) 15 15
631 38s. "Madonna and Child" (Ralph Laban and Fetalaiga Fareni) 40 30
632 $1 "Mother and Child" (Panapa Pouesi) . . . . . 90 2·25
MS633 130 × 119 mm. Nos. 629/32 1·60 2·75

186 Satellite View of Australasia

1983. Commonwealth Day. Multicoloured.
634 14s. Type **186** 10 10
635 29s. Flag of Samoa 25 20
636 43s. Harvesting copra 25 25
637 $1 Head of State Malietoa Tanumafili II 50 80

187 Douglas DC-1

1983. Bicentenary of Manned Flight and 50th Anniv of Douglas Commercial Aircraft. Sheet, 215 × 113 mm, containing horiz designs as T **187**. Multicoloured.
MS638 32s. × 10, each design showing a different Douglas aircraft from the DC-1 to the DC-10 . . . . 3·25 3·25

188 Pole vaulting

189 Lime

1983. South Pacific Games. Multicoloured.
639 8s. Type **188** 35 10
640 15s. Netball 45 20
641 25s. Tennis 70 50
642 32s. Weightlifting 70 50
643 35s. Boxing . . . . 75 1·00
644 46s. Football . . . . 90 1·40
645 48s. Golf . . . . 2·25 1·50
646 56s. Rugby . . . . 1·40 1·75

1983. Fruit. Multicoloured.
647 1s. Type **189** . . . . 10 1·00
648 2s. Starfruit . . . . 10 1·25
649 3s. Mangosteen . . . . . . 10 1·25
650 4s. Lychee . . . . 10 1·25
651 7s. Passion fruit . . . . . . 15 1·25
652 8s. Mango . . . . 15 1·25
653 11s. Pawpaw . . . . 20 1·00
654 13s. Pineapple . . . . 20 1·00
655 14s. Breadfruit . . . . . . 20 1·00
656 15s. Banana . . . . 30 1·00
657 21s. Cashew nut . . . . . . 2·00 2·00
658 25s. Guava . . . . 2·00 1·00
659 32s. Water melon . . . . . 2·50 1·75
660 48s. Sasalapa . . . . 2·25 2·50
661 56s. Avocado . . . . 2·25 2·50
662 $1 Coconut . . . . 2·25 2·00
663 $2 Vi apple (25x35½ mm) . . 2·50 3·00
664 $4 Grapefruit (25x35½ mm) 2·50 4·50
665 $5 Orange (25x35½ mm) . . 3·00 4·75

190 On Parade

192 Apia Harbour

191 Togitogiga Falls, Upolu

1983. Centenary of Boys' Brigade. Sheet 120 × 83 mm.
MS668 **190** $1 multicoloured . . 2·50 2·00

1984. Scenic Views. Multicoloured.
669 25s. Type **191** 30 15
670 32s. Lano Beach, Savai'i . . 40 60
671 48s. Mulinu'u Point, Upolu 55 1·10
672 56s. Nu'utele Island . . . . 55 1·75

1984. 250th Anniv of "Lloyd's List" (newspaper). Multicoloured.
673 32s. Type **192** 25 20
674 48s. Apia hurricane, 1889 . . 50 45
675 60s. "Forum Samoa" (container ship) 45 50
676 $1 "Matua" (inter-island freighter) 75 80

1984. Universal Postal Union Congress, Hamburg. No. 662 optd **19th U.P.U. CONGRESS HAMBURG 1984**.
677 $1 Coconut . . . . 1·40 80

194 Olympic Stadium

1984. Olympic Games, Los Angeles. Multicoloured.
678 25s. Type **194** 20 20
679 32s. Weightlifting 20 25
680 48s. Boxing 30 45
681 $1 Running 60 80
MS682 170 × 120 mm. Nos. 678/81 1·40 1·60

195 Government Aircraft Factory N24A Nomad

1984. "Ausipex" International Stamp Exhibition, Melbourne. Sheet 131 × 80 mm.
MS683 **195** $2.50 multicoloured 4·75 6·00

196 "Faith"

1984. Christmas. "The Three Virtues" (Raphael). Multicoloured.
684 25s. Type **196** 40 15
685 35s. "Hope" 50 40
686 $1 "Charity" . . . . 1·75 3·25
MS687 63 × 76 mm. Nos. 684/6 2·75 4·00

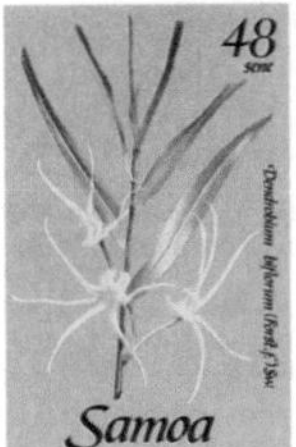

197 "Dendrobium biflorum"

199 "Dictyophora indusiata"

198 Ford "Model A", 1903

1985. Orchids (1st series). Multicoloured.
688 48s. Type **197** 45 35
689 56s. "Dendrobium vaupelianum Kraenzl" . . 50 45
690 67s. "Glomera montana" . . 60 70
691 $1 "Spathoglottis plicata" . . 80 1·40
See also Nos. 818/21.

1985. Veteran and Vintage Cars. Multicoloured.
692 48s. Type **198** . . . . 1·50 60
693 56s. Chevrolet "Tourer", 1912 . . . . 1·60 85
694 67s. Morris "Oxford", 1913 1·75 1·75
695 $1 Austin "Seven", 1923 . . 2·25 3·25

1985. Fungi. Multicoloured.
696 48s. Type **199** . . . . 1·10 55
697 56s. "Ganoderma tornatum" 1·25 85
698 67s. "Mycena chlorophos" 1·60 1·75
699 $1 "Mycobonia flava" . . . 2·25 3·50

200 The Queen Mother at Liverpool Street Station

201 Map of Pacific and Exhibition Logo

1985. Life and Times of Queen Elizabeth the Queen Mother. Multicoloured.
700 32s. At Glamis Castle, aged 9 50 25
701 48s. At Prince Henry's christening with other members of the Royal Family 60 35
702 56s. Type **200** . . . . 2·50 1·25
703 $1 With Prince Henry at his christening (from photo by Lord Snowdon) . . . . . 80 2·25
MS704 91 × 73 mm. $2 Arriving at Tattenham Corner Station with the Queen . . . . 3·25 1·75

1985. "Expo '85" World Fair, Japan. Sheet 70 × 45 mm.
MS705 **201** $2 multicoloured . . 1·50 2·00

202 I.Y.Y. Emblem and Map (Alaska–Arabian Gulf)

1985. International Youth Year. Designs showing background map and emblem (Nos. 706 and 710) or raised arms (others). Multicoloured.
706 60s. Type **202** 40 70
707 60s. Raised arms (Pakistan–Mexico) 40 70
708 60s. Raised arms (Central America–China) 40 70
709 60s. Raised arms (Japan–Greenland) 40 70
710 60s. Type **202** (Iceland–Siberia) 40 70
Nos. 706/10 were printed together in horizontal strips of 5, the background forming a composite design of three continuous world maps.

203 "System"

204 "Hypolimnas bolina"

1985. Christmas. Designs showing illustrations by Millicent Sowerby for R. L. Stevenson's "A Child's Garden of Verses". Multicoloured.
711 32s. Type **203** 20 25
712 48s. "Time to Rise" 30 35
713 56s. "Auntie's Skirts" 35 40
714 $1 "Good Children" . . . . 65 1·75
MS715 87 × 109 mm. Nos. 711/14 2·25 4·00

1986. Butterflies. Multicoloured.
716 25s. Type **204** 35 35
717 32s. "Belenois java" 40 35
718 48s. "Deudorix epijarbas" . . 60 50
719 56s. "Badamia exclamationis" 65 90
720 60s. "Danaus hamata" . . . 65 90
721 $1 "Catochrysops taitensis" 1·00 2·00

205 Halley's Comet over Apia

1986. Appearance of Halley's Comet. Mult.
722 32s. Type **205** 40 20
723 48s. Edmond Halley 50 35
724 60s. Comet passing Earth . . 60 50
725 $2 Preparing "Giotto" spacecraft . . . . 1·25 2·00

1986. 60th Birthday of Queen Elizabeth II. As T **145a** of St. Helena. Multicoloured.
726 32s. Engagement photograph, 1947 . . . . 15 20
727 48s. Queen with Liberty Bell, U.S.A., 1976 . . . . . . 15 35
728 56s. At Apia, 1977 . . . . . 20 40
729 67s. At Badminton Horse Trials, 1978 . . . . . . 30 45
730 $2 At Crown Agents Head Office, London, 1983 . . . 60 1·25

206 U.S.S. "Vincennes" (frigate)

1986. "Ameripex '86" International Stamp Exhibition, Chicago. Multicoloured.
731 48s. Type **206** 35 40
732 56s. Sikorsky S-42A flying boat 40 50
733 60s. U.S.S. "Swan" (patrol boat) 40 50
734 $2 "Apollo 10" descending 1·00 2·50

207 Vailima

1986. "Stampex '86" Stamp Exhibition, Adelaide. Sheet 158 × 97 mm.
MS735 **207** $3 multicoloured . . 4·00 4·00

208 High-finned Grouper

1986. Fishes. Multicoloured.
736 32s. Type **208** 50 40
737 48s. Scarlet-finned squirrelfish 70 45
738 60s. Yellow-edged lyretail ("Lunartail grouper") . . . 80 90
739 67s. Yellow-striped snapper 85 1·50
740 $1 Big-scaled soldierfish . . . 1·10 2·25

209 Samoan Prime Ministers, American Presidents and Parliament House

1986. Christmas. 25th Anniv of United States Peace Corps. Multicoloured.
741 45s. Type **209** 25 40
742 60s. French and American Presidents, Samoan Prime Minister and Statue of Liberty 35 60
MS743 131 × 72 mm. Nos. 741/2 3·00 4·50
No. **MS**743 also commemorates the Centenary of the Statue of Liberty.

210 "Hibiscus rosa-sinensis" and Map of Samoa

1987. 25th Anniv of Independence. Mult.
744 15s. Type **210** 25 10
745 45s. Parliament Building, Apia 40 30
746 60s. Longboat race at Independence celebration 45 40
747 70s. Peace dove and laurel wreath 50 70
748 $2 Head of State Malietoa Tanumafili II and national flag (horiz) . . . . 1·25 2·25

211 Gulper ("Eurypharynx")

1987. Deep Ocean Fishes. Multicoloured.
749 45s. Type **211** 45 30
750 60s. Hatchetfish 60 60
751 70s. Bearded angelfish . . . 70 1·00
752 $2 Swallower ("Saccopharynx") . . . . 1·40 3·25

212 Workmen trimming Logs and building Fale (traditional house)

1987. "Capex 87" International Stamp Exhibition, Toronto. Sheet 122 × 66 mm.
MS753 **212** $3 multicoloured . . 1·90 1·90

213 Lefaga Beach, Upolu

1987. Coastal Scenery. Multicoloured.
754 45s. Type **213** 70 30
755 60s. Vaisala Beach, Savaii . . 90 40
756 70s. Solosolo Beach, Upolu 95 75
757 $2 Neiafu Beach, Savaii . . . 1·75 3·50

214 Abel Tasman

1987. Bicentenary of Australian Settlement (1988) (1st issue). Explorers of the Pacific. Mult.
758 40s. Type **214** 50 25
759 45s. Capt. James Cook . . . 65 40
760 80s. Comte Louis-Antoine de Bougainville 80 80
761 $2 Comte Jean de la Perouse 1·40 3·00
MS762 90 × 73 mm. No. 761 . . 1·40 1·75
See also Nos. 768/72.

1987. "Hafnia" International Stamp Exhibition, Copenhagen. No. **MS**762 optd with Hafnia emblem.
MS763 90 × 73 mm. $2 Comte Jean de la Perouse . . . . 2·50 2·25

216 Christmas Tree

217 Samoa Coat of Arms and Australia Post Logo

1987. Christmas. Multicoloured.
764 40s. Type **216** 30 30
765 45s. Family going to church 40 35
766 50s. Bamboo fire-gun 45 40
767 80s. Inter-island transport . . 1·10 1·25

1988. Bicentenary of Australian Settlement (2nd issue). Postal Services. Multicoloured.
768 45s. Type **217** 80 90
769 45s. Samoan mail van and Boeing 727 airplane . . . 80 90
770 45s. Loading Boeing 727 mail plane 80 90
771 45s. Australian mail van and Boeing 727 . . . . 80 90
772 45s. "Congratulations Australia" message on airmail letter 80 90
Nos. 768/72 were printed together, se-tenant, Nos. 769/71 forming a composite design.

218 Airport Terminal and Douglas DC-9 Airliner taking off

1988. Opening of Faleolo Airport. Mult.
773 40s. Type **218** 60 40
774 45s. Boeing 727 . . . . 65 40
775 60s. De Havilland D.H.C.6 Twin Otter 80 70
776 70s. Boeing 737 . . . . 90 1·40
777 80s. Boeing 727 and control tower . . . . 1·00 1·50
778 $1 Douglas DC-9 over "fale" (house) . . . . 1·10 1·75

219 "Expo '88" Pacific Islands Village   221 Athletics

220 Mormon Temple, Apia

1988. "Expo '88" World Fair, Brisbane. Mult.
779 45s. Type **219** 30 30
780 70s. Expo Complex and monorail . . . . 1·25 1·25
781 $2 Map of Australia showing Brisbane . . . . 2·00 2·75

1988. Centenary of Arrival of the Latter-Day Saints in Samoa. Sheet 86 × 77 mm.
MS782 **220** $3 multicoloured . . 1·50 2·00

1988. Olympic Games, Seoul. Multicoloured.
783 15s. Type **221** 10 10
784 60s. Weightlifting 30 35
785 80s. Boxing 40 45
786 $2 Olympic stadium . . . . 1·10 1·25
MS787 85 × 100 mm. Nos. 783/6 1·90 2·40

222 Spotted Triller ("Polynesian Triller")   223 Forest

1988. Birds. Multicoloured.
788 10s. Type **222** . . . . . . 1·25 45
789 15s. Samoan wood rail . . . 1·50 40
790 20s. Flat-billed kingfisher . . 1·75 1·25
791 25s. Samoan fantail . . . . . 1·75 50
797a 25s. Many-coloured fruit dove (25 × 40 mm) . . . 6·00 2·00
792 35s. Scarlet robin . . . . . 1·75 1·00
793 40s. Black-breasted honeyeater ("Mao") . . . 1·75 1·40
794 50s. Cardinal honeyeater . . 2·00 50
795 65s. Yellow-fronted whistler ("Samoan Whistler") . . 2·00 60
796 75s. Many-coloured fruit dove . . . . 2·50 2·25
798 75s. Silver gull (45 × 28 mm) 2·00 1·50
797 85s. White-throated pigeon 2·50 1·00
799 85s. Great frigate bird (45 × 28 mm) . . . . . . 2·00 1·50
800 90s. Reef heron ("Eastern Reef Heron") (45 × 28 mm) . . . . . . 3·50 1·25
801 $3 Short-tailed albatross (45 × 28 mm) . . . . . . 1·50 1·60
802 $10 White tern ("Common Fairy Tern") (45 × 28 mm) 4·00 5·50
803 $20 Shy albatross (45 × 28 mm) . . . . . . 8·25 12·00
See also No. **MS**1004.

1988. National Conservation Campaign. Mult.
807 15s. Type **223** 80 15
808 40s. Samoan handicrafts . . 55 30
809 45s. Forest wildlife . . . . . 2·50 45
810 50s. Careful use of water (horiz) . . . . 1·00 55
811 60s. Fishing (horiz) . . . . . 1·25 75
812 $1 Coconut plantation (horiz) 1·25 1·50

224 Congregational Church of Jesus, Apia   225 "Phaius flavus"

1988. Christmas. Samoan Churches. Mult.
813 15s. Type **224** 15 10
814 40s. Roman Catholic Church, Leauva'a 35 25
815 45s. Congregational Christian Church, Moataa 40 30
816 $2 Baha'i Temple, Vailima 1·50 2·50
MS817 143 × 64 mm. Nos. 813/16 2·75 2·75

1989. Orchids (2nd series). Multicoloured.
818 15s. Type **225** 15 10
819 45s. "Calanthe triplicata" . . 35 30
820 60s. "Luisia teretifolia" . . . 40 35
821 $3 "Dendrobium mohlianum" . . . . 1·75 2·00

226 "Eber" (German gunboat)

1989. Cent of Great Apia Hurricane. Mult.
822 50s. Type **226** . . . . 1·75 1·75
823 65s. "Olga" (German corvette) . . . . 1·90 1·90
824 85s. H.M.S. "Calliope" (screw corvette) . . . . . 2·00 2·00
825 $2 U.S.S. "Vandalia" (corvette) . . . . 2·25 2·25

227 Samoan Red Cross Youth Group on Parade

1989. 125th Anniv of Int Red Cross. Mult.
826 50s. Type **227** 30 30
827 65s. Blood donors 40 45
828 75s. Practising first aid . . . 45 55
829 $3 Red Cross volunteers carrying patient . . . . . 1·60 2·25

1989. 20th Anniv of First Manned Landing on Moon. As T **50a** of St. Kitts. Multicoloured.
830 18s. Saturn rocket on mobile launcher 40 15
831 50s. Crew of "Apollo 14" (30 × 30 mm) 60 35
832 65s. "Apollo 14" emblem (30 × 30 mm) 75 45
833 $2 Tracks of lunar transporter . . . . 1·60 1·75
MS834 100 × 83 mm. $3 Aldrin with U.S. flag on Moon . . . . . . 3·50 4·00

228 Virgin Mary and Joseph

1989. Christmas. Multicoloured.
835 18s. Type **228** 30 10
836 50s. Shepherds 75 30
837 55s. Donkey and ox 80 35
838 $2 Three Wise Men . . . . 2·50 4·25

1989. "World Stamp Expo '89" International Stamp Exhibition, Washington. Sheet 91 × 105 mm containing designs as Nos. 824/5. Multicoloured. Imperf.
MS839 85s. H.M.S. "Calliope" $2 U.S.S. "Vandalia" . . . . . . 3·75 4·50

229 Pao Pao Outrigger

1990. Local Transport. Multicoloured.
840 18s. Type **229** 35 20
841 55s. Fautasi (large canoe) . . 85 65
842 60s. Polynesian Airlines De Havilland Twin Otter aircraft . . . . 1·75 1·40
843 $3 "Lady Samoa" (ferry) . . 3·75 5·50

230 Bismarck and Brandenburg Gate, Berlin

1990. Treaty of Berlin, 1889, and Opening of Berlin Wall, 1989. Multicoloured.
844 75s. Type **230** . . . . 2·00 3·00
845 $3 "Adler" (German steam gunboat) . . . . 6·00 7·00
Nos. 844/5 were printed together, se-tenant, forming a composite design showing Berliners on the Wall near the Brandenburg Gate.

231 Penny Black and Alexandra Palace, London (½-size illustration)

1990. "Stamp World London 90" Int Stamp Exn.
846 **231** $3 multicoloured . . . . 3·00 3·75

232 Visitors' Bureau

1990. Tourism. Multicoloured.
847 18s. Type **232** 30 10
848 50s. Village resort 55 30
849 65s. Aggie's Hotel 70 60
850 $3 Swimming pool, Tusitala Hotel . . . . 2·50 4·50

233 1964 2nd Anniv of Treaty of Friendship 3s. Commemorative and "NZ 1990" Logo (⅔-size illustration)

1990. "New Zealand 1990" International Stamp Exhibition, Auckland. Sheet 130 × 85 mm.
MS851 **233** $3 multicoloured . . . 3·00 4·00

234 "Virgin and Child" (Bellini)   236 Black-capped Lory

235 William Draper III (administrator) and 40th Anniv Logo

1990. Christmas. Paintings. Multicoloured.
852 18s. Type **234** 30 10
853 50s. "Virgin and Child with St. Peter and St. Paul" (Bouts) 70 30
854 55s. "School of Love" (Correggio) 75 35
855 $3 "Virgin and Child" (Cima) 3·25 5·50
The 55s. value should have shown "The Madonna of the Basket" by the same artist and is so inscribed.

1990. 40th Anniv of United Nations Development Programme.
856 **235** $3 multicoloured . . . . 2·50 3·75

1991. Parrots. Multicoloured.
857 18s. Type **236** 75 40
858 50s. Eclectus parrot . . . . 1·25 60
859 65s. Scarlet macaw . . . . . 1·25 85
860 $3 Palm cockatoo . . . . . 2·75 4·50

1991. 65th Birthday of Queen Elizabeth II and 70th Birthday of Prince Philip. As T **165a** of St. Helena. Multicoloured.
861 75s. Prince Philip in the countryside . . . . 90 1·25
862 $2 Queen wearing yellow lei 2·40 3·00

237 Peter Fatialofa (Samoan captain)

1991. World Cup Rugby Championships. Sheet 121 × 75 mm.
MS863 **237** $5 multicoloured . . 8·50 9·00

238 "O Come All Ye Faithful"

1991. Christmas. Carols (1st series). Mult.
864 20s. Type **238** 55 10
865 60s. "Joy to the World" . . 95 40
866 75s. "Hark the Herald Angels Sing" . . . . 1·25 70
867 $4 "We wish you a Merry Christmas" . . . . 4·25 6·50
See also Nos. 886/9 and 907/11.

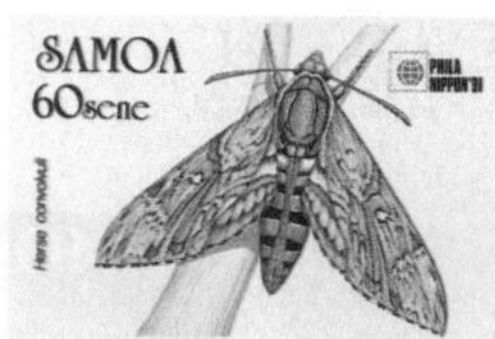

239 "Herse convolvuli"

1991. "Phila Nippon '91" International Stamp Exhibition, Tokyo. Samoan Hawkmoths. Mult.
868 60s. Type **239** . . . . 1·00 70
869 75s. "Gnathothlibus erotus" 1·10 80
870 85s. "Deilephila celerio" . . 1·25 1·00
871 $3 "Cephonodes armatus" . . 4·00 5·25

240 Head of State inspecting Guard of Honour

1992. 30th Anniv of Independence. Mult.
872 50s. Type **240** 70 30
873 65s. Siva ceremony 75 50
874 $1 Commemorative float . . 1·25 1·50
875 $3 Raising Samoan flag . . . 3·75 5·00

1992. 40th Anniv of Queen Elizabeth II's Accession. As T **168a** of St. Helena. Mult.
876 20s. Queen and Prince Philip with umbrellas 55 15
877 60s. Queen and Prince Philip on Royal Yacht . . . . . 1·50 80
878 75s. Queen in multicoloured hat . . . . 1·00 75
879 85s. Three portraits of Queen Elizabeth . . . . 1·10 85
880 $3 Queen Elizabeth II . . . 2·25 3·50

241 Samoa Express 1d. Stamp, 1877   242 Weightlifting

1992. 500th Anniv of Discovery of America by Columbus. Sheet 91 × 70 mm.
MS881 **241** $4 multicoloured . . 3·00 4·00

1992. Olympic Games, Barcelona. Multicoloured.
882 60s. Type **242** 80 70
883 75s. Boxing 90 80

884 85s. Running . . . . 1·00 1·00
885 $3 Montjuic Olympic Stadium, Barcelona . . . . 3·00 4·00

1992. Christmas. Carols (2nd series). As T **238**. Multicoloured.
886 50s. "God rest you Merry Gentlemen" 55 30
887 60s. "While Shepherds watched their Flocks by Night" 65 55
888 75s. "Away in a Manger, no Crib for a Bed" 75 70
889 $4 "O Little Town of Bethlehem" . . . . 3·25 5·00

243 Narrow-banded Batfish

1993. Fishes. Multicoloured.
890 60s. Type **243** 70 60
891 75s. Clown surgeonfish . . . 85 85
892 $1 Black-tailed snapper . . . 1·25 1·75
893 $3 Long-nosed emperor . . . 2·75 4·25

244 Samoan Players performing Traditional War Dance

1993. Rugby World Cup Seven-a-Side Championship, Edinburgh. Multicoloured.
894 60s. Type **244** . . . . 1·25 65
895 75s. Two players (vert) . . . 1·40 75
896 85s. Player running with ball and badge (vert) . . . . . 1·50 1·10
897 $3 Edinburgh Castle . . . . 4·25 6·00

245 Flying Foxes hanging from Branch

1993. Endangered Species. Flying Foxes. Mult.
898 20s. Type **245** 90 30
899 50s. Flying fox with young 1·40 70
900 60s. Flying foxes hunting for food . . . . 1·60 1·00
901 75s. Flying fox feeding from plant . . . . 1·75 1·60

246 Exhibition Emblem

1993. "Taipei '93" Asian International Stamp Exhibition, Taiwan. Sheet 137 × 64 mm.
MS902 **246** $5 yellow, blue and black 8·00 9·00

247 Globe, Letter and Flowers

1993. World Post Day. Multicoloured.
903 60s. Type **247** 55 45
904 75s. Post Office counter . . . 70 80
905 85s. Hands exchanging letter 80 90
906 $4 Globe, national flags and letter . . . . 3·50 6·00

1993. Christmas Carols (3rd series). As T **238**. Multicoloured.
907 20s. "Silent Night" 35 10
908 60s. "As with Gladness Men of Old" 75 45
909 75s. "Mary had a Baby yes, Lord" 90 55
910 $1.50 "Once in Royal David's City" . . . . 1·75 2·50
911 $3 "Angels from the Realms of Glory" . . . . 4·00 5·50

248 "Alveopora allingi"

1994. Corals. Multicoloured.
912 20s. Type **248** 30 10
913 60s. "Acropora polystoma" 65 45
914 90s. "Acropora listeri" . . . 90 90
915 $4 "Acropora grandis" . . . 2·75 5·00

1994. "Hong Kong '94" International Stamp Exhibition. Nos. 912/15 optd **HONG KONG '94** and emblem.
916 20s. Type **248** 35 10
917 60s. "Acropora polystoma" 65 45
918 90s. "Acrophora listeri" . . . 90 90
919 $4 "Acropora grandis" . . . 2·75 5·00

249 Samoan Rugby Management Team

1994. Samoan National Rugby Team. Mult.
920 70s. Type **249** 70 60
921 90s. Test match against Wales 80 80
922 95s. Test match against New Zealand 80 80
923 $4 Apia Park Stadium . . . 3·50 6·00

250 "Anaphaeis java" and "Acraea andromacha" (butterflies)

1994. "Philakorea '94" International Stamp Exhibition, Seoul. Sheet 99 × 82 mm.
MS924 **250** $5 multicoloured . . 3·75 5·00

251 Solo Singer and Choir

1994. Teuila Tourism Festival. Multicoloured.
925 70s. Type **251** . . . . 1·00 45
926 90s. Fire dancer . . . . . . 1·10 65
927 95s. Festival float . . . . . 1·10 65
928 $4 Band outside hotel . . . . 5·50 7·00

252 "Equator" (schooner)

253 Santa Claus on House

1994. Death Centenary of Robert Louis Stevenson (author). Multicoloured.
929 70s. Type **252** 60 50
930 90s. Robert Louis Stevenson 70 80
931 $1.20 Stevenson's tomb, Mt. Vaea . . . . 95 1·25
932 $4 Vailima House (horiz) . . 3·25 5·50

1994. Christmas. Children's Paintings. Mult.
933 70s. Type **253** 60 50
934 95s. Star over house and palm trees 70 70
935 $1.20 Family outing . . . . 95 1·25
936 $4 "Merry Christmas" . . . 3·25 6·00

254 Lotofaga Beach, Aleipata

1995. Scenic Views. Multicoloured.
937 5s. Type **254** 15 50
938 10s. Nuutele Island 15 50
939 30s. Satuiatua, Savaii 15 40
940 50s. Sinalele, Aleipata 30 40
941 60s. Paradise Beach, Lefaga 35 40
942 70s. Houses at Piula Cave . . 45 40
943 80s. Taga blowholes 45 50
944 90s. View from East Coast road 45 50
945 95s. Outrigger canoes, Leulumoega 45 50
946 $1 Parliament Building . . . 50 50

255 Under-12s Rugby Players

1995. World Cup Rugby Championship, South Africa. Multicoloured.
957 70s. Type **255** 55 55
958 90s. Secondary school players 70 70
959 $1 Samoan and New Zealand test match 75 75
960 $4 Ellis Park Stadium, Johannesburg . . . . . . 2·75 4·75

1995. 50th Anniv of End of Second World War. As T **182a** of St. Helena. Multicoloured.
961 70s. Vought Sikorsky OS2U Kingfisher (seaplane) . . . 65 55
962 90s. Chance Vought F4U Corsair (fighter) 80 70
963 95s. American transport ship and landing craft 85 75
964 $3 American marines landing on Samoa . . . . 3·00 4·50
MS965 75 × 85 mm. $4 Reverse of 1939–45 War Medal (vert) . . 2·40 2·75

256 Leatherback Turtle

257 *Phaius tankervilleae*

1995. Year of the Sea Turtle. Multicoloured.
966 70s. Type **256** 55 55
967 90s. Loggerhead turtle . . . 70 70
968 $1 Green turtle 75 75
969 $4 Pacific ridley turtle . . . 2·75 4·25

1995. "Singapore '95" International Stamp Exhibition. Orchids. Sheet 76 × 100 mm.
MS970 **257** $5 multicoloured . . 3·25 4·25
See also No. MS1006.

1995. 50th Anniv of United Nations. As T **201a** of St. Lucia. Multicoloured.
971 70s. Hospital lorry, Bosnia, 1995 . . . . 85 55
972 90s. Bell Sioux helicopter and ambulance, Korea, 1952 1·40 85
973 $1 Bell 212 helicopter, Bosnia, 1995 . . . . . . 1·60 1·00
974 $4 R.N.Z.A.F. Hawker Siddeley Andover, Somalia, 1995 . . . . 3·50 5·00

258 Madonna and Child

259 Hands cupped under Waterfall and Bird

1995. Christmas. Multicoloured.
975 25s. Type **258** 20 10
976 70s. Wise Man wearing green turban 60 50
977 90s. Wise Man with Child in manger 75 65
978 $5 Wise Man wearing red turban . . . . 3·50 6·50

1996. Environment. Water Resources. Mult.
979 70s. Type **259** 50 50
980 90s. Young girl and "WATER FOR LIFE" slogan 65 65
981 $2 Village and waterfall . . . 1·40 2·50
982 $4 Irrigation system . . . . 2·75 4·25

1996. 70th Birthday of Queen Elizabeth II. As T **55** of Tokelau each incorporating a different photograph of the Queen. Multicoloured.
983 70s. Main Street, Apia . . . 50 40
984 90s. Beach scene, Neiafu . . 65 50
985 $1 Vailima House (Head of State's residence) 75 60
986 $3 Parliament Building . . . 2·00 3·75
MS987 64 × 66 mm. $5 Queen Elizabeth II . . . . 3·25 4·00

260 Moon Hare preparing Elixir of Life

1996. Moon Festival. Sheet 103 × 83 mm.
MS988 **260** $2.50 multicoloured 1·75 2·50
No. MS988 also includes the "CHINA '96" International Stamp Exhibition logo on the sheet margin.

261 Meeting Venue

1996. 63rd Session of the EU-ACP Council of Ministers. Sheet 135 × 71 mm.
MS989 **261** $5 multicoloured . . 3·25 4·50

262 Boxing

263 Festival Logo

1996. Centenary of Modern Olympic Games. Mult.
990 70s. Type **262** 60 40
991 90s. Running 70 55
992 $1 Weightlifting 80 60
993 $4 Throwing the javelin . . . 2·75 5·00

1996. 7th Pacific Festival of Arts, Apia. Mult.
994 60s. Type **263** 40 35
995 70s. Decorated pottery . . . 50 40
996 80s. Textile pattern 55 55
997 90s. Traditional dancing . . 60 60
998 $1 Carved poles 70 70
999 $4 Man wearing traditional headdress and necklace . . 2·00 4·25

264 Young Children

1996. 50th Anniv of UNICEF. Multicoloured.
1000 70s. Type **264** 45 40
1001 90s. Children in hospital . . 60 60
1002 $1 Child receiving injection 70 70
1003 $4 Mothers and children . . 2·00 4·00

1997. "HONG KONG '97" International Stamp Exhibition. Sheet, 130 × 90 mm, containing No. 797a.
MS1004 $3 Many-coloured Fruit Dove . . . . 1·75 2·25

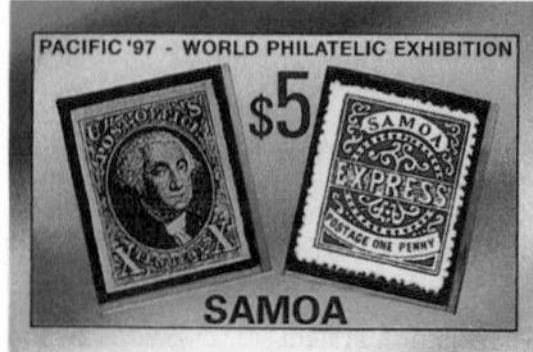

266 First U.S.A. and Samoa Postage Stamps

1997. "Pacific '97" International Stamp Exhibition, San Francisco. Sheet 96 × 70 mm.
MS1005 **266** $5 multicoloured . . 2·75 3·50

1997. Return of Hong Kong to China. Sheet 130 × 90 mm, containing design as T **257**, but with new value.
MS1006 **257** $2.50, multicoloured 1·50 2·25

1997. Golden Wedding of Queen Elizabeth and Prince Philip. As T **192a** of St. Lucia. Mult.
1007 70s. Queen Elizabeth . . . 1·00 1·25
1008 70s. Prince Philip carriage-driving at Royal Windsor Horse Show, 1996 . . . . 1·00 1·25
1009 90s. Queen Elizabeth and horse . . . . 1·10 1·40
1010 90s. Prince Philip laughing 1·10 1·40
1011 $1 Prince Philip and Prince Edward with Zara Phillips on horseback, 1993 . . . 1·25 1·50
1012 $1 Queen Elizabeth and Prince William . . . . . 1·25 1·50
MS1013 111 × 70 mm. $5 Queen Elizabeth and Prince Philip in landau (horiz) . . . . 4·00 4·50
Nos. 1007/8, 1009/10 and 1011/12 respectively were printed together, se-tenant, with the backgrounds forming composite designs.

267 Dolphin on Surface

1997. 26th Anniv of Greenpeace (environmental organization). Multicoloured.
1014 50s. Type **267** 45 35
1015 60s. Two dolphins swimming underwater . . 55 45
1016 70s. Heads of two dolphins underwater 60 65
1017 $1 Dolphin "laughing" . . . 75 1·25
MS1018 113 × 91 mm. $1.25 × 4. As Nos. 1014/17 . . . . 2·75 3·50

268 Christmas Bells

1997. Christmas. Multicoloured.
1019 70s. Type **268** 45 35
1020 80s. Christmas bauble . . . 50 40
1021 $2 Candle . . . . 1·40 2·00
1022 $3 Christmas star . . . . . 1·60 2·75

269 Mangrove Fruit

1998. Mangroves. Multicoloured.
1023 70s. Type **269** 40 35
1024 80s. Mangrove seedlings . . 45 40
1025 $2 Mangrove roots . . . . 1·25 2·00
1026 $4 Mangrove tree on seashore . . . . 2·25 3·50

1998. Diana, Princess of Wales Commemoration. As T **98** of Tokelau. Multicoloured.
1027 50s. Wearing red jacket, 1990 . . . . 30 40
MS1028 145 × 70 mm. $1.40 As 50s.; $1.40 Wearing tweed jacket, 1981; $1.40 Wearing red dress, 1988; $1.40 Carrying bouquets, 1993 (sold at $5.60+75s. charity premium) . . . . 2·75 3·25

270 Westland Wallace

1998. 80th Anniv of the Royal Air Force. Mult.
1029 70s. Type **270** 60 35
1030 80s. Hawker Fury Mk I . . 60 40
1031 $2 Vickers Varsity . . . . . 1·50 1·75
1032 $5 BAC Jet Provost . . . . 3·00 4·50
MS1033 110 × 77 mm. $2 Norman Thompson N.T.2b; $2 Nieuport 27 Scout; $2 Miles Magister; $2 Bristol Bomber . . . . 5·00 5·50

271 Christmas Star

1998. Christmas. Multicoloured.
1034 70s. Type **271** 50 35
1035 $1.05 Bell 70 60
1036 $1.40 Bauble 85 80
1037 $5 Cross . . . . 3·25 5·00

272 Outrigger Canoe

1999. "Australia '99" World Stamp Exhibition, Melbourne. Maritime Heritage. Multicoloured.
1038 70s. Type **272** 40 35
1039 90s. "Heemskerk" and "Zeehan" (Tasman), 1642 90 55
1040 $1.05 H.M.S. "Resolution" and H.M.S. "Adventure" (Cook), 1773 . . . . . . 1·25 1·00
1041 $6 New Zealand scow schooner, 1880 . . . . . 3·75 5·50

1999. Royal Wedding. Vert designs as T **197a** of St. Helena. Multicoloured.
1042 $1.50 Photographs of Prince Edward and Miss Sophie Rhys-Jones 75 75
1043 $6 Engagement photograph 3·00 4·25

1999. 30th Anniv of First Manned Landing on Moon. As T **94a** of St. Kitts. Multicoloured.
1044 70s. Lift-off 40 35
1045 90s. Lunar lander separating from service module . . . 45 40
1046 $3 Buzz Aldrin on Moon's surface . . . . 1·50 2·25
1047 $5 Command module descending on parachutes 2·50 3·50
MS1048 90 × 80 mm. $5 Earth as seen from Moon (circular, 40 mm diam) . . . . 2·75 3·50

1999. "Queen Elizabeth the Queen Mother's Century". As T **199** of St. Helena. Multicoloured.
1049 70s. Talking to air-raid victims, 1940 . . . . . . 60 35
1050 90s. King, Queen and Princess Elizabeth at garden party, South Africa, 1947 . . . . . . 70 40
1051 $2 Reviewing scouts at Windsor, 1991 . . . . . . 1·25 1·50
1052 $6 With Princess Eugenie, 1998 . . . . 2·75 4·50
MS1053 145 × 70 mm. $5 Lady Elizabeth Bowes-Lyon, 1923, and Charlie Chaplin film . . . . . 2·75 3·50

273 Hibiscus and Star

1999. Christmas and Millennium. Multicoloured.
1054 70s. Type **273** 50 35
1055 90s. Poinsettia and star . . 60 40
1056 $2 Christmas cactus and star 1·40 1·40
1057 $6 Southern Cross constellation and Samoan flag . . . . 3·50 5·00

274 Sunrise

2000. New Millennium. Multicoloured.
1058 70s. Type **274** . . . . . . 1·00 90
1059 70s. Sunset . . . . 1·00 90

274a The Count on Ladder

2000. "Sesame Street" (children's T.V. programme). Multicoloured.
1060 90s. Type **274a** 45 60
1061 90s. Ernie on trapeze . . . 45 60
1062 90s. Grover swinging on rope 45 60
1063 90s. Cookie Monster singing and Prairie Dawn playing piano 45 60
1064 90s. Bert with bucket on his head, Elmo and Zoe . . . 45 60
1065 90s. Big Bird dressed as tree 45 60
1066 90s. Little Bear writing and Telly 45 60
1067 90s. Mumiford coming through trap door 45 60
1068 90s. Oscar the Grouch and Slimey 45 60
MS1069 139 × 86 mm. $3 Cookie Monster eating popcorn . . . 1·50 2·00
Nos. 1060/8 were printed together, se-tenant, with the backgrounds forming a composite design.

275 Fire Dancing

2001. Siva afi Fire Dancing. Multicoloured.
1070 25s. Type **275** 20 10
1071 50s. Dancer with torch . . . 30 25
1072 90s. Dancer with arms crossed 45 40
1073 $1 Three dancers 50 45
1074 $4 Pati Levasa, World Fire Dance Champion . . . . 1·90 3·00

276 *Vagrans egista*

2001. Butterflies. Multicoloured. Self-adhesive.
1075 70s. Type **276** 45 50
1076 $1.20 *Jamides bochus* . . . 70 90
1077 $1.40 *Papilio godeffroyi* . . . 75 1·00
1078 $2 *Acraea andromacha* . . . 1·00 1·50
1079 $3 *Eurema hecabe* . . . . . 1·40 2·00

277 Snorkellers

2002. U.N. Year of Eco Tourism. Multicoloured.
1080 60s. Type **277** 45 60
1081 95s. Canoeists 70 90
1082 $1.90 Wood-carver and children . . . . 1·00 1·25
1083 $3 Children by waterfall . . 1·40 1·60
Nos. 1080/3 were printed together, se-tenant, in horizontal strips of 4 and a central label showing the U.N. symbol, with the backgrounds forming a composite design.

278 Buses, Traditional Huts and Man with Baseball Bat

2000. 40th Anniv of Independence. Designs showing the Samoan flag in the background. Multicoloured. Self-adhesive.
1084 25s. Type **278** 50 15
1085 70s. Local dancers and conch blower 40 35
1086 95s. Ferry, aircraft and office workers . . . . . 1·00 55
1087 $5 Church, police parade and rugby player . . . . 4·00 4·00
MS1088 110 × 85 mm. No. 1087 3·50 4·00

279 Woman holding Fish

280 Local Couple on Rock

2002. Faces of Samoa. Multicoloured.
1089 5s. Type **279** 10 10
1090 10s. Boy with grandparents selling fruit 10 10
1091 20s. Young men collecting wood 10 10
1092 25s. Two young boys laughing 10 15
1093 35s. Mother and daughter 15 20
1094 50s. Baby boy 20 25
1095 60s. Male traditional dancer 25 30
1096 70s. Female traditional dancer 25 30
1097 80s. Woman laughing . . . 30 35
1098 90s. Women's choir 35 40
1099 95s. Two women with flowers in their hair . . . 35 40
1100 $1 Young boy under shower 40 45
1101 $1.20 Young girl with pigtails 45 50
1102 $1.85 Man in shirt and tie 75 80
1103 $10 Children awaiting confirmation . . . . . . 4·00 4·25

2002. Samoan Scenes. Multicoloured.
1104 95s. Type **280** 60 45
1105 $1.20 Local couple on beach 70 60
1106 $1.40 Waterfall . . . . . . 1·00 90
1107 $2 Local girl in sea . . . . 1·10 1·60
MS1108 120 × 920 mm. Nos. 1105 and 1107 . . . . 1·75 2·25

281 *Alpinia pupurata*

2002. Ginger Flowers. Multicoloured.
1109 25s. Type **281** 25 10
1110 $1.05 *Alpinia samoensis* . . 75 55
1111 $1.20 *Etlingeria cevuga* . . 85 60
1112 $4 *Hedychium flavescens* . . 2·50 3·25

282 "Return to Paradise" Bus

2003. Buses. Multicoloured. Self-adhesive.
1113 25s. Type **282** 70 15
1114 70s. "Misileti Fatu" bus . . 1·25 45
1115 90s. "Jungle Boys" bus . . 1·40 75
1116 95s. "Sun Rise Transport" bus . . . . 1·40 80
1117 $4 "Laifoni" bus . . . . . 2·75 3·50

283 Turtles, Aleipata

2003. Establishment of Marine Protected Areas. Multicoloured.
1118 25s. Type **283** 50 10
1119 $5 Crab and mangrove, Safata . . . . 2·75 3·50

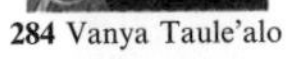

284 Vanya Taule'alo **286** Bicoloured Angelfish

285 David Tua (boxing)

2003. Art of Samoa (1st series). Showing artists and their work. Multicoloured.
1120 25s. Type **284** 20 15
1121 70s. Michel Tuffery 35 30
1122 90s. Momoe von Reiche . . 40 40
1123 $1 Fatu Feu'u 45 45
1124 $4 Lily Laita . . . . 1·60 2·00

2003. Sporting Legends of Samoa. Multicoloured.
1125 25s. Type **285** 20 15
1126 70s. Beatrice Faumuina (discus) 35 30
1127 90s. Michael Jones (rugby) 40 40
1128 95s. Rita Fatialofa (netball) 35 40
1129 $4 Jesse Sapolu (American football) . . . . 1·60 2·00

2003. Angelfish. Multicoloured.
1130 25s. Type **286** 25 15
1131 60s. Flame angelfish 35 30
1132 90s. Regal angelfish 45 40
1133 $5 Emperor angelfish . . . 2·25 3·00
MS1134 123 × 98 mm. $5 No. 1133 2·25 3·00

287 *Heliconia caribaea*

2004. Flowers of the Tropics. Multicoloured.
1135 70s. Type **287** 25 30
1136 80s. *Heliconia psittacorum* "Andromeda" 30 35
1137 90s. *Hibiscus rosa-sinensis* var. 35 40
1138 $4 *Plumeria rubra var. acutifolia* . . . . 1·60 1·75

288 Black-naped Tern

2004. Sea Birds. Multicoloured.
1139 25s. Type **288** 10 15
1140 60s. Crested tern 25 30
1141 70s. Common noddy (vert) 25 30
1142 90s. Lesser frigate bird (vert) 35 40
1143 $4 Reef heron . . . . . . 1·60 1·70
MS1144 191 × 92 mm. Nos. 1139/43 2·50 2·75

289 *Chaetodon meyeri*

2004. Butterfly Fish. Multicoloured.
1145 50s. Type **289** 20 25
1146 90s. *Chaetodon punctatofasciatus* (horiz) 35 40
1147 $1 *Chaetodon ephippium* (horiz) 40 45
1148 $4 *Chaetodon flavirostris* . . 1·60 1·70
MS1149 100 × 61 mm. $4 As No. 1148 . . . . 1·60 1·70
The top right corner of No.**MS**1149 is die-cut round the shape of a sea anemone.

290 Samoan Woman

2004. Samoan Women. Multicoloured.
1150 25s. Type **290** 10 15
1151 70s. Two women and beach scene (vert) 25 30
1152 90s. Woman resting head on hands 35 40
1153 $4 Woman during Kava ceremony (vert) . . . . . 1·60 1·70

291 Three Children in Canoe

2005. Island of Savaii. Multicoloured.
1154 25s. Type **291** 10 15
1155 70s. Tourists on steps to building 25 30
1156 90s. Walkway through forest (vert) 35 40
1157 $4 Coastline (vert) . . . . . 1·60 1·70

SAN MARINO Pt. 8

An independent republic lying near the east coast of the Italian peninsula.

1877. 100 centesimi = 1 lira.
2002. 100 cents = 1 euro.

1 2

1877.
1 **1** 2c. green . . . . 17·00 3·00
18 2c. blue . . . . 11·50 2·75
32 2c. purple . . . . 9·50 3·25
2 **2** 5c. yellow . . . . £130 8·00
33 5c. green . . . . 5·25 1·70
3 10c. blue . . . . £140 8·00
20 10c. green . . . . 7·00 1·70
34 10c. red . . . . 5·25 2·20
21 15c. red . . . . 85·00 22·00
4 20c. red . . . . 30·00 3·25
35 20c. lilac . . . . 6·00 2·75
5 25c. purple . . . . £150 7·25
36 25c. blue . . . . 5·25 2·50
6 30c. brown . . . . £1100 36·00
22 30c. yellow . . . . 7·00 36·00
7 40c. mauve . . . . £1100 36·00
23 40c. brown . . . . 7·00 2·75
24 45c. green . . . . 7·00 3·00
25 65c. brown . . . . 7·00 2·50
26 1l. red and yellow £2000 £325
37 1l. blue £2000 £275
27 2l. brown and buff £2000 £275
28 5l. red and blue £190 £100

1892. Surch **Cmi.** and figure of value.
10c **2** 5c. on 10c. blue . . . . . . 49·00 11·50
12 5c. on 30c. brown . . . . . £475 35·00
16 10c. on 20c. red . . . . . 80·00 4·00

1892. Surch **10 10.**
17 **2** 10(c.) on 20c. red . . . . . £475 4·50

13 Government Palace **14** Government Palace

15 Interior of Government Palace **17** Statue of Liberty

1894. Opening of Government Palace and Installation of Captains-Regent.
29 **13** 25c. purple and blue . . . . 4·50 70
30 **14** 50c. purple and red . . . . 18·00 2·40
31 **15** 1l. purple and green . . . . 14·50 3·25

1899.
38 **17** 2c. brown . . . . 2·00 75
39 5c. orange . . . . 4·25 1·40
See also Nos. 86/91.

18 **19** Mt. Titano

1903.
40 **18** 2c. lilac . . . . 9·50 2·00
73 2c. brown . . . . 1·30 40
74 **19** 5c. green . . . . 2·10 40
111 5c. purple 60 20
42 10c. pink . . . . 5·50 85
75 10c. orange . . . . 1·50 40
112 10c. green 60 20
76 15c. green . . . . 1·30 40
113 15c. purple 60 20
43 20c. orange . . . . £110 15·00
77 20c. brown . . . . 1·50 40
114 20c. green 60 20
44 25c. blue . . . . 12·00 2·20
78 25c. grey . . . . 1·50 40
115 25c. violet 60 20
45 30c. red . . . . 6·50 4·25
79 30c. mauve . . . . 1·30 40
116 30c. orange . . . . 24·00 65
46 40c. red . . . . 9·50 5·25
80 40c. pink . . . . 1·20 40
117 40c. brown 60 20
47 45c. yellow . . . . 9·50 5·50
81 50c. purple . . . . 1·90 60
118 50c. grey 60 20
119 60c. red . . . . 1·00 20
48 65c. brown . . . . 9·50 5·50
82 80c. blue . . . . 2·50 1·60
83 90c. brown . . . . 3·00 1·60
49 1l. green . . . . 23·00 7·50
120 1l. blue . . . . 1·00 40
50 2l. violet £375 £130
85 2l. red . . . . 13·50 10·50
121 2l. green . . . . 9·00 3·00
122 5l. blue . . . . 24·00 10·25

1905. Surch **1905 15.**
52 **19** 15c. on 20c. orange . . . . 10·50 2·75

22 **23** **26** Statue of Liberty

1907.
53a **22** 1c. brown . . . . 11·00 1·40
54 **23** 15c. grey . . . . 15·00 1·80

1917. For Combatants. Surch **1917 Pro combattenti** and value.
55 **18** 25c. on 2c. lilac . . . . . . 7·00 2·00
56 **19** 50c. on 2l. violet . . . . . 39·00 20·00

1918. Surch **Cent. 20 1918.**
57 **23** 20c. on 15c. grey . . . . . 3·25 1·40

1918. War Casualties Fund. Inscr as in T **26**.
58 **26** 2c.(+5c.) black and lilac . . 1·20 40
59 5c.(+5c.) black and green . . 1·20 40
60 10c.(+5c.) black and red . . 1·20 40
61 20c.(+5c.) black and orange 1·20 40
62 25c.(+5c.) black and blue . . 1·40 40
63 45c.(+5c.) black and brown 1·40 40
64 – 1l.(+5c.) black and green . . 14·00 10·00
65 – 2l.(+5c.) black and lilac . . 15·00 6·75
66 – 3l.(+5c.) black and red . . . 15·00 6·75

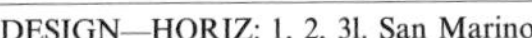
DESIGN—HORIZ: 1, 2, 3l. San Marino.

1918. Italian Victory over Austria and Premium for War Casualties Fund. Optd **3 Novembre 1918.**
67 **26** 20c.(+5c.) black and orange 2·20 1·40
68 25c.(+5c.) black and blue . . 2·20 1·40
69 45c.(+5c.) black and brown 2·20 1·40
70 – 1l.(+5c.) black and green . . 6·00 2·50
71 – 2l.(+5c.) black and lilac . . 13·50 6·75
72 – 3l.(+5c.) black and red . . . 13·50 6·25
DESIGN—HORIZ: 1, 2, 3l. As Nos. 64/66.

1922. Re-issue of T **17**. Colours changed.
86 **17** 2c. purple 25 20
87 5c. green 35 20
88 10c. brown 35 20
89 20c. brown 35 20
90 25c. blue 75 40
91 45c. red . . . . 1·70 80

30 Arbe (Rab) **31** St. Marinus

1923. Delivery to San Marino of Italian Flag flown on Arbe, after the island returned to Yugoslavia.
92 **30** 50c. green 45 30

1923. San Marino Mutual Aid Society.
93 **31** 30c. brown 45 25

32 Mt. Titano **33** "Liberty" **34**

1923. Red Cross Fund.
94 **32** 5c.+5c. green 55 20
95 10c.+5c. orange 75 20
96 15c.+5c. green 55 20
97 25c.+5c. red 75 40
98 40c.+5c. purple . . . . . 7·00 1·20
99 50c.+5c. grey . . . . . . 3·75 20
100 **33** 1l.+5c. blue and black . . 8·25 2·75

1923. San Marino Volunteers in the Great War.
101 **34** 1l. brown . . . . 11·50 6·00

35 Garibaldi **36**

1924. 75th Anniv of Garibaldi's Refuge in San Marino.
102 **35** 30c. purple . . . . 2·20 70
103 50c. brown . . . . 3·75 1·60
104 60c. red . . . . 5·50 2·00
105 **36** 1l. blue . . . . 6·50 3·50
106 2l. green . . . . 8·75 4·00

1924. Red Cross stamps of 1918 surch.
107 **26** 30c. on 45c. black & brown 1·50 60
108 – 60c. on 1l. black and green 3·00 2·75
109 – 1l. on 2l. black and lilac 13·50 8·75
110 – 2l. on 3l. black and red . . 14·50 7·25

1926. Surch.
123 **19** 75c. on 80c. blue . . . . . 1·60 60
124 1l.20 on 90c. brown . . . 1·60 60
125 1l.25 on 90c. brown . . . 3·50 1·60
126 2l.50 on 80c. blue . . . . 8·25 4·00

40 Onofri **44** San Marino War Memorial

1926. Death Centenary of Antonio Onofri, "Father of the Country".
127 **40** 10c. black and blue 30 20
128 20c. black and green . . . 95 50
129 45c. black and violet . . . 55 60
130 65c. black and green . . . 55 60
131 1l. black and orange . . . 4·25 2·40
132 2l. black and mauve . . . 4·25 2·40

1926. No. E92 surch **Lire 1,85**.
133 **19** 1l.85 on 60c. violet 45 40

1927. Surch.
134 **40** "1,25" on 1l. black & orge 5·50 2·00
135 "2,50" on 2l. black & mauve . . . . 8·50 4·00
136 "5" on 2l. black and mauve . . . . 33·00 28·00

1927. Unissued Express stamp (No. 115 surch **ESPRESSO 50**) surch **L. 1,75**.
137 **19** 1l.75 on 50c. on 25c. violet 95 60

1927. War Cenotaph Commemoration.
138 **44** 50c. purple . . . . 1·40 80
139 1l.25 blue . . . . 2·50 1·20
140 10l. violet . . . . 24·00 12·50

45 Franciscan Convent and Capuchin Church

1928. 700th Death Anniv of St. Francis of Assisi.
141 **45** 50c. red . . . . 23·00 1·90
142 1l.25 blue . . . . 9·50 2·50
143 – 2l.50 brown . . . . 9·50 3·00
144 – 5l. violet . . . . 27·00 18·00
DESIGN: 2l.50, 5l. Death of St. Francis.

46 La Rocca Fortress

47 Government Palace

48 Statue of Liberty

1929.
145 **46** 5c. blue and purple . . . . 1·40 40
146 10c. mauve and blue . . . 2·00 40
147 15c. green and orange . . 1·70 40
148 20c. red and blue . . . . 1·70 40
149 25c. black and green . . . 1·70 40
150 30c. red and grey . . . . 1·70 40
151 50c. green and purple . . . 1·70 40
152 75c. grey and red . . . . 1·70 40
153 **47** 1l. green and brown . . . 2·00 40
154 1l.25 black and blue . . . 2·00 40
155 1l.75 orange and green . . 3·25 80
156 2l. red and blue . . . . . 2·50 80
157 2l.50 blue and red . . . . 2·50 80
158 3l. blue and orange . . . . 2·50 80
159 3l.70 purple and green . . 90 1·00
160 **48** 5l. green and violet . . . . 2·75 1·00
161 10l. blue and brown . . . 9·25 4·00
162 15l. purple and green . . . 46·00 48·00
163 20l. red and blue £300 £200

50 Mt. Titano

1931. Air.
164 **50** 50c. green . . . . 6·25 4·00
165 80c. red . . . . 6·25 4·00
166 1l. brown . . . . 2·50 1·20
167 2l. purple . . . . 2·50 1·60
168 2l.60 blue . . . . 20·00 20·00
169 3l. grey . . . . 20·00 20·00
170 5l. green . . . . 2·50 3·25
171 7l.70 brown . . . . 6·50 4·00
172 9l. orange . . . . 6·50 6·00
173 10l. blue £275 £225

51 G.P.O., San Marino

52 San Marino Railway Station

1932. Inauguration of New G.P.O.
174 **51** 20c. green . . . . 8·50 2·40
175 50c. red . . . . 11·50 4·75
176 1l.25 blue . . . . £170 50·00
177 1l.75 brown . . . . 90·00 28·00
178 2l.75 violet . . . . 38·00 13·00

1932. Opening of San Marino Electric Railway, Rimini.
179 **52** 20c. green . . . . 2·00 80
180 50c. red . . . . 2·30 1·20
181 1l.25 blue . . . . 7·25 4·00
182 5l. brown . . . . 48·00 30·00

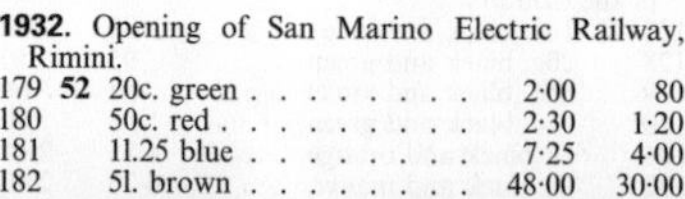

53 Garibaldi

1932. 50th Death Anniv of Garibaldi.
183 **53** 10c. brown . . . . 2·30 60
184 20c. violet . . . . 2·30 60
185 25c. green . . . . 2·30 80
186 50c. brown . . . . 4·50 2·75
187 – 75c. red . . . . 6·25 3·25
188 – 1l.25 blue . . . . 14·50 6·00
189 – 2l.75 orange . . . . 41·00 18·00
190 – 5l. green £225 £200
DESIGN: 75c. to 5l. Garibaldi's arrival at San Marino.

1933. Air. "Graf Zeppelin". Surch **ZEPPELIN 1933** under airship and new value.
191 **50** 3l. on 50c. orange . . . . 1·30 48·00
192 5l. on 80c. green . . . . . 24·00 48·00
193 10l. on 1l. blue . . . . . 24·00 60·00
194 12l. on 2l. brown . . . . . 24·00 90·00
195 15l. on 2l.60 red . . . . . 24·00 95·00
196 20l. on 3l. green . . . . . 24·00 £100

1933. 20th Italian Philatelic Congress. Surch **28 MAGGIO 1933 CONVEGNO FILATELICO** and new value.
197 **51** 25c. on 2l.75 violet . . . . 5·50 4·00
198 50c. on 1l.75 brown . . . 13·50 8·00
199 75c. on 2l.75 violet . . . 23·00 18·00
200 1l.25 on 1l.75 brown . . . £275 £200

1934. Philatelic Exn. Surch **12-27 APRILE 1934 MOSTRA FILATELICA** and value with wheel.
201 **51** 25c. on 1l.25 blue . . . . 2·20 80
202 50c. on 1l.75 brown . . . 2·75 1·20
203 75c. on 50c. red . . . . . 5·00 4·00
204 1l.25 on 20c. green . . . . 24·00 18·00

1934. Surch with value and wheel.
205 **51** 3l.70 on 1l.25 blue . . . . 55·00 40·00
206 3l.70 on 2l.75 violet . . . 65·00 50·00

58 Ascent to Mt. Titano

59 Delfico

1935. 12th Anniv of San Marino Fascist Party.
207 **58** 5c. black and brown . . . 30 20
208 10c. black and violet . . . 30 20
209 20c. black and orange . . . 30 20
210 25c. black and green . . . 30 20
211 50c. black and bistre . . . 40 20
212 75c. black and red . . . . 2·75 1·00
213 1l.25 black and blue . . . 4·25 2·75

1935. Death Centenary of Melchiorre Delfico (historian of San Marino).
214 **59** 5c. black and purple . . . 1·40 25
215 7½c. black and brown . . . 1·30 30
216 10c. black and green . . . 1·50 25
217 15c. black and red . . . . 11·00 1·60
218 20c. black and orange . . . 2·75 60
219 25c. black and green . . . 2·75 60
220 – 30c. black and violet . . . 2·75 50
221 – 50c. black and green . . . 4·25 1·60
222 – 75c. black and red . . . . 7·00 4·00
223 – 1l.25 black and blue . . . 3·50 1·20
224 – 1l.50 black and brown . . 47·00 22·00
225 – 1l.75 black and orange . . 65·00 36·00
DESIGN—25 × 35 mm: 30c. to 1l.75, Statue of Delfico.

1936. Surch. (a) Postage.
226 **40** 80c. on 45c. black & violet 3·50 2·00
227 80c. on 65c. black & green 3·50 2·00
228 **45** 2l.05 on 1l.25 blue . . . . 7·25 3·25
229 – 2l.75 on 2l.50 brown (No. 143) . . . . 16·00 14·50

(b) Air.
230 **50** 75c. on 50c. green . . . . 2·50 2·40
231 75c. on 80c. red . . . . . 8·50 8·00

63 St. Marinus and St. Leo

1937. Independence Monument. Sheet 125 × 105 mm.
MS232 **63** 5l. . . . . 14·50 10·50

64 Abraham Lincoln

1938. Dedication of Bust of Abraham Lincoln. Sheets (each 125 × 105 mm).
MS232a **64** 3l. blue . . . . . . 4·25 2·00
MS232b 5l. red . . . . 25·00 16·00

1941. Surch **10**.
233 **19** 10c. on 15c. purple 15 20
234 10c. on 30c. orange 85 50

1942. Air. Surch **Lire 10** and bars.
235 **50** 10l. on 2l.60 blue . . . . 85·00 75·00
236 10l. on 3l. grey . . . . . 21·00 16·00

67 Gajarda Tower, Arbe, and Flags of Italy and San Marino

1942. Restoration of Italian Flag to Arbe (Rab) annexed by Italy in 1941.
237 **67** 10c. red and bistre (postage) 25 10
238 15c. red and brown 25 10
239 20c. grey and green 25 10
240 25c. blue and green 25 10
241 50c. brown and red 25 10
242 75c. grey and red 25 10
243 – 1l.25 light blue and blue 25 10
244 – 1l.75 grey and brown . . . 25 20
245 – 2l.75 blue and bistre . . . 40 30
246 – 5l. brown and green . . . 2·75 2·00
247 – 25c. grey and brown (air) 25 10
248 – 50c. brown and green . . . 25 10
249 – 75c. brown and blue . . . 25 10
250 – 1l. brown and bistre . . . 60 45
251 – 5l. blue and bistre . . . . 7·50 3·25
DESIGNS—HORIZ: Nos. 243/6, Galleon in Arbe Harbour. VERT: Nos. 247/51, Granda Belfry, Arbe.

1942. Italian Philatelic Congress. Surch **GIORNATA FILATELICA RIMINI - SAN MARINO 3 AGOSTO 1942 (1641 d. F. R.) C. – 30.**
252 **67** 30c. on 10c. red and bistre 10 20

1942. Surch.
253 **67** 30c. on 20c. grey and green 15 25
254 – 20l. on 75c. black and red (No. 222) . . . . 13·50 8·75

71 Printing Press

1943. Press Propaganda.
255 **71** 10c. green 15 15
256 15c. brown 15 15
257 20c. brown 15 15
258 30c. purple 15 15
259 50c. blue 15 15
260 75c. red 15 15
261 **72** 1l.25 blue 15 15
262 1l.75 violet 15 15
263 5l. blue 85 40
264 10l. brown . . . . 5·25 2·50

72 Newspapers

1943. Philatelic Exhibition. Optd **GIORNATA FILATELICA RIMINI - SAN MARINO 5 LUGLIO 1943 (1642 d. F. R.).**
265 **71** 30c. purple 10 15
266 50c. blue 10 15

74 Gateway

75 War Memorial

1943. Fall of Fascism. Unissued series for 20th Anniv of Fascism optd **28 LVGLIO 1943 1642 d. F.R.** (the "d." is omitted on T **74**) and bars cancelling commemorative inscription.
267 **74** 5c. brown (postage) . . . 10 20
268 10c. orange 10 20
269 20c. blue 10 20
270 25c. green 10 20
271 30c. purple 10 20
272 50c. violet 10 20
273 75c. red 10 20
274 **75** 1l.25 blue 10 20
275 1l.75 orange 10 20
276 2l.75 brown 75 30
277 5l. green . . . . 1·30 60
278 10l. violet . . . . 1·70 80
279 20l. blue . . . . 4·00 2·50
280 – 25c. brown (air) 25 20
281 – 50c. purple 25 20
282 – 75c. brown 25 20
283 – 1l. purple 25 20
284 – 2l. blue 25 20
285 – 5l. orange . . . . 1·90 65
286 – 10l. green . . . . 2·10 90
287 – 20l. black . . . . 6·25 3·00
DESIGN—Air: Nos. 280/7, Map of San Marino.

1943. Provisional Govt. Optd **GOVERNO PROVVISORIO** over ornamentation.
288 **74** 5c. brown (postage) . . . 35 20
289 10c. orange 35 20
290 20c. blue 35 20
291 25c. green 35 20
292 30c. purple 35 20
293 50c. violet 35 20
294 75c. red 35 20
295 **75** 1l.25 blue 35 20
296 1l.75 orange 35 20
297 5l. green . . . . 1·30 60
298 20l. blue . . . . 2·10 1·80
299 – 25c. brown (air) 50 20
300 – 50c. red 50 20
301 – 75c. brown 50 20
302 – 1l. purple 50 20
303 – 5l. orange 85 20
304 – 20l. black . . . . 2·75 3·00

78 St. Marinus

79 Mt. Titano

1944.
305 **78** 20l.+10l. brown (postage) 1·70 1·10
306 **79** 20l.+10l. green (air) . . . 1·70 70

80 Govt Palace

81 Govt Palace

1945. 50th Anniv of Government Palace.
307 **80** 25l. purple (postage) . . . 7·25 4·00
308 **81** 25l. brown (air) . . . . . 7·25 3·50
MS308a 180 × 120 mm comprising 10l. blue and15l. green (angels and crowd scene, horiz); 25l. red (Palace, vert). Perf or imperf £110 65·00

82 Arms of Montegiardino

83 Arms of San Marino

1945. Arms Types.
309 – 10c. blue 25 20
310 **82** 20c. red 25 20
311 – 40c. orange 25 20
312 **82** 60c. grey 25 20
313 – 80c. green 25 20
314 – 1l. red 25 20
315 – 1l.20 violet 25 20
316 – 2l. brown 25 20
317 – 3l. blue 25 20
317a – 4l. orange 25 20
318 – 5l. brown 25 20
319 – 10l. red and brown . . . 2·00 1·40
318a – 15l. blue . . . . 2·30 1·40
320 – 20l. red and blue . . . . 4·75 1·60
321 – 20l. brown and blue . . . 9·50 2·00
322 **82** 25l. blue and brown . . . 7·50 2·40
323 **83** 50l. blue and green . . . 16·00 8·00
DESIGNS (Arms of San Marino and villages in the Republic): 10c., 1l., 1l.20, 15l. Faetano; 40c., 5l. San Marino; 80c., 2, 3, 4l. Fiorentino; 10l. Borgomaggiore; 20l. (2) Serravalle.

84 U.N.R.R.A. Aid for San Marino

1946. U.N.R.R.A.
324 **84** 100l. red, purple and orange . . . . 8·00 3·50

85 Airplane and Mt. Titano

1946. Air.
325 – 25c. grey 15 15
326 **85** 75c. red 15 15
327 – 1l. brown 15 15
328 **85** 2l. green 15 15
329 3l. violet 15 15
330 – 5l. blue 15 20
331 – 10l. red 15 20
334 – 20l. purple . . . . 65 1·60
332 – 35l. red . . . . 3·50 3·25
335 – 50l. green . . . . 7·50 5·25
333 – 100l. brown . . . . 1·10 1·20
DESIGNS—HORIZ: 25c., 1, 10l. Wings over Mt. Titano; 100l. Airplane over globe. VERT: 5, 20, 35, 50l. Four aircraft over Mt. Titano.

1946. Stamp Day. Surch **L.10**.
336 **83** 50l.+10l. blue and green . . 14·00 8·25

1946. National Philatelic Convention. Nos. 329/31 but colours changed and without "POSTA AEREA" surch **CONVEGNO FILATELICO 30 NOVEMBRE 1946** and premium.
336a **85** 3l.+25l. brown 55 80
336b – 5l.+25l. orange 55 80
336c – 10l.+50l. blue . . . . . 6·75 6·25

87 Quotation from F.D.R. on Liberty

88 Franklin D. Roosevelt

1947. In Memory of President Franklin D. Roosevelt.
336d **87** 1l. brn & ochre (postage) 10 20
336e **88** 2l. brown and blue . . . 10 20
336f – 5l. multicoloured 10 20
336g – 15l. multicoloured 10 20
336h **87** 50l. brown and red . . . 65 20
336i **88** 100l. brown and violet . . 1·10 80
DESIGN—HORIZ: 5l., 15l. Roosevelt and flags of San Marino and U.S.A.

336j – 1l. brown and blue (air) 10 20
336k – 2l. brown and red 10 20
336l – 5l. multicoloured 10 15
336m – 20l. brown and purple . . 25 20
336n – 31l. brown and orange . . 75 30
336o – 50l. brown and red . . . 1·20 55
336p – 100l. brown and blue . . 3·25 1·00
336q – 200l. multicoloured . . . 26·00 13·50
DESIGNS—HORIZ: 1, 3, 50l. Roosevelt and eagle; 2, 20, 100l. Roosevelt and San Marino arms. VERT: 5, 200l. Roosevelt and flags of San Marino and U.S.A.

1947. Surch in figures.
336r **87** 3 on 1l. brown and ochre (postage) 20 25
336s **88** 4 on 2l. brown and blue 20 25
336t – 6 on 5l. mult (No. 336f) 20 25
336u – 3 on 1l. brown and blue (No. 336j) (air) 20 30
336v – 4 on 2l. brown and red (No. 336k) 20 30
336w – 6 on 5l. mult (No. 336l) 20 30

1947. No. 317a surch.
337 6l. on 4l. orange 10 20
338 21l. on 4l. orange 50 60

91 St. Marinus founding Republic

94 Mt. Titano, Statue of Liberty and 1847 U.S.A. Stamp

95 Mt. Titano and 1847 U.S.A. Stamp

1947. Reconstruction.
339 **91** 1l. mauve & green (postage) 10 20
340 2l. green and mauve . . . 10 20
341 4l. green and brown . . . 10 20
342 10l. blue and orange . . . 10 20
343 25l. mauve and red . . . . 50 1·00
344 50l. brown and green . . . 21·00 10·50
345 25l. blue and orange (air) 1·50 1·60
346 50l. blue and brown . . . 2·10 2·40
Nos. 343/6 are larger (24½ × 32 mm) and have two rows of ornaments forming the frame.

1947. Air. Rimini Philatelic Exhibition. No. 333 optd **Giornata Filatelica Rimini - San Marino 8 Luglio 1947**.
347 100l. brown . . . . 1·10 85

1947. Reconstruction. Surch **+** and value in figures.
348 **91** 1l.+1 mauve and green . . 10 20
349 1l.+2 mauve and green . . 10 20
350 1l.+3 mauve and green . . 10 20
351 1l.+4 mauve and green . . 10 20
352 1l.+5 mauve and green . . 10 20
353 2l.+1 green and mauve . . 10 20
354 2l.+2 green and mauve . . 10 20
355 2l.+3green and mauve . . 10 20
356 2l.+4green and mauve . . 10 20
357 2l.+5 green and mauve . . 10 20
358 4l.+1green and brown . . 2·75 2·10
359 4l.+2 green and brown . . 2·75 2·10

1947. Centenary of First U.S.A. Postage Stamp.
360 **94** 2l. brown & pur (postage) 10 20
361 – 3l. grey, red and blue . . . 10 20
362 **94** 6l. green and blue 10 20
363 – 15l. violet, red and blue . . 30 35
364 – 35l. brown, red and blue . . 1·40 1·10
365 – 50l. green, red and blue . . 1·40 1·10
366 **95** 100l. brown and violet (air) 9·25 7·00

DESIGNS: 3, 35l. U.S.A. stamps, 5c. and 10c. of 1847 and 90c. of 1869 and flags of U.S.A. and San Marino; 15, 50l. Similar but differently arranged.

96 Worker and San Marino Flag

1948. Workers' Issue.
367 **96** 5l. brown 10 20
368 8l. green 10 20
369 30l. red 25 20
370 50l. brown and mauve . . 1·60 1·60
371 100l. blue and violet . . . 49·00 28·00
See also Nos. 506/7.

1948. Surch **L.100** between circular ornaments.
372 **59** 100l. on 15c. black and red 48·00 30·00

1948. Air. Surch **POSTA AEREA 200**.
373 **91** 200l. on 25l. mauve and red (No. 343) . . . . . 32·00 14·00

99 Faetano

100 Mt. Titano

1949.
374 – 1l. blue and black . . . 10 20
375 – 2l. red and purple . . . 10 20
376 **99** 3l. blue and violet . . . 10 20
377 – 4l. violet and black . . . 15 20
378 – 5l. brown and purple . . 15 20
379 **99** 6l. black and blue . . . 50 20
380 **100** 8l. brown and deep brown 30 20
381 – 10l. blue and black . . . 30 20
382 – 12l. violet and red . . . 65 40
383 – 15l. red and violet . . . 3·75 2·10
383a **99** 20l. brown and blue . . . 21·00 1·20
384 – 35l. violet and green . . 9·25 2·40
385 – 50l. brown and red . . . 3·75 2·25
385a – 55l. green and blue . . . 48·00 17·00
386 **100** 100l. green and brown 70·00 40·00
387 – 200l. brown and blue . . 70·00 50·00
DESIGNS—HORIZ: 1, 5, 35l. Guaita Tower and walls; 2, 12, 50l. Serravalle and Mt. Titano; 4, 15, 55l. Franciscan Convent and Capuchin Church. VERT: 10, 200l. Guaita Tower.
For similar stamps see Nos. 491/5, 522a/7a and 794/9.

1949. Stamp Day. Optd **Giornata Filatelica San Marino-Riccione 28-6-1949**.
388 **91** 1l. mauve and green . . . 20 20
389 2l. green and mauve . . . 20 20

104 Garibaldi

105 Garibaldi in San Marino

1949. Centenary of Garibaldi's Retreat from Rome.
(a) Postage. Portraits as T **104**. (i) Size 22 × 28 mm.
390 – 1l. red and black . . . 35 20
391 – 2l. blue and brown . . . 35 20
392 **104** 3l. green and red 35 20
393 – 4l. brown and blue . . . 35 20
(ii) Size 27 × 37 mm.
394 – 5l. brown and mauve . . 35 20
395 – 15l. blue and red 55 80
396 – 20l. red and violet . . . . 1·10 1·40
397 **104** 50l. violet and purple . . 15·00 11·50
(b) Air. (i) Size 28 × 22 mm.
398 **105** 2l. blue and purple . . . 15 20
399 3l. black and green . . . 15 20
400 5l. green and blue . . . 15 20
(ii) Size 37 × 27 mm.
401 **105** 25l. violet and green . . . 3·25 1·90
402 65l. black and green . . . 13·50 5·75
PORTRAITS—VERT: 1, 20l. Francesco Nullo; 2, 5l. Anita Garibaldi; 4, 15l. Ugo Bassi.
See also Nos. 538/44.

106 Mail Coach and Mt. Titano

1949. 75th Anniv of U.P.U.
403 **106** 100l. purple & blue (postage) . . . . 10·50 7·50
404 200l. blue (air) . . . . . 1·20 1·30
405 300l. brown, light brown and purple . . . . . . 23·00 12·50

107 Mt. Titano from Serravalle

108 Second and Guaita Towers

109 Guaita Tower

1950. Air. Views.
406 **107** 2l. green and violet . . . 20 20
407 – 3l. brown and blue . . . 20 25
408 **108** 5l. red and brown (22 × 28 mm) 20 25
409 – 10l. blue and green . . . 1·20 60
410 – 15l. violet and black . . . 1·30 80
411 – 55l. green and blue . . . 20·00 12·00
412 **107** 100l. black and red (37 × 27 mm) . . . . . 15·00 6·75
413 **108** 250l. brown and violet . . 70·00 28·00
414 **109** 500l. brown and green (37 × 27 mm) . . . . . 65·00 55·00
415 500l. purple, green and blue . . . . 90·00 65·00
DESIGNS—As Type **107**: 3l. Distant view of Domagnano; 10l. Domagnano; 15l. San Marino from St. Mustiola. 27 × 37 mm: 55l. Borgo Maggiore.

1950. Air. 28th Milan Fair. As Nos. 408, 410 and 411 but in different colours, optd **XXVIII FIERA INTERNAZIONALE DI MILANO APRILE 1950**.
416 5l. green and blue 15 20
417 15l. black and red 60 55
418 55l. brown and violet . . . . 3·75 2·75

111 Government Palace

1951. Red Cross.
419 **111** 25l. purple, red and brown . . . . 6·25 4·75
420 – 75l. brown, red & lt brown . . . . 8·75 6·00
421 – 100l. black, red and brown . . . . 9·50 7·25
DESIGNS—HORIZ: 75l. Archway of Murata Nuova. VERT: 100l. Guaita Tower.

1951. Air. Stamp Day. No. 415 surch **Giornata Filatelica San Marino - Riccione 20-8-1951 L. 300**.
422 **109** 300l. on 500l. purple, green and blue . . . . 38·00 28·00

113 Flag, Douglas DC-6 Airliner and Mt. Titano

1951. Air.
423 **113** 1000l. blue and brown . . £375 £325

1951. Air. Italian Flood Relief Fund. Surch **Pro-alluvionati italiani 1951 L. 100** and bars.
424 **108** 100l. on 250l. brown and violet . . . . 3·25 3·25

115 "Columbus at the Council of Salamanca" (after Barabino)

1952. 500th Birth Anniv (1951) of Christopher Columbus.
425 **115** 1l. orange & grn (postage) 20 20
426 – 2l. brown and violet . . . 20 20
427 – 3l. violet and brown . . . 20 20
428 – 4l. blue and brown . . . 20 20
429 – 5l. green and turquoise . . 45 20
430 – 10l. brown and black . . 70 40
431 – 15l. red and black 95 60
432 – 20l. blue and green . . . 1·40 1·00
433 – 25l. purple and brown . . 5·75 3·50
434 **115** 60l. brown and violet . . 8·00 6·25
435 – 80l. grey and black . . . 24·00 15·00
436 – 200l. green and blue . . . 49·00 31·00

437 – 200l. blue and black (air) 29·00 19·00
DESIGNS—HORIZ: 2, 25l. Columbus and fleet; 3, 10, 20l. Landing in America; 4, 15, 80l. Red Indians and American settlers; 5, 200l. (No. 436) Columbus and Map of America; 200l. (No. 437) Columbus, Statue of Liberty (New York) and skyscrapers.

1952. Trieste Fair. As Columbus issue of 1952, but colours changed, optd **FIERA DI TRIESTE 1952.**
438 1l. violet and brown (postage) 10 20
439 2l. red and black 10 25
440 3l. green and turquoise . . . 10 25
441 4l. brown and black 10 30
442 5l. mauve and violet 15 40
443 10l. blue and brown 85 75
444 15l. brown and blue . . . . 3·00 2·50

445 200l. brown and black (air) 36·00 26·00

117 Rose

118 Cyclamen, Douglas DC-6 Airliner, Rose, San Marino and Riccione

1952. Air. Stamp Day and Philatelic Exhibition.
446 – 1l. purple and violet . . . 10 20
447 – 2l. green and blue 10 20
448 **117** 3l. red and brown 10 20
449 **118** 5l. brown and purple . . 10 20
450 25l. green and violet . . . 35 80
451 200l. multicoloured . . . 60·00 26·00
DESIGNS—As Type **117**: 1l. Cyclamen; 2l. San Marino and Riccione.

119 Airplane over San Marino

1952. Air. Aerial Survey of San Marino.
452 **119** 25l. green and yellow . . 1·70 1·60
453 – 75l. violet and brown . . 5·25 3·25
DESIGN: 75l. Airplane over Mt. Titano.

120 "The Discus Thrower"

121 Tennis

1953. Sports.
454 **120** 1l. black & brn (postage) 10 20
455 **121** 2l. brown and black . . . 10 20
456 – 3l. blue and black 10 20
457 – 4l. blue and green 10 20
458 – 5l. green and brown . . . 10 20
459 – 10l. red and blue 25 20
460 – 25l. brown and black . . 1·90 1·00
461 – 100l. black and brown . . 6·50 3·50

462 – 200l. turquoise & grn (air) 46·00 34·00
DESIGNS—As Type **120**: 3l. Running. As Type **121**: HORIZ: 4l. Cycling; 5l. Football; 100l. Roller skating; 200l. Skiing. VERT: 10l. Model glider flying; 25l. Shooting.
See also No. 584.

1953. Stamp Day and Philatelic Exn. As No. 461 but colour changed, optd **GIORNATA FILATELICA S. MARINO - RICCIONE 24 AGOSTO 1953.**
463 100l. green and turquoise . . 15·00 11·00

123 Narcissus

1953. Flowers.
464 **123** 1l. blue, green and yellow 10 20
465 – 2l. blue, green and yellow 10 20
466 – 3l. blue, green and yellow 10 20
467 – 4l. blue, green and yellow 10 20
468 – 5l. green and red 10 20
469 – 10l. blue, green and yellow 10 20
470 – 25l. blue, green and pink 1·80 1·60
471 – 80l. blue, green and red 14·00 14·50
472 – 100l. blue, green and pink 22·00 55·00
FLOWERS: 2l. "Parrot" tulip; 3l. Oleander; 4l. Cornflower; 5l. Carnation; 10l. Iris; 25 l; Cyclamen; 80l. Geranium; 100l. Rose.

124 Douglas DC-6 Airliner over Mt. Titano and Arms

1954. Air.
473 **124** 1000l. brown and blue . . 75·00 70·00

125 Walking

126 Statue of Liberty

1954. Sports.
474 **125** 1l. mauve and violet . . . 10 15
475 – 2l. violet and green . . . 10 15
476 – 3l. chestnut and brown . . 10 15
477 – 4l. blue and turquoise . . 10 15
478 – 5l. brown and green . . . 10 15
479 – 8l. lilac and purple . . . 10 20
480 – 12l. red and black 10 20
481 – 25l. green and blue . . . 60 25
482 **125** 80l. green and blue . . . 1·50 45
483 – 200l. brown and lilac . . 7·00 2·40
484 – 250l. multicoloured . . . 39·00 30·00
DESIGNS—HORIZ: 2l. Fencing; 3l. Boxing; 5l. Motor-cycle racing; 8l. Throwing the javelin; 12l. Car racing. VERT: 4, 200, 250l. Gymnastics; 25l. Wrestling.
The 200l. measures 27 × 37 mm and the 250l. 28 × 37½ mm.

1954.
485 **126** 20 l. blue & brn (postage) 20 25
486 60l. green and red 65 45

487 120l. brown and blue (air) 1·10 75

127 Hurdling

1955. Air. 1st Int Exhibition of Olympic Stamps.
488 **127** 80l. black and red 75 60
489 – 120l. red and green . . . 1·20 1·40
DESIGN—HORIZ: 120l. Relay racing.

128 Yacht

129 Ice Skating

1955. 7th International Philatelic Exhibition.
490 **128** 100l. black and blue . . . 2·75 2·40
See also No. 518.

1955. Views as T **99**.
491 5l. brown and blue 10 10
492 10l. green and orange 10 10
493 15l. red and green 10 10
494 25l. violet and brown 25 15
495 35l. red and lilac 20 15
DESIGNS—HORIZ: 5, 25l. Archway of Murata Nuova. VERT: 10, 35l. Guaita Tower; 15l. Government Palace.
See also Nos. 519/21 and 797/9.

1955. Winter Olympic Games, Cortina D'Ampezzo.
496 **129** 1l. brown & yell (postage) 10 10
497 – 2l. blue and red 10 10
498 – 3l. black and brown . . . 10 10
499 – 4l. brown and green . . . 10 10
500 – 5l. blue and red 10 10
501 – 10l. blue and pink 10 15
502 – 25l. black and red 60 50
503 – 50l. brown and blue . . . 1·20 1·00
504 – 100l. black and green . . 4·00 3·00

505 – 200l. black and orange (air) . . . . 19·00 13·00
DESIGNS—HORIZ: 2, 25l. Skiing; 3, 50l. Bobsleighing; 5, 100l. Ice hockey; 200l. Ski jumping. VERT: 4l. Slalom racing; 10l. Figure skating.

1956. Winter Relief Fund. As T **96** but additionally inscr "ASSISTENZA INVERNALE".
506 50l. green . . . . 4·75 5·25

1956. 50th Anniv of "Arengo" (San Marino Parliament). As T **96** but additionally inscr "50° ANNIVERSARIO ARENGO 25 MARZO 1906".
507 50l. blue . . . . 5·75 5·25

130 Pointer

1956. Dogs. 25l. to 100l. have multicoloured centres.
508 **130** 1l. brown and blue . . . 10 20
509 – 2l. grey and red 10 20
510 – 3l. brown and blue . . . 10 20
511 – 4l. grey and blue 10 20
512 – 5l. brown and red 10 20
513 – 10l. brown and blue . . . 10 20
514 – 25l. blue 75 60
515 – 60l. red . . . . 5·75 3·00
516 – 80l. blue . . . . 8·25 3·75
517 – 100l. red . . . . 13·50 8·50
DOGS: 2l. Borzoi; 3l. Sheepdog; 4l. Greyhound; 5l. Boxer; 10l. Great Dane; 25l. Irish setter; 60l. Alsatian; 80l. Rough collie; 100l. Foxhound.

1956. Philatelic Exn. As T **128** but inscr "1956".
518 **128** 100l. brown and green . . 1·10 1·20

1956. International Philatelic Congress. Designs as Nos. 491/5 but larger and new values inscr "CONGRESSO INTERNAZ. PERITI FILATELICI SAN MARINO SALSO-MAGGIORE 6–8 OTTOBRE 1956".
519 20l. brown and blue 55 20
520 80l. red and violet . . . . . 1·50 1·00
521 100l. green and orange . . . 2·10 1·60
SIZES—26½ × 37 mm: 20l. Guaita Tower; 100l. Government Palace. (36½ × 27 mm): 8l. Archway of Murata Nuova.

1956. Air. No. 504 optd with an airplane and **POSTA AEREA.**
522 100l. black and green . . . . 1·40 1·40

1957. Views as T **99**.
522a 1l. green and deep green . . 10 10
523 2l. red and green 10 10
524 3l. brown and blue 10 10
524a 4l. blue and brown 10 15
525 20l. green and deep green . . 10 10
525a 30l. violet and brown . . . 35 25
526 60l. violet and brown . . . 60 80
526a 115l. brown and blue . . . 20 40
527 125l. blue and black 40 25
527a 500l. black and green . . . 65·00 50·00
DESIGNS—VERT: 2l. Borgo Maggiore Church; 3, 30l. Town gate, San Marino; 4, 125l. View of San Marino from southern wall; 20, 115l. Borgo Maggiore market place. HORIZ: 1, 60l. View of San Marino from Hospital Avenue. 37½ × 28 mm: 500l. Panorama of San Marino.
See also Nos. 794/6.

132 Marguerites

134 St. Marinus and Fair Entrance

1957. Flowers. Multicoloured.
528 1l. Type **132** 10 15
529 2l. Polyanthuses 10 15
530 3l. Lilies 10 15
531 4l. Orchid 10 15
532 5l. Lilies of the valley 10 15
533 10l. Poppies 10 15
534 25l. Pansies 10 15
535 60l. Gladiolus 30 45
536 80l. Wild roses 65 65
537 100l. Anemones . . . . . . 1·10 1·10

1957. 150th Birth Anniv of Garibaldi. As T **104** but inscr "COMMEMORAZIONE 150° NASCITA G. GARIBALDI 1807 1957. (a) Size 22 × 28 mm.
538 – 2l. blue and violet (as No. 391) 15 15
539 – 3l. green and red (as No. 390) 15 15
540 **104** 5l. drab and brown . . . 15 15

(b) Size 26½ × 37 mm.
541 – 15l. violet and blue (as No. 395) 15 20
542 – 25l. black and green (as No. 396) 15 25
543 – 50l. brown and violet (as No. 394) . . . . 95 1·20
544 **104** 100l. violet and brown . . 95 1·20

1958. 36th Milan Fair.
545 **134** 15l. yellow & bl (postage) 20 10
546 – 60l. green and red 30 35

547 – 125l. blue and brown (air) 2·40 2·50
DESIGNS—HORIZ: 60l. Italian pavilion and giant arch. VERT: 125l. Bristol 173 Rotocoach helicopter and airplane over fair.

135 Exhibition Emblem, Atomium and Mt. Titano

137 Wheat

136 View of San Marino

1958. Brussels International Exhibition.
548 **135** 40l. sepia and green . . . 10 20
549 60l. lake and blue 25 30

1958. Air.
550 **136** 200l. blue and brown . . 2·75 1·90
551 – 300l. violet and red . . . 2·75 1·90
DESIGN: 300l. Mt. Titano.

1958. Fruit and Agricultural Products.
552 **137** 1l. yellow and blue . . . 10 15
553 – 2l. red and green 10 15
554 – 3l. orange and blue . . . 10 15
555 – 4l. red and green 10 15
556 – 5l. yellow, green and blue 10 15
557 **137** 15l. yellow, brown & blue 10 15
558 – 25l. multicoloured 10 15
559 – 40l. multicoloured 40 25
560 – 80l. multicoloured 55 50
561 – 125l. multicoloured . . . 2·75 2·10
DESIGNS: 2, 125l. Maize; 3, 80l. Grapes; 4, 25l. Peaches; 5, 40l. Plums.

138 Naples 10 grana stamp of 1858 and Bay of Naples

1958. Centenary of First Naples Postage Stamps.
562 **138** 25l. brown & blue (postage) 25 20
563 125l. brown and bistre (air) . . . . 1·80 1·40
The Naples stamp on No. 563 is the 50gr.

139 Mediterranean Gull

140 P. de Coubertin (founder)

1959. Air. Native Birds.
564 **139** 5l. black and green . . . 20 15
565 – 10l. brown, black and blue 20 15
566 – 15l. multicoloured 20 15
567 – 120l. multicoloured . . . 85 40
568 – 250l. black, yellow & green . . . . 1·90 1·60
BIRDS: 10l. Common kestrel; 15l. Mallard; 120l. Feral rock dove; 250l. Barn swallow.

1959. Pre-Olympic Games Issue.
569 **140** 2l. black & brn (postage) 10 15
570 – 3l. sepia and mauve . . . 10 15
571 – 5l. green and blue . . . 10 15
572 – 30l. black and violet . . . 10 10
573 – 60l. sepia and green . . . 10 15
574 – 80l. green and lake . . . 10 15
575 – 120l. brown (air) . . . . 2·40 1·60
PORTRAITS—As Type **140**: 3l. A. Bonacossa; 5l. A. Brundage; 30l. C. Montu; 60l. J. S. Edstrom; 80l. De Baillet-Latour. HORIZ: (36 × 21½ mm): 120l. De Coubertin and Olympic Flame. All, except the founder, De Coubertin are executives of the Olympic Games Committee.

141 Vickers Viscount 700 Airliner over Mt. Titano

1959. Air. Alitalia Inaugural Flight, Rimini–London.
576 **141** 120l. violet . . . . 1·10 1·20

142 Abraham Lincoln and Scroll

1959. Abraham Lincoln's 150th Birth Anniv. Inscr "ABRAMO LINCOLN 1809–1959".
577 **142** 5l. brn & sepia (postage) 10 15
578 – 10l. green and blue . . . 10 15
579 – 15k. grey and green . . . 10 15
580 – 70k. violet 20 25
581 – 200l. blue (air) . . . . 3·25 1·90
DESIGNS—Portraits of Lincoln with: HORIZ: 10l. Map of San Marino; 15l. Govt Palace, San Marino; 200l. Mt. Titano. VERT: 70l. Mt. Titano.

143 1859 Romagna ½b. stamp and Arch of Augustus, Rimini

1959. Romagna Stamp Centenary. Inscr "1859–1959".
582 **143** 30l. brown & sepia (postage) 15 20
583 – 120l. green and black (air) 1·10 1·20
DESIGN: 120 l. 1989 Romagna 3l. stamp and view of Bologna.

1959. World University Games, Turin. Inscr "UNIVERSITY TORINO 1959".
584 **120** 30l. red 30 45

144 Portal of Messina Cathedral and ½gr. Sicily stamp

146 Putting the Shot

145 Golden Oriole

1959. Centenary of First Sicilian Postage Stamp.
585 **144** 1l. brown & yell (postage) 10 10
586 – 2l. red and green 10 10
587 – 3l. slate and blue 10 10
588 – 4l. brown and red 10 10
589 – 5l. purple and blue . . . 10 10
590 – 25l. multicoloured 10 15
591 – 60l. multicoloured 10 20
592 – 200l. multicoloured (air) 1·10 90
DESIGNS—VERT: 2l. Selinunte Temple (1gr.); 3l. Erice Church (2gr.); 4l. "Concordia" Temple, Agrigento (5gr.); 5l. "Castor and Pollux" Temple, Agrigento (10gr.); 25l. "St. John of the Hermits" Church, Palermo (20gr.). HORIZ: 60l. Taormina (50gr.); 200l. Bay of Palermo (50gr.).

1960. Birds.
593 **145** 1l. yellow, olive and blue 10 15
594 – 2l. brown, red and green 10 15
595 – 3l. red, brown and green 10 15
596 – 4l. black, brown and green 10 20
597 – 5l. red, brown and green 10 15
598 – 10l. multicoloured 10 20
599 – 25l. multicoloured 35 20
600 – 60l. multicoloured . . . . 95 1·00
601 – 80l. multicoloured . . . . 2·75 2·10
602 – 110l. multicoloured . . . 3·00 3·00
DESIGNS—VERT: 2l. Nightingale; 4l. Hoopoe; 10l. Eurasian goldfinch; 25l. River kingfisher; 80l. Green woodpecker; 110l. Red-breasted flycatcher. HORIZ: 3l. Eurasian woodcock; 5l. Red-legged partridge; 60l. Common pheasant.

1960. Olympic Games.
603 **146** 1l. violet and red (postage) 10 10
604 – 2l. orange and black . . . 10 10
605 – 3l. violet and brown . . . 10 10
606 – 4l. brown and red 10 10
607 – 5l. blue and brown . . . 10 10
608 – 10l. blue and brown . . . 10 10
609 – 15l. violet and green . . . 10 15
610 – 25l. orange and green . . . 10 15
611 – 60l. brown and green . . 10 15
612 – 110l. red, black and green 10 20
613 – 20l. violet (air) 10 15
614 – 40l. red and brown . . . 10 15
615 – 80l. yellow and blue . . . 10 15
616 – 125l. brown and red . . . 25 25
MS616a 90 × 125 mm. 1, 2, 3, 60l. brown, green and light green 2·10 1·60
MS616b 90 × 127 mm. 4, 10, 20, 40l. brown, red and light red . . . 2·10 1·60
MS616c 145 × 100 mm. 5, 15, 25, 80, 110, 125l. brown, deep brown and light green . . . . 3·25 3·50
DESIGNS—VERT: 2l. Gymnastics; 3l. Long-distance walking; 4l. Boxing; 10l. Cycling; 20l. Handball; 40l. Breasting the tape; 60l. Football. HORIZ: 5l. Fencing; 15l. Hockey; 25l. Rowing; 80l. Diving; 110l. Horse-jumping; 125l. Rifle shooting.

147 Melvin Jones (founder) and Lions International H.Q.

1960. Lions International Commemoration.
617 – 30l. brown and violet (postage) 10 20
618 **147** 45l. brown and violet . . 35 20
619 – 60l. red and blue 10 20
620 – 115l. green and black . . 40 40
621 – 150l. brown and violet . . 1·40 2·10
622 – 200l. blue and green (air) 4·00 5·50
DESIGNS—VERT: 30l. Mt. Titano; 60l. San Marino Government Palace. HORIZ: 115l. Pres. Clarence Sturm; 150l. Vice-Pres. Finis E. Davis; 200l. Globe. All designs except Type **147** bear the Lions emblem.

148 Riccione

1960. 12th Riccione–San Marino Stamp Day. Centres multicoloured.
623 **148** 30l. red (postage) 15 20
624 125l. blue (air) 85 80

149 "Youth with Basket of Fruit"

1960. 350th Death Anniv of Caravaggio (painter).
625 **149** 200l. multicoloured . . . 4·75 5·00

150 Hunting Roe Deer

1961. Hunting (1st issue). Historical Scenes.
626 **150** 1l. blue and mauve . . . 10 10
627 – 2l. red and brown 10 10
628 – 3l. black and red 10 10
629 – 4l. red and blue 10 10
630 – 5l. brown and green . . . 10 10
631 – 10l. violet and orange . . 10 10
632 – 30l. blue and yellow . . . 10 10
633 – 60l. brown, orange & black 10 15
634 – 70l. red, purple and green 10 15
635 – 115l. blue, purple & black 30 25
DESIGNS—VERT: 2l. 16th-cent falconer; 10l. 16th-cent falconer (mounted); 60l. 17th-century hunter with rifle and dog. HORIZ: 3l. 16th-cent wild boar hunt; 4l. Duck-shooting with crossbow (16th-cent); 5l. 16th-cent stag hunt with bow and arrow; 30l. 17th-cent huntsman with horn and dogs; 70l. 18th-cent hunter and beater; 115l. Duck-shooting with bow and arrow (18th-cent).
See also Nos. 679/88.

151 Bell 47J Ranger Helicopter near Mt. Titano

1961. Air.
636 **151** 1000l. red . . . . 30·00 29·00

152 Guaita Tower, Mt. Titano and 1858 Sardinian Stamp

1961. Centenary of Italian Independence Philatelic Exhibition, Turin.
637 **152** 30l. multicoloured 35 35
638 70l. multicoloured 50 40
639 200l. multicoloured . . . 40 55

153 Mt. Titano

1961. Europe.
640 **153** 500l. green and brown . . 28·00 9·00

155 King Enzo's Palace, Bologna

1961. Bologna Stamp Exn. Inscr "BOLOGNA".
641 **155** 30l. black and blue . . . 10 10
642 – 70l. black and myrtle . . 10 15
643 – 100l. black and brown . . 10 20
DESIGNS: 70l. Gateway of Merchant's Palace; 100l. Towers of Garisenda and Asinelli, Bologna.

156 Duryea, 1892

1962. Veteran Motor Cars.
644 **156** 1l. blue and brown . . . 10 15
645 – 2l. orange and blue . . . 10 15
646 – 3l. orange and black . . . 10 15
647 – 4l. red and black 10 15
648 – 5l. orange and violet . . . 10 15
649 – 10l. orange and black . . 10 15
650 – 15l. red and black 10 15
651 – 20l. blue and black . . . 10 20
652 – 25l. orange and black . . 10 20
653 – 30l. buff and black . . . 10 20
654 – 50l. mauve and black . . 10 20
655 – 70l. green and black . . . 15 20
656 – 100l. red, yellow and black 15 35
657 – 115l. green, orange & black 20 40
658 – 150l. yellow, orange & black 45 60
MOTOR CARS—HORIZ: 2l. Panhard and Levassor, 1895; 3l. Peugeot "Vis-a-vis", 1895; 4l. Daimler, 1899; 10l. Decauville, 1900; 15l. Wolseley, 1901; 20l. Benz, 1902; 25l. Napier, 1903; 50l. Oldsmobile, 1904; 100l. Isotta Fraschini, 1908; 115l. Bianchi, 1910; 150l. Alfa, 1910. VERT: 5l. F.I.A.T., 1899; 30l. White, 1903; 70l. Renault, 1904.

157 Wright Type A Biplane

1962. Vintage Aircraft.
659 **157** 1l. black and yellow . . . 10 15
660 – 2l. brown and green . . . 10 15
661 – 3l. brown and green . . . 10 15
662 – 4l. black and bistre . . . 10 15
663 – 5l. red and blue 10 15
664 – 10l. brown and green . . 10 15
665 – 30l. bistre and blue . . . 10 20
666 – 60l. bistre and violet . . . 10 25
667 – 70l. black and orange . . 20 30
668 – 115l. bistre, black & green 50 60
DESIGNS: 2l. Archdeacon-Voisin "Boxkite" float glider; 3l. Albert and Emile Bonnet-Labranche biplane; 4l. Glenn Curtiss "June Bug"; 5l. Henri Farman H.F.III biplane; 10l. Bleriot XI, 30l. Hubert Latham's Antoinette IV; 60l. Alberto Santos-Dumont's biplane "14 bis"; 70l. Alliott Verdon Roe's Triplane II; 115l. Faccioli's airplane.

158 Roping Down

1962. Mountaineering.
669 **158** 1l. bistre and black . . . 10 15
670 – 2l. turquoise and black . . 10 15
671 – 3l. purple and black . . . 10 15
672 – 4l. blue and black 10 15
673 – 5l. orange and black . . . 10 15
674 – 15l. yellow and black . . 10 15
675 – 30l. red and black 10 15
676 – 40l. blue and black . . . 10 15
677 – 85l. green and black . . . 10 20
678 – 115l. blue and black . . . 20 40
DESIGNS: 2l. Sassolungo; 3l. Mt. Titano; 4l. Three Lavaredo peaks; 5l. The Matterhorn; 15l. Skier; 30l. Climber negotiating overhang; 40l. Step-cutting in ice; 85l. Aiguille du Geant; 115l. Citadel on Mt. Titano.

159 Hunter and Retriever

1962. Hunting (2nd issue). Modern scenes.
679 **159** 1l. deep purple and green 10 15
680 – 2l. blue and orange . . . 10 15
681 – 3l. black and blue 10 15
682 – 4l. sepia and brown . . . 10 15
683 – 5l. brown and green . . . 10 15
684 – 15l. black and green . . . 10 15
685 – 50l. sepia and green . . . 10 20
686 – 70l. turquoise and red . . 10 20
687 – 100l. black and red . . . 20 20
688 – 150l. green and lilac . . . 20 35

DESIGNS—HORIZ: 3l. Marsh ducks (with decoys); 4l. Roe deer; 5l. Grey partridge; 15l. Northern lapwing; 50l. Partridge; 70l. Marsh geese; 100l. Wild boar. VERT: 2l. Huntsman and hounds; 150l. Hunter shooting pheasant.

160 Arrows encircling "Europa"

1962. Europa.
689 **160** 200l. red and black . . . 75 80

161 Egyptian Merchant Ship, 2000 B.C.

1963. Historical Ships.
690 **161** 1l. blue and orange . . . 10 15
691 – 2l. sepia and purple . . . 10 15
692 – 3l. sepia and mauve . . . 10 15
693 – 4l. dull purple and grey 10 15
694 – 5l. sepia and yellow . . . 10 15
695 – 10l. brown and green . . 10 15
696 – 30l. sepia and blue . . . 45 35
697 – 60l. blue and green . . . 50 35
698 – 70l. red and deep grey . . 40 35
699 – 115l. brown and blue . . 1·10 1·20
DESIGNS—HORIZ: 2l. Greek trier, 5th-cent, B.C.; 3l. Roman trireme, 1st-cent, B.C.; 4l. Viking longship, 10th-cent; 5l. The "Santa Maria"; 30l. Gallery, c. 1600; 115l. "Duncan Dunbar" (full-rigged merchantman), 1550. VERT: 10l. Carrack, c. 1550; 60l. "Sovereign of the Seas" (English galleon), 1637; 70l. "Fyn" (Danish ship of the line), c. 1750.

162 "The Fornarina" (or "The Veiled Woman")
163 Saracen Game, Arezzo

1963. Paintings by Raphael. Multicoloured.
700 30l. Type **162** 10 20
701 70l. Self portrait 10 15
702 100l. Sistine Madonna (detail of woman praying) 10 20
703 200l. "Portrait of a Young Woman" (Maddalena Strozzi) 10 25
The 200l. is larger, 27 × 44 mm.

1963. Ancient Tournaments.
704 **163** 1l. mauve 10 15
705 – 2l. black 10 15
706 – 3l. black 10 15
707 – 4l. violet 10 15
708 – 5l. violet 10 15
709 – 10l. green 10 15
710 – 30l. red 10 15
711 – 60l. blue 10 15
712 – 70l. brown 10 20
713 – 115l. black 15 25
TOURNAMENTS—HORIZ: 2l. 14th-century, French cavaliers; 4l. 15th-century, Presenting arms to an English cavalier; 30l. Quintana game, Foligno; 70l. 15th-century, Cavaliers (from castle mural, Malpaga). VERT: 3l. Crossbow Champion-ships, Gubbio; 5l. 16th-century, Cavaliers, Florence; 10l. Quintana game, Ascoli Piceno; 60l. Palio (horse-race), Siena; 115l. 13th-century, The Crusades: cavaliers' challenge.

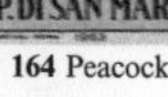

164 Peacock
165 Corner of Government Palace, San Marino

1963. Butterflies. Multicoloured.
714 25l. Type **164** 15 15
715 30l. "Nessaea obrinus" . . . 15 15
716 60l. Large tortoiseshell . . . 15 15
717 70l. Peacock (horiz) 15 30
718 115l. "Papilio blumei" (horiz) . . . 25 35

1963. San Marino–Riccione Stamp Fair.
719 **165** 100l. black and blue . . . 15 15
720 – 100l. blue and sepia . . . 15 15
DESIGN: No. 720, Fountain, Riccione.

166 Pole Vaulting

1963. Olympic Games, Tokyo (1964) (1st issue).
721 – 1l. purple and orange . . 10 10
722 **166** 2l. sepia and green . . . 10 10
723 – 3l. sepia and blue 10 10
724 – 4l. sepia and blue 10 10
725 – 5l. sepia and red 10 10
726 – 10l. mauve and purple . . 10 10
727 – 30l. purple and grey . . . 10 10
728 – 60l. sepia and yellow . . 10 10
729 – 70l. sepia and blue . . . 10 10
730 – 115l. sepia and green . . 10 10
SPORTS—HORIZ: 1l. Hurdling; 3l. Relay-racing; 4l. High jumping (men); 5l. Football; 10l. High jumping (women); 60l. Throwing the javelin; 70l. Water polo; 115l. Throwing the hammer. VERT: 30l. Throwing the discus.
See also Nos. 743/52.

167 "E" and Flag of San Marino

1963. Europa.
731 **167** 200l. blue and brown . . 45 30

168 Tupolev Tu-104A Jetliner

1963. Air. Contemporary Aircraft.
732 **168** 5l. purple, brown and blue 10 10
733 – 10l. blue and red 10 15
734 – 15l. red, mauve and violet 10 10
735 – 25l. red, mauve and violet 10 10
736 – 50l. red and blue 10 10
737 – 75l. orange and green . . 10 10
738 – 120l. red and blue 10 20
739 – 200l. black and yellow . . 10 10
740 – 300l. black and orange . . 10 25
741 – 500l. multicoloured . . . 3·00 3·00
742 – 1000l. multicoloured . . . 1·50 1·50
DESIGNS—HORIZ: 15l. Douglas DC-8 jetliner; 25, 1000l. Boeing 707 jetliner (different views); 50l. Vickers Viscount 837 airliner; 120l. Vickers VC-10; 200l. Hawker Siddley Comet 4C jetliner; 300l. Boeing 727-100 jetliner. VERT: 10l. Boeing 707 jetliner; 75l. Sud Aviation Caravelle jetliner; 500l. Rolls Royce Dart 527 turboprop engine.

169 Running

1964. Olympic Games, Tokyo (2nd issue).
743 **169** 1l. brown and green . . . 15 10
744 – 2l. brown and sepia . . . 15 10
745 – 3l. brown and black . . . 15 10
746 – 4l. blue and red 15 10
747 – 5l. brown and blue . . . 15 10
748 – 15l. purple and orange . . 15 10
749 – 30l. blue and light blue 15 10
750 – 70l. brown and green . . 15 10
751 – 120l. brown and blue . . 15 10
752 – 150l. purple and red . . 15 20
DESIGNS—VERT: 2l. Gymnastics; 3l. Basketball; 120l. Cycling; 150l. Fencing. HORIZ: 4l. Pistol-shooting; 5l. Rowing; 15l. Long jumping; 30l. Diving; 70l. Sprinting.

1964. "Towards Tokyo" Sports Stamp Exn, Rimini. As Nos. 749/50, but inscr "VERSO TOKIO" and colours changed.
753 30l. blue and violet 10 10
754 70l. brown and turquoise . . 10 10

170 Murray Blenkinsop Rack Locomotive (1812)

1964. "Story of the Locomotive".
755 **170** 1l. black and buff 10 10
756 – 2l. black and green . . . 10 10
757 – 3l. black and violet . . . 10 10
758 – 4l. black and yellow . . . 10 10
759 – 5l. black and salmon . . 10 10
760 – 15l. black and green . . . 15 10
761 – 20l. black and pink . . . 15 15
762 – 50l. black and blue . . . 30 15
763 – 90l. black and orange . . 35 15
764 – 110l. black and blue . . . 35 35
LOCOMOTIVES: 2l. "Puffing Billy" (1813–14); 3l. "Locomotion" (1825); 4l. "Rocket" (1829); 5l. "Lion" (1838); 15l. "Bayard" (1839); 20l. Crampton type No. 125, France (1849); 50l. "Little England" (1851); 90l. "Spitfire", Canada (1855); 110l. Rogers, U.S.A. (c. 1865).

171 Baseball Players

1964. 7th European Baseball Championships, Milan.
765 **171** 30l. sepia and green . . . 10 15
766 – 70l. black and red 10 25
DESIGN: 70l. Player pitching ball.

172 "E" and Part of Globe

1964. Europa.
767 **172** 200l. red, blue & light blue 25 45

173 Pres. Kennedy giving Inaugural Address

1964. 1st Death Anniv of John F. Kennedy (President of U.S.A.). Multicoloured.
768 70l. Type **173** 10 10
769 130l. Pres. Kennedy and U.S. flag (vert) 10 30

174 Cyclists at Government Palace
176 Rooks on Chessboard

175 Brontosaurus

1965. Cycle Tour of Italy.
770 **174** 30l. sepia 10 10
771 – 70l. purple 10 10
772 – 200l. red 10 20
DESIGNS—Cyclists passing: 70l. "The Rock"; 200l. Mt. Titano.

1965. Prehistoric Animals.
773 **175** 1l. purple and green . . . 10 15
774 – 2l. black and blue . . . 10 15
775 – 3l. yellow and green . . . 10 15
776 – 4l. brown and blue . . . 10 15
777 – 5l. purple and green . . . 10 15
778 – 10l. purple and green . . 10 15
779 – 75l. blue and turquoise . . 25 15
780 – 100l. purple and green . . 40 25
781 – 200l. purple and green . . 70 40
ANIMALS—VERT: 2l. Brachyosaurus. HORIZ: 3l. Pteranodon; 4l. Elasmosaurus; 5l. Tyrannosaurus; 10l. Stegosaurus; 75l. Thamatosaurus Victor; 100l. Iguanodon; 200l. Triceratops.

1965. Europa.
782 **176** 200l. multicoloured . . . 45 35

177 Dante

1965. 700th Anniv of Dante's Birth.
783 **177** 40l. sepia and blue . . . 10 15
784 – 90l. sepia and red 10 15
785 – 130l. sepia and brown . . 10 15
786 – 140l. sepia and blue . . . 10 25
DESIGNS: 90l. "Hell"; 130l. "Purgatory"; 140l. "Paradise".

178 Mt. Titano and Flags

1965. Visit of Pres. Saragat of Italy.
787 **178** 115l. multicoloured . . . 15 25

179 Trotting

1966. Equestrian Sports. Multicoloured.
788 10l. Type **179** 15 15
789 20l. Cross-country racing (vert) 15 15
790 40l. Horse-jumping 15 15
791 70l. Horse-racing 15 15
792 90l. Steeple-chasing 15 20
793 170l. Polo (vert) 15 20

1966. New values in previous designs.
794 5l. brown and blue (as No. 522a) 15 10
795 10l. green and black (as No. 524) 15 10
796 15l. violet and brown (as No. 524a) 15 10
797 40l. red and lilac (as No. 491) 15 10
798 90l. blue and black (as No. 492) 15 10
799 140l. orange and violet (as No. 493) 15 10

180 "La Bella"

1966. Paintings by Titian. Multicoloured.
800 40l. Type **180** 10 15
801 90l. "The Three Graces" . . 10 15
802 100l. "The Three Graces" . . 10 20
803 170l. "Sacred and Profane Love" 10 25
The 90 and 100l. show different details from the picture.

181 Stone Bass

1966. Sea Animals. Multicoloured.

804	1l. Type **181**	15	15
805	2l. Cuckoo wrasse	15	15
806	3l. Common dolphin	15	15
807	4l. John Dory	15	15
808	5l. Octopus (vert)	15	15
809	10l. Red scorpionfish	15	15
810	40l. Eyed electric ray (vert)	15	15
811	90l. Medusa (vert)	15	15
812	115l. Long-snouted seahorse (vert)	15	20
813	130l. Dentex seabream	15	25

182 Our Lady of Europe

183 Peony

1966. Europa.

814 **182**	200l. multicoloured	30	25

1967. Flowers. Multicoloured.

815	5l. Type **183**	10	15
816	10l. Campanula	10	15
817	15l. Pyrenean poppy	10	15
818	20l. Purple deadnettle	10	15
819	40l. Hemerocallis	10	15
820	140l. Gentian	10	15
821	170l. Thistle	10	20

Each flower has a different background view of Mt. Titano.

184 St. Marinus

185 Map of Europe

1967. Paintings by Francesco Barbieri (Guercino). Multicoloured.

822	40l. Type **184**	10	20
823	170l. "St. Francis"	15	20
824	190l. "Return of the Prodigal Son" (45 × 37 mm)	15	20

1967. Europa.

825 **185**	200l. green and orange	40	30

186 Caesar's Mushroom

1967. Fungi. Multicoloured.

826	5l. Type **186**	15	10
827	15l. The Miller	15	10
828	20l. Parasol mushroom	15	10
829	40l. Cep	15	10
830	50l. "Russula paludosa"	15	10
831	170l. St. George's mushroom	15	20

187 Salisbury Cathedral

1967. Gothic Cathedrals.

832 –	20l. violet on cream	15	15
833 –	40l. green on cream	15	10
834 –	80l. blue on cream	15	10
835 **187**	90l. sepia on cream	15	10
836 –	170l. red on cream	15	15

DESIGNS: 20l. Amiens; 40l. Siena; 80l. Toledo; 170l. Cologne.

188 Cimabue Crucifix, Florence

1967. Christmas.

837 **188**	300l. brown and violet	30	40

189 Arms of San Marino

190 Europa "Key"

1968. Arms of San Marino Villages. Mult.

838	2l. Type **189**	10	15
839	3l. Penna Rossa	10	15
840	5l. Fiorentino	10	15
841	10l. Montecerreto	10	15
842	25l. Serravalle	10	15
843	35l. Montegiardino	10	15
844	50l. Faetano	10	15
845	90l. Borgo Maggiore	10	15
846	180l. Montelupo	10	20
847	500l. State crest	20	30

1968. Europa.

848 **190**	250l. brown	40	35

191 "The Battle of San Romano" (detail, P. Uccello)

1968. 671st Birth Anniv of Paolo Uccello (painter).

849 **191**	50l. black on lilac	10	15
850 –	90l. black on lilac (vert)	10	15
851 –	130l. black on lilac	10	20
852 –	230l. black on pink	10	30

All stamps show details of "The Battle of San Romano".

192 "The Nativity" (detail, Botticelli)

1968. Christmas.

853 **192**	50l. blue	10	15
854	90l. red	10	15
855	180l. sepia	10	25

193 "Peace"

1969. "The Good Government" (frescoes) by Ambrogio Lorenzetti.

856 **193**	50l. blue	10	10
857 –	80l. sepia	10	10
858 –	90l. violet	10	10
859 –	180l. red	10	15

DESIGNS—VERT: 80l. "Justice"; 90l. "Temperance". HORIZ: 180l. View of Siena.

194 "Young Soldier" (Bramante)

1969. 525th Birth Anniv of Donato Bramante (architect and painter). Multicoloured.

860	50l. Type **194**	10	15
861	90l. "Old Soldier" (Bramante)	10	10

195 Colonnade

1969. Europa.

862 **195**	50l. green	25	15
863	180l. purple	25	15

196 Benched Carriage ("Char-a-banc")

1969. Horses and Carriages. Multicoloured.

864	5l. Type **196**	10	15
865	10l. Barouche	10	15
866	25l. Private drag	10	15
867	40l. Hansom cab	10	15
868	50l. Curricle	10	15
869	90l. Wagonette	10	15
870	180l. Spider phaeton	10	20

197 Mt. Titano

1969. Paintings by R. Viola. Multicoloured.

871	20l. Type **197**	15	15
872	180l. "Pier at Rimini"	15	25
873	200l. "Pier at Riccione" (horiz)	15	25

198 "Faith"

1969. Christmas. "The Theological Virtues" by Raphael.

874 **198**	20l. violet and orange	10	15
875 –	180l. violet and green	10	25
876 –	200l. violet and buff	10	25

DESIGNS: 180l. "Hope"; 200l. "Charity".

199 "Aries"

1970. Signs of the Zodiac. Multicoloured.

877	1l. Type **199**	10	15
878	2l. "Taurus"	10	15
879	3l. "Gemini"	10	15
880	4l. "Cancer"	10	15
881	5l. "Leo"	10	15
882	10l. "Virgo"	10	15
883	15l. "Libra"	10	15
884	20l. "Scorpio"	10	15
885	70l. "Sagittarius"	10	15
886	90l. "Capricorn"	15	25
887	100l. "Aquarius"	15	25
888	180l. "Pisces"	20	35

200 "Flaming Sun"

1970. Europa.

889 **200**	90l. red and green	15	20
890	180l. red and yellow	30	25

201 "The Fleet in the Bay of Naples" (Pieter Brueghel the Elder)

1970. 10th "Europa" Stamp Exhibition, Naples.

891 **201**	230l. multicoloured	15	25

202 St. Francis' Gate

1970. 65th Anniv of Rotary International and 10th Anniv of San Marino Rotary Club. Multicoloured.

892	180l. Type **202**	10	20
893	220l. "Rocco" Fort, Mt. Titano	25	40

203 "Girl with Mandolin"

204 Black Pete

1970. Death Bicentenary of Giambattista Tiepolo (painter).

894	50l. Type **203**	15	20
895	180l. "Girl with Parrot"	15	25
896	220l. "Rinaldo and Armida Surprised"	20	30

SIZES: 180l. As Type **203**; 220l. 57 × 37 mm.

1970. 4th Death Anniv of Walt Disney (film producer). Cartoon Characters. Multicoloured.

897	1l. Type **204**	15	15
898	2l. Gyro Gearloose	15	15
899	3l. Pluto	15	15
900	4l. Minnie Mouse	15	15
901	5l. Donald Duck	15	15
902	10l. Goofy	15	15
903	15l. Scrooge McDuck	10	20
904	50l. Hewey, Dewey and Louie	35	25
905	90l. Mickey Mouse	60	65
906	220l. Walt Disney and scene from "The Jungle Book" (horiz)	3·75	2·50

205 "Customs House, Venice"

1971. "Save Venice" Campaign. Paintings by Canaletto. Multicoloured.
907 20l. Type **205** 10 15
908 180l. "Grand Canal, Balbi Palace and Rialto Bridge, Venice" 15 35
909 200l. "St. Mark's and Doge's Palace" 20 40

206 Congress Building and San Marino Flag

1971. Italian Philatelic Press Union Congress, San Marino. Multicoloured.
910 20l. Type **206** 10 10
911 90l. Government Palace door and emblems (vert) 10 10
912 180l. Type **206** 10 15

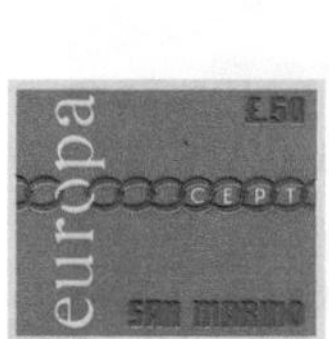

207 Europa Chain **209** Day Lily

208 "Duck" Jug with "Lasa" Decoration

1971. Europa.
913 **207** 50l. blue and yellow . . . 20 15
914 90l. orange and blue . . . 20 20

1971. Etruscan Art (1st series).
915 **208** 50l. black and orange . . 10 15
916 – 80l. black and green . . . 10 15
917 – 90l. black and green . . . 10 20
918 – 180l. black and orange . . 10 20
DESIGNS—VERT: 80l. Head of Hermes (bust); 90l. Man and Wife (relief on sarcophagus). HORIZ: 180l. Chimera (bronze).
See also Nos. 1018/21.

1971. Flowers. Multicoloured.
919 1l. Type **209** 10 10
920 2l. "Phlox paniculata" . . . 10 10
921 3l. Wild pink 10 10
922 4l. Globe flower 10 10
923 5l. "Centaurea dealbata" . . 10 10
924 10l. Peony 10 10
925 15l. Christmas rose 10 10
926 50l. Pasque flower 10 10
927 90l. "Gaillardia aristata" . . 10 10
928 220l. "Aster dumosus" . . . 15 15

210 "Allegory of Spring" (detail, Botticelli) **211** "Communications"

1972. "Allegory of Spring" by Sandro Botticelli. Multicoloured.
929 50l. Type **210** 10 15
930 190l. The Three Graces (27 × 37 mm) 15 25
931 220l. Flora 25 25

1972. Europa.
932 **211** 50l. multicoloured 20 10
933 90l. multicoloured 20 10

212 "Taming the Bear"

1972. "Life of St. Marinus". 16th-century paintings from former Government Palace.
934 **212** 25l. black and buff . . . 10 10
935 – 55l. black and orange . . 10 10
936 – 100l. black and blue . . . 10 10
937 – 130l. black and yellow . . 10 10
DESIGNS: 55l. "The Conversion of Donna Felicissima"; 100l. "Hostile archers turned to stone"; 130l. "Mount Titano given to St. Marinus".

213 House Sparrow **214** "Healthy Man"

1972. Birds. Multicoloured.
938 1l. Type **213** 15 10
939 2l. Firecrest 15 10
940 3l. Blue tit 15 10
941 4l. Ortulan bunting 15 10
942 5l. Bluethroat 15 10
943 10l. Northern bullfinch . . . 15 10
944 25l. Linnet 15 10
945 50l. Black-eared wheatear . . 15 10
946 90l. Sardinian warbler . . . 15 10
947 220l. Western greenfinch . . 15 10

1972. World Heart Month. Multicoloured.
948 50l. Type **214** 15 10
949 90l. "Sick Man" (horiz) . . . 15 10

215 Veterans Emblem **216** Plane over Mt. Titano

1972. "Veterans of Philately" Award of Italian Philatelic Federation.
950 **215** 25l. gold and blue 10 20

1972. Air.
951 **216** 1000l. multicoloured . . . 1·00 1·00

217 Five-Cent Coin of 1864

1972. San Marino Coinage.
952 **217** 5l. bronze, black and grey 45 10
953 – 10l. bronze, black & orge 45 10
954 – 15l. silver, black and red 45 10
955 – 20l. silver, black and purple 45 10
956 – 25l. silver, black and blue 45 15
957 – 50l. silver, black and blue 10 10
958 – 55l. silver, black and ochre 15 10
959 – 220l. gold, black and green 20 10
COINS (obverse and reverse on each stamp): 10l. 10c. of 1935; 15l. 1l. of 1906; 20l. 5l. of 1898; 25l. 5l. of 1937; 50l. 10l. of 1932; 55l. 20l. of 1938; 220l. 20l. of 1925.

218 New York, 1673

1973. "Interpex" Stamp Exhibition and Important Cities of the World (1st series). New York.
960 **218** 200l. brown, grey & black 25 20
961 – 300l. blue, lilac & deep lilac 35 30
DESIGN: 300l. New York, 1973.
See also Nos. 1032/3, 1075/6, 1144/5, 1160/1, 1197/8, 1215/16, 1230/1, 1259/60, 1271/2, 1306/7, 1331/2, 1358/9 and 1524/5.

219 Printing Press **220** "Sportsmen"

1973. Tourist Press Congress.
962 **219** 50l. multicoloured 10 20

1973. Youth Games.
963 **220** 100l. multicoloured . . . 15 20

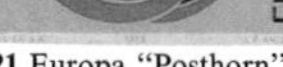
221 Europa "Posthorn" **222** Grapes

1973. Europa.
964 **221** 20l. green, blue and flesh 35 20
965 180l. mauve, red and blue 35 40

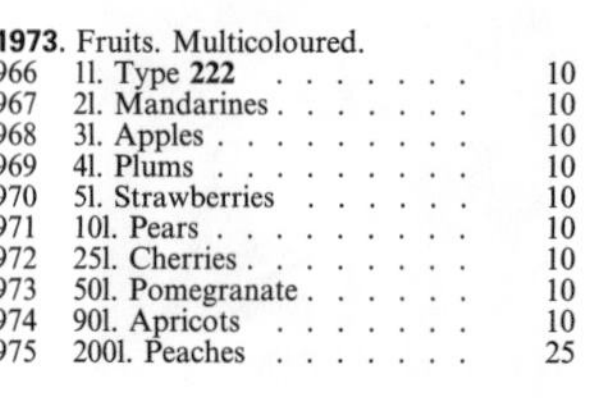

1973. Fruits. Multicoloured.
966 1l. Type **222** 10 10
967 2l. Mandarines 10 10
968 3l. Apples 10 10
969 4l. Plums 10 10
970 5l. Strawberries 10 10
971 10l. Pears 10 15
972 25l. Cherries 10 10
973 50l. Pomegranate 10 10
974 90l. Apricots 10 10
975 200l. Peaches 25 20

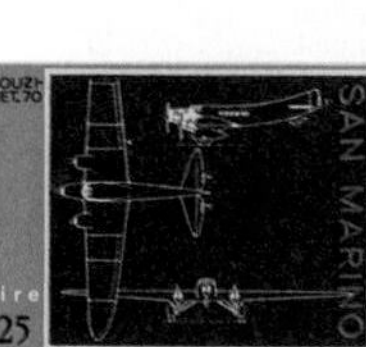

223 Couzinet 70 "Arc en Ciel" **224** Crossbowman, Serravalle Castle

1973. Aircraft.
976 **223** 25l. blue, yellow and gold 10 15
977 – 55l. blue, grey and gold 10 10
978 – 60l. blue, pink and gold 10 10
979 – 90l. blue, bistre and gold 10 10
980 – 220l. blue, orange and gold 10 15
AIRCRAFT: 55l. Macchi Castoldi MC-72-181 seaplane; 60l. Tupolev ANT-9; 90l. Ryan NYP "Spirit of St. Louis" (Charles Lindburgh's plane); 220l. Handley Page H.P.42.

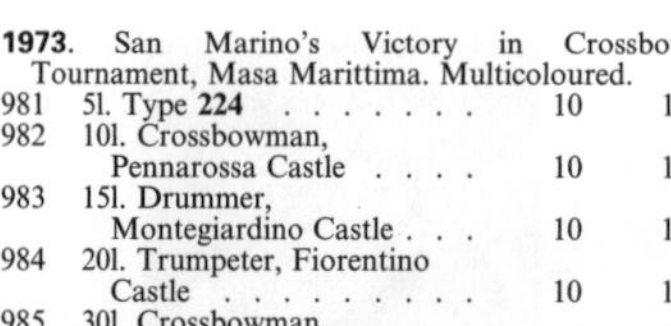

1973. San Marino's Victory in Crossbow Tournament, Masa Marittima. Multicoloured.
981 5l. Type **224** 10 10
982 10l. Crossbowman, Pennarossa Castle 10 10
983 15l. Drummer, Montegiardino Castle . . . 10 10
984 20l. Trumpeter, Fiorentino Castle 10 10
985 30l. Crossbowman, Montecerreto Castle . . . 10 10
986 40l. Crossbowman, Borgo Maggiore Castle 10 10
987 50l. Trumpeter, Guaita Castle 10 10
988 80l. Crossbowman, Faetano Castle 10 10
989 200l. Crossbowman, Montelupo Castle 10 15

225 "Adoration of the Magi" (detail) **226** Combat Shield (16th-century)

1973. Christmas. 600th Birth Anniv of Gentile da Fabriano. Details of Gentile's altarpiece "Adoration of the Magi".
990 **225** 5l. multicoloured 10 10
991 – 30l. multicoloured 10 10
992 – 115l. multicoloured . . . 10 10
993 – 250l. multicoloured . . . 10 20

1974. Ancient Weapons from "Cesta" Museum, San Marino.
994 **226** 5l. black brown and green 10 10
995 – 10l. black, blue & brown 10 10
996 – 15l. black, blue & lt blue 10 10
997 – 20l. black, blue & brown 10 10
998 – 30l. black, brown & blue 10 10
999 – 50l. black, blue and pink 10 10
1000 – 80l. black, blue and lilac 10 10
1001 – 250l. black and yellow 10 10
DESIGNS: 10l. German armour (16th-century); 15l. Crested morion (16th-century); 20l. Horse head-armour (15th–16th century); 30l. Italian morion with crest (16th–17th century); 50l. Gauntlets and sword pommel (16th-century); 80l. Sallet helmet (16th-century); 250l. Sforza shield (16th-century).

227 "The Joy of Living" (Emilio Greco)

1974. Europa. Sculpture.
1002 **227** 100l. black and brown 35 20
1003 – 200l. black and green . . 35 25
DESIGN: 200l. "The Joy of Living" (complete sculpture).

228 "Sea and Mountains" **229** Arms of Sansepolcro

1974. San Marino–Riccione Stamp Fair.
1004 **228** 50l. multicoloured . . . 15 20

1974. 9th Crossbow Tournament, San Marino. Arms. Multicoloured.
1005 15l. Type **229** 35 15
1006 20l. Massa Marittima . . . 35 15
1007 50l. San Marino 35 15
1008 115l. Gubbio 35 25
1009 300l. Lucca 35 05

230 U.P.U. Emblem and Shadow

1974. Centenary of Universal Postal Union.
1010 **230** 50l. multicoloured . . . 10 10
1011 90l. multicoloured . . . 10 10

231 Glider

1974. Air. 50th Anniv of Gliding in Italy.
1012 **231** 40l. blue, green and brown 15 10
1013 – 120l. blue, lt blue & pur 15 15
1014 – 500l. violet, mauve & purple 25 40

DESIGNS: 120, 500l. Gliders in "air currents" (both different).

232 Mt. Titano and Verses of Hymn

1974. Death Centenary of Niccolo Tommaseo (writer).
1015 **232** 50l. black, green and red . . 10 10
1016 – 150l. black, yellow & blue 10 15
DESIGN: 150l. Portrait of Tommaseo.

233 "Madonna and Child" (4th-century painting)

1974. Christmas.
1017 **233** 250l. multicoloured . . . 25 30

234 "Dancing Scene", Tomb of the Leopards, Tarquinia

1975. Etruscan Art (2nd series). Tomb Paintings. Multicoloured.
1018 20l. Type **234** 10 10
1019 30l. "Chariot Race", Tomb of the Hill, Chiusi 10 10
1020 180l. "Achilles and Troillus", Tomb of the Bulls, Tarquinia 15 15
1021 220l. "Dancers", Tomb of the Triclinium, Tarquinia 15 25

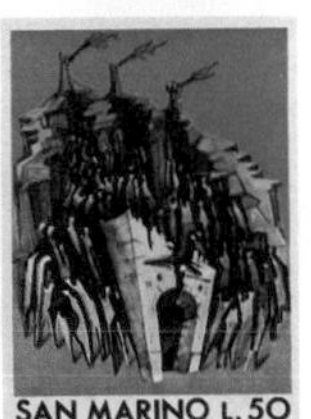

235 "Escape Tunnel" **236** "The Blessing"

1975. 30th Anniv of Escape of 100,000 Italian War Refugees to San Marino.
1022 **235** 50l. multicoloured . . . 10 20

1975. Europa. Details from "St. Marinus" by Guercino. Multicoloured.
1023 100l. Type **236** 35 15
1024 200l. "St. Marinus" 40 25

237 "The Virgin Mary" **238** "Aphrodite" (sculpture)

1975. Holy Year. Details from Frescoes by Giotto from Scrovegni Chapel, Padua. Multicoloured.
1025 10l. Type **237** 10 15
1026 40l. "Virgin and Child" . . 10 15
1027 50l. "Heads of Angels" . . 10 15
1028 100l. "Mary Magdalene" (horiz) 10 15
1029 500l. "Heads of Saints" (horiz) 15 35

1975. 15th Europa Stamp Exhibition, Naples.
1030 **238** 50l. black, grey and violet 10 20

239 Congress Emblem

1975. "Eurocophar" International Pharmaceutical Congress, San Marino.
1031 **239** 100l. multicoloured . . . 15 20

240 Tokyo, 1835

1975. Important Cities of the World (2nd series). Tokyo. Multicoloured.
1032 200l. Type **240** 20 20
1033 300l. Tokyo, 1975 . . . . . 30 45

241 "Woman on Balcony" **242** "Head of the Child" (detail)

1975. International Women's Year. Paintings by Gentilini. Multicoloured.
1034 50l. Type **241** 05 10
1035 150l. "Heads of Two Women" (horiz) 15 15
1036 230l. "Profile of Girl" . . . 15 30

1975. Christmas. 500th Birth Anniv of Michelangelo. Painting "Doni Madonna" and details. Multicoloured.
1037 50l. Type **242** 10 10
1038 100l. "Head of Virgin" (detail) 10 15
1039 250l. "Doni Madonna" . . 20 25

243 "Modesty" **244** Capitol, Washington

1976. "The Civil Virtues". Sketches by Emilio Greco.
1039a – 5l. black and lilac . . . 10 10
1040 **243** 10l. black and stone . . 10 10
1041 – 20l. black and lilac . . 10 15
1041a – 35l. black and stone . . 10 10
1042 – 50l. black and green . . 10 10
1043 – 70l. black and pink . . 10 10
1044 – 90l. black and pink . . 10 10
1045 – 100l. black and pink . . 10 10
1046 – 120l. black and blue . . 10 10
1047 – 150l. black and lilac . . 10 10
1048 – 160l. black and green 10 10
1049 – 170l. black and flesh . . 10 10
1050 – 220l. black and grey . . 10 15
1051 – 250l. black and yellow 10 20
1052 – 300l. black and grey . . 15 25
1053 – 320l. black and mauve 15 25
1054 – 500l. black and stone 20 40
1055 – 1000l. black and blue 40 80
1055a – 2000l. black and cream 1·30 1·80
DESIGNS: 5l. "Wisdom"; 20, 160l. "Temperance"; 35l. "Love"; 50, 70l. "Fortitude"; 90, 220l. "Prudence"; 100, 120l. "Altruism"; 150, 170l. "Hope"; 250l. "Justice"; 300, 320l. "Faith"; 500l. "Honesty"; 1000l. "Industry"; 2000l. "Faithfulness".

1976. Bicentenary of American Revolution and "Interphil 1976" International Stamp Exhibition, Philadelphia. Multicoloured.
1056 70l. Type **244** 10 10
1057 150l. Statue of Liberty, New York 10 15
1058 180l. Independence Hall, Philadelphia 15 25

245 Emblem and Maple Leaf

1976. Olympic Games, Montreal.
1059 **245** 150l. black and red . . . 15 25

246 Polychrome Plate (U. Bruno)

1976. Europa. Handicrafts. Multicoloured.
1060 150l. Type **246** 40 20
1061 180l. Silver plate (A. Ruscelli) 40 25

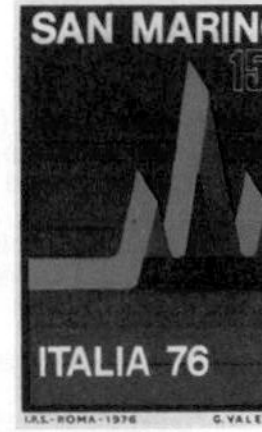

247 S.U.M.S. Emblem **249** "San Marino"

248 Children of Different Races

1976. Centenary of San Marino Social Welfare Union.
1062 **247** 150l. red, yellow and lilac 15 25

1976. 30th Anniv of UNESCO.
1063 **248** 180l. brown, orange & blue 10 20
1064 220l. brown, buff & sepia 15 35

1976. "Italia '76" International Stamp Exhibition, Milan.
1065 **249** 150l. multicoloured . . . 15 25

250 "The Annunciation" **251** Mount Titano and Emblem

1976. Christmas. 400th Death Anniv of Titian. Multicoloured.
1066 150l. Type **250** 20 15
1067 300l. "The Nativity" 30 35

1977. "San Marino 77" International Stamp Exhibition (1st issue).
1068 **251** 80l. red, green and olive (postage) 10 10
1069 170l. yellow, violet & blue 10 15
1070 200l. orange, ultram & blue 15 20
1071 200l. ochre, green and blue (air) 15 75
See also No. 1082.

252 "San Marino" (Ghirlandaio) **253** Leonardo da Vinci's Drawing of "Helicopter"

1977. Europa. Landscapes. Multicoloured.
1072 170l. Type **252** 45 25
1073 200l. "San Marino" (Guercino) 45 35

1977. Centenary of Enrico Forlanini's First Vertical Flight Experiment.
1074 **253** 120l. multicoloured . . . 15 20

254 University Square, 1877

1977. Centenary of Rumanian Independence. Important Cities of the World (3rd series). Bucharest.
1075 **254** 200l. green and blue . . 25 20
1076 – 400l. brown and stone 35 30
DESIGN: 400l. City centre, 1977.

255 Design of First San Marino Stamp **256** "St. Marinus Blessing" (Retrosi)

1977. Centenary of San Marino Postage Stamps.
1077 **255** 40l. green 10 10
1078 70l. blue 10 10
1079 170l. red 10 15
1080 500l. brown 35 40
1081 1000l. lilac 50 75

1977. "San Marino 1977" International Stamp Exhibition (2nd issue).
1082 **256** 1000l. multicoloured . . 90 1·20

257 Medicinal Plants **259** Angel

258 Woman gripped by Octopus

1977. Italian Pharmacists' Union Congress.
1083 **257** 170l. multicoloured . . . 15 25

1977. World Rheumatism Year.
1084 **258** 200l. multicoloured . . . 15 30

1977. Christmas.
1085 **259** 170l. black, grey & silver 15 15
1086 – 230l. black, grey & silver 15 20
1087 – 300l. black, grey & silver 25 25
DESIGNS: 230l. Palm tree and olive; 300l. The Virgin.

260 Baseball Player **261** San Francesco Gate

1978. World Baseball Championships.
1088 **260** 90l. black, blue and ultramarine 10 15
1089 120l. black, light green and green 10 20

1978. Europa. Architecture.
1090 **261** 170l. blue and light blue 45 25
1091 – 200l. brown and stone 50 30
DESIGN: 200l. Ripa Gate.

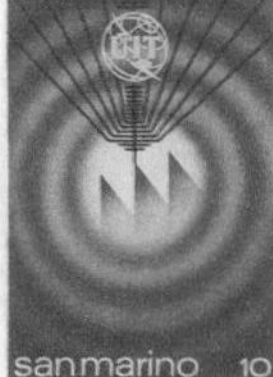

262 Feather **263** Mt. Titano and Antenna

1978. World Hypertension Month.
1092 **262** 320l. black, blue and red 20 40

1978. San Marino's Admission to the I.T.U.
1093 **263** 10l. yellow and red . . . 10 10
1094 200l. blue and violet . . 20 15

264 Hawk and Slender-billed Gull

1978. 30th San Marino–Riccione Stamp Fair.
1095 **264** 120l. multicoloured . . . 10 15
1096 170l. multicoloured . . . 20 25

265 Wright Flyer I **266** Allegory of Human Rights

1978. Air. 75th Anniv of First Powered Flight.
1097 **265** 10l. multicoloured . . . 15 10
1098 50l. multicoloured . . . 15 10
1099 200l. multicoloured . . . 15 10

1978. 30th Anniv of Declaration of Human Rights.
1100 **266** 200l. multicoloured . . . 15 25

267 Holly

1978. Christmas. Multicoloured.
1101 10l. Type **267** 10 10
1102 120l. Star 10 10
1103 170l. Snowflakes 10 15

268 Albert Einstein

1979. Birth Cent of Albert Einstein (physicist).
1104 **268** 120l. brown, sepia and grey 15 25

269 Motor-coach, 1915

1979. Europa. Multicoloured.
1105 170l. Type **269** 30 40
1106 220l. Horse-drawn stage-coach 40 55

270 San Marino Crossbowmen Federation Emblem **271** Maigret (G. Simenon)

1979. 14th Crossbow Tournament.
1107 **270** 120l. multicoloured . . . 15 15

1979. Fictional Detectives. Multicoloured.
1108 10l. Type **271** 10 15
1109 80l. Perry Mason (S. Gardner) 10 15
1110 150l. Nero Wolfe (R. Stout) 10 15
1111 170l. Ellery Queen (F. Dannay and M. B. Lee) 10 20
1112 220l. Sherlock Holmes (A. Conan Doyle) 10 25

272 Water Skiing

1979. Water Skiing Championships, Castelgandolfo.
1113 **272** 150l. green, blue & black 15 25

273 St. Apollonia **275** Horse Chestnut and Red Deer

274 "Knowledge"

1979. 13th International Stomatology Congress.
1114 **273** 170l. multicoloured . . . 15 25

1979. International Year of the Child. Mult.
1115 20l. Type **274** 15 10
1116 120l. "Friendship" 15 10
1117 170l. "Equality" 15 15
1118 220l. "Love" 15 25
1119 350l. "Existence" 25 35

1979. Environment Protection. Trees and Animals. Multicoloured.
1120 5l. Type **275** 20 10
1121 10l. Cedar of Lebanon and golden eagle 20 10
1122 35l. Flowering dogwood and common racoon 20 15
1123 50l. Banyan and tiger . . . 20 10
1124 70l. Stone pine and hoopoe 20 10
1125 90l. Larch and yellow-throated marten 20 10
1126 100l. Tasmanian blue gum and koala 20 10
1127 120l. Date palm and dromedary 20 10
1128 150l. Silver maple and American beaver 20 10
1129 170l. Baobab and African elephant 20 15

276 "Disturbing Muses" **277** St. Joseph

1979. 1st Death Anniv of Giorgio de Chirico (painter). Multicoloured.
1130 40l. Type **276** 10 10
1131 150l. "Ancient Horses" . . 10 15
1132 170l. "Self-portrait" 10 20

1979. Christmas. "The Holy Family" (fresco) by Antonio Alberti or details from it.
1133 80l. Type **277** 15 15
1134 170l. Infant Jesus 15 15
1135 220l. Magus 15 25
1136 320l. "The Holy Family" . . 20 35

278 St. Benedict of Nursia **279** Cigarette Ends

1980. 1500th Birth Anniv of Saint Benedict of Nursia (founder of Benedictine Order).
1137 **278** 170l. multicoloured . . . 15 25

1980. Anti-smoking Campaign. Multicoloured.
1138 120l. Type **279** 15 20
1139 220l. Face hidden by cigarettes 15 25
1140 520l. Face wreathed in smoke 25 45

280 Naples

1980. "Europa" Stamp Exhibition, Naples.
1141 **280** 170l. multicoloured . . . 15 25

281 Giovanbattista Belluzzi (military architect)

1980. Europa. Multicoloured.
1142 170l. Type **281** 50 25
1143 220l. Antonio Orafo (silver and goldsmith) 60 30

282 London, 1850

1980. "London 1980" International Stamp Exhibition and Important Cities of the World (4th series). London.
1144 **282** 200l. brown and green 15 25
1145 – 400l. blue and lilac . . . 40 35
DESIGN: 400l. London, 1980.

283 Cycling

1980. Olympic Games, Moscow.
1146 **283** 70l. black, emerald & green 10 15
1147 – 90l. black, orange & brown 10 15
1148 – 170l. black, red & mauve 10 20
1149 – 350l. black, blue & dp blue 20 35
1150 – 450l. black, violet & blue 25 45
DESIGNS: 90l. Basketball; 170l. Running; 350l. Gymnastics; 450l. High jumping.

284 Stolz and Score of "Philatelic Waltz"

1980. Birth Centenary of Robert Stolz (composer).
1151 **284** 120l. blue and black . . 15 20

285 Weightlifting **286** City Fortifications

1980. European Junior Weightlifting Championship.
1152 **285** 170l. red, black and green 15 25

1980. World Tourism Conference, Manila.
1153 **286** 220l. multicoloured . . . 15 30

287 "The Annunciation" (detail) **288** St. Joseph's Eve Bonfire

1980. Christmas. Details of Paintings by Andrea del Sarto. Multicoloured.
1154 180l. "Madonna of the Harpies" (detail) 15 25
1155 250l. "Annunciation" (Mary) 25 25
1156 500l. Type **287** 40 50

1981. Europa. Multicoloured.
1157 200l. Type **288** 45 25
1158 300l. National Day fireworks 70 35

289 Hands holding Broken Branch

1981. International Year of Disabled Persons.
1159 **289** 300l. yellow, green and light green 10 40

290 "St. Charles' Square, 1817" (Jakob Alt)

1981. "WIPA 1981" International Stamp Exn and Important Cities of the World (5th series). Vienna. Multicoloured.
1160 200l. Type **290** 10 20
1161 300l. St. Charles' Square, 1981 . . . . 20 35

291 Motor Cyclist **292** Girl playing Pipes

1981. San Marino Motor Cycle Grand Prix.
1162 **291** 200l. multicoloured . . . 15 35

1981. Birth Bimillenary of Virgil (poet).
1163 **292** 300l. grey and silver . . 35 35
1164 – 550l. grey and silver . . 45 55
1165 – 1500l. grey and silver . . 70 1·40
DESIGNS: 550l. Soldier; 1500l. Shepherd.

293 House **294** Judo

1981. Urban Development Scheme. Multicoloured.
1167 20l. Type **293** 10 15
1168 80l. Tree (provision of green belts) 10 15
1169 400l. Gas flame (power plants) 15 40

1981. European Junior Judo Championships, San Marino.
1170 **294** 300l. multicoloured . . . 20 40

295 "Girl with Dove" (Picasso) **296** Bread

1981. Birth Centenary of Pablo Picasso (artist). Multicoloured.
1171 150l. Type **295** 15 25
1172 200l. "Homage to Picasso" (detail, Renato Guttuso) 15 30

1981. World Food Day.
1173 **296** 300l. multicoloured . . . 20 40

297 King presenting Gift **298** Cancellation and "San Marino 82" Emblem

1981. Christmas. 500th Birth Anniv of Benvenuto Tisi da Garofalo (artist). Details from "Adoration of the Magi and St. Bartholomew". Multicoloured.
1174 200l. Type **297** 15 15
1175 300l. Kneeling King 20 25
1176 600l. Virgin and Child . . . 35 60

1982. Centenary of Postal Stationery.
1177 **298** 200l. multicoloured . . . 10 25

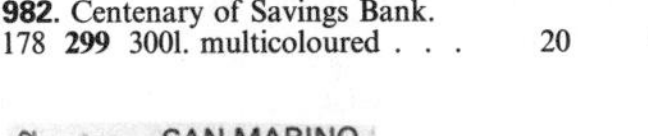
299 "The Cicada and the Ant" (Aesop fable)

1982. Centenary of Savings Bank.
1178 **299** 300l. multicoloured . . . 20 40

300 Assembly of Heads of Families, 1906 **301** Archimedes

1982. Europa. Multicoloured.
1179 300l. Type **300** . . . . . . 2·10 55
1180 450l. Napoleon at the border of San Marino, 1797 . . . . 1·60 75

1982. Pioneers of Science.
1181 **301** 20l. red and black . . . 10 10
1182 – 30l. blue and black . . . 10 10
1183 – 40l. brown and black . . 10 10
1184 – 50l. green and black . . 10 10
1185 – 60l. red and black . . . 10 10
1186 – 100l. brown and black 10 10
1187 – 150l. brown and black 10 15
1188 – 200l. brown and black 20 15
1189 – 250l. red and black . . . 45 15
1190 – 300l. green and black . . 15 20
1191 – 350l. green and black . . 25 20
1192 – 400l. red and black . . . 35 30
1193 – 450l. red and black . . 30 40
1194 – 1000l. red and black . . 55 60
1195 – 1400l. red and black . . 75 1·00
1196 – 5000l. black and blue . . 2·50 3·75
DESIGNS: 30l. Copernicus; 40l. Isaac Newton; 50l. Antoine Lavoisier; 60l. Marie Curie; 100l. Robert Koch; 150l. Alexander Fleming; 200l. Thomas Edison; 250l. Alessandro Volta; 300l. Guglielmo Marconi; 350l. Evangelista Torricelli; 400l. Carl Linnaeus; 450l. Hippocrates; 1000l. Pythagoras; 1400l. Leonardo da Vinci; 5000l. Galileo.

302 "Notre Dame", 1806 (J. Hill)

1982. "Philexfrance 82" International Stamp Exhibition and Important Cities of the World (6th series). Paris.
1197 **302** 300l. buff and black . . 25 25
1198 – 450l. multicoloured . . . 30 35
DESIGN: 450l. Notre Dame and Ile de Cite, 1982.

303 Hands and Birds **304** Pope John Paul II

1982. 800th Birth Anniv of St. Francis of Assisi.
1199 **303** 200l. multicoloured . . . 10 30

1982. Visit of Pope John Paul II to San Marino.
1200 **304** 900l. purple, deep green and green 60 95

305 Globe encircled by Flag Stamps **306** Face besplattered with Blood

1982. 5th Anniv of International Association of Stamp Philatelic Catalogue Editors (ASCAT).
1201 **305** 300l. multicoloured . . . 20 40

1982. 15th International Congress of Amnesty International, Rimini.
1202 **306** 700l. red and black . . . 45 75

307 "Accipe Lampadam Ardentem" (detail) **308** Refugee

1982. Christmas. Paintings by Gregorio Sciltian. Multicoloured.
1203 200l. Type **307** 15 15
1204 300l. "Madonna della Citta" (detail) 25 35
1205 450l. Angel (detail, "Accipe Sal Sapientiae") 30 50

1982. "For Refugees".
1206 **308** 300l.+100l. mult 20 40

309 Begni Building and Quill **310** Formula One Racing Cars

1983. Centenary of Secondary School.
1207 **309** 300l. multicoloured . . . 20 40

1983. San Marino Formula One Grand Prix.
1208 **310** 50l. multicoloured . . . 10 10
1209 350l. multicoloured . . . 30 50

311 Auguste Piccard and Stratosphere Balloon "F.N.R.S." **312** Amateur Radio Operator

1983. Europa. Multicoloured.
1210 400l. Type **311** . . . . . . 1·50 1·00
1211 500l. Piccard and bathyscaphe . . . . . . 1·70 1·30

1983. World Communications Year.
1212 **312** 400l. black, blue and red 30 45
1213 – 500l. black, brown & red 30 60
DESIGN: 500l. Postman on bicycle.

313 Montgolfier Balloon

1983. Bicentenary of Manned Flight.
1214 **313** 500l. multicoloured . . . 35 60

314 "Rio de Janeiro, 1845" (Richard Bate)

1983. "Brasiliana 83" International Stamp Exhibition and Important Cities of the World (7th series). Rio de Janeiro. Multicoloured.
1215 400l. Type **314** 30 35
1216 1400l. Rio de Janeiro, 1983 1·00 1·10

315 Feeding Colt

1983. World Food Programme.
1217 **315** 500l. multicoloured . . . 35 60

316 "Madonna of the Grand Duke" **317** Demetrius Vikelas

1983. Christmas. 500th Birth Anniv of Raphael. Multicoloured.
1218 300l. Type **316** 25 25
1219 400l. "Madonna of the Goldfinch" (detail) . . . 35 35
1220 500l. "Madonna of the Chair" (detail) 45 40

1984. 90th Anniv of International Olympic Committee. I.O.C. Presidents.
1221 **317** 300l. black and green . . 40 40
1222 – 400l. purple and blue . . 50 45
1223 – 550l. lilac and green . . 60 60
DESIGNS: 400l. Lord Killanin; 550l. Juan Samaranch.

318 Bridge

1984. Europa. 25th Anniv of C.E.P.T.
1224 **318** 400l. yellow, violet & black . . . . 1·30 90
1225 550l. yellow, red & black 2·00 1·20

319 Flag Waver **320** Male Athlete

1984. Flag Wavers. Multicoloured.
1226 300l. Type **319** 20 35
1227 400l. Waver with two flags 55 50

1984. Olympic Games, Los Angeles. Sheet 151 × 110 mm containing T **320** and similar vert designs. Multicoloured.
MS1228 550l. Type **320**; 1000l. Female athlete . . . . 1·60 1·60

321 Motocross

1984. World Motocross Championship.
1229 **321** 450l. multicoloured . . . 35 60

322 Collins Street, 1839

1984. "Ausipex 84" International Stamp Exhibition, and Important Cities of the World (8th series). Melbourne. Multicoloured.
1230 1500l. Type **322** . . . . . 1·20 1·20
1231 2000l. Collins Street, 1984 1·50 1·60

323 Pres. Pertini and San Marino City

1984. Visit of President Sandro Pertini of Italy.
1232 **323** 1950l. multicoloured . . 1·30 1·60

324 "Universe" **325** Angel with Book

1984. Youth Philately. Multicoloured.
1233 50l. Type **324** 10 15
1234 100l. Caveman and modern man framed by television ("The Evolution of Life") 15 15
1235 150l. Pipe smoker driving car ("The World in which we Live") 15 15
1236 200l. Man with fig leaf and snake with apple ("Mankind") 15 20
1237 450l. Scientist with H-bomb ("Science") 20 50
1238 550l. Man in barrel with books and candle ("Philosophy") 30 60

1984. Christmas. Designs showing details of "Madonna of San Girolamo" by Correggio. Mult.
1239 400l. Type **325** 40 55
1240 450l. Virgin and Child . . . 50 60
1241 550l. Attendant 60 75

326 Johann Sebastian Bach and Score **327** State Flags, Stadium and Swimming Pictogram

1985. Europa.
1242 **326** 450l. black and brown 1·30 95
1243 – 600l. black and green . . 2·00 1·30
DESIGN: 600l. Vincenzo Bellini and score.

1985. 1st Small States Games. Multicoloured.
1244 50l. Type **327** 10 10
1245 350l. Flags, stadium and running pictogram . . . 20 25
1246 400l. Flags, stadium and shooting pictogram . . . 25 35
1247 450l. Flags, stadium and cycling pictogram 30 40
1248 600l. Flags, stadium and handball pictogram . . . 40 55

328 Sunset and Birds **329** Face and Hand holding Dove

1985. Emigration.
1249 **328** 600l. multicoloured . . . 45 60

1985. International Youth Year.
1250 **329** 400l. yellow, blue and gold 30 40
1251 – 600l. gold, blue and yellow 40 60
DESIGN: 600l. Girl's face, dove and horse's head.

330 Camera and San Marino **331** Sun breaking through Clouds and Sapling

1985. 18th Int Federation of Photographic Art Congress.
1252 **330** 450l. multicoloured . . . 35 50

1985. 10th Anniv of Helsinki European Security and Co-operation Conference.
1253 **331** 600l. multicoloured . . . 45 65

332 Don Abbondio and Don Rodrigo's Henchmen

1985. Birth Bicentenary of Alessandro Manzoni (writer). Scenes from "I Promessi Sposi".
1254 **332** 400l. green 25 35
1255 – 450l. brown 30 45
1256 – 600l. blue 40 60
DESIGNS: 450l. Forcing curate to bless wedding; 600l. Plague in Milan.

333 Common Carp caught on Hook

1985. World Angling Championships, River Arno, Florence.
1257 **333** 600l. multicoloured . . . 45 60

334 Cat (after Pompeian mosaic)

1985. International Feline Federation Congress.
1258 **334** 600l. multicoloured . . . 45 60

335 Colosseum, 85 A.D.

1985. "Italia 85" International Stamp Exhibition, and Important Cities of the World (9th series). Rome. Multicoloured.
1259 1000l. Type **335** 65 80
1260 1500l. Colosseum, 1985 . . 90 1·20

336 Flying Angel

1985. Christmas. Multicoloured.
1261 400l. Type **336** 55 50
1262 450l. Madonna and Child 75 55
1263 600l. Angel resting 85 75

337 Aerial View of Cailungo Hospital

1986. 30th Anniv of Social Security Institute (450l.) and World Health Day (650l.). Mult.
1264 450l. Type **337** 30 55
1265 650l. Front view of Cailungo hospital 40 70

338 "Giotto" Space Probe

1986. Appearance of Halley's Comet. Mult.
1266 550l. Type **338** 45 60
1267 1000l. "Adoration of the Magi" (Giotto) . . . . . 75 1·20

339 Player and Emblem **340** Deer

1986. World Table Tennis Championships, Rimini.
1268 **339** 450l. blue, ultram & red 35 65

1986. Europa. Multicoloured.
1269 550l. Type **340** . . . . . . 6·75 4·50
1270 650l. Common kestrel . . . 9·00 5·00

341 Water Tower, 1870 (lithograph, Charles Shober)

1986. "Ameripex" International Stamp Exhibition, and Important Cities of the World (10th series). Chicago. Multicoloured.
1271 2000l. Type **341** . . . . . 1·50 1·60
1272 3000l. Water tower, 1986 . . 1·90 2·50

342 Swallows

343 Head of Soldier

1986. International Peace Year.
1273 **342** 550l. multicoloured . . . 40 70

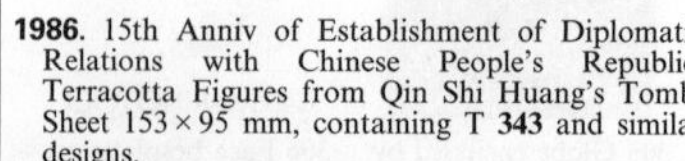
1986. 15th Anniv of Establishment of Diplomatic Relations with Chinese People's Republic. Terracotta Figures from Qin Shi Huang's Tomb. Sheet 153 × 95 mm, containing T **343** and similar designs.
MS1274 550l. black and blue; 650l. black and brown; 2000l. black and magenta . . . . 3·50 3·50
DESIGNS—VERT: 650l. Head of horse. VERT: 2000l. Head of soldier (different).

344 "Apollo dancing with the Muses" (detail, Giulio Romano)

1986. 25th Anniv of San Marino Choral Society.
1275 **344** 450l. multicoloured . . . 35 50

345 Boules Player

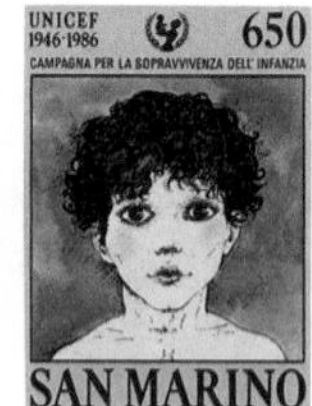

346 Boy

1986. European Boules Championships, San Marino.
1276 **345** 550l. multicoloured . . . 40 60

1986. 40th Anniv of UNICEF. Child Survival Campaign.
1277 **346** 650l. multicoloured . . . 45 80

347 "St. John the Baptist"

349 Sketch of Church

348 Motor Car and Route Map (Paris–Peking Rally, 1907)

1986. Christmas. Triptych by Hans Memling. Mult.
1278 450l. Type **347** 55 60
1279 550l. "Madonna and Child" 70 65
1280 650l. "St. John the Evangelist" 75 80

1987. Motor Rallies. Multicoloured.
1281 500l. Type **348** 35 45
1282 600l. Peugeot "205" (15th San Marino Rally) . . . 35 55
1283 700l. Motor car and crowds (60th anniv of Mille Miglia) 55 65

1987. Europa. Architecture. Our Lady of Consolation Church, Borgomaggiore (Giovanni Michelucci).
1284 **349** 600l. black and red . . . 7·75 3·50
1285 – 700l. black and yellow 9·00 4·50
DESIGN: 700l. Church interior.

350 Modern Sculpture (Reffi Busignani)

351 "Chromatic Invention" (Corrado Cagli)

1987. Modern Sculptures in San Marino. Designs showing works by artists named. Multicoloured.
1286 50l. Type **350** 10 15
1287 100l. Bini 10 15
1288 200l. Guguianu 15 20
1289 300l. Berti 15 35
1290 400l. Crocetti 30 40
1291 500l. Berti 30 55
1292 600l. Messina 40 65
1293 1000l. Minguzzi . . . . . 55 1·10
1294 2200l. Greco . . . . . . 1·20 2·30
1295 10000l. Sassu . . . . . . 7·25 11·50

1987. Art Biennale.
1300 – 500l. blue, black and red 35 55
1301 **351** 600l. multicoloured . . . 40 70
DESIGN: 500l. "From My Brazilian Diary—Virgin Forest" (Emilio Vedova).

352 Baroudeur Microlight, San Marino Air Club

354 Olympic Rings and Hurdler in "Stamp"

353 Bust of Mahatma Gandhi in Gandhi Square, San Marino

1987.
1302 **352** 600l. multicoloured . . . 45 65

1987. "A Society based on Non-violence".
1303 **353** 500l. multicoloured . . . 40 60

1987. "Olymphilex" Olympic Stamp Exhibition and World Light Athletics Championships, Rome.
1304 **354** 600l. multicoloured . . . 50 90

355 Sports Pictograms

357 "The Annunciation" (detail)

356 "View from Round Tower, 1836" (anon)

1987. Mediterranean Games, Syria.
1305 **355** 700l. red, blue and black 50 80

1987. "Hafnia 87" International Stamp Exhibition, and Important Cities of the World (11th series). Copenhagen. Multicoloured.
1306 1200l. Type **356** . . . . . 1·10 1·20
1307 2200l. View from Round Tower, 1987 . . . . . . 2·00 2·30

1987. Christmas. 600th Birth Anniv of Fra Giovanni of Florence (Beato Angelico). Mult.
1308 600l. Type **357** 85 60
1309 600l. Madonna and Child (detail, Triptych of Cortona) 90 60
1310 600l. Saint (detail, "The Annunciation") 90 60

358 1923 30c., 1944 20l.+10l. and 1975 200l. Stamps of St. Marinus

359 Maglev Monorail Train and Globe

1988. Thematic Collecting. Multicoloured.
1311 50l. Type **358** 10 10
1312 150l. Aerogramme and 1933 3l. "Graf Zeppelin" stamp (transport) 10 15
1313 300l. 1954 5l. and 1981 200l. motor cycle racing stamps and 1986 meter mark showing motor cycle (sport) 20 35
1314 350l. 1978 200l. human rights stamp on cover and 1982 200l. St. Francis of Assisi stamp (art) 25 35
1315 1000l. 1949 50l. Garibaldi stamp, 1985 450l. Europa stamp and 1952 1l. Columbus stamp (famous people) . . . . 70 1·10
See also Nos. 1340/4 and 1393/7.

1988. Europa. Transport and Communications. Multicoloured.
1316 600l. Type **359** . . . . . . 4·50 2·30
1317 700l. Optical fibres and globe . . . . 7·25 3·00

360 Carlo Malagola and Palazzo della Mercanzia

361 "La Strada"

1988. 900th Anniv of Bologna University. Mult.
1318 550l. Type **360** 45 45
1319 650l. Pietro Ellero and Palazzo del Podesta . . . 50 55
1320 1300l. Giosue Carducci and Pala dei Mercanti . . . . 80 1·20
1321 1700l. Giovanni Pascoli and Atheneum . . . . 95 1·50

1988. Award of Celebrities of Show Business Prize to Federico Fellini (film director). Film posters. Multicoloured.
1322 300l. Type **361** 20 40
1323 900l. "La Dolce Vita" . . . 70 1·00
1324 1200l. "Amarcord" . . . . 80 1·40

362 Mt. Titano from Beach

1988. 40th Riccione Stamp Fair.
1325 **362** 750l. blue, green and mauve 50 80

363 Healthy Tree with Diseased Roots

1988. Present Day Problems. International AIDS Congress, San Marino.
1326 **363** 250l. multicoloured . . . 25 25
1327 – 350l. red and black . . . 25 30
1328 – 650l. multicoloured . . . 50 60
1329 – 1000l. multicoloured . . 75 95
DESIGNS: 350l. "AIDS" crumbling; 650l. Knotted cord and emblem of virus; 1000l. Printed information.

364 Man Running

1988. Olympic Games, Seoul. Sheet 118 × 103 mm containing T **364**and similar vert designs, each black, magenta and yellow.
MS1330 650l. Type **364**; 750l. Hurdling; 1300l. Woman running 2·75 2·75

365 "Kurhaus, Scheveningen, 1885" (anon)

1988. "Filacept" International Stamp Exhibition, and Important Cities of the World (12th series). The Hague. Multicoloured.
1331 1600l. Type **365** . . . . . 1·20 1·20
1332 3000l. Kurhaus, Scheveningen, 1988 . . . 2·10 2·50

366 "Angel with Violin"

368 Sledging

367 Bird in Tree (Federica Sparagna)

1988. Christmas. 550th Birth Anniv of Melozzo da Forli. Multicoloured.
1333 650l. Type **366** 85 60
1334 650l. "Angel of the Annunciation" (20 × 37 mm) 85 60
1335 650l. "Angel with Mandolin" 85 60

1989. "Nature is Beautiful. Nature is Useful. Nature is ...". Multicoloured.
1336 200l. Type **367** 20 20
1337 500l. Birds beneath tree (Giovanni Monteduro) . . 50 55
1338 650l. Landscape (Rosa Mannarino) 70 70
Nos. 1336/8 depict the first three winning entries in a children's drawing competition.

1989. Europa. Children's Games. Sheet 115 × 80 mm containing T **368** and similar vert design. Multicoloured.
MS1339 60l. Type **368**; 750l. Hopscotch . . . . 5·50 5·50

1989. Postal History. As T **358**. Multicoloured.
1340 100l. "San Marino 1977" Exhibition 1000l. stamp on cover (postal tariffs) 10 10
1341 200l. 1988 350l. stamp on cover (cancellations) . . . 10 20
1342 400l. Parcel receipt (parcel post) 30 35
1343 500l. Essay by Martin Riester, 1865 . . . . . . 40 45
1344 1000l. 1862 handstamp on cover (pre-stamp period) 1·40 95

369 Emblem

1989. Sport. Multicoloured.
1345 650l. Type **369** (30th anniv of San Marino Olympic Committee) 70 70
1346 750l. Emblems (admission of San Marino Football Federation to UEFA and FIFA) 75 75
1347 850l. Tennis racquet and ball (San Marino championships) 55 75
1348 1300l. Formula 1 racing car (San Marino Grand Prix, Imola) . . . . 80 1·40

370 Oath of the Tennis Court

1989. Bicentenary of French Revolution. Mult.
1349 700l. Type **370** 55 75
1350 1000l. Arrest of Louis XVI 80 90
1351 1800l. Napoleon's army . . 1·40 1·60

371 "Marguerite and Armand"

372 "Angel of the Annunciation"

1989. Award of Celebrities of Show Business Prize to Rudolph Nureyev (ballet dancer). Mult.
1352 1200l. Type **371** . . . . . 70 1·40
1353 1500l. "Apollo Musagete" 1·10 1·60
1354 1700l. Ken Russell's film "Valentino" . . . . . . 1·40 1·90

1989. Christmas. Details of the polyptych in Church of Servants of Mary. Multicoloured.
1355 650l. Type **372** 55 60
1356 650l. "Nativity" (50 × 40 mm) 55 60
1357 650l. Mary ("Annunciation") 55 60

373 Capitol, 1850

1989. "World Stamp Expo '89" Int Stamp Exhibition, and Important Cities of the World (13th series). Washington D.C. Multicoloured.
1358 2000l. Type **373** . . . . . 1·60 1·20
1359 2500l. Capitol, 1989 . . . . 1·90 1·90

374 Old Post Office

375 "Martyrdom of St. Agatha" (Tiepolo) and Cardinal Alberoni leaving City

1990. Europa. Post Office Buildings. Mult.
1360 700l. Type **374** . . . . . . 1·20 95
1361 800l. Dogana Post Office . . 1·60 1·20

1990. 250th Anniv of End of Cardinal Alberoni's Occupation of San Marino.
1362 **375** 3500l. multicoloured . . 2·40 3·00

376 Map pinpointing San Marino

377 Statue, Government Palace

1990. European Tourism Year. Multicoloured.
1366 50l. Type **377** 10 10
1367 50l. Liberty Statue and English inscription . . . 10 10
1368 50l. Government Palace and German inscription . . . 10 10
1369 50l. Man with flag and French inscription 10 10
1363 600l. Type **376** 35 65
1364 600l. Aerial view showing villages 35 65
1365 600l. First Tower 35 65
See also Nos. 1424/7.

378 West Germany (winners 1954, 1974)

1990. World Cup Football Championship, Italy. Previous Winners. Sheet 120 × 114 mm containing T **378** and similar vert designs. Multicoloured.
MS1373 700l Type **378**; 700l. Italy (1934, 1938, 1982); 700l. England (1966); 700l. Uruguay (1930, 1950); 700l. Brazil (1958, 1962, 1970); 700l. Argentina (1978, 1986) . . . . 4·25 4·25

379 Olivier in "Hamlet" 381 Pinocchio

380 Mt. Titano and State Flags

1990. Award of Celebrities of Show Business Prize to Laurence Olivier (actor). Multicoloured.
1374 600l. Type **379** 55 80
1375 700l. "Richard III" . . . . 65 1·00
1376 1500l. "The Runner" . . . 1·30 1·90
Nos. 1374/6 are wrongly inscribed "Lawrence".

1990. Visit of President Francesco Cossiga of Italy.
1377 **380** 600l. multicoloured . . . 40 60

1990. Death Centenary of Carlo Collodi (writer). Characters from "Pinocchio". Multicoloured.
1378 250l. Type **381** 25 25
1379 400l. Geppetto 25 40
1380 450l. Blue fairy 40 55
1381 600l. Cat and wolf 40 70

382 Pre-Columbian Civilizations

1990. 500th Anniv (1992) of Discovery of America by Columbus (1st issue). Multicoloured.
1382 1500l. Type **382** . . . . . 1·10 1·20
1383 2000l. Produce of the New World . . . . 1·40 1·90
See also Nos. 1401/2 and 1417/18.

383 Mary and Two Kings **384** Swallowtail on "Ephedra major"

1990. Christmas. Details of Cuciniello Crib. Mult.
1384 750l. Type **383** 85 75
1385 750l. Baby Jesus in manger and third King 80 75
Nos. 1384/5 were issued together, se-tenant, forming a composite design.

1990. Flora and Fauna. Multicoloured.
1386 200l. Type **384** 15 15
1387 300l. "Apoderus coryli" (weevil) and hazelnut . . 25 30
1388 500l. Garden dormouse and acorns of holm oak . . . 40 55
1389 1000l. Green lizard and "Ophrys bertolonii" (orchid) . . . . 70 1·00
1390 2000l. Firecrest on black pine . . . . 1·40 2·10

385 Launch of "Ariane-4"

1991. Europa. Europe in Space. Multicoloured.
1391 750l. Type **385** . . . . . . 2·30 1·90
1392 800l. "E.R.S.-1." survey satellite . . . . 2·30 2·30

1991. World of Stamps. As T **358**. Multicoloured.
1393 100l. Stamp shop 15 10
1394 150l. Stamp club 15 15
1395 200l. Exhibition 15 20
1396 450l. Stamp album and catalogues 95 40
1397 1500l. Philatelic publications (25th anniv of Italian Philatelic Press Union) . . 1·10 1·40

386 Torch Bearer leaving Athens **387** Cat

1991. Olympic Games, Barcelona (1992) (1st issue). Multicoloured.
1398 400l. Type **386** 30 40
1399 600l. Torch bearer passing through San Marino . . . 40 60
1400 2000l. Torch bearer arriving in Barcelona . . . . . . 1·80 2·10
See also No. **MS**1434.

1991. 500th Anniv (1992) of Discovery of America by Columbus (2nd issue). As T **382**. Mult.
1401 750l. Navigational dividers, quadrant, hour-glass, compass and route map 70 80
1402 3000l. "Santa Maria", "Nina" and "Pinta" . . . 2·75 2·75

1991. Pets. Multicoloured.
1403 500l. Type **387** 30 45
1404 550l. Hamster on wheel . . 30 55
1405 750l. Great Dane and Pomeranian 50 75
1406 1000l. Aquarium fishes . . . 80 1·10
1407 1200l. Canaries in cage . . . 90 1·30

388 Players, Balls and Baskets

1991. Centenary of Basketball. Multicoloured.
1408 650l. Type **388** 55 70
1409 750l. James Naismith (inventor) and players . . 60 95

389 James Clerk-Maxwell (physicist)

1991. 100 Years of Radio (1st issue).
1410 **389** 750l. multicoloured . . . 45 1·10
Clerk-Maxwell formulated the theory of electromagnetic radiation.
See also Nos. 1431, 1452, 1479 and 1521/2.

390 Dove and Broken Chain (unification of Germany) **391** Keep

1991. "Birth of a New Europe". Sheet 120 × 72 mm containing T **390** and similar vert designs. Multicoloured.
MS1411 1500l. Type **390**; 1500l. Pres. Gorbachev of Soviet Union, Pres. Bush of United States and rainbow (stategic arms talks); 1500l. Flower breaking through barbed wire (Eastern European democracy) . . . . 4·00 3·75

1991. Christmas. La Rocca Fortress. Multicoloured.
1412 600l. Type **391** (postage) . . 55 60
1413 750l. Inland view of fortress 70 75
1414 1200l. Fortress on crag (air) 95 1·30

392 "Bianca and Falliero" (Pesaro production)

1992. Birth Bicentenary of Gioachino Rossini (composer). Scenes from productions of his operas. Multicoloured.
1415 750l. Type **392** 60 80
1416 1200l. "The Barber of Seville" (La Scala Theatre, Milan) . . . . . 90 1·20

1992. 500th Anniv of Discovery of America by Columbus (3rd issue). As T **382**. Multicoloured.
1417 1500l. Amerindians watching fleet . . . . 90 1·60
1418 2000l. Route map of the four voyages . . . . . . 1·40 2·10

393 Roses **394** Courting Couple

1992. Plants. Multicoloured.
1419 50l. Type **393** 10 15
1420 200l. Ficus as house plant 10 15
1421 300l. Orchid in conservatory 20 30
1422 450l. Cacti in pots 30 40
1423 5000l. Pelargoniums in trough . . . . 3·75 5·00

1992. Tourism. Multicoloured. (a) As T **377**.
1424 50l. Man with crossbow and Italian inscription 10 10
1425 50l. Tennis player and English inscription . . . 10 10
1426 50l. Motor cycle rider and French inscription 10 10
1427 50l. Ferrari racing car and German inscription . . . 10 10

(b) As T **394**.
1428 600l. Type **394** 45 55
1429 600l. Man in restaurant . . 45 55
1430 600l. Woman reading on veranda 45 55

1992. 100 Years of Radio (2nd issue). As T **389**. Multicoloured.
1431 750l. Heinrich Rudolf Hertz (physicist) 45 90
Hertz proved Clerk-Maxwell's theory.

395 Egg-shaped Globe and Caravel **396** Football

1992. Europa. 500th Anniv of Discovery of America. Multicoloured.
1432 750l. Type **395** 70 80
1433 850l. Caravel and island inside broken egg . . . . 70 1·00

1992. Olympic Games, Barcelona (2nd Issue). Sheet 137 × 105 mm containing T **396** and similar multicoloured designs.
MS1434 1250l. Type **396**; 1250l. Shooting (horiz); 1250l. Swimming; 1250l. Running . . 5·00 4·75

397 Inedible Mushrooms

1992. 3rd Titano Mycological Exhibition, Borgo Maggiore. Multicoloured.
1435 250l. Type **397** 25 35
1436 250l. Inedible mushrooms (different) 25 35
1437 350l. Edible mushrooms in bowl 35 40
1438 350l. Edible mushrooms on cloth 35 40
Stamps of the same value were issued together, se-tenant, each pair forming a composite design.

398 View and Arms of San Marino **399** "La Sacra Conversazione"

1992. Admission of San Marino to United Nations Organization. Multicoloured.
1439 1000l. Type **398** 70 80
1440 1000l. View of San Marino (different) and United Nations emblem 70 80

1992. Christmas. 500th Death Anniv of Piero della Francesca (artist). Multicoloured.
1441 750l. Type **399** 70 60
1442 750l. Close-up of Madonna 70 70
1443 750l. Close-up of shell decoration 70 60

400 Tennis Player **401** Stars

1993. Sporting Events. Multicoloured.
1444 300l. Type **400** (Italian and San Marino Youth Games) 15 25
1445 400l. Cross-country skiers (European Youth Olympic Days (winter), Aosta, Italy) 20 40
1446 550l. Runners (European Youth Olympic Days (summer), Eindhoven, Netherlands) 30 45
1447 600l. Fisherman (Freshwater Angling Clubs World Championship, Ostellato, Italy) 35 55
1448 700l. Runners breasting tape (Small States Games, Malta) 55 70
1449 1300l. Sprinters (Mediterranean Games, Rousillon, France) . . . 80 1·20

1993. Europa. Contemporary Art.
1450 **401** 750l. multicoloured . . . 65 90
1451 – 850l. blue and orange . . 80 1·00
DESIGN: 850l. Silhouette.

1993. 100 Years of Radio (3rd issue). As T **389**. Multicoloured.
1452 750l. Edouard Branly (physicist) and his "radioconductor" 65 95
Branly developed a method of revealing Hertzian waves.

402 Finish of World Championship 100 Metres Race, Tokyo, 1991

1993. Inauguration of State Television. Sheet 140 × 70 mm containing T **402** and similar horiz designs. Multicolored.
MS1453 2000l. Type **402**; 2000l. Hologram of satellite over San Marino by night; 2000l. Neil Armstrong on the Moon, 1969 . . . 5·75 5·75

404 Scarce Swallowtail ("Iphidides podalirius") on Wild Apple
405 Denmark

1993. Butterflies. Multicoloured.
1454 250l. Type **404** 20 25
1455 250l. Clouded yellow ("Colias crocea") on wild vetch 20 25
1456 250l. Glanville's fritillary ("Melitaea anxia") . . . 20 25
1457 250l. Camberwell beauty ("Nymphalis antiopa") on white willow 20 25

1993. "The European Village". Sheet 145 × 170 mm containing T **405**and similar vert designs, each representing a European Community member. Multicoloured.
MS1458 750l. Type **405**; 750l. England; 750l. Eire; 750l. Luxembourg; 750l. Germany; 750l. Netherlands; 750l. Belgium; 750l. Portugal; 750l. Italy; 750l. Spain; 750l. France; 750l. Greece 9·00 9·00

GOLDONI
1707-1793
SAN MARINO 550

406 Carlo Goldoni
407 San Marino

1993. Death Anniversaries. Multicoloured.
1459 550l. Type **406** (dramatist, bicentenary) 30 40
1460 650l. Horace (Quintus Horatius Flaccus) (poet) (2000th anniv) 30 50
1461 850l. Scene from opera "Orpheus" by Claudio Monteverdi (composer, 350th anniv) (horiz) . . . 55 70
1462 1850l. Guy de Maupassant (writer, centenary) (horiz) 1·10 1·50

1993. Christmas. Multicoloured.
1463 600l. Type **407** 30 55
1464 750l. "Adoration of the Child" (Gerrit van Honthorst) (horiz) 45 65
1465 850l. "Adoration of the Shepherds" (Van Honthorst) 65 80

408 Long-haired Dachshund

1994. 10th International Dog Show. Multicoloured.
1466 350l. Type **408** 25 25
1467 400l. Afghan hound 25 40
1468 450l. Belgian tervuren shepherd dog 25 40
1469 500l. Boston terrier 25 40
1470 550l. Mastiff 30 50
1471 600l. Malamute 35 55

409 Ernst Vettori (90 metre ski jumping)

1994. Winter Olympic Games, Lillehammer, Norway. 1992 Gold Medal Winners. Sheet 164 × 112 mm containing T **409** and similar square designs. Multicoloured.
MS1472 750l. × 2, Type **409**; 750l. × 2, Patrick Ortlieb (downhill skiing); 750l. × 2, Alberto Tomba (giant slalom); 750l. Natalia Mishkutionok and Arthur Dmitriev (pairs figure skating) 5·50 5·50

410 Gate
411 Olympic Flags

1994. Gardens. Multicoloured.
1473 100l. Type **410** 10 15
1474 200l. Pergola 10 20
1475 300l. Well 20 25
1476 450l. Gazebo 20 40
1477 1850l. Pond . . . . 95 1·60

1994. Centenary of International Olympic Committee.
1478 **411** 600l. multicoloured . . . 55 70

1994. 100 Years of Radio (4th issue). As T **389**. Multicoloured.
1479 750l. Aleksandr Stepanovich Popov 50 80
Popov was the first to use a suspended wire as an aerial.

412 Players
413 Route Map

1994. World Cup Football Championship, U.S.A. Multicoloured.
1480 600l. Type **412** 30 50
1481 600l. Player kicking ball . . 30 50
1482 600l. Player heading ball . . 30 50
1483 600l. Players tackling . . . 30 50
1484 600l. Goalkeeper saving goal 30 50

1994. Europa. Discoveries. Exploration of Sun by "Ulysses" Space Probe. Multicoloured.
1485 750l. Type **413** 40 85
1486 850l. "Ulysses" approaching Sun . . . . 50 1·10

414 Government Palace
416 Angels playing Musical Instruments

415 St. Mark's Basilica

1994. Centenary of Government Palace. Mult.
1487 150l. Type **414** 10 20
1488 600l. Tower and San Marino from ramparts . . 30 50
1489 650l. Clock-tower 30 60
1490 1000l. Government chamber (horiz) 55 90

1994. 900th Anniv of Dedication of St. Mark's Basilica, Venice.
1491 **415** 750l. multicoloured . . . 2·75 4·00
MS1492 80 × 115 mm. No. 1491 together with No. 2276 of Italy 1·30 2·75

1994. Christmas. 500th Death Anniv of Giovanni Santi (painter). Details of "The Enthroned Madonna and Child with Saints". Multicoloured.
1493 600l. Type **416** 30 50
1494 750l. Madonna and Child 40 65
1495 850l. Angel playing harp . . 45 75

417/420 "Italy on the Road in a Sea of Flowering Greenery"

1994. Centenary of Italian Touring Club.
1496 **417** 1000l. multicoloured . . 50 60
1497 **418** 1000l. multicoloured . . 50 60
1498 **419** 1000l. multicoloured . . 50 60
1499 **420** 1000l. multicoloured . . 50 60
Nos. 1496/9 were issued together, se-tenant, forming the composite design illustrated.

421 Cyclist
422 Flora and Fauna

1995. Sporting Events. Multicoloured.
1500 100l. Type **421** (Junior World Cycling Championships, Italy and San Marino) 10 20
1501 500l. Volleyball (centenary) 30 40
1502 650l. Skater (Men's Speed-skating Championships, Baselga di Pine, Italy) . . 30 55
1503 850l. Sprinter (World Athletics Championships, Gothenburg, Sweden) . . 50 75

1995. European Nature Conservation Year. Mult.
1504 600l. Type **422** 30 45
1505 600l. Frog, lizard and water lily 30 65
1506 600l. Water lily, bird and ladybirds 30 40
1507 600l. Butterfly, white-headed duckling and frog 30 40
1508 600l. Mallard and duckling 30 40
Nos. 1504/8 were issued together, se-tenant, forming a composite design of river life.

423 U.N. Emblem

1995. 50th Anniv of U.N.O. Multicoloured.
1509 550l. Type **423** 35 45
1510 600l. Rose with emblem . . 30 50
1511 650l. Hourglass 35 60
1512 1200l. Rainbow and emblem forming "50" . . . . . . 65 1·10

424 Mute Swans over Coastline

1995. Europa. Peace and Freedom. Multicoloured.
1513 750l. Type **424** 35 75
1514 850l. Landscape 40 85

425 Basilica and "Legend of the True Cross" (detail of fresco, Agnolo Gaddi)

1995. 700th Anniv of Santa Croce Basilica, Florence. Multicoloured.
1515 1200l. Type **425** . . . . . 75 1·00
1516 1250l. Pazzi Chapel and "Madonna and Child with Saints" (Andrea della Robbia) . . . . 75 1·10

426 Eye and Airplane

1995. 20th Anniv of World Tourism Organization. Multicoloured.
1517 600l. Type **426** 30 50
1518 750l. Five ribbons (continents) around La Rocca fortress 40 65
1519 850l. Airplane and postcards circling globe 50 75
1520 1200l. Five ribbons around globe 75 95

427 Guglielmo Marconi and Transmitter

1995. 100 Years of Radio (5th issue). Centenary of First Radio Transmission. Multicoloured.
1521 850l. Type **427** 50 60
1522 850l. Radio frequency dial 50 60

428 *The General*, 1928 (1)

1995. Centenary of Motion Pictures. Sheet 187 × 120 mm containing T **428** and similar horiz designs. Black "*The General*" or multicoloured (others).
MS1523 250l. × 4, Buster Keaton in *The General*; 250l. × 4, Burt Lancaster and Claudia Cardinale in *The Leopard*; 250l. × 4, Bruno Bozzetto's *Allegro non Troppo* (animated film); 250l. × 4, Mel Gibson in *Braveheart* . . . . . 3·75 3·75
Each film is represented by four different frames, numbered from 1 to 4.

429 Qianmen Complex, 1914

1995. "Beijing 1995" International Stamp and Coin Exhibition, Peking, and Important Cities of the World (14th series). Multicoloured.
1524 1500l. Type **429** . . . . . . 90 1·30
1525 1500l. Qianmen complex, 1995 . . . . 90 1·30

430 "The Anunciation" (detail of illuminated MS)

1995. "Neri of Rimini" Art and Literature Exn.

1526	**430**	650l. multicoloured . . .	50	55

431 Reindeer pulling Sleigh **433** Throwing the Discus

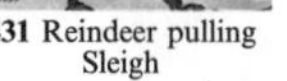

432 Cheetah

1995. Christmas. Multicoloured.

1527	750l. Type **431**	55	75
1528	750l. Children dancing around Christmas tree . .	55	75
1529	750l. Wise Men approaching stable with crib	55	75

Nos. 1527/9 were issued together, se-tenant, forming a composite design.

1995. Inaug of San Marino Express Mail Service.

1530	**432**	6000l. multicoloured . .	3·75	5·25

1996. Centenary of Modern Olympic Games. Mult.

1531	100l. Type **433**	10	15
1532	500l. Wrestling	35	40
1533	650l. Long jumping	35	55
1534	1500l. Throwing the javelin	65	1·30
1535	2500l. Running	1·00	2·00

434 Dolphin swimming

1996. 3rd "Nature World" Exhibition, Rimini. Mult.

1536	50l. Type **434**	10	15
1537	100l. Frog on leaf	10	15
1538	150l. Emperor penguins in snow	10	30
1539	1000l. Butterfly on flower	55	80
1540	3000l. Mallards flying over water	1·70	2·50

435 Mother Teresa of Calcutta

1996. Europa. Famous Women.

1541	**435**	750l. multicoloured . . .	1·00	1·00

436 Marco Polo and Palace in the Forbidden City

1996. 700th Anniv (1995) of Marco Polo's Return from Asia and "China '96" International Stamp Exhibition, Peking.

1542	**436**	1250l. multicoloured . .	1·20	1·10

437 Great Wall of China

1996. 25th Anniv of San Marino–China Diplomatic Relations. Multicoloured.

1543	750l. Type **437**	60	50
1544	750l. Walled rampart, San Marino	60	50
MS1545	110 × 75 mm. Nos. 1543/4	1·50	1·50

Nos. 1543/4 were issued together, se-tenant, forming a composite design.

438 Traditional Weaving **439** Front Page

1996. "Medieval Days" Traditional Festival. Mult.

1546	750l. Type **438**	45	60
1547	750l. Potter	45	60
1548	750l. Traditional craftswoman	45	60
1549	750l. Playing traditional game	45	60
1550	750l. Trumpeters (horiz) . .	45	60
1551	750l. Flag display (horiz) . .	45	60
1552	750l. Crossbow tournament (horiz)	45	60
1553	750l. Dancing and playing musical instruments (horiz)	45	60

1996. Centenary of "La Gazzetta dello Sport" (newspaper).

1554	**439**	1850l. multicoloured . .	1·30	1·60

440 Applauding Crowd

1996. 33rd "Festivalbar" Song Festival.

1555	**440**	2000l. multicoloured . .	1·75	1·30

441 Enrico Caruso and "O Sole Mio"

1996. Italian Music. Singers and Their Songs. Multicoloured.

1556	750l. Type **441**	45	55
1557	750l. Armando Gill and "Come Pioveva"	45	55
1558	750l. Ettore Petrolini and "Gastone"	45	55
1559	750l. Vittorio de Sica and "Parlami d'Amore Mariu"	45	55
1560	750l. Odoardo Spadaro and "La porti un bacione a Firenze"	45	55
1561	750l. Alberto Rabagliati and "O mia bela Madonina"	45	55
1562	750l. Beniamino Gigli and "Mamma"	45	55
1563	750l. Claudio Villa and "Luna rossa"	45	55
1564	750l. Secondo Casadei and "Romagna Mia"	45	55
1565	750l. Renato Rascel and "Arrivederci Roma" . . .	45	55
1566	750l. Fred Buscaglione and "Guarda che luna" . . .	45	55
1567	750l. Domenico Modugno and "Nel blu, dipinto di blu"	45	55

442 Yellowstone National Park, United States

1996. 50th Anniv of UNESCO. World Heritage Sites. Multicoloured.

1568	450l. Type **442**	25	35
1569	500l. Prehistoric cave paintings, Vezere Valley, France	40	40
1570	650l. San Gimignano, Italy	50	55
1571	1450l. Wies Pilgrimage Church, Germany	95	1·20

443 Hen and Chicks

1996. 50th Anniv of UNICEF. Multicoloured.

1572	550l. Type **443**	35	45
1573	1000l. Chicks in nest	70	85

444 Playing Lotto

1996. Christmas. Multicoloured.

1574	750l. Type **444**	40	55
1575	750l. Hanging decoration . .	40	55
1576	750l. Father Christmas on sleigh and child reading book	40	55
1577	750l. Christmas tree	40	55
1578	750l. Bowls of fruit and nuts	40	55
1579	750l. Snowflakes and shooting star	40	55
1580	750l. Children's toys	40	55
1581	750l. Presents	40	55
1582	750l. Hanging Father Christmas decoration . .	40	55
1583	750l. Nativity scene	40	55
1584	750l. Mistletoe	40	55
1585	750l. Stocking hanging on mantelpiece	40	55
1586	750l. Family celebrating . .	40	55
1587	750l. Christmas tree outside window and party	40	55
1588	750l. Snowman outside window and party	40	55
1589	750l. Calendar pages and bottle of champagne (New Year's celebrations) . . .	40	55

Nos. 1574/89 were issued together, se-tenant, forming a composite design.

445 Hong Kong, 1897

1997. Important Cities of the World (15th series). Sheet 84 × 94 mm containing T **445** and similar horiz design. Multicoloured.

MS1590	750l. Type **445**; 750l. Hong Kong, 1997	1·50	1·50

446/449 Championship Races

1997. World Skiing Championships, Sestriere.

1591	**446**	1000l. multicoloured . .	55	80
1592	**447**	1000l. multicoloured . .	55	80
1593	**448**	1000l. multicoloured . .	55	80
1594	**449**	1000l. multicoloured . .	55	80

Nos. 1591/4 were issued together, se-tenant, forming the composite design illustrated.

450 Acquaviva

1997. Communes. Multicoloured.

1595	100l. Type **450**	10	10
1596	200l. Borgomaggiore	10	15
1597	250l. Chiesanuova	10	20
1598	400l. Domagnano	25	35
1599	500l. Faetano	30	40
1600	550l. Fiorentino	35	45
1601	650l. Montegiardino	45	55
1602	750l. Serravalle	50	60
1603	5000l. San Marino	2·75	4·00

451 St. Marinus tames the Bear

1997. Europa. Tales and Legends. Multicoloured.

1604	650l. Type **451**	45	75
1605	750l. Felicissima begs St. Marinus to cure her son Verissimus	55	80

452 Bicycle and Stopwatch

1997. Sporting Events in San Marino. Each with Mt. Titano in the background. Multicoloured.

1606	500l. Type **452** (80th Giro d'Italia cycle race)	20	40
1607	550l. Tennis racket and ball (men's tennis championships)	30	45
1608	750l. Ferrari Formula One racing car (17th San Marino Grand Prix) . . .	30	60
1609	850l. Juventus badge, football and trophy (Republic of San Marino Trophy football championship)	45	70
1610	1000l. Boules (World Petanque Championship)	55	80
1611	1250l. Motor cycle (World 250cc Motocross Championship)	80	1·00
1612	1500l. Car dashboard (Mille Miglia (classic car rally))	1·10	1·20

453 Scanning the Heavens **454** Stone Pine

1997. 5th International Symposium on Unidentified Flying Objects and Associated Phenomena, San Marino.

1613	**453**	750l. multicoloured . . .	45	60

1997. Trees. Multicoloured.

1614	50l. Type **454**	15	10
1615	800l. White oak	50	65
1616	1800l. Walnut	1·10	1·60
1617	2000l. Pear	1·30	1·80

455 Count Giovanni Barbavera di Grevellona

1997. 120th Anniv of First San Marino Postage Stamp.

1618	**455**	800l. brown and green	50	60
1619	–	800l. brown and blue . .	50	60
1620	–	800l. brown and mauve	50	60
1621	–	800l. brown and red . .	50	60

DESIGNS: No. 1618, Type **455** (Director-General of Italian Post Office and co-signatory of postal convention between Italy and San Marino); 1619, Italian Government Printing Works, Turin, and Enrico Repettati (chief engraver); 1620, "San Marino-Philatelist" (monthly magazine) and Otto Bickel (collectables dealer) holding illustrated envelopes; 1621, Alfredo Reffi (stamp dealer and postcard publisher) and postcard.

456 First Tower and Dal Monte

1997. Beatification of Father Bartolomeo Maria dal Monte.
1622 **456** 800l. multicoloured . . . 50 65

457 Quadratino (Antonio Rubino)

1997. Italian Comic Strips. Multicoloured.
1623 800l. Type **457** 50 65
1624 800l. Signor Bonaventura (Sergio Tofano) 50 65
1625 800l. Kit Carson (Rino Albertarelli) 50 65
1626 800l. Cocco Bill (Benito Jacovitti) 50 65
1627 800l. Tex Willer (Gian Bonelli and Aurelio Galleppini) 50 65
1628 800l. Diabolik (Angela and Luciana Giussani and Franco Paludetti) 50 65
1629 800l. Valentina (Guido Crepax) 50 65
1630 800l. Corto Maltese (Hugo Pratt) 50 65
1631 800l. Sturmtruppen (Franco Bonvicini) 50 65
1632 800l. Alan Ford (Max Bunker) 50 65
1633 800l. Lupo Alberto (Guido Silvestri) 50 65
1634 800l. Pimpa (Francesco Tullio Altan) 50 65
1635 800l. Bobo (Sergio Staino) 50 65
1636 800l. Zanardi (Andrea Pazienza) 50 65
1637 800l. Martin Mystere (Alfredo Castelli and Giancarlo Alessandrini) 50 65
1638 800l. Dylan Dog (Tiziano Sclavi and Angelo Stano) 50 65

458 St. Francis of Assisi and Dove

1997. Voluntary and Charitable Service. Mult.
1639 550l. Type **458** (voluntary aid after Assisi earthquake) 30 45
1640 650l. Mariele Ventre (organizer of Zecchino d'Oro) and children (40th anniv of Antoniano in Bologna (charitable organization)) 40 55
1641 800l. Children around globe (40th anniv of Zecchino d'Oro (children's song festival)) 45 70

459 "Adoration of the Magi" (detail of altarpiece by Giorgio Vasari, San Fortunato Abbey, Rimini)

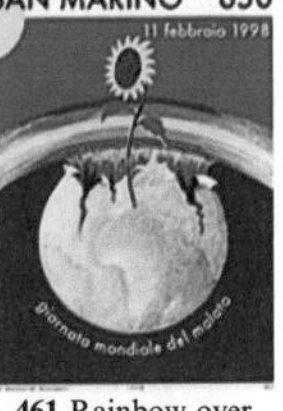

461 Rainbow over Grass and Sunflower erupting from Globe

460 Beetle

1997. Christmas.
1642 **459** 800l. multicoloured . . . 55 70

1997. 60th Anniv of Volkswagen (motor manufacturer). Sheet 154×115 mm containing T **460** and similar horiz designs. Multicoloured.
MS1643 800l. Type **460**; 800l. Golf Mk I; 800l. New Beetle; 800l. Golf Mk IV . . . . 3·00 3·00

1998. World Day of the Sick. Multicoloured.
1644 650l. Type **461** 40 55
1645 1500l. Dove and rainbow over waves and globe . . 85 1·20

462 125S Racing Car, 1947

1998. Birth Centenary of Enzo Ferrari (motor manufacturer). Racing Cars. Multicoloured.
1646 800l. Type **462** 50 65
1647 880l. Model 375, 1950 (wrongly inscr "500 F2, 1952") 50 65
1648 800l. Lancia D50, 1956 (wrongly inscr "801") . . 50 65
1649 800l. Racing car (wrongly inscr "246 Dino") 50 65
1650 800l. Model 156, 1961 . . . 50 65
1651 800l. John Surtees' 158, 1964 . . . . 50 65
1652 800l. Niki Lauda's 312T, 1975 . . . . 50 65
1653 800l. Jody Scheckter's 312T4, 1979 . . . . . . 50 65
1654 800l. Model 126C, 1981 . . 50 65
1655 800l. Michelo Alboreto's 156/85, 1985 . . . . . . 50 65
1656 800l. Model 639, 1989 . . . 50 65
1657 800l. Michael Schumacher's F310, 1996 . . . . 50 65

463 Verse of "Infinity", 1819

1998. Birth Bicentenary of Giacomo Leopardi (poet). Multicoloured.
1658 550l. Type **463** 40 50
1659 650l. "A Village Saturday", 1829 . . . . 40 60
1660 900l. "Nocturne of a Wandering Asian Shepherd", 1822–30 . . . 60 75
1661 2000l. "To Sylvia", 1828 . . 1·30 1·60

464 Installation of Captains Regent

466 Goalkeeper reaching for Ball

465 Emigrants on Ship, Passport and Ticket

1998. Europa. National Festivals. Multicoloured.
1662 650l. Type **464** 45 60
1663 1200l. Religious procession (Feast Day of Patron Saint) . . . . 75 1·10

1998. Museum of the Emigrant. Multicoloured.
1664 800l. Type **465** 65 65
1665 1500l. Emigrants working, restaurant, work permit, pay slip, money and residency permit . . . . 1·10 1·20

1998. World Cup Football Championship, France. Multicoloured.
1666 650l. Type **466** 60 60
1667 800l. Two players challenging for ball . . . 90 80
1668 900l. Three players challenging for ball . . . 1·10 85

467 Launch of Space Shuttle, Cape Canaveral

1998. San Marino Flag in Space. Sheet 140×70 mm containing T **467** and similar horiz designs. Multicoloured.
MS1669 2000l. Type **467**; 2000l, Space capsule in orbit and San Marino flag; 2000l. Space shuttle returning to Earth . . . . . . 5·00 5·00

468 "20,000 Leagues Under the Sea" (Jules Verne)

469 Sailing Dinghy and Factory Chimneys

1998. Science Fiction Novels. Multicoloured.
1670 800l. Type **468** 45 65
1671 800l. "War of the Worlds" (H. G. Wells) (centenary of publication) 45 65
1672 800l. "Brave New World" (Aldous Huxley) 45 65
1673 800l. "1984" (George Orwell) 45 65
1674 800l. "Foundation Trilogy" (Isaac Asimov) 45 65
1675 800l. "City" (Clifford D. Simak) 45 65
1676 800l. "Fahrenheit 451" (Ray Bradbury) 45 65
1677 800l. "The Seventh Victim" (Robert Sheckley) 45 65
1678 800l. "The Space Merchants" (Frederik Pohl and Cyril Kornbluth) 45 65
1679 800l. "The Coming Dark Age" (Roberto Vacca) . . 45 65
1680 800l. "Stranger in a Strange Land" (Robert Heinlein) 45 65
1681 800l. "A Clockwork Orange" (Anthony Burgess) 45 65
1682 800l. "The Drowned World" (James Ballard) 45 65
1683 800l. "Dune" (Frank Herbert) 45 65
1684 800l. "2001 A Space Odyssey" (Arthur Clarke) 45 65
1685 800l. "Do Androids Dream of Electric Sheep?" (Philip K. Dick) 45 65

1998. International Stamp Fair, Riccione. Mult.
1686 800l. Type **469** 45 65
1687 1500l. Dolphin jumping through stamp and factory chimneys . . . . 90 1·20

470 Pope John Paul II

1998. "Italia 98" International Stamp Exhibition, Milan (1st issue).
1688 **470** 800l. multicoloured . . . 70 65
See also No. 1695.

471 Boy and Tree of Santa Clauses

472 Woman

1998. Christmas. Multicoloured.
1689 800l. Type **471** 50 75
1690 800l. Pacific Island child . . 50 75
1691 800l. Boy in clogs and rabbit 50 75
1692 800l. Girl and dog 50 75
Nos. 1689/92 were issued together, se-tenant, forming a composite design of a tree of Santa Clauses bearing gifts.

1998. 50th Anniv of Universal Declaration of Human Rights. Multicoloured.
1693 900l. Type **472** 65 75
1694 900l. Man 65 75
Nos. 1693/4 were issued together, se-tenant, forming a composite design.

473 "The Joy of Living" (Emilio Greco)

475 Hand writing with Quill Pen

474 "The Coronation of Poppea" (Claudio Monteverdi)

1998. "Italia 98" International Stamp Exhibition (2nd issue). Art Day.
1695 **473** 1800l. multicoloured . . 1·10 1·50

DENOMINATION. From No. 1696 San Marino stamps are denominated both in lire and in euros. As no cash for the latter is in circulation, the catalogue continues to use the lira value.

1999. 400 Years of Opera. Multicoloured.
1696 800l. Type **474** 50 65
1697 800l. "Dido and Aeneas" (Henry Purcell) 50 65
1698 800l. "Orpheus and Eurydice" (Christoph Willibald Gluck) 50 65
1699 800l. "Don Juan" (Wolfgang Amadeus Mozart) 50 65
1700 800l. "The Barber of Seville" (Gioacchino Rossini) 50 65
1701 800l. "Norma" (Vincenzo Bellini) 50 65
1702 800l. "Lucia di Lammermoor" (Gaetano Donizetti) 50 65
1703 800l. "Aida" (Giuseppe Verdi) 50 65
1704 800l. "Faust" (Charles Gounod) 50 65
1705 800l. "Carmen" (Georges Bizet) 50 65
1706 800l. "The Ring of the Nibelung" (Richard Wagner) 50 65
1707 800l. "Boris Godunov" (Modest Musorgsky) . . . 50 65
1708 800l. "Tosca" (Giacomo Puccini) 50 65
1709 800l. "The Love for Three Oranges" (Sergei Prokofiev) 50 65
1710 800l. "Porgy and Bess" (George Gershwin) . . . 50 65
1711 800l. "West Side Story" (Leonard Bernstein) . . . 50 65

1999. 12th World Hang-gliding Championship, Montecucco, Italy. Multicoloured.
1712 800l. Type **475** 45 65
1713 1800l. Hang-glider with balloon . . . . 1·10 1·50

476 Mountain Pine

1999. San Marino Bonsai Exhibition. Mult.
1714 50l. Type **476** 15 10
1715 300l. Olive 15 25
1716 350l. Scots pine 20 30
1717 500l. Pedunculate oak . . . 25 40

477 Eastern Slopes of Mount Titano

1999. Europa. Parks and Gardens. Multicoloured.
1718 650l. Type **477** 45 65
1719 1250l. Cesta Tower, Mount Titano . . . . 70 1·20

478 Emblem and Town Hall, Treviso

1999. World Cycling Championships, Treviso and Verona, Italy. Multicoloured.
1720 900l. Type **478** 55 75
1721 3000l. Emblem and amphitheatre, Verona . . 1·80 2·50

479 Article 1 of First Treaty (1874) and Swiss Parliament Building

1999. 125th Anniv of Universal Postal Union. Multicoloured.
1722 800l. Type **479** 50 65
1723 3000l. World map highlighting original U.P.U. signatories, 1875 1·80 2·50

480 Garibaldi (after Lorusso) and Crowds in front of the Quirinale, Rome

1999. 150th Anniv of Garibaldi's Refuge in San Marino after Fall of the Roman Republic.
1724 **480** 1250l. multicoloured . . 75 1·00

481 "50" and People climbing Ladder to Council Emblem

1999. 50th Anniv of Council of Europe.
1725 **481** 1300l. multicoloured . . 80 1·10

482 European Brown Hare

1999. Animals. Multicoloured.
1726 500l. Type **482** 30 40
1727 650l. Eurasian red squirrel 45 55
1728 1100l. Eurasian badger . . . 65 90
1729 1250l. Red fox . . . . . . 70 1·00
1730 1850l. North African crested porcupine . . . . 1·10 1·50

483 Pilgrimage Route Map and Canterbury Cathedral

1999. Holy Year 2000. Multicoloured.
1731 650l. Type **483** 45 55
1732 800l. Priest blessing pilgrim (fresco, Novalesa Abbey) and Rheims Cathedral . . 50 65
1733 900l. Hospice welcoming pilgrims (fresco, St. James's Chapel, Briancon) and Pavia Cathedral 55 75
1734 1250l. Pilgrims on the road (bas-relief, Fidenza Cathedral) and Fidenza Cathedral . . . . 70 1·00
1735 1500l. "Mount of Joy" (Sir Charles Eastlake) and St. Peter's Cathedral, Rome . . . . 85 1·20

484 Fregoso Castle, Sant'Agata Feltria

1999. Architecture of Montefeltro. Multicoloured.
1736 50l. Type **484** 10 10
1737 250l. Feltresca Castle, San Leo 15 30
1738 650l. Ducal Palace, Urbino 40 65
1739 1300l. Ubaldinesca Castle, Sassocorvaro . . . . . . 75 1·30
1740 6000l. Il Montale and La Rocca fortress, San Marino . . . . 3·50 5·50

485 St. Martin tearing Cloak in Half

1999. 50th Anniv of San Marino Red Cross.
1741 **485** 800l. multicoloured . . . 50 75

486 Team Photograph (Italian championship, 1901)

1999. Centenary of A. C. Milan Football Club. Sheet 155 × 115 mm containing T **486** and similar horiz designs. Multicoloured.
MS1742 800l. Type **486**; 800l. Players Gren, Nordahl and Liedholm, 1950s; 800l. Team photograph, Wembley (goalkeeper in front row) (European Championship, 1963); 800l. Team photograph, Vienna (goalkeeper in back row), 1990; 800l. Team and children celebrating Italian Championship, 1994; 800l. Team with trophy (Italian Championship, 1999) . . . . . 3·75 3·50

487 Nativity

1999. Christmas.
1743 **487** 800l. multicoloured . . . 50 75

488 18/50 h.p. Horch

1999. Centenary of Audi (car manufacturer). Sheet 155 × 115 mm containing T **488** and similar horiz designs. Multicoloured.
MS1744 1500l. Type **488**; 1500l. Audi TT; 1500l. Audi A8; 1500l. Auto Union racing car . . . . 4·50 4·50

489 Tank, Soldiers and Civilians (First and Second World Wars)

2000. The Twentieth Century. Multicoloured.
1745 650l. Type **489** 40 55
1746 650l. Syringe being filled, scanner and DNA molecular structure (science and medicine) . . 40 55
1747 650l. Washing machine, underground train and lamp (electricity) . . . .
1748 650l. Switchboard operators, radio and computer (telecommunications) . . 40 55
1749 650l. Airplanes, airship and astronaut on Moon (conquest of space) . . . 40 55
1750 650l. Factory chimneys and rubbish (pollution) . . . 40 55
1751 650l. Sports car, lorry and traffic jam (development of motor vehicles) 40 55
1752 650l. Submarine and mushroom cloud (atomic energy) 40 55
1753 650l. Charlie Chaplin in *Modern Times*, comic strip and chair (cinema, comics and design) 40 55
1754 650l. Crossword puzzle, art gallery and car towing caravan (leisure activities) 40 55
1755 650l. Advertising posters (publicity) 40 55
1756 650l. Cyclist, stadium and footballers (sport) 40 55

490 St. John Lateran Basilica, Rome, Pilgrim (detail of engraving by G. Perugino) and Mt. Titano

2000. Holy Year 2000. Sheet 155 × 115 mm containing T **490** and similar horiz designs. Multicoloured.
MS1757 1000l. Type **490**; 1000l. St. Paul without the Walls Basilica, Rome, St. Marinus (statue) and La Rocca fortress; 1000l. St. Mary Major Basilica, Rome, with Madonna and Child; 1000l. St. Peter's Basilica, Rome, and St. Marinus (detail of painting by Pompeo Batoni) . . . . . 3·00 3·00

491 Emblem and La Rocca Fortress

492 I.I.S.A. Emblem, Government Palace, Fiera di Bologna Towers and Statue of Liberty, San Marino

2000. 40th Anniv of San Marino Rotary Club. Mult.
1758 650l. Type **491** 35 65
1759 800l. Government Palace, Arms and Statue of Liberty, San Marino . . . 55 75

2000. International Institute of Administrative Science Conference, Bologna (1760) and European City of Culture (others). Multicoloured.
1760 650l. Type **492** 30 65
1761 800l. Guglielmo Marconi's workbench, radio aerial, San Pietro Cathedral, clock tower, Tubertini dome and St. Petronius Basilica 40 75
1762 1200l. Microchip, musical instruments, St. Petronius Basilica, Santa Maria della Vita Church and Asinelli and Garisenda Towers . . . . 65 1·10
1763 1500l. Books, detail of still life by Giorgio Morandi, campanile and apse of St. Giacomo Maggiore and St. Francis Churches and Arengo Tower . . . 1·10 1·40

493 Vincenzo Muccioli (founder of San Patrignano Community) and Drug Addict

2000. 5th Anniv of Rainbow International Association Against Drugs. Multicoloured.
1764 650l. Type **493** 35 55
1765 1200l. Blocks spelling "rainbow" in sky . . . . 65 1·10
1766 2400l. Muccioli and reformed addicts . . . . 1·60 2·20

494 "Building Europe"

496 Dog and Butterfly

495 "2000"

2000. Europa.
1767 **494** 800l. multicoloured . . . 30 75

2000. "Stampin' the Future". Winning Entries in Children's International Painting Competition.
1768 **495** 800l. multicoloured . . . 50 75

2000. Olympic Games, Sydney. Multicoloured.
1769 1000l. Type **496** 70 95
1770 1000l. Hippopotamus and penguin 70 95
1771 1000l. Elephant and ladybird 70 95
1772 1000l. Rabbit and snail . . 70 95

497 Bicycles

2000. Centenary of International Cycling Union.
1773 **497** 1200l. multicoloured . . 70 1·10

498 Child hiding beneath Soldier's Helmet

2000. 10th Anniv of International Convention on Children's Rights. Multicoloured.
1774 650l. Type **498** 40 55
1775 800l. Child cowering away from frightening shadow 50 75
1776 1200l. Child in flower . . . 75 1·10
1777 1500l. Childhood fantasies tumbling from book . . . 90 1·50

499 Council Emblem and child's face

2000. 50th Anniv of the European Convention on Human Rights.
1778 **499** 800l. multicoloured . . . 50 75

500 Basilica of the Saint

2000. Churches of Montefeltro. Multicoloured.
1779 650l. Type **500** 40 55
1780 800l. Church of St. Mary of Antico, Maiolo 55 75
1781 1000l. St. Lawrence's Church, Talamello . . . 60 95
1782 1500l. Parish Church, San Leo . . . . 90 1·40
1783 1800l. Sanctuary of Our Lady of Graces, Pennabilli . . . . 1·10 1·70

501 "Virgin and Child" (Ludovico Carracci)

2000. Christmas.
1784 **501** 800l. multicoloured . . . 1·90 75

502 Melchiorre Delfico (author of *History of the Republic of San Marino*) and Title Page

2000. 1700th Anniv of San Marino (1st issue). Multicoloured.
1785 800l. Type **502** 50 75
1786 800l. Guiseppe Garibaldi (painting) 50 75
1787 800l. Abraham Lincoln and passage from his letter to the Captains Regent, 1861 50 75
1788 800l. Refugees arriving in San Marino, 1943–45 . . 50 75
1789 800l. Roman jewels 50 75
1790 800l. 1463 map of San Marino 50 75
1791 800l. Napoleon Bonaparte 50 75
1792 800l. "L'Arengo" (detail) (postcard, 1906) 50 75
1793 800l. Child, class and swimming pool 50 75
1794 800l. Young man, construction site and computers 50 75
1795 800l. Woman, street scene and church 50 75
1796 800l. Man, dancers and building 50 75
1797 1200l. St. Marinus (detail) (Francesco Manzocchi di Forl) . . . . 75 1·20
1798 1200l.15 th-century painting of St. Marinus . . . . . 75 1·20
1799 1200l. St. Marinus (painting, School of Guercino) . . . 75 1·20
1800 1200l. "St. Marinus in glory" (anon) . . . . . . 75 1·20
1801 1200l. Double throne of Captains Regent . . . . 75 1·20
1802 1200l. Title page of 17th-century edition of Republican Statutes . . . 75 1·20
1803 1200l. Parade of Palace guards . . . . 75 1·20
1804 1200l. Flags . . . . 75 1·20
See also Nos. 1846/9.

503 Michael Schumacher and Ferrari Racing Car

2001. Michael Schumacher Drivers' Champion and Ferrari. Constructors' Champion (2000). Sheet 110 × 75 mm containing T **503** and similar horiz designs. Multicoloured.
MS1805 1500l. Type **503**; 1500l. Schumacher, racing car and engineers . . . . 2·50 2·50

504 Verdi and Scene from *Nabucco*

2001. Death Centenary of Guiseppe Verdi (composer). Scenes from named operas. Multicoloured.
1806 800l. Type **504** 50 75
1807 800l. *Ernani* 50 75
1808 800l. *Rigoletto* 50 75
1809 800l. *Il Trovatore* 50 75
1810 800l. *La Traviata* 50 75
1811 800l. *I Vespri Siciliani* . . . 50 75
1812 800l. *Un Ballo in Maschera* 50 75
1813 800l. *La Forza del Destino* 50 75
1814 800l. *Don Carlos* 50 75
1815 800l. *Aida* 50 75
1816 800l. *Otello* 50 75
1817 800l. *Falstaff* 50 75

505 Malatestian Temple (by Leon Battista Alberti), Rimini

2001. Commemoration of Malatesta Family (Lords of Rimini). Multicoloured.
1818 800l. Type **505** 50 75
1819 1200l. "Christ's Devotion" (Giovanni Bellini) . . . . 70 1·10

506 Yacht

507 Bowls and Athletics

2001. 10th Anniv of "San Marino 24 Hour Yacht Race". Multicoloured.
1820 1200l. Type **506** . . . . . 70 1·10
1821 1200l. Yacht with green and purple spinnaker . . . . 70 1·10
1822 1200l. Yacht with brown and white sails . . . . . 70 1·10
1823 1200l. Yacht with white spinnaker . . . . 70 1·10

2001. 9th European Small States Games. Multicoloured.
1824 800l. Type **507** 50 75
1825 800l. Swimming 50 75
1826 800l. Cycling 50 75
1827 800l. Target and skeet shooting 50 75
1828 800l. Judo 50 75
1829 800l. Tennis and table tennis 50 75
1830 800l. Basketball and volleyball 50 75
1831 800l. RASTA (mascot) . . . 50 75

508 Safe containing Water and Forest

509 *Santa Maria* and *Dahlia variablis*

2001. Europa. Water Resources. Multicoloured.
1832 800l. Type **508** 55 75
1833 1200l. Mountain, tap and running water . . . . . 80 1·10

2001. "Euroflora 2001" International Flower Show, Genoa. Multicoloured.
1834 800l. Type **509** 50 75
1835 1200l. *Santa Maria* and *Zantedeschia aethiopica* 70 1·10
1836 1500l. *Santa Maria* and rose "Helen Troubel" . . . . 90 1·40
1837 2400l. Faro Tower, Genoa and *Amaryllis hippeastrum* . . . . 1·40 2·30

510 Ellis Island Immigration Museum, New York

2001. "Emigration of the Sammarinese" Exhibition, New York and 25th Anniv of San Marino Social Club, Detroit. Multicoloured.
1838 1200l. Type **510** . . . . . 70 1·10
1839 2400l. San Marino Social Club, Detroit . . . . . . 1·40 2·20

511 Early Stringed Instrument and Ceramics

2001. Inauguration of State Museum. Multicoloured.
1840 550l. Type **511** 35 45
1841 800l. Painting and gallery 50 75
1842 1500l. Ancient ceramics . . 90 1·40
1843 2000l. European artifacts . . 2·75 1·90

512 Figure reaching Downwards

2001. 50th Anniv of United Nations High Commissioner for Refugees. Multicoloured.
1844 1200l. Type **512** . . . . . 70 1·10
1845 1200l. Figure reaching upwards . . . . 70 1·10
Nos. 1844/5 were issued together, se-tenant, forming a composite design.

513 Mount Titan

2001. 1700th Anniv of San Marino (2nd issue). Scenes of Mount Titan. Multicoloured.
1846 1200l. Type **513** . . . . . 70 1·10
1847 1200l. Three Towers, Mount Titan . . . . 70 1·10
1848 1200l. Fields below Mount Titan . . . . 70 1·10
1849 1200l. Urban infrastructure below Mount Titan . . . 70 1·10

514 Old Bakery Mill Silo and Woman surrounded by People

2001. 125th Anniv of San Marino Social Welfare Union (S.U.M.S.). Multicoloured.
1850 1200l. Type **514** 70 70
1851 1200l. New Bakery Mill Silo headquarters and woman giving sheaves of corn to crowd 70 70

515 Banner

2001. "Defence of Nature" Exhibition of Works by Joseph Beuys (artist), San Marino.
1852 **515** 2400l. multicoloured . . 1·40 2·30

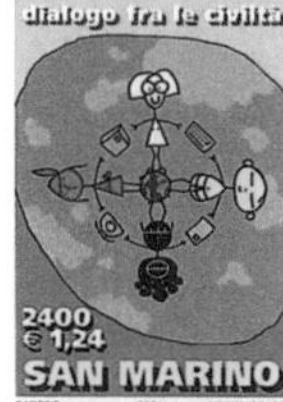

516 Children encircling Globe

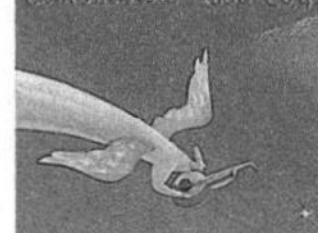
517 Angel playing Lute

2001. United Nations Year of Dialogue among Civilizations.
1853 **516** 2400l. multicoloured . . 1·40 2·30

2001. Christmas. Multicoloured.
1854 800l. Type **517** 50 45
1855 800l. Woman with basket and king riding on camel 50 45
1856 800l. King riding camel, woman leading sheep, and woman with parcel . . . 50 45
1857 800l. Man with parcel and Holy Family on Mount Titano 50 45
1858 800l. Sheep, birds and man with lantern 50 45
1859 800l. Ascending angel with trumpet 50 45
1860 800l. Angel with lyre . . . 50 45
1861 800l. King with blue crown riding camel 50 45
1862 800l. Women with parcel, basket and dog 50 45
1863 800l. Shepherd and sheep 50 45
1864 800l. Descending angel with trumpet 50 45
1865 800l. Woman with parcel and angel with trumpet 50 45
1866 800l. Angel playing violin 50 45
1867 800l. Man with parcels on sledge 50 45
1868 800l. Woman with parcel in right hand 50 45
1869 800l. Angel playing drum 50 45
Nos. 1854/69 were issued together, se-tenant, forming a composite design.

518 Coins and Map of Euro Zone

2001. Introduction of Euro Coins and Banknotes (2002). Multicoloured.
1870 1200l. Type **518** 50 70
1871 2400l. Banknotes and map of Euro Zone . . . . . . 1·40 1·40

New Currency 100 cents = 1 euro

519 Rabbits

520 Hippopotamus Ice Skating

2002. New Currency. Multicoloured.
1872 1c. Type **519** 10 10
1873 2c. Sunset 10 10
1874 5c. Cactus flower 10 10
1875 10c. Field of grain 15 15
1876 25c. Alpine landscape . . . 40 40
1877 50c. Olive leaves 75 75
1878 €1 Sparrows . . . . 1·40 1·40
1879 €5 Baby . . . . 7·25 7·25

2002. Winter Olympic Games, Salt Lake City. Multicoloured.
1885 41c. Type **520** 60 60
1886 41c. Dog skiing 60 60
1887 41c. Elephant playing ice hockey 60 60
1888 41c. Rabbit cross-country skiing 60 60

521 Poggiali racing

2002. Manuel Poggiali—2001 125cc. Motorcycle World Champion. Multicoloured.
1889 62c. Type **521** 90 90
1890 62c. Side view of Poggiali racing 90 90

522 Trapeze Artist

2002. Europa. Circus. Multicoloured.
1891 36c. Type **522** 55 55
1892 62c. Equestrienne performer 90 90

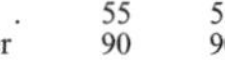

523 Players and Ball (finals, 1934)

2002. World Cup Football Championship, Japan and South Korea. Winning Italian Teams. Sheet 155 × 116 mm, containing T **523** and similar horiz designs. Multicoloured.
MS1893 41c. Type **523** (score wrongly inscr as 4-2); 41c. Player heading ball (finals, 1938) (score wrongly inscr as 1-0); 41c. Players jumping (semi-finals, 1970); 41c. Italy and Brazil players at goal mouth (finals, 1982); 41c. Player tackling (third-place playoff, 1990); 41c. Italy and Nigeria (No 10 players at goal (second round, 1994)) . . . . 3·75 3·50

524 Cyclist

2002. Priority Mail Stamps. Multicoloured.
1894 62c. Type **524** 90 90
1895 €1.24 Hurdler . . . . . . 1·80 1·80

525 Three Towers, Mount Titano — **527** 1877 2c. and 10c. Stamps

526 Map of Europe as Tree

2002. International Year of Mountains. Mult.
1896 41c. Type **525** 60 60
1897 41c. Tower and wall on Mount Titano 60 60
1898 41c. Tower on peak 60 60

2002. 10th Anniv of Maastricht Treaty.
1899 **526** €1.24 multicoloured . . 1·80 1·80

2002. 125th Anniv of First San Marino Stamps. Sheet 140 × 71 mm, containing T **527** and similar square designs depicting stamps (issued in 1877). Multicoloured.
MS1900 €1.24, Type **527**; €1.24, 10c. and 20c. stamps; €1.24, 20c. and 30c. stamps; €1.24, 30c. and 40c. stamps . . . . 10·00 10·00

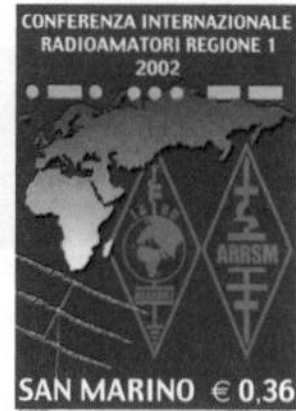

528 Blacksmith working at Anvil — **529** Emblems, World Map, Aerial and Morse Code Notation

2002. Traditional Crafts. Multicoloured.
1901 26c. Type **528** 40 40
1902 36c. Broom-maker tying grass bundle 55 55
1903 41c. Chair-mender repairing chair seat 60 60
1904 77c. Scribe writing at table 1·10 1·10
1905 €1.24 Knife-grinder sharpening knife at wheel 1·80 1·80
1906 €1.55 Charcoal burner and wood clamp . . . . . . 2·20 2·20

2002. International Amateur Radio Union Region 1 Conference. Multicoloured.
1907 36c. Type **529** 65 55
1908 62c. Emblems, national flag, world map, aerial and Morse code notation . . . 90 90

530 Government Palace — **531** Woman's Mouth

2002. Tourism. Sheet 150 × 116 mm, containing T **530** and similar multicoloured designs showing places of interest.
MS1909 62c. Type **530**; 62c. Guaita (First Tower), Mount Titan (44 × 30 mm); 62c. Cesta (Second Tower) and Montale (Third Tower), Mount Titan (44 × 30 mm); 62c. Basilicia del Santo and San Pietro Church; 62c. Capuchin Church; 62c. St. Francis gate (39 × 39 mm) . . . . . . 5·25 5·25

2002. Greetings Stamps. Multicoloured.
1910 41c. Type **531** 60 60
1911 41c. Child's face and "Hello" 60 60
1912 41c. Man's face and "best wishes" 60 60
1913 41c. Baby's face and "Ehi" 60 60
1914 41c. Man's perplexed face 60 60
1915 41c. Hand covering smiling face and "sorry" 60 60

532 Child's and Adults Hands

2002. Christmas. Sheet 185 × 144 mm, containing T **532** and similar vert designs. Multicoloured.
MS1916 41c. Type **532**; 41c. Mother wearing earrings and baby; 41c. Baby at breast; 41c. Mother and baby sleeping; 41c. Adult hands holding baby; 41c. Mother and baby wrapped in shawl; 41c. Wakeful baby against mother's left shoulder; 41c. Baby with finger in mouth laughing with mother; 41c. Baby asleep against mother's left shoulder; 41c. Baby looking away from smiling mother; 41c. Baby with arm extended towards mother's face; 41c. Two babies 7·00 7·00

533 Mushrooms and Artichokes

2003. Italian Cuisine. Multicoloured.
1917 41c. Type **533** 60 60
1918 41c. Cooked meats 60 60
1919 41c. Spaghetti 60 60
1920 41c. Cappelletti 60 60
1921 41c. Prawns 60 60
1922 41c. Mixed seafood 60 60
1923 41c. Ravioli 60 60
1924 41c. Tagliatelle 60 50
1925 41c. Chicken and potatoes 60 60
1926 41c. Fish 60 60
1927 41c. Fruit tart 60 60
1928 41c. Chocolate pudding . . 60 60
1929 41c. Scrambled eggs 60 60
1930 41c. Pancetta 60 60
1931 41c. Pastries 60 60
1932 41c. Brandy snap basket . . 60 60

534 "Woman with Mango" (Paul Gauguin)

2003. Artists' Anniversaries. Multicoloured.
1933 52c. Type **534** (death centenary) 75 70
1934 62c. "Wheat-field with flight of crows" (Vincent Van Gogh) (150th birth anniv) 90 90
1935 €1.55 "Portrait of a young woman" (Parmigianino) (500th birth anniv) . . . 2·20 2·20

535 Combination Skiing

2003. World Nordic Skiing Championship, Val di Femme. Sheet 156 × 116 mm containing T **535** and similar vert designs. Multicoloured.
MS1936 Type **535**; 77c. Ski jumping; 77c. Cross-country skiing . . . . 3·50 3·50

536 Molvedo (horse) — **537** Partially submerged Woman's Head (Armando Testa)

2003. Horse Racing. Showing champion race horses. Multicoloured.
1937 11c. Type **536** 15 15
1938 15c. Tornese 20 20
1939 26c. Ribot 35 35
1940 €1.55 Varenne . . . . . . 2·20 2·20

2003. Europa. Poster Art. Multicoloured.
1941 28c. Type **537** 35 35
1942 77c. "Jane Avril" (Toulouse Latrec) . . . . 1·00 1·00

538 Girolamo Fracastoro

2003. 550th Death Anniv of Girolamo Fracastoro (writer and scientist) Centenary of Veronafil Exhibition.
1943 **538** 77c. multicoloured . . . 1·00 1·00

539 Bridge over Winter Canal

2003. 300th Anniv of St. Petersburg. Multicoloured.
1944 15c. Type **539** 20 20
1945 26c. Bartolomeo Francesco Rastrelli (architect) . . . 35 35
1946 36c. Trinity bridge over River Neva 45 45
1947 41c. Aleksander Sergeyevich Pushkin (writer) 55 55
1948 77c. Queen Catherine II . . 1·00 1·00
1949 €1.55 Tsar Peter I . . . . 2·20 2·20

540 Wright *Flyer I*

2003. Centenary of Powered Flight. Multicoloured.
1950 36c. Type **540** 45 45
1951 41c. Bleriot XI 55 55
1952 62c. Aermacchi MB339 . . 80 80
1953 77c. Frecce Tricolori (Italian acrobatic flying team) . . 1·00 1·00

541 Stagecoach on Road

2003. 120th Anniv of First Daily Mail Coach between Rimini and San Marino. Multicoloured.
1954 41c. Type **541** 55 55
1955 77c. Stagecoach in town . . 1·00 1·00

542 Chain Wheel (Tour de France)

2003. Centenary of Tour de France Cycle Race. Hamilton 2003 World Championship Road Race, Hamilton, Canada. Sheet 155 × 115 mm containing T **542** and similar circular design. Multicoloured.
MS1956 77c. Type **542**; 77c. Front wheel (Hamilton 2003) . . . . 2·20 2·20

543 Go-Carting

2003. Children's Games. Multicoloured.
1957 36c. Type **543** 45 45
1958 41c. Blind man's buff . . . 55 55
1959 62c. Hoops 80 80
1960 77c. Marbles . . . . 1·00 1·00
1961 €1.24 Dance . . . . 1·60 1·60
1962 €1.55 Tug-of-war . . . . . 2·20 2·20

544 Masked Puppet

2003. Puppetry. Multicoloured.
1963 41c. Type **544** 55 55
1964 41c. Blowing trumpet . . . 55 55
1965 41c. Male puppet offering flower to female 55 55
1966 41c. Two puppets with sticks 55 55
Nos. 1963/6 were issued together, se-tenant, forming a composite design of a puppet theatre.

545 Two Players and Ball
547 Theatre Emblem

546 Angel

2003. Rugby World Cup Championship, Australia. Multicoloured.
1967 41c. Type **545** 55 55
1968 62c. Player about to throw ball 80 80
1969 77c. Two players fighting for possession . . . . 1·00 1·00
1970 €1.55 Player with ball . . . 2·20 2·20

2003. Christmas. Sheet 186 × 143 mm containing T **546** and similar horiz designs. Multicoloured.
MS1971 41c. × 16, Type **546** (1/2); Shepherds and three kings (3/4); Holy family (5/6); Christmas cards (7/8); Decorated tree (9); Filled stocking (10); Wreath (11/12); Child and snowman (13/14); Father Christmas (15/16); Children and toys (17/18); Toys (19); Angels singing (20/21); Children and cake (22); Girl and games (23); Cornucopia (24); San Marino arms (25) . . . . . . 8·75 8·75
MS1971 was arranged in the shape of a snakes and ladders board, with seven stamps (1/2; 3/4; 5/6; 7/8; 20/21; 22; 23) reversed and two (9; 10) at right angles. The numbers on the board are given in brackets.

2003. Reopening of La Fenice Theatre, Venice.
1972 **547** $3.72 multicoloured . . 5·00 5·00

548 "Ballet" (Edgar Degas) and Tango Dancers

2004. 50th Anniv of Latin Union (inter-government organization). Multicoloured.
1973 41c. Type **548** 55 55
1974 77c. "Don Quixote" (Miguel De Cervantes) and "Donna Flor and her Two Husbands" (Jorge Amado) . . . . 1·00 1·00
1975 €1.55 "Susanna and the Elders" (Tintoretto) and "Sunday Afternoon" (Fernando Botero) . . . 2·10 2·10

549 Building Facade and Coloured Spheres

2004. Venice Carnival. Multicoloured.
1976 77c. Type **549** . . . . . . 1·00 1·00
1977 €1.55 Masked woman . . . 2·10 2·10

550 Manuel Poggiali

2004. Manuel Poggiali—2003 250cc. Motorcycle World Champion.
1978 **550** €1.55 multicoloured . . 2·10 2·10
See also 1889/90.

551 Bonsai Tree

2004. 20th European Bonsai Association Convention, San Marino.
1979 45c. Type **551** 60 65
1980 60c. Bonsai (different) . . . 80 80

552 Government Palace, San Marino and Tian-An-Men Palace, China

2004. 55th Anniv of People's Republic of China. Sheet 180 × 166 mm containing T **552** and similar horiz designs. Multicoloured.
MS1981 80c. × 3, Type **552**; San Marino mountain and Great Wall, China; Temple of Heaven Pagoda, China and San Marino Tower 3·25 3·25

553 Emblem
554 "Autoshipplane"

2004. Centenary of FIFA (Federation Internationale de Football Association).
1982 **553** €2.80 multicoloured . . 3·75 3·75

2004. Europa. Tourism. Multicoloured.
1983 45c. Type **554** 60 65
1984 80c. "Boatcampertrainbus" (horiz) . . . . 1·10 1·10

555 Chariot Racing, Boxers and Javelin Thrower

2004. Olympic Games 2004, Athens. Multicoloured.
1985 90c. Type **555** . . . . . . 1·20 1·20
1986 90c. Runner, discus thrower and wrestlers . . . . . . 1·20 1·20
1987 90c. Relay runner, cyclist and golfer . . . . 1·20 1·20
1988 90c. Racquet player, weightlifter and gymnasts 1·20 1·20
Nos. 1985/8 were issued together, se-tenant, forming a composite design.

556 Volkswagen Golf

2004. 50th Anniv of Volkswagen (car manufacturers). Multicoloured.
1989 €1.50 Type **556** (30th anniv of Golf) . . . . 2·00 2·00
1990 €1.50 Early and modern Beetles ("50" upright) . . 2·00 2·00
1991 €1.50 Early and modern Beetles ("50" diagonal) 2·00 2·00
1992 €1.50 Golf (different) . . . 2·00 2·00

557 *Hansel and Gretel* (Jakob and Wilhelm Grimm)
558 Francesco Petrarca (Petrarch)

2004. Fairytales.
1993 45c. Type **557** 60 60
1994 60c. *Little Red Riding Hood* (Jakob and Wilhelm Grimm) 80 80
1995 80c. *Pinocchio* (Carlo Collodi) . . . . 1·10 1·10
1996 €1 *Puss in Boots* (Charles Perrault) . . . . 1·30 1·30

2004. Writers' Anniversaries. Multicoloured.
1997 45c. Type **558** (700th birth anniv) 60 60
1998 €1.50 Oscar Wilde (150th birth anniv) . . . . . . 2·00 2·00
1999 €2.20 Anton Chekov (death centenary) . . . . 3·00 3·00

559 Manuel de Nobrega and Josa Anchieta (founders)

2004. 450th Anniv of Founding of San Paulo, Brazil. Multicoloured.
2000 60c. Type **559** 80 80
2001 80c. Mario Andrade and Antonio Machado (writers) . . . . 1·10 1·10
2002 €1.40 Modern San Paulo and Imaculada Conceicao da Luz monastery . . . . 1·90 1·90

560 Three Men

2004. 25th Meeting for Friendship Among Peoples, Rimini, Italy (Meeting Rimini). Sheet 155 × 115 mm containing T **560** and similar horiz designs. Multicoloured.
MS2003 €1 × 4 Type **560**; Two women and child; Family; Priests 5·25 5·25
The stamps and margin of No.**MS**2003 form a composite design.

561 "Rebecca at the Well" (Giovanni Battista Piazzetta)

2004. Artists' Anniversaries. Multicoloured.
2004 45c. Type **561**(250th death anniv) 60 60
2005 €1.40 "Piazza Navona" (Scipione Gino Bonichi) (birth centenary) . . . . 1·90 1·90
2006 €1.70 "The Persistence of Memory" (Salvador Dali) (birth centenary) . . . . 2·30 2·30

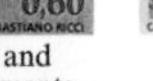

562 Cherubs and Musical Instruments
564 Manuel Fangio (1956)

563 Antonio Salieri and 18th-century Auditorium (½-size illustration)

2004. Christmas. Designs showing cherubs. Multicoloured.
2007 60c. Type **562** 80 80
2008 60c. Holding bag of presents 80 80
2009 60c. Carrying Christmas tree 80 80
2010 60c. Holding cornucopia . . 80 80

2004. Re-opening of La Scala Theatre, Milan. Sheet 132 × 172 mm containing T **563** and similar horiz designs. Multicoloured.
MS2011 $1.50 × 3, Type **563**; 19th-century and modern theatre building facade; Ricardo Muti and modern auditorium . . . . . 6·00 6·00
The stamps of No.**MS**2011 merge with the score of "Europa riconosciuta" (opera by Antonio Salieri) in the margin to form a composite design.

2005. Ferrari—World Champion Racing Team. Showing World Champions and their cars. Multicoloured.
2012 1c. Type **564** 10 10
2013 4c. Niki Lauda (1975—77) 10 10
2014 5c. John Surtees (1964) . . 10 10
2015 45c. Michael Schumacher (2000—04) 60 65
2016 62c. Race car 80 80
2017 €1.50 Alberto Ascari (1952—53) . . . . 2·00 2·00

566 "In the Hollow of a Wave off the Coast at Kanagawa" (Hokusai Katsushika) and Faces of Victims

2005. Support For Victims of the Tsunami Disaster.
2020 **566** €1.50 multicoloured . . 2·00 2·00

567 Weightlifter

2005. Centenary of International Weightlifting Federation.
2021 **567** €2.20 multicoloured . . 3·00 3·00

EXPRESS LETTER STAMPS

E 22 Mt. Titano and "Liberty"

1907.
E53 **E 22** 25c. pink . . . . 19·00 6·75

1923. Optd **ESPRESSO**.
E92 **19** 60c. violet 50 40

1923. Surch **Cent. 60**.
E93 **E 22** 60c. on 25c. pink . . . 50 40

E 34

1923. Red Cross.

E101	E **34**	60c.+5c. red	1·10	1·20

1926. No. E92 surch **Lire 1,25**.

E134	E **19**	1l.25 on 60c. violet	90	60

1927. No. E93 surch **L. 1,25** and bars over old surch.

E138	E **22**	1l.25 on 60c. on 25c. pink	65	55

E **50** Statue of Liberty and View of San Marino

1929. As Type E **50** but without "**UNION POSTALE UNIVERSELLE**" and inscr "ESPRESSO".

E164	E **50**	1l.25 green	20	15

1929. Optd **UNION POSTALE UNIVERSELLE** as in Type E **50**.

E165	E **50**	2l.50 blue	75	65

E 78

1943.

E305	E **78**	1l.25 green	10	15
E306		2l.50 orange	10	15

E **79** Mt. Titano

1945.

E307	E **79**	2l.50 green	10	15
E308		5l. orange	10	15
E309		5l. red	60	70
E310		10l. blue	1·30	1·20
E419		60l. red	7·75	5·50

E **87** Pegasus and Mt. Titano

1946.

E337	E **87**	30l. blue	4·75	3·75
E420		80l. blue	9·25	5·50

1947. Surch.

E339	E **79**	15l. on 5l. red	15	25
E340		15l. on 10l. blue	15	25
E374	E **87**	35l. on 30l. blue	41·00	29·00
E341		60l. on 30l. blue	2·30	3·50
E545	E **79**	75l. on 60l. red	1·90	1·90
E375	E **87**	80l. on 30l. blue	20·00	15·00
E546		100l. on 80l. blue	1·90	1·80
E783	E **180**	120l. on 75l. black and yellow	15	15
E784		135l. on 100l. black and orange	15	15

E **180** Crossbow and Three "Castles"

1966.

E800	E **180**	75l. black and yellow	10	10
E801		80l. black and purple	10	10
E802		100l. black and orange	10	10

No. E800 has crossbow in white without "shadows".

PARCEL POST STAMPS

Unused and used prices are for complete pairs.

P 46

1928.

P145	P **46**	5c. purple and blue	30	20
P146		10c. blue and light blue	30	20
P147		20c. black and blue	30	20
P148		25c. red and blue	30	20
P149		30c. ultramarine & blue	30	20
P150		30c. orange and blue	30	20
P151		60c. red and blue	30	20
P152		1l. violet and red	30	20
P153		2l. green and red	85	40
P154		3l. bistre and red	1·00	80
P155		4l. grey and red	1·20	1·00
P156		10l. mauve and red	4·00	1·60
P157		12l. lake and red	14·00	5·75
P158		15l. green and red	23·00	12·50
P159		20l. purple and red	30·00	19·00

1945.

P309	P **46**	5c. purple and red	10	10
P310		10c. brown and black	10	10
P311		20c. red and green	10	10
P312		25c. yellow and black	10	10
P313		30c. mauve and red	10	10
P314		50c. violet and black	10	10
P315		60c. red and black	10	10
P316		1l. brown and blue	10	10
P317		2l. brown and blue	10	10
P318		3l. grey and brown	10	10
P319		4l. green and brown	10	10
P320		10l. grey and violet	10	10
P770		10l. green and red	20	15
P321		12l. green and blue	4·00	1·90
P322		15l. green and violet	1·90	1·60
P323		20l. violet and brown	1·80	1·60
P324		25l. red and blue	34·00	25·00
P771		50l. yellow and red	25	41·00
P455		300l. violet and red	£110	£110
P773		300l. violet and brown	30	35
P526		500l. brown and red	1·90	3·75
P775		1000l. green and brown	55	1·00

1948. Nos. P324 and P771 surch in figures and wavy lines on each half of design.

P524	P **46**	100l. on 50l. yellow and red	60	45
P375		200l. on 25l. red & blue	1·90	£110

POSTAGE DUE STAMPS

D 18 D 82

1897.

D38	D **18**	5c. brown and green	20	25
D39		10c. brown and green	20	25
D40		30c. brown and green	1·40	60
D41		50c. brown and green	3·00	1·20
D42		60c. brown and green	14·50	4·50
D43		1l. brown and pink	5·75	2·75
D44		3l. brown and pink	19·00	10·50
D45		5l. brown and pink	70·00	29·00
D46		10l. brown and pink	26·00	19·00

1924.

D102	D **18**	5c. brown and red	20	40
D103		10c. brown and red	20	40
D104		30c. brown and red	25	40
D105		50c. brown and red	1·50	80
D106		60c. brown and red	7·50	4·00
D107		1l. brown and green	10·50	6·25
D108		3l. brown and green	22·00	21·00
D109		5l. brown and green	34·00	24·00
D110		10l. brown and green	£300	£200

1925.

D111	D **18**	5c. brown and red	25	20
D113		10c. brown and red	25	20
D114		15c. brown and blue	20	80
D115		20c. brown and blue	25	20
D116		25c. brown and blue	30	40
D117		30c. brown and blue	70	20
D118		40c. brown and blue	4·00	1·60
D119		50c. brown and blue	50	40
D120		60c. brown and blue	1·50	60
D121		1l. brown and orange	7·25	60
D122		2l. brown and orange	1·80	1·20
D123		3l. brown and orange	95·00	21·00
D124		5l. brown and orange	24·00	4·00
D125		10l. brown and orange	36·00	6·25
D126		15l. brown and orange	1·00	20
D127		25l. brown and orange	60·00	12·50
D128		30l. brown and orange	9·00	5·25
D129		50l. brown and orange	12·00	6·50

1931. As Type D **18** but with centre obliterated in black and new value superimposed in silver.

D164	D **18**	15c. on 5c. blue	25	20
D165		15c. on 10c. blue	25	20
D166		15c. on 30c. blue	25	20
D167		20c. on 5c. blue	25	20
D168		20c. on 10c. blue	25	20
D169		20c. on 30c. blue	25	20
D170		25c. on 5c. blue	1·50	40
D171		25c. on 10c. blue	1·30	40
D172		25c. on 30c. blue	16·00	4·00
D173		40c. on 10c. blue	1·30	20
D174		40c. on 10c. blue	1·50	20
D175		40c. on 30c. blue	1·50	20
D176		2l. on 5c. blue	80·00	25·00
D177		2l. on 10c. blue	£120	43·00
D178		2l. on 30c. blue	95·00	33·00

1936. Surch in figures and words and bars. Nos. D233/8 and D242 are brown and blue; the rest brown and orange.

D233	D **18**	10c. on 5c.	65	60
D234		25c. on 30c.	14·00	7·00
D236		50c. on 5c.	10·50	7·00
D237		1l. on 30c.	50·00	5·00
D238		1l. on 40c.	8·00	4·00
D239		1l. on 3l.	50·00	2·10
D240		1l. on 25l.	£110	11·50
D241		2l. on 15l.	38·00	14·50
D242		3l. on 20c.	26·00	16·00
D243		25l. on 50l.	2·30	1·60

1945.

D309	D **82**	5c. green	10	10
D310		10c. brown	10	10
D311		15c. red	10	10
D312		20c. blue	10	10
D313		25c. violet	10	10
D314		30c. mauve	10	10
D315		40c. yellow	10	10
D316		50c. grey	10	10
D317		60c. brown	10	10
D318		1l. orange	10	10
D319		2l. red	10	10
D320		5l. violet	10	10
D321		10l. blue	15	60
D322		20l. green	9·50	6·25
D323		25l. brown	9·50	6·25
D324		50l. brown	9·50	6·25

SANTANDER Pt. 20

One of the states of the Granadine Confederation. A department of Colombia from 1886, now uses Colombian stamps.

100 centavos = 1 peso.

1

2

1884. Imperf.

1	**1**	1c. blue	15	15
2		5c. red	30	25
3		10c. violet	50	50

1886. Imperf.

4	**2**	1c. blue	40	40
5		5c. red	15	15
6		10c. lilac	20	20

1887. As T **1** but inscr "REPUBLICA DE COLOMBIA". Imperf.

7		1c. blue	15	15
8		5c. red	45	45
9		10c. violet	1·50	1·50

3

4

5 6 7

1890. Perf.

10	**3**	1c. blue	15	15
11	**4**	5c. red	60	60
12	**5**	10c. violet	25	25

1895.

14	**6**	5c. red on buff	35	30

1895.

15	**7**	5c. brown	60	60
16		5c. green	60	60

8 9 10

1899.

17	**8**	1c. black on green	20	20
18	**9**	5c. black on red	20	20
19	**10**	10c. blue	35	35

F 11

1903. Fiscal stamp as Type F **11** optd **Provisional. Correos de Santander.** Imperf.

21	F **11**	50c. red	20	20

SARAWAK Pt. 1

Formerly an independent state on the north coast of Borneo under British protection. Under Japanese occupation from 1941 until 1945. A Crown Colony from 1946 until September 1963, when it became a state of the Federation of Malaysia.

100 cents = 1 dollar (Malayan or Malaysian).

1 Sir James Brooke

2 Sir Charles Brooke

1869.

1	**1**	3c. brown on yellow	48·00	£225

1871.

3	**2**	2c. mauve on lilac	7·00	17·00
2		3c. brown on yellow	1·75	3·50
4		4c. brown on yellow	3·25	3·00
5		6c. green on green	3·75	3·50
6		8c. blue on blue	3·75	3·50
7		12c. red on red	7·50	6·50

4 Sir Charles Brooke

11 Sir Charles Brooke

1888.

8	**4**	1c. purple and black	2·00	50
9		2c. purple and red	3·25	1·75
10		3c. purple and blue	3·50	3·25
11		4c. purple and yellow	18·00	50·00
12		5c. purple and green	13·00	2·75
13		6c. purple and brown	15·00	55·00
14		8c. green and red	11·00	3·25
15		10c. green and purple	38·00	14·00
16		12c. green and blue	9·00	9·00
17		16c. green and orange	45·00	75·00
18		25c. green and brown	42·00	40·00
19		32c. green and black	30·00	55·00
20		50c. green	42·00	90·00
21		$1 green and black	75·00	85·00

1889. Surch in words (1c.) or figures (others).

27	**2**	1c. on 3c. brown on yellow (surch **ONE CENT**)	1·40	2·00
22	**4**	1c. on 3c. purple and blue (surch **One Cent.**)	45·00	29·00
23		1c. on 3c. purple and blue (surch **one cent.**)	3·00	2·75
24		2c. on 8c. green and red	3·00	5·50
25		5c. on 12c. green and blue	24·00	45·00

1895. Various frames.

28c	**11**	2c. red	11·00	4·50
29		4c. black	8·50	3·50
30		6c. violet	10·00	9·00
31		8c. green	27·00	6·00

1889. Surch in figures and words.

32	**2**	2c. on 3c. brown on yellow	1·60	1·75
33		2c. on 12c. red on red	2·75	3·00
34		4c. on 6c. green on green	27·00	70·00
35		4c. on 8c. blue on blue	3·50	7·50

1899. As T **4**, but inscr "POSTAGE POSTAGE".

36		1c. blue and red	1·25	1·25
37		2c. green	2·00	90
38		3c. purple	9·50	65
39a		4c. red	2·50	15
40		8c. yellow and black	2·00	80
41		10c. blue	2·50	1·00
42		12c. mauve	4·75	4·50
43		16c. brown and green	3·50	1·75
44		20c. brown and mauve	5·50	4·00
45		25c. brown and blue	5·50	5·00
46		50c. green and red	21·00	26·00
47		$1 red and green	50·00	£110

17 Sir Charles Vyner Brooke

19 Sir Charles Vyner Brooke

1918.

76	**17**	1c. blue and red	1·50	35
51		2c. green	2·50	1·50
77		2c. purple	2·00	1·25
52		3c. purple	3·25	2·75
64		3c. green	1·75	1·25
53		4c. red	4·00	3·25
79		4c. purple	1·75	10
66		5c. orange	1·75	90
81		6c. purple	1·25	30
54		8c. yellow and black	12·00	60·00
82		8c. red	3·25	17·00
55		10c. blue	3·00	3·25
83		10c. black	1·75	1·25
56		12c. purple	12·00	28·00
84		12c. blue	3·25	24·00
85		16c. brown and green	3·25	4·00
86		20c. bistre and violet	3·25	5·50
87		25c. brown and blue	5·50	8·50
71		30c. brown and grey	3·75	4·25
89		50c. green and red	5·50	15·00
90		$1 pink and green	15·00	24·00

1923. Surch in words.

72	**17**	1c. on 10c. blue	10·00	55·00
73		2c. on 12c. purple	6·50	42·00

1932.

91	**19**	1c. blue	80	1·00
92		2c. green	1·00	1·50
93		3c. violet	4·00	1·00
94		4c. orange	3·50	75
95		5c. lake	6·50	1·25
96		6c. red	7·00	9·50
97		8c. yellow	8·50	8·50
98		10c. black	2·25	3·25
99		12c. blue	4·00	9·50
100		15c. brown	6·50	8·50
101		20c. orange and violet	6·50	8·00
102		25c. yellow and brown	10·00	22·00
103		30c. brown and red	9·50	25·00
104		50c. red and olive	14·00	13·00
105		$1 green and red	22·00	35·00

21 Sir Charles Vyner Brooke

23 Sir James Brooke, Sir Charles Vyner Brooke and Sir Charles Brooke

1934.

106	**21**	1c. purple	1·25	10
107		2c. green	1·50	10
107a		2c. black	3·75	1·60
108		3c. black	1·25	10
108a		3c. green	7·00	4·50
109		4c. purple	1·75	15
110		5c. violet	1·75	10
111		6c. red	2·75	60
111a		6c. brown	7·50	8·00
112		8c. brown	2·25	10
112a		8c. red	8·00	10
113		10c. red	2·50	40
114		12c. blue	3·00	25
114a		12c. orange	6·00	4·75
115		15c. orange	4·00	10·00
115a		15c. blue	8·50	15·00
116		20c. green and red	4·00	1·25
117		25c. violet and orange	4·00	1·50
118		30c. brown and violet	4·00	2·50
119		50c. violet and red	4·50	75
120		$1 red and brown	1·75	75
121		$2 purple and violet	15·00	12·00
122		$3 red and green	29·00	32·00
123		$4 blue and red	29·00	55·00
124		$5 red and brown	35·00	55·00
125		$10 black and yellow	23·00	60·00

1945. Optd B M A.

126	**21**	1c. purple	1·25	60
127		2c. black	1·50	1·25
128		3c. green	1·25	1·50
129		4c. purple	1·50	30
130		5c. violet	2·25	1·00
131		6c. brown	2·75	75
132		8c. red	13·00	13·00
133		10c. red	1·25	70
134		12c. orange	1·75	3·75
135		15c. blue	3·75	40
136		20c. green and red	2·50	2·50
137		25c. violet and orange	2·75	2·75
138		30c. brown and violet	6·00	2·75
139		50c. violet and red	1·25	35
140		$1 red and brown	2·50	1·75
141		$2 purple and violet	9·00	11·00
142		$3 red and green	18·00	60·00
143		$4 blue and red	26·00	45·00
144		$5 red and brown	£160	£190
145		$10 black and yellow	£150	£200

1946. Centenary Issue.

146	**23**	8c. red	1·50	1·00
147		15c. blue	1·50	2·00
148		50c. black and red	1·75	2·50
149		$1 black and brown	2·50	20·00

1947. Optd with the Royal Cypher.

150	**21**	1c. purple	15	30
151		2c. black	15	15
152		3c. green	15	15
153		4c. purple	15	15
154		6c. brown	20	90
155		8c. red	75	10
156		10c. red	20	20
157		12c. orange	20	1·00
158		15c. blue	20	40
159		20c. green and red	2·00	50
160		25c. violet and orange	40	30
161		50c. violet and red	40	40
162		$1 red and brown	1·00	90
163		$2 purple and violet	2·00	3·25
164		$5 red and brown	3·00	3·25

1948. Silver Wedding. As T **33b/c** of St. Helena.

165		8c. red	30	30
166		$5 brown	32·00	40·00

1949. U.P.U. As T **33d/g** of St. Helena.

167		8c. red	1·25	60
168		15c. blue	3·00	2·50
169		25c. green	2·00	1·50
170		50c. violet	2·00	5·00

25 "Trogonoptera brookiana"

26 Western Tarsier **27** Kayan Tomb

1950.

171	**25**	1c. black	40	30
172	**26**	2c. orange	20	40
173	**27**	3c. green	20	60
174	–	4c. brown	20	20
175	–	6c. blue	20	15
176	–	8c. red	20	30
177	–	10c. orange	1·25	4·00
186	–	10c. orange	1·75	50
178	–	12c. violet	3·50	1·50
179	–	15c. blue	2·50	15
180	–	20c. brown and orange	2·00	30
181	–	25c. green and red	3·25	30
182	–	50c. brown and violet	4·00	25
183	–	$1 green and brown	20·00	4·50
184	–	$2 blue and red	26·00	15·00
185	–	$5 multicoloured	19·00	15·00

DESIGNS—VERT: 4c. Kayan boy and girl; 6c. Beadwork; 50c. Iban woman. HORIZ: 8c. Dayak dancer; 10c. (No. 177) Malayan Pangolin; 10c. (No. 186) Map of Sarawak; 12c. Kenyah boys; 15c. Fire-making; 20c. Kelemantan rice barn; 25c. Pepper vines; $1 Kelabit smithy; $2 Map of Sarawak; $5 Arms of Sarawak.

1953. Coronation. As T **33h** of St. Helena.

187		10c. black and blue	1·25	1·50

47 Barong Panau (sailing prau)

51 Queen Elizabeth II

52 Queen Elizabeth II (after Annigoni)

1955.

188	–	1c. green	10	30
189	–	2c. orange	30	55
190	–	4c. brown	45	60
191	–	6c. blue	3·25	3·00
192	–	8c. red	30	30
193	–	10c. green	20	10
194	**47**	12c. plum	3·75	55
195	–	15c. blue	1·00	30
196	–	20c. olive and brown	1·00	10
197	–	25c. sepia and green	6·50	20
198	**51**	30c. brown and lilac	5·50	30
199		50c. black and red	2·00	30
200	**52**	$1 green and brown	8·00	1·50
201		$2 violet and green	15·00	3·75
202	–	$5 multicoloured	16·00	12·00

DESIGNS—VERT (as Type **47**): 1c. Logging; 2c. Young orang-utan; 4c. Kayan dancing. HORIZ: 6c. Malabar pied hornbill ("Hornbill"); 8c. Shield with spears; 10c. Kenyah ceremonial carving; 15c. Turtles; 20c. Melanau basket-making; 25c. Astana, Kuching; $5 Arms of Sarawak.

1963. Freedom from Hunger. As T **63a** of St. Helena.

203		12c. sepia	1·50	1·00

53 "Vanda hookeriana"

1965. As Nos. 155/21 of Kedah, but with Arms of Sarawak inset as in T **53**.

212	**53**	1c. multicoloured	10	1·10
213	–	2c. multicoloured	20	2·00
214	–	5c. multicoloured	45	10
215	–	6c. multicoloured	60	2·00
216	–	10c. multicoloued	80	10
217	–	15c. multicoloured	1·50	10
218	–	20c. multicoloured	2·00	50

The higher values used in Sarawak were Nos. 20/7 of Malaysia (National issues).

54 "Precis orithya"

1971. Butterflies. As Nos. 124/30 of Kedah, but with Sarawak Arms as in T **54**.
219 – 1c. multicoloured . . . . . 65 2·00
220 – 2c. multicoloured . . . . . 70 2·00
221 – 5c. multicoloured . . . . . 1·75 10
222 – 6c. multicoloured . . . . . 1·75 2·50
223 – 10c. multicoloured . . . . 1·75 10
224 **54** 15c. multicoloured . . . . 2·75 10
225 – 20c. multicoloured . . . . 2·75 1·25
The higher values in use with this issue were Nos. 64/71 of Malaysia (National issues).

55 "Precis orithya" (different crest at right)

1977. As Nos. 219/21 and 223/5, but showing new State Crest.
226 – 1c. multicoloured . . . . . 6·50 13·00
227 – 2c. multicoloured . . . . . 11·00 9·50
228 – 5c. multicoloured 80 70
230 – 10c. multicoloured 50 30
231 **55** 15c. multicoloured . . . . 1·25 20
232 – 20c. multicoloured . . . . 3·00 2·25

56 "Rhododendron scortechinii"

57 Coffee

1979. As Nos. 135/41 of Kedah, but with Arms of Sarawak as in T **56**.
233 1c. "Rafflesia hasseltii" . . . 10 50
234 2c. "Pterocarpus indicus" . . 10 50
235 5c. "Lagerstroemia speciosa" 20 70
236 10c. "Durio zibethinus" . . . 20 10
237 15c. "Hibiscus rosa-sinensis" 20 10
238 20c. Type **56** 30 10
239 25c. "Etlingera elatior" (inscr "Phaeomeria speciosa") . . 50 70

1986. As Nos. 152/8 of Kedah, but with Arms of Sarawak as in T **57**.
247 1c. Type **57** 10 10
248 2c. Coconuts 10 10
249 5c. Cocoa 10 10
250 10c. Black pepper 10 10
251 15c. Rubber 10 10
252 20c. Oil palm 10 10
253 30c. Rice 10 15
Nos. 247/53 exist with slightly different versions to state arms at right.

JAPANESE OCCUPATION

府政國帝本日大
(**1**) "Imperial Japanese Government"

1942. Stamps of Sarawak optd with T **1**.
J 1 **21** 1c. purple . . . . 32·00 75·00
J 2 2c. green £100 £170
J 3 2c. black . . . . 95·00 £120
J 4 3c. black £375 £375
J 5 3c. green . . . . 55·00 95·00
J 6 4c. purple . . . . 75·00 95·00
J 7 5c. violet . . . . 85·00 95·00
J 8 6c. red £140 £140
J 9 6c. brown . . . . 85·00 95·00
J10 8c. brown £375 £375
J11 8c. red . . . . 75·00 £120
J12 10c. red . . . . 80·00 £100
J13 12c. blue £160 £180
J14 12c. orange £160 £190
J15 15c. orange £375 £375
J16 15c. blue £100 £120
J17 20c. green and red . . . . 60·00 £100
J18 25c. violet and orange . . 95·00 £100
J19 30c. brown and violet . . . 65·00 £100
J20 50c. violet and red . . . . 70·00 £100
J21 $1 red and brown £100 £140
J22 $2 purple and violet . . . £200 £300
J23 $3 red and green £1500 £1600
J24 $4 blue and red £225 £375
J25 $5 red and brown £250 £375
J26 $10 black and yellow . . . £250 £375

SARDINIA Pt. 8

A former Italian kingdom, including the island of Sardinia, a large part of the mainland and parts of what is now south-east France. The Kingdom of Italy was formed by the adhesion of other Italian states to Sardinia, whose king became the first ruler of united Italy.

100 centesimi = 1 lira.

1 Victor Emmanuel II

2 Victor Emmanuel II

1851. Imperf.
1 **1** 5c. black £6000 £1700
3 20c. blue £6000 £130
7 40c. pink £8000 £3500

1853. Embossed on coloured paper. Imperf.
9 **1** 5c. on green £9500 £1000
10 20c. on blue £11000 £120
11 40c. on pink £7500 £800

1854. Embossed on white paper. Imperf.
13 **1** 5c. green £29000 £500
15 20c. blue £12000 £100
18 40c. red £86000 £2500

1855. Head embossed. Imperf.
28 **2** 5c. green . . . . 5·50 12·50
40 10c. bistre . . . . 5·50 12·00
39 10c. brown . . . . 85·00 70·00
35 10c. grey . . . . 28·00 90·00
47 20c. blue . . . . 90·00 10·00
55 40c. red . . . . 20·00 30·00
59 80c. yellow . . . . 17·00 £225
61 3l. bronze £350 £2500
For Type **2** perf, see Italy Nos. 1/4.

NEWSPAPER STAMPS

N **3**

1861. Numerals embossed. Imperf.
N62 N **3** 1c. black . . . . 5·75 10·00
N63 2c. black . . . . £130 90·00
For 2c. stamps of similar types in yellow see Italy No. N5.

SASENO Pt. 3

An island off the W. coast of Albania, temporarily occupied by Italy.

100 centesimi = 1 lira.

1923. Stamps of Italy optd **SASENO**.
1 **38** 10c. red . . . . 9·00 14·00
2 15c. grey . . . . 9·00 14·00
3 **41** 20c. orange . . . . 9·00 14·00
4 **39** 25c. blue . . . . 9·00 14·00
5 30c. brown . . . . 9·00 14·00
6 50c. mauve . . . . 9·00 14·00
7 60c. red . . . . 9·00 14·00
8 **34** 1l. brown and green . . . . 9·00 14·00

SAUDI ARABIA Pt. 19

Formerly under Turkish rule, the Hejaz became an independent kingdom in 1916 but was conquered in 1925 by the Sultan of Nejd. In 1926 the two kingdoms were combined. In 1932 the name of the state was changed to the Saudi Arabian Kingdom.

1916. 40 paras = 1 piastre.
1929. 110 guerche = 10 riyal = 1 gold sovereign.
1952. 440 guerche = 40 riyal = 1 gold sovereign.
1960. 100 halalah = 20 guerche = 1 riyal.
(1 piastre = 1 guerche.)

A. HEJAZ

5 From Stucco Work over Entrance to Cairo Railway Station

1916. As T **5** (various Arabic designs). Perf or roul.
11 **5** 1pa. purple . . . . 4·00 1·10
12 – ⅛pi. yellow . . . . 4·50 2·00
13 – ¼pi. green . . . . 4·50 2·20
14 – ½pi. red . . . . 5·00 3·00
15 – 1pi. blue . . . . 5·00 3·00
16 – 2pi. purple . . . . 23·00 9·75

الحكومة العربية الهاشمية
١٣٤٠ ١٣٤٠
(**7** "1340 Hashemite Kingdom 1340")

1921. Optd with T **7**.
21 1pa. purple . . . . 32·00 18·00
22 ⅛pi. yellow . . . . 65·00 18·00
23 ¼pi. green . . . . 12·50 6·25
24 ½pi. red . . . . 15·00 7·50
26 1pi. blue . . . . 12·50 7·25
28 2pi. purple . . . . 18·00 9·75

نصف قرش
(**8**) (½pi.)

قرش واحد
(**9**) (1pi.)

1921. No. 21 surch with T **8** or **9**.
29 **5** ½pi. on 1pa. purple £350 £160
30 1pi. on 1pa. purple £350 £160

(**10** "1340 Hashemite Kingdom 1340")

1922. Nos. 11 to 16 optd with T **10**.
31 **5** 1pa. purple . . . . 3·25 3·00
32 – ⅛pi. yellow . . . . 9·75 8·50
33 – ¼pi. green . . . . 4·00 3·00
34 – ½pi. red . . . . 2·50 2·30
35 – 1pi. blue . . . . 2·50 90
36 – 2pi. claret . . . . 7·25 6·75

1922. No. 31 surch with T **8** or **9**.
37 **5** ½pi. on 1pa. purple . . . . . 27·00 15·00
38 1pi. on 1pa. purple . . . . . 2·50 1·00

11 Meccan Sherifian Arms

1922.
39 **11** ⅛pi. brown . . . . 2·00 55
57 ¼pi. green . . . . 6·25 6·25
41 ½pi. red . . . . 2·00 45
42 1pi. blue . . . . 2·00 45
43 1½pi. lilac . . . . 2·00 55
44 2pi. orange . . . . 2·30 65
45 3pi. brown . . . . 2·00 55
46 5pi. green . . . . 2·00 55
58 – 10pi. purple and mauve . . 5·00 5·00
DESIGN: 10pi. As T **11** but with different corner ornaments in the centre motif.

ربع قرش
(**12**) (¼pi.)

عشرة قروش
(**13**) (10pi.)

1923. Surch with T **12** or **13**.
47 **11** ¼pi. on ⅛pi. brown . . . . . 41·00 36·00
49 10pi. on 5pi. olive . . . . . 32·00 30·00

تذكار الخلافة
شعبان
١٣٤٢
(**14**)

1924. Proclamation of King Hussein as Caliph. Optd with T **14**.
50 **11** ⅛pi. brown . . . . 5·00 3·25
51 ½pi. red . . . . 3·25 1·60
52 1pi. blue . . . . 5·00 3·25
53 1½pi. lilac . . . . 5·00 3·25
54 2pi. orange . . . . 5·00 3·25
55 3pi. brown . . . . 5·00 3·25
56 5pi. green . . . . 6·75 5·00

(**15** "Hejaz Government. 4th October, 1924")

1924. Optd with T **15**.
66 1pa. purple (No. 11) . . . . . 13·50 13·50
77 1pa. purple (No. 31) £180 £180
59 ⅛pi. yellow (No. 12) . . . . . 18·00 18·00
78 ⅛pi. yellow (No. 32) £2750 £2000
68 ¼pi. green (No. 13) . . . . . 22·00 22·00
79 ¼pi. green (No. 33) . . . . . 75·00 70·00
71 ½pi. red (No. 14) . . . . . . 31·00 31·00
76 ½pi. red (No. 24) £2750
80 ½pi. red (No. 34) . . . . . . £100 90·00
86 ½pi. red (No. 41) £1100 £1100
84 ½pi. on 1pa. purple (No. 37) . . £100 £100
73 1pi. blue (No. 15) . . . . . . 36·00 36·00
81 1pi. blue (No. 35) £150 £120
85 1pi. on 1pa. purple (No. 38) . . 80·00 80·00
74 2pi. purple (No. 16) . . . . . 40·00 36·00
83 2pi. purple (No. 36) £180 £180
87 10pi. purple and mauve (No. 58) £2000 £2000

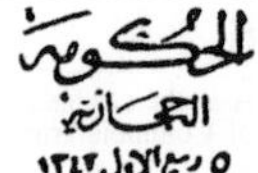
(**16** "Hejaz Government, 4th October, 1924")

1924. Optd with T **16** (or smaller size). (a) On No. 13.
90 – ¼pi. green . . . . 75·00 65·00

(b) On Nos. 39 etc.
105 **11** ⅛pi. brown . . . . 6·25 6·25
96 ¼pi. green . . . . 18·00 18·00
116 ½pi. red . . . . 5·00 5·00
98 1pi. blue . . . . 9·00 9·00
99 1½pi. lilac . . . . 5·00 5·00
119 2pi. orange . . . . 7·50 7·50
120 3pi. brown . . . . 7·50 6·25
103 5pi. green . . . . 11·00 8·00
104 – 10pi. purple and mauve . . 18·00 18·00

(c) On Nos. 50/6.
136 **11** ⅛pi. brown . . . . 45·00 45·00
137 ½pi. red . . . . 90·00 90·00
138 1pi. blue . . . . 65·00 60·00
139 1½pi. lilac . . . . 75·00 70·00
134 2pi. orange £120 £100
146 3pi. brown £120 £120
142 5pi. green . . . . 41·00 41·00
For similar overprint see Nos. 172/6.

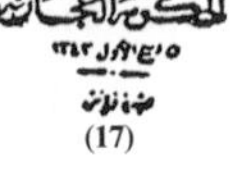
(**17**)

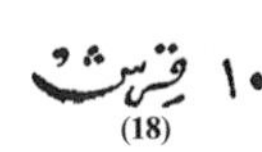
(**18**)

1925. Stamps of 1922 surch as Type **17**.
148 **11** ¼pi. on ⅛pi. brown £110
149 ¼pi. on ½pi. red £110
150 1pi. on 2pi. orange £110
151 1pi. on 3pi. brown £110
153 10pi. on 5pi. green £110

1925. Nos. 148/53 further surch with values in larger type as Type **18**.
154 **11** ¼pi. on ¼pi. on ⅛pi. brown 55·00 55·00
155 ¼pi. on ¼pi. on ½pi. red . . 32·00 32·00
157 1pi. on 1pi. on 2pi. orange 32·00 32·00
158 1pi. on 1pi. on 3pi. brown 25·00 25·00
160 10pi. on 10pi. on 5pi. green 18·00 18·00

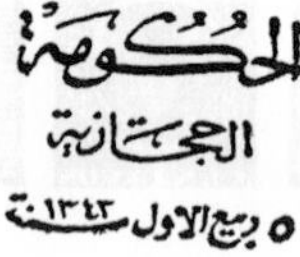
(**19**)

1925. Stamps of 1922 surch as T **19**.
165 **11** ⅛pi. on ½pi. red . . . . . 15·00 11·50
166 ¼pi. on ½pi. red . . . . . 15·00 11·50
167 1pi. on ½pi. red . . . . . 15·00 11·50
173c 1pi. on 1½pi. lilac . . . . 9·00 9·00
174 1pi. on 2pi. orange . . . . 9·00 9·00
175 1pi. on 3pi. brown . . . . 9·00 9·00
176 10pi. on 5pi. green . . . 15·00 15·00

20

(**24**)

1925. As T **20** (various Arabic designs) optd with T **24**.
177 ⅛pi. brown . . . . 1·80 1·80
178 ¼pi. blue . . . . 1·80 1·80
179 ½pi. red . . . . 1·80 1·80
180 1pi. green . . . . 2·00 2·00
181 1½pi. orange . . . . 2·00 2·00
182 2pi. blue . . . . 6·25 6·25
183 3pi. green . . . . 6·25 6·25
184 5pi. brown . . . . 6·25 6·25
185 10pi. green and red . . . . . 9·50 9·50

B. NEJDI OCCUPATION OF HEJAZ

(**25**) "Nejd Sultanate Post 1343"

1925. Various stamps optd with T **25**. (A.) Stamps of Turkey.
190 **30** 5pa. bistre (No. 583) . . . 23·00 16·00
191 10pa. green (No. 503) . . . 16·00 12·50

26

27

(B.) Hejaz Fiscal stamps. (i) Notarial stamps.
192 **26** 1pi. violet 20·00 20·00
193a 1pi. blue 25·00 25·00

(ii) Bill stamp.
194 **27** 1pi. violet 14·00 14·00

28

(iii) Railway Tax stamps.
195 **28** 1pi. blue 16·00 16·00
196 2pi. orange 21·00 21·00
197 3pi. lilac 25·00 25·00

(C.) Hejaz Postage stamps (1922 issue).
198 **11** ⅛pi. brown 21·00 21·00
198ca ⅛pi. red 25·00 25·00
199a ½pi. red 16·00 16·00
200 1½pi. lilac 21·00 21·00
201 2pi. orange 35·00 35·00
202 3pi. red 21·00 21·00

(**29**) "1343 Commemoration of First Pilgrimage under Sultan of Nejd"

(**30**) "W-ednesday"

(**31**)

1925. Pilgrimage Commemoration. Various stamps optd with T **29** and **30** and surch as T **31**. (a) 1914 pictorial stamps of Turkey.
210 1pi. on 10pa. green (No. 503) 70·00 55·00
211 5pi. on 1pi. blue (No. 518) 70·00 55·00

(b) 1916 stamps of Hejaz.
212 2pi. on 1pa. purple 90·00 70·00
213 4pi. on ⅛pi. yellow £300 £160

(c) Railway Tax stamp of Hejaz.
214 **28** 3pi. lilac £225 80·00

(**32**) "Nejd Sultanate Post"

1925. Various stamps optd with T **32**. (A.) Stamps of Turkey.
215 **30** 5pa. bistre 10·50 9·75
216 – 10pa. green (No. 503) 14·00 12·50

(B.) Hejaz Fiscal stamps. (i) Notarial stamp.
217 **26** 2pi. blue 20·00 16·00

(ii) Railway Tax Stamps.
218b **28** 1pi. blue 28·00 9·75
219 2pi. orange 25·00 9·75
220 3pi. lilac 21·00 14·00
221 5pi. green 20·00 11·50

(C.) Hejaz Postage stamps. (i) Nos. 35/6.
222 1pi. blue 33·00 33·00
223 2pi. purple 55·00 55·00

(ii) Stamps of 1922 (some in new colours).
224 **11** ⅛pi. brown £3750
225 ½pi. red 14·00 6·25
226 1pi. violet 16·00 14·00
227 1½pi. pink 28·00 18·00
228 2pi. orange 80·00 55·00
229 2pi. purple 41·00 28·00
230 3pi. red 21·00 16·00
231 5pi. red 28·00 25·00

(**33**) (1pi.)

(**34**) (1½pi.)

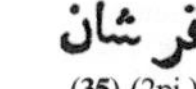
(**35**) (2pi.)

1925. Stamps optd with T **32** further surch with T **33/5**.
239 **11** 1pi. on ½pi. red 7·00 2·10
241 1½pi. on ½pi. red 8·25 2·10
243 2pi. on 3pi. red 14·00 2·75

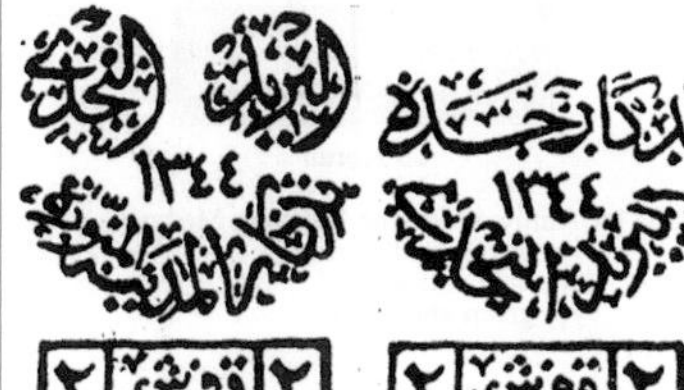
(**36**) "Postage of Nejd, 1344, Commemoration of Medina"

(**37**) "Commemoration of Jeddah, 1344, Postage of Nejd"

1925. Capture of Medina. Railway Tax stamps of Hejaz optd with T **36**.
244 **28** 1pi. on 10pi. mauve and violet 75·00 49·00
245 2pi. on 50pi. red and blue 75·00 49·00
246 3pi. on 100pi. brown 75·00 49·00
247 4pi. on 500pi. red 75·00 49·00
248 5pi. on 1000pi. violet and red 75·00 49·00

1925. Capture of Jeddah. Optd with T **37**.
249 **28** 1pi. on 10pi. mauve and violet 75·00 49·00
250 2pi. on 50pi. red and blue 75·00 49·00
251 3pi. on 100pi. brown 75·00 49·00
252 4pi. on 500pi. red 75·00 49·00
253 5pi. on 1000pi. violet and red 75·00 49·00

C. HEJAZ AND NEJD

38

39

1926.
254 **38** ¼pi. violet 19·00 12·00
261 ¼pi. orange 14·00 1·60
255 ½pi. grey 19·00 12·00
262 ½pi. green 8·00 95
256 1pi. blue 21·00 14·00
263 1pi. red 7·00 95
257 **39** 2pi. green 19·00 12·00
264 2pi. purple 7·00 95
259 3pi. pink 28·00 18·00
265 3pi. blue 7·00 95
266 5pi. brown 14·00 1·60

(**40**) "Islamic Congress, 1 June, 1926"

1926. Pan-Islamic Congress, Cairo. Optd with T **40**.
275 **38** ¼pi. orange 9·75 4·00
276 ½pi. green 9·75 4·00
277 1pi. red 9·75 4·00
278 **39** 2pi. purple 9·75 4·00
279 3pi. blue 9·75 4·00
280 5pi. brown 9·75 4·00

41 Tougra of Ibn Saud

(**42** "25th Rajab 1345")

1926.
284 **41** ⅛pi. brown 7·00 50
285 ¼pi. green 7·00 1·10
286 ½pi. red 7·00 1·10
287 1pi. purple 7·00 1·10
288 1½pi. blue 10·50 1·90
289 3pi. green 10·50 3·75
290 5pi. brown 18·00 4·75
291 10pi. brown 55·00 5·25

1927. Establishment of Kingdom. Optd with T **42**.
294 **41** ⅛pi. brown 9·75 4·75
295 ¼pi. green 9·75 4·75
296 ½pi. red 9·75 4·75
297 1pi. purple 9·75 4·75
298 1½pi. blue 9·75 4·75
299 3pi. green 9·75 4·75
300 5pi. brown 9·75 4·75
301 10pi. brown 9·75 4·75

43

44

1929.
302 **43** 1¾g. blue 16·00 2·10
303 20g. violet 45·00 8·00
304 30g. green 80·00 14·00

1930. 4th Anniv of King Ibn Saud's Accession.
305 **44** ½g. red 14·00 3·00
306 1½g. violet 14·00 2·00
307 1¾g. blue 14·00 2·75
308 3½g. green 14·00 3·25
309 5g. purple 14·00 5·25

45

46

1931.
310 **45** ⅛g. yellow 14·00 2·10
311 ¼g. green 14·00 1·50
312 1¾g. blue 41·00 2·10

1932.
313 **46** ¼g. green 16·00 1·90
314a ½g. red 41·00 2·75
315 2¼g. blue 70·00 2·00

D. SAUDI ARABIA

47

1932. Proclamation of Emir Saud as Heir Apparent.
316 **47** ¼g. green 6·00 3·75
317 ½g. red 6·00 4·00
318 1½g. blue 12·00 12·00
319 3g. green 15·00 15·00
320 3½g. blue 18·00 6·00
321 5g. yellow 32·00 26·00
322 10g. orange 65·00
323 20g. violet 80·00
324 30g. violet £120
325 ¼s. purple £160
326 ½s. brown £350
327 1s. purple £800

48

1934. Charity Tax. Fund for Wounded in War with Yemen.
328 **48** ½g. red £130 8·00

49

1934.
329 **49** ⅛g. yellow 3·75 40
330 ¼g. green 4·75 40
331a ½g. red 2·50 10
332 ⅞g. blue 5·25 55
333a 1g. green 3·25 30
334 2g. green 12·00 1·80
335 2⅞g. violet 5·25 55
336b 3g. blue 4·00 25
337 3½g. blue 16·00 1·80
338a 5g. orange 4·00 50
339b 10g. violet 14·00 1·40
340a 20g. purple 20·00 90
341 100g. mauve 65·00 4·00
342a 200g. brown 80·00 5·25

50 General Hospital, Mecca

1936. Charity. Medical Aid. Perf or roul. (a) Three palm trees.
345 **50** ⅛g. red (37 × 20 mm) £475 14·00
346 ⅛g. red (30½ × 18 mm) 70·00 1·50

(b) One palm tree.
348 **50** ⅛g. red (30½ × 18 mm) 55·00 55
351 ¼g. red (30½ × 18 mm) 7·00 15

53 Egyptian Royal Yacht "Fakhr el Bihar", Radhwa

54 Map of Saudi Arabia, Flags and Emblem

1945. Meeting of King Ibn Saud and King Farouk of Egypt at Radhwa.
352 **53** ½g. red 8·00 1·10
353 3g. blue 9·00 3·50
354 5g. violet 29·00 7·00
355 10g. purple 65·00 14·00

1946. Obligatory Tax. Return of King Ibn Saud from Egypt.
356a **54** ½g. mauve 17·00 1·00

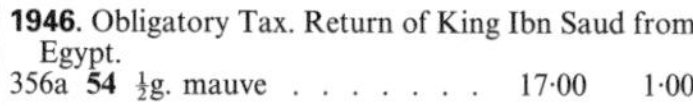

55 Airliner

1949. Air.
357 **55** 1g. green 3·50 10
358 3g. blue 4·50 15
359 4g. orange 4·50 15
360 10g. violet 12·00 40
361 20g. brown 11·50 1·60
362 100g. purple £110 11·50

56 Arms of Saudi Arabia and Afghanistan

1950. Visit of King Mohamed Zahir Shah of Afghanistan.
363 **56** ½g. red 7·00 90
364 3g. blue 11·50 90

57 Al-Murabba Palace, Riyadh

1950. 50th Anniv of Capture of Riyadh by King Abdulaziz Ibn Saud. Centres in purple.
365 **57** ½g. purple 6·50 1·40
366 1g. blue 9·75 2·00
367 3g. violet 16·00 3·75
368 5g. orange 31·00 6·00
369 10g. green 55·00 13·00

58 Arms of Saudi Arabia and Jordan

1951. Visit of King Talal of Jordan.
370 **58** ½g. red 4·75 90
371 3g. blue 15·00 1·60

59 Arabs and Diesel Goods Train

60 Arms of Saudi Arabia and Lebanon

1952. Inaug of Dammam–Riyadh Railway.
372 **59** ½g. brown 9·00 3·00
373 1g. green 10·50 3·25
374 3g. mauve 18·00 3·00
375 10g. red 36·00 12·00
376 20g. blue 75·00 28·00

1953. Visit of President Chamoun of Lebanon.
377 **60** ½g. red 4·00 1·10
378 3g. blue 10·50 2·50

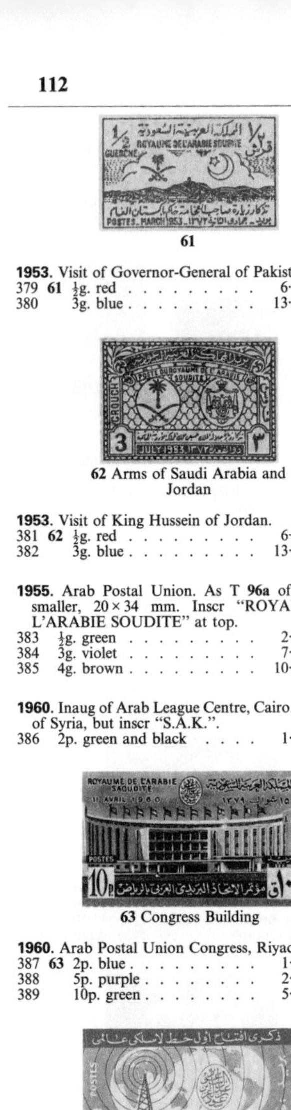

61

1953. Visit of Governor-General of Pakistan.
379 **61** ½g. red 6·50 1·10
380 3g. blue 13·00 2·50

62 Arms of Saudi Arabia and Jordan

1953. Visit of King Hussein of Jordan.
381 **62** ½g. red 6·50 1·10
382 3g. blue 13·00 2·50

1955. Arab Postal Union. As T **96a** of Syria but smaller, 20 × 34 mm. Inscr "ROYAUME DE L'ARABIE SOUDITE" at top.
383 ½g. green 2·50 65
384 3g. violet 7·25 1·20
385 4g. brown 10·50 3·50

1960. Inaug of Arab League Centre, Cairo. As T **154a** of Syria, but inscr "S.A.K.".
386 2p. green and black 1·80 95

63 Congress Building

1960. Arab Postal Union Congress, Riyadh.
387 **63** 2p. blue 1·20 80
388 5p. purple 2·75 1·20
389 10p. green 5·75 2·40

64 Radio Mast and Globe

1960. Inauguration of Direct Radio Service.
390 **64** 2p. red and black 1·20 80
391 5p. purple and claret 2·75 2·75
392 10p. indigo and blue 5·75 2·40

65 Refugee Camp

1960. World Refugee Year.
393 **65** 2p. blue 25 15
394 8p. violet 25 15
395 10p. green 1·10 50

66 Gas Oil Plant

67 Wadi Hanifa Dam, near Riyadh

68 Vickers Viscount 800

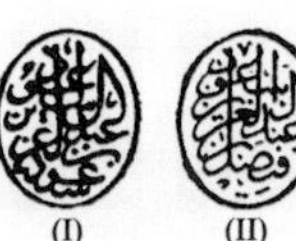

(I) (II)

1960. Cartouche of King Saud as Type I. Size 27½ × 22 mm. (a) Postage. (i) Type **66**.
396 ½p. orange and red 1·20 25
397 1p. red and blue 1·20 25
398 2p. blue and red 1·20 25
399 3p. green and violet 1·20 25
400 4p. purple and green 1·20 25
401 5p. red and purple 1·20 25
471 5p. red and brown 11·50 50
402 6p. lilac and brown 1·20 25
534 6p. chocolate and brown 55·00 4·75
403 7p. green and violet 1·20 25
404 8p. black and green 2·00 25
405 9p. brown and blue 3·50 25
406 10p. red and blue 1·80 30
539 11p. orange and green 32·00 1·80
540 12p. green and brown 4·00 30
541 13p. blue and mauve 4·00 40
542 14p. brown and lilac 5·75 40
543 15p. brown and mauve 6·50 50
544 16p. red and green 8·00 50
545 17p. brown and mauve 13·00 1·50
546 18p. blue and black 8·00 55
547 19p. yellow and brown 8·00 55
407 20p. black and brown 6·50 50
549 23p. red and orange 7·75 65
550 24p. yellow and green 8·00 75
551 26p. brown and purple 11·50 75
552 27p. black and red 11·50 75
553 31p. red and green 20·00 1·50
554 33p. black and brown 18·00 1·50
408 50p. green and brown 18·00 1·50
409 75p. purple and red 29·00 3·00
410 100p. brown and blue 45·00 2·50
411 200p. green and black 80·00 6·00

(ii) Type **67**.
412 ½p. orange and bistre 1·30 25
413 1p. purple and olive 1·30 15
414 2p. brown and blue 1·30 15
415 3p. blue and brown 1·30 15
416 4p. chestnut and brown 1·30 15
417 5p. purple and black 1·30 15
418 6p. red and black 1·30 15
419 7p. green and red 1·30 15
563 7p. black and brown 11·50 30
420 8p. purple and blue 1·30 25
564 8p. brown and blue 65·00 4·75
421 9p. red and brown 1·50 30
422 10p. lake and green 1·50 25
567 11p. green and red 5·25 1·80
568 12p. blue and orange 5·25 40
569 13p. mauve and green 5·25 40
570 14p. green and brown 5·25 40
571 15p. green and brown 5·25 1·80
572 16p. lilac and red 6·50 40
573 17p. blue and purple 6·50 2·10
574 18p. blue and green 6·50 40
575 19p. brown and black 8·00 50
423 20p. green and brown 3·75 40
480 20p. green and red 21·00 1·50
577 23p. purple and brown 7·00 1·80
578 24p. blue and red 8·00 55
579 26p. yellow and green 10·50 65
580 27p. purple and blue 10·50 65
581 31p. blue and black 10·50 75
582 33p. purple and green 10·50 75
424 50p. brown and black 21·00 2·00
425 75p. grey and brown 60·00 3·75
426 100p. turquoise and blue 55·00 2·50
427 200p. green and purple 90·00 7·00

(b) Air. Type **68**.
428 1p. green and purple 55 15
429 2p. purple and green 55 15
430 3p. blue and red 55 15
431 4p. purple and blue 55 15
432 5p. red and green 55 15
433 6p. violet and brown 95 25
484 6p. green and orange 9·00 90
434 8p. green and red 1·10 25
435 9p. brown and violet 1·80 25
436 10p. purple and black 4·75 50
437 15p. brown and blue 4·75 30
438 20p. green and brown 4·75 40
439 30p. green and brown 11·50 1·20
440 50p. blue and green 24·00 80
441 100p. brown and grey 49·00 2·40
442 200p. black and purple 75·00 4·00

Some values vary in size.

For similar design to Type **68** with King Saud cartouche but with different airplane, see Nos. 585/610c.

For designs with Type II cartouche, see Nos. 755 etc (1966 issue).

69 Globe, Pylon and Telegraph Pole

1960. 6th Anniv (1959) of Arab Telecommunications Union.
443 **69** 3p. purple 1·30 25
444 6p. black 2·10 50
445 8p. brown 3·50 65

71 Damman Port

72 Campaign Emblem

1961. Opening of Damman Port Extension.
446 **71** 3p. violet 1·50 15
447 6p. blue 2·00 65
448 8p. green 3·50 40

1962. Arab League Week. As T **178** of Syria but larger, 25 × 41 mm. Inscr "S.A.K.".
449 3p. green 1·20 10
450 6p. mauve 2·40 25
451 8p. green 3·75 30

1962. Malaria Eradication.
452 **72** 3p. red and blue 90 15
453 6p. green and blue 1·50 30
454 8p. black and purple 2·10 40
MS455 89 × 110 mm. Imperf 20·00 20·00

73 Koran

1963. 1st Anniv of Islamic Institute, Medina.
456 **73** 2½p. purple and orange 95 25
457 7½p. blue and green 1·10 30
458 9½p. green and black 2·00 50

74 Emblem within Hands

1963. Freedom From Hunger.
459 **74** 2½p. mauve and orange 95 25
460 7½p. purple and pink 1·10 30
461 9p. brown and blue 2·00 50

75 Boeing 707 over Airport

76 "Flame of Freedom"

1963. Opening of Dhahran Airport and Inauguration of Jet Service.
462 **75** 1p. violet and brown 95 15
463 3½p. blue and green 3·00 30
464 6p. green and red 4·75 50
465 7½p. mauve and blue 4·75 55
466 9½p. red and violet 6·50 65

1964. 15th Anniv of Declaration of Human Rights.
493 **76** 3p. blue, violet and orange 3·00 30
494 6p. blue, green & light blue 3·50 65
495 9p. blue, brown and pink 7·25 95

77 Arms and King Faisal

1964. Installation of King Faisal.
496 **77** 4p. blue and green 4·00 40

80 Boeing 720-B

81 Kaaba, Mecca

1964. Air. Type **80**. Cartouche of King Saud as Type **1** (illus next to T **68**).
585 1p. green and purple 80·00 2·75
586 2p. purple and green £2750 95·00
587 3p. blue and red 9·75 25
588 4p. purple and blue 5·75 25
589 5p. red and green £1800 £400
590 6p. grey and brown £110 1·80
591 7p. green and mauve 6·50 40
592 8p. green and red 80·00 1·80
593 9p. brown and violet 5·75 30
594 10p. purple and black 80·00 5·75
595 11p. buff and green 80·00 19·00
596 12p. grey and orange 5·75 30
597 13p. green and myrtle 4·50 30
598 14p. orange and blue 4·50 40
599 15p. brown and blue 80·00 5·75
600 16p. blue and black 6·50 50
601 17p. brown and ochre 5·25 40
602 18p. green and blue 5·25 40
603 19p. orange and mauve 5·75 50
604 20p. green and brown £150 6·50
605 23p. brown and green £150 11·50
606 24p. brown and blue 5·25 50
607 26p. green and red 5·25 50
608 27p. green and brown 6·00 50
609 31p. red and mauve 7·75 55
610 33p. purple and red 9·75 55
610a 50p. blue and green
610b 100p. brown and grey
610c 200p. brown and purple

For Type **80** with Type II cartouche, see Nos. 806 etc (1966 issue).

1965. Moslem League Conference, Mecca.
611 **81** 4p. black and brown 3·75 40
612 6p. black and mauve 5·25 65
613 10p. black and green 7·25 95

82 Arms of Saudi Arabia and Tunisia

1965. Visit of President Bourguiba of Tunisia.
614 **82** 4p. silver and mauve 2·30 75
615 8p. silver and violet 4·50 1·50
616 10p. silver and blue 5·75 1·90

83 Highway

1965. Opening of Arafat–Taif Highway.
617 **83** 2p. black and red 1·50 15
618 4p. black and blue 3·00 40
619 6p. black and violet 4·00 65
620 8p. black and green 5·25 80

84 I.C.Y. Emblem

1965. International Co-operation Year.
621 **84** 1p. brown and yellow 50 15
622 2p. green and orange 95 30
623 3p. green and blue 1·50 50
624 4p. black and green 1·90 65
625 10p. purple and orange 4·75 1·60

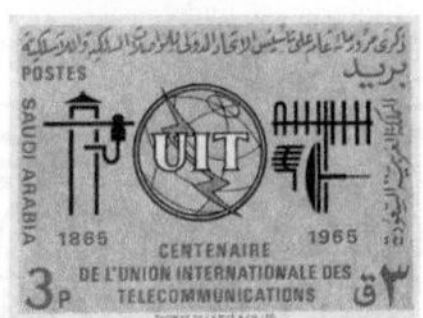

85 I.T.U. Symbol and Emblems

1965. Centenary of I.T.U.
626 **85** 3p. black and blue 95 25
627 4p. green and violet 1·30 30
628 8p. brown and green 2·50 65
629 10p. green and orange 3·25 80

86 Lamp and Burning Library

1966. Burning of Algiers Library in 1962.
630 **86** 1p. red 1·10 10
631 2p. red 2·10 15
632 3p. purple 3·00 30
633 4p. violet 4·00 40
634 5p. mauve 4·75 50
635 6p. red 6·00 55

87 A.P.U. Emblem

88 Dagger on Deir Yassin, Palestine

1966. 10th Anniv (1964) of Arab Postal Union's Permanent Office, Cairo.
636 **87** 3p. green and purple 1·20 30
637 4p. green and blue 1·20 30
638 6p. green and purple 3·75 65
639 7p. olive and green 3·75 65

1966. Deir Yassin Massacre.
640 **88** 2p. black and green 1·60 30
641 4p. black and brown 3·00 65
642 6p. black and blue 4·00 95
643 8p. black and orange 6·00 1·30

89 Scout Badges

1966. Arab Scout Jamboree.
644 **89** 4p. multicoloured 4·00 1·40
645 8p. multicoloured 4·00 1·40
646 10p. multicoloured 8·00 2·10

90 W.H.O. Building

1966. Inaug of W.H.O. Headquarters, Geneva.
647 **90** 4p. multicoloured 1·20 50
648 6p. multicoloured 2·40 75
649 10p. multicoloured 4·50 1·20

91 UNESCO Emblem
92 Radio Mast, Telephone and Map

1966. 20th Anniv of UNESCO.
650 **91** 1p. multicoloured 1·40 10
651 2p. multicoloured 1·40 25
652 3p. multicoloured 1·80 30
653 4p. multicoloured 1·80 40
654 10p. multicoloured 2·50 95

1966. 8th Arab Telecommunications Union Congress, Riyadh.
655 **92** 1p. multicoloured 80 15
656 2p. multicoloured 1·50 30
657 4p. multicoloured 3·00 55
658 6p. multicoloured 4·50 90
659 7p. multicoloured 4·75 1·10

1966. As 1960 and 1964 issues, but with cartouche of King Faisal as Type II (see above No. 396). (a) Postage. (i) Type **66**.
755 1p. red and blue 9·75 95
756 2p. blue and red 6·00 50
662 3p. green and violet 14·50 55
663 4p. purple and green 8·00 30
759 5p. red and purple 21·00 1·50
760 6p. chocolate and brown 26·00 1·80
666 7p. green and lilac 34·00 1·80
667 8p. green and turquoise 5·75 30
668 9p. brown and blue 4·00 30
669 10p. red and blue 4·75 55
765 11p. orange and green 32·00 1·80
671 12p. green and brown 4·75 75
672 13p. blue and mauve 45·00 30
673 14p. brown and lilac 41·00 2·40
674 15p. brown and mauve 11·50 65
675 16p. red and green 14·50 75
676 17p. brown and mauve 13·00 1·60
677 18p. blue and black 14·50 1·60
678 19p. yellow and brown 16·00 1·60
679 20p. brown and light brown 13·00 1·60
680 23p. red and orange 21·00 1·80
681 24p. yellow and green 9·75 75
681a 26p. brown and purple £160
682 27p. black and red 37·00 3·75
683 31p. red and green 11·50 75
684 33p. black and brown 21·00 1·10
685 50p. green and brown £375 £150
686 100p. brown and blue £300 41·00
687 200p. green and black £375 60·00

(ii) Type **67**.
688 1p. purple and green 95·00 17·00
689 2p. brown and blue 20·00 1·60
690 3p. blue and brown 11·50 80
691 4p. orange and brown 16·00 40
782 5p. purple and black 26·00 1·80
783 6p. red and black 24·00 1·50
694 7p. black and brown 19·00 1·80
695 8p. brown and blue 11·50 50
696 9p. red and brown 8·00 80
697 10p. brown and green 16·00 1·50
698 11p. green and red 11·50 1·50
699 12p. purple and orange 7·00 1·50
700 13p. mauve and green 24·00 1·50
701 14p. green and brown 20·00 1·50
702 15p. green and brown 20·00 1·80
703 16p. lilac and red 29·00 3·50
704 17p. blue and purple 34·00 1·80
705 18p. blue and green 24·00 2·50
706 19p. brown and black 7·75 80
707 20p. green and brown 75·00 2·40
708 23p. purple and brown £275 4·75
708a 24p. blue and red 55·00 5·75
709 26p. yellow and green 7·25 75
711 27p. purple and blue 8·00 80
712 33p. purple and green 45·00 2·40
713 50p. brown and black £180 37·00
714 100p. blue and deep blue £300 75·00

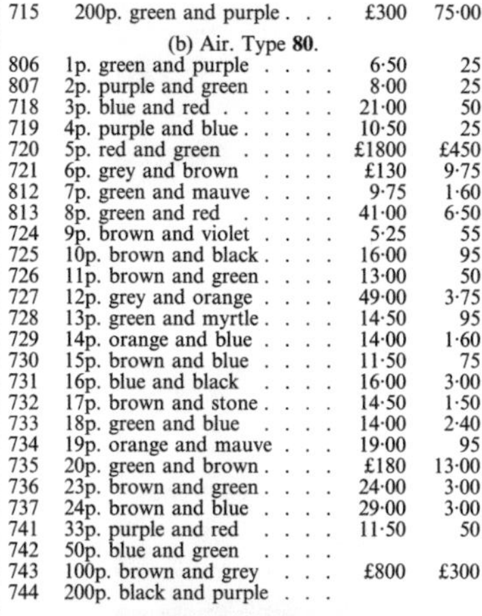
715 200p. green and purple £300 75·00

(b) Air. Type **80**.
806 1p. green and purple 6·50 25
807 2p. purple and green 8·00 25
718 3p. blue and red 21·00 50
719 4p. purple and blue 10·50 25
720 5p. red and green £1800 £450
721 6p. grey and brown £130 9·75
812 7p. green and mauve 9·75 1·60
813 8p. green and red 41·00 6·50
724 9p. brown and violet 5·25 55
725 10p. brown and black 16·00 95
726 11p. brown and green 13·00 50
727 12p. grey and orange 49·00 3·75
728 13p. green and myrtle 14·50 95
729 14p. orange and blue 14·00 1·60
730 15p. brown and blue 11·50 75
731 16p. blue and black 16·00 3·00
732 17p. brown and stone 14·50 1·50
733 18p. green and blue 14·00 2·40
734 19p. orange and mauve 19·00 95
735 20p. green and brown £180 13·00
736 23p. brown and green 24·00 3·00
737 24p. brown and blue 29·00 3·00
741 33p. purple and red 11·50 50
742 50p. blue and green
743 100p. brown and grey £800 £300
744 200p. black and purple

93 Moot Emblem
94 Meteorological Apparatus

1967. 2nd Rover Moot, Mecca.
745 **93** 1p. multicoloured 2·10 55
746 2p. multicoloured 2·10 55
747 3p. multicoloured 3·25 55
748 4p. multicoloured 4·00 55
749 10p. multicoloured 9·00 1·60

1967. World Meteorological Day.
750 **94** 1p. mauve 95 15
751 2p. violet 2·00 15
752 3p. green 2·00 25
753 4p. green 6·50 25
754 10p. blue 9·00 55

96 Route Map and Dates
97 The Prophet's Mosque, Medina

98 Prophet's Mosque Extension
99 Ancient Wall Tomb, Madayin Saleh

100 Colonnade, Sacred Mosque, Mecca
101 Camels and Oil Derrick

102 Arab Stallion
103 Holy Ka'aba, Mecca

1968. Inauguration of Dammam–Jeddah Highway.
834 **96** 1p. multicoloured 1·50 25
835 2p. multicoloured 1·50 25
836 3p. multicoloured 3·00 25
837 4p. multicoloured 3·00 50
838 10p. multicoloured 8·00 80

1968. (a) Type **97**.
839 **97** 1p. green and orange 2·40 30
840 2p. green and brown 6·50 30
857 3p. green and violet 3·50 40
945 4p. green and brown 6·50 30
843 5p. green and purple 13·00 95
860 6p. green and black 13·00 95
948 10p. green and brown 13·00 95
949 20p. green and brown 16·00 1·80
864 50p. green and purple 20·00 6·00
865 100p. green and blue 20·00 6·00
866 200p. green and red 20·00 6·50

(b) Type **98**.
952 **98** 1p. green and orange 5·25 25
953 2p. green and brown 7·75 25
954 3p. green and black 6·50 40
868 4p. green and red 9·00 50
851 5p. green and red 4·75 75
852 6p. green and blue 6·50 55
870a 8p. green and red 24·00 1·80
871 10p. green and brown 11·50 65
940 20p. green and violet 19·00 2·40

(c) Type **99**.
876 **99** 2p. brown and blue 21·00 3·75
878 4p. cinnamon and brown 5·25 75
880 7p. brown and orange 41·00 9·75
881 10p. brown and green 12·00 1·80
883 20p. brown and purple 14·50 1·50

(d) Type **100**.
887 **100** 3p. grey and red £375 95·00
888 4p. grey and green 6·00 50
891 10p. grey and purple 9·00 90

(e) Type **101**.
898 **101** 4p. red and lilac 16·00 3·75
901 10p. red and blue 20·00 3·00

(f) Type **102**.
908 **102** 4p. brown and purple 5·75 75
911 10p. brown and black 14·50 3·00
912 14p. brown and blue 24·00 6·00
913 20p. brown and green 8·00 1·80

(g) Type **103**.
918 **103** 4p. black and green 8·00 75
920 6p. black and purple 4·75 40
924 8p. black and red 29·00 3·00
921 10p. black and red 18·00 1·50

104 Saker Falcon
105 Traffic Signals

1968. Air.
1022 **104** 1p. brown and green 75·00 30
1023 4p. brown and red £250 11·50
1024 10p. brown and blue 36·00 3·00
1025 20p. brown and green 70·00 5·75

1969. Traffic Day.
1026 **105** 3p. blue, green and red 2·10 25
1027 4p. brown, green and red 2·10 25
1028 10p. purple, green and red 4·00 80

106 Scout Emblem, Camp and Flag

1969. 3rd Arab Rover Moot, Mecca.
1029 **106** 1p. multicoloured 1·20 55
1030 4p. multicoloured 4·00 1·10
1031 10p. multicoloured 11·50 4·50

107 W.H.O. Emblem

1969. 20th Anniv (1968) of W.H.O.
1032 **107** 4p. yellow, blue and deep blue 9·00 55

108 Conference Emblem

1970. Islamic Foreign Ministers' Conf, Jeddah.
1033 **108** 4p. black and blue 2·50 25
1034 10p. black and brown 3·75 40

109 Satellite, Dish Aerial and Open Book
112 Emblem and Arab Archway

110 Steel Rolling-mill

1970. World Telecommunications Day.
1035 **109** 4p. blue, mauve and ultramarine 4·50 40
1036 10p. blue, mauve & green 9·00 1·30

1970. Inauguration (1967) of First Saudi Arabian Steel Rolling-mill.
1037 **110** 3p. multicoloured 2·50 25
1038 4p. multicoloured 4·00 30
1039 10p. multicoloured 7·00 65

1971. 4th Arab Rover Moot, Mecca.
1049 **112** 10p. multicoloured 8·00 80

113 Global Emblem

1971. World Telecommunications Day.
1050 **113** 4p. black and blue 2·10 25
1051 10p. black and lilac 4·50 50

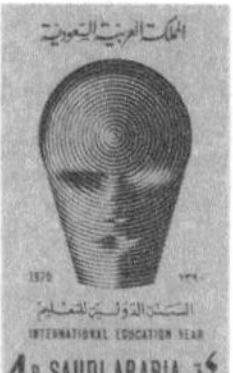
114 University "Tower" Emblem
115 I.E.Y. Emblem

1971. 4th Anniv of Inauguration of King Abdulaziz National University.
1052 **114** 3p. black and green 1·60 25
1053 4p. black and brown 3·25 50
1054 10p. black and blue 6·00 95

1971. International Education Year (1970).
1055 **115** 4p. red and green 5·25 25

116 Arab League Emblem
117 O.P.E.C. Emblem

1971. Arab Propaganda Week.
1056 **116** 10p. multicoloured 6·00 80

1971. 10th Anniv of O.P.E.C.
1057 **117** 4p. blue . . . . 6·00 25
O.P.E.C. = Organization of Petroleum Exporting Countries.

118 Globe

1972. World Telecommunications Day.
1058 **118** 4p. multicoloured . . . 6·00 25

119 Telephone within Dial

1972. Inauguration of Automatic Telephone System (1969).
1059 **119** 1p. black, green and red 2·10 25
1060 4p. black, turquoise & green . . . . 2·10 25
1061 5p. black, green & mauve . . . . 4·00 30
1062 10p. black, green & brn 7·25 75

120 Writing in Book

1973. World Literacy Day (1972).
1063 **120** 10p. multicoloured . . . 8·00 55

121 Mosque, Mecca, and Moot Emblem

1973. 5th Arab Rover Moot, Mecca. Mult.
1064 4p. Type **121** . . . . . . 3·25 65
1065 6p. Holy Ka'aba, Mecca . . 6·50 95
1066 10p. Rover encampment . . 9·75 2·40

122 Globe and Map of Palestine

1973. Universal Palestine Week.
1067 **122** 4p. red, yellow and grey 3·75 15
1068 10p. red, yellow and blue 6·50 80

123 Leaf and Emblem

1973. International Hydrological Decade.
1069 **123** 4p. multicoloured . . . 5·75 25

124 A.P.U. Emblem

1973. 25th Anniv of Founding of Arab Postal Union at Sofar Conference.
1070 **124** 4p. multicoloured . . . 4·50 25
1071 10p. multicoloured . . . 9·75 1·20

125 Balloons **126** U.P.U. Monument and Postal Emblem

1973. Universal Childen's Day (1971).
1072 **125** 4p. multicoloured . . . 7·25 25

1974. Centenary of U.P.U.
1073 **126** 3p. multicoloured . . . 36·00 4·00
1074 4p. multicoloured . . . 49·00 6·50
1075 10p. multicoloured . . . 60·00 8·00

127 Handclasp and UNESCO Emblem

1974. International Book Year (1972).
1076 **127** 4p. multicoloured . . . 1·40 20
1077 10p. multicoloured . . . 5·75 50

128 Desalination Works

1974. Inauguration of Sea-water Desalination Plant, Jeddah (1971).
1078 **128** 4p. blue and orange . . 2·00 25
1079 6p. lilac and green . . . 4·00 30
1080 10p. black and red . . . 6·50 75

129 Interpol Emblem **130** Tower, Emblem and Hand with Letter

1974. 50th Anniv (1973) of International Criminal Police Organization (Interpol).
1081 **129** 4p. blue and red . . . . 6·50 30
1082 10p. blue and green . . 13·00 1·50

1974. 3rd Session of Arab Postal Studies Consultative Council, Riyadh.
1083 **130** 4p. multicoloured . . . 6·50 25

131 New Headquarters Building

1974. Inauguration (1970) of New U.P.U. Headquarters, Berne.
1084 **131** 3p. multicoloured . . . 3·00 30
1085 4p. multicoloured . . . 5·75 50
1086 10p. multicoloured . . . 8·00 1·60

132 Armed Forces and Flame

1974. King Faisal Military Cantonment (1971).
1087 **132** 3p. multicoloured . . . 2·10 15
1088 4p. multicoloured . . . 4·00 30
1089 10p. multicoloured . . . 10·50 1·60

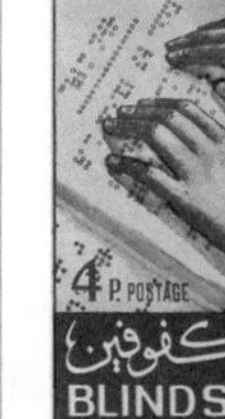

133 Red Crescent "Flower" **135** Reading Braille

134 Scout Emblem and Minarets

1974. 10th Anniv (1973) of Saudi Arabian Red Crescent Society.
1090 **133** 4p. multicoloured . . . 1·60 30
1091 6p. multicoloured . . . 4·50 80
1092 10p. multicoloured . . . 9·00 1·60

1974. 6th Arab Rover Moot, Mecca.
1093 **134** 4p. multicoloured . . . 4·50 30
1094 6p. multicoloured . . . 9·00 55
1095 10p. multicoloured . . . 13·00 1·60

1975. Day of the Blind.
1096 **135** 4p. multicoloured . . . 3·75 30
1097 10p. multicoloured . . . 7·00 65

136 Anemometer and U.N. Emblem as Weather Balloon

1975. Centenary (1973) of World Meteorological Organization.
1098 **136** 4p. multicoloured . . . 8·00 40

137 King Faisal **138** Conference Emblem

1975. King Faisal Memorial Issue.
1099 **137** 4p. purple and green . . 2·50 30
1100 16p. green and violet . . 3·50 65
1101 23p. violet and green . . 7·00 1·10
MS1102 71 × 80 mm. 40p. As T **137** but larger £300 £300

1975. 6th Islamic Conference of Foreign Ministers, Jeddah.
1103 **138** 10p. black and brown . . 4·75 50

139 Wheat and Sun

1975. 29th Anniv of Charity Society.
1104 **139** 4p. multicoloured . . . 3·00 25
1105 10p. multicoloured . . . 8·00 40

140 Kaaba, Handclasp and Globe

1975. Moslem Organizations Conference, Mecca.
1106 **140** 4p. multicoloured . . . 6·50 25
1107 10p. multicoloured . . . 14·50 40

141 Lockheed TriStar and Douglas DC-3 Aircraft

1975. 30th Anniv of National Airline "Saudia".
1108 **141** 4p. multicoloured . . . 8·00 30
1109 10p. multicoloured . . . 13·00 50

142 Mecca and Riyadh

1975. Conference Locations.
1110 **142** 10p. multicoloured . . . 9·75 50

143 Friday Mosque, Medina, and Juwatha Mosque, Al-Hasa

1975. Islamic Holy Places.
1111 **143** 4p. multicoloured . . . 5·75 25
1112 10p. multicoloured . . . 8·00 50

144 F.A.O. Emblem

1975. 10th Anniv (1973) of World Food Programme.
1113 **144** 4p. multicoloured . . . 4·50 15
1114 10p. multicoloured . . . 12·00 50

145 Conference Emblem

1976. Islamic Solidarity Conference of Science and Technology, Mecca.
1115 **145** 4p. multicoloured . . . 14·50 40

146 Map and T.V. Screen

1976. 10th Anniv (1975) of Saudi Arabian Television Service.
1116 **146** 4p. multicoloured . . . 19·00 40

147 Ear of Wheat, Atomic Symbol and Graph

1976. 2nd Five-year Plan.
1117 **147** 20h. multicoloured . . . 4·00 25
1118 50h. multicoloured . . . 6·50 50

148 Quba Mosque, Medina

149 Holy Kaaba, Mecca

150 Oil Rig, Al-Khafji

1976. Size 36 × 26 mm. (a) Type **148**.
1122 20h. grey and orange . . . 2·10 25
1128 50h. lilac and green . . . 2·75 25

(b) Type **149**.
1137 5h. black and lilac 25 25
1138 10h. black and lilac 25 25
1139 15h. black and orange . . . 40 25
1140 20h. black and blue . . . . 4·00 25
1141 25h. black and yellow . . . 1·10 25
1142 30h. black and green . . . 1·50 25
1143 35h. black and brown . . . 80 25
1144 40h. black and green . . . 3·50 25
1145 45h. black and purple . . . 1·10 25
1146 50h. black and red . . . . 1·10 25
1149 65h. black and blue . . . . 1·30 25
1151 1r. black and green . . . . 1·80 30
1152 2r. black and green . . . . 7·00 40

(c) Type **150**.
1167 5h. blue and orange . . . 25 25
1168 10h. green and orange . . 25 25
1169 15h. brown and orange . . 25 25
1170 20h. green and orange . . 25 25
1171 25h. purple and orange . . 25 25
1172 30h. blue and orange . . . 25 25
1173 35h. brown and orange . . 30 25
1174 40h. purple and orange . . 30 25
1175 45h. mauve and orange . . 40 25
1176b 50h. pink and orange . . . 50 25
1177 55h. green and orange . . 21·00 3·75
1179 65h. brown and orange . . 1·10 40
1180 1r. green and orange . . . 1·50 55
1181 2r. purple and red . . . . 3·25 95
For smaller designs see Nos. 1283/1325 and 1435/7.

151 Globe and Telephones

1976. Telephone Centenary.
1191 **151** 50h. multicoloured . . . 6·50 40

152 Emblem and Heads of State

1976. Arab League Summit Conference.
1192 **152** 20h. green and blue . . 4·00 25

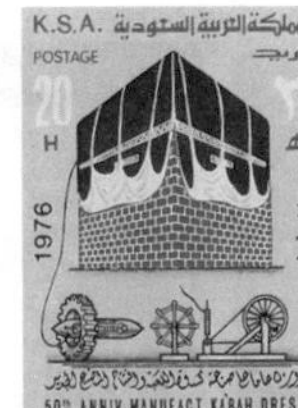

153 Kaaba and Spinning Wheel

1976. 50th Anniv of Manufacture of Kaaba Covering.
1193 **153** 20h. multicoloured . . . 7·25 40

154 Eye and W.H.O. Emblem

1976. World Health Day. Prevention of Blindness.
1194 **154** 20h. multicoloured . . . 9·75 40

155 Emblem

1976. Islamic Jurisprudence Conference.
1195 **155** 20h. multicoloured . . . 7·25 40

156 Emblem **157** King Khaled

1977. 25th Anniv of Sharia Law College, Mecca.
1196 **156** 4p. green, yellow and mauve . . . . 6·50 40

1977. 2nd Anniv of Installation of King Khaled.
(a) With incorrect dates at foot.
1197 **157** 20h. brown and green . . 16·00 16·00
1198 80h. black and green . . 16·00 16·00

(b) With corrected dates.
1199 **157** 20h. brown and green . . 1·80 25
1200 80h. black and green . . 3·75 30
On Nos. 1197/8 the two Arabic dates end with the same characters. On the correct version of the design, the characters differ.

158 Diesel Train and Route Map

1977. 25th Anniv (1976) of Dammam–Riyadh Railway.
1201 **158** 20h. multicoloured . . . 21·00 1·60

159/62 "The Four Imams" (½-size illustration)

1977.
1202 **159** 20h. blue, yellow and grey . . . . 6·50 75
1203 **160** 20h. blue, yellow and grey . . . . 6·50 75
1204 **161** 20h. blue, yellow and grey . . . . 6·50 75
1205 **162** 20h. blue, yellow and grey . . . . 6·50 75
Nos. 1202/5 were issued together, se-tenant, forming the composite design illustrated.

163 Moenjodaro Ruins, Pakistan

1977. "Save Moenjodaro" Campaign.
1206 **163** 50h. multicoloured . . . 7·25 40

164 Map by al-Idrisi

1977. 1st International Arab History Symposium.
1207 **164** 20h. multicoloured . . . 2·50 25
1208 50h. multicoloured . . . 5·25 40

165 King Faisal Hospital, Riyadh

1977. Opening of King Faisal Hospital.
1209 **165** 20h. multicoloured . . . 3·00 25
1210 50h. multicoloured . . . 4·75 40

166 A.P.U. Emblem

1977. 25th Anniv of Arab Postal Union.
1211 **166** 20h. multicoloured . . . 1·60 25
1212 80h. multicoloured . . . 3·50 50

167 Kaaba, Book and Lighthouse

1977. 1st World Conference on Muslim Education.
1213 **167** 20h. blue and yellow . . 4·00 40

168 Taif–Abha–Jizan Road and Route Map

1978. Opening of Taif–Abha–Jizan Road.
1214 **168** 20h. multicoloured . . . 1·60 15
1215 80h. multicoloured . . . 3·50 40

169 Mount Arafat, Pilgrims and Kaaba

1978. Pilgrimage to Mecca.
1216 **169** 20h. multicoloured . . . 1·60 15
1217 80h. multicoloured . . . 3·50 40

170 Posthorn Dhow

1979. 2nd Gulf Postal Organization Conf, Dubai.
1218 **170** 20h. multicoloured . . . 1·30 15
1219 50h. multicoloured . . . 2·50 30

171 5g. Stamp of 1930

1979. 50th Anniv of First Commemorative Stamp Issue.
1220 **171** 20h. multicoloured . . . 1·50 15
1221 50h. multicoloured . . . 3·25 25
1222 115h. multicoloured . . 4·75 80
MS1223 100 × 75 mm. **171** 100h. multicoloured. Imperf . . . . 80·00 80·00

172 Crown Prince Fahd

1979. Crown Prince Fahd's Birthday.
1224 **172** 20h. multicoloured . . . 1·80 15
1225 50h. multicoloured . . . 3·75 30

173 Dome of the Rock, Jerusalem

1979. Soldarity with Palestinians.
1226 **173** 20h. multicoloured . . . 1·80 40
For similar design see No. 1354.

174 Golden Door of Kaaba, Mecca

1979. Installation of New Gold Doors on Kaaba.
1227 **174** 20h. multicoloured . . . 1·50 15
1228 80h. multicoloured . . . 3·25 40

175 The Kaaba, Mecca

1979. Pilgrimage to Mecca.
1229 **175** 20h. multicoloured . . . 95 15
1230 50h. multicoloured . . . 2·50 40

176 "Birds in a Forest"

1980. International Year of the Child. Children's Paintings. Multicoloured.
1231 20h. Type **176** . . . . . . 9·00 25
1232 50h. "Paper Lanterns" . . . 14·50 80

177 King Abdulaziz Ibn Saud

1980. 80th Anniv of Saudi Armed Forces.
1233 **177** 20h. multicoloured . . . 1·30 15
1234 80h. multicoloured . . . 3·25 50

178 Emblem

179 Globe and Books

1980. 35th Anniv of Arab League.
1235 **178** 20h. green, black and blue . . . . 1·60 25

1980. 50th Anniv of Int Bureau of Education.
1236 **179** 50h. multicoloured . . . 2·00 25

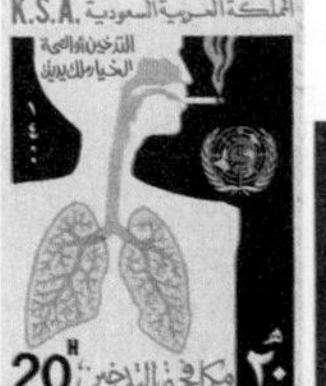

180 Polluted Air Passages and W.H.O. Emblem

181 O.P.E.C. Emblem and Globe

1980. Anti-smoking Campaign.
1237 **180** 20h. multicoloured . . . 4·00 15
1238 – 50h. black, red and blue 3·75 40
DESIGN: 50h. Cigarette crossed through and W.H.O. emblem.

1980. 20th Anniv of Organization of Petroleum Exporting Countries. Multicoloured.
1239 20h. Type **181** . . . . . . 1·50 15
1240 50h. Figures supporting O.P.E.C. emblem . . . . 2·40 40

182 Pilgrims leaving Airplane

1980. Pilgrimage to Mecca.
1241 **182** 20h. multicoloured . . . 90 15
1242 50h. multicoloured . . . 1·60 40

183 Kaaba, Mecca

1981. 3rd Islamic Summit Conference, Mecca. Multicoloured, frame colours given in brackets.
1243 20h. Type **183** (mauve) . . . 90 25
1244 20h. Prophet's Mosque, Medina (blue) 90 25
1245 20h. Dome of the Rock, Jerusalem (black) 90 25
1246 20h. Conference emblem (35 × 35 mm) 90 25

184 Thour Cave, Mecca, and Quba Mosque, Medina, on Map

1981. 1400th Anniv of Hegira.
1247 **184** 20h. multicoloured . . . 65 15
1248 50h. multicoloured . . . 1·30 30
1249 80h. multicoloured . . . 2·75 40

185 Royal Corporation of Jubeil and Yanbou Emblem

1981. Industry Week.
1250 **185** 20h. brown, orange & silver 65 25
1251 80h. brown, orge & gold 2·10 40

186 Satellite Earth Station

1981. Telecommunications Achievements.
1252 – 20h. gold, black and blue 40 25
1253 – 80h. multicoloured . . . 2·30 40
1254 **186** 115h. multicoloured . . 2·50 50
DESIGNS—As T **186**: 20h. Modern telephone and graph. 36 × 36 mm: 80h. Microwave antenna on map of Saudi Arabia.

187 Emblem of Arab Towns Organization

189 Flags of participating Countries and Saudi Team Emblem

188 Douglas DC-9-80 Super Eighty Jetliner

1981. Arab Towns Day.
1255 **187** 20h. multicoloured . . . 40 25
1256 65h. multicoloured . . . 1·10 40
1257 80h. multicoloured . . . 1·50 40
1258 115h. multicoloured . . 2·00 55

1981. Inauguration of King Abdulaziz International Airport, Jeddah. Multicoloured.
1259 20h. Type **188** 55 25
1260 80h. Airplane over departure halls in form of tents . . 2·30 40

1981. World Cup Football Championship Preliminary Round, Riyadh.
1261 **189** 20h. multicoloured . . . 1·80 25
1262 80h. multicoloured . . . 3·50 40

190 Blind Person reading Braille

191 Wheat and Cogwheel on Graph

1981. Int Year of Disabled Persons. Mult.
1263 20h. Type **190** . . . . . . 1·60 25
1264 50h. Disabled person in wheelchair weaving on loom . . . . 2·50 30

1981. 3rd Five-year Plan.
1265 **191** 20h. multicoloured . . . 1·30 25

192 King Abdulaziz Ibn Saud and Map of Saudi Arabia

1981. 50th Anniv of Unification of Saudi Arabia.
1266 **192** 5h. multicoloured . . . 25 25
1267 10h. multicoloured . . . 25 25
1268 15h. multicoloured . . . 25 25
1269 20h. multicoloured . . . 30 25
1270 50h. multicoloured . . . 65 30
1271 65h. multicoloured . . . 95 40
1272 80h. multicoloured . . . 2·40 40
1273 115h. multicoloured . . 3·00 50
MS1274 100 × 74 mm. 10r. King Abdulaziz Ibn Saud, map and unification decree. Imperf . . . 80·00 80·00

193 Pilgrims passing through Almasa'a Arcade

1981. Pilgrimage to Mecca.
1275 **193** 20h. multicoloured . . . 1·30 15
1276 65h. multicoloured . . . 2·50 40

194 Tractor

1981. World Food Day.
1277 **194** 20h. multicoloured . . . 2·10 25
For similar design see No. 1343.

195 Conference Emblem

1981. 2nd Session of Gulf Co-operation Council Summit Conference, Riyadh.
1278 **195** 20h. multicoloured . . . 65 25
1279 80h. multicoloured . . . 2·10 50

196 University Emblem

1982. 25th Anniv of King Saud University.
1280 **196** 20h. multicoloured . . . 80 25
1281 50h. multicoloured . . . 1·80 40

1982. As T **149/150** but in smaller size, 25 × 20 mm.
(a) Type **149**.
1283 10h. black and lilac . . . 25 25
1284 15h. black and orange . . 25 25
1285d 20h. black and blue . . . 25 25
1291c 50h. black and red 30 25
1294c 65h. black and blue . . . 65 25
1301c 1r. black and green . . . . 1·50 25

(b) Type **150**.
1306a 5h. blue and orange . . . 25 15
1307c 10h. green and orange . . 25 25
1308c 15h. brown and orange . . 25 25
1309c 20h. green and orange . . 25 25
1310 25h. purple and orange . . 25 25
1315c 50h. red and orange . . . 30 25
1318c 65h. brown and orange . . 40 25
1325c 1r. green and orange . . . 50 30

197 Riyadh Postal Building

198 Riyadh Television Centre

1982. New Postal Buildings. Multicoloured.
1330 20h. Type **197** 40 25
1331 65h. Jeddah 95 40
1332 80h. Dammam . . . . . . 1·40 40
1333 115h. Postal mechanized sorting . . . . 1·80 55
MS1334 Four sheets, each 8 × 70 mm. (a) No. 1330; (b) No. 1331; (c) No. 1332; (d) No. 1333. Imperf (each sold at 3000h.) . . . . 80·00 80·00

1982. Riyadh Television Centre.
1335 **198** 20h. multicoloured . . . 1·10 25

199 Football and King's Cup

200 A.P.U. Emblem and Map

1982. 25th Anniv of King's Cup Football Championship.
1336 **199** 20h. multicoloured . . . 80 25
1337 65h. multicoloured . . . 1·60 40

1982. 30th Anniv of Arab Postal Union. Mult.
1338 20h. A.P.U. Emblem and Arabic "30" 65 25
1339 65h. Type **200** . . . . . . 1·80 40

201 Pilgrims at Muzdalefa looking for Stones to stone the Devil

1982. Pilgrimage to Mecca.
1340 **201** 20h. multicoloured . . . 65 25
1341 50h. multicoloured . . . 1·80 40

202 Saudi Arabian and World Standards Organizations Emblems

1982. World Standards Day.
1342 **202** 20h. multicoloured . . . 1·30 30

203 Tractor

1982. World Food Day.
1343 **203** 20h. multicoloured . . . 1·10 25
For similar design see No. 1277.

204 King Fahd

1983. Installation of King Fahd.
1344 **204** 20h. multicoloured . . . 30 15
1345 50h. multicoloured . . . 65 30
1346 65h. multicoloured . . . 95 40
1347 80h. multicoloured . . . 1·10 50
1348 115h. multicoloured . . 1·80 65

205 Crown Prince Abdullah

1983. Installation of Crown Prince.
1349 **205** 20h. multicoloured . . . 30 15
1350 50h. multicoloured . . . 65 30
1351 65h. multicoloured . . . 95 40
1352 80h. multicoloured . . . 1·10 50
1353 115h. multicoloured . . 1·80 65

206 Dome of the Rock, Jerusalem

1983. Solidarity with Palestinians.
1354 **206** 20h. multicoloured . . . 65 30
For similar design but inscribed "K.S.A." see No. 1226.

207 Container Ship "Bar'zan"

1983. 6th Anniv of United Arab Shipping Company. Multicoloured.
1355 20h. Type **207** 50 25
1356 65h. "Al Drieya" (container ship) . . . . 1·80 55

208 Stoning the Devil

1983. Pilgrimage to Mecca.
1357 **208** 20h. multicoloured . . . 40 25
1358 65h. multicoloured . . . 1·30 25

209 Saudi Arabia Post and U.P.U. Emblems

211 Wheat and F.A.O. Emblem

210 Terminal Building

1983. World Communications Year. Mult.
1359 20h. Type **209** 30 25
1360 80h. Saudi Arabia telephone and I.T.U. emblems . . . 1·30 30

1983. Opening of King Khaled International Airport, Riyadh. Multicoloured.
1361 20h. Type **210** 30 25
1362 65h. Embarkation wing of terminal . . . . 1·30 30

1983. World Food Day.
1363 **211** 20h. multicoloured . . . 1·30 25

212 Al Aqsa Mosque, Jerusalem

1983. Solidarity with Palestinians.
1364 **212** 20h. brown, blue & green 50 25

213 Riyadh

214 Shobra Palace, Taif

215 Jeddah

216 Dammam

217 Abha

1984. Saudi Cities. (a) Riyadh.
1365 **213** 20h. multicoloured . . . 25 25
1366 50h. multicoloured . . . 30 25
1370 75h. multicoloured . . . 65 40
1371 150h. multicoloured . . 1·60 80

(b) Taif.
1367 **214** 20h. multicoloured . . . 25 25
1368 50h. multicoloured . . . 65 40
1374 75h. multicoloured . . . 65 40
1375 150h. multicoloured . . 1·60 80

(c) Jeddah.
1377 **215** 50h. multicoloured . . . 95 50
1378 75h. multicoloured . . . 95 50
1379 150h. multicoloured . . 1·60 80

(d) Dammam.
1380 **216** 50h. multicoloured . . . 50 30
1381 75h. multicoloured . . . 65 40
1382 150h. multicoloured . . 1·30 65

(e) Abha.
1383 **217** 1r. multicoloured 80 80
1384 2r. multicoloured . . . . 1·60 1·60

223 Family and House

1984. 10th Anniv of Estate Development Fund.
1385 **223** 20h. multicoloured . . . 50 25

224 Solar Panels and Symbols

1984. Al-Eyenah Solar Village. Multicoloured.
1386 20h. Type **224** 40 25
1387 80h. Sun and solar panels 1·10 30
MS1388 Two sheets, each 80 × 80 mm. Imperf. (a) 100h. As Type **224**; (b) As No. 1387, but both larger . . . . 55·00 55·00

225 Al-Kheef Mosque, Mina

1984. Pilgrimage to Mecca. Multicoloured.
1389 20h. Type **225** 50 15
1390 65h. Al-Kheef Mosque, Mina (different) . . . . . 1·50 30

226 Olympic and Saudi Football Federation Emblems

1984. Qualification of Saudi Football Team for Olympic Games.
1391 **226** 20h. multicoloured . . . 1·20 30
1392 115h. multicoloured . . 5·25 95
Nos. 1391/2 have the incorrect spellings "Gamos" and "Olympied".

227 Wheat and F.A.O. Emblem

1984. World Food Day.
1393 **227** 20h. green, buff and black 50 25

228 Olympic Rings and "90"

1984. 90th Anniv of Int Olympic Committee.
1394 **228** 20h. multicoloured . . . 95 30
1395 50h. multicoloured . . . 2·30 50

229 "Arabsat" and Globe

1985. Launch of "Arabsat" Satellite.
1396 **229** 20h. multicoloured . . . 1·80 25

230 Emblem and Koran

1985. International Koran Reading Competition.
1397 **230** 20h. multicoloured . . . 40 25
1398 65h. multicoloured . . . 95 40

231 King Fahd and Jubail Industrial Complex

1985. Five Year Plan. Multicoloured.
1399 20h. Type **231** 40 25
1400 50h. King Fahd, T.V. tower, dish aerial and microwave tower 95 25
1401 65h. King Fahd and agricultural landscape . . 1·10 25
1402 80h. King Fahd and Yanbu industrial complex . . . . 1·60 30

232 I.Y.Y. Emblem

1985. International Youth Year.
1403 **232** 20h. multicoloured . . . 30 25
1404 80h. multicoloured . . . 1·10 30

233 Map and Wheat

235 "Arabsat 2" Satellite and Launch of "Discovery" (space shuttle)

234 Loading Berth, Yanbu

1985. "Self Sufficiency in Wheat Production".
1405 **233** 20h. multicoloured . . . 50 25

1985. Abqaiq–Yanbu Oil Pipeline. Multicoloured.
1406 20h. Type **234** 50 25
1407 65h. Pipeline and map . . . 1·30 40

1985. 1st Arab Astronaut, Prince Sultan Ibn Salman Al-Saud. Multicoloured.
1408 20h. Type **235** 80 40
1409 115h. Space shuttle and mission emblem (51 × 26 mm) . . . . . . 4·50 2·00

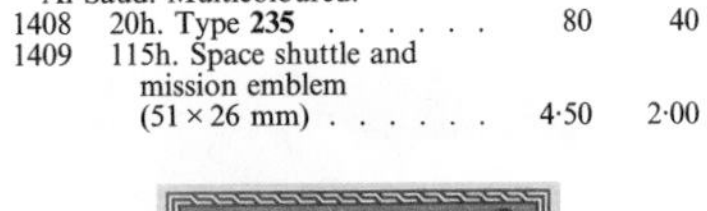

236 "40" and U.N. Emblem

1985. 40th Anniv of U.N.O.
1410 **236** 20h. light blue, blue and green 55 25

237 Highway and Map of Route

1985. Mecca–Medina Highway.
1411 **237** 20h. multicoloured . . . 40 25
1412 65h. multicoloured . . . 1·10 30

238 Coded Envelope and Post Emblem

1985. Post Code Publicity.
1413 **238** 20h. multicoloured . . . 50 25

239 Trophy and Football

1985. Victory in 8th (1984) Asian Football Cup Championship.
1414 **239** 20h. multicoloured . . . 40 15
1415 65h. multicoloured . . . 1·20 40
1416 115h. multicoloured . . 2·10 75

240 Pilgrims around Kaaba

1985. Pilgrimage to Mecca.
1417 **240** 10h. multicoloured . . . 25 25
1418 15h. multicoloured . . . 25 25
1419 20h. multicoloured . . . 30 25
1420 65h. multicoloured . . . 75 25

241 Olympic Rings and Council Emblem

1985. 1st Arabian Gulf Co-operation Council Olympic Day.
1421 **241** 20h. multicoloured . . . 40 25
1422 115h. multicoloured . . 1·80 40

242 Irrigation System

1985. World Food Day.
1423 **242** 20h. multicoloured . . . 80 40
1424 65h. multicoloured . . . 2·40 80

243 King Abdulaziz and Horsemen

1985. International Conference on King Abdulaziz.
1425 **243** 15h. multicoloured . . . 15 15
1426 20h. multicoloured . . . 25 15
1427 65h. multicoloured . . . 50 40
1428 80h. multicoloured . . . 95 50
MS1429 120 × 100 mm. Nos. 1425/8. Imperf (sold at 10r.) . . . . . 20·00 20·00

244 Building within Roll of Printed Paper

1985. King Fahd Holy Koran Press Compound, Medina. Multicoloured.
1430 20h. Type **244** 25 25
1431 65h. Open book sculpture within roll of printed paper . . . . 1·10 30

245 O.P.E.C. Emblem and "25"

1985. 25th Anniv of Organization of Petroleum Exporting Countries.
1432 **245** 20h. sepia, brown and black 30 25
1433 65h. multicoloured . . . 1·50 30

246 Doves and I.P.Y. Emblem — 248 Child in Droplet

247 Riyadh

1986. International Peace Year.
1434 **246** 20h. multicoloured . . . 95 40

1986. As T **149** but size 29 × 19 mm.
1435 10h. black and violet . . . 6·00 6·00
1436 20h. black and blue . . . . 9·75 9·75
1437 50h. black and red . . . . 20·00 16·00

1986. 50th Anniv of Riyadh Municipality.
1438a **247** 20h. multicoloured . . 30 25
1439 65h. multicoloured . . 95 30

1986. World Health Day.
1440 **248** 20h. multicoloured . . . 30 25
1441 50h. multicoloured . . . 95 30

249 Electricity Pylon and Flashes

1986. 10th Anniv of General Electricity Corporation.
1442 **249** 20h. multicoloured . . . 30 25
1443 65h. multicoloured . . . 95 30

250 Route Map of Cable

1986. Inauguration of Singapore–Marseilles Communications Cable.
1444 **250** 20h. blue, black and green 50 25
1445 50h. multicoloured . . . 95 30

251 Houses and Soldier — 252 Holy Kaaba

1986. National Guards Housing Project, Riyadh.
1446 **251** 20h. multicoloured . . . 30 25
1447 65h. multicoloured . . . 95 30

1986.
1448 **252** 30h. black and green 25 25
1449 40h. black and mauve 30 25
1450 50h. black and green 65 40
1451a 75h. black and blue . . 80 40
1451b 100h. black and green 95 55
1452a 150h. black and mauve 95 50
1454 2r. black and blue . . . 1·80 95

253 Mount Arafat, Pilgrims and Kaaba

1986. Pilgrimage to Mecca. Multicoloured.
1460 20h. Type **253** . . . . . . 1·60 1·20
1461 20h. Pilgrims leaving jet airliner . . . . 1·60 1·20
1462 20h. Stoning the Devil . . . 1·60 1·20
1463 20h. Pilgrims at Muzdalefa looking for stones to stone the Devil . . . . . 1·60 1·20
1464 20h. Pilgrims passing through Almasa'a Arcade 1·60 1·20
1465 20h. Kaaba, Mecca . . . . 1·60 1·20
1466 20h. Pilgrims around Kaaba 1·60 1·20
1467 20h. Al-Kheef Mosque, Mina . . . . 1·60 1·20

254 Refinery — 255 Palm Tree and Wheat in Globe

1986. 50th Anniv of Discovery of Oil in Saudi Arabia. Multicoloured.
1468 20h. Type **254** 40 25
1469 65h. Oil derrick on map . . 1·20 30

1986. World Food Day. Multicoloured.
1470 20h. Type **255** 25 25
1471 115h. Corn cob and wheat in leaves of flower . . . . 1·10 55

256 Scroll behind Dagger and Pool of Blood

1986. 4th Anniv of Massacre of Palestinian Refugees at Sabra and Shatila Camps, Lebanon.
1472 **256** 80h. multicoloured . . . 75 40
1473 115h. multicoloured . . 1·20 55

257

258

259 — 260

261

262

263

1986. University Crests. (a) Imam Mohammed ibn Saud Islamic University, Riyadh.
1474 **257** 15h. black and green . . 25 25
1475 20h. black and blue . . 25 25
1476 50h. black and blue . . 40 30
1477 65h. black and blue . . 55 30
1478 75h. black and blue . . 65 40
1479 100h. black and pink . . 75 40
1480 150h. black and red . . 1·50 65

(b) Umm al-Qura University, Mecca.
1481 **258** 50h. black and blue . . 55 30
1482 65h. black and blue . . 65 30
1483 75h. black and blue . . 65 40
1484 100h. black and pink . . 1·10 55
1485 150h. black and red . . 1·60 80

(c) King Saud University, Riyadh.
1487 **259** 50h. black and blue . . 55 30
1488 75h. black and blue . . 65 40
1489 100h. black and pink . . 1·10 55
1490 150h. black and pink . . 1·50 65

(d) King Abulaziz University, Jeddah.
1493 **260** 50h. black and blue . . 40 30
1494 75h. black and blue . . 65 40
1496 150h. black and pink . . 1·50 65

(e) King Faisal University, Al-Hasa.
1499 **261** 50h. black and blue . . 40 30
1500 75h. black and blue . . 65 40
1502 150h. black and red . . 1·50 50

(f) King Fahd University of Petroleum and Minerals, Dhahran.
1505 **262** 50h. black and blue . . 40 30
1506 75h. black and blue . . 65 40
1508 150h. black and pink . . 1·30 65

(g) Islamic University, Medina.
1511 **263** 50h. black and blue . . 50 25
1512 75h. black and blue . . 65 40
1514 150h. black and red . . 1·30 30

264 Road Bridge and Aerial View of Causeway (left)

1986. Saudi Arabia–Bahrain Causeway. Mult.
1515 20h. Type **264** 80 30
1516 20h. Road bridge and aerial view of causeway (right) 80 30

265 Olympic Torch and Rings

1986. 90th Anniv of Modern Olympic Games.
1517 **265** 20h. multicoloured . . . 95 25
1518 100h. multicoloured . . 5·25 1·40

266 Oil Derrick and Refinery

1987. 25th Anniv of General Petroleum and Mineral Organization.
1519 **266** 50h. multicoloured . . . 55 30
1520 100h. multicoloured . . 1·10 55

267 Mosque and Model of Extension

1987. Restoration and Extension of Quba Mosque, Medina.
1521 **267** 50h. multicoloured . . . 65 30
1522 75h. multicoloured . . . 95 40

268 Drill-press Operator

1987. Technical and Vocational Training. Mult.
1523 50h. Type **268** . . . . . . 1·40 65
1524 50h. Lathe operator . . . . 1·40 65
1525 50h. Laboratory technician 1·40 65
1526 50h. Welder . . . . 1·40 65
Nos. 1523/6 were printed together, se-tenant, each block forming an overall design of a cogwheel.

269 Pyramid, Riyadh T.V. Tower, King Khaled International Airport and Fort
270 Dish Aerials and Satellite

1987. "Saudi Arabia—Yesterday and Today" Exhibition, Cairo.
1527 **269** 50h. multicoloured . . . 55 30
1528 75h. multicoloured . . . 1·10 50

1987. King Fahd Space Communications City, Umm al Salam, Jeddah. Multicoloured.
1529 50h. Type **270** 55 30
1530 75h. Dish aerials and City buildings (51 × 26 mm) . . 1·10 50

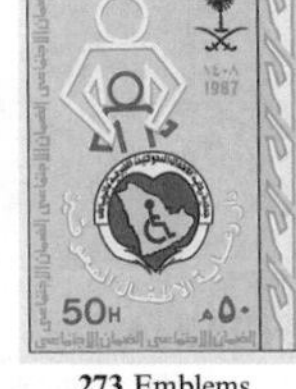
271 Map and Rifleman
273 Emblems

272 Mosque and Pilgrims

1987. Afghan Resistance to Occupation.
1531 **271** 50h. multicoloured . . . 55 30
1532 100h. multicoloured . . 1·10 55

1987. Pilgrimage to Mecca.
1533 **272** 50h. multicoloured . . . 65 30
1534 75h. multicoloured . . . 95 40
1535 100h. multicoloured . . 1·10 55

1987. 1st Anniv of Disabled Children's Care Home.
1536 **273** 50h. multicoloured . . . 55 30
1537 75h. multicoloured . . . 80 40

274 Emblems and Hands writing on Airmail Envelope

1987. World Post Day.
1538 **274** 50h. multicoloured . . . 55 30
1539 150h. multicoloured . . 1·50 75

275 Combine Harvester within Leaf

1987. World Food Day.
1540 **275** 50h. multicoloured . . . 65 30
1541 75h. multicoloured . . . 95 40

276 Woman and Children in Hand
277 Dome of the Rock, Jerusalem

1987. 25th Anniv of First Social Welfare Society.
1542 **276** 50h. multicoloured . . . 65 30
1543 100h. multicoloured . . 1·30 55

1987.
1544 **277** 75h. multicoloured . . . 1·60 40
1545 150h. multicoloured . . 3·25 80

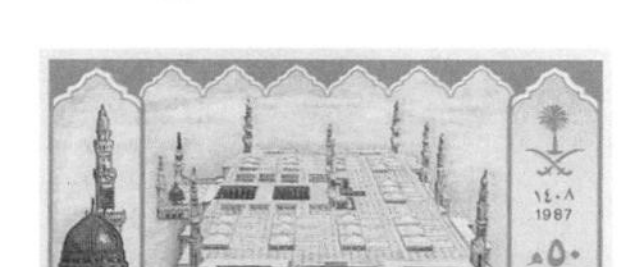
278 Mosque

1987. Expansion of Prophet's Mosque, Medina.
1546 **278** 50h. multicoloured . . . 65 30
1547 75h. multicoloured . . . 95 40
1548 150h. multicoloured . . 1·80 75
MS1549 110 × 70 mm. Imperf (sold at 300h.) . . . . 41·00 41·00

279 Dome of the Rock, Horseman and Battle Scene

1987. 800th Anniv of Battle of Hattin.
1550 **279** 75h. multicoloured . . . 1·60 40
1551 150h. multicoloured . . 3·25 80

280 Emblem
281 Road as "3" and Ship

1987. 8th Supreme Council Session of Gulf Co-operation Council, Riyadh.
1552 **280** 50h. multicoloured . . . 65 30
1553 75h. multicoloured . . . 1·10 40

1988. 3rd International Roads Federation (Middle East Region) Meeting, Riyadh.
1554 **281** 50h. multicoloured . . . 90 50
1555 75h. multicoloured . . . 1·30 65

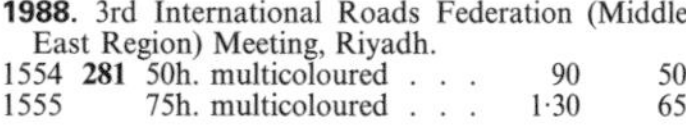

282 Aerial View of Stadium and Sports Pictograms

1988. Inauguration of International King Fahd Stadium, Riyadh. Multicoloured.
1556 50h. Type **282** 65 30
1557 150h. Side view of stadium and sports pictograms (51 × 26 mm) . . . . . . 2·10 90

283 Anniversary Emblem and W.H.O. Building

1988. World Health Day. 40th Anniv of W.H.O.
1558 **283** 50h. multicoloured . . . 80 30
1559 75h. multicoloured . . . 90 40

284 Blood Transfusion and Blood Drop
286 Clean Air, Land and Sea

285 Mosque, Holy Kaaba and King Fahd

1988. Blood Donation.
1560 **284** 50h. multicoloured . . . 65 30
1561 75h. multicoloured . . . 90 40

1988. Appointment of King Fahd as Custodian of Two Holy Mosques.
1562 **285** 50h. multicoloured . . . 50 30
1563 75h. multicoloured . . . 65 40
1564 150h. multicoloured . . 1·50 65
MS1565 120 × 85 mm. As No. 1563 but 63 × 32 mm (sold at 3r.) . . 49·00 49·00

1988. Environmental Protection.
1566 **286** 50h. multicoloured . . . 75 30
1567 75h. multicoloured . . . 1·10 40

287 Palestinian Flag, Hand holding Stone and Crowd

1988. Palestinian "Intifada" Movement.
1568 **287** 75h. multicoloured . . . 1·10 40
1569 150h. multicoloured . . 2·10 80

288 Pilgrims at al-Sail al-Kabir Miqat

1988. Pilgrimage to Mecca.
1570 **288** 50h. multicoloured . . . 80 30
1571 75h. multicoloured . . . 1·30 50

289 Ear of Wheat

1988. World Food Day.
1572 **289** 50h. multicoloured . . . 95 50
1573 75h. multicoloured . . . 1·50 75

290 Mosque

1988. Expansion of Qiblatayn Mosque, Medina.
1574 **290** 50h. multicoloured . . . 75 30
1575 75h. multicoloured . . . 1·10 40

291 Footballer and Trophy on Globe

1989. World Youth Football Cup, Saudi Arabia.
1576 **291** 75h. multicoloured . . . 1·20 55
1577 150h. multicoloured . . 2·40 1·10

292 W.H.O. Emblem and Means of Communications

1989. World Health Day.
1578 **292** 50h. multicoloured . . . 80 30
1579 75h. multicoloured . . . 1·30 40

293 Shuaibah Desalination Plant, Red Sea

1989. 1st Anniv of Sea Water Desalination and Electricity Power Station.
1580 **293** 50h. multicoloured . . . 55 30
1581 75h. multicoloured . . . 80 50

294 Palestinian Flag and Dome of the Rock, Jerusalem

1989. "Freedom of Palestine".
1582 **294** 50h. multicoloured . . . 65 25
1583 75h. multicoloured . . . 1·10 30

295 Attan'eem Miqat, Mecca

1989. Pilgrimage to Mecca.

1584	**295**	50h. multicoloured	65	25
1585		75h. multicoloured	95	30

296 Ears of Wheat encircling Globe

1989. World Food Day.

1586	**296**	75h. multicoloured	55	40
1587		150h. multicoloured	1·10	80

297 Hands holding Trophy aloft

299 Emblem and Arabic Letters

298 Mosque after Expansion

1989. 3rd World Under-16 JVC Cup Soccer Championship, Scotland.

1588	**297**	75h. multicoloured	80	40
1589		150h. multicoloured	1·60	80

1989. Expansion of Holy Mosque, Mecca.

1590	**298**	50h. multicoloured	55	30
1591		75h. multicoloured	80	50
1592		150h. multicoloured	1·60	80
MS1593		105 × 80 mm. 5r. As T **298** but larger. Imperf or perf	28·00	28·00

1990. International Literacy Year.

1595	**299**	50h. multicoloured	75	30
1596		75h. multicoloured	1·10	40

300 "Aloe sheilaa"

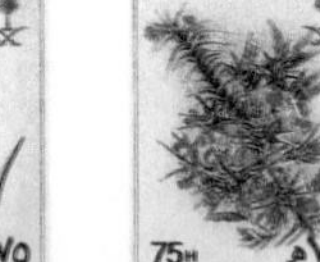

301 "Blopharis ciliaris"

302 "Pergularia tormentosa"

303 "Talinam cuneifolium"

304 "Echium horridum"

305 "Cleome arabica"

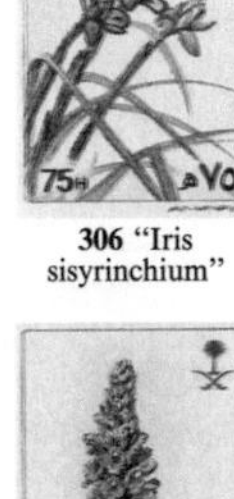

306 "Iris sisyrinchium"

307 "Senecio desfontaini"

308 "Cistanche phelypaea"

309 "Plumbago zeylanica"

310 "Cappario cartilaginea"

311 "Peganum harmala"

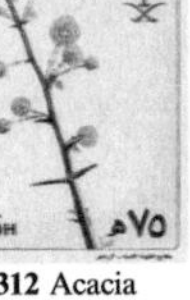

312 Acacia

313 "Cagea reticulata"

314 "Diplotakis harra"

315 "Anvillea garcini"

316 "Striga asiatica"

317 "Rhanterium eppaposum"

318 "Oenostachys abyssinica"

319 "Roemeria dodecandra"

320 Poppy

1990. Flowers.

1597	**300**	50h. multicoloured	40	25
1598	**301**	50h. multicoloured	40	25
1599	**302**	50h. multicoloured	40	25
1600	**303**	50h. multicoloured	40	25
1601	**304**	50h. multicoloured	40	25
1602	**305**	50h. multicoloured	40	25
1603	**306**	50h. multicoloured	40	25
1604	**307**	50h. multicoloured	40	25
1605	**308**	50h. multicoloured	40	25
1606	**309**	50h. multicoloured	40	25
1607	**310**	50h. multicoloured	40	25
1608	**311**	50h. multicoloured	40	25
1609	**312**	50h. multicoloured	40	25
1610	**313**	50h. multicoloured	40	25
1611	**314**	50h. multicoloured	40	25
1612	**315**	50h. multicoloured	40	25
1613	**316**	50h. multicoloured	40	25
1614	**317**	50h. multicoloured	40	25
1615	**318**	50h. multicoloured	40	25
1616	**319**	50h. multicoloured	40	25
1617	**320**	50h. multicoloured	40	25
1618	**300**	75h. multicoloured	55	30
1619	**301**	75h. multicoloured	55	30
1620	**302**	75h. multicoloured	55	30
1621	**303**	75h. multicoloured	55	30
1622	**304**	75h. multicoloured	55	30
1623	**305**	75h. multicoloured	55	30
1624	**306**	75h. multicoloured	55	30
1625	**307**	75h. multicoloured	55	30
1626	**308**	75h. multicoloured	55	30
1627	**309**	75h. multicoloured	55	30
1628	**310**	75h. multicoloured	55	30
1629	**311**	75h. multicoloured	55	30
1630	**312**	75h. multicoloured	55	30
1631	**313**	75h. multicoloured	55	30
1632	**314**	75h. multicoloured	55	30
1633	**315**	75h. multicoloured	55	30
1634	**316**	75h. multicoloured	55	30
1635	**317**	75h. multicoloured	55	30
1636	**318**	75h. multicoloured	55	30
1637	**319**	75h. multicoloured	55	30
1638	**320**	75h. multicoloured	55	30
1639	**300**	150h. multicoloured	1·10	65
1640	**301**	150h. multicoloured	1·10	65
1641	**302**	150h. multicoloured	1·10	65
1642	**303**	150h. multicoloured	1·10	65
1643	**304**	150h. multicoloured	1·10	65
1644	**305**	150h. multicoloured	1·10	65
1645	**306**	150h. multicoloured	1·10	65
1646	**307**	150h. multicoloured	1·10	65
1647	**308**	150h. multicoloured	1·10	65
1648	**309**	150h. multicoloured	1·10	65
1649	**310**	150h. multicoloured	1·10	65
1650	**311**	150h. multicoloured	1·10	65
1651	**312**	150h. multicoloured	1·10	65
1652	**313**	150h. multicoloured	1·10	65
1653	**314**	150h. multicoloured	1·10	65
1654	**315**	150h. multicoloured	1·10	65
1655	**316**	150h. multicoloured	1·10	65
1656	**317**	150h. multicoloured	1·10	65
1657	**318**	150h. multicoloured	1·10	65
1658	**319**	150h. multicoloured	1·10	65
1659	**320**	150h. multicoloured	1·10	65

321 "20" within Crescent and Circle

1990. 20th Anniv of Islamic Conference Organization.

1660	**321**	75h. multicoloured	55	30
1661		150h. multicoloured	1·10	55

322 Globe and W.H.O. Emblem

1990. World Health Day.

1662	**322**	75h. multicoloured	80	40
1663		150h. multicoloured	1·60	75

323 White Horse

1990. 25th Anniv of Horsemanship Club. Mult.

(a) Size 38 × 29 mm.

1664	50h. Type **323**	80	30
1665	50h. Brown horse	80	30
1666	50h. White horse with dark muzzle	80	30
1667	50h. Chestnut horse	80	30

(b) Size 36 × 27 mm.

1668	50h. As No. 1667	80	30
1669	75h. As No. 1665	95	50
1670	100h. Type **323**	1·30	65
1671	150h. As No. 1666	1·90	95

324 El Johfah Miqat, Rabegh

1990. Pilgrimage to Mecca.

1672	**324**	75h. multicoloured	80	40
1673		150h. multicoloured	1·60	80

325 T.V. Tower and Centre

1990. 25th Anniv of Saudi Television.

1674	**325**	75h. multicoloured	80	40
1675		150h. multicoloured	1·60	80

326 Ornament

1990. Islamic Heritage Year. Multicoloured.

1676	75h. Type **326**	80	50
1677	75h. Mosque	80	50
1678	75h. Arabic script	80	50
1679	75h. Decoration with stylized minarets	80	50

Nos. 1676/9 were issued together, se-tenant, each block having a composite design of a stylized rosette in the centre.

327 Boeing 747-300/400 and International Flights Route Map

1990. 45th Anniv of Saudi Airlines. Multicoloured.

1680	75h. Type **327**	65	40
1681	75h. Douglas DC-10 airliner and domestic flights route map	65	40
1682	150h. Type **327**	1·30	80
1683	150h. As No. 1681	1·30	80

328 Anniversary Emblem

1990. 30th Anniv of Organization of Petroleum Exporting Countries.

1684	**328**	75h. multicoloured	1·10	40
1685		150h. multicoloured	2·10	1·20

329 World Map

1990. World Food Day.

1686	**329**	75h. multicoloured	80	40
1687		150h. multicoloured	1·80	80

330 Industrial Site, Irrigation System and Oil Refinery

1990. 5th Five Year Plan. Multicoloured.

No.	Type	Description		
1688		75h. Type **330**	95	50
1689		75h. Radio tower, road and mine	95	50
1690		75h. Monument, sports stadium and vocational training	95	50
1691		75h. Television tower, environmental protection and modern building	95	50

331 Arabic Script and Decoration

1991. Battle of Badr, 624 A.D.

No.	Type	Description		
1692	**331**	75h. green and orange	75	40
1693		150h. dp blue, blue & green	1·50	75

332 Tidal Wave, Erupting Volcano and Earthquake-damaged House

1991. World Health Day. Natural Disasters Relief.

No.	Type	Description		
1694	**332**	75h. multicoloured	75	40
1695		150h. multicoloured	1·50	75

333 Mountain Gazelle

334 Ibex

335 Arabian Oryx

336 Sand Fox

337 Bat

338 Striped Hyena

339 Sand Cat

340 Dugong

341 Arabian Leopard

342 Flag and Map of Kuwait

1991. Animals.

No.	Type	Description		
1696	**333**	25h. multicoloured	30	15
1697	**334**	25h. multicoloured	30	15
1698	**335**	25h. multicoloured	30	15
1699	**336**	25h. multicoloured	30	15
1700	**337**	25h. multicoloured	30	15
1701	**338**	25h. multicoloured	30	15
1702	**339**	25h. multicoloured	30	15
1703	**340**	25h. multicoloured	30	15
1704	**341**	25h. multicoloured	30	15
1705	**333**	50h. multicoloured	65	40
1706	**334**	50h. multicoloured	65	40
1707	**335**	50h. multicoloured	65	40
1708	**336**	50h. multicoloured	65	40
1709	**337**	50h. multicoloured	65	40
1710	**338**	50h. multicoloured	65	40
1711	**339**	50h. multicoloured	65	40
1712	**340**	50h. multicoloured	65	40
1713	**341**	50h. multicoloured	65	40
1714	**333**	75h. multicoloured	95	65
1715	**334**	75h. multicoloured	95	65
1716	**335**	75h. multicoloured	95	65
1717	**336**	75h. multicoloured	95	65
1718	**337**	75h. multicoloured	95	65
1719	**338**	75h. multicoloured	95	65
1720	**339**	75h. multicoloured	95	65
1721	**340**	75h. multicoloured	95	65
1722	**341**	75h. multicoloured	95	65
1723	**333**	100h. multicoloured	1·30	80
1724	**334**	100h. multicoloured	1·30	80
1725	**335**	100h. multicoloured	1·30	80
1726	**336**	100h. multicoloured	1·30	80
1727	**337**	100h. multicoloured	1·30	80
1728	**338**	100h. multicoloured	1·30	80
1729	**339**	100h. multicoloured	1·30	80
1730	**340**	100h. multicoloured	1·30	80
1731	**341**	100h. multicoloured	1·30	80
1732	**333**	150h. multicoloured	1·90	1·30
1733	**334**	150h. multicoloured	1·90	1·30
1734	**335**	150h. multicoloured	1·90	1·30
1735	**336**	150h. multicoloured	1·90	1·30
1736	**337**	150h. multicoloured	1·90	1·30
1737	**338**	150h. multicoloured	1·90	1·30
1738	**339**	150h. multicoloured	1·90	1·30
1739	**340**	150h. multicoloured	1·90	1·30
1740	**341**	150h. multicoloured	1·90	1·30

1991. Liberation of Kuwait.

No.	Type	Description		
1741	**342**	75h. multicoloured	80	55
1742		150h. multicoloured	1·80	1·10

343 Rainbow and Arrows

1991. World Telecommunications Day.

No.	Type	Description		
1743	**343**	75h. multicoloured	75	40
1744		150h. multicoloured	1·50	75

344 Thee el Halifa Miqat, Medina

1991. Pilgrimage to Mecca.

No.	Type	Description		
1745	**344**	75h. multicoloured	75	40
1746		150h. multicoloured	1·50	75

345 Blackboard and I.L.Y. Emblem

346 Olive Branch and F.A.O. Emblem

1991. International Literacy Year.

No.	Type	Description		
1747	**345**	75h. multicoloured	1·10	55
1748		150h. multicoloured	2·10	1·10

1991. World Food Day.

No.	Type	Description		
1749	**346**	75h. multicoloured	75	40
1750		150h. multicoloured	1·50	80

347 Child's Profile and Emblem

1991. World Children's Day.

No.	Type	Description		
1751	**347**	75h. multicoloured	1·10	65
1752		150h. multicoloured	2·10	1·30

348 Arabian Woodpecker

349 Arabian Bustard

350 Crested Lark

351 Turtle Dove

352 Western Reef Heron

353 Arabian Chukar

354 Hoopoe

355 Peregrine Falcon

356 Houbara Bustard

357 Heart and Cardiograph

1992. Birds.

No.	Type	Description		
1753	**348**	25h. multicoloured	40	25
1754	**349**	25h. multicoloured	40	25
1755	**350**	25h. multicoloured	40	25
1756	**351**	25h. multicoloured	40	25
1757	**352**	25h. multicoloured	40	25
1758	**353**	25h. multicoloured	40	25
1759	**354**	25h. multicoloured	40	25
1760	**355**	25h. multicoloured	40	25
1761	**356**	25h. multicoloured	40	25
1762	**348**	50h. multicoloured	80	50
1763	**349**	50h. multicoloured	80	50
1764	**350**	50h. multicoloured	80	50
1765	**351**	50h. multicoloured	80	50
1766	**352**	50h. multicoloured	80	50
1767	**353**	50h. multicoloured	80	50
1768	**354**	50h. multicoloured	80	50
1769	**355**	50h. multicoloured	80	50
1770	**356**	50h. multicoloured	80	50
1771	**348**	75h. multicoloured	95	55
1772	**349**	75h. multicoloured	95	55
1773	**350**	75h. multicoloured	95	55
1774	**351**	75h. multicoloured	95	55
1775	**352**	75h. multicoloured	95	55
1776	**353**	75h. multicoloured	95	55
1777	**354**	75h. multicoloured	95	55
1778	**355**	75h. multicoloured	95	55
1779	**356**	75h. multicoloured	95	55
1780	**348**	100h. multicoloured	1·80	1·20
1781	**349**	100h. multicoloured	1·80	1·20
1782	**350**	100h. multicoloured	1·80	1·20
1783	**351**	100h. multicoloured	1·80	1·20
1784	**352**	100h. multicoloured	1·80	1·20
1785	**353**	100h. multicoloured	1·80	1·20
1786	**354**	100h. multicoloured	1·80	1·20
1787	**355**	100h. multicoloured	1·80	1·20
1788	**356**	100h. multicoloured	1·80	1·20
1789	**348**	150h. multicoloured	2·75	1·80
1790	**349**	150h. multicoloured	2·75	1·80
1791	**350**	150h. multicoloured	2·75	1·80
1792	**351**	150h. multicoloured	2·75	1·80
1793	**352**	150h. multicoloured	2·75	1·80
1794	**353**	150h. multicoloured	2·75	1·80
1795	**354**	150h. multicoloured	2·75	1·80
1796	**355**	150h. multicoloured	2·75	1·80
1797	**356**	150h. multicoloured	2·75	1·80

1992. World Health Day.

No.	Type	Description		
1798	**357**	75h. multicoloured	80	40
1799		150h. multicoloured	1·60	80

358 Arabic Script

1992. Battle of Mt. Uhod (between Mecca and Medina, 625 A.D.) Commemoration.

No.	Type	Description		
1800	**358**	75h. green and orange	75	40
1801		150h. dp blue, blue & green	1·50	80

359 Mosque, Yalamlam Miqat

1992. Pilgrimage to Mecca.

No.	Type	Description		
1802	**359**	75h. multicoloured	80	40
1803		150h. multicoloured	1·60	80

360 Human Pyramid inside House

1992. Population and Housing Census.

No.	Type	Description		
1804	**360**	75h. multicoloured	55	40
1805		150h. multicoloured	1·10	75

361 Vegetables

1992. World Food Day. Multicoloured.

No.	Type	Description		
1806		75h. Type **361**	80	40
1807		150h. Fruits	1·80	75

362 Decree of Regional System

363 Decree of Consultative Council

364 Decree of Essential Governing

365 Flags, Globe and King Fahd Stadium

1992. Declaration of Basic Law of Government.

No.	Type	Description		
1808	**362**	75h. black, silver & green	55	30
1809	**363**	75h. black, silver & green	55	30
1810	**364**	75h. black, silver & green	55	30
1811	**362**	150h. multicoloured	1·20	65
1812	**363**	150h. multicoloured	1·20	65
1813	**364**	150h. multicoloured	1·20	65

1993. Continental Cup Football Championship, Saudi Arabia.

No.	Type	Description		
1815	**365**	75h. multicoloured	1·10	40
1816		150h. multicoloured	2·10	50

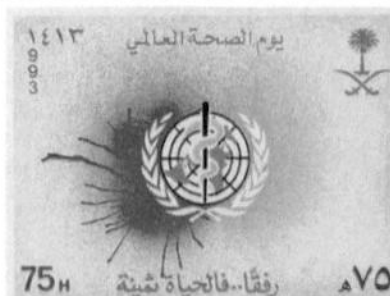
366 Blood Spot and W.H.O. Emblem

1993. World Health Day.
1817 **366** 75h. multicoloured . . . 75 40
1818 150h. multicoloured . . 1·50 75

367 Arabic Script

1993. Battle of Khandaq (between Mecca and Medina, 627 A.D.) Commemoration.
1819 **367** 75h. green and orange 65 40
1820 150h. dp blue, blue & green . . . . 1·50 75

368 I.T.U. Emblem

370 Desert, Oasis, Mountains and Sea Environments

369 That Irq Miqat

1993. 25th Anniv of World Telecommunications Day.
1821 **368** 75h. multicoloured . . . 65 40
1822 150h. multicoloured . . 1·10 75

1993. Pilgrimage to Mecca.
1823 **369** 75h. multicoloured . . . 65 40
1824 150h. multicoloured . . 1·10 75

1993. World Food Day.
1825 **370** 75h. multicoloured . . . 80 40
1826 150h. multicoloured . . 1·80 75

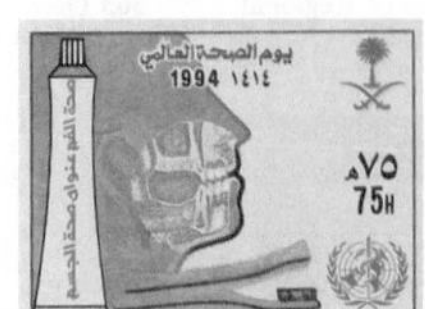
371 X-ray of Teeth and Cleaning Implements

1994. World Health Day.
1827 **371** 75h. multicoloured . . . 75 40
1828 150h. multicoloured . . 1·50 75

372 "100" and Olympic Rings

1994. Centenary of International Olympic Committee.
1829 **372** 75h. multicoloured . . . 80 40
1830 150h. multicoloured . . 1·80 75

373 Namirah Mosque and Tents

1994. Pilgrimage to Mecca.
1831 **373** 75h. multicoloured . . . 65 40
1832 150h. multicoloured . . 1·10 75

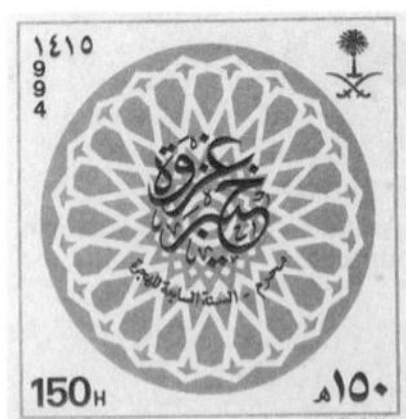
374 Arabic Script

1994. Battle of Khaibar Commemoration.
1833 **374** 75h. green and gold . . 75 40
1834 150h. blue, silver and green . . . . 1·50 75

375 Flag, International and Saudi Football Federation Emblems and Player

1994. Qualification of Saudi Arabian Team to Final Rounds of World Cup Football Championship, U.S.A. Multicoloured.
1835 75h. Type **375** 75 40
1836 150h. Maps of United States and Saudi Arabia and player (51 × 27 mm) . . . 1·50 75

376 Council Building

1994. Establishment of Consultative Council (advisory body). Multicoloured.
1837 75h. Type **376** 75 40
1838 150h. Council building (closer view) . . . . . . 1·50 75
MS1839 120 × 80 mm. Nos. 1837/8. Imperf (sold at 5r.) . . . . . 26·00 26·00

377 King Abdul Aziz Port, Dammam

378 Islam Port, Jeddah

379 Jubail Port

380 Yanbu Port

1994. Saudi Ports. (a) Dammam.
1839a **377** 25h. multicoloured . . 55 30
1839b 50h. multicoloured . . 55 30
1840 75h. multicoloured . . 75 40
1841 100h. multicoloured . . 95 50
1842 150h. multicoloured . . 1·50 75

(b) Jeddah.
1845 **378** 25h. multicoloured . . . 40 25
1846 50h. multicoloured . . . 80 50
1847 75h. multicoloured . . . 1·20 75
1848 100h. multicoloured . . 1·60 95
1849 150h. multicoloured . . 2·40 1·50

(c) Jubail.
1853 **379** 2r. multicoloured . . . . 2·40 1·10
1854 4r. multicoloured . . . . 2·00 95

(d) Yanbu.
1856 **380** 100h. multicoloured . . 55 30
1858 2r. multicoloured . . . . 2·00 1·10

385 Crops inside Greenhouse

1994. World Food Day. Multicoloured.
1880 75h. Type **385** . . . . . . 1·10 40
1881 150h. Crops on globe (36 × 37 mm) . . . . . . 2·30 80

386 U.N. Emblem

1995. 50th Anniv of U.N.O. Multicoloured.
1882 75h. Type **386** 75 40
1883 150h. U.N. headquarters, New York (26 × 52 mm) 1·50 75

387 Emblem and Map of Member Countries

1995. 50th Anniv of Arab League.
1884 **387** 75h. yellow, mauve and green 65 40
1885 – 150h. gold and green . . 1·30 75
DESIGN—36 × 27 mm: 150h. Anniversary emblem.

388 Emblem and Family

1995. Protection of Refugees.
1886 **388** 75h. multicoloured . . . 65 40
1887 150h. multicoloured . . 1·30 75

389 Mish'ar el Haram Mosque, Muzdalefah

1995. Pilgrimage to Mecca.
1888 **389** 75h. multicoloured . . . 65 40
1889 150h. multicoloured . . 1·30 75

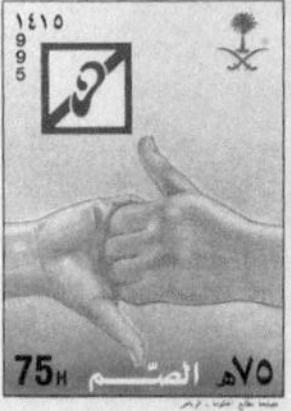
390 Hand Sign and International Symbol

391 Anniversary Emblem

1995. Deaf Week. Multicoloured.
1890 75h. Type **390** 75 40
1891 150h. International symbol (ear) and hand sign . . . 1·50 75

1995. 50th Anniv of Saudia (national airline). Mult.
1892 75h. Type **391** 75 40
1893 150h. Tailfins (horiz) . . . 1·50 75

392 Ears of Wheat and Anniversary Emblem

1995. 50th Anniv of F.A.O. Multicoloured.
1894 75h. Type **392** . . . . . . 1·10 40
1895 150h. Anniversary emblem illuminating globe . . . . 2·10 80

393 Al-Khaif Mosque, Mecca

1996. Pilgrimage to Mecca.
1896 **393** 150h. multicoloured . . 1·60 80
1897 2r. multicoloured . . . . 2·00 1·10
1898 3r. multicoloured . . . . 3·25 1·60

394 Emblems and Pictograms

1996. Olympic Games, Atlanta, U.S.A.
1899 **394** 150h. multicoloured . . 1·60 80
1900 2r. multicoloured . . . . 2·40 1·10

395 Sunrise over City

1996. World Health Day.
1901 **395** 2r. multicoloured . . . . 1·80 95
1902 3r. multicoloured . . . . 3·00 1·50

396 River and Emblem

1996. 50th Anniv (1995) of F.A.O.
1903 **396** 2r. multicoloured . . . . 2·50 1·10
1904 3r. multicoloured . . . . 4·00 1·60

397 Anniversary Emblem

1996. 50th Anniv of UNICEF.

1905 **397** 150h. multicoloured . . 1·50 75
1906 2r. multicoloured . . . . 2·00 95

398 Power Station

1997. Opening of Rabigh Power Station. Mult.

1907 150h. Type **398** . . . . . 1·50 75
1908 2r. Power station and pylon (54 × 29 mm) . . . . . . 2·00 95

399 Emblem and Map

1997. 25th Anniv of King Abdul Aziz Research Centre.

1909 **399** 150h. multicoloured . . 1·50 75
1910 2r. multicoloured . . . . 2·00 95

400 Sunrise and Arabic Inscription

1997. Mecca.

1911 **400** 1r. green, yellow and black 95 50
1912 2r. multicoloured . . . . 2·00 95

401 Skeleton

1997. Anti-drugs Campaign.

1913 **401** 150h. multicoloured . . 2·40 1·60
1914 2r. multicoloured . . . . 3·25 2·10

402 King Fahd

1997. 74th Birthday of King Fahd.

1915 **402** 100h. multicoloured . . 95 50
1916 150h. multicoloured . . 1·50 75
1917 2r. multicoloured . . . . 2·00 95
MS1918 103 × 117 mm. **402** 5r. multicoloured . . . . 13·00 13·00

403 Arabic Script

1997. Battle of Honain, 630.

1919 **403** 150h. multicoloured . . 1·50 75
1920 2r. multicoloured . . . . 2·00 95

404 Shrine

1997. Pilgrimage to Mecca. Multicoloured.

1921 1r. Type **404** 95 50
1922 2r. Shrine and Kaaba (39 × 39 mm) . . . . . . 2·00 95

405 W.H.O. Emblem

1997. World Health Day.

1923 **405** 150h. multicoloured . . 1·50 75
1924 2r. multicoloured . . . . 2·00 95

406 Library

1997. Inauguration of King Fahd National Library. Multicoloured.

1925 1r. Type **406** 95 50
1926 2r. Books and library emblem . . . . 2·00 95

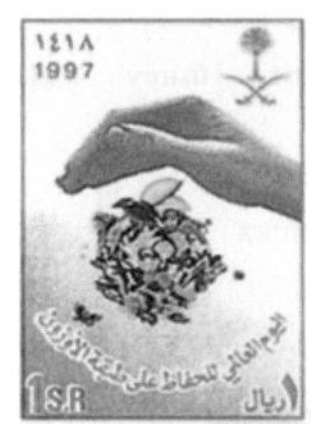

407 Hand over Globe of Flora and Fauna

408 Emblem

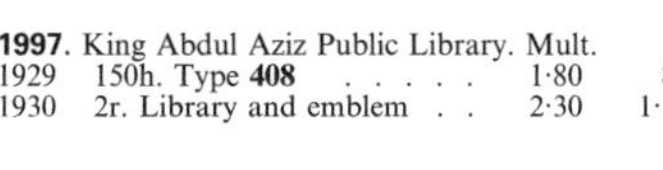

1997. International Anti-ozone Day. 10th Anniv of Montreal Protocol.

1927 **407** 1r. multicoloured 95 55
1928 2r. multicoloured . . . . 2·00 95

1997. King Abdul Aziz Public Library. Mult.

1929 150h. Type **408** . . . . . 1·80 80
1930 2r. Library and emblem . . 2·30 1·10

409 Emblem

1997. 3rd Gulf Co-operation Council Stamp Exhibition, Riyadh.

1931 **409** 1r. multicoloured . . . . 1·10 55

410 Emblem

1998. Prince Salman Centre.

1932 **410** 1r. multicoloured . . . . 1·10 55

411 Arabic Script

1998. Battle of Tabuk Commemoration.

1933 **411** 1r. multicoloured 95 55

412 Globe as Vegetable

413 Mother and Child, House and Sun

1998. World Food Day.

1934 **412** 2r. multicoloured . . . . 2·00 1·10

1998. Disabled Persons Day.

1935 **413** 1r. multicoloured 95 55

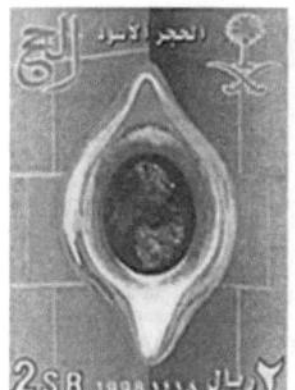

414 Detail of Corner of Kaaba

415 Bishah-Tal Reservoir

1998. Pilgrimage to Mecca.

1936 **414** 2r. multicoloured . . . . 2·00 95

1998. Inauguration of King Fahd Dam.

1937 **415** 1r. multicoloured 95 50

416 Mother with Child and W.H.O. Emblem

417 Emblem and Flag

1998. World Health Day.

1938 **416** 1r. multicoloured 95 50

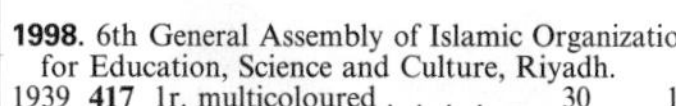

1998. 6th General Assembly of Islamic Organization for Education, Science and Culture, Riyadh.

1939 **417** 1r. multicoloured 30 15

418 Dove with Envelope over Globe

419 Horses

1998. Arabic Stamp Day.

1940 **418** 2r. multicoloured . . . . 1·80 95

1999. Centenary of Saud Dynasty. Multicoloured.

1941 1r. Type **419** . . . . 1·60 1·10
1942 1r. Restored buildings in Riyadh (51 × 27 mm) . . 1·60 1·10
1943 1r. Emblem of National Cultural Festivals and traditional buildings . . . 1·60 1·10
1944 1r. Airplane, tanks, ships and armed forces coat of arms (36 × 37 mm) . . . 1·60 1·10
1945 1r. Fort . . . . 1·60 1·10
1946 2r. King Abdul Aziz, emblem and outline map of Saudi Arabia . . . . . 3·25 2·10
MS1947 Five sheets. Imperf (with simulated perforations). (a) 121 × 81 mm. No. 1941; (b0 125 × 85 mm. No. 1942; (c) 124 × 94 mm. No. 1943; (d) 120 × 90 mm. No. 1944; (e) 121 × 92 mm. Nos. 1945/6 (set sold at 25r.) . . . . 80·00 80·00

420 Airplane over Airport

1999. Inauguration of King Fahd International Airport. Multicoloured.

1948 1r. Type **420** 90 50
1949 2r. Air traffic control tower and airplane (26 × 37 mm) 1·80 90

421 Hand holding Globe as Apple

1999. World Food Day.

1950 **421** 1r. multicoloured . . . . 1·80 80

422 Zam-Zam Fountain and Holy Kaaba

1999. Pilgrimage to Mecca.

1951 **422** 2r. multicoloured . . . . 1·80 90

423 Emblem on Open Book

424 Emblem and Traffic Lights

1999. Academy for Security Sciences.

1952 **423** 150h. multicoloured . . 1·50 75

1999. Gulf Co-operation Council Traffic Week.

1953 **424** 1r. multicoloured 95 50

425 Emblem

1999. International Koran Reading Competition.

1954 **425** 1r. multicoloured 30 15

426 Emblem

1999. 125th Anniv of the Universal Postal Union.
1955 **426** 1r. multicoloured . . . . 1·80 80

2000. Flowers. As T **300/20**.
1956 **300** 1r. multicoloured 80 40
1957 **301** 1r. multicoloured . . . . 1·60 80
1958 **302** 1r. multicoloured 95 50
1959 **303** 1r. multicoloured . . . . 1·20 80
1960 **304** 1r. multicoloured . . . . 1·20 80
1961 **305** 1r. multicoloured . . . . 1·20 80
1962 **306** 1r. multicoloured 80 40
1963 **307** 1r. multicoloured 40 40
1964 **308** 1r. multicoloured 40 40
1965 **309** 1r. multicoloured 80 80
1966 **310** 1r. multicoloured 80 80
1967 **311** 1r. multicoloured . . . . 1·60 1·60
1968 **312** 1r. multicoloured . . . . 1·60 1·60
1969 **313** 1r. multicoloured 55 55
1970 **314** 1r. multicoloured 40 40
1971 **315** 1r. multicoloured 80 80
1972 **316** 1r. multicoloured . . . . 1·60 1·60
1973 **317** 1r. multicoloured . . . . 1·60 80
1974 **318** 1r. multicoloured 40 40
1975 **319** 1r. multicoloured 80 80
1976 **320** 1r. multicoloured . . . . 1·60 1·60

427 Medina

2000. Pilgrimage to Mecca.
1998 **427** 1r. multicoloured 80 80
1999 2r. multicoloured 80 80

428 Organization Emblem

2000. 50th Anniv of World Meteorological Organization.
2000 **428** 1r. multicoloured 80 80

429 Door and Dome

430 Tap enclosed in Water Droplet

2000. 75th Anniv of Council of State.
2001 **429** 1r. multicoloured 80 80

2000. Water Conservation Campaign.
2002 **430** 1r. multicoloured 80 80

431 Rainbow, Palm Tree and Wall

432 Emblem

2000. Ryadh, Arabian Cultural Capital, 2000.
2003 **431** 1r. multicoloured 80 80

2000. Altaif 2000. 24th Arab Scout Camp.
2004 **432** 1r. multicoloured 80 80

433 Aerial View of City

434 City enclosed in Oval

2000. Buraydah City.
2005 **433** 50h. multicoloured . . . 80 80
2006 **434** 50h. multicoloured . . . 80 80
2007 **433** 1r. multicoloured . . . . 1·60 1·60
2008 **434** 1r. multicoloured 80 80
2009 **433** 2r. multicoloured . . . . 1·60 1·60
2010 **434** 2r. multicoloured 80 80

435 Al Khafji Oil Rig

436 Port Tower

2000.
2011 **435** 25h. lilac and orange . . 80 80

2000. Jazan Port.
2012 **436** 50h. multicoloured . . . 80 80
2013 1r. multicoloured 80 80
2014 2r. multicoloured 80 80

437 Anniversary Emblem

2000. 50th Anniv of United Nations High Commissioner for Refugees.
2015 **437** 2r. multicoloured 80 50

438 Printing Press and Building

2000. King Fahd Koran Printing Complex.
2016 **438** 50h. multicoloured . . . 80 50
2017 1r. multicoloured 80 50
2018 2r. multicoloured 80 50

439 Emblem

2000. King Abdul Aziz Science and Technology City.
2019 **439** 1r. multicoloured 80 50

440 University Emblem

2000. King Khaled University.
2020 **440** 1r. multicoloured 80 50

441 Mosque and Pilgrims

2001. Pilgrimage to Mecca. Designs showing Hajj sites. Multicoloured.
2021 1r. Type **441** 80 50
2022 1r. Holy Kabba 80 50
2023 1r. Attan'eem Miqat, Mecca 80 50
2024 1r. El Johfah Miqat, Rabergh 80 50
2025 1r. Thee el Haifa, Miqat . . 80 50
2026 1r. Al-Kheef Mosque . . . 80 50
2027 1r. That Irq Miqat 80 50
2028 1r. Mosque, Yalamlam . . . 80 50

442 Profiles

2001. King Aziz Institute for Persons of Talent.
2029 **442** 1r. multicoloured . . . . 1·30 75

443 Mohammed Al Durra and Father

2001. Al Asqa Intifada. Multicoloured.
2030 1r. Type **443** . . . . 1·30 75
2031 2r. Father and child enclosed in barbed wire (vert) . . . . 1·30 75
MS2032 110 × 95 mm. 5r. No. 1988 enlarged. Imperf . . . . 28·00 28·00

444 Building Facade

2001. King Abdul Aziz History Centre. Multicoloured.
2033 1r. Type **444** . . . . 1·30 75
2034 1r. Corner of building . . . 1·30 75
2035 1r. Towers and wall . . . . 1·30 75
2036 1r. Aerial view of complex 1·30 75

445 Buildings

2001. Folk Art. Multicoloured.
2037 1r. Type **445** 80 80
2038 1r. Horse 80 80
2039 1r. Doorways 80 80
2040 1r. Desert 80 80
2041 1r. Gate 80 80

446 Handshake

2001. World Teachers' Day.
2042 **446** 1r. multicoloured 80 80

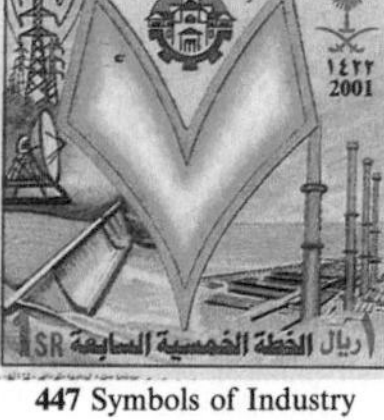

447 Symbols of Industry

2002. Seventh Five Year Plan.
2043 **447** 1r. multicoloured 80 80

448 Islamic Education, Scientific and Culture Organization (ISESCO) Emblem

2002. First Conference of Islamic Ministers of Higher Education and Scientific Research.
2044 **448** 1r. multicoloured 80 80

449 Tents and Pilgrims

2002. Pilgrimage to Mecca.
2045 **449** 1r. multicoloured 80 80

450 King Fahd

2002. 20th Anniv of King Fahd's Accession to the Throne. Multicoloured.
2046 1r. Type **450** 80 80
MS2047 98 × 128 mm. 3r. As Type **450** plus a montage of other stamps issued during his reign. Imperf . . . . 2·40 2·40

451 King Fahd Port, Yanbu

2002.
2048 **451** 1r. multicoloured 80 80
2049 2r. multicoloured . . . . 1·60 1·60

452 Ship at Dockside, King Fahd Port, Jubail

2002. King Fahd Port, Jubail.
2050 **452** 1r. multicoloured 80 80
2051 2r. multicoloured . . . . 1·60 1·60

453 Pilgrims and Tunnel, Mecca   **454** Water Droplet

2003. Pilgrimage to Mecca.

2052	**453**	1r. multicoloured	80	80

2003. Water Conservation. Multicoloured.

2053		1r. Type **454**	80	80
2054		1r. Two droplets (vert) . . .	80	80

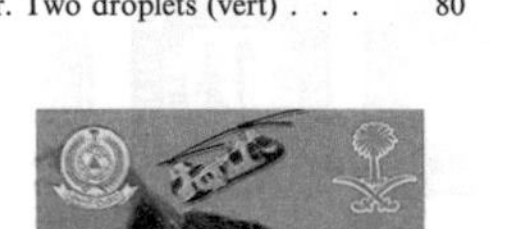

455 Fire Fighters

2003. Civil Defence.

2055	**455**	1r. multicoloured	80	80

456 Emblem and Red Crescent Workers

2003. Saudi Red Crescent (aid organization).

2056	**456**	1r. multicoloured	80	80

457 *Cirrhilabrus rubriventralis*

2003. Red Sea Fish. Multicoloured.

2057		1r. Type **457**	80	75
2058		1r. *Cryptocentrus caeruleopunctatus*	80	75
2059		1r. *Plesiops nigricans*	80	75
2060		1r. Arabian angelfish (*Pomacanthus asfur*) . . .	80	75
2061		1r. *Cheilinus abudjubbe* . . .	80	75
2062		1r. *Pomacentrus albicaudatus*	80	75
2063		1r. *Caesio suevicus*	80	75
2064		1r. *Chaetodon austriacus* . .	80	75
2065		1r. *Thalassoma klumzinger* (inscr "klumzingeri") . .	80	75
2066		1r. *Oxymonacanthus halli* . .	80	75
2067		1r. Two-banded anemonefish (*Amphiprion bicinctus*) . .	80	75
2068		1r. *Canthigaster pygmaea* . .	80	75
2069		2r. *Cirrhilabrus rubriventralis*	80	75
2070		2r. *Cryptocentrus caeruleopunctatus*	80	75
2071		2r. *Plesiops nigricans*	80	75
2072		2r. Arabian angelfish (*Pomeacanthus asfur*) . .	80	75
2073		2r. *Cheilinus abudjubbe* . . .	80	75
2074		2r. *Pomacentrus albicaudatus*	80	75
2075		2r. *Caesio suevicus*	80	75
2076		2r. *Chaetodon austriacus* . .	80	75
2077		2r. *Thalassoma klumzingeri* . .	80	75
2078		2r. *Oxymonacanthus halli* . .	80	75
2079		2r. Two-banded anemonefish (*Amphiprion bicinctus*) . .	80	75
2080		2r. *Canthigaster pygmaea* . .	80	75

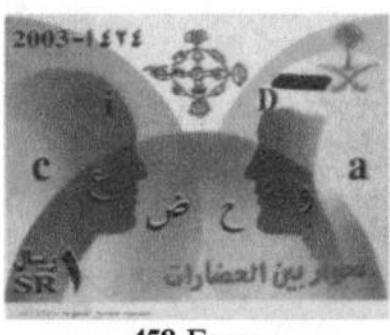

458 Faces

2003. Dialogue among Civilzations.

2081	**458**	1r. multicoloured	80	75

459 Hands enclosing Light Bulb

2003. Electricity Consumption Campaign.

2082	**459**	1r. multicoloured	80	75

460 Envelope and Postman

2003. Post Day.

2083	**460**	1r. multicoloured	80	75

461 "9" enclosing Emblem and Fireworks   **463** Adult and Child

462 1930 Hedjaz and Nedjde 5g. Stamp

2003. Ninth Gulf Co-operation Council Philatelic Exhibition, Riyadh.

2084	**461**	1r. multicoloured	80	75

2003. 75th Anniv of First Saudi Stamp.

2085	**462**	1r. multicoloured	80	75

2003. Council for the Disabled.

2086	**463**	1r. multicoloured	80	75

464 Horse Race

2003. King Abdul Aziz Equestrian Centre, Riyadh.

2087	**464**	1r. multicoloured	80	75

465 Pilgrims at Airport

2003. Pilgrimage to Mecca.

2088	**465**	1r. multicoloured	80	75

466 Mosque

467 Mosque

468 Mosque

469 Mosque

470 Mosque

471 Mosque

472 Mosque

473 Mosque

2003. Mosques of Saudi Arabia.

2089	**466**	1r. multicoloured	80	75
2090	**467**	1r. multicoloured	80	75
2091	**468**	1r. multicoloured	80	75
2092	**469**	1r. multicoloured	80	75
2093	**470**	1r. multicoloured	80	75
2094	**471**	1r. multicoloured	80	75
2095	**472**	1r. multicoloured	80	75
2096	**473**	1r. multicoloured	80	75
2097	**466**	2r. multicoloured	80	75
2098	**467**	2r. multicoloured	80	75
2099	**468**	2r. multicoloured	80	75
2100	**469**	2r. multicoloured	80	75
2102	**470**	2r. multicoloured	80	75
2103	**471**	2r. multicoloured	80	75
2104	**472**	2r. multicoloured	80	75
2105	**473**	2r. multicoloured	80	75

474 McDonnell-Douglas MD 11-F

2004. Aircraft. Multicoloured.

2106		1r. Type **474**	80	75
2107		1r. Boeing 747-400	80	75
2108		1r. Boeing 777-268	80	75
2109		1r. McDonnell-Douglas MD-90-30	80	75

475 Rose and Town Square

2004. Tabuk.

2110	**475**	1r. multicoloured	80	75
2111		2r. multicoloured	80	75

476 Scales and Book

2004. Legal System.

2112	**476**	1r. multicoloured	30	15

477 Tower and City Walls

2004. Hail City.

2113	**477**	1r. multicoloured	30	15
2114		2r. multicoloured	60	30

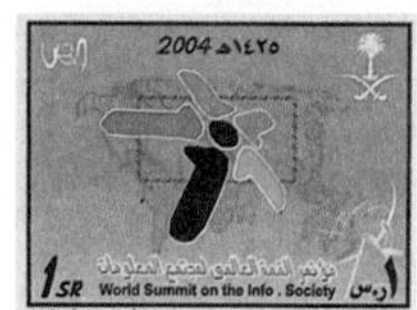

478 World Map and Binary Code

2004. World Conferences on Information Technology, Geneva and Tunis.

2115	**478**	1r. multicoloured	30	15

480 Clasped Hands

2004. Peace.

2120	**480**	2r. multicoloured	60	30

NEWSPAPER STAMPS
NEJDI OCCUPATION OF HEJAZ

(N 29)

1925. Nos. 198 and 199a optd with Type N **29**.

N208	**11**	$\frac{1}{4}$pi. brown	£1400
N209		$\frac{1}{2}$pi. red	£3500

OFFICIAL STAMPS
SAUDI ARABIA

O 52   O 72

1939.

O347	**O 52**	3g. blue	3·25	1·60
O348		5g. mauve	4·75	2·00
O349		20g. brown	8·00	4·50
O350		50g. turquoise	16·00	8·00
O351		100g. olive	70·00	36·00
O352		200g. purple	55·00	26·00

1961. Size $18\frac{1}{2} \times 22\frac{1}{2}$ mm.

O449	**O 72**	1p. black	95	25
O450		2p. green	1·60	40
O451		3p. bistre	2·30	65
O452		4p. blue	3·00	80

O453		5p. red	3·50	1·10
O454		10p. purple	4·75	2·10
O455		20p. violet	9·75	4·00
O456		50p. brown	24·00	10·50
O457		100p. green	49·00	21·00

1964. Size 21 × 26 mm.

O497	O 72	1p. black	1·50	50
O498		2p. green	2·50	90
O504		3p. ochre	3·75	1·50
O505		4p. blue	3·75	1·50
O501		5p. red	7·00	2·30
O507		6p. purple	7·25	1·80
O508		7p. green	7·25	1·80
O509		8p. red	7·25	1·80
O510		9p. red	£160	
O511		10p. brown	29·00	1·80
O512		11p. green	55·00	
O513		12p. violet	£300	
O514		13p. blue	9·75	2·75
O515		14p. violet	9·75	2·75
O516		15p. orange	£180	
O517		16p. black	£180	
O518		17p. green	£180	
O519		18p. yellow	£180	
O520		19p. purple	£180	
O520a		20p. blue		
O521		23p. blue	£250	
O522		24p. green	£180	
O523		26p. bistre	£180	
O524		27p. lilac	£180	
O525		31p. brown	£250	
O526		33p. green	£180	
O527		50p. green	£375	
O528		100p. green	£800	

O 111

1970.

O1040	O 111	1p. brown	3·00	95
O1041		2p. green	3·00	95
O1042		3p. mauve	3·75	1·50
O1043		4p. blue	4·75	1·80
O1044		5p. red	4·75	1·80
O1045		6p. orange	4·75	1·80
O1046		7p. red	£150	00
O1047		8p. violet		
O1048		9p. blue		
O1049		10p. blue	6·50	3·00
O1050		11p. green		
O1050a		12p. brown		
O1051		20p. blue	14·50	4·75
O1051b		23p. brown	£375	
O1052		31p. purple	49·00	20·00
O1053		50p. brown		
O1054		100p. green		

POSTAGE DUE STAMPS
A. HEJAZ

D 7 From Old Door at El Ashra Barsbai, Shari El Ashrafuga, Cairo

(D 11)

1917.

D17	D 7	20pa. red	2·75	1·90
D18		1pi. blue	2·75	1·90
D19		2pi. purple	2·75	1·90

1921. Nos. D17/19 optd with T 7.

D31	D 7	20pa. red	16·00	2·75
D33		1pi. blue	5·75	3·75
D34		2pi. purple	9·75	7·00

1922. Nos. D17/19 optd with T 10.

D39	D 7	20pa. red	23·00	26·00
D40		1pi. blue	3·25	3·25
D41		2pi. purple	3·25	3·25

1923. Optd with Type D 11.

D47	11	½pi. red	3·75	1·30
D48		1pi. blue	6·50	1·40
D49		2pi. orange	3·75	1·80

1924. Nos. D47/9 optd with T 14.

D57	11	½pi. red	£3000	
D58		1pi. blue	£3000	
D59		2pi. orange	£3000	

1925. Nos. D17/19 optd with T 15.

D88		20pa. red	£350	£375
D91		1pi. blue	28·00	24·00
D92		2pi. purple	14·00	14·00

1925. Nos. D17/19 optd with T 16.

D93a		20pa. red	£300	
D94		1pi. blue	23·00	23·00
D96		2pi. claret	18·00	26·00

No. D93a has the overprint inverted.

(D 17)

1925. Stamps of 1924 (optd T 16) optd with Type D 17.

D149	11	½pi. red (No. 116)	95·00	
D150		1½pi. lilac (No. 99)	95·00	
D151		2pi. orange (No. 119)	£140	
D152		3pi. brown (No. 120)	95·00	
D153		5pi. green (No. 103)	95·00	

(D 18) D 25

1925. Stamps of 1922 optd with Type D 18.

D154	11	⅛pi. brown	35·00	
D155		½pi. red	41·00	
D156		1pi. blue	41·00	
D157		1½pi. lilac	41·00	
D158		2pi. orange	41·00	
D160		3pi. brown	41·00	
D161		5pi. green	55·00	
D162	–	10pi. purple and mauve	55·00	

1925. Nos. D154/62 optd with Type D 17.

D163	11	⅛pi. brown	20·00	18·00
D164		½pi. red	24·00	24·00
D165		1pi. blue	18·00	18·00
D166		1½pi. lilac	20·00	18·00
D167		2pi. orange	20·00	19·00
D169		3pi. brown	45·00	45·00
D170		5pi. green	20·00	19·00
D171	–	10pi. purple and mauve	28·00	24·00

1925. Optd with T 24.

D186	D 25	½pi. blue	2·75	
D187		1pi. orange	2·75	
D188		2pi. brown	2·75	
D189		3pi. pink	2·75	

These stamps without overprint were not officially issued.

B. NEJDI OCCUPATION OF HEJAZ

1925. Nos. D47/9 of Hejaz optd with T 25.

D203	11	½pi. red	24·00	
D204c		1pi. blue	70·00	
D205c		2pi. orange	70·00	

(D 29) (D 33)

1925. Hejaz Postage Stamps of 1922 optd with Type D 29.

D206	11	½pi. red	28·00	
D207		3pi. red	28·00	

1925. Postage stamps optd with T 32 further optd with Type D 33.

D232	28	1pi. blue	20·00	
D233		2pi. orange	20·00	
D234	11	3pi. red	16·00	
D236	28	5pi. green	34·00	

1925. No. D40 of Hejaz optd with T 32.

D238	D 7	1pi. blue	95·00	

C. HEJAZ AND NEJD

D 40 D 42 Tougra of Ibn Saud

1926.

D267	D 40	½pi. red	3·50	1·40
D270		2pi. orange	3·50	1·40
D272		6pi. brown	3·50	1·40

1926. Pan-Islamic Congress, Cairo. Optd with T 40.

D281	D 40	½pi. red	7·00	4·75
D282		2pi. orange	7·00	4·75
D283		6pi. brown	7·00	4·75

1927.

D292	D 42	1pi. grey	9·75	1·40
D293		2pi. violet	12·00	1·40

D. SAUDI ARABIA

1935. No. 331a optd **T** in a circle.

D343	49	½g. red	£225	

D 52 D 72

1937.

D347	D 52	½g. brown	13·00	13·00
D348		1g. blue	13·00	13·00
D349		2g. purple	18·00	8·00

1961.

D449	D 72	1p. violet	5·25	5·25
D450		2p. green	9·00	4·00
D451		4p. red	10·50	10·50

SAXONY Pt. 7

A former kingdom in S. Germany. Stamps superseded in 1868 by those of the North German Federation.

10 pfennige = 1 neugroschen;
30 neugroschen = 1 thaler.

1 2 3 Friedrich August II

1850. Imperf.

1	1	3pf. red	£6000	£6000

1851. Imperf.

7	2	3pf. green	£120	£110

1851. Imperf.

10	3	½ngr. black on grey	80·00	11·50
12		1ngr. black on pink	£110	9·75
13		2ngr. black on blue	£275	55·00
14		3ngr. black on yellow	£180	20·00

4 King Johann I 5 6

1855. Imperf.

16	4	½ngr. black on grey	10·50	2·75
18		1ngr. black on pink	10·50	2·75
20		2ngr. black on blue	21·00	9·75
23		3ngr. black on yellow	22·00	7·00
24		5ngr. red	£100	70·00
28		10ngr. blue	£275	£250

1863. Perf.

31	5	3pf. green	2·00	27·00
36		½ngr. orange	1·10	2·10
39	6	1ngr. pink	1·20	1·80
40		2ngr. blue	2·20	6·25
42		3ngr. brown	3·00	10·50
45		5ngr. blue	18·00	44·00
46		5ngr. purple	35·00	55·00
47		5ngr. grey	27·00	£275

SCHLESWIG-HOLSTEIN Pt. 7

Two former Duchies of the King of Denmark which, following a revolt, established a Provisional Government in 1848. Danish stamps were in use from 1851 in Schleswig and 1853 in Holstein.

The Duchies were invaded by Prussia and Austria in 1864 and, by the Convention of Gastein in 1865, were placed under joint sovereignty of those countries, with Holstein administered by Austria.

The Duchies were annexed by Prussia in 1867 and from 1868 used the stamps of the North German Confederation.

96 skilling = 1 Rigsbankdaler (Danish).
16 schilling = 1 mark.

SCHLESWIG-HOLSTEIN

1 2

1850. Imperf.

2	1	1s. blue	£325	£5500
4		2s. pink	£600	£7000

1865. Inscr "SCHLESWIG-HOLSTEIN". Roul.

6	2	½s. pink	32·00	47·00
7		1¼s. green	19·00	23·00
8		1⅓s. mauve	47·00	£130
9		2s. blue	47·00	£225
10		4s. bistre	60·00	£1300

SCHLESWIG

1864. Inscr "HERZOGTH. SCHLESWIG". Roul.

24	2	½s. green	32·00	55·00
21		1¼s. green	47·00	21·00
25		1¼s. lilac	60·00	26·00
27		1⅓s. pink	30·00	65·00
28		2s. blue	30·00	50·00
22		4s. red	£110	£475
29		4s. bistre	34·00	85·00

HOLSTEIN

6 9 10

1864. Imperf.

51	6	1¼s. blue	50·00	60·00

1864. Roul.

59	9	1¼s. blue	38·00	21·00

1865. Roul.

61	10	½s. green	65·00	£100
62		1¼s. mauve	47·00	26·00
63		1⅓s. pink	65·00	47·00
64		2s. blue	55·00	50·00
65		4s. bistre	60·00	85·00

On the 1⅓s. and 4s. the word "SCHILLING" is inside the central oval.

1868. Inscr "HERZOGTH. HOLSTEIN". Roul.

66	2	1¼s. purple	70·00	26·00
67		2s. blue	£150	£150

SELANGOR Pt. 1

A state of the Federation of Malaya, incorporated in Malaysia in 1963.

100 cents = 1 dollar (Straits or Malayan).

1881. Stamps of Straits Settlements optd **SELANGOR**.

3	5	2c. brown	£100	£100
35		2c. red	10·00	2·75

1882. Straits Settlements stamp optd **S.**

8	5	2c. brown	—	£2500

1891. Stamp of Straits Settlements surch **SELANGOR Two CENTS**.

44	5	2c. on 24c. green	28·00	65·00

40 42

43

1891.

49	40	1c. green	1·50	25
50		2c. red	3·50	1·00
51		2c. orange	2·50	80
52		5c. blue	24·00	2·75

1894. Surch **3 CENTS**.

53	40	3c. on 5c. red	3·50	50

1895.

54	42	3c. purple and red	6·50	30
55		5c. purple and yellow	5·00	30
56		8c. purple and blue	48·00	7·00
57		10c. purple and orange	9·50	1·75
58		25c. green and red	80·00	50·00
60		50c. green and black	£400	£120
59		50c. purple and black	65·00	23·00
61	43	$1 green	50·00	£130
62		$2 green and red	£200	£200
63		$3 green and yellow	£475	£375
64		$5 green and blue	£250	£300
65		$10 green and purple	£600	£750
66		$25 green and orange	£2750	

1900. Surch in words.

66a	42	1c. on 5c. purple & yellow	60·00	£120
66b		1c. on 50c. green and black	2·75	22·00
67		3c. on 50c. green and black	4·00	22·00

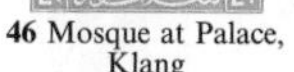

46 Mosque at Palace, Klang — 47 Sultan Suleiman

1935.

68 46 1c. black 30 10
69 2c. green 90 10
70 2c. orange . . . . 3·50 75
71a 3c. green . . . . 1·25 8·00
72 4c. orange 50 10
73 5c. brown 70 10
74 6c. red . . . . 5·50 10
75 8c. grey 60 10
76 10c. purple 60 10
77 12c. blue . . . . 1·00 10
78 15c. blue . . . . 12·00 32·00
79 25c. purple and red . . . . 1·00 60
80 30c. purple and orange . . 1·00 85
81 40c. red and purple . . . . 1·50 1·00
82 50c. black on green . . . . 1·00 15
83 47 $1 black and red on blue 7·50 90
84 $2 green and red . . . . . 24·00 8·00
85 $5 green and red on green 70·00 23·00

48 Sultan Hisamud-din Alam Shah — 49 Sultan Hisamud-din Alam Shah

1941.

86 48 $1 black and red on blue . . 16·00 6·00
87 $2 green and red . . . . . 48·00 27·00

1948. Silver Wedding. As T **33b/c** of St. Helena.
88 10c. violet 20 20
89 $5 green . . . . 27·00 16·00

1949.

90 49 1c. black 10 60
91 2c. orange 10 70
92 3c. green . . . . 1·75 1·50
93 4c. brown 20 10
94a 5c. purple 30 60
95 6c. grey 20 40
96 8c. red 35 65
97 8c. green . . . . 65 1·75
98 10c. purple 10 10
99 12c. red . . . . 80 3·50
100 15c. blue . . . . 4·25 10
101 20c. black and green . . . 2·50 35
102 20c. blue 80 10
103 25c. purple and orange . . 2·00 20
104 30c. red and purple . . . 2·00 2·25
105 35c. red and purple . . . 70 1·50
106 40c. red and purple . . . 7·00 6·00
107 50c. black and blue . . . 2·25 10
108 $1 blue and purple . . . 3·00 60
109 $2 green and red . . . . 13·00 60
110 $5 green and brown . . . 45·00 2·25

1949. U.P.U. As T **33d/g** of St. Helena.
111 10c. purple 30 10
112 15c. blue . . . . 2·00 2·50
113 25c. orange . . . . 35 3·50
114 50c. black . . . . 1·00 3·50

1953. Coronation. As T **33h** of St. Helena.
115 10c. black and purple . . . . 1·50 10

1957. As Nos. 92/102 of Kedah but inset portrait of Sultan Hisamud-din Alam Shah.
116 1c. black . . . . 10 2·25
117 2c. red . . . . 30 1·00
118 4c. sepia 10 10
119 5c. lake 10 10
120 8c. green . . . . 1·10 3·00
121 10c. sepia 65 10
122 10c. purple . . . . 4·75 10
123 20c. blue . . . . 2·25 20
124a 50c. black and blue 50 10
125 $1 blue and purple . . . . 2·00 10
126 $2 green and red . . . . . 2·50 1·25
127a $5 brown and green . . . . 7·50 1·25

50 Sultan Salahuddin Abdul Aziz Shah — 51 Sultan Salahuddin Abdul Aziz Shah

1961. Coronation of the Sultan.
128 50 10c. multicoloured 20 10

1961. As Nos. 116 etc but with inset portrait of Sultan Salahuddin Abdul Aziz as in T **51**.
129 1c. black . . . . 20 1·50
130 2c. red . . . . 20 1·90
131 4c. sepia 85 10
132 5c. lake 85 10
133 8c. green . . . . 3·00 4·50
134 10c. purple 50 10
135 20c. blue . . . . 5·50 1·00

52 "Vanda hookeriana"

1965. As Nos. 115/21 of Kedah but with inset portrait of Sultan Salahuddin Abdul Aziz Shah as in T **52**.
136 52 1c. multicoloured 10 20
137 – 2c. multicoloured . . . . . 10 1·75
138 – 5c. multicoloured 15 10
139 – 6c. multicoloured 15 10
140 – 10c. multicoloured 15 10
141 – 15c. multicoloured . . . . 1·25 10
142 – 20c. multicoloured . . . . 1·90 70

The higher values used in Selangor were Nos. 20/7 of Malaysia (National issues).

53 "Parthenos sylvia"

1971. Butterflies. As Nos. 124/30 of Kedah, but with portrait of Sultan Salahuddin Abdul Aziz Shah as in T **53**.
146 – 1c. multicoloured . . . . . 75 2·00
147 – 2c. multicoloured . . . . . 1·50 2·00
148 53 5c. multicoloured . . . . . 1·50 20
149 – 6c. multicoloured . . . . . 1·50 2·00
150 – 10c. multicoloured . . . . 1·50 10
151 – 15c. multicoloured . . . . 1·50 10
152 – 20c. multicoloured . . . . 1·50 50

The higher values in use with this issue were Nos. 64/71 of Malaysia (National issues).

54 "Lagerstroemia speciosa"

1979. Flowers. As Nos. 135/41 of Kedah but with portrait of Sultan Salahuddin Abdul Aziz Shah as in T **54**.
158 1c. "Rafflesia hasseltii" . . . 10 1·00
159 2c. "Pterocarpus indicus" . . 10 1·00
160 5c. Type **54** 10 10
161 10c. "Durio zibethinus" . . . 15 10
162 15c. "Hibiscus rosa sinensis" 15 10
163 20c. "Rhododendron scortechinii" 20 10
164 25c. "Etlingera elatior" (inscr "Phaeomeria speciosa") . . 40 10

55 Sultan Salahuddin Abdul Aziz Shah and Royal Crest — 56 Black Pepper

1985. Silver Jubilee of Sultan.
173 55 15c. multicoloured . . . . 1·50 10
174 20c. multicoloured . . . . 1·50 15
175 $1 multicoloured . . . . . 6·00 8·50

1986. As Nos. 152/8 of Kedah but with portrait of Sultan Salahuddin Abdul Aziz Shah as in T **56**.
176 1c. Coffee 10 10
177 2c. Coconuts 10 10
178 5c. Cocoa 10 10
179 10c. Type **56** 10 10
180 15c. Rubber 10 10
181 20c. Oil palm 10 10
182 30c. Rice 10 15

SENEGAL — Pt. 6; Pt. 14

A French colony incorporated in French West Africa in 1944. In 1958 Senegal became an autonomous State within the French Community and in 1959 joined the Sudan to form the Mali Federation. In 1960 the Federation broke up with Mali and Senegal becoming independent republics.

100 centimes = 1 franc.

1887. Stamps of French Colonies, "Commerce" type, surch in figures.
1 J 5 on 20c. red on green . . . £130 £150
2 5 on 30c. brown on drab . . £200 £200
3 10 on 4c. brown on green . . 60·00 60·00
4a 10 on 20c. red on green . . . £400 £400
5 15 on 20c. red on green . . . 50·00 50·00

1892. Stamps of French Colonies, "Commerce" type, surch **SENEGAL** and new value.
6 J 75 on 15c. blue on blue . . . £350 £130
7 1f. on 5c. green on green . . . £350 £150

1892. "Tablet" key-type inscr "SENEGAL ET DEPENDANCES".
8 D 1c. black and red on blue . . 50 80
9 2c. brown and blue on buff 3·00 2·50
10 4c. red and blue on grey . . 90 1·00
21 5c. green and red . . . . . 2·25 40
12 10c. black and blue on lilac 5·25 3·50
22 10c. red and blue . . . . . 4·50 40
13 15c. blue and red . . . . . 8·00 80
23 15c. grey and red . . . . . 3·75 80
14 20c. red and blue on green 4·50 5·25
15 25c. black and red on pink 3·25 1·25
24 25c. blue and red . . . . . 28·00 45·00
16 30c. brown & blue on drab 8·00 10·00
17 40c. red and blue on yellow 30·00 26·00
18 50c. red and blue on pink 13·50 32·00
25 50c. brown and red on blue 45·00 48·00
19 75c. brown & red on orange 10·50 20·00
20 1f. green and red . . . . . 15·00 18·00

1903. Surch.
26 D 5 on 40c. red & blue on yell 11·50 18·00
27 10 on 50c. red and blue on pink . . . . 19·00 21·00
28 10 on 75c. brown and red on orange . . . . 22·00 21·00
29 10 on 1f. green and red . . 70·00 95·00

1906. "Faidherbe". "Palms" and "Balay" key types inscr "SENEGAL".
33 I 1c. grey and red 70 75
34 2c. brown and red 70 30
34a 2c. brown and blue . . . . 4·00 5·00
35 4c. brown and red on blue 1·90 1·10
36 5c. green and red . . . . . 3·00 15
37 10c. pink and blue . . . . 11·00 15·00
38 15c. violet and red . . . . 9·50 3·50
39 J 20c. black and red on blue 3·75 2·50
40 25c. blue and red . . . . . 2·25 65
41 30c. brown and red on pink 4·75 6·00
42 35c. black and red on yellow . . . . 1·40 1·25
43 40c. red and blue on blue 8·00 10·00
44 45c. brown & red on green 13·00 11·50
45 50c. violet and red . . . . 7·50 5·25
46 75c. green & red on orange 5·50 5·75
47 K 1f. black and red on blue 18·00 25·00
48 2f. blue and red on pink . . 25·00 38·00
49 5f. red and blue on yellow 50·00 60·00

1912. Surch.
58 D 05 on 15c. grey and red . . 15 65
59 05 on 20c. red and blue on green . . . . 30 3·25
60 05 on 30c. brown and blue on drab . . . . 20 2·75
61 10 on 40c. red and blue on yellow . . . . 30 2·50
62 10 on 50c. red and blue . . 3·25 4·75
63 10 on 75c. brown and red on orange . . . . 4·75 9·00

33 Market

1914.

64 33 1c. violet and brown . . . 10 10
65 2c. blue and black 10 10
66 4c. brown and grey 10 10
67 5c. green and light green 10 10
91 5c. red and black 35 40
68 10c. pink and red 65 10
92 10c. green and light green 35 35
113 10c. blue and purple . . . 40 10
69 15c. purple and brown . . 10 10
70 20c. grey and brown . . . 15 70
114 20c. green . . . . 50 2·25
115 20c. blue and grey . . . . 1·75 15
71 25c. blue and ultramarine 1·90 10
93 25c. black and red . . . . 1·60 1·10
72 30c. pink and black . . . 10 75
94 30c. carmine and red . . . 2·00 3·00
116 30c. blue and grey 80 15
117 30c. green and olive . . . 2·00 95
73 35c. violet and orange . . 1·25 1·40
74 40c. green and violet . . . 1·60 10
75 45c. brown and blue . . . 90 3·50
95 45c. blue and red 15 35
118 45c. red and carmine . . . 65 1·25
119 45c. red and brown . . . . 6·25 5·00
76 50c. blue and purple . . . 2·50 2·75
96 50c. blue and ultramarine 60 50
120 50c. green and red . . . . 1·60 10
121 60c. violet on pink . . . . 50 2·75
122 65c. green and red . . . . 2·75 3·50
77 75c. pink and grey . . . . 1·90 2·25
123 75c. light blue and blue . . 20 1·00
124 75c. blue and pink . . . . 2·25 70
125 90c. carmine and red . . . 2·75 3·25
78 1f. black and violet . . . . 1·90 70
126 1f. blue 40 30
127 1f. blue and black . . . . 2·25 20
128 1f.10 black and green . . . 4·25 5·00
129 1f.25 red and green . . . . 1·75 1·25
130 1f.50 light blue and blue 2·75 70
131 1f.75 green and brown . . 9·00 1·50
79 2f. blue and pink . . . . . 1·75 3·75
97 2f. brown and blue . . . . 3·00 40
132 3f. mauve on pink . . . . 3·50 35
80 5f. violet and green . . . . 3·75 90

1915. Surch **5c** and red cross.
89 33 10c.+5c. pink and red . . . 1·00 3·25
90 15c.+5c. purple & brown . . 1·00 3·50

1922. Surch.
102 33 0,01 on 15c. purple & brn 25 2·75
103 0,02 on 15c. purple & brn 15 2·75
104 0,04 on 15c. purple & brn 15 2·75
105 0,05 on 15c. purple & brn 15 2·75
106 25c. on 5f. violet on green 1·75 3·00
98 60 on 15c. purple and pink 70 30
99 65 on 15c. purple & brown 2·25 3·50
100 85 on 15c. purple & brown 1·50 3·50
101 85 on 75c. pink and grey 2·50 3·25
107 90c. on 75c. pink and red 1·60 3·00
108 1f.25 on 1f. blue . . . . . 30 2·50
109 1f.50 on 1f. lt blue & blue 95 50
110 3f. on 5f. brown and purple . . . . 1·50 50
111 10f. on 5f. red and blue . . 4·75 2·75
112 20f. on 5f. brown & mauve 8·00 6·75

1931. "Colonial Exhibition" key-types.
135 E 40c. green and black . . . 3·25 3·00
136 F 50c. mauve and black . . . 3·00 3·50
137 G 90c. red and black . . . . 2·50 3·25
138 H 1f.50 blue and black . . . 3·50 3·75

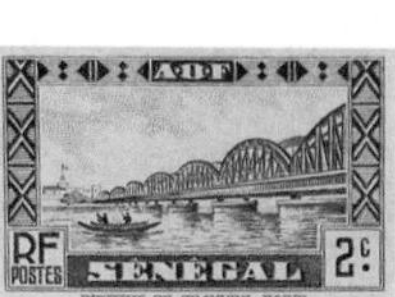

38 Faidherbe Bridge, Dakar — 39 Senegalese Girl

1935.

139 38 1c. blue (postage) . . . . 10 2·50
140 2c. brown . . . . 10 2·25
141 3c. violet . . . . 10 2·75
142 4c. blue . . . . 10 2·75
143 5c. orange . . . . 10 1·60
144 10c. purple . . . . 10 1·75
145 15c. black 10 90
146 20c. red . . . . 35 2·00
147 25c. brown 85 55
148 30c. green . . . . 45 2·50
149 39 35c. green . . . . 1·25 2·50
150 38 40c. red . . . . 65 1·00
151 45c. green . . . . 20 2·50
152 A 50c. orange 10 10
153 39 55c. brown . . . . 1·60 2·25
154 A 60c. violet . . . . 40 2·50
155 65c. violet . . . . 1·60 10
156 70c. brown . . . . 1·75 2·75
157 75c. brown . . . . 1·25 95
158 39 80c. violet . . . . 1·90 1·90
159 A 90c. red . . . . 80 2·25
160 39 90c. violet . . . . 1·40 2·00
161 A 1f. violet . . . . 12·00 3·75
162 39 1f. red 80 95
163 1f. brown 25 70
164 A 1f.25 brown . . . . 95 3·00
165 1f.25 red . . . . 25 3·25
166 1f.40 green . . . . 40 3·00
167 1f.50 blue 75 80
168 1f.60 blue . . . . 1·50 2·50
169 1f.75 green . . . . 1·60 1·25
170 39 1f.75 blue . . . . 1·75 2·75
171 A 2f. blue . . . . 1·90 75
172 39 2f.25 blue . . . . 2·00 2·50
173 2f.50 black . . . . 1·00 2·75
174 A 3f. green . . . . 15 1·75
175 5f. brown . . . . 1·75 1·00
176 10f. red . . . . 2·75 1·50
177 20f. grey . . . . 1·25 40

178 B 25c. brown (air) . . . . . 80 2·25
179 50c. red . . . . 70 2·75
180 1f. purple 45 70
181 1f.25 green . . . . 1·25 2·50
182 1f.90 blue . . . . 1·25 2·75
183 2f. blue . . . . 1·50 40
184 2f.90 red . . . . 1·40 3·00
185 3f. green . . . . 1·75 1·40
186 C 3f.50 violet . . . . 1·60 1·25
187 B 4f.50 green . . . . 1·10 2·75
188 C 4f.75 orange . . . . . . 1·25 2·75
189 B 4f.90 brown . . . . 1·75 2·75
190 C 6f.50 blue . . . . 80 2·25
191 B 6f.90 orange . . . . . . 1·75 3·00
192 C 8f. black . . . . 2·00 2·75
193 15f. red . . . . 2·00 2·75

DESIGNS—HORIZ: A, Djourbel Mosque; B, Airplane over village; C, Airplane over camel caravan.

1937. International Exhibition, Paris. As Nos. 168/73 of St.-Pierre et Miquelon.
194 20c. violet . . . . 70 3·00
195 30c. green . . . . 1·00 3·00
196 40c. red . . . . 60 2·50
197 50c. brown . . . . 35 3·00
198 90c. red . . . . 1·10 2·25
199 1f.50 blue . . . . 80 3·25
MS200 120 × 100 mm. 3f. purple. Imperf . . . . 5·75 14·00

1938. International Anti-cancer Fund. As T **38** of St.-Pierre et Miquelon.
201 1f.75+50c. blue . . . . . . 3·75 12·50

40 Rene Caillie (explorer)

1939. Death Centenary of Rene Caillie (explorer).
202 **40** 90c. orange 25 25
203 2f. violet 35 30
204 2f.25 blue 35 35

1939. New York World's Fair. As T **41** of St.-Pierre et Miquelon.
205 1f.25 red . . . . 60 1·10
206 2f.25 blue . . . . 75 3·00

1939. 150th Anniv of French Revolution. As T **42** of St.-Pierre et Miquelon.
207 45c.+25c. green and black (postage) . . . . 4·25 11·50
208 70c.+30c. brown and black 4·25 11·50
209 90c.+35c. orange and black 4·25 11·50
210 1f.25+1f. red and black . . . 5·25 11·50
211 2f.25+2f. blue and black . . 4·25 12·00
212 4f.75+4f. black & orge (air) 8·00 14·00

1941. National Defence Fund. Surch **SECOURS NATIONAL** and value.
213 +1f. on 50c. (No. 152) . . . 2·75 1·60
214 +2f. on 80c. (No. 158) . . . 4·00 6·75
215 +2f. on 1f.50 (No. 167) . . . 5·75 9·00
216 +3f. on 2f. (No. 171) . . . . 5·25 8·00

1942. Air. Colonial Child Welfare Fund. As Nos. 98g/i of Niger.
216a 1f.50+3f.50 green . . . . . 15 1·10
216b 2f.+6f. brown . . . . 25 1·25
216c 3f.+9f. red . . . . 15 1·10

40c "Vocation"

1942. Air. "Imperial Fortnight".
216d **40c** 1f.20+1f.80 blue and red 15 3·25

40d Aeroplane over Camel Caravan

1942. Air. As T **40d**, but inscr "SENEGAL" and similar design.
217 **40d** 50f. green and yellow . . 1·60 3·00
218 – 100f. blue and red . . . . 1·75 2·75
DESIGN—48 × 26 mm: 100f. Twin-engined airliner landing.

1944. Stamps of 1935 surch.
219 **38** 1f.50 on 15c. black 25 25
220 A 1f.50 on 65c. violet 20 45
221 **38** 4f.50 on 15c. black 35 25
222 5f.50 on 2c. brown . . . . 65 1·60
223 A 5f.50 on 65c. violet 85 80
224 **38** 10f. on 15c. black 70 55
225 A 50f. on 65c. violet . . . . 75 1·25

1944. No. 202 surch.
226 20f. on 90c. orange . . . . . 45 3·00
227 50f. on 90c. orange . . . . . 4·25 2·50

42 African Buffalo

1960. Niokolo-Koba National Park.
228 – 5f. purple, black and green 20 10
229 **42** 10f. purple, black and green 45 15
230 – 15f. purple, brown and sepia 50 30
231 – 20f. brown, green & chest 70 30
232 – 25f. brown, choc & green 1·00 40
233 – 85f. multicoloured . . . . 2·25 1·00
ANIMALS—VERT: 5f. Roan antelope; 15f. Warthog; 20f. Giant eland; 85f. Waterbuck. HORIZ: 25f. Bushbuck.

43 African Fish Eagle

1960. Air.
234 – 50f. multicoloured . . . . 2·50 90
235 – 100f. multicoloured . . . . 5·50 1·40
236 – 200f. multicoloured . . . . 10·50 4·50
237 – 250f. multicoloured . . . . 13·50 5·50
238 **43** 500f. multicoloured . . . . 29·00 7·50
BIRDS—VERT: 50f. Carmine bee-eater; 200f. Violet turaco; 250f. Red bishop. HORIZ: 100f. Abyssinian roller.

44 Mother and Child

1961. Independence Commemoration.
239 **44** 25f. brown, blue and green 55 20

45 Pirogue Race

1961. Sports.
240 – 50c. brown, blue and sepia 10 10
241 **45** 1f. purple, turquoise & green 10 10
242 – 2f. sepia, bistre and blue 10 10
243 – 30f. purple and red 90 55
244 – 45f. black, blue and brown 1·50 65
DESIGNS: 50c. African wrestling; 2f. Horse race; 30f. African dancers; 45f. Lion game.

46 Senegal Flag, U.N. Emblem and H.Q. Building

1962. 1st Anniv of Admission of Senegal to U.N.O.
245 **46** 10f. red, ochre and green 15 15
246 30f. green, ochre and red 30 25
247 85f. multicoloured . . . . 1·10 55

47 I.T.U. Emblems, African Map and Telephonist

47b Campaign Emblem

47a European, African and Airliners

1962. 1st I.T.U. African Plan Sub-Committee Meeting, Dakar.
248 **47** 25f. multicoloured 55 20

1962. Air. "Air Afrique" Airline.
249 **47a** 25f. purple, brown & green 35 20

1962. Malaria Eradication.
250 **47b** 25f.+5f. turquoise 40 35

47c Union Flag

1962. 1st Anniv of Union of African and Malagasy States.
251 **47c** 30f. turquoise 40 35

47d Globe and Emblem

1963. Freedom from Hunger.
252 **47d** 25f.+5f. olive, brn & vio 35 35

48 Boxing

50 "Charaxes varanes"

49 Main Motif of U.P.U. Monument, Berne

1963. Dakar Games. Inscr as in T **48**. Centres brown; inscr and frame colours given.
253 **48** 10f. red and green 15 10
254 – 15f. ochre and blue 20 15
255 – 20f. red and blue 25 15
256 – 25f. green and blue 40 20
257 – 30f. red and green 85 25
258 – 85f. blue . . . . 1·75 1·00
DESIGNS—HORIZ: 15f. Diving; 20f. High-jumping. VERT: 25f. Football; 30f. Basketball; 85f. Running.

1963. 2nd Anniv of Admission to U.P.U.
259 **49** 10f. red and green 20 15
260 15f. brown and blue . . . 20 20
261 30f. blue and brown . . . 45 25

1963. Butterflies. Butterflies in natural colours; inscr in black; background colours given.
262 **50** 30f. blue . . . . 1·00 40
263 – 45f. orange . . . . 1·75 60
264 – 50f. yellow . . . . 1·75 1·00
265 – 85f. red . . . . 4·25 1·75
266 – 100f. blue . . . . 5·50 2·50
267 – 500f. green . . . . 17·00 7·50
BUTTERFLIES: 45f. "Papilio nireus"; 10f. "Colotis danae"; 85f. "Epiphora bauhiniae"; 100f. "Junonia hierta"; 500f. "Danaus chrysippus".

1963. Air. 2nd Anniv of African and Malagasian Posts and Telecommunications Union. As No. 36 of Rwanda.
268 85f. multicoloured . . . . . 1·10 55

51 G. Berger, Owl and "Prospective" (book)

1963. 3rd Death Anniv of Prof. Gaston Berger (educationalist).
269 **51** 25f. multicoloured 55 20

51a Airline Emblem

1963. Air. 1st Anniv of "Air Afrique" and "DC-8" Service Inauguration.
270 **51a** 50f. multicoloured . . . . 1·25 55

52 Globe, Scales of Justice and Flag

53 Mother and Child

1963. 15th Anniv of Declaration of Human Rights.
271 **52** 60f. multicoloured 90 40

1963. Senegalese Red Cross.
272 **53** 25f. multicoloured 55 25

54 Temple Gods, Abu Simbel

1964. Air. Nubian Monument Preservation Fund.
273 **54** 25f.+5f. brown, green and turquoise . . . . 1·40 70

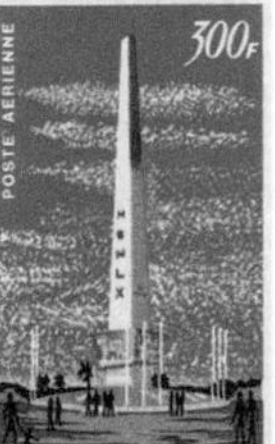

55 Independence Monument

57 Titanium Sand Dredger

56 Allegorical Figures of Twin Towns

1964. Air.
274 **55** 300f. multicoloured . . . . 4·00 2·00

1964. Air. World Twin Towns Federation Congress, Dakar.
275 **56** 150f. brown, black & turq 3·25 1·40

1964. Senegal Industries.
276 **57** 5f. brown, turquoise & lake 15 15
277 – 10f. blue, brown and green 15 10
278 – 15f. brown, green and blue 20 10
279 – 20f. purple, bistre and blue 25 10
280 – 25f. black, ochre and blue 65 10
281 – 85f. brown, blue and red 2·25 1·10
DESIGNS: 10f. Titanium sorting works; 15f. Rufisque cement works; 20f. Loading phosphate at Pallo; 25f. Working phosphate at Taiba; 85f. Mineral wharf, Dakar.

58 "Supporting the Globe"

1964. Air. "Europafrique".
282 **58** 50f. multicoloured . . . . 1·25 55

59 Basketball

60 "Syncom 2" Satellite and Rocket

1964. Air. Olympic Games, Tokyo.
283 **59** 85f. brown and blue . . . 2·00 70
284 – 100f. purple and green . . 2·25 90
DESIGN: 100f. Pole-vaulting.

1964. Air. Space Telecommunications.
285 **60** 150f. blue, brown and green . . . . 2·25 1·25

60a "Co-operation"

61 Church of Ste. Therese, Dakar

1964. French, African and Malagasy Co-operation.
286 **60a** 100f. brown, red and green . . . . 1·75 90

1964. Religious Buildings.
287 **61** 5f. lake, green and blue . . 10 10
288 – 10f. brown, black and blue 15 10
289 – 15f. slate, brown and blue 45 15
DESIGNS—HORIZ: 10f. Touba Mosque. VERT: 15f. Dakar Mosque.

62 Pres. Kennedy

63 Child and Microscope

1964. Air. Pres. Kennedy Commemoration.
290 **62** 100f. brown, yellow & green . . . . 2·00 1·00

1965. Anti-leprosy Campaign.
292 **63** 20f. black, green and brown 25 20
293 – 65f. multicoloured 90 45
DESIGN: 65f. Peycouk Village.

64 Haute Casamance

1965. Senegal Landscapes.
294 **64** 25f. green, brown and blue (postage) 25 15
295 – 30f. blue, green and brown 30 15
296 – 45f. turquoise, green & brown 75 55
297 – 100f. black, green and bistre (air) . . . . 1·50 1·10
DESIGNS: 30f. Sangalkam; 45f. Senegal River forest region; 100f. Banks of Gambia River, East Senegal (48 × 27 mm).

65 A. Seck (Director of Posts, 1873–1931)

66 Berthon-Ader Telephone

1965. Postal Services Commemoration.
298 **65** 10f. black and brown . . . 15 15
299 – 15f. brown and green . . . 20 15
DESIGN—HORIZ: 15f. P.T.T. Headquarters, Dakar.

1965. I.T.U. Centenary.
300 **66** 50f. brown, bistre and green 50 30
301 – 60f. red, green and blue . . 1·00 60
302 – 85f. purple, red and blue 1·10 50
DESIGNS: 60f. Cable-ship "Alsace"; 85f. Picard's submarine telegraph cable relay apparatus.

67 Ploughing with Oxen

1965. Rural Development.
303 **67** 25f. brown, violet and green 35 25
304 – 60f. multicoloured 90 45
305 – 85f. black, red and green 1·25 55
DESIGNS—VERT: 50f. Millet cultivation. HORIZ: 85f. Rice cultivation, Casamance.

68 Goree Pirogue under Sail

1965. Senegal Pirogues. Multicoloured.
306 10f. Type **68** 20 15
307 20f. Large pirogue at Seumbedioune 35 15
308 30f. One-man pirogue at Fadiouth Island 85 20
309 45f. One-man pirogue on Senegal River . . . . . . 1·50 65

69 Woman holding Child and U.N. Emblems

70 "Fruit of Cashew Tree"

1965. Air. International Co-operation Year.
310 **69** 50f. brown, green and blue 90 30

1965. Fruits. Multicoloured.
311 10f. Type **70** 15 10
312 15f. Papaw 20 15
313 20f. Mango 25 10
314 30f. Groundnuts 65 15

71 "The Gentleman of Fashion"

72 Tom-tom Player

1966. Goree Puppets.
315 **71** 1f. blue, brown and red . . 10 10
316 – 2f. orange, brown and blue 10 10
317 – 3f. blue, brown and red . . 10 10
318 – 4f. green, brown and violet 10 10
PUPPETS: 2f. "The Lady of Fashion"; 3f. "The Pedlar"; 4f. "The Pounder".

1966. World Festival of Negro Arts, Dakar ("Announcement").
319 **72** 30f. brown, red and green 75 15
See also Nos. 327/30.

73 Rocket "Diamant"

1966. Air. French Satellites.
320 **73** 50f. red, blue and brown 70 40
321 – 50f. black, brown and green 70 40
322 – 90f. blue, brown and slate 1·75 75
DESIGNS: No. 321, Satellite "A1"; 322, Rocket "Scout" and satellite "FR1".

74 Little Tuna

76 Arms of Senegal

75 Satellite "D1"

1966. Senegal Fishes. Multicoloured.
323 20f. Type **74** 50 25
324 30f. White grouper 90 35
325 50f. Peacock wrasse . . . . 1·90 65
326 100f. West African parrotfish 3·50 1·25

1966. World Festival of Negro Arts, Dakar. As T **72**.
327 15f. lake, orange and blue . . 15 15
328 30f. lake, yellow and blue . . 35 20
329 75f. black, lake and blue . . 1·25 55
330 90f. lake, black and orange 1·40 65
DESIGNS: 15f. Statuette ("Sculpture"); 30f. Musical instrument ("Music"); 75f. Carving ("Dance"); 90f. Ideogram.

1966. Air. Launching of Satellite "D 1".
332 **75** 100f. blue, lake and violet 1·50 65

1966.
333 **76** 30f. multicoloured 55 15

76a Douglas DC-8F Jet Trader and "Air Afrique" Emblem

1966. Air. Inauguration of DC-8F Air Services.
334 **76a** 30f. yellow, black & brown 55 20

77 "Argemone mexicana"

79 Port of Ile de Goree

78 Couzinet 70 "Arc en Ciel"

1966. Flowers. Multicoloured.
335 45f. Type **77** . . . . 1·00 20
336 55f. "Dichrostachys glomerata" . . . . 1·00 25
337 60f. "Haemanthus multiflorus" . . . . 1·25 35
338 90f. "Adansonia digitata" . . 1·75 50

1966. Air. 30th Anniv of Disappearance of Jean Mermoz (aviator).
339 **78** 20f. slate, purple and blue 70 20
340 – 35f. slate, brown and green 85 20
341 – 100f. lake, emerald & green 1·50 45
342 – 150f. lake, black and blue 3·00 1·00
DESIGNS—HORIZ: 35f. Latecoere 300 flying boat "Croix du Sud"; 100f. Map of Mermoz's last flight across Atlantic Ocean. VERT: 150f. Jean Mermoz.

1966. Tourism.
343 **79** 20f. lake, blue and black 20 15
344 – 25f. sepia, green and red 1·75 30
345 – 30f. blue, red and green . . 30 10
346 – 50f. blue, green and red . . 50 20
347 – 90f. black, green and blue 1·10 45
DESIGNS: 25f. Liner "France" at Dakar; 30f. N'Gor Hotel and tourist cabins; 50f. N'Gor Bay and Hotel; 90f. Town Hall, Dakar.

80 Laying Water Mains

1967. International Hydrological Decade.
348 **80** 10f. blue, green and brown 15 15
349 – 20f. brown, green and blue 30 20
350 – 30f. blue, orange and black 35 20
351 – 50f. lake, flesh and blue . . 75 20
DESIGNS—HORIZ: 20f. Cattle at trough. VERT: 30f. Decade emblem; 50f. Obtaining water from primitive well.

81 Terminal Building, Dakar-Yoff Airport

1967. Air.
352 **81** 200f. indigo, blue & brown 2·75 1·00

82 Lions Emblem

1967. 50th Anniv of Lions International.
353 **82** 30f. multicoloured 65 45

83 Blaise Diagne

1967. 95th Birth Anniv of Blaise Diagne (statesman).
354 **83** 30f. brown, green & purple 55 20

84 Spiny Mimosa

1967. Air. Flowers. Multicoloured.
355 100f. Type **84** . . . . 2·50 75
356 150f. Barbary fig . . . . . . 3·50 1·40

85 "Les Demoiselles d'Avignon" (Picasso)

86 Carved Eagle and Kudu's Head

1967. Air.
357 **85** 100f. multicoloured . . . . 3·00 1·10

1967. "EXPO 67" World Fair, Montreal.
358 **86** 90f. black and red . . . . 1·50 50
359 – 150f. multicoloured . . . . 2·00 75
DESIGN: 150f. Maple leaf and flags.

86a Map, Letters and Pylons

1967. Air. 5th Anniv of UAMPT.
360 **86a** 100f. red, green and violet 90 50

87 I.T.Y. Emblem

88 Currency Tokens

1967. International Tourist Year.
361 **87** 50f. black and blue 80 35
362 – 100f. black, green & orange 2·75 1·00
DESIGN: 100f. Tourist photographing hippopotamus.

1967. 5th Anniv of West African Monetary Union.
363 **88** 30f. violet, purple and grey 25 15

89 "Lyre" Stone, Kaffrine

90 Nurse feeding Baby

1967. 6th Pan-American Prehistory Congress, Dakar.
364 **89** 30f. red, blue and green . . 90 15
365 – 70f. red, brown and blue 1·60 90
DESIGN: 70f. Ancient bowl, Bandiala.

1967. Senegalese Red Cross.
366 **90** 50f. lake, red and green . . 50 25

91 Human Rights Emblem

92 Chancellor Adenauer

1968. Human Rights Year.
367 **91** 30f. gold and green 35 20

1968. Air. Adenauer Commemoration.
368 **92** 100f. sepia, red and green 1·40 55

93 Weather Balloon, Flourishing Plants and W.M.O. Emblem

95 Spiny Lobster

94 Parliament Building, Dakar

1968. Air. World Meteorological Day.
370 **93** 50f. green, blue and black 90 40

1968. Inter-Parliamentary Union Meeting, Dakar.
371 **94** 30f. red 55 15

1968. Marine Crustacea. Multicoloured.
372 10f. Type **95** 15 10
373 20f. Sea crawfish 25 15
374 35f. Prawn 75 20
375 100f. Gooseneck barnacle . . 2·40 1·00

96 Lesser Pied Kingfisher

98 Hurdling

97 Ox and Syringe

1968. Birds. Multicoloured.
376 5f. Type **96** (postage) 35 10
377 15f. African jacana 65 10
378 70f. African darter . . . . . 2·25 1·10
379 250f. Village weaver (air) . . 6·75 1·50
380 300f. Comb duck . . . . . . 10·50 2·50
381 500f. Bateleur . . . . 18·00 6·75
Nos. 379/81 are 45½ × 26 mm.

1968. Campaign for Prevention of Cattle Plague.
382 **97** 30f. red, green and blue . . 55 20

1968. Air. Olympic Games, Mexico.
383 **98** 20f. brown, green and blue 45 15
384 – 30f. brown, ochre & purple 65 15
385 – 50f. lake, brown and blue 1·25 35
386 – 75f. bistre, brown and green . . . . 2·00 60
DESIGNS: 30f. Throwing the javelin; 50f. Judo; 75f. Basketball.

98a "Young Girl reading a Letter" (J. Raoux)

99 Senegalese Boy

1968. Air. "Philexafrique". Stamp Exhibition, Abidjan (1st issue) (1969).
387 **98a** 100f. multicoloured . . . 3·00 2·25

1968. 20th Anniv of W.H.O.
388 **99** 30f. black, red and green 25 25
389 45f. black, green and brown 60 20

101 Faculty Building

1969. Faculty of Medicine and Pharmaceutics, and Sixth "Medical Days", Dakar.
391 **101** 30f. blue and green . . . 55 20
392 – 50f. green, red and brown 60 25
DESIGN—VERT: 50f. Emblem of "Medical Days".

101a Modern Dakar and Senegal Stamp of 1935

1969. Air. "Philexafrique". Stamp Exhibition, Abidjan, Ivory Coast (2nd issue).
393 **101a** 50f. violet, slate and green . . . . 1·25 1·25

102 Panet, Camels and Route-map

1969. 150th Birth Anniv of Leopold Panet, first Explorer of the Mauritanian Sahara.
394 **102** 75f. brown and blue . . . 1·50 75

103 AITY Emblem

1969. Air. African International Tourist Year.
395 **103** 100f. red, green and blue 1·10 45

104 I.L.O. Emblem

105 Pres. Lamine Gueye

1969. 50th Anniv of I.L.O.
396 **104** 30f. black and turquoise 25 15
397 45f. black and red 40 20

1969. Air. President Gueye Memorial.
398 **105** 30f. black, buff and brown 25 15
399 – 45f. black, blue and brown 65 20
DESIGN: 45f. Pres. Lamine Gueye (different).

106 Arms of Casamance

107 Bank Emblem

1969. Senegal Arms. Multicoloured.
401 15f. Type **106** 15 10
402 20f. Arms of Ile de Goree . . 45 15

1969. 5th Anniv of African Development Bank.
403 **107** 30f. brown, green and slate 25 15
404 45f. brown and green . . 35 20

108 Mahatma Gandhi

109 "Transmission of Thought" (O. Faye)

1969. Birth Centenary of Mahatma Gandhi.
405 **108** 50f. multicoloured 45 25

1969. Air. Tapestries. Multicoloured.
407 25f. Type **109** 60 20
408 30f. "The Blue Cock" (Mamadou Niang) 35 20
409 45f. "The Fairy" (Papa Sidi Diop) . . . . 1·25 50
410 50f. "Fari" (A. N'Diaye) . . 1·50 75
411 75f. "Lunaris" (J. Lurcat) . . 2·00 70
SIZES—VERT: 30f., 45f. 37 × 49 mm. HORIZ: 50f. 49 × 37 mm.

110 Baila Bridge

1969. Air. Europafrique.
412 **110** 100f. multicoloured . . . 1·25 45

111 Rotary Emblem and "Sailing Ship"

1969. 30th Anniv of Dakar Rotary Club.
413 **111** 30f. yellow, black and blue 35 20

112 Airliner, Map and Airport

1969. 10th Anniv of ASECNA.
414 **112** 100f. slate 90 35

113 Cape Skiring, Casamance

115 Bottle-nosed Dolphins

114 Lecrivain, Latecoere 25 Airplane and Route

1969. Tourism.
415 **113** 20f. green, lake and blue 45 15
416 – 30f. lake, brown and blue 65 15
417 – 35f. black, brown and blue . . . . 2·50 65
418 – 45f. lake and blue . . . . 1·10 55
DESIGNS: 30f. Tourist camp, Niokolo-Koba; 35f. Herd of African elephants, Niokolo-Koba Park; 45f. Millet granaries on stilts, Fadiouth Island.

1970. Air. 40th Anniv of Disappearance of Emile Lecrivain (aviator).
419 **114** 50f. lake, slate and green 1·00 40

1970.
420 **115** 50f. multicoloured . . . . 2·50 1·10

116 R. Maran (Martinique)

1970. Air. Negro Celebrities (1st series).
421 **116** 30f. brown, green and lake 25 15
422 – 45f. brown, blue and pink 65 25
423 – 50f. brown, green & yellow 75 35
PORTRAITS: 45f. M. Garvey (Jamaica); 50f. Dr. P. Mars (Haiti).
See also Nos. 457/60.

117 Sailing Pirogue and Obelisk

118 Lenin

1970. Air. 10th Anniv of Independence.
424 **117** 500f. multicoloured . . . 6·50 3·25

1970. Birth Centenary of Lenin.
426 **118** 30f. brown, stone and red 1·40 55

119 Bay of Naples, and Post Office, Dakar

1970. Air. 10th "Europa" Stamp Exn, Naples.
428 **119** 100f. multicoloured . . . 1·25 55

1970. New U.P.U. Headquarters Building, Berne. As T **101** of St. Pierre et Miquelon.
429 30f. plum, blue and lake . . 25 15
430 45f. brown, lake and green 45 20

121 Nagakawa and Mt. Fuji

1970. Air. World Fair "EXPO 70", Osaka, Japan.
431 – 25f. red, green and lake 45 15
432 **121** 75f. red, blue and green 1·25 30
433 – 150f. red, brown and blue 1·90 70
DESIGNS—VERT: 25f. "Woman playing guitar" (Hokusai) and Sun tower; 150f. "Nanboku Beauty" (Shuncho).

122 Harbour Quayside, Dakar

1970. Air. Industrial and Urban Development.
434 **122** 30f. blue, black and red 75 15
435 – 100f. brown, green & slate 1·40 45
DESIGN: 100f. Aerial view of city centre, Dakar.

123 Beethoven, Napoleon and "Evocation of Eroica" Symphony

1970. Air. Birth Bicentenary of Beethoven.
436 **123** 50f. brown, orange and green . . . . 1·25 35
437 – 100f. red and blue . . . . 2·50 1·25
DESIGN: 100f. Beethoven with quillpen and scroll.

124 Heads of Four Races

1970. Air. 25th Anniv of U.N.O.
438 **124** 100f. multicoloured . . . 1·60 90

125 Looms and Textile Works, Thies

1970. "Industrialization".
439 **125** 30f. red, blue and green 30 15
440 – 45f. blue, brown and red 65 20
DESIGN: 45f. Fertilizer plant, Dakar.

126 Scouts in Camp

127 Three Heads and Sun

1970. 1st African Scouting Conference, Dakar. Multicoloured.
441 30f. Type **126** 30 20
442 100f. Scout badge, Lord Baden-Powell and map . . 1·40 45

1970. International Education Year.
443 **127** 25f. brown, blue & orange 25 15
444 – 40f. multicoloured 45 20
DESIGN: 40f. Map of Africa on Globe, and two heads.

128 Arms of Senegal

129 De Gaulle, Map, Ears of Wheat and Cogwheel

1970.
445 **128** 30f. multicoloured . . . 35 15
446 35f. multicoloured . . . 35 15
446a 50f. multicoloured . . . 35 15
446b 65f. multicoloured . . . 35 15
803 95f. multicoloured . . . 35 30

1970. Air. "De Gaulle the De-colonizer". Mult.
447 50f. Type **129** . . . . 1·25 90
448 100f. De Gaulle, and map within "sun" . . . . . . 3·00 1·90

130 Refugees

1971. 20th Anniv of U.N. High Commissioner for Refugees. Multicoloured.
449 40f. Type **130** (postage) . . . 65 20
450 100f. Building house (air) . . 1·10 80
No. 450 is 46 × 27 mm.

131 "Mbayang" Horse

1971. Horse-breeding Improvement Campaign. Multicoloured.
451 25f. "Madjiguene" 65 40
452 40f. Type **131** 90 45
453 100f. "Pass" . . . . 2·25 1·50
454 125f. "Pepe" . . . . 2·75 1·60

132 European Girl and African Boy

133 Phillis Wheatley

1971. Racial Equality Year. Multicoloured.
455 30f. Type **132** 25 15
456 50f. People of four races (horiz) (37 × 30 mm) . . . 80 25

1971. Air. Negro Celebrities (2nd series). Mult.
457 25f. Type **133** 20 15
458 40f. J. E. K. Aggrey 35 20
459 60f. A. Le Roy Locke . . . 80 25
460 100f. Booker T. Washington 1·10 45

134 "Telephones"

135 "Napoleon as First Consul" (Ingres)

1971. World Telecommunications Day.
461 **134** 30f. brown, green & purple 25 15
462 – 40f. brown, red and blue 65 20
DESIGN: 40f. "Telecommunications" theme.

1971. Air. 150th Death Anniv of Napoleon. Mult.
463 15f. Type **135** 55 25
464 25f. "Napoleon in 1809" (Lefevre) 70 30
465 35f. "Napoleon on his Death-bed" (Rouget) . . . . . . 1·25 45
466 50f. "The Awakening to Immortality" (bronze by Rude) . . . . 2·25 1·10

136 Pres. Nasser

138 A. Nobel

137 Hayashida (drummer)

1971. Air. Nasser Commemoration.
467 **136** 50f. multicoloured 45 25

1971. 13th World Scout Jamboree, Asagiri, Japan. Multicoloured.
468 35f. Type **137** 65 15
469 50f. Japonica 90 45
470 65f. Judo . . . . 1·25 55
471 75f. Mt. Fuji . . . . 1·60 90

1971. Air. 75th Death Anniv of Alfred Nobel (scientist and philanthropist).
472 **138** 100f. multicoloured . . . 1·50 60

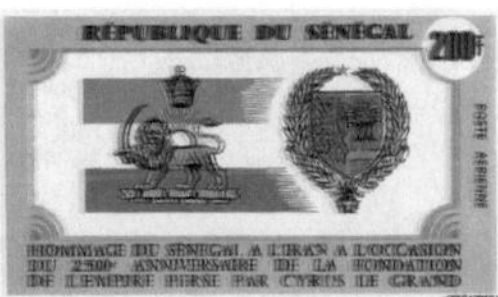
139 Persian Flag and Senegal Arms

1971. Air. 2500th Anniv of Persian Empire.
473 **139** 200f. multicoloured . . . 2·25 1·00

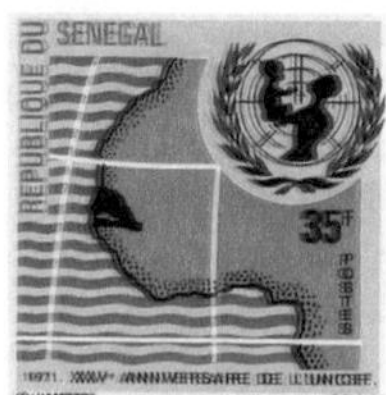
140 Map and Emblem

1971. 25th Anniv of UNICEF. Multicoloured.
474 35f. Type **140** 35 20
475 100f. Nurse, children and UNICEF emblem . . . . 1·25 55

141 UAMPT Headquarters, Brazzaville, and arms of Senegal

1971. Air. 10th Anniv of UAMPT.
476 **141** 100f. multicoloured . . . 1·10 40

142 Louis Armstrong

143 Trying for Goal

1971. Air. Louis Armstrong Commemoration.
477 **142** 150f. brown and gold . . 3·75 1·60

1971. 6th African Basketball Championships, Dakar. Multicoloured.
478 35f. Type **143** 55 15
479 40f. Players reaching for ball 75 25
480 75f. Championships emblem 1·25 60

144 Ice-skating

1971. Air. Winter Olympic Games, Sapporo, Japan. Multicoloured.
481 5f. Type **144** 15 10
482 10f. Bobsleighing 15 10
483 125f. Alpine skiing . . . . . 1·75 60

145 "Il Fonteghetto della Farina" (detail, Canaletto)

1972. Air. UNESCO "Save Venice" Campaign. Multicoloured.
484 50f. Type **145** 90 55
485 100f. "Giudecca e S. Giorgio Maggiore" (detail, Guardi) (vert) . . . . 1·90 1·10

146 "Albouri and Queen Seb Fall" (scene from "The Exile of Albouri")

1972. International Theatre Day. Multicoloured.
486 35f. Type **146** (postage) . . . 65 20
487 40f. Scene from "The Merchant of Venice" . . . 65 25
488 150f. Daniel Sorano as "Shylock" ("The Merchant of Venice") (vert) (air) . . 3·25 1·50

147 Human Heart

1972. World Heart Month.
489 **147** 35f. brown and blue . . . 25 15
490 – 40f. purple, green & emerald 55 20
DESIGN: 40f. Doctor and patient.

148 Vegetation in Desert

1972. U.N. Environmental Conservation Conf, Stockholm. Multicoloured.
491 35f. Type **148** (postage) . . . 65 20
492 100f. Oil slick on shore (air) 1·60 60

149 Tartarin of Tarascon shooting Lion

1972. 75th Death Anniv of Alphonse Daudet (writer).
493 **149** 40f. red, green and brown 1·10 30
494 – 100f. brown, lt blue & blue . . . . 1·25 50
DESIGN: 100f. Daudet and scene from "Tartarin de Tarascon".

151 Wrestling 152 Emperor Haile Selassie and Flags

1972. Olympic Games, Munich. Multicoloured.
496 15f. Type **151** 20 15
497 20f. Running (100 m) 45 15
498 100f. Basketball . . . . . . 1·40 45
499 125f. Judo . . . . 1·75 55

1972. Air. Emperor Haile Selassie's 80th Birthday.
501 **152** 100f. multicoloured . . . 1·25 55

153 Children reading Book 154 "Senegalese Elegance"

1972. International Book Year.
502 **153** 50f. multicoloured 45 20

1972. (1st issue).
502a **154** 5f. blue 10 10
502b 10f. red 15 10
502c 15f. orange 15 10
502d 20f. purple 15 10
503 25f. black 20 10
503a 30f. brown 15 10
504 40f. blue 55 10
504a 45f. orange 10 10
504b 50f. red 35 10
504c 60f. green 60 10
504d 75f. purple 55 35
504e 90f. red 65 35
504f 125f. blue 80 20
504g 145f. orange 90 25
504h 180f. blue . . . . 1·10 45
See also Nos. 1334/45 and 1544/6.

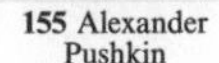

155 Alexander Pushkin 157 "Amphicraspedum murrayanum"

156 Africans and 500f. Coin

1972. Pushkin (writer) Commemoration.
505 **155** 100f. purple and pink . . 1·50 50

1972. 10th Anniv of West African Monetary Union.
506 **156** 40f. brown, grey and blue 60 15

1972. Protozoans and Marine Life. Multicoloured.
507 5f. Type **157** (postage) . . . 10 10
508 10f. "Pterocanium tricolpum" 15 10
509 15f. "Ceratospyris polygona" 75 10
510 20f. "Cortiniscus typicus" . . 20 10
511 30f. "Theopera cortina" . . . 75 10
512 50f. Swordfish (air) . . . . . 1·40 50
513 65f. Killer whale . . . . . . 1·75 65
514 75f. Whale shark . . . . . . 2·50 1·25
515 125f. Fin whale . . . . . . 4·25 1·50
Nos. 512/15 are size 45 × 27 mm.

1972. No. 353 surch **1872-1972** and value.
516 **83** 100f. on 30f. brown, green and chestnut . . . . . . 1·40 60

159 Melchior 160 "Sharing the Load"

1972. Christmas. Nativity Scene and Three Kings. Multicoloured.
517 10f. Type **159** 15 15
518 15f. Gaspard 20 15
519 40f. Balthazar 90 20
520 60f. Joseph . . . . 1·10 40
521 100f. Mary and Baby Jesus (African representation) . . 1·50 65

1973. Europafrique.
522 **160** 65f. black and green . . . 1·00 30

161 Palace of the Republic

1973. Air.
523 **161** 100f. multicoloured . . . 1·10 60

162 Station and Aerial

1973. Inauguration of Satellite Earth Station, Gandoul.
524 **162** 40f. multicoloured 35 20

163 Hotel Teranga

1973. Air. Opening of Hotel Teranga, Dakar.
525 **163** 100f. multicoloured . . . 1·10 60

164 "Lions" African Emblem

1973. Air. 15th Lions International District 403 Congress, Dakar.
526 **164** 150f. multicoloured . . . 1·75 85

165 Stages of Eclipse

1973. Eclipse of the Sun. Multicoloured.
527 35f. Type **165** 55 15
528 65f. Eclipse in diagramatic form 90 25
529 150f. Eclipse and "Skylab 1" 1·90 75

166 Symbolic Torch 169 "Riccione 1973"

168 "Couple with Mimosa" (Chagall)

1973. 10th Anniv of Organization of African Unity.
530 **166** 75f. multicoloured 80 40

1973. "Drought Relief". African Solidarity. No. 451 surch **SECHERESSE SOLIDARITE AFRICAINE** and value.
531 100f. on 25f. multicoloured 1·50 75

1973. Air.
532 **168** 200f. multicoloured . . . 5·00 2·25

1973. Air. Int Stamp Exhibition, Riccione (Italy).
533 **169** 100f. violet, green and red 1·50 55

170 Crane with Letter and Telecommunications Emblem

1973. 12th Anniv of African and Malagasy Posts and Telecommunications Union.
534 **170** 100f. violet, green and red 1·10 35

171 W.H.O. Emblem and Child

1973. Centenary of W.M.O.
535 **171** 50f. multicoloured 35 15

172 Interpol H.Q., Paris 174 Flame Emblem and People

1973. 50th Anniv of International Criminal Police Organization (Interpol).
536 **172** 75f. brown, blue and green . . . . 1·00 40

1973. 25th Anniv of Declaration of Human Rights. Multicoloured.
538 35f. Type **174** 55 15
539 65f. Emblem and drummer 70 25

175 R. Follereau (rehabilitation pioneer) and Map

1973. Air. Cent of Discovery of Leprosy Bacillus.
540 **175** 40f. brown, green & violet 75 15
541 – 100f. purple, red and green . . . . 1·50 50
DESIGN: 100f. Dr. G. Hansen (discoverer of leprosy bacillus) and laboratory equipment.

176 "Key" Emblem 177 Amilcar Cabral and Weapons

1973. Air. World Twinned Towns Congress, Dakar. Multicoloured.
542 50f. Type **176** 75 20
543 125f. Arms of Dakar and meeting of citizens (horiz) 1·50 50

1974. Amilcar Cabral (Guinea Bissau guerilla leader) Commemoration.
544 **177** 75f. multicoloured 90 40

178 Peters's Finfoot

1974. Air. Birds of Djoudj Park. Multicoloured.
545 1f. Type **178** 15 10
546 2f. White spoonbills 15 10
547 3f. Crowned cranes 15 10
548 4f. Little egret 30 10
549 250f. Greater flamingos (gold value) . . . . 6·50 2·25
550 250f. Greater flamingos (black value) . . . . . . 6·50 2·25

179 "Tiger attacking Wild Horse"

1974. Air. Paintings by Delacroix. Multicoloured.
551 150f. Type **179** . . . . 2·25 80
552 200f. "Tiger-hunting" . . . . 2·75 1·25

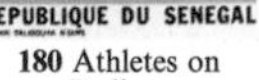

180 Athletes on Podium

182 U.P.U. Emblem, Letters and Transport

181 World Cup, Footballers and "Munich"

1974. National Youth Week. Multicoloured.
553 35f. Type **180** 50 15
554 40f. Dancer with mask . . . 50 20

1974. World Cup Football Championship. Footballers and locations.
555 25f. Type **181** 15 10
556 40f. "Hamburg" 40 15
557 65f. "Hanover" 60 20
558 70f. "Stuttgart" . . . . . . 1·00 25

1974. Centenary of U.P.U.
559 **182** 100f. green, blue and lilac 1·75 75

183 Archway, and Africans at Work

184 Dakar, "Gateway to Africa"

1974. 1st Dakar International Fair.
560 **183** 100f. brown, orange and blue (postage) . . . . 1·00 35
561 **184** 350f. silver (air) . . . . . 4·50
562 1500f. gold . . . . 20·00
Nos. 561/2 are embossed on foil.

1975. West Germany's Victory in World Cup Football Championship, Munich. No. 566 surch **200F ALLEMAGNE RFA–HOLLANDE 2 – 1**.
563 200f. on 40f. multicoloured 2·00 1·25

186 Pres. Senghor and King Baudouin

1975. Visit of King Baudouin of the Belgians.
564 **186** 65f. blue and purple . . . 50 25
565 100f. green and orange . . 1·25 45

187 I.L.O. Emblem

1975. Labour Day.
566 **187** 125f. multicoloured . . . 1·10 45

188 "Apollo" and "Soyuz" Spacecraft

1975. Air. "Apollo"–"Soyuz" Space Co-operation Project.
567 **188** 125f. green, blue and red 1·25 60

189 Spanish "Stamp", Globe and Letters

1975. "Espana 75" (Madrid) and "Arphila 75" (Paris) International Stamp Exhibitions.
568 **189** 55f. red, blue and green 85 30
569 – 95f. light brown and brown . . . . 2·00 70
DESIGN: 95f. Head of Apollo and "Arphila" Emblem.

190 Classroom and Tractor

1975. Technical Education.
570 **190** 85f. brown, blue and black 75 30

191 Dr. Schweitzer

1975. Birth Centenary of Dr. Albert Schweitzer.
571 **191** 85f. lilac and green . . . 90 55

192 Soldier, Flag and Map of Sinai Desert 1973–74

1975. Senegalese Battalion with U.N.
572 **192** 100f. multicoloured . . . 90 40

193 Stamps and Map of Italy

194 Woman pounding Maize

1975. Air. Riccione Stamp Exhibition.
573 **193** 125f. brown, red and lilac 1·25 75

1975. International Women's Year. Multicoloured.
574 55f. Type **194** 65 20
575 75f. Mother and child with woman doctor (horiz) . . . 90 25

1975. Air. "Apollo"–"Soyuz" Space Link. Optd **JONCTION 17 Juil. 1975**.
576 **188** 125f. green, blue and red 1·40 60

196 Stylized Caduceus

1975. French Medical Congress, Dakar.
577 **196** 50f. multicoloured 55 15

197 "Massacre of Boston" (A. Chappel)

1975. Air. Bicentenary of American Revolution. (1st issue).
578 **197** 250f. brown, red and blue 2·75 1·00
579 – 500f. red and blue . . . . 5·50 2·75
DESIGN: 500f. Siege of Yorktown.
See also No. 593.

198 Emblem on Map of Africa

1976. International "Rights of Man" and Namibia Conferences, Dakar.
580 **198** 125f. multicoloured . . . 60 30

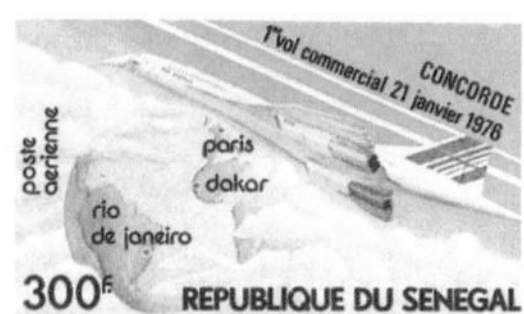

199 Concorde and Flight Locations

1976. Air. Concorde's 1st Commercial Flight.
581 **199** 300f. multicoloured . . . 4·50 2·25
See also No. 641.

200 Deep-sea Fishing

1976. "Expo", Okinawa. Multicoloured.
582 140f. Type **200** . . . . . . 3·25 1·60
583 200f. Yacht-racing . . . . . 2·25 1·25

201 Serval

1976. Basse Casamance National Park. Fauna. Multicoloured.
584 2f. Type **201** 10 10
585 3f. Bar-tailed godwit (marsh bird) 60 10
586 4f. Bush pig 10 10
587 5f. African fish eagle . . . . 1·60 30
588 250f. Sitatunga (males) . . . 3·25 1·50
589 250f. Sitatunga (females) . . 3·25 1·50

202 Alexander Graham Bell

1976. Telephone Centenary.
590 **202** 175f. multicoloured . . . 1·40 85

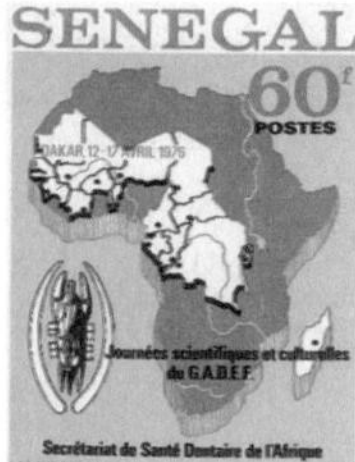

203 Map of Africa

1976. G.A.D.E.F. Scientific and Cultural Days.
591 **203** 60f. multicoloured 35 20

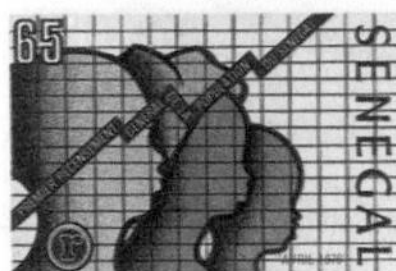

204 Heads on Graphs

1976. 1st Population Census.
592 **204** 65f. multicoloured 65 25

205 Jefferson reading Independence Declaration

1976. Bicentenary of American Revolution (2nd issue).
593 **205** 50f. black, red and blue 65 20

206 Plant Cultivation

1976. Operation "Sahel Vert".
594 **206** 60f. multicoloured 35 20

207 Scouts around Campfire

1976. 1st All African Scouts Jamboree, Jos, Nigeria. Multicoloured.
595 80f. Type **207** 45 35
596 100f. Emblem and map (vert) 90 45

208 Swimming

1976. Olympic Games, Montreal. Multicoloured.
597 5f. Type **208** (postage) . . . 10 10
598 10f. Weightlifting 10 10
599 15f. Hurdling (horiz) . . . 15 10
600 20f. Horse-jumping (horiz) 15 10
601 25f. Steeplechasing (horiz) 15 10
602 50f. Wrestling (horiz) . . . 55 15
603 60f. Hockey 55 20
604 65f. Running 65 20
605 70f. Gymnastics 75 25
606 100f. Cycling (horiz) . . . . 1·10 30

607 400f. Boxing (horiz) (air) . . 3·75 40
607a 500f. Judo . . . . 4·50 1·10
608 1000f. Basketball (41 × 41 mm) . . . . . . 7·25 3·75
608a 1500f. Running (41 × 41 mm) . . . . . . 11·00 5·50

210 Emblem and Map

1976. President Senghor's 70th Birthday. Mult.
610 40f. Type **210** 25 20
611 60f. Star over world map . . 35 25
612 70f. Technicians and symbol 75 30
613 200f. President Senghor and extended hands . . . . . 1·90 75

211 Harvesting Tomatoes

1976. Tomato Production.
614 **211** 180f. multicoloured . . . 2·25 1·25

212 Concorde and Route Plan

1976. Air. Dakar International Fair.
615 **212** 500f. silver . . . . 5·50
616 – 1500f. gold . . . . 20·00

213 Black Peoples' "Charter"   214 Mohammed Ali and Joe Frazier

1977. Black Peoples' Day.
617 **213** 60f. multicoloured 65 25

1977. World Boxing Championship.
618 **214** 60f. black and blue . . . 50 15
619 – 150f. black and green . . 1·75 50
DESIGN—HORIZ: 150f. Mohammed Ali landing punch.

215 Dancer and Musicians

1977. 2nd World Black and African Festival of Arts and Culture, Lagos (Nigeria). Multicoloured.
620 50f. Type **215** 40 20
621 75f. Statuette and masks . . 85 25
622 100f. Statuette and dancers 1·00 45

216 Cog Wheels

1977. 1st Anniv of Dakar Industrial Zone.
623 **216** 70f. brown and green . . 40 20

217 Hauling in Net   218 Burnt Tree in "Flame"

1977. Fishing. Multicoloured.
624 25f. Type **217** (postage) . . .
625 5f. Fishing by trawl-line (air)
626 10f. Harpooning . . . . . .
627 15f. Pirogue breasting wave
628 20f. Displaying prize catch

1977. Fight Against Forest Fires. Multicoloured.
629 40f. Type **218** 55 15
630 60f. Firefighting vehicle (horiz) . . . . 1·00 55

219 Industrial and Pre-Industrial Communication

1977. World Telecommunications Day. Mult.
631 80f. Type **219** 45 35
632 100f. Printed circuit (vert) . . 70 45

220 Arms of Senegal

1977. 10th Anniv of International French Language Council. Multicoloured.
633 65f. Type **220** 35 20
634 250f. As No. 831 of Rwanda 2·00 1·00

221 Woman rowing on River

1977. "Amphilex 1977" International Stamp Exhibition, Amsterdam. Multicoloured.
635 50f. Type **221** 30 25
636 125f. Senegalese woman . . . 1·00 45

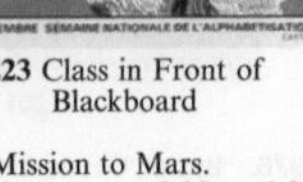
222 "Viking" and Control Centre   223 Class in Front of Blackboard

1977. Air. "Viking" Space Mission to Mars.
637 **222** 300f. multicoloured . . . 2·25 1·25

1977. Literacy Week. Multicoloured.
638 60f. Type **223** 35 25
639 65f. Man with alphabet table 35 25

224 "Mercury and Argus" (Rubens)   226 "Adoration of the Kings"

1977. Paintings. Multicoloured.
640 20f. Type **224** 10 10
641 25f. "Daniel and the Lions" (Rubens) 15 10
642 40f. "The Empress" (Titian) 20 15
643 60f. "Flora" (Titian) 55 20
644 65f. "Jo la belle Irlandaise" (Courbet) 75 20
645 100f. "The Painter's Studio" (Courbet) . . . . 1·40 55

1977. Air. 1st Paris–New York Commercial Flight of Concorde. Optd **22.11.77 PARIS NEW-YORK**.
646 **199** 300f. multicoloured . . . 4·25 2·25

1977. Christmas. Multicoloured.
647 20f. Type **226** 10 10
648 25f. Fanal (celebration) . . . 15 10
649 40f. Family Christmas tree 55 15
650 100f. "Three Wise Men" (horiz) . . . . 1·00 40

227 Wrestler   228 Dakar Cathedral and Parthenon, Athens

1978. Tourism. Multicoloured.
651 10f. Type **227** 10 10
652 30f. Soumbedioun Regatta (canoes) 20 15
653 65f. Soumbedioun Regatta (race) (horiz) 45 25
654 100f. Dancers (horiz) 95 50

1978. UNESCO Campaign for Protection of Monuments.
655 **228** 75f. multicoloured 35 25

229 Solar Pump

1978. Sources of Energy. Multicoloured.
656 50f. Type **229** 25 15
657 95f. Electricity power station 75 30

230 Caspian and Royal Terns

1978. Saloum Delta National Park. Multicoloured.
658 5f. Type **230** 20 15
659 10f. Pink-backed pelicans . . 50 15
660 15f. Grey Heron and warthog 1·00 40
661 20f. Greater flamingoes . . . 1·00 40
662 150f. Grey heron and royal terns . . . . 5·00 1·50
663 150f. Abyssinian ground hornbill and warthog . . . 5·00 1·50

231 Dome of the Rock   232 Mahatma Gandhi

1978. Palestine Freedom-Fighters.
664 **231** 60f. multicoloured 55 20

1978. Apostles of Non-violence. Multicoloured.
665 125f. Type **232** 85 50
666 150f. Martin Luther King . . 1·25 60

233 Jenner and Vaccination of Children

1978. Global Eradication of Smallpox.
668 **233** 60f. multicoloured 55 20

234 Players, and Flags of Group 1 Countries

1978. World Cup Football Championship, Argentina. Multicoloured.
669 25f. Type **234** 15 10
670 40f. Players and flags of Group 2 countries 30 15
671 65f. Players and flags of Group 3 countries 45 20
672 100f. Players and flags of Group 4 countries 85 30

235 Symbols of Technology, Equipment and Industrialization

1978. 3rd International Fair, Dakar.
674 **235** 110f. multicoloured . . . 75 30

236 Wright Brothers and Wright Type A

1978. Conquest of Space. Multicoloured.
675 75f. Type **236** (75th anniv of first powered flight) 65 20
676 100f. Yuri Gagarin (10th death anniv of first cosmonaut) . . . . 1·00 30
677 200f. "Apollo 8" (10th anniv of first manned moon orbit) . . . . 1·60 85

237 Henri Dunant and Children's Ward

1978. 150th Birth Anniv of Henri Dunant (founder of the Red Cross).
679 **237** 5f. blue, black and red . . 10 10
680 – 20f. multicoloured 15 10
DESIGN: 20f. Henri Dunant and scenes of Red Cross aid.

237a Western Capercaillie and Schleswig-Holstein 1850 1s. stamp

1978. Air. "Philexafrique" Stamp Exhibition, Libreville, Gabon and International Stamp Fair, Essen, West Germany. Multicoloured.

681 100f. Type **237a** . . . . . . 2·25 1·60
682 100f. Lion and Senegal 1960 200f. Violet turaco stamp 2·25 1·60

238 Telecommunications

1978. Post Office Achievements. Multicoloured.

683 50f. Type **238** 25 15
684 60f. Social welfare 30 20
685 65f. Travelling post offce . . 55 20

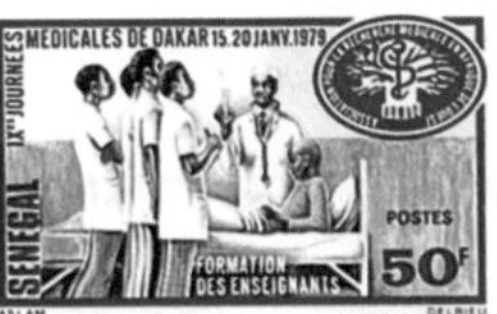

239 Doctor with Students

1979. 9th Medical Days, Dakar. Multicoloured.

686 50f. Type **239** 25 15
687 100f. Problems of pollution 70 45

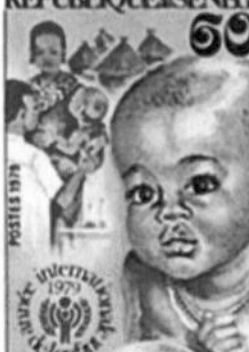

240 Agriculture **242** Young Child

241 Open Air Class

1979. Professional Pride. Multicoloured.

688 30f. Type **240** 15 10
689 150f. Symbols of progress . . 1·00 45

1979. S.O.S. Children's Village. Multicoloured.

690 40f. Type **241** 20 15
691 60f. View of village 30 20

1979. International Year of the Child. Mult.

692 60f. Type **242** 30 20
693 65f. Children with book . . . 30 20

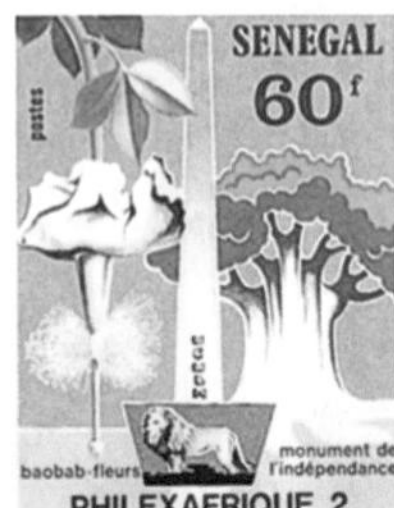

243 Baobab Flower and Tree and Independence Monument

1979. "Philexafrique" Stamp Exhibition, Libreville, Gabon. Multicoloured.

694 60f. Type **243** . . . . 1·25 90
695 150f. Drum, early telegraph apparatus and dish aerial (square, 36 × 36 mm) . . . 2·50 1·60

244 Children ushered into Open Book

1979. 50th Anniv of International Bureau of Education.

696 **244** 250f. multicoloured . . . 1·40 80

245 Hill and Senegal 100f. Stamp of 1960

1979. Death Centenary of Sir Rowland Hill.

697 **245** 500f. multicoloured . . . 4·75 2·75

246 "Black Trees" **247** Start of Race

1979. Paintings by Friedensreich Hundertwasser. Multicoloured.

698 60f. Type **246** . . . . 1·10 65
699 100f. "Head" . . . . 2·25 1·00
700 200f. "Rainbow Windows" 3·25 1·60

1980. 1st African Athletic Championships. Mult.

702 20f. Type **247** 15 10
703 25f. Javelin 15 10
704 50f. Passing the relay baton 25 10
705 100f. Discus 75 30

248 Musicians

1980. Mudra African Arts Festival.

706 50f. Type **248** 40 15
707 100f. Dancers 85 25
708 200f. Dancers and drummer 1·50 70

249 Lions Emblem

1980. 22nd Congress of Lions' Club District 403, Dakar.

709 **249** 100f. multicoloured . . . 75 25

250 Chimpanzees

1980. Niokolo-Koba National Park. Multicoloured.

710 40f. Type **250** 25 10
711 60f. African elephants 45 20
712 65f. Giant elands 75 20
713 100f. Spotted hyenas . . . . 1·00 30
714 200f. Wildlife on the savannah . . . . 3·00 70
715 200f. Simenti Hotel . . . . . 3·00 70

Nos. 714/15 were issued together, se-tenant, forming a composite deisgn.

251 Watering Sapling

1980. Tree Planting Year.

717 **251** 60f. multicoloured 75 25
718 65f. multicoloured 95 30

252 Women with Bowls of Rice Flour and Electric Mill **253** Wrestling

1980. Rural Women. Multicoloured.

719 50f. Street market (horiz) . . 25 15
720 100f. Type **252** 90 30
721 200f. Drawing water (horiz) 1·50 70

1980. Olympic Games, Moscow. Multicoloured.

722 60f. Type **253** 30 20
723 65f. Running 30 20
724 70f. Games emblems 35 25
725 100f. Judo 45 30
726 200f. Basketball . . . . . . 1·25 70

254 Dabry, Gimie, Mermoz and Seaplane "Comte de la Vaulx"

1980. Air. 50th Anniv of First South Atlantic Airmail Flight.

728 **254** 300f. multicoloured . . . 2·50 1·00

255 Caspian Tern, Eastern White Pelicans and Grey-headed Gulls (Pointe Kalissaye Bird Sanctuary)

1981. National Parks. Multicoloured.

729 50f. Type **255** . . . . 2·25 50
730 70f. Slender-billed gulls and gull-billed tern (Langue de Barbarie) . . . . 2·25 75
731 85f. Turtle and crab (Madeline Islands) 50 25
732 150f. White-breasted cormorant and red-billed tropic bird (Madeline Islands) . . . . 4·75 1·60

256 Healthy Activities **257** Fair Visitors beneath Tree

1981. Anti-smoking Campaign. Multicoloured.

734 75f. Type **256** 30 30
735 80f. Cancerous mouth with pipe 35 35

1981. 4th International Fair, Dakar.

736 **257** 80f. multicoloured 35 35

258 Lat Dior Damel Teigne **259** "Nymphaea lotus"

1982. National Heroes. Lat Dior. Multicoloured.

737 80f. Type **258** 35 25
738 500f. Lat Dior on horseback 3·25 1·25

1982. Flowers. Multicoloured.

739 50f. Type **259** 50 20
740 75f. "Strophanthus sarmentosus" 75 30
741 200f. "Crinum moorei" . . . 1·75 75
742 225f. "Cochlospermum tinctorium" . . . . 2·00 1·00

260 "Euryphrene senegalensis" (male and female)

1982. Butterflies. Multicoloured.

743 45f. Type **260** 60 35
744 55f. "Hypolimnas salmacis, Precis octavia" and "Salamis cytora" 75 45
745 75f. "Cymothoe caenis" and "Cyrestis camillus" 90 55
746 80f. "Precis cebrene, Junonia terea" and "Salamis parhassus" . . . . 1·10 70

261 "Rhaguva albipunctella" **263** Black-tailed Godwit

262 Flags and Three-dimensional Map of Senegambia

1982. Harmful Insects. Multicoloured.

748 75f. Type **261** 75 45
749 80f. "Amsacta moloneyi, Tolyposporium penicillariae" and "Sclerospore graminicola" (horiz) . . . . 1·50 45
750 100f. "Amsacta moloneyi" 1·10 60

1982. Senegambia Confederation. Multicoloured.

751 225f. Type **262** . . . . 1·60 60
752 350f. Arms of Senegal and Gambia . . . . 2·25 90

1982. Birds. Multicoloured.

753 45f. Type **263** 45 30
754 75f. Saddle-bill stork 95 40
755 80f. Double-spurred francolin 1·10 45
756 500f. Tawny eagle . . . . . 5·75 3·25

264 Footballer and Emblem **265** Flag "Stamp" and Ribbon

1982. World Cup Football Championship, Spain. Multicoloured.
757 30f. Type **264** 15 15
758 50f. Footballer 20 20
759 75f. Football 55 30
760 80f. World Cup and emblem 60 35

1982. "Philexfrance 82" International Stamp Exhibition, Paris. Multicoloured.
762 100f. Type **265** 40 25
763 500f. Arms "stamp" between circling arrows . . . . . . 3·25 1·50

266 Exhibition Poster

1983. Stamp Exhibition, Dakar. Multicoloured.
764 60f. Type **266** 25 20
765 70f. Butterfly stamps 65 20
766 90f. Stamps and magnifying glass 75 25
767 95f. Exhibition hall and Dakar arms on stamp . . 75 30

267 Light Bulb **268** Torch on Map of Africa

1983. Energy Conservation. Multicoloured.
768 90f. Type **267** 90 30
769 95f. Cars queueing for petrol 1·00 30
770 260f. Woman cooking . . . 1·60 85

1983. "For Namibian Independence". Mult.
771 90f. Type **268** 55 30
772 95f. Clenched fist and broken chain on map of Africa . . 60 30
773 260f. Woman with torch on map of Africa . . . . . . 2·25 85

269 Agency Building, Ziguinchor **270** Dakar Rotary Banner

1983. 20th Anniv of West African Monetary Union. Multicoloured.
774 60f. Type **269** 25 20
775 65f. Headquarters building, Dakar (vert) 25 25

1983. 1st Anniv of Dakar Alizes Rotary Club.
776 **270** 70f. multicoloured 50 25
777 500f. multicoloured . . . 3·50 1·75

271 Customs Council Headquarters **272** Anniversary Emblem

1983. 30th Anniv of Customs Co-operation Council.
778 **271** 90f. multicoloured 30 30
779 300f. multicoloured . . . 2·25 1·00

1984. 25th Anniv of Economic Commission for Africa.
780 **272** 90f. multicoloured 60 30
781 95f. multicoloured 60 30

273 Village

1984. S.O.S. Children's Village. Multicoloured.
782 90f. Type **273** 55 30
783 95f. Foster-mother and child (vert) 65 30
784 115f. Foster-family 80 40
785 260f. House (vert) . . . . . 2·00 85

274 Scout Salute **275** Javelin-throwing

1984. 75th Anniv of Boy Scout Movement. Mult.
786 60f. Type **274** 45 15
787 70f. Scout badge 55 20
788 90f. Scouts of different nations 60 30
789 95f. Lord Baden-Powell (founder) 65 35

1984. Olympic Games, Los Angeles. Multicoloured.
790 90f. Type **275** 35 30
791 95f. Hurdling 65 35
792 165f. Football . . . . 1·10 70

276 Basket of Food, Fishing and Farming

1984. World Food Day. Multicoloured. Inscr "16 OCTOBRE 1983".
794 65f. Type **276** 25 20
795 70f. Woman cooking and child (vert) 60 20
796 225f. Group and food . . . 1·90 1·25

1984. Drought Aid. No. 785 optd **Aide au Sahel 84**.
797 260f. multicoloured . . . . . 2·00 1·25

278 William Ponty School

1984. World Heritage. Goree Island.
798 **278** 90f. multicoloured 75 30
799 – 95f. black and blue 90 35
800 – 250f. multicoloured . . . 2·25 85
801 – 500f. multicoloured . . . 4·50 2·25
DESIGN—HORIZ: 95f. Map of Goree; 500f. Slaves' House. VERT: 250f. Goree Historical Museum.

279 Pump and Sprinkler **280** Globe, Envelopes and Map

1985. Irrigation Project. Multicoloured.
810 40f. Type **279** 45 15
811 50f. Tap and dam 55 15
812 90f. Storage tanks and cattle 1·00 55
813 250f. Women at water pump 2·40 1·10

1985. World Communication Year (1984).
814 **280** 90f. multicoloured 55 25
815 – 95f. blue, green and brown 60 30
816 – 350f. multicoloured . . . 2·75 1·50
DESIGNS: 95f. Maps of Africa and Senegal and aerial; 350f. Globe, dove and map of Senegal.

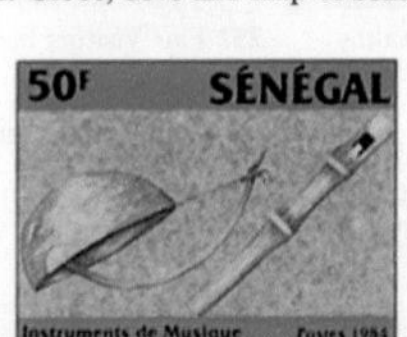

281 Stringed Instrument and Flute

1985. Musical Instruments. Multicoloured.
817 50f. Type **281** 65 15
818 85f. Drums and stringed instrument . . . . 1·00 25
819 125f. Musician, stringed instruments, xylophone and drums . . . . 1·50 40
820 250f. Stringed instruments . . 2·50 1·10

282 Seaplane "Comte de la Vaulx" and Map

1985. Air. 55th Anniv of 1st Airmail Flight across South Atlantic.
821 **282** 250f. multicoloured . . . 2·50 1·10

283 People and Broken Chain

1985. "Philexafrique" Int Stamp Exn, Lome, Togo. "Youth and Development". Multicoloured.
822 100f. Type **283** (political and civic education) 45 40
823 125f. Carpenter and draughtsman (professional education) 75 45
824 150f. Couple looking at planets (general education) 90 60
825 175f. Farm workers (food self-sufficiency) . . . . . . 1·40 80

284 Laboratory and Farm Workers

1985. International Youth Year. Multicoloured.
826 40f. Type **284** 20 15
827 50f. Young people, forms of communication and globe 20 15
828 90f. Youth building "Peace" monument 65 35
829 125f. Youth, football and globe 90 45

285 Man, Woman and Boy

1985. National Costumes. Multicoloured.
830 40f. Type **285** 20 15
831 95f. Man in straw hat and striped gown (vert) 65 35
832 100f. Seated gown (vert) . . 75 40
833 150f. Man and woman (vert) 1·25 60

286 Men bringing Boat Ashore

1986. Fishing at Kayar. Multicoloured.
834 40f. Type **286** 20 15
835 50f. Women waiting on shore 20 15
836 100f. Man with large fish (vert) . . . . 1·00 55
837 125f. Sorting the catch (vert) 1·50 65
838 150f. View of beach . . . . 1·75 90

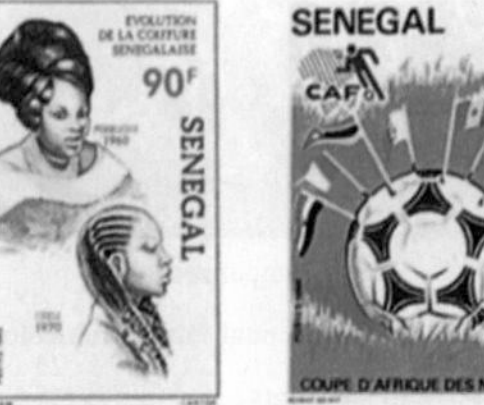

287 Perruque and Ceeli **288** Flags and Football

1986. Hairstyles. Multicoloured.
839 90f. Type **287** 40 30
840 125f. Ndungu, Kearly and Rasta 75 40
841 250f. Jamono, Kura and Kooraa . . . . 1·50 60
842 300f. Mbaram and Jeere . . 2·00 70

1986. African Football Cup, Cairo. Multicoloured.
843 115f. Type **288** 70 35
844 125f. Footballer and map . . 75 45
845 135f. Lion rampant with torch ascending pyramid (horiz) . . . . 1·10 50
846 165f. Lions rampant beneath flag (horiz) . . . . 1·25 65

1986. 5th Convention of District 403 of Lions Int. No. 818 surch **Ve CONVENTION MULTI-DISTRICT 8-10 MAI 1988.**
847 165f. on 85f. Drums and stringed instrument . . . . 1·00 65

290 Doe and Calf

1986. Ndama Gazelle. Multicoloured.
848 15f. Type **290** 10 10
849 45f. Group of gazelle resting 75 15
850 85f. Gazelle among dead trees 1·25 30
851 125f. Gazelle running . . . . 1·75 90

291 Immunizing Child **294** Ostriches

292 Trophy, Footballers and Terracotta Offertory Vessel

1986. UNICEF Child Survival Campaign. Multicoloured.
852 50f. Type **291** 20 15
853 85f. Child drinking from bowl 40 35

1986. World Cup Football Championship, Mexico. Multicoloured. (a) As T **292**.
854 125f. Type **292** 75 45
855 135f. Trophy, footballers and stucco Maya head from Palenque 80 50
856 165f. Gold breastplate, footballers and trophy . . 1·00 65
857 340f. Teotihuacan porcelain mask, footballers and trophy . . . . 2·00 90

(b) Nos. 854/7 optd **ARGENTINA 3 R.F.A. 2.**
858 125f. Type **292** 75 45
859 135f. Trophy, footballers and stucco Maya head from Palenque 80 50
860 165f. Gold breastplate, footballers and trophy . . 1·00 65
861 340f. Teotihuacan porcelain mask, footballers and trophy . . . . 2·00 90

1986. Guembeul Nature Reserve. Multicoloured.
862 50f. Type **294** . . . . 1·25 35
863 65f. Gazelles 55 20
864 85f. Giraffes 60 30
865 100f. Ostrich, buffalo, gazelle and giraffe . . . . 2·00 75
866 150f. Buffalo . . . . 1·40 60

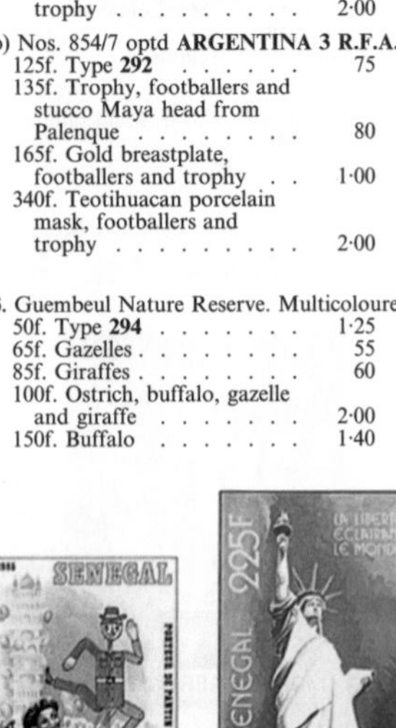
295 Man with Puppet (Xuusmaanapaa)

296 Statue of Liberty

1986. Christmas. Customs. Multicoloured.
867 70f. Type **295** 25 20
868 85f. Setting up fanal (Fente) (horiz) 65 25
869 150f. Decorating fanal (Jebele) 90 55
870 250f. Boy praying before candle and Nativity scene (horiz) 1·50 75

1986. Centenary of Statue of Liberty.
871 **296** 225f. multicoloured 1·50 80

297 Jellyfish and Coral

1987. Marine Fauna. Multicoloured.
872 50f. Type **297** 30 15
873 85f. Sea urchin and starfish 75 25
874 100f. Norway lobster 1·10 35
875 150f. Common dolphin 1·50 55
876 200f. Octopus 2·25 1·10

298 Motor Cyclist and Lorry

299 Hands over Antelope

1987. Paris–Dakar Rally. Multicoloured.
877 115f. Type **298** 1·10 40
878 125f. Thierry Sabine, helicopter, motor cyclist, lorry and car (horiz) 1·50 60
879 135f. Sabine and motor car (horiz) 1·50 45
880 340f. Eiffel Tower, car and huts 2·75 1·10

1987. Endangered Fauna in Ferlo National Park. Multicoloured.
881 55f. Type **299** 20 15
882 70f. Ostriches 1·25 35
883 85f. Warthog 75 25
884 90f. Elephant 75 30

300 Spacecraft above Earth

1987. 10th Anniv of "Gemini 8"–Agena Flight.
885 **300** 320f. multicoloured 2·25 1·40

301 International Express Mail Emblem

1987. Centenary of First Senegal Stamp. Mult.
887 100f. Type **301** 65 35
888 130f. 1892 4c. Senegal and Dependencies stamp 75 45
889 140f. 1961 Senegal independence stamp 80 50
890 145f. 1935 30c. and 1f.25 Senegal stamps 85 50
891 320f. Senegal 1887 15c. on 20c. stamp and cancellation 2·25 1·10

302 Hand gripping Bloodied Claw above Map of South Africa

1987. Anti-Apartheid Campaign. Multicoloured.
892 130f. Type **302** 80 45
893 140f. Broken and bloodied chain in fist (vert) 85 50
894 145f. Skeleton with scythe, dove and globe 85 50

303 Emblem

1987. 20th Anniv of Intelsat. Multicoloured.
895 50f. Type **303** 20 15
896 125f. Satellite and emblem 75 45
897 150f. Emblem and globe 90 55
898 200f. Globe and satellite 1·25 75

304 Emblem and Crowd

305 Yacht and Sun

1987. West African Cities Organization. Mult.
899 40f. Type **304** 15 15
900 125f. Emblem and clasped hands 75 45

1987. 45th Anniv of Dakar Rotary Club.
901 **305** 500f. multicoloured 4·00 1·50

306 U.N. Building, New York

307 Fr. Daniel Brottier (founder) and Angel

1987. 40th Anniv (1985) of U.N.O. Multicoloured.
902 85f. Type **306** 60 25
903 95f. Emblem 65 35
904 150f. Hands of different races and emblem 90 55

1987. 50th Anniv of Cathedral of African Remembrance. Multicoloured.
905 130f. Type **307** 85 45
906 140f. Cathedral in 1936 and 1986 85 50

308 Hand pouring Grain into Globe

1987. World Food Day. Multicoloured.
907 130f. Type **308** 80 45
908 140f. Ear of wheat and F.A.O. emblem rising as sun (horiz) 1·10 50
909 145f. Emblem 1·25 50

309 Servals

1987. Basse Casamance National Park. Mult.
910 115f. Type **309** 1·00 40
911 135f. Demidoff's galagos 1·40 45
912 150f. Bush pig 1·50 55
913 250f. Leopards 2·75 1·25
914 300f. Little egrets 11·00 3·50
915 300f. Carmine bee eaters 11·00 3·50

310 Wrestlers

1987. Senegalese Wrestling. Multicoloured.
916 115f. Type **310** 80 40
917 125f. Wrestlers and musicians 80 45
918 135f. Wrestlers (vert) 1·00 45
919 165f. Referee, wrestlers and crowd (vert) 1·25 55

311 African Open-bill Stork

312 Boy dreaming of Father Christmas's Visit

1987. Djoudj National Park. Multicoloured.
920 115f. Type **311** 1·75 85
921 125f. Greater flamingos (horiz) 1·75 1·25
922 135f. Pink-backed pelican and greater flamingos (horiz) 2·60 1·25
923 300f. Pink-backed pelicans 4·75 2·00
924 350f. As No. 921 5·00 2·50
925 350f. As No. 922 5·00 2·50

1987. Christmas. Multicoloured.
926 145f. Type **312** 85 50
927 150f. Star behind Virgin gazing at Child 90 55
928 180f. Nativity scene above people praying in church 1·25 65
929 200f. Nativity scene in candle glow 1·25 75

313 Battle of Dekhele

1988. Death Centenary of Lat-Dior. Multicoloured.
930 130f. Type **313** 1·00 45
931 160f. Lat-Dior on his horse "Maalaw" 1·00 60

314 10th Anniv Emblem and Map

1988. Dakar International Fair.
932 **314** 125f. multicoloured 75 45

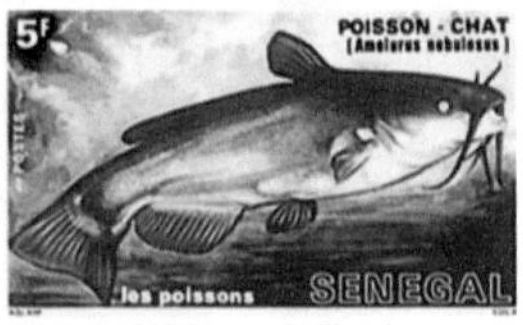

315 Brown Bullhead

1988. Fishes. Multicoloured.
933 5f. Type **315** 10 10
934 100f. Pennant coralfish 50 45
935 145f. Common barberfish 1·10 70
936 180f. Common carp 1·90 1·25

316 W.M.O. Emblem and Means of Conveying Information

1988. World Meteorology Day.
937 **316** 145f. multicoloured 90 30

317 Motor Cyclist

1988. 10th Anniv of Paris–Dakar Rally. Mult.
938 145f. Type **317** 1·25 50
939 180f. Rally car and emblem 1·50 65
940 200f. Rally cars and man 1·75 70
941 410f. Thierry Sabine and motor cyclist 3·50 1·90

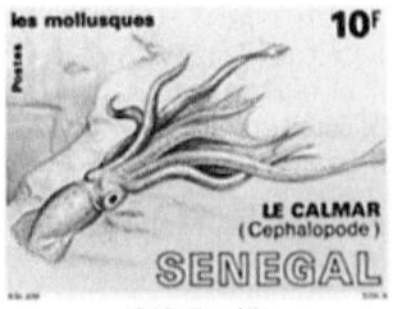

318 Squid

1988. Molluscs. Multicoloured.
942 10f. Type **318** 15 10
943 20f. Truncate donax (bivalve) 15 10
944 145f. Giant East African snail 1·40 65
945 165f. Banded snail 1·75 75

319 Football, Cup and Map

1988. Africa Cup Football Championship, Rabat. Multicoloured.
946 80f. Type **319** 55 25
947 100f. Player's leg and ball (vert) 75 35
948 145f. Match scene and map of Africa (vert) 90 50
949 180f. Emblem and cup (vert) 1·25 65

320 Corps Member and Children

321 "Dictyota atomaria"

1988. 25th Anniv of American Peace Corps in Senegal.
950 **320** 190f. multicoloured 1·25 65

1988. Marine Flora. Multicoloured.
951 10f. Type **321** 10 10
952 65f. "Agarum gmelini" 75 20
953 145f. "Saccorrhiza bulbosa" 1·10 55
954 180f. "Rhodymenia palmetta" 1·75 65

1988. Riccione Stamp Fair. No. 891 optd **RICCIONE 88 27-29-08-89.**
955 320f. multicoloured 2·25 1·25

323 Hodori (mascot) and Stadium

325 Thies Phosphate Mine

324 Thierno Saidou Nourou Tall Centre

1988. Olympic Games, Seoul. Multicoloured.

956 5f. Type **323** 10 10
957 75f. Athletics, swimming and football 55 25
958 300f. Hodori, flame and sports pictograms . . . . 2·10 1·00
959 410f. Emblem and athletics pictogram . . . . 2·75 1·40

1988.

960 **324** 125f. multicoloured . . . 70 60

1988. Senegal Industries. Multicoloured.

961 5f. Type **325** . . . . 1·00 50
962 20f. Chemical industry . . . 10 10
963 145f. Diourbel factory . . . 85 50
964 410f. Mbao refinery . . . . 3·00 1·75

326 Children and Government Palace

1988. Postcards of 1900. Multicoloured.

965 20f. Type **326** 10 10
966 145f. Wrestlers and St. Louis Grand Mosque . . . . . 1·10 50
967 180f. Old Dakar railway station and young woman 2·25 1·25
968 200f. Goree Governor's residence and young woman . . . . 1·60 70

327 "Packia biglobosa" **328** Mask, Rally Car and Eiffel Tower

1988. Flowers. Multicoloured.

969 20f. Type **327** 10 10
970 60f. "Euphorbia pulcherrima" 20 15
971 65f. "Cyrtosperma senegalense" 25 20
972 410f. "Bombax costatum" . . 3·00 1·40

1989. 11th Paris–Dakar Rally. Multicoloured.

973 10f. Type **328** 10 10
974 145f. Crash helmet and sand dunes . . . . 1·25 55
975 180f. Turban and motor cyclist . . . . 1·50 70
976 220f. Motor cyclist and Thierry Sabine . . . . . . 2·00 85

329 Teranga Hotel **330** Senegal Tourism Emblem

1989. Tourism (1st series). Multicoloured.

977 10f. Type **329** 10 10
978 80f. Thatched hut and shades on beach 55 25
979 100f. Saly hotel 65 35
980 350f. Dior hotel . . . . . . 2·50 1·25

1989. Tourism (2nd series). Multicoloured.

981 130f. Type **330** 75 45
982 140f. Rural tourism (horiz) 85 50
983 145f. Fishing (horiz) . . . . 1·40 70
984 180f. Water sports (horiz) . . 1·25 70

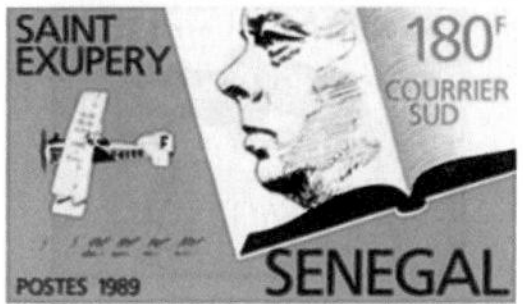

331 Saint-Exupery and Scene from "Courrier Sud"

1989. 45th Anniv of Disappearance of Antoine de Saint-Exupery (pilot and writer).

985 **331** 180f. black, orange and grey . . . . 1·40 50
986 – 220f. black, blue and grey 1·75 75
987 – 410f. multicoloured . . . 3·50 1·25

DESIGNS: 220f. Scene from "Vol de Nuit"; 410f. Scene from "Pilote de Guerre".

332 Presentation of Lists of Grievances by People of St. Louis

1989. Bicentenary of French Revolution. Mult.

988 180f. Type **332** . . . . . . 1·25 1·00
989 220f. Declaration of Rights of Man, quill pen in hand and phrygian cap (vert) . . . . 1·25 1·10
990 300f. Revolutionaries and flag 2·75 1·50

333 Arts and Culture **335** Stamps

1989. 3rd Francophone Summit. Multicoloured.

991 5f. Type **333** 10 10
992 30f. Education (horiz) 15 10
993 100f. Communication (horiz) 65 35
994 200f. Development (horiz) . . 1·25 75

1989. No. 960 surch.

995 555f. on 125f. multicoloured 3·50 1·25

1989. "Philexfrance 89" International Stamp Exhibition, Paris. Multicoloured.

996 10f. Type **335** 10 10
997 25f. Stamp on map of France (vert) 10 10
998 75f. Couple viewing stamp on easel (vert) 55 25
999 145f. Sticking stamp on envelope (vert) . . . . . . 1·10 55

336 "30" Dish Aerial and Envelope **337** Record Stacks and 1922 Postcard

1989. 30th Anniv Meeting of West African Post and Telecommunications Administrations Conference, Dakar. Multicoloured.

1000 25f. Type **336** 10 10
1001 30f. Telephone handset, punched tape and map on stamp 15 10
1002 180f. Map of Africa, stamp and telephone earpiece . . 1·40 70
1003 220f. Stamp, satellite, globe and map of Africa . . . 1·50 85

1989. 75th Anniv (1988) of Senegal Archives. Mult.

1004 15f. Type **337** 10 10
1005 40f. 1825 document 15 10
1006 145f. 1825 document and archive building . . . . . 1·10 55
1007 180f. Bound volume . . . . . 1·25 70

338 Jar with Lid **339** Nehru

1989. Pottery. Multicoloured.

1008 15f. Type **338** 10 10
1009 30f. Potter at work 15 10
1010 75f. Stacked pots 65 25
1011 145f. Woman carrying pots 1·25 55

1989. Birth Centenary of Jawaharlal Nehru (Indian statesman).

1012 **339** 220f. multicoloured . . . 1·25 85
1013 – 410f. black, red & yellow 2·75 1·40

DESIGN—HORIZ: 410f. Nehru (different).

340 Swimming Crab

1989. Marine Life. Multicoloured.

1014 10f. Type **340** 10 10
1015 60f. Long-snouted seahorse (vert) 60 25
1016 145f. Barnacles . . . . . . 1·25 55
1017 220f. Sand-hopper . . . . . 1·50 85

341 Clasped Hand and People of Different Races **342** Pilgrims

1989. World AIDS Day. Multicoloured.

1018 5f. Type **341** 10 10
1019 100f. People under umbrella 40 35
1020 145f. Fist smashing AIDS virus 85 55
1021 180f. Hammer smashing AIDS virus . . . . 1·10 70

1989. Centenary of Pilgrimage to Our Lady of Popenguine. Multicoloured.

1022 145f. Type **342** 90 55
1023 180f. Our Lady of Popenguine Church . . . 1·40 70

343 White-breasted Cormorant and African Darter, Djoudj

1989. National Parks. Multicoloured.

1024 10f. Type **343** 25 15
1025 45f. Grey-headed gulls, Langue de Barbarie . . . 90 35
1026 100f. Blue-checked bee eater and long-crested eagle, Basse Casamance . . . . 1·50 85
1027 180f. Western reef herons, Saloum . . . . 4·25 1·75

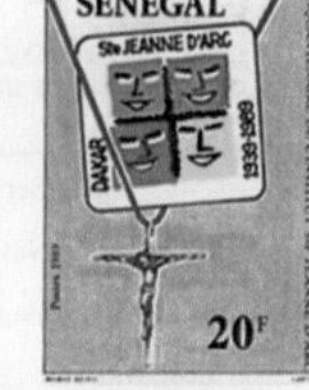

344 Boy looking at Christmas Tree **345** Crucifix and Anniversary Emblem

1989. Christmas. Multicoloured.

1028 10f. Type **344** 10 10
1029 25f. Teddy bear and bauble hanging from tree 10 10
1030 30f. Animals around Baby Jesus 15 10
1031 200f. Madonna and Child 1·25 75

1989. 50th Anniv of St. Joan of Arc Institute, Dakar. Multicoloured.

1032 20f. Type **345** 10 10
1033 500f. Emblem and Institute building . . . . 3·50 1·40

346 "Hydravion"

1989. 79th Anniv of First Flight of Henri Fabre's Seaplane. Multicoloured.

1034 125f. Type **346** 75 55
1035 130f. Fabre working on engine of "Hydravion" . . 1·10 55
1036 475f. Technical drawings and Fabre (vert) . . . . 3·50 1·00

347 Basketball

1990. Olympic Games, Barcelona (1992). Mult.

1038 10f. Type **347** 10 10
1039 130f. High jumping 50 20
1040 180f. Throwing the discus 1·00 35
1041 190f. Running . . . . 1·10 45
1042 315f. Lawn tennis . . . . . 2·00 55
1043 475f. Show jumping . . . . 2·75 65

348 Rally Car

1990. 12th Paris–Dakar Rally. Multicoloured.

1045 20f. Type **348** 10 10
1046 25f. Motor cycle and sidecar 10 10
1047 180f. Crowd cheering winning driver . . . . . 1·40 70
1048 200f. Thierry Sabine and car 1·40 75

349 Piazza della Signoria, Florence, and Footballer

1990. World Cup Football Championship, Italy. Multicoloured.

1049 45f. Type **349** 20 15
1050 140f. Piazza Navona, Rome 1·00 25
1051 180f. "Virgin with St. Anne and Infant Jesus" (Leonardo da Vinci) . . . 1·25 30
1052 220f. "Giuseppe Garibaldi" (oil painting) . . . . . . 1·40 55
1053 300f. "Sistine Madonna" (Raphael) . . . . 2·00 75
1054 415f. "Virgin and Child" (Danielle da Volterra) . . 2·75 1·10

350 Footballer **351** Facsimile Telegraphy

1990. African Nations Cup Football Championship, Algeria. Multicoloured.

1056 20f. Type **350** 10 10
1057 60f. Goalkeeper 25 20
1058 100f. Clasped hands and pennants 75 35
1059 500f. Trophy . . . . 3·50 1·75

1990. Postal Services. Multicoloured.

1060 5f. Type **351** 10 10
1061 15f. Express mail service . . 10 10
1062 100f. Postal cheques 65 35
1063 180f. Savings . . . . 1·25 40

352 Hands and Umbrella protecting Children **353** Envelopes on Map

1990. Louga S.O.S. Children's Village. Mult.

1064 5f. Type **352** 10 10
1065 500f. Children under umbrella . . . . 3·25 1·25

1990. 20th Anniv of Multinational Postal Training School, Abidjan. Multicoloured.

1066 145f. Type **353** . . . . . . 1·00 55
1067 180f. Man carrying wreath containing envelope . . . 1·25 70

354 Excursion by Pirogue, Basse-Casamance

1990. Tourism. Multicoloured.

1068 10f. Type **354** 10 10
1069 25f. Hotel and beach, Goree 10 10
1070 30f. Houses on stilts, Fadiouth 15 10
1071 40f. Rose Lake and salt drying 15 10

355 Camp

1990. Scouting. Multicoloured.

1072 30f. Type **355** 15 10
1073 100f. Scouts trekking alongside lake 75 35
1074 145f. Scouts trekking through hilly landscape 1·00 55
1075 200f. Scout and emblem (vert) . . . . 1·25 75

356 "Cassia tora" **357** Angels and Tree

1990. Medicinal Plants. Multicoloured.

1076 95f. Type **356** 65 35
1077 105f. "Tamarind" 75 40
1078 125f. "Cassia occidentalis" 90 45
1079 175f. "Leptadenia hastata" 1·25 65

1990. Christmas.

1080 **357** 25f. multicoloured . . . 10 10
1081 – 145f. multicoloured . . . 1·00 55
1082 – 180f. orange, red & black . . . . 1·25 70
1083 – 200f. multicoloured . . . 1·40 75

DESIGNS: 145f. Angel trumpeting stars; 180f. Adoration of Three Kings; 200f. Donkey and cow gazing at Child.

358 Anniversary Emblem

1991. 125th Anniv (1988) of International Red Cross and 25th Anniv of Senegal Red Cross.

1084 **358** 180f. multicoloured . . . 1·25 45

359 Rally Car

1991. 13th Paris–Dakar Rally. Multicoloured.

1085 15f. Type **359** 10 10
1086 15f. Car and motor cycle at night 75 35
1087 180f. Rally car (different) . . 1·25 75
1088 220f. Motor cycles . . . . 1·60 90

360 African Python

1991. Reptiles. Multicoloured.

1089 15f. Type **360** 10 10
1090 60f. Common green turtle 65 15
1091 100f. Nile crocodile . . . . 1·10 25
1092 180f. Senegal chameleon . . 1·75 90

361 Sphinx, House of Slaves, Frescoes, Kirdi Houses and Mohammed's Tomb **362** Nobel

1991. "Fespaco". 12th Pan-African Cinema and Television Festival. Multicoloured.

1093 30f. Type **361** 10 10
1094 60f. Dogon mask, B. Dioulasso Mosque, drawing of Osiris, and camel rider 25 15
1095 100f. Rabat, "Seated Scribe" (Egyptian statue), drum and camels 75 25
1096 180f. Pyramids of Egypt, Djenne Mosque, Guinean mask, Moroccan architecture and Moorish door decorations . . . . 1·25 75

1991. 95th Death Anniv of Alfred Nobel (founder of Nobel prizes). Multicoloured. Self-adhesive.

1097 145f. Type **362** . . . . . . 1·00 75
1098 180f. Nobel and prize presentation (horiz) . . . 1·25 90

363 Oribi

1991. National Parks. Multicoloured.

1099 5f. Type **363** 10 10
1100 10f. Dorcas gazelle 10 10
1101 180f. Kob . . . . 1·25 45
1102 555f. Hartebeest . . . . . 4·50 2·25

364 Cashew

1991. Trees and their Fruit. Multicoloured.

1103 90f. Type **364** 65 25
1104 100f. Mango 75 25
1105 125f. Sugar-palm (vert) . . 90 35
1106 145f. Oil palm (vert) . . . . 1·00 45

365 Ader, Motor Car and Telephone

1991. Air. Centenary (1990) of First Heavier than Air Powered Flight. Multicoloured.

1107 145f. Type **365** . . . . . . 1·10 40
1108 180f. Clement Ader and his monoplane "Eole" . . . 1·25 55
1109 615f. "Eole" and Ader (vert) 4·25 2·00

366 Columbus and Haitians

1991. 500th Anniv (1992) of Discovery of America by Columbus. Multicoloured.

1111 100f. Type **366** 65 25
1112 145f. Arms of Castile and Leon (vert) 90 40
1113 180f. "Santa Maria" and Columbus . . . . 1·10 45
1114 200f. Vicente Yanez Pinzon and "Nina" . . . . . . 1·25 55
1115 220f. Martin Alonzo Pinzon and "Pinta" . . . . . . 1·40 60
1116 500f. Details of charts . . . 3·25 1·25
1117 625f. Compass rose and Columbus with charts . . 4·00 1·75

367 Armstrong

1991. 20th Death Anniv of Louis Armstrong (musician). Multicoloured.

1118 10f. Type **367** 10 10
1119 145f. Armstrong singing . . 90 40
1120 180f. Armstrong and trumpets . . . . 1·40 45
1121 220f. Armstrong playing trumpet . . . . 2·00 90

368 Yuri Gagarin and "Vostok 1"

1991. 30th Anniv of First Man in Space. Mult.

1125 15f. Type **368** 10 10
1126 145f. "Vostok 1" and Gagarin in spacesuit . . . 90 40
1127 180f. Gagarin in spacesuit and "Vostok 1" (different) 1·25 45
1128 220f. Globe, "Vostok 1" and Gagarin in flying kit 1·50 90

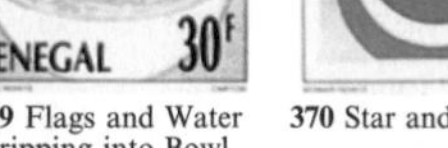

369 Flags and Water dripping into Bowl **370** Star and Crescents

1991. "Water, Source of Life". Senegal–Saudi Arabia Rural Water Supply Co-operation. Mult.

1129 30f. Type **369** 10 10
1130 145f. Tap and village . . . 90 40
1131 180f. Tap dripping and flags 1·25 45
1132 220f. Water tower and village . . . . 1·50 90

1991. 6th Summit Meeting of Islamic Conference Organization, Dakar. Multicoloured.

1133 15f. Type **370** 10 10
1134 145f. Hands 90 40
1135 180f. Conference centre and accommodation . . . . . 1·25 45
1136 220f. Grand Mosque, Dakar 1·50 90

371 Player shooting at Basket **372** Giving Blessing

1991. Centenary of Basketball. Multicoloured.

1137 125f. Type **371** 75 35
1138 145f. Player approaching basket . . . . 1·00 40
1139 180f. King and Queen of the Basket . . . . 1·10 45
1140 220f. Lion, trophies and ball 1·50 60

1991. Christmas. Multicoloured.

1141 5f. Type **372** 10 10
1142 145f. Madonna and Child 90 40
1143 160f. Angels and star . . . 1·25 45
1144 220f. Animals and Baby Jesus . . . . 1·50 90

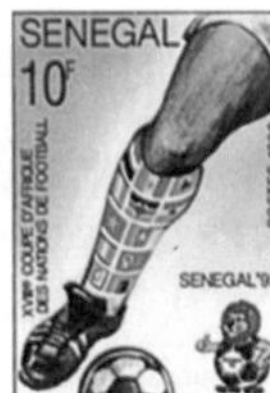

373 Bust of Mozart and Score **374** Flags on Player's Sock

1991. Death Bicentenary of Wolfgang Amadeus Mozart (composer). Multicoloured.

1145 5f. Type **373** 10 10
1146 150f. Mozart conducting . . 1·00 40
1147 180f. Mozart at keyboard 1·25 45
1148 220f. Mozart and score . . 1·50 90

1992. 18th African Nations Cup Football Championship. Multicoloured.

1149 10f. Type **374** 10 10
1150 145f. Footballs forming "92" 70 45
1151 200f. Cup and mascot . . . 1·25 65
1152 220f. Players . . . . . . 1·50 1·00

1992. Papal Visit. No. 1143 surch **VISITE DU PAPE JEAN PAUL II AU SENEGAL 19-23/02/92 180F.**

1153 180f. on 160f. multicoloured 1·60 1·10

376 Saloum Delta

1992. National Parks. Multicoloured.

1154 10f. Type **376** 35 15
1155 125f. Djoudj . . . . 1·50 60
1156 145f. Niokolo-Koba . . . . 2·10 65
1157 220f. Basse Casamance . . . 3·00 1·75

377 Oil Wells, Flag and Bombs **378** Frozen Fish

1992. Participation of Senegal Contingent in Gulf War. Multicoloured.

1158 30f. Type **377** 15 10
1159 145f. Senegalese officer . . . 70 45
1160 180f. Kaaba and Senegalese guard . . . . 1·10 55
1161 220f. Map, dove and flag . . 1·50 75

1992. Fish Products. Multicoloured.

1162	5f. Type **378**	10	10
1163	60f. Sandwich seller and platters of fish	40	20
1164	100f. Woman filleting fish	1·10	40
1165	150f. Women packing prawns	1·10	75

379 Niokolo Complex

1992. Tourist Sites. Multicoloured.

1166	5f. Type **379**	10	10
1167	10f. Basse Casamance	10	10
1168	150f. Dakar	1·10	45
1169	200f. Saint-Louis	1·60	80

380 Teacher and Pupils carrying Saplings

1992. Reforestation by Schoolchildren. Mult.

1170	145f. Type **380**	1·00	45
1171	180f. Planting sapling	1·25	55
1172	200f. Planting saplings (different)	1·40	90
1173	220f. Watering-in sapling (vert)	1·75	1·10

381 People with Cleaning Materials

1992. Manpower Services Operation, Setal. Mult.

1174	25f. Type **381**	10	10
1175	145f. Clearing road	70	45
1176	180f. Sweeping streets (vert)	1·10	55
1177	220f. Painting kerbstones (vert)	1·50	1·00

382 Education

1992. Rights of the Child. Multicoloured.

1178	20f. Type **382**	10	10
1179	45f. Vocational training	20	15
1180	165f. Instruction	1·10	55
1181	180f. Health	1·25	55

383 Customs Post (Free Trade)

1992. African Integration. Multicoloured.

1182	10f. Type **383**	10	10
1183	30f. Silhouettes (youth activities)	15	10
1184	145f. Communications equipment	1·10	45
1185	220f. Women's movements	1·50	75

384 Rings and Map of Spain

1992. Olympic Games, Barcelona. Multicoloured.

1186	145f. Type **384**	70	45
1187	180f. Runner (vert)	1·10	55
1188	200f. Sprinter	1·40	90
1189	300f. Athlete carrying torch (vert)	2·00	1·50

385 Passenger Carriages

1992. "The Blue Train". Multicoloured.

1190	70f. Type **385**	45	30
1191	145f. Diesel locomotives and carriages	1·00	55
1192	200f. Train and track on map	1·40	90
1193	220f. Railway station	1·50	1·00

386 Sealife around Map of Antarctic

1992. International Maritime Heritage Year.

1194	**386**	25f. black, blue & yellow	10	10
1195	–	100f. multicoloured	70	25
1196	–	180f. multicoloured	1·25	55
1197	–	220f. multicoloured	1·50	75

DESIGNS—VERT: 100f. Marine life caught in sun ray; 180f. United Nations seminar; 220f. Fish, ship, flags and hands holding globe.

387 Coral

1992. Corals.

1198	**387**	50f. multicoloured	35	15
1199	–	100f. multicoloured	90	25
1200	–	145f. multicoloured (vert)	1·25	45
1201	–	220f. multicoloured	2·00	1·00

DESIGNS: 100f. to 220f. Different corals.

388 Adenauer **389** Crab

1992. 25th Death Anniv of Konrad Adenauer (German statesman). Multicoloured.

1202	5f. Type **388**	10	10
1203	145f. Schaumburg Palace and flags (horiz)	1·00	45
1204	180f. German flag and handshake (horiz)	1·25	55
1205	220f. Map, flag and emblem of Germany (horiz)	1·50	75

1992. Crustaceans. Multicoloured.

1206	20f. Type **389**	10	10
1207	30f. Sea spider	25	10
1208	180f. Crayfish	1·50	55
1209	200f. King prawn	1·75	1·00

390 "Parkia biglobosa"

1992. Flowers and their Fruits. Multicoloured.

1210	10f. Type **390**	10	10
1211	50f. Desert date	35	15
1212	200f. "Parinari macrophylla"	1·50	65
1213	220f. Cactus	1·75	1·00

391 Rocket and Earth

1992. 30th Anniv of First American Manned Orbit of the Earth. Multicoloured.

1214	15f. Type **391**	10	10
1215	145f. American flag and John Glenn	1·00	55
1216	180f. Rocket launch and globe	1·25	90
1217	200f. Astronaut and rocket on launch-pad (vert)	1·40	1·00

392 Bakari II and Map from 14th-century Catalan Atlas

1992. Bakari II. Multicoloured.

1218	100f. Type **392**	65	25
1219	145f. Giant Mexican carved head and map from 15th-century atlas	1·00	45

393 Picture Frame and Obelisk **394** Children dancing round Decorated Globe

1992. Dakar Biennale. Multicoloured.

1220	20f. Type **393**	10	10
1221	50f. Mask hanging from window frame	35	10
1222	145f. Open book	1·00	65
1223	220f. Traditional string instrument	1·75	1·00

1992. Christmas. Multicoloured.

1224	15f. Type **394**	10	10
1225	145f. People around tree (vert)	1·00	55
1226	180f. Jesus (vert)	1·25	65
1227	200f. Father Christmas (vert)	1·40	90

1993. 15th Paris–Dakar Rally. Nos. 941 and 975 surch **Dakar le 17-01-93** and new value.

1228	145f. on 180f. multicoloured	1·10	90
1229	220f. on 410f. multicoloured	1·60	1·10

396 First Aid Post

1993. Accident Prevention Campaign. Mult.

1230	20f. Type **396** (prevention, security and first aid)	10	10
1231	25f. The Sonacos incident (reinforcement of preventative measures) (36 × 28 mm)	10	10
1232	145f. Chemical accident (need for vigilance and security) (36 × 28 mm)	1·00	55
1233	200f. Helicopter rescue (rapid and efficient intervention at air disasters)	1·25	90

397 Seck **398** Spotted Hyena

1993. 120th Birth Anniv of Abdoulaye Seck (Director of Posts and Telecommunications).

1234	**397**	220f. multicoloured	1·50	65

1993. Wild Animals. Multicoloured.

1235	30f. Type **398**	10	10
1236	50f. Lioness	10	10
1237	70f. Leopard	25	10
1238	150f. Giraffe (vert)	50	25
1239	180f. Stag	75	30

399 Decorated Tree, Children playing and Father Christmas

1993. Christmas. Multicoloured.

1240	5f. Type **399**	10	10
1241	80f. Children decorating tree and Father Christmas	20	15
1242	145f. Children visiting Father Christmas	35	25
1243	150f. Girl tugging Father Christmas's beard	35	25

400 U.S. Flag and Kennedy

1993. 30th Anniv of Assassination of President John F. Kennedy of the United States. Mult.

1244	80f. Type **400**	20	15
1245	555f. Kennedy and White House	1·90	95

402 Vehicles and Tree at Sunset

1994. 16th Anniv of Paris–Dakar Rally. Mult.

1250	145f. Type **402**	50	25
1251	180f. Boys with camel	60	30
1252	220f. Rally cars	75	35

403 Diplodocus

1994. Prehistoric Animals. Multicoloured.

1253	100f. Type **403**	25	15
1254	175f. Brontosaurus	40	25
1255	215f. Triceratops	50	35
1256	290f. Stegosaurus	1·25	45
1257	300f. Tyrannosaurus	1·75	1·10

404 Black-headed Herons

1994. Birds of Kalissaye National Park. Mult.

1258	100f. Type **404**	50	20
1259	275f. Caspian terns	1·10	45
1260	290f. Little egrets	1·25	45
1261	380f. Pink-backed pelicans (horiz)	1·75	1·10

405 Dried Moray Fat

1994. Produce of the Sea. Multicoloured.
1262 5f. Type **405** 10 10
1263 90f. Sifting shellfish 20 15
1264 100f. Salted shark 40 25
1265 200f. Smoking small fry 70 40

406 "Stop Sand Extraction"

1994. Coastal Protection. Multicoloured.
1266 5f. Type **406** 10 10
1267 75f. Prevention of sand dunes 20 15
1268 100f. Horizontal and vertical barrages 25 15
1269 200f. Cleanliness of beaches 50 35

407 Water Store, Goree, and Railway Station, Rufisque

1994. Preservation of Heritage Sites. Mult.
1270 100f. Type **407** 30 20
1271 175f. Soudan House 40 25
1272 215f. Goree Island 50 35
1273 275f. Pinet Laprade Fort, Sedhiou 90 45

408 Red-flowered Kapok

409 Breguet 14 Biplane over Route Map

1994. Flowers. Multicoloured.
1274 30f. Type **408** 10 10
1275 75f. Golden trumpet 20 15
1276 100f. Rose periwinkle 25 15
1277 1000f. Glory-bower 3·50 2·10

1994. 10th Toulouse–Saint-Louis Aerial Rally (1993). Multicoloured.
1278 100f. Type **409** 40 15
1279 145f. Henri Guillaumet and route map 50 25
1280 180f. Jean Mermoz and route map 60 30
1281 220f. Antoine Saint-Exupery and route map 75 35

410 Head of Elephant with Ear forming Map of Africa

1994. S.O.S. Elephant Conservation Programme. Multicoloured.
1282 30f. Type **410** 20 10
1283 60f. Elephant within "SOS" 25 10
1284 90f. Pair of elephants with trunks forming "SOS" 40 15
1285 145f. Dead elephant and tusks 50 25

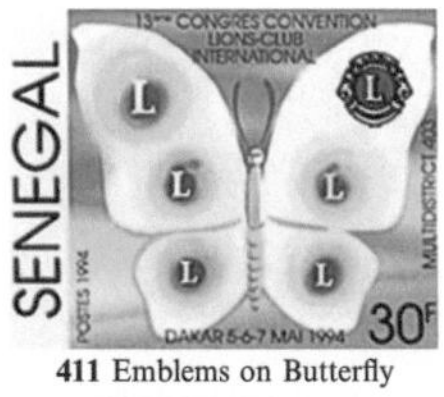

411 Emblems on Butterfly

1994. 13th Congress of District 403 of Lions Clubs International, Dakar. Multicoloured.
1286 30f. Type **411** 20 10
1287 60f. Emblem over butterfly 30 10
1288 175f. "L"s and emblem 60 25
1289 215f. Emblem on rainbow 90 35

412 "Stamp" showing Children playing

1994. African Children's Day. Children's Drawings. Multicoloured.
1290 175f. Type **412** 40 25
1291 215f. Preparing meal outside house 50 35

413 Flags and Football

1994. World Cup Football Championship, U.S.A. Multicoloured.
1292 45f. Type **413** 10 10
1293 175f. World map forming part of football 65 25
1294 215f. Player dribbling ball (horiz) 75 35
1295 665f. Players with ball (horiz) 2·10 1·10

414 Slave House

1994. World Heritage Site, Goree.
1296 **414** 500f. multicoloured 1·60 1·10

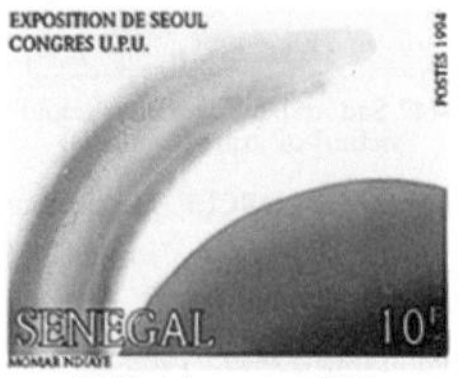

415 Rainbow over Globe

1994. 21st Universal Postal Union Congress and "Philakorea 1994" International Stamp Exhibition, Seoul. Multicoloured.
1297 10f. Type **415** 10 10
1298 175f. "Stamp" forming wing of dove 40 25
1299 260f. "Stamp" forming sail of boat 65 45
1300 300f. Globe, hands and airmail envelope 75 50

416 Peace Dove, People of Different Cultures and Flags

1994. International Year of the Family. Mult.
1301 5f. Type **416** 10 10
1302 175f. People of different cultures, flags and globe 65 25
1303 215f. Globe and mothers with children 75 35
1304 290f. Globe, dove and family 1·00 45

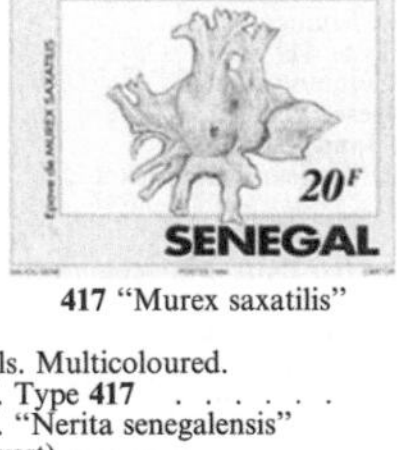

417 "Murex saxatilis"

1994. Shells. Multicoloured.
1305 20f. Type **417** 10 10
1306 45f. "Nerita senegalensis" (vert) 10 10
1307 75f. "Polymita picea" 20 15
1308 175f. "Scalaria pretiosa" (vert) 65 25
1309 215f. Glory of the sea cone (vert) 75 65

418 Golden Jackal

1994. Animals. Multicoloured.
1310 60f. Type **418** 25 10
1311 70f. African clawless otter 25 10
1312 100f. Egyptian mongoose 40 15
1313 175f. Giant ground pangolin 90 25
1314 215f. Nile monitor 1·00 35

419 Pierre de Coubertin (founder) and Anniversary Emblem

1994. Centenary of International Olympic Committee. Multicoloured.
1315 175f. Type **419** 40 25
1316 215f. Coubertin within wreath and anniversary emblem 50 35
1317 275f. Coubertin over anniversary emblem (vert) 90 45
1318 290f. Coubertin within anniversary emblem and Olympic rings (vert) 1·10 45

420 Africans greeting Portuguese

1994. 550th Anniv of First Portuguese Landing in Senegal.
1319 **420** 175f. multicoloured 65 25

421 Father Christmas and Children with Presents

1994. Christmas. Multicoloured.
1320 175f. Type **421** 40 25
1321 215f. Madonna and Child and Christmas trees 50 35
1322 275f. Adoration of the Wise Men (horiz) 90 45
1323 290f. Madonna and Child 1·10 45

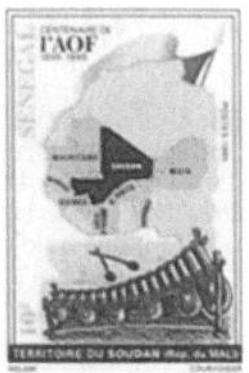

422 Emblem and Ribbons

423 Sudan and Xylophone

1995. Conference of District 9100 of Rotary International. Multicoloured.
1324 260f. Type **422** 90 45
1325 275f. Emblem and dove in flight 90 45

1995. Centenary of Formation of French Governate-General of French West Africa. Map highlighting featured country. Multicoloured.
1326 10f. Type **423** 10 10
1327 15f. Dahomey and canoes 10 10
1328 30f. Ivory Coast and elephant 10 10
1329 70f. Mauritania and camel 15 10
1330 175f. Guinea, stringed instrument and plants 40 25
1331 180f. Upper Volta, cow and produce 45 30
1332 215f. Niger and Cross of Agadez 75 35
1333 225f. Senegal and lions 80 35

1995. As Nos. 502a/504h but size 21 × 26 mm.
1334 **154** 5f. orange 10 10
1335 10f. green 10 10
1336 20f. red 10 10
1337 25f. green 10 10
1338 30f. green 10 10
1339 40f. green 10 10
1340 50f. green 10 10
1341 60f. green 10 10
1342 70f. green 15 10
1343 80f. green 15 10
1344 100f. blue 25 15
1345 150f. blue 35 25
1346 175f. brown 40 25
1347 190f. green 40 30
1348 200f. black 50 35
1349 215f. blue 45 30
1350 225f. blue 45 30
1351 240f. brown 50 35
1352 250f. red 60 40
1353 260f. brown 50 35
1354 275f. red 65 45
1355 300f. purple 60 40
1356 320f. mauve 60 40
1357 350f. brown 70 50
1358 410f. red and brown 80 55
1363 500f. purple 1·00 70
1366 1000f. red 2·00 1·40

424 Communications, Map of West Africa and Energy Sources

425 Pasteur developing Rabies Vaccine

1995. 1st Economic Community of West African States Trade Fair. Multicoloured.
1370 175f. Type **424** 40 25
1371 215f. Members' flags, banknotes and crops (horiz) 50 35

1995. Death Centenary of Louis Pasteur (chemist). Multicoloured.
1372 275f. Type **425** 1·10 45
1373 500f. Pasteur working on pasteurization 1·60 85

426 Scene from "L'Arroseur Arrose" (dir. Lumiere Brothers)

1995. Centenary of Motion Pictures. Multicoloured.
1374 100f. Type **426** 25 15
1375 200f. First public film screening by Lumiere brothers 75 35
1376 250f. Auguste and Louis Lumiere watching screening of "Arrival by Train" 90 40
1377 275f. Presentation on cinematography by Antoine Lumiere, 1895 1·25 90

427 Animal Welfare

428 People of Different Cultures

1995. 50th Anniv of F.A.O. Multicoloured.
1378 175f. Type **427** 40 25
1379 215f. Teaching new skills to rural communities 50 35
1380 260f. Aquaculture 1·00 45
1381 275f. Nourishment of children 1·10 90

1995. 50th Anniv of U.N.O.
1382 **428** 275f. blue, violet and black 1·10 45
1383 – 1000f. multicoloured 3·25 2·10
DESIGN: 1000f. "ONU 50" and U.N. Headquarters, New York.

429 Figures dancing around Book

1995. 25th Anniv of Agency for Cultural and Technical Co-operation in French-speaking Countries. Multicoloured.
1384 150f. Type **429** 35 25
1385 500f. Panels of contestants (victory of St. Louis Military Academy in 1994 competition) . . . . . . 1·60 1·10

430 African buffalo

1995. Animals. Multicoloured.
1386 90f. Type **430** 20 15
1387 150f. Warthog 50 25
1388 175f. Bushbuck . . . . . . 1·00 25
1389 275f. African spurred tortoise . . . . 1·25 45
1390 300f. North African crested porcupine . . . . 1·25 50

431 Caspian Tern

1995. Endangered Birds. Terns. Multicoloured.
1391 90f. Type **431** 20 15
1392 145f. Gull-billed tern . . . 35 25
1393 150f. Royal tern 65 25
1394 180f. Common tern 75 55

432 "Meganostoma eurydice"

1995. Butterflies. Multicoloured.
1395 45f. Type **432** 10 10
1396 100f. "Luehdorfia japonica" 40 15
1397 200f. Great orange-tip . . . 1·00 35
1398 220f. Small tortoiseshell . . 1·25 65

433 Bassari Festivals

1995. Cultural Tourism. Multicoloured.
1399 100f. Type **433** 25 15
1400 175f. "Baawnann" (vert) . . 40 25
1401 220f. Pyramid-roofed houses 55 35
1402 500f. Turu Dance . . . . . 1·60 1·10

434 Rally Car and Profiles

435 Sea-island Cotton

1996. Paris–Granada–Dakar Motor Rally. Mult.
1403 215f. Type **434** 50 35
1404 275f. Motor cyclists (vert) 65 45
1405 290f. Landmarks and vehicles 65 45
1406 665f. Rally cars . . . . . . 1·75 1·10

1996. Flowers. Multicoloured.
1407 175f. Type **435** 40 30
1408 275f. Sorrel 75 45
1409 290f. Wood sorrel 75 45
1410 500f. Lotus water-lily . . . 1·25 75

436 Diop in Youth and "Sphinx" (Dominique Denon)

1996. 10th Death Anniv of Cheikh Anta Diop. Mult.
1411 175f. Type **436** 40 30
1412 215f. Diop engaged in Carbon 14 dating tests . . 50 35

437 Saloum Delta National Park

1996. National Parks. Multicoloured.
1413 175f. Type **437** 40 30
1414 200f. Niokolo Koba 45 30
1415 220f. Madeleine Islands . . . 50 35
1416 275f. Basse Casamance . . . 65 45

438 Boxing

1996. Sport. Multicoloured.
1417 125f. Type **438** 30 20
1418 215f. Judo 50 35
1419 275f. Throwing the javelin 65 45
1420 320f. Throwing the discus 75 55

439 Woman

1996. Improvement of World. Multicoloured.
1421 215f. Type **439** (campaign against poverty) 50 35
1422 500f. "Drop of Hope" (balloon) over landscape (Rio de Janeiro, 1992–Dakar, 1996) . . . . . . 1·10 75

440 "Choose Corridor 1"

1996. "Hall of Pearls" by Serge Correa (painter). Multicoloured.
1423 260f. Type **440** 60 40
1424 320f. "Choose Symphony 1" 75 55

441 Man with Globe rejecting Drugs

1996. United Nations Decade against the Abuse and Trafficking of Drugs. Multicoloured.
1425 175f. Type **441** 40 30
1426 215f. U.N. emblem and hand holding up stop sign to drugs 50 35

442 Competitors and Statue

1996. Centenary of Modern Olympic Games.
1427 **442** 215f. multicoloured . . . 50 35

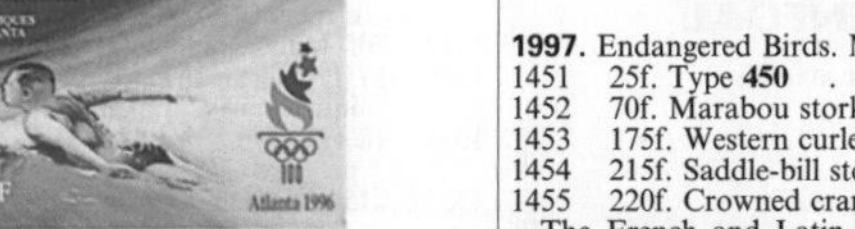

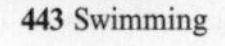

443 Swimming

1996. Olympic Games, Atlanta, U.S.A. Mult.
1428 10f. Type **443** 10 10
1429 80f. Gymnastics 30 15
1430 175f. Running 60 30
1431 260f. Hurdling 75 40

444 "90" and Senghor

1996. 90th Birthday of Leopold Senghor (President, 1960–81). Multicoloured.
1432 175f. Type **444** 40 30
1433 275f. Senghor as young and older man (vert) 65 45

445 Sack of Food and Boy eating

446 Savanna Monkey

1996. Senegalese Red Cross.
1434 **445** 275f. multicoloured . . . 65 45

1996. Primates. Multicoloured.
1435 10f. Type **446** 20 10
1436 30f. Patas monkey 25 10
1437 90f. Campbell's monkey . . 40 15
1438 215f. Chimpanzee 75 35
1439 260f. Guinea baboon . . . 1·00 40

447 Sad and Injured Boys (child victims of armed conflicts)

1996. 50th Anniv of UNICEF. Multicoloured.
1440 75f. Type **447** 15 10
1441 275f. Nurse and child, mother feeding baby, smiling boy and boy at tap (primary health care) and breastfeeding 65 45

448 Lorry

450 White Spoonbill

449 Praying Mantis

1997. Dakar–Agades–Dakar Motor Rally. Mult.
1442 25f. Type **448** 25 10
1443 75f. Man pushing car . . . 50 10
1444 215f. Rally car 75 30
1445 300f. Motor cyclist . . . . 1·00 45

1997. Insects. Multicoloured.
1446 10f. Type **449** 20 10
1447 50f. Common earwig . . . 20 10
1448 75f. Desert locust 25 10
1449 215f. Sand tiger beetle . . . 75 30
1450 220f. European field cricket 75 30

1997. Endangered Birds. Multicoloured.
1451 25f. Type **450** 10 10
1452 70f. Marabou stork 25 10
1453 175f. Western curlew . . . 50 25
1454 215f. Saddle-bill stork . . . 1·00 30
1455 220f. Crowned crane . . . . 1·00 30

The French and Latin inscriptions on Nos. 1453 and 1455 have been transposed.

451 Acacia

1997. Trees and their Fruits. Multicoloured.
1456 80f. Type **451** 40 10
1457 175f. Eucalyptus 50 25
1458 220f. "Khaya senegalensis" 75 30
1459 260f. Horse-tail tree . . . . 1·00 40

452 Goree Island

1997. Unissued stamp with part of inscription deleted by bar as in T **452**.
1460 **452** 180f. multicoloured . . . 85 30

453 African Buffaloes

1997. Mammals. Multicoloured.
1461 25f. Type **453** 20 10
1462 90f. Antelopes 35 15
1463 100f. Gnus 40 15
1464 200f. African hunting dogs 75 30
1465 240f. Cheetahs . . . . . . 1·00 35

454 African Fish Eagle

1997. Niokolo-Badiar National Park. Mult.
1466 30f. Type **454** 50 10
1467 90f. Hippopotamus 50 15
1468 240f. African elephant . . . 75 35
1469 300f. Giant eland . . . . . 1·00 45

455 West African Helmet

456 Von Stephan

1997. Shells. Multicoloured.
1470 15f. Type **455** 20 10
1471 40f. "Pugilina meria" . . . 30 10
1472 190f. Map cowrie 60 30
1473 200f. "Natica adansoni" . . 75 30
1474 300f. "Bullia miran" . . . . 1·00 45

There are errors of spelling in the Latin inscriptions.

1997. Death Centenary of Heinrich von Stephan (founder of U.P.U.).
1475 **456** 310f. multicoloured . . . 75 45

457 Cereal Stockpiles

1997. Security of Food Supplies. Multicoloured.
1476 190f. Type **457** 70 30
1477 200f. Woman weighing herself (post-weaning nutritional vulnerability) 90 30

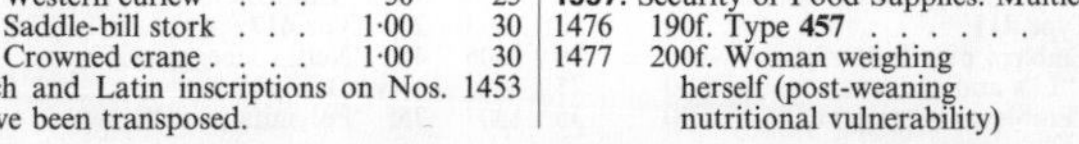

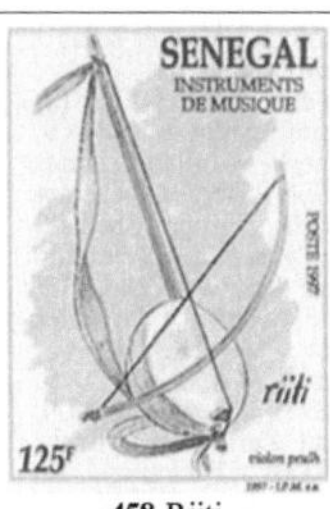

458 Riiti

1997. Musical Instruments. Multicoloured.
1478 125f. Type **458** 40 20
1479 190f. Kora (stringed instrument) 70 30
1480 200f. Tama (double-ended drum) 75 30
1481 240f. Dioung dioung (royal ceremonial drum) . . . . 1·00 35

459 Da Gama and Ship's Hold containing Spices (Spice Route)
460 Planche Mask, Burkina Faso

1997. 500th Anniv of Vasco da Gama's Voyage to India via the Cape of Good Hope. Multicoloured.
1482 40f. Type **459** 20 10
1483 75f. Map of Africa, scales and Da Gama (port of call at Zanzibar) 25 10
1484 190f. "Sao Gabriel" (flagship) and Da Gama (development of caravel) 90 30
1485 200f. Compass rose over map of Africa and printing press (introduction of compass and printed maps) 90 30

1997. Traditional Masks. Multicoloured.
1486 45f. Type **460** 25 10
1487 90f. Kpeliyehe mask, Senufo, Ivory Coast . . . 40 15
1488 200f. Nimba mask, Baga, Guinea 80 30
1489 240f. Walu mask, Dogon, Mali 90 35
1490 300f. Dogon mask, Bandiagara, Mali . . . . 1·00 45

461 Series CC2400 Diesel-electric Locomotive

1997. Trains. Multicoloured.
1491 15f. Type **461** 25 10
1492 90f. Diesel goods locomotive 45 15
1493 100f. Mountain steam locomotive 50 15
1494 240f. Maquinista diesel locomotive 85 35
1495 310f. Series 151-A steam locomotive and goods wagons . . . . 1·00 45

462 Cat

1997. The African Golden Cat. Multicoloured.
1496 45f. Type **462** 25 10
1497 100f. Standing on branch . . 50 15
1498 240f. Lying on branch . . . 75 35
1499 300f. One cat grooming another . . . . 1·00 45

463 Lorry crossing Sahara

1998. Dakar–Dakar Motor Rally. Multicoloured.
1500 20f. Type **463** 20 10
1501 45f. Motor cycle at Lac Rose 40 10
1502 190f. Off-road vehicle crossing Mauritanian desert 75 30
1503 240f. Rally car by River Senegal . . . . 1·00 35

464 Hut and Children

1998. 25th Anniv of Aldiana Club. Multicoloured.
1504 290f. Type **464** 90 55
1505 320f. Canoe, woman and fish 95 60

465 Children

1998. SOS Children's Village, Ziguinchor. Multicoloured.
1506 190f. Type **465** 60 35
1507 240f. Girl and huts 95 60

466 Diana, Princess of Wales

1998. Diana, Princess of Wales Commemoration. Multicoloured.
1508 240f. Diana wearing hat with veil 95 60
MS1509 Five sheets. (a) 141 × 198 mm. 200f. T **466** and different designs showing Diana, Princess of Wales; (b) 141 × 198 mm. 25f. As No. 1508 and 8 different designs showing Diana; (c) 131 × 94 mm. 1000f. With head on hand; (d) 131 × 94 mm. 1500f. With Princes William and Harry (e) 138 × 100 mm. 2000f. Wearing tiara Set of 5 sheets . . . . . 26·00 14·00

467 Slave House, Goree Island

1998. 150th Anniv of Abolition of Slavery. Multicoloured.
1510 20f. Type **467** 15 10
1511 40f. Frederick Douglas (American abolitionist) . . 15 10
1512 190f. Mother, child and slave ship 60 35
1513 290f. Victor Schoelcher (French abolitionist and politician) 90 55

468 Museum Emblem, Museum Building and Reyane Henriette Bathily (founder)

1998. 4th Anniv of Henriette Bathily Women's Museum. Multicoloured.
1514 190f. Type **468** 60 25
1515 270f. Emblem, building and Henriette Bathily (different) 95 60

469 Brazilian Player with Football

1998. World Cup Football Championships, France. Multicoloured.
1516 25f. Type **469** 15 10
1517 50f. Mascot, legs, ball and trophy 15 10
1518 150f. Mascot, trophy and ball 45 25
1519 300f. Flags of competing countries 95 60

470 House and Car

1998. Children's Paintings. SOS Children's Village, Ziguinchor. Multicoloured.
1520 30f. Type **470** 10 10
1521 50f. Trees and rainbow . . 15 10
1522 180f. Sunrise and flowers . . 60 35
1523 300f. House, road and eyes 95 60

471 Buoy with Siren

1998. Lighthouses and Buoys. Multicoloured.
1524 50f. Type **471** 15 15
1525 100f. Mammelles lighthouse 30 20
1526 190f. Luminescent buoy . . 60 35
1527 240f. Port entrance lighthouse 75 45

472 Alberto Asgari

1998. Ferrari Formula I Racing Team. Two sheets containing T **472** and similar horiz designs. Multicoloured.
MS1528 (a) 158 × 125 mm. 100f. × 6 Type **472**, Guiseppe Farina, Ricardo Patrese, Michele Alboreto, Elio de Angelis, Andrea de Cesaris; (b) 81 × 100 mm. 1000f. Ferrari race car Set of two sheets 7·75 4·50

473 Leaning Tower, Pisa

1998. Italia '98 International Stamp Exhibition, Milan (1st issue).
1529 **473** 290f. multicoloured . . . 95 60
See also No. **MS**1559 and **MS**1607.

474 Seagull, Dolphin and Undersea Fauna

1998. International Year of the Ocean. Multicoloured.
1530 190f. Type **474** 60 35
1531 790f. Fish . . . . 2·60 1·50

475 Emblem and Beach

1998. Palm Beach Hotel. 50th Anniv of FRAM (travel company). Multicoloured.
1532 240f. Type **475** 75 45
1533 300f. Women and beach scene 95 60

476 Woman wearing Turban

1998. Women's Hair Styles and Headdresses.
1534 **476** 40f. brown, chocolate and black 10 10
1535 – 100f. green, deep green and black 30 20
1536 – 240f. violet, deep violet and black 75 45
1537 – 300f. blue, deep blue and black 95 60
DESIGNS: Type **476**; 100f. Long braided hair; 240f. Braided hair with beads; 300f. Turban tied in front.

477 Figure behind Bars and United Nations Emblem

1998. 50th Anniv of United Nations Declaration of Human Rights. Multicoloured.
1538 200f. Type **477** 60 35
1539 350f. Women and emblem 1·00 60

478 Seagull, Fish and Net
479 Smiling Woman

1998. Marine Protection. Multicoloured.
1540 50f. Type **478** 15 10
1541 100f. Fish and effluent pipe 30 20
1542 310f. Dynamite and dead fish 90 55
1543 365f. Fish and oil pollution 1·00 60

1998. "Senegalese Elegance" (3rd series).
1544 **479** 125f. olive 45 25
1545 290f. purple 90 55
1546 310f. purple 95 60

480 Repairing Rally Car

1999. 21st Paris—Dakar Rally. Multicoloured.
1555 150f. Type **480** 45 25
1556 175f. Digging out of sand dune 50 30
1557 240f. Motorcycle crash . . . 75 45
1558 290f. Motorcycle and car sunk in sand 95 60

481 Romy Schneider

1999. Italia '98 International Stamp Exhibition, Milan (2nd issue). Film Actors. Three sheets containing T **481** and similar horiz designs. Multicoloured.
MS1559 (a) 140 × 195 mm. 200f. × 9, Type **481**; Yves Montand; Catherine Deneuve; Gina Lollobrigida; Marcello Mastroianni; Sophia Loren; Frank Sinatra; Dean Martin; Marilyn Monroe; (b) 144 × 116 mm. 1500f. Marilyn Monroe (different); (c) 144 × 116 mm. 2000f. Marcello Masstroianni (different) . . . . 4·50 2·75

482 Black Coupe

1999. 40th Anniv of De Tomaso (car manufacturer). Sheet 153 × 103 mm containing T **482** and similar horiz designs. Multicoloured.
MS1560 250f. × 4, Type **482**; White coupe; Dark blue coupe; Red coupe . . . . 3·00 1·75

483 Elvis Presley

1999. Elvis Presley (entertainer) Commemoration. Sheet 130 × 175 mm containing T **483** and similar vert designs. Multicoloured.
MS1561 250f. Type **483** and 8 designs showing Elvis Presley 6·00 3·50

484 Stamp and Flags

1999. PhilexFrance '99 International Stamp Exhibition, Paris. 150th Anniv of First French Stamp.
1562 **484** 240f. multicoloured . . . 95 60

485 Ayrton Senna

1999. Formula 1 Racing Drivers. Multicoloured.
1563 200f. Type **485** 80 50
MS1564 (a) 157 × 120 mm. 200f. × 9, Juan Manuel Fangio; Alberto Ascari; Graham Hill; Jim Clark; Jack Brabham; Jackie Stewart; Niki Lauda; Type **485** (design enlarged); Alain Prost; (b) 112 × 82 mm. 2000f. Ayrton Senna (different) (50 × 36 mm) . . . . 6·00 3·50

486 Knight on Horseback and Knight (chess piece)

1999. Chess. Multicoloured.
1565 250f. Knight and chess piece (different) 95 60
MS1566 Three sheets, each 140 × 200 mm. (a) 200f. Type **486** and 8 different designs showing soldiers of the Crusades and chess pieces; (b) 250f. × 9 Soldiers and chess pieces; (c) 400f. × 9 Soldiers and chess pieces (different) Set of 3 sheets . . . . 25·00 15·00

487 Jackie Robinson

1999. Jackie Robinson (baseball player) Commemoration. Multicoloured.
1567 250f. Type **487** 95 60
MS1568 Three sheets. (a) 132 × 177 mm. 1000f. Type **487** and 8 different designs showing Jackie Robinson; (b) 88 × 138 mm. 1500f. Looking left (36 × 42 mm); (c) 88 × 138 mm. 2000f. With raised bat Set of 3 sheets . . . 7·50 4·50

488 Ludger Beerbaum (show jumper)

1999. Equestrian Competitors. Multicoloured.
1569 300f. Type **488** . . . . . . 1·10 65
MS1570 Two sheets. (a) 120 × 156 mm. 300f. × 9, Martin Schaudi; Klaus Balkenhols; Nadine Capellmann Bifar; Willi Melliger; Type **488**; Ulrich Kirchhoff; Sally Clark; Bettina Overesch Boker; Karen O' Connor; (b) 112 × 82 mm. 1500f. German equestrian team (50 × 36 mm) Set of 2 sheets . . 8·50 5·00

489 Mohammed Ali

1999. 25th Anniv of Mohammed Ali—George Forman Boxing Match. Multicoloured.
1571 300f. Type **489** 95 60
MS1572 Three sheets. (a) 132 × 177 mm. 300f. Type **489** and 8 different designs showing Mohammed Ali; (b) 88 × 138 mm. 1000f. Wearing robe (36 × 42 mm) (c) 88 × 138 mm. 2000f. With raised fists (36 × 42 mm) . . . 7·50 4·50

490 Pete Sampras

1999. Racquet Sports. Multicoloured.
1573 400f. Type **490** . . . . . . 1·30 80
MS1574 Two sheets. (a) 120 × 156 mm. 400f. × 9, Liu Guoliang (tennis player); Martina Hingis (tennis); Deng Yaping (table tennis player); Andre Agassi (tennis); Jean-Philippe Gatien (table tennis); Anna Kournikova (tennis); Mikael Appelgren (table tennis); Type **490** (tennis); Jan-Ove Waldner (table tennis); (b) 112 × 82 mm. 2000f. Vladimir Samsonov, Deng Yaping and Jörg Rosskopf (table tennis players) (50 × 36 mm) Set of 2 sheets . . 12·00 7·00

491 Racing Yachts

1999. Transport. Multicoloured.
1575 250f. Type **491** 95 60
1576 325f. Bentley coupe . . . . 1·00 60
1577 350f. Prussian locomotive S10 . . . . 1·10 65
1578 375f. Ducati 900 SS motorbike . . . . 1·20 70
1579 500f. Concorde super sonic aircraft . . . . 1·50 90
MS1580 Ten sheets. (a) 155 × 119 mm. Ships:—250f. × 9, *France* (liner); United States (liner); *Finnjet* (ferry); *Chusan* (liner); *Cheers* (inscr "Sheers") (catamaran); *Vendredi 13* (racing yacht); Type **491**; *Pen Duick II* (transatlantic ketch); *Jester* (transatlantic yacht); (b) 155 × 119 mm. Cars:—325f. × 9, Duryea (1893); Menon (1897); Renault; Fiat Zero (1912); Inscr "Spa" (1913); Packard; As No.1525; Mercedes Benz; Morris Minor (1930); (c) 155 × 119 mm Steam trains:—350f. × 9, *Mikado*; French locomotive 241 P (1948); French locomotive 230 K; The Milwaukee road class A locomotive (1935) Russian locomotive class 1.5; Prussian locomotive G12; As No. 1526; Inscr "Austrian locomotive KK SEB series 310"; French locomotive *Outrance* (1877) (d) 155 × 119 mm. 375f. × 9, Zenith motorcycle and sidecar (1913) Brough Superior motor cycle (1920); Motor cycle racing, 1903; As No.1257; Dave Thorpe (motocross rider); Suzuki 500 motorcycle; Michaux bicycle (1865); Modern solid wheel racing cycle; Woman cyclist (e) 155 × 119 mm. High speed trains: —450f. × 9, Acela, USA; Class 332 Britain; I.C.E., Germany; Trans Europe Express locomotive, Luxembourg; California–Nevada Super Speed monorail, USA; Inter City 250, Britain; Korean high speed locomotive; Eurostar locomotive, Britain; TGV Thalys PBA, France (f) 155 × 119 mm. Aircraft:—500f. × 9, USA; USA Maglifter launch catapult; Inscr "S.M." (USA); Concorde; Inscr "T.U. 144" (URSS); Inscr "Futur X USA"; USA X 33; Type **491**; USA X 34 space vehicle (g) 121 × 92 mm. 1000f. Eric Tabarly and *Pen Duick VI* (51 × 36 mm) (h) 121 × 92 mm.1500f. Walter Chrysler and Chrysler (1924) (i) 122 × 92 mm. 1500f. Marc Seguin and steam locomotive (36 × 51 mm) (j) 112 × 82 mm. 2000f. Bobby Julich (cycle racer) (51 × 36 mm) (k) 122 × 92 mm. TGV locomotive *Atlantique*, TGV *Mediterranee* and *Etienne Chambron* (l) 122 × 92 mm. 2000f. Concorde (51 × 36 mm) Set of 10 sheets . . . . 65·00 38·00

492 Evacuation of Sinking Ship

1999. Sinking of *Titanic* (liner), 1912. Multicoloured.
1581 300f. Type **492** 95 60
MS1582 155 × 119 mm. 300f. × 9, In shipyard; At the dockside; Pulled by tugboat; At sea; Collision with iceberg; Type **492**; Expedition to wreck; Couple lost in accident; Captain John Smith . . . . . 9·00 5·00

493 Russian R.D. 107 Rocket

1999. Spacecraft. Two sheets containing T **493** and similar multicoloured designs.
MS1583 (a) 140 × 200 mm. 400f. × 9, Type **493**; Russian Soyuz; Russian Proton; USA Atlas-Centaur; USA Atlas-Agena; USA Atlas-mercury; USA Titan 2; USA Juno 2; USA Saturn I; (b) 122 × 92 mm. Neil Armstrong (51 × 36 mm) Set of 2 sheets . . . . 12·00 7·00

494 Book, Men and National Colours

1999. International Year of the Elderly. Multicoloured.
1584 30f. Type **494** 15 10
1585 150f. Blacksmith 45 25
1586 290f. Musicians 90 55
1587 300f. Scientist (vert) 95 60

495 Death Cap (*Amanita phalloides*) (inscr "Amanite phalloide")

1999. Fungi. Senegal Scouts. Multicoloured.
1588 60f. Type **495** 20 10
1589 175f. Common ink cap (*Coprinus atramantarius*) 60 35
1590 220f. Destroying angel (*Amanita virosa*) (inscr "Amanite vireuse") . . . 75 45
1591 250f. Field mushroom (*Agaricus campestri*) (inscr "campester") 95 60

496 Astronauts and Flag on Moon

1999. 30th Anniv of First Moon Landing. Multicoloured.
1592 25f. Type **496** 15 10
1593 145f. Neil Armstrong, flag and astronaut (vert) . . . 45 25
1594 180f. Astronaut, flag and rocket (vert) 55 30
1595 500f. Astronaut and space shuttle (vert) . . . . . . 1·50 90

497 Roan Antelope (*Hippotragus equines*)

1999. Fauna. Multicoloured.
1596 60f. Type **497** 20 10
1597 90f. Oyster catcher (*Haematopus ostralegus*) 30 20
1598 300f. White-face whistling duck (*Dendrocygna viduata*) (inscr "viduada") 95 60
1599 320f. Leatherback turtle (*Dermochelys coriacea*) . . 95 60

498 Mother Teresa and Child **499** Emblem and Rainbows

1999. 20th Anniv of Award of Nobel Peace Prize to Mother Teresa (humanitarian). Multicoloured.
1600 75f. Type **498** 20 10
1601 100f. With children 45 25
1602 290f. With priest 80 50
1603 300f. Holding laughing child 1·00 60

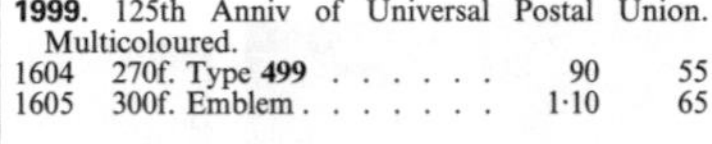
1999. 125th Anniv of Universal Postal Union. Multicoloured.
1604 270f. Type **499** 90 55
1605 300f. Emblem . . . . 1·10 65

500 "Mont Sainte-Victoire seen from Bibemus Quarry"

1999. Art. Four sheets containing T **500** and similar multicoloured designs showing paintings by artists named.
MS1606 (a) Horiz. 195 × 141 mm. Paul Cezanne. 200f. × 9, Type **500**; "Sea at l'Estaque"; "Landscape"; "Still Life"; "Still Life with Basket"; "Still Life with Apples and Peaches"; "Bibemus Quarry"; "Woods with Millstone"; "Lake Annecy". (b) Vert. 113 × 163 mm. Paul Gauguin. 250f. × 4, "Te Faaturuma (Brooding Woman)"; "The Cellist (Portrait of Upaupa Scheklud)"; "Self-portrait with Halo"; "When are you getting Married?". (c) Vert. 113 × 163 mm. Pablo Picasso. 375f. × 4, "Cavalier with Pipe"; "Rembrandt Figure and Eros"; "Female Nude and Smoker"; "The Doves". (d) Vert. 156 × 120 mm. Vincent van Gogh. 2000f. "Dr. Paul Gachet" Set of 4 sheets . . . . 12·50 7·50

501 Clark Gable

1999. Italia '98 International Stamp Exhibition, Milan (3rd issue). Film Actors. Four sheets containing T **501** and similar vert designs. Multicoloured.
MS1607 (a) 136 × 196 mm. 250f. × 9, Type **501**; Rudolph Valentino; Errol Flynn; Cary Grant; Robert Taylor; Gary Cooper; James Dean; Humphrey Bogart; Marlon Brando. (b) 136 × 196 mm. 425f. × 9, Grace Kelly; Marilyn Monroe; Audrey Hepburn; Greta Garbo; Jean Harlow; Loretta Young; Jane Russell; Dorothy Lamour; Veronica Lake. (c) 140 × 200 mm. 450f. × 9, Ginger Rogers and Fred Astaire; Cary Grant, Katherine Hepburn and James Stewart; Melvyn Douglas and Greta Garbo; Vivien Leigh and Clark Gable; Burt Lancaster and Deborah Kerr; Humphrey Bogart and Lauren Bacall; Steve McQueen and Jacqueline Bisset; Gene Kelly and Rita Hayworth; Ingrid Bergman and Cary Grant. (d) 116 × 143 mm. 2000f. Grace Kelly (different) Set of 4 sheets 24·00 14·50

502 Betty Boop holding Microphone

1999. Betty Boop (cartoon character created by Max Fleischer). Multicoloured.
1608 250f. Type **502** 50 30
1609 250f. Holding guitar 50 30
1610 400f. Seated 80 50
MS1611 Five sheets. (a) 132 × 177 mm. 250f. × 9, Holding saxophone; Playing tambourine; 1609; Playing guitar; Wearing top hat; Holding drum sticks; Wearing headphones; 1608; Wearing patterned trousers. (b) 132 × 177 mm. 400f. × 9, Wearing red dress; Wearing flowered earrings, bracelets and belt; Wearing ruffled blouse and waistcoat; Wearing purple dress; 1610; Wearing black outfit; Wearing fringed waistcoat; Wearing black sleeveless dress; Wearing purple jacket and trousers. (c) 89 × 140 mm. 1000f. Head and shoulders. (d) 89 × 140 mm. 1500f. With folded arms. (e) 89 × 140 mm. 2000f. Wearing purple jacket Set of 5 sheets . . . . 20·00 12·00

503 Lucy (Lucille Ball)

1999. *I Love Lucy* (Television comedy series). Multicoloured.
1612 300f. Type **503** 60 40
1613 300f. Fred Mertz (William Fawley), Ethel Mertz (Vivian Vance) and Lucy 60 40
MS1614 Four sheets. (a) Vert. 137 × 182 mm. 330f. × 9, Lucy holding telephone; No. 1612; Wearing green dress with black tie; With hand raised; Wearing pearl necklace and black hat; Holding medicine bottle; Wearing hat, glasses and fur stole; Wearing purple hat; Wearing top hat. (b) Horiz. 177 × 132 mm. 330f. × 9, With Ethel holding boxes; Desi Arnaz, Lucy, Fred and Ethel; Fred, Ethel and Lucy wearing headscarf; Lucy and chicks; Fred, Ethel, Lucy and Desi seated at table; Ethel and Lucy; Lucy dancing wearing rolled up trousers; As No. 1613; Lucy, Ethel and Fred seated at table. (c) 89 × 127 mm. 1000f. Lucy holding box (36 × 51 mm). (d) 117 × 89 mm. 2000f. Lucy holding paper bag (36 × 51 mm) Set of 4 sheets . . . . 18·00 11·00

504 Three Stooges

1999. *The Three Stooges* (comedy series starring Moe Howard, Larry Fine and Curly Howard). Multicoloured.
1615 400f. Type **504** 80 50
MS1616 Three sheets. (a) Horiz. 175 × 140 mm. 400f. × 9, Moe and Larry lying on bed; Moe, Larry and Curly; Moe and Larry listening to telephone ("False Alarms"); Holding scissors; As No. 1615; With surgical trolley ("Dizzy Doctors"); Larry and Curly holding Moe down; Holding step ladder; Holding plank ("Tassels in the Air"). (b) Vert. 140 × 89 mm. 1000f. Curly and Moe with feathers. (c) Vert. 140 × 89 mm. 1500f. Curly as cowboy Set of 3 sheets . . . . 12·00 7·25

505 Participants and Pyramids

2001. 22nd Paris—Dakar Rally. Multicoloured.
1617 75f. Type **505** 15 10
1618 100f. Truck, four-wheel drive and rally car 20 10
1619 220f. Truck and motorcycle 45 25
1620 320f. Camel and motorcycle 65 40

506 Motorcyclist and Rally Emblem

2001. 23rd Paris—Dakar Rally. Multicoloured.
1621 190f. Type **506** 40 25
1622 220f. Emblem as face (vert) 45 25
1623 240f. Emblem containing camel (vert) 50 30
1624 790f. Emblem and four-wheel drive car . . . . . 1·60 95

507 Festival of Arts and Culture Emblem **508** Swimmer and Weightlifter

2001. Third Millennium. Multicoloured.
1625 20f. Type **507** 10 10
1626 100f. Pan African Plastic Arts festival emblem . . . 20 10
1627 150f. National Heritage Day emblem 30 20
1628 300f. Memorial, Goree Island (anti-slavery memorial) (horiz) 60 35

2001. Olympic Games, Sydney (2000). Multicoloured.
1629 40f. Type **508** 10 10
1630 80f. Taekwondo 15 10
1631 240f. Runners finishing 200m race 50 30
1632 290f. Handball match . . . 60 35

509 Flower Seller **511** *Maytenus senegalensis*

510 Satellite Dish, Globe and Weather Station

2001. Craft Market, Kermel. Multicoloured.
1633 50f. Type **509** 10 10
1634 90f. Wooden carvings . . . 20 10
1635 250f. Bowls and pendants (horiz) 50 30
1636 350f. Carvings and flower seller 70 40

2001. 50th Anniv of World Meteorological Organization. Multicoloured.
1637 100f. Type **510** 20 10
1638 790f. Weather station (vert) 1·60 95

2001. Medicinal Plants. Multicoloured.
1639 240f. Type **511** 50 30
1640 320f. *Boscia senegalensis* . . 65 40
1641 350f. *Euphorbia hirta* . . . 70 40
1642 500f. *Guiera senegalensis* . . 1·00 60

512 Outline of Senegal

2001. 19th Lions International District 403 Congress, Dakar. Multicoloured.
1643 190f. Type **512** 40 25
1644 300f. Lion (vert) 60 35

513 Emblem, Tank and Runners

2001. 50th Anniv of United Nations High Commissioner for Refugees. Multicoloured.

1645		240f. Type **513**	50	30
1646		320f. Emblem, globe and runner (vert)	65	40

514 Hands holding Book

2001. International Teachers' Day. Multicoloured.

1647		225f. Type **514**	45	25
1648		290f. Man writing and world map (horiz)	60	35

515 Drummer

2001. Tourism. Multicoloured.

1649		145f. Type **515**	30	20
1650		290f. Tree, windsurfer, and beach (vert)	60	35

516 Antelope and Lioness

2001. National Parks. Multicoloured.

1651		75f. Type **516**	15	10
1652		125f. Heron and marabou stork	25	15
1653		275f. Crowned cranes and elephant	55	35
1654		300f. Zebra (vert)	60	35

OFFICIAL STAMPS

O 45 Arms of Dakar

O 78 Baobab Tree

1961. Figures of value in black.

O240	O **45**	1f. black and blue	10	10
O241		2f. blue and yellow	10	10
O242		5f. lake and green	10	10
O243		10f. red and blue	10	10
O244		25f. blue and red	45	15
O245		50f. red and grey	75	30
O246		85f. purple and orange	1·40	45
O247		100f. red and green	2·25	1·10

1966.

O 339	O **78**	1f. black and yellow	10	10
O 340		5f. black and orange	10	10
O 341		10f. black and red	10	10
O 342		20f. black and purple	15	10
O 342a		25f. black and mauve	15	10
O 343		30f. black and blue	15	10
O 344		35f. black and blue	45	10
O 344a		40f. black and blue	20	10
O1122		50f. black and red	20	15
O 345		55f. black and green	65	20
O 345a		60f. black and green	45	20
O 346		90f. black and green	1·00	35
O 347		100f. black & brown	1·10	40
O1123		145f. black and green	1·00	35
O1124		180f. black & orange	1·10	45

1969. No. O345 surch.

O390	O **78**	60f. on 55f. black & grn	1·10	10

POSTAGE DUE STAMPS

1903. Postage Due stamps of French Colonies surch.

D30	U	10 on 50c. purple	80·00	80·00
D31		10 on 60c. brown on buff	80·00	80·00
D32		10 on 1f. pink on buff	£300	£300

1906. "Natives" key-type.

D50	L	5c. green and red	2·25	3·50
D51		10c. purple and blue	4·50	3·50
D52		15c. blue and red on blue	4·75	9·00
D53		20c. black & red on yellow	5·25	3·00
D54		30c. red and blue on cream	11·00	11·50
D55		50c. violet and red	8·00	12·00
D56		60c. black and red on buff	14·00	16·00
D57		1f. black and red on pink	16·00	30·00

1915. "Figure" key-type.

D81	M	5c. green	20	2·50
D82		10c. red	50	1·60
D83		15c. grey	25	2·00
D84		20c. brown	55	2·00
D85		30c. blue	1·60	1·75
D86		50c. black	1·25	2·25
D87		60c. orange	2·25	3·75
D88		1r. violet	2·00	1·00

1927. Surch in figures.

D133	M	2f. on 1f. purple	2·50	6·75
D134		3f. on 1f. brown	3·50	6·00

D 40

1935.

D194	D **40**	5c. green	10	2·50
D195		10c. orange	15	2·50
D196		15c. violet	20	2·75
D197		20c. olive	25	2·25
D198		30c. brown	30	2·75
D199		50c. purple	20	2·75
D200		60c. yellow	1·60	3·00
D201		1f. black	50	3·00
D202		2f. blue	2·25	3·75
D203		3f. red	1·10	3·25

D 43

D 77 Lion's Head

1961.

D239	D **43**	1f. orange and red	10	10
D240		2f. blue and red	10	10
D241		5f. brown and red	10	10
D242		20f. green and red	25	25
D243		25f. purple and red	65	65

1966. Head in gold and black; value in black.

D339	D **77**	1f. red	15	15
D340		2f. brown	15	15
D341		5f. violet	20	20
D342		10f. blue	40	40
D343		20f. green	50	50
D344		30f. grey	65	65
D345		60f. blue	65	65
D346		90f. purple	75	75

SENEGAMBIA AND NIGER Pt. 6

A French colony later re-named Upper Senegal and Niger, and later French Sudan.

100 centimes = 1 franc.

1903. "Tablet" key-type inscr "SENEGAMBIE ET NIGER" in red (1, 5, 15, 25, 75c., 1f.) or blue (others).

22	D	1c. black on blue	75	3·00
23		2c. brown on buff	1·00	2·75
24		4c. brown on grey	2·40	4·00
25		5c. green	4·25	2·25
26		10c. red	4·75	2·50
27		15c. grey	13·00	8·50
28		20c. red on green	14·00	16·00
29		25c. blue	20·00	23·00
30		30c. brown on drab	11·00	23·00
31		40c. red on yellow	20·00	35·00
32		50c. brown on blue	35·00	50·00
33		75c. brown on orange	35·00	60·00
34		1f. green	50·00	75·00

SERBIA Pt. 3

A kingdom in the Balkans, S.E. Europe. Part of Yugoslavia since 1918, except during the Second World War when stamps were issued by a German sponsored Government.

1866. 40 para = 1 grosch.
1880. 100 para = 1 dinar.

2 Prince Michael (Obrenovic III)

3 Prince Milan (Obrenovic IV)

5 King Milan I

1866. Perf.

12	**2**	10p. orange	75·00	£120
15		20p. red	7·25	10·00
14		40p. blue	45·00	30·00

1869. Perf.

42	**3**	10p. brown	3·25	1·75
45		10p. orange	1·90	4·50
31c		15p. orange	55·00	9·00
46		20p. blue	1·90	2·75
39b		25p. red	1·90	4·25
34c		35p. green	4·50	6·75
47		40p. mauve	1·90	4·50
36		50p. green	5·75	16·00

1880. Perf.

54a	**5**	5p. green	1·00	30
55		10p. red	1·75	30
56		20p. orange	50	50
57a		25p. blue	1·00	75
58		50p. brown	1·50	2·75
59		1d. violet	6·75	7·50

6 King Alexander (Obrenovic V)

7 King Alexander (Obrenovic V)

10 King Alexander (Obrenovic V)

1890.

60	**6**	5p. green	30	10
61		10p. red	60	10
62		15p. lilac	60	10
63		20p. orange	50	10
64		25p. blue	1·00	25
65		50p. brown	2·50	2·50
66		1d. lilac	12·00	10·00

1894.

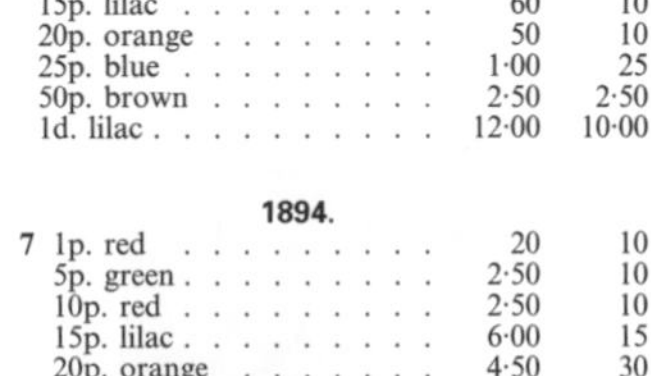

75	**7**	1p. red	20	10
76		5p. green	2·50	10
68		10p. red	2·50	10
69		15p. lilac	6·00	15
79		20p. orange	4·50	30
80		25p. blue	4·25	35
81a		50p. brown	14·00	1·00
73		1d. green	1·50	3·00
74		1d. brown on blue	18·00	3·50

1900. Surch.

82	**7**	10p. on 20p. red	2·75	10
84		15p. on 1d. brown on blue	4·50	1·50

1901.

85a	**10**	5p. green	35	10
86		10p. red	10	10
87		15p. purple	10	10
88		20p. yellow	10	10
89		25p. blue	15	10
90		50p. yellow	35	30
91	–	1d. brown	1·00	1·75
92a	–	3d. pink	6·00	8·00
93a	–	5d. violet	6·00	10·00

The 1d. to 5d. are larger.

12 King Alexander I (Obrenovic V)

14 Karageorge and Petar I

1903. Optd with shield.

94	**12**	1p. black and red	50	75
95		5p. black and green	40	10
96		10p. black and red	25	10
97		15p. black and grey	25	10
98		20p. black and yellow	35	15
99		25p. black and blue	35	15
100		50p. black and grey	3·50	90
101		1d. black and green	10·00	3·75
102		3d. black and lilac	2·25	2·75
103		5d. black and brown	2·25	3·00

1903. Surch with arms and new value.

104	**12**	1p. on 5d. black and brown	1·00	2·75

1904. Coronation. Centenary of Karageorgevic Dynasty. Dated "1804 1904".

108	**14**	5p. green	20	10
109		10p. red	20	10
110		15p. purple	25	15
111		25p. blue	50	30
112		50p. brown	65	65
113	–	1d. bistre	1·25	2·50
114	–	3d. green	2·25	4·75
115	–	5d. violet	3·00	6·00

DESIGN: 1, 3, 5d. Karageorge and insurgents, 1804.

16 Petar I

17 Petar I

1905.

116	**16**	1p. black and grey	25	10
117		5p. black and green	40	10
118		10p. black and red	1·75	10
119		15p. black and mauve	1·90	10
120		20p. black and yellow	3·50	10
121		25p. black and blue	4·25	10
122		30p. black and green	3·00	15
123		50p. black and brown	3·25	30
135		1d. black and bistre	75	25
136		3d. black and green	75	75
137		5d. black and violet	2·75	2·00

1911.

146	**17**	1p. black	10	10
147		2p. violet	10	10
169		5p. green	10	10
170		10p. red	10	10
150		15p. purple	35	10
171		15p. black	10	10
151		20p. yellow	35	10
172		20p. brown	50	30
173		25p. blue	10	10
153		30p. green	35	30
173a		30p. bronze	10	20
154		50p. brown	50	30
174		50p. red	10	20
155		1d. orange	20·00	40·00
175		1d. green	1·25	5·00
156		3d. lake	28·00	80·00
176		3d. yellow	90·00	£750
177		5d. violet	2·50	20·00

19 King Petar I on the Battlefield

20 King Petar I and Prince Alexander

1915.

178	**19**	5p. green	15	5·00
179		10p. red	15	5·00
179a		15p. grey	5·00	
179b		20p. brown	75	
179c		25p. blue	10·00	
179d		30p. green	6·00	
179e		50p. brown	24·00	

1918.

194	**20**	1p. black	10	10
195		2p. olive	10	10
196		5p. green	10	10
197		10p. red	10	10
198		15p. sepia	10	10
199		20p. brown	10	10
208		20p. mauve	2·00	1·00
200		25p. blue	10	10
201		30p. olive	10	10
202		50p. mauve	10	10
220		1d. brown	35	15
204		3d. slate	1·00	75
205		5d. brown	1·50	1·00

NEWSPAPER STAMPS

1 State Arms

4 King Milan

1866. Imperf.

N7	**1**	1p. green and pink	40·00	
N2		2p. green and blue	£500	
N6		2p. brown and blue	£100	

1867. Perf.

N17	**2**	1p. green	14·00	£550
N18		2p. brown	25·00	£500

1868. Imperf.

N19	**2**	1p. green	40·00	
N20		2p. brown	65·00	

1869. Perf.

N49a	**3**	1p. yellow	4·00	£275

1872. Imperf.

N51	**3**	1p. yellow	3·75	13·50
N53	**4**	2p. black	1·90	50

POSTAGE DUE STAMPS

D 8

D 21

1895.

D87 D 8 5p. mauve 50 30
D83 10p. blue 5·00 35
D91 20p. brown 45 80
D85 30p. green 50 75
D86 50p. red 60 35

1918.

D227 D 21 5p. red 20 20
D232 5p. brown 20 50
D228 10p. green 20 20
D229 20p. brown 20 20
D230 30p. blue 20 20
D233 30p. grey 50 1·00
D231 50p. brown 50 1·00

GERMAN OCCUPATION

1941. Stamps of Yugoslavia on paper with coloured network optd **SERBIEN** reading downwards.

G 1 99 25p. black 10 1·75
G 2 50p. orange 10 50
G 3 1d. green 10 50
G 4 1d.50 red 10 50
G 5 2d. red 10 50
G 6 3d. brown 75 6·75
G 7 4d. blue 15 1·10
G 8 5d. blue 45 3·00
G 9 5d.50 violet 45 3·00
G10 6d. blue 45 3·00
G11 8d. brown 70 5·00
G12 12d. violet 70 5·00
G13 16d. purple 1·00 17·00
G14 20d. blue 1·00 70·00
G15 30d. pink 5·00 £200

1941. Air. Stamps of Yugoslavia on paper with coloured network, optd **SERBIEN**.

G16 80 50p. brown 5·75 65·00
G17 – 1d. green (No. 361) 5·75 65·00
G18 – 2d. blue (No. 362) 5·75 65·00
G19 – 2d.50 red (No. 363) 5·75 65·00
G20 80 5d. violet 5·75 65·00
G21 – 10d. red (No. 365) 5·75 65·00
G22 – 20d. green (No. 366) 5·75 65·00
G23 – 30d. blue (No. 367) 7·50 65·00
G24 – 40d. green (No. 443) 13·00 £300
G25 – 50d. blue (No. 444) 16·00 £450

1941. Air. As last, but without network opt, surch **SERBIEN** and value.

G26 – 1d. on 10d. red (No. 365) 1·75 50·00
G27 – 3d. on 20d. grn (No. 366) 1·75 50·00
G28 – 6d. on 30d. blue (No. 367) 1·75 50·00
G29 – 8d. on 40d. grn (No. 443) 3·50 £110
G30 – 12d. on 50d. blue (No. 444) 5·00 £250

1941. As Nos. G1/15, but with **SERBIEN** reading upwards.

G31 99 25p. black 10 5·00
G32 50p. orange 10 1·00
G33 1d. green 15 1·00
G34 1d.50 red 15 1·00
G35 2d. red 15 1·00
G36 3d. brown 35 5·00
G37 4d. blue 25 1·00
G38 5d. blue 25 2·00
G39 5d.50 violet 45 4·00
G40 6d. blue 55 4·00
G41 8d. brown 70 4·00
G42 12d. violet 1·00 4·00
G43 16d. purple 1·00 23·00
G44 20d. blue 1·00 60·00
G45 30d. pink 6·00 £175

G 4 Smederovo Fortress

G 6 Christ and the Virgin Mary

1941. Smederovo Explosion Relief Fund. (a).

G46 G 4 0.50d.+1d. brown 25 1·40
G47 – 1d.+2d. green (Refugees) 25 1·75
G48 – 1.50d.+3d. purple (Refugees) 45 3·00
G49 G 4 2d.+4d. blue 65 4·00

(b) Sheets 149 × 109 mm comprising Nos. G47 and G49, colours changed and with high premiums.

MSG49a 1d.+49d. red; 2d.+48d. green. P 11½ 40·00 £300
MSG49b 1d.+49d. green; 2d.+48d. red. Imperf 40·00 £300

1941. Prisoners of War Fund.

G50 G 6 0.50d.+1.50d. red 30 5·00
G51 1d.+3d. green 30 5·00
G52 2d.+6d. red 30 5·00
G53 4d.+12d. blue 30 5·00

This set also exists with an optd network, both plain and incorporating a large "E", this letter being either normal or reversed.

G 7

G 8

1942. Anti-Masonic Exn. Dated "22.X.1941".

G54 G 7 0.50d.+1.50d. brown 25 1·25
G55 – 1d.+1d. green 25 1·25
G56 G 8 2d.+2d. red 30 2·50
G57 – 4d.+4d. blue 30 2·50

DESIGNS—HORIZ: 1d. Hand grasping snake. VERT: 4d. Peasant demolishing masonic symbols.

G 9 Kalenic

G 11 Mother and Children

1942. Monasteries.

G58 – 0d.50 violet 10 30
G59 G 9 1d. red 10 30
G60 – 1d.50 brown 70 3·00
G61 – 1d.50 green 10 30
G62 – 2d. purple 10 30
G63 – 3d. blue 70 3·00
G64 – 3d. pink 10 30
G65 – 4d. blue 10 30
G66 – 7d. green 10 30
G67 – 12d. red 15 1·50
G68 – 16d. black 75 2·00

DESIGNS—VERT: 0d.50, Lazarica; 1d.50, Ravanica; 12d. Gornjak; 16d. Studenica. HORIZ: 2d. Manasija; 3d. Ljubostinja; 4d. Sopocani; 7d. Zica.

1942. As Nos. G50/53, colours changed.

G68a G 6 0.50d.+1.50d. brown 60 3·25
G68b 1d.+3d. green 60 3·25
G68c 2d.+6d. red 60 3·25
G68d 4d.+12d. blue 60 3·25

1942. Air. 1939 issue of Yugoslavia surch with airplane, "SERBIA" in cyrillic characters and new value.

G69 99 2 on 2d. mauve 15 1·50
G70 4 on 4d. blue 15 1·50
G71 10 on 12d. violet 15 2·75
G72 14 on 20d. blue 15 2·75
G73 20 on 30d. pink 50 13·00

1942. War Orphans Fund.

G74 G 11 2d.+6d. violet 1·50 4·75
G75 4d.+8d. blue 1·50 4·75
G76 7d.+13d. green 1·50 4·75
G77 20d.+40d. red 1·50 4·75

G 12 Broken Sword

G 13 Post Rider

1943. War Invalids' Relief Fund.

G78 G 12 1.50d.+1.50d. brown 40 1·25
G79 – 2d.+3d. green 40 1·25
G80 – 3d.+5d. mauve 75 2·50
G81 – 4d.+10d. blue 1·00 3·75

MSG81a Two sheets, each 149 × 110 mm. Thick paper. P 11½. (a) 1d.50+48d.50, 4d.+46d. (b) 2d.+48d., 3d.+47d. 60·00 £4000

DESIGNS—HORIZ: 2d. Fallen standard bearer; 3d. Wounded soldier (seated). VERT: 4d. Nurse tending soldier.

1943. Postal Centenary. Inscr "15.X.1843–15.X.1943".

G82 G 13 3d. red and lilac 30 1·50
G83 – 8d. red and green 30 1·50
G84 – 9d. green and brown 90 1·50
G85 – 30d. brown and green 30 1·50
G86 – 50d. blue and red 30 1·50

DESIGNS: 8d. Horse wagon; 9d. Railway mail van; 30d. Postal motor van; 50d. Junkers Ju 52/3m mail plane.

1943. Bombing of Nish Relief Fund. Monasteries issue of 1942 on paper with network, surch with Serbian inscr **20-X-1943** and value.

G87 0d.50+2d. violet 10 20·00
G88 1d.+3d. red 10 20·00
G89 1d.50+4d. green 10 20·00
G90 2d.+5d. purple 15 20·00
G91 3d.+7d. pink 15 20·00
G92 4d.+9d. blue 15 20·00
G93 7d.+15d. green 45 20·00
G94 12d.+25d. red 45 £100
G95 16d.+33d. black 85 £180

OFFICIAL STAMP

GO 12

1943.

GO78 GO 12 3d. red 60 2·00

POSTAGE DUE STAMPS

GD 2

GD 3

1941. Unissued Postage Due stamps optd **SERBIEN**.

GD16 GD 2 0d.50 violet 50 13·50
GD17 1d. red 50 13·50
GD18 2d. blue 50 13·50
GD19 3d. red 65 20·00
GD20 GD 3 4d. blue 85 50·00
GD21 5d. orange 85 50·00
GD22 10d. violet 2·50 £100
GD23 20d. green 6·50 £350

1942. Types GD 2 and GD 3 without opt. Bottom inscription on white background.

GD69 GD 2 1d. red and green 35 5·00
GD70 2d. blue and red 35 5·00
GD71 3d. red and blue 40 8·00
GD72 GD 3 4d. blue and red 40 8·00
GD73 5d. orange and blue 50 10·00
GD74 10d. violet and red 55 16·00
GD75 20d. green and red 1·50 60·00

GD 13

1943.

GD82 GD 13 0d.50 black 20 3·00
GD83 3d. violet 20 3·00
GD84 4d. blue 20 3·00
GD85 5d. green 20 3·00
GD86 6d. orange 35 8·50
GD87 10d. red 50 12·50
GD88 20d. blue 1·75 30·00

SERBIAN OCCUPATION OF HUNGARY Pt. 2

BARANYA

100 filler = 1 korona.

1919. Stamps of Hungary optd **1919 Baranya** or surch also. (a) "Turul" Type.

1 7 6f. drab 15 15
2 50f. red on blue 10 10
3 60f. green on red 35 35
4 70f. brown on green 10 10
5 80f. violet 35 35

(b) War Charity stamp of 1915.

6 7 50+2f. red on blue 4·75 4·75

(c) War Charity stamps of 1916.

8 20 10f. (+ 2f.) red 10 10
9 – 15f. (+ 2f.) violet 10 10

(d) Harvesters and Parliament Types.

10 18 2f. brown 10 10
11 3f. purple 10 10
12 5f. green 10 10
13 6f. blue 10 10
14 15f. purple 10 10
15 20f. brown 5·00 5·00
16 25f. blue 1·25 1·25
17 35f. brown 1·90 1·90
18 40f. green 5·00 5·00
19 45 on 2f. brown 40 40
20 45 on 5f. green 10 10
21 45 on 15f. purple 45 45
22 19 50f. purple 25 25
23 75f. blue 10 10
24 80f. green 15 15
25 1k. red 15 15
26 2k. brown 15 15
27 3k. grey and violet 15 15
28 5k. light brown and brown 65 65
29 60k. mauve and brown 1·25 1·25

(e) Charles and Zita stamps.

30 27 10f. pink 10 10
31 20f. brown 10 10
32 25f. blue 40 40
33 28 40f. green 50 50

(f) Stamps optd **KOZTARSASAG**. (i) Harvesters Type.

34 18 2f. brown 1·40 1·40
35 45 on 2f. brown 40 40

(ii) Zita stamp.

36 28 40f. green 5·00 5·00

1919. Stamps of Hungary surch **BARANYA** and value. (a) Harvesters and Parliament Types.

42 18 20 on 2f. brown 2·00 2·00
43 50 on 5f. green 1·00 1·00
44 150 on 15f. purple 65 65
45 19 200 on 75f. blue 65 65

(b) Harvesters Type inscr "MAGYAR POSTA".

46 18 20 on 2f. brown 10 10
47 30 on 6f. blue 35 35
48 50 on 5f. green 10 10
49 100 on 25f. blue 10 10
50 100 on 40f. green 10 10
51 100 on 45f. orange 40 40
52 150 on 20f. brown 40 40

(c) Charles stamp optd **KOZTARSASAG**.

53 27 150 on 15f. purple 65 65

EXPRESS LETTER STAMPS

1919. No. E245 of Hungary surch **1919 Baranya 105**.

E37 E 18 105 on 2f. green and red 65 65

1919. No. E245 of Hungary surch **BARANYA 10**.

E55 E 18 10 on 2f. olive and red 40 40

NEWSPAPER STAMP

1919. No. N136 of Hungary surch **BARANYA 10**.

N54 N 9 10 on 2(f). orange 35 35

POSTAGE DUE STAMPS

1919. Nos. D191 etc of Hungary optd **1919 BARANYA** or surch also.

D38 D 9 2f. red and green 2·00 2·00
D39 10f. red and green 40 40
D40 20f. red and geen 40 40
D41 40 on 2f. red and green 40 40

SAVINGS BANK STAMP

1919. No. B199 of Hungary surch **BARANYA 10**.

B56 B 17 10 on 10f. purple 45 45

TEMESVAR

Temesvar was later occupied by Rumania which issued stamps for this area. It was then incorporated in Rumania and renamed Timosoara.

100 filler = 1 korona.

1919. Stamps of Hungary surch. (a) War Charity stamps of 1916.

1 20 45f. on 10f.(+2f.) red 10 10

(b) Harvesters Type.

2 18 10f. on 2f. brown 10 10
3 30f. on 2f. brown 10 10
4 1k.50 on 15f. purple 15 15

(c) Charles Stamp.

5 27 50f. on 20f. brown 10 10

POSTAGE DUE STAMPS

1919. No. D191 of Hungary surch.

D6 D 9 40f. on 2f. red and green 40 40
D7 60f. on 2f. red and green 40 40
D8 100f. on 2f. red and green 40 40

SEYCHELLES Pt. 1

A group of islands in the Indian Ocean, east of Africa.

100 cents = 1 rupee.

1

6

1890.

9 1 2c. green and red 2·50 1·00
28 2c. brown and green 2·00 1·25
22 3c. purple and orange 1·50 50
10 4c. red and green 2·50 1·00
29 6c. red 3·50 50
11 8c. purple and blue 8·00 1·75
12 10c. blue and brown 9·50 3·25
23 12c. brown and green 2·50 60
13 13c. grey and black 3·25 1·75
24 15c. olive and lilac 4·50 2·00
30 15c. blue 5·50 3·50
6 16c. brown and blue 6·50 4·25
31 18c. blue 5·00 1·00
32 36c. brown and red 27·00 4·50
25 45c. brown and red 23·00 35·00
7 48c. bistre and green 20·00 10·00
33 75c. yellow and violet 55·00 70·00
8 96c. mauve and red 55·00 48·00
34 1r. mauve and red 13·00 4·25

35 1r.50 grey and red . . . . . 70·00 85·00
36 2r.25 mauve and green . . . £100 85·00

1893. Surch in figures and words in two lines.
15 **1** 3c. on 4c. red and green . . 1·10 1·50
16 12c. on 16c. brown and blue 2·00 3·75
19 15c. on 16c. brown and blue 15·00 3·00
20 45c. on 48c. brown and green 25·00 5·50
21 90c. on 96c. mauve and red 55·00 32·00

1896. Surch in figures and words in one line.
26 **1** 18c. on 45c. brown and red 7·00 2·75
27 36c. on 45c. brown and red 8·00 50·00

1901. Surch in figures and words.
41 **1** 2c. on 4c. red and green . . 1·75 2·75
37 3c. on 10c. blue and brown 1·50 60
38 3c. on 16c. brown and blue 3·00 4·25
39 3c. on 36c. brown and red . . 70 80
40 6c. on 8c. purple and blue . . 2·00 3·00
42 30c. on 75c. yellow and violet 1·50 4·00
43 30c. on 1r. mauve and red . . 6·50 29·00
44 45c. on 1r. mauve and red . . 3·50 32·00
45 45c. on 2r.25 mauve and green . . . . 42·00 90·00

1903.
46 **6** 2c. brown and green . . . . 1·75 2·00
47 3c. green . . . . 1·00 1·25
62 6c. red . . . . 2·00 80
49 12c. brown and green . . . . 2·75 2·50
64 15c. blue . . . . 3·00 2·00
65 18c. olive and red . . . . 3·00 6·50
66 30c. violet and green . . . . 6·00 8·00
67 45c. brown and red . . . . . 3·00 6·50
54 75c. yellow and violet . . . . 10·00 28·00
69 1r.50 black and red . . . . 55·00 60·00
70 2r.25 purple and green . . . 35·00 60·00

1903. Surch **3 cents**.
57 **6** 3c. on 15c. blue . . . . . . 1·00 3·25
58 3c. on 18c. olive and red . . 2·75 38·00
59 3c. on 45c. brown and red . . 3·00 3·25

9 11

1912. Inscr "POSTAGE POSTAGE".
71 **9** 2c. brown and green . . . . 70 5·50
72 3c. green . . . . 2·25 60
73 6c. red . . . . 4·25 70
74 12c. brown and green . . . . 1·25 4·00
75 15c. blue . . . . 3·75 1·00
76 18c. olive and red . . . . 3·25 6·00
77 30c. violet and green . . . . 5·50 1·25
78 45c. brown and red . . . . . 2·75 35·00
79 75c. yellow and violet . . . . 2·75 5·50
80 1r.50 black and red . . . . 7·50 1·00
81 2r.25 purple and green . . . 55·00 2·50

1917. Inscr "POSTAGE & REVENUE".
98 **11** 2c. brown and green . . . 25 15
99 3c. green . . . . 1·75 15
100 3c. black . . . . 1·00 30
101 4c. green . . . . 1·00 2·50
102 4c. olive and red . . . . 6·50 17·00
103 5c. brown . . . . 75 5·50
85 6c. red . . . . 2·25 1·50
105 6c. mauve 60 10
106 9c. red . . . . 3·25 4·25
86 12c. grey . . . . 1·00 1·00
108 12c. red . . . . 1·25 30
110 15c. blue . . . . 2·00 55
111 15c. yellow . . . . 1·00 2·75
112 18c. purple on yellow . . 2·50 12·00
113 20c. blue . . . . 1·50 35
89b 25c. black & red on yellow . . . . 1·75 9·50
90 30c. purple and olive . . 1·50 8·50
116 45c. purple and orange . . 1·25 5·00
117 50c. purple and black . . 2·50 2·25
93 75c. black on green . . . 1·60 15·00
119 1r. purple and red . . . . 14·00 18·00
121 1r.50 purple & blue on bl 14·00 22·00
122 2r.25 green and violet . . 13·00 14·00
123 5r. green and blue . . . . 85·00 £170

1935. Silver Jubilee. As T **32a** of St. Helena.
128 6c. blue and black . . . . . 1·00 2·00
129 12c. green and blue . . . . 3·00 1·50
130 20c. brown and blue . . . . 2·50 2·75
131 1r. grey and purple . . . . 6·50 15·00

1937. Coronation. As T **32b** of St. Helena.
132 6c. green 35 15
133 12c. orange 50 50
134 20c. blue . . . . 70 1·00

14 Coco-de-mer Palm

1938.
135 a **14** 2c. brown . . . . 30 1·75
136 – 3c. green . . . . 8·50 1·75
136ab – 3c. orange . . . . . . 55 1·50
137 – 6c. orange . . . . . . 8·50 3·50
137ab – 6c. green . . . . 55 2·25
138 **14** 9c. red . . . . 10·00 2·25
138ac – 9c. blue . . . . 6·50 2·50
139 – 12c. mauve . . . . . . 42·00 1·25
139ab – 15c. red . . . . 6·50 3·00
139ca **14** 18c. red . . . . 6·50 2·75
140 – 20c. blue . . . . 42·00 6·00
140ab – 20c. yellow . . . . . . 2·50 3·00
141 **14** 25c. brown . . . . . . 50·00 14·00
142 – 30c. red . . . . 50·00 10·00
142ab – 30c. blue . . . . 2·25 3·25
143 a – 45c. brown . . . . . . 2·75 1·75
144 b **14** 50c. violet . . . . . . 2·25 2·25
145 – 75c. blue . . . . 85·00 38·00
145ab – 75c. mauve . . . . . . 2·25 3·00
146 – 1r. green . . . . £100 55·00
146ab – 1r. black . . . . 1·50 3·25
147 a **14** 1r.50 blue . . . . . . 4·50 7·50
148 a – 2r.25 olive . . . . . . 20·00 22·00
149 – 5r. red . . . . 11·00 8·50
DESIGNS—VERT: 3, 12, 15, 30, 75c., 2r.25, Giant tortoise. HORIZ: 6, 20, 45c., 1, 5r. Fishing pirogue.

1946. Victory. As T **33a** of St. Helena.
150 9c. blue 10 10
151 30c. blue 30 10

1948. Silver Wedding. As T **33b/c** of St. Helena.
152 9c. blue 15 60
153 5r. red . . . . 12·00 29·00

1949. U.P.U. As T **33d/g** of St. Helena.
154 18c. mauve 15 25
155 50c. purple . . . . 1·75 1·00
156 1r. grey 25 20
157 2r.25 olive . . . . 30 1·00

17 Sailfish **21** "La Pierre de Possession"

1952. Full face portrait.
158 **17** 2c. lilac 60 70
159 – 3c. orange 60 30
160 – 9c. blue . . . . 60 1·75
161 – 15c. green 50 75
162 – 18c. lake . . . . 1·25 20
163 – 20c. yellow . . . . 1·00 1·50
164 – 25c. red . . . . 70 1·50
165 **17** 40c. blue . . . . 1·00 1·25
166 – 45c. brown 70 30
167 – 50c. violet . . . . 1·25 1·75
168 – 1r. black . . . . 3·00 2·75
169 – 1r.50 blue . . . . 7·00 12·00
170 – 2r.25 olive . . . . 11·00 12·00
171 – 5r. red . . . . 11·00 14·00
172 **17** 10r. green . . . . 19·00 30·00
DESIGNS—VERT: 2, 25c., 2r.25, Giant tortoise; 9, 50c., 1r.50, Coco-de-mer palm. HORIZ: 15, 20, 45c. Fishing pirogue; 18c., 1, 5r. Map of Indian Ocean.

1953. Coronation. As T **33h** of St. Helena.
173 9c. black and blue 60 70

1954. Designs as 1952 but with portrait of Queen Elizabeth II.
174 2c. lilac 10 10
175 3c. orange 10 10
175a 5c. violet . . . . 2·00 30
176 9c. blue 10 10
176a 10c. blue (as 9c.) . . . . . 50 2·25
177 15c. green 30 30
178 18c. lake 10 10
179 20c. yellow 75 20
180 25c. red . . . . 60 1·00
180a 35c. lake (as 18c.) . . . . . 4·50 1·75
181 40c. blue 50 25
182 45c. brown 20 15
183 50c. violet 30 80
183a 70c. brown (as 45c.) . . . . 5·50 1·25
184 1r. black 50 40
185 1r.50 blue . . . . 3·50 6·50
186 2r.25 olive . . . . 3·50 8·00
187 5r. red . . . . 18·00 9·00
188 10r. green . . . . 28·00 18·00
NEW DESIGN: 5c. Seychelles flying fox.

1956. Bicent of "La Pierre de Possession".
189 **21** 40c. blue 15 15
190 1r. black 15 15

1957. No. 182 surch **5 cents** and bars.
191 5c. on 45c. brown 15 10

23 Mauritius 6d. Stamp with Seychelles "B 64" Cancellation

1961. Cent of First Seychelles Post Office.
193 **23** 10c. blue, black and purple 25 10
194 35c. blue, black and green 40 10
195 2r.25 blue, black & brown 70 45

24 Black Parrot **40** Colony's Badge

1962. Multicoloured.
233 5c. Type **24** . . . . 35 2·25
234 10c. Vanilla vine 30 15
198 15c. Fisherman 30 10
199 20c. Denis Is. Lighthouse . . 30 10
200 25c. Clock Tower, Victoria 30 10
200a 30c. Anse Royale Bay . . . 5·00 5·00
201 35c. Anse Royale Bay . . . 1·75 1·50
202 40c. Government House . . 20 1·50
203 45c. Fishing pirogue . . . . 3·50 5·00
204 50c. Cascade Church . . . 40 25
236 60c. red, blue and brown (Flying fox) . . . . 1·75 45
205 70c. ultramarine and blue (Sailfish) . . . . 6·00 3·00
206 75c. Coco-de-mer palm . . 2·25 4·25
237 85c. ultramarine and blue (Sailfish) . . . . 1·00 40
207 1r. Cinnamon 30 10
208 1r.50 Copra . . . . 5·50 6·50
209 2r.25 Map . . . . 5·50 7·00
210 3r.50 Land settlement . . . 2·25 6·50
211 5r. Regina Mundi Convent 3·50 2·50
212 10r. Type **40** . . . . 12·00 4·00
The 30, 35, 40, 85c., 1, 1r.50, 2r.25, 3r.50 and 5r. are horiz.
No. 236 is 23 × 25 mm.

1963. Freedom from Hunger. As T **63a** of St. Helena.
213 70c. violet 60 25

1963. Cent of Red Cross. As T **63b** of St. Helena.
214 10c. red and black 20 10
215 75c. red and blue 50 60

1965. Surch.
216 45c. on 35c. (No. 201) . . . 10 15
217 75c. on 70c. (No. 205) . . . 20 15

1965. Cent of I.T.U. As T **64a** of St. Helena.
218 5c. orange and blue 10 10
219 1r.50 mauve and green . . . 50 25

1965. I.C.Y. As T **64b** of St. Helena.
220 5c. purple and turquoise . . 15 10
221 40c. green and lavender . . . 35 30

1966. Churchill Commemoration. As T **64c** of St. Helena.
222 5c. blue 15 20
223 15c. green 35 10
224 75c. brown 60 10
225 1r.50 violet . . . . 90 1·00

1966. World Cup Football Championship. As T **64d** of St. Helena.
226 15c. multicoloured 20 25
227 1r. multicoloured 35 40

1966. Inauguration of W.H.O. Headquarters, Geneva. As T **64e** of St. Helena.
228 20c. black, green and blue . . 20 10
229 30c. black, purple and ochre 40 20

1966. 20th Anniv of UNESCO. As T **64f** of St. Helena.
230 15c. multicoloured 20 10
231 1r. yellow, violet and olive . . 35 10
232 5r. black, purple and orange 80 1·00

1967. Universal Adult Suffrage. Nos. 198, 203, 206 and 210 optd **UNIVERSAL ADULT SUFFRAGE 1967.**
238 15c. multicoloured 10 10
239 45c. multicoloured 10 10
240 75c. multicoloured 10 10
241 3r.50 multicoloured 20 50

44 Money Cowrie, Mole Cowrie and Tiger Cowrie

1967. International Tourist Year. Mult.
242 15c. Type **44** 20 10
243 40c. Beech cone, textile or cloth of gold cone and Virgin cone 25 10
244 1r. Arthritic spider conch . . 35 10
245 2r.25 Subulate auger and trumpet triton shells . . . 60 1·25

1968. Nos. 202/3 and 206 surch.
246 30c. on 40c. multicoloured . . 10 10
247 60c. on 45c. multicoloured . . 15 10
248 85c. on 75c. multicoloured . . 20 15

49 Farmer with Wife and Children at Sunset

1968. Human Rights Year.
249 **49** 20c. multicoloured 10 10
250 50c. multicoloured 10 10
251 85c. multicoloured 10 10
252 2r.25 multicoloured . . . . 25 1·60

50 Expedition landing at Anse Possession **54** Apollo Launch

1968. Bicent of First Landing on Praslin. Mult.
253 20c. Type **50** 35 10
254 50c. French warships at anchor (vert) 40 15
255 85c. Coco-de-mer and Black parrot (vert) 90 25
256 2r.25 French warships under sail . . . . 90 2·75

1969. First Man on the Moon. Multicoloured.
257 5c. Type **54** 10 50
258 20c. Module leaving mother ship for the Moon 15 10
259 50c. Astronauts and Space Module on the Moon . . . 20 15
260 65c. Tracking station 25 15
261 2r.25 Moon craters with Earth on the "Horizon" . . 45 1·60

59 Picault's Landing, 1742

1969. Multicoloured.
262 5c. Type **59** 10 10
263 10c. U.S. satellite-tracking station 10 10
264 15c. "Konigsberg I" (German cruiser) at Aldabra, 1914 . . . . . 3·00 2·00
265 20c. Fleet re-fuelling off St. Anne, 1939–45 . . . . 1·75 10
266 25c. Exiled Ashanti King, Prempeh 20 10
267 30c. Laying Stone of Possession, 1756 . . . . 1·00 4·00
268 40c. As 30c. . . . . 2·75 1·25
269 50c. Pirates and treasures 30 15
270 60c. Corsairs attacking merchantman . . . . . . 1·00 1·50
271 65c. As 60c. . . . . 6·00 8·00
272 85c. Impression of proposed airport . . . . 3·50 1·75
273a 95c. As 85c. . . . . 5·50 3·25
274 1r. French Governor capitulating to British naval officer, 1794 . . . . 35 15
275 1r.50 H.M.S. "Sybille" (frigate) and "Chiffone" (French frigate) in battle, 1801 . . . . 1·75 2·00
276 3r.50 Visit of the Duke of Edinburgh, 1956 . . . . 1·00 2·25
277 5r. Chevalier Queau de Quincy . . . . 1·00 2·75
278 10r. Indian Ocean chart, 1574 . . . . 2·75 8·00
279 15r. Badge of Seychelles . . 4·25 12·00
NOTE: The design of No. 264 incorrectly shows the vessel "Konigsberg II" and date "1915".

74 White Terns, French Warship and Island

1970. Bicentenary of First Settlement, St. Anne Island. Multicoloured.
280 20c. Type **74** 70 10
281 50c. Spot-finned flyingfish, ship and island 45 10
282 85c. Compass and chart . . . 45 10
283 3r.50 Anchor on sea-bed . . 70 1·25

78 Girl and Optician's Chart

1970. Centenary of British Red Cross. Mult.
284 20c. Type **78** 30 10
285 50c. Baby, scales and milk bottles 30 10
286 85c. Woman with child and umbrella (vert) 30 10
287 3r.50 Red Cross local headquarters building 1·25 2·75

79 Pitcher Plant **81** Piper Navajo

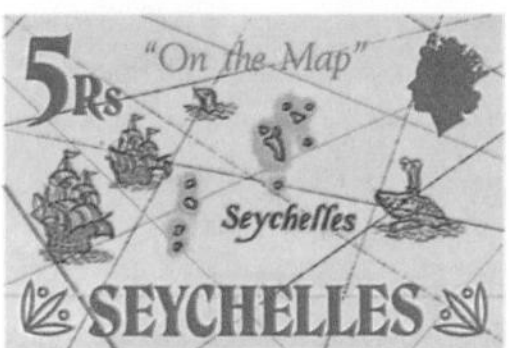

80 Seychelles "On the Map"

1970. Flowers. Multicoloured.
288 20c. Type **79** 25 15
289 50c. Wild vanilla 30 15
290 85c. Tropic-bird orchid 80 30
291 3r.50 Vare hibiscus 1·00 2·25
MS292 81 × 133 mm. Nos. 288/91 2·75 13·00

1971. "Putting Seychelles on the Map". Sheet 152 × 101 mm.
MS293 **80** 5r. multicoloured 1·75 9·00

1971. Airport Completion. Multicoloured.
294 5c. Type **81** 30 50
295 20c. Westland Wessex HAS-1 helicopter 65 10
296 50c. Consolidated Catalina amphibian (horiz) 70 10
297 60c. Grumman Albatross 75 10
298 85c. Short "G" Class flying boat "Golden Hind" (horiz) 80 10
299 3r.50 Vickers Supermarine Walrus Mk I amphibian (horiz) 2·25 3·50

82 Santa Claus delivering Gifts (Jean-Claude Waye Hive)

1971. Christmas. Multicoloured.
300 10c. Type **82** 10 10
301 15c. Santa Claus seated on turtle (Edison Theresine) 10 10
302 3r.50 Santa Claus landing on island (Isabelle Tirant) 40 2·00

1971. Nos. 267, 270 and 272 surch.
303 40c. on 30c. multicoloured 30 55
304 65c. on 60c. multicoloured 40 75
305 95c. on 85c. multicoloured 45 1·00

1972. Royal Visit. Nos. 265 and 277 optd **ROYAL VISIT 1972.**
306 20c. multicoloured 15 20
307 5r. multicoloured 1·00 3·00

85 Seychelles Brush Warbler **86** Fireworks Display

1972. Rare Seychelles Birds. Multicoloured.
308 5c. Type **85** 60 70
309 20c. Bare-legged scops owl ("Seychelles Scoops Owl") 2·25 70
310 50c. Seychelles blue pigeon 2·25 70
311 65c. Seychelles magpie robin 2·75 75
312 95c. Seychelles paradise flycatcher ("Black Paradise Flycatcher") 3·00 2·50
313 3r.50 Seychelles kestrel 8·00 12·00
MS314 144 × 162 mm. Nos. 308/13 20·00 27·00

1972. "Festival '72". Multicoloured.
315 10c. Type **86** 10 10
316 15c. Pirogue race (horiz) 10 10
317 25c. Floats and costumes 10 10
318 5r. Water skiing (horiz) 60 1·25

1972. Royal Silver Wedding. As T **103** of St. Helena, but with Giant Tortoise and Sailfish in background.
319 95c. blue 15 10
320 1r.50 brown 15 10

1973. Royal Wedding. As T **103a** of St. Helena. Multicoloured, background colours given.
321 95c. brown 10 10
322 1r.50 blue 10 10

88 Seychelles Squirrelfish

1974. Fishes. Multicoloured.
323 20c. Type **88** 25 15
324 50c. Harlequin filefish 35 15
325 95c. Pennant coralfish ("Papillon") 40 40
326 1r.50 Oriental sweetlips ("Peau d'ane canal") 85 2·50

89 Globe and Letter

1974. Centenary of U.P.U. Multicoloured.
327 20c. Type **89** 10 10
328 50c. Globe and radio beacon 20 10
329 95c. Globe and postmark 35 40
330 1r.50 Emblems within "UPU" 50 1·25

90 Sir Winston Churchill

1974. Birth Centenary of Sir Winston Churchill. Multicoloured.
331 95c. Type **90** 20 20
332 1r.50 Profile portrait 35 80
MS333 81 × 109 mm. Nos. 331/2 60 1·75

1975. Visit of Liner "Queen Elizabeth II". Nos. 265, 269, 273a and 275 optd **VISIT OF Q.E. II** and silhouette of liner.
334 20c. multicoloured 15 15
335 50c. multicoloured 20 20
336 95c. multicoloured 25 40
337 1r.50 multicoloured 35 1·75

1975. Internal Self-Government. Nos. 265, 271, 274 and 276 optd **INTERNAL SELF-GOVERNMENT OCTOBER 1975.**
338 20c. multicoloured 15 15
339 65c. multicoloured 25 30
340 1r. multicoloured 30 35
341 3r.50 multicoloured 75 2·50

93 Queen Elizabeth I **94** Map of Praslin and Postmark

1975. International Women's Year. Mult.
342 10c. Type **93** 10 25
343 15c. Gladys Aylward 10 25
344 20c. Elizabeth Fry 10 10
345 25c. Emmeline Pankhurst 10 10
346 65c. Florence Nightingale 25 20
347 1r. Amy Johnson 40 35
348 1r.50 Joan of Arc 50 1·50
349 3r.50 Eleanor Roosevelt 1·00 3·50

1976. Rural Posts. Multicoloured.
350 20c. Type **94** 30 10
351 65c. La Digue 40 20
352 1r. Mahe with Victoria postmark 50 25
353 1r.50 Mahe with Anse Royale postmark 60 2·00
MS354 166 × 127 mm. Nos. 350/3 1·50 3·00
Nos. 350/53 show maps and postmarks.

95 First Landing, 1609 (inset portrait of Premier James Mancham)

1976. Independence. Multicoloured.
355 20c. Type **95** 15 10
356 25c. The Possession Stone 15 10
357 40c. First settlers, 1770 15 15
358 75c. Chevalier Queau de Quincy 15 40
359 1r. Sir Bickham Sweet-Escott 15 20
360 1r.25 Legislative Building 20 70
361 1r.50 Seychelles badge 20 80
362 3r.50 Seychelles flag 60 2·00

96 Flags of Seychelles and U.S.A.

1976. Seychelles Independence and American Bicent of Independence. Multicoloured.
363 1r. Type **96** 30 15
364 10r. Statehouses of Seychelles and Philadelphia 70 3·00

97 Swimming

1976. Olympic Games, Montreal.
365 **97** 20c. blue, lt blue & brown 10 10
366 – 65c. lt green, green & grey 35 10
367 – 1r. brown, blue and grey 35 10
368 – 3r.50 light red, red & grey 50 2·75
DESIGNS: 65c. Hockey; 1r. Basketball; 3r.50, Football.

98 Seychelles Paradise Flycatcher

1976. 4th Pan-African Ornithological Congress, Seychelles. Multicoloured.
369 20c. Type **98** 40 20
370 1r.25 Seychelles sunbird (horiz) 1·10 1·00
371 1r.50 Seychelles brown white eye ("The Seychelles White-eye") (horiz) 1·50 1·50
372 5r. Black parrot ("The Seychelles Black Parrot") 2·50 5·50
MS373 161 × 109 mm. Nos. 369/72 6·50 9·00

1976. Independence. Nos. 265, 269, 271, 273a, 274 and 276/9 optd **Independence 1976** or surch also.
374 20c. Fleet re-fuelling off St. Anne, 1939–45 70 2·50
375 50c. Pirates and treasure 60 2·50
376 95c. Impression of proposed airport 2·25 2·25
377 1r. French Governor capitulating to British naval officer, 1794 55 2·25
378 3r.50 Visit of Duke of Edinburgh, 1956 2·75 4·50
379 5r. Chevalier Queau de Quincy 1·75 7·50
380 10r. Indian Ocean chart, 1574 2·50 12·00
381 15r. Badge of Seychelles 2·75 12·00
382 25r. on 65c. Corsairs attacking merchantman 3·00 16·00

100 Inauguration of George Washington

1976. Bicentenary of American Revolution.
383 **100** 1c. deep red and red 10 10
384 – 2c. violet and lilac 10 10
385 – 3c. light blue and blue 10 10
386 – 4c. brown and yellow 10 10
387 – 5c. green and yellow 10 10
388 – 1r.50 brown & light brown 30 35
389 – 3r.50 blue and green 35 70
390 – 5r. brown and yellow 40 80
391 – 10r. blue and light blue 65 1·50
MS392 141 × 141 mm. 25r. purple and mauve 3·00 6·50
DESIGNS: 2c. Jefferson and Louisiana Purchase; 3c. William Seward and Alaska Purchase; 4c. Pony Express, 1860; 5c. Lincoln's Emancipation Proclamation; 1r.50, Trans-continental Railroad, 1869; 3r.50, Wright Brothers flight, 1903; 5r. Henry Ford's assembly-line, 1913; 10r. J. F. Kennedy and 1969 Moon-landing; 25r. Signing Independence Declaration, 1776.

101 Silhouette of the Islands

1977. Silver Jubilee. Multicoloured.
393 20c. Type **101** 10 10
394 40c. Silhouette (different) 10 10
395 50c. The Orb (vert) 10 10
396 1r. St. Edward's Crown (vert) 10 10
397 1r.25 Ampulla and Spoon (vert) 10 15
398 1r.50 Sceptre with Cross (vert) 10 15
399 5r. Silhouette (different) 25 30
400 10r. Silhouette (different) 45 60
MS401 133 × 135 mm. 20c., 50c., 1r., 10r. 55 1·40

102 Cruiser "Aurora" and Flag

1977. 60th Anniv of Russian Revolution.
402 **102** 1r.50 multicoloured 55 30
MS403 101 × 129 mm. No. 402 80 1·10

103 Coral Scene

1977. Marine Life. Rupee face values shown as "Re" or "Rs". Multicoloured.
404A 5c. Reef fish 30 2·00
405B 10c. Hawksbill turtle 20 10
406B 15c. Coco-de-mer 20 15
407A 20c. Wild vanilla orchid 1·50 20
408A 25c. "Hypolimnas misippus" (butterfly) 1·50 1·50
409B 40c. Type **103** 20 10
410A 50c. Giant tortoise 30 10
411A 75c. Crayfish 40 10
412A 1r. Madagascar red fody ("Madagascar Fody") 1·25 10
413A 1r.25 White tern ("Fairy Tern") 1·25 20
414A 1r.50 Seychelles flying fox 1·00 20
736 3r. Green gecko 5·50 5·50
415A 3r.50 As 3r. 75 3·25
416A 5r. Octopus 1·50 40
417A 10r. Tiger cowrie 1·50 2·50
418A 15r. Pitcher plant 1·50 2·50
419A 20r. Coat of arms 1·50 2·50
The 40c., 1r., 1r.25 and 1r.50 values are horizontal, 31 × 27 mm. The 5, 10, 15 and 20r. are vertical, 28 × 36 mm. The others are horizontal, 29 × 25 mm.
Nos. 405/12 and 414 exist with or without imprint date at foot.

For similar designs with rupee face values shown as "R" see Nos. 487a/94.

104 St. Roch Roman Catholic Church, Bel Ombre

1977. Christmas. Multicoloured.
420 20c. Type **104** 10 10
421 1r. Anglican cathedral, Victoria 10 10
422 1r.50 Roman Catholic cathedral, Victoria 15 10
423 5r. St. Mark's Anglican church, Praslin 30 45

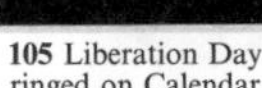

105 Liberation Day ringed on Calendar

106 Stamp Portraits of Edward VII, George V and George VI

1978. Liberation Day. Multicoloured.
424 40c. Type **105** 10 10
425 1r.25 Hands holding bayonet, torch and flag 15 10
426 1r.50 Fisherman and farmer 15 15
427 5r. Soldiers and rejoicing people 35 40

1978. 25th Anniv of Coronation. Multicoloured.
428 40c. Type **106** 10 10
429 1r.50 Queen Victoria and Elizabeth II 15 10
430 3r. Queen Victoria Monument 25 25
431 5r. Queen's Building, Victoria 35 35
MS432 87 × 129 mm. Nos. 428/31 75 85

107 Gardenia

1978. Wildlife. Multicoloured.
433 40c. Type **107** 15 10
434 1r.25 Seychelles magpie robin ("Magpie Robin of Fregate Island") . . . . 1·50 70
435 1r.50 Seychelles paradise flycatcher . . . . 1·50 70
436 5r. Green turtle . . . . . . 1·25 1·50

108 Possession Stone

1978. Bicentenary of Victoria. Multicoloured.
437 20c. Type **108** 10 10
438 1r.25 Plan of 1782 "L' Etablissement" 15 15
439 1r.50 Clock Tower 15 15
440 5r. Bust of Pierre Poivre . . 40 1·75

109 Seychelles Fody **110** Patrice Lumumba

1979. Birds (1st series). Multicoloured.
441 2r. Type **109** 55 50
442 2r. Green-backed heron . . . 55 50
443 2r. Thick-billed bulbul ("Seychelles Bulbul") . . . 55 50
444 2r. Seychelles cave swiftlet . . 55 50
445 2r. Grey-headed lovebird . . 55 50
See also Nos. 463/7, 500/4 and 523/7.

1979. Africa Liberation Heroes.
446 **110** 40c. black, violet and lilac 10 10
447 – 2r. black, blue & light blue 20 25
448 – 2r.25 black, brown & orange 20 30
449 – 5r. black, olive and green 45 1·25
DESIGNS: 2r. Kwame Nkrumah; 2r.25, Dr. Eduardo Mondlane; 5r. Hamilcar Cabral.

111 1978 5r. Liberation Day Commemorative and Sir Rowland Hill

113 The Herald Angel

112 Child with Book

1979. Death Cent of Sir Rowland Hill. Mult.
450 40c. Type **111** 10 10
451 2r.25 1972 50c. Seychelles blue pigeon commemorative 25 70
452 3r. 1962 50c. definitive . . . 35 95
MS453 112 × 88 mm. 5r. 1892 4c. definitive 50 55

1979. International Year of the Child. Mult.
454 40c. Type **112** 10 10
455 2r.25 Children of different races 15 30
456 3r. Young child with ball (vert) 20 50
457 5r. Girl with glove puppet (vert) 35 70

1979. Christmas. Multicoloured.
458 20c. Type **113** 10 10
459 2r.25 The Virgin and Child 30 40
460 3r. The Three Kings (horiz) 40 60
MS461 87 × 75 mm. 5r. The Flight into Egypt (horiz) 50 70

1980. No. 415 surch **R.1.10.**
462 1r.10 on 3r.50 Green gecko 30 50

115 Seychelles Kestrel **117** Sprinting

116 10 Rupees Banknote

1980. Birds (2nd series). Seychelles Kestrel. Mult.
463 2r. Type **115** 80 60
464 2r. Pair of Seychelles kestrels 80 60
465 2r. Seychelles kestrel with eggs 80 60
466 2r. Seychelles kestrel on nest with chick 80 60
467 2r. Seychelles kestrel chicks in nest 80 60

1980. "London 1980" International Stamp Exhibition. Currency Notes. Multicoloured.
468 40c. Type **116** 15 10
469 1r.50 25 rupees 30 15
470 2r.25 50 rupees (vert) 40 25
471 5r. 100 rupees (vert) 80 75
MS472 119 × 102 mm. Nos. 468/71 2·00 1·60

1980. Olympic Games, Moscow. Multicoloured.
473 40c. Type **117** 10 10
474 2r.25 Weightlifting 20 20
475 3r. Boxing 30 30
476 5r. Sailing 60 50
MS477 90 × 121 mm. Nos. 473/6 1·40 2·25

118 Boeing 747-200 Airliner

1980. Int Tourism Conference, Manila. Mult.
478 40c. Type **118** 10 10
479 2r.25 Bus 25 30
480 3r. Cruise liner 35 40
481 5r. "La Belle Coralline" (tourist launch) 55 65

119 Female Palm **121** Male White Tern

120 Vasco da Gama's "Sao Gabriel", 1497

1980. Coco-de-mer (palms). Multicoloured.
482 40c. Type **119** 10 10
483 2r.25 Male palm 25 20
484 3r. Artefacts 40 35
485 5r. Fisherman's gourd . . . 55 55
MS486 82 × 140 mm. Nos. 482/5 1·60 1·60

1981. As Nos. 412/14, 415 (with new value), and 416/19 but face values redrawn as "R" instead of "Re" or "Rs".
487 1r. Madagascar red fody ("Madagascar Fody") . . 1·00 50
488 1r.10 Green gecko 70 80
489 1r.25 White tern ("Fairy Tern") . . . . 2·75 1·25
490 1r.50 Seychelles flying fox . . 50 75
491 5r. Octopus . . . . 1·25 1·40
492 10r. Tiger cowrie . . . . . . 3·25 3·50
493 15r. Pitcher plant . . . . . 4·00 4·50
494 20r. Seychelles coat of arms 5·00 6·00

1981. Ships. Multicoloured.
495 40c. Type **120** 15 10
496 2r.25 Mascarenhas' caravel, 1505 . . . . 50 55
497 3r.50 Darwin's H.M.S. "Beagle", 1831 . . . . . 55 1·00
498 5r. "Queen Elizabeth 2" (liner), 1968 . . . . . . 60 1·40
MS499 141 × 91 mm. Nos. 495/8 1·50 3·50

1981. Birds (3rd series). White Tern. Mult.
500 2r. Type **121** . . . . 1·00 65
501 2r. Pair of white terns . . . 1·00 65
502 2r. Female white tern . . . . 1·00 65
503 2r. Female white tern on nest and egg . . . . 1·00 65
504 2r. White tern and chick . . 1·00 65

1981. Royal Wedding. Royal Yachts. As T **14a/b** of St. Kitts. Multicoloured.
505 1r.50 "Victoria and Albert I" 15 25
506 1r.50 Prince Charles and Lady Diana Spencer . . . 65 75
507 5r. "Cleveland" 35 60
513 5r. As No. 506 . . . . 1·25 2·00
509 10r. "Britannia" . . . . . . 60 1·50
510 10r. As No. 506 . . . . . . 1·75 3·00
MS511 120 × 109 mm. 7r.50 As No. 506 . . . . 1·00 1·00

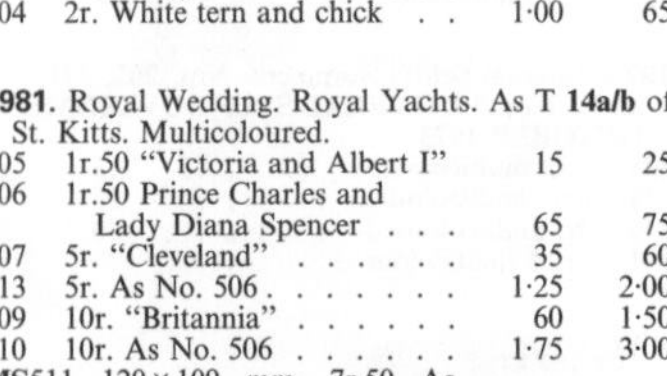

122 Britten Norman Islander

1981. 10th Anniv of Opening of Seychelles International Airport. Aircraft. Multicoloured.
514 40c. Type **122** 15 10
515 2r.25 Britten Norman "long nose" Trislander 40 45
516 3r.50 Vickers Super VC-10 airliner 60 70
517 5r. Boeing 747-100 airliner 75 1·00

123 Seychelles Flying Foxes in Flight

124 Chinese Little Bittern (male)

1981. Seychelles Flying Fox (Roussette). Mult.
518 40c. Type **123** 10 10
519 2r.25 Flying fox eating . . . 30 45
520 3r. Flying fox climbing across tree branch 45 70
521 5r. Flying fox hanging from tree branch . . . . 55 1·00
MS522 95 × 130 mm. Nos. 518/21 1·50 3·75

1982. Birds (4th series). Chinese Little Bittern. Multicoloured.
523 3r. Type **124** . . . . 2·00 1·00
524 3r. Chinese little bittern (female) . . . . 2·00 1·00
525 3r. Hen on nest . . . . . . 2·00 1·00
526 3r. Nest and eggs . . . . . 2·00 1·00
527 3r. Hen with chicks . . . . . 2·00 1·00

125 Silhouette Island and La Digue

1982. Modern Maps. Multicoloured.
528 40c. Type **125** 15 10
529 1r.50 Denis and Bird Islands 25 25
530 2r.75 Praslin 30 65
531 7r. Mahe . . . . 50 2·25
MS532 92 × 128 mm. Nos. 528/31 1·10 5·00

126 "Education"

1982. 5th Anniv of Liberation. Multicoloured.
533 40c. Type **126** 10 10
534 1r.75 "Health" 25 25
535 2r.75 "Agriculture" 30 45
536 7r. "Construction" . . . . . 80 1·40
MS537 128 × 120 mm. Nos. 533/6 2·25 6·50

127 Tourist Board Emblem

1982. Tourism. Multicoloured.
538 1r.75 Type **127** 20 35
539 1r.75 Northolme Hotel . . . 20 35
540 1r.75 Reef Hotel 20 35
541 1r.75 Barbarous Beach Hotel 20 35
542 1r.75 Coral Strand Hotel . . 20 35
543 1r.75 Beau Vallon Bay Hotel 20 35
544 1r.75 Fisherman's Cove Hotel 20 35
545 1r.75 Mahe Beach Hotel . . 20 35

128 Tata Bus

1982. Land Transport. Multicoloured.
546 20c. Type **128** 10 10
547 1r.75 Mini-Moke 20 30
548 2r.75 Ox-cart 25 65
549 7r. Truck . . . . 80 2·75

129 Radio Seychelles Control Room

1983. World Communications Year. Mult.
550 40c. Type **129** 10 10
551 2r.75 Satellite Earth station 30 50
552 3r.50 Radio Seychelles television control room 45 75
553 5r. Postal services sorting office 60 1·25

130 Agricultural Experimental Station

1983. Commonwealth Day. Multicoloured.
554 40c. Type **130** 10 10
555 2r.75 Food processing plant 25 40
556 3r.50 Unloading fish catch 40 60
557 7r. Seychelles flag 65 1·40

131 Denis Island Lighthouse

1983. Famous Landmarks. Multicoloured.
558 40c. Type **131** 10 10
559 2r.75 Victoria Hospital 30 45
560 3r.50 Supreme Court 35 65
561 7r. State House 55 1·40
MS562 110 × 98 mm. Nos. 558/61 2·75 7·00

132 "Royal Vauxhall" Balloon, 1836

1983. Bicentenary of Manned Flight. Mult.
563 40c. Type **132** 15 10
564 1r.75 De Havilland D.H.50J 30 30
565 2r.75 Grumman Albatros flying boat 35 55
566 7r. Swearingen Merlin IIIA 55 1·75

133 Douglas DC-10-30

1983. 1st International Flight of Air Seychelles.
567 **133** 2r. multicoloured 1·75 2·00

134 Swamp Plant and Moorhen **137** Victoria Port

136 Coconut Vessel

1983. Centenary Visit to Seychelles by Marianne North (botanic artist). Multicoloured.
568 40c. Type **134** 25 10
569 1r.75 "Wormia flagellaria" 45 30
570 2r.75 Asiatic pancratium 55 75
571 7r. Pitcher plant 95 2·50
MS572 90 × 121 mm. Nos. 568/71 2·75 6·50

1983. Nos. 505/7, 509/10 and 513 surch.
573 50c. on 1r.50 "Victoria and Albert I" 15 30
574 50c. on 1r.50 Prince Charles and Lady Diana Spencer 40 1·50
575 2r.25 on 5r. "Clevland" 45 70
576 2r.25 on 5r. As No. 574 1·25 3·00
577 3r.75 on 10r. "Britannia" 75 1·10
578 3r.75 on 10r. As No. 574 1·60 3·50

1984. Traditional Handicrafts. Multicoloured.
579 50c. Type **136** 15 10
580 2r. Scarf and doll 30 70
581 3r. Coconut-fibre roses 35 1·00
582 10r. Carved fishing boat and doll 90 4·50

1984. 250th Anniv of "Lloyd's List" (newspaper). Multicoloured.
583 50c. Type **137** 25 10
584 2r. "Boissevain" (cargo liner) 65 55
585 3r. "Sun Viking" (liner) 90 90
586 10r. Loss of R.F.A. "Ennerdale II" (tanker) 2·40 3·50

138 Old S.P.U.P. Office

1984. 20th Anniv of Seychelles People's United Party. Multicoloured.
587 50c. Type **138** 10 10
588 2r. Liberation statue (vert) 25 50
589 3r. New S.P.U.D. office 35 85
590 10r. President Rene (vert) 1·00 4·00

139 1949 U.P.U. 2r 25 Stamp

1984. Universal Postal Union Congress, Hamburg. Sheet 70 × 85 mm.
MS591 **139** 5r. green, pink and black 1·40 2·50

140 Long Jumping

1984. Olympic Games, Los Angeles. Mult.
592 50c. Type **140** 10 10
593 2r. Boxing 40 45
594 3r. Swimming 60 75
595 10r. Weightlifting 1·75 2·50
MS596 100 × 100 mm. Nos. 592/5 3·00 5·50

141 Sub-aqua Diving

1984. Water Sports. Multicoloured.
597 50c. Type **141** 30 10
598 2r. Paraskiing 90 45
599 3r. Sailing 1·00 75
600 10r. Water-skiing 2·40 2·50

142 Humpback Whale

1984. Whale Conservation. Multicoloured.
601 50c. Type **142** 1·50 20
602 2r. Sperm whale 2·75 1·75
603 3r. Black right whale 3·00 2·50
604 10r. Blue whale 6·00 9·00

143 Two Bare-legged Scops Owls in Tree **144** Giant Tortoises

1985. Birth Bicentenary of John J. Audubon (ornithologist). Bare-legged Scops Owl. Mult.
605 50c. Type **143** 1·75 50
606 2r. Owl on branch 2·50 2·25
607 3r. Owl in flight 2·75 2·75
608 10r. Owl on ground 5·50 8·50

1985. "Expo '85" World Fair, Japan. Mult.
609 50c. Type **144** 70 30
610 2r. White terns ("Fairy Tern") 2·00 1·75
611 3r. Windsurfing 2·00 2·50
612 5r. Coco-de-mer 2·00 5·00
MS613 130 × 80 mm. Nos. 609/12 8·50 9·50
See also No. MS650.

145 The Queen Mother with Princess Anne and Prince Andrew, 1970 **147** Agriculture Students

146 Boxing

1985. Life and Times of Queen Elizabeth the Queen Mother. Multicoloured.
614 50c. The Queen Mother in 1930 20 10
615 2r. Type **145** 50 50
616 3r. On her 75th Birthday 70 75
617 5r. With Prince Henry at his christening (from photo by Lord Snowdon) 90 1·50
MS618 91 × 73 mm. 10 r. Arriving at Blenheim Palace by Westland Wessex helicopter 3·00 2·25

1985. 2nd Indian Ocean Islands Games. Mult.
619 50c. Type **146** 15 10
620 2r. Football 55 50
621 3r. Swimming 75 75
622 10r. Windsurfing 2·40 2·75

1985. Acquisition of First Air Seychelles "Airbus". As No. 413A, but additionally inscribed "AIR SEYCHELLES FIRST AIRBUS".
623 1r.25 White tern ("Fairy Tern") 2·50 2·25

1985. International Youth Year. Multicoloured.
624 50c. Type **147** 10 10
625 2r. Construction students building wall 55 50
626 3r. Carpentry students 70 1·00
627 10r. Science students 2·25 5·00

148 Ford "Model T" (1919)

1985. Vintage Cars. Multicoloured.
628 50c. Type **148** 50 20
629 2r. Austin "Seven" (1922) 1·50 1·00
630 3r. Morris "Oxford" (1924) 1·60 1·75
631 10r. Humber "Coupe" (1929) 3·00 6·00

149 Five Foot Transit Instrument **150** Ballerina

1986. Appearance of Halley's Comet. Mult.
632 50c. Type **149** 30 10
633 2r. Eight foot quadrant 75 70
634 3r. Comet's orbit 75 95
635 10r. Edmond Halley 1·25 3·00

1986. Visit of Ballet du Louvre Company, "Giselle". Multicoloured.
636 2r. Type **150** 50 75
637 3r. Male dancer 60 1·50
MS638 80 × 90 mm. 10r. Pas de deux 1·40 2·40

1986. 60th Birthday of Queen Elizabeth II. As T **145a** of St. Helena. Multicoloured.
639 50c. Wedding photograph, 1947 10 10
640 1r.25 At State Opening of Parliament, 1982 25 35
641 2r. Queen accepting bouquet, Seychelles, 1972 30 50
642 3r. On board Royal Yacht "Britannia", Qatar, 1979 40 75
643 5r. At Crown Agents Head Office, London, 1983 60 1·25

151 Ferry to La Digue

1986. "Ameripex '86" Int Stamp Exhibition, Chicago. Inter-island Communications. Mult.
644 50c. Type **151** 60 10
645 2r. Telephone kiosk (vert) 1·25 70
646 3r. Post Office counter, Victoria (vert) 1·40 1·10
647 7r. Air Seychelles Britten Norman "short nose" Trislander aircraft 4·00 3·50

152 Crests of Seychelles and Knights of Malta

1986. Seychelles Knights of Malta Day.
648 **152** 5r. multicoloured 1·10 1·60
MS649 101 × 81 mm. No. 648 2·25 4·00

1986. Seychelles Philatelic Exhibition, Tokyo. Miniature sheet, 130 × 80 mm, containing stamps as Nos. 609/12, but without "Expo '85" inscription and emblem.
MS650 As Nos. 609/12 1·75 3·00

1986. Royal Wedding. As T **146a** of St. Helena. Multicoloured.
651 2r. Prince Andrew and Miss Sarah Ferguson 35 50
652 10r. Prince Andrew boarding Wessex helicopter, 1983 1·40 3·00

1986. International Creole Day. No. 487 optd **LAZOURNEN ENTERNASYONAL KREOL.**
653 1r. Madagascar red fody 2·75 2·50

154 Pope John Paul at Seychelles Airport

1986. Visit of Pope John Paul II. Designs showing Pope and Seychelles scenes. Multicoloured.
654 50c. Type **154** 75 30
655 2r. Catholic Cathedral, Victoria 2·00 1·25
656 3r. Baie Lazare Parish Church 2·50 2·25
657 10r. Aerial view of People's Stadium 4·25 8·00
MS658 95 × 106 mm. Nos. 654/7 11·00 13·00

155 "Melanitis leda"

1987. Butterflies. Multicoloured.
659 1r. Type **155** . . . . 1·00 30
660 2r. "Phalanta philiberti" . . 1·60 1·25
661 3r. "Danaus chrysippus" . . 1·90 1·90
662 10r. "Euploea mitra" . . . . 5·00 8·00

156 Royal Oak Scallop 157 Statue of Liberation

1987. Sea Shells. Multicoloured.
663 1r. Type **156** . . . . 1·25 30
664 2r. Golden thorny oyster . . 2·00 1·00
665 3r. Ventral or single harp and ornate pitar venus . . . . 2·25 1·60
666 10r. Silver conch . . . . . . 5·50 8·00

1987. 10th Anniv of Liberation. Multicoloured.
667 1r. Type **157** 20 25
668 2r. Seychelles hospital (horiz) 35 50
669 3r. Orphanage village (horiz) 45 75
670 10r. Proposed Sail-fish Monument . . . . 1·00 2·50

158 Seychelles Savings Bank, Praslin

1987. Centenary of Banking in Seychelles.
671 **158** 1r. deep green and green 20 25
672 – 2r. brown and orange . . 35 50
673 – 10r. deep blue and blue 1·00 2·50
DESIGNS: 2r. Development Bank; 10r. Central Bank.

1987. Royal Ruby Wedding. Nos. 639/43 optd **40TH WEDDING ANNIVERSARY.**
674 50c. Wedding photograph, 1947 . . . . 15 15
675 1r.25 At State Opening of Parliament, 1982 . . . . . 25 65
676 2r. Queen accepting bouquet, Seychelles, 1972 . . . . . 30 65
677 3r. On board Royal Yacht "Britannia", Qatar, 1979 40 1·10
678 5r. At Crown Agents Head Office, London, 1983 . . . 60 2·00

159 Tuna-canning Factory

1987. Seychelles Fishing Industry. Mult.
679 50c. Type **159** 15 15
680 2r. Trawler 45 55
681 3r. Weighing catch . . . . . 70 1·00
682 10r. Unloading net . . . . . 2·25 3·50

160 Water Sports

1988. Tourism. Multicoloured.
683 1r. Type **160** 55 25
684 2r. Speedboat and yachts . . 85 65
685 3r. Yacht at anchor . . . . 1·40 1·40
686 10r. Hotel at night . . . . . 3·25 6·00

161 Young Turtles making for Sea 162 Shot Put

1988. The Green Turtle. Multicoloured.
687 2r. Type **161** . . . . 1·50 2·00
688 2r. Young turtles hatching . . 1·50 2·00
689 3r. Female turtle leaving sea 1·75 2·25
690 3r. Female laying eggs . . . 1·75 2·25
Nos. 687/8 and 689/90 were printed together, se-tenant, each pair forming a composite design.

1988. Olympic Games, Seoul. Multicoloured.
691 1r. Type **162** 30 25
692 2r. Type **162** 55 90
693 2r. High jump 55 90
694 2r. Gold medal winner on podium 55 90
695 2r. Athletics 55 90
696 2r. Javelin 55 90
697 3r. As No. 694 . . . . 60 90
698 4r. As No. 695 . . . . 80 1·10
699 5r. As No. 696 . . . . 1·00 1·25
MS700 121 × 52 mm. 10r. Tennis 4·00 6·50

1988. 300th Anniv of Lloyd's of London. As T **152a** of St. Helena. Multicoloured.
701 1r. Leadenhall Street, 1928 60 25
702 2r. "Cinq Juin" (travelling post office) (horiz) . . . . 1·60 75
703 3r. "Queen Elizabeth 2" (liner) (horiz) . . . . . 3·00 1·50
704 10r. Loss of "Hindenburg" (airship), 1937 . . . . . . 6·00 5·00

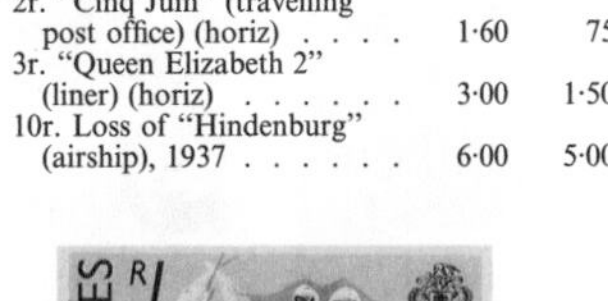

163 Police Motorcyclists

1988. 1st Anniv of Defence Forces Day. Mult.
705 1r. Type **163** . . . . 2·75 50
706 2r. Hindustan Aircraft Chetak helicopter . . . . 4·00 2·25
707 3r. "Andromanche" (patrol boat) . . . . 4·00 2·75
708 10r. BRDM armoured car . . 7·50 10·00

164 Father Christmas with Basket of Presents 165 "Dendrobium sp."

1988. Christmas. Multicoloured.
709 50c. Type **164** 15 10
710 2r. Bird and gourd filled with presents 70 70
711 3r. Father Christmas basket weaving 90 90
712 10r. Christmas bauble and palm tree . . . . 2·50 4·00

1988. Orchids (1st series). Multicoloured.
713 1r. Type **165** . . . . 1·25 25
714 2r. Arachnis" hybrid (horiz) 1·75 70
715 3r. "Vanda caerulea" . . . . 2·00 1·25
716 10r. "Dendrobium phalaenopsis" (horiz) . . . 4·00 6·50
See also Nos. 767/70 and 795/8.

166 India 1976 25p. Nehru Stamp

1989. Birth Centenary of Jawaharlal Nehru (Indian statesman). Each showing flags of Seychelles and India. Multicoloured.
724 2r. Type **166** . . . . 1·25 50
725 10r. Jawaharlal Nehru . . . 3·25 5·00

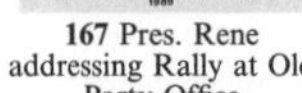

167 Pres. Rene addressing Rally at Old Party Office 169 Black Parrot and Map of Praslin

168 British Red Cross Ambulance, Franco-Prussian War, 1870

1989. 25th Anniv of Seychelles People's United Party. Multicoloured.
742 1r. Type **167** 25 25
743 2r. Women with Party flags and Maison du Peuple . . 60 50
744 3r. President Rene making speech and Torch of Freedom 70 80
745 10r. President Rene, Party flag and Torch of Freedom 2·25 4·00

1989. 20th Anniv of First Manned Landing on Moon. As T **50a** of St. Kitts. Multicoloured.
746 1r. Lift off of "Saturn 5" rocket 45 25
747 2r. Crew of "Apollo 15" (30 × 30 mm) 75 75
748 3r. "Apollo 15" emblem (30 × 30 mm) . . . . . . 90 1·10
749 5r. James Irwin saluting U.S. flag on Moon . . . . . . 1·50 2·25
MS750 100 × 83 mm. 10r. Aldrin alighting from "Apollo 11" on Moon . . . . 5·00 6·50

1989. 125th Anniv of International Red Cross.
751 **168** 1r. black and red . . . . 2·50 35
752 – 2r. black, green and red 3·00 1·50
753 – 3r. black and red . . . 3·50 2·50
754 – 10r. black and red . . . . 9·00 12·00
DESIGNS: 2r. "Liberty" (hospital ship), 1914–18; 3r. Sunbeam "Standard" army ambulance, 1914–18; 10r. "White Train" (hospital train), South Africa, 1899–1902.

1989. Island Birds. Multicoloured.
755 50c. Type **169** . . . . 2·25 55
756 2r. Sooty tern and Ile aux vaches . . . . 3·25 1·75
757 3r. Seychelles magpie robin ("Magpie Robin") and Fregate . . . . 4·00 3·00
758 5r. Roseate tern and Aride 4·25 7·50
MS759 83 × 109 mm. Nos. 755/8 14·00 15·00

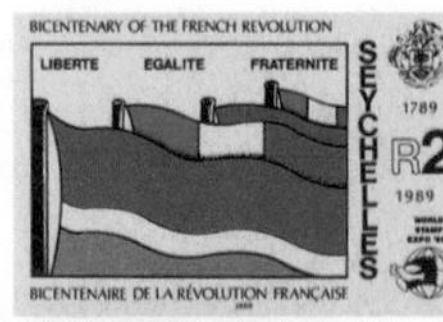

170 Flags of Seychelles and France

1989. Bicentenary of French Revolution and "World Stamp Expo '89". International Stamp Exhibition, Washington.
760 **170** 2r. multicoloured . . . . 3·50 1·50
761 – 5r. black, blue and red . . 4·00 6·00
MS762 78 × 100 mm. 10r. mult 5·00 7·00
DESIGN: 5r. Storming the Bastille, Paris, 1789; 10r. Reading Revolutionary proclamation, Seychelles, 1791.

171 Beau Vallon School

1989. 25th Anniv of African Development Bank. Multicoloured.
763 1r. Type **171** 45 25
764 2r. Seychelles Fishing Authority Headquarters . . 80 1·00
765 3r. "Variola" (fishing boat) (vert) . . . . 2·75 2·50
766 10r. "Deneb" (fishing boat) (vert) . . . . 6·50 10·00

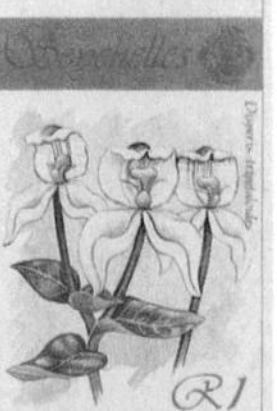

172 "Disperis tripetaloides" 174 Fumiyo Sako

173 Seychelles 1903 2c. and Great Britain 1880 1½d. Stamps

1990. Orchids (2nd series). Multicoloured.
767 1r. Type **172** . . . . 2·50 50
768 2r. "Vanilla phalaenopsis" . . 3·00 1·50
769 3r. "Angraecum eburneum" subsp. "superbum" . . . . 3·50 2·50
770 10r. "Polystachya concreta" 7·00 11·00

1990. "Stamp World London '90" International Stamp Exhibition. Each showing stamps. Mult.
771 1r. Type **173** 75 25
772 2r. Seychelles 1917 25c. and G.B. 1873 1s. . . . . . . 1·25 1·25
773 3r. Seychelles 1917 2c. and G.B. 1874 6d. . . . . . . 1·75 2·25
774 5r. Seychelles 1890 2c. and G.B. 1841 1d. red . . . . 2·50 4·50
MS775 88 × 60 mm. 10r. Seychelles 1961 Post Office Centenary 2r.25 and G.B. 1840 Penny Black . . 10·00 11·00

1990. "EXPO 90" International Garden and Greenery Exhibition, Osaka. Multicoloured.
776 2r. Type **174** . . . . 1·75 1·00
777 3r. Male and female coco-de-mer palms . . . . 2·00 1·50
778 5r. Pitcher plant and Aldabra lily . . . . 3·00 3·50
779 7r. Arms of Seychelles and gardenia . . . . 3·75 6·00
MS780 130 × 85 mm. Nos. 776/9 8·50 11·00

175 Air Seychelles Boeing 767-200ER over Island

1990. Air Seychelles "Boeing 767-200ER" World Record-breaking Flight (1989).
781 **175** 3r. multicoloured . . . . 4·25 3·75

1990. 90th Birthday of Queen Elizabeth the Queen Mother. As T **161a** of St. Helena.
782 2r. multicoloured . . . . . . 1·25 75
783 10r. black and violet . . . . 3·25 4·50
DESIGNS—(21 × 36 mm): 2r. Queen Elizabeth in Coronation robes, 1937. (29 × 37 mm): 10r. Queen Elizabeth visiting Lord Roberts Workshops, 1947.

176 Adult Class 177 Sega Dancers

1990. International Literacy Year. Mult.
784 1r. Type **176** 75 25
785 2r. Reading a letter . . . . . 1·50 1·25
786 3r. Following written instructions . . . . 2·00 2·00
787 10r. Typewriter, calculator and crossword . . . . . . 5·00 8·50

1990. Kreol Festival. Sega Dancing. Mult.
788 2r. Type **177** . . . . 2·25 2·50
789 2r. Dancing couple (girl in yellow dress) . . . . . . 2·25 2·50
790 2r. Female Sega dancer . . . 2·25 2·50
791 2r. Dancing couple (girl in floral pattern skirt) . . . . 2·25 2·50
792 2r. Dancing couple (girl in red patterned skirt) . . . . 2·25 2·50

178 Beach

1990. 1st Indian Ocean Regional Seminar on Petroleum Exploration. Multicoloured.
793 3r. Type **178** 1·75 1·50
794 10r. Geological map 5·75 7·50

1991. Orchids (3rd series). As T **172**. Mult.
795 1r. "Bullbophyllum intertextum" 1·75 45
796 2r. "Agrostophyllum occidentale" 2·25 1·75
797 3r. "Vanilla planifolia" 2·50 2·50
798 10r. "Malaxis seychellarum" 6·00 7·50

1991. 65th Birthday of Queen Elizabeth II and 70th Birthday of Prince Philip. As T **165a** of St. Helena. Multicoloured.
799 4r. Queen in evening dress 1·60 2·25
800 4r. Prince Philip in academic robes 1·60 2·25

179 "Precis rhadama"

1991. "Phila Nippon '91" International Stamp Exhibition, Tokyo. Butterflies. Multicoloured.
801 1r.50 Type **179** 2·00 85
802 3r. "Lampides boeticus" 2·50 2·25
803 3r.50 "Zizeeria knysna" 2·75 2·50
804 10r. "Phalanta phalantha" 7·25 7·50
MS805 78 × 81 mm. 10r. "Eagris sabadius" 7·00 7·50

180 "The Holy Virgin, Joseph, The Holy Child and St. John" (S. Vouillemont after Raphael)

1991. Christmas. Woodcuts.
806 **180** 50c. black, brown and red 50 15
807 – 1r. black, brown and green 90 25
808 – 2r. black, brown and blue 1·75 1·10
809 – 7r. black, brown and blue 4·50 7·00
DESIGNS: 1r. "Holy Virgin, the Child and Angel" (A. Blooting after Van Dyck); 2r. "The Holy Family, St. John and St. Anna" (L. Vorsterman after Rubens); 7r. "The Holy Family, Angel and St. Cathrin" (C. Bloemaert).

1992. 40th Anniv of Queen Elizabeth II's Accession. As T **168a** of St. Helena. Mult.
810 1r. Seychelles coastline 65 25
811 1r.50 Clock Tower, Victoria 80 40
812 3r. Victoria harbour 1·50 1·50
813 3r.50 Three portraits of Queen Elizabeth 1·60 1·75
814 5r. Queen Elizabeth II 1·75 2·75

181 Seychelles Brush Warbler ("Bush Warbler")

1993. Flora and Fauna. Multicoloured.
815 10c. Type **181** 1·00 90
816 25c. Bronze gecko (vert) 10 10
817 50c. Seychelles tree frog 65 20
818 1r. Seychelles splendid palm (vert) 65 25
819 1r.50 Seychelles skink (vert) 80 80
820 2r. Giant tenebrionid beetle 40 45
821 3r. Seychelles sunbird 2·00 1·25
822 3r.50 Seychelles killifish 70 75
823 4r. Seychelles magpie robin ("Magpie Robin") 75 80
824 5r. Seychelles vanilla (plant) (vert) 1·75 1·75
825 10r. Tiger chameleon 1·90 2·00
826 15r. Coco-de-mer (vert) 3·00 3·25
827 25r. Seychelles paradise flycatcher ("Paradise Flycatcher") (vert) 4·75 5·00
828 50r. Giant tortoise 16·00 18·00

182 Archbishop George Carey and Anglican Cathedral, Victoria

1993. First Visit of an Archbishop of Canterbury to Seychelles. Multicoloured.
834 3r. Type **182** 2·50 1·50
835 10r. Archbishop Carey with Air France Boeing 747-400 and Air Seychelles Boeing 737-200 airliners 6·00 8·50

183 Athletics

184 "Scotia" (cable ship) off Victoria, 1893

1993. 4th Indian Ocean Island Games. Mult.
836 1r.50 Type **183** 65 55
837 3r. Football 1·25 1·00
838 3r.50 Cycling 2·00 1·75
839 10r. Sailing 3·25 6·00

1993. Century of Telecommunications. Mult.
840 1r. Type **184** 1·75 60
841 3r. Eastern Telegraph Co office, Victoria, 1904 2·50 1·75
842 4r. HF Transmitting Station, 1971 2·75 3·00
843 10r. New Telecoms House, Victoria, 1993 5·00 7·50

1994. "Hong Kong '94" Int Stamp Exhibition. Nos. 62, 64 and 66/7 of Zil Elwannyen Sesel surch **HONG KONG '94**, emblem and value.
844 1r. on 2r.10 Souimanga sunbird 50 30
845 1r.50 on 2r.75 Sacred ibis 75 60
846 3r.50 on 7r. Seychelles kestrel (vert) 1·60 2·25
847 10r. on 15r. Comoro blue pigeon (vert) 3·00 5·00

186 "Eurema floricola"

1994. Butterflies. Multicoloured.
848 1r.50 Type **186** 1·75 75
849 3r. "Coeliades forestan" 2·50 2·00
850 3r.50 "Borbo borbonica" 2·75 2·75
851 10r. "Zizula hylax" 5·50 7·50

187 Lady Elizabeth Bowes-Lyon

1995. 95th Birthday of Queen Elizabeth the Queen Mother. Multicoloured.
852 1r.50 Type **187** 75 40
853 3r. Duchess of York on wedding day, 1923 1·40 1·00
854 3r.50 Queen Elizabeth 1·60 1·40
855 10r. Queen Elizabeth the Queen Mother 3·50 6·00

188 Female Seychelles Paradise Flycatcher feeding Chick

189 Swimming

1996. Endangered Species. Seychelles Paradise Flycatcher. Multicoloured.
856 1r. Type **188** 70 95
857 1r. Male bird in flight 70 95
858 1r. Female bird on branch 70 95
859 1r. Male bird on branch 70 95
MS860 60 × 53 mm. 10r. Pair on branch 6·50 7·50

1996. Centenary of Modern Olympic Games. Mult.
861 50c. Type **189** 40 20
862 1r.50 Running 60 45
863 3r. Sailing 1·25 1·50
864 5r. Boxing 1·90 3·00

190 Archbishop Makarios at Table

191 Comoro Blue Pigeon

1996. 40th Anniv of Exile of Archbishop Makarios of Cyprus to Seychelles. Multicoloured.
865 3r. Type **190** 1·50 1·00
866 10r. Archbishop Makarios in priest's robes 3·25 6·00

1996. Birds. Multicoloured.
867 3r. Type **191** 1·25 1·50
868 3r. Seychelles blue pigeon 1·25 1·50
869 3r. Souimanga sunbird 1·25 1·50
870 3r. Seychelles sunbird 1·25 1·50
871 3r. Mascarene fody ("Aldabra Red-headed Fody") 1·25 1·50
872 3r. Seychelles fody 1·25 1·50
873 3r. Madagascar white eye 1·25 1·50
874 3r. Seychelles brown white-eye ("Seychelles White eye") 1·25 1·50
Nos. 867/8, 869/70, 871/2 and 873/4 respectively were printed together, se-tenant, with the background of each pair forming a composite design showing a regional map.

1997. "HONG KONG '97" International Stamp Exhibition. No. 226 of Zil Elwannyen Sesel surch **R1.50** and emblem.
875 1r.50 on 2r. Little egret ("Dimorphic Little Egret") 2·50 2·50

1997. Golden Wedding of Queen Elizabeth and Prince Philip. As T **192a** of St. Helena. Mult.
876 1r. Queen Elizabeth wearing red and white suit 65 90
877 1r. Prince Philip driving carriage 65 90
878 1r.50 Prince Philip 75 1·10
879 1r.50 Queen Elizabeth with horse 75 1·10
880 3r. Prince Charles and Princess Anne on horseback 1·40 1·75
881 3r. Prince Philip and Queen Elizabeth 1·40 1·75
MS882 110 × 70 mm. 10r. Queen Elizabeth and Prince Philip in landau (horiz) 4·00 4·50
Nos. 876/7, 878/9 and 880/1 respectively were printed together, se-tenant, with the backgrounds forming composite designs.

1998. Diana, Princess of Wales Commemoration. Sheet, 145 × 70 mm, containing vert designs as T **62a** of Tokelau. Multicoloured.
MS883 3r. Wearing red jacket, 1992; 3r. Wearing floral dress, 1981; 3r. Wearing blue and black jacket, 1993; 3r. Wearing white dress, Nepal 1993 (sold at 12r.+2r. charity premium) 3·50 4·00

193 Powderblue Surgeonfish

1998. International Year of the Ocean. Mult.
884 3r. Type **193** 90 1·25
885 3r. Shoal of soldierfish 90 1·25
886 3r. Lionfish 90 1·25
887 3r. School of fish 90 1·25
888 3r. Coral 90 1·25
889 3r. Turtle 90 1·25

194 "Vierge du Cap" (galleon), 1721

1999. 18th-century Ships. Multicoloured.
890 1r.50 Type **194** 55 35
891 3r. "L'Elizabeth" (corvette), 1741 1·25 1·00
892 3r.50 "Curieuse" (sloop), 1768 1·25 1·75
893 10r. "La Fleche" (frigate), 1801 2·75 4·25
MS894 105 × 70 mm. 20r. "Le Cheval Marin" (French merchantman), 1774 (vert) 6·00 7·50
No. **MS**894 also includes the "Australia '99" World Stamp Exhibition, Melbourne, emblem on the sheet margin.

195 Royal Couple on Steps of Chapel Royal, Windsor

197 Lady Elizabeth Bowes-Lyon

196 Cathedral of the Immaculate Conception

1999. Royal Wedding. Multicoloured.
895 3r. Type **195** 1·00 75
896 15r. In landau 4·50 6·50

1999. New Millennium. Multicoloured.
897 1r. Type **196** 40 30
898 1r.50 White tern at sunrise 1·50 1·00
899 2r.50 Dolphin and island 1·75 1·50
900 10r. Comet over beach 4·00 5·50

2000. Queen Elizabeth the Queen Mother's 100th Birthday.
901 **197** 3r. multicoloured 90 70
902 – 5r. black and brown 1·50 1·50
903 – 7r. black and lilac 2·00 2·75
904 – 10r. multicoloured 2·50 3·25
DESIGNS: 5r. Queen Elizabeth in East End of London during Second World War; 7r. Visiting Seychelles with King George VI and Princess Elizabeth; 10r. Wearing blue hat and outfit.

198 Arrival of Jacobin Deportees (Bicentenary)

2001. Milestones in Seychelles History. Mult.
905 1r. Type **198** 55 30
906 1r.50 Victoria (160th anniv as capital) 65 40
907 3r. Father Leon des Avanchers (150th anniv of arrival) 1·25 1·00
908 3r.50 Victoria Fountain (centenary) (vert) 1·25 1·25
909 5r. Botanical Gardens (centenary) 1·90 2·00
910 10r. Independence monument (25th anniv) (vert) 2·50 3·50

199 Ruddy Shelduck

2001. Bird Life World Bird Festival. Migrant Ducks and Bare-legged Scops Owl (No. **MS**915). Multicoloured.
911 3r. Type **199** 1·40 1·50
912 3r. White-faced whistling duck 1·40 1·50
913 3r. Northern Shoveler 1·40 1·50
914 3r. Garganey 1·40 1·50
MS915 171 × 78 mm. 3r. Bare-legged scops owl ("Seychelles Scops Owl") in flight (35 × 30 mm); 3r. Chick in tree hole (35 × 30 mm); 3r. Adult tufts down (30 × 35 mm); 3r. Adult tufts erect (30 × 35 mm); 3r. Immature (35 × 30 mm) 6·25 7·50

2002. Queen Elizabeth the Queen Mother Commemoration. Sheet, 145 × 70 mm, containing vert designs as T **215** of St. Helena.
MS916 5r. brown, gold and black; 10r. multicoloured . . . . . . 4·25 4·50
DESIGNS 5r. Lady Elizabeth Bowes-Lyon, 1923; 10r. Queen Mother on her birthday, 1986.

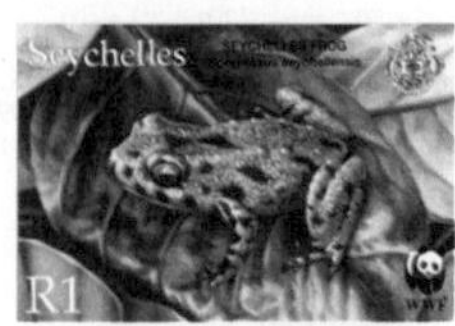

200 Seychelles Frog

2003. Endangered Species. Frogs. Multicoloured.
917 1r. Type **200** 65 65
918 1r. Palm frog 65 65
919 1r. Thomasset's frog 65 65
920 1r. Gardiner's frog 65 65
MS921 65 × 65 mm. 20r. Seychelles tree frog . . . . 7·50 8·00

201 Seychelles Blenny

2003. Marine Life. Multicoloured.
922 10c. Type **201** 10 10
924 50c. Seychelles anemonefish 10 15
925 1r. Indian butterflyfish . . . 20 25
926 1r.50 Goldbar wrasse 30 35
928 3r. Seychelles squirrelfish . . 60 65
931 5r. Green-beaked parrotfish ("Greenthroat Parrotfish") 95 1·00
935 50r. Whale shark . . . . . . 9·75 10·00

202 Emblem

2004. 20th Anniv of the Indian Ocean Commission.
936 **202** 10r. multicoloured . . . . 1·90 2·00

2004. Flora and Fauna. Nos. 819, 821 and 824/8 surch.
937 1r. on 1r.50 Seychelles skink (vert) 20 25
938 2r. on 3r. Seychelles sunbird 40 45
939 3r.50 on 5r. Seychelles vanilla (vert) 70 75
940 3r.50 on 10r. Tiger chameleon 70 75
941 3r.50 on 15r. Coco-de-mer (vert) 70 75
942 4r. on 25r. Paradise flycatcher (vert) 75 80
943 4r. on 50r. Giant tortoise . . 75 80

POSTAGE DUE STAMPS

D **1**

1951. Value in red.
D1 D **1** 2c. red and carmine . . . 80 1·50
D2 3c. red and green . . . . 2·00 1·50
D3 6c. red and bistre . . . . 2·00 1·25
D4 9c. red and orange . . . 2·00 1·25
D5 15c. red and violet . . . 1·75 12·00
D6 18c. red and blue . . . . 1·75 12·00
D7 20c. red and brown . . . 1·75 12·00
D8 30c. red and claret . . . 1·75 7·50

1980. As Type D **1** but 18 × 22 mm.
D11 D **1** 5c. red and mauve . . . 15 1·00
D12 10c. red and green . . . 15 1·00
D13 15c. red and bistre . . . 20 1·00
D14 20c. red and brown . . . 20 1·00
D15 25c. red and violet . . . 20 1·00
D16 75c. red and maroon . . 30 1·00
D17 80c. red and blue . . . . 30 1·00
D18 1r. red and purple . . . 30 1·00

SHAHPURA Pt. 1

One of the Indian Feudatory States. Now uses Indian stamps.

12 pies = 1 anna; 16 annas = 1 rupee.

RAJ
SHAHPURA
Postage 1 pice
1

1914. Perf (No. 1) or imperf (No. 2).
1 **1** 1p. red on grey . . . . — £750
2 1p. red on brown . . . . . . — £1000

1920. As T **1** but "Postage" omitted. Imperf.
3 1p. red on brown . . . . . . — £1300
4 1a. black on pink . . . . . . — £1500

SHANGHAI Pt. 17

A seaport on the E. coast of China, which for a time had a separate postal system.

1865. 10 cash = 1 candareen;
100 candareens = 1 tael.
1890. 100 cents = 1 dollar (Chinese).

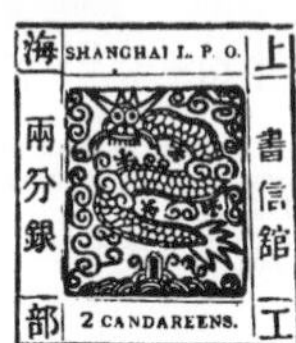

1 Dragon

1865. Value in candareens. Imperf. (a) "CANDAREEN" in singular.
28 **1** 1ca. blue . . . . 80·00 £3250
12 2ca. black £200 £6000
29 3ca. brown . . . . 80·00 £3750
13 4ca. yellow £225 £7000
14 8ca. green £180
15 16ca. red £225

(b) "CANDAREENS" in plural.
30 **1** 2ca. black . . . . 75·00
31 3ca. brown . . . . 75·00 £2250
3 4ca. yellow £200 £7000
18 6ca. brown £100
20 6ca. red £160
4 8ca. green £225 £7500
21 12ca. brown £100
22 16ca. red £100

2

6

1866. Value in cents. Frames differ. Perf.
32 **2** 2c. red . . . . 8·50 18·00
33 4c. lilac . . . . 18·00 32·00
34 8c. blue . . . . 20·00 32·00
35 16c. green . . . . 30·00 48·00

1867. Value in candareens. Frames differ.
37 **6** 1ca. brown . . . . 6·00 8·00
59 1ca. yellow on yellow . . . 12·00 15·00
62 1ca. yellow . . . . 8·00 10·00
73 1ca. red £650 £1200
38 3ca. yellow . . . . 16·00 25·00
60 3ca. pink on pink . . . . 12·00 15·00
63 3ca. red . . . . 40·00 50·00
39 6ca. grey . . . . 16·00 48·00
64 6ca. green . . . . 60·00 £100
65 9ca. grey . . . . 80·00 £140
40 12ca. brown . . . . 24·00 48·00

1873. Surch with value in English and Chinese.
41 **2** 1ca. on 2c. red . . . . . . 28·00 38·00
44 1ca. on 4c. lilac . . . . . 11·00 12·50
46 1ca. on 8c. blue . . . . . 18·00 18·00
48 1ca. on 16c. green £2000 £1200
50 3ca. on 2c. red £100 £100
52 3ca. on 16c. green £1200 £1800

1873. Surch with value in English and Chinese.
53 **6** 1ca. on 3ca. yellow £12000 £7500
67 1ca. on 3ca. red . . . . . 45·00 38·00
68 1ca. on 3ca. pink on pink . . £200 £180
54 1ca. on 6ca. grey £300 £250
69 1ca. on 6ca. green . . . . £120 85·00
70 1ca. on 9ca. grey £200 £160
56 1ca. on 12ca. brown £300 £250
58 3ca. on 12ca. brown £2500 £1500

1877. Value in cash.
74 **6** 20 cash blue . . . . 5·00 4·00
75 20 cash lilac . . . . 4·50 3·75
93 20 cash green . . . . . . 4·00 3·25
114 20 cash grey . . . . 2·50 3·25
81 40 cash pink . . . . 7·00 9·00
94 40 cash brown . . . . . . 5·00 4·75
107 40 cash black . . . . . . 5·00 3·25
82 60 cash green . . . . . . 8·50 10·00
95 60 cash violet . . . . . . 6·50 5·50
108 60 cash red . . . . 7·50 6·50
83 80 cash blue . . . . 10·00 12·00
96 80 cash brown . . . . . . 6·00 6·00
109 80 cash green . . . . . . 7·00 5·50
84 100 cash brown . . . . . . 10·00 12·00
97 100 cash yellow . . . . . . 6·50 6·00
110 100 cash blue . . . . 10·00 8·50

1879. Surch in English and Chinese.
89 **6** 20 cash on 40 cash pink . . 9·00 10·00
103 20 cash on 40 cash brown 16·00 15·00
105 20 cash on 80 cash brown 10·00 7·50
111 20 cash on 80 cash green . . 7·50 6·00
112 20 cash on 100 cash blue . . 7·50 6·00
100 40 cash on 80 cash brown 6·00 7·00
101 40 cash on 100 cash yellow 6·00 6·50
90 60 cash on 80 cash blue . . 18·00 20·00
88 60 cash on 100 cash brown 24·00 22·00
102 60 cash on 100 cash yellow 8·00 7·50

1886. Surch **20 CASH** in English and Chinese in double-lined frame.
104 **6** 20 cash on 40 cash brown 20·00 14·00

1889. Surch **100 CASH** over **20 CASH** in English and Chinese in double-lined frame.
113 **6** 100 cash on 20 cash on 100 cash yellow . . . . 60·00 85·00

16

25

1890. Value in cents.
119 **16** 2c. brown . . . . 2·50 1·50
142 2c. green . . . . 2·00 1·50
120 5c. pink . . . . 6·75 3·75
143 5c. red . . . . 5·00 4·50
122 10c. black . . . . 9·00 6·50
144 10c. orange . . . . 15·00 16·00
123 15c. blue . . . . 11·00 10·00
145 15c. mauve . . . . 9·00 7·50
124 20c. mauve . . . . 8·75 7·50
146 20c. brown . . . . 9·00 7·50

1892. Surch **2 Cts** and in Chinese.
141 **16** 2c. on 5c. pink . . . . . . 75·00 40·00

1893. Surch in words in English and Chinese.
147 **16** ½c. on 15c. mauve . . . . 8·00 6·50
148 1c. on 20c. brown . . . . 8·00 6·50

1893. Surch **½Ct.** or **1 Ct.**
149 **16** ½c. on half of 5c. pink . . 6·00 5·50
152 ½c. on half of 5c. red . . 6·00 5·00
155 1c. on half of 2c. brown . 2·50 2·00
156 1c. on half of 2c. green . . 8·50 7·50

1893. Inscriptions in outer frame in black.
165 **25** ½c. orange 30 25
166 1c. brown 30 25
187 2c. red 25 50
188 4c. orange on yellow . . . 1·50 2·25
161 5c. blue 70 75
189 6c. red on pink . . . . . 2·25 2·75
167 10c. green . . . . 70 1·25
163 15c. yellow . . . . 1·25 2·50
168 20c. mauve . . . . 1·10 2·00

26

1893. Jubilee of First Settlement.
176 **26** 2c. red and black 90 75

1893. Optd **1843 Jubilee 1893**. Inscriptions in outer frame in black.
177 **25** ½c. orange 25 20
178 1c. brown 30 25
179 2c. red 50 35
180 5c. blue . . . . 2·25 1·75
181 10c. green . . . . 3·00 2·75
182 15c. yellow . . . . 4·50 3·75
183 20c. mauve . . . . 4·25 3·75

1896. Surch in English and Chinese.
184 **25** 4c. on 15c. yellow . . . . 5·50 4·25
185 6c. on 20c. mauve . . . . 5·50 4·00

POSTAGE DUE STAMPS

1892. T **16** optd **Postage Due**.
D134 2c. brown . . . . 2·50 1·75
D135 5c. pink . . . . 6·00 4·50
D130 10c. black . . . . 18·00 15·00
D138 10c. orange . . . . 10·00 8·50
D131 15c. blue . . . . 16·00 14·00
D139 15c. mauve . . . . 20·00 16·00
D132 20c. mauve . . . . 11·00 11·00
D140 20c. brown . . . . 22·00 16·00

D **26**

1893. Inscriptions in outer frame in black.
D169 D **26** ½c. orange 40 25
D170 1c. brown 40 15
D171 2c. red 40 40
D172 5c. blue 40 65
D173 10c. green . . . . . . 55 1·25
D174 15c. yellow . . . . . 65 1·75
D175 20c. mauve . . . . . 1·10 1·50

SHARJAH Pt.19

One of the Trucial States on the Persian Gulf. Embodies the principalities of Dibbah, Khor Fakkan and Khor al-Kalba.

On 2 December 1971, Sharjah, together with six other Gulf Shaikdoms, formed the United Arab Emirates.

1963. 100 naye paise = 1 rupee.
1966. 100 dirhams = 1 riyal.

IMPERFORATE STAMPS. Some sets also exist imperf in limited quantities.

1 Shaikh Saqr bin Sultan al Qasimi, Flag and Map

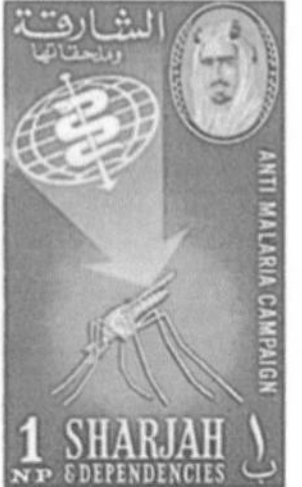

2 Mosquito and W.H.O. Emblem

1963. Multicoloured.
1 **1** 1n.p. (postage) 10 10
2 2n.p. 10 10
3 3n.p. 10 10
4 4n.p. 10 10
5 5n.p. 10 10
6 6n.p. 10 10
7 8n.p. 10 10
8 10n.p. 20 20
9 16n.p. 40 20
10 20n.p. 50 20
11 30n.p. 70 30
12 40n.p. 80 50
13 50n.p. . . . . 1·10 60
14 75n.p. . . . . 2·00 1·30
15 100n.p. . . . . 2·50 2·00
16 1r. (air) . . . . 1·20 60
17 2r. . . . . 2·20 1·00
18 3r. . . . . 2·40 1·60
19 4r. . . . . 4·00 2·20
20 5r. . . . . 5·50 3·00
21 10r. . . . . 9·75 5·75

The air stamps are as T **1** but additionally inscr "AIRMAIL" in English and Arabic, and with a hawk in flight.

1963. Malaria Eradication.
22 **2** 1n.p. turquoise 10 10
23 2n.p. blue 10 10
24 3n.p. blue 20 10
25 4n.p. green 30 20
26 90n.p. brown . . . . 3·25 1·50
MS26a 64 × 90 mm. **2** 100n.p. greenish blue (40 × 67mm). Imperf 4·50 2·00

3 "Red Crescent"

1963. Red Cross Centenary.
27 **3** 1n.p. red and purple 10 10
28 2n.p. red and turquoise . . . 10 10
29 3n.p. red and blue 10 10
30 4n.p. red and green 10 10
31 5n.p. red and brown 10 10
32 85n.p. red and green . . . . 1·70 70
MS32a 90 × 64 mm. **3** 100n.p. red and purple (67 × 40 mm). Imperf 4·50 2·40

4 Campaign Emblem between Hands

1963. Freedom from Hunger.

33	4	1n.p. green	10	10
34		2n.p. brown	10	10
35		3n.p. green	10	10
36		4n.p. blue	10	20
37		90n.p. red	2·20	1·00
MS37a		64 × 90 mm. **4** 100n.p. plum (40 × 67 mm). Imperf	3·00	2·00

1963. Surch.

38	4	10n.p. on 1n.p. green	30	30
39		20n.p. on 2n.p. brown	60	50
40		30n.p. on 3n.p. green	1·00	80
41		40n.p. on 4n.p. blue	1·30	1·20
42		75n.p. on 90n.p. red	2·40	2·00
43		80n.p. on 90n.p. red	3·00	2·20
44	2	1r. on 90n.p. brown	4·00	3·25

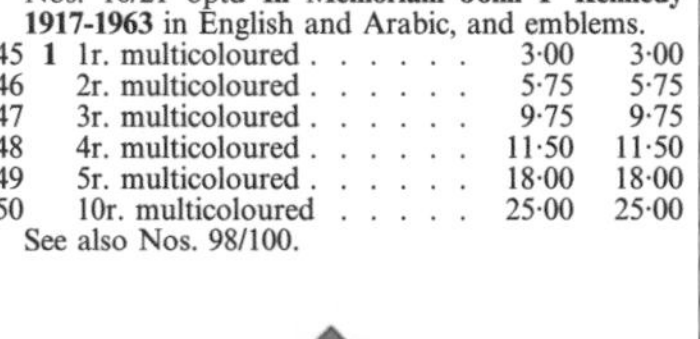

1964. Air. Pres. Kennedy Memorial Issue (1st issue). Nos. 16/21 optd **In Memoriam John F Kennedy 1917-1963** in English and Arabic, and emblems.

45	1	1r. multicoloured	3·00	3·00
46		2r. multicoloured	5·75	5·75
47		3r. multicoloured	9·75	9·75
48		4r. multicoloured	11·50	11·50
49		5r. multicoloured	18·00	18·00
50		10r. multicoloured	25·00	25·00

See also Nos. 98/100.

7 Orbiting Astronomical Observatory

1964. Scientific Space Research.

51	7	1n.p. blue	10	10
52		2n.p. green and brown	10	10
53		3n.p. blue and black	10	10
54		4n.p. black and bistre	10	10
55		5n.p. bistre and violet	10	10
56		35n.p. violet and blue	1·00	80
57		50n.p. brown and green	2·00	1·20
MS57a		112 × 80 mm. 100n.p. multicoloured (Various satellites). Imperf	6·75	2·00

DESIGNS: 2n.p. "Nimbus" weather satellite; 3n.p. "Pioneer V" space probe; 4n.p. "Explorer XIII" satellite; 5n.p. "Explorer XII" satellite; 35n.p. Project "Relay" satellite; 50n.p. Orbiting solar observatory.

8 Running

1964. Olympic Games, Tokyo (1st issue).

58	8	1n.p. blue, green and yellow	10	10
59	–	2n.p. red and turquoise	10	10
60	–	3n.p. brown and green	10	10
61	–	4n.p. green and brown	10	10
62	–	20n.p. blue and brown	50	20
63	–	30n.p. bistre and pink	80	40
64	–	40n.p. violet and yellow	1·00	50
65	–	1r. brown and blue	2·40	1·50
MS65a		102 × 102 mm. 1r. sepia and cobalt (67 × 67 mm) (As No. 65). Imperf	9·75	5·00

DESIGNS: 2n.p. Throwing the discus; 3n.p. Hurdling; 4n.p. Putting the shot; 20n.p. High jumping; 30n.p. Weightlifting; 40n.p. Throwing the javelin; 1r. High diving.

See also Nos. 90/7.

9 Flame and World Map

1964. Air. Human Rights Day.

66	9	50n.p. brown	60	30
67		1r. violet	1·20	70
68		150n.p. green	2·20	1·20
MS68a		90 × 64 mm. **9** 3r. rosine (67 × 40 mm). Imperf	4·00	2·40

10 Girl Scouts Marching

1964. Sharjah Girl Scouts.

69	10	1n.p. green	10	10
70		2n.p. green	10	10
71		3n.p. blue	20	20
72		4n.p. violet	20	20
73		5n.p. mauve	30	20
74		2r. brown	3·25	2·20
MS74a		103 × 76 mm. **10** 2r. vermilion (67 × 40 mm). Imperf	5·00	3·50

11 Khor Fakkan

1964. Air. Multicoloured.

75	10n.p. Type **11**	20	20
76	20n.p. Bedouin camp, Beni Qatab	30	20
77	30n.p. Dhaid oasis	40	20
78	40n.p. Kalba Castle	50	30
79	75n.p. Street and Wind tower, Sharjah	1·10	40
80	100n.p. Fortress	2·00	50

12 "Mr. Gus" (oil rig) 13 Scout at Attention

1964. Air. New York World's Fair. Multicoloured.

81	20n.p. Type **12**	60	20
82	40n.p. Unisphere	1·00	30
83	1r. New York skyline (85½ × 44½ mm)	2·40	70
MS83a	76 × 108 mm. 40n.p. multicoloured (40 × 67 mm) (As No. 82). Imperf	4·00	1·70

1964. Sharjah Boy Scouts.

84	13	1n.p. green	10	10
85	–	2n.p. green	10	10
86	–	3n.p. blue	10	10
87	13	4n.p. violet	50	40
88	–	5n.p. mauve	60	50
89	–	2r. brown	2·20	1·50
MS89a		77 × 103 mm. 2r. vermilion (40 × 67 mm) (As No. 86). Imperf	5·00	3·50

DESIGNS—HORIZ: 2, 5n.p. Scouts marching. VERT: 3n.p., 2r. Boy scout.

14 Olympic Torch

1964. Olympic Games, Tokyo (2nd issue).

90	14	1n.p. green	10	10
91		2n.p. blue	10	10
92		3n.p. brown	10	10
93		4n.p. turquoise	10	10
94		5n.p. violet	10	10
95		40n.p. blue	40	10
96		50n.p. brown	70	30
97		2r. brown	3·50	1·80
MS97a		108 × 76 mm. **14** 2r. green (57 × 82 mm). Imperf	9·75	7·75

15 Pres. Kennedy and Statue of Liberty

1964. Air. Pres. Kennedy Commemoration (2nd issue). Inscr in gold.

98	15	40n.p. blue, brown & green	2·00	1·00
99		60n.p. brown, green & blue	2·00	1·00
100		100n.p. green, blue & brown	2·00	1·00
MS100a		108 × 76 mm. Nos. 98/100. Imperf	9·75	7·75

16 Feral Rock Pigeon ("Rock Dove")

1965. Air. Birds. Multicoloured.

101	30n.p. Type **16**	80	20
102	40n.p. Red junglefowl	1·00	30
103	75n.p. Hoopoe	1·50	50
104	150n.p. Type **16**	3·00	1·00
105	2r. Red junglefowl	4·00	1·20
106	3r. Hoopoe	5·00	2·00

17 Early Telephone

1965. "Science, Transport and Communications".

107	17	1n.p. black and red	10	10
108	A	1n.p. black and red	10	10
109	B	2n.p. blue and orange	10	10
110	C	2n.p. blue and orange	10	10
111	D	3n.p. brown and green	10	10
112	E	3n.p. brown and green	10	10
113	F	4n.p. violet and green	10	10
114	G	4n.p. violet and green	10	10
115	H	5n.p. brown and green	10	10
116	I	5n.p. brown and green	10	10
117	J	30n.p. indigo and blue	20	20
118	K	30n.p. indigo and blue	20	20
119	L	40n.p. blue and yellow	40	20
120	M	40n.p. blue and yellow	40	20
121	N	50n.p. brown and blue	50	30
122	O	50n.p. brown and blue	50	30
123	P	75n.p. brown and green	50	30
124	Q	75n.p. brown and green	50	30
125	R	1r. blue and yellow	2·40	1·00
126	S	1r. blue and yellow	2·40	1·00
MS126a		Two sheets each 153 × 77 mm. Nos. 119/20 and 125/6. Imperf	7·50	4·25

DESIGNS: A, Modern teleprinter; B, 1895 Car; C, 1964 American car; D, Early X-ray apparatus; E, T.V. X-ray machine; F, Early mail coach; G, "Telstar" satellite; H, Medieval ship; I, Nuclear- powered freighter "Savannah"; J, Early astronomers; K, Jodrell Bank radio-telescope; L, Greek messengers; M, "Relay" satellite; N, "Man's early flight" (Lilienthal biplane glider); O, Sud Aviation Caravelle jetliner; P, Persian waterwheel; Q, Hydro-electric dam; R, Locomotive "Fitzwilliam", 1849, Great Britain; S, Modern diesel train.

1965. Air. Churchill Commemoration (1st issue). Optd **In Memoriam Sir Winston Churchill 1874-1965** in English and Arabic.

127	15	40n.p. multicoloured	1·00	40
128		60n.p. multicoloured	1·50	50
129		100n.p. multicoloured	2·00	60
MS129a		108 × 76 mm. Nos. 127/9. Imperf	11·50	9·75

See also Nos. 201/4.

18a A.P.U. Emblem

1965. 10th Anniv (1964) of Arab Postal Union's Permanent Office.

130	18a	5n.p. blue and yellow	10	10
131		30n.p. blue and red	60	30
132		65n.p. green and orange	1·50	90

1965. Various issues of Shaikh Saqr with portrait obliterated with bars. (a) Postage. Nos. 5, 8/13.

150	1	5n.p. multicoloured	10	10
151		10n.p. multicoloured	10	10
152		16n.p. multicoloured	20	20
153		20n.p. multicoloured	30	20
154		30n.p. multicoloured	40	20
155		40n.p. multicoloured	40	30
156		50n.p. multicoloured	50	40

(b) Air. (i) Nos. 16, 18/21.

157	1	1r. multicoloured	80	60
158		3r. multicoloured	2·40	2·00
159		4r. multicoloured	3·25	2·40
160		5r. multicoloured	4·00	3·00
161		10r. multicoloured	8·25	5·00

(ii) Nos. 75/80.

144	11	10n.p. multicoloured	30	20
145	–	20n.p. multicoloured	40	20
146	–	30n.p. multicoloured	50	20
147	–	40n.p. multicoloured	60	30
148	–	75n.p. multicoloured	80	30
149	–	100n.p. multicoloured	1·00	40

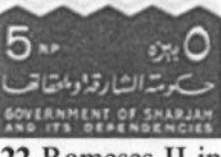

22 Rameses II in War Chariot

23 Cable Ship "Monarch IV" and COMPAC Cable Route Map

1965. Nubian Monuments Preservation.

162	22	5n.p. blue and yellow	10	10
163		10n.p. green and brown	10	10
164		30n.p. blue and orange	60	50
165		55n.p. violet and blue	1·00	70

1965. I.T.U. Centenary. Country name in gold.

166	23	1n.p. brown and blue	10	10
167	–	2n.p. brown and blue	10	10
168	–	3n.p. violet and green	10	10
169	–	4n.p. brown and blue	10	10
170	23	5n.p. brown and violet	20	10
171	–	50n.p. purple and black	50	20
172	–	1r. green and brown	1·00	40
173	–	120n.p. red and green	1·50	60

DESIGNS: 2, 120n.p. "Relay 1" satellite and tracking station, Goonhilly Down; 3, 50n.p. "Telstar" satellite and Atlas-Agena rocket on launching pad; 4n.p., 1r. "Syncom" satellite, Post Office Tower (London) and horn paraboloid reflector aerial.

24 Running

1965. Pan-American Games, Cairo.

174	24	50n.p. turquoise and lilac	70	30
175	–	50n.p. green and brown	70	30
176	–	50n.p. lilac and brown	70	30
177	–	50n.p. brown and green	70	30
178	–	50n.p. brown and turquoise	70	30

SPORTS: No. 175, Pole vaulting; 176, Boxing; 177, High jumping; 178, Long jumping.

25 Flags (reverse of 5r. coin)

1966. Arabian Gulf Area Monetary Conf. Circular designs on silver foil, backed with paper inscr "Walsall Security Paper" in English and Arabic. Imperf. (a) Diameter 41 mm.

179	25	50n.p. black	1·00	1·00
180	–	75n.p. violet	1·10	1·10

(b) Diameter 52 mm.

181	25	1r. purple	1·20	1·20
182	–	3r. blue	3·25	3·25

(c) Diameter 64 mm.

183	25	4r. green	5·00	5·00
184	–	5r. orange	5·50	5·50

COINS: 75n.p., 3r. and 5r. show the obverse (Pres. Kennedy).

1966. Rendezvous in Space. Nos. 33/6 optd **15–12–1965 Rendezvous in SPACE**, two space capsules and four bars obliterating portrait or surch also in English and Arabic.

No.		Description	Mint	Used
185	4	1n.p. green	10	10
186		2n.p. brown	10	10
187		3n.p. green	10	10
188		4n.p. blue	10	10
189		15n.p. on 1n.p. green	30	20
190		30n.p. on 2n.p. brown	40	30
191		50n.p. on 3n.p. green	1·10	70
192		1r. on 4n.p. blue	1·40	80

27 I.C.Y. Emblem and Prime Minister Harold Wilson

1986. International Co-operation Year.

No.		Description	Mint	Used
193	27	80n.p. brown and violet	60	20
194	–	80n.p. brown and green	60	20
195	–	80n.p. green and red	60	20
196	–	80n.p. purple and blue	60	20
197	–	80n.p. blue and orange	60	20
198	–	80n.p. purple and green	60	20
199	–	80n.p. blue and grey	60	20
200	–	80n.p. purple and brown	60	20

DESIGNS—I.C.Y. emblem and "World Leaders": No. 194, Chancellor Erhard (West Germany); 195, Pres. Nasser (Egypt); 196, Pres. Johnson (U.S.A.); 197, Pope Paul VI; 198, Pres. De Gaulle (France); 199, Shaikh Isa bin Sulman al-Khalifa (Bahrain); 200, King Faisal (Saudi Arabia).

28 Sir Winston Churchill, Pen and Ink, and Books

1966. Churchill Commemoration (2nd issue). Multicoloured, printed on gold foil, backed with paper.

No.		Description	Mint	Used
201		2r. Type **28**	1·00	50
202		3r. Churchill and Houses of Parliament, pen and ink	1·20	60
203		4r. Churchill and St. Paul's Cathedral	1·80	80
204		5r. Churchill and "Big Ben" (clock tower, Houses of Parliament) and Tower Bridge	2·00	1·00
MS205		102 × 71 mm. 1, 2, 3, and 4r. stamps in colours and designs of Nos. 201/2, 204 and 203 but smaller	12·50	8·75

29 Pennant Coralfish

1966. Fishes. Multicoloured.

No.		Description	Mint	Used
206		1n.p. Type **29**	30	20
207		2n.p. Sail-finned tang	30	20
208		3n.p. Young emperor angelfish	30	20
209		4n.p. African mouthbrooder	30	20
210		5n.p. Undulate triggerfish	30	20
211		15n.p. Diamond fingerfish	90	20
212		20n.p. Ornate butterflyfish	1·20	20
213		30n.p. Moorish idol	1·20	20
214		40n.p. Regal angelfish	1·20	20
215		50n.p. African mouthbrooder	1·50	20
216		75n.p. Undulate triggerfish	1·80	30
217		1r. Regal angelfish	2·40	30
218		2r. Moorish idol	3·50	55
219		3r. Ornate butterflyfish	4·50	60
220		4r. Diamond fingerfish	5·75	1·10
221		5r. Young emperor angelfish	8·75	1·40
222		10r. Type **29**	18·00	2·75

30 Arms of Munich and "Souvenir Sheet"

34 Pres. Kennedy

33 Greek 6th-cent Ball-player

1966. International Philatelic Federation and International Philatelic Journalists Association Congresses, Munich. Multicoloured.

No.		Description	Mint	Used
223		80n.p. Type **30**	50	20
224		120n.p. Frauenkirche, Munich	70	30
225		2r. Statue and Hall of Fame, Munich (81 × 41 mm)	1·30	60

NEW CURRENCY SURCHARGES. During the latter half of 1966 various issues appeared surcharged in dirhams and riyals. The 1966 definitives with this surcharge are listed below as there is evidence of their postal use. Nos. 102, 107/126, 135, 145, 150/61, 174/84 and 190 also exist with these surcharges.

Earlier in 1966 Nos. 98/100, 171/3, 193/4, 196, 198 and 200/5 appeared surcharged in piastres and rials. As Sharjah did not adopt this currency their status is uncertain.

1966. Nos. 206/22 with currency names changed by overprinting in English and Arabic. (a) Optd. **Dirham** or **Riyal**.

No.		Description	Mint	Used
226	29	1d. on 1n.p. multicoloured	20	20
227	–	2d. on 2n.p. multicoloured	20	20
228	–	3d. on 3n.p. multicoloured	20	20
229	–	4d. on 4n.p. multicoloured	20	20
230	–	5d. on 5n.p. multicoloured	20	20
231	–	15d. on 15n.p. mult	20	20
232	–	20d. on 20n.p. mult	20	20
233	–	30d. on 30n.p. mult	40	40
234	–	40d. on 40n.p. mult	60	40
235	–	50d. on 50n.p. mult	80	60
236	–	75d. on 75n.p. mult	1·20	80
237	–	1r. on 1r. multicoloured	1·60	1·20
238	–	2r. on 2r. multicoloured	3·25	2·40
239	–	3r. on 3r. multicoloured	4·75	3·25
240	–	4r. on 4r. multicoloured	6·25	4·25
241	–	5r. on 5r. multicoloured	6·75	5·00
242	29	10r. on 10r. multicoloured	12·50	11·00

(b) Optd **Dh.**

No.		Description	Mint	Used
242b	–	2d. on 2n.p. multicoloured	20	20
242c	–	3d. on 3n.p. multicoloured	20	20
242f	–	15d. on 15n.p. mult	35	20
242g	–	20d. on 20n.p. mult	40	25
242h	–	30d. on 30n.p. mult	50	20
242i	–	40d. on 40n.p. mult	60	20
242j	–	50d. on 50n.p. mult	60	40
242k	–	75d. on 75n.p. mult	95	60

1966. World Cup Football Championship, England. Printed on coloured metal foil-surfaced paper. Multicoloured.

No.		Description	Mint	Used
243		½r. Type **33**	1·30	20
244		½r. Tsu-chu "Kick-ball" game, China, c. 175 B.C.	1·30	20
245		½r. 14th-cent ball game	1·30	20
246		½r. Blowing up ball-bladder (17th-cent)	1·30	20
247		½r. Football game, Barnet, England, c. 1750	1·30	20
248		½r. England v. Scotland game, Kennington Oval (London), 1879	1·30	20
249		½r. Victorious England team, Wembley, 1966 (56 × 55½ mm)	1·30	20
MS250		Six sheets comprising Nos. 243/8, but smaller, 31 × 36 mm, each block of four	11·50	11·50

1966. 3rd Death Anniv of Pres. Kennedy and Inauguration of Arlington Memorial.

No.		Description	Mint	Used
251		50d. Type **34**	40	20
252		2r. Sharjah 50n.p. Kennedy stamp of 1964	1·60	50
253		2r.50 Pres. Kennedy's grave (77 × 40 mm)	2·00	80
MS254		102 × 126 mm. 3r. President Kennedy's grave (55 × 42 mm)	7·25	7·25

35 Shaikh Khalid bin Mohammed al Qasimi and Arms

1968. Multicoloured.

No.		Description	Mint	Used
255		5d. Type **35** (postage)	20	20
256		10d. Flag	20	20
257		15d. Flag and arms (vert)	30	20
258		20d. Decorative pattern (vert)	30	20
259		35d. Type **35** (air)	50	30
260		40d. As 10d.	50	20
261		60d. As 15d.	70	30
262		75d. As 20d.	90	40
263		1r. Type **35**	1·20	40
264		2r. As 10d.	2·40	1·00
265		3r. As 15d.	3·50	1·80
266		4r. As 20d.	4·50	2·40
267		5r. Type **35**	5·50	2·40
268		10r. As 10d.	9·75	5·75

36 Freighter at Wharf

1970. 5th Anniv of Ruler's Accession. "Progress in Sharjah".

No.		Description	Mint	Used
285	36	5d. deep violet and violet	20	20
286	A	5d. deep blue and blue	20	20
287	B	5d. brown and red	20	20
288	C	5d. brown and green	20	20
289	D	5d. brown and light brown	20	20
290		20d. brown and light brown	20	20
291	36	35d. deep violet and violet	30	30
292	A	35d. deep blue and blue	30	30
293	B	35d. brown and red	30	30
294	C	35d. brown and green	30	30
295	D	35d. brown and light brown	30	30
296	36	40d. deep violet and violet	40	30
297	A	40d. deep blue and blue	40	30
298	B	40d. brown and red	40	30
299	C	40d. brown and green	40	30
300	D	40d. brown and light brown	40	30
301	36	60d. deep violet and violet	60	40
302	A	60d. deep blue and blue	60	40
303	B	60d. brown and red	60	40
304	C	60d. brown and green	60	40
305	D	60d. brown and light brown	60	40

DESIGNS: A, Airport; B, Oil derrick; C, Modern building; D, Shaikh Khalid.

37 Turbines

1971. 6th Anniv of Ruler's Accession. "Progress in Sharjah".

No.		Description	Mint	Used
306	37	5d. bl, vio & grn (postage)		
307	A	5d. mauve, brown & vio		
308	B	5d. multicoloured		
309	C	5d. multicoloured		
310	B	35d. multicoloured (air)		
311	37	75d. blue, violet and green		
312	A	75d. mauve, brown and violet		
313	B	75d. multicoloured		
314	C	75d. multicoloured		
315	37	1r. blue, violet and green		
316	A	1r. mauve, brown and violet		
317	B	1r. multicoloured		
318	C	1r. multicoloured		
319	A	2r. mauve, brown and violet		
320	37	3r. blue, violet and green		
321	A	3r. mauve, brown and violet		
322	B	3r. multicoloured		
323	C	3r. multicoloured		
324		5r. multicoloured		

DESIGNS—HORIZ: A, Mosque. VERT: B, Clock fountain; C, Shaikh Khalid.

38 Shaikh Rashid of Dubai and Shaikh Khalid

1971. Air. Proclamation of United Arab Emirates. Multicoloured.

No.		Description	Mint	Used
325		25d. Type **38**		
326		35d. Shaikh Ahmed of Umm al Qiwain and Shaikh Khalid		
327		65d. United Nations and Arab League emblems		
328		75d. Shaikh Rashid of Ajman and Shaikh Khalid		
329		1r. Shaikh Mohamed of Fujeira and Shaikh Khalid		
330		2r. Shaikh Zaid of Abu Dhabi and Shaikh Khalid		

1971. Various stamps surcharged. (a) 1968 Winter Olympics issue (Appendix).

331 – 35d. on 5d. multicoloured

(b) Nos. 255 and 262.

332 **35** 35 on 5d. mult (postage)
334 – 60 on 75d. multicoloured

(c) 5th Anniv of Ruler's Accession (Nos. 296/300).

335 **36** 5 on 40d. dp vio & vio
336 A 5 on 40d. dp blue & blue
337 B 5 on 40d. brown and red
338 C 5 on 40d. brown and green
339 D 5 on 40d. brn & lt brn

(d) Air. Proclamation of United Arab Emirates (Nos. 325 and 328/30).

340 **38** 65d. on 25d. multicoloured
341 – 65d. on 75d. multicoloured
342 – 65d. on 1r. multicoloured
343 – 65d. on 2r. multicoloured

OFFICIAL STAMPS

1966. Optd **ON STATE SERVICE** in English and Arabic. Multicoloured.

No.		Description	Mint	Used
O101	1	8n.p.	10	10
O102		10n.p.	10	10
O103		16n.p.	20	20
O104		20n.p.	30	30
O105		30n.p.	30	30
O106		40n.p.	50	50
O107		50n.p.	1·30	1·30
O108		75n.p.	3·25	3·25
O109		100n.p.	5·75	5·75

1968. As Nos. 258 and 261 but colours changed and inscr "OFFICIAL".

O269 20d. multicoloured
O270 60d. multicoloured

For later issues see **UNITED ARAB EMIRATES**.

APPENDIX

The following stamps have either been issued in excess of postal needs or have not been available to the public in reasonable quantities at face value. Such stamps may later be given full listing if there is evidence of regular postal use.

1967.

Post Day. Japanese Paintings. 1r. × 3.

22nd Anniv of United Nations. 10, 30, 60d.

Olympics Preparation, Mexico, 1968. Postage 1, 2, 3, 10 d; Air 30, 60d., 2r.

Flowers and Butterflies. Postage 1, 2, 3, 4, 5, 10, 20d.; Air 30, 60d., 1, 2r.

Famous Paintings. Postage 1, 2, 3, 4, 5, 30, 40, 60, 75d.; Air 1, 2, 3, 4, 5r.

1968.

Winter Olympic Games, Grenoble. Postage 1, 2, 3, 4, 5d.; Air 1, 2, 3r.

12th World Jamboree. Postage 1, 2, 3, 4, 5, 10d.; Air 30, 50, 60d., 1r.50.

Grenoble Olympic Medal Winners. Optd on Winter Olympics, Grenoble issue. Postage 1, 2, 3, 4, 5d.; Air 1, 2, 3r.

Mothers' Day. Paintings. Postage 10, 20, 30, 40d.; Air 1, 2, 3, 4r.

American Paintings. Postage 20, 30, 40, 50, 60d.; Air 1, 4, 5r.

Egyptian Art. 15, 25, 35, 45, 55, 65, 75, 95d.

Martyrs of Liberty. Air 35d. × 4, 60d. × 4, 1r. × 4.

Olympic Games, Mexico. 10, 20, 30d., 2r., 2r. 40, 5r.

Previous Olympic Games. Air 25, 50, 75d., 1r. 50, 3, 4r.

Sportsmen and Women. Postage 20, 30, 40, 60d., 1r. 50, 2r. 50; Air 25, 50d., 1, 2r., 3r. 25, 4, 4r.

Robert Kennedy Memorial. Optd on American Paintings issue. Air 4r.

Olympic Medal Winners, Mexico. 35, 50, 60d., 1, 2, 4r.

1969.

Famous Men and Women. Postage 10, 20, 25, 35, 50, 60d.; Air 1, 2, 3, 4, 5, 6r.

"Apollo 8" Moon Mission. Postage 5d. × 6; Air 10, 15, 20d., 2, 3, 4r.

"Apollo 11" Moon Mission (1st series). Postage 5d. × 8; Air 75d. × 8, 1r. × 8.

Post Day. Famous Ships. Postage 5d. × 8; Air 90d. × 8.

"Apollo 12" Moon Mission. Optd on Famous Ships issue. 5d. × 8.

1970.

UNICEF. Paintings of Children. Postage 5d. × 9; Air 20, 25, 35, 40, 50, 60, 75d., 1, 3r.

Animals. Postage 3d. × 14, 10, 10, 15, 15d.; Air 20, 20, 35, 35d., 1, 1, 2, 2r.

"Expo 70" World Fair, Osaka, Japan (1st series). Japanese Paintings. Postage 3d. × 4; Air 1r. × 4.

"Expo 70" World Fair, Osaka, Japan (2nd series). Pavilions. Postage 2, 2, 3, 3d.; Air 40d. × 4.

Paintings of Napoleon. Postage 3d. × 5; Air 20, 30, 40, 60d., 2r.

De Gaulle Commemoration. Postage 3d. × 5; Air 20, 30, 40, 60d., 2r.

"Mercury" and "Vostok" Moon Missions. Postage 1, 2, 3, 4, 5d.; Air 25, 40, 85d., 1, 2r.

"Gemini" Space Programme. Postage 1, 2, 3, 4, 5d.; Air 25, 40, 85d., 1, 2r.

"Apollo", "Voskhod" and "Soyuz" Projects. Postage 1, 2, 3, 4, 5d.; Air 25, 40, 85d., 1, 2r.

Events of 1970. Postage 1d. × 5, 5d.; Air 75d., 1, 2, 3r.

200th Birth Anniv of Beethoven. Postage 3d. × 5; Air 35, 40, 60d., 1, 2r.

Mozart. Postage 3d. × 5; Air 35, 40, 60d., 1, 2r.

The Life of Christ (1st series). Postage 1, 2, 3, 4, 5d.; Air 25, 40, 60d., 1, 2r.

1971.

"Apollo 14" Moon Mission. Optd on 1969 "Apollo 11" issue. Postage 5d. × 4; Air 75d. × 4.

Post Day 1970. Cars. Postage 1, 2, 3, 4, 5d.; Air 25, 50, 60d., 2, 3r.

Post Day (1st series). American Cars. Postage 1, 2, 3, 4, 5d.; Air 35, 50d., 1, 2, 3r.

Post Day (2nd series). Trains. Postage 1, 2, 3, 4, 5d.; Air 25, 50, 60d., 1, 2r.

Pres. Nasser Commemoration. Postage 5d. × 5; Air 20, 35, 40, 60d., 2r.

Safe return of "Apollo 13". Optd on 1969 "Apollo 8" issue. Air 10, 15, 20d., 2, 3, 4r.

De Gaulle Memorial. Postage 3, 4, 5, 6, 7d.; Air 40, 60, 75d., 1, 2r.

Olympics Preparation, Munich, 1972. Postage 2, 3, 4, 5, 6d.; Air 35, 40, 60d., 1, 2r.

Miracles of Christ. Postage 1, 2, 3, 4, 5d.; Air 25, 40, 60d., 1, 2r.

1972.

Sport. Postage 2, 3, 4, 5, 6d.; Air 35, 40, 60d., 1, 2r.

The Life of Christ (2nd series). Postage 1, 2, 3, 4, 5d.; Air 25, 40, 60d., 1, 2r.

Winter Olympics Preparation, Sapporo. Postage 2, 3, 4, 5, 6d.; Air 35, 40, 60d., 1, 2r.

Safe Return of "Apollo 14". Optd on 1969 "Apollo 11" issue. Postage 5d. × 4; Air 1r. × 4.

Previous World Cup Winners. Postage 5, 10, 15, 20, 25d.; Air 35, 75d., 1, 2, 3r.

Sapporo Olympic Medal Winners. Paintings. Postage 5, 10, 15, 20, 25d.; Air 35, 75d., 1, 2, 3r.

Famous People, Churchill, De Gaulle and John Kennedy. Postage 5d. × 4, 10d. × 4, 35d. × 4; Air 75d. × 4, 1r. × 4, 3r. × 4.

Olympic Games, Munich. Postage 5, 10, 15, 20, 25d.; Air 35, 75d., 1, 2, 3r.

Cats. Postage 20, 25d.; Air 75d., 1, 2r.

Birds (1st series). Postage 20, 25, 75d., Air 1, 2r.

"Apollo 11" Moon Mission (2nd series). Postage 1, 1r. Air 1r. × 3.

"Apollo 16" Moon Mission. Postage 1, 1r.; Air 1r. × 3.

Dogs. Postage 20, 25d.; Air 75d., 1, 2r.

"Apollo 17" Moon Mission. Postage 1, 1r.; Air 1r. × 3.

Munich Olympic Medal Winners. Air 5r. × 20.

Horses. Postage 20, 25d.; Air 75d., 1, 2r.

"Apollo 17" Astronauts. Postage 1, 1r.; Air 1r. × 3.

Butterflies. Postage 20, 25d.; Air 75d., 1, 2r.

"Luna 9" Soviet Space Programme. Postage 1, 1r.; Air 1r. × 3.

Monkeys. Postage 20, 25d.; Air 75d., 1, 2r.

Birds (2nd series). Air 25, 25, 35, 35, 50, 50, 65, 65d., 1r. × 6, 3, 3r.

Fish. Air 25, 35, 50, 65d., 1r. × 5, 3r.

Insects. Air 25, 35, 50, 65d., 1, 3r.

Flowers. Postage 25, 35, 50, 65d., 1, 3r.; Air 1r. × 4.

Fruit. Air 1r. × 4.

Children. Air 1r. × 4.

Eastern Antiquities. Air 25, 35, 40, 65, 75d., 1r. × 4, 3r.

Planetary Exploration. Postage 1r. × 3; Air 1, 1r.

13th World Jamboree. Postage 2d. × 3, 3d. × 3, 4d. × 3, 5d. × 3, 6d. × 3; Air 35d. × 3, 75d. × 3, 1r. × 3, 2r. × 3, 3r. × 3.

A number of issues on gold or silver foil also exist, but it is understood that these were mainly for presentation purposes, although valid for postage.

In common with the other states of the United Arab Emirates the Sharjah stamp contract was terminated on 1 August 1972, and further new issues released after that date were unauthorized.

SIBERIA Pt. 10

Various Anti-Bolshevist governments existed in this area, culminating in Kolchak's assumption of power as "Supreme Ruler". The Kolchak Government fell in January 1920, provincial issues followed until the area was incorporated into the Soviet Union in 1922.

100 kopeks = 1 rouble.

1919. Admiral Kolchak Govt. Arms types of Russia surch in figures, or in figures and words (rouble values). Imperf or perf.

No.	T	Description	Unused	Used
5	22	35 on 2k. green	25	1·25
6		50 on 3k. red	25	1·40
3		70 on 1k. orange	30	3·25
8	23	1r. on 4k. red	40	1·40
9	22	3r. on 7k. blue	70	3·50
10	10	5r. on 14k. red and blue	1·25	8·00

1920. Transbaikal Province. Ataman Semyonov regime. Arms types of Russia surch **p. 1 p.** Perf.

No.	T	Description	Unused	Used
11	23	1r. on 4k. red	20·00	30·00
12	14	2r.50 on 20k. red and blue	17·00	24·00
13	22	5r. on 5k. red	10·00	17·00
14	10	10r. on 70k. orange & brn	17·00	27·00

6

1920. Amur Province. Imperf.

No.	T	Description	Unused	Used
15	6	2r. red	1·60	4·50
16		3r. green	1·60	4·50
17		5r. blue	1·60	4·50
18		15r. brown	1·60	4·50
19		30r. mauve	1·60	4·50

FAR EAST REPUBLIC

1920. Vladivostok issue. Optd **DBP** in fancy letters or surch also. Imperf or perf. (a) On Arms types of Russia.

No.	T	Description	Unused	Used
32	22	1k. orange	4·00	6·50
33		2k. green	1·90	2·50
21		3k. red	2·40	3·25
39	10	3k. on 35k. green and purple	4·00	5·00
22	23	4k. red	2·40	4·75
40	10	4k. on 70k. orange & brown	2·50	3·50
41		7k. on 15k. blue and purple	1·25	1·75
23	23	10k. blue	42·00	45·00
44	11	10k. on 3r.50 green & brn	6·00	7·00
24	10	14k. red and blue	10·00	15·00
25		15k. blue and purple	4·25	6·00
26	14	20k. red and blue	50·00	60·00
27	10	20k. on 14k. red and blue	3·50	4·75
28		25k. mauve and green	4·00	8·00
29		35k. green and purple	18·00	26·00
30	14	50k. green and purple	3·25	6·50
35	15	1r. orange and brown	8·00	17·00

(b) On Nos. 5 and 3 of Siberia.

No.	T	Description	Unused	Used
37	22	35k. on 2k. green	2·75	4·00
38		70k. on 1k. orange	2·25	4·00

(c) On Postal Savings Bank stamps of Russia.

No.	T	Description	Unused	Used
45		1k. on 5k. green on buff	8·00	8·00
46		2k. on 10k. brown on buff	10·00	12·00

10

11

13

1921. Chita issue. Imperf.

No.	T	Description	Unused	Used
47	10	1k. orange	50	1·10
48		3k. red	50	60
49	11	4k. brown and red	20	50
50	10	5k. brown	40	70
51b		7k. blue	40	1·00
52	11	10k. red and blue	30	70
53	10	15k. red	40	1·00
54	11	20k. red and blue	40	1·25
55		30k. red and green	45	1·25
56		50k. red and black	1·00	2·00

1922. Vladivostok issue. 5th Anniv of Russian October Revolution. Optd **1917 7-XI 1922**. Imperf.

No.	T	Description	Unused	Used
57	13	2k. green	8·00	10·00
58		4k. red	8·00	10·00
59		5k. brown	9·00	16·00
60		10k. blue	9·00	16·00

PRIAMUR AND MARITIME PROVINCES

Anti-Bolshevist Government

1921. Vladivostok issue. Imperf.

No.	T	Description	Unused	Used
61	13	2k. green	40	2·50
62		4k. red	40	1·50
63		5k. purple	50	1·50
64		10k. blue	95	1·25

(15)

(16 Trans. "Priamur Territory")

Д. В.
коп. 1 коп.
ЗОЛОТОМ
(18)

1922. Anniv of Priamur Provisional Govt. Optd with T **15**.

No.	T	Description	Unused	Used
89	13	2k. green	16·00	17·00
90		4k. red	16·00	17·00
91		5k. purple	16·00	17·00
92		10k. blue	16·00	17·00

1922. Optd or surch as T **16**.

No.	T	Description	Unused	Used
93	13	1k. on 2k. green	2·00	4·00
94		2k. green	3·00	5·00
95		3k. on 4k. red	3·00	5·00
96		4k. red	3·00	5·00
97		5k. purple	3·00	5·00
98		10k. blue	3·00	6·00

1922. Optd as T **16**. Imperf or perf. (a) On Arms types of Russia.

No.	T	Description	Unused	Used
114	22	1k. orange	4·00	6·00
115		2k. green	4·00	7·50
116		3k. red	6·00	13·00
102	23	4k. red	2·50	3·50
118	22	5k. red	12·00	20·00
104		7k. blue	18·00	38·00
105	23	10k. blue	18·00	38·00
106	10	14k. red and blue	60·00	70·00
107		15k. blue and purple	3·00	6·00
108	14	20k. red and blue	6·00	10·00
109	10	20k. on 14k. red and blue	£100	£110
110		25k. mauve and green	16·00	24·00
111		35k. green and purple	3·00	5·00
112	14	50k. green and purple	4·00	6·00
113	10	70k. orange and brown	10·00	18·00
121	15	1r. orange and brown	10·00	17·00

(b) On Nos. 5 and 3 of Siberia.

No.	T	Description	Unused	Used
122	22	35k. on 2k. green	40·00	50·00
123		70k. on 1k. orange	40·00	50·00

1922. Nos. 37 and 38 optd **П.З.К.** and three bars. Imperf and perf.

No.	T	Description	Unused	Used
125	22	35k. on 2k. green	3·00	5·00
126		70k. on 1k. orange	4·00	7·50

SOVIET UNION ISSUE FOR THE FAR EAST

1923. Stamps of Russia surch as T **18**. Imperf or perf.

No.	T	Description	Unused	Used
131	79	1k. on 100r. red	50	1·25
128		2k. on 70r. purple	30	70
129	78	5k. on 10r. blue	30	1·00
130	79	10k. on 50r. brown	50	1·00

SICILY Pt. 8

An island to the south of Italy, which, with Naples, formed the Kingdom of the Two Sicilies, until incorporated in the Kingdom of Italy.

100 grano = 1 ducato.

1 King "Bomba"

1859. Imperf.

No.	T	Description	Unused	Used
1b	1	½g. yellow	£800	£650
2b		1g. olive	£375	£130
3		2g. blue	95·00	75·00
4		5g. red	£450	£300
5		10g. blue	£550	£250
6		20g. grey	£550	£450
7		50g. brown	£550	£3500

SIERRA LEONE Pt. 1

A British colony on the west coast of Africa. Achieved independence within the British Commonwealth in 1961. By vote of the Assembly on 19 April 1971, Sierra Leone was proclaimed a republic.

1859. 12 pence = 1 shilling;
20 shillings = 1 pound.
1964. 100 cents = 1 leone.

1

2

1859.

No.	T	Description	Unused	Used
16	2	½d. brown	2·75	8·00
27		½d. green	2·75	1·75
28		1d. red	4·50	1·00
29		1½d. lilac	3·25	6·50
25		2d. mauve	50·00	8·50
30		2d. grey	35·00	2·50
31		2½d. blue	10·00	1·25
32		3d. yellow	3·25	10·00
21		4d. blue	£170	6·50
33		4d. brown	2·00	1·75
37	1	6d. purple	2·75	7·00
22	2	1s. green	55·00	6·50
34		1s. brown	21·00	11·00

1893. Surch **HALF PENNY**.

No.	T	Description	Unused	Used
39	2	½d. on 1½d. lilac	4·25	3·00

4

6

1896.

No.	T	Description	Unused	Used
41	4	½d. mauve and green	2·50	3·00
42		1d. mauve and red	3·75	1·75
43		1½d. mauve and black	4·00	20·00
44		2d. mauve and orange	2·50	5·00
45		2½d. mauve and blue	2·25	1·25
46		3d. mauve and grey	8·50	7·00
47		4d. mauve and red	9·50	13·00
48		5d. mauve and black	13·00	14·00
49		6d. mauve	8·00	23·00
50		1s. green and black	6·00	19·00
51		2s. green and blue	25·00	60·00
52		5s. green and red	65·00	£180
53		£1 purple on red	£170	£450

1897. T **6** optd **POSTAGE AND REVENUE**.

No.	T	Description	Unused	Used
54	6	1d. purple and green	4·00	3·25

1897. T **6** optd **POSTAGE AND REVENUE** and surch **2½d.** and bars.

No.	T	Description	Unused	Used
55	6	2½d. on 3d. purple and green	11·00	13·00
59		2½d. on 6d. purple and green	8·50	13·00
63		2½d. on 1s. lilac	90·00	65·00
67		2½d. on 2s. lilac	£1700	£2000

15

1903.

No.	T	Description	Unused	Used
73	15	½d. purple and green	3·00	4·50
87		1d. purple and red	1·50	1·00
75		1½d. purple and black	1·25	11·00
89		2d. purple and orange	4·25	4·00
90		2½d. purple and blue	4·50	2·00
78		3d. purple and grey	9·50	13·00
92		4d. purple and red	7·50	7·00
93		5d. purple and black	12·00	26·00
94		6d. purple	4·00	3·25
95		1s. green and black	7·50	9·00
96		2s. green and blue	23·00	27·00
97		5s. green and red	30·00	50·00
85		£1 purple on red	£225	£250

1907.

No.	T	Description	Unused	Used
99	15	½d. green	1·00	50
100a		1d. red	7·50	60
101		1½d. orange	1·25	2·00
102		2d. grey	1·25	1·50
103		2½d. blue	3·75	3·00
104		3d. purple on yellow	7·50	2·75
105		4d. black and red on yellow	2·25	1·60
106		5d. purple and green	10·00	5·00
107		6d. purple and light purple	10·00	8·00
108		1s. black on green	5·50	5·00
109		2s. purple and blue on blue	15·00	19·00
110		5s. green and red on yellow	40·00	55·00
111		£1 purple and black on red	£250	£180

17

20

1912.

No.	T	Description	Unused	Used
131	17	½d. green	1·25	1·00
113		1d. red	2·25	30
132a		1d. violet	3·00	20
114		1½d. orange	2·00	2·50
133		1½d. red	1·75	1·25
134		2d. grey	1·25	20
116a		2½d. blue	1·00	80
116b	20	3d. purple on yellow	3·00	3·25
136	17	3d. blue	1·25	1·25
137		4d. black and red on yellow	2·00	3·25
138		5d. purple and green	1·25	1·25
139		6d. purple and light purple	1·25	2·50
120		7d. purple and orange	3·00	8·50
121		9d. purple and black	5·00	12·00
122		10d. purple and red	3·00	18·00
124a	20	1s. black on green	4·50	3·25
125		2s. blue and purple on blue	13·00	5·50
126		5s. red and green on yellow	13·00	26·00
127		10s. red and green on green	70·00	£120
128		£1 black and purple on red	£150	£225
147		£2 blue and purple	£475	£650
148		£5 orange and green	£1200	£1800

21 Rice Field

22 Palms and Cola Tree

1932.

155	21	½d. green	20	30
156		1d. violet	30	30
157		1½d. red	30	1·25
158		2d. brown	30	30
159		3d. blue	60	1·75
160		4d. orange	60	8·00
161		5d. green	85	3·75
162		6d. blue	60	3·25
163		1s. lake	2·50	7·00
164	22	2s. brown	5·00	5·50
165		5s. blue	12·00	19·00
166		10s. green	60·00	£130
167		£1 purple	£120	£200

23 Arms of Sierra Leone

1933. Cent of Abolition of Slavery and of Death of William Wilberforce. Dated "1833 1933".

168	23	½d. green	1·00	1·25
169	–	1d. black and brown	65	10
170	–	1½d. brown	4·75	4·50
171	–	2d. purple	3·00	20
172	–	3d. blue	3·25	1·75
173	–	4d. brown	6·50	10·00
174	–	5d. green and brown	7·00	13·00
175	–	6d. black and orange	8·00	8·00
176	–	1s. violet	4·75	18·00
177	–	2s. brown and blue	24·00	40·00
178	–	5s. black and purple	£150	£170
179	–	10s. black and olive	£180	£275
180	–	£1 violet and orange	£375	£450

DESIGNS—VERT: 1d. "Freedom"; 1½d. Map of Sierra Leone; 4d. Government sanatorium; 5s. African elephant. HORIZ: 2d. Old Slave Market, Freetown; 3d. Native fruit seller; 5d. Bullom canoe; 6d. Punting near Banana Is; 1s. Government buildings, Freetown; 2s. Bunce Is; 10s. King George V; £1 Freetown Harbour.

1935. Silver Jubilee. As T **32a** of St. Helena.

181	1d. blue and black	1·00	2·50
182	3d. brown and blue	1·25	8·50
183	5d. green and blue	2·00	15·00
184	1s. grey and purple	9·00	5·50

1937. Coronation. As T **32b** of St. Helena.

185	1d. orange	70	1·00
186	2d. purple	90	1·00
187	3d. blue	1·50	3·75

30 Freetown from the Harbour

1938. King George VI.

188	30	½d. black and green	15	40
189		1d. black and lake	40	60
190	–	1½d. red	20·00	1·00
190a	–	1½d. mauve	30	60
191	–	2d. mauve	40·00	2·25
191a	–	2d. red	30	2·00
192	30	3d. black and blue	55	50
193		4d. black and brown	1·25	4·50
194	–	5d. green	5·00	4·00
195	–	6d. grey	1·25	50
196	30	1s. black and green	2·25	70
196a	–	1s.3d. orange	75	60
197	30	2s. black and brown	4·50	2·75
198	–	5s. brown	10·00	9·00
199	–	10s. green	17·00	10·00
200	30	£1 blue	17·00	22·00

DESIGNS: 1½, 2, 5, 6d., 1s.3d., 5s., 10s. Rice harvesting.

1946. Victory. As T **33a** of St. Helena.

201	1½d. lilac	20	10
202	3d. blue	20	30

1948. Silver Wedding. As T **33b/c** of St. Helena.

203	1½d. mauve	15	15
204	£1 blue	18·00	17·00

1949. 75th Anniv of U.P.U. As T **33d/g** of St. Helena.

205	1½d. purple	20	50
206	3d. blue	1·50	4·00
207	6d. grey	35	4·25
208	1s. green	35	1·00

1953. Coronation. As T **33h** of St. Helena.

209	1½d. black and lilac	30	30

32 Cape Lighthouse

1956. Centres in black.

210	32	½d. lilac	1·00	2·25
211	–	1d. olive	90	40
212	–	1½d. blue	1·60	5·50
213	–	2d. brown	70	40
214	–	3d. blue	1·25	10
215	–	4d. slate	2·50	2·25
216	–	6d. violet	1·00	30
217	–	1s. red	1·25	50
218	–	1s.3d. sepia	11·00	30
219	–	2s.6d. brown	14·00	8·50
220	–	5s. green	3·25	3·50
221	–	10s. mauve	3·50	2·75
222	–	£1 orange	14·00	25·00

DESIGNS—HORIZ: 1d. Queen Elizabeth II Quay; 1½d. Piassava workers; 4d. Iron ore production, Marampa; 6d. Whale Bay, York Village; 1s.3d. Bristol 170 Freighter Mk 31 airplane and map; 10s. Law Courts, Freetown; £1 Government House. VERT: 2d. Cotton tree, Freetown; 3d. Rice harvesting; 1s. Bullom canoe; 2s.6d. Orugu railway bridge; 5s. Kuranko chief.

46 Licensed Diamond Miner

1961. Independence.

223	–	½d. brown and turquoise	20	10
224	46	1d. brown and green	1·25	10
225	–	1½d. black and green	20	10
226	–	2d. black and blue	20	10
227	–	3d. brown and blue	20	10
228	–	4d. blue and red	20	10
229	–	6d. black and purple	20	10
230	–	1s. brown and orange	20	10
231	–	1s.3d. blue and violet	20	10
232	46	2s.6d. green and black	2·75	30
233	–	5s. black and red	1·00	1·25
234	–	10s. black and green	1·00	1·25
235	–	£1 red and yellow	8·00	11·00

DESIGNS—VERT: ½d., 1s. Palm fruit gathering; 1½d., 5s. Bundu mask; 2d., 10s. Bishop Crowther and Old Fourah Bay College; £1 Forces bugler. HORIZ: 3d., 6d. Sir Milton Margai; 4d., 1s.3d. Lumley Beach, Freetown.

53 Royal Charter, 1799

55 Old House of Representatives, Freetown, 1924

1961. Royal Visit.

236	53	3d. black and red	15	10
237	–	4d. black and violet	15	1·25
238	55	6d. black and orange	20	10
239	–	1s.3d. black and blue	3·00	1·75

DESIGNS—VERT: 4d. King's Yard Gate, Freetown, 1817. HORIZ: 1s.3d. Royal Yacht "Britannia" at Freetown.

57 Campaign Emblem

58 Fireball Lily

1962. Malaria Eradication.

240	57	3d. red	10	10
241		1s.3d. green	20	10

1963. Flowers in natural colours; background colours given below.

242	58	½d. bistre	10	10
243	–	1d. red	10	10
244	–	1½d. green	20	10
245	–	2d. olive	20	10
246	–	3d. green	20	10
247	–	4d. blue	20	10
248	–	6d. blue	30	10
249	–	1s. green	40	10
250	–	1s.3d. green	1·50	20
251	–	2s.6d. purple	1·25	30
252	–	5s. violet	1·25	80
253	–	10s. purple	2·50	1·50
254	–	£1 blue	6·00	7·00

FLOWERS—VERT: 1½d. Stereospermum; 3d. Beniseed; 4d. Blushing hibiscus; 1s. Beautiful crinum; 2s.6d. Broken hearts; 5s. Ra-ponthi; 10s. Blue plumbago. HORIZ: 1d. Jina-gbo; 2d. Black-eyed Susan; 6d. Climbing lily; 1s.3d. Blue bells; £1 African tulip tree.

71 Threshing Machine and Corn Bins

75 Centenary Emblem

1963. Freedom from Hunger.

255	71	3d. black and ochre	30	10
256	–	1s.3d. sepia and green	35	10

DESIGN: 1s.3d. Girl with onion crop.

1963. 2nd Anniv of Independence. Stamps of 1956 surch **2ND YEAR OF INDEPENDENCE PROGRESS DEVELOPMENT 1963** and value (except 2s.6d.). Centres in black. (a) Postage.

257	3d. on ½d. lilac	40	10
258	4d. on 1½d. blue	15	10
259	6d. on ½d. lilac	30	10
260	10d. on 3d. blue	50	10
261	1s.6d. on 3d. blue	30	20
262	3s.6d. on 3d. blue	40	20

(b) Air. Optd **AIR MAIL** in additon.

263	7d. on 1½d. blue	20	10
264	1s.3d. on 1½d. blue	20	10
265	2s.6d. brown	2·00	40
266	3s. on 3d. blue	40	20
267	6s. on 3d. blue	1·00	20
268	11s. on 10s. mauve	1·10	85
269	11s. on £1 orange	£500	£180

1963. Centenary of Red Cross.

270	75	3d. red and violet	50	10
271	–	6d. red and black	50	15
272	–	1s.3d. red and green	65	20

DESIGNS: 6d. Red Cross emblem; 1s.3d. As T **75** but with lined background and value on left.

1963. Postal Commemorations. (a) Postage. Optd or surch **1853–1859–1963 Oldest Postal Service Newest G.P.O. in West Africa** and value.

273	–	3d. (No. 214)	10	10
274	–	4d. on 1½d. (No. 212)	10	10
275	–	9d. on 1½d. (No. 212)	10	10
276	–	1s. on 1s.3d. (No. 231)	10	10
277	32	1s.6d. on ½d	15	10
278	–	2s. on 3d. (No. 214)	15	10

(b) Air. Optd or surch as above but **Postage Stamp** instead of **Postal Service** and **AIRMAIL** in addition.

279	53	7d. on 3d.	20	50
280	–	1s.3d. (No. 239)	2·00	1·50
281	–	2s.6d. on 4d. (No. 228)	1·25	20
282	52	3s. on 3d.	2·50	2·00
283	55	6s. on 6d.	1·00	1·00
284	–	£1 (No. 222)	18·00	18·00

Commemoration dates:—
1853—"First Post Office".
1859—"First Postage Stamps".
1963—"Newest G.P.O. in West Africa".

80 Lion Emblem and Map

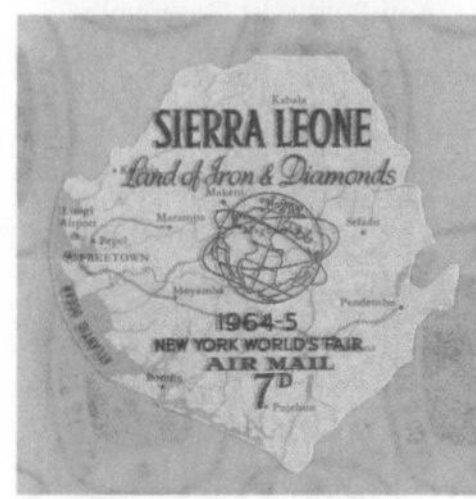

81 Globe and Map

1964. World's Fair, New York. Imperf. Self-adhesive.

285	80	1d. multicoloured (postage)	10	10
286		3d. multicoloured	10	10
287		4d. multicoloured	10	10
288		6d. multicoloured	10	10
289		1s. multicoloured	10	10
290		2s. multicoloured	30	20
291		5s. multicoloured	50	50
292	81	7d. multicoloured (air)	10	10
293		9d. multicoloured	10	10
294		1s.3d. multicoloured	20	10
295		2s.6d. multicoloured	30	15
296		3s.6d. multicoloured	30	20
297		6s. multicoloured	55	60
298		11s. multicoloured	70	1·00

WARNING:—These self-adhesive stamps should be kept mint on their backing paper and used on cover or piece.

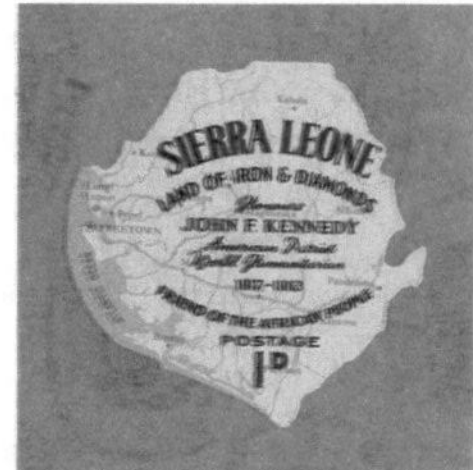

82 Inscription and Map

83 Pres. Kennedy and Map

1964. President Kennedy Memorial Issue. Imperf. Self-adhesive.

299	82	1d. multicoloured (postage)	10	10
300		3d. multicoloured	10	10
301		4d. multicoloured	10	10
302		6d. multicoloured	10	10
303		1s. multicoloured	10	10
304		2s. multicoloured	30	25
305		5s. multicoloured	50	80
306	83	7d. multicoloured (air)	10	10
307		9d. multicoloured	10	10
308		1s.3d. multicoloured	15	10
309		2s.6d. multicoloured	30	25
310		3s.6d. multicoloured	30	25
311		6s. multicoloured	55	1·00
312		11s. multicoloured	70	1·60

The note below No. 298 applies also to the above issue.

1964. Decimal Currency. Various stamps surch. (i) First issue. Surch in figures. (a) Postage.

313	–	1c. on 6d. (No. 248)	10	10
314	53	2c. on 3d. (No. 236)	10	10
315	–	3c. on 3d. (No. 246)	10	10
316	–	5c. on ½d. (No. 223)	10	10
317	71	8c. on 3d. (No. 255)	10	10
318	–	10c. on 1s.3d. (No. 250)	10	10
319	–	15c. on 1s. (No. 249)	15	10
320	55	25c. on 6d. (No. 238)	30	25
321	46	50c. on 2s.6d. (No. 232)	1·50	1·00

(b) Air. Nos. 322/5 additonally optd **AIRMAIL**.

322	–	7c. on 1s.3d. (No. 256)	10	10
323	–	20c. on 4d. (No. 228)	25	20
324	–	30c. on 10s. (No. 234)	40	45
325	–	40c. on 5s. (No. 233)	50	60
326	83	1l. on 1s.3d. (No. 308)	75	1·40
327		2l. on 11s. (No. 312)	1·25	2·75

(ii) Second issue. Surch in figures or figures and words (Nos. 332/3).

328	–	1c. on 3d. (No. 227) (postage)	10	10
329	82	2c. on 1d. (No. 299)	10	10
330		4c. on 3d. (No. 300)	10	10
331	–	5c. on 2d. (No. 245)	10	10
332	–	1l. on 5s. (No. 252)	1·25	2·00
333	–	2l. on £1 (No. 235)	2·25	3·25
334	83	7c. on 7d. (No. 306) (air)	10	10
335		60c. on 9d. (Nos. 307)	50	75

(iii) Third issue. Surch in figures.

336	–	1c. on 1½d. (No. 225) (postage)	10	10
337	82	2c. on 3d. (No. 300)	10	10
338	80	2c. on 4d. (No. 287)	10	10
339	–	3c. on 1d. (No. 243)	10	10
340	–	3c. on 2d. (No. 226)	10	10
341	–	5c. on 1s.3d. (No. 231)	10	10
342	82	15c. on 6d. (No. 302)	80	50
343		15c. on 1s. (No. 303)	1·25	90
344	–	20c. on 6d. (No. 229)	30	15
345	–	25c. on 6d. (No. 248)	35	20
346	–	50c. on 3d. (No. 227)	80	55
347	80	60c. on 5s. (No. 291)	3·25	2·00
348	82	1l. on 4d. (No. 301)	3·75	4·00
349	–	2l. on £1 (No. 235)	7·50	8·00
350	81	7c. on 9d. (air)	15	10

(iv) Fourth issue. Surch in figures.

351	80	1c. on 6d. (postage)	2·50	7·00
352		1c. on 2s.	2·50	7·00
353	82	1c. on 2s.	2·50	7·00
354		1c. on 5s.	2·50	7·00
355	81	2c. on 1s.3d. (air)	2·50	7·00
356	83	2c. on 1s.3d.	2·50	7·00
357		2c. on 3s.6d.	2·50	7·00
358	81	3c. on 7d.	2·50	7·00
359	83	3c. on 9d.	2·50	7·00
360	81	5c. on 2s.6d.	2·50	7·00
361	83	5c. on 2s.6d.	2·50	7·00
362	81	5c. on 3s.6d.	2·50	7·00
363		5c. on 6s.	2·50	7·00
364	83	5c. on 6s.	2·50	7·00

(v) Fifth issue. No. 374 further surch **TWO Leones**.

365	–	2l. on 30c. on 6d. (air)	1·50	1·50

IN MEMORIAM 2c
TWO GREAT LEADERS
SIR MILTON MARGAI 1895-1964
SIR WINSTON CHURCHILL 1874-1965

(91 Margai and Churchill)

1965. Sir Milton Margai and Sir Winston Churchill Commem. Flower stamps of 1963 surch as T **91** on horiz designs or with individual portraits on vert designs as indicated. Multicoloured. (a) Postage.

366 – 2c. on 1d. 10 10
367 – 3c. on 3d. Margai 10 10
368 – 10c. on 1s. Churchill 20 10
369 – 20c. on 1s.3d. 40 10
370 – 50c. on 4d. Margai 90 35
371 – 75c. on 5s. Churchill 2·25 90

(b) Air. Additionally optd **AIRMAIL**.

372 – 7c. on 2d. 20 10
373 **58** 15c. on ½d. Margai 35 10
374 – 30c. on 6d. 1·25 25
375 – 1l. on £1 4·00 1·00
376 – 2l. on 10s. Churchill 11·00 5·00

92 Cola Plant and Nut

1965. Various shapes, backed with paper bearing advertisements. Imperf. Self-adhesive. A. Printed in green, yellow and red on silver foil. Values in colours given.

377 **92** 1c. green (postage) 25 10
378 2c. red 25 10
379 3c. yellow 25 10
380 4c. silver on green 30 10
381 5c. silver on red 30 10

B. Designs 45 × 49 mm showing Arms of Sierra Leone.

382 – 20c. mult on cream (postage) 2·00 60
383 – 50c. multicoloured on cream 3·75 3·75
384 – 40c. mult on cream (air) 3·50 3·75

C. Designs 48 × 44½ mm showing inscription and necklace.

385 – 7c. multicoloured (air) 80 15
386 – 15c. multicoloured 1·25 90

1966. 5th Anniv of Independence. Surch **FIVE YEARS INDEPENDENCE 1961-1966** and value. (a) Postage.

387 – 1c. on 6d. (No. 248) 10 10
388 – 2c. on 4d. (No. 247) 10 10
389 – 3c. on 1½d. (No. 212) 10 10
390 – 8c. on 1s. (No. 249) 15 10
391 – 10c. on 2s.6d. (No. 251) 15 10
392 – 20c. on 2d. (No. 213) 20 10

(b) Air. Surch **AIRMAIL** also.

393 **75** 7c. on 3d. 10 10
394 – 15c. on 1s. (No. 249) 20 10
395 – 25c. on 2s.6d. (No. 251) 65 60
396 – 50c. on 1½d. (No. 244) 1·00 80
397 – 1l. on 4d. (No. 247) 1·60 1·60

97 Lion's Head

1966. First Sierra Leone Gold Coinage Commem. Circular designs, embossed on gold foil, backed with paper bearing advertisements. Imperf. (a) Postage. (i) ¼ golde coin. Diameter 1½ in.

398 **97** 2c. mauve and orange 10 10
399 – 3c. green and purple 10 10

(ii) ½ golde coin. Diameter 2⅛ in.

400 **97** 5c. red and blue 10 10
401 – 8c. turquoise and black 20 20

(iii) 1 golde coin. Diameter 3¼ in.

402 **97** 25c. violet and green 40 35
403 – 1l. orange and red 2·75 3·25

(b) Air. (i) ¼ golde coin. Diameter 1½ in.

404 **97** 7c. orange and red 15 10
405 – 30c. purple and black 20 25

(ii) ½ golde coin. Diameter 2⅛ in.

406 **97** 15c. orange and red 35 35
407 – 30c. purple and black 50 60

(iii) 1 golde coin. Diameter 3¼ in.

408 **97** 50c. green and purple 1·00 1·00
409 – 2l. black and green 4·00 4·50

DESIGN: Nos. 399, 401, 403, 405, 407 and 409, Map of Sierra Leone.

1967. Decimal Currency Provisionals. Nos. 347/8, 369/71 and 383/4 surch.

410 6½c. on 75c. on 5s. (postage) 15 15
411 7½c. on 75c. on 5s. 15 15
412 9½c. on 50c. on 4d. 20 20
413 12½c. on 20c. on 1s.3d. 30 25
414 17½c. on 50c. on 1l. on 4d. 1·75 2·00
415 17½c. on 1l. on 4d. 1·75 2·00
416 18½c. on 1l. on 4d. 1·75 2·00
417 18½c. on 60c. on 5s. 4·75 6·50
418 25c. on 50c. 70 80
419 11½c. on 40c. (air) 25 25
420 25c. on 40c. 70 80

1967. Decimal Currency. Imperf. Self-adhesive. As T **92**, but embossed on white paper, backed with paper bearing advertisements. Background colours given first, and value tablet colours in brackets.

421 **92** ½c. red (red on white) 10 30
422 1c. red (red on white) 15 10
423 1½c. yellow (green on white) 20 15
424 2c. red (green on white) 35 10
425 2½c. green (yellow on white) 60 50
426 3c. red (white on red) 35 10
427 3½c. purple (white on green) 60 50
428 4c. red (white on green) 60 15
429 4½c. green (green on white) 60 50
430 5c. red (yellow on white) 60 15
431 5½c. red (green on white) 60 70

102 Eagle (⅔-size illustration)

1967. T **102** embossed on black paper, backed with paper bearing advertisements, or as No. 382 also with advertisements (No. 433/b).

432 **102** 9½c. red and gold on black 70 70
432a 9½c. blue & gold on black 6·50 6·50
433 – 10c. mult (red frame) 70 70
433b – 10c. mult (black frame) 7·00 7·00
434 **102** 15c. green & gold on black 1·00 1·00
434a 15c. red and gold on black 7·50 7·50

See also Nos. 538/44.

1968. No advertisements on back and colours in value tablet reversed. Background colours given first, and value tablet colours in brackets.

435 **92** ½c. red (white on green) 10 10
436 1c. red (white on red) 15 10
437 2c. red (white on green) 4·50 4·50
438 2½c. green (white on yellow) 5·00 5·00
439 3c. red (red on white) 2·00 65

On Nos. 435 and 438 the figure "½" is larger than on Nos. 421 and 425.

1968. No advertisements on back, colours changed and new value (7c.). Background colours given.

440 **92** 2c. pink (postage) 2·00 1·50
441 2½c. green 2·00 1·50
442 3½c. yellow 2·25 1·60
442a 7c. yellow (air) 7·00 3·50

On Nos. 441/2 the fraction "½" is larger than on Nos. 425 and 427.

103 Outline Map of Africa

1968. Human Rights Year. Each value comes in six types showing the following territories: Portuguese Guinea; South Africa; Mozambique; Rhodesia; South West Africa and Angola. Imperf. Self-adhesive.

443 **103** ½c. multicoloured (postage) 10 10
444 2c. multicoloured 10 10
445 2½c. multicoloured 10 10
446 3½c. multicoloured 10 10
447 10c. multicoloured 15 15
448 11½c. multicoloured 20 20
449 15c. multicoloured 25 25
450 7½c. multicoloured (air) 15 15
451 9½c. multicoloured 20 20
452 14½c. multicoloured 25 25
453 18½c. multicoloured 30 30
454 25c. multicoloured 40 40
455 1l. multicoloured 3·00 5·50
456 2l. multicoloured 9·00 12·00
Set of 84 (6 different territories) 65·00 £100

Nos. 443/56 were issued in sheets of 30 (6 × 5) on backing paper depicting diamonds or the coat-of-arms on the reverse. The six types occur once in each horiz row.

1968. Mexico Olympics Participation. Nos. 383/4 optd **OLYMPIC PARTICIPATION MEXICO 1968** or surch also.

457 6½c. on 50c. mult (postage) 25 20
458 17½c. on 50c. multicoloured 30 25
459 22½c. on 50c. multicoloured 45 40
460 28½c. on 50c. multicoloured 60 90
461 50c. multicoloured 90 1·75
462 6½c. on 40c. mult (air) 25 20
463 17½c. on 40c. multicoloured 30 25
464 22½c. on 40c. multicoloured 45 40
465 28½c. on 40c. multicoloured 60 90
466 40c. multicoloured 90 1·75

105 1859 6d. Stamp

111 1965 15c. Self-adhesive

1969. 5th Anniv of World's First Self-adhesive Postage Stamps. Multicoloured. Self-adhesive. Imperf.

467 1c. Type **105** (postage) 10 10
468 2c. 1965 2c. self-adhesive 10 10
469 3½c. 1961 Independence £1 10 10
470 5c. 1965 20c. self-adhesive 10 10
471 12½c. 1948 Royal Silver Wedding £1 30 15
472 1l. 1923 £2 2·50 1·50
473 7½c. Type **111** (air) 20 10
474 9½c. 1967 9½c. self-adhesive 20 10
475 20c. 1964 1s.3d. self-adhesive 40 25
476 30c. 1964 President Kennedy Memorial 6s. self-adhesive 55 35
477 50c. 1933 Centenary of Abolition of Slavery £1 1·50 75
478 2l. 1963 2nd Anniv of Independence 11s. 9·00 8·00

DESIGNS—As Type **105**, Nos. 468/72; As Type **111**, Nos. 474/8.

All values are on white backing paper with advertisement printed on the reverse.

117 Ore Carrier, Globe and Flags of Sierra Leone and Japan

118 Ore Carrier, Map of Europe and Africa and Flags of Sierra Leone and Netherlands

1969. Pepel Port Improvements. Imperf. Self-adhesive, backed with paper bearing advertisements.

479 **117** 1c. multicoloured (postage) 10 10
480 **118** 2c. multicoloured 10 10
481 – 3½c. multicoloured 10 10
482 – 10c. multicoloured 10 10
483 **118** 18½c. multicoloured 20 25
484 – 50c. multicoloured 80 85
485 **117** 7½c. multicoloured (air) 10 10
486 – 9½c. multicoloured 15 10
487 **117** 15c. multicoloured 20 25
488 **118** 25c. multicoloured 30 35
489 – 1l. multicoloured 1·50 1·75
490 – 2l. multicoloured 2·00 4·00

The 3½, 9½c., 2l., 10, 50c., 1l. show respectively the flags of Great Britain and West Germany instead of the Netherlands.

119 African Development Bank Emblem

1969. 5th Anniv of African Development Bank. Imperf. Self-adhesive, backed with paper bearing advertisements.

491 **119** 3½c. green, gold and black (postage) 25 40
492 9½c. violet, gold & grn (air) 35 70

120 Boy Scouts Emblem in "Diamond"

1969. Boy Scouts Diamond Jubilee. Imperf. Self-adhesive.

493 **120** 1c. multicoloured (postage) 10 10
494 2c. multicoloured 10 10
495 3½c. multicoloured 15 10
496 4½c. multicoloured 15 15
497 5c. multicoloured 15 15
498 75c. multicoloured 5·50 2·75
499 – 7½c. multicoloured (air) 35 20
500 – 9½c. multicoloured 45 25
501 – 15c. multicoloured 70 50
502 – 22c. multicoloured 90 70
503 – 55c. multicoloured 4·00 2·00
504 – 3l. multicoloured 50·00 35·00

DESIGN—OCTAGONAL (65 × 51 mm): Nos. 499/504, Scout saluting, Baden-Powell and badge.

1970. Air. No. 443 surch **AIRMAIL** twice and new value.

505 **103** 7½c. on ½c. multicoloured 20 10
506 9½c. on ½c. multicoloured 20 10
507 15c. on ½c. multicoloured 40 25
508 28c. on ½c. multicoloured 70 55
509 40c. on ½c. multicoloured 1·25 1·50
510 2l. on ½c. multicoloured 5·00 12·00
Set of 36 (6 different territories) 38·00 70·00

122 Expo Symbol and Maps of Sierra Leone and Japan

1970. World Fair, Osaka. Imperf. Self-adhesive.

511 **122** 2c. multicoloured (postage) 10 10
512 3½c. multicoloured 10 10
513 10c. multicoloured 15 10
514 12½c. multicoloured 15 10
515 20c. multicoloured 20 10
516 45c. multicoloured 45 45
517 – 7½c. multicoloured (air) 10 10
518 – 9½c. multicoloured 15 10
519 – 15c. multicoloured 20 10
520 – 25c. multicoloured 40 20
521 – 50c. multicoloured 55 50
522 – 3l. multicoloured 1·75 5·50

DESIGN—CHRYSANTHEMUM (43 × 42 mm): Nos. 517/22, Maps of Sierra Leone and Japan.

123 Diamond

124 Palm Nut

1970. Imperf. Self-adhesive.

No.	Type	Description	Unused	Used
523	123	1c. multicoloured	15	10
524		1½c. multicoloured	10	10
525		2c. multicoloured	15	10
526		2½c. multicoloured	15	10
527		3c. multicoloured	20	10
528		3½c. multicoloured	20	10
529		4c. multicoloured	30	10
530		5c. multicoloured	40	10
531	124	6c. multicoloured	30	10
532		7c. multicoloured	35	15
533		8½c. multicoloured	50	15
534		9c. multicoloured	50	15
535		10c. multicoloured	55	15
536		11½c. multicoloured . . .	65	20
537		18½c. multicoloured . . .	1·10	55

1970. Air. As T **102**, but on white paper.

No.	Type	Description	Unused	Used
538	102	7½c. gold and red	45	10
539		9½c. silver and green . . .	50	10
540		15c. silver and blue . . .	1·00	20
541		25c. gold and purple . . .	1·75	50
542		50c. green and orange . .	3·50	2·00
543		1l. blue and silver	7·00	8·50
544		2l. blue and gold	13·00	18·00

126 Jewellery Box and Sewa Diadem

1970. Diamond Industry. Imperf. Self-adhesive.

No.	Type	Description	Unused	Used
545	126	2c. multicoloured (postage)	35	10
546		3½c. multicoloured	35	10
547		10c. multicoloured	60	15
548		12½c. multicoloured	80	25
549		40c. multicoloured	2·25	1·00
550		1l. multicoloured	12·00	10·00
551	–	7½c. multicoloured (air)	60	10
552	–	9½c. multicoloured	70	10
553	126	15c. multicoloured	1·10	30
554	–	25c. multicoloured	1·50	60
555	–	75c. multicoloured	7·00	5·50
556	–	2l. multicoloured	27·00	24·00

DESIGN—HORIZ (63 × 61 mm): Nos. 551/6, Diamond and curtain.

127 "Traffic Changeover"

1971. Changeover to Driving on the Right of the Road. Imperf. Self-adhesive.

No.	Type	Description	Unused	Used
557	127	3½c. orange, blue and black (postage)	1·50	1·00
558		9½c. blue, orge & blk (air)	2·25	2·50

1971. Air. Various stamps surch **AIRMAIL** and value (Nos. 559/61) or value only (Nos. 562/3).

No.	Description	Unused	Used
559	10c. on 2d. (No. 226)	40	20
560	20c. on 1s. (No. 230)	70	45
561	50c. on 1d. (No. 243)	1·25	1·50
562	70c. on 30c. (No. 476) . . .	2·00	4·00
563	1l. on 30c. (No. 476)	3·00	5·50

129 Flag and Lion's Head

1971. 10th Anniv of Independence. Imperf. Self-adhesive.

No.	Type	Description	Unused	Used
564	129	2c. multicoloured (postage)	10	10
565		3½c. multicoloured	10	10
566		10c. multicoloured	15	10
567		12½c. multicoloured . . .	20	10
568		40c. multicoloured	70	40
569		1l. multicoloured	1·50	2·50
570	–	7½c. multicoloured (air)	15	10
571	–	9½c. multicoloured	15	10
572	–	15c. multicoloured	25	10
573	–	25c. multicoloured	35	35
574	–	75c. multicoloured	1·10	1·50
575	–	2l. multicoloured	3·00	6·50

DESIGN—"Map" shaped as Type **129**: Nos. 570/5, Bugles and lion's head.

130 Pres. Siaka Stevens

1972. Multicoloured. Background colour given.

No.	Type	Description	Unused	Used
576	130	1c. lilac	10	10
577		2c. lavender	10	10
578		4c. blue	10	10
579		5c. brown	10	10
580		7c. pink	15	10
581		10c. brown	15	10
582		15c. green	25	15
583		18c. yellow	25	15
584		20c. blue	30	15
585		25c. orange	35	15
586		50c. green	1·00	55
587		1l. mauve	1·50	1·00
588		2l. pink	2·25	3·50
589		5l. cream	3·75	8·50

131 Guma Valley Dam and Bank Emblem

1975. 10th Anniv of African Development Bank.

No.	Type	Description	Unused	Used
590	131	4c. multicoloured (postage)	50·00	28·00
591		15c. multicoloured (air)	1·00	80

132 Opening Ceremony

1975. New Congo Bridge Opening and 70th Birthday of President Stevens.

No.	Type	Description	Unused	Used
592	132	5c. multicoloured (postage)	1·60	85
593		20c. multicoloured (air)	40	25

133 Presidents Tolbert and Stevens, and Handclasp

1975. 1st Anniv of Mano River Union.

No.	Type	Description	Unused	Used
594	133	4c. multicoloured (postage)	30	40
595		15c. multicoloured (air)	20	20

134 "Quaid-i-Azam" (Mohammed Ali Jinnah)

135 Queen Elizabeth II

1977. Birth Centenary of Mohammed Ali Jinnah (Quaid-i-Azam).

No.	Type	Description	Unused	Used
596	134	30c. multicoloured	75	30

1977. Silver Jubilee.

No.	Type	Description	Unused	Used
597	135	5c. multicoloured	10	10
598		1l. multicoloured	65	80

136 College Buildings

1977. 150th Anniv of Fourah Bay College. Multicoloured.

No.	Description	Unused	Used
599	5c. Type **136**	10	10
600	20c. The old college (vert) . .	35	30

137 St. Edward's Crown and Sceptres

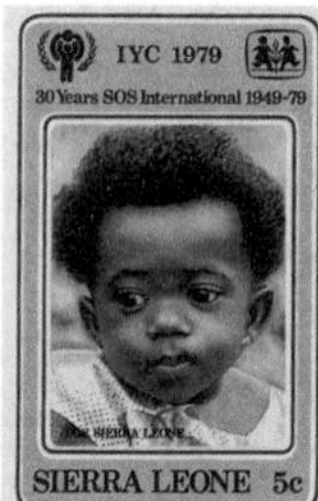

139 Young Child's Face

138 "Myrina silenus"

1978. 25th Anniv of Coronation. Multicoloured.

No.	Description	Unused	Used
601	5c. Type **137**	10	10
602	50c. Queen Elizabeth II in Coronation Coach	20	40
603	1l. Queen Elizabeth II and Prince Philip	35	60

1979. Butterflies (1st series). Multicoloured.

No.	Description	Unused	Used
604	5c. Type **138**	10	10
605	15c. "Papilio nireus"	25	15
606	25c. "Catacroptera cloanthe"	40	15
607	1l. "Druryia antimachus" . .	1·00	1·50

See also Nos. 646/9.

1979. International Year of the Child. 30th Anniv of S.O.S. International. Multicoloured.

No.	Description	Unused	Used
608	5c. Type **139**	10	10
609	27c. Young child with baby	20	25
610	1l. Mother with young child	50	1·10
MS611	114 × 84 mm. No. 610 . .	75	1·75

140 Presidents Stevens (Sierra Leone) and Tolbert (Liberia), Dove with Letter and Bridge

1979. 5th Anniv of Mano River Union and 1st Anniv of Postal Union.

No.	Type	Description	Unused	Used
612	140	5c. brown, orange & yellow	10	10
613		22c. brown, yellow & violet	10	15
614		27c. brown, blue & orange	10	15
615		35c. brown, green and red	15	20
616		1l. brown, violet and blue	50	1·00
MS617		144 × 73 mm. No. 616 . .	55	1·00

141 Great Britain 1848 10d. Stamp

1979. Death Centenary of Sir Rowland Hill.

No.	Type	Description	Unused	Used
618	141	10c. black, brown and blue	15	10
619	–	15c. black, brown and blue	25	15
620	–	50c. black, red and yellow	60	70
MS621		90 × 99 mm. 1l. black, red and pink	60	80

DESIGNS: 15c. 1872 4d. stamp; 50c. 1961 £1 Independence commemorative; 1l. 1912 £1.

142 Green Turaco ("Sierra Leone Turaco")

1980. Birds. Multicoloured.

No.	Description	Unused	Used
622B	1c. Type **142**	30	1·75
623B	2c. Olive-bellied sunbird ("Sierra Leone Olive-billed Sunbird")	40	1·75
624B	3c. Western black-headed oriole ("Sierra Leone Black-headed Oriole") . .	40	1·75
625B	5c. Spur-winged goose . . .	40	75
626A	7c. Didric cuckoo ("White-bellied Didric Cuckoo")	1·25	60
627B	10c. Grey parrot ("Sierra Leone Grey Parrot") (vert)	40	80
628B	15c. Indian Blue quail ("African Blue Quail") (vert)	50	2·00
629B	20c. African wood owl ("West African Wood Owl") (vert)	50	2·25
630B	30c. Greater blue turaco ("Blue Plantain eater") (vert)	50	2·25
631B	40c. Blue-breasted kingfisher ("Nigerian Blue-breasted kingfisher") (vert)	60	2·50
632B	50c. African black crake ("Black Crake") (vert) . .	60	2·50
633A	1l. Hartlaub's duck	1·40	2·50
634A	2l. Black bee eater	2·00	4·00
635B	5l. Denham's Bustard . . .	1·00	11·00

143 Paul P. Harris (founder), President Stevens of Sierra Leone and Rotary Emblem

1980. 75th Anniv of Rotary International.

No.	Type	Description	Unused	Used
636	143	5c. multicoloured	10	10
637		27c. multicoloured	10	10
638		50c. multicoloured	20	25
639		1l. multicoloured	40	55

144 "Maria", 1844

1980. "London 1980" Int Stamp Exhibition. Mult.

No.	Description	Unused	Used
640	6c. Type **144**	30	10
641	31c. "Tarquah", 1902	40	35
642	50c. "Aureol", 1951	50	70
643	1l. "Africa Palm", 1974 . . .	60	1·60

145 Organization for African Unity Emblem

146 "Graphium policenes"

1980. African Summit Conference, Freetown.
644 **145** 20c. black, blue and purple 10 10
645 1l. black, purple and blue 45 45

1980. Butterflies (2nd series). Multicoloured.
646 5c. Type **146** 10 10
647 27c. "Charaxes varanes" . . 30 15
648 35c. "Charaxes brutus" . . . 35 25
649 1l. "Euphaedra zaddachi" . . 1·10 1·40

147 Arrival at Freetown Airport

149 Soldiers (Defence)

148 Servals

1980. Tourism. Multicoloured.
650 6c. Type **147** 10 10
651 26c. Welcome to tourists . . 10 20
652 31c. Freetown cotton tree . . 10 25
653 40c. Beinkongo Falls 20 30
654 50c. Sports facilities 20 40
655 1l. African elephant . . . . 1·00 95

1981. Wild Cats. Multicoloured.
656 6c. Type **148** 20 10
657 6c. Serval cubs 20 10
658 31c. African golden cats . . . 50 30
659 31c. African golden cat cubs 50 30
660 50c. Leopards 70 45
661 50c. Leopard cubs 70 45
662 1l. Lions . . . . 1·00 80
663 1l. Lion cubs . . . . 1·00 80

The two designs of each value were printed together, se-tenant, in horizontal pairs, forming composite designs.

1981. 20th Anniv of Independence and 10th Anniv of Republic. National Services. Multicoloured.
664 6c. Type **149** 55 10
665 31c. Nurses administering first aid, and ambulance (Health) (horiz) . . . . . 1·50 20
666 40c. Traffic (Police Force) . . 2·75 70
667 1l. Patrol boat (Coastguard) (horiz) . . . . 3·00 2·75

150 Wedding Bouquet from Sierra Leone

151 Sandringham

1981. Royal Wedding (1st issue). Mult.
668 31c. Type **150** 10 10
669 45c. Prince Charles as helicopter pilot 15 20
670 1l. Prince Charles and Lady Diana Spencer 20 90

1981. Royal Wedding (2nd issue). Mult.
671 35c. Type **151** 10 15
672 60c. Prince Charles in outdoor clothes 15 25
675 70c. Type **151** 75 90
676 1l.30 As 60c. 75 90
673 1l.50 Prince Charles and Lady Diana Spencer . . . 25 90

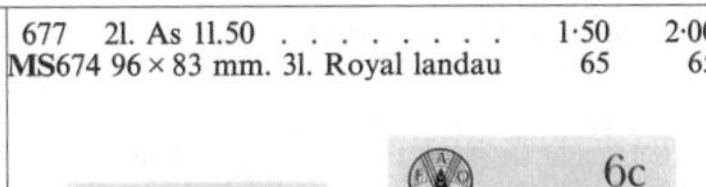

677 2l. As 1l.50 . . . . 1·50 2·00
MS674 96 × 83 mm. 3l. Royal landau 65 65

152 "Physical Recreation"

153 Pineapples

1981. 25th Anniv of Duke of Edinburgh Award Scheme and President's Award Scheme Publicity. Multicoloured.
678 6c. Type **152** 10 10
679 31c. "Community service" . . 15 10
680 1l. Duke of Edinburgh . . . 30 40
681 1l. President Siaka Stevens 30 40

1981. World Food Day. Multicoloured.
682 6c. Type **153** 10 10
683 31c. Ground nuts 15 10
684 50c. Cassava fruits 20 15
685 1l. Rice plants 50 50

154 Groundnut

1981. World Food Day (2nd issue). Agricultural Industry. Multicoloured.
686 6c. Type **154** 10 10
687 31c. Cassava 25 10
688 50c. Rice 40 25
689 1l. Pineapples 65 70

155 Scouts with Cattle

1982. 75th Anniv of Boy Scout Movement. Mult.
690 20c. Type **155** 25 10
691 50c. Scouts picking flowers 50 40
692 1l. Lord Baden-Powell . . . 90 1·00
693 2l. Scouts fishing . . . . . . 1·90 2·00
MS694 101 × 70 mm. 3l. Scouts raising flag . . . . 1·75 3·25

1982. Nos. 668/74 surch.
695 50c. on 31c. Type **150** . . . 70 70
696 50c. on 35c. Type **151** . . . 70 70
697 50c. on 45c. Prince Charles as helicopter pilot 70 70
698 50c. on 60c. Prince Charles in outdoor clothes 70 70
699 90c. on 1l. Prince Charles and Lady Diana Spencer 1·50 85
699a 1l.30 on 60c. Prince Charles in outdoor clothes . . . . 2·25 2·75
699b 2l. on 35c. Type **151** . . . 3·25 3·75
700 2l. on 1l.50 Prince Charles and Lady Diana Spencer 1·75 2·00
700a 8l. on 1l.50 Prince Charles and Lady Diana Spencer 11·00 13·00
MS701 95 × 83 mm. 3l.50 on 3l. Royal landau . . . . 1·00 1·00

157 Heading

158 Prince and Princess of Wales

1982. World Cup Football Championship, Spain. Multicoloured.
702 20c. Type **157** 45 15
703 30c. Dribbling 70 20
704 1l. Tackling . . . . 2·25 2·25
705 2l. Goalkeeping . . . . . . 3·50 3·75
MS706 92 × 75 mm. 3l. Shooting 4·75 3·00

1982. 21st Birthday of Princess of Wales. Mult.
707 31c. Caernarvon Castle . . . 20 15
708 50c. Type **158** 40 15
709 2l. Princess of Wales . . . . 2·50 80
MS710 103 × 75 mm. 3l. Princess of Wales (different) . . . . 1·40 1·00

1982. Birth of Prince William of Wales. Nos. 707/9 optd **ROYAL BABY 21.6.82.**
711 31c. Caernarvon Castle . . . 15 15
712 50c. Type **158** 30 15
713 2l. Princess of Wales . . . . 1·00 80
MS714 103 × 75 mm. 3l. Princess of Wales (different) . . . . 1·25 1·00

159 Washington with Troops

1982. 250th Birth Anniv of George Washington. Multicoloured.
715 6c. Type **159** 10 10
716 31c. Portrait of Washington (vert) 20 20
717 50c. Washington with horse 35 35
718 1l. Washington standing on battlefield (vert) 65 80
MS719 103 × 71 mm. 2l. Washington at home . . . . 75 1·25

160 Temptation of Christ

162 Long Snouted Crocodile

1982. Christmas. Stained-glass Windows. Mult.
720 6c. Type **160** 10 10
721 31c. Baptism of Christ . . . 15 20
722 50c. Annunciation 20 40
723 1l. Nativity 55 90
MS724 74 × 104 mm. 2l. Mary and Joseph . . . . 70 1·10

1982. World Cup Football Championship Winners. Nos. 702/5 optd **WORLD CUP WINNERS ITALY (3) vs. W. GERMANY (1).**
725 20c. Type **157** 30 20
726 30c. Dribbling 30 30
727 1l. Tackling 80 75
728 2l. Goalkeeping . . . . . . 1·25 1·75
MS729 91 × 75 mm. 3l. Shooting 1·00 2·00

1982. Death Cent of Charles Darwin. Mult.
730 6c. Type **162** . . . . 1·50 20
731 31c. Rainbow lizard . . . . 2·25 75
732 50c. River turtle . . . . . . 2·75 2·50
733 1l. Chameleon . . . . 3·75 6·00
MS734 90 × 70 mm. 2l. Royal python (vert) . . . . 1·75 3·00

163 Diogenes

1983. 500th Birth Anniv of Raphael. Details from painting "The School of Athens". Multicoloured.
735 6c. Type **163** 15 10
736 31c. Euclid, Ptolemy, Zoroaster, Raphael and Sodoma 25 30
737 50c. Euclid and his pupils . . 35 45
738 2l. Pythagoras, Francesco Maria della Rovere and Heraclitus . . . . 1·00 1·40
MS739 101 × 126 mm. 3l. Plato and Aristolle (vert) . . . . 1·50 2·00

164 Agricultural Training

1983. Commonwealth Day. Multicoloured.
740 6c. Type **164** 10 10
741 10c. Tourism development . . 10 10
742 50c. Broadcasting training . . 45 45
743 1l. Airport services . . . . . 1·50 1·25

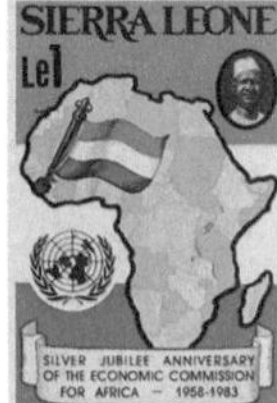

165 Map of Africa and Flag of Sierra Leone

1983. 25th Anniv of Economic Commission for Africa.
744 **165** 1l. multicoloured . . . . 80 1·10

166 Chimpanzees in Tree

1983. Endangered Species. Multicoloured.
745 6c. Type **166** . . . . 1·50 20
746 10c. Three chimpanzees (vert) 1·75 30
747 31c. Chimpanzees swinging in tree (vert) . . . . 3·25 90
748 60c. Group of chimpanzees 5·50 7·50
MS749 115 × 80 mm. 3l. African elephant . . . . 3·00 2·25

167 Traditional Communications

1983. World Communications Year. Mult.
750 6c. Type **167** 10 10
751 10c. Mail via Mano River . . 15 10
752 20c. Satellite ground station 15 10
753 1l. British packet, c. 1805 . . 90 65
MS754 115 × 85 mm. 2l. Telecommunications . . . . . 80 1·25

168 Montgolfier Balloon, Paris, 1783

1983. Bicentenary of Manned Flight. Mult.
755 6c. Type **168** 35 10
756 20c. Wolfert's airship "Deutschland", Berlin, 1879 (horiz) . . . . 1·00 30
757 50c. Amundsen's airship N.1 "Norge", North Pole, 1926 (horiz) . . . . 2·75 2·25
758 1l. "Cap Sierra" sport balloon, Freetown, 1983 . . 2·25 3·00
MS759 115 × 85 mm. 2l. Airship of 21st century . . . . 1·00 1·75

169 Mickey Mouse

1983. Space Ark Fantasy. Walt Disney Cartoon Characters. Multicoloured.
774 1c. Type **169** 10 10
775 1c. Huey, Dewey and Louie 10 10
776 3c. Goofy in spaceship . . . 10 10
777 3c. Donald Duck 10 10
778 10c. Ludwig von Drake . . . 10 10
779 10c. Goofy 10 10
780 2l. Mickey Mouse and Giraffe in spaceship . . . 1·00 1·25
781 3l. Donald Duck floating in space . . . . 1·25 1·75
MS782 140 × 116 mm. 5l. Mickey Mouse leaving spaceship . . . 3·00 3·50

170 Graduates from Union Training Programme

1984. 10th Anniv of Mano River Union. Mult.

783 6c. Type **170** 10 10
784 25c. Intra-Union trade . . . 10 10
785 31c. Member Presidents on map 15 15
786 41c. Signing ceremony marking Guinea's accession 20 20
MS787 75 × 113 mm. No. 786 . . 35 90

171 Gymnastics

1984. Olympic Games, Los Angeles. Mult.

788 90c. Type **171** 30 40
789 1l. Hurdling 30 40
790 3l. Javelin-throwing . . . . 75 1·25
MS791 104 × 71 mm. 7l. Boxing 1·10 2·00

172 "Apollo 11" Liftoff

1984. 15th Anniv of First Moonwalk. Mult.

792 50c. Type **172** 20 20
793 75c. Lunar module 30 30
794 1l.25 First Moonwalk 45 45
795 2l.50 Lunar exploration 85 85
MS796 99 × 69 mm. 5l. Family watching Moonwalk on television (horiz) . . . . 1·60 2·25

173 Concorde

1984. Universal Postal Union Congress, Hamburg. Multicoloured.

797 4l. Type **173** . . . . 2·75 1·75
MS798 100 × 70 mm. 4l. Heinrich von Stephan (founder of U.P.U.) 1·25 1·75

174 Citroen "Traction Avante"

1984. United Nations Decade of African Transport. Multicoloured.

799 12c. Type **174** 50 10
800 60c. Locomotive 80 35
801 90c. A.C. "Ace" 95 45
802 1l. Vauxhall "Prince Henry" 95 45
803 1l.50 Delahaye "135" . . . . 1·00 70
804 2l. Mazda "1105" . . . . . 1·00 90
MS805 107 × 75 mm. 6l. Volkswagen "Beetle" . . . . 3·75 4·50

1984. Nos. 625, 627 and 634 surch.

811 25c. on 10c. Grey parrot (vert) 75 85
812 40c. on 10c. Grey parrot (vert) 50 70
813 50c. on 2l. Black bee eater . . 50 70
814 70c. on 5c. Spur-winged goose 50 70
815 10l. on 5c. Spur-winged goose 3·00 3·50

1984. "Ausipex" International Stamp Exhibition, Melbourne. Nos. 632 and 635 optd **AUSIPEX 84**.

818 50c. African black crake (vert) . . . . 1·50 75
819 5l. Denham's bustard . . . . 3·50 2·00

177 Portuguese Caravel

1984. History of Shipping. Multicoloured.

820B 2c. Type **177** . . . . . . 55 1·50
821B 5c. "Merlin" of Bristol . . 55 80
822B 10c. "Golden Hind" . . . 75 70
823A 15c. "Mordaunt" . . . . 1·75 90
824B 20c. "Atlantic" (sail transport) 80 60
825B 25c. H.M.S. "Lapwing" (frigate), 1785 . . . . . 80 60
826B 30c. "Traveller" (brig) . . 80 60
827B 40c. "Amistad" (schooner) 90 60
828B 50c. H.M.S. "Teazer" (gun vessel), 1868 . . . . . 1·00 60
829B 70c. "Scotia" (cable ship) 1·75 2·00
830B 1l. H.M.S. "Alecto" (paddle-steamer), 1882 1·75 2·00
831B 2l. H.M.S. "Blonde" (cruiser), 1889 . . . . . 2·00 3·00
832B 5l. H.M.S. "Fox" (cruiser), 1895 . . . . . 2·75 4·50
833B 10l. "Accra" (liner) . . . 3·25 5·50
833cA 15l. H.M.S. "Favourite" (sloop), 1829 . . . . . 3·00 4·00
833dA 25l. H.M.S. "Euryalus" (screw frigate), 1883 . . 3·00 4·50

Nos. 820/2 and 824/33 come both with and without imprint dates.

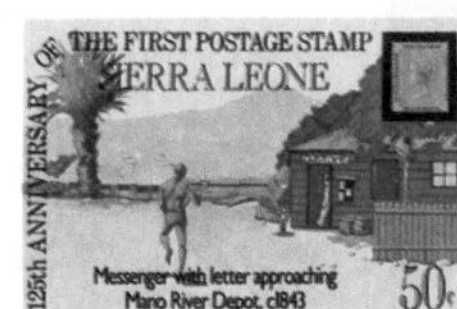

178 Mail Runner approaching Mano River Depot, c. 1843

1984. 125th Anniv of First Postage Stamps. Mult.

834 50c. Type **178** 35 15
835 2l. Isaac Fitzjohn, first Postmaster, receiving letters, 1855 . . . . 1·25 85
836 3l. 1859 packet franked with four 6d. stamps . . . . . 1·75 1·50
MS837 100 × 70 mm. 5l. Sierra Leone 1859 6d. purple and Great Britain 1840 Penny Black stamps 1·50 1·60

179 "Madonna and Child" (Pisanello)

1984. Christmas. Madonna and Child Paintings by artists named. Multicoloured.

838 20c. Type **179** 10 10
839 1l. Memling 40 40
840 2l. Raphael 75 90
841 3l. Van der Werff . . . . . 1·10 1·40
MS842 100 × 69 mm. 6l. Picasso 2·75 2·75

180 Donald Duck in "The Wise Little Hen"

1984. 50th Birthday of Donald Duck. Walt Disney Cartoon Characters. Multicoloured.

843 1c. Type **180** 10 10
844 2c. Mickey Mouse and Donald Duck in "Boat Builders" 10 10
845 3c. Panchito, Donald Duck and Jose Carioca in "The Three Caballeros" 10 10
846 4c. Donald Duck meeting Pythagoras in "Mathmagic Land" 10 10
847 5c. Donald Duck and nephew in "The Mickey Mouse Club" 10 10
848 10c. Mickey Mouse, Goofy and Donald Duck in "Donald on Parade" . . . 10 10
849 1l. Donald Duck riding donkey in "Don Donald" 1·00 1·00
850 2l. Donald Duck in "Donald Gets Drafted" . . . . . . 2·00 2·00
851 4l. Donald Duck meeting children in Tokyo Disneyland . . . . 3·25 3·25
MS852 126 × 102 mm. 5l. Style sheet for Donald Duck . . . . . . 4·50 2·50

181 Fischer's Whydah

1985. Birth Bicentenary of John J. Audubon (ornithologist). Songbirds of Sierra Leone. Mult.

853 40c. Type **181** . . . . 1·75 55
854 90c. Spotted flycatcher . . . 3·00 1·75
855 1l.30 Garden warbler . . . . 3·25 3·50
856 3l. Speke's weaver . . . . . 5·50 7·50
MS857 100 × 70 mm. 5l. Great grey shrike . . . . 3·50 3·00

182 Fishing

1985. International Youth Year. Multicoloured.

858 1l.15 Type **182** 45 55
859 1l.50 Sawing timber 60 75
860 2l.15 Rice farming 75 95
MS861 100 × 70 mm. 5l. Polishing diamonds . . . . 1·75 1·50

183 Eddie Rickenbacker and Spad "XIII", 1918

1985. 40th Anniv of I.C.A.O. Multicoloured.

862 70c. Type **183** . . . . 1·50 75
863 1l.25 Samuel P. Langley and "Aerodrome A", 1903 . . 2·00 1·75
864 1l.30 Orville and Wilbur Wright with Wright Flyer I, 1903 . . . . 2·00 1·75
865 2l. Charles Lindbergh and "Spirit of St. Louis", 1927 2·25 2·75
MS866 100 × 69 mm. 5l. Sierra Leone Airlines Boeing 707-384C 2·00 1·75

184 "Temptation of Christ' (Botticelli)

1985. Easter. Religious Paintings. Mult.

867 45c. Type **184** 30 15
868 70c. "Christ at the Column" (Velasquez) 55 35
869 1l.55 "Pieta" (Botticelli) (vert) 90 75
870 10l. "Christ on the Cross" (Velasquez) (vert) . . . . 4·75 5·00
MS871 106 × 76 mm. 12l. "Man of Sorrows" (Botticelli) . . . . . 4·00 4·00

185 The Queen Mother at St. Paul's Cathedral

189a Viola Pomposa

188 Chater-Lea (1905) at Hill Station House

1985. Life and Times of Queen Elizabeth the Queen Mother. Multicoloured.

872 1l. Type **185** 20 25
873 1l.70 With her racehorse, "Double Star", at Sandown (horiz) 30 40
874 10l. At Covent Garden, 1971 1·75 2·50
MS875 56 × 85 mm. 12l. With Princess Anne at Ascot . . . . 1·75 2·25

1985. 75th Anniv of Girl Guide Movement. Nos. 690/3 surch **75th ANNIVERSARY OF GIRL GUIDES.**

876 70c. on 20c. Type **155** . . . 30 30
877 1l.30 on 50c. Scouts picking flowers 55 55
878 5l. on 1l. Lord Baden-Powell 1·60 1·60
879 7l. on 2l. Scouts fishing . . . 2·25 2·25
MS880 101 × 70 mm. 15l. on 3l. Scouts raising flag . . . . 3·75 4·00

1985. Olympic Gold Medal Winners, Los Angeles. Nos. 788/90 surch.

881 2l. on 90c. Type **171** (surch **Le2 MA YANHONJG CHINA GOLD MEDAL**) 50 55
882 4l. on 1l. Hurdling (surch **Le4 E. MOSES U.S.A. GOLD MEDAL**) . . . . 1·00 1·25
883 8l. on 3l. Javelin-throwing (surch **Le8 A. HAERKOENEN FINLAND GOLD MEDAL**) . . . . 2·00 2·10
MS884 104 × 71 mm. 15l. on 7l. Boxing (surch **M. TAYLOR U.S.A. GOLD MEDAL**) . . . 3·25 3·75

1985. Centenary of Motor Cycle and Decade for African Transport. Multicoloured.

885 1l.40 Type **188** . . . . . . 1·00 1·00
886 2l. Honda "XR 350 R" at Queen Elizabeth II Quay, Freetown . . . . 1·40 1·40
887 4l. Kawasaki "Vulcan" at Bo Clock Tower . . . . . . 2·50 2·50
888 5l. Harley-Davidson "Electra-Glide" in Makeni village 2·75 2·75
MS889 104 × 71 mm. 12l. Millet (1893) . . . . 4·75 4·25

1985. 300th Birth Anniv of Johann Sebastian Bach (composer). Multicoloured (except No. **MS**894).

890 70c. Type **189a** . . . . . . 1·00 25
891 3l. Spinet . . . . 2·50 80
892 4l. Lute . . . . 2·50 1·10
893 5l. Oboe . . . . 2·50 1·40
MS894 103 × 77 mm. 12l. "Johann Sebastian Bach" (Toby E. Rosenthal) (black) . . . . . 5·00 3·50

1985. Nos. 707/10 and 711/14 surch.

895 70c. on 3l. Caernarvon Castle (No. 707) 30 30
899 1l.30 on 3lc. Caernarvon Castle (No. 711) . . . . . . 1·50 1·25
896 4l. on 50c. Type **158** (No. 708) . . . . 2·00 2·50
897 5l. on 2l. Princess of Wales (No. 709) . . . . 2·75 3·00
900 5l. on 50c. Type **158** (No. 712) . . . . 3·00 3·50
901 7l. on 2l. Princess of Wales (No. 713) . . . . 6·00 4·50
MS898 103 × 75 mm. 15l. on 3l. Princess of Wales (different) (No. **MS**710) . . . . 8·00 6·00
MS902 103 × 75 mm. 15l. on 3l. Princess of Wales (different) (No. **MS**714) . . . . 8·00 6·00

190 "Madonna and Child" (Crivelli)

1985. Christmas. "Madonna and Child" Paintings by artists named. Multicoloured.

903 70c. Type **190** 25 10
904 3l. Bouts 80 40
905 4l. Da Messina 95 55
906 5l. Lochner . . . . 1·10 65
MS907 113 × 85mm. 12l. Miniature from Book of Kells . . . . . 1·50 1·60

190a Snow White and Bashful

1985. 150th Birth Anniv of Mark Twain (author). Walt Disney cartoon characters illustrating Mark Twain quotations. Multicoloured.

908 1l.50 Type **190a** 1·00 85

909 3l. Three Little Pigs 1·25 1·40

910 4l. Donald Duck and nephew 1·50 1·60

911 5l. Pinocchio and Figaro the cat 1·60 1·90

MS912 126 × 101 mm. 15l. Winnie the Pooh 4·25 2·50

190b The Miller (Donald Duck) and his daughter (Daisy Duck) meet the King (Uncle Scrooge)

1985. Birth Bicentenaries of Grimm Brothers (folklorists). Walt Disney cartoon characters in scenes from "Rumpelstiltskin". Multicoloured.

913 70c. Type **190b** 20 25

914 1l. The King puts the Miller's daughter to work 35 40

915 2l. Rumpelstiltskin demands payment 50 55

916 10l. The King with gold spun from straw 2·75 3·50

MS917 126 × 100 mm. 15l. The King and Queen with baby 5·50 4·50

190c John Kennedy and 1954 Human Rights 8c. Stamp

1985. 40th Anniv of U.N.O. Showing United Nations (New York) stamps. Multicoloured.

918 2l. Type **190c** 50 70

919 4l. Albert Einstein (scientist) and 1958 Atomic Energy 3c. 1·00 1·60

920 7l. Maimonides (physician) and 1956 W.H.O. 8c. 3·50 4·25

MS921 110 × 85 mm. 12l. Martin Luther King (civil rights leader) (vert) 1·25 1·75

191 Player kicking Ball **191a** Times, Square, 1905

1986. World Cup Football Championship, Mexico. Multicoloured.

922 70c. Type **191** 55 10

923 3l. Player controlling ball 1·00 50

924 4l. Player chasing ball 1·25 70

925 5l. Player kicking ball (different) 1·50 80

MS926 105 × 74 mm. 12l. Player kicking ball (different) 1·50 1·75

1986. Centenary of Statue of Liberty. Mult.

927 40c. Type **191a** 10 10

928 70c. Times Square, 1986 15 10

929 1l. "Tally Ho" coach, c. 1880 (horiz) 35 15

930 10l. Express bus, 1986 (horiz) 2·00 1·90

MS931 105 × 75 mm. 12l. Statue of Liberty 2·50 2·25

191b Johannes Kepler (astronomer) and Paris Observatory

1986. Appearance of Halley's Comet (1st issue). Multicoloured.

932 15c. Type **191b** 30 10

933 50c. N.A.S.A. Space Shuttle landing, 1985 40 10

934 70c. Halley's Comet (from Bayeux Tapestry) 40 15

935 10l. Comet of 530 A.D. and Merlin predicting coming of King Arthur 2·50 1·60

MS936 101 × 70 mm. 12l. Halley's Comet 1·50 1·60

See also Nos. 988/91.

191c Princess Elizabeth Inspecting Guard of Honour, Cranwell, 1951 **192c** Prince Andrew and Miss Sarah Ferguson

192 Chicago–Milwaukee "Hiawatha Express"

1986. 60th Birthday of Queen Elizabeth II.

937 **191c** 10c. black and yellow 20 10

938 – 1l.70 multicoloured 55 35

939 – 10l. multicoloured 2·50 2·75

MS940 120 × 85 mm. 12l. black and brown 2·25 2·00

DESIGNS: 1l.70, In Garter robes; 10l. At Braemar Games, 1970; 12l. Princess Elizabeth, Windsor Castle, 1943.

1986. "Ameripex" International Stamp Exhibition, Chicago. American Trains. Multicoloured.

941 50c. Type **192** 90 40

942 2l. Rock Island Line "The Rocket" 1·75 1·75

943 4l. Rio Grande "Prospector" 2·75 3·25

944 7l. Southern Pacific "Daylight Express" 3·50 5·00

MS945 105 × 85 mm. 12l. Pennsylvania "Broadway Limited" 3·25 2·25

1986. Royal Wedding. Multicoloured.

946 10c. Type **192c** 10 10

947 1l.70 Prince Andrew at clay pigeon shoot 30 35

948 10l. Prince Andrew in naval uniform 1·40 1·75

MS949 88 × 88 mm. 12l. Prince Andrew and Miss Sarah Ferguson (different) 2·25 1·60

193 "Monodora myristica"

1986. Flowers of Sierra Leone. Multicoloured.

950 70c. Type **193** 15 10

951 1l.50 "Gloriosa simplex" 20 15

952 4l. "Mussaenda erythrophylla" 35 25

953 6l. "Crinum ornatum" 50 40

954 8l. "Bauhinia purpurea" 60 60

955 10l. "Bombax costatum" 70 70

956 20l. "Hibiscus rosasinensis" 1·25 1·50

957 30l. "Cassia fistula" 1·75 2·00

MS958 Two sheets, each 101 × 92 mm. (a) 40l. "Clitoria ternatea" (b) 40l. "Plumbago auriculata" Set of 2 sheets 6·00 6·00

194 Handshake and Flags of Sierra Leone and U.S.A.

1986. 25th Anniv of United States Peace Corps.

959 **194** 4l. multicoloured 70 70

195 Transporting Goods by Canoe

1986. International Peace Year. Multicoloured.

960 1l. Type **195** 30 15

961 2l. Teacher and class 40 25

962 5l. Rural post office 80 50

963 10l. Fishermen in longboat 1·60 1·25

1986. Various stamps surch.

968 70c. on 10c. Type **191c** (No. 937) 1·25 30

971 70c. on 10c. Prince Andrew and Miss Sarah Ferguson (No. 946) 10 10

964 30l. on 2c. Type **177** (No. 820) 2·75 2·75

965 40l. on 30c. "Traveller" (brig) (No. 826) 3·25 3·25

969 45l. on 10l. Queen at Braemar Games, 1970 (No. 934) 5·50 2·50

972 45l. on 10l. Prince Andrew in naval uniform (No. 948) 2·40 2·50

966 45l. on 40c. "Amistad" (schooner) (No. 827) 3·50 3·50

967 50l. on 70c. "Scotia" (cable ship) (No. 829) 3·50 3·50

MS970 120 × 85 mm. 50l. on 12l. black and brown (No. **MS**940) 2·50 3·00

MS973 88 × 88 mm. 50l. on 12l. Prince Andrew and Miss Sarah Ferguson (different) (No. **MS**949) 2·50 3·00

1986. World Cup Football Championship Winners, Mexico. Nos. 922/5 optd **WINNERS Argentina 3 W.Germany 2** or surch also.

974 70c. Type **191** 35 10

975 3l. Player controlling ball 75 30

976 4l. Player chasing ball 80 40

977 40l. on 5l. Player kicking ball (different) 6·50 4·50

MS978 105 × 74 mm. 40l. on 12l. Player kicking ball (different) 2·75 2·50

198 Mickey and Minnie Mouse as Jack and Jill

1986. "Stockholmia '86" International Stamp Exn, Sweden. Walt Disney cartoon characters in scenes from nursery rhymes. Multicoloured.

979 70c. Type **198** 10 10

980 1l. Donald Duck as Wee Willie Winkie 15 15

981 2l. Minnie Mouse as Little Miss Muffet 20 20

982 4l. Goofy as Old King Cole 40 40

983 5l. Clarabelle as Mary Quite Contrary 50 50

984 10l. Daisy Duck as Little Bo Peep 90 1·00

985 25l. Daisy Duck and Minnie Mouse in "Polly put the Kettle on" 2·00 2·75

986 35l. Goofy, Mickey Mouse and Donald Duck as the Three Men in a Tub 2·50 3·25

MS987 Two sheets, each 127 × 102 mm. (a) 40l. Aunt Matilda as the Old Woman in the Shoe. (b) 40l. Goofy as Simple Simon Set of 2 sheets 6·50 6·50

(198a) **199** "Virgin and Child with St. Dorothy"

1986. Appearance of Halley's Comet (2nd issue). Nos. 932/5 optd as T **198a**.

988 50c. N.A.S.A. Space Shuttle landing, 1985 30 10

989 70c. Halley's Comet (from Bayeux Tapestry) 30 10

990 1l.50 on 15c. Johannes Kepler (astronomer) and Paris Observatory 30 10

991 45l. on 10l. Comet of 530 A.D. and Merlin predicting coming of King Arthur 6·00 3·75

MS992 101 × 70 mm. 50l. on 12l. Halley's Comet 3·25 3·75

1986. Christmas. Paintings by Titian. Mult.

993 70c. Type **199** 10 10

994 1l.50 "The Gypsy Madonna" (vert) 15 10

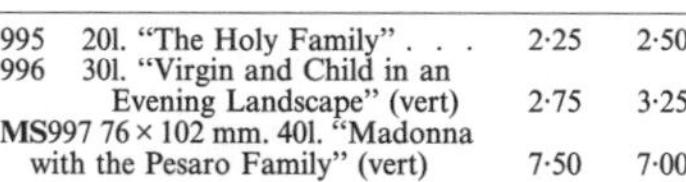

995 20l. "The Holy Family" 2·25 2·50

996 30l. "Virgin and Child in an Evening Landscape" (vert) 2·75 3·25

MS997 76 × 102 mm. 40l. "Madonna with the Pesaro Family" (vert) 7·50 7·00

200 Nomoli (soapstone figure) **201** Removing Top of Statue's Torch

1987. Bicentenary of Sierra Leone. Mult.

998 2l. Type **200** 20 20

999 5l. King's Yard Gate, Royal Hospital, 1817 80 60

MS1000 100 × 70 mm. 60l. Early 19th-century British warship at Freetown 3·25 3·75

1987. Centenary of Statue of Liberty (1986) (2nd issue). Multicoloured.

1001 70c. Type **201** 10 10

1002 1l.50 View of Statue's torch and New York harbour (horiz) 10 10

1003 2l. Crane lifting torch 10 10

1004 3l. Workman steadying torch 10 15

1005 4l. Statue's crown (horiz) 15 20

1006 5l. Statue of Liberty (side view) and fireworks 20 25

1007 10l. Statue of Liberty and fireworks 40 45

1008 25l. Bedloe Island, statue and fireworks (horiz) 1·00 1·40

1009 30l. Statue's face 1·25 1·75

202 Emblem, Mother and Child and Syringe

1987. 40th Anniv of UNICEF.

1010 **202** 10l. multicoloured 50 55

203 "U.S.A.", 1987 **205** "Salamis temora"

204 Mickey Mouse as Mountie and Parliament Building, Ottawa

1987. America's Cup Yachting Championship. Multicoloured.

1011 1l. Type **203** 15 10

1012 1l.50 "New Zealand II", 1987 (horiz) 15 10

1013 2l.50 "French Kiss", 1987 15 10

1014 10l. "Stars and Stripes", 1987 (horiz) 75 45

1015 15l. "Australia II", 1983 1·00 75

1016 25l. "Freedom", 1980 1·75 1·40

1017 30l. "Kookaburra", 1987 (horiz) 1·75 1·60

MS1018 100 × 70 mm. 50l. "Constellation", 1964 2·25 2·50

1987. "Capex '87" International Stamp Exhibition, Toronto. Walt Disney cartoon characters in Canada. Multicoloured.

1019 2l. Type **204** 20 20

1020 5l. Goofy dressed as Mountie and totem poles 35 35

1021 10l. Goofy windsurfing and Donald Duck fishing off Perce Rock 60 45

1022 20l. Goofy with mountain goat in Rocky Mountains 1·00 1·25

1023 25l. Donald Duck and Mickey Mouse in Old Quebec . . . . 1·25 1·40
1024 45l. Goofy emerging from igloo and "Aurora Borealis" . . . . 1·75 2·50
1025 50l. Goofy as gold prospector and post office, Yukon . . . . 2·00 3·00
1026 75l. Dumbo flying over Niagara Falls . . . . . . 3·25 4·50
MS1027 Two sheets, each 127 × 101 mm. (a) 100l. Mickey Mouse driving chuckwagon in Calgary Stampede. (b) 100l. Mickey Mouse and Goofy as Vikings in Newfoundland Set of 2 sheets . . . . 8·00 12·00

1987. Butterflies. Multicoloured, "Sierra Leone" in black.
1028Ac 10c. Type **205** 75 40
1029B 20c. "Stugeta marmorea" 75 75
1030B 40c. "Graphium ridleyanus" 75 50
1031Ac 1l. "Papilio bromius" . . 1·00 40
1032Ac 2l. "Iterus zalmoxis" . . 1·25 60
1033Ac 3l. "Cymothoe sangaris" 1·25 60
1033Bd 3l. As 40c. . . . . 4·00 2·50
1034Ac 5l. "Graphium tynderaeus" . . . . . 1·25 30
1034Bc 9l. As 3l. (No. 1033) . . 5·00 3·50
1035Ac 10l. "Graphium policenes" . . . . . . 1·25 30
1035Bc 12l. Type **205** . . . . . 6·00 3·75
1035Bd 16l. As 20c. . . . . . . 6·00 3·75
1036Ac 20l. "Tanuetheira timon" 1·50 60
1037Ac 25l. "Danaus limniace" 1·50 30
1038Ac 30l. "Papilio hesperus" 1·75 65
1039Ac 45l. "Charaxes smaragdalis" . . . . . 1·75 30
1040Ac 60l. "Charaxes lucretius" 2·00 2·25
1041Ac 75l. "Antanartia delius" 2·25 2·75
1042A 100l. "Abisara talantus" 3·25 6·00
For similar stamps but with "Sierra Leone" in blue, see Nos. 1658/72.

206 Cycling

206b "Apollo 8" Spacecraft (first manned Moon orbit), 1968

206a "The Quarrel"

1987. Olympic Games, Seoul (1988) (1st series). Multicoloured.
1043 5l. Type **206** 20 25
1044 10l. Three-day eventing . . 40 50
1045 45l. Athletics . . . . 1·75 2·00
1046 50l. Tennis . . . . 2·00 2·40
MS1047 73 × 84 mm. 100l. Olympic gold medal . . . . 4·00 4·50
See also Nos. 1137/41.

1987. Birth Centenary of Marc Chagall (artist). Multicoloured.
1048 3l. Type **206a** 15 15
1049 5l. "Rebecca giving Abraham's Servant a Drink" 20 25
1050 10l. "The Village" 40 45
1051 20l. "Ida at the Window" 60 65
1052 25l. "Promenade" . . . . . 1·00 1·10
1053 45l. "Peasants" . . . . . . 2·00 2·25
1054 50l. "Turquoise Plate" (ceramic) . . . . 2·25 2·25
1055 75l. "Cemetery Gate" . . . 3·25 3·75
MS1056 Two sheets, each 110 × 95 mm. (a) 100l. "Wedding Feast" (stage design) (104 × 78 mm). (b) 100l. "The Falling Angel" (104 × 78 mm). Imperf Set of 2 sheets . . . . 9·00 10·00

1987. Milestones of Transportation. Multicoloured.
1057 3l. Type **206b** 40 30
1058 5l. Blanchard's balloon (first U.S. balloon flight), 1793 40 30
1059 10l. Amelia Earhart's Lockheed Vega 5B (first solo transatlantic flight by woman), 1932 . . . . . . 1·25 60
1060 15l. Vicker's Vimy (first non-stop transatlantic flight), 1919 . . . . . . 1·50 80
1061 20l. British "Mk 1" tank (first combat tank), 1916 1·75 1·25
1062 25l. Vought-Sikorsky VS-300 (first U.S. helicopter flight), 1939 . . 2·00 1·60
1063 30l. Wright brothers Flyer I (first powered flight), 1903 2·00 1·60
1064 35l. Bleriot XI (first cross Channel flight), 1909 . . 2·00 2·00
1065 40l. Paraplane (first flexible-wing ultralight), 1983 . . 2·00 2·25
1066 50l. Daimler's first motorcycle, 1885 . . . . 2·00 2·50
MS1067 114 × 83 mm. 100l. "Rhinegold Express" (first electric express service) (horiz) . . . . 3·75 6·50
Nos. 1058/64 are horiz.

207 Evonne Goolagong

1987. Wimbledon Tennis Champions. Mult.
1068 2l. Type **207** 35 35
1069 5l. Martina Navratilova . . 55 55
1070 10l. Jimmy Connors 85 85
1071 15l. Bjorn Borg . . . . . . 1·25 1·25
1072 30l. Boris Becker . . . . . 2·25 2·25
1073 40l. John McEnroe . . . . 2·50 2·50
1074 50l. Chris Evert Lloyd . . . 2·75 2·75
1075 75l. Virginia Wade . . . . 3·50 3·50
MS1076 Two sheets, each 105 × 75 mm. (a) 100l. Boris Becker (different). (b) 100l. Steffi Graf Set of 2 sheets . . . . . 13·00 13·00

208 Ducats, "Santa Maria" and Isaac Abravanel (financier)

1987. 500th Anniv (1992) of Discovery of America by Columbus. Multicoloured.
1077 5l. Type **208** 70 20
1078 10l. Astrolabe, "Pinta" and Abraham Zacuto (astronomer) 80 35
1079 45l. Maravedis (coins), "Nina" and Luis de Santangel (financier) . . . 2·50 3·00
1080 50l. Carib and Spaniard with tobacco plant and Luis de Torres (translator) 2·75 3·25
MS1081 101 × 70 mm. 100l. Christopher Columbus and map 3·00 3·50

209 Cotton Tree

1987. Flora and Fauna. Multicoloured.
1082 3l. Type **209** 15 15
1083 5l. Dwarf crocodile 35 25
1084 10l. Kudu 40 35
1085 20l. Yellowbells 65 65
1086 25l. Hippopotamus and calf 1·75 1·25
1087 45l. Comet orchid . . . . . 3·25 2·50
1088 50l. Baobab tree . . . . . 2·25 2·50
1089 75l. Elephant and calf . . . 4·25 5·00
MS1090 Two sheets, each 100 × 70 mm. (a) 100l. Bananas, Coconut Palm, Papayas and Pineapple. (b) 100l. Leopard Set of 2 sheets . . . . 5·75 7·00

210 Scouts at Ayers Rock

1987. World Scout Jamboree, Australia. Mult.
1091 5l. Type **210** 30 20
1092 15l. Scouts sailing yacht . . 65 65
1093 40l. Scouts and Sydney skyline . . . . 1·75 2·50
1094 50l. Scout, Sydney Harbour Bridge and Opera House 3·25 2·75
MS1095 114 × 78 mm. 100l. Flags of Sierra Leone, Australia and Boy Scouts . . . . 3·00 3·50

210a White House

1987. Bicentenary of U.S. Constitution. Mult.
1096 5l. Type **210a** 15 20
1097 10l. George Washington (Virginia delegate) (vert) 30 35
1098 30l. Patrick Henry (statesman) (vert) 80 95
1099 65l. State Seal, New Hampshire . . . . 1·60 2·40
MS1100 105 × 75 mm. 100l. John Jay (jurist) (vert) . . . . 1·50 3·00

210b Mickey and Minnie Mouse on Space Mountain

1987. 60th Anniv of Mickey Mouse (Walt Disney cartoon character). Cartoon characters at Tokyo Disneyland. Multicoloured.
1101 20c. Type **210b** 10 10
1102 40c. Mickey Mouse at Country Bear Jamboree 10 10
1103 80c. Mickey Mouse as bandleader and Minnie Mouse, Goofy and Pluto as musicians 10 10
1104 1l. Goofy, Mickey Mouse and children in canoe and Mark Twain's river boat 10 10
1105 2l. Mickey Mouse, Goofy and Chip n'Dale on Western River Railroad 10 10
1106 3l. Goofy and Mickey Mouse as Pirates of the Caribbean 15 15
1107 10l. Mickey Mouse, Goofy and children aboard Big Thunder Mountain train 55 55
1108 20l. Mickey Mouse, Morty and Ferdie in boat and Goofy on flying carpet . . 1·25 1·50
1109 30l. Mickey and Minnie Mouse in kimonos at Disneyland entrance . . . 1·75 2·00
MS1110 127 × 102 mm. 65l. Mickey and Minnie Mouse in kimonos at Cinderella's Castle . . . . . . 5·50 4·50

211 "The Annunciation" (detail) (Titian)

1987. Christmas. Religious Paintings by Titian. Multicoloured.
1111 2l. Type **211** 20 10
1112 10l. "Madonna and Child with Saints" 60 35
1113 20l. "Madonna and Child with Saints Ulfus and Brigid" . . . . 1·10 1·25
1114 35l. "The Madonna of the Cherries" . . . . 1·90 2·75
MS1115 70 × 100 mm. 65l. "The Pesaro Altarpiece" (vert) . . . 3·50 4·00

211a Wedding of Princess Elizabeth and Duke of Edinburgh, 1947

212 "Russula cyanoxantha"

1988. Royal Ruby Wedding.
1116 **211a** 2l. brown, black and grey 40 10
1117 – 3l. multicoloured . . . 40 10
1118 – 10l. brown, black and orange 60 35
1119 – 50l. multicoloured . . . 2·50 2·50
MS1120 76 × 100 mm. 65l. mult 3·00 2·75

DESIGNS: 3l. Prince Charles's christening photograph, 1949; 10l. Queen Elizabeth II with Prince Charles and Princess Anne, c. 1951; 50l. Queen Elizabeth, c. 1960; 65l. Wedding photograph, 1947.

1988. Fungi. Multicoloured.
1121 3l. Type **212** 45 30
1122 10l. "Lycoperdon perlatum" 1·10 70
1123 20l. "Lactarius deliciosus" 1·90 2·00
1124 30l. "Boletus edulis" . . . . 2·25 2·75
MS1125 100 × 70 mm. 65l. "Amanita muscaria" . . . . 5·50 4·75

213 Golden Pheasant Panchax

1988. Fishes of Sierra Leone. Multicoloured.
1126 3l. Type **213** 15 15
1127 10l. Banded panchax . . . 30 30
1128 20l. Jewel cichlid 50 75
1129 35l. Freshwater butterflyfish 75 1·40
MS1130 99 × 69 mm. 65l. Long-finned tetra . . . . 2·50 4·00

1988. Stamp Exhibitions. Nos. 1016, 1072 and 1079 optd.
1131 25l. "Freedom", 1980 (optd **INDEPENDENCE 40**, Israel) . . . . 1·10 1·40
1132 30l. Boris Becker (optd **OLYMPHILEX '88**, Seoul) . . . . 1·25 1·75
1133 45l. Maravedis (coins), "Nina" and Luis de Santangel (financier) (optd **PRAGA 88**, Prague) . . . 1·75 2·25

214 Hands holding Coffee Beans and Woman with Cocoa

1988. International Fund for Agricultural Development. Multicoloured.
1134 3l. Type **214** 20 20
1135 15l. Tropical fruits and man climbing palm tree . . . 70 80
1136 25l. Sheaf of rice and harvesters . . . . 1·25 1·50

215 Basketball

216 Swallow-tailed Bee Eater

1988. Olympic Games, Seoul (2nd issue). Mult.
1137 3l. Type **215** 10 10
1138 10l. Judo 30 35
1139 15l. Gymnastics 45 55
1140 40l. Synchronized swimming 1·25 1·75
MS1141 73 × 101 mm. 65l. Sierra Leone athlete . . . . 1·90 2·50

1988. Birds. Multicoloured.
1142 3l. Type **216** 85 75
1143 5l. Double-toothed barbet ("Tooth-billed Barbet") 1·10 1·00
1144 8l. African golden oriole . . 1·40 1·25
1145 10l. Red bishop . . . . . . 1·40 1·25
1146 12l. Red-billed shrike . . . 1·40 1·25
1147 20l. European bee eater . . 1·60 1·40
1148 35l. Common gonolek ("Barbary Shrike") . . . 2·25 2·00
1149 40l. Western black-headed oriole ("Black-headed Oriole") . . . . 2·25 2·25
MS1150 Two sheets, each 111 × 82 mm. (a) 65l. Purple heron. (b) 65l. Saddle-bill stork Set of 2 sheets . . . . 3·75 4·50

217 "Aureol" (liner)

1988. Ships. Multicoloured.
1151 3l. Type **217** 75 30
1152 10l. "Dunkwa" (freighter) 1·75 80

1153 15l. "Melampus" (container ship) . . . . 2·25 1·60
1154 30l. "Dumbaia" (freighter) 2·75 3·00
MS1155 95×95 mm. 65l. Loading container ship, Freetown . . . 2·25 2·50

1988. 500th Birth Anniv of Titian (artist). As T **183a** of St. Vincent. Multicoloured.
1156 1l. "The Concert" (detail) 10 10
1157 2l. "Philip II of Spain" . . 15 15
1158 3l. "Saint Sebastian" (detail) 20 20
1159 5l. "Martyrdom of St. Peter Martyr" 30 30
1160 15l. "St. Jerome" 75 85
1161 20l. "St. Mark enthroned with Saints" . . . . . . 90 1·10
1162 25l. "Portrait of a Young Man" . . . . 1·10 1·40
1163 30l. "St. Jerome in Penitence" . . . . 1·25 1·50
MS1164 Two sheets, each 110×95 mm. (a) 50l. "Self Portrait". (b) 50l. "Orpheus and Eurydice" Set of 2 sheets . . . 4·00 4·50

218 Sikorsky S-58 Helicopter lowering "Mercury" Capsule to Flight Deck

1988. 25th Death Anniv of John F. Kennedy (American statesman). U.S. Space Achievements. Multicoloured.
1165 3l. Type **218** 75 25
1166 5l. "Liberty Bell 7" capsule descending (vert) 75 20
1167 15l. Launch of first manned American capsule (vert) 90 70
1168 40l. "Freedom 7" orbiting Earth . . . . 1·75 2·00
MS1169 98×69 mm. 65l. President Kennedy and quotation . . . 1·90 2·25

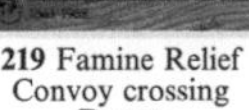

219 Famine Relief Convoy crossing Desert

220 "Adoration of the Magi" (detail)

219a Donald Duck's Nephews playing as Band

1988. 125th Anniv of Int Red Cross. Mult.
1170 3l. Type **219** 70 40
1171 10l. Rifle and map of Battle of Solferino, 1859 . . . . 2·25 90
1172 20l. World War II hospital ship in Pacific . . . . . 2·75 2·00
1173 40l. Red Cross tent and World War I German biplanes . . . . 3·50 3·25
MS1174 100×70 mm. 65l. Henri Dunant (founder), Alfred Nobel and Peace Prize scroll (horiz) 2·40 3·00

1988. Christmas. "Mickey's Christmas Dance". Walt Disney cartoon characters. Multicoloured.
1175 10l. Type **219a** 70 80
1176 10l. Clarabelle 70 80
1177 10l. Goofy 70 80
1178 10l. Scrooge McDuck and Grandma Duck 70 80
1179 10l. Donald Duck 70 80
1180 10l. Daisy Duck 70 80
1181 10l. Minnie Mouse 70 80
1182 10l. Mickey Mouse 70 80
MS1183 Two sheets, each 127×102 mm. (a) 70l. Mickey Mouse dancing the Charleston. (b) 70l. Mickey Mouse jiving Set of 2 sheets . . . . 6·50 6·50
Nos. 1175/82 were printed together, se-tenant, forming a composite design.

1988. Christmas. Religious Paintings by Rubens. Multicoloured.
1184 3l. Type **220** 15 15
1185 3l.60 "Adoration of the Shepherds" (detail) . . . 15 15
1186 5l. "Adoration of the Magi" (detail) 25 25
1187 10l. "Adoration of the Shepherds" (different detail) 40 40
1188 20l. "Virgin and Child surrounded by Flowers" 75 75
1189 40l. "St. Gregory the Great and Other Saints" (detail) 1·60 1·75
1190 60l. "Adoration of the Magi" (detail) . . . . . 2·25 2·75
1191 80l. "Madonna and Child with Saints" (detail) . . . 2·75 3·25
MS1192 Two sheets, each 76×113 mm. (a) 100l. "Virgin and Child enthroned with Saints". (b) 100l. "St. Gregory the Great and Other Saints" Set of 2 sheets 6·00 9·00

1989. Steffi Graf's "Grand Slam" Tennis Victories. No. MS1076b optd **GOLD MEDALIST** (No. MS1193e) or (others), each with different inscription on sheet margin, all in gold.
MS1193 105×75 mm. 100l. Steffi Graf. (a) Optd **AUSTRALIAN OPEN JANUARY 11–24, 1988 GRAF v EVERET**. (b) Optd **FRENCH OPEN MAY 23–JUNE 5, 1988 GRAF v ZVERENA**. (c) Optd **WIMBLEDON JUNE 20–JULY 4, 1988 GRAF v NAVRATILOVA**. (d) Optd **U.S. OPEN AUGUST 29–SEPTEMBER 11, 1988 GRAF v SABATINI**. (e) Optd **SEOUL OLYMPICS 1988 GRAF v SABBATINI** Set of 5 sheets . . 16·00 15·00
Each marginal overprint includes score of match involved.
No. MS1193a overprinted "EVERET" in error for "EVERT".

222 Brazil v. Sweden, 1958

1989. World Cup Football Championship, Italy (1st issue). Designs showing action from previous World Cup finals. Multicoloured.
1194 3l. Type **222** 40 30
1195 6l. West Germany v. Hungary, 1954 . . . . 50 40
1196 8l. England v. West Germany, 1966 . . . . . 60 45
1197 10l. Argentina v. Netherlands, 1978 . . . . 70 50
1198 12l. Brazil v. Czechoslovakia, 1962 . . 75 75
1199 20l. West Germany v. Netherlands, 1974 . . . . 1·00 1·00
1200 30l. Italy v. West Germany, 1982 . . . . 1·40 1·60
1201 40l. Brazil v. Italy, 1970 . . 1·75 1·90
MS1202 Two sheets, each 73×104 mm. (a) 100l. Argentina v. West Germany, 1986. (b) 100l. Uruguay v. Brazil, 1950 Set of 2 sheets . . . . 6·75 6·75
See also Nos. 1455/74.

223 Decathlon (Gold, C. Schenk, East Germany)

1989. Olympic Medal Winners, Seoul (1988). Mult.
1203 3l. Type **223** 70 30
1204 6l. Men's heavyweight judo (Gold, H. Saito, Japan) 1·00 40
1205 10l. Women's cycle road race (Silver, J. Niehaus, West Germany) . . . . . 2·00 75
1206 15l. Men's single sculls (Gold, T. Lange, East Germany) . . . . 1·50 80
1207 20l. Men's 50 metres freestyle swimming (Gold, M. Biondi, U.S.A.) . . . 1·50 1·00
1208 30l. Men's 100 m (Gold, C. Lewis, U.S.A.) . . . . 1·50 1·50
1209 40l. Dressage (Gold, West Germany) . . . . 2·75 2·00
1210 50l. Greco-Roman wrestling (57 kg) (Gold, A. Sike, Hungary) . . . . 2·50 2·75
MS1211 Two sheets, each 70×100 mm. (a) 100l. Olympic gold medal. (b) 100l. Olympic torch and rings Set of 2 sheets 6·75 6·75

224 Map of Union States, Mail Lorry and Post Office

1989. 15th Anniv of Mano River Union. Mult.
1212 1l. Type **224** 60 40
1213 3l. Map of West Africa and Presidents Momoh, Conte and Doe . . . . 1·00 40
1214 10l. Construction of Freetown–Monrovia Highway . . . . 1·60 80
MS1215 96×68 mm. 15l. Presidents signing anniversary metting communique . . . . 1·00 1·00

225 "Richard III"

1989. 425th Birth Anniv of Shakespeare. Mult.
1216 15l. Type **225** 60 60
1217 15l. "Othello" (Iago) . . . 60 60
1218 15l. "Two Gentlemen of Verona" 60 60
1219 15l. "Macbeth" (Lady Macbeth) 60 60
1220 15l. "Hamlet" 60 60
1221 15l. "The Taming of the Shrew" 60 60
1222 15l. "The Merry Wives of Windsor" 60 60
1223 15l. "Henry IV" (Sir John Falstaff) 60 60
1224 15l. "Macbeth" (The Witches) 60 60
1225 15l. "Romeo and Juliet" . . 60 60
1226 15l. "Merchant of Venice" . 60 60
1227 15l. "As You Like It" . . . 60 60
1228 15l. "The Taming of the Shrew" (banquet scene) 60 60
1229 15l. "King Lear" 60 60
1230 15l. "Othello" (Othello and Desdemona) 60 60
1231 15l. "Henry IV" (Justice Shallow) 60 60
MS1232 Two sheets, each 117×82 mm. (a) 100l. Shakespeare and arms (49×36 mm). (b) 100l. Shakespeare (49×36 mm) Set of 2 sheets . . . . 8·00 8·50

226 Centenary Logo

1989. Cent of Ahmadiyya Muslim Society.
1233 **226** 3l. black and blue . . . 30 30

1989. Japanese Art (1st series). Paintings by Seiho. As T **188a** of St. Vincent. Multicoloured.
1234 3l. "Lapping Waves" . . . 60 35
1235 6l. "Hazy Moon" (vert) . . 70 45
1236 8l. "Passing Spring" (vert) 70 45
1237 10l. "Mackerels" 70 45
1238 12l. "Calico Cat" 70 45
1239 30l. "The First Time to be a Model" (vert) . . . . . . 2·00 80
1240 40l. "Kingly Lion" . . . . 2·25 1·25
1241 75l. "After a Shower" (vert) 2·75 2·00
MS1242 Two sheets, each 102×77 mm. (a) 150l. "Dozing in the midst of all the Chirping" (Detail) (vert). (b) 150l. "Domesticated Monkeys and Rabbits" (detail) Set of 2 sheets 8·50 8·50
See also Nos. 1321/50.

227 Robespierre and Bastille

1989. "Philexfrance '89" International Stamp Exhibition, Paris and Bicentenary of French Revolution. Multicoloured.
1243 6l. Type **227** 45 35
1244 20l. Danton and Louvre . . 90 80
1245 45l. Queen Marie Antoinette and Notre Dame . . . . 1·40 1·25
1246 80l. Louis XVI and Palace of Versailles . . . . . . 2·00 2·75
MS1247 77×107 mm. 150l. Celebrating crowd, Paris (vert) 3·25 4·00

228 Sputnik Satellite in Orbit, 1957

1989. History of Space Exploration. As T **228**. Multicoloured.
1248/1301 10l.×27, 15l.×27 Set of 54 . . . . . 22·00 23·00
MS1302 Three sheets, each 112×90 mm. 100l.×3 Set of 3 sheets . . . . 12·00 13·00

229 "Bulbophyllum barbigerum"

1989. Orchids of Sierra Leone. Multicoloured.
1303 3l. Type **229** 55 40
1304 6l. "Bulbophyllum falcatum" 85 60
1305 12l. "Habenaria macrara" 1·25 90
1306 20l. "Eurychone rothchildiana" . . . . . 1·60 1·40
1307 50l. "Calyptrochilum christyanum" . . . . . . 2·25 2·25
1308 60l. "Bulbophyllum distans" 2·50 2·75
1309 70l. "Eulophia guineensis" 2·50 2·75
1310 80l. "Diaphananthe pellucida" . . . . 2·75 3·25
MS1311 Two sheets, each 112×80 mm. (a) 100l. "Cyrtorchis arcuata" and Pagoda, Kew Gardens. (b) 100l. "Eulophia cucullata" Set of 2 sheets . . . 17·00 17·00

230 "Salamis temora"

1989. Butterflies. Multicoloured.
1312 6l. Type **230** 85 75
1313 12l. "Pseudacraea lucretia" 1·25 1·10
1314 18l. "Charaxes boueti" (vert) . . . . 1·60 1·40
1315 30l. "Graphium antheus" (vert) . . . . 2·25 2·00
1316 40l. "Colotis protomedia" 2·50 2·25
1317 60l. "Asterope pechueli" (vert) . . . . 3·00 2·75
1318 72l. "Coenyra aurantiaca" 3·25 3·00
1319 80l. "Precis octavia" (vert) 3·25 3·00
MS1320 Two sheets, each 100×70 mm. (a) 100l. "Charaxes cithaeron" (vert). (b) 100l. "Euphaedra themis" Set of 2 sheets . . . . 14·00 14·00

1989. Japanese Art (2nd series). Paintings by Hiroshige of "The Fifty-three Stations on the Tokaido Road". As T **188a** of St. Vincent. Mult.
1321 25l. "Ferry-boat to Kawasaki" 80 80
1322 25l. "The Hilly Town of Hodogaya" 80 80
1323 25l. "Lute Players at Fujisawa" 80 80
1324 25l. "Mild Rainstorm at Oiso" 80 80
1325 25l. "Lake Ashi and Mountains of Hakone" 80 80
1326 25l. "Twilight at Numazu" 80 80
1327 25l. "Mount Fuji from Hara" 80 80
1328 25l. "Samurai Children riding through Yoshiwara" 80 80
1329 25l. "Mountain Pass at Yui" 80 80
1330 25l. "Harbour at Ejiri" . . 80 80
1331 25l. "Halt at Fujieda" . . . 80 80
1332 25l. "Misty Kanaya on the Oi River" 80 80
1333 25l. "The Bridge to Kakegawa" 80 80
1334 25l. "Teahouse at Fukuroi" 80 80
1335 25l. "The Ford at Mistuke" 80 80

1336 25l. "Coolies warming themselves at Hamamatsu" 80 80
1337 25l. "Imakiri Ford at Maisaka" 80 80
1338 25l. "Pacific Ocean from Shirasuka" 80 80
1339 25l. "Futakawa Street-singers" 80 80
1340 25l. "Repairing Yoshida Castle" 80 80
1341 25l. "The Inn at Akasaka" 80 80
1342 25l. "The Bridge to Okazaki" 80 80
1343 25l. "Samurai's Wife entering Narumi" 80 80
1344 25l. "Harbour at Kuwana" 80 80
1345 25l. "Autumn in Ishiyakushi" 80 80
1346 25l. "Snowfall at Kameyama" 80 80
1347 25l. "The Frontier-station of Seki" 80 80
1348 25l. "Teahouse at Sakanoshita" 80 80
1349 25l. "Kansai Houses at Minakushi" 80 80
1350 25l. "Kusatsu Station" . . . 80 80
MS1351 Two sheets, each 102 × 75 mm. (a) 120l. "Nihom Bridge, Edo". (b) 120l. "Sanjo Bridge, Kyoto" Set of 2 sheets 8·00 8·50

The English captions of the two miniature sheets of No. **MS**1351 are transposed. The sheet showing the Nihom Bridge, Edo, has a group of fishmongers in the left foreground.

231 Formosan Sika Deer

1989. "World Stamp Expo '89" International Stamp Exhibition, Washington (2nd issue). Endangered Fauna. Multicoloured.

1353 6l. Humpback whale 50 40
1354 9l. Type **231** 40 40
1355 16l. Spanish lynx 65 60
1356 20l. Goitred gazelle 60 60
1357 30l. Japanese sea lion . . . 65 65
1358 50l. Long-eared owl . . . . 1·50 1·25
1359 70l. Lady Amherst's ("Chinese Copper") pheasant . . . . 1·50 1·50
1360 100l. Siberian tiger . . . . 2·25 2·50
MS1361 Two sheets, each 103 × 75 mm. (a) 150l. Mauritius kestrel (vert). (b) 150l. Japanese crested ibis (vert) Set of 2 sheets 12·00 11·00

231a Mickey Mouse and Goofy in Rolls-Royce "Phantom II Roadstar", 1934

1989. Christmas. Walt Disney cartoon characters with cars. Multicoloured.

1362 3l. Type **231a** 50 30
1363 6l. Mickey and Minnie Mouse in Mercedes-Benz "500K", 1935 . . . . . . 70 40
1364 10l. Mickey and Minnie Mouse with Jaguar "SS-100", 1938 . . . . . 80 45
1365 12l. Mickey Mouse and Goofy with U.S. army jeep, 1941 . . . . 90 55
1366 20l. Mickey and Minnie Mouse with Buick Roadmaster Sedan "Model 91", 1937 . . . . 1·25 90
1367 30l. Mickey Mouse driving 1948 Tucker . . . . . . 1·50 1·25
1368 40l. Mickey and Minnie Mouse in Alfa Romeo, 1933 . . . . 1·60 1·40
1369 50l. Mickey and Minnie Mouse with 1937 Cord . . 1·75 1·60
MS1370 Two sheets, each 127 × 101 mm. (a) 100l. Mickey in Fiat Topolino, 1938. (b) 100l. Mickey Mouse with gifts and Pontiac "Model 401", 1931 Set of 2 sheets . . . . 6·50 7·00

1989. Christmas. Paintings by Rembrandt. As T **204a** of St. Vincent. Multicoloured.

1371 3l. "The Adoration of the Magi" 50 30
1372 6l. "The Holy Family with a Cat" 60 40
1373 10l. "The Holy Family with Angels" 70 45
1374 15l. "Simeon in the Temple" 85 55
1375 30l. "The Circumcision" . . 1·50 1·10
1376 90l. "The Holy Family" . . 3·00 3·25
1377 100l. "The Visitation" . . . 3·00 3·25
1378 120l. "The Flight into Egypt" . . . . 3·25 3·50
MS1379 Two sheets, each 70 × 95 mm. (a) 150l. "The Adoration of the Shepherds" (detail). (b) 150l. "The Presentation of Jesus in the Temple" (detail) Set of 2 sheets 8·50 8·50

232 Johann Kepler (astronomer)

1990. Exploration of Mars. Designs as T **232** showing astronomers, spacecraft and Martian landscapes.

1380/1415 175l. × 36 multicoloured Set of 36 . . . . . . 65·00 75·00
MS1416 Two sheets, each 105 × 85 mm. (a) 150l. The "Face" on Mars. (b) 150l. Section of space station Set of 2 sheets . . . . 11·00 12·00

1990. 50th Anniv of Second World War. American Aircraft. As T **206a** of St. Vincent. Multicoloured.

1417 1l. Dolittle's North American B-25 Mitchell "Ruptured Duck", 1942 30 10
1418 2l. Consolidated B-24 Liberator 40 10
1419 3l. Douglas A20J Boston attacking Japanese convoy, Bismark Sea, 1943 . . . . 40 10
1420 9l. Lockheed P-38 Lightning 60 35
1421 12l. Martin B-26 Marauder 75 40
1422 16l. Boeing B-17F Flying Fortress bombers 85 55
1423 50l. North American B-25D Mitchell bomber . . . . 2·50 1·75
1424 80l. Boeing B-29 Superfortress . . . . . . 2·75 2·50
1425 90l. Boeing B-17G Flying Fortress bomber . . . . 2·75 2·50
1426 100l. Boeing B-29 Superfortress "Enola Gay" . . . . 3·00 2·75
MS1427 Two sheets, each 106 × 77 mm. (a) 150l. North American B-25 Mitchell "Ruptured Duck" taking off from U.S.S. "Hornet" 1942. (b) 150l. Boeing B-17G Flying Fortress of 447th Bomber Group Set of 2 sheets . . . . 6·50 7·00

233 Mickey Mouse at Bauxite Mine

1990. Sierra Leone Sites and Scenes. Walt Disney cartoon characters. Multicoloured.

1428 3l. Type **233** 30 15
1429 6l. Scrooge McDuck panning for gold 30 15
1430 10l. Minnie Mouse at Lungi Airport 40 20
1431 12l. Mickey Mouse at Old Fourah Bay College . . . 40 20
1432 16l. Mickey Mouse mining bauxite 60 25
1433 20l. Huey, Dewey and Louie harvesting rice 60 30
1434 30l. Mickey and Minnie Mouse admire the Freetown Cotton Tree . . 70 40
1435 100l. Mickey Mouse flying over Rutile Mine . . . . 3·00 2·50
1436 200l. Mickey Mouse fishing at Goderich . . . . . 3·75 4·25
1437 225l. Mickey and Minnie Mouse at Bintumani Hotel . . . . 3·75 4·25
MS1438 Two sheets, each 130 × 100 mm. (a) 250l. Dwarfs with diamonds. (b) 250l. Mickey and Minnie Mouse at King Jimmy Market (vert) Set of 2 sheets 7·00 7·50

234 Olivier as Antony in "Antony and Cleopatra", 1951

235 Penny Black

1990. Sir Laurence Olivier (actor) Commem. Multicoloured.

1439 3l. Type **234** 55 20
1440 9l. As King Henry V in "Henry V", 1943 . . . . 65 30
1441 16l. As Oedipus in "Oedipus", 1945 . . . . 80 35
1442 20l. As Heathcliffe in "Wuthering Heights", 1939 . . . . 85 40
1443 30l. As Szell in "Marathon Man", 1976 . . . . . . 1·00 55
1444 70l. As Othello in "Othello", 1964 . . . . 2·25 1·40
1445 175l. As Michael in "Beau Geste", 1929 . . . . . . 3·00 3·00
1446 200l. As King Richard III in "Richard III", 1956 . . . 3·25 3·25
MS1447 Two sheets, each 98 × 68 mm. (a) 250l. As Hamlet in "Hamlet", 1947. (b) 250l. As Sir Hugh Dowding in "The Battle of Britain", 1969 Set of 2 sheets 9·00 9·00

1990. 150th Anniv of the Penny Black.

1448 **235** 50l. blue . . . . 2·25 1·50
1449 100l. brown . . . . . . 3·00 2·75
MS1450 145 × 106 mm. **235** 250l. black . . . . 4·00 4·50

236 Cameroons World Cup Team

1990. World Cup Football Championship, Italy (2nd issue). Finalists. Multicoloured.

1451/74 15l. × 8 (Type **236**, Colombia, Costa Rica, Egypt, Rumania, South Korea, U.A.E., Yugoslavia) 30l. × 8 (Austria, Belgium, Czechoslovakia, Netherlands, Scotland, Sweden, Uruguay, U.S.S.R.) 45l. × 8 (Argentina, Brazil, England, Ireland, Italy, Spain, U.S.A., West Germany) Set of 24 . . 14·00 15·00

No. 1452 is inscr "COLUMBIA" and No. 1465 "URAGUAY", both in error.

237 Great Crested Grebe

1990. Birds. Multicoloured.

1475 3l. Type **237** 20 20
1476 6l. Green wood hoopoe . . 25 25
1477 10l. African jacana 30 30
1478 12l. Pied avocet ("Avocet") 35 35
1479 20l. Peter's finfoot 40 40
1480 80l. Glossy ibis . . . . . . 1·25 1·50
1481 150l. Hammerkop . . . . . 1·75 2·00
1482 200l. Black-throated honeyguide . . . . 2·00 2·50
MS1483 Two sheets, each 100 × 70 mm. (a) 250l. African palm swift. (b) 250l. Painted snipe Set of 2 sheets . . . . 7·00 8·00

1990. "Stamp World London '90" International Stamp Exhibition. British Costumes. As T **207a** of St. Vincent showing Walt Disney cartoon characters. Multicoloured.

1484 3l. Mickey Mouse as a Yeoman Warder 20 15
1485 6l. Scrooge McDuck as a lamplighter 20 15
1486 12l. Goofy as a medieval knight 30 20
1487 15l. Clarabelle as Ann Boleyn 30 20
1488 75l. Minnie Mouse as Queen Elizabeth I . . . . . . 2·50 2·00
1489 100l. Donald Duck as a chimney sweep . . . . . 2·75 2·25
1490 125l. Pete as King Henry VIII . . . . 3·00 2·50
1491 150l. Clarabell, Minnie Mouse and Daisy Duck as May dancers . . . . . 3·00 2·50
MS1492 Two sheets, each 127 × 102 mm. (a) 250l. Donald Duck as a lawyer (vert). (b) 250l. Minnie Mouse as Queen Boadicea Set of 2 sheets . . . . 7·50 8·50

1990. 90th Birthday of Queen Elizabeth the Queen Mother. As T **208a** of St. Vincent. Mult.

1493 75l. Queen Mother on Remembrance Sunday . . 1·75 1·25
1494 75l. Queen Mother in yellow hat . . . . 1·75 1·25
1495 75l. Waving to crowds on 85th birthday . . . . . . 1·75 1·25
MS1496 90 × 75 mm. 250l. As No. 1495 . . . . 3·25 3·25

238 Golden Cat

1990. Wildlife. Multicoloured.

1497 25l. Type **238** 75 75
1498 25l. White-backed night heron 75 75
1499 25l. Bateleur ("Bateleur Eagle") 75 75
1500 25l. Marabou stork 75 75
1501 25l. White-faced whistling duck 75 75
1502 25l. Aardvark 75 75
1503 25l. Royal antelope 75 75
1504 25l. Pygmy hippopotamus 75 75
1505 25l. Leopard 75 75
1506 25l. Sacred ibis 75 75
1507 25l. Mona monkey 75 75
1508 25l. African darter 75 75
1509 25l. Chimpanzee 75 75
1510 25l. African elephant . . . 75 75
1511 25l. Potto 75 75
1512 25l. African manatee 75 75
1513 25l. African fish eagle . . . 75 75
1514 25l. African spoonbill . . . 75 75
MS1515 106 × 76 mm. 150l. Crowned eagle (vert) . . . . . 7·50 7·50

239 Rabbit

239a Start of Men's 100 m

1990. Fairground Carousel Animals. Mult.

1516 5l. Type **239** 15 15
1517 10l. Horse with panther saddle 20 20
1518 20l. Ostrich 30 30
1519 30l. Zebra 40 40
1520 50l. Horse 55 55
1521 80l. Sea monster 80 80
1522 100l. Giraffe . . . . 1·00 1·00
1523 150l. Armoured horse . . . 1·40 1·40
1524 200l. Camel . . . . 1·75 1·75
MS1525 Two sheets (a) 98 × 68 mm. 300l. Masked horse. (b) 68 × 98 mm. 300l. Baden-Powell as Centaur Set fo 2 sheets . . . . 8·00 9·00

1990. Olympic Games, Barcelona (1992). Mult.

1526 5l. Type **239a** 20 15
1527 10l. Men's 4 × 400 m relay 25 20
1528 20l. Men's 100 m in progress 40 30
1529 30l. Weightlifting 50 40
1530 40l. Freestyle wrestling . . . 55 45
1531 80l. Water polo 80 90
1532 150l. Women's gymnastics 1·40 1·50
1533 200l. Cycling . . . . 2·75 2·25
MS1534 Two sheets, each 103 × 75 mm. (a) 400l. Boxing (horiz). (b) 400l. Olympic flag (horiz) Set of 2 sheets . . . . 7·50 8·50

240 Morty assembling Bicycle by Christmas Tree

1990. Christmas. "The Night before Christmas". As T **240** showing Walt Disney cartoon characters in scenes from Clement Moore's poem. Multicoloured.

1535/58 50l. × 8, 75l. × 8, 100l. × 8 Set of 24 . . . . 20·00 22·00
MS1559 Six sheets, each 129 × 107mm. 400l. × 6 multicoloured Set of 6 sheets 20·00 22·00

Of the stamps in No. **MS**1559 four are horizontal and two vertical.

241 "Holy Family with St. Elizabeth" (Mantegna)

1990. Christmas. Paintings. Multicoloured.
1560 10l. "Holy Family resting" (Rembrandt) 40 15
1561 20l. Type **241** 55 20
1562 30l. "Virgin and Child with an Angel" (Correggio) . . 70 30
1563 50l. "Annunciation" (Bernardo Strozzi) 85 45
1564 100l. "Madonna and Child appearing to St. Anthony" (Lippi) . . 2·00 80
1565 175l. "Virgin and Child" (Giovanni Boltraffio) . . 3·00 3·25
1566 200l. "Esterhazy Madonna" (Raphael) . . . . . . 3·25 3·25
1567 300l. "Coronation of Mary" (Andrea Orcagna) . . . . 3·75 4·25
MS1568 Two sheets, each 75 × 114 mm. (a) 400l. "Adoration of the Shepherds" (Bronzino). (b) 400l. "Adoration of the Shepherds" (Gerard David) Set of 2 sheets . . . . 9·00 9·50

241a Helena Fourment as "Hagar in the Wilderness" (detail)

242 "Chlorophyllum molybdites"

1990. 350th Death Anniv of Rubens (1st issue). Multicoloured.
1569 5l. Type **241a** 15 10
1570 10l. "Isabella Brant" . . . 20 15
1571 20l. "Countess of Arundel and her Party" (detail) . . 30 20
1572 60l. "Countess of Arundel and her Party" (different detail) 70 70
1573 80l. "Nicolaas Rockox" . . 90 90
1574 100l. "Adriana Perez" . . . 1·00 1·00
1575 150l. "George Villiers, Duke of Buckingham" (detail) 1·75 2·00
1576 300l. "Countess of Buckingham" . . . . . . 2·50 2·75
MS1577 Two sheets, each 71 × 100 mm. (a) 350l. "Giovanni Carlo Dorio" (detail). (b) 350l. "Veronica Spinola Dorio" (detail) Set of 2 sheets . . . . 8·00 8·50
See also Nos. 1595/602.

1990. Fungi. Multicoloured.
1578 3l. Type **242** 30 15
1579 5l. "Lepista nuda" 30 15
1580 10l. "Clitocybe nebularis" 40 20
1581 15l. "Cyathus striatus" . . . 50 30
1582 20l. "Bolbitius vitellinus" . . 55 35
1583 25l. "Leucoagaricus naucinus" 55 40
1584 30l. "Suillus luteus" 60 45
1585 40l. "Podaxis pistillaris" . . 70 55
1586 50l. "Oudemansiella radicata" 80 60
1587 60l. "Phallus indusiatus" . . 90 70
1588 80l. "Macrolepiota rhacodes" . . . . 1·00 1·10
1589 100l. "Mycena pura" . . . . 1·25 1·25
1590 150l. "Volvariella volvacea" 1·60 1·75
1591 175l. "Omphalotus olearius" 1·90 2·25
1592 200l. "Sphaerobolus stellatus" . . . . 2·00 2·50
1593 250l. "Schizophyllum commune" . . . . 2·25 2·75
MS1594 Four sheets, each 101 × 70 mm. (a) 350l. "Hypholoma fasciculare" (b) 350l. "Psilocybe coprophila" (c) 350l. "Agaricus campestris" (d) 350l. "Suillus granulatus" Set of 4 sheets . . . . 15·00 15·00

243 "The Flight of St. Barbara" (detail) (Rubens)

1991. Easter. 350th Death Anniv (1990) of Rubens (2nd issue). Multicoloured.
1595 10l. Type **243** 50 15
1596 20l. "The Last Judgement" (detail) 65 20
1597 30l. "St. Gregory of Nazianzus" 75 30
1598 50l. "Doubting Thomas" . . 1·00 45
1599 80l. "The Way to Calvary" (detail) . . . . 1·90 1·10
1600 100l. "St. Gregory with Sts. Domitilla, Maurus and Papianus" . . . . 2·00 1·25
1601 175l. "Sts. Gregory, Maurus and Papianus" . . . . . 3·25 3·50
1602 300l. "Christ and the Penitent Sinners" . . . . 4·50 6·00
MS1603 Two sheets, each 70 × 101 mm. (a) 400l. "The Last Judgement" (different detail). (b) 400l. "The Way to Calvary" (different detail) Set of 2 sheets 8·50 9·00

244 Krauss Class 1400 Steam Locomotive, 1895

1991. "Phila Nippon '91" International Stamp Exhibition, Tokyo. Japanese Trains. Mult.
1604 10l. Type **244** 35 20
1605 20l. Class C55 streamline steam locomotive, 1935 50 25
1606 30l. Class ED17 electric locomotive, 1931 . . . . 70 40
1607 60l. Class EF13 electric locomotive, 1944 . . . . 1·00 85
1608 100l. Baldwin Mikado steam locomotive, 1897 . . . . 1·25 1·25
1609 150l. Class C62 steam locomotive, 1948 . . . . 1·75 2·00
1610 200l. Class Kiha 81 diesel multiple unit, 1960 . . . 2·00 2·25
1611 300l. Schenectady Class 8550 steam locomotive, 1899 . . . . 2·25 2·75
MS1612 Four sheets, each 106 × 76 mm. (a) 400l. Class 9600 steam locomotive, 1913. (b) 400l. Class D51 steam locomotive, 1936. (c) 400l. Class 7000 electric multiple unit. (d) 400l. "Hikari" express train Set of 4 sheets . . 15·00 15·00

245 Turquoise Killifish

1991. Fishes. Multicoloured.
1613 10l. Type **245** 45 20
1614 20l. Red-chinned panchax 65 25
1615 30l. Peters' killifish 80 40
1616 60l. Micro-walkeri killifish 1·40 90
1617 100l. Freshwater butterflyfish . . . . . . 1·60 1·25
1618 150l. Green panchax . . . . 2·00 2·25
1619 200l. Six-banded lyretail . . 2·25 2·50
1620 300l. Nile pufferfish . . . . 2·25 2·50
MS1621 Two sheets, each 96 × 70 mm. (a) 400l. Spot-finned squeaker. (b) 400l. Two-striped panchax Set of 2 sheets . . . . 8·50 8·50

1991. Death Centenary of Vincent van Gogh (artist). As T **215a** of St. Vincent. Multicoloured.
1622 10c. "The Langlois Bridge at Arles" (horiz) 10 10
1623 50c. "Tree in Garden at Saint-Paul Hospital" . . . 10 10
1624 1l. "Wild Flowers and Thistles in a Vase" . . . 10 10
1625 2l. "Still Life: Vase with Oleanders and Books" (horiz) 10 10
1626 5l. "Farmhouses in a Wheatfield near Arles" (horiz) 15 10
1627 10l. "Self-portrait, September 1889" 25 15
1628 20l. "Patience Escalier" . . 45 20
1629 30l. "Doctor Felix Rey" . . 60 30
1630 50l. "The Iris" 90 45
1631 60l. "The Shepherdess" . . 1·00 65
1632 80l. "Vincent's House in Arles" (horiz) . . . . . . 1·40 1·00
1633 100l. "The Road Menders" (horiz) . . . . 1·60 1·10
1634 150l. "The Garden of Saint-Paul Hospital" . . . . . 2·75 3·00
1635 200l. "View of the Church, Saint-Paul-de-Mausole" (horiz) . . . . 3·00 3·25
1636 250l. "Seascape at Saintes-Maries" (horiz) . . . . . 3·25 3·50
1637 300l. "Pieta" . . . . 3·25 3·50
MS1638 Six sheets. (a) 102 × 76 mm. 400l. "Haystacks in Provence" (96 × 70 mm). (b) 102 × 76 mm. 400l. "The Trinquetaille Bridge" (96 × 70 mm). (c) 102 × 76 mm. 400l. "Vineyards with a View of Auvers" (96 × 70 mm). (d) 102 × 76 mm. 400l. "The Garden of Saint-Paul Hospital" (96 × 107 mm). (e) 76 × 102 mm. 400l. "Church at Auvers-sur-Dise" (70 × 96 mm). (f) 76 × 102 mm. 400l. "Two Poplars on a Road through the Hills" (70 × 96 mm). Imperf Set of 6 sheets . . . . 16·00 16·00

1991. 65th Birthday of Queen Elizabeth II. As T **220b** of St. Vincent. Multicoloured.
1639 10l. The Queen and Prince Charles at polo match . . 15 10
1640 30l. The Queen at Windsor, 1989 . . . . 20 20
1641 200l. The Queen and Princess Diana in Nigeria, 1989 . . . . 1·75 2·00
1642 250l. The Queen and Prince Philip . . . . 2·00 2·50
MS1643 68 × 90 mm. 400l. Separate photographs of the Queen and Prince Philip in 1987 and 1988 4·25 3·75

1991. 10th Wedding Anniv of Prince and Princess of Wales. As T **220b** of St. Vincent. Mult.
1644 20l. Prince and Princess of Wales in August, 1987 . . 80 15
1645 80l. Separate photographs of Prince, Princess and sons 2·00 85
1646 100l. Prince Henry in Majorca and Prince William on his first day at school . . . . 1·75 95
1647 300l. Prince Charles at Caister, April, 1988 and Princess Diana in Hyde Park, May, 1989 . . . . 4·25 4·00
MS1648 68 × 90 mm. 400l. Prince, Princess and Prince Henry in Majorca and Prince William going to school . . . . 5·00 4·50

246 "Graphium latreillianus" and "Ancistrochilus rothschildianus"

1991. Butterflies and Flowers. Multicoloured.
1649 10l. Type **246** 75 30
1650 30l. "Euphraedra eleus" and "Clitoria ternatea" . . . 1·25 45
1651 50l. "Graphium antheus" and "Gloriosa simplex" 1·50 60
1652 60l. "Salamis cacta" and "Stenandriopsis guineensis" . . . . 1·75 85
1653 80l. "Kallima rumia" and "Cassia fistula" . . . . . 2·25 1·25
1654 100l. "Hypolimnas salmacis" and "Amorphophallus abyssinicus" . . . . 2·25 1·50
1655 200l. "Danaus formosa" and "Nephthytis afzelii" . . . 3·75 3·75
1656 300l. "Graphium leonidas" and "Clappertonia ficifolia" . . . . 4·50 5·00
MS1657 Four sheets, each 102 × 74 mm. (a) 400l. "Charaxes cynthia" and "Plumbago auriculata" (b) 400l. "Colias electo" and "Combretum grandiflorum" (c) 400l. "Cynandra opis" and "Bombax costatum" (d) 400l. "Eurema brigitta" and "Monodora myristica" Set of 4 sheets . . . . 14·00 14·00

1991. Butterflies. As Nos. 1028/42 but "Sierra Leone" in blue. Multicoloured.
1658 10c. "Danaus limniace" . . 7·50 40
1660 50c. "Graphium ridleyanus" 7·50 30
1661 1l. "Papilio bromius" . . . 7·50 30
1662 2l. "Iterus ("Papilio") zalmoxis" . . . . 7·50 30
1663 5l. "Graphium tynderaeus" — 30
1665 10l. "Graphium policenes" 7·50 30
1666 20l. "Tanuetheira ("Iolaus") timon" . . . . — 40
1667 30l. "Cymothoe sangaris" — 50
1668 50l. Type **205** . . . . . . 7·50 55
1669 60l. "Charaxes lucretius" . . 7·50 70
1670 80l. "Stugeta ("Iolaus") marmorea" . . . . 14·00 1·00
1671 100l. "Abisara talantus" . . — 1·00
1672 300l. "Papilio hesperus" . . 14·00 2·50

247 Audie Murphy in "To Hell and Back"

1991. Films of Second World War. Mult.
1675 2l. Type **247** 15 10
1676 5l. Jack Palance in "Attack" 20 15
1677 10l. Greer Garson and Walter Pidgeon in "Mrs. Miniver" 20 20
1678 20l. Heavy artillery from "The Guns of Navarone" 40 30
1679 30l. Charlie Chaplin and Paulette Goddard in "The Great Dictator" 75 40
1680 50l. Steam locomotive from "The Train" 80 60
1681 60l. Diary and fountain pen from "The Diary of Anne Frank" 90 70
1682 80l. William Holden in "The Bridge on the River Kwai" . . . . 1·25 90
1683 100l. Tallulah Bankhead in "Lifeboat" and Alfred Hitchcock (director) . . . 1·25 1·00
1684 200l. John Wayne in "Sands of Iwo Jima" . . . . . . 2·25 2·25
1685 300l. Van Johnson and Spencer Tracy in "Thirty Seconds over Tokyo" . . 3·00 3·25
1686 350l. Humphrey Bogart and Ingrid Bergman in "Casablanca" . . . . . . 3·25 3·50
MS1687 Three sheets, each 116 × 76 mm. (a) 450l. George C. Scott in "Patton". (b) 450l. Gregory Peck in "Twelve O'clock High". (c) 450l. Burning American cruiser from "Tora! Tora! Tora!" Set of 3 sheets . . . . 11·00 11·00

248 Meissen China Parrot Ornament, Munich Botanic Garden

248a "Mary being Crowned by Two Angels"

1991. Botanical Gardens of the World. Multicoloured.
1688/1735 60l. × 48 Type **248** Set of 48 . . . . . . 24·00 25·00
MS1736 Three sheets, each 97 × 69 mm. (a) 600l. Munich Botanic Garden. (b) 600l. Kyoto Botanic Garden. (c) 600l. Brooklyn Botanic Garden Set of 3 sheets . . . . 12·00 13·00
Issued in 3 sheetlets of 16 stamps, depicting features and plants from Munich (Nos. 1688/1703), Kyoto (Nos. 1704/19) and Brooklyn (Nos. 1720/35).
The single designs in the three miniature sheets of No. **MS**1736 are horiz.

1991. Christmas. Drawings and Paintings by Albrecht Durer.
1737 **248a** 6l. black and mauve . . 15 10
1738 – 60l. black and blue . . 35 30
1739 – 80l. multicoloured . . . 45 40
1740 – 100l. multicoloured . . 65 65
1741 – 200l. multicoloured . . 1·60 1·60
1742 – 300l. multicoloured . . 2·00 2·00
1743 – 700l. multicoloured . . 4·75 5·50
MS1744 Two sheets, each 102 × 127 mm. (a) 600l. multicoloured. (b) 600l. multicoloured Set of 2 sheets 7·50 7·50
DESIGNS: 60l. "St. Christopher"; 80l. "Virgin and Child with St. Anne" (detail); 100l. "Virgin with the Pear" (detail); 200l. "Madonna and Child" (detail); 300l. "The Virgin in Half-Length" (detail); 700l. "The Madonna with the Siskin" (detail); 600l. (No. **MS**1744a) "Virgin and Child with St. Anne"; 600l. (No. **MS**1744b) "The Feast of the Rose Garlands" (detail).

249 National Theatre, Prague

1991. Anniversaries and Events. Multicoloured.
1745 50l. Type **249** 50 20
1746 100l. St. Peter's Abbey, Salzburg 70 35

1747	250l. Sea Scouts learning sailing	1·00	1·00
1748	300l. Sierra Leone scouts emblem and Lord Baden-Powell	1·00	1·00
1749	400l. Scouts playing baseball at Mt. Sorak Jamboree	1·40	1·40
1750	500l. Scene from "Idomeneo"	2·75	3·00
MS1751	Two sheets. (a) 75 × 105 mm. 600l. Bust of Mozart (vert). (b) 89 × 117 mm. 750l. 17th World Scout Jamboree emblem (vert) Set of 2 sheets	10·00	10·00

ANNIVERSARIES AND EVENTS: Nos. 1745/6, 1750, Death bicentenary of Mozart; 1747/9, 50th death anniv of Lord Baden-Powell and World Scout Jamboree, Korea.

250 Aichi D3A "Val" Dive Bomber

1991. 50th Anniv of Japanese Attack on Pearl Harbor. Multicoloured.

1752	75l. Type **250**	55	55
1753	75l. Japanese Aichi D3A "Val" dive bomber and smoke	55	55
1754	75l. Battleship Row burning	55	55
1755	75l. Planes and burning dockyard	55	55
1756	75l. Burning installations	55	55
1757	75l. Two Japanese Aichi D3A "Val" dive bombers	55	55
1758	75l. Burning ships and hangars	55	55
1759	75l. Airfield under attack	55	55
1760	75l. American Curtiss P-40C fighter	55	55
1761	75l. Japanese Mitsubishi A6M Zero-Sen fighter-bombers	55	55
1762	75l. Japanese Mitsubishi A6M Zero-Sen fighter-bombers over suburb	55	55
1763	75l. Japanese Nakajima B5N "Kate" bombers attacking ships	55	55
1764	75l. Japanese Nakajima B5N "Kate" aircraft on fire	55	55
1765	75l. Japanese Nakajima B5N "Kate" bombers over jungle	55	55
1766	75l. Mitsubishi A6M Zero-Sen fighters	55	55

1991. Christmas. Walt Disney Christmas Cards. As T **228** of St. Vincent. Multicoloured.

1767	12l. Mickey Mouse, Donald Duck and characters from "Peter Pan", 1952 (horiz)	30	10
1768	30l. Disney characters reading "Alice in Wonderland", 1950 (horiz)	40	10
1769	60l. Sleepy and animals, 1938 (horiz)	60	25
1770	75l. Mickey, Minnie, Donald and Pluto posting card, 1936 (horiz)	70	30
1771	100l. Disney cartoon characters, 1984 (horiz)	95	45
1772	125l. Mickey and Donald singing carols with Donald's nephews and Pluto reading, 1954 (horiz)	1·25	90
1773	150l. "101 Dalmatians", 1960 (horiz)	1·40	1·10
1774	200l. Mickey and Donald opening presents, 1948 (horiz)	1·75	1·40
1775	300l. Mickey, Minnie, Morte and Ferdie decorating tree, 1983 (horiz)	2·25	2·25
1776	400l. Donald decorating tree and nephews watching television, 1956 (horiz)	2·50	2·75
1777	500l. Characters from Disney films, 1972 (horiz)	2·50	2·75
1778	600l. Mickey, Donald, Pluto and friends singing, 1964 (horiz)	2·50	3·00
MS1779	Three sheets, each 128 × 102 mm. (a) 900l. Mad Hatter's tea party, 1950; (b) 900l. Disneyland, 1955. (c) 900l. Seven Dwarfs in toboggan, 1959 Set of 3 sheets	12·00	13·00

250a Minnie Mouse as Chiquita with Pluto, Cuba

1992. Mickey's World Tour. Walt Disney cartoon characters in different countries. Multicoloured.

1780	6l. Type **250a**	20	10
1781	10l. Goofy as Olympic discus champion, Greece	20	10
1782	20l. Donald and Daisy Duck as flamenco dancers, Spain	30	15
1783	30l. Goofy and Donald as guardsman, England	40	15
1784	50l. Mickey and Minnie at Paris fashion show, France	50	25
1785	100l. Goofy in the Alps, Switzerland	80	50
1786	200l. Daisy and Minnie in grass skirts, Hawaii	1·50	1·75
1787	350l. Mickey, Donald and Goofy as ancient Egyptians (horiz)	2·00	2·25
1788	500l. Daisy and Minnie as cancan dancers, France (horiz)	2·25	2·50
MS1789	Three sheets, each 83 × 105 mm. (a) 700l. Mickey playing bagpipes, Scotland. (b) 700l. Donald the gondolier, Italy. (c) 700l. Mickey and Goofy smashing plates, Greece Set of 3 sheets	12·00	13·00

1992. 40th Anniv of Queen Elizabeth II's Accession. As T **229a** of St. Vincent. Mult.

1790	60l. State House	80	20
1791	100l. Beach	1·40	40
1792	300l. Parliament Building	3·00	2·50
1793	400l. Canoe on beach	3·00	3·00
MS1794	Two sheets, each 75 × 97 mm. (a) 700l. Jungle hillside. (b) 700l. Freetown Set of 2 sheets	11·00	12·00

250b "Visit of St. Thomas Aquinas to St. Bonaventure"

1992. "Granada '92" International Stamp Exhibition, Spain. Paintings by Francisco Zurbaran. Multicoloured.

1795	1l. Type **250b**	10	10
1796	10l. "St. Gregory"	15	10
1797	30l. "St. Andrew"	30	20
1798	50l. "St. Gabriel the Archangel"	40	30
1799	60l. "The Blessed Henry Suso"	40	30
1800	100l. "St. Lucy"	65	40
1801	300l. "St. Casilda"	1·75	1·25
1802	400l. "St. Margaret of Antioch"	2·00	1·75
1803	500l. "St. Apollonia"	2·25	2·25
1804	600l. "St. Bonaventure at Council of Lyons"	2·50	2·75
1805	700l. "St. Bonaventure on his Bier"	2·75	3·00
1806	800l. "The Martyrdom of St. James" (detail)	3·00	3·25
MS1807	Three sheets. (a) 95 × 112 mm. 900l. "The Martyrdom of St. James". (b) 95 × 112 mm. 900l. "The Young Virgin". (c) 112 × 95 mm. 900l. "St. Hugh in the Refectory". Imperf Set of 3 sheets	9·50	10·00

250c Rhamphorhynchus

251 Greater Flamingo

1992. Prehistoric Animals. Multicoloured.

1808	50l. Type **250c**	60	60
1809	50l. Pteranodon	60	60
1810	50l. Dimorphodon	60	60
1811	50l. Pterodactyl	60	60
1812	50l. Archaeopteryx	60	60
1813	50l. Iguanodon	60	60
1814	50l. Hypsilophodon	60	60
1815	50l. Nothosaurus	60	60
1816	50l. Brachiosaurus	60	60
1817	50l. Kentrosaurus	60	60
1818	50l. Plesiosaurus	60	60
1819	50l. Trachodon	60	60
1820	50l. Hesperornis	60	60
1821	50l. Henodus	60	60
1822	50l. Steneosaurus	60	60
1823	50l. Stenopterygius	60	60
1824	50l. Eurhinosaurus	60	60
1825	50l. Placodus	60	60
1826	50l. Mosasaurus	60	60
1827	50l. Mixosaurus	60	60
MS1828	106 × 76 mm. No. 1820	1·75	2·00

Nos. 1808/27 were printed together, se-tenant, forming a composite design.

No. 1811 is inscribed "Pteradactyl" and No. 1826 "Mosasaurs", both in error.

1992. Birds. Multicoloured.

1829	30l. Type **251**	60	50
1830	50l. African white-crested hornbill ("White-crested Hornbill")	75	50
1831	100l. Crested touraco ("Verreaux's Touraco")	1·40	65
1832	170l. Yellow-spotted barbet	2·00	1·25
1833	200l. African spoonbill	2·25	1·25
1834	250l. Saddle-bill stork	2·25	1·50
1835	300l. Red-faced lovebird ("Red Headed Lovebird")	2·50	2·50
1836	600l. Yellow-billed barbet	4·75	7·00
MS1837	Two sheets, each 72 × 101 mm. (a) 1000l. Fire-bellied woodpecker. (b) 1000l. Swallow-tailed bee eater Set of 2 sheets	10·00	10·00

251a Marathon

1992. Olympic Games, Albertville and Barcelona. Multicoloured.

1838	10l. Type **251a**	25	20
1839	20l. Men's parallel bars	30	25
1840	30l. Men's discus	30	25
1841	50l. Men's 110 m hurdles (horiz)	40	30
1842	60l. Women's long jump	40	30
1843	100l. Men's floor exercise (horiz)	55	45
1844	200l. Windsurfing	1·00	80
1845	250l. Women's biathlon	1·25	1·00
1846	300l. Cycle road race	4·50	2·75
1847	400l. Weightlifting	3·00	3·25
1848	500l. Men's speed skating	3·50	3·50
1849	600l. Men's downhill skiing (horiz)	4·50	5·00
MS1850	Three sheets, each 102 × 71 mm. (a) 900l. Football (horiz). (b) 900l. Men's single luge (horiz). (c) 900l. Pairs ice dancing Set of 3 sheets	13·00	14·00

252 Minnie Mouse and Chip decorating Christmas Tree

1992. Christmas. Walt Disney cartoon characters. Multicoloured.

1851	10l. Type **252**	20	10
1852	20l. Goofy as Father Christmas	30	10
1853	30l. Daisy Duck and Minnie decorating Christmas tree	30	10
1854	50l. Mickey Mouse, and Goofy lighting candle	45	20
1855	80l. Big Pete as Father Christmas	70	40
1856	100l. Donald Duck as Father Christmas	75	40
1857	150l. Morty and Ferdie decorating cake	1·50	1·25
1858	200l. Mickey and bauble	1·60	1·40
1859	300l. Goofy and toy Father Christmas	1·90	1·75
1860	500l. Chip and Dale with sledge	2·50	2·50
1861	600l. Donald and Dale with musical instruments	2·50	3·00
1862	800l. Huey, Dewey and Louie making patterns in snow	3·00	4·00
MS1863	Three sheets, each 128 × 102 mm. (a) 900l. Mickey as Father Christmas. (b) 900l. Chip and Christmas tree fairy (horiz). (c) 900l. Mickey and Minnie (horiz) Set of 3 sheets	13·00	14·00

253 Toy Pennsylvania Railroad GG-1 Electric Locomotive No. 6-18306, 1992

254 African Pygmy Goose ("Pigmy Goose")

1992. "Genova '92" International Thematic Stamp Exhibition. Toy Trains. Designs showing electric locomotives and rolling stock manufactured by Lionel. Multicoloured.

1864	150l. Type **253**	1·25	1·25
1865	150l. Wabash Railroad Hudson locomotive No. 8610, 1985	1·25	1·25
1866	150l. Locomotive No. 1911, 1911	1·25	1·25
1867	150l. Chesapeake & Ohio locomotive No. 6-18627, 1992	1·25	1·25
1868	150l. Gang car No. 50, 1954	1·25	1·25
1869	150l. Rock Island & Peoria locomotive No. 8004, 1980	1·25	1·25
1870	150l. Western Maryland Railroad Shay locomotive No. 6-18023, 1992	1·25	1·25
1871	150l. Boston & Albany Railroad Hudson locomotive No. 784, 1986	1·25	1·25
1872	150l. Locomotive No. 6, 1906	1·25	1·25
1873	170l. Special F-3 diesel locomotive, 1947	1·25	1·25
1874	170l. Pennsylvania Railroad diesel switcher locomotive No, 6-18905, 1992	1·25	1·25
1875	170l. No. 1 Trolley, 1913	1·25	1·25
1876	170l. Seaboard Railroad diesel freight locomotive No. 602, 11008	1·25	1·25
1877	170l. Pennsylvania Railroad S-2 turbine locomotive, 1991	1·25	1·25
1878	170l. Western Pacific GP-9 diesel locomotive No. 6-18822, 1992	1·25	1·25
1879	170l. Locomotive No. 10, 1929	1·25	1·25
1880	170l. Locomotive No. 400E, 1931	1·25	1·25
1881	170l. Locomotive No. 384E, 1928	1·25	1·25
1882	170l. Pennsylvania Railroad "Torpedo" locomotive No. 238EW, 1936	1·25	1·25
1883	170l. Denver & Rio Grande Western Type PA diesel locomotive, 1992	1·25	1·25
1884	170l. Locomotive No. 408E, 1930	1·25	1·25
1885	170l. Mickey Mouse 60th Birthday boxcar No. 19241, 1991	1·25	1·25
1886	170l. Polished brass locomotive No. 54, 1913	1·25	1·25
1887	170l. Pennsylvania Railroad "Broadway Limited" locomotive No. 392E, 1936	1·25	1·25
1888	170l. Great Northern Railroad EP-5 electric locomotive No. 18302, 1988	1·25	1·25
1889	170l. Locomotive No. 6, 1918	1·25	1·25
1890	170l. Locomotive No. 400E, 1933	1·25	1·25
MS1891	Three sheets, each 119 × 90 mm. (a) 1000l. Joshua Lionel Cowen commemorative locomotive (50 × 37 mm). (b) 1000l. Trolley No. 300 (50 × 37 mm). (c) 1000l. Locomotive No. 381E, 1928 (50 × 37 mm) Set of 3 sheets	15·00	15·00

Nos. 1874 and 1877 are inscribed "Pennsylvannia" in error.

1992. Birds. Multicoloured.

1892B	50c. Type **254**	25	10
1893A	1l. Spotted eagle owl	70	50
1894A	2l. Crested touraco ("Verraux's Toucan")	70	50
1895A	5l. Saddle-bill stork	70	50
1896A	10l. African golden oriole	70	50
1897A	20l. Malachite kingfisher	1·00	50
1898A	30l. Red-crowned bishop ("Fire-crowned Bishop")	1·00	50
1899A	40l. Fire-bellied woodpecker	1·00	50
1900B	50l. Red-billed fire finch	10	10
1901A	80l. Blue flycatcher ("Blue Fairy Flycatcher")	1·00	50
1902B	100l. Crested malimbe	10	10
1903B	150l. Vitelline masked weaver	1·50	30
1904A	170l. Great blue turaco ("Blue Plantain-eater")	1·50	40
1905B	200l. Superb sunbird	10	15
1906B	250l. Swallow-tailed bee eater	10	15
1907B	300l. Cabanis's yellow bunting ("Cabanis's Yellow Bunting")	15	20
1908B	500l. Egyptian plover ("Crocodile Bird")	20	25
1909A	750l. White-faced scops owl ("White-faced Owl")	35	40

1910B 1000l. African blue cuckoo shrike (Blue Cuckoo-shrike") . . . 45 50
1911B 2000l. White-necked bald crow ("Bare-headed Rock fowl") 90 95
1912B 3000l. African red-tailed buzzard ("Red-tailed Buzzard") . . . . . . 1·30 1·40
1913A 4000l. Grey-headed bush shrike . . . . 1·80 1·90
1914A 5000l. Black-backed puffback . . . . 2·20 2·30
1915A 6000l. Burchell's gonolek ("Crimson-breasted Shrike) . . . . 2·75 3·00
1915Ac 10000l. Northern shrike 4·50 4·75

1992. Christmas. Religious Paintings. As T **241a** of St. Vincent. Multicoloured.
1916 1l. "Virgin and Child" (Fiorenzo di Lorenzo) . . 10 10
1917 10l. "Madonna and Child on a Wall" (School of Bouts) 15 15
1918 20l. "Virgin and Child with the Flight into Egypt" (Master of Hoogstraeten) 25 20
1919 30l. "Madonna and Child before Firescreen" (Robert Campin) 30 20
1920 50l. "Mary in a Rosegarden" (detail) (Hans Memling) 50 25
1921 100l. "Virgin Mary and Child" (Lucas Cranach the Elder) 90 45
1922 170l. "Virgin and Child" (Rogier van der Weyden) 1·60 1·25
1923 200l. "Madonna and Saints" (detail) (Perugino) . . . . 1·75 1·25
1924 250l. "Madonna Enthroned with Sts. Catherine and Barbara" (Master of Hoogstraeten) . . . . . 1·90 1·25
1925 300l. "The Virgin in a Rose Arbour" (Stefan Lochner) 2·25 1·75
1926 500l. "Madonna with Child and Angels" (Botticelli) 3·50 3·75
1927 1000l. "Madonna and Child with young St. John the Baptist" (Fra Bartolommeo) . . . . . 6·00 7·50
MS1928 Three sheets, each 76 × 102 mm. (a) 900l. "Virgin and Child" (detail) (Jan Gossaert). (b) 900l. "Virgin and Child (detail) (Lucas Cranach the Younger). (c) 900l. "The Virgin with the Green Cushion" (detail) (Anrea Solario) Set of 3 sheets . . . . 14·00 14·00

255 Mickey Mouse and Sousaphone (magazine cover, 1936)

1992. Mickey Mouse in Literature. Designs showing Walt Disney cartoon characters on magazine or book covers. Multicoloured.
1929 10l. Type **255** 25 10
1930 20l. Mickey and Minnie Mouse, 1936 . . . . . . 30 10
1931 30l. Mickey and Donald Duck, 1936 . . . . 30 10
1932 40l. Mickey, Minnie and Goofy in car, 1936 . . . 30 15
1933 50l. Mickey as Ringmaster, 1937 . . . . 35 15
1934 60l. Mickey as Father Christmas, 1937 . . . . . 40 25
1935 70l. Donald and Goofy representing 1937 and 1938 . . . . 45 25
1936 150l. Mickey and Minnie steering ship, 1935 . . . . 1·25 1·10
1937 170l. Mickey and Tanglefoot the horse, 1936 . . . . . 1·40 1·10
1938 200l. Mickey tied up . . . . 1·60 1·25
1939 300l. Mickey and Goofy in Jungle . . . . 2·00 1·75
1940 400l. Mickey and Goofy on submarine . . . . 2·25 2·25
1941 500l. Mickey and Minnie singing and dancing, 1931 2·50 2·75
MS1942 Three sheets. (a) 127 × 102 mm. 900l. Mickey reading to Morty and Ferdie, 1933 (horiz). (b) 102 × 127 mm. 900l. Mickey with book, 1935 (horiz). (c) 102 × 127 mm. 900l. Mickey the hunter, 1948 Set of 3 sheets . . 12·00 13·00

256 Emblems

1993. Anniversaries and Events. Multicoloured.
1943 150l. Type **256** 70 70
1944 170l. Cow and cereal with emblems 80 90
1945 170l. Airship LZ-127 "Graf Zeppelin" . . . . 1·50 90
1946 200l. Starving child with W.H.O. emblem . . . . 1·00 1·00
1947 250l. Summit emblem and cottonwood tree . . . . 1·25 1·25
1948 250l. Lions Club emblem and World map . . . . . 1·25 1·25
1949 300l. Emblem and African elephant . . . . 3·00 2·00
1950 300l. Columbus, King Ferdinand and Queen Isabella . . . . 2·50 2·00
1951 500l. Landing in the New World . . . . 3·25 3·00
1952 600l. American space shuttle 3·50 3·75
1953 700l. Construction drawings of "Graf Zeppelin" . . . 3·75 4·00
MS1954 Three sheets. (a) 100 × 70 mm. 900l. Count Ferdinand von Zeppelin (vert). (b) 97 × 67 mm. 900l. Christopher Columbus (vert). (c) 100 × 70 mm. 900l. American astronaut on space walk Set of 3 sheets . . . . . 10·50 11·50
ANNIVERSARIES AND EVENTS: Nos. 1943/4, International Conference on Nutrition, Rome; 1945, 1953, **MS**1954a, 75th death anniv of Count Ferdinand von Zeppelin (airship pioneer); 1946, United Nations World Health Organization Projects; 1947, 1949, Earth Summit '92, Rio; 1948, 75th anniv of International Association of Lions Clubs; 1950/1, **MS**1954b, 500th anniv of discovery of America by Columbus; 1952, **MS**1954c, International Space Year.

257 Joe Louis

1993. Centenary of Modern Boxing (1st issue). World Champions. Multicoloured.
1955 200l. Type **257** . . . . . . 1·25 1·10
1956 200l. Archie Moore . . . . 1·25 1·10
1957 200l. Muhammad Ali . . . . 1·25 1·10
1958 200l. George Foreman . . . 1·25 1·10
1959 200l. Joe Frazier . . . . . 1·25 1·10
1960 200l. Marvin Hagler . . . . 1·25 1·10
1961 200l. Sugar Ray Leonard . . 1·25 1·10
1962 200l. Evander Holyfield . . 1·25 1·10
MS1963 128 × 102 mm. 1000l. Muhamad Ali (different) . . . 4·00 4·25

1993. Centenary of Modern Boxing (2nd issue). Boxing Films. As T **257**. Multicoloured.
1964 200l. Wallace Beery ("The Champ") 80 80
1965 200l. William Holden ("Golden Boy") 80 80
1966 200l. John Garfield ("Body and Soul") 80 80
1967 200l. Kirk Douglas ("Champion") 80 80
1968 200l. Robert Ryan ("The Set-Up") 80 80
1969 200l. Anthony Quinn ("Requiem for a Heavyweight") 80 80
1970 200l. Elvis Presley ("Kid Galahad") 80 80
1971 200l. Jeff Bridges ("Fat City") 80 80
MS1972 Two sheets, each 128 × 102 mm. (a) 1000l. Errol Flynn "Gentleman Jim" (b) 1000l. Sylvester Stallone "Rocky III" Set of 2 sheets . . . . 7·00 7·50

1993. Bicentenary of the Louvre, Paris. Paintings by Delacroix. As T **255a** of St. Vincent. Mult.
1973 70l. "Young Orphan at a Cemetery" 45 50
1974 70l. "Algerian Women in their Apartment" (left detail) 45 50
1975 70l. "Algerian Women in their Apartment" (right detail) 45 50
1976 70l. "Dante and Virgil" . . 45 50
1977 70l. "Self-portrait" 45 50
1978 70l. "Massacre of Chios" (left detail) 45 50
1979 70l. "Massacre of Chios" (right detail) 45 50
1980 70l. "Frederic Chopin" . . 45 50
1981 70l. "Entry of the Crusaders into Constantinople" (left detail) 45 50
1982 70l. "Entry of the Crusaders into Constantinople" (right detail) 45 50
1983 70l. "Jewish Wedding, Morocco" (left detail) . . 45 50
1984 70l. "Jewish Wedding, Morocco" (right detail) 45 50
1985 70l. "Death of Sardanopoulous" (left detail) 45 50
1986 70l. "Death of Sardanopoulous" (right detail) 45 50
1987 70l. "Liberty leading the People" (left detail) . . . 45 50
1988 70l. "Liberty leading the People" (right detail) . . 45 50
MS1989 100 × 70 mm. 900l. "The Sabine Women" (Louis David) (85 × 53 mm) . . . . 5·50 6·00

258 "Amanita flammeola"

259 "Pseudacraea boisduvali"

1993. Mushrooms. Multicoloured.
1990 30l. Type **258** 40 20
1991 50l. "Cantharellus pseudocibarius" 50 20
1992 100l. "Volvariella volvacea" 70 40
1993 200l. "Termitomyces microcarpus" . . . . . . 1·10 90
1994 300l. "Auricularia auricula-judae" . . . . 1·60 1·50
1995 400l. "Lentinus tuber-regium" ("Pleurotus tuberregium") . . . . . 1·75 2·00
1996 500l. "Schizophyllum commune" . . . . 1·90 2·25
1997 600l. "Termitomyces robustus" . . . . 2·00 2·50
MS1998 Two sheets, each 106 × 76 mm. (a) 1000l. "Daldinia concentrica" (b) 1000l. "Phallus rubicundus" Set of 2 sheets . . 10·00 11·00

1993. Butterflies. Multicoloured.
1999 20l. Type **259** 55 20
2000 30l. "Salamis temora" . . . 60 25
2001 50l. "Charaxes jasius" . . . 65 30
2002 100l. "Amblypodia anita" . . 75 40
2003 150l. "Papilio nireus" . . . 90 70
2004 170l. "Danaus chrysippus" 95 85
2005 200l. "Meneris tulbaghia" 1·00 90
2006 250l. "Precis octavia" . . . 1·10 1·00
2007 300l. "Palla ussheri" . . . . 1·40 1·40
2008 500l. "Catacroptera cloanthe" . . . . 1·60 1·75
2009 600l. "Cynthia cardui" . . . 1·75 2·25
2010 700l. "Euphaedra neophron" . . . . 2·00 2·50
MS2011 Three sheets, each 100 × 70 mm. (a) 1000l. "Papilio zalmoxis" (b) 1000l. "Hypolimnas salmacts" (c) 1000l. "Kallimoides rumia" Set of 3 sheets . . . . 11·00 11·00

260 Black Persian

1993. Cats. Multicoloured.
2012 150l. Type **260** 90 80
2013 150l. Blue-point Siamese . . 90 80
2014 150l. American wirehair . . 90 80
2015 150l. Birman 90 80
2016 150l. Scottish fold 90 80
2017 150l. American shorthair red tabby 90 80
2018 150l. Blue and white Persian bicolour 90 80
2019 150l. Havana brown 90 80
2020 150l. Norwegian forest cat 90 80
2021 150l. Brown tortie Burmese 90 80
2022 150l. Angora 90 80
2023 150l. Exotic shorthair . . . 90 80
2024 150l. Somali 90 80
2025 150l. Egyptian mau smoke 90 80
2026 150l. Chocolate-point Siamese 90 80
2027 150l. Mi-Ke Japanese bobtail 90 80
2028 150l. Chinchilla 90 80
2029 150l. Red Burmese 90 80
2030 150l. British shorthair brown tabby 90 80
2031 150l. Blue Persian 90 80
2032 150l. British silver classic tabby 90 80
2033 150l. Oriental ebony 90 80
2034 150l. Red Persian 90 80
2035 150l. British calico shorthair 90 80
MS2036 Two sheets, each 108 × 65 mm. (a) 1000l. American shorthair blue tabby. (B) 1000l. Seal-point colourpoint Set of 2 sheets . . . . 10·00 10·00

261 Gorilla

1993. Wildlife. Multicoloured.
2037 30l. Type **261** 50 30
2038 100l. Bongo 60 35
2039 150l. Potto 70 60
2040 170l. Chimpanzee 90 90
2041 200l. Dwarf galago . . . . 1·00 1·00
2042 300l. African linsang . . . . 1·25 1·25
2043 500l. Banded duiker . . . . 1·75 2·00
2044 750l. Diana monkey . . . . 2·25 3·25
MS2045 Two sheets, each 106 × 77 mm. (a) 1200l. African elephant. (b) 1200l. Leopard Set of 2 sheets . . . . 12·00 12·00

262 "Clerodendrum thomsonae"

1993. Flowers. Multicoloured.
2046 30l. Type **262** 30 20
2047 40l. "Passiflora quadrangularis" 35 25
2048 50l. "Hydrangea macrophylla" 35 25
2049 60l. "Begonia semperflorens" 40 30
2050 100l. "Hibiscus rosa-sinensis" 50 40
2051 150l. "Lagerstroemia indica" 75 75
2052 170l. "Bougainvillea glabra" 85 85
2053 200l. "Plumbago capensis" 1·00 1·00
2054 250l. "Gerbera jamesonae" 1·25 1·25
2055 300l. "Thunbergia alata" . . 1·40 1·50
2056 500l. "Gloriosa superba" . . 1·75 2·25
2057 900l. "Viola odorata" . . . 2·75 4·00
MS2058 Three sheets, each 72 × 102 mm. (a) 1200l. "Hibiscus rosa-sinensis" (different). (b) 1200l. "Passiflora quadrangularis" (different). (c) 1200l. "Gloriosa superba" (different) Set of 3 sheets 12·00 13·00

263 Royal Family

265a Jose Brown with Goalkeeper (Agentina)

265 Donald Duck and Toy Train

1993. Anniversaries and Events. Black (No. 2061) or multicoloured (others).
2059 100l. Type **263** . . . . . . 1·25 40
2060 170l. "Woman with Hat" (Picasso) . . . . 1·50 1·00
2061 200l. Coronation procession 1·50 1·25
2062 200l. "Buste de Femme" (Picasso) . . . . 1·50 1·25
2063 250l. Early telescope . . . . 3·25 2·00
2064 600l. Queen Elizabeth II in Coronation robes (from photograph by Cecil Beaton) . . . . 3·00 3·25
2065 800l. "Maya with a Doll" (Picasso) . . . . 3·50 5·00
2066 800l. Craters on Moon . . . 5·00 5·00
MS2067 Two sheets. (a) 100 × 70 mm. 1000l. "Woman of Algiers" (detail) (Picasso). (b) 73 × 103 mm. 1500l. "Queen Elizabeth II" (detail) (Pietro Annigoni) Set of 2 sheets . . . 11·00 12·00

ANNIVERSARIES AND EVENTS: Nos. 2059, 2061, 2064, **MS**2067b, 40th anniv of Coronation; 2060, 2062, 2065, **MS**2067a, 20th death anniv of Picasso (artist); 2063, 2066, 450th death anniv of Copernicus (astronomer).

1993. Christmas. Religious Paintings. As T **265a** of St. Vincent. Black, yellow and red (Nos. 2071/4) or multicoloured (others).

2068 50l. "Madonna of the Fish" (detail) (Raphael) 30 10
2069 100l. "Madonna of the Fish" (different detail) (Raphael) 50 20
2070 150l. "Madonna and Child enthroned with Five Saints" (detail) (Raphael) 75 30
2071 200l. "The Circumcision" (detail) (Durer) 85 55
2072 250l. "The Circumcision" (different detail) (Durer) 95 75
2073 300l. "The Circumcision" (different detail) (Durer) 1·00 1·00
2074 500l. "Holy Family with Saints and Two Angels playing Music" (detail) (Durer) . . . . 1·90 2·25
2075 800l. "The Holy Family with the Lamb" (detail) (Raphael) . . . . 2·50 4·00
MS2076 Two sheets. (a) 102×127 mm. 1200l. "Madonna of the Fish" (different detail) (Raphael). (b) 127×102 mm. 1200l. "Holy Family with Saints and Two Angels playing Music" (different detail) (Durer) Set of 2 sheets . . . . 8·50 9·00

1993. Christmas. Walt Disney cartoon characters in Christmas scenes. Multicoloured.

2077 50l. Type **265** 45 10
2078 100l. Disney carol singers 65 20
2079 170l. Mickey drinking punch 1·25 70
2080 200l. Pluto with cream-covered bones . . . . . 1·40 85
2081 250l. Goofy eating angel cakes . . . . 1·60 1·25
2082 500l. Donald's nephews decorating Christmas tree 2·75 2·75
2083 600l. Donald dropping Christmas cake on foot 3·00 3·50
2084 800l. Uncle Scrooge and Daisy under mistletoe . . 3·50 4·50
MS2085 Four sheets. (a) 127×102 mm. 1200l. Father Christmas in sleigh. (b) 102×127 mm. 1200l. Disney carol singers in wood (horiz). (c) 127×102 mm. 1200l. Father Christmas (horiz). (d) 127×102 mm. 1200l. Mickey and Minnie with turkey (horiz) Set of 4 sheets . . . . 15·00 16·00

1993. World Cup Football Championship, U.S.A. (1994) (1st issue). Multicoloured.

2086 30l. Type **265a** 50 20
2087 50l. Gary Lineker (England) 75 30
2088 100l. Carlos Valderrama (Colombia) 85 35
2089 250l. Tomas Skuhravy (Czechoslovakia) and Hector Marchena (Costa Rica) . . . . 1·60 1·40
2090 300l. Butragueno (Spain) . . 1·75 1·75
2091 400l. Roger Milla (Cameroun) . . . . . . 2·25 2·50
2092 500l. Roberto Donadoni (Italy) . . . . 2·50 2·75
2093 700l. Enzo Scifo (Belgium) 2·75 3·50
MS2094 Two sheets. (a) 70×100 mm. 1200l. Mark Wright (England) and Stephane Demol (Belgium). (b) 100×70 mm. 1200l. Socrates (Brazil) Set of 2 sheets 13·00 13·00

See also Nos. 2130/5.

1994. "Hong Kong '94" International Stamp Exhibition (1st issue). As T **271a** of St. Vincent. Multicoloured.

2095 200l. Hong Kong 1985 $1.70 Bauhinia stamp and Pagoda, Tiger Baum Garden 65 75
2096 200l. Sierra Leone 1989 70l. Orchid stamp and Aw Par Gardens 65 75

See also Nos. 2097/2102 and 2103/4.

1994. "Hong Kong '94" International Stamp Exhibition (2nd issue). Ching Dynasty Carved Lacquerware. As T **271b** of St. Vincent. Mult.

2097 100l. Bowl 55 70
2098 100l. Four-wheeled box . . . 55 70
2099 100l. Flower container . . . 55 70
2100 100l. Box with human figure design 55 70
2101 100l. Shishi dog 55 70
2102 100l. Box with persimmon design 55 70

1994. "Hong Kong '94" International Stamp Exhibition (3rd issue). Nos. 2013 and 2025 optd **HONG KONG '94** and emblem.

2103 150l. Blue-point Siamese . . 75 75
2104 150l. Egyptian mau smoke 75 75
MS2105 Two sheets, each 108×65 mm. (a) 1000l. American shorthair blue tabby. (b) 1000l. Seal-point colourpoint Set of 2 sheets . . . . 6·50 7·00

On No. **MS**2105 the overprint only appears on the margins of the miniature sheet.

267 Pekingese

1994. Chinese New Year ("Year of the Dog"). Multicoloured.

2106 100l. Type **267** . . . . . . 85 1·10
2107 150l. Dobermann pinscher 1·10 1·25
2108 200l. Tibetan terrier . . . . 1·25 1·40
2109 250l. Weimaraner . . . . . 1·25 1·40
2110 400l. Rottweiler . . . . . . 1·40 1·60
2111 500l. Akita . . . . 1·40 1·60
2112 600l. Schnauzer . . . . . . 1·50 1·75
2113 1000l. Tibetan spaniel . . . 1·75 1·90
MS2114 Two sheets, each 116×88 mm. (a) 1200l. Wire-haired pointing griffon. (b) 1200l. Shih Tzu Set of 2 sheets . . . 6·00 7·00

1994. 50th Anniv of D-Day. As T **284b** of St. Vincent. Multicoloured.

2115 500l. British paratroop drop 1·25 1·25
2116 750l. U.S. paratrooper jumping from aircraft . . 1·75 1·75
MS2117 106×76 mm. 1000l. U.S. paratrooper preparing to jump from Douglas C-47 Dakota . . 2·75 3·25

1994. "Philakorea '94" International Stamp Exn, Seoul. As T **286a** of St. Vincent. Multicoloured.

2118 100l. Traditional wedding 40 25
2119 200l. Tiger and cubs 70 70
2120 200l. Munsa-pasal 70 70
2121 200l. Extinct Korean tiger 70 70
2122 200l. Tiger and bamboo . . 70 70
2123 200l. Tiger, three cubs and magpies 70 70
2124 200l. Tiger, two cubs and black-billed magpies . . . 70 70
2125 200l. Mountain spirit . . . 70 70
2126 200l. Tiger and black-billed magpie 70 70
2127 400l. Royal tombs, Kaesong 1·00 1·00
2128 600l. Terraced fields, Chungmu . . . . 1·50 1·75
MS2129 100×70 mm. 1200l. Tiger hunt . . . . 4·50 4·50

No. **MS**2129 is inscribed "Sierre Leone" in error.

268 Kim Ho (South Korea)

1994. World Cup Football Championship, U.S.A. (2nd issue). Multicoloured.

2130 250l. Type **268** 95 85
2131 250l. Cobi Jones (U.S.A.) ("No. 13") 95 85
2132 250l. Claudio Suarez (Mexico) ("No. 2") . . . 95 85
2133 250l. Tomas Brolin (Sweden) ("No. 11") 95 85
2134 250l. Ruud Gullit (Holland) (red shirt without number) 95 85
2135 250l. Andreas Herzog (Austria) (white shirt without number) 95 85
MS2136 Two sheets. (a) 70×100 mm. 1500l. Player and Giant Stadium, New Jersey. (b) 100×70 mm. 1500l. Sierra Leone national team Set of 2 sheets 8·00 9·00

1994. 25th Anniv of First Manned Moon Landing. As T **284a** of St. Vincent. Multicoloured.

2137 200l. Buzz Aldrin gathering Moon samples 60 60
2138 200l. Lunar Module "Eagle" on Moon's surface . . . 60 60
2139 200l. Tranquility Base . . . 60 60
2140 200l. Aldrin with U.S. flag 60 60
2141 200l. Plaque 60 60
2142 200l. "Apollo 11" crew with stamps 60 60
2143 200l. Edwin Aldrin 60 60
2144 200l. Michael Collins . . . 60 60
2145 200l. Neil Armstrong . . . 60 60
2146 200l. "Apollo 11" lift off . . 60 60
2147 200l. Aldrin descending to Moon's surface 60 60
2148 200l. Reflection in Aldrin's face shield 60 60
MS2149 103×73 mm. 1000l. First lunar footprint (vert) . . . . . . 2·50 3·00

269 White-necked Bald Crow ("Picathartes") feeding Chicks

1994. Birds. Multicoloured.

2150 50l. Type **269** 65 65
2151 100l. Adult white-necked bald crow 75 75
2152 150l. Pair of white-necked bald crows 85 85
2153 200l. Young white-necked bald crow 90 90
2154 250l. Black kite . . . . . . 1·00 1·00
2155 300l. Superb sunbird . . . . 1·10 1·10
2156 500l. Martial eagle . . . . 1·60 2·00
2157 800l. Red bishop . . . . . 2·00 2·75
MS2158 Two sheets, each 90×65 mm. (a) 1200l. Greater flamingo (vert). (b) 1200l. White-necked bald crow (vert) Set of 2 sheets . . . . 9·00 9·50

270 "Aerangis kotschyana"

1994. Orchids. Multicoloured.

2159 50l. Type **270** 40 20
2160 100l. "Brachycorythis kalbreyeri" 50 30
2161 150l. "Diaphananthe pellucida" 65 55
2162 200l. "Eulophia guineensis" 75 65
2163 300l. "Eurychone rothschildiana" . . . . . 1·00 85
2164 500l. "Tridactyle tridactylites" . . . . . . 1·60 1·60
2165 750l. "Cyrtorchis arcuata" 2·25 3·00
2166 900l. "Ancistrochilus rothschildianus" . . . . 2·50 3·50
MS2167 Two sheets, each 117×78 mm. (a) 1500l. "Plectrelminthus caudatus". (b) 1500l. "Polystachaya affinis" Set of 2 sheets . . . . 8·00 9·00

1994. Christmas. Religious Paintings. As T **290** of St. Vincent. Multicoloured.

2168 50l. "The Birth of the Virgin" (Murillo) 35 10
2169 100l. "Education of the Virgin" (Murillo) 45 20
2170 150l. "Annunciation" (detail) (Filippino Lippi) 75 55
2171 200l. "Marriage of the Virgin" (Bernard van Orley) 85 70
2172 250l. "The Visitation" (Nicolas Vleughels) . . . 1·00 90
2173 300l. "Castelfranco Altarpiece" (detail) (Giorgione) . . . . 1·25 1·25
2174 400l. "Adoration of the Magi" (workshop of Bartholome Zeitblom) . . 1·60 1·75
2175 600l. "Presentation of Infant Jesus in the Temple" (Master of the Prado) . . 2·00 3·00
MS2176 Two sheets, each 115×95 mm. (a) 1500l. "Nativity Altarpiece" (detail) (Lorenzo Monaco). (b) 1500l. "Allendale Nativity" (detail) (Giorgione) Set of 2 sheets . . . . 8·00 9·00

271 Family working in Field

1994. International Year of the Family. Mult.

2177 300l. Type **271** 75 80
2178 350l. Family on beach . . . 75 80

272 Mickey Mouse stroking Cat

1995. Christmas. Walt Disney cartoon characters. Multicoloured.

2179 50l. Type **272** 35 10
2180 100l. Goofy with Christmas tree and axe (vert) . . . 45 20
2181 150l. Donald Duck giving Daisy Duck a plant . . . 70 45
2182 200l. Donald finding Chipmunk in stocking (vert) 80 60
2183 250l. Minnie Mouse in airplane 95 85
2184 300l. Goofy in snowball (vert) . . . . 1·25 1·00
2185 400l. Goofy with Chip N' Dale at mail box . . . . 1·40 1·50
2186 500l. Mickey and Donald on sledge (vert) . . . . . . 1·60 1·75
2187 600l. Mickey and Minnie making snowmouse . . . 1·90 2·50
2188 800l. Mickey and Pluto with cake (vert) . . . . 2·25 3·00
MS2189 Two sheets. (a) 108×133 mm. 1500l. Goofy caught up in Christmas lights. (b) 130×108 mm. 1500l. Mickey asleep in armchair (vert) Set of 2 sheets . . . . 9·00 10·00

273 "Madonna Duck" (after Da Vinci)

274 Ragnar Lundberg (Sweden) (1952 pole vault bronze medal)

1995. Donald's Gallery of Old Masters. Donald and Daisy Duck in portraits inspired by famous paintings. Multicoloured.

2190 50l. Type **273** 25 15
2191 100l. "Portrait of a Venetian Duck" (after Tintoretto) 35 25
2192 150l. "Duck with a Glove" (after Frans Hals) 50 50
2193 200l. "Donald with a Pink" (after Massys) 60 60
2194 250l. "Pinkie Daisy" (after Lawrence) 70 70
2195 300l. "Donald's Whistling Mother" (after Whistler) 80 80
2196 400l. "El Quacko" (after El Greco) 90 90
2197 500l. "The Noble Snob" (after Rembrandt) . . . . 1·00 1·00
2198 600l. "The Blue Duck" (after Gainsborough) . . 1·25 1·50
2199 800l. "Modern Quack" (after Picasso) . . . . . 1·40 1·60
MS2200 Two sheets, each 133×108 mm. (a) 1500l. "Soup's On" (detail) (after Brueghel). (b) 1500l. "Two Duck Dancers" (detail) (after Degas) (horiz) Set of 2 sheets . . . . 8·50 9·00

1995. Centenary of International Olympic Committee. Medal Winners. Multicoloured.

2201 75l. Type **274** 45 45
2202 75l. Karin Janz (Germany) (1972 gymnastics silver) 45 45
2203 75l. Matthias Volz (Germany) (1936 gymnastics bronze) . . . 45 45
2204 75l. Carl Lewis (U.S.A.) (1988 long jump gold) . . 45 45
2205 75l. Sara Simeoni (Italy) (1976 high jump silver) . . 45 45
2206 75l. Daley Thompson (Great Britain) (1980 decathlon gold) 45 45
2207 75l. Japan and Britain (1964 football) 45 45
2208 75l. Gabriella Dorio (Italy) (1984 1500 m gold) . . . 45 45
2209 75l. Daniela Hunger (Germany) (1988 swimming gold) 45 45
2210 75l. Kyoko Iwasaki (Japan) (1992 swimming bronze) 45 45
2211 75l. Italian team (1960 water polo gold) 45 45
2212 75l. David Wilkie (Great Britain) (1976 swimming gold) 45 45
2213 200l. Katja Seizinger (Germany) (1994 alpine skiing gold) 55 55
2214 200l. Hot air balloon showing Olympic Rings 55 55
2215 200l. Elvis Stojko (Canada) (1994 figure skating silver) 55 55
2216 200l. Jans Weissflog (Germany) (1994 ski jumping gold) 55 55
2217 200l. Bjorn Daehlie (Norway) (1994 cross-country skiing gold) . . . 55 55
2218 200l. German team (1994 four-man bobsled gold) 55 55
2219 200l. Markus Wasmeier (Germany) (1994 alpine skiing gold) 55 55
2220 200l. Georg Hacki (Germany) (1994 luge gold) 55 55
2221 200l. Jayne Torvill and Christopher Dean (Great Britain) (1994 ice dancing bronze) 55 55
2222 200l. Bonnie Blair (U.S.A.) (1994 speed skating gold) 55 55
2223 200l. Nancy Kerrigan (U.S.A.) (1994 figure skating silver) 55 55

2224 200l. Sweden team (1994 ice hockey gold) 55 55
MS2225 Two sheets, each 100×70 mm. (a) 1000l. Medal winners (1994 women's figure skating) (horiz). (b) 100l. Athlete holding Olympic Torch (horiz) Set of 2 sheets . . . . 5·00 6·00

275 Ceratosaurus

1995. Prehistoric Animals. Multicoloured.
2226 200l. Type **275** 75 75
2227 200l. Brachiosaurus 75 75
2228 200l. Pteranodon 75 75
2229 200l. Stegoceras 75 75
2230 200l. Saurolophus 75 75
2231 200l. Ornithomumus 75 75
2232 200l. Compsognathus . . . 75 75
2233 200l. Deinonychus 75 75
2234 200l. Ornitholestes 75 75
2235 200l. Archaeopteryx 75 75
2236 200l. Heterodontosaurus . . 75 75
2237 200l. Lesothosaurus 75 75
MS2238 130×58 mm. 100l. Triceratops (vert); 250l. Protoceratops (vert); 400l. Monoclonius (vert); 800l. Styracosaurus (vert) . . . . . 3·00 3·25
MS2239 Two sheets, each 99×79 mm. (a) 2500l. Rhamphorynchus (vert). (b) 2500l. Deinonychus (vert) Set of 2 sheets . . . . 5·00 5·50
Nos. 2226/37 were printed together, se-tenant, forming a composite design.

276 Pig (on red panel)

1995. Chinese New Year ("Year of the Pig"). Multicoloured.
2240 100l. Type **276** 50 50
2241 100l. Pig facing right (on green panel) 50 50
2242 100l. Pig facing left (on green panel) 50 50
2243 100l. Pig facing right (on red panel) 50 50
MS2244 77×105 mm. 500l. Two pigs (vert) . . . . 2·00 2·75

276a Black-faced Impalas

1995. Centenary (1992) of Sierra Club (environmental protection society). Endangered Species. Multicoloured.
2245 150l. Type **276a** 50 50
2246 150l. Herd of black-faced impalas 50 50
2247 150l. Black-faced impalas drinking 50 50
2248 150l. Bonobo with young . . 50 50
2249 150l. Black-footed cat in foliage 50 50
2250 150l. Close-up of black-footed cat 50 50
2251 150l. L'Hoest's monkey on all fours 50 50
2252 150l. L'Hoest's monkey squatting 50 50
2253 150l. Pair of mandrills . . . 50 50
2254 150l. L'Hoest's monkey (vert) 50 50
2255 150l. Black-footed cat (vert) 50 50
2256 150l. Head of colobus monkey (vert) 50 50
2257 150l. Colobus monkey in tree fork (vert) 50 50
2258 150l. Head of mandrill (vert) 50 50
2259 150l. Bonobo with young (vert) 50 50
2260 150l. Bonobo asleep on log (vert) 50 50
2261 150l. Mandrill facing right (vert) 50 50
2262 150l. Colobus monkey on log (vert) 50 50

277 Denver and Rio Grande Western Railroad

1995. Railways of the World. Multicoloured.
2263/74 200l. × 12 (Type **277**; Central of Georgia; Seaboard Air Line; Missouri Pacific Lines; Atchison, Topeka and Santa Fe; Chicago, Milwaukee, St. Paul and Pacific; Texas and Pacific; Minneapolis, St. Paul and Sault Ste. Marie; Western Pacific; Great Northern; Baltimore and Ohio; Chicago, Rock Island and Pacific) . . . .
2275/86 200l. × 12 (Southern Pacific; Belgian National; Indian; Southern Australian; Union Pacific; British Railways; German Federal; Japanese National; Pennsylvania; East African; Milwaukee; Paris-Orleans) . . .
2287/98 250l. × 12 (Eurostar; E.T.R. 401 Pendolino express; British Rail Intercity 125; Talgo "Virgen" express, Spain; French National TGV; Amtrak "Southwest Chief" express; French National TGV "Atlantique" express; Greek "Peloponnese Express"; Japanese "Hikari" express train; Canadian National Turbotrain; Australian XPT high-speed train; Chinese SS1 electric locomotive) . . . .
2299/2310 300l. × 12 (Canadian National U1-f locomotive; Union Pacific steam locomotive No. 119; LNER Class A4 No. 4468 "Mallard"; New York Central Class J3a steam locomotive; Canadian National Class U4 locomotive; Australian Class 38 locomotive; Canadian Pacific Class G3c locomotive; Southern Railway Class "West Country" locomotive; Norfolk & Western Class J locomotive; China Class RM locomotive; Russia Class P-36 locomotive; GWR Class "King" locomotive) . . . .
2263/2310 Set of 48 . . . . 26·00 28·00
MS2311 Five sheets, each 107×79 mm. containing larger designs, 56½×42½ mm. (a) 1500l. British Railways No. 45627 "Sierra Leone" locomotive. (b) 1500l. China Railways Class QJ locomotive. (c) 1500l. Denver and Rio Grande Western Railroad "California Zephyr" express. (d) 1500l. China Railways Beijing-Shanghai express. (e) 1500l. China Railways first train across Yangtze Bridge, 1968 Set of 5 sheets . . 13·00 14·00
No. 2290 is inscribed "VIRGIN", No. 2300 "CENTRAL PACIFIC RAILWAY" and No. 2302 "J-32", all in error.

278 National Flag and Scout Emblems

1995. 18th World Scout Jamboree, Netherlands. Multicoloured.
2312 400l. Type **278** . . . . . . 90 1·00
2313 500l. Lord Baden-Powell . . 1·00 1·25
2314 600l. Scout sign . . . . . . 1·10 1·40
MS2315 80×111 mm. 1500l. Scout saluting . . . . 2·75 3·00

1995. 50th Anniv of End of Second World War in Europe. As T **296a** of St. Vincent, showing warships. Multicoloured.
2316 250l. U.S.S. "Idaho" (battleship) 65 65
2317 250l. H.M.S. "Ark Royal" (aircraft carrier) 65 65
2318 250l. Admiral "Graf Spee" (German pocket battleship) 65 65
2319 250l. American destroyer . . 65 65
2320 250l. H.M.S. "Nelson" (battleship) 65 65
2321 250l. U.S.S. "PT 109" (motor torpedo boat) . . 65 65
2322 250l. U.S.S. "Iowa" (battleship) 65 65
2323 250l. "Bismarck" (German battleship) 65 65
MS2324 105×74 mm. 1500l. H.M.S. "Indomitable" (aircraft carrier) (57×42½ mm) . . . . 3·75 4·50
No. 2323 is wrongly inscr "BISMARK".

278a U.N. Emblem above Podium

1995. 50th Anniv of the United Nations. Mult.
2325 300l. Type **278a** 60 70
2326 400l. U Thant (Secretary-General, 1961–71) 70 90
2327 500l. Peace dove and U.N. Building, New York . . . 80 1·00
MS2328 105×74 mm. 1500l. Dag Hammarskjold (Secretary-General, 1953-61) . . . . . . 2·00 2·50
Nos. 2325/7 were printed together, se-tenant, forming a composite design.

1995. 50th Anniv of F.A.O. As T **298** of St. Vincent. Multicoloured.
2329 300l. Fisherman in boat (horiz) 60 70
2330 400l. Boy carrying wood (horiz) 70 90
2331 500l. Woman with fruit (horiz) . . . . 80 1·00
MS2332 76×106 mm. 1500l. Mother and child . . . . 2·00 2·50

1995. 90th Anniv of Rotary International. As T **299** of St. Vincent. Multicoloured.
2333 500l. National flag and Rotary logo . . . . . . 1·10 1·50
MS2334 105×75 mm. 1000l. Paul Harris (founder) and logo . . 1·60 1·75

1995. 95th Birthday of Queen Elizabeth the Queen Mother. As T **323a** of St. Vincent.
2335 400l. brown, lt brown & blk 90 1·00
2336 400l. multicoloured . . . . 90 1·00
2337 400l. multicoloured . . . . 90 1·00
2338 400l. multicoloured . . . . 90 1·00
MS2339 102×127 mm. 1500l. multicoloured . . . . 3·50 3·50
DESIGNS: No. 2335, Queen Elizabeth the Queen Mother (pastel drawing); 2336, Holding bouquet of flowers; 2337, At desk (oil painting); . 2338, Wearing pink evening dress; **MS**2339, wearing blue hat.

1995. 50th Anniv of End of Second World War in the Pacific. As T **296a** of St. Vincent. Mult.
2340 300l. American B-179 bomber 80 80
2341 300l. American B-25 bomber 80 80
2342 300l. American Consolidated B-24 Liberator bomber 80 80
2343 300l. U.S.S. "Missouri" (battleship) 80 80
2344 300l. American Douglas A-20 Boston bomber . . 80 80
2345 300l. American battle fleet in Lingayen Gulf 80 80
MS2346 108×76 mm. 1500l. Nose of B-29 Superfortress . . . . . 3·00 3·50

279 Black-spotted Pufferfish

1995. "Singapore '95" International Stamp Exhibition (1st issue). Marine Life. Multicoloured.
2347 300l. Type **279** 65 65
2348 300l. Coral hind 65 65
2349 300l. Hawksbill turtle . . . 65 65
2350 300l. Hogfish 65 65
2351 300l. Emperor angelfish . . 65 65
2352 300l. Red-tailed butterflyfish 65 65
2353 300l. Lemon butterflyfish . . 65 65
2354 300l. Green-beaked parrotfish 65 65
2355 300l. Spotted reef moray . . 65 65
2356 300l. Pintado petrel ("Cape Pigeons") 65 65
2357 300l. Eastern white pelican ("Pelican") 65 65
2358 300l. Atlantic puffin ("Puffin") 65 65
2359 300l. Humpback whale . . . 65 65
2360 300l. Greater shearwater . . 65 65
2361 300l. Bottlenose dolphin . . 65 65
2362 300l. Gurnards 65 65
2363 300l. Atlantic salmon . . . 65 65
2364 300l. John Dory 65 65
MS2365 Two sheets. (a) 71×101 mm. 1500l. Ocean surgeonfish. (b) 101×71 mm. 1500l. Pennant coralfish ("Angelfish") (vert) Set of 2 sheets 6·00 6·50
Nos. 2347/55 and 2356/64 were printed together, se-tenant, forming composite designs.

280 Flame Lily

1995. "Singapore '95" International Stamp Exhibition (2nd issue). African Flora and Fauna. Multicoloured.
2366 300l. Type **280** 90 90
2367 300l. Grant's gazelle 90 90
2368 300l. Dogbane 90 90
2369 300l. Gold-banded forester 90 90
2370 300l. Horned chameleon . . 90 90
2371 300l. Malachite kingfisher 90 90
2372 300l. Leaf beetle 90 90
2373 300l. Acanthus 90 90
2374 300l. African tulip tree . . . 90 90
2375 300l. Senegal bush locust . . 90 90
2376 300l. Killfish 90 90
2377 300l. Bird of paradise (flower) 90 90
2378 300l. Mandrill 90 90
2379 300l. Painted reed frog . . . 90 90
2380 300l. Large spotted acraea 90 90
2381 300l. Carmine bee eater . . 90 90
MS2382 Two sheets, each 103×73 mm. (a) 1500l. Elephant. (b) 1500l. Lion Set of 2 sheets 6·00 6·50

281 School Building and Emblem

1995. 150th Anniv of Sierra Leone Grammar School.
2383 **281** 300l. brown, mauve and black 70 70

281a "Holy Family" (detail) (Beccafumi)

1995. Christmas. Religious Paintings. Mult.
2384 50l. Type **281a** 25 10
2385 100l. "The Rest on the Flight into Egypt" (detail) (Federico Barocci) 30 10
2386 150l. "The Virgin" (Jacopo Bellini) 40 15
2387 200l. "The Flight" (Cavaliere d'Arpino) . . . 50 25
2388 600l. "Adoration of the Magi" (detail) (Francken) 1·60 2·25
2389 800l. "The Annunciation" (Cima de Conegliano) . . 1·75 2·50
MS2390 Two sheets, each 102×127 mm. (a) 1500l. "Virgin and Child" (detail) (Cranach). (b) 1500l. "Madonna and Child" (detail) (Berlinghiero) Set of 2 sheets . . . . 6·00 6·50

282 Mickey Mouse Doll

1995. Christmas. Disney Toys. Multicoloured.
2391 5l. Type **282** 10 10
2392 10l. Donald Duck drum-major doll 10 10
2393 15l. Donald Duck wind-up toy 15 10
2394 20l. Donald Duck toothbrush holder 15 10
2395 25l. Mickey Mouse telephone 15 10
2396 30l. Mickey Mouse walking toy 15 10
2397 800l. Toy film projector . . 2·50 3·25
2398 1000l. Goofy tricycle toy . . 2·75 3·50
MS2399 Two sheets, each 133 × 107 mm. (a) 1500l. Black Mickey Mouse doll. (b) 1500l. First Mickey Mouse book Set of 2 sheets . . . . 6·00 6·50

283 Andrew Huxley (1963 Medicine)

1995. Cent of Nobel Prize Trust Fund. Mult.
2400/8 250l. × 9 (Type **283**; Nelson Mandela (1993 Peace); Gabriela Mistral (1945 Literature); Otto Diels (1950 Chemistry); Hannes Alfven (1970 Physics); Wole Soyinka (1986 Literature); Hans Dehmelt (1989 Physics); Desmond Tutu (1984 Peace); Leo Esaki (1973 Physics)) . . . . . .
2409/17 250l. × 9 (Tobias Asser (1911 Peace); Andrei Sakharov (1975 Peace); Frederic Passy (1901 Peace); Dag Hammarskjold (1961 Peace); Aung San Suu Kyi (1991 Peace); Ludwig Quidde (1927 Peace); Elie Wiesel (1986 Peace); Bertha von Suttner (1905 Peace); The Dalai Lama (1989 Peace)) . .
2418/26 50l. × 9 (Richard Zsigmondy (1925 Chemistry); Robert Huber (1988 Chemistry); Wilhelm Ostwald (1909 Chemistry); Johann Deisenhofer (1988 Chemistry); Heinrich Wieland (1922 Chemistry); Gerhard Herzberg (1971 Chemistry); Hans von Euler-Chelpin (1929 Chemistry); Richard Willsatter (1915 Chemistry); Fritz Haber (1918 Chemistry)) . . .
2427/35 250l. × 9 (Maria Goeppert Mayer (1963 Physics); Irene Joliot-Curie (1935 Chemistry); Mother Teresa (1979 Peace); Selma Lagerlof (1909 Literature); Rosalyn Yalow (1977 Medicine); Dorothy Hodgkin (1964 Chemistry); Rita Levi-Montalcini (1986 Medicine); Mairead Corrigan (1976 Peace); Betty Williams (1976 Peace)) . . . .
2400/35 Set of 36 . . . . 28·00 28·00
MS2436 Three sheets, each 80 × 110 mm. (a) 1500l. Albert Einstein (1921 Physics). (b) 1500l. Wilhelm Rontgen (1901 Physics). (c) 1500l. Sin-Itiro Tomonaga (1965 Physics) Set of 3 sheets 9·00 11·00

284 Rat

1996. Chinese New Year ("Year of the Rat"). Background colour given.
2437 **284** 200l. multicoloured (brown background) 50 55
2438 – 200l. multicoloured (pink background) 50 55
2439 – 200l. multicoloured (red background) 50 55
2440 – 200l. multicoloured (blue background) 50 55
MS2441 110 × 84 mm. Nos. 2437/40 2·00 2·50
MS2442 76 × 106 mm. 500l. multicoloured (orange background) (vert) . . . . . . 2·00 2·50

285 Mickey Mouse as Magician

1996. Disney Circus Performers. Cartoon Characters. Multicoloured.
2443 100l. Type **285** 50 20
2444 200l. Clarabelle Cow walking tightrope 70 50
2445 250l. Donald Duck and nephews as clowns . . . 80 60
2446 300l. Donald as lion tamer 1·00 75
2447 800l. Minnie Mouse riding bareback . . . . 2·50 3·25
2448 1000l. Goofy on trapeze . . 2·75 3·50
MS2449 Two sheets, each 104 × 125 mm. (a) 1500l. Mickey with dinosaur (horiz). (b) 1500l. Pluto balancing ball on nose (horiz) Set of 2 sheets . . . . 7·00 8·00

286 Lumiere Brothers (cine camera inventors) and Train

1996. Centenary of Cinema. Multicoloured.
2450 250l. Type **286** 70 75
2451 250l. Georges Melies (director) 70 75
2452 250l. Toshiro Mefune (director) 70 75
2453 250l. David O. Selznick (director) 70 75
2454 250l. Character from "Metropolis" 70 75
2455 250l. Akira Kurosawa (director) 70 75
2456 250l. Charlie Chaplin (actor) 70 75
2457 250l. Marlene Dietrich (actress) 70 75
2458 250l. Steven Spielberg (director) 70 75
2459 250l. Film camera 70 75
2460 250l. Pete (dog) 70 75
2461 250l. Silver (horse) 70 75
2462 250l. Rin-Tin-Tin (dog) . . . 70 75
2463 250l. King Kong (gorilla) 70 75
2464 250l. Flipper (dolphin) . . . 70 75
2465 250l. Great White Shark from "Jaws" 70 75
2466 250l. Elsa (lioness) 70 75
2467 250l. Whale from "Moby Dick" 70 75
MS2468 Two sheets, each 109 × 80 mm. (a) 1500l. Cecil B. De Mille (producer). (b) 1500l. Lassie (dog) Set of 2 sheets . . 6·00 6·50
Nos. 2450/8 and 2459/67 respectively were printed together, se-tenant, forming composite designs.

1996. 125th Anniv of Metropolitan Museum of Art, New York. As T **317a** of St. Vincent. Mult.
2469/76 200l. × 8 ("Honfleur" (detail) (Jongkind); "A Boat on the Shore" (detail) (Courbet); "Barges at Pontoise" (detail) (Pissarro); "The Dead Christ with Angels" (Manet); "Salisbury Cathedral" (detail) (Constable); "Lady with a Setter Dog" (detail) (Eakins); "Tahitian Women Bathing" (detail) (Gauguin); "Majas on a Balcony" (detail) (Goya)) . . .
2477/84 200l. × 8 ("In the Meadow"; "By the Seashore" (detail); "Still Life with Peaches and Grapes" (detail); "Marguerite Berard"; "Young Girl in Pink and Black Hat"; "Waitress at Duval's Restaurant" (detail); "A Road in Louveciennes" (detail); "Two Young Girls at the Piano" (detail) (all by Renoir)) . . . . . .
2485/92 200l. × 8 ("Morning, An Overcast Day, Rouen" (detail) (Pissarro); "The Horse Fair" (detail) (Bonheur); "High Tide: The Bathers" (detail) (Homer); "The Dance Class" (Degas); "The Brioche" (detail) (Manet); "The Grand Canal, Venice" (detail) (Turner); "St. Tecia interceding for plague-stricken Este" (detail) (G. B. Tiepolo); "Bridge at Villeneuve" (detail) (Sisley)) . . . . . .
2493/2500 200l. × 8 ("Madame Charpentier" (detail) (Renoir); "Head of Christ" (detail) (Rembrandt); "The Standard-bearer" (detail) (Rembrandt); "Girl Asleep" (Vermeer); "Lady with a Lute" (Vermeer); "Portrait of a Woman" (detail) (Rembrandt); "La Grenouillere" (detail) (Monet); "Woman with Chrysanthemums" (detail) (Degas)) . .
2469/2500 Set of 32 . . . . 14·00 15·00
MS2501 Four sheets, each 95 × 70 mm. (a) 1500l. "The Death of Socrates" (J. L. David) 85 × 56 mm). (b) 1500l. "Battle of Constantine and Licinius" (detail) (rubens) (85 × 56 mm). (c) 1500l. "Samson and Delilah" (detail) (rubens) (85 × 56 mm). (d) 1500l. "The Emblem of Christ appearing to Constantine" (detail) (Rubens) (85 × 56 mm) Set of 4 sheets . . 6·50 7·50

287 Olympic Stadium, Los Angeles, 1932

1996. Olympic Games, Atlanta. Multicoloured.
2502 100l. Type **287** 30 20
2503 150l. Archery 50 50
2504 300l. Hockey 80 90
2505 300l. Swimming 80 90
2506 300l. Equestrian 80 90
2507 300l. Boxing 80 90
2508 300l. Pommel horse exercises 80 90
2509 300l. 100 m running 80 90
2510 500l. Rings exercises . . . . 1·25 1·40
2511 600l. Pole vault . . . . . . 1·40 1·60
MS2512 104 × 75 mm. 1500l. Running (vert) . . . . 3·50 4·00

288 "Cantharellus cinnabarinus"

289 Abyssinian Cat

1996. Fungi. Multicoloured.
2513 50l. Type **288** 35 20
2514 250l. "Poronidulus conchifer" and "Aphyllophorales polyporaceae" 80 85
2515 250l. "Ceratiomyxa fruticulosa" 80 85
2516 250l. "Cortinarius semisanguineus" and "Cortinariaceae agaricales" 80 85
2517 250l. "Volvamella surrecta" and "Pluteaceae agricales" 80 85
2518 250l. "Lepiota cepaestipes" 80 85
2519 250l. "Amanita rubescans" 80 85
2520 250l. "Phyllotopsis nidulans" and "Tricholomataceas agaricales" 80 85
2521 250l. "Lysyrus gardneri" and "Clathraceae phallales" 80 85
2522 250l. "Lactarius indigo" . . 80 85
2523 250l. "Coprinus quadrifidus" 80 85
2524 250l. "Geopyxis carbonaria" 80 85
2525 250l. "Astraeus hygrometricus" 80 85
2526 250l. "Agaicaceae agaricales" 80 85
2527 250l. "Mycena maculata" 80 85
2528 250l. "Lactarius delciosus" 80 85
2529 250l. "Amanita fulva" . . . 80 85
2530 300l. "Suillus grevillci" . . . 90 95
2531 400l. "Morchella esculenta" 1·10 1·25
2532 500l. "Cortinamaceae agaricales" . . . . 1·25 1·40
MS2533 Two sheets, each 110 × 80 mm. (a) 1500l. "Psathyrella epimyces" (horiz). (b) 1500l. "Rhodotus parmatus" (horiz) Set of 2 sheets . . . . 6·00 6·50

1996. Cats. Multicoloured.
2534 200l. Type **289** 65 60
2535 200l. British tabby 65 60
2536 200l. Norwegian forest cat 65 60
2537 200l. Maine coon 65 60
2538 200l. Bengal 65 60
2539 200l. Asian 65 60
2540 200l. American curl 65 60
2541 200l. Devon rex 65 60
2542 200l. Tonkinese 65 60
2543 200l. Egyptian mau 65 60
2544 200l. Burmese 65 60
2545 200l. Siamese 65 60
2546 200l. British shorthair . . . 65 60
2547 200l. Tiffany 65 60
2548 200l. Birman 65 60
2549 200l. Somali 65 60
2550 200l. Malayan 65 60
2551 200l. Japanese bobtail . . . 65 60
2552 200l. Himalayan 65 60
2553 200l. Tortoiseshell 65 60
2554 200l. Oriental 65 60
2555 200l. Ocicat 65 60
2556 200l. Chartreux 65 60
2557 200l. Ragdoll 65 60
MS2558 Two sheets, each 110 × 80 mm. (a) 2000l. Persian. (b) 2000l. Burmilla Set of 2 sheets 6·50 7·00

1996. 70th Birthday of Queen Elizabeth II. As T **323a** of St. Vincent. Different photographs. Multicoloured.
2559 600l. Queen Elizabeth II . . 1·40 1·50
2560 600l. Receiving posy . . . . 1·40 1·50
2561 600l. Carrying bouquets . . 1·40 1·50
MS2562 125 × 103 mm. 1500l. Waving from balcony . . . . 3·75 4·00

290 Three Asian Girls reading

1996. 50th Anniv of UNICEF. Multicoloured.
2563 300l. Type **290** 80 80
2564 400l. African children reading . . . . 90 1·00
2565 500l. Children in class . . . 95 1·10
MS2566 104 × 74 mm. 1500l. Children's faces . . . . 3·00 3·50

291 "Pioneer" Spacecraft in Venus Orbit, 1986–1992

1996. Space Exploration. Multicoloured.
2567 300l. Type **291** 80 75
2568 300l. Hubble space telescope 80 75
2569 300l. "Voyager" space probe 80 75
2570 300l. Space Shuttle "Challenger" 80 75
2571 300l. "Pioneer II" space probe 80 75
2572 300l. "Viking I" Mars lander 80 75
MS2573 104 × 74 mm. 1500l. Space shuttle "Challenger" landing 3·50 3·75
Nos. 2567/72 were printed together, se-tenant, the background forming a composite design.

292 Rat

1996. Chinese Lunar Calendar. Multicoloured.
2574 150l. Type **292** 50 50
2575 150l. Ox 50 50
2576 150l. Tiger 50 50
2577 150l. Hare 50 50
2578 150l. Dragon 50 50
2579 150l. Snake 50 50
2580 150l. Horse 50 50
2581 150l. Sheep 50 50
2582 150l. Monkey 50 50
2583 150l. Cockerel 50 50
2584 150l. Dog 50 50
2585 150l. Pig 50 50

293 "Charaxes pleione"

1996. Butterflies. Multicoloured.
2586 150l. Type **293** 50 35
2587 200l. "Eurema brigitta" 70 50
2588 250l. "Precis orithya" 75 80
2589 250l. "Palla ussheri" 75 80
2590 250l. "Junonia orithya" 75 80
2591 250l. "Cymothoe sangaris" 75 80
2592 250l. "Cyrestis camillus" 75 80
2593 250l. "Precis rhadama" 75 80
2594 250l. "Precis cebrene" 75 80
2595 250l. "Hypolimnas misippus" 75 80
2596 250l. "Colotis danae" 75 80
2597 300l. "Charaxes ameliae" 80 85
2598 500l. "Kallimoides rumia" 1·25 1·40
MS2599 Two sheets, each 100 × 70 mm. (a) 1500l. "Papilio antimachus" (b) 1500l. "Charaxes bohemani" Set of 2 sheets 6·50 7·00

294 "Begonia multiflora" "Rambouillet"

296 "The Sea Dragon's Daughter"

295 Greek War Galley (4th-century B.C.)

1996. Flowers. Multicoloured.
2600 150l. "Tulipa" "Georgette" 40 30
2601 200l. "Helichrysum bracteatum" "Monstrosum" 55 60
2602 200l. Fountain 55 60
2603 200l. Type **294** 55 60
2604 200l. Narcissus "Trumpet Daffodil" 55 60
2605 200l. "Crocus speciosus" 55 60
2606 200l. "Chrysanthemum frutescens" "Marguerite" 55 60
2607 200l. Petunia "Polaris" and "Danaus gilippus" (butterfly) 55 60
2608 200l. "Cosmos pipinnatus" "Sensation" and "Papilio calguanabus" (butterfly) 55 60
2609 200l. "Anemone coronaris" 55 60
2610 200l. "Convolvulus minor" 55 60
2611 300l. "Paphiopedilum" "Claire de Lune" 65 70
2612 300l. "Cymbidium" "Peach Bloom" 65 70
2613 300l. Yacht 65 70
2614 300l. "Mitonia" "Peach Blossom" 65 70
2615 300l. "Parides gundalachianus" (butterfly) 65 70
2616 300l. "Laeliocattleya" "Grand Gate" 65 70
2617 300l. "Lycaste aromatica" 65 70
2618 300l. "Brassolaeliocattleya" "Golden Land" 65 70
2619 300l. "Cymbidium" "Southern Lace" and "Catastica teutila" (butterfly) 65 70
2620 400l. Vida "Pansy" 80 85
2621 500l. "Phalaenopsis" "Pink Beauty" 95 1·10
MS2622 Two sheets, each 80 × 110 mm. (a) 1500l. "Helianthus annuus" (b) 1500l. "Cymbidium" "Lucifer" Set of 2 sheets 6·00 7·00
Nos. 2602/10 and 2611/19 respectively were printed together, se-tenant, with the backgrounds forming composite designs.

1996. History of Ships. Multicoloured.
2623 300l. Type **295** 75 75
2624 300l. Roman war galley (A.D. 50) 75 75
2625 300l. Viking longship (9th-century) 75 75
2626 300l. Flemish carrack (15th-century) 75 75
2627 300l. Merchantman (16th-century) 75 75
2628 300l. Tudor galleon (16th-century) 75 75
2629 300l. Elizabethan galleon (17th-century) 75 75
2630 300l. Dutch warship (17th-century) 75 75
2631 300l. "Maestrale" (18th-century Maltese galley) 75 75
2632 300l. "Cutty Sark" (19th-century clipper) 75 75
2633 300l. "Great Britain", 1846 (steam/sail liner) 75 75
2634 300l. H.M.S. "Dreadnought", 1906 (battleship) 75 75
2635 300l. "Queen Elizabeth", 1940 (liner) 75 75
2636 300l. Ocean-going yacht, 1962 75 75
2637 300l. "United States", 1952 (liner) 75 75
2638 300l. Nuclear-powered submarine, 1950s 75 75
2639 300l. Super tanker, 1960s 75 75
2640 300l. U.S.S. "Enterprise", 1961 (aircraft carrier) 75 75
MS2641 Two sheets, each 96 × 66 mm. (a) 1500l. Egyptian ship (1480 B.C.) (56 × 42 mm). (b) 1500l. "Legend of the Seas" 1996 (cruise ship) (56 × 42 mm) Set of 2 sheets 6·50 7·00
No. 2634 is inscribed "Dreadnaught" in error.

1996. Christmas. Religious Paintings. As T **337** of St.Vincent. Multicoloured.
2642 200l. "Madonna of Humility" (Filippo Lippi) 50 15
2643 250l. "Coronation of the Virgin" (Lippi) 60 25
2644 400l. "The Annunciation" (Lippi) 1·00 90
2645 500l. "Annunciation" (different) (Lippi) 1·10 1·10
2646 600l. "Barbadori Altarpiece" (Lippi) 1·50 2·00
2647 800l. "Coronation of the Virgin" (different) (Lippi) 1·75 2·50
MS2648 Two sheets, each 76 × 106 mm. (a) 2000l. "Adoration of the Magi" (Rubens). (b) 2000l. "Holy Family with St. Anne" (Rubens) Set of 2 sheets 6·50 7·00
No. 2646 is inscribed "Alterpiece" in error.

1996. Legends of the Seas. Forty sheets, each 105 × 75 mm, containing T **296** and similar multicoloured designs.
MS2649 (a) 1500l. Type **296**; (b) 1500l. "Homo aquaticus"; (c) 1500l. Chinese sea fairy; (d) 1500l. Sea totem pole; (e) 1500l. "Turtle" (fantasy submarine) (horiz); (f) 1500l. Mermaid (horiz); (g) 1500l. "How the Whale got its throat" (horiz); (h) 1500l. Killer Whale crest; (i) 1500l. Odysseus and siren (horiz); (j) 1500l. "The Little Mermaid" (Hans Christian Andersen) (horiz); (k) 1500l. Squamish Indians (horiz); (l) 1500l. Boy on Dolphin; (m) 1500l. Atlantis airship (horiz); (n) 1500l. Sea Bishop (horiz); (o) 1500l. "Twenty Thousand Leagues Under the Sea" (Jules Verne); (p) 1500l. "Whale Song" (horiz); (q) 1500l. Arion (horiz); (r) 1500l. Dragonrider of Pern (horiz); (s) 1500l. Kelpie (horiz); (t) 1500l. Natsihlane on Sea Lion (horiz); (u) 1500l. Triton; (v) 1500l. Lang (dragon) (horiz); (w) 1500l. "The Flying Dutchman" (horiz); (x) 1500l. Lilith; (y) 1500l. "Queen of the Orkney Islands"; (z) 1500l. Merman; (za) 1500l. Sea Centaur; (zb) 1500l. Albatross (horiz); (zc) 1500l. "The Rime of the Ancient Mariner" (Samuel Coleridge); (zd) 1500l. Haida Eagle (horiz); (ze) 1500l. Poseidon; (zf) 1500l. Captain Ahab "Moby Dick"; (zg) 1500l. Underwater City; (zh) 1500l. Jonah and the Whale; (zi) 1500l. Waskos (horiz); (zj) 1500l. Tom Swift (horiz); (zk) 1500l. Arthropod sea monsters; (zl) 1500l. Sea Serpant; (zm) 1500l. Aphrodite (horiz); (zn) 1500l. Ship's figurehead Set of 40 sheets 48·00 55·00

297 Ox

1997. Chinese New Year ("Year of the Ox"). Multicoloured.
2650 250l. Type **297** (on purple panel) 40 50
2651 250l. Ox (on green panel) 40 50
2652 250l. Ox (on blue panel) 40 50
2653 250l. Ox (on brown panel) 40 50
MS2654 106 × 76 mm. Nos. 2650/3 1·60 1·75
MS2655 106 × 76 mm. 800l. Ox (vert) 1·40 1·75

298 Aladdin and Jasmine

1997. Christmas. Aladdin. Disney Cartoon Characters. Multicoloured.
2656 10l. Type **298** 20 10
2657 15l. Genie and Santa Claus 20 10
2658 20l. Aladdin and Jasmine on magic carpet 25 10
2659 25l. Genie as a Christmas tree 25 10
2660 30l. Genie as Santa Claus and Aladdin 25 10
2661 100l. Aladdin, Jasmine and Genie on magic carpet 1·00 30
2662 800l. Genie writing letter to Santa Claus 3·25 3·50
2663 1000l. Genie with four heads 3·50 4·00
MS2664 Two sheets, each 127 × 101 mm. (a) 2000l. Aladdin under a pile of gold; (b) 2000l. Aladdin and Jasmine on magic carpet (horiz) Set of 2 sheets 7·50 8·00

299 Hong Kong Skyline by Day

1997. "Hong Kong '97" International Stamp Exhibition. Two sheets, each 125 × 68 mm, containing T **299** and similar vert designs. Multicoloured.
MS2665 (a) 500l. × 4 forming panorama of central Hong Kong by day. (b) 500l. × 4 forming panorama of central Hong Kong by night Set of 2 sheets 7·50 8·00

1997. 50th Anniv of UNESCO. As T **342a** of St. Vincent. Multicoloured.
2666 60l. Church, Kizhi Pogost, Russia 15 10
2667 200l. Durmitor National Park, Yugoslavia 40 15
2668 250l. Nessebar, Bulgaria 60 35
2669 300l. Roros, Norway 75 80
2670 300l. Varsovia city gate, Poland 75 80
2671 300l. Nuestra Senora Cathedral, Luxembourg 75 80
2672 300l. Tower, Vilnius, Lithuania 75 80
2673 300l. Jelling, Denmark 75 80
2674 300l. Petajavesi Church, Finland 75 80
2675 300l. Round house, Sweden 75 80
2676 300l. Berne Cathedral, Switzerland 75 80
2677 300l. Slopes of Mount Kilimanjaro, Tanzania 75 80
2678 300l. Tombs, Fasil Ghebbi, Ethiopia 75 80
2679 300l. Mount Ruwenzori National Park, Uganda 75 80
2680 300l. Nubia Monument, Abu Simbel, Egypt 75 80
2681 300l. Tsingy of Bemaraha Nature Reserve, Madagascar 75 80
2682 300l. House, Djenne, Mali 75 80
2683 300l. Traditional house, Ghana 75 80
2684 300l. House, Abomey, Benin 75 80
2685 400l. Gateway, Bukhara, Uzbekistan 85 90
2686 500l. Monastery, Petchersk, Ukraine 95 1·10
2687 500l. Tower, Himeji-jo, Japan (horiz) 95 1·10
2688 500l. Gateway, Himeji-jo, Japan (horiz) 95 1·10
2689 500l. Outer wall and turrets, Himeji-jo, Japan (horiz) 95 1·10
2690 500l. Village, Himeji-jo, Japan (horiz) 95 1·10
2691 500l. Ornate gables, Himeji-jo, Japan (horiz) 95 1·10
2692 800l. Mountains, Slovakia 1·40 1·60
MS2693 Two sheets, each 127 × 102 mm. (a) 2000l. Djudj National Bird Sanctuary, Senegal (horiz). (b) 2000l. The Acropolis, Athens, Greece (horiz) Set of 2 sheets 7·50 8·00
No. 2676 is inscribed "BERNA", No. 2677 "KILIMANDJARO" and No. 2686 "MONESTRY", all in error.

1997. 300th Anniv of Mother Goose Nursery Rhymes. Two sheets, each 72 × 102 mm, containing horiz designs as T **346a** of St. Vincent.
MS2694 (a) 1500l. "Three Blind Mice". (b) 1500l. Woman in pink dress ("Myself") Set of 2 sheets 5·50 6·00

1997. 10th Anniv of Chernobyl Nuclear Disaster. As T **347** of St. Vincent. Multicoloured.
2695 1000l. Child's face and UNESCO emblem 2·00 2·50
2696 1500l. As 1000l., but inscribed "CHABAD'S CHILDREN OF CHERNOBYL" at foot 2·50 3·00

1997. Golden Wedding of Queen Elizabeth and Prince Philip. As T **347a** of St. Vincent. Multicoloured (except Nos. 2699/2700).
2697 400l. Queen Elizabeth II 1·50 1·50
2698 400l. Royal coat of arms 1·50 1·50
2699 400l. Queen Elizabeth with Prince Philip in military uniform (black) 1·50 1·50
2700 400l. Queen Elizabeth with Prince Philip in naval mess dress (black) 1·50 1·50
2701 400l. St. James's Palace 1·50 1·50
2702 400l. Prince Philip 1·50 1·50
MS2703 100 × 70 mm. 1500l. Queen Elizabeth with Prince Philip in naval uniform 2·50 2·75

1997. Birth Bicentenary of Hiroshige (Japanese painter). "One Hundred Famous Views of Edo". As T **347d** of St. Vincent. Multicoloured.
2704 400l. "Hatsune Riding Grounds, Bakuro-cho" 85 85
2710 400l. "Mannen Bridge, Fukagawa" 85 85
2706 400l. "Ryogoku Bridge and the Great Riverbank" 85 85
2707 400l. "Asakusa River, Great Riverbank, Miyato River" 85 85
2708 400l. "Silk-goods Lane, Odenma-cho" 85 85
2709 400l. "Mokuboji Temple, Uchigawa Inlet, Gozensaihata" 85 85
MS2710 Two sheets, each 102 × 127 mm. (a) 1500l. "Nihonbashi Bridge and Edobashi Bridge". (b) 1500l. "Tsukudajima from Eitai Bridge" Set of 2 sheets 5·00 5·50

300 Hong Kong Skyline

1997. Return of Hong Kong to China.
2711 **300** 400l. multicoloured . . . 85 90
2712 – 500l. multicoloured . . . 95 1·00
2713 – 550l. multicoloured . . . 1·00 1·10
2714 – 600l. multicoloured . . . 1·10 1·25
2715 – 650l. multicoloured . . . 1·25 1·40
2716 – 800l. multicoloured . . . 1·50 1·60
DESIGNS: 500l. to 650l. Different views of modern Hong Kong; 800l. Deng Xiaoping.

301 Calgary Stadium, 1988

1997. Winter Olympic Games, Nagano, Japan (1998). Multicoloured.
2717 250l. Type **301** 60 40
2718 300l. Freestyle Skiing Aerials, 1994 (vert) . . . 75 80
2719 300l. Peggy Fleming (U.S.A.) (figure skating, 1968) (vert) 75 80
2720 300l. Japanese competitor (Nordic combined-ski jump, 1992/4) (vert) . . . 75 80
2721 300l. German team (two-man luge, 1968 to 1992) (vert) 75 80
2722 300l. Frank-Peter Roetsch (East Germany) (biathlon, 1988) (vert) 75 80
2723 500l. Ice Hockey (vert) . . . 1·25 1·40
2724 800l. Dan Jansen (U.S.A.) (speed skating, 1994) (vert) . . . . 1·50 1·60
MS2725 Two sheets. (a) 106 × 76 mm. 1500l. Jamaican bobsleigh team (vert). (b) 76 × 106 mm. 1500l. Johann Olav Koss (Norway) (speed skating, 1992/4) (vert) Set of 2 sheets 5·00 5·50

301a Stabile, Uruguay

1997. World Cup Football Championship, France (1998).
2726 **301a** 100l. black 30 20
2727 – 150l. black 40 30
2728 – 200l. black 50 30
2729 – 250l. black 60 40
2730 – 300l. multicoloured . . 80 85
2731 – 300l. multicoloured . . 80 85
2732 – 300l. multicoloured . . 80 85
2733 – 300l. multicoloured . . 80 85
2734 – 300l. multicoloured . . 80 85
2735 – 300l. multicoloured . . 80 85
2736 – 300l. multicoloured . . 80 85
2737 – 300l. multicoloured . . 80 85
2738 – 500l. black . . . . . . 95 1·10
2739 – 600l. black . . . . . . 1·10 1·25
MS2740 Two sheets, each 127 × 102 mm. (a) 1500l. brown (b) 1500l. multicoloured Set of 2 sheets . . . . 6·50 6·50
DESIGNS—VERT: No. 2727, Schavio, Italy; 2728, Kocsis, Hungary; 2729, Nejedly, Czechoslovakia; 2730, Dwight Yorke, Trinidad and Tobago; 2731, Dennis Bergkamp, Netherlands; 2732, Steve McManaman, England; 2733, Ryan Giggs, Wales; 2734, Romario, Brazil; 2735, Faustino Asprilla, Colombia; 2736, Roy Keane, Republic of Ireland; 2737, Peter Schmeichel, Denmark; 2738, Leonidas, Brazil; 2739, Ademir, Brazil. HORIZ: No. **MS**2740a, Pele, Brazil; **MS**2740b, Lato, Poland.

302 "Vindula erota"

1997. Butterflies of the World. Multicoloured.
2741 150l. Type **302** 40 20
2742 200l. "Pereute leucodrosime" 55 20
2743 250l. "Dynastor napolean" 60 25
2744 300l. "Thauria aliris" . . . 70 50
2745 500l. "Lycaena dispar" . . 95 1·00
2746 500l. "Graphium sarpedon" 95 1·00
2747 500l. "Euploe core" . . . . 95 1·00
2748 500l. "Papilio cresphontes" 95 1·00
2749 500l. "Colotis danae" . . . 95 1·00
2750 500l. "Battus philenor" . . 95 1·00
2751 600l. "Papilio aegeus" . . . 1·10 1·25
2752 600l. "Mylothris chloris" . . 1·10 1·25
2753 600l. "Argynnis lathonia" 1·10 1·25
2754 600l. "Elymnias agondas" 1·10 1·25
2755 600l. "Palla ussheri" . . . . 1·10 1·25
2756 600l. "Papilio glaucus" . . . 1·10 1·25
2757 600l. "Cercyonis pegala" . . 1·10 1·25
2758 800l. "Amblypodia anita" 1·50 1·60
2759 1500l. "Kallimoides rumia" 2·75 3·25
2760 2000l. "Papilio dardanas" 3·25 3·75
MS2761 Two sheets, each 74 × 103 mm. (a) 3000l. "Hebomoia glaucippe" (horiz). (b) 3000l. "Colias eurytheme" (horiz) Set of 2 sheets . . . . 9·00 10·00
Nos. 2745/50 and 2752/7 respectively were printed together, se-tenant, with the backgrounds forming composite designs.

303 Lon Chaney in "Phantom of the Opera", 1925

1997. Famous Films. Horror classics (Nos. 2762/70) or the films of Alfred Hitchcock (Nos. 2771/9). Multicoloured.
2762 300l. Type **303** 80 80
2763 300l. Boris Karloff in "The Mummy", 1932 . . . . . 80 80
2764 300l. Fredric March in "Dr. Jekyll and Mr Hyde", 1932 . . . . . 80 80
2765 300l. Lon Chaney Jr. in "The Wolf Man", 1941 80 80
2766 300l. Charles Laughton in "Island of Lost Souls", 1933 . . . . 80 80
2767 300l. Lionel Atwill in "Mystery of the Wax Museum", 1933 . . . . 80 80
2768 300l. Bela Lugosi in "Dracula", 1931 . . . . 80 80
2769 300l. Vincent Price in "The Haunted Palace", 1963 . . 80 80
2770 300l. Elsa Lanchester in "Bride of Frankenstein", 1935 . . . . 80 80
2771 350l. Ray Milland in "Dial M for Murder", 1954 . . 80 80
2772 350l. James Stewart and Kim Novak in "Vertigo", 1958 . . . . 80 80
2773 350l. Cary Grant, Ingrid Bergman and Claude Rains in "Notorious", 1946 . . . . 80 80
2774 350l. Farley Granger and John Dall in "Rope", 1948 . . . . 80 80
2775 350l. Cary Grant in "North by Northwest", 1959 . . 80 80
2776 350l. James Stewart and Grace Kelly in "Rear Window", 1954 . . . . . 80 80
2777 350l. Joan Fontaine and Laurence Olivier in "Rebecca", 1940 . . . . 80 80
2778 350l. Tippi Hedren in "The Birds", 1963 . . . . . . 80 80
2779 350l. Janet Leigh in "Psycho", 1960 . . . . . 80 80
MS2780 Two sheets. (a) 72 × 102 mm. 1500l. Alfred Hitchcock. (b) 82 × 82 mm. 3000l. Boris Karloff in "Son of Frankenstein" 1939 Set of 2 sheets 8·50 9·00
Nos. 2762/70 and 2771/9 respectively were printed together, se-tenant, with the backgrounds forming composite designs.

304 Shetland Sheepdog

305 "Ansellia africana"

1997. Dogs and Cats. Multicoloured.
2781 100l. Type **304** 30 15
2782 150l. American shorthair tabby cat 45 25
2783 250l. British shorthair cat 55 45
2784 250l. Alaskan husky 55 45
2785 400l. Basset hound 70 70
2786 400l. Irish setter 70 70
2787 400l. St. Bernard 70 70
2788 400l. German shepherd . . 70 70
2789 400l. Dalmatian 70 70
2790 400l. Cocker spaniel 70 70
2791 400l. Chartreux cat 70 70
2792 400l. Abyssinian cat 70 70
2793 400l. Burmese cat 70 70
2794 400l. White angora cat . . . 70 70
2795 400l. Japanese bobtail cat 70 70
2796 400l. Cymric cat 70 70
2797 500l. Turkish angora cat . . 80 80
2798 600l. Jack Russell terrier . . 90 1·10
MS2799 Two sheets, each 106 × 75 mm. (a) 1500l. Boxer (31 × 63 mm). (b) 1500l. Egyptian mau cat (63 × 31 mm) Set of 2 sheets . . . . 5·50 6·00

1997. Orchids of the World. Multicoloured.
2800 150l. Type **305** 50 25
2801 200l. "Maxillaria praestans" 60 30
2802 250l. "Cymbidium mimi" . . 65 35
2803 300l. "Dendrobium bigibbum" 70 40
2804 400l. "Laelia anceps" . . . 80 85
2805 400l. "Paphiopedilum fairrieanum" 80 85
2806 400l. "Restrepia lansbergii" 80 85
2807 400l. "Yamadara cattleya" 80 85
2808 400l. "Cleistes divaricata" 80 85
2809 400l. "Calypso bulbosa" . . 80 85
2810 500l. "Encyclia vitellina" . . 90 90
2811 800l. "Epidendrum prismatocarpum" . . . . 1·50 1·75
MS2812 Two sheets, each 76 × 106 mm. (a) 1500l. "Paphiopedilum tonsum" (b) 1500l. "Odontoglossum schieperianum" Set of 2 sheets 5·50 5·50

306 Daisy Duck

1997. Christmas. Disney Holidays. Multicoloured.
2813 50l. Type **306** 20 20
2814 50l. Huey, Dewey and Louie 20 20
2815 50l. Donald Duck 20 20
2816 50l. Minnie Mouse 20 20
2817 50l. Morty and Ferdie . . . 20 20
2818 50l. Mickey Mouse 20 20
2819 150l. As No. 2814 . . . . . 60 60
2820 200l. As No. 2817 . . . . . 75 75
2821 250l. Type **306** 90 90
2822 300l. As No. 2816 . . . . . 1·10 1·10
2823 400l. As No. 2818 . . . . . 1·25 1·40
2824 500l. As No. 2815 . . . . . 1·50 1·60
2825 600l. Pluto . . . . 1·75 2·00
2826 800l. Goofy . . . . 2·25 2·50
MS2827 Two sheets. (a) 114 × 140 mm. 2000l. Mickey Mouse in sleigh. (b) 140 × 114 mm. 2000l. Mickey, Donald and Daisy (horiz) Set of 2 sheets . . . . 11·00 12·00

307 Benoist Type XIV

308a With Daffodils

308 "The Annunciation" (Titian)

1997. Development of the Civil Airliner. Mult.
2828 600l. Type **307** . . . . . . 1·25 1·25
2829 600l. Douglas DC-3 . . . . 1·25 1·25
2830 600l. Junkers JU52/3m seaplane . . . . 1·25 1·25
2831 600l. Sikorsky S-42 flying boat . . . . 1·25 1·25
2832 600l. Sud Caravelle 6 . . . 1·25 1·25
2833 600l. Boeing 707 . . . . . 1·25 1·25
2834 600l. De Havilland Comet 1·25 1·25
2835 600l. Airbus Industrie A300 1·25 1·25
MS2836 Two sheets, each 121 × 96 mm. (a) 2000l. Lockheed L.1649A Starliner (91 × 34 mm). (b) 2000l. Concorde (91 × 34 mm) Set of 2 sheets . . . . 8·00 8·50

1997. Christmas. Religious Paintings. Mult.
2837 100l. Type **308** 30 10
2838 150l. "The Annunciation" (Titian) (different) 40 20
2839 200l. "Madonna of Foligno" (Raphael) 50 20
2840 250l. "The Annunciation" (Michelino) 60 25
2841 500l. "The Prophet Isaiah" (Michelangelo) . . . . . 1·10 1·40
2842 600l. "Three Angels" (Master of the Rhenish Housebook) . . . . . . 1·40 1·60
MS2843 Two sheets, each 105 × 95 mm. (a) 2000l. "The Fall of the Rebel Angels" (Bruegel the Elder) (horiz). (b) 2000l. Angel and Monk (Anon) (horiz) Set of 2 sheets . . . . 6·00 7·00

1998. Diana, Princess of Wales Commemoration. Multicoloured (except Nos. 2844, 2849, 2854 and 2856).
2844 400l. Type **308a** (violet and black) 80 80
2845 400l. Carrying bouquet . . 80 80
2846 400l. With Mother Teresa 80 80
2847 400l. Wearing green and black jacket 80 80
2848 400l. With shawl over head 80 80
2849 400l. In evening dress (red and black) 80 80
2850 400l. Wearing choker and earrings 80 80
2851 400l. With Prince William 80 80
2852 400l. Wearing blue jacket and hat 80 80
2853 400l. Wearing white jacket 80 80
2854 400l. Wearing hat (brown and black) 80 80
2855 400l. Wearing black evening dress 80 80
2856 400l. Laughing (blue and black) 80 80
2857 400l. Wearing blue and white jacket and hat . . . 80 80
2858 400l. Wearing green jacket with arms folded 80 80
2859 400l. Wearing black and white hat 80 80
2860 400l. Wearing open white shirt 80 80
2861 400l. Getting out of car . . 80 80
MS2862 Three sheets. (a) 100 × 70 mm. 1500l. Spooning food into bowl. (b) 100 × 70 mm. 1500l. Wearing grey-blue hat and jacket. (c) 70 × 100 mm. 1500l. Inspecting guard of honour Set of 3 sheets . . . . 8·00 8·50

309 Tiger

1998. Chinese New Year ("Year of the Tiger"). Designs with the tiger in the colour given.
2863 **309** 250l. mult (mauve) . . . 10 15
2864 – 250l. mult (lake) 10 15
2865 – 250l. mult (purple) . . . 10 15
2866 – 250l. mult (red) 10 15
MS2867 76 × 106 mm. 800l. multicoloured (vert) 35 40

310 "Metagyrphus nitens"

311 Hypsilophodon

1998. Fauna and Flora. Multicoloured.
2868 200l. Type **310** 10 15
2869 250l. Lord Derby's parakeet 10 15
2870 300l. Narcissus 15 20
2871 400l. "Barbus tetrazona" (fish) (horiz) 20 25
2872 450l. Japanese white-eyes (bird) (horiz) 20 25
2873 450l. Rhododendron (horiz) 20 25
2874 450l. Slow loris (horiz) . . . 20 25
2875 450l. Gentiana (flower) (horiz) 20 25
2876 450l. "Orthetrum albistylum" (dragonfly) (horiz) 20 25

2877 450l. "Coluber jugularis" (snake) (horiz) 20 25
2878 450l. Cheetah (horiz) . . . 20 25
2879 450l. "Ornithogalum thyrsoides" (plant) (horiz) 20 25
2880 450l. Ostrich (horiz) 20 25
2881 450l. Common chameleon (horiz) 20 25
2882 450l. Fennec fox (horiz) . . 20 25
2883 450l. "Junonia hierta cebrene" (butterfly) (horiz) 20 25
2884 500l. "Agalychnis callidryas" (frog) (horiz) 20 25
2885 600l. Wolverine (horiz) . . . 25 30
MS2886 Two sheets (a) 70 × 100 mm. 2000l. Louisiana heron ("Tricoloured Heron") (b) 100 × 70 mm. 2000l. "Atheris squamiger" (snake) (horiz) Set of 2 sheets . . . . 1·80 1·90

Nos. 2872/7 and 2878/83 respectively were printed together, se-tenant, with the backgrounds forming composite designs.

1998. Prehistoric Animals. Multicoloured.
2887 200l. Type **311** 10 15
2888 400l. Lambeosaurus 20 25
2889 500l. Corythosaurus 20 25
2890 500l. Tyrannosaurus (horiz) 20 25
2891 500l. Tenontosaurus (horiz) 20 25
2892 500l. Deinonychus (horiz) 20 25
2893 500l. Triceratops (horiz) . . 20 25
2894 500l. Maiasaura with eggs (horiz) 20 25
2895 500l. Struthiomimus (horiz) 20 25
2896 500l. Plateosaurus 20 25
2897 500l. Tyrannosaurus 20 25
2898 500l. Brachiosaurus 20 25
2899 500l. Iguanodon 20 25
2900 500l. Styracosaurus 20 25
2901 500l. Hadrosaurus 20 25
2902 600l. Stegosaurus 25 30
2903 800l. Antrodemus (horiz) . . 35 40
MS2904 Two sheets. (a) 73 × 103 mm. 2000l. Triceratops (horiz). (b) 83 × 108 mm. 2000l. Tyrannosaurus (horiz) Set of 2 sheets . . . . 1·80 1·90

Nos. 2890/5 and 2896/2901 respectively were printed together, se-tenant, with the backgrounds forming composite designs.

312 Phoenician Galley

1998. Ships of the World. Multicoloured.
2905 300l. Type **312** 15 20
2906 300l. Viking longship . . . 15 20
2907 300l. Carrack 15 20
2908 300l. Venetian galley 15 20
2909 300l. Galeasse 15 20
2910 300l. Chebeck 15 20
2911 300l. Junk 15 20
2912 300l. H.M.S. "Victory" (ship of the line, 1765) 15 20
2913 300l. "Savannah" (paddle-steamer) 15 20
2914 300l. Gaissa (sailing canoe) 15 20
2915 300l. H.M.S. "Warrior" (ironclad) 15 20
2916 300l. "Preussen" (full-rigged ship) 15 20
MS2917 Two sheets, each 108 × 83 mm. (a) 2000l. "Santa Maria" (Columbus) (56 × 41 mm). (b) 2000l. "Titanic" (liner) (56 × 41 mm) Set of 2 sheets . . 1·80 1·90

1998. 70th Birthday of Mickey Mouse. Nos. 2813/18 and **MS**2827. Optd with Mickey Mouse and **HAPPY BIRTHDAY 1998**.
2918 50l. Type **306** 50 50
2919 50l. Huey, Dewey and Louie 50 50
2920 50l. Donald Duck 50 50
2921 50l. Minnie Mouse 50 50
2922 50l. Morty and Ferdie . . . 50 50
2923 50l. Mickey Mouse 50 50
MS2924 Two sheets. (a) 114 × 140 mm. 2000l. Mickey Mouse in sleigh. (b) 140 × 114 mm. 2000l. Mickey, Donald and Daisy (horiz) Set of 2 sheets . . . . 11·00 12·00

No. **MS**2924 are overprinted on the sheet margins which are additionally overprinted "MICKEY & MINNIE — 70th ANNIVERSARY".

314 Kiara and Butterfly

1998. Disney's "Lion King" (cartoon film). Multicoloured.
2925 500l. Type **314** . . . . . . 1·25 1·25
2926 500l. Timon and Pumbaa 1·25 1·25
2927 500l. Kiara . . . . 1·25 1·25
2928 500l. Kiara and Kovu lying down . . . . 1·25 1·25
2929 500l. Kovu with bird . . . 1·25 1·25
2930 500l. Kiara sitting with Kovu . . . . 1·25 1·25
2931 500l. Kiara and bird . . . . 1·25 1·25
2932 500l. Pumbaa . . . . 1·25 1·25
2933 500l. Kiara and Kovu side by side . . . . 1·25 1·25
2934 500l. Kovu . . . . 1·25 1·25
2935 500l. Kiara and Kovu back to back . . . . 1·25 1·25
2936 500l. Timon . . . . 1·25 1·25
MS2937 Two sheets, each 130 × 104 mm. (a) 2500l. Pumbaa and Timon. (b) 2500l. Kiara, Kovu and butterflies (horiz). 12·00 13·00

315 "Mary Magdalen Penitent" (Titian)

1998. Christmas. Religious Paintings. Mult.
2938 200l. Type **315** 10 15
2939 500l. "Lamentation of Christ" (Veronese) . . . 20 25
2940 1500l. "Building of Noah's Ark" (Guido Reni) . . . 65 70
2941 2000l. "Abraham and Isaac" (Rembrandt) 90 95
MS2942 Two sheets, each 70 × 100 mm. (a) 3000l. "The Assumption of the Virgin" (Murillo). (b) 3000l. "Adoration of the Shepherds" (Murillo) Set of 2 sheets . . . . 2·75 3·00

1998. 25th Death Anniv of Pablo Picasso (painter). As T **373** of St. Vincent. Multicoloured.
2943 400l. "Man with Straw Hat and Ice Cream Cone" (vert) 20 25
2944 600l. "Woman in a Red Armchair" (vert) 25 30
2945 800l. "Nude in a Garden" 35 40
MS2946 101 × 127 mm. 2000l. "Girl holding a Dove" (vert) 90 95

315a Dan Beard and Lord Baden-Powell, 1937

1998. 19th World Scout Jamboree, Chile. Multicoloured (except No. 2950).
2947 1500l. Type **315a** 65 70
2948 1500l. Kuwaiti Scouts . . . 65 70
2949 1500l. Scout leader feeding bear cub 65 70
2950 1500l. William D. Boyce (founder of Lone Scouts) (purple, brown and black) (vert) 65 70
2951 1500l. Guion S. Bluford (astronaut and former Eagle scout) (vert) 65 70
2952 1500l. Ellison S. Onizuka (astronaut and former Eagle scout) (vert) 65 70
MS2953 Two sheets, each 70 × 100 mm. (a) 3000l. Lord and Lady Baden-Powell, 1932. (b) 3000l. Feeding bear cub from bottle Set of 2 sheets . . . . . 2·75 3·00

315b Mahatma Gandhi

316a Diana, Princess of Wales

316 "Rocks and a Small Valley"

1998. 50th Death Anniv of Mahatma Gandhi.
2954 **315b** 600l. multicoloured . . 25 30
MS2955 98 × 59 mm. 2000l. brown and black (horiz) 90 95

1998. 80th Anniv of Royal Air Force. As T **373d** of St. Vincent. Multicoloured.
2956 800l. McDonnell Douglas FRG2 Phantom 35 40
2957 800l. Pair of Panavia Tornado GR1s 35 40
2958 800l. Sepecat Jaguar GR1A 35 40
2959 800l. Lockheed C-130 Hercules 35 40
MS2960 Two sheets, each 92 × 70 mm.(a) 2000l. Lysander (reconnaissance) and Eurofighter EF-2000. (b) 2000l. Common buzzard and Bristol F2B fighter Set of 2 sheets . . . . 1·80 1·90

1998. Birth Bicentenary of Eugene Delacroix (painter). Multicoloured.
2961 400l. Type **316** 20 25
2962 400l. "Jewish Musicians from Magador" 20 25
2963 400l. "Moroccans travelling" 20 25
2964 400l. "Women of Algiers in their Apartment" 20 25
2965 400l. "Moroccan Military Training" 20 25
2966 400l. "Arabs skirmishing in the Mountains" 20 25
2967 400l. "Arab Chieftain reclining on a Carpet" . . 20 25
2968 400l. "Procession in Tangier" 20 25
MS2969 85 × 100 mm. 400l. "Self-portrait" (vert) 20 25

1998. 1st Death Anniv of Diana, Princess of Wales. Multicoloured.
2970 **316a** 600l. multicoloured . . 25 30

317 Rabbit

1998. Chinese New Year ("Year of the Rabbit"). Designs with the rabbit in the colour given.
2971 **317** 700l. mult (red) 30 35
2972 – 700l. mult (purple) . . . 30 35
2973 – 700l. mult (blue) 30 35
2974 – 700l. mult (violet) . . . 30 35
MS2975 76 × 106 mm. 1500l. multicoloured (vert) 65 70

318 Powder-blue Surgeonfish

1999. International Year of the Ocean. Mult.
2976 150l. Type **318** 10 10
2977 250l. Frilled anemone . . . 10 15
2978 400l. Reef heron ("Eastern Reef Heron") 20 25
2979 400l. Dolphins 20 25
2980 400l. Humpback whale and sailing ship 20 25
2981 400l. Green-winged macaw ("Red and Green Macaw") 20 25
2982 400l. Blue tangs 20 25
2983 400l. Guitarfish and blue-striped pipefish 20 25
2984 400l. Manatees 20 25
2985 400l. Hammerhead shark . . 20 25
2986 400l. Blue shark 20 25
2987 400l. Lemon goby and moorish idol 20 25
2988 400l. Ribbon moray ("Ribbon Eels") 20 25
2989 400l. Loggerhead turtle . . 20 25
2990 500l. Blue shark 20 25
2991 500l. Tiger shark 20 25
2992 500l. Bull shark 20 25
2993 500l. Great white shark . . 20 25
2994 500l. Scalloped hammerhead shark 20 25
2995 500l. Oceanic white-tipped shark 20 25
2996 500l. Zebra shark 20 25
2997 500l. Leopard shark 20 25
2998 500l. Horn shark 20 25
2999 500l. Hector's dolphin . . . 20 25
3000 500l. Tucuxi 20 25
3001 500l. Hourglass dolphin . . 20 25
3002 500l. Bottlenose dolphin . . 20 25
3003 500l. Gray's beaked whale 20 25
3004 500l. Bowhead whale . . . 20 25
3005 500l. Fin whale 20 25
3006 500l. Gray whale 20 25
3007 500l. Blue whale 30 35
3008 600l. Red beard sponge . . 25 30
3009 800l. Dusky batfish ("Red-finned Batfish") 35 40
MS3010 Three sheets, each 110 × 85 mm. (a) 3000l. Purple fire goby ("Purple Fire-fish"). (b) 3000l. Spotted eagle ray. (c) 3000l. Leather-back turtle Set of 3 sheets 4·00 4·25

Nos. 2978/89, 2990/8 and 2999/3007 were each printed together, se-tenant, with the backgrounds forming composite designs.

319 Grumman X-29

1999. Aircraft. Multicoloured.
3011 200l. Type **319** 10 15
3012 300l. Bell XS-1 rocket aircraft 15 20
3013 400l. Mikoyan Gurevich MiG-21 . . . . 20 25
3014 600l. Bleriot XI 25 30
3015 600l. Nieuport 11 "Bebe" 25 30
3016 600l. D.H.100 Vampire . . 25 30
3017 600l. Aerospatiale/Aeritalia ATR 72 . . . . 25 30
3018 600l. Fiat CR-32 . . . . . 25 30
3019 600l. Curtiss P-6E Hawk . . 25 30
3020 600l. SAAB JA 37 Viggen 25 30
3021 600l. Piper PA-46 Malibu 25 30
3022 600l. Grumman F-14 Tomcat 25 30
3023 600l. Grumman F3F-1 . . . 25 30
3024 600l. North American F-86A Sabre 25 30
3025 600l. Cessna 377 Super Skymaster 25 30
3026 600l. General Dynamics F-16 Fighting Falcon . . 25 30
3027 600l. "Voyager" experimental aircraft . . . 25 30
3028 600l. Fairchild A10A Thunderbolt II 25 30
3029 600l. Wiley Post's Lockheed Vega, 1933 . . . . 25 30
3030 600l. Amelia Earhart's Lockheed Vega, 1930 . . 25 30
3031 600l. Sopwith Tabloid . . . 25 30
3032 600l. Vickers F.B.5 "Gun Bus" 25 30
3033 600l. Savoia-Marchetti S.M. 79-II Sparviero 25 30
3034 600l. Mitsubishi A6M3 "Zero Sen" 25 30
3035 600l. Morane-Saulnier L . . 25 30
3036 600l. Shorts 360 . . . . . 25 30
3037 600l. Tupolev TU-160 . . . 25 30
3038 600l. Mikoyan-Gurevich MiG-15 . . . . 25 30
3039 800l. Fokker F.VIIa/3m "Southern Cross" 35 40
3040 1500l. Supermarine S6B (seaplane) 65 70
MS3041 Two sheets, each 98 × 68 mm. (a) 3000l. Ryan NYP Special "Spirit of St. Louis" (56 × 42 mm). (b) 3000l. Canadair CL-215 (fire-fighting amphibian) (56 × 42 mm) Set of 2 sheets . . 2·75 3·00

No. 3023 is inscribed "GUMMAN F3F-1", No. 3027 "NICK" and No. 3030 "Amella Earhart", all in error.

320 "Geranium wallichianum"

1999. "Australia '99" World Stamp Exhibition, Melbourne. Flowers. Multicoloured.
3042 150l. Type **320** 10 10
3043 200l. "Osmanthus x burkwoodii" 10 15
3044 250l. "Iris pallida dalmatica" (vert) 10 15
3045 500l. Rhododendron (vert) 20 25
3046 600l. Rose (vert) 25 30
3047 600l. "Clematis hybrida" (vert) 25 30
3048 600l. "Cardiospermum halicacabum" (vert) . . . 25 30
3049 600l. "Fritillaria imperialis" (vert) 25 30
3050 600l. "Iris foetidiissima" (vert) 25 30
3051 600l. Pyracantha (vert) . . . 25 30
3052 600l. "Hepatica transsilvanica" (vert) . . . 25 30
3053 600l. "Aquilegia olympica" 25 30
3054 600l. Lilium (orange) . . . 25 30
3055 600l. "Magnolia grandiflora" 25 30
3056 600l. "Polygonatum x hybridum" 25 30
3057 600l. "Clematis montana" 25 30
3058 600l. "Vinca minor" 25 30
3059 600l. "Jack Snipe" 25 30
3060 600l. "Alstroemeria ligtu" 25 30
3061 600l. Lilium (yellow) 25 30
3062 600l. "Marjorie fair" 25 30
3063 600l. "Anemone coronaria" 25 30
3064 600l. "Clematis ranncu lanaceae" 25 30
3065 600l. "Colchicum speciosum" 25 30
3066 600l. "Scandere" 25 30
3067 600l. "Helianthus annuus" 25 30
3068 600l. "Lady Kerkrade" . . . 25 30
3069 600l. "Clematis x durandii" 25 30
3070 600l. "Lilium regale" 25 30
3071 800l. Papoose (vert) 35 40
3072 1500l. "Viola labradorica" (vert) 65 70

3073 2000l. "Rosa banksiae lutea" (vert) 90 95
MS3074 Four sheets. (a) 100×74 mm. 4000l. "Clerodendrum trichotomum fargesii" (b) 75×100 mm. 4000l. "Rubus fruitcosus" (vert). (c) 75×100 mm. 4000l. "Crocus angustifolius" (vert). (d) 75×100 mm. 4000l. "Holboellia" Set of 4 sheets 7·00 7·25

Nos. 3047/52, 3053/8 and 3071/3 were printed together, se-tenant, with the backgrounds forming a composite design.

Only Nos. 3042/6 and 3071/3 show the "Australia '99" emblem actually printed on the stamp.

No. 3043 is inscribed "Osmanthus burkwoodu" and No. 3069 "Clematix x durandii", both in error.

321 Red-headed Malimbe
322 Diana Monkey

1999. Birds of Africa. Multicoloured.
3075 400l. Type **321** 20 25
3076 500l. Common kestrel 20 25
3077 600l. Little owl 25 30
3078 600l. Eastern white pelican ("Great White Pelican") 25 30
3079 600l. Superb starling 25 30
3080 600l. Red-throated bee eater 25 30
3081 600l. Woodland kingfisher 25 30
3082 600l. Purple swamphen 25 30
3083 600l. Lesser pied kingfisher ("Pied Kingfisher") 25 30
3084 600l. African spoonbill 25 30
3085 600l. Egyptian plover ("Crocodilebird") 25 30
3086 600l. Cattle egret 25 30
3087 600l. White-fronted bee eater 25 30
3088 600l. Gray parrot ("African Grey Parrot") 25 30
3089 600l. Cinnamon-chested bee eater 25 30
3090 600l. Malachite kingfisher 25 30
3091 600l. White-throated bee eater 25 30
3092 600l. Yellow-billed stork 25 30
3093 600l. Hildebrandt's starling 25 30
3094 600l. White-faced whistling duck (horiz) 25 30
3095 600l. Black-headed heron (horiz) 25 30
3096 600l. Black-headed gonolek (horiz) 25 30
3097 600l. Malachite kingfisher (horiz) 25 30
3098 600l. African fish eagle ("Fish-eagle") (horiz) 25 30
3099 600l. African spoonbill (horiz) 25 30
3100 600l. African skimmer (horiz) 25 30
3101 600l. Black heron (horiz) 25 30
3102 600l. Allen's gallinule (horiz) 25 30
3103 600l. Montagu's harrier (horiz) 25 30
3104 600l. Booted eagle (horiz) 25 30
3105 600l. Yellow-crested helmet shrike (horiz) 25 30
3106 600l. Red-tufted malachite sunbird ("Scarlet-tufted Malachite Sunbird") (horiz) 25 30
3107 600l. Pin-tailed whydah (horiz) 25 30
3108 600l. Red-headed weaver ("Red-headed Malimbe") (horiz) 25 30
3109 600l. Violet-backed sunbird (horiz) 25 30
3110 600l. Yellow white eye (horiz) 25 30
3111 600l. Brubru shrike (horiz) 25 30
3112 600l. African paradise flycatcher ("African Paradise Monarch") (horiz) 25 30
3113 600l. Lilac-breasted roller (horiz) 25 30
3114 600l. Scops owl ("European Scops Owl") (horiz) 25 30
3115 600l. African emerald cuckoo (horiz) 25 30
3116 600l. Blue flycatcher ("Blue Monarch") (horiz) 25 30
3117 600l. African golden oriole (horiz) 25 30
3118 600l. White-throated bee eater (horiz) 25 30
3119 600l. Black-bellied seedcracker (horiz) 25 30
3120 600l. Hoopoe (horiz) 25 30
3121 600l. Scimitar-bill (horiz) 25 30
3122 600l. Bateleur (horiz) 25 30
3123 600l. Village weaver ("Black-headed Weaver") (horiz) 25 30
3124 600l. Variable sunbird (horiz) 25 30
3125 600l. Blue swallow (horiz) 25 30
3126 600l. Red-crowned bishop ("Black-winged Red Bishop") (horiz) 25 30
3127 600l. Namaqua dove (horiz) 25 30
3128 600l. Golden-breasted bunting (horiz) 25 30
3129 600l. Hartlaub's bustard (horiz) 25 30
MS3130 Six sheets, each 85×110 mm (3000l.) or 73×98 mm (4000l.). (a) 3000l. African fish eagle. (b) 3000l. Baglafecht weaver ("Richenow's Weaver"). (c) 4000l. African Pygmy kingfisher. (d) 4000l. Ruwenzori turaco. (e) 4000l. Crowned crane ("Grey Crowned Crane") (f) 4000l. Whale-headed stork ("Shoebill") Set of 6 sheets 9·75 10·00

Nos. 3078/85, 3086/93, 3094/102, 3103/11, 3112/20 and 3121/9 were each printed together, se-tenant, with the backgrounds forming composite designs.

No. 3077 is inscribed "LITLE OWL", No. 3087 "BMerops bullockoides", No. 3112 "Terpsiphonevirdis", No. 3121 "Scimitarbill", No. 3124 "Nectarina", No. 3126 "hordeaceus" and No. **MS**3130d ("Rwenzori"), all in error.

1999. Wildlife. Multicoloured.
3131 300l. Type **322** 15 20
3132 800l. Bush pig 35 40
3133 900l. Flap-necked chameleon 40 45
3134 900l. Golden oriole 40 45
3135 900l. European bee eater 40 45
3136 900l. Leopard 40 45
3137 900l. Lion 40 45
3138 900l. Chimpanzee 40 45
3139 900l. Senegal galago 40 45
3140 900l. Hoopoe 40 45
3141 900l. Long-tailed pangolin 40 45
3142 900l. Hippopotamus 40 45
3143 900l. African elelphant 40 45
3144 900l. Red-billed hornbill 40 45
3145 1500l. Lioness 65 70
MS3146 Two sheets, each 85×110 mm. (a) 3000l. Grey parrot. (b) 3000l. West African linsang Set of 2 sheets 2·75 3·00

Nos. 3133/8 and 3139/44 were each printed together, se-tenant, forming composite designs.

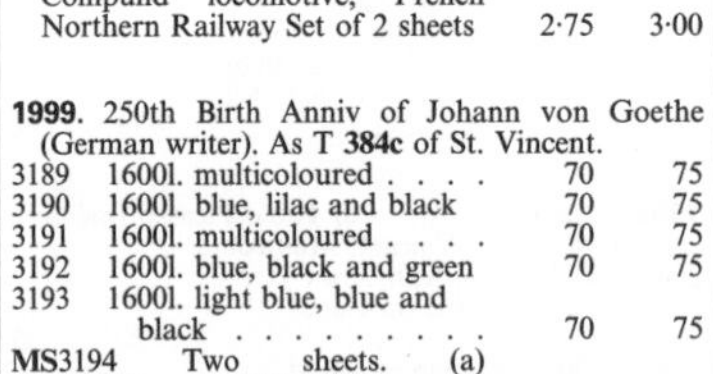

323 Steam Locomotive, Benguela Railway, Angola

1999. Famous Trains. Multicoloured.
3147 100l. The "Rocket" (vert) 10 10
3148 150l. Type **323** 10 10
3149 200l. Class 310 steam locomotive, Sudan 10 15
3150 250l. Steam locomotive, Chicago, Burlington and Quincy Railway, U.S.A. 10 15
3151 300l. Class "Terrier" tank locomotive, Great Britain 15 20
3152 400l. Dublin to Cork express train, Ireland 20 25
3153 500l. Steam locomotive "George Stephenson", Scotland 20 25
3154 600l. Shay steam locomotive 25 30
3155 800l. Class 19D, Africa 35 40
3156 800l. Double-headed train on viaduct over Kaaiman River, Africa 35 40
3157 800l. Bo-Bo electric locomotive, Egypt 35 40
3158 800l. Gmam Garratt steam locomotive, South Africa 35 40
3159 800l. Passenger train at Rabat, Morocco 35 40
3160 800l. Class 14A Garratt, Rhodesia 35 40
3161 800l. Western type steam locomotive, U.S.A. 35 40
3162 800l. "The Flying Scotsman" express, Scotland 35 40
3163 800l. Steam locomotive "Lord Nelson" 35 40
3164 800l. Steam locomotive "Mallard" 35 40
3165 800l. Steam locomotive "Evening Star" 35 40
3166 800l. Indian Railways Class WP steam locomotive No. 7418 35 40
3167 1500l. "South Wind" express, U.S.A. (horiz) 65 70
MS3168 Two sheets. (a) 76×106 mm. 3000l. Railcar on an Alpine rack railway (vert). (b) 106×76 mm. 3000l. Royal train, Rhodesia Set of 2 sheets 2·75 3·00

No. 3166 is inscribed "THE BRITIANIA" and No. **MS**3168a "MOUNTAIN CLASS GARRATT/AFRICA", both in error.

1999. "iBRA '99" International Stamp Exhibition, Nuremburg. As T **384a** of St. Vincent. Mult.
3169 1500l. "Claud Hamilton" steam locomotive, Germany 65 70
3170 2000l. "Borsig" steam locomotive, 1835, Germany 90 95

1999. 150th Death Anniv of Katsushika Hokusai (Japanese artist). As T **384b** of St. Vincent. Multicoloured.
3171 1000l. "People admiring Mount Fuji from a Tea House" 45 50
3172 1000l. "People on a Temple Balcony" 45 50
3173 1000l. "Sea Life" (shrimp) 45 50
3174 1000l. "Sea Life" (shells) 45 50
3175 1000l. "The Pontoon Bridge at Sano in Winter" 45 50
3176 1000l. "A Shower below the Summit" 45 50
3177 1000l. "The Hanging Cloud Bridge" 45 50
3178 1000l. "The Timber Yard by the Tate River" 45 50
3179 1000l. "Bird Drawings" (owl) 45 50
3180 1000l. "Bird Drawings" (ducks) 45 50
3181 1000l. "Travellers crossing the Oi River" 45 50
3182 1000l. "Travellers on the Tokaido Road at Hodogaya" 45 50
MS3183 Two sheets, each 100×70 mm. (a) 3000l. "A view of Mount Fuji and Travellers by a Bridge" (vert). (b) 3000l. "A Sudden Gust of Wind at Ejiri" (vert) Set of 2 sheets 2·75 3·00

1999. 10th Anniv of United Nations Rights of the Child Convention. As T **348d** of St. Vincent. Multicoloured.
3184 1600l. Japanese girl holding candle 70 75
3185 1600l. Two Japanese children 70 75
3186 1600l. Japanese girl in kimono 70 75
MS3187 110×85 mm. 3000l. Baby boy (horiz) 1·30 1·40

1999. "PhilexFrance '99" International Stamp Exhibition, PAris. railway Locomotives. Two sheets, each 106×76 mm containing horiz designs as T **385d** of St. Vincent. Multicoloured.
MS3188 (a) 3000l. Crampton locomotive, French Eastern Railway. (b) 3000l. De Glehn Compund locomotive, French Northern Railway Set of 2 sheets 2·75 3·00

1999. 250th Birth Anniv of Johann von Goethe (German writer). As T **384c** of St. Vincent.
3189 1600l. multicoloured 70 75
3190 1600l. blue, lilac and black 70 75
3191 1600l. multicoloured 70 75
3192 1600l. blue, black and green 70 75
3193 1600l. light blue, blue and black 70 75
MS3194 Two sheets. (a) 106×76 mm. 3000l. brown and black. (b) 76×106 mm. 3000l. brown and black Set of 2 sheets 2·75 3·00

DESIGNS—HORIZ: No. 3189, Helena with her Chorus; 3190, Goethe and Schiller; 3191, Faust seated beside Helena; 3192, The Witch beseeching Faust to drink her fiery brew; 3193, Margaret placing flowers before the niche of Mater Dolorosa; No. **MS**3191a, Angelic spirit. VERT: No. **MS**3194b, Ariel.

No. 3192 is inscribed "BESEIGES" in error.

1999. "Queen Elizabeth the Queen Mother's Century". As T **386b** of St. Vincent.
3195 1300l. black and gold 60 65
3196 1300l. multicoloured 60 65
3197 1300l. black and gold 60 65
3198 1300l. multicoloured 60 65
MS3199 153×157 mm. 4000l. multicoloured 1·80 1·90

DESIGNS: No. 3195, Duke and Duchess of York and Princess Elizabeth, 1926; 3196, Queen Mother, 1979; 3197, Queen Mother visiting Nairobi, 1959; 3198, Queen Mother holding bouquet, 1991. 37×50 mm: No. **MS**3199, Queen Elizabeth in Coronation robes, 1937.

No. **MS**3199 also shows the Royal Arms embossed in gold.

324 "Interpretation of a Poem of Shi-Tao" (Fu Baoshi)

326 Sophie Rhys-Jones

325 Macao Skyline inside "MACAU"

1999. "China '99" International Stamp Exhibition, Beijing. Paintings of Fu Baoshi (Chinese artist). Multicoloured.
3200 400l. Type **324** 20 25
3201 400l. "Autumn of Ho-Pao" 20 25
3202 400l. "Landscape in Rain" (bridge at bottom right) 20 25
3203 400l. "Landscape in Rain" (mountain peaks) 20 25
3204 400l. "Landscape in Rain" (mountain rest house) 20 25
3205 400l. "Portrait of To-Fu" 20 25
3206 400l. "Classic Lady" (amongst green trees) 20 25
3207 400l. "Portrait of Li-Pai" 20 25
3208 400l. "Sprite of the Mountain" 20 25
3209 400l. "Classic Lady" (amongst bare trees) 20 25
MS3210 138×105 mm. 800l. "Four Seasons–Winter" (51×39 mm) (vert); 1500l. "Four Seasons–Summer" (51×39 mm) (vert) 1·00 1·10

1999. Return of Macao to China.
3211 **325** 1200l. multicoloured 55 60

1999. Royal Wedding. Multicoloured.
3212 2000l. Type **326** 90 95
3213 2000l. Prince Edward (wearing striped shirt and black jacket) 90 95
3214 2000l. Sophie Rhys-Jones (different) 90 95
3215 2000l. Prince Edward 90 95
MS3216 117×115 mm. 4000l. Sophie Rhys-Jones and Prince Edward (horiz) 1·80 1·90

327 Dragon

2000. Chinese New Year ("Year of the Dragon"). Multicoloured.
3217 1500l. Type **327** 65 70
3218 1500l. Dragon ("LUNAR NEW YEAR" bottom right) 65 70
3219 1500l. Dragon ("LUNAR NEW YEAR" bottom left) 65 70
3220 1500l. Dragon ("LUNAR NEW YEAR" top right) 65 70
MS3221 76×106 mm. 4000l. Dragon (vert) 1·80 1·90

328 Sammy Davis Jr.

2000. 75th Birth Anniv of Sammy Davis Jr. (American entertainer).
3222 – 1000l. brown and black 45 50
3223 – 1000l. brown and black 45 50
3224 **328** 1000l. multicoloured 45 50
3225 – 1000l. multicoloured 45 50
3226 – 1000l. red and black 45 50
3227 – 1000l. red and black 45 50
MS3228 130×130 mm. 5000l. brown and black 2·20 2·30

DESIGNS: No. 3222, As young boy; 3223, Arms outstretched in front of motorcycle; 3225, Holding microphone and singing; 3226, With foot on chair: 3227, Singing with cigarette. **MS**3228, Wearing sunglasses, white shirt and waistcoat.

329 Betty Boop

2000. Betty Boop (cartoon character). Mult.
3229 800l. Wearing short flowered dress 35 40
3230 800l. Out shopping 35 40
3231 800l. Wearing baseball cap 35 40
3232 800l. Type **329** 35 40
3233 800l. Sitting on chair 35 40
3234 800l. In duffle coat and carrying book 35 40
3235 800l. Playing guitar 35 40
3236 800l. As cowgirl with lasso 35 40

3237 800l. Holding flower 35 40
MS3238 Two sheets (a) 140 × 101 mm. 5000l. Riding bicycle. (b) 101 × 140 mm. 5000l. Wearing purple coat Set of 2 sheets . . . . 4·50 4·75
Nos. 3229/37 were printed, se-tenant, with the backgrounds forming a composite design.

330 Lucille Ball in Hotel Uniform

2000. "I Love Lucy" (American T.V. comedy series). Multicoloured.
3239 800l. Type **330** 35 40
3240 800l. Behind medicine counter with hands crossed 35 40
3241 800l. In bed 35 40
3242 800l. Poking tongue out . . 35 40
3243 800l. Inside television set . . 35 40
3244 800l. Behind counter with bottle in left hand 35 40
3245 800l. Behind medicine counter with hands by sides 35 40
3246 800l. Leaning on counter holding bottle in right hand 35 40
3247 800l. Tipping medicine away 35 40
MS3248 Two sheets, each 101 × 140 mm. (a) 5000l. Lucy inside television set. (b) 5000l. Lucy pinching man's face Set of 2 sheets . . . . 4·50 4·75

330a Tsar Michael Romanov of Russia (elected 1613)

2000. New Millennium. People and Events of Seventeenth Century (1600–1650). Multicoloured.
3249 400l. Type **330a** 20 25
3250 400l. William Shakespeare ("Hamlet", published 1603) 20 25
3251 400l. "Thousand Peaks and Myriad Ravines" (Kung Hsien, 1620–89) 20 25
3252 400l. Francis Bacon and title page (works published 1605) 20 25
3253 400l. Captain John Smith and colonists (Jamestown, founded 1607) 20 25
3254 400l. Versailles and courtiers (succession of Louis XIV, 1643) 20 25
3255 400l. Flag, map and waterfall (French foundation of Quebec, 1608) 20 25
3256 400l. Isaac Newton (born 1642) 20 25
3257 400l. "The Rape of the Sabine Women" (Nicolas Poussin), 1636 . . . . . 20 25
3258 400l. Johannes Kepler ("The New Astronomy" published 1609) 20 25
3259 400l. Colonists at Cape Cod (arrival of "Mayflower" in America, 1620) 20 25
3260 400l. King James I of England and title page of Bible (King James Bible, published 1611) 20 25
3261 400l. Activities of Dutch East India Company (introduction of tea to Europe, 1610) 20 25
3262 400l. Rene Descartes and sketch of boy (doctrine "I think, therefore I am", 1641) 20 25
3263 400l. Galileo (proves Earth orbits Sun, 1632) 20 25
3264 400l. Queen Elizabeth I (died 1603) (59 × 39 mm) 20 25
3265 400l. Miguel de Cervantes and title page (publication of "Don Quixote", 1605) 20 25

330b Flowers forming Top of Head

2000. Faces of the Millennium: Diana, Princess of Wales. Showing collage of miniature flower photographs. Multicoloured.
3266 800l. Type **330b** (face value at left) 35 40
3267 800l. Top of head (face value at right) 35 40
3268 800l. Ear (face value at left) 35 40
3269 800l. Eye and temple (face value at right) 35 40
3270 800l. Cheek (face value at left) 35 40
3271 800l. Cheek (face value at right) 35 40
3272 800l. Blue background (face value at left) 35 40
3273 800l. Chin (face value at right) 35 40
Nos. 3266/73 were printed together, se-tenant, in sheetlets of 8 with the stamps arranged in two vertical columns separated by a gutter also containing miniature photographs. When viewed as a whole, the sheetlet forms a portrait of Diana, Princess of Wales.

331 Colonel Lloyd (Lionel Barrymore) and his Granddaughter (Shirley Temple)

2000. Shirley Temple in "The Little Colonel". Showing scenes from the film. Multicoloured.
3274 1200l. Type **331** 55 60
3275 1200l. Lloyd (Shirley Temple) and Walker (Bill Robinson) 55 60
3276 1200l. Lloyd with Henry Clay and May Lily . . . 55 60
3277 1200l. Lloyd with soldiers 55 60
3278 1200l. Lloyd with her mother and Mom Beck 55 60
3279 1200l. Lloyd hugging her grandfather 55 60
3280 1500l. Lloyd with her grandfather's servants . . 65 70
3281 1500l. Walker and Lloyd tap dancing 65 70
3282 1500l. Lloyd standing in bushes 65 70
3283 1500l. Lloyd and the Colonel 65 70
MS3284 107 × 76 mm. 5000l. Lloyd saluting . . . . 2·20 2·30

332 Mario Andretti in Saloon Car

2000. 60th Birthday of Mario Andretti (U.S. racing driver). Multicoloured (except Nos. 3285 and 3288).
3285 600l. Type **332** (black, yellow and red) 25 30
3286 600l. Wearing racing helmet 25 30
3287 600l. Being congratulated . . 25 30
3288 600l. In car number 26 (black and red) 25 30
3289 600l. Changing wheel . . . 25 30
3290 600l. Wearing white T-shirt 25 30
3291 600l. Shirtless 25 30
3292 600l. Driving GT Ferrari . . 25 30
MS3293 128 × 151 mm. 5000l. As young man with friends and first car . . . . 2·20 2·30

2000. 400th Birth Anniv of Sir Anthony Van Dyck (Flemish painter). As T **394c** of St. Vincent. Mult.
3294 1000l. "Taking of Christ" (detail) 45 50
3295 1000l. "Ecce Homo" (1625–26) 45 50
3296 1000l. "Christ carrying the Cross" (soldier in black helmet) 45 50
3297 1000l. "Raising of Christ on the Cross" 45 50
3298 1000l. "The Crucifixion" (c. 1627) 45 50
3299 1000l. "The Lamentation" (c. 1616) 45 50
3300 1000l. "Taking of Christ" (complete painting) . . . 45 50
3301 1000l. "The Mocking of Christ" 45 50
3302 1000l. "Ecce Homo" (1628–32) 45 50
3303 1000l. "Christ carrying the Cross" (soldier in red helmet) 45 50
3304 1000l. "The Crucifixion" (1629–30) 45 50
3305 1000l. "The Lamentation" (1618–20) 45 50
3306 1000l. "Portrait of a Man" 45 50
3307 1000l. "Anna Wake, Wife of Peeter Stevens" 45 50
3308 1000l. "Peeter Stevens" . . 45 50
3309 1000l. "Adriaen Stevens" . . 45 50
3310 1000l. "Maria Bosschaerts, Wife of Adriaen Stevens" 45 50
3311 1000l. "Portrait of a Woman" 45 50
3312 1000l. "Self-portrait" (1617–18) 45 50
3313 1000l. "Self-portrait" (1620–21) 45 50
3314 1000l. "Self-portrait" (1622–23) 45 50
3315 1000l. "Andromeda chained to the Rock" 45 50
3316 1000l. "Self-portrait" (late 1620s–early 1630s) . . . 45 50
3317 1000l. "Mary Ruthven" . . . 45 50
3318 1000l. "The Duchess of Croy with her Son" . . . 45 50
3319 1000l. "Susanna Fourment and her Daughter" . . . 45 50
3320 1000l. "Geronima Brignole-Sale with her Daughter Maria Aurelia" 45 50
3321 1000l. "Woman with her Daughter" 45 50
3322 1000l. "Genoese Noblewoman with her Child" 45 50
3323 1000l. "Paola Adorno and her Son" 45 50
MS3324 Six sheets. (a) 102 × 127 mm. 5000l. "Young Woman with a Child". (b) 102 × 127 mm. 5000l. "Pozia Imperiale and her Daughter Maria Frencesca". (c) 102 × 127 mm. 5000l. "Portrait of Mother and Daughter". (d) 127 × 102 mm. 5000l. "Self-portrait with Endymion Porter". (e) 127 × 102 mm. 5000l. "Self-portrait with Sunflower". (f) 102 × 127 mm. 5000l. "Woman and Child" (horiz) Set of 6 sheets 13·50 14·00
No. 3311 is inscribed "Protrait of a Women" in error.

333 Grey Parrot ("African Grey Parrot")

2000. "The Stamp Show 2000" International Stamp Exhibition, London. Parrots and Parakeets. Mult.
3325 200l. Type **333** 10 15
3326 800l. Monk parakeet . . . 35 40
3327 800l. Lesser sulphur-crested cockatoo ("Citron-crested Cockatoo") 35 40
3328 800l. Golden conure ("Queen of Bavaria Conure") 35 40
3329 800l. Budgerigar 35 40
3330 800l. Canary-winged parakeet ("Yellow-chevroned Parakeet") . . 35 40
3331 800l. Cockatiel 35 40
3332 800l. Green-checked amazon ("Amazon Parrot") . . . 35 40
3333 800l. Sun conure 35 40
3334 800l. Malabar parakeet . . 35 40
3335 800l. Eclectus parrot ("Grand Eclectus Parrot") 35 40
3336 800l. Jandaya conure ("Sun Parakeet") 35 40
3337 800l. Hawk-headed parrot ("Red fan Parakeet") . . 35 40
3338 800l. Fischer's lovebird . . . 35 40
3339 800l. Masked lovebird ("Blue-masked Lovebird") 35 40
3340 800l. White-bellied caique ("White-bellied Rosella") 35 40
3341 800l. Plum-headed parakeet 35 40
3342 800l. Striated lorikeet . . . 35 40
3343 800l. Eastern rosella ("Gold-mantled Rosella") 35 40
3344 1500l. Sulphur-crested cockatoo 65 70
MS3345 120 × 81 mm. 4000l. Blue and yellow macaw ("Blue and Gold Macaw") (37 × 50 mm) 1·80 1·90
Nos. 3326/34 and 3335/43 were each printed together, se-tenant, with the backgrounds forming composite designs.
No. 3327 is inscribed "Cockatto" and No. 3344 "Sulfur Crested Cockatto", both in error.

334 Herring Gull

2000. Seabirds of the World. Multicoloured.
3346 400l. Type **334** 20 25
3347 600l. Caspian tern (standing by rock) 25 30
3348 800l. Grey phalarope ("Red Phalarope") 35 40
3349 1000l. Wandering albatross 45 50
3350 1000l. Fork-tailed storm petrel 45 50
3351 1000l. Greater shearwater 45 50
3352 1000l. Blue-footed booby . . 45 50
3353 1000l. Great cormorant . . 45 50
3354 1000l. Atlantic puffin . . . 45 50
3355 1000l. Caspian tern (fishing) 45 50
3356 1000l. Glaucous gull 45 50
3357 1000l. Northern gannet . . 45 50
3358 1000l. Long-tailed skua ("Long-tailed Jaeger") . . 45 50
3359 1000l. Brown pelican . . . 45 50
3360 1000l. Great skua 45 50
3361 2000l. Magnificent frigate bird 90 95
MS3362 Two sheets, each 56 × 66 mm. (a) 5000l. red-billed tropic bird ("Red-tailed Tropic Bird") (vert). (b) 5000l. Brown booby (vert) Set of 2 sheets . . 4·50 4·75
No. MS3362b is inscribed "Brown Boobie" in error".
Nos. 3349/54 and 3355/60 were each printed together, se-tenant, with the backgrounds forming composite designs.

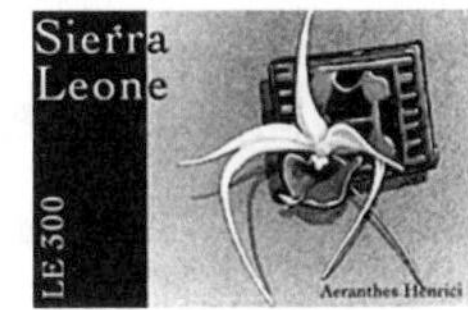

335 *Aeranthes henrici*

2000. Orchids. Multicoloured.
3363 300l. Type **335** 15 20
3364 500l. *Ophrys apifera* 20 25
3365 600l. *Disa crassicornis* . . . 25 30
3366 1100l. *Oeleoclades maculata* (vert) 50 55
3367 1100l. *Polystachya campyloglossa* (vert) . . . 50 55
3368 1100l. *Polystachya pubescens* (vert) 50 55
3369 1100l. *Tridactyle bicaudata* (vert) 50 55
3370 1100l. *Angraecum veitcii* (vert) 50 55
3371 1100l. *Sobennikoffia robusta* (vert) 50 55
3372 1100l. *Aerangis curnowiana* (vert) 50 55
3373 1100l. *Aerangis fastudsa* (vert) 50 55
3374 1100l. *Angraecum magdalenae* (vert) 50 55
3375 1100l. *Angraecum sororium* (vert) 50 55
3376 1100l. *Eulophia speciosa* (vert) 50 55
3377 1100l. *Ansellia africana* (vert) 50 55
3378 2000l. *Aeranthes grandiflora* 90 95
MS3379 Two sheets, each 74 × 64 mm. (a) 4000l. *Angraecum eburneum* (vert). (b) 4000l. *Angraecum compactum* (vert) Set of 2 sheets . . . . 3·50 3·75
Nos. 3366/71 and 3372/7 were each printed together, se-tenant, with the backgrounds forming composite designs.
No. 3367 is inscribed "Ploystachya" in error.

2000. 18th Birthday of Prince William. As T **395a** of St. Vincent. Multicoloured.
3380 1100l. Prince William laughing 50 55
3381 1100l. Wearing blue shirt and grey suit 50 55
3382 1100l. In dark jacket and red-patterned tie 50 55
3383 1100l. Wearing white shirt and blue suit 50 55
MS3384 100 × 80 mm. 5000l. Holding bouquet of flowers (37 × 50 mm) . . . . 2·20 2·30

335a "Apollo 18"

335c Albert Einstein holding Pipe

335b Johann Sebastian Bach

2000. 25th Anniv of "Apollo–Soyuz" Joint Project. Multicoloured.
3385 1200l. Type **335a** 55 60
3386 1200l. "Soyuz 19" 55 60
3387 1200l. "Apollo 18" and "Soyuz 19" docked in orbit 55 60
MS3388 94 × 84 mm. 5000l. "Apollo 18" and "Soyuz 19" docking 2·20 2·30

2000. 50th Anniv of Berlin Film Festival. As T **395c** of St. Vincent. Showing film scenes. Multicoloured.
3389 1100l. *Las Palabras de Max*, 1978 50 55
3390 1100l. *Ascendancy*, 1983 50 55
3391 1100l. *Deprisa, Deprisa*, 1981 50 55
3392 1100l. *Die Sehnsucht der Veronika Voss*, 1982 50 55
3393 1100l. *Heartland*, 1980 50 55
3394 1100l. *La Colmena*, 1983 50 55
MS3395 97 × 103 mm. 5000l. *Las Truches*, 1978 2·20 2·30

2000. 175th Anniv of Stockton and Darlington Line (first public railway). As T **395d** of St. Vincent. Multcoloured.
3396 3000l. George Stephenson and *Locomotion No. 1* 1·30 1·40
3397 3000l. James Watt's original design for separate condenser engine, 1789 1·30 1·40
No. 3397 is inscribed "comdensor" in error.

2000. 250th Death Anniv of Johann Sebastian Bach (German composer). Sheet, 104 × 101 mm.
MS3398 **335b** 5000l. multicoloured 2·20 2·30

2000. Election of Albert Einstein (mathematical physicist) as *Time Magazine* "Man of the Century". Sheet 117 × 91 mm.
MS3399 **335c** 5000l. multicoloured 2·20 2·30

2000. Centenary of First Zeppelin Flight. As T **396a** of St. Vincent. Multicoloured.
3400 2000l. LZ-129 *Hindenburg*, 1936 90 95
3401 2000l. LZ-4, 1908 90 95
3402 2000l. LZ-6 *Delag*, 1909 90 95
MS3403 116 × 76 mm. 4000l. LZ-127 *Graf Zeppelin*, 1928 (50 × 37 mm) 1·80 1·90
No. 3400 is inscribed "Hindenberg" in error.

2000. Olympic Games, Sydney. As T **396b** of St. Vincent. Multicoloured.
3404 1500l. Forrest Smithson (hurdling), London (1908) 65 70
3405 1500l. Football 65 70
3406 1500l. Olympic Stadium, Helsinki (1952) with Finnish flag 65 70
3407 1500l. Ancient Greek wrestlers 65 70

336 Richard Petty sitting on Car with Trophy

2000. Richard Petty (stock car driver) Commem. Multicoloured.
3408 800l. Type **336** 35 40
3409 800l. In cream overalls and cap 35 40
3410 800l. In stetson and sunglasses (blue collar) 35 40
3411 800l. In plain white shirt (blue background) 35 40
3412 800l. In stetson and sunglasses (red collar) 35 40
3413 800l. Squatting with cap alongside No. 43 35 40
3414 800l. Leaning on car 35 40
3415 800l. Crouching with arm in car 35 40
3416 800l. Looking out of car No. 43 35 40
3417 800l. Car in pits 35 40
3418 800l. Standing with family 35 40
3419 800l. Standing by car with helmet on door 35 40
3420 800l. In Pontiac cap 35 40
3421 800l. In white stetson and sunglasses (green background) 35 40
3422 800l. In STP cap 35 40
3423 800l. Standing up in blue car 35 40
3424 800l. In white stetson (with STP epaulettes) 35 40
3425 800l. Sitting watching race 35 40
3426 800l. Being interviewed 35 40
3427 800l. In plain white shirt (brown background) 35 40
3428 800l. Wearing orange cap and sunglasses 35 40
3429 800l. Sitting in car (interior view) 35 40
3430 800l. Timing a race 35 40
3431 800l. In blue and red helmet 35 40
3432 800l. In white stetson and sunglasses (blue overalls) 35 40
3433 800l. Holding trophy in blue, red and white overalls 35 40
3434 800l. Sitting in white stetson and sunglasses 35 40
MS3435 Two sheets, each 110 × 76 mm. (a) 5000l. As No. 3423. (b) 5000l. Car No. 43 during race (horiz) Set of 2 sheets 4·50 4·75

337 Worns (German player)

2000. "Euro 2000" Football Championship. Mult.
3436 1300l. Type **337** 60 65
3437 1300l. German team 60 65
3438 1300l. Babbel (German player) 60 65
3439 1300l. Franz Beckenbauer, 1972 60 65
3440 1300l. Selessin Stadium, Liege 60 65
3441 1300l. Stefan Kuntz, (German player), 1996 60 65
3442 1300l. Walter Zenga (Italian player) 60 65
3443 1300l. Italian team 60 65
3444 1300l. Roberto Bettega (Italian player), 1980 60 65
3445 1300l. Totti (Italian player) 60 65
3446 1300l. Philips Stadium, Eindhoven 60 65
3447 1300l. Vieri (Italian player) 60 65
3448 1300l. Dimas (Portuguese player) 60 65
3449 1300l. Portuguese team 60 65
3450 1300l. Pinto (Portuguese player) 60 65
3451 1300l. Santos (Portuguese player) 60 65
3452 1300l. Gelredome Stadium, Arnhem 60 65
3453 1300l. Sousa (Portuguese player) 60 65
3454 1300l. Munteanu (Rumanian player) 60 65
3455 1300l. Rumanian team 60 65
3456 1300l. Petre (Rumanian player) 60 65
3457 1300l. Petrescu (Rumanian player) 60 65
3458 1300l. Popescu (Rumanian player) 60 65
MS3459 Four sheets, each 145 × 95 mm. (a) 5000l. Erich Ribbeck (German trainer) (vert). (b) 5000l. Dino Zoff (Italian trainer) (vert). (c) 5000l. Humberto Coelho (Portuguese trainer) (vert). (d) 5000l. Emerich Jenei (Rumanian trainer) (vert) Set of 4 sheets 8·75 9·00

337a Emperor Hung-Wu of China

2000. Monarchs of the Millennium.
3460 **337a** 1100l. multicoloured 50 55
3461 – 1100l. multicoloured 50 55
3462 – 1100l. multicoloured 50 55
3463 – 1100l. black, stone & brn 50 55
3464 – 1100l. multicoloured 50 55
3465 – 1100l. black, stone & brn 50 55
MS3466 116 × 131 mm.–5000l. multicoloured 2·20 2·30
DESIGNS: No. 3461, Emperor Hsuan-Te of China; 3462, King Sejong of Korea; 3463, Emperor T'ung Chin of China; 3464, Emperor T'ai-Tsu of China; 3465, Empress Yung Ching of China; **MS**3466, Kublai Khan, Great Khan of the Mongols.

2000. Popes of the Millennium. As T **337a**. Each black, yellow and green (Nos. 3467/78 or black, yellow and brown (No. **MS**3479).
3467 1100l. Gregory VI 50 55
3468 1100l. Celestine V 50 55
3469 1100l. Honorius IV 50 55
3470 1100l. Innocent IV 50 55
3471 1100l. Innocent VII 50 55
3472 1100l. John XXII 50 55
3473 1100l. Martin IV 50 55
3474 1100l. Nicholas II 50 55
3475 1100l. Nicholas IV 50 55
3476 1100l. Urban IV 50 55
3477 1100l. Urban V 50 55
3478 1100l. Urban VI 50 55
MS3479 Two sheets, each 116 × 136 mm. (a) 5000l. Nicholas IV. (b) 5000l. Clement XI Set of 2 sheets 4·50 4·75

338 Bulldog

2000. Dogs and Cats. Multicoloured.
3480 500l. Type **338** 20 25
3481 800l. Brown tabby 35 40
3482 1000l. Red tabby stumpy manx 45 50
3483 1000l. Red self 45 50
3484 1000l. Maine coon 45 50
3485 1000l. Black smoke 45 50
3486 1000l. Chinchilla 45 50
3487 1000l. Russian blue cat 45 50
3488 1000l. Beagle 45 50
3489 1000l. Scottish terrier 45 50
3490 1000l. Bloodhound 45 50
3491 1000l. Greyhound 45 50
3492 1000l. German shepherd 45 50
3493 1000l. Cocker spaniel 45 50
3494 1100l. Singapura 50 55
3495 1100l. Himalayan 50 55
3496 1100l. Abyssinian 50 55
3497 1100l. Black cat 50 55
3498 1100l. Siamese 50 55
3499 1100l. North African wild cat 50 55
3500 1100l. Pointer 50 55
3501 1100l. Doberman pinscher 50 55
3502 1100l. Collie 50 55
3503 1100l. Chihuahua 50 55
3504 1100l. Afghan hound 50 55
3505 1100l. Boxer 50 55
3506 1500l. Burmese 50 55
3507 2000l. Dachshund 90 95
MS3508 Two sheets, each 48 × 62 mm. (a) 5000l. Calico cat (vert). (b) 5000l. Fox terrier (vert) Set of 2 sheets 4·50 4·75
Nos. 3482/7 (cats), 3489/93 (dogs), 3494/9 (cats) and 3500/505 (dogs) were printed together, se-tenant, with the backgrounds forming composite designs.

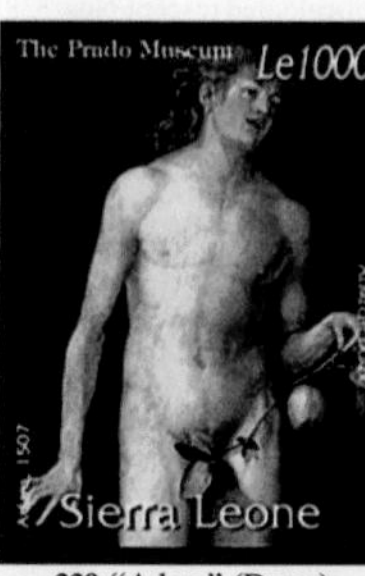

339 "Adam" (Durer)

2000. "Espana 2000" International Stamp Exhibition, Madrid. Paintings from the Prado. Multicoloured.
3509 1000l. Type **339** 45 50
3510 1000l. "Moor" (M. Vives) 45 50
3511 1000l. "Eve" (Durer) 45 50
3512 1000l. "Gypsy" (R. de Madrazo y Garreta) 45 50
3513 1000l. "Maria Guerrero" (J. Sorolla y Bastida) 45 50
3514 1000l. "Aline Masson with a White Mantilla" (R. de Madrazo y Garreta) 45 50
3515 1000l. "Madonna and Child between Sts. Catherine and Ursula" (G. Bellini) (left detail) 45 50
3516 1000l. "Madonna and Child between Sts. Catherine and Ursula" (centre detail) 45 50
3517 1000l. "Madonna and Child between Sts. Catherine and Ursula" (right detail) 45 50
3518 1000l. "Giovanni Mateo Ghiberti" (B. India) 45 50
3519 1000l. "The Marchioness of Santa Cruz" (A. Esteve) 45 50
3520 1000l. "Self Portrait" (O. Borgianni) 45 50
3521 1000l. "The Transport of Mary Magdalen" (J. Antolinez) 45 50
3522 1000l. "The Holy Family" (Goya) 45 50
3523 1000l. "Our Lady of the Immaculate Conception" (J. Antolinez) 45 50
3524 1000l. "Charles IV as Prince" (A. Mengs) 45 50
3525 1000l. "Louis XIII of France" (P. de Champaigne) 45 50
3526 1000l. "Prince Ferdinand VI" (J. Ranc) 45 50
3527 1000l. "Feliciana Bayeu" (F. Bayeu) 45 50
3528 1000l. "Tomas de Iriarte" (J. Inza) 45 50
3529 1000l. "St. Elizabeth of Portugal" (F. de Zurbaran) 45 50
3530 1000l. "The Vision of St. Francis at Porziuncola" (Murillo) (Christ with cross) 45 50
3531 1000l. "The Vision of St. Francis at Porziuncola" (St. Francis) 45 50
3532 1000l. "The Vision of St. Francis at Porziuncola" (Two women) 45 50
3533 1000l. "The Holy Family with a Little Bird" (Murillo) (Virgin Mary) 45 50
3534 1000l. "The Holy Family with a Little Bird" (Holy Child) 45 50
3535 1000l. "The Holy Family with a Little Bird" (St. Joseph) 45 50
3536 1000l. "Cardinal Carlos de Borja" (A. Procaccini) 45 50
3537 1000l. "St. Dominic de Guzman" (C. Coello) 45 50
3538 1000l. "The Dead Christ Supported by an Angel" (A. Cano) 45 50
3539 1000l. "The Seller of Fans" (woman) (J. del Castillo) 45 50
3540 1000l. "Allegory of Summer" (M. Maella) 45 50
3541 1000l. "The Seller of Fans" (man) 45 50
3542 1000l. "Portrait of a Girl" (C. de Ribera y Fieve) 45 50
3543 1000l. "The Poultry Keeper" (Il Pensionante del Saraceni) 45 50
3544 1000l. "The Death of Cleopatra" (G. Reni) 45 50
MS3545 Six sheets, each 110 × 91 mm. (a) 5000l. "The Two Friends" (J. Agrasot y Juan) (horiz). (b) 5000l. "The Finding of Joseph's Cup in Benjamin's Sack" (J. Amiconi). (c) 5000l. "The Execution of Tprrijos and His Companions" (A. Gisbert Pirez). (d) 5000l. "The Concert" (V. Palmaroli Gonzalez). (e) 5000l. "Lot and His Daughters" (F. Furini). (f) 5000l. "Vulcan's Forge" (Velazquez) Set of 6 sheets 13·50 14·00

2000. Faces of the Millennium: Pope John Paul II. As T **330b**, showing collage of miniature religious photographs. Multicoloured.
3546 900l. Top of head (face value at left) 40 45
3547 900l. Top of head (face value at right) 40 45
3548 900l. Ear (face value at left) 40 45
3549 900l. Eye and temple (face value at right) 40 45
3550 900l. Back of neck (face value at left) 40 45
3551 900l. Cheek (face value at right) 40 45
3552 900l. Collar and top of cassock (face value at left) 40 45
3553 900l. Hand (face value at right) 40 45
Nos. 3546/53 were printed together, se-tenant, in sheetlets of 8 with the stamps arranged in two vertical columns separated by a gutter also containing miniature photographs. When viewed as a whole, the sheetlet forms a portrait of Pope John Paul II.

2000. Faces of the Millennium: Queen Elizabeth, The Queen Mother. As T **330b**, showing collage of miniature flower photographs. Multicoloured.

3554 800l. Top of forehead and hat (face value at left) . . 35 40
3555 800l. Hat (face value at right) 35 40
3556 800l. Eye (face value at left) 35 40
3557 800l. Side of face and hat (face value at right) . . . 35 40
3558 800l. Cheek (face value at left) 35 40
3559 800l. Cheek (face value at right) 35 40
3560 800l. Chin (face value at left) 35 40
3561 800l. Chin and neck (face value at right) 35 40

Nos. 3554/61 were printed together, se-tenant, in sheetlets of 8 with the stamps arranged in two vertical columns separated by a gutter also containing miniature photographs. When viewed as a whole, the sheetlet forms a portrait of The Queen Mother.

340 *Tuberus polypore*

2001. Fungi. Multicoloured.

3562 600l. Type **340** 25 30
3563 900l. *Cultivated agaricus* . . 40 45
3564 1000l. Armed stinkhorn (vert) 45 50
3565 1000l. *Red-staining inocybe* (vert) 45 50
3566 1000l. Grisette (*Amanitopsis vaginata*) (vert) 45 50
3567 1000l. *Inocybe jurana* (vert) 45 50
3568 1000l. *Xerula longipes* (vert) 45 50
3569 1000l. Matsu-take mushroom (*Tricholoma matsutake*) (vert) 45 50
3570 1000l. Orange-staining mycena (vert) 45 50
3571 1000l. *Russula amoema* (vert) 45 50
3572 1000l. *Cinnabar chanterelle*(vert) 45 50
3573 1000l. *Calodon aurantiacum* (vert) 45 50
3574 1000l. Scaly lentinus (*Lentinus lepideus*) (vert) 45 50
3575 1000l. *Gomphidius roseus* (vert) 45 50
3576 1200l. Scarlet wax cap . . . 55 60
3577 2500l. Blue-green psilocybe 1·10 1·20
MS3578 Two sheets. (a) 98 × 74 mm. 5000l. Orange latex lactarius. (b) 74 × 98 mm. 5000l. Common morel (vert) Set of 2 sheets . . 4·50 4·75

Nos. 3564/9 and 3570/575 were each printed together, se-tenant, with the backgrounds forming a composite design.

No. 3567 is inscribed "Inoeybe" in error.

341 Kahat Shor (shooting coach)

2000. Israel Olympic Team Members killed at Munich (1972) Commemoration. Multicoloured.

3579 500l. Type **341** 20 25
3580 500l. Andrei Schpitzer (fencing referee) 20 25
3581 500l. Joseph Romano (weightlifter) 20 25
3582 500l. Yaakov Springer (weightlifting referee) . . 20 25
3583 500l. Eliazer Halffin (wrestler) 20 25
3584 500l. Amitsur Shapira (athletics coach) 20 25
3585 500l. Moshe Weinberg (wrestling referee) 20 25
3586 500l. Mark Slavin (wrestler) 20 25
3587 500l. Flag and runner with Olympic Torch 20 25
3588 500l. Joseph Gottfreund (wrestling referee) 20 25
3589 500l. Ze'ev Friedman (weightlifter) 20 25
3590 500l. David Berger (weightlifter) 20 25
MS3591 116 × 80 mm. 5000l. Runner with Olympic Torch (vert) . . 2·20 2·30

342 Tightrope Cyclist

2000. Circus. Multicoloured.

3592 800l. Type **342** 35 40
3593 1000l. Bear with ball 45 50
3594 1100l. Polar bear 50 55
3595 1100l. Gorilla 50 55
3596 1100l. Clown (green background) 50 55
3597 1100l. Tightrope walker . . 50 55
3598 1100l. Sealions 50 55
3599 1100l. Camel 50 55
3600 1100l. Clown (brown background) 50 55
3601 1100l. Tiger on tightropes 50 55
3602 1100l. Chimpanzee 50 55
3603 1100l. Dancing dogs 50 55
3604 1100l. Bear on skates with hockey stick 50 55
3605 1100l. Trapeze artists . . . 50 55
3606 1100l. Acrobat (vert) . . . 50 55
3607 1100l. Giraffe (vert) 50 55
3608 1100l. Bear on stilts (vert) 50 55
3609 1100l. Elephant (vert) . . . 50 55
3610 1100l. Rearing horse (vert) 50 55
3611 1100l. Fire-eater (vert) . . . 50 55
3612 1500l. Tiger on ball 65 70
3613 2000l. Camels 90 95
MS3614 Three sheets, each 70 × 90 mm. (a) 5000l. Tiger leaping through flames (vert). (b) 5000l. Human cannonball (vert). (c) 5000l. Ringmaster standing on elephant (vert) Set of 3 sheets 6·75 7·00

2000. Queen Elizabeth the Queen Mother's 100th Birthday. As T **405** of St. Vincent. Multicoloured.

3615 1100l. Queen Mother in blue hat 50 55

343 Decorative Snake

2001. Chinese New Year. "Year of the Snake". Decorative snakes. Multicoloured.

3616 800l. Type **343** (blue frame) 35 40
3617 800l. Snake (pink frame) . . 35 40
3618 800l. Snake (lilac frame) . . 35 40
3619 800l. Snake (green frame) 35 40
MS3620 65 × 95 mm. 2500l. Snake (vert) . . . . 1·10 1·20

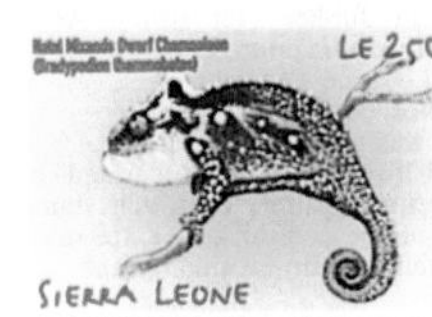

344 Natal Mixands Dwarf Chameleon

2001. African Reptiles. Multicoloured.

3621 250l. Type **344** 10 15
3622 400l. Cape cobra 20 25
3623 500l. Western sand lizard . . 20 25
3624 600l. Pan-hinged terrapin . . 25 30
3625 800l. Many-horned adder . . 35 40
3626 1200l. Reticulated desert lizard 55 60
3627 1200l. Ball python 55 60
3628 1200l. Gabon viper 55 60
3629 1200l. Dumeril's boa . . . 55 60
3630 1200l. Common egg-eater 55 60
3631 1200l. Helmet turtle 55 60
3632 1200l. Saw-scaled viper . . 55 60
3633 1200l. Namibian sand snake 55 60
3634 1200l. Angolan gartersnake 55 60
3635 1200l. Striped skaapsteker 55 60
3636 1200l. Brown housesnake . . 55 60
3637 1200l. Shield-nosed cobra 55 60
3638 1500l. Hawequa flat gecko 65 70
MS3639 Two sheets, each 86 × 56 mm. (a) 5000l. Flat-necked chameleon. (b) 5000l. Green water snake Set of 2 sheets . . . . . 4·50 4·75

Nos. 3626/31 and 3632/7 were each printed together, se-tenant, with the backgrounds forming a composite map of Africa.

No. 3621 is inscribed "Chamaeleon" in error.

345 Sleeping Car No. 507, 1897

2001. "The Orient Express". Multicoloured.

3640 1000l. First sleeping car, 1872 . . . . 45 50
3641 1000l. Dining car No. 193, 1886 . . . . 45 50
3642 1000l. Dining car No. 2422, 1913 . . . . 45 50
3643 1000l. Sleeping car Type S1 45 50
3644 1000l. Metal sleeping car No. 2645, 1922 . . . . . 45 50
3645 1000l. Metal sleeping car No. 2644, 1922 . . . . . 45 50
3646 1000l. Dining car series No. 8341 . . . . 45 50
3647 1000l. Dining car series No. 3342 . . . . 45 50
3648 1000l. Sleeping car series Type Z, No. 3312 . . . . 45 50
3649 1000l. Sleeping car series No. 3879, 1950 . . . . . 45 50
3650 1000l. Sleeping car series, Type Z, No. 3311 . . . . 45 50
3651 1000l. Dining car series No. 3785, 1932 . . . . . 45 50
3652 1100l. Type **345** 50 55
3653 1100l. Sleeping car No. 438, 1894 . . . . 50 55
3654 1100l. Sleeping car No. 313, 1880 . . . . 50 55
3655 1100l. Sleeping car No. 190, 1886 . . . . 50 55
3656 1100l. Sleeping car No. 102, 1882 . . . . 50 55
3657 1100l. Sleeping car No. 77, 1881 . . . . 50 55
3658 1100l. Steam locomotive, Ostend–Vienna Express, 1910 . . . . 50 55
3659 1100l. Steam locomotive East 230 No. 3175 . . . 50 55
3660 1100l. Dual-cylinder steam locomotive 50 55
3661 1100l. Steam locomotive, Simplon Orient Express, 1919 . . . . 50 55
3662 1100l. Steam locomotive East 220 No. 2405 . . . 50 55
3663 1100l. Brake van of Simplon Express, c. 1906 . . . . 50 55
MS3664 Four sheets, each 106 × 81 mm. (a) 5000l. Agatha Christie (author) (vert). (b) 5000l. Georges Nagelmackers (company founder) (vert). (c) 5000l. Mata Hari (spy) (vert). (d) 5000l. "Orient Express" leaving Constantinople Set of 4 sheets 8·75 9·00

346 Candle-bearers from "David playing the Harp" (Jan de Bray)

2001. Bicentenary of Rijksmuseum, Amsterdam. Dutch Paintings. Multicoloured.

3665 1100l. Type **346** 50 55
3666 1100l. Women and children from "St. Paul healing the Cripple at Lystra" Karel Dujardin) 50 55
3667 1100l. Two pikemen (one wearing hat) from "The Meagre Company" (Frans Hals and Pieter Codde) 50 55
3668 1100l. "The Grey" (Philips Wouwermans) 50 55
3669 1100l. "Elegant Couple in an Interior" (Eglon van der Neer) 50 55
3670 1100l. "The Hut" (Adriaen van der Velde) 50 55
3671 1100l. "Lady reading a Letter" (Gabriel Metsu) 50 55
3672 1100l. "Portrait of Titus" (Rembrandt) 50 55
3673 1100l. "Gerard de Lairesse" (Rembrandt) 50 55
3674 1100l. "Family in an Interior" (Emanuel de Witte) 50 55
3675 1100l. "The Letter" (Gerard ter Borch) 50 55
3676 1100l. "Three Women and a Man in a Courtyard" (Pieter de Hooch) 50 55
3677 1100l. "Gentleman writing a Letter" (Gabriel Metsu) 50 55
3678 1100l. "Self-portrait" (Carel Fabritius) 50 55
3679 1100l. "Windmill at Wijk bij Duurstede" (Jacob van Ruisdael) 50 55
3680 1100l. "Bentheim Castle" (Jacob van Ruisdael) . . 50 55
3681 1100l. "Ships on a Stormy Sea" (Willem van der Velde the Younger) . . . 50 55
3682 1100l. David from "David playing the Harp" (Jan de Bray) 50 55
3683 1100l. St. Paul from "St. Paul healing the Cripple at Lystra" (Karel Dujardin) 50 55
3684 1100l. Two pikemen (both bare-headed) from "The Meagre Company" (Frans Hals and Pieter Codde) 50 55
3685 1100l. Man from "Elegant Couple in an Interior" (Eglon van der Neer) . . 50 55
3686 1100l. "Laid Table with Cheese and Fruit" (Floris van Dijck) 50 55
3687 1100l. "Bacchanal" (Moses van Uyttenbroeck) . . . 50 55
3688 1100l. The cripple from "St. Paul healing the Cripple at Lystra" (Karel Dujardin) 50 55
MS3689 Four sheets. (a) 118 × 73 mm. 5000l. "Road in the Dunes with a Coach" (Salomon van Ruysdael) (horiz) (b) 118 × 73 mm. 5000l. "Cows in the Meadow" (Albert Gerard Bilders) (horiz). (c) 118 × 78 mm. 5000l. "Lot and his Daughters" (Hendrick Goltzius) (horiz). (d) 118 × 83 mm. 5000l. "Arrival of Queen Wilhelmina at the Frederiksplein, Amsterdam (Otto Eerelman) (horiz) Set of 4 sheets 8·75 9·00

347 "Song of Simeon"

2001. Biblical Drawings and Paintings by Rembrandt.

3690 **347** 1000l. deep brown, brown and grey . . . 45 50
3691 – 1000l. deep brown, brown and grey . . . 45 50
3692 – 1000l. deep brown, brown and grey . . . 45 50
3693 – 1000l. blue, brown and grey 45 50
3694 – 1000l. deep brown, brown and grey . . . 45 50
3695 – 1000l. blue and brown 45 50
3696 – 1000l. red, brown and grey 45 50
3697 – 1000l. deep brown, brown and red 45 50
3698 – 1000l. deep brown, brown and red 45 50
3699 – 1000l. deep brown, brown and grey . . . 45 50
3700 – 1000l. deep brown, brown and grey . . . 45 50
3701 – 1000l. deep brown, brown and grey . . . 45 50
MS3702 Four sheets 86 × 110 mm. (a) 5000l. multicoloured. (b) 5000l. multicoloured. (c) 5000l. multicoloured. (d) 5000l. multicoloured Set of 4 sheets 8·75 9·00

DESIGNS—HORIZ: No. 3690, Type **347**; 3691, Study for "Adoration of the Magi"; 3692, "Mary with the Child by a Window"; 3693, "The Rest on the Flight into Egypt"; 3694, "The Circumcision"; 3695, "The Shepherds worship the Child"; 3696, "The Angel rises up in the Flame of Manoah's Sacrifice"; 3697, "Tobias frightened by the Fish"; 3698, "The Angel of the Lord stands in Balaam's Path"; 3699, "The Angel appears to Hagar in the Desert"; 3700, "Jacob's Dream"; 3701, "The Healing of Tobit"; **MS**3702a, "The Angel prevents the Sacrifice of Isaac"; **MS**3702b, "Simeon's Prophecy to Mary". VERT: No. **MS**3702c, "The Adoration of the Magi"; **MS**3702d, "The Angel leaves Tobit and His Family".

2001. 60th Anniv of the Battle of Britain. As T **413** of St. Vincent. Multicoloured.

3703 1000l. St. Paul's Cathedral, London 45 50
3704 1000l. Evacuating bombed building 45 50
3705 1000l. Winston Churchill being cheered by British troops 45 50
3706 1000l. Rescuing British pilot by boat 45 50
3707 1000l. Boy Scout and children 45 50
3708 1000l. British anti-aircraft gun 45 50
3709 1000l. Searchlight and crew 45 50
3710 1000l. Royal Observer Corps post 45 50
3711 1000l. Bombed houses 45 50
3712 1000l. Sheltering in underground station . . . 45 50
3713 1000l. Firemen 45 50
3714 1000l. Home Guard at drill 45 50
3715 1000l. ARP warden and blackout sign 45 50
3716 1000l. Pilots on stand-by . . 45 50
3717 1000l. Brendan "Paddy" Finucane (fighter pilot) . . 45 50
3718 1000l. Hawk 75 (fighter) . . 45 50
3719 1000l. Tower Bridge, London 45 50
3720 1000l. Surrey Home Guard 45 50
3721 1000l. Cruiser tank MK III 45 50
3722 1000l. Newfoundland gun crew 45 50
3723 1000l. Bomb damage in Plymouth 45 50
3724 1000l. Winston Churchill . . 45 50
3725 1000l. Bomb damage at Westminster Hall 45 50
3726 1000l. Radar screen 45 50
3727 1000l. Female telephone engineer and W.A.A.F. 45 50
3728 1000l. Women munitions workers 45 50
3729 1000l. Winston Churchill at desk 45 50
3730 1000l. Dornier DO17 (German bomber) 45 50
3731 1000l. Church fire 45 50

3732 1000l. Searchlights over London 45 50
3733 1000l. Lunch in the underground 45 50
3734 1000l. Sing song in the underground 45 50
MS3735 Four sheets. (a) 76×106 mm. 6000l. London skyline. (b) 76×106 mm. 6000l. Winston Churchill and his wife, Clementine. (c) 106×76 mm. 6000l. Supermarine Spitfire. (d) 106×76 mm. 6000l. British bomber crew preparing for mission (vert) Set of 4 sheets 10·50 11·00

No. 3719 is inscribed "LONDON BRIDGE", 3720 "SURRY", 3727 "WAFF", 3729 "DEFINSE" and MS3735c "SUBMARINE SPITFIRE", all in error.

348 "Piebald" from National Velvet (Enid Bagnold)

2001. Horses from Literature and Mythology. Multicoloured.

3736 1100l. Type **348** 50 55
3737 1100l. "Strider" (Tolstoy) 50 55
3738 1100l. "Black Beauty" (Anna Sewell) 50 55
3739 1100l. "Red Pony" (John Steinbeck) 50 55
3740 1100l. "Black Stallion" (Walter Farley) 50 55
3741 1100l. "Misty" from *Misty of Chincoteague* (Marguerite Henry) 50 55
3742 1100l. "Arvak" and "Alsvid" pulling Sun (Norse myth) 50 55
3743 1100l. "Pegasus" (Greek myth) 50 55
3744 1100l. Odin on "Sleipnir" (Norse myth) 50 55
3745 1100l. Roland on "Veillantif" from the "Song of Roland" 50 55
3746 1100l. Sigurd with "Grani" (Norse myth) 50 55
3747 1100l. Hector on "Galathe" from *Troilus and Cressida* (Shakespeare) 50 55
MS3748 Two sheets, each 97×67 mm. (a) 5000l. Don Quixote on "Rocinante" (Cervantes). (b) 5000l. "Xanthus" and "Balius" pulling Achilles chariot (greek myth) Set of 2 sheets 4·50 4·75

Nos. 3736/41 and 3742/7 were each printed together, se-tenant, the backgrounds forming composite designs.

No. 3745 is inscribed "Veillanfif" and No. 3747 "Truilus", both in error.

349 "Native Dancer", 1950 (racehorse)

350 Acrocanthosaurus

2001. Racehorses. Multicoloured.

3749 200l. Type **349** 10 15
3750 500l. "Citation", 1945 20 25
3751 1200l. "Arkle", 1957 55 60
3752 1200l. "Golden Miller", 1927 55 60
3753 1200l. "Phar Lap", 1927 55 60
3754 1200l. "Battleship", 1927 55 60
3755 1200l. "Kelso", 1957 55 60
3756 1200l. "Nijinski", 1967 55 60
3757 1200l. "Red Rum", 1965 55 60
3758 1200l. "Sir Ken", 1947 55 60
3759 1200l. "War Admiral", 1934 55 60
3760 1200l. "Troytown", 1913 55 60
3761 1200l. "Shergar", 1981 55 60
3762 1200l. "Allez France", 1970 55 60
3763 1500l. "Spectre", 1899 65 70
3764 2000l. "Carbine", 1885 90 95
MS3765 Four sheets. (a) 100×74 mm. 5000l. "Cigar". (b) 100×74 mm. 5000l. Racing trophy. (c) 100×74 mm. 5000l. French racecourse. (horiz) (d) 74×100 mm. 5000l. "Desert Orchid" Set of 4 sheets 8·75 9·00

2001. "Hong Kong 2001" International Stamp Exhibition. Dinosaurs. Multicoloured.

3766 1000l. Type **350** 45 50
3767 1000l. Edmontosaurus 45 50
3768 1000l. Archaeopteryx 45 50
3769 1000l. Hadrosaurus 45 50
3770 1000l. Mongolian avimimus 45 50
3771 1000l. Pachyrhinosaurus 45 50
3772 1000l. Iguanadons and log 45 50
3773 1000l. Iguanadons 45 50
3774 1000l. Albertosaurus (horiz) 45 50
3775 1000l. Pteranadon ingens (horiz) 45 50
3776 1000l. Asiatic Iguanadon (horiz) 45 50
3777 1000l. Sordes (horiz) 45 50
3778 1000l. Coelophysis (horiz) 45 50
3779 1000l. Saichania (horiz) 45 50
3780 1000l. Bactrosaurus (horiz) 45 50
3781 1000l. Triceratops (horiz) 45 50
MS3782 Five sheets. (a) 85×110 mm. 5000l. Dryosaurus. (b) 110×85 mm. 5000l. Diplodocus. (c) 110×85 mm. 5000l. Allosaurus (horiz). (d) 71×90 mm. 5000l. Stenonychosaurus. (e) 71×90 mm. 5000l. Corythosaurus Set of 5 sheets 11·00 11·50

Nos. 3771, 3774 and MS3782b are inscribed "PACHYRMINOSAURUS", "ALBERTO-SAUR" or "DIPLODOCIDS", all in error.

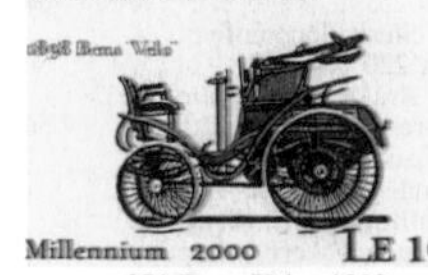

351 Benz Velo, 1898

2001. Cars. Multicoloured.

3783 1000l. Type **351** 45 50
3784 1000l. Rolls-Royce Silver Ghost, 1909 45 50
3785 1000l. Ford Model T, 1912 45 50
3786 1000l. Duesenberg SJ, 1937 45 50
3787 1000l. Grosse Mercedes, 1938–40 45 50
3788 1000l. CitroëLight 15, 1938 45 50
3789 1000l. Lincoln Zephyr, 1939 45 50
3790 1000l. Volkswagen Beetle, 1947 45 50
3791 1000l. Jaguar Mark II, 1959 45 50
3792 1000l. Ford Mustang GT500, 1968 45 50
3793 1000l. Opel/Vauxhall Senator, 1987-94 45 50
3794 1000l. Mercedes Maybach, 2002 45 50
MS3795 Two sheets, each 110×75 mm. (a) 5000l. 3-Litre Bentley Short Chassis Tourer, 1928. (b) 5000l. Ferrari 360 Modena, 1999 Set of 2 sheets 4·50 4·75

No. 3783 is inscribed "Bena" in error.

352 *Teinopalpus imperialis*

2001. Butterflies of the World. Multicoloured.

3796 1100l. Type **352** 50 55
3797 1100l. *Papilio mochaon* 50 55
3798 1100l. *Heliconius doris* 50 55
3799 1100l. *Delias argenthona* 50 55
3800 1100l. *Danaus formosa* 50 55
3801 1100l. *Precis octavia* 50 55
3802 1100l. *Danaus chrysippus* 50 55
3803 1100l. *Tithorea harmonia* 50 55
3804 1100l. *Morpho cypris* 50 55
3805 1100l. *Castnia licusi* 50 55
3806 1100l. *Dismorphia nemesis* 50 55
3807 1100l. *Saintpaulia ionanthe* 50 55
MS3808 Two sheets, each 75×55 mm. (a) 5000l. *Iphiclides podalirius*. (b) 5000l. *Colias crocea* (vert) Set of 2 sheets 4·50 4·75

Nos. 3796/8001 and 3802/7 were each printed together, se-tenant, with the backgrounds forming composite designs.

No. MS3808a is inscribed "podoliruis" in error.

353 *Eurema floricola*

2001. Butterflies of Africa. Multicoloured.

3809 250l. Type **353** 10 15
3810 400l. *Papilio dardanus* 20 25
3811 800l. *Amauris nossima* 35 40
3812 1100l. *Charaxes lucretia* 50 55
3813 1100l. *Euxanthe crossleyi* 50 55
3814 1100l. *Charaxes phoenix* 50 55
3815 1100l. *Charaxes acraeades* 50 55
3816 1100l. *Charaxes protoclea* 50 55
3817 1100l. *Charaxes lydiae* 50 55
3818 1100l. *Papilio dardanus* 50 55
3819 1100l. *Cymothoe sangaris* 50 55
3820 1100l. *Epiphora albida* 50 55
3821 1100l. African giant swallowtail 50 55
3822 1100l. *Papilio nobilis* 50 55
3823 1100l. *Charaxes hadrianus* 50 55
3824 1500l. *Gideona lucasi* 65 70
MS3825 Two sheets, each 110×85 mm. (a) 5000l. *Colotis zoe*. (b) 5000l. *Acraea ranaualona* (vert) Set of 2 sheets 4·50 4·75

Nos. 3812/17 and 3818/23 were each printed together, se-tenant, with the backgrounds forming composite designs based on the map of Africa.

Nos. 3813, 3814, 3819, 3823 and MS3825a are inscribed "CLOSSEX", "PHENIX", "CYMOTOE", "HADNANUS" and "CLOTIS", all in error.

2001. 25th Death Anniv of Mao Tse-tung (Chinese leader). As T **426** of St. Vincent. Multicoloured.

3826 1100l. Young Mao wearing blue 50 55
3827 1100l. Mao in green People's Army uniform 50 55
3828 1100l. Mao in blue cap 50 55
3829 1100l. Mao in khaki uniform 50 55
3830 1100l. Mao in open-necked shirt 50 55
3831 1100l. Mao in grey cap 50 55
MS3832 Two sheets, each 90×119 mm. (a) 5000l. Mao in traditional robe. (b) 5000l. Mao in blue tunic Set of 2 sheets 4·50 4·75

2001. 75th Death Anniv of Claude-Oscar Monet (French painter). As T **427** of St. Vincent. Mult.

3833 1500l. "Road to Vetheuil, Winter, 1879" 65 70
3834 1500l. "Church at Vetheuil, 1879" 65 70
3835 1500l. "Breakup of Ice near Vetheuil, 1880" 65 70
3836 1500l. "Boulevard de Pontoise, Argenteuil, 1875" 65 70
MS3837 137×110 mm. 5000l. "Irises by Pool, 1914–17" (vert) 2·20 2·30

2001. 75th Birthday of Queen Elizabeth II. As T **428** of St. Vincent. Multicoloured.

3838 2000l. Princess Elizabeth in A.T.S. uniform 90 95
3839 2000l. Princess Elizabeth and Prince Charles 90 95
3840 2000l. Queen Elizabeth in evening dress 90 95
3841 2000l. Princess Elizabeth in Girl Guide uniform 90 95
MS3842 80×110 mm. 5000l. Queen Elizabeth in evening dress (37×50 mm) 2·20 2·30

2001. Golden Jubilee (1st issue). As T **429** of St. Vincent. Multicoloured.

3843 1000l. Queen Elizabeth II 45 50

See also Nos. 3960/4.

No. 3843 was printed in sheetlets of 8, containing two vertical rows of four, separated by a large illustrated central gutter. Both the stamp and the illustration on the central gutter are made up of a collage of miniature flower photographs.

2001. Death Centenary of Giuseppe Verdi (Italian composer). As T **430** of St. Vincent showing scenes from *Aida* (opera). Multicoloured.

3844 1700l. Vladimir Popov 75 80
3845 1700l. Enrico Caruso 75 80
3846 1700l. Rudolf Bockelmann 75 80
3847 1700l. Scene from *Aida* 75 80
MS3848 79×110 mm. 5000l. Aprile Millo as Aida and Barseq Tumayan as Amonasro 2·20 2·30

2001. Death Centenary of Henri de Toulouse-Lautrec (French painter). As T **431** of St. Vincent. Multicoloured.

3849 2200l. "A la Mie" 95 1·00
3850 2200l. "Corner of the Moulin de la Galette" 95 1·00
3851 2200l. "Start of the Quadrille" 95 1·00
MS3852 68×109 mm. 5000l. "La Gouloue" (vert) 2·20 2·30

2001. Centenary of Royal Navy Submarine Service. As T **107** of St. Kitts. Multicoloured.

3853 1100l. C29 (submarine) 50 55
3854 1100l. H.M.S. *Spartan* (submarine) 50 55
3855 1100l. H.M.S. *Exeter*(cruiser) 50 55
3856 1100l. H.M.S. *Chatham* (frigate) 50 55
3857 1100l. H.M.S. *Verdun* (destroyer) 50 55
3858 1100l. H.M.S. *Marlborough* (frigate) 50 55
MS3859 70×55 mm. 5000l. H.M.S. *Vanguard* (missle submarine) 2·20 2·30

Nos. 3854 and 3857 are inscribed "SPARTON" or "VERDUM",both in error.

354 Marlene Dietrich in Black Dress

2001. Birth Centenary of Marlene Dietrich (actress and singer).

3860 **354** 2000l. black, purple and red 90 95
3861 – 2000l. multicoloured 90 95
3862 – 2000l. black, purple and red 90 95
3863 – 2000l. black, purple and red 90 95

DESIGNS: No. 3861, Marlene Dietrich in evening dress; 3862, Wearing white fur coat; 3863, Smoking.

2001. "Philanippon '01" International Stamp Exhibition, Tokyo. Japanese Art. As T **432** of St. Vincent. Multicoloured.

3864 50l. "Iziu Chinuki No Hi" (Hokkei) (horiz) 10 10
3865 100l. "Visit to Enoshima" (Torii Kiyonaga) (horiz) 10 10
3866 150l. "Inn on a Harbour" (Sadahide) (horiz) 10 10
3867 200l. "Entrance to Foreigners' Establishment" (Sadahide) (horiz) 10 15
3868 250l. "Courtesans at Cherry Blossom Time" (Kiyonaga) (horiz) 10 15
3869 300l. "Cherry Blossom Viewing at Ueno" (Toyohara Chikanobu) (horiz) 15 20
3870 400l. "Summer Evening at Restaurant by the Sumida River" (Kiyonaga) (horiz) 20 25
3871 500l. "Ichikana Yaozo I as Samurai" (Buncho) 20 25
3872 600l. "Nakamura Noshoi II as Street Walker" (Katsukawa Shunzan) 25 30
3873 800l. "Arashi Sangoro II Hosoban" (Shokosai) 35 40
3874 1500l. "Bando Mitsuguro I" (Shunko) 65 70
3875 2000l. "Matsumoto Koshiro II" (Masanobu) 90 95
3876 2000l. "Young Woman attended by Maid" (Suzuki Harunobu) 90 95
3877 2000l. "Lovers by Lespedeza Bush" (Harunobu) 90 95
3878 2000l. "Girl contemplating a Landscape" (Harunobu) 90 95
3879 2000l. "Young Man unrolling a Hanging Scroll" (Harunobu) 90 95
3880 2000l. "Promenade" (Harunobu) 90 95
3881 2000l. "Wine Tasters" (Harunobu) 90 95
3882 2000l. "Rain in May" (Harunobu) 90 95
3883 2000l. "Lovers by the Wall" (Harunobu) 90 95
3884 2000l. "Six Girls" (standing figure with orange sash) (Eisho) 90 95
3885 2000l. "Courtesan on a Bench" (Eiri) 90 95
3886 2000l. "Courtesan and her Two Kamuro" (Harunobu) 90 95
3887 2000l. "Clearing Weather at Awazu" (Shigemasa) 90 95
3888 2000l. "Nakamura Shikan II and Nakamura Baiko" (Shigeharu) 90 95
3889 2000l. "Women making Rice Cakes" (Shunsho) 90 95
3890 2000l. "Youth sending Letter by Arrow" (Harushige) 90 95
3891 2000l. "Six Girls" (standing figure with green sash) (Eisho) 90 95
MS3892 Five sheets, each 85×120 mm. (a) 5000l. "Courtesan and Two Kamuro". (b) 5000l. "Searching for the Hermit". (c) 5000l. "Girl contemplating a Landscape" (different). (d) 5000l. "Drying Clothes". (e) 5000l. "Komachi praying for Rain". All by Harunobu Set of 5 sheets 11·00 11·50

355 General Ulysses S. Grant

2001. American Civil War. Multicoloured.

3893 2000l. Type **355** 90 95
3894 2000l. General John Hood 90 95
3895 2000l. General Jeb Stuart 90 95
3896 2000l. General Robert E. Lee 90 95
3897 2000l. General Joshua Chamberlain 90 95
3898 2000l. General "Stonewall" Jackson 90 95
3899 2000l. General George McClellan 90 95
3900 2000l. Admiral David Farragut 90 95
3901 2000l. Battle of Fredericksburg, 1862 90 95

3902 2000l. Battle of Gettysburg, 1863 . . . . 90 95
3903 2000l. Naval Battle of Mobile Bay, 1864 . . . . 90 95
3904 2000l. Bombardment of Fort Sumter, 1861 . . . . . . 90 95
3905 2000l. Battle of Shiloh, 1862 90 95
3906 2000l. Battle of Bull Run, 1861 and 1862 . . . . . 90 95
3907 2000l. Battle of Fair Oaks, 1863 . . . . 90 95
3908 2000l. Battle of Chattanooga, 1863 . . . 90 95
MS3909 Four sheets. (a) 109 × 157 mm. 5000l. General George Custer. (b) 109 × 157 mm. 5000l. General William T. Sherman. (c) 109 × 157 mm. 5000l. Battle of Vicksburg, 1863. (d) 157 × 109 mm. 5000l. Battle of Antietam, 1862 Set of 4 sheets 8·75 9·00
No. 3900 is inscribed "ADMRIAL" in error.

356 Ferrari 360 Challenge, 2001

2001. Ferrari Racing Cars. Multicoloured.
3910 100l. Type **356** 10 10
3911 500l. 712 Can Am, 1971 . . 20 25
3912 600l. 512M, 1970 . . . . . 25 30
3913 1000l. F40, 1988 . . . . . 45 50
3914 1500l. 365 GT4/BB, 1982 . . 65 70
3915 2000l. 365 GTB/4, 1972 . . 90 95

357 Chinese Character with Symbolic Horse ("2002" in green)

2001. Chinese New Year ("Year of the Horse"). Each incorporating the same character and a symbolic horse. Multicoloured.
3916 1200l. Type **357** 55 60
3917 1200l. "2002" in red 55 60
3918 1200l. "2002" in orange . . 55 60
3919 1200l. "2002" in blue . . . 55 60
MS3920 97 × 69 mm. 1200l. European toy horse on wheels (37 × 24 mm); 1200l. Chinese toy horse and rider (37 × 24 mm) 1·10 1·20

358 British Newspaper Article, Brazil, 1950

2001. World Cup Football Championship, Japan and Korea (2002). Multicoloured.
3921 1400l. Type **358** 60 65
3922 1400l. Jules Rimet (F.I.F.A. President), Switzerland, 1954 . . . . 60 65
3923 1400l. Pele and other members of Brazilian team, Sweden, 1958 . . . 60 65
3924 1400l. Vava (Brazil) and Schroiff (Czechoslovakia), Chile, 1962 . . . . 60 65
3925 1400l. Bobby Charlton (England), England, 1966 60 65
3926 1400l. Pele (Brazil), Mexico, 1970 . . . . 60 65
3927 1400l. Daniel Passarella (Argentina) with World Cup, Argentina, 1978 . . 60 65
3928 1400l. Karl-Heinz Rummenigge (West Germany), Spain, 1982 . . 60 65
3929 1400l. Diego Maradona (Argentina), Mexico, 1986 60 65
3930 1400l. Roger Milla (Cameroon), Italy, 1990 60 65
3931 1400l. Romario (Brazil), U.S.A., 1994 . . . . . . 60 65
3932 1400l. Zinedine Zidane (France), France, 1998 . . 60 65
MS3933 Two sheets, each 88 × 75 mm. (a) 5000l. Detail of Jules Rimet Trophy, Uruguay, 1930. (b) 5000l. Detail of World Cup Trophy, Japan/Korea 2002 Set of 2 sheets . . . . 4·50 4·75
No. 3922 is inscribed "Rimmet" in error.

359 "Madonna of Humility" (Filippo Lippi)

2001. Christmas. Religious Paintings by Filippo Lippi. Multicoloured.
3934 300l. Type **359** 15 20
3935 600l. "Annunciation" . . . 25 30
3936 1500l. "Annunciation" (different) (vert) 65 70
3937 2000l. "Adoration of the Child and Saints" (vert) 90 95
MS3938 136 × 106 mm. 5000l. "Barbadori Altarpiece" (vert) 2·20 2·30
No. **MS**3938 is inscribed "Alterpiece" in error.

360 Early Steam Fire Engine

2002. Technological Development from Steam to Electricity. Multicoloured.
3939 1100l. Type **360** 50 55
3940 1100l. Dial telephone . . . 50 55
3941 1100l. Luxury liner 50 55
3942 1100l. Electrical battery . . 50 55
3943 1100l. Steam carriage, 1770 50 55
3944 1100l. Modern electric locomotive 50 55
3945 1100l. Robert Fulton and early steam ship 50 55
3946 1100l. Thomas Edison and early electric light bulb . . 50 55
3947 1100l. Class T9 steam locomotive, 1899 . . . . 50 55
3948 1100l. Early radio and transmitting masts 50 55
3949 1100l. James Watt and diagram of steam engine 50 55
3950 1100l. Alexander Graham Bell and early telephone 50 55
3951 1100l. *The Rocket* (steam locomotive), 1829 . . . . 50 55
3952 1100l. Modern TGV train 50 55
3953 1100l. Firefighting steam pump, 1863 . . . . 50 55
3954 1100l. Early electric tram . . 50 55
3955 1100l. Steam car, 1893 . . . 50 55
3956 1100l. Modern electric monorail 50 55
MS3957 Three sheets, each 70 × 100 mm (a) 5000l. Class T9 steam locomotive, 1899. (b)5000l. Telephone, radio and light bulb. (c) 5000l. Benjamin Franklin (vert) Set of 3 sheets . . . . 6·75 7·00

361 S.O.S. Children's Village Logo

363 Jerusalem Artichoke Flower and Butterfly

362 Curling

2002. S.O.S. Children's Villages (Kinderdorf International).
3958 **361** 2000l. multicoloured . . 90 95

2002. "United We Stand". Support for Victims of 11 September 2001 Terrorist Attacks. As T **445** of St. Vincent. Multicoloured.
3959 2000l. U. S. flag as Statue of Liberty and Sierra Leone flag 90 95

2002. Golden Jubilee (2nd issue). As T **110** of St. Kitts Multicoloured.
3960 2000l. Queen Elizabeth with Prince Charles and Princess Anne 90 95
3961 2000l. Queen Elizabeth in red dress and fur stole . . 90 95
3962 2000l. Queen Elizabeth wearing tiara and fur . . 90 95
3963 2000l. Queen Elizabeth wearing beige hat and coat 90 95
MS3964 76 × 108 mm. 5000l. Queen Elizabeth wearing grey hat and coat . . . . 2·20 2·30

2002. Winter Olympic Games, Salt Lake City. Multicoloured.
3965 2000l. Type **362** 90 95
3966 2000l. Ice hockey 90 95
MS3967 88 × 118 mm. Nos. 3965/6 1·80 1·90

2002. Flowers of Sierra Leone. Multicoloured.
3968 400l. Type **363** 20 25
3969 500l. Painted trillium and bee 20 25
3970 600l. Bell flower ("Bluebells") and moth 25 30
3971 1000l. Rough-fruited cinquefoil and moth . . . 45 50
3972 1300l. Laevigata iris (43 × 29 mm) 60 65
3973 1300l. Wild iris ("Dietes") (43 × 29 mm) 60 65
3974 1300l. Day lily (43 × 29 mm) 60 65
3975 1300l. Cardinal flower (43 × 29 mm) 60 65
3976 1300l. Mountain pink (43 × 29 mm) 60 65
3977 1300l. Seaside gentian (43 × 29 mm) 60 65
3978 1300l. Hepatica americana (43 × 29 mm) 60 65
3979 1300l. Star of Bethlehem (43 × 29 mm) 60 65
3980 1300l. Wood lily (43 × 29 mm) 60 65
3981 1300l. Wild geranium (43 × 29 mm) 60 65
3982 1300l. Hedge bindweed (43 × 29 mm) 60 65
3983 1300l. Gloxinia (43 × 29 mm) 60 65
3984 1500l. Wake-robin and wasp 65 70
3985 2000l. Seashore mallow and butterfly 90 95
MS3986 Two sheets, each 117 × 107 mm. (a) 5000l. Dame's rocket (29 × 43 mm). (b) 5000l. Pinxter flower (29 × 43 mm) Set of 2 sheets . . . . 4·50 4·75
Nos. 3972/7 and 3978/83 were each printed together, se-tenant, with the backgrounds forming composite designs.

364 African Buffalo

2002. Sierra Leone Wildlife. Multicoloured.
3987 200l. Giraffe (vert) 10 15
3988 400l. L'Host's guenon (vert) 20 25
3989 1100l. Type **364** 50 55
3990 1100l. Wild dog 50 55
3991 1100l. Black-backed jackal 50 55
3992 1100l. Aardvark 50 55
3993 1100l. Impala 50 55
3994 1100l. Waterbuck 50 55
3995 1100l. Kudu 50 55
3996 1100l. Caracal 50 55
3997 1100l. Oribis 50 55
3998 1100l. Aardwolf 50 55
3999 1100l. Bushpig 50 55
4000 1100l. Meerkat ("Suricates") 50 55
4001 1500l. Jentink's duiker . . . 65 70
MS4002 Two sheets, each 117 × 107 mm. (a) 8000l. Springbok (vert). (b) (b) 8000l. Vervet monkey (vert) Set of 2 sheets . . . . 7·00 7·25
Nos. 3989/94 and 3995/4000 were each printed together, se-tenant, with the backgrounds forming composite designs. Nos. 3991, 3997 and 4001 are inscribed "Jackel", "Orbis" and "Jentik's", all in error.

2002. Queen Elizabeth the Queen Mother Commemoration. Nos. 2335/9 surch.
4003 800l. on 400l. Queen Mother (brown, light brown and black) 35 40
4004 800l. on 400l. Holding bouquet 35 40
4005 800l. on 400l. Sitting at desk 35 40
4006 800l. on 400l. Wearing pink evening dress 35 40
MS4007 103 × 127 mm. 5000l. on 1500l. Wearing blue hat . . . 2·20 2·30

2002. Shirley Temple in *Wee Willie Winkie*. As T **411** of St. Vincent showing scenes from the film. Multicoloured.
4008 1100l. Meeting Khoda Khan 50 55
4009 1100l. Priscilla looking in mirror 50 55
4010 1100l. With drummer boy 50 55
4011 1100l. Priscilla being admonished by Indian servant 50 55
4012 1100l. Priscilla with grandfather 50 55
4013 1100l. Exchanging letter with Khoda Khan in prison 50 55
4014 1300l. Priscilla and mother (vert) 60 65
4015 1300l. Examining Khoda Khan's locket (vert) . . . 60 65
4016 1300l. Priscilla with mother and grandfather (vert) . . 60 65
4017 1300l. Priscilla with colour sergeant, holding rifle (vert) 60 65
MS4018 106 × 76 mm. 5000l. Priscilla on parade (vert) . . . 2·20 2·30

2002. International Year of Mountains. As T **115** of St. Kitts. Multicoloured.
4019 2000l. Mount Etna, Italy . . 90 95
4020 2000l. Mount Cotopaxi, Ecuador 90 95
4021 2000l. Mount Everest, Nepal 90 95
4022 2000l. Mount Popocatepetl, Mexico 90 95
MS4023 118 × 68 mm. 5000l. Mount Machhapuchare, Nepal . . . . 2·20 2·30

2002. U.N. Year of Eco Tourism. As T **449** of St.Vincent, but horiz. Multicoloured.
4024 1300l. Bullom boats 60 65
4025 1300l. Dinkongor Falls . . . 60 65
4026 1300l. Sailing canoe on River Rokel 60 65
4027 1300l. Pigmy hippopotamus 60 65
4028 1300l. Soa Chiefdom hills 60 65
4029 1300l. Long Beach 60 65
MS4030 88 × 103 mm. 5000l. Photo safari . . . . 2·20 2·30

366 *Spirit of St. Louis*

2002. 75th Anniv of First Solo Transatlantic Flight, by Charles Lindbergh.
4031 **366** 2500l. lake and red . . . 1·10 1·20
4032 – 2500l. green and red . . 1·10 1·20
4033 – 2500l. lilac and red . . . 1·10 1·20
MS4034 116 × 85 mm. 2500l. multicoloured (vert) . . . . . 1·10 1·20
DESIGNS—HORIZ: No. 4032, *Spirit of St. Louis*, Curtisfield, 1927; 4033, Taking off from Roosevelt Field, 1927. VERT: No. **MS**4034, Charles Lindbergh.

367 Chiune Sugihara

369 Elvis Presley

368 Popeye and Olive Oyl at Helm

2002. Chiune Sugihara, Japanese Consul-general to Lithuania, 1939–40, Commemoration.
4035 **367** 2000l. multicoloured . . 90 95

2002. 20th World Scout Jamboree, Thailand. As T **116** St. Kitts, but vert. Multicoloured.
4036 2000l. Scouts on rocks . . . 90 95
4037 2000l. Scouts of all nations 90 95
4038 2000l. Two scouts in river, holding fish 90 95
4039 2000l. Watching demonstration 90 95
MS4040 107 × 122 mm. 5000l. Sailing on lake . . . . 2·20 2·30

2002. "Pokemon" (children's cartoon series). As T **417** of St. Vincent. Multicoloured.
4041 1500l. "Sudowoodo No. 185" 65 70
4042 1500l. "Aipom No. 190" . . 65 70
4043 1500l. "Shuckle No. 213" 65 70
4044 1500l. "Miltank No. 241" 65 70
4045 1500l. "Hitmontop No. 237" 65 70
4046 1500l. "Ledian No. 166" . . 65 70
MS4047 67 × 91 mm. 5000l. "Lugia No. 249" . . . . 2·20 2·30

2002. "Popeye" (cartoon character) in New York. Multicoloured.
4048 1300l. Type **368** 60 65
4049 1300l. Popeye giving Olive Oyl spinach 60 65
4050 1300l. By Brooklyn Bridge 60 65
4051 1300l. Popeye near Statue of Liberty 60 65

4052 1300l. At the Flatiron building 60 65
4053 1300l. In front of Empire State Building 60 65
MS4054 128 × 89 mm. 5000l. Popeye and Olive Oyl ice skating (78 × 51 mm) . . . . 2·20 2·30

2002. 25th Death Anniv of Elvis Presley (American entertainer). Each black and brown.
4055 1000l. Type **369** 45 50
4056 1000l. Playing bi-coloured guitar 45 50
4057 1000l. Sitting in director's chair 45 50
4058 1000l. Wearing polo neck jumper 45 50
4059 1000l. In Hispanic suit . . . 45 50
4060 1000l. Playing dark guitar 45 50

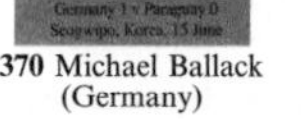

370 Michael Ballack (Germany)

371 "Madonna and Child between Sts. John the Baptist and Catherine of Alexandria" (Perugino)

2002. World Cup Football Championship, Japan and Korea. Multicoloured.
4061 1400l. Type **370** 60 65
4062 1400l. Oliver Kahn (Germany) 60 65
4063 1400l. Miroslav Klose (Germany) 60 65
4064 1400l. Diego Gavilan (Paraguay) 60 65
4065 1400l. Jose Luis Chilavert (Paraguay) 60 65
4066 1400l. Guido Alvarenga (Paraguay) 60 65
4067 1400l. Rafael Marquez (Mexico) 60 65
4068 1400l. Oscar Perez (Mexico) 60 65
4069 1400l. Jared Borgetti (Mexico) 60 65
4070 1400l. Landon Donovan (U.S.A.) 60 65
4071 1400l. Brad Friedel (U.S.A.) 60 65
4072 1400l. DaMarcus Beasley (U.S.A.) 60 65
4073 1400l. Jesper Gronkjaer (Denmark) 60 65
4074 1400l. Thomas Helveg (Denmark) 60 65
4075 1400l. Dennis Rommedahl (Denmark) 60 65
4076 1400l. Michael Owen (England) 60 65
4077 1400l. David Seaman (England) 60 65
4078 1400l. Rio Ferdinand (England) 60 65
4079 1400l. Ryuzo Morioka (Japan) 60 65
4080 1400l. Kazuyuki Toda (Japan) 60 65
4081 1400l. Atsushi Yanagisawa (Japan) 60 65
4082 1400l. Fatih Akyel (Turkey) 60 65
4083 1400l. Yildiray Basturk (Turkey) 60 65
4084 1400l. Umit Davala (Turkey) 60 65
MS4085 Eight sheets, each 82 × 82 mm. (a) 2500l. Rudi Voeller (coach) (Germany); 2500l. Dietmar Hamann (Germany). (b) 2500l. Julio Cesar Caceres (Paraguay); 2500l. Cesare Maldini (coach) (Paraguay). (c) 2500l. Javier Aguirre (coach) (Mexico); 2500l. Jesus Arellano (Mexico). (d) 2500l. Brian McBride (U.S.A.); 2500l. Bruce Arena (coach) (U.S.A.). (e) 2500l. Morten Olsen (coach) (Denmark); 2500l. Jon Dahl Tomasson (Denmark). (f) 2500l. David Beckham (England); 2500l. Sven Goran Eriksson (coach) (England). (g) 2500l. Philippe Troussier (coach) (Japan); 2500l. Junichi Inamoto (Japan). (h) 2500l. Vildiray Basturk (Turkey); 2500l. Senol Gunes (coach) (Turkey) Set of 8 sheets 8·75 9·00

2002. Christmas. Religious Paintings. Mult.
4086 50l. Type **371** 10 10
4087 100l. "Madonna and Child enthroned between Angels and Saints" (Ghirlandaio) 10 10
4088 150l. "The Virgin" (Giovanni Bellini) 10 10
4089 500l. "The Birth of Mary" (Ghirlandaio) 20 25

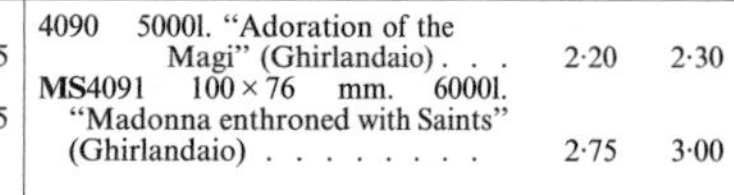

4090 5000l. "Adoration of the Magi" (Ghirlandaio) . . . 2·20 2·30
MS4091 100 × 76 mm. 6000l. "Madonna enthroned with Saints" (Ghirlandaio) . . . . 2·75 3·00

372 Teddy Bear with Green and Gold Bow

373 Princess Diana

2002. Centenary of the Teddy Bear (1st issue). Two sheets containing T **372** and similar vert designs. Multicoloured.
MS4092 107 × 115 mm. 1700l. Type **372**; 1700l. Jester teddy bear; 1700l. Bear with red and gold headband; 1700l. Bear with sash 3·00 3·25
MS4093 148 × 158 mm. 2000l. Baby girl bear; 2000l. School girl bear; 2000l. Bear in denim overalls; 2000l. Bear in pyjamas . . . . 3·50 3·75
See also Nos. **MS**4128/9.

2002. 5th Death Anniv of Diana, Princess of Wales. Two sheets, each 120 × 130 mm, containing T **373** and similar vert design. Multicoloured.
MS4094 1700l. × 4 Type **373** . . 3·00 3·25
MS4095 1700l. × 4 Princess Diana (wearing tiara) . . . . 3·00 3·25

374 President John F. Kennedy

375 Great Blue Turaco

2002. Presidents John F. Kennedy (Commemoration) and Ronald Reagan. Miniature sheets containing vert designs as T **374**. Multicoloured.
MS4096 122 × 135 mm. 1700l. Type **374**; 1700l. John Kennedy reading newspaper; 1700l. John Kennedy (looking ahead); 1700l. John Kennedy (looking left) . . 3·00 3·25
MS4097 114 × 129 mm. 1700l. John and Jacqueline Kennedy in evening dress; 1700l. John and Jacqueline Kennedy; 1700l. With John Jnr; 1700l. Jacqueline Kennedy in pink hat and coat 3·00 3·25
MS4098 143 × 110 mm. 1700l. × 4 containing two different portraits of Ronald Reagan . . . . . . 3·00 3·25
MS4099 137 × 165 mm. 1700l. × 4 containing two different portraits of Ronald Reagan . . . . . . 3·00 3·25

2003. Fauna and Flora of Africa. Miniature sheets containing T **375** and similar multicoloured designs.
MS4100 139 × 100 mm. 1300l. Type **375**; 1300l. Helmet bird ("Helmet Vanga"); 1300l. Red-tufted malachite sunbird ("Scarlet-tufted Malachite Sunbird"); 1300l. African pitta; 1300l. African jacana; 1300l. Carmine bee eater 3·50 3·75
MS4101 139 × 100 mm. 1300l. *Ancistrochilus rothschildianus*; 1300l. *Oeceoclades maculate*; 1300l. *Eulophia guineensis*; 1300l. *Angraecum distichum*; 1300l. *Disa uniflora*; 1300l. *Vanilla imperialis* 3·50 3·75
MS4102 139 × 100 mm. 1300l. Panther-spotted grasshopper; 1300l. Basker moth; 1300l. *Charaxes samagdalis* (butterfly); 1300l. Carpenter ant; 1300l. Worker bee; 1300l. *Libellula pulchella* (ten-spot dragonfly) 3·50 3·75
MS4103 Three sheets. (a) 63 × 87 mm. 5000l. European robin. (b) 87 × 63 mm. 5000l. *Bulbophyllum lepidum*. (c) 87 × 63 mm. 5000l. Common dotted border (butterfly) (horiz) Set of 3 sheets . . . . . . 6·75 7·00
No. **MS**4100 shows birds, **MS**4101 shows flowers and **MS**4102 insects.

376 Green Symbolic Ram

377 David Brown

2003. Chinese New Year ("Year of the Ram"). Sheet 109 × 128 mm, containing T **376** and similar vert designs. Multicoloured.
MS4104 900l. Type **376**; 900l. × 3 Carved ram; 900l. Red symbolic ram. 900l. Magenta symbolic ram 2·00 2·10

2003. *Columbia* Space Shuttle Commemoration. Sheet 184 × 145 mm, containing T **377** and similar vert designs showing crew members. Multicoloured.
MS4105 1000l. Type **377**; 1000l. Commander Rick Husband; 1000l. Laurel Clark; 1000l. Kalpana Chawla; 1000l. Payload Commander Michael Anderson; 1000l. Pilot William McCool; 1000l. Ilan Ramon . . . . . . 3·00 3·25

2003. Centenary of the Teddy Bear (2nd issue). Embroidered Fabric Teddy Bears. As T **464** of St. Vincent. Self-adhesive. Imperf.
4106 12000l. ochre, silver and black . . . . 3·50 3·75
MS4107 126 × 157 mm. No. 4106 × 4 . . . . 14·00 14·50

378 "Priest Raigo tranformed into a Rat" (Tsukioka Yoshitoshi)

2003. Japanese Art. Ghosts and Demons. Multicoloured.
4108 800l. Type **378** 35 40
4109 1000l. "The Spirit of Tamichi as a Great Snake" (Tsukioka Yoshitoshi) 45 50
4110 1500l. "The Gathering and Gossiping of Various Tools" (Utagawa Kuniyoshi) 65 70
4111 2500l. "Caricatures of Actors as Three Animals playing Ken" (Utagawa Kuniyoshi) . . . . 1·10 1·20
MS4112 148 × 148 mm. 2000l. "The Fox Woman leaving her Child"; 2000l. "Fox Cry"; 2000l. "The Lucky Teakettle of Morin Temple"; 2000l. "The Ghost of Okiku" (all Tsukioka Yoshitoshi) 3·50 3·75
MS4113 88 × 118 mm. 5000l. "Fox in a Thunderstorm" (Utagawa Kunisada) . . . . 2·20 2·30

2003. 30th Death Anniv of Pablo Picasso (artist). As T **465** of St. Vincent, but vert. Multicoloured.
4114 400l. "Verres Pipe, Carte a Jouer" 20 25
4115 500l. "Gueridon devant un Balcon" 20 25
4116 600l. "Femme au Chapeau a Plumes" 25 30
4117 700l. "Gueridon et Guitare" 30 35
4118 1000l. "Femme en Pied" . . 45 50
4119 3000l. "Femme Acrobate" 1·30 1·40
MS4120 205 × 140 mm. 2000l. "Portrait de Face"; 2000l. "Femme au Fauteuil Rouge"; 2000l. "Femme au Petit Chapeau Rond, Assise (Dora Maar)"; 2000l. "Femme aux Mains Croisees" . . . . 3·50 3·75
MS4121 (a) 82 × 105 mm. 5000l. "Garcon au Calecon noir". Imperf. (b) 102 × 81 mm. 5000l. "Les Baigneuses". Imperf . . . 4·50 4·75

2003. Paintings by Rembrandt. As T **466** of St. Vincent. Multicoloured.
4122 800l. "Young Man with Pointed Beard" 35 40
4123 1000l. "Old Man with Book" 45 50
4124 1200l. "The Shipbuilder Jan Rijcksen and his Wife, Griet Jans" (horiz) . . . 55 60
4125 2000l. "Portrait of a Young Jew" 90 95
MS4126 185 × 183 mm. 1700l. "Juno"; 1700l. "Bellona, Goddess of War"; 1700l. "Artemisia" (detail); 1700l. "Esther preparing to Intercede with Ahasuerus" (detail) (all 35 × 47 mm) . . . 3·25 3·50
MS4127 110 × 130 mm. 5000l. "Two Scholars Disputing" . . . . . 2·20 2·50

379 Teddy Bear wearing Apron and Hat

380 Prince William

2003. Centenary of the Teddy Bear (2nd issue). German Teddy Bears. Multicoloured.
MS4128 183 × 129 mm. 1500l. Type **379**; 1500l. Bear wearing waistcoat, hat and water bottle; 1500l. Bear wearing pink dress 1500l. Bear with trumpet and score 2·75 3·00
MS4129 98 × 72 mm. 5000l. Bear in Volkswagon Beetle car (horiz) 2·20 2·30

2003. 50th Anniv of Coronation. As T **462** of St. Vincent. Multicoloured.
4130 1500l. Queen Elizabeth II holding Sovereign's Sword 65 70
4131 1500l. Ampulla and spoon 65 75
4132 1500l. Queen presented with Holy Bible 65 70
4133 1500l. Crowning of Queen 65 70
4134 1500l. Queen signing Oath 65 70
4135 1500l. Anointing of Queen 65 70
4136 1500l. Orb and Sceptre . . . 65 70
4137 1500l. Crowd at Palace gates and Royal Family on balcony 65 70
MS4138 9 × 67 mm. 5000l. Queen Elizabeth II (38 × 50 mm) . . . 2·20 2·30

2003. 21st Birthday of Prince William of Wales. Multicoloured.
MS4139 146 × 85 mm. 2500l. Type **380**; 2500l. Prince William (wearing black jacket and tie); 2500l. Wearing grey sweatshirt 3·25 3·50
MS4140 96 × 67 mm. 5000l. Prince William . . . . 3·25 3·40

381 Peggy Williams

382 "Mona Lisa"

2003. Centenary of Circus Clowns. Multicoloured.
MS4141 116 × 196 mm. 2000l. Type **381**; 2000l. Nico; 2000l. Steve TJ Tatter Smith; 2000l. Uncle Dippy . . . . 3·50 3·75
MS4142 145 × 217 mm. 2000l. Caracal (cat) ; 2000l. Chairs (gymnast); 2000l. Elena Panova on trapeze; 2000l. Chinese Circus performer . . . . 2·75 3·00

2003. 500th Anniv of "Mona Lisa" (painting, Da Vinci).
MS4143 100 × 77 mm. 2000l. Type **382** (black and grey); 2000l. "Mona Lisa (black, deep brown and brown); 2000l. "Mona Lisa" (multicoloured) . . . . . . 2·75 3·00
MS4144 67 × 97 mm. 5000l. "Mona Lisa" (detail) (multicoloured) 2·20 2·30

383 Waterfalls of Mount Tonkour

2003. International Year of Freshwater. Multicoloured.
MS4145 96 × 138 mm. 2000l. Type **383**; 2000l. Tagbaladougou Falls; 2000l. Cascades d,Ouzoud 2·75 3·00
MS4146 67 × 97 mm. 5000l. Little Scarcies . . . . 2·20 2·40

384 Rotarian and People in Canoe

2003. 40th Anniv of Rotary Club in Sierra Leone. Multicoloured.
MS4147 105 × 77 mm. 2500l. Type **384**; 2500l. People of Sierra Leone and cacheted first day cover; 2500l. Paul Harris (founder) and girl with flowers . . . . . 3·25 3·50
MS4148 97 × 67 mm. 6000l. Bhichai Rattakul (Rotary President) . . 2·75 3·00

385 Wright Brothers First Plane (USA), 1903

2003. Centenary of Powered Flight. Multicoloured.
MS4149 176 × 96 mm. 1500l. Wright Brothers' First Plane (U.S.A.), 1903; 1500l. Voisin-Farmin (France), 1907 (grey background); 1500l. Levavasseur Antoinette (France), 1909 (No. 29 on fuselage); 1500l. Nieuport (France) 1910 . . . . 2·40 2·50
MS4150 176 × 96 mm. 1500l. Curtiss Triad, 1911 (inscr "Wright Brothers First Plane (U.S.A.) 1903"; 1500l. Avro Biplane, 1911 (inscr "Voisin-Farmin (France) 1907") (blue-grey background); 1500l. Curtiss America, 1913 (inscr "Levavasseur Antoinette (France) 1909"); 1500l. Farnborough Be-2, 1913 (inscr "Nieuport (France) 1910") (No. 345 on tail) . . . 2·75 3·00
MS4150a 176 × 96 mm. 1500l. Curtiss Triad (U.S.A.), 1911; 1500l. Avro Biplane (British), 1911; 1500l. Curtiss America (U.S.A.), 1913; 1500l. Farnborough Be-2 (British), 1913 2·75 3·00
MS4151 Two sheets, each 106 × 76 mm. (a) 5000l. Voisin-Farman plane crossing finish line, Aero Club, 1908. (b) 5000l. Roland Garros and Morane-Saulnier monoplane after first non-stop Mediterranean crossing, 1913 Set of 2 sheets . . . . . 4·50 4·75
No. **MS**4150 was issued with the incorrect aircraft inscriptions and **MS**4150a was issued subsequently with the correct inscriptions.

2003. Centenary of Tour de France Cycle Race. As T **470** of St.Vincent. Multicoloured.
MS4152 157 × 97 mm. 1500l. Ferdinand Kubler (1950); 1500l. Hugo Koblet (1951); 1500l. Fausto Coppi (1952); 1500l. Louison Bobet (1953) . . . . 2·75 3·00
MS4153 157 × 97 mm. 1500l. Louison Bobet 1954); 1500l. Louison Bobet (1955); 1500l. Roger Walkowiak (1956); 1500l. Jacques Anquetil (1957) . . . 2·75 3·00
MS4154 157 × 97 mm. 1500l. Eddy Merckx (1970); 1500l. Eddy Merckx (1971); 1500l. Eddy Merckx (1972); 1500l. Luis Ocana (1973) . . . . 2·75 3·00
MS4155 Two sheets, each 106 × 77 mm. (a) 5000l. Louison Bobet (1953, 1954, 1955). (b) 5000l. Jacques Anquetil (1957). (c) 5000l. Bernard Hinault (1978) Set of 2 Sheets . . . . 4·50 4·75

386 Forrest Smithson (110 metre hurdles), USA, 1908

2003. Olympic History. Gold Medal Winners. Multicoloured.

4156	300l. Type **386**	15	20
4157	400l. Hannes Kolehmainen (10000 metres, 5000 metres and cross-country), Finland, 1912	20	25
4158	500l. Larisa Latynina (gymnastics–floor exercises), URS, 1964 . .	20	25
4159	800l. Klaus Dibiasi (10 metre platform diving), Italy, 1976	35	40
4160	1000l. Archie Hahn (100 metres and 200 metres), USA, 1904	45	50
4161	1500l. Marcus Hurley (cycling), USA, 1904 . . .	65	70
4162	2000l. Ray Ewry (standing high jump, standing long jump and standing triple jump), USA, 1900	90	95
4163	3000l. Henry Taylor (swimming–1500 metres and 400 metres freestyle), Great Britain, 1908 . . .	1·30	1·40

387 "Madonna and Child with St. Anne and Four Saints" (detail)

2003. Christmas. Paintings by Fiorentino. Multicoloured.

4164	100l. Type **387**	10	10
4165	150l. "Madonna and Child with Two Saints" (detail)	10	10
4166	500l. "Madonna and Child enthroned with Four Saints" (detail) (Ognissanti Altarpiece) . .	20	25
4167	4000l. "Madonna enthroned between Two Saints" (detail)	1·80	1·90

MS4168 99 × 110 mm. 5000l. "Madonna with Saints" . . . 2·20 2·30

388 Camarasaurus

2004. Prehistoric Animals. Multicoloured.
MS4169 138 × 99 mm. 2000l. Type **388**; 2000l. Iystrosaurus; 2000l. Ankylosaurus; 2000l. Herrerasaurus . . . . 3·50 3·75
MS4170 125 × 106 mm. 2000l. Apatosaurus (vert); 2000l. Styracosaurus (vert); 2000l. Plateosaurus (vert); 2000l. Pachyrhinosaurus (vert) . . . 3·50 3·75
MS4171 Two sheets (a) 97 × 67 mm. 5000l. Archaeopteryx. (b) 67 × 96 mm. 5000l. Dunklosteus (vert) . . . . 4·50 4·75
No. **MS**4171a is incorrectly inscr "Archaeopterxy".

389 Monkey eating Fruit

2004. Chinese New Year ("Year of the Monkey"). Multicoloured.
MS4173 85 × 70 mm. 1200l. Type **389** (ochre background); 1200l. Type **389** (blue background); 1200l. Monkey eating fruit (facing right, mauve background); 1200l. Monkey eating fruit (facing right, orange background) . . . . 2·20 2·30
MS4174 66 × 96 mm. 2500l. Monkey holding fruit (42 × 28 mm) . . 1·30 1·40

390 "Taoist Ritual at the Imperial Court"

2004. Hong Kong 2004 International Stamp Exhibition. Paintings by Chiao Ping-chen. Multicoloured.
MS4175 136 × 139 mm. 2000l. Type **390**; 2000l. Landscape of mountains, river and lake; 2000l. "Court Ladies" (by pavilion); 2000l. "Court Ladies" (poling raft) 3·50 3·75
MS4176 90 × 90 mm. 5000l. "The Beauty of Traditional Chinese Architecture in Painting". Imperf 2·20 2·30

391 Cabani's Yellow Bunting

2004. 60th Anniv of British Council in Sierra Leone.

4177	**391**	500l. multicoloured . . .	20	25
4178		1000l. multicoloured . .	45	50
4179		2000l. multicoloured . .	90	95
4180		3000l. multicoloured . .	1·30	1·40

392 Lion Emblem and Map

2004. 40th Anniv of First Self-adhesive Stamps. As T **80** (World's Fair, New York of 1964) but redrawn with face value in leones as T **392**. Self-adhesive. Imperf.

4181	**392**	1000l. multicoloured . .	45	50

393 "Ice Cream Carrier"

2004. 25th Death Anniv of Norman Rockwell (artist) (2003). Multicoloured.
MS4182 150 × 180 mm. 2000l. Type **393**; 2000l. "The Voyeur"; 2000l. "Teacher's Birthday"; 2000l. Fisk Tires advertisement, 1919 . . . . 3·50 3·75
MS4183 90 × 97 mm. 5000l. "Cousin Reginald plays Pirate" . . . . 2·20 2·30

394 Concorde over River, Rio de Janeiro

2004. Last Flight of Concorde (2003). Multicoloured.
MS4184 90 × 131 mm. 3000l. Type **394**; 3000l. Concorde over Brazil flag (top left of blue circle); 3000l. Concorde over Brazil flag (bottom left of blue circle) . .
MS4185 90 × 129 mm. 3000l. Concorde (pink background); 3000l. Concorde and pyramid (red background); 3000l. Concorde and pyramid (dark brown background) . . . . 4·00 4·25
MS4186 131 × 90 mm. 3000l. Concorde and Nairobi skyline; 3000l. Concorde over Kenyan bush (black and red background) 3000l. Concorde over Kenyan bush (red and green background) 4·00 4·25
No. **MS**4184 shows Concorde 206 G-BOAA over Rio de Janeiro, **MS**4185 Concorde G-AXDN and Egyptian pyramid and **MS**4186 Concorde G-AXDN Aircraft No. 101 over Kenya.

395 "The Birth of John the Baptist" (detail) (Tintoretto)

396 Marilyn Monroe

2004. 300th Anniv of St. Petersburg. "Treasures of the Hermitage". Multicoloured.
MS4187 144 × 144 mm. 1400l. Type **395**; 1400l. "Penitent Mary Magdalen" (Titian); 1400l. "The Death of St. Petronilla" (Simone Pignoni); 1400l. "The Assumption of the Virgin" (Murillo); 1400l. "St. Jerome Hears the Trumpet" (Jusepe de Ribera); 1400l. "St. George and the Dragon" (Tintoretto) . . . . 2·50 2·75
MS4187a 160 × 140 mm. 2000l. "Countess A. S. Stroganova and Her Son" (Louise-Elisabeth Vigee-Lebrun); 2000l. "Count G. I. Chernyshev Holding a Mask (Louise-Elisabeth Vigee-Lebrun)"; 2000l. "Self Portrait" (Louise-Elisabeth Vigee-Lebrun); 2000l. "Baron G. A. Stroganov" (Louise-Elisabeth Vigee-Lebrun) . . . 3·50 3·75
MS4188 Two sheets. (a) 62 × 81 mm. 5000l. "The Apostles Peter and Paul" (El Greco). (b) 100 × 69 mm. 5000l. "A Visit to the Priest" (Jean-Baptiste Greuze). Both imperf . . . . 2·20 2·30

2004. Marilyn Monroe (actress) Commemoration. Multicoloured.

4189	1000l. Type **396**	45	50
4190	1000l. With short hair and sparkly earrings (cobalt background)	45	50
4191	1000l. As No. 4190 but with lavender background . .	45	50
4192	1000l. Wearing pink patterned shirt	45	50

MS4193 113 × 112 mm. 2000l. Wearing strapless top; 2000l. With arms above head; 2000l. Leaning back with shoulders hunched; 2000l. Wearing scoop-necked top 3·50 3·75

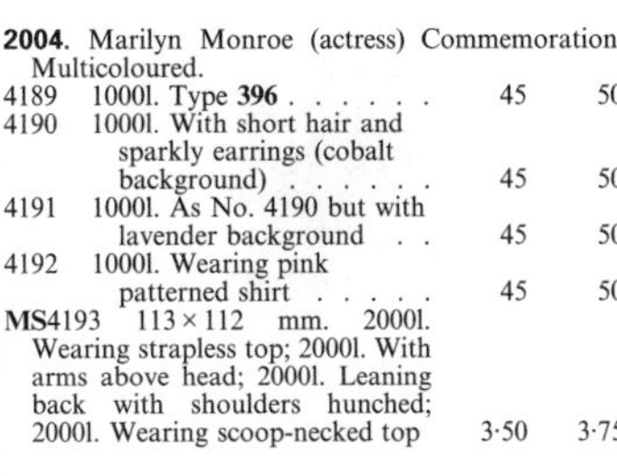

397 Yang Liwei (Chinese Astronaut)

2004. Astronauts. Multicoloured.

4194	900l. Type **397**	40	45
4195	900l. Yang Liwei wearing uniform	40	45
4196	900l. Yang Liwei wearing space suit	40	45
4197	900l. Yang Liwei showing "victory" sign	40	45
4198	1200l. "Vostok 1" (vert) . .	55	60
4199	1200l. John Glenn (American astronaut) (vert)	55	60
4200	1200l. Launch of "Friendship 7" (vert) . .	55	60
4201	1200l. Yuri Gagarin (Russian astronaut) (vert)	55	60
4202	1200l. Launch of "Shenzhou 5" (vert)	55	60
4203	1200l. Yang Liwei (vert) . .	55	60

MS4204 Two sheets, each 100 × 70 mm. (a) 5000l. John Glenn. (b) 5000l. Yang Liwei Set of 2 sheets . . . . 4·50 4·75

398 Lo Moth

2004. Butterflies and Moths. Multicoloured.
4205 200l. Type **398** 10 10
4206 300l. Hackberry butterfly . . 15 20
4207 400l. Red admiral 20 25
4208 4000l. Spangled fritillary . . 1·80 1·90
MS4209 Two sheets. (a) 144 × 118 mm. 1700l. Pearl crescent; 1700l. Pipevine swallowtail; 1700l. Alfalfa looper; 1700l. Tiger swallowtail. (b) 66 × 65 mm. 5000l. Cecropia moth Set of 2 sheets . . . . 5·00 5·25

399 *Catasetum pileatum*

2004. Orchids. Multicoloured.
4210 150l. Type **399** 10 10
4211 400l. *Cattleya araguainsis* . . 20 25
4212 400l. *Barkeria spectabilis* . . 20 25
4213 1700l. *Odontonia vesta* . . . 75 80
4214 1700l. *Ancistro rothschildianus* 75 80
4215 1700l. *Ansellia Africana* . . 75 80
4216 1700l. *Aspasia epidendroides* 75 80
4217 3500l. *Catasetum fimbriatum* 1·50 1·60
MS4218 68 × 73 mm. 5000l. *Bulbophyllum lobbii* . . . . . 2·20 2·30

400 Banded Sculpin

2004. Marine Life. Multicoloured.
4219 800l. Type **400** 35 40
4220 1100l. Black durgon 50 55
4221 1400l. Atlantic spadefish . . 60 65
4222 1400l. Queen triggerfish . . 60 65
4223 1700l. Peacock flounder . . 75 80
4224 1700l. Northern puffer . . . 75 80
4225 1700l. Sea raven 75 80
4226 1700l. Tiger shark 75 80
MS4227 68 × 74 mm. 5000l. Sea lamprey (vert) . . . . 2·20 2·30

401 Ruddy Somali

2004. Cats. Multicoloured.
4228 100l. Type **401** 10 10
4229 800l. Bombay (walking right) 35 40
4230 1200l. Burmese (walking left) 55 60
4231 1700l. Persian (vert) 75 80
4232 1700l. Colorpoint shorthair (vert) 75 80
4233 1700l. Cornish Rex (vert) . . 75 80
4234 1700l. Blue Point Balinese (vert) 75 80
4235 3000l. Blue British shorthair 1·30 1·40
MS4236 83 × 63 mm. 5000l. Devon Rex . . . . 2·20 2·30

402 Great Pyrenees

2004. Dogs. Multicoloured.
4237 250l. Type **402** 10 10
4238 600l. Kerry blue terrier . . . 25 30
4239 1300l. Mastiff 60 65
4240 1700l. Sealyham terrier . . . 75 80
4241 1700l. Norwich terrier . . . 75 80
4242 1700l. Wheaton terrier . . . 75 80
4243 1700l. Bull terrier 75 80
4244 1800l. English sheepdog . . 80 85
MS4245 70 × 79 mm. 5000l. Greyhound . . . . 2·20 2·30

403 Belted Kingfisher 405 Deng Xiaoping

404 Pope John Paul II

2004. Birds. Multicoloured.
4246 500l. Type **403** 20 25
4247 1000l. Burrowing owl . . . 45 50
4248 1500l. Crested caracara . . 65 70
4249 1700l. Snail kite (horiz) . . 75 80
4250 1700l. Avocet (horiz) . . . 75 80
4251 1700l. Greater flamingo (horiz) 75 80
4252 1700l. Bald eagle (horiz) . . 75 80
4253 2000l. Red headed finch . . 90 95
MS4254 84 × 64 mm. 5000l. Ring neck pheasant . . . . 2·20 2·30

2004. 25th Anniv of the Pontificate of Pope John Paul II. Sheet 95 × 118 mm containing T **404** and similar horiz designs. Multicoloured.
MS4255 2000l. Type **404**; 2000l. Pope and John Bonica (President of International Association for the Study of Pain); 2000l. Pope in Croatia; 2000l. Pope presiding over Mass . . . . 3·50 3·75

2004. Birth Centenary of Deng Xiaoping (leader of China, 1978–89). Sheet 96 × 67 mm.
MS4256 **405** 5000l. multicoloured 2·20 2·30

406 Marathon, 1908

2004. Olympic Games, Athens. Multicoloured.
4257 250l. Type **406** 10 10
4258 300l. Demetrius Vikelas (President of International Olympic Committee 1894–1896) 10 10
4259 1500l. Detail of gold medal, Athens (1896) 65 70
4260 2000l. Discobolus (Greek sculpture) 90 95

407 General Dwight D. Eisenhower 408 "Mona Lisa"

2004. 60th Anniv of D-Day Landings. Multicoloured.
4261 1400l. Type **407** 60 65
4262 1400l. Rear Admiral Don. P. Moon 60 65
4263 1400l. Lieutenant General Omar N. Bradley . . . 60 65
4264 1400l. Rear Admiral Alan G. Kirk 60 65
4265 1400l. Major General Clarence R. Huebner . . 60 65
4266 1400l. Major General Maxwell D. Taylor . . . 60 65
MS4267 Six sheets each 200 × 117 mm. (a) 950l. × 8, LST landing craft; M4 Sherman tank; US soldier on tank; Gun of tank; 70th Tank Battalion patch; Soldier aiming rifle; 743rd Tank Battalion patch; 741st Tank Battalion patch. (b) 1000l. × 8, P-51 Mustang; Parachutists; Map of troop movements; P-38 Lightning; M4 Sherman tank and explosion; Soldiers; LCM landing craft; U.S. light cruiser. (c) 1000l. × 8, Spitfire; Typhoon; Tail of Typhoon; P-51 Mustang; C-47 Skytrain; War plane and wing of Typhoon; P-38 Lightning; U.S. Airforce patch. (d) 1000l. × 8, P-47 Thunderbolt; Parachutists, map and planes; Tank and map of troop movements; Map showing Dieppe and soldier aiming rifle; U.S. heavy cruiser; U.S. light cruiser and bow of heavy cruiser; Destroyer and bow and stern of ships; U.S. Destroyer escort. (e) 1100l. × 8 U.S. light cruiser and airships; LST landing craft and airships; Bow of LST landing craft; Hull of LST landing craft; U.S. armoured car; Soldiers; U.S. medical transport; U.S. armoured car and landing craft. (f) 1100l. × 8 Soldier aiming rifle and map of parachutists' descent; Badge of 101st Airborne "Screaming Eagles"; Parachutist and tail of plane; Cockpit of plane; General Dwight D. Eisenhower; Bernard Montgomery; 82nd Airborne Division; C-47 Skytrain and parachutists Set of 6 sheets . . 21·00 22·00

2004. 500th Anniv of the "Mona Lisa".
4268 **408** 2000l. multicoloured . . 90 95

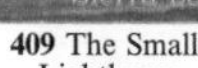
409 The Smalls Lighthouse 410 Arapaho Pipe Bag

2004. Lighthouses of Great Britain. Multicoloured.
4269 1800l. Type **409** 80 85
4270 2000l. Needles Rock lighthouse 90 95
4271 2500l. St. John's Point lighthouse . . . . 1·10 1·20
4272 3500l. Bell Rock lighthouse 1·50 1·60
4273 4000l. Eddystone lighthouse 1·80 1·90

2004. American Indians. Multicoloured.
4274/82 Decorative Artifacts. 1000l. × 9, Type **410**; Apache basket; Blackfoot parfleche; Crow Elkhide robe; Iroquois moccasins; Hopi canteen; Sioux parfleche; Navajo rug; nez Perce cradle . . . 4·00 4·25
4283/8 Chiefs and Warriors. 1500l. × 6, Ne-O-Mon-Ne; Ma-Has-Kah; Moa-Na-Hon-Ga; Tah-Ro-Hon; Not-Chi-Mi-Ne; Shau-Hau-Napo-Tinia . . . . 4·00 4·25

SINGAPORE Pt. 1

An island to the south of the Malay peninsula, formerly part of the Straits Settlement but became a separate Crown Colony on 1 April 1946. From 1 August 1958 an internally self-governing territory designated the State of Singapore. From 16 September 1963 part of the Malaysian Federation until 9 August 1965, when it became an independent republic within the Commonwealth.

100 cents = 1 dollar.

1948. As T **58** of Straits Settlements, but inscr "MALAYA SINGAPORE".
1 1c. black . . . . 15 1·00
2 2c. orange 15 50
3 3c. green 50 75
4 4c. brown . . . . 20 1·25
19a 5c. mauve . . . . 3·00 1·75
5 6c. grey 40 80
6 8c. red 50 80
21a 8c. green . . . . 7·50 3·25
7 10c. purple 30 10
22a 12c. red . . . . 9·00 10·00
8 15c. blue . . . . 11·00 10
9 20c. black and green . . . 5·50 40
24a 20c. blue . . . . 4·50 10
25 25c. purple and orange . . . 1·00 10
25a 35c. red and purple . . . . . 4·50 1·00
11 40c. red and purple . . . . . 9·50 5·00
12 50c. black and blue . . . . . 3·25 10
13 $1 blue and purple . . . . . 10·00 3·50
14 $2 green and red . . . . . . 48·00 4·50
15 $5 green and brown . . . . £110 5·50

1948. Silver Wedding. As T **32a** of St. Helena.
31 10c. violet 75 70
32 $5 brown . . . . £110 42·00

1949. 75th Anniv of U.P.U. As T **33d/g** of St Helena.
33 10c. purple 75 60
34 15c. blue . . . . 6·00 3·00
35 25c. orange . . . . 6·00 3·00
36 50c. black . . . . 6·00 3·25

1953. Coronation. As T **33h** of St. Helena.
37 10c. black and purple . . . . 2·00 30

1 Chinese Sampan 16 The Singapore Lion

3 Singapore River

1955.
38 **1** 1c. black . . . . 10 1·00
39 – 2c. orange . . . . 2·00 1·25
40 – 4c. brown . . . . 1·00 15
41 – 5c. purple 65 40
42 – 6c. blue 65 70
43 – 8c. turquoise . . . . 1·25 1·00
44 – 10c. lilac . . . . 3·00 10
45 – 12c. red . . . . 3·00 2·75
46 – 20c. blue . . . . 2·25 10
47 – 25c. orange and violet . . . 7·00 1·50
48 – 30c. violet and lake . . . . . 3·75 10
49 – 50c. blue and black . . . . . 2·25 10
50 – $1 blue and purple . . . . . 30·00 30
51 **3** $2 green and red . . . . . . 42·00 1·75
52 – $5 multicoloured . . . . . . 42·00 5·00
DESIGNS—HORIZ (as Type **1**) (2c. to 20c. are sailing craft): 2c. Malay kolek; 4c. Twa-kow lighter; 5c. Lombok sloop; 6c. Trengganu pinas; 8c. Palari schooner; 10c. Timber tongkong; 12c. Hainan junk; 20c. Cocos-Keeling schooner; 25c. Douglas DC-4M2 "Argonaut" aircraft; 30c. Oil tanker; 50c. "Chusan III" (liner). VERT (as Type **3**): $1 Raffles statue; $5 Arms of Singapore.

1959. New Constitution. Lion in yellow and sepia.
53 **16** 4c. red 65 75
54 10c. purple . . . . 1·00 40
55 20c. blue . . . . 2·25 3·00
56 25c. green . . . . 2·50 2·25
57 30c. violet . . . . 2·50 3·25
58 50c. slate . . . . 3·25 3·25

17 State Flag

1960. National Day.
59 **17** 4c. red, yellow and blue . . 1·50 1·50
60 10c. red, yellow and grey . . 2·75 30

18 Clasped Hands

1961. National Day.
61 **18** 4c. black, brown and yellow 1·00 1·50
62 10c. black, green and yellow 1·25 10

19 "Arachnis" "Maggie Oei" (orchid) 20 Yellow Seahorse

1962. Orchids, Fishes and Birds.
63 **19** 1c. multicoloured . . . . . 30 1·00
64 **20** 2c. brown and green . . . 30 2·00
65 – 4c. black and red . . . . 30 1·25
66 – 5c. red and black 20 10
67 – 6c. black and yellow . . . 55 1·25
68 – 8c. multicoloured . . . . . 1·25 3·50
69 – 10c. orange and black . . 40 10
70 – 12c. multicoloured . . . . 1·25 3·50
70a – 15c. multicoloured . . . . 2·75 10
71 – 20c. orange and blue . . . 40 10
72 – 25c. black and orange . . 75 10
73 – 30c. multicoloured . . . . 1·25 10
74 – 50c. multicoloured . . . . 1·25 10
75 – $1 multicoloured . . . . . 18·00 60
76 – $2 multicoloured . . . . . 9·00 1·00
77 – $5 multicoloured . . . . . 18·00 6·50
DESIGNS—HORIZ (as Type **20**): 4c. Tiger barb; 5c. Orange clownfish; 10c. Harlequinfish; 25c. Three-spotted gourami. (As Type **19**): 50c. White-rumped shama; $1 White-throated kingfisher.VERT (as Type **20**): 6c. Archerfish; 20c. Copper-banded butterflyfish. (As Type **19**): 8c. "Vanda" "Tan Chay Yan" (orchid); 12c. "Grammatophyllum speciosum" (orchid); 15c. Black-naped tern; 30c. "Vanda" "Miss Joaquim" (orchid); $2 Yellow-bellied sunbird; $5 White-bellied sea eagle.

34 "The Role of Labour in Nation-Building"

1962. National Day.
78 **34** 4c. yellow, red and black . . 1·25 2·25
79 10c. yellow, blue and black 1·50 75

35 Blocks of Flats, Singapore

1963. National Day.
80 **35** 4c. multicoloured 50 80
81 10c. multicoloured . . . . . 1·75 20

36 Dancers in National Costume

1963. South East Asia Cultural Festival.
82 **36** 5c. multicoloured 50 50

37 Workers

1966. 1st Anniv of Republic.
89 **37** 15c. multicoloured 75 30
90 20c. multicoloured . . . . . 1·00 1·25
91 30c. multicoloured . . . . . 1·25 2·00

38 Flag Procession

1967. National Day.
92 **38** 6c. red, brown and slate . . 50 90
93 15c. purple, brown and slate 80 10
94 50c. blue, brown and slate 1·50 1·60
Nos. 92/4 are respectively inscr "Build a Vigorous Singapore" in Chinese, Malay and Tamil, in additon to the English inscr.

39 Skyscrapers and Afro-Asian Map

1967. 2nd Afro-Asian Housing Congress.
95 **39** 10c. multicoloured 30 10
96 25c. multicoloured . . . . . 75 1·00
97 50c. multicoloured . . . . . 1·40 1·60

40 Symbolical Figure wielding Hammer and Industrial Outline of Singapore

45 Sword Dance

43 Mirudhangam

1968. National Day. Inscription at top in Chinese (6c.), Malay (15c.) or Tamil (50c.).
98 **40** 6c. red, black and gold . . 35 65
99 15c. green, black and gold 45 15
100 50c. blue, black and gold 1·00 1·25

1968.
101 **43** 1c. multicoloured . . . . . 15 2·25
102 – 4c. multicoloured . . . . . 60 2·75
103 **45** 5c. multicoloured . . . . . 60 1·75
104 – 6c. black, lemon and orange . . . . 1·75 2·25
105 – 10c. multicoloured 20 10
106 – 15c. multicoloured 60 10
107 – 20c. multicoloured . . . . 1·00 1·75
108 – 25c. multicoloured . . . . 1·25 1·75
109 – 30c. multicoloured . . . . 40 1·50
110 – 50c. black, red and brown 50 60
111 – 75c. multicoloured . . . . 3·00 4·25
112 – $1 multicoloured . . . . . 4·50 1·25
113 – $2 multicoloured . . . . . 3·50 1·00
114 – $5 multicoloured . . . . . 13·00 1·50
115 – $10 multicoloured . . . . 38·00 15·00
DESIGNS—VERT (as Type **43**): 4c. Pi Pa; $2 Rebab; $10 Ta Ku. (As Type **45**): 6c. Lion Dance; 10c. Bharatha Natyam; 15c. Tari Payong; 20c. Kathak Kali; 25c. Lu Chih Shen and Lin Chung; 50c. Tari Lilin; 75c. Tarian Kuda Kepang; $1 Yao Chi. HORIZ (as Type **43**): $5 Vine. (As Type **45**): 30c. Dragon dance.

58 E.C.A.F.E. Emblem

1969. Plenary Session of Economic Commission for Asia and the Far East.
116 **58** 15c. black, silver and blue 35 20
117 30c. black, silver and red 65 1·25
118 75c. black, silver and violet 1·00 2·50

59 "100000" and Slogan as Block of Flats

60 Aircraft over Silhouette of Singapore Docks

1969. Completion of "100000 Homes for the People" Project.
119 **59** 25c. black and green . . . 1·00 50
120 50c. black and blue . . . . 1·25 1·25

1969. 150th Anniv of Founding of Singapore.
121 **60** 15c. black, red and yellow 2·50 70
122 – 30c. black and blue . . . . 2·50 1·75
123 – 75c. multicoloured . . . . 4·50 2·00
124 – $1 black and red . . . . . 9·00 10·00
125 – $5 red and black . . . . . 30·00 55·00
126 – $10 black and green . . . 40·00 55·00
MS127 120 × 120 mm. Nos. 121/6 £450 £475
DESIGNS: 30c. U.N. emblem and outline of Singapore; 75c. Flags and outline of Malaysian Federation; $1 Uplifted hands holding crescent and stars; $5 Tail of Japanese aircraft and searchlight beams; $10 Bust from statue of Sir Stamford Raffles.

61 Sea Shells

1970. World Fair, Osaka. Multicoloured.
128 15c. Type **61** . . . . 1·50 15
129 30c. Veil-tailed guppys . . . 2·75 90
130 75c. Greater flamingo and helmeted hornbill . . . . 7·50 3·75
131 $1 Orchid . . . . 7·50 6·00
MS132 94 × 154 mm. Nos. 128 × 31 24·00 24·00

62 "Kindergarten"

63 Soldier charging

1970. 10th Anniv of People's Association.
133 **62** 15c. brown and orange . . 85 20
134 – 50c. blue and orange . . . 2·25 2·75
135 – 75c. purple and black . . . 3·50 4·50
DESIGNS: 50c. "Sport"; 75c. "Culture".

1970. National Day. Multicoloured.
136 15c. Type **63** . . . . 1·25 20
137 50c. Soldier on assault course 3·75 3·50
138 $1 Soldier jumping . . . . . 5·00 11·00

64 Sprinters

1970. Festival of Sports.
139 **64** 10c. mauve, black and blue 2·00 3·25
140 – 15c. black and orange . . 2·50 3·50
141 – 25c. black, orange and green . . . . 2·75 3·75
142 – 50c. black, green and mauve . . . . 3·00 3·75
DESIGNS: 15c. Swimmers; 25c. Tennis players; 50c. Racing cars.

65 "Neptune Aquamarine" (freighter)

1970. Singapore Shipping.
143 **65** 15c. multicoloured . . . . 2·75 65
144 – 30c. yellow and blue . . . 6·00 5·50
145 – 75c. yellow and red . . . . 10·00 10·00
DESIGNS: 30c. Container berth; 75c. Shipbuilding.

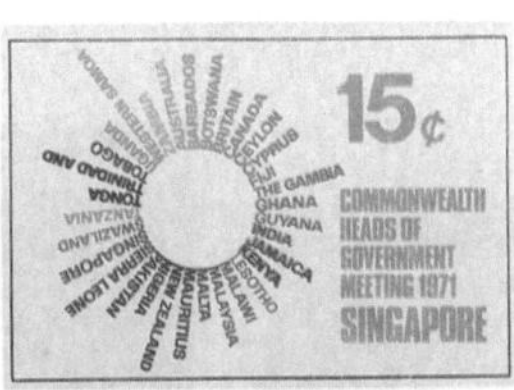

66 Country Names in Circle

1971. Commonwealth Heads of Government Meeting, Singapore. Multicoloured.
146 15c. Type **66** 90 20
147 30c. Flags in circle . . . . . 1·25 80
148 75c. Commonwealth flags . . 2·25 4·00
149 $1 Commonwealth flags linked to Singapore (63 × 61 mm) . . . . . . 3·00 7·00

67 Bicycle Rickshaws

1971. Tourism. ASEAN Year. (ASEAN = Association of South East Asian Nations).
150 **67** 15c. black, violet and orange 80 25
151 – 20c. indigo, orange & blue 1·10 1·00
152 – 30c. red and purple . . . . 1·40 1·75
153 – 50c. multicoloured . . . . 4·75 8·00
154 – 75c. multicoloured . . . . 6·50 10·00
DESIGNS—SQUARE: 20c. Houseboat "village" and boats; 30c. Bazaar. HORIZ (68 × 18 mm): 50c. Modern harbour skyline; 75c. Religious buildings.

68 Chinese New Year

69 "Dish" Aerial

1971. Singapore Festivals. Multicoloured.
155 15c. Type **68** . . . . 1·25 15
156 30c. Hari Raya . . . . . . 3·00 2·50
157 50c. Deepavali . . . . . . 4·00 6·50
158 75c. Christmas . . . . 5·00 7·50
MS159 150 × 125 mm. Nos. 155/8 75·00 48·00

1971. Opening of Satellite Earth Station.
160 **69** 15c. multicoloured . . . . 3·00 1·50
161 – 30c. multicoloured . . . . 11·00 12·00
162 – 30c. multicoloured . . . . 11·00 12·00
163 – 30c. multicoloured . . . . 11·00 12·00
164 – 30c. multicoloured . . . . 11·00 12·00
DESIGNS: Nos. 161/4 were printed in se-tenant blocks of four throughout the sheet, the four stamps forming a composite design similar to Type **69**. They can be identified by the colour of the face values which are: yellow (No. 161), green (No. 162), red (No. 163) or orange (No. 164).

70 "Singapore River and Fort Canning, 1843–7" (Lieut. E. A. Porcher)

1971. Art. Multicoloured.
165 10c. Type **70** . . . . 2·50 2·50
166 15c. "The Padang, 1851" (J. T. Thomson) . . . . . 3·50 4·00
167 20c. "Singapore Waterfront, 1848–9" . . . . 4·50 4·50
168 35c. "View from Fort Canning 1846" (J. T. Thomson) . . . . 9·00 9·00
169 50c. "View from Mt. Wallich, 1857" (P. Carpenter) . . . 13·00 14·00
170 $1 "Singapore Waterfront, 1861" (W. Gray) . . . . . 16·00 19·00
The 50c. and $1 are larger, 69 × 47 mm.

71 One Dollar of 1969

1972. Coins.
171 – 15c. orange, black and green . . . . 1·25 35
172 **71** 35c. black and red . . . . 2·75 3·25
173 – $1 yellow, black and blue 5·00 8·50
DESIGNS: 15c. One-cent coin of George V; $1 One hundred and fifty dollar gold coin of 1969.

72 "Moon Festival" (Seah Kim Joo)

1972. Contemporary Art. Multicoloured.
174 15c. Type **72** 80 30
175 35c. "Complimentary Forces" (Thomas Yeo) (36 × 54 mm) . . . . . . 2·00 3·00
176 50c. "Rhythm in Blue" (Yusman Aman) (36 × 54 mm) . . . . . . 2·50 4·50
177 $1 "Gibbons" (Chen Wen Hsi) . . . . 4·50 7·50

73 Lanterns and Fish

75 "Maria Rickmers" (barque)

74 Student Welding

1972. National Day. Designs symbolizing Festivals. Multicoloured.
178 15c. Type **73** 75 20
179 35c. Altar and candles . . . 1·40 2·75
180 50c. Jug, bowl and gifts . . . 2·00 4·00
181 75c. Candle . . . . 3·00 6·00

1972. Youth.
182 **74** 15c. multicoloured 80 30
183 – 35c. multicoloured . . . . 2·00 3·50
184 – $1 orange, violet and green 3·75 8·00
DESIGNS: 35c. Sport; $1 Dancing.

1972. Shipping. Multicoloured.
185 15c. "Neptune Ruby" (container ship) (42 × 29 mm) . . . . . . 2·25 80
186 75c. Type **75** . . . . 7·50 8·00
187 $1 Chinese junk . . . . . . 8·00 9·00
MS188 152 × 84 mm. Nos. 185/7 45·00 45·00

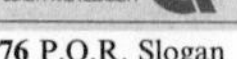

76 P.Q.R. Slogan

77 Jurong Bird Park

1973. "Prosperity Through Quality and Reliability" Campaign. Multicoloured.
189 15c. Type **76** 60 15
190 25c. Badge . . . . 1·50 3·25
191 75c. Text (different) . . . . 1·75 3·75
192 $1 Seal . . . . 1·75 5·00

1973. Singapore Landmarks.
193 **77** 15c. black and orange . . 1·00 15
194 – 35c. black and green . . 2·50 3·25
195 – 50c. black and brown . . 3·25 4·25
196 – $1 black and purple . . . 5·00 6·50
DESIGNS: 35c. National Theatre; 50c. City Hall; $1 Fullerton Building and Singapore River.

78 Aircraft Tail-fins

1973. Aviation. Multicoloured.
197 10c. Type **78** 50 10
198 35c. Emblems of Singapore Airlines and destinations 1·50 2·00
199 75c. Emblem on tail-fin . . . 1·75 2·50
200 $1 Emblems encircling the globe . . . . 2·25 3·50

79 "Culture"

80 Athletics, Judo and Boxing

1973. National Day.
201 **79** 10c. orange and black . . 1·50 2·25
202 – 35c. orange and black . . 1·50 2·75
203 – 50c. orange and black . . 1·75 3·00
204 – 75c. orange and black . . 2·00 3·50
Nos. 201/4 were printed in se-tenant blocks of four within the sheet, and form a composite design representing Singapore's culture.

1973. 7th S.E.A.P.* Games.
205 **80** 10c. gold, silver and blue 55 20
206 – 15c. gold and black . . . . 1·75 1·50
207 – 25c. gold, silver and black 1·50 1·75
208 – 35c. gold, silver and blue 3·00 3·50
209 – 50c. multicoloured . . . . 2·00 4·25
210 – $1 silver, blue and green 3·25 7·50
MS211 130 × 111 mm. Nos. 205/10 32·00 35·00
DESIGNS—SQUARE (as Type **80**): 15c. Cycling, weight-lifting, pistol-shooting and sailing; 25c. Footballs; 35c. Table-tennis bat, shuttlecock, tennis ball and hockey stick. HORIZ (41 × 25 mm): 50c. Swimmers; $1 Stadium.
*S.E.A.P. = South East Asian Peninsula.

81 Agave

82 Mangosteen

1973. Multicoloured. (a) Flowers and plants as T **81**.
212 1c. Type **81** . . . . 1·00 1·50
213 5c. "Coleus blumei" 10 50
214 10c. "Vinca rosea" 15 10
215 15c. "Helianthus angustifolius" . . . . . . 1·50 10
216 20c. "Licuala grandis" . . . 45 60
217 25c. "Wedelia trilobata" . . 3·75 55
218 35c. "Chrysanthemum frutescens" . . . . 1·00 1·00
219 50c. "Costus malorticanus" 1·00 55
220 75c. "Gerbera jamesonii" . . 2·50 1·00

(b) Fruits as T **82**.
221 $1 Type **82** . . . . 1·50 40
222 $2 Jackfruit . . . . 3·00 1·25
223 $5 Coconut . . . . 3·00 6·00
224 $10 Pineapple . . . . 4·50 10·00

83 Tiger and Orang-Utans

84 Delta Guppy

1973. Singapore Zoo. Multicoloured.
225 5c. Type **83** 85 85
226 10c. Leopard and waterbuck 1·00 45
227 35c. Leopard and thamin . . 4·50 6·00
228 75c. Horse and lion . . . . 6·00 9·00

1974. Tropical Fish. Multicoloured.
229 5c. Type **84** 70 60
230 10c. Half-black delta guppy 70 15
231 35c. Delta guppy (different) 2·75 4·00
232 $1 Black delta guppy . . . . 4·75 10·00

85 Scout Badge within "9"

86 U.P.U. Emblem and Multiple "Centenary"

1974. 9th Asian-Pacific Scout Conference.
233 **85** 10c. multicoloured 30 10
234 75c. multicoloured . . . . 1·00 2·00

1974. Centenary of U.P.U.
235 **86** 10c. brown, purple and gold 15 10
236 – 35c. blue, deep blue & gold 40 1·60
237 – 75c. multicoloured . . . . 80 2·75
DESIGNS: 35c. U.P.U. emblem and multiple U.N. symbols; 75c. U.P.U. emblem and multiple peace doves.

87 Family Emblem

88 "Tree and Sun" (Chia Keng San)

1974. World Population Year. Multicoloured.
238 10c. Type **87** 30 10
239 35c. Male and female symbols . . . . 80 1·60
240 75c. World population map 1·75 3·25

1974. Universal Children's Day. Mult.
241 5c. Type **88** 40 65
242 10c. "My Daddy and Mummy" (Angeline Ang) 40 20
243 35c. "A Dump Truck" (Si-Hoe Yeen Joong) . . . . 2·50 3·75
244 50c. "My Aunt" (Raymond Teo) . . . . 2·75 4·50
MS245 138 × 100 mm. Nos. 241/4 23·00 28·00

89 Street Scene

1975. Singapore Views. Multicoloured.
246 15c. Type **89** 80 20
247 20c. Singapore River . . . . 1·50 1·50
248 $1 "Kelong" (fish-trap) . . . 4·00 7·50

90 Emblem and Lighters' Prows

1975. 9th Biennial Conference of Int Association of Ports and Harbours, Singapore. Multicoloured.
249 5c. Type **90** 30 15
250 25c. Freighter and ship's wheel . . . . 1·75 1·50
251 50c. Oil-tanker and flags . . 2·25 3·00
252 $1 Container-ship and propellers . . . . 3·50 6·50

91 Satellite Earth Station, Sentosa

92 "Homes and Gardens"

1975. "Science and Industry". Mult.
253 10c. Type **91** 35 10
254 35c. Oil refineries (vert) . . . 2·50 3·00
255 75c. "Medical Sciences" . . . 2·75 4·25

1975. 10th National Day. Multicoloured.
256 10c. Type **92** 20 10
257 35c. "Shipping and Shipbuilding" . . . . . . 1·75 2·00
258 75c. "Communications and Technology" . . . . . . 2·00 3·50
259 $1 "Trade, Commerce and Industry" . . . . 2·00 4·00

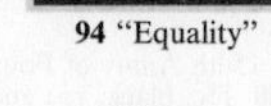

93 South African Crowned Cranes

94 "Equality"

1975. Birds. Multicoloured.
260 5c. Type **93** . . . . 1·75 80
261 10c. Great Indian hornbill . . 1·75 30
262 35c. White-throated kingfishers and white-collared kingfisher . . . . 9·50 9·50
263 $1 Sulphur-crested cockatoo and blue and yellow macaw . . . . 14·00 16·00

1975. International Women's Year. Mult.
264 10c. Type **94** 25 10
265 35c. "Development" . . . . 1·75 3·00
266 75c. "Peace" . . . . 2·25 6·00
MS267 128 × 100 mm. Nos. 264/6 15·00 20·00

95 Yellow Flame

96 "Arachnis hookeriana x Vanda" Hilo Blue

1976. Wayside Trees. Multicoloured.
268 10c. Type **95** 60 10
269 35c. Cabbage tree . . . . . 2·50 3·50
270 50c. Rose of India . . . . . 2·75 3·50
271 75c. Variegated coral tree . . 3·25 6·25

1976. Singapore Orchids. Multicoloured.
272 10c. Type **96** . . . . 1·50 10
273 35c. "Arachnis Maggie Oei x Vanda insignis" . . . . . 4·00 4·00
274 50c. "Arachnis Maggie Oei x Vanda" Rodman . . . . . 4·75 4·50
275 75c. "Arachnis hookeriana x Vanda" Dawn Nishimura 6·00 8·00

97 Festival Symbol and Band

1976. 10th Anniv of Singapore Youth Festival. Multicoloured.
276 10c. Type **97** 20 10
277 35c. Athletes . . . . 1·25 1·75
278 75c. Dancers . . . . 1·40 2·75

98 "Queen Elizabeth Walk"

1976. Paintings of Old Singapore. Mult.
279 10c. Type **98** 50 20
280 50c. "The Padang" . . . . . 2·00 4·00
281 $1 "Raffles Place" . . . . . 3·75 6·00
MS282 164 × 91 mm. Nos. 279/81 18·00 23·00

99 Chinese Costume

100 Radar, Missile and Soldiers

1976. Bridal Costumes. Multicoloured.
283 10c. Type **99** 65 10
284 35c. Indian costume . . . . 1·75 2·50
285 75c. Malay costume . . . . 2·75 5·75

1977. 10th Anniv of National Service. Multicoloured.
286 10c. Type **100** 65 10
287 50c. Tank and soldiers . . . 2·50 2·50
288 75c. Soldiers, wireless operators, pilot and Douglas A-4 Skyhawk aircraft . . . . 3·50 4·50

101 Lyrate Cockle

102 Spotted Hermit Crab

1977. Multicoloured. (a) Shells as T **101**.
289 1c. Type **101** . . . . 1·00 2·00
290 5c. Folded or plicate scallop 20 10
291 10c. Marble cone 20 10

292 15c. Scorpion conch . . . . 1·00 40
293 20c. Amplustre or royal paper bubble . . . . . . 1·00 10
294 25c. Spiral babylon . . . . . 1·25 2·50
295 35c. Royal thorny or spiny oyster . . . . 1·50 1·50
296 50c. Maple-leaf triton or winged frog shell . . . . . 2·00 10
297 75c. Troschel's murex . . . . 3·00 20

(b) Fish and Crustaceans as T **102**.
298 $1 Type **102** . . . . 2·25 15
299 $2 Zuge's stingray . . . . . 2·25 75
300 $5 Cuttlefish . . . . 2·25 3·00
301 $10 Lionfish . . . . 3·25 5·50

103 Shipbuilding
104 Keyhole and Banknotes

1977. Labour Day. Multicoloured.
302 10c. Type **103** 30 10
303 50c. Building construction . . 1·25 2·00
304 75c. Road construction . . . 1·75 2·50

1977. Cent of Post Office Savings Bank. Mult.
305 10c. Type **104** 30 10
306 35c. On-line banking service 75 50
307 75c. GIRO service . . . . . 1·75 1·50

105 Flags of Member Nations
106 "Chingay Procession" (Liang Yik Yin)

1977. 10th Anniv of ASEAN (Association of South-East Asian Nations). Multicoloured.
308 10c. Type **105** 30 10
309 35c. "Agriculture" 75 75
310 75c. "Industry" . . . . . . 1·75 1·75

1977. Children's Art. Multicoloured.
311 10c. Type **106** 30 10
312 35c. "At the Bus Stop" (Chong Khing Ann) (horiz) 1·00 50
313 75c. "Playground" (Yap Li Hwa) (horiz) . . . . . . 2·25 2·75
MS314 160 × 97 mm. Nos. 311/13 13·00 18·00

107 "Life Sciences"
108 Botanical Gardens and Esplanade, Jurong Bird Park

1977. Singapore Science Centre. Mult.
315 10c. Type **107** 10 10
316 35c. "Physical sciences" . . . 45 30
317 75c. "Science and technology" . . . . 1·25 1·75
318 $1 Singapore Science Centre 1·50 1·75

1978. Parks and Gardens. Multicoloured.
319 10c. Type **108** 20 10
320 35c. Lagoon, East Coast Park (vert) 80 80
321 75c. Botanical Gardens (vert) 1·50 2·25

109 Red-whiskered Bulbul
111 Map of South East Asia showing Cable Network

110 Thian Hock Keng Temple

1978. Singing Birds. Multicoloured.
322 10c. Type **109** 60 20
323 35c. Oriental white-eye ("White eye") . . . . . . 1·75 1·50
324 50c. White-rumped shama . . 2·00 2·50
325 75c. White-crested laughing thrush and melodious laughing thrush ("China Thrush") . . . . 2·25 3·50

1978. National Monuments. Multicoloured.
326 10c. Type **110** 55 80
327 10c. Hajjah Fatimah Mosque 55 80
328 10c. Armenian Church . . . 55 80
329 10c. Sri Mariamman Temple 55 80
MS330 173 × 86 mm. 35c. × 4, as Nos. 326/9 . . . . 4·25 3·75
Stamps from No. **MS**330 are similar in design to Nos. 326/9 but have no borders and the inscriptions are slightly larger.

1978. A.S.E.A.N. Submarine Cable (1st issue). Philippines–Singapore Section.
331 **111** 10c. multicoloured 15 10
332 35c. multicoloured 60 85
333 50c. multicoloured . . . . 80 1·50
334 75c. multicoloured . . . . 90 2·00
See also Nos. 385/8 and 458/61.

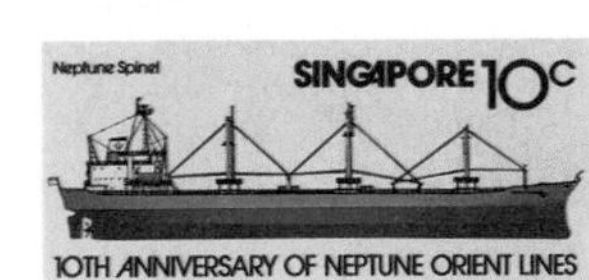

112 "Neptune Spinel" (bulk carrier)

1978. 10th Anniv of Neptune Orient Shipping Lines. Multicoloured.
335 10c. Type **112** 70 20
336 35c. "Neptune Aries" (tanker) . . . . 1·75 1·75
337 50c. "Anro Temasek" (container ship) . . . . . 2·00 2·75
338 75c. "Neptune Pearl" (container ship) . . . . . 2·50 4·25

113 Concorde

1978. Aviation. Multicoloured.
339 10c. Type **113** . . . . 1·00 30
340 35c. Boeing 747-200 . . . . 1·00 1·25
341 50c. Vickers Vimy . . . . . 1·25 2·50
342 75c. Wright Brothers' Flyer I 1·50 4·00

114 10-Kilometre Marker
115 Vanda Hybrid

1979. Metrication. Multicoloured.
343 10c. Type **114** 15 10
344 35c. Tape measure 30 50
345 75c. Weighing scales . . . . 65 1·25

1979. Orchids.
346 **115** 10c. multicoloured 30 10
347 – 35c. multicoloured 60 75
348 – 50c. multicoloured . . . . 70 1·00
349 – 75c. multicoloured . . . . 80 1·40
DESIGNS—HORIZ: 35c. VERT: 50, 75c. Different varieties of vanda hybrid.

116 Envelope with new Singapore Postcode

1979. Postal Code Publicity.
350 **116** 10c. multicoloured 10 10
351 – 50c. multicoloured 60 90
The 50c. design is as Type **116**, but the envelope is addressed to the Philatelic Bureau, General Post Office and has the postcode "Singapore 0104".

117 Early Telephone and Overhead Cables

1979. Centenary of Telephone Service.
352 **117** 10c. brown and blue . . . 15 10
353 – 35c. orange and violet . . 30 40
354 – 50c. blue, turquoise & grn 45 70
355 – 75c. green and orange . . 65 1·25
DESIGNS: 35c. Telephone dial and world map; 50c. Modern telephone and city scene; 75c. Latest computerized telephone and circuit diagram.

118 "Lantern Festival" (Eng Chun-Ngan)

1979. International Year of the Child. Children's Drawings. Multicoloured.
356 10c. Type **118** 10 10
357 35c. "Singapore Harbour" (Wong Chien Chien) . . . 30 40
358 50c. "Use Your Hands" (Leong Choy Yeen) . . . 40 70
359 75c. "Soccer" (Tan Cheong Hin) . . . . 60 1·25
MS360 154 × 98 mm. Nos. 356/9 4·75 4·25

119 View of Gardens

1979. 120th Anniv of Botanic Gardens.
361 **119** 10c. multicoloured 30 10
362 – 50c. multicoloured . . . . 1·00 1·50
363 – $1 multicoloured . . . . 1·50 2·50
DESIGNS: 50c., $1 Different views of Botanic Gardens.

120 Hainan Junk

1980. Ships. Multicoloured.
364 1c. Type **120** . . . . 1·00 2·00
365 5c. Full-rigged clipper 30 55
366 10c. Fujian junk 30 10
367 15c. Golekkan (sailing craft) 40 15
368 20c. Palari (sailing craft) . . 70 40
369 25c. East Indiaman 80 50
370 35c. Galleon 90 50
371 50c. Caravel 60 70
372 75c. Jiangsu trading junk . . 1·00 1·50
373 $1 "Kedah" (coaster) . . . . 70 1·00
374 $2 "Murex" (tanker) . . . . 1·00 1·60
375 $5 "Chusan" (screw steamer) 2·00 3·50
376 $10 "Braganza" (paddle-steamer) . . . . 3·50 6·50
Nos. 373/6 are 42 × 25 mm.

121 Straits Settlements 1867 1½c. Stamp and Map of Singapore, 1843

1980. "London 1980" International Stamp Exn. Mult.
377 10c. Type **121** 20 10
378 35c. Straits Settlements 1906 $500 stamp and treaty between Johore and British Colony of Singapore . . . 35 25
379 $1 1948 $2 stamp and map of Malaysia . . . . 60 1·10
380 $2 1969 150th Anniv of Singapore $10 commemorative and letter to Col. Addenbrooke from Sir Stamford Raffles . . . 1·00 2·25
MS381 148 × 104 mm. Nos. 377/80 2·00 4·50

122 C.P.F. Emblem and "Keys to Retirement Benefits"
123 Map of South East Asia showing Cable Network

1980. 25th Anniv of Central Provident Fund Board. Multicoloured.
382 10c. Type **122** 10 10
383 50c. "C.P.F. savings for home ownership" 40 40
384 $1 "C.P.F. savings for old-age" . . . . 75 1·25

1980. A.S.E.A.N. (Association of South-East Asian Nations) Submarine Cable Network (2nd issue). Completion of Indonesia–Singapore Section.
385 **123** 10c. multicoloured 10 10
386 35c. multicoloured 50 50
387 50c. multicoloured . . . . 60 1·10
388 75c. multicoloured . . . . 75 2·00

124 A.S.E.A.N. Trade Fair Emblem

1980. A.S.E.A.N. (Association of South-East Asian Nations) Trade Fair.
389 **124** 10c. multicoloured 15 10
390 35c. multicoloured 35 30
391 75c. multicoloured . . . . 60 1·00

125 Ixora

1980. National Tree Planting Day. Flowers. Multicoloured.
392 10c. Type **125** 10 10
393 35c. Allamanda 40 45
394 50c. Sky vine 50 70
395 75c. Bougainvillea . . . . . 60 1·10

126 International Currency Symbols
128 Woodwork

1981. 10th Anniv of Singapore Monetary Authority.
396 **126** 10c. black, red and yellow 10 10
397 35c. multicoloured 30 30
398 75c. multicoloured . . . . 55 1·25

1981. No. 65 surch **10 CENTS**.
399 10c. on 4c. black and red . . 30 40

1981. Technical Training. Multicoloured.
400 10c. Type **128** 10 10
401 35c. Building construction . . 25 25
402 50c. Electronics 40 60
403 75c. Precision machining . . 50 1·10

129 Figures representing various Sports
130 "The Right to Environmental Aids"

1981. "Sports for All".
404 **129** 10c. multicoloured 30 10
405 – 75c. multicoloured . . . . 2·00 2·50
406 – $1 multicoloured . . . . 2·50 3·50
DESIGNS: 75c. and $1 Figures representing different sports.

1981. International Year for Disabled Persons. Multicoloured.
407 10c. Type **130** 10 10

408 35c. "The right to social integration" 30 25
409 50c. "The right to education" 45 50
410 75c. "The right to work" . . 60 90

131 Control Tower and Passenger Terminal Building, Changi Airport

132 "Parthenos sylvia"

1981. Opening of Changi Airport.
411 131 10c. multicoloured 10 10
412 35c. multicoloured 20 30
413 50c. mutlicoloured 30 75
414 75c. multicoloured . . . . 40 1·50
415 $1 multicoloured . . . . 45 1·60
MS416 154 × 105 mm. Nos. 411/15 2·25 4·50
The background emblem differs for each value.

1982. Butterflies. Multicoloured.
417 10c. Type **132** 40 15
418 50c. "Danaus vulgaris" . . . 1·25 75
419 $1 "Trogonoptera brookiana" . . . . 1·75 1·75

133 A.S.E.A.N. Emblem

134 Football and Stylized Player

1982. 15th Anniv of A.S.E.A.N. (Association of South-East Asian Nations).
420 133 10c. multicoloured 10 10
421 35c. multicoloured 30 35
422 – 50c. multicoloured 40 65
423 – 75c. multicoloured . . . . 60 1·00
The 50 and 75c. values are as Type **133** but are inscribed "15th ASEAN Ministerial Meeting".

1982. World Cup Football Championship, Spain.
424 134 10c. black, light blue & bl 20 10
425 – 75c. multicoloured . . . . 75 1·50
426 – $1 multicoloured . . . . 95 1·50
DESIGNS: 75c. Football and World Cup, Asian Four emblem; $1 Football and globe.

135 Sultan Shoal Lighthouse, 1896

1982. Lighthouses of Singapore. Mult.
427 10c. Type **135** 50 15
428 75c. Horsburgh Lighthouse, 1855 . . . . 1·40 1·75
429 $1 Raffles Lighthouse, 1855 1·50 2·00
MS430 148 × 104 mm. Nos. 427/9 4·00 5·50

136 Yard Gantry Cranes

1982. 10th Anniv of Container Terminal. Multicoloured.
431 10c. Type **136** 10 10
432 35c. Computer 25 40
433 50c. Freightlifter 35 85
434 75c. Straddle carrier . . . . 65 1·75

137 Scouts on Parade

138 Productivity Movement Slogans

1982. 75th Anniv of Boy Scout Movement. Multicoloured.
435 10c. Type **137** 15 10
436 35c. Scouts hiking 30 25
437 50c. Scouts building tower . . 50 35
438 75c. Scouts canoeing 60 80

1983. Productivity Movement.
439 138 10c. orange and green . . 10 10
440 – 35c. brown and blue . . . 25 50
441 – 50c. red, yellow and grey 40 90
442 – 75c. red and yellow . . . 55 1·25
DESIGNS: 35c. Family and housing ("Benefits of Productivity"); 50c. Works meeting ("Quality Control Circles"); 75c. Aspects of Singapore business ("Everybody's Business").

139 Commonwealth Logo and Country Names

140 Soccer

1983. Commonwealth Day.
443 139 10c. multicoloured 10 10
444 35c. multicoloured 20 35
445 75c. multicoloured . . . . 45 1·10
446 $1 multicoloured . . . . 65 1·40

1983. 12th South-East Asia Games. Mult.
447 10c. Type **140** 10 10
448 35c. Racket games 20 25
449 75c. Athletics 45 50
450 $1 Swimming 65 70

141 Policeman and Family

142 1977 A.S.E.A.N. Stamps and Statue of King Chulalongkorn

1983. Neighbourhood Watch Scheme. Mult.
451 10c. Type **141** 15 10
452 35c. Policeman and children 55 55
453 75c. Policeman and inhabitants with linked arms . . . . 1·00 2·00

1983. Bangkok Int Stamp Exhibition. Mult.
454 10c. Type **142** 20 10
455 35c. 1980 A.S.E.A.N. stamps and map of South-east Asia 55 50
456 $1 1982 A.S.E.A.N. stamps and signatures of Heads of State . . . . 1·25 1·60
MS457 147 × 104 mm. Nos. 454/6 4·25 6·50

143 Map of South-East Asia showing Cable Network

145 Blue-breasted Banded Rail ("Slaty-breasted Rail")

144 Teletex Service (½-size illustration)

1983. A.S.E.A.N. (Association of South-East Asian Nations) Submarine Cable Network (3rd issue). Completion of Malaysia–Singapore–Thailand section.
458 143 10c. multicoloured 15 10
459 35c. multicoloured 55 75
460 50c. multicoloured . . . . 80 1·25
461 75c. multicoloured . . . . 1·25 2·00
MS462 146 × 100 mm. Nos. 331, 388, 458/61 . . . . 4·75 6·00

1983. World Communications Year.
463 144 10c. yellow, green & black 20 15
464 – 35c. yellow, red and brown 55 75
465 – 75c. green, blue & dp blue 1·10 1·75
466 – $1 yellow, brown and black . . . . 1·50 2·75
DESIGNS: 35c. World telephone numbering plan; 75c. Satellite transmission; $1 Sea communications.

1984. Coastal Birds. Multicoloured.
467 10c. Type **145** 60 15
468 35c. Black bittern . . . . . 1·50 1·50
469 50c. Brahminy kite . . . . . 1·75 2·25
470 75c. Moorhen ("Common Moorhen") . . . . 2·00 3·25

146 House of Tan Yeok Nee

147 1970 $1 National Day Stamp

1984. National Monuments. Multicoloured.
471 10c. Type **146** 15 10
472 35c. Thong Chai building . . 40 65
473 50c. Telok Ayer market . . . 55 1·10
474 $1 Nagore Durgha shrine . . 80 2·50

1984. "25 Years of Nation Building". Multicoloured.
475 10c. Type **147** 15 10
476 35c. 1981 $1 "Sports for All" stamp 50 70
477 50c. 1969 25c. "100, 000 Homes for the People" stamp . . . . 60 1·00
478 75c. 1976 10c. Wayside Trees stamp . . . . 70 1·25
479 $1 1981 $1 Opening of Changi Airport stamp . . 80 1·75
480 $2 1981 10c. Monetary Authority stamp . . . . . 1·40 4·00
MS481 132 × 106 mm. Nos. 475/80 7·00 7·50

148 Schoolchildren

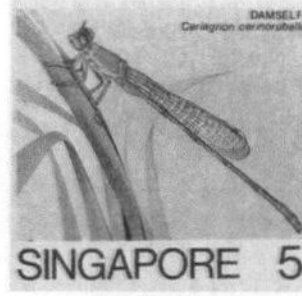

150 "Ceriagrion cerinorubellum" (damselfly)

149 Coleman Bridge

1984. "Total Defence".
482 148 10c. brown and red . . . 15 40
483 – 10c. brown, olive and blue 15 40
484 – 10c. brown, violet and salmon 15 40
485 – 10c. brown, light brown and mauve 15 40
486 – 10c. brown, yellow & olive 15 40
DESIGNS: No. 483, People of Singapore; 484, Industrial workers; 485, Civil Defence first aid worker; 486, Anti-aircraft gun crew.

1985. Bridges of Singapore.
487 10c. black (Type **149**) 15 10
488 35c. black (Cavenagh Bridge) 30 40
489 75c. black (Elgin Bridge) . . 55 70
490 $1 black (Benjamin Sheares Bridge) 70 90

1985. Insects. Multicoloured.
491 5c. Type **150** . . . . 1·25 50
492 10c. "Apis javana" (bee) . . . 1·25 65
493 15c. "Delta arcuata" (wasp) 1·50 1·50
494 20c. "Xylocopa caerulea" (bee) . . . . 1·00 1·75
495 25c. "Donacia javana" (water beetle) . . . . 1·00 1·50
496 35c. "Heteroneda reticulata" (ladybird) . . . . 1·50 30
497 50c. "Catacanthus nigripes" (bug) . . . . 1·50 1·25
498 75c. "Chremistica pontianaka" (cicada) . . . 1·50 2·50
499 $1 "Homoexipha lycoides" (cricket) (35 × 30 mm) . . . 2·75 60
500 $2 "Traulia azureipennis" (grasshopper) (35 × 30 mm) 2·00 1·50
501 $5 "Trithemis aurora" (dragonfly) (35 × 30 mm) 2·75 4·00
502 $10 "Scambophyllum sanguinolentum" (grasshopper) (35 × 30 mm) 5·75 7·50

151 Tennis, Canoeing, Judo and Children Playing

1985. 25th Anniv of People's Assn. Mult.
503 10c. Type **151** 25 10
504 35c. Lion dance, martial arts and athletes with flags . . 30 35
505 50c. Tae-kwon-do, Indian dance and Dragon dance 40 50
506 75c. Boxing, table tennis, basketball and dancing . . 75 90

152 Modern Housing Estate and Squatter Settlement

1985. 25th Anniv of Housing and Development Board. Designs show different aspects of housing at left. Multicoloured.
507 10c. Type **152** 15 10
508 35c. Singapore family (home-ownership) 30 45
509 50c. Group of residents (community development) 40 1·00
510 75c. Construction workers (building technology) . . . 55 1·75
MS511 126 × 105 mm. Nos. 507/10 3·75 5·00

153 Brownies

154 Badges and Emblems of Singapore Youth Organizations

1985. 75th Anniv of Girl Guide Movement. Multicoloured.
512 10c. Type **153** 15 10
513 35c. Guides practising first aid 35 40
514 50c. Senior Branch 45 60
515 75c. Adult leaders and guides 65 90

1985. International Youth Year. Multicoloured.
516 10c. Type **154** 15 10
517 75c. Hand protecting sapling 80 65
518 $1 Stylized figures and dove 1·00 85

155 Guava

156 Laboratory Technician and Salesmen with Bar Graph

1986. Singapore Fruits. Multicoloured.
519 10c. Type **155** 30 10
520 35c. Jambu air 85 65
521 50c. Rambutan . . . . . . 1·10 1·25
522 75c. Ciku . . . . 1·40 2·00

1986. 25th Anniv of National Trades Union Congress. Multicoloured.
523 10c. Type **156** 30 50
524 10c. Computer operator and welder 30 50
525 10c. Draughtsmen and surveyors 30 50
526 10c. Group of workers . . . 30 50
MS527 148 × 100 mm. As Nos. 523/6, but each stamp with a face value of 35c. . . . . . . 4·00 6·00

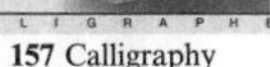

157 Calligraphy **158** Industrial Automation

1986. "Expo '86" World Fair, Vancouver. Multicoloured.
528 50c. Type **157** 55 75
529 75c. Garland maker 70 95
530 $1 Batik printer . . . . . . 85 1·25

1986. 25th Anniv of Economic Development Board. Multicoloured.
531 10c. Type **158** 10 10
532 35c. Manufacture of aircraft components 25 30
533 50c. Electronics industry . . 30 50
534 75c. Biotechnology industry 50 90

159 Map showing Route of Cable and "Vercors" (cable ship)

1986. SEA-ME-WE Submarine Cable Project.
535 **159** 10c. multicoloured 40 10
536 35c. multicoloured 85 55
537 50c. multicoloured . . . . 1·10 90
538 75c. multicoloured . . . . 1·40 2·00

160 Stylized Citizens **161** Peace Doves and People of Different Races

1986. 21st Anniv of Citizens' Consultative Committees.
539 **160** 10c. multicoloured 30 45
540 – 35c. multicoloured 45 60
541 – 50c. multicoloured 55 70
542 – 75c. multicoloured 75 85
DESIGN: 35c. to 75c. Citizens.
Nos. 539/42 were printed together, se-tenant, forming a composite design.

1986. International Peace Year. Multicoloured.
543 10c. Type **161** 15 10
544 35c. Doves and map of A.S.E.A.N. countries . . . 50 70
545 $1 Doves and globe . . . . 1·25 2·50

162 Orchard Road

1987. Singapore Skyline. Multicoloured.
546 10c. Type **162** 15 10
547 50c. Central Business District 50 65
548 75c. Marina Centre and Raffles City . . . . 75 1·50

163 Flags of Members Nations and Logo **164** Soldier with Rocket Launcher and Tank

1987. 20th Anniv of Association of South-east Asian Nations.
549 **163** 10c. multicoloured 15 10
550 35c. multicoloured 35 40
551 50c. multicoloured 55 65
552 75c. multicoloured 65 90

1987. 20th Anniv of National Service. Multicoloured (except No. **MS**557).
553 10c. Type **164** 55 70
554 10c. Radar operator and patrol boat 55 70
555 10c. Fighter pilot and General Dynamics Fighting Falcon and Douglas A-4 Skyhawk aircraft 55 70
556 10c. Servicemen pledging allegiance 55 70
MS557 148 × 100 mm. 35c. × 5. As Nos. 553/6 and Singapore lion symbol (red and black) . . . . 4·25 5·50

165 Singapore River and Dragon Boats

1987. River Conservation. Multicoloured.
558 10c. Type **165** 30 10
559 50c. Kallang Basin, canoe and fishing punt . . . . . 80 1·25
560 $1 Kranji Reservoir, athletes and cyclist . . . . 2·25 4·25

166 Majapahit Gold Bracelet and Museum

1987. Centenary of National Museum. Each showing different drawings of Museum. Multicoloured.
561 10c. Type **166** 30 10
562 75c. Ming fluted kendi (water vessel) . . . . 1·25 1·75
563 $1 Patani hulu pekakak keris (sword) . . . . 1·40 3·00

167 Omni-theatre

1987. 10th Anniv of Singapore Science Centre. Multicoloured.
564 10c. Type **167** 15 10
565 35c. Omni planetarium . . . 1·50 1·25
566 75c. Model of body cell . . . 1·50 2·75
567 $1 Physical sciences exhibits 1·50 3·25

168 Modern Anti-aircraft Gun

1988. Centenary of Singapore Artillery. Mult.
568 10c. Type **168** 55 15
569 35c. 25-pounder field gun firing salute . . . . 1·40 1·25
570 50c. Gunner and 12-pounder gun, c. 1920 . . . . 1·50 2·00
571 $1 Gunner and Maxim gun, 1889 . . . . 2·25 4·50

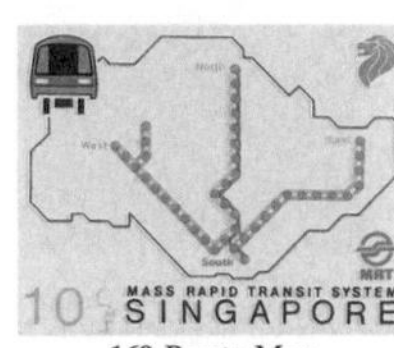

169 Route Map

1988. Singapore Mass Rapid Transit System. Multicoloured.
572 10c. Type **169** . . . . 1·00 15
573 50c. Train on elevated section 2·25 2·25
574 $1 Train in tunnel . . . . . 3·75 5·00

170 Camera, Film and Outside Broadcast Van

1988. 25th Anniv of Television in Singapore. Multicoloured.
575 10c. Type **170** 40 10
576 35c. Camera, studio lights and microphone 80 75
577 75c. Television set and transmitter . . . . 1·25 1·50
578 $1 Globe on TV screen and dish aerial . . . . 1·75 2·25

171 Water Droplet and Blocks of Flats

1988. 25th Anniv of Public Utilities Board. Multicoloured.
579 10c. Type **171** 20 10
580 50c. Electric light bulb and city centre . . . . 1·10 1·00
581 $1 Gas flame and factories 2·00 2·50
MS582 116 × 75 mm. Nos. 579/81 4·50 6·00

172 Greeting Neighbours

1988. 10th Anniv of National Courtesy Campaign. Each showing campaign mascot "Singa". Multicoloured.
583 10c. Type **172** 20 10
584 30c. Queueing at checkout . . 50 55
585 $1 Helping the elderly . . . 1·50 2·75

173 Modern 30 Metre Turntable Fire Appliance

1988. Centenary of Fire Service. Multicoloured.
586 10c. Type **173** . . . . . . 1·00 25
587 $1 Steam fire engine, c. 1890 3·25 3·25

174 Container Ships and Warehouses **175** "Sago Street"

SINGAPORE 10c

1989. 25th Anniv of Singapore Port Authority. Multicoloured.
588 10c. Type **174** 55 10
589 30c. Shipping and oil storage depot . . . . 1·00 50
590 75c. Container ships and Singapore skyline . . . . 1·50 1·50
591 $1 Container port at night . . 1·60 1·60

1989. Paintings of Chinatown by Choo Keng Kwang. Multicoloured.
592 10c. Type **175** 40 15
593 35c. "Pagoda Street" . . . . 1·25 1·00
594 75c. "Trengganu Street" . . 2·00 2·75
595 $1 "Temple Street" . . . . . 2·25 3·25

176 North-west Singapore City, 1920

1989. Maps of Singapore. Multicoloured.
596 15c. Type **176** (top left) . . . 1·50 1·75
597 15c. North-east Singapore (top right) . . . . 1·50 1·75
598 15c. South-west Singapore (bottom left) . . . . 1·50 1·75
599 15c. South-east Singapore (bottom right) . . . . . . 1·50 1·75
600 50c. Singapore Island and Dependencies, 1860s . . . 2·25 2·00
601 $1 British Settlement of Singapore, 1820s . . . . . 3·00 3·50

Nos. 596/9 were printed together, se-tenant, forming a composite design.
Individual stamps can be identifed by the position of the lion emblem which is quoted in brackets.

177 Clown Triggerfish **178** "Hari Raya Puasa" (Loke Yoke Yum)

1989. Fishes. Multicoloured.
602 15c. Type **177** . . . . 1·50 20
603 30c. Blue-girdled angelfish . . 2·25 1·25
604 75c. Emperor angelfish . . . 3·50 4·50
605 $1 Regal angelfish . . . . . 4·00 5·50

1989. Festivals of Singapore Children's Drawings. Multicoloured.
606 15c. Type **178** 40 10
607 35c. "Chinese New Year" (Simon Koh) 70 65
608 75c. "Thaipusam" (Henry Setiono) . . . . 1·40 1·40
609 $1 "Christmas" (Wendy Ang Lin Min) . . . . 1·75 1·75
MS610 126 × 75 mm. Nos. 606/9 4·00 4·00

179 North Entrance of Stadium

1989. Opening of Singapore Indoor Stadium. Multicoloured.
611 30c. Type **179** 85 30
612 75c. Arena . . . . 1·75 1·50
613 $1 East entrance . . . . . . 2·00 1·75
MS614 104 × 104 mm. Nos. 611/13 4·50 4·50

180 "Singapore River, 1839" (Louis le Breton)

1990. Lithographs of 19th-century Singapore. Multicoloured.
615 15c. Type **180** 70 15
616 30c. "Chinatown, 1837" (Barthelemy Lauvergne) . . 1·25 70
617 75c. "Singapore Harbour, 1837" (Barthelemy Lauvergne) . . . . 2·25 2·25
618 $1 "View from the French Resident's House, 1824" (Deroy) . . . . 2·50 2·75

181 1969 150th Anniv of Singapore Stamp Issue

1990. 150th Anniv of the Penny Black. Mult.
619 50c. Type **181** . . . . 1·00 60
620 75c. Indian stamps, including bisect, used from Singapore in 1859 . . . . 1·25 1·50
621 $1 Indian stamps used from Singapore in 1854 . . . . 1·90 1·90
622 $2 Penny Black and Two Pence Blue . . . . 3·00 5·00
MS623 134 × 90 mm. Nos. 619/22 8·50 7·50
No. **MS**623 also commemorates the "Stamp World London 90" international stamp exhibition.

182 Zoological Gardens

183 Chinese Opera Singer and Siong Lim Temple

1990. Tourism. Multicoloured. (a) As T **182**.
624 5c. Type **182** 30 40
625 15c. Sentosa Island 30 10
626 20c. Singapore River 30 20
627 25c. Dragon Boat Festival . . 55 75
628 30c. Raffles Hotel 70 30
629 35c. Coffee shop bird singing contest . . . . 1·25 75
630 40c. Jurong Bird Park . . . 2·00 1·00
631 50c. Chinese New Year boat float . . . . 1·25 45
632 75c. Peranakan Place . . . . 1·75 70

(b) As T **183**.
633 $1 Type **183** . . . . 4·50 1·25
634 $2 Malay dancer and Sultan Mosque . . . . 6·00 2·25
635 $5 Indian dancer and Sri Mariamman Temple . . . 8·00 7·00
636 $10 Ballet dancer and Victoria Memorial Hall . . 12·00 11·00

184 Armed Forces Personnel

1990. 25th Anniv of Independence. Mult.
637 15c. Type **184** . . . . . . 1·00 20
638 35c. Inhabitants of Singapore 1·50 1·00
639 75c. Workers and technological achievements 2·25 2·50
640 $1 Cultural activities . . . . 2·50 3·75

185 Stag's Horn Fern

1990. Ferns. Multicoloured.
641 15c. Type **185** 25 10
642 35c. Maiden hair fern 60 75
643 75c. Bird's nest fern . . . . 1·25 2·00
644 $1 Rabbit's foot fern . . . . 1·60 2·50

186 Carved Dragon Pillar, Hong San See Temple

1991. National Monuments. Multicoloured.
645 20c. Type **186** 50 80
646 20c. Hong San See Temple (40 × 25 mm) 50 80
647 50c. Interior of dome, Abdul Gaffoor Mosque . . . . . 80 1·10
648 50c. Abdul Gaffoor Mosque (40 × 25 mm) . . . . . . 80 1·10
649 75c. Statue of Vishnu, Sri Perumal Hindu Temple . . 1·10 1·50
650 75c. Sri Perumal Temple (40 × 25 mm) . . . . . . 1·10 1·50
651 $1 Stained glass window, St. Andrew's Cathedral . . 1·25 1·75
652 $1 St. Andrew's Cathedral (40 × 25 mm) . . . . . . 1·25 1·75

187 "Vanda Miss Joaquim"

188 Changi Airport Terminal II, 1991, and Boeing 747-400

1991. "Singapore '95" International Stamp Exhibition. Orchids (1st issue). Mult.
653 $2 Type **187** . . . . 4·00 5·00
654 $2 "Dendrobium anocha" . . 4·00 5·00
MS655 123 × 80 mm. Nos. 653/4 9·50 11·00
See also Nos. 674/5, 725/6, 755/6, 795/6 and **MS**817.

1991. Singapore Civil Aviation. Mult.
656 20c. Type **188** . . . . 1·25 25
657 75c. Changi Airport Terminal I, 1981, and Boeing 747-200 . . . . 2·50 2·00
658 $1 Paya Lebar Airport, 1955–1981, and Concorde . . . 2·50 2·25
659 $2 Kallang Airport, 1937–1955, and Douglas DC-2 3·75 6·00

189 "Arachnopsis Eric Holttum"

190 Long-tailed Tailor Bird ("Common Tailorbird")

1991. Orchid Dress Motifs. Multicoloured.
660 20c. Type **189** . . . . 1·00 25
661 30c. "Cattleya meadii" . . . 1·25 1·50
662 $1 "Calanthe vestita" . . . . 3·00 5·00

1991. Garden Birds. Multicoloured.
663 20c. Type **190** 45 25
664 35c. Scarlet-backed flowerpecker . . . . 1·50 1·50
665 75c. Black-naped oriole . . . 2·25 3·25
666 $1 Common iora . . . . 2·50 3·75

191 Productivity Discussion

192 Railway Creeper

1991. 10th Anniv of Productivity Movement. Multicoloured.
667 20c. Type **191** 40 30
668 $1 Construction workers . . 1·10 2·50

1992. "Phila Nippon '91" International Stamp Exhibition, Tokyo. Wild Flowers. Mult.
669 30c. Type **192** 75 25
670 75c. Asystasia . . . . 1·25 1·25
671 $1 Singapore rhododendron 1·50 2·00
672 $2 Coat buttons . . . . . . 2·50 5·25
MS673 132 × 90 mm. Nos. 669/72 7·50 8·50

1992. "Singapore '95" International Stamp Exn. Orchids (2nd issue). As T **187**. Mult.
674 $2 "Dendrobium Sharifah Fatimah" . . . . 2·75 4·25
675 $2 "Phalaenopsis Shim Beauty" . . . . 2·75 4·25
MS676 123 × 80 mm. Nos. 674/5 9·50 10·00

193 "Singapore Waterfront" (Georgette Chen Liying)

1992. Local Artists (1st series). Multicoloured.
677 20c. Type **193** 40 20
678 75c. "Kampung Hut" (Lim Cheng Hoe) . . . . 85 1·25
679 $1 "The Bridge" (Poh Siew Wah) . . . . 1·10 1·40
680 $2 "Singapore River" (Lee Boon Wang) . . . . . . 2·25 4·50
See also Nos. 818/21.

194 Football

1992. Olympic Games, Barcelona. Mult.
681 20c. Type **194** 25 20
682 35c. Athletics 35 30
683 50c. Swimming 55 65
684 75c. Basketball . . . . 1·25 1·25
685 $1 Tennis . . . . 1·50 1·50
686 $2 Sailing . . . . 2·00 2·75
MS687 132 × 90 mm. Nos. 681/6 9·50 11·00

195 Chinese Family and Samfu Pattern

1992. Singapore Costumes of 1910. Mult.
688 20c. Type **195** 40 20
689 35c. Malay family and sarong pattern 50 45
690 75c. Indian family and sari pattern . . . . 1·00 1·25
691 $2 Straits Chinese family and belt pattern . . . . 2·00 3·50

196 Infantryman, Air Force Pilot and Navy Gunner

1992. 25th Anniv of National Service. Mult.
692 20c. Type **196** 60 30
693 35c. Navy diver, General Dynamics F-16 Fighting Falcon and FH-88 155 mm howitzer 85 75
694 $1 General Dynamics F-16 Fighting Falcon in flight, corvette and AMX-13SM1 tank . . . . 2·50 4·00

197 Crafts from A.S.E.A.N. Countries

1992. 25th Anniv of A.S.E.A.N. (Association of South-East Asian Nations). Multicoloured.
695 20c. Type **197** 40 20
696 35c. National dances . . . . 90 1·00
697 $1 National landmarks . . . 2·00 3·75

198 Mosaic Crab

1992. Crabs. Multicoloured.
698 20c. Type **198** 35 25
699 50c. Johnson's freshwater crab . . . . 1·00 1·25
700 75c. Singapore freshwater crab . . . . 1·50 2·25
701 $1 Swamp forest crab . . . . 1·75 3·00

199 Coins

1992. 25th Anniv of Singapore Currency. Mult.
702 20c. Type **199** . . . . 75 1·50
703 75c. Currency note from "orchid" series . . . . . . 1·50 2·50
704 $1 Currency note from "ship" series . . . . 1·75 2·75
705 $2 Currency note from "bird" series . . . . 2·25 3·00
Nos. 702/5 were printed together, se-tenant, forming a composite design.

200 Sun Bear

1993. South-East Asian Mammals. Mult.
706 20c. Type **200** 30 20
707 30c. Orang-utan 60 65

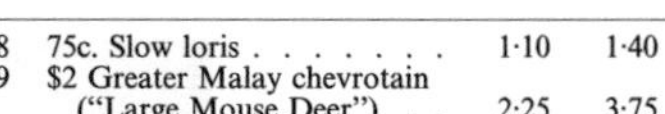
708 75c. Slow loris . . . . 1·10 1·40
709 $2 Greater Malay chevrotain ("Large Mouse Deer") . . 2·25 3·75

201 "Thank You"

203 "Cranes" (painting) (Chen Wen Hsi)

202 Shophouses

1993. Greetings Stamps. Multicoloured.
710 20c. Type **201** 60 90
711 20c. "Congratulations" . . . 60 90
712 20c. "Best Wishes" 60 90
713 20c. "Happy Birthday" . . . 60 90
714 20c. "Get Well Soon" . . . 60 90

1993. Conservation of Tanjong Pagar District. Multicoloured.
715 20c. Type **202** 35 20
716 30c. Jinrikisha Station . . . 2·00 70
717 $2 View of Tanjong Pagar . . 3·50 4·00

1993. "Indopex '93" International Stamp Exhibition, Surabaya.
718 **203** $2 multicoloured . . . . 2·75 4·00

204 Football

205 "Danaus chrysippus"

1993. 17th South-East Asian Games, Singapore. Mult.
719 20c. Type **204** 30 20
720 35c. Basketball 70 60
721 50c. Badminton . . . . . . 90 1·25
722 75c. Athletics . . . . 1·00 1·50
723 $1 Water polo . . . . 1·40 2·00
724 $2 Yachting . . . . 2·25 4·00

1993. "Singapore '95" International Stamp Exhibition. Orchids (3rd issue). As T **187** but 25 × 35 mm. Multicoloured.
725 $2 "Phalaenopsis amabilis" 3·00 4·00
726 $2 "Vanda sumatrana" . . . 3·00 4·00
MS727 123 × 80 mm. Nos. 725/6 6·50 7·50
No. **MS**727 also commemorates "Taipei '93" Asian International Stamp Exhibition, Taiwan.

1993. Butterflies. Multicoloured.
728 20c. Type **205** 30 30
729 50c. "Cethosia hypsea" . . . 65 65
730 75c. "Amathusia phidippus" 90 1·50
731 $1 "Papilio demolion" . . . 1·25 2·00

206 Papaya

207 Egrets drinking

1993. "Bangkok '93" International Stamp Exhibition. Local Fruits. Multicoloured.
732 20c. Type **206** 40 20
733 35c. Pomegranate 60 50
734 75c. Starfruit . . . . 1·25 1·50
735 $2 Durian . . . . 2·25 4·00
MS736 120 × 89 mm. Nos. 732/5 4·00 5·50

1993. Endangered Species. Swinhoe's Egret ("Chinese Egret"). Multicoloured.
737 20c. Type **207** 50 85
738 25c. Egrets eating 55 90
739 30c. Egrets searching for fish 65 1·00
740 35c. Egrets in flight . . . . . 70 1·10

Nos. 737/40 were printed together, se-tenant, with the background forming a composite design.

208 Palm Tree **209** Tiger Cowrie

1993. Self-adhesive. Imperf.
741 **208** (20c.) multicoloured . . . 30 40
No. 741 was only valid for use on mail to local addresses and was initially sold at 20c.

1994. Reef Life (1st series). Multicoloured.
742 5c. Type **209** 30 30
743 20c. Sea-fan 30 75
744 25c. Tunicate 40 25
745 30c. Clown anemonefish . . 40 50
746 35c. Ruppell's nudibranch . . 50 75
747 40c. Sea-urchin . . . . . . 60 1·50
748 50c. Soft coral 70 50
749 75c. Pin cushion star . . . . 1·00 70
750 $1 Knob coral (31 × 27 mm) 3·50 1·75
751 $2 Mushroom coral (31 × 27 mm) . . . . . . 5·50 3·50
752 $5 Bubble coral (31 × 27 mm) 9·00 7·50
753 $10 Octopus coral (31 × 27 mm) . . . . . . 13·00 12·00
See also No. 784.

1994. "Singapore '95" International Stamp Exhibition. Orchids (4th issue). As T **187** but each 25 × 35 mm. Multicoloured.
755 $2 "Paphiopedilum victoriaregina" . . . . . . 4·00 4·50
756 $2 "Dendrobium smillieae" 4·00 4·50
MS757 123 × 80 mm. Nos. 755/6 7·50 8·00
No. **MS**757 also commemorates "Hong Kong'94" International Stamp Exhibition.

210 Dancers

1994. Singapore Festival of Arts. Mult.
758 20c. Type **210** 35 20
759 30c. Actors and puppet . . . 55 55
760 50c. Musicians . . . . 75 1·00
761 $1 Artists . . . . 1·40 2·50

211 Civilian taking Pledge, National Day Parade and Soldier with Anti-tank Missile

1994. 25th Anniv of Operationally-ready National Servicemen. Multicoloured.
762 20c. Type **211** 60 30
763 30c. Serviceman on beach with family and on jungle patrol . . . . 70 1·00
764 35c. Serviceman relaxing at home and with machine gun . . . . 85 1·00
765 75c. National Service officer at work and commanding patrol . . . . 1·75 3·00

212 Black-crowned Night Heron **214** Balloons

213 Traditional and Modern Education

1994. Care for Nature. Herons. Multicoloured.
766 20c. Type **212** 50 60
767 50c. Green-heron ("Little Heron") 70 85
768 75c. Purple heron . . . . . 85 1·00
769 $1 Grey heron . . . . 95 1·25
Nos. 766/9 were printed together, se-tenant, forming a composite design.

1994. 175th Anniv of Modern Singapore. Mult.
770 20c. Type **213** 25 25
771 50c. Rickshaws and Mass Rapid Transit train 70 75
772 75c. Sampans and modern container port . . . . . . 1·00 1·40
773 $1 Victorian buildings and modern skyline . . . . . 1·25 2·00
MS774 135 × 95 mm. Nos. 770/3 3·50 4·00

1994. Self-adhesive Greetings Stamps. Multicoloured.
775 (20c.) Type **214** 55 80
776 (20c.) Fireworks 55 80
777 (20c.) Gift-wrapped parcel . . 55 80
778 (20c.) Bouquet of flowers . . 55 80
779 (20c.) Birthday cake 55 80

215 Logo and Globe

1994. 50th Anniv of I.C.A.O. Multicoloured.
780 20c. Type **215** 20 20
781 35c. Boeing 747 and Changi Airport control tower . . . 60 60
782 75c. Projected hypersonic aircraft over airport . . . 85 1·25
783 $2 Control tower, satellite and Boeing 747 . . . . . 2·00 3·25

1994. Reef Life (2nd series). Multicoloured design as T **209**, but inscr "FOR LOCAL ADDRESSES ONLY".
784 (20c.) Blue-spotted stingray 25 30
No. 784 exists with either ordinary or self-adhesive gum.

216 Singapore International Convention and Exhibition Centre, Suntec City

1995. Opening of Singapore International Convention and Exhibition Centre. Multicoloured.
786 (20c.) Type **216** 20 20
787 75c. Suntec City skyline . . . 85 85
788 $1 Temasek Boulevard . . . 1·10 1·40
789 $2 Fountain Terrace . . . . 1·75 2·75
No. 786 is inscr "FOR LOCAL ADDRESSES ONLY".

217 "Love, LOVE, Love"

1995. Self-adhesive Greetings Stamps.
790 **217** (20c.) multicoloured . . . 60 90
791 – (20c.) red and black . . . 60 90
792 – (20c.) multicoloured . . . 60 90
793 – (20c.) multicoloured . . . 60 90
794 – (20c.) multicoloured . . . 60 90
DESIGNS: No. 791, "LOVE" forming spiral around heart; No. 792, "LOVE, LOVE"; No. 793, "Love" in four different languages; No. 794, Geometric symbols.

1995. "Singapore '95" International Stamp Exhibition. Orchids (5th issue). As T **187**. Multicoloured.
795 $2 Vanda "Marlie Dolera" 2·00 3·00
796 $2 "Vanda limbata" . . . . 2·00 3·00
MS797 123 × 80 mm. Nos. 795/6 with sheet margins showing animals from Singapore Zoo 9·00 9·00
See also No. **MS**817.

218 Ribbons and "My Singapore, My Country, Happy Birthday" **219** Rejoicing Crowd and 1945 B.M.A. $5 Stamp

1995. 30th Anniv of Independence. Multicoloured.
798 (22c.) Type **218** 20 20
799 50c. Chinese inscr and 1985 Housing and Development 50c. stamp (horiz) 65 80
800 75c. National anthem, Civil Aviation 20c. and inscr in Malay (horiz) . . . . . . 90 1·50
801 $1 National flag, 1986 Economic Development Board and inscr in Tamil 1·25 2·25
MS802 120 × 78 mm. Nos. 798/801 4·75 6·00
No. 798 is inscribed "For Local Addresses Only".

1995. 50th Anniv of End of Second World War. Multicoloured.
803 (22c.) Type **219** 30 20
804 60c. Lord Mountbatten accepting Japanese surrender at Singapore and 1945 B.M.A. 15c. stamp 1·00 1·00
805 70c. Emergency food kitchen (horiz) . . . . 80 1·25
806 $2 Police road block during State of Emergency (horiz) 2·75 4·00
No. 803 is inscribed "For Local Addresses Only".

220 Yellow-faced Angelfish

1995. Marine Fishes. Multicoloured.
807 (22c.) Type **220** 35 25
808 60c. Harlequin sweetlips . . . 80 1·00
809 70c. Lionfish . . . . 90 1·50
810 $1 Pennant coralfish ("Longfin bannerfish") . . 1·25 2·25
No. 807 is inscribed "For Local Addresses Only".

221 Envelope, Stamps and Museum

1995. Opening of Singapore Philatelic Museum. Each showing Museum. Multicoloured.
811 (22c.) Type **221** 40 25
812 50c. Stamps and stamp booklet 90 65
813 60c. Stamps and philatelic equipment . . . . 1·00 1·25
814 $2 Museum displays . . . . 3·00 4·00
No. 811 is inscribed "FOR LOCAL ADDRESSES ONLY".

222 Two, Four and Six Digit Post Codes

1995. Introduction of Six Digit Postal Codes. Mult.
815 (22c.) Type **222** 30 25
816 $2 Six empty post code boxes 2·25 3·50
No. 815 is inscribed "For local addresses only".

1995. "Singapore '95" International Stamp Exhibition. Orchids (6th issue). Sheet 123 × 80 mm, containing Nos. 795/6 with sheet margins showing Sentosa Gardens.
MS817 $2 × 2 multicoloured . . . 7·00 8·00

223 "Tropical Fruits" (Georgette Chen Liying)

1995. Local Artists (2nd series). Multicoloured.
818 (22c.) Type **223** 30 25
819 30c. "Bali Beach" (Cheong Soo Pieng) 40 40
820 70c. "Gibbons" (Chen Wen Hsi) . . . . 80 1·25
821 $2 "Shi (Lion)" (Pan Shou) ($22\frac{1}{2} \times 38\frac{1}{4}$ mm) . . . . . 2·25 3·75
No. 818 is inscribed "FOR LOCAL ADDRESSES ONLY".

224 Bukit Pasoh, Chinatown

1996. Architectural Conservation. Multicoloured.
822 (22c.) Type **224** 35 25
823 35c. Jalan Sultan, Kampong Glam 50 50
824 70c. Dalhousie Lane, Little India . . . . 80 1·25
825 $1 Supreme Court, Civic District . . . . 1·10 2·25
No. 822 is inscribed "FOR LOCAL ADDRESSES ONLY".

225 Pair of Rats

1996. Chinese New Year ("Year of the Rat"). Multicoloured.
826 (22c.) Type **225** 30 25
827 $2 Rat holding orange . . . 2·25 3·50
No. 826 is inscribed "FOR LOCAL ADDRESSES ONLY".
See also Nos. **MS**832/3 and **MS**838.

226 The Straits of Singapore, 1794 (Thomas Jefferys)

1996. Old Maps. Multicoloured.
828 (22c.) Type **226** 35 25
829 60c. Singapore (19th-century) 65 75
830 $1 Singapore by James Duncan, 1835 . . . . . . 1·00 1·50
831 $2 Singapore by J. B. Tassin, 1839 . . . . 2·00 3·25
No. 828 is inscribed "FOR LOCAL ADDRESSES ONLY".

1996. "Indonesia 96" International Youth Stamp Exhibition, Bandung. Sheet 123 × 80 mm.
MS832 22c. As Type **225**; $2 No. 827 7·50 8·50

1996. "CHINA '96" 9th Asian International Stamp Exhibition, Peking. Sheet 123 × 80 mm.
MS833 22c. As Type **225**; $2 No. 827 7·50 8·50

227 17th-century Chinese Calligraphy by Zhang Ruitu and Museum Building

1996. Inauguration of Asian Civilizations Museum. Each including museum building. Multicoloured.
834 (22c.) Type **227** 35 25
835 60c. Javanese divination manuscript, 1842 . . . . . 70 70
836 70c. 19th-century temple hanging, South India . . . 80 1·00
837 $2 17th to 19th-century calligraphic implements, Iran and Turkey . . . . . 2·00 3·50
No. 834 is inscribed "FOR LOCAL ADDRESSES ONLY".

1996. "CAPEX '96" International Stamp Exhibition, Toronto. Sheet 123 × 80 mm.
MS838 22c. As Type **225**; $2 No. 827 8·50 9·50

228 "Children in Library" (Ivan Chang) **229** Wind Surfing and Dinghy Sailing

1996. Self-adhesive Greetings Stamps. "Courtesy". Children's Drawings. Multicoloured.
839 (22c.) Type **228** 30 30
840 35c. "Children crossing Road" (Cheong Kah Yin) 50 60

841 50c. "Waiting for Bus" (Jeannie Fong) 65 80
842 60c. "In the Rain" (Liew Cai Yun) 75 95
843 $1 "On the Train" (Yong Wan Quan) . . . . 1·25 1·60
MS844 200 × 130 mm. 22c. As Type **228** and Nos. 840/3 . . . 4·75 5·50
No. 839 is inscribed "For Local Addresses Only".

1996. Olympic Games, Atlanta. Multicoloured.
845 (22c.) Type **229** 35 25
846 60c. Tennis and football . . 90 80
847 70c. Pole vaulting and hurdling . . . . 90 1·10
848 $2 Diving and swimming . . 2·25 3·50
MS849 120 × 70 mm. 22c. As Type **229** and Nos. 846/8 . . . 4·00 5·00
No. 845 is inscribed "For Local Addresses Only".

230 "Cinnamomum iners"

1996. Singapore Trees. Multicoloured.
850 (22c.) Type **230** 30 25
851 60c. "Hibiscus tiliaceus" . . 70 90
852 70c. "Parkia speciosa" . . . 80 1·25
853 $1 "Terminalia catappa" . . 1·25 1·75
No. 850 is inscribed "FOR LOCAL ADDRESSES ONLY".

231 Panmen Gate, Suzhou, China

1996. Singapore–China Joint Issue. Multicoloured.
854 (22c.) Type **231** 30 25
855 60c. Singapore waterfront . . 80 1·25
MS856 120 × 78 mm. 22c. As Type **231** and No. 855 . . . . 1·40 2·00
No. 854 is inscribed "FOR LOCAL ADDRESSES ONLY".

232 Conference Logo

1996. Inaugural Ministerial Conference of World Trade Organization.
857 **232** (22c.) multicoloured . . . 30 30
858 60c. multicoloured . . . . 70 1·25
859 $1 multicoloured . . . . 1·25 1·90
860 $2 multicoloured . . . . 2·25 3·75
No. 857 is inscribed "For local addresses Only".

233 Ox

1997. Chinese New Year ("Year of the Ox").
861 **233** (22c.) multicoloured . . . 15 20
862 – $2 multicoloured . . . . 1·75 2·25
DESIGN: $2 Stylized ox.
No. 861 is inscribed "FOR LOCAL ADDRESSES ONLY".

1997. "HONG KONG '97" International Stamp Exhibition. Chinese New Year ("Year of the Ox"). sheet 123 × 80 mm.
MS863 22c. As Type **233**; $2 No. 862 5·00 6·00

234 Shuttlecock

1997. "SINGPEX '97" International Stamp Exhibition. Traditional Games. Multicoloured.
864 (22c.) Type **234** 20 20
865 35c. Marbles 40 40
866 60c. Tops 55 75
867 $1 Fivestones . . . . 80 1·50
MS868 140 × 75 mm. 22c. As Type **234** and Nos. 865/7 . . . 1·50 2·00
No. 864 is inscribed "For Local Addresses Only".

235 Bullock Cart

236 Taxi

1997. Transportation. Multicoloured. Ordinary or self-adhesive gum (No. 871), ordinary gum (others).
(a) As T **235**.
869 5c. Type **235** 15 30
870 20c. Bicycle (vert) 65 40
871 (22c.) Jinrickshaw (vert) . . . 30 20
872 30c. Electric tram 50 30
873 35c. Trolley bus 60 30
874 40c. Trishaw (vert) 50 50
875 50c. Vintage car (vert) . . . 75 45
876 60c. Horse-drawn carriage . . 1·00 50
877 70c. Fire engine . . . . . . 1·50 60
MS878 132 × 76 mm. 22c. As No. 871 and Nos. 869/70, 872/7 2·50 2·75
(b) As T **236**.
879 $1 Type **236** . . . . 1·00 80
880 $2 Bus (43 × 24 mm) . . . . 2·00 1·60
881 $5 Mass Rapid Transit train 4·00 4·25
882 $10 Light Rapid Transit carriages (43 × 24 mm) . . 7·75 8·50
MS883 119 × 71 mm. Nos. 879/82 11·50 12·00
No. 871 is inscribed "For Local Addresses Only".

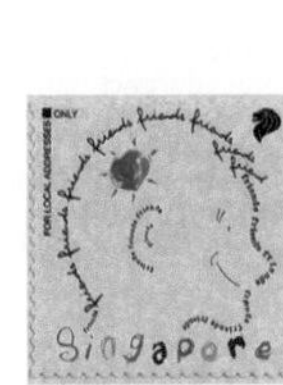

237 Man's Head **238** Family with Car

1997. Self-adhesive Greeting Stamps. "Friends". Multicoloured.
885 (22c.) Type **237** 45 60
886 (22c.) Hands holding umbrella 45 60
887 (22c.) Two emperor penguins 45 60
888 (22c.) Two butterflies 45 60
889 (22c.) Cup and saucer 45 60
890 (22c.) Large flower 45 60
891 (22c.) Candle 45 60
892 (22c.) Tree 45 60
893 (22c.) Jar with stars 45 60
894 (22c.) Simple telephone . . . 45 60
Nos. 885/94 are inscribed "FOR LOCAL ADDRESSES ONLY".

1997. "Pacific '97" International Stamp Exhibition, San Francisco. sheet 123 × 80 mm, containing designs as Nos. 861/2.
MS895 22c. As Type **233**; $2 No. 862 6·50 7·50

1997. Renovation of Housing and Development Board Estates. Multicoloured.
896 (22c.) Type **238** 20 20
897 30c. Family at playground . . 30 35
898 70c. Couple walking through garden 60 80
899 $1 Family on balcony . . . . 80 1·50
No. 896 is inscribed "FOR LOCAL ADDRESSES ONLY".

239 Globe and Hand Clasp

240 Flower and Tree ("Clean Environment")

1997. 30th Anniv of A.S.E.A.N. (Association of Southeast Asian Nations). Multicoloured.
900 (22c.) Type **239** 20 20
901 35c. Dancers, kite flying and decorated truck 35 40
902 60c. Dish aerial and map . . 55 70
903 $1 National landmarks . . . 80 1·50
No. 900 is inscribed "FOR LOCAL ADDRESSES ONLY".

1997. 25th Anniv of the Ministry of the Environment. Multicoloured.
904 (22c.) Type **240** 20 20
905 60c. Fish and river ("Clean Waters") 55 60
906 70c. Bird and sky ("Clean Air") 60 70
907 $1 Dustbin and block of flats ("Clean Homes") . . . . 80 1·25
No. 904 is inscribed "FOR LOCAL ADDRESSES ONLY".

241 "Drupa morum"

1997. Singapore—Thailand Joint Issue. Sea Shells. Multicoloured.
908 (22c.) Type **241** 20 20
909 35c. "Nerita chamaeleon" . . 30 40
910 60c. "Littoraria melanostoma" 45 60
911 $1 "Cryptospira elegans" . . 70 1·10
MS912 125 × 80 mm. 22c. As Type **241** and Nos. 909/11 . . 1·75 2·50
No. 908 is inscribed "FOR LOCAL ADDRESSES ONLY".

1997. "Shanghai '97" International Stamp and Coin Exhibition. Sheet 123 × 80 mm.
MS913 22c. As Type **233**; $2 No. 862 3·25 4·00

242 Tiger

243 Pentaceratops

1998. Chinese New Year ("Year of the Tiger").
914 **242** (22c.) multicoloured . . . 15 20
915 – $2 multicoloured . . . . 1·50 2·00
DESIGN: $2 Stylized tigers.
No. 914 is inscribed "FOR LOCAL ADDRESSES ONLY".

1998. Dinosaurs. Multicoloured. Self-adhesive. Imperf.
916 (22c.) Type **243** 25 30
917 (22c.) Apatosaurus 25 30
918 (22c.) Albertosaurus 25 30
Nos. 916/18 are inscribed "For Local Addresses Only".

244 Lesser Green Leafbird

1998. Songbirds. Multicoloured.
919 (22c.) Type **244** 35 20
920 60c. Magpie robin 70 65
921 70c. Straw-crowned bulbul ("Straw-headed bulbul") 80 80
922 $2 Yellow-bellied prinia . . . 1·60 2·25
No. 919 is inscribed "For Local Addresses Only".

1998. "Israel 98" International Stamp Exhibition. Sheet 122 × 80 mm.
MS923 22c. As Type **242**; $2 No. 915 2·25 3·25

245 "Hello" in Yellow and Orange Bubble

246 Rhino Beetle

1998. Self-adhesive Greetings Stamps. Multicoloured.
924 (22c.) Type **245** 50 65
925 (22c.) "hello" in red and yellow bubble 50 65
926 (22c.) "hello" in yellow and green bubble 50 65
927 (22c.) "Hello" in violet and blue bubble 50 65
928 (22c.) "Hello" in black, red and yellow bubble 50 65
Nos. 924/8 are inscribed "FOR LOCAL ADDRESSES ONLY".

1998. 25th Anniv of Singapore Zoological Gardens and Launch of New "Fragile Forest" Display. Multicoloured. Self-adhesive.
929 (22c.) Type **246** 50 65
930 (22c.) Surinam horned frog 50 65
931 (22c.) Green iguana 50 65
932 (22c.) Atlas moth 50 65
933 (22c.) Giant scorpion 50 65
934 (22c.) Hissing cockroach . . 50 65
935 (22c.) Two-toed sloth 50 65
936 (22c.) Cobalt blue tarantula 50 65
937 (22c.) Archer fish 50 65
938 (22c.) Greater mousedeer . . 50 65
Nos. 929/38 are inscribed "FOR LOCAL ADDRESSES ONLY".

247 Students and Workers Demonstrating, 1955–59

1998. "The Singapore Story" Exhibition. Mult.
939 (22c.) Type **247** 25 20
940 60c. Self-government, 1959–63 . . . . 55 55
941 $1 Creation of Malaysian Federation, 1961–65 . . . 80 90
942 $2 Celebrating Independence, 1965 . . . . 1·60 2·25
MS943 214 × 105 mm. 22c. As Type **247** and Nos. 940/2 (sold at $7) . . . . 8·50 9·50
No. **MS**943, which also commemorates "SINGPEX '98" National Stamp Exhibition, was only available in a special folder.
No. 939 is inscribed "FOR LOCAL ADDRESSES ONLY".

248 "Phalaenopsis rosenstromii"

249 "Canna" Hybrid

1998. Singapore–Australia Joint Issue. Orchids. Multicoloured.
944 (22c.) Type **248** 35 20
945 70c. "Arundina graminifolia" 80 65
946 $1 "Grammatophyllum speciosum" 85 90
947 $2 "Dendrobium phalaenopsis" . . . . . . 1·60 2·25
MS948 134 × 73 mm. 22c. As Type **248** and Nos. 945/7 . . . 3·75 4·50
No. 944 is inscribed "For Local Addresses Only".

1998. Flowers of Singapore. Multicoloured.
949 (22c.) Type **249** 30 30
950 (22c.) "Caesalpinia pulcherrima" 30 30
951 (22c.) "Wedilia trilobata" . . 30 30
952 (22c.) "Dillenia suffruticosa" 30 30
953 35c. "Zephyranthes rosea" 45 50
954 35c. "Cassia alata" 45 50
955 60c. "Heliconia rostrata" . . 60 70
956 60c. "Allamanda cathartica" . . 60 70
MS957 206 × 82 mm. Nos. 949/56 2·25 2·75
Nos. 949/52 are inscribed "FOR LOCAL ADDRESSES ONLY".

250 Hari Raya Aidilfitri (Muslim)

1998. Festivals. Multicoloured.
958 (22c.) Type **250** 35 35
959 (22c.) Christmas 35 35
960 (22c.) Chinese New Year . . 35 35
961 (22c.) Deepavali (Hindu) . . 35 35
962 30c. Boy and decorations (Hari Raya Aidilfitri) (20 × 39 mm) 45 50
963 30c. Girl with holly (Christmas) (20 × 39 mm) 45 50
964 30c. Boy with lanterns (Chinese New Year) (20 × 39 mm) 45 50
965 30c. Girl with oil lamps (Deepavali) (20 × 39 mm) 45 50

Nos. 958/61 are inscribed "For Local Addresses Only" and come with either ordinary or self-adhesive gum.

Nos. 958/61 were printed together, se-tenant, forming a composite design.

1998. "Italia 98" International Stamp Exhibition, Milan. Sheet 123 × 80 mm.
MS970 22c. As Type **242**; $2 No. 915 2·50 3·50

251 Parliament House, 1827

1998. Historical Buildings. Multicoloured.
971 (22c.) Type **251** 30 20
972 70c. Chapel of former Convent of the Holy Infant Jesus, 1903 . . . . 70 65
973 $1 Hill Street Building, 1934 85 95
974 $2 Sun Yat Sen Nanyang Memorial Hall, 1900 . . . 1·60 2·25

No. 971 is inscribed "For Local Addresses Only".

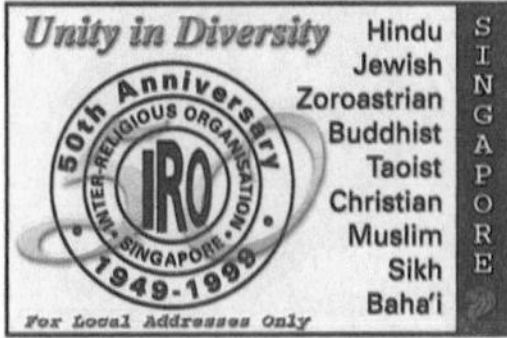

252 Anniversary Logo and List of Religions

1999. 50th Anniv of Inter-Religious Organization.
975 **252** (22c.) multicoloured . . . 30 20
976 60c. multicoloured 55 55
977 $1 multicoloured . . . . 85 1·10

No. 975 is inscribed "For Local Addresses Only".

253 Rabbit

1999. Chinese New Year ("Year of the Rabbit").
978 **253** (22c.) multicoloured . . . 25 20
979 – $2 multicoloured . . . . 1·50 2·00

DESIGN: $2 Stylized rabbits.

No. 978 is inscribed "FOR LOCAL ADDRESSES ONLY".

254 Clipper, Tank Locomotive and Tongkang Junk

1999. Maritime Heritage. Multicoloured.
980 (22c.) Type **254** 40 20
981 70c. Twakow (barge) and Sampan Kotek (vert) . . . 85 65
982 $1 Fujian junk (vert) . . . 1·25 1·10
983 $2 Maduran golekkan (sailing vessel) . . . . 1·75 2·25
MS984 200 × 67 mm. 22c. As Type **254** and Nos. 981/3 . . . 3·50 4·00

No. **MS**984 also includes the "Australia '99" World Stamp Exhibition, Melbourne, emblem on the sheet margin.

No. 980 is inscribed "For Local Addresses Only".

1999. "iBRA '99" International Stamp Exhibtion, nuremberg. Sheet 123 × 80 mm.
MS985 22c. As Type **253**; $2 No. 979 2·00 2·75

255 Washing Lines ("Think of others")

256 Hong Kong Harbour

1999. Self-adhesive Greeting Stamps. "Try a Little Kindness". Multicoloured.
986 (22c.) Type **255** 35 45
987 (22c.) Man throwing litter ("Do not litter") 35 45
988 (22c.) Girl feeding cat and dog ("Be kind to animals") 35 45
989 (22c.) Man watching television ("Be considerate") 35 45
990 (22c.) Boy putting money in collection tin ("Be generous") 35 45

Nos. 986/90 are inscribed "FOR LOCAL ADDRESSES ONLY".

1999. Singapore–Hong Kong, China Joint Issue. Multicoloured.
991 (22c.) Type **256** 25 20
992 35c. Singapore skyline . . . 45 40
993 50c. Giant Buddha, Lantau Island, Hong Kong 60 55
994 60c. Merlion statue, Sentosa Island, Singapore 70 75
995 70c. Street scene, Hong Kong 75 80
996 $1 Bugis Junction, Singapore 1·00 1·10
MS997 125 × 93 mm. 22c. As Type **256** and Nos. 992/6 . . . 3·25 4·00

No. 991 is inscribed "FOR LOCAL ADDRESSES ONLY".

1999. "PhilexFrance '99" International Stamp Exhibtion, Paris. Sheet 123 × 80 mm.
MS998 22c. As Type **253**; $2 No. 979 2·00 2·50

257 Peacock Butterfly

1999. Singapore–Sweden Joint Issue. Butterflies. Multicoloured.
999 (22c.) Type **257** 55 20
1000 70c. Blue pansy . . . . . . 1·00 65
1001 $1 Great egg-fly . . . . . . 1·25 95
1002 $2 Red admiral . . . . . . 2·00 2·50
MS1003 129 × 75 mm. 22c. As Type **257** and Nos. 1000/2 . . 4·25 4·50

No. 999 is inscribed "FOR LOCAL ADDRESSES ONLY".

1999. "China '99" International Stamp Exhibition, Peking. sheet 123 × 80 mm.
MS1004 22c. As Type **253**; $2 As No. 979 . . . . 2·25 2·75

258 Pres. Yusof bin Ishak

1999. Yusof bin Ishak (first President of Singapore) Commemoration.
1005 **258** $2 multicoloured . . . . 1·60 1·75

259 Green Turtle

1999. Amphibians and Reptiles. Multicoloured.
1006 (22c.) Type **259** 30 20
1007 60c. Green crested lizard . . 60 60
1008 70c. Copper-cheeked frog 70 70
1009 $1 Water monitor . . . . . 90 1·25

No. 1006 is inscribed "For Local Addresses Only".

260 New Parliament House from North

1999. Opening of New Parliament House. Mult.
1010 (22c.) Type **260** 30 20
1011 60c. North-east view 60 60
1012 $1 South-east view . . . . 90 1·00
1013 $2 West view . . . . 1·60 2·25

No. 1010 is inscribed "For Local Addresses Only".

The lion's head emblem on these stamps is printed in optically variable ink which changes colour when viewed from different angles.

261 Sir Stamford Raffles and Sir Frank Swettenham (British Governers) and Raffles Museum

1999. New Millennium (1st issue). 20th Century Singapore. Multicoloured.
1014 (22c.) Type **261** 30 35
1015 (22c.) Past and present schooling 30 35
1016 35c. Street scene, 1900, and Samsui woman 45 55
1017 35c. Parliament (Government) 45 55
1018 60c. British surrender, 1942, and Lord Mountbatten celebrating Japanese surrender, 1945 . . . . . 60 70
1019 60c. Soldiers firing missile and fighter aircraft . . . 60 70
1020 70c. Singapore River, 1902, and modern forms of transportation 70 80
1021 70c. Festival scenes 70 80
1022 $1 Housing, past and present . . . . 95 1·10
1023 $1 Skyscrapers . . . . . . 95 1·10

Nos. 1014/15 are inscribed "for Local addresses only".

See also Nos. 1027/30.

262 Dragon

263 Information Technology Equipment

2000. Chinese New Year ("Year of the Dragon"). Multicoloured.
1024 (22c.) Type **262** 25 20
1025 $2 Dragon curled around spheres . . . . 1·75 2·25
MS1026 105 × 65 mm. $10 As No. 1025 . . . . 8·00 9·50

No. 1024 is inscribed "FOR LOCAL ADDRESSES ONLY".

No. **MS**1026 was only sold in a decorative hongbao (envelope).

2000. New Millennium (2nd issue). Singapore in 2000. Multicoloured.
1027 (22c.) Type **263** 25 20
1028 60c. Symbols of Arts and Culture 60 60
1029 $1 Heritage artifacts . . . . 95 1·10
1030 $2 Modern global communications . . . . . 1·60 2·25
MS1031 140 × 75 mm. 22c. As Type **263** and Nos. 1028/30 . . 2·75 3·75

No. 1027 is inscribed "For local addresses only".

264 Post Office from across Singapore River, 1854

2000. Opening of Singapore Post Centre. Postal Landmarks. Multicoloured.
1032 (22c.) Type **264** 25 20
1033 60c. General Post Office, c. 1873 . . . . . 60 60
1034 $1 G.P.O. Fullerton Building, 1928 . . . . . 95 1·00
1035 $2 Singapore Post Centre, 2000 . . . . 1·90 2·25
MS1036 110 × 94 mm. 22c. As Type **264** and Nos. 1033/5 . . 2·75 3·50

No. 1032 is inscribed "FOR LOCAL ADDRESSES ONLY".

2000. "Bangkok 2000" International Stamp Exhibition. Sheet 123 × 75 mm. Multicoloured.
MS1037 22c. As Type **262**; $2 No. 1025 . . . . 1·75 2·25

265 "yipee"

267 "Future Lifestyle" (Liu Jiang Wen)

266 Singapore River, 1920s

2000. Self-adhesive Greetings Stamps. Multicoloured.
1038 (22c.) Type **265** 45 60
1039 (22c.) "yeah" 45 60
1040 (22c.) "hurray" 45 60
1041 (22c.) "yes" 45 60
1042 (22c.) "happy" 45 60

Nos. 1038/42 are inscribed "For Local Addresses Only".

2000. "The Stamp Show 2000" International Stamp Exhibition, London. Sheet, 123 × 75 mm, containing Nos. 1024/5. Multicoloured.
MS1043 22c. As Type **262**; $2 No. 1025 . . . . 1·90 2·40

2000. "naba 2000" National Stamp Exhibition, St. Gallen, Switzerland. Sheet, 123 × 75 mm, containing Nos. 1024/5. Multicoloured.
MS1044 22c. As Type **262**; $2 No. 1025 . . . . 1·90 2·40

2000. "A Century on Singapore River". Showing scenes and common map section. Multicoloured.
1045 (22c.) Type **266** 35 40
1046 (22c.) South Boat Quay, 1930s 35 40
1047 (22c.) Social gathering, 1950s 35 40
1048 (22c.) Skyscrapers, 1980s . . 35 40
1049 (22c.) River Regatta, 1900s 35 40
1050 60c. Sampans at river mouth, 1990s 50 60
1051 60c. Stevedores, 1910s . . . 50 60
1052 60c. Lighters, 1940s 50 60
1053 60c. Men at work on junk, 1960s 50 60
1054 60c. Unloading with crane, 1970s 50 60

Nos. 1045/9 are inscribed "For local addresses only".

Nos. 1045/54 were printed together, se-tenant, with the backgrounds forming a composite design.

2000. "Stampin' the Future" (children's stamp design competition). Multicoloured.
1055 (22c.) Type **267** 25 20
1056 60c. "Future Homes" (Shaun Yew Chuan Bin) 60 60
1057 $1 "Home Automation" (Gwendolyn Soh) . . . . 90 1·00
1058 $2 "Floating City" (Dawn Koh) . . . . 1·60 2·25
MS1059 125 × 80 mm. Nos. 1055/8 3·00 3·50

No. 1055 is inscribed "FOR LOCAL ADDRESSES ONLY".

268 Archer Fish

2000. Wetland Wildlife. Multicoloured.
1060 (22c.) Type **268** 35 30
1061 (22c.) Smooth otter and cubs 35 30
1062 $1 White-collared kingfisher ("Collared Kingfisher") 1·10 1·25
1063 $1 Orange fiddler crab . . . 1·10 1·25
MS1064 294 × 210 mm. Nos. 1060/3, both perf and imperf in se-tenant blocks of 4 . . . . 4·25 5·00

Nos. 1060/1 are inscribed "For Local Addresses Only".

Nos. 1060/3 were printed together, se-tenant, with the backgrounds forming composite designs.

269 High Jump and Swimming

2000. Olympic Games, Sydney. Designs showing a sport within the outline of another. Multicoloured.
1065 (22c.) Type **269** 25 20
1066 60c. Discus and badminton 60 60

1067 $1 Hurdles and football . . 90 1·00
1068 $2 Gymnastics and table tennis . . . . 1·75 2·25
No. 1065 is inscribed "For local addresses only".

270 Chinese New Year

2000. Festivals. Multicoloured. (a) Normal gum.
1069 (22c.) Type **270** 30 35
1070 (22c.) Hari Raya Aidilfitri 30 35
1071 (22c.) Deepavali 30 35
1072 (22c.) Christmas 30 35
1073 30c. Chinese New Year (different) (diamond, 36 × 23 mm) 40 45
1074 30c. Hari Raya Aidilfitri (different) (diamond, 36 × 23 mm) 40 45
1075 30c. Deepavali (different) (diamond, 36 × 23 mm) 40 45
1076 30c. Christmas (different) (diamond, 36 × 23 mm) 40 45

(b) Self-adhesive.
1077 (22c.) Type **270** 60 65
1078 (22c.) As No. 1070 . . . . 60 65
1079 (22c.) As No. 1071 . . . . 60 65
1080 (22c.) As No. 1072 . . . . 60 65
Nos. 1069/72 and 1077/80 are inscribed "FOR LOCAL ADDRESSES ONLY".

2000. "Guangzhou 2000" International Stamp and Coin Exhibition, China. Sheet 123 × 75 mm. Multicoloured.
MS1081 (22c.) As Type **262**; $2 No. 1025 . . . . 2·00 2·50

271 Snake

2001. Chinese New Year ("Year of the Snake"). Mult.
1082 (22c.) Type **271** 15 20
1083 $2 Two snakes . . . . . . 1·40 1·50
No. 1082 is inscribed "FOR LOCAL ADDRESSES ONLY".

2001. "Hong Kong 2001" Stamp Exhibition. Sheet 123 × 75 mm. Multicoloured.
MS1084 22c. As Type **271**; $2 No. 1083 . . . . 2·25 2·50

272 Tan Tock Seng **273** People holding Hands ("Co-operation")

2001. Famous Citizens of Singapore. Multicoloured.
1085 $1 Type **272** . . . . 1·00 1·10
1086 $1 Eunos bin Abdullah . . 1·00 1·10
1087 $1 P. Govindasamy Pillai 1·00 1·10
1088 $1 Edwin John Tessensohn 1·00 1·10

2001. 25th Anniv of Commonwealth Day. Mult.
1089 (22c.) Type **273** 25 20
1090 60c. People using computers ("Education") 60 60
1091 $1 Sporting activities ("Sports") . . . . 90 1·00
1092 $2 Dancers and musicians ("Arts and Culture") . . 1·75 2·25
No. 1089 is inscribed "FOR LOCAL ADDRESSES ONLY".

274 Balloons **275** "Music" ("a")

2001. Self-adhesive Greetings Stamps. "Occasions". Multicoloured.
1093 (22c.) Type **274** 30 40
1094 (22c.) Stars 30 40
1095 (22c.) Tulips 30 40
1096 (22c.) Parcels 30 40
1097 (22c.) Musical instruments 30 40
Nos. 1093/7 are inscribed "FOR LOCAL ADDRESSES ONLY".

2001. Arts Festival. Multicoloured.
1098 (22c.) Type **275** 25 20
1099 60c. "Painting" ("r") . . . 55 45
1100 $1 "Dance" ("t") . . . . . 90 1·00
1101 $2 "Theatre" ("s") . . . . 1·75 2·00
No. 1098 is inscribed "For Local Addresses Only".

2001. "BELGICA 2001" International Stamp Exhibtion, Brussels. Sheet 123 × 75 mm. Multicoloured.
MS1102 (22c) Type **271**; $2 No. 1083 2·00 2·50

276 Cockatiels **277**

2001. "Singpex '01" National Stamp Exhibition. Pets. (a) Multicoloured.
1103 (22c.) Type **276** 25 35
1104 (22c.) Fish in tank 25 35
1105 (22c.) Tortoise 25 35
1106 (22c.) Ducklings 25 35
1107 (22c.) Cat looking at mouse (24 × 34 mm) 25 35
1108 (22c.) Dog looking at fish in bowl (24 × 34 mm) . . . 25 35
1109 50c. West Highland white terrier and bird (24 × 41 mm) 55 65
1110 50c. Two cats (24 × 41 mm) 55 65
1111 $1 Green-winged macaw and Senegal parrot (24 × 41 mm) 85 90
1112 $1 Cat in basket and rabbit (24 × 41 mm) 85 90

(b) T **277** and similar multicoloured frame. Self-adhesive.
1113 (22c.) Type **277** (24 × 24 mm) 30 30
1114 (22c.) As Type **277**, but 24 × 34 mm 30 30
Nos. 1103/8 and 1113/14 are inscribed "For local addresses only".
Nos. 1103/12 were printed together, se-tenant, forming a composite picture of household pets.

2001. "Philanippon '01" International Stamp Exhibition, Tokyo. Sheet 123 × 75 mm. Multicoloured.
MS1115 (22c.) Type **271**; $2 No. 1083 . . . . 2·00 2·50

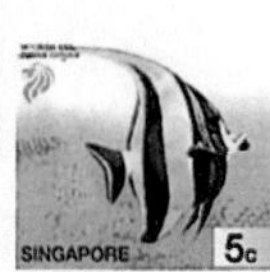

278 Young Ah Meng **280** Moorish Idol

279 *Melastoma malabathricum*

2001. Orang Utan Conservation. Designs showing Ah Meng. Multicoloured. (a) Ordinary gum.
1116 (22c.) Type **278** 25 20
1117 60c. Ah Meng with mate . . 55 45
1118 $1 Ah Meng with offspring 85 90
1119 $1 Three generations of Ah Meng's family 85 90
MS1120 190 × 180 mm. Nos. 1116/19 (sold for $3.90) . . . . 3·25 3·50

(b) Self-adhesive.
1121 (22c.) Type **278** 30 30
Nos. 1116 and 1121 are inscribed "For Local Addresses Only".
No. **MS**1120 is in the shape of a seated orang utan.

2001. Singapore–Switzerland Joint Issue. Flowers. Multicoloured.
1122 (22c.) Type **279** 25 20
1123 60c. *Leontopodium alpinum* 60 60
1124 $1 *Saraca cauliflora* . . . . 90 1·00
1125 $2 *Gentiana clusii* . . . . . 1·75 2·25
MS1126 98 × 68 mm. Nos. 1122/5 3·25 3·50
No. 1122 is inscribed "FOR LOCAL ADDRESSES ONLY".
Two types of 50c.:
I. Inscribed "xanthometopon" in error.
II. Correctly inscribed "xanthometapon".

2001. Tropical Marine Fish. Multicoloured. Size 26 × 19mm. (a) Ordinary gum.
1127 5c. Type **280** 10 10
1128 20c. Thread-finned butterflyfish 15 20
1129 (22c.) Copper-banded butterflyfish 15 20
1130 30c. Pearl-scaled butterflyfish 20 25
1130a 31c. Eight-banded butterflyfish 20 25
1131 40c. Melon butterflyfish ("Rainbow Butterflyfish") 25 30
1132 50c. Yellow-faced angelfish 30 35
1133 60c. Emperor angelfish . . 40 45
1134 70c. Sail-finned tang . . . 45 50
1135 80c. Palette surgeonfish ("Palette Tang") 50 55
MS1136 149 × 90 mm. Nos. 1127/35 3·50 4·00

(b) Size 29 × 24½ mm.
1137 $1 Blue turquoise 65 70
1138 $2 Brown discus . . . . . 1·30 1·40
1139 $5 Red alenguer . . . . . 3·25 3·50
1140 $10 Red turquoise . . . . . 6·50 6·75
MS1141 128 × 75 mm. Nos. 1137/40 16·00 17·00

(c) Self-adhesive.
1142 (22c.) As No. 1129 . . . . 15 20
1142c (23c.) As No. 1129 . . . . 15 20
Nos. 1129 and 1142 are inscribed "FOR LOCAL ADDRESSES ONLY". No. 1142c is inscribed "1st Local".

281 Horse

2002. Chinese New Year ("Year of the Horse"). Multicoloured.
1143 (22c.) Type **281** 15 20
1144 (22c.) As Type 290 but horse embossed in silver 15 20
1145 $2 Two horses rearing . . . 1·30 1·40
1146 $2 As No. 1145, but horses embossed in gold . . . . 1·30 1·40
Nos. 1143/4 are inscribed "FOR LOCAL ADDRESSES ONLY" and were sold for 22c. each.

282 Long-tailed Porcupine

2002. Natural History Drawings from The William Farquhar Collection (1st series). Animals, Reptiles, Fruits and Plants. Multicoloured. Ordinary or self-adhesive gum.
1147 (22c.) Type **282** 25 30
1148 (22c.) Tapir 25 30
1149 (22c.) "Landak Kelubu" . . 25 30
1150 (22c.) Slow loris 25 30
1151 (22c.) "Biawak Tanah" (lizard) 25 30
1152 (22c.) Flying fox 25 30
1153 (22c.) Small-clawed otter . . 25 30
1154 (22c.) "Biawak Pasir" (lizard) 25 30
1155 (22c.) "Tupai Kerawak" (mouse) (vert) 25 30
1156 (22c.) Mouse deer (vert) . . 25 30
1157 (22c.) "Buah rumenia" . . . 25 30
1158 (22c.) "Manggis Hutan" . . 25 30
1159 (22c.) "Cempedak" 25 30
1160 (22c.) "Bunga Dedap" . . . 25 30
1161 (22c.) "Jeringau" (vert) . . . 25 30
1162 (22c.) "Rotang" (vert) . . . 25 30
1163 (22c.) "Tuba" (vert) 25 30
1164 (22c.) "Tebu Gagak" (vert) 25 30
1165 (22c.) "Temu Kunci" (vert) 25 30
1166 (22c.) "Rambutan" (vert) . . 25 30
Nos. 1147/56 (animals and reptiles), 1157/66 (fruits and plants), and are inscribed "For Local Addresses Only". Each stamp was sold for 22c.

2002. Natural History Drawings from The William Farquhar Collection (2nd series). Birds and Fish. As T **282**. Multicoloured. Ordinary or self-adhesive gum.
1187 (22c.) "Burung Gaji-gaji" 15 20
1188 (22c.) "Kuau Cermin" . . . 15 20
1189 (22c.) "Ayam Kolam" . . . 15 20
1190 (22c.) "Kelengking" 15 20
1191 (22c.) "Burung Kuang" . . 15 20
1192 (22c.) "Puhung" 15 20
1193 (22c.) "Burung Kunyit" (vert) 15 20
1194 (22c.) "Burung Pacap Sayat Biru" (vert) 15 20
1195 (22c.) "Burung Murai" (vert) 15 20
1196 (22c.) "Burung Berek-Berek" (vert) 15 20
1197 (22c.) "Ikan Tenggiri Papan" 15 20
1198 (22c.) "Ikan Kertang" . . . 15 20
1199 (22c.) "Ikan Kakatua" . . . 15 20
1200 (22c.) "Ikan Bambangan" 15 20
1201 (22c.) "Ikan Parang" . . . 15 20
1202 (22c.) "Ikan Buntal Pisang" 15 20
1203 (22c.) "Ikan Ketang" . . . 15 20
1204 (22c.) "Pari Hitam" 15 20
1205 (22c.) "Telinga Gajah" . . . 15 20
1206 (22c.) "Ikan Babi" 15 20
Nos. 1187/96 (birds), 1197/206 (fish), and are inscribed "For Local Addresses Only". Each stamp was sold for 22c.

283 Lego Town

2002. Toys. Multicoloured.
1227 (22c.) Type **283** 15 20
1228 60c. Cowboy, Indian, soldier and robot 40 45
1229 70c. Dolls 45 50
1230 $1 Racing cars and bike . . 65 70
No. 1227 is inscribed "For local addresses only" and was sold for 22c.

284 Red-throated Sunbird

2002. Singapore – Malaysia Joint Issue. Birds. Multicoloured.
1231 (22c.) Type **284** 15 20
1232 60c. Asian fairy bluebird . . 40 45
1233 $1 Black-naped oriole . . . 65 70
1234 $2 White-bellied woodpecker 1·30 1·40
MS1235 135 × 94 mm Nos. 1231/4 3·75 4·25

2002. "Philakorea 2002" International Stamp Exhibition, Seoul.
MS1236 123 × 75 mm. Nos. 1143 and 1145 . . . . 2·25 2·50

285 Kolam (doorstep decoration), Deepavali

286 Kolam (doorstep decoration), Deepavali

2002. Festivals. Multicoloured. (a) T **285**. Ordinary or self-adhesive gum.
1237 (22c.) Type **285** 30 30
1238 (22c.) Ketupat (rice cake) wrapper, Hari Raya Aidilfitri 30 30
1239 (22c.) Snowflake in bauble, Christmas 30 30
1240 (22c.) Fish paper decoration, Chinese New Year . . . 30 30

(b) T **286**.
1245 50c. Type **286** 50 55
1246 50c. Ketupat (rice cake) wrapper, Hari Raya Aidilfitri 50 55
1246 50c. Snowflake in bauble, Christmas 50 55
1248 50c. Fish paper decoration, Chinese New Year . . . 50 55
Nos. 1237/44 are inscribed "For Local Addresses Only" and each stamp was sold for 22c.
The central designs on Nos. 1237/48 are foil holograms.

287 Flame of the Forest **289** Two Yachts

288 Esplanade, Performing Arts Centre, Marina Bay

2002. Heritage Trees Scheme. Multicoloured.

No.	Description		
1249	(22c.) Type **287**	15	20
1250	60c. Rain Tree	40	45
1251	$1 Kapok Tree	65	70
1252	$1 Tembusu	65	70

No. 1249 also comes self-adhesive.
Nos. 1249 and 1253 are inscribed "FOR LOCAL ADDRESSES ONLY" and were sold for 22c.

2002. Esplanade, Theatres on the Bay. Esplanade from different angles. Multicoloured.

No.	Description		
1254	(22c.) Type **288**	15	20
1255	60c. With brown background	40	45
1256	$1 Single shell of Esplanade	65	70
1257	$2 Aerial view of both shells	1·30	1·40
MS1258	104 × 80 mm. Nos. 1254/7	2·50	2·75

2002. Singapore-A Global City. (1st series). Leisure and Lifestyle. Multicoloured.

No.	Description		
1259	$2 Type **289**	1·30	1·40
1260	$2 Conductor's hands and baton	1·30	1·40
MS1261	135 × 95 mm. Nos. 1259/60	5·00	6·00

See also Nos. 1277/**MS**1279 and 1405/**MS**1407.

290 Goat

2003. Chinese New Year ("Year of the Goat"). Multicoloured.

No.	Description		
1262	(22c.) Type **290**	15	20
1263	$2 Goat butting tree	1·30	1·40

No. 1262 is inscribed "FOR LOCAL ADDRESSES ONLY" and was sold for 22c.

291 Empress Place Building as Government Offices

2003. Opening of Asian Civilizations Museum in Empress Place Building. Multicoloured.

No.	Description		
1264	(22c.) Type **291**	15	20
1265	60c. Empress Place Building as Registrar's Office	40	45
1266	$1 Empress Place Museum	65	70
1267	$2 Empress Place Building, as Asian Civilizations Museum	1·30	1·40

No. 1264 is inscribed "For local addresses only" and was sold for 22c.

292 Tarsier

2003. Creatures of the Night. Multicoloured.

No.	Description		
1268	(22c.) Type **292**	15	20
1269	40c. Barn owl	25	30
1270	$1 Babirusa	65	70
1271	$2 Clouded leopard	1·30	1·40
MS1272	136 × 94 mm. Nos. 1268/71	3·50	4·00

No. 1268 is inscribed "FOR LOCAL ADDRESSES ONLY" and was sold for 22c.

293 Community Policewomen and Block of Flats

2003. Singapore Police Force. Multicoloured No. 1273 is inscribed "For Local Addresses Only" and was sold at 22c.

No.	Description		
1273	(22c.) Type **293**	15	20
1274	40c. Traffic policeman with motor-cycle	25	30
1275	£1 Maritime policeman and launch	65	70
1276	£2 Singapore police on U.N. peacekeeping duties	1·30	1·40

294 Satellite

2003. Singapore–A Global City (2nd series). Communications and Technology. Multicoloured.

No.	Description		
1277	$2 Type **294**	1·30	1·40
1278	$2 Robot	1·30	1·40
MS1279	135 × 95 mm. Nos. 1277/8	2·50	2·75

295 Cheshire Cat ("Joy!")

297 National Flag

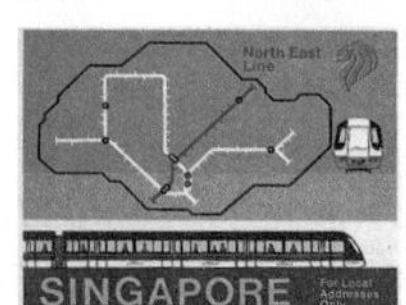

296 Map of Singapore Mass Rapid Transit System

2003. Greetings Stamps. "Joy and Caring". Multicoloured. Ordinary or self-adhesive gum.

No.	Description		
1280	(22c.) Type **295**	15	20
1281	(22c.) Heart with smiling face ("joy!")	15	20
1282	(22c.) Teddy bear ("joy!")	15	20
1283	(22c.) Woman laughing ("joy")	15	20
1284	(22c.) Ostrich ("joy!")	15	20
1285	(22c.) Apple ("caring")	15	20
1286	(22c.) Hand with painted heart ("Helping Hands")	15	20
1287	(22c.) Multicoloured hearts ("Togetherness")	15	20
1288	(22c.) Daisy ("Beauty of a caring heart")	15	20
1289	(22c.) Night sky ("KEEPING IN TOUCH KEEPS US GOING")	15	20

Nos. 1280/9 are inscribed "For local addresses only", and were sold for 22c. each.

2003. Opening of North East Line of Singapore Mass Rapid Transit System. Multicoloured.

No.	Description		
1300	(22c.) Type **296**	15	20
1301	60c. Passengers	40	45
1302	$2 Control centre	1·30	1·40
MS1303	135 × 93 mm. 10c. Type **169**; 60c. As No. 573; $2 As No. 574 and Nos. 1300/2	3·50	3·75

No. 1300 is inscribed "For Local Addresses Only" and were sold at 22c. each.

2003. National Day. Multicoloured.

No.	Description		
1304	(22c.) Type **297**	15	20
1305	60c. *Vanda* "Miss Joaquim"	40	45
1306	$1 "Merlion" statue and Singapore skyline	65	70
1307	$2 Children	1·30	1·40
MS1308	140 × 75 mm. Nos. 1304/7	2·50	2·75

No. 1305 is inscribed "For local addresses only" and were sold for 22c. each.

298 Alouette III (helicopter)

2003. Centenary of Powered Flight. Multicoloured. Ordinary or self-adhesive gum.

No.	Description		
1309	(22c.) Type **298**	15	20
1310	(22c.) E-2C Hawkeye	15	20
1311	(22c.) Hawker Hunter	15	20
1312	(22c.) Super Puma AS-332M (helicopter)	15	20
1313	(22c.) Hercules C-130H	15	20
1314	(22c.) F-16 C/D Fighting Falcon	15	20
1315	(22c.) AH-64D Apache (helicopter)	15	20
1316	(22c.) KC-135R Stratotanker	15	20
1317	(22c.) Cessna 172	15	20
1318	(22c.) F-5E Tiger II	15	20
1319	(22c.) A340-500	15	20
1320	(22c.) B747-400	15	20
1321	(22c.) B777-200	15	20
1322	(22c.) B747-400 Freighter	15	20
1323	(22c.) A320	15	20
1324	(22c.) Concorde	15	20
1325	(22c.) B737-100	15	20
1326	(22c.) Comet IV	15	20
1327	(22c.) Viscount	15	20
1328	(22c.) Airspeed Consul	15	20
1349	(22c.) Airspeed Consul		
MS1329	282 × 188 mm. Nos. 1309/28	2·75	3·00

Nos. 1309/28, and are inscribed "For local addresses only" and were sold at 22c. each.

2003. "Bangkok 2003" World Stamp Exhibition, Thailand. Sheet 123 × 75 mm. Multicoloured.

No.	Description		
MS1350	(22c.) Type **290**; $2 No. 1263	1·40	1·50

299 Singapore Botanic Gardens

2003. Parks and Gardens. Multicoloured. (a) Ordinary gum.

No.	Description		
1351	(22c.) Type **299**	15	20
1352	60c. Fort Canning Park	40	45
1353	$1 Marina City Park	65	70
1354	$1 Stork's nest, Sungei Buloh Wetland Reserve	65	70

Nos. 1351 and 1355 are inscribed "FOR LOCAL ADDRESSES ONLY" and were sold for 22c.

(b) Self-adhesive gum.

No.	Description		
1355	(22c.) Type **299**	15	20

2003. "China 2003" International Stamp Exhibition, Mianyang. Sheet 122 × 75 mm.

No.	Description		
MS1356	(22c.) Type **290**; $2 No. 1263	1·40	1·50

300 Monkey with Heart

2004. Chinese New Year ("Year of the Monkey"). Multicoloured.

No.	Description		
1357	(23c.) Type **300**	15	20
1358	$2 Two monkeys	1·30	1·40

No. 1357 is inscribed "FOR LOCAL ADDRESSES ONLY" and was sold for 22c.

2004. Hong Kong 2004 International Stamp Exhibition. Sheet 123 × 75 mm. Multicoloured.

No.	Description		
MS1359	(23c.) Type **300**; $2 No. 1358	1·40	1·50

301 "Farmer's House" (Liu Kang)

2004. Paintings by Liu Kang and Ong Kim Seng. Multicoloured. Ordinary or self-adhesive gum.

No.	Description		
1360	(23c.) Type **301**	15	20
1361	(23c.) "Artist and Model" (Liu Kang)	15	20
1362	(23c.) "Lanterns Galore" (Liu Kang)	15	20
1363	(23c.) "Enjoying a Smoke, Kashmir" (Liu Kang)	15	20
1364	(23c.) "Life by the River" (Liu Kang)	15	20
1365	(23c.) "Tenth Trip up to Huangshan" (Liu Kang)	15	20
1366	(23c.) "My Young Wife" (Liu Kang) (vert)	15	20
1367	(23c.) "Kek Lok Si, Penang" (Liu Kang) (vert)	15	20
1368	(23c.) "Souri" (Liu Kang) (vert)	15	20
1369	(23c.) "Siesta in Bali" (Liu Kang) (vert)	15	20
1370	(23c.) "Kampong Tengah, Singapore" (Ong Kim Seng)	15	20
1371	(23c.) "Gyantse Market" (Ong Kim Seng)	15	20
1372	(23c.) "Sebatu Spring, Bali" (Ong Kim Seng)	15	20
1373	(23c.) "Jetty, Bangkok" (Ong Kim Seng)	15	20
1374	(23c.) "Resort, Bali" (Ong Kim Seng)	15	20
1375	(23c.) "Dance Studio, Bali" (Ong Kim Seng)	15	20
1376	(23c.) "Telok Ayer Market" (Ong Kim Seng)	15	20
1377	(23c.) "Kathmandu, Nepal" (Ong Kim Seng)	15	20
1378	(23c.) "Portofino, Italy" (Ong Kim Seng) (vert)	15	20
1379	(23c.) "Boats at Rest" (Ong Kim Seng) (vert)	15	20

Nos. 1360/79 are inscribed "For local addresses only" and were sold for 23c. each.

302 "Harmony" Sculpture and Suzhou Industrial Park

2004. 10th Anniv of Suzhou Industrial Park.

No.	Description		
1400	**302** 60c. multicoloured	40	45

303 Colonial and Modern Buildings

2004. Singapore Skyline. Multicoloured.

No.	Description		
1401	(23c.) Type **303**	15	20
1402	60c. Merlion statue and waterfront	40	45
1403	70c. Singapore skyline	45	50
MS1404	Two sheets, each 113 × 80 mm. (a) $1 Singapore from the Roads, c. 1900 (95 × 35 mm). (b) $5 Singapore skyline, 2004 (95 × 35 mm) Set of 2 sheets	3·75	4·00

No. 1401 is inscribed "1st Local" and was sold for 23c.

304 Containers

2004. Singapore—A Global City (3rd series). Trade and Industry. Multicoloured.

No.	Description		
1405	$2 Type **304**	1·30	1·40
1406	$2 Oil refinery	1·30	1·40
MS1407	135 × 95 mm. Nos. 1405/6 and double stamp-size label	2·50	2·75

305 Football Field

306 Three Candles (Deepavali)

2004. Centenary of FIFA (Federation Internationale de Football Association). Multicoloured.

No.	Description		
1408	30c. Type **305**	20	25
1409	60c. Football	40	45
1410	$1 Football shirt	65	70
1411	$2 World map	1·30	1·40

2004. Festivals. Multicoloured. Ordinary or self-adhesive gum (23c.).

No.	Description		
1412	(23c.) Type **306**	15	20
1413	(23c.) One candle (Hari Raya Aidilfitri)	15	20
1414	(23c.) Toy Father Christmas and Rudolph (Christmas)	15	20
1415	(23c.) Plum blossom and oranges (Chinese New Year)	15	20
1416	50c. Woman and oil lamp (Deepavali)	30	35
1417	50c. Girl holding sparkler (Hari Raya Aidilfitri)	30	35
1418	50c. Carol singers (Christmas)	30	35
1419	50c. Woman wearing orange kimono	30	35

Nos. 1412/19 are inscribed "1st LOCAL" and were sold at 23c. each.

307 Column, City Hall

2004. National Day. Monuments. Multicoloured.
1424 (23c.) Type **307** 15 20
1425 (23c.) City Hall (41 × 27 mm) 15 20
1426 30c. Concert Hall bell tower 20 25
1427 30c. Victoria Theatre and Concert Hall (41 × 27 mm) 20 25
1428 60c. Dome of courthouse . . 40 45
1429 60c. Supreme Court (41 × 27 mm) 40 45
1430 $1 Detail of gate, the Istana 65 70
1431 $1 The Istana (41 × 27 mm) 65 70
MS1432 140 × 70 mm. Nos. 1425, 1427, 1429 and 1431 . . . . . 1·40 1·50
Nos. 1424/5 are inscribed "1st Local" and were sold for 23c. each.

308 Running

2004. Olympic Games, Athens, Greece. Designs showing Olympic sports depicted on pebbles. Multicoloured.
1433 (23c.) Type **308** 15 20
1434 30c. Swimming 20 25
1435 $1 Weight-lifting 65 70
1436 $2 Sailing . . . . 1·30 1·40

2004. World Stamp Championship, Singapore. Sheet 161 × 85 mm containing Nos. 1259/60, 1277/8 and 1405/6. Multicoloured.
MS1437 $2 Containers; $2 Oil refinery; $2 Two yachts; $2 Conductor's hands and baton; $2 Satellite; $2 Robot . . . . . . 7·75 8·00

309 Linked Wrists and Singapore Post Centre

2004. 150th Anniv of Introduction of Stamps. Designs showing early Singapore stamps and postmarks. Multicoloured.
1438 (23c.) Type **309** 15 20
1439 60c. King George VI and General Post Office, Fullerton Building 40 45
1440 $1 King Edward VII and General Post Office . . . 65 70
1441 $2 Queen Victoria and the Post Office, Singapore River . . . . 1·30 1·40
MS1442 135 × 94 mm. Nos. 1438/41 2·50 2·75
No. 1438 is inscribed "1st Local" and was sold for 23c.

310 Seashore Nutmeg 312 Balloon Dog

311 Rooster

2004. Wildlife of Chek Jawa. Multicoloured. Ordinary gum.
1443 (23c.) Type **310** 15 20
1444 (23c.) Oriental pied hornbill 15 20
1445 $1 Knobbly Sea stars . . . 65 70
1446 $1 Common seahorses . . . 65 70

2004. Self-adhesive.
1447 (23c.) Type **310** 15 20
1448 (23c.) Oriental pied hornbill 15 20
Nos. 1443/6 were printed together, se-tenant, the backgrounds forming a composite design.
Nos. 1443/4 and 1447/8 were each inscribed "1st Local" and sold for 23c. each.

2005. Chinese New Year ("Year of the Rooster"). Multicoloured.
1449 (23c.) Type **311** 15 20
1450 $2 Rooster and hen . . . . 1·30 1·40
No. 1449 is inscribed "1st Local" and was sold for 23c.

2004. Greetings. Multicoloured. (a) Ordinary gum.
1451 (23c.) Type **312** 15 20
1452 (23c.) Lily 15 20
1453 (23c.) Gift box 15 20
1454 (23c.) Love heart and bears flower arrangement . . . 15 20
1455 (23c.) Candle 15 20

(b) Size 30 × 25 mm. Self-adhesive.
1456 (23c.) Candle 15 20
1457 (23c.) Love heart and bears flower arrangement . . . 15 20
1458 (23c.) Gift box 15 20
1459 (23c.) Lily 15 20
1460 (23c.) Balloon dog 15 20
Nos. 1451/60 were each inscribed "1st Local" and sold for 23c.

POSTAGE DUE STAMPS

The postage due stamps of Malayan Postal Union were in use in Singapore from 1948 until replaced by the following issue.

D 1

D 2

1968.
D1 D 1 1c. green . . . . 60 2·00
D2 2c. red . . . . 1·60 2·50
D3 4c. orange . . . . 2·00 5·50
D4 8c. brown . . . . 1·00 2·00
D5 10c. mauve . . . . 1·00 90
D6 12c. violet . . . . 2·75 3·25
D7 20c. blue . . . . 2·00 3·50
D8 50c. green . . . . 11·00 5·50

1978.
D16a D 2 1c. green . . . . 15 4·25
D17a 4c. orange . . . . . . 20 6·00
D18a 10c. blue . . . . . . 50 2·00
D19a 20c. blue . . . . . . 65 2·25
D20a 50c. green . . . . . . 90 2·75

D 3

1989.
D21 D 3 1c. green . . . .
D22 4c. brown . . . .
D23 5c. mauve 20 50
D24 10c. red 20 40
D25 20c. blue 30 60
D26 50c. green . . . . 60 1·00
D27 $1 brown . . . . 3·00 4·00

SIRMOOR Pt. 1

A state of the Punjab, India. Now uses Indian stamps.

12 pies = 1 anna; 16 annas = 1 rupee.

1

2

1876.
1 1 1pice green . . . . 13·00 £275
2 1pice blue . . . . 4·25 £160

1892.
3b 2 1pice green 75 75
4 1pice blue 90 80

3 Raja Shamsher Parkash 4

1885.
5a 3 3p. brown 30 35
6a 3p. orange 30 20
7c 6p. green 60 35
8d 1a. blue . . . . 50 2·25
9a 2a. red . . . . 3·50 3·00

1895.
22 4 3p. orange . . . . 2·75 30
23 6p. green 75 30
24 1a. blue . . . . 4·00 1·60
25 2a. red . . . . 2·50 1·00
26 3a. green . . . . 20·00 38·00
27 4a. green . . . . 12·00 20·00
28 8a. blue . . . . 15·00 25·00
29 1r. red . . . . 32·00 60·00

5 Raja Shamsher Parkash

1899.
30 5 3a. green . . . . 3·00 22·00
31 4a. green . . . . 4·00 18·00
32 8a. blue . . . . 6·00 14·00
33 1r. red . . . . 9·50 42·00

OFFICIAL STAMPS

1890. Optd **On S. S. S.**
60 3 3p. orange 60 50
79 6p. green 50 45
80 1a. blue 35 60
63a 2a. red . . . . 7·00 7·00

SLESVIG Pt. 11

Stamps issued during the plebiscite of 1920.

100 pfennig = 1 German mark.
100 ore = 1 Danish krone.

1 Arms

3 Rural View

1920.
1 1 $2\frac{1}{2}$pf. grey 10 10
2 5pf. green 10 10
3 $7\frac{1}{2}$pf. brown 10 10
4 10pf. red 10 10
5 15pf. purple 10 10
6 20pf. blue 10 10
7 25pf. orange 25 60
8 35pf. brown . . . . 1·10 1·50
9 40pf. violet 25 95
10 75pf. green . . . . 1·25 2·40
11 3 1m. brown . . . . 95 3·00
12 2m. blue . . . . 2·40 6·00
13 5m. green . . . . 4·00 9·25
14 10m. red . . . . 10·50 23·00

1920. Values in Danish currency and optd **1. ZONE.**
29 1 1ore grey 20 35
30 5ore green 20 25
31 7ore brown 20 40
32 10ore red 20 40
33 15ore purple 20 40
34 20ore blue 20 70
35 25ore orange . . . . 30 3·25
36 35ore brown . . . . 90 5·25
37 40ore violet . . . . 75 1·40
38 75ore green . . . . 50 3·50
39 3 1k. brown . . . . 75 5·25
40 2k. blue . . . . 1·60 26·00
41 5k. green . . . . 2·75 32·00
42 10k. red . . . . 8·50 60·00

OFFICIAL STAMPS

1920. Nos. 1/14 optd **C.I.S.** (= "Comission Interalliee Slesvig").
O15 1 $2\frac{1}{2}$pf. grey . . . . 50·00 55·00
O16 5pf. green . . . . 50·00 55·00
O17 $7\frac{1}{2}$pf. brown . . . . . . 50·00 55·00
O18 10pf. red . . . . 50·00 60·00
O19 15pf. red . . . . 50·00 48·00
O20 20pf. blue . . . . 50·00 48·00
O21 25pf. orange . . . . . . 70·00 80·00
O22 35pf. brown . . . . . . 70·00 80·00
O23 40pf. violet . . . . . . 75·00 55·00
O24 75pf. green . . . . . . 70·00 £150
O25 3 1m. brown £110 £160
O26 2m. blue £120 £180
O27 5m. green £190 £300
O28 10m. red £350 £450

SLOVAKIA Pt. 5

Formerly part of Hungary, Slovakia joined with Bohemia and Moravia in 1918 to form Czechoslovakia. From 1939 to 1945 they were separate states.

In 1993 the federation of Czechoslovakia was dissolved and Slovakia became an independent republic.

100 haleru = 1 koruna.

A. REPUBLIC OF SLOVAKIA

1939. Stamps of Czechoslovakia optd **Slovensky stat 1939**.
2 34 5h. blue 45 80
3 10h. brown 10 10
4 20h. red 10 10
5 25h. green . . . . 75 1·60
6 30h. purple 10 10
7 59 40h. blue 10 25
8 60a 50h. green 10 10
9 66 50h. green 10 10
10 60a 60h. violet 10 10
11 60h. blue . . . . 6·00 9·50
12 61 1k. purple 10 10
13 – 1k.20 purple (No. 354) . . 20 30
14 64 1k.50 red 20 30
15 – 1k.60 green (No. 355a) . . 1·40 2·40
16 – 2k. green (No. 356) . . . . 1·40 2·40
17 – 2k.50 blue (No. 357) . . . 30 45
18 – 3k. brown (No. 358) . . . 30 60
19 – 3k.50 violet (No. 359) . . . 14·00 23·00
20 65 4k. violet . . . . 6·00 13·00
21 – 5k. green (No. 361) . . . . 7·50 14·00
22 – 10k. blue (No. 362) . . . . 60·00 80·00

4 Father Hlinka

7 Krivan

8 Chamois

9 Mgr. Tiso

10 Weaving

11 Sawyer

12 Presidential Palace, Bratislava

1939. As T **4**, but inscr "CESKO-SLOVENSKO SLOVENSKA POSTA", optd **SLOVENSKY STAT**.
23 4 50h. green . . . . 1·00 60
24 1k. red . . . . 1·00 60

1939. Perf or imperf (20, 30h.), perf (others).
25 4 5h. blue 25 45
26 10h. green 45 65
27a 20h. red 30 65
28 30h. violet 45 85
29 50h. green 40 65
33 1k. red 45 50
31 2k.50 blue 45 30
35a 3k. sepia 75 75
See also No. 81.

1939.
40 – 5h. green 10 20
41 7 10h. brown 10 15
42 – 20h. grey 10 10
43 8 25h. brown 40 20
44 – 30h. brown 15 20
45 9 50h. green 10 25
46 70h. brown 30 10
47 10 2k. green . . . . 2·25 45
48 11 4k. brown 55 65
49 – 5k. red 55 30
50 12 10k. blue 55 60
DESIGNS—As Type **7**: 5h., Zelene Pleso; 20h. Kvety Satier (Edelweiss); 30h. Javorina. As Type **11**: 5k. Woman filling ewer at spring.
For 10 to 50h. values in larger size, see Nos. 125/9.

13 Rev. J. Murgas and Wireless Masts

1939. 10th Death Anniv of Rev. J. Murgas.
53 13 60h. violet 10 20
52 1k.20 grey 40 20

1939. Child Welfare. As No. 45 but larger (24 × 30 mm) and inscr "+2.50 DETOM".
54 2k.50+2k.50 blue . . . . . . 1·90 2·25

14 Heinkel He 111C over Lake Csorba

15 Heinkel He 116A over Tatra Mountains

16 Eagle and Aero A-204

1939. Air.
55 **14** 30h. violet 20 30
56 50h. green 20 30
57 1k. red 25 30
58 **15** 2k. green 40 45
59 3k. brown 75 85
60 4k. blue . . . . 1·40 1·75
62 **16** 5k. purple . . . . 85 1·25
63 10k. grey . . . . 1·10 1·50
64 20k. green . . . . 1·40 1·90

17 Stiavnica Castle

18 S. M. Daxner and Bishop Moyses

1941.
65 **17** 1k.20 purple 15 10
66 – 1k.50 red (Lietava) 15 10
67 – 1k.60 blue (Spissky Hrad) . . . 20 10
68 – 2k. green (Bojnice) 15 10

1941. 80th Anniv of Presentation of Slovak Memorandum to Emperor Francis Joseph.
69 **18** 50h. green . . . . 70 1·10
70 1k. blue . . . . 3·00 4·25
71 2k. black . . . . 3·00 4·25

19 Wounded Soldier and Red Cross Orderly

1941. Red Cross Fund.
72 **19** 50h.+50h. green 25 30
73 1k.+1k. purple 30 40
74 2k.+1k. blue . . . . . . 85 1·00

20 Mother and Child

21 Soldier with Hlinka Youth Member

1941. Child Welfare Fund.
75 **20** 50h.+50h. green 45 60
76 1k.+1k. brown 45 60
77 2k.+1k. violet 45 60

1942. Hlinka Youth Fund.
78 **21** 70h.+1k. brown 20 20
79 1k.30+1k. blue 25 30
80 2k.+1k. red 60 65

1942. Father Hlinka. As T **4** but inscr "SLOVENSKO" (without "POSTA").
81 1k.30 violet 25 15

22 Boy Stamp Collector

23 Dove and St. Stephen's

1942. Philatelic Exhibition, Bratislava.
82 – 30h. green 55 85
83 **22** 70h. red 55 85
84 – 80h. violet 55 85
85 – 1k.30 brown 55 85
DESIGNS: 30h., 1k.30, Posthorn, round various arms, above Bratislava; 80h. Postmaster-General examining stamps.

1942. European Postal Congress.
86 **23** 70h. green 60 60
87 1k.30 green 60 90
88 2k. blue . . . . 1·25 1·75

24 Inaugural Ceremony

25 L. Stur

1942. 15th Anniv of Foundation of National Literacy Society.
89 **24** 70h. black 10 10
90 1k. red 10 10
91 1k.30 blue 10 10
92 2k. brown 10 10
93 3k. green 30 30
94 4k. violet 30 30

1943.
95 **25** 80h. green 10 10
96 – 1k. red 10 15
97 – 1k.30 blue 10 10
PORTRAITS: 1k. M. Razus; 1k.30, Father Hlinka.

27 National Costumes

30 Railway Tunnel

29 Infantry

1943. Winter Relief Fund.
98 **27** 50h.+50h. green 10 25
99 – 70h.+1k. red 10 25
100 – 80h.+2k. blue 10 30
DESIGNS: 70h. Mother and child; 80h. Mother and two children.

1943. Fighting Forces.
106 **29** 70h.+2k. red 30 60
107 – 1k.30+2k. blue 45 85
108 – 2k.+2k. green 35 70
DESIGNS—HORIZ: 2k. Artillery. VERT: 1k.30, Air Force.

1943. Opening of the Strazke–Presov Railway.
109 – 70h. purple 35 45
110 – 80h. blue 45 45
111 **30** 1k.30 black 45 55
112 – 2k. brown 60 75
DESIGNS—HORIZ: 70h. Route map and Presov Church; 2k. Railway viaduct. VERT: 80h. Steam locomotive.

32 "The Slovak Language is our Life"

33 National Museum

1943. Culture Fund.
113 **32** 30h.+1k. brown 25 30
114 **33** 70h.+1k. green 30 35
115 – 80h.+2k. blue 25 30
116 – 1k.30+2k. brown 25 30
DESIGNS—HORIZ: 80h. Matica Slovenska College. VERT: 1k.30, Agricultural student.

34 Prince Pribina Okolo

35 Footballer

1944. 5th Anniv of Declaration of Independence.
117 **34** 50h. green 10 10
118 – 70h. mauve 10 10
119 – 80h. brown 10 10
120 – 1k.30 blue 10 10
121 – 2k. blue 10 30
122 – 3k. brown 25 30
123 – 5k. violet 45 45
124 – 10k. black . . . . 1·25 1·50
DESIGNS: 70h. Prince Mojmir; 80h. Prince Ratislav; 1k.30, King Svatopluk; 2k. Prince Kocel; 3k. Prince Mojmir II; 5k. Prince Svatopluk II; 10k. Prince Braslav.

1944. As 1939 issue but larger ($18\frac{1}{2} \times 22\frac{1}{2}$ mm).
125 **7** 10h. red 10 20
126 – 20h. blue 10 20
127 **8** 25h. purple 10 20
128 – 30h. purple 10 20
129 – 50h. green 10 20
DESIGN: 50h. Zelene Pleso (as No. 40).

1944. Sports.
130 **35** 70h.+70h. green 30 50
131 – 1k.+1k. violet 40 55
132 – 1k.30+1k.30 green 40 55
133 – 2k.+2k. brown 40 65
DESIGNS—VERT: 1k. Skiing; 1k.30, Diving. HORIZ: 2k. Running.

36 Symbolic of "Protection"

1944. Protection Series.
134 **36** 70h.+4k. blue 55 85
135 1k.30+4k. brown 55 85
136 2k. green 20 25
137 3k.80 purple 20 25

37 Children Playing

38 Mgr. Tiso

1944. Child Welfare.
138 **37** 2k.+4k. blue . . . . 1·50 1·90

1945.
139 **38** 1k. orange 75 40
140 1k.50 brown 20 15
141 2k. green 25 40
142 4k. red 75 60
143 5k. blue 75 40
144 10k. purple 55 30

B. SLOVAK REPUBLIC

39 State Arms

40 Ruzomberok

1993.
145 **39** 3k. multicoloured 35 30
146 8k. mult (26 × 40 mm) . . 3·75 3·75

1993.
146a – 50h. lilac and blue . . . 10 10
146b – 2k. pink, black and blue 20 10
146c – 3k. black, blue and red 30 10
146d – 4k. black, green and blue 30 10
146e – 4k. green, black and red 30 10
147 **40** 5k. blue and red 35 20
147a – 5k. black, yellow and blue 35 10
147b – 6k. blue, red and yellow 45 25
147c – 7k. black and pink . . . 45 25
147d – 8k. black, blue and red 65 25
147e – 9k. black, yellow and green 65 35
148 – 10k. lilac and orange . . 75 45
148a – 10k. black, blue and red 75 45
148b – 16k. black and blue . . . 1·25 50
149 – 20k. blue and ochre . . . 1·00 50
150 – 30k. black, blue and red 1·75 75
150a – 40k. ochre and black . . 1·10 65
151 – 50k. black, orange & bl 3·75 1·90
152 – 50k. black, blue and red 1·40 80
DESIGNS—VERT: 50h. Bardejov; 2k. Nitra; 4k. (146c) Nova Bana; 4k. (146d) Presov; 5k. Trnava; 6k. Arms of Senica; 7k. St Martin's Church, Martin; 9k. Zilina; 10k. Kosice; 10k. (148a) Kezmarok; 20k. Roznava Watchtower; 50k. (151) Bratislava; 50k. (152) Komarno. HORIZ: 3k. Banska Bystrica; 8k. Trencin; 16k. Levoca; 30k. Suden Castle; 40k. Piestany.

41 Pres. Michal Kovac

42 St. John and Charles Bridge, Prague

1993.
156 **41** 2k. black 10 10
157 3k. brown and mauve . . . 20 10

1993. 600th Death Anniv of St. John of Nepomuk (patron saint of Bohemia).
158 **42** 8k. multicoloured 65 35

43 Pedunculate Oak

44 Jan Levoslav Bella (composer)

1993. Trees. Multicoloured.
159 3k. Type **43** 20 10
160 4k. Hornbeam 30 20
161 10k. Scots pine 80 55

1993. Anniversaries.
162 **44** 5k. cream, brown and blue 35 25
163 – 8k. brown, sepia and red 65 35
164 – 20k. buff, blue and orange 1·50 75
DESIGNS: 5k. Type **44** (150th birth anniv); 8k. Alexander Dubcek (statesman) (1st death anniv); 20k. Jan Kollar (poet and scholar) (birth bicent).

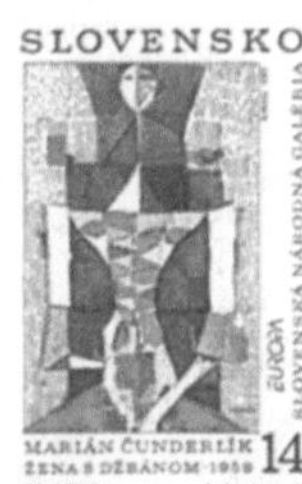

45 "Woman with Jug" (Marian Cunderlik)

1993. Europa. Contemporary Art.
165 **45** 14k. multicoloured . . . . 6·00 4·00

46 Sun

47 Arms of Dubnica nad Vahom

1993. Anniversaries. Multicoloured.
166 2k. Type **46** (150th anniv of Slovakian written language) 20 10
167 8k. Sts. Cyril and Methodius (1130th anniv of arrival in Moravia) 65 35

1993.
168 **47** 1k. silver, black and blue 10 10

48 "The Big Pets" (Lane Smith)

1993. 14th Biennial Exhibition of Book Illustrations for Children, Bratislava.
169 **48** 5k. multicoloured 35 15

49 Canal Lock, Gabcikovo

1993. Rhine—Main—Danube Canal.
170 **49** 10k. multicoloured 90 35

50 Child's Face in Blood-drop

51 "Madonna and Child" (Jozef Klemens)

1993. Red Cross.
171 **50** 3k.+1k. red and blue . . . 30 30

1993. Christmas.
172 **51** 2k. multicoloured 10 10

52 Milan Stefanik's Tomb, Bradlo

1993. Sheet 70 × 90 mm.
MS173 **52** 16k. multicoloured . . 1·60 1·50

53 "The Labourer's Spring" (Jozef Kostka)

1993. Art (1st series).
174 **53** 9k. multicoloured . . . . 3·00 1·90
See also Nos. 198/9, 227/8, 246/8, 271/3, 297, 300/1, 326/7, 351/2, 374/6, 400 and 412.

54 Ski Jumping **55** Family

1994. Winter Olympic Games, Lillehammer, Norway.
175 **54** 2k. black, mauve and blue 10 10

1994. International Year of the Family.
176 **55** 3k. multicoloured 20 15

56 Antoine de Saint-Exupery (writer and pilot) (50th death) **57** Jozef Murgas (radio-telegraphy pioneer)

1994. Anniversaries.
177 – 8k. red and blue 70 45
178 **56** 9k. multicoloured 70 45
DESIGNS: 8k. Janos Andras Segner (mathematician and physicist) (290th birth).

1994. Europa. Inventions.
179 **57** 28k. multicoloured . . . . 2·25 2·25

58 Cigarettes **59** Football Pitch as Tie

1994. World No Smoking Day.
180 **58** 3k. multicoloured 20 10

1994. World Cup Football Championship, U.S.A.
181 **59** 2k. multicoloured 10 10

60 Ancient Greek Runner passing Baton to Modern Athlete

1994. Centenary of International Olympic Committee.
182 **60** 3k. multicoloured 20 25

61 Golden Eagle **63** Rowing Boat with Stamp for Sail

62 Prince Svatopluk

1994. Birds. Multicoloured.
183 4k. Type **61** 35 50
184 5k. Peregrine falcon 55 30
185 7k. Eagle owl 60 45

1994. 1100th Death Anniv of Prince Svatopluk of Moravia.
186 **62** 12k. brown, buff and black 1·10 1·10

1994. 120th Anniv of Universal Postal Union.
187 **63** 8k. multicoloured 65 30

64 Generals Rudolf Viest and Jan Golian

1994. 50th Anniv of Slovak Uprising.
188 **64** 6k. blue, pink and yellow 35 30
189 – 8k. multicoloured 60 35
DESIGNS: 8k. French volunteers and their Memorial.

65 Janko Matuska (lyricist and Allegory of "As Well She Dug" (melody)

1994. "Over The Tatras Lightning Breaks" (national anthem). Sheet 66 × 79 mm.
MS190 **65** 34k. multicoloured . . 3·00 3·00

66 Medal (O. Spaniel) and Faculty Emblems **68** St. George's Church, Kostolany pod Tribecom

67 Tajar (winner of first race)

1994. 75th Anniv of Comenius University, Bratislava.
191 **66** 12k. gold, black and red 90 50

1994. 180th Anniv of Mojmirovce Horse Race.
192 **67** 2k. blue and yellow 10 10

1994.
193 **68** 20k. multicoloured . . . . 1·50 75

69 "Nativity" (early 19th-century glass painting)

1994. Christmas.
194 **69** 2k. multicoloured 10 10

70 Chattam Sofer, Rabbi of Bratislava

1994. Anniversaries. Multicoloured.
195 5k. Type **70** (165th death) . . 35 25
196 6k. Wolfgang Kempelen (conducted study into human speech) (190th death) 45 25
197 10k. Stefan Banic (inventor of parachute) (125th birth (1995)) 75 40

1994. Art (2nd series). As T **53**. Multicoloured.
198 7k. "Girls" (Janko Alexy) (horiz) 45 60
199 14k. "Bulls" (Vincent Hloznik) . . . . 1·25 1·25

71 Container Ship

1994. Ships. Multicoloured.
200 5k. Type **71** 45 25
201 8k. "Ryn" (freighter) 60 35
202 10k. Passenger liner 65 35

72 Samuel Jurkovic (founder) **73** "Ciminalis clusii"

1995. 150th Anniv of Landlords' Association.
203 **72** 9k. multicoloured 80 35

1995. European Nature Protection Year. Flowers. Multicoloured.
204 2k. Type **73** 20 10
205 3k. "Pulsatilla slavica" . . . 30 10
206 8k. "Onosma tornense" . . . 1·25 45

74 Theatre Masks

1995. 75th Anniv of Slovak National Theatre..
207 **74** 10k. pink, black and blue 75 35

75 Ice Hockey Equipment

1995. World Cup Ice Hockey Championship Group B Qualifying Round, Bratislava.
208 **75** 5k. yellow and blue 45 20

76 Bela Bartok (composer, 50th death)

1995. Anniversaries. Multicoloured.
209 3k. Type **76** 30 10
210 6k. Jan Bahyl (inventor, 80th death (1996)) and helicopter design 45 30
MS211 68 × 90 mm. 16k. Ludovit Stur (180th birth) (40 × 26 mm) 1·40 1·40

77 Allegory of Freedom

1995. Europa. Peace and Freedom.
212 **77** 8k. multicoloured . . . . 60 1·10

78 Concentration Camp Victims

1995. 50th Anniv of Liberation of Concentration Camps.
213 **78** 12k. multicoloured 90 50

79 Scout

1995.
214 **79** 5k. multicoloured 35 25

80 Pope John Paul II, Map and Arms **82** Banska Stiavnica

81 "Stamps"

1995. Papal Visit.
215 **80** 3k. red and pink 30 10

1995. Centenary of Album Kremnica Philatelic Association. Sheet 80 × 87 mm.
MS216 **81** 3k. × 2 grey, black and blue 60 60

1995. UNESCO World Heritage Sites. Multicoloured.
217 7k. Type **82** 45 25
218 10k. Spis Castle (horiz) . . . 75 30
219 15k. Vlkolinec (horiz) . . . . 1·10 50

83 Player **84** Sad Clown (Lorenzo Mattotti)

1995. Centenary of Volleyball.
220 **83** 9k. blue, black and yellow 75 45

1995. 15th Biennial Exhibition of Book Illustrations for Children, Bratislava. Multicoloured.
221 2k. Type **84** 15 10
222 3k. Thin and fat men with long noses (Dusan Kallay) 20 10

85 Tree, Arch and Association Emblem

1995. St. Adalbert Association.
223 **85** 4k. black, green and pink . . . 35 10

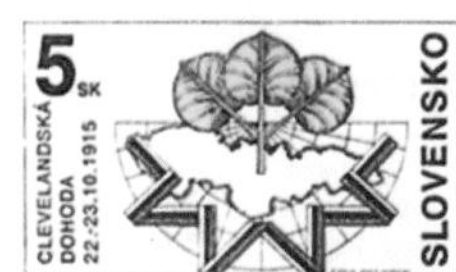

86 Map of Czechoslovakia, Linden Leaves and National Colours

1995. 80th Anniv of Cleveland Agreement.
224 **86** 5k. yellow, blue and red . . 45 10

87 Allegory of Celebration and Peace

1995. 50th Anniv of United Nations Organization.
225 **87** 8k. multicoloured 75 75

88 Christmas Crib (Peter Palka)

1995. Christmas.
226 **88** 2k. multicoloured 15 10

1995. Art (3rd series). As T **53**. Multicoloured.
227 8k. "Hlohovec Nativity" . . 65 60
228 16k. "Two Women" (Mikulas Galanda) . . . . 1·40 1·25

89 Jozef Ciger-Hronsky (writer)
90 Alojz Szokol, Athens, 1896

1996. Anniversaries. Multicoloured.
229 3k. Type **89** (death centenary) 30 10
230 4k. Jozef Ludovit Holuby (botanist, 160th birth anniv) 30 10

1996. Centenary of Modern Olympic Games.
231 **90** 9k. multicoloured 75 35

91 Dousing Woman in Water
93 Izabela Textorisova (botanist)

92 Child replenishing Desertland

1996. Easter.
232 **91** 2k. multicoloured 15 10

1996. Year for the Eradication of Poverty. Sheet 74×90 mm.
MS233 **92** 7k. multicoloured . . 60 60

1996. Europa. Famous Women. Multicoloured.
234 8k. Type **93** 75 60
235 8k. Botanist holding thistle 75 60

94 Handshake breaking through Boxing Gloves

1996. Olympic Games, Atlanta. Sheet 70×79 mm.
MS236 **94** 12k.+2k. black, rose and ultramarine . . . . 1·10 1·10

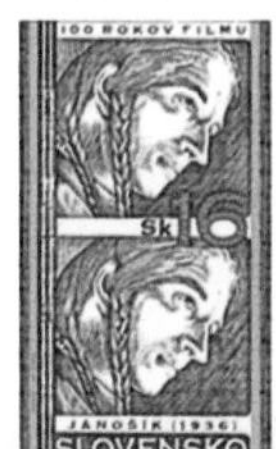

95 Palo Bielik in "Janosik"

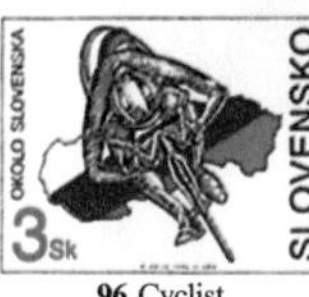

96 Cyclist
97 Page and Mountains

1996. Centenary of Motion Pictures. Sheet 80×89 mm.
MS237 **95** 16k. indigo, orange and blue . . . . 1·40 1·25

1996. Round Slovakia Cycle Race.
238 **96** 3k. black, blue and red . . 20 10

1996. 150th Anniv of "Slovenske Pohl'ady" ("Slovak Perspectives" (review)).
239 **97** 18k. black, red and blue 1·50 75

98 European Bison
99 Popradske

1996. Mammals. Multicoloured.
240 4k. Type **98** 35 10
241 4k. Mouflon ("Ovis musimon") 35 10
242 4k. Chamois ("Rupicapra rupicapra") 35 10

1996. Mountain Lakes. Multicoloured.
243 4k. Type **99** 30 10
244 8k. Skalnate 65 30
245 12k. Strbsky . . . . 1·10 45

1996. Art (4th series). As T **53**.
246 7k. multicoloured 60 60
247 10k. deep blue, lilac and blue 80 75
248 14k. multicoloured . . . . 1·00 1·25
DESIGNS: 7k. "Queen Ntombi Twala" (Andy Warhol); 10k. "Suppressed Laughter" (Franz Messerschmidt); 14k. Baroque chair (Endre Nemes).

100 Horse Tram and Bratislava and Trnava Stations
101 Snow-covered Village, Kysuce

1996. Technological Monuments. Multicoloured.
249 4k. Type **100** 30 30
250 6k. Andrej Kvasz and his airplane 50 30

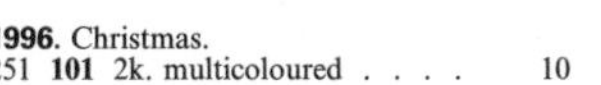

1996. Christmas.
251 **101** 2k. multicoloured 10 10

102 Unissued Stamp Design and Benka

1996. Stamp Day. 25th Death Anniv of Martin Benka (stamp designer).
252 **102** 3k. buff and blue 20 10

103 Michal Martikan

1996. Slovak Achievements at Olympic Games, Atlanta.
253 **103** 3k. brown and stone . . . 20 10

104 Bishop Stefan Moyses
105 Biathlon

1997. Birth Anniversaries of National Activists. Multicoloured.
254 3k. Type **104** (first chairman of Matican Slovenska, bicentenary) 20 10
255 4k. Svetozar Vajansky (writer, 150th) 30 10

1997. World Biathlon Championship, Osrblie.
256 **105** 6k. multicoloured 45 30

106 Collecting Dew
107 Church

1997. Folk Traditions.
257 **106** 3k. multicoloured 20 10

1997. 700th Anniv of Franciscan Church, Bratislava.
258 **107** 16k. black, orange and blue . . . . 1·10 60

108 Guglielmo Marconi and Radio Waves

1997. Centenary of Wireless Telegraphy.
259 **108** 10k. black, blue and yellow 75 45

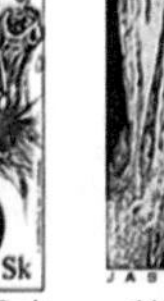

109 Miraculous Rain of Hron
110 Domica Cave

1997. Europa. Tales and Legends.
260 **109** 9k. black, orange and blue 65 75

1997. Caves. Multicoloured.
261 6k. Type **110** 45 45
262 8k. Argonite Cave, Ochtinska 60 60

111 Couple dancing

1997. Folklore Festival, Vychodna. Sheet 66×79 mm.
MS263 **111** 11k. multicoloured . . . 85 1·00

112 "Dance" (Martin Jonas)

1997. Naive Art Triennale.
264 **112** 3k. multicoloured 20 10

113 Woman
114 Cherubs blowing Horns (J. Kiselova-Sitekova)

1997. International Slovak Year.
265 **113** 9k. multicoloured 65 45

1997. 16th Biennial Exhibition of Book Illustrations for Children, Bratislava.
266 **114** 3k. multicoloured 20 10

115 Water Mill, Jelka
116 Flag, Arms and Linden Leaves

1997.
267 **115** 4k. multicoloured 25 10

1997. 5th Anniv of Constitution.
268 **116** 4k. multicoloured 25 10

117 Runners
118 Bronze Boletus ("Boletus aereus")

1997. 6th World Half-marathon Championship, Kosice.
269 **117** 9k. multicoloured 65 45

1997. Endangered Fungi. Sheet 154×102 mm containing T **118** and similar vert designs. Multicoloured.
MS270 9k. Type **118**; 9k. Common morel ("Morchella esculenta"); 9k. "Cathelasma Imperialie" . . . 1·90 1·50

1997. Art (5th series). As T **53**.
271 9k. multicoloured 65 45
272 10k. multicoloured 75 60
273 12k. buff, black and red . . . 90 75
DESIGNS—VERT: 9k. "Self-portrait with Wife" (Jan Kupecky); 12k. "For Aim" (Koloman Sokol). HORIZ: 10k. "St. Lucy and St. Peter" (detail of Bojnice altarpiece, Nardo di Cione).

119 Weeping Woman and Church
120 Nativity

1997. 90th Anniv of Cernova Massacre.
274 **119** 4k. lilac and green 25 10

1997. Christmas.
275 **120** 3k. multicoloured 20 10

121 Nepela

122 Risen Christ amongst Disciples

1997. Ondrej Nepela (figure skater).
276 **121** 5k. black, mauve and green 30 10

1997. Spiritual Regeneration.
277 **122** 4k. multicoloured 25 10

123 Burin as Posthorn

1997. Stamp Day.
278 **123** 4k. brown and blue . . . 25 10

124 Bratislava and Arms of District Towns

1998. 5th Anniv of Independence.
279 **124** 4k. multicoloured 25 10

125 Martin Razus

127 Banishing of Moraine

126 Ice Hockey

1998. Writers' Anniversaries. Multicoloured.
280 4k. Type **125** (110th birth anniv) 25 10
281 4k. Jozef Skultety and Slovak Cultural Society building (50th death anniv) 25 10
282 4k. Jan Smrek (birth centenary) 25 10

1998. Winter Olympic Games, Nagano, Japan.
283 **126** 19k. yellow, black and blue . . . . 1·25 90

1998. Folk Traditions.
284 **127** 3k. multicoloured 20 10

128 Budatin Castle

1998. Castles. Multicoloured.
285 6k. Type **128** 45 25
286 11k. Krasna Hoka castle . . 75 40
MS287 76×82 mm. 18k. Nitra castle 1·40 1·50

129 "Sending Down of the Holy Spirit" (Vincent Hloznik)

130 Tekov Wedding

1998. Spiritual Renewal.
288 **129** 4k. multicoloured 25 10

1998. Europa. National Festivals.
289 **130** 12k. multicoloured . . . 90 60

131 "Butterfly and Rainbow" (Livia Merenicova)

132 Viktor Kolibrik (revolutionary)

1998. Children's Centre.
290 **131** 3k. multicoloured 20 10

1998. 80th Anniv of Kragujevac Uprising.
291 **132** 3k. multicoloured 20 10

133 Rebels

1998. 150th Anniv of Slovak Insurrection.
292 **133** 4k. black, blue and red 25 10

134 Steam Locomotive

136 Stone and Butterfly

135 European Mud minnow ("Umbra krameri") (B8)

1998. 150th Anniv of Railway in Slovakia.
293 **134** 4k. black, red and blue 25 10
294 – 10k. black, yellow and blue 65 45
295 – 15k. black, yellow and brown . . . . 1·10 60
DESIGNS: 10k. Electric locomotive; 15k. Diesel locomotive.

1998. Fishes. Sheet 109×165 mm containing T **135** and similar horiz designs. Multicoloured.
MS296 4k. Type **135**; 11k. Zingel ("Zingel zingel"); 16k. Common carp ("Cyprinus carpio") . . . 2·40 2·75

1998. Art (6th series). As T **53**. Multicoloured.
297 18k. "Pieta" (sculpture in Basilica of Virgin Mary, Sastin) . . . . 1·25 75

1998. Anti-drugs Campaign.
298 **136** 3k. multicoloured 20 10

137 Sunflower

138 Adoration of the Magi

1998. 25th Anniv of Ekotopfilm.
299 **137** 4k. orange, yellow and blue 25 10

1998. Art (7th series). As T **53**. Multicoloured.
300 10k. "Countryside at Terchova" (Martin Benka) 75 60
301 12k. "Fishermen" (Ludovit Fulla) 95 60

1998. Christmas.
302 **138** 3k. multicoloured 20 10

139 Postman on Bicycle

1998. Stamp Day.
303 **139** 4k. multicoloured 25 10

140 Snowboarders

1999. 19th World University and Fourth EYOD Winter Games, Poprad-Tatry.
304 **140** 12k. black, blue and red 90 40

141 Matej Bel (historian, 250th death)

142 Automatic Sorting Machine

1999. Anniversaries.
305 **141** 3k. black, yellow and brown 25 10
306 – 4k. deep lilac, yellow and lilac 25 10
307 – 11k. purple, orange and blue 80 45
DESIGNS: 4k. Cardinal Juraj Haulik (130th death); 11k. Pavol Orszagh (pseudonym) Hviezdoslav (poet, 150th birth).

1999. 125th Anniv of Universal Postal Union.
308 **142** 4k. multicoloured 25 10

143 Cajkov

144 "Transfiguration"

1999. Women's Traditional Bonnets. Multicoloured.
309 4k. Type **143** 20 10
310 15k. Hel'pa . . . . 1·00 70
311 18k. Madunice . . . . 1·25 1·00

1999. Spiritual Renewal.
312 **144** 5k. multicoloured 35 10

145 High Tatras National Park (right-hand detail)

1999. Europa. Parks and Gardens. Multicoloured.
313 9k. Type **145** . . . . 50 1·00
314 11k. High Tatras National Park (left-hand detail) . . 95 1·10
Nos. 313/14 were issued together, se-tenant, forming a composite design.

146 Face within Council Emblem

1999. 50th Anniv of Council of Europe.
315 **146** 16k. ultramarine, blue and yellow . . . . 1·50 1·50
MS316 66×85 mm. No. 315 . . 1·50 1·50

147 Nightingale, Score and Violin Head

148 Hands of Three Generations

1999. 50th Anniv of Slovak Philharmonic Orchestra.
317 **147** 4k. multicoloured 25 10

1999. International Year of the Elderly.
318 **148** 5k. black, flesh and green 30 10
MS319 **148** 12k. multicoloured 90 1·25

150 Zilina University, Open Book and Keyboard

151 Spotlights on Theatre Stage

1999. 125th Anniv of Universal Postal Union. Multicoloured.
320 12k. Type **150** 55 60
321 16k. Globe and Slovak postal emblem 65 75

1999. 50th Anniv of University of Fine Arts, Bratislava.
322 **151** 4k. black, blue and pink 25 10

152 "Man's Head" (Martin Jarrie)

154 Bearded Reedling (*Panurus biarmicus*) (B8)

153 Water Pillar Machine (J. K. Hell)

1999. 17th Biennial Exhibition of Book Illustrations for Children, Bratislava.
323 **152** 5k. multicoloured 30 10

1999. Technical Monuments.
324 **153** 7k. yellow and brown . . 45 10

1999. Songbirds. Sheet 154×102 mm containing T **154** and similar horiz designs. Multicoloured.
MS325 14k. Type **154**; 15k. Red-backed shrike (*Lanius collurio*); 16k. Redstart (*Phoenicurus phoenucurus*) . . . . 3·25 4·50

1999. Art (8th series). As T **53**. Multicoloured.
326 13k. "Malatina" (Milos Alexander Bazovsky) (horiz) . . . . 1·10 1·00
327 14k. "Study of the Resting Blacksmith" (Dominik Skutecky) . . . . 1·10 1·10

155 Children playing in Snow (Stanislav Sekeres)

1999. Christmas.
328 **155** 4k. multicoloured 25 10

156 Woman's Head

1999. 10th Anniv of Velvet Revolution.
329 **156** 5k. blue, red and black 40 20

157 18th-century Urn showing Visit to Sick Man

1999. Museum of Jewish Culture, Bratislava. Multicoloured.
330 12k. Type **157** . . . . . . 95 1·10
331 18k. 18th-century urn showing funeral procession 1·40 1·75

158 Albin Brunovsky (stamp designer) and "Czechoslovakia"

1999. Stamp Day.
332 **158** 5k. brown, stone and green 30 10

159 Dunajec Gap

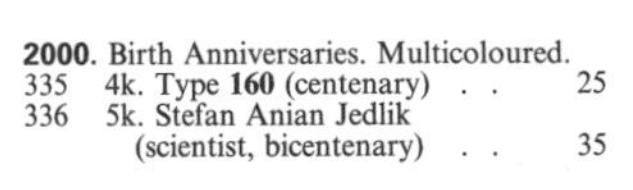
160 Hana Melickova (actress)

2000. Valleys. Multicoloured.
333 10k. Type **159** . . . . . . 80 1·00
334 12k. Vah Gap . . . . 90 1·00

2000. Birth Anniversaries. Multicoloured.
335 4k. Type **160** (centenary) . . 25 10
336 5k. Stefan Anian Jedlik (scientist, bicentenary) . . 35 10

161 Christ's Head (detail of altar panel), St. Jacob's Church, Levoca

162 Globe as Basketball in Net

2000. Easter.
337 **161** 4k. brown 25 10

2000. Women's European Basketball Championship, Ruzomberok.
338 **162** 4k. multicoloured 25 10

163 Juraj Hronec and Stefan Schwarz (mathematicians)

2000. World Mathematics Year.
339 **163** 5k. multicoloured 30 10

164 Jan Holly (poet and priest)

165 "Building Europe"

2000.
340 **164** 5k.50 black, blue and red 30 10

2000. Europa.
341 **165** 12k. multicoloured . . . 1·00 50

166 "Animals from Rainbow" (Alexandra Baníkova)

167 Postman, Austria 1850 2k. Stamp

2000. United Nations Children's Fund.
342 **166** 5k.50 multicoloured . . . 35 10

2000. First Stamps Used in Slovakia.
343 **167** 10k. multicoloured . . . 75 60

168 Pres. Rudolf Schuster

169 Rifle Shooting

2000.
344 **168** 5k.50 brown 15 10

2000. Olympic Games, Sydney.
345 **169** 18k. multicoloured . . . 50 25

170 Emblem

2000. 25th Anniv of Organization for Security and Co-operation in Europe.
346 **170** 4k. black and blue . . . 10 10

171 Timber Bridge, Klukava

172 Wild Raspberry (*Rubus idaeus*) (B26)

2000.
347 **171** 6k. multicoloured 20 10

2000. Berries. Sheet 156 × 103 mm containing T **172** and similar vert designs. Multicoloured.
MS348 11k. Type **172**; 13k. Common strawberry (*Fragaria vescal*); 15k. Bilberry (*Vaccinium myrtillus*) . . . . 1·10 65

173 Mary and Jesus

174 Emblem

2000. Holy Year 2000. Christmas.
349 **173** 4k. multicoloured 10 10

2000. Agreement between the Postal Administration of the Slovak Republic and the Sovereign Order of the Knights of St. John.
350 **174** 10k. multicoloured . . . 25 15

2000. Art (9th series). As T **53**. Multicoloured.
351 18k. Nativity (detail) (altar panel, Spisska-Stara Ves Church) 50 30
352 20k. "Descent from the Cross" (mural, Kocelovce Church) (horiz) 55 30

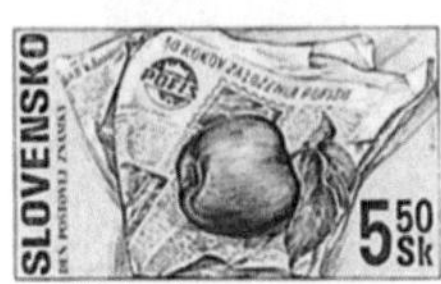
175 Apple on Newspaper

2000. Stamp Day.
353 **175** 5k.50 multicoloured . . . 15 10

176 Maria Theresa

2000. History of Postal Law.
354 **176** 20k. multicoloured . . . 55 30

177 Rococo Mantle Clock

178 Blaho

2001.
355 **177** 13k. multicoloured . . . 35 20

2001. Birth Centenary of Janko Blaho (opera singer).
356 **178** 5k.50 multicoloured . . . 15 10

179 Ice Skater

180 Male

2001. European Figure Skating Championships, Bratislava.
357 **179** 16k. multicoloured . . . 40 25

2001. Traditional Costumes of Detva. Multicoloured.
358 5k.50 Type **180** 15 10
359 6k. Woman in costume, Detva 15 10

181 Woman with Apple

2001. 50th Anniv of Central Control and Check Agricultural Institute, Bratislava.
360 **181** 12k. multicoloured . . . 30 20

182 1st-century Gate and Celtic Coins, Liptovska Mara, Havranok

2001. Archaeological Sites. Multicoloured.
361 12k. Type **182** 30 20
362 15k. 9th-century courtyard, jewellery and button, Ducove, Kostelec 40 25

183 Studenovodsky Waterfall

2001. Europa. Water Resources.
363 **183** 18k. multicoloured . . . 50 30

184 Prince Pribina (800–861) (P91)

2001. Moravian Rulers. Sheet 110 × 165 mm containing T **184** and similar horiz designs. Each cinnamon and sepia.
MS364 6k. Type **184**; 9k. Prince Rastislav (820–870); 11k. Prince Kocel (9th-century); 14k. Prince Svtopluk (840–894) . . . . . 1·60 1·60

185 Brown Bear (*Ursus arctos*) (P95)

2001. Nature Protection. Carnivores. Sheet 118 × 165 mm containing T **185** and similar vert designs. Multicoloured.
MS365 14k. Type **185**; 15k. Wolf (*Canis lupus*); 16k. European lynx (*Lynx lynx*) . . . . 1·40 1·40

186 Guitar and Map of United States

2001. Dobro Resonator Guitar.
366 **186** 19k. multicoloured . . . 50 30

187 Man in Boat (Peter Uchnar)

2001. 18th Biennial Exhibition of Book Illustrations for Children, Bratislava.
367 **187** 7k. multicoloured 20 10

188 Face and Hand

2001. Memorial Day for Victims of the Holocaust.
368 **188** 14k. multicoloured . . . 40 25

189 Dubcek

2001. 9th Death Anniv of Alexander Dubcek (statesman). Sheet 65 × 82 mm.
MS369 **189** 18k. multicoloured 55 55

190 Flowers

2001. Political Trials.
370 **190** 10k. multicoloured . . . 25 15

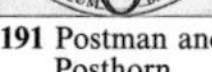

191 Postman and Posthorn **192** Nativity

2001. Opening of Slovak Postal Museum, Banska Bystrica.
371 **191** 6k. multicoloured 15 10

2001. Christmas.
372 **192** 5k.50 multicoloured . . . 15 10

193 Sturovo–Ostrihom Bridge

2001.
373 **193** 10k. multicoloured . . . 25 15

2001. Art (10th series). As T **53**.
374 16k. multicoloured 40 25
375 18k. green and brown 50 30
376 20k. multicoloured 55 30
DESIGNS: 16k. "Raftsman's Dream" (Imrich Weiner-Kral); 18k. "Light of the Soul" (Albin Brunovsky); 20k. "St. Michael the Archangel with the Group of Saints" (icon).

194 Juraj Papanek **196** Dogs pulling Sledge

195 Skiers

2002. Anniversaries. Multicoloured.
377 10k. Type **194** (historian, death bicentenary) 35 20
378 14k. Bjornstjerne Bjornson (writer and poet, 170th birth anniv) 45 30

2002. Winter Olympic Games, Salt Lake City, U.S.A.
379 **195** 18k. multicoloured . . . 60 35

2002. European Sled Dog Race Championship, Donovaly.
380 **196** 6k. multicoloured 20 10

197 Jesus and Flowers (Karol Ondreicka) **198** Martin Gymnasium and Open Book

2002. Easter.
381 **197** 5k.50 multicoloured . . . 20 10

2002. Educational Anniversaries. Multicoloured.
382 12k. Type **198** (140th anniv) 40 25
383 13k. Revuca Gymnasium (140th anniv) 45 30
384 15k. Klastor pod Znievom Gymnasium (133rd anniv) 50 30

199 "Clown with Trumpet" (Emil Bacík)

2002. Europa. Circus.
385 **199** 18k. multicoloured . . . 60 35

200 Beer Barrel and Kegs

2002. Industrial Technology. Multicoloured.
386 7k. Type **200** 25 15
387 9k. Wine press and grapes . . 30 20

201 Southern Festoon (*Zerynthia polyxena*)

2002. Endangered Species. Butterflies. Sheet 109 × 165 mm containing T **201** and similar horiz designs. Multicoloured.
MS388 10k. Type **201**; 16k. Peacock (*Inachis io*); 25k. Swallowtail (*Papilio machaon*) . . . . . . 1·75 1·75

202 Two Doves

2002. Greetings Stamp. "Congratulations".
389 **202** 6k. multicoloured 20 10

203 Player and Trophy

2002. Slovakia–Winners of World Ice Hockey Championship, Sweden.
390 **203** 10k. multicoloured . . . 35 20

204 Rudnay **205** Congtai Pavilion, Handan

2002. 171st Death Anniv of Alexander Rudnay (Archbishop of Esztergom). Sheet 81 × 108 mm.
MS391 **204** 17k. multicoloured 55 55

2002. Castles. Multicoloured.
392 6k. Type **205** 20 20
393 12k. Bojnice Castle 40 40
Stamps of a similar design were issued by China.

206 Emblem **207** Angel (detail), Rajecka Lesna Nativity (sculpture) (Jozef Pekara)

2002. 50th Anniv of Kosice Technical College.
394 **206** 6k. multicoloured 20 20

2002. Christmas.
395 **207** 5k.50 multicoloured . . . 25 25

208 St. Michael's Church, Klizske Hradiste

2002. Churches. Multicoloured.
396 7k. Type **208** 25 25
397 14k. St. George's Church, Skalica 45 45
398 22k. St. Martin's Cathdral, Spisska Kapitula 75 75

209 Moonwalk

2002. 30th Anniv of Flight of *Apollo 17*. Sheet 81 × 101 mm.
MS399 **209** 20k. multicoloured 65 65

2002. Art (11th series). As T **53**. Multicoloured.
400 23k. "In the Atelier" (Koloman Sokol) 75 75

210 Kingfisher

2002. "NITRAFILA 2003" International Stamp Exhibition, Nitra.
401 **210** 10k. multicoloured . . . 35 35

2002. Art (12th series). As T **53**. Multicoloured.
402 20k. "Decollation of St. James the Older" (Master Paul of Levoca) 65 65

211 Family **212** Girl carrying the Lesola (decorated twigs) on Palm Sunday

2003. 10th Anniv of Republic.
403 **211** 20k. multicoloured . . . 65 65

2003. As T **168** but with colour changed.
404 **168** 7k. blue 25 25

2003. Easter.
405 **212** 7k. multicoloured 25 25

213 Kremnica (town) **214** St. Cyril

2003.
406 **213** 18k. black and orange . . 60 60

2003. 25th Anniv of Slovak Ecclesiastical Province. Sheet 166 × 105 mm containing T **214** and similar vert design.
MS407 17k. black, lemon and ochre; 22k. black, lemon and blue . . 1·30 1·30
DESIGNS: 17k. Type **214**; 22k. St. Metod.

215 Ludwig van Beethoven (composer and musician)

2003.
408 **215** 15k. multicoloured . . . 50 50

216 Bouquet

2003. Greetings Stamp.
409 **216** 7k. multicoloured 25 25

217 Milan Stefanik

2003. Milan Rastislav Stefanik Commemoration (founder of Czechoslovakia).
410 **217** 14k. black, blue and red 45 45

218 Don Juan Poster (Vladislav Rostoka) **219** St. Benedict and St. Andrej Svorad

2003. Europa. Poster Art.
411 **218** 14k. black, red and pink 45 45

2003. Art (12th series). As T **53**. Multicoloured.
412 18k. multicoloured 60 60
DESIGN: 18k. "The Brook by the Barn" (Ladislav Mednansky) (horiz).

2003. St. Benedict and St. Andrej Svorad.
413 **219** 13k. black, yellow and orange 45 45

220 Team Members

2003. Slovakia, World Ice Hockey Championship Bronze Medallists, Finland 2003.
414 **220** 20k. multicoloured . . . 65 65

221 Matko and Kubko (L. Capek)
222 Wild Cat

2003. International Children's Day. Characters from book by Marianna Grznarova.
415 **221** 7k. multicoloured 25 25

2003. Endangered Species. Wild Cat (*Felis silvestris*). Sheet 158 × 103 mm containing T **222** and similar vert designs. Multicoloured.
MS416 13k. Type **222**; 14k. Wild cat with bird; 16k. Two wild cats; 18k. Wild cat (different) . . . . . 2·10 2·10

223 Martina Moravcova (world champion swimmer)
225 "Palculienka" (Jana Kiselova-Sitekova)

224 Lake Klinger

2003. World Swimming Championships, Barcelona.
417 **223** 11k. multicoloured . . . 35 35

2003. UNESCO World Heritage Site. Banska Stiavnica. Multicoloured.
418 9k. Type **224** 30 30
419 12k. Lake Rozgrund 40 40

2003. 19th Biennial Exhibition of Book Illustrations for Children, Bratislava.
420 **225** 12k. multicoloured . . . 40 40

NEWSPAPER STAMPS

1939. Nos. of Czechoslovakia optd **1939 SLOVENSKY STAT.**
N25 2h. brown 20 30
N26 5h. blue 20 30
N27 7h. red 20 30
N28 9h. green 20 30
N29 10h. red 20 30
N30 12h. blue 20 30
N31 20h. green 40 60
N32 50h. brown . . . . 1·25 1·50
N33 1k. green . . . . 4·50 7·00

N 7
N 29 Printer's Type

1939. Imperf.
N40 **N 7** 2h. brown 10 10
N65 5h. blue 10 25
N42 7h. red 10 25
N43 9h. green 10 25
N66 10h. red 10 10
N45 12h. blue 70 75
N67 15h. purple 15 10
N68 20h. green 30 50
N69 25h. blue 30 50
N70 40h. red 30 50
N71 50h. brown 55 60
N72 1k. green 55 60
N73 2k. green . . . . 1·00 1·10

1943. Imperf.
N101 **N 29** 10h. green 10 10
N102 15h. brown 10 10
N103 20h. blue 10 10
N104 50h. red 10 10
N105 1k. green 25 30
N106 2k. blue 45 50

PERSONAL DELIVERY STAMPS

P 17

1940. Imperf.
P65 **P 17** 50h. blue . . . . 45 1·25
P66 50h. red . . . . 45 1·25

POSTAGE DUE STAMPS

D 13
D 24

1939.
D51 **D 13** 5h. blue 20 40
D52 10h. blue 20 35
D53 20h. blue 20 35
D54 30h. blue . . . . 1·00 1·40
D55 40h. blue 35 40
D56 50h. blue 35 60
D57 60h. blue 35 65
D58 1k. red 40 65
D59 2k. red . . . . 5·00 5·00
D60 5k. red . . . . 1·10 1·75
D61 10k. red . . . . 1·00 1·75
D62 20k. red . . . . 6·00 6·00

1942.
D 89 **D 24** 10h. brown 10 10
D 90 20h. brown 10 10
D 91 40h. brown 10 10
D 92 50h. brown 45 45
D 93 60h. brown 10 10
D 94 80h. brown 10 10
D 95 1k. red 10 10
D 96 1k.10 red 25 40
D 97 1k.30 red 20 10
D 98 1k.60 red 25 10
D 99 2k. red 30 10
D100 2k.60 red 60 60
D101 3k.50 red . . . . . . 3·75 5·25
D102 5k. red . . . . 1·40 1·50
D103 10k. red . . . . . . 1·75 2·00

SLOVENIA Pt. 3

Formerly part of Austria, in 1918 Slovenia was combined with other areas to form Yugoslavia. Separate stamps were issued during the Second World War whilst under Italian and German Occupation. In 1991 Slovenia seceded and became an independent state.

1941. 100 paras = 1 dinar.
1991. 100 stotinas = 1 tolar.

ITALIAN OCCUPATION, 1941

1941. Nos. 330/1 and 414/26 of Yugoslavia optd **Co. Ci.**
1 **99** 25p. black 30 50
2 50p. orange 30 50
3 1d. green 30 50
4 1d.50 red 30 50
5 2d. red 30 50
6 3d. brown 30 50
7 4d. blue 30 50
8 5d. blue 30 50
9 5d.50 violet 30 50
10 6d. blue 50 50
11 8d. brown 50 75
12 **70** 10d. violet 35 75
13 **99** 12d. violet . . . . 1·00 75
14 **70** 15d. olive £100 £120
15 **99** 16d. purple . . . . 1·00 1·00
16 20d. blue . . . . 3·00 3·50
17 30d. pink . . . . 15·00 18·00

1941. Nos. 330 and 414/26 of Yugoslavia optd **R.Commissariato Civile Territori Sloveni occupati LUBIANA**, with four lines of dots at foot.
23 **99** 25p. black 30 50
24 50p. orange 30 50
25 1d. green 30 50
26 1d.50 red 30 50
27 2d. red 30 50
28 3d. brown 30 50
29 4d. blue 30 50
30 5d. blue 60 65
31 5d.50 violet 35 65
32 6d. blue 35 65
33 8d. brown 35 65
34 **70** 10d. violet . . . . 1·50 1·25
35 **99** 12d. violet 50 65
36 16d. purple . . . . 1·25 1·25
37 20d. blue . . . . 2·50 2·75
38 30d. pink . . . . 30·00 24·00

1941. Nos. 446/9 of Yugoslavia optd as Nos. 23/38 but with only three lines of dots at foot.
45 50p.+50p. on 5d. violet . . . 4·00 5·00
46 1d.+1d. on 10d. lake . . . . 4·00 5·00
47 1d.50+1d.50 on 20d. green . . 4·00 5·00
48 2d.+2d. on 30d. blue . . . . 4·00 5·00

1941. Air. Nos. 360/7 and 443/4 of Yugoslavia optd as Nos. 23/38, with three or four (No. 57) lines of dots at foot.
49 50p. brown . . . . 1·10 2·00
50 1d. green . . . . 1·10 2·00
51 2d. blue . . . . 1·25 2·00
52 2d.50 red . . . . 1·25 2·00
53 5d. violet . . . . 3·00 3·00
54 10d. lake . . . . 3·00 3·00
55 20d. green . . . . 14·00 15·00
56 30d. blue . . . . 30·00 30·00
57 40d. green . . . . 70·00 80·00
58 50d. blue . . . . 70·00 70·00

1941. Nos. 26 and 29 surch.
59 **99** 0d.50 on 1d.50 red 25 35
60 0d.50 on 1d.50 red £400 £650
61 1d. on 4d. blue 25 35

POSTAGE DUE STAMPS

1941. Postage Due stamps of Yugoslavia, Nos. D89/93 optd Co. Ci.
D18 **D 56** 50p. violet 35 50
D19 1d. mauve 35 50
D20 2d. blue 35 50
D21 5d. orange . . . . . . 4·00 3·75
D22 10d. brown . . . . . . 4·00 3·75

Optd as Nos. 23/38, but with four lines of dots at top.
D40 **D 56** 50p. violet 30 50
D41 1d. mauve 30 50
D42 2d. blue 60 75
D43 5d. orange . . . . . . 16·00 18·00
D44 10d. brown . . . . . . 7·00 8·00

Optd as Nos. D40/44, but with narrower lettering.
D62 **D 56** 50p. violet 65 90
D63 1d. mauve . . . . . . 1·00 1·50
D64 2d. blue . . . . 12·50 16·00

GERMAN OCCUPATION, 1943–45

(3)
(4)

1944. Stamps of Italy optd with Types **3** or **4**. (a) On Postage stamps of 1929.
65 **4** 5c. brown . . . . 20 1·10
66 **3** 10c. brown . . . . 20 1·10
67 **4** 15c. green . . . . 20 1·10
68 **3** 20c. red . . . . 20 1·10
69 **4** 25c. green . . . . 20 1·10
70 **3** 30c. brown . . . . 20 1·10
71 **4** 35c. blue . . . . 35 1·10
72 **3** 50c. violet . . . . 35 1·75
73 **4** 75c. red . . . . 30 2·40
74 **3** 1l. violet . . . . 30 2·40
75 **4** 1l.25 blue . . . . 30 1·40
76 **3** 1l.75 orange . . . . 1·00 11·50
77 **4** 2l. red . . . . 30 2·50
78 **3** 10l. violet . . . . 5·50 35·00

Surch with new value.
79 – 2l.55 on 5c. brown . . . . . 85 6·00
80 **4** 5l. on 25c. green . . . . . 85 8·00
81 20l. on 20c. red . . . . . 4·75 40·00
82 **3** 25l. on 2l. red . . . . . . 5·50 85·00
83 **4** 50l. on 1l.75 orange . . . . 15·00 £130
In No. 79 the overprint inscriptions are at each side of the eagle.

(b) On Air stamps, Nos. 270, etc.
84 **4** 25c. green . . . . 3·00 17·00
85 **3** 50c. brown . . . . 5·25 70·00
86 **4** 75c. brown . . . . 2·75 23·00
87 **3** 1l. violet . . . . 6·25 70·00
88 **4** 2l. blue . . . . 4·00 60·00
89 **3** 5l. green . . . . 4·00 70·00
90 **4** 10l. red . . . . 3·25 60·00

(c) On Air Express stamp.
E91 **3** 2l. black (No. E370) . . . . 6·25 60·00

(d) On Express Letter stamp.
E92 **3** 1l.25 green (No. E350) . . . 2·00 10·00

1944. Red Cross. Express Letter stamps of Italy surch as Types **3** or **4** with a red cross and new value alongside.
102 **E 132** 1l.25+50l. green . . . . 15·00 £325
103 2l.50+50l. orange . . . 15·00 £325

1944. Homeless Relief Fund. Express Letter stamps of Italy surch as Types **3** and **4**, but in circular frame, and **BREZDOMCEM DEN OBDACHLOSEN** alongside with new value between.
104 **E 132** 1l.25+50l. green . . . . 15·00 £325
105 2l.50+50l. orange . . . 15·00 £325

1944. Air. Orphans' Fund. Air stamps of Italy Nos. 270, etc., surch as Types **3** and **4**, but in circular frame between **DEN WAISEN SIROTAM** and new value.
106 – 25c.+10l. green . . . . . 8·00 £200
107 **110** 50c.+10l. brown . . . . . 8·00 £200
108 – 75c.+20l. brown . . . . . 8·00 £200
109 – 1l.+20l. violet . . . . . . 8·00 £200
110 **113** 2l.+20l. blue . . . . . . 8·00 £200
111 **110** 5l.+20l. green . . . . . . 8·00 £200

1944. Air. Winter Relief Fund. Air stamps of Italy Nos. 270, etc., surch as Types **3** and **4**, but between **ZIMSKA POMOC WINTERHILFE** and new value.
112 – 25c.+10l. green . . . . . 8·00 £200
113 **110** 50c.+10l. brown . . . . . 8·00 £200
114 – 75c.+20l. brown . . . . . 8·00 £200
115 – 1l.+20l. violet . . . . . . 8·00 £200
116 **113** 2l.+20l. blue . . . . . . 8·00 £200
117 **110** 5l.+20l. green . . . . . . 8·00 £200

9 Railway Viaduct, Borovnice
10 Church in Novo Mesto

1945. Inscr "PROVINZ LAIBACH".
118 – 5c. brown . . . . 35 2·40
119 – 10c. orange . . . . 35 2·40
120 **9** 20c. brown . . . . 35 2·40
121 – 25c. green . . . . 35 2·40
122 **10** 50c. violet . . . . 35 2·40
123 – 75c. red . . . . 35 2·40
124 – 1l. green . . . . 35 2·40
125 – 1l.25 blue . . . . 35 5·25
126 – 1l.50 green . . . . 35 5·25
127 – 2l. blue . . . . 60 6·50
128 – 2l.50 brown . . . . 60 6·50
129 – 3l. mauve . . . . 95 12·00
130 – 5l. brown . . . . 1·25 12·00
131 – 10l. green . . . . 2·25 60·00
132 – 20l. blue . . . . 11·00 £160
133 – 30l. red . . . . 55·00 £700
DESIGNS—VERT: 5c. Stalagmites, Krizna Jama; 1l.25, Kocevje; 1l.50, Borovnice Falls; 3l. Castle, Zuzemberg; 30l. View and Tabor Church. HORIZ: 10c. Zirknitz Lake; 25c. Farm near Ljubljana; 75c. View from Ribnica; 1l. Old Castle, Ljubljana; 2l. Castle, Kostanjevica; 2l.50, Castle, Turjak; 5l. View on River Krka; 10l. Castle, Otocec; 20l. Farm at Dolenjskom.

POSTAGE DUE STAMPS

(D 5)
(D 6)

1944. Postage Due stamps of Italy, Nos. D395, etc., optd as Type **D 5**.
D93 **D 141** 5c. brown . . . . . 1·10 50·00
D94 10c. blue . . . . . 1·10 50·00
D95 20c. red . . . . . . 35 1·40
D96 25c. green . . . . . 35 1·40
D97 50c. violet . . . . . 30 1·40
D98 **D 142** 1l. orange . . . . . 1·00 60·00
D99. 2l. green . . . . . 1·00 60·00

Surch as Type **D 6**.
D100 **D 141** 30c. on 50c. violet . . 50 1·40
D101 40c. on 5c. brown . . 50 1·40

INDEPENDENT STATE

11 Parliament Building
12 Arms

1991. Declaration of Independence.
134 **11** 5d. multicoloured 75 60

1991.
135 **12** 1t. multicoloured 10 10
136 4t. multicoloured 15 15
137 5t. multicoloured 20 15
138 11t. multicoloured 45 40

13 Ski Jumping

1992. Winter Olympic Games, Albertville. Multicoloured.
139 30t. Type **13** 90 90
140 50t. Slalom . . . . 1·60 1·60

14 Arms
15 Opera House

1992. Multicoloured, background colours given.
141 **14** 1t. brown 10 10
142 2t. purple 10 10
143 4t. green 15 15

144 5t. red 20 15
145 6t. yellow 30 20
146 11t. orange 35 25
147 15t. blue 40 30
148 20t. violet 65 50
149 50t. green . . . . 1·00 85
150 100t. grey . . . . 2·25 1·90

1992. Centenary of Ljubljana Opera House.
155 **15** 20t. multicoloured 60 60

16 Tartini and Violins

1992. 300th Birth Anniv of Giuseppe Tartini (violinist and composer).
156 **16** 27t. multicoloured 70 70

17 Map and Marko Anton Kappus preaching to Amerindians

18

1992. 500th Anniv of Discovery of America by Columbus. Multicoloured.
157 27t. Type **17** . . . . 1·00 1·00
158 47t. Map and "Santa Maria" 1·75 1·75

1992. Obligatory Tax. Red Cross.
159 **18** 3t. black, red and blue . . 50 40

19 Collapsible Chair by Niko Kralj and Map

1992. 17th World Industrial Design Congress, Ljubljana.
160 **19** 41t. multicoloured 85 65

20 Slomsek

1992. 130th Death Anniv of Anton Slomsek, Bishop of Maribor.
161 **20** 41t. multicoloured 20 20

21 Wreckage

22 Rescuing Mountaineer

1992. Obligatory Tax. Solidarity Week. Perf and imperf.
162 **21** 3t. brown, black and red 40 30

1992. 80th Anniv of Alpine Rescue Service.
164 **22** 41t. multicoloured 80 70

23 River Jousting

24 Linden Leaf and Flowers

1992. 900th Anniv of River Jousting in Ljubljana.
165 **23** 6t. multicoloured 20 20

1992. 1st Anniv of Independence.
166 **24** 41t. multicoloured 70 70

25 Leon Stukelj and Medals

1992. Olympic Games, Barcelona. Multicoloured.
167 40t. Type **25** 85 85
168 46t. Head of Apoxymenos repeated in three Slovene colours . . . . 1·25 1·25

26 Sheepdog

1992. "Psov '92" World Dog-training Championships, Ljubljana.
169 **26** 40t. multicoloured 80 80

27 Hand crushing Cigarettes

28 Kogoj and scene from "Black Masks" (opera)

1992. Obligatory Tax. Red Cross. Anti-smoking Week.
170 **27** 3t. multicoloured 35 20

1992. Birth Centenary of Marij Kogoj (composer).
171 **28** 40t. multicoloured 75 75

29 Langus (self-portrait)

1992. Birth Bicentenary of Matevz Langus (painter).
172 **29** 40t. multicoloured 75 75

30 Nativity

1992. Christmas. Multicoloured.
173 6t. Type **30** 10 10
174 7t. Type **30** 15 15
175 41t. "Madonna and Child" (stained-glass window by V. Sorli-Puc in St. Mary's Church, Bovec) (vert) . . . 85 75

31 Potocnik, View of Earth from Space and Satellite

1992. Birth Centenary of Herman Potocnik (space flight pioneer).
176 **31** 46t. multicoloured 85 85

32 Illustration from "Solzice"

1993. Birth Centenary of Prezihov Voranc (writer).
177 **32** 7t. multicoloured 15 15

33 "Underneath the Birches"

1993. 50th Death Anniv of Rihard Jakopic (painter).
178 **33** 44t. multicoloured 70 70

34 Bust of Stefan (J. Savinsek)

35 Honey-cake from Skofja Loka

1993. Death Centenary of Jozef Stefan (physicist).
179 **34** 51t. multicoloured 80 80

1993. Slovene Culture.
180 **35** 1t. brown, ochre & dp brn 10 10
181 – 2t. green and light green 10 10
182 – 5t. dp grey, grey & mauve 10 10
183 – 6t. lt green, green & yellow 10 10
184 – 7t. red, crimson and grey 10 10
185 – 8t. green, dp green & olive 10 10
186 – 9t. red, brown and grey 15 10
187 – 10t. brown and light brown 15 10
188 – 11t. green, lt green & yell 15 10
189 – 12t. red, orange and grey 15 10
189 a – 13t. green, black & dp grn 15 10
189 b – 14t. red, brown and grey 20 10
189 c – 15t. black, drab and red 10 10
189 d – 16t. brown, blue and orange 15 10
189 e – 17t. chocolate, yellow & brn 20 10
189 f – 18t. brown, black and blue 25 10
190 – 20t. green and grey . . . 35 25
191 – 44t. blue, dp blue & blk 50 35
192 – 50t. purple and mauve 65 45
193 – 55t. black, grey & orge 45 30
194 – 65t. ochre, brown & pink 55 35
195 – 70t. grey, brown and green 65 45
196 – 75t. green, blue and lilac 65 45
197 – 80t. multicoloured . . . 70 45
197 a – 90t. brown, red and grey 75 50
198 – 100t. brown, red & lt brn . . . . 1·00 85
198 a – 300t. chestnut and brown . . . . 2·75 1·90
198ab – 200t. purple, green and blue . . . . 1·40 1·40
198 b – 400t. red and brown . . 3·75 2·50
198 c – 500t. violet, orge & grey 3·25 3·25

DESIGNS: 2t. Reed pipes; 5t. Double hay-drying frame; 6t. Shepherd's hut, Velika Planina; 7t. Zither; 8t. Mill on the Mur; 9t. Sledge; 10t. Earthenware double-bass; 11t. Hay basket; 12t. Boy on horse (statuette), Ribnica; 13t. Wind-operated bird-scarer, Prlekija; 14t. Hen-shaped wine jug, Sentjernej; 15t. Blast furnace, Zelezniki; 16t. Windmill, Stari, Gori; 17t. Maize store, Ptujskopolje; 18t. Accordion, Kranjska Gora; 20t. Farmhouse, Prekmurje; 44t. House, Karst; 50t. Wind-propelled pump, Secovlje salt-pans; 55t. Easter eggs, Bela Krajina; 65t. Lamp, Trzic; 70t. Ski; 75t. Wrought iron window lattice; 80t. Palm Sunday bundle, Ljubljana; 90t. Apiary; 100t. Nut cake; 200t. Bootjack in shape of stag beetle; 300t. Straw sculpture; 400t. Wine press; 500t. Decorated table.

36 Mountains and Founder Members

1993. Centenary of Alpine Association.
199 **36** 7t. multicoloured 15 15

37 Cop's Route up Triglav

38 Chainbreaker (1919 stamp design)

1993. Birth Centenary of Joza Cop (climber and mountain rescuer).
200 **37** 44t. multicoloured 70 70

1993. 75th Anniv of Slovenian Postal Service.
201 **38** 7t. multicoloured 15 15

39 "St. Nicholas" (altar painting, Tintoretto)

40 "Table in Pompeii" (Marij Pregelj)

1993. 500th Anniv of College Chapter of Novo Mesto. Multicoloured.
202 7t. Type **39** 15 15
203 44t. Arms 65 65

1993. Europa. Contemporary Art. Multicoloured.
204 44t. Type **40** . . . . 1·00 60
205 159t. "Girl with Toy" (Gabrijel Stupica) . . . . 2·75 2·10

41 "Schwagerina carniolica"

42

1993. Fossils.
206 **41** 44t. multicoloured 65 65

1993. Obligatory Tax. Red Cross.
207 **42** 3t.50 black, red and blue 10 10

43 6th-century B.C. Vase

44 Red Cross Rescue Workers

1993. 1st Anniv of Admission to United Nations Organization.
208 **43** 62t. multicoloured 85 85

1993. Obligatory Tax. Solidarity Week.
209 **44** 3t.50 multicoloured 10 10

45 Basketball, Johann and Swimming

1993. Mediterranean Games, Roussillon (Languedoc).
210 **45** 36t. multicoloured 50 50

46 "Battle of Sisak" (Johann Valvasor)

1993. 400th Anniv of Battle of Sisak.
211 **46** 49t. multicoloured 65 65

47 "Monolistra spinosissima"

1993. Cave Fauna. Multicoloured.
212 7t. Type **47** 15 15
213 40t. "Aphaenopidius kamnikensis" (insect) . . . 50 50
214 55t. "Proteus anguinus" . . . 70 70
215 65t. "Zospeum spelaeum" (mollusc) 90 90

48 Horse and Diagram of Movements — **49** Boy smoking and Emblem

1993. European Dressage Championships, Lipica.
216 **48** 65t. multicoloured 85 85

1993. Obligatory Tax. Red Cross. Anti-smoking Week.
217 **49** 4t.50 multicoloured 10 10

50 Valvasor Arms

1993. 300th Anniversaries.
218 **50** 9t. black, lilac and gold . . 15 15
219 – 65t. black, stone and gold 75 75
DESIGN: 9t. Type **50** (death anniv of Johann Valvasor (historian)); 65t. Arms of Academia Operosorum.

51 "Slovenian Family at Christmas Crib" (M. Gaspari)

1993. Christmas. Multicoloured.
220 9t. Type **51** 15 15
221 65t. Dr. Joze Pogacnik (archbishop) (after B. Jakac) and seal 75 75

52 Illustration from "The Vagabond" — **53** Hearts

1994. 150th Anniversaries. Multicoloured.
222 8t. Type **52** (birth anniv of Josip Juncic (writer)) . . . 10 10
223 9t. Nightingale and bridge over river (birth anniv of Simon Gregorcic, poet) . . 15 15
224 55t. Book showing Slovenian vowels (birth anniv of Stanislav Skrabec, philologist) 80 80
225 65t. Cover of grammar book (death anniv of Jernei Kopitar, philologist) . . . 90 90

1994. Greetings Stamp.
226 **53** 9t. multicoloured 15 15

54 Cross-country Skiing

1994. Winter Olympic Games, Lillehammer, Norway. Multicoloured.
227 9t. Type **54** 15 15
228 65t. Slalom skiing 75 75

55 Ski Jumping

1994. 60th Anniv of Ski Jumping Championships, Planica.
229 **55** 70t. multicoloured 80 80

56 Town Names

1994. 850th Anniv of First Official Record of Ljubljana.
230 **56** 9t. multicoloured 15 15

57 Janez Puhar and Camera

1994. Europa. Discoveries and Inventions. Multicoloured.
231 70t. Type **57** (invention of glass-plate photography) 75 75
232 215t. Moon, natural logarithm diagram and Jurij Vega (mathematician) 2·50 2·50

58 Balloons

1994. Obligatory Tax. Red Cross.
233 **58** 4t.50 multicoloured 10 10

59 "Primula carniolica"

1994. Flowers. Multicoloured.
234 9t. Type **59** 10 10
235 44t. "Hladnikia pastinacifolia" 50 50
236 60t. "Daphne blagayana" . . 70 70
237 70t. "Campanula zoysii" . . 95 95

60 Red Cross Worker with Child — **61** Inflating "Globe" Football

1994. Obligatory Tax. Solidarity Week.
238 **60** 4t.50 multicoloured 10 10

1994. World Cup Football Championship, U.S.A.
239 **61** 44t. multicoloured 50 50

62 Globes in Olympic Colours and Flags — **63** Mt. Ojstrica

1994. Centenary of International Olympic Committee.
240 **62** 100t. multicoloured . . . . 1·25 1·25

1994.
241 **63** 12t. multicoloured 20 20

64 Maks Pletersnik (compiler) and University of Laibach Professors

1994. Centenary of First Slovenian–German Dictionary.
242 **64** 70t. multicoloured 85 85

65 Roman Infantry

1994. 1600th Anniv of Battle of Frigidus.
243 **65** 60t. red, black and grey . . 70 70

66 Post Office

1994. Centenary of Maribor Post Office.
244 **66** 70t. multicoloured 80 80

67 Series kkStB Steam Locomotive No. 5722

1994. Centenary of Ljubljana Railway.
245 **67** 70t. multicoloured . . . . 1·25 1·25

68 Orchestra Venue and Music

1994. Bicentenary of Ljubljana Philharmonic Society. Multicoloured.
246 12t. Type **68** 15 15
247 70t. Ludwig van Beethoven, Johannes Brahms, Antonin Dvorak and Joseph Haydn (composers) and Niccolo Paganini (violinist) 75 75

69 Christmas Tree, Window and Candles — **70** "Madonna and Child" (statue, Loreto Basilica)

1994. Christmas and International Year of the Family.
248 **69** 12t. multicoloured 15 15
249 – 70t. cream, black and blue 75 75
DESIGN: 70t. "Children with Christmas Tree" (F. Kralj) and I.Y.F. emblem.

1994. 700th Anniv of Loreto.
250 **70** 70t. multicoloured 80 80

71 Ivan Hribar, Mihajlo Rostohar and Danilo Majaron (founders) and University

1994. 75th Anniv of Ljubljana University.
251 **71** 70t. multicoloured 80 80

72 Postal Emblem — **73** Lili Novy (writer, 110th birth)

1995.
252 **72** 13t. multicoloured 15 15

1995. Anniversaries.
253 **73** 20t. red, black and grey . . 25 25
254 – 70t. yellow, black and gold 85 85
255 – 70t. multicoloured 85 85
DESIGNS—HORIZ: No. 253, Silhouettes of figures and signature of Anton Tomasz Linhart (dramatist, death bicentenary). VERT: No. 255, Detail of facade of Zadruzna Co-operative Bank, Ljubljana (110th birth anniv (1994) of Ivan Vurnik (architect)).

74 Cats and Hearts (Jure Kos) — **75** Allegory

1995. Greetings Stamp.
256 **74** 20t. multicoloured 30 30

1995. 50th Anniv of End of Second World War.

257 **75** 13t. multicoloured 15 15

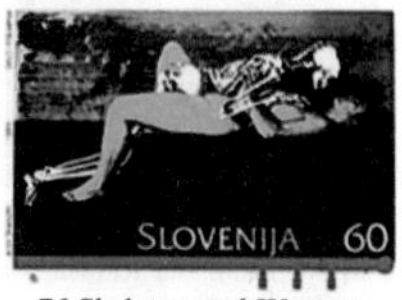

76 Skeleton and Woman

1995. Europa. Peace and Freedom. Multicoloured.

258 60t. Type **76** (50th anniv of liberation of concentration camps) 75 75

259 70t. Woman running free . . 1·00 1·00

77 "Karavankina schellwieni"

1995. Fossils.

260 **77** 70t. multicoloured 90 90

78 Alpine Iris, Triglav National Park and Alpine Poppy

1995. European Nature Conservation Year.

261 **78** 70t. multicoloured 80 80

79 Child painting Red Cross

80 First Aiders tending Casualty

1995. Obligatory Tax. Red Cross.

262 **79** 6t. multicoloured 10 10

1995. Obligatory Tax. Solidarity Week.

263 **80** 6t.50 multicoloured 10 10

81 Lesser Kestrel

1995. Birds. Multicoloured.

264 13t. Type **81** 25 25

265 60t. European roller 90 90

266 70t. Lesser grey shrike . . . 1·10 1·10

267 215t. Black-headed bunting 2·50 2·50

82 Radovljica

1995. 500th Anniv of Radovljica.

268 **82** 44t. multicoloured 60 60

83 Class KRB 37 Steam Locomotive "Podnart"

1995. 125th Anniv of Ljubljana–Jesenice Railway.

269 **83** 70t. black, red and yellow 1·10 1·10

84 Mountain and Presbytery

1995. Centenary of Jakob Aljaz Presbytery, Mount Triglav.

270 **84** 100t. blue, black and red 1·40 1·40

85 Scouts around Campfire

1995. Scouting.

271 **85** 70t. multicoloured 90 90

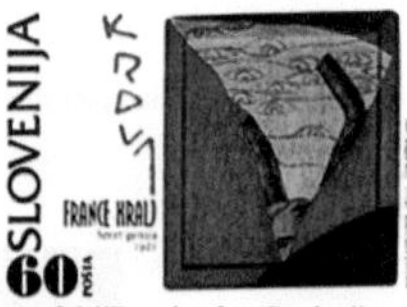

86 "Death of a Genius"

1995. Birth Centenary of France Kralz (artist). Multicoloured.

272 60t. Type **86** 75 75

273 70t. "Family of Horses" . . 85 85

87 Handshake, Anniversary Emblem and Different Nationalities

88 "Winter" (Marlenka Stupica)

1995. 50th Anniversaries of U.N.O. (274) and F.A.O. (275). Multicoloured.

274 70t. Type **87** 85 85

275 70t. Foodstuffs, anniversary emblem and different nationalities 85 85

1995. Christmas. Paintings. Multicoloured.

276 13t. Type **88** 20 20

277 70t. "Madonna and Child" (Leopold Layer) 80 80

89 Birds and Heart (Karmen Podgornik)

1996. Greetings Stamp.

278 **89** 13t. multicoloured 20 15

90 Swimming

1996. The European Pond Turtle. Multicoloured.

279 13t. Type **90** 25 25

280 50t. On bank 70 70

281 60t. In water 80 80

282 70t. Pair of turtles climbing up bank 95 95

91 Ptujsko Polje

1996. Masked Costumes. Multicoloured.

283 13t. Type **91** 20 20

284 70t. Dravsko Polje 80 80

92 Steam Locomotive "Aussee"

1996. 150th Anniv of Slovenian Railways.

285 **92** 70t. multicoloured . . . . 1·10 1·10

93 Fran Finzgar (writer)

1996. Birth Anniversaries. Multicoloured.

286 13t. Type **93** (125th anniv) 10 10

287 100t. Ita Rina (actress) (89th anniv) . . . . 1·25 1·25

94 Child feeding Birds and Children of different Nationalities

95 "Vase of Dahlias"

1996. 50th Anniv of UNICEF.

288 **94** 65t. multicoloured 70 70

1996. Europa. Famous Women. 70th Death Anniv of Ivana Koblica (painter). Multicoloured.

289 65t. "Children in the Grass" (detail) 75 75

290 75t. Type **95** 85 85

96 Pope John Paul II

97 Anniversary Emblem

1996. Papal Visit.

291 **96** 75t. multicoloured 85 85

MS292 60×90 mm. **96** 200t. multicoloured . . . . 2·10 2·10

1996. Obligatory Tax. 130th Anniv of Slovenian Red Cross.

293 **97** 7t. multicoloured 10 10

98 Clasped Hands

1996. Obligatory Tax. Solidarity Week.

294 **98** 7t. multicoloured 10 10

99 Gallenberg Castle

1996. 700th Anniv of Zagorje ob Savi.

295 **99** 24t. multicoloured 25 25

100 Cyclists

1996. World Youth Cycling Championships, Novo Mesto.

296 **100** 55t. multicoloured 55 55

101 Stars over Mountains

103 Rowing and Canoeing

102 Chanterelle (*Cantharellus cibarius*)

1996. 5th Anniv of Independence.

297 **101** 75t. multicoloured 75 75

1996. Fungi. Sheet 114 × 90 mm containing T **102** and similar horiz designs. Multicoloured.

MS298 65t. Type **102**; 75t. *Boletus aestivalis* . . . . 1·50 1·50

1996. Centenary of Modern Olympic Games and Olympic Games, Atlanta. Multicoloured.

299 75t. Type **103** 75 75

300 100t. High jumping and hurdling . . . . 1·00 1·00

104 Corner

106 Cave

105 "Moscon Family"

1996. Traditional Lace Designs from Idria.

301 **104** 1t. brown 10 10

302 – 1t. brown 10 10

303 – 2t. red 10 10

304 – 2t. red 10 10

305 – 5t. blue 10 10

306 – 5t. blue 10 10

307 – 10t. mauve 10 10

308 – 10t. mauve 10 10

309 – 12t. green 15 15

310 – 12t. green 15 15

311 – 13t. red 15 15

312 – 13t. red 15 15

313 – 20t. violet 15 15

314 – 20t. violet 15 15

315 – 44t. blue 30 30

316 – 44t. blue 30 30

317 – 50t. purple 50 50

318 – 50t. purple 50 50

325 – 100t. brown 70 70

326 – 100t. brown 70 70

DESIGNS: No. 302, Corner (different); 303, Rounded collar incorporating scrolls; 304, Pointed collar with scalloped edging; 305, Flowers and leaves forming circular design; 306, Framed rose; 307, Oval with flower in centre; 308, "Q"-shaped with trefoil in centre; 309, Flower; 310, Diamond with flower in centre; 311, Square enclosing diamonds containing "flowers"; 312, Square containing circular motifs; 313, Butterfly; 314, Diamond; 315, Square; 316, Circle; 317, Heart-shaped edging; 318, Ornate edging; 325, Leaf; 326, Insect.

1996. 130th Death Anniv of Jozef Tominc (painter).
331 **105** 65t. multicoloured 60 60

1996. UNESCO World Heritage Sites. Skocjan Cave.
332 **106** 55t. multicoloured 50 50

107 Gimbals

1996. 250th Anniv of Novo Mesto School.
333 **107** 55t. multicoloured 50 50

108 Heart

109 Post Office Building, Ljubljana, and Doves carrying Letter

1996. Centenary of Modern Cardiology.
334 **108** 12t. red, brown and cream 15 15

1996. Centenary of Post and Telecommunications Office.
335 **109** 100t. multicoloured . . . 90 90

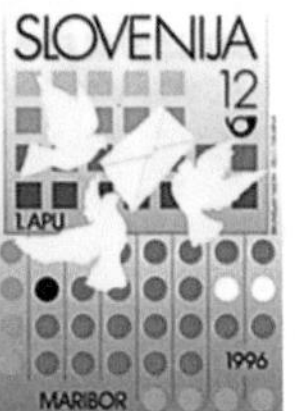

110 Doves carrying Letter and Stylized Letter Sorting

1996. Introduction of Automatic Letter Sorting.
336 **110** 12t. black, red and orange 15 15

111 Children and Christmas Tree on Sledge

1996. Christmas. Multicoloured.
337 12t. Type **111** 15 15
338 65t. "Adoration of the Wise Men" (Stefan Subic) . . . 55 55

112 Cupids

1997. Greeting Stamp.
339 **112** 15t. multicoloured 15 15

113 Mt. Sneznik

1997.
340 **113** 20t. multicoloured 15 15

114 "Ta Terjast"

1997. Masked Costumes. Multicoloured.
341 20r. Type **114** 15 15
342 80r. "Pust" 70 70

115 Marbled Trout

1997. Fishes. Multicoloured.
343 12t. Type **115** 10 10
344 13t. Streber 10 10
345 80t. Zahrte 70 70
346 90t. European mudminnow 75 75
MS347 113 × 79 mm. As Nos. 343/6 but with inscriptions rearranged and fishes enlarged (tails in margin) . . . . 1·60 1·60

116 The Golden Horns

1997. Europa. Tales and Legends.
348 **116** 80t. multicoloured 70 70

117 Wulfenite

1997. Minerals.
349 **117** 80t. multicoloured 70 70

118 Brick

1997. Red Cross.
350 **118** 7t. multicoloured 10 10

119 Matija Cop (scholar)

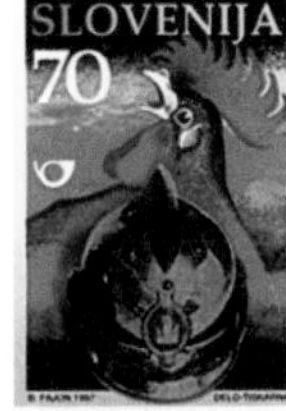

120 Cockerel and Fireman's Helmet

1997. Birth Anniversaries. Multicoloured.
351 13t. Type **119** (bicentenary) 10 10
352 24t. Ziga Zois (naturalist, 250th) 20 20
353 80t. Skof Baraga (missionary, bicentenary) 70 70

1997. Fire Service.
354 **120** 70t. multicoloured 60 60

121 Series SZ Steam Locomotive

1997. 140th Anniv of Ljubljana–Trieste Railway.
355 **121** 80t. black, yellow and red 70 70

124 Girl with Dog (Andrejka Cufer)

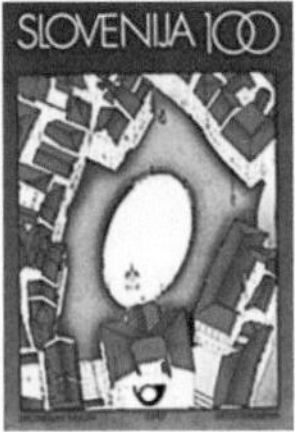

123 Centre of Piran

122 Red Cross

1997. Obligatory Tax. Solidarity Week.
356 **122** 7t. multicoloured 10 10

1997. European Summit, Piran. Sheet 134 × 115 mm containing T **123** and similar vert designs. Multicoloured.
MS357 100t. Type **123**; 200t. Arms of participating states . . . . 2·50 2·50

1997. Children's Week.
358 **124** 14t. multicoloured 10 10

125 "The Shy Lover"

1997. Birth Centenary of France Gorse (sculptor). Multicoloured.
359 70t. Type **125** 50 50
360 80t. "The Farmer's Wife" . . 55 55

126 Judo Bout

127 Venezia Guilia and Istria 1945 Stamp, Anchor and Rose

1997. European Youth Judo Championships, Ljubljana.
361 **126** 90t. multicoloured 65 65

1997. 50th Anniv of Incorporation of Istria and Slovene Coast into Yugoslavia.
362 **127** 50t. multicoloured 40 40

128 Children watching Birds

1997. Christmas and New Year. Multicoloured.
363 14t. Type **128** 10 10
364 90t. Crib (Liza Hribar), Church of the Blessed Virgin, Krope 65 65

129 Globe, Golden Vixen and Skier

130 Dove, Envelope and Postal Centre

1997. World Cup Alpine Skiing Championships.
365 **129** 90t. multicoloured 65 65

1997. Inauguration of New Postal Centre, Ljubljana.
366 **130** 30t. multicoloured 20 20

131 Guests and Attendants

1998. Traditional Pine Brush Wedding. Mult.
367 20t. Type **131** 15 15
368 80t. Priest, accordionist and bride and groom 60 60
Nos. 367/8 were issued together, se-tenant, forming a composite design.

132 Figure Skating

1998. Winter Olympic Games, Nagano, Japan. Multicoloured.
369 70t. Type **132** 50 50
370 90t. Biathlon 65 65

133 Airplane, Air Traffic Controllers and Flight Paths

1998. 35th Anniv of Eurocontrol Convention (on regional aviation safety co-operation).
371 **133** 90t. multicoloured 65 65

134 Lakotnik eating Potato

1998. Cartoon Characters by Miki Muster. Multicoloured.
372 14t. Type **134** 10 10
373 105t. Trdonja (turtle) in sea 75 75
374 118t. Zvitorepec (fox) walking through meadow 85 85
MS375 172 × 100 mm. Nos. 372/4, each × 2 . . . . 3·50 3·50

135 Louis Adamic and Maps highlighting Birthplace and American Residence

1998. Birth Anniversaries. Multicoloured.
376 26t. Type **135** (writer, centenary) 20 20
377 90t. Altar figure from Zagreb Cathedral and fountain (300th anniv of Francesco Robba (sculptor)) 65 65

136 St. George's Festival

1997. Europa. National Festivals.
378 **136** 90t. multicoloured 65 65

137 Red Cross and Blood Drop
138 Red Cross

1998. Obligatory Tax. Red Cross.
379 **137** 7t. red and black 10 10

1998. Obligatory Tax. Solidarity Week. Each red and black.
380 7t. Type **138** 10 10
381 7t. Red cross (value at right) 10 10
Nos. 380/1 were issued together, se-tenant, forming a composite design.

139 Mt. Boc
140 Common Juniper (*Juniperus communis*)

1998.
382 **139** 14t. multicoloured 10 10

1998. Conifers. Sheet 134 × 114 mm containing T **140** and similar vert designs. Multicoloured.
MS383 14t. Type **140**; 15t. Norway spruce (*Picea abies*); 80t. Corsican pine (*Pinus nigra*); 90t. European larch (*Larix decdua*) . . . . . 1·20 1·20

141 Series SZ 06-018 Steam Locomotive
142 Victory Sign

1998.
384 **141** 80t. multicoloured 60 60

1998. 10th Anniv of Committee for Protection of Human Rights.
385 **142** 15t. multicoloured 10 10

143 Map of Slovenia

1998. 150th Anniv of Movement for the Independence of Slovenia.
386 **143** 80t. multicoloured 60 60

144 St. Bernard of Clairvaux, Sticna Monastery Church and Foundation Document

1998. 900th Anniv of Cistercian Order and Centenary of Return of Cistercians to Sticna.
387 **144** 14t. multicoloured 10 10

145 Sound Waves and European Cuckoo

1998. 70th Anniv of Cuckoo Emblem of Radio Ljubljana.
388 **145** 50t. multicoloured 35 35

146 "The Banker" (watercolour and collage)

1998. Birth Centenary of August Cernigoj (artist). Multicoloured.
389 70t. Type **146** 50 50
390 80t. "El" (sculpture) 60 60

147 Hands cradling Sleeping Infant
149 Stukelj

148 Children with Candle (Marjanca Bozic)

1998. 50th Anniv of Universal Declaration of Human Rights.
391 **147** 100t. multicoloured . . . 70 70

1998. Christmas and New Year. Multicoloured.
392 15t. Type **148** 10 10
393 90t. "Adoration of the Wise Men" (fresco, St. Nicholas's Church, Mace) 60 60

1998. Birth Centenary of Leon Stukelj (gymnast). Sheet 135 × 115 mm containing T **149** and similar multicoloured designs.
MS394 100t. Type **149**; 100t. Floor exercise; 100t. With Juan Antonio Samaranch (president of International Olympic Committee) (57 × 40 mm) . . . . 2·10 2·10

150 Peter Kozler (cartographer)

1999. Anniversaries. Multicoloured.
395 14t. Type **150** (125th birth anniv) 10 10
396 15t. Bozidar Lavric (surgeon, birth centenary) 10 10
397 70t. General Rudolf Maister (125th birth anniv) 45 45
398 80t. France Preseren (writer, 150th death anniv) 50 50

151 White Horses, Planets and Hearts

1999. Greetings Stamp.
399 **151** 15t. multicoloured 10 10

152 Carnival Procession

1999. Skoromati Carnival. Multicoloured.
400 20t. Type **152** 15 15
401 80t. Horn-blower and procession 50 50
Nos. 400/1 were issued together, se-tenant, forming a composite design.

153 Mt. Golica

1999.
402 **153** 15t. multicoloured 10 10

154 1919 20v. and 1997 14t. Stamps

1999. 50th Anniv of Slovenian Philatelic Society.
403 **154** 16t. multicoloured 10 10

155 Cinnabarite

1999. Minerals.
404 **155** 80t. multicoloured 50 50

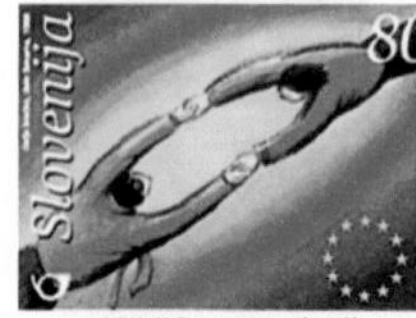

156 "Co-operation"

1999. 50th Anniv of Council of Europe.
405 **156** 80t. multicoloured 50 50

157 Triglav National Park

1999. Europa. Parks and Gardens.
406 **157** 90t. multicoloured 60 60

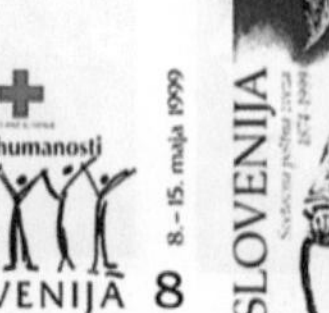

158 Figures with Raised Arms
159 Early Postman and Moon

1999. Obligatory Tax. Red Cross.
407 **158** 8t. black and red 10 10

1999. 125th Anniv of Universal Postal Union. Multicoloured.
408 30t. Type **159** 20 20
409 90t. Astronaut on moon, posthorn and Earth 60 60

160 Slovenian Coldblood

1999. Horses. Multicoloured.
410 60t. Type **160** 45 45
411 70t. Ljutomer trotting horse 45 45
412 120t. Slovenian warmblood (show jumping) 80 80
413 350t. Lipizzaner . . . . . . 2·25 2·25
MS414 113 × 80 mm. Nos. 410/13 4·00 4·00

161 Dogs and Handlers

1999. World Rescue Dogs Championship.
415 **161** 80t. multicoloured 50 50

162 Children's Toys

1999. Year 2000. Multicoloured.
416 20t. Type **162** 15 15
417 70t. Forms of communication 45 45
418 80t. Symbols of science and culture 50 50
419 90t. Tree with symbols of education 60 60

163 "Self-portrait" and "Unravelling the Mysteries of Life"

1999. Birth Centenary of Bozidar Jakac (artist). Multicoloured.
420 70t. Type **163** 45 45
421 80t. "Self-portrait" and "Novo Mesto" 50 50

164 Terglou Locomotive

1999. 150th Anniv of Arrival of First Train in Ljubljana.
422 **164** 80t. multicoloured 50 50

165 Slomsek
166 Family watching Fireworks

1999. Beatification of Bishop Anton Martin Slomsk.
423 **165** 90t. multicoloured 60 60

1999. Obligatory Tax. Solidarity Week. As T **138**. Each orange, black and red.
424 9t. Red cross (value at left) 10 10
425 9t. Red cross (value at right) 10 10
Nos. 424/5 were issued together, se-tenant, each pair forming a composite design of a link in a chain.

1999. Christmas. Multicoloured.
426 17t. Type **166** 10 10
427 18t. Type **166** 10 10

428 80t. Letter "h" illuminated with Nativity scene (Kranj antiphonary) 45 45
429 90t. As No. 428 . . . . . . 50 50

167 Teddy Bear and Baby's Bottle

169 Sailing Ship and Tone Seliskar (writer)

168 Masqueraders

2000. Greetings Stamp.
430 **167** 34t. multicoloured 20 20

2000. Pustovi Carnival Masks. Multicoloured.
431 34t. Type **168** 20 20
432 80t. Four masqueraders . . . 45 45

2000. Birth Centenaries. Multicoloured.
433 64t. Type **169** 35 35
434 120t. Elvira Kralj (actress) and actors holding masks 65 65

170 Stage Coach

172 Muri the Tom Cat

171 Mt. Storzic

2000. 500th Anniv of Postal Service in Slovenia.
435 **170** 500t. multicoloured . . . 2·75 2·75

2000.
436 **171** 18t. multicoloured 10 10

2000. Characters from Children's Books. Multicoloured. Ordinary or self-adhesive gum.
437 20t. Type **172** 15 15
438 20t. Mojca Pokrajculja . . . 15 15
439 20t. Pedenjped 15 15

173 Swallows

2000. 55th Anniv of Return of Slovene Exiles.
443 **173** 25t. multicoloured 15 15

174 Trilobite

176 Predjama Castle

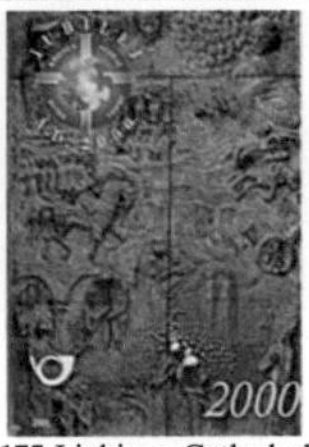

175 Ljubjana Cathedral Doors

2000. Fossil and Mineral. Multicoloured.
444 80t. Type **174** 45 45
445 90t. Magnesium-tourmaliae 50 50

2000. Holy Year 2000. Sheet 60 × 90 mm.
MS446 **175** 2000t. multicoloured 14·00 14·00

2000. Castles.
447 **176** 1t. brown and bistre . . . 10 10
448 – 1t. brown and bistre . . . 10 10
449 – 100t. deep brown and brown 55 55
450 – 100t. deep brown and brown 55 55
DESIGNS: No. 448, Velenje Castle; 449, Podsreda Castle; 450, Bled Castle.

177 Apple Blossom Weevil on Flower Bed

179 Red Cross

2000. The Apple. Multicoloured.
451 10t. Type **177** 10 10
452 10t. Apple blossom 10 10
453 10t. Apple 10 10

2000. No. 189e surch **19.00.**
454 19t. on 17t. choc, yell & brn 10 10

2000. Obligatory Tax. Red Cross Week.
455 **179** 10t. red and black 10 10

180 Globe and Radio Operator

2000. 3rd World Radiosport Team Championship and 50th Anniv of Amateur Radio in Slovenia.
456 **180** 20t. multicoloured 10 10

181 Chicken and Football

183 "Building Europe"

182 Racing Dinghies

2000. European Football Championship, Belgium and The Netherlands.
457 **181** 40t. multicoloured 20 20

2000. Olympic Games, Sydney. Multicoloured.
458 80t. Type **182** 45 45
459 90t. Sydney Opera House . . 50 50
Nos. 458/9 were issued together, se-tenant, forming a composite design.

2000. Europa.
460 **183** 90t. multicoloured 50 50

184 Flowers, Frog, Dragonfly and Plants within Life Ring

2000. World Environment Day.
461 **184** 90t. multicoloured 50 50

185 Lightning, Weather Vane and Carline Thistle

186 Cherry Blossom

2000. World Meteorological Day. 150th Anniv of Meteorological Observation in Slovenia.
462 **185** 150t. multicoloured . . . 75 75

2000. The Cherry. Multicoloured.
463 5t. Type **186** 10 10
464 5t. European cherry fruit fly 10 10
465 5t. Vigred sweet cherries . . 10 10

187 Ptuj Castle

188 Zelen Grape

2000. Castles and Manor Houses (1st series).
466 **187** A (18t.) brown and yellow 10 10
467 – A (18t.) brown and yellow 10 10
468 – B (19t.) brown and green 10 10
469 – B (19t.) brown and green 10 10
DESIGNS: No. 466, Type **187**; 467, Otocec Castle; 468, Zuzemberk Castle; 469, Turjak Castle.
See also Nos. 520/3 and 646.

2000. Wine Grapes. Multicoloured.
470 20t. Type **188** 10 10
471 40t. Ranfol 20 20
472 80t. Zametovka 45 45
473 130t. Rumeni plavec 70 70
MS474 134 × 100 mm. Nos. 470/3 1·50 1·50

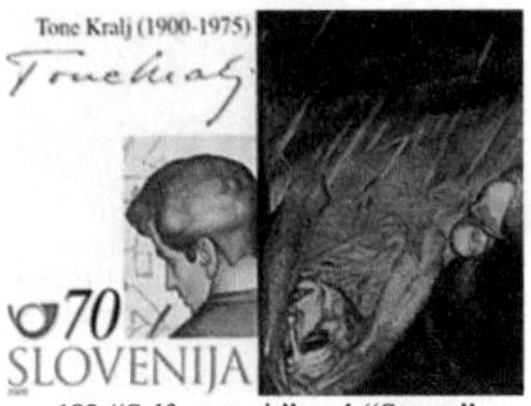

189 "Self-portrait" and "Storm"

2000. Birth Centenary of Tone Kralj (artist). Multicoloured.
475 70t. Type **189** 40 40
476 80t. "Self-portrait" and "Judita" 45 45

190 Iztok Cop and Luka Spik (coxless pairs)

2000. Olympic Gold Medal Winners. Multicoloured.
477 21t. Type **190** 20 20
478 21t. Rajmond Debevec (rifle-shooting) 20 20

2000. Obligatory Tax. Solidarity Week. As T **138**. Each grey, black and red.
479 10t. Type **191** 10 10
480 10t. Red Cross (value at right) 10 10
Nos. 479/80 were issued together, se-tenant, forming a composite design.

191 Healthy and Damaged Environments

2000. New Millennium. "EXPO 2000" World's Fair, Hanover, Germany.
481 **191** 40t. multicoloured 20 20

192 Open Book and Tree

194 Bucket (Dragotin Kette (poet))

193 Children

2000. 450th Anniv of First Printed Book in Slovenian Language.
482 **192** 50t. multicoloured 30 30

2000. Christmas. Multicoloured. Ordinary or self-adhesive gum.
483 B (21t.) Type **193** 10 10
484 90t. Baby Jesus 50 50

2001. Birth Anniversaries. Multicoloured.
487 A(24t.) Type **194** (125th anniv) 15 15
488 95t. Jar of flowers (Ivan Tavcar (politician and writer)) (150th anniv) . . . 50 50
489 107t. Cup of coffee (Ivan Cankar (writer)) (125th anniv) 60 60

195 Bride and Groom riding Bicycle

2001. Wedding Greetings Stamp.
490 **195** B (2t.) multicoloured . . 10 10

196 Colourful Headdresses

2001. Dobrepolje Folk Masks. Multicoloured.
491 50t. Type **196** 30 30
492 95t. Procession 50 50

197 Mt. Jalovec

198 Cowboy Pipec

2001.
493 **197** B (25t.) multicoloured . . 15 15

2001. Cowboy Pipec (cartoon character) by Bozo Kos. Multicoloured. Ordinary or self-adhesive gum.
494 B (25t.) Type **198** 15 15
495 B (25t.) Beetroot (Native American boy) 15 15

199 Fluorite

2001.
498 **199** 95t. multicoloured 55 55

200 Fossilized Starfish

2001.
499 **200** 107t. multicoloured . . . 65 65

201 Stars, Goddess Europa and Bull

2001. Europe Day (9 May).
500 **201** 221t. multicoloured . . . 1·25 1·25

202 Soca River and Bridge, Solkan

2001. Millenary of Solkan.
501 **202** 261t. multicoloured . . . 1·60 1·60

203 Dove with Lime Leaf

2001. 60th Anniv of Liberation Front.
502 **203** 24t. multicoloured 15 15

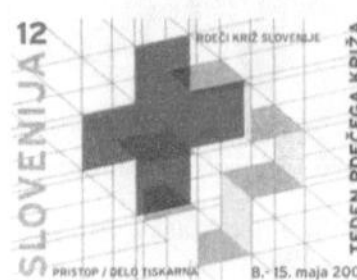
204 Red Cross

2001. Obligatory Tax. Red Cross Week.
503 **204** 12t. red and grey 10 10

205 Worker Bee gathering Nectar

2001. The Carniolan Honey Bee (*Apis mellifera carnica*). Sheet 113 × 80 mm containing T **205** and similar horiz designs. Multicoloured.
MS504 24t. Type **205**; 48t. Queen bee and drones; 95t. Queen, workers and drones on edge of honeycomb; 170t. Building and swarm . . . . 2·00 2·00

206 Flag

2001. 10th Anniv of Independence.
505 **206** 100t. multicoloured . . . 60 60

207 Gospodicna Spring, Gorjanci

2001. Europa. Water Resources.
506 **207** 107t. multicoloured . . . 65 85

208 Tramcar No. 5

2001. Centenary of Introduction of Trams to Ljubljana.
507 **208** 113t. multicoloured . . . 70 70

209 Maxi-Ball and Ljubljana Skyline

2001. 6th World Maxi-Basketball Championship, Ljubljana.
508 **209** 261t. multicoloured . . . 1·60 1·60

210 American and Russian Flags behind Bridge, Ljubljana

211 Peach Blossom Dragon

2001. 1st Summit Meeting between Pres. George W. Bush of America and Pres. Vladimir Putin of Russian Federation, Brdo Castle, Kranj.
509 **210** 107t. multicoloured . . . 65 65
MS510 60 × 90 mm. No. 509 . . 65 65

2001. Peach Cultivation. Multicoloured.
511 50t. Type **211** 30 30
512 50t. Green peach aphid . . . 30 30
513 50t. Redhaven peach 30 30

212 "Mohorjev koledar" 1920 Calendar Cover

2001. 150th Anniv of "Mohorjeva Druzba" Publishing House.
514 **212** B (31t.) multicoloured . . 20 20

213 Logarithms, Building and Globe

2001. Centenary of Jurij Vega Grammar School, Idrija.
515 **213** A (26t.) multicoloured . . 15 15

214 Score and Blaz Arnic

2001. Composers. Multicoloured.
516 95t. Type **214** 55 55
517 107t. Lucijan Marija Skerjanc and score 65 65

215 Cat

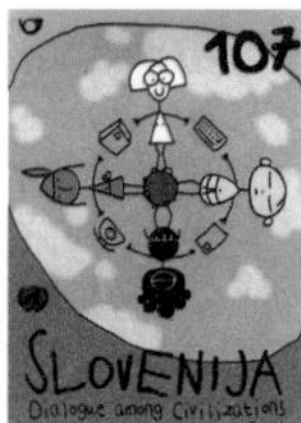
216 Children encircling Globe

2001. World Animal Day (4th October).
518 **215** 107t. multicoloured . . . 65 65

2001. United Nations Year of Dialogue among Civilizations.
519 **216** 107t. multicoloured . . . 65 65

2001. Castles and Manor Houses (2nd series). As T **187**.
520 C (95t.) brown and vermilion 55 55
521 C (95t.) brown and red . . . 55 55
522 D (107t.) deep blue and blue 65 65
523 D (107t.) indigo and blue . . 65 65
DESIGNS: No. 520, Dobrovo Manor; 521, Brezice Castle; 522, Olimje Manor; 523, Murska Sobota Manor.

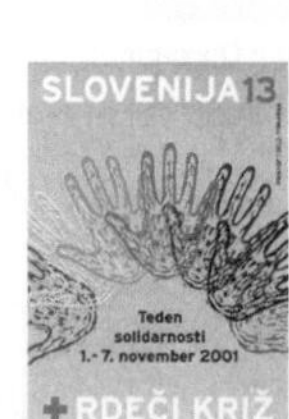
217 Handprints

218 Christmas Tree

2001. Obligatory Tax. Solidarity Week.
524 **217** 13t. multicoloured 10 10

2001. Christmas. Multicoloured. Ordinary or self-adhesive gum.
525 B (31t.) Type **218** 20 20
526 D (107t.) Nativity 65 65

219 Wood Carving

220 Rusa (animal) Mask

2002. Greetings Stamp.
529 **219** B (31t.) multicoloured . . 20 20

2002. Folk Masks. Multicoloured.
530 56t. Type **220** 35 35
531 95t. Picek (cockerel) mask . . 55 55

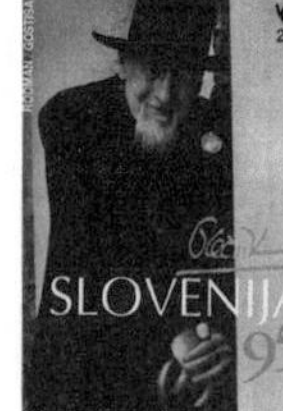
221 Joze Plecnik

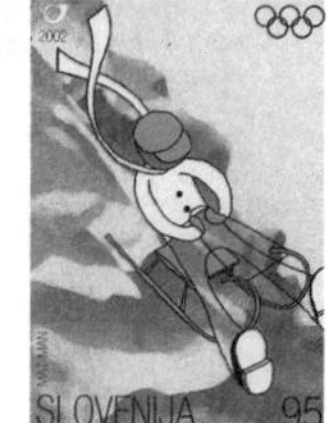
222 Toboggan

2002. Birth Anniversaries. Multicoloured.
532 95t. Type **221** (architect) (130th) 55 55
533 107t. Janko Kersnik (writer and politician) (150th) . . 60 60

2002. Winter Olympic Games, Salt Lake City. Multicoloured.
534 95t. Type **222** 55 55
535 107t. Skier 60 60

223 Easter Eggs

225 Martin Krpan carrying his horse

224 Alpine clematis (*Clematis alpine*) Martuljek Mountains, Triglav National Park

2002. Easter (B) and Palm Sunday (D). Multicoloured.
536 B (31t.) Type **223** 20 20
537 D (107t.) Butarice 60 60

2002. Mountains. Multicoloured.
538 A (30t.) Type **224** 20 20
539 D (107t.) Carniolan lily (*Lilium carniolicum*) and Mt. Spik 60 60

2002. Martin Krpan (character from book by Fran Levstik). Multicoloured. Ordinary or self-adhesive gum.
540 B (31t.) Type **225** 20 20
541 B (31t.) Martin Krpan at forge 20 20
542 B (31t.) Martin Krpan in Ljubljana 20 20

226 Fossilized Fly

2002.
546 **226** C (95t.) multicoloured . . 55 55

227 Monastery and view of Kostanjevica

2002. 750th Anniv of First Written Record of Kostanjevica on the Krka.
547 **227** D (107t.) multicoloured 60 60

228 Man carrying Heart

229 Dog Rose (*Rosa canina*)

2002. Obligatory Tax. Red Cross Week.
548 **228** 15t. multicoloured 10 10

2002. Medicinal Plants. Multicoloured.
549 A (30t.) Type **229** 15 15
550 B (31t.) Camomile (*Chamomilla recutita*) . . . 20 20
551 C (95t.) Valerian (*Valeriana officinalis*) 55 55
MS552 60 × 70 mm. D (107t.) Sweet violet (*Viola odorata*) 60 60

230 Mouse supporting Elephant

2002. Europa. Circus.
553 **230** D (107t.) multicoloured 60 60

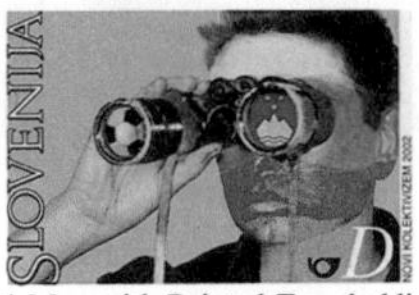

231 Man with Painted Face holding Binoculars

2002. World Cup Football Championships, Japan and South Korea.
554 **231** D (107t.) multicoloured 60 60

232 Lake Bled enclosed in Map of Central Europe

2002. 9th Central European States Presidential Conference, Bled. Sheet 65 × 87 mm containing T **232** and similar horiz design.
MS555 D (107t.) Type **232**; D (107t.) Central Europe map and Brdo Castle (conference venue) . . . 60 60

233 Bilberry Flowers

2002. The Bilberry (*Vaccinium myrtillus*). Multicoloured.
556 150t. Type **233** 85 85
557 150t. Winter moth (pest) . . 85 85
558 150t. Bilberry fruit 85 85

234 Horse and Competition Emblem

2002. 35th Chess Olympiad, Bled. Sheet 70 × 70 mm containing T **234** and similar horiz design.
MS559 C (95t.) Type **234**; D (107t.) Fields and emblem . . . . . . 1·10 1·10

235 "Kolo" (dance)

2002. Matija Jama (artist) Commemoration. Multicoloured.
560 95t. Type **235** 55 55
561 214t. "Village in Winter" . . 1·20 1·20

236 Profiles  **237** Snowman

2002. Obligatory Tax. Solidarity Week.
562 **236** 15t. multicoloured 10 10

2002. Christmas. Multicoloured. Ordinary or Self-adhesive gum.
563 B (31t.) Type **237** 20 20
564 D (107t.) Girl and house . . 60 60

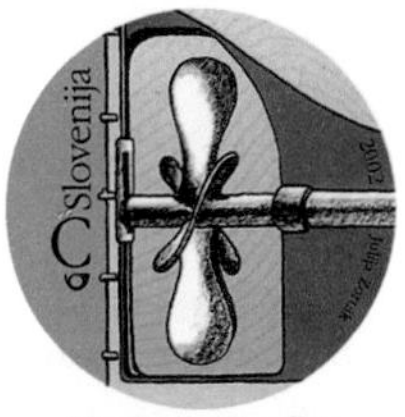

238 Screw Propeller

2002. 175th Anniv of Patenting of the Screw Propeller by Josef Ressel.
567 **238** C (95t.) multicoloured . . 55 55

239 Couple

2003. National Costumes. Slovene Istria.
568 **239** A (30t.) multicoloured . . 15 15

240 Cover of "Observationes Astromice" and Chinese Sextant

2003. Birth Anniversaries. Multicoloured.
569 107t. Type **240** (Ferdinand Augustin Hellerstein, missionary and astronomer) (300th) . . . 60 60
570 221t. Cover of "Flora Exiccata Carniocola" (Alfonz Paulin, botanist and writer) (150th) . . . . 1·20 1·20

241 Couple on Heart-shaped Balloon

2003. Greetings Stamp.
571 **241** 180t. multicoloured . . . 1·00 1·00

No. 571 was perforated in a heart-shape contained within an outer perforated square and impregnated with the scent of roses which is released when the stamp is rubbed.

242 Three Vixens

2003. Folk Tales. Multicoloured. Ordinary or Self-adhesive gum.
572 B (31t.) Type **242** 20 20
573 B (31t.) The Golden Bird (vert) 20 20

243 Avenue of Stalactites

2003. Vilenica Cave, Lokev.
576 **243** D (107t.) multicoloured 60 60

244 Barite

2003.
577 **244** D (107t.) multicoloured 60 60

245 Kamen Castle, Begunje

2003.
578 **245** 1000t. slate and blue . . . 5·50 5·50

246 Red Droplet  **247** Poster, Bucket of Paste and Brush

2003. Obligatory Tax. Red Cross Week.
579 **246** 19t. red and slate 10 10

2003. Europa. Poster Art.
580 **247** D (107t.) multicoloured 60 60

248 Kresnik (fire spirit)  **249** Goddess Europa riding Bull (Zeus)

2003. Mythology.
581 **248** 110t. multicoloured . . . 60 60

2003. European Water Polo Championships, Kranj and Ljubljana.
582 **249** 180t. multicoloured . . . 1·00 1·00

250 Vilko and Slavko Avsenik

2003. 50th Anniv of Avsenik (music) Ensamble (founded by Slavko Avsenik). Sheet 60 × 70 mm.
MS583 **250** 180t. multicoloured 1·00 1·00

251 Painted Beehive Panel

2003. Bee Keeping.
584 **251** 218t. multicoloured . . . 1·20 1·20

252 Letters showing Franking Marks

2003. Pre-Stamp Postage.
585 **252** A (30t.) multicoloured . . 15 15

253 Olive Flowers  **254** Fallen Knight

2003. The Olive Tree. Multicoloured.
586 B (31t.) Type **253** 20 20
587 B (31t.) Olive fruit fly (pest) 20 20
588 B (31t.) Olives 20 20

2003. Illustrations from Gasper Lamberger's Tournament Book. Multicoloured.
589 76t. Type **254** 40 40
590 570t. Gasper Lamberger . . 3·00 3·00

Nos. 589/90 were issued together, se-tenant, forming a composite design of two pages from the book.

255 Black-belted (Krsko polje) Pig

2003. Indigenous Farm Animals. Multicoloured.
591 95t. Type **255** 55 55
592 107t. Solcava sheep 60 60
593 107t. Cica cattle 60 60
MS594 60 × 70 mm. 368t. Styrian poultry (vert) . . . . 2·00 2·00

257 Automatic Sorting Machine and "www.posta.si"

2003. Mail Sorting and Logistics Centre, Maribor.
596 **257** 221t. multicoloured . . . 1·20 1·20

258 Post Office Door, Zgormji Otok

2003. Cultural Heritage. Multicoloured.
597 A (38t.) Type **258** 20 20
598 B (44t.) Fishing boat, Piran 25 25
599 C (95t.) Scythe, Ljubno ob Savinji 50 50
600 D (107t.) Horse-collar comb 60 60

259 Parcel, Flowers, Bell, Bauble and Fir Twig

2003. Christmas. Multicoloured. Ordinary or self-adhesive gum.
601 B (44t.) Type **259** 25 25
602 D (107t.) The Nativity . . . 60 60

260 Hospital

2003. 60th Anniv of Franja Partisan Hospital.
605 **260** 76t. sepia and bronze . . 40 40

261 Parizar (cart)

2003.
606 **261** 221t. multicoloured . . . 1·20 1·20

262 Couple, Vipava Valley

2004. National Costumes.
607 **262** A (38t.) multicoloured . . 20 20

263 Soldiers marching through Snow

2004. 60th Anniv of 14th Division's March to Stajerska.
608 **263** B (44t.) multicoloured . . 25 25

264 Edvard Kocbek and Script

2004. Birth Centenary of Edvard Kocbek (writer and politician).
609 **264** D (107t.) multicoloured 60 60

265 Two Cats

2004. Greeting Stamp.
610 **265** 180t. multicoloured . . . 1·00 1·00

266 Players **268** Keckec

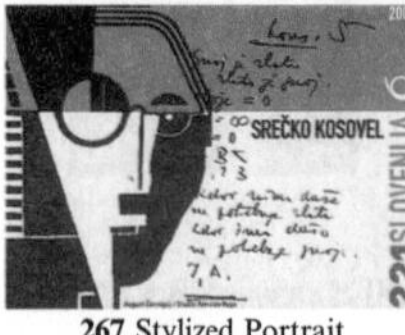

267 Stylized Portrait

2004. Sixth European Men's Handball Championships, Slovenia.
611 **266** 221t. multicoloured . . . 1·20 1·20

2004. Birth Centenary of Srecko Kosovel (writer).
612 **267** 221t. vermilion and black 1·20 1·20

2004. Keckec (character from children's stories created by Josip Vandot). Multicoloured.
613 B (44t.) Type **268** 25 25
614 B (44t.) Pehta 25 25
615 B (44t.) Kosobrin 25 25

269 Gymnast (⅔-size illustration)

2004. European Men's Artistic Gymnastic Championship, Ljubljana.
616 **269** D (107t.) multicoloured 60 60

270 Fossilized Fish **271** Bled Castle

2004.
617 **270** D (107t.) multicoloured 60 60

2004.
618 **271** 218t. multicoloured . . . 1·20 1·20

272 NATO Emblem

2004. Slovenia's Accession to North Atlantic Treaty Organization (NATO).
619 **272** D (107t.) blue and yellow 60 60

273 Stars and New Member's Flags

2004. Slovenia's Accession to European Union.
620 **273** 95t. multicoloured 50 50

274 Iovrenc Kosir and Birthplace

2004. Birth Bicentenary of Iovrenc Kosir (postage stamp pioneer).
621 **274** B (48t.) multicoloured . . 25 25

275 Discus

2004. Olympic Games, Athens. Multicoloured.
622 C (95t.) Type **275** 50 50
623 D (107t.) Long jump 60 60
Nos. 622/3 were issued together, se-tenant, forming a composite design.

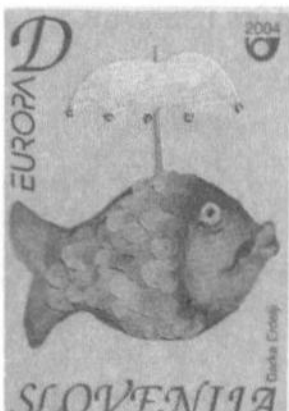

276 Fish with Umbrella

2004. Europa. Holidays.
624 **276** D (107t.) multicoloured 60 60

277 Bicycle Chain Wheel

2004. Puch Bicycles (bicycle manufacture pioneer).
625 **277** 110t. multicoloured . . . 60 60

278 Miller and Wife (1869)

2004. Painted Beehive Panels.
626 **278** 218t. multicoloured . . . 1·20 1·20

279 Town House, Trbovlje **280** Posthorn

2004.
627 **279** B (48t.) multicoloured . . 25 25

2004.
628 **280** B (48t.) blue and yellow 25 25

281 Crni Kal Viaduct

2004. Completion of Crni Kal Viaduct between Ljubljana and Klanec-Srmin. Sheet 70 × 60 mm.
MS629 **281** 95t. multicoloured . . 50 50

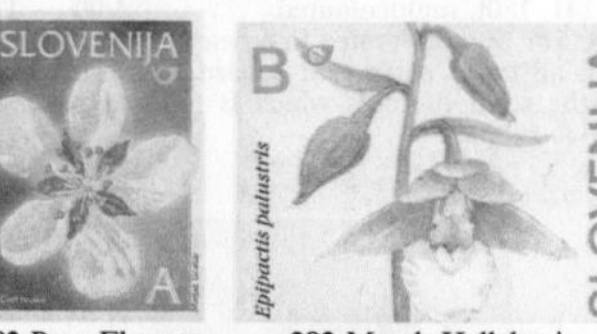

282 Pear Flowers **283** Marsh Helleborine (Epipactis palustris)

2004. William Pear (fruit tree). Multicoloured.
630 A (45t.) Type **282** 25 25
631 A (45t.) Fruit fly (pest) . . . 25 25
632 A (45t.) Pear 25 25

2004. Cultural Heritage. As T **258**. Multicoloured.
633 D (107t.) Cupa (fishing boat) 60 60

2004. Orchids. Multicoloured.
634 B (52t.) Type **283** 30 30
MS635 70 × 60 mm. D (107t.) Spider orchid (*Ophrys holosericea*) . . 60 60

284 "750"

2004. 750th Anniversary of First Documentation of Maribor Town.
636 **284** C (95t.) multicoloured . . 50 50

285 Illuminated Writing

2004. Romanesque Art. Multicoloured.
637 107t. Type **285** 60 60
638 107t. Illuminated writing (different) 60 60

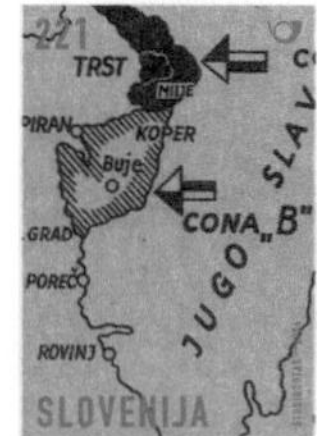

286 Map of Southern Europe **287** Children under Umbrella

2004. 50th Anniv of London Memorandum (Italy—Slovenia border demarcation agreement). Sheet 60 × 70 mm.
MS639 **286** 221t. multicoloured 1·20 1·20

2004. Christmas. Multicoloured. Ordinary or self-adhesive gum.
640 A (45t.) Type **287** 25 25
641 C (95t.) Baby Jesus enclosed in tree 50 50

288 Prekmurje Pie Cake

2004. Gastronomy. Multicoloured.
644 52t. Type **288** 30 30
645 52t. Bogra Goulash 30 30

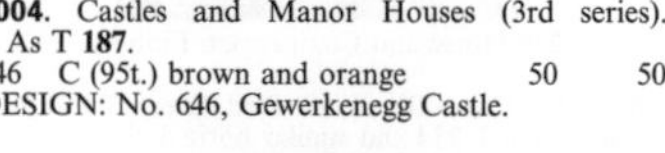

2004. Castles and Manor Houses (3rd series). As T **187**.
646 C (95t.) brown and orange 50 50
DESIGN: No. 646, Gewerkenegg Castle.

289 Rojenice and Sojenice (Fates)

2004. Mythology.
647 **289** 180t. multicoloured . . . 1·00 1·00

SOLOMON ISLANDS Pt. 1

A group of islands in the west Pacific, east of New Guinea.

1907. 12 pence = 1 shilling;
20 shillings = 1 pound.
1966. 100 cents = $1 Australian.

1 2

1907.
1 1 ½d. blue 9·00 14·00
2 1d. red 23·00 25·00
3 2d. blue 30·00 30·00
4 2½d. yellow 32·00 42·00
5 5d. green 55·00 65·00
6 6d. brown 50·00 60·00
7 1s. purple 70·00 75·00

1908.
8 2 ½d. green 1·50 1·00
9 1d. red 1·25 1·00
10 2d. grey 1·25 1·00
11 2½d. blue 3·75 2·00
11a 4d. red on yellow 3·25 11·00
12 5d. olive 9·00 6·00
13 6d. red 10·00 6·50
14 1s. black on green 8·50 6·00
15 2s. purple on blue 40·00 55·00
16 2s.6d. red on blue 48·00 70·00
17 5s. green on yellow 75·00 £100

3

5 Spears and Shield

1913. Inscr "POSTAGE POSTAGE".
18 3 ½d. green 80 3·50
19 1d. red 1·50 14·00
42 1½d. red 2·25 60
20 3d. purple on yellow 80 4·00
21 11d. purple and red 3·00 12·00

1914. Inscr "POSTAGE REVENUE".
39 3 ½d. green 30 3·50
24 1d. red 1·50 1·25
41 1d. violet 1·00 7·50
26 2d. grey 3·00 9·00
27 2½d. blue 2·25 5·00
28 3d. purple on yellow 20·00 85·00
44 3d. blue 70 4·50
29 4d. black and red on yellow 2·00 2·50
45a 4½d. brown 3·00 20·00
46 5d. purple and green 3·00 27·00
32 6d. purple 6·00 14·00
33 1s. black on green 4·75 7·00
34 2s. purple and blue on blue 7·00 10·00
35 2s.6d. black and red on blue 9·50 20·00
36 5s. green and red on yellow 32·00 48·00
37 10s. green and red on green 80·00 65·00
38 £1 purple and black on red £250 £120

1935. Silver Jubilee. As T **32a** of St. Helena.
53 1½d. blue and red 1·00 1·00
54 3d. brown and blue 3·00 6·00
55 6d. blue and green 9·50 12·00
56 1s. grey and purple 7·50 10·00

1937. Coronation. As T **32b** of St. Helena.
57 1d. violet 30 1·25
58 1½d. red 30 60
59 3d. blue 50 50

1939. Portrait of King George VI.
60 5 ½d. blue and green 15 1·00
61 – 1d. brown and violet 30 1·50
62 – 1½d. green and red 70 1·25
63a – 2d. brown and black 30 1·50
64 – 2½d. mauve and olive 2·75 2·25
65 – 3d. black and blue 1·25 1·50
66 – 4½d. green and brown 4·00 13·00
67 – 6d. violet and purple 75 1·00
68 – 1s. green and black 1·25 1·00
69 – 2s. black and orange 8·00 5·50
70 – 2s.6d. black and violet 28·00 4·50
71 – 5s. green and red 32·00 11·00
72 – 10s. green and mauve 4·00 8·50
DESIGNS—VERT: 1d. Native constable and chief; 4½d., 10s. Native house, Reef Islands; 6d. Coconut plantation. HORIZ: 1½d. Artificial Island., Malaita; 2½d. Roviana canoe; 1s. Breadfruit; 5s. Malaita canoe. LARGER (35½ × 22 mm): 2d. Canoe house; 3d. Roviana canoes; 2s. Tinakula volcano; 2s.6d. Bismarck scrub fowl.

1946. Victory. As T **33a** of St. Helena.
73 1½d. red 15 1·25
74 3d. blue 15 20

1949. Silver Wedding. As T **33b/c** of St. Helena.
75 2d. grey 50 50
76 10s. mauve 10·00 8·00

1949. 75th Anniv of U.P.U. As T **33d/g** of St. Helena.
77 2d. brown 50 1·00
78 3d. blue 2·25 1·50
79 5d. green 50 1·75
80 1s. black 50 1·75

1953. Coronation. As T **33h** of St. Helena.
81 2d. black and grey 50 1·25

17 Ysabel Canoe

1956. Portrait of Queen Elizabeth II.
82 17 ½d. orange and purple 15 50
83 – 1d. green & brn (as No. 65) 15 15
84 – 1½d. slate and red (No. 62) 15 80
105 – 2d. sepia and green (No. 63) 20 20
86 – 2½d. black and blue 60 50
106 – 3d. green and red (No. 71) 55 15
88 – 5d. black and blue 30 55
89 – 6d. black and green 50 25
90 – 8d. blue and black 25 15
108 – 9d. green and black 40 35
91 – 1s. slate and brown 50 50
109 – 1s.3d. black and blue 60 70
110 – 2s. black and red (No. 69) 1·00 5·50
93 – 2s.6d. green & pur (No. 66) 7·50 45
94 – 5s. brown 15·00 4·50
95 – 10s. sepia (No. 61) 20·00 5·50
96 – £1 black and blue 30·00 35·00
DESIGNS—VERT: 2½d. Prow of Roviana canoe. 10s. Similar to No. 61, but constable in different uniform, without rifle; HORIZ: 5d., 1s.3d. Map; 6d. "Miena" (Schooner); 8d., 9d. Henderson Airfield, Guadalcanal; 1s. Chart showing voyage of H.M.S. "Swallow" in 1767; 5s. Mendana and "Todos los Santos"; £1 Arms of the Protectorate.

32 Great Frigate Bird

1961. New Constitution, 1960.
97 32 2d. black and turquoise 10 30
98 3d. black and red 10 10
99 9d. black and purple 15 30

1963. Freedom from Hunger. As T **63a** of St. Helena.
100 1s.3d. blue 75 35

1963. Cent of Red Cross. As T **63b** of St. Helena.
101 2d. red and black 25 20
102 9d. red and blue 50 90

33 Makira Food Bowl

1965. Central design in black; background colours given.
112 33 ½d. blue and light blue 10 1·40
113 – 1d. orange and yellow 70 60
114 – 1½d. blue and green 35 50
115 – 2d. ultramarine and blue 60 1·25
116 – 2½d. brown and light brown 10 1·25
117 – 3d. green and light green 10 10
118 – 6d. mauve and orange 35 80
119 – 9d. green and yellow 40 15
120 – 1s. brown and mauve 1·00 15
121 – 1s.3d. red 4·00 2·25
122 – 2s. purple and lilac 8·00 2·75
123 – 2s.6d. brown and light brown 1·00 70
124 – 5s. blue and violet 12·00 4·00
125 – 10s. green and yellow 15·00 3·00
126 – £1 violet and pink 9·00 4·00
DESIGNS: 1d. "Dendrobium veratrifolium" (orchid); 1½d. Chiragra spider conch; 2d. Blyth's hornbill ("Hornbill"); 2½d. Ysabel shield; 3d. Rennellese club; 6d. Moorish idol (fish); 9d. Lesser frigate bird ("Frigate Bird"); 1s. "Dendrobium macrophyllum" (orchid); 1s.3d. "Dendrobium spectabilis" (orchid); 2s. Sanford's sea eagle ("Sanford's Eagle"); 2s.6d. Malaita belt; 5s. "Ornithoptera victoreae" (butterfly); 10s. Ducorp's cockatoo ("White Cockatoo"); £1 Western canoe figurehead.

1965. Cent of I.T.U. As T **64a** of St. Helena.
127 2d. red and turquoise 20 15
128 3d. turquoise and drab 20 15

1965. I.C.Y. As T **64b** of St. Helena.
129 1d. purple and turquoise 10 10
130 2s.6d. green and lavender 45 20

1966. Churchill Commemoration. As T **64c** of St. Helena.
131 2d. blue 15 10
132 9d. green 25 10
133 1s.3d. brown 35 10
134 2s.6d. violet 40 25

1966. Decimal Currency. Nos. 112/26 surch.
135A 1c. on ½d. 10 10
136A 2c. on 1d. 10 10
137A 3c. on 1½d. 10 10
138A 4c. on 2d. 15 10
139A 5c. on 6d. 15 10
140B 6c. on 2½d. 10 10
141B 7c. on 3d. 10 10
142B 8c. on 9d. 15 10
143A 10c. on 1s. 30 10
144B 12c. on 1s.3d. 65 10
145A 13c. on 1s.3d. 2·50 15
146B 14c. on 3d. 40 10
147A 20c. on 2s. 2·50 25
148A 25c. on 2s.6d. 60 40
149B 35c. on 2d. 2·00 25
150A 50c. on 5s. 4·50 1·50
151A $1 on 10s. 2·50 1·50
152A $2 on £1 2·25 3·00

1966. World Cup Football Championship. As T **64d** of St. Helena.
153 8c. multicoloured 15 15
154 35c. multicoloured 30 15

1966. Inauguration of W.H.O. Headquarters. Geneva. As T **64e** of St. Helena.
155 3c. black, green and blue 20 10
156 50c. black, purple and ochre 60 20

1966. 20th Anniv of UNESCO. As T **64f/h** of St. Helena.
157 3c. multicoloured 15 10
158 25c. yellow, violet and olive 30 15
159 $1 black, purple and orange 75 70

49 Henderson Field

1967. 25th Anniv of Guadalcanal Campaign (Pacific War). Multicoloured.
160 8c. Type **49** 15 15
161 35c. Red Beach landings 15 15

51 Mendana's "Todos los Santos" off Point Cruz

1968. 400th Anniv of Discovery of the Solomon Is. Multicoloured.
162 3c. Type **51** 20 10
163 8c. Arrival of missionaries 20 10
164 35c. Pacific Campaign, World War II 40 10
165 $1 Proclamation of the Protectorate 60 1·00

55 Vine Fishing

1968.
166 55 1c. blue, black and brown 10 10
167 – 2c. green, black and brown 10 10
168 – 3c. green, myrtle and black 10 10
169 – 4c. purple, black and brown 15 10
170 – 6c. multicoloured 30 10
171 – 8c. multicoloured 25 10
172 – 12c. ochre, red and black 65 30
173 – 14c. red, brown and black 2·50 3·50
174 – 15c. multicoloured 80 80
175 – 20c. blue, red and black 4·50 3·00
176 – 24c. red, black and yellow 2·00 3·25
177 – 35c. multicoloured 2·00 30
178 – 45c. multicoloured 1·50 30
179 – $1 blue, green and black 2·50 1·50
180 – $2 multicoloured 6·00 3·50
DESIGNS: 2c. Kite fishing; 3c. Platform fishing; 4c. Net fishing; 6c. Gold lip shell diving; 8c. Night fishing; 12c. Boat building; 14c. Cocoa; 15c. Road building; 20c. Geological survey; 24c. Hauling timber; 35c. Copra; 45c. Harvesting rice; $1 Honiara Port; $2 Internal air service.

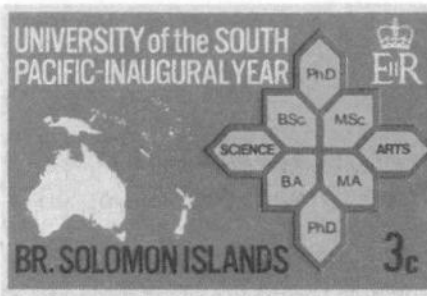

70 Map of Australasia and Diagram

1969. Inaugural Year of South Pacific University.
181 70 3c. multicoloured 10 10
182 12c. multicoloured 10 10
183 35c. multicoloured 15 10

71 Basketball Player **75** South Sea Island with Star of Bethlehem

1969. 3rd South Pacific Games, Port Moresby. Multicoloured.
184 3c. Type **71** 10 10
185 8c. Footballer 10 10
186 14c. Sprinter 10 10
187 45c. Rugby player 20 15
MS188 126 × 120 mm. Nos. 184/7 2·75 8·00

1969. Christmas.
189 75 8c. black, violet and green 10 10
190 – 35c. multicoloured 20 20
DESIGN; 35c. Southern Cross, "PAX" and frigate bird (stained glass window).

77 "Paid" Stamp, New South Wales 1896–1906 2d. Stamp and 1906–07 Tulagi Postmark

1970. New G.P.O., Honiara.
191 77 7c. mauve, blue and black 15 15
192 – 14c. green, blue and black 20 15
193 – 18c. multicoloured 20 15
194 – 23c. multicoloured 20 20
DESIGNS: 14c. 1906–07 2d. stamp and C. M. Woodford; 18c. 1910–14 5s. stamp and Tulagi postmark, 1913; 23c. New G.P.O., Honiara.

81 Coat of Arms

1970. New Constitution.
195 81 18c. multicoloured 15 10
196 – 35c. green, blue and ochre 35 20
DESIGN—HORIZ: 35c. Map.

83 British Red Cross H.Q., Honiara

1970. Centenary of British Red Cross.
197 83 3c. multicoloured 10 10
198 – 35c. blue, red and black 25 20
DESIGN—VERT: 35c. Wheelchair and map.

86 Reredos (Altar Screen)

1970. Christmas.
199 – 8c. ochre and violet 10 10
200 86 45c. chestnut, orange and brown 25 20
DESIGN—HORIZ: 8c. Carved angel.

87 La Perouse and "La Boussole"

1971. Ships and Navigators (1st series). Mult.
201 3c. Type **87** 45 20
202 4c. Astrolabe and Polynesian reed map 45 20

203 12c. Abel Tasman and "Heemskerk" 60 30
204 35c. Te puki canoe, Santa Cruz 70 50
See also Nos. 215/18, 236/9, 254/7 and 272/5.

88 J. Atkin, Bishop Patteson and S. Taroaniara

1971. Death Cent of Bishop Patteson. Mult.
205 2c. Type **88** 10 10
206 4c. Last landing at Nukapu 10 10
207 14c. Memorial Cross and Nukapu (vert) 10 10
208 45c. Knotted leaf and canoe (vert) 20 10

89 Torch Emblem and Boxers

1971. South Pacific Games, Tahiti. Mult.
209 3c. Type **89** 10 25
210 8c. Emblem and footballers 10 25
211 12c. Emblem and runner . . 10 40
212 35c. Emblem and skin-diver 15 20

90 Melanesian Lectern

1971. Christmas. Multicoloured.
213 9c. Type **90** 10 10
214 45c. "United we Stand" (Margarita Bara) 20 20

1972. Ships and Navigators (2nd series). As T **87**. Multicoloured.
215 4c. Bougainville and "La Boudeuse" 30 10
216 9c. Horizontal planisphere and ivory backstaff 35 10
217 15c. Philip Carteret and H.M.S. "Swallow" 60 15
218 45c. Malaita canoe 70 90

91 "Cupha woodfordi"

1972. Multicoloured.
219 1c. Type **91** 15 50
220 2c. "Ornithoptera priamus" 25 50
221 3c. "Vindula sapor" 25 60
222 4c. "Papilio ulysses" 25 60
223 5c. Big-eyed trevally 25 30
224 8c. Australian bonito 40 50
225 9c. Blue demoiselle 50 65
226 12c. "Costus speciosus" . . 1·25 90
227 15c. Clown anemonefish ("Orange anenome fish") 1·25 1·00
228 20c. "Spathoglottis plicata" 3·00 1·75
229 25c. "Ephemerantha comata" . . . . 3·00 1·50
230 35c. "Dendrobium cuthbertsonii" . . . . . 3·00 2·25
231 45c. "Heliconia salomonica" 2·50 3·00
232 $1 Dotty triggerfish . . . . 3·00 4·50
233 $2 "Ornithoptera alottei" 9·00 15·00
233a $5 Great frigate bird . . . . 14·00 16·00
The 2, 3, 4c. and $2 are butterflies; the 5, 8, 9, 15c. and $1 are fishes, and the 12, 20, 25, 35, 45c. are flowers.

1972. Royal Silver Wedding. As T **103** of St. Helena, but with Greetings and Message Drum in background.
234 8c. red 10 10
235 45c. green 20 20

1973. Ships and Navigators (3rd series). As T **87**. Multicoloured.
236 4c. D'Entrecasteaux and "La Recherche" 30 20
237 9c. Ship's hour-glass and chronometer 35 20
238 15c. Lt. Shortland and H.M.S. "Alexander" . . . 70 30
239 35c. Tomoko (war canoe) . . 75 1·10

93 Pan Pipes

1973. Musical Instruments. Multicoloured.
240 4c. Type **93** 10 10
241 9c. Castanets 10 10
242 15c. Bamboo flute 15 10
243 35c. Bauro gongs 20 25
244 45c. Bamboo band 20 30

1973. Royal Wedding. As T **74a** of Pitcairn Islands.
245 4c. blue 10 10
246 35c. blue 15 10

94 "Adoration of the Kings" (Jan Brueghel)

1973. Christmas. "Adoration of the Kings" by the artists listed. Multicoloured.
247 8c. Type **94** 10 10
248 22c. Pieter Brueghel (vert) . . 20 25
249 45c. Botticelli (48 × 35 mm) 50 50

95 Queen Elizabeth II and Map

1974. Royal Visit.
250 **95** 4c. multicoloured 25 10
251 9c. multicoloured 25 10
252 15c. multicoloured 30 20
253 35c. multicoloured . . . . 50 1·25

1974. Ships and Navigators (4th series). As T **87**. Multicoloured.
254 4c. Commissioner landing from S.S. "Titus" 20 10
255 9c. Radar scanner 20 10
256 15c. Natives being transported to a "Blackbirder" brig 25 15
257 45c. Lieut. John F. Kennedy's "P.T. 109" 1·00 90

96 "Postman"

1974. Centenary of U.P.U.
258 **96** 4c. green, dp green & black 10 10
259 – 9c. lt brown, brown & black 10 10
260 – 15c. mauve, purple & black 15 10
261 – 45c. blue, deep blue & black . . . . 35 1·60
DESIGNS (Origami figures)—HORIZ: 9c. Carrier-pigeon; 45c. Pegasus. VERT: 15c. St. Gabriel.

97 "New Constitution" Stamp of 1970

1974. New Constitution.
262 **97** 4c. multicoloured 10 10
263 – 9c. red, black and brown 10 10
264 – 15c. red, black and brown 15 10
265 **97** 35c. multicoloured 30 50
MS266 134 × 84 mm. Nos. 262/5 1·50 3·50
DESIGNS: 9 c, 15c. "New Constitution" stamp of 1961 (inscr "1960").

98 Mangrove Golden Whistler ("Golden Whislter")

1975. Birds. Multicoloured.
267 1c. Type **98** 45 85
268 2c. River kingfisher . . . . . 50 1·00
269 3c. Red-bibbed fruit dove ("Red-throated Fruit Dove") . . . . 55 1·00
270 4c. Red-backed button quail ("Button Quail") 55 85
271 $2 Duchess lorikeet . . . . . 7·00 10·50
See also Nos. 305/20.

1975. Ships and Navigators (5th series). As T **87**. Multicoloured.
272 4c. "Walande" (coaster) . . . 30 10
273 9c. "Melanesian" (coaster) . . 35 10
274 15c. "Marsina" (container ship) 50 15
275 45c. "Himalaya" (liner) . . . 75 1·50

99 800 Metres Race

1975. 5th South Pacific Games. Multicoloured.
276 4c. Type **99** 10 10
277 9c. Long jump 10 10
278 15c. Javelin-throwing 15 10
279 45c. Football 45 45
MS280 130 × 95 mm. Nos. 276/9 3·50 4·00

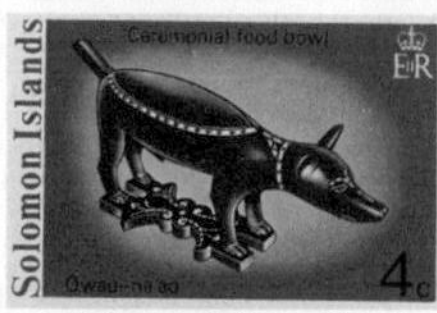

100 Nativity Scene and Candles

1975. Christmas. Multicoloured.
281 15c. Type **100** 15 10
282 35c. Shepherds, angels and candles 30 15
283 45c. The Magi and candles 40 40
MS284 140 × 130 mm. Nos. 281/3 3·50 5·00

1975. Nos. 267/70, 223/32, 271 and 233a with obliterating bar over "BRITISH". Mult.
285 1c. Type **98** 60 55
286 2c. River kingfisher . . . . . 1·00 55
287 3c. Red-bibbed fruit dove . . 70 55
288 4c. Red-backed button quail 1·00 55
289 5c. Big-eyed trevally 50 55
290 8c. Australian bonito 50 60
291 9c. Blue demoiselle 50 60
292 12c. "Costus speciosus" . . . 1·50 1·00
293 15c. Clown anemonefish ("Orange anemone fish") 1·50 1·25
294 20c. "Spathoglottis plicata" 1·50 1·50
295 25c. "Ephemerantha comata" 1·50 1·75
296 35c. "Dendrobium cuthbertsonii" . . . . . . 1·50 1·25
297 45c. "Heliconia salomonica" 1·25 2·00
298 $1 Dotty triggerfish . . . . . 1·00 1·25
299 $2 Duchess lorikeet . . . . . 3·50 6·00
300 $5 Great frigate bird . . . . 3·25 8·00

102 Ceremonial Food-bowl

1975. Artefacts (1st series). Multicoloured.
301 4c. Type **102** 10 10
302 15c. Chieftains' money . . . 10 10
303 35c. Nguzu-nguzu (canoe protector spirit) (vert) . . . 25 20
304 45c. Nguzu-nguzu canoe prow 30 25
See also Nos. 337/40, 353/6 and 376/9.

103 Mangrove Golden Whistler

1976. Multicoloured.
305 1c. Type **103** 50 50
306 2c. River kingfisher . . . . . 1·00 80
307 3c. Red-bibbed fruit dove . . 85 50
308 4c. Red-backed button quail 85 50
309 5c. Willie wagtail . . . . . . 1·00 80
310 6c. Golden cowrie 70 50
311 10c. Glory of the sea cone . . 70 60
312 12c. Rainbow lory . . . . . 1·00 80
313 15c. Chambered or pearly nautilus 65 40
314 20c. Venus comb murex . . . 1·00 45
315 25c. Commercial trochus . . 70 50
316 35c. Blood-red volute 80 50
317 45c. Orange spider conch . . 80 60
318 $1 Trumpet triton . . . . . 1·00 1·75
319 $2 Duchess lorikeet . . . . . 2·50 3·50
320 $5 Great frigate bird . . . . 1·75 3·75

104 Coastwatchers, 1942

1976. Bicent of American Revolution. Mult.
321 6c. Type **104** 20 10
322 20c. "Amagiri" (Japanese destroyer) ramming U.S.S. "PT109" and Lt. J. F. Kennedy 45 30
323 35c. Henderson Airfield . . . 50 40
324 45c. Map of Guadalcanal . . 50 70
MS325 95 × 115 mm. Nos. 321/4 6·50 9·00

105 Alexander Graham Bell

107 The Communion Plate

106 B.A.C. One Eleven 200/400

1976. Centenary of Telephone.
326 **105** 6c. multicoloured 10 10
327 – 20c. multicoloured 15 10
328 – 35c. brown, orange and red 20 15
329 – 45c. multicoloured 25 35
DESIGNS: 20c. Radio telephone via satellite; 35c. Ericson's magneto telephone; 45c. Stick telephone and first telephone.

1976. 50th Anniv of First Flight to Solomon Is. Multicoloured.
330 6c. Type **106** 35 10
331 20c. Britten Norman Islander 65 15
332 35c. Douglas DC-3 . . . . . 90 20
333 45c. De Havilland D.H.50A Seaplane A8-1 . . . . . . 95 55

1977. Silver Jubilee. Multicoloured.
334 6c. Queen's visit, 1974 . . . 10 10
335 35c. Type **107** 15 20
336 45c. The Communion 25 45

108 Carving from New Georgia

110 The Shepherds

109 Spraying Roof and Mosquito

1977. Artefacts (2nd series). Carvings.
337 **108** 6c. multicoloured 10 10
338 – 20c. multicoloured 10 10
339 – 35c. black, grey and red 20 15
340 – 45c. multicoloured 25 30
DESIGNS: 20c. Sea adaro (spirit); 35c. Shark-headed man; 45c. Man from Ulawa or Malaita.

1977. Malaria Eradication. Multicoloured.
341 6c. Type **109** 10 10
342 20c. Taking blood samples 15 10
343 35c. Microscope and map . . 20 15
344 45c. Delivering drugs 30 40

1977. Christmas. Multicoloured.
345 6c. Type **110** 10 10
346 20c. Mary and Jesus in stable 10 10
347 35c. The Three Kings 20 15
348 45c. "The Flight into Egypt" 25 25

111 Feather Money

1977. Introduction of Solomon Islands Coins and Bank-notes. Multicoloured.
349 6c. Type **111** 10 10
350 6c. New currency coins . . . 10 10
351 45c. New currency notes . . 25 25
352 45c. Shell money 25 25

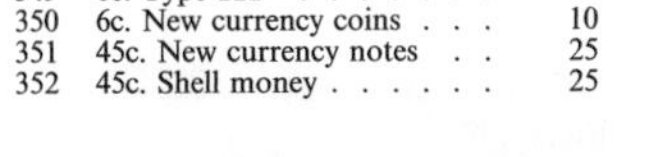

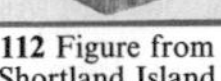

112 Figure from Shortland Island **113** Sanford's Sea Eagle

1977. Artefacts (3rd series).
353 **112** 6c. multicoloured 10 10
354 – 20c. multicoloured 10 10
355 – 35c. brown, black & orge 20 15
356 – 45c. multicoloured 25 30
DESIGNS: 20c. Ceremonial shield; 35c. Santa Cruz ritual figure; 45c. Decorative combs.

1978. 25th Anniv of Coronation. Multicoloured.
357 – 45c. black, red and silver 15 25
358 – 45c. multicoloured 15 25
359 **113** 45c. black, red and silver 15 25
DESIGNS: No. 357, King's Dragon; 358, Queen Elizabeth II.

114 National Flag **115** John

1978. Independence. Multicoloured.
360 6c. Type **114** 15 10
361 15c. Governor-General's flag 20 10
362 35c. The Cenotaph, Honiara 35 30
363 45c. National coat of arms 40 50

1978. 450th Death Anniv of Durer. Detail's from "Four Apostles". Multicoloured.
364 6c. Type **115** 10 10
365 20c. Peter 15 10
366 35c. Paul 20 15
367 45c. Mark 30 30

116 Firelighting

1978. 50th Anniv of Scouting in Solomon Islands. Multicoloured.
368 6c. Type **116** 15 10
369 20c. Camping 20 20
370 35c. Solomon Islands scouts 40 40
371 45c. Canoeing 50 70

117 H.M.S. "Discovery"

1979. Bicentenary of Captain Cook's Voyages, 1768–79.
372 **117** 8c. multicoloured 25 10
373 – 18c. multicoloured 25 15
374 – 35c. black, green and grey 30 25
375 – 45c. multicoloured 30 40
DESIGNS: 18c. Portrait of Captain Cook by Nathaniel Dance; 35c. Sextant; 45c. Flaxman/Wedgwood medallion of Captain Cook.

118 Fish Net Float

1979. Artefacts (4th series).
376 **118** 8c. multicoloured 10 10
377 – 20c. multicoloured 10 10
378 – 35c. black, grey and red 15 15
379 – 45c. black, brown & green 20 30
DESIGNS—VERT: 20c. Armband of shell money; 45c. Forehead ornament. HORIZ: 35c. Ceremonial food bowl.

119 Running **120** 1908 6d. Stamp

1979. South Pacific Games, Fiji. Multicoloured.
380 8c. Type **119** 10 10
381 20c. Hurdling 10 10
382 35c. Football 15 15
383 45c. Swimming 25 35

1979. Death Centenary of Sir Rowland Hill.
384 **120** 8c. red and pink 10 10
385 – 20c. mauve & pale mauve 15 30
386 – 35c. multicoloured 25 45
MS387 121 × 121 mm. 45c. red, green and pink 45 65
DESIGNS: 20c. Great Britian 1856 6d.; 35c. 1978 45c. Independence commemorative.

121 Sea Snake **122** "Madonna and Child" (Morando)

1979. Reptiles. Multicoloured.
388A 1c. Type **121** . . . . . . 10 1·00
389A 3c. Red-banded tree snake 10 1·25
390A 4c. Whip snake . . . . . 10 1·25
391A 6c. Pacific boa . . . . . 10 1·25
392A 8c. Skink 10 80
393A 10c. Gecko . . . . 10 1·00
394Bw 12c. Monitor . . . . . . 30 1·00
395A 15c. Anglehead . . . . . 10 1·25
396A 20c. Giant toad 30 60
397Bw 25c. Marsh frog . . . . . 30 1·00
398A 30c. Horned frog . . . . 1·50 1·00
399A 35c. Tree frog . . . . . . 30 1·00
399cB 40c. Burrowing snake . . 45 1·75
400A 45c. Guppy's snake . . . 30 1·25
400cB 50c. Tree gecko . . . . . 50 1·25
401B $1 Large skink . . . . . 1·50 75
402A $2 Guppy's frog . . . . . 60 1·50
403A $5 Estuarine crocodile . . 1·00 1·75
403cB $10 Hawksbill turtle . . . 4·00 5·50

1979. International Year of the Child. "Madonna and Child" paintings by various artists. Mult.
404 4c. Type **122** 10 10
405 20c. Luini 15 15
406 35c. Bellini 20 15
407 50c. Raphael 30 70
MS408 92 × 133 mm. Nos. 404/7 1·00 1·50

123 H.M.S. "Curacoa" (frigate), 1839

1980. Ships and Crests (1st series). Mult.
409 8c. Type **123** 30 20
410 20c. H.M.S. "Herald" (survey ship), 1854 . . . . 45 40
411 35c. H.M.S. "Royalist" (screw corvette), 1889 . . . 65 80
412 45c. H.M.S. "Beagle" (survey schooner), 1878 . . . . . 70 1·75
See also Nos. 430/3.

124 "Solomon Fisher" (fishery training vessel)

1980. Fishing. Ancillary Craft. Multicoloured.
413 8c. Type **124** 15 10
414 20c. "Solomon Hunter" (fishery training vessel) . . 20 20
415 45c. "Ufi Na Tasi" (refrigerated fish transport) 35 40
416 80c. Research vessel . . . . 60 1·75

125 "Comliebank" (cargo-liner) and 1935 Tulagi Registered Letter Postmark

1980. "London 1980" International Stamp Exhibition. Mail-carrying Transport. Multicoloured.
417 45c. Type **125** 30 45
418 45c. Douglas C-47 Skytrain (U.S. Army Postal Service, 1943) 30 45
419 45c. B.A.C. One Eleven airliner and 1979 Honiara postmark 30 45
420 45c. "Corabank" (container ship) and 1979 Auki postmark 30 45

126 Queen Elizabeth the Queen Mother

1980. 80th Birthday of The Queen Mother.
421 **126** 45c. multicoloured 30 35

127 Angel with Trumpet **129** Francisco Antonio Maurelle

128 "Parthenos sylvia"

1980. Christmas. Multicoloured.
422 8c. Type **127** 10 10
423 20c. Angel with fiddle 10 10
424 45c. Angel with trumpet (different) 25 25
425 80c. Angel with lute 40 45

1980. Butterflies (1st series). Multicoloured.
426 8c. Type **128** 35 10
427 20c. "Delias schoenbergi" . . 45 20
428 45c. "Jamides cephion" . . . 70 40
429 80c. "Ornithoptera victoriae" 1·00 1·40
See also Nos. 456/9 and 610/13.

1981. Ships and Crests (2nd series). As T **123**. Multicoloured.
430 8c. H.M.S. "Mounts Bay" (frigate), 1959 . . . . . . 15 10
431 20c. H.M.S. "Charybdis" (frigate), 1970 . . . . . . 20 20
432 45c. H.M.S. "Hydra" (survey ship), 1972 . . . . . . 30 30
433 $1 Royal Yacht "Britannia", 1974 . . . . 75 1·90

1981. Bicentenary of Maurelle's Visit and Production of Bauche's Chart, 1791.
434 **129** 8c. black, brown and yellow 15 10
435 – 10c. black, red and yellow 20 10
436 – 45c. multicoloured 60 65
437 – $1 multicoloured . . . . 1·00 1·10
MS438 126 × 91 mm. 25c. × 4, each black, red and stone . . . . . 65 1·10
DESIGNS—HORIZ: 10c. Bellin's map of 1742 showing route of "La Princesa"; 45c. "La Princesa". VERT: $1 Spanish compass cards, 1745; **MS**438 "Chart of a part of the South Sea" (each stamp 44 × 28 mm).
The stamps in No. **MS**438 form a composite design.

130 Netball **131** Prince Charles as Colonel-in-Chief, Royal Regiment of Wales

1981. Mini South Pacific Games. Multicoloured.
439 8c. Type **130** 10 10
440 10c. Tennis 15 15
441 25c. Running 25 25
442 30c. Football 25 25
443 45c. Boxing 40 40
MS444 102 × 67 mm. $1 Stylised athletes 70 75

1981. Royal Wedding. Multicoloured.
445 8c. Wedding bouquet from Solomon Islands 10 10
446 45c. Type **131** 15 15
447 $1 Prince Charles and Lady Diana Spencer 45 70

132 "Music" **135** Pair of Sanford's Sea Eagles constructing Nest

133 Primitive Church

1981. 25th Anniv of Duke of Edinburgh Award Scheme. Multicoloured.
448 8c. Type **132** 10 10
449 25c. "Handicrafts" 10 10
450 45c. "Canoeing" 15 10
451 $1 Duke of Edinburgh . . . 35 60

1981. Christmas. Churches.
452 **133** 8c. black, buff and blue 10 10
453 – 10c. multicoloured 10 10
454 – 25c. black, buff and green 10 10
455 – $2 multicoloured . . . . 45 1·25
DESIGNS: 10c. St. Barnabas Anglican Cathedral, Honiara; 25c. Early church; $2 Holy Cross Cathedral, Honiara.

1982. Butterflies (2nd series). As T **128**. Mult.
456 10c. "Doleschallia bisaltide" 25 10
457 25c. "Papilio bridgei" 45 25
458 35c. "Taenaris phorcas" . . . 50 30
459 $1 "Graphium sarpedon" . . 1·10 1·50

1982. Cyclone Relief Fund. No. 447 surch **50 CENTS SURCHARGE CYCLONE RELIEF FUND 1982.**

460 $1+50c. Prince Charles and Lady Diana Spencer . . . 75 2·00

1982. Sanford's Sea Eagle. Multicoloured.

461 12c. Type **135** 35 60
462 12c. Egg and chick 35 60
463 12c. Hen feeding chicks . . . 35 60
464 12c. Fledgelings 35 60
465 12c. Young bird in flight . . 35 60
466 12c. Pair of birds and village dwellings 35 60

136 Wedding Portrait

137 Flags of Solomon Islands and United Kingdom

1982. 21st Birthday of Princess of Wales. Multicoloured.

467 12c. Solomon Islands coat of arms 10 10
468 40c. Lady Diana Spencer at Broadlands, May 1981 . . 30 25
469 50c. Type **136** 50 50
470 $1 Formal portrait . . . . . 1·00 1·75

1982. Royal Visit (Nos. 471/2) and Commonwealth Games, Brisbane (Nos. 473/4). Multicoloured.

471 12c. Type **137** 15 20
472 12c. Queen and Prince Philip 15 20
473 25c. Running 30 45
474 25c. Boxing 30 45
MS475 123 × 123 mm. Nos. 471/2 and $1 Royal Yacht "Britannia" 1·75 2·50
MS476 123 × 123 mm. Nos. 473/4 and $1 Royal Yacht "Britannia" 1·75 2·50

138 Boy Scouts

1982. 75th Anniv of Boy Scout Movement (Nos. 477, 479, 481, 483) and Centenary of Boys' Brigade (others). Multicoloured.

477 12c. Type **138** 10 15
478 12c. Boys' Brigade cadets . . 10 15
479 25c. Lord Baden-Powell . . . 15 40
480 25c. Sir William Smith . . . 15 40
481 35c. Type **138** 15 50
482 35c. As No. 478 . . . . . . 15 50
483 50c. As No. 479 . . . . . . 20 1·10
484 50c. As No. 480 . . . . . . 20 1·10

139 Leatherback Turtle

1983. Turtles. Multicoloured.

485 18c. Type **139** 35 25
486 35c. Loggerhead turtle . . . 45 45
487 45c. Pacific ridley turtle . . . 50 60
488 50c. Green turtle 50 65

140 Black Olive, General Cone and Troschell's Murex

1983. Commonwealth Day. Shells. Mult.

489 12c. Type **140** 15 15
490 35c. Romu, Kurila, Kakadu and money belt 35 40
491 45c. Shells from "Bride-price" necklaces 50 60
492 50c. Commercial trochus polished and in its natural state 55 65

141 Montgolfier Balloon

1983. Bicentenary of Manned Flight. Mult.

493 30c. Type **141** 25 40
494 35c. R.A.A.F. Lockheed Hercules 30 45
495 40c. Wright Brothers' Type A 35 55
496 45c. Space shuttle "Columbia" 40 60
497 50c. Beech C55 Baron . . . 40 65

142 Weto Dancers

1983. Christmas. Multicoloured.

498 12c. Type **142** 10 10
499 15c. Custom wrestling . . . 10 20
500 18c. Girl dancers 15 20
501 20c. Devil dancers 15 20
502 25c. Bamboo band 20 35
503 35c. Gilbertese dancers . . . 25 45
504 40c. Pan pipers 25 55
505 45c. Girl dancers 30 65
506 50c. Cross surrounded by flowers 30 70
MS507 153 × 112 mm. Nos. 498/506 1·00 3·00

Stamps from No. **MS**507 are without the inscription, "Christmas 1983", on Nos. 498/506.

143 Earth Satellite Station

1983. World Communications Year. Mult.

508 12c. Type **143** 15 15
509 18c. Ham radio operator . . 15 20
510 25c. 1908 2½d. Canoe stamp 15 30
511 $1 1908 6d. Canoe stamp . . 40 3·00
MS512 131 × 103 mm. No. 511 1·40 2·25

144 "Calvatia gardneri"

146 "Olivebank" (barque), 1882

145 Cross surrounded by Flowers

1984. Fungi. Multicoloured.

513 6c. Type **144** 10 10
514 18c. "Marasmiellus inoderma" 20 25
515 35c. "Pycnoporus sanguineus" 35 45
516 $2 "Filoboletus manipularis" 1·75 3·25

1984. Visit of Pope John Paul II.

517 **145** 12c. multicoloured 20 15
518 50c. multicoloured . . . . 65 1·40

1984. 250th Anniv of "Lloyds List" (newspaper). Multicoloured.

519 12c. Type **146** 70 15
520 15c. "Tinhow" (freighter), 1906 . . . . 75 40
521 18c. "Oriana" (liner) at Point Cruz, Honiara 85 60
522 $1 "Silwyn Range" (container ship), Point Cruz, Honiara 1·40 3·25

1984. Universal Postal Union Congress, Hamburg. As No. **MS**512 but with changed sheet inscriptions and U.P.U. logo in margin. Multicoloured.

MS523 $1 1908 6d. Canoe stamp 1·75 1·60

147 Village Drums

1984. 20th Anniv of Asia-Pacific Broadcasting Union. Multicoloured.

524 12c. Type **147** 15 15
525 45c. Radio City, Guadalcanal 35 60
526 60c. S.I.B.C. studios, Honiara 50 80
527 $1 S.I.B.C. Broadcasting House . . . . 60 1·40

148 Solomon Islands Flag and Torch-bearer

149 Little Pied Cormorant

1984. Olympic Games, Los Angeles. Multicoloured.

528 12c. Type **148** 15 10
529 25c. Lawson Tama Stadium, Honiara (horiz) 15 10
530 50c. Honiara Community Centre (horiz) 20 25
531 95c. Alick Wickham inventing crawl stroke, Bronte Baths, New South Wales, 1898 (horiz) . . . . 9·00 12·00
532 $1 Olympic Stadium, Los Angeles (horiz) 30 75

1984. "Ausipex" International Stamp Exhibition, Melbourne. Birds. Multicoloured.

533 12c. Type **149** 50 50
534 18c. Pacific black duck ("Australian Grey Duck") 65 60
535 35c. Nankeen night heron . . 90 60
536 $1 Eastern broad-billed roller ("Dollar-bird") . . . . . 1·60 4·25
MS537 130 × 96 mm. Nos. 533/6 3·00 4·50

150 The Queen Mother with Princess Margaret at Badminton Horse Trials

1985. Life and Times of Queen Elizabeth the Queen Mother. Multicoloured.

538 12c. With Winston Churchill at Buckingham Palace, VE Day, 1945 . . . . 50 10
539 25c. Type **150** 40 30
540 35c. At St. Patrick's Day parade 40 35
541 $1 With Prince Henry at his christening (from photo by Lord Snowdon) 80 95
MS542 91 × 73 mm. $1.50 In a gondola, Venice, 1985 . . . . 1·10 1·50

151 Japanese Memorial Shrine, Mount Austen, Guadalcanal

1985. "Expo '85" World Fair, Japan. Multicoloured.

543 12c. Type **151** 10 10
544 25c. Digital telephone exchange equipment . . . 20 30
545 45c. Fishing vessel "Soltai No. 7" 50 55
546 85c. Coastal village scene . . 60 1·40

152 Titiana Village

1985. Christmas. "Going Home for the Holiday". Multicoloured.

547 12c. Type **152** 10 10
548 25c. Sigana, Santa Isabel . . 25 30
549 35c. Artificial Island and Langa Lagoon 30 35

153 Girl Guide Activities

1985. 75th Anniv of Girl Guide Movement (12, 45c.) and International Youth Year (others). Mult.

550 12c. Type **153** 60 10
551 15c. Boys playing and child in wheelchair (Stop Polio) 65 40
552 25c. Runners and Solomon Island scenes 90 70
553 35c. Runners and Australian scenes ("Run Round Australia") . . . . 1·10 80
554 45c. Guide colour party and badges . . . . 1·25 90
MS555 100 × 75 mm. Nos. 552/3 1·50 1·50

154 Osprey

155 Water-powered Generator, Iriri

1985. Birth Bicentenary of John J. Audubon (ornithologist). Sheet 121 × 107 mm containing T **154** and similar vert design.

MS556 45c. black, gold and blue; 50c. (× 2) multicoloured . . . . 3·25 4·25

DESIGNS: 45c. John J. Audubon.

1986. Village Hydro-electric Schemes. Sheet 109 × 135 mm. containing T **155** and similar vert design. Multicoloured.

MS557 30c. Type **155**; 60c. Domestic lighting 75 80

156 Building Red Cross Centre, Gizo

158 "Freedom" (winner, 1980)

157 U.S. Memorial Obelisks, Henderson Airfield, Guadalcanal

1986. Operation Raleigh (volunteer project). Multicoloured.

558 18c. Type **156** 80 20
559 30c. Exploring rainforest . . 1·50 45
560 60c. Observing Halley's Comet . . . . 2·25 1·40
561 $1 "Sir Walter Raleigh" (support ship) and "Zebu" (brigantine) . . . . 2·75 2·00

1986. 60th Birthday of Queen Elizabeth II. As T **145a** of St. Helena. Multicoloured.

562 5c. Princess Elizabeth and Duke of Edinburgh at Clydebank Town Hall, 1947 . . . . 10 10
563 18c. At St. Paul's Cathedral for Queen Mother's 80th birthday service, 1980 . . . 15 20
564 22c. With children, Solomon Islands, 1982 . . . . . 20 25
565 55c. At Windsor Castle on her 50th birthday, 1976 . . 40 45
566 $2 At Crown Agents Head Office, London, 1983 . . . 1·40 1·50

1986. "Ameripex '86" International Stamp Exhibition, Chicago. International Peace Year. Sheet 100 × 75 mm containing T **157** and similar horiz design. Multicoloured.
MS567 55c. Type **157**; $1.65 Peace Corps emblem, President Kennedy and Statue of Liberty (25th anniv of Peace Corps) . . . . 1·10 1·25

1986. Royal Wedding. As T **146a** of St. Helena. Multicoloured.
568 55c. Prince Andrew and Miss Sarah Ferguson 40 55
569 60c. Prince Andrew at helm of yacht "Bluenose II" off Nova Scotia, 1985 . . . . 45 70

1986. America's Cup Yachting Championship (1987).
570 **158** 18c. multicoloured 20 45
571 – 30c. multicoloured . . . . 75 2·50
572 – $1 multicoloured . . . . 50 1·25
Nos. 570/2 were issued as a sheet of 50, each horizontal strip of 5 being separated by gutter margins. The sheet contains 20 different designs at 18c., 10 at 30c. and 20 at $1. Individual stamps depict yachts, charts, the America's Cup or the emblem of the Royal Perth Yacht Club.
See also No. **MS**575.

1986. Cyclone Relief Fund. No. 541 surch **+ 50c Cyclone Relief Fund 1986**.
573 $1+50c. Queen Mother with Prince Henry at his christening . . . . 75 1·25
MS574 100 × 75 mm. 55c.+25c. Type **157**; $1.65+75c. Peace Corps emblem, President Kennedy and Statue of Liberty (25th anniv of Peace Corps) . . . . 3·50 3·00
The surcharges on No. **MS**574 do not include "1986".

1987. America's Cup Yachting Championship (2nd issue). Sheet 111 × 75 mm, containing vert design as T **158**. Multicoloured.
MS575 $5 "Stars and Stripes" (1987 winner) . . . . 3·50 4·50

160 "Dendrophyllia gracilis"

1987. Corals. Multicoloured.
576 18c. Type **160** 20 15
577 45c. "Dendronephthya sp." 40 50
578 60c. "Clavularia sp." . . . . 55 1·40
579 $1.50 "Melithaea squamata" 1·10 3·50

161 "Cassia fistula"

1987. Flowers. Multicoloured.
580 1c. Type **161** 10 70
581 5c. "Allamanda cathartica" 20 80
582 10c. "Catharanthus roseus" 30 80
583 18c. "Mimosa pudica" . . . 50 15
584 20c. "Hibiscus rosa-sinensis" 50 15
585 22c. "Clerodendrum thomsonae" 50 15
586 25c. "Bauhinia variegata" . . 50 30
587 28c. "Gloriosa rothschildiana" 55 30
588 30c. "Heliconia solomonensis" 60 30
589 40c. "Episcia" hybrid 70 30
590 45c. "Bougainvillea" hybrid 70 30
591 50c. "Alpinia purpurata" . . 70 30
592 55c. "Plumeria rubra" . . . 75 35
593 60c. "Acacia farnesiana" . . 85 60
594 $1 "Ipomea purpurea" . . . 2·00 80
595 $2 "Dianella ensifolia" . . . 3·00 4·50
596 $5 "Passiflora foetida" . . . 4·50 8·50
597 $10 "Hemigraphis sp" . . . 7·00 13·00

162 Mangrove Kingfisher on Branch

163 "Dendrobium conanthum"

1987. Mangrove Kingfisher. Multicoloured.
598 60c. Type **162** . . . . 2·40 3·00
599 60c. Kingfisher diving . . . . 2·40 3·00
600 60c. Entering water . . . . . 2·40 3·00
601 60c. Kingfisher with prey . . 2·40 3·00
Nos. 598/601 were printed together, se-tenant, forming a composite design.

1987. Christmas. Orchids (1st series). Mult.
602 18c. Type **163** 85 10
603 30c. "Spathoglottis plicata" . . 1·50 20
604 55c. "Dendrobium gouldii" 1·75 50
605 $1.50 "Dendrobium goldfinchii" . . . . 3·75 3·75
See also Nos. 640/3 and 748/51.

164 Telecommunications Control Room and Satellite

1987. Asia-Pacific Transport and Communications Decade. Multicoloured.
606 18c. Type **164** 20 15
607 30c. De Havilland Twin Otter 300 mail plane 45 20
608 60c. Guadalcanal road improvement project . . . 50 60
609 $2 Beech 80 Queen Air and Henderson Control Tower 2·00 2·50

165 Pupa of "Ornithoptera victoriae"

166 Student and National Agriculture Training Institute

1987. Butterflies (3rd series). "Ornithoptera victoriae" (Queen Victoria's Birdwing). Mult.
610 45c. Type **165** . . . . 3·50 3·50
611 45c. Larva . . . . 3·50 3·50
612 45c. Female butterfly . . . . 3·50 3·50
613 45c. Male butterfly . . . . . 3·50 3·50

1988. 10th Anniv of International Fund for Agricultural Development. Multicoloured.
614 50c. Type **166** 40 55
615 50c. Students working in fields 40 55
616 $1 Transport by lorry . . . 50 1·00
617 $1 Canoe transport . . . . . 50 1·00
Nos. 614/15 and 616/17 were printed together, se-tenant, each pair forming a composite design.

167 Building Fishing Boat

1988. "Expo '88" World Fair, Brisbane. Mult.
618 22c. Type **167** 20 15
619 80c. War canoe 50 45
620 $1.50 Traditional village . . 95 85
MS621 130 × 53 mm. Nos. 618/20 1·50 1·40

168 "Todos los Santos" in Estrella Bay, 1568

1988. 10th Anniv of Independence. Mult.
622 22c. Type **168** 90 15
623 55c. Raising the Union Jack, 1893 . . . . 1·40 45
624 80c. High Court Building . . 1·25 1·10
625 $1 Dancers at traditional celebration . . . . 1·40 1·40

169 "Papuan Chief" (container ship)

1988. "Sydpex '88" National Stamp Exhibition, Sydney and Bicentenary of Australian Settlement. Multicoloured.
626 35c. Type **169** . . . . 1·00 25
627 60c. "Nimos" (container ship) 1·40 40
628 70c. "Malaita" (liner) . . . . 1·40 65
629 $1.30 "Makambo" (inter-island freighter) . . . . . 1·75 1·50
MS630 140 × 76 mm. Nos. 626/9 2·50 2·00

170 Archery

171 "Bulbophyllum dennisii"

1988. Olympic Games, Seoul. Multicoloured.
631 22c. Type **170** 75 20
632 55c. Weightlifting 85 45
633 70c. Athletics . . . . 1·00 65
634 80c. Boxing . . . . 1·10 70
MS635 100 × 80 mm. $2 Olympic Stadium (horiz) . . . . 1·25 1·25

1988. 300th Anniv of Lloyd's of London. As T **152a** of St. Helena.
636 22c. black and brown 30 15
637 50c. multicoloured . . . . . 1·10 30
638 65c. multicoloured . . . . . 1·25 55
639 $2 multicoloured . . . . . . 2·75 1·75
DESIGNS—VERT: 22c. King George V and Queen Mary laying foundation stone of Leadenhall Street Building, 1925; $2 "Empress of China" (liner), 1911. HORIZ: 50c. "Forthbank" (container ship); 65c. Soltel satellite com-munications station.

1989. Orchids (2nd series). Multicoloured.
640 22c. Type **171** 75 20
641 35c. "Calanthe langei" . . . 90 35
642 55c. "Bulbophyllum blumei" 1·25 55
643 $2 "Grammatophyllum speciosum" . . . . 2·00 4·50

172 Red Cross Workers with Handicapped Children

1989. 125th Anniv of Int Red Cross. Mult.
644 35c. Type **172** 35 35
645 35c. Handicapped Children Centre minibus 35 35
646 $1.50 Blood donor . . . . . 1·25 1·25
647 $1.50 Balance test . . . . . 1·25 1·25
Nos. 644/5 and 646/7 were each printed together, se-tenant, each pair forming a composite design.

173 Varicose Nudibranch

1989. Nudibranchs (Sea Slugs). Multicoloured.
648 22c. Type **173** 80 20
649 70c. Bullock's nudibranch . . 2·00 1·50
650 80c. "Chromodoris leopardus" . . . . 2·00 1·60
651 $1.50 "Phidiana indica" . . . 2·50 3·50

1989. 20th Anniv of First Manned Landing on Moon. As T **50a** of St. Kitts. Multicoloured.
652 22c. "Apollo 16" descending by parachute 45 20
653 35c. Launch of "Apollo 16" (30 × 30 mm) 70 45
654 70c. "Apollo 16" emblem (30 × 30 mm) . . . . . . 1·25 1·75
655 80c. Ultra-violet colour photograph of Earth . . . 1·40 2·00
MS656 100 × 83 mm. $4 Moon's surface seen from Space . . . 3·00 3·00

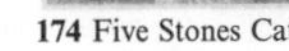

174 Five Stones Catch

176 Man wearing Headband, Necklace and Sash

175 Fishermen and Butterfly

1989. "World Stamp Expo '89". International Stamp Exhibition, Washington. Children's Games. Multicoloured.
657 5c. Type **174** 15 40
658 67c. Blowing soap bubbles (horiz) . . . . 1·25 1·40
659 73c. Coconut shell game (horiz) . . . . 1·25 1·40
660 $1 Seed wind sound . . . . 1·75 2·00
MS661 72 × 72 mm. $3 Softball 7·00 7·50

1989. Christmas. Multicoloured.
662 18c. Type **175** 40 10
663 25c. The Nativity 55 20
664 45c. Hospital ward at Christmas . . . . 1·00 30
665 $1.50 Village tug-of-war . . . 2·50 4·50

1990. Personal Ornaments. Multicoloured.
666 5c. Type **176** 30 75
667 12c. Pendant 40 30
668 18c. Man wearing medallion, nose ring and earrings . . 40 30
669 $2 Forehead ornament . . . 4·00 7·00

177 Spindle Cowrie or Tokio's Volva

1990. Cowrie Shells. Multicoloured.
670 4c. Type **177** 30 75
671 20c. All-red map cowrie . . . 75 30
672 35c. Sieve cowrie . . . . . . 1·00 35
673 50c. Umbilical ovula or little egg cowrie . . . . 1·40 1·60
674 $1 Valentine or prince cowrie 2·25 3·25

1990. 90th Birthday of Queen Elizabeth the Queen Mother. As T **161a** of St. Helena.
675 25c. multicoloured 75 25
676 $5 black and red . . . . . . 3·75 4·75
DESIGNS—21 × 36 mm: 25c. Queen Mother, 1987. 29 × 37 mm: $5 King George VI and Queen Elizabeth inspecting bomb damage to Buckingham Palace, 1940.

178 Postman with Mail Van

1990. 150th Anniv of the Penny Black. Mult.
677 35c. Type **178** . . . . 1·40 35
678 45c. General Post Office . . . 1·50 40
679 50c. 1907 ½d. stamp . . . . 1·75 1·75
680 55c. Child collecting stamps 1·90 2·25
681 60c. Penny Black and Solomon Islands 1913 1d. stamp . . . . 2·00 3·25

179 Purple Swamphen

1990. "Birdpex '90" Stamp Exhibition, Christchurch, New Zealand. Multicoloured.
682 10c. Type **179** 65 80
683 25c. Mackinlay's cuckoo dove ("Rufous Brown Pheasant Dove") . . . . 1·00 50
684 30c. Superb fruit dove . . . 1·25 55
685 45c. Cardinal honeyeater . . 1·40 60
686 $2 Finsch's pygmy parrot ("Pigmy Parrot") . . . . . 2·25 4·50

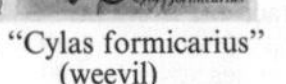

180 "Cylas formicarius" (weevil)

182 Volleyball

181 Child drinking from Coconut

1991. Crop Pests. Multicoloured.

687 7c. Type **180** 60 40
688 25c. "Dacus cucurbitae" (fruit-fly) 90 30
689 40c. "Papuana uninodis" (beetle) 1·40 45
690 90c. "Pantorhytes biplagiastus" (weevil) 2·00 2·25
691 $1.50 "Scapanes australis" (beetle) 2·50 3·50

1991. 65th Birthday of Queen Elizabeth II and 70th Birthday of Prince Philip. As T **165a** of St. Helena. Multicoloured.

692 90c. Prince Philip in evening dress 1·00 1·25
693 $2 Queen Elizabeth II 2·40 3·00

1991. Health Campaign. Multicoloured.

694 5c. Type **181** 20 60
695 75c. Mother feeding child 1·25 1·25
696 80c. Breast feeding 1·40 1·60
697 90c. Local produce 1·60 1·75

1991. 9th South Pacific Games. Multicoloured.

698 25c. Type **182** 1·00 25
699 40c. Judo 1·40 55
700 65c. Squash 2·00 2·00
701 90c. Bowling 2·25 3·00
MS702 92 × 112 mm. $2 Games emblem 6·00 8·00

183 Preparing Food for Christmas

1991. Christmas. Multicoloured.

703 10c. Type **183** 30 10
704 25c. Christmas Day church service 60 15
705 65c. Christmas Day feast 1·50 85
706 $2 Cricket match 3·75 5·00
MS707 138 × 110 mm. Nos. 703/6 7·00 9·00

184 Yellow-finned Tuna

1991. "Phila Nippon '91" International Stamp Exhibition, Tokyo. Tuna Fishing. Mult.

708 5c. Type **184** 10 20
709 30c. Pole and line tuna fishing boat 60 25
710 80c. Pole and line fishing 1·50 1·75
711 $2 Processing "arabushi" (smoked tuna) 2·75 4·00
MS712 101 × 80 mm. 80c. Plate of "tori nanban" (25 × 42 mm); 80c. Bowl of "aka miso" (25 × 42 mm) 1·75 2·00

1992. 40th Anniv of Queen Elizabeth II's Accession. As T **122c** of Pitcairn Islands. Multicoloured.

713 5c. Aerial view of Honiara 25 50
714 20c. Sunset across lagoon 50 20
715 40c. Honiara harbour 75 40
716 60c. Three portraits of Queen Elizabeth 80 1·00
717 $5 Queen Elizabeth II 3·25 4·50

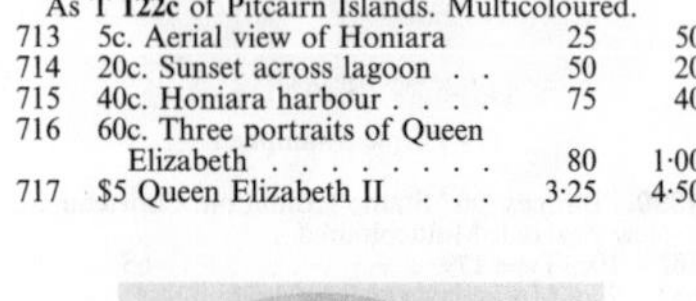

185 Mendana's Fleet in Thousand Ships Bay, 1568

1992. "Granada '92" International Stamp Exhibition, Spain. Mendana's Discovery of Solomon Islands. Multicoloured.

718 10c. Type **185** 65 40
719 65c. Map of voyage 1·25 60
720 80c. Alvaro Mendana de Niera 1·25 1·50
721 $1 Settlement at Graciosa Bay 1·60 2·00
722 $5 Mendana's fleet at sea 4·00 4·50

186 Sgt-major Jacob Vouza

187 Solomon Airlines Domestic Routes

1992. Birth Centenary of Sgt-major Jacob Vouza (war hero). Multicoloured.

723 25c. Type **186** 50 30
724 70c. Vouza in U.S. Marine Corps battle dress 1·00 1·25
725 90c. Vouza in U.S. Marine Corps uniform 1·00 1·40
726 $2 Statue of Vouza 1·25 2·25
MS727 113 × 76 mm. $4 Sgt-major Vouza in ceremonial uniform 7·00 6·00

1992. 500th Anniv of Discovery of America by Columbus and "World Columbian Stamp Expo '92" Exhibition, Chicago. Multicoloured.

728 25c. Type **187** 60 20
729 80c. Solomon Airlines Boeing 737-400 "Guadalcanal" 1·40 1·25
730 $1.50 Solomon Airlines international routes 2·00 2·25
731 $5 Columbus and "Santa Maria" 4·75 6·00
MS732 120 × 94 mm. Nos. 728/31 8·00 9·00

188 Japanese Troops landing at Esperance

1992. 50th Anniv of Battle of Guadalcanal. Multicoloured.

733 30c. Type **188** 80 80
734 30c. American troops in landing craft 80 80
735 30c. H.M.A.S. "Hobart" (cruiser) 80 80
736 30c. U.S. Navy post office 80 80
737 30c. R.N.Z.A.F. Consolidated PBY-5A Catalina flying boat 80 80
738 80c. U.S. Marine Corps Grumman F4F Wildcat fighters 1·00 1·00
739 80c. Henderson Field 1·00 1·00
740 80c. U.S.S. "Quincy" (heavy cruiser) 1·00 1·00
741 80c. H.M.A.S. "Canberra" (heavy cruiser) 1·00 1·00
742 80c. U.S. Marine Corps landing craft 1·00 1·00
743 80c. "Ryujo" (Japanese aircraft carrier) 1·00 1·00
744 80c. Japanese Mitsubishi A6M Zero-Sen fighters 1·00 1·00
745 80c. Japanese Mitsubishi G4M "Betty" bombers 1·00 1·00
746 80c. Japanese destroyer 1·00 1·00
747 80c. "Chockai" (Japanese heavy cruiser) 1·00 1·00

189 "Dendrobium" hybrid

1992. Orchids (3rd series). Multicoloured.

748 15c. Type **189** 50 20
749 70c. "Vanda Amy Laycock" 1·00 90
750 95c. "Dendrobium mirbelianum" 1·25 1·25
751 $2.50 "Dendrobium macrophyllum" 2·00 3·50

190 Stalk-eyed Ghost Crab

1993. Crabs. Multicoloured.

752 5c. Type **190** 20 60
753 10c. Red-spotted crab 20 60
754 25c. Flat crab 25 60
755 30c. Land hermit crab 25 20
756 40c. Grapsid crab 25 30
757 45c. Red and white painted crab 25 30
758 55c. Swift-footed crab 30 30
759 60c. Spanner crab 30 30
760 70c. Red hermit crab 30 40
761 80c. Red-eyed crab 40 40
762 90c. Rathbun red crab 40 50
763 $1 Coconut crab 50 50
764 $1.10 Red-spotted white crab 50 60
765 $4 Ghost crab 1·75 3·00
766 $10 Mangrove fiddler crab 3·25 5·50

191 U.S. War Memorial, Skyline Ridge

1993. 50th Anniv of Second World War. Multicoloured.

767 30c. Type **191** 35 20
768 80c. National flags at half mast 1·00 1·10
769 95c. Major-general Alexander Vandegrift and map 1·10 1·25
770 $4 Aerial dogfight, U.S. carrier and Solomon Islands scouts 4·00 5·00

1993. 14th World Orchid Conference, Glasgow. As Nos. 748 and 751, but different face values, additionally inscr "World Orchid Conference". Multicoloured.

771 20c. Type **189** 40 25
772 $3 "Dendrobium macrophyllum" 2·00 2·75

1993. "Indopex '93" International Stamp Exhibition, Surabaya. As Nos. 749/50, but different face values, additionally inscr "Indopex '93" Exhibition". Multicoloured.

773 85c. "Vanda Amy Laycock" 90 1·00
774 $1.15 "Dendrobium mirbelianum" 1·00 1·25

192 U.S.S. "PT 109" being rammed by "Amagiri" (Japanese destroyer)

1993. 50th Anniv of Sinking of U.S.S. "PT 109" (motor torpedo-boat commanded by John F. Kennedy). Multicoloured.

775 30c. Type **192** 45 25
776 50c. Kennedy thanking islander 60 45
777 95c. Message in coconut shell and islanders in canoe 80 1·00
778 $1.10 Pres. Kennedy and medal 1·00 1·60
MS779 77 × 43 mm. $5 U.S.S. "PT 109" 4·75 6·00

1993. "Taipei '93" Asian International Stamp Exhibition Taiwan. No. **MS**732 optd "TAIPEI '93" and emblem on sheet margin.

MS780 120 × 94 mm. Nos. 728/31 4·50 6·00

193 Nicobar Pigeon

1993. Endangered Species. Nicobar Pigeon. Multicoloured.

781 30c. Type **193** 35 20
782 50c. Pigeon on ground 50 35
783 65c. Pair of pigeons perched on branches 60 50
784 70c. Pigeon on branch looking left 65 60
785 $1.10 Pigeon on branch looking right 1·00 1·25
786 $3 Pigeons in flight 2·25 3·25

194 Pair of Dachshunds

1994. "Hong Kong '94" Int Stamp Exn. Chinese New Year ("Year of the Dog"). Mult.

787 30c. Type **194** 50 30
788 80c. German shepherd dog 80 1·10
789 95c. Pair of Dobermann pinschers 90 1·40
790 $1.10 Australian cattle dog 1·00 1·60
MS791 70 × 55 mm. $4 Boxer 6·50 7·50

195 Striped Dolphin

1994. Dolphins. Multicoloured.

792 75c. Type **195** 70 65
793 85c. Risso's dolphin 80 80
794 $1.15 Common dolphin 1·10 1·40
795 $2.50 Spinner dolphin 2·25 3·25
796 $3 Bottlenose dolphin 2·50 3·50

196 "Vindula sapor"

1994. "Philakorea '94" International Stamp Exhibition, Seoul. Butterflies. Multicoloured.

797 70c. Type **196** 50 70
798 70c. "Papilio aegeus" 50 70
799 70c. "Graphium hicetaon" 50 70
800 70c. "Graphium mendana" 50 70
801 70c. Exhibition logo 50 70
802 70c. "Graphium meeki" 50 70
803 70c. "Danaus schenkii" 50 70
804 70c. "Papilio ptolychus" 50 70
805 70c. "Phaedyma fissizonata vella" 50 70

197 Girl in Brisbane writing letter to Family in Santa Isabel

1994. Int Year of the Family. Mult.

806 $1.10 Type **197** 80 1·25
807 $1.10 Boeing 737-400 leaving Brisbane 80 1·25
808 $1.10 Boeing 737-400 at Henderson Airfield and De Havilland D.H.C.6 Twin Otter leaving for Santa Isabel 80 1·25
809 $1.10 De Havilland D.H.C.6 Twin Otter at Fera Airfield, Santa Isabe 80 1·25
810 $1.10 Family reunited 80 1·25
MS811 160 × 75 mm. Nos. 806/10 3·50 5·00

198 Cook Island Volcano, 1967

1994. Volcanoes. Multicoloured.

812 30c. Type **198** 30 25
813 70c. Kavachi underwater eruption, 1977 50 90
814 80c. Kavachi volcano forming temporary island, 1978 60 1·00
815 90c. Tinakula volcanic island 80 1·40
MS816 130 × 60 mm. $2 Map of Solomon Islands volcanoes; $2 Diagram showing formation of volcanic islands 2·50 3·00

199 La Perouse with King Louis XVI and Map

1994. Loss of the La Perouse Expedition, Santa Cruz Islands, 1788. Multicoloured.

817 30c. Type **199** 40 20
818 80c. Map of Ile de La Perouse 90 80
819 95c. "L'Astrolabe" 1·10 1·00
820 $1.10 "La Boussole" 1·25 1·25
821 $3 "L'Astrolabe" foundering on reef 2·25 4·00

200 Hermit Crab, Shells and Dancers

1995. Visit South Pacific Year. Multicoloured.
822 30c. Type **200** 20 20
823 50c. "Dendrobium rennellii" (orchid) and "Danaus plexippus" (butterfly) . . . 50 45
824 95c. Scuba diver and fish . . 60 1·10
825 $1.15 Grapsid crab, canoes, rusty Second World War gun and catamaran . . . . 65 1·25
MS826 98 × 81 mm. $4 Yellow-bibbed lory . . . . 6·50 7·50

201 Emblem and Bananas

1995. 50th Anniv of F.A.O. Fruits. Multicoloured.
827 70c. Type **201** . . . . 1·00 90
828 75c. Paw paws . . . . 1·00 90
829 95c. Pomelos . . . . 1·40 1·25
830 $2 Star fruits . . . . 2·75 4·00
MS831 90 × 75 mm. $3 Mangos 1·90 3·00

1995. 50th Anniv of End of Second World War. As T **182a** of St. Helena. Multicoloured.
832 95c. Vice-Admiral Nagumo and "Akagi" (Japanese aircraft carrier) . . . . . 1·00 1·00
833 $1 Rear-Admiral Fletcher and U.S.S. "Yorktown" (aircraft carrier) . . . . . 1·00 1·00
834 $2 Vice-Admiral Ghormley and U.S.S. "Wasp" (aircraft carrier) . . . . . 1·75 2·75
835 $3 Vice-Admiral Halsey and U.S.S. "Enterprise" (aircraft carrier) . . . . . 2·50 3·50
MS836 75 × 85 mm. $5 Reverse of 1939-45 War Medal (vert) . . 2·25 2·75

202 "Calanthe triplicata"

204 Marconi demonstrating Radio Transmitter, Salisbury Plain, 1896

203 Start of Canoe Race

1995. Orchids. Mutlicoloured.
837 45c. Type **202** . . . . 1·50 30
838 75c. "Dendrobium mohlianum" . . . . 1·75 1·10
839 85c. "Flickingeria comata" 1·75 1·50
840 $1.15 "Dendrobium spectabile" . . . . 2·25 2·50
MS841 75 × 90 mm. $4 "Coelogyne asperata" . . . . 3·00 4·00
No. **MS**841 includes the "Singapore '95" International Stamp Exhibition emblem on the sheet margin.

1995. Christmas. Local Festivities. Multicoloured.
842 90c. Type **203** 70 60
843 $1.05 Pan-pipe players and Christmas Tree . . . . . 70 1·00
844 $1.25 Picnic on the beach . . 80 1·10
845 $1.45 Church service and infant Jesus . . . . 1·00 1·60

1996. Centenary of Radio. Multicoloured.
846 $1.05 Type **204** 70 80
847 $1.20 Ship's radio room, 1900 80 1·00
848 $1.35 Wireless transmitter, Croydon Aerodrome, 1920 90 1·50
849 $1.45 Marconi in Japan, 1933 1·00 1·75

205 Palm Lorikeet

1996. Birds. Multicoloured.
850 75c. Type **205** 70 55
851 $1.05 Duchess lorikeet . . . 85 75
852 $1.20 Yellow-bibbed lory . . 90 1·00
853 $1.35 Cardinal lory . . . . . 1·25 1·75
854 $1.45 Meek's lorikeet . . . . 1·25 1·75
MS855 94 × 69 mm. $3 Rainbow lory ("Rainbow Lorikeet") . . 4·00 4·25

206 Dug-out Canoe on Beach and Canoe with Outboard Motor

1996. "CAPEX '96" International Stamp Exhibition, Toronto. Mail Transport. Multicoloured.
856 40c. Type **206** 35 20
857 90c. Postman with bicycle . . 1·00 80
858 $1.20 Post van . . . . 1·00 1·00
859 $1.45 "Tulagi Express" (cruise launch) . . . . . 1·50 2·25
MS860 88 × 73 mm. $4 "Tepuke" (traditional canoe) . . . . . . 1·90 3·00

207 Tokyo 1964 Poster

209 Sanford's Sea Eagle

208 Suiesi and Map of Makira Bay

1996. Centenary of Modern Olympic Games. Promotional Posters from Previous Games.
861 90c. Type **207** 50 40
862 $1.20 Los Angeles, 1932 . . . 60 70
863 $1.35 Paris, 1924 . . . . . . 65 85
864 $2.50 London, 1908 . . . . 1·10 2·25

1996. 150th Anniv of First Christian Mission. Multicoloured.
865 40c. Type **208** 30 20
866 65c. Surimahe and sketches of artefacts by Revd. L. Verguet 45 45
867 $1.35 Bishop Espalle and grave, Isabel . . . . 60 1·25
868 $1.45 John Claude Colin and Makira Mission . . . . . 65 1·40

1996. "Taipei '96" 10th Asian International Stamp Exhibition, Taiwan. Sheet 100 × 80 mm.
MS869 **209** $1.50, multicoloured 1·00 1·50

210 Children eating Fruit

1996. 50th Anniv of UNICEF. Multicoloured.
870 40c. Type **210** 25 20
871 $1.05 Children in canoes . . 50 50
872 $1.35 Doctor and child . . . 60 75
873 $2.50 Teacher and child . . . 1·00 2·50

1997. "HONG KONG '97" International Stamp Exhibition. Sheet 130 × 90 mm, containing design as No. 765. Multicoloured.
MS874 $4 Ghost crab . . . . . 1·75 2·25

1997. "Singpex '97" International Stamp Exhibition. No. 797 optd **SINGPEX '97 FEBRUARY 21–23 SINGAPORE** and logo within "perforation" frame across the entire sheetlet.
875 70c. Type **196** 70 80
876 70c. "Papilio aegeus" 70 80
877 70c. "Graphium hicetaon" . . 70 80
878 70c. "Graphium mendana" 70 80
879 70c. "Exhibition logo" . . . 70 80
880 70c. "Graphium meeki" . . . 70 80
881 70c. "Danaus schenkii" . . . 70 80
882 70c. "Papilio ptolychus" . . 70 80
883 70c. "Phaedyma fissizonata vella" 70 80
Individual stamps show parts of the overprint only.

211 Common Phalanger

1997. Common Phalanger ("Northern Common Cuscus"). Multicoloured.
884 15c. Type **211** 20 15
885 60c. Common phalanger eating fruit 30 30
886 $2.50 Common phalanger hanging on branch . . . . 85 1·40
887 $3 Two common phalangers 95 1·60

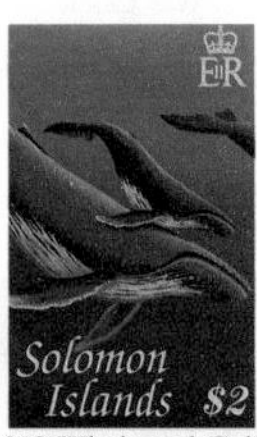

212 Whale and Calf

1997. "Pacific '97" International Stamp Exhibition, San Francisco. Sheet 96 × 74 mm, containnig T **212** and similar multicoloured design.
MS888 $2 Type **212**; $2 Whale breaking surface (horiz) . . . 2·00 2·50

1997. Golden Wedding of Queen Elizabeth and Prince Philip. As T **192a** of St. Helena. Multicoloured.
889 $3 Prince Philip playing polo 2·50 2·75
890 $3 Queen Elizabeth . . . . . 2·50 2·75
891 $3 Queen Elizabeth leading two horses . . . . 2·50 2·75
892 $3 Prince Philip . . . . . . 2·50 2·75
MS893 110 × 70 mm. $3 Queen Elizabeth and Prince Philip in landau (horiz) . . . . 2·00 2·50
Nos. 889/90 and 891/2 respectively were printed together, se-tenant, with the backgrounds forming composite designs.

213 Turtle laying Eggs

1997. 50th Anniv of the South Pacific Commission. Common Green Turtle. Multicoloured.
894 50c. Type **213** 30 20
895 90c. Young turtles heading towards sea 50 50
896 $1.50 Four turtles swimming under water . . . . 70 1·25
897 $2 Pair of turtles swimming 85 1·60

214 Oni Mako Player

1997. Christmas. Multicoloured.
898 $1.10 Type **214** 50 35
899 $1.40 Ysabel dancing women 60 70
900 $1.50 Pan pipers from Small Malaita 60 90
901 $1.70 Western bamboo band 75 1·50

215 Golden Whistler

216 Black Marlin

1997. "Bangkok '97" China Stamp Exhibition, Thailand. Christmas. Sheet 135 × 87 mm, containing T **215** and similar vert design. Multicoloured.
MS902 $1.50 Type **215**; $1.50 "Papilio aegeus" and "Graphium meeki" (butterflies) . . . . . . 4·00 4·50

1998. Billfishes. Multicoloured.
903 50c. Type **216** 60 20
904 $1.20 Shortbill swordfish . . 95 75
905 $1.40 Swordfish . . . . . . 1·10 1·10
906 $2 Indo-Pacific sailfish . . . 1·60 2·25
See also No. **MS**922.

1998. Diana, Princess of Wales Commemoration. As T **62a** of Tokelau. Multicoloured.
907 $2 Wearing pearl earrings . . 60 75
MS908 145 × 70 mm. $2.50 As No. 907; $2.50 Wearing white hat; $2.50 In evening dress; $2.50 Accepting flowers from children (sold at $10+50c. charity premium) . . . . 3·25 3·50

217 Water Melon Cultivation

1998. Technical Co-operation between Solomon Islands and Republic of China (Taiwan). Multicoloured.
909 50c. Type **217** 20 20
910 $1.50 Harvesting rice 55 95
MS911 105 × 60 mm. 80c. Growing cucumbers; $1.20 Inspecting tomato plants . . . . 1·00 1·50

218 War Dance

1998. Melanesian Trade and Culture Show. Multicoloured.
912 50c. Type **218** 40 55
913 50c. Islanders with bows and arrows 40 55
914 50c. Man on beach 40 55
915 $1.20 War dance (different) 50 65
916 $1.20 Warrior in mask . . . 50 65
917 $1.20 Woman wearing shell necklace and headband . . 50 65
918 $1.50 Dance with poles . . . 55 70
919 $1.50 Hunter with spear, shield and axe 55 70
920 $1.50 Man with nose and ear ornaments 55 70

219 New National Parliament Building

1998. 20th Anniv of Independence. Sheet 110 × 79 mm.
MS921 **219** $4 multicoloured . . 1·50 2·50

1998. "Singpex 98" International Stamp Exhibition and International Year of the Ocean. Sheet 90 × 60 mm, containing No. 906. Multicoloured.
MS922 $2 Indo-pacific sailfish . . 1·25 1·75

220 H.M.S. "Endeavour" (Cook), 1770

1999. "Australia '99" World Stamp Exhibition, Melbourne. Maritime History. Sheet, 96 × 55 mm, containing T 220 and similar horiz design. Multicoloured.
MS923 $10 Type **220**; $10 "Los Reyes" (Alvare Mendana) careened at Guadalcanal, 1568 6·50 8·00

221 Beach

1999. "PhilexFrance '99" International Stamp Exhibition, Paris. Marine Life. Multicoloured.

924 $1 Type **221** 50 60
925 $1 Great frigate bird 50 60
926 $1 Coconut crab 50 60
927 $1 Green turtle 50 60
928 $1 Royal Spanish dancer nudibranch 50 60
929 $1 Sun noon and stars butterflyfish 50 60
930 $1 Striped sweetlips 50 60
931 $1 Saddle-back butterflyfish 50 60
932 $1 Cuttlefish 50 60
933 $1 Giant clam 50 60
934 $1 Lionfish 50 60
935 $1 Spiny lobster 50 60

Nos. 924/35 were printed together, se-tenant, with the backgrounds forming a composite design.

1999. 30th Anniv of First Manned Landing on Moon. As T **94a** of St. Kitts. Multicoloured.

936 50c. Lift-off 25 20
937 $1.50 Lunar module above Moon's surface 60 60
938 $2.50 Buzz Aldrin with American flag on Moon . . 90 1·40
939 $3.40 Command module splashdown . . . . 1·25 1·90
MS940 90 × 80 mm. $4 Earth as seen from Moon (circular, 40 mm diam) . . . . 1·40 1·75

1999. "Queen Elizabeth the Queen Mother's Century". As T **199** of St. Helena. Multicoloured (except $5).

941 $1 Inspecting bomb damage at Portsmouth, 1941 . . . 50 30
942 $1.50 At the Derby, 1983 . . 65 55
943 $2.30 Receiving birthday bouquets from children . . 80 1·10
944 $4.90 Inspecting Royal Army Medical Corps parade . . 1·50 2·50
MS945 145 × 70 mm. $5 Duchess of York, 1920s, and with King George VI and Prime Minister Winston Churchill, VE Day, 1945 (black) . . . . 1·75 2·75

1999. "China '99" International Stamp Exhibition, Beijing. No. 687 optd **SOLOMON ISLANDS: 21-30 NAUGUST CHINA 1999.**

946 7c. Type **180** 30 30

223 Ferrari 212 E

1999. Birth Centenary of Enzo Ferrari (car designer) (1998). Racing Cars. Multicoloured.

947 $1 Type **223** 55 35
948 $1.50 250 TR 65 50
949 $3.30 250 LM . . . . 1·25 1·75
950 $4.20 612 CAN-AM . . . . 1·40 2·00

224 Bishop George Augustus Selwyn

1999. Christmas. 150th Anniv of Melanesian Mission. Multicoloured (except $3.30).

951 $1 Type **224** 40 60
952 $1 Bishop John Coleridge Patteson 40 60
953 $1.50 Stained glass windows 50 70
954 $1.50 "Southern Cross" (missionary ship) and religious symbols 50 70
955 $3.30 "150 YEARS MELANESIAN MISSION" (black) . . . . 75 1·25

Nos. 951/5 were printed together, se-tenant, with the $3.30 in the centre, throughout the sheet with the backgrounds forming a composite design.

225 National Flags at Half Mast

1999. Second World War Veterans' Millennium Visit. Multicoloured.

956 30c. Type **225** 35 45
957 30c. The Cenotaph, Honiara 35 45
958 30c. Solomon Peace Memorial Park 35 45
959 30c. U.S. War Memorial, Skyline Ridge 35 45
960 30c. "Ocean Pearl" (cruise ship) 35 45

It was originally intended to issue Nos. 956/60 as part of the 1992 50th Anniv of Battle of Guadalcanal set, Nos. 733/47. This strip of 5 designs was removed from the sheet and was not placed on sale until late 1999.

226 Munda Lighthouse and War Canoe

2000. New Millennium. Multicoloured.

961 $1 Type **226** . . . . 1·25 80
962 $4 Tulagi Lighthouse and launch . . . . 3·50 4·00
MS963 96 × 74 mm. Nos. 961/2 4·75 5·00

227 Islanders

2000. Commonwealth Youth Ministers' Meeting, Honiara. Sheet 130 × 90 mm.

MS964 **227** $6 multicoloured . . 6·50 7·50

2000. "EXPO 2000". International Stamp Exhibition, Anaheim, U.S.A. No. **MS**940 optd **"WORLD STAMP EXPO 2000 - USA VALUE $5.00"** on the sheet margin.

MS965 90 × 80 mm. $4 Earth as seen from Moon . . . . 1·75 2·50

228 Dragon

2000. Chinese New Year ("Year of the Dragon"). Multicoloured.

966 $1 Type **228** 50 30
967 $3.90 Dragon roaring . . . . 1·75 2·25
MS968 131 × 85 mm. Nos. 966/7 2·25 2·50

229 Rennell Island from the Sea

2000. Declaration of East Rennell Island as World Heritage Site. Multicoloured.

969 50c. Type **229** 30 40
970 $3.40 Canoe on Lake Tegano 1·25 1·40
971 $4 Rennell shrikebill . . . . 2·50 2·75
972 $4.90 Endemic orchid . . . . 3·00 3·25

230 Woman running

2000. Olympic Games, Sydney. Multicoloured.

973 $1 Type **230** 85 30
974 $4.50 Man running . . . . . . 2·75 3·25
MS975 105 × 90 mm. Nos. 973/4 3·50 3·75

231 Yellow-throated White-Eye

2001. Birds. Multicoloured.

976 5c. Type **231** 10 10
977 20c. Purple swamphen . . . 15 10
978 50c. Blyth's hornbill 20 10
979 80c. Yellow-faced myna . . . 25 15
980 90c. Blue-faced parrot finch 30 20
981 $1 Greater crested tern ("Crested Tern") 30 20
982 $2 Rainbow lory ("Rainbow Lorikeet") 50 35
983 $3 Eclectus parrot 65 50
984 $4 Dwarf kingfisher 80 65
985 $10 Australian stone-curlew ("Beach Thick-knee") . . . 1·75 1·75
986 $20 Brahminy kite (46 × 37 mm) . . . . . . 3·00 3·25
987 $50 Superb fruit-dove (46 × 37 mm) . . . . . . 7·25 7·50

232 Snake and Exhibition Emblem

2001. "Hong Kong 2001" Stamp Exhibition.

988 **232** $1.70 multicoloured . . . 1·00 1·00
989 $2.30 multicoloured . . . 1·10 1·25
MS990 115 × 85 mm. $5 multicoloured (as No. 972) . . 3·50 4·00

233 Refugees

2001. 50th Anniv of U.N. High Commission for Refugees.

991 **233** 50c. blue and black . . . 20 15
992 – $1 red and black 40 20
993 – $1.90 green and black . . 75 80
994 – $2.30 brown and black . . 85 90

DESIGNS: $1 Red Cross volunteers distributing medical aid; $1.90 Temporary tent accommodation; $2.30 Refugee family.

2001. Chinese New Year ("Year of the Snake"). Sheet, 140 × 75 mm, containing designs as Nos. 389/91 and 400, each 24½ × 35 mm and inscr "YEAR OF THE SNAKE 2001". Multicoloured.

MS995 $1 Red-banded tree snake; $1 Whip snake; $1 Pacific boa; $1 Guppy's snake . . . . 2·00 2·50

234 *Amphiprion chrysopterus* (fish)

2001. Reef Fish. Multicoloured.

996 70c. Type **234** 50 25
997 90c. *Amphiprion perideraion* 55 30
998 $1 *Premnas biaculeatus* . . . 60 30
999 $1.50 *Amphiprion melanopus* 85 60
1000 $2.10 *Amphiprion clarkii* . . 1·00 1·10
1001 $4.50 *Dascyllus trimaculatus* 1·90 2·75
MS1002 160 × 85 mm. Nos. 996/1001 4·75 5·00

235 Grey Cuscus on Branch

2002. Endangered Species. Grey Cuscus. Multicoloured.

1003 $1 Type **235** 60 25
1004 $1.70 Grey Cuscus on branch 85 65
1005 $2.30 Grey Cuscus in leaves 1·10 1·10
1006 $5 Grey Cuscus in leaves . . 2·25 2·75

2002. Golden Jubilee. As T **211** of St. Helena.

1007 $1 black, red and gold . . . 55 30
1008 $1.90 multicoloured 90 90
1009 $2.10 black, red and gold 95 1·00
1010 $2.30 multicoloured . . . . 1·00 1·10
MS1011 162 × 95 mm. Nos. 1002/5 and $10 multicoloured . . . . 6·00 7·00

DESIGNS—HORIZ (as Type **211** of St. Helena): $1 Princess Elizabeth with doll's pram, 1933; $1.90, Queen Elizabeth wearing sunglasses; $2.10, Queen Elizabeth in evening dress, 1955; $2.30, Queen Elizabeth in blue hat. VERT (38 × 51 mm): $10 Queen Elizabeth after Annigoni

Designs as nos. 1002/5 in No. **MS**1011 omit the gold frame around each stamp and the "Golden Jubilee 1952-2002" inscription.

236 Old School Building, Western Solomons

2002. Centenary of Methodist Mission. Multicoloured.

1012 $1 Type **236** 35 20
1013 $1.70 Mrs. Goldie in canoe 55 45
1014 $2.10 Tandanya (missionary schooner) 70 70
1015 $2.30 Revd J Goldie with local chiefs 85 90
MS1016 140 × 80 mm. $5 Revd. J. Goldie with Sam Aqarao (vert) 2·00 2·50

2002. "United We Stand". Support for Victims of 11 September 2001 Terrorist Attacks. As T **445** of St. Vincent. Multicoloured.

1017 $2.10 US flag as Statue of Liberty and Solomon Islands flag . . . . 1·00 1·25

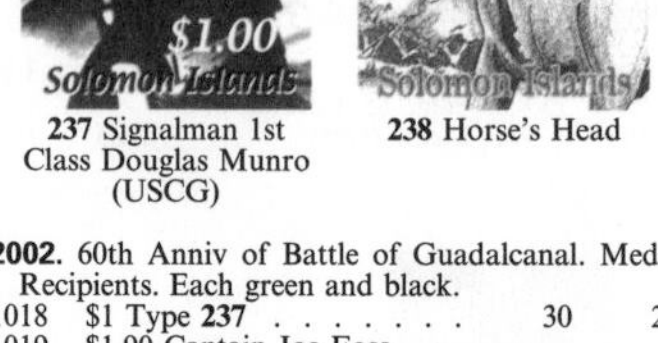

237 Signalman 1st Class Douglas Munro (USCG)   **238** Horse's Head

2002. 60th Anniv of Battle of Guadalcanal. Medal Recipients. Each green and black.

1018 $1 Type **237** 30 20
1019 $1.90 Captain Joe Foss (USMC) 55 45
1020 $2.10 Platoon Sergeant Mitchell Paige (USMC) 65 65
1021 $2.30 Rear Admiral Norman Scott (USN) 70 75
MS1022 127 × 181 mm. Nos. 1018/19, but each with a face value of $5 . . . . 5·50 6·50

2002. Chinese New Year ("Year of the Horse"). Sheet, 140 × 80 mm, containing T **238** and similar design, each brown and green.

MS1023 $4 Type **238**; $4 Horse (horiz) . . . . 2·00 2·50

239 Sieve Cowrie Shell

2002. "Philakorea 2002" International Stamp Exhibition, Seoul. Cowrie Shells. Multicoloured.

1024 $1 Type **239** 25 30
1025 $1 Kitten cowrie 25 30
1026 $1 Eroded cowrie and stolid cowrie 25 30
1027 $1.90 Tapering cowrie . . . 45 55
1028 $1.90 Tiger cowrie 45 55
1029 $1.90 Lynx cowrie 45 55
1030 $2.30 Map cowrie 60 70
1031 $2.30 Pacific deer cowrie . . 60 70
1032 $2.30 Tortoise cowrie 60 70
MS1033 88 × 58 mm. $10 Golden cowrie . . . . 3·25 4·00

2002. Queen Elizabeth the Queen Mother Commemoration. As T **215** of St. Helena.

1034 $1 brown, gold and purple 60 25
1035 $2.30 multicoloured . . . . 1·25 1·40
MS1036 145 × 70 mm. $5 black and gold; $5 multicoloured . . . . 4·00 4·50

DESIGNS: $1 Duchess of York, 1930; $2.30, Queen Mother at Royal Caledonian School, Bushey; $5 (black and gold) Queen Mother in evening dress, 1954; $5 (multicoloured) Queen Mother at St. Paul's Cathedral, 1997. Designs in No. **MS**1036 omit the "1900–2002" inscription and the coloured frame.

240 "Christmas Night" **244** Queen Elizabeth II

243 Ram

2002. Christmas. Religious Paintings. Mult.

1037	$1 Type **240**	40	20
1038	$2.10 "Madonna and Child" (Giovanni Bellini)	75	50
1039	$2.30 "Nativity" (Perugino) (horiz)	80	60
1040	$5 "Madonna and Child" (Simone Martini)	1·75	2·25

2003. World Aids Day. No. 872 surch **$1.35** and pink ribbon.

1041	$1.35+$3 Doctor and child	1·40	1·60

2003. Cyclones Zoe and Beni Relief Fund. No. 907 surch **Cyclones Zoe and Beni Relief Fund Surcharge - $5.00.**

1042	$5 on $2 Princess Diana wearing pearl earrings	1·00	1·25

2003. Chinese New Year ("Year of the Ram").

MS1043	100×101 mm. **243** $3 ×4 multicoloured	1·75	2·00

2003. Golden Jubilee (2nd issue). Multicoloured.

MS1044	156×93 mm. $9 Type **244**; $9 Wearing green outfit; $9 Wearing blue outfit	4·00	4·25
MS1045	106×76 mm. $15 Queen Elizabeth II	2·20	2·30

245 U.S. Air Force Medal of Honour **246** Prince William

2003. Medals of Honour. Multicoloured.

1046	$1 Type **245**	15	20
1047	$1.90 U.S. Navy medal of Honour	30	35
1048	$2.10 U.S. Army medal of Honour	30	35
1049	$2.30 Medal of Honour ribbon	35	40

2003. 21st Birthday of Prince William. Multicoloured.

MS1050	155×93 mm. $9 Type **246**; $9 Wearing red polo shirt; $9 Wearing suit and tie (different)	4·00	4·25
MS1051	75×105 mm. $15 Prince William	2·20	2·30

247 Harvesting Rice

2003. 20th Anniv of Diplomatic Relations with Republic of China. Multicoloured.

1052	$1.50 Type **247**	20	25
1053	$2.10 Hospital	30	35

248 Boeing 747

2003. Centenary of Powered Flight. Multicoloured.

MS1054	108×178 mm. $4 Type **248**; $4 Boeing 707; $4 Lockheed Model 649; $4 Boeing Model 247D; $4 Fokker F.VII; $4 Orville and Wilbur Wright	3·50	3·75
MS1055	105×76 mm. $15 Mach 2 Concorde	2·20	2·30

The backgrounds of the stamps in No. **MS**1054 form a composite design.

249 Pope John Paul II **250** Start of Race

2004. 20th Anniv of Papal Visit. Sheet 104×65 mm containing T **249** and similar vert design. Multicoloured.

MS1056	$5 Type **249**; $10 With head bowed	2·20	2·30

2004. Olympic Games, Athens. Multicoloured.

1057	$1.50 Type **250**	20	25
1058	$2 Running	30	35
1059	$2.20 Winning race	30	35
1060	$10 Solomon Islands flag and Olympic emblem	1·50	1·60

251 *Calanthe triplicate*

2004. Orchids. Multicoloured.

1061	$2.60 Type **251**	40	45
1062	$2.60 *Dendrobium johnsoniae*	40	45
1063	$2.60 *Dendrobium capituliflorum*	40	45
1064	$2.60 *Spathoglottis plicata*	40	45
1065	$2.60 *Dendrobium mirbelianum*	40	45
1066	$5 *Dendrobium polysema*	75	80
1067	$5 *Paphiopedilum bougainvilleanum*	75	80
1068	$5 *Coelogyne asperata*	75	80
1069	$5 *Dendrobium macrophyllum*	75	80
1070	$5 *Dendrobium spectabile*	75	80

252 Ronald Reagan

2004. Ronald Reagan Commemoration.

MS1071	124×76 mm. **252** $5 ×4 blue, red and grey	3·00	3·25

2004. Merchant Ships. As T **227** of St. Helena. Multicoloured.

1072	$1.50 MV *Bilikiki*	20	25
1073	$2.20 MV *Spirit of Solomons*	30	35
1074	$3 SS *Oceana*	45	50
1075	$20 RMS *Queen Elizabeth II*	3·00	3·25

253 Football Player

2004. Centenary of FIFA (Federation Internationale de Football Association). Multicoloured.

1076	$2.10 Type **253**	30	35
1077	$2.10 Two players	30	35
1078	$10 Player No. 3 and opponent	1·50	1·60
1079	$10 Player No. 16 with ball	1·50	1·60

Nos. 1076/7 and 1078/9 were each printed together, se-tenant, with the backgrounds showing composite designs.

254 Rufous-tailed Waterhen

2004. Birds. Multicoloured.

MS1080	Three sheets, each 148×85 mm. (a) $2.10 Type **254**; $2.10 Buff-banded rail; $2.10 Purple swamphen; $2.10 Woodford's rail; $2.10 Roviana rail; $2.10 Makira moorhen. (b) $5 Solomon Islands hawk-owl from side; $5 Great "White-Throated") eared nightjar in flight; $5 Solomon Islands hawk-owl from front; $5 Great ("White-throated") eared nightjar perched; $5 Marbled frogmouth; $5 Fearful owl. (c) $7.50 Beach kingfisher; $7.50 Collared kingfisher; $7.50 Ultramarine kingfisher; $7.50 Moustached kingfisher; $7.50 Mangrove ("Little") kingfisher; $7.50 Dwarf ("Variable") kingfisher Set of 3 sheets	13·00	13·50

The backgrounds of Nos. **MS**1080a/c form composite designs.

255 "Adoration of the Magi" (Rubens)

2004. Christmas. Religious Paintings. Multicoloured.

1081	10c. Type **255**	10	10
1082	50c. "Madonna della Tenda" (Raphael) (vert)	10	10
1083	$1.50 "Madonna and Child" (Titian) (vert)	20	25
1084	$2.60 "Madonna by the Arch" (Dürer) (vert)	40	45
1085	$3 "Holy Family" (Floris)	45	50
1086	$10 "Madonna and Child"	1·50	1·60

POSTAGE DUE STAMPS

D 1

1940.

D1	D 1	1d. green	6·50	7·00
D2		2d. red	7·00	7·00
D3		3d. brown	7·00	11·00
D4		4d. blue	11·00	11·00
D5		5d. olive	12·00	21·00
D6		6d. purple	12·00	15·00
D7		1s. violet	14·00	26·00
D8		1s.6d. green	29·00	48·00

SOMALIA Pt. 8; Pt. 14

A former Italian colony in East Africa on the Gulf of Aden, including Benadir (S. Somaliland), and Jubaland. Under British Administration 1943–50 (for stamps issued during this period see volume 1). Then under United Nations control with Italian Administration. Became independent on 1 July 1960. Following a revolution in October 1969, the country was designated "Somali Democratic Republic". See also British Post Office in Italian Colonies.

1903. 64 besa = 16 annas = 1 rupia.
1905. 100 centesimi = 1 lira.
1922. 100 besa = 1 rupia.
1926. 100 centesimi = 1 lira.
1950. 100 centesimi = 1 somalo.
1961. 100 cents = 1 Somali shilling.

1 African Elephant **2** Somali Lion

1903.

1	**1**	1b. brown	29·00	5·50
2		2b. green	1·00	3·00
3	**2**	1a. red	1·00	4·75
4		2a. brown	1·90	10·00
5		2½a. blue	1·00	10·00
6		5a. yellow	1·90	21·00
7		10a. lilac	1·90	21·00

1905. Surch with new value without bars at top.

10	**1**	2c. on 1b. brown	6·50	11·00
11		5c. on 2b. green	6·50	7·50
12	**2**	10c. on 1a. red	6·50	7·50
13		15c. on 2a. brown	6·50	7·50
8		15c. on 5a. yellow	£2500	£600
13a		20c. on 2a. brown	£300	7·50
14		25c. on 2½a. blue	11·00	7·50
9		40c. on 10a. lilac	£600	£190
15		50c. on 5a. yellow	19·00	19·00
16		1l. on 10a. lilac	19·00	26·00

For stamps with bars at top, see Nos. 68, etc.

1916. Nos. 15 and 16 re-surcharged and with bars cancelling original surcharge.

17	**2**	5c. on 50c. on 5a. yellow	31·00	30·00
18		20c. on 1l. on 10a. lilac	5·50	21·00

1916. Red Cross stamps of Italy optd **SOMALIA**.

19	**53**	10c.+5c. red	8·00	21·00
20	**54**	15c.+5c. grey	25·00	26·00
21		20c.+5c. orange	25·00	42·00
22		20 on 15c.+5c. grey	8·00	22·00

1922. Nos. 12, etc., again surch at top.

23	**1**	3b. on 5c. on 2b. green	9·25	15·00
24	**2**	6b. on 10c. on 1a. red	17·00	11·00
25		9b. on 15c. on 2a. brown	17·00	15·00
26		15b. on 25c. on 2½a. blue	19·00	11·00
27		30b. on 50c. on 5a. yellow	21·00	28·00
28		60b. on 1l. on 10a. lilac	21·00	50·00

1922. Victory stamps of Italy surch **SOMALIA ITALIANA** and new value.

29	**62**	3b. on 5c. green	1·30	5·50
30		6b. on 10c. red	1·30	5·50
31		9b. on 15c. grey	1·30	7·50
32		15b. on 25c. blue	1·30	7·50

1923. Nos. 11 to 16 re-surcharged with new values and bars (No. 33 is optd with bars only at bottom).

33	**1**	bars on 2c. on 1b. brown	7·50	21·00
34		2 on 2c. on 1b. brown	7·50	21·00
35		3 on 2c. on 1b. brown	7·50	12·00
36	**2**	5b. on 50c. on 5a. yellow	7·50	10·00
37	**1**	6 on 5c. on 2b. green	13·00	10·00
38	**2**	18b. on 10c. on 1a. red	13·00	10·00
39		20b. on 15c. on 2a. brown	13·50	10·00
40		25b. on 15c. on 2a. brown	16·00	10·00
41		30b. on 25c. on 2½a. blue	17·00	14·50
42		60b. on 1l. on 10a. lilac	17·00	30·00
43		1r. on 1l. on 10a. lilac	30·00	38·00

1923. Propaganda of Faith stamps of Italy surch **SOMALIA ITALIANA** and new value.

44	**66**	6b. on 20c. orange & green	4·50	20·00
45		13b. on 30c. orange and red	4·50	20·00
46		20b. on 50c. orange & violet	3·00	22·00
47		30b. on 1l. orange and blue	3·00	30·00

1923. Fascist March on Rome stamps of Italy surch **SOMALIA ITALIA** and new value.

48	**73**	3b. on 10c. green	5·50	8·25
49		13b. on 30c. violet	5·50	8·25
50		20b. on 50c. red	5·50	9·25
51	**74**	30b. on 1l. blue	5·50	24·00
52		1r. on 2l. brown	5·50	28·00
53	**75**	3l. on 5l. black and blue	5·50	40·00

1924. Manzoni stamps of Italy surch **SOMALIA ITALIANA** and new value.

54	**77**	6b. on 10c. black and purple	5·50	22·00
55		9b. on 15c. black and green	5·50	22·00
56		13b. on 30c. black	5·50	22·00
57		20b. on 50c. black & brown	5·50	22·00
58		30b. on 1l. black and blue	45·00	£170
59		3r. on 5l. black and purple	£450	£1500

1925. Holy Year stamps of Italy surch **SOMALIA ITALIANA** and new value.

60	–	6b.+3b. on 20c.+10c. brown and green	3·00	13·00
61	**81**	13b.+6b. on 30c.+15c. brown and chocolate	3·00	15·00
62	–	15b.+8b. on 50c.+25c. brown and violet	3·00	13·00
63	–	18b.+9b. on 60c.+30c. brown and red	3·00	17·00
64	–	30b.+15b. on 1l.+50c. purple and blue	3·00	22·00
65	–	1r.+50b. on 5l.+2l.50 purple and red	3·00	34·00

1925. Royal Jubilee stamps of Italy optd **SOMALIA ITALIANA**.

66A	**82**	60c. red	75	4·50
67B		1l. blue	1·50	6·75
67aA		1l.25 blue	35	11·00

1926. Nos. 10/13 and 13a/16 optd with bars at top.

68	**1**	2c. on 1b. brown	21·00	30·00
69		5c. on 2b. green	13·00	17·00
70	**2**	10c. on 1a. pink	8·25	5·50
71		15c. on 2a. brown	8·25	7·50
72		20c. on 2a. brown	9·50	7·50
73		25c. on 2½a. blue	9·25	11·00
74		50c. on 5a. yellow	13·00	19·00
75		1l. on 10a. lilac	21·00	24·00

1926. St. Francis of Assisi stamps of Italy optd **SOMALIA ITALIANA** (76/8) or **Somalia** (79/80).

76	**83**	20c. green	1·70	7·75
77		40c. violet	1·70	7·75
78		60c. red	1·70	13·00
79		1l.25 blue	1·70	21·00
80		5l.+2l.50 green	4·75	40·00

21

24

1926. Italian Colonial Institute.
81 **21** 5c.+5c. brown . . . . . . 70 4·50
82 10c.+5c. olive . . . . . . 70 4·50
83 20c.+5c. green . . . . . . 70 4·50
84 40c.+5c. red . . . . . . 70 4·50
85 60c.+5c. orange . . . . . 70 4·50
86 1l.+5c. blue . . . . . . 70 7·50

1926. Italian stamps optd **SOMALIA ITALIANA.**
87 **31** 2c. brown . . . . . . 1·90 3·50
88 **37** 5c. green . . . . . . 1·90 3·50
89 **92** 7½c. brown . . . . . . 17·00 30·00
90 **37** 10c. pink . . . . . . 1·30 40
91 **39** 20c. purple . . . . . . 1·30 1·50
92 **34** 25c. green and light green 1·30 1·20
92a **39** 30c. black . . . . . . 10·50 19·00
93 **91** 50c. grey and brown . . . 18·00 5·50
94 **92** 50c. mauve . . . . . . 26·00 32·00
95 **39** 60c. orange . . . . . . 3·00 5·25
96 **34** 75c. red and carmine . . 90·00 19·00
97 1l. brown and green . . . 3·00 75
98 1l.25 blue & ultram . . . 7·50 1·90
99 **91** 1l.75 brown . . . . . . 60·00 13·00
100 **34** 2l. green and orange . . . 21·00 10·00
101 2l.50 green and orange . . 21·00 13·00
102 5l. blue and pink . . . . 55·00 28·00
103 10l. green and pink . . . 55·00 45·00

1927. 1st National Defence issue of Italy (lira colours changed) optd **SOMALIA ITALIANA.**
104 **89** 40c.+20c. black & brown 2·10 17·00
105 – 60c.+30c. brown and red 2·10 17·00
106 – 1l.25+60c. black & blue . . 2·10 35·00
107 – 5l.+2l.50 black & green . . 3·75 45·00

1927. Centenary of Volta Stamps of Italy (colours changed) optd **Somalia Italiana.**
108 **90** 20c. violet . . . . 4·75 21·00
109 50c. orange . . . . . . 7·50 13·00
110 1l.25 blue . . . . 10·00 30·00

1928. 45th Anniv of Italian–African Society.
111 **24** 20c.+5c. green . . . . . . 1·90 6·00
112 30c.+5c. red . . . . . . 1·90 6·00
113 50c.+10c. violet . . . . . 1·90 10·50
114 1l.25+20c. blue . . . . . 2·10 12·00

1929. 2nd National Defence issue of Italy (colours changed) optd **SOMALIA ITALIANA.**
115 **89** 30c.+10c. black and red . . 3·50 12·00
116 – 50c.+20c. grey and lilac . . 3·50 14·00
117 – 1l.25+50c. blue & brown 4·25 22·00
118 – 5l.+2l. black and green . . 4·25 40·00

1929. Montecassino Abbey stamps of Italy (colours changed) optd **Somalia Italiana** (10l.) or **SOMALIA ITALIANA** (others).
119 **104** 20c. green . . . . 4·25 10·00
120 – 25c. red . . . . 4·25 10·00
121 – 50c.+10c. red . . . . . 4·25 11·00
122 – 75c.+15c. brown . . . . 4·50 11·00
123 **104** 1l.25+25c. purple . . . . 8·00 19·00
124 – 5l.+1l. blue . . . . . . 8·00 22·00
125 – 10l.+2l. brown . . . . . 8·00 30·00

1930. Royal Wedding stamps of Italy (colours changed) optd **SOMALIA ITALIANA.**
126 **109** 20c. green . . . . 1·20 3·50
127 50c.+10c. red . . . . . . 1·00 4·75
128 1l.25+25c. red . . . . . 1·00 10·50

1930. Ferrucci stamps of Italy (colours changed) optd **SOMALIA ITALIANA.**
129 **114** 20c. violet . . . . 1·90 2·00
130 – 25c. green (No. 283) . . . 1·90 1·90
131 – 50c. black (No. 284) . . . 1·90 3·75
132 – 1l.25 blue (No. 285) . . . 1·90 7·50
133 – 5l.+2l. red (No. 286) . . . 5·50 15·00

1930. 3rd National Defence issue of Italy (colours changed) optd **SOMALIA ITALIANA.**
134 **89** 30c.+10c. green & dp grn 15·00 19·00
135 – 50c.+10c. purple & green 15·00 22·00
136 – 1l.25+30c. brown and deep brown . . . . 15·00 35·00
137 – 5l.+1l.50 green and blue . . 48·00 75·00

29 Irrigation Canal

1930. 25th Anniv (1929) of Colonial Agricultural Institute.
138 **29** 50c.+20c. brown . . . . . 2·75 11·00
139 1l.25+20c. blue . . . . . 2·75 11·00
140 1l.75+20c. green . . . . . 2·75 13·50
141 2l.55+50c. violet . . . . . 3·75 22·00
142 5l.+1l. red . . . . 3·75 32·00

1930. Bimillenary of Virgil stamps of Italy (colours changed) optd **SOMALIA.**
143 15c. grey . . . . 1·00 4·50
144 20c. brown . . . . 1·00 2·20
145 25c. green . . . . 1·00 1·90
146 30c. brown . . . . 1·00 2·20
147 50c. purple . . . . 1·00 1·90
148 75c. red . . . . 1·00 3·50
149 1l.25 blue . . . . 1·00 4·50
150 5l.+1l.50 purple . . . . . 3·50 24·00
151 10l.+2l.50 brown . . . . . 3·50 38·00

1931. Stamps of Italy optd **SOMALIA ITALIANA.**
152 – 25c. green (No. 244) . . . 9·25 11·00
153 **103** 50c. violet . . . . 9·25 3·75

1931. St. Antony of Padua stamps of Italy optd **Somalia** (75c., 5l.) or **SOMALIA** (others).
154 **121** 20c. brown . . . . 1·50 9·25
155 – 25c. green . . . . 1·50 3·75
156 – 30c. brown . . . . 1·50 3·75
157 – 50c. purple . . . . 1·50 3·75
158 – 75c. grey . . . . 1·50 9·25
159 – 1l.25 blue . . . . 1·50 19·00
160 – 5l.+2l.50 brown . . . . . 4·25 42·00

32 Tower at Mnara-Ciromo

33 Hippopotamus

1932.
161a – 5c. brown . . . . 2·10 3·50
162a – 7½c. violet . . . . . . 11·00 8·00
163a – 10c. black . . . . . . 4·50 35
164 – 15c. green . . . . . . 1·50 95
165a **32** 20c. red £170 25
166a 25c. green . . . . . . 1·50 35
167a 30c. brown . . . . . . 15·00 1·00
168 – 35c. blue . . . . . . 2·75 4·50
169a – 50c. violet . . . . . . £250 4·50
170 – 75c. red . . . . 1·90 60
171 – 1l.25 blue . . . . . . 9·25 50
172 – 1l.75 red . . . . . . 4·50 60
173 – 2l. red . . . . 1·90 40
174 – 2l.55 blue . . . . . . 15·00 38·00
175a – 5l. red . . . . 7·25 2·30
176 **33** 10l. violet . . . . . . 19·00 11·00
177 – 20l. green . . . . . . 48·00 48·00
178 – 25l. blue . . . . . . 48·00 75·00
DESIGNS—HORIZ: 5, 7½, 10, 15c. Francesco Crispi Lighthouse, Cape Guardafui; 35, 50, 75c. Governor's Residence, Mogadishu; 25l. Lioness. VERT: 1l.25, 1l.75, 2l. Termitarium (ant-hill); 2l.55, 5l. Ostrich; 20l. Lesser kudu.

1934. Honouring the Duke of the Abruzzi. Stamps of 1932 (some colours changed) optd **ONORANZE AL DUCA DEGLI ABRUZZI.**
179 – 10c. brown . . . . 7·00 12·00
180 **32** 25c. green . . . . 6·75 12·00
181 – 50c. purple . . . . 4·50 12·00
182 – 1l.25 blue . . . . 4·50 12·00
183 – 5l. black . . . . 4·50 12·00
184 **33** 10l. red . . . . 6·75 19·00
185 – 20l. blue . . . . 6·50 19·00
186 – 25l. green . . . . 6·50 19·00

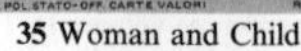
35 Woman and Child

37 King Victor Emmanuel III

36

1934. 2nd Int Colonial Exhibition, Naples.
187 **35** 5c. green & brown (postage) . . . . 3·50 10·50
188 10c. brown and black . . . 3·50 10·00
189 20c. red and blue . . . . 3·50 8·25
190 50c. violet and brown . . . 3·50 8·25
191 60c. brown and slate . . . 3·50 11·00
192 1l.25 blue and green . . . 3·50 19·00
193 – 25c. blue and orange (air) 3·50 10·00
194 – 50c. green and blue . . . 3·50 8·25
195 – 75c. brown and orange . . 3·50 8·25
196 – 80c. brown and green . . . 3·50 10·00
197 – 1l. red and green . . . . 3·50 11·00
198 – 2l. blue and brown . . . 3·50 19·00
DESIGNS: 25c. to 75c. Caproni Ca 101 airplane over River Juba; 80c. to 2l. Cheetahs watching Caproni Ca 101 airplane.

1934. Air. Rome–Mogadishu Flight.
199 **36** 25c.+10c. green . . . . . 3·50 5·50
200 50c.+10c. brown . . . . . 3·50 5·50
201 75c.+15c. red . . . . . . 3·50 5·50
202 80c.+15c. black . . . . . 3·50 5·50
203 1l.+20c. brown . . . . . 3·50 5·50
204 2l.+20c. blue . . . . . . 3·50 5·50
205 3l.+25c. violet . . . . . 18·00 48·00
206 5l.+25c. red . . . . . . 18·00 48·00
207 10l.+30c. purple . . . . . 18·00 48·00
208 25l.+2l. green . . . . . . 18·00 48·00

1934. King of Italy's Visit to Italian Somaliland.
209 **37** 5c.+5c. black . . . . . . 1·90 11·00
210 7½c.+7½c. purple . . . . . 1·90 11·00
211 15c.+10c. green . . . . . 1·90 11·00
212 20c.+10c. red . . . . . . 1·90 11·00
213 25c.+10c. green . . . . . 1·90 11·00
214 30c.+10c. brown . . . . . 1·90 11·00
215 50c.+10c. violet . . . . . 1·90 11·00
216 75c.+15c. red . . . . . . 1·90 11·00
217 1l.25+15c. blue . . . . . 1·90 11·00
218 1l.75+25c. orange . . . . 1·90 11·00
219 2l.75+25c. blue . . . . . 12·50 38·00
220 5l.+1l. purple . . . . . . 12·50 38·00
221 10l.+1l.80 brown . . . . . 12·50 38·00
222 – 25l.+2l.75 sepia & brn . . £120 £190
DESIGN—36 × 44 mm: 25l. King Victor Emmanuel III on horseback.

38a Native Girl and Macchi Castoldi MC-94 Flying Boat

1936. Air.
223 – 25c. green . . . . 1·25 3·00
224 – 50c. brown 25 25
225 – 60c. orange . . . . 1·90 5·50
226 – 75c. brown . . . . 1·20 1·50
227 **38a** 1l. blue 25 25
228 – 1l.50 violet . . . . 1·20 75
229 – 2l. blue . . . . 4·25 1·20
230 **38a** 3l. red . . . . 13·00 5·00
231 – 5l. green . . . . 15·00 9·25
232 – 10l. red . . . . 19·00 15·00
DESIGNS: 25c., 1l.50, Banana trees; 50c., 2l. Native woman in cotton plantation; 60c., 5l. Orchard; 75c., 10l. Native women harvesting.

ITALIAN TRUST TERRITORY

40 Tower at Mnara-Ciromo

41 Ostrich

42 Governor's Residence, Mogadishu

43 River Scene

1950.
233 **40** 1c. black 10 10
234 **41** 5c. red 75 25
235 **42** 6c. violet 15 10
236 **40** 8c. green 15 10
237 **42** 10c. green 10 10
238 **41** 20c. green . . . . 1·25 20
239 **40** 35c. red 35 20
240 **42** 55c. blue 45 15
241 **41** 60c. violet . . . . 1·75 35
242 **40** 65c. brown 70 15
243 **42** 1s. orange 85 15

1950. Air.
244 **43** 30c. brown 30 30
245 45c. red 30 30
246 65c. violet 30 30
247 70c. blue 30 30
248 90c. brown 30 30
249 1s. purple 45 30
250 1s.35 violet 70 70
251 1s.50 green 85 50
252 3s. blue . . . . 7·00 2·25
253 5s. brown . . . . 8·00 3·00
254 10s. orange . . . . 9·50 2·25

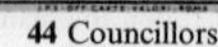
44 Councillors

45 Symbol of Fair

1951. 1st Territorial Council.
255 **44** 20c. brown & grn (postage) 2·00 20
256 55c. violet and brown . . . 3·75 3·50
257 – 1s. blue and violet (air) . . 2·25 70
258 – 1s.50 brown and green . . 3·75 2·75
DESIGN—VERT: 1s., 1s.50, Flags and Savoia Marchetti S.M.95C airliner over Mogadiscio.

1952. 1st Somali Fair, Mogadiscio.
259 **45** 25c. brown & red (postage) 1·75 1·75
260 55c. brown and blue . . . 1·75 1·75
261 – 1s.20 blue and bistre (air) 2·00 2·00
DESIGN: 1s.20, Palm tree, Douglas DC-4 airliner and minaret.

46 Mother and Baby

47 Somali and Entrance to Fair

1953. Anti-tuberculosis Campaign.
262 **46** 5c. brown & violet (postage) 10 10
263 25c. brown and red 15 10
264 50c. brown and blue . . . 70 70
265 1s.20 brown and green (air) 85 85

1953. 2nd Somali Fair, Mogadiscio.
266 **47** 25c. green & grey (postage) 20 20
267 60c. blue and grey 40 40
268 – 1s.20 red and pink (air) . . 40 40
269 – 1s.50 brown and buff . . . 40 40
DESIGN: 1s.20, 1s.50, Palm, airplane and entrance.

48 Stamps of 1903 and Map

1953. 50th Anniv of First Stamps of Italian Somaliland. (a) Postage.
270 **48** 25c. brown, red and lake 25 25
271 35c. brown, red and green 25 25
272 60c. brown, red and orange 25 25

(b) Air. Aeroplane on Map.
273 **48** 60c. brown, red & chestnut 45 45
274 1s. brown, red and black 45 45

49 Airplane and Constellations

1953. Air. 75th Anniv of U.P.U.
275 **49** 1s.20 red and buff 35 35
276 1s.50 brown and buff . . . 40 40
277 2s. green and blue 45 40

50 Somali Bush Country

51 Alexander Island and River Juba

1954. Leprosy Relief Convention.
278 **50** 25c. green & blue (postage) 30 30
279 60c. sepia and brown . . . 30 30
280 **51** 1s.20 brown & green (air) 40 40
281 2s. purple and red 55 65

52 Somali Flag

52a "Adenium somalense"

1954. Institution of Somali Flag.
282 **52** 25c. multicoloured (postage) 25 25
283 1s.20 multicoloured (air) 25 25

1955. Floral Designs.
284 **52a** 1c. red, black and blue 10 10
285 – 5c. mauve, green and blue 10 10
290c – 10c. yellow, green & lilac 10 10
290d – 15c. multicoloured . . . 20 20
290e – 25c. yellow, green & brn 15 10
290f – 50c. multicoloured . . . 30 30
288 – 60c. red, green and black 10 15

289 – 1s. yellow, green & purple 15 20
290 – 1s.20 yellow, green & brn 20 20
FLOWERS: 5c. Blood lily; 10c. "Grinum scabrum"; 15c. Baobab; 25c. "Poinciana elata"; 50c. Glory lily; 60c. "Calatropis procera"; 1s. Sea lily; 1s.20, "Sesamothamnus bussernus".

54 Oribi **54a** Lesser Kudu

1955. Air. Antelopes. (a) As T **54**. Heads in black and orange.
291 **54** 35c. green 30 20
292 – 45c. violet . . . . 1·25 35
293 – 50c. violet 30 20
294 – 75c. red 65 25
295 – 1s.20 green 65 25
296 – 1s.50 blue 75 45
ANTELOPES: 45c. Salt's dik-dik; 50c. Speke's gazelle; 75c. Gerenuk; 1s.20, Soemmering's gazelle; 1s.50, Waterbuck.

(b) As T **54a**.
296a **54a** 3s. purple and brown . . 1·00 85
296b – 5s. yellow and black . . 1·00 85
DESIGN: 5s. Hunter's hartebeest.

55 Native Weaver **56** Voters and Map

1955. 3rd Somali Fair.
297 **55** 25c. brown (postage) . . . 25 25
298 – 30c. green 25 25
299 – 45c. brown and orange (air) 25 25
300 – 1s.20 blue and pink 35 35
DESIGNS: 30c. Cattle fording river; 45c. Camels around well; 1s.20, Native woman at well.

1956. 1st Legislative Assembly.
301 **56** 5c. brown & green (postage) 10 10
302 10c. sepia and brown . . . 10 10
303 25c. brown and red 10 10
304 60c. brown and blue (air) 15 15
305 1s.20 brown and orange . . 20 20

57 Somali Arms **58** Falcheiro Barrage

1957. Inauguration of National Emblem. Arms in blue and brown.
306 **57** 5c. brown (postage) . . . 10 10
307 25c. red 15 15
308 60c. violet 15 15
309 45c. blue (air) 20 20
310 1s.20 green 25 25

1957. 4th Somali Fair.
311 **58** 5c. lilac & brown (postage) 10 10
312 – 10c. green and bistre . . . 10 10
313 – 25c. blue and red 15 15
314 – 60c. brown and blue (air) 25 25
315 – 1s.20 black and red 25 25
DESIGNS—HORIZ: 10c. Juba River bridge; 25c. Silos at Margherita; 60c. Irrigation canal. VERT: 1s.20, Oil well.

59 Somali Nurse with Baby **60** Track Running

1957. Tuberculosis Relief Campaign.
316 **59** 10c.+10c. brown and red (postage) 15 15
317 25c.+10c. brown & green 15 15
318 55c.+20c. brown and blue (air) 20 20
319 1s.20c.+20c. brown and violet 30 30

1958. Sports.
320 **60** 2c. lilac (postage) 10 10
321 – 4c. green (Football) . . . 10 10
322 – 5c. red (Discus) 10 10
323 – 6c. black (Motor-cycling) 10 10
324 – 8c. blue (Fencing) 10 10
325 – 10c. orange (Archery) . . . 10 10
326 – 25c. green (Boxing) 10 10
327 – 60c. brown (Running) (air) 10 10
328 – 1s.20 blue (Cycling) . . . 15 15
329 – 1s.50 red (Basketball) . . . 20 15
The 4, 6, 10 and 25c. are horiz.

61 The Constitution and Assembly Building, Mogadishu **62** White Stork

1959. Opening of Constituent Assembly. Inscr "ASSEMBLEA CONSTITUENTE".
330 **61** 5c. blue and green (postage) 10 10
331 25c. blue and brown . . . 10 10
332 – 1s.20 blue and brown (air) 25 25
333 – 1s.50 blue and green . . . 25 25
MS333a 150 × 200 mm. Nos. 330/3 (sold at 4s.50) . . . . 1·90 2·75
DESIGNS—HORIZ: 1s.20, 1s.50, Police bugler.

1959. Somali Water Birds.
334 **62** 5c. black, red and yellow (postage) 20 10
335 – 10c. red, yellow and brown 20 10
336 – 15c. black and orange . . 20 10
337 – 25c. black, orange and red 20 10
338 – 1s.20 black, red and violet (air) . . . . 1·10 50
339 – 2s. red and blue . . . . . 1·10 50
BIRDS—VERT: 10c. Saddle-bill stork; 15c. Sacred ibis; 25c. Pink-backed pelicans. HORIZ: 1s.20, Marabou stork; 2s. Great egret.

63 Incense Tree **64** Institute Badge

1959. 5th Somali Fair.
340 **63** 20c. black & orge (postage) 10 10
341 – 60c. black, red and orange 20 20
342 – 1s.20 black and red (air) 25 25
343 – 2s. black, brown and blue 40 40
DESIGNS—VERT: 60c. Somali child with incense-burner. HORIZ: 1s.20, Ancient Egyptian transport of incense; 2s. Incense-burner and Mogadishu Harbour.

1960. Opening of University Institute of Somalia, Mogadishu.
344 **64** 5c. red and brown (postage) 10 10
345 – 50c. brown and blue . . . 10 10
346 – 80c. black and red 20 20
347 – 45c. brown, black and green (air) 20 20
348 – 1s.20 blue, black & lt blue 35 35
DESIGNS—HORIZ: 45c., 1s.20, Institute build-ings; 50c. Map of Africa. VERT: 80c. Institute emblem.

65 "The Horn of Africa"

1960. World Refugee Year.
349 **65** 10c. green, black and brown (postage) 10 10
350 – 60c. brown, ochre and black 10 10
351 – 80c. green, black and pink 10 10
352 – 1s.50 red, blue and green (air) 60 60
DESIGNS—HORIZ: 60c. Similar to Type **65**. VERT: 80c. Palm; 1s.50, White stork.

REPUBLIC

1960. Optd **Somaliland Independence 26 June 1960.**
353 10c. yellow, green and lilac (No. 290c) (postage) . . . 12·00 12·00
354 50c. black, orange and violet (No. 293) (air) . . . . . . 22·00 17·00
355 1s.20 blk, orge & turq (No. 295) . . . . 19·00 17·00
Nos. 353/5 were only issued in the former British protectorate, which united with Somalia when the latter became independent on 1 July 1960.

67 Gazelle and Map of Africa **68** Olympic Flame and Somali Flag

1960. Proclamation of Independence.
356 **67** 5c. brn, bl & lilac (postage) 20 20
357 – 25c. blue 35 35
358 – 1s. brown, red & green (air) 40 20
359 – 1s.80 blue and orange . . . 1·10 90
DESIGNS—VERT: 25c. U.N. Flag and Headquarters Building. HORIZ: 1s. Chamber of Deputies, Montecitorio Palace, Rome; 1s.80, Somali Flag.

1960. Olympic Games. Inscr "1960".
360 **68** 5c. blue and green (postage) 15 10
361 – 10c. blue and yellow . . . 15 10
362 – 45c. blue and lilac (air) . . 10 15
363 – 1s.80 blue and red . . . . 1·10 95
DESIGNS: 10c. Relay race; 45c. Runner breasting tape; 1s.80, Runner.

69 Child drawing Giraffe **70** Girl harvesting Papaws

1960. Child Welfare. Inscr "PRO INFANZIA".
364 **69** 10c. black, brown and green (postage) 10 10
365 – 15c. black, light green & red 15 15
366 – 25c. brown, black & yellow 30 30
367 – 3s. orange, black, blue and green (air) . . . . 1·60 1·10
ANIMALS: 15c. Common zebra; 25c. Black rhinoceros; 3s. Leopard.

1961. Multicoloured. Designs each show a girl harvesting.
368 5c. Type **70** 10 10
369 10c. Girl harvesting durra . . 10 10
370 20c. Cotton 15 15
371 25c. Sesame 15 15
372 40c. Sugar cane 20 20
373 50c. Bananas 35 35
374 75c. Groundnuts (horiz) . . . 55 55
375 80c. Grapefruit (horiz) . . . 1·10 1·10

71 "Amauris hyalites" **72** Shield, Bow and Arrow, Quiver and Dagger

1961. Air. Butterflies. Multicoloured.
376 60c. Type **71** 25 15
377 90c. "Euryphura chalcis" . . 30 20
378 1s. "Papilio lormieri" . . . . 3·25 25
379 1s.80 "Druryia antimachus" 75 45
380 3s. "Danaus formosa" . . . 90 60
381 5s. "Papilio phorcas" . . . . 3·25 90
382 10s. "Charaxes cynthia" . . . 6·75 2·40

1961. 6th Somali Trade Fair.
383 **72** 25c. yellow, black and red (postage) 10 10
384 – 45c. yellow, black and green 20 20
385 – 1s. yellow, black & bl (air) 55 45
386 – 1s.80 brown, black & yell 1·10 65

DESIGNS—Handicrafts—VERT: 45c. "Tungi" wooden vase and pottery. HORIZ: 1s. National head-dress, support and comb; 1s.80, Statuettes of camel and man, and balancing novelty.

73 Girl embroidering **75** Auxiliaries tending Casualty

74 Mosquito

1962. Child Welfare. Tropical Fishes. Inscr "PRO INFANZIA". Multicoloured.
387 15c. Type **73** (postage) . . . 15 15
388 25c. Semicircle angelfish . . . 15 15
389 40c. Dragon wrasse 80 80
390 2s.70 Emperor snapper (air) 2·50 1·10

1962. Malaria Eradication. Inscr "MONDO UNITO CONTRO LA MALARIA".
391 **74** 10c. green and red (postage) 15 15
392 – 25c. brown and mauve . . 30 30
393 – 1s. brown and black (air) 55 20
394 – 1s.80 green and black . . . 1·10 90
DESIGNS—VERT: 25c. Insecticide sprayer; 1s., 1s.80, Campaign emblem and mosquitoes.

1963. Women's Auxiliary Forces Formation. Multicoloured.
395 5c. Policewoman (postage) . . 10 10
396 10c. Army auxiliary 20 20
397 25c. Policewomen with patrol car 35 35
398 75c. Type **75** 45 45
399 1s. Policewomen marching with flag (air) 55 35
400 1s.80 Army auxiliaries at attention with flag . . . . 1·40 80
The 5c., 10c. and 25c. are horiz.

76 Wooden Spoon and Fork

1963. Freedom from Hunger.
401 **76** 75c. brown & grn (postage) 45 45
402 – 1s. multicoloured (air) . . 1·10 65
DESIGN: 1s. Sower.

77 Pres. Osman and Arms **78** Open-air Theatre

1963. 3rd Anniv of Independence. Arms in blue and yellow.
403 **77** 25c. sepia & blue (postage) 30 15
404 1s. sepia and red (air) . . . 65 35
405 1s.80 sepia and green . . . 1·00 55

1963. 7th Somali Fair.
406 **78** 25c. green (postage) . . . 20 20
407 – 55c. red 65 45
408 – 1s.80 blue (air) . . . . . 1·40 90
DESIGNS: 55c. African Trade Building; 1s.80, Government Pavilion.

79 Credit Bank, Mogadishu

1964. 10th Anniv of Somali Credit Bank. Multicoloured.
409 60c. Type **79** (postage) . . . 45 20
410 1s. Map of Somalia and globe (air) 90 45
411 1s.80 Bank emblem . . . . . 1·40 90

80 Running

1964. Olympic Games, Tokyo. Each sepia, brown and blue.
412 10c. Type **80** (postage) . . . 15 15
413 25c. High-jumping 20 20
414 90c. Diving (air) 55 45
415 1s.80 Footballer . . . . . . 1·10 65

81 Douglas DC-3 Airliner

1964. Inauguration of Somali Airlines.
416 **81** 5c. blue and red (postage) 20 35
417 – 20c. blue and orange . . . 65 35
418 – 1s. ochre and green (air) 1·10 55
419 – 1s.80 blue and black . . . 2·25 1·60
DESIGNS: 20c. Passengers disembarking from DC-3; DC-3 in flight over: 1s. African elephants; 1s.80, Mogadishu.

82 Refugees **83** I.T.U. Emblem on Map of Africa

1964. Somali Refugees Fund.
420 **82** 25c.+10c. red and blue (postage) 55 20
421 – 75c.+20c. purple, black and red (air) 45 45
422 – 1s.80+50c. green, black and bistre . . . . 1·50 1·25
DESIGNS—HORIZ: 75c. Ruined houses. VERT: 1s.80, Soldier with child refugees.

1965. I.T.U. Centenary.
423 **83** 25c. blue & orange (postage) 45 10
424 1s. black and green (air) 85 55
425 1s.80 brown and mauve . . 1·60 1·10

84 Tanning

1965. Somali Industries.
426 **84** 10c. sepia and buff (postage) 15 15
427 – 25c. sepia and pink 20 15
428 – 35c. sepia and blue 35 15
429 – 1s.50 sepia and green (air) 1·10 55
430 – 2s. sepia and mauve . . . 2·25 1·10
DESIGNS: 25c. Meat processing and canning; 35c. Fish processing and canning; 1s.50, Sugar—cutting cane and refining; 2s. Dairying—milking and bottling.

85 Hottentot Fig and Gazelle

1965. Somali Flora and Fauna. Multicoloured.
431 20c. Type **85** 10 10
432 60c. African tulips and giraffes 20 10
433 1s. White lotus and greater flamingoes 75 55
434 1s.30 Pervincia and ostriches 1·60 1·40
435 1s.80 Bignonia and common zebras . . . . 2·25 80

86 Narina's Trogon

1966. Somali Birds. Multicoloured.
436 25c. Type **86** 35 25
437 35c. Bateleur (vert) 50 25
438 50c. Ruppell's griffon 65 55
439 1s.30 European roller . . . . 1·40 1·25
440 2s. Vulturine guineafowl (vert) . . . . 1·50 1·40

87 Globe and U.N. Emblem

1966. 21st Anniv of U.N.O. Multicoloured.
441 35c. Type **87** 35 15
442 1s. Map of Africa and U.N. emblem 45 20
443 1s.50 Map of Somalia and U.N. emblem 90 45

88 Woman sitting on Crocodile

1966. Somali Art. Showing Paintings from Garesa Museum, Mogadishu. Multicoloured.
444 25c. Type **88** 10 10
445 1s. Woman and warrior . . . 20 10
446 1s.50 Boy leading camel . . . 45 20
447 2s. Women pounding grain 90 55

89 UNESCO Emblem and Palm **90** Oribi

1966. 20th Anniv of UNESCO.
448 **89** 35c. black, red and grey . . 10 10
449 1s. black, green and yellow 15 10
450 1s.80 black, blue and red 85 45

1967. Antelopes.
451 **90** 35c. ochre, black and blue 10 10
452 – 60c. brown, black & orange 15 15
453 – 1s. bistre, black and red . . 30 20
454 – 1s.80 ochre, black & green 1·10 60
ANTELOPES: 60c. Kirk's dik-dik; 1s. Gerenuk gazelle; 1s.80, Soemmering's gazelle.

91 Somali Dancers **92** Badge and Scout Saluting

1967. "Popular Dances". Designs showing dancers.
455 **91** 25c. multicoloured 10 10
456 – 50c. multicoloured 10 10
457 – 1s.30 multicoloured 35 30
458 – 2s. multicoloured . . . . . 1·10 60

1967. World Scout Jamboree. Multicoloured.
459 35c. Type **92** 10 10
460 50c. Scouts and flags 15 10
461 1s. Camp scene 40 20
462 1s.80 Jamboree emblem . . . 1·00 65

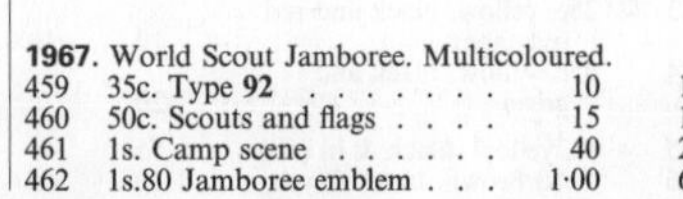

93 Pres. Schermarche and King Faisal

1967. Visit of King Faisal of Saudi Arabia.
463 **93** 50c. black & blue (postage) 20 10
464 – 1s. multicoloured 45 35
465 – 1s.80 multicoloured (air) 90 55
DESIGNS: 1s. Somali and Saudi Arabian flags; 1s.80, Kaaba, Mecca and portraits as Type **93**.

94 Black-spotted Sweetlips

1967. Fishes. Multicoloured.
466 35c. Type **94** 10 10
467 50c. Blue-cheeked butterflyfish 20 10
468 1s. Catalufa 50 35
469 1s.80 Summana grouper . . . 1·10 55

95 Inoculation **96** Somali Girl with Lemons

1968. 20th Anniv of W.H.O.
470 **95** 35c. multicoloured 10 10
471 – 1s. black, brown and green 20 20
472 – 1s.80 black brown & orge 90 55
DESIGNS: 1s. Chest examination; 1s.80, Heart examination.

1968. Agricultural Produce. Multicoloured.
473 5c. Type **96** 10 10
474 10c. Oranges 10 10
475 25c. Coconuts 10 10
476 35c. Papaws 15 10
477 40c. Mangoes 15 10
478 50c. Grapefruit 15 10
479 1s. Bananas 55 20
480 1s.30 Cotton bolls 85 45
Each design includes a Somali girl.

97 Waterbuck **98** Throwing the Javelin

1968. Somali Antelopes. Multicoloured.
481 1s.50 Type **97** 35 20
482 1s.80 Speke's gazelle 45 35
483 2s. Lesser kudu 60 35
484 5s. Hunter's hartebeest . . . 1·40 80
485 10s. Dibatag gazelle . . . . 4·50 1·60

1968. Olympic Games, Mexico.
486 **98** 35c. black, brown & lemon 10 10
487 – 50c. black, brown and red 10 10
488 – 80c. black, brown & purple 20 20
489 – 1s.50 black, brown & green 1·40 65
DESIGNS: 50c. Running; 80c. Pole-vaulting; 1s.50, Basketball.

99 Great Egret **100** "Pounding Meal"

1968. Air. Birds. Multicoloured.
491 35c. Type **99** 25 25
492 1s. Carmine bee eater 70 70
493 1s.30 Yellow-bellied green pigeon 90 90
494 1s.80 Paradise whydah . . . 2·75 2·75

1968. Somali Art.
495 **100** 25c. brown, black and lilac 15 10
496 – 35c. brown, black and red 15 10
497 – 2s.80 brown, black & grn 20 20
DESIGNS (wood-carvings): 35c. "Preparing food"; 2s.80, "Rug-making".

101 Cornflower **102** Workers at Anvil

1969. Flowers. Multicoloured.
498 40c. Type **101** 10 10
499 80c. Sunflower 20 15
500 1s. Oleander 55 30
501 1s.80 Chrysanthemum . . . 1·40 85

1969. 50th Anniv of I.L.O. Multicoloured.
502 25c. Type **102** 10 10
503 1s. Ploughing with oxen . . . 20 20
504 1s.80 Drawing water for irrigation 80 45

103 Gandhi, and Hands releasing Dove

1969. Birth Centenary of Mahatma Gandhi.
505 – 35c. purple 10 10
506 **103** 1s.50 orange 45 30
507 – 1s.80 brown . . . . 1·10 70
DESIGNS—VERT—(Size 25½ × 36 mm): 35c. Mahatma Gandhi; 1s.80, Gandhi seated.

SOMALI DEMOCRATIC REPUBLIC

An issue for the "Apollo 11" Moon Landing was prepared in 1970, but not issued.

104 "Charaxes varanes" **105** Lenin with Children

1970. Butterflies. Multicoloured.
508 25c. Type **104** 15 10
509 50c. "Cethosia lamarcki" . . 40 10
510 1s.50 "Troides aeacus" . . . 55 45
511 2s. "Chrysiridia ripheus" . . 1·40 55

1970. Birth Centenary of Lenin.
512 **105** 25c. multicoloured 10 10
513 – 1s. multicoloured 20 15
514 – 1s.80 black, orange and brown 80 55
DESIGNS—VERT: 1s. Lenin making speech. HORIZ: 1s.80, Lenin at desk.

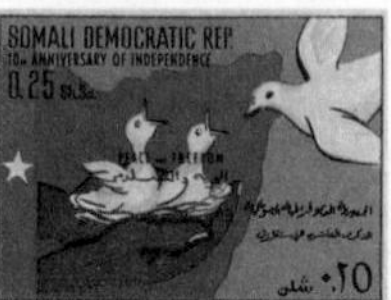

106 Dove feeding Young

1970. 10th Anniv of Independence.
515 25c. Type **106** 10 10
516 35c. Dagahtur Memorial . . 10 10
517 1s. Somali arms (vert) . . . 35 20
518 2s.80 Camel and star (vert) 1·10 90

107 Tractor and Produce

1970. 1st Anniv of 21 October Revolution.
519 **107** 35c. multicoloured 10 10
520 – 40c. black and blue . . . 10 10
521 – 1s. black and brown . . . 35 20
522 – 1s.80 multicoloured . . . 80 45

DESIGNS: 40c. Soldier and flag; 1s. Hand on open book; 1s.80, Emblems of Peace, Justice and Prosperity.

108 African within Snake's Coils

1971. Racial Equality Year.
523 **108** 1s.30 multicoloured . . . 45 20
524 – 1s.80 black, red & brown 65 45
DESIGN: 1s.80, Human figures, chain and barbed wire.

109 I.T.U. Emblem

1971. World Telecommunications Day.
525 **109** 25c. black, ultram & bl 10 10
526 – 2s.80 black, blue & green 1·10 65
DESIGN: 2s.80, Global emblem.

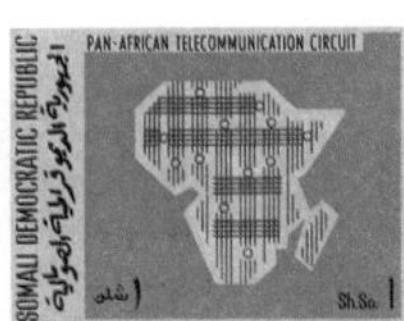

110 Telecommunications Map

1971. Pan-African Telecommunications Network.
527 **110** 1s. green, black and blue 35 20
528 – 1s.50 black, green & yell 80 35
DESIGN: 1s.50, similar to Type **110** but with different network pattern.

111 White Rhinoceros

1971. Wild Animals.
529 **111** 35c. multicoloured 20 20
530 – 1s. multicoloured 35 35
531 – 1s.30 black, yellow and violet 90 90
532 – 1s.80 multicoloured . . . 1·40 1·40
DESIGNS: 1s. Cheetahs; 1s.30, Common zebras; 1s.80, Lion attacking dromedary.

112 Ancient Desert City

1971. East and Central African Summit Conference, Mogadishu.
533 **112** 1s.30 brown, black & red 55 55
534 – 1s.50 multicoloured . . . 95 95
DESIGN: 1s.50, Headquarters building, Mogadishu.

113 Memorial

1971. 2nd Anniv of Revolution.
535 **113** 10c. black, cobalt and blue 10 10
536 – 1s. multicoloured 30 30
537 – 1s.35 multicoloured . . . 1·00 1·00
DESIGNS: 1s. Agricultural workers; 1s.35, Building workers.

114 Inoculating Cattle

1971. Rinderpest Control Programme. Multicoloured.
538 40c. Type **114** 55 35
539 1s.80 Herdsmen with cattle 1·10 80

115 A.P.U. Emblem and Back of Airmail Envelope

1972. 10th Anniv of African Postal Union.
540 1s.50 A.P.U. emblem and dove with letter (postage) 80 55
541 1s.30 Type **115** (air) 90 65

116 Mother and Child

1972. 25th Anniv of UNICEF.
542 **116** 50c. black, brown and light brown 20 10
543 – 2s.80 multicoloured . . . 1·40 1·00
DESIGNS—HORIZ: 2s.80, UNICEF emblem and schoolchildren.

117 Dromedary

1972. Domestic Animals.
544 **117** 5c. multicoloured 10 10
545 – 10c. multicoloured 10 10
546 – 20c. multicoloured 10 10
547 – 40c. black, brown and red 20 20
548 – 1s.70 black, green & black 1·60 1·60
DESIGNS: 10c. Cattle on quayside; 20c. Bull; 40c. Black-headed sheep; 1s.70, Goat.

118 Child within Cupped Hands

1972. 3rd Anniv of 21 October Revolution. Multicoloured.
549 70c. Type **118** 20 10
550 1s. Parade of standards . . . 30 15
551 1s.50 Youth Camps emblem 90 55

119 Folk Dancers

1973. Folk Dances. Multicoloured.
552 5c. Type **119** 10 10
553 40c. Pair of dancers (vert) . . 10 10
554 1s. Team of dancers (vert) . . 45 20
555 2s. Three dancers . . . . . 1·00 55

120 Old Alphabet in Flames

121 Soldiers and Chains within O.A.U. Emblem

1973. Introduction of New Somali Script.
556 **120** 40c. multicoloured 10 10
557 – 1s. multicoloured 20 15
558 – 2s. black, stone and yellow 80 55
DESIGNS—HORIZ: 1s. Alphabet in sun's rays; 2s. Writing new script.

1974. 10th Anniv (1973) of Organization of African Unity. Multicoloured.
559 40c. Type **121** 20 10
560 2s. Spiral on map of Africa 90 65

122 Hurdling

1974. Sports.
561 **122** 50c. black, red and orange 15 10
562 – 1s. black, grey and green 35 20
563 – 1s.40 black, grey and olive 90 55
DESIGNS—HORIZ: 1s. Running. VERT: 1s.40, Basketball.

123 Somali Youth and Girl

1974. Guulwade Youth Movement. Multicoloured.
564 40c. Type **123** 10 10
565 2s. Guulwade members helping old woman . . . . 1·00 65

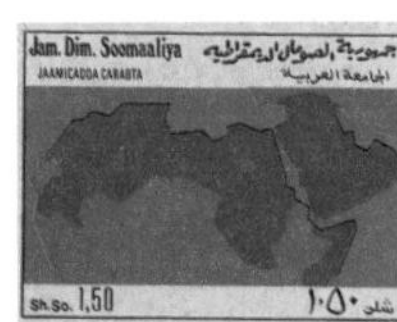

124 Map of League Members

1974. 30th Anniv (1975) of Arab League. Multicoloured.
566 1s.50 Type **124** 55 35
567 1s.70 Flags of Arab League countries 85 55

125 Desert Landscape

1975. 5th Anniv of 21 October Revolution. Multicoloured.
568 40c. Type **125** 20 15
569 2s. Somali villagers reading books (vert) 90 65

126 Doves **128**

1975. Centenary of U.P.U. Multicoloured.
570 50c. Type **126** 30 10
571 3s. Mounted postman . . . . 2·00 1·00

1975. African Postal Union. As T **126**. Multicoloured.
572 1s. Maps of Africa (repetitive motif) 35 20
573 1s.50 Dove with letter . . . 1·00 65

1975. Traditional Costumes.
574 **128** 10c. multicoloured 10 10
575 – 40c. multicoloured 10 10
576 – 50c. multicoloured 15 10
577 – 1s. multicoloured 35 20
578 – 5s. multicoloured . . . . 2·10 85
579 – 10s. multicoloured . . . . 4·50 2·50
DESIGNS: 40c. to 10s. Various costumes.

129 Independence Square, Mogadishu

1976. Int Women's Year. Multicoloured.
580 50c. Type **129** 30 10
581 2s.30 I.W.Y. emblem (horiz) 1·40 1·00

130 Hassan Statue

1976. Sayed M. A. Hassan Commemoration. Mult.
582 50c. Type **130** 15 10
583 60c. Hassan directing warriors (vert) 20 10
584 1s.50 Hassan inspiring warriors (vert) 55 35
585 2s.30 Hassan leading attack 1·60 55

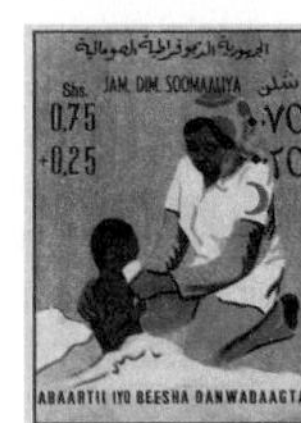

131 Nurse and Child

1976. Famine Relief. Multicoloured.
586 75c.+25c. Type **131** 45 45
587 80c.+20c. Devastated land (horiz) 45 45
588 2s.40+10c. Somali family with produce 80 80
589 2s.90+10c. Relief emblem and medical officer (horiz) . . . 1·60 1·60

132 Noted Graceful Cowrie

1976. Somali Sea Shells. Multicoloured.
590 50c. Type **132** 30 15
591 75c. "Charonia bardayi" . . 30 15
592 1s. Townsend's scallop . . . 50 25
593 2s. Ranzani's triton . . . . . 1·25 60
594 2s.75 Clay cone . . . . . . 1·50 95
595 2s.90 Old's conch . . . . . 2·25 95

133 Benin Head and Hunters

1977. Second World Black and African Festival of Arts and Cultures, Lagos, Nigeria. Multicoloured.
597 50c. Type **133** 20 15
598 75c. Handicrafts 35 30
599 2s. Dancers 85 65
600 2s.90 Musicians . . . . 1·60 1·10
The Benin Head appears on all designs.

134 Somali Flags

1977. 1st Anniv of Somali Socialist Revolutionary Party. Multicoloured.

601	75c. Type **134**	20	10
602	1s. Somali Arms (horiz)	35	20
603	1s.50 Pres. Barre and globe (horiz)	55	35
604	2s. Arms over rising sun	85	45

135 Hunting Dog

1977. Protected Animals. Multicoloured.

605	50c. Type **135**	15	10
606	75c. Lesser bushbaby	20	10
607	1s. African ass	45	20
608	1s.50 Aardwolf	55	35
609	2s. Greater kudu	1·10	55
610	3s. Giraffe	2·00	90

136 Leonardo da Vinci's Drawing of Helicopter

1977. 30th Anniv of I.C.A.O. Multicoloured.

612	1s. Type **136**	35	25
613	1s.50 Montgolfier Brothers' balloon	45	35
614	2s. Wright Flyer I	65	45
615	2s.90 Boeing 720B of Somali Airlines	1·40	65

137 Dome of the Rock

1978. Palestine Freedom-Fighters.

617 **137**	75c. black, green and pink	20	10
618	2s. black, red and blue	90	55

138 Stadium and Footballer

1978. World Cup Football Championship, Argentina. Multicoloured.

619	1s.50 Type **138**	45	35
620	4s.90 Stadium and goalkeeper	1·50	1·00
621	5s.50 Stadium and footballer (different)	2·00	1·40

139 "Acacia tortilis"

1978. Trees. Multicoloured.

623	40c. Type **139**	15	10
624	50c. "Ficus sycomorus" (vert)	30	20
625	75c. "Terminalia catapa" (vert)	45	35
626	2s.90 "Adansonia digitata"	1·40	65

140 "Hibiscus rosa-sinensis"

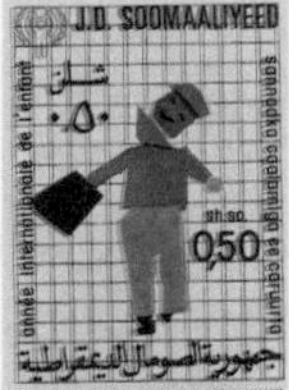

142 "Child going to School" (Ahmed Dahir Mohamed)

141 Fishing from Punt and Marbled Rabbitfish

1978. Flowers. Multicoloured.

627	50c. Type **140**	20	10
628	1s. "Cassia baccarinii"	45	20
629	1s.50 "Kigelia somalensis"	80	45
630	2s.30 "Dichrostachys glomerata"	1·40	65

1979. Fishing. Multicoloured.

632	75c. Type **141**	25	10
633	80c. Fishing from felucca and black-spotted sweetlips	30	15
634	2s.30 Fishing fleet and leerfish	1·40	55
635	2s.50 Trawler and narrow-barred Spanish mackerel	1·90	85

1979. International Year of the Child. Children's Paintings. Multicoloured.

636	50c. Type **142**	15	10
637	75c. "Sailboat" (M. A. Mohamed)	20	15
638	1s.50 "House in the Country" (A. M. Ali)	45	30
639	3s. "Bird on Blossoming Branch" (A. A. Siyad)	1·10	65

143 University Students and Open-air Class

1979. 10th Anniv of Revolution. Multicoloured.

641	20c. Type **143**	10	10
642	50c. Housing construction	10	10
643	75c. Children at play	20	10
644	1s. Health and agriculture	35	20
645	2s.40 Hydro-electric power	80	45
646	3s. Telecommunications	1·25	65

144 Devecchi's Cave Barb

1979. Fish. Multicoloured.

647	50c. Type **144**	25	10
648	90c. Andruzzi's caveminnow	70	20
649	1s. Somali blind catfish	90	35
650	2s.50 Tarabini's catfish	1·50	65

145 Taleh Fortress

1980. 1st International Congress of Somali Studies.

652 **145**	2s.25 multicoloured	85	45
653	3s.50 multicoloured	1·10	65

146 Marka

1980. Landscapes (1st series). Multicoloured.

654	75c. Type **146**	20	10
655	1s. Gandershe	35	20
656	2s.30 Afgooye	85	35
657	3s.50 Mogadishu	1·10	65

See also Nos. 673/6.

147 Pygmy Puff-back Flycatcher

148 Parabolic Antenna and Shepherd

1980. Birds. Multicoloured.

658	1s. Type **147**	80	60
659	2s.25 Golden-winged grosbeak	2·00	1·40
660	5s. Red-crowned bush shrike	3·25	3·25

1981. World Telecommunications Day.

662 **148**	1s. multicoloured	40	20
663	– 3s. blue, black and red	1·00	55
664	– 4s.60 multicoloured	1·40	90

DESIGNS: 3s., 4s.60, Ribbons forming caduceus, I.T.U. and W.H.O. emblems.

149 F.A.O. Emblem and Stylized Wheat

150 Refugee Family

1981. World Food Day. Multicoloured.

665	75c. Type **149**	20	15
666	3s.25 F.A.O. emblem on stylized field (horiz)	1·10	55
667	5s.50 Type **149**	2·00	95

1981. Refugee Aid.

668 **150**	2s.+50c. multicoloured	70	45
669	6s.80+50c. multicoloured	2·50	1·25

151 Mosques, Mecca and Medina

153 Footballer

1981. 1500th Anniv of Hejira.

671 **151**	1s.50 multicoloured	45	35
672	3s.80 multicoloured	1·50	80

1982. Landscapes (2nd series). As T **146**. Multicoloured.

673	2s.25 Balcad	80	45
674	4s. Jowhar	1·40	90
675	5s.50 Golaleey	1·60	1·10
676	8s.30 Muqdisho	2·75	2·00

1982. World Cup Football Championship, Spain. Multicoloured.

677	1s. Type **153**	35	20
678	1s.50 Footballer running to right	80	45
679	3s.25 Footballer running to left	1·60	1·00

154 I.T.U. Emblem

1982. I.T.U. Delegates' Conference, Nairobi.

681 **154**	75c. multicoloured	20	15
682	3s.25 multicoloured	1·10	65
683	5s.50 multicoloured	2·00	1·10

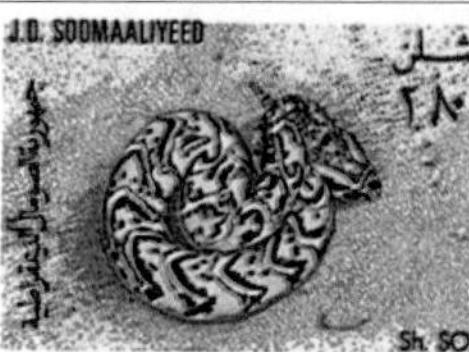

155 "Bitis arietans somalica"

1982. Snakes. Multicoloured.

684	2s.80 Type **155**	1·10	45
685	3s.20 "Psammophis punctulatus trivirgatus"	1·60	65
686	4s.60 "Rhamphiophis oxyrhynchis rostratus"	2·25	1·10

156 Bacillus, Microscope and Dr. Robert Koch

1982. Centenary of Discovery of Tubercle Bacillus.

688 **156**	4s.60+60c. mult	1·10	1·10
689	5s.80+60c. mult	1·40	1·40

157 Somali Woman

158 W.C.Y. Emblem

1982.

690 **157**	1s. multicoloured	15	10
691	5s.20 multicoloured	80	35
692	5s.80 multicoloured	1·00	45
693	6s.40 multicoloured	1·10	60
694	9s.40 multicoloured	1·60	1·00
695	25s. multicoloured	4·25	1·60

1983. World Communications Year.

696 **158**	5s.20 multicoloured	45	35
697	6s.40 multicoloured	85	40

159 View of Hamburg

1983. 2nd International Congress of Somali Studies, Hamburg. Multicoloured.

698	5s.20 Type **159**	85	65
699	6s.40 View of Hamburg (different)	1·25	1·00

160 Air Force Uniform

1983. Military Uniforms. Multicoloured.

700	3s.20 Type **160**	1·00	55
701	3s.20 Women's Auxiliary Corps	1·00	55
702	3s.20 Border Police	1·00	55
703	3s.20 People's Militia	1·00	55
704	3s.20 Infantry	1·00	55
705	3s.20 Custodial Corps	1·00	55
706	3s.20 Police Force	1·00	55
707	3s.20 Navy	1·00	55

161 Barawe

1983. Landscapes. Multicoloured.

No.	Type	Description	Unused	Used
708		2s.80 Type **161**	55	35
709		3s.20 Bur Hakaba	65	45
710		5s.50 Baydhabo	1·00	60
711		8s.60 Dooy Nuunaay	1·60	1·10

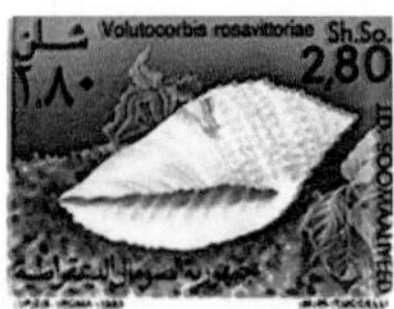

162 "Volutocorbis rosavittoriae"

1984. Shells. Multicoloured.

No.	Type	Description	Unused	Used
712		2s.80 Type **162**	80	40
713		3s.20 Valdiva bonnet	1·25	50
714		5s.50 Glory of India cone	3·00	1·00

163 Running

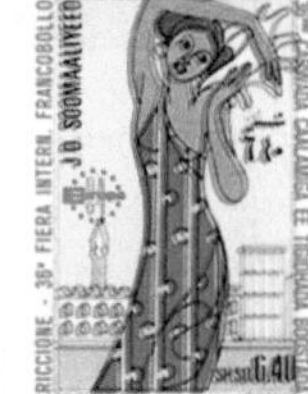

165 Girl holding Spider Conch to Ear

164 North African Crested Porcupine

1984. Olympic Games, Los Angeles. Multicoloured.

No.	Type	Description	Unused	Used
716		1s.50 Type **163**	35	20
717		3s. Throwing the discus	80	45
718		8s. High jumping	2·25	1·00

1984. Mammals. Multicoloured.

No.	Type	Description	Unused	Used
720		1s. Type **164**	20	20
721		1s.50 White-tailed mongoose	35	20
722		2s. Banded mongoose	55	35
723		4s. Ratel	1·10	65

1984. 36th International Fair, Riccione.

No.	Type	Description	Unused	Used
725	**165**	5s.20 multicoloured	2·00	65
726		6s.40 multicoloured	2·75	1·10

166 Emblem within Winged Horse

1985. 40th Anniv of International Civil Aviation Organization.

No.	Type	Description	Unused	Used
727	**166**	3s. multicoloured	65	35
728		6s.40 multicoloured	1·10	80

167 Aquila

169 Woman and Posthorn

168 Ras Kiambone

1985. Constellations. Illustrations from "The Book of Stars" by Abd al-Rahman al-Sufi. Multicoloured.

No.	Type	Description	Unused	Used
730		4s.30 Type **167**	55	20
731		11s. Taurus	1·40	65
732		12s.50 Aries	1·60	80
733		13s. Orion	2·00	1·10

1985. Architecture (1st series). Multicoloured.

No.	Type	Description	Unused	Used
734		2s. Type **168**	20	20
735		6s.60 Hannassa	90	35
736		10s. Mnarani	1·10	65
737		18s.60 Ras Kiambone (different)	2·25	1·25

See also Nos. 758/61.

1985. "Italia '85" Stamp Exhibition, Rome.

No.	Type	Description	Unused	Used
738	**169**	2s. multicoloured	55	35
739		20s. multicoloured	2·75	1·40

170 Persian Leaf-nosed Bat

1985. Bats. Multicoloured.

No.	Type	Description	Unused	Used
741		2s.50 Type **170**	55	35
742		4s.50 Heart-nosed false vampire bat	85	55
743		16s. Wrinkle-lipped bat	2·25	1·40
744		18s. Mozambique sheath-tailed bat	2·50	1·60

171 Kenyan and Somali Presidents, Solar System and Industry

1986. Trade Agreement with Kenya.

No.	Type	Description	Unused	Used
746	**171**	9s. multicoloured	65	45
747		14s.50 multicoloured	1·60	65

172 Flower Arrangement

173 Seated Man holding Pottery Flask

1986. "Euroflora" International Flower Exhibition, Genoa. Multicoloured.

No.	Type	Description	Unused	Used
748		10s. Type **172**	65	55
749		15s. Flower arrangement (different)	1·60	1·10

1986. 3rd International Somali Studies Conference, Rome.

No.	Type	Description	Unused	Used
751	**173**	11s.35 multicoloured	65	45
752		20s. multicoloured	1·60	90

174 Footballers

1986. World Cup Football Championship, Mexico. Footballing Scenes.

No.	Type	Description	Unused	Used
753	**174**	3s.60 multicoloured	35	20
754	–	4s.80 multicoloured	45	20
755	–	6s.80 multicoloured	90	45
756	–	22s.60 multicoloured	1·50	1·10

1986. Architecture (2nd series). As T **168**. Multicoloured.

No.	Type	Description	Unused	Used
758		10s. Bulaxaar ruins	55	30
759		15s. Saylac mosque	85	45
760		20s. Saylac mosque (different)	1·40	65
761		31s. Jasiiradaha Jawaay tomb	2·25	1·10

175 Rehabilitation Centre, Mogadishu

176 Runner

1987. Norwegian Red Cross in Somalia.

No.	Type	Description	Unused	Used
762	**175**	56s. multicoloured	2·75	2·25

1987. "Olymphilex '87" Olympic Stamps Exhibition, Rome. Multicoloured.

No.	Type	Description	Unused	Used
764		20s. Type **176**	85	55
765		40s. Javelin thrower	2·00	1·10

177 Modern and Shanty Towns

178 Western Indian Ocean 160,000,000 Years Ago

1987. International Year of Shelter for the Homeless.

No.	Type	Description	Unused	Used
767	**177**	53s. multicoloured	1·40	65
768		72s. multicoloured	2·00	1·10

1987. "Geosom 87" Geological Evolution of Western Indian Ocean Symposium. Multicoloured.

No.	Type	Description	Unused	Used
769		10s. Type **178**	20	10
770		20s. 60,000,000 years ago	55	20
771		40s. 15,000,000 years ago	90	45
772		50s. Today	1·60	90

179 Baby receiving Oral Vaccination (Italian inscr)

180 Somali Hare

1988. 40th Anniv of W.H.O.

No.	Type	Description	Unused	Used
774	**179**	50s. multicoloured	45	20
775		168s. multicoloured (English inscr)	1·75	90

1989. Animals. Multicoloured.

No.	Type	Description	Unused	Used
776		75s. Type **180**	45	20
777		198s. African buffalo	1·10	35
778		200s. Hamadryas baboon (horiz)	1·25	45
779		216s. Hippopotamus (horiz)	1·60	65

181 Water Lily and Boys playing Football

1989. 20th Anniv of 21 October Revolution. Multicoloured.

No.	Type	Description	Unused	Used
781		70s. Type **181**	35	20
782		100s. Boys playing on swing	45	20
783		150s. Girls on see-saw	90	35
784		300s. Girl skipping and boy rolling hoop	1·60	65

182 Dove and Broken Chain

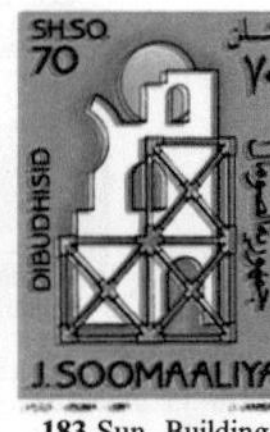

183 Sun, Building and Scaffolding

1991. Liberation. (a) Type **182** (without opt).

No.	Type	Description	Unused	Used
785	**182**	150s. multicoloured	85	35
786		300s. multicoloured	1·60	80

(b) No. 785 additionally optd **"FREEDOM"**.

No.	Type	Description	Unused	Used
787	**182**	150s. multicoloured	3·00	2·75

1991. Reconstruction.

No.	Type	Description	Unused	Used
788	**183**	70s. multicoloured	35	20
789		100s. multicoloured	55	35
790		150s. multicoloured	80	45
791		300s. multicoloured	1·60	65

EXPRESS LETTER STAMPS

1923. Express Letter stamps of Italy surch **Somalia Italiana** and value.

No.	Type	Description	Unused	Used
E44	E **12**	30b. on 60c. red	24·00	17·00
E45	E **13**	60b. on 1l.20 blue & pink	35·00	34·00

E 17

1924.

No.	Type	Description	Unused	Used
E60	E **17**	30b. brown and red	9·25	10·00
E61		60b. pink and blue	14·00	18·00

No. E61 is inscr "EXPRES".

1926. Nos. E60/1 surch.

No.	Type	Description	Unused	Used
E104		70c. on 30b. brown and red	10·00	13·00
E106		1l.25 on 30b. brown and red	12·00	9·25
E105		2l.50 on 60b. blue and pink	13·00	15·00

E 44 Grant's Gazelle

1950.

No.	Type	Description	Unused	Used
E255	E **44**	40c. green	5·00	3·50
E256		80c. violet	8·00	6·00

E 54 "Gardenia lutea"

1955.

No.	Type	Description	Unused	Used
E291	E **54**	50c. yellow, grn & lilac	40	85
E292	–	1s. red, green and blue	75	1·10

FLOWER: 1s. Coral tree.

E 61 Young Gazelles

1958. Air.

No.	Type	Description	Unused	Used
E330	E **61**	1s.70 red and black	1·90	1·50

OFFICIAL STAMPS

1934. Air. Rome–Mogadishu Flight. As No. 208, but colour changed, optd **SERVIZIO DI STATO** and crown.

No.	Type	Description	Unused	Used
O209	**36**	25l.+2l. pink	£1900	£2750

1934. Air. No. 193 optd **11 NOV. 1934-XIII SERVIZIO AEREO SPECIALE** and crown.

No.	Type	Description	Unused	Used
O210		25c. blue and orange	£2000	£2500

PARCEL POST STAMPS

Nos. P23 to P122 are Parcel Post stamps of Italy optd or surch on each half of stamp.

Unused prices are for complete pairs, used prices for a half stamp.

1920. Optd **SOMALIA ITALIANA**.

No.	Type	Description	Unused	Used
P23	P **53**	5c. brown	1·50	21·00
P24		10c. blue	2·20	15·00
P82		20c. black	34·00	24·00
P26		25c. red	5·50	28·00
P84		50c. orange	34·00	20·00
P28		1l. violet	24·00	24·00
P29		2l. green	34·00	38·00
P87		3l. yellow	10·00	24·00
P88		4l. grey	10·00	24·00
P89		10l. purple	19·00	32·00
P90		12l. brown	19·00	32·00
P91		15l. green	19·00	45·00
P92		20l. purple	19·00	45·00

1922. Optd **SOMALIA**.

No.	Type	Description	Unused	Used
P32	P **53**	25c. red	38·00	12·50
P33		50c. orange	48·00	3·75
P34		1l. violet	48·00	4·50
P35		2l. green	60·00	5·75
P36		3l. yellow	75·00	10·50
P37		4l. grey	75·00	11·50

1923. Surch **SOMALIA ITALIANA** and value.
P44 P 53 3b. on 5c. brown . . . . 3·50 13·00
P45 5b. on 5c. brown . . . . 3·50 13·00
P46 10b. on 10c. blue . . . 2·00 11·00
P47 25b. on 25c. red . . . . 3·00 19·00
P48 50b. on 50c. orange . . 3·25 28·00
P49 1r. on 1l. violet . . . . 3·50 28·00
P50 2r. on 2l. green . . . . 6·50 37·00
P51 3r. on 3l. yellow . . . . 9·00 37·00
P52 4r. on 4l. grey . . . . . 14·00 37·00

1928. Optd **SOMALIA ITALIANA**.
P111 P 92 5c. brown . . . . . . 1·20 3·75
P112 10c. blue . . . . 1·50 3·75
P113 25c. red . . . . 30·00 13·00
P114 30c. blue . . . . 60 1·50
P115 50c. orange . . . . . £12000 95·00
P116 60c. red . . . . 60 1·90
P127 1l. violet . . . . 32·00 3·25
P128 2l. green . . . . 32·00 3·25
P119 3l. yellow . . . . . . 1·90 6·75
P120 4l. black . . . . 1·90 6·75
P121 10l. mauve £300 £300
P122 20l. purple £300 £300

P 44

1950.
P255 P 44 1c. red . . . . 1·50 1·50
P256 3c. violet . . . . 1·50 1·50
P257 5c. purple . . . . . . 1·50 1·50
P258 10c. orange . . . . . 1·50 1·50
P259 20c. brown . . . . . . 1·50 1·50
P260 50c. green . . . . . . 3·75 3·75
P261 1s. violet . . . . 15·00 15·00
P262 2s. brown . . . . . . 19·00 19·00
P263 3s. blue . . . . 30·00 30·00

POSTAGE DUE STAMPS

Nos. D17 to D199 are Postage Due stamps of Italy optd or surch.

1906. Optd **Somalia Italiana Meridionale**.
D17 D 12 5c. mauve and orange 6·25 22·00
D18 10c. mauve and orange 34·00 28·00
D19 20c. mauve and orange 24·00 36·00
D20 30c. mauve and orange 21·00 40·00
D21 40c. mauve and orange £170 40·00
D22 50c. mauve and orange 40·00 48·00
D23 60c. mauve and orange 38·00 48·00
D24 1l. mauve and blue . . £750 £190
D25 2l. mauve and blue . . £700 £190
D26 5l. mauve and blue . . £700 £225
D27 10l. mauve and blue . . £120 £190

1909. Optd **Somalia Italiana**.
D28 D 12 5c. mauve and orange 3·00 12·50
D29 10c. mauve and orange 3·00 12·50
D30 20c. mauve and orange 7·50 21·00
D31 30c. mauve and orange 22·00 21·00
D32 40c. mauve and orange 22·00 24·00
D33 50c. mauve and orange 22·00 40·00
D34 60c. mauve and orange 32·00 34·00
D35 1l. mauve and blue . . 85·00 40·00
D36 2l. mauve and blue . . £110 £100
D48 5l. mauve and blue . . £110 £120
D38 10l. mauve and blue . . 22·00 45·00

1923. Stamps without figures of value, surch **Somalia Italiana** and value in "besa" or "rupia" in figures and words.
D49 D 12 1b. orange . . . . . . 95 3·50
D50 2b. orange . . . . . . 95 3·50
D51 3b. orange . . . . . . 95 3·50
D52 5b. orange . . . . . . 1·90 3·50
D53 10b. orange . . . . . 1·90 3·50
D54 20b. orange . . . . . 1·90 3·50
D55 40b. orange . . . . . 1·90 3·50
D56 1r. blue . . . . 3·00 19·00

1926. Optd **Somalia Italiana** and surch with figures only.
D76 5c. orange . . . . 15·00 17·00
D77 10c. orange . . . . 15·00 9·25
D78 20c. orange . . . . 15·00 17·00
D79 30c. orange . . . . 15·00 9·25
D80 40c. orange . . . . 15·00 9·25
D81 50c. orange . . . . 19·00 9·25
D82 60c. orange . . . . 19·00 9·25
D83 1l. blue . . . . 32·00 17·00
D84 2l. blue . . . . 45·00 17·00
D85 5l. blue . . . . 50·00 25·00
D86 10l. blue . . . . 48·00 32·00

1934. Optd **SOMALIA ITALIANA**.
D187 D 141 5c. brown . . . . . 60 1·90
D188 10c. blue . . . . . . 60 1·90
D189 20c. red . . . . . . 2·20 3·75
D190 25c. green . . . . . 2·20 3·75
D191 30c. red . . . . . . 5·50 6·75
D192 40c. brown . . . . . 5·50 9·25
D193 50c. violet . . . . . 11·00 2·75
D194 60c. blue . . . . . . 15·00 21·00
D195 D 142 1l. orange . . . . . 17·00 7·50
D196 2l. green . . . . . . 32·00 21·00
D197 5l. violet . . . . . . 45·00 38·00
D198 10l. blue . . . . . . 45·00 40·00
D199 20l. red . . . . . . 40·00 48·00

D 44

1950.
D255 D 44 1c. violet 75 75
D256 2c. blue 75 75
D257 5c. green 75 75
D258 10c. purple 75 75
D259 40c. violet . . . . . . 4·50 4·50
D260 1s. brown . . . . . . 6·75 6·75

SOMALILAND PROTECTORATE Pt. 1

A British protectorate in north-east Africa on the Gulf of Aden. Amalgamated with the Somalia Republic on 1 July 1960, whose stamps it now uses.

1903. 16 annas = 1 rupee.
1951. 100 cents = 1 shilling.

1903. Stamps of India (Queen Victoria) optd **BRITISH SOMALILAND**.
1 23 ½a. green . . . . 2·75 4·00
2 – 1a. red . . . . 2·75 3·75
3 – 2a. lilac . . . . 2·25 1·50
4 – 2½a. blue . . . . 2·00 1·75
5 – 3a. orange . . . . 3·25 3·00
6 – 4a. green (No. 96) . . . . 3·50 2·75
7 – 6a. brown (No. 80) . . . . 5·00 4·50
8 – 8a. mauve . . . . 3·75 5·00
9 – 12a. purple on red . . . . 3·25 7·00
21 37 1r. green and red . . . . 4·00 11·00
11 38 2r. red and orange . . . . 26·00 42·00
12 3r. brown and green . . . . 22·00 48·00
13 5r. blue and violet . . . . . 38·00 55·00

1903. Stamps of India of 1902 (King Edward VII) optd **BRITISH SOMALILAND**.
25 ½a. green (No. 122) . . . . . 2·25 55
26 1a. red (No. 123) . . . . . . 1·25 30
27 2a. lilac . . . . 1·75 2·50
28 3a. orange . . . . 2·50 2·50
29 4a. olive . . . . 1·50 4·00
30 8a. mauve . . . . 1·75 2·25

2

1904.
32 2 ½a. green . . . . 1·75 4·25
46a 1a. black and red . . . . . 11·00 1·60
59 1a. red . . . . 2·50 2·00
34 2a. purple . . . . 1·75 2·25
35 2½a. blue . . . . 3·75 3·75
36 3a. brown and green . . . . 2·00 2·50
37 4a. green and black . . . . 2·00 4·75
38 6a. green and violet . . . . 4·75 17·00
39 8a. black and blue . . . . . 3·75 5·50
53 12a. black and orange . . . 6·50 10·00
41 1r. green . . . . 12·00 40·00
42 2r. purple . . . . 40·00 75·00
43 3r. green and black . . . . 40·00 85·00
44 5r. black and red . . . . . 40·00 85·00
The rupee values are larger, 26 × 31 mm.

1912. As 1904, but portrait of King George V.
60 ½a. green . . . . 65 8·00
61 1a. red . . . . 2·50 50
75 2a. purple . . . . 4·25 1·00
76 2½a. blue . . . . 1·00 4·50
64 3a. brown and green . . . . 2·25 6·50
78 4a. green and black . . . . 2·50 7·50
66 6a. green and violet . . . . 2·50 5·00
80 8a. black and blue . . . . . 2·00 5·50
81 12a. black and orange . . . . 8·50 15·00
69 1r. green . . . . 11·00 16·00
83 2r. purple . . . . 23·00 50·00
84 3r. green and black . . . . 35·00 £100
72 5r. black and red . . . . . 55·00 £160

1935. Silver Jubilee. As T **32a** of St. Helena.
86 1a. blue and red . . . . . . 2·25 3·50
87 2a. blue and grey . . . . . . 2·75 3·50
88 3a. brown and blue . . . . . 2·25 14·00
89 1r. grey and purple . . . . . 7·00 14·00

1937. Coronation. As T **32b** of St. Helena.
90 1a. red 15 25
91 2a. grey . . . . 55 2·00
92 3a. blue . . . . 1·10 1·00

6 Berbera Blackhead Sheep

9 Berbera Blackhead Sheep

8 Somaliland Protectorate

1938. Portrait faces left.
93 6 ½a. green . . . . 50 5·00
94 1a. red . . . . 50 2·00
95 2a. purple . . . . 2·50 2·50
96 3a. blue . . . . 9·50 12·00
97 – 4a. brown . . . . 5·50 10·00
98 – 6a. violet . . . . 8·50 12·00
99 – 8a. grey . . . . 1·75 12·00
100 – 12a. orange . . . . 8·00 18·00
101 8 1r. green . . . . 8·50 55·00
102 2r. purple . . . . 18·00 55·00
103 3r. blue . . . . 19·00 35·00
104 5r. black . . . . 21·00 35·00
DESIGN—As T **6**: 4a. to 12a. Lesser kudu antelope.

1942. As Nos. 93/104 but with full-face portraits as in T **9**.
105 9 ½a. green 20 40
106 1a. red 20 10
107 2a. purple 50 20
108 3a. blue . . . . 2·00 20
109 – 4a. brown . . . . 3·00 30
110 – 6a. violet . . . . 3·00 20
111 – 8a. grey . . . . 3·25 20
112 – 12a. orange . . . . 3·25 40
113 – 1r. green . . . . 2·00 70
114 – 2r. purple . . . . 2·00 4·50
115 – 3r. blue . . . . 3·25 8·00
116 – 5r. black . . . . 7·50 7·50

1946. Victory. As T **33a** of St. Helena.
117 1a. red 10 10
118 3a. blue 10 10

1949. Silver Wedding. As T **33b/c** of St. Helena.
119 1a. red 10 10
120 5r. black . . . . 3·50 3·50

1949. 75th Anniv of U.P.U. As T **33d/g** of St. Helena.
121 1a. on 10c. red 20 30
122 3a. on 30c. blue . . . . . . 1·25 1·25
123 6a. on 50c. purple . . . . . 35 1·50
124 12a. on 1s. orange . . . . . 35 1·00

1951. 1942 issue surch with figures and **Cents** or **Shillings**.
125 5c. on ½a. green . . . . . . 30 1·50
126 10c. on 2a. purple 30 60
127 15c. on 3a. blue . . . . . . 1·75 1·75
128 20c. on 4a. brown . . . . . 2·00 20
129 30c. on 6a. violet . . . . . 1·75 75
130 50c. on 8a. grey . . . . . . 2·50 20
131 70c. on 2a. orange . . . . . 4·00 4·50
132 1s. on 1r. green . . . . . . 2·00 75
133 2s. on 2r. purple . . . . . . 5·50 14·00
134 2s. on 3r. blue . . . . 6·50 6·00
135 5s. on 5r. black . . . . . . 8·50 8·00

1953. Coronation. As T **33h** of St. Helena.
136 15c. black and green 30 20

12 Camel and Gurgi

13 Sentry, Somaliland Scouts

1953.
137 12 5c. black 15 50
138 13 10c. orange . . . . 2·25 60
139 12 15c. green 60 60
140 20c. red 60 40
141 13 30c. brown . . . . 2·25 40
142 – 35c. blue . . . . 5·50 1·75
143 – 50c. brown and red . . . . 5·50 55
144 – 1s. blue 65 30
145 – 1s.30 blue and black . . . 10·00 3·25
146 – 2s. brown and violet . . . 27·00 6·00
147 – 5s. brown and green . . . 27·00 6·50
148 – 10s. brown and violet . . . 17·00 19·00
DESIGNS—HORIZ: 35c., 2s. Somali pigeon; 50c., 5s. Martial eagle; 1s. Berbera blackhead sheep; 1s.30, Sheikh Isaaq's Tomb, Mait; 10s. Taleh Fort.

1957. Opening of Legislative Council. Optd **OPENING OF THE LEGISLATIVE COUNCIL 1957**.
149 12 20c. red 10 15
150 – 1s. blue (No. 144) 30 15

1960. Legislative Council's Unofficial Majority. Optd **LEGISLATIVE COUNCIL UNOFFICIAL MAJORITY, 1960**.
151 12 20c. red 10 15
152 – 1s.30 blue and black (No. 145) . . . . 1·50 15

OFFICIAL STAMPS

1903. Official stamps of India (Queen Victoria) (optd **O.H.M.S.**) further optd **BRITISH SOMALILAND**.
O1 23 ½a. turquoise . . . . . . 6·50 48·00
O2 – 1a. red . . . . 15·00 8·50
O3 – 2a. lilac . . . . 8·00 48·00
O4 – 8a. mauve . . . . 10·00 £375
O5 37 1r. green and red . . . . 10·00 £550

1904. Stamps of 1904 optd **O.H.M.S.**
O10 2 ½a. green . . . . 4·00 48·00
O11 1a. black and red . . . . . 3·25 7·00
O12 2a. purple . . . . £180 65·00
O13 8a. black and blue . . . . 60·00 £140
O15 – 1r. green (No. 41) £170 £600

SORUTH Pt. 1

A state of India. In 1948 the Saurashtra Union was formed which included Jasdan, Morvi, Nawanagar and Wadhwan as well as Soruth. Now uses Indian stamps.

12 pies = 1 anna; 16 annas = 1 rupee.

JUNAGADH

1

2 (1a.)

1864. On paper of various colours. Imperf.
1 1 1a. black . . . . £650 70·00

1867. (Nos. 11 and 13 are on paper of various colours). Imperf.
11 2 1a. black . . . . 75·00 8·50
13 1a. red . . . . 19·00 20·00
15 4a. black £120 £140

6

7

1877. Imperf or perf.
40 7 3p. green . . . . 1·00 35
19 6 1a. green 40 15
41 1a. red . . . . 1·25 1·75
20 7 4a. red . . . . 1·75 75

1913. Surch in words in English and in native characters.
33 6 3p. on 1a. green 15 20
34 7 1a. on 4a. red . . . . 2·25 6·00

(14)

13 Nawab Mahabat Khan III

1923. Surch as T **14**.
43 13 3p. on 1a. red . . . . 4·00 7·00

1924. Imperf or perf.
44 13 3p. mauve 35 45
46b 1a. red . . . . 3·50 3·75
The 1a. is smaller.

15 Junagadh City

17 Nawab Mahabat Khan III

1929. Inscr "POSTAGE".
49 15 3p. black and green . . . . 1·00 10
50 – ½a. black and blue . . . . 5·50 10
51 17 1a. black and red . . . . . 5·00 1·00
52 – 2a. black and orange . . . 12·00 2·00
53 15 3a. black and red . . . . . 5·50 9·50
54 – 4a. black and purple . . . . 13·00 24·00
55 – 8a. black and green . . . . 11·00 22·00
56 17 1r. black and blue . . . . . 8·00 24·00
DESIGNS—HORIZ: ½a., 4a. Lion; 2a., 8a. Kathi horse.

1936. Inscr "POSTAGE AND REVENUE".
57 17 1a. black and red . . . . . 6·50 1·00

OFFICIAL STAMPS

1929. Nos. 49/56 optd **SARKARI**.
O1a 15 3p. black and green . . . 1·25 10
O2 – ½a. black and blue . . . . 2·75 10
O3a 17 1a. black and red . . . . 2·50 15
O4 – 2a. black and orange . . . 2·50 1·00
O5 15 3a. black and red 75 30
O6 – 4a. black and purple . . . 3·50 45
O7 – 8a. black and green . . . 3·50 2·50
O8 17 1r. black and blue . . . . 2·75 19·00

1938. No. 57 optd **SARKARI**.
O13a 17 1a. black and red . . . . 13·00 1·50

UNITED STATE OF SAURASHTRA

1949. Surch **POSTAGE & REVENUE ONE ANNA.**
61 **15** 1a. on 3p. black and green . . 40·00 55·00
58 – 1a. on ½a. black & bl (No. 50) . . . . 9·50 4·75

1949. Surch **Postage & Revenue ONE ANNA.**
59 1a. on 2a. grey & yell (No. 52) 13·00 22·00

21

1949.
60 **21** 1s. purple . . . . 10·00 9·50

1948. Official stamps of 1929 surch **ONE ANNA.**
O14 1a. on 2a. grey and yellow £8500 26·00
O15 1a. on 3a. black and red . . £2250 65·00
O16 1a. on 4a. black and purple £350 55·00
O17 1a. on 8a. black and green £325 42·00
O19 1a. on 1r. black and blue . . £700 45·00

1949. No. 59 optd **SARKARI.**
O22 1a. on 2a. grey and yellow 75·00 24·00

SOUTH AFRICA Pt. 1

The Union of South Africa consisted of the Provinces of the Cape of Good Hope, Natal, the Orange Free State and the Transvaal. It became an independent republic outside the Commonwealth on 31 May 1961. Rejoined the Commonwealth on 1 June 1994.

1910. 12 pence = 1 shilling;
20 shillings = 1 pound.
1961. 100 cents = 1 rand.

1

2

1910.
2 **1** 2½d. blue . . . . 1·75 1·40

1913.
3 **2** ½d. green . . . . 1·25 30
4 1d. red . . . . 1·75 10
5 1½d. brown 80 10
6 2d. purple . . . . 1·75 10
7 2½d. blue . . . . 3·75 1·25
8 3d. black and red . . . . . 9·50 30
9 3d. blue . . . . 3·50 1·75
10a 4d. orange and green . . . 6·50 55
11 6d. black and violet . . . 5·50 60
12 1s. orange . . . . 16·00 80
13 1s.3d. violet . . . . 13·00 7·00
14 2s.6d. purple and green . . 55·00 1·50
15 5s. purple and blue . . . . £110 7·50
16 10s. blue and olive . . . . £180 7·50
17 £1 green and red £600 £350

5 De Havilland D.H.9 Biplane

1925. Air.
26 **5** 1d. red . . . . 3·75 10·00
27 3d. blue . . . . 7·00 10·00
28 6d. mauve . . . . 9·00 11·00
29 9d. green . . . . 23·00 55·00

NOTE—"Bilingual" in heading indicates that the stamps are inscribed alternately in English and Afrikaans throughout the sheet. Our prices for such issues are for mint bilingual pairs and used single stamps of either inscription.

6 Springbok

7 "Dromedaris" (Van Riebeeck's ship)

8 Orange Tree

10 "Hope"

11 Union Buildings, Pretoria

12 Groot Schuur

1926. Bilingual pairs ("SUIDAFRIKA" in one word on Afrikaans stamps). No. 33 is imperf.
42w **6** ½d. black and green . . . 3·50 10
31 **7** 1d. black and red . . . . 2·00 10
34 **11** 2d. grey and purple . . . 11·00 60
44cw 2d. grey and lilac . . . 17·00 20
44d 2d. blue and violet . . . £300 2·50
35 **12** 3d. black and red . . . . 15·00 60
45cw 3d. blue . . . . 6·00 10
33 **10** 4d. blue . . . . 1·75 1·25
46c – 4d. brown . . . . 3·75 10
47 **8** 6d. green and orange . . 13·00 10
36 – 1s. brown and blue . . . 30·00 1·00
49 – 2s.6d. green and brown £100 3·25
49b – 2s.6d. blue and brown . . 26·00 20
38 – 5s. black and green . . . £225 35·00
39 – 10s. blue and brown . . . £150 10·00
DESIGNS—As Type **11**: 4d. (No. 118) A native kraal; 1s. Black and blue wildebeest; 2s.6d. Ox-wagon inspanned; 5s. Ox-wagon outspanned; 10s. Cape Town and Table Bay.

On No. 33 the English and Afrikaans inscriptions are on separate sheets and our price is for a single stamp of either language.

For these designs with Afrikaans stamps inscr "SUID-AFRIKA", see Nos. 114 etc (issued 1933). For ½d., 1d., 2d., 3d. and 10s. in similar designs see Nos. 105/6, 107a, 116/17 and 64ba respectively.

17 De Havilland D.H.60 Cirrus Moth

18 Church of the Vow

1929. Air.
40 **17** 4d. green . . . . 5·50 2·50
41 1s. orange . . . . 16·00 13·00

1933. Voortrekker Memorial Fund. Inscr as in T **18**. Bilingual pairs.
50 **18** ½d.+½d. green . . . . 3·50 50
51 – 1d.+½d. black and pink . . 2·75 25
52 – 2d.+1d. green and purple . . 3·50 55
53 – 3d.+1½d. green and blue . . 5·50 70
DESIGNS: 1d. The "Great Trek" (C. Michell); 2d. Voortrekker man; 3d. Voortrekker woman.

22 Gold Mine

1933. As Nos. 42 etc but with Afrikaans stamps inscr "SUID-AFRIKA" (with hyphen) and new design. Bilingual pairs.
114 **6** ½d. grey and green . . . 2·00 10
56i **7** 1d. grey and red 70 10
57bw **22** 1½d. green and gold . . 1·50 10
58 **11** 2d. blue and violet . . . 70·00 75
58a 2d. grey and purple . . 50·00 1·25
118 – 4d. brown . . . . . . 3·50 10
119a **8** 6d. green and red . . . 3·25 10
120 – 1s. brown and blue . . 10·00 10
121 – 2s.6d. green and brown 10·00 1·00
64b – 5s. black and green . . 38·00 35

24

1935. Silver Jubilee. Bilingual pairs.
65 **24** ½d. black and green . . . . 2·50 10
66 1d. black and red . . . . . 2·50 10
67 3d. blue . . . . 14·00 2·25
68 6d. green and orange . . . 27·00 3·25
The positions of Afrikaans and English inscriptions are transposed on alternate stamps.

1936. Johannesburg International Philatelic Exhibition. Optd

MS69 **6** ½d. grey and green (No. 114) 3·50 10·00
MS70 **7** 1d. grey and red (No. 56) 2·75 7·00
Issued each in miniature sheet of six stamps.

25 King George VI

1937. Coronation. Bilingual pairs.
71 **25** ½d. grey and green 80 10
72 1d. grey and red 80 10
73 1½d. orange and green . . . 80 10
74 3d. blue . . . . 1·50 10
75 1s. brown and blue . . . . 2·25 15

27 Wagon crossing Drakensberg

28 Signing of Dingaan-Retief Treaty

1938. Voortrekker Centenary Memorial Fund. Dated "1838 1938". Bilingual pairs.
76 – ½d.+½d. blue and green . . 12·00 30
77 **27** 1d.+1d. blue and red . . . 13·00 40
78 **28** 1½d.+1½d. brown and green 18·00 80
79 – 3d.+3d. blue . . . . 19·00 1·00
DESIGNS—As T **27**: ½d. Voortrekker ploughing. As T **28**: 3d. Voortrekker Monument.

31 Voortrekker Family

1938. Voortrekker Commem. Bilingual pairs.
80 – 1d. blue and red . . . . . 6·50 30
81 **31** 1½d. blue and brown . . . . 8·50 30
DESIGN: 1d. Wagon wheel.

22a Groot Schuur

23 Groot Constantia

1939. Bilingual pairs.
117 **22a** 3d. blue . . . . 2·75 10
64ca **23** 10s. blue and brown . . 42·00 30

32 Old Vicarage, Paarl, now a Museum

33 Symbol of the Reformation

34 Huguenot Dwelling, Drakenstein Mountain Valley

34a Gold Mine

1939. 250th Anniv of Landing of Huguenots in South Africa. Bilingual pairs.
82 **32** ½d.+½d. brown and green . . 4·75 30
83 **33** 1d.+1d. green and red . . . 11·00 30
84 **34** 1½d.+1½d. green and purple 26·00 1·00

1941. Bilingual pair.
87 **34a** 1½d. green and buff . . . . 2·00 1·25

35 Infantry
Us sheet

38 Sailor, Destroyer and Lifebelts

39 Women's Auxiliary Services

1941. War Effort. Bilingual pairs except the 2d. and 1s. which are inscr in both languages on each stamp.
88 **35** ½d. green . . . . 1·50 10
89 – 1d. red . . . . 2·00 10
90 – 1½d. green . . . . 1·50 10
95 **38** 2d. violet . . . . 1·00 75
91 **39** 3d. blue . . . . 23·00 70
92 – 4d. brown . . . . 22·00 15
93 – 6d. orange . . . . 12·00 15
96 – 1s. brown . . . . 3·75 1·00
94a – 1s.3d. brown . . . . . . 4·00 20
DESIGNS—As Type **35**: 1d. Nurse and ambulance; 1½d. Airman; 1s.3d. Signaller. As Type **38**: 4d. Artillery; 6d. Welding. As Type **39**: 1s. Tank corps.

43 Infantry

54 Union Buildings, Pretoria

1942. War Effort. Reduced size. Bilingual except 4d. and 1s. which are inscr in both languages on each stamp.
97 **43** ½d. green . . . . 2·00 10
98a – 1d. red . . . . 1·00 10
99 – 1½d. brown 65 10
100 – 2d. violet 90 10
101 – 3d. blue . . . . 7·00 10
103 – 4d. green . . . . 18·00 10
102 – 6d. orange . . . . 2·00 10
104 – 1s. brown . . . . 15·00 10
DESIGNS—VERT: 1d. Nurse; 1½d. Airman; 2d. Sailor; 6d. Welder. HORIZ: 3d. Women's Auxiliary Services; 6d. Heavy gun; 1s. Tanks.

Our unused prices for Nos. 97, 98, 101 and 103 are for units of three. The other stamps are in units of two.

1943. As 1926, but in single colours and with plain background to central oval. Bilingual pairs.
105 **6** ½d. green . . . . 2·50 20
106 **7** 1d. red . . . . 3·25 15

1945. Type **11** redrawn. Bilingual pairs.
107a **54** 2d. slate and violet . . . 3·25 15
116 2d. blue and purple . . . 2·50 10

55 "Victory"

58 King George VI

59 King George VI and Queen Elizabeth

1945. Victory. Bilingual pairs.
108 **55** 1d. brown and red 20 10
109 – 2d. blue and violet 20 10
110 – 3d. blue 20 10
DESIGNS: 2d. Man and oxen ploughing ("Peace"); 3d. Man and woman gazing at a star ("Hope").

1947. Royal Visit. Bilingual pairs.
111 **58** 1d. black and red 10 10
112 **59** 2d. violet 15 10
113 – 3d. blue 15 10
DESIGN—As Type **59**: 3d. Queen Elizabeth II when Princess and Princess Margaret.

61 Gold Mine

62 King George VI and Queen Elizabeth

1948. Bilingual.
124 **61** 1½d. green and buff . . . . 2·50 10
The price for No. 124 is for a unit of four stamps.

1948. Royal Silver Wedding. Bilingual pair.
125 **62** 3d. blue and silver 50 10

63 "Wanderer" (emigrant ship) entering Durban

64 Hermes

1949. Centenary of Arrival of British Settlers in Natal. Bilingual pair.
127 **63** 1½d. brown 80 10

1949. 75th Anniv of U.P.U. Bilingual pairs.
128 **64** ½d. green 50 10
129 1½d. red 50 10
130 3d. blue 60 10

65 Wagons approaching Bingham's Berg

68 Union Buildings, Pretoria

1949. Inauguration of Voortrekker Monument, Pretoria.
131 **65** 1d. mauve 10 10
132 – 1½d. green 10 10
133 – 3d. blue 15 15
DESIGNS: 1½d. Voortrekker Monument, Pretoria; 3d. Bible, candle and Voortrekkers.

1950. Bilingual pair.
134 **68** 2d. blue and violet 40 10

INSCRIPTIONS. In all later issues except Nos. 167 and 262/5, the stamps are inscribed in both Afrikaans and English. Our prices are for single examples, unused and used.

70 "Maria de la Quellerie" (D. Craey)

76 Queen Elizabeth II

1952. Tercentenary of Landing of Van Riebeeck. Dated "1652–1952".
136 – ½d. purple and sepia 10 10
137 **70** 1d. green 10 10
138 – 2d. violet 50 10
139 – 4½d. blue 10 10
140 – 1s. brown 40 10
DESIGNS—HORIZ: ½d. Seal and monogram; 2d. Arrival of Van Riebeeck's ships; 1s. Landing at the Cape (D. Craey). VERT: 4½d. "Jan van Riebeeck" (D. Craey).

1952. South African Tercentenary Stamp Exn, Cape Town. No. 137 optd **SATISE** and No. 138 optd **SADIPU**.
141 **70** 1d. green 20 1·75
142 – 2d. violet 50 1·25

1953. Coronation.
143 **76** 2d. blue 30 10

77 1d. Cape Triangular Stamp

1953. Stamp Cent of Cape of Good Hope.
144 **77** 1d. sepia and red 10 10
145 – 4d. indigo and blue 50 20
DESIGN: 4d. as Type **77** but reproducing 4d. "Triangular".

79 Merino Ram

1953.
146 **79** 4½d. purple and yellow 20 10
147 – 1s.3d. brown 1·25 10
148 – 1s.6d. red and green 60 55

DESIGNS: 1s.3d. Springbok; 1s.6d. Aloes.

82 Arms of Orange Free State and Scroll

1954. Centenary of Orange Free State.
149 **82** 2d. sepia and red 10 10
150 4½d. purple and grey 20 50

83 Warthog

87 White Rhinoceros

1954. Wild Animals.
151 **83** ½d. green 10 10
152 – 1d. lake 10 10
153 – 1½d. sepia 10 10
154 – 2d. plum 10 10
155 **87** 3d. brown and blue 1·00 10
156 – 4d. blue and green 1·00 10
157 – 4½d. indigo and blue 60 1·00
158 – 6d. sepia and orange 50 10
159 – 1s. brown and light brown 1·25 10
160 – 1s.3d. brown and green 2·25 10
161 – 1s.6d. brown and pink 1·75 60
162 – 2s.6d. sepia and green 3·50 20
163 – 5s. sepia and buff 8·00 1·60
164 – 10s. black and blue 13·00 4·50
DESIGNS—VERT (as Type **83**): 1d. Black wildebeest; 1½d. Leopard; 2d. Mountain zebra. (As Type **87**): 4d. African elephant; 4½d. Hippopotamus; 1s. Greater kudu; 1s.6d. Gemsbok; 2s.6d. Nyala; 5s. Giraffe; 10s. Sable antelope. HORIZ (as Type **87**): 6d. Lion; 1s.3d. Springbok.

97 President Kruger

99 A. Pretorius, Church of the Vow and Flag

1955. Centenary of Pretoria.
165 **97** 3d. green 10 10
166 – 6d. purple (Pres. M. Pretorius) 10 30

1955. Voortrekker Covenant Celebrations Pietermaritzburg. Bilingual pair.
167 **99** 2d. blue and red 45 10

100 Settlers' Block- wagon and House

1958. Centenary of Arrival of German Settlers in South Africa.
168 **100** 2d. brown and purple 10 10

101 Arms of the Academy

1959. 50th Anniv of South African Academy of Science and Art, Pretoria.
169 **101** 3d. blue and turquoise 10 10

103 Globe and Antarctic Scene

104 Union Flag

1959. South African National Antarctic Expedition.
178 **103** 3d. turquoise and orange 20 10

1960. 50th Anniv of Union of South Africa.
179 **104** 4d. orange and blue 30 10
180 – 6d. red, brown and green 30 10
181 – 1s. blue and yellow 30 10
182 – 1s.6d. black and blue 70 2·25
DESIGNS—VERT: 6d. Union arms. HORIZ: 1s. "Wheel of Progress"; 1s.6d. Union Festival emblem.
See also Nos. 190 and 192/3.

108 Steam Locomotives "Natal" (1860) and Class 25 (1950s)

1960. Centenary of South African Railways.
183 **108** 1s.3d. blue 1·10 30

109 Prime Ministers Botha, Smuts, Hertzog, Malan, Strijdom and Verwoerd

1960. Union Day.
184 **109** 3d. brown and light brown 15 10

1961. Types as before but new currency.
185 **83** ½c. turquoise 10 10
186 – 1c. lake (as No. 152) 10 10
187 – 1½c. sepia (as No. 153) 10 10
188 – 2c. plum (as No. 154) 10 80
189 **109** 2½c. brown 20 10
190 **104** 3½c. orange and blue 15 2·00
191 – 5c. sepia & orge (as No. 158) 20 10
192 – 7½c. red, brown and green (as No. 180) 20 2·50
193 – 10c. bl & yell (as No. 181) 40 50
194 – 12½c. brown and green (as No. 160) 1·00 1·25
195 – 20c. brown and pink (as No. 161) 2·25 2·75
196 – 50c. sepia and buff (as No. 163) 4·50 10·00
197 – 1r. black & blue (as No. 164) 14·00 24·00

110 African Pygmy Kingfisher

115 Burchell's Gonolek

1961. Republic Issue.
198 **110** ½c. blue, red and brown 10 10
199 – 1c. red and grey 10 10
200 – 1½c. lake and purple 10 10
241 – 2c. blue and yellow 20 10
230 – 2½c. violet and green 10 10
243 **115** 3c. red and blue 30 10
288 – 4c. violet and green 40 50
204 – 5c. yellow and turquoise 30 10
290 – 6c. brown and green 70 30
205 – 7½c. brown and green 60 10
292 – 9c. red, yellow and green 1·25 30
233 – 10c. sepia and green 40 10
247 – 12½c. red, yellow and green 1·00 40
248 – 15c. black, olive & orange 85 25
234 – 20c. turq, red & salmon 1·00 80
250 – 50c. black and blue 1·25 40
251 – 1r. orange, green and blue 1·25 1·00
DESIGNS—VERT (as Type **110**): 1c. Kafferboom flower (As Type **115**): 2½, 4c. Groot Constantia; 5c. Baobab tree; 6, 7½c. Maize; 9, 12½c. Protea (flower); 10c. Cape Town Castle entrance; 15c. Industry; 20c. Secretary bird. HORIZ (as Type **110**): 1½c. Afrikander bull. (As Type **115**) 2c. Pouring gold; 50c. Cape Town harbour; 1r. Strelitzia (flower).
Most values exist in two forms showing differences in the size of the inscriptions and figures of value.
See also Nos. 276/7.

123 Bleriot XI Monoplane and Boeing 707 Airliner over Table Mountain

124 Folk-dancers

1962. 50th Anniv of First South African Aerial Post.
220 **123** 3c. blue and red 50 10

1962. 50th Anniv of Volkspele (folk-dancing) in South Africa.
221 **124** 2½c. red and brown 15 10

125 "The Chapman" (emigrant ship)

1962. Unveiling of Precinct Stone, British Settlers Monument, Grahamstown.
222 **125** 2½c. green and purple 50 10
223 12½c. blue and brown 2·00 1·25

126 Red Disa (orchid), Castle Rock and Gardens

128 Centenary Emblem and Nurse

1963. 50th Anniv of Kirstenbosch Botanic Gardens, Cape Town.
224 **126** 2½c. multicoloured 20 10

1963. Cent of Red Cross. Inscr "1863–1963".
225 **128** 2½c. red, black and purple 20 10
226 – 12½c. red and blue 2·25 1·00
DESIGN—HORIZ: 12½c. Centenary emblem and globe.

130 Assembly Building, Umtata

145 "Springbok" Badge of Rugby Board

1963. First Meeting of Transkei Legislative Assembly.
237 **130** 2½c. sepia and green 10 10

1964. 75th Anniv of South African Rugby Board.
252 **145** 2½c. brown and green 15 10
253 – 12½c. black and green 3·00 3·75
DESIGN—HORIZ: 12½c. Rugby footballer.

147 Calvin

148 Nurse's Lamp

1964. 400th Death Anniv of Calvin (Protestant reformer).
254 **147** 2½c. cerise, violet & brown 10 10

1964. 50th Anniv of South African Nursing Association.
255 **148** 2½c. blue and gold 10 10
257 – 12½c. blue and gold 2·25 1·75
DESIGN—HORIZ: 12½c. Nurse holding lamp.

150 I.T.U. Emblem and Satellites

152 Pulpit in Groote Kerk, Cape Town

1965. Centenary of I.T.U.
258 **150** 2½c. orange and blue 25 10
259 – 12½c. purple and green 1·25 1·00
DESIGN: 12½c. I.T.U. emblem and symbols.

1965. Tercentenary of Nederduites Gereformeerde Kerk (Dutch Reformed Church) in South Africa.
260 **152** 2½c. brown and yellow . . 15 10
261 – 12½c. black, orange & blue 70 85
DESIGN—HORIZ: 12½c. Church emblem.

155 Bird in Flight

1965. 5th Anniv of Republic. Bilingual pairs.
262 – 1c. black, green and yellow 45 10
263 **155** 2½c. blue, indigo and green 85 10
264 – 3c. red, yellow and brown 3·00 10
265 – 7½c. blue, ultram & yell 3·75 20
DESIGNS—VERT: 1c. Diamond; 3c. Maize plants. HORIZ: 7½c. Mountain landscape.

158 Verwoerd and Union Buildings, Pretoria

161 "Martin Luther" (Cranach the Elder)

1966. Verwoerd Commemoration.
266 **158** 2½c. brown and turquoise 10 10
267 – 3c. brown and green . . . 10 10
268 – 12½c. brown and blue . . 60 60
DESIGNS: 3c. "Dr. H. F. Verwoerd" (I. Henkel); 12½c. Verwoerd and map of South Africa.

1967. 450th Anniv of Reformation.
269 **161** 2½c. black and red 10 10
270 – 12½c. black and orange 1·25 2·00
DESIGN: 12½c. Wittenberg Church door.

163 "Profile of Pres. Fouche" (I. Henkel)

165 Hertzog in 1902

1968. Inauguration of President Fouche.
271 **163** 2½c. brown 10 10
272 – 12½c. blue . . . . 60 1·00
DESIGN: 12½c. Portrait of Pres. Fouche.

1968. Inauguration of General Hertzog Monument, Bloemfontein.
273 **165** 2½c. black, brown & yellow 10 10
274 – 3c. multicoloured 15 10
275 – 12½c. black, red and orange . . . . 1·50 1·50
DESIGNS—HORIZ: 3c. Hertzog in 1924. VERT; 12½c. Hertzog Monument.

168 African Pygmy Kingfisher

170 Springbok and Olympic Torch

1969.
276 **168** ½c. blue, red and ochre . . 10 30
277 – 1c. red and brown 10 10
DESIGN—VERT: 1c. Kafferboom flower.

1969. South African Games, Bloemfontein.
278 **170** 2½c. black, red and green 15 10
279 12½c. black, red and brown . . . . 70 1·50

171 Professor Barnard and Groote Schuur Hospital

1969. World's First Heart Transplant and 47th South African Medical Association Congress.
280 **171** 2½c. purple and red . . . 15 10
281 – 12½c. red and blue . . . . 1·25 2·00
DESIGN: 12½c. Hands holding heart.

173 Mail Coach

1969. Centenary of First Stamps of the South African Republic (Transvaal).
297 **173** 2½c. yellow, blue & brown 15 10
298 – 12½c. green, gold & brown 2·75 3·50
DESIGN—VERT: 12½c. Transvaal stamp of 1869.

175 "Water 70" Emblem

177 "The Sower"

1970. Water 70 Campaign.
299 **175** 2½c. green, blue and brown 30 10
300 – 3c. blue and buff 30 20
DESIGN—HORIZ: 3c. Symbolic waves.

1970. 150th Anniv of Bible Society of South Africa.
301 **177** 2½c. multicoloured 15 10
302 – 12½c. gold, black and blue 1·50 2·00
DESIGN—HORIZ: 12½c. "Biblia" and open book.

178 J. G. Strijdom and Strijdom Tower

179 Map and Antarctic Landscape

1971. "Interstex" Stamp Exhibition, Cape Town.
303A **178** 5c. blue, black and yellow 20 10

1971. 10th Anniv of Antarctic Treaty.
304 **179** 12½c. black, blue and red 1·50 4·00

180 "Landing of British Settlers, 1820" (T. Baines)

1971. 10th Anniv of Republic of South Africa.
305 **180** 2c. flesh and red 15 20
306 – 4c. green and black . . . 15 10
DESIGN—VERT: 4c. Presidents Steyn and Kruger and Treaty of Vereeniging Monument.

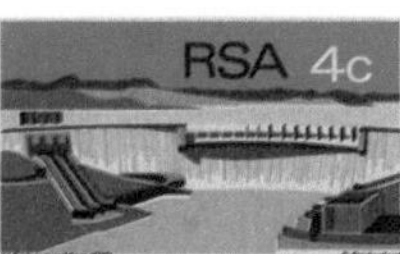

181 View of Dam

1972. Opening of Hendrik Verwoerd Dam. Multicoloured.
307 4c. Type **181** 20 10
308 5c. Aerial view of dam . . . 25 10
309 10c. Dam and surrounding country (58 × 21 mm) . . . 1·50 2·50

182 Sheep

183 Black and Siamese Cats

1972. Sheep and Wool Industry.
310 **182** 4c. multicoloured 30 10
311 – 15c. stone, dp blue & blue 2·25 20
DESIGN: 15c. Lamb.

1972. Centenary of Societies for the Prevention of Cruelty to Animals.
312 **183** 5c. multicoloured . . . . 1·25 10

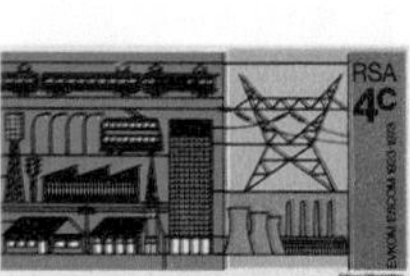

184 Transport and Industry

185 University Coat of Arms

1973. 50th Anniv of ESCOM (Electricity Supply Commission). Multicoloured.
326 4c. Type **184** 20 10
327 5c. Pylon (21 × 28 mm) . . . 30 10
328 15c. Cooling towers (21 × 28 mm) . . . . . . 3·00 3·50

1973. Centenary of University of South Africa.
329 **185** 4c. multicoloured 20 10
330 – 5c. multicoloured 30 15
331 – 15c. black and gold . . . 3·00 3·50
DESIGNS—HORIZ (38 × 21 mm): 5c. University Complex, Pretoria. VERT (as Type **185**): 15c. Old University Building, Cape Town.

186 Rescuing Sailors

1973. Bicentenary of Rescue by Wolraad Woltemade.
332 **186** 4c. brown, green and black 20 10
333 – 5c. olive, green and black 40 10
334 – 15c. brown, green & black 5·00 6·50
DESIGNS: 5c. "De Jonge Thomas" foundering; 15c. "De Jonge Thomas" breaking up and sailors drowning.

187 C. J. Langenhoven

1973. Birth Cent of C. J. Langenhoven (politician and composer of national anthem).
335 **187** 4c. multicoloured 25 10
336 – 5c. multicoloured 35 10
337 – 15c. multicoloured . . . . 3·50 5·00
Nos. 336/7 are as Type **187** but with motifs rearranged. The 5c. is vert, 21 × 38 mm, and the 15c. is horiz, 38 × 21 mm.

188 Communications Map

1973. World Communications Day.
338 **188** 15c. multicoloured . . . . 50 1·40

189 Restored Buildings

190 Burgerspond (obverse and reverse)

1974. Restoration of Tulbagh. Multicoloured.
340 4c. Type **189** 15 10
341 5c. Restored Church Street (58 × 21 mm) 40 90

1974. Centenary of Burgerspond (coin).
342 **190** 9c. brown, red and olive 60 1·00

191 Dr. Malan

192 Congress Emblem

1974. Birth Centenary of Dr. D. F. Malan (Prime Minister).
343 **191** 4c. blue and light blue . . 20 10

1974. 15th World Sugar Congress, Durban.
344 **192** 15c. blue and silver . . . 75 1·40

193 "50" and Radio Waves

1974. 50th Anniv of Broadcasting in South Africa.
345 **193** 4c. red and black 10 10

194 Monument Building

1974. Inauguration of British Settlers' Monument, Grahamstown.
346 **194** 5c. red and black 10 10

195 Stamps of the South African Provinces

1974. Centenary of Universal Postal Union.
347 **195** 15c. multicoloured 70 80

196 Iris

197 Bokmakierie Shrikes

1974. Multicoloured. (a) As Type **196**.
348 1c. Type **196** 10 10
349a 2c. Wild heath 10 10
350a 3c. Geranium 10 10
351a 4c. Arum lily 10 10
352 5c. Cape gannet (horiz) . . 20 10
353 6c. Galjoen (fish) (horiz) . . 1·00 10
354 7c. Bontrok seabream (horiz) 25 10
355 9c. Dusky batfish (horiz) . . 30 30
356 10c. Moorish idol (horiz) . . 30 10
357 14c. Roman seabream (horiz) 30 10
358 15c. Greater double-collared sunbird (horiz) 30 10
359 20c. Southern yellow-billed hornbill (horiz) 45 10
360 25c. Barberton daisy 45 10

(b) As Type **197**.
361 30c. Type **197** . . . . 7·00 70
362 50c. Stanley cranes . . . . . 1·00 35
363 1r. Bateleurs . . . . 4·00 3·00

1974. Coil Stamps. As Nos. 348/9a, 352 and 356. Colours changed.
370a **196** 1c. violet and pink . . . 55 60
371 – 2c. green and yellow . . 80 60
372 – 5c. black and blue . . . 1·75 80
373a – 10c. violet and blue . . . 4·00 5·25

198 Voortrekker Monument and Encampment

1974. 25th Anniv of Voortrekker Monument, Pretoria.
374 **198** 4c. multicoloured 20 30

199 SASOL Complex

1975. 25th Anniv of South African Coal, Oil and Gas Corporation Ltd (SASOL).
375 **199** 15c. multicoloured . . . . 75 1·50

200 President Diederichs

201 Jan Smuts

1975. Inauguration of State President.
376 **200** 4c. brown and gold . . . 10 10
377 15c. blue and gold . . . 50 1·25

1975. Smuts Commemoration.
378 **201** 4c. black and grey 10 10

202 "Dutch East Indiaman, Table Bay"

1975. Death Centenary of Thomas Baines (painter). Multicoloured.
379 5c. Type **202** 15 10
380 9c. "Cradock, 1848" 15 15
381 15c. "Thirsty Flat, 1848" . . 25 25
382 30c. "Pretoria, 1874" . . . . 40 1·50
MS383 120 × 95 mm. Nos. 379/82 1·00 3·75

203 Gideon Malherbe's House, Paarl

1975. Cent of Genootskap van Regte Afrikaners (Afrikaner Language Movement).
384 **203** 4c. multicoloured 10 10

204 "Automatic Sorting"

205 Title Page of "Die Afrikaanse Patriot"

1975. Postal Mechanization.
385 **204** 4c. multicoloured 10 10

1975. Inaug of Language Monument, Paarl.
386 **205** 4c. black, brown & orange 10 10
387 – 5c. multicoloured 10 10
DESIGN: 5c. "Afrikaanse Taalmonument".

206 Table Mountain

1975. Tourism. Multicoloured.
388 15c. Type **206** . . . . . . 2·00 3·00
389 15c. Johannesburg . . . . 2·00 3·00
390 15c. Cape vineyards . . . . 2·00 3·00
391 15c. Lions in Kruger National Park . . . . . . 2·00 3·00

207 Globe and Satellites

1975. Satellite Communication.
392 **207** 15c. multicoloured 30 30

208 Bowls

210 "Picnic under a Baobab Tree"

1976. Sporting Commemorations.
393 **208** 15c. black and green . . . 20 75
394 – 15c. black and green . . . 50 1·00
395 – 15c. black and green . . . 20 60
396 – 15c. black and green . . . 50 60
MS397 161 × 109 mm. Nos. 393/6 1·50 4·00
DESIGNS AND EVENTS: No. 393, Type **208** (World Bowls Championships, Johannesburg); 394, Batsman (Centenary of organized cricket in South Africa); 395, Polo player; 396, Gary Player (golfer).

1976. South Africa's Victory in World Bowls Championships. Optd **WERELDKAMPIOENE WORLD CHAMPIONS.**
398 **208** 15c. black and green . . . 30 1·00

1976. Birth Cent of Erich Mayer (painter). Mult.
399 4c. Type **210** 15 10
400 10c. "Foot of the Blaawberg" 25 20
401 15c. "Harteespoort Dam" . . 30 90
402 20c. "Street scene, Doornfontein" . . . . . . 40 1·25
MS403 121 × 95 mm. Nos. 399/402 1·50 4·00

211 Cheetah

1976. World Environment Day. Multicoloured.
404 3c. Type **211** 15 10
405 10c. Black rhinoceros 40 30
406 15c. Blesbok 40 40
407 20c. Mountain zebra 45 75

212 "Emily Hobhouse" (H. Naude)

214 Family with Globe

213 "Donrobin Castle" (mail ship), 1876

1976. 50th Death Anniv of Emily Hobhouse (welfare worker).
408 **212** 4c. multicoloured 10 10

1976. Centenary of Ocean Mail Service.
409 **213** 10c. multicoloured . . . . 60 1·00

1976. Family Planning and Child Welfare.
410 **214** 4c. brown and orange . . 10 10

215 Glasses of Wine

216 Dr. Jacob du Toit

1977. International Wine Symposium, Cape Town.
411 **215** 15c. multicoloured . . . . 40 1·25

1977. Birth Centenary of J. D. du Toit (theologian and poet).
412 **216** 4c. multicoloured 10 10

217 Palace of Justice

1977. Centenary of Transvaal Supreme Court.
413 **217** 4c. brown 10 10

218 "Protea repens"

219 Gymnast

1977. Succulents. Multicoloured.
414 1c. Type **218** 10 10
431 1c. "Leucadendron argenteum" . . . . . 35 1·00
415 2c. "P. punctata" 15 50
432 2c. "Mimetes cucullatus" . . 35 1·00
416 3c. "P. neriifolia" 10 10
417 4c. "P. longifolia" 10 10
418 5c. "P. cynaroides" 10 10
433 5c. "Serruria florida" . . . 35 1·00
419b 6c. "P. canaliculata" 30 80
420b 7c. "P. lorea" 20 80
421a 8c. "P. mundii" 15 10
422 9c. "P. roupelliae" 20 70
423 10c. "P. aristata" 30 10
434 10c. "Leucadendron sessile" 35 1·00
424 15c. "P. eximia" 25 10
425 20c. "P. magnifica" 30 10
426c 25c. "P. grandiceps" 40 75
427 30c. "P. amplexicaulis" . . 45 10
428a 50c. "Leucospermum cordifolium" 45 15
429a 1r. "Paranomus reflexus" 50 75
430a 2r. "Orothamnus zeyheri" 60 1·00

1977. 8th Congress of Int Assn of Physical Education and Sports for Girls and Women.
435 **219** 15c. black, red and yellow 30 30

220 Metrication Symbol on Globe

1977. Metrication.
436 **220** 15c. multicoloured 30 30

221 Atomic Diagram

1977. Uranium Development.
437 **221** 15c. multicoloured 40 30

222 National Flag

224 Dr. Andrew Murray

223 Walvis Bay, 1878

1977. 50th Anniv of National Flag.
438 **222** 5c. multicoloured 10 10

1977. Centenary of Annexation of Walvis Bay.
439 **223** 15c. multicoloured 60 60

1978. 150th Birth Anniv of Dr. Andrew Murray (church statesman).
440 **224** 4c. multicoloured 10 10

225 Steel Rail

1978. 50th Anniv of I.S.C.O.R. (South African Iron and Steel Industrial Corporation).
441 **225** 15c. multicoloured 30 30

226 Richards Bay

1978. Harbours. Multicoloured.
442 15c. Type **226** . . . . 50 1·00
443 15c. Saldanhabaai . . . . . 50 1·00

227 "Shepherd's Lonely Dwelling, Riversdale"

1978. 125th Birth Anniv of J. E. A. Volschenk (painter). Multicoloured.
444 10c. Type **227** 15 20
445 15c. "Clouds and Sunshine, Laneberg Range, Riversdale" 20 30
446 20c. "At the Foot of the Mountain" 30 75
447 25c. "Evening on the Veldt" 35 1·40
MS448 124 × 90 mm. Nos. 444/7 1·25 4·00

228 Pres. B. J. Vorster

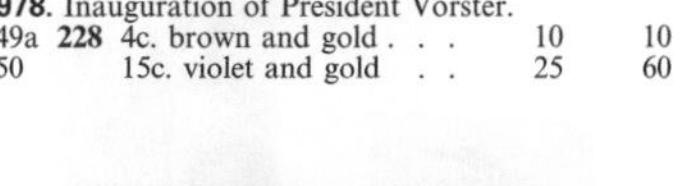

1978. Inauguration of President Vorster.
449a **228** 4c. brown and gold . . . 10 10
450 15c. violet and gold . . 25 60

229 Golden Gate

1978. Tourism. Multicoloured.
451 10c. Type **229** 15 10
452 15c. Blyde River Canyon . . 25 35
453 20c. Amphitheatre, Drakensberg . . . . . . 40 1·10
454 25c. Cango Caves . . . . . 55 1·50

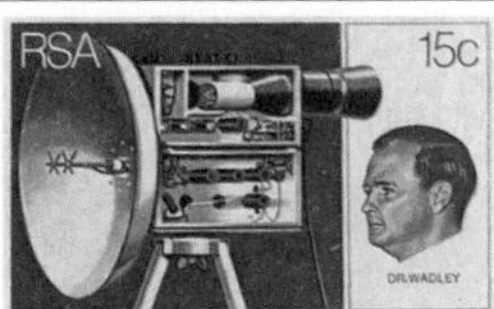

230 Dr. Wadley (inventor) and Tellurometer

1979. 25th Anniv of Tellurometer (radio distance measurer).
455 **230** 15c. multicoloured 20 20

231 1929 4d. Airmail Stamp

1979. 50th Anniv of Stamp Production in South Africa.
456 **231** 15c. green, cream and grey 30 20

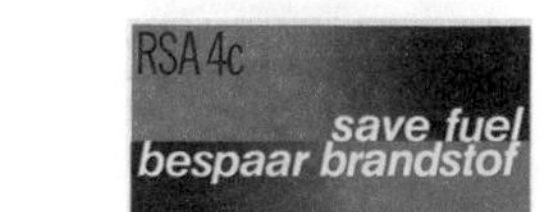

232 "Save Fuel"

1979. Fuel Conservation.
457 **232** 4c. black and red 25 65
458 – 4c. black and red 25 65
No. 458 is as Type **232** but with face value and country initials in bottom left-hand corner, and Afrikaans inscription above English.

233 Isandlwana

1979. Centenary of Zulu War.
459 **233** 4c. black and red 20 10
460 – 15c. black and red 55 50
461 – 20c. black and red . . . . 70 1·00
MS462 125 × 90 mm. Nos. 459/61 2·25 3·50
DESIGNS: 15c. Ulundi; 20c. Rorke's Drift.

234 "Health Care"

1979. Health Year.
463 **234** 4c. multicoloured 10 10

235 Children looking at Candle

1979. 50th Anniv of Christmas Stamp Fund.
464 **235** 4c. multicoloured 10 10

236 University of Cape Town **237** "Gary Player"

1979. 50th Anniv of University of Cape Town.
465a **236** 4c. multicoloured 15 15

1979. "Rosafari 1979" World Rose Convention, Pretoria. Multicoloured.
466 4c. Type **237** 15 10
467 15c. "Prof. Chris Barnard" 30 40
468 20c. "Southern Sun" 40 60
469 25c. "Soaring Wings" 40 85
MS470 100 × 125 mm. Nos. 466/9 1·40 2·50

238 University of Stellenbosch

1979. 300th Anniv of Stellenbosch (oldest town in South Africa). Multicoloured.
471 4c. Type **238** 10 10
472 15c. Rhenish Church on the Braak 20 40

239 F.A.K. Emblem **240** "Still-life with Sweet Peas"

1979. 50th Anniv of F.A.K. (Federation of Afrikaans Cultural Societies).
473 **239** 4c. multicoloured 10 15

1980. Paintings by Pieter Wenning. Multicoloured.
474 5c. Type **240** 10 10
475 25c. "House in the Suburbs, Cape Town" (44½ × 37 mm) 40 60
MS476 94 × 121 mm. Nos. 474/5 1·00 1·60

241 "Cullinan II" **242** C. L. Leipoldt

1980. World Diamond Congresses, Johannesburg. Multicoloured.
477 15c. Type **241** 60 60
478 20c. "Cullinan I (Great Star of Africa)" 65 65

1980. Birth Centenary of C. L. Leipoldt (poet).
479 **242** 5c. multicoloured 10 10

243 University of Pretoria

1980. 50th Anniv of University of Pretoria.
480 **243** 5c. multicoloured 10 10

244 "Marine with Shipping" (Willem van de Velde)

1980. Paintings from South African National Gallery, Cape Town. Multicoloured.
481 5c. Type **244** 15 10
482 10c. "Firetail and his Trainer" (George Stubbs) 20 25
483 15c. "Lavinia" (Thomas Gainsborough) (vert) . . 25 50
484 20c. "Classical Landscape" (Pieter Post) 30 80
MS485 126 × 90 mm. Nos. 481/4 1·00 1·75

245 Joubert, Kruger and M. Pretorius (Triumvirate Government)

1980. Centenary of Paardekraal Monument (cairn commemorating formation of Boer Triumvirate Government). Multicoloured.
486 5c. Type **245** 10 10
487 10c. Paardekraal Monument (vert) 20 65

246 Boers advancing up Amajuba Mountain

1981. Centenary of Battle of Amajuba. Mult.
488 5c. Type **246** 20 10
489 15c. British troops defending hill (horiz) 40 75

247 Ballet "Raka"

1981. Opening of State Theatre, Pretoria. Multicoloured.
490 20c. Type **247** 25 30
491 25c. Opera "Aida" 40 35
MS492 110 × 90 mm. Nos. 490/1 65 70

248 Former Presidents C. R. Swart, J. J. Fouche, N. Diederichs and B. J. Vorster

1981. 20th Anniv of Republic.
493 **248** 5c. black, green and brown 15 10
494 – 15c. multicoloured 30 30
DESIGN—28 × 22 mm: 15c. President Marais Viljoen.

249 Girl with Hearing Aid **250** Microscope

1981. Centenary of Institutes for Deaf and Blind, Worcester. Multicoloured.
495 5c. Type **249** 10 10
496 15c. Boy reading braille . . . 20 50

1981. 50th Anniv of National Cancer Association.
497 **250** 5c. multicoloured 10 10

251 "Calanthe natalensis" **252** Voortrekkers in Uniform

1981. 10th World Orchid Conference, Durban. Multicoloured.
498 5c. Type **251** 10 10
499 15c. "Eulophia speciosa" . . 20 35
500 20c. "Disperis fanniniae" . . 20 75
501 25c. "Disa uniflora" . . . . 25 1·10
MS502 120 × 91 mm. Nos. 498/501 2·25 2·00

1981. 50th Anniv of Voortrekker Movement (Afrikaans cultural youth organization).
503 **252** 5c. multicoloured 10 10

253 Lord Baden-Powell **254** Dr. Robert Koch

1982. 75th Anniv of Boy Scout Movement.
504 **253** 15c. multicoloured 30 30

1981. Cent of Discovery of Tubercle Bacillus.
505 **254** 20c. multicoloured 20 30

255 "Maria van Riejbeck" submarine

1982. 25th Anniv of Simonstown as South African Naval Base. Multicoloured.
506 8c. Type **255** 15 10
507 15c. Missile patrol vessel . . 20 30
508 20c. "Durban" (minesweeper) 25 60
509 25c. Harbour patrol boats . . 30 85
MS510 125 × 90 mm. Nos. 506/9 2·00 2·00

256 Old Provost, Grahamstown **257** Bradysaurus

1982. South African Architecture.
511 **256** 1c. brown 15 20
512b – 2c. green 10 20
513 – 3c. violet 30 30
514 – 4c. green 20 15
515 – 5c. red 30 30
515a – 5c. purple 10 10
516 – 6c. green 45 40
517 – 7c. green . . . . 30 1·00
518a – 8c. blue 40 10
519 – 9c. mauve 40 20
520 – 10c. red 40 55
520a – 10c. brown 35 10
520b – 11c. mauve 40 20
520c – 12c. blue 70 10
520d – 14c. brown . . . . . . 1·75 10
521 – 15c. blue 30 15
521a – 16c. red . . . . 1·00 1·25
522 – 20c. red 65 30
522a – 20c. black 80 10
523 – 25c. brown 50 50
524 – 30c. brown 50 30
525 – 50c. blue 50 30
526 – 1r. violet 50 15
527 – 2r. red 65 40
DESIGNS—(28 × 20 mm): 2c. Tuynhuys, Cape Town; 3c. Appelhof, Bloemfontein; 4c. Raadsaal, Pretoria; 5c. Cape Town Castle; 6c. Goewermentsgebou, Bloemfontein; 7c. Drostdy, Graaff-Reinet; 8c. Leeuwenhof, Cape Town; 9c. Libertas, Pretoria; 10c. City Hall, Pietermaritzburg; 11c. City Hall, Kimberley; 12c. City Hall, Port Elizabeth; 14c. City Hall, Johannesburg; 15c. Matjesfontein; 16c. City Hall, Durban; 20c. Post Office, Durban; 25c. Melrose House, Pretoria. (45 × 28 mm): 30c. Old Legislative Asembly Building, Pietermaritzburg; 50c. Raadsaal, Bloemfontein; 1r. Houses of Parliament, Cape Town; 2r. Uniegebou, Pretoria.

1982. Coil Stamps. As T **256**.
528 1c. brown 30 70
529 2c. green 30 75
530 5c. brown 30 75
531 10c. brown 30 80
DESIGNS: 1c. Drostdy, Swellendam; 2c. City Hall, East London; 5c. Head Post Office, Johannesburg; 10c. Morgenster, Somerset West.

1982. Karoo Fossils. Multicoloured.
532 8c. Type **257** 30 10
533 15c. Lystrosaurus 35 60
534 20c. Euparkeria 40 75
535 25c. Thrinaxodon 45 90
MS536 107 × 95 mm. Nos. 532/5 1·50 3·25

258 Gough Island Base

1983. Weather Stations. Multicoloured.

537 8c. Type **258** 20 10
538 20c. Marion Island base . . . 30 45
539 25c. Taking meteorological readings 30 50
540 40c. Launching weather balloon, Sanae 40 90

259 Class S2 Krupp Locomotive, 1952 **260** Rugby

1983. Steam Railway Locomotives. Multicoloured.

541 10c. Type **259** 30 10
542 20c. Class 16E Henschel express locomotive, 1935 50 70
543 25c. Class 6H locomotive, 1901 . . . . 55 80
544 40c. Class 15F locomotive, 1939 . . . . 65 1·50

1983. Sport in South Africa. Multicoloured.

545 10c. Type **260** 15 10
546 20c. Soccer (horiz) 20 30
547 25c. Yachting 25 40
548 40c. Horse-racing (horiz) . . 40 80

261 Plettenberg Bay

1983. Tourism Beaches. Multicoloured.

549 10c. Type **261** 10 10
550 20c. Durban 20 30
551 25c. West coast 20 35
552 40c. Clifton 35 65
MS553 128 × 90 mm. Nos. 549/52 1·50 2·50

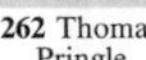
262 Thomas Pringle **263** Manganese

1984. South African English Authors.

554 **262** 10c. brown, lt brn & grey 10 10
555 – 20c. brown, green and grey 20 40
556 – 25c. brown, pink and grey 20 50
557 – 40c. brown, lt brn & grey 35 85

DESIGNS: 20c. Pauline Smith; 25c. Olive Schreiner; 40c. Sir Percy Fitzpatrick.

1984. Strategic Minerals. Multicoloured.

558 11c. Type **263** 30 10
559 20c. Chromium 45 60
560 25c. Vanadium 50 80
561 30c. Titanium 60 90

264 Bloukrans River Bridge

1984. South African Bridges. Multicoloured.

562 11c. Type **264** 25 10
563 25c. Durban four-level interchange 40 60
564 30c. Mfolozi railway bridge 45 75
565 45c. Gouritz River bridge . . 55 1·40

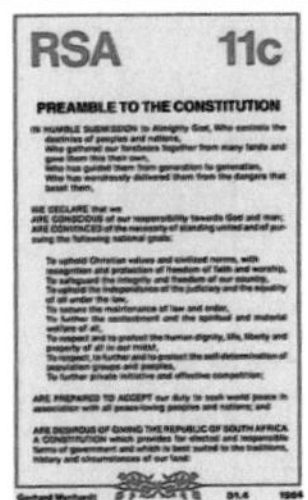

265 Preamble to the Constitution in Afrikaans **266** Pres. P. W. Botha

1984. New Constitution.

566 – 11c. stone, black and bistre . . . . 70 1·25
567 **265** 11c. stone, black and bistre . . . . 70 1·25
568 – 25c. stone, purple and bistre 45 50
569 – 30c. multicoloured 45 50

DESIGNS: No. 566, Preamble to the Constitution in English; 568, Last two lines of National Anthem; 569, South African coat of arms.

1984. Inauguration of President Botha.

570 **266** 11c. multicoloured 30 10
571 25c. multicoloured 55 40

267 Pro Patria Medal **268** "Reflections" (Frans Oerder)

1984. Military Decorations. Multicoloured.

572 11c. Type **267** 20 10
573 25c. De Wet decoration . . . 30 45
574 30c. John Chard decoration 30 65
575 45c. Honoris Crux (Diamond) decoration . . 35 1·10
MS576 71 × 116 mm. Nos. 572/5 1·50 3·00

1985. Paintings by Frans Oerder. Multicoloured.

577 11c. Type **268** 20 15
578 25c. "Ladies in a Garden" 25 35
579 30c. "Still-life with Lobster" 25 45
580 50c. "Still-life with Marigolds" 40 70
MS581 129 × 74 mm. Nos. 577/80 1·50 3·00

269 Cape Parliament Building **270** Freesia

1985. Centenary of Cape Parliament Building. Multicoloured.

582 12c. Type **269** 15 10
583 25c. Speaker's Chair 25 30
584 30c. "National Convention 1908–9" (Edward Roworth) 25 40
585 50c. Republic Parliamentary emblem . . . . 40 1·10

1985. Floral Emigrants. Multicoloured.

586 12c. Type **270** 15 10
587 25c. Nerine 25 30
588 30c. Ixia 25 45
589 50c. Gladiolus . . . . 40 1·25

271 Sugar Bowl

1985. Cape Silverware. Multicoloured.

590 12c. Type **271** 20 10
591 25c. Teapot 30 30
592 30c. Loving cup (vert) . . . 30 45
593 50c. Coffee pot (vert) . . . 45 1·50

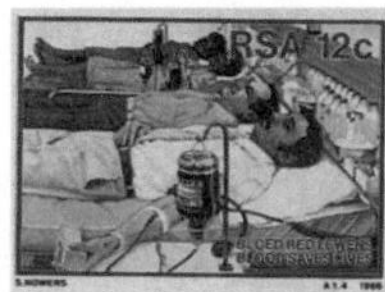
272 Blood Donor Session

1986. Blood Donor Campaign. Multicoloured.

594 12c. Type **272** 45 10
595 20c. Baby receiving blood transfusion 75 80
596 25c. Operation in progress . . 80 95
597 30c. Ambulanceman and accident victim . . . . . . 95 1·60

273 National Flag

1986. 25th Anniv of Republic of South Africa.

598 14c. Type **273** . . . . 75 1·00
599 14c. As Type **273**, but inscr "UNITY IS STRENGTH" 75 1·00

274 Drostdyhof, Graaff-Reinet

1986. Restoration of Historic Buildings. Multicoloured.

600 14c. Type **274** 30 10
601 20c. Pilgrim's Rest mining village 55 70
602 25c. Strapp's Store, Bethlehem 60 90
603 30c. Palmdene, Pietermaritzburg . . . . . 75 1·40

275 Von Brandis Square, Johannesburg, c. 1900

1986. Centenary of Johannesburg. Multicoloured.

604 14c. Type **275** 35 10
605 20c. Gold mine (26 × 20 mm) 1·25 1·25
606 25c. Johannesburg skyline, 1986 . . . . 1·00 1·60
607 30c. Gold bars (26 × 20 mm) 1·75 2·50

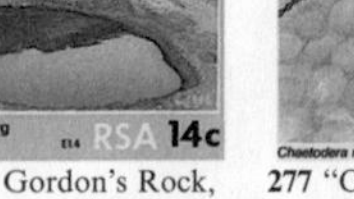
276 Gordon's Rock, Paarlberg **277** "Cicindela regalis"

1986. Rock Formations. Multicoloured.

608 14c. Type **276** 45 10
609 20c. The Column, Drakensberg 70 80
610 25c. Maltese Cross, Sederberge . . . . 75 1·00
611 30c. Bourke's Luck Potholes, Blyde River Gorge . . . . 85 1·50

1987. South African Beetles. Multicoloured.

612 14c. Type **277** 40 10
613 20c. "Trichostetha fascicularis" 55 60
614 25c. "Julodis viridipes" . . . 65 90
615 30c. "Ceroplesis militaris" . . 75 1·75

278 Eland, Sebaaieni Cave

1987. Rock Paintings. Multicoloured.

616 16c. Type **278** 40 10
617 20c. Leaping lion, Clocolan 60 65
618 25c. Black wildebeest, uMhlwazini Valley 75 90
619 30c. Bushman dance, Floukraal . . . . 80 1·60

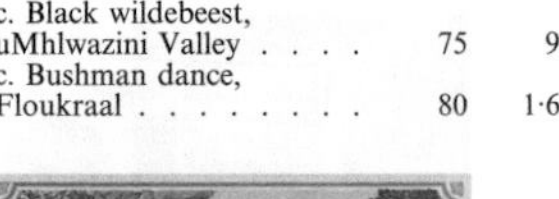

279 Oude Pastorie, Paarl

1987. 300th Anniv of Paarl. Multicoloured.

620 16c. Type **279** 20 10
621 20c. Grapevines 35 55
622 25c. Wagon-building 40 65
623 30c. KWV Cathedral Wine Cellar . . . . 45 1·25

1987. Natal Flood Relief Fund (1st issue). No. 521a surch.

624 16c.+10c. red (surch **VLOEDRAMP NATAL +10c**) 30 80
625 16c.+10c. (surch **NATAL FLOOD DISASTER +10c**) 30 80

See also Nos. 629/30 and 635/6.

281 "Belshazzar's Feast" (Rembrandt)

1987. The Bible Society of South Africa. Multicoloured.

626 16c. "The Bible" in 75 languages (54 × 34 mm) . . 30 10
627 30c. Type **281** 45 60
628 50c. "St. Matthew and the Angel" (Rembrandt) (vert) 75 1·40

1987. Natal Flood Relief Fund (2nd issue). No. 626 surch.

629 16c.+10c. multicoloured (surch as No. 625) 45 70
630 16c.+10c. multicoloured (surch as No. 624) 45 70

282 Bartolomeu Dias and Cape of Good Hope

1988. 500th Anniv of Discovery of Cape of Good Hope by Bartolomeu Dias. Multicoloured.

631 16c. Type **282** 60 10
632 30c. Kwaaihoek Monument 80 85
633 40c. Caravels . . . . 1·40 1·50
634 50c. Martellus map, c. 1489 1·75 2·25

1988. Natal Flood Relief Fund (3rd issue). No. 631 surch.

635 16c.+10c. multicoloured (surch as No. 624) 45 70
636 16c.+10c. multicoloured (surch as No. 625) 45 70

283 Huguenot Monument, Franschhoek

1988. 300th Anniv of Arrival of First French Huguenots at the Cape. Multicoloured.

637 16c. Type **283** 30 10
638 30c. Map of France showing Huguenot areas 85 80
639 40c. Title page of French/ Dutch New Testament of 1672 . . . . 85 1·25
640 50c. St. Bartholomew's Day Massacre, Paris, 1572 . . . 1·10 1·50

1988. National Flood Relief Fund Nos. 637/40 surch in English (**National Flood Disaster +10c**) (E) or in Afrikaans (**Nasionale Vloedramp +10c**) (A).

641 16c.+10c. multicoloured (E) 40 65
642 16c.+10c. multicoloured (A) 40 65
643 30c.+10c. multicoloured (A) 55 75
644 30c.+10c. multicoloured (E) 55 75
645 40c.+10c. multicoloured (A) 70 90
646 40c.+10c. multicoloured (E) 70 90
647 50c.+10c. multicoloured (E) 90 1·25
648 50c.+10c. multicoloured (A) 90 1·25

285 Pelican Point Lighthouse, Walvis Bay

1988. Lighthouses. Multicoloured.
649 16c. Type **285** 50 10
650 30c. Green Point, Cape Town 70 70
651 40c. Cape Agulhas . . . . . 90 1·25
652 50c. Umhlanga Rocks, Durban . . . . 1·25 1·75
MS653 132 × 112 mm. Nos. 649/52 4·50 4·25

286 "Huernia zebrina" **287** Map of Great Trek Routes

1988. Succulents. Multicoloured.
654 1c. Type **286** 10 10
655 2c. "Euphorbia symmetrica" 10 10
656 5c. "Lithops dorotheae" . . 10 10
657 7c. "Gibbaeum nebrownii" 15 10
658 10c. "Didymaotus lapidiformis" 15 10
659 16c. "Vanheerdea divergens" 60 10
659a 18c. "Faucaria tigrina" . . 50 10
660 20c. "Conophytum mundum" 80 10
660a 21c. "Gasteria armstrongii" 40 10
661 25c. "Cheiridopsis peculiaris" 80 10
662 30c. "Tavaresia barklyi" . . 60 20
663 35c. "Dinteranthus wilmotianus" . . . . . . 1·00 20
664 40c. "Frithia pulchra" . . . 1·00 25
665 50c. "Lapidaria margaretae" 1·00 25
666 90c. "Dioscorea elephantipes" . . . . . . 1·25 45
667 1r. "Trichocaulon cactiforme" . . . . 1·00 50
668 2r. "Crassula columnaris" 1·25 90
668a 5r. "Anacampseros albissima" . . . . 2·25 2·40
See also No. 778.

1988. Coil stamps. As T **286**. Multicoloured.
669 1c. "Adromischus marianiae" 1·00 1·50
670 2c. "Titanopsis calcarea" . . 50 60
671 5c. "Dactylopsis digitata" . . 50 60
672 10c. "Pleiospilos bolusii" . . 55 70

1988. 150th Anniv of Great Trek. Multicoloured.
673 16c. Type **287** 60 10
674 30c. "Exodus" (tapestry by W. Coetzer) (56 × 20 mm) 90 90
675 40c. "Crossing the Drakensberg" (tapestry by W. Coetzer) (77 × 20 mm) 1·10 1·10
676 50c. "After the Service, Church of the Vow" (J. H. Pierneef) (horiz) . . . . . 1·40 1·75

288 Coelacanth

1989. 50th Anniv of Discovery of Coelacanth. Multicoloured.
677 16c. Type **288** 75 15
678 30c. Prof. J. L. B. Smith and Dr. M. Courtenay-Latimer examining Coelacanth . . 1·10 1·25
679 40c. J. L. B. Smith Institute of Ichthyology, Grahamstown . . . . . . 1·40 1·60
680 50c. Coelacanth and "GEO" midget submarine . . . . 1·50 2·25

289 Man-made Desert

1989. National Grazing Strategy. Multicoloured.
681 18c. Type **289** 40 15
682 30c. Formation of erosion gully 65 75
683 40c. Concrete barrage in gully . . . . 70 1·00
684 50c. Reclaimed veldt . . . . 80 1·40

290 South Africa v. France Match, 1980

1989. Cent of South African Rugby Board. Mult.
685 18c. Type **290** 80 15
686 30c. South Africa v. Australia, 1963 . . . . . 1·25 90
687 40c. South Africa v. New Zealand, 1937 . . . . . . 1·40 1·50
688 50c. South Africa v. British Isles, 1896 . . . . 1·40 2·00

291 "Composition in Blue" **292** Pres. F. W. de Klerk

1989. Paintings by Jacob Hendrik Pierneef. Multicoloured.
689 18c. Type **291** 45 15
690 30c. "Zanzibar" 70 60
691 40c. "The Bushveld" . . . . . 90 1·10
692 50c. "Cape Homestead" . . . 1·00 1·50
MS693 114 × 86 mm. Nos. 689/92 2·25 2·75

1989. Inaug of President F. W. de Klerk. Mult.
694 18c. Type **292** 50 15
695 45c. F. W. de Klerk (different) . . . . 75 1·40

293 Gas-drilling Rig, Mossel Bay

1989. Energy Sources. Multicoloured.
696 18c. Type **293** 40 10
697 30c. Coal to oil conversion plant 70 70
698 40c. Nuclear power station 80 85
699 50c. Thermal electric power station . . . . 90 1·25

294 Electric Goods Train and Map of Railway Routes

1990. Co-operation in Southern Africa. Mult.
700 18c. Cahora Bassa Hydro-electric Scheme, Mozambique, and map of transmission lines (68 × 26 mm) 70 25
701 30c. Type **294** 90 70
702 40c. Projected dam on upper Orange River, Lesotho, and map of Highlands Water Project (68 × 26 mm) 1·10 1·10
703 50c. Cow, syringe and outline map of Africa . . . . . . 1·40 1·25
MS704 136 × 78 mm. Nos. 700/3 3·25 2·75

295 Great Britain 1840 Penny Black **296** Green Turaco

1990. National Stamp Day. Multicoloured.
705 21c. Type **295** 40 50
706 21c. Cape of Good Hope 1853 4d. triangular pair . . 40 50
707 21c. Natal 1857 1s. 40 50
708 21c. Orange Free State 1868 1s. 40 50
709 21c. Transvaal 1869 1s. . . . 40 50

1990. Birds. Multicoloured.
710 21c. Type **296** 70 20
711 35c. Red-capped robin chat 90 80
712 40c. Rufous-naped bush lark 90 1·10
713 50c. Bokmakierie shrike . . . 1·25 1·50

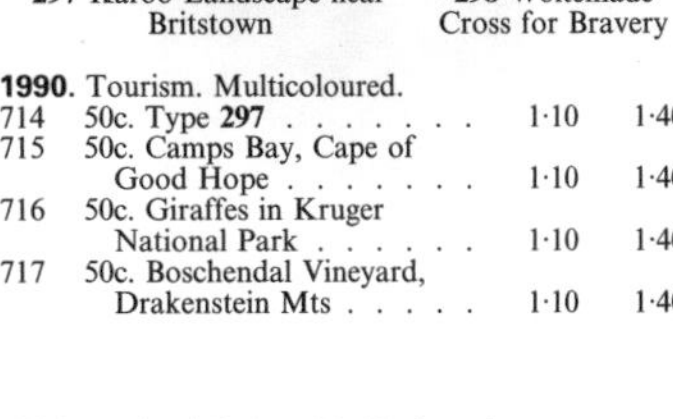

297 Karoo Landscape near Britstown **298** Woltemade Cross for Bravery

1990. Tourism. Multicoloured.
714 50c. Type **297** . . . . 1·10 1·40
715 50c. Camps Bay, Cape of Good Hope . . . . 1·10 1·40
716 50c. Giraffes in Kruger National Park . . . . . . 1·10 1·40
717 50c. Boschendal Vineyard, Drakenstein Mts . . . . . 1·10 1·40

1990. National Orders. Multicoloured.
718 21c. Type **298** 50 60
719 21c. Order of the Southern Cross 50 60
720 21c. Order of the Star of South Africa 50 60
721 21c. Order for Meritorious Service 50 60
722 21c. Order of Good Hope . . 50 60
MS723 143 × 70 mm. Nos. 718/22 2·25 2·75

299 Boer Horses **300** Diagram of Human Heart and Transplant Operation

1991. Animal Breeding in South Africa. Mult.
724 21c. Type **299** 70 70
725 21c. Bonsmara bull 70 70
726 21c. Dorper sheep 70 70
727 21c. Ridgeback dogs 70 70
728 21c. Putterie racing pigeons 70 70

1991. 30th Anniv of Republic. Scientific and Technological Achievements. Multicoloured.
729 25c. Type **300** 20 10
730 40c. Matimba Power Station (horiz) 35 35
731 50c. Dolos design breakwater (horiz) 45 45
732 60c. Western Deep Levels gold mine 60 60

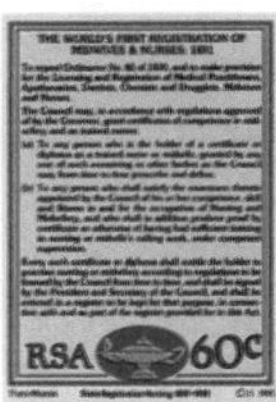

301 State Registration of Nurses Act, 1891 **302** South Africa Post Office Ltd Emblem

1991. Centenary of State Registration for Nurses and Midwives.
733 **301** 60c. multicoloured 60 60

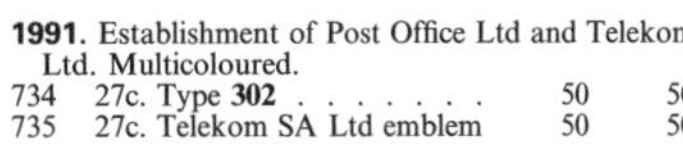

1991. Establishment of Post Office Ltd and Telekom Ltd. Multicoloured.
734 27c. Type **302** 50 50
735 27c. Telekom SA Ltd emblem 50 50

303 Sir Arnold Theiler (veterinarian)

1991. South African Scientists. Multicoloured.
736 27c. Type **303** 30 15
737 45c. Sir Basil Schonland (physicist) 60 60
738 65c. Dr. Robert Broom (palaeontologist) 80 90
739 85c. Dr. Alex du Toit (geologist) . . . . 1·00 1·75

304 "Agulhas" (Antarctic research ship)

1991. 30th Anniv of Antarctic Treaty. Mult.
740 27c. Type **304** . . . . 1·00 20
741 65c. Chart showing South African National Antarctic Expedition base . . . . . 1·50 80

305 Soil Conservation

1992. Environmental Conservation. Mult.
742 27c. Type **305** 50 15
743 65c. Water pollution . . . . 1·25 1·10
744 85c. Air pollution . . . . . 1·50 1·50

306 Dutch Fleet approaching Table Bay **307** Queen Anne Settee, c. 1750

1992. National Stamp Day. Cape of Good Hope Postal Stones. Multicoloured.
745 35c. Type **306** 60 60
746 35c. Landing for water and provisions 60 60
747 35c. Discovering a postal stone 60 60
748 35c. Leaving letters under a stone 60 60
749 35c. Reading letters 60 60

1992. Antique Cape Furniture. Multicoloured.
750 35c. Type **307** 50 50
751 35c. Stinkwood settee, c. 1800 50 50
752 35c. Canopy bed, c. 1800 (vert) 50 50
753 35c. 19th-century rocking cradle 50 50
754 35c. Water butt, c. 1800 (vert) 50 50
755 35c. Flemish style cabinet, c. 1700 (vert) . . . 50 50
756 35c. Armoire, c. 1780 (vert) 50 50
757 35c. Late 17th-century church chair (vert) 50 50
758 35c. Tub chair, c. 1770 (vert) 50 50
759 35c. Bible desk, c. 1750 (vert) 50 50

308 Grand Prix Motor Racing **309** "Women's Monument" (Van Wouw)

1992. Sports. Multicoloured.
760 35c. Type **308** 30 25
761 35c. Football 30 25
762 55c. Total Paris–Cape Motor Rally 45 35
763 70c. Athletics 55 50
764 90c. Rugby 75 65
765 1r.05 Cricket . . . . 1·25 1·00
MS766 167 × 69 mm. Nos. 760/5 3·50 3·00

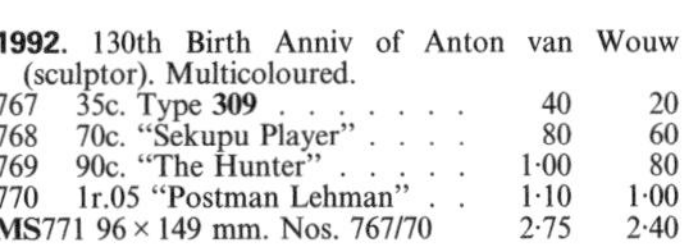

1992. 130th Birth Anniv of Anton van Wouw (sculptor). Multicoloured.
767 35c. Type **309** 40 20
768 70c. "Sekupu Player" 80 60
769 90c. "The Hunter" . . . . . 1·00 80
770 1r.05 "Postman Lehman" . . 1·10 1·00
MS771 96 × 149 mm. Nos. 767/70 2·75 2·40

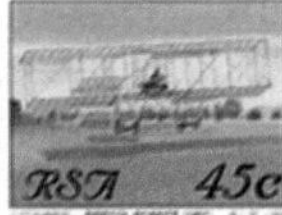

310 Walvis Bay Harbour **311** Bristol "Boxkite", 1907

1993. South African Harbours. Multicoloured.
772 35c. Type **310** 35 20
773 55c. East London 45 35
774 70c. Port Elizabeth 70 50
775 90c. Cape Town 90 75

776 1r.05 Durban 95 95
MS777 147 × 112 mm. Nos. 772/6 2·75 2·50

1993. Succulents. As T **286**, but inscr "Standardised mail" in English and Afrikaans.
778 (–) "Stapelia grandiflora" . . 60 10
No. 778 was sold at 45c.

1993. Aviation in South Africa. Multicoloured.
779 45c. Type **311** 65 60
780 45c. Voisin "Boxkite", 1909 65 60
781 45c. Bleriot XI, 1911 . . . . 65 60
782 45c. Paterson No. 2 biplane, 1913 . . . . 65 60
783 45c. Henri Farman H.F.27, 1915 . . . . 65 60
784 45c. Royal Aircraft Factory B.E.2.E, 1918 . . . . . . 65 60
785 45c. Vickers Vimy "Silver Queen II", 1920 . . . . . 65 60
786 45c. Royal Aircraft Factory S.E.5.A, 1921 . . . . . . 65 60
787 45c. Avro 504k, 1921 . . . . 65 60
788 45c. Armstrong Whitworth Atalanta, 1930 . . . . . . 65 60
789 45c. De Havilland D.H.66 Hercules, 1931 . . . . . . 65 60
790 45c. Westland Wapiti, 1931 65 60
791 45c. Junkers F-13, 1932 . . . 65 60
792 45c. Handley Page H.P.42, 1933 . . . . 65 60
793 45c. Junkers Ju 52/3m, 1934 65 60
794 45c. Junkers Ju 86, 1936 . . 65 60
795 45c. Hawker Hartbees, 1936 65 60
796 45c. Short Empire "C" Class flying boat "Canopus", 1937 . . . . 65 60
797 45c. Miles Master II and Airspeed A.S 10 Oxford, 1940 . . . . 65 60
798 45c. North American Harvard Mk IIa, 1942 . . 65 60
799 45c. Short Sunderland flying boat, 1945 . . . . 65 60
800 45c. Avro Type 685 York, 1946 . . . . 65 60
801 45c. Douglas DC-7B, 1955 65 60
802 45c. Sikorsky S-55c helicopter, 1956 . . . . . 65 60
803 45c. Boeing 707-344, 1959 . . 65 60

312 Table Mountain Ghost Frog

313 Dragoons carrying Mail between Cape Town and False Bay, 1803

1993. Endangered Fauna. Multicoloured. (a) Face values as T **312**.
804 1c. Type **312** (I) 10 10
804c 1c. Type **312** (II) 20 20
805 2c. Smith's dwarf chameleon (I) 10 10
805c 2c. Smith's dwarf chameleon (II) 20 20
806 5c. Giant girdle-tailed lizard (I) 10 10
807 10c. Geometric tortoise (I) 10 10
807c 10c. Geometric tortoise (II) 30 30
808 20c. Southern African hedgehog (I) 10 10
913 20c. Southern African hedgehog (II) 10 10
809 40c. Riverine rabbit (I) . . . 20 10
809c 40c. Riverine rabbit (II) . . 20 10
810 50c. Samango monkey (I) 25 20
914 50c. Samango monkey (II) 25 10
811 55c. Aardwolf (I) 20 10
811c 55c. Aardwolf (II) 30 30
812 60c. Cape hunting dog (I) 40 20
915 60c. Cape hunting dog (II) 30 10
813 70c. Roan antelope (I) . . . 55 25
813c 70c. Roan antelope (II) . . 30 20
814 75c. African striped weasel (I) 30 20
815 80c. Kori bustard (I) . . . 1·00 25
815a 85c. Lemon-breasted seedeater (I) . . . . . . 1·00 25
816 90c. Jackass penguin (I) . . 1·10 30
816c 90c. Jackass penguin (II) . . 1·00 30
817 1r. Wattled crane (I) . . . . 1·10 30
916 1r. Wattled crane (II) . . . 80 25
818 2r. Blue swallow (I) . . . . 1·25 55
818c 2r. Blue swallow (II) . . . . 1·25 55
819 5r. Martial eagle (I) . . . . 2·00 1·40
819c 5r. Martial eagle (II) . . . . 1·75 1·40
820 10r. Bateleur (I) . . . . . . 3·00 2·10
917 20r. African fish eagle (II) 4·00 4·25

(b) Inscr "Standardised mail" in Afrikaans and English (Nos. 821 and 918b) or "Airmail postcard rate" (others).
821 (–) Black rhinoceros (III) . . 50 25
821b (–) Black rhinoceros (IV) . . 50 35
821c (1r.) White rhinoceros (II) 50 30
821d (1r.) Buffalo (II) 50 30
821e (1r.) Lion (II) 50 30
821f (1r.) Leopard (II) 50 30
821g (1r.) African elephant (II) 50 30

I and III. Species name in Latin. II and IV. Species name in English, No. 821 has a small rhinoceros and No. 821b a larger rhinoceros; they were sold at 45c. at first but this was later increased to the prevailing rates.

For redrawn designs without frame and inscribed "South Africa" only, see Nos. 1029/44.

1993. National Stamp Day. Early 19th-century Postal Services. Multicoloured.
822 45c. Type **313** 30 25
823 65c. Ox wagon carrying Stellenbosch to Cape Town mail, 1803 . . . . 45 50
824 85c. Khoi-Khoin mail runners from Stellenbosch, 1803 . . . . 65 70
825 1r.05 Mounted postmen, 1804 80 90

314 Flowers from Namaqualand

1993. Tourism. Multicoloured.
826 85c. Type **314** (Afrikaans inscr) 65 70
827 85c. North Beach, Durban (English inscr) 65 70
828 85c. Lion (German inscr) . . 65 70
829 85c. "Appel Express" on Van Staden's Bridge (Dutch inscr) 65 70
830 85c. Gemsbok (antelope) (French inscr) 65 70

315 Grapes and Packing Bench

1994. Export Fruits. Multicoloured.
831 85c. Type **315** 55 50
832 90c. Apple and picker . . . 55 50
833 1r.05 Plum and fork-lift truck 65 60
834 1r.25 Orange and tractor with trailer 75 70
835 1r.40 Avocado and loading freighter 85 80

316 "Children of Different Races" (Nicole Davies)

1994. Peace Campaign. Children's Paintings. Multicoloured.
836 45c. Type **316** 25 20
837 70c. "Dove and Tree" (Robynne Lawrie) 40 40
838 95c. "Children and Dove" (Batami Nothmann) . . . 55 55
839 1r.15 "Multi-racial Crowd" (Karen Uys) 75 80

317 Pres. Mandela

1994. Inaug of President Nelson Mandela. Mult.
840 45c. Type **317** 45 20
841 70c. South African national anthems 80 60
842 95c. New national flag . . . 1·10 1·40
843 1r.15 Union Buildings, Pretoria . . . . 1·25 1·75

318 Tug "T.S. McEwen" towing "Winchester Castle" (liner), 1935

1994. Tugboats. Multicoloured.
844 45c. Type **318** 35 20
845 70c. "Sir William Hoy" with "Karanja" (liner), 1970 . . 55 40
846 95c. "Sir Charles Elliott" and wreck of "Dunedin Star" (liner), 1942 . . . . 70 55
847 1r.15 "Eland" and freighter at wharf, 1955 . . . . . . 95 75
848 1r.35 "Pioneer" (paddle tug) and sailing ships, 1870 . . 1·10 90
MS849 163 × 84 mm. Nos. 844/8 3·25 2·50

319 "Mother hands out Work" (Emile du Toit)

1994. International Year of the Family. Children's Paintings. Multicoloured.
850 45c. Type **319** 45 45
851 45c. "My Friends and I at Play" (Patrick Mackenzie) 45 45
852 45c. "Family Life" (Michelle du Pisani) 45 45
853 45c. "Sunday in Church" (Elizabeth Nel) 45 45
854 45c. "I visit my Brother in Hospital" (Zwelinzema Sam) 45 45

320 Hands holding Invoice and Bulk Mail Envelope

1994. National Stamp Day. Multicoloured.
855 50c. Type **320** 30 25
856 70c. Certified mail 40 40
857 95c. Registered mail 50 55
858 1r.15 Express Delivery mail 60 65

321 "Erica tenuifolia"

1994. Heathers. Multicoloured.
859 95c. Type **321** 65 65
860 95c. "Erica urna-viridis" . . 65 65
861 95c. "Erica decora" 65 65
862 95c. "Erica aristata" 65 65
863 95c. "Erica dichrus" 65 65

322 Warthogs (Eastern Transvaal) and Map (⅔-size illustration)

1995. Tourism. Multicoloured. (a) With face value.
864 50c. Type **322** 60 25
865 50c. Lost City resort (North-West Province) 60 25

(b) Inscr "Standardised mail" in English and Afrikaans
866 (60c.) White rhinoceros and calf (KwaZulu/Natal) . . . 60 25
867 (60c.) Cape Town waterfront (Western Cape) 60 25
868 (60c.) Baobab tree (Northern Transvaal) 60 40
869 (60c.) Highland Route (Free State) 60 40
870 (60c.) Augrabies Falls (Northern Cape) 60 40
871 (60c.) Herd of elephants, Addo National Park (Eastern Cape) 60 40
872 (60c.) Union Buildings, Pretoria (Gauteng) 60 40

323 De Havilland D.H.9 Biplane and Cheetah D Jet Fighter

1995. Aviation Anniversaries. Multicoloured.
873 50c. Type **323** (75th anniv of South African Air Force) 55 30
874 95c. Vickers Vimy "Silver Queen II" (75th anniv of first Trans-African flight) 80 75

324 Player running with Ball and Silhouettes

1995. World Cup Rugby Championship, South Africa. Multicoloured.
875 (60c.) Type **324** 30 25
876 (60c.) Player running with ball and silhouettes (vert) 30 25
877 1r.15 Player taking ball from scrum (68 × 26½ mm) . . . 75 85
MS878 109 × 61 mm. No. 876 . . 75 75
Nos. 875/6 are inscribed "STANDARD POSTAGE" in English and Afrikaans.

325 Rural Water Purification System

1995. 50th Anniv of C.S.I.R. (technological research organization).
879 **325** (60c.) multicoloured . . . 45 45
No. 879 is inscribed "Standardised mail" in English and Afrikaans.

326 Player with Ball

1995. South Africa's Victory in Rugby World Cup. Multicoloured.
880 (60c.) Type **326** 40 40
881 (60c.) South African player holding trophy aloft (vert) 40 40
Nos. 880/1 are inscribed "STANDARD POSTAGE" in English and Afrikaans.

327 Dr. John Gilchrist, South African Pilchards and "Africana" (oceanographic research ship)

328 Singapore Lion

1995. Centenary of Marine Science in South Africa.
882 **327** (60c.) multicoloured . . . 30 30
No. 882 is inscribed "Standard Postage" in English and Afrikaans.

1995. "Singapore '95" International Stamp Exhibition. Sheet 71 × 55 mm.
MS883 **328** (60c.) multicoloured 75 1·00
No. **MS**883 is inscribed "STANDARD POSTAGE" in English and Afrikaans.

329 People building Flag Wall

1995. Masakhane Campaign.
884 **329** (60c.) multicoloured (34 × 24 mm) 20 20
884b (60c.) multicoloured (26 × 20 mm) 20 20
Nos. 884 and 884b are inscribed "STANDARD POSTAGE" in English and Afrikaans.

330 Papal Arms

1995. Visit of Pope John Paul II.
885 **330** (60c.) multicoloured . . . 65 30
No. 885 is inscribed "STANDARD POSTAGE" in English and Afrikaans.

331 Gandhi wearing Suit

332 Traditional African Postman

1995. 125th Birth Anniv (1994) of Mahatma Gandhi.
886 **331** (60c.) violet 65 25
887 – 1r.40 brown 85 85
MS888 71 × 71 mm. No. 887 . . 1·40 1·40
DESIGN: 1r.40, Gandhi wearing dhoti.
No. 886 is inscribed "STANDARD POSTAGE" in English and Afrikaans.

1995. World Post Day.
889 **332** (60c.) multicoloured . . . 30 30
No. 889 is inscribed "STANDARD POSTAGE" in English and Afrikaans.

1995. "Total Stampex '95" and "Ilsapex '98" Stamp Exhibitions. Sheet, 70 × 66 mm, containing **T 332** and "ILSAPEX '98" logo. Imperf.
MS890 5r. multicoloured . . . . 2·00 2·25

333 "50" and U.N. Emblem

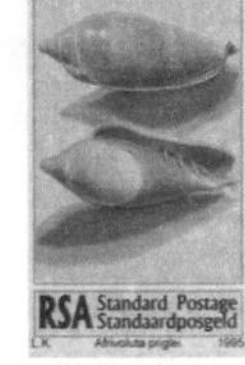

334 "Afrivoluta pringlei"

1995. 50th Annivs of United Nations and UNESCO. Multicoloured.
891 **333** (60c.) multicoloured . . . 30 30
MS892 101 × 78 mm. (60c.) Traditional village (30 × 47 mm) 30 30
No. 891 is inscribed "STANDARD POSTAGE" in English and Afrikaans.

1995. Sea Shells. Multicoloured.
893 (60c.) Type **334** 40 40
894 (60c.) "Lyria africana" . . . 40 40
895 (60c.) "Marginella mosaica" 40 40
896 (60c.) "Conus pictus" 40 40
897 (60c.) "Gypreaea fultoni" . . 40 40
Nos. 893/7 are inscribed "STANDARD POSTAGE" in English and Afrikaans.
No. 893 is inscribed "priglei" in error.

335 Map of Africa and Player

336 South African Player, Map and Trophy

1996. African Nations Football Championship, South Africa. Map and Players.
898 **335** (60c.) multicoloured ("RSA" in blue) . . . 55 55
899 – (60c.) multicoloured ("RSA" in brown) . . 55 55
900 – (60c.) multicoloured ("RSA" in red) 55 55
901 – (60c.) multicoloured ("RSA" in grey) . . . 55 55
902 – (60c.) multicoloured ("RSA" in green) . . . 55 55
MS903 75 × 55 mm. (60c.) multicoloured (young player) 50 60
Nos. 898/903 are inscribed "STANDARD POSTAGE" in English and Afrikaans.

1996. South Africa's Victory in African Nations Football Championship.
904 **336** (60c.) multicoloured . . . 40 30
No. 904 is inscribed "STANDARD POSTAGE" in English and Afrikaans.

337 Historical Buildings, Bloemfontein

1996. 150th Anniv of City of Bloemfontein.
905 **337** (60c.) multicoloured . . . 50 20
No. 905 is inscribed "Standard Postage" in English and Afrikaans.

338 Rat

1996. "CHINA '96" 9th Asian International Stamp Exhibition, Peking. Sheet 109 × 85 mm.
MS906 **338** 60c. multicoloured 70 70

339 "Man in a Donkey Cart" (Gerard Sekoto)

1996. Gerard Sekoto (artist) Commemoration. Multicoloured.
907 1r. Type **339** 30 30
908 2r. "Song of the Pick" . . . 80 80
MS909 108 × 70 mm. 2r. "Yellow Houses, Sophiatown" (detail) (vert) . . . . 1·00 1·10

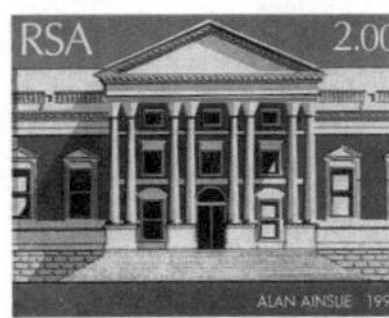

340 Parliament Building, Cape Town

1996. "CAPEX '96" International Stamp Exhibition, Toronto. Sheet 72 × 49 mm.
MS910 **340** 2r. multicoloured . . 1·00 1·10

341 Children playing

1996. Youth Day.
911 **341** (60c.) multicoloured . . . 30 20
No. 911 is inscribed "STANDARD POSTAGE" in English and Afrikaans.

342 Marathon Runners

1996. 75th Anniv of Comrades Marathon.
912 **342** (60c.) multicoloured . . . 30 20
No. 912 is inscribed "Standard postage" in English and Afrikaans.

343 Cycling

344 Constitutional Assembly Logo

1996. Olympic Games, Atlanta. Multicoloured.
919 (70c.) Type **343** 40 40
920 (70c.) Swimming 40 40
921 (70c.) Boxing 40 40
922 (70c.) Running 40 40
923 (70c.) Pole vaulting 40 40
924 1r.40 South African Olympic emblem 40 40
Nos. 919/24 are inscribed "STANDARD POSTAGE" in English and Afrikaans.

1996. New Democratic Constitution.
925 **344** (70c.) green, red and black 30 30
926 (70c.) blue, violet, and black 30 30
927 (70c.) violet, yellow and black 30 30
928 (70c.) blue, red and black 30 30
929 (70c.) red, yellow and black 30 30
Nos. 925/9 are inscribed "Standard Postage" in English and Afrikaans.

345 "Sea Pioneer" (bulk carrier)

1996. 50th Anniv of South African Merchant Marine. Multicoloured.
930 (70c.) Type **345** 75 65
931 (70c.) "Winterberg" (container ship) 75 65
932 1r.40 "Langkloof" (freighter) 1·10 95
933 1r.40 "Vaal" (liner) . . . . . 1·10 95
MS934 102 × 63 mm. 2r. "Constantia" (freighter) and tug (71 × 30 mm) (inscr "SOUTH AFRICAN MERCHANT MARINE 1946–1996" on top margin) . . . . 1·00 1·00
No. **MS**934 also comes with the top margin inscription replaced by "Safmarine" and logo.
Nos. 930/1 are inscribed "Standard Postage" in English and Afrikaans.

346 "Xhosa Woman" (G. Pemba)

347 Postman delivering Letters

1996. National Women's Day.
935 **346** 70c. multicoloured 30 25

1996. World Post Day.
936 **347** 70c. multicoloured 30 25

348 Candles and Holly

1996. Christmas.
937 **348** 70c. multicoloured 30 25

349 "Liner "Oranje" at cape Town" (E. Wale) (¾-size illustration)

1996. "Bloemfontein 150" National Stamp Show. Sheet 86 × 56 mm.
MS938 **349** 2r. multicoloured . . 1·50 1·50

350 Max Theiler (Medicine, 1951)

352 Lion

351 Early Motor Car

1996. South African Nobel Laureates.
939 **350** (70c.) violet and purple 45 45
940 – (70c.) green, purple and violet 45 45
941 – (70c.) purple and violet 45 45
942 – (70c.) green, purple and violet 45 45
943 – (70c.) violet and purple 45 45
944 – (70c.) violet and purple 45 45
945 – (70c.) green, purple and violet 45 45
946 – (70c.) purple and violet 45 45
947 – (70c.) green, purple and violet 45 45
948 – (70c.) violet and purple 45 45
DESIGNS: No. 940, Albert Luthuli (Peace, 1961); 941, Alfred Nobel; 942, Allan Cormack (Medicine, 1979); 943, Aaron Klug (Chemistry, 1982); 944, Desmond Tutu (Peace, 1984); 945, Nadine Gordimer (Literature, 1991); 946, Nobel Prizes symbol; 947, Nelson Mandela (Peace, 1993); 948, F. W. de Klerk (Peace, 1993).
Nos. 939/48 are inscribed "Standard Postage" in English and Afrikaans.

1997. Centenary of Motoring in South Africa.
949 **351** (70c.) multicoloured . . . 75 35
No. 949 is inscribed "STANDARD POSTAGE" in English and Afrikaans.

1997. "Hong Kong '97" International Stamp Exhibition. Sheet 82 × 68 mm.
MS950 **352** 3r. blue, gold and red 1·40 1·40

353 Vegetables and Water Pump

355 Election Day Poster

354 S.A.S. "Umkomaas" (minesweeper)

1997. National Water Conservation. Multicoloured.
951 (70c.) Type **353** 40 30
952 (70c.) Flowers and watering can 40 40
953 (70c.) Child in bath 40 40
954 (70c.) Building tools 40 40
955 (70c.) Water cart and stand pipe 40 40
Nos. 951/5 are inscribed "STANDARD POSTAGE".

1997. 75th Anniv of South African Navy. Multicoloured.
956 (70c.) Type **354** 60 60
957 (70c.) S.A.S. "Emily Hobhouse" (submarine) and S.A.S. "President Steyn" (frigate) 60 60
958 (70c.) S.A.S. "Kobie Coetsee" (fast attack craft) 60 60
959 (70c.) S.A.S. "Protea" (hydrographic survey ship) 60 60
Nos. 956/9 are inscribed "Standard Postage" in English and Afrikaans.

1997. Freedom Day. Each black and red.
960 (1r.) Type **355** 40 40
961 (1r.) People queueing 40 40
962 (1r.) People registering . . . 40 40
963 (1r.) Voting booth 40 40
964 (1r.) Woman placing vote in ballot box 40 40
Nos. 960/4, which are inscribed "STANDARD POSTAGE", were printed together, se-tenant, forming a composite design.

356 Brahman Bull

1997. Chinese New Year ("Year of the Ox"). "SAPDA '97" Stamp Exhibition, Johannesburg. Sheet 107 × 61 mm.
MS965 **356** 4r.50 multicoloured 1·00 1·00

357 Zulu Baskets

359 White-breasted Cormorant

358 Grocott's, Muirhead and Gowie Buildings, Grahamstown

1997. Year of Cultural Experiences. Multicoloured.
966 (1r.) Type **357** 40 40
967 (1r.) Southern Sotho figure 40 40
968 (1r.) South Ndebele figure . . 40 40
969 (1r.) Venda door 40 40
970 (1r.) Tsonga medicine gourd 40 40
971 (1r.) Wooden pot, Northern Cape 40 40
972 (1r.) Khoi walking stick . . . 40 40
973 (1r.) Tswana knife handle . . 40 40
974 (1r.) Xhosa pipe 40 40
975 (1r.) Swazi vessel 40 40
Nos. 966/75 are inscribed "Standard Postage".

1997. "Pacific '97" International Stamp Exhibition, San Francisco. Sheet 94 × 49 mm.
MS976 **358** 5r. multicoloured . . 1·25 1·25

1997. World Environment Day. Waterbirds. Multicoloured.
977 (1r.) Type **359** 40 40
978 (1r.) Hamerkop 40 40
979 (1r.) Lesser pied kingfisher ("Pied Kingfisher") 40 40
980 (1r.) Purple heron 40 40
981 (1r.) Black-headed heron . . 40 40
982 (1r.) African darter ("Darter") 40 40
983 (1r.) Green-backed heron . . 40 40
984 (1r.) White-face whistling duck ("White-faced Duck") 40 40
985 (1r.) Saddle-billed stork . . . 40 40
986 (1r.) Water dikkop 40 40
Nos. 977/86 are inscribed "STANDARD POSTAGE".

360 Double-headed Class 6E 1 Electric Locomotives

1997. Inaurguration of Revived Blue Train Service. Multicoloured.
987 (1r.20) Type **360** 70 70
988 (1r.20) Double-headed Class 6E 1 electric locomotives (different) 70 70
989 (1r.20) Double-headed Class 25NC steam locomotives, 1960s 70 70
990 (1r.20) Double-headed Class 34,900 diesel locomotives on Modder River bridge 70 70
991 (1r.20) Double-headed Class 34 diesel locomotives and baobab tree 70 70
Nos. 987/91 are inscribed "AIRMAIL POSTAGE RATE".

361 Nguni Breed

1997. Cattle Breeds. Multicoloured.
992 (1r.) Type **361** 50 50
993 (1r.) Bonsmara 50 50
994 (1r.) Afrikander 50 50
995 (1r.) Drakensberger 50 50
Nos. 992/5 are inscribed "Standard Postage" in English and Afrikaans.

362 Leopard Seal

1997. Antarctic Fauna. Multicoloured.
996 (1r.) Type **362** 35 25
997 1r.20 Antarctic skua 65 40
998 1r.70 King penguin . . . . . 1·00 70
No. 996 is inscribed "Standard Postage" in English and Afrikaans.

363 Enoch Sontonga and Verse from "Nkosi Sikelel'i Afrika"

1997. Heritage Day. Centenary of "Nkosi Sikele'i Afrika" (National Anthem). Multicoloured.
999 (1r.) Type **363** 50 50
1000 (1r.) As Type **363** but portrait at right 50 50
Nos. 999/1000 are inscribed "Standard Postage".

364 Horse-drawn Postcart delivering Mail

1997. "Cape Town '97" National Stamp Show. Sheet 85 × 64 mm.
MS1001 **364** 4r.50 multicoloured 1·50 1·50

365 Modern Postbox

366 Bethlehem

1997. World Post Day. Sheet, 108 × 69 mm.
MS1002 **365** (1 r.) multicoloured 70 70
No. **MS**1002 is inscribed "STANDARD POSTAGE".

1997. Christmas. 50th Anniv of S.A.N.T.A. (South African National Tuberculosis Association). Charity Labels. Multicoloured.
1003 (1r.) Type **366** 35 35
1004 (1r.) Cross of Lorraine and candles 35 35
1005 (1r.) Cross of Lorraine, angels and candles . . . 35 35
1006 (1r.) Angel kneeling before Cross of Lorraine 35 35
1007 (1r.) Father Christmas carrying sack 35 35
1008 (1r.) Mary and Jesus 35 35
1009 (1r.) Christmas trees 35 35
1010 (1r.) Wise men on camels . . 35 35
1011 (1r.) Christmas bell 35 35
1012 (1r.) Child kneeling 35 35
Nos. 1003/12 are inscribed "STANDARD POSTAGE".

367 Black Rhinoceros

368 Tiger (woodcut)

1997. Endangered Fauna (3rd series). Redrawn values as 1993–97 issue and new designs (Nos. 1030/4), all without frame and inscr "South Africa" only as T **367**. Multicoloured. (a) Designs as Nos. 806/20, and some new values, redrawn.
1012a 5c. Giant girdle-tailed lizard 10 20
1013 10c. Geometric tortoise . . 10 20
1014 20c. Southern African hedgehog 10 20
1015 30c. Spotted hyena 10 20
1016 40c. Riverine rabbit . . . 15 20
1017 50c. Samango monkey . . . 15 10
1018 60c. Cape hunting dog . . 20 15
1019 70c. Roan antelope 20 20
1020 80c. Kori bustard . . . . 1·25 20
1021 90c. Jackass penguin . . . 1·40 25
1022 1r. Wattled crane . . . . 1·25 25
1022a 1r.50 Tawny eagle (20 × 37 mm) . . . . . 1·75 30
1023 2r. Blue swallow . . . . . 1·50 45
1023a 2r.30 Cape vulture (20 × 37 mm) . . . . . 2·00 45
1024 3r. Giraffe . . . . 2·00 65
1025 5r. Martial eagle . . . . . 2·25 1·10
1026 10r. Bateleur (34 × 24 mm) 2·75 2·25
1028 20r. African fish eagle ("Fish Eagle") (34 × 24 mm) . . . . . 4·75 4·25

(b) Inscr "Standard Postage" (No. 1029) or "standard postage" (others).
1029 (1r.) Type **367** 30 25
1030 (1r.) Eland (vert) 30 25
1031 (1r.10) Greater kudu (vert) 30 25
1032 (1r.10) Impala (vert) 30 25
1033 (1r.10) Waterbuck (vert) . . 30 25
1034 (1r.10) Blue wildebeest (vert) 30 25

(d) Inscr "Airmail Postcard".
1040 (1r.20) White rhinoceros . . 50 55
1041 (1r.20) Buffalo 50 55
1042 (1r.20) Lion 50 55
1043 (1r.20) Leopard 50 55
1044 (1r.20) African elephant . . 50 55

1998. Chinese New Year ("Year of the Tiger"). Sheet 67 × 85 mm.
MS1051 **368** 5r. red, black and green 1·50 1·50

369 "Rescue 8" (lifeboat)

1998. 30th Anniv (1997) of National Sea Rescue Institute.
1052 **369** (1r.) multicoloured . . . 65 30

370 Leopard

371 Football Player

1998. "SAPDA '98" National Stamp Exhibition, Johannesburg. sheet 64 × 84 mm.
MS1053 **370** 5r. multicoloured . . 1·50 1·50

1998. World Cup Football Championship, France.
1054 **371** (1r.10) multicoloured . . 60 30
No. 1054 is inscribed "STANDARD POSTAGE".

372 Stone Age Hand Axe

373 Pale Chanting Goshawk

1998. Early South African History. Multicoloured.
1055 (1r.10) Type **372** 40 40
1056 (1r.10) Musuku (altar) . . . 40 40
1057 (1r.10) San rock engravings 40 40
1058 (1r.10) Early iron age pot 40 40
1059 (1r.10) Khoekhoe pot . . . 40 40
1060 (1r.10) Florisbad skull . . . 40 40
1061 (1r.10) San rock painting . . 40 40
1062 (1r.10) Mapungubwe gold rhinoceros and pot . . . 40 40
1063 (1r.10) Lydenburg head (ceremonial mask) 40 40
1064 (1r.10) Taung skull 40 40
Nos. 1055/64 are inscribed "standard postage".

1998. South African Raptors. Multicoloured.
1065 (1r.10) Type **373** 50 50
1066 (1r.10) Augur buzzard ("Jackal Buzzard") . . . 50 50
1067 (1r.10) Lanner falcon . . . 50 50
1068 (1r.10) Lammergeier ("Bearded Vulture") . . . 50 50
1069 (1r.10) Black harrier 50 50
1070 (1r.10) Cape vulture 50 50
1071 (1r.10) Bateleur 50 50
1072 (1r.10) Spotted eagle owl . . 50 50
1073 (1r.10) White-headed vulture 50 50
1074 (1r.10) African fish eagle . . 50 50
Nos. 1065/74 are inscribed "standard postage".

1998. Endangered Fauna. Antelopes. Designs as Nos. 1030/4, but self-adhesive.
1075 (1r.10) Eland (vert) 50 50
1076 (1r.10) Greater kudu (vert) 50 50
1077 (1r.10) Impala (vert) 50 50
1078 (1r.10) Waterbuck (vert) . . 50 50
1079 (1r.10) Blue wildebeest (vert) 50 50
The above are inscribed "standard postage".

374 Shepherd's Tree

1998. Trees. Multicoloured.
1080 (1r.10) Type **374** 60 60
1081 (1r.10) Karee 60 60
1082 (1r.10) Baobab 60 60
1083 (1r.10) Umbrella thorn . . . 60 60
Nos. 1080/3 are inscribed "Standard Postage".

375 Sandstone Cliffs, Cape Point

1998. "Explore South Africa" (1st series). Multicoloured. (a) Western Cape.
1084 (1r.30) Type **375** 90 70
1085 (1r.30) Robben Island . . . 90 70
1086 (1r.30) Ostrich farming, Pinehurst Homestead . . 90 70
1087 (1r.30) Victoria and Alfred Waterfront, Capetown . . 90 70
1088 (1r.30) Homestead, Boschendal Wine Estate 90 70

(b) KwaZulu-Natal.
1089 (1r.30) Drakensberg waterfall 90 70
1090 (1r.30) Zulu women preparing food 90 70
1091 (1r.30) Eastern white pelicans and rhinoceros 90 70
1092 (1r.30) Rickshaw driver . . 90 70
1093 (1r.30) Indian dancers . . . 90 70
Nos. 1084/8 and 1089/93 are inscribed "AIRMAIL POSTCARD".
See also Nos. 1338/42.

376 Angel

377 African Harrier Hawk

1998. Christmas. Multicoloured.
1094 (1r.10) Type **376** 60 60
1095 (1r.10) Christmas bell . . . 60 60
1096 (1r.10) Present 60 60
1097 (1r.10) Christmas tree . . . 60 60
1098 (1r.10) Star 60 60
Nos. 1094/8 are inscribed "STANDARD POSTAGE".

1998. World Post Day. Sheet 67 × 85 mm.
MS1099 **377** 5r. multicoloured . . 1·50 1·50

378 London Pictorial Essay, 1927

380 Emblem and Building

379 Cuvier's Beaked Whale

1998. "ILSAPEX '98" International Stamp Exhibition, Johannesburg. Sheet, 108 × 80 mm, containing T **378** and similar vert design.
MS1100 5r. green, red and cream (Type **378**); 5r. black, green and cream (as Type **378**, but "SOUTH AFRICA" at top) . . . . . . 2·25 2·50

1998. Endangered Species. Whales of the Southern Ocean. Multicoloured.
1101 (1r.30) Type **379** 75 55
1102 (1r.30) Minke whale 75 55
1103 (1r.30) Bryde's whale . . . 75 55
1104 (1r.30) Pygmy right whale . . 75 55
MS1105 103 × 68 mm. 5r. Blue whale 1·75 1·75

Nos. 1101/4 are inscribed "airmail postcard".
No. **MS**1105 forms part of joint issue with Namibia and Norfolk Island.

1998. 50th Anniv of Universal Declaration of Human Rights.
1106 **380** (1r.10) multicoloured . . 55 35
No. 1106 is inscribed "Standard Postage".

381 Dennis Mail Van, 1913

1999. 125th Anniv of Universal Postal Union. Multicoloured.
1107 (1r.10) Type **381** 60 45
1108 (1r.10) Ford V8 post van, 1935 . . . . 60 45
1109 (1r.10) Mobile Post Office, 1937 . . . . 60 45
1110 (1r.10) Trojan Post Office van, 1927 . . . . 60 45
Nos. 1107/10 are inscribed "Standard Postage".

382 Rabbit

1999. Chinese New Year ("Year of the Rabbit"). Sheet 85 × 67 mm.
MS1111 **382** 5r. multicoloured . . 1·50 1·50

383 "Discovery" (Scott)

1999. Famous Ships. Multicoloured.
1112 (1r.10) Type **383** 65 50
1113 (1r.10) "Heemskerk" (Tasman) 65 50
1114 (1r.10) H.M.S. "Endeavour" (Cook) 65 50
1115 (1r.10) H.M.S. "Beagle" (Darwin) 65 50
Nos. 1112/15 are inscribed "standard postage".

384 "Lawhill" (barque)

385 Traditional Nguni Love Token with AIDS Ribbon

1999. "Australia '99" International Stamp Exhibition, Melbourne. Sheet 65 × 85 mm.
MS1116 **384** 5r. multicoloured . . 1·50 1·50

1999. AIDS Awareness Campaign.
1117 **385** (1r.20) multicoloured (violet background) . . 50 50
1118 (1r.20) multicoloured (green background) . . 50 50
Nos. 1117/18 are inscribed "Standard Postage".

386 African Elephant

1999. "iBRA '99" International Stamp Exhibition, Nuremburg. Sheet 100 × 68 mm.
MS1119 **386** 5r. multicoloured . . 1·90 1·50

387 Class 19D Steam Locomotive, South African Railways
388 Nurse

1999. "SAPDA '99" Stamp Show, Johannesburg. Sheet 100 × 75 mm.
MS1120 **387** 5r. multicoloured . . 1·75 1·50

1999. Workers' Day. Multicoloured.
1121 (1r.20) Type **388** 50 50
1122 (1r.20) Cleaner with mop . . 50 50
1123 (1r.20) Forester with axe . . 50 50
1124 (1r.20) Farmer with spade 50 50
1125 (1r.20) Chef with sieve . . . 50 50
1126 (1r.20) Fisherman with net 50 50
1127 (1r.20) Construction worker with scaffolding 50 50
1128 (1r.20) Miner with pick . . 50 50
1129 (1r.20) Postman with mail 50 50
1130 (1r.20) Road worker with pneumatic drill 50 50

389 President Thabo Mbeki
390 Nelson Mandela in Mantle of Order

1999. Inauguration of President Thabo Mbeki.
1131 **389** (1r.20) multicoloured . . 70 35
No. 1131 is inscribed "standard postage".

1999. 900th Anniv of Order of St. John of Jerusalem. sheet 108 × 68 mm.
MS1132 **390** 2r. multicoloured . . 1·00 1·00

391 Actress with Drama Masks
392 North Ndebele Wall Pattern

1999. 25th Anniv of Standard Bank National Arts Festival. Multicoloured.
1133 (1r.20) Type **391** 55 55
1134 (1r.20) Woman with roll of film 55 55
1135 (1r.20) Woman playing guitar 55 55
1136 (1r.20) Woman dancing . . 55 55
1137 (1r.20) Painter 55 55
Nos. 1133/7 are inscribed "STANDARD POSTAGE".

1999. "Explore South Africa" (2nd series). Mpumalanga and Northern Province. As T **375**. Multicoloured.
1138 (1r.70) Blyde River Canyon 80 60
1139 (1r.70) Lone Creek Falls, Sabie 80 60
1140 (1r.70) Ndebele women in traditional dress 80 60
1141 (1r.70) Pilgrim's Rest (historic town) 80 60
1142 (1r.70) Elephants, Kruger National Park 80 60
Nos. 1138/42 are inscribed "AIRMAIL POSTCARD".

1999. Traditional Wall Art. Designs showing sections of wall art. Multicoloured.
1143 (1r.20) Type **392** 50 50
1144 (1r.20) South Ndebele . . . 50 50
1145 (1r.20) Swazi 50 50
1146 (1r.20) Venda 50 50
1147 (1r.20) South Sotho 50 50
1148 (1r.20) Xhosa 50 50
1149 (1r.20) North Sotho 50 50
1150 (1r.20) Tsonga 50 50
1151 (1r.20) Zulu 50 50
1152 (1r.20) Tswana 50 50
Nos. 1143/52 are inscribed "STANDARD POSTAGE".

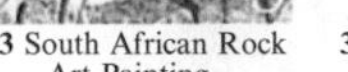

393 South African Rock Art Painting
395 Barn Swallow

394 Strelitzia reginae (flower)

1999. China '99 International Stamp Exhibition, Beijing. Sheet 154 × 85 mm.
MS1153 **393** 5r. multicoloured . . 1·75 1·75

1999. "JOPEX '99" National Stamp Exhibition, Johannesburg. Sheet 65 × 85 mm.
MS1154 **394** 5r. multicoloured . . 1·75 1·75

1999. Migratory Species of South Africa. Multicoloured.
1155 (1r.20) Type **395** 55 50
1156 (1r.20) Great white shark . . 55 50
1157 (1r.20) Lesser kestrel 55 50
1158 (1r.20) Common dolphin . . 55 50
1159 (1r.20) European bee-eater 55 50
1160 (1r.20) Loggerhead turtle . . 55 50
1161 (1r.20) Curlew sandpiper . . 55 50
1162 (1r.20) Wandering albatross 55 50
1163 (1r.20) Springbok 55 50
1164 (1r.20) Lesser flamingo . . . 55 50
Nos. 1155/64 are inscribed "Standard Postage".

396 Boers leaving for Commando

1999. Centenary of Anglo-Boer War (1st issue). Multicoloured.
1165 (1r.20) Type **396** 75 60
1166 (1r.20) British soldiers . . . 75 60
See also Nos. 2003/4, 1343/4 and **MS**1384.

397 Landscape

2000. New Millennium.
1167 **397** (1r.20) multicoloured . . 70 40
No. 1167 is inscribed "Standard Postage".

398 National Lottery Logo
399 Family inside Heart

2000. 1st National Lottery.
1168 **398** (1r.20) multicoloured . . 65 30
No. 1168 is inscribed "STANDARD POSTAGE".

2000. National Family Day.
1169 **399** (1r.30) multicoloured . . 65 30
No. 1169 is inscribed "Standard Postage".

400 Green Turaco ("Knysna Lourie")

2000. "The Stamp Show 2000" International Stamp Exhibition, London. Sheet 108 × 68 mm.
MS1170 **400** 4r.60 multicoloured 2·00 1·75

401 Banded Stream Frog

2000. Frogs of South Africa. Multicoloured.
1171 1r.30 Type **401** 50 50
1172 1r.30 Yellow-striped reed frog 50 50
1173 1r.30 Natal leaf-folding frog 50 50
1174 1r.30 Paradise toad 50 50
1175 1r.30 Table Mountain ghost frog 50 50
1176 1r.30 Banded rubber frog 50 50
1177 1r.30 Dwarf grass frog . . . 50 50
1178 1r.30 Long-toed tree frog . . 50 50
1179 1r.30 Namaqua rain frog . . 50 50
1180 1r.30 Bubbling kassina . . . 50 50

402 Forest Tree Frog

2000. "JUNASS 2000" National Junior Stamp Show, Baksburg. Sheet 108 × 68 mm.
MS1181 **402** 4r.60 multicoloured 1·75 1·75

403 Stalked Bulbine
404 Athelete with South African Flag

2000. Medicinal Plants. Multicoloured.
1182 1r.30 Type **403** 45 45
1183 1r.30 Wild dagga 45 45
1184 1r.30 Wild garlic 45 45
1185 1r.30 Pig's ear 45 45
1186 1r.30 Wild ginger 45 45
1187 2r.30 Red paintbrush . . . 60 60
1188 2r.30 Cancer bush 60 60
1189 2r.30 Yellow star 60 60
1190 2r.30 Bitter aloe 60 60
1191 2r.30 Sour fig 60 60

2000. Olympic Games, Sydney. Multicoloured.
1192 1r.30 Type **404** 50 25
1193 1r.50 Elana Meyer (medal winner, 1992) 50 35
1194 2r.20 Joshua Thugwane (medal winner, 1996) . . 70 60
1195 2r.30 Olympic rings and South African flag 85 65
1196 6r.30 Penny Heyns (medal winner, 1996) . . . . . . 1·75 2·25

405 Globe and Peace Doves

2000. United Nations International Year of Peace.
1197 **405** 1r.30 multicoloured . . . 65 30

406 Robben Island

2000. UNESCO World Heritage Sites. Mult.
1198 1r.30 Type **406** 55 35
1199 1r.30 Greater St. Lucia Wetland Park 55 35
1200 1r.30 Early skull from Sterkfontein 55 35

407 Dragon

2000. Chinese New Year ("Year of the Dragon"). Sheet 85 × 65 mm.
MS1201 **407** 4r.60 multicoloured 1·50 1·50

408 Heart and Envelope

2000. World Post Day.
1202 **408** 1r.30 multicoloured . . . 70 40

409 Sol Plaatje and Johanna Brandt

2000. Centenary of Anglo-Boer War (2nd issue). Authors. Multicoloured.
1203 1r.30 Type **409** 20 25
1204 4r.40 Arthur Conan Doyle and Winston Churchill . . 2·00 1·50

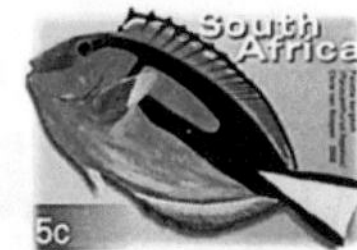

410 Palette Surgeonfish

2000. Flora and Fauna (1st issue). Multicoloured.
1205 5c. Type **410** 10 10
1206 10c. Clown surgeonfish ("Bluebanded Surgeon") 10 10
1207 20c. Regal angelfish 10 10
1208 30c. Emperor angelfish . . . 10 10
1209 40c. Picasso triggerfish ("Blackbar triggerfish") 10 10
1210 50c. Coral hind ("Coral rockcod") 10 10
1211 60c. Powder-blue surgeonfish 15 15
1212 70c. Thread-finned butterflyfish 15 15
1213 80c. Long-horned cowfish 15 15
1214 90c. Forceps butterflyfish ("Longnose butterflyfish") 20 20
1215 1r. Two-spined angelfish ("Coral Beauty") 25 20
1216 1r.30 Botterblom (vert) . . . 30 25
1217 1r.30 Blue marguerite (vert) 30 25
1218 1r.30 Karoo violet (vert) . . 30 25
1219 1r.30 Tree pelargonium (vert) 30 25
1220 1r.30 Black-eyed susy (vert) 30 25
1221 1r.40 Gold-banded forester 35 25
1222 1r.50 Brenton blue 40 30
1223 1r.90 Silver-barred charaxes 50 35
1224 2r. Lilac-breasted roller (vert) 70 35
1225 2r.30 Citrus butterfly . . . 70 40

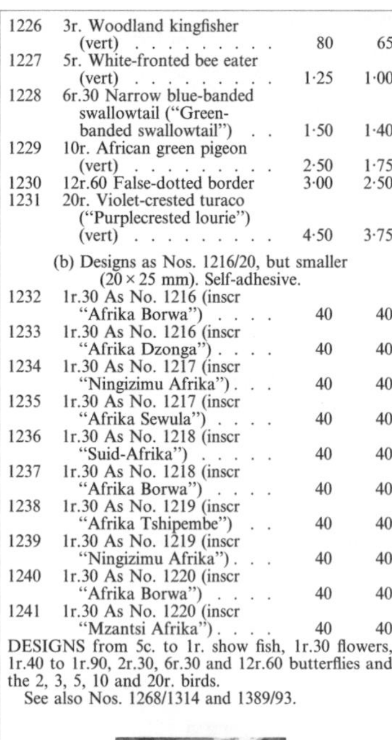

1226 3r. Woodland kingfisher (vert) 80 65
1227 5r. White-fronted bee eater (vert) . . . . 1·25 1·00
1228 6r.30 Narrow blue-banded swallowtail ("Green-banded swallowtail") . . 1·50 1·40
1229 10r. African green pigeon (vert) . . . . 2·50 1·75
1230 12r.60 False-dotted border 3·00 2·50
1231 20r. Violet-crested turaco ("Purplecrested lourie") (vert) . . . . 4·50 3·75

(b) Designs as Nos. 1216/20, but smaller (20 × 25 mm). Self-adhesive.
1232 1r.30 As No. 1216 (inscr "Afrika Borwa") 40 40
1233 1r.30 As No. 1216 (inscr "Afrika Dzonga") 40 40
1234 1r.30 As No. 1217 (inscr "Ningizimu Afrika") . . . 40 40
1235 1r.30 As No. 1217 (inscr "Afrika Sewula") 40 40
1236 1r.30 As No. 1218 (inscr "Suid-Afrika") 40 40
1237 1r.30 As No. 1218 (inscr "Afrika Borwa") 40 40
1238 1r.30 As No. 1219 (inscr "Afrika Tshipembe") . . 40 40
1239 1r.30 As No. 1219 (inscr "Ningizimu Afrika") . . . 40 40
1240 1r.30 As No. 1220 (inscr "Afrika Borwa") 40 40
1241 1r.30 As No. 1220 (inscr "Mzantsi Afrika") 40 40

DESIGNS from 5c. to 1r. show fish, 1r.30 flowers, 1r.40 to 1r.90, 2r.30, 6r.30 and 12r.60 butterflies and the 2, 3, 5, 10 and 20r. birds.
See also Nos. 1268/1314 and 1389/93.

411 The Rain Bull

2001. South African Myths and Legends. Mult.
1242 1r.30 Type **411** 30 25
1243 1r.50 The Grosvenor Treasure 35 30
1244 2r.20 Seven Magic Birds . . 50 45
1245 2r.30 The Hole in the Wall 55 55
1246 6r.30 Van Hunks and the Devil . . . . 1·40 1·60

412 African Tree Snake

2001. Chinese New Year ("Year of the Snake") and "Hong Kong 2001" Stamp Exhibition. Sheet 65 × 85 mm.
MS1247 **412** 4r.60, multicoloured 1·50 1·50

413 Ernie Els (golf)

2001. South African Sporting Heroes. Multicoloured.
1248 1r.40 Type **413** 50 45
1249 1r.40 Lucas Radebe (soccer) 50 45
1250 1r.40 Francois Pienaar (rugby) 50 45
1251 1r.40 Terrence Parkin (swimming) 50 45
1252 1r.40 Rosina Magola (netball) 50 45
1253 1r.40 Hestrie Cloete (high-jumping) 50 45
1254 1r.40 Hezekiel Sepeng (athletics) 50 45
1255 1r.40 Jonty Rhodes (cricket) 50 45
1256 1r.40 Zanele Situ (paralymic javelin) 50 45
1257 1r.40 Vuyani Bungu (boxing) 50 45

414 Elephant

2001. Wildlife. Multicoloured. (a) Designs 34 × 26 mm.
1258 (2r.10) Type **414** 40 40
1259 (2r.10) Lion 40 40
1260 (2r.10) Rhinoceros 40 40
1261 (2r.10) Leopard 40 40
1262 (2r.10) Buffalo 40 40

(b) Designs 29 × 24 mm. Self-adhesive.
1263 (2r.10) Buffalo 40 40
1264 (2r.10) Leopard 40 40
1265 (2r.10) Rhinoceros 40 40
1266 (2r.10) Lion 40 40
1267 (2r.10) Type **414** 40 40

Nos. 1258/67 are inscribed "AIRMAIL POSTCARD RATE" and were initially valid for 2r.10.

2001. Flora and Fauna (2nd issue). Multicoloured. (a) As T **410**.
1268 5c. Type **410** 10 10
1269 10c. Clown surgeonfish ("Bluebanded Surgeon") 10 10
1270 20c. Regal angelfish . . . 10 10
1271 30c. Emperor angelfish . . 10 10
1272 40c. Picasso triggerfish . . 10 10
1273 50c. Coral hind ("Coral rockcod") 10 10
1274 60c. Powder-blue surgeonfish 10 15
1275 70c. Thread-finned butterflyfish 15 15
1276 80c. Long-horned cowfish 15 15
1277 90c. Forceps butterflyfish ("Longnose butterflyfish") 20 20
1278 1r. Two-spined angelfish ("Coral Beauty") 25 20
1279 1r.40 Botterblom (vert) . . 20 25
1280 1r.40 Blue marguerite (vert) 20 25
1281 1r.40 Karoo violet (vert) 20 25
1282 1r.40 Tree pelargonium (vert) 20 25
1283 1r.40 Black-eyed susy (vert) 20 25
1284 1r.60 Yellow pansy butterfly 25 30
1284a (1r.65) Botterblom (vert) 25 30
1284b (1r.65) Blue marguerite (vert) 25 30
1284c (1r.65) Karoo violet (vert) 25 30
1284d (1r.65) Tree pelargonium (vert) 25 30
1284e (1r.65) Black-eyed Susy (vert) 25 30
1285 1r.90 Large-spotted acraea 30 35
1286 2r. Lilac-breasted roller (vert) 35 40
1287 2r.10 Kopje charaxes . . . 35 40
1288 2r.50 Common grass-yellow 40 45
1289 3r. Woodland kingfisher (vert) 50 55
1290 5r. White-fronted bee-eater (vert) 85 90
1291 7r. Southern milkweed . . 1·20 1·30
1292 10r. African green pigeon (vert) . . . . 1·70 1·80
1293 14r. Lilac-tip . . . . . . 2·30 2·40
1294 20r. Purple-crested turacao ("Purplecrested lourie") (vert) . . . . 3·25 3·50

(b) Designs as Nos. 1279/83, but 20 × 25 mm and inscr "Standard Postage" instead of face value. Self-adhesive.
1295 (1r.40) As No. 1280 (inscr "Afrika Borwa") 20 25
1296 (1r.40) As No. 1280 (inscr "Afrika Dzonga") 20 25
1297 (1r.40) As No. 1281 (inscr "Ningizimu Afrika") . . . 20 25
1298 (1r.40) As No. 1281 (inscr "Afrika Sewula") 20 25
1299 (1r.40) As No. 1282 (inscr "Suid-Afrika") 20 25
1300 (1r.40) As No. 1282 (inscr "Afrika Borwa") 20 25
1301 (1r.40) As No. 1283 (inscr "Afrika Tshipembe") . . 20 25
1302 (1r.40) As No. 1283 (inscr "Ningizimu Afrika") . . . 20 25
1303 (1r.40) As No. 1284 (inscr "Afrika Borwa") 20 25
1304 (1r.40) As No. 1284 (inscr "Mzantsi Afrika") 20 25

Nos. 1284, 1285, 1287/8, 1291 and 1293 show butterflies.
Nos. 1284a/e and 1295/1304 are inscribed "Standard Postage" and were initially valid for 1r.65 and 1r.40 respectively.

415 Gemsbok

2001. Kgalagadi Transfrontier Wildlife Park. Joint Issue with Botswana. Multicoloured.
1315 1r.40 Type **415** 40 25
1316 2r.50 Cheetah 70 55
1317 2r.90 Sociable weaver (bird) 80 80
1318 3r.60 Meercat . . . . 1·00 1·00
MS1319 114 × 78 mm. Nos. 1316/17 1·50 1·50

416 Adult holding Child's Hand

2001. "no excuse for child abuse" Campaign.
1320 **416** 1r.40 multicoloured . . . 50 55

417 Victims of Soweto Uprising

419 Conference Logo

418 Cape Horseshoe Bat

2001. 25th Anniv of Soweto Uprising.
1321 **417** 1r.40 multicoloured . . . 50 35

2001. Bats of South Africa. Multicoloured. Self-adhesive.
1322 1r.40 Type **418** 30 30
1323 1r.40 Welwitsch's hairy bat 30 30
1324 1r.40 Schreiber's long-fingered bat 30 30
1325 1r.40 Wahlberg's epauletted fruit bat 30 30
1326 1r.40 Short-eared trident bat 30 30
1327 1r.40 Common slit-faced bat 30 30
1328 1r.40 Egyptian fruit bat . . 30 30
1329 1r.40 Egyptian free-tailed bat (vert) 30 30
1330 1r.40 De Winton's long-eared bat 30 30
1331 1r.40 Large-eared free-tailed bat 30 30

Nos. 1322/31 were printed in sheetlets of 10 with the background forming a composite design. Descriptions of the various species are printed on the reverse of the backing paper.

2001. 3rd U.N. World Conference Against Racism, Durban.
1332 **419** 1r.40 mult (inscr as in T **419**) 30 30
1333 1r.40 mult (inscr "ningizimu afrika" and "kubeketelelana" at foot) 30 30
1334 1r.40 mult (inscr "suid-afrika") 30 30
1335 1r.40 mult (inscr "afrika tshipembe") 30 30
1336 1r.40 mult (inscr "afrika borwa" and "kutlwisiso" at foot) 30 30
1337 1r.40 mult (inscr "afrika dzonga") 30 30
1338 1r.40 mult (inscr "afrika sewula") 30 30
1339 1r.40 mult (inscr "afrika borwa" and "kgothlelelo" at foot) 30 30
1340 1r.40 mult (inscr "ningizimu afrika" and "ukubekezelelana" at foot) 30 30
1341 1r.40 mult (inscr "mzantsi afrika") . . 30 30
1342 – 2r.10 mult (logo and South Africans) . . . 50 50

420 Dominee J. D. Kestell

2001. Centenary of Anglo-Boer War (3rd issue). Angels of Mercy. Multicoloured.
1343 1r.40 Type **420** 50 25
1344 3r. Captain Thomas Crean V.C., R.A.M.C. . . . . . . 1·00 85

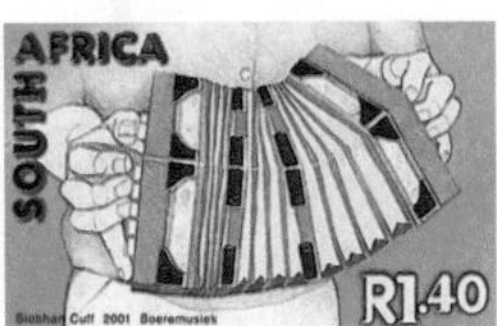
421 Boere Concertina

2001. Musical Instruments. Multicoloured.
1345 1r.40 Type **421** 35 25
1346 1r.90 Trumpet 45 45
1347 2r.50 Electric guitar 60 55
1348 3r. African drum 65 65
1349 7r. Cello . . . . 1·60 1·75

422 Fields of Flowers, Namaqualand

2001. Natural Wonders of South Africa. Multicoloured.
1350 (2r.10) Type **422** 45 45
1351 (2r.10) Cango Caves 45 45
1352 (2r.10) Richtersveld Desert 45 45
1353 (2r.10) Rocks on West Coast 45 45
1354 (2r.10) Snow covered mountains near Elliot . . 45 45
1355 (2r.10) Table Mountain . . 45 45
1356 (2r.10) Tsitsikamma Forest 45 45
1357 (2r.10) Augrabies Waterfall 45 45
1358 (2r.10) Cape Mountain Zebra 45 45
1359 (2r.10) Vineyards, Stellenbosch 45 45
Nos. 1350/9 are inscribed "Airmail Postcard Rate" and were initially valid at 2r.10 each.

423 Tree of Life decorated with Christmas Lights

2001. Christmas. Multicoloured.
1360 2r. Type **423** 50 35
1361 3r. Angel 60 50

424 Frame

2001. Greetings Stamps. Self-adhesive.
1362 **424** (1r.40) multicoloured . . 30 20
No. 1362 is inscribed "Standard Postage" and was initially valid for 1r.40.

425 Class Volvo 60 Yacht

426 International Cricket Council Logo

2001. Volvo Round the World Ocean Race. Multicoloured.
1363 **425** 1r.40 multicoloured . . . 60 35
MS1364 55×85 mm. 6r. Volvo 60 yacht (horiz) . . . . 1·25 1·25

2001. Cricket World Cup (2003) (1st issue).
1365 **426** (1r.40) black, gold and silver 50 30
No. 1365 is inscribed "Standard Postage" and was initially valid for 1r.40.
See also Nos. 1394/9 and **MS**1417.

427 Horse's Head

2001. Chinese New Year ("Year of the Horse").
1366 **427** 6r. multicoloured . . . . 1·75 1·75

428 Scalloped Hammerhead Sharks

2001. Marine Life. Multicoloured. Self-adhesive.
1367 1r.40 Type **428** 30 30
1368 1r.40 Loggerhead turtle (vert) 30 30
1369 1r.40 Clown triggerfish (vert) 30 30
1370 1r.40 Cape fur seals (vert) 30 30
1371 1r.40 Bottlenosed dolphins 30 30
1372 1r.40 Crowned seahorses (vert) 30 30
1373 1r.40 Blue-spotted ribbontail ray (vert) 30 30
1374 1r.40 Moorish idols 30 30
1375 1r.40 Octopus 30 30
1376 1r.40 Coral rock cod 30 30
Nos. 1367/76 were printed together, se-tenant, with the background forming a composite design. Descriptions of the various species are printed on the reverse of the backing paper.

429 Child laughing

2002. World Summit for Sustainable Development, Johannesburg. Multicoloured. Ordinary gum.
1377 (1r.40) Type **429** 30 30
1378 (1r.40) Globe in rainforest 30 30
1379 (1r.40) Trees in sunset . . . 30 30
1380 (3r.) Globe and South African landmarks (48×30 mm) 60 60
See also Nos. 1386/9.

2002. (b) Designs 20×25 mm. Self-adhesive.
1381 (1r.50) Type **429** 35 35
1382 (1r.50) As No. 1378 . . . . 35 35
1383 (1r.50) As No. 1379 . . . . 35 35

430 Earl Kitchener

2002. Centenary of Anglo-Boer War (4th issue). Treaty of Vereeniging. Sheet, 105×65 mm, containing T **430** and similar square design. Multicoloured.
MS1384 1r.50 Type **430**; 3r.30 Boer representative signing Treaty 1·00 1·00

431 African Union Logo

2002. 1st African Union Summit, Durban.
1385 **431** 1r.50 multicoloured . . . 60 40

432 Water, Sanitation and Energy

2002. World Summit on Sustainable Development (2nd issue). Multicoloured.
1386 (1r.50) Type **432** 35 30
1387 (3r.) Child with hands raised to globe (Environment) 60 55
1388 (3r.30) Hands holding seedling (Food) 70 70
No. 1386 is inscribed "standard postage", No. 1387 "airmail postcard rate" and No. 1388 "international letter rate". The stamps were initially sold at the values quoted above.

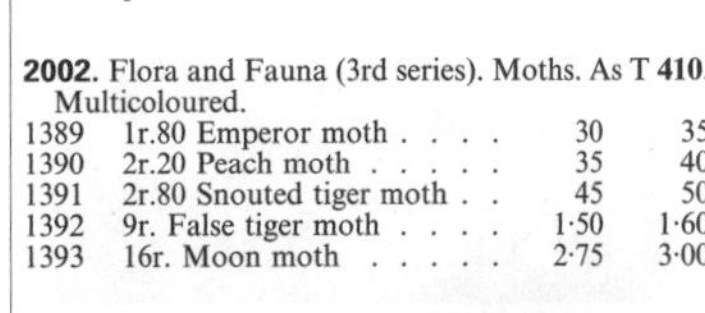

2002. Flora and Fauna (3rd series). Moths. As T **410**. Multicoloured.
1389 1r.80 Emperor moth 30 35
1390 2r.20 Peach moth 35 40
1391 2r.80 Snouted tiger moth . . 45 50
1392 9r. False tiger moth . . . . 1·50 1·60
1393 16r. Moon moth . . . . . 2·75 3·00

433 "Dazzler" Mascot as Batsman (running)

435 Steve Biko

434 Postal Stone

2002. Cricket World Cup (2003) (2nd issue). Designs showing "Dazzler" zebra mascot. Multicoloured.
1394 (1r.50) Type **433** 25 30
1395 (1r.50) Bowler (after releasing ball) 25 30
1396 (1r.50) Fielder 25 30
1397 (1r.50) Batsman (on one knee) 25 30
1398 (1r.50) Bowler (running with ball) 25 30
1399 (1r.50) Batsman (standing) 25 30

2002. World Post Day. Sheet 105×65 mm.
MS1400 **434** 4r.75 multicoloured 85 90

2002. 25th Death Anniv of Steve Biko (anti-apartheid campaigner). Sheet 105×65 mm.
MS1401 **435** 4r.75 black, red and cinnamon 85 90

436 *Pristis microdon*

2002. "Algoapex" (**MS**1402) and "JUNASS" (**MS**1403) National Stamp Show. Sawfish. Two sheets containing horiz designs as T **436**. Multicoloured.
MS1402 104×65 mm. 7r. Type **436** . . . . 1·20 1·30
MS1403 106×65 mm. 7r. *Pristis pectinata* . . . . 1·20 1·30

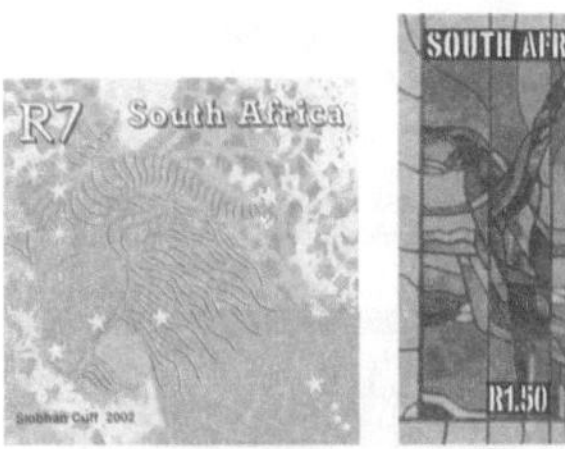
437 Stylised Goat

438 "The Tree of Life"

2002. Chinese New Year ("Year of the Goat"). Star-shaped sheet, 105×105 mm.
MS1404 **437** 7r. multicoloured . . 1·20 1·30

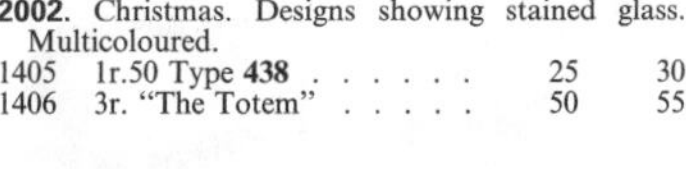

2002. Christmas. Designs showing stained glass. Multicoloured.
1405 1r.50 Type **438** 25 30
1406 3r. "The Totem" 50 55

439 Man wearing Sunglasses

440 Total Eclipse

2002. AIDS Prevention. Self-adhesive.
1407 (1r.50) Type **439** 25 30
1408 (1r.50) Woman with AIDS ribbon on headband . . . 25 30
1409 (1r.50) Woman wearing sunglasses and hat 25 30
1410 (1r.50) Hand holding purple candle and "STOP" . . . 25 30
1411 (1r.50) Woman's face and "AiDS" 25 30
1412 (1r.50) Man holding purple candle and "Be safe" . . 25 30
1413 (1r.50) Hand touching AIDS ribbon and green candle 25 30
1414 (1r.50) Raised palm of hand and "AIDS" 25 30
1415 (1r.50) Woman's face in glass jar 25 30
1416 (1r.50) Hand catching anti-HIV drugs and AIDS ribbon in heart 25 30
Nos. 1407/16 are inscribed "Standard Postage" and were initially valid for 1r.50. They form a composite design.

2002. Total Solar Eclipse, 4 December 2002. Sheet 105×65 mm.
MS1417 **440** 4r.75 black, orange and red 85 90

441 Traditional Thatched Huts

2003. Cricket World Cup (3rd issue). South African Scenes. Multicoloured.
MS1418 174×90 mm. (1r.50) Type **441**; (1r.50) Man wearing brimmed hat on horse; (1r.50) Four cricketers and settlement houses; (1r.50) Passengers inside bus and on roof; (1r.50) Woman and baby; (1r.50) Double-decker bus . . . . 1·50 1·75
Stamps from **MS**1418 are inscribed "STANDARD POSTAGE" and were initially valid for 1r.50 each.

442 Chris Hani

443 Women carrying Water Drums

2003. 10th Death Anniv of Chris Hani (former Secretary-general of South African Communist Party). Sheet 105×65 mm.
MS1419 **442** (1r.50) brown and red 25 30
No. **MS**1419 is inscribed "Standard Postage" and was initially valid for 1r.50.

2003. Life in Informal Settlements. Multicoloured.
1420 (1r.65) Type **443** 25 30
1421 (1r.65) Boy playing musical instrument 25 30
1422 (1r.65) Workman laying road 25 30
1423 (1r.65) Seamstress 25 30
1424 (1r.65) Two schoolchildren 25 30
1425 (1r.65) Shopkeeper with customer 25 30
1426 (1r.65) Shoemakers 25 30
1427 (1r.65) Woman wearing green hat 25 30
1428 (1r.65) Teenager leaning on tyre 25 30
1429 (1r.65) Mother and child . . 25 30
Nos. 1420/9 are inscribed "STANDARD POSTAGE" and were initially valid for 1r.65 each.

444 Outline Map of Africa **445** Oliver Tambo

2003. Africa Day. Sheet 105 × 65 mm.
MS1430 **444** 11r.70 multicoloured . . . 1·90 2·00

2003. 10th Death Anniv of Oliver Tambo. Sheet, 105 × 65 mm.
MS1431 **445** (1r.65) multicoloured . . . 25 30
No. **MS**1431 is inscribed "Standard Postage" and was initially valid for 1r.65.

446 Salsa Dancers

2003. Dances. Multicoloured.

No.	Description		
1432	1r.65 Type **446**	35	25
1433	2r.20 Rumba	50	45
1434	2r.80 Waltz	65	70
1435	3r.30 Foxtrot	80	90
1436	3r.80 Tango	1·00	1·10

447 African Dog

2003. Dogs. Sheet 100 × 100 mm containing T **447** and similar square designs. Multicoloured.
MS1437 (1r.65) Type **447**; (1r.65) Rhodesian ridgeback; (1r.65) Boerboel; (1r.65) Basenji . . . . 1·75 1·75
The stamps of No. **MS**1437 are each inscribed "standard postage" and were sold for 1r.65.

448 Robert Mangaliso Sobukwe **449** Walter Max Ulyate Sisulu

2003. 25th Death Anniv of Robert Mangaliso Sobukwe (nationalist leader and founder of the Pan-Africanist Congress). Sheet 105 × 65 mm.
MS1438 **448** 11r.70 multicoloured . . . 3·25 3·25

2003. Walter Max Ulyate Sisulu (political activist and member of the African National Congress) Commemoration. Sheet 105 × 65 mm.
MS1439 **449** 11r.70 multicoloured . . . 3·25 3·25

450 Shaka

2003. Shaka (Warrior King of the Zulu) Commemoration.
1440 **450** (3r.) multicoloured . . . 80 80
No. 1440 was inscribed "Airmail Postcard" and sold for 3r. each stamp.

451 Football Supporter and Globe

2003. World Cup Football Bid. Multicoloured.

No.	Description		
1441	(3r.80) Type **451**	1·00	1·00
1442	(4r.25) Supporter and children playing football	1·10	1·10

No. 1441 is inscribed "International Airmail Rate Small Letter" and was sold for 3r.80. No. 1442 is inscribed "B4 Domestic Large" and was sold for 4r.25.

452 Stamp of Fortune and Post Office Logos and Cars **454** Pot created by Afrikania Job Creation Project

453 Shangweni Dam Kwa-Zulu

2003. Television and Post Office Joint Issue.
1443 **452** (1r.65) multicoloured . . . 35 35
No. 1443 is inscribed "Standard Postage" and was sold for 1r.65.

2003. Engineering and Postal Communication. Sheet 90 × 143 mm containing T **453** and similar multicoloured designs.
MS1444 (3r.30) Type **453**; (3r.30) Kimberly Microwave Tower (30 × 48 mm); (3r.30) Northern Cape Legislature (30 × 24 mm); (3r.30) Community Bridge, Limpopo (30 × 24 mm); (3r.30) Durban Westville Interchange (30 × 48 mm); (3r.30) Nelson Mandela Bridge, Gauteng (60 × 24 mm) . . . . 5·50 5·50

2003. 10th Anniv of Diplomatic Relations with India. Sheet 105 × 65 mm.
MS1445 **454** 3r.35 multicoloured . . . 1·00 1·00

455 "Hope"

2003. 150th Anniv of the Cape Triangular Stamp. Design as T **10** but with face value as T **455**.
1446 **455** (1r.65) blue 35 35

456 Joseph with Mary on Donkey **457** Star

2003. Christmas. Multicoloured. (a) As T **456**.

No.	Description		
1447	(1r.65) Type **456**	50	50
1448	(1r.65) Angels	50	50
1449	(1r.65) Three Wise Men . .	50	50
1450	(1r.65) Mary and Jesus . . .	50	50
1451	(1r.65) Dove carrying holly	50	50
	(b) As T **457**.		
1452	3r.80 Type **457**	1·00	1·00

Nos. 1447/51 are each inscribed "Standard Postage" and were sold for 1r.65.

458 African Elephant

2003. 10th Anniv of Diplomatic Relations with Thailand. Multicoloured.

No.	Description		
1453	3r.35 Type **458**	1·00	1·00
1454	3r.35 Indian elephant . . .	1·00	1·00

459 Paterson Biplane

2003. Centenary of Powered Flight. Multicoloured.

No.	Description		
1455	(1r.65) Type **459**	50	50
1456	(1r.65) Silver Queen Vickers Vimy	50	50
1457	(1r.65) Wapiti	50	50
1458	(1r.65) De Havilland DH 9	50	50
1459	(1r.65) Junkers Ju52/53 . .	50	50
1460	(1r.65) Sikorsky S-55 . . .	50	50
1461	(1r.65) Boeing 707	50	50
1462	(1r.65) Rooivalk	50	50
1463	(1r.65) SUNSAT Micro satellite	50	50
1464	(1r.65) Mark Shuttleworth (astronaut)	50	50

Nos. 1455/64 are inscribed "Standard Postage" and were sold for 1r.65 each.

460 Monkey

2004. Chinese New Year ("Year of the Monkey"). Sheet 105 × 65 mm.
MS1465 **460** 11r.70 multicoloured . . . 3·00 3·25

461 Patrol Sign and Pedestrian

2004. "Drive Alive" Road Safety Campaign. Multicoloured.

No.	Description		
1466	(1r.65) Type **461**	50	50
1467	(1r.65) Slippery road sign and alcohol	50	50
1468	(1r.65) Service sign and car in disrepair	50	50
1469	(1r.65) Slow lorry sign and steering wheel	50	50
1470	(1r.65) Danger sign and sleeping driver	50	50

Nos. 1466/70 are inscribed "Standard Postage" and were initially sold for 1r.65 each.

462 Dove and Outline of Africa

2004. 10th Anniv of Democracy. Multicoloured.

No.	Description		
1471	(1r.65) Type **462**	45	45
1472	(1r.65) Voters	45	45
1473	(1r.65) Accessing services (water, electricity)	45	45
1474	(1r.65) Sports supporters . .	45	45
1475	(1r.65) Traditional arts and crafts	45	45

Nos. 1471/5 are inscribed "Standard Postage" and were initially sold for 1r.65 each.

463 Slave Lodge, Cape Town

2004. The Legacy of Slaves. Multicoloured.

No.	Description		
1476	(1r.70) Type **463**	50	50
1477	(1r.70) First book written in Arabic and Afrikaans . .	50	50
1478	(1r.70) Stinkwood Tulback chair and Jonkmans cupboard	50	50
1479	(1r.70) Traditional food . .	50	50
1480	(1r.70) Labourers on sugar cane farm	50	50
1481	(1r.70) Miners	50	50

Nos. 1476/81 are inscribed "Standard Postage" and were initially sold for 1r.70 each.

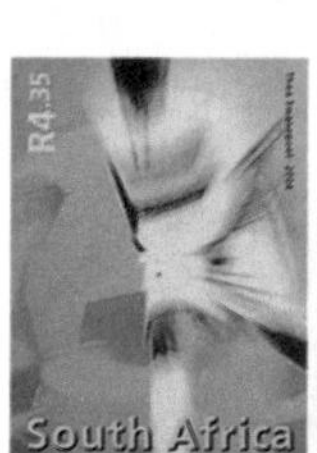

464 Abstract Footballer **466** Archery

465 Penguins (Environmental Helpers)

2004. Centenary of FIFA (Federation Internationale de Football Association). Sheet 105 × 65 mm.
MS1482 **464** 4r.35 multicoloured . . . 1·25 1·40

2004. Volunteers. Multicoloured.

No.	Description		
1483	(1r.70) Type **465**	55	55
1484	(1r.70) Volunteer assisting elderly person (Caring for the elderly)	55	55
1485	(1r.70) Child with building blocks (Education) . . .	55	55
1486	(1r.70) Paramedics (Medical and ambulance services)	55	55
1487	(1r.70) Life guards (Surf life saving)	55	55
1488	(1r.70) Volunteer with dogs (Helping abandoned pets)	55	55
1489	(1r.70) Child in cot (Caring for orphans)	55	55
1490	(1r.70) Rescuing someone from fire (Fire fighters)	55	55
1491	(1r.70) Group gardening (Community gardens) . .	55	55
1492	(1r.70) Blind person and volunteer recording tape (Tape aids for the blind)	55	55

Nos. 1483/92 are inscribed "Standard Postage" and were sold for 1r.70 each.

2004. Sport. Multicoloured.

No.	Description		
1493	(1r.70) Type **466**	55	55
1494	(1r.70) Sprinting	55	55
1495	(1r.70) Show jumping . . .	55	55
1496	(1r.70) Cycling	55	55
1497	(1r.70) Gymnastics	55	55
1498	(1r.70) Canoeing	55	55
1499	(1r.70) Football	55	55
1500	(1r.70) Swimming	55	55
1501	(1r.70) Boxing	55	55
1502	(1r.70) Tennis	55	55

Nos. 1493/1502 are inscribed "Standard Postage" and were sold for 1r.70 each.

467 Cape Sugarbird **469** Virgin "Hodigitria"

468 Children sharing Letters

2004. Ecology of Table Mountain. Sheet 172 × 233 mm containing T **467** and similar multicoloured designs. Self-adhesive.
MS1503 (4r.) Type **467**; (4r.) Dark opal butterflies (horiz); (4r.) King protea (flower) (horiz); (4r.) Cape rock hyrax (horiz); (4r.) Cuckoo wasp (horiz); (4r.) Ghost frog (horiz); (4r.) Cockroaches (horiz); (4r.) *Staavia dodii* (flower); (4r.) Spotted skaapsteker (snake) (horiz); (4r.) *Duvalia immaculate* (horiz) . . . . 7·00 7·50
The stamps in No. **MS**1503 were each inscribed "International Airmail Rate Small Letter" and sold for 4r.

2004. Universal Postal Union Congress, Romania.
1504 **468** 3r.45 multicoloured . . . 1·00 1·00
No. 1504 was inscribed "Airmail Postcard" and sold for 3r.45.

2004. Christmas. Multicoloured.

No.	Type	Description	Mint	Used
1505		(1r.70) Type **469**	50	15
1506		(4r.) Christ Pantocrator (Almighty)	1·00	1·00

No. 1505 is inscribed "Standard Postage" and was initially sold for 1r.70. No. 1506 is inscribed "International Airmail Letter" and was initially sold for 4r.

470 Stylized Dove

2004. World Post Day.

No.	Type	Description	Mint	Used
MS1507	**470**	12r.50 multicoloured	3·25	3·50

470a African Fish Eagle (Namibia)

2004. First Joint Issue of Southern Africa Postal Operators Association Members. Sheet 170×95 mm containing T **470a** and similar hexagonal designs showing national birds of Association members. Multicoloured.

No.	Type	Description	Mint	Used
MS1508		12r.50 Type **470a**; 12r.50 Two African fish eagles perched (Zimbabwe); 12r.50 Peregrine falcon (Angola); 12r.50 Cattle egret (Botswana); 12r.50 Purple-crested turaco ("Lourie") (Swaziland); 12r.50 Stanley ("Blue") crane (South Africa); 12r.50 Bar-tailed trogon (Malawi) (inscribed "apaloderma vittatum"); 12r.50 Two African fish eagles in flight (Zambia)	17·00	18·00

The stamp depicting the Bar-tailed trogon is not inscribed with the country of which the bird is a national symbol.

Miniature sheets of similar designs were also issued by Namibia, Zimbabwe, Angola, Botswana, Swaziland, Malawi and Zambia.

471 South African Large Telescope

472 South African Police Service Badge

2004. South African Large Telescope. Multicoloured.

No.	Type	Description	Mint	Used
1509		4r. Type **471**	85	85
1510		4r. Cross-section of observatory	85	85
1511		4r. View of the Southern Cross	85	85
1512		4r. Telescope	85	85
1513		4r. Telescope inside observatory	85	85

2004. South African Police Service (SAPS). Self-adhesive. Multicoloured.

No.	Type	Description	Mint	Used
1514		1r.70 Type **472**	55	55
1515		1r.70 Handcuffed hands and drugs (Fight Against Drugs)	55	55
1516		1r.70 Police helicopter (SAPS Air Wing)	55	55
1517		1r.70 Microscope (Fingerprint and Forensic Science Units)	55	55
1518		1r.70 Parachutists (Special Task Force)	55	55
1519		1r.70 Child and officer (Family Violence, Child Protection and Sexual Offences Unit)	55	55
1520		1r.70 Officers and map (Sector Policing)	55	55
1521		1r.70 Three police officers (The Dignified Blue)	55	55
1522		1r.70 Officer on horse (SAPS Mounted Unit)	55	55
1523		1r.70 Officer and police dog (SAPS Dog Unit)	55	55

Nos. 1514/23 are inscribed "Standard Postage" and were initially sold for 1r.70 each.

OFFICIAL STAMPS

Prices for bilingual stamps are for mint pairs and used singles.

1926. Optd **OFFICIAL. OFFISIEEL.** (with full points). (a) On stamp of 1913.

No.	Type	Description	Mint	Used
O1	3	2d. purple	21·00	1·75

(b) On pictorial issues.

No.	Type	Description	Mint	Used
O2	6	½d. black and green	7·50	1·50
O3	7	1d. black and red	4·00	50
O4	8	6d. green and orange	£550	10·00

1928. Optd **OFFICIAL OFFISIEEL** (without full points).

No.	Type	Description	Mint	Used
O 7	6	½d. black and green (No. 42)	2·50	35
O39		½d. black and green (No. 114)	70	15
O 8	7	1d. black and red (No. 31)	3·00	45
O21aw		1d. grey and red (No. 56)	3·00	20
O22aw	22	1½d. green and gold	28·00	1·00
O44	34a	1½d. green and buff	2·00	30
O 5a	11	2d. grey and purple (No. 34)	6·00	1·50
O14		2d. grey and lilac (No. 44)	7·50	1·50
O15		2d. blue and violet (No. 44d)	£120	9·00
O30		2d. grey and purple (No. 58a)	14·00	2·25
O36	54	2d. slate and violet	5·50	1·90
O45	68	2d. blue and violet	1·00	20
O16	8	6d. green and orange (No. 47)	8·50	85
O46		6d. green and red (No. 119a)	1·25	35
O10	–	1s. brown and blue (No. 36)	38·00	9·50
O47	–	1s. brown and blue (No. 120)	5·50	2·00
O18a	–	2s.6d. green and brown (No. 49)	50·00	8·50
O48	–	2s.6d. green and brown (No. 121)	8·50	3·50
O19	–	2s.6d. blue and brown (No. 49a)	42·00	6·50
O50	–	5s. black and green (No. 64a)	65·00	6·50
O51	–	10s. blue and brown (No. 39)	75·00	22·00

POSTAGE DUE STAMPS

D 1 D 2

1914. Perf or roul.

No.	Type	Description	Mint	Used
D11	D 1	½d. black and green	80	1·75
D12		1d. black and red	90	15
D13		1½d. black and brown	1·00	1·25
D14		2d. black and violet	1·00	70
D 4		3d. black and blue	2·25	60
D 5		5d. black and brown	4·00	25·00
D16		6d. black and grey	12·00	2·50
D 7		1s. red and black	60·00	£150

1927.

No.	Type	Description	Mint	Used
D17	D 2	½d. black and green	1·00	3·25
D18		1d. black and red	1·25	30
D19		2d. black and mauve	1·25	30
D23		2d. black and purple	10·00	2·50
D20		3d. black and blue	8·50	24·00
D28		3d. indigo and blue	8·00	30
D21		6d. black and grey	21·00	3·50
D29		6d. green and brown	25·00	5·00
D29a		6d. green and orange	14·00	3·00

D 3 D 5

1943.

No.	Type	Description	Mint	Used
D30	D 3	½d. green	11·00	30
D31		1d. red	10·00	10
D32		2d. violet	6·50	15
D33		3d. blue	48·00	1·25

The above mint prices are for horiz units of three.

1948. Frame as Type D 2, but with bolder figures of value and capital "D".

No.	Type	Description	Mint	Used
D34		½d. black and green	6·00	13·00
D39		1d. black and red	70	30
D40		2d. black and violet	50	20
D41		3d. indigo and blue	4·50	2·25
D42		4d. turquoise and green	12·00	15·00
D43		6d. green and orange	7·00	9·00
D44		1s. brown and purple	12·00	15·00

1961.

No.	Type	Description	Mint	Used
D45	D 5	1c. black and red	20	3·50
D46		2c. black and violet	35	3·50
D47		4c. turquoise and green	80	8·00
D48		5c. indigo and blue	1·75	8·00
D49		6c. green and orange	6·50	8·50
D50		10c. sepia and brown	7·00	10·00

D 6 D 8

1961. (A) Inscr as in Type D 6; (B) English at top and left, Afrikans at bottom and right.

No.	Type	Description	Mint	Used
D59	D 6	1c. black and red (A)	20	55
D60		1c. black and red (B)	20	30
D61		2c. black and violet (A)	30	1·50
D53		2c. black and violet (B)	40	55
D54		4c. myrtle and green (A)	2·25	2·25
D54a		4c. myrtle and green (B)	12·00	22·00
D63		4c. black and green (A)	32·00	32·00
D64		4c. black and green (B)	32·00	32·00
D55		5c. indigo and blue (B)	2·00	4·25
D65		5c. black and blue (A)	50	50
D66		5c. black and blue (B)	50	50
D67		6c. green & salmon (A)	3·50	10·00
D68		6c. green and salmon (B)	3·50	10·00
D58		10c. sepia & brown (B)	2·75	1·75
D69		10c. black and brown (A)	1·00	2·75
D70		10c. black and brown (B)	1·00	2·75

1972.

No.	Type	Description	Mint	Used
D75	D 8	1c. green	50	2·25
D76		2c. orange	70	3·00
D77		4c. plum	1·75	3·50
D78		6c. yellow	1·75	4·75
D79		8c. blue	2·00	5·00
D80		10c. red	6·00	7·50

SOUTH ARABIAN FEDERATION Pt. 1

Comprising Aden and most of the territories of the former Western Aden Protectorate plus one from the Eastern Aden Protectorate. The South Arabian Federation became fully independent on 30 November 1967.

1963. 100 cents = 1 shilling.
1965. 1000 fils = 1 dinar.

1963. Cent of Red Cross. As T **63b** of St. Helena, but without portrait. Value in English and Arabic.

No.	Type	Description	Mint	Used
1		15c. red and black	30	30
2		1s.25 red and blue	70	95

2 Federal Crest

3 Federal Flag

1965.

No.	Type	Description	Mint	Used
3	2	5f. blue	20	10
4		10f. lavender	20	10
5		15f. green	20	10
6		20f. green	20	10
7		25f. brown	20	10
8		30f. bistre	20	10
9		35f. brown	20	10
10		50f. red	20	10
11		65f. green	30	30
12		75f. red	30	10
13	3	100f. multicoloured	30	10
14		250f. multicoloured	5·00	1·25
15		500f. multicoloured	9·00	1·25
16		1d. multicoloured	16·00	15·00

4 I.C.Y. Emblem

1965. International Co-operation Year.

No.	Type	Description	Mint	Used
17	4	5f. purple and turquoise	20	10
18		65f. green and lavender	80	20

5 Sir Winston Churchill and St. Paul's Cathedral in Wartime

1966. Churchill Commem. Designs in black, cerise and gold with background in colours given.

No.	Type	Description	Mint	Used
19	5	5f. blue	10	10
20		10f. green	30	10
21		65f. brown	80	20
22		125f. violet	1·25	1·75

6 Footballer's Legs, Ball and Jules Rimet Cup

1966. World Cup Football Championship, England.

No.	Type	Description	Mint	Used
23	6	10f. multicoloured	50	10
24		50f. multicoloured	1·50	20

7 W.H.O. Building

1966. Inaug of W.H.O. Headquarters, Geneva.

No.	Type	Description	Mint	Used
25	7	10f. black, green and blue	50	10
26		75f. black, purple and brown	1·25	45

8 "Education"

1966. 20th Anniv of U.N.E.S.C.O.

No.	Type	Description	Mint	Used
27	8	10f. multicoloured	30	20
28	–	65f. yellow, violet and olive	1·25	1·40
29	–	125f. black, purple and orange	3·25	4·75

DESIGNS: 65f. "Science"; 125f. "Culture".

For later issues see **SOUTHERN YEMEN** and **YEMEN PEOPLE'S DEMOCRATIC REPUBLIC**.

SOUTH AUSTRALIA Pt. 1

A state of the Australian Commonwealth whose stamps it now uses.

12 pence = 1 shilling;
20 shillings = 1 pound.

1

1855. Imperf.

No.	Type	Description	Mint	Used
1	1	1d. green	£3500	£450
2		2d. red	£550	80·00
3		6d. blue	£2250	£160
12		1s. orange	£4500	£400

3 **4**

1858. Roul or perf.

No.	Type	Description	Mint	Used
20	1	1d. green	50·00	28·00
26		2d. red	60·00	3·25
112	3	3d. on 4d. blue	85·00	19·00
138		4d. purple	45·00	2·75
141	1	6d. blue	55·00	2·00
118	4	8d. on 9d. brown	90·00	7·00
124		9d. purple	10·00	3·50
35		10d. on 9d. orange	£225	35·00
38	1	1s. yellow	£500	28·00
130		1s. brown	25·00	3·00
151	3	2s. red	25·00	11·00

The 3d., 8d. and 10d. are formed by surcharges: **3-PENCE**, **8 PENCE** and **TEN PENCE** (curved).

15 **11** **12**

1868. Various frames.

No.	Type	Description	Mint	Used
191	15	½d. brown	2·75	30
173	11	1d. green	11·00	1·00
176		1d. red	4·25	20
177	12	2d. orange	5·50	10
178		2d. violet	4·25	10
229b	–	2½d. on 4d. green	8·00	1·75

192a – 3d. green 5·00 1·75
193 – 4d. violet 6·00 50
230a – 5d. on 6d. brown 16·00 4·75
194 – 6d. blue 7·00 1·50

Nos. 230 and 231 are surch in figures over straight or curved line.

1882. Surch **HALF-PENNY** in two lines.
181 **11** ½d. on 1d. green 11·00 8·00

19 — 24 G.P.O., Adelaide

22 Red Kangaroo — 23

1886.
195a **19** 2s.6d. mauve 38·00 7·00
196a 5s. pink 48·00 16·00
197a 10s. green £120 45·00
198a 15s. brown £400 £170
199a £1 blue £250 £120

1894.
241 **24** ½d. green 2·00 50
236 **22** 2½d. violet 18·00 70
237 2½d. blue 6·00 1·75
238a **23** 5d. purple 6·50 75

1902. Inscr "POSTAGE" at top.
268 **19** 3d. green 6·50 2·00
299 4d. orange 10·00 2·25
270 6d. green 7·00 2·00
271 8d. blue 8·00 8·00
273 9d. red 8·50 4·50
274 10d. orange 12·00 8·50
303b 1s. brown 10·00 5·00
276a 2s.6d. violet 23·00 13·00
290 5s. red 50·00 30·00
278 10s. green £120 65·00
292a £1 blue £150 £120

OFFICIAL STAMPS

1874. Various postage issues optd **O.S.** A. Issue of 1858.
O 6 **1** 1d. green £1300 £200
O 7 **3** 3d. on 4d. blue £2500 £1200
O17 4d. mauve 38·00 2·50
O19 **1** 6d. blue 65·00 4·50
O26 **4** 8d. on 9d. brown £1800 £850
O11 9d. purple £1200 £650
O33 **1** 1s. brown 32·00 5·50
O35 **3** 2s. red 75·00 10·00

B. Issues of 1868–82.
O63 **15** ½d. brown 17·00 7·00
O48 **11** ½d. on 1d. green 65·00 15·00
O56 1d. green 12·00 1·25
O81 1d. red 14·00 1·60
O44 **12** 2d. orange 8·50 1·00
O82 2d. violet 17·00 80
O71 – 2½d. on 4d. green 38·00 13·00
O61 – 4d. violet 50·00 3·50
O72 – 5d. on 6d. brown 45·00 18·00
O62 – 6d. blue 21·00 2·50

C. Issue of 1886.
O86 **19** 2s.6d. violet £3500 £3000
O87 5s. pink £3500 £3000

D. Issue of 1894.
O80 **24** ½d. green 16·00 6·00
O75 **22** 2½d. blue 50·00 7·00
O74 **23** 5d. purple 70·00 11·00

SOUTH GEORGIA Pt. 1

An island in the Antarctic. From May 1980 to 1985 used stamps inscribed FALKLAND ISLANDS DEPENDENCIES and thereafter those of South Georgia and the South Sandwich Islands (q.v.).

1963. 12 pence = 1 shilling;
20 shillings = 1 pound.
1971. 100 pence = 1 pound.

1 Reindeer

1963.
1 **1** ½d. red 50 1·25
2 – 1d. blue 1·50 1·25
3 – 2d. blue 1·25 1·25
4 – 2½d. black 5·50 2·50
5 – 3d. bistre 2·75 30
6 – 4d. green 5·00 1·50
7 – 5½d. violet 2·50 30
8 – 6d. orange 75 50
9 – 9d. blue 5·50 2·00
10 – 1s. purple 75 30
11 – 2s. olive and blue 25·00 6·50
12 – 2s.6d. blue 24·00 4·00
13 – 5s. brown 22·00 4·00
14 – 10s. pink 42·00 10·00
15 – £1 blue 90·00 48·00
16 – £1 black 10·00 16·00

DESIGNS—HORIZ: 2½d. King penguins and Bearded penguin ("Chinstrap Penguin"); 4d. Fin whale; 5½d. Southern elephant-seal; 9d. Whale-catcher; 1s. Leopard seal; 2s. Shackleton's Cross; 2s.6d. Wandering albatross; 5s. Southern elephant seal and South American fur seal; £1 (No. 15) Blue whale. VERT: 1d. South Sandwich Islands map; 2d. Sperm whale; 3d. South American fur seal; 6d. Light-mantled sooty albatross ("Sooty Albatross"); 10s. Plankton and krill; £1 (No. 16) King penguins.

1971. Decimal Currency. Nos. 1/14 surch.
18a ½p. on ½d. red 1·00 1·00
19 1p. on 1d. blue 1·50 55
55 1½p. on 5½d. violet 90 1·75
21 2p. on 2d. blue 70 50
22 2½p. on 2½d. black 2·25 40
23 3p. on 3d. bistre 1·00 50
24 4p. on 4d. green 1·00 50
25 5p. on 6d. orange 2·00 30
26 6p. on 9d. blue 1·50 70
27 7½p. on 1s. purple 1·50 70
63w 10p. on 2s. olive and blue 1·00 5·00
64w 15p. on 2s.6d. blue 1·50 5·50
65w 25p. on 5s. brown 1·00 5·50
66 50p. on 10s. pink 1·00 5·00

6 "Endurance" beset in Weddell Sea

1972. 50th Death Anniv of Sir Ernest Shackleton. Multicoloured.
32 1½p. Type **6** 1·00 1·50
33 5p. Launching of the longboat "James Caird" 1·25 2·00
34 10p. Route of the "James Caird" 1·75 2·25
35 20p. Sir Ernest Shackleton and the "Quest" 2·00 2·50

1972. Royal Silver Wedding. As T **103** of St. Helena, but with Elephant Seal and King Penguins in background.
36 5p. green 75 35
37 10p. violet 75 35

1973. Royal Wedding. As T **103a** of St. Helena. Background colours given. Multicoloured.
38 5p. brown 30 10
39 15p. lilac 40 20

8 Churchill and Westminster Skyline

1974. Birth Cent of Sir Winston Churchill. Mult.
40 15p. Type **8** 1·00 1·25
41 25p. Churchill and warship 1·25 1·25
MS42 122 × 98 mm. Nos. 40/1 6·00 6·00

9 Captain Cook — 10 "Discovery" and Biological Laboratory

1975. Bicentenary of Possession by Captain Cook.
43 2p. Type **9** 2·25 1·00
44 8p. H.M.S. "Resolution" (horiz) 3·50 1·50
45 16p. Possession Bay (horiz) 3·75 1·75

1976. 50th Anniv of "Discovery" Investigations. Multicoloured.
46 2p. Type **10** 1·50 45
47 8p. "William Scoresby" and water-sampling bottles 1·75 60
48 11p. "Discovery II" and plankton net 2·00 65
49 25p. Biological station and krill 2·50 95

11 The Queen and Retinue after Coronation

1977. Silver Jubilee. Multicoloured.
50 6p. Visit by Prince Philip, 1957 50 30
51 11p. Queen Elizabeth and Westminster Abbey 70 35
52 33p. Type **11** 80 50

12 Fur Seal — 13 H.M.S. "Resolution"

1978. 25th Anniv of Coronation.
67 – 25p. deep blue, blue and silver 40 1·10
68 – 25p. multicoloured 40 1·10
69 **12** 25p. deep blue, blue and silver 40 1·10

DESIGNS: No. 67, Panther of Henry VI; No. 68, Queen Elizabeth II.

1979. Bicentenary of Captain Cook's Voyages, 1768–79. Multicoloured.
70 3p. Type **13** 1·50 80
71 6p. "Resolution" and Map of South Georgia and S. Sandwich Isles showing route 1·50 70
72 11p. King penguin (from drawing by George Forster) 1·75 1·40
73 25p. Flaxman/Wedgwood medallion of Capt. Cook 2·00 1·75

SOUTH GEORGIA AND THE SOUTH SANDWICH ISLANDS Pt. 1

Under the new constitution, effective 3 October 1985, South Georgia and the South Sandwich Islands ceased to be dependencies of the Falkland Islands.

100 pence = 1 pound.

1986. 60th Birthday of Queen Elizabeth II. As T **145a** of St. Helena. Multicoloured.
153 10p. Four generations of Royal Family at Prince Charles's christening, 1948 35 50
154 24p. With Prince Charles and Lady Diana Spencer, Buckingham Palace, 1981 60 75
155 29p. In robes of Order of the British Empire, St. Paul's Cathedral, London 60 80
156 45p. At banquet, Canada, 1976 80 1·00
157 58p. At Crown Agents Head Office London, 1983 1·00 1·25

25a Prince Andrew and Miss Sarah Ferguson at Ascot — 26a I.G.Y. Logo

26 Southern Black-backed Gull ("Dominican Gull")

1986. Royal Wedding. Multicoloured.
158 17p. Type **25a** 75 1·00
159 22p. Wedding photograph 85 1·25
160 29p. Prince Andrew with Westland Lynx helicopter on board H.M.S. "Brazen" 1·50 1·50

1987. Birds. Multicoloured.
161 1p. Type **26** 1·00 1·50
162 2p. South georgia cormorant ("Blue-eyed cormorant") 1·25 1·75
163 3p. Snowy sheathbill ("Wattled Sheatbill") (vert) 1·50 2·00
164 4p. Skua antarctic ("Brown Skua") (vert) 1·25 2·00
165 5p. Pintado petrel ("Coupe Pigeon") 1·25 2·00
166 6p. Georgian diving petrel ("South Georgia Diving Petrel") 1·25 2·00
167 7p. South Georgia pipit (vert) 1·50 2·00
168 8p. Georgian teal ("South Georgian Pintail") (vert) 1·50 2·00
169 9p. Fairy prion 1·50 2·00
170 10p. bearded penguin ("Chinstrap Penguin") 1·50 2·00
171 20p. Macaroni penguin (vert) 1·75 2·25
172 25p. Light-mantled sooty albatross (vert) 1·75 2·25
173 50p. Giant petrel ("Southern Giant Petrel") (vert) 2·00 2·50
174 £1 Wandering albatross 2·25 3·75
175 £3 King penguin (vert) 6·00 8·00

1987. 30th Anniv of International Geophysical Year.
176 **26a** 24p. black and blue 70 55
177 – 29p. multicoloured 75 60
178 – 58p. multicoloured 1·40 1·25

DESIGNS: 29p. Grytviken; 58p. Glaciologist using hand-drill to take core sample.

27 "Gaimardia trapesina"

1988. Sea Shells. Multicoloured.
179 10p. Type **27** 65 30
180 24p. "Margarella tropidophoroides" 1·00 60
181 29p. "Trophon geversianus" 1·10 65
182 58p. "Chlanidota densesculpta" 1·60 1·25

1988. 300th Anniv of Lloyd's of London. As T **192** of Samoa.
183 10p. black and brown 60 40
184 24p. multicoloured 85 75
185 29p. black and green 90 80
186 58p. black and red 1·40 1·60

DESIGNS—VERT: 10p. Queen Mother at opening of new Lloyd's building, 1957; 58p. "Horatio" (tanker) on fire, 1916. HORIZ: 24p. "Lindblad Explorer" (cruise liner); 29p. Whaling station, Leith Harbour.

28 Glacier Headwall

1989. Glacier Formations. Multicoloured.
187 10p. Type **28** 40 35
188 24p. Accumulation area 80 70
189 29p. Ablation area 90 80
190 58p. Calving front 1·60 1·40

29 Retracing Shackleton's Trek — 30 "Brutus", Prince Olav Harbour

1989. 25th Anniv of Combined Services Expedition to South Georgia. Multicoloured.
191 10p. Type **29** 40 35
192 24p. Surveying at Royal Bay 90 70
193 29p. H.M.S. "Protector" (ice patrol ship) 1·00 80
194 58p. Raising Union Jack on Mount Paget 1·60 1·40

1990. 90th Birthday of Queen Elizabeth the Queen Mother. As T **161a** of St. Helena.
195 26p. multicoloured 1·00 1·75
196 £1 black and blue 2·75 3·75

DESIGNS—(21 × 36 mm): 26p. Queen Mother. (29 × 37 mm): King George VI and Queen Elizabeth with A.R.P. wardens, 1940.

1990. Wrecks and Hulks. Multicoloured.
197 12p. Type **30** 55 40
198 26p. "Bayard", Ocean Harbour 1·00 80
199 31p. "Karrakatta", Husvik 1·10 95
200 62p. "Louise", Grytviken 1·90 1·75

1991. 65th Birthday of Queen Elizabeth II and 70th Birthday of Prince Philip. As T **165a** of St. Helena. Multicoloured.

201 31p. Queen Elizabeth II 1·40 1·75
202 31p. Prince Philip in Grenadier Guards uniform 1·40 1·75

31 Contest between two Bull Elephant Seals

1991. Elephant Seals. Multicoloured.

203 12p. Type **31** 50 50
204 26p. Adult elephant seal 1·00 1·00
205 29p. Seal throwing sand 1·10 1·10
206 31p. Head of elephant seal 1·10 1·10
207 34p. Seals on beach 1·25 1·25
208 62p. Cow seal with pup 2·00 2·00

1992. 40th Anniv of Queen Elizabeth II's Accession. As T **168a** of St. Helena. Multicoloured.

209 7p. Ice-covered mountains 40 40
210 14p. Zavodovski Island 65 65
211 29p. Gulbrandsen Lake 1·00 1·00
212 34p. Three portraits of Queen Elizabeth 1·10 1·25
213 68p. Queen Elizabeth II 1·60 1·75

32 Adult Teal and Young Bird

1992. Endangered Species. Georgian Teal ("South Georgia Teal"). Multicoloured.

214 2p. Type **32** 50 20
215 6p. Adult with eggs 60 30
216 12p. Teals swimming 80 50
217 20p. Adult and two chicks 1·00 90

1992. 10th Anniv of Liberation. As T **169** of St. Helena. Multicoloured.

218 14p.+6p. King Edward Point 70 70
219 29p.+11p. "Queen Elizabeth 2" (liner) in Cumberland Bay 1·50 1·25
220 34p.+16p. Royal Marines hoisting Union Jack on South Sandwich Islands 1·90 1·60
221 68p.+32p. H.M.S. "Endurance" (ice patrol ship) and Westland Wasp helicopter 3·50 3·00
MS222 116 × 116 mm. Nos. 218/21 7·00 6·00

33 Disused Whale Factory, Grytviken

1993. Opening of South Georgia Whaling Museum. Multicoloured.

223 15p. Type **33** 65 60
224 31p. Whaler's lighter and whale bones 1·10 1·10
225 36p. Aerial view of King Edward Cove 1·40 1·40
226 72p. Museum building 2·50 2·75

34 Pair of Swimming Penguins

1993. Macaroni Penguin. Multicoloured.

227 16p. Type **34** 70 45
228 34p. Group of penguins 1·40 1·00
229 39p. Two juvenile penguins 1·60 1·25
230 78p. Two adult penguins 2·50 2·25

35 Hourglass Dolphin

1994. Whales and Dolphins. Multicoloured.

231 1p. Type **35** 75 75
232 2p. Southern right whale dolphin 1·00 1·00
233 5p. Long-finned pilot whale 1·50 1·10
234 8p. Southern bottlenose whale 1·75 1·10
235 9p. Killer whale 1·75 1·10
236 10p. Minke whale 1·75 1·10
237 20p. Sei whale 2·50 1·50
238 25p. Humpback whale 2·50 1·50
239 50p. Southern right whale 3·25 1·75
240 £1 Sperm whale 4·25 3·00
241 £3 Fin whale 7·50 7·00
242 £5 Blue whale 12·00 11·00

1994. "Hong Kong '94" International Stamp Exhibition. Nos. 227/30 optd **HONG KONG '94** and emblem.

243 16p. Type **34** 80 1·25
244 34p. Group of penguins 1·40 2·25
245 39p. Two juvenile penguins 1·60 2·50
246 78p. Two adult penguins 2·50 3·25

36 Bull Elephant Seals

1994. "Life in the Freezer". Scenes from the B.B.C. Natural History Unit series. Multicoloured.

247 17p. Type **36** 50 75
248 35p. Young fur seal (vert) 90 1·50
249 40p. Pair of grey-headed albatrosses 1·60 1·75
250 65p. King penguins in courtship display (vert) 2·50 2·75

37 Map of Jason Harbour

1994. Centenary of C. A. Larsen's First Voyage to South Georgia. Multicoloured.

251 17p. Type **37** 60 75
252 35p. "Castor" (whaling ship), 1886 1·10 1·50
253 40p. "Hertha" (whaling ship), 1886 1·25 1·60
254 65p. "Jason" (whaling ship), 1881 2·25 2·75

1994. 50th Anniv of Second World War. As T **182a** of St. Helena. Multicoloured.

255 50p. H.M.S. "Queen of Bermuda" (armed merchant cruiser), Leith Harbour 2·25 2·50
256 50p. 4-inch coastal gun, Hansen Point 2·25 2·50
MS257 75 × 85 mm. £1 Reverse of 1939–45 war medal (vert) 2·25 2·50

Nos. 255/6 were printed together, se-tenant, forming a composite design.

38 "Damien II" (research schooner)

1995. Sailing Ships. Multicoloured.

258 35p. Type **38** 1·25 1·75
259 40p. "Curlew" (cutter) 1·40 1·75
260 76p. "Mischief" (yacht) 2·25 2·75

39 Sir Ernest Shackleton and Ridge 2493

1996. 80th Anniv of Sir Ernest Shackleton's Trek across South Georgia. Multicoloured.

261 15p. Type **39** 85 90
262 20p. Frank Worsley and King Haakon Bay 90 1·00
263 30p. Map of route 1·10 1·25
264 65p. Tom Crean and Manager's villa, Stromness whaling station 1·40 1·75

40 Bearded Penguin swimming

1996. Bearded Penguins ("Chinstrap Penguins"). Multicoloured.

265 17p. Type **40** 55 55
266 35p. Mutual display 90 90
267 40p. Adult feeding chicks 1·10 1·10
268 76p. Feeding on krill 1·90 1·90

1997. Return of Hong Kong to China Sheet 130 × 90 mm, containing No. 268.

MS269 76p. Feeding on krill 2·00 2·25

1997. Golden Wedding of Queen Elizabeth and Prince Philip. As T **192a** of St. Helena. Multicoloured.

270 15p. Queen Elizabeth wearing red hat, 1996 75 50
271 15p. Prince Philip in carriage-driving at Royal Windsor Horse Show 75 50
272 17p. Queen Elizabeth with show jumping team, 1993 80 55
273 17p. Prince Philip smiling 80 55
274 40p. Princess Anne on horseback and Queen Elizabeth 1·75 1·40
275 40p. Zara Phillips horse riding and Prince Philip 1·75 1·40
MS276 110 × 70 mm. £1.50 Queen Elizabeth and Prince Philip in landau (horiz) 3·50 3·75

Nos. 270/1, 272/3 and 274/5 respectively were printed together, se-tenant, with the backgrounds forming composite designs.

41 Reindeer

1998. Wildlife. Sheet, 138 × 84 mm, containing T **41** and similar horiz designs. Multicoloured.

MS277 35p. Type **41**; 35p. Antartic tern; 35p. Grey-headed albatross; 35p. King penguin; 35p. Prickly burr; 35p. Fur seal 6·50 5·00

1998. Diana, Princess of Wales Commemoration. Sheet, 145 × 70 mm, containing vert designs as T **194** of St. Helena. Multicoloured.

MS278 35p. Laughing, 1983; 35p. In eveing dress, 1996; 35p. Wearing red jacket, 1991; 35p. Wearing white jacket, 1996 (sold at £1.40 + 20p. charity premium) 4·25 3·50

42 "Explorer" (cruise ship)

1998. Tourism. Multicoloured.

279 30p. Type **42** 1·50 1·10
280 35p. Wandering albatross 1·75 1·25
281 40p. Elephant seal 1·75 1·25
282 65p. Post Office at King Edward Point 2·00 1·75

43 Grytviken and Sugartop Mountain

1999. Island Views. Multicoloured.

283 9p. Type **43** 85 60
284 17p. "Dias" and "Albatros" (abandoned sealing ships), Grytviken 1·10 85
285 35p. King Edward Point 1·50 1·25
286 40p. South Georgia from the sea 1·50 1·25
287 65p. Grytviken Church 2·00 1·50

44 H.M.S. "Resolution" in Antartic, 1773

45 Bearded Penguins ("Chinstrap Penguins")

1999. "Australia '99" World Stamp Exhibition, Melbourne. Sheet 120 × 83 mm.

MS288 **44** £1.50 multicoloured 7·00 4·50

1999. "Queen Elizabeth the Queen Mother's Century". As T **199** of St. Helena. Multicoloured. (except 30p., £1).

289 25p. Visiting air-raid shelter, 1940 1·25 1·25
290 30p. With grandchildren, 1970 (black) 1·40 1·40
291 35p. With Prince William, 1994 1·50 1·50
292 40p. Presenting colour to Royal Anglian Regt 1·60 1·60
MS293 145 × 70 mm. £1 Lady Elizabeth Boewes-Lyon, 1914, and funeral of Queen Victoria, 1901 (black) 4·75 5·50

1999. Birds. Multicoloured.

294 1p. Type **45** 45 60
295 2p. White-chinned petrel (horiz) 50 60
296 5p. Grey-backed storm petrel 60 70
297 10p. South Georgia pipit 75 75
298 11p. Grey-headed albatross (horiz) 75 75
299 30p. Blue petrel 1·50 1·50
300 35p. Black-browed albatross (horiz) 1·50 1·50
301 40p. Georgian diving petrel ("South Georgia Diving Petrel") (horiz) 1·50 1·50
302 50p. Macaroni penguin 1·75 1·75
303 £1 Light-mantled sooty albatross (horiz) 3·00 3·25
304 £3 Georgian teal ("South Georgia Pintail") (horiz) 7·00 8·00
305 £5 King penguin 11·00 12·00

46 Sunrise

1999. New Millennium. Multicoloured.

306 11p. Type **46** 1·00 1·00
307 11p. Grytviken Church 1·00 1·00
308 11p. Nesting black-browed and grey-headed albatross 1·00 1·00
309 35p. Sunset 1·75 1·75
310 35p. Reindeer 1·75 1·75
311 35p. Macaroni penguins and chicks 1·75 1·75

47 Shackleton in "James Caird" crossing Scotia Sea

2000. Shackleton's Trans-Antarctic Expedition, 1914–17, Commemoration. Multicoloured.

312 35p. Type **47** 1·75 1·75
313 40p. Shackleton and party approaching Stromness Whaling Station 1·90 1·90
314 65p. Shackleton's Cross at Hope Point 2·75 2·75

48 Prince William at Zurich Airport, 1994

2000. 18th Birthday of Prince William. Multicoloured.

315 25p. Type **48** 1·50 1·50
316 30p. Skiing in Klosters, Switzerland, 1994 1·60 1·60
317 35p. Prince William in 1997 (horiz) 1·75 1·75

318 40p. Prince William waving, 1999 (horiz) . . . . 1·90 1·90
MS319 175 × 95 mm. 50p. In Parachute Regiment uniform, 1986 (horiz) and Nos. 315/18 8·50 7·00

49 King Penguins swimming

2000. King Penguins. Multicoloured.
320 37p. Type **49** . . . . 1·90 1·90
321 37p. Adult penguin with chicks . . . . 1·90 1·90
322 43p. Penguins courting . . . 2·25 2·25
323 43p. Penguins on nests . . . 2·25 2·25

50 R.F.A. *Tidespring* (tanker)

2001. Royal Fleet Auxiliary Vessels. Multicoloured.
324 37p. Type **50** . . . . 1·90 1·90
325 37p. R.F.A. *Sir Percivale* (landing ship) . . . . . . 1·90 1·90
326 43p. R.F.A. *Diligence* (maintenance ship) . . . . 2·25 2·25
327 43p. R.F.A. *Gold Rover* (tanker) . . . . 2·25 2·25

51 Mackerel Icefish

2001. 20th Anniv of Convention for the Conservation of Antarctic Marine Resources. Marine Life. Multicoloured.
328 33p. Type **51** . . . . . . 1·50 1·50
329 37p. Spiney back crab . . . 1·75 1·75
330 37p. Krill (vert) . . . . . . 1·75 1·75
331 43p. Blenny rockcod ("Toothfish") (vert) . . . . 1·90 1·90

2002. Golden Jubilee. As T **211** of St. Helena.
332 20p. brown, turquoise and gold . . . . 1·10 1·10
333 37p. multicoloured . . . . . 1·75 1·75
334 43p. black, turquoise and gold . . . . 1·90 1·90
335 50p. multicoloured . . . . . 2·25 2·25
MS336 162 × 95 mm. Nos. 332/5 and 50p. multicoloured . . . . . . 8·50 9·00
DESIGNS—HORIZ (as Type **211** of St. Helena): 20p. Queen Elizabeth with corgi, 1952; 37p. Queen Elizabeth and Prince Philip in evening dress; 43p. Princess Elizabeth looking at stamp album, 1946; 50p. Queen Elizabeth at garden party, 1999. VERT (38 × 51 mm.): 50p. Queen Elizabeth after Annigoni.
Designs as Nos. 332/5 in No. **MS**336 omit the gold frame around each stamp and the "Golden Jubilee 1952-2002" inscription.

52 Fin Whale

2002. South Atlantic Sea Mammals. Multicoloured.
337 10p. Type **52** 90 90
338 10p. Blue whale 90 90
339 20p. Sperm whale . . . . . 1·40 1·40
340 37p. Head of leopard seal . . 1·60 1·60
341 37p. Leopard seal on ice floe 1·60 1·60
342 43p. Elephant seal . . . . . 1·75 1·75
MS343 90 × 67 mm. £1.50 Elephant seal . . . . 6·00 7·00

2002. Queen Elizabeth the Queen Mother Commemoration. As T **215** of St. Helena.
344 22p. brown, gold and purple 1·00 1·00
345 40p. multicoloured . . . . . 1·40 1·40
346 45p. black, gold and purple 1·50 1·50
347 95p. multicoloured . . . . . 2·50 2·50
MS348 145 × 70 mm. Nos. 346/7 5·50 6·50
DESIGNS: 22p. Queen Elizabeth at British Red Cross Society, London; 40p. Queen Mother at Birthday Variety Show, 1990; 45p. Duchess of York and corgi, 1936; 95p. Queen Mother at Royal College of Music, 1989.

Designs in No. **MS**348 omit the "1900–2002" inscription and the coloured frame.

53 Antarctic Fur Seals on Ice

2002. Fur Seals. Multicoloured.
349 40p. Type **53** . . . . 1·90 1·90
350 40p. Fur seal underwater . . 1·90 1·90
351 45p. Fur seal in winter coat 1·90 1·90
352 45p. Competing males . . . 1·90 1·90

54 Pair of Grey-headed Albatrosses on Nest

2003. Endangered Species. Grey-headed Albatross. Multicoloured.
353 40p. Type **54** . . . . 1·40 1·40
354 45p. Adult with chick . . . . 1·50 1·50
355 45p. Two adults . . . . . . 1·50 1·50
356 70p. Grey-headed Albatross in flight . . . . 2·00 2·00

2003. As T **220** of St. Helena.
361 £2 black, yellow and brown 5·50 5·50

55 Prince William at Golden Jubilee Church Service and at Queen Mother's 101st Birthday

2003. 21st Birthday of Prince William of Wales. Multicoloured.
362 70p. Type **55** . . . . 2·25 2·25
363 70p. On Raleigh International Expedition and in Prefect's Common Room, Dr. Gailey's . . . . 2·25 2·25

56 HMS *Sappho* (cruiser), Grytviken, 1906

2004. Aspects of South Georgia. Multicoloured.
364 40p. Type **56** 80 85
365 40p. Norwegian reindeer, introduced 1911 . . . . . 80 85
366 40p. Largest blue whale landed, 1912 . . . . 80 85
367 40p. Shackleton's island crossing, 1916 . . . . . . 80 85
368 40p. Shackleton's memorial cross, Grytviken, 1922 . . 80 85
369 40p. *Discovery* I on expedition to study whale populations, 1925 . . . . 80 85
370 40p. First powered flight over South Georgia, 1938 . . . 80 85
371 40p. Operation Tabarin, 1943 80 85
372 40p. Duke of Edinburgh (with penguins), 1957 . . . 80 85
373 40p. Bird Island Research Station, 1958 . . . . . . 80 85
374 40p. Ascent of Mount Paget, 1964 . . . . 80 85
375 40p. Royal Navy ship, Liberation of South Georgia, 1982 . . . . . . 80 85
376 40p. Royal Charter and Crest, 1985 . . . . 80 85
377 40p. Inauguration of South Georgia Musuem, Grytviken, 1992 . . . . . 80 85
378 40p. Applied fishery research, 2001 . . . . 80 85
379 40p. Remedial work at old whaling station, Grytviken, 2003 . . . . 80 85

Nos. 364/79 were printed together, se-tenant, each horizontal row of stamps forming a composite background design of Grytviken (Nos. 364/7), Bird Island (Nos. 368/71), Drygalski Fjord (Nos. 372/5) or King Haakon Bay (Nos. 376/9).

57 HMS *Ajax*

2004. Royal Navy Frigates and Cruisers. Multicoloured.
380 10p. Type **57** 30 40
381 25p. HMS *Amazon* 70 70
382 45p. HMS *Dartmouth* . . . 1·25 1·40
383 50p. HMS *Penelope* . . . . 1·25 1·40
384 70p. HMS *St. Austell Bay* 1·75 1·90
385 £1 HMS *Plymouth* . . . . . 2·25 2·40

2004. Merchant Ships. As T **227** of St. Helena. Multicoloured.
386 42p. MS *Endeavour* 85 90
387 42p. RMS *Queen Elizabeth II* 85 90
388 50p. MS *Lindblad Explorer* 1·00 1·10
389 75p. SS *Canberra* . . . . . 1·50 1·60

58 Antarctic Skua 59 Captain C. A. Larsen

2004. Juvenile Fauna. Multicoloured designs.
(a) Ordinary gum.
390 1p. Type **58** 10 10
391 2p. Reindeer 10 10
392 3p. Dove ("Antarctic") prion (horiz) 10 10
393 5p. Humpback whale (horiz) 10 15
394 10p. Gentoo penguin 20 25
395 25p. Antarctic fur seal . . . 50 55
396 50p. South Georgia pintail (horiz) . . . . 1·00 1·10
397 75p. Light-mantled sooty albatross . . . . 1·50 1·60
398 £1 Weddell seal . . . . . . 2·00 2·10
399 £2 King penguin (horiz) . . . 4·00 4·25
400 £3 Southern right whale (horiz) . . . . 6·00 6·25
401 £5 Wandering albatross . . . 10·00 10·50

(b) Size 39 × 26 mm. Self-adhesive.
402 (42p.) Elephant seal pup . . 85 90
No. 402 is inscribed "Airmail Postcard" and was sold for 42p. each.

2004. Centenary of Grytviken (first settlement). Multicoloured.
403 24p. Type **59** 50 55
404 42p. View of Grytviken from Mount Hodges 85 90
405 50p. *Fortuna* (whaling ship) 1·00 1·10
406 £1 Ski jump . . . . 2·00 2·10

SOUTH KASAI Pt. 14

100 centimes = 1 franc.

Region of Zaire around the town of Bakwanga. The area was declared autonomous in 1960, during the upheaval following independence, but returned to the control of the central government in October 1962.

Various stamps of Belgian Congo were overprinted "ETAT AUTONOME DU SUD-KASAI" and some surcharged in addition with new values. These were put on sale at the Philatelic Bureau in Brussels and were also valid for use in South Kasai but no supplies were sent out.

1 Leopard's Head and "V" 2 A. D. Kalonji

1961.
1 **1** 1f. multicoloured 10 10
2 1f.50 multicoloured 10 10
3 3f.50 multicoloured 15 15
4 8f. multicoloured 25 25
5 10f. multicoloured 30 30

1961.
6 **2** 6f.50 brown, blue and black 20 20
7 9f. light brown, brown & black 25 25
8 14f.50 brown, green and black 40 40
9 20f. multicoloured . . . . . . 45 1·45

SOUTH RUSSIA Pt. 10

Stamps of various anti-Bolshevist forces and temporary governments in S. Russia after the revolution.

100 kopeks = 1 rouble.

A. KUBAN TERRITORY: COSSACK GOVERNMENT

1918. Arms type of Russia surch. Imperf or perf.
8 **22** 25k. on 1k. orange 25 45
2 50k. on 2k. green 15 25
23 70k. on 1k. orange 30 55
10 70k. on 5k. red 45 75
11 1r. on 3k. red 20 50
13 **23** 3r. on 4k. red . . . . 9·00 11·00
14 10r. on 4k. red . . . . . . 4·00 5·00
15 **10** 10r. on 15k. blue and purple 70 1·10
16 **22** 25r. on 3k. red . . . . . . 4·00 3·00
17 25r. on 7k. blue . . . . . . 30·00 60·00
18 **10** 25r. on 14k. red and blue 70·00 £100
19 25r. on 25k. mauve & green 35·00 65·00

1919. Postal Savings Bank stamps of Russia surch.
20 10r. on 1k. red on buff . . . 40·00 70·00
21 10r. on 5k. green on buff . . . 40·00 70·00
22 10r. on 10k. brown on buff . . 75·00 £225

B. DON TERRITORY: COSSACK GOVERNMENT

1919. Arms type of Russia surch in figures only. Imperf or perf.
25 **22** 25k. on 1k. orange 20 45
29 25k. on 2k. green 20 40
30 25k. on 3k. red 25 60
31 **23** 25k. on 4k. red 20 45
32 **22** 50k. on 7k. blue . . . . . 1·75 2·75

10 T. Ermak (16th century Cossack Ataman) 13

1919. Currency stamp with arms and seven-line print on back used for postage.
33 **10** 20k. green . . . . 18·00 £150

C. CRIMEA: REGIONAL GOVERNMENT

1919. Arms type of Russia surch **35 Kon.** Imperf.
34 **22** 35k. on 1k. orange 15 40

1919. Currency and postage stamp. Arms and inscription on back. Imperf.
35 **13** 50k. brown on buff . . . . 25·00 80·00

D. SOUTH RUSSIA: GOVERNMENT OF GENERAL DENIKIN

1919. Nos. G6 and G10 of Ukraine surch in figs.
36 G **1** 35k. on 10s. brown . . . 15·00 30·00
37 G **5** 70k. on 50s. red . . . . 30·00 50·00

15 16

1919. Imperf or perf.
38 **15** 5k. yellow 10 15
39 10k. green 10 15
40 15k. red 10 15
41 35k. blue 10 15
42 70k. blue 10 15
43 **16** 1r. red and brown 15 35
44 2r. yellow and lilac 35 55
45 3r. green and brown 35 60
46 5r. violet and blue . . . . . 1·00 1·50
47 7r. pink and green . . . . . 80 1·75
48 10r. grey and red . . . . . 1·50 2·00
Higher values similar to Type **16** are bogus.

E. SOUTH RUSSIA: GOVERNMENT OF GENERAL WRANGEL

5 ПЯТЬ рублей. (17)

ЮГЪ РОССИИ. 100 рублей. (18)

1920. Crimea issue. Surch with T **17**. (a) On Arms types of Russia. Imperf or perf.
52 **22** 5r. on 5k. red 2·00 3·75
54 **14** 5r. on 20k. red and blue 2·00 3·75

(b) On No. 41 of South Russia.
55 **15** 5r. on 35k. blue 7·50 12·00

1920. Arms type of Russia surch with T **18**.
56 **22** 100r. on 1k. orange 2·50

SOUTH WEST AFRICA Pt. 1

A territory in S.W. Africa formerly the German Colony of German South West Africa (q.v. in Volume 2). Administered by South Africa until 1990 when it became independent as Namibia.

1923. 12 pence = 1 shilling;
20 shillings = 1 pound.
1961. 100 cents = 1 rand.

NOTE. Stamps overprinted for South West Africa are always of South Africa, except where otherwise indicated. "Bilingual" in heading indicates that the stamps are inscribed alternately in English and Afrikaans throughout the sheet, "Bilingual" is not repeated in the heading where bilingual stamps of South Africa are overprinted. Our prices for surch issues are for mint bilingual pairs and used single stamps of either inscription.

1923. Optd **South West Africa.** or **Zuid-West Afrika.** alternately.
1 **2** ½d. green 2·50 1·00
2 1d. red 3·25 1·00
3 2d. purple 4·25 1·50
4 3d. blue 7·50 2·75
5 4d. orange and green 13·00 4·00
6 6d. black and violet 8·00 4·00
7 1s. yellow 23·00 5·00
8 1s.3d. violet 30·00 5·50
9 2s.6d. purple and green 60·00 18·00
13 5s. purple and blue £140 45·00
14 10s. blue and green £500 £140
12 £1 green and red £700 £250

1923. Optd **Zuidwest Afrika.** or **South West Africa.*** alternately.
16 **2** ½d. green 7·00 3·75
30 1d. red 3·25 1·40
31 2d. purple 5·00 1·75
19 3d. blue 5·00 1·25
20 4d. yellow and green 6·00 2·75
34 6d. black and violet 9·00 5·00
35 1s. yellow 11·00 5·00
36 1s.3d. violet 15·00 5·00
37 2s.6d. purple and green 29·00 10·00
38 5s. purple and blue 42·00 14·00
39 10s. blue and green 70·00 20·00
40 £1 green and red £250 55·00
*The English overprint is the same, for the purposes of this catalogue, as that on Nos. 1/12.

1926. Optd **South West Africa.** (on stamps inscr in English) or **Suidwes Afrika.** (on stamps inscr in Afrikaans) alternately.
41 **6** ½d. black and green 4·25 1·00
42 **7** 1d. black and red 3·50 80
49 **11** 2d. grey and purple 4·75 1·75
50 – 3d. black and red 4·75 2·50
43 **8** 6d. green and orange 26·00 7·00
51 – 1s. brown and blue 15·00 4·00
52 – 2s.6d. green and brown 35·00 13·00
53 – 5s. black and green 75·00 20·00
54 – 10s. blue and brown 65·00 20·00

1926. Optd **SOUTH WEST AFRICA** in two lines or **SUIDWES-AFRIKA** in one line. Imperf or perf.
44A **10** 4d. blue 75 3·00

1927. Optd as Nos. 41/2 and 43 but with Afrikaans opt on stamp inscr in English and vice versa.
45 **6** ½d. black and green 2·00 80
46 **7** 1d. black and red 2·50 50
47 **8** 6d. green and orange 11·00 3·00

1927. Optd **SOUTH WEST AFRICA** in one line. Imperf.
48 **10** 4d. blue 6·00 19·00

1927. Optd **S.W.A.**
56 **2** 1s.3d. violet 1·25 6·50
57 £1 olive and red 90·00 £160

1927. Optd **S.W.A.**
58 **6** ½d. black and green 2·50 80
59 **7** 1d. black and red 1·25 55
60 **11** 2d. grey and purple 9·00 1·50
61 – 3d. black and red 6·00 3·25
62 – 4d. brown 15·00 7·00
63 **8** 6d. green and orange 11·00 2·75
64 – 1s. brown and blue 20·00 5·00
65 – 2s.6d. green and brown 40·00 12·00
66 – 5s black and green 60·00 18·00
67 – 10s. blue and brown £100 28·00

1930. Air. Optd **S.W.A.**
72 **17** 4d. green 1·25 6·00
73 1s. orange 3·75 15·00

12 Kori Bustard

1931. Bilingual pairs.
74 **12** ½d. black and green 2·25 10
75 – 1d. blue and red 2·25 10
76 – 2d. blue and brown 70 15
77 – 3d. dull blue and blue 70 15
78 – 4d. green and purple 1·75 20
79 – 6d. blue and brown 1·50 20
80 – 1s. brown and blue 1·50 25
81 – 1s.3d. violet and yellow 7·50 50
82 – 2s.6d. red and grey 20·00 1·75
83 – 5s. green and brown 16·00 2·75
84 – 10s. brown and green 45·00 6·00
85 – £1 lake and green 70·00 10·00
DESIGNS: 1d. Cape Cross; 2d. Bogenfels; 3d. Windhoek; 4d. Waterberg; 6d. Luderitz Bay; 1s. Bush scene; 1s.3d. Elands; 2s.6d. Mountain zebra and wildebeests; 5s. Herero huts; 10s. Welwitschia plant; £1 Okuwahaken Falls.

24 Fokker Monoplane over Windhoek

1931. Air. Bilingual pairs.
86 **24** 3d. brown and blue 25·00 2·50
87 – 10d. black and brown 35·00 5·00
DESIGN: 10d. Handley Page H.P.25 Hendon biplane over Windhoek.

26

1935. Silver Jubilee.
88 **26** 1d. black and red 1·00 25
89 2d. black and brown 1·00 25
90 3d. black and blue 7·50 20·00
91 6d. black and purple 3·00 10·00

1935. Voortrekker Memorial. Nos. 50/3 of South Africa optd **S.W.A.**
92 ½d.+½d. black and green 1·50 75
93 1d.+½d. black and pink 1·50 40
94 2d.+1d. green and purple 5·50 80
95 3d.+1½d. green and blue 16·00 4·00

27 Mail Transport **28**

1937. Bilingual pair.
96 **27** 1½d. brown 24·00 30

1937. Coronation. Bilingual pairs.
97 **28** ½d. black and green 40 15
98 1d. black and red 40 15
99 1½d. black and orange 40 15
100 2d. black and brown 40 15
101 3d. black and blue 50 10
102 4d. black and purple 50 10
103 6d. black and yellow 50 20
104 1s. black and grey 55 25

1938. Voortrekker Centenary Fund. Nos. 76/9 of South Africa optd **S.W.A.**
105 ½d.+½d. blue and green 8·50 1·75
106 1d.+1d. blue and red 21·00 1·00
107 1½d.+1½d. brown and green 23·00 2·75
108 3d.+3d. blue 48·00 7·50

1938. Voortrekker Commem. Nos. 80/1 of South Africa optd **S.W.A.**
109 1d. blue and red 10·00 1·50
110 1½d. blue and brown 15·00 1·75

1939. 250th Anniv of Landing of Huguenots in South Africa. Nos. 82/4 of South Africa optd **S.W.A.**
111 ½d.+½d. brown and green 14·00 1·10
112 1d.+1d. green and red 17·00 1·25
113 1½d.+1½d. green and purple 25·00 1·25

1941. War Effort. Nos. 88/94a of South Africa optd **SWA**.
114a ½d. green 65 15
115 1d. red 55 15
116 1½d. green 55 15
121 2d. violet 50 1·00
117 3d. blue 22·00 1·00
118 4d. brown 6·50 1·00
119 6d. orange 3·00 50
122 1s. brown 70 1·00
120 1s.3d. brown 13·00 1·25

1943. War Effort. Nos. 97/104 of South Africa optd **SWA**.
123 ½d. green (T) 50 10
124 1d. red (T) 2·50 10
125 1½d. brown (P) 50 10
126 2d. violet (P) 7·50 10
127 3d. blue (T) 3·25 45
129 4d. green (T) 2·00 45
128 6d. orange (P) 6·00 30
130b 1s. brown (P) 4·00 30
The units refered to above consist of pairs (P) or triplets (T).

1945. Victory. Nos. 108/10 of South Africa optd **SWA**.
131 1d. brown and red 25 10
132 2d. blue and violet 30 10
133 3d. blue 1·50 10

1947. Royal Visit. Nos. 111/13 of South Africa optd **SWA**.
134 1d. black and red 10 10
135 2d. violet 10 10
136 3d. blue 15 10

1948. Silver Wedding. No. 125 of South Africa optd **SWA**.
137 3d. blue and silver 1·00 10

1949. 75th Anniv of U.P.U. Nos 128/30 of South Africa optd **SWA**.
138 ½d. mauve 75 25
139 1½d. red 75 15
140 3d. blue 1·25 25

1949. Inauguration of Voortrekker Monument Pretoria. Nos. 131/3 of South Africa optd **S W A**.
141 1d. mauve 10 10
142 1½d. green 10 10
143 3d. blue 15 60

1952. Tercentenary of Landing of Van Riebeeck. Nos. 136/40 of South Africa optd **SWA**.
144 ½d. purple and sepia 10 50
145 1d. green 10 10
146 2d. violet 50 10
147 4½d. blue 30 2·75
148 1s. brown 75 20

33 Queen Elizabeth II and "Catophracies alexandri"
34 "Two Bucks" (rock painting)

1953. Coronation. Native Flowers.
149 **33** 1d. red 40 10
150 – 2d. green ("Bauhinia macrantha") 40 10
151 – 4d. mauve ("Caralluma nebrownii") 50 30
152 – 6d. blue ("Gloriosa virescens") 50 60
153 – 1s. brown ("Rhigozum tricholotum") 65 20

1954.
154 **34** 1d. red 30 10
155 – 2d. brown 35 10
156 – 3d. purple 1·25 10
157 – 4d. black 1·50 10
158 – 4½d blue 70 40
159 – 6d. green 70 70
160 – 1s. mauve 70 50
161 – 1s.3d. red 2·00 1·00
162 – 1s.6d. purple 2·00 50
163 – 2s.6d. brown 4·50 70
164 – 5s. blue 6·00 2·75
165 – 10s. green 32·00 15·00
DESIGNS—VERT: 2d. "White Lady" (rock painting); 4½d. Karakul lamb; 6d. Ovambo woman blowing horn; 1s. Ovambo woman; 1s. 3d. Herero woman; 1s. 6d. Ovambo girl; 2s. 6d. Lioness; 5s. Gemsbok; 10s. African elephant. HORIZ: 3d. "Rhinoceros Hunt" (rock painting); 4d. "White Elephant and Giraffe" (rock painting).

46 G.P.O., Windhoek

59 "Agricultural Development"

1961.
171 **46** ½c. brown and blue 60 10
172 – 1c. brown and lilac 15 10
173 – 1½c. violet and orange 20 10
174 – 2c. green and yellow 75 60
175 – 2½c. brown and blue 35 10
176 – 3c. blue and red 4·25 40
177 – 3½c. blue and green 85 15
209 – 4c. brown and blue 1·50 2·50
178 – 5c. red and blue 6·50 10
211 – 6c. sepia and yellow 7·00 9·00
179 – 7½c. brown and lemon 70 15
213 – 9c. blue and yellow 7·50 10·00
180 – 10c. blue and yellow 1·75 60
181 – 12½c. blue and yellow 60 40
182 – 15c. brown and blue 14·00 3·25
183 – 20c. brown and orange 4·00 30
184 – 50c. green and orange 6·00 1·50
185 – 1r. yellow, purple and blue 10·00 15·00
DESIGNS—VERT: 1c. Finger Rock; 1½c. Mounted Soldier Monument; 2c. Quivertree; 3c. Greater flamingoes and Swakopmund Lighthouse; 3½c. Fishing industry; 5c. Greater flamingo; 6c., 7½c. German Lutheran Church, Windhoek; 10c. Diamond; 20c. Topaz; 50c. Tourmaline; 1r. Heliodor. HORIZ: 2½c., 4c. S.W.A. House, Windhoek; 9c., 12½c. Fort Namutoni; 15c. Hardap Dam.
See also Nos. 224/26.

1963. Opening of Hardap Dam.
192 **59** 3c. brown and green 30 15

61 Centenary Emblem and part of Globe

62 Interior of Assembly Hall

1963. Centenary of Red Cross.
193 – 7½c. red, black and blue 4·00 5·00
194 **61** 15c. red, black and brown 6·00 8·00
DESIGN: 7½c. Centenary emblem and map.

1964. Opening of Legislative Assembly Hall, Windhoek.
195 **62** 3c. blue and orange 50 30

63 Calvin

64 Mail Runner of 1890

1965. 400th Death Anniv of Calvin (Protestant reformer).
196 **63** 2½c. purple and gold 50 15
197 15c. green and gold 2·25 3·75

1965. 75th Anniv of Windhoek.
198 **64** 3c. sepia and red 50 15
199 – 15c. brown and green 90 1·75
DESIGN: 15c. Kurt von Francois (founder).

66 Dr. H. Vedder

70 Pres. Swart

67 Camelthorn Tree

1966. 90th Birth Anniv of Dr. H. Vedder (philosopher and writer).
200 **66** 3c. green and orange 30 15
201 15c. brown and blue 70 40

1967. Verwoerd Commemoration.
217 **67** 2½c. black and green 15 10
218 – 3c. brown and blue 15 10
219 – 15c. brown and purple 55 45
DESIGNS—VERT: 3c. Waves breaking against rock; 15c. Dr. H. F. Verwoerd.

1968. Swart Commemoration. Inscr in German, Afrikaans or English.
220 **70** 3c. red, blue and black 30 15
221 – 15c. red, green and olive 1·00 1·25
DESIGN: 15c. Pres. and Mrs. Swart.

1970. Water 70 Campaign. As Nos. 299/300 of South Africa, but inscr "SWA".
222 2½c. green, blue and brown 50 30
223 3c. blue and buff 50 30

1970. As Nos. 171 etc, but with "POSGELD" "INKOMSTE" omitted and larger figure of value.
224 **46** ½c. brown and blue 1·50 30
225 – 1½c. violet and orange 13·00 16·00
226 – 2c. green and yellow 5·00 40

1970. 150th Anniv of Bible Society of South Africa. As Nos. 301/2 of South Africa. Inscr "SWA".

228	2½c. multicoloured	1·50	10
229	12½c. gold, black and blue	5·00	6·00

1971. "Interstex" Stamp Exhibition, Cape Town. As No. 303 of South Africa. Inscr "SWA".

230	5c. blue, black and yellow	3·25	1·50

1971. 10th Anniv of Antarctic Treaty. As No. 304 of South Africa. Inscr "SWA".

231	12½c. black, blue and red	20·00	16·00

1971. 10th Anniv of South African Republic. As Nos. 305/6 of South Africa. Inscr "SWA".

232	2c. flesh and red	3·25	75
233	4c. green and black	3·25	75

1972. Centenary of S.P.C.A. As No. 312 of South Africa. Inscr "SWA".

234	5c. multicoloured	3·00	1·00

73 "Red Sand-dunes, Eastern South-West Africa"

1973. Scenery. Paintings by Adolph Jentsch. Multicoloured.

235	2c. Type **73**	75	75
236	4c. "After the Rain"	85	1·00
237	5c. "Barren Country"	1·00	1·25
238	10c. "Schaap River" (vert)	1·25	1·75
239	15c. "Namib Desert" (vert)	2·25	3·25

74 "Sarcocaulon rigidum" 75 "Euphorbia virosa"

1973. Succulents. Multicoloured. (a) As T **74**.

241	1c. Type **74**	15	10
242a	2c. "Lapidaria margaretae"	20	10
243	3c. "Titanopsis schwantesii"	20	10
244	4c. "Lithops karasmontana"	25	10
245b	5c. "Caralluma lugardii"	50	20
246	6c. "Dinteranthus mircospermus"	2·00	2·50
247	7c. "Conophytum gratum"	1·25	2·50
248	9c. "Huernia oculata"	65	50
249b	10c. "Gasteria pillansii"	40	30
250	14c. "Stapelia pedunculata"	1·75	3·00
251	15c. "Fenestraria aurantiaca"	65	30
252	20c. "Decabelone grandiflora"	5·00	3·50
253	25c. "Hoodia bainii"	4·75	3·00
	(b) As T **75**.		
254	30c. Type **75**	75	80
255a	50c. "Pachypodium namaquanum" (vert)	75	1·25
256	1r. "Welwitschia bainesii"	1·00	5·00

1973. As Nos. 241/2a and 245. Colours changed.

257	**18** 1c. black and mauve	70	60
258	– 2c. black and yellow	50	50
259a	– 5c. black and red	1·00	60

76 Chat-shrikes 77 Giraffe, Antelope and Spoor

1974. Rare Birds. Multicoloured.

260	4c. Type **76**	3·25	1·00
261	5c. Peach-faced lovebirds	4·00	1·50
262	10c. Damaraland rock jumper	7·50	5·50
263	15c. Ruppell's parrots	10·00	9·50

1974. Twyfelfontein Rock-engravings. Mult.

264	4c. Type **77**	1·50	50
265	5c. Elephant, hyena, antelope and spoor	1·50	80
266	15c. Kudu cow (38 × 21 mm)	5·50	7·50

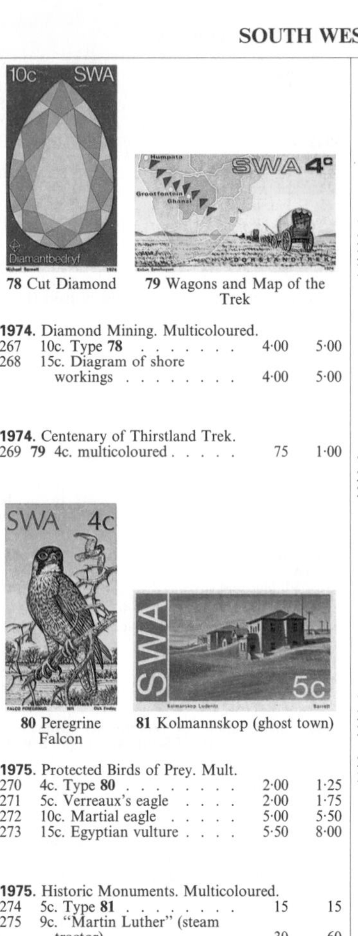

78 Cut Diamond 79 Wagons and Map of the Trek

1974. Diamond Mining. Multicoloured.

267	10c. Type **78**	4·00	5·00
268	15c. Diagram of shore workings	4·00	5·00

1974. Centenary of Thirstland Trek.

269	**79** 4c. multicoloured	75	1·00

80 Peregrine Falcon 81 Kolmannskop (ghost town)

1975. Protected Birds of Prey. Mult.

270	4c. Type **80**	2·00	1·25
271	5c. Verreaux's eagle	2·00	1·75
272	10c. Martial eagle	5·00	5·50
273	15c. Egyptian vulture	5·50	8·00

1975. Historic Monuments. Multicoloured.

274	5c. Type **81**	15	15
275	9c. "Martin Luther" (steam tractor)	30	60
276	15c. Kurt von Francois and Old Fort, Windhoek	50	75

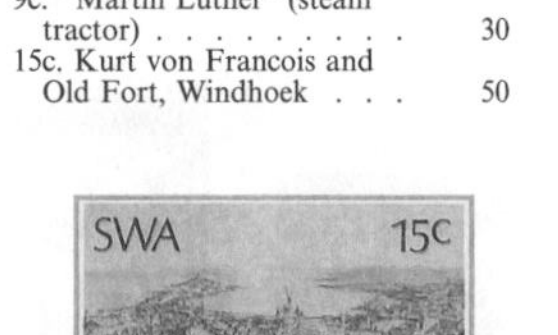

82 "View of Luderitz"

1975. Otto Schroder (painter). Multicoloured.

277	15c. Type **82**	30	60
278	15c. "View of Swakopmund"	30	60
279	15c. "Harbour Scene"	30	60
280	15c. "Quayside, Walvis Bay"	30	60
MS281	122 × 96 mm. Nos. 277/80	1·00	3·50

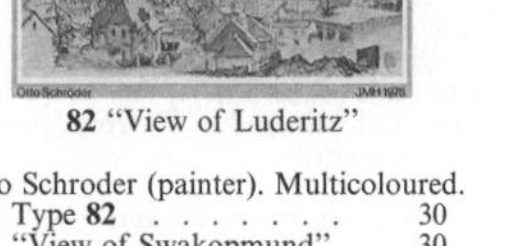

83 Elephants

1976. Prehistoric Rock Paintings. Mult.

282	4c. Type **83**	30	15
283	10c. Rhinoceros	30	60
284	15c. Antelope	35	70
285	20c. Man with bow and arrow	40	1·00
MS286	121 × 95 mm. Nos. 282/5	1·25	3·50

84 Schwerinsburg

1976. Castles. Multicoloured.

287	10c. Type **84**	20	30
288	15c. Schloss Duwisib	30	50
289	20c. Heynitzburg	30	70

85 Large-toothed Rock Hyrax

1976. Fauna Conservation. Multicoloured.

290	4c. Type **85**	30	20
291	10c. Kirk's dik-dik	50	75
292	15c. Kuhl's tree squirrel	75	1·60

86 The Augustineum, Windhoek

1976. Modern Buildings.

293	**86** 15c. black and yellow	30	60
294	– 20c. black and yellow	40	80

DESIGN: 20c. Katutura Hospital, Windhoek.

87 Ovambo Water Canal System

1976. Water and Electricity Supply. Mult.

295	15c. Type **87**	30	50
296	20c. Ruacana Falls Power Station	40	75

88 Coastline, near Pomona

1977. Namib Desert. Multicoloured.

297	4c. Type **88**	15	15
298	10c. Bush and dunes, Sossusvlei	20	20
299	15c. Plain near Brandberg	35	35
300	20c. Dunes, Sperr Gebiet	40	40

89 Kraal

1977. The Ovambo People.

301	**89** 4c. multicoloured	10	10
302	– 10c. black, orange & brown	20	15
303	– 15c. multicoloured	25	20
304	– 20c. multicoloured	25	35

DESIGNS: 10c. Grain baskets; 15c. Pounding grain; 20c. Women in tribal dress.

90 Terminal Buildings

1977. J. G. Strijdom Airport, Windhoek.

305	**90** 20c. multicoloured	40	30

91 Drostdy, Luderitz

1977. Historic Houses. Multicoloured.

306	5c. Type **91**	15	10
307	10c. Woermannhaus, Swakopmund	25	30
308	15c. Neu-Heusis, Windhoek	30	35
309	20c. Schmelenhaus, Bethanie	40	40
MS310	122 × 96 mm. Nos. 306/9	1·00	2·00

92 Side-winding Adder

1978. Small Animals. Multicoloured.

311	4c. Type **92**	15	10
312	10c. Grant's desert golden mole	25	20
313	15c. Palmato gecko	25	25
314	20c. Namaqua chameleon	25	25

93 Ostrich Hunting

1978. The Bushmen. Each brown, stone and black.

315	4c. Type **93**	30	10
316	10c. Woman carrying ostrich eggs	30	20
317	15c. Hunters kindling fire	40	20
318	20c. Woman with musical instrument	40	30

94 Lutheran Church, Windhoek

1978. Historic Churches.

319	**94** 4c. black and brown	10	10
320	– 10c. black and brown	15	20
321	– 15c. black and pink	20	25
322	– 20c. black and blue	30	35
MS323	125 × 90 mm. Nos. 319/22	75	1·75

DESIGNS: 10c. Lutheran Church, Swakopmund; 15c. Rhenish Mission Church, Otjimbingwe; 20c. Rhenish Missionary Church, Keetmanshoop.

1978. Universal Suffrage. Nos. 244/5, 249b and 251/3 optd **ALGEMENE STEMREG** (Afrikaans), **UNIVERSAL SUFFRAGE** (English) or **ALLGEMEINES WAHLRECHT** (German).

324	4c. "Lithops karasmontana"	10	10
325	5c. "Caralluma lugardii"	10	10
326	10c. "Gasteria pillansii"	10	10
327	15c. "Fenestraria aurantiaca"	10	15
328	20c. "Decabelone grandiflora"	10	15
329	25c. "Hoodia bainii"	15	15

Nos. 324/9 were issued in se-tenant strips of three, each stamp in the strip being optd in either Afrikaans, English or German. The same prices apply for any of the three languages.

96 Greater Flamingo 98 Killer Whale

97 Silver Topaz

1979. Water Birds. Multicoloured.

330	4c. Type **96**	20	10
331	15c. White-breasted cormorant	35	25
332	20c. Chestnut-banded sand plover	35	35
333	25c. Eastern white pelican	35	40

1979. Gemstones. Multicoloured.

334	4c. Type **97**	30	10
335	15c. Aquamarine	65	20
336	20c. Malachite	70	25
337	25c. Amethyst	70	30

1980. Whales. Multicoloured.

338	4c. Type **98**	25	20
339	5c. Humpback whale (38 × 22 mm)	25	20
340	10c. Black right whale (38 × 22 mm)	35	30
341	15c. Sperm whale (58 × 22 mm)	45	75
342	20c. Fin whale (58 × 22 mm)	55	90
343	25c. Blue whale (88 × 22 mm)	65	1·25
MS344	202 × 95 mm. Nos. 338/43	2·75	5·00

99 Impala

1980. 25th Anniv of Division of Nature Conservation and Tourism. Antelopes. Mult.

345	5c. Type **99**	15	10
346	10c. Topi	15	10
347	15c. Roan antelope	25	15
348	20c. Sable antelope	25	20

100 Black-backed Jackal

101 Meerkat

1980. Wildlife. Multicoloured.
349 1c. Type **100** 15 10
350 2c. Hunting dog 15 10
351 3c. Brown hyena 15 10
352 4c. Springbok 15 10
353 5c. Gemsbok 15 10
354 6c. Greater kudu 15 10
355 7c. Mountain zebra (horiz) 40 20
356 8c. Cape porcupine (horiz) 20 10
357 9c. Ratel (horiz) 20 10
358 10c. Cheetah (horiz) 30 10
358a 11c. Blue wildebeest 40 30
358b 12c. African buffalo (horiz) 70 1·50
358c 14c. Caracal (horiz) 3·00 2·25
359 15c. Hippopotamus (horiz) 30 10
359b 16c. Warthog (horiz) 1·75 1·75
360 20c. Eland (horiz) 30 10
361 25c. Black rhinoceros (horiz) 50 20
362 30c. Lion (horiz) 50 20
363 50c. Giraffe 50 30
364 1r. Leopard 50 55
365 2r. African elephant 50 90

1980. Wildlife.
366 **101** 1c. brown 20 20
367 – 2c. blue 20 20
368 – 5c. green 30 30
DESIGNS: 2c. Savanna monkey; 5c. Chacma baboon.

102 Von Bach

1980. Water Conservation. Dams. Mult.
369 5c. Type **102** 10 10
370 10c. Swakoppoort 10 10
371 15c. Naute 15 20
372 20c. Hardap 15 25

103 View of Fish River Canyon

1981. Fish River Canyon.
373 – 5c. multicoloured 10 10
374 – 15c. multicoloured 15 20
375 – 20c. multicoloured 20 25
376 **103** 25c. multicoloured 20 30
DESIGNS: 5c. to 20c. Various views of Canyon.

104 "Aloe erinacea"

1981. Aloes. Multicoloured.
377 5c. Type **104** 15 10
378 15c. "Aloe viridiflora" 35 25
379 20c. "Aloe pearsonii" 40 25
380 25c. "Aloe littoralis" 50 30

105 Paul Weiss-Haus

1981. Historic Buildings of Luderitz.
381 5c. Type **105** 10 10
382 15c. Deutsche Afrika Bank 15 20
383 20c. Schroederhaus 20 30
384 25c. Altes Postamt 20 35
MS385 125 × 90 mm. Nos. 381/4 65 1·00

106 Salt Pan

1981. Salt Industry. Multicoloured.
386 5c. Type **106** 10 10
387 15c. Dumping and washing 20 20
388 20c. Loading by conveyor 25 30
389 25c. Dispatch to refinery 30 35

107 Kalahari Starred Tortoise ("Psammobates oculifer")

1982. Tortoises. Multicoloured.
390 5c. Type **107** 15 10
391 15c. Leopard tortoise ("Geochelone pardalis") 25 25
392 20c. Angulate tortoise ("Chersina angulata") 30 35
393 25c. Speckled padloper ("Homopus signatus") 40 45

108 Mythical Sea-monster

1982. Discoveries of South West Africa (1st series). Multicoloured.
394 15c. Type **108** 20 20
395 20c. Bartolomeu Dias and map of Africa showing voyage 40 30
396 25c. Dias' caravel 65 40
397 30c. Dias erecting commemorative cross, Angra das Voltas, 25 July 1488 70 45
See also Nos. 455/8.

109 Brandberg

1982. Mountains of South West Africa. Mult.
398 6c. Type **109** 10 10
399 15c. Omatako 20 20
400 20c. Die Nadel 25 30
401 25c. Spitzkuppe 30 35

110 Otjikaeva Headdress of Herero Woman

1982. Traditional Headdresses of South West Africa (1st series). Multicoloured.
402 6c. Type **110** 10 10
403 15c. Ekori headdress of Himba 20 35
404 20c. Oshikoma hair-piece and iipanda plaits of Ngandjera 25 45
405 25c. Omhatela headdress of Kwanyama 25 60
See also Nos. 427/30.

111 Fort Vogelsang

1983. Centenary of Luderitz.
406 **111** 6c. black and red 10 10
407 – 20c. black and brown 15 20
408 – 25c. black and brown 20 25
409 – 30c. black and purple 20 30
410 – 40c. black and green 25 50
DESIGNS—VERT (23 × 29 mm): 20c. Chief Joseph Fredericks; 30c. Heinrich Vogelsang (founder); 40c. Adolf Luderitz (colonial promoter). HORIZ (as T **111**): 25c. Angra Pequena.

112 Searching for Diamonds, Kolmanskop, 1908

1983. 75th Anniv of Discovery of Diamonds.
411 **112** 10c. deep brown & brown 15 15
412 – 20c. red and brown 30 40
413 – 25c. blue and brown 35 45
414 – 40c. black and brown 55 85
DESIGNS—HORIZ (34 × 19 mm): 20c. Digging for diamonds, Kolmanskop, 1908. VERT (19 × 26 mm): 25c. Sir Ernest Oppenheimer (industrialist); 40c. August Stauch (prospector).

113 "Common Zebras drinking" (J. van Ellinckhuijzen)

1983. Painters of South West Africa. Mult.
415 10c. Type **113** 15 15
416 20c. "Rossing Mountain" (H. Henckert) 20 30
417 25c. "Stampeding African Buffalo" (F. Krampe) 20 35
418 40c. "Erongo Mountains" (J. Blatt) 30 55

114 The Rock Lobster

1983. The Lobster Industry. Multicoloured.
419 10c. Type **114** 15 15
420 20c. Mother ship and fishing dinghies 20 30
421 25c. Netting lobsters from a dinghy 20 35
422 40c. Packing lobsters 30 55

115 Hohenzollern House

1984. Historic Buildings of Swakopmund.
423 **115** 10c. black and brown 15 15
424 – 20c. black and blue 20 25
425 – 25c. black and green 20 30
426 – 30c. black and brown 25 30
DESIGNS: 20c. Railway Station; 25c. Imperial District Bureau; 30c. Ritterburg.

1984. Traditional Headdresses of South West Africa (2nd series). As T **110**. Multicoloured.
427 11c. Eendjushi headdress of Kwambi 15 15
428 20c. Bushman woman 20 25
429 25c. Omulenda headdress of Kwaluudhi 20 35
430 30c. Mbukushu women 20 35

116 Map and German Flag

1984. Cent of German Colonization. Mult.
431 11c. Type **116** 25 15
432 25c. Raising the German flag, 1884 50 50
433 30c. German Protectorate boundary marker 50 60
434 45c. "Elizabeth" and "Leipzig" (German corvettes) 1·25 1·75

117 Sweet Thorn

118 Head of Ostrich

1984. Spring in South West Africa. Mult.
435 11c. Type **117** 15 15
436 25c. Camel thorn 20 35
437 30c. Hook thorn 20 35
438 45c. Candle-pod acacia 25 50

1985. Ostriches. Multicoloured.
439 11c. Type **118** 40 10
440 25c. Ostrich on eggs 60 30
441 30c. Newly-hatched chick and eggs 70 50
442 50c. Mating dance 90 75

119 Kaiserstrasse

1985. Historic Buildings of Windhoek.
443 **119** 12c. black and brown 15 10
444 – 25c. black and green 20 25
445 – 30c. black and brown 20 30
446 – 50c. black and brown 25 70
DESIGNS: 25c. Turnhalle; 30c. Old Supreme Court Building; 50c. Railway Station.

120 Zwilling Locomotive

1985. Narrow-gauge Railway Locomotives. Mult.
447 12c. Type **120** 25 10
448 25c. Feldspur side-tank locomotive 45 25
449 30c. Jung and Henschel side-tank locomotive 40 35
450 50c. Henschel Hd locomotive 60 60

121 Lidumu-dumu (keyboard instrument)

1985. Traditional Musical Instruments. Mult.
451 12c. Type **121** 10 10
452 25c. Ngoma (drum) 15 20
453 30c. Okambulumbumbwa (stringed instrument) 20 25
454 50c. //Gwashi (stringed instrument) 25 35

122 Erecting Commemorative Pillar at Cape Cross, 1486

1986. Discoverers of South West Africa (2nd series). Diogo Cao.
455 **122** 12c. black, grey and green 25 10
456 – 20c. black, grey and brown 40 25
457 – 25c. black, grey and blue 60 35
458 – 30c. black, grey and purple 70 60
DESIGNS: 20c. Diogo Cao's coat of arms; 25c. Caravel; 30c. Diogo Cao.

123 Ameib, Erongo Mountains

1986. Rock Formations. Multicoloured.
459 14c. Type **123** 35 15
460 20c. Vingerklip, near Outjo 40 25
461 25c. Petrified sand dunes, Kuiseb River 45 40
462 30c. Orgelpfeifen, Twyfelfontein 50 55

124 Model wearing Swakara Coat

125 Pirogue, Lake Liambezi

1986. Karakul Industry. Multicoloured.
463 14c. Type **124** 15 15
464 20c. Weaving karakul wool carpet 25 30

465 25c. Flock of karakul ewes in veld 25 45
466 30c. Karakul rams 30 60

1986. Life in the Caprivi Strip. Mult.
467 14c. Type **125** 30 15
468 20c. Ploughing with oxen . . 50 80
469 25c. Settlement in Eastern Caprivi . . . . 60 1·25
470 30c. Map of Caprivi Strip . . 1·00 2·00

126 "Gobabis Mission Station", 1863

1987. Paintings by Thomas Baines. Multicoloured.
471 14c. Type **126** 30 15
472 20c. "Outspan at Koobie", 1861 . . . . 55 80
473 25c. "Outspan under Oomahaama Tree", 1862 70 1·50
474 30c. "Swakop River", 1861 80 2·25

127 "Garreta nitens" (beetle)

1987. Useful Insects. Multicoloured.
475 16c. Type **127** 40 15
476 20c. "Alcimus stenurus" (fly) 60 80
477 25c. "Anthophora caerulea" (bee) . . . . 75 1·50
478 30c. "Hemiempusa capensis" (mantid) . . . . 1·10 2·00

128 Okaukuejo

1987. Tourist Camps. Multicoloured.
479 16c. Type **128** 25 15
480 20c. Daan Viljoen 40 55
481 25c. Ai-Ais . . . . 45 1·25
482 30c. Hardap . . . . 50 1·40

129 Wreck of "Hope" (Dutch whaling schooner, 1804) **130** Bartolomeu Dias

1987. Shipwrecks. Multicoloured.
483 16c. Type **129** 50 15
484 30c. "Tilly" (brig), 1885 . . . 75 80
485 40c. "Eduard Bohlen" (steamer), 1909 . . . . . 1·00 2·00
486 50c. "Dunedin Star" (liner), 1942 . . . . 1·25 2·50

1988. 500th Anniv of Discovery of Cape of Good Hope by Bartolomeu Dias. Multicoloured.
487 16c. Type **130** 35 15
488 30c. Caravel 70 55
489 40c. Map of South West Africa, c. 1502 . . . . . . 80 70
490 50c. King Joao II of Portugal 80 75

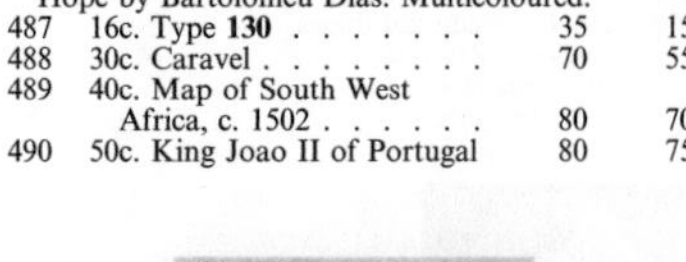

131 Sossusvlei

1988. Landmarks of South West Africa. Multicoloured.
491 16c. Type **131** 30 15
492 30c. Sesriem Canyon 60 65
493 40c. Hoaruseb "clay castles" 70 1·25
494 50c. Hoba meteorite . . . . 80 1·50

132 First Postal Agency, Otyimbingue, 1888

1988. Centenary of Postal Service in South West Africa. Multicoloured.
495 16c. Type **132** 30 15
496 30c. Post Office, Windhoek, 1904 . . . . 60 55
497 40c. Mail-runner and map . . 70 75
498 50c. Camel mail, 1904 . . . 80 1·00

133 Herero Chat **134** Dr. C. H. Hahn and Gross-Barmen Mission

1988. Birds of South West Africa. Mult.
499 16c. Type **133** 80 25
500 30c. Gray's lark . . . . . . 1·25 80
501 40c. Ruppell's bustard . . . 1·40 1·25
502 50c. Monteiro's hornbill . . . 1·40 1·40

1989. Missionaries. Multicoloured.
503 16c. Type **134** 20 10
504 30c. Revd. J. G. Kronlein and Berseba Mission . . . 35 60
505 40c. Revd. F. H. Kleinschmidt and Rehoboth Mission 40 70
506 50c. Revd. J. H. Schmelen and Bethanien Mission . . 40 85

135 Beech Commuter 1900

1989. 75th Anniv of Aviation in South West Africa. Multicoloured.
507 18c. Type **135** 55 20
508 30c. Ryan Navion 90 60
509 40c. Junkers F-13 . . . . . 1·00 65
510 50c. Pfalz Otto biplane . . . 1·25 85

136 Barchan Dunes

1989. Namib Desert Sand Dunes. Mult.
511 18c. Type **136** 20 15
512 30c. Star dunes (36 × 20 mm) 30 40
513 40c. Transverse dunes 35 60
514 50c. Crescentic dunes (36 × 20 mm) 40 80

137 Ballot Box and Outline Map of South West Africa

1989. South West Africa Constitutional Election.
515 **137** 18c. brown and orange . . . 15 15
516 35c. blue and green . . . 25 40
517 45c. purple and yellow . . 35 60
518 60c. green and ochre . . . 45 80

138 Gypsum **140** Arrow Poison

139 Oranjemund Alluvial Diamond Field

1989. Minerals. Multicoloured.
519 1c. Type **138** 15 30
520 2c. Fluorite 20 30
521 5c. Mimetite 30 30
522 7c. Cuprite 45 45
523 10c. Azurite 50 20
524 18c. Boltwoodite 70 10
525 20c. Dioptase 75 15
526 25c. Type **139** . . . . 1·25 15
527 30c. Tsumeb lead and copper complex . . . . 1·00 20
528 35c. Rosh Pinah zinc mine 1·00 20
529 40c. Diamonds . . . . 1·25 30
530 45c. Wulfenite . . . . 1·00 30
531 50c. Uis tin mine . . . . . . 1·25 40
532 1r. Rossing uranium mine . . 1·75 1·00
533 2r. Gold . . . . 2·75 2·00

The 1, 2, 5, 7, 10, 18, 20, 40, 45c. and 2r. are vert as T **138**, and the remainder horiz as T **139**.

1990. Flora. Multicoloured.
534 18c. Type **140** 20 10
535 35c. Baobab flower 35 40
536 45c. Sausage tree flowers . . 40 50
537 60c. Devil's claw 45 90

OFFICIAL STAMPS

Prices are for pairs mint and for single stamps used.

1927. Pictorial and portrait (2d.) stamps alternately optd **OFFICIAL South West Africa.** or **OFFISIEEL Suidwes Afrika.**
O1 **6** ½d. black and green . . . . 75·00 30·00
O2 **7** 1d. black and red . . . . . 75·00 30·00
O3 **2** 2d. purple . . . . £170 45·00
O4 **8** 6d. green and orange . . . . 95·00 30·00

1929. Pictorial stamps alternately optd **OFFICIAL S.W.A.** or **OFFISIEEL S.W.A.** horizontally or vertically.
O 9 **6** ½d. black and green . . . 75 2·75
O10 1d. black and red . . . . 1·00 2·75
O11 **11** 2d. grey and purple . . . 1·00 3·25
O 8 **8** 6d. green and orange . . . 2·00 3·75

1931. Optd alternately **OFFICIAL** or **OFFISIEEL**.
O13 **12** ½d. black and green . . . 11·00 3·50
O14 – 1d. blue and red (No. 75) 1·00 3·50
O25 **27** 1½d. brown . . . . 24·00 5·00
O15 – 2d. blue and brown (No. 76) . . . . 2·25 2·25
O16 – 6d. blue and brown (No. 79) . . . . 3·50 3·25

POSTAGE DUE STAMPS

Prices for Nos. D1/46 are for pairs mint and for single stamps used.

1923. Optd **South West Africa.** or **Zuid-West Afrika.** alternately. (i) On Postage Due stamps of Transvaal.
D1 **D 1** 5d. black and violet . . . 4·00 11·00
D2 6d. black and brown . . . 17·00 11·00

(ii) On Postage Due stamps of South Africa.
D 6 **D 1** ½d. black and green . . 6·00 5·50
D 7 1d. black and pink . . . 7·00 6·00
D 8 1½d. black and brown . . 1·25 2·75
D 9 2d. black and violet . . 3·50 5·00
D12 3d. black and blue . . . 7·50 5·50
D 5 6d. black and grey . . . 27·00 13·00

1923. Optd **South West Africa.*** or **Zuidwest Afrika.**
(i) on Postage Due stamps of Transvaal.
D25 **D 1** 5d. black and violet . . 2·75 3·50
D14 6d. black and brown . . 21·00 20·00

(ii) On Postage Due stamps of South Africa.
D23 **D 1** ½d. black and green . . 3·00 6·50
D28 1d. black and pink . . . 2·00 1·60
D29 1½d. black and brown . . 4·50 6·50
D30 2d. black and violet . . 2·50 3·50
D31 3d. black and blue . . . 4·50 3·75
D20 6d. black and grey . . . 2·25 9·00

*The English overprint is the same, for the purposes of this catalogue, as that on the previous set.

1927. Optd **South West Africa.*** or **Suidwes Afrika.**
(a) On Postage Due stamps of Transvaal.
D33 **D 1** 5d. black and violet . . 19·00 23·00

(b) On Postage Due stamps of South Africa.
D39 **D 2** 1d. black and red . . . 1·00 2·25
D34 **D 1** 1½d. black and brown . . 1·00 3·50
D35 2d. black and violet . . 4·75 3·25
D37 3d. black and blue . . . 13·00 11·00
D38 6d. black and grey . . . 7·50 8·50

*The English overprint is the same, for the purposes of this catalogue, as that on Nos. D33 and D34/8 of the previous sets.

1928. Postage Due stamps of South Africa optd **S.W.A.** (a) On Nos. D4 and D16.
D40 **D 1** 3d. black and blue . . . 1·50 15·00
D41 6d. black and grey . . . 6·00 28·00

(b) On Nos. D 17 etc.
D42 **D 2** ½d. black and green . . 50 8·00
D43 1d. black and red . . . 50 3·25
D44 2d. black and mauve . . 50 4·50
D45 3d. black and blue . . . 2·25 26·00
D46 6d. black and grey . . . 1·50 20·00

D 3

1931. Size 19 × 23½ mm.
D47 **D 3** ½d. black and green . . 1·00 9·00
D48 1d. black and red . . . 1·00 1·25
D49 2d. black and violet . . 1·00 2·75
D50 3d. black and blue . . 4·25 17·00
D51 6d. black and slate . . . 13·00 27·00

1959. As Type D 3 but smaller, 17½ × 21 mm.
D55 1d. black and red . . . . . 1·50 3·00
D53 2d. black and violet . . . . 1·50 15·00
D56 3d. black and blue . . . . . 1·50 3·75

1961. As Nos. D55, etc. but values in cents.
D57 1c. black and turquoise . . . 70 3·75
D58 2c. black and red . . . . . 70 3·75
D59 4c. black and violet . . . . 70 6·00
D60 5c. black and blue . . . . . 1·00 4·25
D61 6c. black and green . . . . 1·25 6·50
D62 10c. black and yellow . . . 4·00 9·00

1972. As Type D 8 of South Africa. Inscr "S.W.A.".
D63 1c. green . . . . 75 5·00
D64 8c. blue . . . . 3·00 8·50

For subsequent issues see **NAMIBIA**.

SOUTHERN NIGERIA Pt. 1

A British possession on the west coast of Africa. In 1914 joined with Northern Nigeria to form Nigeria (q.v.).

12 pence = 1 shilling;
20 shillings = 1 pound.

1

1901.
1 **1** ½d. black and green . . . . . 1·75 2·25
2 1d. brown and red . . . . 1·40 1·50
3 2d. black and brown . . . . 3·25 3·75
4 4d. black and green . . . . 2·75 18·00
5 6d. black and purple . . . . 2·75 6·50
6 1s. green and black . . . . 8·00 26·00
7 2s.6d. black and brown . . . 45·00 80·00
8 5s. black and yellow . . . . 48·00 £110
9 10s. black and purple on yellow . . . . 90·00 £180

2 3

1903.
21 **2** ½d. black and green . . . 60 10
11 1d. black and red . . . . 1·25 70
23 2d. black and brown . . . 2·50 45
24 2½d. black and blue . . . 1·00 1·00
25 3d. brown and purple . . . 9·50 1·25
14 4d. black and green . . . 2·75 5·50
15 6d. black and purple . . . 4·25 8·00
28 1s. green and black . . . . 3·25 3·50
29 2s.6d. black and brown . . 24·00 17·00
30 5s. black and yellow . . . 40·00 75·00
19 10s. black & purple on yell 29·00 90·00
32ab £1 green and violet £170 £225

1907.
33 **2** ½d. green . . . . 2·25 20
34ab 1d. red 75 10
35 2d. grey . . . . 2·50 70
36 2½d. blue . . . . 2·25 3·75
37 3d. purple on yellow . . . 2·00 30
38 4d. black and red on yellow . . . . 2·25 80
39 6d. purple . . . . 25·00 3·25
40 1s. black on green . . . . 7·00 40
41 2s.6d. black and red on blue . . . . 5·00 1·00
42 5s. green and red on yellow 38·00 48·00
43 10s. green and red on green . . . . 65·00 95·00
44 £1 purple and black on red £190 £225

1912.
45 **3** ½d. green . . . . 2·25 10
46 1d. red . . . . 2·00 10
47 2d. grey 75 85
48 2½d. blue . . . . 2·75 2·75
49 3d. purple on yellow . . . 1·00 30
50 4d. black and red on yellow 1·25 2·00
51 6d. purple . . . . 1·25 1·25
52 1s. black on green . . . . 2·75 75
53 2s.6d. black and red on blue 8·00 32·00

54		5s. green and red on yellow	20·00	75·00
55		10s. green and red on green	45·00	90·00
56		£1 purple and black on red	£170	£225

SOUTHERN RHODESIA Pt. 1

A Br. territory in the N. part of S. Africa, S. of the Zambesi. In 1954 became part of the Central African Federation which issued its own stamps inscribed "Rhodesia and Nyasaland" (q.v.), until 1964 when it resumed issuing after the break-up of the Federation. In October 1964, Southern Rhodesia was renamed Rhodesia.

12 pence = 1 shilling;
20 shillings = 1 pound.

1

1924.

1	1	½d. green	2·00	10
2		1d. pink	1·75	10
3		1½d. brown	2·00	80
4		2d. black and grey	2·50	70
5		3d. blue	2·25	3·00
6		4d. black and red	2·50	2·75
7		6d. black and mauve	2·00	4·00
8		8d. purple and green	11·00	42·00
9		10d. blue and pink	11·00	48·00
10		1s. black and blue	5·00	6·00
11		1s.6d. black and yellow	19·00	32·00
12		2s. black and brown	17·00	17·00
13		2s.6d. black and brown	30·00	60·00
14		5s. blue and green	60·00	£140

2 King George V

3 Victoria Falls

1931.

15a	2	½d. green	65	20
16b		1d. red	50	20
16d		1½d. brown	2·50	80
17	3	2d. black and brown	4·00	1·40
18		3d. blue	10·00	11·00
19	2	4d. black and red	1·25	1·50
20		6d. black and mauve	2·25	3·00
21		8d. violet and green	1·75	3·25
21b		9d. red and green	6·00	9·00
22		10d. blue and red	7·00	2·25
23		1s. black and blue	2·00	2·50
24		1s.6d. black and yellow	10·00	17·00
25		2s. black and brown	21·00	6·50
26a		2s.6d. blue and brown	28·00	30·00
27		5s. blue and green	48·00	48·00

4

1932.

29	4	2d. green and brown	4·00	1·00
30		3d. blue	4·00	1·75

5 Victoria Falls

1935. Silver Jubilee.

31	5	1d. green and red	3·25	2·00
32		2d. green and brown	5·50	5·50
33		3d. violet and blue	5·50	10·00
34		6d. black and purple	8·00	15·00

1935. As Nos. 29/30, but inscr "POSTAGE AND REVENUE".

35a	4	2d. green and brown	2·25	10
35b		3d. blue	4·00	50

6 Victoria Falls and Railway Bridge

1937. Coronation.

36	6	1d. olive and red	60	70
37		2d. green and brown	60	1·75
38		3d. violet and blue	3·25	8·00
39		6d. black and purple	1·75	3·75

7 King George VI

10 Cecil John Rhodes (after S. P. Kendrick)

8 British South Africa Co's Arms

1937.

40	7	½d. green	50	10
41		1d. red	50	10
42		1½d. brown	1·00	30
43		4d. orange	1·50	10
44		6d. black	1·50	50
45		8d. green	2·00	2·50
46		9d. blue	1·50	70
47		10d. purple	2·25	2·75
48		1s. black and green	2·00	10
49		1s.6d. black and yellow	11·00	2·25
50		2s. black and brown	15·00	55
51		2s.6d. blue and purple	9·00	5·00
52		5s. blue and green	18·00	2·25

1940. Golden Jubilee of British South Africa Company.

53	8	½d. violet and green	10	65
54	–	1d. blue and red	10	10
55	10	1½d. black and brown	15	80
56	–	2d. green and violet	30	70
57	–	3d. black and blue	30	1·50
58	–	4d. green and brown	2·25	2·50
59	–	6d. brown and green	1·00	2·00
60	–	1s. blue and green	1·00	2·00

DESIGNS—HORIZ: 1d. Fort Salisbury, 1890; 2d. Fort Victoria; 3d. Rhodes makes peace, 1896; 1s. Queen Victoria, King George VI, Lobengula's kraal and Govt. House, Salisbury. VERT: 4d. Victoria Falls Bridge; 6d. Statue of Sir Charles Coghlan.

16 Mounted Pioneer

20 King George VI

17 Queen Elizabeth II when Princess, and Princess Margaret

1943. 50th Anniv of Occupation of Matabeleland.

61	16	2d. brown and green	20	1·00

1947. Royal Visit.

62	17	½d. black and green	30	60
63	–	1d. black and red	30	60

DESIGN: 1d. King George VI and Queen Elizabeth.

1947. Victory.

64	–	1d. red	10	10
65	20	2d. slate	10	10
66	–	3d. blue	85	1·00
67	–	6d. orange	30	1·40

PORTRAITS: 1d. Queen Elizabeth; 3d. Queen Elizabeth II when Princess; 6d. Princess Margaret.

1949. 75th Anniv of U.P.U. As T **33d/g** of St. Helena.

68		2d. green	70	20
69		3d. blue	80	3·50

23 Queen Victoria, Arms and King George VI

1950. Diamond Jubilee of S. Rhodesia.

70	23	2d. green and brown	50	1·00

24 "Medical Services"

27 "Water Supplies"

1953. Birth Centenary of Cecil Rhodes. Inscr "RHODES CENTENARY".

71	24	½d. blue and sepia	15	2·00
72	–	1d. chestnut and green	15	10
73	–	2d. green and violet	15	10
74	27	4½d. green and blue	75	2·75
75	–	1s. black and brown	3·00	1·00

DESIGNS: 1d. "Agriculture"; 2d. "Building"; 4½d. "Water Supplies"; 1s. "Transport".

No. 74 also commemorates the Diamond Jubilee of Matabeleland.

1953. Rhodes Centenary Exhibition, Bulawayo. As No. 59 of Northern Rhodesia.

76		6d. violet	30	75

30 Queen Elizabeth II

1953. Coronation.

77	30	2s.6d. red	4·75	6·00

31 Sable Antelope

33 Rhodes's Grave

43 Balancing Rocks

1953.

78	31	½d. grey and claret	30	50
79	–	1d. green and brown	30	10
80	33	2d. brown and violet	30	10
81	–	3d. brown and red	55	1·75
82	–	4d. red, green and blue	3·25	30
83	–	4½d. black and blue	2·50	4·00
84	–	6d. olive and turquoise	3·00	1·00
85	–	9d. blue and brown	3·00	4·00
86	–	1s. violet and blue	1·25	10
87	–	2s. purple and red	11·00	4·50
88	–	2s.6d. olive and brown	5·00	5·00
89	–	5s. brown and green	7·00	6·50
90	43	10s. brown and olive	9·00	21·00
91	–	£1 red and black	14·00	27·00

DESIGNS—VERT (as Type **31**): 1d Tobacco planter. (As Type **33**): 6d. Baobab tree; 5s. Basket maker. HORIZ (as Type **33**): 3d. Farm worker; 4d. Flame lily; 4½d. Victoria Falls; 9d. Lion; 1s. Zimbabwe ruins; 2s. Birchenough Bridge; 2s.6d. Kariba Gorge. (As Type **43**): £1 Coat of arms.

45 Maize

50 Flame Lily

56 Cattle

1964.

92	45	½d. yellow, green and blue	20	2·25
93	–	1d. violet and ochre	15	10
94	–	2d. yellow and violet	60	10
95	–	3d. brown and blue	20	10
96	–	4d. orange and green	30	10
97	50	6d. red, yellow and green	40	10
98	–	9d. brown, yellow and green	2·50	1·50
99	–	1s. green and ochre	3·25	30
100	–	1s.3d. red, violet and green	3·00	10
101	–	2s. blue and ochre	2·50	2·75
102	–	2s.6d. blue and red	4·00	1·00
103	56	5s. multicoloured	3·50	2·25
104	–	10s. multicoloured	11·00	6·50
105	–	£1 multicoloured	6·00	16·00

DESIGNS—As Type **45**: 1d. African buffalo; 2d. Tobacco; 3d. Greater kudu; 4d. Citrus. As Type **50**: 9d. Ansellia orchid; 1s. Emeralds; 1s.3d. Aloe; 2s. Lake Kyle; 2s.6d. Tigerfish. As Type **56**: 10s. Helmeted guineafowl; £1 Coat of arms.

Similar designs inscribed "RHODESIA" are listed under that heading.

POSTAGE DUE STAMPS

1951. Postage due stamps of Great Britain optd **SOUTHERN RHODESIA**.

D1	D 1	½d. green	3·25	16·00
D2		1d. blue	3·00	2·00
D3		2d. black	2·50	1·75
D4		3d. violet	2·75	2·75
D5		4d. blue	1·75	3·50
D6		4d. green	£190	£550
D7		1s. blue	2·50	4·00

For later issues see **RHODESIA**.

SOUTHERN YEMEN Pt. 19

PEOPLE'S REPUBLIC

Independent Republic comprising the areas formerly known as Aden, the Aden States and the South Arabian Federation.

From 30 November 1970, the country was renamed The People's Democratic Republic of Yemen.

1000 fils = 1 dinar.

1968. Stamps of South Arabian Federation optd **PEOPLE'S REPUBLIC OF SOUTHERN YEMEN** in English and Arabic.

1	2	5f. blue	10	10
2		10f. blue	10	10
3		15f. green	15	10
4		20f. green	15	15
5		25f. brown	25	15
6		30f. bistre	30	45
7		35f. brown	45	35
8		50f. red	50	45
9		65f. green	70	60
10		75f. red	70	60
11	3	100f. multicoloured	1·30	1·00
12		250f. multicoloured	2·50	2·10
13		500f. multicoloured	4·75	4·25
14		1d. multicoloured	11·00	9·25

3 National Flag across Globe

1968. Independence. Multicoloured.

15		10f. Type **3**	15	15
16		15f. Revolutionary (vert)	15	15
17		50f. Aden harbour	60	60
18		100f. Cotton-picking	1·70	1·70

4 Girl Guides

1968. Aden Girl Guides' Movement.

19	–	10f. brown and blue	50	50
20	–	25f. blue and brown	70	70
21	4	50f. multicoloured	1·40	1·40

DESIGNS—HORIZ: 10f. Guides around camp-fire. VERT: 25f. Brownies.

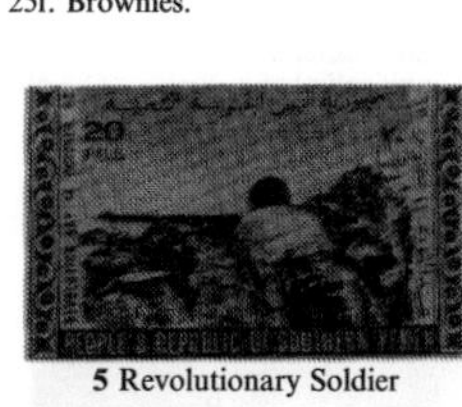

5 Revolutionary Soldier

1968. Revolution Day.

22	5	20f. brown and blue	25	25
23	–	30f. brown and green	45	45
24	–	100f. red and yellow	1·20	1·20

DESIGNS—HORIZ: 30f. Radfan Mountains ("where first martyr fell"). VERT: 100f. Open book and torch ("Freedom, Socialism and Unity").

6 Sculptured Plaque "Assyrian influence")

1968. Antiquities.
25 – 5f. yellow and green 10 10
26 – 35f. blue and purple 50 50
27 **6** 50f. buff and blue . . . . . 1·20 95
28 – 65f. green and purple . . . . 1·40 1·20
DESIGNS—VERT: 5f. King Yusdqil Far'am of Ausan (statue); 35f. Sculptured figure ("African-inspired"). HORIZ: 65f. Bull's head ("Moon God").

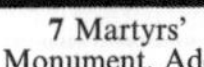

7 Martyrs' Monument, Aden

8 Albert Thomas Memorial, Geneva

1969. Martyrs' Day.
29 **7** 15f. multicoloured 15 15
30 35f. multicoloured 45 45
31 100f. multicoloured . . . . . 1·30 1·10

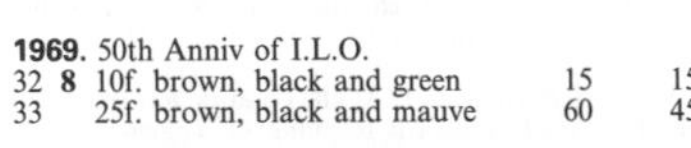

1969. 50th Anniv of I.L.O.
32 **8** 10f. brown, black and green 15 15
33 25f. brown, black and mauve 60 45

9 Teacher and Class

1969. International Literacy Day.
34 **9** 35f. multicoloured 60 45
35 100f. multicoloured . . . . . 1·50 1·30

10 Mahatma Gandhi

1969. Birth Centenary of Mahatma Gandhi.
36 **10** 35f. purple and blue . . . . 1·70 85

11 Yemeni Family

1969. Family Day.
37 **11** 25f. multicoloured 60 45
38 75f. multicoloured . . . . . 1·50 1·10

12 U.N. Headquarters, New York

1969. United Nations Day.
39 **12** 20f. multicoloured 50 35
40 65f. multicoloured . . . . . 1·40 85

13 Map and Flag

1969. 2nd Anniv of Independence. Multicoloured.
41 15f. Type **13** 25 25
42 35f. Type **13** 50 45
43 40f. Bulldozers (37 × 37 mm) 60 50
44 50f. As No. 43 . . . . 1·00 70

14 Arab League Flag, Emblem and Map

1970. 25th Anniv of Arab League.
45 **14** 35f. multicoloured 70 45

15 Lenin

16 Palestinian Guerrilla

1970. Birth Centenary of Lenin.
46 **15** 75f. multicoloured . . . . . 1·50 1·00

1970. Palestine Day. Multicoloured.
47 15f. Type **16** 15 15
48 35f. Guerrilla and attack on airliner 50 45
49 50f. Guerrillas and Palestinan flag (horiz) . . . . 1·00 70

17 New Headquarters Building, Berne

1970. Inauguration of New U.P.U. Headquarters Building, Berne.
50 **17** 15f. green and orange . . . 70 25
51 65f. red and buff . . . . . 1·20 75

18 Girl with Pitcher

1970. National Costumes. Multicoloured.
52 10f. Type **18** 35 15
53 15f. Woman in veil 45 35
54 20f. Girl in burnous 60 45
55 50f. Three Yemeni men . . . 1·30 60

19 Dromedary and Calf

1970. Fauna. Multicoloured.
56 15f. Type **19** 45 25
57 25f. Goats 70 45
58 35f. Arabian oryx and kid . . 1·40 85
59 65f. Socotran dwarf cows . . 2·20 1·40

20 Torch and Flags

1970. 7th Revolution Day. Multicoloured.
60 25f. Type **20** 45 25
61 35f. National Front Headquarters (57 × 27 mm) 70 60
62 50f. Farmer and soldier (42 × 25 mm) . . . . 2·10 1·50

21 U.N. H.Q., New York, and Emblem

1970. 25th Anniv of United Nations.
63 **21** 10f. orange and blue 50 15
64 65f. mauve and blue . . . . 1·60 1·00

For later issues see **YEMEN PEOPLE'S DEMOCRATIC REPUBLIC**.

SPAIN Pt. 9

A kingdom in south-west Europe; a republic between 1873 and 1874, and from 1931 until 1939.

1850. $8\frac{1}{2}$ (later 8) cuartos = 1 real.
1866. 80 cuartos = 100 centimos de escudo = 1 escudo.
1867. 1000 milesimas = 100 centimos de escudo = 80 cuartos = 1 escudo.
1872. 100 centimos = 1 peseta.
2002. 100 cents = 1 euro.

1 Queen Isabella II

2 Queen Isabella II

3 Queen Isabella II

1850. Imperf.
2 **1** 6c. black . . . . £375 14·00
3 **2** 12c. lilac £2000 £250
4 5r. red £2250 £250
5 6r. blue £2750 £700
6 10r. green £4000 £2000

1851. Imperf.
9 **3** 6c. black . . . . £225 2·75
10 12c. lilac £3750 £160
11 2r. red £17000 £9500
12 5r. pink £2250 £225
13 6r. blue £3500 £900
14 10r. green £2500 £450

4

5

7 Arms of Castile and Leon

1852. Imperf.
16 **4** 6c. pink . . . . £325 2·40
17 12c. purple £1700 £130
18 2r. red £14000 £4750
19 5r. green £1900 £110
20 6r. blue £3000 £450

1853. Imperf.
22 **5** 6c. red . . . . £375 1·90
23 12c. purple £1900 £110
24 2r. red £9500 £3000
25 5r. green £2000 £110
26 6r. blue £2750 £375

1854. Imperf.
32 **7** 2c. green £1800 £450
33 4c. red . . . . £350 1·90
34 6c. red . . . . £300 1·30
35 1r. blue £3000 £300
36 2r. red . . . . £1400 95·00
37 5r. green . . . . £1300 95·00
38 6r. blue £2250 £275

9

12

13

1855. Imperf.
54 **9** 2c. green . . . . £450 37·00
55a 4c. red . . . . 3·75 25
61 1r. blue . . . . 18·00 21·00
57 2r. purple . . . . 60·00 21·00

1860. Imperf.
63 **12** 2c. green on green . . . . . £300 18·00
64 4c. orange on green . . . . 35·00 65
65 12c. red on buff . . . . . . £300 11·50
66 19c. brown on brown . . . £2500 £1300
67 1r. blue on green . . . . . £250 11·00
68 2r. lilac on lilac . . . . . . £325 9·50

1862. Imperf.
69a **13** 2c. blue on yellow . . . . 32·00 9·50
70 4c. brown on brown . . . 2·00 55
70b 4c. brown on white . . . . 19·00 4·75
71 12c. blue on pink . . . . 39·00 7·75
72 19c. red on lilac £160 £200
72a 19c. red on white £190 £225
73a 1r. brown on yellow . . . 55·00 18·00
74 2r. green on pink . . . . 32·00 11·50

14

15

16

1864. Imperf.
75 **14** 2c. blue on lilac . . . . . 45·00 17·00
75b 2c. blue on white . . . . . 65·00 25·00
76b 4c. red on red . . . . . . 2·00 65
76c 4c. pink on white . . . . 15·00 11·50
77a 12c. green on pink . . . . 38·00 11·50
78 19c. lilac on lilac £170 £180
79 1r. brown on green . . . . £170 75·00
80 2r. blue on pink . . . . . 40·00 12·00
80b 2r. blue on white . . . . . 75·00 17·00

1865. Imperf.
81a **15** 2c. red . . . . £275 29·00
82 12c. pink and blue . . . . £350 18·00
83 19c. pink and brown . . . £1300 £650
84 1r. green . . . . £375 55·00
85 2r. mauve . . . . £350 29·00
85c 2r. red . . . . £375 65·00
85e 2r. yellow . . . . £375 34·00

1865. Perf.
86 **15** 2c. red £425 £110
87 4c. blue . . . . 32·00 65
88 12c. pink and blue . . . . £500 50·00
89 19c. pink and brown . . . £3250 £2000
90 1r. green £1500 £450
91 2r. lilac £1000 £200
91b 2r. orange £1200 £275

1866. Perf.
92 **16** 2c. pink . . . . £225 27·00
93a 4c. blue . . . . 37·00 65
94a 12c. orange . . . . £200 11·00
95 19c. brown £950 £375
96 10c. de e. green . . . . . £250 23·00
97 20c. de e. lilac . . . . . . £170 18·00

1866. As T **14**, but dated "1866", and perf.
98 20c. de e. lilac . . . . £950 65·00

19

25

26

1867. Inscr "CORREOS DE ESPANA". Various frames.
99a **19** 2c. brown . . . . £375 39·00
100 4c. blue . . . . 21·00 85
101a 12c. orange . . . . £180 6·75
102 19c. pink £1200 £350
150 19c. brown £2000 £450
103 10c. de e. green . . . . . £225 20·00
104 20c. de e. lilac . . . . . £100 8·75

1867. Various frames.
105 **25** 5m. green . . . . 37·00 14·50
106 10m. brown . . . . . . 37·00 14·50
107 **26** 25m. pink and blue . . . £200 21·00
145 25m. blue . . . . £225 14·00
108 50m. brown . . . . . . 17·00 65
146a **19** 50m. purple . . . . . . 21·00 50
147 100m. brown . . . . . . £450 65·00
148 200m. green . . . . . . £160 11·00

1868. Various stamps optd **HABILITADO POR LA NACION**.
109 **25** 5m. green . . . . 18·00 6·25
110 10m. brown . . . . 10·00 4·25
111 **26** 25m. pink and blue . . . . 32·00 12·00
151 25m. blue . . . . 29·00 10·00
112 50m. brown . . . . 8·00 4·50
152 **19** 50m. purple . . . . 8·50 3·25
153 100m. brown . . . . 65·00 29·00
154 200m. green . . . . 24·00 10·00
113 10c. de e. green . . . . . 31·00 13·00
114 20c. de e. lilac . . . . . 23·00 7·75
115 12c. orange . . . . 33·00 8·50
116 19c. pink £450 £130
156 19c. brown £650 £180

36 38a 38

1870.

No.	Type	Description	Mint	Used
172	36	1m. brown on buff	7·00	7·75
173		2m. black on buff	8·75	9·50
174		4m. brown	18·00	14·00
175		10m. red	19·00	7·00
176a		25m. mauve	60·00	7·00
177a		50m. blue	11·50	30
178b		100m. brown	32·00	6·00
179		200m. brown	32·00	6·00
180		400m. green	£275	26·00
181		12c. red	£250	7·75
182		19c. green	£350	£200
183a		1e.60m. lilac	£1400	£900
184		2e. blue	£1300	£550

1872. Imperf.

No.	Type	Description	Mint	Used
185	38a	¼c. blue	2·00	2·00
186	38	¼c. green	1·20	1·20
187	38a	¼c. green	15	15

1872. As T **25**, but currency in centavos de peseta and bottom panel inscr "COMUNICS".

No.	Type	Description	Mint	Used
192	25	2c. lilac	20·00	14·00
193		5c. green	£150	70·00

40 King Amadeo

41

42 Allegorical Figure of Peace

1872.

No.	Type	Description	Mint	Used
194	40	5c. pink	21·00	6·75
195b		6c. blue	£130	48·00
196		10c. lilac	£300	£250
197		10c. blue	6·00	30
199		12c. lilac	14·00	1·80
200		20c. lilac	£120	65·00
201		25c. brown	47·00	7·75
202		40c. brown	60·00	7·75
203		50c. green	90·00	8·75
204	41	1p. lilac	90·00	44·00
205		4p. brown	£500	£450
206		10p. green	£1900	£2000

1873.

No.	Type	Description	Mint	Used
207	42	2c. orange	14·00	7·00
208		5c. pink	34·00	7·00
209		10c. green	7·75	30
210		20c. black	95·00	30·00
211		25c. brown	33·00	7·00
212		40c. purple	37·00	7·00
213		50c. blue	14·00	7·00
214a		1p. lilac	48·00	33·00
215		4p. brown	£600	£450
216		10p. purple	£2000	£2000

43 Allegorical Figure of Justice

44

45 King Alfonso XII

1874.

No.	Type	Description	Mint	Used
217	43	2c. yellow	21·00	9·50
218a		5c. mauve	33·00	7·75
219		10c. blue	11·50	30
220		20c. green	£160	47·00
221		25c. brown	33·00	7·75
222a		40c. mauve	£375	8·75
223		50c. orange	£120	8·75
224		1p. green	85·00	42·00
225		4p. red	£700	£450
226		10p. black	£2750	£2000

1874.

No.	Type	Description	Mint	Used
227	44	10c. brown	21·00	65

1875.

No.	Type	Description	Mint	Used
228	45	2c. brown	18·00	9·50
229		5c. lilac	65·00	11·00
230		10c. blue	7·75	30
231		20c. brown	£250	£120
232		25c. pink	55·00	6·75
233		40c. brown	£100	34·00
234		50c. mauve	£160	30·00
235		1p. black	£170	75·00
236		4p. green	£450	£450
237		10p. blue	£1400	£1500

46 King Alfonso XII

48

49

1876.

No.	Type	Description	Mint	Used
238	46	5c. brown	11·00	3·00
239		10c. blue	3·25	30
240		20c. green	19·00	14·00
241		25c. brown	7·00	4·50
242		40c. brown	70·00	90·00
250		50c. green	13·50	5·75
244		1p. blue	19·00	8·75
245		4p. purple	50·00	60·00
246		10p. red	£120	£130

1878.

No.	Type	Description	Mint	Used
253	48	2c. mauve	33·00	11·00
254a		5c. yellow	38·00	11·00
255		10c. brown	7·00	40
256		20c. black	£160	£120
257		25c. green	20·00	2·10
258		40c. brown	£150	£140
259		50c. green	85·00	8·75
260		1p. grey	70·00	18·00
261		4p. violet	£190	£120
262a		10p. blue	£375	£375

1879.

No.	Type	Description	Mint	Used
263	49	2c. black	7·75	3·50
264		5c. green	11·00	90
265		10c. pink	10·50	30
266		20c. brown	£110	14·50
267		25c. grey	13·50	30
268		40c. brown	25·00	4·50
269b		50c. yellow	£100	4·50
270		1p. red	£120	1·80
271		4p. grey	£650	33·00
272		10p. bistre	£1600	£200

50 King Alfonso XII

51 King Alfonso XIII

52

1882.

No.	Type	Description	Mint	Used
273	50	15c. pink	7·50	15
273b		15c. yellow	60·00	1·30
274		30c. mauve	£275	5·00
275		75c. lilac	£250	5·00

1889.

No.	Type	Description	Mint	Used
276	51	2c. green	4·50	30
289		2c. black	25·00	5·25
277		5c. blue	7·75	15
290		5c. green	90·00	1·00
278		10c. brown	12·50	15
291		10c. red	£170	3·25
279		15c. brown	3·25	15
280		20c. green	32·00	3·25
281		25c. blue	13·50	15
282		30c. grey	50·00	3·50
283		40c. brown	50·00	2·10
284		50c. red	50·00	1·50
285		75c. orange	£180	3·25
286		1p. purple	38·00	30
287		4p. red	£550	37·00
288		10p. red	£850	90·00

For 15c. yellow see No. O289.

1900.

No.	Type	Description	Mint	Used
292a	52	2c. brown	3·25	15
293b		5c. green	5·75	15
294		10c. red	8·25	15
295		15c. black	14·50	15
296		15c. mauve	11·00	15
297		15c. violet	5·75	15
298		20c. black	34·00	2·30
299		25c. blue	5·50	15
300		30c. green	34·00	30
301		40c. bistre	£120	4·25
302		40c. pink	£275	3·50
303		50c. blue	34·00	50
304		1p. purple	32·00	50
305		4p. purple	£250	18·00
306		10p. orange	£250	70·00

54 Quixote setting out

1905. Tercentenary of Publication of Cervantes' "Don Quixote".

No.	Type	Description	Mint	Used
307	54	5c. green	1·30	1·00
308	–	10c. red	2·50	1·50
309	–	15c. violet	2·50	1·50
310	–	25c. blue	7·00	3·25
311	–	30c. green	42·00	7·75
312	–	40c. red	90·00	28·00
313	–	50c. grey	19·00	6·25
314	–	1p. red	£300	80·00
315	–	4p. purple	£110	80·00
316	–	10p. orange	£180	£140

DESIGNS: 10c. Quixote attacking windmill; 15c. Meeting country girls; 25c. Sancho Panza tossed in a blanket; 30c. Don Quixote knighted by innkeeper; 40c. Tilting at the flock of sheep; 50c. On the wooden horse; 1p. Adventure with lions; 4p. In the bullock-cart; 10p. The enchanted lady.

64

66

67 G.P.O., Madrid

1909.

No.	Type	Description	Mint	Used
344	64	2c. brown	65	65
330		5c. green	1·50	15
331		10c. red	1·90	15
332		15c. violet	9·50	15
343		15c. yellow	4·50	15
334		20c. green	55·00	70
335		20c. violet	39·00	15
336		25c. blue	3·75	15
337		30c. green	9·50	15
338		40c. pink	14·50	55
339a		50c. blue	12·50	30
340		1p. red	33·00	30
341		4p. purple	90·00	11·00
342		10p. orange	£110	21·00

1920. Air. Optd **CORREO AEREO**.

No.	Type	Description	Mint	Used
353	64	5c. green	1·30	90
354		10c. red	1·90	1·30
355		25c. blue	2·75	2·50
356		50c. blue	12·00	7·00
357		1p. red	38·00	29·00

1920. Imperf.

No.	Type	Description	Mint	Used
358	66	1c. green	20	20

1920. U.P.U. Congress, Madrid.

No.	Type	Description	Mint	Used
361	67	1c. black and green	15	15
362		2c. black and brown	15	15
363		5c. black and green	1·00	85
364		10c. black and red	1·00	85
365		15c. black and yellow	1·70	1·30
366		20c. black and violet	1·90	1·30
367		25c. black and blue	2·50	2·50
368		30c. black and green	7·00	3·75
369		40c. black and red	27·00	6·75
370		50c. black and blue	32·00	19·00
371		1p. black and pink	32·00	15·00
372		4p. black and brown	£100	75·00
373		10p. black and orange	£200	£160

68

69

1922.

No.	Type	Description	Mint	Used
374	68	2c. green	90	15
375		5c. purple	4·25	15
376		5c. red	1·90	15
377		10c. red	1·90	95
378a		10c. green	1·80	15
380		15c. blue	7·75	15
382		20c. violet	4·25	15
383a		25c. red	4·25	15
387		30c. brown	14·00	15
388		40c. blue	4·50	15
389		50c. orange	19·00	15
391	69	1p. grey	18·00	15
392		4p. red	85·00	3·75
393		10p. brown	33·00	14·00

70 Princesses Maria Cristina and Beatriz

71 King Alfonso XIII

1926. Red Cross.

No.	Type	Description	Mint	Used
394	70	1c. black	2·00	2·00
395	–	2c. blue	2·00	2·00
396	–	5c. purple	4·50	4·50
397	–	10c. green	4·00	4·00
398	70	15c. blue	1·50	1·50
399	–	20c. violet	1·50	1·50
400	71	25c. red	25	25
401	70	30c. green	38·00	38·00
402	–	40c. blue	23·00	23·00
403	–	50c. red	21·00	21·00
404	–	1p. grey	1·50	1·50
405	–	4p. red	1·30	1·30
406	71	10p. brown	1·30	1·30

DESIGNS—VERT: 2, 50c. Queen Victoria Eugenie as nurse; 5, 40c., 4p. Queen Victoria Eugenie; 10, 20c., 1p. Prince of the Asturias.

75 CASA-built Dornier Do-J Wal Flying Boat "Plus Ultra"

76 Route Map and Gallarza and Loriga's Breguet 19A2 Biplane

1926. Air. Red Cross and Trans-Atlantic and Madrid-Manila Flights.

No.	Type	Description	Mint	Used
407	75	5c. violet and black	1·70	1·70
408		10c. black and blue	2·10	2·10
409	76	15c. blue and red	30	30
410		20c. red and green	30	30
411	75	25c. black and red	30	30
412	76	30c. brown and blue	30	30
413		40c. green and brown	30	30
414	75	50c. black and red	30	30
415		1p. green and black	2·50	2·50
416	76	4p. red and yellow	95·00	95·00

1927. 25th Anniv of Coronation. Red Cross stamps of 1926 variously optd or surch **17-V 1902 17-V 1927 A XIII** or **17-V-1902 17-V-1927 ALFONSO XIII** or **17 MAYO 17 1902 1927 ALFONSO XIII** with ornaments. (a) Postage stamps of Spain optd only.

No.	Type	Description	Mint	Used
417	70	1c. black	5·50	5·50
418	–	2c. blue	10·50	10·50
419	–	5c. purple	2·75	2·75
420	–	10c. green	65·00	65·00
421	70	15c. blue	1·70	1·70
422	–	20c. violet	3·75	3·75
423	71	25c. red	65	65
424	70	30c. green	1·00	1·00
425	–	40c. blue	1·00	1·00
426	–	50c. red	1·00	1·00
427	–	1p. grey	1·70	1·70
428	–	4p. red	10·00	10·00
429	71	10p. brown	38·00	38·00

(b) Postage stamps of Spain also surch with new value.

No.	Type	Description	Mint	Used
430	–	3c. on 2c. blue	9·25	9·25
431	–	4c. on 2c. blue	9·25	9·25
432	71	10c. on 25c. red	45	45
433		25c. on 25c. red	45	45
434	–	55c. on 2c. blue	85	85
435	–	55c. on 10c. green	55·00	55·00
436	–	55c. on 20c. violet	55·00	55·00
437	70	75c. on 15c. blue	65	65
438		75c. on 30c. green	£190	£190
439	–	80c. on 5c. purple	48·00	48·00
440	–	2p. on 40c. blue	85	85
441	–	2p. on 1p. grey	85	85
442	–	5p. on 50c. red	1·70	1·70
443	–	5p. on 4p. red	2·40	2·40
444	71	10p. on 10p. brown	21·00	21·00

(c) Air stamps of Spain optd only.

No.	Type	Description	Mint	Used
445	75	5c. violet and black	1·50	1·50
446		10c. black and blue	3·25	3·25
447	76	15c. blue and red	30	30
448		20c. red and green	30	30
449	75	25c. black and red	30	30
450	76	30c. brown and blue	30	30
451		40c. green and brown	30	30
452	75	50c. black and red	30	30
453		1p. green and black	2·75	2·75
454	76	4p. red and yellow	£120	£120

(d) Air stamps of Spain also surch with new value.

No.	Type	Description	Mint	Used
455	75	75c. on 5c. violet and black	5·00	5·00
456		75c. on 10c. black and blue	23·00	23·00
457		75c. on 25c. black and red	44·00	44·00
458		75c. on 50c. black and red	18·00	18·00

(e) Nos. 24/5 of Spanish Post Offices in Tangier.

No.	Type	Description	Mint	Used
460		1p. on 10p. violet	£100	£100
461		4p. bistre	38·00	38·00

(f) Nos. 122/3 of Spanish Morocco.

No.	Type	Description	Mint	Used
462		55c. on 4p. bistre	20·00	20·00
463		80c. on 10p. violet	20·00	20·00

(g) Nos. 34 and 35 of Cape Juby.

No.	Type	Description	Mint	Used
464		5p. on 4p. bistre	65·00	65·00
465		10p. on 10p. violet	38·00	38·00

(h) Nos. 231/2 of Spanish Guinea.

No.	Type	Description	Mint	Used
466		1p. on 10p. violet	20·00	20·00
467		2p. on 4p. bistre	20·00	20·00

(i) Nos. 23/4 of Spanish Sahara.

No.	Type	Description	Mint	Used
468		80c. on 10p. violet	29·00	29·00
469		2p. on 4p. bistre	20·00	20·00

82 Pope Pius XI and King Alfonso XIII

1928. Rome Catacombs Restoration Fund.

No.	Type	Description	Mint	Used
470	82	2c. black and violet	30	30
471		2c. black and purple	40	40
486		2c. red and black	30	30
487		2c. red and blue	40	40
472		3c. violet and black	30	30
473		3c. violet and blue	40	40
488		3c. blue and bistre	30	30
489		3c. blue and green	40	40
474		5c. violet and green	75	75
490		5c. red and purple	75	75
475		10c. black and green	1·30	1·30
491		10c. blue and green	1·30	1·30
476		15c. violet and green	4·50	4·50
492		15c. red and blue	4·50	4·50
477		25c. violet and red	4·50	4·50
493		25c. blue and brown	4·50	4·50
478		40c. black and blue	30	30
494		40c. red and blue	30	30
479		55c. violet and brown	30	30
495		55c. blue and brown	30	30
480		80c. black and red	30	30
496		80c. red and black	30	30
481		1p. violet and grey	30	30
497		1p. red and yellow	30	30
482		2p. black and brown	6·25	6·25
498		2p. blue and grey	6·25	6·25
483		3p. violet and pink	6·25	6·25
499		3p. red and violet	6·25	6·25
484		4p. black and purple	6·25	6·25

500 4p. red and purple . . . . 6·25 6·25
485 5p. violet and black . . . 6·25 6·25
501 5p. blue and yellow . . . . 6·25 6·25

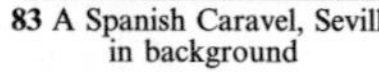

83 A Spanish Caravel, Seville in background **84** Miniature of Exhibition Poster

1929. Seville and Barcelona Exhibitions. Inscr "EXPOSICION GENERAL (or GRAL.) ESPANOLA".
502 **83** 1c. green . . . . 2·00 2·00
503 **84** 2c. green 25 25
504 – 5c. red 40 40
505 – 10c. green 40 40
506 **83** 15c. blue 70 70
507 **84** 20c. violet 50 50
508 **83** 25c. red 50 50
509 – 30c. brown . . . . 4·00 4·00
510 – 40c. blue . . . . 7·00 7·00
511 **84** 50c. orange . . . . 4·00 4·00
512 – 1p. grey . . . . 11·00 11·00
513 – 4p. purple . . . . 24·00 24·00
514 – 10p. brown . . . . 60·00 60·00
DESIGNS—VERT: 5, 30c., 1p. View of exhibition. HORIZ: 10, 40c., 4, 10p. Alfonso XIII and Barcelona.

87 "Spirit of St. Louis" over Coast

1929. Air. Seville and Barcelona Exhibitions.
515 **87** 5c. brown . . . . 5·50 5·50
516 10c. red . . . . 5·75 5·75
517 25c. blue . . . . 6·25 6·25
518 50c. violet . . . . 7·50 7·50
519 1p. green . . . . 35·00 35·00
520 4p. black . . . . 25·00 25·00

1929. Meeting of Council of League of Nations at Madrid. Optd **Sociedad de las Naciones LV reunion del Consejo Madrid.**
521 **66** 1c. green 65 65
522 **68** 2c. green 65 65
523 5c. red 65 65
524 10c. green 65 65
525 15c. blue 65 65
526 20c. violet 65 65
527 25c. red 65 65
528 30c. brown . . . . 2·75 2·75
529 40c. blue . . . . 2·75 2·75
530 50c. orange . . . . 2·75 2·75
531 **69** 1p. grey . . . . 13·50 13·50
532 4p. red . . . . 13·50 13·50
533 10p. brown . . . . 46·00 46·00

89 Class 4601 Steam Locomotive, 1924 **90** Stinson Junior over Congress Emblem

1930. 11th Int Railway Congress, Madrid.
534 **89** 1c. green (postage) 55 55
535 2c. green 55 55
536 5c. purple 55 55
537 10c. green 55 55
538 15c. blue 55 55
539 20c. violet 55 55
540 25c. red 55 55
541 30c. brown . . . . 1·90 1·90
542 40c. blue . . . . 1·90 1·90
543 50c. orange . . . . 3·75 3·75
544 – 1p. grey . . . . 4·50 4·50
545 – 4p. red . . . . 90·00 90·00
546 – 10p. brown £350 £350
DESIGN: 1p. to 10p. Class 1301 steam locomotive (1914) at points.

547 **90** 5c. brown (air) . . . . . . 5·50 5·50
548 10c. red . . . . 5·50 5·50
549 25c. blue . . . . 5·50 5·50
550 50c. violet . . . . 13·50 13·50
551 1p. green . . . . 27·00 27·00
552 4p. black . . . . 27·00 27·00

91 Francisco Goya (after Lopez) **92**

93 "The Naked Maja"

1930. Death Cent of Goya (painter). (a) Postage.
553 **91** 1c. yellow 15 15
554 2c. brown 15 15
555 **92** 2c. green 15 15
556 **91** 5c. mauve 15 15
557 **92** 5c. violet 15 15
558 **91** 10c. green 15 15
559 15c. blue 15 15
560 20c. purple 15 15
561 25c. red 15 15
562 **92** 25c. red 30 30
563 **91** 30c. brown . . . . 5·00 5·00
564 40c. blue . . . . 5·00 5·00
565 50c. red . . . . 5·00 5·00
566 1p. black . . . . 6·25 6·25
567 **93** 1p. purple 90 90
568 4p. black 65 65
569 10p. brown . . . . 14·00 14·00

94 "Flight" **97** King Alfonso XIII

(b) Air. Designs show works by Goya, all with curious flying figures.
570 **94** 5c. yellow and red 15 15
571 – 5c. blue and green 15 15
572 – 10c. green and turquoise 15 15
573 – 15c. red and black 15 15
574 – 20c. red and blue 15 15
575 **94** 25c. red and purple 20 20
576 – 30c. violet and brown . . . 40 40
577 – 40c. blue and ultramarine 40 40
578 – 50c. green and red 40 40
579 – 1p. violet and purple . . . 40 40
580 – 4p. black and purple . . . 2·50 2·50
581 – 4p. blue and light blue . . 2·50 2·50
582 – 10p. brown and sepia . . . 9·50 9·50
DESIGNS—VERT: 5, 10, 20, 40c. Asmodeus and Cleofas; 1, 4 (581), 10p. Woman and dwarfs in flight. HORIZ: 30, 50c., 4p. (580), Weird flying methods.

1930.
583 **97** 2c. brown 15 15
584 5c. brown 70 15
585 10c. green . . . . 3·75 15
586 15c. green . . . . 12·00 15
587 20c. violet . . . . 7·00 65
588 25c. red 70 15
589 30c. red . . . . 14·50 1·80
590 40c. blue . . . . 30·00 1·20
592 50c. orange . . . . 20·00 7·00

98 The "Santa Maria" **99**

100 "Santa Maria", "Pinta" and "Nina"

101 The Departure from Palos

1930. Columbus issue.
593 **98** 1c. brown 30 15
594 2c. green 30 15
595 **99** 2c. green 30 15
596 **98** 5c. purple 30 15
597 **99** 5c. purple 30 15
598 10c. green 95 95
599 **98** 15c. blue 95 95
600 **99** 20c. violet . . . . 1·40 1·40
601 **100** 25c. red . . . . 1·40 1·40
602 **101** 30c. brown, blue and sepia . . . . 6·75 6·75
603 **100** 40c. blue . . . . 5·75 5·75
604 **101** 50c. violet, blue and purple . . . . 8·75 8·75
605 **100** 1p. black . . . . 8·75 8·75
606 – 4p. black and blue . . . 9·50 9·50
607 – 10p. brown and purple . . 40·00 40·00
DESIGNS—As Type **101**: 4, 10p. Arrival in America.

103 Monastery of La Rabida

104 Martin Pinzon

106 Columbus

1930. "Columbus" Air stamps (for Europe and Africa).
608 **103** 5c. red 15 15
609 5c. brown 15 15
610 10c. green 25 25
611 15c. violet 25 25
612 20c. blue 25 25
613 **104** 25c. red 25 25
614 – 30c. brown . . . . 1·90 1·90
615 **104** 40c. blue . . . . 1·90 1·90
616 – 50c. orange . . . . 1·90 1·90
617 **104** 1p. violet . . . . 1·90 1·90
618 **106** 4p. green . . . . 1·90 1·90
619 10p. brown . . . . 11·50 11·50
DESIGNS—As Type **104**: 30, 50c. Vincent Pinzon.

107 Monastery of La Rabida

108 Columbus **109** Columbus and the brothers Pinzon

1930. "Columbus" Air stamps (for America and Philippines).
620 **107** 5c. red 15 15
621 10c. green 15 15
622 **108** 25c. red 15 15
623 50c. grey . . . . 2·30 2·30
624 1p. brown . . . . 2·30 2·30
625 **109** 4p. blue . . . . 2·30 2·30
626 10p. purple . . . . 11·00 11·00

110 Arms of Bolivia and Paraguay

113 Sidar and Douglas 0-2-M Biplane **114** Breguet 19GR "Jesus del Gran Poder" over "Santa Maria"

1930. Spanish-American Exhibition. Views of pavilions of various countries.
627 **110** 1c. green (postage) . . . 15 15
628 – 2c. brown (C. America) 15 15
629 – 5c. brown (Venezuela) . . 15 15
630 – 10c. green (Colombia) . . 30 30
631 – 15c. blue (Dominican Republic) 30 30
632 – 20c. violet (Uruguay) . . 30 30
633 – 25c. red (Argentina) . . . 30 30
634 – 25c. red (Chile) 30 30
635 – 30c. purple (Brazil) . . . 1·80 1·80
636 – 40c. blue (Mexico) . . . . 1·00 1·00
637 – 40c. blue (Cuba) . . . . 1·00 1·00
638 – 50c. orange (Peru) . . . . 1·80 1·80
639 – 1p. blue (U.S.A.) . . . . 2·50 2·50
640 – 4p. purple (Portugal) . . 34·00 34·00
641 – 10p. brown . . . . 2·50 2·50
The 10p. shows King Alfonso and Queen Victoria, maps of S. America and Spain, and the Giralda, Seville. The 2, 5c., 4, 10p. are vert.

643 – 5c. black (air) 90 90
644 – 10c. green 90 90
645 – 25c. blue 90 90
646 – 50c. blue . . . . 1·80 1·80
647 **113** 50c. black . . . . 1·80 1·80
648 – 1p. red . . . . 4·50 4·50
649 – 1p. purple . . . . 80·00 80·00
650 – 1p. green . . . . 4·50 4·50
651 **114** 4p. blue . . . . 8·25 8·25
DESIGNS—HORIZ: 5c. Alberto Santos Dumont and Wright Flyer I over Rio de Janeiro; 10c. Teodoro Fels and Douglas 0-2-M biplane; 25c. Dagoberto Godoy and Nieuport 17 biplane; 50c. Admiral Gago Coutinha, Sacadura Cabral and Fairey IIID seaplane; 1p. (650) Charles Lindbergh and "Spirirt of St. Louis". VERT: 1p. (648/9) Jimenez Iglesias and Breguet 19GR "Jesus de Gran Poder".

115 **121** The Fountain of the Lions

1930.
652 **115** 5c. black . . . . 6·00 15

1931. Optd **REPUBLICA**. (a) Postage.
660 **66** 1c. green 15 15
673 **97** 2c. brown 15 15
662 5c. brown 15 15
671 **115** 5c. black . . . . 1·80 1·80
675 **97** 10c. green 30 15
664 15c. green 65 65
677 20c. violet 50 50
678 25c. red 50 50
667 30c. red . . . . 4·50 4·50
668 40c. blue . . . . 1·60 1·60
669 50c. orange . . . . 1·60 1·60
670 **69** 1p. grey . . . . 7·50 7·50

(b) Air. On Nos. 353/6.
683 **64** 5c. green . . . . 8·75 8·75
684 10c. red . . . . 8·75 8·75
685 25c. blue . . . . 12·50 20
686 50c. blue . . . . 26·00 26·00

1931. Optd **Republica Espanola** in two lines continuously.
687 **97** 2c. brown 15 15
688 5c. brown 25 15
689 10c. green 25 15
690 15c. green . . . . 3·25 15
691 20c. violet . . . . 1·40 1·10
692 25c. red 45 15
693 30c. red . . . . 4·50 1·10

694 40c. blue 4·50 65
695 50c. orange 7·25 65
696 69 1p. grey 50·00 90

1931. 3rd Pan-American Postal Union Congress. (a) Postage.
697 121 5c. purple 15 15
698 – 10c. green 45 45
699 – 15c. violet 45 45
700 – 25c. red 45 45
701 – 30c. green 45 45
702 121 40c. blue 1·30 1·30
703 – 50c. red 1·30 1·30
704 – 1p. black 2·40 2·40
705 – 4p. purple 11·50 11·50
706 – 10p. brown 38·00 38·00
DESIGNS—VERT: 10, 25, 50c. Cordoba Cathedral. HORIZ: 15c., 1p. Alcantara Bridge, Toledo; 30c. Dr. F. Garcia y Santos; 4, 10p. Revolutionaries hoisting Republican flag, 14 April, 1931.

123 Royal Palace and San Francisco el Grande

(b) Air.
707 123 5c. purple 15 15
708 10c. green 15 15
709 25c. red 15 15
710 – 50c. blue 50 50
711 – 1p. violet 75 75
712 – 4p. black 10·50 10·50
DESIGNS—HORIZ: 50c., 1p. G.P.O. and Cibeles Fountain; 4p. Calle de Alcala.

125a Montserrat Arms 125b Airplane above Montserrat

1931. 900th Anniv of Montserrat Monastery.
713 125a 1c. green (postage) 1·40 1·50
714 2c. brown 85 65
715 5c. brown 1·00 85
716 10c. green 1·00 85
717 – 15c. green 1·40 1·00
718 – 20c. purple 3·25 2·40
719 – 25c. purple 4·25 3·50
720 – 30c. red 46·00 38·00
721 – 40c. blue 26·00 18·00
722 – 50c. orange 60·00 46·00
723 – 1p. blue 60·00 46·00
724 – 4p. mauve £500 £425
725 – 10p. brown £400 £350
DESIGNS: 15, 50c. Monks planning Monastery; 20, 30c. "Black Virgin" (full length); 25c., 1, 10p. "Black Virgin" (profile); 40c., 4p. Monastery.

726 125b 5c. brown (air) 55 55
727 10c. green 2·75 2·75
728 25c. purple 10·50 10·50
729 50c. orange 38·00 38·00
730 1p. blue 25·00 25·00

126 Blasco Ibanez 127 Pi y Margall 128 Joaquin Costa

129 Mariana Pineda 130 Nicolas Salmeron 131 Concepcion Arenal

132 Ruiz Zorilla 133 Pablo Iglesias 134 Ramon y Cajal

135 Azcarate 136 Jovellanos 137 Pablo Iglesias

138 Emilio Castelar 139 Pablo Iglesias 140 Velazquez

141 F. Salvoechea 142 Cuenca

1931.
738 126 2c. brown 15 15
731 127 5c. brown 3·25 30
740 126 5c. brown 15 15
741 128 10c. green 5·50 15
742 129 10c. green 15 15
744 130 15c. green 80 15
745 131 15c. green 25 15
747 15c. black 85 15
748 127 20c. violet 30 15
734 133 25c. red 41·00 15
750 132 25c. red 65 15
751 133 30c. red 2·30 15
752 134 30c. brown 8·25 1·70
753 135 30c. red 9·25 25
755 136 30c. red 15 15
756 137 30c. red 15 15
757 139 30c. red 1·40 50
758 138 40c. blue 15 15
759 40c. red 1·40 50
760 139 45c. red 15 15
761 130 50c. orange 34·00 75
762 50c. blue 1·30 65
763 140 50c. blue 15 15
764 138 60c. green 15 15
765 141 60c. blue 1·00 1·30
766 60c. orange 7·75 8·75
767c 142 1p. black 15 15
768c – 4p. mauve 40 30
769c – 10p. brown 65 65
DESIGNS—As Type 142: 4p. Castle of Segovia; 10p. Sun Gate, Toledo.

143 144

1933. Imperf (1c.), perf (others).
770 143 1c. green 15 15
771 2c. brown 15 15
772 144 2c. brown 15 15
773 143 5c. brown 15 15
774 10c. green 15 15
775 15c. green 15 15
776a 20c. violet 15 15
777a 25c. mauve 15 15
778 30c. red 15 15

145 Cierva C.30A Autogyro over Seville

1935.
780 145 2p. blue 15 15

146 Lope De Vega's Book-plate 148 Scene from "Peribanez"

1935. 300th Death Anniv of Lope de Vega (author).
781 146 15c. green 7·50 30
782 – 30c. red 3·25 20
783 – 50c. blue 14·50 2·50
784 148 1p. black 25·00 1·70
DESIGN—As Type 146: 30, 50c. Lope de Vega (after Tristan).

149 Old-time Map of the Amazon

1935. Iglesias' Amazon Expedition.
785 149 30c. red 2·40 80

150 M. Moya 153 Airplane over Press Association Building

151 House of Nazareth and Rotary Press

152 Pyrenean Eagle and Newspapers

1936. 40th Anniv of Madrid Press Association.
786 150 1c. red (postage) 15 15
787 – 2c. brown 15 15
788 – 5c. brown 15 15
789 – 10c. green 15 15
790 150 15c. green 15 15
791 – 20c. violet 15 15
792 – 25c. mauve 15 15
793 – 30c. red 15 15
794 150 40c. orange 55 15
795 – 50c. blue 25 15
796 – 60c. green 65 25
797 – 1p. black 65 25
798 151 2p. blue 8·25 3·25
799 4p. purple 8·25 5·75
800 10p. red 20·00 14·00
PORTRAITS: 2, 20, 50c. T. L. de Tena; 5, 25, 60c. J. F. Rodriguez; 10, 30c., 1p. A. Lerroux.
SIZES: 1c. to 10c. 22 × 27 mm; 15c. to 30c. 24 × 30 mm; 40c. to 1p. 26 × 31½ mm.

801 152 1c. red (air) 15 15
802 153 2c. brown 15 15
803 152 5c. brown 15 15
804 153 10c. green 15 15
805 – 15c. blue 15 15
806 152 20c. violet 15 15
807 153 25c. mauve 15 15
808 – 30c. red 15 15
809 152 40c. orange 55 30
810 50c. blue 40 30
811 153 60c. green 80 30
812 – 1p. black 80 30
813 – 2p. blue 5·50 3·50
814 – 4p. purple 6·00 5·50
815 – 10p. red 15·00 11·50
DESIGNS—VERT: 15, 30, 50c., 1p. Cierva C.30A autogyro over House of Nazareth. HORIZ: 2, 4, 10p. Don Quixote on wooden horse.

155 Gregorio Fernandez 156

1936. 300th Birth Anniv of Gregorio Fernandez (sculptor).
816 155 30c. red 1·40 85

1936. 1st National Philatelic Exhibition, Madrid. Imperf. (a) Postage.
817 156 10c. brown 47·00 47·00
818 15c. green 47·00 47·00

(b) Air. Optd **CORREO AEREO**.
819 156 10c. red £160 £160
820 15c. blue £160 £160

1936. Manila–Madrid Flight of Arnaiz and Calvo. Optd **VUELO MANILA MADRID 1936 ARNAIZ CALVO.**
821 137 30c. red 5·50 5·50

159 160a Republican Symbol

1937. Fiscal stamp of Austrias and Leon surch.
822 159 25c. on 5c. red 10·00 8·25
823 45c. on 5c. red 5·50 10·00
824 60c. on 5c. red 25 45
825 1p. on 5c. red 25 40

1938. Surch **45 centimos.**
826 143 45c. on 1c. green (imperf) 10·50 7·00
827 45c. on 1c. green (perf) 45 30
830 45c. on 2c. brown 18·00 15·00
831 144 45c. on 2c. brown 15 15
832 126 45c. on 2c. brown 36·00 36·00

1938.
833 160a 40c. pink 15 15
834 45c. red 15 15
835 50c. blue 15 15
836 60c. blue 55 30

1938. 7th Anniv of Republic. Nos. 308/9 surch **14 ABRIL 1938 VII Aniversario de la Republica** and values. (a) Postage.
837 45c. on 15c. violet 14·00 14·00

(b) Air. Additionally optd **CORREO AEREO.**
838 2p.50 on 10c. red £100 £100

163 Defence of Madrid

1938. Defence of Madrid Relief Fund. (a) Postage.
839 163 45c.+2p. blue & lt blue 65 65
MS840 120 × 105 mm. No. 839 24·00 35·00

(b) Air. Surch **AEREO + 5 Pts.**
841 163 45c.+2p.+5p. blue and light blue £300 £300
MS842 120 × 105 mm. No. 841 £4000 £5000

1938. Labour Day. Surch **FIESTA DEL TRABAJO 1 MAYO 1938** and values.
843 54 45c. on 15c. violet 3·25 3·25
844 1p. on 15c. violet 6·00 6·00

167 Statue of Liberty and Flags

1938. 150th Anniv of U.S. Constitution. (a) Postage.
845 167 1p. multicoloured 18·00 18·00
MS846 120 × 105 mm. No. 845 30·00 30·00

(b) Air. Surch **AEREO + 5 Pts.**
847 167 1p.+5p. multicoloured £250 £250
MS848 120 × 105 mm. No. 847 £900 £1100

169  172 Steelworks

1938. Red Cross. (a) Postage.
849 169 45c.+5p. red 55 55

(b) Air. Surch **+3 Pts. Aereo.**
850 169 45c.+5p.+3p. red 10·00 9·50

1938. Air. No. 719 surch with two airplanes, **CORREO AEREO** twice and value.
851 50c. on 25c. purple 34·00 34·00
852 1p. on 25c. purple 1·30 1·30
853 1p.25 on 25c. purple 1·30 1·30
854 1p.50 on 25c. purple 1·30 1·30
855 2p. on 25c. purple 34·00 34·00

1938. Workers of Sagunto.
856 **172** 45c. black 15 15
857 – 1p.25 blue 15 15
DESIGN: 1p.25, Blast furnace and air raid victims.

173 "Isaac Peral"

1938. Submarine Service.
857a **173** 1p. blue 4·50 4·50
857b – 2p. brown 9·50 9·50
857c – 4p. orange 10·00 10·00
857d – 6p. blue 21·00 21·00
857e – 10p. purple 39·00 39·00
857f – 15p. green £425 £425
MS857g 150×118 mm. 4p. black and red; 6p. black and blue; 15p. black and green £450 £450
DESIGNS: 2, 6p. "Narciso Monturiol". 4, 10p. "B-2".

174 Troops on the Alert

1938. In Honour of 43rd Division. Perf or imperf.
858 **174** 25c. green 10·00 10·00
859 – 45c. brown 10·00 10·00
DESIGN—VERT: 45c. Two soldiers on guard.

1938. 2nd Anniv of Defence of Madrid. Optd **SEGUNDO ANIVERSARIO DE LA HEROICA DEFENSA DE MADRID 7 NOV. 1938.**
860 **163** 45c.+2p. blue and light blue 3·25 3·25

1938. No. 719 surch **2'50 PTAS.**, bars and ornaments.
861 2p.50 on 25c. purple 15 15

176a Man and Woman in Firing Position

1938. In honour of the Militia.
861b **176a** 5c. brown 3·25 3·25
861c 10c. purple 3·25 3·25
861d 25c. green 3·25 3·25
861e – 45c. red 3·25 3·25
861f – 60c. blue 6·00 6·00
861g – 1p.20 black £120 £120
861h – 2p. orange 37·00 37·00
861i – 5p. brown £225 £225
861j – 10p. green 41·00 41·00
DESIGNS—HORIZ: 45, 60c., 1p.20, Militia with machine gun. VERT: 2, 5, 10p. Grenade-thrower.

NATIONAL STATE

The Civil War began on 17 July 1936. Until it ended on 1 April 1939, the stamps listed below were current only in areas held by the forces of General Franco.

177 Seville Cathedral

178 Xavier Castle, Navarre

1936. Junta of National Defence.
862 – 5c. brown 65 65
863 – 15c. green 65 65
864 **177** 25c. red 65 65
865 **178** 30c. red 65 65
867 – 1p. black 6·00 4·50
DESIGNS—VERT: 5c. Burgos Cathedral. HORIZ: 15c. Zaragoza Cathedral; 1p. Alcantara Bridge and Alcazar, Toledo.

179

180 Cordoba Cathedral

1936.
868 **179** 1c. green (imperf) 6·00 5·75
869 2c. brown 65 65
870 – 10c. green 65 65
871 – 50c. blue 15·00 11·50
872 **180** 60c. green 1·10 90
873 – 4p. lilac, red and yellow 60·00 35·00
874 – 10p. brown 60·00 35·00
DESIGNS (As T **180**)—HORIZ: 10c. Salamanca University; 50c. Court of Lions, Granada; 10p. Troops disembarking at Algeciras. VERT: 4p. National flag at Malaga.

181 **182**

183 "El Cid" **184** Isabella the Catholic

1937.
875 **181** 1c. green (imperf) 15 15
876 **182** 2c. brown 15 15
902 **183** 5c. brown 15 15
879 10c. green 15 15
903 10c. red 15 15
896 15c. green 15 15
880 **184** 15c. black 15 15
881 20c. violet 40 15
882 25c. red 30 15
883 30c. red 55 15
885 40c. orange 2·00 15
886 50c. blue 2·00 15
887 60c. yellow 30 15
897 70c. blue 65 15
888 1p. blue 19·00 45
889 4p. mauve 23·00 5·75
891 **183** 10p. blue 33·00 14·50
See also No. 1113.

186 Santiago Cathedral

189

188 Alcazar, Toledo (before Siege)

1937. Holy Year of Compostela.
905 – 15c. brown 1·30 1·00
906 **186** 30c. red 6·50 55
908 – 1p. orange and blue 19·00 3·25
DESIGNS—VERT: 15c. St. James of Compostela. HORIZ: 1p. Portico de la Gloria.

1937. 1st Anniv of National Uprising. Sheets 140×110 mm containing T **909** and similar designs.
MS909 **188** 2p. (+2p.) orange 21·00 21·00
MS910 Imperf £400 £400
MS911 – 2p. (+2p.) green 21·00 21·00
MS912 – Imperf £400 £400
DESIGN: No. **MS**911/12 Alcazar in ruins.

1937. Anti-tuberculosis Fund. Cross in red.
913 **189** 10c. blue and black 7·75 5·00

189a Covadonga Monastery

1938. Historic Monuments. Sheet 140×100 mm containing T **189a**and similar designs.
MS914 20c. violet, 30c. red, 50c. blue, 1p. green (sold at 4p.) 65·00 65·00
MS915 Imperf 85·00 85·00
DESIGNS—VERT: 30c. Cathedral, Palma de Mallorca; 50c. Alcazar, Segovia. VERT 1p. Leon Cathedral.

190 Ferdinand the Catholic

191a Soldier with Flag

1938.
917 **190** 15c. green 1·50 15
918 20c. violet 10·00 2·30
919 25c. red 70 15
921 30c. red 5·00 15

1938. Air. Optd **correo aereo.**
922 **190** 50c. blue 1·00 65
923 1p. blue 3·25 65

1938. Honouring Army and Navy. Sheet 175×132 mm containing designs as T **191a** (various frames).
MS924 2c. violet (Type **191a**), 2c. violet (a), 3c. blue (b), 3c. blue (c), 5c. sepia (a), 5c. sepia (Type **191a**), 10c. green (b), 10c. green (c), 30c. orange (b), 30c. orange (c). Two of each stamp (sold at 4p.) 35·00 35·00
MS925 Imperf £170 £170
DESIGNS: (a) Cruiser *Almirante Cervera*; (b) Trenches near Teruel; (c)General Franco's Moorish bodyguard.

192

193 Isabella the Catholic

1938. 2nd Anniv of National Uprising.
926 **192** 15c. green and light green 5·00 4·50
927 25c. red and pink 5·00 4·50
928 30c. blue and light blue 2·75 2·50
929 1p. brown and yellow £100 95·00

1938.
930 **193** 20c. violet 65 15
931 25c. red 7·00 65
932 30c. red 25 15
933 40c. mauve 25 25
934 50c. blue 32·00 2·40
935 1p. blue 10·00 1·10

193a Don Juan of Austria

194

1938. Battle of Lepanto. Sheets each 90×75 mm containing T **193a** and another design.
MS936 **193a** 30c. carmine (perf) 19·00
MS937 – 50c. blue 19·00
MS938 **193a** 30c. violet (imperf) £400
MS939 – 50c. green £400
DESIGN—(36½×23 mm): 50c. Naval Battle of Lepanto.

1938. Anti-tuberculosis Fund. Cross in red.
940 **194** 10c. blue and black 5·00 2·00

195 Juan de la Cierva and Cierva C.30A Autogyro

196 General Franco

1939. Air.
1010 **195** 20c. orange 25 15
1011 25c. red 25 15
943 35c. mauve 65 30
1013 50c. brown 40 10
945 1p. blue 65 20
1015 2p. green 1·70 10
1016 4p. blue 5·00 25
1017 10p. violet 3·75 65

1939.
960 **196** 5c. brown 45 15
961 10c. red 2·00 70
962 15c. green 55 15
1114 20c. violet 15 15
1115 25c. purple 15 15
950 30c. red 30 15
1116 30c. blue 15 15
1117 35c. blue 25 15
951 40c. green 25 15
966 40c. grey 45 15
952 45c. red 2·30 2·10
1119 45c. blue 15 15
1120 50c. grey 15 15
1121 60c. orange 15 15
955 70c. blue 45 15
956 1Pts. black 14·00 15
974 1PTA. black 6·50 15
975 1PTS. grey 60·00 70
957 2Pts. brown 20·00 1·30
1124 2PTAS. brown 3·75 15
958 4Pts. purple £110 15·00
1125 4PTAS. red 6·25 15
959 10Pts. brown 55·00 37·00
978 10PTS. brown £150 3·75
1126 10PTAS. brown 1·50 50
For 10c. brown imperf, see No. 981.

197 "Spain" and Wreath of Peace

1939. Homage to the Army.
980 **197** 10c. blue 15 15

1939. Anti-tuberculosis Fund. Imperf.
981 **196** 10c. brown 15 15

198 Ruins of Belchite

1940. Zaragoza Cathedral Restoration Fund and 19th Centenary of Apparition of Virgin of El Pilar at Zaragoza. (a) Postage.
982 **198** 10c.+5c. brown and blue 15 15
983 – 15c.+10c. green and lilac 15 15
984 – 20c.+10c. blue & violet 15 15
985 – 25c.+10c. brown & red 15 15
986 – 40c.+10c. purple & grn 15 15
987 – 45c.+15c. red and blue 30 30
988 **198** 70c.+20c. black & brn 30 30
989 – 80c.+20c. violet and red 45 45
990 – 1p.+30c. purple & black 45 45
991 – 1p.40+40c. black & vio 38·00 38·00
992 – 1p.50+50c. purple & bl 55 55
993 – 2p.50+50c. blue & pur 55 55
994 – 4p.+1p. grey and lilac 13·00 13·00
995 – 10p.+4p. brown & blue £180 £180
DESIGNS—HORIZ: 15, 80c. Procession of the Rosary; 20c., 1p.50, El Pilar; 25c., 1p. Mother Rafols praying; 40c., 2p.50, Sanctuary of the Virgin; 45c., 1p.40, Oath of the besieged; 4p. Miracle of Calanda; 10p. Virgin appearing to St. James.

(b) Air.
996 25c.+5c. grey and purple 25 25
997 50c.+5c. violet and red 25 25
998 65c.+15c. blue and violet 25 25
999 70c.+15c. violet and grey 25 25
1000 90c.+20c. red and brown 25 25
1001 1p.20+30c. purple & violet 25 25
1002 1p.40+40c. brown & blue 25 25
1003 2p.+50c. violet and purple 45 45
1004 4p.+1p. purple and green 10·50 10·50
1005 10p.+4p. blue and brown £250 £250
DESIGNS—VERT: 25, 70c. Prayer during bombardment; 50c., 1p.40, Caravel and Image of the Virgin; 65, 90c. The Assumption; 1p.20, 2p. Coronation of the Virgin; 4p. "The Cave", after Goya; 10p. Bombing of Zaragoza Cathedral.

199 Gen. Franco

200 Knight and Cross of Lorraine

1940. Anti-tuberculosis Fund.
1006 **199** 10c. violet and red (post) 15 15
1007 20c.+5c. green and red 70 70
1008 40c.+10c. blue and red 1·00 40
1009 10c. pink and red (air) 90 90

1941. Anti-tuberculosis Fund.
1018 **200** 10c. black and red (post) 15 15
1019 20c.+5c. violet and red 65 30
1020 40c.+10c. grey and red 65 25
1021 10c. blue and red (air) 25 25

201 Gen. Franco

202 St. John of the Cross

1942.
1022 **201** 40c. brown 30 15
1023 75c. blue 3·25 65

1024a 90c. green . . . . . . 1·00 15
1025b 1p.35 violet 85 50

1942. 400th Birth Anniv of St. John of the Cross.
1026 **202** 20c. violet 75 15
1027 40c. orange . . . . . . 1·70 30
1028 75c. blue . . . . 2·00 1·90

203 Arms and Lorraine Cross

1942. Anti-T.B. Fund. Inscr "1942–43".
1029 **203** 10c. orange and red (postage) 15 15
1030 20c.+5c. brown and red 1·70 1·70
1031 40c.+10c. green and red 1·00 30
1032 – 10c. orange and red (air) 90 55
DESIGN—HORIZ: No. 1032, Lorraine Cross and two doves in flight.

204 St. James of Compostela

205

1943. Holy Year. Inscr "ANO SANTO 1943".
1033 **204** 20c. blue 25 15
1034 – 20c. red 25 15
1035 – 20c. lilac 25 15
1036 – 40c. brown 65 15
1037 **205** 40c. green 55 15
1038 – 40c. brown 65 15
1039 – 75c. blue . . . . 2·40 2·00
1040 – 75c. blue . . . . 3·00 2·10
1041 – 75c. blue . . . . 34·00 37·00
DESIGNS—VERT: Nos. 1034 and 1040. Details of pillars in Santiago Cathedral; No. 1036, St. James enthroned; No. 1038, Portal of Santiago Cathedral; No. 1039, Censer; No. 1041, Santiago Cathedral. HORIZ: No. 1035, Tomb of St. James.

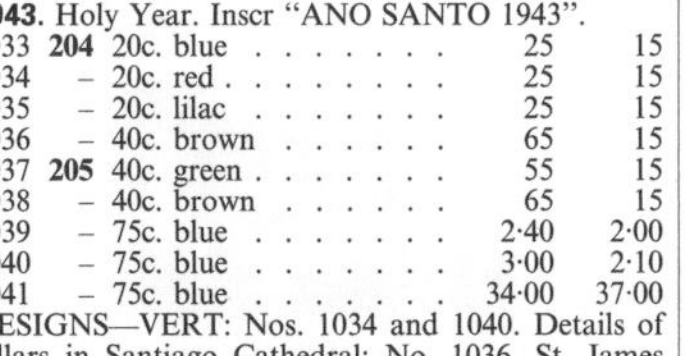

206

1943. Anti-Tuberculosis Fund. Inscr "1943–1944".
1042 **206** 10c. violet & red (postage) 30 25
1043 20c.+5c. green and red 3·75 1·70
1044 40c.+10c. blue and red 2·50 1·30
1045 – 10c. violet and red (air) 1·10 1·20
DESIGN: No. 1045. Lorraine Cross and outline of bird.

207 10th-cent Tower

208 Arms of Soria

1944. Millenary of Castile. Arms designs as T **208** inscr "MILENARIO DE CASTILLA".
1046 **207** 20c. lilac 25 25
1047 **208** 20c. lilac 25 25
1048 – 20c. lilac 25 25
1049 – 40c. brown . . . . . . 3·25 70
1050 – 40c. brown . . . . . . 3·25 70
1051 – 40c. brown . . . . . . 2·50 70
1052 – 75c. blue . . . . 3·25 3·75
1053 – 75c. blue . . . . 3·25 3·75
1054 – 75c. blue . . . . 3·50 4·25
DESIGNS: No. 1048, Avila (Shield at left); No. 1049, Castile (Arms in centre); No. 1050, Segovia (Shield at left); No. 1051, Burgos (Shield at right); No. 1052, Avila (Shield at left); No. 1053, Fernan Gonzalez, founder of Castile (Helmet, bow and arrows at left); No. 1054, Santander (Shield at right).

209 "Dr. Thebussem" (M. P. de Figueroa, author and postal historian)

1944. Air. Stamp Day.
1055 **209** 5p. blue . . . . 18·00 17·00

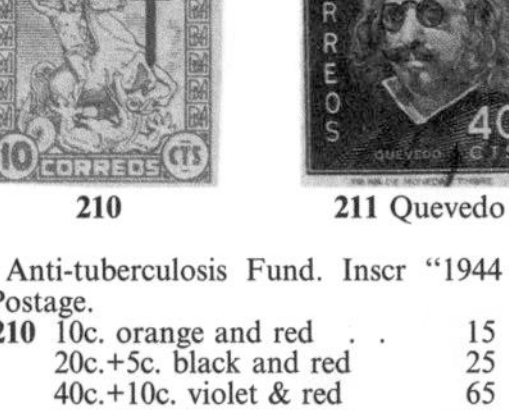
210 **211** Quevedo

1944. Anti-tuberculosis Fund. Inscr "1944 1945". (a) Postage.
1056 **210** 10c. orange and red . . 15 15
1057 20c.+5c. black and red 25 25
1058 40c.+10c. violet & red 65 65
1059 80c.+10c. blue and red 9·50 9·50

(b) Air. Inscr "CORRESPONDENCIA AEREA".
1060 – 25c. orange and red . . . 4·25 4·25
DESIGN—HORIZ: No. 1060, Hospital.

1945. 300th Death Anniv of Francisco de Quevedo (author).
1061 **211** 40c. brown 70 70

212 Conde de San Luis, Mail Vehicle of 1850 and Airplane

1945. Air. Stamp Day.
1062 **212** 10p. green . . . . 21·00 18·00

213 Carlos de Haya Gonzalez

214 J. Garcia Morato

1945. Air. Civil War Air Aces.
1063 **213** 4p. red . . . . 11·50 6·75
1064 **214** 10p. purple . . . . . . 26·00 7·75

215 St. George and Dragon

216 Lorraine Cross and Eagle

1945. Anti-T.B. Fund.
1065 **215** 10c. orge & red (postage) 15 15
1066 20c.+5c. green and red 25 15
1067 40c.+10c. violet and red 30 15
1068 80c.+10c. blue and red 9·50 9·25
1069 **216** 25c. red (air) . . . . . 1·60 1·40

217 E. A. de Nebrija (compiler of first Spanish Grammar)

219 Statue of Fray Bartolome de las Casas and native Indian

1946. Stamp Day and Day of the Race.
1070 **217** 50c. red (postage) . . . 50 15
1071 – 75c. blue 55 50
1072 **219** 5p.50 green (air) . . . . 2·50 2·40
DESIGN—As Type **217**: 75c. Salamanca University and signature of F. F. de Vitoria (founder of International Law).

220 Self-portrait of Goya

221 Woman and Child

1946. Birth Bicentenary of Goya (painter).
1073 **220** 25c. red 15 15
1074 50c. green 15 15
1075 75c. blue 70 65

1946. Anti-tuberculosis Fund. Dated "1946 1947".
1076 **221** 5c. violet and red (postage) 15 15
1077 10c. green and red . . . 15 15
1078 – 25c. orange and red (air) 15 15
DESIGN—HORIZ: 25c. Eagle.

222 B. J. Feijoo y Montenegro

1947.
1079 **222** 50c. green 65 65

223 Don Quixote in Library

224 Don Quixote

1947. Stamp Day and 400th Birth Anniv of Cervantes.
1080 **223** 50c. brown (postage) . . 25 15
1081 **224** 75c. blue 50 45
1082 – 5p.50 violet (air) . . . . 5·50 4·50
DESIGN—HORIZ: 5p.50, Quixote on Wooden Horse (after Gustav Dore).

226 Manuel de Falla (composer)

228 Lorraine Cross

1947. Air.
1083 **226** 25p. purple . . . . . . 34·00 21·00
1084 – 50p. red . . . . £130 39·00
PORTRAIT: 50p. Ignacio Zuloaga (painter).

1947. Anti-tuberculosis Fund. Dated "1947 1948".
1085 **228** 5c. brown & red (postage) 15 15
1086 – 10c. blue and red 15 15
1087 – 25c. mauve and red (air) 15 15
DESIGNS—VERT: 10c. Deckchair in garden. HORIZ: 25c. Sanatorium.

229 General Franco

230 Hernando Cortes

1948.
1088 **229** 5c. brown 15 15
1088a 5c. green 15 15
1089 15c. green 15 15
1090 50c. brown 15 15
1091 80c. red . . . . 3·25 15

1948.
1092 **230** 35c. black 15 15
1093 – 70c. purple . . . . . . 2·30 2·10
PORTRAIT: 70c. M. Aleman (writer).

232 Gen. Franco and Castillo de la Mota

233 Ferdinand III of Castile

1948.
1094 **232** 25c. orange 15 15
1095 30c. green 15 15
1096 35c. green 15 15
1097 40c. brown 65 15
1099 45c. red 25 15
1100 50c. purple . . . . . . 1·20 15
1101 70c. violet . . . . . . 1·90 15
1102 75c. blue . . . . 1·70 15
1103 1p. red . . . . 5·75 15

1948. 700th Anniv of Institution of Castilian Navy.
1104 **233** 25c. violet 25 15
1105 – 30c. red (Admiral R. de Bonifaz) 15 15

235 Marquis of Salamanca

236 Series ABJ Diesel Railcar (1936) and Lockheed Constellation Airliner

1948. Stamp Day and Spanish Railway Centenary Inscr "F.F.C.C. ESPANOLES 1848 1948".
1106 **235** 50c. brown (postage) . . 55 15
1107 – 5p. green . . . . 1·70 15
1108 **236** 2p. red (air) . . . . . . 2·10 2·00
DESIGN—HORIZ: 5p. Garganta de Pancorbo Viaduct.

238 Aesculapius

240 Globe and Buildings

1948. Anti-tuberculosis Fund. Dated "1948 1949".
1109 **238** 5c. brown & red (postage) 15 15
1110 10c. green and red . . 15 15
1111 50c.+10c. brown & red 90 85
1112 – 25c. blue and red (air) 30 25
DESIGN: 25c. Lockheed Constellation airliner over sanatorium.

1949. Relief of War Victims. As T **183**, but larger and inscr "AUXILIO A LAS VICTIMAS DE LA GUERRA 1946".
1113 5c. violet 15 15

1949. 75th Anniv of U.P.U.
1127 **240** 50c. brown (postage) . . 55 15
1128 75c. blue 50 45
1129 4p. green (air) 30 25

241 Galleon

242 San Juan de Dios and Leper

1949. Anti-tuberculosis Fund. Inscr "1949 1950".
1130 **241** 5c. violet & red (postage) 15 15
1131 10c. green and red . . . 15 15
1132 50c.+10c. brown & red 55 25
1133 – 25c. brown and red (air) 15 15
DESIGN: 25c. Bell.

1950. 400th Death Anniv of San Juan de Dios.
1134 **242** 1p. violet . . . . 11·50 6·50

243 Calderon de la Barca (dramatist)

244 Isabella II

1950. Portraits.
1135 **243** 5c. brown 15 15
1136 – 10c. purple 15 15
1137 – 15c. green 20 15
1138 – 20c. violet 15 15
1139 – 2p. blue . . . . 19·00 25
1140 – 4p.50 purple . . . . . . 1·30 1·30
PORTRAITS—VERT: 10c. Lope de Vega (author); 15c. Tirso de Molina (poet); 20c. Ruiz de Alarcon (author); 2p. Dr. Ramon y Cajal (physician); 4p.50, Dr. Ferran y Clua (bacteriologist).

1950. Stamp Centenary. Imperf. (a) Postage. Reproduction of T **1**.
1141 **244** 50c. violet . . . . 10·50 6·00
1142 75c. blue . . . . 10·50 6·00
1143 10p. green £160 £120
1144 15p. red £160 £120

(b) Air. Reproduction of T **2**.
1145 – 1p. purple . . . . 10·50 6·00
1146 – 2p.50 brown . . . . . . 10·50 6·00
1147 – 20p. blue £160 £120
1148 – 25p. green £160 £120

1950. Gen. Franco's Canary Is Visit. Nos. 1100 and 1103 surch **VISITA DEL CAUDILLO A CANARIAS OCTUBRE 1950 SOBRETASA: DIEZ CTS** and No. 1083 with **Correspondencia por avion** also.
1149 **232** 10c. on 50c. purple (postage) . . . . . . 70·00 44·00
1150 10c. on 1p. red . . . . 70·00 44·00
1151 **226** 10c. on 25p. purple (air) £325 £300

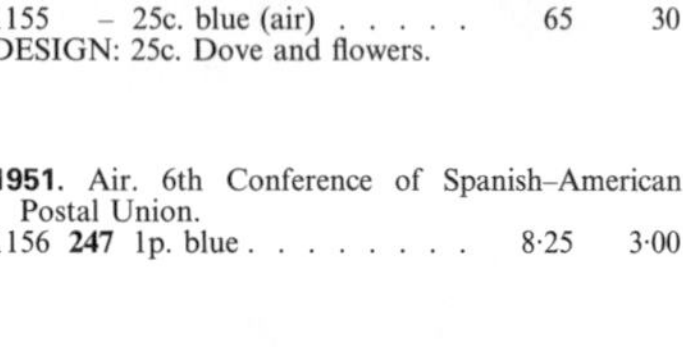

246 Candle and Conifer **247** Map

1950. Anti-T.B. Fund. Cross in red. Inscr "1950 1951".
1152 **246** 5c. violet (postage) . . . 20 15
1153 10c. green 20 15
1154 50c.+10c. brown . . . . 2·50 1·30
1155 – 25c. blue (air) 65 30
DESIGN: 25c. Dove and flowers.

1951. Air. 6th Conference of Spanish–American Postal Union.
1156 **247** 1p. blue . . . . 8·25 3·00

248 Isabella the Catholic **248a** St. Antonio Claret

1951. 5th Centenary of Birth of Isabella.
1157 **248** 50c. brown . . . . . . 1·10 40
1158 75c. blue . . . . 1·60 40
1159 90c. purple 70 25
1160 1p.50 orange . . . . . 18·00 8·25
1161 2p.80 olive . . . . . . 39·00 24·00

1951. Stamp Day.
1162 **248a** 50c. blue . . . . 5·75 3·25

249 Children on Beach **250** Isabella the Catholic

1951. Anti-tuberculosis Fund. Cross in red.
1163 **249** 5c. red (postage) 20 15
1164 10c. green 75 15
1165 – 25c. brown (air) 90 15
DESIGN: 25c. Nurse and child.

1951. Air. Stamp Day and 500th Birth Anniv of Isabella the Catholic.
1166 **250** 60c. green . . . . 8·50 55
1167 90c. yellow . . . . . . 1·10 70
1168 1p.30 red . . . . 12·00 6·25
1169 1p.90 sepia . . . . . . 8·50 6·75
1170 2p.30 blue . . . . 5·75 3·25

251 Ferdinand the Catholic **252** St. Maria Micaela

1952. 500th Birth Anniv of Ferdinand the Catholic.
1171 **251** 50c. green . . . . 1·00 30
1172 75c. blue . . . . 7·50 1·70
1173 90c. purple 65 30
1174 1p.50 orange . . . . . 17·00 9·00
1175 2p.80 brown . . . . . . 27·00 19·00

1952. 35th International Eucharistic Congress, Barcelona.
1176 **252** 90c. red (postage) . . . 20 15
1177 – 1p. green (air) . . . . . 4·50 45
DESIGN: 1p. "The Eucharist" (Tiepolo).

252a St. Francis Xavier **254** Nurse and Baby

1952. Air. 400th Death Anniv of St. Francis Xavier.
1178 **252a** 2p. blue . . . . 35·00 26·00

1952. Air. Stamp Day and 500th Anniv of Birth of Ferdinand the Catholic. As T **250** but interior scene and portrait of Ferdinand the Catholic.
1179 60c. green 30 15
1180 90c. orange 30 15
1181 1p.30 red . . . . 1·00 90
1182 1p.90 brown . . . . 3·50 2·75
1183 2p.30 blue . . . . 17·00 11·00

1953. Anti-tuberculosis Fund. Cross in red.
1184 **254** 5c. lake (postage) . . . 65 15
1185 10c. green . . . . 2·00 15
1186 – 25c. brown (air) . . . . 7·50 6·25
DESIGN: 25c. Girl and angel.

255 J. Sorolla (painter)

1953. Air.
1187 **255** 50p. violet . . . . . . £650 26·00

256 Bas-relief **257** Fray Luis de Leon

1953. Stamp Day and 700th Anniv of Salamanca University. Inscr "UNIVDAD DE SALAMANCA".
1188 **256** 50c. red 55 15
1189 **257** 90c. green . . . . 2·75 2·75
1190 – 2p. brown . . . . 21·00 5·50
DESIGN—As Type **185**—HORIZ: 2p. Salamanca University.

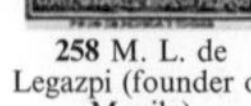

258 M. L. de Legazpi (founder of Manila) **259** "St. Mary Magdalene"

1953. Air. Signing of Filipino–Spanish Postal Convention.
1191 **258** 25p. black . . . . £150 38·00

1954. Death Tercentenary of Ribera (painter).
1192 **259** 1p.25 lake 15 15

260 St. James of Compostela **261** "Purity" (after Cano)

1954. Holy Year.
1193 **260** 50c. brown 65 30
1194 – 3p. blue . . . . 65·00 4·50
DESIGN: 3p. Santiago Cathedral.

1954. Marian Year.
1195 **261** 10c. red 20 15
1196 – 15c. green 20 15
1197 – 25c. violet 20 15
1198 – 30c. brown 20 15
1199 – 50c. green 85 15
1200 – 60c. black 20 15
1201 – 80c. green . . . . 3·75 15
1202 – 1p. violet . . . . 3·75 15
1203 – 2p. brown . . . . 1·20 15
1204 – 3p. blue . . . . 1·30 1·00
DESIGNS: 15c. Virgin of Begona, Bilbao; 25c. Virgin of the Abandoned, Valencia Cathedral; 30c. The "Black Virgin" of Montserrat; 50c. El Pilar Virgin, Zaragoza; 60c. Covadonga Virgin; 80c. Virgin of the Kings, Seville Cathedral; 1p. Almudena Virgin, Madrid; 2p. Virgin of Africa; 3p. Guadalupe Virgin.

262 M. Menendez Pelayo (historian) **263** Gen. Franco

1954. Stamp Day.
1205 **262** 80c. green . . . . 7·50 15

1955.
1206 **263** 10c. red 20 15
1207 15c. ochre 20 15
1208 20c. green 20 15
1209 25c. violet 20 15
1210 30c. brown 20 15
1211 40c. purple 20 15
1212 50c. brown 20 15
1213 60c. purple 20 15
1214 70c. green 20 15
1215 80c. turquoise 20 15
1216 1p. orange 20 15
1217 1p.40 mauve 20 15
1218 1p.50 turquoise 20 15
1219 1p.80 green 20 15
1220 2p. red . . . . 22·00 85
1221 2p. mauve 20 15
1222 3p. blue 20 15
1222a 4p. red 15 15
1223 5p. brown 20 15
1224 6p. black 20 15
1224a 7p. blue 15 15
1225 8p. violet 20 15
1226 10p. green 20 15
1226a 12p. green 15 15
1226b 20p. red 20 15

264 Torres Quevedo (engineer and inventor) **265** St. Ignatius of Loyola

1955. Air.
1229 – 25p. black . . . . 30·00 85
1230 **264** 50p. violet . . . . . . 10·50 2·00
PORTRAIT: 25p. Fortuny

1955. Stamp Day and 4th Centenary of Death of St. Ignatius of Loyola.
1231 **265** 25c. slate 20 15
1232 – 60c. ochre 85 50
1233 **265** 80c. green . . . . 3·25 50
DESIGN—HORIZ: 60c. St. Ignatius and Loyola Castle.

266 Lockheed L.1049 Super Constellation and Caravel

1955. Air.
1234 **266** 20c. green 20 15
1235 25c. violet 20 15
1236 50c. brown 20 15
1237 1p. red 20 15
1238 1p.10 green 20 15
1239 1p.40 mauve 20 15
1240 3p. blue 20 15
1241 4p.80 yellow 20 15
1242 5p. brown . . . . 1·70 15
1243 7p. mauve 80 15
1244 10p. green 60 20

267 "T-elecommunications" **269** "The Holy Family" (after El Greco)

1955. Centenary of Telegraphs in Spain.
1245 **267** 15c. brown 65 20
1246 80c. green . . . . 11·50 25
1247 3p. blue . . . . 22·00 1·10

1955. 500th Anniv of Canonization of St. Vincent Ferrer. As T **259** but portrait of the Saint (after C. Vilar).
1248 15c. ochre 20 20

1955. Christmas.
1249 **269** 80c. myrtle . . . . . . 2·40 65

270 **272** The "Black Virgin"

271 "Ciudad de Toledo" (cargo liner)

1956. 20th Anniv of Civil War.
1250 **270** 15c. brown and bistre . . 20 15
1251 50c. olive and green . . 85 45
1252 80c. grey and mauve . . 8·50 25
1253 3p. blue and ultramarine 11·50 2·30

1956. 1st Floating Exhibition of National Products.
1254 **271** 3p. blue . . . . 5·75 2·40

1956. 75th Anniv of "Black Virgin" of Montserrat.
1255 **272** 15c. brown 20 15
1256 – 60c. purple 30 20
1257 **272** 80c. green 45 40
DESIGN—VERT: 60c. Montserrat Monastery.

273 Archangel Gabriel **274** "Statistics"

1956. Stamp Day.
1258 **273** 80c. green 65 40

1956. Centenary of Statistics in Spain.
1259 **274** 15c. ochre 40 30
1260 80c. green . . . . 5·25 60
1261 1p. red . . . . 5·25 60

275 Hermitage and Monument **276** Refugee Children

1956. 20th Anniv of Gen. Franco's Assumption of Office as Head of State.
1262 **275** 80c. green . . . . 2·40 35

1956. Hungarian Children's Relief.
1263 **276** 10c. lake 20 15
1264 15c. brown 20 15
1265 50c. sepia 40 20
1266 80c. green . . . . 5·00 25

1267 1p. red . . . . 5·00 25
1268 3p. blue . . . . 14·00 2·50

277 Apparition of the Sacred Heart
278 "The Great Captain"

1957. Stamp Day and Centenary Feast of the Sacred Heart.
1269 **277** 15c. brown 20 15
1270 60c. purple 25 15
1271 80c. green 25 15

1958. 5th Birth Cent of Gonzalves de Cordoba.
1272 **278** 1p.80 green 15 15

279 Francisco Goya after Lopez
280 Exhibition Emblem

1958. Stamp Day and Goya (painter) Commem. Frames in gold.
1273 – 15c. ochre 20 15
1274 – 40c. purple 20 15
1275 – 50c. green 20 15
1276 – 60c. purple 20 15
1277 – 70c. green 20 15
1278 **279** 80c. green 20 15
1279 – 1p. red 20 15
1280 – 1p.80 green 20 15
1281 – 2p. purple 40 25
1282 – 3p. blue . . . . 1·00 45
PAINTINGS—HORIZ: 15c. "The Sunshade"; 3p. "The Drinker". VERT: 40c. "The Bookseller's Wife"; 50c. "The Count of Fernan-Nunez"; 60c. "The Crockery Vendor"; 70c. "Dona Isabel Cobos de Porcel"; 1p. "The Carnival Doll"; 1p.80, "Marianito Goya"; 2p. "The Vintage".
For similar designs see Nos. 1301/10, 1333/42, 1391/1400, 1479/88, 1495/8, 1559/68, 1627/36, 1718/27, 1770/9, 1837/46, 1912/21, 1968/77, 2021/30, 2077/84, 2135/42 and 2204/11.

1958. Brussels International Exhibition.
1283 **280** 80c. brown, red and deep brown 20 15
1284 3p. blue, red and black 90 85

1958. Brussels Exhibition, Madrid. Sheets each 49 × 83 mm containing Nos. 1283/4 in new colours.
MS1285 80c. green, red and brown (sold at 2p.) . . . . 35·00 25·00
MS1286 3p. violet, orange and brown (sold at 5p.) . . . . . 35·00 25·00

281 Emperor Charles V (after Strigell)

1958. 4th Death Cent of Emperor Charles V.
1287 **281** 15c. brown and ochre . . 20 15
1288 – 50c. olive and green . . 20 15
1289 – 70c. green and drab . . 20 15
1290 – 80c. green and brown . . 20 15
1291 **281** 1p. red and buff 20 15
1292 – 1p.80 emerald and green 20 15
1293 – 2p. purple and grey . . . 65 55
1294 – 3p. blue and brown . . . 1·70 1·30
PORTRAITS of Charles V: 50c., 1p.80, At Battle of Muhlberg (after Titian); 70c., 2p. (after Leoni); 80c., 3p. (after Titian).

282 Talgo II Articulated Train and Escorial

1958. 17th Int Railway Congress, Madrid. Inscr "XVII CONGRESO", etc.
1295 **282** 15c. ochre 20 15
1296 – 60c. plum 20 15
1297 – 80c. green 20 15
1298 **282** 1p. orange 65 15
1299 – 2p. purple 65 15
1300 – 3p. blue . . . . 2·20 1·30
DESIGNS—VERT: 60c., 2p. Class 1600 diesel-electric locomotive on viaduct, Despenaperros Gorge. HORIZ: 80c., 3p. Class 242F steam locomotive and Castillo de La Mota.

1959. Stamp Day and Velazquez Commem. Designs as T **279**. Frames in gold.
1301 15c. sepia 15 15
1302 40c. purple 15 15
1303 50c. olive 15 15
1304 60c. sepia 15 15
1305 70c. green 15 15
1306 80c. myrtle 15 15
1307 1p. brown 15 15
1308 1p.80 green 15 15
1309 2p. purple 30 30
1310 3p. blue 45 45
PAINTINGS—HORIZ: 15c. "The Drunkards". VERT: 40c. "The Spinners" (detail); 50c. "The Surrender of Breda"; 60c. "Las Meninas"; 70c. "Balthasar Don Carlos"; 80c. Self-portrait; 1p. "The Coronation of the Virgin"; 1p.80, "Aesop"; 2p. "The Forge of Vulcan"; 3p. "Menippus".

284 The Holy Cross of the Valley of the Fallen

1959. Completion of Monastery of the Holy Cross of the Valley of the Fallen.
1311 **284** 80c. green and brown . . 15 10

285 Mazarin and Luis de Haro (after tapestry by Lebrun)
286 Monastery from Courtyard

1959. 300th Anniv of Treaty of the Pyrenees.
1312 **285** 1p. brown and gold . . 15 15

1959. 50th Anniv of Entry of Franciscan Community into Guadeloupe Monastery.
1313 **286** 15c. brown 20 15
1314 – 80c. myrtle 20 15
1315 – 1p. red 20 15
DESIGNS: 80c. Exterior view of monastery; 1p. Entrance doors of church.

287 "The Holy Family" (after Goya)
288 Pass with Muleta

1959. Christmas.
1316 **287** 1p. brown 15 15

1960. Bullfighting.
1317 – 15c. brown and ochre (postage) 15 15
1318 – 20c. violet and blue . . . 15 15
1319 – 25c. black 15 15
1320 – 30c. brown and bistre . . 15 15
1321 – 50c. brown and violet . . 15 15
1322 – 70c. green and brown . . 15 15
1323 **288** 80c. emerald and green 15 15
1324 – 1p. brown and red . . . 25 15
1325 – 1p.40 purple and brown 20 15
1326 – 1p.50 green and blue . . 20 15
1327 – 1p.80 blue and green . . 20 15
1328 – 5p. red and brown . . . 65 55
1329 – 25c. dp pur & pur (air) 20 15
1330 – 50c. blue and turquoise 20 15
1331 – 1p. red and vermilion . . 20 15
1332 – 5p. violet and purple . . 65 45
DESIGNS—HORIZ: No. 1317, Fighting bull; No. 1318, Rounding-up bull; No. 1327, Placing darts from horseback; No. 1330, Pass with cape; No. 1332, Bull-ring. VERT: No. 1319, Corralling bulls at Pamplona; No. 1320, Bull entering ring; No. 1321, As No. 1330 (different pass); No. 1322, Banderillero placing darts; No. 1323/6, As Type **288** (different passes with muleta); No. 1328, Old-time bull-fighter; No. 1329, Village bull-ring; No. 1331, Dedicating the bull.

1960. Stamp Day and Murillo Commemoration. (painter). Designs as T **279**. Frames in gold.
1333 25c. violet 20 15
1334 40c. purple 20 15
1335 50c. olive 20 15
1336 70c. green 20 15
1337 80c. turquoise 20 15
1338 1p. brown 20 15
1339 1p.50 turquoise 20 15
1340 2p.50 red 20 15
1341 3p. blue . . . . 1·40 65
1342 5p. brown 40 25
PAINTINGS—VERT: 25c. "The Good Shepherd"; 40c. "Rebecca and Elizer"; 50c. "The Virgin of the Rosary"; 70c. "The Immaculate Conception"; 80c. "Children with Shells"; 1p. Self-portrait; 2p.50, "The Dice Game"; 3p. "Children Eating"; 5p. "Children with Coins". HORIZ: 1p.50, "The Holy Family with Bird".

289 "Christ of Lepanto"
290 Pelota Player

1960. International Philatelic Congress and Exhibition, Barcelona. Inscr "CIF".
1343 **289** 70c. lake & green (postage) . . . . . . 1·60 1·30
1344 – 80c. black and sage . . . 1·60 1·30
1345 **289** 1p. purple and red . . . 1·60 1·30
1346 – 2p.50 slate and violet . . 1·60 1·30
1347 **289** 5p. sepia and bistre . . . 1·60 1·30
1348 – 10p. sepia and ochre . . 1·60 1·30
1349 **290** 1p. black and red (air) 4·75 3·00
1350 5p. red and brown . . . 4·75 3·00
1351 6p. red and purple . . . 4·75 3·00
1352 10p. red and green . . . 4·75 3·00
DESIGN—VERT: Nos. 1344, 1346, 1348, Church of the Holy Family, Barcelona.

291 St. John of Ribera
292 St. Vincent de Paul

1960. Canonization of St. John of Ribera.
1353 **291** 1p. brown 20 15
1354 2p.50 mauve 20 15

1960. Europa. 1st Anniv of European Postal and Telecommunications Conference. As T **144a** of Switzerland but size 38½ × 22 mm.
1355 1p. drab and green 40 20
1356 5p. red and brown 55 75

1960. 300th Death Anniv of St. Vincent de Paul.
1357 **292** 25c. violet 15 15
1358 1p. brown 15 15

293 Menendez de Aviles
294 Running

1960. 400th Anniv of Discovery and Colonization of Florida.
1359 **293** 25c. blue and light blue 20 15
1360 – 70c. green and orange 20 15
1361 – 80c. green and stone . . 20 15
1362 – 1p. brown and yellow . . 20 15
1363 **293** 2p. red and pink 35 15
1364 – 2p.50 mauve and green 55 15
1365 – 3p. blue and green . . . 3·25 75
1366 – 5p. brown and bistre . . 2·10 1·20
PORTRAITS: 70c., 2p.50, Hernando de Soto; 80c., 3p. Ponce de Leon; 1, 5p. Cabeza de Vaca.

1960. Sports.
1367 **294** 25c. brn and bl (postage) 20 15
1368 – 40c. orange and violet 20 15
1369 – 70c. red and green . . . 35 15

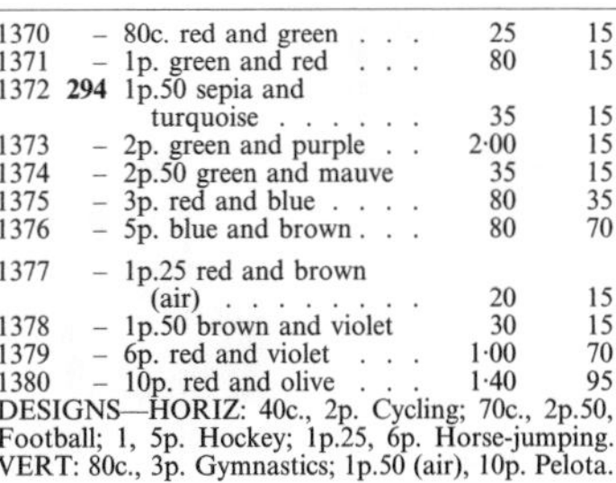

1370 – 80c. red and green . . . 25 15
1371 – 1p. green and red . . . 80 15
1372 **294** 1p.50 sepia and turquoise 35 15
1373 – 2p. green and purple . . 2·00 15
1374 – 2p.50 green and mauve 35 15
1375 – 3p. red and blue 80 35
1376 – 5p. blue and brown . . . 80 70
1377 – 1p.25 red and brown (air) 20 15
1378 – 1p.50 brown and violet 30 15
1379 – 6p. red and violet . . . 1·00 70
1380 – 10p. red and olive . . . 1·40 95
DESIGNS—HORIZ: 40c., 2p. Cycling; 70c., 2p.50, Football; 1, 5p. Hockey; 1p.25, 6p. Horse-jumping. VERT: 80c., 3p. Gymnastics; 1p.50 (air), 10p. Pelota.

295 Albeniz
296 Cloisters

1960. Birth Cent of Isaac Albeniz (composer).
1381 **295** 25c. violet 20 15
1382 1p. brown 20 15

1960. Samos Monastery.
1383 **296** 80c. turquoise and green 20 15
1384 – 1p. lake and brown . . . 1·20 15
1385 – 5p. sepia and bistre . . . 1·30 95
DESIGNS—VERT: 1p. Fountain; 5p. Portico and facade.

297 "The Nativity" (Velazquez)
298 "The Flight to Egypt" (after Bayeu)

1960. Christmas.
1386 **297** 1p. brown 30 15

1961. World Refugee Year.
1387 **298** 1p. brown 20 15
1388 5p. brown 45 35

299 L. F. Moratin (after Goya)
301 Velazquez (Prado Memorial)

1961. Birth Bicentenary of Moratin (poet and dramatist).
1389 **299** 1p. red 15 15
1390 1p.50 turquoise 15 15

1961. Stamp Day and El Greco (painter) Commem. Designs as T **279**. Frames in gold.
1391 25c. purple 15 15
1392 40c. purple 15 15
1393 70c. green 20 15
1394 80c. turquoise 15 15
1395 1p. purple . . . . 2·50 15
1396 1p.50 turquoise 15 15
1397 2p.50 lake 20 15
1398 3p. blue . . . . 1·90 95
1399 5p. sepia . . . . 4·25 2·30
1400 10p. violet 60 40
PAINTINGS: 25c. "St. Peter"; 40c. Madonna (detail, "The Holy Family" ("Madonna of the Good Milk")); 70c. Detail of "The Agony in the Garden"; 80c. "Man with Hand on Breast"; 1p. Self-portrait; 1p.50, "The Baptism of Christ"; 2p.50, "The Holy Trinity"; 3p. "Burial of the Count of Orgaz"; 5p. "The Spoliation"; 10p. "The Martyrdom of St. Maurice".

1961. 300th Death Anniv of Velazquez.
1401 **301** 80c. green and blue . . . 1·30 20
1402 – 1p. brown and red . . . 6·50 20
1403 – 2p.50 violet and blue . . 85 55
1404 – 10p. green and light green . . . . 9·00 2·00
PAINTINGS—VERT: 1p. "The Duke of Olivares"; 2p.50, "Princess Margarita". HORIZ: Part of "The Spinners".

Sheets each 71 × 86 mm. Colours changed. Imperf.
MS1405 80c. slate and brown . . 7·50 8·00
MS1406 1p. violet and blue . . . 7·50 8·00
MS1407 2p.50 blue and green . . 7·50 8·00
MS1408 10p. blue and slate . . . 7·50 8·00
Sold at 1p.10, 1p.40, 3p.50 and 14p. respectively.

302 "Stamp" and "Postmark" **303** Vazquez de Mella

1961. World Stamp Day.
1409 **302** 25c. black and red . . . 15 15
1410 1p. red and black . . . 1·10 15
1411 10p. green and purple . . 1·20 60

1961. Birth Centenary of Juan Vazquez de Mella (politician and writer).
1412 **303** 1p. red 40 15
1413 2p.30 purple 15 15

304 Gen. Franco **305** "Portico de la Gloria" (Cathedral of Santiago de Compostela)

1961. 25th Anniv of National Uprising. Mult.
1414 70c. Angel and flag 15 15
1415 80c. Straits of Gibraltar . . 15 15
1416 1p. Knight and Alcazar, Toledo 15 15
1417 1p.50 Victory Arch 15 15
1418 2p. Knight crossing River Ebro 15 15
1419 2p.30 Soldier, flag and troops 15 15
1420 2p.50 Shipbuilding 15 15
1421 3p. Steelworks 30 35
1422 5p. Map of Spain showing electric power stations (horiz) . . . . 2·40 1·30
1423 6p. Irrigation (woman beside dam) . . . . 1·80 1·80
1424 8p. Mine 75 75
1425 10p. Type **304** 65 70

1961. Council of Europe's Romanesque Art Exhibition. Inscr as in T **305**.
1426 **305** 25c. violet and gold . . 15 15
1427 – 1p. brown and gold . . 15 15
1428 – 2p. purple and gold . . 40 15
1429 – 3p. multicoloured . . . 40 50
DESIGNS: 1p. Courtyard of Dominican Monastery, Santo Domingo de Silos; 2p. Madonna of Irache; 3p. "Christos Pantocrator" (from Tahull Church fresco).

306 L. de Gongora (after Velazquez) **308** Burgos Cathedral

307 Doves and C.E.P.T. Emblem

1961. 400th Birth Anniv of De Gongora (poet).
1430 **306** 25c. violet 15 15
1431 1p. brown 20 15

1961. Europa.
1432 **307** 1p. red 15 15
1433 5p. brown 40 40

1961. 25th Anniv of Gen. Franco as Head of State.
1434 **308** 1p. green and gold . . . 15 15

309 S. de Belalcazar **310** Courtyard

1961. Explorers and Colonizers of America (1st series).
1435 **309** 25c. violet and green . . 15 15
1436 – 70c. green and buff . . . 15 15
1437 – 80c. green and pink . . 15 15
1438 – 1p. blue and flesh . . . 45 15
1439 **309** 2p. red and blue . . . . 3·50 20
1440 – 2p.50 purple and mauve 90 55
1441 – 3p. blue and grey . . . 2·10 90
1442 – 5p. brown and yellow . . 2·10 1·20
PORTRAITS: 70c., 2p.50, B de Lezo; 80c., 3p. R. de Bastidas; 1, 5p. N. de Chaves.
See also Nos. 1515/22, 1587/94, 1683/90, 1738/45, 1810/17, 1877/84, 1947/51, 1997/2001 and 2054/8.

1961. Escorial.
1443 – 70c. green and turquoise 20 15
1444 **310** 80c. slate and green . . 15 15
1445 – 1p. red and brown . . . 55 15
1446 – 2p.50 purple and violet 30 15
1447 – 5p. sepia and ochre . . . 1·60 90
1448 – 6p. purple and blue . . . 2·40 2·20
DESIGNS—VERT: 70c. Patio of the Kings; 2p.50, Grand Staircase; 6p. High Altar. HORIZ: 1p. Monks' Garden; 5p. View of Escorial.

311 King Alfonso XII Monument **312** Santa Maria del Naranco Church

1961. 400th Anniv of Madrid as Capital of Spain.
1449 **311** 25c. purple and green . . 15 15
1450 – 1p. brown and bistre . . 30 15
1451 – 2p. purple and grey . . . 30 15
1452 – 2p.50 violet and red . . 15 15
1453 – 3p. black and blue . . . 65 45
1454 – 5p. blue and brown . . . 1·40 85
DESIGNS—VERT: 1p. King Philip II (after Pantoja); 5p. Plaza, Madrid. HORIZ: 2p. Town Hall, Madrid; 2p.50, Fountain of Cybele; 3p. Portals of Alcala Palace.

1961. 1200th Anniv of Oviedo.
1455 **312** 25c. violet and green . . 15 15
1456 – 1p. brown and bistre . . 35 15
1457 – 2p. sepia and purple . . 1·00 15
1458 – 2p.50 violet and purple 15 15
1459 – 3p. black and blue . . . 85 45
1460 – 5p. brown and green . . 85 90
DESIGNS: 1p. Fruela (portrait); 2p. Cross of the Angels; 2p.50, Alfonso II; 3p. Alfonso III; 5p. Apostles of the Holy Hall, Oviedo Cathedral.

313 "The Nativity" (after Gines) **314** Cierva C.30A Autogyro

1961. Christmas.
1461 **313** 1p. plum 25 15

1961. 50th Anniv of Spanish Aviation.
1462 **314** 1p. violet and blue . . . 15 15
1463 – 2p. green and lilac . . . 30 15
1464 – 3p. black and green . . 1·40 75
1465 – 5p. purple and slate . . 3·25 1·30
1466 – 10p. brown and blue . . 1·50 50
DESIGNS—HORIZ: 2p. CASA-built Dornier Do-J Wal flying boat "Plus Ultra"; 3p. Breguet 19GR airplane "Jesus del Gran Poder" (Madrid-Manila Flight). VERT: 5p. Avro 504K biplane hunting great bustard; 10p. Madonna of Loreto (patron saint) and North American F-86F Sabre jet fighters.

315 Arms of Alava **316** "Ecstasy of St. Teresa" (Bernini)

1962. Arms of Provincial Capitals. Multicoloured.
1467 5p. Type **315** 15 15
1468 5p. Albacete 15 15
1469 5p. Alicante 25 25
1470 5p. Almeria 25 25
1471 5p. Avila 25 25
1472 5p. Badajoz 15 15
1473 5p. Baleares 15 15
1474 5p. Barcelona 15 15
1475 5p. Burgos 65 50
1476 5p. Caceres 40 35
1477 5p. Cadiz 55 40
1478 5p. Castellon de la Plana . . 4·75 2·20
See also Nos. 1542/53, 1612/23, 1692/1703 and 1756/64.

1962. Stamp Day and Zurbaran (painter) Commem. As T **279**. Frames in gold.
1479 25c. olive 15 15
1480 40c. purple 15 15
1481 70c. green 15 15
1482 80c. turquoise 15 15
1483 1p. sepia . . . . 7·50 15
1484 1p.50 turquoise 65 15
1485 2p.50 lake 65 15
1486 3p. blue . . . . 1·30 95
1487 5p. brown . . . . 3·25 1·80
1488 10p. olive . . . . 3·25 1·80
PAINTINGS—HORIZ: 25c. "Martyr". VERT: 40c. "Burial of St. Catalina"; 70c. "St. Casilda"; 80c. "Jesus crowning St. Joseph"; 1p. Self-portrait; 1p.50, "St. Hieronymus"; 2p.50, "Madonna of the Grace"; 3p. Detail from "Apotheosis of St. Thomas Aquinas"; 5p. "Madonna as a Child"; 10p. "The Immaculate Madonna".

1962. 4th Centenary of Teresian Reformation.
1489 – 25c. violet 15 15
1490 **316** 1p. brown 15 15
1491 – 3p. blue . . . . 1·20 40
DESIGNS—As Type **316**: 25c. St. Joseph's Monastery, Avila. (22 × 38½ mm): 3p. "St. Teresa of Avila" (Velazquez).

317 Mercury **318** St. Benedict

1962. World Stamp Day.
1492 **317** 25c. pink, purple & violet 15 15
1493 1p. yellow, brown and bistre 15 15
1494 10p. green and turquoise 1·80 95

1962. Rubens Paintings. As T **279**. Frames in gold.
1495 25c. violet 25 15
1496 1p. brown . . . . 3·50 15
1497 3p. turquoise . . . . . . 5·50 2·50
1498 10p. green . . . . 6·25 2·40
PAINTINGS—As Type **279**: 25c. Ferdinand of Austria; 1p. Self-portrait; 3p. Philip II. (26 × 39 mm): 10p. Duke of Lerma.

1962. 400th Death Anniv of Alonso Berruguete (sculptor). Sculptures by Berruguete.
1499 **318** 25c. mauve and blue . . 15 15
1500 – 80c. green and brown . . 20 15
1501 – 1p. red and stone . . . 40 15
1502 – 2p. mauve and stone . . 3·25 15
1503 – 3p. blue and mauve . . 1·40 1·00
1504 – 10p. brown and pink . . 1·40 1·20
SCULPTURES: 80c. "The Apostle"; 1p. "St. Peter"; 2p. "St. Christopher and Child Jesus"; 3p. "Ecce Homo"; 10p. "St. Sebastian".

319 El Cid (R. Diaz de Vivar), after statue by J. Cristobal **321** Throwing the Discus

320 Honey Bee and Honeycomb

1962. El Cid Campeador Commem. Inscr "EL CID".
1505 **319** 1p. drab and green . . . 15 15
1506 – 2p. violet and sepia . . 1·50 15
1507 – 3p. green and blue . . . 4·25 2·30
1508 – 10p. green and yellow . . 2·75 1·40
DESIGNS—VERT: 2p. El Cid (equestrian statue by A. Huntington). HORIZ: 3p. El Cid's treasure chest; 10p. Oath-taking ceremony of Santa Gadea.

1962. Europa.
1509 **320** 1p. red 20 15
1510 5p. green . . . . 1·20 40

1962. 2nd Spanish–American Athletic Games, Madrid.
1511 **321** 25c. blue and pink . . . 15 15
1512 – 80c. green and yellow . . 20 15
1513 – 1p. brown and pink . . 15 15
1514 – 3p. blue and light blue 20 30
DESIGNS: 80c. Running; 1p. Hurdling; 3p. Start of sprint.

1962. Explorers and Colonizers of America (2nd series). As T **309**.
1515 25c. mauve and grey 15 15
1516 70c. green and pink 65 15
1517 80c. green and yellow . . . 40 15
1518 1p. brown and green 90 15
1519 2p. red and blue . . . . . 3·25 30
1520 2p.50 violet and brown . . 60 35
1521 3p. blue and pink . . . . . 8·00 1·80
1522 5p. brown and yellow . . . 3·75 2·50
PORTRAITS: 25c., 2p. A. de Mendoza; 70c., 2p.50, J. de Quesada; 80c., 3p. J. de Garay; 1, 5p. P. de la Gasca.

322 U.P.A.E. Emblem **323** "The Annunciation" (after Murillo)

1962. 50th Anniv of Postal Union of the Americas and Spain.
1523 **322** 1p. brown, grn & dp grn 15 15

1962. Mysteries of the Rosary.
1524 **323** 25c. brn & vio (postage) 15 15
1525 – 70c. turquoise and green 15 15
1526 – 80c. turquoise and olive 15 15
1527 – 1p. sepia and green . . . 4·75 60
1528 – 1p.50 blue and green . . 15 15
1529 – 2p. sepia and violet . . . 1·10 45
1530 – 2p.50 red and purple . . 15 15
1531 – 3p. black and violet . . 15 15
1532 – 5p. lake and brown . . . 85 85
1533 – 8p. black and purple . . 70 80
1534 – 10p. green and myrtle . . 70 40
1535 – 25c. violet and slate (air) 15 15
1536 – 1p. olive and purple . . 15 20
1537 – 5p. lake and purple . . . 60 40
1538 – 10p. yellow, green & grey . . . . 1·40 1·00
PAINTINGS—"Joyful Mysteries": No. 1525, "Visit of Elizabeth" (Correa); 1526, "The Birth of Christ" (Murillo); 1527, "Christ shown to the Elders" (Campana); 1528, "Jesus lost and found in the Temple" (unknown artist). "Sorrowful Mysteries": 1529, "Prayer on the Mount of Olives" (Giaquinto); 1530, "Scourging" (Cano); 1531, "The Crown of Thorns" (Tiepolo); 1532, "Carrying the Cross" (El Greco); 1533, "The Crucifixion" (Murillo). "Glorious Mysteries": 1534, "The Resurrection" (Murillo); 1535, "The Ascension" (Bayeu); 1536, "The Sending-forth of the Holy Ghost" (El Greco); 1537, "The Assumption of the Virgin" (Cerezo); 1538, "The Coronation of the Virgin" (El Greco).

324 "The Nativity" (after Pedro de Mena) **325** Campaign Emblem and Swamp

1962. Christmas.
1539 **324** 1p. olive 30 15

1962. Malaria Eradication.
1540 **325** 1p. black, yellow & green 15 15

326 Pope John and Dome of St. Peter's **327** "St. Paul" (after El Greco)

1962. Ecumenical Council. Vatican City (1st issue).
1541 **326** 1p. slate and purple . . 15 15
See also Nos. 1601 and 1755.

1963. Arms of Provincial Capitals. As T **315**. Multicoloured.
1542 5p. Ciudad Real 55 50
1543 5p. Cordoba . . . . 4·25 1·90
1544 5p. Coruna 55 60
1545 5p. Cuenca 55 45
1546 5p. Fernando Poo . . . . 85 1·10
1547 5p. Gerona 15 15
1548 5p. Gran Canaria 15 15
1549 5p. Granada 55 35
1550 5p. Guadalajara 55 35
1551 5p. Guipuzcoa 15 15

1552 5p. Huelva 15 15
1553 5p. Huesca 15 15

1963. 1900th Anniv of Arrival of St. Paul in Spain.
1554 **327** 1p. sepia, olive and brown 20 15

328 Poblet Monastery

329 Mail Coach

1963. Poblet Monastery.
1555 **328** 25c. purple, sepia & green 15 15
1556 – 1p. orange and red . . . 40 15
1557 – 3p. blue and violet . . . 1·20 35
1558 – 5p. ochre and brown . . 2·20 1·70
DESIGNS—VERT: 1p. Tomb; 5p. Arch. HORIZ: 3p. Aerial view of monastery.

1963. Stamp Day and Ribera (painter) Commem. As T **279**. Frames in gold.
1559 25c. violet 15 15
1560 40c. purple 15 15
1561 70c. green 40 15
1562 80c. turquoise 40 15
1563 1p. brown 40 15
1564 1p.50 turquoise 40 15
1565 2p.50 red . . . . 2·40 15
1566 3p. blue . . . . 3·75 70
1567 5p. brown . . . . 12·00 2·75
1568 10p. brown and purple . . . 4·50 1·50
PAINTINGS: 25c. "Archimedes"; 40c. "Jacob's Flock"; 70c. "Triumph of Bacchus"; 80c. "St. Christopher"; 1p. Self-portrait; 1p.50, "St. Andrew"; 2p.50, "St. John the Baptist"; 3p. "St. Onofrius"; 5p. "St. Peter"; 10p. "The Madonna".

1963. Centenary of Paris Postal Conference.
1569 **329** 1p. multicoloured . . . 15 15

330 Globe

1963. World Stamp Day.
1570 **330** 25c. multicoloured . . . 15 15
1571 1p. multicoloured . . . 15 15
1572 10p. multicoloured . . . 1·00 65

331 "Give us this day our daily bread"

1963. Freedom from Hunger.
1573 **331** 1p. multicoloured . . . 15 15

332 Pillars and Globes

1963. Spanish Cultural Institutions Congress. Multicoloured.
1574 25c. Type **332** 15 15
1575 80c. "Santa Maria", "Pinta" and "Nina" 40 15
1576 1p. Columbus 40 15

333 Civic Seals

334 "St. Maria of Europe"

1963. 150th Anniv of San Sebastian.
1577 **333** 25c. blue and green . . . 15 15
1578 – 80c. red and purple . . . 15 15
1579 – 1p. green and bistre . . 15 15
DESIGNS: 80c. City aflame; 1p. View of San Sebastian, 1836.

1963. Europa.
1580 **334** 1p. brown and bistre . . 15 15
1581 5p. sepia and green . . . 55 45

335 Arms of the Order of Mercy

336 Scenes from Parable of the Good Samaritan

1963. 75th Anniv of the Order of Mercy.
1582 **335** 25c. red, gold and black 25 15
1583 – 80c. sepia and green . . 15 15
1584 – 1p. purple and blue . . . 15 15
1585 – 1p.50 brown and blue . . 15 15
1586 – 3p. black and violet . . 15 15
DESIGNS: 80c. King Jaime I; 1p. Our Lady of Mercy; 1p.50, St. Pedro Nolasco; 3p. St. Raimundo de Penafort.

1963. Explorers and Colonizers of America (3rd series). As T **309**.
1587 25c. deep blue and blue . . 15 15
1588 70c. green and salmon . . . 15 15
1589 80c. green and cream . . . 45 15
1590 1p. blue and salmon 55 15
1591 2p. red and blue . . . . . 1·70 15
1592 2p.50 violet and flesh . . . 1·30 15
1593 3p. blue and pink . . . . . 2·40 1·30
1594 5p. brown and cream . . . 3·25 2·50
PORTRAITS: 25c., 2p. Brother J. Serra; 70c., 2p.50, Vasco Nunez de Balboa; 80c., 3p. J. de Galvez; 1, 5p. D. Garcia de Paredes.

1963. Red Cross Centenary.
1595 **336** 1p. violet, red and gold 15 15

337 "The Nativity" (after sculpture by Berruguete)

338 Fr. Raimundo Lulio

1963. Christmas.
1596 **337** 1p. green 15 15

1963. Famous Spaniards (1st series).
1597 **338** 1p. black & vio (postage) 15 15
1598 – 1p.50 violet and sepia . . 15 15
1599 – 25p. purple and red (air) 90 35
1600 – 50p. black and green . . 1·70 50
PORTRAITS: 1p.50, Cardinal Belluga; 25p. King Recaredo; 50p. Cardinal Cisneros.
See also Nos. 1714/17.

339 Pope Paul and Dome of St. Peter's

1963. Ecumenical Council, Vatican City (2nd issue).
1601 **339** 1p. black and turquoise 15 15

340 Alcazar de Segovia

1964. Tourist Series.
1602 – 40c. brown, blue & green 15 15
1603 – 50c. sepia and blue . . . 15 15
1604 – 70c. blue and green . . . 15 15
1605 – 70c. brown and lilac . . 15 15
1606 – 80c. black and blue . . . 15 15
1607 **340** 1p. lilac and violet . . . 15 15
1608 – 1p. red and purple . . . 15 15
1609 – 1p. black and green . . . 15 15
1610 – 1p. red and purple . . . 15 15
1611 – 1p.50 brown, green and blue 15 15
DESIGNS—HORIZ: No. 1602, Potes; 1604, Crypt of St. Isidore (Leon); 1608, Lion Court of the Alhambra (Granada); 1611, Gerona. VERT: 1603, Leon Cathedral; 1605, Costa Brava; 1606, "Christ of the Lanterns" (Cordoba); 1609, Drach Caves (Majorca); 1610, Mosque (Cordoba).
See also Nos. 1704/13, 1786/95, 1798/1805, 1860/6, 1867/74, 1933/42, 1985/9, 1993/6, 2035/9, 2040/5, 2311/6, 2379/84, 2466/7, 2575/8, 2696/2700, 2744/8, 2858/9, 2870/1 and 2915/18.

1964. Arms of Provincial Capitals. As T **315**. Multicoloured.
1612 5p. Ifni 15 15
1613 5p. Jaen 15 15
1614 5p. Leon 15 15
1615 5p. Lerida 15 15
1616 5p. Logrono 15 15
1617 5p. Lugo 15 15
1618 5p. Madrid 15 15
1619 5p. Malaga 15 15
1620 5p. Murcia 15 15
1621 5p. Navarra 15 15
1622 5p. Orense 15 15
1623 5p. Oviedo 15 15

341 Santa Maria Monastery

1964. Monastery of Santa Maria, Huerta.
1624 – 1p. bronze and green . . 15 15
1625 – 2p. sepia, black & turq 20 15
1626 **341** 5p. slate and violet . . . 1·30 75
DESIGNS—VERT: 1p. Great Hall; 2p. Cloisters.

1964. Stamp Day and Sorolla (painter) Commem. As T **279**. Frames in gold.
1627 25c. violet 15 15
1628 40c. purple 15 15
1629 70c. green 15 15
1630 80c. turquoise 15 15
1631 1p. brown 15 15
1632 1p.50 turquoise 15 15
1633 2p.50 mauve 15 15
1634 3p. blue 40 40
1635 5p. brown . . . . 1·30 1·00
1636 10p. green 65 30
PAINTINGS—VERT: 25c. "The Earthen Jar"; 70c. "La Mancha Types"; 80c. "Valencian Fisherwoman"; 1p. Self-portrait; 5p. "Pulling the Boat"; 10p. "Valencian Couple on Horse". HORIZ: 40c. "Castillan Oxherd"; 1p.50, "The Cattlepen"; 2p.50, "And people say fish is dear" (fish market); 3p. "Children on the Beach".

342 "25 Years of Peace"

1964. 25th Anniv of End of Spanish Civil War.
1637 **342** 25c. gold, green and black 15 15
1638 – 30c. red, blue and green 15 15
1639 – 40c. black and gold . . . 15 15
1640 – 50c. multicoloured . . . 15 15
1641 – 70c. multicoloured . . . 15 15
1642 – 80c. multicoloured . . . 15 15
1643 – 1p. multicoloured . . . 20 15
1644 – 1p.50 olive, red and blue 15 15
1645 – 2p. multicoloured . . . 15 15
1646 – 2p.50 multicoloured . . 15 15
1647 – 3p. multicoloured . . . 85 95
1648 – 5p. red, green and gold 30 30
1649 – 6p. multicoloured . . . 40 45
1650 – 10p. multicoloured . . . 50 60
DESIGNS—VERT: 30c. Athletes ("Sport"); 50c. Apartment-houses ("National Housing Plan"); 1p. Graph and symbols ("Economic Development"); 1p.50, Rocks and tower ("Construction"); 2p.50, Wheatear and dam ("Irrigation"); 5p. "Tree of Learning" ("Scientific Research"); 10p. Gen. Franco. HORIZ: 40c. T.V. screen and symbols ("Radio and T.V."); 70c. Wheatears, tractor and landscape ("Agriculture"); 80c. Tree and forests ("Reafforestation"); 2p. Forms of transport ("Transport and Communications"); 3p. Pylon and part of dial ("Electrification"); 6p. Ancient buildings ("Tourism").

343 Spanish Pavilion at Fair

344 6c. Stamp of 1850 and Globe

1964. New York World's Fair.
1651 **343** 1p. green and turquoise 15 15
1652 – 1p.50 brown and red . . 15 15
1653 – 2p.50 green and blue . . 15 15
1654 – 5p. red 25 25
1655 – 50p. blue and grey . . . 80 35
DESIGNS—VERT: 1p.50, Bullfighting; 2p.50, Castillo de la Mota; 5p. Spanish dancing; 50p. Pelota.

1964. World Stamp Day.
1656 **344** 25c. red and purple . . . 15 15
1657 1p. green and blue . . . 15 15
1658 10p. orange and red . . 35 30

345 Macarena Virgin

346 Medieval Ship

1964. Canonical Coronation of Macarena Virgin.
1659 **345** 1p. green and yellow . . 15 15

1964. Spanish Navy Commemoration.
1660 **346** 15c. slate and purple . . 15 15
1661 – 25c. green and orange 15 15
1662 – 40c. grey and blue . . 15 15
1663 – 50c. green and slate . . 15 15
1664 – 70c. violet and blue . . . 15 15
1665 – 80c. blue and green . . . 15 15
1666 – 1p. purple and brown . . 15 15
1667 – 1p.50 sepia and red . . . 15 15
1668 – 2p. black and green . . 65 15
1669 – 2p.50 red and violet . . 15 15
1670 – 3p. blue and brown . . . 15 15
1671 – 5p. blue and green . . . 85 85
1672 – 6p. violet and turquoise 70 75
1673 – 10p. red and orange . . 30 35
SHIPS—VERT: 25c. Carrack; 1p. Ship of the line "Santissima Trinidad"; 1p.50, Corvette "Atrevida". HORIZ: 40c. "Santa Maria"; 50c. Galley; 70c. Galleon; 80c. Xebec; 2p. Steam frigate "Isabel II"; 2p.50, Frigate "Numancia"; 3p. Destroyer "Destructor"; 5p. Isaac Peral's submarine; 6p. Cruiser "Baleares"; 10p. Cadet schooner "Juan Sebastian de Elcano".

347 Europa "Flower"

348 "The Virgin of the Castle"

1964. Europa.
1674 **347** 1p. ochre, red and green 30 15
1675 5p. blue, purple and green 90 85

1964. 700th Anniv of Reconquest of Jerez.
1676 **348** 25c. brown and buff . . 15 15
1677 1p. blue and grey . . . 15 15

349 Putting the Shot

350 "Adoration of the Shepherds" (after Zurbaran)

1965. Olympic Games, Tokyo and Innsbruck. Olympic rings in gold.
1678 **349** 25c. blue and orange . . 15 15
1679 – 80c. blue and green . . 15 15
1680 – 1p. blue and light blue 15 15
1681 – 3p. blue and buff . . . 15 15
1682 – 5p. blue and violet . . 20 15
DESIGNS: 80c. Long jumping; 1p. Skiing (slalom); 3p. Judo; 5p. Throwing the discus.

1964. Explorers and Colonizers of America (4th series). As T **309**. Inscr "1964" at foot.
1683 25c. violet and blue . . . 15 15
1684 70c. olive and pink . . . 15 15
1685 80c. green and buff . . . 30 20
1686 1p. violet and buff . . . 30 15
1687 2p. olive and blue 30 15
1688 2p.50 purple and turquoise 20 20
1689 3p. blue and grey . . . . 3·00 1·10
1690 5p. brown and cream . . . 1·70 1·40
PORTRAITS: 25c., 2p. D. de Almagro; 70c., 2p.50, F. de Toledo; 80c., 3p. T. de Mogrovejo; 1, 5p. F. Pizarro.

1964. Christmas.
1691 **350** 1p. brown 15 15

1965. Arms of Provincial Capitals. As T **315**. Multicoloured.
1692 5p. Palencia 15 15
1693 5p. Pontevedra 15 15
1694 5p. Rio Muni 15 15
1695 5p. Sahara 15 15
1696 5p. Salamanca 15 15
1697 5p. Santander 15 15
1698 5p. Segovia 15 15
1699 5p. Seville 15 15
1700 5p. Soria 15 15
1701 5p. Tarragona 15 15
1702 5p. Tenerife 15 15
1703 5p. Teruel 15 15

1965. Tourist Series. As T **340**.
1704 25c. black and blue 15 15
1705 30c. brown and turquoise 15 15
1706 50c. purple and red 15 15
1707 70c. indigo and blue 15 15
1708 80c. purple and mauve . . . 15 15
1709 1p. mauve, red and sepia . . 15 15
1710 2p.50 purple and brown . . 15 15
1711 2p.50 olive and blue 15 15
1712 3p. purple and purple . . . 15 15
1713 6p. violet and slate 15 15
DESIGNS—VERT: 25c. Columbus Monument, Barcelona; 30c. Santa Maria Church, Burgos; 50c. Synagogue, Toledo; 80c. Seville Cathedral; 1p. Cudillero Port; 2p.50, (No. 1710), Burgos Cathedral (interior); 3p. Bridge at Cambados (Pontevedra); 6p. Ceiling, Lonja (Valencia). HORIZ: 70c. Zamora; 2p.50, (No. 1711), Mogrovejo (Santander).

1965. Famous Spaniards (2nd series). As T **338**.
1714 25c. sepia and turquoise . . 15 15
1715 70c. deep blue and blue . . 15 15
1716 2p.50 sepia and bronze . . . 15 15
1717 5p. bronze and green . . . 15 15
PORTRAITS: 25c. Donoso Cortes; 70c. King Alfonso X (the Saint); 2p.50, G. M. de Jovellanos; 5p. St. Dominic de Guzman.

1965. Stamp Day and J. Romero de Torres Commem. As T **279**. Frames in gold.
1718 25c. purple 15 15
1719 40c. purple 15 15
1720 70c. green 15 15
1721 80c. turquoise 15 15
1722 1p. brown 15 15
1723 1p.50 turquoise 15 15
1724 2p.50 mauve 15 15
1725 3p. blue 35 30
1726 5p. brown 35 30
1727 10p. green 35 30
PAINTINGS (by J. Romero de Torres): 25c. "Girl with Jar"; 40c. "The Song"; 70c. "The Virgin of the Lanterns"; 80c. "Girl with Guitar"; 1p. Self-portrait; 1p.50, "Poem of Cordoba"; 2p.50, "Marta and Maria"; 3p. "Poem of Cordoba" (different); 5p. "A Little Charcoal-maker"; 10p. "Long Live the Hair!".

351 Bull and Stamps

352 I.T.U. Emblem and Symbols

1965. World Stamp Day.
1728 **351** 25c. multicoloured . . . 15 15
1729 1p. multicoloured . . . 15 15
1730 10p. multicoloured . . . 40 30

1965. Centenary of I.T.U.
1731 **352** 1p. red, black and pink 15 15

353 Pilgrim

354 Spanish Knight and Banners

1965. Holy Year of Santiago de Compostela. Multicoloured.
1732 1p. Type **353** 15 15
1733 2p. Pilgrim (profile) 15 15

1965. 400th Anniv of Florida Settlement.
1734 **354** 3p. black, red and yellow 15 15

355 St. Benedict (after sculpture by Pereira)

356 Sports Palace, Madrid

1965. Europa.
1735 **355** 1p. green and emerald 15 15
1736 5p. violet and purple . . 40 30

1965. Int Olympic Committee Meeting, Madrid.
1737 **356** 1p. brown, gold and grey 15 15

1965. Explorers and Colonizers of America (5th series). As T **309**. Inscr "1965" at foot.
1738 25c. violet and green 15 15
1739 70c. brown and pink 15 15
1740 80c. green and cream . . . 15 15
1741 1p. violet and buff 15 15
1742 2p. brown and blue 15 15
1743 2p.50 purple and turquoise 15 15
1744 3p. blue and grey 95 40
1745 5p. brown and yellow . . . 95 35
PORTRAITS: 25c., 2p. Don Fadrique de Toledo; 70c., 2p.50, Padre Jose de Anchieta; 80c., 3p. Francisco de Orellana; 1p., 5p. St. Luis Beltran.

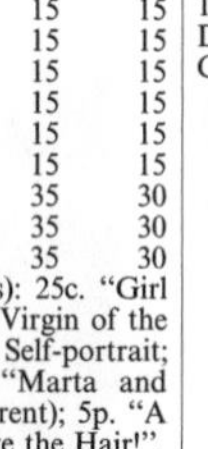

357 Cloisters

1965. Yuste Monastery.
1746 **357** 1p. blue and sepia . . . 15 15
1747 – 2p. sepia and brown . . 15 15
1748 – 5p. green and blue . . . 20 20
DESIGNS—VERT: 2p. Charles V room. HORIZ: 5p. Courtyard.

358 Spanish 1r. Stamp of 1865

360 Madonna of Antipolo

359 "The Nativity" (after Mayno)

1965. Centenary of Spanish Perforated Stamps.
1749 **358** 80c. green and bronze 15 15
1750 – 1p. brown and purple . . 15 15
1751 – 5p. brown and sepia . . 15 15
DESIGNS: 1p. 1865 19c. stamp; 5p. 1865 2r. stamp.

1965. Christmas.
1752 **359** 1p. green and blue . . . 15 15

1965. 400th Anniv of Christianity in the Philippines.
1753 **360** 1p. brown, black and buff 15 15
1754 – 3p. blue and grey . . . 15 15
DESIGN: 3p. Father Urdaneta.

361 Globe

362 Admiral Alvaro de Bazan

1965. 21st Ecumenical Council, Vatican City (3rd issue).
1755 **361** 1p. multicoloured . . . 15 15

1966. Arms of Provincial Capitals. As T **315**. Multicoloured.
1756 5p. Toledo 15 15
1757 5p. Valencia 15 15
1758 5p. Valladolid 15 15
1759 5p. Vizcaya 15 15
1760 5p. Zamora 15 15
1761 5p. Zaragoza 15 15
1762 5p. Ceuta 15 15
1763 5p. Melilla 15 15
1764 10p. Spain (26 × 38½ mm) 15 15

1966. Celebrities (1st series).
1765 **362** 25c. black and blue (postage) 15 15
1766 – 2p. violet and purple . . 15 15
1767 – 25p. bronze & green (air) 1·10 20
1768 – 50p. grey and blue . . . 1·90 55
PORTRAITS: 2p. Benito Daza de Valdes (doctor); 25p. Seneca; 50p. St. Damaso.
See also Nos. 1849/52.

363 Exhibition Emblem

364 Luno Church

1966. Graphic Arts Exn, "Graphispack", Barcelona.
1769 **363** 1p. green, blue and red 15 15

1966. Stamp Day and J. M. Sert Commem. Designs as T **279**. Frames in gold.
1770 25c. violet 15 15
1771 40c. purple 15 15
1772 70c. green 15 15
1773 80c. bronze 15 15
1774 1p. brown 15 15
1775 1p.50 blue 15 15
1776 2p.50 red 15 15
1777 3p. blue 15 15
1778 5p. sepia 15 15
1779 10p. green 15 15
PAINTINGS (by J. M. Sert)—VERT: 25c. "The Magic Ball"; 70c. "Christ Addressing the Disciples"; 80c. "The Balloonists"; 1p. Self-portrait; 1p.50, "Audacity"; 2p.50, "Justice"; 3p. "Jacob's Struggle with the Angel"; 5p. "The Five Parts of the World"; 10p. "St. Peter and St. Paul". HORIZ: 40c. "Memories of Toledo".

1966. 600th Anniv of Guernica. Multicoloured.
1780 80c. Type **364** 15 15
1781 1p. Arms of Guernica . . . 15 15
1782 3p. "Tree of Guernica" . . 15 15

365 Postmarked 6 cuartos Stamp of 1850

1966. World Stamp Day.
1783 **365** 25c. multicoloured . . . 15 15
1784 – 1p. multicoloured . . . 15 15
1785 – 10p. multicoloured . . . 15 15
DESIGNS—POSTMARKED STAMPS: 1p. 5r. stamp of 1850; 10p. 10r. stamp of 1850.

1966. Tourist Series. As T **340**.
1786 10c. emerald and green . . 15 15
1787 15c. bistre and green . . . 15 15
1788 40c. brown and chestnut . . 15 15
1789 50c. purple and red 15 15
1790 80c. purple and mauve . . . 15 15
1791 1p. turquoise and blue . . . 15 15
1792 1p.50 black and blue . . . 15 15
1793 2p. brown and blue 15 15
1794 3p. brown and blue 15 15
1795 10p. blue and turquoise . . 15 15
DESIGNS—VERT: 10c. Bohi waterfalls (Lerida); 40c. Sigena monastery (Huesca); 50c. Santo Domingo Church (Soria); 80c. Golden Tower (Seville); 1p. El Teide (Canaries); 10p. Church of St. Gregory (Valladolid). HORIZ: 15c. Torla (Huesca); 1p.50, Cathedral, Guadalupe; 2p. University, Alcala de Henares; 3p. La Seo Cathedral (Lerida).

366 Tree and Globe

1966. World Forestry Congress.
1796 **366** 1p. green, brown and deep brown 15 15

367 Crown and Anchor

368 Butron Castle (Vizcaya)

1966. Naval Week, Barcelona.
1797 **367** 1p. blue and grey . . . 15 15

1966. Spanish Castles (1st series).
1798 – 10c. sepia and blue . . . 15 15
1799 – 25c. purple and violet . . 15 15
1800 – 40c. green and turquoise 15 15
1801 – 50c. blue and indigo . . 15 15
1802 – 70c. blue and ultramarine 15 15
1803 **368** 80c. green and violet . . 15 15
1804 – 1p. olive and brown . . 15 15
1805 – 3p. purple and red . . . 15 15
CASTLES—HORIZ: 10c. Guadamur (Toledo); 25c. Alcazar (Segovia); 40c. La Mota (Medina del Campo); 50c. Olite (Navarra); 70c. Monteagudo (Murcia); 1p. Manzanares (Madrid). VERT: 3p. Almansa (Albacete).

369 Don Quixote, Dulcinea and Aldonza Lorenzo

1966. 4th World Psychiatric Congress, Madrid.
1806 **369** 1p.50 multicoloured . . 15 15

370 "Europa and the Bull"

371 Horseman in the Sky

1966. Europa.
1807 **370** 1p. multicoloured . . . 15 15
1808 5p. multicoloured . . . 25 20

1966. 17th Int Astronautics Federation Congress, Madrid.
1809 **371** 1p.50 red, black and blue 15 15

1966. Explorers and Colonizers of America (6th series). As T **309**. Inscr "1966" at foot.
1810 30c. bistre and brown . . . 15 15
1811 50c. red and green 15 15
1812 1p. violet and blue 15 15
1813 1p.20 slate and grey 15 15
1814 1p.50 myrtle and green . . . 15 15
1815 3p. blue 15 15
1816 3p.50 violet and lilac . . . 15 15
1817 6p. brown and buff 15 15
DESIGNS: 30c. A. de Mendoza; 50c. Title page of Dominican Fathers' "Christian Doctrine"; 1p. J. A. Manso de Velasco; 1p.20, Coins of Lima Mint (1699); 1p.50, M. de Castro y Padilla; 3p. Oruro Convent; 3p.50, M. de Amat; 6p. Inca postal runner.

372 R. del Valle Inclan

373 Monastery Facade

1966. Spanish Writers.
1818 **372** 1p.50 green and black 15 15
1819 – 3p. violet and black . . 15 15
1820 – 6p. blue and black . . . 15 15
WRITERS: 3p. Carlos Arniches; 6p. J. Benavente y Martinez.
See also Nos. 1888/91.

1966. St. Mary's Carthusian Monastery, Jerez.
1821 **373** 1p. indigo and blue . . . 15 15
1822 – 2p. light green and green 15 15
1823 – 5p. plum and purple . . 15 15
DESIGNS—HORIZ: 2p. Cloisters; 5p. Gateway.

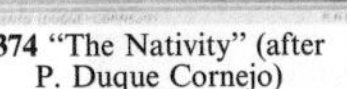

374 "The Nativity" (after P. Duque Cornejo) **375** Alava Costume

1966. Christmas.
1824 **374** 1p.50 multicoloured . . 15 15

1967. Provincial Costumes. Multicoloured.
1825 6p. Type **375** 15 15
1826 6p. Albacete 15 15
1827 6p. Alicante 15 15
1828 6p. Almeria 15 15
1829 6p. Avila 15 15
1830 6p. Badajoz 15 15
1831 6p. Baleares 15 15
1832 6p. Barcelona 15 15
1833 6p. Burgos 15 15
1834 6p. Caceres 15 15
1835 6p. Cadiz 15 15
1836 6p. Castellon de la Plana . . 15 15
See also Nos. 1897/1908, 1956/67, 2007/18 and 2072/6.

376 Archers

1967. Stamp Day. Cave Paintings. Multicoloured.
1837 40c. Type **376** 15 15
1838 50c. Boar-hunting 15 15
1839 1p. Trees (vert) 15 15
1840 1p.20 Bison 15 15
1841 1p.50 Hands 15 15
1842 2p. Hunter (vert) 15 15
1843 2p.50 Deer (vert) 15 15
1844 3p.50 Hunters 15 15
1845 4p. Chamois-hunters (vert) . . 15 15
1846 6p. Deer-hunter (vert) . . . 15 15

377 Cathedral, Palma de Mallorca, and Union Emblem

1967. Interparliamentary Union Congress, Palma de Mallorca.
1847 **377** 1p.50 green 15 15

378 Wilhelm Rontgen (physicist)

1967. Radiology Congress, Barcelona.
1848 **378** 1p.50 green 15 15

1967. Celebrities (2nd series). As T **362**.
1849 1p.20 violet and purple . . 15 15
1850 3p.50 purple 15 15
1851 4p. sepia and brown 15 15
1852 25p. grey and blue 15 15
PORTRAITS: 1p.20, Averroes (physician and philosopher); 3p.50, Acosta (poet); 4p. Maimonides (physician and philosopher); 25p. Andres Laguna (physician).

379 Cogwheels **381** Spanish 5r. Stamp of 1850 with Numeral Postmark

380 Fair Building

1967. Europa.
1853 **379** 1p.50 green, brown & red 15 15
1854 6p. violet, blue & purple 15 15

1967. 50th Anniv of Valencia Int Samples Fair.
1855 **380** 1p.50 green 15 15

1967. World Stamp Day.
1856 **381** 40c. brown, blue & black 15 15
1857 – 1p.50 lake, blue and green 15 15
1858 – 6p. blue, red and black 15 15
DESIGNS: 1p.50, Spanish 12c. stamp of 1850 with crowned "M" (Madrid) postmark; 6p. Spanish 6r. stamp of 1850 with "1.R." postmark.
See also Nos. 1927/8, 1980/1, 2032, 2091, 2150 and 2185.

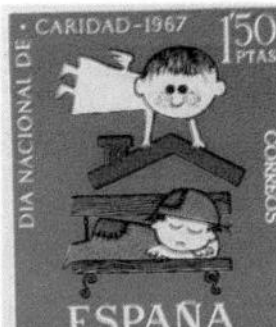

382 Sleeping Vagrant and "Guardian Angel" **383** I.T.Y. Emblem

1967. National Day for Caritas Welfare Organization.
1859 **382** 1p.50 multicoloured . . 15 15

1967. Tourist Series and Int Tourist Year.
1860 – 10c. black and blue . . . 15 15
1861 – 1p. black and blue . . . 15 15
1862 – 1p.50 black and brown 15 15
1863 – 2p.50 blue and turquoise 15 15
1864 **383** 3p.50 blue and purple . . 15 15
1865 – 5p. bronze and green . . 15 15
1866 – 6p. purple and mauve . . 15 15
DESIGNS: 10c. Betanzos Church (Corunna); 1p. St. Miguel's Tower (Palencia); 1p.50, Castellers (acrobats); 2p.50, Columbus Monument (Huelva); 5p. "Enchanted City" (Cuenca); 6p. Church of our Lady, Sanlucar (Cadiz).

1967. Spanish Castles (2nd series). As T **368**.
1867 50c. brown and grey 15 15
1868 1p. violet and grey 15 15
1869 1p.50 green and blue . . . 15 15
1870 2p. brown and red 15 15
1871 2p.50 brown and green . . . 15 15
1872 5p. blue and purple 15 15
1873 6p. sepia and brown 15 15
1874 10p. green and blue 15 15
CASTLES—HORIZ: 50c. Balsareny (Barcelona); 1p. Jarandilla (Caceres); 1p.50, Almodovar (Cordoba); 2p.50, Peniscola (Castellon); 5p. Coca (Segovia); 6p. Loarre (Huesca); 10p. Belmonte (Cuenca). VERT: 2p. Ponferrada (Leon).

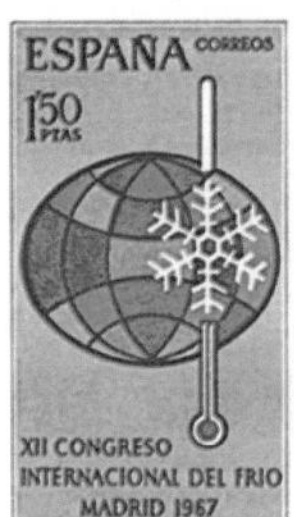

384 Globe and Snow Crystal **385** Map of the Americas, Spain and the Philippines

1967. 12th Int Refrigeration Congress, Madrid.
1875 **384** 1p.50 blue 15 15

1967. 4th Spanish, Portuguese, American and Philippine Municipalities Congress, Barcelona.
1876 **385** 1p.50 violet 15 15

1967. Explorers and Colonizers of America (7th series). As T **309**. Inscr "1967" at foot.
1877 40c. olive and orange . . . 15 15
1878 50c. agate and grey 15 15
1879 1p. mauve and blue 15 15
1880 1p.20 green and cream . . . 15 15
1881 1p.50 green and flesh . . . 15 15
1882 3p. violet and buff 15 15
1883 3p.50 blue and pink 15 15
1884 6p. brown 15 15
DESIGNS—VERT: 40c. J. Francisco de la Bodega y Quadra; 50c. Map of Nutka coast; 1p. F. A. Mourelle; 1p.50, E. J. Martinez; 3p.50, Cayetano Valdes y Florez. HORIZ: 1p.20, View of Nutka; 3p. Map of Californian coast; 6p. San Elias, Alaska.

387 Ploughing with Oxen **388** Main Portal, Veruela Monastery

1967. 2000th Anniv of Caceres. Multicoloured.
1885 1p.50 Statue and archway 15 15
1886 3p.50 Type **387** 15 15
1887 6p. Roman coins 15 15
Nos. 1885 and 1887 are vert.

1967. Anniversaries. Portraits as T **372**.
1888 1p.20 brown and black . . . 15 15
1889 1p.50 green and black . . . 15 15
1890 3p.50 violet and black . . . 15 15
1891 6p. blue and black 15 15
DESIGNS: 1p.20, P. de S. Jose Bethencourt (founder of Bethlehemite Order, 300th death anniv); 1p.50, Enrique Granados (composer, birth cent); 3p.50, Ruben Dario (poet, birth centenary); 6p. San Ildefonso, Archbishop of Toledo (after El Greco) (1900th death anniv).

1967. Veruela Monastery.
1892 **388** 1p.50 blue & ultramarine 15 15
1893 – 3p.50 grey and green . . 15 15
1894 – 6p. purple and brown . . 15 15
DESIGNS—HORIZ: 3p.50, Aerial view of monastery; 6p. Cloisters.

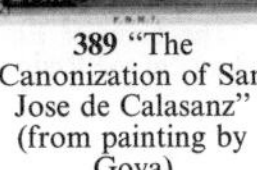

389 "The Canonization of San Jose de Calasanz" (from painting by Goya) **390** "The Nativity" (Salzillo)

1967. Bicentenary of Canonization of San Jose de Calasanz.
1895 **389** 1p.50 multicoloured . . 15 15

1967. Christmas.
1896 **390** 1p.50 multicoloured . . 15 15

1968. Provincial Costumes. As T **375**. Mult.
1897 6p. Ciudad Real 15 15
1898 6p. Cordoba 15 15
1899 6p. Coruna 15 15
1900 6p. Cuenca 15 15
1901 6p. Fernando Poo 15 15
1902 6p. Gerona 15 15
1903 6p. Las Palmas (Gran Canaria) 15 15
1904 6p. Granada 15 15
1905 6p. Guadalajara 15 15
1906 6p. Guipuzcoa 15 15
1907 6p. Huelva 15 15
1908 6p. Huesca 15 15

391 Slalom

1968. Winter Olympic Games, Grenoble. Multicoloured.
1909 1p.50 Type **391** 15 15
1910 3p.50 Bobsleighing (vert) . . 15 15
1911 6p. Ice hockey 15 15

1968. Stamp Day and Fortuny Commemoration As T **279**. Frames in gold.
1912 40c. purple 15 15
1913 50c. green 15 15
1914 1p. brown 15 15
1915 1p.20 violet 15 15
1916 1p.50 green 15 15
1917 2p. brown 15 15
1918 2p.50 red 15 15
1919 3p.50 brown 15 15
1920 4p. olive 15 15
1921 6p. blue 15 15
Fortuny Paintings—HORIZ: 40c. "The Vicarage"; 1p.20, "The Print Collector"; 6p. "Queen Christina". VERT: 50c. "Fantasia"; 1p. "Idyll"; 1p.50, Self-portrait; 2p. "Old Man Naked to the Sun"; 2p.50, "Typical Calabrian"; 3p.50, "Portrait of Lady"; 4p. "Battle of Tetuan".

392 Beatriz Galindo

1968. Famous Spanish Women. With background scenes.
1922 **392** 1p.20 brown and bistre 15 15
1923 – 1p.50 blue and turquoise 15 15
1924 – 3p.50 violet 15 15
1925 – 6p. black and blue . . . 15 15
WOMEN: 1p.50, Agustina de Aragon; 3p.50, Maria Pacheco; 6p. Rosalia de Castro.

393 Europa "Key"

1968. Europa.
1926 **393** 3p.50 gold, brn & blue 15 15

1968. World Stamp Day. As T **381**, but stamps and postmarks changed. Inscr "1968".
1927 1p.50 black, brown and blue 15 15
1928 3p.50 blue, black and green 15 15
DESIGNS: 1p.50, Spanish 6c. stamp of 1850 with Puebla (Galicia) postmark; 3p.50, Spanish 6r. stamp of 1850 with Serena postmark.

394 Emperor Galba's Coin **395** Human Rights Emblem

1968. 1900th Anniv of Foundation of Leon by VIIth Roman Legion.
1929 – 1p. brown and purple . . 15 15
1930 – 1p.50 brown and yellow 15 15
1931 **394** 3p.50 green and ochre 20 20
DESIGNS—VERT: 1p. Inscribed tile and town map of Leon (26 × 47 mm); 1p.50, Legionary with standard (statue).

1968. Human Rights Year.
1932 **395** 3p.50 red, green and blue 15 15

1968. Tourist Series. As T **340**.
1933 50c. brown 15 15
1934 1p.20 green 15 15
1935 1p.50 blue and green . . . 15 15
1936 2p. purple 15 15
1937 3p.50 purple 15 15
DESIGNS—VERT: 50c. Count Benavente's Palace, Baeza; 1p.50, Sepulchre, St. Vincent's Church, Avila; 3p.50, Main portal, Church of Santa Maria, Sanguesa (Navarra). HORIZ: 1p.20, View of Salamanca; 2p. "The King's Page" (statue), Siguenza Cathedral.

1968. Spanish Castles (3rd series). As T **368**.
1938 40c. sepia and blue 15 15
1939 1p.20 purple 15 15
1940 1p.50 black and bistre . . . 15 15
1941 2p.50 bronze and green . . 15 15
1942 6p. turquoise and blue . . . 15 15
DESIGNS—HORIZ: 40c. Escalona; 1p.20, Fuensaldana; 1p.50, Penafiel; 2p.50, Villas and obroso. VERT: 6p. Frias.

396 Rifle-shooting

1968. Olympic Games, Mexico. Multicoloured.
1943 1p0. Type **396** 15 15
1944 1p.50 Horse-jumping . . . 15 15
1945 3p.50 Cycling 15 15
1946 6p. Yachting (vert) 15 15

1968. Explorers and Colonisers of America (8th series). As T **309** but inscr "1968" at foot.
1947 40c. blue and light blue . . 15 15
1948 1p. purple and blue 15 15
1949 1p.50 green and flesh . . . 15 15
1950 3p.50 blue and mauve . . . 20 20
1951 6p. brown and yellow . . . 20 20
DESIGNS—VERT: 40c. Map of Orinoco missions; 1p. Diego de Losada (founder of Caracas); 1p.50, Arms of the Losadas; 3p.50, Diego de Henares (builder of Caracas). HORIZ: 6p. Old plan of Santiago de Leon de Caracas.

397 Monastery Building

398 "The Nativity" (Barocci)

1968. Santa Maria del Parral Monastery.
1952 **397** 1p.50 lilac and blue . . . 15 15
1953 – 3p.50 brown & chocolate 15 15
1954 – 6p. brown and red . . . 15 15
DESIGNS—VERT: 3p.50, Cloisters; 6p. "Santa Maria del Parral".

1968. Christmas.
1955 **398** 1p.50 multicoloured . . 15 15

1969. Provincial Costumes. As T **375**. Mult.
1956 6p. Ifni 15 15
1957 6p. Jaen 15 15
1958 6p. Leon 15 15
1959 6p. Lerida 15 15
1960 6p. Logrono 15 15
1961 6p. Lugo 15 15
1962 6p. Madrid 15 15
1963 6p. Malaga 15 15
1964 6p. Murcia 15 15
1965 6p. Navarra 15 15
1966 6p. Orense 15 15
1967 6p. Oviedo 15 15

1969. Stamp Day and Alonso Cano Commem. Various paintings as T **279**. Frames gold: centre colours below.
1968 40c. red 15 15
1969 50c. green 15 15
1970 1p. sepia 15 15
1971 1p.50 green 15 15
1972 2p. brown 15 15
1973 2p.50 mauve 15 15
1974 3p. blue 15 15
1975 3p.50 purple 15 15
1976 4p. purple 15 15
1977 6p. blue 15 15
Alonso Cano paintings—VERT: 40c. "St. Agnes"; 50c. "St. Joseph"; 1p. "Christ supported by an Angel"; 1p.50, "Alonso Cano" (Velazquez); 2p. "The Holy Family"; 2p.50, "The Circumcision"; 3p. "Jesus and the Samaritan"; 3p.50, "Madonna and Child"; 6p. "The Vision of St. John the Baptist". HORIZ: 4p. "St. John Capistrano and St. Bernardin".

399 Molecules and Diagram

1969. 6th European Biochemical Congress.
1978 **399** 1p.50 multicoloured . . 15 15

400 Colonnade

1969. Europa.
1979 **400** 3p.50 multicoloured . . 15 15

1969. World Stamp Day. As T **381**.
1980 1p.50 black, red and green 15 15
1981 3p.50 green, red and blue 15 15
DESIGNS: 1p.50, Spanish 6c. stamp of 1851 with "A 3 1851" postmark; 3p.50, Spanish 10r. stamp of 1851 with "CORVERA" postmark.

401 Spectrum

1969. 15th Int Spectroscopical Conf, Madrid.
1982 **401** 1p.50 multicoloured . . 15 15

402 Red Cross Symbols and Globe

1969. 50th Anniv of League of Red Cross Societies.
1983 **402** 1p.50 multicoloured . . 15 15

403 Capital, Lugo Cathedral

1969. 300th Anniv of Dedication of Galicia to Jesus Christ.
1984 **403** 1p.50 brown, blk & grn 15 15

1969. Spanish Castles (4th series). As T **368**.
1985 1p. purple and green 15 15
1986 1p.50 blue and violet . . . 15 15
1987 2p.50 lilac and blue 15 15
1988 3p.50 brown and green . . . 20 15
1989 6p. drab and green 15 15
CASTLES—HORIZ: 1p. Turegano; 1p.50, Villalonso; 2p.50, Velez Blanco; 3p.50, Castilnovo; 6p. Torrelobaton.

404 Franciscan Friar and Child

405 Rock of Gibraltar

1969. Bicentenary of San Diego (California).
1990 **404** 1p.50 multicoloured . . 15 15

1969. Aid for Spanish "ex-Gibraltar" Workers.
1991 **405** 1p.50 blue 15 15
1992 – 2p. purple 15 15
DESIGN: 2p. Aerial view of Rock.

1969. Tourist Series. As T **340**.
1993 1p.50 green and turquoise 15 15
1994 3p. turquoise and green . . 15 15
1995 3p.50 blue and green . . . 15 15
1996 6p. violet and green 15 15
DESIGNS—HORIZ: 1p.50, Alcaniz (Teruel). VERT: 3p. Murcia Cathedral; 3p.50, "The Lady of Elche" (sculpture); 6p. Church of Our Lady of the Redonda, Logrono.

1969. Explorers and Colonizers of America (9th series). Chile. As T **309**. Inscr "1969" at foot.
1997 40c. brown on blue 15 15
1998 1p.50 violet on flesh . . . 15 15
1999 2p. green on mauve 15 15
2000 3p.50 green on cream . . . 35 30
2001 6p. brown on cream 25 20
DESIGNS—VERT: 40c. Convent of Santo Domingo, Santiago de Chile; 2p. Ambrosio O'Higgins; 3p.50, Pedro de Valdivia (founder of Santiago de Chile). HORIZ: 1p.50, Chilean Mint; 6p. Cal y Canto Bridge.

406 "Adoration of the Three Kings" (Maino)

1969. Christmas. Multicoloured.
2002 1p.50 Type **406** 15 15
2003 2p. "The Nativity" (Gerona Cathedral) 15 15

407 Las Huelgas Monastery

1969. Las Huelgas Monastery, Burgos.
2004 **407** 1p.50 slate and green . . 15 15
2005 – 3p.50 blue 40 40
2006 – 6p. olive and green . . . 20 15
DESIGNS—HORIZ: 3p.50, Tombs. VERT: 6p. Cloisters.

1970. Provincial Costumes. As T **375**. Multicoloured.
2007 6p. Palencia 15 15
2008 6p. Pontevedra 15 15
2009 6p. Sahara 15 15
2010 6p. Salamanca 15 15
2011 6p. Santa Cruz de Tenerife 15 15
2012 6p. Santander 15 15
2013 6p. Segovia 15 15
2014 6p. Seville 15 15
2015 6p. Soria 15 15
2016 6p. Tarragona 15 15
2017 6p. Teruel 15 15
2018 6p. Toledo 15 15

408 Blessed Juan of Avila (after El Greco)

409 "St. Stephen"

1970. Spanish Celebrities.
2019 **408** 25p. blue and lilac . . . 4·25 15
2020 – 50p. brown and orange 1·90 20
DESIGN: 25p. Type **408** (400th death anniv); 50p. Cardinal Rodrigo Ximenes de Rada (after J. de Borgena) (800th birth anniv).
See also Nos. 2129/31.

1970. Stamp Day and Luis de Morales Commem. Various paintings. Multicoloured.
2021 50c. Type **409** 15 15
2022 1p. "The Annunciation" . . 15 15
2023 1p.50 "Virgin and Child with St. John" 15 15
2024 2p. "Virgin and Child" . . 15 15
2025 3p. "The Presentation of the Infant Christ" 15 15
2026 3p.50 "St. Jerome" 15 15
2027 4p. "St. John of Ribera" . . 15 15
2028 5p. "Ecce Homo" 15 15
2029 6p. "Pieta" 15 15
2030 10p. "St. Francis of Assisi" 15 15
See also Nos. 2077/84, 2135/42, 2204/11, 2261/8, 2420/7, 2478/85, 2529/36 and 2585/90.

410 "Flaming Sun"

1970. Europa.
2031 **410** 3p.50 gold & ultramarine 15 15

1970. World Stamp Day. As T **381** but stamp and postmark changed.
2032 2p. red, black and green . . 15 15
DESIGN: 2p. Spanish 12c. stamp of 1860 with railway cachet.

411 Fair Building

1970. 50th Anniv of Barcelona Fair.
2033 **411** 15p. multicoloured . . . 20 15

412 Gen. Primo de Rivera

1970. Birth Cent of General Primo de Rivera.
2034 **412** 2p. green, brown and buff 15 15

1970. Spanish Castles (5th series). As T **368**.
2035 1p. black and blue 35 15
2036 1p.20 blue and turquoise . . 15 15
2037 3p.50 brown and green . . . 15 15
2038 6p. violet and brown . . . 20 15
2039 10p. brown and chestnut . . 80 15
CASTLES—HORIZ: 1p. Valencia de Don Juan; 1p.20, Monterrey; 3p.50, Mombeltran; 6p. Sadaba; 10p. Bellver.

1970. Tourist Series. As T **340**.
2040 50c. lilac and blue 15 15
2041 1p. brown and ochre . . . 15 15
2042 1p.50 green and blue . . . 15 15
2043 2p. blue and deep blue . . . 15 15
2044 3p.50 blue and violet . . . 15 15
2045 5p. brown and blue 15 15
DESIGNS—HORIZ: 50c. Alcazaba, Almeria; 1p. Malaga Cathedral; 2p. St. Francis' Convent, Orense. VERT: 1p.50, Our Lady of the Assumption, Lequeitio; 3p.50, The Lonja, Zaragoza; 5p. The Portalon, Vitoria.

413 17th-century Tailor

1970. International Tailoring Congress.
2046 **413** 2p. violet, red and brown 15 15

414 Diver on Map

1970. 12th European Swimming, Diving and Water-polo Championships, Barcelona.
2047 **414** 2p. brown, blue and green 15 15

415 Concha Espina

417 "The Adoration of the Shepherds" (El Greco)

416 Survey Map of Southern Spain and North Africa

1970. Spanish Writers.
2048 **415** 50c. blue, brown and buff 15 15
2049 – 1p. violet, green and drab 15 15
2050 – 1p.50 green, blue & drab 15 15
2051 – 2p. olive, green and buff 15 15
2052 – 2p.50 pur, vio & ochre 15 15
2053 – 3p.50 red, brown & lilac 15 15
WRITERS: 1p. Guillen de Castro; 1p.50, J. R. Jimenez; 2p. G. A. Becquer; 2p.50, Miguel de Unamuno; 3p.50, J. M. Gabriel y Galan.

1970. Explorers and Colonizers of America (10th series). Mexico. As T **309**.
2054 40c. green on light green . . 15 15
2055 1p.50 brown on blue 15 15
2056 2p. violet on cream 50 15
2057 3p.50 green on light green 15 15
2058 6p. blue on pink 25 15
DESIGNS—VERT: 40c. House in Queretaro; 2p. Vasco de Quiroga; 3p.50, F. Juan de Zumarraga; 6p. Morelia Cathedral. HORIZ: 1p.50, Cathedral, Mexico City.

1970. Centenary of Spanish Geographical and Survey Institute.
2059 **416** 2p. multicoloured . . . 15 15

1970. Christmas. Multicoloured.
2060 1p.50 Type **417** 15 15
2061 2p. "The Adoration of the Shepherds" (Murillo) . . 15 15

418 U.N. Emblem and New York Headquarters

1970. 25th Anniv of United Nations.
2062 **418** 8p. multicoloured . . . 15 15

419 Ripoll Monastery

420 Pilgrims' Route Map

1970. Ripoll Monastery.
2063 – 2p. purple and violet . . 45 15
2064 **419** 3p.50 purple and orange 15 15
2065 – 5p. green and slate . . . 90 15
DESIGNS: 2p. Entrance; 5p. Cloisters.

1971. Holy Year of Compostela (1st issue). "St. James in Europe".
2066 **420** 50c. brown and blue . . 15 15
2067 – 1p. black and brown . . 15 15
2068 – 1p.50 purple and green 20 15
2069 – 2p. brown and purple . . 15 15
2070 – 3p. deep blue and blue 20 15
2071 – 4p. olive 40 15
DESIGNS—VERT: 1p. Statue of St. Brigid, Vadstena (Sweden); 1p.50, St. Jacques' Church tower, Paris; 2p. "St. James" (carving from altar, Pistoia, Italy). HORIZ: 3p. St. David's Cathedral, Wales; 4p. Carving from Ark of Charlemagne (Aachen, West Germany).
See also Nos. 2105/11 and 2121/8.

1971. Provincial Costumes. As T **375**. Mult.
2072 6p. Valencia 15 15
2073 8p. Valladolid 40 15
2074 8p. Vizcaya 40 15
2075 8p. Zamora 40 15
2076 8p. Zaragoza 40 15

1971. Stamp Day and Ignacio Zuloaga Commem. Paintings as T **409**. Multicoloured.
2077 50c. "My Uncle Daniel" . . 15 15
2078 1p. "Segovia" (horiz) . . . 15 15
2079 1p.50 "The Duchess of Alba" 15 15
2080 2p. "Ignacio Zuloaga" (self-portrait) 20 15
2081 3p. "Juan Belmonte" . . . 20 15
2082 4p. "The Countess of Noailles" 15 15
2083 5p. "Pablo Uranga" 20 15
2084 8p. "Boatmen's Houses, Lerma" (horiz) 20 15

421 Amadeo Vives (composer)

1971. Spanish Celebrities. Multicoloured.
2085 1p. Type **421** 15 15
2086 2p. St. Teresa of Avila (mystic) 20 15
2087 8p. B. Perez Galdos (writer) 20 20
2088 15p. R. Menendez Pidal (writer) 15 15

422 Europa Chain

1971. Europa.
2089 **422** 2p. brown, violet and blue 50 15
2090 8p. brown, light green and green 40 40

1971. World Stamp Day. As T **381**, but with different stamp and postmark.
2091 2p. black, blue and green . . 15 15
DESIGN: 2p. Spanish 6c. stamp of 1850 with "A.s." postmark.

423 Gymnast on Vaulting-horse

1971. 9th European Male Gymnastics Cup Championships, Madrid. Multicoloured.
2092 1p. Type **423** 15 15
2093 2p. Gymnast on bar 15 15

424 Great Bustard

1971. Spanish Fauna (1st series). Mult.
2094 1p. Type **424** 20 20
2095 2p. Lynx 15 15
2096 3p. Brown bear 15 15
2097 5p. Red-legged partridge (vert) 40 30
2098 8p. Spanish ibex (vert) . . . 40 40
See also Nos. 2160/4, 2192/6, 2250/4, 2317/21, 2452/6 and 2579/83.

426 Legionaries in Battle

1971. 50th Anniv of Spanish Foreign Legion. Multicoloured.
2101 1p. Type **426** 15 15
2102 2p. Ceremonial parade . . . 20 15
2103 5p. Memorial service . . . 20 15
2104 8p. Officer and mobile column 30 30

1971. Holy Year of Compostela (2nd issue). "En Route to Santiago". As T **420**.
2105 50c. purple and blue 15 15
2106 6p. blue 15 15
2107 7p. purple and deep purple 40 15
2108 7p.50 red and purple . . . 15 15
2109 8p. purple and green 20 20
2110 9p. violet and green 20 20
2111 10p. brown and green . . . 35 15
DESIGNS—HORIZ: 50c. Pilgrims' route map of northern Spain; 7p.50, Cloisters, Najera Monastery; 9p. Eunate Monastery. VERT: 6p. "Pilgrims" (sculpture, Royal Hospital, Burgos); 7p. Gateway, St. Domingo de la Calzada Monastery; 8p. Statue of Christ, Puente de la Reina; 10p. Cross of Roncesvalles.

427 "Children of the World"

1971. 25th Anniv of UNICEF.
2112 **427** 8p. multicoloured . . . 15 15

428 "Battle of Lepanto" (after L. Valdes)

1971. 400th Anniv of Battle of Lepanto.
2113 – 2p. green & brown (vert) 40 15
2114 **428** 5p. chocolate and brown 75 15
2115 – 8p. blue and red (vert) 65 65
DESIGNS: 2p. "Don John of Austria" (S. Coello); 8p. Standard of the Holy League.

429 Hockey Players

431 "The Nativity" (detail from altar, Avia)

430 De Havilland D.H.9B over Seville

1971. World Hockey Cup Championships, Barcelona.
2116 **429** 5p. multicoloured . . . 50 15

1971. 50th Anniv of Spanish Airmail Services. Multicoloured.
2117 2p. Type **430** 25 15
2118 15p. Boeing 747-100 airliner over Madrid 25 15

1971. Christmas. Multicoloured.
2119 2p. Type **431** 15 15
2120 8p. "The Birth" (detail from altar, Saga) 15 15

1971. Holy Year of Compostela (3rd issue). As T **420**.
2121 1p. black and green 15 15
2122 1p.50 violet and purple . . 15 15
2123 2p. blue and green 80 15
2124 2p.50 violet and red 15 15
2125 3p. purple and red 40 15
2126 3p.50 green and pink . . . 15 15
2127 4p. brown and blue 15 15
2128 5p. black and green 35 15
DESIGNS—VERT: 1p. Santiago Cathedral; 2p. Lugo Cathedral; 3p. Astorga Cathedral; 4p. San Tirso, Sahagun. HORIZ: 1p.50, Pilgrim approaching Santiago de Compostela; 2p.50, Villafranca del Bierzo; 3p.50, San Marcos, Leon; 5p. San Martin, Fromista.

1972. Spanish Celebrities. As T **408**.
2129 15p. green and brown . . . 20 15
2130 25p. black and green . . . 25 15
2131 50p. brown and red 50 15
CELEBRITIES: 15p. Emilia Pardo Bazan (novelist); 25p. Jose de Espronceda (poet); 50p. Fernan Gonzalez (first King of Castile).

432 Ski Jumping

433 Title-page of "Don Quixote" (1605)

1972. Winter Olympic Games, Sapporo, Japan. Multicoloured.
2132 2p. Type **432** 30 15
2133 15p. Figure skating (vert) 15 15

1972. International Book Year.
2134 **433** 2p. red and brown . . . 15 15

1972. Stamp Day and Solana Commem. Paintings by Solana. As T **409**. Multicoloured.
2135 1p. "Clowns" (vert) . . . 15 15
2136 2p. "Solana and Family" (self-portrait) 35 15
2137 3p. "Blind Musician" . . . 35 15
2138 4p. "Return of the Fishermen" 15 15
2139 5p. "Decorating Masks" . . 1·00 30
2140 7p. "The Bibliophile" . . . 50 15
2141 10p. "Merchant Navy Captain" 50 15
2142 15p. "Pombo Reunion" (vert) 50 20

434 "Abies pinsapo"

435 "Europeans"

1972. Spanish Flora (1st series). Multicoloured.
2143 1p. Type **434** 15 15
2144 2p. Strawberry tree 30 15
2145 3p. Maritime pine 35 15
2146 5p. Holm oak 50 15
2147 8p. "Juniperus thurifera" . . . 30 25
See also Nos. 2178/82, 2278/82 and 2299/303.

1972. Europa. Multicoloured.
2148 2p. Type **435** . . . . . . 1·50 15
2149 8p. "Communications" . . . 55 40

436 Cordoba Pre-stamp Postmark

1972. World Stamp Day.
2150 **436** 2p. red, black and brown 15 15

1972. Spanish Castles (6th series). As T **368**.
2151 1p. brown and green 40 35
2152 2p. brown and green 70 15
2153 3p. brown and red 70 15
2154 5p. green and blue 70 15
2155 10p. violet and blue . . . . 2·10 15
CASTLES—VERT: 1p. Sajazarra. HORIZ: 2p. Santa Catalina; 3p. Biar; 5p. San Servando; 10p. Pedraza.

437 Fencing

1972. Olympic Games, Munich. Multicoloured.
2156 1p. Type **437** 15 15
2157 2p. Weightlifting (vert) . . . 25 15
2158 5p. Rowing (vert) 15 15
2159 8p. Pole vaulting (vert) . . . 20 20

438 Chamois

439 Brigadier M. A. de Ustariz

1972. Spanish Fauna (2nd series). Mult.
2160 1p. Pyrenean desman . . . 15 15
2161 2p. Type **438** 15 15
2162 3p. Wolf 20 15
2163 5p. Egyptian mongoose (horiz) 45 15
2164 7p. Small-spotted genet (horiz) 35 15

1972. "Spain in the New World" (1st series). 450th Anniv of Puerto Rico. Multicoloured.
2165 1p. Type **439** 15 15
2166 2p. View of San Juan, 1870 (horiz) 20 15
2167 5p. View of San Juan, 1625 (horiz) 35 15
2168 8p. Map of Plaza de Bahia, 1792 (horiz) 35 35
See also Nos. 2212/5, 2271/4, 2338/41 and 2430/3.

440 Facade of Monastery

441 Grand Lyceum Theatre

1972. Monastery of St.Thomas, Avila.
2169 **440** 2p. green and blue . . . 75 15
2170 – 8p. purple and brown . . 65 30
2171 – 15p. blue and purple . . 40 15
DESIGNS—VERT: 8p. Interior of monastery. HORIZ: 15p. Cloisters.

1972. 125th Anniv of Grand Lyceum Theatre, Barcelona.
2172 **441** 8p. brown and blue . . . 20 15

442 "The Nativity"

1972. Christmas. Murals in Royal Collegiate Basilica of San Isidoro, Leon. Multicoloured.
2173 2p. Type **442** 15 15
2174 8p. "The Annunciation" . . 15 15

443 J. de Herrera and Escorial

1973. Spanish Architects (1st series).
2175 **443** 8p. green and sepia . . . 45 15
2176 – 10p. blue and brown . . 1·50 1·70
2177 – 15p. blue and green . . 35 15
DESIGNS: 10p. J. de Villanueva and Prado; 15p. V. Rodriguez and Apollo Fountain, Madrid.
See also Nos. 2295/7.

444 "Apollonias canariensis"

1973. Spanish Flora (2nd series). Canary Islands. Multicoloured.
2178 1p. Type **444** 15 15
2179 2p. "Myrica faya" 50 15
2180 4p. "Phoenix canariensis" 15 15
2181 5p. "Ilex canariensis" . . . 50 20
2182 15p. "Dracaena draco" . . 25 15
Nos. 2179/82 are vert.

445 Roman Mosaic 446 Iznajar Dam

1973. Europa.
2183 **445** 2p. multicoloured . . . 40 15
2184 – 8p. blue, red and black 35 15
DESIGN—HORIZ (37×26 mm): 8p. Europa "Posthorn".

1973. World Stamp Day. As T **381**, but with different stamp and postmark.
2185 2p. red, blue and black . . 15 15
DESIGN: 2p. Spanish 6r. stamp of 1853 with Madrid postmark.

1973. 11th Congress of Int High Dams Commission, Madrid.
2186 **446** 8p. multicoloured . . . 15 15

1973. Tourist Series. As T **340**.
2187 1p. brown and green 15 15
2188 2p. green and dark green . . 50 15
2189 3p. brown and light brown 50 15
2190 5p. violet and blue . . . . 1·40 15
2191 8p. red and green 60 15
DESIGNS—HORIZ: 1p. Gateway, Onate University, Guipuzcoa; 2p. Town Square, Lugo; 5p. Columbus' House, Las Palmas; 8p. Windmills, La Mancha. VERT: 3p. Llerena Square, Badajoz.

447 Black-bellied Sandgrouse

1973. Spanish Fauna (3rd series). Birds. Mult.
2192 1p. Type **447** 15 15
2193 2p. Black stork 30 15
2194 5p. Azure-winged magpie (vert) 45 40
2195 7p. Imperial eagle 55 15
2196 15p. Red-crested pochard (vert) 20 20

448 Hermandad Standard-bearer, Castile, 1488

1973. Spanish Military Uniforms (1st series). Multicoloured.
2197 1p. Type **448** 15 15
2198 2p. Mounted knight, Castile, 1493 (horiz) . . . . . . 40 1·70
2199 3p. Arquebusier, 1534 . . . 40 15
2200 7p. Mounted arquebusier, 1560 . . . . 30 15
2201 8p. Infantry sergeant, 1567 30 20

See also Nos. 2225/7, 2255/9, 2290/4, 2322/6, 2410/14, 2441/5, 2472/6 and 2499/503.

449 Fishes in Net and Trawler

1973. World Fishing Fair and Congress, Vigo.
2202 **449** 2p. multicoloured . . . 15 15

450 Conference Building

1973. I.T.U. Conference, Torremolinos.
2203 **450** 8p. multicoloured . . . 15 15

1973. Stamp Day and Vicente Lopez Commem. Paintings. As T **409**. Multicoloured.
2204 1p. "Ferdinand VII" . . . 15 15
2205 2p. Self-portrait 20 15
2206 3p. "La Senora de Carvallo" 20 15
2207 4p. "M. de Castelldosrrius" 15 15
2208 5p. "Isabella II" 15 15
2209 7p. "Goya" 15 15
2210 10p. "Maria Amalia of Saxony" 20 15
2211 15p. "Felix Lopez, the Organist" 20 15

451 Leon Cathedral, Nicaragua 452 Pope Gregory XI receiving St. Jerome's Petition

1973. "Spain in the New World" (2nd series). Nicaragua. Multicoloured.
2212 1p. Type **451** 15 15
2213 2p. Subtiava Church 25 15
2214 5p. Colonial-style house (vert) 45 20
2215 8p. Rio San Juan Castle . . 25 25

1973. 600th Anniv of Order of St. Jerome.
2216 **452** 2p. multicoloured . . . 15 15

453 Courtyard 454 "The Nativity" (pillar capital, Silos)

1973. Monaster of Santo Domingo de Silos, Burgos.
2217 **453** 2p. purple and brown . . 40 15
2218 – 8p. purple and blue . . . 15 15
2219 – 15p. blue and green . . 20 15
DESIGNS—HORIZ: 8p. Cloisters. VERT: 15p. "Three Saints" (statue).

1973. Christmas. Multicoloured.
2220 2p. Type **454** 15 15
2221 8p. "Adoration of the Kings" (bas-relief, Butrera) (horiz) 15 15

455 Map of Spain and the Americas

1973. 500th Anniv of Spanish Printing.
2222 **455** 1p. blue and green . . . 25 15
2223 – 7p. violet and blue . . . 15 15
2224 – 15p. green and purple . . 20 15
DESIGNS—VERT: 7p. "Teacher and pupils" (ancient woodcut); 15p. "Los Sinodales" (manuscript).

1974. Spanish Military Uniforms (2nd series). As T **448**. Multicoloured.
2225 1p. Mounted arquebusier, 1603 . . . . 15 15
2226 2p. Arquebusier, 1632 . . . 45 15
2227 3p. Mounted cuirassier, 1635 65 15
2228 5p. Mounted drummer, 1677 90 20
2229 9p. Musketeers, "Viejos Morados" Regiment, 1694 20 20

456 14th-century Nautical Chart

1974. 50th Anniv of Spanish Higher Geographical Council.
2230 **456** 2p. multicoloured . . . 15 15

457 Miguel Biada (construction engineer) and Locomotive "Mataro"

1974. 125th Anniv of Barcelona–Mataro Railway.
2231 **457** 2p. multicoloured . . . 15 15

458 Stamp Collector, Album and Magnifier

1974. "ESPANA 75" Int Stamp Exhibition, Madrid.
2232 **458** 2p. multicoloured . . . 15 15
2233 – 5p. blue, black and brown 35 35
2234 – 8p. multicoloured . . . 30 30
DESIGNS—DIAMOND (43×43 mm): 5p. Exhibition emblem; 8p. Globe and arrows.

459 "Woman with Offering"

1974. Europa. Stone Sculptures. Multicoloured.
2235 2p. Type **459** 45 15
2236 8p. "Woman from Baza" . . 20 20

460 2r. Stamp of 1854 with Seville Postmark

1974. World Stamp Day.
2237 **460** 2p. multicoloured . . . 15 15

461 Jaime Balmes (philosopher) and Monastery 462 Bramante's "Little Temple", Rome

1974. Spanish Celebrities.
2238 **461** 8p. brown and blue . . . 15 15
2239 – 10p. brown and red . . 55 55
2240 – 15p. blue and brown . . 15 15
DESIGNS: 10p. Pedro Poveda (educationalist) and mountain village; 15p. Jorge Juan (cosmographer and mariner) and shipyard.

1974. Centenary of Spanish Fine Arts Academy, Rome.
2241 **462** 5p. multicoloured . . . 15 15

463 Roman Aqueduct, Segovia

1974. Spain as a Province of the Roman Empire.
2242 **463** 1p. black and brown . . 15 15
2243 – 2p. brown and green . . 25 15
2244 – 3p. brown & light brown 15 15
2245 – 4p. blue and green . . . 15 15
2246 – 5p. purple and blue . . . 15 15
2247 – 7p. purple and green . . 15 15
2248 – 8p. green and red . . . 15 15
2249 – 9p. brown and purple . . 15 15
DESIGNS—HORIZ: 2p. Roman Bridge, Alcantara; 3p. Martial (poet) giving public reading; 5p. Theatre, Merida; 7p. Ossio, 1st Bishop of Cordoba, addressing the Synod. VERT: 4p. Triumphal Arch, Bara; 8p. Ruins of Curia, Talavera la Vieja; 9p. Statue of Emperor Trajan.

464 Tortoise

1974. Spanish Fauna (4th series). Reptiles. Mult.
2250 1p. Type **464** 15 15
2251 2p. Chameleon 25 15
2252 5p. Gecko 55 50
2253 7p. Green lizard 40 20
2254 15p. Adder 15 15

1974. Spanish Military Uniforms (3rd series). As T **448**. Multicoloured.
2255 1p. Dismounted trooper, Hussars de la Muerte, 1705 . . . . 15 15
2256 2p. Officer, Royal Regiment of Artillery, 1710 . . . . 40 15
2257 3p. Drummer and fifer, Granada Regiment, 1734 40 15
2258 7p. Guidon-bearer, Numancia Dragoons, 1737 . . . . 35 15
2259 8p. Ensign with standard, Zamora Regiment, 1739 15 15

465 Swimmer making Rescue

1974. 18th World Life-saving Championships. Barcelona.
2260 **465** 2p. multicoloured . . . 15 15

1974. Stamp Day and Eduardo Rosales. Commemoration. Various paintings as T **409**. Multicoloured.
2261 1p. "Tobias and the Angel" 15 15
2262 2p. Self-portrait 15 15
2263 3p. "Testament of Isabella the Catholic" (horiz) . . . 15 15
2264 4p. "Nena" 15 15
2265 5p. "Presentation of Don Juan of Austria" (horiz) 15 15
2266 7p. "The First Steps" (horiz) 15 15
2267 10p. "St. John the Evangelist" 25 15
2268 15p. "St. Matthew the Evangelist" 15 15

466 Figure with Letter and Posthorns

1974. Centenary of U.P.U. Multicoloured.
2269 2p. Type **466** 15 15
2270 8p. U.P.U. Monument, Berne 15 15

467 Sobremonte's House, Cordoba

1974. "Spain in the New World" (3rd series). Argentina. Multicoloured.

2271 1p. Type **467** 15 15
2272 2p. Town Hall, Buenos Aires (1929) 35 15
2273 5p. Ruins of St. Ignacio de Mini (vert) 30 15
2274 10p. "The Gaucho" (M. Fierro) (vert) 20 15

468 "Nativity" (detail, Valdavia Church)

1974. Christmas. Church Fonts. Multicoloured.

2275 2p. Type **468** 15 15
2276 3p. "Adoration of the Kings", Valcobero Church (vert) 15 15
2277 8p. As No. 2276 . . . . . 15 1·70

469 "Teucrium lanigerum"

471 Spanish 6c. and 5p. Stamps of 1850 and 1975

470 Leyre Monastery

1974. Spanish Flora (3rd series). Multicoloured.

2278 1p. Type **469** 15 15
2279 2p. "Hypericum ericoides" 15 15
2280 4p. "Thymus longiflorus" 15 15
2281 5p. "Anthyllis onobrychioides" 20 15
2282 8p. "Helianthemum paniculatum" 15 15

The 1p. and 8p. are wrongly inscribed "Teucriun" and "Heliantheum" respectively.

1974. Leyre Monastery.

2283 **470** 2p. grey and green . . . 40 15
2284 – 8p. red and brown . . . 15 15
2285 – 15p. deep green and green 30 15

DESIGNS—VERT: 8p. Pillars and bas-relief. HORIZ: 15p. Crypt.

1975. 125th Anniv of Spanish Postage Stamps.

2286 **471** 2p. blue 30 30
2287 – 3p. brown and green . . 40 40
2288 – 8p. mauve and violet . . 95 45
2289 – 10p. green and purple . . 45 40

DESIGNS—HORIZ: 3p. Mail coach, 1850; 8p. Sail packet of West Indian service. VERT: 10p. St. Mark's Chapel.

1975. Spanish Military Uniforms (4th series). As T **448**. Multicoloured.

2290 1p. Toledo Regiment, 1750 15 15
2291 2p. Royal Corps of Artillery, 1762 . . . . . 15 15
2292 3p. Queen's Regt of the Line, 1763 . . . . 1·50 20
2293 5p. Vitoria Regt of Fusiliers, 1766 . . . . 40 15
2294 10p. Dragoon of Saguntо Regt, 1775 . . . . 1·30 20

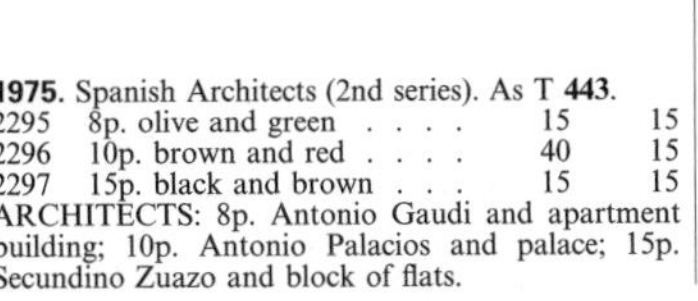

1975. Spanish Architects (2nd series). As T **443**.

2295 8p. olive and green 15 15
2296 10p. brown and red 40 15
2297 15p. black and brown . . . 15 15

ARCHITECTS: 8p. Antonio Gaudi and apartment building; 10p. Antonio Palacios and palace; 15p. Secundino Zuazo and block of flats.

472 Agate Casket

1975. "Espana 75" International Stamp Exhibition, Madrid (2nd issue). Two sheets, 124 × 88 mm or 88 × 124 mm, containing T **472** and similar designs.

MS2298 (a) 2p. blue and brown; 8p. brown and blue; 15p. red and brown; 50p. red, brown and deep brown. (b) 3p. green and brown; 10p. green, brown and deep brown; 12p. blue and brown; 25p. blue, brown and deep brown 15·00 15·00

473 Almonds

1975. Spanish Flora (4th series). Multicoloured.

2299 1p. Type **473** 15 15
2300 2p. Pomegranates (vert) . . 20 15
2301 3p. Oranges (vert) 20 15
2302 4p. Chestnuts (vert) 15 15
2303 5p. Apples (vert) 15 15

474 Woman and Pitcher, La Aranya

475 Early Leon Postmark

1975. Europa. Primitive Cave Paintings.

2304 **474** 3p. red, brown and stone 20 15
2305 – 12p. mauve, black & brn 30 20

DESIGN—HORIZ: 12p. Horse, Tito Bustillo.

1975. World Stamp Day.

2306 **475** 3p. multicoloured . . . 15 15

476 Emblem and Inscription

1975. 1st General Assembly of World Tourism Organization, Madrid.

2307 **476** 3p. blue 15 15

477 Farm Scene

1975. 25th Anniv of "Feria del Campo".

2308 **477** 3p. multicoloured . . . 15 15

478 Heads of Different Races

1975. International Women's Year.

2309 **478** 3p. multicoloured . . . 15 15

479 Virgin of Cabeza Sanctuary and Forces Emblems

1975. Defence of Virgin of Cabeza Sanctuary during Civil War Commemoration.

2310 **479** 3p. multicoloured . . . 15 15

1975. Tourist Series. As T **340**.

2311 1p. lilac and purple 15 15
2312 2p. deep brown and brown 15 15
2313 3p. black and blue 15 15
2314 4p. mauve and orange . . . 15 15
2315 5p. black and green 15 15
2316 7p. indigo and blue 35 15

DESIGNS—HORIZ: 1p. Cervantes' cell, Argamasilla de Alba; 2p. St. Martin's Bridge, Toledo; 3p. St. Peter's Church, Tarrasa. VERT: 4p. Alhambra archway, Granada; 5p. Mijas village, Malaga; 7p. St. Mary's Chapel, Tarrasa.

480 Salamander Lizard

1975. Spanish Fauna (5th series). Reptiles and Amphibians. Multicoloured.

2317 1p. Type **480** 15 15
2318 2p. Triton lizard 20 15
2319 3p. Tree-frog 20 15
2320 6p. Toad 15 15
2321 7p. Frog 15 15

1975. Spanish Military Uniforms (5th series). As T **448**. Multicoloured.

2322 1p. Montesa Regt. 1788 . . 15 15
2323 2p. Asturias Regt of Fusiliers, 1789 . . . . . 40 15
2324 3p. Infantry of the Line, 1802 . . . . 15 15
2325 4p. Royal Corps of Artillery, 1803 . . . . . 15 15
2326 7p. Royal Engineers Regt, 1809 . . . . 15 15

481 Child

1975. Child Welfare.

2327 **481** 3p. multicoloured . . . 15 15

482 Scroll

1975. Latin Notaries' Congress, Barcelona.

2328 **482** 3p. multicoloured . . . 15 15

483 "Blessing the Birds"

1975. Stamp Day and Millenary of Gerona Cathedral. Beatitude Miniatures. Multicoloured.

2329 1p. Type **483** 15 15
2330 2p. "Angel and River of Life" (vert) 15 15
2331 3p. "Angel at Gates of Paradise" (vert) 15 15
2332 4p. "Fox seizing Cockerel" 15 15
2333 6p. "Daniel with the Lions" 15 15
2334 7p. "Blessing the Multitude" (vert) 20 20
2335 10p. "The Four Horsemen of the Apocalypse" (vert) 15 15
2336 12p. "Peacock and Snake" (vert) 15 15

484 Industry Emblems

1975. Spanish Industry.

2337 **484** 3p. violet and purple . . 15 15

485 El Cabildo, Montevideo

1975. "Spain in the New World" (4th series). 150th Anniv of Uruguayan Independence. Multicoloured.

2338 1p. Type **485** 15 15
2339 2p. Ox wagon 15 15
2340 3p. Fortress, St. Teresa . . 20 15
2341 8p. Cathedral, Montevideo (vert) 15 15

486 San Juan de la Pena Monastery

1975. San Juan de la Pena Monastery Commem.

2342 **486** 3p. brown and green . . 25 15
2343 – 8p. violet and mauve . . 15 15
2344 – 10p. red and mauve . . 20 15

DESIGNS—HORIZ: 8p. Cloisters. VERT: 10p. Pillars.

487 "Virgin and Child"

1975. Christmas. Navarra Art. Multicoloured.

2345 3p. Type **487** 15 15
2346 12p. "The Flight into Egypt" (horiz) 15 15

488 King Juan Carlos I

489 Virgin of Pontevedra

1975. Proclamation of King Juan Carlos I. Multicoloured.

2347 3p. Type **488** 15 15
2348 3p. Queen Sophia 15 15
2349 3p. King Juan Carlos and Queen Sophia (33 × 33 mm) 15 15
2350 12p. As No. 2349 . . . . . 15 15

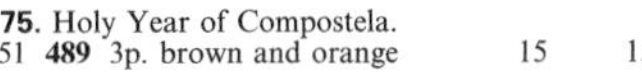

1975. Holy Year of Compostela.

2351 **489** 3p. brown and orange 15 15

490 Mountain Scene and Emblems

491 Cosme Damian Churruca and "San Juan Nepomucendo"

1976. Centenary of Catalunya Excursion Centre.

2352 **490** 6p. multicoloured . . . 15 15

1976. Spanish Navigators.
2353 **491** 7p. black and brown . . 1·30 20
2354 – 12p. violet 15 15
2355 – 50p. brown and green . . 50 15
NAVIGATORS—VERT: 12p. Luis de Requesens. HORIZ: 50p. Juan Sebastian del Cano and "Vitoria".

492 Alexander Graham Bell and Telephone Equipment

1976. Telephone Centenary.
2356 **492** 3p. multicoloured . . . 15 15

493 Crossing the Road

1976. Road Safety. Multicoloured.
2357 1p. Type **493** 15 15
2358 3p. Dangerous driving (vert) 30 15
2359 5p. Wearing of seat-belts . . 15 15

494 St. George on Horseback

1976. 700th Anniv of St. George's Guardianship of Alcoy.
2360 **494** 3p. multicoloured . . . 15 1·70

495 Talavera Pottery

1976. Europa. Spanish Handicrafts. Multicoloured.
2361 3p. Type **495** 65 15
2362 12p. Camarinas lace-making 80 25

496 Spanish 1851 6r. Stamp with Coruna Postmark

1976. World Stamp Day.
2363 **496** 3p. red, blue and black 15 15

497 Coins

1976. Bimillenary of Zaragoza. Roman Antiquities.
2364 **497** 3p. brown and black . . 1·80 15
2365 – 7p. blue and black . . . 90 25
2366 – 25p. brown and black . . 45 15
DESIGNS—HORIZ: 7p. Plan of site and coin. VERT: 25p. Mosaic.

498 Rifle, 1757

1976. Bicentenary of American Revolution.
2367 **498** 1p. blue and brown . . . 15 15
2368 – 3p. brown and green . . 90 15
2369 – 5p. green and brown . . 40 15
2370 – 12p. brown and green . . 40 25
DESIGNS: 3p. Bernado de Galvez and emblem; 5p. Richmond $1 banknote of 1861; 12p. Battle of Pensacola.

499 Customs-house, Cadiz

1976. Spanish Customs Buildings.
2371 **499** 1p. brown and black . . 15 15
2372 – 3p. brown and green . . 50 15
2373 – 7p. purple and brown . . 1·00 35
BUILDINGS: 3p. Madrid; 7p. Barcelona.

500 Savings Jar and "Industry"

1976. Spanish Post Office. Multicoloured.
2374 1p. Type **500** 15 15
2375 3p. Railway mail-sorting van 35 15
2376 6p. Mounted postman (horiz) 15 15
2377 10p. Automatic letter sorting equipment (horiz) 20 15

501 King Juan Carlos I, Queen Sophia and Map of the Americas

1976. Royal Visit to America (1st issue).
2378 **501** 12p. multicoloured . . . 20 15
See also No. 2434.

1976. Tourist Series. As T **340**.
2379 1p. brown and blue 15 15
2380 2p. green and blue 65 15
2381 3p. chocolate and brown . . 40 15
2382 4p. blue and brown 20 15
2383 7p. brown and blue 75 30
2384 12p. purple and red 95 15
DESIGNS—HORIZ: 1p. Cloisters, San Marcos, Leon; 2p. Las Canadas, Tenerife; 4p. Cruz de Tejeda, Las Palmas; 7p. Gredos, Avila; 12p. La Arruzafa, Cordoba. VERT: 3p. Hospice of the Catholic Kings, Santiago de Compostela.

502 Rowing

1976. Olympic Games, Montreal. Multicoloured.
2385 1p. Type **502** 15 15
2386 2p. Boxing 30 15
2387 3p. Wrestling (vert) 20 15
2388 12p. Basketball (vert) . . . 20 15

503 King Juan Carlos I

504 "Giving Blood"

1976.
2389 **503** 10c. orange 15 15
2390 25c. yellow 15 15
2391 30c. blue 15 15
2392 50c. purple 15 15
2393 1p. green 15 15
2394 1p.50 red 15 15
2395 2p. blue 15 15
2396 3p. green 15 15
2397 4p. turquoise 15 15
2398 5p. red 15 15
2399 6p. turquoise 15 15
2400 7p. olive 15 15
2401 8p. blue 15 15
2402 10p. red 15 15
2403 12p. brown 15 20
2403a 13p. brown 20 15
2403b 14p. orange 20 15
2404 15p. violet 25 15
2405 16p. brown 25 15
2405a 17p. blue 30 15
2406 19p. orange 30 15
2407 20p. red 30 15
2408 30p. green 40 15
2409 50p. red 85 15
2409a 60p. blue 75 15
2409b 75p. green 90 25
2409c 85p. grey . . . . . . 1·10 40
2409d – 100p. brown . . . . . 1·30 15
2409e – 200p. green . . . . . 2·50 15
2409f – 500p. blue . . . . . . 6·00 50
Nos. 2409d/f are as Type **503**, but larger, 25 × 30 mm.

1976. Spanish Military Uniforms (6th series). As T **448**. Multicoloured.
2410 1p. Alcantara Regiment, 1815 . . . . 15 15
2411 2p. Regiment of the line, 1821 . . . . 75 15
2412 3p. Gala Engineers, 1825 . . 25 15
2413 7p. Artillery Regiment, 1828 20 20
2414 25p. Light Infantry Regiment, 1830 . . . . . 25 15

1976. Blood Donors Publicity.
2415 **504** 3p. red and black . . . 15 15

505 Batitales Mosaic

506 Parliament House, Madrid

1976. Bimillenary of Lugo.
2416 **505** 1p. purple and black . . 15 15
2417 – 3p. brown and black . . 15 15
2418 – 7p. red and green . . . 40 20
DESIGNS: 3p. Old City Wall; 7p. Roman coins.

1976. 63rd Inter-Parliamentary Union Congress, Madrid.
2419 **506** 12p. brown and green . . 15 15

1976. Stamp Day and Luis Menendez Commemoration. Paintings as T **409**. Mult.
2420 1p. "Jug, Cherries, Plums and Cheese" 15 15
2421 2p. "Jar, Melon, Oranges and Savouries" 15 15
2422 3p. "Barrel, Pears and Melon" 15 15
2423 4p. "Pigeons, Basket and Bowl" 15 15
2424 6p. "Fish and Oranges" (horiz) 15 15
2425 7p. "Melon and Bread" (horiz) 25 20
2426 10p. "Jug, Plums and Bread" (horiz) 20 15
2427 12p. "Pomegranates, Apples and Grapes" (horiz) . . . 25 15

507 "The Nativity"

508 Nicoya Church

1976. Christmas. Statuettes. Multicoloured.
2428 3p. Type **507** 65 15
2429 12p. St. Christopher carrying Holy Child (vert) 1·40 40

1976. "Spain in the New World" (5th series). Costa Rica. Multicoloured.
2430 1p. Type **508** 15 15
2431 2p. Juan Vazquez de Coronado 20 15
2432 3p. Orosi Mission (horiz) . . 15 15
2433 12p. Tomas de Acosta . . . 20 15

1976. Royal Visit to America (2nd issue). As T **501**. Multicoloured.
2434 12p. "Santa Maria" and South America 25 15

510 San Pedro de Alcantara Monastery

1976. Monastery of San Pedro de Alcantara.
2435 **510** 3p. brown and purple . . 15 15
2436 – 7p. purple and blue . . . 25 15
2437 – 20p. chocolate and brown 25 15
DESIGNS—VERT: 7p. High Altar; 20p. San Pedro de Alcantara.

511 Hand releasing Doves

1976. Civil War Invalids' Association Commem.
2438 **511** 3p. multicoloured . . . 15 15

512 Pablo Casals and Cello

1976. Birth Centenaries.
2439 **512** 3p. black and blue . . . 15 15
2440 – 5p. green and red . . . 15 15
DESIGN: 5p. Manuel de Falla and "Fire Dance".

1977. Spanish Military Uniforms (7th series). Vert designs as T **448**. Multicoloured.
2441 1p. Calatrava Regiment of Lancers, 1844 . . . . . . 15 15
2442 2p. Engineers' Regiment, 1850 . . . . 30 15
2443 3p. Light Infantry Regiment, 1861 . . . . 15 15
2444 4p. Infantry of the Line, 1861 . . . . 15 15
2445 20p. Horse Artillery, 1862 20 15

513 King James I and Arms of Aragon

1977. 700th Death Anniv of King James I.
2446 **513** 4p. brown and violet . . 15 15

514 Jacinto Verdaguer (poet)

516 Atlantic Salmon

515 King Charles III

1977. Spanish Celebrities.
2447 **514** 5p. red and purple . . . 20 15
2448 – 7p. green and brown . . 15 15
2449 – 12p. green and blue . . 15 15
2450 – 50p. brown and green . . 50 15
DESIGNS: 7p. Miguel Servet (theologian and physician); 12p. Pablo Sarasate (violinist); 50p. Francisco Tarrega (guitarist).

1977. Bicentenary of Economic Society of the Friends of the Land.
2451 **515** 4p. brown and green . . 15 15

1977. Spanish Fauna (6th series). Freshwater Fishes. Multicoloured.
2452 1p. Type **516** 15 15
2453 2p. Brown trout (horiz) . . 15 15
2454 3p. European eel (horiz) . . 15 15
2455 4p. Common carp (horiz) . . 15 15
2456 6p. Barbel (horiz) 15 15

517 Skiing

1977. World Ski Championships, Granada.
2457 **517** 5p. multicoloured . . . 15 15

518 La Cuadra, 1902

1977. Vintage Cars. Multicoloured.
2458 2p. Type **518** 15 15
2459 4p. Hispano Suiza, 1916 . . 15 15
2460 5p. Elizade, 1915 . . . . . 15 15
2461 7p. Abadal, 1914 . . . . . 15 15

519 Donana

1977. Europa. Landscapes, National Parks. Multicoloured.
2462 3p. Type **519** 15 15
2463 12p. Ordesa 15 15

520 Plaza Mayor, Madrid and Stamps

1977. 50th Anniv of Philatelic Bourse on Plaza Mayor, Madrid.
2464 **520** 3p. green, red and violet 15 15

521 Enrique de Osso (founder)

1977. Centenary of Society of St. Theresa of Jesus.
2465 **521** 8p. multicoloured . . . 15 15

1977. Tourist Series. As T **340**.
2466 1p. brown and orange . . . 15 15
2467 2p. grey and brown 15 15
2468 3p. purple and blue 15 15
2469 4p. green and blue 15 15
2470 7p. grey and brown 15 15
2471 12p. brown and violet . . . 15 15
DESIGNS—HORIZ: 1p. Toledo Gate, Ciudad Real; 2p. Roman Aqueduct, Almunecar; 7p. Ampudia Castle, Palencia; 12p. Bisagra Gate, Toledo. VERT: 3p. Jaen Cathedral; 4p. Bridge and Gate, Ronda Gorge, Malaga.

1977. Spanish Military Uniforms (8th series). As T **448**. Multicoloured.
2472 1p. Administration officer, 1875 . . . . 15 15
2473 2p. Lancer, 1883 . . . . . 15 15
2474 3p. General Staff commander, 1884 . . . . 15 15
2475 7p. Trumpeter, Divisional Artillery, 1887 . . . . . 15 15
2476 25p. Medical Corps officer, 1895 . . . . 25 15

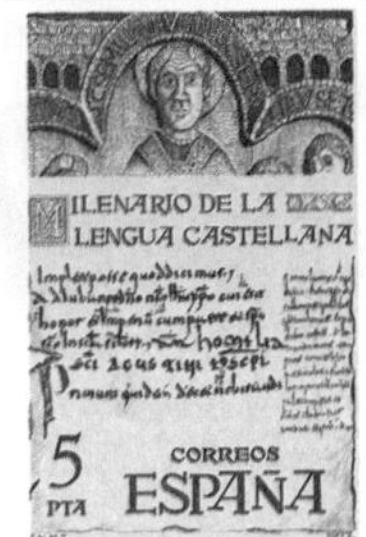

522 San Marino de la Cogalla (carving) and Early Castilian Manuscript

1977. Millenary of Castilian Language.
2477 **522** 5p. brown, green & pur 15 15

1977. Stamp Day and F. Madrazo (painter) Commemoration. Portraits. As T **409**. Mult.
2478 1p. "The Youth of Florez" 15 15
2479 2p. "Duke of San Miguel" 15 15
2480 3p. "C. Coronado" 15 15
2481 4p. "Campoamor" 15 15
2482 6p. "Marquesa de Montelo" 15 15
2483 7p. "Rivadeneyra" 15 15
2484 10p. "Countess of Vilches" 15 15
2485 15p. "Gomez de Avellaneda" 15 15

523 West Indies Sailing Packet and Map of Mail Routes to America

1977. Bicentenary of Mail to the Indies, and "Espamer 77" Stamp Exhibition, Barcelona.
2486 **523** 15p. green and brown . . 15 15

524 St. Francis's Church

1977. Spanish–Guatemalan Relations. Guatemala City Buildings. Multicoloured.
2487 1p. Type **524** 15 15
2488 3p. High-rise flats 15 15
2489 7p. Government Palace . . 15 15
2490 12p. Monument, Columbus Square 15 15

525 Monastery Building

1977. St. Peter's Monastery, Cardena Commem.
2491 **525** 3p. grey and blue . . . 15 15
2492 – 7p. red and brown . . . 15 15
2493 – 20p. grey and green . . 20 15
DESIGNS: 7p. Cloisters; 20p. El Cid (effigy).

526 Adoration of the Kings

1977. Christmas. Miniatures from Manuscript "Romanico de Huesca". Multicoloured.
2494 5p. Type **526** 15 15
2495 12p. Flight into Egypt (vert) 15 15

527 Rohrbach Ro.VII Roland, 1927, and Douglas DC-10

1977. 50th Anniv of Iberia (State Airline).
2496 **527** 12p. multicoloured . . . 15 15

528 Crown Prince Felipe

529 Judo

1977. Felipe de Borbon, Prince of Asturias.
2497 **528** 5p. multicoloured . . . 15 15

1977. 10th World Judo Championships.
2498 **529** 3p. black, red and brown 15 15

1977. Spanish Military Uniforms (9th series). Multicoloured. Vert designs as T **448**.
2499 1p. Standard bearer, Royal Infantry Regiment, 1908 15 15
2500 2p. Lieutenant-Colonel, Pavia Hussars', 1909 . . . 15 15
2501 3p. Lieutenant, Horse Artillery, 1912 . . . . . 15 15
2502 5p. Engineers' Captain, 1921 15 15
2503 12p. Captain-General of the Armed Forces, 1925 . . . 15 15

530 Hilarion Eslava (composer)

531 "The Deposition of Christ" (detail Juan de Juni)

1977. Spanish Celebrities.
2504 **530** 5p. black and purple . . 15 15
2505 – 8p. black and green . . 15 15
2506 – 25p. black and green . . 25 15
2507 – 50p. purple and brown 50 15
DESIGNS: 8p. Jose Clara (sculptor); 25p. Pio Baroja (writer); 50p. Antonio Machado (writer).

1978. Anniversaries of Artists.
2508 **531** 3p. multicoloured . . . 15 15
2509 – 3p. multicoloured . . . 15 15
2510 – 3p. mauve and violet . . 15 15
2511 – 5p. multicoloured . . . 15 15
2512 – 5p. multicoloured . . . 15 15
2513 – 5p. brown and black . . 15 15
2514 – 8p. multicoloured . . . 15 15
2515 – 8p. multicoloured . . . 15 15
2516 – 8p. pink and green . . . 15 15
DESIGNS—As T **531**. No. 2510, Portrait of Juan de Juni (sculptor, 400th death anniv); No. 2511, Detail of "Rape of the Sabines" (Rubens); No. 2513, Artist's palette and Ruben's signature; No. 2514, Detail of "Bacchanal" (Titian); No. 2516, Artist's palette and Titian's initial. 46 × 25 mm: No. 2509, Different detail of "Deposition of Christ" and sculptor's tools; No. 2512, Different detail of "Rape of the Sabines" and portrait of Rubens (400th birth anniv); No. 2515, Different detail of "Bacchanal" and portrait of Titian (500th birth anniv).

532 Edelweiss in the Pyrenees

1978. Protection of the Environment. Mult.
2517 3p. Type **532** 15 15
2518 5p. Brown trout and red-breasted merganser . . . 15 15
2519 7p. Forest (fire prevention) 15 15
2520 12p. Tanker, oil rig and industrial complex (protection of the sea) . . 15 15
2521 20p. Audouin's gull and Mediterranean monk seal (vert) 20 15

533 Palace of Charles V, Granada

1978. Europa.
2522 **533** 5p. green and light green 15 15
2523 – 12p. red and green . . . 15 15
DESIGN: 12p. Exchange building, Seville.

534 Council Emblem and Map of Spain

1978. Membership of the Council of Europe.
2524 **534** 12p. multicoloured . . . 15 15

535 Columbus Hermitage

1978. 500th Anniv of Las Palmas, Gran Canaria. Multicoloured.
2525 3p. 16th-century plan of city (horiz) 15 15
2526 5p. Type **535** 15 15
2527 12p. View of Las Palmas (16th century) (horiz) . . 15 15

536 Post Box, Stamp, U.P.U. Emblem and Postal Transport

1978. World Stamp Day.
2528 **536** 5p. green and deep green 15 15

1978. Stamp Day and Picasso Commemoration. As T **409**. Multicoloured.
2529 3p. "Portrait of Senora Canals" 15 15
2530 5p. Self-portrait 15 15
2531 8p. "Portrait of Jaime Sabartes" 15 15
2532 10p. "The End of the Number" 15 15
2533 12p. "Science and Charity" (horiz) 15 15
2534 15p. "Las Meninas" (horiz) 15 15
2535 20p. "The Pigeons" 20 15
2536 25p. "The Painter and Model" (horiz) 25 15

537 Jose de San Martin

1978. Latin-American Heroes.
2537 **537** 7p. brown and red . . . 15 15
2538 – 12p. violet and red . . . 15 15
DESIGNS: 12p. Simon Bolivar.

538 Flight into Egypt

1978. Christmas. Capitals from Santa Maria de Nieva. Multicoloured.
2539 5p. Type **538** 15 15
2540 12p. The Annunciation . . 15 15

539 Aztec Calendar

1978. Royal Visits to Mexico, Peru and Argentina. Multicoloured.
2541 5p. Type **539** 15 15
2542 5p. Macchu Piccu, Peru . . 15 15
2543 5p. Pre-Columbian pots, Argentina 15 15

540 Philip V

1978. Spanish Kings and Queens of the House of Bourbon.
2544 **540** 5p. red and blue 15 15
2545 – 5p. deep green and green 15 15
2546 – 8p. lake and blue 15 15
2547 – 10p. black and green . . 15 15
2548 – 12p. lake and brown . . 15 15
2549 – 15p. blue and green . . 15 15
2550 – 20p. blue and olive . . . 15 15
2551 – 25p. violet and blue . . 15 15
2552 – 50p. brown and red . . 15 15
2553 – 100p. violet and blue . . 15 15
DESIGNS: 5p. (No. 2545), Luis I; 8p. Ferdinand VI; 10p. Charles III; 12p. Charles IV; 15p. Ferdinand VII; 20p. Isabel II; 25p. Alfonso XII; 50p. Alfonso XIII; 100p. Juan Carlos I.

541 Miniatures from Bible

1978. Millenary of Consecration of Third Basilica of Santa Maria, Ripoll.
2554 **541** 5p. multicoloured . . . 15 15

542 Flag, First Lines of Constitution and Cortes Building

1978. New Constitution.
2555 **542** 5p. multicoloured . . . 15 15

543 Car and Oil Drop

545 Jorge Manrique (poet)

544 St. Jean Baptiste de la Salle (founder)

1979. Energy Conservation. Multicoloured.
2556 5p. Type **543** 15 15
2557 8p. Insulated house and thermometer 15 15
2558 10p. Hand removing electric plug 15 15

1979. Centenary of Brothers of the Christian Schools in Spain.
2559 **544** 5p. brown, blue & mauve 15 15

1979. Spanish Celebrities.
2560 **545** 5p. brown and green . . 15 15
2561 – 8p. blue and red 15 15
2562 – 10p. violet and brown 15 15
2563 – 20p. green and bistre . . 20 15
DESIGNS: 8p. Fernan Caballero (novelist); 10p. Francisco Villaespesa (poet); 20p. Gregorio Maranon (writer).

546 Running and Jumping

1979. Sport for All.
2564 **546** 5p. red, green and black 15 15
2565 – 8p. blue, ochre and black 15 15
2566 – 10p. brown, blue & black 15 15
DESIGNS: 8p. Football, running, skipping and cycling; 10p. Running.

547 School Library (child's drawing)

1979. International Year of the Child.
2567 **547** 5p. multicoloured . . . 15 15

548 Cabinet Messenger and Postilion, 1761

549 Wave Pattern and Television Screen

1979. Europa.
2568 **548** 5p. deep brown and brown on yellow . . . 15 15
2569 – 12p. green and brown on yellow 15 15
DESIGN—HORIZ: 12p. Manuel de Ysasi (postal reformer).

1979. World Telecommunications Day. Mult.
2570 5p. Type **549** 15 15
2571 8p. Satellite and receiving aerial (horiz) 15 15

550 First Bulgarian Stamp and Exhibition Hall

1979. "Philaserdica 79" Stamp Exhibition, Sofia.
2572 **550** 12p. multicoloured . . . 15 15

551 Tank, "Roger de Lauria" (destroyer) and Hawker Siddeley Matador Jet Fighter

1979. Armed Forces Day.
2573 **551** 5p. multicoloured . . . 15 15

552 King receiving Messenger

1979. Stamp Day.
2574 **552** 5p. multicoloured . . . 15 15

1979. Tourist Series. As T **340**.
2575 5p. lilac and blue 15 15
2576 8p. brown and blue 15 15
2577 10p. green and myrtle . . . 15 15
2578 20p. sepia and brown . . . 15 15
DESIGNS—VERT: 5p. Daroca Gate, Zaragoza; 8p. Gerona Cathedral; 10p. Interior of Carthusian Monastery Church, Granada; 20p. Portal of Marques de Dos Aguas Palace, Valencia.

553 Turkey Sponge

1979. Spanish Fauna (7th series). Invertebrates. Multicoloured.
2579 5p. Type **553** 15 15
2580 7p. Crayfish 15 15
2581 8p. Scorpion 15 15
2582 20p. Starfish 20 15
2583 25p. Sea anemone 25 15

554 Antonio Gutierrez

1979. Defence of Tenerife, 1797.
2584 **554** 5p. multicoloured . . . 15 15

1979. Stamp Day and J. de Juanes (painter) Commemoration. Religious Paintings as T **409**. Multicoloured.
2585 8p. "Immaculate Conception" 15 15
2586 10p. "Holy Family" 15 15
2587 15p. "Ecce Homo" 15 15
2588 20p. "St. Stephen in the Synagogue" 20 15
2589 25p. "The Last Supper" (horiz) 25 15
2590 50p. "Adoration of the Mystic Lamb" (horiz) . . 50 15

555 Cathedral and Statue of Virgin and Child, Zaragoza

1979. 8th Mariological Congress, Zaragoza.
2591 **555** 5p. multicoloured . . . 15 15

556 St. Bartholomew's College, Bogota

1979. Latin-American Architecture.
2592 **556** 7p. green, blue and brown 15 15
2593 – 12p. indigo, purple & brn 15 15
DESIGN: 12p. University of San Marcos, Lima.

557 Hands and Governor's Palace, Barcelona

1979. Catalonian Autonomy.
2594 **557** 8p. multicoloured . . . 15 15

558 Autonomy Statute

1979. Basque Autonomy.
2595 **558** 8p. multicoloured . . . 15 15

559 Prince of Asturias and Hospital

1979. Centenary of Hospital of the Child Jesus, Madrid.
2596 **559** 5p. multicoloured . . . 15 15

560 Barcelona Tax Stamp, 1929

1979. 50th Anniv of Barcelona Exhibition Tax Stamps.
2597 **560** 5p. multicoloured . . . 15 15

561 The Nativity

1979. Christmas. Capitals from San Pedro el Viejo, Huesca. Multicoloured.
2598 8p. Type **561** 15 15
2599 19p. Flight into Egypt . . . 15 15

562 Charles I

1979. Spanish Kings of the House of Hapsburg.
2600 **562** 15p. green and blue . . 15 15
2601 – 20p. blue and mauve . . 20 15
2602 – 25p. violet and brown 25 15
2603 – 50p. brown and green . . 50 15
2604 – 100p. mauve and brown 1·00 30
DESIGNS: 20p. Philip II; 25p. Philip III; 50p. Philip IV; 100p. Charles II.

563 Olive Plantation and Harvester

1979. International Olive Oil Year.
2605 **563** 8p. multicoloured . . . 15 15

564 Electric Train

1980. Public Transport.
2606 **564** 3p. lake and brown . . . 15 15
2607 – 4p. blue and brown . . . 15 15
2608 – 5p. green and brown . . 15 15
DESIGNS: 4p. Motorbus; 5p. Underground train.

565 Steel Products

1980. Spanish Exports (1st series). Multicoloured.
2609 5p. Type **565** 15 15
2610 8p. Tankers 15 15
2611 13p. Footwear 15 15
2612 19p. Industrial machinery 20 15
2613 25p. Factory buildings, bridge and symbols of technology 25 15
See also Nos. 2653/5.

566 Federico Garcia Lorca

1980. Europa. Writers.
2614 **566** 8p. violet and green . . 15 15
2615 – 19p. brown and green . . 15 15
DESIGN: 19p. J. Ortega y Gasset.

567 Footballers

1980. World Cup Football Championship, Spain (1982) (1st issue). Multicoloured.
2616 8p. Type **567** 15 15
2617 19p. Football and flags . . 15 15
See also Nos. 2640/1, 2668/9 and 2683/**MS**2685.

568 Armed Forces

1980. Armed Forces Day.
2618 **568** 8p. multicoloured . . . 15 15

569 Bourbon Arms, Ministry of Finance, Madrid

1980. Public Finances under the Bourbons.
2619 **569** 8p. deep brown & brown 15 15

570 Helen Keller

1980. Birth Centenary of Helen Keller.
2620 **570** 19p. red and green . . . 20 15

571 Postal Courier (14th century)

1980. Stamp Day.
2621 **571** 8p. brown, stone and red 15 15

572 King Alfonso XIII and Count of Maceda at Exhibition

1980. 50th Anniv of First National Stamp Exhibition.
2622 **572** 8p. multicoloured . . . 15 15

573 Altar of the Virgin, La Palma Cathedral — 574 Ramon Perez de Ayala

1980. 300th Anniv of Appearance of the Holy Virgin at La Palma.
2623 **573** 8p. brown and black . . 15 15

1980. Birth Centenary of Ramon Perez de Ayala (writer).
2624 **574** 100p. green and brown 15 15

575 Manuel Falla, Ruins of Atlantis and Bonampak Musicians

1980. "Espamer '80" International Stamp Exhibition, Madrid. Sheet 150 × 100 mm containing T **575** and similar horiz designs.
MS2625 25p. × 2, 50p., 100p. each brown, green and blue (sold at 250p.) . . . . 2·00 2·00
DESIGNS: 25p. Type **575**; 25p. Sun Gate, Tiahuanaco and Roman arch, Medinaceli; 50p. Alonos de Ercilla, Garcilaso de la Vega and title pages from *La Araucana* and *Commentarios Reales*; 100p. Virgin of Quito and Virgin of Seafarers.

576 Juan de Garay and Founding of Buenos Aires (after Moreno Carbonero)

1980. 400th Anniv of Buenos Aires.
2626 **576** 19p. blue, green and red 15 15

577 Tapestry Detail

1980. The Creation Tapestry, Gerona. Sheet 132 × 106 mm containing T **577** and similar designs showing tapestry details.
MS2627 25p. × 3 (each 33 × 26 mm), 50p. × 3, multicoloured . . . . 2·30 1·80

578 Palace of Congresses, Madrid — 579 "Nativity" (mural from Church of Santa Maria de Cuina, Oza de los Rios)

1980. European Security and Co-operation Conference, Madrid.
2628 **578** 22p. multicoloured . . . 20 15

1980. Christmas. Multicoloured.
2629 10p. Type **579** 15 15
2630 22p. "Adoration of the Kings" (doorway of Church of St. Nicholas of Cines, Oza de los Rios) (horiz) 20 15

580 Pedro Vives and Farman H.F.III Biplane

1980. Aviation Pioneers. Multicoloured.
2631 5p. Type **580** 15 15
2632 10p. Benito Loygorri and Farman H.F.20 type biplane 15 15
2633 15p. Alfonso de Orleans and Caudron G-3 . . . . . . 15 15
2634 22p. Alfredo Kindelan and biplane 20 15

581 Games Emblem and Skier

1981. Winter University Games.
2635 **581** 30p. multicoloured . . . 30 15

582 "Homage to Picasso" (Joan Miro)

1981. Birth Centenary of Pablo Picasso (artist).
2636 **582** 100p. multicoloured . . 1·00 15

583 Newspaper, Camera, Notepaper and Pen

1981. The Press.
2637 **583** 12p. multicoloured . . . 15 15

584 Map of Galicia, Arms and National Anthem — 585 Mosaic forming Human Figure

1981. Galician Autonomy.
2638 **584** 12p. multicoloured . . . 15 15

1981. International Year of Disabled Persons.
2639 **585** 30p. multicoloured . . . 30 15

586 Heading Ball

588 King Juan Carlos reviewing Army

587 La Jota (folk dance)

1981. World Cup Football Championship (1982) (2nd issue). Multicoloured.
2640 12p. Type **586** 15 15
2641 30p. Kicking ball (horiz) . . 30 15

1981. Europa.
2642 **587** 12p. black and brown . . 15 15
2643 – 30p. deep lilac and lilac 30 15
DESIGN: 30p. Procession of the Virgin of Rocio.

1981. Armed Forces Day.
2644 **588** 12p. multicoloured . . . 15 15

589 Gabriel Miro (writer) — 590 Messenger (14th-century woodcut)

1981. Spanish Celebrities.
2645 **589** 6p. violet and green . . 15 15
2646 – 12p. brown and violet 15 15
2647 – 30p. green and brown . . 30 15
DESIGNS: 12p. Francisco de Quevedo (writer); 30p. St. Benedict.

1981. Stamp Day.
2648 **590** 12p. pink, brown & green 15 15

591 Map of the Balearic Islands (from Atlas of Diego Homem, 1563)

1981. Spanish Islands. Multicoloured.
2649 7p. Type **591** 15 15
2650 12p. Map of the Canary Islands (from map of Mateo Prunes, 1563) . . . 15 15

592 Alfonso XII, Juan Carlos and Arms

1981. Century of Public Prosecutor's Office.
2651 **592** 50p. brown, green & blue 50 15

593 King Sancho VI of Navarre with Foundation Charter

1981. 800th Anniv of Vitoria.
2652 **593** 12p. multicoloured . . . 15 15

594 Citrus Fruit

1981. Spanish Exports (2nd series). Multicoloured.
2653 6p. Type **594** 15 15
2654 12p. Wine 15 15
2655 30p. CASA C-212 Aviocar airplane, car and lorry . . 30 15

595 Foodstuffs

1981. World Food Day.
2656 **595** 30p. multicoloured . . . 30 15

596 "Guernica" (½-size illustration)

1981. Birth Centenary of Pablo Picasso (2nd issue) and Return of "Guernica" to Spain. Sheet 163 × 105 mm.
MS2657 **596** 200p. black, grey and green . . . . 2·00 2·00

597 Congress Palace, Buenos Aires

1981. "Espamer 81" International Stamp Exhibition, Buenos Aires.
2658 **597** 12p. red and blue . . . 15 15

598 "Adoration of the Kings" (from Cervera de Pisuerga)

1981. Christmas. Multicoloured.
2659 12p. Type **598** 15 15
2660 30p. "Nativity" (from Paredes de Nava) 30 15

599 Plaza de Espana, Seville

1981. Air.
2661 **599** 13p. green and blue . . 15 15
2662 – 20p. blue and brown . . 20 15
DESIGN: 20p. Rande Bridge, Ria de Vigo.

600 Telegraph Operator

1981. Postal and Telecommunications Museum, Madrid.
2663 **600** 7p. green and brown . . 15 15
2664 – 12p. brown and violet 15 15
MS2665 135 × 100 mm. Nos. 2663/4; 50p. violet and green; 100p. green and brown . . . . 1·70 1·70
DESIGNS: 12p. Post wagon; 50p. Emblem of Spanish American and Philippines Postal Academy; 100p. Cap, pouch, posthorn, books and cancellation.

601 Royal Mint, Seville

1981. Financial Administration by the Bourbons in Spain and the Indies.
2666 **601** 12p. brown and grey . . 15 15

602 Iparraguirre **603** Publicity Poster by Joan Miro

1981. Death Centenary of Jose Maria Iparraguirre.
2667 **602** 12p. blue and black . . 15 15

1982. World Cup Football Championship, Spain (3rd issue). Multicoloured.
2668 14p. Type **603** 15 15
2669 33p. World Cup trophy and championship emblem . . 35 15

604 Andres Bello (author and philosopher) (birth bicent) **605** St. James of Compostela (Codex illustration)

1982. Anniversaries (1981).
2670 **604** 30p. deep green and green 30 15
2671 – 30p. green and blue . . 30 15
2672 – 50p. violet and black . . 50 15
DESIGNS: No. 2671, J. R. Jimenez (author, birth centenary); 2672, P. Calderon (playwright, 300th death anniv).

1982. Holy Year of Compostela.
2673 **605** 14p. multicoloured . . . 15 15

606 Manuel Fernandez Caballero **608** Swords, Arms and Flag

607 Arms, Seals and Signatures (Unification of Spain, 1479)

1982. Masters of Operetta (1st series). As T **606** (2674, 2676, 2678) or T **625** (others). Multicoloured.
2674 3p. Type **606** 15 15
2675 3p. Scene from "Gigantes y Cabezudos" (horiz) . . . 15 15
2676 6p. Amadeo Vives Roig . . 15 15
2677 6p. Scene from "Maruxa" (horiz) 15 15
2678 8p. Tomas Breton y Hernandez 15 15
2679 8p. Scene from "La Verbena de la Paloma" (horiz) . . . 15 15
See also Nos. 2713/8 and 2772/7.

1982. Europa. Multicoloured.
2680 14p. Type **607** 15 15
2681 33p. Symbolic ship, Columbus map of "La Spanola" and signature (Discovery of America) 35 15

1982. Armed Forces Day and Centenary of General Military Academy.
2682 **608** 14p. multicoloured . . . 15 15

609 Tackling

1982. World Cup Football Championship, Spain (4th issue). Multicoloured.
2683 14p. Type **609** 15 15
2684 33p. Goal 35 35
MS2685 163 × 105 mm. 9p. Handshake; 14p. Type **609**; 33p. As No. 2684; 100p. Players with cup . . . . 1·60 1·60

610 "St. Andrew and St. Francis" **612** "Transplants"

611 Map of Tenerife and Letter

1982. Air. Paintings by El Greco. Multicoloured.
2686 13p. Type **610** 15 15
2687 20p. "St. Thomas" 20 15

1982. Stamp Day.
2688 **611** 14p. multicoloured . . . 15 15

1982. Organ Transplants.
2689 **612** 14p. multicoloured . . . 15 15

613 White Storks and Diesel Locomotive

1982. 23rd International Railway Congress, Malaga. Multicoloured.
2690 9p. Type **613** 15 15
2691 14p. Steam locomotive "Antigua" (37 × 26 mm) 15 15
2692 33p. Steam locomotive "Montana" (wrongly inscr "Santa Fe") (37 × 26 mm) 35 15

614 La Fortaleza, San Juan

1982. "Espamer 82" Stamp Exhibition, San Juan, Puerto Rico.
2693 **614** 33p. blue and lilac . . . 35 15

615 St. Theresa of Avila (sculpture by Gregorio Hernandez)

1982. 400th Death Anniv of St. Theresa of Avila.
2694 **615** 33p. brown, blue and green 35 15

616 Pope John Paul II

1982. Papal Visit.
2695 **616** 14p. blue and brown . . 15 15

1982. Tourist Series. As T **340**.
2696 4p. blue and grey 15 15
2697 6p. grey and blue 15 15
2698 9p. lilac and blue 15 15
2699 14p. lilac and blue 15 15
2700 33p. brown and red 35 15
DESIGNS—VERT: 4p. Arab water-wheel, Alcantarilla; 9p. Dying Christ, Seville; 14p. St. Martin's Tower, Teruel; 33p. St. Andrew's Gate, Villalpando. HORIZ: 6p. Bank of Spain, Madrid.

617 "Adoration of The Kings" (sculpture, Covarrubias Collegiate Church)

1982. Christmas. Multicoloured.
2701 14p. Type **617** 15 15
2702 33p. "The Flight into Egypt" (painting) 35 15

618 "The Prophet" **619** St. John Bosco (founder) and Children

1982. Birth Centenary of Pablo Gargallo (sculptor).
2703 **618** 14p. green and blue . . 15 15

1982. Centenary of Salesian Schools in Spain.
2704 **619** 14p. multicoloured . . . 15 15

620 Arms of Spain

1983.
2705 **620** 14p. multicoloured . . . 15 15

621 Sunrise over Andalusia

1983. Andalusian Autonomy.
2706 **621** 14p. multicoloured . . . 20 15

622 Arms of Cantabria, Mountains and Monuments

1983. Cantabrian Autonomy.
2707 **622** 14p. multicoloured . . . 20 15

623 National Police

1983. State Security Forces. Multicoloured.
2708 9p. Type **623** 15 15
2709 14p. Civil Guard 15 15
2710 33p. Superior Police Corps 35 15

624 Cycling

1983. Air. Sports. Multicoloured.
2711 13p. Type **624** 15 15
2712 20p. Bowling (horiz) 20 15

625 Scene from "La Parranda"

1983. Masters of Operetta (2nd series). As T **625** (2714, 2716, 2718) or T **606** (others). Multicoloured.
2713 4p. Francisco Alonso (vert) 15 15
2714 4p. Type **625** 15 15
2715 6p. Jacinto Guerrero (vert) 15 15
2716 6p. Scene from "La Rosa del Azafran" 15 15
2717 9p. Jesus Guridi (vert) . . . 15 15
2718 9p. Scene from "El Caserio" 15 15

626 Cervantes and Scene from "Don Quixote"

1983. Europa.
2719 **626** 16p. red and green . . . 15 15
2720 – 38p. sepia and brown . . 40 15
DESIGN: 38p. Torres Quevedo and Niagara cable-car.

627 Francisco Salzillo (artist)

628 W.C.Y. Emblem

1983. Spanish Celebrities.
2721 **627** 16p. purple and green . . 15 15
2722 – 38p. blue and brown . . 40 15
2723 – 50p. blue and brown . . 50 15
2724 – 100p. brown and violet 1·00 20
DESIGNS: 38p. Antonio Soler (composer); 50p. Joaquin Turina (composer); 100p. St. Isidro Labrador (patron saint of Madrid).

1983. World Communications Year.
2725 **628** 38p. multicoloured . . . 40 15

629 Leaves

1983. Riojan Autonomy.
2726 **629** 16p. multicoloured . . . 20 15

630 Army Monument, Burgos

1983. Armed Forces Day.
2727 **630** 16p. multicoloured . . . 15 15

631 Burgos Setter

1983. Spanish Dogs.
2728 **631** 10p. blue, brown and red 15 15
2729 – 16p. multicoloured . . . 15 15
2730 – 26p. multicoloured . . . 35 20
2731 – 38p. multicoloured . . . 45 15
DESIGNS: 16p. Spanish mastiff; 26p. Ibiza spaniel; 38p. Navarrese basset.

632 Juan-Jose and Fausto Elhuyar y de Suvisa

1983. Anniversaries. Multicoloured.
2732 16p. Type **632** (bicentenary of discovery of wolfram) 15 15
2733 38p. Scout camp (75th anniv of Boy Scout Movement) 40 15
2734 50p. University of Zaragoza (400th anniv) 55 15

633 Arms of Murcia

1983. Murcian Autonomy.
2735 **633** 16p. multicoloured . . . 20 15

634 Covadonga Basilica and Victory Cross

1983. Autonomy of Asturias.
2736 **634** 14p. multicoloured . . . 20 15

635 National Statistical Institute, Madrid

1983. 44th International Institute of Statistics Congress.
2737 **635** 38p. multicoloured . . . 40 15

636 Roman Horse-drawn Mail Cart

1983. Stamp Day.
2738 **636** 16p. pink and brown . . 30 25

637 Palace and Arms of Valencia

1983. Valencian Autonomy.
2739 **637** 16p. multicoloured . . . 20 15

638 Seville (Illustration from "Floods of Guadalquivir" by Francisco Palomo)

1983. America–Spain.
2740 **638** 38p. violet and blue . . 40 15

639 "Biblical King" (Leon Cathedral)

1983. Stained Glass Windows. Multicoloured.
2741 10p. Type **639** 15 15
2742 16p. "Epiphany" and Gerona Cathedral 20 15
2743 38p. "St. James" and Santiago de Compostela Hospital 40 15

1983. Tourist Series. As T **340**.
2744 3p. blue and green 15 15
2745 6p. indigo 15 15
2746 16p. violet and red 15 15
2747 38p. red and brown 40 20
2748 50p. red and brown 50 15
DESIGNS: 3p. Church and tower, Llivia, Gerona; 6p. Santa Maria del Mar, Barcelona; 16p. Ceuta Cathedral; 38p. Bridge gateway, Melilla; 50p. Charity Hospital, Seville.

640 "Nativity" (altarpiece, Tortosa)

641 Indalecio Prieto

1983. Christmas. Multicoloured.
2749 16p. Type **640** 15 15
2750 38p. "Adoration of the Kings" (altarpiece, Vich) 40 15

1983. Birth Centenary of Indalecio Prieto (politician).
2751 **641** 16p. brown and black . . 15 15

642 Worker falling from Scaffolding

1984. Safety at Work. Multicoloured.
2752 7p. Type **642** 15 15
2753 10p. Burning factory and extinguisher 15 15
2754 16p. Electric plug and wiring, cutters, gloved hands and warning sign 15 15

643 Tree

1984. Extremaduran Autonomy.
2755 **643** 16p. multicoloured . . . 20 15

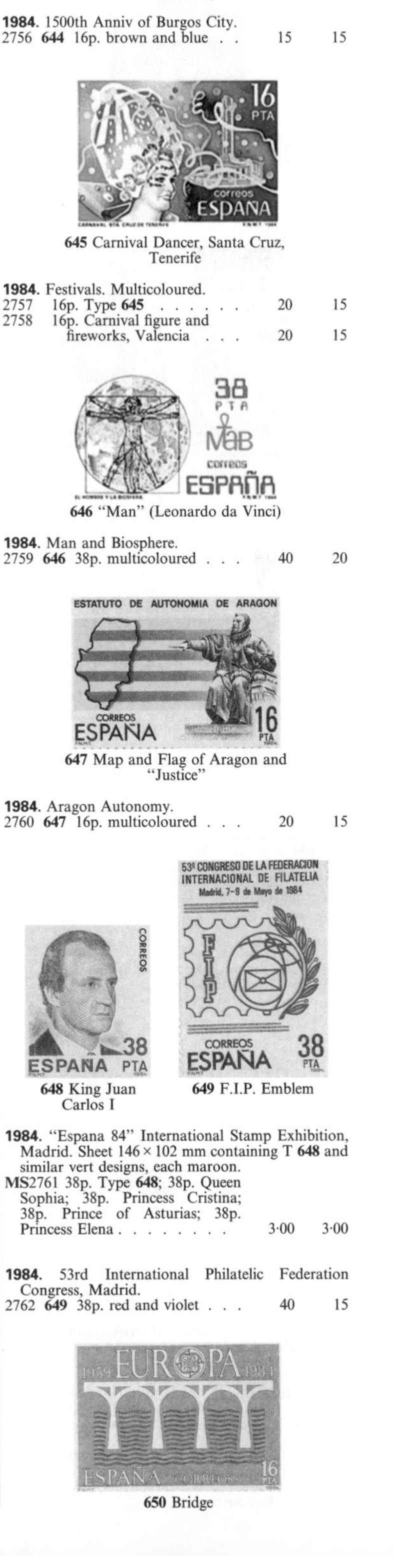

644 Burgos Cathedral and Coat of Arms

1984. 1500th Anniv of Burgos City.
2756 **644** 16p. brown and blue . . 15 15

645 Carnival Dancer, Santa Cruz, Tenerife

1984. Festivals. Multicoloured.
2757 16p. Type **645** 20 15
2758 16p. Carnival figure and fireworks, Valencia . . . 20 15

646 "Man" (Leonardo da Vinci)

1984. Man and Biosphere.
2759 **646** 38p. multicoloured . . . 40 20

647 Map and Flag of Aragon and "Justice"

1984. Aragon Autonomy.
2760 **647** 16p. multicoloured . . . 20 15

648 King Juan Carlos I

649 F.I.P. Emblem

1984. "Espana 84" International Stamp Exhibition, Madrid. Sheet 146 × 102 mm containing T **648** and similar vert designs, each maroon.
MS2761 38p. Type **648**; 38p. Queen Sophia; 38p. Princess Cristina; 38p. Prince of Asturias; 38p. Princess Elena . . . . 3·00 3·00

1984. 53rd International Philatelic Federation Congress, Madrid.
2762 **649** 38p. red and violet . . . 40 15

650 Bridge

1984. Europa.
2763 **650** 16p. red 15 15
2764 38p. blue 40 20

651 Monument to the Alcantara Cazadores Regiment, Valladolid (Mariano Benlliure)

1984. Armed Forces Day.
2765 **651** 17p. multicoloured . . . 15 15

652 Arms of Canary Islands

1984. Autonomy of Canary Islands.
2766 **652** 16p. multicoloured . . . 20 15

653 Arms of Castilla-La Mancha

655 "James III confirming Grants"

654 King Alfonso X, the Wise, of Castile and Leon (700th death anniv)

1984. Autonomy of Castilla-La Mancha.
2767 **653** 17p. multicoloured . . . 20 15

1984. Anniversaries.
2768 **654** 16p. red, blue and black 20 15
2769 – 38p. blue, red and black 40 15
DESIGN: 38p. Ignacio Barraquer (opthalmologist, birth centenary).

1984. Autonomy of Balearic Islands.
2770 **655** 17p. multicoloured . . . 20 15

656 Running before Bulls

1984. Pamplona Festival, San Fermin.
2771 **656** 17p. multicoloured . . . 20 15

1984. Masters of Operetta (3rd series). Horiz designs as T **625** (2772, 2775/6) or vert designs as T **606** (others). Multicoloured.
2772 6p. Scene from "El Nino Judio" 15 15
2773 6p. Pablo Luna 15 15
2774 7p. Ruperto Chapi 15 15
2775 7p. Scene from "La Revoltosa" 15 15
2776 10p. Scene from "La Reina Mora" 15 15
2777 10p. Jose Serrano 15 15

657 Bronze of Swimmer ready to Dive

1984. Olympic Games, Los Angeles. Mult.
2778 1p. Roman quadriga (horiz) 15 15
2779 2p. Type **657** 15 15
2780 5p. Bronze of two wrestlers (horiz) 15 15
2781 8p. "The Discus-thrower" (statue, Miron) 15 15

658 Arms and Map of Navarra

1984. Autonomy of Navarra.
2782 **658** 17p. multicoloured . . . 20 15

659 Cyclist

661 Women gathering Grapes

660 Arms (Levante Building Salamanca University)

1984. International Cycling Championship, Barcelona.
2783 **659** 17p. multicoloured . . . 15 15

1984. Autonomy of Castilla y Leon.
2784 **660** 17p. multicoloured . . . 20 15

1984. Vintage Festival, Jerez.
2785 **661** 17p. multicoloured . . . 20 15

662 Egeria on Donkey and Map of Middle East

1984. 1600th Anniv of Nun Egeria's Visit to Middle East.
2786 **662** 40p. multicoloured . . . 40 20

663 Arab Courier

1984. Stamp Day.
2787 **663** 17p. multicoloured . . . 15 15

664 Father Junipero Serra

1984. Death Bicentenary of Father Junipero Serra (missionary).
2788 **664** 40p. red and blue . . . 40 15

665 "Adoration of the Kings" (Miguel Moguer) (Campos altarpiece)

1984. Christmas. Multicoloured.
2789 17p. "Nativity" (15th-century retable) (horiz) 15 15
2790 40p. Type **665** 40 15

666 Arms, Buildings and Trees

1984. Autonomy of Madrid.
2791 **666** 17p. multicoloured . . . 20 15

667 Flags and Andean Condor

1985. 15th Anniv (1984) of Andes Pact.
2792 **667** 17p. multicoloured . . . 15 15

668 "Virgin of Louvain" (attr Jan Gossaert)

669 College Porch and Tympanum

1985. "Europalia 85 Espana" Festival.
2793 **668** 40p. multicoloured . . . 40 20

1985. 500th Anniv of Santa Cruz College, Valladolid University.
2794 **669** 17p. yellow, brown & red 15 15

670 Flames and "Olymphilex '85"

1985. "Olymphilex 85" International Olympic Stamps Exhibition, Lausanne.
2795 **670** 40p. red, yellow & black 40 15

671 Havana Cathedral

1985. "Espamer '85" International Stamp Exhibition, Havana, Cuba.
2796 **671** 40p. blue and purple . . 40 20

672 Couple in Traditional Dress on Horseback

1985. April Fair, Seville.
2797 **672** 17p. multicoloured . . . 20 15

673 Heads as Holder for Flames

1985. International Youth Year.
2798 **673** 17p. green, black and red 15 15

674 Moors and Christians fighting

1985. Festival of Moors and Christians, Alcoy.
2799 **674** 17p. multicoloured . . . 20 15

675 Don Antonio de Cabezon (organist)

1985. Europa.
2800 **675** 18p. red, black and blue on yellow 20 15
2801 – 45p. red, black and green on yellow 45 20
DESIGN: 45p. Musicians of National Youth Orchestra.

676 Capitania General Headquarters, La Coruna

1985. Armed Forces Day.
2802 **676** 18p. multicoloured . . . 20 15

677 Carlos III's Arms, 1785 Decree and "Santissima Trinidad" (ship of the line)

1985. Bicentenary of National Flag. Mult.
2803 18p. Type **677** 20 15
2804 18p. State arms, 1978 constitution and lion (detail from House of Deputies) 20 15

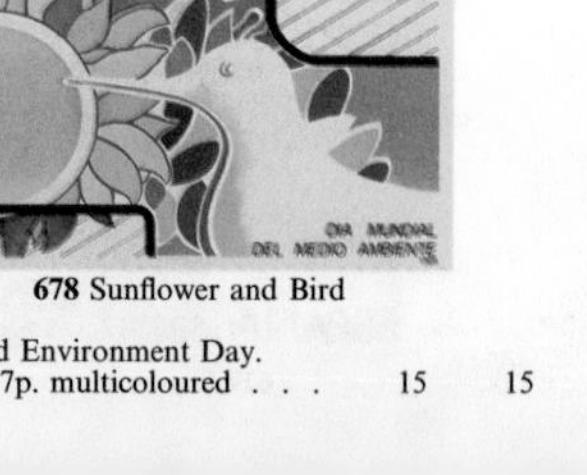

678 Sunflower and Bird

1985. World Environment Day.
2805 **678** 17p. multicoloured . . . 15 15

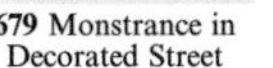

679 Monstrance in Decorated Street

680 King Juan Carlos I

1985. Corpus Christi Festival, Toledo.
2806 **679** 18p. multicoloured . . . 20 15

1985.

2807	**680**	10c. blue	15	15
2808		50c. green	15	15
2809		1p. blue	15	15
2810		2p. green	15	15
2811		3p. brown	15	15
2812		4p. bistre	15	15
2813		5p. purple	15	15
2814		6p. brown	15	15
2815		7p. violet	15	15
2816		7p. green	15	15
2817		8p. grey	15	15
2818		10p. red	15	15
2819		12p. red	15	15
2820		13p. blue	15	15
2821		15p. green	15	15
2822		17p. orange	15	15
2823		18p. green	20	15
2824		19p. brown	20	15
2825		20p. mauve	20	15
2825a		25p. green	25	15
2825b		27p. mauve	25	15
2826		30p. blue	30	15
2827		45p. green	45	15
2828		50p. blue	50	15
2828a		55p. brown	25	15
2829		60p. red	60	15
2830		75p. mauve	75	15

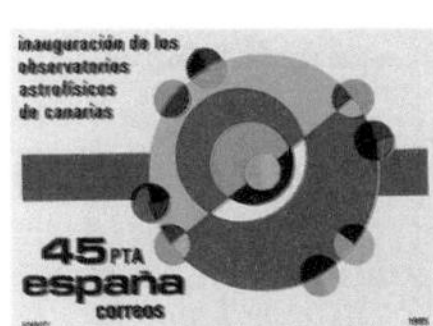

681 Planetary System

1985. Inauguration of Astrophysical Observatories, Canary Islands.
2831 **681** 45p. multicoloured . . . 45 15

682 Ataulfo Argenta (conductor)

1985. European Music Year. Multicoloured.
2832 12p. Type **682** 15 15
2833 17p. Tomas Luis de Victoria (composer) 20 15
2834 45p. Fernando Sor (guitarist and composer) 45 15

683 Bernal Diaz del Castillo (conquistador)

1985. Celebrities.
2835 **683** 7p. red, black and green on yellow 15 15
2836 – 12p. red, black and blue on yellow 15 15
2837 – 17p. green, red and black on yellow 20 15
2838 – 45p. green, black and brown on yellow . . . 50 15
DESIGNS: 12p. Esteban Terradas (mathema-tician); 17p. Vicente Aleixandre (poet); 45p. Leon Felipe Camino (poet).

684 Canoeist

1985. "Descent down the Sella" Canoe Festival, Asturias.
2839 **684** 17p. multicoloured . . . 20 15

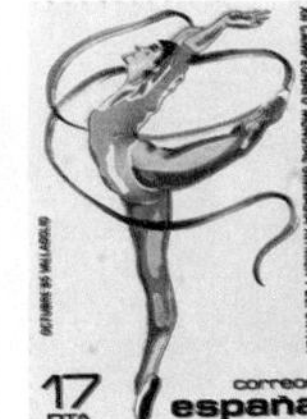

685 Monk returning with Rotulet to Savigni Abbey, 1122

686 Ribbon Exercise

1985. Stamp Day.
2840 **685** 17p. multicoloured . . . 20 15

1985. 12th World Rhythmic Gymnastics Championship, Valladolid. Multicoloured.
2841 17p. Type **686** 15 15
2842 45p. Hoop exercise 45 20

687 Prado Museum and "la Alcacofa" Fountain

1985. "Exfilna '85" National Stamp Exhibition, Madrid. Sheet 120 × 80 mm.
MS2843 17p. multicoloured . . . 40 40

688 "Virgin and Child" (Escalas Chapel, Seville Cathedral)

690 Subalpine Warbler

689 "Nativity" (detail of altarpiece by Ramon de Mur)

1985. Stained Glass Windows. Multicoloured.
2844 7p. Type **688** 15 15
2845 12p. Monk (Toledo Cathedral) 15 15
2846 17p. King Enrique II of Castile and Leon (Alcazar of Segovia) 15 15

1985. Christmas. Multicoloured.
2847 17p. Type **689** 15 15
2848 45p. "Adoration of the Magi" (embroidered frontal, after Jaume Huguet) 45 15

1985. Birds. Multicoloured.
2849 6p. Type **690** 15 15
2850 7p. Rock thrush 15 15
2851 12p. Spotless starling . . . 15 15
2852 17p. Bearded reedling . . . 25 15

691 Count of Penaflorida

1985. Death Bicentenary of Count of Penaflorida (founder of Economic Society of Friends of the Land).
2853 **691** 17p. blue 15 15

692 Royal Palace, Madrid

1986. Admission of Spain and Portugal to European Economic Community. Multicoloured.
2854 7p. Type **692** 15 15
2855 17p. Map and flags of member countries 15 15
2856 30p. Hall of Columns, Royal Palace 30 15
2857 45p. Flags of Portugal and Spain uniting with flags of other members 55 20

1986. Tourist Series. As T **340**.
2858 12p. black and red 15 15
2859 35p. brown and blue 40 15
DESIGNS: 12p. Lupiana Monastery, Guadalajara; 35p. Balcony of Europe, Nerja.

693 Merino

1986. 2nd World Conference on Merinos.
2860 **693** 45p. multicoloured . . . 45 15

694 "Revellers" (detail, F. Hohenleiter)

1986. Cadiz Carnival.
2861 **694** 17p. multicoloured . . . 20 15

695 Helmets and Flower

1986. International Peace Year.
2862 **695** 45p. multicoloured . . . 45 15

696 Organ Pipes

1986. Religious Music Week, Cuenca.
2863 **696** 17p. multicoloured . . . 20 15

697 "Swearing in of Regent, Queen Maria Cristina" (detail, Joaquin Sorolla y Bastida)

1986. Centenary of Chambers of Commerce, Industry and Navigation.
2864 **697** 17p. black and green . . 15 15

698 Man with Suitcase

1986. Emigration.
2865 **698** 45p. multicoloured . . . 45 15

699 Boy and Birds

1986. Europa. Multicoloured.
2866 17p. Type **699** 15 15
2867 45p. Woman watering young tree 50 15

700 Our Lady of the Dew

1986. Our Lady of the Dew Festival, Rocio, near Almonte.
2868 **700** 17p. multicoloured . . . 20 15

701 Capitania General Building, Tenerife

1986. Armed Forces Day.
2869 **701** 17p. multicoloured . . . 15 15

1986. Tourist Series. As T **340**. Multicoloured.
2870 12p. black and blue 15 15
2871 35p. brown and blue 40 15
DESIGNS: 12p. Ciudad Rodrigo Cathedral, Salamanca; 35p. Calella lighthouse, Barcelona.

702 Hands and Ball

1986. 10th World Basketball Championship.
2872 **702** 45p. multicoloured . . . 45 15

703 Francisco Loscos (botanist)

704 Apostles awaiting Angels carrying Virgin's Soul

1986. Celebrities.
2873 **703** 7p. green and black . . 15 15
2874 – 11p. red and black . . . 15 15
2875 – 17p. brown and black . . 15 15
2876 – 45p. purple, orange and black 45 20
DESIGNS: 11p. Salvador Espriu (writer); 17p. Azorin (Jose Martinez Ruiz) (writer); 45p. Juan Gris (artist).

1986. Elche Mystery Play.
2877 **704** 17p. multicoloured . . . 20 15

705 Swimmer

1986. 5th World Swimming, Water Polo, Leap and Synchronous Swimming Championships.
2878 **705** 45p. multicoloured . . . 45 15

706 Pelota Player

1986. 10th World Pelota Championship.
2879 **706** 17p. multicoloured . . . 20 15

707 King's Messenger with Letter summoning Nobleman to Court

1986. Stamp Day.
2880 **707** 17p. multicoloured . . . 15 15

708 Man releasing Dove and Cordoba Mosque

1986. "Exfilna '86" National Stamp Exhibition, Corosba. Sheet 120 × 80 mm.
MS2881 **708** 17p. multicoloured 20 20

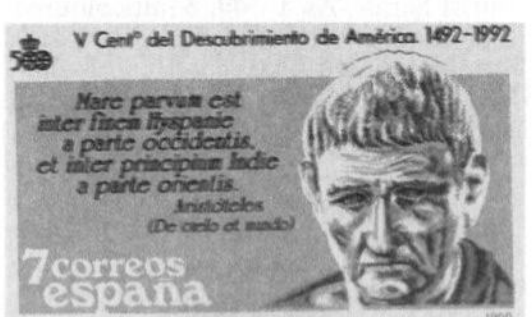

709 Aristotle

1986. 500th Anniv (1992) of Discovery of America by Columbus (1st issue). Designs showing historic figures and prophecies of discovery of New World.
2882 **709** 7p. black and mauve . . 15 15
2883 – 12p. black and lilac . . 15 15
2884 – 17p. black and yellow . . 15 15
2885 – 30p. black and mauve 30 15
2886 – 35p. black and green . . 35 15
2887 – 45p. black and orange 45 15
DESIGNS: 12p. Seneca and quote from "Medea"; 17p. St. Isidoro of Seville and quote from "Etymologies"; 30p. Cardinal Pierre d'Ailly and quote from "Imago Mundi"; 35p. Mayan and quote from "Chilam Balam" books; 45p. Conquistador and quote from "Chilam Balam" books.
See also Nos. 2932/7, 2983/8, 3035/40, 3079/82, 3126/9, **MS**3147, 3175/6, **MS**3177 and 3190.

710 Gaspar de Portola

711 "Holy Family" (detail, Diego de Siloe)

1986. Death Bicentenary of Gaspar de Portola (first Governor of California).
2888 **710** 22p. blue, red and black 20 15

1986. Christmas. Wood Carvings. Multicoloured.
2889 19p. Type **711** 20 15
2890 48p. "Nativity" (detail, Toledo Cathedral altarpiece, Felipe de Borgona) (horiz) 50 15

712 Abd-er Rahman II and Cordoba Mosque

1986. Hispanic Islamic Culture.
2891 **712** 7p. brown and red . . . 15 15
2892 – 12p. brown and red . . 15 15
2893 – 17p. blue and black . . 15 15
2894 – 45p. green and black . . 45 15
DESIGNS: 12p. Ibn Hazm (writer) and burning book; 17p. Al-Zarqali (astronomer) and azophea (astrolabe); 45p. King Alfonso VII of Castile and Leon and scholars of Toledo School of Translators.

713 "The Good Curate"

1986. Birth Centenary of Alfonso Castelao (artist and writer).
2895 **713** 32p. multicoloured . . . 35 15

714 Chateau de la Muette (headquarters)

1987. 25th Anniv of Organization for Economic Co-operation and Development.
2896 **714** 48p. multicoloured . . . 50 15

715 Abstract Shapes

1987. "Expo 92" World's Fair, Seville (1st issue). Multicoloured.
2897 19p. Type **715** 30 15
2898 48p. Moon surface, Earth and symbol 90 15
See also Nos. 2941/2, 2951/2, 3004/7, 3052/5, 3094/7, 3143 and 3148/**MS**3172.

716 Francisco de Vitoria

1987. 500th Birth Anniv of Francisco de Vitoria (jurist).
2899 **716** 48p. brown 50 15

717 18th-century Warship and Standard Bearer

718 University

1987. 450th Anniv of Marine Corps.
2900 **717** 19p. multicoloured . . . 20 15

1987. Centenary of Deusto University.
2901 **718** 19p. red, green and black 20 15

719 Breastfeeding Baby

1987. UNICEF Child Survival Campaign.
2902 **719** 19p. brown and deep brown 20 15

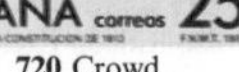
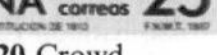
720 Crowd

721 15th-century Pharmacy Jar, Manises

1987. 175th Anniv of Constitution of Cadiz. Multicoloured.
2903 25p. Type **720** 25 15
2904 25p. Crowd and herald on steps 25 15
2905 25p. Dignitaries on dais . . 25 20
2906 25p. Crown and Constitution 25 15
Nos. 2903/6 were printed together, se-tenant, the first three stamps forming a composite design showing "The Promulgation of the Constitution of 1812" by Salvador Viniegra.

1987. Ceramics. Multicoloured.
2907 7p. Type **721** 15 15
2908 14p. 20th-century glazed figure, Sargadelos 15 15
2909 19p. 18th-century vase, Buen Retiro 20 15
2910 32p. 20th-century pot, Salvatierra de los Barros 35 15
2911 40p. 18th-century jar, Talavera 40 15
2912 48p. 18–19th century jug, Granada 50 15

722 "Procession at Dawn, Zamora" (Gallego Marquina)

723 Bilbao Bank, Madrid (Saenz de Oiza)

1987. Holy Week Festivals. Multicoloured.
2913 19p. Type **722** 20 15
2914 48p. Gate of Pardon, Seville Cathedral and "Passion" (statue by Martinez Montanes) 50 15

1987. Tourist Series. As T **340**.
2915 14p. green and blue 15 15
2916 19p. deep green and green 20 15
2917 40p. brown 40 15
2918 48p. black 50 15
DESIGNS—HORIZ: 14p. Ifach Rock, Calpe, Alicante; 19p. Ruins of Church of Santa Maria d'Ozo, Pontevedra; 40p. Palace of Sonanes, Villacarriedo, Santander. VERT: 48p. 11th-century monastery of Sant Joan de les Abadesses, Gerona.

1987. Europa. Architecture.
2919 **723** 19p. multicoloured . . . 20 15
2920 – 48p. brown, bistre & grn 50 15
DESIGN—HORIZ: 14p. National Museum of Roman Art, Merida (Rafael Moneo).

724 Horse's Head and Harnessed Pair

1987. Jerez Horse Fair.
2921 **724** 19p. multicoloured . . . 20 15

725 Carande

1987. Birth Centenary of Ramon Carande (historian and Honorary Postman).
2922 **725** 40p. black and brown . . 40 15

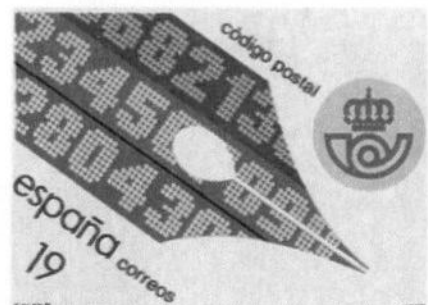

726 Numbers on Pen Nib

1987. Postal Coding.
2923 **726** 19p. multicoloured . . . 20 15

727 Arms and School

1987. 75th Anniv of Eibar Armoury School.
2924 **727** 20p. multicoloured . . . 20 15

728 Batllo House Chimneys (Antonio Gaudi)

1987. Nomination of Barcelona as 1992 Olympic Games Host City. Multicoloured.
2925 32p. Type **728** 35 15
2926 65p. Athletes 70 15

729 Festival Poster (Fabri)

1987. 25th Pyrenees Folklore Festival, Jaca.
2927 **729** 50p. multicoloured . . . 50 15

730 Monturiol (after Marti Alsina) and Diagrams of Submarine "Ictineo"

1987. Death Cent of Narcis Monturiol (scientist).
2928 **730** 20p. black and brown . . 20 15

731 Detail from Jaime II of Majorca's Law appointing Couriers

1987. Stamp Day.
2929 **731** 20p. multicoloured . . . 20 15

732 18th-century Pre-stamp Letter

1987. "Espamer '87" Stamp Exhibition, La Coruna. Maritime Post to America. Sheet 149 × 83 mm containing T **732** and similar horiz designs.
MS2930 8p. Type **732**; 12p. 19th-century engraving of La Coruna harbour; 20p. 18th-century view of Havana harbour; 50p. 18th-century sailing packets running between La Coruna and Havana (sold at 180p.) . . . . 3·25 3·25

No. MS2930 included an entrance coupon divided from the sheet by a line of rouletting. Price quoted is for the sheet with coupon attached.

733 "Aesculapius" and Olympic Torch Bearer

1987. "Exfilna '87" National Stamp Exhibition, Gerona. Sheet 120 × 80 mm.
MS2931 **733** 20p. multicoloured 20 20

734 Amerigo Vespucci

1987. 500th Anniv (1992) of Discovery of America by Columbus (2nd issue). Explorers. Multicoloured.

2932	14p. Type **734**	15	15
2933	20p. King Ferdinand and Queen Isabella the Catholic and arms on ships	20	15
2934	32p. Juan Perez and departing ships	35	15
2935	40p. Juan de la Cosa and ships	40	15
2936	50p. Map, ship and Christopher Columbus	50	15
2937	65p. Native on shore, approaching ships and Martin Alonzo and Vincente Yanez Pinzon	65	15

735 Star and Baubles

736 Macho (self-sculpture)

1987. Christmas. Multicoloured.

2938	20p. Type **735**	20	15
2939	50p. Zambomba and tambourine	50	15

1987. Birth Centenary of Victorio Macho (sculptor).
2940 **736** 50p. brown and black 50 15

1987. "Expo '92" World's Fair, Seville (2nd issue). As Nos. 2897/8 but values changed. Multicoloured.

2941	20p. Type **715**	20	15
2942	50p. As No. 2898	50	15

737 Queen Sofia

739 Speed Skating

738 Campoamor

1988. 50th Birthdays of King Juan Carlos I and Queen Sofia. Each brown, yellow and violet.

2943	20p. Type **737**	20	15
2944	20p. King Juan Carlos I	20	15

1988. Birth Centenary of Clara Campoamor (politician and women's suffrage campaigner).
2945 **738** 20p. multicoloured 20 15

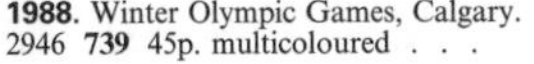

1988. Winter Olympic Games, Calgary.
2946 **739** 45p. multicoloured 45 15

740 "Christ tied to the Pillar" (statue) and Valladolid Cathedral

742 Globe and Stylized Roads

741 Ingredients for and Dish of Paella

1988. Holy Week Festivals. Multicoloured.

2947	20p. Type **740**	20	15
2948	50p. Float depicting Christ carrying the Cross, Malaga	50	15

1988. Tourist Series. Multicoloured.

2949	18p. Type **741**	20	15
2950	45p. Covadonga National Park (70th anniv of National Parks)	45	15

1988. "Expo '92" World's Fair, Seville (3rd issue).

2951	8p. Type **742**	15	15
2952	45p. Compass rose and globe (horiz)	45	15

743 18th-Century Valencian Chalice

744 Francis of Taxis (organiser of European postal service, 1505)

1988. Glassware. Multicoloured.

2953	20p. Type **743**	20	15
2954	20p. 18th-century pitcher, Cadalso de los Vidrios, Madrid	20	15
2955	20p. 18th-century crystal sweet jar, La Granja de San Ildefonso	20	15
2956	20p. 18th-century Andalusian two-handled jug, Castril	20	15
2957	20p. 17th-century Catalan four-spouted jug	20	15
2958	20p. 20th-century bottle, Balearic Islands	20	15

1988. Stamp Day.
2959 **744** 20p. violet and brown 20 15

745 Pablo Iglesias (first President)

1988. Centenary of General Workers' Union.
2960 **745** 20p. multicoloured 20 15

746 Steam Locomotive, 1837, Cuba

1988. Europa. Transport and Communications.

2961	**746** 20p. red and black	20	15
2962	– 50p. green and black	50	15

DESIGN: 50p. Light telegraph, Philippines, 1818.

747 Monnet

749 Couple in Granada

748 Emblem

1988. Birth Cent of Jean Monnet (statesman).
2963 **747** 45p. blue 45 15

1988. Centenary of 1888 Universal Exhibition, Barcelona.
2964 **748** 50p. multicoloured 50 15

1988. International Festival of Music and Dance, Granada.
2965 **749** 50p. multicoloured 50 15

750 Bull

1988. "Expo 88" World's Fair, Brisbane.
2966 **750** 50p. multicoloured 50 15

751 "Virgin of Hope"

1988. Coronation of "Virgin of Hope", Malaga.
2967 **751** 20p. multicoloured 20 15

752 Plan of Pamplona Palace

1988. "Exfilna '87" National Stamp Exhibition, Pamplona. Sheet 120 × 81 mm.
MS2968 **752** 20p. multicoloured 20 20

753 Orreo (agricultural store), Cantabria

1988. Tourist Series.

2969	**753** 18p. green, brown & blue	20	15
2970	– 45p. black, brn & ochre	45	15

DESIGN: 45p. Dulzaina (wind instrument), Castilla y Leon.

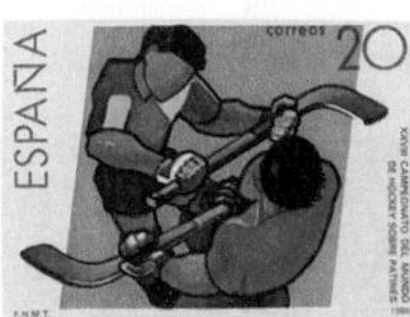

754 Players

1988. 28th World Roller Skate Hockey Championship, La Coruna.
2971 **754** 20p. multicoloured 20 15

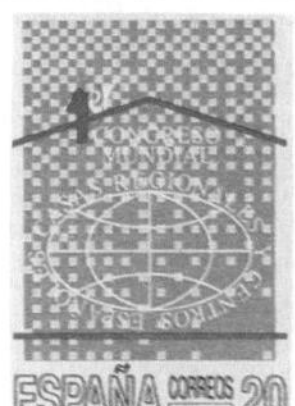

755 Congress Emblem

756 "Olympic" Class Yacht

1988. 1st Spanish Regional Homes and Centres World Congress, Madrid.
2972 **755** 20p. multicoloured 20 15

1988. Olympic Games, Seoul.
2973 **756** 50p. multicoloured 50 15

757 Borrell II, Count of Barcelona

1988. Millenary of Catalonia.
2974 **757** 20p. multicoloured 20 15

758 King Alfonso IX of Leon (detail of Codex of "Toxos Outos")

1988. 800th Anniv of 1st Leon Parliament.
2975 **758** 20p. multicoloured 20 15

759 Emblem on Band around Peace Year Stamps

1988. 25th Anniv of Spanish Philatelic Associations Federation.
2976 **759** 20p. multicoloured 20 15

760 Games Emblem

1988. Olympic Games, Barcelona (1992) (1st issue). Designs showing stylized representations of sports. Multicoloured.

2977	8p. Type **760**	15	15
2978	20p.+5p. Athletics	30	30
2979	45p.+5p. Badminton	55	55
2980	50p.+5p. Basketball	65	65

See also Nos. 3008/11, 3031/3, 3056/8, 3076/8, 3098/3100, 3123/5, 3144/6, 3180/2 and 3183/5.

761 Palace of the Generality, Valencia, and Seal of Jaime I

762 Manuel Alonso Martinez (statesman)

1988. 750th Anniv of Re-conquest of Valencia by King Jaime I of Aragon.
2981 **761** 20p. multicoloured . . . 20 15

1988. Centenary of Civil Code.
2982 **762** 20p. multicoloured . . . 20 15

763 Hernan Cortes and Quetzalcoatl Serpent

1988. 500th Anniv (1992) of Discovery of America by Columbus (3rd issue). Each red, blue and orange.
2983 10p. Type **763** 15 15
2984 10p. Vasco Nunez de Balboa and waves 15 15
2985 20p. Francisco Pizarro and guanaco 20 15
2986 20p. Ferdinand Magellan, Juan Sebastian del Cano and globe 20 15
2987 50p. Alvar Nunez Cabeza de Vaca and river 50 15
2988 50p. Andres de Urdaneta and maritime currents . . 50 15

764 Enrique III of Castile and Leon (first Prince of Asturias)

1988. 600th Anniv of Title of Prince of Asturias.
2989 **764** 20p. multicoloured . . . 20 15

765 Snowflakes

1988. Christmas. Multicoloured.
2990 20p. Type **765** 20 15
2991 50p. Shepherd carrying sheep (vert) 50 15

766 Cordoba Mosque

1988. UNESCO World Heritage Sites.
2992 **766** 18p. brown 20 15
2993 – 20p. blue 20 15
2994 – 45p. brown 50 15
2995 – 50p. green 60 15
DESIGNS—VERT: 20p. Burgos Cathedral. HORIZ: 45p. San Lorenzo Monastery, El Escorial; 50p. Alhambra, Granada.

767 Representation of Political Parties

1988. 10th Anniv of Constitution.
2996 **767** 20p. multicoloured . . . 20 15

768 Courtiers in Palace Grounds

1988. Death Bicentenary of King Charles III. Sheet 100 × 80 mm.
MS2997 **768** 45p. green and black 50 50

769 Blind Person

1988. 50th Anniv of National Organization for the Blind.
2998 **769** 20p. multicoloured . . . 20 15

770 Luis de Granada **772** Abstract

771 Olympic Rings and Sails (Natalia Barrio Fernandez)

1988. 400th Death Anniv of Brother Luis de Granada (mystic).
2999 **770** 20p. multicoloured . . . 20 15

1989. Children's Stamp Designs. Multicoloured.
3000 20p. Type **771** 20 15
3001 20p. Magnifying glass on stamp (Jose Luis Villegas Lopez) (vert) 20 15

1989. Bicentenary of French Revolution.
3002 **772** 45p. red, blue and black 45 15

773 Maria de Maeztu

1989. 107th Birth Anniv of Maria de Maeztu (educationist).
3003 **773** 20p. multicoloured . . . 20 15

774 London, 1851

1989. "Expo '92" World's Fair, Seville (4th issue). Great Exhibitions. Multicoloured.
3004 8p.+5p. Type **774** 15 15
3005 8p.+5p. Paris, 1889 . . . . 15 15
3006 20p.+5p. Brussels, 1958 . . 25 25
3007 20p.+5p. Osaka, 1970 . . . 25 25

1989. Olympic Games, Barcelona (1992) (2nd issue). As T **760**. Multicoloured.
3008 8p.+5p. Handball 15 15
3009 18p.+5p. Boxing 30 30
3010 20p.+5p. Cycling 30 30
3011 45p.+5p. Show jumping . . 55 55

775 Uniforms, 1889

1989. Centenary of Post Office.
3012 **775** 20p. multicoloured . . . 20 15

776 International Postal Service Treaty, 1601 **777** Entrance Door

1989. Stamp Day.
3013 **776** 20p. black 20 15

1989. Cordon House, Burgos.
3014 **777** 20p. black 20 15

778 Skittles **780** "Holy Family with St. Anne" (El Greco)

779 European Flag

1989. Europa. Children's Toys. Multicoloured.
3015 40p. Type **778** 40 15
3016 50p. Spinning top 50 15

1989. Spanish Presidency of European Economic Community.
3017 **779** 45p. multicoloured . . . 45 15

1989. "Exfilna '89" National Stamp Exhibition, Toledo. Sheet 105 × 78 mm.
MS3018 **780** 20p. multicoloured 20 20

781 Manuscript and Portrait

1989. Birth Centenary of Gabriela Mistral (poet).
3019 **781** 50p. multicoloured . . . 55 15

782 Flags forming Ballot Box

1989. European Parliament Elections.
3020 **782** 45p. multicoloured . . . 50 15

783 Catalonia

1989. Lace. Typical designs from named region.
3021 **783** 20p. blue and brown . . 20 15
3022 – 20p. blue and brown . . 20 15
3023 – 20p. blue 20 15
3024 – 20p. blue 20 15
3025 – 20p. blue and brown . . 20 15
3026 – 20p. blue and brown . . 20 15
DESIGNS: No. 3022, Andalucia; 3023, Extremadura; 3024, Canary Islands; 3025, Castilla-La Mancha; 3026, Galicia.

784 Pope John Paul II and Youths

1989. 3rd Papal Visit.
3027 **784** 50p. green, brown & blk 50 15

785 Foot leaving Starting Block

1989. World Cup Athletics Championships, Barcelona.
3028 **785** 50p. multicoloured . . . 50 15

786 Chaplin **787** 1p. Stamp

1989. Birth Centenary of Charlie Chaplin (actor).
3029 **786** 50p. multicoloured . . . 50 15

1989. Centenary of First King Alfonso XIII Stamps.
3030 **787** 50p. brown, grey and red 50 15

1989. Olympic Games, Barcelona (1992) (3rd issue). As T **760**.
3031 18p.+5p. Fencing 60 60
3032 20p.+5p. Football 60 60
3033 45p.+5p. Gymnastics . . . 1·10 1·10

788 Fr. Andres Manjon (founder)

1989. Centenary of Ave Maria Schools.
3034 **788** 20p. multicoloured . . . 20 15

789 Maize

1989. 500th Anniv (1992) of Discovery of America by Columbus (4th issue). Multicoloured.
3035 8p.+5p. Type **789** 15 15
3036 8p.+5p. Cacao nut 15 15
3037 20p.+5p. Tomato 25 15
3038 20p.+5p. Horse 25 15
3039 50p.+5p. Potato 55 15
3040 50p.+5p. Turkey 55 15

790 Inca irrigating Corn (from "New Chronicle" by Waman Puma)

791 "Navidad 89"

1989. America. Pre-Columbian Life.
3041 **790** 50p. multicoloured . . . 50 15

1989. Christmas. Multicoloured.
3042 20p. Type **791** 20 15
3043 45p. Girl with Christmas present (horiz) 45 15

792 Altamira Caves

1989. World Heritage Sites. Multicoloured.
3044 20p. Type **792** 20 15
3045 20p. Segovia Aqueduct . . . 20 15
3046 20p. Santiago de Compostela 20 15
3047 20p. Guell Park and Palace and Mila House 20 15

793 San Lorenzo Monastery, El Escorial

1989. National Heritage. Royal Palaces. Sheet 162 × 92 mm containing T **793** and similar horiz designs. Multicoloured.
MS3048 45p. Type **793**; 45p. Aranjuez; 45p. La Granja de San Ildefonso; 45p. Madrid . . . . 1·80 1·80

794 Olympic Rings, Compass Rose, Church of Holy Family, Barcelona, and Seville

795 Getxo City Hall and Competitor

1990. Children's Stamp Design.
3049 **794** 20p. multicoloured . . . 20 15

1990. World Cyclo-cross Championship, Getxo.
3050 **795** 20p. multicoloured . . . 20 15

796 Victoria Kent

1990. 3rd Death Anniv of Victoria Kent (prison reformer).
3051 **796** 20p. lilac 20 15

797 Curro (mascot) flying over Path of Discoveries

1990. "Expo '92" World's Fair, Seville (5th issue). Multicoloured.
3052 8p.+5p. Type **797** 15 15
3053 20p.+5p. Curro and Exhibition building . . . 25 25
3054 45p.+5p. Curro and view of Project Cartuja '93 . . . 55 55
3055 50p.+5p. Curro crossing bridge in Project Cartuja '93 . . . . 65 65

1990. Olympic Games, Barcelona (1992) (4th issue). As T **760**. Multicoloured.
3056 18p.+5p. Weightlifting . . . 25 25
3057 20p.+5p. Hockey 25 25
3058 45p.+5p. Judo 50 50

798 Rafael Alvarez Sereix (Honorary Postman)

1990. Stamp Day.
3059 **798** 20p. flesh, brown & green 20 15

799 Vitoria Post Office

1990. Europa. Post Office Buildings.
3060 20p. Type **799** 20 15
3061 50p. Malaga Post Office (vert) 50 15

800 "Hispasat" Communications Satellite

1990. 125th Anniv of I.T.U.
3062 **800** 8p. multicoloured . . . 15 15

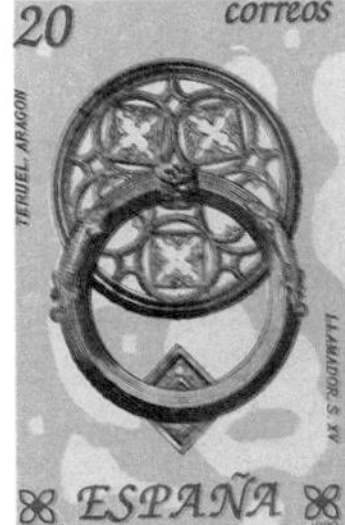

801 Door Knocker, Aragon

802 Infanta's Patio, Zaragoza

1990. Wrought Ironwork. Each black, grey and red.
3063 20p. Type **801** 20 15
3064 20p. Door knocker, Andalucia 20 15
3065 20p. Pistol, Catalonia . . . 20 15
3066 20p. Door knocker, Castilla-La Mancha 20 15
3067 20p. Mirror with lock, Galicia 20 15
3068 20p. Basque fireback 20 15

1990. "Exfilna '90" National Stamp Exhibition, Zaragoza. Sheet 105 × 78 mm.
MS3069 **802** 20p. chestnut . . . 20 20

803 "Charity" (Lopez Alonso)

805 Poster

804 St. Antolin's Crypt, Palencia Cathedral

1990. Anniversaries.
3070 **803** 8p. multicoloured . . . 15 15
3071 – 20p. multicoloured . . . 25 15
3072 – 45p. orange and brown 55 15
3073 – 50p. red and blue . . . 60 15
DESIGNS—VERT: 8p. Type **803** (bicent of arrival in Spain of Daughters of Charity); 50p. Page of book (500th anniv of publication of "Tirant lo Blanch" by Joanot Martorell and Marti Joan de Galba). HORIZ: 20p. Score of "Leilah" and Jose Padilla (composer, birth centenary (1989)); 45p. Palace of Kings of Navarre (900th anniv of grant of privileges to Estella).

1990. "Filatem '90" Third National Thematic Stamps Exhibition, Palencia. Sheet 105 × 77 mm.
MS3074 **804** 20p. brown 20 20

1990. 17th International Historical Sciences Congress, Madrid.
3075 **805** 50p. multicoloured . . . 50 15

1990. Olympic Games, Barcelona (1992) (5th issue). As T **760**. Multicoloured.
3076 8p.+5p. Wrestling 15 15
3077 18p.+5p. Swimming 35 35
3078 20p.+5p. Baseball 40 40

806 Caravel and Compass Rose

1990. 500th Anniv of Discovery of America by Columbus (5th issue). Multicoloured.
3079 8p.+5p. Type **806** 15 15
3080 8p.+5p. Caravels 15 15
3081 20p.+5p. Caravel 25 25
3082 20p.+5p. Galleons 25 25

807 Puerto Rican Todys

808 Sun

1990. America. The Natural World.
3083 **807** 50p. multicoloured . . . 50 15

1990. Christmas. Details of "Cosmic Poem" by Jose Antonio Sistiaga. Multicoloured.
3084 25p. Type **808** 25 15
3085 45p. Moon (horiz) 45 15

809 "Flemish Soldiers" (after Philips Wouvermans)

1990. Tapestries. Sheet 105 × 151 mm containing T **809** and similar vert designs. Multicoloured.
MS3086 20p. × 4: "Calvary" (Peter Pannemaker, after Jan van Roome and Bernard van Orley); Type **809**; "Wreck of the Telemach" (Urbano Leyniers after Miguel Houasse); "Flower Sellers" (Antonio Morena and Eusebio de Candano, after Goya) 85 85

810 Tourism Logo (Joan Miro)

811 Church of St. Miguel de Lillo, Oviedo

1990. European Tourism Year.
3087 **810** 45p. multicoloured . . . 45 15

1990. World Heritage Sites. Multicoloured.
3088 20p. Type **811** 20 15
3089 20p. St. Peter's Tower, Teruel 20 15
3090 20p. Bujaco Tower, Caceres (horiz) 20 15
3091 20p. St. Vincent's Church, Avila (horiz) 20 15

812 Conductor and Orchestra

1990. Spanish National Orchestra.
3092 **812** 25p. green, turq & blk 25 15

813 Maria Moliner

1991. 10th Death Anniv of Maria Moliner (philologist).
3093 **813** 25p. multicoloured . . . 30 15

814 La Cartuja (Santa Maria de las Cuevas Monastery)

1991. "Expo 92" World's Fair, Seville (6th issue). Views of Seville. Multicoloured.
3094 15p.+5p. Type **814** 20 20
3095 25p.+5p. The Auditorium 35 35
3096 45p.+5p. La Cartuja bridge 60 60
3097 55p.+5p. La Barqueta bridge 70 70

1991. Olympic Games, Barcelona (1992) (6th series). As T **760**.
3098 15p.+5p. grey, black and red 25 25
3099 25p.+5p. multicoloured . . 35 35
3100 45p.+5p. multicoloured . . 60 60
DESIGNS: 15p. Modern pentathlon; 25p. Canoeing; 45p. Rowing.

815 Olympic Rings and Yachts

817 Juan de Tassis y Peralta (Chief Courier to Kings Philip III and IV)

816 Loja Gate

1991. Children's Stamp Design.
3101 **815** 25p. multicoloured . . . 30 15

1991. "Granada '92" International Thematic Stamp Exhibition (1st issue)and 500th Anniv of Santa Fe. Sheet 106 × 78 mm.
MS3102 **816** 25p. purple and gold 30 30
See also No. **MS**3174.

1991. Stamp Day.
3103 **817** 25p. black 30 15

818 Talavera Apothecary Jar

1991. Porcelain and Ceramics. Sheet 106 × 150 mm containing T **818** and similar vert designs. Multicoloured.
MS3104 25p. Type **818**; 25p. Buen Retiro figurine; 25p. Pickman bottle; 25p. La Moncloa plate 1·20 1·20

819 Dish Aerials, INTA-NASA Earth Station, Robledo de Chavela

1991. Europa. Europe in Space. Multicoloured.
3105 25p. Type **819** 30 15
3106 45p. "Olympus I" telecommunications satellite 50 15

820 Brother Luis Ponce de Leon (translator and poet, 400th death anniv)

822 Choir (after mural mosaic, Palau de la Musica)

821 Apollo Fountain

1991. Anniversaries.
3107 – 15p. multicoloured . . . 15 15
3108 **820** 15p. orange, red & black 15 15
3109 – 25p. multicoloured . . . 30 30
3110 – 25p. multicoloured . . . 30 30
DESIGNS—HORIZ: No. 3107, Table and chair (400th death anniv of St. John of the Cross). VERT: No. 3109, Banner and cap (500th birth anniv of St. Ignatius de Loyola (founder of Society of Jesus)); 3110, Abd-er Rahman III, Emir of Cordoba (1100th birth anniv).

1991. Madrid. European City of Culture (1st issue). Multicoloured.
3111 15p.+5p. Type **821** 20 20
3112 25p.+5p. "Don Alvaro de Bazan" (statue, Mariano Benlliure) 35 35
3113 45p.+5p. Bank of Spain . . 55 55
3114 55p.+5p. Cloisters, St. Isidro Institute 65 65
See also Nos. 3195/8.

1991. Centenary of Orfeo Catala (Barcelona choral group).
3115 **822** 25p. multicoloured . . . 30 15

823 Basque Drug Cupboard

824 Hands holding Net

1991. Furniture. Multicoloured.
3116 25p. Type **823** 30 15
3117 25p. Kitchen dresser, Castilla y Leon 30 15
3118 25p. Chair, Murcia 30 15
3119 25p. Cradle, Andalucia . . 30 15
3120 25p. Travelling chest, Castilla-La Mancha . . . 30 15
3121 25p. Bridal chest, Catalonia 30 15

1991. World Fishing Exhibition, Vigo.
3122 **824** 55p. multicoloured . . . 60 15

1991. Olympic Games, Barcelona (1992) (7th series). As T **760**. Multicoloured.
3123 15p.+5p. Tennis 40 40
3124 25p.+5p. Table tennis . . . 55 55
3125 55p.+5p. Shooting . . . . . 1·20 1·20

825 Garcilaso de la Vega (Spanish-Inca poet)

1991. 500th Anniv of Discovery of America by Columbus (6th issue). Multicoloured.
3126 15p.+5p. Type **825** 20 20
3127 25p.+5p. Pope Alexander VI 35 35
3128 45p.+5p. Luis de Santangel (banker) 55 55
3129 55p.+5p. Brother Toribio Motolinia (missionary) . . 65 65

826 Nocturlabe

827 "Nativity" (from "New Chronicle" by Guaman Poma de Ayala)

1991. America. Voyages of Discovery.
3130 **826** 55p. brown and purple 60 15

1991. Christmas.
3131 **827** 25p. buff and brown . . 30 15
3132 – 45p. multicoloured . . . 50 15
DESIGN: 45p. "Nativity" (16th-century Russian icon).

828 "The Meadow of San Isidro" (Francisco Goya)

1991. "Exfilna '91" National Stamp Exhibition, Madrid. Sheet 106 × 78 mm.
MS3133 **828** 25p. multicoloured 30 30

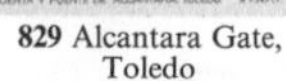
829 Alcantara Gate, Toledo

830 Gen. Carlos Ibanez de Ibero (cartographer)

1991. World Heritage Sites.
3134 **829** 25p. agate and brown . . 35 15
3135 – 25p. black and brown . . 35 15
3136 – 25p. brown and blue . . 35 15
3137 – 25p. violet and green . . 35 15
DESIGNS—VERT: No. 3135, Casa de las Conchas, Salamanca. HORIZ: No. 3136, Seville Cathedral; 3137, Aeonio (flower) and Garajonay National Park, Gomera.

1991. Anniversaries and Events. Multicoloured.
3138 25p. Type **830** (death centenary) 30 15
3139 55p. "Las Palmas" (Antarctic survey ship) (signing of Antarctic Treaty protocol of Madrid declaring the Antarctic a nature reserve) 60 15

831 Margarita Xirgu

1992. 23rd Death Anniv of Margarita Xirgu (actress).
3140 **831** 25p. brown and red . . 30 15

832 "Expo 92, Seville"

1992. Children's Stamp Design.
3141 **832** 25p. multicoloured . . . 30 15

833 Pedro Rodriguez, Count of Campomanes (administrator and postal consultant)

1992. Stamp Day.
3142 **833** 27p. multicoloured . . . 30 15

834 Spanish Pavilion

1992. "Expo '92" World's Fair, Seville (7th issue).
3143 **834** 27p. grey, black & brown 35 15

1992. Olympic Games, Barcelona (8th issue). As T **760**. Multicoloured.
3144 15p.+5p. Archery 35 35
3145 25p.+5p. Sailing 50 50
3146 55p.+5p. Volleyball . . . . 1·00 1·00

835 Columbus's Fleet

1992. 500th Anniv of Discovery of America by Columbus (7th issue). Sheet 164 × 94 mm reproducing 1930 Columbus design.
MS3147 **835** 17p.+5p. red; 17p.+5p. blue; 17p.+5p. black 90 90

836 Cable-cars

1992. "Expo '92" World's Fair, Seville (8th issue). Multicoloured.
3148 17p. Exhibition World Trade Centre 30 15
3149 17p. Type **836** 30 15
3150 17p. Fourth Avenue 30 15
3151 17p. Barqueta entrance . . 30 15
3152 17p. Nature pavilion 30 15
3153 17p. Bioclimatic sphere . . 30 15
3154 17p. Alamillo bridge 30 15
3155 17p. Press centre 30 15
3156 17p. Pavilion of the 15th century 30 15
3157 17p. Expo harbour 30 15
3158 17p. Tourist train 30 15
3159 17p. One-day entrance ticket showing bridge 30 15
3160 27p. Santa Maria de las Cuevas Carthusian monastery 45 15
3161 27p. Palisade 45 15
3162 27p. Monorail 45 15
3163 27p. Avenue of Europe . . 45 15
3164 27p. Pavilion of Discovery 45 15
3165 27p. Auditorium 45 15
3166 27p. First Avenue 45 15
3167 27p. Square of the Future 45 15
3168 27p. Italica entrance 45 15
3169 27p. Last avenue 45 15
3170 27p. Theatre 45 15
3171 27p. Curro (official mascot) 45 15
MS3172 105 × 77 mm. 17p.+5p. View of 16th-century Seville (after A. Sanchez Coello) 30 30

837 Wheelchair Sports

1992. Paralympic (Physically Handicapped) Games, Barcelona.
3173 **837** 27p. multicoloured . . . 35 15

838 Arrival in America

1992. "Granada '92" International Thematic Stamp Exhibition (2nd issue). Sheet 114 × 105 mm reproducing 1930 Columbus stamps.
MS3174 **835** 250p. black; **838** 250p. brown . . . . 5·75 5·75

839 "Preparation before leaving Palos" (R. Espejo)

841 "Water and the Environment"

840 Columbus soliciting Aid of Isabella

1992. Europa. 500th Anniv of Discovery of America by Columbus (7th issue).
3175 **839** 17p. multicoloured . . . 20 15
3176 – 45p. grey and brown . . 55 15
DESIGN: 45p. Map of the Americas, Columbus's fleet and Monastery of Santa Maria de La Rabida.

1992. 500th Anniv of Discovery of America by Columbus (9th issue). Six sheets, each 107 × 91 mm, containing horiz designs as T **840** reproducing scenes from United States 1893 Columbian Exposition issue.
MS3177 Six sheets. (a) 60p. brown (Type **840**); (b) 60p. blue (Columbus sighting land); (c) 60p. brown (Landing of Columbus); (d) 60p. violet (Columbus welcomed at Barcelona); (e) 60p. black (Columbus presenting natives); (f) 60p. black ("America", Columbus and "Liberty") Set of 6 sheets 6·00 6·00

1992. World Environment Day.
3178 **841** 27p. blue and yellow . . 35 15

842 "Albertville", Olympic Rings and "Barcelona"

1992. Winter Olympic Games, Albertville, and Summer Games, Barcelona.
3179 **842** 45p. multicoloured . . . 55 15

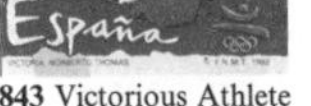

843 Victorious Athlete

845 Cobi holding Magnifying Glass and Stamp Album

844 Olympic Stadium

1992. Olympic Games, Barcelona (9th issue). Multicoloured.
3180 17p.+5p. Type **843** 30 30
3181 17p.+5p. Cobi (official mascot) 30 30
3182 17p.+5p. Olympic torch (horiz) 30 30

1992. Olympic Games, Barcelona (10th issue). Multicoloured.
3183 27p.+5p. Type **844** 40 40
3184 27p.+5p. San Jordi sports arena 40 40
3185 27p.+5p. I.N.E.F. sports university 40 40

1992. "Olymphilex 92" International Stamp Exhibition, Barcelona. Multicoloured.
3186 17p.+5p. Type **845** 30 30
3187 17p.+5p. Church of the Holy Family, Barcelona, and exhibition emblem . . 30 30

846 Athletes

1992. Paralympic (Mentally Handicapped) Games, Madrid.
3188 **846** 27p. blue and red . . . 35 15

847 St. Paul's Church

1992. "Exfilna '92" National Stamp Exhibition, Valladolid. Sheet 105 × 78 mm.
MS3189 **814** 27p. brown 35 35

848 Quarterdeck of "Santa Maria"

1992. America. 500th Anniv of Discovery of America by Columbus (8th issue).
3190 **848** 60p. brown, cinnamon and ochre 65 15

849 Luis Vives (philosopher)

850 Helmet of Mercury and European Community Emblem

1992. Anniversaries. Multicoloured.
3191 17p. Type **849** (500th birth anniv) 20 15
3192 27p. Pamplona Choir (centenary) (horiz) 35 15

1992. European Single Market.
3193 **850** 45p. blue and yellow . . 55 15

851 "Nativity" (Obdulia Acevedo)

852 Municipal Museum

1992. Christmas.
3194 **851** 27p. multicoloured . . . 35 15

1992. Madrid, European City of Culture (2nd issue). Multicoloured.
3195 17p.+5p. Type **852** 30 20
3196 17p.+5p. Queen Sofia Art Museum 30 20
3197 17p.+5p. Prado Museum . . 30 20
3198 17p.+5p. Royal Theatre . . 30 20

853 Huitzilopochtli, Mexican God of War

1992. Codices. Sheet 106 × 151 mm containing T **853**and similar vert designs. Multicoloured.
MS3199 27p. Type **853** (Codex Veitia); 27p. "Mounted Spaniard" (Bishop Baltasar Jaime's *History of the Diocese of El Trujillo del Peru*); 27p. 13th-century miniature from King Alfonso X's *Book of Chess, Dice and Tablings*; 27p. "Of the Months and the Festivals" from Bernardino de Sahagun's *General History of the Matters of New Spain* . . . . 1·20 1·20

854 Bird, Sun, Leaves and Silhouettes

855 Maria Zambrano

1993. Public Services. Protection of the Environment.
3200 **854** 28p. blue and green . . 40 15

1993. 2nd Death Anniv of Maria Zambrano (writer).
3201 **855** 45p. multicoloured . . . 65 15

856 Figures and Blue Cross

857 Segovia

1993. Public Services. Health and Sanitation.
3202 **856** 65p. blue and green . . 85 15

1993. Birth Centenary of Andres Segovia (guitarist).
3203 **857** 65p. black and brown . . 95 15

858 Post-box, Cadiz, 1908

1993. Stamp Day.
3204 **858** 28p. multicoloured . . . 40 15

859 Parasol Mushroom ("Lepiota procera")

861 Road Safety

860 Holy Week Procession

1993. Fungi (1st series). Multicoloured.
3205 17p. Type **859** 35 15
3206 17p. Caesar's mushroom ("Amanita caesarea") . . 35 15
3207 28p. "Lactarius sanguifluus" 40 15
3208 28p. The charcoal burner ("Russula cyanoxantha") 40 15
See also Nos. 3256/9 and 3312/13.

1993. "Exfilna '93" National Stamp Exhibition, Alcaniz. Sheet 105 × 78 mm.
MS3209 **860** 100p. multicoloured 1·40 1·40

1993. Public Services.
3210 **861** 17p. green and red . . . 35 15

863 "Fusees"

1993. Europa. Contemporary Art. Paintings by Joan Miro.
3212 **863** 45p. black and blue . . 65 15
3213 – 65p. multicoloured . . . 95 15
DESIGN—VERT: 65p. "La Bague d'Aurore".

864 "Translation of Body from Palestine to Galicia" (detail of altarpiece, Santiago de Compostela Cathedral)

1993. St. James's Holy Year (1st issue). Mult.
3214 17p. Type **864** 35 15
3215 28p. "Discovery of St. James's tomb by Bishop Teodomiro" (miniature from "Tumbo A" (codex)) 40 15
3216 45p. "St. James" (illuminated initial letter from Bull issued by Pope Alexander III declaring Holy Years of St. James) 65 15
See also No. 3218/**MS**3219.

865 Letters, Map and Satellite

1993. World Telecommunications Day.
3217 **865** 28p. multicoloured . . . 40 15

866 Bagpipe Player (Isaac Diaz Pardo)

867 King Juan Carlos I

1993. St. James's Holy Year (2nd issue). Multicoloured.
3218 28p. Type **866** 40 15
MS3219 106 × 82 mm. 100p. Pilgrim under the star tree (Eugenio Granel) (vert) . . . . 1·40 60

1993.

3220	**867**	1p. blue and gold . . .	15	15
3221		2p. green and gold . .	15	15
3222		10p. red and gold . . .	15	15
3222b		15p. green and gold . .	20	15
3223		16p. brown and gold	15	15
3224		17p. orange and gold	20	15
3225		18p. turquoise and gold	25	15
3226		19p. brown and gold	30	15
3226a		20p. mauve and gold	25	15
3227		21p. green and gold . .	25	15
3229		28p. brown and gold	40	15
3230		29p. green and gold . .	40	15
3231		30p. blue and gold . .	40	15
3232		32p. green and gold . .	40	15
3233		35p. red and gold . .	40	15
3234		45p. green and gold . .	60	15
3235		55p. brown and gold	75	15
3236		60p. red and gold . . .	80	30
3237		65p. orange and gold	85	15
3238		70p. red and gold . . .	80	15

868 "Water and the Environment"

869 Count of Barcelona (after Ricardo Macarrion)

1993. World Environment Day.
3240 **868** 28p. multicoloured . . . 40 15

1993. Juan de Borbon, Count of Barcelona (King Juan Carlos's father) Commemoration.
3241 **869** 28p. multicoloured . . . 40 15

870 Tank Locomotive

1993. Centenary of Igualada–Martorell Railway.
3242 **870** 45p. green and black . . 65 15

871 "The Mint" (lithograph, Pic de Leopold, 1866)

1993. Cent of National Coin and Stamp Mint.
3243 **871** 65p. blue 95 15

872 Alejandro Malaspina (navigator)

1993. Explorers. Multicoloured.
3244 45p. Type **872** 65 15
3245 65p. Jose Celestino Mutis (naturalist) (vert) 95 15

873 "Road to Santiago"

1993. Children's Stamp Design.
3246 **873** 45p. multicoloured . . . 65 15

874 Black Stork

1993. America. Endangered Animals.
3247 **874** 65p. black and orange 95 15
3248 – 65p. black and red . . . 95 15
DESIGN: No. 3248, Lammergeier.

875 Old and Young Hands

1993. European Year of Senior Citizens and Solidarity between Generations.
3249 **875** 45p. multicoloured . . . 65 15

876 Star and Three Wise Men

1993. Christmas. Multicoloured.
3250 17p. Type **876** 30 15
3251 28p. Holy Family (vert) . . 40 15

877 Guillen

1993. Birth Centenary of Jorge Guillen (poet).
3252 **877** 28p. green 40 15

878 Santa Maria de Poblet Monastery, Tarragona

1993. World Heritage Sites.
3253 **878** 50p. brown, blue & green 75 15

879 Luis Bunuel and Camera

1994. Spanish Cinema (1st series). Multicoloured.
3254 29p. Type **879** 40 15
3255 55p. Segundo de Chomon and scene from "Goblin House" 80 15
See also Nos. 3308/9 and 3419/20.

1994. Fungi (2nd series). As T **859**. Multicoloured.
3256 18p. Cep ("Boletus edulis") 30 15
3257 18p. Satan's mushroom ("Boletus satanas") . . . 30 15
3258 29p. Death cap ("Amanita phalloides") 40 15
3259 29p. Saffron milk cap ("Lactarius deliciosus") 40 15

880 Cinnabar

1994. Minerals (1st series).
3260 **880** 29p. multicoloured . . . 45 15
3261 – 29p. multicoloured . . . 45 15
3262 – 29p. multicoloured . . . 45 15
3263 – 29p. black and blue . . 45 15
DESIGNS: 3261, Blende (inscr "Esfalerita"); 3262, Pyrites; 3263, Galena.
See also Nos. 3314/16 and 3366/7.

881 Barristers' Mailbox, Barcelona

1994. Stamp Day.
3264 **881** 29p. brown and cinnamon 40 15

882 Worker (detail of sculpture), I.L.O. Building, Geneva.

1994. 75th Anniv of I.L.O., Geneva.
3265 **882** 65p. multicoloured . . . 95 15

883

1994. 90th Birth Anniv of Salvador Dali (painter). Multicoloured.
3266 18p. Type **883** 30 15
3267 18p. "Portrait of Gala" (horiz) 30 15
3268 29p. "Port Alguer" 40 15
3269 29p. "The Great Masturbator" (horiz) . . 40 15
3270 55p. "The Bread Basket" . . 80 15
3271 55p. "Soft Self-portrait" . . 80 15
3272 65p. "Galatea of the Spheres" . . . . 1·00 15
3273 65p. "The Enigma without End" (horiz) . . . . 1·00 15

884 Pla

1994. 13th Death Anniv of Josep Pla (writer).
3274 **884** 65p. green and red . . . 95 15

885 "Martyrdom of St. Andrew" (Peter Paul Rubens)

886 "Foundation of Santa Cruz de Tenerife" (Gonzalez Mendez)

1994. 400th Anniv of Carlos de Amberes Foundation (philanthropic organization).
3275 **885** 55p. multicoloured . . . 80 15

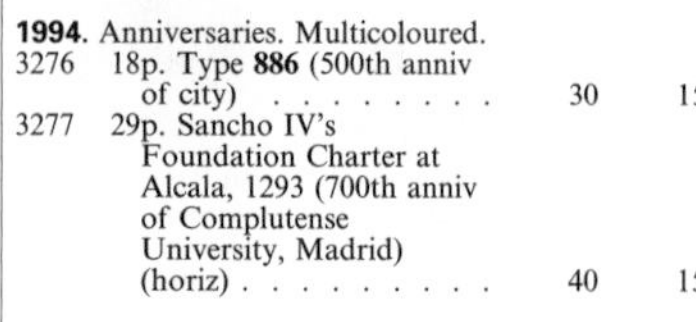

1994. Anniversaries. Multicoloured.
3276 18p. Type **886** (500th anniv of city) 30 15
3277 29p. Sancho IV's Foundation Charter at Alcala, 1293 (700th anniv of Complutense University, Madrid) (horiz) 40 15

887 Severo Ochoa (biochemist)

1994. Europa. Discoveries. Multicoloured.
3278 55p. Type **887** (research into DNA) 80 15
3279 65p. Miguel Catalan (spectrochemist) (research into atomic structures) . . 95 15

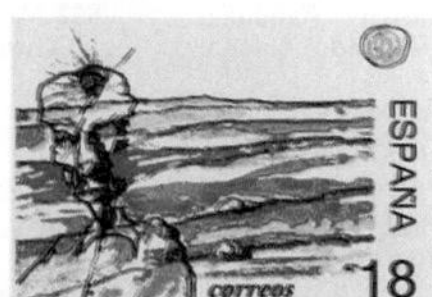

888 "Family of Pascual Duarte"

1994. Spanish Literature. Works of Camilo Jose Cela. Multicoloured.
3280 18p. Type **888** 30 15
3281 29p. Walker and horse rider ("Journey to Alcarria") 40 15

889 Sancho I Ramirez

1994. 900th Death Anniv of King Sancho I Ramirez of Aragon (3282) and 500th Anniv of Treaty of Tordesillas (defining Portuguese and Spanish spheres of influence) (others).
3282 **889** 18p. red, yellow and blue 30 15
3283 – 29p. multicoloured . . . 40 15
3284 – 55p. green, orange and brown 80 15
DESIGN—HORIZ: 29p Compass rose and arms of Tordesillas; 55p. Treaty House, Tordesillas.

890 St. Anne's Cathedral

1994. "Exfilna '94" National Stamp exhibition, Las Palmas, Gran Canaria. Sheet 105 × 78 mm.
MS3285 **890** 100p. multicoloured 1·40 65

891 "Giralda" (yacht)

893 Knight of Swords (14th-century Catalan deck)

892 Forum Caryatid and Tablet bearing Roman Name of Merida

1994. Ships sailed by Count of Barcelona. Multicoloured.
3286 16p. Type **891** 30 15
3287 29p. "Saltillo" (schooner) 40 15

1994. World Heritage Site. Merida.
3288 **892** 55p. brn, cinnamon & red 80 15

1994. Playing Card Museum, Vitoria. Multicoloured.
3289 18p. Type **893** 30 15
3290 29p. Jack of Clubs (Catalan Tarot deck, 1900) 40 15
3291 55p. King of Cups (Spanish deck by Juan Barbot, 1750) 80 15
3292 65p. "Mars", Jack of Diamonds (English deck by Stopforth, 1828) . . . 1·00 15

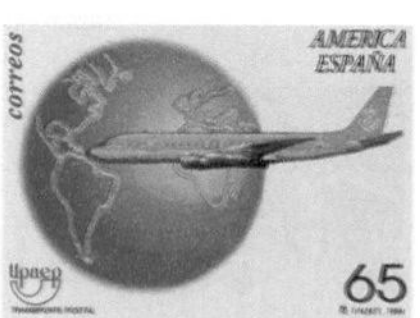

894 Globe and Douglas DC-8

1994. America. Postal Transport.
3293 **894** 65p. multicoloured . . . 85 15

895 Civil Guard (150th anniv)

1994. Public Services.
3294 – 18p. red and blue . . . 30 15
3295 **895** 29p. multicoloured . . . 40 15
DESIGN—As T **854**: 18p. Underground train (75th anniv of Madrid Metro).

896 Map of Member Countries

1994. 40th Anniv of Western European Union.
3296 **896** 55p. multicoloured . . . 80 15

897 Running

1994. Centenary of International Olympic Committee. Spanish Olympic Gold Medal Sports. Multicoloured.
3297 29p. Type **897** 40 15
3298 29p. Cycling 40 15
3299 29p. Skiing 40 15
3300 29p. Football 40 15
3301 29p. Show jumping 40 15
3302 29p. Hockey 40 15
3303 29p. Judo 40 15
3304 29p. Swimming 40 15
3305 29p. Archery 40 15
3306 29p. Yachting 40 15
See also Nos. 3332/45 and 3373/81.

898 "Adoration of the Kings" (detail of Ripoll altarpiece, Esteve Bover)

1994. Christmas.
3307 **898** 29p. multicoloured . . . 40 15

899 "Belle Epoque" (dir. Fernando Trueba)

1995. Spanish Cinema (2nd series). Film posters. Multicoloured.
3308 30p. Type **899** 40 15
3309 60p. "Volver a Empezar" (dir. Jose Luis Garci) . . 90 30

900 Logrono

1995. 900th Anniv of Logrono Law Code.
3310 **900** 30p. multicoloured . . . 40 15

901 Snow Star

1995. "Filatem '95" National Thematic Stamp Exhibition, Granada, and Worl Alpine Skiing Championships, Sierra Nevasa. Sheet 105 × 78 mm.
MS3311 **901** 130p. multicoloured 1·80 85

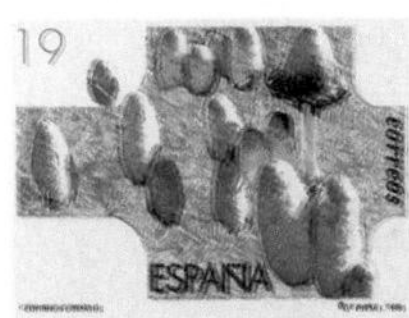

902 Shaggy Ink Cap

1995. Fungi (3rd series). Multicoloured.
3312 19p. Type **902** 35 15
3313 30p. "Dermocybe cinnamomea" 40 15

1995. Minerals (2nd series). As T **880**. Mult.
3314 30p. Aragonite 40 15
3315 30p. Advanced Mining Engineering Technical School and Mining Museum, Madrid 40 15
3316 30p. Dolomite 40 15

903 19th-century Lion's Head Letter Box

1995. Stamp Day.
3317 **903** 30p. brown and green . . 40 15

904 Goicoechea and Talgo Train

1995. Birth Centenary of Alejandro Goicoechea (inventor of Talgo articulated train).
3318 **904** 30p. multicoloured . . . 40 15
3319 – 60p. blue and brown . . 90 30
DESIGN: 60p. Goicoechea and "Virgen del Pilar" articulated train.

905 Globe as Tree on Hand

906 *"San Juan Nepomuceno"*

1995. European Nature Conservation Year.
3320 **905** 60p. multicoloured . . . 65 35

1995. Ships Paintings by AlejoBerlinquero de la y Gallego. Two sheets, each 87 × 164 mm, containing vert designs as T **906**. Multicoloured.
MS3321 Two sheets. (a) 19p. × 4, Type **906**; (b) 30p. × 4, *"San Telmo"* . . . . 2·75 1·70

907 Angel (from illuminated manuscript)

1995. 900th Anniv of Monastery of Liebana. Multicoloured.
3322 30p. Type **907** 40 15
3323 60p. Liebana landscape . . 90 30

908 Miguel Hernandez and part of "El Nino Yuntero"

1995. Literature.
3324 **908** 19p. multicoloured . . . 35 15
3325 – 30p. blue, green and black 40 15
DESIGN—VERT: 30p. Juan Valera and scene from "Juanita la Larga".

909 Marti

1995. Death Centenary of Jose Marti (Cuban poet).
3326 **909** 60p. multicoloured . . . 90 30

910 Captain Trueno

1995. Comic Strip Characters. Multicoloured.
3327 30p. Type **910** 40 15
3328 60p. Carpanta (vert) 90 30

911 Chain and Laurel Twig

1995. Europa. Peace and Freedom.
3329 **911** 60p. multicoloured . . . 90 30

912 Lumiere Brothers

1995. Centenary of Motion Pictures.
3330 **912** 19p. brown 30 15

913 Typewriter, Pen and Camera

1995. Centenary of Madrid Press Association.
3331 **913** 30p. multicoloured . . . 40 15

1995. Spanish Olympic Silver Medal Sports. As T **897**. Multicoloured.
3332 30p. Type **897** 40 15
3333 30p. Basketball 40 15
3334 30p. Boxing 40 15
3335 30p. As No. 3300 . . . . . 40 15
3336 30p. Gymnastics 40 15
3337 30p. As No. 3301 . . . . . 40 15
3338 30p. As No. 3302 . . . . . 40 15
3339 30p. Canoeing 40 15
3340 30p. Polo 40 15
3341 30p. Rowing 40 15
3342 30p. Tennis 40 15
3343 30p. Shooting 40 15
3344 30p. As No. 3306 . . . . . 40 15
3345 30p. Water polo 40 15

914 King Juan Carlos I at National Assembly, 1986

1995. Anniversaries. Multicoloured.
3346 60p. Type **914** (50th anniv of U.N.O.) 90 30
3347 60p. Anniversary emblem, globes and wheat ears (50th anniv of F.A.O.) (vert) 90 30
3348 60p. Emblem and coloured bands (20th anniv of World Tourism Organization) 90 30

915 Presidency Emblem

916 Spotlight on Woman

1995. Spanish Presidency of the European Union.
3349 **915** 60p. red, yellow and blue 90 30

1995. 4th U.N. Conference on Women, Peking.
3350 **916** 60p. multicoloured . . . 90 30

917 Cover Illustration of National Atlas of Spain

1995. 17th International Cartography Conference, Barcelona. Sheet 105 × 78 mm.
MS3351 **917** 130 p. multicoloured 1·70 85

918 Entrance to Hospital de la Azabacheria

1995. 500th Anniv of University of Santiago de Compostela.
3352 **918** 30p. multicoloured . . . 40 15

919 Royal Monastery of Santa Maria, Guadalupe

920 The Peddler" (sculpture, Jamie Pimentel)

1995. World Heritage Sites.
3353 **919** 60p. brown 60 35
3354 – 60p. multicoloured . . . 60 35
DESIGN—HORIZ: No. 3354, Route map of Spanish section of road to Santiago de Compostela and statue of pilgrim.

1994. "Exfilna '95" National Stamp Exhibition, Malaga. Sheet 105 × 78 mm.
MS3355 **920** 130p. green . . . . 1·70 85

921 Red-crested pochard, Mallard and Lagoon of La Mancha

1995. America. Environmental Protection.
3356 **921** 60p. multicoloured . . . 80 30

922 La Cueva de Menga, Malaga (Bronze Age)

1995. Archaeology. Multicoloured.
3357 30p. Type **922** 40 15
3358 30p. La Taula de Torralba (c. 700 B.C.) 40 15

923 Reciation

1995. Art. Sheet 145 × 95 mm containing details of "The Contemporary Poets" by Antonio Wsquivel. Multicoloured.
MS3359 19, 30, 60, 60p. Composite design of painting . . . . . . 2·30 1·30

925 King Juan Carlos

924 "Adoration of the Kings" (capital, Collegiate Church, San Martin de Elines)

1995. Christmas.
3360 **924** 30p. multicoloured . . . 30 20

1995. 20th Anniv of Accession of King Juan Carlos I.
3361 **925** 1000p. violet . . . . . 11·50 2·10
See also Nos. 3408/11.

926 Cordoba Station, Plaza de Armas, Seville (venue)

1995. "Espamer" Spanish–Latin American and "Aviation and Space" Stamp Exhibitions, Seville. Multicoloured.
3362 60p. Type **926** 80 30
3363 60p. Dr. Lorenzo Galindez de Carvajal (Master Courier of the Indies and Terra Firma of the Ocean Sea, 1514) 80 30
See also No. **MS**3382.

927 "Leaving Mass at Pilar de Zaragoza" (first Spanish film, 1896)

1996. Centenary of Motion Pictures.
3364 **927** 30p. brown, mauve and black 40 15
3365 – 60p. multicoloured . . . 80 30
DESIGN: 60p. "Bienvenido, Mister Marshall!" (poster).

928 Miner's Lamp

1996. Minerals (3rd series). Multicoloured.
3366 30p. Type **928** 40 15
3367 60p. Amber fluorite 80 30

929 Jose Mathe Aragua (General Director) and Telegraph Tower

1996. Stamp Day. 150th Anniv of Madrid–Irun Telegraph Signal Line.
3368 **929** 60p. green and red . . . 80 30

930 Columbus (statue), "B" and Arch of Triumph

1996. 10th Anniv (1995) of Start of Barcelona Urbanization Programme.
3369 **930** 30p. multicoloured . . . 40 15

931 Brown Bear with Cubs

932 *Real Phelipe* (ship of the line)

1996. Endangered Species.
3370 **931** 30p. multicoloured . . . 40 15

1996. 18th-century Ships. Two sheets each 87 × 165 mm containing vert designs as T **932**. Multicoloured.
MS3371 Two sheets. (a) 30p. × 4, Type **932**; (b) 60p. × 4, *El Catalan* (after Rafael Moleon) . . . . 4·50 2·50

933 Scales

1996. 400th Anniv of Madrid Bar Assocation.
3372 **933** 19p. multicoloured . . . 30 15

1996. Spanish Olympic Bronze Medal Sports. As T **897**. Multicoloured. Dated "1996".
3373 30p. Type **897** 40 15
3374 30p. As No. 3334 . . . . . 40 15
3375 30p. As No. 3299 . . . . . 40 15
3376 30p. As No. 3302 . . . . . 40 15
3377 30p. As No. 3304 . . . . . 40 15
3378 30p. As No. 3339 . . . . . 40 15
3379 30p. As No. 3342 . . . . . 40 15
3380 30p. As No. 3343 . . . . . 40 15
3381 30p. As No. 3306 . . . . . 40 15

934 Map of Seville—Larache Postal Route

1996. "Espaamer" Spanish-Latin American and "Aviation and Space" Stamp Exhibitions, Seville (2nd issue). Two sheets, each 164 × 87 mm containing T **934** and similar horiz designs (sheet a) or single stamp (b). Multicoloured.
MS3382 Two sheets. (a) 100p. Type **934**; 100p. Cover flown by airship *Graf Zeppelin*, 1930; 100p. Rocket launch, El Arenosillo, Huelva; 100 p. Hispano HA200 Saeta jet fighter. (b) 400p. The Royal Family (78 × 54 mm) . . 5·25 2·50

935 Carmen Amaya (flamenco dancer)

1996. Europa. Famous Women.
3383 **935** 60p. multicoloured . . . 80 30

936 El Jabato (Victor Mora and Francisco Darnis)

937 "General Don Antonio Ricardos"

1996. Comic Strip Characters. Multicoloured.
3384 19p. Type **936** 30 15
3385 30p. Reporter Tribulete (Guillermo Cifre) (horiz) 40 15

1996. 250th Birth Anniv of Francisco de Goya (artist). Multicoloured.
3386 19p. Type **937** 30 15
3387 30p. "The Milkmaid of Bordeaux" 40 15
3388 60p. "Boys with Mastiffs" (horiz) 85 30
3389 130p. "3rd of May 1808 in Madrid" (horiz) . . . . . 1·80 65

938 Magnifying Glass and Stamp Album

1996. 50th Anniv of Philatelic Service.
3390 **938** 30p. multicoloured . . . 40 15

939 Jose Monge Cruz (Camaron de la Isla)

1996. Flamenco Artistes.
3391 **939** 19p. multicoloured . . . 30 15
3392 – 30p. purple and red . . 40 15
DESIGN—HORIZ: 30p. Lola Flores.

940 Lanuza Market, Zaragoza (Felix Navarro Perez)

1996. 19th International Architects Congress, Barcelona. Metallic Buildings.
3393 **940** 30p. multicoloured . . . 40 15

941 Gerardo Diego and Pen (poet, birth centenary)

1996. Anniversaries.
3394 **941** 19p. violet and red . . . 25 15
3395 – 30p. multicoloured . . . 40 15
3396 – 60p. black, red and blue 75 30
DESIGNS—HORIZ: 30p. Joaquin Costa and birthplace (politician and historian, 150th birth anniv). VERT: 60p. The five senses (50th anniv of UNICEF.).

942 Naveta (tomb) des Tudons, Minorca

1996. Archaeology. Multicoloured.
3397 30p. Type **942** 40 15
3398 30p. Cabezo de Alcala de Azila, Teruel 40 15

944 Salamancan Costumes

945 Albaicin Quarter, Granada

1996. America. Traditional Costumes.
3400 **944** 60p. multicoloured . . . 60 40

1996. World Heritage Sites.
3401 **945** 19p. blue 25 15
3402 – 30p. purple 40 15
3403 – 60p. blue 75 30
DESIGNS—HORIZ: 30p. Tiberiades Square and statue of Maimonides (centre of Cordova). VERT: 60p. Deer, Donana National Park.

946 Oviedo Cathedral, Leopoldo Alas and Quotation from "La Regenta"

947 "Nativity" (Fernando Gallego)

1996. Literature.
3404 **946** 30p. blue and purple . . 40 15
3405 – 60p. blue and purple . . 75 30
DESIGN—HORIZ: 60p. Scene from "Don Juan Tenorio" by Jose Zorrilla.

1996. Christmas.
3406 **947** 30p. multicoloured . . . 40 15

948 Map (½-size illustration)

1996. Autonomous Communities of Spain. Sheet 164 × 87 mm.
MS3407 **948** 130p. multicoloured 1·60 85

1996. King Juan Carlos I.
3408 **925** 100p. brown . . . . . . 1·10 15
3409 200p. green . . . . . . 2·30 20
3410 300p. purple . . . . . . 4·50 40
3411 500p. blue . . . . 7·25 1·00

949 Genet

950 Exhibition Poster (Jose Sanchez)

1997. Endangered Species.
3416 **949** 32p. multicoloured . . . 40 15

1997. "Juvenia '97" National Youth Stamp Exhibition, El Puerto de Santa Maria.
3417 **950** 32p. multicoloured . . . 40 15

951 Stone Post Box, Madrid

1997. Stamp Day.
3418 **951** 65p. blue and red . . . 75 35

952 "The Journey to Nowhere" (dir. Fernando Fernan)

953 La Caprichosa and Bano de Diana Waterfalls, Monastery of Piedra Park

1997. Spanish Cinema (3rd series). Posters. Multicoloured.
3419 21p. Type **952** 25 15
3420 32p. "The South" (dir. Victor Erice) 40 15

1997. World Water Day.
3421 **953** 65p. multicoloured . . . 75 35

954 *Asturias* (frigate)

1997. 19th-century Ships. Two sheets each 87×164 mm containing similar vert designs as T **954**. Multicoloured.
MS3422 Two sheets (a) 21p. ×4, Type **954**; (b) 32p. ×4, 16-gun brigantine (after Rodriguez and Gasco) . . . . 2·40 1·30

955 Vizcaya Bridge

1997. Anniversaries. Metal Structures. Mult.
3423 32p. Type **955** (centenary of Engineering School, Bilbao) 40 15
3424 194p. Atocha railway station and AVE locomotive (fifth anniv of AVE high speed train) . . . . 2·20 95

956 Joint and Trueta

1997. Birth Centenary of Josep Trueta i Raspall (orthopaedic surgeon).
3425 **956** 32p. multicoloured . . . 40 15

957 Prince and Princess, Castle and Forest

958 Lazaro with Blind Beggar

1997. Europa. Tales and Legends.
3426 **957** 65p. multicoloured . . . 75 35

1997. Spanish Literature.
3427 **958** 21p. black and green . . 25 15
3428 – 32p. brown and blue . . 40 15
DESIGNS—VERT: 21p. Type **958** ("Life of Lazarillo de Tormes and his Fortunes and Setbacks"). HORIZ: 32p. Jose Maria Peman and character El Seneca.

959 Anxel Fole (writer) (after Siro Lopez Lorenzo)

1997. Galician Literature Day.
3429 **959** 65p. multicoloured . . . 75 35

960 The Ulysses Family (Mariano Benejam)

1997. Comic Strip Characters. Multicoloured.
3430 21p. Type **960** 25 15
3431 32p. The Masked Warrior (Manuel Gago) 40 15

961 Manolete (Manuel Rodriguez Sanchez) (matador)

1997. Anniversaries. Multicoloured.
3432 32p. Type **961** (50th death anniv) 40 15
3433 65p. Charlie Rivel (Josep Andreu i Lasserre) (clown, birth centenary (1996)) . . 75 35

962 "The Annunciation" (from Church of Our Lady of Sorrow, Agreda)

1997. Sixth "The Ages of Man" Exhibition. El Burgo de Osma. Sheet 92×148 mm containing T **962** and similar vert designs. Multicoloured.
MS3434 21p. Type **962**; 32p. El Burgo de Osma Cathedral;65p. Illustration from Codex, 1086; 140p. Santo Domingo de Silos (17-century statue) . . . . 3·00 1·70

963 Championship Poster (Manel Esclusa)

1997. 30th Men's European Basketball Championship, Barcelona, Girona and Badalona.
3435 **963** 65p. multicoloured . . . 75 35

964 Cibeles Fountain, Madrid

1997. North Atlantic Co-operation Council Summit, Madrid.
3436 **964** 65p. multicoloured . . . 75 35

965 Grape Harvest Monument (Jose Esteve Edo)

966 Antonio Canovas del Castillo (author of 1876 Constitution)

1997. 50th Anniv of Grape Harvest Festival, Requena.
3437 **965** 32p. multicoloured . . . 40 15

1997. Anniversaries. Multicoloured.
3438 21p. Type **966** (death centenary) 25 15
3439 32p. Roman coin and arrival of "Virgin of the Assumption" (statue) (2000th anniv of Elche) 40 15
3440 65p. Ships attacking city (after contemporary painting) (bicentenary of defence of Tenerife) (horiz) 75 35

967 Blue Ribbon

968 Mariano Benlliure and "Breath of Life"

1997. Campaign for Peaceful Co-existence.
3441 **967** 32p. blue and black . . 40 15

1997. Spanish Art.
3442 **968** 32p. multicoloured . . . 40 15
3443 – 65p. black and stone . . 75 35
DESIGNS: 32c. Type **968** (sculptor, 50th death anniv); 65c. "Basque Rower" (photograph by Jose Ortiz Echague).

969 Net and Boat

1997. 4th World Fishing Fair, Vigo.
3444 **969** 32p. blue, deep blue and gold 40 15

970 City

1997. Anniversaries.
3445 **970** 21p. multicoloured . . . 25 15
3446 – 32p. multicoloured . . . 40 15
3447 – 65p. violet and red . . . 75 35
DESIGNS—VERT: 21p. Type **970** (500th anniv of Spanish administration of Melilla); 32p. St. Pascual Baylon (after Vincente Carducho) (centenary of proclamation as World Patron of Eucharistic Congresses). HORIZ: 65p. Ausias March (after Jacomart) (poet, 600th birth anniv).

971 San Julian de los Prados Church, Oviedo

1997. World Heritage Sites.
3448 **971** 21p. brown, blue and green 25 15
3449 – 32p. brown, blue and green 40 15
DESIGN: 32p. Santa Cristina de Lena.

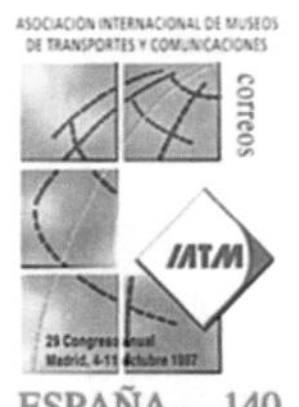

972 Emblem

973 Statue of Don Palayo (Jose Maria Lopez)

1997. 29th Annual Congress of International Transport and Communications Museums Association, Madrid.
3450 **972** 140p. multicoloured . . 1·60 70

1997. "Exfilna '97" National Stamp Exhibition, Gijon. Sheet 105×78 mm.
MS3451 **973** 140p. multicoloured 1·60 85

974 Postman

1997. America. Postal Delivery.
3452 **974** 65p. multicoloured . . . 75 35

975 Miguel Fleta (tenor)

976 Town Arms

1997. Re-opening of Royal Theatre, Madrid.
3453 **975** 21p. brown 25 15
3454 – 32p. brown 40 15
DESIGNS: 21p. Type **975** (birth centenary); 32p. Theatre facade.

1997. 500th Anniv of San Cristobal de la Laguna, Tenerife.
3455 **976** 32p. multicoloured . . . 40 15

977 Emblem

1997. 6th World Downs Syndrome Congress, Madrid.
3456 **977** 65p. blue and yellow . . 75 35

978 School

1997. 150th Anniv of Cordoba Veterinary School.
3457 **978** 21p. green and blue . . 25 15

979 "Adoration of the Kings" (detail, Pedro Berruguete)

1997. Christmas.
3458 **979** 32p. multicoloured . . . 40 15

980 New Gate, Ribadavia

1997. Jewish Quarters.
3459 **980** 21p. brown and black . . 25 15
3460 – 32p. violet and black . . 40 15
3461 – 32p. brown and black . . 40 15
3462 – 65p. violet and black . . 75 35
DESIGNS: No. 3460, Women's Gallery, Cordoba Synagogue; 3461, Facade of 15th-century building, St. Anthony's Quarter, Caceres; 3462, Street, El Call, Girona.

981 Ball in Net **982** Emblem

1997. Spanish Sporting Success. Zarra's Winning Goal in Spain v England Match, World Cup Football Championship, Brazil, 1950.
3463 **981** 32p. multicoloured . . . 85 25

1998. St. James's Holy Year (1999).
3464 **982** 35p. orange, grey and black 40 15

983 Lynx **985** Clever and Smart (Francisco Ibanez)

984 Club Flag and Emblem

1998. Endangered Species.
3465 **983** 35p. multicoloured . . . 40 15

1998. Centenary of Athletic Bilbao Football Club.
3466 **984** 35p. multicoloured . . . 40 20

1998. Comic Strip Characters. Multicoloured.
3467 35p. Type **985** 40 20
3468 70p. Zipi and Zape (Josep Escobar) (horiz) 80 40

986 Gredos Parador

1998. 70th Anniv of Paradores (state hotels).
3469 **986** 35p. multicoloured . . . 40 20

987 St. Philip's Fort and Harbour, Ceuta

1998. 3rd Anniv of Autonomy of Ceuta and Melilla. Multicoloured.
3470 150p. Type **987** . . . . . 1·70 75
3471 150p. Plaza de Menendez Pelayo, Melilla (horiz) . . 1·70 75

988 1898 Generation

1998. 1898 Generation of Spanish Writers.
3472 **988** 70p. multicoloured . . . 80 40
The writers depicted are Azorin, Pio Baroja, Miguel de Unamuno, Ramiro de Maeztu, Antonio Machado and Valle Inclan.

989 Pedro Abarca de Bolea, Count of Aranda **990** "The Celestine" (Fernando de Rojas)

1998. Death Bicentenary of Pedro Abarca de Bolea, Count of Aranda (politician).
3473 **989** 35p. multicoloured . . . 40 20

1998. Spanish Literature.
3474 **990** 35p. deep green and green 40 20
3475 – 70p. green and red . . . 80 40
DESIGN: 70p. "Fortunata and Jecinta" (Benito Perez Galdos).

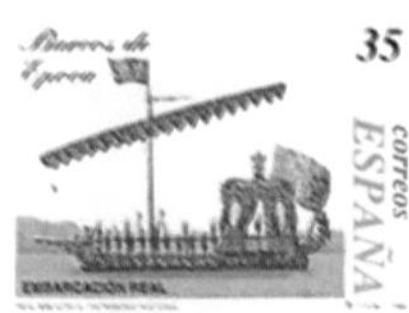

991 Royal Barge

1998. Ship Paintings by Carlos Broschi from "Royal Celebrations in Reign of Fernando VI". Multicoloured.
3476 35p. Type **991** 40 20
3477 70p. Tajo xebec (for court officials) 80 40

992 St. John's Bonfires, Alicante

1998. Europa. National Festivals.
3478 **992** 70p. multicoloured . . . 80 40

993 Jimenez Diaz

1998. Centenary of Professional Institute of Doctors of Madrid and Birth Centenary of Carlos Jimenez Diaz (physician).
3479 **993** 35p. black and blue . . 40 20

994 Felix Rodriguez de la Fuente (naturalist, 70th anniv)

1998. Birth Anniversaries.
3480 **994** 35p. multicoloured . . . 40 20
3481 – 70p. orange and red . . . 80 40
DESIGN—VERT: 70p. Fofo (Alfonso Aragon) (clown, 75th anniv).

995 Philip II (after Antonio Moro) **996** Lorca

1998. 400th Death Anniv of King Philip II.
3482 **995** 35p. multicoloured . . . 40 20

1998. Birth Centenary of Federico Garcia Lorca (writer).
3483 **996** 35p. multicoloured . . . 40 20

997 Antonio Manso Fernandez and 1978 Queen Isabel II Stamp

1998. Spanish Engravers.
3484 **997** 35p. brown, blue and deep blue 40 20
3485 – 70p. purple, blue and black 80 40
DESIGN: 70p. Jose Luis Sanchez Toda and 1935 Mariana Pineda stamp.

998 Spanish and Philippine Flags, Cebu Basilica (after M. Miguel) and "Holy Child" (statuette)

1998. Centenary of Philippine Independence.
3486 **998** 70p. multicoloured . . . 80 40

999 "Foster Brothers" (sculpture, Aniceto Marinas)

1998. Spanish Art.
3487 **999** 35p. multicoloured . . . 40 20

1000 "Union of the Oceans"

1998. "Expo '98" World's Fair, Lisbon.
3488 **1000** 70p. multicoloured . . 80 40

1001 Computer, Computer Disk and Letter

1998. 20th International Data Protection Conference, Santiago de Compostela.
3489 **1001** 70p. multicoloured . . 80 40

1002 Barcelona Cathedral

1998. "Exfilna '98" National Stamp Exhibition, Barcelona. Sheet 106 × 88 mm.
MS3490 **1002** 150p. black and blue 1·60 1·60

1003 Fortified City, Cuenca

1998. World Heritage Sites.
3491 **1003** 35p. brown and blue . . 40 20
3492 – 70p. brown and red . . 80 40
DESIGN: 70p. Silk Exchange, Valencia.

1004 Man writing with Quill

1998. School Correspondence Programme. Scenes from "Don Quixote" (novel by Cervantes). Multicoloured.
3493 20p. Type **1004** 25 15
3494 20p. Man reading book . . 25 15
3495 20p. Priest dubbing Quixote 25 15
3496 20p. Quixote riding off at dawn (angel blowing trumpet) 25 15
3497 20p. Man beating Quixote with stick 25 15
3498 20p. Investigator burning books 25 15
3499 20p. Quixote and Sancho on horseback 25 15
3500 20p. Quixote and horse on sail of windmill 25 15
3501 20p. Quixote watching Sancho fly through air . . 25 15
3502 20p. Quixote charging through flock of sheep . . 25 15
3503 20p. Quixote and galley slaves 25 15
3504 20p. Quixote piercing goat-skins of wine 25 15
3505 20p. Quixote in cage 25 15
3506 20p. Quixote and Sancho on knees and woman on donkey 25 15
3507 20p. Quixote on foot holding sword to Knight of the Mirrors 25 15
3508 20p. Lion escaping cage . . 25 15
3509 20p. Quixote attacking birds 25 15
3510 20p. Quixote on wooden horse 25 15
3511 20p. Sancho as governor at meal 25 15
3512 20p. Quixote surprised in bed by Dona Rodriguez 25 15
3513 20p. Sancho and donkey . . 25 15
3514 20p. Quixote and Sancho looking over lake 25 15
3515 20p. Quixote on horse holding sword to Knight of the White Moon . . . 25 15
3516 20p. Quixote and Sancho returning home at night 25 15

1005 Angel Ganivet (writer, death centenary)

1998. Anniversaries.
3517 **1005** 35p. brown and violet 40 20
3518 – 70p. brown and blue . . 80 40
DESIGN—VERT: 70p. Giralda Tower, Seville (800th anniv).

1006 Ladies' Tower and El Partal Gardens, Alhambra, Granada

1998. Aga Khan 1998 Architecture Award.
3519 **1006** 35p. brown and green 40 20

1007 U.P.U. Emblem

1998. World Stamp Day.
3520 **1007** 70p. blue and green . . 80 40

1008 Maria Guerrero (actress) and Scene from "The Lioness of Castille" by Francisco Villaespesa

1998. America. Famous Women.
3521 **1008** 70p. multicoloured . . 80 40

1009 Steam Locomotive "Mataro" (1848) and Euromed Electric Train (1998)

1998. 150th Anniv of Spanish Railways.
3522 **1009** 35p. blue and black . . 40 20

1010 Antarctic Base

1998. 10th Anniv of Juan Carlos I Antarctic Base.
3523 **1010** 35p. multicoloured . . 40 20

1011 Altarpiece (detail) **1012** Chestnut Seller

1998. Restoration of San Salvador's Cathedral, Zaragoza. Details of Altarpiece by Hans of Swabia. Sheet 105 × 122 mm containing T **1011** and similar vert design. Multicoloured.
MS3524 35p. Type **1011**; 35p. Adoration of the Wise Men (detail) 85 65

1998. Christmas. Multicoloured.
3525 35p. Type **1012** 40 20
3526 70p. "Wedding of Virgin Mary and Joseph" (detail of capital from Oviedo Cathedral) 80 40

1013 Juan de Onate (expedition leader)

1998. 400th Anniv of Foundation of Spanish Province of New Mexico. Multicoloured.
3527 35p. Type **1013** 40 20
3528 70p. Map and arms of New Mexico 80 40

1014 House, Hervas

1998. Jewish Quarters.
3529 **1014** 35p. purple and blue . . 40 20
3530 – 35p. green and blue . . 40 20
3531 – 70p. purple and blue . . 80 40
3532 – 70p. green and blue . . 80 40
DESIGNS: No. 3530, Bust of Benjamin Tudela (travel writer); 3531, Corpus Christi Church (former synagogue), Segovia; 3532, Santa Maria la Blanca synagogue, Toledo.

1015 Alaior and Mt. Toro

1998. UNESCO Biosphere Reserve, Minorca.
3533 **1015** 35p. multicoloured . . 40 20

1016 Bust of Plato and Ancient Greek Amphora

1998. 30th Anniv of Spanish Olympic Academy.
3534 **1016** 70p. multicoloured . . 80 40

1017 Angel Sanz Briz (diplomat)

1998. 50th Anniv of Universal Declaration of Human Rights. Multicoloured.
3535 35p. Type **1017** 40 20
3536 70p. Fingerprints forming heart (painting, Javier Valmaseda Calvo) 80 40

1018 Mare and Foal

1998. "Espana 2000" International Stamp Exhibition (1st issue). La Cartuja-Hierro del Bocado Horses. Multicoloured.
3537 20p. Type **1018** (emblem bottom right) 25 15
3538 20p. Type **1018** (emblems top left and top right) . . 25 15
3539 35p. Brown horse (emblem top right) 40 20
3540 35p. As No. 3538 (emblem bottom left) 40 20
3541 70p. Horse's head (emblems bottom left and bottom right) 80 40
3542 70p. As No. 3541 (emblem top left) 80 40
3543 100p. Mare and foal (different) (emblems top left and top right) . . . . 1·20 50
3544 100p. As No. 3543 (emblem bottom right) . . . . . . 1·20 50
3545 150p. Grey (emblem bottom left) . . . . 1·70 85
3546 150p. As No. 3545 (emblem top right) . . . . 1·70 85
3547 185p. Two white horses (emblem top left) . . . . 2·20 1·00
3548 185p. As No. 3547 (emblems bottom left and bottom right) . . . . 2·20 1·00
See also Nos. 3612/23 and 3662/3.

1019 Giant Lizard, El Hierro Island

1999. Endangered Species. Multicoloured.
3549 35p. Type **1019** 40 15
3550 70p. Osprey (vert) 80 40
3551 100p. Manx shearwater . . 1·20 50

1020 Stone Cross, Perelada, Galicia **1021** Poster (Antoni Tapies)

1999. St. James's Holy Year. Multicoloured.
3552 35p. Type **1020** 40 20
3553 70p. Figure of St. James on tympanum, St. James's Church, Sanguesa, Navarra (horiz) 85 40
3554 100p. Stone cross and Cizur bridge, Pamplona, Navarra . . . . 1·20 50
3555 185p. Jurisdictional stone pillar, Boadilla del Camino, Palencia . . . . 2·20 90

1999. Centenary of Barcelona Football Club.
3556 **1021** 35p. multicoloured . . 40 20

1022 "Alaior" (Aroa Vidal)

1999. "Juvenia'99" National Youth Stamp Exhibition, Alaior, Minorca.
3557 **1022** 35p. black, red and yellow 40 20

1023 Police Moped, Helicopter and Men in Protective Suits

1999. 175th Anniv of Spanish Police Force.
3558 **1023** 35p. multicoloured . . 40 20

1024 Aljaferia Palace, Zaragoza **1026** Emblem and Athletes

1025 Radio Transmitter and Receiver

1999. "Exfilna '99" National Stamp Exhibition, Zaragoza. Sheet 106 × 79 mm.
MS3559 **1024** 185p. green and chestnut . . . . 2·10 1·00

1999. 50th Anniv of Spanish Amateur Radio Union.
3560 **1025** 70p. multicoloured . . 80 40

1999. 7th World Athletics Championship, Seville.
3561 **1026** 70p. multicoloured . . 80 40

1027 Monfrague Nature Park, Caceres, and Wild Cat

1999. Europa. Parks and Gardens.
3562 **1027** 70p. multicoloured . . 80 40

1028 Underground Train

1999. 75th Anniv of Barcelona Metro.
3563 **1028** 70p. multicoloured . . 80 40

1029 "King Solomon" (detail of reredos from Becerril de Campos Church)

1999. "The Ages of Man" Exhibition, Palencia. Multicoloured.
3564 35p. Type **1029** 40 20
3565 70p. Detail of choir railing, Palencia Cathedral . . . 80 40

1030 European Community Flag

1999. The Euro (European single currency). Showing maps of the participating countries and the appropriate exchange rate. Multicoloured.
3566 166p. Type **1030** . . . . . 1·90 85
3567 166p. Germany . . . . . . 1·90 85
3568 166p. Austria . . . . 1·90 85
3569 166p. Belgium . . . . . . 1·90 85
3570 166p. Spain . . . . 1·90 85
3571 166p. Finland . . . . . . 1·90 85
3572 166p. France . . . . 1·90 85
3573 166p. Netherlands . . . . . 1·90 85
3574 166p. Republic of Ireland 1·90 85
3575 166p. Italy . . . . 1·90 85
3576 166p. Luxembourg . . . . 1·90 85
3577 166p. Portugal . . . . . . 1·90 85

1031 Footballers and Club Badge

1999. Real Club Recreativo (Royal Recreation Club) of Huelva.
3578 **1031** 35p. multicoloured . . 40 20

1032 Dona Urraca (Jorge (Miguel Bernet Toledano)) **1033** Games Emblem

1999. Comic Strip Characters. Multicoloured.
3579 35p. Type **1032** 40 20
3580 70p. El Coyote (Jose Mallorqui and Francisco Batet) 80 40

1999. World University Summer Games and Fifth National Thematic Stamps Exhibition, Palma de Mallorca. Sheet 105 × 78 mm.
MS3581 **1033** 185p. multicoloured 2·10 1·00

1034 Attack of Dutch Navy (after De Bry) and Arms of Las Palmas

1999. 400th Anniv of Defence of Las Palmas, Gran Canaria.
3582 **1034** 70p. black and yellow 80 40

1035 Cangas de Onis Parador (former Monastery of San Pedro de Villanueva)

1999. Paradores (state hotels).
3583 **1035** 35p. multicoloured . . 40 20

1036 Old Bridge

1037 Society and Anniversary Emblems

1999. 800th Anniv of Granting of Township Rights to Balmaseda.
3584 **1036** 35p. multicoloured . . 40 20

1999. Centenary of Society of Authors and Publishers.
3585 **1037** 70p. multicoloured . . 80 40

1038 Illuminated Fountain

1999. Birth Centenary of Carles Buigas (engineer).
3586 **1038** 70p. multicoloured . . 80 40

1039 Queen Isabel II, Geological Map of Spain and Founding Decree

1999. 150th Anniv of Spanish Technical Institute of Geology and Mining.
3587 **1039** 150p. multicoloured . . 1·80 75

1040 El Cid (after Vela Zanetti)

1042 "The Jester Don Sebastian de Morra"

1041 "Winter"

1999. 900th Death Anniv of El Cid (Rodrigo Diaz de Vivar).
3588 **1040** 35p. multicoloured . . 40 20

1999. Spanish Art. Paintings by Vela Zanetti. Multicoloured.
3589 70p. Type **1041** 80 40
3590 150p. "The Harvest" (vert) 1·70 75

1999. 400th Birth Anniv of Diego de Silva Velazquez (artist). Multicoloured.
3591 35p. Type **1042** 30 20
3592 70p. "A Sibyl" 60 40

1043 Emblem, Couple, Man and Baby

1999. International Year of the Elderly.
3593 **1043** 35p. multicoloured . . 40 20

1044 Oix Castle

1999. Catalan Lower Pyrenees Region.
3594 **1044** 70p. brown and blue . . 80 40

1045 St. Millan of Yuso Monastery, La Rioja

1999. World Heritage Sites.
3595 **1045** 35p. brown, green and blue 40 20
3596 – 70p. brown, green and blue 80 40
DESIGN: 70p. St. Millan of Suso Monastery, La Rioja.

1046 U.P.U. Monument, Berne

1999. Stamp Day. 125th Anniv of Universal Postal Union.
3597 **1046** 70p. multicoloured . . 80 40

1047 First Spanish Stamp, 1850

1999. School Correspondence Programme. Designs showing a stamp performing various activities. Multicoloured.
3598 20p. Type **1047** 25 15
3599 20p. Watching airliner taking off over city . . . 25 15
3600 20p. As postman delivering letter 25 15
3601 20p. Writing letter 25 15
3602 20p. Reading book 25 15
3603 20p. With bird, butterfly and fish (nature) . . . 25 15
3604 20p. Viewing historical buildings (heritage) . . . 25 15
3605 20p. Painting portrait . . . 25 15
3606 20p. With football, tennis racquet and sailboard . . 25 15
3607 20p. With baton, cello and saxophone 25 15
3608 20p. Holding magnifying glass over 40c. stamp . . 25 15
3609 20p. On horseback 25 15

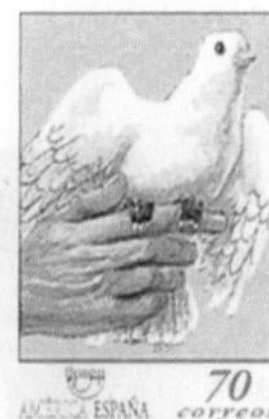
1048 Dove on Hand

1999. America. A New Millennium without Arms.
3610 **1048** 70p. multicoloured . . 80 40

1049 "The Money Changer and his Wife" (Marinus Reymerswaele)

1999. National Money Museums Congress, Madrid.
3611 **1049** 70p. brown and blue . . 80 40

1050 Horse and Rider

1999. "Espana 2000" International Stamp Exhibition, Madrid (2nd issue). La Cartuja-Hierro del Bocado Horses. Paintings by Jose Manuel Gomez. Multicoloured.
3612 20p. Type **1050** (emblem bottom right) 25 15
3613 20p. Type **1050** (emblem top left) 25 15
3614 35p. Exhibition emblem and horses (emblems top left and right) 40 20
3615 35p. As No. 3614 (emblems top left and right but transposed) 40 20
3616 70p. Exhibition emblem (emblems bottom left and right) 80 40
3617 70p. As No. 3616 (emblems bottom left and right but transposed) 80 40
3618 100p. White horses (emblem top right) . . . . 1·20 50
3619 100p. As No. 3618 (emblem bottom left) . . . . . . 1·20 50
3620 150p. Heads of two white horses (emblem bottom left) . . . . 1·70 85
3621 150p. As No. 3620 (emblem top right) . . . . 1·70 85
2622 185p. Men inspecting horse (emblem top left) . . . . 2·20 1·00
3623 185p. As No. 3622 (emblem bottom right) . . . . . . 2·20 1·00

1051 "The Epiphany" (altarpiece, Toledo Cathedral)

1999. Christmas. Multicoloured.
3624 35p. Type **1051** 40 20
3625 70p. "Christmas" (Isabel Guerra) (horiz) 80 40

1052 King Juan Carlos and 1850 12c. Stamp

2000. 150th Anniv of First Spanish Stamp. Mult.
3626 35p. Type **1052** 40 20
3627 35p. King Juan Carlos and 6c. stamp 40 20
3628 35p. King Juan Carlos and 5r. stamp 40 20
3629 35p. King Juan Carlos and 6r. stamp 40 20
3630 35p. Anniversary emblem and 6c. stamp 40 20
3631 35p. King Juan Carlos and 10r. stamp 40 20
3632 35p. King Juan Carlos and State arms 40 20

1053 Apollo

2000. Endangered Butterflies. Multicoloured.
3633 35p. Type **1053** 40 15
3634 70p. *Agriades zullichi* . . . 80 40

1054 Virgin Mary and Baby Jesus (xylographic engraving, Juan Luschner)

1055 "Charles V as Sovereign Master of the Order of the Golden Fleece" (anon)

2000. 500th Anniv of the Monastery of Santa Maria of Montserrat Printing House.
3635 **1054** 35p. multicoloured . . 40 20

2000. 500th Birth Anniv of King Charles V, Holy Roman Emperor. Multicoloured.
3636 35p. Type **1055** 40 20
3637 70p. "Charles V" (Corneille da la Haye) 80 40
MS3638 126 × 91 mm. 150p. "Charles V on Horseback" (40 × 49 mm) . . . . 1·70 95

1056 The Virgin de al Majestad (12th-century statue), Astorga Cathedral

2000. "The Age of Man" Exhibition, Astorga, Leon. Multicoloured.
3639 70p. Type **1056** 80 40
3640 100p. 12th-century Lignum Crucis and 10th-century Arab perfume bottle) . . 1·10 50

1057 Sos del Rey Catolico, Saragossa

2000. Paradores (state hotels).
3641 **1057** 35p. multicoloured . . 40 20

1058 Lleida University

2000. University Anniversaries.
3642 **1058** 35p. brown and mauve 40 20
3643 – 70p. brown and blue . . 80 40
DESIGNS: 35p. Type **1058** (700th anniv); 70p. Valencia (500th anniv (1999)).

1059 Emblem

1060 Maria de las Mercedes (painting, Ricardo Macarron)

2000. Centenary of Reial Club Deportiu Espanyol Football Club, Barcelona.
3644 **1059** 35p. multicoloured . . 30 20

2000. Maria de las Mercedes de Borbon y Orleans (mother of King Juan Carlos I) Commemoration.
3645 **1060** 35p. multicoloured . . 40 20

1061 "Building Europe"

2000. Europa.

3646 **1061** 70p. multicoloured . . 80 20

1062 Emblem

2000. World Mathematics Year (3648) and Science (others). Multicoloured.

3647 35p. Type **1062** (300th anniv of Royal Academy of Medicine, Seville) 40 20

3648 70p. Julio Rey Pastor (mathematician) (painting, Pedro Piug Adam) and mathematical equation . . 80 40

3649 100p. School of Pharmacy, Granada (150th anniv) (vert) . . . . 1·10 50

3650 185p. Prince Felipe Science Museum, Valencia . . . . 2·10 90

1063 Hermenegilda and Leovigilda (Manuel Vazquez Gallego)

2000. Comic Strip Characters. Multicoloured.

3651 35p. Type **1063** 40 20

3652 70p. Roberto Alcazar and Pedrin (Eduardo Vano and Juan Bautista Puerto Belda) (vert) 80 40

1064 Guggenheim Museum

2000. 700th Anniv of Bilbao.

3653 **1064** 70p. multicoloured . . 80 40

1065 "Prayer in the Garden" (detail, Francisco Salzillo)

1066 Water Fountain

2000. Spanish Art.

3654 **1065** 70p. multicoloured . . 80 40

2000. "Exfilna '2000" National Philatelic Exhibition, Aviles. Sheet 105 × 78 mm.

MS3655 **1066** 185p. brown and blue 2·00 1·00

1067 Wild Pine (*Pinus silvestris*)

2000. Trees (1st series). Multicoloured.

3656 70p. Type **1067** 80 40

3657 150p. Holm oak (*Quercus ilex*) . . . . 1·70 75

See also Nos. 3757/8, 3837/8, 3994/5 and 4021.

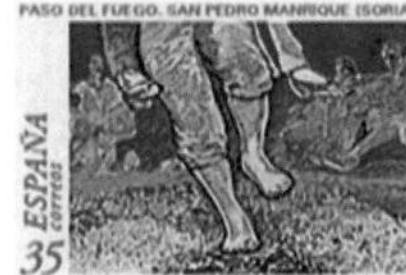

1068 Fire Walking, San Pedro Manrique, Soria

2000. Festivals (1st series). Multicoloured.

3658 35p. Type **1068** 40 20

3659 70p. Rearing horse, crowd and flag (700th anniv of Chivalry Festival of San Juan, Ciudadela, Menorca) 80 40

See also Nos 3760/1.

1069 Escriva

2000. 25th Death Anniv of Josemaria Escriva de Balaguer (founder of Opus Dei (religious organization)).

3660 **1069** 70p. black and orange 80 40

1070 Detail of Chart (½-size illustration)

2000. 500th Anniv of Chart by Juan de la Cosa (sailor and cartographer) (first chart showing the Americas). Sheet 164 × 87 mm.

MS3661 **1070** 150p. multicoloured 1·70 95

1071 Horse and Emblem

2000. "Espana 2000" International Stamp Exhibition, Madrid (3rd issue). La Carbija-Hierro de Bocado Horses. Multicoloured.

3662 20p. Type **1071** (emblem bottom right) 25 15

3663 20p. Type **1071** (emblems top right) 25 15

3664 35p. Horse on beach (emblem top right) . . . 40 20

3665 35p. As No. 3664 (emblem bottom left) 40 20

3666 70p. Galloping horses and horse's head (emblems bottom left and right) . . 80 40

3667 70p. As No. 3666 (emblem top left) 80 40

3668 100p. Two horses' heads (emblems top left and right) . . . . 1·20 50

3669 100p. As No. 3668 (emblem bottom right) . . . . . . 1·20 50

3670 150p. Horse and horse's head (emblem bottom left) 1·70 85

3671 150p. As No. 3671 (emblem top right) . . . . 1·70 85

3672 185p. Horse outside stable (emblem top left) . . . . 2·20 1·00

3673 185p. As No. 3672 (emblems bottom left and right) . . 2·20 1·00

Nos. 3662/73 were issued together in se-tenant sheetlets of 12 stamps. Two different emblems were each printed twice in orange within the sheet, occurring in each case at the intersection of four stamps so that each stamp carries only part of one or two emblems as described in brackets.

1072 Las Medulas, Leon

2000. UNESCO World Heritage Sites.

3674 **1072** 35p. multicoloured . . 40 20

3675 – 70p. brown and blue (vert) 80 40

3676 – 150p. red and brown 1·70 75

DESIGNS: 70p. Mount Perdido, Pyrenees; 150p. Catalan Music Palace, Barcelona.

1073 Atapuercan Man wearing Football Scarf

2000. School Correspondence Programme (1st series). Spanish History. Multicoloured.

3677 20p. Type **1073** 25 15

3678 20p. Cave artists, Altamira 25 15

3679 20p. Phoenician ship 25 15

3680 20p. Question marks in Roman helmets (Tartessos) 25 15

3681 20p. Celtic and Iberian men 25 15

3682 20p. "The Lady of Elche" listening to music 25 15

3683 20p. Elephant on low-loader (Carthage) (first Punic war) 25 15

3684 20p. Romans 25 15

3685 20p. Viriathus (leader) attacking Roman (uprising in northern Spain) 25 15

3686 20p. Roman preparing to kick football into net full of Numanians (fall of the city of Numantia) 25 15

3687 20p. Aqueduct of Segova . . 25 15

3688 20p. Roman facing Vandal, Suevian and Alani (invasion, 409) 25 15

3689 20p. Visigoth kings Teodoredo I, Wallia, Sigerico and Ataulfo . . . 25 15

3690 20p. King Recaredo I (conversion to Christianity, 589) 25 15

3691 20p. Map showing extent of Arab rule (conquest by Arab forces, 711) 25 15

3692 20p. Pelayo (Visigoth soldier), Covadonga, 722 (victory over the Moors) 25 15

3693 20p. Horseman (discovery of Tomb of the Apostle, 813) 25 15

3694 20p. Kings (union of Castille and Navarre) 25 15

3695 20p. Death of El Cid (soldier), 1099 . . . . . 25 15

3696 20p. Battle of Las Navas de Tolosa represented by chess game 25 15

3697 20p. Accession of Alfonso X (1252) 25 15

3698 20p. Enrique II and slain Pedro I foundation of House of Trastamara (Kingdom of Castille and Leon), 1396 . . . . 25 15

3699 20p. Monk with magnifying glass (The Inquisition, established 1478) 25 15

3700 20p. Two crowns (unification of Kingdoms of Castile and Aragon 1479) 25 15

See also Nos. 3775/86 and 3882/93.

1074 Record and Hand (Julio Iglesias, singer)

2000. "Espana 2000" International Stamp Exhibition, Madrid (4th issue). Eleven sheets 105 × 78 mm containing T **1074** and similar multicoloured designs.

MS3701 Eleven sheets (a) 200p. Type **1074**; (b) 200p. Record and signature (Alejandro Sanz, singer-songwriter); (c) 200p. Film projector (Antonio Banderas, actor); (d) 200p. Designers mannequin (Jesus de Pozo, designer and couturier); (e) 200p. Football (Raul Gonzalez Blanco, footballer); (f) 200p. Cycle wheel (Miguel Indurain, cyclist); (g) 200p. Hands (Joquin Cortes, dancer and choreographer); (h) 200p. Dancing feet (Sara Baras, Flamenco dancer); (i) 200p Emblem (televisin); (j) 200p. Radio mast; (k) 200p. Newspaper titles (the press) . . . . 24·00 12·50

1075 Boy putting up Poster

1076 Portrait and Treble Clef

2000. America. A.I.D.S. Awareness.

3702 **1075** 70p. multicoloured . . 80 40

2000. 1st Death Anniv of Alfred Kraus (tenor).

3703 **1076** 70p. multicoloured . . 80 40

1077 The Adoration of Jesus (triptych) (Cristiane Hemmerich)

1078 Building Facade

2000. Christmas. Multicoloured.

3704 35p. Type **1077** 40 20

3705 70p. "Birth of Christ" (Conrad von Soest) . . . 80 40

2000. Millenary of Santa María la Real Church, Aranda de Duero.

3706 **1078** 35p. brown 40 20

1079 Couple in Orange Grove (*Etre Naranjos*, Vicente Blasco Ibanez)

2000. Literature.

3707 35p. Type **1079** 40 20

3708 70p. Troubadour with lute, figures and castle (*La Venganza de Don Mendo*, Pedro Munzo Seca) . . . 80 40

3709 100p. Soldiers (*El Alcalde Zalamea*, Pedro Calaeron de la Barca) . . . . . . 1·10 50

1080 "Tribute to Broker" (sculpture) (Francisco Lopez Hernandez) and Emblem

1081 Firefighters

2001. 75th Anniv of Brokers' Schools.

3710 **1080** 40p. multicoloured . . 40 15

2001.

3711 **1081** 75p. multicoloured . . 75 15

1082 Soldier, Building and Emblem

2001. 150th Anniv of Infantry College, Toledo.

3712 **1082** 120p. multicoloured . . 1·20 20

1083 Emblem

2001. Campaign Against Domestic Violence.
3713 **1083** 155p. multicoloured . . 1·50 20

1084 First Post Box in Spain, Mayorga (1793)

2001. Stamp Day.
3714 **1084** 155p. black . . . . . . 1·50 20

1085 Young Couple and Yacht

2001. "Juvenia 2001" Youth Stamp Exhibition, Cadiz.
3715 **1085** 12p. multicoloured . . 1·20 20

1086 Plasencia Hotel (former monastery of San Vicente Ferrer)

2001. Paradores (state hotels).
3716 **1086** 40p. multicoloured . . 40 15

1087 Joaquin Rodrigo (composer, birth centenary)

2001. Personalities.
3717 **1087** 40p. violet 40 15
3718 – 75p. brown and blue . . 75 15
DESIGNS: 75p. Rafael Alberti (poet and dramatist, first death anniv).

1088 Zuda Castle, Tortosa

1089 Books forming Flower

2001. Castles. Multicoloured.
3719 40p. Type **1088** 40 15
3720 75p. Castle of El Cid, Jadraque (horiz) 75 15
3721 155p. San Fernando Castle, Figueres (horiz) . . . . . 1·50 20
3722 260p. Montesquiu Castle (horiz) . . . . 2·75 40

2001. World Book Day.
3723 **1089** 40p. multicoloured . . 40 15

1090 Dornier Do-J Wal Flying Boat, *Plus Ultra* and Map of South America

2001. 75th Anniv of Spanish Aviation. Multicoloured.
3724 40p. Type **1090** (flight from Palos de Fontera, Spain to Buenos Aires, 1926) . . 40 20
3725 75p. Breguet 19A2 and map of Europe (flight by Gallariza and Loruga from Madrid to Manilla, 1926) 75 25
3726 155p. Dornier flying boat and map of Africa (flight from Melilla to Santa Isabel, Equatorial Guinea, 1926) . . . . 1·50 40
3727 260p. C-295 (transport) (commemorative flight) . . 2·75 60
Nos. 3724/7 were issued together, se-tenant, the backgrounds forming the composite design of a map.

1091 Decorated Ceiling and Emblem

1092 King Juan Carlos I

2001. 154th Anniv of Liceu Theatre.
3728 **1091** 120p. multicoloured . . 1·20 15

2001.
3729 5p. red and silver . . . 15 15
3730 **1092** 40p. green and silver . . 40 15
3744 75p. violet and silver 75 15
3748 100p. brown and silver 1·00 15

1093 Garden

1094 Church Facade (church of San Martino, Noia)

2001. Europa. Water Resources.
3750 **1093** 75p. multicoloured . . 75 15

2001. Architecture.
3751 **1094** 40p. brown and blue . . 40 15
3752 – 75p. multicoloured . . 75 15
3753 – 155p. blue and brown 1·50 20
DESIGNS: 75p. Tui Cathedral, Pontevedra; 155p. Dovecote, Villaconcha, Frechilla.

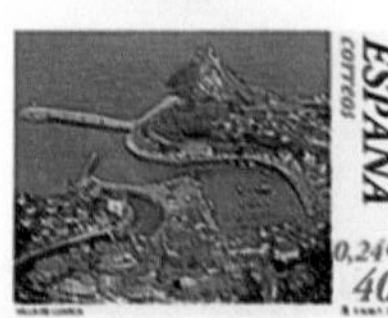

1095 Peninsula, Marina and Bay

2001. Luarca.
3754 **1095** 40p. multicoloured . . 40 15

1096 De Castro (statue, Juan de Bologna) and School of Our Lady of Antigua

2001. 400th Death Anniv of Cardinal Rodrigo de Castro (Supreme Counsellor of The Inquisition).
3755 **1096** 40p. multicoloured . . 40 15

1097 Children and Calf (*Adios Corderia*, Leopodo Alas ("Clarin"))

2001. Literature.
3756 **1097** 75p. multicoloured . . 75 15

2001. Trees (2nd series). As T **1067**. Multicoloured.
3757 40p. Olive 40 15
3758 75p. Beech 75 15

1098 Emblem and Shield

2001. 25th Anniv of Copa del Rey Football Championship.
3759 **1098** 40p. multicoloured . . 40 20

1099 Hooded Dancer being pelted with Tomatoes, Zaragoza

2001. Festivals (2nd series). Multicoloured.
3760 40p. Type **1099** 40 15
3761 70p. Giants, Barcelona (vert) 1·20 20

1100 Gracian

2001. 400th Birth Anniv of Baltasar Gracian (philosopher and writer).
3762 **1100** 120p. multicoloured . . 1·20 20

1101 Our Lady of Calva (statue), Zamora Cathedral

1102 Boy looking up (Grandmothers' Day)

2001. "Ages of Man Exhibition", Zamora.
3763 **1101** 120p. mauve and red 1·20 15
3764 – 155p. red and black . . 1·50 20
DESIGN: 155p. Cupola and cathedral.

2001. Social Activities. Multicoloured.
3765 40p. Type **1102** 40 15
3766 75p. Nun and building (Servants of Jesus for Charity (social relief organization)) 75 15

1103 View of City (½-size illustration)

2001. Salamanca, European City of Culture, 2002 .
3767 **1103** 75p. multicoloured . . 75 20

1104 Covadonga Basilica

2001. Centenary of Consecration of Basilica of Covadonga.
3768 **1104** 40p. multicoloured . . 40 20

1105 Emblem

2001. Formation of State Post and Telegraph Company.
3769 **1105** 40p. multicoloured . . 40 15

1106 View of Vigo

2001. "EXFILNA 2001" National Philatelic Exhibition, Vigo. Sheet 105 × 78 mm.
MS3770 **1106** 260p. ultramarine and deep ultramarine . . . . . . 2·75 1·70

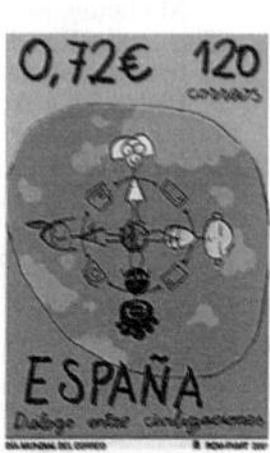

1107 Musicians

1108 Children encircling Globe

2001. Birth Millenary of St. Dominic of Silos (Benedictine monk and abbot).
3771 **1107** 40p. multicoloured . . 40 20
MS3772 106 × 79 mm. No. 3771 4·25 4·25

2001. United Nations Year of Dialogue among Civilizations.
3773 **1108** 120p. multicoloured . . 1·20 20

1109 Grasses, Ses Salines Nature Reserve

2001. America. UNESCO World Heritage Sites.
3774 **1109** 155p. multicoloured . . 1·50 20

2001. School Correspondence Programme. Spanish History (2nd series). As T **1073** but with currency inscribed in both euros and pesetas. Multicoloured.
3775 25p. Christopher Columbus juggling eggs (discovery of America, 1492) 25 15
3776 25p. Spanish and Portuguese boys each holding balloons showing maps (Treaty of Tordesillas, 1494) 25 15
3777 25p. King Carlos I of Spain (elected Emperor Charles V, 1519) 25 15
3778 25p. Hernan Cortes and Mexican musicians (conquest of Mexico, 1519) 25 15
3779 25p. Juan Sebastian Elcano (first circumnavigation of globe, 1522) 25 15
3780 25p. Inca city and bull on mountain (Francisco Pizarro's conquest of Peru, 1532) 25 15
3781 25p. King Felipe II with globe shaped as map of Spain (accession, 1556) . . 25 15
3782 25p. King Felipe II drawing plans (commencement of Monastery San Lorenzo de El Escorial, 1563) . . . 25 15
3783 25p. Severed arm attacking Turk (Battle of Lepanto, 1571) 25 15
3784 25p. St John of the Cross, St. Teresa of Avila and El Greco being drawn up into spacecraft 25 15
3785 25p. Lope de Vega Carpio using his open skull as inkwell (Spanish playwright, died 1593) . . 25 15
3786 25p. King Felipe III surrounded by buckets collecting water (accession, 1598) 25 15

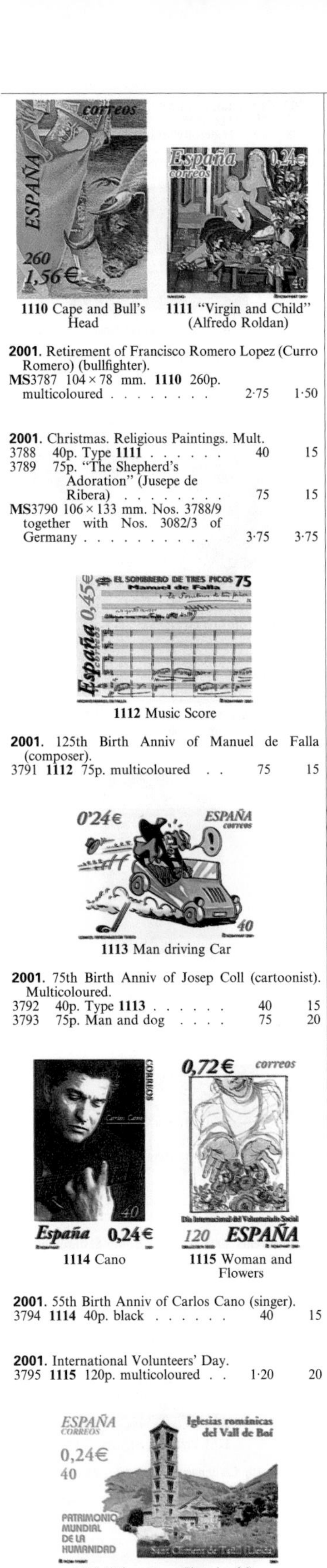

1110 Cape and Bull's Head

1111 "Virgin and Child" (Alfredo Roldan)

2001. Retirement of Francisco Romero Lopez (Curro Romero) (bullfighter).
MS3787 104 × 78 mm. **1110** 260p. multicoloured . . . . 2·75 1·50

2001. Christmas. Religious Paintings. Mult.
3788 40p. Type **1111** 40 15
3789 75p. "The Shepherd's Adoration" (Jusepe de Ribera) 75 15
MS3790 106 × 133 mm. Nos. 3788/9 together with Nos. 3082/3 of Germany . . . . 3·75 3·75

1112 Music Score

2001. 125th Birth Anniv of Manuel de Falla (composer).
3791 **1112** 75p. multicoloured . . 75 15

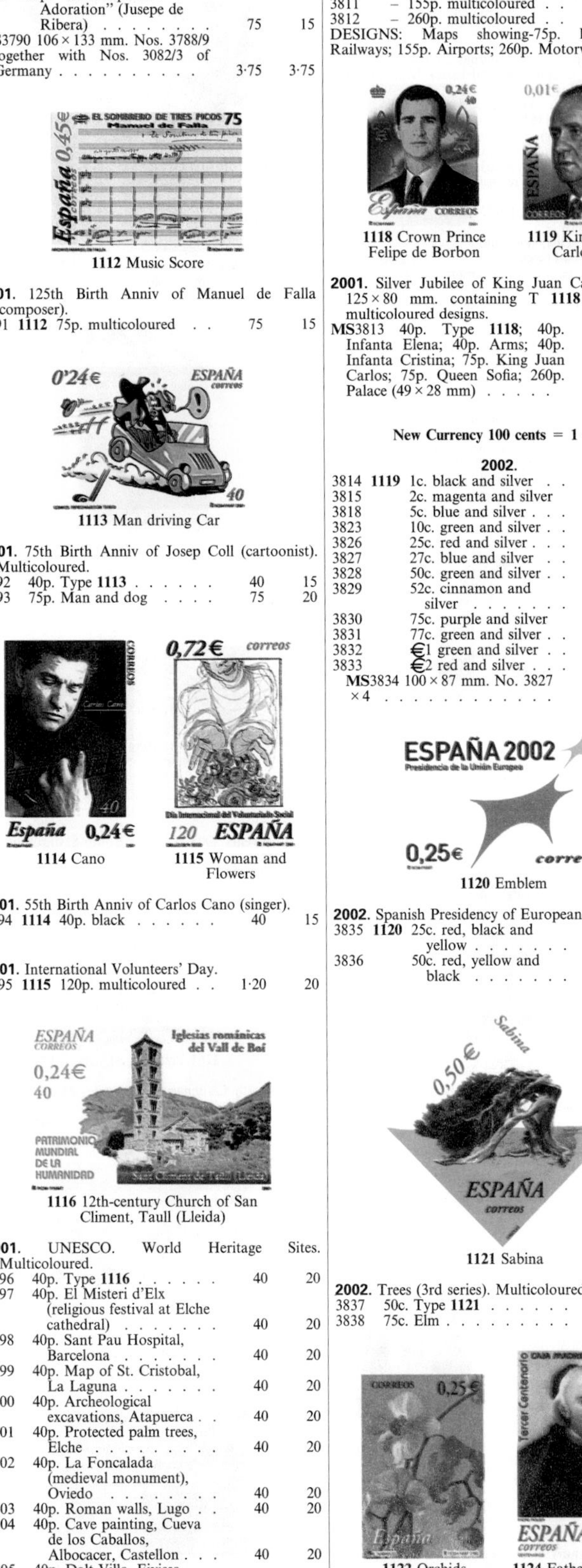

1113 Man driving Car

2001. 75th Birth Anniv of Josep Coll (cartoonist). Multicoloured.
3792 40p. Type **1113** 40 15
3793 75p. Man and dog 75 20

1114 Cano

1115 Woman and Flowers

2001. 55th Birth Anniv of Carlos Cano (singer).
3794 **1114** 40p. black 40 15

2001. International Volunteers' Day.
3795 **1115** 120p. multicoloured . . 1·20 20

1116 12th-century Church of San Climent, Taull (Lleida)

2001. UNESCO. World Heritage Sites. Multicoloured.
3796 40p. Type **1116** 40 20
3797 40p. El Misteri d'Elx (religious festival at Elche cathedral) 40 20
3798 40p. Sant Pau Hospital, Barcelona 40 20
3799 40p. Map of St. Cristobal, La Laguna 40 20
3800 40p. Archeological excavations, Atapuerca . . 40 20
3801 40p. Protected palm trees, Elche 40 20
3802 40p. La Foncalada (medieval monument), Oviedo 40 20
3803 40p. Roman walls, Lugo . . 40 20
3804 40p. Cave painting, Cueva de los Caballos, Albocacer, Castellon . . . 40 20
3805 40p. Dalt Villa, Eivissa, Ibiza 40 20
3806 40p. Roman amphitheatre, Tarraco 40 20
3807 40p. Renaissance university building, Alcala de Henares 40 20

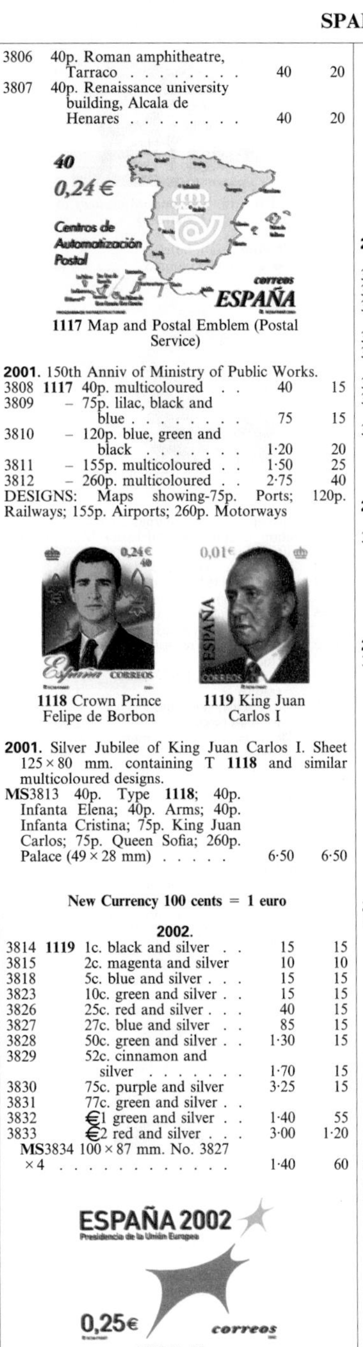

1117 Map and Postal Emblem (Postal Service)

2001. 150th Anniv of Ministry of Public Works.
3808 **1117** 40p. multicoloured . . 40 15
3809 – 75p. lilac, black and blue 75 15
3810 – 120p. blue, green and black . . . . 1·20 20
3811 – 155p. multicoloured . . 1·50 25
3812 – 260p. multicoloured . . 2·75 40
DESIGNS: Maps showing-75p. Ports; 120p. Railways; 155p. Airports; 260p. Motorways

1118 Crown Prince Felipe de Borbon

1119 King Juan Carlos I

2001. Silver Jubilee of King Juan Carlos I. Sheet 125 × 80 mm. containing T **1118** and similar multicoloured designs.
MS3813 40p. Type **1118**; 40p. Infanta Elena; 40p. Arms; 40p. Infanta Cristina; 75p. King Juan Carlos; 75p. Queen Sofia; 260p. Palace (49 × 28 mm) . . . . . 6·50 6·50

New Currency 100 cents = 1 euro

2002.
3814 **1119** 1c. black and silver . . 15 15
3815 2c. magenta and silver 10 10
3818 5c. blue and silver . . . 15 15
3823 10c. green and silver . . 15 15
3826 25c. red and silver . . . 40 15
3827 27c. blue and silver . . 85 15
3828 50c. green and silver . . 1·30 15
3829 52c. cinnamon and silver . . . . 1·70 15
3830 75c. purple and silver 3·25 15
3831 77c. green and silver . .
3832 €1 green and silver . . 1·40 55
3833 €2 red and silver . . . 3·00 1·20
MS3834 100 × 87 mm. No. 3827 × 4 . . . . 1·40 60

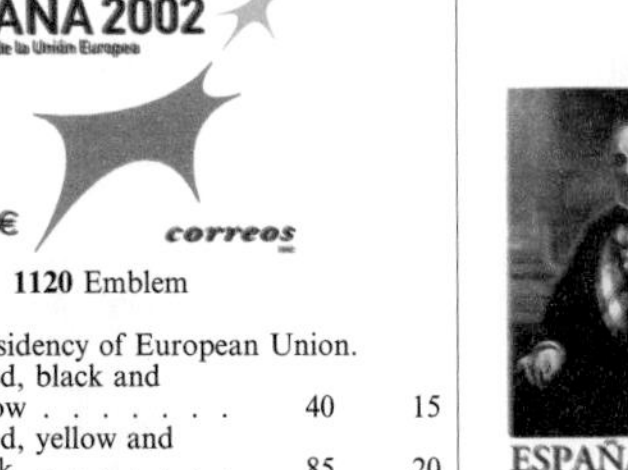

1120 Emblem

2002. Spanish Presidency of European Union.
3835 **1120** 25c. red, black and yellow 40 15
3836 50c. red, yellow and black 85 20

1121 Sabina

2002. Trees (3rd series). Multicoloured.
3837 50c. Type **1121** 85 15
3838 75c. Elm . . . . 1·30 20

1122 Orchids

1124 Father Francisco Piquer (founder)

1123 Emblem

2002. Flowers.Depicting paintings by Eduardo Naranjo. Multicoloured. Self-adhesive.
3839 25c. Type **1122** 40 20
3840 25c. Gardenia in vase . . . 40 20
3841 25c. Hands holding white rose 40 20
3842 25c. Iris 40 20
3843 25c. Two white orchid blooms 40 20
3844 25c. Pink-tinged rose in vase 40 20
3845 25c. Two pink orchid blooms 40 20
3846 25c. Three pink orchid blooms on one stem . . . 40 20

2002. "Espana 2002" International Youth Stamp Exhibition, Salamanca (1st issue). Multicoloured.
3847 50c. Type **1123** 85 20
MS3848 80 × 105 mm. £1.80 Salamanca Cathedral . . . . . 3·00 1·70
See also Nos. 2913/22.

2002. 300th Anniv of Caja Madrid Savings Bank.
3849 **1124** 25c. multicoloured . . . 40 15

1125 Anniversary Emblem

2002. Centenary of Real Madrid Football Club.
3850 **1125** 75c. yellow and grey . . 1·30 20

1126 Town Hall Portico, Tarazona

2002. "PHILAIBERIA '02" Spanish-Portuguese Stamp Exhibition, Tarazona. Sheet 106 × 80 mm.
MS3851 **1126** €2.10 multicoloured 3·50 1·80

1127 Mon

1128 Stylized Coin

2002. Birth Centenary (2001) of Alejandro Mon (politician).
3852 **1127** 25c. multicoloured . . . 40 15

2002. "Homage to the Peseta".
3853 **1128** 25c. multicoloured . . . 40 15

1129 Canon do Sil, Ribeira Sacra

1130 Cadets on Parade, 1886

2002. Nature. Multicoloured.
3854 75c. Type **1129** . . . . . . 1·30 20
3855 €2.10 Cabo de Gata, Nijer Park, Almeria (horiz) . . 3·50 85

2002. 75th Anniv of Military Academy, Zaragoza.
3856 **1130** 25c. multicoloured . . . 40 15

1131 Emblem

2002. Centenary of Real Union Irun Football Club.
3857 **1131** 50c. multicoloured . . . 85 20

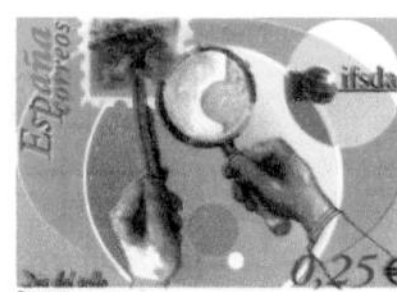

1132 Tweezers, Stamp and Magnifying Glass

2002. Stamp Day.
3858 **1132** 25c. multicoloured . . . 40 15

1133 Banyeres de Mariola Castle, Alicante

2002. Castles.
3859 **1133** 25c. brown and blue . . 40 15
3860 – 50c. black 85 20
3861 – 75c. black . . . . . . 1·30 25
DESIGNS: 50c. Soutomaior Castle, Pontevedra; 75c. Calatorao Castle, Zaragoza.

1134 View across River

2002. Anniversaries. Multicoloured.
3862 75c. Type **1134** (1200th anniv of Tuleda) . . . . 1·30 20
3863 €1.80 View through pillars (millennium of St. Cugat Monastery) . . . . 3·00 65

1135 Luis Cernuda

2002. Birth Anniversaries. Multicoloured.
3864 50c. Type **1135** (poet, centenary) 85 20
3865 50c. Dr. Federico Rubio and nurses (175th anniv) . . . 85 20

1136 Clown (Sara Blanco Quintas)

2002. Europa. The Circus.
3866 **1136** 50c. multicoloured . . . 85 20

1137 Soldiers on Horseback

2002. Bicentenary of Inclusion of Menorca under Spanish Rule.
3867 **1137** 50c. multicoloured . . . 85 20

1138 Driving

2002. World Equestrian Games, Jerez. Mult.
3868 25c. Type **1138** 40 20
3869 25c. Hunting 40 20
3870 25c. Dressage 40 20
3871 25c. Reining 40 20
3872 25c. Acrobats 40 20
3973 75c. Racing . . . . 1·30 25
3874 €1.80 Show jumping . . . 3·00 85

1139 Maria de las Dolores

2002. 108th Death Anniv of Maria "La Dolores" de las Dolores.
3875 **1139** 50c. multicoloured . . . 85 20

1140 Plaza Mayor, Salamanca

2002. "EXFILNA 2002" National Stamp Exhibition, Salamanca. European City of Culture. Sheet 155 × 94 mm, containing T **1140** and similar horiz design. Multicoloured (€1.80) or orange and blue (others).
MS3876 25c. Type **1140**; 25c. Centre view of Plaza; 25c. Right side of Plaza; €1.80 Aerial view of Plaza 4·25 4·25

1141 Rohrbach R-VIII Aircraft, 1927

2002. 75th Anniv of IBERIA Airlines. Multicoloured.
3877 25c. Type **1141** 40 15
3878 50c. Boeing 747 . . . . . . 85 20

1142 Grapes (Rias Baixas)
1143 Grapes and Glass of Red Wine (Rioja)

2002. Wine Regions (1st series).
3879 **1142** 25c. multicoloured . . . 40 15

2002. Wine Regions (2nd series). Multicoloured.
3880 50c. Type **1143** 85 20
3881 75c. Grapes, wine bottle and glass of sherry (Manzanilla) . . . . . . 1·30 25

2002. School Correspondence Programme. Spanish History (3rd series). As T **1073** but with currency inscribed in euros. Multicoloured.
3882 10c. Man being knighted with pen (*Don Quixote* by Miguel de Cervantes) . . 15 15
3883 10c. Felipe IV and the Count-Duke of Olivares (accession, 1621) 15 15
3884 10c. Quevedo and Gongora pulling on rope of words (literary rivalry) 15 15
3885 10c. Velazquez (artist) sitting at easel 15 15
3886 10c. Carlos II and witch holding apple 15 15
3887 10c. Man rolling out carpet and Felipe V (start of War of the Spanish Succession) 15 15
3888 10c. Fernando VI (accession, 1746) 15 15
3889 10c. Carlos III holding architectural drawings (accession, 1759) 15 15
3890 10c. Bull and toreador (Riot of Esquilanche) 15 15
3891 10c. Book escaping from bird cage 15 15
3892 10c. Carlos IV (accession, 1788) and Napoleon . . . 15 15
3893 10c. Manuel de Godoy (politician) and open door 15 15

1144 Temple Expiatori de la Sagrada Famíla, Barcelona

2002. 150th Birth Anniv of Antonio Gaudi (architect).
3894 **1144** 50c. blue and black . . 85 15

1145 Musicians

2002. Music. Designs depicting paintings by G. Dominguez. Multicoloured. Self-adhesive.
3895 25c. Type **1145** 40 20
3896 25c. Vase of flowers and lute 40 20
3897 25c. Woman holding lute . . 40 20
3898 25c. Flowers and open book of music 40 20
3899 25c. Vase of flowers, clock and violin 40 20
3900 25c. Man holding lute with woman 40 20
3901 25c. Flowers, violin, compass and sheet music 40 20
3902 25c. Woman wearing blue dress holding lute 40 20

1146 Alphabet Jigsaw Puzzle

2002. America. Education and Literacy Campaign.
3903 **1146** 75c. multicoloured . . . 1·30 20

1147 Cordoba Mosque and Silhouette of Almanzor

2002. Death Millenary of Abu Amir Muhammad al-Ma'afiri (Almanzor) (Arab ruler).
3904 **1147** 75c. multicoloured . . . 1·30 20

1148 Basket
1149 Cupola, Aranjuez

2002. Dijous Bo Fair, Inca, Mallorca.
3905 **1148** 75c. multicoloured . . . 1·30 20

2002. UNESCO. World Heritage Sites. Multicoloured.
3906 25c. Type **1149** 40 15
3907 25c. Santa Maria church, Calatayud, Aragon . . . 40 15
3908 50c. San Martin church, Teruel, Aragon 85 15
3909 75c. Santa Maria church, Tobed, Aragon . . . . . 1·30 20
3910 €1.80 Santa Tecla church, Cervera de la Canada, Aragon . . . . 3·00 65
3911 €2.10 San Pablo church, Zaragoza, Aragon . . . . 3·50 85

1150 Alcaniz (former Monastery of Calatrava)

2002. Paradores (state hotels).
3912 **1150** 25c. multicoloured . . . 40 15

1151 Capitan Alatriste (Arturo Perez-Reverte)

2002. "Espana 2002" International Youth Stamp Exhibition, Salamanca (2nd issue). Multicoloured. (a) Self-adhesive gum.
3913 50c. As No. 3847 . . . . . 85 40
3914 75c. Type **1151** (comic strip character) . . . . 1·30 65
3915 75c. Television screen and emblem (television) . . . 1·30 65
3916 75c. Hand and record (music) . . . . 1·30 65
3917 75c. Radio and music score (radio) . . . . 1·30 65
3918 75c. Cyclist, skier and football (sport) . . . . . 1·30 65
3919 75c. Person holding camera (the press) . . . . 1·30 65
3920 75c. Film clapper board (film) . . . . 1·30 65
3921 €1.80 Salamanca Cathedral (vert) . . . . 3·00 1·50

2002. (b) Ordinary gum.
MS3922 Six sheets 79 × 106 mm (g) or 106 × 79 mm (others) (a) 75c. As No. 3920; (b) 75c. As 3915; (c) 75c. As 3919; (d) 75c. As 3917; (e) 75c. As 3918; (f) 75c. As 3916; (g) 75c. As 3914 Set of 6 sheets . . 12·50 12·50

1152 San Jorge Church, Alicante

2002.
3923 **1152** 75c. multicoloured . . . 1·30 20

1153 Cruceiro do Hio (crucifix) (Jose Cervino) Hio, Galicia

2002. Historical Monuments. Multicoloured.
3924 50c. Type **1153** 40 15
3925 50c. Herreria de Compludo (smithy), Leon (horiz) . . 85 20

1154 Mary (detail, stained glass window)
1155 "Adoration of Kings" (Carlos Munoz de Pablos) (alterpiece, Calzadilla de Barros Church)

2002. 140th Anniv of St. Mary's Cathedral, Vitoria-Gasteiz. Sheet 106 × 79 mm.
MS3926 **1154** 50c. multicoloured 85 40

2002. Christmas. Multicoloured.
3927 25c. Type **1155** 40 15
3928 50c. "Maternity" (Goyo Dominguez) 85 15

1156 Somport Tunnel Entrance

2003. Spain–France Tunnel through Pyrenees.
3929 **1156** 51c. multicoloured . . . 90 15

1157 Costumes from Anso (Huesca)
1158 Fingerprints forming Flower

2003. Traditional Costumes.
3930 **1157** 76c. multicoloured . . . 1·30 20

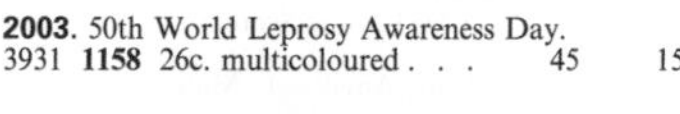

2003. 50th World Leprosy Awareness Day.
3931 **1158** 26c. multicoloured . . . 45 15

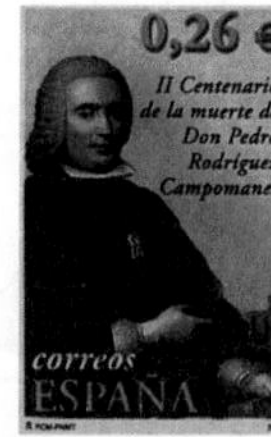

1159 Pedro Campomanes

2003. Death Bicentenary of Pedro Rodriguez Campomanes (statesman and writer).
3932 **1159** 26c. multicoloured . . . 45 15

1160 Benissa Cathedral

2003. Juvenia 2003 National Youth Stamp, Benissa, Alicante.
3933 **1160** 51c. Multicoloured . . 90 15

1161 Praxedes Sagasta

2003. Death Centenary of Praxedes Mateo Sagasta (politician).
3934 **1161** 26c. brown and blue . . 45 15

1162 "ABC"

2003. Centenary of "ABC" (newspaper).
3935 **1162** €2.15 multicoloured 3·50 65

1163 Santiago Ramon y Cajal (1906)

2003. Nobel Prize Winners for Medicine. Multicoloured.
3936 51c. Type **1163** 90 15
3937 76c. Severo Ochoa (1959) 1·30 20
Stamps of the same design were issued by Sweden.

1164 Tui Bridge to Valenca do Minho (Portugal)

2003. Bicentenary of School of Civil Engineers, Madrid. Multicoloured.
3938 26c. Type **1164** 45 15
MS3939 106 × 78 mm. 26c. Type **1164**; 51c. Murcia valley; 76c. Gigon . . . . 2·50 2·50

1165 Anniversary Emblem

2003. Centenary of "La Laverdad" (Catholic newspaper).
3940 **1165** 26c. multicoloured . . . 45 15

1166 "La Hoz de Priego"

2003. Paintings. Designs depicting paintings by Chico Montilla. Multicoloured. Self-adhesive.
3941 26c. Type **1166** 45 20
3942 26c. "Fields of Gold" . . . 45 20
3943 26c. "Los Tornos Gorge" 45 20
3944 26c. "Armilla Countryside" 45 20
3945 26c. "Nenufar" 45 20
3946 26c. "What Colour is the Wind?" 45 20
3947 51c. "Pastrana Countryside" 90 30
3948 76c. "Early Flowers" . . . 90 40

1167 Ramon Sender and Book Cover

2003. Ramon Jose Sender (writer) Commemoration.
3949 **1167** €2.15 brown, yellow and deep brown . . . 3·50 65

1168 Blackboard and Pupil

2003. Rural Schools.
3950 **1168** 26c. multicoloured . . . 3·00 50

1169 Pillar Capital, Lron Patio, Alhambra, Granada

2003. Exfilna 2003 National Stamp Exhibition, Granada. Sheet 79 × 106 mm.
MS3951 **1169** €2.15 brown and green . . . . 3·50 2·10

1170 Valdecarzana Palace, Aviles, Asturias

2003. Avilés Villa Millenary.
3952 **1170** 51c. multicoloured . . . 3·25 50

1171 Anniversary Emblem

2003. Stamp Day. 25th Anniv of Spanish Philatelic Academy.
3953 **1171** €1.85 multicoloured 90 15

1172 Toy Cars (Jimenez Carrero)

2003. Europa. Poster Art.
3954 **1172** 76c. multicoloured . . . 1·30 20

1173 Centenary Emblem

2003. Centenary of Athletic Club of Madrid.
3955 **1173** 26c. red and blue . . . 45 15

1174 Roman Amphitheatre, Zaragoza

2003.
3956 **1174** €1.85 multicoloured 3·25 50

1175 Map of Europe, Faces and Wheelchair User

2003. European Year of the Disabled.
3957 **1175** 76c. multicoloured . . . 1·30 40
No. 3957 has "correos" written in Braille across it.

1176 San Felipe Castle, Ferrol, Coruna

2003. Castles.
3958 **1176** 26c. maroon and blue 45 15
3959 – 51c. brown and green 90 15
3960 – 76c. orange and black 1·30 20
DESIGNS: 21c. Type **1176**; 51c. Cuellar Castle, Segovia; 76c. Montilla Castle, Cordoba (500th Anniv of Battles of Cerinola and Garellano).

1177 Swimmer 1178 Max Aub

2003. Barcelona '03 International Swimming Championship. Multicoloured.
3961 26c. Type **1177** 35 10
3962 51c. Diver 70 10
MS3963 115 × 106 mm. 26c. Type **1177**; 51c. No. 3962; 76c. Synchronised swimmers; €1.85 Freestyle swimmer; €2.15 Water polo . . . . 7·25 7·25

2003. Birth Centenary of Max Aub (writer).
3964 **1178** 76c. black and red . . . 1·00 40

1179 Football and Club Emblem 1180 Juan Murillo

2003. Centenary of Centre D'Esports Sabadell Football Club.
3965 **1179** 76c. multicoloured . . . 1·00 40

2003. Birth Bicentenary of Juan Bravo Murillo (politician).
3966 **1180** 51c. multicoloured . . . 70 10

1181 Newspaper Vendor

2003. 135th Anniv of "Diario de Cadiz" Newspaper.
3967 **1181** 26c. multicoloured . . . 35 10

1182 Dodge Dart Barreiros (1967)

2003. Centenary of Royal Automobile Club (RACE). Sheet 106 × 80 mm containing T **1182** and similar horiz designs. Multicoloured.
MS3968 26c. Type **1182**; 51c.Seat 600 (1967–73); 76c. Hispano Suiza 20/30 HP (1907); €1.85 Pegaso Z102 Touring Berlinetta (1953) 4·50 4·50

1183 5c. Chile Stamp of 1853 1184 "El Diario Montanes"

2003. 150th Anniv of First Chilean Stamp.
3969 **1183** 76c. brown and black 1·00 40

2003. Centenary of "El Diario Montanes" Newspaper.
3970 **1184** 26c. multicoloured . . . 35 10

1185 Santa Catalina Castle

2003. Paradores (state hotels).
3971 **1185** 25c. multicoloured . . . 35 10

1186 Front Page

2003. Centenary of "Diario de Navarra" Newspaper.
3972 **1186** 26c. multicoloured . . . 35 10

1187 Doorway

2003. 800th Anniv of Seu Vella Old Cathedral, Lleida, Segria.
3973 **1187** €1.85 sepia, violet and brown . . . . 2·50 1·00

1188 Stylized Hat and Newspaper 1189 Woman attaching Flowers to Hat

2003. 120th Anniv of "El Adelanto de Salamanca" Newspaper.
3974 **1188** 26c. multicoloured . . . 35 10

2003. Paintings. No value expressed. Designs depicting portraits of women and flowers by Alfredo Roldan. Multicoloured. Self-adhesive.
3975 A (26c.) Type **1189** 35 10
3976 A (26c.) With bouquet . . . 35 10
3977 A (26c.) Stood behind lilies 35 10
3978 A (26c.) With raised arms arranging flowers in hair 35 10
3979 A (26c.) Wearing flowers in hair 35 10
3980 A (26c.) Woman lying with fruit and flowers 35 10
3981 A (26c.) Wearing dark dress putting flowers in hair 35 10
3982 A (26c.) With vase of flowers 35 10

1190 Building Interior, Ferrol

2003. 25th Anniv of "El Correo Gallego" Newspaper.
3983 **1190** 26c. multicoloured . . . 35 10

1191 Masthead

2003. 125th Anniv of "El Comercio" Newspaper.
3984 **1191** 26c. multicoloured . . . 35 10

1192 Reliquary, Chapel of La Vera Cruz 1194 Wine Glass (Penedes)

1193 49er Dinghy, Map and Statue

2003. Granting of Perpetual Jubilee to Caravaca de la Cruz.
3985 **1192** 76c. multicoloured . . . 1·00 40

2003. ISAF World Sailing Championship, Cadiz.
3986 **1193** 76c. multicoloured . . . 1·00 40

2003. Wine. Multicoloured.
3987 26c. Type **1194** 35 10
3988 51c. Angel holding wine dipper (Montilla-Moriles) 60 10

3989 76c. Grapes and hands holding wine glass (Valdepenas) . . . . . . 1·00 40
3990 $1.85 Bottles (Bierzo) . . . 2·50 1·00

1195 College Building and Emblem

2003. Bicentenary of Military Engineering College, Madrid.
3991 **1195** 51c. multicoloured . . . 60 10

1196 Stained Glass Window (detail)

2003. 700th Anniv of Leon Cathedral. Sheet 105 × 78 mm.
MS3992 **1196** 76c. multicoloured 1·00 1·00

1197 Society Emblem and Map (detail)

2003. Centenary of Real Geographic Society. Sheet 105 × 78 mm.
MS3993 **1197** €1.85 multicoloured 2·50 2·50

1198 *Ficus Macrophylla*

2003. Trees (4th issue). Multicoloured.
3994 26c. Type **1198** 35 10
3995 51c. Pedunculate oak (*Quercus robur*) 60 10

1199 College Building

2003. 75th Anniv of Aircraft Engineering Technical College, Madrid.
3996 **1199** 51c. multicoloured . . . 60 10

1200 Type 1-2-0 Engine Madrilena (1851)

2003. America. Railways.
3997 **1200** 76c. multicoloured . . . 1·00 40

1201 "El Virjo y el Pajaro"

2003. 93rd Birth Anniv of Luis Seoane (artist).
3998 **1201** €1.85 multicoloured 2·50 1·00

1202 "La Voz de Galicia"

2003. Newspaper Anniversaries.
3999 **1202** 26c. red and black . . . 35 10
4000 – 26c. red, orange and black 35 10
4001 – 26c. multicoloured . . . 35 10
DESIGNS: Type **1202** (120th anniv (2002); "El Correo de Andalucia" (centenary (1999)); "Faro de Vigo" (150th anniv).

1203 Camilo Jose Cela

1204 Donkey and Child (Los Reyes Magos festival, Alcoy)

2003. 1st Death Anniv of Camilo Jose Cela Trulock (writer (winner of 1989 Nobel Prize for Literature)).
4002 **1203** 26c. multicoloured . . . 35 10

2003. Christmas. Multicoloured.
4003 26c. Type **1204** 35 10
4004 51c. "Christmas" (Raquel Farinas) 60 10

1205 Exhibition Emblem

2003. Espana 2004 International Stamp Exhibition, Valencia. Multicoloured.
4005 76c. Type **1205** . . . . . . 1·00 40
MS4006 78 × 106 mm. €1.85 City of Arts and Sciences Building, Valencia . . . . 2·50 2·50

1206 Organos de Montoro, Teruel Mountains

2003.
4007 **1206** 51c. multicoloured . . . 60 10

1207 Geological Map

2003. New National Geological Survey. Sheet 106 × 79 mm.
MS4008 **1207** 26c. multicoloured 35 35

1208 Blindfolded Woman

2003. 25th Anniv of Constitution. Ten sheets, each 78 × 105 mm containing T **1208** and similar multicoloured designs.
MS4009 (a) 26c. Type **1208** (Juan Bautista Nieto) (judicial power); (b) 26c. Dove and doors (J. Carrero) (general courts); (c) 26c. Ship (Araceli Alarcon) (state territorial organization) (horiz); (d) 26c. Families (R. Seco) (economy and property) (horiz); (e) 26c. King Juan Carlos (horiz); (f) 26c. Boy writing (fundamental rights and duties) (horiz); (g) 26c. Woman and bird (Goyo Domínguez) (relations between government and courts); (h) 26c. Flower and window (Galicia) (constitutional reform) (horiz); (i) 26c. Scales containing child and couple (J. Carrero) (Constitutional Court) (horiz); (j) 26c. Seated woman holding Arms (Fesanpe) (government and administration) (horiz) . . . . 3·50 3·50

1209 Control Tower, Four Winds Aerodrome, Madrid and Biplane

2003. Centenary of Powered Flight.
4010 **1209** 76c. brown and blue . . 1·00 40

1210 Ironwork, Santa Maria de Iguacel, Jaca

2004. Romanic Architecture, Aragon. No value expressed. Multicoloured. Self-adhesive.
4011 A (26c.) Type **1210** 35 10
4012 A (26c.) Bible (detail), Huesca 35 10
4013 A (26c.) Apostles (fresco) . . . 35 10
4014 A (26c.) Cloister, San Juan Bautista de Ruesta . . . 35 10
4015 A (26c.) Jacobean dinars . . 35 10
4016 A (26c.) Column capital, La Iglesia de Santiago . . . 35 10
4017 A (26c.) Sarcophagus of Dona Sancha 35 10
4018 A (26c.) Crucifix, Jaca Cathedral 35 10

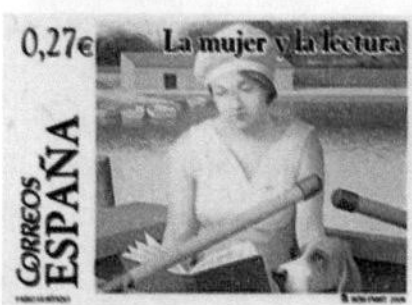

1211 Woman Reading whilst Boating

2004. Women and Reading. Two sheets, each 106 × 79 mm containing T **1211** and similar horiz designs showing women reading. Multicoloured.
MS4019 (a) 27c. Type **1211**; 52c. With head resting in hand; 77c. Reading newspaper; (b) 27c. Lying facing left; 52c. Lying facing right; 77c. Looking over top of book Set of 2 sheets . . . . 4·25 1·70

1212 Hand and Damaged Leaf

2004. 50th (2003) Anniv of Spanish Cancer Association.
4020 **1212** 27c. multicoloured . . . 35 10

1213 "La Terrona" (oak tree), Zarza de Montánchez

2004. Trees (5th series).
4021 **1213** 52c. multicoloured . . . 70 10

1214 Stylized Canoe

2004. World Rowing Championship, Banyoles.
4022 **1214** 77c. multicoloured . . . 1·00 40

1215 Woman standing on Cliff

2004. School Correspondence Programme. *Trazo y Tiza* (graphic novel by Miguelanxo Prado). Sheet 183 × 145 mm containing T **1215** and similar horiz designs. Multicoloured.
MS4023 27c. × 4, Type **1215**; Yacht and lighthouse; Seagull, yacht, lighthouse and woman; Lighthouse . . . . 1·40 60

1216 Stairs and Arches

1218 19th-century Bronze Clock (La Almudaina Palace, Palma De Mallorca)

1217 Emblem

2004. Saint Maria de Carracedo Monastery. Sheet 80 × 105 mm.
MS4024 **1216** €1.90 multicoloured 2·50 1·00

2004. 36th Chess Olympiad, Calvia, Mallorca.
4025 **1217** 77c. multicoloured . . . 1·00 40

2004. Cultural Heritage. Clocks. Sheet 106 × 151 mm containing T **1218** and similar vert designs. Each brown, blue and gold.
MS4026 27c. Type **1218**; 52c. 18th-century bronze (La Granja Palace, Segovia); 77c. 19th-century bronze clock (La Granja Palace, Segovia); €1.90 18th-century bronze clock (El Pardo Palace, Madrid) . . . . 4·50 1·80

1219 Newspaper Vendor (statue)

1220 Ribbon

2004. Centenary (2001) of "Diario de Burgos" Newspaper.
4027 **1219** 27c. multicoloured . . . 35 10

2004. European Day (11 March) for Victims of Terrorism. (a) Ordinary gum.
4028 **1220** 27c. black 35 10

(b) No value expressed. Self-adhesive gum.
4029 **1220** A (27c.) black 35 10

1221 Eggs

2004. Painted Eggs Festival.
4030 **1221** 27c. multicoloured . . . 35 10

1222 Floral Shawl and Shell

2004. Shawls. Sheet 80 × 105 mm containing T **1222** and similar vert designs showing details of paintings by Soledad Fernandez. Multicoloured.
MS4031 27c. Type **1222**; 52c. Hands across dark shawl; 77c. Gladioli and part of shawl; €1.90 Shawl draped over chair . . . . . . 4·50 1·80

1223 Saint Domingo de la Calzada

2004. 150th Anniv of Public Technical Engineering Works.
4032 **1223** 52c. multicoloured . . . 70 10

1224 Cable Ingles Bridge, Almeria

2004. Centenary of Cable Ingles Bridge, Almeria.
4033 **1224** 52c. multicoloured . . . 70 10

1225 Historical Buildings (Sagrada Familia, Barcelona, Antoni Gaudi's Church, Fuente de Cibeles, Madrid, Giralda and Torre del Oro, Seville) and Parasols on Beach

2004. Europa. Holidays.
4034 **1225** 77c. multicoloured . . . 1·00 40

1226 "e" enclosing Figures

2004. Enlargement of European Union.
4035 **1226** 52c. multicoloured . . . 70 10

1227 "Self Portrait with Neck of Raphael"

2004. Birth Centenary of Salvador Dali (artist).
4036 **1227** 77c. multicoloured . . . 1·00 40

1228 "100" containing Football and FIFA Emblem

2004. Centenary of FIFA (Federation Internationale de Football Association).
4037 **1228** 77c. multicoloured . . . 1·00 40

1229 Bourbon Royal Arms

2004. Wedding of Crown Prince Felipe de Bourbon and Letizia Ortiz.
4038 **1229** 27c. multicoloured . . . 35 10

1230 Vincente Martin y Soler

2004. Espana 2004 International Stamp Exhibition, Madrid (1st issue). 350th Birth Anniv of Vincente Martin y Soler (musician).
4039 27c. Type **1230** 35 10
4040 52c. Saxophone and drum 70 10
See also Nos. **MS**4041, 4042/3, **MS**4044 and 4045/6.

1231 Crown Prince Felipe and Princess Letizia

2004. Espana 2004 International Stamp Exhibition, Madrid (2nd issue). The Royal Family. Sheet 151 × 86 mm containing T **1231** and similar horiz designs.
MS4041 27c. multicoloured; 77c. multicoloured; €6 blue and deep blue . . . . 9·25 3·75
DESIGNS: 27c. Type **1231**; 77c. Prince Felipe; €6 King Juan Carlos and Queen Sophia.

1232 Entry of the Bulls

2004. Espana 2004 International Stamp Exhibition, Madrid (3rd issue). Festivals.
4042 27c. Type **1232** 35 10
4043 52c. Lance taurino (bullfighter's cape pass) 70 10

1233 Tennis Player (¾-size illustration)

2004. Espana 2004 International Stamp Exhibition, Madrid (4th issue). Sport. Sheet 232 × 86 mm containing T **1233** and similar horiz designs.
MS4044 35c. Type **1233**; 52c. Ricardo Tormo (motorcyclist) and Valencia circuit; €1.90 Golf course . . . . 3·75 1·50

1234 *Bravo Espana* (yacht)

2004. Espana 2004 International Stamp Exhibition, Madrid (5th issue). Valencia.
4045 27c. Type **1234** 35 10
4046 52c. Architectural heritage 70 10

1235 Newsboy and Masthead

2004. 214th Anniv of "Diario de Valencia" Newspaper.
4047 **1235** 27c. multicoloured . . . 35 10

1236 Portico de la Gloria and Nave, Santiago Cathedral

2004. Xacobeo 2004 Holy Year (St. James jubilee year).
4048 **1236** 52c. multicoloured . . . 70 10

1237 Lerma (former Ducal palace)

2004. Paradores (state hotels).
4049 **1237** 52c. multicoloured . . . 70 10

1238 Granadilla Castle, Caceres

2004. Castles.
4050 27c. orange and red 35 10
4051 52c. brown 70 10
4052 77c. green . . . . 1·00 40
4053 €1.90 black (vert) . . . . 2·50 1·00
DESIGNS: 27c. Type **1238**; 52c. Aguas Mansas, Agoncillo; 77c. Mota, Alcala la Real, Jaen; €1.90 Villafuerte de Esgueva, Valladolid.

1239 Danforth Anchor

1240 Pot with Handles and Lid

2004. Salinas Anchor Museum, Castrillon, Asturias.
4054 **1239** €1.90 multicoloured 2·50 1·00

2004. Paintings. Designs depicting paintings of ceramics by Antonio Miguel Gonzalez. Multicoloured. Self-adhesive.
4055 A (27c.) Type **1240** 35 10
4056 A (27c.) Tall pot with handles, wide-necked pot and pot containing brushes 35 10
4057 A (27c.) Pot with central handle, bread and figs 35 10
4058 A (27c.) Pot with long neck and decorated body . . 35 10
4059 A (27c.) Broken bread, onions, tall pot and pentagon 35 10
4060 A (27c.) Decorated vase . . 35 10
4061 A (27c.) Fruit and jug . . . 35 10
4062 A (27c.) Decorated storage jar 35 10

1241 Building Facade

2004. Centenary of the Circulo Oscense Building, Huesca.
4063 **1241** 52c. multicoloured . . . 70 10

1242 Virgin and Celebrating Crowds

1243 Grapes and Bottle (Ribeiro)

2004. White Virgin Festival, Vitoria-Gasteiz.
4064 **1242** 27c. multicoloured . . . 35 10

2004. Wine. Multicoloured.
4065 27c. Type **1243** 35 10
4066 52c. Glass and bottle (Malaga) 70 10

1244 1854 Philippine Stamp and Postmark

2004. 150th Anniv of First Philippine Stamp.
4067 **1244** 77c. multicoloured . . . 1·00 40

1245 Mural (detail)

2004. 109th Anniv of "Heraldo de Aragon" Newspaper.
4068 **1245** 27c. multicoloured . . . 35 10

1246 Jorge Juan (sailor and scientist)

2004. 250th Anniv of Nautical Astronomy.
4069 **1246** €1.90 multicoloured 2·50 1·00

EXPRESS LETTER STAMPS

E **53** Pegasus and Arms

1905.
E308 E **53** 20c. red . . . . 36·00 85

E **77** Spanish Royal Family

1926. Red Cross.
E417 E **77** 20c. purple and deep purple . . . . 7·50 7·50

1927. 25th Anniv of Coronation. No. E417 optd **17-V-1902 17-V-1927 ALFONSO XIII.**
E459 E **77** 20c. purple and deep purple . . . . 6·50 6·50

E **88** Gazelle

E **89**

1929. Seville and Barcelona Exhibitions.
E521 E **88** 20c. brown . . . . . . 16·00 16·00

1929.
E522 E **89** 20c. red . . . . 16·00 3·25

1929. Optd **Sociedad de las Naciones LV reunion del Consejo Madrid.**
E534 E **89** 20c. red . . . . 15·00 15·00

1930. Optd **URGENCIA**.
E535 E **89** 20c. red . . . . 14·00 3·25

E **91** Class 7201 Electric Locomotive

1930. 11th Int Railway Congress, Madrid.
E553 E **91** 20c. red . . . . 50·00 50·00

1930. "Goya" types optd **URGENTE**.
E570 **91** 20c. mauve (postage) . . 25 25
E583 – 20c. brown and blue (as No. 574) (air) 25 25

1930. "Columbus" type optd **URGENTE**.
E608 **99** 20c. purple . . . . 1·80 1·80

E **113** Seville Exhibition

1930. Spanish–American Exhibition.
E643 E **113** 20c. orange 50 50

1931. Optd **REPUBLICA**.
E660 E **89** 20c. red (No. E535) . . 14·00 3·25
E672 20c. red (No. E522) . . 4·00 4·00

1931. Optd **Republica Espanola** in two lines continuously.
E697 E **89** 29c. red (No. E522) . . 7·00 2·40

E **126** E **152** Newspaper Boy

E **145**

1931. 900th Anniv of Montserrat Monastery.
E731 E **126** 20c. red . . . . . . 23·00 24·00

1934.
E779 E **145** 20c. red 15 15

1936. 40th Anniv of Madrid Press Association.
E801 E **152** 20c. red 30 30

E **185** Pegasus

1937.
E906 E **185** 20c. brown . . . . . 5·50 85

E **198** Pegasus

1939.
E1022 E **198** 25c. red 15 15

E **199**

1940. 19th Centenary of Apparition of Virgin of El Pilar at Zaragoza.
E1006 E **199** 25c.+5c. red & buff 30 30

E **270** "Speed" E **271** Centaur

1956.
E1250 E **270** 2p. red 20 10
E1251 3p. red 15 10
E1252 E **271** 4p. mauve and black 20 10
E1253 E **270** 5p. red 15 10
E1254 E **271** 6p.50 red and violet 15 10

E **425** Roman Chariot

1971.
E2099 E **425** 10p. green, blk & red 15 10
E2100 – 15p. blue, black & red 15 10
DESIGN—VERT: 15p. Letter encircling globe.

E **862** Communications

1993. Public Services.
E3211 E **862** 180p. red and yellow 2·50 30

FRANK STAMPS

F **36** F **50**

1869. For use on "Cartilla Postal de Espana" (book) by Senor Castell.
F172 F **36** (–) blue . . . . 55·00 50·00

1881. For use on book by A. F. Duro.
F273 F **50** (–) black on buff . . . 40·00 18·00

F **163**

1938. For use by Agencia Filatelica Oficial, Barcelona.
F839 F **163** (–) blue . . . . 4·00
F840 (–) lilac . . . . 4·00
F841 (–) green . . . . . . 4·00
F842 (–) brown . . . . . . 4·00
F843 (–) black . . . . . . 4·00

OFFICIAL STAMPS

O **9** O **10**

1854. Imperf.
O46 O **9** ½ onza black on orange 2·40 2·50
O47 1 onza black on pink . . 3·00 3·50
O48 4 onza black on green 8·50 10·50
O49 1 libra black on blue . . 60·00 65·00

The face values of Nos. O46/53 are expressed in onzas (ounces) and libra (pound) which refer to the maximum weight for which each value could prepay postage.

1855. Imperf.
O50 O **10** ½ onza black on yellow 1·80 2·20
O55 1 onza black on pink 1·80 2·20
O52 4 onza black on green 3·50 4·25
O53 1 libra black on blue . . 17·00 20·00

O **52**

1895. For use by Members of Chamber of Deputies.
O289 **51** 15c. yellow . . . . . 8·50 3·50
O290 O **52** (–) pink . . . . 2·00 22·00
O291 (–) blue . . . . 7·25 36·00

O **66** National Library

O **67** Cervantes (from painting by J. de Jauregui) O **68** Statue of Cervantes by A. Sola

1916. Death Tercentenary of Cervantes. (a) For use by Members of the Chamber of Deputies.
O353 – (–) black and violet . . 1·00 1·00
O354 O **66** (–) black and green . . 1·00 1·00
O355 O **67** (–) black and violet . . 1·00 1·00
O356 O **68** (–) black and red . . . 1·00 1·00

(b) For use by Members of the Senate.
O357 – (–) black and green . . 1·00 1·00
O358 O **66** (–) black and red . . . 1·00 1·00
O359 O **67** (–) black and brown 1·00 1·00
O360 O **68** (–) black and brown 1·00 1·00
DESIGN—As Type O **66**: Chamber of Deputies.

1931. 3rd Pan-American Postal Union Congress. T **121** etc optd **Oficial**.
O707 5c. purple 25 25
O708 10c. green 25 25
O709 15c. violet 25 25
O710 25c. red 25 25
O711 30c. green 25 25
O712 40c. blue 50 50
O713 50c. orange 50 50
O714 1p. grey 50 50
O715 4p. mauve . . . . 11·00 11·00
O716 10p. brown . . . . . . 26·00 26·00

Air. T **123** etc optd **OFICIAL**.
O717 5c. brown 15 15
O718 10c. green 15 15
O719 25c. red 15 15
O720 50c. blue 15 15
O721 1p. lilac 15 15
O722 4p. grey . . . . 4·25 4·25

WAR TAX STAMPS

W **42** W **48** W **49**

1874. The 5c. perf or imperf.
W217 W **42** 5c. de p. black . . . 9·50 1·10
W218 10c. de p. blue . . . 11·50 1·90

1875. As Type W **42**, but large figures in bottom corners.
W228a 5c. de p. green . . . . 5·75 65
W229 10c. de p. mauve . . . . 12·00 3·25

1876. 2nd Carlist War (1873–76) and Cuban War (1868–78).
W253 W **48** 5c. de p. green . . . 4·25 65
W254 10c. de p. blue . . . 4·25 65
W255 25c. de p. black . . . 32·00 12·00
W256 1p. lilac . . . . . . £375 85·00
W257 5p. pink £600 £250

1877. Cuban War (1868–78).
W258 W **49** 15c. de p. purple . . 20·00 65
W259 50c. de p. yellow . . £600 80·00

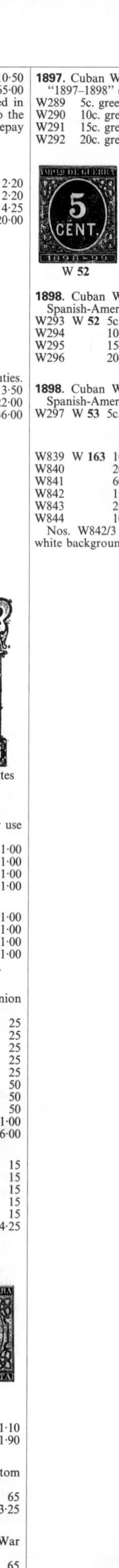

1897. Cuban War of Independence (1895–98). Inscr "1897–1898" (15c.) or "1897 A 1898" (others).
W289 5c. green . . . . 3·25 2·00
W290 10c. green . . . . 3·25 2·00
W291 15c. green £400 £200
W292 20c. green . . . . 7·50 3·50

W **52** W **53** W **163**

1898. Cuban War of Independence (1895–98) and Spanish-American War (1898). Inscr "1898–99".
W293 W **52** 5c. black . . . . . . 2·50 2·00
W294 10c. black . . . . . 2·50 2·00
W295 15c. black . . . . . 50·00 10·50
W296 20c. black . . . . . 4·00 3·50

1898. Cuban War of Independence (1895–98) and Spanish-American War (1898).
W297 W **53** 5c. black . . . . . . 8·50 65

1938.
W839 W **163** 10c. red . . . . . . 40 1·20
W840 20c. blue 40 80
W841 60c. pink . . . . . 1·40 3·25
W842 1p. blue 40 95
W843 2p. green 40 95
W844 10p. blue . . . . . 2·00 4·75

Nos. W842/3 have coloured figures of value on white backgrounds.

SPANISH GUINEA Pt. 9

A Spanish colony consisting of the islands of Fernando Poo, Annobon and the Corisco Islands off the west coast of Africa and Rio Muni on the mainland. In 1959 it was divided into the two Spanish Overseas Provinces of Fernando Poo and Rio Muni.

100 centimos = 1 peseta.

1902. "Curly Head" key-type inscr "GUINEA ESPANOLA 1902".
1 Z 5c. green 11·00 7·25
2 10c. grey 11·00 7·25
3 25c. red 80·00 55·00
4 50c. brown 80·00 55·00
5 75c. lilac 80·00 55·00
6 1p. red £130 55·00
7 2p. green £140 £120
8 5p. red £250 £225

1903. Fiscal stamps inscr "POSESIONES ESPANOLAS DE AFRICA OCCIDENTAL", surch **HABILITADO PARA CORREOS 10 cen de peseta**.
9 10c. on 25c. black £475 £180
10 10c. on 50c. orange £100 30·00
11 10c. on 1p.25 pink £650 £300
12 10c. on 2p. red £700 £450
13a 10c. on 2p.50 brown £1100 £600
14a 10c. on 5p. black £1300 £400
15 10c. on 10p. brown £950 £400
16 10c. on 5p. lilac £750 £400
17 10c. on 25p. blue £750 £600
18 10c. on 50p. brown £950 £650
19 10c. on 70p. violet £1100 £600
20 10c. on 100p. green £1500 £650

1903. "Curly Head" key-type inscr "GUINEA CONTIAL-ESPANOLA PARA 1903".
21 Z ¼c. black 1·20 85
22 ½c. green 1·20 85
23 1c. purple 1·20 70
24 2c. green 1·20 70
25 3c. brown 1·20 70
26 4c. red 1·20 70
27 5c. black 1·20 70
28 10c. brown 1·90 85
29 15c. blue 7·00 6·75
30 25c. orange 7·00 6·75
31 50c. red 12·50 14·50
32 75c. lilac 17·00 14·50
33 1p. green 27·00 22·00
34 2p. green 27·00 22·00
35 3p. red 75·00 30·00
36 4p. blue 90·00 50·00
37 5p. purple £170 75·00
38 10p. red £275 £100

1905. "Curly Head" key-type inscr as above but dated "1905".
39 Z 1c. black 20 15
40 2c. green 20 15
41 3c. red 20 15
42 4c. green 20 15
43 5c. brown 20 15
44 10c. red 1·20 70
45 15c. brown 3·75 2·20
46 25c. brown 3·75 2·20
47 50c. blue 8·25 5·25
48 75c. orange 9·25 5·25
49 1p. red 9·25 5·25
50 2p. lilac 20·00 11·00
51 3p. green 50·00 23·00
52 4p. green 50·00 33·00
53 5p. red 85·00 36·00
54 10p. blue £140 £110

1905. No. 19/34 of Elobey optd **CONTINENTAL GUINEA CORREOS ASSOBLA**.
55 Z 1c. pink 5·75 4·00
56 2c. purple 5·75 4·00
57 3c. black 5·75 4·00
58 4c. red 5·75 4·00
59 5c. green 5·75 4·00
60 10c. green 11·50 8·25
61 15c. lilac 21·00 12·00
62 25c. red 21·00 12·00
63 50c. orange 28·00 14·50
64 75c. blue 33·00 17·00
65 1p. brown 65·00 30·00
66 2p. brown 90·00 36·00
67 3p. red £130 60·00
68 4p. brown £475 £170
69 5p. green £475 £170
70 10p. red £2000 £850

1907. As Nos. 18/33 of Rio de Oro, but inscr "GUINEA CONTIAL ESPANOLA".
71 1c. green 60 15
72 2c. blue 60 15
73 3c. lilac 60 15
74 4c. green 60 15
75 5c. red 60 15
76 10c. bistre 3·25 1·30
77 15c. brown 2·40 80
78 25c. blue 2·40 80
79 50c. brown 2·40 80
80 75c. green 2·40 80
81 1p. orange 4·25 1·50
82 2p. brown 7·25 6·50
83 3p. black 7·25 6·50
84 4p. red 10·00 6·50
85 5p. green 10·00 9·50
86 10p. purple 16·00 12·00

1908. Surch **HABILITADO PARA** and value in figures and **CTMS**.
87 3 05c. on 1c. green 4·50 2·50
88 05c. on 2c. blue 4·50 2·50
89 05c. on 3c. lilac 4·50 2·50
90 05c. on 4c. green 4·50 2·50
91 05c. on 10c. bistre 4·50 2·50
92 15c. on 10c. bistre 16·00 10·50

1909. Fiscal stamps inscr "TERRITORIOS ESPANOLES DEL AFRICA OCCIDENTAL", surch **HABILITADO PARA CORREOS 10 cen de peseta**.
93 10c. on 50c. green 85·00 60·00
94 10c. on 1p.25 violet £250 £150
95 10c. on 2p. brown £600 £425
96 10c. on 5p. mauve £600 £425
97 10c. on 25p. brown £900 £600
98 10c. on 50p. red £3000 £1500
99 10c. on 75p. pink £3000 £1500
100 10c. on 100p. orange £3000 £1500

1909. As Nos. 47/59 of Rio de Oro, but inscr "TERRITORIOS ESPANOLES DEL GOLFO DE GUINEA".
101 1c. brown 15 15
102 2c. red 15 15
103 5c. green 1·00 15
104 10c. red 30 15
105 15c. brown 30 15
106 20c. mauve 50 30
107 25c. blue 50 30
108 30c. brown 70 15
109 40c. red 40 15
110 50c. lilac 40 15
111 1p. green 11·00 5·75
112 4p. orange 2·50 3·50
113 10p. orange 2·50 3·50

1911. Nos. 101/13 optd **GUINEA 1911** in oval.
114 1c. brown 30 30
115 2c. red 30 30
116 5c. green 1·20 40
117 10c. red 80 45
118 15c. brown 1·20 85
119 20c. mauve 1·60 1·30
120 25c. blue 1·90 2·50
121 30c. brown 2·50 3·25
122 40c. red 2·75 3·50
123 50c. lilac 4·75 5·25
124 1p. green 43·00 14·00
125 4p. orange 20·00 13·50
126 10p. orange 27·00 27·00

1912. As Nos. 73/85 of Rio de Oro, but inscr "TERRS. ESPANOLES DEL GOLFO DE GUINEA".
127 1c. black 15 15
128 2c. brown 15 15
129 5c. green 15 15
130 10c. red 25 15
131 15c. red 25 15
132 20c. red 45 15
133 25c. blue 25 15
134 30c. red 2·50 1·70
135 40c. red 1·70 85
136 50c. orange 1·30 35
137 1p. lilac 1·70 1·10
138 4p. mauve 4·00 2·20
139 10p. green 8·00 8·25

1914. As Nos. 86/98 of Rio de Oro, but inscr as 1912 issue.
140 1c. violet 15 15
141 2c. red 15 15
142 5c. green 15 15
143 10c. red 15 15
144 15c. purple 15 15
145 20c. brown 65 40
146 25c. blue 25 25
147 30c. brown 1·10 45
148 40c. green 1·10 45
149 50c. red 50 30
150 1p. orange 1·20 1·60
151 4p. red 4·25 3·50
152 10p. brown 5·75 6·50

1917. Nos. 127/39 optd **1917**.
153 1c. black 85·00 55·00
154 2c. brown 85·00 55·00
155 5c. green 30 15
156 10c. orange 30 15
157 15c. purple 30 15
158 20c. red 30 15
159 25c. blue 15 15
160 30c. red 30 15
161 40c. pink 50 30
162 50c. orange 25 15
163 1p. brown 50 30
164 4p. violet 6·50 3·50
165 10p. green 6·50 3·50

1918. Stamps of 1912 surch **HTADO 1917** and value in figures and words.
166 11 5c. on 40c. pink 29·00 10·50
167 10c. on 4p. violet 29·00 10·50
168 15c. on 20c. red 55·00 18·00
169 25c. on 10p. green 55·00 18·00

12 13 14 Nipa House

1919.
170 12 1c. violet 80 40
171 2c. red 80 40
172 5c. red 80 40
173 10c. purple 1·20 40
174 15c. brown 1·20 45
175 20c. blue 2·50 80
176 25c. green 1·20 80
177 30c. orange 1·20 80
178 40c. orange 3·50 80
179 50c. red 3·50 80
180 1p. green 3·50 2·40
181 4p. red 7·25 9·00
182 10p. brown 13·00 16·00

1920. As Nos. 125/37 of Rio de Oro, but inscr as T **12**.
183 1c. brown 15 15
184 2c. red 15 15
185 5c. green 15 15
186 10c. red 15 15
187 15c. orange 15 15
188 20c. yellow 15 15
189 25c. blue 50 30
190 30c. green 27·00 18·00
191 40c. brown 45 25
192 50c. purple 1·20 30
193 1p. brown 1·20 30
194 4p. red 4·00 4·25
195 10p. violet 6·00 9·00

1922.
196 13 1c. brown 50 25
197 2c. red 50 25
198 5c. green 50 25
199 10c. red 3·50 30
200 15c. orange 50 25
201 20c. mauve 2·30 95
202 25c. blue 3·50 1·20
203 30c. violet 3·50 1·30
204 40c. blue 2·50 60
205 50c. red 2·50 60
206 1p. green 2·50 60
207 4p. brown 10·00 11·50
208 10p. yellow 20·00 23·00

1925.
209 14 5c. blue and brown 15 15
210 10c. blue and green 15 15
211 15c. black and red 15 15
212 20c. black and violet 15 15
213 25c. black and red 35 15
214 30c. black and orange 35 15
215 40c. black and blue 35 15
216 50c. black and red 35 15
217 60c. black and brown 35 15
218 1p. black and violet 1·40 15
219 4p. black and blue 3·50 1·60
220 10p. black and green 7·25 3·50

1926. Red Cross stamps of Spain optd **GUINEA ESPANOLA**.
221 – 5c. brown 9·50 9·50
222 – 10c. green 9·50 9·50
223 70 15c. violet 2·20 2·20
224 – 20c. purple 2·20 2·20
225 71 25c. red 2·20 2·20
226 70 30c. green 2·20 2·20
227 – 40c. blue 45 45
228 – 50c. red 45 45
229 71 60c. green 45 45
230 – 1p. red 45 45
231 – 4p. bistre 1·80 1·80
232 71 10p. violet 6·25 6·25

1929. Seville and Barcelona Exhibition stamps of Spain (1929) optd **GUINEA**.
233 5c. red 30 30
234 10c. green 30 30
235 15c. blue 30 30
236 20c. violet 30 30
237 25c. red 30 30
238 30c. brown 30 30
239 40c. blue 50 50
240 50c. orange 50 50
241 1p. grey 9·00 9·00
242 4p. red 19·00 19·00
243 10p. brown 36·00 36·00

17 Porter 24 26 Gen. Franco

1931.
244 17 1c. green 15 15
245 2c. brown 15 15
246 5c. black 15 15
318 5c. grey 2·20 15
247 10c. green 15 15
248 15c. black 15 15
290 15c. green 3·25 15
249 20c. lilac 15 15
250 – 25c. red 15 15
251 – 30c. red 25 15
252 – 40c. blue 70 50
320 – 40c. green 85 15
253 – 50c. orange 1·20 80
292 – 50c. blue 8·75 70
254 – 80c. blue 3·25 1·90
255 – 1p. black 5·25 4·25
256 – 4p. mauve 36·00 20·00
257 – 5p. brown 14·50 14·50
DESIGNS: 25c. to 50c. Native drummers; 80c. to 5p. King Alfonso XIII and Queen Victoria.

1931. Optd **REPUBLICA ESPANOLA** horiz.
258 17 1c. green 15 15
259 2c. brown 15 15
260 5c. grey 15 15
261 10c. green 15 15
262 15c. blue 15 15
263 20c. violet 15 15
264 – 25c. red 15 15
265 – 30c. red 50 20
266 – 40c. blue 1·60 50
267 – 50c. orange 11·00 6·00
268 – 80c. blue 3·50 1·80
269 – 1p. black 11·00 4·00
270 – 4p. red 19·00 11·50
271 – 5p. brown 19·00 11·50

1933. Optd **Republica Espanola**.
272 17 1c. green 15 15
273 2c. brown 15 15
274 5c. grey 15 15
275 10c. green 15 15
276 15c. blue 15 15
277 20c. violet 50 15
278 – 25c. red 45 25
279 – 30c. red 40 25
280 – 40c. blue 3·25 70
281 – 50c. orange 11·50 3·50
282 – 80c. blue 5·75 3·25
283 – 1p. black 12·00 3·25
284 – 4p. red 40·00 16·00
285 – 5p. brown 46·00 16·00

1937. Surch **HABILITADO 30 Cts**.
293 30c. on 40c. (No. 252) 4·00 2·40
294 30c. on 40c. (No. 266) 16·00 3·50
295 30c. on 40c. (No. 280) 60·00 18·00

1939. Stamps of Spain, 1937, optd **Territorios Espanoles del Golfo de Guinea** in script type.
296 183 10c. green 1·60 50
297 184 15c. black 1·60 50
298 20c. violet 3·50 1·70
299 25c. red 3·50 1·70

1939. Surch **Habilitado 40 cts**.
300 40c. on 80c. (No. 268) 12·00 8·00
301 40c. on 80c. (No. 282) 12·00 4·25

1940. Fiscal stamps as T **24** inscr "ESPECIAL MOVIL", "TIMBRE MOVIL" or "IMPUESTO SOBRE CONTRATOS" and surch or optd **Habilitado Correos**.
302 5c. red 4·25 1·60
304 5c. on 35c. green 5·25 1·70
307 10c. on 75c. brown 6·25 2·50
308 15c. on 1p.50 violet 5·25 2·40
305 25c. on 60c. brown 5·25 2·40
306 50c. on 75c. brown 6·25 2·50
310 1p. bistre 80·00 33·00
303 1p. on 15c. green 21·00 6·75
316 1p. on 17p. red 37·00 12·50
315 1p. on 40p. green 12·50 4·00

1940.
311 26 5c. brown 3·25 85
312 40c. blue 4·25 85
314 50c. green 5·50 85

1941. Air. Fiscal stamp as T **24** inscr "IMPUESTO SOBRE CONTRATOS" surch **Habilitado para Correo Aereo Intercolonial Una Peseta** and bar.
317a 1p. on 17p. red 30·00 7·50

1942. No. 249 surch **Habilitado 3 Pesetas**.
321 17 3p. on 20c. violet 10·00 1·60
1939,

1942. Stamps of Spain, 1939, optd **Golfo de Guinea**.
322 196 1PTA. black 45 15
323 4PTAS. pink 9·00 70

1942. Air. Air stamp of Spain optd **Golfo de Guinea**.
324 195 1p. blue 1·60 15

1943. Stamp of Spain, 1939, optd **Territorios espanoles del Golfo de Guinea.**
325 196 2PTAS. brown 85 15

1948. Air. Ministerial Visit. No. 323 optd **CORREO AEREO Viaje Ministerial 10-19 Enero 1948**.
326 196 4PTAS. pink 9·00 3·00

1949. Nos. 322 and 325 surch **Habilitado para** and value in words.
327 196 5c. on 1PTA. black 25 15
328 15c. on 2PTAS. brown 25 15

33 Natives in Pirogue

1949. 75th Anniv of U.P.U.
329 33 4p. violet 1·30 65

34 Count Argalejo and San Carlos Bay

1949. Air. Colonial Stamp Day.
330 34 5p. green 1·30 65

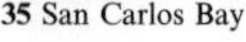

35 San Carlos Bay **36** Manuel Iradier y Bulfy

1949.

331 **35** 2c. brown 15 15
332 – 5c. violet 15 15
333 – 10c. blue 15 15
334 – 15c. green 15 15
335 **35** 25c. brown 15 15
336 – 30c. yellow 15 15
337 – 40c. green 15 15
338 – 45c. purple 15 15
339 **35** 50c. orange 15 15
340 – 75c. blue 15 15
341 – 90c. green 25 15
342 – 1p. black . . . . 1·60 15
343 **35** 1p.35 violet . . . . . . 6·00 1·20
344 – 2p. brown . . . . 16·00 2·75
345 – 5p. mauve . . . . 22·00 9·00
346 **35** 10p. brown . . . . 90·00 34·00
DESIGNS: 5, 30, 75c., 2p. Benito River rapids; 10, 40, 90c., 5p. Coast scene and Clarence Peak, Fernando Poo; 15, 45, 1p. Niepan, Benito River.

1950. Air. Colonial Stamp Day.
347 **36** 5p. brown . . . . 3·00 1·60

37 Hands and Natives **38** Mt. Mioco

1951. Native Welfare.
348 **37** 50c.+10c. blue 40 15
349 1p.+25c. green . . . . . . 12·50 4·25
350 6p.50+1p.65 orange . . . 3·25 2·50

1951. Air.
351 – 25c. yellow 15 15
352 **38** 50c. mauve 15 15
353 – 1p. green 15 15
354 – 2p. blue 25 15
355 **38** 3p.25 violet 75 15
356 – 5p. sepia . . . . 6·25 2·40
357 – 10p. red . . . . 24·00 8·25
DESIGNS: 25c., 2, 10p. Benito Rapids; 1, 5p. Santa Isabel Bay.

1951. Air. 500th Birth Anniv of Isabella the Catholic. As T **9a** of Spanish Sahara.
358 5p. blue . . . . 19·00 8·00

39 Leopard **40** Native and Map

1951. Colonial Stamp Day.
359 **39** 5c.+5c. brown 20 20
360 10c.+5c. orange 20 20
361 60c.+15c. olive 40 40

1951. International West African Conference.
362 **40** 50c. orange 25 20
363 5p. blue . . . . 7·00 1·40

41 Native Man **42** "Crinum giganteum"

1952.
364 **41** 5c. brown 15 15
365 50c. olive 20 20
366 5p. violet . . . . 2·00 50

1952. Native Welfare Fund.
367 **42** 5c.+5c. brown 20 20
368 50c.+10c. black 20 20
369 2p.+30c. blue . . . . . . 1·20 1·20

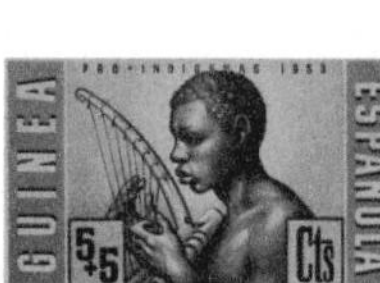

43 Ferdinand the Catholic **44** Brown-cheeked Hornbills

1952. Air. 500th Birth Anniv of Ferdinand the Catholic.
370 **43** 5p. brown . . . . 25·00 8·00

1952. Colonial Stamp Day.
371 **44** 5c.+5c. brown 20 20
372 10c.+5c. purple 20 20
373 60c.+15c. green 40 40

45 Native Musician **46** Native Woman and Dove

1953. Native Welfare Fund. Inscr "PRO INDIGENAS 1953".
374 **45** 5c.+5c. lake 20 20
375 – 10c.+5c. purple 20 20
376 **45** 15c. olive 20 20
377 – 60c. brown 20 20
DESIGN: 10, 60c. Musician facing right.

1953.
378 **46** 5c. orange 15 15
379 10c. purple 15 15
380 60c. brown 20 20
381 – 1p. lilac 80 20
382 – 1p.90 green . . . . 2·10 50
DESIGN: 1, 1p.90, Native drummer.

47 "Tragocephala nobilis" (longhorn beetle) **48** Hunting with Bow and Arrow

1953. Colonial Stamp Day. Inscr "DIA DEL SELLO COLONIAL 1953".
383 **47** 5c.+5c. blue 20 20
384 – 10c.+5c. purple 20 20
385 **47** 15c. green 25 25
386 – 60c. brown 35 35
DESIGN: 10, 60c. African giant swallowtail (butterfly).

1954. Native Welfare Fund. Inscr "PRO-INDIGENAS 1954".
387 **48** 5c.+5c. lake 20 20
388 – 10c.+5c. lilac 20 20
389 **48** 15c. green 25 25
390 – 60c. brown 35 35
DESIGN: 10, 60c. Native hunting elephant with spear.

49 Turtle

1954. Colonial Stamp Day. Inscr "DIA DEL SELLO COLONIAL 1954".
391 **49** 5c.+5c. red 20 20
392 – 10c.+5c. purple 20 20
393 **49** 15c. green 25 25
394 – 60c. brown 35 35
DESIGN: 10, 60c. Barbelled houndshark (fish).

50 M. Iradier y Bulfy **51** Native Priest

1955. Birth Centenary of Iradier (explorer).
395 **50** 60c. brown 20 20
396 1p. violet . . . . 2·50 80

1955. Centenary of Apostolic Prefecture in Fernando Poo.
397 **51** 10c.+5c. purple 20 10
398 – 25c.+10c. violet 20 20
399 **51** 50c. olive 20 20
DESIGN: 25c. "Baptism".

52 Footballers **53** El Pardo Palace, Madrid

1955. Air.
400 **52** 25c. grey 20 20
401 50c. olive 20 20
402 1p.50 brown 85 20
403 4p. red . . . . 2·50 40
404 10p. green . . . . 1·60 60

1955. Treaty of Pardo, 1778.
405 **53** 5c. brown 20 20
406 15c. red 20 20
407 80c. green 20 20

54 Moustached Monkeys **55** "Orquidea"

1955. Colonial Stamp Day. Inscr "DIA DEL SELLO COLONIAL 1955".
408 **54** 5c.+5c. lake and brown . . 20 20
409 – 15c.+5c. sepia and lake . . 20 20
410 **54** 70c. blue and slate 40 40
DESIGN—HORIZ: 15c. Talapoin and young.

1956. Native Welfare Fund. Inscr "PRO INDIGENAS 1956".
411 **55** 5c.+5c. olive 20 20
412 – 15c.+5c. ochre 20 20
413 **55** 20c. turquoise 20 20
414 – 50c. brown 20 20
DESIGN: 15, 50c. "Strophantus kombe".

56 Arms of Santa Isabel **57** Grey Parrot

1956. Colonial Stamp Day. Inscr "DIA DEL SELLO 1956".
415 **56** 5c.+5c. brown 20 20
416 – 15c.+5c. violet 20 20
417 **56** 70c. green 20 20
DESIGN—HORIZ: 15c. Arms of Bata and natives.

1957. Native Welfare Fund. Inscr "PRO INDIGENAS 1957".
418 **57** 5c.+5c. purple 20 20
419 – 15c.+5c. ochre 20 20
420 **57** 70c. green 20 20
DESIGN—HORIZ: 15c. Grey parrot in flight.

58 "Flight"

1957. Air. 30th Anniv of Spain–Fernando Poo Flight by "Atlantida" Seaplane Squadron.
421 **58** 25p. sepia and bistre . . . 7·25 1·60

59 African Elephant and Calf

1957. Colonial Stamp Day.
422 **59** 10c.+5c. mauve 20 20
423 – 15c.+5c. brown 20 20
424 **59** 20c. turquoise 20 20
425 – 70c. green 20 20
DESIGN—VERT: 15, 70c. African elephant trumpeting.

60 Doves and Arms of Valencia and Santa Isabel

1958. "Aid for Valencia".
426 **60** 10c.+5c. brown 20 20
427 15c.+10c. ochre 20 20
428 50c.+10c. brown 20 20

61 Boxing

1958. Sports.
429 **61** 5c. brown 15 15
430 – 10c. brown 15 15
431 – 15c. brown 15 15
432 – 80c. green 15 15
433 **61** 1p. red 15 15
434 – 2p. purple 20 15
435 – 2p.30 lilac 30 20
436 – 3p. blue 30 20
DESIGNS—VERT: 10c., 2p. Basketball; 80c., 3p. Running. HORIZ: 15c., 2p.30, Long jumping.

62 Missionary holding Cross **63** African Monarchs

1958. Native Welfare Fund. Inscr "1883 PRO-INDIGENAS 1958".
437 **62** 10c.+5c. brown 20 20
438 – 15c.+5c. ochre 20 20
439 **62** 20c. turquoise 20 20
440 – 70c. green 20 20
DESIGN: 15, 70c. The Crucifixion.

1958. Colonial Stamp Day. Inscr "1958".
441 **63** 10c.+5c. red 20 20
442 – 25c.+10c. violet 20 20
443 – 50c.+10c. olive 20 20
DESIGNS: 25, 50c. Different views of butterflies on plants.

64 Digitalis **65** Boy on "Penny-farthing" Cycle

1959. Child Welfare Fund. Floral designs as T **64**. Inscr "PRO-INFANCIA 1959".
444 **64** 10c.+5c. lake 20 20
445 – 15c.+5c. ochre 20 20
446 – 20c. myrtle 20 20
447 **64** 70c. green 20 20
DESIGN: 15, 20c. Castor bean.

1959. Colonial Stamp Day. Inscr "1959".
448 **65** 10c.+5c. lake 20 20
449 – 20c.+5c. myrtle 20 20
450 – 50c.+20c. olive 20 20
DESIGNS: 20c. Racing cyclists; 50c. Winning cyclist.

EXPRESS LETTER STAMP

E **38** Fernando Poo

1951.
E358 E **38** 25c. red 25 10

SPANISH MOROCCO Pt. 9

100 centimos = 1 peseta.

I. SPANISH POST OFFICES IN MOROCCO.

Nos. 2/150, except Nos. 93/8 and 124/37 are all stamps of Spain overprinted.

1903. Optd **CORREO ESPANOL MARRUECOS.**
2 **38a** ½c. green 50 25

1903. Optd **CORREO ESPANOL MARRUECOS.**
3 **52** 2c. brown . . . . 1·20 1·20
4 5c. green . . . . 1·30 60
5 10c. red . . . . 1·70 25
6 15c. violet . . . . 2·20 65
7 20c. black . . . . 8·25 3·00
8 25c. blue 70 65
9 30c. green . . . . 5·00 3·00
10 40c. pink . . . . 9·00 5·00
11 50c. blue . . . . 5·00 4·75
12 1p. purple . . . . 10·50 7·00
13 4p. purple . . . . 26·00 12·00
14 10p. orange . . . . 26·00 30·00

1908. Stamps of Spain handstamped **TETUAN**.
15 **38a** ½c. green . . . . 13·50 5·25
16 **52** 2c. brown . . . . 55·00 21·00
17 5c. green . . . . 70·00 32·00
18 10c. red . . . . 70·00 36·00
19 15c. violet . . . . 70·00 35·00
20 20c. black £250 £180
21 25c. blue . . . . £110 55·00
22 30c. green £250 £110
23 40c. bistre £300 £180

1908. Nos. 2/5 and 7/8 handstamped **TETUAN**.
24 **38a** ½c. green . . . . 21·00 13·50
25 **52** 2c. brown £180 £100
26 5c. green . . . . £170 60·00
27 10c. red . . . . £170 60·00
28 20c. grey £375 £170
29 25c. blue . . . . £150 50·00

1909. Optd **CORREO ESPANOL MARRUECOS.**
30 **64** 2c. brown 50 15
31 5c. green . . . . 2·50 15
32 10c. red . . . . 3·25 15
33 15c. violet . . . . 7·50 35
34 20c. green . . . . 19·00 75
35 25c. blue £110
36 30c. green . . . . 6·00 35
37 40c. pink . . . . 6·00 35
38 50c. blue . . . . 10·50 10·00
39 1p. lake . . . . 23·00 21·00
40 4p. purple £110
41 10p. orange £110

After the appearance of Nos. 42/54 for the Spanish Protectorate in 1914, the use of Nos. 30/41 was restricted to Tangier.

II. SPANISH PROTECTORATE (excluding Tangier).

1914. Optd **MARRUECOS**.
42 **38a** ½c. green 10 10
43 **64** 2c. brown 10 10
44 5c. green 30 25
45 10c. red 30 25
46 15c. violet . . . . 1·10 85
47 20c. green . . . . 2·10 1·50
48 25c. blue . . . . 2·10 1·20
49 30c. green . . . . 4·00 2·10
50 40c. pink . . . . 9·50 3·00
51 50c. blue . . . . 5·00 2·10
52 1p. red . . . . 5·00 3·00
53 4p. purple . . . . 2·75 21·00
54 10p. orange . . . . 37·00 28·00

1915. Optd **PROTECTORADO ESPANOL EN MARRUECOS.**
55 **38a** ½c. green 40 20
56 **64** 2c. brown 20 20
57 5c. green 50 20
58 10c. red 40 20
59 15c. violet 55 20
60 20c. green . . . . 1·50 20
61 25c. blue . . . . 1·50 30
62 30c. green . . . . 1·60 35
63 40c. pink . . . . 2·50 35
64 50c. blue . . . . 4·25 30
65 1p. red . . . . 4·25 30
66 4p. purple . . . . 31·00 21·00
67 10p. orange . . . . 45·00 23·00

1916. Optd **ZONA DE PROTECTORADO ESPANOL EN MARRUECOS.**
68 **38a** ½c. green . . . . 1·20 30
69 **66** 1c. green . . . . 1·40 10
70 **64** 2c. brown . . . . 1·20 30
71 5c. green . . . . 5·00 30
72 10c. red . . . . 6·25 30
73 15c. orange . . . . 7·00 30
74 20c. violet . . . . 9·25 10
75 25c. blue . . . . 21·00 3·50
76 30c. green . . . . 27·00 22·00
77 40c. red . . . . 24·00 65
78 50c. blue . . . . 13·00 35
79 1p. red . . . . 29·00 2·40
80 4p. purple . . . . 46·00 33·00
81 10p. orange . . . . £100 75·00

1920. Optd **PROTECTORADO ESPANOL EN MARRUECOS** perf through centre and each half surch in figures and words.
82 **64** 10c.+10c. on 20c. green . . 3·75 1·80
83 15c.+15c. on 30c. green . . 9·00 6·75

1920. No. E68 perf through centre, and each half surch **10 centimos**.
E84 **53** 10c.+10c. on 20c. red . . . 10·50 6·25

1920. Fiscal stamps showing figure of Justice, bisected and surch **CORREOS** and value.
93 5c. on 5p. blue . . . . . . 8·00 1·50
94 5c. on 10p. green 20 10
95 10c. on 25p. green 20 10
96 10c. on 50p. grey 35 25
97 15c. on 100p. red 35 25
98 15c. on 500p. red . . . . . . 10·50 5·25

1923. Optd **ZONA DE PROTECTORADO ESPANOL EN MARRUECOS.**
101 **68** 2c. green 70 10
102 5c. purple 70 10
103 10c. green . . . . 2·75 10
105 15c. blue . . . . 2·75 10
106 20c. violet . . . . 6·25 10
107 25c. red . . . . 12·50 1·30
108 40c. blue . . . . 12·50 4·25
109 50c. orange . . . . 33·00 7·50
110 **69** 1p. grey . . . . 49·00 4·25

1926. Red Cross stamps optd **ZONA PROTECTORADO ESPANOL.**
111 **70** 1c. orange . . . . 7·25 7·25
112 – 2c. red . . . . 10·00 12·00
113 – 5c. brown . . . . 3·75 10·50
114 – 10c. green . . . . 3·75 3·75
115 **70** 15c. violet 70 70
116 – 20c. purple 70 70
117 **71** 25c. red 70 70
118 **70** 30c. green 70 70
119 – 40c. blue 15 15
120 – 50c. red 15 15
121 – 1p. red 15 15
122 – 4p. bistre 70 70
123 **71** 10p. violet . . . . 2·50 2·50

11 Mosque of Alcazarquivir
12 Moorish Gateway, Larache

1928.
124 **11** 1c. red 10 10
126 2c. violet 30 25
127 3c. blue 15 15
128 10c. green 15 15
129 15c. brown 35 15
130 **12** 20c. olive 35 15
131 25c. red 35 15
132 30c. brown . . . . 1·30 10
133 40c. blue . . . . 1·70 10
134 50c. purple . . . . 3·25 10
135 – 1p. green . . . . 5·00 30
136 – 2p.50 purple . . . . . . 16·00 6·75
137 – 4p. blue . . . . 12·00 4·25
DESIGNS—HORIZ: 1p. Well at Alhucemas; 2p.50, Xauen; 4p. Tetuan.

1929. Seville–Barcelona Exhibition stamps, Nos. 502/14 optd **PROTECTORADO MARRUECOS.**
138 1c. blue 25 25
139 2c. green 25 25
140 5c. red 25 25
141 10c. green 25 25
142 15c. blue 25 25
143 20c. violet 25 25
144 25c. red 25 25
145 30c. brown 60 60
146 40c. blue 60 60
147 50c. orange 60 60
148 1p. grey . . . . 5·25 5·25
149 4p. red . . . . 12·50 12·50
150 10p. brown . . . . 25·00 25·00

14 Xauen
15 Market-place, Larache

1933.
151 **14** 1c. red 10 10
152 – 2c. green 10 10
153 – 5c. mauve 10 10
154 – 10c. green 40 30
155 – 15c. yellow . . . . 2·10 1·50
156 **14** 20c. green 45 25
157 – 25c. red . . . . 22·00 16·00
165 – 25c. violet . . . . 1·30 85
158 – 30c. lake . . . . 4·75 30
166 – 30c. red . . . . 13·00 25
159 **15** 40c. blue . . . . 10·50 30
167 – 40c. red . . . . 7·00 30
160 – 50c. red . . . . 31·00 8·25
168 – 50c. blue . . . . 7·00 30
169 – 60c. green . . . . 7·00 30
161 – 1p. grey . . . . 11·00 30
170 – 2p. lake . . . . 35·00 9·25
162 – 2p.50 brown . . . . 20·00 8·25
163 – 4p. green . . . . 20·00 8·25
164 – 5p. black . . . . 27·00 8·25
DESIGNS—HORIZ: 2c., 1p. Xauen; 5c., 2p.50, Arcila; 25c. (No. 157), 5p. Sultan and bodyguard; 30c. (No. 166), 50c. (No. 168), 2p. Forest at Ketama. VERT: 10c., 30c. (No. 158), Tetuan; 15c., 4p. Alcazarquivir; 25c. (No. 165), 40c. (No. 167), Wayside scene at Arcila.
See also Nos. 177/83 and 213/6.

1936. Air. No. 157 surch with new value and **18-7-36.**
171 25c.+2p. on 25c. red . . . . 28·00 6·25

1936. Surch.
172 – 1c. on 4p. blue (137) . . 25 10
173 – 2c. on 2p.50 pur (136) 25 10
174 **12** 5c. on 25c. red (131) . . 10 10
175 – 10c. on 1p. green (135) 8·25 4·00
176 E **12** 15c. on 20c. black . . . 6·75 2·00

1937. Pictorials as T **14/15**.
177 1c. green 10 10
178 2c. mauve 10 10
179 5c. orange 10 10
180 15c. violet 10 10
181 30c. red 50 25
182 1p. blue . . . . 4·75 30
183 10p. brown . . . . 55·00 27·00
DESIGNS—VERT: 1, 15c. Caliph and Viziers; 30c. Tetuan; 1p. Arcila; 10p. Caliph on horseback. HORIZ: 2c. Bokoia; 5c. Alcazarquivir.

Sheets each 105 × 95 mm comprising Nos. 177/83
MS183a 1, 2, 5c., 1p. . . . . . 14·00 14·00
MS183b 2, 5, 30c. . . . . 14·00 14·00

18 Legionaries
19 General Franco

1937. 1st Anniv of Civil War.
184 – 1c. blue 10 10
185 **18** 2c. brown 10 10
186 – 5c. mauve 10 10
187 – 10c. green 10 10
188 – 15c. blue 10 10
189 – 20c. purple 10 10
190 – 25c. mauve 10 10
191 – 30c. red 10 10
192 – 40c. orange 10 10
193 – 50c. blue 10 10
194 – 60c. green 10 10
195 – 1p. violet 10 10
196 – 2p. blue . . . . 9·00 8·25
197 – 2p.50 black . . . . 9·00 8·25
198 – 4p. brown . . . . 9·00 8·25
199 – 10p. black . . . . 9·00 8·25
DESIGNS—VERT: 1c. Sentry; 5c. Trooper; 10c. Volunteers; 15c. Colour bearer; 20c. Desert halt; 25c. Ifni mounted riflemen; 30c. Trumpeters; 40c. Cape Juby Camel Corps; 50c. Infantryman; 60c., 1, 2, 4p. Sherifian Guards; 2p.50, Cavalryman. HORIZ: 10p. "Road to Victory".

1937. Obligatory Tax. Disabled Soldiers in N. Africa.
200 **19** 10c. brown 45 10
201 10c. blue 45 10

Sheets each 120 × 100 mm containing blocks of four. Imperf.
MS202a **19** 10c. sepia . . . . . 3·75 2·50
MS202b 10c. brown . . . . 3·75 2·50
MS202c 10c. blue . . . . 3·75 2·50

20 Yellow-billed Stork over Mosque
22 Soldier on Horseback

1938. Air.
203 – 5c. brown 10 10
204 **20** 10c. green 10 10
205 – 25c. red 10 10
206 – 40c. blue . . . . 2·00 60
207 – 50c. mauve 10 10
208 – 75c. blue 10 10
209 – 1p. brown 10 10
210 – 1p.50 violet 60 45
211 – 2p. red 45 10
212 – 3p. black . . . . 1·50 30
DESIGNS—VERT: 5c. Mosque de Baja, Tetuan; 25c. Straits of Gibraltar; 40c. Desert natives; 1p. Mounted postman; 1p.50, Farmers; 2p. Sunset; 3p. Shadow of airplane over city. HORIZ: 50c. Airplane over Tetuan; 75c. Airplane over Larache.

1939. Pictorials as T **14**.
213 5c. orange 10 10
214 10c. green 10 10
215 15c. brown 35 10
216 20c. blue 35 10
DESIGNS: 5c. "Carta de Espana'; 10c. "Carta de Marruecos"; 15c. Larache; 20c. Tetuan.

1940. Pictorials as T **14**, inscr "ZONA" on back.
217 1c. brown 10 10
218 2c. olive 10 10
219 5c. blue 10 10
220 10c. lilac 10 10
221 15c. green 10 10
222 20c. violet 10 10
223 25c. sepia 10 10
224 30c. green 10 10
225 40c. green . . . . 1·40 10
226 45c. orange 55 10
227 50c. brown 55 10
228 70c. blue 55 10
229 1p. brown and blue . . . . 1·80 10
230 2p.50 green and brown . . . 10·50 3·75
231 5p. sepia and purple . . . . 1·80 25
232 10p. brown and olive . . . . 19·00 7·00
DESIGNS—VERT: 1c. Postman; 2c. Pillar-box; 5c. Winter landscape; 10c. Alcazar street; 15c. Castle wall, Xauen; 20c. Palace sentry, Tetuan; 25c. Caliph on horseback; 30c. Market-place, Larache; 40c. Gateway, Tetuan; 45c. Gateway, Xauen; 50c. Street, Alcazarquivir; 70c. Post Office; 1p. Spanish War veterans.

1940. 4th Anniv of Civil War. Nos. 184/99 optd **17-VII-940 4º ANIVERSARIO**.
233 1c. blue 55 55
234 2c. brown 55 55
235 5c. mauve 55 55
236 10c. green 55 55
237 15c. blue 55 55
238 20c. purple 55 55
239 25c. mauve 55 55
240 30c. red 55 55
241 40c. orange 85 85
242 50c. blue 85 85
243 60c. green 85 85
244 1p. violet 85 85
245 2p. blue . . . . 36·00 36·00
246 2p.50 black . . . . 36·00 36·00
247 4p. brown . . . . 36·00 36·00
248 10p. black . . . . 36·00 36·00

1941. Obligatory Tax for Disabled Soldiers.
249 **22** 10c. green . . . . 3·50 15
250 10c. pink . . . . 3·50 15
251 10c. red . . . . 3·50 15
252 10c. blue . . . . 3·50 15

23 Larache
25 General Franco

1941.
253 **23** 5c. brown and deep brown 10 10
263 – 5c. blue 10 10
254 – 10c. deep red and red . . . 10 10
255 – 15c. yellow and green . . . 10 10
256 – 20c. blue and deep blue . . 35 10
264 – 40c. brown . . . . 55·00 30
257 – 40c. red and purple . . . . 1·10 10
DESIGNS: 5c. blue, 10c. Alcazarquivir; 15, 40c. brown, Larache market; 20c. Moorish house; 40c. purple, Gateway, Tangier.

1942. Air. New designs as T **14**, optd **Z**.
258 5c. blue 10 10
259 10c. brown 10 10
260 15c. green 10 10
261 90c. red 10 10
262 5p. black 80 40

DESIGNS—VERT: 5c. Atlas mountains; 10c. Mosque at Tangier; 15c. Velez fortress; 90c. Sanjurjo harbour; 5p. Straits of Gibraltar.

1943. Obligatory Tax for Disabled Soldiers.
265 **25** 10c. grey . . . . 7·00 10
266 10c. blue . . . . 7·00 10
267 10c. brown . . . . 7·00 10
268 10c. violet . . . . 7·00 10
283 10c. brown and mauve . . 6·25 10
284 10c. green and orange . . 6·25 10
295 10c. brown and blue . . . 6·25 10
296 10c. lilac and grey . . . . 6·25 10

26 Homeward Bound

1944. Agricultural Scenes.
269 – 1c. blue and brown 10 10
270 – 2c. green 10 10
271 **26** 5c. black and brown . . . 10 10
272 – 10c. orange and blue . . . 10 10
273 – 15c. green 10 10
274 – 20c. black and red 10 10
275 – 25c. brown and blue . . . 15 10
276 – 30c. blue and green 15 10
277 – 40c. purple and brown . . 10 10
278 **26** 50c. brown and blue . . . 35 10
279 – 75c. blue and green 45 10
280 – 1p. brown and blue 45 10
281 – 2p.50 blue and black . . . 5·75 2·30
282 – 10p. black and orange . . 9·50 5·50
DESIGNS—HORIZ: 1, 30c. Ploughing; 2, 40c. Harvesting; 10, 75c. Threshing; 15c., 1p. Vegetable garden; 20c., 2p.50, Gathering oranges; 25c., 10p. Shepherd and flock.

27 Dyers

28 Sanatorium

1946. Craftsmen.
285 – 1c. brown and purple . . . 10 10
286 **27** 2c. violet and green 10 10
287 – 10c. blue and orange . . . 10 10
288 **27** 15c. green and blue 10 10
289 – 25c. blue and green 10 10
290 – 40c. brown and blue . . . 10 10
291 **27** 45c. red and black 50 40
292 **27** 1p. blue and green 65 50
293 – 2p.50 green and orange . . 1·90 1·40
294 – 10p. grey and blue . . . . 3·50 2·50
DESIGNS: 1, 10, 25c. Potters; 40c. Blacksmiths; 1p. Cobblers; 2p.50, Weavers; 10p. Metal workers.

1946. Anti-T.B. Fund.
297 – 10c. green and red 10 10
298 **28** 25c. brown and red 10 10
299 – 25c.+5c. violet and red . . 10 10
300 – 50c.+10c. blue and red . . 25 10
301 – 90c.+10c. brown and red 65 35
DESIGNS: 10c. Emblem and arabesque ornamentation; 25c.+5c. Mountain roadway; 50c.+10c. Fountain; 90c.+10c. Wayfarers.

29 Sanatorium

30 Steam Goods Train

1947. Anti-T.B. Fund.
302 – 10c. blue and red 10 10
303 **29** 25c. brown and red 10 10
304 – 25c.+5c. lilac and red . . . 10 10
305 – 50c.+10c. blue and red . . 25 20
306 – 90c.+10c. brown and red 70 50
DESIGNS: 10c. Emblem, mosque and palm tree; 25c.+5c. Hospital ward; 50c.+10c. Nurse and children; 90c.+10c. Arab swordsman.

1948. Transport and Commerce.
307 **30** 2c. brown and violet . . . 10 10
308 – 5c. violet and red 10 10
309 – 15c. green and blue 10 10
310 – 25c. green and black . . . 10 10
311 – 35c. black and blue 10 10
312 – 50c. violet and orange . . 10 10
313 – 70c. blue and green 10 10
314 – 90c. green and red 10 10
315 – 1p. violet and blue 50 30
316 **30** 2p.50 green and purple . . 1·40 30
317 – 10p. blue and black . . . 3·25 1·20
DESIGNS: 5, 35c. Road transport; 15, 70c. Urban market; 25, 90c. Rural market; 50c., 1p. Camel caravan; 10p. "Arango" (freighter) at quay.

31 Emblem

32 Herald

1948. Anti-T.B. Fund.
318 **31** 10c. green and red 10 10
319 – 25c. green and red . . . . 1·50 70
320 **32** 50c.+10c. purple and red 20 10
321 – 90c.+10c. black and red . . 1·10 40
322 – 2p.50+50c. brown & red 8·50 3·00
323 – 5p.+1p. violet and red . . 9·50 5·75
DESIGNS: 25c. Airplane over sanatorium; 90c. Arab swordsman; 2p.50, Natives sitting in the sun; 5p. Airplane over Ben Karrich.

33 Market Day

34 Caliph on Horseback

1949. Air.
324 – 5c. green and purple . . . 10 10
325 **33** 10c. mauve and black . . . 10 10
326 – 30c. grey and blue 10 10
327 – 1p.75 blue and black . . . 10 10
328 **33** 3p. black and blue 15 10
329 – 4p. red and black 40 15
330 – 6p.50 brown and green . . 1·20 20
331 – 8p. blue and mauve . . . 1·90 50
DESIGNS—VERT: 5c., 1p.75, Straits of Gibraltar; 30c., 4p. Kebira Fortress; 6p.50, Arrival of mail plane; 8p. Galloping horseman.

1949. Caliph's Wedding Celebrations.
332 **34** 50c.+10c. red (postage) . . 30 10
333 – 1p.+10c. black (air) 80 20
DESIGN: 1p. Wedding crowds in palace grounds.

35 Emblem

36 Postman, 1890

1949. Anti-T.B. Fund.
334 **35** 5c. green and red 10 10
335 – 10c. blue and red 10 10
336 – 25c. black and red 50 25
337 – 50c.+10c. brown and red 30 70
338 – 90c.+10c. green and red . . 90 40
DESIGNS: 10c. Road to recovery; 25c. Palm tree and tower; 50c. Flag and followers; 90c. Moorish horseman.

1950. 75th Anniv of U.P.U.
339 **36** 5c. blue and brown 10 10
340 – 10c. black and blue 10 10
341 – 15c. green and black . . . 10 10
342 – 35c. black and violet . . . 10 10
343 – 45c. mauve and red 10 10
344 **36** 50c. black and green . . . 10 10
345 – 75c. blue and deep blue . . 10 10
346 **36** 90c. red and black 10 10
347 – 1p. green and purple . . . 10 10
348 – 1p.50 blue and red 50 40
349 – 5p. purple and black . . . 95 75
350 – 10p. blue and violet . . . 27·00 19·00
DESIGNS: 10, 45c., 1p. Mounted postman; 15c., 1p.50, Mail coach; 35, 75c., 5p. Mail van; 10p. Steam mail train.

37 Morabito

38 Hunting

1950. Anti-T.B. Fund.
351 – 5c. black and red 10 10
352 – 10c. green and red 10 10
353 – 25c. blue and red 50 30
354 – 50c.+10c. brown and red 20 10
355 **37** 90c.+10c. green and red . . 50 30
DESIGNS: 5c. Arab horseman; 10c. Fort; 25c. Sanatorium; 50c. Crowd at Fountain of Life.

1950.
356 **38** 5c. mauve and brown . . . 10 10
357 – 10c. grey and red 10 10
358 **38** 50c. sepia and green . . . 10 10
359 – 1p. red and violet 35 10
360 – 5p. violet and red 55 10
361 – 10p. red and green . . . . 1·80 45
DESIGNS: 10c., 1p. Hunters and hounds; 5p. Fishermen; 10p. Carabo (fishing boat).

39 Emblem

40 Mounted Riflemen

1951. Anti-T.B. Fund.
362 **39** 5c. green and red 10 10
363 – 10c. blue and red 10 10
364 – 25c. black and red 55 35
365 – 50c.+10c. brown and red 10 10
366 – 90c.+10c. blue and red . . 30 10
367 – 1p.+5p. blue and red . . . 7·50 3·25
368 – 1p.10+25c. sepia and red 2·75 1·60
DESIGNS: 10c. Natives and children; 25c. Airplane over Nubes; 50c. Moorish horsemen; 90c. Riverside fortress; 1p. Brig "Hernan Cortes"; 1p.10, Airplane over caravan.

1952.
369 **40** 5c. brown and blue 10 10
370 – 10c. mauve and sepia . . . 10 10
371 – 15c. green and black . . . 10 10
372 – 20c. purple and green . . . 10 10
373 – 25c. blue and red 10 10
374 – 35c. orange and olive . . . 10 10
375 – 45c. red 10 10
376 – 50c. green and red 10 10
377 – 75c. blue and purple . . . 10 10
378 – 90c. purple and blue . . . 10 10
379 – 1p. brown and blue 10 10
380 – 5p. blue and red . . . . 1·20 30
381 – 10p. black and green . . . 1·90 40
DESIGNS—HORIZ: 10c. Grooms leading horses; 15c. Parade of horsemen; 20c. Peasants; 25c. Monastic procession; 35c. Native band; 45c. Tribesmen; 50c. Natives overlooking roof tops; 75c. Inside a tea house; 90c. Wedding procession; 1p. Pilgrims on horseback; 5p. Storyteller and audience; 10p. Natives talking.

41 Road to Tetuan

1952. Air. Tetuan Postal Museum Fund.
382 **41** 2p. blue and black 10 10
383 – 4p. red and black 30 10
384 – 8p. green and black . . . 40 20
385 – 16p. brown and black . . . 2·10 1·00
DESIGNS: 4p. Moors watching airplane; 8p. Horseman and airplane; 16p. Shadow of airplane over Tetuan.

42 Natives at Prayer

43 Sidi Saidi

1952. Anti-T.B. Fund. Frame in red.
386 **42** 5c. green 10 10
387 – 10c. brown 10 10
388 – 25c. blue 30 20
389 – 50c.+10c. black 10 10
390 – 60c.+25c. green 55 30
391 – 90c.+10c. purple 55 30
392 – 1p.10+25c. violet . . . . 1·60 75
393 – 5p.+2p. black . . . . . . 4·00 2·00
DESIGNS: 10c. Beggars outside doorway; 25c. Airplane over cactus; 50c. Natives on horseback; 60c. Airplane over palms; 90c. Hilltop fortress; 1p.10, Airplane over agaves; 5p. Mounted warrior.

1953. Air.
394 – 35c. red and blue 10 10
395 **43** 60c. green and lake 10 10
396 – 1p.10 black and blue . . . 20 10
397 – 4p.50 brown and lake . . . 70 15
DESIGNS: 35c. Carabo (fishing boat); 1p.10, Le Yunta (ploughing); 4p.50, Fortress, Xauen.

1953. Air. No. 208 surch **50.**
398 50c. on 75c. blue 25 10

1953. Anti-T.B. Fund. As T **32** but inscr "PRO TUBERCULOSOS 1953". Frame in red.
400 5c. green 10 10
401 10c. purple 10 10
402 25c. green 70 40
403 50c.+10c. violet 10 10
404 60c.+25c. brown . . . . . . 1·50 80
405 90c.+10c. black 50 30
406 1p.10+25c. brown . . . . . 2·50 1·30
407 5p.+2p. blue . . . . 9·00 5·25
DESIGNS: 5c. Herald; 10c. Moorish horseman; 25c. Airplane over Ben Karrich; 50c. Mounted warrior; 60c. Airplane over sanatorium; 90c. Moorish horseman; 1p.10, Airplane over sea; 5p. Arab swordsman.

46

47 Water-carrier

1953.
408 **46** 5c. red 10 10
409 10c. green 10 10

1953. 25th Anniv of 1st Pictorial Stamps of Spanish Morocco.
410 – 25c. purple and green . . . 10 10
411 **47** 50c. green and red 10 10
412 – 90c. orange and blue . . . 10 10
413 – 1p. green and brown . . . 10 10
414 – 1p.25 mauve and green . . 10 10
415 – 2p. blue and purple 25 15
416 **47** 2p.50 orange and grey . . 55 20
417 – 4p.50 green and mauve . . 3·25 50
418 – 10p. black and green . . . 4·00 90
DESIGNS—VERT: 35c., 1p.25, Mountain women; 90c., 2p. Mountain tribesmen; 1, 4p.50, Veiled Moorish women; 10p. Arab dignitary.

1954. Anti-T.B. Fund. As T **32**, but inscr "PRO TUBERCULOSOS 1954". Frame in red.
419 5c. turquoise 10 10
420 5c.+5c. purple 10 10
421 10c. sepia 10 10
422 25c. blue 15 10
423 50c.+10c. green 60 35
424 5p.+2p. black . . . . 7·50 3·75
DESIGNS: 5c. Convent; 5c.+5c. White stork on a tower; 10c. Moroccan family; 25c. Airplane over Spanish coast; 50c. Father and child; 5p. Chapel.

48 Saida Gate

49 Celebrations

1955. Frames in black.
425 – 15c. green 10 10
426 **48** 25c. purple 10 10
427 – 80c. blue 10 10
428 **48** 1p. mauve 20 10
429 – 15p. turquoise . . . . . . 3·00 1·00
DESIGNS: 15c., 80c. Queen's Gate; 15p. Ceuta Gate.

1955. 30th Anniv of Caliph's Accession.
430 **49** 15c. olive and brown . . . 10 10
431 – 25c. lake and purple . . . 10 10
432 – 30c. green and sepia . . . 10 10
433 **49** 70c. green and myrtle . . . 10 10
434 – 80c. brown and olive . . . 10 10
435 – 1p. brown and blue 10 10
436 **49** 1p.80 violet and black . . 15 10
437 – 3p. grey and blue 15 10
438 – 5p. brown and myrtle . . . 1·10 35
439 – 15p. green and brown . . . 2·50 1·20
DESIGNS: 25c., 80c., 3p. Caliph's portrait; 30c., 1, 5p. Procession; 15p. Coat of Arms.

EXPRESS LETTER STAMPS

Express Letter Stamps of Spain overprinted.

1914. Optd **MARRUECOS.**
E55 E **53** 20c. red . . . . 4·25 2·10

1915. Optd **PROTECTORADO ESPANOL EN MARRUECOS.**
E68 E **53** 20c. red . . . . 3·50 1·60

1923. Optd **ZONA DE PROTECTORADO ESPANOL EN MARRUECOS.**
E111 E **53** 20c. red . . . . 10·50 9·25

1926. Red Cross. Optd **ZONA PROTECTORADO ESPANOL.**
E124 E **77** 20c. black and blue . . 2·00 2·00

E 12 Moorish Courier   E 16

1928.
E138 E 12 20c. black . . . . . . 3·25 3·25

1935.
E171 E 16 20c. red . . . . 1·60 30

E 19 Moorish Courier   E 21

1937. 1st Anniv of Civil War.
E200 E 19 20c. red 10 10

1940.
E233 E 21 25c. red 30 25

1940. No. E200 optd as Nos. 233/48 and surch also.
E249 E 19 25c. on 20c. red . . . 10·50 10·50

E 37 Air Mail 1935   E 41 Moorish Courier

1950. 75th Anniv of U.P.U.
E351 E 37 25c. black and red . . 27·00 19·00

1952.
E382 E 41 25c. red 10 10

E 48 Moorish Courier   E 49 Tangier Gate

1953. 25th Anniv of First Pictorial Stamps of Spanish Morocco.
E419 E 48 25c. mauve and blue 20 10

1955.
E430 E 49 2p. violet and black . . 10 10

For later issues see **MOROCCO**.

SPANISH POST OFFICES IN TANGIER Pt. 9

See note below No. 41 of Spanish P.O.s in Morocco, concerning the exclusive use of Nos. 30/41 in Tangier after 1914.

Postage stamps of Spain overprinted.

1921. Optd **CORREO ESPANOL MARRUECOS**.
1 66 1c. green 15 10
2 64 2c. brown £300
3 15c. yellow . . . . 1·10 10
4 20c. violet . . . . 1·90 10

1939. Optd as 1921.
5 68 2c. green . . . . 3·75 15
6 5c. purple . . . . 3·75 15
7 5c. red . . . . 3·75 15
8a 10c. green . . . . 4·25 15
10 20c. violet . . . . 7·50 90
11 50c. orange . . . . 32·00 6·50
12 69 10p. brown . . . . 4·25 4·25

1926. Red Cross stamps optd **CORREO ESPANOL TANGER**.
13 70 1c. orange . . . . 6·25 6·25
14 – 2c. red . . . . 6·25 6·25
15 – 5c. grey . . . . 3·00 3·00
16 – 10c. green . . . . 3·00 3·00
17 70 15c. violet . . . . 1·25 1·25
18 – 20c. purple . . . . 1·25 1·25
19 71 25c. red . . . . 1·25 1·25
20 70 30c. olive . . . . 1·25 1·25
21 – 40c. blue 25 25
22 – 50c. brown 25 25
23 – 1p. red 55 55
24 – 4p. brown 55 55
25 71 10p. lilac . . . . 3·00 3·00

1929. Seville–Barcelona Exhibition stamps, Nos. 504/14 optd **TANGER**.
27 5c. red 25 25
28 10c. green 25 25
29 15c. blue 25 25
30 20c. violet 25 25
31 25c. red 25 25
32 30c. brown 25 25
33 40c. blue 70 70
34 50c. orange 70 70
35 1p. grey . . . . 7·00 7·00
36 4p. red . . . . 19·00 19·00
37 10p. brown . . . . 28·00 28·00

1930. Optd as 1921.
38 97 10c. green . . . . 2·40 30
39 15c. turquoise . . . . . . £110 1·25
40 20c. violet . . . . 2·50 50
41 30c. red . . . . 2·75 1·25
42 40c. blue . . . . 10·00 6·50

1933. Optd **MARRUECOS**.
43 143 1c. green (imperf) 15 15
44 2c. brown 15 15
45 127 5c. brown 15 15
46 128 10c. green 15 15
47 130 15c. blue 15 15
48 127 20c. violet 15 15
49 132 25c. red 15 15
50 133 30c. red . . . . 45·00 5·50
51 138 40c. blue 25 15
52 130 50c. orange 60 15
53 138 60c. green 60 15
54 142 1p. black 60 25
55 – 4p. mauve . . . . 1·60 2·40
56 – 10p. brown . . . . 2·40 5·50

1937. Optd **TANGER**.
58 143 1c. green (imperf) 30 15
59 2c. brown 30 15
60 127 5c. brown 30 15
61 128 10c. green 30 15
62 130 15c. blue 40 15
63 127 20c. violet 40 40
64 132 25c. red 40 40
65 136 30c. red 40 15
66 138 40c. blue . . . . 1·10 50
67 130 50c. orange . . . . 3·25 50
68 142 1p. black . . . . 6·00 3·00
69 – 4p. mauve (No. 768c) . . . £160
70 – 10p. brown (No. 769c) . . £200

1938. Optd **Correo Espanol Tanger**.
71 143 5c. brown . . . . 1·60 90
72 10c. green . . . . 1·60 90
73 15c. green . . . . 1·60 90
74 20c. violet . . . . 1·60 60
75 25c. mauve . . . . 1·60 60
76 30c. red . . . . 6·50 3·00
77 160a 40c. red . . . . 3·25 1·40
78 45c. red . . . . 1·10 40
79 50c. blue . . . . 1·10 40
80 60c. blue . . . . 3·25 1·40
81 145 2p. blue . . . . 20·00 8·00
82 – 4p. mauve (No. 768c) . . 20·00 8·00

1938. Air. Optd **Correo Aereo TANGER**.
83 143 25c. mauve 85 45
84 160a 50c. blue 85 45

1938. Air. Optd **CORREO AEREO TANGER**.
86 142 1p. black 85 45
85 145 2p. blue . . . . 6·50 2·50
87 – 4p. mauve (No. 768c) . . 6·50 2·50
88 – 10p. brown (No. 769c) . . 48·00 30·00

1939. Optd **Tanger**.
89 143 5c. brown 60 40
90 10c. green 60 40
91 15c. green 60 40
92 20c. violet 60 40
93 25c. mauve 60 40
94 30c. red 60 40
95 160a 40c. red 60 40
96 45c. red 60 40
97 50c. blue . . . . 1·60 1·00
98 60c. blue 80 40
99 142 1p. black . . . . 1·10 60
100 145 2p. blue . . . . 21·00 12·50
101 – 4p. mauve (No. 768c) . . 21·00 12·50
102 – 10p. brown (No. 769c) . . 21·00 12·50

1939. Air. Optd **Via Aerea Tanger**.
103 143 5c. brown 85 80
104 10c. green 85 80
105 15c. green 80 65
106 20c. violet 80 65
107 25c. mauve 80 65
108 30c. red . . . . 1·40 95
109 160a 40c. red . . . . 38·00
110 45c. red 40 40
111 50c. blue . . . . 80·00
112 60c. blue . . . . 80·00 16·00
113 142 1p. black . . . . 25·00
114 – 4p. mauve (No. 768c) . . 40·00 24·00
115 – 10p. brown (No. 769c) . . £110

1939. Air. Express Letter stamp optd **Via Aerea Tanger**.
116 E 145 20c. red . . . . 2·75 1·40

1939. Various fiscal types inscr "DERECHOS CONSULARES ESPANOLES" optd **Correo Tanger**.
117 50c. pink . . . . 17·00 17·00
118 1p. pink . . . . 4·25 4·25
119 2p. pink . . . . 4·25 4·25
120 5p. red and green . . . . . 4·75 4·25
121 10p. red and violet . . . . . 20·00 20·00

1939. Air. Various fiscal types inscr "DERECHOS CONSULARES ESPANOLES" optd **Correo Aereo Tanger**.
122 1p. blue . . . . 48·00 48·00
123 2p. blue . . . . 48·00 48·00
124 5p. blue . . . . 80·00 80·00
125 10p. blue . . . . 6·00 6·00

15 Moroccan Woman   16 Douglas DC-3

1948.
126 – 1c. green 10 10
127 – 2c. orange 10 10
128 – 5c. purple 10 10
129 – 10c. blue 10 10
130 – 20c. sepia 10 10
131 – 25c. green 10 10
132 – 30c. grey 25 10
133 – 45c. red 25 10
134 15 50c. red 25 10
135 – 75c. blue 50 10
136 – 90c. green 40 10
137 – 1p.35 red . . . . 1·75 30
138 15 2p. violet . . . . 3·25 30
139 – 10p. green . . . . 3·75 60
DESIGNS: 1, 2c. Woman's head facing right; 5, 25c. Palm tree; 10, 20c. Woman's head facing left; 30c., 1p.35, Old map of Tangier; 45c., 10p. Street scene; 75, 90c. Head of Moor.

1949. Air.
140 – 20c. brown 50 10
141 16 25c. red 50 10
142 – 35c. green 50 10
143 – 1p. violet . . . . 1·50 10
144 16 2p. green . . . . 2·50 30
145 – 10p. purple . . . . 3·50 1·10
DESIGNS: 20c., 1p. Lockheed Constellation and map; 35c., 10p. Boeing 377 Stratocruiser in clouds.

EXPRESS LETTER STAMPS

Express Letter Stamps of Spain overprinted.

1926. Red Cross. Optd **CORREO ESPANOL TANGER**.
E26 E 77 20c. black and blue . . 3·00 3·00

1933. No. E17 optd **MARRUECOS**.
EE57 145 20c. red . . . . 1·10 35

E 17 Courier

1949.
E146 E 17 25c. red 55 30

SPANISH SAHARA Pt. 9

Former Spanish territory on the north-west coast of Africa, previously called Rio de Oro. Later divided between Morocco and Mauritania.

100 centimos = 1 peseta.

1 Tuareg and Camel

1924.
1 1 5c. green . . . . 2·00 75
2 10c. green . . . . 2·00 75
3 15c. blue . . . . 2·00 75
4 20c. violet . . . . 2·00 1·10
5 25c. red . . . . 2·00 1·10
6 30c. brown . . . . 2·00 1·10
7 40c. blue . . . . 2·00 1·10
8 50c. orange . . . . 2·00 1·10
9 60c. purple . . . . 2·00 1·10
10 1p. red . . . . 10·00 5·75
11 4p. brown . . . . 48·00 29·00
12 10p. purple . . . . £110 90·00

1926. Red Cross stamps of Spain optd **SAHARA ESPANOL**.
13 – 5c. grey . . . . 8·00 8·00
14 – 10c. green . . . . 8·00 8·00
15 70 15c. violet . . . . 2·40 2·40
16 – 20c. purple . . . . 2·40 2·40
17 71 25c. red . . . . 2·40 2·40
18 70 30c. olive . . . . 2·40 2·40
19 – 40c. blue 20 20
20 – 50c. brown 20 20
21 71 60c. green 20 20
22 – 1p. red 20 20
23 – 4p. brown . . . . 2·40 2·40
24 71 10p. lilac . . . . 5·50 5·50

1929. Seville and Barcelona Exn stamps of Spain. Nos. 504/14, optd **SAHARA**.
25 5c. red 20 20
26 10c. green 20 20
27 15c. blue 20 20
28 20c. violet 20 20
29 25c. red 20 20
30 30c. brown 20 20
31 40c. blue 45 45
32 50c. orange 45 45
33 1p. grey . . . . 2·75 2·75
34 4p. red . . . . 20·00 20·00
35 10p. brown . . . . 38·00 38·00

1931. Optd **Republica Espanola**.
36 1 5c. green 60 60
37 10c. green 60 60
38 15c. blue 60 60
39 20c. violet 60 60
40 25c. red 75 60
41 30c. brown 75 60
42 40c. blue . . . . 3·25 95
43 50c. orange . . . . 3·25 2·20
44 60c. purple . . . . 3·25 2·20
45 1p. red . . . . 3·25 2·20
46 4p. brown . . . . 34·00 23·00
47 10p. purple . . . . 65·00 46·00

1941. Stamps of Spain optd **SAHARA ESPANOL**.
47a 181 1c. green . . . . 1·60 1·60
47b 182 2c. brown . . . . 1·60 1·60
48 183 5c. brown 45 45
49 10c. red . . . . 1·60 1·60
50 15c. green 45 45
51 196 20c. violet 45 45
52 25c. red . . . . 1·10 85
53 30c. blue . . . . 1·10 1·10
54 40c. green 45 45
55 50c. blue . . . . 5·50 1·20
56 70c. blue . . . . 3·75 2·00
57 1PTA. black . . . . . . 17·00 2·75
58 2PTAS. brown . . . . . . £100 65·00
59 4PTAS. red £225 £150
60 10PTS. brown £650 £250

6 Dorcas Gazelles   7 Ostriches

1943.
61 6 1c. mauve & brown (postage) 15 15
62 – 2c. blue and green 15 15
63 – 5c. blue and red 15 15
64 6 15c. green and myrtle . . . 15 15
65 – 20c. brown and mauve . . . 15 15
66 6 40c. mauve and purple . . . 15 15
67 – 45c. red and purple 20 20
68 – 75c. blue and indigo 20 20
69 6 1p. brown and red 70 70
70 – 3p. green and violet . . . . 1·30 1·30
71 – 10p. black and sepia . . . 22·00 20·00
DESIGNS—VERT: 2, 20, 45c., 3p. Camel caravan; 5, 75c., 10p. Camel troups.

72 7 5c. brown and red (air) . . . 20 15
73 – 25c. olive and green 20 15
74 7 50c. turquoise and blue . . . 20 15
75 – 1p. blue and mauve 20 15
76 7 1p.40 blue and green 20 15
77 – 2p. brown and purple . . . . 1·10 85
78 7 5p. mauve and brown . . . . 1·60 1·20
79 – 6p. green and blue . . . . . 23·00 17·00
DESIGN: 25c., 1, 2, 6p. Airplane and camels.

8 Boy carrying Lamb   9 Diego de Herrera

1950. Child Welfare.
80 8 50c.+10c. brown 20 20
81 1p.+25c. red . . . . 8·75 8·75
82 6p.50+1p.65 green . . . . . 4·75 4·75

1950. Air. Colonial Stamp Day.
83 9 5p. violet . . . . 2·00 2·00

9a Woman and Dove

9b General Franco

1951. Air. 500th Birth Anniv of Isabella the Catholic.
84 **9a** 5p. green . . . . 19·00 7·25

1951. Visit of General Franco.
85 **9b** 50c. orange 30 30
86 1p. brown 45 45
87 5p. turquoise . . . . 28·00 28·00

10 Dromedary and Calf

11 Native Woman

1951. Colonial Stamp Day.
88 **10** 5c.+5c. brown 20 20
89 10c.+5c. orange 20 20
90 60c.+15c. olive 35 35

1952. Child Welfare Fund.
91 **11** 5c.+5c. brown 20 20
92 50c.+10c. black 20 20
93 2p.+30c. blue . . . . 1·30 1·30

12 Morion, Sword and Banner

13 Head of Ostritch

1952. Air. 500th Birth Anniv of Ferdinand the Catholic.
94 **12** 5p. brown . . . . 22·00 7·25

1952. Colonial Stamp Day.
95 **13** 5c.+5c. brown 20 20
96 10c.+5c. red 20 20
97 60c.+15c. green 35 35

14 "Geography"

15 Woman Musician

1953. 75th Anniv of Royal Geographical Society.
98 **14** 5c. red 20 20
99 35c. green 20 20
100 60c. brown 20 20

1953. Child Welfare Fund. Inscr "PRO INFANCIA 1953".
101 **15** 5c.+5c. brown 20 20
102 – 10c.+5c. purple 20 20
103 **15** 15c. olive 20 20
104 – 60c. brown 20 20
DESIGN: 10, 60c. Native man musician.

16 Red Scorpionfish

1953. Colonial Stamp Day. Inscr "DIA DEL SELLO COLONIAL 1953".
105 **16** 5c.+5c. violet 20 20
106 – 10c.+5c. green 20 20
107 **16** 15c. olive 20 20
108 – 60c. orange 20 20
DESIGN—HORIZ: 10, 60c. Zebra seabreams.

17 Hurdlers

1954. Child Welfare Fund. Inscr "PRO INFANCIA 1954".
109 **17** 5c.+5c. brown 20 20
110 – 10c.+5c. violet 20 20
111 **17** 15c. green 20 20
112 – 60c. brown 20 20
DESIGN—VERT: 10, 60c. Native runner.

18 Atlantic Flyingfish

1954. Colonial Stamp Day. Inscr "DIA DEL SELLO COLONIAL 1954".
113 **18** 5c.+5c. red 20 20
114 – 10c.+5c. purple 20 20
115 **18** 15c. green 20 20
116 – 60c. brown 20 20
DESIGN—HORIZ: 10, 60c. Gilthead seabream.

19 E. Bonelli

1955. Birth Centenary of Bonelli (explorer).
117 **19** 10c.+5c. purple 20 20
118 – 25c.+10c. violet 20 20
119 **19** 50c. olive 20 20
DESIGN: 25c. Bonelli and felucca.

20 Scimitar Oryx

21 "Antirrhinum ramosissimum"

1955. Colonial Stamp Day. Inscr "DIA DEL SELLO COLONIAL 1955".
120 **20** 5c.+5c. brown 20 20
121 – 15c.+5c. bistre 20 20
122 **20** 70c. green 20 20
DESIGN: 15c. Scimitar oryx's head.

1956. Child Welfare Fund. Inscr "PRO-INFANCIA 1956".
123 **21** 5c.+5c. olive 20 20
124 – 15c.+5c. ochre 20 20
125 **21** 20c. turquoise 20 20
126 – 50c. brown 20 20
DESIGN: 15, 50c. "Sesuvium portulacastrum" (wrongly inscr "Sesiviun").

22 Arms of Aaiun and Native on Camel

23 Dromedaries

1956. Colonial Stamp Day. Inscr "DIA DEL SELLO 1956".
127 **22** 5c.+5c. black and violet . . 20 20
128 – 15c.+5c. green and ochre 20 20
129 **22** 70c. brown and green . . . 20 20
DESIGN—VERT: 15c. Arms of Villa Cisneros and native chief.

1957. Animals.
130 **23** 5c. violet 15 15
131 – 15c. ochre 15 15
132 – 50c. brown 20 15
133 **23** 70c. green 60 15
134 – 80c. turquoise 60 15
135 – 1p.80 mauve 75 30
DESIGNS: 15, 80c. Ostrich; 50c., 1p.80, Dorcas gazelle.

24 Golden Eagle

25 Head of Striped Hyena

1957. Child Welfare Fund. Inscr "PRO-INFANCIA 1957".
136 **24** 5c.+5c. brown 20 20
137 – 15c.+5c. bistre 20 20
138 **24** 70c. green 20 20
DESIGN: 15c. Tawny eagle in flight.

1957. Colonial Stamp Day. Inscr "DIA DEL SELLO 1957".
139 **25** 10c.+5c. purple 20 20
140 – 15c.+5c. ochre 20 20
141 **25** 20c. green 20 20
142 – 70c. myrtle 20 20
DESIGN: 15, 70c. Striped hyena.

26 White Stork and Arms of Valencia and Aaiun

27 Cervantes

1958. Aid for Valencia.
143 **26** 10c.+5c. brown 20 20
144 15c.+10c. ochre 20 20
145 50c.+10c. brown 20 20

1958. Child Welfare Fund. Inscr "1958".
146 **27** 10c.+5c. brown & chest . . 20 20
147 – 15c.+5c. myrtle & orange 20 20
148 – 20c. green and brown . . . 20 20
149 **27** 70c. blue and green 20 20
DESIGNS—VERT: 15c. Don Quixote and Sancho Panza on horseback. HORIZ: 20c. Don Quixote and the lion.

28 Hoopoe Lark

29 Lope de Vega (author)

1958. Colonial Stamp Day. Inscr "1958".
150 **28** 10c.+5c. red 20 20
151 – 25c.+10c. violet 20 20
152 – 50c.+10c. olive 20 20
DESIGNS—HORIZ: 25c. Hoopoe lark feeding young. VERT: 50c. Fulvous babbler.

1959. Child Welfare Fund. Inscr "PRO INFANCIA 1959".
153 **29** 10c.+5c. olive and brown 20 20
154 – 15c.+5c. brown and bistre 20 20
155 – 20c. sepia and green . . . 20 20
156 **29** 70c. myrtle and green . . . 20 20
DESIGNS—Characters from the comedy "The Star of Seville": 15c. Spanish lady; 20c. Caballero.

30 Grey Heron

31 Sahara Postman

1959. Birds.
157 **30** 25c. violet 70 15
158 – 50c. green 15 15
159 – 75c. sepia 15 15
160 **30** 1p. red 15 15
161 – 1p.50 green 20 15
162 – 2p. purple 70 15
163 **30** 3p. blue 75 20
164 – 5p. brown . . . . 1·30 20
165 – 10p. olive . . . . 7·00 3·75
DESIGNS: 50c., 1p.50, 5p. Northern sparrow hawk; 75c., 2, 10p. Herring gull.

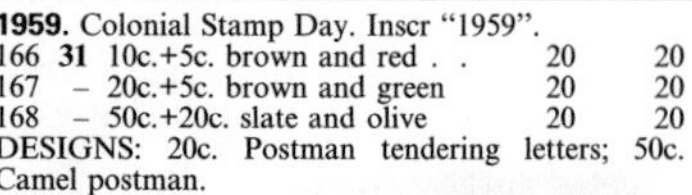
1959. Colonial Stamp Day. Inscr "1959".
166 **31** 10c.+5c. brown and red . . 20 20
167 – 20c.+5c. brown and green 20 20
168 – 50c.+20c. slate and olive 20 20
DESIGNS: 20c. Postman tendering letters; 50c. Camel postman.

32 F. de Quevedo (writer)

33 Leopard

1960. Child Welfare Fund. Inscr "PRO-INFANCIA 1960".
169 **32** 10c.+5c. purple 20 20
170 – 15c.+5c. bistre 20 20
171 – 35c. green 20 20
172 **32** 80c. turquoise 20 20
DESIGNS—VERT: (representing Quevedo's works): 15c. Winged railway wheel and hour-glass; 25c. Man in plumed hat wearing cloak and sword.

1960. Stamp Day. Inscr "1960".
173 **33** 10c.+5c. mauve 20 20
174 – 20c.+5c. myrtle 20 20
175 – 30c.+10c. brown 20 20
176 – 50c.+20c. brown 20 20
DESIGNS: 20c. Fennec fox; 30c. Golden eagle defying leopard; 50c. Red fox.

34 Houbara Bustard

35 Cameleer and Airplane

1961.
177 **34** 25c. violet 15 15
178 – 50c. brown 15 15
179 **34** 75c. dull purple 15 15
180 – 1p. red 15 15
181 **34** 1p.50 green 15 15
182 – 2p. mauve 60 15
183 **34** 3p. blue 80 20
184 – 5p. brown 95 25
185 **34** 10p. olive . . . . 2·50 1·40
DESIGN: 50c., 1, 2, 5p. Feral rock doves.

1961. Air.
186 **35** 25p. sepia . . . . 2·10 1·10

36 Dorcas Gazelle

37

1961. Child Welfare. Inscr "PRO-INFANCIA 1961".
187 **36** 10c.+5c. red 20 20
188 – 25c.+10c. violet 20 20
189 **36** 80c.+20c. green 20 20
DESIGN: 25c. One dorcas gazelle.

1961. 25th Anniv of Gen. Franco as Head of State.
190 – 25c. grey 20 20
191 **37** 50c. olive 20 20
192 – 70c. green 20 20
193 **37** 1p. orange 20 20
DESIGNS—VERT: 25c. Map; 70c. Aaiun Chapel.

38 A. Fernandez de Lugo

39 "Neurada procumbres linn"

1961. Stamp Day. Inscr "DIA DEL SELLO 1961".
194 **38** 10c.+5c. salmon 20 20
195 – 25c.+10c. plum 20 20
196 **38** 30c.+10c. brown 20 20
197 – 1p.+10c. orange 20 20
PORTRAIT: 25c., 1p. D. de Herrera.

1962. Flowers.

198 **39** 25c. violet 15 15
199 – 50c. sepia 15 15
200 – 70c. green 15 15
201 **39** 1p. orange 15 15
202 – 1p.50 turquoise 30 15
203 – 2p. purple 90 15
204 **39** 3p. blue . . . . 1·70 25
205 – 10p. olive . . . . 3·75 1·20

FLOWERS: 50c., 1p.50, 10p. "Anabasis articulata moq"; 70c., 2p. "Euphorbia resinifera".

40 Hoefler's Butterflyfish   **42** Seville Cathedral

41 Goats

1962. Child Welfare.

206 **40** 25c. violet 20 20
207 – 50c. green 20 20
208 **40** 1p. brown 20 20

DESIGN—HORIZ: 50c. Dungat groupers.

1962. Stamp Day.

209 **41** 15c. green 20 20
210 – 35c. purple 20 20
211 **41** 1p. brown 20 20

DESIGN: 35c. Sheep.

1963. Seville Flood Relief.

212 **42** 50c. olive 20 20
213 1p. brown 20 20

43 Cameleer and Camel   **44** Dove in Hands

1963. Child Welfare. Inscr "PRO-INFANCIA 1963".

214 – 25c. violet 20 20
215 **43** 50c. grey 20 20
216 – 1p. red 20 20

DESIGN: 25c., 1p. Three camels.

1963. "For Barcelona".

217 **44** 50c. turquoise 20 20
218 1p. brown 20 20

45 John Dory

1964. Stamp Day. Inscr "DIA DEL SELLO 1963".

219 **45** 25c. violet 20 20
220 – 50c. olive 20 20
221 **45** 1p. brown 20 20

FISH—VERT: 50c. Plain bonito.

46 Striped Hawk Moth   **47** Mounted Dromedary and Microphone

1964. Child Welfare.

222 **46** 25c. violet 20 20
223 – 50c. olive 20 20
224 **46** 1p. red 20 20

DESIGN—VERT: 50c. Goat moths.

1964.

225 **47** 25c. purple 15 15
226 – 50c. olive 15 15
227 – 70c. green 15 15
228 **47** 1p. purple 15 15
229 – 1p.50 turquoise 15 15
230 – 2p. turquoise 20 15
231 – 3p. blue 20 15
232 – 10p. lake . . . . 1·30 75

DESIGNS: 50c., 1p.50, 3p. Flute-player; 70c., 2, 10p. Women drummer.

48 Barbary Ground Squirrel

1964. Stamp Day.

233 – 50c. olive 20 20
234 **48** 1p. lake 20 20
235 – 1p.50 green 20 20

DESIGN—VERT: 50c., 1p.50, Eurasian red squirrel eating.

49 Doctor tending Patient, and Hospital

1965. 25th Anniv of End of Spanish Civil War.

236 – 50c. olive 20 20
237 **49** 1p. red 20 20
238 – 1p.50 blue 20 20

DESIGNS—VERT: 50c. Saharan woman; 1p.50, Desert installation and cameleer.

50 "Anthia sexmaculata" (ground beetle)   **51** Handball

1965. Child Welfare. Insects.

239 **50** 50c. blue 20 20
240 – 1p. green 20 20
241 **50** 1p.50 brown 20 20
242 – 3p. blue 90 90

INSECTS—VERT: 1, 3p. "Blepharopsis mendica" (praying mantis).

1965. Stamp Day.

243 **51** 50c. red 20 20
244 – 1p. purple 20 20
245 **51** 1p.50 blue 20 20

DESIGN: 1p. Arms of Spanish Sahara.

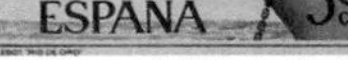

52 Bows of "Rio de Oro"

1966. Child Welfare.

246 **52** 50c. olive 20 20
247 1p. brown 20 20
248 – 1p.50 green 20 20

DESIGN: 1p.50, Freighter "Fuerta Ventura".

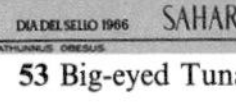

53 Big-eyed Tuna   **54** Fig

1966. Stamp Day.

249 **53** 10c. blue and yellow . . . 20 20
250 – 40c. grey and salmon . . 20 20
251 **53** 1p.50 brown and green . . 20 20
252 – 4p. purple and green . . 20 20

DESIGN—VERT: 40c., 4p. Ocean sunfish.

1967. Child Welfare.

253 **54** 10c. yellow and blue . . . 20 20
254 – 40c. purple and green . . 20 20
255 **54** 1p.50 yellow and green . . 20 20
256 – 4p. orange and blue . . . 20 20

DESIGN: 40c., 4p. Lupin.

55 Quay, Aaiun

1967. Inauguration of Sahara Ports.

257 **55** 1p.50 brown and blue . . . 15 15
258 – 4p. ochre and blue 20 20

DESIGN: 4p. Port of Villa Cisneros.

56 Ruddy Shelduck

1968. Stamp Day.

259 **56** 1p. brown and green . . . 20 20
260 – 1p.50 mauve and black . . 20 20
261 – 3p.50 lake and brown . . 30 30

DESIGNS—VERT: 1p.50, Greater flamingo. HORIZ: 3p.50, Rufous scrub robin.

56a Scorpio (scorpion)   **57** Dove, and Stamp within Posthorn

1968. Child Welfare. Signs of the Zodiac.

262 **56a** 1p. mauve on yellow . . . 20 20
263 – 1p.50 brown on pink . . 20 20
264 – 2p.50 violet on yellow . . 30 30

DESIGNS: 1p.50, Capricorn (goat); 2p.50, Virgo (virgin).

1968. Stamp Day.

265 **57** 1p. blue and purple 20 20
266 – 1p.50 green and light green 20 20
267 – 2p.50 blue and orange . . 30 30

DESIGNS: 1p.50, Postal handstamp, stamps and letter; 2p.50, Saharan postman.

58 Head of Dorcas Gazelle

1969. Child Welfare.

268 **58** 1p. brown and black . . . 20 20
269 – 1p.50 brown and black . . 20 20
270 – 2p.50 brown and black . . 20 20
271 – 6p. brown and black . . . 35 35

DESIGNS: 1p.50, Dorcas gazelle tending young; 2p.50, Dorcas gazelle and camel; 6p. Dorcas gazelle leaping.

59 Woman beating Drum   **61** Dorcas Gazelle and Arms of El Aaiun

60 "Grammodes boisdeffrei" (moth)

1960. Stamp Day.

272 **59** 50c. brown and bistre . . . 20 20
273 – 1p.50 turquoise and green 20 20
274 – 2p. blue and brown 20 20
275 – 25p. brown and green . . . 90 90

DESIGNS—VERT: 1p.50, Man playing flute. HORIZ: 2p. Drum and mounted cameleer; 25p. Flute.

1970. Child Welfare. As T **58**.

276 50c. ochre and blue 20 20
277 2p. brown and blue 20 20
278 2p.50 ochre and blue . . . 20 20
279 6p. ochre and blue 35 35

DESIGNS: 50c. Fennec fox; 2p. Fennec fox walking; 2p.50, Head of fennec fox; 6p. Fennec fox family.

1970. Stamp Day. Butterflies. Multicoloured.

280 50c. Type **60** 20 20
281 1p. Type **60** 20 20
282 2p. African monarch 20 20
283 5p. As 2p. 30 30
284 8p. Spurge hawk moth . . . 55 55

1971. Child Welfare.

285 **61** 1p. multicoloured 20 20
286 – 2p. green and olive 20 20
287 – 5p. blue, brown and grey 30 30
288 – 25p. green, grey and blue 90 90

DESIGNS—VERT: 25p. Smara Mosque. HORIZ: 2p. Tourist inn, Aaiun; 5p. Assembly House, Aaiun.

63 Trumpeter Finch

1971. Stamp Day. Multicoloured.

290 1p.50 Type **63** 20 20
291 2p. Type **63** 20 20
292 5p. Cream-coloured courser 30 30
293 24p. Lanner falcon 90 90

64 Seated Woman   **65** Tuareg Woman

1972. Saharan Nomads.

294 **64** 1p. black, pink and blue 20 20
295 – 1p.50 slate, lilac and brown 20 20
296 – 2p. black, flesh and green 20 20
297 **64** 5p. purple, olive and green 20 20
298 – 8p. violet, green and black 35 20
299 – 10p. green, grey and black 35 20
300 – 12p. multicoloured 35 30
301 – 15p. multicoloured 35 30
302 – 24p. multicoloured 90 55

DESIGNS: 1p.50, 2p. Squatting nomad; 8, 10p. Head of nomad; 12p. Woman with bangles; 15p. Nomad with rifle; 24p. Woman displaying trinkets.

1972. Child Welfare. Multicoloured.

303 8p. Type **65** 35 35
304 12p. Tuareg elder 35 35

66 Mother and Child

1972. Stamp Day. Multicoloured.

305 4p. Type **66** 30 30
306 15p. Nomad 35 35

67 Sahara Desert

1973. Child Welfare. Multicoloured.

307 2p. Type **67** 20 20
308 7p. City Gate, El Aaiun . . . 35 35

68 Villa Cisneros

1973. Stamp Day. Multicoloured.

309	2p. Type **68**	20	20
310	7p. Tuareg (vert)	30	20

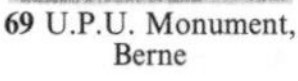

69 U.P.U. Monument, Berne

70 Archway, Smara Mosque

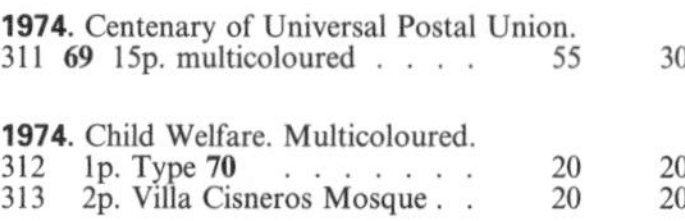

1974. Centenary of Universal Postal Union.

311 **69**	15p. multicoloured	55	30

1974. Child Welfare. Multicoloured.

312	1p. Type **70**	20	20
313	2p. Villa Cisneros Mosque	20	20

71 Desert Eagle Owl

1974. Stamp Day. Multicoloured.

314	2p. Type **71**	20	20
315	5p. Lappet-faced vulture	30	30

72 "Espana" Emblem and Spanish Sahara Stamp

74 Tuareg Elder

73 Desert Conference

1975. "Espana 75" International Stamp Exhibition, Madrid.

316 **72**	8p. yellow, blue and black	35	35

1975. Child Welfare. Multicoloured.

317	1p.50 Type **73**	20	20
318	3p. Desert oasis	20	20

1975.

319 **74**	3p. purple, green and black	20	20

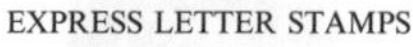

EXPRESS LETTER STAMPS

1943. Design as No. 63, inscr "URGENTE".

E80	25c. red and myrtle	90	65

E 62 Despatch-rider

1971.

E289 **E 62**	10p. brown and red	55	55

SPANISH WEST AFRICA Pt. 9

100 centimos = 1 peseta.

Issues for use in Ifni and Spanish Sahara.

1 Native

2 Isabella the Catholic

1949. 75th Anniv of U.P.U.

1 **1**	4p. green	2·00	90

1949. Air. Colonial Stamp Day.

2 **2**	5p. brown	1·70	90

3 Tents

1950.

3 **3**	2c. brown	15	15
4 –	5c. violet	15	15
5 –	10c. blue	15	15
6 –	15c. black	15	15
7 **3**	25c. brown	15	15
8 –	30c. yellow	15	15
9 –	40c. olive	15	15
10 –	45c. red	15	15
11 **3**	50c. orange	15	15
12 –	75c. blue	15	15
13 –	90c. green	20	15
14 –	1p. grey	20	15
15 **3**	1p.35 violet	60	45
16 –	2p. sepia	1·10	85
17 –	5p. mauve	11·00	3·00
18 **3**	10p. brown	24·00	20·00

DESIGNS: 5, 30, 75c., 2p. Palm trees, Lake Tinzgarrentz; 10, 40, 90c., 5p. Camels and irrigation; 15, 45c., 1p. Camel transport.

8 Camel Train

1951. Air.

19 –	25c. yellow	15	15
20 **8**	50c. mauve	15	15
21 –	1p. green	20	15
22 –	2p. blue	60	15
23 **8**	3p.25 violet	1·30	1·00
24 –	5p. sepia	13·00	3·25
25 –	10p. red	27·00	19·00

DESIGNS: 25c., 2, 10p. Desert camp; 1, 5p. Four camels.

EXPRESS LETTER STAMP

E 10 Port Tilimenzo

1951.

E26 **E 10**	25c. red	30	25

SRI LANKA Pt. 1

Ceylon became a republic within the British Commonwealth on 22 May 1972 and changed its name to Sri Lanka (= "Resplendent Island").

100 cents = 1 rupee.

208 National Flower and Mountain of the Illustrious Foot

1972. Inaug of Republic of Sri Lanka.

591 **208**	15c. multicoloured	30	30

209 Map of World with Buddhist Flag

1972. 10th World Fellowship of Buddhists Conf.

592 **209**	5c. multicoloured	30	60

210 Book Year Emblem

211 Emperor Angelfish

1972. International Book Year.

593 **210**	20c. orange and brown	20	50

1972. Fishes. Multicoloured.

594	2c. Type **211**	10	1·25
595	5c. Green chromide	10	1·25
596	30c. Skipjack tuna	1·25	30
597	2r. Black ruby barb	3·50	5·25

212 Memorial Hall

1973. Opening of Bandaranaike Memorial Hall.

598 **212**	15c. cobalt and blue	30	30

213 King Vessantara giving away his Children

1973. Rock and Temple Paintings. Mult.

599	35c. Type **213**	35	10
600	50c. The Prince and the grave-digger	40	10
601	90c. Bearded old man	60	85
602	1r.55 Two female figures	70	2·00
MS603	115 × 141 mm. Nos. 599/602	3·00	3·00

214 Bandaranaike Memorial Conference Hall

215 Prime Minster Bandaranaike

1974. 20th Commonwealth Parliamentary Conf, Colombo.

604 **214**	85c. multicoloured	30	30

1974.

605 **215**	15c. multicoloured	15	10

216 "U.P.U." and "100"

1974. Centenary of U.P.U.

606 **216**	50c. multicoloured	1·00	75

217 Sri Lanka Parliament Building

1975. Inter-Parliamentary Meeting.

607 **217**	1r. multicoloured	30	50

218 Sir Ponnambalam Ramanathan (politician)

219 D. J. Wimalasurendra (engineer)

1975. Ramanathan Commemoration.

608 **218**	75c. multicoloured	30	80

1975. Wimalasurendra Commemoration.

609 **219**	75c. black and blue	30	80

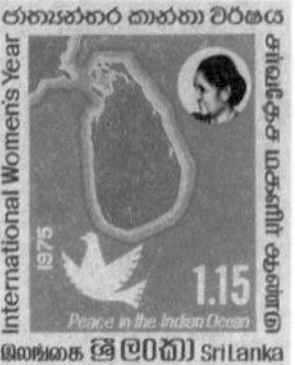
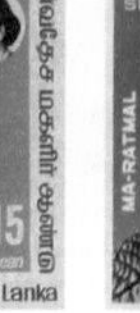

220 Mrs. Bandaranaike, Map and Dove

221 Ma-ratmal

1975. International Women's Year.

610 **220**	1r.15 multicoloured	2·25	1·25

1976. Indigenous Flora. Multicoloured.

611	25c. Type **221**	10	10
612	50c. Binara	10	10
613	75c. Daffodil orchid	15	15
614	10r. Diyapara	3·00	4·50
MS615	153 × 153 mm. Nos. 611/14	12·00	16·00

222 Mahaweli Dam

1976. Mahaweli River Diversion.

616 **222**	85c. turquoise, bl & azure	30	1·00

223 Dish Aerial

1976. Opening of Satellite Earth Station, Padukka.

617 **223**	1r. multicoloured	65	1·00

224 Conception of the Buddha

1976. Vesak. Multicoloured.

618	5c. Type **224**	10	90
619	10c. King Suddhodana and the astrologers	10	90
620	1r.50 The astrologers being entertained	90	95
621	2r. The Queen in a palanquin	1·00	95
622	2r.25 Royal procession	1·10	1·90
623	5r. Birth of the Buddha	1·60	3·25
MS624	161 × 95 mm. Nos 618/23	9·50	13·00

Nos. 618/23 show paintings from the Dambava Temple.

225 Blue Sapphire

1976. Gems of Sri Lanka. Multicoloured.

625	60c. Type **225**	4·50	30
626	1r.15 Cat's eye	7·00	1·50
627	2r. Star sapphire	8·00	3·25
628	5r. Ruby	11·00	11·00
MS629	152 × 152 mm. Nos. 625/8	35·00	26·00

226 Prime Minister Mrs. S. Bandaranaike
227 Statue of Liberty

1976. Non-aligned Summit Conf, Colombo.
630 **226** 1r.15 multicoloured . . . 25 50
631 2r. multicoloured . . . . 40 1·00

1976. Bicent of American Revolution.
632 **227** 2r.25 blue and indigo . . 65 1·50

228 Bell, Early Telephone and Telephone Lines
229 Maitreya (pre-carnate Buddha)

1976. Centenary of Telephone.
633 **228** 1r. multicoloured 60 20

1976. Centenary of Colombo Museum. Mult.
634 50c. Type **229** 25 15
635 1r. Sundara Murti Swami (Tamil psalmist) 30 30
636 5r. Tara (goddess) . . . . . 2·25 4·50

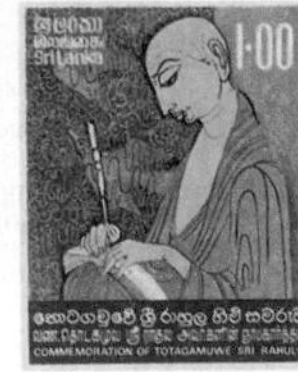

230 Kandyan Crown
231 Sri Rahula Thero (poet)

1977. Regalia of the Kings of Kandy. Mult.
637 1r. Type **230** 50 40
638 2r. Throne and footstool . . 1·10 3·25

1977. Sri Rahula Commemoration.
639 **231** 1r. multicoloured . . . . 75 1·00

232 Sir Ponnambalam Arunachalam
233 Brass Lamps

1977. Sir Ponnambalam Arunachalam (social reformer) Commemoration.
640 **232** 1r. multicoloured . . . . 50 1·00

1977. Handicrafts. Multicoloured.
641 20c. Type **233** 15 15
642 25c. Jewellery box 15 15
643 50c. Caparisoned elephant . . 30 20
644 5r. Mask . . . . 1·60 3·25
MS645 205 × 89 mm. Nos. 641/4 3·50 4·25

234 Siddi Lebbe (author and educationist)
235 Girl Guide

1977. Siddi Lebbe Commemoration.
646 **234** 1r. multicoloured . . . . 30 1·00

1977. 60th Anniv of Sri Lanka Girl Guides Association.
647 **235** 75c. multicoloured 85 30

236 Parliament Building and "Wheel of Life"
237 Youths Running

1978. Election of New President.
648 **236** 15c. gold, green & emerald 20 10
For similar design in a smaller format, see Nos. 680/c.

1978. National Youth Service Council.
649 **237** 15c. multicoloured 30 70

238 Prince Siddhartha's Renunciation

1978. Vesak. Rock Carvings from Borobudur Temple.
650 **238** 15c. buff, brown and blue 75 30
651 – 50c. buff, brown and blue 1·00 1·50
DESIGN: 50c. Prince Siddhartha shaving his hair.

1978. Surch.
652 5c. on 90c. Bearded old man (No. 601) . . . . 2·00 3·25
653 10c. on 35c. Type **213** . . . 50 50
654 25c. on 15c. Type **215** . . . 4·25 4·25
655 25c. on 15c. Type **236** . . . 4·25 4·25
656 25c. on 15c. Type **237** . . . 4·25 4·25
657 1r. on 1r.55 Two female figures (No. 602) . . . . . 1·25 45

240 Veera Puran Appu
241 "Troides helena"

1978. 130th Death Anniv of Veera Puran Appu (revolutionary).
658 **240** 15c. multicoloured 20 35

1978. Butterflies. Multicoloured.
659 25c. Type **241** 55 10
660 50c. "Cethosia nietneri" . . . 1·00 10
661 5r. "Kallima horsfieldi" . . . 1·75 1·25
662 10r. "Papilio polymnestor" . . 1·75 2·50
MS663 203 × 147 mm. Nos. 659/62 11·00 7·00

1979. No. 486 of Ceylon surch **SRI LANKA 15**.
664 15c. on 10c. green . . . . . 2·75 1·75

243 Prince Danta and Princess Hema Mala bringing the Sacred Tooth Relic from Kalinga
244 Piyadasa Sirisena

1979. Vesak. Kelaniya Temple Paintings. Mult.
665 25c. Type **243** 10 10
666 1r. Theri Sanghamitta bringing the Bodhi Tree branch to Sri Lanka . . . 15 15
667 10r. King Kirti Sri Rajasinghe offering fan of authority to the Sangha Raja . . . . 1·50 2·75
MS668 120 × 80 mm. Nos. 665/7 2·50 3·75

1979. Piyadasa Sirisena (writer) Commem.
669 **244** 1r.25 multicoloured . . . 40 40

245 Wrestlers
246 Dudley Senanayake

1979. Wood Carvings from Embekke Temple.
670 **245** 20r. brown, ochre & green 1·00 1·25
671 – 50r. agate, yellow & green 1·50 2·75
DESIGN: 50r. Dancer.

1979. Dudley Senanayake (former Prime Minister) Commemoration.
672 **246** 1r.25 green 15 20

247 Mother with Child

1979. International Year of the Child. Mult.
673 5c. Type **247** 10 10
674 3r. Superimposed heads of children of different races 40 1·10
675 5r. Children playing . . . . 50 1·40

248 Ceylon 1857 6d. Stamp and Sir Rowland Hill

1979. Death Centenary of Sir Rowland Hill.
676 **248** 3r. multicoloured . . . . 30 1·25

249 Conference Emblem and Parliament Building

1979. International Conference of Parliamentarians on Population and Development, Colombo.
677 **249** 2r. multicoloured . . . . 70 1·50

250 Airline Emblem on Aircraft Tail-fin
251 Coconut Tree

1979. Inauguration of "Airlanka" Airline.
678 **250** 3r. black, blue and red . . 80 1·75

1979. 10th Anniv of Asian and Pacific Coconut Community.
679 **251** 2r. multicoloured . . . . 1·00 1·75

1979. As No. 648, but 20 × 24 mm.
680 **236** 25c. gold, green and emerald 30 20
680a 50c. gold, green and emerald . . . . 2·50 10
680b 60c. gold, green and emerald . . . . 9·00 1·25
680c 75c. gold, green and emerald 10 10

252 Swami Vipulananda
253 Inscription and Crescent

1979. Swami Vipulananda (philosopher) Commem.
681 **252** 1r.25 multicoloured . . . 30 60

1979. 1500th Anniv of Hegira (Mohammedan religion).
682 **253** 3r.75 black, deep green and green . . . . . . 35 2·00

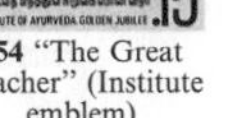

254 "The Great Teacher" (Institute emblem)
255 Ceylon Blue Magpie

1979. 50th Anniv of Institute of Ayurveda (school of medicine).
683 **254** 15c. multicoloured 30 70

1979. Birds (1st series). Multicoloured.
684 10c. Type **255** . . . . 10 1·00
685 15c. Ceylon hanging parrot 1·00 10
686 75c. Ceylon whistling thrush 15 15
687 1r. Ceylon spurfowl 15 15
688 5r. Yellow-fronted barbet . . 75 1·75
689 10r. Yellow-tufted bulbul . . 75 1·75
MS690 151 × 151 mm. Nos. 684/9 5·50 6·50
See also Nos. 827/30, 985/8 and 1242/5.

256 Rotary International Emblem and Map of Sri Lanka
257 A. Ratnayake

1980. 75th Anniv of Rotary International and 50th Anniv of Sri Lanka Rotary Movement.
691 **256** 1r.50 multicoloured . . . 70 2·00

1980. 80th Birth Anniv of A. Ratnayake (politician).
692 **257** 1r.25 green 20 30

1980. No. 680 surch **.35**.
693 **236** 35c. on 25c. gold, green and emerald 15 15

259 Tank and Stupa (symbols of Buddhist culture)
260 Colonel Olcott

1980. 60th Anniv of All Ceylon Buddhist Congress. Multicoloured.
694 10c. Type **259** . . . . 25 1·50
695 35c. Bo-leaf wheel and fan 25 20

1980. Centenary of Arrival of Colonel Olcott (campaigner for Buddhism).
696 **260** 2r. multicoloured . . . . 80 1·75

261 Patachara's Journey through Forest
262 George E. de Silva

1980. Vesak. Details from Temple Paintings, Purvaramaya, Kataluwa. Multicoloured.
697 35c. Type **261** 30 15
698 1r.60 Patachara crossing river 1·25 2·50

1980. George E. de Silva (politician) Commem.
699 **262** 1r.60 multicoloured . . . 30 30

263 Dalada Maligawa

1980. UNESCO—Sri Lanka Cultural Triangle Project.
700 **263** 35c. claret 15 40
701 – 35c. grey 15 40
702 – 35c. red 15 40

703 – 1r.60 olive . . . . 45 1·10
704 – 1r.60 green . . . . 45 1·10
705 – 1r.60 brown . . . . . . 45 1·10
MS706 215 × 115 mm. Nos. 700/5 1·40 3·25
DESIGNS: No. 701, Dambulla; 702, Alahana Pirivena; 703, Jetavanarama; 704, Abhayagiri; 705, Sigiri.

264 Co-operation Symbols

266 The Holy Family

265 Lanka Mahila Samiti Emblem

1980. 50th Anniv of Co-operative Department.
707 **264** 20c. multicoloured 10 30

1980. 50th Anniv of Lanka Mahila Samiti (Rural Women's Movement).
708 **265** 35c. violet, red and yellow 15 65

1980. Christmas. Multicoloured.
709 35c. Type **266** 10 10
710 3r.75 The Three Wise Men 60 1·75
MS711 125 × 75 mm. Nos. 709/10 1·25 2·00

267 Colombo Public Library

1980. Opening of Colombo Public Library.
712 **267** 35c. multicoloured 10 10

268 Flag of Walapane Disawa

269 Fishing Cat

1980. Ancient Flags.
713 **268** 10c. black, green & purple 10 10
714 – 25c. black, yellow & purple 10 10
715 – 1r.60 black, yellow & purple 15 20
716 – 20r. black, yellow & purple . . . . 85 2·50
MS717 215 × 140 mm. Nos. 713/16 1·00 3·00
DESIGNS: 25c. Flag of the Gajanayaka Huduhumpola, Kandy; 1r.60, Sinhala royal flag; 20r. Sinhala royal flag, Ratnapura.

1981. Animals. Multicoloured.
718 2r.50 on 1r.60 Type **269** . . 25 15
719 3r. on 1r.50 Golden palm civet 25 20
720 4r. on 2r. Indian-spotted chevrotain 25 30
721 5r. on 3r.75 Rusty-spotted cat 35 45
MS722 165 × 89 mm. Nos. 718/21 1·00 2·50
Nos. 718/21 are previously unissued stamps surcharged as in T **269**.
For stamps with revised face values see Nos. 780/3.

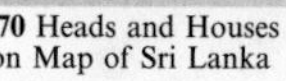

270 Heads and Houses on Map of Sri Lanka

271 Sri Lanka Light Infantry Regimental Badge

1981. Population and Housing Census.
723 **270** 50c. multicoloured . . . . 75 1·25

1981. Centenary of Sri Lanka Light Infantry.
724 **271** 2r. multicoloured . . . . 1·00 1·50

272 Panel from "The Great Stupa" in Honour of the Buddha, Sanci, India, 1st-century A.D.

274 Rev. Polwatte Sri Buddadatta

273 St. John Baptist de la Salle

1981. Vesak.
725 **272** 35c. black, dp green & green 10 10
726 – 50c. multicoloured 10 10
727 – 7r. black and pink . . . . 1·75 4·00
MS728 147 × 108mm. Nos. 725/7 3·50 3·75
DESIGNS: 50c. Silk banner representing a Bodhisattva from "Thousand Buddhas", Tun-Huang, Central Asia; 7r. Bodhisattva from Fondukistan, Afghanistan.

1981. 300th Anniv of De La Salle Brothers (Religious Order of the Brothers of the Christian Schools).
729 **273** 2r. pink, light blue & blue 1·50 2·25

1981. National Heroes.
730 **274** 50c. brown . . . . 60 1·25
731 – 50c. pink . . . . 60 1·25
732 – 50c. mauve . . . . 60 1·25
DESIGNS: No. 731, Rev. Mohottiwatte Gunananda; 732, Dr. Gnanaprakasar (each a scholar, writer and Buddhist campaigner).

275 Dr. Al-Haj T. B. Jayah

276 Dr. N. M. Perera

1981. Dr. Al-Haj T. B. Jayah (statesman) Commemoration.
733 **275** 50c. green . . . . 70 1·25

1981. Dr. N. M. Perera (campaigner for social reform) Commemoration.
734 **276** 50c. red . . . . 70 1·25

277 Stylized Disabled Person and Globe

1981. International Year for Disabled Persons.
735 **277** 2r. red, black and grey . . 1·10 2·00

278 Hand placing Vote into Ballot Box

1981. 50th Anniv of Universal Franchise. Mult.
736 50c. Type **278** 25 15
737 7r. Ballot box and people forming map of Sri Lanka (vert) . . . . 1·75 3·00

279 T. W. Rhys Davids (founder)

1981. Centenary of Pali Text Society.
738 **279** 35c. stone, dp brown & brown 70 30

280 Federation Emblem and "25"

1981. 25th Anniv of All-Ceylon Buddhist Students' Federation.
739 **280** 2r. black, yellow and red 1·00 1·00

281 "Plan for Happiness"

282 Dove Symbol with Acupuncture Needle and "Yin-Yang" (Chinese universe duality emblem)

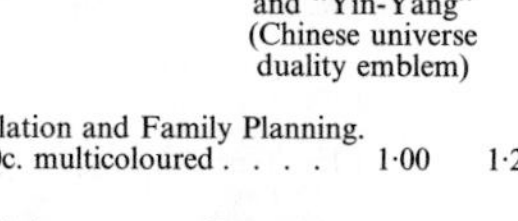

1981. Population and Family Planning.
740 **281** 50c. multicoloured . . . . 1·00 1·25

1981. World Acupuncture Congress.
741 **282** 2r. black, yellow & orange 2·75 3·50

283 Union and Sri Lanka Flags

1981. Royal Visit.
742 **283** 50c. multicoloured 50 25
743 5r. multicoloured . . . . 1·75 4·00
MS744 165 × 90 mm. Nos. 742/3 2·25 4·00

284 "Conserve our Forests"

285 Sir James Peiris

1981. Forest Conservation.
745 **284** 35c. multicoloured 15 10
746 – 50c. brown and stone . . 20 20
747 – 5r. multicoloured . . . . 1·90 3·75
MS748 180 × 90 mm. Nos. 745/7 1·50 3·75
DESIGNS: 50c. "Plant a tree"; 5r. Jak (tree).

1981. Birth Centenary of Sir James Peiris (politician).
749 **285** 50c. brown . . . . 60 1·00

286 F. R. Senanayaka

287 Philip Gunawardhane

1982. Birth Centenary of F. R. Senanayaka (national hero).
750 **286** 50c. brown . . . . 70 1·25

1982. 10th Death Anniv of Philip Gunawardhane (politician).
751 **287** 50c. red . . . . 70 1·25

288 Department of Inland Revenue Building, Colombo

289 Rupavahini Emblem

1982. 50th Anniv of Department of Inland Revenue.
752 **288** 50c. black, blue & orange 70 1·25

1982. Inauguration of Rupavahini (national television service).
753 **289** 2r.50 yellow, brn & grey 2·25 3·50

290 Cricketer and Ball

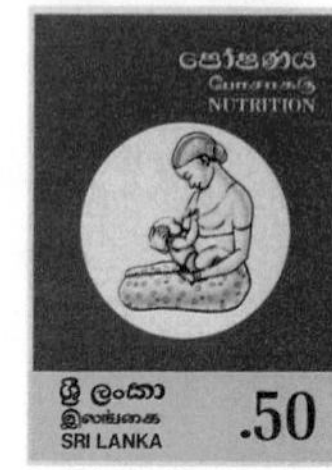

292 Mother breast-feeding Child

291 "Obsbeckia wightiana"

1982. 1st Sri Lanka–England Test Match, Colombo.
754 **290** 2r.50 multicoloured . . . 4·25 4·50

1982. Flowers. Multicoloured.
755 35c. Type **291** 10 10
756 2r. "Mesua nagassarium" . . 20 20
757 7r. "Rhodomyrtus tomentosa" . . . . 50 1·25
758 20r. "Phaius tancarvilleae" 1·40 4·00
MS759 180 × 110 mm. Nos.755/8 6·00 7·50

1982. Food and Nutrition Policy Planning.
760 **292** 50c. multicoloured . . . . 1·50 1·50

293 Conference Emblem

1982. World Hindu Conference.
761 **293** 50c. multicoloured . . . . 1·00 1·25

294 King Vessantara giving away Magical, Rain-making White Elephant

1982. Vesak. Legend of Vessantara Jataka. Details of Cloth Painting from Arattana Rajamaha Vihara (temple), Hanguranketa, District of Nuwara Eliya. Multicoloured.
762 35c. Type **294** 45 10
763 40c. King Vessantara with family in Vankagiri Forest 55 15
764 2r.50 Vessantara giving away his children as slaves . . . 2·00 2·25
765 5r. Vessantara and family returning to Jetuttara in royal chariot . . . . . . 2·75 3·50
MS766 160 × 115 mm. Nos. 762/5 7·00 7·00

295 Parliament Buildings, Sri Jayawardanapura

1982. Opening of Parliament Building Complex, Sri Jayawardanapura, Kotte.
767 **295** 50c. multicoloured . . . . 1·00 1·25

296 Dr. C. W. W. Kannangara

298 Dr. G. P. Malalasekara

297 Lord Baden-Powell

1982. Dr. C. W. W. Kannangara ("Father of Free Education") Commemoration.
768 **296** 50c. green . . . . 1·00 1·25

1982. 125th Birth Anniv of Lord Baden-Powell.
769 **297** 50c. multicoloured . . . . 1·75 1·25

1982. Dr. G. P. Malalasekara (founder of World Fellowship of Buddhists) Commemoration.
770 **298** 50c. green . . . . 1·00 1·25

299 Wheel encircling Globe

1982. World Buddhist Leaders Conference.
771 **299** 50c. multicoloured . . . . 1·00 1·50

300 Wildlife

1982. World Environment Day.
772 **300** 50c. multicoloured . . . . 1·90 1·50

301 Sir Waitialingam Duraiswamy

303 Rev. Weliwita Sri Saranankara Sangharaja

302 Y.M.C.A. Emblem

1982. Sir Waitialingam Duraiswamy (statesman and educationalist) Commemoration.
773 **301** 50c. deep brown and brown . . . . 1·00 1·25

1982. Centenary of Colombo Y.M.C.A.
774 **302** 2r.50 multicoloured . . . 3·00 4·25

1982. Rev. Weliwita Sri Saranankara Sangharaja (Buddhist leader) Commemoration.
775 **303** 50c. brown and orange . . 1·00 1·25

304 Maharagama Sasana Sevaka Samithiya Emblem

1982. 25th Anniv of Maharagama Sasana Sevaka Samithiya (Buddhist Social Reform Movement).
776 **304** 50c. multicoloured . . . . 1·40 1·40

305 Dr. Robert Koch

1982. Centenary of Robert Koch's Discovery of Tubercle Bacillus.
777 **305** 50c. multicoloured . . . . 2·00 1·50

306 Sir John Kotelawala

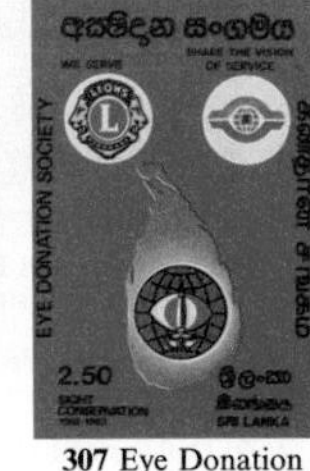

307 Eye Donation Society and Lions Club Emblems

1982. 2nd Death Anniv of Sir John Kotelawala.
778 **306** 50c. green . . . . 1·00 1·25

1982. World-Wide Sight Conservation Project.
779 **307** 2r.50 multicoloured . . . 3·00 4·25

1982. As Nos. 718/21 but without surcharges and showing revised face values.

780	2r.50 Type **269**	30	20
781	3r. Golden palm civet* . . .	3·75	3·75
1081	3r. Golden palm civet* . . .	1·40	30
782	4r. Indian-spotted chevrotain	30	30
783	5r. Rusty-spotted cat . . .	35	30

*No. 781 has the face value and inscriptions in brown, No. 1081 in black.

308 1859 4d. Rose and 1948 15c. Independence Commemorative

1982. 125th Anniv of First Postage Stamps. Mult.

784	50c. Type **308**	50	50
785	2r.50 1859 1s.9d. green and 1981 50c. "Just Society" stamp	1·75	3·00
MS786	59 × 84 mm. Nos. 784/5 (sold at 5r.)	2·00	3·25

309 Goonetilleke

1983. 4th Death Anniv of Sir Oliver Goonetilleke (statesman).
787 **309** 50c. grey, brown and black . . . . 60 1·25

310 Sarvodaya Emblem

1983. 25th Anniv of Sarvodaya Movement.
788 **310** 50c. multicoloured . . . . 1·00 1·25

311 Morse Key, Radio Aerial and Amateur Radio Society Emblem

1983. Amateur Radio Society.
789 **311** 2r.50 multicoloured . . . 2·75 4·50

312 Customs Co-operation Council Emblem and Sri Lanka Flag

1983. 30th Anniv of International Customs Day.
790 **312** 50c. multicoloured 50 40
791 – 5r. multicoloured . . . . 3·00 6·00

313 Bottle-nosed Dolphin

1983. Marine Mammals.

792	**313**	50c. black, blue and green	40	20
793	–	2r. multicoloured	60	80
794	–	2r.50 black, blue and grey	1·75	2·00
795	–	10r. multicoloured	4·00	7·00

DESIGNS: 2r. Dugongs; 2r.50, Humpback whale; 10r. Sperm whale.

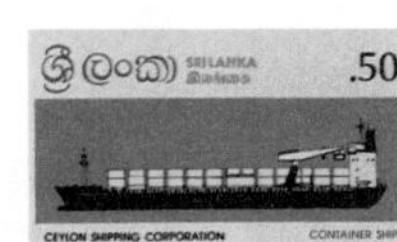

314 "Lanka Athula" (container ship)

1983. Ships of the Ceylon Shipping Corporation. Multicoloured.

796	50c. Type **314**	25	15
797	2r.50 Map of routes	90	70
798	5r. "Lanka Kalyani" (freighter)	1·25	1·60
799	20r. "Tammanna" (tanker)	2·00	6·00

315 Woman with I.W.D. Emblem and Sri Lanka Flag

1983. International Women's Day. Mult.

800	50c. Type **315**	20	25
801	5r. Woman, emblem, map and symbols of progress	80	2·75

316 Waterfall

1983. Commonwealth Day. Multicoloured.

802	50c. Type **316**	10	10
803	2r.50 Tea plucking	15	25
804	5r. Harvesting rice	25	40
805	20r. Decorated elephants . .	80	2·00

317 Lions Club International Badge

1983. 25th Anniv of Lions Club International in Sri Lanka.
806 **317** 2r.50 multicoloured . . . 2·50 2·50

318 "The Dream of Queen Mahamaya"

1983. Vesak. Life of Prince Siddhartha at Gotami Vihara. Multicoloured.

807	35c. Type **318**	10	10
808	50c. "Prince Siddhartha given to Maha Brahma"	10	10
809	5r. "Prince Siddhartha and the Sleeping Dancers" . .	85	1·50
810	10r. "The Meeting with Mara"	1·40	3·25
MS811	150 × 90 mm. Nos. 807/10	2·00	4·00

319 First Telegraph Transmission, Colombo to Galle, 1858

1983. 125th Anniv of Telecommunications in Sri Lanka (2r.) and World Communications Year (10r.). Multicoloured.

812	2r. Type **319**	50	60
813	10r. World Communications Year emblem	2·25	4·50

320 Henry Woodward Amarasuriya (philanthropist)

1983. National Heroes.

814	**320**	50c. green	30	1·00
815	–	50c. blue	30	1·00
816	–	50c. mauve	30	1·00
817	–	50c. green	30	1·00

DESIGNS: No. 815, Father Simon Perera (historian); 816, Charles Lorenz (lawyer and newspaper editor); 817, Noordeen Abdul Cader (first President of All-Ceylon Muslim League).

321 Family and Village

1983. Gam Udawa (Village Re-awakening Movement). Multicoloured.

818	50c. Type **321**	10	25
819	5r. Village view	55	2·00

322 Caravan of Bulls

1983. Transport. Multicoloured.
820 35c. Type **322** 10 10
821 2r. Steam train . . . . 2·00 1·75
822 2r.50 Ox and cart . . . . . 1·00 2·25
823 5r. Ford motor car . . . . . 2·25 4·25

323 Sir Tikiri Banda Panabokke

1983. 20th Death Anniv of Adigar Sir Tikiri Banda Panabokke.
824 **323** 50c. red . . . . 1·00 1·25

324 C. W. Thamotheram Pillai **325** Arabi Pasha

1983. C. W. Thamotheram Pillai (Tamil scholar) Commemoration.
825 **324** 50c. brown . . . . 1·00 1·25

1983. Centenary of Banishment of Arabi Pasha (Egyptian nationalist).
826 **325** 50c. green . . . . 1·00 1·25

326 Sri Lanka Wood Pigeon

1983. Birds (2nd series). Multicoloured.
827 25c. Type **326** . . . . . . 70 1·25
828 35c. Large Sri Lanka white-eye 70 70
829 2r. Sri Lanka dusky blue flycatcher . . . . 1·00 40
829a 7r. As 35c. 50 30
830 20r. Ceylon coucal . . . . 1·50 3·00
MS831 183 × 93 mm. Nos. 827/9 and 830 . . . . 2·25 6·50

327 Pelene Siri Vajiragnana **328** Mary praying over Jesus and St. Joseph welcoming Shepherds

1983. Pelene Siri Vajiragnana (scholar) Commem.
832 **327** 50c. brown . . . . 1·50 1·50

1983. Christmas.
833 **328** 50c. multicoloured 10 15
834 5r. multicoloured . . . . 30 1·75
MS835 85 × 141 mm. Nos. 833/4 65 2·00

1983. No. 680a surch **.60**.
836 **236** 60c. on 50c. gold, green and emerald . . . . . 3·50 1·75

331 Paddy Field, Globe and F.A.O. Emblem

1984. World Food Day.
838 **331** 3r. multicoloured . . . . 45 1·75

332 Modern Tea Factory

1984. Centenary of Colombo Tea Auctions. Mult.
839 1r. Type **332** 15 15
840 2r. Logo 30 45
841 5r. Girl picking tea . . . . . 75 1·75
842 10r. Auction in progress . . 1·50 3·50

333 Students and University

1984. 4th Anniv of Mahapola Scheme for Development and Education. Multicoloured.
843 60c. Type **333** 10 15
844 1r. Teacher with Gnana Darsana class 10 15
845 5r.50 Student with books and microscope . . . . 35 1·75
846 6r. Mahapola lamp symbol 40 1·75

334 King Daham Sonda instructing Angels

1984. Vesak. The Story of King Daham Sonda from Ancient Casket Paintings. Multicoloured.
847 35c. Type **334** 20 10
848 60c. Elephant paraded with gift of gold 55 25
849 5r. King Daham Sonda leaps into mouth of God Sakra 1·40 2·75
850 10r. God Sakra carrying King Daham Sonda . . . 1·75 4·50
MS851 154 × 109 mm. Nos. 847/50 2·25 4·50

335 Development Programme Logo **336** Dodanduwe Siri Piyaratana Tissa Mahanayake Thero (Buddhist scholar)

1984. Sri Lanka Lions Clubs' Development Programme.
852 **335** 60c. multicoloured . . . . 1·40 1·00

1984. National Heroes.
853 **336** 60c. bistre 30 90
854 – 60c. green 30 90
855 – 60c. green 30 90
856 – 60c. red 30 90
857 – 60c. brown 30 90
DESIGNS: No. 854, G. P. Wickremarachchi (physician); 855, Sir Mohamed Macan Markar (politician); 856, Dr. W. Arthur de Silva (philanthropist); 857, K. Balasingham (lawyer).

337 Association Emblem

1984. Centenary of Public Service Mutual Provident Association.
858 **337** 4r.60 multicoloured . . . 60 2·00

338 Sri Lanka Village

1984. 6th Anniv of "Gam Udawa" (Village Re-awakening Movement).
859 **338** 60c. multicoloured 30 75

339 World Map showing A.P.B.U. Countries

1984. 20th Anniv of Asia-Pacific Broadcasting Union.
860 **339** 7r. multicoloured . . . . 2·00 3·50

340 Drummers and Elephant carrying Royal Instructions

1984. Esala Perahera (Procession of the Tooth), Kandy. Multicoloured.
861 4r.60 Type **340** . . . . . . 1·10 1·90
862 4r.60 Dancers and elephants 1·10 1·90
863 4r.60 Elephant carrying Tooth Relic . . . . 1·10 1·90
864 4r.60 Custodian of the Sacred Tooth and attendants . . . 1·10 1·90
MS865 223 × 108 mm. Nos. 861/4 3·75 7·00
Nos. 861/4 were printed together, se-tenant, forming a composite design.

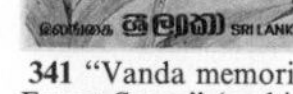

341 "Vanda memoria Ernest Soysa" (orchid) **342** Symbolic Athletes and Stadium

1984. 50th Anniv of Ceylon Orchid Circle. Mult.
866a 60c. Type **341** . . . . . . 1·00 1·25
867a 4r.60 "Acanthephippium bicolor" . . . . 2·00 3·75
868a 5r. "Vanda tessellata var. rufescens" . . . . 1·25 3·75
869 10r. "Anoectochilus setaceus" . . . . 4·00 6·00
MS870 115 × 110 mm. Nos. 866/9 7·00 10·00

1984. 1st National School Games.
871 **342** 60c. black, grey and blue 1·75 1·50

343 D. S. Senanayake, Temple and Fields

1984. Birth Centenary of D. S. Senanayake (former Prime Minister). Multicoloured.
872 35c. Type **343** 10 10
873 60c. Senanayake and statue 10 10
874 4r.60 Senanayake and irrigation project 40 50
875 6r. Senanayake and House of Representatives 55 60

344 Lake House **345** Agricultural Workers and Globe

1984. 150th Anniv of "Observer" Newspaper.
876 **344** 4r.60 multicoloured . . . 2·25 3·50

1984. 20th Anniv of World Food Programme.
877 **345** 7r. multicoloured . . . . 1·50 1·25

346 College Emblem **347** Dove and Stylized Figures

1984. Cent of Baari Arabic College, Weligama.
878 **346** 4r.60 green, turquoise & blue . . . . 1·25 3·25

1985. International Youth Year. Multicoloured.
879 4r.60 Type **347** 50 60
880 20r. Dove, stylized figures and flower . . . . 2·00 3·00

348 Religious Symbols **349** College Crest

1985. World Religion Day.
881 **348** 4r.60 multicoloured . . . 2·25 3·25

1985. 150th Anniv of Royal College, Colombo.
882 **349** 60c. yellow and blue . . . 20 25
883 – 7r. multicoloured . . . . 2·00 3·50
DESIGN: 7r. Royal College.

350 Banknotes, Buildings, Ship and "Wheel of Life" **351** Wariyapola Sri Sumangala Thero

1985. 5th Anniv of Mahapola Scheme.
884 **350** 60c. multicoloured . . . . 1·00 1·50

1985. Wariyapola Sri Sumangala Thero (Buddhist priest and patriot) Commemoration.
885 **351** 60c. brown, yellow & black . . . . 70 1·25

352 Victoria Dam

1985. Inaug of Victoria Hydro-electric Project. Multicoloured.
886 60c. Type **352** 75 50
887 7r. Map of Sri Lanka enclosing dam and power station (vert) . . . . . . 4·25 6·00

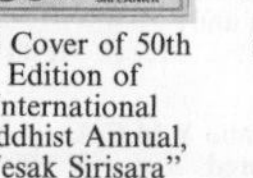

353 Cover of 50th Edition of International Buddhist Annual, "Vesak Sirisara" **354** Ven. Waskaduwe Sri Subhuthi (priest and scholar)

1985. Centenary of Vesak Poya Holiday. Mult.
888 35c. Type **353** 10 10
889 60c. Buddhists worshipping at temple 10 10
890 6r. Buddhist Theosophical Society Headquarters, Colombo . . . . 60 1·25
891 9r. Buddhist flag . . . . . . 1·25 2·25
MS892 180 × 110 mm. Nos. 888/91 4·00 6·00

1985. Personalities.
893 **354** 60c. black, orange & brown 30 75
894 – 60c. black, orange & mauve 30 75
895 – 60c. black, orange & brown 30 75
896 – 60c. black, orange & green 30 75
DESIGNS: No. 894, Revd. Fr. Peter A. Pillai (educationist and social reformer); 895, Dr. Senarath Paranavitane (scholar); 896, A. M. Wapche Marikar (architect and educationist).

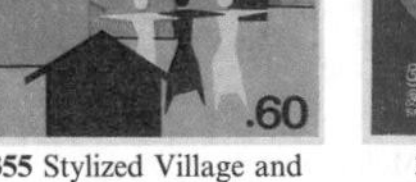

355 Stylized Village and People **356** Emblem

1985. Gam Udawa '85 (Village Re-awakening Movement).
897 **355** 60c. multicoloured . . . . 1·00 1·00

1985. 50th Anniv of Colombo Young Poets' Association.
898 **356** 60c. multicoloured . . . . 1·25 1·50

357 Kothmale Dam and Reservoir

1985. Inauguration of Kothmale Hydro-electric Project. Multicoloured.
899 60c. Type **357** 75 25
900 6r. Kothmale Power Station 3·25 4·00

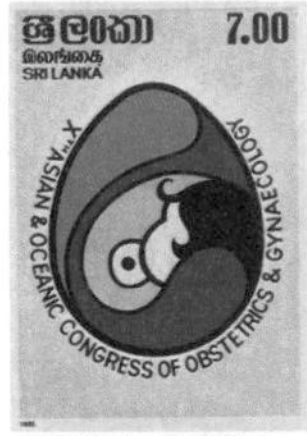

358 Federation Logo **359** Breast-feeding

1985. 10th Asian and Oceanic Congress of Obstetrics and Gynaecology.
901 **358** 7r. multicoloured . . . . 3·25 4·00

1985. UNICEF Child Survival and Development Programme. Multicoloured.
902 35c. Type **359** 30 10
903 60c. Child and oral rehydration salts 45 30
904 6r. Weighing child (growth monitoring) . . . . 2·25 3·50
905 9r. Immunization . . . . . . 2·75 5·00
MS906 99 × 180 mm. Nos. 902/5 4·00 6·00

360 Blowing Indian Chank Shell

1985. 10th Anniv of World Tourism Organization. Multicoloured.
907 1r. Type **360** 30 10
908 6r. Parliamentary Complex, Jayawardhanapura, Kotte 90 90
909 7r. Tea plantation . . . . . . 1·00 1·10
910 10r. Ruwanveliseya (Buddhist shrine), Anuradhapura . . 1·60 1·75
MS911 179 × 89 mm. Nos. 907/10 3·25 2·75

361 Casket containing Land Grant Deed **362** Koran and Map of Sri Lanka

1985. 50th Anniv of Land Development Ordinance.
912 **361** 4r.60 multicoloured . . . 2·00 3·50

1985. Translation of The Koran into Sinhala.
913 **362** 60c. violet and gold . . . 1·75 1·50

363 "Our Lady of Matara" Statue

1985. Christmas. Multicoloured.
914 60c. Type **363** 30 15
915 9r. "Our Lady of Madhu" Statue . . . . 1·50 2·75
MS916 180 × 100 mm. Nos. 914/15 5·50 7·00

1985. Nos. 680b, 780, 828, 860 and 879 surch.
917 **236** 75c. on 60c. gold, green and emerald 20 10
918 **347** 1r. on 4r.60 mult . . . . 5·50 3·00
919 **339** 1r. on 7r. multicoloured 7·50 3·00
920 **269** 5r.75 on 2r.50 mult . . . 3·50 1·50
921 – 7r. on 35c. mult (No. 828) 5·50 1·25

365 Linked Arms and Map of S.A.A.R.C. Countries

1985. 1st Summit Meeting of South Asian Association for Regional Co-operation, Dhaka, Bangladesh. Multicoloured.
922 60c. Type **365** . . . . 3·75 6·50
923 5r.50 Logo and flags of member countries . . . . 3·75 4·00

366 "Viceroy Special" Train

1986. Inaugural Run of "Viceroy Special" Train from Colombo to Kandy.
924 **366** 1r. multicoloured . . . . 60 1·50

367 Girl and Boy Students

1986. 6th Anniv of Mahapola Scheme.
925 **367** 75c. multicoloured 50 75

368 Wijewardena

1986. Birth Centenary of D. R. Wijewardena (newspaper publisher).
926 **368** 75c. brown and green . . 30 75

369 Ven. Welitara Gnanatillake Maha Nayake Thero **370** Red Cross Flag and Personnel

1986. Ven. Welitara Gnanatillake Maha Nayake Thero (scholar) Commemoration.
927 **369** 75c. multicoloured . . . . 70 1·00

1986. 50th Anniv of Sri Lanka Red Cross Society.
928 **370** 75c. multicoloured . . . . 2·00 1·75

371 Comet depicted as Goddess visiting Sun-god **372** Woman lighting Lamp

1986. Appearance of Halley's Comet. Mult.
929 50c. Type **371** 15 20
930 75c. Comet and constellations of Scorpius and Sagittarius 15 20
931 6r.50 Comet's orbit . . . . . 30 1·50
932 8r.50 Edmond Halley . . . . 55 2·25
MS933 180 × 115 mm. Nos. 929/32 5·00 10·00

1986. Sinhalese and Tamil New Year. Mult.
934 50c. Type **372** 15 20
935 75c. Woman and festive foods 15 20
936 6r.50 Women playing drum 30 2·00
937 8r.50 Anointing and making offerings at temple . . . . 55 2·50
MS938 178 × 108 mm. Nos. 934/7 1·75 5·50

373 The King donating Elephant to the Brahmin

1986. Vesak. Wall paintings from Samudragiri Temple, Mirissa. Multicoloured.
939 50c. Type **373** 10 20
940 75c. The Bodhisattva in the Vasavarthi heaven 10 20
941 5r. The offering of milk rice by Sujatha . . . . 45 2·00
942 10r. The offering of parched corn and honey by Thapassu and Bhalluka . . 50 3·00

374 Ven. Kalukondayave Sri Prajnasekhara Maha Nayake Thero (Buddhist leader and social refomer) **375** Stylized Village and People

1986. National Heroes. Multicoloured.
943 75c. Type **374** 15 80
944 75c. Brahmachari Walisinghe Harischandra (social reformer) (birth centenary) 15 80
945 75c. Martin Wickramasinghe (author and scholar) . . . 15 80
946 75c. G. G. Ponnambalam (politician) 15 80
947 75c. A. M. A. Azeez (Islamic scholar) (75th birth anniv) 15 80

1986. Gam Udawa '86 (Village Re-awakening Movement).
948 **375** 75c. multicoloured . . . . 1·50 1·75

376 Co-op Flag and Emblem **377** Arthur V. Dias

1986. 75th Anniv of Sri Lanka Co-operative Movement.
949 **376** 1r. multicoloured . . . . 1·00 2·00

1986. Birth Centenary of Arthur V. Dias (philanthropist).
950 **377** 1r. brown and blue . . . 1·50 2·25

378 Bull Elephant

1986. Sri Lanka Wild Elephant. Multicoloured.
951 5r. Type **378** . . . . 9·00 6·50
952 5r. Cow elephant and calf . . 9·00 6·50
953 5r. Cow elephant . . . . . . 9·00 6·50
954 5r. Elephants bathing . . . . 9·00 6·50

379 Congress Logo **381** Anniversary Logo

380 Map showing Route of Cable and Telephone Receiver

1986. 2nd Indo-Pacific Congress on Legal Medicine and Forensic Sciences.
955 **379** 8r.50 multicoloured . . . 2·25 3·00

1986. SEA-ME-WE Submarine Cable Project.
956 **380** 5r.75 multicoloured . . . 4·75 2·75

1986. 25th Anniv of Dag Hammarskjold Award.
957 **381** 2r. multicoloured . . . . 1·25 1·00

382 Logo on Flag **383** Logo

1986. 2nd National School Games.
958 **382** 1r. multicoloured . . . . 2·75 1·90

1986. 60th Anniv of Surveyors' Institute of Sri Lanka.
959 **383** 75c. brown & light brown 60 1·25

384 College Building and Crest

1986. Centenary of Ananda College, Colombo.
960 **384** 75c. multicoloured 10 10
961 – 5r. multicoloured 30 80
962 – 5r.75 multicoloured . . . 35 80
963 – 6r. red, gold and lilac . . 40 1·25
DESIGNS: 5r. Sports field and college crest; 5r.75, Col. H. S. Olcott (founder), Ven. Migettuwatte Gunananda, Ven. Hikkaduwe Sri Sumangala (Buddhist leaders) and Buddhist flag; 6r. College flag.

385 Mangrove Swamp

1986. Mangrove Conservation. Multicoloured.

964 35c. Type **385** 70 20
965 50c. Mangrove tree 80 30
966 75c. Germinating mangrove flower 90 30
967 6r. Fiddler crab . . . . . . 6·50 8·00

386 Family and Housing Estate

1987. International Year of Shelter for the Homeless.
968 **386** 75c. multicoloured . . . . 1·75 50

387 Ven. Ambagahawatte I- n- dasabhawaragnanasamy Thero

388 Proctor John de Silva

1987. Ven. Ambagahawatte Indasabhawaragnanasamy Thero (Buddhist monk) Commemoration.
969 **387** 5r.75 multicoloured . . . 2·50 1·00

1987. Proctor John de Silva (playwright) Commemoration.
970 **388** 5r.75 multicoloured . . . 70 70

389 Mahapola Logo and Aspects of Communication

1987. 7th Anniv of Mahapola Scheme.
971 **389** 75c. multicoloured . . . . 75 1·50

390 Dr. R. L. Brohier

1987. Dr. Richard L. Brohier (historian and surveyor) Commemoration.
972 **390** 5r.75 multicoloured . . . 2·00 1·40

391 Tyre Corporation Building, Kelaniya, and Logo

1987. 25th Anniv of Sri Lanka Tyre Corporation.
973 **391** 5r.75 black, red and orange 50 70

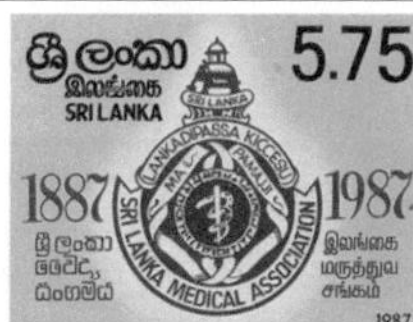

392 Logo

1987. Centenary of Sri Lanka Medical Association.
974 **392** 5r.75 brown, yellow and black . . . . 2·00 3·00

393 Clasped Hands, Farmer and Paddy Field

394 Exhibition Logo

1987. Inauguration of Farmers' Pension and Social Security Benefit Scheme.
975 **393** 75c. multicoloured . . . . 1·00 1·50

1987. Mahaweli Maha Goviya Contest and Agro Mahaweli Exhibition.
976 **394** 75c. multicoloured 30 30

395 Young Children with W.H.O. and Immunization Logos

1987. World Health Day.
977 **395** 1r. multicoloured . . . . 2·50 1·00

396 Girls playing on Swing

1987. Sinhalese and Tamil New Year. Mult.
978 75c. Type **396** 10 10
979 5r. Girls with oil lamp and sun symbol 50 50

397 Lotus Lanterns

1987. Vesak. Multicoloured.
980 50c. Type **397** 10 10
981 75c. Octagonal lanterns . . . 10 10
982 5r. Star lanterns 35 30
983 10r. Gok lanterns 60 65
MS984 150 × 90 mm. Nos. 980/3 1·00 1·00

398 Emerald-collared Parakeet ("Layard's Parakeet")

1987. Birds (3rd series). Multicoloured.
985A 50c. Type **398** 50 10
986A 1r. Legge's flowerpecker . . 75 10
987A 5r. Ceylon white-headed starling ("Sri Lanka White-headed Starling") 1·10 1·50
988A 10r. Ceylon jungle babbler ("Sri Lanka Rufous Babbler") . . . . 1·40 2·50
MS989A 140 × 80 mm. Nos. 985A/8A . . . . 5·50 5·50

399 Ven. Heenatiyana Sri Dhammaloka Maha Nayake Thero (Buddhist monk)

1987. National Heroes. Multicoloured.
990 75c. Type **399** 40 40
991 75c. P. de S. Kularatne (educationist) 40 40
992 75c. M. C. Abdul Rahuman (legislator) 40 40

400 Peasant Family and Village

1987. Gam Udawa '87 (Village Re-awakening Movement).
993 **400** 75c. multicoloured 30 30

401 "Mesua nagassarium"

1987. Forest Conservation. Multicoloured.
994 75c. Type **401** 10 10
995 5r. Elephants in forest . . . 1·25 1·25

402 Dharmaraja College, Crest and Col. Olcott (founder)

1987. Centenary of Dharmaraja College, Kandy.
996 **402** 75c. multicoloured . . . . 2·25 30

403 Youth Sevices Logo

1987. 20th Anniv of National Youth Services.
997 **403** 75c. multicoloured 20 20

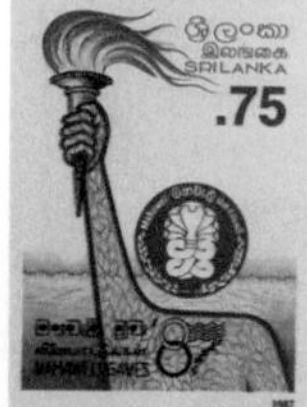

404 Arm holding Torch and Mahaweli Logo

405 Open Bible and Logo

1987. Mahaweli Games.
998 **404** 75c. multicoloured . . . . 3·00 2·25

1987. 175th Anniv of Ceylon Bible Society.
999 **405** 5r.75 multicoloured . . . 40 40

406 Hurdler and Committee Symbol

1987. 50th Anniv of National Olympic Committee.
1000 **406** 10r. multicoloured . . . 2·50 1·25

407 Madonna and Child, Flowers and Oil Lamp

408 Sir Ernest de Silva

1987. Christmas. Multicoloured.
1001 75c. Type **407** 10 10
1002 10r. Christ Child in manger, star and dove 35 40
MS1003 145 × 82 mm. Nos. 1001/2 60 70

1987. Birth Centenary of Sir Ernest de Silva (philanthropist and philatelist).
1004 **408** 75c. multicoloured . . . 30 30

409 Society Logo

410 University Flag and Graduates

1987. 150th Anniv of Kandy Friend-in-Need Society.
1005 **409** 75c. multicoloured . . . 30 30

1987. 1st Convocation of Buddhist and Pali University.
1006 **410** 75c. multicoloured . . . 30 30

411 Father Joseph Vaz

412 Wheel of Dhamma, Dagaba and Bo Leaf

1987. 300th Anniv of Arrival of Father Joseph Vaz in Kandy.
1007 **411** 75c. multicoloured . . . 30 30

1988. 30th Anniv of Buddhist Publication Society, Kandy.
1008 **412** 75c. multicoloured . . . 30 30

413 Dharmayatra Lorry

414 Society Logo

1988. 5th Anniv of Mahapola Dharmayatra Service.
1009 **413** 75c. multicoloured . . . 30 30

1988. Centenary of Ceylon Society of Arts.
1010 **414** 75c. multicoloured . . . 30 30

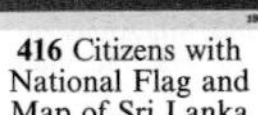

415 National Youth Centre, Maharagama

416 Citizens with National Flag and Map of Sri Lanka

1988. Opening of National Youth Centre, Maharagama.
1011 **415** 1r. multicoloured . . . . 3·25 30

1988. 40th Anniv of Independence. Multicoloured.
1012 75c. Type **416** 10 10
1013 8r.50 "40" in figures and lion emblem 90 90

417 Graduates, Clay Lamp and Open Book

419 Ven. Weligama Sri Sumangala Maha Nayake Thero

418 Bus and Logo

1988. 8th Anniv of Mahapola Scheme.
1014 **417** 75c. multicoloured . . . 20 20

1988. 30th Anniv of Sri Lanka Transport Board.
1015 **418** 5r.75 multicoloured . . . 55 55

1988. Ven. Weligama Sri Sumangala Maha Nayake Thero (Buddhist monk) Commemoration.
1016 **419** 75c. multicoloured . . . 20 20

420 Regimental Colour

1988. Centenary of Regiment of Artillery.
1017 **420** 5r.75 multicoloured . . . 2·50 80

421 Chevalier I. X. Pereira

423 Father Ferdinand Bonnel (educationist)

422 Invitation to the Deities and Brahmas

1988. Birth Centenary of Chevalier I. X. Pereira (politician).
1018 **421** 5r.75 multicoloured . . . 30 30

1988. Vesak. Paintings from Narendrarama Rajamaha Temple, Suriyagoda. Multicoloured.
1019 50c. Type **422** 15 15
1020 75c. Bodhisathva at the Seventh Step 15 15
MS1021 150 × 92 mm. Nos. 1019/20 1·50 1·50

1988. National Heroes. Multicoloured.
1022 75c. Type **423** 15 20
1023 75c. Sir Razik Fareed (politician) 15 20
1024 75c. W. F. Gunawardhana (scholar) 15 20
1025 75c. Edward Nugawela (politician) 15 20
1026 75c. Chief Justice Sir Arthur Wijeyewardene 15 20

424 Stylized Figures and Re-awakened Village

1988. 10th Anniv of Gam Udawa (Village Re-awakening Movement).
1027 **424** 75c. multicoloured . . . 20 20

425 Maliyadeva College, Kurunegala, and Crest

1988. Cent of Maliyadeva College, Kurunegala.
1028 **425** 75c. multicoloured . . . 20 20

426 M. J. M. Lafir, Billiard Game and Trophy

1988. Mohamed Junaid Mohamed Lafir (World Amateur Billiards Champion, 1973) Commem.
1029 **426** 5r.75 multicoloured . . . 45 45

427 Flags of Australia and Sri Lanka, Handclasp and Map of Australia

1988. Bicentenary of Australian Settlement.
1030 **427** 8r.50 multicoloured . . . 50 50

428 Ven. Kataluwe Sri Gunaratana Maha Nayake Thero

429 Athlete, Rice and Hydro-electric Dam

1988. Ven. Kataluwe Sri Gunaratana Maha Nayake Thero (Buddhist monk) Commemoration.
1031 **428** 75c. multicoloured . . . 20 20

1988. Mahaweli Games.
1032 **429** 75c. multicoloured . . . 20 20

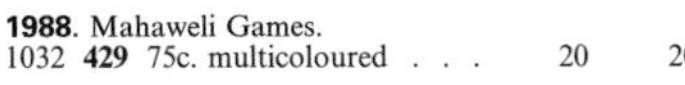

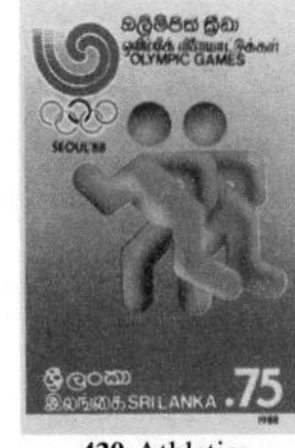

430 Athletics

431 Outline Map of Sri Lanka and Anniversary Logo

1988. Olympic Games, Seoul. Multicoloured.
1033 75c. Type **430** 10 10
1034 1r. Swimming 10 10
1035 5r.75 Boxing 40 40
1036 8r.50 Map of Sri Lanka and logos of Olympic Committee and Seoul Games 70 70
MS1037 181 × 101 mm. Nos. 1033/6 1·10 1·40

1988. 40th Anniv of W.H.O.
1038 **431** 75c. multicoloured . . . 20 20

432 Games Logo

1988. 3rd National School Games.
1039 **432** 1r. black, gold and mauve . . . . 2·50 25

433 Mahatma Gandhi

1988. 40th Death Anniv of Mahatma Gandhi.
1040 **433** 75c. multicoloured . . . 75 20

434 Globe with Forms of Transport and Communications

1988. Asia-Pacific Transport and Communications Decade.
1041 **434** 75c. multicoloured . . . 50 10
1042 – 5r.75 mauve, blue & blk 2·50 1·60
DESIGN: 5r.75, Antenna tower with dish aerials and forms of transport.

435 Woman with Rice Sheaf and Hydro-electric Project

1988. Commissioning of Randenigala Project. Multicoloured.
1043 75c. Type **435** 10 10
1044 5r.75 Randenigala Dam and reservoir 60 60

436 Handicrafts and Centre Logo in Cupped Hands

437 Angel, Dove, Olive Branch and Globe

1988. Opening of Gramodaya Folk Art Centre, Colombo.
1045 **436** 75c. multicoloured . . . 20 20

1988. Christmas. Multicoloured.
1046 75c. Type **437** 10 10
1047 8r.50 Shepherds and Star of Bethlehem 60 75
MS1048 175 × 100 mm. Nos. 1046/7 1·00 1·00

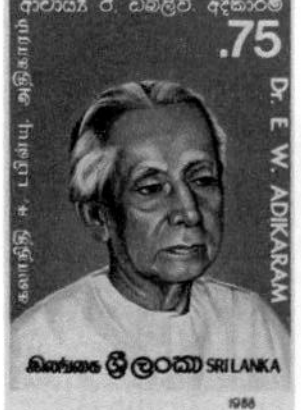

438 Dr. E. W. Adikaram

439 Open Book in Tree and Children reading

1988. Dr. E. W. Adikaram (educationist) Commemoration.
1049 **438** 75c. multicoloured . . . 20 20

1989. 10th Anniv of Free Distribution of School Text Books.
1050 **439** 75c. multicoloured . . . 20 20

440 Wimalaratne Kumaragama

441 Logo and New Chamber of Commerce Building

1989. Poets of Sri Lanka. Multicoloured.
1051 75c. Type **440** 15 20
1052 75c. G. H. Perera 15 20
1053 75c. Sagara Palansuriya . . 15 20
1054 75c. P. B. Alwis Perera . . 15 20

1989. 150th Anniv of Ceylon Chamber of Commerce.
1055 **441** 75c. multicoloured . . . 20 20

442 Bodhisatva at Lunch and Funeral Pyre

1989. Vesak. Wall Paintings from Medawala Monastery, Harispattuwa. Multicoloured.
1056 50c. Type **442** 10 10
1057 75c. Rescue of King Vessantara's childen by god Sakra 10 10
1058 5r. Bodhisatva ploughing and his son attacked by snake 30 40
1059 5r.75 King Vessantara giving away his children 30 55
MS1060 150 × 90 mm. Nos. 1056/9 1·00 1·00

443 Parawahera Vajiragnana Thero (Buddhist monk)

444 College Crest

1989. National Heroes. Multicoloured.
1061 75c. Type **443** 25 25
1062 75c. Fr. Maurice Jacques Le Goc (educationist) 25 25
1063 75c. Hemapala Munidasa (author) 25 25
1064 75c. Ananda Samarakoon (composer) 25 25
1065 75c. Simon Casie Chitty (scholar) (horiz) 25 25

1989. 150th Anniv of Harley College, Point-Pedro (1988).
1066 **444** 75c. multicoloured . . . 20 20

445 Dramachakra, Lamp, Buddhist Flag and Map

1989. Establishment of Ministry of Buddha Sasana.
1067 **445** 75c. multicoloured . . . 20 20

446 Hands holding Brick and Trowel, House and Family

1989. Gam Udawa '89 (Village Re-awakening Movement).
1068 **446** 75c. multicoloured . . . 20 20

447 Two Families and Hand turning Cogwheel

448 Dunhinda Falls

1989. Janasaviya Development Programme.
1069 **447** 75c. multicoloured . . . 20 20
1070a 1r. multicoloured . . . 10 10

1989. Waterfalls. Multicoloured.
1071 75c. Type **448** 10 10
1072 1r. Rawana Falls 10 10
1073 5r.75 Laxapana Falls . . . 45 45
1074 8r.50 Diyaluma Falls . . . 60 60

449 Rev. James Chater (missionary) and Baptist Church

1989. 177th Anniv of Baptist Church in Sri Lanka.
1075 **449** 5r.75 multicoloured . . . 30 30

450 Bicentenary Logo

1989. Bicentenary of French Revolution.
1076 **450** 8r.50 black, blue and red 70 70

451 Old and New Bank Buildings and Logo

452 Water Lily, Dharma Chakra and Books

1989. 50th Anniv of Bank of Ceylon. Mult.
1077 75c. Type **451** 10 10
1078 5r. "Bank of Ceylon orchid and logo" 45 45

1989. State Literary Festival.
1079 **452** 75c. multicoloured . . . 20 20

453 Wilhelm Geiger

454 H. V. Perera, Q.C.

1989. Wilhelm Geiger (linguistic scholar) Commemoration.
1080 **453** 75c. multicoloured . . . 20 20

1989. Constitutional Pioneers. Multicoloured.
1082 75c. Type **454** 20 20
1083 75c. Prof. Ivor Jennings . . 20 20

455 Sir Cyril de Zoysa

456 Map of South-east Asia and Telecommunications Equipment

1989. Sir Cyril de Zoysa (Buddhist philanthropist) Commemoration.
1084 **455** 75c. multicoloured . . . 20 20

1989. 10th Anniv of Asia-Pacific Telecommunity.
1085 **456** 5r.75 multicoloured . . . 50 50

457 Members with Offerings and Water Lily on Map of Sri Lanka

458 "Apollo 11" Blast- off and Astronauts

1989. 50th Anniv of Sri Sucharitha Welfare Movement.
1086 **457** 75c. multicoloured . . . 20 20

1989. 20th Anniv of First Manned Landing on Moon. Multicoloured.
1087 75c. Type **458** 15 10
1088 1r. Armstrong leaving lunar module "Eagle" 20 10
1089 2r. Astronaut on Moon . . 35 30
1090 5r.75 Lunar surface and Earth from Moon 60 70
MS1091 100 × 160 mm. Nos. 1087/90 1·40 1·40

459 Shepherds

460 Ven. Sri Devananda Nayake Thero

1989. Christmas. Multicoloured.
1092 75c. Type **459** 10 10
1093 8r.50 Magi with gifts . . . 60 2·25
MS1094 160 × 100 mm. Nos. 1092/3 1·25 2·25

1989. Ven. Sri Devananda Nayake Thero (Buddhist monk) Commemoration.
1095 **460** 75c. multicoloured . . . 30 20

461 College Building, Crest and Revd. William Ault (founder)

1989. 175th Anniv of Methodist Central College, Batticaloa.
1096 **461** 75c. multicoloured . . . 20 20

462 Golf Ball, Clubs and Logo

1989. Cent of Nuwara Eliya Golf Club. Mult.
1097 75c. Type **462** . . . . . . 2·00 25
1098 8r.50 Course and club house 6·50 6·00

463 "Raja"

464 College Building and G. Wickremarachchi (founder)

1989. "Raja" Royal Ceremonial Elephant, Kandy Commemoration.
1099 **463** 75c. multicoloured . . . 3·25 65

1989. 60th Anniv of Gampaha Wickremarachchi Institute of Ayurveda Medicine.
1100 **464** 75c. multicoloured . . . 20 20

465 Ven. Udunuwara Sri Sarananda Thero

467 Cardinal Thomas Cooray

466 Diesel Train on Viaduct, Ella–Demodara Line

1989. Ven. Udunuwara Sri Sarananda Thero (Buddhist monk) Commemoration.
1101 **465** 75c. multicoloured . . . 20 20

1989. 125 Years of Sir Lanka Railways. Mult.
1102 75c. Type **466** 65 20
1103 2r. Diesel train at Maradana Station . . . . 1·40 30
1104 3r. Steam train and semaphore signal . . . . 1·60 55
1105 7r. Steam train leaving station, 1864 . . . . . . 2·00 1·25

1989. Cardinal Thomas Cooray Commemoration.
1106 **467** 75c. multicoloured . . . 1·25 30

468 Farmer and Wife with Dagaba and Dam

1989. Agro Mahaweli Development Programme.
1107 **468** 75c. multicoloured . . . 20 20

469 Justin Wijayawardena

470 Ven. Induruwe Uttarananda Mahanayake Thero

1990. Justin Wijayawardena (scholar) Commem.
1108 **469** 1r. multicoloured . . . . 2·00 25

1990. Surch.
1108a 25c. on 5r.75 King Vessantara giving away his children (No. 1059) 60 20
1109a 1r. on 75c. Type **447** . . . 1·40 1·25

1990. 4th Death Anniv of Ven. Induruwe Uttarananda Mahanayake Thero (Buddhist theologian).
1109 **470** 1r. multicoloured . . . . 1·40 1·25

471 Two Graduates, Lamp and Open Book

1990. 9th Anniv of Mahapola Scheme.
1110 **471** 75c. multicoloured . . . 20 20

472 Traditional Drums

1990. 25th Anniv of Laksala Traditional Handicrafts Organization. Multicoloured.
1111 1r. Type **472** 25 10
1112 2r. Silverware 45 15
1113 3r. Lacquerware 65 20
1114 8r. Dumbara mats . . . . . 1·50 1·50

473 King Maha Prathapa visiting Queen Chandra

1990. Vesak. Wall Paintings from Buduraja Maha Viharaya, Wewurukannala. Multicoloured.
1115 75c. Type **473** 10 10
1116 1r. Execution of Prince Dharmapala 10 10
1117 2r. Prince Mahinsasaka with the Water Demon 20 20
1118 8r. King Dahamsonda with the God Sakra disguised as a demon 75 75
MS1119 160 × 99 mm. Nos. 1115/18 1·00 1·00

474 Father T. Long (educationist)

476 Gold Reliquary

475 Janasaviya Workers

1990. National Heroes. Multicoloured.
1120 1r. Type **474** 40 25
1121 1r. Prof. M. Ratnasuriya (37 × 25 mm) 40 25
1122 1r. D. Wijewardene (patriot) (37 × 25 mm) 40 25
1123 1r. L. Manjusri (artist) (37 × 25 mm) 40 25

1990. 12th Anniv of Gam Udawa and Opening of Janasaviya Centre, Pallekele.
1124 **475** 1r. multicoloured . . . . 1·50 30

1990. Cent of Department of Archaeology.
1125 **476** 1r. black and yellow . . 30 10
1126 – 2r. black and grey . . . 50 15
1127 – 3r. black, green & brown 70 35
1128 – 8r. black and brown . . 1·40 1·25
DESIGNS: 2r. Statuette of Ganesh; 3r. Terrace of the Bodhi-tree, Isurumuniya Vihara; 8r. Inscription of King Nissankamalla.

477 Male Tennis Player at Left

1990. 75th Anniv of Sri Lanka Tennis Association. Multicoloured.

1129 1r. Type **477** 65 65
1130 1r. Male tennis player at right 65 65
1131 8r. Male tennis players . . . 2·25 2·25
1132 8r. Female tennis players . . 2·25 2·25

Nos. 1129/30 and 1131/2 were each printed together, se-tenant, each pair forming a composite design of a singles (1r.) or doubles (8r.) match.

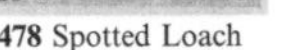

478 Spotted Loach **479** Rukmani Devi

1990. Endemic Fishes. Multicoloured.

1133 25c. Type **478** 10 10
1134 2r. Spotted gourami ("Ornate paradise fish") 40 10
1135 8r. Mountain labeo . . . . 95 1·25
1136 20r. Cherry barb . . . . . . 1·75 3·25
MS1137 150 × 90 mm. Nos. 1133/6 2·75 4·00

1990. 12th Death Anniv of Rukmani Devi (actress and singer).

1138 **479** 1r. multicoloured . . . . 2·50 1·25

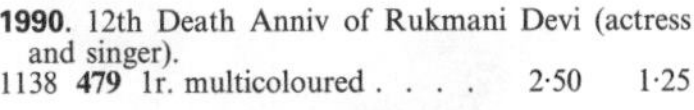

480 Innkeeper turning away Mary and Joseph

1990. Christmas. Multicoloured.

1139 1r. Type **480** 50 10
1140 10r. Adoration of the Magi 3·50 4·00
MS1141 190 × 114 mm. Nos. 1139/40 4·00 4·25

481 Health Worker talking to Villagers

1990. World AIDS Day. Multicoloured.

1142 1r. Type **481** 60 15
1143 8r. Emblem and Aids virus 3·00 3·50

482 Main College Building and Flag **483** Peri Sundaram

1990. 50th Anniv of Dharmapala College, Pannipitiya.

1144 **482** 1r. multicoloured . . . . 2·50 1·25

1990. Birth Centenary of Peri Sundaram (lawyer and politician).

1145 **483** 1r. brown and green . . 2·50 1·25

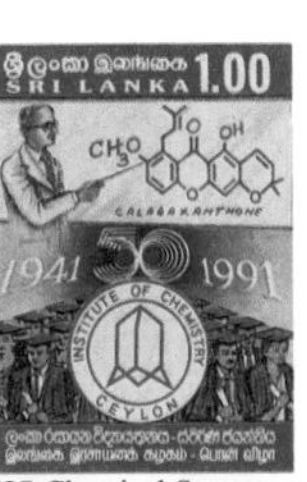

484 Letter Box, Galle, 1904 **485** Chemical Structure Diagram, Graduating Students and Emblem

1990. 175th Anniv of Sri Lanka Postal Service. Multicoloured.

1146 1r. Type **484** 60 10
1147 2r. Mail runner, 1815 . . . 1·10 30
1148 5r. Mail coach, 1832 . . . . 2·25 1·75
1149 10r. Nuwara-Eliya Post Office, 1894 . . . . . . 3·00 3·50

1991. 50th Anniv of Institute of Chemistry.

1150 **485** 1r. multicoloured . . . . 2·50 1·25

486 Kastavahana on Royal Elephant

1991. Vesak. Temple Paintings from Karagampitiya Subodarama. Multicoloured.

1151 75c. Type **486** 25 10
1152 1r. Polo Janaka in prison 25 10
1153 2r. Two merchants offering food to Buddha 55 35
1154 11r. Escape of Queen . . . 2·50 5·00
MS1155 150 × 90 mm. Nos. 1151/4 3·50 5·00

487 Narada Thero (Buddhist missionary) **488** Society Building

1991. National Heroes. Multicoloured.

1156 1r. Type **487** 50 60
1157 1r. Wallewatta Silva (novelist) 50 60
1158 1r. Sir Muttu Coomaraswamy (lawyer and politician) 50 60
1159 1r. Dr. Andreas Nell (ophthalmic surgeon) . . 50 60

1991. Centenary of Maha Bodhi Society.

1160 **488** 1r. multicoloured . . . . 1·25 1·00

489 Women working at Home

1991. 13th Anniv of Gam Udawa Movement.

1161 **489** 1r. multicoloured . . . . 2·00 80

490 Globe and Plan Symbol **492** Ven. Henpitagedera Gnanaseeha Nayake Thero

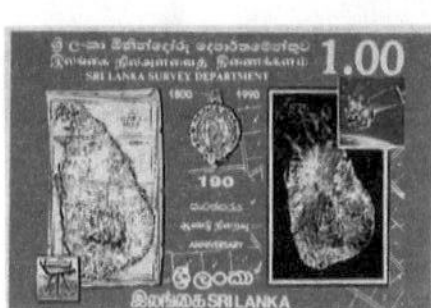

491 17th-century Map and Modern Satellite Photo of Sri Lanka

1991. 40th Anniv of Colombo Plan.

1162 **490** 1r. violet and blue . . . 2·25 80

1991. 190th Anniv of Sri Lanka Survey Department.

1163 **491** 1r. multicoloured . . . . 1·75 80

1991. 10th Death Anniv of Ven. Nayak Henpitagedera Gnanaseeha Nayake Thero (Buddhist theologian).

1164 **492** 1r. multicoloured . . . . 1·75 80

493 Police Officers of 1866 and 1991 with Badge

1991. 125th Anniv of Sri Lanka Police Force.

1165 **493** 1r. multicoloured . . . . 1·00 60

494 Kingswood College

1991. Centenary of Kingswood College, Kandy.

1166 **494** 1r. multicoloured 50 30

495 The Annunciation **496** Early Magneto Telephone

1991. Christmas. Multicoloured.

1167 1r. Type **495** 20 20
1168 10r. The Presentation of Jesus in the Temple . . . 1·10 2·25
MS1169 90 × 150 mm. Nos. 1167/8 1·25 2·25

1991. Inauguration of Sri Lankan Telecom Corporation. Multicoloured.

1170 1r. Type **496** 20 10
1171 2r. Manual switchboard and telephonist 25 15
1172 8r. Satellite communications system . . . . 55 1·40
1173 10r. Fibre optics cable and mobile phone . . . . . . 70 1·40

497 S.A.A.R.C. Logo and Bandaranaike Memorial Hall

1991. 6th South Asian Association for Regional Co-operation Summit, Colombo. Multicoloured.

1174 1r. Type **497** 15 10
1175 8r. Logo and hall surrounded by national flags . . . . 45 1·50

498 "Pancha" (Games mascot)

1991. 5th South Asian Federation Games. Mult.

1176 1r. Type **498** 25 10
1177 2r. Games logo 45 20
1178 4r. Sugathadasa Stadium . . 85 1·25
1179 11r. Asia map on globe and national flags . . . . . . 1·75 3·75

499 Crate, Boeing 747-300/400 Airliner and Container Ship

1992. Exports Year.

1180 **499** 1r. multicoloured . . . . 1·50 80

500 Plucking Tea **501** General Ranjan Wijeratne

1992. 125th Anniv of Tea Industry. Mult.

1181 1r. Type **500** 40 10
1182 2r. Healthy family, tea and tea estate 70 20
1183 5r. Ceylon tea symbol . . . 2·00 2·00
1184 10r. James Taylor (founder) 2·50 3·75

1992. 1st Death Anniv of General Ranjan Wijeratne.

1185 **501** 1r. multicoloured 30 20

502 Olcott Hall, Mahinda College

1992. Centenary of Mahinda College, Galle.

1186 **502** 1r. multicoloured 20 20

503 Newstead College and Logo

1992. 175th Anniv (1991) of Newstead Girls' College, Negombo.

1187 **503** 1r. multicoloured 20 20

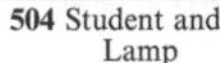

504 Student and Oil Lamp **506** Ven. Devamottawe Amarawansa (Buddhist missionary)

505 Sama's Parents leaving for Forest

1992. 11th Anniv of Mahapola Scholarship Fund.

1188 **504** 1r. multicoloured 20 20

1992. Vesak Festival. Sama Jataka Paintings from Kottimbulwala Cave Temple. Multicoloured.

1189 75c. Type **505** 15 10
1190 1r. Sama and parents in forest 15 10
1191 8r. Sama leading blind parents . . . . 1·10 1·50
1192 11r. Sama's parents grieving for wounded son . . . . 1·50 2·25
MS1193 151 × 91 mm. Nos. 1189/92 2·40 4·00

1992. National Heroes. Multicoloured.

1194 1r. Type **506** 15 25
1195 1r. Richard Mirando (Buddhist philanthropist) 15 25
1196 1r. Gate Mudaliyar N. Canaganayagam (Buddhist social reformer) 15 25
1197 1r. Abdul Azeez (Moorish social reformer) 15 25

507 Map of Sri Lanka, Flag and Symbol
508 Family in House

1992. 2300th Anniv of Arrival of Buddhism in Sri Lanka.
1198 **507** 1r. multicoloured 20 20

1992. 14th Anniv of Gam Udawa Movement.
1199 **508** 1r. multicoloured 20 20

509 Postal Activities and Award
510 Narilata Mask

1992. Postal Service Awards. Multicoloured.
1200 1r. Type **509** 30 10
1201 10r. Medals and commemorative cachet . . 2·25 2·75

1992. Kolam Dance Masks. Multicoloured.
1202 1r. Type **510** 20 10
1203 2r. Mudali mask 30 10
1204 5r. Queen mask 60 70
1205 10r. King mask . . . . . . 1·00 1·75
MS1206 150 × 90 mm. Nos. 1202/5 1·50 2·25

511 19th and 20th-century Players and Match of 1838
512 Running

1992. 160th Anniv of Cricket in Sri Lanka.
1207 **511** 5r. multicoloured . . . . 2·50 2·25

1992. Olympic Games, Barcelona. Multicoloured.
1208 1r. Type **512** 20 10
1209 11r. Shooting . . . . 1·40 2·00
1210 13r. Swimming . . . . . . 1·75 2·50
1211 15r. Weightlifting . . . . . 1·90 2·75
MS1212 91 × 151 mm. Nos. 1208/11 4·50 7·00

513 Vijaya Kumaratunga
514 College Building and Crest

1992. Vijaya Kumaratunga (actor) Commem.
1213 **513** 1r. multicoloured 30 20

1992. Centenary of Al-Bahjathhul Ibraheemiyyah Arabic College.
1214 **514** 1r. multicoloured 30 20

515 Official Church Seal
516 Nativity

1992. 350th Anniv of Dutch Reformed Church in Sri Lanka.
1215 **515** 1r. black, green & yellow 1·00 40

1992. Christmas. Multicoloured.
1216 1r. Type **516** 15 10
1217 9r. Family going to church 1·60 2·25
MS1218 150 × 90 mm. Nos. 1216/17 1·50 2·50

517 Fleet of Columbus

1992. 500th Anniv of Discovery of America by Columbus. Multicoloured.
1219 1r. Type **517** 50 10
1220 11r. Columbus landing in New World . . . . . . 1·25 1·50
1221 13r. Wreck of "Santa Maria" . . . . 1·50 2·00
1222 15r. Columbus reporting to Queen Isabella and King Ferdinand . . . . 1·50 2·25
MS1223 155 × 95 mm. Nos. 1219/22 3·75 5·50

1992. No. 684 surch **2.00**.
1224 **255** 2r. on 10c. multicoloured 2·25 50

519 Ven. Sumedhankara Thero and Dagoba

1992. Birth Centenary of Ven. Dambagasare Sumedhankara Nayake Thero.
1225 **519** 1r. multicoloured 20 20

520 University Logo, Students and Building

1992. 50th Anniv of University Education in Sri Lanka (1st issue).
1226 **520** 1r. multicoloured 20 20
See also No. 1227.

521 University of Colombo Building and Logo

1993. 50th Anniv of University Education in Sri Lanka (2nd issue).
1227 **521** 1r. multicoloured 75 20

522 College Building and Crest

1993. Centenary of Zahira College, Colombo.
1228 **522** 1r. multicoloured 75 30

523 Magandiya being presented to Buddha
524 Girl Guide, Badge and Camp

1993. Vesak Festival. Verses from the "Dhammapada". Multicoloured.
1229 75c. Type **523** 15 10
1230 1r. Kisa Gotami carrying her dead baby 20 10
1231 3r. Patachara and her dying family 50 70
1232 10r. Angulimala praying . . 1·25 2·00
MS1233 180 × 101 mm. Nos. 1229/32 1·75 2·50

1993. 75th Anniv of Sri Lanka Girl Guides Association. Multicoloured.
1234 1r. Type **524** 50 10
1235 5r. Girl Guide activities . . 1·50 2·00

525 Ven. Yagirala Pagnananda Maha Nayaka Thero (scholar)
526 Family arriving at New Home

1993. National Heroes. Multicoloured.
1236 1r. Type **525** 30 40
1237 1r. Charles de Silva (politician) 30 40
1238 1r. Wilmot A. Perera (politician) 30 40
1239 1r. Abdul Caffoor (philanthropist) 30 40

1993. "Gam Udawa '93".
1240 **526** 1r. multicoloured . . . . 1·25 30

527 Consumer Movement Flag and Logo

1993. 50th Anniv (1992) of Co-operative Consumer Movement.
1241 **527** 1r. multicoloured . . . . 1·50 30

528 Ashy-headed Laughing Thrush

1993. Birds (4th series). Multicoloured.
1242 3r. Type **528** 40 20
1243 4r. Brown-capped jungle babbler ("Ceylon Brown-capped Babbler") 40 20
1244 5r. Red-faced malkoha . . . 50 55
1245 10r. Ceylon grackle ("Ceylon Hill-Mynah") 95 1·40
MS1246 151 × 121 mm. Nos. 1242/5 2·75 3·50

529 Talawila Church

1993. 150th Anniv of Talawila Church.
1247 **529** 1r. multicoloured . . . . 1·00 30

530 Rosette and Mail Delivery
531 College and Flag

1993. Sri Lanka Post Excellent Service Awards.
1248 **530** 1r. multicoloured . . . . 1·00 30

1993. Centenary of Musaeus College.
1249 **531** 1r. multicoloured . . . . 1·75 30

532 Presentation of Jesus in the Temple

1993. Christmas. Multicoloured.
1250 1r. Type **532** 10 10
1251 17r. Boy Jesus with the Jewish teachers . . . . . 1·25 2·25
MS1252 180 × 102 mm. Nos. 1250/1 1·25 2·25

533 Healthy Youth and Drug Addict

1993. Youth and Health Campaign.
1253 **533** 1r. multicoloured 50 30

534 Maradana Technical College Building and Emblems
535 Trinity College Logo

1993. Centenary of Technical Education.
1254 **534** 1r. multicoloured . . . . 1·00 30

1994. Centenary of Trinity College, Kandy, Old Boys' Association.
1255 **535** 1r. multicoloured 30 20

536 College Flag

1994. 150th Anniv of St. Thomas' College, Matara.
1256 **536** 1r. brown and blue . . . 30 20

537 Ven. Siyambalangamuwe Sri Gunaratana Thero

1994. Ven. Siyambalangamuwe Sri Gunaratana Thero (educationist) Commemoration.
1257 **537** 1r. multicoloured . . . . 1·50 30

538 College Building and Arms

1994. 125th Anniv of St. Joseph's College, Trincomalee.
1258 **538** 1r. multicoloured 30 20

539 Man distributing Water

1994. Vesak Festival. Dasa Paramita (Ten Virtues). Multicoloured.
1259 1r. Type **539** 20 10
1260 2r. Man and elephant . . . 1·00 40
1261 5r. Man surrounded by women . . . . 1·00 90
1262 17r. Ruler with snake charmer . . . . 2·00 3·25
MS1263 162/88 mm. Nos. 1259/62 3·00 4·50

540 I.L.O. Monument, Geneva, Logo and Workers

1994. 75th Anniv of I.L.O.
1264 **540** 1r. multicoloured . . . . 1·00 30

541 Mahakavindra Dhammaratana Thero (Buddhist theologian)

1994. National Heroes. Multicoloured.
1265 1r. Type **541** 20 25
1266 1r. Ranasinghe Premadasa (former President) 20 25
1267 1r. Dr. Colvin de Silva (trade union leader) . . . 20 25
1268 1r. E. Periyathambipillai (Tamil poet) 20 25

542 Conference Logo

1994. 13th International Federation of Social Workers World Conference, Colombo.
1269 **542** 8r. multicoloured . . . . 2·25 2·25

543 Ven. Sri Somaratana Thero and Temple

1994. 10th Death Anniv of Ven. Sri Somaratana Thero (Buddhist religious leader).
1270 **543** 1r. multicoloured . . . . 1·50 40

544 Communication Technology and Logo

1994. "INFOTEL LANKA '94" International Computers and Telecommunications Exhibition.
1271 **544** 10r. multicoloured . . . 2·25 2·50

545 Veddah Tribesman stringing Bow

546 Luca Pacioli (pioneer), Logo and Equipment inside "500"

1994. Year of Indigenous People (1993). Mult.
1272 1r. Type **545** 25 10
1273 17r. Veddah artist and rock paintings . . . . 3·25 3·75

1994. 500th Anniv of Accountancy.
1274 **546** 1r. multicoloured . . . . 1·50 40

547 Society Emblem

1994. Centenary of Wildlife and Nature Society of Sri Lanka.
1275 **547** 1r. green and black . . . 15 10
1276 – 2r. multicoloured 60 20
1277 – 10r. multicoloured . . . 1·75 1·75
1278 – 17r. multicoloured . . . 2·50 3·50
MS1279 130 × 96 mm. Nos. 1275/8 3·50 5·00
DESIGNS: 2r. Horned lizard; 10r. Giant squirrel; 17r. Sloth bear.

548 Airliner, I.C.A.O. Logo and Globe

1994. 50th Anniv of I.C.A.O.
1280 **548** 10r. multicoloured . . . 2·75 2·75

549 Christmas Crib

1994. Christmas. Multicoloured.
1281 1r. Type **549** 20 10
1282 17r. St. Joseph's carpentry workshop, Nazareth . . . 2·50 3·00
MS1283 145 × 81 mm. Nos. 1281/2 2·25 3·00

550 Map of Sri Lanka and Aspects of Science

1994. 50th Anniv of Sri Lankan Association for the Advancement of Science.
1284 **550** 1r. multicoloured . . . . 2·00 50

551 College Building and Arms

1994. Cent of Richmond College Old Boys' Assn.
1285 **551** 1r. black, red and blue 20 20

552 "Dendrobium maccarthiae"

554 Blue Water Lily

553 Father Joseph Vaz and Pope John Paul II

1994. 60th Anniv of Orchid Circle of Ceylon. Multicoloured.
1286 50c. Type **552** 20 10
1287 1r. "Cottonia peduncularis" 25 10
1288 5r. "Bulbophyllum wightii" 55 50
1289 17r. "Habenaria crinifera" 1·10 2·25
MS1290 127 × 95 mm. Nos. 1286/9 2·25 3·00

1995. Papal Visit and Beatification of Father Joseph Vaz.
1291 **553** 1r. multicoloured . . . . 2·00 50

1995.
1292 **554** 1r. multicoloured 60 10

555 College Building and Arms

1995. Centenary of St. Joseph's College, Colombo.
1293 **555** 1r. multicoloured . . . . 1·00 35

556 Sirimavo Bandaranaike and National Flag

1995. Election of Sirimavo Banadaranaike as Prime Minister.
1294 **556** 2r. multicoloured . . . . 1·50 80

557 Man offering Water to Crew of Outrigger Canoe

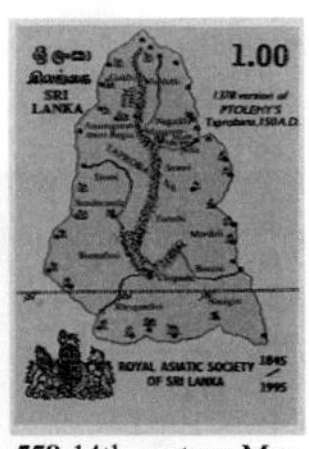

558 14th-century Map of Sri Lanka and Society Arms

1995. Vesak Festival. Dasa Paramita (Ten Virtues). Multicoloured.
1295 1r. Type **557** 20 10
1296 2r. Catching falling man . . 25 15
1297 10r. Teacher with students 1·00 1·10
1298 17r. Stopping man digging 1·75 2·50
MS1299 170 × 90 mm. Nos. 1295/8 2·50 3·50

1995. 150th Anniv of Royal Asiatic Society of Sri Lanka.
1300 **558** 1r. multicoloured . . . . 2·00 65

559 Abdul Cader

1995. 120th Birth Anniv of Abdul Cader (lawyer).
1301 **559** 2r. multicoloured . . . . 1·50 85

560 College Building

1995. Centenary of St. Aloysius's College, Galle.
1302 **560** 2r. multicoloured . . . . 1·50 80

561 Tikiri Ilangaratna

1995. Tikiri Bandara Ilangaratna (politician and author) Commemoration.
1303 **561** 2r. multicoloured . . . . 1·50 80

562 Lamps and Schools Flag

1995. Centenary of Dhamma Schools Movement.
1304 **562** 2r. multicoloured . . . . 1·50 80

563 G.P.O. Building

1995. Centenary of General Post Office, Colombo.
1305 **563** 1r. multicoloured . . . . 1·00 35

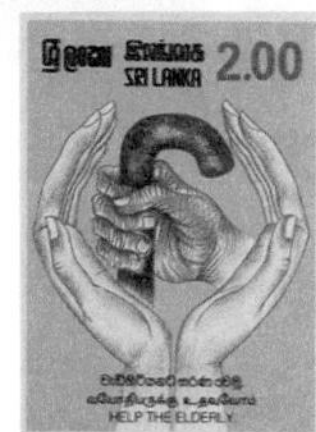

564 Young Hands surrounding Old Hand

1995. International Day for the Elderly.
1306 **564** 2r. multicoloured . . . . 1·50 80

565 Sri Lankan Parliament Building and C.P.A. Logo

1995. 41st Commonwealth Parliamentary Conf, Colombo.
1307 **565** 2r. multicoloured . . . . 1·50 80

566 Anniversary Emblem and Map of Sri Lanka

567 Money falling into Globe Money Box

1995. 50th Anniv of United Nations.
1308 **566** 2r. multicoloured . . . . 1·50 1·00

1995. 71st Anniv of World Thrift Day and 110th Anniv of National Savings Bank.
1309 **567** 2r. multicoloured . . . . 1·50 80

568 Diocesan Arms of Colombo and Kurunegala

1995. Christmas. 150th Anniv of Anglican Diocese of Colombo. Multicoloured.
1310 2r. Type **568** 20 10
1311 20r. Nativity scene and hands surrounding map 2·25 3·00
MS1312 150 × 90 mm. Nos. 1310/11 2·25 3·50

569 Flags of Member Countries
570 School Emblem

1995. 10th Anniv of South Asian Association for Regional Co-operation.
1313 **569** 2r. multicoloured . . . . 1·75 1·00

1996. 175th Anniv of Vincent Girls' High School, Batticaloa.
1314 **570** 2r. multicoloured . . . 1·50 80

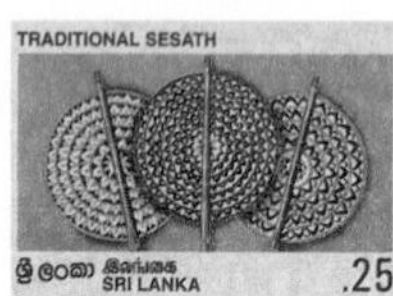

571 Little Basses Lighthouse
572 Traditional Sesath (umbrellas)

1996. Lighthouses. Multicoloured.
1315 50c. Type **571** 30 15
1316 75c. Great Basses 35 15
1317 2r. Devinuwara 60 25
1317a 2r.50 As 2r. 60 35
1318 20r. Galle . . . . 2·00 2·50
MS1319 151 × 91 mm. Nos. 1315/17 and 1318 . . . . 2·25 3·00

1996. Traditional Handicrafts. Multicoloured.
1320 25c. Type **572** 10 10
1321 8r.50 Pottery 40 45
1322 10r.50 Mats 55 70
1323 17r. Lace . . . . 75 1·40
MS1324 150 × 90 mm. Nos. 1320/3 2·50 3·00

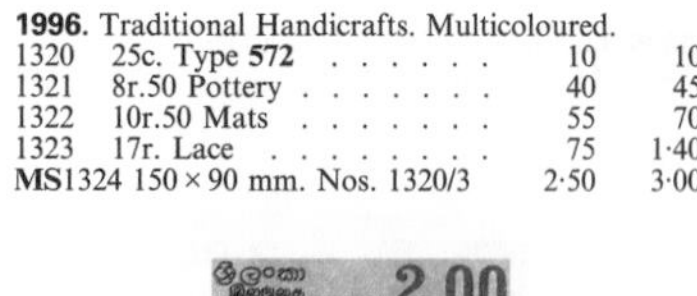

573 School Emblem and Trees

1996. Centenary of Chundikuli Girls' College, Jaffna.
1325 **573** 2r. multicoloured . . . . 1·50 80

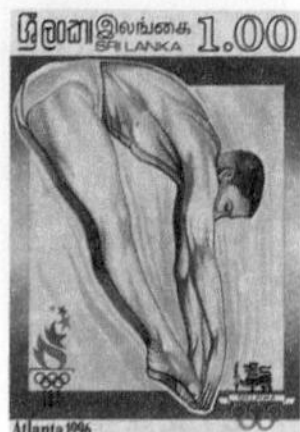

574 Upaka and Capa
575 Diving

1996. Vesak Festival. Multicoloured.
1326 1r. Type **574** 15 10
1327 2r. Dantika and elephant . . 40 15
1328 5r. Subha removing her eye 60 65
1329 10r. Punna and the Brahmin 85 1·25
MS1330 170 × 90 mm. Nos. 1326/9 1·50 2·25

1996. Olympic Games, Atlanta. Multicoloured.
1331 1r. Type **575** 20 10
1332 2r. Tennis 70 10
1333 5r. Rifle shooting (horiz) . . 1·00 80
1334 17r. Running (horiz) . . . . 1·75 3·00

576 Bowler

1996. Sri Lanka's Victory in World Cup Cricket Tournament. Multicoloured.
1335 2r. Type **576** 45 25
1336 10r.50 Wicket-keeper . . . 80 90
1337 17r. Batsman . . . . 1·25 1·75
1338 20r. World Cup trophy . . 1·40 2·00
MS1339 150 × 90 mm. Nos. 1335/8 3·00 4·25

577 Main Building, Jaffna Central College

1996. 180th Anniv of Jaffna Central College.
1340 **577** 2r. multicoloured . . . . 1·50 80

578 Globe in Flowers and White Dove
579 Jesus washing the Disciples' Feet

1996. 50th Anniv of UNESCO.
1341 **578** 2r. multicoloured . . . . 1·75 1·00

1996. Christmas. Murals by David Paynter from Trinity College Chapel, Kandy. Multicoloured.
1342 2r. Type **579** 10 10
1343 17r. Parable of the Good Samaritan . . . . 1·25 1·50
MS1344 150 × 90 mm. Nos. 1342/4 1·25 1·75

580 Cupped Hands holding Child
581 Swami Vivekananda and Globe

1996. 50th Anniv of UNICEF.
1345 **580** 5r. multicoloured 60 85

1997. Centenary of Swami Vivekananda's Visit to Sri Lanka.
1346 **581** 2r.50 multicoloured . . . 70 70

1997. No. 1317 surch **2.50**.
1347 2r.50 on 2r. multicoloured 2·00 50

586 Venerable Welivitiye Sorata Thero (scholar)
589 Thuparama Stupa, 3rd-century B.C.

1997. National Heroes (1st series). Multicoloured.
1351 2r. Type **586** 60 60
1352 2r. Mahagama Sekera (writer and artist) 60 60
1353 2r. Dr. S. A. Wickremasinghe (physician) 60 60
1354 2r. Lt. Gen. Denzil Kobbekaduwa 60 60
See also Nos. 1373/6.

1997. No. 1322 surch **11.00**.
1355 11r. on 10r.50 multicoloured 2·75 2·75

1997. Vesak Festival. Anuradhapura Sites. Mult.
1357 1r. Type **589** 10 10
1358 2r.50 Ruwanvalisaya stupa, 61–137 B.C. 15 10
1359 3r. Abhayagiri Dagaba, 103–102 B.C. 15 15
1360 17r. Jethavana Dagaba, 276–303 A.D. . . . . . . 80 1·25
MS1361 170 × 90 mm. Nos. 1357/60 1·00 1·75

590 Don Johannes Kumarage

1997. Birth Centenary of D. J. Kumarage (Buddhist teacher).
1362 **590** 2r.50 multicoloured . . . 1·00 60

591 "Munronia pinnata"

1997. Medicinal Herbs. Multicoloured.
1363 2r.50 Type **591** 20 10
1364 14r. "Rauvolfia serpentina" 80 1·25

592 Tourist Board Logo, Airliner and Holiday Resorts

1997. Visit Sri Lanka.
1365 **592** 20r. multicoloured . . . 2·00 2·50

1997. No. 1321 surch **1.00**.
1366 1r. on 8r.50 Pottery . . . . 3·50 40

594 Lyre Head Lizard

1997. Reptiles. Multicoloured.
1367 2r.50 Type **594** 10 10
1368 5r. Boie's roughside (snake) 20 20
1369 7r. Common Lanka skink 55 70
1370 20r. Great forest gecko . . 60 1·25
MS1371 170 × 90 mm. Nos. 1367/70 1·50 2·25

595 St. Servatius' College, Matara

1997. Centenary of St. Servatius' College, Matara.
1372 **595** 2r.50 multicoloured . . . 45 20

1997. National Heroes (2nd series). As T **586**. Multicoloured.
1373 2r.50 Sri Indasara Nayake Thero (Buddhist leader) 20 25
1374 2r.50 Abdul Aziz (trade union leader) 20 25
1375 2r.50 Prof. Subramaniam Vithiananthan 20 25
1376 2r.50 Vivienne Goonewardene (politician) 20 25

596 The Nativity

1997. Christmas. Multicoloured.
1377 2r.50 Type **596** 10 10
1378 20r. Visit of the Three Kings 90 1·40
MS1379 170 × 90 mm. Nos. 1377/8 1·00 1·40

597 Young Men's Buddhist Association Building, Colombo

1998. Centenary of Young Men's Buddhist Association, Colombo.
1380 **597** 2r.50 multicoloured . . . 30 25

598 Sri Jayawardenapura Vidyalaya School

1998. 175th Anniv of Sri Jayawardenapura Vidyalaya School, Kotte.
1381 **598** 2r.50 multicoloured . . . 30 25

599 Children and Mathematical Symbols

1998. 50th Anniv of Independence. Multicoloured.
1382 2r. Type **599** 30 10
1383 2r.50 Flag and 1949 4c. Independence stamp (38 × 28 mm) 50 40
1384 2r.50 People with technological and industrial symbols 40 40
1385 5r. Dancers with arts and music symbols 50 55
1386 10r. Women with cultural and historical symbols . . 70 90

600 Scouts raising Flag and Jamboree Logo
601 W.H.O. Emblem in "50" and Flag of Sri Lanka

1998. 5th National Scout Jamboree, Kandy. Mult.
1387 2r.50 Type **600** 50 10
1388 17r. Scout saluting and Jamboree emblem . . . . 1·60 2·50

1998. 50th Anniv of W.H.O.
1389 **601** 2r.50 multicoloured . . . 40 15

602 Chunam Box
603 Kelani River and Stupa

1998. Traditional Jewellery and Crafts. Mult.
1390 2r.50 Type **602** 20 10
1391 5r. Agate necklace 30 20
1392 10r. Bangle and hairpin . . 50 60
1393 17r. Sigiri ear-ring . . . . . 80 1·25
MS1394 151 × 91 mm. Nos. 1390/3 1·50 2·00

1998. Vesak Festival. Wall Paintings from Kelaniya Temple. Multicoloured.
1395 1r. Type **603** 10 10
1396 2r.50 Crown Prince Mahanaga and his court on way to Magampura . . 20 10
1397 4r. Mahanaga and wife with baby Yatala Tissa 35 30
1398 17r. Prince Mahanaga with King's minister . . . . . 80 1·10
MS1399 170 × 90 mm. Nos. 1395/8 1·25 1·75

604 School Building and Emblem

1998. 175th Anniv of St. John's College, Jaffna.
1400 **604** 2r.50 multicoloured . . . 20 15

605 Elephants in River

1998. Elephants. Multicoloured.
1401 2r.50 Type **605** 45 15
1402 10r. Cow and calf 75 50
1403 17r. Family group . . . . . 1·00 1·10
1404 50r. Bull elephant . . . . . 1·75 3·50
MS1405 105 × 90 mm. Nos. 1401/4 3·25 4·00

606 S.A.A.R.C. Flags and Logo

1998. 10th Anniv of South Asian Association for Regional Co-operation.
1406 **606** 2r.50 multicoloured . . . 55 25

607 William Gopallawa

1998. William Gopallawa (first President of Sri Lanka) Commemoration.
1407 **607** 2r.50 multicoloured . . . 30 15

608 Satellite and Computer

1998. Year of Information Technology.
1408 **608** 2r.50 multicoloured . . . 30 15

609 Ven. Kotahene Pannakitti Nayaka Thero (Buddhist scholar)

610 Flag of Sri Lanka and Lions Club Emblem

1998. Distinguished Personalities. Multicoloured.
1409 2r.50 Type **609** 20 20
1410 2r.50 Prof. Ediriweera Sarachchandra (scholar) 20 20
1411 2r.50 Sir Nicholas Attygalle (medical pioneer) 20 20
1412 2r.50 Dr. Samuel Fisk Green (Tamil scholar) . . 20 20

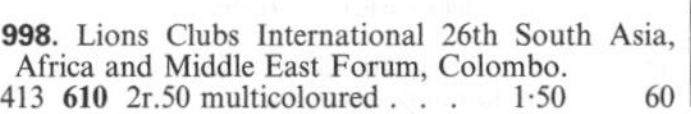

1998. Lions Clubs International 26th South Asia, Africa and Middle East Forum, Colombo.
1413 **610** 2r.50 multicoloured . . . 1·50 60

611 "50" and Meteorological Symbols

1998. 50th Anniv of Department of Meteorology.
1414 **611** 2r.50 multicoloured . . . 50 25

612 Virgin Mary and the Infant Jesus

613 S. W. Bandaranaike as a Young Man

1998. Christmas. Multicoloured.
1415 2r.50 Type **612** 10 10
1416 20r. The Annunciation . . . 90 1·40
MS1417 90 × 150 mm. Nos. 1415/16 1·00 1·40

1999. Birth Centenary of S. W. Bandaranaike. Multicoloured.
1418 3r.50 Type **613** 65 65
1419 3r.50 Bandaranaike as Prime Minister 65 65
MS1420 81 × 100 mm. Nos. 1418/19 1·25 1·50

614 Traditional Dancer

615 Sir Arthur C. Clarke (author) and Spacecraft

1999.
1422 **614** 1r. brown 10 10
1423 2r. blue 10 10
1424 3r. purple 15 10
1425 3r.50 blue 15 10
1426 4r. red 15 10
1427 5r. green 15 10
1428 10r. violet 25 20
1429 13r.50 red 30 20
1430 17r. green 35 25
1431 20r. brown 40 30
1431a – 50r. brown and orange 65 70
1431b – 100r. brown and ochre 1·25 1·40
1431c – 200r. lavender and blue 2·50 2·75
DESIGNS—(25 × 30mm): 50, 100 and 200r. As T **614** but with background of scroll work.
The 5r. to 20r. are larger, 21 × 26 mm.

1999. 50 Years of Communication Improvement. Multicoloured.
1432 3r.50 Type **615** 65 65
1433 3r.50 Sir Arthur C. Clarke with spacecraft orbiting Earth 65 65
Nos. 1432/3 were printed together, se-tenant, forming a composite design.

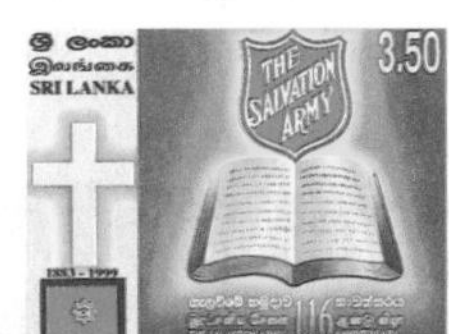

616 Salvation Army Badge, Bible and Cross

1999. 116th Anniv of Salvation Army in Sri Lanka.
1434 **616** 3r.50 multicoloured . . . 45 40

617 Activities of British Council

618 "Birth of Prince Siddhartha"

1999. 50th Anniv of British Council.
1435 **617** 3r.50 multicoloured . . . 40 30

1999. Vesak Festival. Multicoloured.
1436 2r. Type **618** 10 10
1437 3r.50 "The Enlightenment" 15 15
1438 13r.50 "The Maha Parinirvana" 45 70
1439 17r. Celebrating Vesak . . . 55 90
MS1440 151 × 90 mm. Nos. 1436/9 1·25 1·75

619 Dish Aerial and Transmitting Tower

620 Sumithrayo Logo

1999. 20th Anniv of Independent Television.
1441 **619** 3r.50 multicoloured . . . 30 25

1999. 25th Anniv of Sumithrayo (humanitarian charity).
1442 **620** 3r.50 multicoloured . . . 30 25

621 Scene from "Handaya" and Camera Crew

623 Hector Kobbekaduwa

622 Vidyodaya Pirivena

1999. 50 Years of Sri Lankan Cinema. Mult.
1443 3r.50 Type **621** 10 10
1444 4r. Scene from "Nidhanaya" and film societies' emblems 10 10
1445 10r. Scene from "Gamperaliya" and camera crew 30 30
1446 17r. Two scenes from "Kadawunu Poronduwa" 85 1·40
MS1447 109 × 183 mm. Nos. 1443/6 1·25 1·50

1999. 125th Anniv of Vidyodaya Pirivena (Buddhist education foundation).
1448 **622** 3r.50 multicoloured . . . 30 25

1999. Hector Kobbekaduwa (former Minister of Agriculture and Lands) Commemoration.
1449 **623** 3r.50 multicoloured . . . 30 25

624 Hands holding Emblem, Fountain Pen and Magazine

1999. Centenary of *Bhakthi Prabodanaya* (religious magazine).
1450 **624** 3r.50 multicoloured . . . 30 25

625 Army Emblem and Flags

626 Emblem and Scenery within Segments of Circle

1999. 50th Anniv of Sri Lankan Army.
1451 **625** 3r.50 multicoloured . . . 50 30

1999. 50th Anniv of Sri Lankan National Commission for UNESCO.
1452 **626** 13r.50 multicoloured . . 1·75 2·00

627 Two Children on Globe within Hands

628 Ven. Balangoda Ananda Maitreya

1999. 10th Anniv of United Nations Rights of the Child Convention.
1453 **627** 3r.50 multicoloured . . . 80 45

1999. Ven. Balangoda Ananda Maitreya (Buddhist monk and teacher).
1454 **628** 3r.50 multicoloured . . . 30 25

629 The Nativity

1999. Christmas. Multicoloured.
1455 3r.50 Type **629** 25 10
1456 20r. Visit of Three Wise Men . . . . 1·40 1·60
MS1457 150 × 90 mm. Nos. 1455/6 1·60 1·75

630 Sunil Santha

632 Dr. Pandithamani Kanapathipillai

1999. 85th Birth Anniv of Sunil Santha (musician and teacher).
1458 **630** 3r.50 multicoloured . . . 1·25 60

1999. No. 1317a surch **2.00**.
1459 2r. on 2r.50 Devinawara Lighthouse . . . . 2·00 55

1999. Birth Centenary of Dr. Pandithamani Kanapathipillai (Tamil scholar).
1460 **632** 3r.50 multicoloured . . . 75 40

633 Emblem, Figures and Inscriptions

1999. Bicentenary of State Audit Department.
1461 **633** 3r.50 multicoloured . . . 50 35

634 Dr. Badiudin Mahmud

635 "Christian Family" (David Paynter)

1999. 95th Birth Anniv of Dr. Badiudin Mahmud (Islamic polititian).
1462 **634** 3r.50 multicoloured . . . 75 40

1999. Sri Lankan Paintings. Multicoloured.
1463 3r.50 Type **635** 20 10
1464 4r. "Sri Lankan Woman" (Justin Daraniyagala) . . 20 10
1465 17r. "Waiting for the Fishermen" (Ivan Peries) 70 85
1466 20r. "Composing the 'Tripitaka'" (Soliyas Mendis) . . . . 80 1·00
MS1467 150 × 91 mm. Nos. 1463/6 1·50 1·75

636 Kumar Anandan swimming Palk Strait

1999. Sporting Achievements. Multicoloured.

1468	1r. Type **636**	20	10
1469	3r.50 Batsman and trophy (One Day Cricket World Champions, 1996) (vert)	50	25
1470	13r.50 Athletics (vert)	1·00	1·50

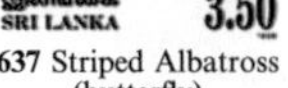

637 Striped Albatross (butterfly)

638 Doves at Nest and Religious Symbols

1999. Butterflies. Multicoloured.

1471	3r.50 Type **637**	35	10
1472	13r.50 Ceylon tiger	75	75
1473	17r. Three-spot grass yellow	90	1·00
1474	20r. Great orange tip	1·00	1·25
MS1475	90 × 148 mm. Nos. 1471/4	2·50	3·00

2000. New Millennium. Multicoloured.

1476	10r. Type **638**	40	25
1477	100r. Girl reading within hands, Scales of Justice and Red Cross	2·75	3·50
1478	100r. Man using computer, airliner and dish aerial	2·75	3·50
1479	100r. People within open cupped hands	2·75	3·50
MS1480	148 × 90 mm. Nos. 1476/9	7·50	9·50

639 Cathedral Church, Kurunagala

2000. 50th Anniv of Diocese of Kurunagala.

1481	**639**	13r.50 multicoloured	1·00	1·10

640 College Logo and Figures around Globe

2000. 125th Anniv of Wesley College, Colombo.

1482	**640**	3r.50 multicoloured	30	25

641 Buddhist Monk and Temple

2000. Centenary of Saddharmakara Pirivena (Buddhist college), Panadura.

1483	**641**	3r.50 multicoloured	30	25

642 Boulder Coral

2000. Corals. Multicoloured.

1484	3r.50 Type **642**	35	10
1485	13r.50 Blue-tipped coral	90	1·00
1486	14r. Brain-boulder coral	90	1·00
1487	22r. Elk-horn coral	1·10	1·40
MS1488	148 × 90 mm. Nos. 1484/7	2·75	3·25

643 Arrival of Cutting from Jaya Sri Maha Bodhi (sacred tree)

2000. Vesak Festival. Multicoloured.

1489	2r. Type **643**	15	10
1490	3r.50 King Devanampiyatissa carrying Jaya Sri Maha Bodhi	25	15
1491	10r. Venerating the Java Sri Maha Bodhi	55	65
1492	13r.50 Planting the cutting at Anuradhapura	75	95
MS1493	98 × 166 mm. Nos 1489/92	1·50	1·75

644 Bar Association Logo and Courts

2000. 25th Anniv of Sri Lanka Bar Association.

1494	**644**	3r.50 multicoloured	30	25

645 C.W.E. Emblem and People in Supermarket

2000. 50th Anniv of Co-operative Wholesale Establishment.

1495	**645**	3r.50 multicoloured	30	25

2000. No. 1135 surch **.50**.

1496	50c. on 8r. Mountain labeo	2·00	1·25

647 St. Patrick's College

2000. 150th Anniv of St. Patrick's College, Jaffna.

1497	**647**	3r.50 multicoloured	75	40

648 Surveyors at Work

2000. Bicentenary of Survey Department, Sri Lanka.

1498	**648**	3r.50 multicoloured	30	25

649 Central Bank of Sri Lanka

2000. 50th Anniv of Central Bank of Sri Lanka.

1499	**649**	3r.50 multicoloured	30	30

650 Dr. Maria Montessori

2000. 130th Birth Anniv of Dr. Maria Montessori (educator).

1500	**650**	3r.50 multicoloured	30	25

651 "2" with Olympic Rings and Maps

2000. Olympic Games, Sydney. Multicoloured.

1501	10r. Type **651**	50	60
1502	10r. Running	50	60
1503	10r. Olympic flame	50	60
1504	10r. Hurdling	50	60
MS1505	172 × 96 mm. Nos. 1501/4	1·75	2·25

652 Association Flag and Conference Hall

2000. 50th Anniv of All Ceylon Young Men's Muslim Association Conference.

1506	**652**	3r.50 multicoloured	30	25

653 Beach, Hotel and Bay-headed Bee Eaters

2000. 25th Anniv of Modern Hotel Industry.

1507	**653**	10r. multicoloured	1·25	1·00

654 Airliner, Ship and Globe

2000. 50th Anniv of Dept of Immigration and Emigration.

1508	**654**	3r.50 multicoloured	45	30

655 Saumiyamoorthy Thondaman

656 Baddegama Siri Piyaratana Nayake Thero (Buddhist educator)

2000. Saumiyamoorthy Thondaman (politician) Commemoration.

1509	**655**	3r.50 multicoloured	30	25

2000. Distinguished Personalities. Multicoloured.

1510	3r.50 Type **656**	25	25
1511	3r.50 Aluthgamage Simon de Silva (novelist)	25	25
1512	3r.50 Desigar Ramanujam (trade unionist)	25	25

657 Journey to Bethlehem

2000. Christmas. Multicoloured.

1513	2r. Type **657**	20	10
1514	17r. The Nativity	1·40	1·60
MS1515	150 × 91 mm. Nos. 1513/14	1·60	1·75

658 Lalith Athulathmudali

2000. Lalith Athulathmudali (politician) Commem.

1516	**658**	3r.50 multicoloured	30	25

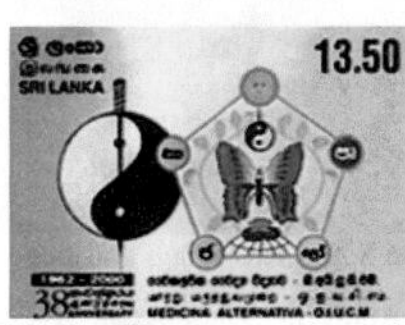

659 Five Elements and Butterfly

2000. 38th Anniv of Medicina Alternativa (alternative medicine society).

1517	**659**	13r.50 multicoloured	1·00	1·25

660 Chapel of Hope of the World

2000. Centenary of Ladies' College, Colombo.

1518	**660**	3r.50 multicoloured	30	25

661 Patrol Boat

2000. 50th Anniv of Sri Lanka Navy.

1519	**661**	3r.50 multicoloured	65	40

662 Peliyagoda Vidyalankara Pirivena Building

2000. 125th Anniv of Peliyagoda Vidyalankara Pirivena (Buddhist university).

1520	**662**	3r.50 multicoloured	30	25

663 Bishop's College

2001. 125th Anniv of Bishop's College, Colombo.

1521	**663**	3r.50 multicoloured	30	25

664 St. Thomas' College

2001. 150th Anniv of St. Thomas' College, Mount Lavinia.
1522 **664** 3r.50 multicoloured . . . 30 25

665 Woman with Basket of Vegetables and Logo

2001. 70th Anniv of Lanka Mahili Samiti (rural women's society).
1523 **665** 3r.50 multicoloured . . . 30 25

666 Air Force Crest and Aircraft

2001. 50th Anniv of Sri Lanka Air Force.
1524 **666** 3r.50 multicoloured . . . 65 40

667 St. Lawrence's School

2001. Centenary (2000) of St. Lawrence's School, Wellawatta.
1525 **667** 3r.50 multicoloured . . . 30 25

668 Bernard Soysa

669 Nagadeepa Stupa, Jaffna

2001. Bernard Soysa (politician) Commemoration.
1526 **668** 3r.50 multicoloured . . . 30 25

2001. Vesak Festival. Buddhist shrines. Mult.
1527 2r. Type **669** 10 10
1528 3r.50 Muthiyangana Chaithya, Badulla 15 10
1529 13r.50 Kirivehera Stupa, Kataragama 55 65
1530 17r. Temple of the Tooth, Kandy 75 90
MS1531 179 × 99 mm. Nos. 1527/30 1·25 1·50

670 "Hansa Jataka" (George Keyt) (½-size illustration)

2001. Birth Centenary of George Keyt (painter).
1532 **670** 13r.50 multicoloured . . 1·00 1·10

671 Gold Kahavanu Coin (9th century)

2001. Sri Lanka Coins. Multicoloured.
1533 3r.50 Type **671** 20 10
1534 13r.50 Silver coin of Vijayabahu I (11th-12th century) 60 55
1535 17r. Copper Sethu coin from Jaffna (13th-14th century) 85 90
1536 20r. Silver commemorative five rupee coin (1957) . . 1·00 1·10
MS1537 155 × 95 mm. Nos. 1533/6 2·40 2·75

672 Colombo Plan Emblem

674 Lance-Corporal Gamini Kularatne and Attack on Tank

673 Flags of Sri Lanka and U.S.A.

2001. 50th Anniv of Colombo Plan.
1538 **672** 10r. multicoloured . . . 50 65

2001. 150th Anniv of Bi-lateral Relations with U.S.A.
1539 **673** 10r. multicoloured . . . 50 65

2001. 10th Death Anniv of Gamini Kularatne (war hero).
1540 **674** 3r.50 multicoloured . . . 30 25

2001. No. 630 surch.
1541 **226** 5r. on 1r.15 multicoloured 30 30
1542 10r. on 1r.15 multicoloured . . . . 1·00 1·00

676 Prince and Princess of Wales Colleges, Moratuwa

2001. 125th Anniv of Prince and Princess of Wales Colleges, Moratuwa.
1543 **676** 3r.50 multicoloured . . . 30 25

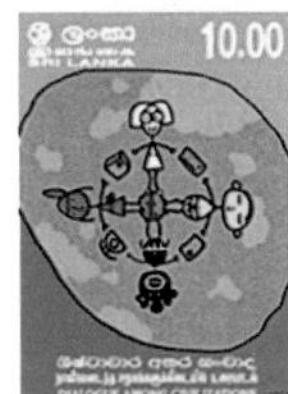

677 Congress Building

2001. All-Ceylon Buddhist Congress National Awards Ceremony.
1544 **677** 3r.50 multicoloured . . . 40 25

678 Children encircling Globe

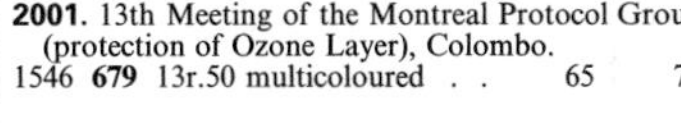

679 Hand protecting Globe from Harmful Rays

2001. U.N. Year of Dialogue among Civilizations.
1545 **678** 10r. multicoloured . . . 50 65

2001. 13th Meeting of the Montreal Protocol Group (protection of Ozone Layer), Colombo.
1546 **679** 13r.50 multicoloured . . . 65 75

680 Ramakrishna Mission Students' Home, Batticaloa

2001. 75th Anniv of Ramakrishna Mission Students' Home, Batticaloa.
1547 **680** 3r.50 multicoloured . . . 30 25

681 Daul Drummer

2001. Drummers.
1548 **680** 1r. red 10 10
1549 – 2r. green 10 10
1550 – 3r. brown 10 10
1551 – 3r.50 blue 10 10
1552 – 4r. pink 10 10
1553 – 5r. orange 10 10
1554 – 10r. violet 10 15
1555 – 13r.50 violet 15 20
1555a – 16r.50 violet 20 25
1556 – 17r. orange 20 25
1557 – 20r. blue 20 25
DESIGNS: (18 × 23 mm.)–1r. to 3r.50, Type **680**. (23 × 28 mm.)–4r. to 10r. Kandyan drummer; 13r.50 to 20r. Low Country drummer.

682 Bandaranaike Memorial International Conference Hall, Colombo

2001. 25th Anniv of S.W.R.D. Bandaranaike National Memorial Foundation.
1558 **682** 3r.50 multicoloured . . . 30 25

683 Jesus with Children

2001. Christmas. Multicoloured.
1559 3r.50 Type **683** 15 10
1560 17r. Angel Gabriel appearing to Mary . . . 50 65
MS1561 150 × 120 mm. Nos. 1559/60 65 80

684 Conical Wart Pygmy Tree-frog

2001. 4th World Congress of Herpetology. Frogs. Multicoloured.
1562 3r.50 Type **684** 20 10
1563 13r.50 Sharp-snout saddle tree-frog 40 35
1564 17r. Round-snout pygmy tree-frog 55 65
1565 20r. Sri Lanka wood frog 65 75
MS1566 180 × 120 mm. Nos. 1562/5 1·50 1·75

685 St. Bridget's Convent

2002. Centenary of St. Bridget's Convent, Colombo.
1567 **685** 3r.50 multicoloured . . . 25 20

686 Front Page from First Edition of Ceylon Government Gazette, 1802

2002. Bicentenary of Ceylon Government Gazette.
1568 **686** 3r.50 multicoloured . . . 25 20

687 Prime Minister D. Senanayake

2002. 50th Death Anniv of D. Senanayake (first Sri Lankan Prime Minister).
1569 **687** 3r.50 multicoloured . . . 25 20

688 Gamini Dissanayake and Victoria Dam

2002. 60th Birth Anniv of Gamini Dissanayake (former government minister).
1570 **688** 3r.50 multicoloured . . . 25 20

689 Lester James Peries and Awards

2002. Lester James Peries (film director).
1571 **689** 3r.50 multicoloured . . . 10 10

690 Sinharaja Forest Reserve

2002. Natural Beauty of Sri Lanka. Multicoloured.
1572 5r. Type **690** 10 10
1573 10r. Horton Plains National Park 10 10
1574 13r.50 Knuckles Range . . 15 20
1575 20r. Rumassala Cliff and Bonavista Coral Reef . . 20 25

691 Mount Fuji and Flags of Sri Lanka and Japan

2002. 50th Anniv of Sri Lanka–Japan Diplomatic Relations.
1576 **691** 16r.50 multicoloured . . 20 25

692 President Ranasinghe Premadasa and Modern Housing Development

2002. 9th Death Anniv of Ranasinghe Premadasa (President 1989–93).
1577 **692** 4r.50 multicoloured . . . 10 10

693 Queen Mahamaya's Dream

2002. Vesak. Dambulla Raja Maha Vihara Rock Paintings. Multicoloured.

1578 3r. Type **693** 10 10

1579 4r.50 Birth of Prince Siddhartha 10 10

1580 16r.50 Prince Siddhartha demonstrating his archery skills 20 25

1581 23r. Ordination of Prince Siddhartha 25 30

MS1582 150 × 93 mm. Nos. 1578/81 65 75

694 Madihe Pamasiha Maha Nayaka Thera

2002. 90th Birthday of Most Venerable Madihe Pamasiha Maha Nayaka Thera (Supreme Patriarch of Sri Lanka Amarapura Maha Nikaya).

1583 **694** 4r.50 multicoloured . . . 10 10

695 Buddhist Monk with Pen and Scroll and Society Emblem

2002. Centenary of Sri Lanka Oriental Studies Society.

1584 **695** 4r.50 multicoloured . . . 10 10

696 Anniversary Emblem and Association Headquarters

2002. 125th Anniv of Rifai Thareeq Association of Sri Lanka.

1585 **696** 4r.50 multicoloured . . . 10 10

697 Discus Thrower

2002. 14th Asian Athletic Championships, Colombo. Multicoloured.

1586 4r.50 Type **697** 10 10

1587 16r.50 Sprinter 20 25

1588 23r. Hurdler 30 35

1589 26r. Long jumper 30 35

698 Carved Stone Lion of 12th Century (squatting)

2002. 125th Anniv of National Museum, Colombo. Multicoloured.

1590 4r.50 Type **698** 10 10

1591 4r.50 Carved stone lion of 12th century (standing) . . 10 10

Nos. 1590/1 were printed together, se-tenant, forming a composite design.

699 "Sapu Mudra" Logo of Sri Lanka Tourist Board

700 Dr. A. C. S. Hameed

2002. Tourism. "Sri Lanka A land like no other".

1592 **699** 10r. multicoloured . . . 10 10

2002. 3rd Death Anniv of Dr. A. C. S. Hameed (Foreign Minister 1977–92).

1593 **700** 4r.50 multicoloured . . . 10 10

701 Freemasons Hall, Colombo

2002. Centenary of Freemasons Hall (Victoria Masonic Temple), Colombo (2001).

1594 **701** 4r.50 multicoloured . . . 10 10

702 Holy Cross College, Kalutara

2002. Centenary of Holy Cross College, Kalutara.

1595 **702** 4r.50 multicoloured . . . 10 10

703 Berlin Buddhist Vihara (temple)

704 Images from Children's Paintings

2002. 50th Anniv of German Dharmaduta Society.

1596 **703** 4r.50 multicoloured . . . 10 10

2002. International Children's Day.

1597 **704** 4r.50 multicoloured . . . 10 10

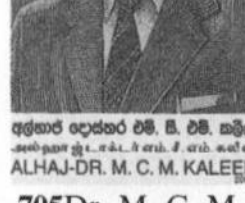

705 Dr. M. C. M. Kaleel

707 Dr. Wijayananda Dahanayake

706 College Entrance, Arms and Building

2002. Al-Haj Dr. M. C. M. Kaleel Commemoration.

1598 **705** 4r.50 green 10 10

2002. 150th Anniv of Uduppiddy American Mission College.

1599 **706** 4r.50 multicoloured . . . 10 10

2002. Birth Centenary of Dr. Wijayananda Dahanayake (politician and educational reformer).

1600 **707** 4r.50 brown 10 10

708 Meeting of King of Kandy and Admiral van Spilbergen, 1602 (from painting by C. L. Beling)

2002. 400th Anniv of Sri Lanka–Netherlands Relations.

1601 **708** 16r.50 multicoloured . . . 20 25

709 Virgin and Child

2002. Christmas. Design showing stained glass windows. Multicoloured.

1602 4r.50 Type **709** 10 10

1603 26r. Holy Family 30 35

MS1604 190 × 130 mm. Nos. 1602/3 40 45

710 Woman harvesting Rubber and Chinese Rice Farmer

2002. 50th Anniv of Ceylon–China Rubber–Rice Pact.

1605 **710** 4r.50 multicoloured . . . 10 10

711 Kopay Christian College

2002. 150th Anniv of Kopay Christian College.

1606 **711** 4r.50 multicoloured . . . 10 10

712 Teacher and Class

2003. Centenary of Teachers' College, Maharagama.

1607 **712** 4r.50 lticoloured 10 10

713 Stained Glass Window

2003. Centenary of Holy Family Convent, Bambalapitiya.

1608 **713** 4r.50 multicoloured . . . 10 10

2003. No. 1556 surch **.50**.

1609 50c. on 17r. orange 10 10

715M. D. Banda and Rice Fields

2003. 30th Death Anniv (2004) of M. D. Banda (politician).

1610 **715** 4r.50 multicoloured . . . 10 10

716 Scholar and Buildings

2003. Centenary of Balagalle Saraswati Maha Pirivena.

1611 **716** 4r.50 multicoloured . . . 10 10

717 D. B. Welagedara

718 Children paying Obeisance to Parents

2003. D. B. Welagedara (politician) Commemoration.

1612 **717** 4r.50 multicoloured . . . 10 10

2003. Vesak. Multicoloured.

1613 2r.50 Type **718** 10 10

1614 3r. Dhamma school 10 10

1615 4r.50 Bhikku on alms round 10 10

1616 23r. Meditation 30 35

MS1617 93 × 152 mm. Nos. 1613/16 60 65

719 Stupa

720 Emblem

2003. Features of Construction of Dagobas in Ancient Sri Lanka. Multicoloured.

1618 4r.50 Type **719** 10 10

1619 16r.50 Guard stones and flight of steps (57 × 28 mm) 10 10

1620 50r. Moonstone (horiz) . . 50 55

MS1621 155 × 116 mm. Nos. 1618/20 70 75

2003. Second World Hindu Conference, Sri Lanka.

1622 **720** 4r.50 multicoloured . . . 10 10

721 Nurses carrying Lamps and Florence Nightingale

2003. International Nursing Day.

1623 **721** 4r.50 multicoloured . . . 10 10

722 Sirimavo Bandaranaike Memorial Exhibition Centre and Mrs. Bandaranaike (former Prime Minister)

2003. Opening of Sirimavo Bandaranaike Memorial Exhibition Centre. Joint issue with People's Republic of China.

1624 **722** 4r.50 multicoloured . . . 10 10

723 Al-Haj H. S. Ismail

2003. Al-Haj H. S. Ismail (former Speaker of Parliament) Commemoration.

1625 **723** 4r.50 multicoloured . . . 10 10

724 Plantation Workers, Port, Cogwheels and Computer

2003. 25th Anniv of Board of Investment of Sri Lanka.

1626 **724** 4r.50 multicoloured . . . 10 10

725 Pidurutalagala Mountain Range

2003. World Bio-diversity Day. Multicoloured.
1627 4r. Type **725** 10 10
1628 4r.50 Seven Maidens Mountain Range 10 10
1629 16r.50 Kirigalpoththa Mountain 20 25
1630 23r. Ritigala Mountain . . . 30 35

726 College Arms

2003. Centenary of G/Gonapinuwala Saralankara College.
1631 **726** 4r.50 multicoloured . . . 10 10

727 Masjidul Abrar Jummah Mosque (central section)

728 Healthy People and Drug Addicts

2003. 1st Arab Settlement in Sri Lanka, Beruwala. Multicoloured.
1632 4r.50 Type **727** 10 10
1633 23r. Masjidul Abrar Jummah Mosque, Beruwala (57 × 22 mm) . . 30 35

2003. Anti Narcotic Week.
1634 **728** 4r.50 multicoloured . . . 10 10

729 Malwathu Maha Viharaya

2003. 250th Anniv of Buddhist Higher Ordination in Sri Lanka. Multicoloured.
1635 4r.50 Type **729** 10 10
1636 4r.50 Asgiri Maha Viharaya 10 10

730 Two Cow Elephants with Calves

2003. Elephant Orphanage, Pinnawala. Multicoloured.
1637 4r.50 Type **730** 10 10
1638 16r.50 Keeper hand feeding milk to young elephant 20 25
1639 23r. Young elephant and calf 30 35
1640 26r. Tusker 30 35
MS1641 183 × 100 mm. Nos. 1637/40 90 1·00

731 Emblem and Mother with Children looking at Stamp Album

2003. "Lanka Philex 2003" Stamp Exhibition, Colombo. 25th Anniv of Philatelic Society of Sri Lanka.
1642 **731** 16r.50 multicoloured . . 20 25
MS1643 111 × 92 mm. **731** 16r.50 multicoloured 20 25

732 Dr. Ananda Tissa de Alwis

2003. Dr Ananda Tissa de Alwis (first Speaker of New Parliament, Kotte) Commemoration.
1644 **732** 4r.50 multicoloured . . . 10 10

733 Ven Mohottiwatte Gunananda Thero, Wheel and Globe

734 Ven Haldanduwana Dhammarakkitha Thero

2003. 130th Anniv of the Great Panadura Controversy (debate between Buddhists and Christians).
1645 **733** 4r.50 multicoloured . . . 10 10

2003. Ven Haldanduwana Dhammarakkitha Thero (Chief Sanganayake and Buddhist philosopher) Commemoration.
1646 **734** 4r.50 multicoloured . . . 10 10

735 Shrine in Procession

2003. 75th Anniv of Poson Maha Perahara (cultural pageant).
1647 **735** 4r.50 multicoloured . . . 10 10

736M. H. M. Ashraff

738 Black-necked Stork

737 Convent of Sisters of the Holy Angels

2003. M. H. M. Ashraff (leader of National Unity Alliance) Commemoration.
1648 **736** 4r.50 multicoloured . . . 10 10

2003. Centenary of the Sisters of the Holy Angels.
1649 **737** 4r.50 multicoloured . . . 10 10

2003. Resident Birds of Sri Lanka. Multicoloured.
1650 4r.50 Type **738** 10 10
1651 4r.50 Purple swamphen . . 10 10
1652 4r.50 Grey heron 10 10
1653 4r.50 White-throated kingfisher 10 10
1654 4r.50 Black-crowned night heron 10 10
1655 4r.50 Scarlet minivet 10 10
1656 4r.50 White-rumped shama 10 10
1657 4r.50 Malabar trogon . . . 10 10
1658 4r.50 Asiatic paradise flycatcher 10 10
1659 4r.50 Little green bee eater 10 10
1660 4r.50 Brown wood owl . . . 10 10
1661 4r.50 Crested serpent eagle 10 10
1662 4r.50 Asian crested goshawk 10 10
1663 4r.50 Jungle owlet 10 10
1664 4r.50 Chestnut-bellied hawk eagle ("Rufous-bellied Eagle") 10 10
1665 4r.50 Chestnut mannikin ("Black-headed Munia") 10 10
1666 4r.50 Pompadour green pigeon 10 10
1667 4r.50 Plum-headed parakeet 10 10
1668 4r.50 Crimson-breasted barbet ("Coppersmith Barbet") 10 10
1669 4r.50 Emerald dove 10 10
1670 4r.50 Blue-faced Malkoha 10 10
1671 4r.50 Travancore scimitar babbler 10 10
1672 4r.50 Painted partridge ("Painted Francolin") . . 10 10
1673 4r.50 Lesser flame-backed woodpecker ("Red-backed Woodpecker") 10 10
1674 4r.50 Malabar pied hornbill 10 10

739 Globe and City

2003. World Habitat Day.
1675 **739** 4r.50 multicoloured . . . 10 10

740 Globe, Post, Computer, Fax and Telephone

2003. World Post Day.
1676 **740** 23r. multicoloured . . . 10 10

741 Blue Sapphire

742 Pope John Paul II

2003. National Gem Stone of Sri Lanka (Blue Sapphire).
1677 **741** 4r.50 multicoloured . . . 10 10

2003. 25th Anniv of the Pontificate of Pope John Paul II.
1678 **742** 4r.50 multicoloured . . . 10 10

743 Couple with Candle and Sacred Cow

744 Ramboda Waterfall

2003. Deepavali Festival.
1679 **743** 4r.50 multicoloured . . . 10 10

2003. Waterfalls of Sri Lanka. Multicoloured.
1680 2r.50 Type **744** 10 10
1681 4r.50 Saint Clair Waterfall 10 10
1682 23r. Bopath Ella Waterfall 30 35
1683 50r. Devon Waterfall . . . 50 55

745 Hon. U. B. Wanninayake

2003. Hon. U. B. Wanninayake (Minister of Finance, 1965–70) Commemoration.
1684 **745** 4r.50 multicoloured . . . 10 10

746 St. Philipnery Church, Katukurunda, Kalutara

2003. Christmas. Multicoloured.
1685 4r.50 Type **746** 10 10
1686 16r.50 Angel and shepherds (vert) 20 25

747 Dr. Pandith Amaradeva

2003. Sri Lankan Artists' Day. Dr. Pandith W. D. Amaradeva (musician).
1687 **747** 4r.50 multicoloured . . . 10 10

748 Gangarama Seemamalakaya

2003. Sri Jinaratana Vocational Training Centre.
1688 **748** 4r.50 multicoloured . . . 10 10

749 Pushparamaya Temple, Malegoda

2003. Daham Pahana (Buddhist Religious Ceremony).
1689 **749** 4r.50 multicoloured . . . 20 15

750 Jummah Mosque, Beruwala

2004. 140th Anniv of Shazuliyathul Fassiya Tharika.
1690 **750** 18r. multicoloured . . . 35 40

751 Emblem of Chavakachcheri Hindu College

753 D. B. Wijetunga

752 Cricket Match

2004. Centenary of Chavakachcheri Hindu College.
1691 **751** 4r.50 multicoloured . . . 20 15

2004. 125th Cricket Match between The Royal and S. Thomas Colleges.

1692	**752**	4r.50 multicoloured	20	15

2004. 82nd Birth Anniv of D. B. Wijetunga (President 1993–94).

1693	**753**	4r.50 multicoloured	10	10

754 Old and Young Trees

2004. 150th Anniv of Inauguration of the Planters Association.

1694	**754**	4r.50 multicoloured	10	10

755 Mapalagama Vipulasara Thero (artist)

756 Cricket Player, Ball and Emblems

2004. Distinguished Personalities. Multicoloured.

1695	3r.50 Type **755**	10	10
1696	3r.50 Cathiravelu Sittampalam (politician)	10	10
1697	3r.50 Maithripala Senanayeke (politician)	10	10
1698	3r.50 M. G. Mendis (politician)	10	10

2004. 75th Anniv of Ananda and Nalanda Cricket Matches. "Battle of the Maroons".

1699	**756**	4r.50 multicoloured	10	10

757 Anthony's College, Kandy

2004. 150th Anniv of St. Anthony's College, Kandy.

1700	**757**	4r.50 multicoloured	10	10

758 Sucharita going to Pandit Vidhura

2004. Vesak. Multicoloured.

1701	4r. Type **758**	10	10
1702	4r.50 Sucharita meeting with Pandit Vidhura	10	10
1703	16r.50 Sucharita introduced to Badraka by Pandit Vidhura	20	25
1704	20r. Sucharita going to Sanjaya, who advises meeting Prince Sambava	20	25
MS1705	122 × 81 mm. 26r. Sucharita meeting Badraka and Sanjaya	30	35

759 "Gongalegoda Banda"

760 Stylized Figure in Blood Droplet and Globe

2004. 155th Death Anniv of Wansapurna Deva David "Gongalegoda Banda" (leader of 1848 Rebellion).

1706	**759**	4r.50 multicoloured	10	10

2004. World Blood Donor Day (14th June).

1707	**760**	4r.50 multicoloured	10	10

761 Swimming

2004. Olympic Games, Athens. Multicoloured.

1708	4r.50 Type **761**	10	10
1709	16r.50 Woman sprinting	20	25
1710	17r. Shooting	20	25
1711	20r. Men's athletics	20	25

762 Sri Chandraratne Manawasinghe

2004. 40th Death Anniv of Sri Chandraratne Manawasinghe (writer).

1712	**762**	4r.50 multicolored	10	10

POSTAL FISCALS

1952. As T **57** but inscr " REVENUE" at sides.

F1	10r. green and orange	60·00	28·00

F 1 Republic Crest

1979. As Type F **1** but with additional Sinhala and Tamil inscriptions on either side of crest.

F2	20r. green	5·00	2·75
F3	50r. violet	13·00	7·00
F4	100r. red	23·00	22·00

1984.

F8	F **1**	100r. purple	2·00	3·00

1998.

F 9	F **1**	50r. orange	65	70
F10		100r. brown	1·25	1·40

F 4

2002.

F11	F **4**	50r. blue and brown	55	60
F12		100r. blue and green	1·10	1·20

STELLALAND Pt. 1

A temporary Boer republic annexed by the British in 1885 and later incorporated in Br. Bechuanaland.

12 pence = 1 shilling;
20 shillings = 1 pound.

1 Arms of the Republic

1884.

1	**1**	1d. red	£180	£325
2		3d. orange	22·00	£325
3		4d. blue	21·00	£350
4		6d. mauve	22·00	£350
5		1s. green	48·00	£600

1885. Surch **Twee**.

6	**1**	2d. on 4d. blue	£3500	

STRAITS SETTLEMENTS Pt. 1

A British Crown colony which included portions of the mainland of the Malay Peninsula and islands off its coasts, and the island of Labuan off the N. coast of Borneo.

100 cents = 1 dollar (Straits).

1867. Stamps of India surch with crown and value.

1	**11**	1½c. on ½a. blue	90·00	£200
2		2c. on 1a. brown	£130	80·00
3		3c. on 1a. brown	£130	85·00
4		4c. on 1a. brown	£250	£250
5		6c. on 2a. orange	£550	£225
6		8c. on 2a. orange	£190	42·00
7		12c. on 4a. green	£950	£300
8		24c. on 8a. red	£425	80·00
9		32c. on 2a. orange	£350	90·00

1869. No. 1 with "THREE HALF" deleted and "2" written above in manuscript.

10	**11**	2 on 1½c. on ½c. blue	£11000	£5000

5

8

9

1867.

11	**5**	2c. brown	29·00	4·50
98		4c. red	5·00	1·25
66a		6c. lilac	2·00	4·00
52		8c. orange	3·00	1·00
15		12c. blue	£110	6·50
68a		24c. green	4·50	3·75
69	**8**	30c. red	10·00	11·00
70	**9**	32c. red	7·00	2·75
71		96c. grey	75·00	50·00

1879. Surch in words.

20	**5**	5c. on 8c. orange	£100	£150
21	**9**	7c. on 32c. red	£120	£150

1880. Surch in figures and words.

47	**5**	5c. on 4c. red	£275	£300
42		5c. on 8c. orange	£120	£150
44		10c. on 6c. lilac	60·00	6·00
45a		10c. on 12c. blue	50·00	9·00
23	**8**	10c. on 30c. red	£350	75·00

1880. Surch in figures only.

33	**8**	"10" on 30c. red	£170	50·00

18

19

1882.

63a	**5**	2c. red	7·50	85
64		4c. brown	26·00	1·50
65	**18**	5c. blue	13·00	1·00
99		5c. brown	6·00	1·00
100		5c. mauve	2·25	2·00
101	**5**	8c. blue	4·50	50
53	**19**	10c. grey	5·50	1·25
102	**5**	12c. purple	13·00	8·50

1883. Surch in words in one line horiz (No. 109) or vert.

57	**5**	2c. on 8c. orange	£130	80·00
59	**9**	2c. on 32c. orange	£700	£190
109	**18**	4c. on 5c. red	1·00	30

1883. Surch with figures over words in two lines.

61	**5**	2c. on 4c. red	75·00	85·00
62		2c. on 12c. blue	£275	£140
82	**18**	3c. on 5c. blue	£130	£225
84		3c. on 5c. purple	£200	£225
106		4c. on 5c. brown	2·75	4·75
73		4c. on 5c. blue (A)*	£120	£100
107		4c. on 5c. blue (B)*	4·25	14·00
108b	**5**	4c. on 8c. blue	1·00	1·00
74		8c. on 12c. blue	£475	£140
75		8c. on 12c. purple	£350	£130

*(A) "Cents" in italics. (B) "cents" (with small "c") in roman type.

1884. Surch **TWO CENTS** vert.

76	**18**	2c. on 5c. blue	£130	£140

1884. No. 75 additionally surch with large figure **8**.

80	**5**	8 on 8c. on 12c. purple	£250	£275

1885. Surch with words in one line and thick bar.

93	**5**	1c. on 8c. green	1·00	1·50
83a	**9**	3c. on 32c. purple	1·25	1·00
94		3c. on 32c. red	2·25	70

1887. Surch **2 Cents** in one line.

85	**18**	2c. on 5c. blue	24·00	70·00

1891. Surch **10 CENTS** in one line and thin bar.

86	**5**	10c. on 24c. green	3·25	1·25

1891. Surch with words in two lines and thin bar.

88	**5**	1c. on 2c. red	2·00	3·75
89		1c. on 4c. brown	5·00	5·50
90		1c. on 6c. lilac	1·40	5·50
91		1c. on 8c. orange	1·00	1·25
92		1c. on 12c. purple	5·00	9·00
87	**9**	30c. on 32c. orange	8·00	3·50

33

37

1892.

95	**33**	1c. green	4·00	70
96		3c. red	11·00	40
97b		3c. brown	5·00	60
103c		25c. purple and green	24·00	6·00
104		50c. olive and red	20·00	2·50
105		$5 orange and red	£325	£250

1902.

110	**37**	1c. green	2·75	3·00
111		3c. purple and orange	3·50	20
112		4c. purple on red	4·75	30
113		5c. purple	5·50	85
157		5c. orange	2·75	2·50
114		8c. purple on blue	4·25	20
132		10c. purple & black on yellow	8·00	80
159		10c. purple on yellow	8·00	1·00
116		25c. purple and green	13·00	6·00
161		25c. purple	15·00	8·00
117		30c. grey and red	18·00	8·00
162		30c. purple and yellow	42·00	4·25
118		50c. green and red	20·00	20·00
164		50c. black on green	5·00	5·00
136a		$1 green and black	48·00	18·00
165		$1 black and red on blue	15·00	5·50
120		$2 purple and black	75·00	75·00
166		$2 green and red on yellow	24·00	24·00
138a		$5 green and orange	£200	£150
167		$5 green and red on green	£130	75·00
139		$25 green and black	£1700	£1700

39

42

46

47

1903.

127	**39**	1c. green	3·00	10
128		3c. purple	2·25	30
153		3c. red	3·75	10
125		4c. purple on red	5·50	30
154		4c. red	6·00	2·50
156		4c. purple	2·25	80
131a	**42**	8c. purple on blue	25·00	2·75
158		8c. blue	3·50	60
160	**46**	21c. purple	6·50	38·00
163		45c. black on green	2·50	4·00
168	**47**	$25 purple and blue	£1600	£1200

1907. Stamps of Labuan (Crown type) optd **Straits Settlements**. (10c.) or **STRAITS SETTLEMENTS** (others) or surch in words also.

141	**18**	1c. black and purple	65·00	£180
142a		2c. black and green	£180	£325
143		3c. black and brown	20·00	85·00
144		4c. on 12c. black & yellow	2·75	6·00
145		4c. on 16c. green & brown	5·00	8·00
146		4c. on 18c. black & brown	2·75	6·50
147		8c. black and orange	3·50	8·00
148		10c. brown and blue	8·00	8·00
149		25c. green and blue	17·00	40·00
150		50c. purple and lilac	17·00	70·00
151		$1 red and orange	48·00	£120

48

54

52

53

1912.
193 **48** 1c. green . . . . 7·00 1·25
196a 3c. red . . . . 2·50 10
197 4c. purple . . . . 1·75 60
225 **54** 5c. orange . . . . 1·50 15
227 **52** 6c. purple . . . . 2·00 15
201 8c. blue . . . . 2·50 80
202 **54** 10c. purple on yellow . . 1·50 1·00
204 **53** 21c. purple . . . . 6·00 9·50
234b **54** 25c. purple and mauve . . 5·00 1·75
235a 30c. purple and orange . . 2·00 1·25
208b **53** 45c. black on green . . . 3·25 13·00
238 **54** 50c. black on green . . . 1·75 40
239 $1 black and red on blue 6·00 65
240 $2 green and red on yellow . . . . 10·00 8·00
240a $5 green and red on green 90·00 32·00
240b – $25 purple and blue on blue £750 £120
No. 240b is as Type **47** but with head of King George V.

1917. Surch **RED CROSS 2c.**
216 **48** 2c. on 3c. red . . . . . . 2·50 27·00
217 2c. on 4c. purple . . . . . 3·50 27·00

1919.
218 **48** 1c. black 50 10
219 **52** 2c. green 50 10
220 2c. brown . . . . 7·00 2·50
221 **48** 3c. green . . . . 1·50 80
198 4c. red . . . . 2·00 15
223 4c. violet 60 10
224 4c. orange . . . . 1·00 10
226 **54** 5c. brown . . . . 2·75 10
227 **52** 6c. red . . . . 2·00 15
230 **54** 10c. blue . . . . 1·75 3·00
232 **52** 12c. blue . . . . 1·00 20
236a **53** 35c. purple and orange . . 3·50 5·50
237 35c. red and purple . . . 10·00 7·00

1922. Optd **MALAYA-BORNEO EXHIBITION.**
250 **48** 1c. black . . . . 3·00 14·00
251 **52** 2c. green . . . . 2·50 14·00
252 **48** 4c. red . . . . 3·50 30·00
243 **54** 5c. orange . . . . 5·50 19·00
244 **52** 8c. blue . . . . 1·75 8·00
254 **54** 10c. blue . . . . 2·25 26·00
245 25c. purple and mauve . . 3·25 35·00
246 **53** 45c. black on green . . . . 3·00 29·00
255 **54** $1 black and red on blue 20·00 £130
248 $2 green and red on yellow 26·00 £120
249 $5 green and red on green £250 £450

1935. Silver Jubilee. As T **32a** of St. Helena.
256 5c. blue and grey . . . . . 3·00 30
257 8c. green and blue . . . . . 3·00 3·25
258 12c. brown and blue . . . . 3·00 4·50
259 25c. grey and purple . . . . 3·25 5·50

57

58

1936.
260 **57** 1c. black . . . . 1·00 20
261 2c. green . . . . 1·25 70
262 4c. orange . . . . 2·25 70
263 5c. brown . . . . 1·00 30
264 6c. red . . . . 1·25 1·10
265 8c. grey . . . . 2·00 70
266 10c. purple . . . . 2·25 60
267 12c. blue . . . . 2·00 2·50
268 25c. purple and red . . . . 1·25 50
269 30c. purple and orange . . 1·25 3·25
270 40c. red and purple . . . . 1·25 2·50
271 50c. black and green . . . 4·50 1·25
272 $1 black and red on blue 19·00 1·75
273 $2 green and red . . . . 45·00 10·00
274 $5 green and red on green £100 10·00

1937. Coronation. As T **32b** of St. Helena.
275 4c. orange 40 10
276 8c. grey . . . . 1·00 10
277 12c. blue . . . . 2·00 75

1937.
278 **58** 1c. black . . . . 7·00 10
279 2c. green . . . . 18·00 20
294 2c. orange . . . . 2·00 13·00
295 3c. green . . . . 5·00 4·00
280 4c. orange . . . . 18·00 20
281 5c. brown . . . . 20·00 30
282 6c. red . . . . 11·00 50
283 8c. grey . . . . 38·00 10
284 10c. purple . . . . 8·00 10
285 12c. blue . . . . 8·00 50
298 15c. blue . . . . 6·00 10·00
286 25c. purple and red . . . . 42·00 1·10
287 30c. purple and orange . . 20·00 2·00
288 40c. red and purple . . . . 12·00 2·25
289 50c. black on green . . . . 11·00 10
290 $1 black and red on blue 15·00 20
291 $2 green and red . . . . . 32·00 6·50
292 $5 green and red on green 25·00 3·50
For Japanese issues see **JAPANESE OCCUPATION OF MALAYA** and for British military administration see **MALAYA.**

POSTAGE DUE STAMPS

D 1

1924.
D1 **D 1** 1c. violet . . . . 5·00 6·50
D2 2c. black . . . . 3·25 1·25
D3 4c. green . . . . 2·00 4·75
D4 8c. red . . . . 4·50 55
D5 10c. orange . . . . 6·00 85
D6 12c. blue . . . . 7·00 65
For later issues see **MALAYAN POSTAL UNION.**

SUDAN Pt. 1; Pt. 14

A territory in Africa, extending south from Egypt towards the Equator, jointly administered by Gt. Britain and Egypt until 1954 when the territory was granted a large measure of self-government. Became independent on 1 January 1956.

1897. 1000 milliemes = 100 piastres = £1 Sudanese.
1993. dinar.

1897. Stamps of Egypt optd **SOUDAN** in English and Arabic.
1 **18** 1m. brown . . . . 2·25 2·00
3 2m. green . . . . 1·25 1·75
4 3m. yellow . . . . 1·40 1·50
5 5m. red . . . . 2·00 70
6 **10** 1p. blue . . . . 7·00 2·00
7 – 2p. orange . . . . 55·00 16·00
8 – 5p. grey . . . . 50·00 19·00
9 **18** 10p. mauve . . . . 32·00 42·00

2 Arab Postman

6

1898.
18 **2** 1m. brown and red . . . . 1·25 65
19 2m. green and brown . . . 1·75 10
20 3m. mauve and green . . . 2·25 25
21 4m. blue and brown . . . . 1·50 2·50
22 4m. red and brown . . . . 1·50 75
23 5m. red and black . . . . 2·00 10
24 1p. blue and brown . . . . 2·25 30
25 2p. black and blue . . . . 24·00 1·75
44 2p. purple and orange . . . 2·25 10
44b 3p. brown and blue . . . . 3·00 10
44c 4p. blue and black . . . . 3·50 10
45 5p. brown and green . . . 1·25 10
45b 6p. blue and black . . . . 6·50 1·25
45c 8p. green and black . . . 6·50 2·75
46 10p. black and mauve . . . 4·00 10
46b 20p. blue . . . . 5·00 10

1903. Surch **5 Milliemes.**
29 **2** 5m. on 5p. brown and green 6·50 9·50

1921.
37 **6** 1m. black and orange . . . 70 10
38 2m. yellow and brown . . . 75 10
39 3m. mauve and green . . . 70 10
40 4m. green and brown . . . 60 10
41 5m. brown and black . . . 60 10
42 10m. red and black . . . . 1·50 10
43a 15m. blue and brown . . . 1·50 10
For stamps as Type **2** and **6** with different Arabic inscriptions see issue of 1948.

1931. Air. Nos. 41/2 and 44 optd **AIR MAIL.**
47 **6** 5m. brown and black 35 70
48 10m. red and black . . . . . 85 11·00
49 **2** 2p. purple and yellow . . . . 85 7·50

10 Statue of General Gordon

1931. Air.
49b **10** 3m. green and brown . . . 2·50 6·50
50 5m. black and green . . . 1·00 10
51 10m. black and red . . . . 1·00 20
52 15m. brown 40 10
53 2p. black and orange . . . 30 10
53d 2½p. mauve and blue . . . 3·00 10
54 3p. black and grey 60 15
55 3½p. black and violet . . . 1·50 80
56 4½p. brown and grey . . . 10·00 15·00
57 5p. black and blue . . . . 1·00 30
57c 7½p. green . . . . 4·00 10·00
57d 10p. brown and blue . . . 9·00 1·75

1932. Air. Surch **2½ 2½ AIR MAIL** and value in Arabic figures.
58 **2** 2½p. on 2p. purple and orange . . . . 1·40 3·50

12 General Gordon (after C. Ouless)

13 Gordon Memorial College, Khartoum

1935. 50th Death Anniv of Gen. Gordon.
59 **12** 5m. green 35 10
60 10m. brown 85 25
61 13m. blue . . . . 85 11·00
62 15m. red . . . . 1·75 25
63 **13** 2p. blue . . . . 1·25 20
64 5p. orange . . . . 1·25 40
65 10p. purple . . . . 7·50 8·50
66 – 20p. black . . . . 22·00 50·00
67 – 50p. brown . . . . 80·00 £110
DESIGN—(44 × 20 mm): 20, 50p. Gordon Memorial Service, Khartoum.

1935. Air. Stamps of 1931 surch in English and Arabic.
74 **10** 5m. on 2½p. mauve and blue 3·50 10
68 15m. on 10m. black and red 40 10
69 2½p. on 3m. green & brown 85 4·50
70 2½p. on 5m. black and green 50 1·50
75 3p. on 3½p. black and violet 35·00 48·00
71 3p. on 4½p. brown and grey 1·75 17·00
76 3p. on 7½p. green . . . . . 7·00 6·50
77 5p. on 10p. brown and blue 1·75 4·75
72 7½p. on 4½p. brown and grey . . . . 6·50 48·00
73 10p. on 4½p. brown and grey . . . . 6·50 48·00

1940. No. 42 surch **5 Mills.** and in Arabic.
78 **6** 5m. on 10m. red and black 60 30

1940. Nos. 41 surch **4½ PIASTRES** and No. 45c surch **4½ Piastres** in English and Arabic.
79 **6** 4½p. on 5m. brown and black 48·00 6·50
80 **2** 4½p. on 8p. green and black 40·00 9·00

20 Tuti Island, R. Nile near Khartoum

1941.
81 **20** 1m. black and orange . . . 1·75 4·00
82 2m. orange and brown . . . 1·75 4·00
83 3m. mauve and green . . . 2·00 20
84 4m. green and brown . . . 80 60
85 5m. brown and black . . . 30 10
86 10m. red and black . . . . 8·50 2·50
87 15m. blue and brown . . . 1·00 10
88 2p. purple and yellow . . . 6·50 60
89 3p. brown and blue . . . . 1·00 10
90 4p. blue and black . . . . 2·00 10
91 5p. brown and green . . . 5·00 9·00
92 6p. blue and black . . . . 18·00 40
93 8p. green and black . . . . 14·00 45
94 10p. slate and purple . . . 65·00 75
95 20p. blue . . . . 60·00 35·00
The piastre values are larger, 30 × 25 mm.

22 Arab Postman

23 Arab Postman

1948.
96 **22** 1m. black and orange . . . 35 3·75
97 2m. orange and brown . . 80 4·50
98 3m. mauve and green . . . 30 4·75
99 4m. green and brown . . . 50 50
100 5m. brown and black . . . 5·50 2·00
101 10m. red and black . . . . 5·50 10
102 15m. blue and brown . . . 5·00 10
103 **23** 2p. purple and yellow . . . 8·00 2·50
104 3p. brown and blue . . . . 7·00 30
105 4p. blue and black . . . . 4·00 1·75
106 5p. orange and green . . . 4·00 2·75
107 6p. blue and black . . . . 4·50 3·00
108 8p. green and black . . . . 4·50 3·00
109 10p. black and mauve . . . 11·00 4·75
110 20p. blue . . . . 4·50 30
111 50p. red and blue . . . . 6·50 2·50
In this issue the Arabic inscriptions below the camel differ from those in Types **2** and **6**.

24 Arab Postman

25 Arab Postman

1948. Golden Jubilee of "Camel Postman" design.
112 **24** 2p. black and blue 20 10

1948. Opening of Legislative Assembly.
113 **25** 10m. red and black 50 10
114 5p. orange and green . . . 1·00 1·50

26 Blue Nile Bridge, Khartoum

1950. Air.
115 **26** 2p. black and green . . . 4·50 1·50
116 – 2½p. blue and orange . . . 75 1·25
117 – 3p. purple and blue . . . . 3·00 1·25
118 – 3½p. sepia and brown . . . 2·50 3·00
119 – 4p. brown and blue . . . . 1·50 2·75
120 – 4½p. black and blue . . . . 2·50 3·75
121 – 6p. black and red . . . . 2·25 3·25
122 – 20p. black and purple . . . 2·25 5·50
DESIGNS: 2½p. Kassala Jebel; 3p. Sagia (water wheel); 3½p. Port Sudan; 4p. Gordon Memorial College; 4½p. "Gordon Pasha" (Nile mail boat); 6p. Suakin; 20p. G.P.O. Khartoum.

34 Ibex

35 Cotton Picking

1951.
123 **34** 1m. black and orange . . . 1·75 1·50
124 – 2m. black and blue . . . . 1·75 1·00
125 – 3m. black and green . . . 6·50 3·50
126 – 4m. black and green . . . 1·50 3·50
127 – 5m. black and purple . . . 2·25 10
128 – 10m. black and blue . . . 30 10
129 – 15m. black and brown . . 3·75 10
130 **35** 2p. blue 30 10
131 – 3p. brown and blue . . . . 8·50 10
132 – 3½p. green and brown . . . 2·25 10
133 – 4p. blue and black . . . . 1·25 10
134 – 5p. brown and green . . . 50 10
135 – 6p. blue and black . . . . 8·50 2·50
136 – 8p. blue and brown . . . . 14·00 3·50
137 – 10p. black and green . . . 1·50 30
138 – 20p. turquoise and black . . 5·50 2·25
139 – 50p. red and black . . . . 13·00 2·25
DESIGNS—VERT (As Type **34**): 2m. Whale-headed stork ("Shoebill");, 3m. Giraffe; 4m. Baggara girl; 5m. Shilluk warrior; 10m. Hadendowa; 15m. Policeman. (As Type **35**): 50p. Camel postman. HORIZ (As Type **35**): 3p. Ambatch reed canoe; 3½p. Nuba wrestlers; 4p. Weaving; 5p. Saluka farming; 6p. Gum tapping; 8p. Darfur chief; 10p. Stack Laboratory; 20p. Nile lechwe (antelope).

51 Camel Postman

52 "Independent Sudan"

1954. Self-Government.
140 **51** 15m. brown and green . . 50 1·25
141 3p. blue and indigo . . . . 50 1·90
142 5p. black and purple . . . 50 1·50
Stamps as Type **51** but dated "1953" were released in error at the Sudan Agency in London. They had no postal validity.

1956. Independence Commemoration.
143 **52** 15m. orange and purple . . 15 10
144 3p. orange and blue . . . 35 15
145 5p. orange and green . . . 50 35

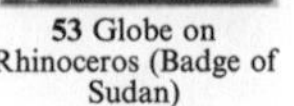

53 Globe on Rhinoceros (Badge of Sudan) — **54** Sudanese Soldier and Farmer

1958. Arab Postal Congress, Khartoum.
146 **53** 15m. orange and purple . . 20 10
147 3p. orange and blue . . . 35 15
148 5p. orange and green . . . 80 35

1959. 1st Anniv of Army Revolution.
149 **54** 15m. yellow, blue & brown 15 10
150 3p. multicoloured 50 20
151 55m. multicoloured 65 40

1960. Inauguration of Arab League Centre, Cairo. As T **154a** of Syria.
152 15m. black and green 15 10

55 Refugees — **56** Football

1960. World Refugee Year.
153 **55** 15m. blue, black and brown 15 15
154 55m. red, black and sepia 55 45

1960. Olympic Games, Rome.
155 **56** 15m. multicoloured 20 10
156 3p. multicoloured 45 25
157 55m. multicoloured 65 35

57 Forest — **58** King Ta'rhaqa

1960. 5th World Forestry Congress, Seattle.
158 **57** 15m. green, brown and red 15 10
159 3p. green, brown and deep green 35 20
160 55m. multicoloured 60 35

1961. Sudanese Nubian Monuments Preservation Campaign.
161 **58** 15m. brown and green . . 20 10
162 3p. violet and orange . . . 35 20
163 55m. brown and blue . . . 60 35

59 Girl with Book — **60** "The World United against Malaria"

1961. "50 Years of Girls' Education in the Sudan".
164 **59** 15m. mauve, purple & blue 15 10
165 3p. blue, orange and black 40 20
166 55m. brown, green & black 55 40

1962. Malaria Eradication.
167 **60** 15m. violet, blue and black 15 10
168 55m. green, emerald & blk 50 35

60a League Centre, Cairo and Emblem

1962. Arab League Week.
169 **60a** 15m. orange 15 10
170 55m. turquoise 45 35

62 Republican Palace — **63** Nile Felucca

64 Camel Postman — **65** Campaign Emblem and "Millet" Cobs

1962.
185 **62** 5m. blue 10 10
186 – 10m. purple and blue . . 10 10
187 – 15m. purple, orange & bistre 10 10
188 **62** 2p. purple 10 10
189 – 3p. brown and green . . . 20 10
190 – 35m. brown, dp brown & green 55 10
191 – 4p. mauve, red and blue 55 10
192 – 55m. black and green . . 55 20
193 – 6p. brown and blue . . . 65 20
194 – 8p. green 65 20
195 **63** 10p. brown, bistre and blue 80 35
196 – 20p. green and bronze . . 1·75 55
194a – 25p. brown and green . . 10 10
197 – 50p. green, blue and black 4·75 1·25
469 **64** £S1 brown and green . . 9·25 4·25
198 – £S5 green and brown . . 11·00 1·75
199 **63** £S10 orange and green . . 22·00 3·75

DESIGNS: As Type **62**—HORIZ: 15m. "Tabbaque" (food cover); 55m., 6, 25p. Cattle; 8p. Date palms. VERT: 10m., 3p. Cotton picking; 35m., 4p. Wild game. As Type **63**—HORIZ: 20p., £S5 Bohein Temple; 50p. Sennar Dam.

1963. Freedom from Hunger.
226 **65** 15m. green and brown . . 15 15
227 55m. violet, lilac and blue 55 35

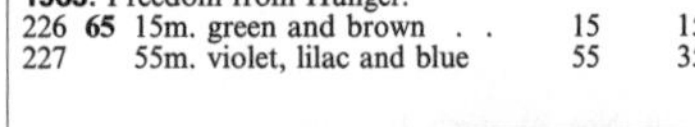

66 Centenary Emblem and Medallions — **67** "Knight"

1963. Centenary of Red Cross.
228 **66** 15m. multicoloured 35 15
229 55m. multicoloured 65 35

1964. Nubian Monuments Preservation. Frescoes from Faras Church, Nubia. Multicoloured.
230 15m. Type **67** 20 15
231 30m. "Saint" (horiz) 35 20
232 55m. "Angel" 85 55

68 Sudan Map — **69** Chainbreakers and Mrs. E. Roosevelt

1964. New York World's Fair. Multicoloured.
233 15m. Khashm el Girba Dam 10 10
234 3p. Sudan Pavilion 20 15
235 55m. Type **68** 50 30
Nos. 233/4 are horiz.

1964. 80th Birth Anniv of Mrs. Eleanor Roosevelt (Human Rights pioneer).
236 **69** 15m. blue and black . . . 10 10
237 3p. violet and black . . . 30 15
238 55m. brown and black . . 45 30

70 Postal Union Emblem — **71** I.T.U. Symbol and Emblems

1964. 10th Anniv of Arab Postal Unions' Permanent Bureau.
239 **70** 15m. black, gold and red 10 10
240 3p. black, gold and green 30 15
241 55m. black, gold and violet 45 30

1965. Centenary of I.T.U.
242 **71** 15m. brown and gold . . . 10 10
243 3p. black and gold 30 15
244 55m. green and gold . . . 45 30

72 Gurashi (martyr) and Demonstrators

1965. 1st Anniv of 21 October Revolution.
245 **72** 15m. black and brown . . 10 10
246 3p. black and red 20 15
247 55m. black and grey . . . 45 30

73 I.C.Y. Emblem — **74** El Siddig El Mahdi

1965. International Co-operation Year.
248 **73** 15m. lilac and black . . . 10 10
249 3p. green and black . . . 20 15
250 55m. red and black 45 30

1966. 5th Death Anniv of Imam El Siddig El Mahdi.
251 **74** 15m. violet and blue . . . 35 15
252 3p. brown and orange . . 50 35
253 55m. brown and grey . . . 1·10 60

75 M. Zaroug (politician)

1966. Mubarak Zaroug Commemoration.
254 **75** 15m. olive and pink . . . 35 15
255 3p. green and light green 50 35
256 55m. brown and chestnut 1·10 55

76 W.H.O. Building — **77** Crests of Upper Nile, Blue Nile and Kassala Provinces

1966. Inaug of W.H.O. Headquarters, Geneva.
257 **76** 15m. blue 10 10
258 3p. purple 20 15
259 55m. brown 45 30

1967. "The Month of the South".
260 **77** 15m. multicoloured 10 10
261 – 3p. multicoloured 20 10
262 – 55m. multicoloured 80 40
DESIGNS (Crests of): 3p. Equatoria, Kordofan and Khartoum Provinces; 55m. Bahr El Gazal, Darfur and Northern Provinces.

78 Giraffe and Tourist Emblem — **79** Handclasp Emblem

1967. International Tourist Year.
263 **78** 15m. multicoloured 20 10
264 3p. multicoloured 45 25
265 55m. multicoloured 70 25

1967. Arab Summit Conference, Khartoum.
266 **79** 15m. multicoloured 10 10
267 3p. green and orange . . . 20 10
268 55m. violet and yellow . . 45 20

80 P.L.O. Shoulder Flash

1967. Palestine Liberation Organization.
269 **80** 15m. multicoloured 10 10
270 3p. multicoloured 20 10
271 55m. multicoloured 45 20

81 Mohamed Nur El Din

1968. Nur El Din (politician) Commemoration.
272 **81** 15m. green and blue . . . 35 15
273 3p. bistre and blue 50 30
274 55m. ultramarine and blue 1·10 50

82 Abdullahi El Fadil El Mahdi

1968. Abdullahi El Fadil El Mahdi (Ansar leader) Commemoration.
275 **82** 15m. violet and blue . . . 35 15
276 3p. green and blue 50 30
277 55m. green and orange . . 1·10 50

83 Ahmed Yousif Hashim

1968. 10th Death Anniv of Ahmed Yousif Hashim (journalist).
278 **83** 15m. brown and green . . 35 10
279 3p. brown and blue 50 10
280 55m. violet and blue . . . 1·10 30

84 Mohamed Ahmed El Mardi

1968. Mohamed Ahmed El Mardi (politician) Commemoration.
281 **84** 15m. ultramarine and blue 35 15
282 3p. orange, blue and pink 50 35
283 55m. brown and blue . . . 1·10 55

85 Douglas DC-3 Airliner

1968. 20th Anniv of Sudan Airways. Mult.
284 15m. Type **85** 10 10
285 2p. De Havilland Dove . . . 20 10
286 3p. Fokker Friendship . . . 40 20
287 55m. Hawker Siddeley Comet 4C 65 45

87 Anniversary and Bank Emblems

1969. 5th Anniv of African Development Bank.
288 87 2p. black and gold 15 10
289 4p. red and gold 30 15
290 65m. green and gold . . . 45 20

88 I.L.O. Emblem

1969. 50th Anniv of Int Labour Organization.
291 88 2p. black, red and blue . . 15 10
292 4p. black, blue and yellow 30 15
293 65m. black, mauve & green 45 20

89 "Solidarity of the People"

1970. 1st Anniv of 25 May Revolution (1st issue).
294 89 2p. multicoloured . . . .
295 4p. multicoloured . . . .
296 65m. multicoloured . . .
Set of 3 . . . . 50·00

Nos. 294/6 were withdrawn on day of issue (25 May) as being unsatisfactory. They were later replaced by Nos. 297/9 and the 1st issue may be easily distinguished by the figures of value which appear on the extreme left of the design.

90 "Solidarity of the People"

1970. 1st Anniv of 25 May Revolution (2nd issue).
297 90 2p. brown, green and red 15 10
298 4p. blue, green and red . . 35 15
299 65m. green, blue and red 50 25

91 Map of Egypt, Libya and Sudan

92 I.E.Y. Emblem

1971. 1st Anniv of Tripoli Charter.
300 91 2p. green, black and red 20 10

1971. International Education Year.
301 92 2p. multicoloured 15 10
302 4p. multicoloured 30 10
303 65m. multicoloured 45 20

93 Laurel and Bayonets on Star

94 Emblems of Arab League and Sudan Republic

1971. 2nd Anniv of 25 May Revolution.
304 93 2p. black, green and yellow 15 10
305 4p. black, green and blue 35 15
306 10½p. black, green and grey 60 35

1972. 25th Anniv of Arab League.
307 94 2p. black, yellow and green 15 10
308 4p. multicoloured 35 15
309 10½p. multicoloured . . . 70 35

95 U.N. Emblem and Text

96 Cogwheel Emblem

1972. 25th Anniv of United Nations.
310 95 2p. green, orange and red 15 10
311 4p. blue, orange and red 35 15
312 10½p. black, orange and red 70 40

1972. World Standards Day.
313 96 2p. multicoloured 15 10
314 4p. multicoloured 40 20
315 10½p. multicoloured . . . 85 55

97 Sudanese Arms and Pres. Nemery

1972. Presidential Elections.
316 97 2p. multicoloured 15 10
317 4p. multicoloured 35 15
318 10½p. multicoloured . . . 70 40

98 Arms and Emblem

1972. Socialist Union's Founding Congress.
319 98 2p. black, yellow and blue 10 10
320 4p. mauve, yellow and black 20 15
321 10½p. black, yellow & green 65 25

99 Airmail Envelope and A.P.U. Emblem

1972. 10th Anniv of African Postal Union (1971).
322 99 2p. multicoloured 10 10
323 4p. multicoloured 20 15
324 10½p. multicoloured . . . 80 30

100 Provincial Emblems

1973. National Unity.
325 100 2p. multicoloured 10 10
326 – 4p. brown and black . . . 20 10
327 – 10½p. green, orange & silver 80 35

DESIGNS—HORIZ: 4p. Revolutionary Council. VERT: 10½p. Entwined trees.

101 Emperor Haile Selassie of Ethiopia

1973. 80th Birthday of Emperor Haile Selassie.
328 101 2p. multicoloured 20 15
329 4p. multicoloured 50 20
330 10½p. multicoloured . . . 1·10 45

102 President Nasser

1973. 3rd Death Anniv of Pres. Nasser.
331 102 2p. black 10 10
332 4p. black and green . . . 20 10
333 10½p. black and violet . . 65 35

103 Ancient Gateway

1973. 10th Anniv of World Food Programme.
334 103 2p. multicoloured 10 10
335 4p. multicoloured 20 10
336 10½p. multicoloured . . . 80 45

104 Scout Emblem

1973. World Scout Conference, Nairobi and Addis Ababa.
337 104 2p. multicoloured 30 10
338 4p. multicoloured 45 20
339 10½p. multicoloured . . . 95 55

105 Interpol Emblem

1974. 50th Anniv of International Criminal Police Organization (Interpol).
340 105 2p. multicoloured 10 10
341 4p. multicoloured 30 15
342 10½p. multicoloured . . . 70 35

106 K.S.M. Building, Khartoum University

1974. 50th Anniv of Faculty of Medicine, Khartoum University.
343 106 2p. multicoloured 15 10
344 4p. green, brown and red 35 10
345 10½p. red, brown and green 70 45

107 African Postal Union Emblem

1974. Centenary of Universal Postal Union. Mult.
346 2p. Type 107 . . . . 10 10
347 4p. Arab Postal Union emblem 20 15
348 10½p. Universal Postal Union emblem 80 35

108 A. A. Latif and A. F. Elmaz (revolution leaders)

1975. 50th Anniv of 1924 Revolution.
349 108 2½p. green and blue . . . 10 10
350 4p. red and blue 20 10
351 10½p. brown and blue . . 80 35

109 Bank and Commemorative Emblems

1975. 10th Anniv of African Development Bank.
352 109 2½p. multicoloured . . . 10 10
353 4p. multicoloured 20 10
354 10½p. multicoloured . . . 80 35

110 Earth Station and Camel Postman

1976. Inauguration of Satellite Earth Station.
355 110 2½p. multicoloured . . . 15 10
356 4p. multicoloured 30 15
357 10½p. multicoloured . . . 65 35

111 Woman, Flag and IWY Emblem

1976. International Women's Year.
358 111 2½p. multicoloured . . . 10 10
359 4p. multicoloured 30 15
360 10½p. multicoloured . . . 70 35

112 Arms of Sudan and "Gold Medal"

113 "Unity"

1976. Olympic Games, Montreal.
361 112 2½p. multicoloured . . . 40 10
362 4p. multicoloured 45 20
363 10½p. multicoloured . . . 1·10 55

1977. 5th Anniv of National Unity.
364 113 2½p. red, black and blue 10 10
365 4p. red, black and green 20 15
366 10½p. red, black and brown 65 30

114 Archbishop Capucci

1977. Archbishop Capucci's Imprisonment Commemoration.
367 114 2½p. black 45 10
368 4p. black and green . . . 65 20
369 10½p. black and red . . . 1·10 45

115 Fair Emblem and Flags

1978. International Fair, Khartoum.
370 **115** 3p. multicoloured 20 10
371 4p. multicoloured 35 15
372 10½p. multicoloured . . . 55 25

117 Commemorative and A.P.U. Emblems

1978. Silver Jubilee of Arab Postal Union.
373 **117** 3p. black, silver and red 15 10
374 4p. black, silver and green 30 10
375 10½p. black, silver and blue 65 35

118 Jinnah and Sudanese Flag

1978. Birth Cent of Mohammed Ali Jinnah (first Governor-General of Pakistan).
376 **118** 3p. multicoloured 20 10
377 4p. multicoloured 35 15
378 10½p. multicoloured . . . 55 25

119 Desert Scene

1978. U.N. Conference on Desertification.
379 **119** 3p. black, yellow and green 20 10
380 4p. black, pink and green 35 15
381 10½p. black, brown & green 85 45

120 Lion God Apedemek and O.A.U. Emblem

1978. 15th African Summit Conference, Khartoum.
382 **120** 3p. black, yellow & purple 15 10
383 4p. black, yellow and blue 30 15
384 10½p. black, yellow & green 55 30

121 Sudanese Flag

122 I.B.E. and UNESCO Emblems

1979. 10th Anniv of May Revolution.
385 **121** 3½p. multicoloured . . . 15 10
386 6p. multicoloured 35 15
387 13p. multicoloured . . . 60 30

1980. 50th Anniv of International Bureau of Education (1979).
388 **122** 4½p. black and orange . . 20 15
389 8p. black and green . . . 45 25
390 15½p. black and blue . . 90 40

123 I.Y.C. Emblem and Hands carrying Child

1980. International Year of the Child (1979).
391 **123** 4½p. multicoloured . . . 20 15
392 8p. multicoloured 40 25
393 15½p. multicoloured . . . 70 40

124 National Flag, Arms and Sudanese Warrior

1982. 25th Anniv of Independence.
396 **124** 60m. multicoloured . . . 20 10
397 120m. multicoloured . . . 45 20
398 250m. multicoloured . . . 90 45

125 Hands reaching for F.A.O. Emblem on Map of Sudan

1983. World Food Day.
399 **125** 60m. blue, green and black 20 10
400 – 120m. green, black and red 45 20
401 – 250m. green, black and red 90 45
DESIGNS: 120m. F.A.O. emblem, crops and cattle; 250m. Emblem, crops and cattle on map of Sudan.

126 Commission Emblem

127 Warrior on Horseback

1984. 25th Anniv of Economic Commission for Africa.
402 **126** 10p. lilac and silver . . . 20 15
403 25p. blue and silver . . . 55 35
404 40p. green and silver . . . 1·00 60

1984. Centenary of Shaykan Battle, Kordofan.
405 **127** 10p. multicoloured . . . 20 15
406 25p. multicoloured . . . 55 35
407 40p. multicoloured . . . 90 50

128 Sudan Olympic Committee Emblem

129 Emblem and Flags

1984. 1st Olympic Week.
408 **128** 10p. multicoloured . . . 20 15
409 25p. multicoloured . . . 60 30
410 40p. multicoloured . . . 1·10 55

1984. 2nd Anniv of Sudan–Egypt Co-operation Treaty.
411 **129** 10p. multicoloured . . . 20 15
412 25p. multicoloured . . . 55 35
413 40p. multicoloured . . . 90 50

130 Institute Emblem

131 Map and Broken Chain

1985. 50th Anniv of Bakht Erruda Teacher Training Institute, Eddueim Town.
414 **130** 10p. multicoloured . . . 20 15
415 25p. multicoloured . . . 55 35
416 40p. multicoloured . . . 90 50

1986. 1st Anniv of 6 April Rising.
417 **131** 5p. black, green and brown 10 10
418 25p. black, green and blue 55 30
419 40p. black, green and brown 90 45

132 Fishermen hauling in Nets

1988. World Food Day (1986).
420 **132** 25p. black, silver and brown 40 15
421 – 30p. green and black . . 45 15
422 – 50p. multicoloured . . . 55 35
423 – 75p. black, deep blue and blue . . . . 1·00 45
424 – 300p. blue, black and silver . . . . 3·50 1·40
DESIGNS—VERT: 30p. Two fishes. HORIZ: 50p. Plant and globe; 75p. Outline of fish and waves; 300p. Shoal of fish.

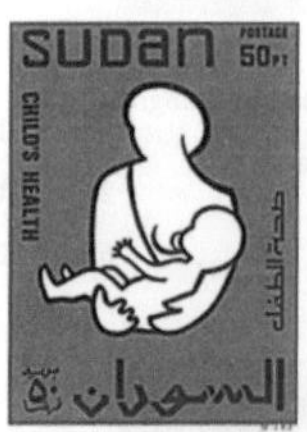

133 Mother breast-feeding Baby

134 Emblem

1988. Child Health Campaign.
426 **133** 50p. black and mauve . . 55 20
427 – 75p. multicoloured . . . 85 35
428 – 100p. multicoloured . . . 1·10 45
429 – 150p. multicoloured . . . 1·60 65
DESIGNS—HORIZ: No. 427, Mother spoon-feeding child; 428, Child being given oral vaccination; 429, Children on scales.

1988. 30th Anniv of Sudan Red Crescent.
431 **134** 40p. black, yellow and red 40 30
432 – 100p. black, red and green 90 60
433 – 150p. black, red and blue 1·25 80
DESIGNS: 100p. Candle; 150p. Figure with crescent on head.

135 Anniversary Emblem

1988. 75th Anniv of Bank of Khartoum. Mult.
434 40p. Type **135** 40 20
435 100p. Bubbles and medal . . 90 45
436 150p. Inscription and emblem 1·25 65

136 Plough

1988. World Food Day. The Small Farmer. Mult.
437 40p. Type **136** 40 20
438 100p. Farmer ploughing . . . 90 45
439 150p. Farmer drawing water from river . . . . 1·25 65

137 Emblem

138 Crowd of Youths

1989. "Freedom of Palestine".
440 **137** 100p. multicoloured . . . 50 20
441 150p. multicoloured . . . 80 35
442 200p. multicoloured . . . 95 55

1989. Palestinian "Intifada" Movement.
443 **138** 100p. multicoloured . . . 50 20
444 150p. multicoloured . . . 80 35
445 200p. multicoloured . . . 95 55

139 Emblem

1989. 25th Anniv of African Development Bank.
446 **139** 100p. green, black & silver 50 20
447 150p. blue, black and silver 80 35
448 200p. purple, black & sil 95 55

140 Map

142 Pied Hornbill ("Zande Hornbill")

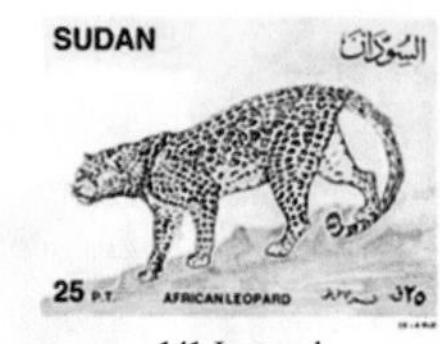

141 Leopard

1990. 34th Anniv of Independence.
449 **140** 50p. blue and yellow . . . 20 10
450 100p. brown and yellow 50 20
451 150p. mauve and yellow 80 35
452 200p. mauve and yellow 1·00 55

1990. Mammals. Multicoloured.
453 25p. Type **141** 15 10
454 50p. African elephant . . . 35 20
455 75p. Giraffe (vert) 45 35
456 100p. White rhinoceros . . . 60 45
457 125p. Addax (vert) 65 55

1990. Birds. Multicoloured.
458 25p. Type **142** 25 10
459 50p. Marabou stork 60 20
460 75p. Crested bustard ("Buff-crested Bustard") 85 35
461 100p. Saddle-bill stork ("Saddle-bill") . . . . . . 1·10 50
462 150p. Waldrapp ("Bald-headed Ibis") . . . . . . 1·50 60

143 Mardoum Dance

1990. Traditional Dances. Multicoloured.
463 25p. Type **143** 15 10
464 50p. Zandi dance (vert) . . . 35 20
465 75p. Kambala dance (vert) 45 35
466 100p. Nubian dance (vert) . . 60 45
467 125p. Sword dance 65 55

1990. No. 195 surch with new value in Arabic.
468 **63** £S1 on 10p. brown, bistre & blue . . . . 2·50 1·50

146 Flag

1991. 1st Anniv of "National Salvation Revolution".
470 **146** 150p. multicoloured . . . 75 55
471 200p. multicoloured . . . 1·00 75
472 250p. multicoloured . . . 1·25 1·00
473 £S5 multicoloured . . . . 2·50 2·10
474 £S10 multicoloured . . . 5·00 4·50

147 Whale-headed Stork ("Shoebill") **148** Camel Postman

1991. (a) As T **147**. Multicoloured.
475 25p. Type **147** 10 10
476 50p. Sunflower 10 10
477 75p. Collecting gum arabic 35 20
478 100p. Cotton 50 35
479 125p. South African crowned crane 60 40
480 150p. Kenana Sugar Co Ltd (29½ × 25 mm) 75 50
481 175p. Secretary bird (24 × 30½ mm) 85 60
482 £S2 Atbara Cement Factory (29½ × 25 mm) 95 70
483 250p. King Taharka (statue) (26 × 37 mm) . . . . . . 1·25 90
484 £S3 Republican Palace (26 × 37 mm) . . . . . . 1·50 1·10
485 £S4 Hug (scent container) (24 × 30½ mm) . . . . . . 1·90 1·40
486 £S5 Gabanah (coffee pot) (24 × 30½ mm) . . . . . . 2·40 2·00
(b) As T **148**. Multicoloured.
487 £S8 Lionfish (horiz) . . . . 3·75 3·00
488 £S10 Goat, ox and camel (horiz) . . . . 4·75 4·00
489 £S15 Nubian ibex . . . . . 7·25 6·25
490 £S20 Type **148** . . . . . . 9·75 8·00

150 Campaign Emblem (**151**)

1991. Pan-African Campaign against Rinderpest.
507 **150** £S1 black and green . . . 50 35
508 £S2 violet and green . . . 95 60
509 £S5 orange and green . . 2·40 1·40

1993. Various stamps handstamped as T **151**.
510 – 1d. on 100p. multicoloured (No. 478) 2·50 1·75
511 – 2d. on £S2 mult (No. 482) 5·00 3·25
512 **147** 2½d. on 25p. multicoloured (No. 475) 6·25 3·75
513 – 3d. on £S3 mult (No. 484) 7·75 4·75
514 – 4d. on £S4 mult (No. 485) 10·00 6·50

152 Emblem **153** Arabic Script and Hearts

1993. 500th Anniv of Fung Sultanate and Abdalab Islamic Shaikhdom. Multicoloured.
515 £S4 Type **152** 60 40
516 £S5 Arabic script on bottle 75 50
517 750p. Arabic script in cartouche and helmet (horiz) . . . . 1·10 75
Nos. 515/17 were sold at 4, 5 and 7½ dinars respectively.

1993. International Human Rights Day.
518 **153** £S4 multicoloured 60 40
519 – £S5 multicoloured 75 50
520 – 750p. black, green and red 1·10 75
DESIGNS—HORIZ: £S5 Rainbow breaking through chains. VERT: 750p. Rose and Arabic script.
Nos. 518/20 were sold at 4, 5 and 7½ dinars respectively.

154 Feeding Young **155** Olympic Flag

1994. The Wild Ass. Multicoloured.
521 4d. Type **154** 15 10
522 8d. Adult 35 20
523 10d. Adult galloping 70 25
524 15d. Head of adult . . . . . 1·10 60

1994. Cent of International Olympic Committee.
525 **155** 5d. multicoloured 20 10
526 7d. multicoloured 30 20
527 15d. multicoloured . . . 85 35

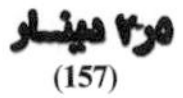
156 Anniversary Emblem (**157**)

1994. 50th Anniv of I.C.A.O.
528 **156** 5d. purple, yellow & black 20 10
529 7d. brown, yellow & black 30 20
530 15d. blue, yellow and black 60 35

1995. Various stamps handstamped as T **157**.
531 2½d. on 25p. green and brown (No. 194a) . . . . 1·75 1·25
532 15d. on 150p. multicoloured (No. 480) 45 25
533 20d. on 75p. multicoloured (No. 477) 60 35

158 Goalkeeper **159** Map and Emblem

1995. World Cup Football Championship, U.S.A. (1994). Multicoloured.
534 4d. Type **158** 10 10
535 5d. Type **158** 15 10
536 7d. Player in green shirt . . . 15 10
537 8d. As No. 536 but red shirt 20 10
538 10d. Player heading ball . . . 25 15
539 15d. Brazilian player 40 25
540 20d. German player 50 30
541 25d. American player 60 35
542 35d. As No. 537 . . . . . . 85 50

1995. 50th Anniv of Arab League.
544 **159** 15d. green and black . . 25 15
545 25d. blue and black . . . 40 25
546 30d. violet and black . . 45 25

160 Emblem **162** Rahman

1996. Common Market for Eastern and Southern Africa.
547 **160** 15d. multicoloured . . . 15 10
548 25d. multicoloured . . . 25 15
549 30d. multicoloured . . . 35 20

1997. 42nd Death Anniv of Abdel Rahman al Mahadi.
557 **162** 25d. black and violet . . 20 10
558 35d. black and red . . . 25 15
559 50d. black and brown . . 40 25

163 Hands reaching to Dove **164** Stripes

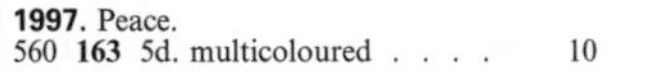
1997. Peace.
560 **163** 5d. multicoloured 10 10

1997. 25th Anniv of Police Force.
561 **164** 25d. multicoloured . . . 20 10
562 35d. multicoloured . . . 25 15
563 50d. silver, green and black 40 25

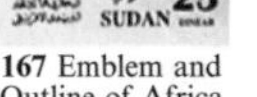
165 Mosque (**166**)

1997. 5th Anniv of Reconstruction of Sheikh Quribulla's Mosque, Omdurman. Multicoloured.
564 25d. Type **165** 20 10
565 35d. Close-up of facade . . . 25 15
566 50d. Distant view of facade (vert) 40 25

1997. Nos. 476, 483 and 487 surch as T **166**.
567 5d. on 50p. multicoloured . . 10 10
568 25d. on 250p. multicoloured 20 10
569 35d. on £S8 multicoloured . . 25 15
The size of surcharge differs for each value.

167 Emblem and Outline of Africa **168** Faras Church Fresco (detail)

1998. 18th Anniv of Pan-African Postal Union.
570 **167** 25d. multicoloured . . . 15 10
571 35d. multicoloured . . . 20 10
572 50d. multicoloured . . . 30 20

1998. Archaeological Finds. Multicoloured.
573 50d. Type **168** 30 20
574 50d. Drinking cup 30 20
575 50d. Faras Church fresco (different) 30 20
576 60d. Decorated dish (2000 B.C.) 40 25
577 75d. Statue of King Natakamani (vert) 45 25
578 75d. Meroe decorated pot (4000 B.C.) 45 25
579 100d. Bowl (2000 B.C.) . . . 60 35

169 Arab Postman Design **170** Soldier with Flag and Cannon

1998. Centenary of First Sudanese Stamp.
580 **169** 100d. multicoloured . . . 60 35

1999. Centenary of Battle of Kerreri.
581 **170** 75d. multicoloured . . . 35 25
582 100d. multicoloured . . . 50 30
583 150d. multicoloured . . . 75 45

171 Factory Ruins **172** Elderly Women and Children

1999. 1st Anniv of Bombing of Shifa Pharmaceutical Factory. Multicoloured.
584 75d. Type **171** 35 25
585 100d. Shifa emblem (22 × 27 mm) 50 30
586 150d. Effects of bombing . . 75 45

1999. International Year of the Elderly Person. Multicoloured.
587 75d. Type **172** 40 25
588 100d. Emblem (vert) 55 35
589 150d. Elderly man and children 80 50

173 Emblems

1999. 50th Anniv of S.O.S. Children's Villages.
590 **173** 75d. multicoloured . . . 40 25
591 100d. multicoloured . . . 55 35
592 150d. multicoloured . . . 80 50

175 UPU Emblem, Fortified Gate and Camels **176** Map of Africa

2000. 125th Anniv of Universal Postal Union (1999).
595 **175** 75d. multicoloured . . . 35 20
596 100d. multicoloured . . . 40 25
597 150d. multicoloured . . . 60 35

2000. 7th Anniv of Africa Free Trade Area (COMESA).
598 **176** 100d. multicoloured . . . 40 25
599 150d. multicoloured . . . 60 35
600 200d. multicoloured . . . 85 50

177 Anniversary Emblem **178** Children encircling Globe

2001. 50th Anniv of United Nations High Commissioner for Refugees.
601 **177** 100d. black and light green 40 25
602 150d. black and red . . . 60 35
603 200d. black and violet . . 85 50

2002. United Nations Year of Dialogue among Civilizations.
604 **178** 100d. multicoloured . . . 40 25
605 150d. multicoloured . . . 60 35
606 200d. multicoloured . . . 85 50

179 Scientific Symbols and Al-Zubair

2002. Al-Zubair Prize for Innovation and Scientific Excellence.
607 **179** 100d. multicoloured . . . 40 25
608 150d. multicoloured . . . 60 35
609 200d. multicoloured . . . 85 50

180 Atomic Symbol, Computer and Crescent

2002. Association for the Promotion of Scientific Innovation. .
610 **180** 100d. black and blue . . 40 25
611 150d. black, red and blue 60 35
612 200d. black, green and blue 85 50

181 Mohamed Dorra and Father

2002. Mohamed Dorra Commemoration.
613 **181** 100d. multicoloured . . . 40 25
614 150d. multicoloured . . . 60 35
615 200d. multicoloured . . . 85 50

182 Worm emerging from Foot

2002. Guinea Worm Eradication Campaign. Multicoloured.
616 100d. Type **182** 40 25
617 150d. Emblem (Eradication programme managers meeting, Khartoum) 60 35
618 200d. Child 85 50

(183) **186** Nile Perch

184 Conference Emblem and Map of Africa

2003. No. 479 surch with T **183**.
619 100d. on 125p. multicoloured 45 25

2003. Annual Conference of Association of Banknote and Security Document Printers, Khartoum. Multicoloured.
620 100d. Type **184** 45 25
621 150d. Emblem and national arms 65 40
622 200d. Ruins 90 55

2003. National Symbols. Multicoloured.
627 50d. Type **186** 20 10
628 50d. Mango (vert) 20 10
629 75d. Cattle 35 20
630 100d. Marchers carrying flags 45 25
631 100d. Al Imam El Mahadi 45 25
632 125d. Butterfly fish 55 35
633 150d. Amon Ra temple (vert) 65 40
634 150d. Leafless baobab tree (vert) 65 40
635 150d. Doum palm (vert) 65 40
636 150d. Sheep (vert) 65 40
637 200d. Wellhead (Sudan petrol) (vert) 90 55
638 200d. Grapefruit (vert) 90 55
639 300d. Tomb 1·30 80
640 500d. Camel postman (vert) 2·20 1·30

187 Anniversary Emblem

2004. 50th Anniv of National Parliament.
641 **187** 100d. multicoloured 45 25
642 200d. multicoloured 90 55
643 250d. multicoloured 1·10 65

188 Council Building

2004. 50th Anniv of General Secretariat of Council of Ministers.
644 **188** 100d. multicoloured 45 25
645 200d. multicoloured 90 55
646 250d. multicoloured 1·10 65

189 Veiled Woman

2004. Rural Women Innovation.
647 **189** 100d. multicoloured 45 25
648 200d. multicoloured 90 55
649 250d. multicoloured 1·10 65

190 Arms

2004. 50th Anniv of Armed Forces.
650 **190** 100d. multicoloured 45 25
651 200d. multicoloured 90 55
652 250d. multicoloured 1·10 65

ARMY SERVICE STAMPS

1905. Optd **ARMY OFFICIAL**.
A1 **2** 1m. brown and red 3·00 2·00

1906. Optd **ARMY SERVICE**.
A 6 **2** 1m. brown and red 1·50 20
A 7 2m. green and brown 13·00 1·00
A 8 3m. mauve and green 17·00 40
A 9 5m. red and black 1·50 10
A10 1p. blue and brown 13·00 15
A11 2p. black and blue 55·00 13·00
A12 5p. brown and green £120 65·00
A16 10p. black and mauve £140 £400

OFFICIAL STAMPS

1902. Optd **O.S.G.S.**
O 5 **2** 1m. brown and red 50 10
O 6 3m. mauve and green 2·50 15
O 7 5m. red and black 2·50 10
O 8 1p. blue and brown 2·75 10
O 9 2p. black and blue 22·00 20
O10 5p. brown and green 2·00 30
O 4 10p. black and mauve 13·00 25·00

1936. Optd **S.G.**
O32 **6** 1m. black and orange 2·50 9·50
O33 2m. yellow and brown 1·50 5·00
O34 3m. mauve and green 3·00 10
O35 4m. green and brown 3·50 2·75
O36 5m. brown and black 2·50 10
O37 10m. red and black 1·00 10
O38 15m. blue and brown 7·50 30
O39 2p. purple and orange 14·00 10
O39b 3p. brown and blue 6·50 2·75
O39c 4p. blue and black 29·00 4·75
O40 5p. brown and green 17·00 10
O40b 6p. blue and black 8·00 7·00
O40c **2** 8p. green and black 5·50 30·00
O41 10p. black and mauve 32·00 12·00
O42 20p. blue 28·00 24·00

1948. Optd **S.G.**
O43 **22** 1m. black and orange 30 3·75
O44 2m. orange and brown 1·25 10
O45 3m. mauve and green 3·50 7·00
O46 4m. green and brown 3·25 4·25
O47 5m. brown and black 3·25 10
O48 10m. red and black 3·25 1·75
O49 15m. blue and brown 3·50 10
O50 **23** 2p. purple and yellow 3·50 10
O51 3p. brown and blue 3·50 10
O52 4p. blue and black 3·25 10
O53 5p. orange and green 4·25 10
O54 6p. blue and black 3·25 10
O55 8p. green and black 3·25 3·00
O56 10p. black and mauve 5·50 20
O57 20p. blue 4·50 25
O58 50p. red and blue 65·00 60·00

1950. Air. Nos. 115/22 optd **S.G.**
O59 2p. black and green 15·00 3·25
O60 2½p. blue and orange 1·50 1·75
O61 3p. purple and blue 80 1·00
O62 3½p. sepia and brown 80 7·50
O63 4p. brown and blue 80 7·50
O64 4½p. black and blue 4·00 17·00
O65 6p. black and red 1·00 4·25
O66 20p. black and purple 4·00 12·00

1951. Nos. 123/39 optd **S.G.**
O67 1m. black and orange 40 3·75
O68 2m. black and blue 50 1·00
O69 3m. black and green 5·50 15·00
O70 4m. black and green 10 5·50
O71 5m. black and purple 10 10
O72 10m. black and blue 10 10
O73 15m. black and brown 30 10
O74 2p. blue 10 10
O75 3p. brown and blue 10·00 10
O76 3½p. green and brown 25 10
O77 4p. blue and black 1·50 10
O78 5p. brown and green 25 10
O79 6p. blue and black 50 2·75
O80 8p. blue and brown 75 10
O81 10p. black and green 50 10
O82 20p. turquoise and black 1·25 30
O83 50p. red and black 3·50 1·25

(O **65** "S.G.") (O **161**)

1962. Nos. 171/84 optd with Type O **65** (larger on 10p. to £S10).
O185 **62** 5m. blue 10 10
O186 – 10m. purple and blue 10 10
O187 – 15m. purple, orge & bis 10 10
O188 **62** 2p. violet 10 10
O189 – 3p. brown and green 45 10
O190 – 35m. brown, deep brown and green 55 20
O191 – 4p. purple, red and blue 65 20
O192 – 55m. brown and green 90 20
O193 – 6p. brown and blue 90 35
O194 – 8p. green 1·10 55
O222 **63** 10p. brown, black & blue 1·10 55
O223 – 20p. green and olive 2·75 90
O223a – 25p. brown and green 10 10
O224 – 50p. green, blue & black 4·50 2·00
O198 **64** £S1 brown and green 14·00 9·00
O226 – £S5 green and brown 6·50 4·00
O227 **63** £S10 orange and blue 14·00 8·50

1991. Nos. 475/90 optd similarly to Type O **65**.
O491 25p. multicoloured 10 10
O492 50p. multicoloured 10 10
O493 75p. multicoloured 35 20
O494 100p. multicoloured 45 20
O495 125p. multicoloured 55 25
O496 150p. multicoloured 65 30
O497 175p. multicoloured 80 50
O498 £S2 multicoloured 90 60
O499 250p. multicoloured 1·10 75
O500 £S3 multicoloured 1·25 90
O501 £S4 multicoloured 1·75 1·25
O502 £S5 multicoloured 2·10 1·50
O503 £S8 multicoloured 3·50 3·00
O504 £S10 multicoloured 4·25 3·50
O505 £S15 multicoloured 6·50 5·50
O506 £S20 multicoloured 8·50 7·00

1996. Nos. O494, O496, O498 and O500/2 handstamped. (a) As Type O **161**.
O550 2d. on £S2 multicoloured
O551 3d. on £S3 multicoloured
O552 4d. on £S4 multicoloured
O553 5d. on £S5 multicoloured
O554 15d. on 100p. multicoloured
O555 15d. on 150p. multicoloured

(b) As T **151**.
O556 2d. on £S2 multicoloured

O **185** National Arms

2003.
O623 O **185** 50d. black, green and red 20 10
O624 100d. black, green and red 45 25
O625 200d. black, green and red 90 55
O626 300d. black, green and red 1·30 80

POSTAGE DUE STAMPS

1897. Postage Due Stamps of Egypt optd **SOUDAN** in English and Arabic.
D1 D **23** 2m. green 1·75 5·00
D2 4m. purple 1·75 5·00
D3 1p. blue 10·00 3·50
D4 2p. orange 10·00 7·00

D **1** Gunboat "Zafir" D **2** Gunboat "Zafir"

1901.
D 5 D **1** 2m. black and brown 55 60
D10 4m. brown and green 1·00 80
D11 10m. green and mauve 1·25 1·60
D 8 20m. blue and red 3·25 3·25

1948.
D12 D **2** 2m. black and brown 1·00 35·00
D13 4m. brown and green 2·00 38·00
D14 10m. green and mauve 18·00 20·00
D15 20m. blue and red 18·00 32·00
The Arabic inscription in Type D **2** differs from that in Type D **1**.

SUNGEI UJONG Pt. 1

A native state of the Malay Peninsula, later incorporated in Negri Sembilan.

100 cents = 1 dollar (Straits).

1878. Stamp of Straits Settlements optd with Crescent, Star and **SU** in an oval.
1 **5** 2c. brown £2500 £2750

1881. Stamps of Straits Settlements optd **SUNGEI UJONG**.
28 **5** 2c. brown 48·00 £110
43 2c. red 8·50 12·00
22 4c. red £1400 £1500
34 4c. brown £225 £300
24 8c. orange £1600 £1200
26 **19** 10c. grey £500 £475

1882. Stamps of Straits Settlements optd **S.U.** (2c. with or without stops).
13 **5** 2c. brown £275 £325
14 4c. red £2750 £3000

1891. Stamp of Straits Settlements surch **SUNGEI UJONG Two CENTS**.
49 **5** 2c. on 24c. green £160 £180

35 Tiger **37** Tiger

1891.
50 **35** 2c. red 30·00 27·00
51 2c. orange 1·75 4·25
55 **37** 3c. purple and red 11·00 3·50
52 **35** 5c. blue 5·00 6·50

1894. Surch in figures and words.
53 **35** 1c. on 5c. green 1·00 70
54 3c. on 5c. red 2·50 4·75

SURINAM Pt. 4; Pt. 20

A Netherlands colony on the north-east coast of South America. In December 1954 Surinam became an autonomous state within the Kingdom of the Netherlands. Became an independent state in November 1975.

100 cents = 1 gulden.

1 King William III **3**

1873. No gum.
25 **1** 1c. grey 2·50 2·50
26 2c. yellow 1·40 1·40
14 2½c. red 1·40 1·40
15 3c. green 20·00 16·00
16 5c. lilac 17·00 5·50
17 10c. bistre 3·50 3·50
27 12½c. blue 16·00 7·25
18 15c. grey 22·00 7·00
19 20c. green 35·00 29·00
20 25c. blue 85·00 9·00
22 30c. brown 35·00 35·00
23 40c. brown 32·00 29·00
12 50c. brown 30·00 18·00
28 1g. grey and brown 50·00 50·00
13 2½g. brown and green 70·00 65·00
The gulden values are larger.

1890.
44 **3** 1c. grey 2·00 1·25
45 2c. brown 3·00 2·40
46 2½c. red 2·40 2·00
47 3c. green 5·50 3·75
48 5c. blue 25·00 1·25

1892. Surch **2½ CENT.**
53 **1** 2½c. on 50c. brown £275 11·00

5 **6** Queen Wilhelmina

1892. No gum.
56 **5** 2½c. black and yellow 1·60 90

1892.
63 **6** 10c. bistre 40·00 3·00
64 12½c. mauve 45·00 5·75
65 15c. grey 4·00 2·50
66 20c. green 4·25 3·00
67 25c. blue 10·00 3·75
68 30c. brown 5·50 4·00

1898. Surch **10 CENT.**
69 **1** 10c. on 12½c. blue 25·00 3·50
70 10c. on 15c. grey 65·00 50·00
71 10c. on 20c. green 4·75 4·75
72 10c. on 25c. blue 10·50 6·00
74 10c. on 30c. brown 4·75 4·75

1900. Stamps of Netherlands surch **SURINAME** and value.
77 **13** 50c. on 50c. red and green 22·00 7·50
78 **11** 1g. on 1g. green 20·00 12·50
79 2½g. on 2½g. lilac 16·00 10·50

1900. Surch.
83 **1** 25c. on 40c. brown 2·75 2·50

84 25c. on 50c. brown 2·75 1·90
86 50c. on 1g. grey and brown 30·00 27·00
82 50c. on 2½g. brown and green £140 £150

11 (shaded background)
12

1902.
87 11 ½c. lilac 90 75
88 1c. green 1·90 1·25
89 2c. brown 10·00 3·50
90 2½c. green 4·50 35
91 3c. yellow 7·25 4·25
92 5c. red 4·25 35
93 7½c. grey 15·00 7·00
94 12 10c. slate 10·00 90
95 12½c. blue 3·75 30
96 15c. brown 26·00 9·00
97 20c. green 25·00 4·50
98 22½c. green and brown 19·00 10·50
99 25c. violet 17·00 1·10
100 30c. brown 40·00 7·75
101 50c. brown 32·00 7·75

13

1907.
102 13 1g. purple 50·00 14·50
103 2½g. slate 50·00 50·00

14
17

1909. Roul or perf. No gum.
104 14 5c. red 10·00 8·25

1911. Surch with crown and value.
106 3 ½c. on 1c. grey 1·60 1·00
107 ½c. on 2c. brown 9·00 7·25
108 6 15c. on 25c. blue 65·00 55·00
109 20c. on 30c. brown 9·50 7·25
110 – 30c. on 2½g. on 2½g. purple (No. 79) £120 £100

1912. No gum.
113 17 ½c. lilac 95 95
114 2½c. green 95 95
115 5c. red 7·25 7·25
116 12½c. blue 9·00 9·00

18 (unshaded background)
19

20
21

1913. With or without gum.
117 18 ½c. lilac 35 30
118 1c. green 35 20
119 1½c. blue 35 20
120 2c. brown 1·40 1·25
121 2½c. green 90 20
122 3c. yellow 75 55
123 3c. green 2·75 2·40
125 4c. blue 7·25 4·25
126 5c. pink 1·50 20
127 5c. green 1·90 90
128 5c. violet 1·40 20
129 6c. buff 2·50 2·40
130 6c. red 2·00 50
131 7½c. brown 1·00 35
132 7½c. red 1·25 35
133 7½c. yellow 8·00 8·00
134 10c. lilac 4·50 4·50
135 10c. red 3·50 55
136 19 10c. red 1·25 55
137 12½c. blue 1·60 55
138 12½c. red 1·90 2·00
139 15c. green 55 65
140 15c. blue 6·75 4·25
142 20c. blue 2·10 1·90
143 20c. green 3·00 2·75
144 22½c. orange 2·50 2·40
145 25c. mauve 3·50 35
146 30c. grey 4·25 1·00
147 32½c. violet and orange 13·50 17·00
148 35c. blue and orange 4·50 4·50
149 20 50c. green 4·00 75
150 1g. brown 5·25 55
151 1½g. purple 30·00 30·00
152a 2½g. pink 26·00 24·00

1923. Queen's Silver Jubilee.
169a 21 5c. green 90 65
170 10c. red 1·40 1·40
171 20c. blue 3·00 2·50
172a 50c. orange 16·00 19·00
173 1g. purple 23·00 12·50
174 2g.50 grey 65·00 £190
175 5g. brown 80·00 £225

1925. Surch.
176 18 3c. on 5c. green 90 90
177 19 10c. on 12½c. red 1·75 1·60
180 12½c. on 22½c. orange 22·00 24·00
178 15c. on 12½c. blue 1·25 1·25
179 15c. on 20c. blue 1·25 1·25

1926. Postage Due stamps surch **Frankeerzegel 12½ CENT SURINAME.** (a) In three lines with bars.
181 D 6 12½c. on 40c. mve & blk 2·50 2·50

(b) In four lines without bars.
182 D 6 12½c. on 40c. lilac 24·00 24·00

28
29

1927.
183 28 10c. red 80 35
184 12½c. orange 1·60 1·60
185 15c. blue 1·90 55
186 20c. blue 1·90 75
187 21c. brown 15·00 14·50
188 22½c. brown 7·25 9·00
189 25c. purple 2·50 65
190 30c. green 2·50 1·00
191 35c. sepia 2·75 2·75

1927. Green Cross Fund. Various designs incorporating green cross.
192 29 2c.+2c. green and slate 1·10 1·00
193 – 5c.+3c. green and purple 1·10 1·00
194 – 10c.+3c. green and red 1·90 1·60

1927. Unissued Marine Insurance stamps (as Type M 22 of Netherlands but inscr "SURINAME") surch **FRANKEER ZEGEL** and value.
195 3c. on 15c. green 40 35
196 10c. on 60c. red 40 35
197 12½c. on 75c. brown 40 35
198 15c. on 1g.50 blue 2·10 2·00
199 25c. on 2g.25 brown 4·75 4·25
200 30c. on 4½g. black 10·50 8·50
201 50c. on 7½g. red 4·50 4·25

32 Indigenous Disease
33 The Good Samaritan

1928. Governor Van Heemstrastichting Medical Foundation Fund.
202 32 1½c.+1½c. blue 5·00 4·50
203 2c.+2c. green 5·00 4·50
204 5c.+3c. violet 5·00 4·50
205 7½c.+2½c. red 5·00 4·50

1929. Green Cross Fund.
206 33 1½c.+1½c. green 6·25 6·25
207 2c.+2c. red 6·25 6·25
208 5c.+3c. blue 6·25 6·25
209 6c.+4c. black 6·25 6·25

1930. No. 132 surch **6.**
210 18 6c. on 7½c. red 1·90 95

35 Mercury and Posthorn
37 Mother and Child

1930. Air.
276 35 10c. red 2·50 35
212 15c. blue 3·25 65
213 20c. green 10 20
214 40c. red 20 30
215 60c. purple 50 35
216 1g. black 1·25 1·40
217 1½g. brown 1·40 1·60
281 2½g. yellow 12·50 11·00
282 5g. green £275 £300
283 10g. bistre 30·00 45·00

1931. Air. "Dornier 10" Flight. Optd **Vlucht Do. X 1931.**
218 35 10c. red 18·00 15·00
219 15c. blue 19·00 15·00
220 20c. green 19·00 15·00
221 40c. red 28·00 23·00
222 60c. purple 55·00 50·00
223 1g. black 70·00 60·00
224 1½g. brown 70·00 65·00

1931. Child Welfare.
225 37 1½c.+1½c. black 4·50 4·00
226 2c.+2c. red 4·50 4·00
227 5c.+3c. blue 4·50 4·00
228 6c.+4c. green 4·50 4·00

37a William I (after Key)
38 "Supplication"

1933. 400th Birth Anniv of William I of Orange.
229 37a 6c. red 5·50 1·60

1935. Bicent of Moravian Mission in Surinam.
230 38 1c.+½c. brown 2·25 1·90
231 2c.+1c. blue 2·25 1·90
232 – 3c.+1½c. green 2·75 2·50
233 – 4c.+2c. orange 2·75 2·50
234 – 5c.+2½c. black 3·00 3·00
235 38 10c.+5c. red 3·00 3·00
DESIGN: 3, 4, 5c. Cross and clasped hands.

39 "Johannes van Walbeeck" (galleon)
40 Queen Wilhelmina

1936.
236 39 ½c. brown 25 30
237 1c. green 35 20
238 1½c. blue 50 35
239 2c. brown 55 30
240 2½c. green 25 20
241 3c. blue 55 35
242 4c. orange 55 65
243 5c. grey 55 20
244 6c. red 2·25 1·75
245 7½c. purple 25 20
246 40 10c. red 75 20
247 12½c. green 3·00 1·25
248 15c. blue 1·10 55
249 20c. orange 1·90 55
250 21c. black 2·75 2·75
251 25c. red 2·00 90
252 30c. purple 3·00 90
253 35c. bistre 3·50 3·50
254 50c. green 3·50 1·60
255 1g. blue 6·50 2·00
256 1g.50 brown 18·00 14·50
257 2g.50 red 11·00 7·25
Nos. 254/7 are larger, 22 × 33 mm.

41 "Infant Support"

1936. Child Welfare.
258 41 2c.+1c. green 2·25 2·25
259 3c.+1½c. blue 2·25 2·25
260 5c.+2½c. black 3·00 3·00
261 10c.+5c. red 3·00 3·00

42 "Emancipation"
42a Surinam Girl

1938. 75th Anniv of Liberation of Slaves in Surinam and Paramaribo Girls' School Funds.
262 42 2½c.+2c. green 1·75 1·40
263 42a 3c.+2c. black 1·75 1·40
264 5c.+3c. brown 1·90 1·60
265 7½c.+5c. blue 1·90 1·60

42b Queen Wilhelmina
44 Creole

1938. 40th Anniv of Coronation.
266 42b 2c. violet 35 30
267 7½c. red 90 90
268 15c. blue 2·40 2·25

1940. Social Welfare Fund.
269 44 2½c.+2c. green 2·50 1·90
270 – 3c.+2c. red 2·50 1·90
271 – 5c.+3c. blue 2·50 1·90
272 – 7½c.+5c. red 2·50 1·90
DESIGNS: 3c. Javanese woman; 5c. Hindu woman; 7½c. Indian woman.

44a Netherlands Coat of Arms
44b Queen Wilhelmina

1941. Prince Bernhard and "Spitfire" Funds.
273 44a 7½c.+7½c. blue & orge 2·50 2·75
274 15c.+15c. blue and red 3·00 3·00
275 1g.+1g. blue and grey 23·00 20·00

1941.
342 44b 12½c. blue 90 20
284 15c. blue 18·00 6·25

1942. Red Cross. Surch with red cross and new values.
289 39 2c.+2c. brown (postage) 1·90 1·90
291 2½c.+2c. green 1·90 1·90
292 7½c.+5c. purple 1·90 1·90
293 35 10c.+5c. red (air) 4·25 1·25

44d Dutch Royal Family

1943. Birth of Princess Margriet.
294 44d 2½c. orange 55 50
295 7½c. red 55 10
296 15c. black 2·40 1·90
297 40c. blue 3·00 2·10

1945. Surch.
298 39 ½c. on 1c. green 10 20
299 1½c. on 7½c. purple 25 20
300 2½c. on 7½c. purple 1·90 2·00
301 40 2½c. on 10c. red 1·00 30
302 5c. on 10c. red 65 50
303 7½c. on 10c. red 75 50

1945. Air. Surch.
304 35 22½c. on 60c. purple 80 80
305 1g. on 2½g. yellow 12·50 12·00
306 5g. on 10g. bistre 18·00 19·00

1945. National Welfare Fund. Surch **CENT VOOR HET NATIONAAL STEUNFONDS** and premium.
307 49 7½c.+5c. orange 3·25 2·25
308 50 15c.+10c. brown 2·50 2·25
309 20c.+15c. green 2·50 2·25
310 22½c.+20c. grey 2·50 2·25
311 40c.+35c. red 2·50 2·25
312 60c.+50c. violet 2·50 2·25

49 Sugar-cane Train

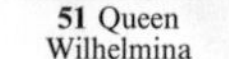

50 Queen Wilhelmina
51 Queen Wilhelmina
53 Star

1945.

313 – 1c. red 30 30
314 – 1½c. red . . . . 1·00 1·00
315 – 2c. violet 50 35
316 – 2½c. brown 50 35
317 – 3c. green . . . . 1·00 55
318 – 4c. brown . . . . 1·00 65
319 – 5c. blue . . . . 1·00 30
320 – 6c. olive . . . . 1·90 1·25
321 **49** 7½c. orange 65 30
322 **50** 10c. blue . . . . 1·25 20
323 15c. brown . . . . 1·60 30
324 20c. green . . . . 2·75 20
325 22½c. grey . . . . 3·00 75
326 25c. red . . . . 8·50 3·50
327 30c. olive . . . . 8·25 50
328 35c. blue . . . . 13·50 5·75
329 40c. red . . . . 8·25 30
330 50c. red . . . . 8·25 30
331 60c. violet . . . . 8·25 75
332 **51** 1g. brown . . . . 10·00 30
333 1g.50 lilac . . . . 9·00 65
334 2g.50 brown . . . . . . 17·00 75
335 5g. red . . . . 35·00 10·00
336 10g. orange . . . . 90·00 19·00

DESIGNS—As Type **49**: 1c. Bauxite mine, Moengo; 1½c. Natives in canoes; 2c. Native and stream; 2½c. Road in Coronie; 3c. River Surinam near Berg en Dal; 4c. Government Square, Paramaribo; 5c. Mining gold; 6c. Street in Paramaribo.

1946. Air. Anti-tuberculosis Fund. Surch **LUCHT POST** and premium.
340 **50** 10c.+40c. blue . . . . . . 1·10 1·10
341 15c.+60c. brown . . . . . 1·10 1·10

1947. Anti-leprosy Fund.
343 **53** 7½c.+12½c. orange (postage) . . . . . . 2·75 2·40
344 12½c.+37½c. blue . . . . . 2·75 2·40
345 22½c.+27½c. grey (air) . . . 2·75 2·40
346 27½c.+47½c. green . . . . 2·75 2·40

54

54a Queen Wilhelmina

1948.

347 **54** 1c. red 20 20
348 1½c. purple 20 20
349 2c. violet 30 20
350 2½c. green . . . . 1·25 20
351 3c. green 20 20
352 4c. brown 20 20
353 5c. blue . . . . 1·25 20
355 **54a** 5c. blue 35 20
356 6c. green 90 65
354 **54** 7½c. orange . . . . 2·75 1·10
357 **54a** 7½c. red 35 20
358 10c. blue 55 20
359 12½c. blue . . . . 1·00 90
360 15c. brown . . . . 1·50 35
361 17½c. purple . . . . . . 1·60 1·25
362 20c. green . . . . 1·25 20
363 22½c. blue . . . . 1·25 65
364 25c. red . . . . 1·25 30
365 27½c. red . . . . 1·25 20
366 30c. green . . . . 1·60 20
367 37½c. brown . . . . 2·50 1·75
368 40c. purple . . . . 1·90 30
369 50c. orange . . . . 2·00 30
370 60c. violet . . . . 2·00 35
371 70c. black . . . . 2·25 55

54b Queen Wilhelmina
54c Queen Juliana

1948. Queen Wilhelmina's Golden Jubilee.
372 **54b** 7½c. orange 80 65
373 12½c. blue 80 65

1948. Accession of Queen Juliana.
374 **54c** 7½c. orange . . . . 2·75 2·50
375 12½c. blue . . . . 2·75 2·50

55 Women of Netherlands and Surinam
55a Posthorns and Globe

1949. Air. 1st K.L.M. Flight on Paramaribo–Amsterdam Service.
376 **55** 27½c. brown . . . . 6·00 2·75

1949. 75th Anniv of U.P.U.
377 **55a** 7½c. red . . . . 6·00 2·75
378 27½c. blue . . . . 6·00 2·00

56 Marie Curie

1950. Cancer Research Fund.
379 **56** 7½c.+7½c. violet . . . . . 14·50 7·75
380 – 7½c.+22½c. green . . . . 14·50 7·75
381 – 27½c.+12½c. blue . . . . 14·50 7·75
382 **56** 27½c.+97½c. brown . . . . 14·50 7·75
PORTRAIT: Nos. 380/1, Wilhelm Rontgen.

1950. Surch **1 Cent** and bars.
383 **49** 1c. on 7½c. orange 80 65

57a Queen Juliana
57b Queen Juliana

1951.

395 **57a** 10c. blue 40 20
396 15c. brown 95 30
397 20c. turquoise . . . . . 2·40 20
398 25c. red . . . . 1·60 35
399 27½c. lake . . . . 1·40 20
400 30c. green . . . . 1·40 35
401 35c. olive . . . . 1·60 1·00
402 40c. mauve . . . . 1·90 35
403 50c. orange . . . . 2·40 35
404 **57b** 1g. brown . . . . 24·00 35

1953. Netherlands Flood Relief Fund. Nos. 374/5 surch **STORMRAMP NEDERLAND 1953** and premium.
405 12½c.+7½c. on 7½c. orange . . 2·75 2·50
406 20c.+10c.on 12½c. blue . . . 2·75 2·50

60 Fisherman
61 Surinam Stadium

1953.

407 – 2c. brown 20 20
408 **60** 2½c. green 30 20
409 – 5c. grey 30 20
410 – 6c. blue . . . . 1·60 1·10
411 – 7½c. violet 20 20
412 – 10c. red 20 20
413 – 12½c. blue . . . . 1·60 1·25
414 – 15c. red 60 30
415 – 17½c. brown . . . . . . 2·50 1·90
416 – 20c. green 50 20
417 – 25c. green . . . . 2·40 75
MS418 112 × 147 mm. Nos. 413/15 and 417 . . . . 55·00 30·00

DESIGNS—HORIZ: 2c. Native shooting fish; 10c. Woman gathering fruit. VERT: 5c. Bauxite mine; 6c. Log raft; 7½c. Ploughing with buffalo; 12½c. Brown hoplo (fish); 15c. Blue and yellow macaw; 17½c. Nine-banded armadillo; 20c. Poling pirogue; 25c. Iguana.

1953. Sports Week.
419 **61** 10c.+5c. red . . . . 10·00 7·25
420 15c.+7½c. brown . . . . . 10·00 7·25
421 30c.+15c. green . . . . . 10·00 7·25

62 Posthorn and Globe
63 Native Children and Youth Centre

1954. Air. 25th Anniv of Surinam Airlines.
422 **62** 15c. blue . . . . 1·25 1·10

1954. Child Welfare Fund.
423 **63** 7½c.+3c. purple . . . . . 5·50 4·50
424 10c.+5c. green . . . . . . 5·50 4·50
425 15c.+7½c. brown . . . . . 5·50 4·50
426 30c.+15c. blue . . . . . . 5·50 4·50

63a Queen Juliana

1954. Ratification of Statute for the Kingdom.
427 **63a** 7½c. purple 55 55

64 Doves of Peace
65 Gathering Bananas

1955. 10th Anniv of Liberation of Netherlands and War Victims Relief Fund.
428 **64** 7½c.+3½c. red . . . . . . 2·40 2·40
429 15c.+8c. blue . . . . . . 2·40 2·40

1955. 4th Caribbean Tourist Assn Meeting.
430 **65** 2c. green . . . . 1·60 1·25
431 – 7½c. yellow . . . . 2·50 1·90
432 – 10c. brown . . . . 2·50 1·90
433 – 15c. blue . . . . 2·75 1·90
DESIGNS: 7½c. Pounding rice; 10c. Preparing cassava; 15c. Fishing.

66 Caduceus and Globe
67 Queen Juliana and Prince Bernhard

1955. Surinam Fair.
434 **66** 5c. blue 40 35

1955. Royal Visit.
435 **67** 7½c.+2½c. olive 55 55

68 Flags and Caribbean Map
69 Facade of 19th-century Theatre

1956. 10th Anniv of Caribbean Commission.
447 **68** 10c. blue and red 30 30

1958. 120th Anniv of "Thalia" Amateur Dramatic Society.
448 **69** 7½c.+3c. blue and black . . 50 50
449 – 10c.+5c. purple & black . . 50 50
450 – 15c.+7½c. green & black . . 50 50
451 – 20c.+10c. orange & black . 50 50
DESIGNS: 10c. Early 20th-century theatre; 15c. Modern theatre; 20c. Performance on stage.

1959. No. 399 surch **8 C**.
452 8c. on 27½c. red 20 20

71 Queen Juliana
72 Symbolic Plants

1959.

453 **71** 1g. purple . . . . 1·50 20
454 1g.50 brown . . . . . . 2·25 50
455 2g.50 red . . . . 3·00 30
456 5g. blue . . . . 6·00 30

1959. 5th Anniv of Ratification of Statute for the Kingdom.
457 **72** 20c. multicoloured . . . . 2·50 1·50

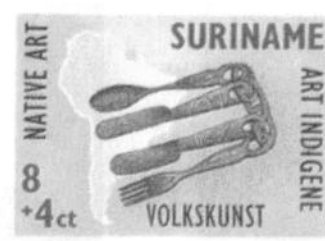

73 Wooden Utensils

1960. Surinam Handicrafts.
458 **73** 8c.+4c. multicoloured . . . 90 90
459 – 10c.+5c. red, blue & brn 90 90
460 – 15c.+7c. green, brn & red 90 90
461 – 20c.+10c. multicoloured . . 90 90
DESIGNS: 10c. Indian chief's headgear; 15c. Clay pottery; 20c. Wooden stool.

74 Boeing 707

1960. Opening of Zanderij Airport Building.
462 – 8c. blue . . . . 1·10 1·10
463 – 10c. green . . . . 1·60 1·60
464 – 15c. red . . . . 1·60 1·60
465 – 20c. lilac . . . . 2·00 2·00
466 **74** 40c. brown . . . . 2·75 2·75
DESIGNS: 8c. Charles Lindbergh's seaplane, 1929; 10c. Fokker "De Snip", 1934; 15c. Cessna 170A, 1954; 20c. Lockheed Super Constellation, 1957.

75 "Uprooted Tree"
76 Surinam Flag

1960. World Refugee Year.
467 **75** 8c.+4c. green and brown 20 20
468 10c.+5c. green and blue . . 20 20

1960. Freedom Day. Multicoloured.
469 10c. Type **76** 55 55
470 15c. Coat-of-arms (30 × 26 mm) 55 55

77 Putting the Shot
78 Bananas

1960. Olympic Games, Rome.
471 **77** 8c.+4c. brown, blk & grey 80 65
472 – 10c.+5c. brown, blk & orge 80 65
473 – 15c.+7c. brown, blk & vio 1·00 90
474 – 20c.+10c. brown, blk & bl 1·00 90
475 – 40c.+20c. brown, blk & grn 1·10 90
DESIGNS: 10c. Basketball; 15c. Running; 20c. Swimming; 40c. Football.

1961. Local Produce.
476 **78** 1c. yellow, black and green 15 10
477 – 2c. green, black and yellow 15 10
478 – 3c. brown, black & choc 15 10
479 – 4c. yellow, black and blue 15 10
480 – 5c. red, black and brown 15 10
481 – 6c. yellow, black and green 15 10
482 – 8c. yellow, black and blue 15 10
DESIGNS: 2c. Citrus fruit; 3c. Cocoa; 4c. Sugar-cane; 5c. Coffee; 6c. Coconuts; 8c. Rice.

79 Treasury
80 Commander Shepard, Rocket and Globe

1961. Surinam Buildings. Multicoloured.
483 10c. Type **79** 30 20
484 15c. Court of Justice 25 20
485 20c. Concordia Masonic Lodge 30 20
486 25c. Neve Shalom Synagogue 55 40
487 30c. Lock Gate, Nieuw Amsterdam 1·50 1·25
488 35c. Government Building 1·50 1·40
489 40c. Governor's House 80 65
490 50c. Legislative Assembly 80 30
491 60c. Old Dutch Reform Church 90 90
492 70c. Fort Zeelandia (1790) 90 1·00
The 10, 15, 20 and 30c. are vert and the rest horiz.

1961. Air. "Man in Space". Multicoloured.
493 15c. Globe and astronaut in capsule 90 90
494 20c. Type **80** 90 90

81 Girl Scout saluting **82** Dag Hammarskjold

1961. Caribbean Girl Scout Jamborette. Mult.
495 8c.+2c. Semaphoring (horiz) 45 35
496 10c.+3c. Type **81** 45 35
497 15c.+4c. Brownies around a "toadstool" (horiz) 45 35
498 20c.+5c. Campfire sing-song 55 50
499 25c.+6c. Lighting fire (horiz) 50 50

1962. Dag Hammarskjold Memorial Issue.
500 **82** 10c. black and blue 20 20
501 20c. black and violet 20 20

82a Queen Juliana and Prince Bernhard

1962. Royal Silver Wedding.
502 **82a** 20c. green 30 30

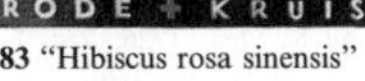

83 "Hibiscus rosa sinensis" **84** Campaign Emblem

1962. Red Cross Fund. Flowers in natural colours. Background colours given.
503 **83** 8c.+4c. olive 50 30
504 – 10c.+5c. blue 50 30
505 – 15c.+6c. brown 50 30
506 – 20c.+10c. violet 50 30
507 – 25c.+12c. turquoise 50 30
FLOWERS: 10c. "Caesalpinia pulcherrima"; 15c. "Heliconia psittacorum"; 20c. "Lochnera rosea"; 25c. "Ixora macrothyrsa".

1962. Malaria Eradication.
508 **84** 8c. red 20 20
509 10c. blue 20 20

85 Stoelmans Guesthouse

1962. Opening of New Hotels. Multicoloured.
510 10c. Type **85** 35 35
511 15c. Torarica Hotel 35 35

86 Sisters' Residence **87** Wildfowl

1962. Nunnery and Hospital of the Deaconesses. Multicoloured.
512 10c. Type **86** 35 35
513 20c. Hospital building 35 35

1962. Animal Protection Fund.
514 **87** 2c.+1c. red and blue 30 20
515 – 8c.+2c. red and black 30 20
516 – 10c.+3c. black and green 30 20
517 – 15c.+4c. black and red 30 20
ANIMALS: 8c. Dog; 10c. Donkey; 15c. Horse.

88 Emblem in Hands

1963. Freedom from Hunger.
518 **88** 10c. red 20 20
519 – 20c. blue 20 20
DESIGN—VERT: 20c. Tilling the land.

89 "Freedom"

1963. Centenary of Abolition of Slavery in Dutch West Indies.
520 **89** 10c. black and red 20 20
521 20c. black and green 20 20

90 Indian Girl **90a** William of Orange at Scheveningen

1963. Child Welfare Fund.
522 **90** 8c.+3c. green 30 20
523 – 10c.+4c. brown 30 20
524 – 15c.+10c. blue 30 20
525 – 20c.+10c. red 30 20
526 – 40c.+20c. purple 30 20
MS527 95 × 131 mm. Nos. 522/3 (two of each) 1·25 1·25
PORTRAITS OF CHILDREN: 10c. Bush negro; 15c. Hindustani; 20c. Indonesian; 40c. Chinese.

1963. 150th Anniv of Kingdom of the Netherlands.
528 **90a** 10c. black, bistre and blue 20 20

91 North American X-15

1964. Aeronautical and Astronomical Foundation, Surinam.
529 3c.+2c. sepia and lake 40 20
530 8c.+4c. sepia, indigo & blue 40 20
531 10c.+5c. sepia and green 40 20
532 15c.+7c. sepia and brown 40 20
533 20c.+10c. sepia and violet 40 20
DESIGNS: 3, 15c. Type **91**; 8c. Foundation flag; 10, 20c. Agena B-Ranger rocket.

92 "Camp Fire" **93** Skipping

1964. Scout Jamborette, Paramaribo, and 40th Anniv of Surinam Boy Scouts Association.
534 **92** 3c.+1c. lt yell, yell & bis 40 20
535 8c.+4c. brn, bl & dp bl 40 20
536 10c.+5c. brn, red & dp red 40 20
537 20c.+10c. brn, grn & bl 40 20

1964. Child Welfare.
538 **93** 8c.+3c. blue 20 20
539 – 10c.+4c. red 20 20
540 – 15c.+9c. green 20 20
541 – 20c.+10c. purple 20 20
MS542 139 × 96 mm. Nos. 538/9 (two of each) 80 80
DESIGNS: 10c. Children swinging; 15c. Child on scooter; 20c. Child with hoop.

94 Crown and Wreath **95** Expectant Mother ("Prenatal Care")

1964. 10th Anniv of Statute of the Kingdom.
543 **94** 25c. multicoloured 20 20

1965. 50th Anniv of "Het Groene Kruis" (The Green Cross).
544 **95** 4c.+2c. green 20 20
545 – 10c.+5c. brown and green 20 20
546 – 15c.+7c. blue and green 20 20
547 – 25c.+12c. violet and green 20 20
DESIGNS: 10c. Mother and baby ("Infant care"); 15c. Young girl ("Child care"); 25c. Old man ("Care in old age").

96 Abraham Lincoln **97** I.C.Y. Emblem

1965. Death Centenary of Abraham Lincoln.
548 **96** 25c. purple and bistre 20 20

1965. International Co-operation Year.
549 **97** 10c. orange and blue 20 20
550 15c. red and blue 20 20

98 Surinam Waterworks **99** Bauxite Mine, Moengo

1965. Air. Size 25 × 18 mm.
551 **98** 10c. green 20 20
552 – 15c. ochre 20 20
553 – 20c. green 20 20
554 – 25c. indigo 25 20
555 – 30c. turquoise 25 20
556 – 35c. red 30 20
557 – 40c. orange 30 20
558 – 45c. red 30 20
559 – 50c. red 30 20
560 **98** 55c. green 30 20
561 – 65c. yellow 35 30
562 – 75c. blue 35 30
DESIGNS: 15, 65c. Brewery; 20c. River scene; 25, 75c. Timber yard; 30c. Bauxite mine; 35, 50c. Poelepantje Bridge; 40c. Shipping; 45c. Jetty.
For same designs but size 22 × 18 mm, see Nos. 843a/h.

1965. Opening of Brokopondo Power Station.
563 **99** 10c. ochre 20 20
564 – 15c. green 20 20
565 – 20c. blue 20 20
566 – 25c. red 20 20
DESIGNS: 15c. Alum-earth works, Paranam; 20c. Power station and dam, Afobaka; 25c. Aluminium smeltery, Paranam.

100 Girl with Leopard **101** Red-breasted Blackbird

100a "Help them to a safe haven" (Queen Juliana)

1965. Child Welfare.
567 **100** 4c.+4c. black, turquoise and green 20 20
568 – 10c.+5c. black, brown and light brown 20 20
569 – 15c.+7c. black, orange and red 20 20
570 – 25c.+10c. black, blue and cobalt 20 20
MS571 140 × 96 mm. Nos. 567 and 569 (two of each) 80 80
DESIGNS: 10c. Boy with monkey; 15c. Girl with tortoise; 25c. Boy with rabbit.

1966. Intergovernmental Committee for European Migration (I.C.E.M.) Fund.
572 **100a** 10c.+5c. green & black 20 20
573 25c.+10c. red and black 20 20
MS574 117½ × 43 mm. Nos. 572 (× 2), 573 55 55

1966. Birds. Multicoloured.
575 1c. Type **101** 30 20
576 2c. Great kiskadee 30 20
577 3c. Silver-beaked tanager 30 20
578 4c. Ruddy ground dove 30 20
579 5c. Blue-grey tanager 30 20
580 6c. Straight-billed hermit 30 20
581 8c. Turquoise tanager 30 20
582 10c. Pale-breasted thrush 30 20

102 Hospital Building **103** Father P. Donders

1966. Opening of Central Hospital, Paramaribo. Multicoloured.
583 10c. Type **102** 20 20
584 15c. Different view 20 20

1966. Centenary of Redemptorists Mission.
585 **103** 4c. black and brown 20 20
586 – 10c. black, brown and red 20 20
587 – 15c. black and ochre 20 20
588 – 25c. black and lilac 20 20
DESIGNS: 10c. Batavia Church, Coppename; 15c. Mgr. J. B. Swinkels; 25c. Paramaribo Cathedral.

104 Mary Magdalene and Disciples **105** "Century Tree"

1966. Easter Charity.
589 **104** 10c.+5c. black, red and gold 20 20
590 15c.+8c. black, violet and blue 20 20
591 20c.+10c. black, yellow and blue 20 20
592 25c.+12c. black, green and gold 20 20
593 30c.+15c. black, blue and gold 20 20
On Nos. 590/3 the emblems at bottom left differ for each value. These represent various welfare organizations.

1966. Centenary of Surinam Parliament.
594 **105** 25c. black, green and red 20 20
595 30c. black, red and green 20 20

106 TV Mast, Eye and Globe **107** Boys with Bamboo Gun

1966. Inauguration of Surinam Television Service.
596 **106** 25c. red and blue 20 20
597 30c. red and brown 20 20

1966. Child Welfare. Multicoloured.
598 10c.+5c. Type **107** 15 15
599 15c.+8c. Boy pouring liquid on another 20 20
600 20c.+10c. Children rejoicing 20 20
601 25c.+12c. Children on merry-go-round 20 20
602 30c.+15c. Children decorating room 20 20
MS603 96 × 76 mm. Nos. 598 (× 2) and 600 55 55
The designs symbolize New Year's Eve, the End of Lent, Liberation Day, Queen's Birthday and Christmas respectively.

108 Mining Bauxite, 1916

109 "The Good Samaritan"

1966. 50th Anniv of Surinam Bauxite Industry.
604 **108** 20c. black, orange & yell . . . 20 20
605 – 25c. black, orange and blue 20 20
DESIGN: 25c. Modern bauxite plant.

1967. Easter Charity. Printed in black, background colours given.
606 **109** 10c.+5c. yellow 20 20
607 – 15c.+8c. blue 20 20
608 – 20c.+10c. ochre 20 20
609 – 25c.+12c. pink 20 20
610 – 30c.+15c. green 20 20
DESIGNS: 15 to 30c. Various episodes illustrating the parable of "The Good Samaritan".

110 Central Bank

1967. 10th Anniv of Surinam Central Bank.
611 **110** 10c. black and yellow . . 15 10
612 – 25c. black and lilac . . . 15 10
DESIGN: 25c. Aerial view of Central Bank.

111 Amelia Earhart and Lockheed 10E Electra Airplane

112 Siva Nataraja and Ballerina's Foot

1967. 30th Anniv of Visit of Amelia Earhart to Surinam.
613 **111** 20c. red and yellow . . . 15 10
614 25c. green and yellow . . 15 10

1967. 20th Anniv of Surinam Cultural Centre. Multicoloured.
615 10c. Type **112** 15 10
616 25c. "Bashi-Lele" mask and violin scroll 15 10

113 Fort Zeelandia, Paramaribo (c. 1670)

114 Stilt-walking

1967. 300th Anniv of Treaty of Breda. Mult.
617 10c. Type **113** 25 20
618 20c. Nieuw Amsterdam (c. 1660) 25 20
619 25c. Breda Castle (c. 1667) 25 20

1967. Child Welfare. Multicoloured.
620 10c.+5c. Type **114** 30 20
621 15c.+8c. Playing marbles . . 30 20
622 20c.+10c. Playing dibs . . . 30 20
623 25c.+12c. Kite-flying 30 20
624 30c.+15c. "Cooking" game 30 20
MS625 96 × 76 mm. Nos. 620 (× 2) and 622 . . . . 95 55

115 "Cross of Ashes"

116 W.H.O. Emblem

1968. Easter Charity.
626 10c.+5c. grey and violet . . . 30 20
627 15c.+8c. green and red . . . 30 20
628 20c.+10c. green and yellow 30 20
629 25c.+12c. black and grey . . 30 20
630 30c.+15c. brown and yellow 30 20
DESIGNS: 10c. Type **115** (Ash Wednesday); 15c. Palm branches (Palm Sunday); 20c. Cup and wafer (Maundy Thursday); 25c. Cross (Good Friday); 30c. Symbol of Christ (Easter).

1968. 20th Anniv of W.H.O.
631 **116** 10c. blue and purple . . . 10 10
632 25c. violet and blue . . . 20 20

117 Chandelier, Reformed Church

119 Map of Joden Savanne

118 Missionary Shop, 1768

1968. 300th Anniv of Reformed Church, Paramaribo.
633 **117** 10c. blue 10 10
634 – 25c. green 20 20
DESIGN: 25c. No. 633 reversed; chandelier on left.

1968. Bicentenary of Evangelist Brothers' Missionary Store, G. Kersten and Co.
635 **118** 10c. black and yellow . . 10 10
636 – 25c. black and blue . . . 20 20
637 – 30c. black and mauve . . 20 20
DESIGNS: 25c. Paramaribo Church and Kersten's store, 1868; 30c. Kersten's modern store, Paramaribo.

1968. Restoration of Joden Savanne Synagogue. Multicoloured.
638 20c. Type **119** 35 35
639 25c. Synagogue, 1685 . . . . 35 35
640 30c. Gravestone at Joden Savanne, dated 1733 . . . 35 35

120 Playing Hopscotch

121 Western Hemisphere illuminated by Full Moon

1968. Child Welfare.
641 **120** 10c.+5c. black & brown 30 20
642 – 15c.+8c. black and blue 30 20
643 – 20c.+10c. black & pink 30 20
644 – 25c.+12c. black & green 30 20
645 – 30c.+15c. black & lilac . . 30 30
MS646 98 × 76 mm. Nos. 641 (× 2) and 643 . . . . 85 55
DESIGNS: 15c. Forming "pyramids"; 20c. Playing ball; 25c. Handicrafts; 30c. Tug-of-war.

1969. Easter Charity.
647 **121** 10c.+5c. blue & lt blue . . 30 30
648 15c.+8c. grey & yellow . . 30 30
649 20c.+10c. turq & green . . 30 30
650 25c.+12c. brown & buff 30 30
651 30c.+15c. violet & grey 30 30

122 Cayman

123 Mahatma Gandhi

1969. Opening of Surinam Zoo, Paramaribo. Mult.
652 10c. Type **122** . . . . 50 3·00
653 20c. Common squirrel-monkey (vert) 50 30
654 25c. Nine-banded armadillo 50 30

1969. Birth Centenary of Mahatma Gandhi.
655 **123** 25c. black and red 30 30

124 I.L.O. Emblem

125 Pillow Fight

1969. 50th Anniv of Int Labour Organization.
656 **124** 10c. green and black . . . 20 20
657 25c. red and black 30 20

1969. Child Welfare.
658 10c.+5c. purple and blue . . 30 20
659 15c.+8c. brown and yellow 30 20
660 20c.+10c. blue and grey . . . 30 20
661 25c.+12c. blue and pink . . . 30 20
662 30c.+15c. brown and green 30 20
MS663 97 × 76 mm. Nos. 658 × 2 and 660 . . . . 90 90
DESIGNS: 10c. Type **125**; 15c. Eating contest; 20c. Pole-climbing; 25c. Sack-race; 30c. Obstacle-race.

126 Queen Juliana and "Sunlit Road"

1969. 15th Anniv of Statute for the Kingdom.
664 **126** 25c. multicoloured 30 25

127 "Flower"

128 "1950–1970"

1970. Easter Charity. "Wonderful Nature". Mult.
665 10c.+5c. Type **127** 50 50
666 15c.+8c. "Butterfly" 50 50
667 20c.+10c. "Bird" 50 50
668 25c.+12c. "Sun" 50 50
669 30c.+15c. "Star" 50 50

1970. 20th Anniv of Secondary Education in Surinam.
670 **128** 10c. yellow, green and brown 15 15
671 25c. yellow, blue and green 15 15

129 New U.P.U. Headquarters Building

130 U.N. "Diamond"

1970. New U.P.U. Headquarters Building.
672 **129** 10c. violet, blue & turq 15 15
673 – 25c. black and red 20 20
DESIGN: 25c. Aerial view of H.Q. Building.

1970. 25th Anniv of United Nations.
674 **130** 10c. multicoloured 20 20
675 25c. multicoloured 20 20

131 Aircraft over Paramaribo Town Plan

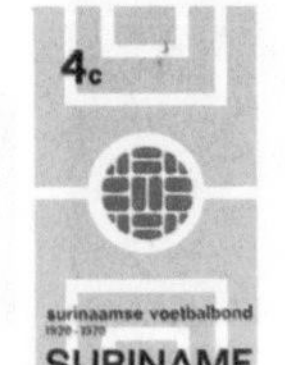

132 Football Pitch (ball in centre)

1970. "40 Years of Inland Airmail Flights".
676 **131** 10c. grey, ultramarine & blue 40 30
677 – 20c. grey, red and yellow 40 30
678 – 25c. grey, red and pink 40 30
DESIGNS: As Type **131**, but showing different background maps—20c. Totness; 25c. Nieuw-Nickerie.

1970. 50th Anniv of Surinam Football Association.
679 **132** 4c. brown, yellow & black 30 20
680 – 10c. brown, olive and black 30 20
681 – 15c. brown, green & black 30 20
682 – 25c. brown, green & black 30 20
DESIGNS: As Type **132**, but with ball: 10c. in "corner"; 15c. at side ("throw-in"); 25c. at top ("goal").

133 Beethoven (1786)

134 Grey Heron

1970. Child Welfare. Birth Bicentenary of Beethoven (composer).
683 **133** 10c.+5c. yellow, drab and green 55 50
684 – 15c.+8c. yellow, drab and red 55 50
685 – 20c.+10c. yellow, drab and blue 55 50
686 – 25c.+12c. yellow, drab and orange 55 50
687 – 30c.+15c. yellow, drab and violet 55 50
MS688 97 × 76 mm. Nos. 683 × 2 and 685 . . . . 1·25 1·10
DESIGNS—Beethoven: 15c. 1804; 20c. 1812; 25c. 1814; 30c. 1827.

1971. 25th Anniv of Netherlands–Surinam–Netherlands Antilles Air Service. Multicoloured.
689 15c. Type **134** 45 35
690 20c. Greater flamingo 45 35
691 25c. Scarlet macaw 45 35

135 Donkey and Palm

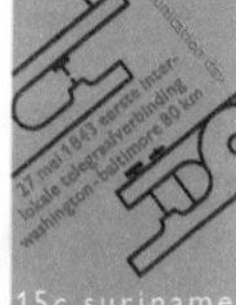

136 Morse Key

1971. Easter. The Bible Story. Multicoloured.
692 10c.+5c. Type **135** 50 50
693 15c.+8c. Cockerel 50 50
694 20c.+10c. Lamb 50 50
695 25c.+12c. Crown of Thorns 50 50
696 30c.+15c. Sun ("The Resurrection") 50 50

1971. World Telecommunications Day. Mult.
697 15c. Type **136** 35 35
698 20c. Telephones 35 35
699 25c. Lunar module and telescope 35 35
EVENTS: 15c. First national telegraph, Washington–Baltimore, 1843; 20c. First international telephone communication, England–Sweden, 1926; 25c. First interplanetary television communication, Earth–Moon, 1969.

137 Prince Bernhard

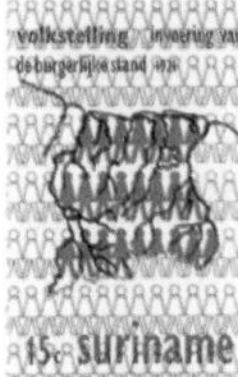

138 Population Map

1971. Prince Bernhard's 60th Birthday.
700 **137** 25c. multicoloured 30 30

1971. 50th Anniv of 1st Census and Introduction of Civil Registration.
701 **138** 15c. blue, black and red 20 20
702 30c. red, black and blue 30 30
DESIGN: 30c. "Individual" representing civil registration.

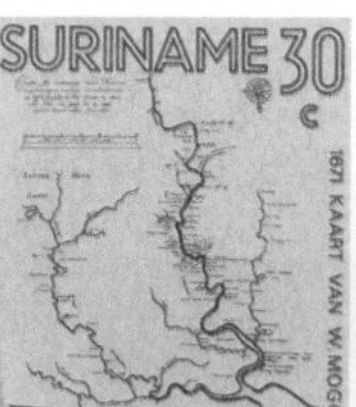

139 William Mogge's Map of Surinam

1971. 300th Anniv of First Surinam Map.
703 **139** 30c. brown on yellow . . 55 50

140 Leap-frog **141** Plan of Albina

1971. Child Welfare. Details from Brueghel's "Children's Games". Multicoloured.
704 10c.+5c. Type **140** 50 50
705 15c.+8c. Strewing flowers . . 50 50
706 20c.+10c. Rolling hoop . . . 50 50
707 25c.+12c. Playing ball . . . 50 50
708 30c.+15c. Stilt-walking . . . 50 50

1971. 125th Anniv of Albina Settlement.
710 **141** 15c. black on blue 35 35
711 – 20c. black on green 35 35
712 – 25c. black on yellow . . . 35 35
DESIGNS—HORIZ: 20c. Albina and River Marowijne. VERT: 25c. August Kappler (naturalist and founder).

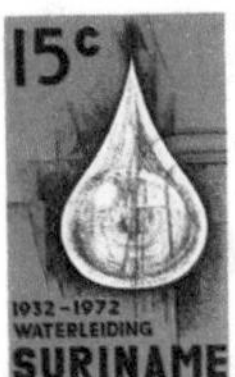

142 Drop of Water **143** Easter Candle

1972. 40th Anniv of Surinam Waterworks.
713 **142** 15c. black and violet . . . 30 30
714 – 30c. black and blue . . . 35 35
DESIGN: 30c. Water tap.

1972. Easter Charity. Multicoloured.
715 10c.+5c. Type **143** 50 50
716 15c.+8c. "Christ teaching the Apostles" 50 50
717 20c.+10c. Hands holding cup ("Christ in Gethsemane") 50 50
718 25c.+12c. Fishes in net ("Miracle of the Fishes") 50 50
719 30c.+15c. Pieces of silver ("Judas's Betrayal") . . . 50 50

144 "Eucyane bicolor" **145** Air-letter Motif

1972. Moths and Butterflies. Multicoloured.
720 15c. Type **144** 25 20
721 20c. Gold drop 25 20
722 25c. Orange swallowtail . . . 25 20
723 30c. White tailed page . . . 30 20
724 35c. "Stalachtis calliope" . . 30 20
725 40c. "Stalachtis phlegia" . . 30 20
726 45c. Malachite 30 20
727 50c. Spear-winged cattle heart 40 20
728 55c. Red anartia 55 55
729 60c. Five continent butterfly 55 75
730 65c. Doris 65 35
731 70c. "Nessaea obrinus" . . . 65 55
732 75c. Cracker 65 35

1972. 50th Anniv of 1st Airmail in Surinam.
733 **145** 15c. red and blue 20 20
734 30c. blue and red 30 30

146 Doll and Toys (kindergarten) **147** Giant Tree

1972. Child Welfare. Multicoloured.
735 10c.+5c. Type **146** 50 50
736 15c.+8c. Clock and abacus (primary education) . . . 50 50
737 20c.+10c. Blocks (primary education) 50 50
738 25c.+12c. Molecule complex (secondary education) . . . 50 50
739 30c.+15c. Wrench and blue-print (technical education) 50 50
MS740 96×78 mm. Nos. 735 ×2 and 737 . . . . 1·40 1·40

1972. 25th Anniv of Surinam Forestry Commission.
741 **147** 15c. brown and yellow . . 25 20
742 – 20c. brown, black and blue 25 20
743 – 30c. chocolate, brn & grn 30 35
DESIGNS: 20c. Aerial transport of logs; 30c. Planting tree.

148 "The Storm on the Lake" **149** Hindu Peasant Woman

1973. Easter Charity. Jesus's Life and Death. Mult.
744 10c.+5c. Type **148** 50 50
745 15c.+8c. "Washing the Disciples' Feet" 50 50
746 20c.+10c. "Jesus taken to Execution" 50 50
747 25c.+12c. The Cross 50 50
748 30c.+15c. "The Men of Emmaus" 50 50

1973. Centenary of Arrival of Indian Immigrants in Surinam.
749 **149** 15c. violet and yellow . . 30 30
750 – 25c. red and grey 30 30
751 – 30c. orange and blue . . 35 35
DESIGNS: 25c. J. F. A. Cateau van Rosevelt, Head of Department of Immigration, holding map; 30c. Symbols of immigration.

150 Queen Juliana

1973. Silver Jubilee of Queen Juliana's Reign.
752 **150** 30c. black, orange & silver 65 55

151 Florence Nightingale and Red Cross **152** Interpol Emblem

1973. 30th Anniv of Surinam Red Cross.
753 **151** 30c.+10c. multicoloured 75 75

1973. 50th Anniv of International Criminal Police Organization (Interpol). Multicoloured.
754 15c. Type **152** 20 20
755 30c. Emblem within passport stamp 30 30

153 Flower **154** Carrier-pigeons

1973. Child Welfare.
756 **153** 10c.+5c. multicoloured . . 50 50
757 – 15c.+8c. green, brown and emerald 50 50
758 – 20c.+10c. violet, blue and green 50 50
759 – 25c.+12c. multicoloured 50 50
760 – 30c.+15c. multicoloured 50 50
MS761 97×76 mm. Nos. 756 ×2 and 758 . . . . 1·10 1·10
DESIGNS: 15c. Tree; 20c. Dog; 25c. House; 30c. Doll.

1973. Stamp Centenary.
762 **154** 15c. green and blue . . . 20 20
763 – 25c. multicoloured 30 30
764 – 30c. multicoloured 50 50
DESIGNS: 25c. Postman; 30c. Map and postal routes.

155 "Quassia amara" **156** Nurse and Blood Transfusion Equipment

1974. Easter Charity Flowers. Multicoloured.
765 10c.+5c. Type **155** 55 50
766 15c.+8c. "Passiflora quadrangularis" 55 50
767 20c.+10c. "Combretum rotundifolium" 55 50
768 25c.+12c. "Cassia alata" . . 55 50
769 30c.+15c. "Asclepias curassavica" 55 50

1974. 75th Anniv of Surinam Medical School. Multicoloured.
770 15c. Type **156** 20 20
771 30c. Microscope slide and oscilloscope scanner . . . 30 30

157 Aerial Crop-spraying **158** Commemorative Text superimposed on Early Newspaper

1974. 25th Anniv of Mechanized Agriculture. Multicoloured.
772 15c. Type **157** 20 30
773 30c. Fertilizer plant 20 30

1974. Bicentenary of Surinam's "Weekly Wednesday" Newspaper.
774 **158** 15c. multicoloured 20 20
775 30c. multicoloured 30 30

159 Scout and Tent **160** G.P.O., Paramaribo

1974. "50 Years of Scouting in Surinam". Mult.
776 10c.+5c. Type **159** 45 35
777 15c.+8c. Jamboree emblem 45 35
778 20c.+10c. Scouts and badge 45 35

1974. Centenary of Universal Postal Union.
779 **160** 15c. black and brown . . 20 20
780 – 30c. black and blue . . . 30 30
DESIGN: 30c. G.P.O., Paramaribo (different view).

161 Girl with Fruit

1974. Child Welfare.
781 **161** 10c.+5c. green, emerald and pink 50 50
782 – 15c.+8c. brown, mauve and green 50 50
783 – 20c.+10c. yellow, orange and mauve 50 50
784 – 25c.+12c. brown, lilac and yellow 50 50
785 – 30c.+15c. cobalt, blue and lilac 50 50
MS786 76×97 mm. Nos. 781 ×2 and 783 . . . . 1·40 1·40
DESIGNS: 15c. Birds and nest; 20c. Mother and child with flower; 25c. Young boy in cornfield; 30c. Children at play.

162 Panning for Gold **163** "I am the Good Shepherd"

1975. Centenary of Prospecting Concession Policy.
787 **162** 15c. brown and bistre . . 20 20
788 – 30c. purple and red . . . 30 30
DESIGN: 30c. Claws of modern excavator.

1975. Easter Charity.
789 **163** 15c.+5c. yellow and green 50 50
790 – 20c.+10c. yellow and blue 50 50
791 – 30c.+15c. yellow and red 50 50
792 – 35c.+20c. blue and violet 50 50
DESIGNS—Quotations from the New Testament: 20c. "I do not know the man"; 30c. "He is not here; He has been raised again"; 35c. "Because you have seen Me you have found faith. Happy are they who never saw Me and yet have found faith".

164 "Looking to Equality, Education and Peace" **165** "Weights and Measures"

1975. International Women's Year.
793 **164** 15c.+5c. blue and green 50 50
794 30c.+15c. violet & mve . . 50 50

1975. Centenary of Metre Convention.
795 **165** 15c. multicoloured . . . 35 35
796 25c. multicoloured . . . 35 35
796a 30c. multicoloured . . . 35 35

166 Caribbean Water Jug **167** "Labour and Technology"

1975. Child Welfare. Multicoloured.
797 15c.+5c. Type **166** 50 50
798 20c.+10c. Indian arrowhead 50 50
799 30c.+15c. "Maluana" (protection against evil spirits) 50 50
800 35c.+20c. Indian arrowhead (different) 50 50
MS801 97×77 mm. Nos. 797 ×2 and 798 . . . . 1·40 1·40

1975. Independence. "Nation in Development". Multicoloured.
802 25c. Type **167** 20 20
803 50c. Open book ("Education and Art") 50 50
804 75c. Hands with ball ("Physical Training") . . . 70 70

168 Central Bank, Paramaribo **169** "Oncidium lanceanum"

1975.
805 **168** 1g. black, mauve & purple 90 25
806 1½g. black, orange & brn 1·50 25
807 2½g. black, red and brown 2·75 35
808 5g. black, emerald & green . . . . 5·50 55
809 10g. black, blue & dp blue 11·00 1·10

1976. Surinam Orchids. Multicoloured.
809 1c. Type **169** 10 10
810 2c. "Epidendrum stenopetalum" 10 10
811 3c. "Brassia lanceana" 10 10
812 4c. "Epidendrum ibaguense" 10 10
813 5c. "Epidendrum fragrans" . . 10 10

170 Surinam Flag   171 "Feeding the Hungry"

1976. Multicoloured.
814 25c. Type **170** 30 30
815 35c. Surinam arms 35 35

1976. Easter. Paintings in Alkmaar Church. Mult.
816 20c.+10c. Type **171** 30 30
817 25c.+15c. "Visiting the Sick" 35 35
818 30c.+15c. "Clothing the Naked" 40 40
819 35c.+15c. "Burying the Dead" 45 55
820 50c.+25c. "Refreshing the Thirsty" 70 80

172 Semicircle Angelfish

1976. Fishes. Multicoloured.
822 1c. Type **172** (postage) . . . 10 10
823 2c. Diadem squirrelfish . . . 10 10
824 3c. Zebra goby 10 10
825 4c. Queen triggerfish 10 10
826 5c. Black-barred soldierfish 10 10
827 35c. Teardrop butterflyfish (air) 50 40
828 60c. Flame angelfish 90 65
829 95c. Red-tailed butterflyfish 1·40 1·00

173 Early Telephone and Switchboard

1976. Telephone Centenary.
830 20c. Type **173** 25 20
831 35c. Globe, satellite and modern telephone 40 35

174 "Anansi Tori" (A. Baag)

1976. Paintings by Surinam Artists. Mult.
832 20c. Type **174** 25 20
833 30c. "Surinam Now" (R. Chang) 35 30
834 35c. "Lamentation" (N. Hatterman) (vert) 45 40
835 50c. "Chess-players" (Q. Jan Telting) 60 55

175 "Join or Die" (Franklin's "Divided Snake" poster of 1754)

1976. Bicentenary of American Revolution.
836 **175** 20c. black, green & cream 25 20
837 60c. black, red and cream 75 75

176 Pekinese   177 "Ionopsis utricularioides"

1976. Child Welfare. Pet Dogs.
838 20c.+10c. Type **176** 40 40
839 25c.+10c. Alsatian 45 45
840 30c.+10c. Dachshund 55 55
841 35c.+15c. Surinam breed . . 60 60
842 50c.+25c. Mongrel 85 85

1976. As Nos. 551/7 and new values but size 22 × 18 mm.
843a – 5c. brown 10 10
843b **98** 10c. green 15 10
843c – 20c. green 25 15
843d – 25c. blue 25 15
843e – 30c. green 30 15
843f – 35c. red 35 20
843g – 40c. orange 50 25
843h – 60c. red 75 35
NEW VALUES: 5c. Brewery; 60c. Jetty.

1977. Surinam Orchids. Multicoloured.
844 20c. Type **177** 30 25
845 30c. "Rodriguezia secunda" 45 40
846 35c. "Oncidium pusillum" . . 50 45
847 55c. "Sobralia sessilis" . . . 75 65
848 60c. "Octomeria surinamensis" 80 70

178 Javanese Costume   179 Triptych, left panel (Jan Mostaert)

1977. Surinam Costumes (1st series). Mult.
849 10c. Type **178** 15 10
850 15c. Forest Negro 20 15
851 35c. Chinese 40 35
852 60c. Creole 75 65
853 75c. Aborigine Indian 95 85
854 1g. Hindustani . . . . 1·25 1·25
DESIGNS: 15c. to 1g. Various women's festival costumes.
See also Nos. 906/11.

1977. Easter. Multicoloured.
855 20c.+10c. Type **179** 25 30
856 25c.+15c. Right panel 35 40
857 30c.+15c. Right panel 40 45
858 35c.+15c. Centre panel (30 × 38 mm.) 50 55
859 50c.+25c. Left panel 70 80
The 20c. and 25c. show the triptych closed, the 30c. and 50c. show designs on the reverse of the doors, and the 35c. shows the centre panel.

180 Green Honeycreeper

1977. Air. Birds. Multicoloured.
860 20c. Red-breasted blackbird 60 35
861 25c. Type **180** 70 40
862 30c. Paradise tanager . . . 75 45
863 40c. Spot-tailed nightjar . . 90 55
864 45c. Yellow-backed tanager 95 60
865 50c. White-tailed goldenthroat . . . . . . 1·00 70
866 55c. Grey-breasted sabrewing . . . . 1·10 75
867 60c. Caica parrot (vert) . . 1·10 80
868 65c. Red-billed toucan (vert) 1·25 90
869 70c. Crimson-hooded manakin (vert) . . . . . 1·40 95
870 75c. Hawk-headed parrot (vert) . . . . 1·50 1·00
871 80c. Spangled cotinga (vert) 1·75 1·10
872 85c. Black-tailed trogon (vert) . . . . 1·90 1·25
872a 90c. Orange-winged amazon (vert) . . . . 1·75 1·10
873 95c. Black-banded owl (vert) 2·00 1·40

181 Candy Basslet

1977. Fishes. Multicoloured.
875 1c. Type **181** (postage) . . . 10 10
876 2c. Queen angelfish 10 10
877 3c. Yellow-headed jawfish . . 10 10
878 4c. Porkfish 10 10
879 5c. Royal gramma 10 10
880 60c. Banded butterflyfish (air) 75 65
881 90c. Spot-finned hogfish . . . 1·10 95
882 120c. Cherub angelfish . . . 1·75 1·40

182 Edison's Phonograph, 1877

1977. Centenary of Sound Reproduction. Mult.
883 20c. Type **182** 25 20
883a 60c. Modern gramophone turntable 75 75

183 Paddle Steamer "Curacao"   185 Dog

1977. 150th Anniv of Regular Passenger Steam Service with Netherlands.
884 **183** 5c. blue and light blue . . 25 10
885 – 15c. red and orange . . . 45 15
886 – 30c. black and ochre . . . 40 35
887 – 35c. black and olive . . . 50 40
888 – 60c. black and lilac . . . 80 70
889 – 95c. green and light green 1·75 1·75
DESIGNS: 15c. Hellevoetsluis port; 30c. Chart of steamer route from Hellevoetsluis to Paramaribo; 35c. Log of "Curacao"; 60c. Chart of Paramaribo and 1852 postmark; 95c. Passenger liner "Stuyvesant".

1977. Surch.
890 – 1c. on 25c. mult (No. 722) 10 10
891 **144** 4c. on 15c. multicoloured 10 10
892 – 4c. on 30c. mult (No. 723) 10 10
893 – 5c. on 40c. mult (No. 725) 10 10
894 – 10c. on 75c. mult (No. 732) 15 15
The word "LUCHTPOST" ("AIR-MAIL") on the original stamp is obliterated by bars.

1977. Child Welfare. Multicoloured.
895 20c.+10c. Type **185** 30 35
896 25c.+15c. Monkey 40 45
897 30c.+15c. Rabbit 45 50
898 35c.+15c. Cat 50 55
899 50c.+25c. Parrot 75 80

186 "Passiflora quadrangularis"   187 Javanese Costumes

1978. Flowers. Multicoloured.
901 20c. Type **186** 25 20
902 30c. "Centropogon surinamensis" 35 30
903 55c. "Gloxinia perennis" . . 65 55
904 60c. "Hydrocleys nymphoides" 70 60
905 75c. "Clusia grandiflora" . . . 85 75

1978. Surinam Costumes (2nd series). Mult.
906 10c. Type **187** 15 10
907 20c. Forest Negro 25 20
908 35c. Chinese 40 35
909 60c. Creole 75 60
910 75c. Aborigine Indian 85 75
911 1g. Hindustani . . . . 1·25 1·25

188 Cross and Halo   189 Municipal Church, 1783

1978. Easter Charity.
912 **188** 20c.+10c. multicoloured 30 35
913 – 25c.+15c. brown, yellow and red 45 50
914 – 30c.+15c. brown, red and yellow 50 55
915 – 35c.+15c. brown, violet and red 55 60
916 – 60c.+30c. brown, yellow and green . . . . . . 1·00 1·10
DESIGNS: 25c. Serpent and cross; 30c. Blood and lamb; 35c. Passover dish and chalice; 60c. Eclipse and crucifix.

1978. Bicentenary of Church of Evangelistic Brothers Community.
917 **189** 10c. brown, black and blue 10 10
918 – 20c. black and grey . . . 20 20
919 – 55c. black and purple . . 55 55
920 – 60c. black and orange . . 70 70
DESIGNS: 20c. Brother Johannes King, 1830–1899; 55c. Modern Municipal Church; 60c. Brother Johannes Raillard, 1939–1954.

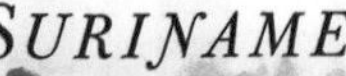

190 Golden-eyed Cichlid   192 Coconuts

1978. Tropical Fish. Multicoloured.
921 1c. Type **190** (postage) . . . 10 10
922 2c. Banded leporinus 10 10
923 3c. X-ray tetra 10 10
924 4c. Golden pencilfish 10 10
925 5c. Agila rivulus 10 10
926 60c. Two-spotted astyanax (air) 85 75
927 90c. Blue-spotted corydoras 1·25 1·10
928 120c. River hatchetfish . . . 1·75 1·50

1978. Fruits. Multicoloured.
930 5c. Type **192** 10 10
931 10c. Citrus 10 10
932 15c. Papaya 15 15
933a 20c. Bananas 15 15
934 25c. Sour-sop 25 25
934b 30c. Cacao 25 25
935 35c. Water melons 35 35

193 Children's Heads and Kittens   194 Daedalus and Icarus

1978. Child Welfare.
936 **193** 20c.+10c. multicoloured 25 30
937 – 25c.+15c. multicoloured 35 40
938 – 30c.+15c. multicoloured 40 45
939 – 35c.+15c. multicoloured 40 45
940 – 60c.+30c. multicoloured 80 90
DESIGNS: 25c. to 60c. Different designs showing kittens at play.

1978. 75th Anniv of First Powered Flight. Mult.
942 20c. Type **194** 25 20
943 60c. Wright Flyer I (horiz) 60 50
944 95c. Douglas DC-8-63 (horiz) 85 70
945 125c. Concorde (horiz) . . . 1·25 1·25

195 Black Curassow   196 "Rodriguezia candida"

1979. Air.
946 **195** 5g. purple . . . . 8·00 6·00

1979. Orchids. Multicoloured.
947 10c. Type **196** 15 10
948 20c. "Stanhopea grandiflora" 25 20

949 35c. "Scuticaria steelei" . . . 40 35
950 60c. "Bollea violacea" . . . 65 60

197 Javanese Dance

198 Church, Chalice and Cross

1979. Dancing Costumes. Multicoloured.
951 5c. Type **197** 10 10
952 10c. Forest Negro 10 10
953 15c. Chinese 20 15
954 20c. Creole 20 20
955 25c. Aborigine Indian 25 20
956 25c. Hindustani 35 35

1979. Easter Charity.
957 **198** 20c.+10c. multicoloured 25 30
958 – 30c.+15c. multicoloured 35 40
959 – 35c.+15c. multicoloured 40 45
960 – 40c.+20c. multicoloured 45 50
961 – 60c.+30c. multicoloured 70 80
DESIGNS: 30c. to 60c. Different churches.

199 Spotted Drum

1979. Fishes. Multicoloured.
962 1c. Type **199** (postage) . . . 10 10
963 2c. Barred cardinalfish . . . 10 10
964 3c. Porkfish 10 10
965 5c. Spanish hogfish 10 10
966 35c. Yellow-tailed damselfish 45 40
967 60c. White-spotted filefish (air) 75 70
968 90c. Long-spined squirrelfish 1·10 1·00
969 120c. Rock beauty . . . . . 1·50 1·40

200 Javanese Wooden Head

1979. Art Objects. Multicoloured.
970 20c. Type **200** 20 20
971 35c. American Indian hair ornament 30 30
972 60c. Javanese horse's head . . 55 55

201 S.O.S. Children's Village and Emblem

202 Sir Rowland Hill

1979. International Year of the Child. Mult.
973 20c. Type **201** 20 15
974 60c. Different view of Village, and emblem 55 55

1979. Death Centenary of Sir Rowland Hill.
975 **202** 1g. green and yellow . . . 1·00 1·00

203 Bird, Running Youth and Blood Transfusion Bottle

204 Javanese

1979. Child Welfare.
976 **203** 20c.+10c. blk, vio & red 25 30
977 30c.+15c. blk, red & vio 40 45
978 35c.+15c. multicoloured 45 50
979 40c.+20c. multicoloured 50 55
980 60c.+30c. multicoloured 70 80

1980. Children's Costumes. Multicoloured.
982 10c. Type **204** 10 10
983 15c. Forest Negro 15 15
984 25c. Chinese 25 20
985 60c. Creole 55 55
986 90c. Indian 80 80
987 1g. Hindustani 85 85

205 Handshake and Rotary Emblem

206 Church Interior

1980. 75th Anniv of Rotary International. Each blue and yellow.
988 20c. Type **205** 20 20
989 60c. Globe and Rotary emblem 50 50

1980. Easter Charity. Various Easter symbols.
990 **206** 20c.+10c. multicoloured 25 30
991 – 30c.+15c. multicoloured 40 45
992 – 40c.+20c. multicoloured 50 55
993 – 50c.+25c. multicoloured 60 70
994 – 60c.+30c. multicoloured 70 80

207 Mail Coach

208 Weightlifting

1980. "London 1980" International Stamp Exhibition.
995 **207** 50c. yellow, black and blue 40 40
996 – 1g. yellow, black & purple 80 80
997 – 2g. pink, black & turq . . 1·60 1·60
DESIGNS: 1g. Sir Rowland Hill; 2g. People posting letters.

1980. Olympic Games, Moscow.
999 **208** 20c. multicoloured . . . 20 20
1000 – 30c. multicoloured . . . 25 25
1001 – 50c. green, yellow and red 40 40
1002 – 75c. multicoloured . . . 60 60
1003 – 150c. multicoloured . . . 1·25 1·25
DESIGNS: 30c. Diving; 50c. Gymnastics; 75c. Basketball; 150c. Running.

209 Arawana

210 Anansi disguised as Spider

1980. Tropical Fishes. Multicoloured.
1005 10c. Type **209** (postage) . . 10 10
1006 15c. Colossoma 15 15
1007 25c. Garnet tetra 30 20
1008 30c. False rummy-nosed tetra 35 25
1009 45c. Red-spotted tetra . . . 50 40
1010 60c. Red discus (air) 70 55
1011 75c. Flag acara 80 65
1012 90c. Wimple piranha . . . 95 75

1980. Child Welfare. "The Story of Anansi and his Creditors".
1013 **210** 20c.+10c. bistre and yellow 30 35
1014 – 25c.+15c. yellow, brown and orange 35 40
1015 – 30c.+15c. brown, red and orange 40 45
1016 – 35c.+15c. green, light green and yellow . . . 45 50
1017 – 60c.+30c. multicoloured 80 90
DESIGNS—(Anansi in various disguises): 25c. Bear; 30c. Cockerel; 35c. Hunter; 60c. Beetle.

212 Old Woman reading

213 "Passiflora laurifolia"

1980. Welfare of the Aged. Multicoloured.
1020 25c.+10c. Type **212** 30 35
1021 50c.+15c. Old man tending flowers 50 60
1022 75c.+20c. Grandfather and grandchildren 80 90

1981. Flower Drawings by Maria Sibylle Merian. Multicoloured.
1023 20c. Type **213** 20 20
1024 30c. "Aphelandra pectinata" 30 25
1025 60c. "Caesalpinia pulcherrima" 55 55
1026 75c. "Hibiscus mutabilis" 70 70
1027 1g.25 "Hippeastrum puniceum" . . . . 1·25 1·25

214 Justice and Text "Renewal of the Governmental and Political Order"

215 Christ with Jug

1981. The Four Renewals.
1028 – 30c. yellow, brown and deep yellow 25 25
1029 – 60c. orange, brown & red 50 50
1030 – 75c. green, deep green and olive 60 60
1031 **214** 1g. deep yellow, green and yellow 80 80
DESIGNS: 30c. "Renewal of the Economic Order"; 60c. "Renewal of the Educational Order"; 75c. "Renewal of the Social Order".

1981. Easter Charity. Multicoloured.
1033 20c.+10c. Type **215** 25 30
1034 30c.+15c. Christ and pointing hand 40 45
1035 50c.+25c. Christ and Roman soldier 60 65
1036 60c.+30c. Christ wearing crown of thorns 70 80
1037 75c.+35c. Christ and Mary 80 90

218 "Phyllomedusa hypochondrialis"

1981. Frogs. Multicoloured.
1040 40c. Type **218** (postage) . . 40 35
1041 50c. "Leptodactylus pentadactylus" 45 40
1042 60c. "Hyla boans" 55 50
1043 75c. "Phyllomedusa burmeisteri" (vert) (air) 70 65
1044 1g. "Dendrobates tinctorius" (vert) 90 85
1045 1g.25 "Bufo guttatus" (vert) 1·25 1·25

219 Deaf Child

1981. International Year of Disabled Persons.
1046 **219** 50c. yellow and green . . 40 40
1047 – 100c. yellow and green . . 80 80
1048 – 150c. yellow and red . . 1·25 1·25
DESIGNS: 100c. Child reading braille; 150c. Woman in wheelchair.

220 Planter's House on the Parakreek River

221 Indian Girl

1981. Illustrations to "Journey to Surinam" by P. I. Benoit. Multicoloured.
1049 20c. Type **220** 20 20
1050 30c. Saramecca Street, Paramaribo 25 25
1051 75c. Negro hamlet, Paramaribo 60 60
1052 1g. Fish market, Paramaribo 80 80
1053 1g.25 Blaauwe Berg Cascade 1·00 1·00

1981. Child Welfare. Multicoloured.
1055 20c.+10c. Type **221** 25 30
1056 30c.+15c. Negro girl 40 45
1057 50c.+25c. Hindustani girl . . 60 70
1058 60c.+30c. Javanese girl . . . 70 80
1059 75c.+35c. Chinese girl . . . 80 90

222 Satellites orbiting Earth

1982. Peaceful Uses of Outer Space. Mult.
1061 35c. Type **222** 35 30
1062 65c. Space shuttle 60 55
1063 1g. U.S.–Russian space link 85 85

223 "Caretta caretta"

224 Pattern from Stained Glass Window

1982. Turtles. Multicoloured.
1064 5c. Type **223** (postage) . . . 10 10
1065 10c. "Chelonia mydas" . . 10 10
1066 20c. "Dermochelys coriacea" 20 20
1067 25c. "Eretmochelys imbricata" 25 25
1068 35c. "Lepidochelys olivacea" 30 30
1069 65c. "Platemys platycephala" (air) . . . 60 60
1070 75c. "Phrynops gibba" . . . 75 75
1071 125c. "Rihnoclemys punctularia" . . . . . . 1·10 1·10

1982. Easter. Stained-glass Windows, Church of Saints Peter and Paul, Paramaribo.
1072 **224** 20c.+10c. multicoloured 25 30
1073 – 35c.+15c. multicoloured 40 45
1074 – 50c.+25c. multicoloured 60 70
1075 – 65c.+30c. multicoloured 75 85
1076 – 75c.+35c. multicoloured 80 90
DESIGNS: 35c. to 75c. Different patterns.

225 Lions Emblem

226 Father Donders with the Sick

1982. 25th Anniv of Surinam Lions Club.
1077 **225** 35c. multicoloured . . . 30 30
1078 70c. multicoloured . . . 60 60

1982. Beatification of Father Peter Donders.
1079 **226** 35c. multicoloured . . . 30 30
1080 – 65c. silver, black and red 50 50
DESIGN: 65c. Portrait, birthplace, Tilburg, and map of South America.

227 Stamp Designer

228 Dr. Robert Koch

1982. "Philexfrance 82" International Stamp Exhibition, Paris. Multicoloured.
1082 50c. Type **227** 40 40
1083 100c. Stamp printing . . . 80 80
1084 150c. Stamp collector . . . 1·25 1·25

1982. Cent of Discovery of Tubercle Bacillus.
1086 **228** 35c. yellow and green . . 35 30
1087 – 65c. orange and brown 60 55
1088 – 150c. light blue, blue and red . . . . 1·50 1·50
DESIGNS: 65c. Dr. Koch and microscope; 150c. Dr. Koch and Bacillus.

229 Sugar Mill

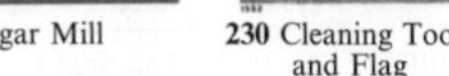

230 Cleaning Tools and Flag

1982. Cent of Marienburg Sugar Company.
1089 229 35c. yellow, green and black 30 30
1090 – 65c. orange and brown 50 50
1091 – 100c. light blue, blue and black . . . . 2·10 2·10
1092 – 150c. lilac and purple . . 1·25 1·25
DESIGNS: 65c. Workers in cane fields; 100c. Sugar-cane railway; 150c. Mill machinery.

1982. Child Welfare. "Keep Surinam Tidy" (children's paintings). Multicoloured.
1093 20c.+10c. Type **230** 25 30
1094 35c.+15c. Man with barrow 40 45
1095 50c.+25c. Litter bin and cleaning tools 60 70
1096 65c.+30c. Spraying weeds 75 85
1097 75c.+35c. Litter bin 85 95

231 Municipal Church, Paramaribo

1982. 250th Anniv of Moravian Church Mission in the Caribbean.
1099 231 35c. multicoloured . . . 30 30
1100 – 65c. light blue, black and blue 50 50
1101 – 150c. multicoloured . . . 1·25 1·25
DESIGNS—HORIZ: 65c. Aerial view of St. Thomas Monastery. VERT: 150c. Johann Leonhardt Dober (missionary).

232 "Erythrina fusca"

1983. Flower Paintings by Maria Sibylle Merian. Multicoloured.
1102 1c. Type **232** 10 10
1103 2c. "Ipomoea acuminata" 10 10
1104 3c. "Heliconia psittacorum" 10 10
1105 5c. "Ipomoea" 10 10
1106 10c. "Herba non denominata" 10 10
1107 15c. "Anacardium occidentale" 15 15
1108 20c. "Inga edulis" (vert) . . 20 15
1109 25c. "Abelmoschus moschatus" (vert) 25 20
1110 30c. "Argemone mexicana" (vert) 30 25
1111 35c. "Costus arabicus" (vert) 35 30
1112 45c. "Muellera frutescens" (vert) 45 45
1113 65c. "Punica granatum" (vert) 60 60

233 Scout Anniversary Emblem
234 Dove of Peace

1983. Year of the Scout.
1114 233 40c. mauve, violet & green 45 40
1115 – 65c. lt grey, blue & grey 70 60
1116 – 70c. multicoloured . . . 80 70
1117 – 80c. blue, lt green & green 85 80
DESIGNS: 65c. Lord Baden-Powell; 70c. Tent and campfire; 80c. Axe in tree trunk.

1983. Easter. Multicoloured.
1118 234 10c.+5c. Type 15 15
1119 15c.+5c. Bread 20 25
1120 25c.+10c. Fish 30 35
1121 50c.+25c. Eye 60 70
1122 65c.+30c. Chalice . . . 75 85

235 Drawing by Raphael

1983. 500th Birth Anniv of Raphael.
1123 235 5c. multicoloured 10 10
1124 – 10c. multicoloured . . . 10 10
1125 – 40c. multicoloured . . . 35 35
1126 – 65c. multicoloured . . . 60 60
1127 – 70c. multicoloured . . . 65 65
1128 – 80c. multicoloured . . . 70 70
DESIGNS: 10c. to 80c. Drawings by Raphael.

236 1c. Coin
237 "25" on Map of Surinam

1983. Coins and Banknotes. Multicoloured.
1129 5c. Type **236** 10 10
1130 10c. 5c. coin 10 10
1131 40c. 10c. coin 45 40
1132 65c. 25c. coin 65 65
1133 70c. 1g. note 70 70
1134 80c. 2½g. note . . . . . . 1·50 90

1983. 25th Anniv of Department of Construction. Multicoloured.
1135 25c. Type **237** 25 25
1136 50c. Construction vehicles on map 45 45

238 "Papilio anchisiades"
239 Montgolfier Balloon "Le Martial", 1783

1983. Butterfly Paintings by Maria Sibylle Merian. Multicoloured.
1137 1c. Type **238** 10 10
1138 2c. "Urania leilus" 10 10
1139 3c. "Morpho deidamia" . . . 10 10
1140 5c. "Thysania agrippina" . . 10 10
1141 10c. "Morpho sp." 20 10
1142 15c. "Philaethria dido" . . . 30 20
1143 20c. "Morpho menelaus" (horiz) 40 25
1144 25c. "Protoparce rustica" (horiz) 50 30
1145 30c. "Rothschildia aurota" (horiz) 60 40
1146 35c. "Phoebis sennae" (horiz) 80 50
1147 45c. "Papilio androgeos" (horiz) 90 70
1148 65c. "Dupo vitis" (horiz) . . 1·40 1·00

1983. Bicentenary of Manned Flight. Mult.
1149 5c. Type **239** 10 10
1150 10c. Montgolfier balloon (1st manned free flight by D'Arlandes and Pilatre de Rozier, 1783) 10 10
1151 40c. Charles's hydrogen balloon, 1783 . . . . . . 40 40
1152 65c. Balloon "Armand Barbes", 1870 . . . . . 65 65
1153 70c. Balloon "Double Eagle II" (transatlantic flight, 1978) 70 70
1154 80c. Hot-air balloons at International Balloon Festival, Albuquerque, U.S.A. 75 75

240 Calabash Pitcher
241 Martin Luther

1983. Child Welfare. Caribbean Artifacts. Mult.
1155 10c.+5c. Type **240** 15 15
1156 15c.+5c. Umari (headdress) 15 20
1157 25c.+10c. Maraka (medicine man's rattle) 20 35
1158 50c.+25c. Manari (sieve) . . 60 70
1159 65c.+30c. Pasuwa/pakara (basket) 70 80

1983. 500th Birth Anniv of Martin Luther (Protestant reformer).
1161 241 25c. yellow, brown and black 20 20
1162 – 50c. pink, purple & black 40 40
DESIGN: 50c. Selling of indulgences.

242 "Catasetum discolor"
243 Atlantic Turkey Wing

1983. Orchids. Multicoloured.
1163 5c. Type **242** 10 10
1164 10c. "Menadenium labiosum" 10 10
1165 40c. "Comparettia falcata" 45 40
1166 50c. "Rodriguezia decora" 70 60
1167 70c. "Oncidium papilio" . . 80 70
1168 75c. "Epidendrum porpax" 85 75

1984. Sea Shells. Multicoloured.
1169 40c. Type **243** 45 45
1170 65c. American prickly cockle 80 80
1171 70c. Sunrise tellin 80 80
1172 80c. Knorr's worm shell . . 95 95

244 Cross and Flower
245 Sikorsky S-40 Flying Boat

1984. Easter. Multicoloured.
1173 10c.+5c. Type **244** 15 15
1174 15c.+5c. Cross and gate of cemetery 15 20
1175 25c.+10c. Candle flames . . 30 35
1176 50c.+25c. Cross and crown of thorns 60 70
1177 65c.+30c. Lamp 70 80

1984. 40th Anniv of I.C.A.O. Multicoloured.
1178 35c. Type **245** 40 40
1179 65c. Surinam Airways De Havilland Twin Otter 200/300 . . . . 85 85

246 Running
247 Emblem of 8th Caribbean Scout Jamboree

1984. Olympic Games, Los Angeles. Multicoloured.
1180 2c. Type **246** 10 10
1181 3c. Javelin, discus and long jump 10 10
1182 5c. Massage 10 10
1183 10c. Rubbing with ointment 10 10
1184 15c. Wrestling 15 15
1185 20c. Boxing 20 20
1186 30c. Horse-racing 30 30
1187 35c. Chariot-racing 35 35
1188 45c. Temple of Olympia . . 40 40
1189 50c. Entrance to Stadium, Olympia 45 45
1190 65c. Stadium, Olympia . . . 60 60
1191 75c. Zeus 70 70

1984. 60th Anniv of Scouting in Surinam. Mult.
1193 30c.+10c. Type **247** 40 40
1194 35c.+10c. Scout saluting . . 50 50
1195 50c.+10c. Scout camp . . . 65 65
1196 90c.+10c. Campfire and map 95 95

248 Ball entering Basket
249 Red Square, Moscow

1984. International Military Sports Council Basketball Championship. Multicoloured.
1197 50c. Type **248** 50 45
1198 90c. Ball leaving basket . . 85 75

1984. World Chess Championship, Moscow.
1199 249 10c. brown 10 10
1200 – 15c. green and light green 15 15
1201 – 30c. light brown & brown 30 30
1202 – 50c. brown and purple . . 50 50
1203 – 75c. brown & light brown 80 80
1204 – 90c. green and blue . . . 90 90
DESIGNS: 15c. Knight, king and pawn on board; 30c. Gary Kasparov; 50c. Start of game and clock; 75c. Anatoly Karpov; 90c. Position during Andersen–Kizeritski game.

250 Children collecting Milk from Cow
251 Kite

1984. World Food Day. Multicoloured.
1206 50c. Type **250** 50 45
1207 90c. Platter of food 85 75

1984. Child Welfare. Multicoloured.
1208 5c.+5c. Type **251** 10 10
1209 10c.+5c. Kites 15 15
1210 30c.+10c. Pingi-pingi-kasi (game) 40 40
1211 50c.+25c. Cricket 85 85
1212 90c.+30c. Peroen, peroen (game) . . . . 1·10 1·10

252 Leaf Cactus

1985. Cacti. Multicoloured.
1215 5c. Type **252** 10 10
1216 10c. Melocactus 10 10
1217 30c. Pillar cactus 25 25
1218 50c. Fig cactus 45 45
1219 75c. Night queen 70 70
1220 90c. Segment cactus 80 80

253 "Peace" and Star
254 Crosses

1985. 5th Anniv of Revolution. Multicoloured.
1221 5c. Type **253** 10 10
1222 30c. "Unity in labour" and manual workers 20 20
1223 50c. "5 years of Steadfastness" and flower 40 40
1224 75c. "Progress" and wheat as flower 60 60
1225 90c. "Unity", flower and dove 70 70

1985. Easter. Multicoloured.
1227 5c.+5c. Type **254** 10 10
1228 10c.+5c. Crosses (different) 10 10
1229 30c.+15c. Sun's rays illuminating crosses . . . 30 30
1230 50c.+25c. Crosses (different) 55 65
1231 90c.+30c. Crosses and leaves (Resurrection) 75 85

255 Emblem
256 U.N. Emblem and State Arms

1985. 75th Anniv of Chamber of Commerce and Industry.
1232 255 50c. yellow, green and red 40 40
1233 – 90c. green, blue & yellow 70 70
DESIGN: 90c. Chamber of Commerce building.

1985. 40th Anniv of U.N.O.
1234 256 50c. multicoloured . . . 40 40
1235 90c. multicoloured . . . 70 70

257 Sugar-cane Train (detail of 1945 stamp)

1985. Railway Locomotives.
1236 **257** 5c. orange and blue . . 10 10
1237 – 5c. green, red and blue 10 10
1238 – 10c. multicoloured . . . 20 15
1239 – 10c. multicoloured . . . 20 15
1240 – 20c. multicoloured . . . 45 30
1241 – 20c. multicoloured . . . 45 30
1242 – 30c. multicoloured . . . 80 45
1243 – 30c. multicoloured . . . 80 45
1244 – 50c. multicoloured . . . 1·40 80
1245 – 50c. multicoloured . . . 1·40 80
1246 – 75c. multicoloured . . . 1·75 1·25
1247 – 75c. multicoloured . . . 1·75 1·25
DESIGNS: No. 1237, Monaco 3f. Postage due train stamp; 1238, Steam locomotive "Dam"; 1239, Modern electric railcars; 1240, Steam locomotive No. 3737, Netherlands; 1241, Electric railcar Type IC-III, Netherlands; 1242, Stephenson's "Rocket"; 1243, TGV express train, France; 1244, Stephenson "Adler", Germany; 1245, Double-deck UB2N train, France; 1246, "General", U.S.A.; 1247, "Hikari" express train, Japan.

258 American Purple Gallinule
259 German Letterbox, 1900

1985. Birds. Multicoloured.
1248 1g. Type **258** . . . . 1·25 1·00
1249 1g.50 Rufescent tiger heron 1·60 1·40
1250 2g.50 Scarlet ibis . . . . . 3·00 2·50
1251 5g. Guianan cock of the rock . . . . 3·75 3·00
1252 10g. Harpy eagle . . . . . 8·00 7·00

1985. Old Letterboxes. Multicoloured.
1254 15c. Type **259** 15 15
1255 30c. French letterbox, 1900 20 20
1256 50c. English pillar box, 1932 35 35
1257 90c. Dutch letterbox, 1850 55 55

260 Emblem on Map
261 Studying

1985. 25th Anniv of Evangelical Brotherhood in Surinam.
1258 **260** 30c.+10c. multicoloured 30 30
1259 – 50c.+10c. red, yellow and brown 45 45
1260 – 90c.+20c. yellow, brown and red 75 75
DESIGNS: 50c. Different population groups around cross and clasped hands emblem; 90c. List of work undertaken by Brotherhood.

1985. Child Welfare. Multicoloured.
1261 5c.+5c. Type **261** 10 10
1262 10c.+5c. Writing alphabet on board 15 15
1263 30c.+10c. Writing 30 30
1264 50c.+25c. Reading 55 55
1265 90c.+30c. Thinking 80 80

1985. Victory of Kasparov in World Chess Championship. No. 1201 optd **KACTTAPOB Wereldkampioen 9 nov. 1985.**
1267 30c. light brown and brown 30 20

263 Agriculture
264 "Epidendrum ciliare"

1985. 10th Anniv of Independence.
1268 **263** 50c. yellow and green . . 40 40
1269 – 90c. orange and brown 70 70
DESIGN: 90c. Industry.

1986. Orchids. Multicoloured.
1271 5c. Type **264** 35 35
1272 15c. "Cycnoches chlorochilon" . . . . . . 1·10 1·10
1273 30c. "Epidendrum anceps" 1·75 1·75
1274 50c. "Epidendrum vespa" 3·25 3·25

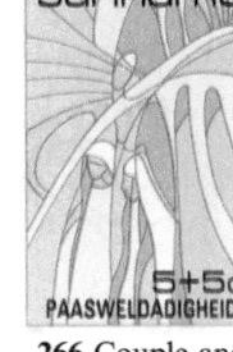

265 Bayeux Tapestry (detail)
266 Couple and Palm Leaves

1986. Appearance of Halley's Comet. Mult.
1275 50c. Type **265** 35 35
1276 110c. Comet 75 75

1986. Easter.
1277 **266** 5c.+5c. multicoloured . . 10 10
1278 10c.+5c. multicoloured 15 15
1279 30c.+15c. multicoloured 30 30
1280 50c.+25c. multicoloured 55 55
1281 90c.+30c. multicoloured 80 80

1986. Nos. 1244/5 surch.
1282 15c. on 50c. multicoloured 1·25 90
1283 15c. on 50c. multicoloured 1·25 90

268 Cathedral
270 National Forestry Emblem

1986. Centenary of St. Peter and St. Paul's Cathedral, Paramaribo.
1284 **268** 30c.+10c. brown and ochre 30 30
1285 – 50c.+10c. brown and red 50 50
1286 – 110c.+30c. deep brown and brown . . . . . 1·10 1·10
DESIGNS: 50c. Relief of St. Peter and St. Paul; 110c. Font.

1986. 150th Anniv of Finance Building. No. 1133 surch **30 c 150 jaar FINANCIENGEBOUW.**
1287 30c. on 70c. multicoloured 30 30

1986. Centenary of Foresters' Court Charity. Mult.
1288 50c.+20c. Type **270** 60 60
1289 110c.+30c. First Court building . . . . 1·25 1·25

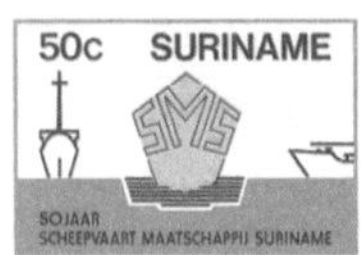

271 Emblem

1986. 50th Anniv of Surinam Shipping Line. Mult.
1290 50c. Type **271** 40 40
1291 110c. Container ship "Saramacca" . . . . . . 2·75 1·10

1986. No. 862 surch **15ct.**
1292 15c. on 30c. multicoloured 70 25

273 Children playing Hopscotch

1986. Child Welfare. Multicoloured.
1293 5c.+5c. Type **273** 10 10
1294 10c.+5c. Ballet class 15 15
1295 30c.+10c. Children boarding library bus 35 35
1296 50c.+25c. Boys at display of craftwork 65 65
1297 110c.+30c. Children in class 1·10 1·10

274 Red Howler

1987. Monkeys. Multicoloured.
1299 35c. Type **274** 30 30
1300 60c. Night monkey 55 55
1301 110c. Common squirrel-monkey 85 85
1302 120c. Red uakari 90 90

275 Emblem

1987. Centenary of Esperanto (invented language). Multicoloured.
1303 60c. Type **275** 55 55
1304 110c. Dove holding "Esperanto" banner across world map 85 85
1305 120c. L. L. Zamenhof (inventor) 90 90

1987. Various stamps surch.
1306 – 10c. on 85c. multicoloured (No. 872) 70 20
1307 – 10c. on 95c. multicoloured (No. 873) 70 20
1308 **168** 50c. on 1½g. black, orange and brown . . 45 45
1309 60c. on 2½g. black, red and brown 55 55

277 "Crucifixion"
278 Mushroom (Brownie emblem)

1987. Easter. Etchings by Rembrandt. Each light mauve, mauve and black.
1310 5c.+5c. Type **277** 10 10
1311 10c.+5c. "Christ on the Cross" 15 15
1312 35c.+15c. "Descent from the Cross" 35 35
1313 60c.+30c. "Christ carried to His Tomb" 65 65
1314 110c.+50c. "Entombment of Christ" . . . . 1·10 1·10

1987. 40th Anniv of Surinam Girl Guides.
1315 **278** 15c.+10c. mult 20 20
1316 – 60c.+10c. mult 50 50
1317 – 110c.+10c. mult 80 80
1318 – 120c.+10c. green, black and yellow 90 90
DESIGNS: 60c. Cloverleaf and star (Guide emblem); 110c. Campfire (Rangers emblem) on Guide trefoil; 120c. Ivy leaves (Captain's emblem).

279 Football
280 Commission Emblem

1987. 10th Pan-American Games, Indianapolis.
1319 **279** 90c. blue, green and brown 80 80
1320 – 110c. blue, light blue and brown 90 90
1321 – 150c. blue, mauve and brown . . . . 1·25 1·25
DESIGNS: 110c. Swimming; 150c. Basketball.

1987. 40th Anniv of Forestry Commission. Mult.
1322 90c. Type **280** 80 80
1323 120c. Loading tree trunks for export 95 95
1324 150c. Green-winged macaw in forest . . . . 2·50 1·25

282 Boy and Tents
283 Banana

1987. International Year of Shelter for the Homeless (90, 120c.) and Centenary of Salvation Army in the Caribbean Territory (150c.). Multicoloured.
1331 90c. Type **282** 70 70
1332 120c. Shanty town and man 85 85
1333 150c. William and Catherine Booth and emblem . . . 1·10 1·10

1987. Fruits. Multicoloured.
1334 10c. Type **283** 10 10
1335 15c. Cacao bean 15 15
1336 20c. Pineapple 15 15
1337 25c. Papaya 20 20
1338 35c. China orange 30 30

284 Jacob Degen's Balloon-assisted "Ornithopter", 1808

1987. Aircraft. Multicoloured.
1339 25c. Type **284** 20 20
1340 25c. Microlight airplane . . 20 20
1341 35c. Ellehammer II, 1906 . . 30 30
1342 35c. Concorde 30 30
1343 60c. Fokker F.VII (inscr "F.7"), 1924 . . . . . . 50 50
1344 60c. Fokker F28 Friendship 50 50
1345 90c. Fokker monoplane "Haarlem Spin", 1910 . . 75 75
1346 90c. Douglas DC-10 . . . . 75 75
1347 110c. Lockheed 9 Orion, 1932 . . . . 80 80
1348 110c. Boeing 747 . . . . . 80 80
1349 120c. 1967 Amelia Earhart 25c. stamp 95 95
1350 120c. 1978 Douglas DC-8-63 95c. stamp 95 95

285 Herring-bone Design
287 Ganges Gavial

1987. Child Welfare. Indian Weaving.
1351 **285** 50c.+25c. green & blk 65 65
1352 – 60c.+30c. orange and black 70 70
1353 – 110c.+50c. red & black 1·25 1·25
DESIGNS: 60c. Tortoise-back design; 110c. Concentric diamonds design.

1987. Nos. 869 and 805 surch.
1356 – 25c. on 70c. mult 75 40
1357 **168** 35c. on 1g. black, mauve and purple 60 60

1988. Reptiles. Multicoloured.
1358 50c. Type **287** 40 40
1359 60c. Nile crocodile 50 50
1360 90c. Black cayman 70 70
1361 110c. Mississippi alligator 80 80

288 Javanese Costumes
290 Cross and Chalice

1988. Wedding Costumes. Multicoloured.
1362 35c. Type **288** 30 30
1363 60c. Bushman 50 50
1364 80c. Chinese 65 65
1365 110c. Creole 80 80
1366 120c. Amerindian 85 85
1367 130c. Hindustan 90 90

1988. Various stamps surch.
1368 – 60c. on 75c. mult (No. 1246) . . . . . 1·75 1·25
1369 – 60c. on 75c. mult (No. 1247) . . . . . 1·75 1·25
1370 **168** 125c. on 10g. black, blue and deep blue . . . . 1·75 1·75

1988. Easter.
1371 **290** 50c.+25c. mult 65 65
1372 60c.+30c. mult 75 75
1373 110c.+50c. mult . . . . 1·40 1·40

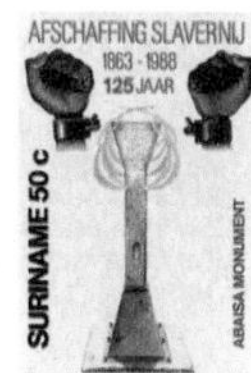

291 Relay
292 Abaisa Monument

1988. Olympic Games, Seoul. Multicoloured.
1374 90c. Type **291** 80 80
1375 110c. Football 90 90
1376 120c. Pole vaulting . . . . 1·00 1·00
1377 250c. Tennis . . . . 2·00 2·00

1988. 125th Anniv of Abolition of Slavery. Mult.
1379 50c. Type **292** 50 50
1380 110c. Kwakoe monument 90 90
1381 120c. Anton de Kom's house . . . . 1·10 1·10

293 Combine Harvester
294 Egypt 1906 4m. Stamp 

1988. 10th Anniv of International Agricultural Development Fund. "For a World without Hunger". Multicoloured.
1382 105c. Type **293** 90 90
1383 110c. Fishing 95 95
1384 125c. Cultivation . . . . . 1·25 1·25

1988. "Filacept" International Stamp Exhibition, The Hague.
1385 **294** 120c. red, black & orange . . . . 1·00 1·00
1386 – 150c. green, black & blue 1·25 1·25
1387 – 250c. red, black & deep red . . . . 2·25 2·25
DESIGNS: No. 1386, Netherlands 1952 10c. Stamp Centenary stamp; 1387, Surinam 1949 7½c. U.P.U. stamp.

295 Anniversary Emblem
296 Symbolic Representation of Butterfly Stroke 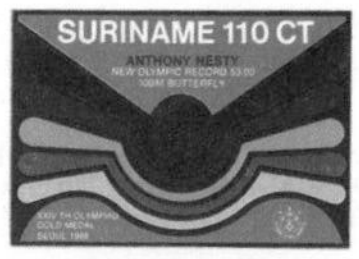

1988. 125th Anniv of Red Cross. Multicoloured.
1389 60c.+30c. Type **295** 85 85
1390 120c.+60c. Anniversary emblem and red cross in blood drop . . . . 1·60 1·60

1988. Anthony Nesty, Seoul Olympic Gold Medal Winner for 100 m Butterfly.
1391 **296** 110c. multicoloured . . . 95 95

297 "Man and Animal"

1988. 25th Anniv of Child Welfare Stamps. Mult.
1392 50c.+25c. Type **297** 70 70
1393 60c.+30c. "The Child in Nature" 85 85
1394 110c.+50c. Children helping each other ("Stop Drugs") 1·50 1·50

1988. Nos. 1238/9 and 1244/5 surch.
1396 2c. on 10c. mult (No. 1238) 55 60
1397 2c. on 10c. mult (No. 1239) 55 60
1398 3c. on 50c. mult (No. 1244) 55 60
1399 3c. on 50c. mult (No. 1245) 55 60

299 Otter on Rock
300 "The Passion" (left wing) 

1989. Otters. Multicoloured.
1400 10c. Type **299** 10 10
1401 20c. Two otters 20 10
1402 25c. Two otters (different) 25 25
1403 30c. Otter with fish 50 30
1404 185c. Two otters (vert) (air) 1·60 1·60

1989. Easter. Altarpiece by Tamas of Koloszvar. Multicoloured.
1405 60c.+30c. Type **300** 85 85
1406 105c.+50c. "Crucifixion" (centre panel) (28 × 36 mm) . . . . . . 1·50 1·50
1407 110c.+55c. "Resurrection" (right wing) . . . . . . 1·50 1·50

301 Mercedes Touring Car, 1930

1989. Motor Cars. Multicoloured.
1408 25c. Type **301** 15 15
1409 25c. Mercedes Benz "300 E", 1985 . . . . 15 15
1410 60c. Daimler, 1897 . . . . 40 40
1411 60c. Jaguar "Sovereign", 1986 . . . . 40 40
1412 90c. Renault "Voiturette", 1898 . . . . 60 60
1413 90c. Renault "25 TX", 1989 60 60
1414 105c. Volvo "Jacob", 1927 70 70
1415 105c. Volvo "440", 1989 . . 70 70
1416 110c. Left-half of 1961 1f. Monaco stamp 75 75
1417 110c. Right-half of 1961 1f. Monaco stamp 75 75
1418 120c. Toyota "AA", 1936 80 80
1419 120c. Toyota "Corolla" saloon, 1988 . . . . . . 80 80

303 Joseph Nicephore Niepce (pioneer)
304 Jade Statuette 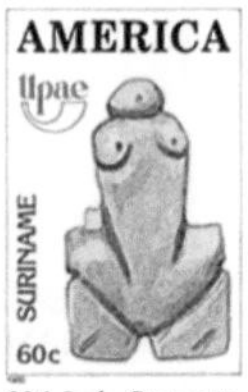

1989. 150th Anniv of Photography. Mult.
1421 60c. Type **303** 40 40
1422 110c. First camera using daguerreotype process . . 75 75
1423 120c. Louis Jacques Mande Daguerre (inventor of daguerreotype process) . . 80 80

1989. America. Pre-Columbian Artifacts. Mult.
1424 60c. Type **304** 40 40
1425 110c. Statuette of pregnant woman 75 75

305 1976 25c. Surinam Stamp
306 "Children Helping Each Other" (Gianna Karg) 

1989. "World Stamp Expo '89" International Stamp Exhibition, Washington, D.C. Mult.
1426 110c. Type **305** 75 75
1427 150c. 1950 3c. U.S.A. White House stamp . . . . . . 1·00 1·00
1428 250c. 1976 60c. Surinam "Divided Snake" stamp 1·75 1·75

1989. Child Welfare. Children's Paintings. Mult.
1430 60c.+30c. Type **306** 60 60
1431 105c.+50c. "Child and Nature" (Tamara Busropan) . . . . 1·00 1·00
1432 110c.+55c. "In the School Bus" (Cindy Kross) . . . 1·10 1·10

307 Local Emblem
308 Temple 

1990. International Literacy Year. Multicoloured.
1434 60c. Type **307** 40 40
1435 110c. I.L.Y. emblem 75 75
1436 120c. Emblems and boy reading 80 80

1990. 60th Anniv of Arya Dewaker Temple.
1437 **308** 60c. brown, red and black 40 40
1438 110c. violet and black . . 75 75
1439 200c. green and black . . 1·40 1·40

309 Mary and Baby Jesus
310 Surinam 1930 10c. Air Stamp 

1990. Easter. Multicoloured.
1440 60c.+30c. Type **309** 55 55
1441 105c.+50c. Jesus teaching . . 90 90
1442 110c.+55c. Jesus's body taken from cross . . . . 1·00 1·00

1990. "Stamp World London 90" International Stamp Exhibition, London, and 150th Anniv of the Penny Black. Multicoloured.
1443 110c. Type **310** 65 65
1444 200c. Penny Black . . . . . 1·25 1·25
1445 250c. G.B. 1929 2½d. Postal Union Congress stamp . . 1·50 1·50

311 Couple carrying Goods 
313 Swamp

312 Pomegranate

1990. Centenary of Javanese Immigration. Mult.
1447 60c. Type **311** 35 35
1448 110c. Woman 65 65
1449 120c. Man 70 70

1990. Flowers. Paintings by Maria Sibylle Merian. Multicoloured.
1450 25c. Type **312** 15 15
1451 25c. Passion flower 15 15
1452 35c. "Hippeastrum puniceum" 20 20
1453 35c. Sweet potato 20 20
1454 60c. Rose of Sharon 35 35
1455 60c. Jasmine 35 35
1456 105c. Blushing hibiscus . . . 60 60
1457 105c. "Musa serapionis" . . 60 60
1458 110c. Frangipani 65 65
1459 110c. "Hibiscus diversifolius" 65 65
1460 120c. Annatt ("Bixa orellana") 70 70
1461 120c. Dwarf poinciana ("Caesalpinia pulcherima") 70 70

1990. America. Natural World.
1462 **313** 60c. multicoloured . . . 35 35
1463 110c. multicoloured . . . 65 65

314 Anniversary Emblem
315 Fish and Flag as Map 

1990. Centenary of Organization of American States.
1464 **314** 100c. multicoloured . . . 65 65

1990. 15th Anniv of Independence. Multicoloured.
1465 10c. Type **315** 15 10
1466 60c. Passion flower and flag as map 35 35
1467 110c. Dove and flag as map 65 65

316 Painting by Janneke Fleskens

1990. Child Welfare. The Child in Nature. Paintings by children named. Multicoloured.
1468 60c.+30c. Type **316** 55 55
1469 105c.+50c. Tahlita Zuiverloon 90 90
1470 110c.+55c. Samuel Jensen 1·00 1·00

317 Green Aracari

1991. Birds. Multicoloured.
1472 10c. Type **317** 10 10
1473 15g. Blue and yellow macaw 9·75 9·75
1542 25g. Barn owl . . . . . . 19·00 19·00

318 Christ carrying Cross
319 Shipping Company Store 

1991. Easter. Multicoloured.
1474 60c.+30c. Type **318** 60 60
1475 105c.+50c. Christ wearing crown of thorns . . . . . 1·00 1·00
1476 110c.+55c. Woman cradling Christ's body . . . . . . 1·10 1·10

1991. Buildings.
1478 **319** 35c. black, blue & lt blue 20 20
1479 – 60c. black, green and emerald 40 40
1480 – 75c. black, yell & lemon 50 50
1481 – 105c. black, orange and light orange 70 70
1482 – 110c. black, pink and red 70 70
1483 – 200c. black, deep mauve and mauve . . . . . 1·25 1·25
DESIGNS: 60c. Upper class house; 75c. House converted into Labour Inspection offices; 105c. Plantation supervisor's house; 110c. Ministry of Labour building; 200c. Houses.

320 Puma
321 Route Map to Bahamas via San Salvador 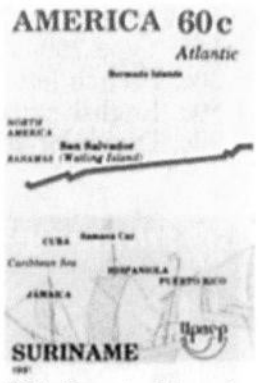

1991. The Puma. Multicoloured.
1484 10c. Type **320** (postage) . . 10 10
1485 20c. Stalking 15 15
1486 25c. Stretching 15 15
1487 30c. Licking nose 20 20
1488 125c. Lying down (horiz) (air) 80 80
1489 500c. Leaping (horiz) . . . 3·25 3·25

1991. America. Voyages of Discovery. Each red, blue and black.
1490 60c. Type **321** 80 80
1491 110c. Route map from Canary Islands . . . . . 1·40 1·40
Nos. 1490/1 were printed together, se-tenant, forming a composite design.

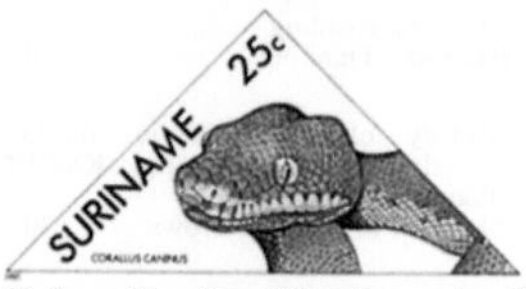

322 Green Tree Boa ("Corallus caninus")

1991. Snakes. Multicoloured.
1492 25c. Type **322** 15 15
1493 25c. Garden tree boa ("Corallus enydris") . . . 15 15
1494 35c. Boa constrictor 20 20
1495 35c. Bushmaster ("Lachesis muta") 20 20
1496 60c. South American rattlesnake ("Crotalus durissus") 40 40
1497 60c. Surinam coral snake ("Micrurus surinamensis") 40 40
1498 75c. Mussurana ("Clelia cloelia") 50 50
1499 75c. Anaconda ("Eunectes murinus") 50 50
1500 110c. Rainbow boa ("Epicrutes cenchris") . . 70 70
1501 110c. Sipo ("Chrironius carinatus") 70 70
1502 200c. Black and yellow rat snake ("Spilotes pullatus") 1·25 1·25
1503 200c. Vine snake ("Oxybelis argenteus") . . . . 1·25 1·25

323 Child in Wheelchair **324** "Cycnoches haagii"

1991. Child Welfare. Multicoloured.
1504 60c.+30c. Type **323** 60 60
1505 105c.+50c. Trees and girl . . 1·10 1·00
1506 110c.+55c. Girls playing in yard . . . . 1·10 1·10

1992. Orchids. Multicoloured.
1508 50c. Type **324** 30 30
1509 60c. "Lycaste cristata" . . . 40 40
1510 75c. "Galeandra dives" (horiz) 50 50
1511 125c. "Vanilla mexicana" 80 80
1512 150c. "Cyrtopodium glutiniferum" . . . . . . 1·00 1·00
1513 250c. "Gongora quinquenervis" . . . . . 1·60 1·60

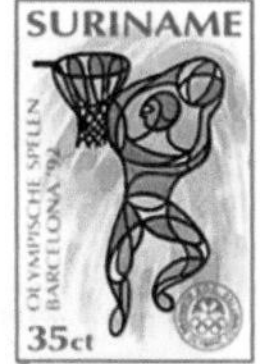

325 Crucifixion **327** Basketball

1992. Easter. Multicoloured.
1514 60c.+30c. Type **325** 70 70
1515 105c.+50c. Women taking away Christ's body . . . 1·10 1·10
1516 110c.+55c. The Resurrection 1·25 1·25

1992. Olympic Games, Barcelona. Multicoloured.
1518 35c. Type **327** 25 25
1519 60c. Volleyball 45 45
1520 75c. Sprinting 55 55
1521 125c. Football 95 95
1522 150c. Cycling . . . . . . 1·10 1·10
1523 250c. Swimming . . . . . 1·90 1·90

328 Emblems

1992. 50th Anniv of Young Women's Christian Association.
1525 **328** 60c. multicoloured . . . 45 45
1526 250c. multicoloured . . . 1·90 1·90

1992. Nos. 1236/7 surch **1 c.**
1527 1c. on 5c. orange and blue 65 65
1528 1c. on 5c. green, red and blue 65 65

330 Nau **331** Matzeliger and Shoe-lasting Machine

1992. 500th Anniv of Expulsion of Jews from Spain.
1529 **330** 250c. multicoloured . . . 2·50 2·50

1992. 140th Birth Anniv of Jan E. Matzeliger (inventor).
1530 **331** 60c. multicoloured . . . 45 45
1531 250c. multicoloured . . . 1·90 1·90

332 Amerindian Ornament **333** Tree with Child's Face

1992. America. 500th Anniv of Discovery of America by Columbus.
1532 **332** 60c. multicoloured . . . 45 45
1533 250c. multicoloured . . . 1·90 1·90

1992. Child Welfare. Multicoloured.
1534 60c.+30c. Type **333** 70 70
1535 105c.+50c. Tree with child's face beside flower . . . . 1·10 1·10
1536 110c.+55c. Children hanging from tree . . . . 1·25 1·25

334 Star and Holly **336** "Costus arabicus"

1992. Christmas. Multicoloured.
1538 10c. Type **334** 10 10
1539 60c. Candle 45 45
1540 250c. Parcels . . . . 1·90 1·90
1541 400c. Crown . . . . 3·00 3·00

1993. Air. No. 865 surch **35 ct.**
1543 35c. on 50c. multicoloured 25 25

1993. Medicinal Plants. Multicoloured.
1544 50c. Type **336** 40 40
1545 75c. "Quassia amara" . . . 55 55
1546 125c. "Combretum rotundifolium" (horiz) . . 95 95
1547 500c. "Bixa orellana" (horiz) 3·75 3·75

337 Christ and Cross **339** 90r. "Bull's Eye" Stamp

338 Long-horned Beetle ("Macrodontia cervicornis")

1993. Easter. Multicoloured.
1548 60c.+30c. Type **337** 70 70
1549 110c.+50c. Crucifixion . . . 1·25 1·25
1550 125c.+60c. Resurrection . . 1·40 1·40

1993. Insects. Multicoloured.
1551 25c. Type **338** 20 20
1552 25c. Locust 20 20
1553 35c. Weevil ("Curculionidae") 25 25
1554 35c. Grasshopper ("Acrididae") 25 25
1555 50c. Goliath beetle ("Euchroma gigantea") 40 40
1556 50c. Bush cricket ("Tettigonidae") 40 40
1557 100c. "Tettigonidae" 75 75
1558 100c. Scarab beetle ("Phanaeus festivus") . . 75 75
1559 175c. Cricket ("Grylllidae") 1·25 1·25
1560 175c. Dung beetle ("Phanaeus lancifer") . . 1·25 1·25
1561 220c. "Tettigonidae" (different) . . . . 1·60 1·60
1562 220c. Longhorn beetle ("Batus barbicornis") . . 1·60 1·60

1993. 150th Anniv of First Brazilian Stamps and "Brasiliana 93" International Stamp Exhibition, Rio de Janeiro.
1563 **339** 50c. black and violet . . 40 40
1564 – 250c. black and blue . . 1·90 1·90
1565 – 500c. black and green . . 3·75 3·75
DESIGNS: 250c. 60r. "Bull's eye" stamp; 500c. 30r. "Bull's eye" stamp.

340 Dwarf Cayman **341** Afro-Caribbean Angel

1993. America. Endangered Animals. Multicoloured.
1567 **340** 50c. multicoloured . . . 40 40
1568 100c. multicoloured . . . 75 75

1993. Christmas. Multicoloured.
1569 25c. Type **341** 20 20
1570 45c. Asian angel 35 35
1571 50c. Oriental angel 40 40
1572 150c. Amerindian angel . . 1·10 1·10

342 Hopscotch **344** Sambura

1993. Child Welfare. Children's Games.
1573 **342** 25g.+10g. brown & grn 25 25
1574 – 35g.+10g. brown & blue 35 35
1575 – 50g.+25g. brown & grn 55 55
1576 – 75g.+25g. brown & blue 75 75
DESIGNS: 35g. Hopscotch (different); 50g. Djoel (variant of hopscotch); 75g. Djoel (different).

1993. Nos. 1252 and 1473 surch **f 5.-**.
1578 5g. on 10g. multicoloured 3·75 3·75
1579 5g. on 15g. multicoloured 3·75 3·75

1994. Traditional Drums. Multicoloured.
1580 25g. Type **344** 20 20
1581 50g. Apinti 40 40
1582 75g. Terbangan 60 60
1583 100g. Dhol 80 80

345 Roseate Spoonbill

1994.
1584 **345** 1300g. multicoloured . . 10·00 10·00

1994. Air. No value expressed. Nos. 864 and 866/7 optd **Port Paye.**
1585 (–) on 45c. multicoloured 35 35
1586 (–) on 55c. multicoloured 45 45
1587 (–) on 60c. multicoloured 55 55

347 Smoking Chimneys **348** Goalkeeper's Gloves and Ball

1994. Environmental Protection. Multicoloured.
1588 50g. Type **347** 40 40
1589 350g. Dead fish in polluted sea . . . . 2·75 2·75

1994. World Cup Football Championship, U.S.A. Multicoloured.
1590 100g. Type **348** 30 30
1591 250g. Boot on ball 80 80
1592 300g. Goal net on ball . . . 95 95

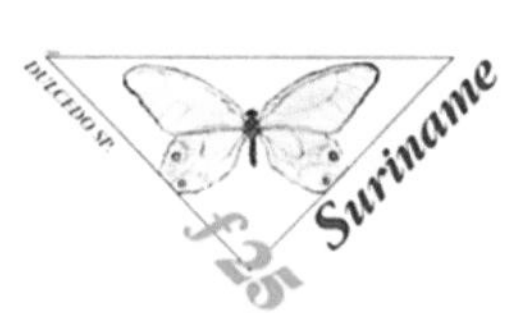

349 Anniversary Emblem

1994. Cent of International Olympic Committee.
1594 **349** 250g. multicoloured . . 80 80

350 "Dulcedo sp."

1994. Butterflies. Multicoloured.
1595 25g. Type **350** 10 10
1596 25g. "Ithomia sp." 10 10
1597 30g. "Danaus sp." (brown wings) 10 10
1598 30g. "Danaus sp." (black and gold wings) 10 10
1599 45g. "Bithijs sp." 15 15
1600 45g. "Echenais sp." 15 15
1601 75g. White peacock ("Anartia jatrophae") . . 25 25
1602 75g. Caribbean buckeye ("Junonia evarete") . . . 25 25
1603 250g. Small postman ("Heliconius erato") . . . 80 80
1604 250g. "Heliconius sp." . . . 80 80
1605 300g. "Parides sp." 95 95
1606 300g. "Eurytides sp." . . . 95 95

351 Netherlands 1943 Stamp Day Issue

1994. "Fepapost 94" European Stamp Exhibition, The Hague. Multicoloured.
1607 250g. Type **351** 80 80
1608 300g. Surinam 1936 1c. stamp 95 95

352 Canoe and Airplane

1994. America. Postal Transport. Multicoloured.
1610 50g. Type **352** 15 15
1611 400g. Donkey-cart and motor van . . . . 1·25 1·25

353 Mother reading to Children **354** Hands and Globes

1994. Christmas. Multicoloured. (a) Value indicated by letter "A".
1612 A Angel hovering over pine forest 25 25

(b) With face value.
1613 250g. Type **353** 80 80
1614 625g. Woman praying . . . 2·00 2·00

1995. Centenary of Volleyball. Multicoloured.
1616 375g. Type **354** . . . . . . 1·25 1·25
1617 650g. Balls . . . . 2·10 2·10

355 "Stachytarpheta jamaicense"

1995. Medicinal Plants. Multicoloured.
1619 30g. Type **355** 10 10
1620 30g. "Ruellia tuberosa" . . 10 10
1621 50g. Sweet basil ("Ocimum sanctum") 15 15
1622 50g. "Peperomia pellucida" 15 15
1623 75g. "Phyllanthus amarus" 25 25
1624 75g. "Portulaca oleracea" 25 25
1625 250g. "Wulffia baccata" . . 80 80
1626 250g. Sesame ("Sesamum indicum") 80 80
1627 500g. Blood flower ("Asclepias curassavica") 1·60 1·60
1628 500g. "Heliotropium indicum" . . . . 1·60 1·60
1629 600g. "Wedelia tribolata" 1·90 1·90
1630 600g. "Lantana camara" . . 1·90 1·90

356 Jaguarundi **357** Emblem, Dove and "50"

1995. Big Cats. Multicoloured.
1631 25g. Type **356** (postage) . . 10 10
1632 30g. Head of jaguarundi . . 10 10
1633 50g. Tiger cat 15 15
1634 100g. Head of tiger cat . . . 30 30
1635 1000g. Tree ocelot (air) . . 3·25 3·25
1636 1200g. Head of tree ocelot 3·75 3·75

1995. 50th Anniv of U.N.O. Multicoloured.
1637 135g. Type **357** 45 45
1638 740g. As T **357** but dove flying towards right . . . 2·40 2·40

358 Emblem

1995. Centenary of Surinam Police Force.

1639 **358** 875g. multicoloured . . 2·75 2·75

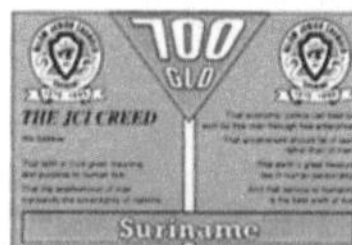

359 Emblem and Creed

1995. 25th Anniv of Nilom Junior Chamber.

1640 **359** 700g. orange, blue and deep blue . . . . . . 2·25 2·25

360 Channel-billed Toucan

1995. Birds. Multicoloured.

1641 1780g. Type **360** . . . . . 5·75 5·75

1642 2225g. Rufous-throated sapphire . . . . 7·00 7·00

1643 2995g. Hoatzin . . . . . . 9·50 9·50

See also Nos. 1679/81, 1736/9, 1767/70 and 1826/7.

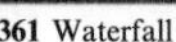

361 Waterfall

362 Shepherds and Star of Bethlehem

1995. America. Environmental Protection. Mult.

1644 135g. Forest floor 45 45

1645 1500g. Type **361** . . . . . 4·75 4·75

1995. Christmas. Multicoloured.

1646 70g. Type **362** 20 20

1647 135g. Joseph with Mary on donkey 45 45

1648 295g. Three wise men bearing gifts 95 95

1649 1000g. Wise men adoring child Jesus (horiz) . . . . 3·25 3·25

363 Jester and Bird

365 Hawk-headed Parrot

364 "Cyrtopodium cristatum"

1995. Paintings by Corneille. Multicoloured.

1651 135g. Type **363** 45 45

1652 615g. Jester and cat . . . . 1·90 1·90

1996. Flowers. Multicoloured.

1653 10g. Type **364** 10 10

1654 10g. "Epidendrum cristatum" 10 10

1655 75g. "Cochleanthes guianensis" 25 25

1656 75g. "Otostylis lepida" . . . 25 25

1657 135g. "Catasetum longifolium" 40 40

1658 135g. "Rudolfiella aurantiaca" 40 40

1659 250g. "Encyclia granitica" 75 75

1660 250g. "Maxillaria splendens" 75 75

1661 300g. "Brassia caudata" . . 90 90

1662 300g. "Catasetum macrocarpum" 90 90

1663 750g. "Maxillaria rufescens" 2·25 2·25

1664 750g. "Vanilla grandiflora" 2·25 2·25

1996.

1665 **365** 2000g. multicoloured . . 6·00 6·00

366 Traditional Huts

367 Radio Apparatus

1996. Eco-tourism. Multicoloured.

1666 70g. Type **366** 20 20

1667 70g. Butterfly on leaf . . . 20 20

1668 135g. Men in traditional costumes 40 40

1669 135g. Woman hand-spinning 40 40

1996. Centenary of Guglielmo Marconi's Patented Wireless-Telegraph. Multicoloured.

1670 135g. Type **367** 40 40

1671 615g. Marconi and world map (horiz) . . . . . . 1·90 1·90

368 Basketball

370 Women

1996. Olympic Games, Atlanta. Multicoloured.

1672 70g. Type **368** 20 20

1673 135g. Running 40 40

1674 195g. Badminton 60 60

1675 200g. Swimming 60 60

1676 900g. Cycling . . . . 2·75 2·75

1677 1000g. Hurdling . . . . . . 3·00 3·00

1996. Birds. As T **360**. Multicoloured.

1679 75g. Green kingfisher . . . 25 25

1680 160g. Bat falcon 50 50

1681 1765g. Red-legged honey-creeper . . . . 5·25 5·25

1996. America. Traditional Costumes. Mult.

1682 135g. Type **370** 40 40

1683 990g. Young women . . . . 3·00 3·00

Nos. 1682/3 were issued together, se-tenant, forming a composite design.

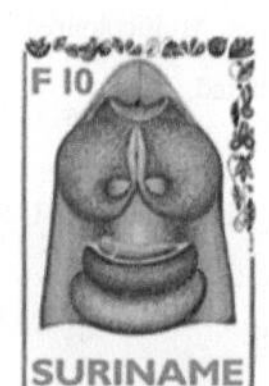

371 Mother praying over Child in Crib

373 Brown Dog and Injured Boy

1996. Christmas. Multicoloured.

1684 10g. Type **371** 10 10

1685 70g. Mother kneeling beside child 20 20

1686 135g. Mother with backpack kneeling beside "eye" on mouth/cushion 40 40

1687 285g. Mother playing with child on floor 85 85

1688 750g. Mother and child rocking on floor . . . . 2·25 2·25

1996. Nos. 1603/6 surch.

1690 50g. on 250g. mult (No. 1603) 15 15

1691 50g. on 250g. mult (No. 1604) 15 15

1692 100g. on 300g. mult (No. 1605) 30 30

1693 100g. on 300g. mult (No. 1606) 30 30

1996. No value expressed. Nos. 1648/9 optd **Port Paye**.

1694 (–) on 295g. multicoloured 1·40 1·40

1695 (–) on 1000g. multicoloured . . . . 1·40 1·40

1996. Child Welfare. Paintings by Jan Telting. Multicoloured.

1696 135g. Type **373** 40 40

1697 865g. White dog and injured boy . . . . 2·75 2·75

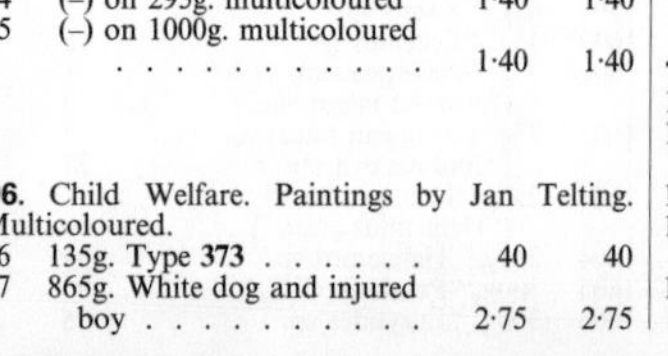

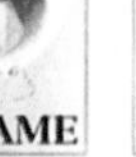

374 August Kappier (founder)

375 Inauguration of Aluminium Smelter, Paranam, 1965

1996. 150th Anniv of Town of Albina.

1698 **374** 875g. multicoloured . . 2·75 2·75

1996. 80th Anniv of Bauxite Industry. Paintings by Michel Pawiroredjo. Multicoloured.

1699 10g. Type **375** 10 10

1700 70g. Drilling blasting holes, Moengo, 1947 . . . . . 20 20

1701 130g. Labourers' huts, Moengo, 1919 . . . . . 40 40

1702 150g. Loading "Tarpon" with alumina, Paranam, 1995 . . . . 45 45

1703 160g. Construction of dam and power station, 1960 50 50

1704 730g. "Moengo" (schooner), 1922 . . . . 2·25 2·25

376 Von Stephan

1997. Death Centenary of Heinrich von Stephan (founder of U.P.U.).

1705 **376** 275g. multicoloured . . 85 85

1706 475g. multicoloured . . 1·40 1·40

377 Weeper Capuchin ("Cebus nigrivittatus")

1997. Primates. Multicoloured.

1707 25g. Type **377** 10 10

1708 25g. Black-capped capuchin ("Cebus apella") 10 10

1709 75g. Yellow-handed marmoset ("Saguinus midas") 25 25

1710 75g. Black spider monkey ("Ateles paniscus") . . . 25 25

1711 100g. Black-handed spider monkey ("Ateles geoffroyi panamensis") 30 30

1712 100g. Black-handed spider monkey ("Ateles geoffroyi frontatus") 30 30

1713 275g. Bald uakari ("Cacajao calvus") 85 85

1714 275g. Hendee's woolly monkey ("Lagothrix flavicauda") 85 85

1715 300g. Bare-faced tamarin ("Saguinus bicolor") . . . 90 90

1716 300g. Cotton-headed tamarin ("Saguinus oedipus") 90 90

1717 725g. Red howler monkey ("Alouatta seniculus") . . 2·25 2·25

1718 725g. Common squirrel monkey ("Saimiri sciureus") . . . . 2·25 2·25

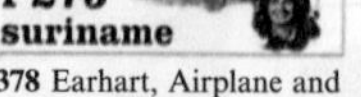

378 Earhart, Airplane and Finch

379 "Selenipedium steyermarkii"

1997. Linda Finch's Reconstruction of Amelia Earhart's Last Flight.

1719 **378** 275g. multicoloured . . 85 85

1997. Orchids. Multicoloured.

1720 25g. Type **379** 10 10

1721 50g. "Phragmipedium schlimii" 15 15

1722 75g. "Criosanthes arietina" 25 25

1723 200g. "Cypripedium margaritaceum" 60 60

1724 775g. "Paphiopedilum gratrixianum" . . . . . 2·40 2·40

380 Museum

382 Great Mosque, Isfahan, Iran

1997. 50th Anniv of Surinam Museum.

1725 **380** 625g. multicoloured . . 1·90 1·90

1997. Mosques. Multicoloured.

1727 50g. Type **382** 15 15

1728 125g. Dome of the Rock, Jerusalem 40 40

1729 175g. Ulugh Beg's Mosque, Samarkand, Uzbekistan 55 55

1730 225g. Taj Mahal, Agra, India 70 70

1731 275g. Mosque on Keizerstraat, Paramaribo, Surinam 85 85

1732 325g. Suleiman Mosque, Istanbul, Turkey . . . . 1·00 1·00

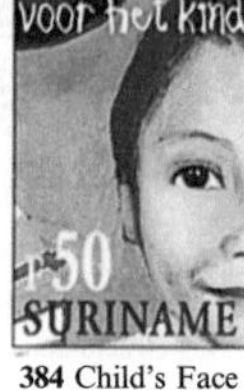

383 Tower

384 Child's Face (left side)

1997. 17th Anniv of State Oil Company. Mult.

1734 50g. Type **383** 15 15

1735 125g. Oil derrick and butterfly 40 40

1736 275g. Tank 85 85

1737 275g. Pressure gauge in field 85 85

1997. Birds. As T **360**. Multicoloured.

1738 50g. Spectacled owl 15 15

1739 125g. Rufous pigeon 40 40

1740 275g. Blaack-crested antshrike 85 85

1741 3150g. Red-crested finch . . 9·50 9·50

1997. Child Welfare. Multicoloured.

1742 50g. Type **384** 15 15

1743 100g. Child's face (right side) 30 30

1744 175g. Child with shoulder-length hair (left side) . . 55 55

1745 225g. Child with shoulder-length hair (right side) . . 70 70

1746 350g. Faces of the two children . . . . 1·10 1·10

385 Madonna and Child

386 Motor Cycle Courier

1997. Christmas. Multicoloured.

1748 125g. Type **385** 40 40

1749 225g. Children and baby . . 70 70

1750 450g. Angel and candle . . 1·40 1·40

1997. America. Postal Workers. Multicoloured.

1752 170g. Type **386** 50 50

1753 230g. Postal worker carrying parcel 70 70

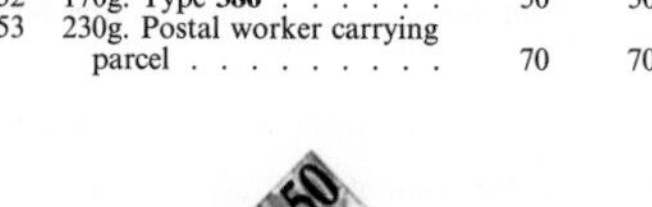

387 "Alcandor"

1998. Butterflies. Multicoloured.

1754 50g. Type **387** 15 15

1755 50g. "Achilles" 15 15

1756 75g. "Alphenor" 25 25

1757 75g. "Ceres" 25 25

1758 100g. "Cecropia" 30 30

1759 100g. "Helenor" 30 30

1760 175g. "Promothea" 55 55

1761 175g. "Cassiae" 55 55

1762 275g. "Ino" 85 85

1763 275g. "Phidippus" 85 85

1764 725g. "Palamedes" . . . . 2·25 2·25

1765 725g. "Helenor" . . . . . 2·25 2·25

1998. Birds. As T **360**. Multicoloured.
1767 50g. Blue-headed parrot . . 15 15
1768 225g. Bicoloured sparrowhawk falcon . . . 70 70
1769 2425g. Red-fronted woodpecker (vert) . . . . 6·75 6·75
1770 3800g. Green-backed heron 11·25 11·25

388 Immigrants and Lala Rooch (painting)

1998. 125th Anniv of Arrival of First Hindu Immigrants. Multicoloured.
1771 175g. Type **388** 55 55
1772 200g. "Baba and Mai" (statue) (first immigrants from India) 65 65

389 Tanden Temple, Sri Lanka

390 Sophie Redmond

1998. Temples. Multicoloured.
1773 50g. Type **389** 15 15
1774 75g. Golden Pagoda, Myanmar (vert) 20 20
1775 275g. Swayambhunath, Nepal (vert) 85 85
1776 325g. Borobudur, Indonesia 95 95
1777 400g. Phra Kaew, Thailand (vert) . . . . 1·25 1·25
1778 450g. Peking, China (vert) 1·40 1·40

1998. America. Famous Women. Multicoloured.
1780 400g. Type **390** . . . . . . 1·25 1·25
1781 1000g. Grace Ruth Schneiders-Howard . . . 2·75 2·75

391 1951 20c. Queen Juliana Stamp

1998. International Stamp Exhibition, The Hague, Netherlands. Multicoloured.
1782 400g. Type **391** . . . . . . 1·25 1·25
1783 800g. 1946 12½c. Queen Wilhelmina stamp . . . 2·50 2·50

392 "Canawaima" (ferry)

1998. Surinam–Guyana Ferry.
1785 **392** 275g. multicoloured . . 85 85
1786 400g. multicoloured . . 1·25 1·25

393 Holy Family

394 Boy flying Kite

1998. Christmas. Multicoloured.
1787 50g. Type **393** 15 15
1788 325g. Angel with banner, Holy Family and stable of animals 95 95
1789 400g. Holy family and animals . . . . 1·25 1·25
1790 1225g. Nativity . . . . . . 3·50 3·50

1998. Child Welfare. Multicoloured.
1792 375g. Type **394** . . . . . . 1·00 1·00
1793 400g. Girl flying kite . . . . 1·25 1·25
1794 1225g. Child holding kite . . 3·50 3·50

395 Mother and Child and Food

1998. 50th Anniv of W.H.O. "Mother and Child Care". Multicoloured.
1795 400g. Type **395** . . . . . . 1·25 1·25
1796 1000g. Mother and baby . . 2·75 2·75

396 "Heliconia pastazae"

1999. Flora. Multicoloured.
1797 50g. Type **396** 10 10
1798 50g. "Heliconia caribaea 'Kawauchi'" 10 10
1799 200g. "Heliconia rostrata" 30 30
1800 200g. "Heliconia 'Sexy Pink'" 30 30
1801 300g. "Heliconia collinsiana" 45 45
1802 300g. "Heliconia wagneriana" 45 45
1803 400g. "Heliconia 'Jaded Forest'" 60 60
1804 400g. "Heliconia 'Bihai-nappi'" 60 60
1805 750g. "Heliconia 'Golden Torch'" . . . . 1·10 1·10
1806 750g. "Heliconia latispatha 'Red Yellow Gyro'" . . . 1·10 1·10
1807 1300g. "Heliconia 'Sexy Pink'" (different) . . . . 2·00 2·00
1808 1300g. "Heliconia 'Nappi Yellow'" . . . . 2·00 2·00

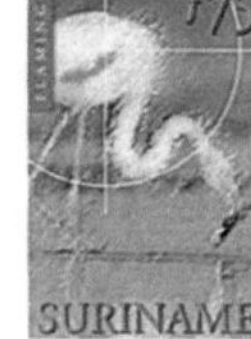

397 Katwijk Plantation

398 Greater Flamingo

1999. Plantation Houses.
1809 **397** 75g. black 10 10
1810 – 300g. purple and black 45 45
1811 – 400g. yellow and black 60 60
1812 – 2225g. blue and black . . 3·25 3·25
DESIGNS: 300g. Sorgvliet Plantation; 400g. Peperpot Plantation; 2225g. Speiringshoek Plantation.

1999. Endangered Species. Multicoloured.
1813 75g. Type **398** 10 10
1814 375g. Orang-utan 55 55
1815 450g. Elephant 70 70
1816 500g. Whale 75 75
1817 850g. Frog . . . . 1·25 1·25
1818 900g. Rhinoceros . . . . . 1·25 1·25
1819 1600g. Giant panda . . . . 2·50 2·50
1820 7250g. Tiger . . . . 11·00 11·00

399 Coppename Bridge

400 STINASU Emblem

1999. Coppename Bridge.
1821 **399** 850g. green, lt grn & blk 1·25 1·25
1822 2250g. blue, dp bl & blk 3·50 3·50

1999. Conservation. Multicoloured.
1823 850g. Type **400** (30th anniv of Surinam Nature Protection Society) . . . 1·25 1·25
1824 2650g. Map and rainforest (first anniv of Surinam Central Forest Nature Reserve) . . . . 4·00 4·00

1999. Birds. As T **360**. Multicoloured.
1826 1000g. Blue-grey tanager . . 1·50 1·50
1827 5500g. Wattled jacana . . . 8·00 8·00

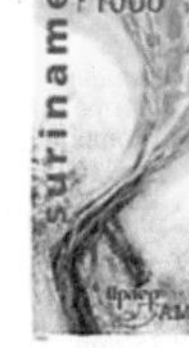

401 Earth, Letter and Satellite

402 Gun firing Streamers and Flowers

1999. 125th Anniv of Universal Postal Union. Multicoloured.
1828 950g. Type **401** . . . . . . 1·40 1·40
1829 1000g. Satellite, letter and ringed planet . . . . . . 1·50 1·50

1999. America. A Millennium without Arms. Mult.
1830 1000g. Type **402** . . . . . 1·50 1·50
1831 2250g. Flowers . . . . . . 3·50 3·50
Nos. 1830/1 were issued together, se-tenant, forming a composite design.

403 Star over Stable

404 Child's Painting

1999. Christmas. Multicoloured.
1832 500g. Type **403** 75 75
1833 850g. Christmas tree . . . . 1·25 1·25
1834 900g. Angel . . . . 1·25 1·25
1835 1000g. Candle . . . . . . 1·50 1·50

1999. Child Welfare.
1837 **404** 1100g. multicoloured . . 1·60 1·60
1838 – 1400g. multicoloured . . 2·10 2·10
1839 – 1600g. multicoloured . . 2·40 2·40
DESIGNS: 1400g. to 1600g. Different children's paintings.

405 Tennis Players, House and Car (Tahirih van Kanten)

406 One Way Sign

2000. "Stampin' the Future". Children's Drawings. Multicoloured.
1841 1000g. Type **405** . . . . . 1·40 1·40
1842 2500g. Sunflower (Tirsa Braaf) (vert) . . . . . . 3·50 3·50

2000. Traffic Signs (1st series).
1843 **406** 2000g. multicoloured . . 2·75 2·75
See also Nos. 1858, 1861, 1868, 1874, 1903, 1917, 1921, 1936, 1937, 1952 and 1960.

407 Watermelon

2000. Tropical Fruits. Multicoloured.
1844 50g. Type **407** (postage) . . 10 10
1845 50g. Papaya (*Carica papaya*) 10 10
1846 175g. Mango (*Mangifera indica*) 25 25
1847 175g. Mangosteen (*Garcinia mangostana*) 25 25
1848 200g. Banana (*Musa nana*) 30 30
1849 200g. Grapefruit (*Citrus paradisi*) 30 30
1850 250g. *Punika granatum* . . 35 35
1851 250g. Pineapple (*Ananas comosus*) 35 35
1852 325g. Coconut (*Cocos nucifera*) 45 45
1853 325g. Giant granadilla (*Passiflora quadrangularis*) 45 45
1854 5000g. Sweet orange (*Citrus sinensis*) (air) . . . . . . 7·00 7·00
1855 5000g. Avocado (*Persea gratissima*) . . . . 7·00 7·00

408 Red-billed Whistling Duck

409 Double Bend Sign

2000. Birds. Multicoloured.
1856 1100g. Type **408** . . . . . 1·50 1·50
1857 4425g. Ringed kingfisher . . 6·00 6·00

2000. Traffic Signs (2nd series).
1858 **409** 2000g. multicoloured . . 3·00 3·00

410 Bridge over Suriname River

411 No Overtaking

2000.
1859 **410** 1100g. multicoloured . . 1·60 1·60
1860 1700g. multicoloured . . 2·50 2·50

2000. Traffic Signs (3rd series).
1861 **411** 2000g. multicoloured . . 3·00 3·00

413 Running

2000. Olympic Games, Sydney. Multicoloured.
1863 1100g. Type **413** . . . . . 1·60 1·60
1864 1100g. Football . . . . . . 1·60 1·60
1865 3900g. Swimming . . . . . 5·50 5·50
1866 3900g. Tennis . . . . 5·50 5·50

414 Roundabout Ahead

415 Foot stamping on "AIDS"

2000. Traffic Signs (4th series).
1868 **414** 2000g. multicoloured . . 3·00 3·00

2000. America. AIDS Awareness Campaign. Multicoloured.
1869 1100g. Type **415** . . . . . 1·60 1·60
1870 6400g. Stylized figures holding condoms (vert) 9·00 9·00

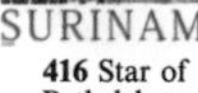

416 Star of Bethelehem

417 No Parking

2000. Christmas. Multicoloured.
1871 1100g. Type **416** . . . . . 1·60 1·25
1872 3900g. Mary and Jesus . . . 6·00 4·75
MS1873 72×51 mm. 3000g. Three Kings bearing gifts . . . . . . 4·50 3·50

2000. Traffic (5th series).
1874 **417** 2000g. multicoloured . . 3·00 2·40

418 Currency Notes

419 Emblem

2000. 25th Anniv of International Philatelic Agency for Surinam Stamps. Multicoloured.
1875 125g. Type **418** 10 10
1876 5900g. Stamps . . . . . . 9·00 7·25
MS1877 75 × 73 mm. Nos. 1875/7 9·00 9·00

2000. 25th Anniv of Independence.
1878 **419** 1100g. multicoloured . . 1·60 1·25
1879 4900g. multicoloured . . 7·50 6·00

420 Toddler
423 Silver-beaked Tanager (*Ramphocelus carbo*)

2000. Child Care. Multicoloured.
1880 1100g. Type **420** . . . . . 1·60 1·25
1881 3900g. Baby at breast . . . 6·00 4·75
MS1882 72 × 51 mm. 2000g. Baby 3·00 2·40

2000. Nos. 1551/2 surch **F 3100**.
1883 3100g. on 35c. multicoloured 4·75 3·75
1884 3100g. on 35c. multicoloured 4·75 3·75

2001. Nos. 1551/2 surch **F 1000**.
1885 1000g. on 25c. multicoloured 1·20 1·20
1886 1000g. on 25c. multicoloured 1·20 1·20

2001. Birds. Multicoloured.
1887 50g Type **423** (postage) . . 10 10
1888 50g Yellow-bellied elaenia (*Elaenia flavogaster*) . . . 10 10
1889 175g Green-backed heron (*Butorides striatus*) . . . 15 15
1890 175g Black-throated mango (*Athracothorax nigricollis*) 15 15
1891 200g Everglade kite (*Rostrhamus sociabilis*) . . 15 15
1892 200g. *Veniliornis sanguineus* 15 15
1893 250g. Spangled cotinga (Cotinga cayana) 25 25
1894 250g. *Bucco tamatia* 25 25
1895 825g. *Tapera naevia* 70 70
1896 825g. Green aracari (*Pteroglossus viridis*) . . . 70 70
1897 7500g. Pompadour cotinga (*Xipholena punicea*) (air) 7·25 7·25
1898 7500g. *Caprimulgus nigrescens* . . . . 7·25 7·25

424 Male and Female Symbols
425 Musician (Bhoelai Surender Kumar)

2001. United Nations Women's Rights Campaign ("A life free from violence"). Multicoloured.
1899 1400g. Type **424** . . . . . 1·20 1·20
1900 4600g. Woman . . . . . . 4·50 4·50

2001. Youth Philately. Winning Entries in Children's Design a Stamp Competition. Multicoloured.
1901 650g. Type **425** 80 80
1902 5350g. Children (Sharon Cameron) . . . . 4·75 4·75

426 Moveable Bridge
427 Collared Plover (*Charadrius collaris*)

2001. Traffic (6th series).
1903 **417** 4000g. multicoloured . . 3·50 3·50

2001. Birds. Multicoloured.
1904 4500g. Type **427** . . . . . 4·00 4·00
1905 9000g. Great horned owl (*Bubo virginianus*) . . . . 9·00 9·00

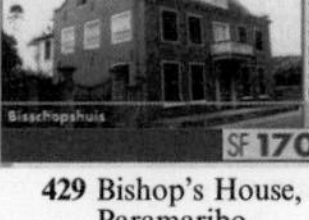
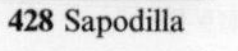

428 Sapodilla
429 Bishop's House, Paramaribo

2001. Fruit. Multicoloured.
1906 150g. Type **428** 15 15
1907 200g. Noni 25 25
1908 800g. Banana . . . . 1·10 90
1909 1200g. Mopé . . . . 1·70 1·40
1910 1700g. Pomerac . . . . . . 2·40 1·90

2001. America. Cultural Heritage. Multicoloured.
1911 1700g. Type **429** . . . . . 1·70 1·70
1912 7300g. Presidential Palace, Paramaribo . . . . . . 7·25 7·25
MS1913 72 × 75 mm. Nos. 1912/13 9·00 9·00

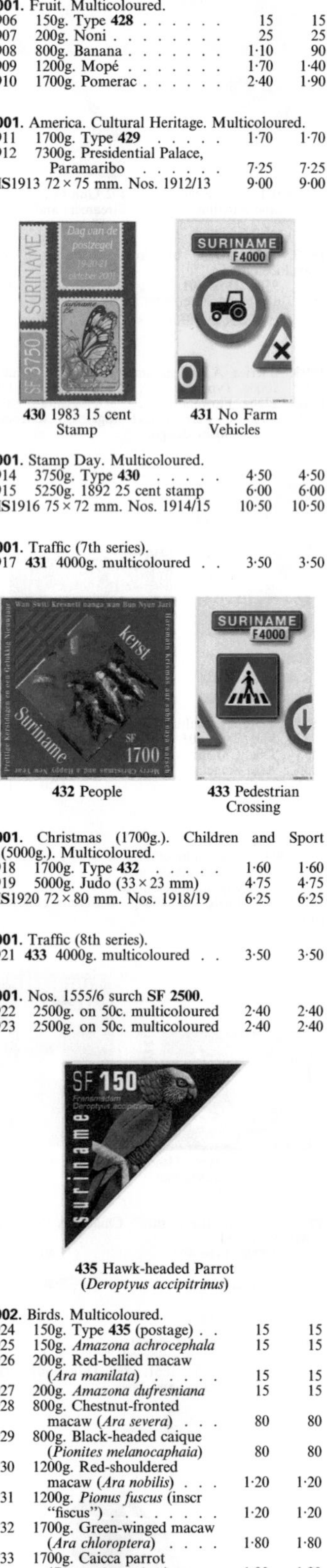

430 1983 15 cent Stamp
431 No Farm Vehicles

2001. Stamp Day. Multicoloured.
1914 3750g. Type **430** . . . . . 4·50 4·50
1915 5250g. 1892 25 cent stamp 6·00 6·00
MS1916 75 × 72 mm. Nos. 1914/15 10·50 10·50

2001. Traffic (7th series).
1917 **431** 4000g. multicoloured . . 3·50 3·50

432 People
433 Pedestrian Crossing

2001. Christmas (1700g.). Children and Sport (5000g.). Multicoloured.
1918 1700g. Type **432** . . . . . 1·60 1·60
1919 5000g. Judo (33 × 23 mm) 4·75 4·75
MS1920 72 × 80 mm. Nos. 1918/19 6·25 6·25

2001. Traffic (8th series).
1921 **433** 4000g. multicoloured . . 3·50 3·50

2001. Nos. 1555/6 surch **SF 2500**.
1922 2500g. on 50c. multicoloured 2·40 2·40
1923 2500g. on 50c. multicoloured 2·40 2·40

435 Hawk-headed Parrot (*Deroptyus accipitrinus*)

2002. Birds. Multicoloured.
1924 150g. Type **435** (postage) . . 15 15
1925 150g. *Amazona achrocephala* 15 15
1926 200g. Red-bellied macaw (*Ara manilata*) 15 15
1927 200g. *Amazona dufresniana* 15 15
1928 800g. Chestnut-fronted macaw (*Ara severa*) . . . 80 80
1929 800g. Black-headed caique (*Pionites melanocaphaia*) 80 80
1930 1200g. Red-shouldered macaw (*Ara nobilis*) . . . 1·20 1·20
1931 1200g. *Pionus fuscus* (inscr "fiscus") . . . . 1·20 1·20
1932 1700g. Green-winged macaw (*Ara chloroptera*) . . . . 1·80 1·80
1933 1700g. Caicca parrot (*Pionopsitta caicca*) . . . 1·80 1·80
1934 5325g. Scarlet macaw (*Ara macao*) (air) . . . . . . 4·75 4·75
1935 5325g. Mealy amazon (*Amazona farinose*) . . . 4·75 4·75

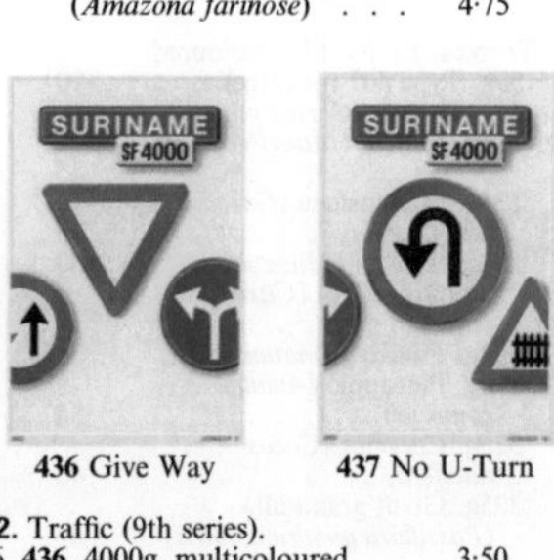
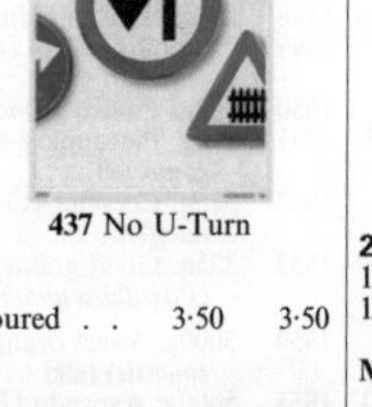

436 Give Way
437 No U-Turn

2002. Traffic (9th series).
1936 **436** 4000g. multicoloured . . 3·50 3·50

2002. Traffic (10th series).
1937 **437** 4000g. multicoloured . . 3·50 3·50

438 Man wearing Fez and Shell Decoration
440 Children Crossing

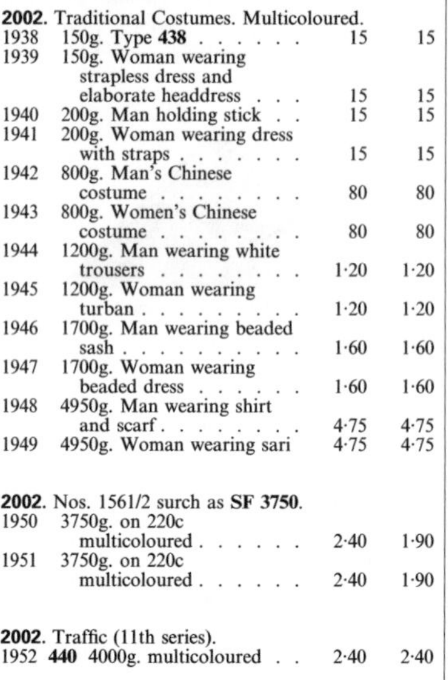

2002. Traditional Costumes. Multicoloured.
1938 150g. Type **438** 15 15
1939 150g. Woman wearing strapless dress and elaborate headdress . . . 15 15
1940 200g. Man holding stick . . 15 15
1941 200g. Woman wearing dress with straps 15 15
1942 800g. Man's Chinese costume 80 80
1943 800g. Women's Chinese costume 80 80
1944 1200g. Man wearing white trousers . . . . 1·20 1·20
1945 1200g. Woman wearing turban . . . . 1·20 1·20
1946 1700g. Man wearing beaded sash . . . . 1·60 1·60
1947 1700g. Woman wearing beaded dress . . . . . . 1·60 1·60
1948 4950g. Man wearing shirt and scarf . . . . 4·75 4·75
1949 4950g. Woman wearing sari 4·75 4·75

2002. Nos. 1561/2 surch as **SF 3750**.
1950 3750g. on 220c multicoloured . . . . . . 2·40 1·90
1951 3750g. on 220c multicoloured . . . . . . 2·40 1·90

2002. Traffic (11th series).
1952 **440** 4000g. multicoloured . . 2·40 2·40

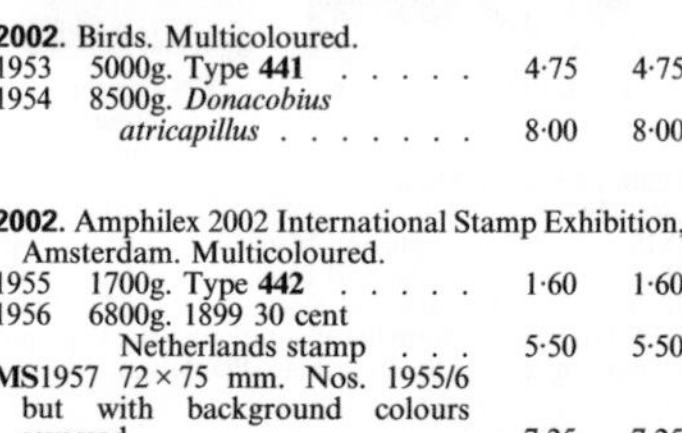

441 Royal Flycatcher (*Onychorhynchus coronatus*)
442 1942 2½ cent Netherlands Stamp

2002. Birds. Multicoloured.
1953 5000g. Type **441** . . . . . 4·75 4·75
1954 8500g. *Donacobius atricapillus* . . . . 8·00 8·00

2002. Amphilex 2002 International Stamp Exhibition, Amsterdam. Multicoloured.
1955 1700g. Type **442** . . . . . 1·60 1·60
1956 6800g. 1899 30 cent Netherlands stamp . . . 5·50 5·50
MS1957 72 × 75 mm. Nos. 1955/6 but with background colours reversed . . . . 7·25 7·25

443 Head and Question Mark
444 Trains Crossing

2002. America. Literacy Campaign.
1958 1700g. black and red . . . 1·60 1·60
1959 7300g. blue, red and black 6·50 6·50
DESIGNS: Type **443**; 7300g. Text and signature cross.

2002. Traffic (12th series).
1960 **444** 4000g. multicoloured . . 3·50 3·00

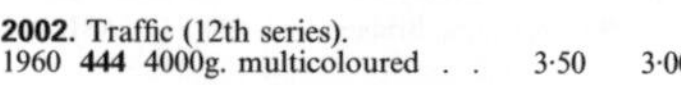

445 Father Christmas and Cut-out Clothes

2002. Christmas. Multicoloured.
1961 1700g. Type **445** . . . . . 1·60 1·60
1962 5000g. Tree, decorations and presents . . . . 4·50 4·50
MS1963 72 × 75 mm. Nos. 1959/60 but with background colours changed . . . . 6·00 6·00

POSTAGE DUE STAMPS

D 2 D 6

1885.
D36b D 2 2½c. mauve and black 2·00 2·00
D37b 5c. mauve and black . . 6·25 6·25
D38a 10c. mauve and black £100 75·00
D39a 20c. mauve and black 6·25 6·25
D40b 25c. mauve and black 7·25 7·25
D41b 30c. mauve and black 2·75 2·75
D42b 40c. mauve and black 4·00 4·00
D43b 50c. mauve and black 2·25 2·25

1892.
D57 D 6 2½c. mauve and black 35 35
D58b 5c. mauve and black . . 90 90
D59 10c. mauve and black 16·00 12·00
D60b 20c. mauve and black 1·90 1·25
D61b 25c. mauve and black 7·00 5·75
D62 40c. mauve and black 2·10 2·50

1911.
D111b D 2 10c. on 30c. mve & blk . . . . 85·00 85·00
D112b 10c. on 50c. mve & blk £110 £110

1913.
D153 D 6 ½c. lilac 20 20
D154 1c. lilac 20 20
D155 2c. lilac 20 20
D156 2½c. lilac 20 20
D157 5c. lilac 20 20
D158 10c. lilac 20 20
D159a 12c. lilac 20 20
D160a 12½c. lilac 20 10
D161 15c. lilac 30 30
D162a 20c. lilac 55 50
D163 25c. lilac 30 20
D164a 30c. lilac 20 35
D165 40c. lilac . . . . . . 9·75 9·50
D166a 50c. lilac 90 70
D167a 75c. lilac 90 90
D168a 1g. lilac . . . . 1·10 90

D 52 D 68

1945.
D337 D 52 1c. purple 55 35
D338 5c. purple . . . . . . 4·00 1·40
D339 25c. purple . . . . . 9·00 20

1950. As Type **D 121** of Netherlands.
D384 1c. purple . . . . 1·60 1·60
D385 2c. purple . . . . 2·75 2·00
D386 2½c. purple . . . . 2·75 1·75
D387 5c. purple . . . . 3·50 35
D388 10c. purple . . . . 2·40 35
D389 15c. purple . . . . 6·75 2·25
D390 20c. purple . . . . 1·90 3·00
D391 25c. purple . . . . 22·00 30
D392 50c. purple . . . . 27·00 1·50
D393 75c. purple . . . . 40·00 30·00
D394 1g. purple . . . . 28·00 6·00

1956.
D436 D 68 1c. purple 10 10
D437 2c. purple 35 20
D438 2½c. purple 35 35
D439 5c. purple 35 35
D440 10c. purple 35 35
D441 15c. purple 55 50
D442 20c. purple 55 55
D443 25c. purple 65 20
D444 50c. purple . . . . . 1·60 35
D445 75c. purple . . . . . 2·25 1·00
D446 1g. purple . . . . . . 3·00 70

1987. Various stamps optd **TE BETALEN**.
D1325 65c. mult (No. 868) . . . 1·75 50
D1326 65c. mult (No. 1132) . . . 50 50
D1327 80c. mult (No. 1134) . . . 1·75 60
D1328 90c. mult (No. 872a) . . . 1·75 70
D1329 95c. mult (No. 873) . . . 2·00 75
D1330 1g. mult (No. 1248) . . . 2·00 75

SWAZILAND Pt. 1

A kingdom in the eastern part of S. Africa. Its early stamps were issued under joint control of Gt. Britain and the S. Africa Republic. Incorporated into the latter state in 1895 it was transferred in 1906 to the High Commissioner for S. Africa. Again issued stamps in 1933. Achieved Independence in 1968.

1961. 100 cents = 1 rand.
1974. 100 cents = 1 lilangeni (plural: emalangeni).

1889. Stamps of Transvaal optd **Swazieland**.
10 **18** ½d. grey . . . . 7·50 16·00
1 1d. red . . . . 17·00 16·00
5 2d. bistre . . . . 17·00 15·00
6 6d. blue . . . . 22·00 42·00
3 1s. green . . . . 10·00 13·00

7 2s.6d. yellow £250 £275
8 5s. blue £150 £190
9 10s. brown £5000 £3250

2 King George V
7 Swazi Married Woman

1933.
11 2 ½d. green 30 30
12 1d. red 30 20
13 2d. brown 30 45
14 3d. blue 45 2·75
15 4d. orange 2·75 3·25
16 6d. mauve 1·25 1·00
17 1s. olive 1·50 2·75
18 2s.6d. violet 15·00 22·00
19 5s. grey 30·00 48·00
20 10s. brown 80·00 £100

1935. Silver Jubilee. As T **32a** of St. Helena.
21 1d. blue and red 50 1·50
22 2d. blue and black 50 1·50
23 3d. brown and blue 55 5·00
24 6d. grey and purple 65 2·00

1937. Coronation. As T **32b** of St. Helena.
25 1d. red 50 2·00
26 2d. brown 50 20
27 3d. blue 50 75

1938. As T **2**, but with portraits of King George VI and inscr "SWAZILAND" only below portrait.
28a ½d. green 30 2·75
29a 1d. red 1·00 1·75
30b 1½d. blue 30 1·00
31a 2d. brown 30 50
32b 3d. blue 3·75 5·00
33a 4d. orange 50 1·40
34b 6d. purple 4·50 1·50
35a 1s. olive 1·25 65
36a 2s.6d. violet 17·00 2·50
37b 5s. grey 28·00 14·00
38a 10s. brown 6·50 6·00

1945. Victory stamps of South Africa (inscr alternately in English or Afrikaans) optd **Swaziland**.
39 **55** 1d. brown and red 55 10
40 – 2d. blue and violet (No. 109) 55 10
41 – 3d. blue (No. 110) 55 20
Unused prices are for bilingual pairs, used prices for single stamps in either language.

1947. Royal Visit. As Nos. 32/5 of Basutoland.
42 1d. red 10 10
43 2d. green 10 10
44 3d. blue 10 10
45 1s. mauve 10 10

1948. Silver Wedding. As T **33b/c** of St. Helena.
46 1½d. blue 50 50
47 10s. purple 25·00 30·00

1949. 75th Anniv of U.P.U. As T **33d/g** of St. Helena.
48 1½d. blue 15 15
49 3d. blue 2·00 2·75
50 6d. mauve 30 60
51 1s. olive 30 1·00

1953. Coronation. As T **33h** of St. Helena.
52 2d. black and brown 20 20

1956.
53 – ½d. black and orange 10 10
54 – 1d. black and green 10 10
55 **7** 2d. black and brown 30 10
56 – 3d. black and red 20 10
57 – 4½d. black and blue 60 10
58 – 6d. black and mauve 1·00 10
59 – 1s. black and olive 20 10
60 – 1s.3d. black and sepia 1·00 2·50
61 – 2s.6d. green and red 1·00 2·00
62 – 5s. violet and grey 7·50 3·00
63 **7** 10s. black and violet 15·00 15·00
64 – £1 black and turquoise 38·00 27·00
DESIGNS—HORIZ: ½d., 1s. Havelock asbestos mine; 1d., 2s.6d. Highveld view. VERT: 3d., 1s.3d. Swazi courting couple; 4½d., 5s. Swazi warrior in ceremonial dress; 6d., £1 Greater kudu.

1961. Stamps of 1956 surch in new currency.
65 ½c. on ½d. black and orange 3·25 4·25
66 1c. on 1d. black and green 10 1·75
67 2c. on 2d. black and brown 10 2·00
68 2½c. on 2d. black and brown 10 1·25
69 2½c. on 3d. black and red 10 10
70 3½c. on 2d. black and brown 10 1·25
71 4c. on 4½d. black and blue 10 10
72 5c. on 6d. black and mauve 10 10
73 10c. on 1s. black and olive 25·00 3·00
74 25c. on 2s.6d. green and red 30 65
75 50c. on 5s. violet and grey 30 60
76 1r. on 10s. black and violet 1·50 60
77a 2r. on £1 black and turquoise 4·50 8·50

1961. As 1956 but values in new currency.
78 ½c. black and orange (as ½d.) 10 1·25
79 1c. black and green (as 1d.) 10 10
80 2c. black and brown (as 2d.) 10 2·50
81 2½c. black and red (as 3d.) 15 10
82 4c. black and blue (as 4½d.) 15 1·50
83 5c. black and mauve (as 6d.) 1·25 15
84 10c. black and olive (as 1s.) 15 10
85 12½c. black and sepia (as 1s.3d.) 1·25 40
86 25c. green and red (as 2s.6d.) 3·00 4·25
87 50c. violet and grey (as 5s.) 2·00 1·40
88 1r. black and violet (as 10s.) 4·50 10·00
89 2r. black and turquoise (as £1) 9·50 11·00

15 Swazi Shields

31 Goods Train and Map of Swaziland Railway

1962.
90 **15** ½c. black, brown and buff 10 10
91 – 1c. orange and black 10 10
92 – 2c. green, black and olive 10 1·50
93 – 2½c. black and red 10 10
94 – 3½c. green and grey 10 40
95 – 4c. black and turquoise 10 10
96 – 5c. black, red and deep red 1·00 10
97 – 7½c. brown and buff 1·00 50
98 – 10c. black and blue 4·00 20
99 – 12½c. red and olive 1·25 3·25
100 – 15c. black and mauve 1·50 70
101 – 20c. black and green 40 90
102 – 25c. black and blue 50 70
103 – 50c. black and red 13·00 4·25
104 – 1r. green and ochre 2·50 2·25
105 – 2r. red and blue 14·00 9·50
DESIGNS—VERT: 1c. Battle axe; 2c. Forestry; 2½c. Ceremonial headdress; 3½c. Musical instrument; 4c. Irrigation; 5c. Long-tailed whydah ("Widowbird"); 7½c. Rock paintings; 10c. Secretary bird; 12½c. Pink arum; 15c. Swazi married woman; 20c. Malaria control; 25c. Swazi warrior; 1r. Aloes. HORIZ: 50c. Southern ground hornbill ("Ground Hornbill"); 2r. Msinsi in flower.

1963. Freedom from Hunger. As T **63a** of St. Helena.
106 15c. violet 50 15

1963. Cent of Red Cross. As T **63b** of St. Helena.
107 2½c. red and black 30 10
108 15c. red and blue 70 90

1964. Opening of Swaziland Railway.
109 **31** 2½c. green and purple 55 10
110 3½c. blue and olive 55 1·00
111 15c. orange and brown 70 70
112 25c. yellow and blue 85 80

1965. Cent of I.T.U. As T **64a** of St. Helena.
113 2½c. blue and bistre 15 10
114 15c. purple and red 35 20

1965. I.C.Y. As T **64b** of St. Helena.
115 ½c. purple and turquoise 10 10
116 15c. green and lavender 40 20

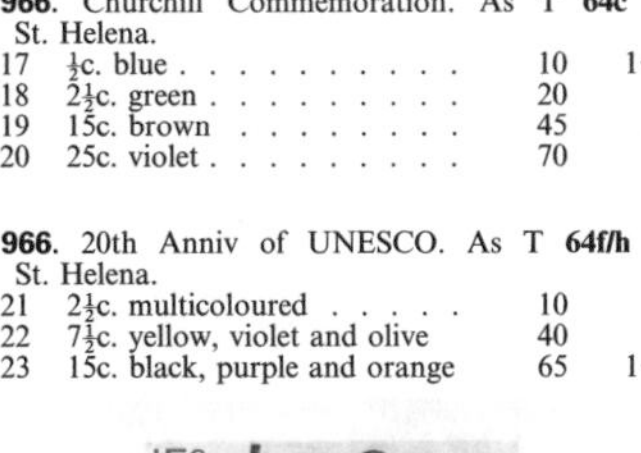

1966. Churchill Commemoration. As T **64c** of St. Helena.
117 ½c. blue 10 1·25
118 2½c. green 20 10
119 15c. brown 45 25
120 25c. violet 70 70

1966. 20th Anniv of UNESCO. As T **64f/h** of St. Helena.
121 2½c. multicoloured 10 10
122 7½c. yellow, violet and olive 40 60
123 15c. black, purple and orange 65 1·25

32 King Sobhuza II and Map

1967. Protected State.
124 **32** 2½c. multicoloured 10 10
125 – 7½c. multicoloured 15 15
126 **32** 15c. multicoloured 20 30
127 – 25c. multicoloured 25 40
DESIGN—VERT: 7½, 25c. King Sobhuza II.

1967. 1st Conferment of University Degrees. As Nos. 234/7 of Botswana.
128 2½c. sepia, blue and orange 10 10
129 7½c. sepia, blue and turquoise 15 15
130 15c. sepia, blue and red 25 30
131 25c. sepia, blue and violet 30 35

35 Incwala Ceremony

1968. Traditional Customs.
132 **35** 3c. silver, red and black 10 10
133 – 10c. multicoloured 10 10
134 **35** 15c. gold, red and black 15 20
135 – 25c. multicoloured 15 20
DESIGN—VERT: 10, 25c. Reed dance.

1968. No. 96 surch **3c.**
136 3c. on 5c. black, red & dp red 1·50 10

38 Cattle Ploughing

1968. Independence.
137 **38** 3c. multicoloured 10 10
138 – 4½c. multicoloured 10 45
139 – 17½c. multicoloured 15 70
140 – 25c. slate, black and gold 45 90
MS141 180 × 162 mm. Nos. 137/40 each × 5 14·00 22·00
DESIGNS: 4½c. Overhead cable carrying asbestos; 17½c. Cutting sugar cane; 25c. Iron ore mining and railway map.

1968. Nos. 90/105 optd **INDEPENDENCE 1968** and No. 93 additionally surch **3 c.**
142 **15** ½c. black, brown and buff 10 10
143 – 1c. orange and black 10 10
144 – 2c. green, black and olive 10 10
145a – 2½c. black and red 1·50 10
146 – 3c. on 2½c. black and red 10 10
147 – 3½c. green and grey 15 10
148 – 4c. black and turquoise 10 10
149 – 5c. black, red and deep red 4·00 10
150 – 7½c. brown and buff 50 10
151 – 10c. black and blue 4·25 10
152 – 12½c. red and olive 25 1·00
153 – 15c. black and mauve 25 1·25
154 – 20c. black and green 75 2·00
155 – 25c. black and blue 35 1·25
159 – 50c. black and red 3·50 6·00
157 – 1r. green and ochre 2·00 4·50
160 – 2r. red and blue 5·00 5·00

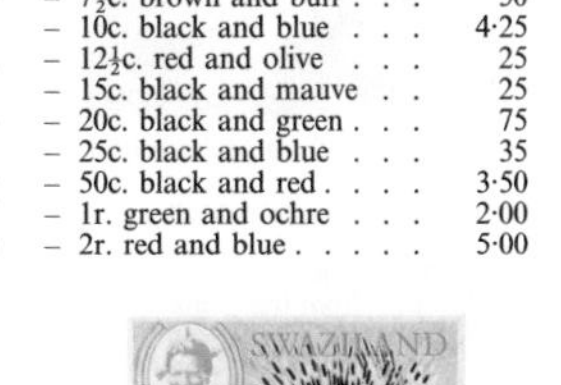

43 Porcupine

1969. Multicoloured.
161 ½c. Caracal 10 10
162 1c. Type **43** 10 10
163 2c. Crocodile 20 10
164 3c. Lion 60 10
165 3½c. African elephant 75 10
166 5c. Bush pig 30 10
167 7½c. Impala 35 10
168 10c. Chacma baboon 45 10
169 12½c. Ratel 70 3·75
170 15c. Leopard 1·25 70
171 20c. Blue wildebeest 95 60
172 25c. White rhinoceros 1·40 1·75
173 50c. Common zebra 1·50 3·25
174 1r. Waterbuck (vert) 3·00 6·50
175 2r. Giraffe (vert) 8·00 11·00
Nos. 164/5 are larger, 35 × 24½ mm.
For designs as Nos. 174/5, but in new currency, see Nos. 219/20.

44 King Sobhuza II and Flags

1969. Swaziland's Admission to the U.N. Multicoloured.
176 3c. Type **44** 10 10
177 7½c. King Sobhuza II, U.N. Building and emblem 15 10
178 12½c. As Type **44** 25 10
179 25c. As 7½c. 40 40

46 Athlete, Shield and Spears

47 "Bauhinia galpinii"

1970. 9th Commonwealth Games. Multicoloured.
180 3c. Type **46** 10 10
181 7½c. Runner 20 10
182 12½c. Hurdler 25 10
183 25c. Procession of Swaziland competitors 35 40

1971. Flowers. Multicoloured.
184 3c. Type **47** 20 10
185 10c. "Crocosmia aurea" 20 10
186 15c. "Gloriosa superba" 30 25
187 25c. "Watsonia densiflora" 40 1·00

48 King Sobhuza II in Ceremonial Dress

49 UNICEF Emblem

1971. Golden Jubilee of King Sobhuza II's Accession. Multicoloured.
188 3c. Type **48** 10 10
189 3½c. Sobhuza II in medallion 10 10
190 7½c. Sobhuza II attending Incwala ceremony 15 10
191 25c. Sobhuza II and aides at opening of Parliament 30 35

1972. 25th Anniv of UNICEF.
192 **49** 15c. black and lilac 15 20
193 – 25c. black and green 20 80
DESIGN: 25c. As Type **49**, but inscription rearranged.

50 Local Dancers

1972. Tourism. Multicoloured.
194 3½c. Type **50** 10 10
195 7½c. Swazi beehive hut 15 15
196 15c. Ezulwini Valley 20 50
197 25c. Fishing, Usutu River 65 1·25

51 Spraying Mosquitoes

1973. 25th Anniv of W.H.O. Multicoloured.
198 3½c. Type **51** 20 20
199 7½c. Anti-malaria vaccination 40 80

52 Mining

1973. Natural Resources. Multicoloured.
200 3½c. Type **52** 55 10
201 7½c. Cattle 25 15
202 15c. Water 30 20
203 25c. Rice 35 50

53 Coat of Arms

1973. 5th Anniv of Independence.
204 **53** 3c. pink and black 10 10
205 – 10c. multicoloured 15 10
206 – 15c. multicoloured 30 75
207 – 25c. multicoloured 40 1·60
DESIGNS: 10c. King Sobhuza II saluting; 15c. Parliament buildings; 25c. National Somhlolo stadium.

54 Flags and Mortar-board

55 King Sobhuza as College Student

1973. 10th Anniv of University of Botswana, Lesotho and Swaziland. Multicoloured.

208	7½c. Type **54**	20	10
209	12½c. University campus	25	10
210	15c. Map of Southern Africa	30	20
211	25c. University badge	40	35

1974. 75th Birth Anniv of King Sobhuza II. Multicoloured.

212	3c. Type **55**	10	10
213	9c. King Sobhuza in middle-age	10	10
214	50c. King Sobhuza at 75 years of age	70	60

56 New Post Office, Lobamba

1974. Centenary of U.P.U. Multicoloured.

215	4c. Type **56**	10	10
216	10c. Mbabane Temporary Post Office, 1902	15	15
217	15c. Carrying mail by cableway	30	50
218	25c. Mule-drawn mail-coach	40	70

1975. As Nos. 174/5, but in new currency.

219	1e. Waterbuck	50	2·00
220	2e. Giraffe	1·10	4·00

57 Umcwasho Ceremony

1975. Swazi Youth. Multicoloured.

221	3c. Type **57**	10	10
222	10c. Butimba (hunting party)	15	10
223	15c. Lusekwane (sacred shrub) (horiz)	40	40
224	25c. Goina Regiment	60	70

58 Control Tower, Matsapa Airport

1975. 10th Anniv of Internal Air Service. Multicoloured.

225	4c. Type **58**	30	10
226	5c. Fire engine	70	20
227	15c. Douglas DC-3	1·25	1·40
228	25c. Hawker Siddeley H.S.748	2·00	2·00

1975. Nos. 167 and 169 surch.

230	3c. on 7½c. Impala	75	1·00
231	6c. on 12½c. Ratel	1·50	2·00

60 Elephant Symbol

1975. International Women's Year.

232 **60**	4c. grey, black and blue	10	10
233 –	5c. multicoloured	10	10
234 –	15c. multicoloured	30	60
235 –	25c. multicoloured	50	90

DESIGNS—HORIZ: 5c. Queen Labotsibeni. VERT: 15c. Craftswoman; 25c. "Women in Service".

61 African Black-headed Oriole ("Black-headed Oriole")

1976. Birds. Multicoloured.

236	1c. Type **61**	75	2·50
237	2c. African green pigeon ("Green Pigeon") (vert)	80	2·50
238	3c. Green-winged pytilia ("Melba Finch")	1·00	1·00
239	4c. Violet starling ("Plum-coloured Starling") (vert)	80	15
240	5c. Black-headed heron (vert)	90	1·75
241	6c. Common stonechat ("Stonechat") (vert)	1·50	2·50
242	7c. Chorister robin chat ("Chorister Robin") (vert)	1·40	2·75
243	10c. Four-coloured bush-shrike ("Gorgeous Bush Shrike") (vert)	1·50	1·75
244	15c. Black-collared barbet (vert)	2·25	55
245	20c. Grey heron (vert)	3·25	2·00
246	25c. Giant kingfisher (vert)	3·50	2·00
247	30c. Verreaux's eagle ("Black Eagle") (vert)	3·50	2·50
248a	50c. Red bishop (vert)	90	1·00
249a	1e. Pin-tailed whydah (vert)	1·40	2·50
250a	2e. Lilac-breasted roller	1·50	5·00

62 Blindness from Malnutrition

1976. Prevention of Blindness. Mult.

251	5c. Type **62**	20	10
252	10c. Infected retina	25	10
253	20c. Blindness from trachoma	45	75
254	25c. Medicines	50	95

63 Marathon

64 Footballer Shooting

1976. Olympic Games, Montreal. Mult.

255	5c. Type **63**	15	10
256	6c. Boxing	20	30
257	20c. Football	45	45
258	25c. Olympic torch and flame	55	65

1976. F.I.F.A. Membership. Multicoloured.

259	4c. Type **64**	20	10
260	6c. Heading	20	10
261	20c. Goalkeeping	50	25
262	25c. Player about to shoot	50	30

65 Alexander Graham Bell and Telephone

1976. Centenary of Telephone.

263 **65**	4c. multicoloured	10	10
264 –	5c. multicoloured	10	10
265 –	10c. multicoloured	10	10
266 –	15c. multicoloured	20	20
267 –	20c. multicoloured	25	30

Nos. 264/7 as Type **65**, but showing different telephones.

66 Queen Elizabeth II and King Sobhuza II

1977. Silver Jubilee. Multicoloured.

268	20c. Type **66**	15	15
269	25c. Coronation Coach at Admiralty Arch	15	15
270	50c. Queen in coach	20	40

67 Matsapa College

1977. 50th Anniv of Police Training. Mult.

271	5c. Type **67**	10	10
272	10c. Policemen and women on parade	50	20
273	20c. Royal Swaziland Police badge (vert)	70	95
274	25c. Dog handling	1·25	1·50

68 Animals and Hunters

1977. Rock Paintings. Multicoloured.

275	5c. Type **68**	25	10
276	10c. Four dancers in a procession	30	10
277	15c. Man with cattle	40	20
278	20c. Four dancers	45	30
MS279	103 × 124 mm. Nos. 275/8	2·00	2·75

69 Timber, Highveld Region

70 Timber, Highveld Region

1977. Maps of the Regions. Multicoloured.

280	5c. Type **69**	50	10
281	10c. Pineapple, Middleveld	60	10
282	15c. Orange and lemon, Lowveld	80	65
283	20c. Cattle, Lubombo region	95	95
MS284	87 × 103 mm. Four 25c. designs as T **70**, together forming a composite map of Swaziland	1·40	1·60

71 Cabbage Tree

1978. Trees of Swaziland.

285 **71**	5c. green, brown and black	15	15
286 –	10c. multicoloured	20	15
287 –	20c. multicoloured	45	1·25
288 –	25c. multicoloured	55	1·40

DESIGNS: 10c. Marula; 20c. Kiaat; 25c. Lucky bean-tree.

72 Rural Electrification at Lobamba

1978. Hydro-electric Power.

289 **72**	5c. black and brown	10	10
290 –	10c. black and green	15	10
291 –	20c. black and blue	25	30
292 –	25c. black and purple	30	35

DESIGNS: 10c. Edwaleni Power Station; 20c. Switch-gear, Magudza Power Station; 25c. Turbine Hall, Edwaleni.

73 Elephant

75 Defence Force

74 Clay Pots

1978. 25th Anniv of Coronation.

293 –	25c. blue, black and green	15	25
294 –	25c. multicoloured	15	25
295 **73**	25c. blue, black and green	15	25

DESIGNS: No. 293, Queen's Lion; No. 294, Queen Elizabeth II.

1978. Handicrafts (1st series). Multicoloured.

296	5c. Type **74**	10	10
297	10c. Basketwork	10	10
298	20c. Wooden utensils	15	15
299	30c. Wooden pot	25	30

See also Nos. 310/13.

1978. 10th Anniv of Independence. Mult.

300	4c. Type **75**	15	10
301	6c. The King's Regiment	15	10
302	10c. Tinkabi tractor (agricultural development)	15	10
303	15c. Water-pipe laying (self-help scheme)	25	10
304	25c. Sebenta adult literacy scheme	30	25
305	50c. Fire emergency service	1·25	50

76 Archangel Gabriel appearing before Shepherds

1978. Christmas. Multicoloured.

306	5c. Type **76**	10	10
307	10c. Wise men paying homage to infant Jesus	10	10
308	15c. Archangel Gabriel warning Joseph	10	10
309	25c. Flight into Egypt	20	20

1979. Handicrafts (2nd series). As T **74**. Mult.

310	5c. Sisal bowls	10	10
311	15c. Pottery	15	10
312	20c. Basket work	20	15
313	30c. Hide shield	30	20

77 Prospecting at Phophonyane

1979. Centenary of Discovery of Gold in Swaziland.

314 **77**	5c. gold and blue	25	10
315 –	15c. gold and brown	45	20
316 –	25c. gold and green	65	30
317 –	50c. gold and red	90	1·50

DESIGNS: 15c. Early 3-stamp battery mill; 25c. Cyanide tanks at Piggs Peak; 50c. Pouring off molten gold.

78 "Girls at the Piano"

1979. International Year of the Child. Paintings by Renoir. Multicoloured.
318 5c. Type **78** 10 10
319 15c. "Madame Charpentier and her Children" 25 10
320 25c. "Girls picking Flowers" 35 15
321 50c. "Girl with Watering Can" 70 55
MS322 123 × 135 mm. Nos. 318/21 1·25 1·75

79 1933 1d. Carmine Stamp and Sir Rowland Hill

1979. Death Centenary of Sir Rowland Hill. Multicoloured.
323 10c. 1945 3d. Victory commemorative 15 10
324 20c. Type **79** 25 25
325 25c. 1968 25c. Independence commemorative 25 30
MS326 115 × 90 mm. 50c. 1956 6d. Great kudu antelope definitive 75 85

80 Obverse and Reverse of 5 Cents

1979. Coins.
327 **80** 5c. black and brown . . . 15 10
328 – 10c. black and blue 20 10
329 – 20c. black and green . . . 35 20
330 – 50c. black and orange . . 50 50
331 – 1e. black and cerise . . . . 75 1·00
DESIGNS: 10c. Obverse and reverse of 10 cents; 20c. Obverse and reverse of 20 cents; 50c. Reverse of 50 cents; 1e. Reverse of 1 lilangeni.

81 Big Bend Post Office

1979. Post Office Anniversaries.
332 **81** 5c. multicoloured 10 10
333 – 15c. multicoloured 15 10
334 – 20c. black, green and red 20 15
335 – 50c. multicoloured 40 60
DESIGNS AND COMMEMORATIONS—HORIZ: 5c. Type **81** (25th anniv of Posts and Telecommunications Services); 20c. 1949 75th anniv of U.P.U. 1s. stamp (10th anniv of U.P.U. membership); 50c. 1974 Centenary of U.P.U. 25c. stamp (10th anniv of U.P.U membership). VERT: 15c. Microwave antenna, Mount Ntondozi (25th anniv of Posts and Telecommunications Services).

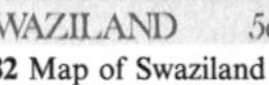

82 Map of Swaziland **83** "Brunsvigia radulosa"

1980. 75th Anniv of Rotary International.
336 **82** 5c. blue and gold 25 10
337 – 15c. blue and gold 45 10
338 – 50c. blue and gold 50 55
339 – 1e. blue and gold . . . . 85 1·25
DESIGNS: 15c. Vitreous cutter and optical illuminator; 50c. Scroll; 1e. Rotary Head-quarters, Evanston, U.S.A.

1980. Flowers. Multicoloured.
340A 1c. Type **83** 10 10
341A 2c. "Aloe suprafoliata" . . 10 10
342A 3c. "Haemanthus magnificus" 10 10
343A 4c. "Aloe marlothii" . . . 10 10
344A 5c. "Dicoma zeyheri" . . . 10 10
345A 6c. "Aloe kniphofioides" . . 15 30
346A 7c. "Cyrtanthus bicolor" . . 10 10
347A 10c. "Eucomis autumnalis" (horiz) 20 10
348A 15c. "Leucospermum gerrardii" (horiz) 15 10
349A 20c. "Haemanthus multiflorus" (horiz) . . . 30 25
350A 30c. "Acridocarpus natalitius" (horiz) 20 20
351A 50c. "Adenium swazicum" (horiz) 20 30
352A 1e. "Protea simplex" . . . 35 60
353A 2e. "Calodendrum capense" 1·10 1·25
354A 5e. "Gladiolus ecklonii" . . 1·50 3·00
Nos. 347A/51A are 42 × 45 mm and Nos. 352A/4A 28 × 38 mm.
Nos. 340A/1A, 343A, 345A, 347A and 349A come with and without date imprint.

84 Mail Runner

1980. "London 1980" International Stamp Exhibition. Multicoloured.
355 10c. Type **84** 15 10
356 20c. Post Office mail truck 25 15
357 25c. Mail sorting office . . . 30 20
358 50c. Ropeway conveying mail at Bulembu 70 70

85 Scaly

1980. River Fishes. Multicoloured.
359 5c. Type **85** 25 10
360 10c. Silver catfish ("Silver barbel") 25 10
361 15c. Tiger fish 40 15
362 30c. Brown squeaker 50 30
363 1e. Red-breasted tilapia ("Bream") . . . . 60 1·40

86 Oribi

1980. Wildlife Conservation. Multicoloured.
364 5c. Type **86** 15 10
365 10c. Nile crocodile (vert) . . 30 10
366 50c. Temminck's ground pangolin 75 70
367 1e. Leopard (vert) . . . . . 1·60 1·50

87 Public Bus Service

1981. Transport. Multicoloured.
368 5c. Type **87** 10 10
369 25c. Royal Swazi National Airways 25 15
370 30c. Swaziland United Transport 30 20
371 1e. Swaziland Railway . . . 1·25 1·75

88 Mantenga Falls

1981. Tourism. Multicoloured.
372 5c. Type **88** 10 10
373 15c. Mananga Yacht Club . . 15 10
374 30c. White rhinoceros in Mlilwane Game Sanctuary 40 30
375 1e. Gambling equipment (casinos) . . . . 1·10 1·60

89 Prince Charles on Hike **91** "Physical Recreation"

90 Installation of King Sobhuza II, 22 December 1921

1981. Royal Wedding. Multicoloured.
376 10c. Wedding bouquet from Swaziland 10 10
377 25c. Type **89** 15 10
378 1e. Prince Charles and Lady Diana Spencer 40 70

1981. Diamond Jubilee of King Sobhuza II. Multicoloured.
379 5c. Type **90** 10 10
380 10c. Royal Visit, 1947 . . . 10 10
381 15c. King Sobhuza II and Coronation of Queen Elizabeth II, 1953 . . . . 15 15
382 25c. King Sobhuza taking Royal Salute, Independence, 1968 . . . . 15 15
383 30c. King Sobhuza in youth 20 20
384 1e. King Sobhuza and Parliament Buildings . . . 50 90

1981. 25th Anniv of Duke of Edinburgh Award Scheme. Multicoloured.
385 5c. Type **91** 10 10
386 20c. "Expeditions" 10 10
387 50c. "Skills" 25 25
388 1e. Duke of Edinburgh in ceremonial dress 50 80

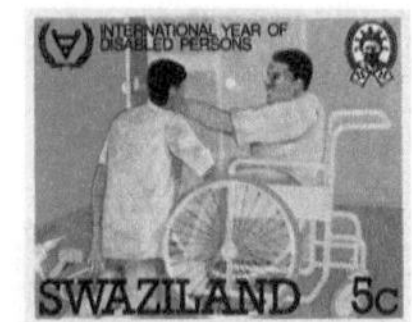

92 Disabled Person in Wheelchair

1981. International Year of Disabled Persons. Multicoloured.
389 5c. Type **92** 30 10
390 15c. Teacher with disabled child (vert) 50 15
391 25c. Disabled craftsman (vert) 75 20
392 1e. Disabled driver in invalid carriage . . . . 2·25 2·75

93 "Papilio demodocus"

1981. Butterflies. Multicoloured.
393 5c. Type **93** 50 10
394 10c. "Charaxes candiope" . . 50 10
395 50c. "Papilio nireus" . . . . 1·50 85
396 1e. "Terias desjardinsii" . . . 2·00 2·00

94 Man holding a Flower after discarding Cigarettes **95** Male Pel's Fishing Owl

1982. Pan-African Conference on Smoking and Health. Multicoloured.
397 5c. Type **94** 50 85
398 10c. Smoker and non-smoker 60 90

1982. Wildlife Conservation (1st series). Pel's Fishing Owl. Multicoloured.
399 35c. Type **95** . . . . 8·00 4·00
400 35c. Female Pel's fishing owl at nest . . . . 8·00 4·00
401 35c. Pair of Pel's fishing owls 8·00 4·00
402 35c. Pel's fishing owl, nest and eggs . . . . 8·00 4·00
403 35c. Adult Pel's fishing owl with youngster . . . . . . 8·00 4·00
See also Nos. 425/29 and 448/52.

96 Swaziland Coat of Arms

1982. 21st Birthday of Princess of Wales. Mult.
404 5c. Type **96** 10 10
405 20c. Princess leaving Eastleigh Airport, Southampton 80 10
406 50c. Bride at Buckingham Palace 90 30
407 1e. Formal portrait . . . . . 2·25 85

97 Irrigation

1982. Sugar Industry. Multicoloured.
408 5c. Type **97** 10 10
409 20c. Harvesting 25 15
410 30c. Mhlume mills 35 25
411 1e. Sugar transportation by train . . . . 1·00 2·00

98 Doctor with Child

1982. Swaziland Red Cross Society (Baphaladi). Multicoloured.
412 5c. Type **98** 10 10
413 20c. Juniors carrying stretcher 25 15
414 50c. Disaster relief 55 75
415 1e. Henri Dunant (founder of Red Cross) . . . . 1·25 2·50

99 Taking the Oath

1982. 75th Anniv of Boy Scout Movement. Multicoloured.
416 5c. Type **99** 10 10
417 10c. Hiking and exploration 15 10
418 25c. Community development 30 30
419 75c. Lord Baden-Powell . . . 1·00 1·25
MS420 107 × 109 mm. 1e. World Scout badge . . . . 1·00 1·40

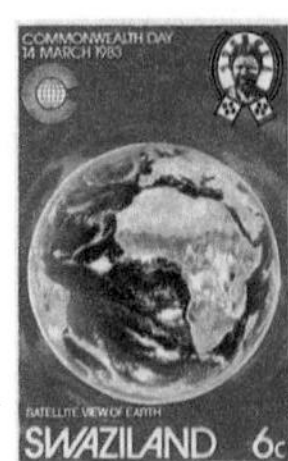

100 Satellite View of Earth **102** Montgolfier Balloon

1982. Commonwealth Day. Multicoloured.
421 6c. Type **100** 10 10
422 10c. King Sobhuza II 10 10
423 50c. Swazi woman and beehive huts (horiz) 35 55
424 1e. Spraying sugar crops (horiz) . . . . 70 1·00

1983. Wildlife Conservation (2nd series). Lammergeier. As T **95**. Multicoloured.
425 35c. Adult male . . . . . . 2·50 2·50
426 35c. Pair . . . . 2·50 2·50
427 35c. Nest and egg . . . . . 2·50 2·50

428 35c. Female at nest . . . . . 2·50 2·50
429 35c. Adult bird with fledgling 2·50 2·50

101 Swaziland National Football Team

1983. Tour of Swaziland by English Football Clubs. Three sheets, 101 × 72 mm, each containing one 75c. stamp as T **101**. Multicoloured.
MS430 75c. Type **101**; 75c. Tottenham Hotspur; 75c. Manchester United Set of 3 sheets 1·50 3·00

1983. Bicentenary of Manned Flight. Mult.
431 5c. Type **102** 10 10
432 10c. Wright brothers' Flyer I (horiz) 15 10
433 25c. Fokker Fellowship (horiz) 35 35
434 50c. Bell XS-1 (horiz) 85 65
MS435 73 × 73 mm. 1e. Space shuttle "Columbia" . . . . 1·00 1·40

103 Dr. Albert Schweitzer (Peace Prize, 1952)

1983. 150th Birth Anniv of Alfred Nobel. Multicoloured.
436 6c. Type **103** . . . . 2·25 70
437 10c. Dag Hammarskjold (Peace Prize, 1961) 85 15
438 50c. Albert Einstein (Physics Prize, 1921) . . . . . . 3·75 2·00
439 1e. Alfred Nobel . . . . . . 3·75 4·25

104 Maize

1983. World Food Day. Multicoloured.
440 6c. Type **104** 20 10
441 10c. Rice 20 10
442 50c. Cattle herding . . . . . 90 1·00
443 1e. Ploughing . . . . 1·60 2·75

105 Women's College

1984. Education. Multicoloured.
444 5c. Type **105** 10 10
445 15c. Technical training school 15 15
446 50c. University 35 60
447 1e. Primary school . . . . . 65 1·10

106 Male on Ledge

1984. Wildlife Conservation (3rd series). Bald Ibis. Multicoloured.
448 35c. Type **106** . . . . 3·00 3·00
449 35c. Male and female . . . . 3·00 3·00
450 35c. Bird and egg . . . . . . 3·00 3·00
451 35c. Female on nest of eggs 3·00 3·00
452 35c. Adult and fledgling . . . 3·00 3·00

107 Mule-drawn Passenger Coach

1984. Universal Postal Union Congress, Hamburg. Multicoloured.
453 7c. Type **107** 30 10
454 15c. Ox-drawn post wagon 45 15
455 50c. Mule-drawn mail coach 90 75
456 1e. Bristol to London mail coach . . . . 1·40 1·75

108 Running

1984. Olympic Games, Los Angeles. Multicoloured.
457 7c. Type **108** 10 20
458 10c. Swimming 10 10
459 50c. Shooting . . . . 45 1·00
460 1e. Boxing . . . . 90 2·00
MS461 100 × 70 mm. Nos. 457/60 3·00 5·00

109 "Suillus bovinus"

1984. Fungi. Multicoloured.
462 10c. Type **109** . . . . 1·50 30
463 15c. "Langermannia gigantea" (vert) . . . . . 2·50 55
464 50c. "Trametes versicolor" ("Coriolus versicolor") (vert) . . . . 2·75 2·75
465 1e. "Boletus edulis" . . . . 3·25 5·25

110 King Sobhuza opening Railway, 1964

1984. 20th Anniv of Swaziland Railways. Multicoloured.
466 10c. Type **110** 30 15
467 25c. Type 15A locomotive at Siweni Yard 55 40
468 30c. Container loading, Matsapha Station 55 40
469 1e. Locomotive No. 268 leaving Alto Tunnel . . . 1·25 2·50
MS470 144 × 74 mm. Nos. 466/9 2·75 6·00

1985. Nos. 340, 342, 343, 345 and 346 surch.
471a 10c. on 4c. "Aloe marlothii" 35 10
472 15c. on 7c. "Cyrtanthus bicolor" 40 20
473 20c. on 3c. "Haemanthus magnificus" 35 15
474 25c. on 6c. "Aloe kniphofioides" 40 20
475 30c. on 1c. Type **83** 50 20
476 30c. on 2c. "Aloe suprafoliata" . . . . . . 2·75 3·75

112 Rotary International Logo and Map of World

1985. 80th Anniv of Rotary International. Multicoloured.
477 10c. Type **112** 50 10
478 15c. Teacher and handicapped children 90 20
479 50c. Youth exchange . . . . 1·25 1·25
480 1e. Nurse and children . . . 2·75 3·50

113 Male Southern Ground Hornbill

114 The Queen Mother in 1975

1985. Birth Bicentenary of John J. Audubon (ornithologist). Southern Ground Hornbills. Multicoloured.
481 25c. Type **113** . . . . 2·25 3·25
482 25c. Male and female ground hornbills . . . . 2·25 3·25
483 25c. Female at nest . . . . . 2·25 3·25
484 25c. Ground hornbill in nest, and egg . . . . 2·25 3·25
485 25c. Adult and fledgling . . . 2·25 3·25

1985. Life and Times of Queen Elizabeth the Queen Mother. Multicoloured.
486 10c. The Queen Mother in South Africa, 1947 . . . . 35 10
487 15c. With the Queen and Princess Margaret, 1985 (from photo by Norman Parkinson) 35 10
488 50c. Type **114** . . . . 1·00 90
489 1e. With Prince Henry at his christening (from photo by Lord Snowdon) . . . . . 1·25 2·00
MS490 91 × 73 mm. 2e. Greeting Prince Andrew . . . . 3·00 1·75

115 Buick "Tourer"

1985. Century of Motoring. Multicoloured.
491 10c. Type **115** 50 10
492 15c. Four cylinder Rover . . 70 20
493 50c. De Dion Bouton . . . . 1·75 2·00
494 1e. "Model T" Ford . . . . 2·25 4·00

116 Youths building Bridge over Ravine

1985. International Youth Year (10, 50c.) and 75th Anniv of Girl Guide Movement (others). Multicoloured.
495 10c. Type **116** 15 10
496 20c. Girl Guides in camp . . 20 15
497 50c. Youth making model from sticks . . . . 45 1·00
498 1e. Guides collecting brushwood . . . . 80 2·00

117 Halley's Comet over Swaziland

1986. Appearance of Halley's Comet.
499 **117** 1e.50 multicoloured . . . 2·75 4·00

1986. 60th Birthday of Queen Elizabeth II. As T **145a** of St. Helena. Multicoloured.
500 10c. Christening of Princess Anne, 1950 . . . . 10 10
501 30c. On Palace balcony after wedding of Prince and Princess of Wales, 1981 . . 15 25
502 45c. Royal visit to Swaziland, 1947 . . . . 15 30
503 1e. At Windsor Polo Ground, 1984 . . . . 30 70
504 2e. At Crown Agents Head Office, London 1983 . . . 60 1·40

118 King Mswati III

119 Emblems of Round Table and Project Orbis (eye disease campaign)

1986. Coronation of King Mswati III.
505 **118** 10c. black and gold . . . 35 25
506 – 20c. multicoloured 70 30
507 – 25c. multicoloured 80 35
508 – 30c. multicoloured 90 50
509 – 40c. multicoloured . . . . 3·25 2·00
510 – 2e. multicoloured . . . . 4·00 7·50
DESIGNS—HORIZ: 20c. Prince with King Sobhuza II at Incwala ceremony; 25c. At primary school; 30c. At school in England; 40c. Inspecting guard of honour at Matsapha Airport; 2e. Dancing the Simemo.

1986. 50th Anniv of Round Table Organization. Designs showing branch emblems. Multicoloured.
511 15c. Type **119** 30 10
512 25c. Ehlanzeni 51 . . . . . 40 20
513 55c. Mbabane 30 . . . . . . 85 70
514 70c. Bulembu 54 . . . . . . 1·10 1·50
515 2e. Manzini 44 . . . . 2·00 3·75

120 "Precis hierta"

1987. Butterflies (1st series). Multicoloured.
516 10c. Type **120** . . . . 55 1·50
517 15c. "Hamanumida daedalus" 65 1·25
518 20c. "Charaxes boueti" . . . 65 90
519 25c. "Abantis paradisea" . . 65 1·75
520 30c. "Acraea anemosa" . . . 65 70
521 35c. "Graphium leonidas" . . 65 75
522 45c. "Graphium antheus" . . 70 1·75
523 50c. "Precis orithya" 70 85
524 55c. "Pinacopteryx eriphia" 70 85
525 70c. "Precis octavia" . . . . 80 1·40
526 1e. "Mylothris chloris" . . . 1·00 3·00
527 5e. "Colotis regina" 85 90
528 10e. "Spindasis natalensis" . 1·70 1·80
For these designs and similar 5c. with different portrait of King Mswati III, see Nos. 606/17.

121 Two White Rhinoceroses

122 Hybrid Tea Rose "Blue Moon"

1987. White Rhinoceros. Multicoloured.
529 15c. Type **121** . . . . 2·00 45
530 25c. Female and calf . . . . 2·75 1·00
531 45c. Rhinoceros charging . . 4·25 3·25
532 70c. Rhinoceros wallowing 6·50 7·50

1987. Garden Flowers. Multicoloured.
533 15c. Type **122** . . . . 1·00 20
534 35c. Rambler rose "Danse du feu" . . . . 2·00 80
535 55c. Pompon dahlia "Odin" 2·25 1·50
536 2e. "Lilium davidii var. willmottiae" . . . . 6·50 11·00

1987. Royal Ruby Wedding. Nos. 501/4 optd **40TH WEDDING ANNIVERSARY.**
537 30c. On Palace balcony after wedding of Prince and Princess of Wales, 1981 . . 30 20
538 45c. Royal visit to Swaziland, 1947 . . . . 40 30
539 1e. At Windsor Polo Ground, 1984 . . . . 75 1·50
540 2e. At Crown Agents Head Office, London, 1983 . . . 1·10 2·75

123 "Zabalius aridus" (grasshopper)

1988. Insects. Multicoloured.
541 15c. Type **123** . . . . 1·40 15
542 55c. "Callidea bohemani" (shieldbug) . . . . 2·75 85
543 1e. "Phymateus viridipes" (grasshopper) . . . . . . 4·75 4·75
544 2e. "Nomadacris septemfasciata" (locust) . . 7·50 9·50

124 Athlete with Swazi Flag and Olympic Stadium

1988. Olympic Games, Seoul. Multicoloured.
545 15c. Type **124** . . . . 1·00 10
546 35c. Taekwondo . . . . . . 1·40 45
547 1e. Boxing . . . . 1·75 2·25
548 2e. Tennis . . . . 3·50 5·00

125 Savanna Monkey

1989. Small Mammals. Multicoloured.
549 35c. Type **125** . . . . 1·75 30
550 55c. Large-toothed rock hyrax . . . . 2·25 75
551 1e. Zorilla . . . . 4·00 4·25
552 2e. African wild cat . . . . 7·00 9·00

126 Dr. David Hynd (founder of Swazi Red Cross)

1989. 125th Anniv of Int Red Cross. Mult.
553 15c. Type **126** 20 15
554 60c. First aid training 55 40
555 1e. Sigombeni Clinic . . . . 90 1·25
556 2e. Refugee camp . . . . . 1·40 2·50

127 King Mswati III with Prince of Wales, 1987

1989. 21st Birthday of King Mswati III. Mult.
557 15c. Type **127** 10 10
558 60c. King with Pope John Paul II, 1988 . . . . . . 30 35
559 1e. Introduction of Crown Prince to people, 1983 . . 50 55
560 2e. King Mswati III and Queen Mother . . . . . . 95 1·00

128 Manzini to Mahamba Road

1989. 25th Anniv of African Development Bank. Multicoloured.
561 15c. Type **128** 10 10
562 60c. Microwave Radio Receiver, Mbabane 30 40
563 1e. Mbabane Government Hospital . . . . 50 1·10
564 2e. Ezulwini Power Station switchyard . . . . 95 2·25

129 International Priority Mail Van

1990. "Stamp World London 90" International Stamp Exhibition. Multicoloured.
565 15c. Type **129** 15 10
566 60c. Facsimile service operators 40 40
567 1e. Rural post office . . . . 75 1·00
568 2e. Ezulwini Earth Station . . 1·40 2·50
MS569 105 × 85 mm. 2e. Mail runner . . . . 4·00 4·50

1990. 90th Birthday of Queen Elizabeth the Queen Mother. As T **161a** of St. Helena.
570 75c. multicoloured 50 50
571 4e. black and green . . . . . 2·25 3·50
DESIGNS—21 × 36 mm: 75c. Queen Mother. 29 × 37 mm: 4e. King George VI and Queen Elizabeth visiting Civil Resettlement Unit, Hatfield House.

130 Pictorial Teaching

1990. International Literacy Year. Mult.
572 15c. Type **130** 10 10
573 75c. Rural class 45 45
574 1e. Modern teaching methods 60 1·00
575 2e. Presentation of certificates 1·10 2·00

131 Rural Water Supply

133 Lobamba Hot Spring

1990. 40th Anniv of United Nations Development Programme. "Helping People to Help Themselves". Multicoloured.
576 60c. Type **131** 35 35
577 1e. Seed multiplication project . . . . 60 1·10
578 2e. Low-cost housing project 1·25 2·25

1990. Nos. 519/20, 522 and 524 surch.
579 10c. on 25c. "Abantis paradisea" 30 30
580 15c. on 30c. "Acraea anemosa" 40 40
580a 15c. on 45c. "Graphium antheus" . . . . 17·00 17·00
581 20c. on 45c. "Graphium antheus" 40 40
582 40c. on 55c. "Pinacopteryx eriphia" 55 55

1991. National Heritage. Multicoloured.
583 15c. Type **133** 30 10
584 60c. Sibebe Rock 75 45
585 1e. Jolobela Falls . . . . . 1·25 1·50
586 2e. Mantjolo Sacred Pool . . 2·00 2·75
MS587 80 × 60 mm. 2e. Usushwana river . . . . 3·75 4·25

134 King Mswati III making Speech

1991. 5th Anniv of King Mswati III's Coronation. Multicoloured.
588 15c. Type **134** 30 10
589 75c. Butimba Royal Hunt . . 1·00 60
590 1e. King and visiting school friends, 1986 . . . . . . 1·25 1·50
591 2e. King opening Parliament 2·00 2·75

1991. 65th Birthday of Queen Elizabeth II and 70th Birthday of Prince Philip. As T **165a** of St. Helena. Multicoloured.
592 1e. Prince Philip . . . . . . 1·50 1·75
593 2e. Queen Elizabeth II . . . 1·75 2·00

135 "Xerophyta retinervis"

136 Father Christmas arriving with Gifts

1991. Indigenous Flowers. Multicoloured.
594 15c. Type **135** 50 10
595 75c. "Bauhinia galpinii" . . . 1·25 80
596 1e. "Dombeya rotundifolia" . 1·50 1·60
597 2e. "Kigelia africana" . . . . 2·25 3·25

1991. Christmas. Multicoloured.
598 20c. Type **136** 15 10
599 70c. Singing carols 65 50
600 1e. Priest reading from Bible 80 1·25
601 2e. The Nativity . . . . . . 1·50 2·50

137 Lubombo Flat Lizard

1992. Reptiles (1st series). Multicoloured.
602 20c. Type **137** 90 20
603 70c. Natal hinged tortoise . . 2·25 1·50
604 1e. Swazi thick-toed gecko . . 2·75 2·75
605 2e. Nile monitor . . . . . . 3·75 5·50
See also Nos. 658/61.

138 "Precis hierta"

1992. Butterflies (2nd series). Nos. 516/26 and new value (5c.) showing different portrait of King Mswati III. Multicoloured.
606 5c. "Colotis antevippe" . . . 10 10
607 10c. Type **138** 10 10
608 15c. "Hamanumida daedalus" 10 10
609 20c. "Charaxes boueti" . . . 10 10
610 25c. "Abantis paradisea" . . 10 10
611 30c. "Acraea anemosa" . . . 10 10
612 35c. "Graphium leonidas" . . 10 10
613 45c. "Graphium antheus" . . 10 10
614 50c. "Precis orithya" 10 10
615 55c. "Pinacopteryx eriphia" . 10 10
616 70c. "Precis octavia" 10 15
617 1e. "Mylothris chloris" . . . 15 20

139 Missionaries visiting King Sobhuza II and Queen Lomawa

140 Calabashes

1992. Centenary of Evangelical Alliance Missions. Multicoloured.
620 20c. Type **139** 40 10
621 1e. Pioneer missionaries . . . 2·00 2·50

1993. Archaeological and Contemporary Artifacts. Multicoloured.
622 20c. Type **140** 45 10
623 70c. Contemporary cooking pot . . . . 1·10 85
624 1e. Wooden bowl and containers . . . . 1·50 1·75
625 2e. Quern for grinding seeds 2·50 3·50

141 King Mswati III as Baby

142 Male and Female Common Waxbills

1993. 25th Birthday of King Mswati III and 25th Anniv of Independence. Mult.
626 25c. Type **141** 20 10
627 40c. King Mswati III addressing meeting 25 20
628 1e. King Sobhuza II receiving Instrument of Independence . . . . . . 75 1·25
629 2e. King Mswati III delivering Coronation speech . . . . 1·40 2·50

1993. Common Waxbill. Multicoloured.
630 25c. Type **142** 40 20
631 40c. Waxbill and eggs in nest 55 25
632 1e. Waxbill on nest . . . . . 1·25 1·50
633 2e. Waxbill feeding chicks . . 2·00 2·75

143 Classroom and Practical Training

144 "Agaricus arvensis"

1994. 25th Anniv of U.S. Peace Corps in Swaziland. Multicoloured.
634 25c. Type **143** 30 10
635 40c. Rural water supply . . . 40 20
636 1e. Americans and Swazis in traditional costumes . . . 1·50 1·50
637 2e. Swazi–American co-operation . . . . 1·75 2·50

1994. Fungi. Multicoloured.
638 30c. Type **144** . . . . 1·25 50
639 40c. "Boletus edulis" . . . . 1·25 50
640 1e. "Russula virescens" . . . 2·50 1·75
641 2e. "Armillaria mellea" . . . 3·50 4·00

145 Emblem and Airliner on Runway

1994. 50th Anniv of I.C.A.O. Multicoloured.
642 30c. Type **145** 40 10
643 40c. Control tower and dish aerial 45 20
644 1e. Crash tenders . . . . . . 1·00 1·25
645 2e. Air traffic controllers . . 1·50 2·50

146 Wooden Bowls

147 Harvesting Maize

1995. Handicrafts. Multicoloured.
646 35c. Type **146** 45 20
647 50c. Chicken nests 65 35
648 1e. Leather crafts . . . . . 1·00 1·10
649 2e. Wood carvings . . . . . 1·75 2·25

1995. 50th Anniv of F.A.O. Multicoloured.
650 35c. Type **147** 20 20
651 50c. Planting vegetables . . . 30 35
652 1e. Herd of cattle 50 75
653 2e. Harvesting sorghum . . . 90 1·75

148 Green Turaco

1995. Turacos ("Louries"). Multicoloured.
654 35c. Type **148** 40 30
655 50c. Green turaco in flight . . 55 45
656 1e. Violet-crested turaco . . . 80 1·00
657 2e. Livingstone's turaco . . . 1·25 2·00

1996. Reptiles (2nd series). As T **137** with King's portrait at right. Multicoloured.
658 35c. Chameleon 55 20
659 50c. Rock monitor 65 35
660 1e. African python . . . . . 1·10 1·25
661 2e. Tree agama . . . . . . 1·75 2·50

149 Waterberry

1996. Trees. Multicoloured.
662 40c. Type **149** 20 15
663 60c. Sycamore fig 25 20

664 1e. Stem fruit 45 80
665 2e. Wild medlar . . . . . . 90 1·60

150 Mahamba Methodist Church

1996. Historic Monuments. Multicoloured.
666 40c. Type **150** 40 15
667 60c. Colonial Secretariat, Mbabane 55 20
668 1e. King Sobhuza II Monument, Lobamba . . . 95 1·10
669 2e. First High Court Building, Hlatikulu . . . . 1·60 2·00

151 Children in Class

1996. 50th Anniv of UNICEF. Multicoloured.
670 40c. Type **151** 15 15
671 60c. Child being inoculated (vert) 20 20
672 1e. Child on crutches (vert) 40 70
673 2e. Mother and children (vert) . . . . 80 1·60

152 Klipspringer **153** Umgaco Costume

1997. Mammals. Multicoloured.
674 50c. Type **152** 30 20
675 70c. Grey duiker 35 30
676 1e. Antbear (horiz) 50 70
677 2e. Cape clawless otter (horiz) 80 1·60

1997. Traditional Costumes. Multicoloured.
678 50c. Type **153** 25 15
679 70c. Sigeja cloak 35 25
680 1e. Umdada kilt 55 65
681 2e. Ligcebesha costume . . . 90 1·40

154 Olive Toad

1998. Amphibians. Multicoloured.
682 55c. Type **154** 25 15
683 75c. African bullfrog 35 25
684 1e. Water lily frog 55 65
685 2e. Bushveld rain frog . . . 90 1·40

155 Aerial View of King Sobhuza II Memorial Park

1998. 30th Anniv of Independence and 30th Birthday of King Mswati III. Multicoloured.
686 55c. Type **155** 25 15
687 75c. King Mswati III taking oath (vert) 35 25
688 1e. King Mswati delivering speech 50 70
689 2e. King Sobhuza II receiving Instrument of Independence . . . . . . 90 1·40

156 Grinding Stone **157** Internet Service

1999. Local Culinary Utensils. Multicoloured.
690 60c. Type **156** 25 15
691 75c. Stirring sticks 30 20
692 80c. Clay pot 35 25
693 95c. Swazi spoons 45 45
694 1e.75 Beer cups 75 85
695 2e.40 Mortar and pestle . . . 1·00 1·25

1999. 125th Anniv of Universal Postal Union. Multicoloured.
696 60c. Type **157** 25 15
697 80c. Cellular phone service 35 25
698 1e. Two post vans exchanging mail (horiz) 70 75
699 2e.40 Training school (horiz) 1·10 1·40

158 Lion and Lioness

2000. Wildlife. Multicoloured.
700 65c. Type **158** 25 15
701 90c. Leopard (horiz) 45 30
702 1e.50 Rhinoceros (horiz) . . 1·25 1·10
703 2e.50 Buffalo . . . . 1·10 1·50

159 Oribi with Young

2001. Endangered Species. Antelopes. Mult.
704 65c. Type **159** 25 15
705 90c. Oribi buck 40 25
706 1e.50 Young klipspringers . . 70 75
707 2e.50 Male and female klipspringers . . . . 1·00 1·25

160 Fighting Forest Fires

2001. Environment Protection. Multicoloured.
708 70c. Type **160** 30 10
709 95c. Tree planting 40 15
710 2e.05 Construction of Maguga Dam . . . . . . 1·00 1·25
711 2e.80 Building embankment 1·25 1·50

2002. Golden Jubilee. As T **211** of St. Helena.
712 70c. agate, violet and gold . . 50 10
713 95c. multicoloured 70 25
714 2e.05 agate, violet and gold 1·10 1·25
715 2e.80 multicoloured . . . . . 1·40 1·50
MS716 162 × 95 mm. Nos. 715/15 and 22e.50 multicoloured . . . 6·00 7·00

DESIGNS—HORIZ (as T **211** of St. Helena): 70c. Princess Elizabeth, Prince Philip, and children, 1951; 95c. Queen Elizabeth in blue and white beret; 2e.05, Queen Elizabeth in evening dress; 2e80, Queen Elizabeth on visit to Norway, 2001. VERT (38 × 51 mm): 50p. Queen Elizabeth after Annigoni.

Designs as Nos. 712/15 in No. **MS**716 omit the gold frame around each stamp and the "Golden Jubilee 1952–2002" inscription.

161 Swazi Village

2002. Tourism. Multicoloured.
717 75c. Type **161** 20 10
718 1e. King Mswati and lions (vert) 30 20
719 2e.05 Crocodile 75 80
720 2e.80 Ostrich with young . . 1·00 1·10

162 Sitolotolo (mouth organ) **164** King Mswati III and Outline of Africa

163 Community Health Worker with AIDS Patient

2003. Musical Instruments. Multicoloured.
721 80c. Type **162** 10 15
722 1e.05 Emafahlawane (rattles) (horiz) 15 20
723 2e.35 Impalampala (Kudu horn trumpet) (horiz) . . 35 40
724 2e.80 Makhoyane (chordphone) 45 50

2004. AIDS Awareness Campaign. Multicoloured.
725 85c. Type **163** 30 15
726 1e.10 Care and Voluntary Counselling and Testing Centre 40 25
727 2e.45 Testing blood (vert) . . 90 95
728 3e.35 Nurse giving injection and sterilizer (vert) . . . . 1·10 1·25

2004. Global 2003 Smart Partnership Movement. Multicoloured.
729 85c. Type **164** 30 15
730 1e.10 Outline of Africa and logos (horiz) 40 25
731 2e.45 Stylized people holding globe 85 95
732 3e.35 King Mswati III and speaker . . . . 1·00 1·10

2004. First Joint Issue of Southern Africa Postal Operators Association Members. Sheet 170 × 95 mm containing hexagonal designs as T **470a** of South Africa showing national birds of Association members. Multicoloured.
MS733 85c. Purple-crested turaco ("Lourie") (Swaziland); 1e.10 Stanley ("Blue") crane (South Africa); 1e.35 Cattle egret (Botswana); 1e.90 Two African fish eagles perched (Zimbabwe); 2e. African fish eagle (Namibia); 2e.45 Bar-tailed trogon (Malawi) (inscribed "apaloderma vittatum"); 3e. Two African fish eagles in flight (Zambia); 3e.35 Peregrine falcon (Angola) . . . 2·75 3·00

The stamp depicting the Bar-tailed trogon is not inscribed with the country of which the bird is a national symbol.

Miniature sheets of similar designs were also issued by Namibia, Zimbabwe, Angola, Botswana, South Africa, Malawi and Zambia.

165 School Child under Car and Children by Road

2005. Road Safety Council. Multicoloured.
734 85c. Type **165** 15 20
735 1e.10 Fire rescue team pulling injured man from car . . . 15 20
736 2e.45 Pedestrians and car approaching stop sign . . 40 45
737 3e.35 Bus and road safety officials 55 60

POSTAGE DUE STAMPS

D 1 D 6

1933.
D1 D 1 1d. red . . . . 30 9·50
D2 2d. violet . . . . 2·00 25·00

1961. Surch **Postage Due 2d.**
D3 7 2d. on 2d. black and brown 1·25 2·75

These prices apply to stamps with large figure measuring 4½ mm high.

1961. As Type D 1 but with value in cents.
D4 1c. red . . . . 15 1·10
D5 2c. violet . . . . 15 1·10
D6 5c. green . . . . 20 1·10

1961. Surch **Postage Due** and value in cents.
D10 7 1c. on 2d. black and brown 70 2·75
D11 2c. on 2d. black and brown 50 2·75
D12 5c. on 2d. black and brown 90 2·25

1971.
D19 D 6 1c. red . . . . 30 1·75
D23 2c. purple 10 25
D24 5c. green 10 25
D25 10c. blue 10 25
D26 25c. brown 10 25

SWEDEN Pt. 11

A kingdom of N. Europe, united to Norway till 1905.

1855. 48 skilling banco = 1 riksdaler.
1858. 100 ore = 1 riksdaler.
1875. 100 ore = 1 krona.

1 2 3

1855.
1 1 3s. green £5500 £225
2 4s. blue . . . . £1000 44·00
3 6s. grey £6500 £800
4 8s. orange £3500 £400
5 24s. red £5000 £1300

1858.
6b 1 5ore green . . . . £150 12·50
7 9ore purple £375 £170
8a 12ore blue . . . . £170 1·60
9 24ore orange . . . . £400 18·00
10a 30ore brown . . . . £400 20·00
11b 50ore red . . . . £550 65·00

1862.
12c 2 3ore brown . . . . £100 9·25
13 3 17ore purple £600 £100
14 17ore grey £750 £600
15b 20ore red . . . . £190 11·00

4 5 **6** King Oscar II

1872.
29 4 2ore orange . . . . 1·70 3·75
30 3ore brown . . . . 10·50 11·50
31 4ore grey . . . . 27·00 85
32 5ore green . . . . 65·00 45
33a 6ore mauve . . . . 23·00 34·00
20 6ore green . . . . £750 42·00
34 6 10ore pink . . . . 60·00 35
21a 4 12ore blue . . . . 23·00 50
35 20ore red £110 45
23a 24ore yellow . . . . 47·00 16·00
36 30ore brown £190 75
37 50ore red . . . . £150 2·40
26 5 1r. blue and bistre . . . . £750 55·00
38 1k. blue and bistre . . . . 95·00 1·60

No. 26 has the value expressed as one riksdaler and No. 38 one krona.

1889. Surch **10 10 TIO ORE** and Arms.
39 4 10ore on 12ore blue . . . . 2·30 3·25
40 10ore on 24ore yellow . . . 7·75 21·00

9 **10** Oscar II 11

1891.
41 9 1ore blue and brown . . . 1·10 40
42a 2ore yellow and blue . . . 4·00 35
43 3ore orange and brown . . 55 85
44a 4ore blue and red . . . . 6·00 30
45c 10 5ore green . . . . 2·75 15
46 8ore purple . . . . 3·00 85
47 10ore red . . . . 3·75 15
48 15ore brown . . . . 25·00 15
49 20ore blue . . . . 25·00 15
56 25ore orange . . . . 25·00 2·75
51a 30ore brown . . . . 60·00 15
53 50ore grey . . . . 95·00 25
54 11 1k. grey and red . . . . . £150 1·10

13 G.P.O., Stockholm **14** **15** Gustav V

1903. Opening of new Post Office.
57 13 5k. blue . . . . £300 20·00

1910.
65 14 1ore black 15 15
66 2ore orange 15 15
67 3ore brown 15 20
68 4ore mauve 15 15
69 15 5ore green . . . . 1·70 15
70 7ore green 30 15
71 8ore purple 30 25
72 10ore red . . . . 2·20 15
73 12ore purple 30 15
74 15ore brown . . . . 4·75 15

75		20ore blue	7·75	15
76		25ore orange	30	15
77		27ore blue	35	50
78		30ore brown	19·00	15
79		35ore violet	17·00	15
80		40ore green	24·00	15
81		50ore grey	55·00	15
82		55ore blue	£1100	£3250
83		65ore green	60	1·30
84		80ore black	£1100	£3250
85		90ore green	55	40
63		1k. black on yellow	65·00	35
64		5k. purple on yellow	2·00	2·20

1916. Clothing Fund for Mobilized Reservists ("Landstorm"). (a) Postage stamps surch **FRIMARKE LANDSTORMEN** and value in figures and words round Arms.

86a	**4**	5+5 on 2ore orange	3·50	4·75
86b		5+5 on 3ore brown	3·50	4·75
86c		5+5 on 4ore grey	3·50	4·75
86d		5+5 on 5ore green	3·50	4·75
86e		5+5 on 6ore mauve	3·50	4·75
86f		10+10 on 12ore blue	3·50	4·75
86g		10+10 on 20ore red	3·50	4·75
86h		10+10 on 24ore yellow	3·50	4·75
86i		10+10 on 30ore brown	3·50	4·75
86j		10+10 on 50ore red	3·50	4·75

(b) Postage Due stamps surch **FRIMARKE SVERIGE** in frame round Arms, **LANDSTORMEN** and value in figures and words.

86k	**D 6**	5+5 on 1ore black	31·00	6·25
86l		5+5 on 3ore red	6·25	3·50
86m		5+5 on 5ore brown	7·50	4·00
86n		5+10 on 6ore orange	4·50	4·50
86o		5+15 on 12ore red	46·00	17·00
86p		10+20 on 20ore blue	12·50	14·50
86q		10+40 on 24ore mauve	55·00	60·00
86r		10+20 on 30ore green	4·75	4·75
86s		10+40 on 50ore brown	20·00	22·00
86t		10+90 on 1k. blue and brown	£130	£250

(c) No. 57 surch **FRIMARKE ORE 10 ORE FRIMARKE LANDSTORMEN KR. 4,90** and Arms.

86u	**13**	10 ore+4k.90 on 5k. blue	£100	£250

1917. Surch in figures only.

87	**15**	7 on 10ore red	25	20
88		12 on 25ore orange	1·90	25
89		12 on 65ore green	80	75
90		27 on 55ore blue	60	1·10
91		27 on 65ore green	1·20	2·40
92		27 on 80ore black	65	1·10
93		1.98k. on 5k. purple on yell	1·00	3·75
94		2.12k. on 5k. purple on yell	1·40	4·25

1918. Landstorm Fund. Nos. 8ba/j surch.

94a	**4**	7+3 on 5ore on 2ore	7·75	7·50
94b		7+3 on 5ore on 3ore	2·10	1·10
94c		7+3 on 5ore on 4ore	2·10	1·10
94d		7+3 on 5ore on 5ore	2·10	1·10
94e		7+3 on 5ore on 6ore	2·10	1·10
94f		12+8 on 10ore on 12ore	2·10	1·10
94g		12+8 on 10ore on 20ore	2·10	1·10
94h		12+8 on 10ore on 24ore	2·10	1·10
94i		12+8 on 10ore on 30ore	2·10	1·10
94j		12+8 on 10ore on 50ore	2·10	1·10

19 Arms

20 Lion (after sculpture by B. Foucquet)

21 Gustav V

22 Emblem of Swedish Post

1920.

95A	**19**	3ore red	25	25
96Bb	**20**	5ore green	1·00	1·40
97A		5ore brown	5·25	25
98B		10ore green	2·30	50
99A		10ore violet	4·25	25
102a	**21**	10ore red	8·50	6·75
103		15ore purple	30	30
104a		20ore blue	41·00	2·10
100A	**20**	25ore orange	12·00	30
101A		30ore brown	35	25
105A	**22**	35ore yellow	49·00	30
106A		40ore green	36·00	1·10
107A		45ore brown	1·00	45
108A		60ore purple	18·00	20
109A		70ore brown	55	1·80
110A		80ore green	35	25
111A		85ore green	4·00	25
112A		90ore blue	65·00	25
113A		1k. orange	7·00	25
114A		110ore blue	55	20
115A		115ore brown	8·75	25
116A		120ore black	60·00	40
117A		120ore mauve	13·00	40
118A		140ore black	45	20
119A		145ore green	7·50	55

23 Gustavus II Adolphus

24 Gustav V (after portrait by E. Osterman)

25 Gustavus Vasa

1920. Tercentenary of Swedish Post between Stockholm and Hamburg.

120A	**23**	20ore blue	3·25	25

1920. Air. Official stamps surch **LUFTPOST** and value.

120a	**O 17**	10 on 3ore brown	2·25	3·50
120b		20 on 2ore yellow	3·75	5·25
120c		50 on 4ore lilac	15·00	17·00

1921.

121	**24**	15ore violet	18·00	20
122a		15ore red	9·50	25
123		15ore brown	4·25	20
124		20ore violet	30	20
125		20ore red	20·00	25
126		20ore orange	30	40
128		25ore red	65	1·20
129		25ore blue	14·00	20
131		25ore orange	33·00	25
133		30ore brown	22·00	20
134		30ore blue	5·50	25
135		35ore purple	14·50	20
136		40ore blue	35	45
137		40ore green	36·00	60
138		45ore brown	4·00	45
139a		50ore black	1·50	35
140		85ore green	10·50	75
141		115ore brown	11·00	1·10
142		145ore green	7·50	1·00

1921. 400th Anniv of Liberation of Sweden.

143	**25**	20ore violet	8·25	16·00
144		110ore blue	50·00	4·75
145		140ore black	28·00	4·75

26 Old City, Stockholm

27 Gustav V

1924. 8th Congress of U.P.U.

146	**26**	5ore brown	1·70	1·90
147		10ore green	1·80	1·90
148		15ore violet	1·80	1·50
149		20ore red	10·50	8·75
150		25ore orange	15·00	14·50
151		30ore blue	14·50	14·00
152		35ore black	18·00	18·00
153		40ore green	26·00	19·00
154		45ore brown	31·00	27·00
155		50ore grey	27·00	22·00
156		60ore purple	42·00	36·00
157		80ore green	34·00	33·00
158	**27**	1k. green	60·00	65·00
159		2k. red	£150	£170
160		5k. blue	£275	£325

28 Post Rider and Friedrichsafen FF-49 Seaplane

29 Carrier-pigeon

1924. 50th Anniv of U.P.U.

161	**28**	5ore brown	2·75	2·75
162		10ore green	2·75	3·75
163		15ore violet	2·50	1·90
164		20ore red	19·00	19·00
165		25ore orange	25·00	21·00
166		30ore blue	24·00	21·00
167		35ore black	31·00	34·00
168		40ore green	28·00	20·00
169		45ore brown	39·00	25·00
170		50ore grey	46·00	37·00
171		60ore purple	48·00	47·00
172		80ore green	40·00	22·00
173	**29**	1k. green	70·00	60·00
174		2k. red	£150	50·00
175		5k. blue	£275	£160

29a King Gustav V

29c Night Flight by Junkers F-13 (with skis) over Stockholm

1928. 70th Birthday of King Gustav V and Cancer Research Fund.

175a	**29a**	5(+5)ore green	2·20	3·75
175b		10(+5)ore violet	2·20	3·75
175c		15(+5)ore red	2·30	2·75
175d		20(+5)ore orange	3·75	1·90
175e		25(+5)ore blue	3·75	2·30

1930. Air.

175f	**29c**	10ore blue	35	40
175g		50ore violet	90	1·10

30 Royal Palace, Stockholm

31 Death of Gustavus Adolphus at Lutzen

1931.

176	**30**	5k. green	95·00	7·00

1932. Death Tercentenary of Gustavus Adolphus.

177	**31**	10ore violet	1·80	25
178a		15ore red	2·40	55
179		25ore blue	5·25	45
180		90ore green	31·00	1·20

32 Allegory of Thrift

33 Stockholm Cathedral

1933. 50th Anniv of Swedish Postal Savings Bank.

181	**32**	5ore green	2·20	60

1935. 500th Anniv of First Swedish Parliament. Stockholm Buildings.

182a	–	5ore green	3·00	50
183	–	10ore violet	3·50	2·40
184	**33**	15ore red	3·50	20
185	–	25ore blue	7·25	50
186	–	35ore purple	11·50	1·60
187	–	60ore purple	18·00	1·00

DESIGNS: 5ore Old City Hall; 10ore Exchange; 25ore House of the Nobility; 35ore Houses of Parliament; 60ore Arms of Engelbrekt and representatives of the Four Estates.

35 A. Oxenstierna (after D. Dumonstier)

38 Junkers W.34 over Scandinavia

1936. Tercentenary of Swedish Post.

188	**35**	5ore green	1·30	25
189	–	10ore violet	1·60	60
190	–	15ore red	2·50	25
191	–	20ore blue	9·00	3·25
192	–	25ore blue	5·75	35
193	–	30ore brown	19·00	2·10
194	–	35ore mauve	5·50	1·20
195	–	40ore green	6·75	1·60
196	–	45ore green	7·75	1·00
197	–	50ore grey	25·00	1·90
198	–	60ore purple	30·00	50
199	–	1k. blue	8·75	5·25

DESIGNS: 10ore Early courier; 15ore Post rider; 20ore Sailing packet "Hiorten"; 25ore Paddle-steamer "Constitutionen"; 30ore Mail coach; 35ore Arms; 40ore Class F steam locomotive and mail train; 45ore A. W. Roos (Postmaster General 1867–89); 50ore Motor bus and trailer; 60ore Liner "Gripsholm"; 1k. Junkers Ju 52/3m seaplane.

For similar designs, but dated "1972" at foot, see Nos. 700/4.

1936. Inauguration of Bromma Aerodrome.

200	**38**	50ore blue	4·00	5·75

39 E. Swedenborg (after P. Krafft)

40 Governor Printz and Red Indian

1938. 250th Birth Anniv of Swedenborg.

201	**39**	10ore violet	1·40	20
202		100ore green	4·75	1·00

1938. 300th Anniv of Founding of New Sweden, U.S.A.

203	**40**	5ore green	75	30
204	–	15ore brown	90	45
205	–	20ore red	1·50	55
206	–	30ore blue	4·50	60
207	–	60ore purple	7·25	30

DESIGNS: 15ore Emigrant ships "Calmare Nyckel" and "Fagel Grip"; 20ore Swedish landing in America; 30ore First Swedish church, Wilmington; 60ore Queen Christina (after S. Bourdon).

41 King Gustav V

42 King Gustav V

43 Small Arms of Sweden

1938. 80th Birthday of King Gustav V.

208	**41**	5ore green	1·00	25
209		15ore brown	1·00	25
210		30ore blue	13·00	70

1939.

234	**42**	5ore green	35	10
299		5ore orange	10	15
235		10ore violet	10	10
300		10ore green	15	15
236b		15ore brown	35	25
237		20ore red	15	10
238		25ore orange	75	15
301		25ore violet	70	15
239		30ore blue	30	10
240		35ore purple	50	15
241		40ore green	45	10
242		45ore brown	45	10
243		50ore grey	2·40	15
301a	**43**	50ore grey	1·20	20
302		55ore brown	45	15
221		60ore red	95	15
302a		65ore green	45	20
302b		70ore blue	1·70	1·00
302c		75ore brown	1·40	55
303		80ore green	40	15
222		85ore green	40	15
303a		85ore brown	2·75	1·10
223		90ore blue	50	15
224		1k. orange	50	10
303b		1k.05 blue	50	20
304		1k.10 violet	2·75	15
225		1k.15 brown	45	15
226		1k.20 purple	1·80	15
304a		1k.20 blue	1·30	1·50
305		1k.40 green	50	20
227		1k.45 green	2·10	55
305a		1k.50 purple	75	70
305b		1k.50 brown	50	15
305c		1k.70 red	70	15
306		1k.75 blue	6·00	5·50
306a		1k.80 blue	50	40
306b		1k.85 blue	1·00	70
306c		2k. purple	60	15
306ca		2k. mauve	50	15
306d		2k.10 blue	5·25	20
306e		2k.15 green	2·30	30
306f		2k.30 brown	3·50	20
306g		2k.50 green	75	15
306h		2k.55 red	1·70	1·60
306i		2k.80 red	85	20
306j		2k.85 orange	2·30	2·50
306k		3k. blue	85	15

44 P. H. Ling (after J. G. Sandberg)

45 Carl von Linne (Linnaeus) (after A. Roslin)

47 Carl Michael Bellman

1939. Death Centenary of P. H. Ling (creator of "Swedish Drill").

228	**44**	5ore green	30	15
229		25ore brown	90	25

1939. Bicent of Swedish Academy of Sciences.

230a	–	10ore violet	1·70	40
231	**45**	15ore brown	15	20
232	–	30ore blue	8·75	40
233	**45**	50ore grey	11·00	75

PORTRAIT: 10ore, 30ore J. J. Berzelius (after O. J. Sodermark).

1940. Birth Bicent of C. M. Bellman (poet).

244	**47**	5ore green	15	20
245		35ore red	55	40

48 Johan Tobias Sergel (self-portrait bust)

49 Reformers presenting Bible to Gustavus Vasa

1940. Birth Bicent of J. T. Sergel (sculptor).

246a	**48**	15ore brown	3·25	30
247		50ore grey	14·50	85

1941. 400th Anniv of First Authorized Version of Bible in Swedish.

248	**49**	15ore brown	15	20
249		90ore blue	16·00	70

50 Hasjo Belfry

50a Royal Palace, Stockholm

1941. 50th Anniv of Foundation of Skansen Open-air Museum.
250a **50** 10ore violet . . . . . . 1·80 35
251 60ore purple . . . . . . 7·25 30

1941.
252 **50a** 5k. blue . . . . 1·40 20

51 A. Hazelius

52 St. Bridget (from altar painting, Vasteras Cathedral)

1941. Artur Hazelius (founder of Skansen Museum).
253 **51** 5ore green 40 20
254 1k. orange . . . . 5·75 2·00

1941. 550th Anniv of Canonization of St. Bridget (Foundress of Brigittine Order of Our Saviour).
255 **52** 15ore brown 20 20
256 120ore purple . . . . . . 20·00 8·50

53 Mute Swans

54 King Gustavus III (after A. Roslin)

1942.
257a **53** 20k. blue . . . . 3·25 30

1942. 150th Anniv of National Museum, Stockholm.
258 **54** 20ore red 75 15
259 – 40ore green . . . . 16·00 75
PORTRAIT: 40ore Carl Gustaf Tessin (architect and chancery president) (after Gustav Lundberg).

55 Count Rudenschold and Nils Mansson

56 Carl Wilhelm Scheele

1942. Centenary of Institution of National Elementary Education.
260a **55** 10ore red 20 25
261 90ore blue . . . . 2·30 3·75

1942. Birth Bicent of C. W. Scheele (chemist).
262 **56** 5ore green 15 15
263 60ore red . . . . 5·75 30

57 King Gustav V

58 Rifle Assn Badge

1943. 85th Birthday of King Gustav V.
264 **57** 20ore red 50 30
265 30ore blue . . . . 90 1·80
266 60ore purple . . . . 1·10 2·10

1943. 50th Anniv of National Voluntary Rifle Association.
267 **58** 10ore purple 15 10
268 90ore blue . . . . 3·00 30

59 O. Montelius (after E. Stenberg)

60 First Swedish Navigators' Chart

1943. Birth Centenary of Oscar Montelius (archaeologist).
269 **59** 5ore green 15 15
270 120ore purple . . . . . . 5·25 1·70

1944. Tercent of First Swedish Marine Chart.
271 **60** 5ore green 20 15
272 60ore red . . . . 3·25 35

61 "Smalands Lejon" (ship of the line)

1944. Swedish Fleet (Tercentenary of Battle of Femern).
273 **61** 10ore violet 20 30
274 – 20ore red 35 15
275 – 30ore blue 45 65
276 – 40ore green 85 95
277 – 90ore grey . . . . 7·00 1·50
DESIGNS—27 × 22½ mm: 30ore "Kung Karl" (ship of the line); 40ore Stern of "Amphion" (royal yacht); 90ore "Gustav V" (cruiser). 18¾ × 20½ mm: 20ore Admiral C. Fleming (after L. Pasch).
See also Nos. 517/22.

62 Red Cross

63 Press Symbols

1945. 80th Anniv of Swedish Red Cross and Birthday of Prince Carl.
278 **62** 20ore red 50 15

1945. Tercentenary of Swedish Press.
279 **63** 5ore green 25 15
280 60ore red . . . . 3·75 25

64 Viktor Rydberg (after A. Edelfelt)

65 Oak Tree, Savings Banks' Symbol

1945. 50th Death Anniv of Viktor Rydberg (author).
281 **64** 20ore red 25 15
282 90ore blue . . . . 3·75 25

1945. 125th Anniv of Swedish Savings Banks.
283 **65** 10ore violet 25 20
284 40ore green 85 75

66 Cathedral Model

67 Lund Cathedral

1946. 800th Anniv of Lund Cathedral.
285 **66** 15ore brown 55 25
286 **67** 20ore red 25 15
287 **66** 90ore blue . . . . 6·25 50

68 Mare and Foal

69 Tegner (after bust by J. N. Bystrom)

70 A. Nobel

1946. Centenary of Swedish Agricultural Show.
288 **68** 5ore green 25 15
289 60ore red . . . . 3·25 20

1946. Death Centenary of Esaias Tegner (poet).
290 **69** 10ore violet 25 15
291 40ore green . . . . 1·00 40

1946. 50th Death Anniv of Alfred Nobel (scientist and creator of Nobel Foundation).
292 **70** 20ore red 55 15
293 30ore blue . . . . 1·50 35

71 E. G. Geijer (after J. G. Sandberg)

72 King Gustav V

73 Ploughman and Skyscraper

1947. Death Centenary of Erik Gustav Geijer (historian, philosopher, poet and composer).
294 **71** 5ore green 25 15
295 90ore blue . . . . 3·00 20

1947. Forty Years Reign of King Gustav V.
296 **72** 10ore violet 25 20
297 20ore red 25 20
298 60ore purple . . . . 85 1·10

1948. Centenary of Swedish Pioneers in U.S.A.
307 **73** 15ore brown 25 15
308 30ore blue 30 40
309 1k. orange . . . . 1·00 70

73a King Gustav V

74 J. A. Strindberg (after R. Bergh)

75 Gymnasts

1948. King Gustav V's 90th Birthday, and Youth Fund.
309a **73a** 10ore+10ore green . . . 40 45
309b 20ore+10ore red 40 60
309c 30ore+10ore blue . . . 30 50

1949. Birth Centenary of Strindberg (dramatist).
310 **74** 20ore red 25 15
311 30ore blue 55 55
312 80ore green . . . . 2·10 40

1949. 2nd Lingiad, Stockholm.
313 **75** 5ore blue 25 25
314 15ore brown 25 20

76 Globe and Hand Writing

77

1949. 75th Anniv of U.P.U.
315 **76** 10ore green 25 20
316 20ore red 25 20
317 **77** 30ore blue 25 40

78 King Gustav VI Adolf

79 Christopher Polhem (after G. E. Schroder)

80

1951. (a) Coloured lettering and figures.
318 **78** 10ore green 15 15
318b 10ore brown 10 15
319 15ore brown 15 25
388 15ore red 15 15
320 20ore red 15 20
391 20ore black 30 15
322a 25ore black 40 30
323 25ore red 85 20
324a 25ore blue 15 15
392 25ore brown 55 25
393 30ore blue 30 15
326 30ore brown 30 30
326a 30ore red . . . . 3·75 20
327 40ore blue 35 20
328 40ore green 40 25

(b) White lettering and figures.
429 **78** 15ore red 15 15
430 20ore black 20 15
431a 25ore brown 15 15
432a 30ore blue 50 15
433 30ore violet 35 15
433b 30ore red 50 70
434 35ore violet 50 15
435a 35ore blue 35 15
436 35ore black 50 20
437 40ore green 35 15
438a 40ore blue 20 15
439a 45ore orange 50 15
439b 45ore blue 50 15
440 50ore green 40 20
440a 50ore green 25 20
440c 55ore red 35 15
441 60ore red 40 50
441a 65ore blue 60 15
441c 70ore mauve 50 15
441d 85ore purple 60 25

1951. Death Bicentenary of Polhem (engineer).
329a **79** 25ore black 30 30
330 45ore brown 25 30

1951.
383 **80** 5ore red 20 15
386 10ore blue 10 15
387a 10ore brown 10 20
389 15ore green 10 20
390a 15ore brown 15 40

81 Olavus Petri Preaching

81a King Gustav VI Adolf

1952. 400th Death Anniv of Petri (reformer).
332 **81** 25ore black 15 25
333 1k.40 brown . . . . 1·70 45

1952. 70th Birthday of King Gustav VI Adolf and Culture Fund.
333a **81a** 10ore+10ore green . . 15 30
333ba 25ore+10ore red . . . 15 40
333c 40ore+10ore blue . . . 20 35

82 Ski Jumping

83 Stockholm, 1650

1953. 50th Anniv of Swedish Athletic Assn.
334 **82** 10ore green 25 20
335 – 15ore brown 25 45
336 – 40ore blue . . . . 85 1·00
337 – 1k.40 mauve . . . . . . 2·75 70
DESIGNS—HORIZ: 1k.40, Wrestling. VERT: 15ore Ice hockey; 40ore Slingball.

1953. 700th Anniv of Stockholm.
338 **83** 25ore blue 15 15
339 – 1k.70 red . . . . 1·60 45
DESIGN: 1k.70, Seal of Stockholm, 1296 (obverse and reverse).

84 "Radio"

85 Skier

1953. Cent of Telecommunications in Sweden.
340 – 25ore blue ("Telephones") 15 20
341 **84** 40ore green . . . . 80 1·00
342 – 60ore red ("Telegraphs") 1·70 1·80

1954. World Skiing Championships.
343 **85** 20ore grey 20 25
344 – 1k. blue (Woman skier) . . 4·25 90

86 Anna Maria Lenngren (after medallion, J. T. Sergel)

87 Rock-carvings

88

1954. Birth Bicentenary of Anna Maria Lenngren (poetess).
345 **86** 20ore grey 15 20
346 65ore brown . . . . 2·30 1·80

1954.
347 **87** 50ore grey 15 15
348 55ore red 65 20
349 60ore red 20 15
350 65ore green 90 15
351 70ore orange 35 15
352 75ore brown . . . . 1·50 20
353 80ore green 35 15
355 90ore blue 35 15
356 95ore violet . . . . 1·80 2·10

1955. Centenary of First Swedish Postage Stamps.
362 **88** 25ore blue 15 15
363 40ore green 85 25

89 Swedish Flag

91 P. D. A. Atterbom (after Fogelberg)

1955. National Flag Day.
364 **89** 10ore yellow, blue & green 15 15
365 15ore yellow, blue and red 20 25

1955. Cent of First Swedish Postage Stamps and "Stockholmia" Philatelic Exn. As T **1** but with two rules through bottom panel.

366 **1** 3ore green . . . . 1·20 3·50
367 4ore blue . . . . 1·20 3·50
368 6ore grey . . . . 1·20 3·50
369 8ore yellow . . . . 1·20 3·50
370 24ore orange . . . . 1·20 3·50

Nos. 366/70 were sold only at the exhibition in single sets, at 2k.45 (45ore face + 2k. entrance fee).

1955. Death Centenary of Atterbom (poet).

371 **91** 20ore blue 15 20
372 1k.40 brown . . . . 2·00 40

92 Greek Horseman, (from Parthenon frieze)
92a Whooper Swans

1956. 16th Olympic Games Equestrian Competitions, Stockholm.

373 **92** 20ore red 20 20
374 25ore blue 20 15
375 40ore green . . . . 1·60 1·40

1956. Northern Countries' Day.

376 **92a** 25ore red 15 20
377 40ore blue 40 45

93 Railway Construction
94 Trawler in Distress and Lifeboat

1956. Centenary of Swedish Railways.

378 **93** 10ore green 35 20
379 – 25ore blue 20 20
380 – 40ore orange . . . . . . 1·80 2·20

DESIGNS: 25ore Steam locomotive, "Fryckstad" and passenger carriage; 40ore Type XOa5 electric train on Arsta Bridge, Stockholm.

1957. 50th Anniv of Swedish Life Saving Service.

381 **94** 30ore blue . . . . 1·60 20
382 1k.40 red . . . . 2·75 1·00

95 Galleon and "Gripsholm II"
96 Bell 47G Helicopter with Floats

1958. Postal Services Commemoration.

395 **95** 15ore red 15 20
396 **96** 30ore blue 15 20
397 **95** 40ore green . . . . 2·30 2·10
398 **96** 1k.40 brown . . . . 2·40 80

97 Footballer
98 Bessemer Tilting-furnace

1958. World Cup Football Championship.

399 **97** 15ore red 40 20
400 20ore green 30 20
401 1k.20 blue . . . . 1·10 55

1958. Centenary of Swedish Steel Industry.

402 **98** 30ore blue 15 20
403 170ore brown . . . . . . 2·75 60

99 Selma Lagerlof (after bust by G. Malmquist)
100 Overhead Power Lines

1958. Birth Centenary of Selma Lagerlof (writer).

404 **99** 20ore red 15 20
405 30ore blue 15 20
406 80ore green 55 70

1959. 50th Anniv of Swedish State Power Board.

407 **100** 30ore blue 20 20
408 – 90ore red . . . . 2·40 1·80

DESIGN—HORIZ: 90ore Dam sluice-gates.

101 Henri Dunant (founder)
102 Heidenstam

1959. Red Cross Centenary.

409 **101** 30ore+10ore red 40 45

1959. Birth Centenary of Verner von Heidenstam (poet).

410 **102** 15ore red 55 20
411 1k. black . . . . 2·00 60

103 Forest Trees
104 S. Arrhenius

1959. Centenary of Crown Lands and Forests Administration.

412 **103** 30ore green 90 20
413 – 1k.40 red . . . . 2·30 45

DESIGN: 1k.40, Forester felling tree.

1959. Birth Centenary of Arrhenius (chemist).

414 **104** 15ore brown 15 20
415 1k.70 blue . . . . 2·30 30

105 Anders Zorn (self-portrait)
106 "Uprooted Tree"

1960. Birth Cent of Zorn (painter and etcher).

416 **105** 30ore grey 15 20
417 80ore brown . . . . . . 2·10 1·20

1960. World Refugee Year.

418 **106** 20ore brown 15 20
419 – 40ore violet 20 20

DESIGN—VERT: 40ore Refugees.

107 Target-shooting
108 G. Froding

1960. Centenary of Voluntary Shooting Organization.

420 **107** 15ore red 15 20
421 – 90ore blue . . . . 2·10 1·10

DESIGN: 90ore Organization members marching, 1860.

1960. Birth Centenary of Gustav Froding (poet).

422 **108** 30ore brown 15 20
423 1k.40 green . . . . 1·80 25

1960. Europa. As T **144a** of Switzerland.

424 40ore blue 30 30
425 1k. red 25 30

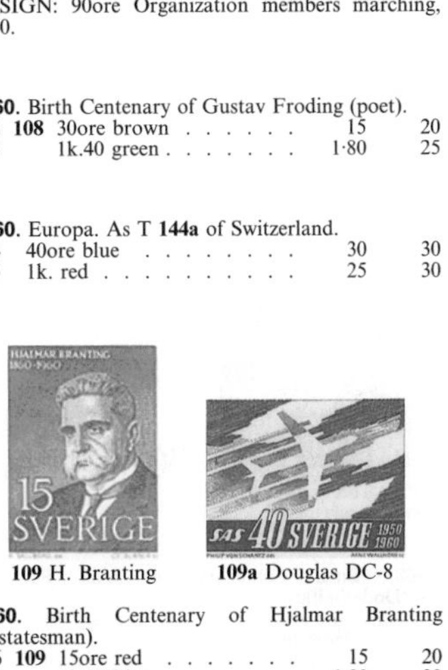

109 H. Branting
109a Douglas DC-8

1960. Birth Centenary of Hjalmar Branting (statesman).

426 **109** 15ore red 15 20
427 1k.70 blue . . . . 1·90 30

1961. 10th Anniv of Scandinavian Airlines System.

428 **109a** 40ore blue 20 20

111 "Coronation of Gustav III" (after Pilo)

1961. 250th Birth Anniv of Carl Gustav Pilo (painter).

442 **111** 30ore brown 15 20
443 1k.40 blue . . . . 2·30 75

112 J. Alstromer (after bust by P. H. l'Archeveque)

113 Printing Works and Library

1961. Death Bicentenary of Jonas Alstromer (industrial reformer).

444 **112** 15ore purple 15 20
445 90ore blue . . . . 1·00 1·20

1961. Tercentenary of Royal Library Regulation.

446 **113** 20ore red 15 20
447 1k. blue . . . . 3·00 60

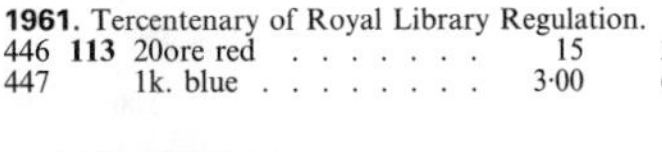

114 Motif on Runic Stone at Oland

115 Nobel Prize Winners of 1901

1961.

448 **114** 10k. purple . . . . 13·50 50

1961. Nobel Prize Winners of 1901.

449 **115** 20ore red 15 20
450 40ore blue 15 20
451 50ore green 15 20

See also Nos. 458/9, 471/2, 477/8, 488/9, 523/4, 546/7 and 573/4.

116 Postman's Footprints

117 Code, Voting Instrument and Mallet

1962. Cent of Swedish Local Mail Delivery Service.

452 **116** 30ore violet 15 20
453 1k.70 red . . . . 2·20 30

1962. Centenary of Municipal Laws.

454 **117** 30ore blue 15 20
455 2k. red . . . . 2·30 20

118 St. George and Dragon, Storkyrkan ("Great Church"), Stockholm

119 Ice Hockey Player

118a King Gustav VI Adolf and Cultural Themes

1962. Swedish Monuments (1st series).

456 **118** 20ore purple 15 20
457 – 50ore green 20 20

DESIGN—HORIZ: 50ore Skokloster Castle.

See also Nos. 469/70 and 479/80.

1962. King Gustav's 80th Birthday and Swedish Culture Fund.

457b **118a** 20ore+10ore brown . . 20 25
457c 35ore+10ore blue . . . 20 25

1962. Nobel Prize Winners of 1902. As T **115** but inscr "NOBELPRIS 1902".

458 25ore red 20 20
459 50ore blue 25 20

PORTRAITS: 25ore Theodor Mommsen (literature) and Sir Ronald Ross (medicine); 50ore Emil Hermann Fischer (chemistry) and Pieter Zeeman and Hendrik Lorentz (physics).

1963. World Ice Hockey Championships.

460 **119** 25ore green 15 20
461 1k.70 blue . . . . 2·00 30

120 Hands reaching for Wheat

121 Engineering and Industrial Symbols

1963. Freedom from Hunger.

462 **120** 35ore mauve 15 20
463 50ore violet 20 20

1963. "Engineering and Industry".

464 **121** 50ore black 20 20
465 1k.05 orange . . . . . . 1·60 2·00

122 Dr. G. F. Du Rietz (after D. K. Ehrenstrahl)

123 Linne's Hammarby (country house)

1963. 300th Anniv of Swedish Board of Health.

466 **122** 25ore brown 20 25
467 35ore blue 20 20
468 2k. red . . . . 2·20 40

1963. Swedish Monuments (2nd series).

469 **123** 20ore red 15 20
470 50ore green 20 20

1963. Nobel Prize Winners of 1903. As T **115** but inscr "NOBELPRIS 1903".

471 25ore green 40 45
472 50ore brown 30 15

PORTRAITS: 25ore Svante Arrhenius (chemistry), Niels Ryberg Finsen (medicine) and Bjornstjerne Bjornson (literature); 50ore Antoine Henri Becquerel and Pierre and Marie Curie (physics).

124 Motif from Poem "Elie Himmelsfard"

125 Seal of Archbishop Stefan

1964. Birth Centenary of E. A. Karlfeldt (poet).

473 **124** 35ore blue 25 15
474 1k.05 red . . . . 2·10 2·75

1964. 800th Anniv of Archbishopric of Uppsala.

475 **125** 40ore green 10 15
476a 60ore brown 20 25

1964. Nobel Prize Winners of 1904. As T **115** but inscr "NOBELPRIS 1904".

477 30ore blue 20 20
478 40ore red 55 20

PORTRAITS: 30ore Jose Echegaray y Eizaguirre and Frederic Mistral (literature) and J. W. Strutt (Lord Rayleigh) (physics); 40ore Sir William Ramsay (chemistry) and Ivan Petrovich Pavlov (medicine).

126 Visby Town Wall

127 Posthorns

128 Telecommunications

1965. Swedish Monuments (3rd series).

479 **126** 30ore mauve 15 20
480 2k. blue . . . . 2·10 20

1965.

481 **127** 20ore blue and yellow . . 15 15

1965. Centenary of I.T.U.

482 **128** 60ore violet 20 20
483 1k.40 blue . . . . 1·50 75

129 Prince Eugen (after D. Tagtstrom) **130** F. Bremer (after O. J. Sodermark)

1965. Birth Centenary of Prince Eugen (painter).
484 **129** 40ore black 15 15
485 1k. brown . . . . 2·20 25

1965. Death Centenary of Fredrika Bremer (novelist).
486 **130** 25ore violet 10 20
487 3k. green . . . . 2·50 25

1965. Nobel Prize Winners of 1905. As T **115** but inscr "NOBELPRIS 1905".
488 30ore blue 20 20
489 40ore red 25 20
PORTRAITS: 30ore Philipp von Lenard (physics) and Johann von Baeyer (chemistry); 40ore Robert Koch (medicine) and Henryk Sienkiewicz (literature).

131 N. Soderblom **132** Skating

1966. Birth Centenary of Nathan Soderblom, Archbishop of Uppsala.
490 **131** 60ore brown 20 20
491 80ore green 65 20

1966. World Men's Speed Skating Championships, Gothenburg.
492 **132** 5ore red 10 20
493 25ore green 25 30
494 40ore blue 35 50

133 Entrance Hall, National Museum **134** Ale's Stones, Ship Grave, Kaseberga

1966. Centenary of Opening of National Museum Building.
495 **133** 30ore violet 15 20
496 2k.30 green 70 80

1966.
498 – 35ore brown and blue . . 15 15
499 **134** 3k.50 grey 90 15
500 – 3k.70 violet . . . . . . 1·00 15
501 – 4k.50 red . . . . 1·30 20
502 – 7k. red and blue . . . . 1·90 30
DESIGNS—HORIZ: 35ore Fjeld (mountains); 7k. Gripsholm Castle. VERT: 3k.70, Lion Fortress, Gothenburg; 4k.50, Uppsala Cathedral (interior).

135 Louis de Geer (advocate of reform)

1966. Cent of Representative Assembly Reform.
510 **135** 40ore blue 15 20
511 3k. red . . . . 2·75 45

136 Theatre Stage **137** Almqvist (after C. P. Mazer)

1966. Bicentenary of Drottningholm Theatre.
512 **136** 5ore red on pink 10 15
513 25ore bistre on pink . . . 10 15
514 40ore purple on pink . . 30 45

1966. Death Centenary of Carl Almqvist (writer).
515 **137** 25ore mauve 15 20
516 1k. green . . . . 1·60 80

1966. National Cancer Fund. Swedish Ships. Designs as T **61**, but with imprint "1966" at foot.
517 10ore red 15 30
518 15ore red 15 30
519 20ore green 15 30
520 25ore blue 15 25
521 30ore red 15 30
522 40ore red 15 30
SHIPS—HORIZ: 10ore "Smalands Lejon"; 15ore "Calmare Nyckel" and "Fagel Grip"; 20ore "Hiorten"; 25ore "Constitutionen"; 30ore "Kung Karl"; 40ore Stern of "Amphion".

1966. Nobel Prize Winners of 1906. As T **115** but inscr "NOBELPRIS 1906".
523 30ore red 20 20
524 40ore green 30 20
PORTRAITS: 30ore Sir Joseph John Thomson (physics) and Giosue Carducci (literature); 40ore Henri Moissan (chemistry) and Camillo Golgi and Santiago Ramon y Cajal (medicine).

138 Handball **139** "E.F.T.A."

1967. World Handball Championships.
525 **138** 45ore blue 15 20
526 2k.70 mauve . . . . . . 2·00 1·00

1967. European Free Trade Assn (E.F.T.A.).
527 **139** 70ore orange 20 20

140 Table Tennis Player **141** Axeman and Beast

1967. World Table Tennis Championships, Stockholm.
528 **140** 35ore mauve 15 20
529 90ore blue 85 40

1967. Iron Age Helmet Decorations, Oland.
530 **141** 10ore blue and brown . . 10 20
531 – 15ore brown and blue . . 15 20
532 – 30ore mauve and brown 15 20
533 – 35ore brown and mauve 15 25
DESIGNS: 15ore Man between two bears; 30ore "Lion man" putting enemy to flight; 35ore Two warriors.

142 "Solidarity" **144** 18th-century Post-rider

143 "Keep to the Right"

1967. Finnish Settlers in Sweden.
534 **142** 10ore multicoloured . . . 10 15
535 35ore multicoloured . . . 15 20

1967. Adoption of Changed Rule of the Road.
536 **143** 35ore black, yellow & blue 15 20
537 45ore black, yellow & grn 15 15

1967.
538 **144** 5ore black and red . . . 10 10
539 – 10ore black and blue . . 10 10
539b – 20ore black on flesh . . 15 15
540 – 30ore red and blue . . . 15 15
541 – 40ore blue, green & black 15 20
541b – 45ore black and blue . . 15 15
542 – 90ore brown and blue 25 15
543 – 1k. green 25 15
DESIGNS—As T **144**. VERT: 10ore "Svent Skepp" (warship); 20ore "St. Stephen" (ceiling painting, Dadesjo Church, Smaland); 30ore Angelica plant on coast. HORIZ: 40ore Haverud Aqueduct, Dalsland Canal. 27½ × 22½ mm: 45ore Floating logs; 90ore Elk; 1k. Dancing cranes.

145 King Gustav VI Adolf **146** Berwald, Violin and Music

1967. 85th Birthday of King Gustav VI Adolf.
544 **145** 45ore blue 15 20
545 70ore green 20 20

1967. Nobel Prize Winners 1907. As T **115**, but inscr "NOBELPRIS 1907".
546 35ore red 45 40
547 45ore blue 20 20
PORTRAITS: 35ore Eduard Buchner (chemistry) and Albert Abraham Michelson (physics); 45ore Charles Louis Alphonse Laveran (medicine) and Rudyard Kipling (literature).

1968. Death Centenary of Franz Berwald (composer).
548 **146** 35ore black and red . . . 20 20
549 2k. black, blue and yellow 2·20 40

147 Bank Seal **148** Butterfly Orchids

1968. 300th Anniv of Bank of Sweden.
550 **147** 45ore blue 15 20
551 70ore black on orange . . 20 20

1968. Wild Flowers.
552 **148** 45ore green 80 30
553 – 45ore green 80 30
554 – 45ore red and green . . . 80 30
555 – 45ore green 80 30
556 – 45ore green 80 30
DESIGNS: No. 553, Wood anemone; 554, Wild rose; 555, Wild cherry; 556, Lily of the valley.

149 University Seal **150** Ecumenical Emblem

1968. 300th Anniv of Lund University.
557 **149** 10ore blue 10 20
558 35ore red 25 35

1968. 4th General Assembly of World Council of Churches, Uppsala.
559 **150** 70ore purple 20 25
560 90ore blue 60 20

151 "The Universe" **152** "Orienteer" crossing Forest

1968. Centenary of the People's College.
561 **151** 45ore red 15 20
562 2k. blue . . . . 2·00 30

1968. World Orienteering Championships, Linkoping.
563 **152** 40ore red and violet . . . 20 20
564 2k.80 violet and green . . 1·50 1·60

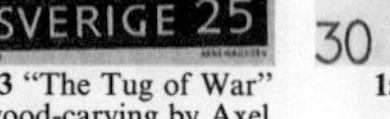

153 "The Tug of War" (wood-carving by Axel Petersson) **154** Red Fox

1968. Birth Centenary of Axel Petersson ("Doderhultarn").
565 **153** 5ore green 10 15
566 25ore brown 35 80
567 45ore brown and sepia . . 10 15

1968. Bruno Liljefors' Fauna Sketches.
568 – 30ore blue 60 50
569 – 30ore black 60 50
570 **154** 30ore brown 60 35
571 – 30ore brown 60 50
572 – 30ore blue 60 50
DESIGNS: No. 568, Arctic hare; 569, Greater black-backed gull; 571, Golden eagle and carrion crows; 572, Stoat.

1968. Nobel Prize Winner of 1908. As T **115**, but inscr "NOBELPRIS 1908".
573 35ore red 30 30
574 45ore green 25 20
PORTRAITS: 35ore Ilya Mechnikov and Paul Ehrlich (medicine) and Lord Rutherford (chemistry); 45ore Gabriel Lippman (physics) and Rudolf Eucken (literature).

154a Viking Ships **155** "The Worker" (A. Amelin)

1969. 50th Anniv of Northern Countries Union.
575 **154a** 45ore brown 20 20
576 70ore blue 75 75

1969. 50th Anniv of I.L.O.
577 **155** 55ore red 15 20
578 70ore blue 50 35

156 Colonnade **157** A. Engstrom with Eagle Owl (self-portrait)

1969. Europa.
579 **156** 70ore multicoloured . . . 95 40
580 1k. multicoloured 95 25

1969. Birth Centenary of Albert Engstrom (painter and writer).
581 **157** 35ore black 15 20
582 55ore blue 20 20

158 "Still Life"

1969. Birth Centenary of Ivan Agueli (painter) Sheet 135 × 90 mm containing multicoloured designs as T **158**.
MS583 45ore "Landscape" (35 × 28 mm); 45ore Type **158**; 45ore "Arab town" (35 × 28 mm); 55ore "Egyptian Girl" (28 × 43 mm); 55ore "Street Scene" (48 × 43 mm); 55ore "Landscape" (28 × 43 mm) (sold at 3k.) . . . . 1·25 1·25

159 Tjorn Bridges **160** Helmeted Figure (carving)

1969. Tjorn Bridges.
584 **159** 15ore blue on blue . . . 70 40
585 – 30ore green and black on blue 70 40
586 – 55ore black and blue on blue 70 35
DESIGNS—As T **159**: 30ore Tjorn Bridges (different). 41 × 19 mm: 55ore Tjorn Bridges (different).

1969. Warship "Wasa" Commemoration.
587 **160** 55ore red 40 35
588 – 55ore brown 40 35
589 – 55ore blue 40 45
590 – 55ore brown 40 35
591 – 55ore red 40 35
592 – 55ore blue 40 45
DESIGNS—As T **160**: No. 588, Crowned lion's head (carving); 590, Lion's head (carving); 591, Carved support. 46 × 28 mm: No. 589, Ship's coat-of-arms; 592, Ship of the line "Wasa", 1628.

161 H. Soderberg (writer)

163 "The Adventures of Nils" by S. Lagerlof (illus by J. Bauer)

162 Lighthouses and Lightship "Cyklop"

1969. Birth Centenaries of Hjalmar Soderberg and Bo Bergman.
593 **161** 45ore brown on cream . . 15 20
594 – 55ore green on green . . 20 20
DESIGN—HORIZ: 55ore Bo Bergman (poet).

1969. 300th Anniv of Swedish Lighthouse Service.
595 **162** 30ore black, red and grey 15 20
596 55ore black, orange & blue 15 20

1969. Swedish Fairy Tales.
597 – 35ore brown, red & orange . . . . 1·30 1·20
598 **163** 35ore brown . . . . . . 1·30 1·20
599 – 35ore brown, red & orange . . . . 1·30 1·20
600 – 35ore brown . . . . . . 1·30 1·20
601 – 35ore red and orange . . 1·30 1·20
DESIGNS: No. 597, "Pelle's New Suit" written and illus by Elsa Beskow; 599, "Pippi Longstocking" by A. Lindgren (illus by I. Vang Nyman); 600, "Vill-Vallareman, the Shepherd" (from "With Pucks and Elves" illus by J. Bauer); 601, "The Cat's Journey" written and illus by I. Arosenius.

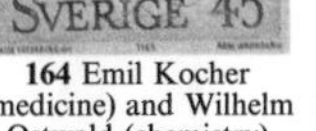

164 Emil Kocher (medicine) and Wilhelm Ostwald (chemistry)

165 Weathervane, Soderala Church

1969. Nobel Prize Winners of 1909.
602 **164** 45ore green 45 30
603 – 55ore black on flesh . . . 35 20
604 – 70ore black 45 50
DESIGNS: 55ore Selma Lagerlof (literature); 70ore Guglielmo Marconi and Ferdinand Braun (physics).

1970. Swedish Forgings.
605 **165** 5ore green and brown . . 30 25
606 – 10 green and brown . . . 30 25
607 – 30 ore black and green . . 30 25
608 – 55 ore brown and green 30 25
DESIGNS—As T **165**: 10ore As Type **165**, but design and country name/figures of value in reverse order; 30ore Memorial Cross, Eksharad Churchyard. 24 × 44 mm: 55ore 14th-century door, Bjorksta Church.

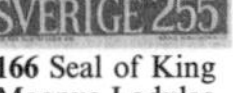

166 Seal of King Magnus Ladulas

167 River Ljungan

1970.
609 **166** 2k.55 blue on cream . . 65 45
610a – 3k. blue on cream . . . 80 15
611a – 5k. green on cream . . . 1·20 15
DESIGNS: 3k. Seal of Duke Erik Magnusson; 5k. Great Seal of Erik IX.

1970. Nature Conservation Year.
612 **167** 55ore multicoloured . . . 20 15
613 70ore multicoloured . . . 45 45

168 View of Kiruna

1970. Sweden within the Arctic Circle.
614 **168** 45ore brown 40 50
615 – 45ore blue 40 50
616 – 45ore green 40 50
617 – 45ore brown 40 50
618 – 45ore blue 40 50
DESIGNS: No. 615, Winter landscape and skiers; 616, Lake and Lapp hut, Stora National Park; 617, Reindeer herd; 618, Rocket-launching.

170 Chinese Palace, Drottningholm

171 Lumber Trucks

1970. Historic Buildings.
619 – 55ore green 15 15
620 **170** 2k. multicoloured . . . . 1·00 15
DESIGN—21 × 27½ mm: 55ore Glimmingehus (15th-century castle).

1970. Swedish Trade and Industry.
621 **171** 70ore brown and blue 1·30 1·70
622 – 70ore blue, brown & pur 1·30 1·70
623 – 70ore purple and blue 1·30 1·70
624 – 70ore blue and purple 1·30 1·70
625 – 70ore blue and purple 1·30 1·50
626 – 70ore brown and purple 1·30 1·70
627a – 1k. black on cream . . . 35 20
DESIGNS—As Type **171**: No. 623, Ship's propeller; 624, Dam and Class Dm3 electric locomotive; 626, Technician and machinery. 44 × 20 mm: No. 622, Loading freighter at quayside; 625, Mine and electric ore train. 26 × 20 mm: No. 627a, Miners at coal face.

173 Three Hearts

1970. 25th Anniv of United Nations.
628 **173** 55ore red, yellow and black 20 20
629 – 70ore green, yellow & blk 25 35
DESIGN: 70ore Three four-leaved clovers.

174 Blackbird

175 Paul Heyse (literature)

1970. Christmas. Birds. Multicoloured.
630 30ore Type **174** 70 70
631 30ore Great tit 70 70
632 30ore Northern bullfinch . . 70 70
633 30ore Western greenfinch . . 70 70
634 30ore Blue tit 70 70

1970. Nobel Prize Winners of 1910.
635 **175** 45ore violet 65 40
636 – 55ore blue 50 20
637 – 70ore black 70 75
PORTRAITS: 55ore Otto Wallach (chemistry) and Johannes van der Waals (physics); 70ore Albrecht Kossel (medicine).

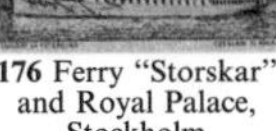
176 Ferry "Storskar" and Royal Palace, Stockholm

178 Kerstin Hesselgren (suffragette)

1971.
638 **176** 80ore black and blue . . 35 15
639 – 4k. black . . . . 1·00 20
639a – 6k. blue . . . . 1·50 20
DESIGN: 4k. 16th-century "Blood Money" coins; 6k. Gustav Vasa's dollar.

1971. 50th Anniv of Swedish Women's Suffrage.
640 **178** 45ore violet on green . . 15 20
641 1k. brown on yellow . . . 45 20

179 Arctic Terns

180 "The Prodigal Son" (painting, Sodra Rada Church)

1971. Nordic Help for Refugees Campaign.
642 **179** 40ore red 40 20
643 55ore blue 40 20

1971.
644 **180** 15ore green on green . . 10 20
645 – 25ore blue and brown . . 15 20
646 – 25ore blue and brown . . 15 20
DESIGNS—HORIZ (Panels from Grodinge Tapestry, Swedish Natural History Museum): No. 645, Griffin; 646, Lion.

182 Container Port, Gothenburg

1971.
647 **182** 55ore violet and blue . . 20 20
648 – 60ore brown on cream . . 25 25
649 – 75ore green on green . . 20 15
DESIGNS—28 × 23 mm: 60ore Timber-sledge; 75ore Windmills, Oland.

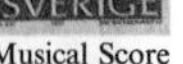

184 Musical Score

186 "The Three Wise Men"

185 "The Mail Coach" (E. Schwab)

1971. Bicent of Swedish Royal Academy of Music.
650 **184** 55ore purple 20 20
651 85ore green 25 20

1971.
652 **185** 1k.20 multicoloured . . . 45 15

1971. Gotland Stone-masons' Art.
653 **186** 5ore violet and brown . . 25 25
654 – 10ore violet and green . . 25 25
655 – 55ore green and brown 25 20
656 – 65ore brown and violet 25 20
DESIGNS—As T **186**: 10ore "Adam and Eve". 40 × 21 mm: 55ore "Winged Knight" and "Samson and the Lion"; 65ore "The Flight into Egypt".

187 Child beside Lorry Wheel

188 State Sword of Gustavus Vasa, c. 1500

1971. Road Safety.
657 **187** 35ore black and red . . . 15 20
658 65ore blue and red . . . 30 20

1971. Swedish Crown Regalia. Multicoloured.
659 65ore Type **188** 45 25
660 65ore Sceptre of Erik XIV, 1561 . . . . 45 25
661 65ore Crown of Erik XIV, 1561 . . . . 45 25
662 65ore Orb of Erik XIV, 1561 45 25
663 65ore Anointing horn of Karl IX, 1606 . . . . 45 25

189 Santa Claus and Gifts

190 "Nils Holgersson on Goose" (from "The Wonderful Adventures of Nils" by Selma Lagerlof)

1971. Christmas. Traditional Prints.
664 **189** 35ore red . . . . 1·00 1·00
665 – 35ore blue . . . . 1·00 1·00
666 – 35ore purple . . . . . . 1·00 1·00
667 – 35ore blue . . . . 1·00 1·00
668 – 35ore green . . . . . . 1·00 1·00
DESIGNS: No. 665, Market scene; 666, Musical evening; 667, Skating; 668, Arriving for Christmas service.

1971.
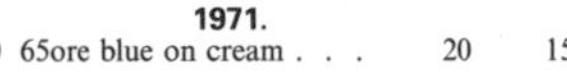
669 **190** 65ore blue on cream . . . 20 15

191 Maurice Maeterlinck (literature)

192 Fencing

1971. Nobel Prize Winners of 1911.
670 **191** 55ore orange 30 25
671 – 65ore green 55 20
672 – 85ore red 55 45
DESIGNS: 65ore Allvar Gullstrand (medicine) and Wilhelm Wien (physics); 85ore Marie Curie (chemistry).

1972. Sportswomen.
673 **192** 55ore purple 55 55
674 – 55ore blue 55 55
675 – 55ore green 55 55
676 – 55ore purple 55 55
677 – 55ore blue 55 55
DESIGNS: No. 674, Diving; 675, Gymnastics; 676, Tennis; 677, Figure-skating.

193 L. J. Hierta (newspaper editor, statue by C. Eriksson)

195 Roe Deer

1972. Anniversaries of Swedish Cultural Celebrities.
678 **193** 35ore multicoloured . . . 15 20
679 – 50ore violet 20 20
680 – 65ore blue 25 20
681 – 85ore multicoloured . . . 35 35
DESIGNS AND ANNIVERSARIES—VERT: 35ore (death cent); 85ore G. Stiernhielm (poet 300th death anniv) (portrait by D. K. Ehrenstrahl). HORIZ: 50ore F. M. Franzen (poet and hymn-writer, birth bicent) (after K. Hultstrom); 65ore Hugo Alfven (composer, birth cent) (granite bust by C. Milles).

1972.
682 **195** 95ore brown on cream . . 25 15

196 Glass-blowing

1972. Swedish Glass Industry.
683 **196** 65ore black 70 45
684 – 65ore blue 70 45
685 – 65ore red 70 45
686 – 65ore black 70 45
687 – 65ore blue 70 45
DESIGNS: No. 684, Glass-blowing (close-up); 685, Shaping glass; 686, Handling glass vase; 687, Bevelling glass vase.

197 Horses, Borgholm Castle (after N. Kreuger)

1972. Tourism in South-east Sweden.
688 **197** 55ore brown on cream . . 25 35
689 – 55ore blue on cream . . . 25 35
690 – 55ore brown on cream . . 25 35
691 – 55ore green on cream . . 25 35
692 – 55ore blue on cream . . . 25 35
DESIGNS: No. 689, Oland Bridge and sailing barque "Meta"; 690, Kalmar Castle; 691, Salmon-fishing, Morrumsan; 692, Cadet schooner "Falken", Karlskrona Naval Base.

198 Conference Emblem and Motto, "Only One Earth"

1972. U.N. Environment Conservation Conference, Stockholm.
693 **198** 65ore blue and red on cream 25 20
694 – 85ore mult on cream . . 45 35
DESIGN—28 × 45 mm: 85ore "Spring" (wooden relief by B. Hjorth).

199 Junkers F-13

201 Early Courier

200 Reindeer and Sledge (woodcut from "Lapponia")

1972. Swedish Mailplanes.
695 **199** 5ore lilac 10 20
696 – 15ore blue 10 30
697 – 25ore blue 10 30
698 – 75ore green 30 25
DESIGNS—45 × 19 mm: 15ore Junkers Ju 52/3m; 25ore Friedrichshafen FF-49 seaplane; 75ore Douglas DC-3.

1972. Centenary of "Lapponia" (book by J. Schefferus).
699 **200** 1k.40 red and blue . . . 40 15

1972. "Stockholmia 74" Stamp Exhibition (1st issue) and Birth Centenary of Olle Hjortzberg (stamp designer).
700 **201** 10ore red 25 45
701 – 15ore green 40 35
702 – 40ore blue 40 45
703 – 50ore brown 35 35
704 – 60ore blue 40 35
DESIGNS: 15ore Post-rider; 40ore Steam train; 50ore Motor bus and trailer; 60ore Liner "Gripsholm".
See also Nos. 779/82.

202 Figurehead of Royal Yacht "Amphion" (Per Ljung)

203 Christmas Candles (J. Wikstrom)

1972. Swedish 18th-century Art.
705 – 75ore green 45 30
706 – 75ore brown 45 30
707 **202** 75ore red 45 30
708 – 75ore red 45 30
709 – 75ore black, brown and red 45 30
710 – 75ore black, blue & purple 45 30
DESIGNS—59 × 24 mm: No. 705, "Stockholm" (F. Martin); 706, "The Forge" (P. Hillestrom). As T **202**: No. 708, "Quadriga" (Sergel). 28 × 37 mm: No. 709, "Lady with a Veil" (A. Roslin); 710, "Sophia Magdalena" (C. G. Pilo).

1972. Christmas. Multicoloured.
711 45ore Type **203** 25 20
712 45ore Father Christmas (E. Flygh) 25 20
713 75ore Carol singers (S. Hagg) (40 × 23 mm) 35 20

204 King Gustav VI Adolf

205 King Gustav with Book

1972.
714 **204** 75ore blue 20 15
715 1k. red 25 15

1972. King Gustav VI Adolf's 90th Birthday.
716 **205** 75ore blue . . . . . . 80 1·70
717 – 75ore green . . . . . . 80 1·70
718 – 75ore red . . . . 80 1·70
719 – 75ore blue . . . . . . 80 1·70
720 – 75ore green . . . . . . 80 1·70
DESIGNS: No. 717, Chinese objets d'art; 718, Opening Parliament; 719, Greek objets d'art; 720, King Gustav tending flowers.

206 Alexis Carrel (medicine)

207 "Tintomara" Stage Set (B-R. Hedwall)

1972. Nobel Prize Winners of 1912.
721 – 60ore brown 45 35
722 **206** 65ore blue 55 35
723 – 75ore violet 65 20
724 – 1k. brown 80 20
DESIGNS—HORIZ: 60ore Paul Sabatier and Victor Grignard (chemistry). VERT: 75ore Nils Gustav Dalen (physics); 1k. Gerhart Hauptmann (literature).

1973. Bicentenary of Swedish Royal Theatre.
725 **207** 75ore green 20 15
726 – 1k. purple 30 20
DESIGN—41 × 23 mm: 1k. "Orpheus" (P. Hillestrom).

208 Modern Mail Coach, Vietas

210 Horse (bas relief)

209 Vasa Ski Race

1973.
727 – 60ore black on yellow . . 20 20
728 **208** 70ore orange, blue & green 20 20
DESIGN: 60ore Mail bus, 1923.

1973. Tourism in Dalecarlia.
729 **209** 65ore green 25 30
730 – 65ore green 25 40
731 – 65ore black 25 40
732 – 65ore green 25 40
733 – 65ore red 25 40
DESIGNS: No. 730, "Going to the Church in Mora" (A. Zorn); 731, Church stables in Rattvik; 732, "The Great Pit"; 733, "Mid-summer Dance" (B. Nordenberg).

1973. Gottland Picture Stones.
734 **210** 5ore purple 10 15
735 – 10 blue 10 15
DESIGN: 10ore Viking longship (bas relief).

211 "Row of Willows" (P. Persson)

1973. Swedish Landscapes.
736 **211** 40ore brown 15 15
737 – 50ore black and brown . . 20 15
738 – 55ore green on cream . . 20 20
DESIGNS—20 × 28 mm: 50ore "View of Trosa" (R. Ljunggren). 27 × 23 mm: 55ore "Spring Birches" (O. Bergman).

212 Lumberman

213 Observer reading Thermometer

1973. 75th Anniv of Swedish Confederation of Trade Unions.
739 **212** 75ore red 20 20
740 1k.40 blue 40 20

1973. Centenary of I.M.O./W.M.O. and Swedish Meteorological Organizations.
741 **213** 65ore green 55 20
742 – 65ore blue and black . . 55 25
DESIGN: No. 742, U.S. satellite weather picture.

214 Nordic House, Reykjavik

1973. Nordic Countries' Postal Co-operation.
743 **214** 75ore multicoloured . . . 35 20
744 1k. multicoloured 45 20

215 C. P. Thunberg, Japanese Flora and Scene

1973. Swedish Explorers.
745 **215** 1k. brown, green and blue 65 75
746 – 1k. multicoloured 65 75
747 – 1k. brown, green and blue 65 75
748 – 1k. multicoloured 65 75
749 – 1k. multicoloured 65 75
DESIGNS: No. 746, Anders Sparrman and Tahiti; 747, Adolf Erik Nordenskiold and the "Vega"; 748, Salomon Andree and wreckage of balloon "Ornen"; 749, Sven Hedin and camels.

216 Team of Oxen

217 Grey Seal

1973. Centenary of Nordic Museum.
750 **216** 75ore black . . . . . . 85 1·20
751 – 75ore brown . . . . . . 85 1·20
752 – 75ore black . . . . . . 85 1·20
753 – 75ore purple . . . . . . 85 1·20
754 – 75ore brown . . . . . . 85 1·20
DESIGNS: No. 751, Braking flax; 752, Potato-planting; 753, Baking bread; 754, Spring sowing.

1973. "Save Our Animals".
755 **217** 10ore green 10 20
756 – 20ore violet 10 15
757 – 25ore blue 10 15
758 – 55ore blue 10 20
759 – 65ore violet 15 15
760 – 75ore green 20 25
DESIGNS: 20ore Peregrine falcon; 25ore Lynx; 55ore European otter; 65ore Wolf; 75ore White-tailed sea eagle.

218 King Gustav VI Adolf

220 "Goosegirl" (E. Josephson)

219 "Country Dance" (J. Nilsson)

1973. King Gustav VI Adolf Memorial Issue.
761 **218** 75ore blue 20 20
762 1k. purple 25 20

1973. Christmas. Peasant Paintings. Mult.
763 45ore Type **219** 30 20
764 45ore "The Three Wise Men" (A. Clemetson) 30 20
765 75ore "Gourd Plant" (B. A. Hansson) (23 × 28 mm) . . 1·30 20
766 75ore "The Rider" (K. E. Jonsson) (23 × 28 mm) . . 1·30 20

1973. Ernst Josephson Commemoration.
767 **220** 10k. multicoloured . . . 2·40 15

221 A. Werner (chemistry) and H. Kamerlingh-Onnes (physics)

1973. Nobel Prize Winners 1913.
768 **221** 75ore violet 40 20
769 – 1k. brown 50 20
770 – 1k.40 green 50 20
DESIGNS—VERT: 1k. Charles Robert Richet (medicine); 1k.40, Rabindranath Tagore (literature).

222 Ski Jumping

1974. "Winter Sports on Skis".
771 **222** 65ore green 35 35
772 – 65ore blue 35 40
773 – 65ore green 35 35
774 – 65ore red 35 40
775 – 65ore blue 35 40
DESIGNS: No 772, Cross-country (man); 773, Relay-racing; 774, Downhill-racing; 775, Cross-country (woman).

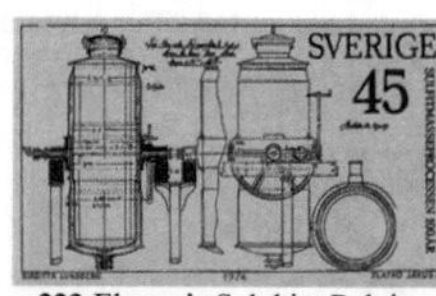
223 Ekman's Sulphite Pulping Machine

1974. Swedish Anniversaries.
776 **223** 45ore brown on grey . . 15 20
777 – 60ore green 20 30
778 – 75ore red 20 20
DESIGNS AND EVENTS: 45ore Type **223** (centenary of first sulphite pulp plant, Bergvik); 60ore Hans Jarta and part of Government Act (birth bicent); 75ore Samuel Owen and engineers (birth bicent).

224 U.P.U. Congress Stamp of 1924

1974. "Stockholmia '74" Stamp Exn (2nd issue).
779 **224** 20ore green 10 25
780 25ore blue 10 25
781 30ore brown 10 25
782 35ore red 10 25
MS783 Four sheets, 120 × 80 mm. containing stamps as Nos. 779/82, each in separate block of four. Colours changed. 20ore yellow; 25ore lilac; 30ore red; 35ore green. Set of 4 sheets . . . . 1·75 3·50

225 Great Falls

226 "Figure in a Storm" (B. Marklund)

1974.
784 **225** 35ore black and blue . . 15 20
785 – 75ore brown 20 20
DESIGN—HORIZ: 75ore Ystad (town).

1974. Europa. Sculptures.
786 **226** 75ore purple 65 20
787 – 1k. green 75 25
DESIGN: 1k. Picasso statue (from "Les Dames de Mougins"), Kristinehamn.

227 King Carl XVI Gustav

228 Central Post Office, Stockholm

1974.
788 **227** 75ore green 20 15
789 90ore blue 25 15
790 1k. purple 25 15
791 1k.10 red 30 15
792 1k.30 green 35 20
793 1k.40 blue 35 15
794 1k.50 mauve 40 15
795 1k.70 orange 45 20
796 2k. brown 50 20

1974. Centenary of Universal Postal Union.
800 **228** 75ore purple 75 15
801 – 75ore purple 75 20
802 – 1k. green 35 20
DESIGNS—As Type **228**: No. 801, Interior of Central Post Office, Stockholm. 40 × 24 mm: No. 802, Rural postman.

229 Regatta

1974. Tourism on Sweden's West Coast.
803 **229** 65ore red 25 35
804 – 65ore blue 25 35

805 – 65ore green 25 35
806 – 65ore green 25 35
807 – 65ore brown 25 35
DESIGNS: No. 804, Vinga Lighthouse; 805, Varberg Fortress; 806, Seine fishing; 807, Mollosund.

230 "Mr. Simmons" (A. Fridell)

231 Thread and Spool

1974. Centenary of Publicists' Club (Swedish press, radio and television association).
808 **230** 45ore black 15 20
809 1k.40 purple 45 20

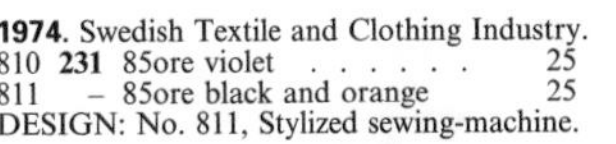

1974. Swedish Textile and Clothing Industry.
810 **231** 85ore violet 25 20
811 – 85ore black and orange . . . 25 20
DESIGN: No. 811, Stylized sewing-machine.

232 Deer

1974. Christmas. Mosaic Embroideries of Mythical Creatures. Each blue, red and green (45ore) or multicoloured (75ore).
812 45ore Type **232** 55 60
813 45ore Griffin 55 60
814 45ore Lion 55 60
815 45ore Griffin 55 60
816 45ore Unicorn 55 60
817 45ore Horse 55 60
818 45ore Lion 55 60
819 45ore Griffin 55 60
820 45ore Lion 55 60
821 45ore Lion-like creature . . . 55 60
822 75ore Deer-like creature . . . 20 20

No. 813 is facing right and has inscr at top, No. 815 faces left with similar inscr and No. 819 has inscr at bottom.

No. 814 has the inscr at top, No. 818 has it at the foot of the design, the lion having blue claws, No. 820 has similar inscr, but white claws.

Nos. 812/22 were issued together, se-tenant, forming a complete design.

233 Tanker "Bill"

1974. Swedish Shipping. Each blue.
823 1k. Type **233** 45 55
824 1k. "Snow Storm" (liner) . . 45 55
825 1k. "Tor" and "Atle" (ice-breakers) 45 55
826 1k. "Skanes" (train ferry) . . 45 55
827 1k. Tugs "Bill", "Bull" and "Starkodder" 45 55

234 Max von Laue (physics)

235 Sven Jerring (first announcer), Children and Microphone

1974. Nobel Prize Winners of 1914.
828 **234** 65ore red 25 25
829 – 70ore green 25 30
830 – 1k. blue 55 20
DESIGNS:—70ore Theodore William Richards (chemistry); 1k. Richard Barany (medicine).

1974. 50th Anniv of Swedish Broadcasting Corporation.
831 **235** 75ore blue and brown . . 40 20
832 – 75ore blue and brown . . 40 20
DESIGN: No. 832, Television camera at Parliamentary debate.

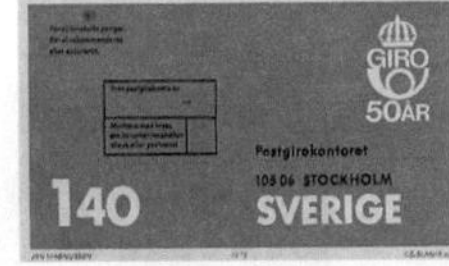

236 Giro Envelope

1975. 50th Anniv of Swedish Postal Giro Office.
833 **236** 1k.40 black and brown . . 40 20

237 Male and Female Engineers

238 Bronze Helmet Decoration, Vendel

1975. International Women's Year.
834 **237** 75ore green 20 20
835 – 1k. purple 25 20
DESIGN—VERT: 1k. Jenny Lind (singer) (portrait by O. J. Sodermark).

1975. Archaeological Discoveries.
836 **238** 10ore red 15 15
837 – 15ore green 15 15
838 – 20ore violet 15 15
839 – 25ore yellow 15 15
840 – 55ore brown 20 15
DESIGNS: 15ore Iron sword hilt and chapel, Vendel; 20ore Iron shield buckle, Vendel; 25ore Embossed gold plates (Gold Men), Eketorp Fortress, Oland; 55ore Iron helmet, Vendel.

239 "New Year's Eve at Skansen" (Eric Hallstrom)

1975. Europa. Paintings. Multicoloured.
841 90ore Type **239** 35 20
842 1k.10 "Inferno" (August Strindberg) (vert) 45 20

240 Metric Tape-measure (centenary of Metre Convention)

241 Western European Hedgehog

1975. Anniversaries.
843 **240** 55ore blue 15 20
844 – 70ore sepia and brown . . 20 25
845 – 75ore violet 20 25
DESIGNS AND EVENTS—44 × 27 mm: 70ore Peter Hernqvist (founder) and title-page of his book "Comprehensive Thesis on Glanders in Horses" (bicent of Swedish Veterinary Service). 24 × 31 mm: 75ore "Folke Filbyter" (birth centenary of Carl Milles (sculptor)).

1975.
846 **241** 55ore black 20 20
847 – 75ore red 20 20
848 – 1k.70 blue 50 20
849 – 2k. purple 65 20
850 – 7k. green . . . . 1·70 20
DESIGNS—HORIZ: 75ore Key-fiddler; 1k.70, Western capercaillie ("cock of the woods"). VERT: 2k. Rok stone (ancient inscribed rock), Ostergotland; 7k. Ballet dancers (from "Romeo and Juliet").

242 Village Buildings, Skelleftea

1975. European Architectural Heritage Year.
851 **242** 75ore black 20 30
852 – 75ore red 20 30
853 – 75ore black 20 30
854 – 75ore red 20 30
855 – 75ore blue 20 30
DESIGNS: No. 852, Engelsberg iron-works, Vastmanland; 853, Gunpowder tower, Visby, Gotland; 854, Iron-mine, Falun; 855, Rommehed military barracks, Dalecarlia.

243 Fire Brigade

1975. "Watch, Guard and Help". Public Services.
856 **243** 90ore red 25 25
857 – 90ore blue 25 25
858 – 90ore red 25 25
859 – 90ore blue 25 25
860 – 90ore green 25 25
DESIGNS: No. 857, Customs service; 858, Police service; 859, Ambulance and hospital service; 860, Shipwreck of "Merkur" (Sea rescue service).

244 "Fryckstad"

1975. Swedish Steam Locomotives.
861 **244** 5ore green 20 15
862 – 5ore blue 20 15
863 – 90ore green 45 15
DESIGNS—As Type **244**: No. 862, "Gotland". 49 × 22 mm: 90ore "Prins August".

245 Canoeing

246 "Madonna" (sculpture), Vikiau church, Gotland

1975. Scouting. Multicoloured.
864 90ore Type **245** 25 25
865 90ore Camping 25 25

1975. Christmas. Religious Art.
866 **246** 55ore multicoloured . . . 15 20
867 – 55ore multicoloured . . . 20 25
868 – 55ore multicoloured . . . 20 25
869 – 90ore brown 30 20
870 – 90ore red 45 20
871 – 90ore blue 45 20
DESIGNS—VERT: No. 867, "Birth of Christ" (embossed copper), Broddetorp church, Vastergotland; 868, "The Sun" (embossed copper), Broddetorp church, Vastergotland; 869, "Mourning Mary" (sculpture), Oja church, Gotland. HORIZ: Noore 870, 871, "Jesse at Foot of Christ's genealogical tree" (retable), Lofta church, Smaland.

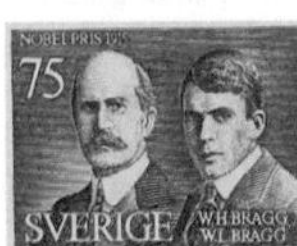

247 W. H. and W. L. Bragg (physics)

248 Bronze Coiled Snake Brooch, Vendel

1975. Nobel Prize Winners of 1915.
872 **247** 75ore purple 20 25
873 – 90ore blue 25 20
874 – 1k.10 green 40 35
DESIGNS: 90ore Richard Willstatter (chemistry); 1k.10, Romain Rolland (literature).

1976.
875 **248** 15ore bistre 10 10
876 – 20ore green 10 10
877 – 30ore purple 15 15
878 – 85ore blue 20 20
879 – 90ore blue 20 15
880 – 1k. purple 10 15
881 – 1k.90 green 50 30
882 – 9k. deep green and green 2·10 20
DESIGNS—21 × 19 mm: 20ore Pilgrim badge. 28 × 21 mm: 30ore Drinking horn; 85ore Common guillemot and razorbills. 28 × 23 mm: 1k.90, "Cave of the Winds" (sculpture) (Eric Grate). 21 × 28 mm: 90ore Chimney sweep; 1k. Bobbin lace-making; 9k. "Girl's Head" (wood-carving) (Bror Hjorth).

249 Early and Modern Telephones

250 Wheat and Cornflower Seed

1976. Telephone Centenary.
883 **249** 1k.30 mauve 35 20
884 3k.40 red 85 35

1976. Swedish Seed-testing Centenary.
885 **250** 65ore brown 15 20
886 – 65ore green and brown 15 20
DESIGN: No. 886, Viable and non-viable plants.

251 Lapp Spoon

253 Ship's Wheel and Cross

252 "View from Ringkallen" (H. Osslund)

1976. Europa. Handicrafts.
887 **251** 1k. black, pink and blue 35 20
888 – 1k.30 multicoloured . . . 45 30
DESIGN: 1k.30, Tile stove (from aquarelle by C. Slania).

1976. Tourism. Angermanland.
889 **252** 85ore green 25 30
890 – 85ore blue 25 30
891 – 85ore brown 25 30
892 – 85ore blue 25 30
893 – 85ore red 25 30
DESIGNS: No. 890, Tug towing timber; 891, Hay-drying racks; 892, Granvagsnipan; 893, Seine-net fishing.

1976. Centenary of Swedish Seamen's Church.
894 **253** 85ore blue 20 25

254 Torgny Segerstedt and "Goteborg Handels-och Sjofarts-tidning"

1976. Birth Centenary of Torgny Segerstedt (newspaper editor).
895 **254** 1k.90 black and brown . . 55 25

255 King Carl XVI Gustav and Queen Silvia

257 Hands and Cogwheels

256 John Ericsson (marine propeller)

1976. Royal Wedding.
896 **255** 1k. red 20 15
897 1k.30 green 35 30

1976. Swedish Technological Pioneers. Mult.
898 1k.30 Type **256** 45 50
899 1k.30 Helge Palmcrantz (hay maker) 45 50
900 1k.30 Lars Magnus Ericsson (telephone improvements) 45 50
901 1k.30 Sven Wingquist (ball bearing) 45 50
902 1k.30 Gustaf de Laval (milk separator and reaction turbine) 45 45

1976. Industrial Safety.
903 **257** 85ore orange and violet 20 20
904 1k. green and brown . . . 25 20

258 Verner von Heidenstam

259 "Archangel Michael Destroying Lucifer" (Flemish prayer book)

1976. Literature Nobel Prize Winner of 1916.
905 **258** 1k. green 25 20
906 1k.30 blue 45 30

1976. Christmas. Mediaeval Book Illustrations. Multicoloured.
907 65ore Type **259** 15 20
908 65ore "St. Nicholas awakening Children from Dead" (Flemish prayer book) 15 20
909 1k. "Mary visiting Elizabeth" (Austrian prayer book) . . 25 20
910 1k. "Prayer to the Virgin" (Austrian prayer book) . . 25 20
Nos. 909/10 are vert, 26 × 44 mm.

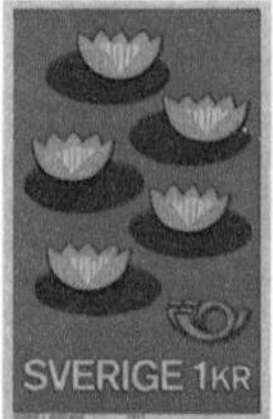

260 Water-lilies

261 Tawny Owl

1977. Nordic Countries Co-operation in Nature Conservation and Environment Protection.
911 **260** 1k. multicoloured 25 20
912 1k.30 multicoloured . . . 35 35

1977.
913 **261** 45ore green 15 20
914 – 70ore blue 20 20
915 – 1k.40 brown 40 25
916 – 2k.10 brown 55 20
DESIGNS—23 × 29 mm: 70ore Norwegian cast-iron stove decoration. 41 × 21 mm: 1k.40, Gotland ponies. 28 × 22 mm: 2k.10, Tailor.

262 "Politeness"

264 Gustavianum Building

263 Skating

1977. Birth Centenary of Oskar Andersson (cartoonist).
917 **262** 75ore black 20 25
918 3k.80 red . . . . 1·00 25

1977. Keep-fit Activities.
919 **263** 95ore blue 20 25
920 – 95ore green 20 30
921 – 95ore red 20 25
922 – 95ore green 20 30
923 – 95ore blue 20 25
DESIGNS: No. 920, Swimming; 921, Cycling; 922, Jogging; 923, Badminton.

1977. 500th Anniv of Uppsala University.
924 **264** 1k.10 black, yellow & blue 25 15

265 Winter Forest Scene

1977. Europa. Landscapes. Multicoloured.
925 1k.10 Type **265** 40 20
926 1k.40 Rapadalen valley, Sarek 55 65

266 Calle Schewen at Breakfast

267 Blackberries

1977. Tourism. Roslagen. Poem "Calle Schewen Waltz" by E. Taube.
927 **266** 95ore green 20 30
928 – 95ore violet 20 30
929 – 95ore black and red . . . 20 30
930 – 95ore blue 20 30
931 – 95ore red 20 30
DESIGNS: No. 928, Black-headed gull; 929, Calle Schewen dancing; 930, Fishing; 931, Sunset.

1977. Wild Berries. Multicoloured.
932 75ore Type **267** 30 30
933 75ore Cowberries 30 30
934 75ore Cloudberries 30 30
935 75ore Bilberries 30 30
936 75ore Strawberries 30 30

268 Horse-drawn Tram

1977. Public Transport.
937 **268** 1k.10 green 30 35
938 – 1k.10 blue 30 35
939 – 1k.10 blue 30 35
940 – 1k.10 blue 30 35
941 – 1k.10 green 30 35
DESIGN: No. 938, Electric tram; 939, Ferry "Djurgarden 6"; 940, Articulated bus; 941, Underground train, Stockholm.

269 H. Pontoppidan and K. A. Gjellerup (literature)

270 Erecting Sheaf for Birds

1977. Nobel Prize Winners of 1917.
942 **269** 1k.10 brown 40 20
943 – 1k.40 green 50 45
DESIGN: 1k.40, Charles Glover Barkla (physics).

1977. Christmas. Seasonal Customs.
944 **270** 75ore violet 20 25
945 – 75ore orange 20 25
946 – 75ore green 20 20
947 – 1k.10 green 20 20
948 – 1k.10 red 20 20
949 – 1k.10 blue 25 20
DESIGNS: No. 945, Making gingersnaps; 946, Bringing in the Christmas tree; 947, Preparing the traditional fish dish; 948, Making straw goats for the pantomime; 949, Candle-making.

271 Brown Bear

272 Orebro Castle

1978.
950 **271** 1k.15 brown 25 15
951 – 2k.50 blue 65 15
DESIGN: 2k.50, "Space without Affiliation" (sculpture by Arne Jones).

1978. Europa.
952 **272** 1k.30 green 40 20
953 – 1k.70 red 55 50
DESIGN—VERT: 1k.70, Doorway, Orebro Castle.

273 Pentecostal Meeting

1978. Independent Christian Associations.
954 **273** 90ore purple 30 45
955 – 90ore black 30 45
956 – 90ore violet 30 45
957 – 90ore green 30 45
958 – 90ore purple 30 45
DESIGNS: No. 955, Minister with children (Swedish Missionary Society); 956, Communion Service, Ethopia (Evangelical National Missionary Society); 957, Baptism (Baptist Society); 958, Salvation Army band.

274 Brosarp Hills

1978. Travels of Carl Linne (botanist).
959 **274** 1k.30 black 30 30
960 – 1k.30 blue 30 35
961 – 1k.30 purple 30 30
962 – 1k.30 red 30 30
963 – 1k.30 blue 30 30
964 – 1k.30 purple 30 30
DESIGNS—58 × 23 mm: No. 960, Pied avocets. 27 × 23 mm: No. 961, Grindstone production (after J. W. Wallander); 962, "Linnaea borealis". 27 × 36 mm: No. 963, Red limestone cliff; 964, Linnaeus wearing Lapp dress and Dutch doctor's hat, and carrying Lapp drum (H. Kingsbury).

275 Glider over Alleberg Plateau

1978. Tourism. Vastergotland.
965 **275** 1k.15 green 30 30
966 – 1k.15 red 30 30
967 – 1k.15 blue 30 30
968 – 1k.15 grey 30 25
969 – 1k.15 black and purple . . 30 30
DESIGNS: No. 966, Common cranes; 967, Fortress on Lacko Island Skara; 968, Rock tomb, Luttra; 969, "Traders of South Vastergotland" (sculpture, N. Sjogren).

276 Diploma and Laurel Wreath

1978. Centenary of Stockholm University.
970 **276** 2k.50 green on brown . . 60 25

277 "The Homecoming" (Carl Kylberg)

1978. Paintings by Swedish Artists. Mult.
971 90ore Type **277** 25 20
972 1k.15 "Standing Model seen from Behind" (Karl Isakson) 35 20
973 4k.50 "Self-portrait with a Floral Wreath" (Ivar Arosenius) . . . . 1·20 45

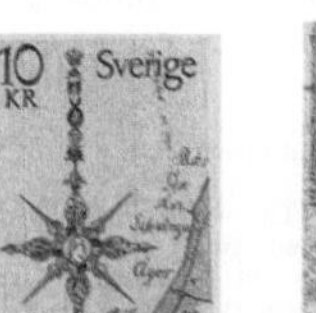

278 Northern Arrow

280 "Russula decolorans"

279 Coronation Carriage, 1699

1978.
974 **278** 10k. mauve . . . . 1·90 15

1978.
975 **279** 1k.70 red on buff 50 45

1978. Edible Mushrooms. Multicoloured.
976 1k.15 Type **280** 30 40
977 1k.15 Common puff-ball ("Lycoperdon perlatum") 30 40
978 1k.15 Parasol mushroom ("Macrolepiota procera") 30 40
979 1k.15 Chanterelle ("Cantharellus cibarius") 30 40
980 1k.15 Cep ("Boletus edulis") 30 40
981 1k.15 Cauliflower clavaria ("Ramaria botrytis") . . . 30 40

281 Dalecarlian Horse

282 Fritz Haber (chemistry)

1978. Christmas. Old Toys.
982 **281** 90ore multicoloured . . . 20 20
983 – 90ore multicoloured . . . 20 20
984 – 90ore green and red . . . 20 15
985 – 1k.30 multicoloured . . . 35 20
986 – 1k.30 multicoloured . . . 35 20
987 – 1k.30 blue 35 15
DESIGNS—VERT: No. 983, Swedish Court doll; 984, Meccano; 987, Teddy bear. HORIZ: No. 985, Tops; 986, Equipage with water barrel (metal toys).

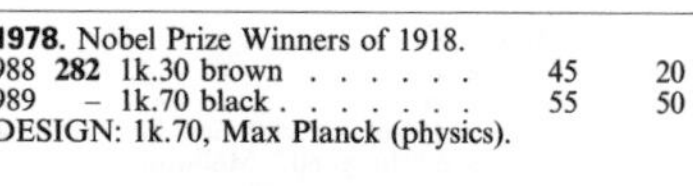

1978. Nobel Prize Winners of 1918.
988 **282** 1k.30 brown 45 20
989 – 1k.70 black 55 50
DESIGN: 1k.70, Max Planck (physics).

283 Bandy Players fighting for Ball

1979. Bandy.
990 **283** 1k.05 blue 25 20
991 2k.50 orange 65 20

284 Child in Gas-mask

285 Wall Hanging

1979. International Year of the Child.
992 **284** 1k.70 blue 55 45

1979.
993 **285** 4k. blue and red 95 15

286 Carrier Pigeon and Hand with Quill

287 Sledge-boat

1979. Rebate Stamp.
994 **286** (1k.) yellow, black and blue 85 15
No. 994 was only issued in booklets of 20 sold at 20k. in exchange for tokens distributed to all households in Sweden. Valid for inland postage only, they represented a rebate of 30ore on the normal rate of 1k.30.

1979. Europa.
995 **287** 1k.30 black and green . . 70 25
996 – 1k.70 black and brown . . 85 65
DESIGN: 1k.70, Hand using telegraph key.

288 Felling Tree

1979. Farming.
997 **288** 1k.30 black, red & green 30 30
998 – 1k.30 green and black 30 30
999 – 1k.30 green and black 30 30
1000 – 1k.30 brown and green 30 30
1001 – 1k.30 red, black & green 30 30
DESIGNS: No. 998, Sowing; 999, Cows; 1000, Harvesting; 1001, Ploughing.

289 Tourist Launch "Juno"

1979. Tourism. Gota Canal.
1002 **289** 1k.15 violet 35 40
1003 – 1k.15 green 35 40
1004 – 1k.15 purple 35 40
1005 – 1k.15 red 35 40
1006 – 1k.15 violet 35 40
1007 – 1k.15 green 35 40
DESIGNS—As T **289**: No. 1003, Borenshult lock. 27 × 23½ mm: No. 1004, Hajstorp roller bridge; 1005, Opening lock gateore 27 × 36½ mm: No. 1006, Motor barge "Wilhelm Tham" in lock; 1007, Kayak in lock.

290 "Aeshna cyanea" (dragonfly)

291 Workers leaving Sawmills

1979. Wildlife.
1008 **290** 60ore violet 30 25
1009 – 65ore green 35 20
1010 – 80ore green 45 30
DESIGNS—41 × 21 mm: 65ore Northern pike. 27 × 22 mm: 80ore Green spotted toad.

1979. Centenary of Sundsvall Strike.
1011 **291** 90ore brown and red 25 25

292 Banner

293 J. J. Berzelius

1979. Cent of Swedish Temperance Movement.
1012 **292** 1k.30 multicoloured 40 25

1979. Birth Bicentenaries of J. J. Berzelius (chemist) and J. O. Wallin (poet and hymn-writer).
1013 **293** 1k.70 brown and green 45 45
1014 – 4k.50 blue 1·20 35
DESIGN: 4k.50, J. O. Wallin and hymn numbers.

294 Pot-pourri Jar

1979. Swedish Rococo. Sheet 143 × 63 mm containing T **294** and similar vert designs.
MS1015 90ore multicoloured; 1k.15 multicoloured; 1k.30 blue, black and pink; 1k.15 multicoloured; 1k.30 blue, black and pink; 1k.70 buff and black (sold at 6k.) 1·10 1·60

295 Atlantic Herrings and Growth Marks

1979. Marine Research.
1016 **295** 1k.70 green and blue 45 50
1017 – 1k.70 brown 45 50
1018 – 1k.70 green and blue 45 50
1019 – 1k.70 brown 45 50
1020 – 1k.70 green and blue 45 50
DESIGNS: No. 1017, Acoustic survey of sea-bed; 1018, Plankton bloom; 1019, Echo-sounding chart of Baltic Sea, October 1978; 1020, Fishery research ship "Argos".

296 Ljusdal Costume

1979. Peasant Costumes and Jewellery.
1021 **296** 90ore multicoloured 30 15
1022 – 90ore multicoloured 30 20
1023 – 90ore blue 30 20
1024 – 1k.30 multicoloured 35 20
1025 – 1k.30 multicoloured 35 20
1026 – 1k.30 red 35 15
DESIGNS: As T **296**: No. 1022, Osteraker costume. 21 × 27 mm: No. 1023, Brooch from Jamtland; 1026, Brooch from Smaland. 23 × 40 mm: No. 1024, Goinge church dress; 1025, Mora church dress.

297 Jules Bordet (chemistry)

298 Wind Power

1979. Nobel Prize Winners of 1919.
1027 **297** 1k.30 mauve 40 25
1028 – 1k.70 blue 50 65
1029 – 2k.50 green 60 25
DESIGNS: 1k.70, Johannes Stark (physics); 2k.50, Carl Spitteler (literature).

1980. Renewable Energy Sources.
1030 **298** 1k.15 blue 40 30
1031 – 1k.15 buff and green 40 30
1032 – 1k.15 orange 40 30
1033 – 1k.15 green 40 30
1034 – 1k.15 green and blue 40 30
DESIGNS: No. 1031, Biological energy; 1032, Solar energy; 1033, Geothermal energy; 1034, Wave energy.

299 King Carl XVI Gustav and Crown Princess Victoria

300 Child's Hand in Adult's

1980. New Order of Succession to Throne.
1035 **299** 1k.30 blue 35 20
1036 1k.70 red 45 40

1980. Care.
1037 **300** 1k.40 brown 35 20
1038 – 1k.60 green 40 20
DESIGN: 1k.60, Aged hand clasping stick.

301 Squirrel

302 Elise Ottesen-Jensen (pioneer of birth control)

1980. Rebate Stamp.
1039 **301** (1k.) yellow, blue & black 80 15
No. 1039 was only issued in booklets of 20 sold at 20k. on production of tokens distributed to all households in Sweden.

1980. Europa.
1040 **302** 1k.30 green 55 20
1041 – 1k.70 red 60 60
DESIGN: 1k.70, Joe Hill (member of workers' movement).

303 Tybling Farm, Tyby

1980. Tourism. Halsingland.
1042 **303** 1k.15 red 45 30
1043 – 1k.15 blue and purple 45 30
1044 – 1k.15 green 45 30
1045 – 1k.15 purple 45 30
1046 – 1k.15 blue 45 30
DESIGNS: No. 1043, Old iron works, Iggesund; 1044, Blaxas ridge, Forsa; 1045, Banga farm, Alfta; 1046, Sunds Canal, Hudiksvall.

304 Chair from Scania (1831)

305 Motif from film "Diagonal Symphony"

1980. Nordic Countries' Postal Co-operation.
1047 **304** 1k.50 green 40 20
1048 – 2k. brown 55 35
DESIGN: 2k. Cradle from North Bothnia (19th century).

1980. Birth Bicentenary of Viking Eggeling (film-maker).
1049 **305** 3k. blue 75 20

306 Gustaf Erikson's Paraffin-driven Car, 1898

1980. Swedish Motor Vehicles. Sheet 120 × 67 mm containing T **306**and similar horiz designs.
MS1050 90ore black and blue; 1k.15 black and ochre; 1k.30 black and blue; 1k.40 black and blue; 1k.50 black and ochre; 1k.70, black and blue (sold at 9k.) 1·75 1·90

307 Bamse

308 "Necken" (Ernst Josephson)

1980. Christmas. Swedish Comic Strips.
1051 **307** 1k.15 blue and red 35 20
1052 – 1k.15 multicoloured 30 20
1053 – 1k.50 black 40 20
1054 – 1k.50 multicoloured 40 20
DESIGNS—As T **307** but VERT: No. 1052, Karlsson; 1053, Adamson. 40 × 23 mm: No. 1054, Kronblom.

1980.
1055 **308** 8k. brown, black and blue 1·90 65

309 Knut Hamsun (literature)

310 Angel blowing Horn

1980. Nobel Prize Winners of 1920.
1056 **309** 1k.40 blue 35 35
1057 – 1k.40 red 35 35
1058 – 2k. green 45 45
1059 – 2k. brown 45 45
DESIGNS: No. 1057, August Krogh (medicine); 1058, Charles-Edouard Guillaume (physics); 1059, Walther Nernst (chemistry).

1980. Christmas.
1060 **310** 1k.25 brown and blue 35 20

311 Ernst Wigforss

312 Thor catching Midgard Serpent

1981. Birth Centenary of Ernst Wigforss (politician).
1061 **311** 5k. red 1·20 25

1981. Norse Mythology.
1062 **312** 10ore black 10 15
1063 – 15ore red 10 15
1064 – 50ore red 15 15
1065 – 75ore green 25 15
1066 – 1k. black 30 15
DESIGNS: 15ore Heimdall blowing horn; 50ore Freya riding boar; 75ore Freya in carriage drawn by cats; 1k. Odin on eight-footed steed.

313 Gyr Falcon

314 Troll

1981.
1067 **313** 50k. brown, black & blue 10·50 90

1981. Europa.
1068 **314** 1k.50 blue and red 50 20
1069 – 2k. red and green 65 25
DESIGN: 2k. The Lady of the Woods.

315 Blind Boy feeling Globe

316 Arms of Bohuslan

1981. International Year of Disabled Persons.
1070 **315** 1k.50 green 40 20
1071 3k.50 violet 65 35

1981. Rebate stamps. Arms of Swedish Provinces (1st series). Multicoloured.
1072 1k.40 Ostergotland 80 15
1073 1k.40 Jamtland 80 15
1074 1k.40 Dalarna 80 15
1075 1k.40 Type **316** 80 15

See also Nos. 1112/15, 1153/6, 1189/92, 1246/9 and 1302/5.

317 King Carl XVI Gustav

318 Boat from Bohuslan

1981.
1076 **317** 1k.65 green 45 15
1077 – 1k.75 blue 45 25
1077a **317** 1k.80 blue 45 15
1077b 1k.90 red 50 20
1078 2k.40 purple 65 25
1078a – 2k.40 green 65 55
1078b **317** 2k.70 purple 70 30
1078c – 3k.20 red 80 35
DESIGN: 1k.75, 2k.40 (1078a), 3k.20, Queen Silvia.

1981. Provincial Sailing Boats.
1079 **318** 1k.65 blue 45 30
1080 – 1k.65 blue 45 30
1081 – 1k.65 blue 45 30
1082 – 1k.65 blue 45 30
1083 – 1k.65 blue 45 30
1084 – 1k.65 blue 45 30
DESIGNS: No. 1080, Boat from Blekinge; 1081, Boat from Norrbotten; 1082, Boat from Halsingland; 1083, Boat from Gotland; 1084, Boat from West Skane.

319 "Night and Day"

320 Par Lagerkvist riding Railway Trolley with Father (illustration from "Guest of Reality")

1981.
1085 **319** 1k.65 violet 40 15

1981.
1086 **320** 1k.50 green 40 20

321 Electric Locomotive

1981. "Sweden in the World".
1087 **321** 2k.40 red 55 55
1088 – 2k.40 red 55 55
1089 – 2k.40 purple 55 55
1090 – 2k.40 violet 55 55
1091 – 2k.40 blue 55 55
1092 – 2k.40 blue 55 55
DESIGNS—As T **321**: No. 1088, Scania trucks with rock drilling equipment; 1089, Birgit Nilsson (opera singer) and Sixten Ehrling (conductor); 1090, North Sea gas rig. 19 × 23 mm: No. 1091, Bjorn Borg (tennis player); 1092, Ingemar Stenmark (skier).

322 Baker's Sign

324 Wooden Bird

323 Olof As in *The Coachman*

1981. Business Mail.
1093 **322** 2k.30 brown 1·40 55
1094 – 2k.30 brown 1·40 55
DESIGN: No. 1094, Pewterer's sign.

1981. Swedish Film History. Sheet 135 × 69 mm containing T **323** and similar horiz designs.
MS1095 1k.50 black and yellow; 1k.50 black and blue; 1k.65 black and yellow; 1k.65 black and blue; 2k.40 multicoloured (sold at 10k.) 2·25 2·75

1981. Christmas.
1096 **324** 1k.40 red 35 20
1097 – 1k.40 green 35 20
DESIGN: No. 1097, Wooden bird (different).

325 Albert Einstein (physics)

1981. Nobel Prize Winners of 1921.
1098 **325** 1k.35 red 35 35
1099 – 1k.65 green 45 20
1100 – 2k.70 blue 55 55
DESIGNS: 1k.65, Anatole France (literature); 2k.70, Frederick Soddy (chemistry).

326 Knight on Horseback **327** Impossible Triangle

1982. Birth Centenary of John Bauer (illustrator of fairy tales).
1101 **326** 1k.65 blue, yellow & lilac 40 25
1102 – 1k.65 multicoloured . . 40 25
1103 – 1k.65 black and yellow 40 25
1104 – 1k.65 yellow and lilac . . 40 25
DESIGNS: No. 1102, "What a wretched pale creature, said the Troll Woman"; 1103, "The Princess beside the Forest Lake"; 1104, "Now it is already twilight Night".

1982.
1105 **327** 25ore brown 15 15
1106 – 50ore brown 15 15
1107 – 75ore blue 20 20
1108 – 1k.35 blue 35 20
1109 – 5k. purple . . . . 1·20 15
DESIGNS: 50, 75ore, Impossible figures (different); 1k.35, Newspaper distributor; 5k. "Graziella wonders if she could be a Model" (etching, Carl Larsson).

328 Villages before and after Land Reform

1982. Europa.
1110 **328** 1k.65 green and black 1·30 20
1111 – 2k.40 green 60 55
DESIGN—26 × 22 mm: 2k.40, Anders Celsius.

1982. Rebate Stamps. Arms of Swedish Provinces (2nd series). As T **316**. Multicoloured.
1112 1k.40 Dalsland 80 15
1113 1k.40 Oland 80 15
1114 1k.40 Vastmanland 80 15
1115 1k.40 Halsingland 80 15

329 Elin Wagner **330** Burgher House

1982. Birth Centenary of Elin Wagner (novelist).
1116 **329** 1k.35 brown on grey . . 35 25

1982. Centenary of Museum of Cultural History, Lund.
1117 **330** 1k.65 brown 50 15
1118 – 2k.70 brown 65 40
DESIGN: 2k.70, Embroidered lace.

331 Lateral Mark

1982. New International Buoyage System.
1119 **331** 1k.65 blue and green . . 55 20
1120 – 1k.65 green and blue . . 55 20
1121 – 1k.65 deep blue and blue 55 20
1122 – 1k.65 blue and green . . 55 20
1123 – 1k.65 deep blue and blue 55 20
DESIGNS: No. 1120, Cardinal mark and Sweden–Finland ferry "Sally"; 1121, Racing yachts and special mark; 1122, Safe-water mark; 1123, Pilot boat, isolated danger mark and lighthouse.

332 Scene from "The Emigrants" (film)

1982. Living Together.
1124 **332** 1k.65 green 40 20
1125 – 1k.65 purple 40 20
1126 – 1k.65 blue 40 20
1127 – 1k.65 red 40 20
DESIGNS: No. 1125, Vietnamese boat people in factory; 1126, Immigrants examining local election literature; 1127, Three girls arm-in-arm.

333 Lady's Slipper (*Cypropedium calceolus*)

1982. Wild Orchids. Sheet 144 × 63 mm containing T **333** and similar vert design.
MS1128 1k.65 Early purple orchid (*Orchis mascula*); 1k.65 Type **333**; 2 k.40 Marsh helleborine (*Epipactris*); 2k.70 Elderflowered orchid (*Dactylorhiza sambucia*) (sold at 10k.) . . . . 2·50 2·40

334 Angel

1982. Christmas. Medieval Glass Paintings from Lye Church. Multicoloured.
1129 1k.40 Type **334** 45 35
1130 1k.40 "The Child in the Temple" 45 35
1131 1k.40 "Adoration of the Magi" 45 35
1132 1k.40 "Tidings to the Shepherds" 45 35
1133 1k.40 "The Birth of Christ" 45 35

335 Quantum Mechanics (Niels Bohr, 1922)

1982. Nobel Prize Winners for Physics.
1134 **335** 2k.40 blue 55 60
1135 – 2k.40 red 55 60
1136 – 2k.40 green 55 60
1137 – 2k.40 lilac 55 60
1138 – 2k.40 red 55 60
DESIGNS: No. 1135, Fuse distribution (Erwin Schrodinger, 1933); 1136, Wave pattern (Louis de Broglie, 1929); 1137, Electrons (Paul Dirac, 1933); 1138, Atomic model (Werner Heisenberg, 1932).

336 Horse Chestnut **337** Ferlin (statue by K. Bejemark)

1983. Fruits.
1139 **336** 5ore brown 10 10
1140 – 10ore green 10 10
1141 – 15ore red 10 10
1142 – 20ore blue 15 15
DESIGNS: 10ore Norway maple; 15ore Dog rose; 20ore Blackthorn.

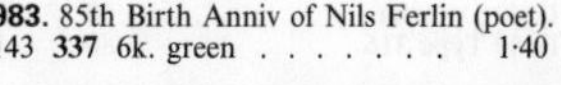
1983. 85th Birth Anniv of Nils Ferlin (poet).
1143 **337** 6k. green . . . . 1·40 15

338 Peace March **340** Family Cycling in Countryside

339 Lead Type

1983. Centenary of Swedish Peace Movement.
1144 **338** 1k.35 blue 35 20

1983. 500th Anniv of Printing in Sweden.
1145 **339** 1k.65 black and brown on stone 40 25
1146 – 1k.65 black, green and red on stone 40 25
1147 – 1k.65 brown and black on stone 40 25
1148 **339** 1k.65 black and brown on stone 40 25
1149 – 1k.65 brown, green and black on stone 40 25
DESIGNS: No. 1146, Ox plough (illustration from "Dialogus creaturarum" by Johan Snell, 1483); 1147, Title page of Karl XII's Bible, 1703; 1148, 18th-century alphabet books; 1149, Laser photocomposition.

1983. Nordic Countries' Postal Co-operation. "Visit the North".
1150 **340** 1k.65 green 40 20
1151 – 2k.40 blue and brown . . 60 40
DESIGN: 2k.40, Yachts at Stockholm.

341 Benjamin Franklin and Great Seal of Sweden

1983. Bicentenary of Sweden–U.S.A. Treaty of Amity and Commerce.
1152 **341** 2k.70 blue, brown & blk 70 40

1983. Rebate Stamps. Arms of Swedish Provinces (3rd series). As T **316**. Multicoloured.
1153 1k.60 Vastergotland 80 15
1154 1k.60 Medelpad 80 15
1155 1k.60 Gotland 80 15
1156 1k.60 Gastrikland 80 15

342 Costume Sketch by Fernand Leger for "Creation du Monde" **343** Essay for Unissued Stamp, 1885

1983. Europa.
1157 1k.65 chocolate and brown 75 20
1158 2k.70 blue . . . . 1·20 70
DESIGNS: 1k.65, Type **342** (Swedish Ballet); 2k.70, J. P. Johansson's adjustable spanner.

1983. "Stockholmia 86" International Exhibition (1st issue). Oscar II stamp designs by Max Mirowsky.
1159 **343** 1k. blue 60 40
1160 – 2k. red 60 45
1161 – 3k. blue 60 55
1162 – 4k. green 60 65
DESIGNS: 2k. Issued stamp of 1885; 3k. Essay for unissued stamp, 1891; 4k. Issued stamp of 1891.
See also Nos. 1199/1202, 1252/5, 1285/8 and 1310/13.

344 Greater Karlso **345** Freshwater Snail

1983.
1163 **344** 1k.60 blue 50 15
1164 **345** 1k.80 green 45 15
1165 – 2k.10 green 45 15
DESIGN—22 × 27 mm: 2k.10, Arctic fox.

346 Bergman **347** Helgeandsholmen, 1580 (after Franz Hogenberg) and Riksdag

1983. Birth Centenary of Hjalmar Bergman (novelist and dramatist).
1166 **346** 1k.80 blue 45 20
1167 – 1k.80 multicoloured . . 45 25
DESIGN: No. 1167, Jac the Clown (novel character).

1983. Return of Riksdag (Parliament) to Helgeandsholmen Island, Stockholm.
1168 **347** 2k.70 purple and blue . . 70 40

348 Red Cross **350** Dancing round the Christmas Tree

349 Wilhelm Stenhammer (after R. Thegerstrom) (classical music)

1983. Swedish Red Cross.
1169 **348** 1k.50 red 40 20

1983. Music in Sweden. Sheet 135 × 69 mm containing T **349** and similar designs.
MS1170 1k.80 green and black (Type **349**); 1k.80 yellow and black (*Aniara*) (opera)); 1k.80 pink and black (Abba (pop)); 2k.70, multicoloured ("Fiddler" (Anders Zorn) (folk music)) (44 × 48 mm) (sold at 11k. 50) . . . . 2·50 2·75

1983. Christmas. Early Christmas Cards. Multicoloured.
1171 1k.60 Type **350** 40 25
1172 1k.60 Straw goats 40 25
1173 1k.60 The Christmas table 40 25
1174 1k.60 Carrying Christmas presents on pole 40 25

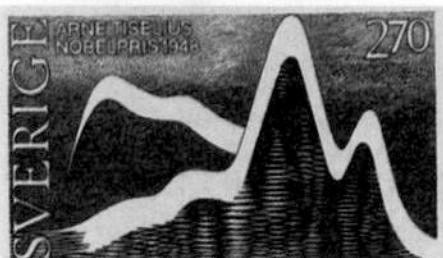

351 Electrophoresis (Arne Tiselius, 1948)

1983. Nobel Prize Winners for Chemistry.
1175 **351** 2k.70 black 65 70
1176 – 2k.70 violet 65 70
1177 – 2k.70 mauve 65 70
1178 – 2k.70 violet 65 70
1179 – 2k.70 black 65 70
DESIGNS: No. 1176, Radioactive isotopes (George de Hevesy, 1943); 1177, Electrolytic dissociation (Svante Arrhenius, 1903); 1178, Colloids (Theodor Svedberg, 1926); 1179, Fermentation of sugar (Hans von Euler-Chelpin, 1929).

352 Three Crowns (detail from Postal Savings Receipt)

1984. Centenary of Postal Savings.
1180 **352** 100ore orange 20 20
1181 – 1k.60 violet 40 40
1182 – 1k.80 mauve 50 20
DESIGNS: 1k.60, 1k.80, Postal Savings badge.

353 Bridge

1984. Europa. 25th Anniv of European Post and Telecommunications Conference.
1183 **353** 1k.80 red 50 20
1184 2k.70 blue . . . . 1·10 70

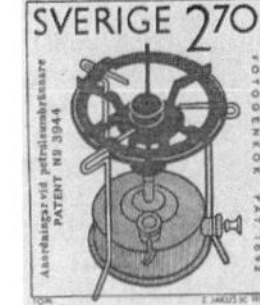

354 Norway Lemming
355 Paraffin Stove (F. W. Lindqvist)

1984. Swedish Mountain World.
1185 **354** 1k.90 brown 45 20
1186 – 1k.90 blue 45 20
1187 – 2k. green 50 15
1188 – 2k.25 black 75 45
DESIGNS: No. 1186, Musk ox; 1187, Garden angelica; 1188, Tolpagorni mountain.

1984. Rebate Stamps. Arms of Swedish Provinces (4th series). As T **316**. Multicoloured.
1189 1k.60 Sodermanland 80 15
1190 1k.60 Blekinge 80 15
1191 1k.60 Vasterbotten 80 15
1192 1k.60 Skane 80 15

1984. "Made in Sweden". Centenary of Patent Office. Patented Swedish Inventions.
1193 **355** 2k.70 red 60 70
1194 – 2k.70 lilac 60 70
1195 – 2k.70 green 60 70
1196 – 2k.70 green 60 70
1197 – 2k.70 lilac 60 70
1198 – 2k.70 blue 60 70
DESIGNS: No. 1194, "ASEA IRB 6" industrial robot for arc welding; 1195, Vacuum cleaner (Axel Wennergren); 1196, "AQ 200" inboard/outboard engine; 1197, Integrated circuit; 1198, Tetrahedron container.

356 King Erik XIV (after S. van der Meulen) and Letter to Queen Elizabeth I of England
358 Genetic Symbols forming "100"

357 Jonkoping

1984. "Stockholmia 86" International Stamp Exhibition (2nd issue).
1199 **356** 1k. brown, blue and ultramarine 50 40
1200 – 2k. multicoloured . . . 60 45
1201 – 3k. multicoloured . . . 65 60
1202 – 4k. multicoloured . . . 75 65
DESIGNS: 2k. Erik Dahlbergh (architect) (after J. H. Stromer) and letter to Sten Bielke (Paymaster General), 1674; 3k. Feather letter, 1843; 4k. Harriet Bosse and letter from her husband, August Strindberg, 1905.

1984. Old Towns. 17th-century views by M. Karl (1207) or Erik Dahlberg (others).
1203 **357** 1k.90 blue 45 35
1204 – 1k.90 brown 45 35
1205 – 1k.90 blue 45 40
1206 – 1k.90 brown 45 40
1207 – 1k.90 blue 45 40
1208 – 1k.90 brown 45 40
DESIGNS: No. 1204, Karlstad; 1205, Gavle; 1206, Sigtuna; 1207, Norrkoping; 1208. Vadstena.

1984. Centenary of Fredrika Bremer Association (for promotion of male/female equal rights).
1209 **358** 1k.50 purple 40 20
1210 6k.50 red . . . . 1·60 45

359 "Viking" in Orbit

1984. Launch of Swedish "Viking" Satellite.
1211 **359** 1k.90 ultramarine, blue and deep blue 50 20
1212 – 3k.20 green, yellow and black 80 70
DESIGN: 3k.20, Dish aerial and rocket pad at Esrange space station.

360 Thulin Type D Biplane, 1915
361 Hawfinch ("Coccothraustes coccothraustes")

1984. Swedish Aviation History. Sheet 132 × 73 mm containing T **360** and similar designs.
MS1213 1k.90 ultramarine and red (Type **360**); 1k.90 ultramarine and orange (SAAB 90 Scandia, 1946); 1k.90 orange, ultramarine and red (Carl Gustaf Cedarstrom ("The Flying Baron") and Bleriot X1 monoplane, 1910); 1k.90 multicoloured (Ahrenberg's Junkers F-13 airplane *The Gnome* 1927); 2k.70 brown, red and dull ultramarine (Carl Nyberg and *The Tiny Fly*, 1900) (43 × 46 mm) (sold at 12k.) . . . . 2·40 2·75

1984. Christmas. Birds. Multicoloured.
1214 1k.60 Type **361** 40 30
1215 1k.60 Bohemian waxwing ("Bombycilla garrulus") 40 30
1216 1k.60 Great-spotted woodpecker ("Dendrocopos major") 40 30
1217 1k.60 Eurasian nuthatch ("Sitta europaea") 40 30

362 Inner Ear (Georg von Bekesy, 1961)

1984. Nobel Prize Winners for Medicine.
1218 **362** 2k.70 blue, black and red 65 65
1219 – 2k.70 blue and black . . 65 65
1220 – 2k.70 red, black and blue 65 65
1221 – 2k.70 blue and black . . 65 65
1222 – 2k.70 red, black and blue 65 65
DESIGNS: No. 1219, Nerve cell activation (John Eccles, Alan Hodgkin and Andrew Huxley, 1963); 1220, Nerve cell signals (Bernard Katz, Ulf von Euler and Julius Axelrod, 1970); 1221, Functions of the brain (Roger Sperry, 1981); 1222, Eye (David Hubel and Torsten Wiesel, 1981).

363 Post Office Emblem
364 King Carl XVI Gustav

1985.
1223 **363** 1k.60 blue 45 20
1224 1k.70 violet 50 20
1326 1k.80 purple 55 20
1225 2k.50 yellow 65 20
1226 2k.80 green 80 40
1327 3k.20 brown 85 60
1227 4k. red 90 20
1328 6k. turquoise . . . . . 1·40 30

1985.
1228 **364** 2k. black 50 15
1229 2k.10 blue 60 15
1230 2k.20 blue 55 20
1230a 2k.30 green 55 20
1230b 2k.50 purple 65 20
1231 2k.70 brown 70 35
1232 2k.90 green 75 35
1233 3k.10 brown 80 45
1234 – 3k.20 blue 80 60
1235 **364** 3k.30 purple . . . . . 1·30 50
1236 – 3k.40 red 85 40
1237 – 3k.60 green 90 50
1238 – 3k.90 blue 90 60
1239 – 4k.60 orange . . . . . 1·10 80
DESIGNS: 3k.20 and 3k.40 to 4k.60, Queen Silvia.

365 Hazel Dormouse ("Muscardinus avellanarius")
366 Jan-Ove Waldner

1985. Nature.
1240 **365** 2k. brown and black . . 50 20
1241 – 2k. orange and black . . 50 20
1242 – 2k.20 red 55 15
1243 – 3k.50 red and green . . 85 20
DESIGNS: No. 1241, Char ("Salvelinus salvelinus"); 1242, Black vanilla orchid ("Nigritella nigra"); 1243, White water-lily ("Nymphaea alba frosea").

1985. World Table Tennis Championships, Gothenburg.
1244 **366** 2k.70 blue 75 35
1245 – 3k.20 mauve 85 60
DESIGN: 3k.20, Cai Zhenhua (Chinese player).

1985. Rebate Stamps. Arms of Swedish Provinces (5th series). As T **316**. Multicoloured.
1246 1k.80 Narke 80 15
1247 1k.80 Angermanland . . . 80 15
1248 1k.80 Varmland 80 15
1249 1k.80 Smaland 80 15

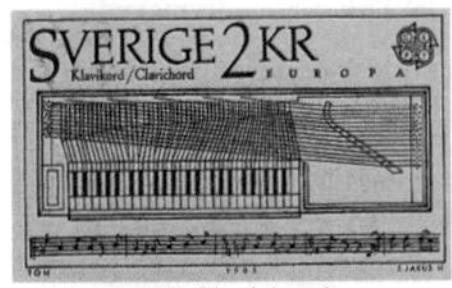

367 Clavichord

1985. Europa. Music Year.
1250 **367** 2k. purple on buff . . . 1·90 20
1251 – 2k.70 brown on buff . . 65 60
DESIGN—28 × 24 mm: 2k.70, Keyed fiddle.

368 "View of Slussen" (Sigrid Hjerten)
369 Syl Hostel, 1920

1985. "Stockholmia 86" International Stamp Exhibition (3rd issue). Multicoloured.
1252 2k. Type **368** 60 50
1253 2k. "Skeppsholmen, Winter" (Gosta Adrian-Nilsson) 60 50
1254 3k. "A Summer's Night by Riddarholmen Canal" (Hilding Linnqvist) . . . 70 60
1255 4k. "Klara Church Tower" (Otte Skold) 80 65

1985. Centenary of Swedish Touring Club.
1256 **369** 2k. blue and black . . . 50 20
1257 – 2k. black and blue . . . 50 20
DESIGN—58 × 24 mm: No. 1257, "Af Chapman" (youth hostel in Stockholm).

370 Canute and Helsingborg
371 Nilsson's Music Shop Sign

1985. 900th Anniv of Saint Canute's Deed of Gift to Lund.
1258 – 2k. blue and black . . . 50 20
1259 **370** 2k. red and black . . . 50 20
DESIGN: No. 1258, Canute and Lund Cathedral.

1985. Trade Signs.
1260 **371** 10ore blue 10 15
1261 – 20ore brown 10 15
1262 – 20ore brown 10 15
1263 – 50ore blue 20 15
1264 – 2k. green 85 15
DESIGNS: No. 1261, Erik Johansson's furrier's sign; 1262, O. L. Sjowals's coppersmith's sign; 1263, Bodecker's hatter's sign; 1264, Berggren's shoemaker's sign.

372 "Otryades" (Johan Tobias Sergel)

1985. 250th Anniv of Royal Academy of Fine Arts.
1265 **372** 2k. blue 50 20
1266 – 7k. brown . . . . 1·70 50
DESIGN—20 × 28 mm: 7k. "Baron Carl Fredrik Adelcrantz" (former Academy president) (Alexander Roslin).

373 Fox and Geese
374 Birger Sjoberg (writer)

1985. Board Games.
1267 **373** 50ore blue 15 15
1268 – 60ore green 15 15
1269 – 70ore yellow 20 20
1270 – 80ore red 20 20
1271 – 90ore mauve 20 20
1272 – 3k. purple 65 15
DESIGNS—As T **373**: 60k. Dominoes; 70k. Ludo; 80k. Chinese checkers; 90k. Backgammon. 23 × 28 mm: 3k. Chess.

1985. Birth Centenaries.
1273 – 1k.60 red and black . . 40 30
1274 **374** 4k. green . . . . 1·00 20
DESIGN—40 × 24 mm: 1k.60, Per Albin Hansson (politician).

375 Boy helping Old Lady collect Leaves (Marina Karlsson)

1985. International Youth Year. Sheet 134 × 64 mm containing T **375** and similar vert designs showing children's drawings. Multicoloured.
MS1275 2k. Type **375**; 2k. Silhouettes and light (Madeleine Andersson); 3k.20 Children on swing (Charlotte Ankar) (sold at 10k) . . . . 2·25 2·00

376 "Annunciation"
377 American Deep South Scene (William Faulkner, 1949)

1985. Christmas. Medieval Church Frescoes by Albertus Pictor.
1276 **376** 1k.80 blue, brown and red 45 25
1277 – 1k.80 brown, blue and red 45 25
1278 – 1k.80 brown, blue and red 45 25
1279 – 1k.80 blue, brown and red 45 25
DESIGNS: No. 1277, "Birth of Christ"; 1278, "Adoration of the Magi"; 1279, "Mary as the Apocalyptic Virgin".

1985. Nobel Prize Winners for Literature.
1280 **377** 2k.70 green 70 70
1281 – 2k.70 brown, blue and green 70 70
1282 – 2k.70 green and brown 70 70
1283 – 2k.70 green and blue . . 70 70
1284 – 2k.70 brown and blue . . 70 70
DESIGNS: No. 1281, Icelandic scene (Halldor Kiljan Laxness, 1955); 1282, Guatemalan scene (Miguel Angel Asturias, 1967); 1283, Japanese scene (Yasunari Kawabata, 1968); 1284, Australian scene (Patrick White, 1973).

378 1879 "20 TRETIO" Error

379 Eiders ("Somaternia mollissima")

1986. "Stockholmia 86" International Stamp Exhibition (4th issue).
1285 **378** 2k. orange, purple & grn . . . 70 50
1286 – 2k. multicoloured . . . 70 45
1287 – 3k. purple, blue and green 75 65
1288 – 4k. multicoloured . . . 75 75
DESIGNS: No. 1286, Sven Ewert (engraver); 1287, Magnifying glass and United States 1938 Scandinavian Settlement 3c. stamp; 1288, Boy soaking stamps.

1986. Water Birds.
1289 **379** 2k.10 blue and brown . . 50 20
1290 – 2k.10 brown 50 20
1291 – 2k.30 blue 55 20
DESIGNS: No. 1290, Whimbrel ("Numenius phaeopus"); 1291, Black-throated diver ("Gavia arctica").

380 Swedish Academy Emblem

381 Jubilee Emblem

1986. Bicentenaries of Swedish Academy and Royal Swedish Academy of Letters, History and Antiquities.
1292 **380** 1k.70 green and red on grey 40 40
1293 – 1k.70 blue and purple on grey 40 40
DESIGN: No. 1293, Royal Swedish Academy emblem.

1986. 350th Anniv of Post Office.
1294 **381** 2k.10 blue and yellow . . 55 15

382 Palme

383 Carl Gustav Birdwatching

1986. Olof Palme (Prime Minister) Commemoration.
1295 **382** 2k.10 purple 55 75
1296 2k.90 black 80 75

1986. 40th Birthday of King Carl XVI Gustav.
1297 **383** 2k.10 black and green 60 35
1298 – 2k.10 gold, mauve and blue 60 35
1299 – 2k.10 deep blue and blue 60 35
1300 – 2k.10 gold, blue and deep blue 60 35
1301 – 2k.10 black and mauve 60 35
DESIGNS: Nos. 1298, 1300, Crowned cypher; 1299, King presenting Nobel Prize for Literature to Czeslaw Milosz; 1301, King and family during summer holiday at Solliden Palace.

1986. Rebate Stamps. Arms of Swedish Provinces (6th series). As T **316**. Multicoloured.
1302 1k.90 Harjedalen 80 20
1303 1k.90 Uppland 80 20
1304 1k.90 Halland 80 20
1305 1k.90 Lappland 80 20

384 Uppsala

385 Forest and Car Fumes

1986. Nordic Countries' Postal Co-operation. Twinned Towns.
1306 **384** 2k.10 green, chestnut and brown 55 20
1307 – 2k.90 green, red & brown 70 55
DESIGN: 2k.90, Eskilstuna.

1986. Europa. Each black, green and red.
1308 2k.10 Type **385** . . . . . 1·10 20
1309 2k.90 Forest and industrial pollution 65 65

386 Tomteboda Sorting Office (20th-century)

388 Olive Branch sweeping away Weapons

387 Ann-Louise Skoglund (400 m. hurdles European Champion, 1982)

1986. "Stockholmia 86" International Stamp Exhibition (5th issue). Multicoloured.
1310 2k.10 19th-century railway sorting carriage . . . . . 1·30 2·10
1311 2k.10 Type **386** . . . . . 1·30 2·10
1312 2k.90 17th-century farmhand postal messenger . . . . 1·30 2·10
1313 2k.90 18th-century post office . . . . 1·30 2·10

1986. Athletics. Sheet 93 × 72 mm containing T **387** and similar horiz designs.
MS1314 2k.10 brown, blue and green (Type **387**); 2k.10 brown and green (Eric Lemming, early Olympic Medal winner, and Dag Wennlund (javelin throwers)); 2k.10 blue and brown (Patrik Sjoberg (high jumper)); 2k.10 green and brown (Anders Garderud, 3000 m. steeplechase world record holder) (sold at 11k.) 2·25 2·50

1986. International Peace Year (1315) and 25th Anniv of Amnesty International (1316).
1315 **388** 3k.40 green and black 80 85
1316 – 3k.40 red and black . . 80 80
DESIGN: No. 1316, Emblem above broken manacles.

389 Bertha von Suttner (founder of Austrian Society of Peace Lovers, 1905)

1986. Nobel Prize Winners for Peace.
1317 **389** 2k.90 black, red and blue 75 75
1318 – 2k.90 black and red . . 75 75
1319 – 2k.90 black, brown and blue 75 75
1320 – 2k.90 brown and black 75 75
1321 – 2k.90 red, black and blue 75 75
DESIGNS: No. 1318, Carl von Ossietzky (anti-Nazi fighter and concentration camp victim, 1935); 1319, Albert Luthuli (South African anti-apartheid leader, 1960); 1320, Martin Luther King (American civil rights leader, 1964); 1321, Mother Teresa (worker amongst poor of Calcutta, 1979).

390 Mail Van

391 Clouded Apollo ("Parnassius mnemosyne")

1986. Christmas. Designs showing a village at Christmas. Multicoloured.
1322 1k.90 Type **390** 45 25
1323 1k.90 Postman on cycle delivering mail 45 25
1324 1k.90 Children and sledge loaded with parcels . . . 45 25
1325 1k.90 Christmas tree, man carrying parcel and child posting letter 45 25
Nos. 1322/5 were printed together, se-tenant, forming a composite design.

1987. Threatened Species of Meadows and Pastures.
1331 **391** 2k.10 black, green and purple 50 20
1332 – 2k.10 black, green and purple 50 20
1333 – 2k.50 brown 65 15
1334 – 4k.20 green and yellow 95 20
DESIGNS: 2k.10 (1332), Field gentian ("Gentianella campestris"); 2k.50, Leather beetle ("Osmoderma eremita"); 4k.20, Arnica ("Arnica montana").

392 SAAB-Fairchild SF-340

393 Boys flying over Rooftops ("Karlsson")

1987. Swedish Aircraft.
1335 **392** 25k. purple . . . . . . 5·50 55

1987. Rebate Stamps. Characters from Children's Books by Astrid Lindgren. Multicoloured.
1336 1k.90 Type **393** 85 15
1337 1k.90 Girl holding doll ("Bullerby Children") . . 85 15
1338 1k.90 Girls dancing ("Madicken") 85 15
1339 1k.90 Boys on horse ("Mio, Min Mio") 85 15
1340 1k. Boy doing handstand ("Nils Karlsson-Pyssling") 85 15
1341 1k.90 Emil picking cherries ("Emil") 85 15
1342 1k.90 "Ronja the Robber's Daughter" 85 15
1343 1k.90 "Pippi Longstocking" 85 15
1344 1k.90 Dragon ("Brothers Lionheart") 85 15
1345 1k.90 "Lotta" 85 15

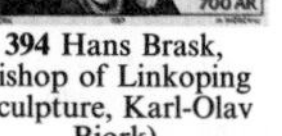
394 Hans Brask, Bishop of Linkoping (sculpture, Karl-Olav Bjork)

395 Stockholm City Library (Gunnar Asplund)

1987. Town Anniversaries. Each brown, blue and black.
1346 2k.10 Type **394** (700th anniv) 50 45
1347 2k.10 Nykoping Castle (800th anniv) 50 45

1987. Europa. Architecture.
1348 **395** 2k.10 brown and blue . . 1·00 20
1349 3k.10 brown and green 70 65
1350 – 3k.10 purple and green 70 65
DESIGN: No. 1350, Marcus Church (Sigurd Lewerentz).

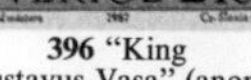
396 "King Gustavus Vasa" (anon)

398 Clowns

397 Raoul Wallenberg (rescuer of Hungarian Jews) and Prisoners

1987. 450th Anniv of Gripsholm Castle.
1351 **396** 2k.10 multicoloured . . 50 25
1352 – 2k.10 multicoloured . . 50 25
1353 – 2k.10 multicoloured . . 50 25
1354 – 2k.10 brown, black and blue 50 25
DESIGNS: No. 1352, "Blue Tiger" (David Klocker Ehrenstrahl); 1353, "Hedvig Charlotta Nordenflycht" (after Johan Henrik Scheffel); 1354, "Gripsholm Castle" (lithograph, Carl Johan Billmark).

1987. "In the Service of Humanity".
1355 **397** 3k.10 blue 65 70
1356 – 3k.10 green 65 70
1357 – 3k.10 brown 65 70
DESIGNS: No. 1356, Dag Hammarskjold (U.N. Secretary-General, 1953–1961); 1357, Folke Bernadotte (leader of "white bus" relief action to rescue prisoners, 1945).

1987. Stamp Day. Bicentenary of Circus in Sweden. Multicoloured.
1358 2k.10 Type **398** 60 65
1359 2k.10 Reino riding one-wheel cycle on wire . . . 60 65
1360 2k.10 Acrobat on horseback 60 65

399 "Victoria cruziana" at Bergian Garden, Stockholm University

400 Porridge left for the Grey Christmas Elf

1987. Bicentenary of Swedish Botanical Gardens.
1361 **399** 2k.10 green, deep green and blue 50 25
1362 – 2k.10 green and brown 50 25
1363 – 2k.10 deep green, green and blue 50 25
1364 – 2k.10 yellow, brown and green 50 25
DESIGNS: No. 1362, Uppsala University Baroque Garden plan and Carl Harleman (architect); 1363, Rock garden, Gothenburg Botanical Garden; 1364, "Liriodendron tulipifera", Lund Botanical Garden.

1987. Christmas. Folk Customs. Multicoloured.
1365 2k. Type **400** 45 30
1366 2k. Staffan ride (watering horses in North-running spring on Boxing Day) . . 45 30
1367 2k. Christmas Day sledge race home from church 45 30
1368 2k. Northern bullfinches on corn sheaf 45 30

401 Pulsars (Antony Hewish, 1974)

1987. Nobel Prize Winners for Physics.
1369 **401** 2k.90 blue 65 65
1370 – 2k.90 black 65 65
1371 – 2k.90 blue 65 65
1372 – 2k.90 blue 65 65
1373 – 2k.90 black 65 65
DESIGNS: No. 1370, Formula of maximum white dwarf star mass (S. Chandrasekhar, 1983); 1371, Heavy atom nuclei construction (William Fowler, 1983); 1372, Temperature of cosmic background radiation (A. Penzias and R. Wilson, 1978); 1373, Radio telescopes receiving radio waves from galaxy (Martin Ryle, 1974).

402 Lake Hjalmaren Fishing Skiff

404 White-tailed Sea Eagle ("Haliaetus albicilla")

403 Bishop Hill and Erik Jansson (founder)

1988. Inland Boats. Each purple on buff.
1374 3k.10 Type **402** 70 70
1375 3k.10 Lake Vattern market boat 70 70
1376 3k.10 River Byske logging boat 70 70
1377 3k.10 Lake Asnen rowing boat 70 70
1378 3k.10 Lake Vanern ice boat 70 70
1379 3k.10 Lake Lockne church longboat 70 70

1988. 350th Anniv of New Sweden (settlement in America).
1380 – 3k.60 multicoloured . . 85 80
1381 **403** 3k.60 multicoloured . . 85 80
1382 – 3k.60 brown 85 80
1383 – 3k.60 blue and brown . . 85 80
1384 – 3k.60 blue, yellow and red 85 80
1385 – 3k.60 black, blue and red 85 80
DESIGNS—As T **403**: No. 1380, Map, settlers, Indians, "Calmare Nyckel" and "Fagel Grip". 27 × 23 mm: No. 1382, Carl Sandburg (American poet) and Jenny Lind (Swedish soprano); 1383, Charles Lindbergh (aviator) and Ryan NYP Special "Spirit of St. Louis". 27 × 37 mm: No. 1384, Alan Bean (astronaut) on Moon with Hasselblad camera; 1385, Ice hockey.

1988. Coastal Wildlife.
1386 **404** 2k.20 brown and red . . 50 20
1387 – 2k.20 brown and blue . . 50 20
1388 – 4k. black, brown and green . . . . 1·00 25
DESIGNS: No. 1387, Grey seal ("Halichoerus gryphus"); 1388, European eel ("Anguilla anguilla").

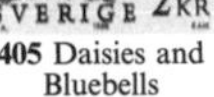

405 Daisies and Bluebells

406 Detail of "Creation" Stained Glass Window (Bo Beskow), Skara Cathedral

1988. Rebate stamps. Midsummer Festival. Multicoloured.
1389 2k. Type **405** 85 20
1390 2k. Garlanded longboat . . 85 20
1391 2k. Children making garlands 85 20
1392 2k. Raising the maypole . . 85 20
1393 2k. Fiddlers 85 20
1394 2k. "Norrskar" (tourist launch) 85 20
1395 2k. Couples dancing 85 20
1396 2k. Accordianist 85 20
1397 2k. Archipelago with decorated landing stage 85 20
1398 2k. Bouquet of seven wild flowers 85 20

1988. Anniversaries.
1399 **406** 2k.20 multicoloured . . 55 20
1400 – 4k.40 red on brown . . 1·00 30
1401 – 8k. red, green and black 1·80 70
DESIGNS: 2k.20, Type **406** (millenary of Skara). 23 × 41 mm: 4k.40, "Falun Copper Mine" (Pehr Hillestrom) (700th anniv of Stora Kopparberg (mining company)); 8k. Scene from play "The Queen's Diamond Ornament" (bicentenary of Royal Dramatic Theatre, Stockholm).

407 "Self-portrait" (Nils Dardel)

408 X2 High-speed Train

1968. Swedish Artists in Paris. Multicoloured.
1402 2k.20 Type **407** 50 45
1403 2k.20 "Autumn, Gubbhuset" (Vera Nilsson) (40 × 43 mm) . . 50 45
1404 2k.20 "Self-Portrait" (Isaac Grunewald) 50 45
1405 2k.20 "Visit to an Eccentric Lady" (Nils Dardel) . . . 50 45
1406 2k.20 "Soap Bubbles" (Vera Nilsson) (40 × 43 mm) . . 50 45
1407 2k.20 "The Singing Tree" (Isaac Grunewald) 50 45

1988. Europa. Transport and Communications.
1408 **408** 2k.20 blue, orange and brown . . . . 1·00 20
1409 3k.10 blue, black and purple 75 75
1410 – 3k.10 black and purple 75 75
DESIGN: No. 1410, Narrow-gauge steam locomotive.

409 Common Swift **410** Andersson

1988.
1411 **409** 20k. purple and mauve 4·25 55

1988. Birth Centenary of Dan Andersson (poet). Each violet, green and blue.
1412 2k.20 Type **410** 50 30
1413 2k.20 Lake, Finnmarken (58 × 24 mm) 50 30

411 Players

412 Angel and Shepherds

1988. Swedish Football. Multicoloured.
1414 2k.20 Type **411** 60 70
1415 2k.20 Three players 60 70
1416 2k.20 Women players . . . 60 70

1988. Christmas. Multicoloured.
1417 2k. Type **412** 45 25
1418 2k. Horse and angel 45 25
1419 2k. Birds singing in trees . . 45 25
1420 2k. Three wise men 45 25
1421 2k. Holy Family 45 25
1422 2k. Shepherds and sheep . . 45 25
Nos. 1417/22 were printed together, se-tenant, forming a composite design.

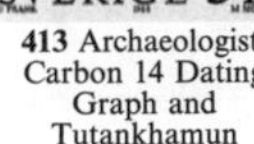

413 Archaeologist, Carbon 14 Dating Graph and Tutankhamun

414 Nidingen 1946 Concrete and 1832 Twin Lighthouses

1988. Nobel Prize Winners for Chemistry. Mult.
1423 3k.10 Type **413** (Willard Frank Libby, 1960) . . . 70 70
1424 3k.10 Plastics molecules (Karl Ziegler and Giulio Natta, 1963) 70 70
1425 3k.10 Electron microscope (Aaron Klug, 1982) . . . 70 70
1426 3k.10 Landscape and symbols (Ilya Prigogine, 1977) 70 70

1989. Lighthouses.
1427 **414** 1k.90 green, brown and black 45 20
1428 – 2k.70 blue, red and deep blue 70 45
1429 – 3k.80 brown, deep blue and blue 90 55
1430 – 3k.90 black, red & brown . . . . 1·00 65
DESIGNS: 2k.70, Soderarm stone lighthouse; 3k.80, Sydostbrotten caisson lighthouse; 3k.90, Sandhammaren iron lighthouse.

415 Wolverine ("Gulo gulo")

1989. Animals in Threatened Habitats.
1431 **415** 2k.30 brown, orange and green 50 20
1432 – 2k.30 brown, green and orange 50 20
1433 – 2k.40 brown, chocolate and red 55 20
1434 – 2k.60 agate, brown and orange 60 25
1435 – 3k.30 deep green, green and brown 70 60
1436 – 4k.60 black, green and orange . . . . 1·00 40
DESIGNS: 2k.30 (1432), Ural owl ("Strix uralensis"): 2k.40, Lesser spotted woodpecker ("Dendrocopos minor"); 2k.60, Dunlin ("Calidris alpina schinzii"); 3k.30, Common tree frog ("Hyla arborea"); 4k.60, Red-breasted flycatcher ("Ficedula parva").

416 Globe Arena

1989. Opening of Globe Arena, Stockholm. Mult.
1437 2k.30 Type **416** 50 25
1438 2k.30 Ice hockey 50 25
1439 2k.30 Gymnastics 50 25
1440 2k.30 Pop concert 50 25

417 Woman's Woollen Bib Front

418 Sailing

1989. Nordic Countries' Postal Co-operation. Traditional Lapp Costumes.
1441 2k.30 Type **417** 60 20
1442 3k.30 Man's belt pouch . . 80 60

1989. Rebate stamps. Summer Activities. Mult.
1443 2k.10 Type **418** 80 25
1444 2k.10 Beach ball 80 25
1445 2k.10 Cycling 80 25
1446 2k.10 Canoeing 80 25
1447 2k.10 Fishing 80 25
1448 2k.10 Camping 80 25
1449 2k.10 Croquet 80 25
1450 2k.10 Badminton 80 25
1451 2k.10 Gardening 80 25
1452 2k.10 Sand castle, bucket and spade 80 25

419 "Protest March" (Nils Kreuger)

420 Playing with Boats

1989. Centenary of Swedish Labour Movement.
1453 **419** 2k.30 black and red . . 55 15

1989. Europa. Children's Games and Toys.
1454 **420** 2k.30 brown 90 20
1455 3k.30 mauve 75 75
1456 – 3k.30 green 75 75
DESIGN: No. 1456, Girl riding kick-sled.

421 Lounger (Varnamo)

422 Researcher in Greenland and Temperature Curve

1989. Industries of Smaland Towns. Each mauve, orange and red.
1457 2k.30 Type **421** 50 55
1458 2k.30 Tools for self-assembly furniture (Almhult) 50 55
1459 2k.30 Sewing machine and embroidery (Huskvarna) 50 55
1460 2k.30 Blowing glass (Afors) 50 55
1461 2k.30 Coathanger hook and clothes-peg spring (Gnosjo) 50 55
1462 2k.30 Match (Jonkoping) . . 50 55

1989. 250th Anniv of Swedish Academy of Sciences. Polar Research. Multicoloured.
1463 3k.30 Type **422** 80 70
1464 3k.30 Abisko Natural Science Station, Lapland (40 × 43 mm) 80 70
1465 3k.30 "Oden" (ice research ship) and researchers . . 80 70
1466 3k.30 Otto Nordenskiold 1901–03 expedition's "Antarctic" and Emperor penguin with chick . . . 80 70
1467 3k.30 1988 Antarctic expedition's vehicles and Hughes Model 500 helicopter (40 × 43 mm) 80 70
1468 3k.30 Geodimeter and South polar skua 80 70

423 Eagle Owl

1989.
1469 **423** 30k. brown, black & mve 5·75 45

424 Arctic Rhododendron ("Rhododendron lapponicum")

425 Jamthund

1989. National Parks (1st series).
1470 **424** 2k.40 mauve, green & bl 55 25
1471 – 2k.40 mauve and green 55 25
1472 – 4k.30 red, black and blue 1·00 75
DESIGNS—HORIZ: No. 1471, Calypso ("Calypso bulbosa"). VERT: No. 1472, Black guillemots at Bla Jungfrun.
See also Nos. 1486/90.

1989. Centenary of Swedish Kennel Club. Mult.
1473 2k.40 Type **425** 75 85
1474 2k.40 Hamilton foxhound 75 85
1475 2k.40 Vastgota sheep dog 75 85

426 Decorated Tree

427 Vinegar Flies (T. H. Morgan, 1933)

1989. Christmas. Multicoloured.
1476 2k.10 Type **426** 55 25
1477 2k.10 Candelabra and food 55 25
1478 2k.10 Star, poinsettia and tureen 55 25
1479 2k.10 Decorated tree and straw goat 55 25
1480 2k.10 Girl watching television 55 25
1481 2k.10 Family with present 55 25
Nos. 1476/81 were issued together, se-tenant, forming a composite design.

1989. Nobel Prize Winners for Medicine.
1482 **427** 3k.60 brown, yellow & bl 80 80
1483 – 3k.60 yellow, blue & red 80 80
1484 – 3k.60 multicoloured . . 80 80
1485 – 3k.60 multicoloured . . 80 80
DESIGNS: No. 1483 X-ray diffractogram and D.N.A. molecule (Francis Crick, James Watson and Maurice Wilkins, 1962); 1484, D.N.A. molecule cut by restriction enzyme (W. Arber, D. Nathans and H. O. Smith, 1978); 1485, Maize kernels (Barbara McClintock, 1983).

428 Angso

429 Lumberjack

1990. National Parks (2nd series).
1486 **428** 2k.50 blue, green and red 55 20
1487 – 2k.50 red, green and blue 55 20
1488 – 3k.70 blue, brown & grn 85 25
1489 – 4k.10 blue, green & brn 95 80
1490 – 4k.80 green, brown & bl 1·20 90
DESIGNS: No. 1487, Pieljekaise; 1488, Muddus; 1489, Padjelanta; 1490, Sanfjallet.

1990. Centenary of Industrial Safety Inspectorate.
1491 **429** 2k.50 blue and brown . . 65 20

430 Postal Museum, Stockholm

431 Carved Bone Head and Cast Dragon Head

1990. Europa. Post Office Buildings.
1492 **430** 2k.50 brown, orange & bl 85 25
1493 – 3k.80 blue, yellow and brown 85 85
1494 – 3k.80 brown, blue and yellow 85 85
DESIGNS: No. 1493, Sollebrunn Post Office; 1494, Vasteras Post Office.

1990. Vikings. Multicoloured.
1495 2k.50 Type **431** 55 55

1496 2k.50 Returning Viking longships (34×29 mm) . . 55 55
1497 2k.50 Wooden houses (34×29 mm) 55 55
1498 2k.50 Bronze figurine of God of Fertility and silver cross 55 55
1499 2k.50 Crosier and gold embroidered deer 55 55
1500 2k.50 Vikings in roundship (34×29 mm) 55 55
1501 2k.50 Viking disembarking (34×29 mm) 55 55
1502 2k.50 Viking swords 55 55
Nos. 1496/7 and 1500/1 form a composite design.

432 Worker collecting Pollen

433 Prow of "Wasa" and Museum

1990. Rebate stamps. Honey Bees. Multicoloured.
1503 2k.30 Type **432** 90 25
1504 2k.30 Worker on bilberry 90 25
1505 2k.30 Worker flying back to hive 90 25
1506 2k.30 Beehive 90 25
1507 2k.30 Bees building honeycombs 90 25
1508 2k.30 Drone 90 25
1509 2k.30 Queen 90 25
1510 2k.30 Swarm on branch . . 90 25
1511 2k.30 Beekeeper collecting frame 90 25
1512 2k.30 Pot of honey 90 25

1990. Opening of New "Wasa" (17th-century ship of the line) Museum.
1513 **433** 2k.50 black and red . . 75 20
1514 – 4k.60 blue and red . . . 1·10 70
DESIGNS: 4k.60, Stern of "Wasa" and museum.

434 Endurance Event

1990. World Equestrian Games, Stockholm. Mult.
1515 3k.80 Type **434** 90 85
1516 3k.80 Mark Todd on Carisma jumping wall (3-day event) 90 85
1517 3k.80 John Whitaker on Next Milton jumping fence (show jumping) . . 90 85
1518 3k.80 Louise Nathorst (dressage) 90 85
1519 3k.80 Team vaulting 90 85
1520 3k.80 Pahlsson brothers driving four-in-hand . . . 90 85

435 Papermaking, 1600

436 "Dearest Brothers, Sisters and Friends"

1990. Centenary of Swedish Pulp and Paper Industry. Multicoloured.
1521 2k.50 Type **435** 55 40
1522 2k.50 Crown watermark . . 55 40
1523 2k.50 Foreign newspapers using Swedish newsprint 55 40
1524 2k.50 Rolls of paper 55 40

1990. 250th Birth Anniv of Carl Michael Bellman (poet) (1525/7) and Birth Centenary of Evert Taube (poet) (1528/30). Designs showing illustrations of their poems.
1525 **436** 2k.50 brown and black 60 55
1526 – 2k.50 multicoloured . . 60 55
1527 – 2k.50 black, blue and red 60 55
1528 – 2k.50 multicoloured . . 60 55
1529 – 2k.50 multicoloured . . 60 55
1530 – 2k.50 multicoloured . . 60 55
DESIGNS—As Type **436**: No. 1527, "Fredman in the Gutter"; 1528, "Happy Baker of San Remo"; 1530, "Violava". 40×43 mm: 1526, "Proud City"; 1529, "At Sea".

437 Oved Castle

1990.
1531 **437** 40k. brown, black and red . . . . 7·50 30

438 Moa Martinson

439 Box Camera with Bellows

1990. Birth Centenary of Moa Martinson (novelist).
1532 **438** 2k.50 black and red . . 60 25
1533 – 2k.50 black and violet 60 25
DESIGN: No. 1533, Fredrika and Sofi bathing (from "Women and Apple Trees").

1990. Photography. Multicoloured.
1534 2k.50 Type **439** 70 75
1535 2k.50 August Strindberg (self-photograph) 70 75
1536 2k.50 Modern 35 mm camera 70 75

440 Cumulus Clouds

441 Christmas Cactus ("Schlumbergera x buckleyi")

1990. Clouds.
1537 **440** 4k.50 multicoloured . . 1·10 25
1538 – 4k.70 black and blue . . 1·20 85
1539 – 4k.90 blue, green & brn 1·20 90
1540 – 5k.20 blue & ultramarine 1·30 80
DESIGNS: 4k.70, Cumulonimbus; 4k.90, Cirus uncinus; 5k.20, Altocumulus lenticularis.

1990. Christmas. Flowers. Multicoloured.
1541 2k.30 Type **441** 60 30
1542 2k.30 Christmas rose ("Helleborus niger") . . . 60 30
1543 2k.30 Azalea ("Rhododenron simsii") . . 60 30
1544 2k.30 Amaryllis ("Hippeastrum × hortorum") 60 30
1545 2k.30 Hyacinth ("Hyacinthus orientalis") 60 30
1546 2k.30 Poinsettia ("Euphorbia pulcherrima") 60 30

442 Par Lagerkvist (1951)

1990. Nobel Prize Winners for Literature.
1547 **442** 3k.80 blue 85 85
1548 – 3k.80 red 85 85
1549 – 3k.80 green 85 80
1550 – 3k.80 violet 85 80
DESIGNS: No. 1548, Ernest Hemingway (1954); 1549, Albert Camus (1957); 1550, Boris Pasternak (1958).

443 Heath of Wels ("Silurus glanis") and Young

444 "Carta Marina", 1572 (Olaus Magnus)

1991. Freshwater Fishes.
1551 **443** 2k.50 black, green & brn 60 20
1552 – 2k.50 black, green & brn 60 20
1553 – 5k. black, blue and brown . . . . 1·10 25
1554 – 5k.40 black, violet & red 1·30 90
1555 – 5k.50 brown and green 1·30 35
1556 – 5k.60 black, blue & orge 1·40 85
DESIGNS: No. 1552, Wels (different); 1553, Spined loach ("Cobitis taeina"); 1554, Gudgeon ("Gobio gobio"); 1555, Stone loach ("Noemacheilus barbataulus"); 1556, Sunbleak ("Leucaspius delineatus").
Nos. 1551/2 form a composite design of two catfish.

1991. Maps. Multicoloured.
1557 5k. Type **444** . . . . . . 1·10 1·10
1558 5k. Sweden, Denmark and Norway, 1662 (A. Bureus and J. Blaeu) (40×43 mm) . . . . . . 1·10 1·10
1559 5k. Star globe, 1759 (Anders Akerman) . . . . 1·10 1·10
1560 5k. Relief map of Areskutan, 1938 . . . . 1·10 1·10
1561 5k. Stockholm old town, 1989 (40×43 mm) . . . . 1·10 1·10
1562 5k. Bed-rock map of Areskutan, 1984 . . . . 1·10 1·10

445 Queen Silvia

447 Seglora Church

446 Drottningholm Palace (after Erik Dahlbergh)

1991.
1564 – 2k.80 blue 75 20
1565 – 2k.90 green 70 20
1566 – 3k.20 violet 80 20
1568 **445** 5k. purple . . . . 1·20 30
1569 6k. red . . . . 1·30 20
1570 6k.50 violet . . . . . . 1·60 55
DESIGN: 2k.80 to 3k.20, King Carl XVI Gustav.

1991. Royal Residence at Drottningholm Palace.
1576 **446** 25k. brown, black & grn 5·00 65

1991. Rebate stamps. Centenary of Skansen Park, Stockholm. Multicoloured.
1577 2k.40 Type **447** 65 25
1578 2k.40 Celebration of Swedish Flag and National Days at Skansen 65 25
1579 2k.40 Wedding at Skansen 65 25
1580 2k.40 Animals, Skansen Zoo 65 25

448 Park Entrance

449 Polar Bears

1991. Centenary of Public Amusement Parks. Each blue.
1581 2k.50 Type **448** 60 30
1582 2k.50 Dancers and violinist 60 30

1991. Nordic Countries' Postal Co-operation. Tourism. Animals in Kolmarden Zoo.
1583 **449** 2k.50 black, brown & bl 65 25
1584 – 4k. red and purple . . 90 60
DESIGN: 4k. Dolphins and trainer.

450 "Hermes" Rocket

1991. Europa. Europe in Space. Multicoloured.
1585 4k. Type **450** . . . . . . 1·00 85
1586 4k. "Freja" Northern Lights research satellite . . . . 1·00 85
1587 4k. "Tele-X" television satellite . . . . 1·00 85

451 Magda Julin (figure skating, Antwerp, 1920)

1991. Olympic Games Gold Medallists (1st issue). Multicoloured.
1588 2k.50 Type **451** 55 40
1589 2k.50 Toini Gustafsson (cross-country skiing, Grenoble, 1968) 55 40
1590 2k.50 Agneta Andersson and Anna Olsson (canoeing, Los Angeles, 1984) 55 40
1591 2k.50 Ulrika Knape (high diving, Munich, 1972) . . 55 40
See also Nos. 1619/22 and 1635/8.

452 Spetal Mine, Norberg (after Carl David af Uhr)

1991. Bergslagen Iron Industry. Multicoloured.
1592 2k.50 Type **452** 65 45
1593 2k.50 Walloon smithy, Forsmark Mill (after J. Wilhem Wallender) . . 65 45
1594 2k.50 Forge (27×24 mm) 65 45
1595 2k.50 Foundry (after Johann Ahlback) (27×24 mm) . . 65 45
1596 2k.50 Dannemora Mine (after Elias Martin) (27×37 mm) 65 45
1597 2k.50 Pershyttan Mill (27×37 mm) 65 45

453 Stromsholm Castle

1991.
1598 **453** 10k. green and black . . 1·90 25

454 Lena Philipsson

455 Close-up of Gustav III

1991. Rock and Pop Music. Multicoloured.
1599 2k.50 Type **454** 55 50
1600 2k.50 Roxette (duo) 55 50
1601 2k.50 Jerry Williams 55 50

1991. 70th Birthday of Czeslaw Slania (engraver). Designs showing "Coronation of King Gustav III" by Carl Gustav Pilo.
1602 **455** 10k. blue . . . . 2·20 1·30
1603 – 10k. violet . . . . . . 2·20 1·30
1604 – 10k. black . . . . . . 2·20 1·30
DESIGNS—As T **455**: No. 1603, Close-up of lowering of crown onto King's head. 76 x 44mm: 1604, Complete picture.

456 "Mans and Mari from Spring to Winter" (Kaj Beckman)

1991. Christmas. Illustrations from children's books. Multicoloured.
1605 2k.30 Type **456** 50 30
1606 2k.30 Family dancing round Christmas tree ("Peter and Lottas's Christmas", Elsa Beskow) 50 30

1607 2k.30 Dressed cat by Christmas tree ("Pettersson gets a Christmas Visit", Sven Nordqvist) 50 30
1608 2k.30 Girl by bed ("Little Anna's Christmas Present", Lasse Sandberg) 50 30

457 Henri Dunant (founder of Red Cross), 1901

1991. Nobel Prize Winners for Peace.
1609 **457** 4k. red 90 70
1610 – 4k. green 90 95
1611 – 4k. blue 90 70
1612 – 4k. lilac 90 70
DESIGNS: No. 1610, Albert Schweitzer (medical missionary), 1953; 1611, Alva Myrdal (disarmament negotiator), 1982; 1612, Andrei Sakharov (human rights activist), 1975.

458 Mulle, the Forest Elf, with Children

459 Roe Buck

1992. Centenary of Outdoor Life Association.
1613 **458** 2k.30 brown, red & grn 55 20

1992. Wildlife.
1614 **459** 2k.80 brown, agate & grn 70 20
1615 – 2k.80 agate, brn & grn 70 20
1617 – 6k. brown and agate . . 1·40 50
1618 – 7k. brown and green . . 1·60 50
DESIGNS—As T **459**: No. 1615, Roe deer ("Capreolus capreolus") with fawn. 20 × 28 mm: No. 1617, Eurasian red squirrel ("Sciurus vulgaris"); 1618, Elk ("Alces alces").

1992. Olympic Games Gold medallists (2nd issue). As T **451**. Multicoloured.
1619 2k.80 Gunde Svan (cross-country skiing, Sarajevo, 1984, and Calgary, 1988) 65 45
1620 2k.80 Thomas Wassberg (cross-country skiing, Lake Placid, 1980, and Sarajevo, 1984) 65 35
1621 2k.80 Tomas Gustafson (speed skating, Sarajevo, 1984, and Calgary, 1988) 65 35
1622 2k.80 Ingemar Stenmark (slalom, Lake Placid, 1980) 65 35

460 Gunnar Nordahl (Sweden)

461 1855 3s. Green

1992. European Football Championship, Sweden. Each blue and green.
1623 2k.80 Type **460** 70 20
1624 2k.80 Lothar Matthaus (Germany) and Tomas Brolin (Sweden) 70 20

1992. Stamp Year.
1625 **461** 2k.80 green, yellow & blk . . . . 1·10 1·60
1626 4k.50 green, yellow & blk . . . . 1·10 1·60
1627 – 5k.50 yellow, grey & blk 1·10 1·10
DESIGN: 5k.50, 1857 3s. yellow error.

462 "Sprengtporten" (frigate), 1785

463 Rabbit (Emma Westerberg)

1992. Europa. 500th Anniv of Discovery of America by Columbus. Multicoloured.
1628 4k.50 Type **462** . . . . . 1·10 1·10
1629 4k.50 "Superb" (brig), 1855 1·10 1·10
1630 4k.50 "Big T" (yacht) (competitor in Discovery Race) . . . . 1·10 1·10

1992. Rebate stamps. Centenary of "Kamratposten" (children's magazine) showing children's drawings. Multicoloured.
1631 2k.50 Type **463** 55 25
1632 2k.50 Horses (Helena Johansson) 55 25
1633 2k.50 Kitten (Sabina Ostermark) 55 25
1634 2k.50 Elephant (Hanna Bengtsson) 55 25

1992. Olympic Games Gold Medallists (3rd series). As T **451**. Multicoloured.
1635 5k.50 Gunnar Larsson (swimming, Munich, 1972) 1·30 1·00
1636 5k.50 Bernt Johansson (cycling, Montreal, 1976) 1·30 1·00
1637 5k.50 Anders Garderud (steeplechase, Montreal, 1976) . . . . 1·30 1·10
1638 5k.50 Gert Fredriksson (canoeing, London, 1948) 1·30 1·10

464 Karlberg Castle

1992.
1639 **464** 20k. black, green and blue . . . . 4·00 35

465 Hand holding Flower

466 Gustaf Dalen's Sun Valve and First Automated Lighthouse, Gasfeten

1992. Greetings Stamps. Multicoloured.
1640 2k.80 Type **465** 65 30
1641 2k.80 Wedge of cheese ("Lyckans ost") 65 30
1642 2k.80 New-born baby ("Lev val!") 65 30
1643 2k.80 Writing with feather ("Gratulerar") 65 30

1992. Centenary of Patent and Registration Office.
1644 **466** 2k.80 black and blue . . 65 20

467 Riksdag (Parliament), Helgeandsholmen Island

1992. 88th Interparliamentary Union Conference, Stockholm.
1645 **467** 2k.80 violet on buff . . 70 20

468 "Kitchen Maid" (Rembrandt)

469 Plateosaurus

1992. Bicentenary of National Museum of Fine Arts. Multicoloured.
1646 5k.50 Type **468** . . . . . 1·20 1·10
1647 5k.50 "Triumph of Venus" (Francois Boucher) (40 × 44 mm) . . . . . . 1·20 1·10
1648 5k.50 "Portrait of a Girl" (Albrecht Durer) . . . . 1·20 1·10
1649 5k.50 Rorstrand vase decorated by Erik Wahlberg . . . . 1·20 1·10
1650 5k.50 "Seine Motif" (Carl Fredrik Hill) (40 × 44 mm) 1·20 1·10
1651 5k.50 "Sergel in his Studio" (Carl Larsson) . . . . . 1·20 1·10

1992. Prehistoric Animals. Mult.
1652 2k.80 Type **469** 75 70
1653 2k.80 Crocodile ("Thoracosaurus scanicus") 75 70
1654 2k.80 Woolly-haired rhino ("Coelodonta antiquitatis") 75 70
1655 2k.80 Mammoth ("Mammuthus primigenius") 75 70

470 Volvo "PV831", 1950

471 Osprey ("Pandion haliaetus")

1992. Swedish Cars.
1656 **470** 4k. blue 90 45
1657 – 4k. green and blue . . . 90 45
DESIGN: No. 1657 Saab "92", 1950.

1992. Birds of the Baltic.
1658 **471** 4k.50 black and blue . . 1·00 85
1659 – 4k.50 brown, black & bl 1·00 85
1660 – 4k.50 deep brown, brown and blue . . . 1·00 95
1661 – 4k.50 black, brown & bl 1·00 85
DESIGNS: No. 1659, Black-tailed godwit ("Limosa limosa"); 1660, Goosander ("Mergus merganser"); 1661, Common shelducks ("Tadorna tadorna").

472 "Meeting of Joachim and Anna"

473 Walcott

1992. Christmas. Icons. Multicoloured.
1662 2k.30 Type **472** 50 30
1663 2k.30 "Madonna and Child" 50 30
1664 2k.30 "Archangel Gabriel" (head) 50 30
1665 2k.30 "Saint Nicholas" ($\frac{1}{2}$-length portrait) 50 30

1992. Award of Nobel Literature Prize to Derek Walcott.
1666 **473** 5k.50 purple, blue & brn 1·20 80
1667 – 5k.50 purple, brown & bl 1·20 80
DESIGN: No. 1667, Palm trees, ocean and text.

474 Brown Bear Cubs

1993. Wildlife.
1668 **474** 2k.90 brown and black 75 20
1669 – 2k.90 brown and black 75 20
1671 – 3k. multicoloured . . . 50 45
1672 – 5k.80 black, grey & brn 1·40 35
1673 – 12k. brown, blue and red 2·50 1·00
DESIGNS—As T **474**: No. 1669, Brown bear. 27 × 21 mm: No. 1671, Polecat; 1672, Wolf. 21 × 27 mm: No. 1673, Lynx.

475 "Big Bird" Glider (World Gliding Championships, Borlange)

476 Gooseberries ("Ribes uva-crispa")

1993. Int Sports Championships in Sweden. Mult.
1674 6k. Type **475** . . . . . 1·30 1·20
1675 6k. Martin Kornbakk (World Wrestling Championships, Stockholm) . . . . 1·30 1·20
1676 6k. Jorgen Persson (World Table Tennis Championships, Gothenburg) . . . . . . 1·30 1·20
1677 6k. Lars Erik Andersson (European Bowling Championships, Malmo) 1·30 1·20
1678 6k. Per Carlen (World Handball Championships, Gothenburg) . . . . . . 1·30 1·20
1679 6k. Marie Helene Westin (World Cross-country Skiing Championships, Falun) . . . . 1·30 1·20
Nos. 1675/9 show Swedish competitors.

1993. Fruits.
1680 **476** 2k.40 green 55 20
1681 – 2k.40 green 55 25
1682 – 2k.40 red 55 25
DESIGNS: No. 1681, Pears ("Prys communis"); 1682, Cherries ("Prunus avium").

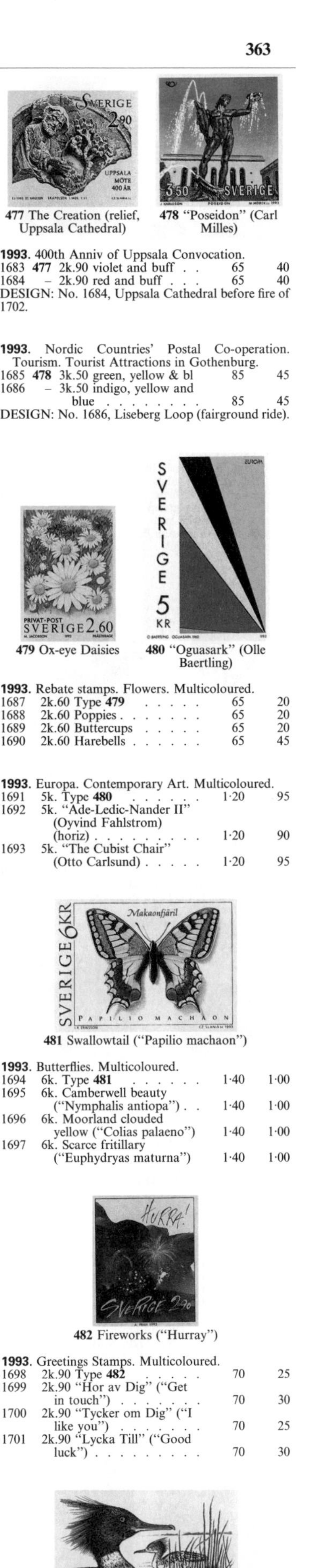

477 The Creation (relief, Uppsala Cathedral)

478 "Poseidon" (Carl Milles)

1993. 400th Anniv of Uppsala Convocation.
1683 **477** 2k.90 violet and buff . . 65 40
1684 – 2k.90 red and buff . . . 65 40
DESIGN: No. 1684, Uppsala Cathedral before fire of 1702.

1993. Nordic Countries' Postal Co-operation. Tourism. Tourist Attractions in Gothenburg.
1685 **478** 3k.50 green, yellow & bl 85 45
1686 – 3k.50 indigo, yellow and blue 85 45
DESIGN: No. 1686, Liseberg Loop (fairground ride).

479 Ox-eye Daisies

480 "Oguasark" (Olle Baertling)

1993. Rebate stamps. Flowers. Multicoloured.
1687 2k.60 Type **479** 65 20
1688 2k.60 Poppies 65 20
1689 2k.60 Buttercups 65 20
1690 2k.60 Harebells 65 45

1993. Europa. Contemporary Art. Multicoloured.
1691 5k. Type **480** . . . . . . 1·20 95
1692 5k. "Ade-Ledic-Nander II" (Oyvind Fahlstrom) (horiz) . . . . 1·20 90
1693 5k. "The Cubist Chair" (Otto Carlsund) . . . . . 1·20 95

481 Swallowtail ("Papilio machaon")

1993. Butterflies. Multicoloured.
1694 6k. Type **481** . . . . . . 1·40 1·00
1695 6k. Camberwell beauty ("Nymphalis antiopa") . . 1·40 1·00
1696 6k. Moorland clouded yellow ("Colias palaeno") 1·40 1·00
1697 6k. Scarce fritillary ("Euphydryas maturna") 1·40 1·00

482 Fireworks ("Hurray")

1993. Greetings Stamps. Multicoloured.
1698 2k.90 Type **482** 70 25
1699 2k.90 "Hor av Dig" ("Get in touch") 70 30
1700 2k.90 "Tycker om Dig" ("I like you") 70 25
1701 2k.90 "Lycka Till" ("Good luck") 70 30

483 Red-breasted Merganser ("Mergus serrator")

1993. Sea Birds. Multicoloured.
1702 5k. Type **483** . . . . . . 1·10 85
1703 5k. Velvet scoter ("Melanitta fusca") . . . . 1·10 85
1704 5k. Tufted duck ("Aythya fuligula") . . . . 1·10 85
1705 5k. Eider ("Somateria mollissima") . . . . . . 1·10 95

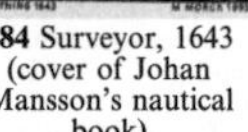

484 Surveyor, 1643 (cover of Johan Mansson's nautical book)

485 King Carl Gustav

1993. 350th Anniv of Hydrographic Service.
1706 **484** 2k.90 brown, blue & blk 70 25
1707 – 2k.90 brown, blue & blk 70 25
DESIGN: No. 1707, Survey ship "Nils Stromcrona", 1993.

1993. 20th Anniv of Accession of King Carl XVI Gustav and Queen Silvia's 50th Birthday.
1708 8k. Type **485** . . . . . . 1·40 1·50
1709 10k. King Carl Gustav wearing medals . . . . . 2·50 1·90
1710 10k. Queen Silvia . . . . . 2·50 1·90
1711 12k. Family group and Stockholm and Drottningholm Palaces (75 × 44 mm) . . . . . . 3·00 2·50

486 Plaited Heart

487 Stockholm City Hall

1993. Christmas.
1712 **486** 2k.40 green 55 20
1713 – 2k.40 red 55 20
DESIGN: No. 1713, Straw goat.

1993. Award of Nobel Literature Prize to Toni Morrison.
1714 **487** 6k. red and blue . . . . 1·30 90
1715 – 6k. brown and red . . . . 1·30 90
DESIGN: No. 1715, Toni Morrison.

488 Victoria Plums

489 North Sweden Horse's Head

1994. Fruits.
1716 **488** 2k.80 multicoloured . . 70 20
1717 – 2k.80 multicoloured . . 70 30
1718 – 2k.80 light green & green 70 30
DESIGNS: No. 1717, Opal plums; 1718, "James Grieve" apples.

1994. Domestic Animals (1st series).
1719 **489** 3k.20 brown, agate and red 75 20
1720 – 3k.20 brown, agate and red 75 20
1721 – 3k.20 black, brown & bl 80 20
1722 – 6k.40 black and green 1·50 40
DESIGNS—VERT: No. 1720, North Sweden horses in harness. HORIZ: 1721, Gotland sheep; 1722, Mountain cow.
See also Nos. 1787/91 and 1802/3.

490 Mother Svea and European Union Emblem

491 Siamese

1994. Single European Market.
1723 **490** 5k. blue . . . . 1·20 35

1994. Cats. Multicoloured.
1724 4k.50 Type **491** . . . . . 1·00 80
1725 4k.50 Persian . . . . 1·00 80
1726 4k.50 European . . . . . . 1·00 85
1727 4k.50 Abyssinian . . . . . 1·00 75

492 Illustration from "Le Roman de la Rose"

1994. Franco–Swedish Cultural Relations. Multicoloured.
1728 5k. Type **492** . . . . . . 1·10 95
1729 5k. Swedish and French flags . . . . 1·10 1·10
1730 5k. Sketch by De la Vallee of Knight's House (40 × 43 mm) . . . . . . 1·10 1·10
1731 5k. "Household Chores" (Pehr Hillestrom) . . . . 1·10 1·10
1732 5k. "Banquet for Gustav III at the Trianon, 1784" (Niclas Lafrensen the younger) (40 × 43 mm) . . 1·10 1·10
1733 5k. "Carl XIV Johan" (Francois Gerard) . . . . 1·10 1·10

493 Martin Dahlin during Match

1994. World Cup Football Championship, U.S.A.
1734 **493** 3k.20 blue and red . . . 80 35

494 Wild Rose ("Rosa dumalis")

495 Lunar Module "Eagle" and Astronauts

1994. Roses. Multicoloured.
1735 3k.20 Type **494** 95 20
1736 3k.20 "Rosa alba maxima" 95 20
1737 3k.20 "Tuscany Superb" . . 95 20
1738 3k.20 "Peace" 95 20
1739 3k.20 "Four Seasons" . . . 95 20

1994. 25th Anniv of First Manned Moon Landing.
1740 **495** 6k.50 orange, black & bl 1·50 1·00

496 Iris Vase (Gunnar Wennerberg), 1897

497 Cat ("Love and Kisses")

1994. 150th Annivs of Stockholm College of Arts, Crafts and Design and of Swedish Society of Crafts and Design. Multicoloured.
1741 6k.50 Type **496** . . . . . 1·50 1·30
1742 6k.50 Wallpaper (Uno Ahren) and Chair (Carl Malmsten), 1917 . . . . 1·50 1·30
1743 6k.50 Aralia cloth, 1920, and cabinet, 1940 (Josef Frank) . . . . 1·50 1·30
1744 6k.50 Crystal bowl engraved with fireworks design (Edward Hald), 1921 . . 1·50 1·30
1745 6k.50 Silver water jug, 1941, and sketch of coffee pot, 1970s (Wiwen Nilsson) . . 1·50 1·30
1746 6k.50 Linen towel (Astrid Sampe), plate (Stig Lindberg) and cutlery (Sigurd Persson), 1955 . . 1·50 1·30

1994. Greetings Stamps. Multicoloured.
1747 3k.20 Type **497** 75 20
1748 3k.20 Snail ("You've got time") 75 20
1749 3k.20 Frog ("You're lovely just as you are") 75 25
1750 3k.20 Dog ("Hi there!") . . . 75 25

498 Musicians (sketch, Johan Silvius) and Opening Bars of "Drottningholm Music"

499 Sepo Raty (javelin)

1994. 300th Birth Anniv of Johan Helmich Roman (composer) (1751) and Inauguration of Gothenburg Opera House (1752).
1751 **498** 3k.20 brown and blue . . 80 25
1752 – 3k.20 multicoloured . . 80 20
DESIGN: No. 1752, Opera House (designed Jan Izikowitz) and opening bars of opera "Aniara" by Karl Birger (inaugural programme).

1994. Sweden-Finland Athletics Meeting, Stockholm. Multicoloured.
1753 4k.50 Type **499** . . . . . 1·00 90
1754 4k.50 Patrik Sjoberg (high jump) . . . . 1·00 90

500 Erland Nordenskiold (South America)

501 Caspian Tern ("Sterna caspia")

1994. Europa. Swedish Explorers. Multicoloured.
1755 5k.50 Type **500** . . . . . . 1·20 1·20
1756 5k.50 Eric von Rosen (Africa) . . . . 1·20 1·20
1757 5k.50 Sten Bergman (Asia and Australasia) . . . . 1·20 1·20

1994. Endangered Birds. Multicoloured.
1758 5k.50 Type **501** . . . . . 1·30 1·10
1759 5k.50 White-tailed sea eagle ("Haliaeetus albicilla") . . 1·30 1·10
1760 5k.50 White-backed woodpecker ("Dendrocopos leucotos") 1·30 1·10
1761 5k.50 Lesser white-fronted goose ("Anser erythropus") . . . . . . 1·30 1·10

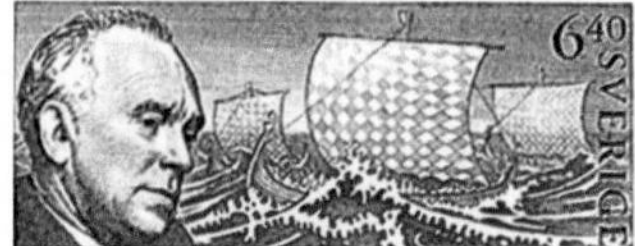

502 Bengtsson and Illustration from "The Longships" (novel)

1994. Birth Centenary of Frans Bengtsson (writer).
1762 **502** 6k.40 violet, red and black . . . . 1·50 70

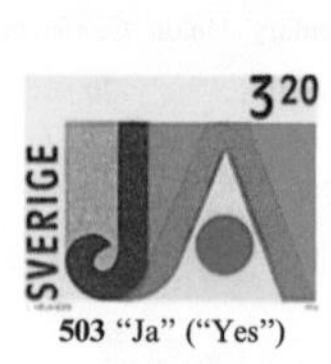

503 "Ja" ("Yes")

504 "The Annunciation"

1994. European Union Membership Referendum (1st issue). Multicoloured.
1763 3k.20 Type **503** 80 25
1764 3k.20 "Nej" ("No") 80 25
See also Nos. 1785/6.

1994. Christmas. Details from Askeby altarpiece. Multicoloured.
1765 2k.80 Type **504** 65 20
1766 2k.80 "Flight into Egypt" 65 20

505 Erik Axel Karlfeldt (1931)

506 King Carl XVI Gustav

1994. Swedish Winners of the Nobel Literature Prize.
1767 **505** 4k.50 brown, dp bl & bl 1·00 70
1768 – 5k.50 deep brn, bl & brn 1·30 90
1769 – 6k.50 brn, dp grn & grn 1·50 1·20
DESIGNS: 5k.50, Eyvind Johnson (1974); 6k.50, Harry Martinsson (1974).

1995.
1772 **506** 3k.70 red 90 25
1773 3k.85 black . . . . . . 1·00 25
1775 – 6k. green . . . . 1·30 65
1776 – 7k.50 purple . . . . . . 1·70 85
1777 – 8k. red . . . . 1·70 80
DESIGN: 6k., 7k.50, 8k. Queen Silvia.

1995. European Union Membership Referendum (2nd issue). Designs as Nos. 1763/4 but colours and values changed. Multicoloured.
1785 3k.70 Type **503** 85 25
1786 3k.70 "Nej" ("No") 85 25

507 Swedish Dwarf Cock

508 Strawberries

1995. Domestic Animals (2nd series).
1787 **507** 3k.10 brown, chocolate and red 80 35
1788 – 3k.70 chestnut, brown and red 85 20
1789 – 3k.70 chestnut, brown and red 85 20
DESIGNS—VERT: No. 1788, Red poll cow; 1789, Goat.

1995. Berries.
1790 **508** 3k.35 red, green and black on cream . . . 1·30 25
1791 – 3k.35 black, green and purple on cream . . . 75 30
1792 – 3k.35 red, green and black on cream . . . 75 30
DESIGNS: No. 1791, Blackberries; 1792, Raspberries.

509 Cottage with Allotment, Sodermanland

1995. Traditional Buildings (1st series). Rural Houses. Multicoloured.
1793 3k.70 Type **509** 75 25
1794 3k.70 Soldier's smallholding, Skanegard 75 25
1795 3k.70 17th-century farmhouse, Scania 75 25
1796 3k.70 19th-century farmhouse, Jamtland . . 75 25
1797 3k.70 18th-century manor house, Dalarna 75 25
See also Nos. 1856/64, 1905/10 and 1961/5.

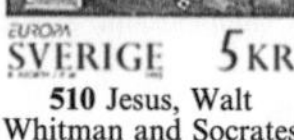

510 Jesus, Walt Whitman and Socrates

511 Scanian Geese

1995. Europa. Peace and Freedom. "Love, Peace and Labour" (wooden relief, Bror Hjorth). Multicoloured.
1798 5k. Type **510** . . . . . . 1·20 1·00
1799 5k. Lumumba, Albert Schweitzer and people of different races . . . . . 1·20 1·00
1800 6k. Type **510** . . . . 1·30 1·20
1801 6k. As No. 1799 . . . . . 1·30 1·20

1995. Domestic Animals.
1802 **511** 7k.40 deep brown, brown and green . . . 1·70 50
1803 – 7k.50 brown, green and blue . . . . 1·80 90
DESIGN: 7k.50, Swedish yellow duck.

512 Members' Flags forming "EU"

1995. Admission of Sweden to European Union.
1804 **512** 6k. multicoloured . . . 1·40 65

513 Ice Hockey

1995. World Ice Hockey Championship, Stockholm and Gavle (1805) and World Athletics Championships, Gothenburg (1806). Mult.

1805	3k.70 Type **513**	1·00	25
1806	3k.70 Erica Johansson (1992 junior long jump champion) (27½ × 28 mm)	90	20

514 Rock Speedwell — **515** "Wilhelm Tham" (motor barge) on Gota Canal

1995. Mountain Flowers. Multicoloured.

1807	3k.70 Type **514**	90	20
1808	3k.70 Cloudberry (white flowers)	90	20
1809	3k.70 Mountain heath (pink flowers) and black bearberry	90	20
1810	3k.70 Alpine arnica (yellow flowers) and crowberry . .	90	20

1995. Nordic Countries' Postal Co-operation. Tourism.

1811	**515** 5k. green	1·10	80
1812	– 5k. violet	1·10	80

DESIGN: No. 1812, Moored yacht, Lake Vattern.

516 English Horse-drawn Tram, Gothenburg

1995. Trams.

1813	**516** 7k.50 red	1·70	1·40
1814	– 7k.50 purple	1·70	1·40
1815	– 7k.50 green	1·70	1·40
1816	– 7k.50 lilac	1·70	1·40
1817	– 7k.50 blue	1·70	1·50

DESIGNS: No. 1814, Electric tram, Norrkoping; 1815, Commuter tram, Helsingborg; 1816, Narrow gauge tram, Kiruna; 1817, Mustang tram, Stockholm.

517 "Non-Violence" (sculpture, Carl Frederik Reutersward) (U.N. Building, New York)

1995. 50th Anniv of U.N.O.

1818	**517** 3k.70 deep blue and blue	1·20	20

518 "The Ball is Yours!" (Mikael Angesjo) — **519** Maria Akraka

1995. Greetings Stamps. Winning Entries in Children's Drawing Competition. Multicoloured.

1819	3k.70 Type **518**	90	20
1820	3k.70 Happy man saying "Hello" (Erica Sandstrom)	90	20
1821	3k.70 Teddy bear saying "I miss you" (Linda Nordenhem)	90	20
1822	3k.70 Shy mussel saying "Hello" (Christoffer Stenbom)	90	25

1995. World Athletics Championships, Gothenburg.

1823	**519** 7k.50 multicoloured . .	1·70	1·10

520 "Soldier Bom" (1948)

1995. Centenary of Motion Pictures. Scenes from Swedish Films. Multicoloured.

1824	6k. Type **520**	1·30	1·10
1825	6k. "Sir Arne's Treasure" (1919)	1·30	1·10
1826	6k. "Wild Strawberries" (1957)	1·30	1·10
1827	6k. "House of Angels" (1992)	1·30	1·10
1828	6k. "One Summer of Happiness" (1951)	1·30	1·10
1829	6k. "The Apple War" (1971)	1·30	1·10

521 Nilsson — **522** Bronze Figures (Bronze Age)

1995. Birth Centenary of Fritiof Nilsson (writer).

1830	**521** 3k.70 blue and red . . .	85	20

1995. Ancient Treasures from Museum of National Antiquities, Stockholm. Multicoloured.

1831	3k.70 Type **522**	85	75
1832	3k.70 Gold collar (400–550 A.D.)	85	70
1833	3k.70 Pendant (400–550 A.D.)	85	70
1834	3k.70 Bronze drum (Bronze Age)	85	70

523 Uraniborg Observatory — **524** Santa Candlestick, Varmland

1995. 450th Birth Anniv of Tycho Brahe (astronomer). Multicoloured.

1835	5k. Type **523**	1·30	70
1836	6k. Instrument for measuring positions in Space	1·40	90

1995. Christmas. Candlesticks. Multicoloured.

1837	3k.35 Type **524**	85	25
1838	3k.35 Apple candlestick, Smaland	85	30
1839	3k.35 Wrought iron candlestick, Dalarna . . .	85	25
1840	3k.35 Three-armed candlestick, Bergslagen . .	85	30

525 Nobel and Will

1995. Centenary of Nobel Prize Trust Fund. Multicoloured.

1841	6k. Type **525**	1·50	1·30
1842	6k. Nobel's home in Paris	1·50	1·30
1843	6k. Laboratory, Bjorkborn Manor, Karlskoga . . .	1·50	1·30
1844	6k. Medal and award ceremony for Wilhelm Rontgen, 1901	1·50	1·20

526 Rose Hips and Juniper — **527** West European Hedgehog ("Erinaceus europaeus")

1996. Winter Berries. Multicoloured.

1845	3k.50 Type **526**	85	40
1846	3k.50 Cowberries and sloes	85	45
1847	3k.50 Holly	85	45
1848	7k.50 Rowan	1·80	90

1996. Wildlife.

1849	**527** 1k. sepia, brown and green	20	20
1850	– 3k.20 multicoloured . .	85	35
1851	– 3k.85 multicoloured . .	90	25
1854	– 3k.85 green, olive and black	90	30
1852	– 7k.70 brown, deep brown and chocolate	1·70	60

DESIGNS—VERT: No. 1850, Eurasian beaver ("Castor fiber"). HORIZ: No. 1851, Stoat ("Mustela erminea"); 1852, Red fox ("Vulpes vulpes"); 1854, European otter ("Lutra lutra").

528 Postal Sorters and Modern Mail Carriage

1996. Discontinuation of Mail Sorting on Train Travelling Post Offices.

1855	**528** 6k. black, blue and red	1·40	95

529 Post Office and Railway Station, Halsingland

1996. Traditional Buildings (2nd series). Business and Commercial Premises. Multicoloured.

1856	3k.85 Type **529**	85	65
1857	3k.85 Motala Assembly Hall, Ostergotland	85	50
1858	3k.85 Parish storehouse, Smaland (27 × 23 mm) . .	85	50
1859	3k.85 Octagonal log barn, Vasterbotten (27 × 23 mm)	85	50
1860	3k.85 Sheep shelter, Gotland (27 × 36 mm)	85	50
1861	3k.85 Old Town Hall, Lidkoping (27 × 36 mm)	85	50

530 King Carl Gustav opening Tyresta National Park, 1993 — **531** Karin Kock (politician)

1996. 50th Birthday of King Carl XVI Gustaf. Multicoloured.

1862	10k. Type **530**	2·20	1·70
1863	10k. In Bernadotte Gallery with painting of King Karl XIV Johan	2·20	1·90
1864	10k. With King Albert of Belgium, 1994	2·20	1·70
1865	20k. With royal family, 1995 (76 × 43 mm)	4·25	3·00

1996. Europa. Famous Women.

1866	**531** 6k. brown and red . . .	1·30	1·10
1867	– 6k. blue and red . . .	1·30	1·10

DESIGN: No. 1867, Astrid Lindgren (children's writer).

532 "Summer" (Sven X:et Erixson)

1996. Summer Paintings. Multicoloured.

1868	3k.85 Type **532**	85	30
1869	3k.85 "Summer Evening in Stora Nassa" (Roland Svensson)	85	30
1870	3k.85 "On The Island" (Eric Hallstrom)	85	30
1871	3k.85 "Rallarros" (Thage Nordholm)	85	30
1872	3k.85 "On the Bridge" (Ragnar Sandberg) . . .	85	30

533 Annika Sorenstam — **534** Theatre Masks

1996. Golf.

1873	**533** 3k.50 green on cream . .	85	50

1996. Greetings Stamps.

1874	**534** 3k.85 multicoloured . .	1·00	35
1875	– 3k.85 blue, yellow and black	1·00	35
1876	– 3k.85 violet, yellow and black	1·00	35
1877	– 3k.85 red, black and pink	1·00	35

DESIGNS: No. 1875, Hearts forming four-leaved clover ("Be Happy!"); 1876, Heart within posthorn; 1877, Girl and hearts ("Do you remember me?").

535 Cep ("Boletus edulis") — **536** Grass Slopes, Haga Park

1996. Fungi. Multicoloured.

1878	3k.85 Type **535**	90	20
1879	5k. "Russula integra" . . .	1·10	55
1880	5k. Chanterelle ("Cantherellus cibarius")	1·10	55
1881	5k. Death trumpets ("Craterellus cornucopioides")	1·10	55
1882	5k. Shaggy ink caps ("Coprinus comatus") . .	1·10	55

1996. The Ecopark, Stockholm. Multicoloured.

1883	7k.50 Type **536**	1·50	1·40
1884	7k.50 Copper tents, Haga Park	1·50	1·40
1885	7k.50 Rosendal Palace . . .	1·50	1·40
1886	7k.50 Herons, Isbladskarret Swamp	1·50	1·40

537 Errand Boy, 1930s — **538** "Baroque Chair" (Endre Nemes)

1996. Four Decades of Youth. Multicoloured.

1887	3k.85 Type **537**	95	1·10
1888	3k.85 Hippy, 1960s	95	1·30
1889	3k.85 Zoot-suiter, 1940s . .	95	1·10
1890	3k.85 Biker, 1950s	95	1·30

1996. Art.

1891	**538** 6k. multicoloured . . .	1·40	95

539 The Annunciation

1996. Christmas. Illustrations from 15th-century Book of Hours. Multicoloured.

1892	3k.50 Type **539**	80	40
1893	3k.50 Nativity	80	35
1894	3k.50 Adoration of the Wise Men	80	40

540 Sune Bergstrom (1982)

1996. Swedish Winners of the Nobel Physiology and Medicine Prize.

1895	**540** 5k. black, blue and green	1·30	80
1896	– 5k. black and green . .	1·30	80
1897	– 5k. black, blue and green	1·30	80
1898	– 5k. blue, green and black	1·30	80

DESIGNS: No. 1896, Bengt Samuelsson (1982); 1897, Hugo Theorell (1955); 1898, Ragnar Granit (1967).

541 Wolverine ("Gulo gulo") — **543** Roses forming Heart

542 Queen Margareta, Coronation Document and Erik of Pommern

1997. Wildlife.
1899 **541** 3k.20 black, green and blue 80 55
1900 – 3k.50 black, green and red 85 50
1901 – 7k.70 black, red and green . . . . 1·80 85
DESIGNS—HORIZ: 3k.50, Snowy owl ("Nyctea scandiaca"). VERT: 7k.70, White stork ("Ciconia ciconia").

1997. 600th Anniv of Kalmar Union (of Sweden, Denmark and Norway).
1902 **542** 3k.85 blue 70 40

1997. Greetings Stamps.
1903 **543** 3k.85 multicoloured (red roses) 80 35
1904 3k.85 multicoloured (pink roses) 80 35

544 Dalby Church

1997. Traditional Buildings (3rd series). Churches. Multicoloured.
1905 3k.85 Type **544** 85 60
1906 3k.85 Vendel 85 60
1907 3k.85 Hagby (27 × 23 mm) 85 65
1908 3k.85 Overtornea (27 × 23 mm) 85 65
1909 3k.85 Varnhem (27 × 37 mm) 85 65
1910 3k.85 Ostra Amtervik (27 × 23 mm) 85 65

545 Cockerel
546 King Carl XVI Gustav

1997. Easter. Inscr "INRIKES BREV". Mult.
1911 (5k.) Type **545** . . . . . . 1·10 45
1912 (5k.) Daffodils . . . . . . 1·10 45
Nos. 1911/12 were for use on domestic first class mail.

1997. Inscr "INRIKES BREV".
1913 **546** (5k.) blue 90 25
No. 1913 was for use on domestic first class mail.

547 Arctic Fox ("Alopex lagopus")
548 Siberian Iris ("Iris sibirica")

1997. Wildlife (2nd series). (a) Inscr "EKONOMIBREV".
1914 **547** (4k.50) black, brn & bl 90 45

(b) Inscr "BREV INRIKES" (1915/16) or "INRIKES BREV" (1917).
1915 – (5k.) brown, black & grn 1·20 25
1916 – (5k.) black and blue . . . 1·20 30
1917 – (5k.) black and red . . . 1·20 30
DESIGNS: No. 1915, Przewalski's horses; 1916, Snow leopard; 1917, Snow leopard cubs.
No. 1914 was for use on domestic second class mail and Nos. 1915/17 on domestic first class mail.

1997. Garden Flowers. Inscr "INRIKES BREV". Multicoloured.
1918 (5k.) Type **548** . . . . . . 1·10 25
1919 (5k.) Honeysuckle ("Lonicera periclymenum") . . . . . . 1·10 25
1920 (5k.) Columbine ("Aquilegia vulgaris") . . . . 1·10 25
1921 (5k.) Day lily ("Hemerocallis flava") . . . . 1·10 25
1922 (5k.) Pansy ("Viola wittrockiana") . . . . . . 1·10 25
Nos. 1918/22 were for use on domestic first class mail.

549 Common Pheasant ("Phasianus colchicus")

1997. Pheasants. Multicoloured.
1923 2k. Type **549** 50 25
1924 2k. Lady Amherst's pheasants ("Chrysolophus amherstiae") 50 25

550 Figurehead from "Carl XIII" (ship of the line)

1997. Inauguration of Naval Museum, Karlskrona.
1925 **550** 6k. blue, brown and red 1·40 80

551 Troll with Treasure Chest ("The Troll and the Gnome Boy")
552 18th-century Compass Rose (Sven Billing)

1997. Europa. Tales and Legends. Illustrations by John Bauer. Multicoloured.
1926 7k. Type **551** . . . . . . 1·90 1·20
1927 7k. Trolls gazing at fairy ("The Boy and the Trolls or the Adventure") . . . 1·90 1·20
1928 7k. Boy before troll ("The Fearless Boy") . . . . . 1·90 1·20

1997. 18th International Cartographic Conference, Stockholm. Multicoloured.
1929 7k. Type **552** . . . . . . 1·70 75
1930 8k. Compass rose, 1568 (from atlas by Diego Homem) . . . . 1·70 85

553 Lesser Panda
554 Bridge

1997. Inscr "FORENINGSBREV".
1931 **553** (3k.50) choc, brn & red 85 55
No. 1931 was for use on bulk rate mail from societies.

1997. Inauguration of High Coast Suspension Bridge. Inscr "INRIKES Brev".
1932 **554** (5k.) blue, green & dp bl 1·30 30
No. 1932 was for use on domestic first class mail.

555 Elk and Mountains

1997. Greeting Stamps. Elk. Inscr "INRIKES BREV".
1933 **555** (5k.) multicoloured . . . 1·10 35
1934 – (5k.) multicoloured . . . 1·10 35
1935 – (5k.) multicoloured . . . 1·10 35
1936 – (5k.) multicoloured . . . 1·10 35
1937 – (5k.) black, yellow and red . . . . 1·10 35
1938 – (5k.) black and red . . . 1·10 35
DESIGNS: No. 1934, Elk-shaped bar code; 1935, Striped elk; 1936, Running elk; 1937, Running elk (different); 1938, Elk and young.
Nos. 1933/8 were for use on domestic first class mail.

556 "Gallery of the Muses" (Peter Hillerstrom)

1997. Gustav III's Museum of Antiquities, Stockholm. Multicoloured.
1939 8k. Type **556** . . . . . . 1·70 1·50
1940 8k. "Endymion" . . . . . 1·70 1·40

557 Volvo "Duett", 1958

1997. Cars. Inscr "INRIKES BREV". Mult.
1941 (5k.) Type **557** . . . . . . 1·10 90
1942 (5k.) Chevrolet "Bel Air", 1955 . . . . 1·10 90
1943 (5k.) Porsche "356", 1959 1·10 90
1944 (5k.) Citroen "B11", 1952 1·10 90
1945 (5k.) Saab "Monte Carlo" (Erik Carlsson's rally car) 1·10 90
1946 (5k.) Jaguar "E-type", 1961 1·10 90
Nos. 1941/6 were for use on domestic first class mail.

558 Alfred Nobel (founder of Prize Fund)

1997. The Nobel Prize.
1947 **558** 7k. black and pink . . . 1·60 1·10
1948 – 7k. black and grey . . . 1·60 1·10
DESIGN: No. 1948, Paul Karrer and molecular structure of Vitamin A (Chemistry Prize, 1937).

559 Heart

1997. Christmas Gingerbread Biscuits. Each brown, ochre and silver on yellow. Inscr "JULPOST".
1949 (3k.50) Type **559** 90 55
1950 (3k.50) Pigs 90 55
1951 (3k.50) Gingerbread men . . 90 50

560 Angels with Pipe and Lute

1997. Christmas. Angels from altarpiece, Litslena Church. Multicoloured.
1952 6k. Type **560** . . . . . . 1·30 95
1953 6k. Angels with pipes and harp . . . . 1·30 95

561 Tiger's Head

1998. Wildlife Photographs by Jan Lindblad. Inscr "FORENINGSBREV". Multicoloured.
1954 (3k.50) Type **561** 85 50
1955 (3k.50) Two tigers on rock 85 50
Nos. 1954/5 were for use on bulk rate mail from societies.

562 "Sponge Sculpture" (Yves Klein)
563 Heart with Love Birds

1998. Modern Art. Inscr "INRIKES BREV". Multicoloured.
1956 (5k.) Type **562** . . . . . . 1·10 70
1957 (5k.) "Skeppsholmen" (Goran Gidenstam) . . . 1·10 70
1958 (5k.) "Monogram" (Robert Rauschenberg) . . . . . 1·10 70
Nos. 1956/8 were for use on domestic first class mail.

1998. St. Valentine's Day. Inscr "INRIKES Brev".
1959 **563** (5k.) red and green . . . 1·10 35
1960 (5k.) mauve and blue . . 1·10 35
Nos. 1959/60 were for use on domestic first class mail.

564 Fire Station, Gavle

1998. Traditional Buildings (4th series). Town Houses. Inscr "INRIKES BREV". Multicoloured.
1961 (5k.) Type **564** . . . . . . 1·10 35
1962 (5k.) Shoe shop, Askersund 1·10 35
1963 (5k.) Fish and delicatessen market hall, Goteborg . . 1·10 35
1964 (5k.) Red Mill Cinema, Halmstad . . . . 1·10 35
1965 (5k.) Stads Hotel, Eksjo . . 1·10 35
Nos 1961/5 were for use on domestic first class mail.

565 Apron, Dalarna
566 Confederation Building, Stockholm (after Birger Lundquist)

1998. Handicrafts. (a) Inscr "EKONOMI BREV INRIKES".
1966 **565** (4k.50) scarlet, blk & red 95 35

(b) Inscr "INRIKES BREV".
1967 – (5k.) black and brown . . 1·20 30

(c) With face value.
1968 – 8k. orange, violet and red 1·40 1·50
1969 – 8k. violet and red . . . . 1·40 1·50
DESIGNS: No. 1967, Iron candlestick, Skane; 1968, Lumberjack's woollen glove; 1969, Decorative wooden box.
No. 1966 was for use on domestic second class mail and No. 1967 on domestic first class mail.

1998. Centenary of Swedish Confederation of Trade Unions. Inscr "Inrikes BREV".
1970 **566** (5k.) black, stone & red 1·20 20
No. 1970 was for use on domestic first class mail.

567 Queen Kristina and Memorial Medal

1998. 350th Anniv of Peace of Westphalia.
1971 **567** 7k. green and red . . . 1·50 95

568 Marsh Violet

1998. Wetland Flowers. Inscr "BREV INRIKES". Multicoloured.
1972 (5k.) Type **568** . . . . . 1·10 25
1973 (5k.) Great willow herb . . 1·10 25
Nos. 1972/3 were for use on domestic first class mail.

569 The Royal Palace

1998. Stockholm, Cultural Capital of Europe, Multicoloured. (a) Inscr "INRIKES BREV".
1974 (5k.) Type **569** . . . . . . 1·10 55
1975 (5k.) Archipelago ferries . . 1·10 55
1976 (5k.) Fisherman in front of Opera House (31 × 26 mm) . . . . . . 1·10 55
1977 (5k.) Yachts (31 × 26 mm) 1·10 55
1978 (5k.) Open-air swimming (31 × 39 mm) . . . . . . 1·10 55
1979 (5k.) City Hall (31 × 39 mm) 1·10 55

(b) With face value.
1980 7k. Type **569** . . . . . . 1·60 1·20
1981 7k. As No. 1975 . . . . . . 1·60 1·20
Nos. 1974/9 were for use on domestic first class mail.

570 "Albatros" (cruise ship) in Stadsgard Harbour

1998. Nordic Countries, Postal Co-operation. Shipping.
1982 **570** 6k. multicoloured . . . 1·40 70

571 Paper Moon and Plate of Crayfish ("Crayfish Party")
572 King Carl XVI Gustav and Coat of Arms

1998. Europa. National Festivals. Multicoloured.
1983 7k. Type **571** . . . . . . 1·60 1·20
1984 7k. Children dancing around midsummer pole . . . . 1·60 1·20

1998. 25th Anniv of Accession of King Carl XVI Gustav. Inscr "INRIKES BREV".
1985 **572** (5k.) purple, green and red . . . . 1·20 25
No. 1985 was for use on domestic first class mail.

573 Moberg and Characters from "The Emigrants" (novel)

1998. Birth Centenary of Vilhelm Moberg (writer). Inscr "BREV INRIKES".
1986 **573** (5k.) multicoloured . . . 1·30 40
No. 1986 was for use on domestic first class mail.

574 Princess Cake

1998. Greetings Stamps. Pastries. Inscr "BREV". Multicoloured.
1987 (5k.) Type **574** . . . . . . 1·10 50
1988 (5k.) Gustav Adolf pastry 1·10 50
1989 (5k.) Napoleon pastry . . . 1·10 50
1990 (5k.) Mocha cake . . . . . 1·10 50
1991 (5k.) National pastry . . . 1·10 50
1992 (5k.) Lent bun . . . . . . 1·10 50
Nos. 1987/92 were for use on domestic first class mail.

575 "Flowers in the window" (Carl Larsson)

1998. The Twentieth Century (1st series). 1900–1938. Inscr "INRIKES BREV". Multicoloured.
1993 (5k.) Type **575** . . . . . 1·20 75
1994 (5k.) Stockholm Stadium and poster (Olympic Games, 1912) . . . . . . 1·20 75
1995 (5k.) Porjus hydro-electric power station and electric iron-ore. train on Lulea (Sweden)–Narvik (Norway) railway line . . 1·20 75
1996 (5k.) Zip, ball-bearing, vacuum cleaner and refrigerator (Swedish inventions) . . . . 1·20 75
1997 (5k.) Map of trans-ocean shipping routes and liner 1·20 75
1998 (5k.) Sven Jerring (first Swedish radio reporter) 1·20 75
1999 (5k.) Jazz musicians and Charleston dancers . . . 1·20 75
2000 (5k.) Ellen Key (writer and suffragist) and Kerstin Hesselgren (first woman member of parliament) . . 1·20 75
2001 (5k.) Arne Borg (swimmer) and Gillis Grafstrom (figure skater) (Olympic and world champions) . . 1·20 75
2002 (5k.) Ernst Rolf (entertainer) 1·20 75
Nos. 1993/2002 were for use on domestic first class mail.
See also Nos. 2026/35 and 2083/92.

576 Nadine Gordimer (1991)
577 "King Sigismund of Sweden and Poland" (Studio of Rubens)

1998. The Nobel Literature Prize.
2003 **576** 6k. violet and blue . . . 90 85
2004 – 6k. violet and red . . . 90 85
DESIGN: No. 2004, Sigrid Undset (1928).

1998. 400th Anniv of Battle of Stangebro.
2005 **577** 7k. multicoloured . . . 1·10 95

578 Hyacinths
579 King Gustav Vasa 1 Daler, 1540

1998. Christmas. Flowers. (a) No value expressed. Inscr "Julpost". Size 21 × 28 mm. Multicoloured.
2006 (4k.) Type **578** 80 30
2007 (4k.) Mistletoe 65 35
2008 (4k.) Amaryllis 65 35

(b) With face value. Size 23 × 27½ mm.
2009 6k. Lingonberry wreath . . 90 70
2010 6k. Azaleas 90 70

1999. Coins. (a) Inscr "Ekonomibrev".
2011 **579** (4k.50) green 80 35

(b) Inscr "Brev inrikes".
2012 – (5k.) blue 90 25
DESIGN: No. 2012, King Carl XIV John 1 riksdaler, 1831–43.
No. 2011 was for use on domestic second class mail and No. 2012 on domestic first class mail.

580 Harbour and Katarina Lift, Stockholm
581 Easter Egg and Rabbit

1999. Centenary of Co-operative Union. Inscr "INRIKES BREV".
2013 **580** (5k.) multicoloured . . . 90 40
No. 2013 was for use on domestic first class mail.

1999. Easter. Inscr "INRIKES Brev". Mult.
2014 (5k.) Type **581** 30 40
2015 (5k.) Easter eggs and chicks 30 40
Nos. 2014/15 were for use on domestic first class mail.

582 Rabbit cooking

1999. Rabbits. Drawings by Eva Eriksson from "Little Sister Rabbit" by Ulf Nilsson. Inscr "INRIKES BREV" Multicoloured.
2016 (5k.) Type **582** 80 45
2017 (5k.) Rabbit feeding baby rabbit 80 45
2018 (5k.) Rabbits dancing . . . 80 45
2019 (5k.) Rabbits running through grass 80 45
Nos. 2016/19 were for use on domestic first class mail.

583 "East Indies" (anon)

1999. "Australia 99" International Stamp Exhibition, Melbourne. Paintings of Ships. Multicoloured.
2020 8k. Type **583** . . . . . . 1·20 1·40
2021 8k. "Mary Anne" (brigantine) (Folke Sjogren) . . . . 1·20 1·50
2022 8k. "Beatrice" (barque) (A. V. Gregory) . . . . . . 1·20 1·40
2023 8k. "Australic" (steamship) (T. G. Purvis) . . . . . 1·20 1·50

584 Pontoon "Swan" at Dresund Bridge

1999. Construction of Oresund Bridge between Sweden and Denmark. (a) Inscr "INRIKES BREV". Multicoloured.
2024 (5k.) Type **584** 90 45

(b) With face value
2025 6k. Bridge under construction (different) . . 1·00 90
No. 2024 was for use on domestic first class mail.

585 Eva Dahlbeck and Gunnar Bjornstrand in "Smiles of a Summer Night" (director Ingmar Bergman), 1955

1999. The Twentieth Century (2nd series). 1939–1969. Inscr "INRIKES BREV". Multicoloured.
2026 (5k.) Type **585** 75 60
2027 (5k.) Vallingby (first satellite town of Stockholm) . . . 75 60
2028 (5k.) Ulla Billquist and scene from "My Soldier somewhere in Sweden" (song) (emergency military service, 1939–45) 75 60
2029 (5k.) Cobra telephone (L.M. Ericsson), three-point seat belt (Nils Bohlins), high voltage cables and Tetra Pak milk carton (Swedish inventions) 75 60
2030 (5k.) Douglas DC-4 airliner (first scheduled flight of state airline SAS) 75 60
2031 (5k.) Jester, Carl-Gustaf Lindstedt, host of "Hyland's Corner", and Prime Minister Tage Erlander (television) . . . 75 60
2032 (5k.) Demonstrators, girl wearing optical-patterned dress and pop group Hep Stars (the 60s) 75 60
2033 (5k.) Volvo Amazon Car and family camping (leisure time) 75 60
2034 (5k.) Ingemar Johansson (world heavy-weight boxing champion), Mora-Nisse Karlsson (skier) and Gunder Hagg (athlete) . . 75 60
2035 (5k.) Alice Babs (jazz singer) and Jussi Bjorling (opera tenor) 75 60
Nos. 2026/35 were for use on domestic first class mail.

586 Postman's Bicycle
587 Pyramidal Orchid ("Salepsrot")

1999. Bicycles. (a) Inscr "FORENINGSBREV".
2036 **586** (3k.50) bl, ultram & yell 80 55

(b) Inscr "INRIKES BREV".
2037 – (5k.) multicoloured 90 35

(c) With face value.
2038 – 6k. blue, purple and black 1·00 90
2039 – 8k. green, lt green & red 1·30 1·20
DESIGNS: No. 2037, Racing cyclist; 2038, City bike; 2039, Bike messenger.
No. 2036 was for use on bulk rate mail from societies; No. 2037 for use on domestic first class mail.

1999. Orchids. Inscr "INRIKES BREV". Multicoloured.
2040 (5k.) Type **587** 80 30
2041 (5k.) Lady's slipper ("Guckusko") 80 30
2042 (5k.) Marsh helleborine ("Karrknipprot") 80 30
2043 (5k.) Green-winged orchid ("Goknycklar") 80 30
Nos. 2040/3 were for use on domestic first class mail.

588 Plant Shoot
589 Eurasian Pygmy Owl and Tyresta National Park

1999. 50th Anniv of Council of Europe.
2044 **588** 7k. multicoloured . . . 1·20 85

1999. Europa. Parks and Gardens. Multicoloured.
2045 7k. Type **589** . . . . . . 1·50 1·30
2046 7k. Pink helleborine and Gotska Sandon National Park . . . . 1·50 1·30

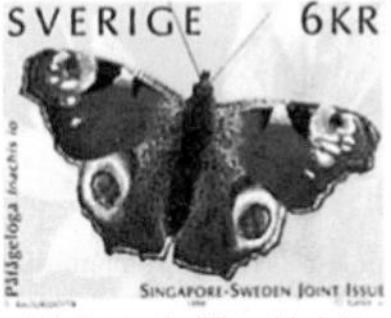

590 Peacock ("Inachis io")

1999. Butterflies. Multicoloured.
2047 6k. Type **590** . . . . . . 95 1·10
2048 6k. Blue argus ("Junonia orithya") . . . . 95 1·10
2049 6k. Common eggfly ("Hypolimnas bolina") . . 95 1·10
2050 6k. Red admiral ("Vanessa atalanta") . . . . 95 1·10

591 "Pisces"

1999. Signs of the Zodiac. Inscr "INRIKES Brev".
2051 **591** (5k.) blue, ultram and orge 90 45
2052 – (5k.) multicoloured . . . 90 45
2053 – (5k.) blue, ultram and orge 90 45
2054 – (5k.) multicoloured . . . 90 45
2055 – (5k.) blue, ultram and orge 90 45
2056 – (5k.) multicoloured . . . 90 45
2057 – (5k.) multicoloured . . . 90 45
2058 – (5k.) blue, ultram and orge 90 45
2059 – (5k.) orange, ultram and bl 90 45
2060 – (5k.) blue, ultram and orge 90 45
2061 – (5k.) orange, ultram and bl 90 45
2062 – (5k.) blue, ultram and orge 90 45
DESIGNS: No. 2052, "Aries"; 2053, "Taurus"; 2054, "Gemini"; 2055, "Cancer"; 2056, "Aquarius"; 2057, "Virgo"; 2058, "Libra"; 2059, "Scorpio"; 2060, "Sagittarius"; 2061, "Capricorn"; 2062, "Leo".
Nos. 2051/62 were for use on domestic first class mail.

592 Auguste Beernaert (Prime Minister of Belgium 1884–94), 1909

594 "Nativity"

593 Thorleifs

1999. Belgian Winners of Nobel Peace Prize.
2063 **592** 7k. blue and gold . . . 1·10 1·30
2064 – 7k. red and gold . . . . 1·10 1·30
DESIGN: No. 2064, Henri la Fontaine (President of International Peace Bureau), 1913.

1999. Swedish Dance Bands. Inscr "INRIKES BREV". Multicoloured.
2065 (5k.) Type **593** 75 50
2066 (5k.) Arvingara 75 50
2067 (5k.) Lotta Engbergs 75 50
2068 (5k.) Sten and Stanley . . . 75 50
Nos. 2065/8 were for use on domestic first class mail.

1999. Christmas. Stained-glass Windows (2069/71) and Wood Sculptures (2072/3). Multicoloured. (a) Inscr "JULPOST".
2069 (4k.) Type **594** 80 35
2070 (4k.) "Nativity" (different) 75 35
2071 (4k.) "Adoration of the Wise Men" 75 35
(b) With face value. Size 27½ × 30 mm.
2072 6k. Crowned Madonna with child 90 70
2073 6k. Madonna (in white cloak) and child 90 70
Nos. 2069/71 were for use on domestic first class mail.

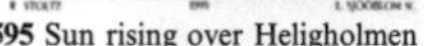

595 Sun rising over Heligholmen

596 Watch Mechanism

1999. Dawning of New Millennium. Multicoloured.
2074 5k. Type **595** . . . . . . 1·30 90
2075 5k. Sun rising over coast at Gotland . . . . 1·30 1·00

2000. Recovery of King Karl XII's Pocket Watch. (a) Inscr "EKONOMIBREV".
2076 **596** (4k.50) blue 80 30
(b) Inscr "INRIKES BREV".
2077 – (5k.) brown 90 20
DESIGN: 5k. Watch face.

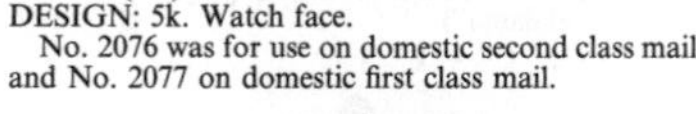

No. 2076 was for use on domestic second class mail and No. 2077 on domestic first class mail.

597 Heart

2000. Valentine's Day. Inscr "INRIKES BREV". Multicoloured.
2078 (5k.) Type **597** 80 45
2079 (5k.) Scribbled line in heart 80 45
Nos. 2078/9 were for use on domestic first class mail.

598 Dragon

2000. Chinese New Year. Year of the Dragon. Illustrations from "The Little Dragon with Red Eyes" by Astrid Lindgren. Inscr "INRIKES BREV". Multicoloured.
2080 (5k.) Type **598** 80 50
2081 (5k.) Dragon with basket . . 80 50
2082 (5k.) Dragon flying 80 50
Nos. 2080/2 were for use on domestic first class mail.

599 Modern Art, Stockholm Underground Railway

2000. The Twentieth Century (3rd series). 1970–1999. Inscr "INRIKES BREV". Multicoloured.
2083 (5k.) Type **599** 80 55
2084 (5k.) Swedish soldiers in United Nations peace-keeping force 80 55
2085 (5k.) Computer screen, mouse and voice-activated mobile phone (Swedish inventions) 80 55
2086 (5k.) Cullberg Ballet dancer and Hans Alfredson and Tage Danielsson (sketch writers) 80 55
2087 (5k.) Jonkoping Railway Station and high-speed train 80 55
2088 (5k.) Punk and Abba (pop group) 80 55
2089 (5k.) European flag and map of Europe (European Union membership, 1994) 80 55
2090 (5k.) Couple in orchard (film "The Apple War, 1971") 80 55
2091 (5k.) Pernilla Wiberg (slalom skier), Ingemar Stenmark (downhill skier) and Björn Borg (tennis player) . . . 80 55
2092 (5k.) Child in womb (photograph, Lennart Nilsson) 80 55
Nos. 2083/92 were for use on domestic first class mail.

600 Parent and Child walking through Forest (public access)

2000. Swedish Forests. Multicoloured. (a) Inscr "Foreningsbrev".
2093 (3k.80) Type **600** 70 55
(b) Inscr "INRIKES BREV".
2094 (5k.) Felled trees and elk (forestry) 80 40
2095 (5k.) Western capercaillie in fir forest 80 70
(c) With face value.
2096 6k. Birch trees . . . . . . 1·00 60
No. 2093 was for use on bulk rate mail from societies. Nos. 2094/5 were for use on domestic first class mail.

601 "Great deeds by Swedish Kings" (David Klocker Ehrenstrahl) (½-size illustration)

2000. 1000th Stamp Engraving by Czeslew Slanis. Sheet 94 × 126 mm.
MS2097 **601** 50k. multicoloured 3·50 2·00

602 Oresund Bridge

2000. Inauguration of Oresund Link (Sweden–Denmark road and rail system). (a) Inscr "INRIKES BREV".
2098 **602** (5k.) black, bl & ultram 90 30
(b) Size 58 × 24 mm.
2099 – 6k. multicoloured . . . . 1·00 1·10
2100 – 6k. ultramarine and green 1·00 1·20
DESIGNS: No. 2099, Oresund Bridge; 2100, Map of Oresund Region.
No. 2098 was for use on domestic first class mail.

603 " A Peck of Apples"

604 " Building Europe"

2000. Modern Paintings by Philip von Schantz. Inscr "INRIKES BREV". Multicoloured.
2101 (5k.) Type **603** 80 45
2102 (5k.) "A Bowl of Blueberries" 80 45
Nos. 2101/2 were for use on domestic first class mail.

2000. Europa.
2103 **604** 7k. multicoloured . . . 1·20 1·10

605 Hurdling

2000. Olympic Games, Sydney. Multicoloured.
2104 8k. Type **605** . . . . . . 1·20 1·50
2105 8k. Archery . . . . 1·20 1·50
2106 8k. Wind surfing . . . . . 1·20 1·50
2107 8k. Beach volleyball . . . . 1·20 1·50

606 Red Sun and Clouds

2000. Weather. Inscr "INRIKES BREV". Multicoloured. Self-adhesive.
2108 (5k.) Type **606** 75 45
2109 (5k.) Lightning 75 50
2110 (5k.) Black clouds 75 50
2111 (5k.) Northern lights 75 50
2112 (5k.) Rainbow 75 50
2113 (5k.) Blue sky and white clouds 75 45
Nos. 2108/13 were for use on domestic first class mail.

607 King Carl Gustaf XVI

608 Wislawa Szymborska (poet), 1996

2000. (a) Inscr "INRIKES Brev".
2114 **607** (5k.) blue 90 30
2115 (5k.50) lake . . . . . . 1·20 1·10
(b) With face values.
2118 – 8k. red . . . . 1·30 1·30
2119 10k. mauve . . . . 2·00 1·50
DESIGN: 8k. Queen Silvia.
No. 2114/15 were for use on domestic first class mail.

2000. Nobel Prize Winners for Literature.
2120 **608** 7k. purple and green . . 1·10 1·20
2121 – 7k. green and purple . . 1·10 1·20
DESIGN: No. 2121, Nelly Sachs (author), 1966.

609 Teddy Bear and Doll

2000. Children's Toys. Booklet stamps. Inscr "BREV". Multicoloured.
2122 (5k.) Type **609** 85 60
2123 (5k.) Skipping rope, marbles and tin soldier 85 60
2124 (5k.) Toy horses pulling cart, doll and flag 85 60
2125 (5k.) Toy cars and policeman 85 60

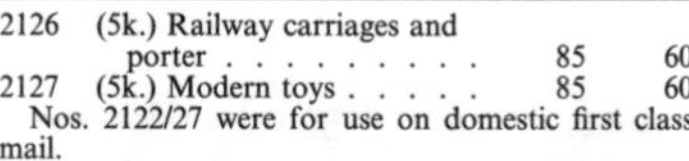

2126 (5k.) Railway carriages and porter 85 60
2127 (5k.) Modern toys 85 60
Nos. 2122/27 were for use on domestic first class mail.

610 Elves drinking

611 Farming

612 Gammelstad Church Village

2000. Christmas. Traditional Songs (2128/32) or Snowflakes (2133/4) (others). (a) No value expressed. Inscr "JULPOST".
2128 (4k.30) Type **610** 80 65
2129 (4k.30) Children dancing around tree (vert) 70 50
2130 (4k.30) Three gingerbread men (vert) 70 50
2131 (4k.30) Fox running (vert) 70 50
2132 (4k.30) Children dancing around candles (vert) . . 70 50
(b) With face value. Size 28 × 29 mm.
2133 6k. silver and blue (face value in blue) 95 70
2134 6k. silver and blue (face value in white) 95 70
DESIGNS: Nos. 2133/34 Snowflakes.
Nos. 2128/32 were for use on domestic first class mail.

2001. UNESCO World Heritage Sites. Rock Carvings, Tanum. (a) Inscr "EKONOMIBREV".
2135 **611** (4k.50) blue on grey . . 80 65
(b) Inscr "INRIKES BREV".
2136 – (5k.) red on grey 90 55
(c) With face value 35 × 28 mm.
2137 6k. Type **612** 95 85
2138 6k. Karlskrona Naval Base 95 1·10
2139 6k. Interior of Drottningholm Palace Theatre . . . . 95 1·10
2140 6k. Ironworks, Engelsberg 95 1·10

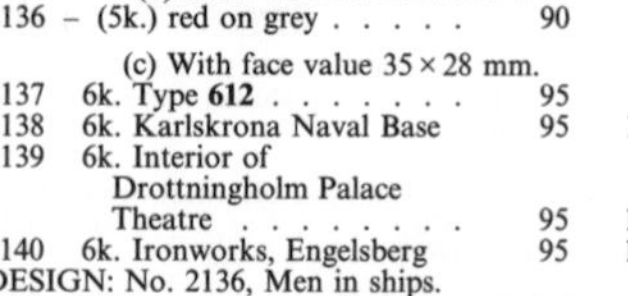

DESIGN: No. 2136, Men in ships.
No. 2135 was for use on domestic second class mail and No. 2136 on domestic first class mail.

613 Rosa

614 Children with Golden Retriever

2001. Chinese New Year. Year of the Snake. Depicting scenes from *Nelson the Snake* (book) by Ulf Stark. Multicoloured. Inscr "INRIKES BREV".
2141 (5k.) Type **613** 80 75
2142 (5k.) Nelson coiled on rock 80 75
Nos. 2141/2 were for use on domestic first class mail.

2001. Working Dogs. Multicoloured. Inscr "INRIKES BREV".
2143 (5k.) Type **614** 80 80
2144 (5k.) German shepherds hunting in snow 80 85
2145 (5k.) Labrador guide dog with blind woman 80 85
2146 (5k.) Dachshunds and man 80 80

615 Northern Lapwing (*Vanellus vanellus*)

617 Waterways of Northern Sweden

616 Yellow Egg

2001. Birds. (a) Inscr "FORENINGSBREV".
2147 **615** (3k.80) blue, green and brown 70 60

(b) Inscr "INRIKES Brev".
2148 – (5k.) blue and black . . . 90 55

(c) With face value.
2149 – 6k. green, black and orange . . . . 1·00 90
2150 – 7k. purple, brown and green . . . . 1·20 1·00

DESIGNS: No. 2148, Black-billed magpie (*Pica pica*); 2149, Herring gull (*Larus argentatus*); 2150, Long-tailed tit (*Aegithalos caudatus*).

No. 2147 was for use on bulk rate mail from societies and No. 2148 for use on domestic first class mail.

2001. Easter. Multicoloured. Self-adhesive. Inscr "INRIKES Brev".
2151 (5k.) Type **616** 80 55
2152 (5k.) Purple egg 80 55
2153 (5k.) Chick 80 55

Nos. 2151/3 were for use on domestic first class mail.

2001. Europa. Water Resources.
2154 **617** 7k. blue, green and black 1·10 1·30
2155 – 7k. blue, green and black 1·10 1·30
2156 – 7k. multicoloured . . . 1·10 1·30
2157 – 7k. multicoloured . . . 1·10 1·30

DESIGNS: No. 2155, Waterways of Southern Sweden; 2156, Freighter entering lock, Trollhatte Canal; 2157 *Juno* (canal boat) leaving lock, Trollhatte Canal.

618 Obverse of Medals and Alfred Nobel (founder)

2001. Centenary of Nobel Prizes (1st issue). Each yellow and brown.
2158 8k. Type **618** . . . . 1·20 1·40
2159 8k. Reverse of medal for Medicine . . . . 1·20 1·40
2160 8k. Reverse of medal for Physics and Chemistry . . 1·20 1·50
2161 8k. Reverse of medal for Literature . . . . 1·20 1·40

See also Nos. 2172/3.

619 Lo-Johansson

620 Fern Leaf Peony

2001. Birth Centenary of Ivar Lo-Johansson (writer). Each indigo, red and blue. Inscr "INRIKES BREV".
2162 (5k.) Type **619** 80 70
2163 (5k.) "The Last Vanload of Furniture of the Agricultural Labourers, 1945" (Svenolov Ehren) 80 70

Nos. 2162/3 were for use on domestic first class mail.

2001. Peonies. Multicoloured. Inscr "INRIKES brev".
2164 (5k.) Type **620** . . . . . . 1·40 55
2165 (5k.) Garden peony "Monsieur Jules Elie" . . 1·40 55
2166 (5k.) Herbaceous peony . . 1·40 55
2167 (5k.) Common peony . . . 1·40 55
2168 (5k.) Tree peony . . . . . 1·40 55

Nos. 2164/8 were for use on domestic first class mail.

621 Eurasian Perch (*Perca fluviatilis*)

2001. Fishes. Illustrations by Wilhelm von Wright from *The Fishes of Scandinavia*. Inscr "INRIKES Brev". Multicoloured. Self-adhesive.
2169 (5k.) Type **621** 80 60
2170 (5k.) Bream (*Abramis brama*) 80 60
2171 (5k.) Four-horned sculpin (*Triglopsis quadricornis*) 80 60

Nos. 2169/71 were for use on domestic first class mail.

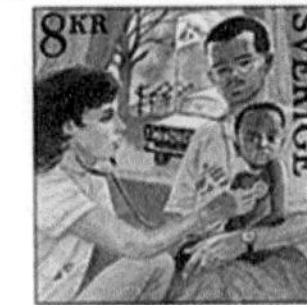

622 Doctors (Medicins sans Frontiers (1999))

2001. Centenary of Nobel Prize (2nd issue). Organizations. Peace Prize Winners. Multicoloured.
2172 8k. Type **622** . . . . 1·20 1·40
2173 8k. Relief workers distributing food (Red Cross (1901, 1917, 1944 and 1963)) . . . . 1·20 1·40

623 Solander

2001. 230th Anniv of Daniel Solander's (botanist) Voyage on H.M.S. *Endeavour*. Multicoloured.
2174 8k. Type **623** . . . . 1·20 1·40
2175 8k. Plant and H.M.S. *Endeavour* . . . . 1·20 1·50

624 Inline Skater and Wall with Graffiti (Emelie Kilstrom)

626 Christmas Tree

625 Otto Lilienthal and Biplane Glider, 1895

2001. Design a Stamp Prize Winners. Inscr "BREV INRIKES". Multicoloured.
2176 (5k.) Type **624** 85 65
2177 (5k.) Letter dropping through letter-box (Thomas Frohling) . . . 85 65

Nos. 2176/7 were for use on domestic first class mail.

2001. Aviation. Multicoloured.
2178 5k. Type **625** 85 85
2179 5k. DFS Weihl glider and emblem of Royal Swedish Flying Club 85 85
2180 5k. SAAB J 29, 1962 . . . 85 85
2181 5k. Freidrichshafen FF49, 1920 . . . . 85 85
2182 5k. Ultra-light trike, 1999 85 85
2183 5k. Douglas DC-3, 1938 . . 85 85

2001. Christmas. Decorations (2184/9) or Presents (2190/1). Multicoloured. (a) Inscr "julpost" (i) Ordinary gum.
2184 (4k.50) Type **626** 75 70

(ii) Size 26 × 20 mm. Self-adhesive.
2185 (4k.50) Star 75 70
2186 (4k.50) Home-made candy 75 70
2187 (4k.50) Angel 75 70
2188 (4k.50) Heart-shaped decoration 75 70
2189 (4k.50) Cone filled with sweets 75 70

(b) With face value. Size 26 × 29 mm. Ordinary gum.
2190 6k. Goat-shaped parcel . . 1·00 85
2191 6k. Christmas tree-shaped parcel . . . . 1·00 85

Nos. 2184/9 were for domestic first class mail.

627 Hockey Players

628 Children riding Horse

2002. World Ice Hockey Championship, Sweden. Inscr "INRIKES BREV".
2192 **627** (5k.) multicoloured . . . 85 70

No. 2192 was for use on domestic first class mail.

2002. Year of the Horse. Showing illustrations from Fairhair the Horse (cartoon character) by Bertil Almquist. Multicoloured. Inscr "INRIKES BREV".
2193 (5k.) Type **628** 85 70
2194 (5k.) Child leading Fairhair 85 70

Nos. 2193/4 were for use on domestic first class mail.

629 Couple in Bed

2002. Illustrations from *Love and Miss Terrified* by Joanna Dranger (book). Self-adhesive.
2195 **629** (5k.) pink, mauve and orange 85 70
2196 (5k.) mauve, pink and orange 85 70
2197 (5k.) orange, mauve and pink 85 70

Nos. 2195/7 were for use on domestic first class mail.

630 Osprey (*Pandion haliaetus*)

2002.
2198 **630** 10k. brown and blue . . 1·60 1·40

631 Scientists, Ship and Seabird

2002. Swedish Antarctic Expedition (1901–03). Multicoloured.
2199 10k. Type **631** . . . . . . 1·60 2·10
2200 10k. Icebergs, ship and gentoo penguin . . . . . 1·60 2·10

632 Pippi Longstocking (Ingrid Vang Nyman)

2002. Astrid Lindgren (children's writer) Commemoration. Depicting book illustrations by named artists.
2201 **632** 5k. multicoloured . . . 75 45
2202 – 5k. multicoloured . . . 75 45
2203 – 5k. multicoloured . . . 75 45
2204 – 5k. brown and black . . 75 45
2205 – 5k. multicoloured . . . 75 45
2206 – 5k. multicoloured . . . 75 45
2207 – 5k. multicoloured . . . 75 45

DESIGNS: No. 2202, Karlsson Pa Taket (Ilon Wikland); 2206, Lotta Pa Brakmakargatan (I. Wikland); 2207, Madicken (I. Wikland). 24 × 31 mm-No. 2203, Broderna Lejonhjarta (I. Wikland); 2205, Emil I Lonneberga (Bjorn Berg). 27 × 31 mm—No. 2204, Astrid Lindgren.

633 Cross (pendant, Birka)

634 Visby

2002. World Heritage Sites. (a) Birka and Hovgarden. (i) Inscr "FORENINGS BREV".
2208 **633** (3k.80) lilac 60 35

(ii) Inscr "EKONOMI BREV".
2209 (4k.50) blue 70 40

(iii) Inscr "INRIKES BREV".
2210 (5k.) brown and mauve . . 75 45

DESIGNS: No. 2209, Runic stone, Hovgarden; 2210, Face-shaped pendant, Birka.

(b) Visby. Multicoloured. Inscr "INRIKES BREV".
2211 (5k.) Type **634** 75 45
2212 (5k.) Part of town wall . . . 75 45
2213 (5k.) Burmeister building . . 75 45
2214 (5k.) Ruins of St. Catherine's Church . . 75 45

No. 2208 was for use on bulk rate mail from societies, No. 2209 was for domestic second class mail and Nos. 2210/14 were for domestic first class mail.

635 "Vadersolstavlan"

2002. 750th Anniv of Stockholm. (a) Inscr "INRIKES BREV".
2215 **635** (5k.) green and mauve 75 45

(b) With face value. Size 30 × 31 mm.
2216 10k. mauve . . . . 1·50 90

DESIGN: 10k. Stadsholmen Island ("Vadersolstavlan" (detail))

636 "Structure" (Takashi Naraha)

637 Charlie Rivel (clown)

2002. Nordic Countries' Postal Co-operation. Modern Art. Sculptures. Multicoloured.
2217 8k. Type **636** . . . . 1·20 70
2218 8k. "Sprung From" (Pal Svensson) . . . . 1·20 70

2002. Europa. Circus. Multicoloured.
2219 8k. Type **637** . . . . 1·20 70
2220 8k. Clown with child (Clowns without Borders) 1·20 70
2221 8k. Man in balloon (Cirkus Cirkor) . . . . 1·20 70
2222 8k. Elephant and rider (Cirkus Scott) . . . . . 1·20 70

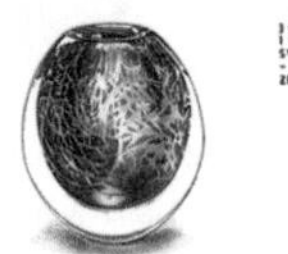

638 "Rain Forest" (glass vase) (Marie and Ola Hoglund)

2002. Artistic Crafts. Joint Issue with New Zealand. Multicoloured.
2223 10k. Type **638** . . . . . . 1·50 90
2224 10k. Flax basket (Willa Rogers) . . . . 1·50 90

Nos. 2223/4 are additionally inscr "JOINT ISSUE SWEDEN–NEW ZEALAND".

639 Haro Warehouse

640 Lighthouse and Cliffs

2002. Bohuslan Province. Inscr "INRIKES BREV". (a) Ordinary gum.
2225 **639** (5k.) multicoloured . . . 75 45

(b) Multicoloured. Self-adhesive.
2226 (5k.) Type **640** . . . . . .
2227 (5k.) Lighthouse, rocks and birds 75 45
2228 (5k.) Yacht and waterfront houses 75 45
2229 (5k.) Dinghy with outboard engine 75 45

Nos. 2225/9 were for use on domestic first class mail.

641 Police Chief

2002. Centenary of *Gronkopings Veckoblad* (satirical newspaper). Inscr "INRIKES Brev". Each blue, buff and red.
2230 (5k.) Type **641** 75 45
2231 (5k.) Postman 75 45

Nos. 2230/1 were for use on domestic first class mail.

642 Charles Emil Hagdahl and Cajsa Warg

2002. Swedish Gastronomy. Chefs. Inscr "INRIKES BREV". Multicoloured.
2232 (5 k.) Type **642** 75 45
2233 (5k.) Marit "Hiram" Huldt 75 45
2234 (5k.) Tore Wretman 75 45
2235 (5k.) Leif Mannerstrom . . 75 45
2236 (5k.) Gert Klotzke 75 45
2237 (5k.) Christer Lingstrom . . 75 45
Nos. 2232/7 were for use on domestic first class mail.

643 The Royal Palace, Stockholm

2002. Palaces. Joint Issue with Thailand. Multicoloured.
2238 5k. Type **643** 75 45
2239 5k. Dusit Maha Prasat Throne Hall 75 45

644 Hakan Carlqvist (motocross)

2002. Motorcycle Sports. Multicoloured.
2240 5k. Type **644** 75 45
2241 5k. Sten Lundin (motocross) 75 45
2242 5k. Anders Eriksson (enduro) 75 45
2243 5k. Ulf Karlsson (trial) . . . 75 45
2244 5k. Ove Fundin (speedway) 75 45
2245 5k. Tony Rickardsson (speedway) 75 45
2246 5k. Peter Linden (road racing) 75 45
2247 5k. Varg-Olle Nygren (road racing) 75 45

645 Karl-Bertil Jonsson and Father **646** Kiruna Church

2002. Christmas. Karl-Bertil Jonsson's Christmas (animated film by Per Ahlin). Scenes from the film. Inscr "julpost" Multicoloured. (a) Ordinary gum.
2248 (4k. 50) Type **645** 70 20
Nos. 2248/52 were for domestic first class mail.

(b) Self-adhesive gum.
2249 (4k.50) With sack of presents 70 20
2250 (4k.50) Asleep wearing cap with feather 70 20
2251 (4k.50) Shaking hands with man 70 20
2252 (4k.50) Surrounded by family 70 20

2002. Christmas. Churches. Multicoloured.
2253 8k. Type **646** . . . . 1·20 70
2254 8k. Habo . . . . 1·20 70
2255 8k. Sundborns . . . . . . 1·20 70
2256 8k. Tensta . . . . 1·20 70

647 Bowline **648** Boy and Teacher

2003. Knots. Coil stamps. (a) Inscr "Forenings brev".
2257 (4k.80) green 70 20

(b) Inscr "Ekonomibrev".
2258 (5k.) blue 75 45

(c) Inscr "Brev inrikes".
2259 (5k.50) redon 80 50
DESIGNS: (5k.) Sheet bend; (5k.50) Reef knot.

No. 2257 was for use on bulk rate mail from societies, No. 2258 was for domestic second-class mail and No. 2259 were for domestic first class mail.

2003. Centenary of Swedish Sports Federation. Multicoloured. Self-adhesive.
2260 (5k.50) Type **648** 80 50
2261 (5k.50) Wheelchair racing 80 50
2262 (5k.50) Snowboarding and deaf sign for sport . . . 80 50
2263 (5k.50) Girl running 80 50
Nos. 2260/3 were for use on domestic first class mail.

649 St. Birgitta (Bridget) (sculpture) (Johannes Stanrat)

2003. 700th Birth Anniv of St. Birgitta (1st issue). Inscr "INRIKES BREV".
2264 **649** (5k.50) sepia and scarlet 80 50
Nos. 2264 was for use on domestic first class mail.

650 "Kaos" (Georg Magnusson)

2003. Europa. Poster Art. Multicoloured.
2265 10k. Type **650** . . . . . . 1·40 85
2266 10k. "Biologika Museum" (Carina Lank) . . . . . 1·40 85
2267 10k. "Aerotransport" (Anders Beckman) . . . . 1·40 85
2268 10k. "Levande Lantbruk" (Owe Gustafson) . . . . 1·40 85

651 Cottage, Narke **652** Hepatica (*Hepatica nobilis*)

2003. Provincial Houses (1st series). Designs from watercolour paintings by Laila Reppen.
2269 **651** 2k. lake, chestnut and green 30 20
2270 – 4k. green, lake and indigo 60 35
2271 – 5k. sepia, blue and emerald 75 45
DESIGNS: 4k. Double cottage, Bohuslan; 5k. Hall house, Medelpad.
See also Nos. 2338/40 and 2357/60.

2003. Flowers. Inscr "INRIKES BREV". Multicoloured. Self-adhesive.
2272 (5k.50) Type **652** 80 50
2273 (5k.50) Cowslip (*Primula veris*) 80 50
2274 (5k.50) Coltsfoot (*Tussilago farfara*) 80 50
Nos. 2272/4 were for use on domestic first class mail.

653 Windmills

2003. World Heritage Sites. Oland. Inscr "INRIKES BREV".
2275 (5k.50) Type **653** 80 50
2276 (5k.50) Stone circle, Stora Alvar 80 50
2277 (5k.50) Village 80 50
2278 (5k.50) Sheep grazing coastal wetlands 80 50
Nos. 2275/8 were for use on domestic first class mail.

654 Santiago Ramon y Cajal (1906)

2003. Nobel Prize Winners for Medicine. Joint Issue with Spain. Multicoloured.
2279 10k. Type **654** . . . . . . 1·40 85
2280 10k. Severo Ochoa (1959) 1·40 85

655 Frederik Blom's 19th-century Folly

2003. Garden Follies. Multicoloured. (a) Ordinary gum.
2281 (5k.50) Type **655** 90 70

(b) Self-adhesive gum.
2282 (5k.50) Emanuel Swedenborg's 18th-century folly 90 70
2283 (5k.50) Ebba Brahe's folly 90 70
2284 (5k.50) Raised folly 90 70
2285 (5k.50) Godegard manor folly, Ostergotland . . . 90 70

656 St. Bridget (⅔-size illustration)

2003. 700th Birth Anniv of St. Bridget. Sheet 94 × 128 mm.
MS2286 **656** 40k. multicoloured 7·00 7·00

657 Red Cabbage, Parsnip, Cucumber, Beetroot and Onion **658** Lion (figurehead)

2003. Harvest. Multicoloured. Self-adhesive.
2287 (5k.50) Type **657** 90 70
2288 (5k.50) Melon, apple, raspberries and pumpkin 90 70
2289 (5k.50) Cabbage, potatoes, carrots and tomato . . . 90 70
2290 (5k.50) Cherries, strawberries, plums and pear 90 70
Nos. 2287/90 form a composite design of a basket of fruit and vegetables.

2003. 250th Anniv of Sinking of Gotheborg (East Indiaman). Reconstruction of Gotheborg. Multicoloured.
2291 5k.50 Type **658** 90 70
2292 5k.50 Interior of hull (44 × 26 mm) 90 70
2293 10k. Side elevation (43 × 53 mm) . . . . . . 1·80 1·10
2294 30k. "Under Sail" (Marc Grieves) . . . . 5·00 4·50

659 Pied Avocet (*Recurvirostra avosetta*)

2003. Water Birds. Multicoloured.
2295 10k. Type **659** . . . . . . 1·80 1·10
2296 10k. Slavonian grebe (*Podiceps auritus*) . . . . 1·80 1·10
2297 10k. Black-throated diver (*Gavia artica*) . . . . . . 1·80 1·10
2298 10k. Great crested grebe (*Podiceps cristatus*) . . . 1·80 1·10
Stamps of the same design were issued by Hong Kong.

660 "Evening Meal"

2003. Christmas. Birth Centenary of Carl Larsson (artist). Paintings. Multicoloured. (a) Inscr "Julpost". (i) Coil stamp. Ordinary gum.
2299 (5k.) Type **660** 85 65

(ii) Size 23 × 27 mm. Self-adhesive.
2300 (5k.) "Esbjorn on Skis" . . 85 65
2301 (5k.) "Brita as Idun" . . . 85 65
2302 (5k.) "Esbjorn" 85 65
2303 (5k.) "Front-yard and Washhouse" (detail) . . . 85 65

(b) With face value. Size 27 × 30 mm. Ordinary gum.
2304 9k. "Martina with Breakfast Tray" . . . . 1·60 1·00
2305 9k. "Kersti's Sleigh Ride" 1·60 1·00

661 Anna Lindh **662** Brace and Bit

2003. Anna Lindh (foreign minister) Commemoration.
2306 **661** (5k.50) purple 90 70
2307 10k. indigo . . . . . . 1·80 1·10

2004. Woodworking Tools. Coil stamps. (a) Inscr "Forenings brev".
2308 **662** (4k.80) green 75 60

(b) Inscr "Ekonomibrev".
2309 – (5k.) blue 85 65

(c) Inscr "Brev inrikes".
2310 – (5k.50) red 90 70
DESIGNS: Saw (5k.); Plane (5k.50).
No. 2308 was for use on bulk rate mail from societies, No. 2309 was for domestic second-class mail and No. 2310 was for domestic first class mail.

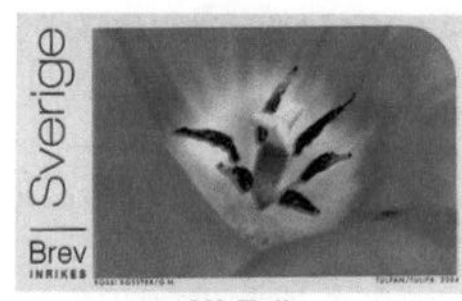

663 Tulip

2004. Flowers. Multicoloured.
2311 (5k.50) Type **663** 90 70
2312 (5k.50) Lily 90 70
2313 (5k.50) Hibiscus 90 70
2314 (5k.50) Amaryllis 90 70
2315 (5k.50) Zantedeschia 90 70

664 Lake and Mountain

2004. World Heritage Sites. Lapona. Multicoloured.
2316 10k. Type **664** . . . . . . 1·80 1·10
2217 10k. Tents . . . . 1·80 1·10

665 Mine Head

2004. World Heritage Sites. Falun. Multicoloured.
2318 (5k.50) Type **665** 90 70
2319 (5k.50) Water tower and buildings 90 70
2320 (5k.50) Doorway 90 70
2321 (5k.50) Miners 90 70

666 Two Footballers (Nils Liedholm)

2004. Centenary of Swedish Football Association. Multicoloured. Self-adhesive.
2322 (5k.50) Type **666** 90 70
2323 (5k.50) Women players (Hanna Ljungberg) . . . 90 70
2324 (5k.50) Two players chasing ball (Fredrik Ljungberg) 90 70
2325 (5k.50) Player with raised arm (Henrik Larsson) . . 90 70
2326 (5k.50) Women players tackling (Victoria Svensson) 90 70
2327 (5k.50) Goalkeeper (Thomas Ravelli) 90 70

667 Returning Warrior 668 Night Fishing

2004. Nordic Mythology. Sheet 104×70 mm containing T **667** and similar multicoloured design.
MS2328 10k. ×2, Type **667**; Welcoming Valkyrie . . . . . 3·50 3·50
Stamps of a similar theme were issued by Aland Islands, Denmark, Faroe Islands, Finland, Greenland, Iceland and Norway.

2004. "Northern Light".
2329 **668** (5k.50) blue 90 70
2330 – (5k.50) brown 90 70
DESIGN: No. 2330 Lighthouse.

669 Yacht and Hut (Gilloga)

2004. Stockholm Archipelago. Multicoloured.
2331 (5k.50) Type **669** 90 70
2332 (5k.50) Rowing boat (Langviksskar) 90 70
2333 (5k.50) Saltsjon (steam boat) (Stora Nassa) 90 70
2334 (5k.50) Yacht and lighthouse (Namdofjarden) 90 70

670 Collared Dove (*Streptopelia decaocto*) 671 Tree, Berries, Fungi and Flowers

2004. Centenary of Swedish Pigeon Society. Coil stamps. (a) Inscr "EKONOMIBREV".
2335 **670** (5k.) blue and agate . . 75 45

(b) Inscr "Brev inrikes".
2336 – (5k.50) multicoloured . . . 90 70

(c) With face value.
2337 – 10k. multicoloured . . . . 1·90 1·10
DESIGNS: (5k.50) Swedish tumbler; 10k Wood pigeon (*Columba palumbus*).
No. 2335 was for use on bulk rate mail from societies and No. 2336 was for domestic second-class mail.

2004. Provincial Houses (2nd series). As T **651** showing watercolour paintings by Laila Reppen.
2338 3k. yellow, red and brown 50 40
2339 6k. red, brown and green . . 1·00 75
2340 8k. deep green, brown and green . . . . 1·50 90
DESIGNS: 3k. Blacksmith's cottage, Uppland; 6k. Dalstand cottage; 8k. Gotland cottage.

2004. Forest Food. Multicoloured. Self-adhesive.
2341 (5k.50) Type **671** 90 70
2342 (5k.50) Tree stump, butterfly and berries 90 70
2343 (5k.50) Basket of fungi . . . 90 70
2344 (5k.50) Flowers, pond, berries and tree 90 70
Nos. 2341/2 and 2343/4, respectively, form composite designs.

672 William Butler Yeats

2004. Irish Winners of Nobel Prize for Literature. Multicoloured.
2345 10k. Type **672** . . . . . 1·80 1·10
2346 10k. George Bernard Shaw 1·80 1·10
2347 10k. Samuel Beckett . . . . 1·80 1·10
2348 10k. Seamus Heaney . . . . 1·80 1·00
Stamps of similar designs were issued by Ireland.

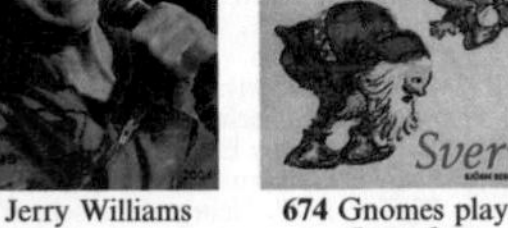

673 Jerry Williams 674 Gnomes playing Leap-frog

2004. Rock 54–04. 50th Anniv of "That's alright Mama" (record by Elvis Presley). Multicoloured.
2349 5k.50 Type **673** 90 70
2350 5k.50 Elvis Presley 90 70
2351 5k.50 Eve Dahlgren 90 70
2352 5k.50 Ulf Lundell 90 70
2353 5k.50 Tomas Leon 90 70
2354 5k.50 Pugh Rogefeldt . . . 90 70
2355 5k.50 Maria Anderson (Sahara Hotnights) . . . 90 70
2356 5k.50 Louise Hoffsten . . . 90 70

2004. Provincial Houses (3rd series). Designs as T **651** showing watercolour paintings by Laila Reppen.
2357 50ore. blue and black (21×24 mm) 10 10
2358 1k. brown, green and black (31×24 mm) 15 10
2359 7k. black, brown and green 1·10 75
2360 9k. black, green and grey . . 1·60 1·00
DESIGNS: 50ore. Log cabin, Lapland; 1k. Miner's house, Vstmanland; 7k. Scanian farm house; 9k. Blekinge cottage.

2004. Christmas. Designs showing gnomes. Multicoloured. Inscr "Julpost". (a) Ordinary gum.
2361 (5k.) Type **674** 85 65

(b) Self-adhesive gum.
2362 (5k.) Talking on cell phone 85 65
2363 (5k.) Carrying tree 85 65
2364 (5k.) Sledding 85 65
2365 (5k.) Collecting post 85 65

675 Great Tit (*Parus major*)

2004. Winter Birds. Multicoloured.
2366 10k. Type **675** . . . . . . 1·80 1·10
2367 10k. Yellowhammer (*Emberiza citronella*) . . . 1·80 1·10
2368 10k. Pine grosbeak (*Pinicola enucleator*) . . . . 1·80 1·10
2369 10k. Bullfinch (*Pyrrhula pyrrhula*) . . . . 1·80 1·10

OFFICIAL STAMPS

O 6 O 17

1874.
O27 **O 6** 2ore orange . . . . . 1·00 1·30
O28 a 3ore bistre . . . . . . 1·00 1·70
O29 c 4ore grey . . . . . . 2·10 40
O30 a 5ore green . . . . . . 1·80 40
O31 a 6ore lilac . . . . . . 29·00 39·00
O32 6ore grey . . . . . . £250 70·00
O33 b 10ore red . . . . . . 1·90 25
O34 a 12ore blue . . . . . . 50·00 7·75
O35 a 20ore red . . . . . . £170 1·50
O36 20ore blue . . . . . . 3·75 25
O37 a 24ore yellow . . . . . 60·00 11·00
O38ca 30ore brown . . . . . 17·50 45
O39 a 50ore red . . . . . . £120 18·00
O40 50ore grey . . . . . 14·50 1·00
O41 d 1k. blue and bistre . . 7·25 1·30

1889. Surch **TJENSTE FRIMARKE**, two crowns, and **TIO 10 ORE** on scroll.
O42 **O 6** 10ore on 12ore blue . . 10·00 10·00
O43 10ore on 24ore yellow . . 15·00 16·00

1910.
O 87 **O 17** 1ore black 30 30
O101 2ore yellow 20 70
O102 3ore brown 30 45
O103 4ore lilac 20 20
O104 5ore green 20 15
O105 7ore green 40 60
O 91 8ore purple 45 65
O107 10ore red 20 15
O108 12ore red 20 20
O109 15ore brown 30 20
O110 20ore blue 25 15
O111 25ore orange 85 30
O112 30ore brown 45 25
O113 35ore violet 65 45
O114 50ore grey . . . . . . 1·20 1·30
O 98 1k. black on yellow . . 7·75 5·25
O 99 5k. purple on yellow 9·75 3·00

POSTAGE DUE STAMPS

D 6

1874.
D27 a **D 6** 1ore black . . . . . 1·90 2·00
D28ab 3ore red . . . . . . 4·00 4·00
D29ba 5ore brown . . . . . 2·75 2·75
D30 a 6ore yellow . . . . . 3·25 2·75
D31 12ore red . . . . . . 6·00 3·25
D32 a 20ore blue . . . . . 3·25 2·75
D33 24ore lilac . . . . . . 39·00 33·00
D34 b 24ore grey . . . . . 11·50 15·00
D35 b 30ore green . . . . . 4·00 3·00
D36 a 50ore brown . . . . . 6·25 3·50
D37 a 1k. blue and bistre . . 31·00 17·00

SWITZERLAND Pt. 8

A federal republic in central Europe between France, Germany and Italy.

100 rappen = 1 franken.
100 centimes = 1 franc.
100 centesimi = 1 franco.

These are expressions of the same currency in three languages.
For the issues under the Cantonal Administrations of Basel, Geneva and Zurich, see Stanley Gibbons' Part 8 (Italy and Switzerland) Catalogue.

1 6

1850. Imperf. (a) Inscr "ORTS-POST".
1 **1** 2½r. black and red £2000 £1000

(b) Inscr "POSTE LOCALE".
3 **1** 2½r. black and red £1600 £950

1850. As T **1** but inscr "RAYON I", "II" or "III". Imperf.
6 **1** 5r. red, black and blue (I) . . £1200 £325
13 5r. red and blue (I) . . . . . £425 85·00
10 10r. red, black and yellow (II) . . . . £700 80·00
24 15rp. red (III) . . . . £1600 75·00
21 15 cts. red (III) £8000 £500

1854. Imperf.
46 **6** 2r. grey £140 £300
47a 5r. brown . . . . £120 10·50
48 10r. blue . . . . £130 8·00
49a 15r. pink . . . . £225 29·00
50 20r. orange . . . . £275 38·00
51 40r. green . . . . £250 36·00
38a 1f. lilac £800 £600

7 9 10

1862. Perf.
52 **7** 2c. grey . . . . 44·00 1·70
61 2c. brown . . . . 1·60 65
61a 2c. bistre . . . . 1·60 60
53 3c. black . . . . 6·25 47·00
54b 5c. brown . . . . 1·70 25
55 10c. blue £225 25
62 10c. pink . . . . 1·90 35
63 15c. yellow . . . . 2·20 18·00
56a 20c. orange . . . . 1·40 1·10
64 25c. green . . . . 1·30 1·20
57 30c. red . . . . £750 18·00
65a 30c. blue . . . . £300 5·25
58 40c. green . . . . £750 27·00
66 40c. grey . . . . 1·50 60·00
67 50c. purple . . . . 35·00 18·00
59 60c. bronze . . . . £500 65·00
60a 1f. gold . . . . 12·00 45·00

1882.
126Bd **9** 2c. brown 65 10
127Bc 3c. brown . . . . 1·10 1·60
128Bd 5c. purple . . . . 11·50 30
196a 5c. green . . . . 3·50 10
130Be 10c. red . . . . 2·30 15
131Be 12c. blue . . . . 4·00 10
132A 15c. yellow . . . . 95·00 9·75
133Bc 15c. violet . . . . 31·00 85

1882.
214 **10** 20c. orange . . . . 1·70 1·10
146B 25c. green . . . . 8·25 55
207 25c. blue . . . . 5·00 60
202 30c. brown . . . . 4·75 1·10
209 40c. grey . . . . 23·00 4·00
150B 50c. blue . . . . 30·00 2·20
218 50c. green . . . . 5·50 1·00
152B 1f. purple . . . . 41·00 1·80
219 1f. red . . . . 21·00 3·25
154B 3f. brown . . . . £120 15·00

11

1900. 25th Anniv of U.P.U.
191 **11** 5c. green . . . . 2·75 60
189 10c. red . . . . 7·00 65
190 25c. blue . . . . 13·00 8·50

15 Tell's Son 16 17

1907.
225 **15** 2c. yellow 30 25
226 3c. brown . . . . 20 5·00
227 5c. green . . . . 2·30 15
228 **16** 10c. red . . . . 1·40 15
229 12c. brown . . . . 30 1·70
230 15c. mauve . . . . 3·75 7·00

1908.
232 **17** 20c. yellow and red . . . 1·10 30
233 25c. blue and deep blue 1·90 20
234 30c. green and brown . . 1·90 20
235 35c. yellow and green . . 1·90 2·20
236 40c. yellow and purple . . 9·75 30
238 40c. blue . . . . 1·50 15
239 40c. green . . . . 23·00 20
240a 50c. green and deep green 5·00 35
241 60c. brown . . . . 6·50 20
242 70c. yellow and brown . . 50·00 5·00
243 70c. buff and violet . . . 13·00 1·00
244 80c. buff and grey . . . . 7·00 40
245 1f. green and purple . . . 4·75 25
246 3f. yellow and bistre . . . £170 85

18 Cord in front of Shaft 19

1908.
247 **18** 2c. bistre 20 50
248 3c. violet . . . . 20 6·75
249 5c. green . . . . 2·00 15
250 **19** 10c. red 55 15
251 12c. brown 70 25
252 15c. mauve . . . . 16·00 45

20a Cord behind Shaft 21 William Tell

1910.
260 **20a** 2c. brown 10 15
261 2½c. purple 15 65
262 2½c. bistre on buff . . . . 30 1·60
254 3c. violet 10 15
255 3c. brown 10 20
256 3c. blue on buff . . . . . 2·40 4·50
263 5c. green . . . . 1·10 15
264 5c. orange on buff 10 20
265 5c. grey on buff 10 15
266 5c. purple on buff 10 20
267 5c. green on buff 30 20
258 7½c. grey . . . . 1·40 20
259 7½c. green on buff . . . . 30 1·90

1914.
279 **21** 10c. red on buff 35 20
280 10c. green on buff 10 15
282 10c. violet on buff . . . . 1·20 20
283 12c. brown on buff . . . . 35 2·40
284 13c. green on buff . . . . 1·20 20
285 15c. purple on buff . . . . 2·00 15
286 15c. red on buff . . . . . 2·50 1·40
287 20c. purple on buff . . . . 1·80 15
289 20c. red on buff 20 15
291 25c. red on buff 60 35
292 25c. brown on buff . . . . 4·25 80
293 30c. blue on buff . . . . . 6·50 15

22 The Mythen

1914. Mountain Views.
294 **22** 3f. green . . . . £550 2·75
295 3f. red . . . . 70·00 45
296 – 5f. blue . . . . 30·00 1·10
297 – 10f. mauve . . . . £110 1·50
337 – 10f. green . . . . £200 29·00
DESIGNS: 5f. The Rutli; 10f. The Jungfrau and girl holding shield.

1915. Surch.
298 **20a** 1c. on 2c. brown 10 55
307 2½c. on 3c. brown 10 25
308 3c. on 2½c. bistre on buff 10 1·50
309 5c. on 2c. brown . . . . 10 2·40
310 5c. on 7½c. grey 10 20
312 5c. on 7½c. green on buff 15 5·25

313 21 10c. on 13c. green on buff . . . . 15 1·40
299 19 13c. on 12c. brown . . . 10 5·25
300 21 13c. on 12c. brn on buff 15 60
314a 20c. on 15c. purple on buff . . . . 80 1·30
315 17 20c. on 25c. bl & dp bl 15 25
301 80c. on 70c. yell & brn 23·00 8·50

1919. Air. Optd with wings and propeller.
302 17 30c. green and brown . . . £100 £900
303 50c. green and deep green 32·00 95·00

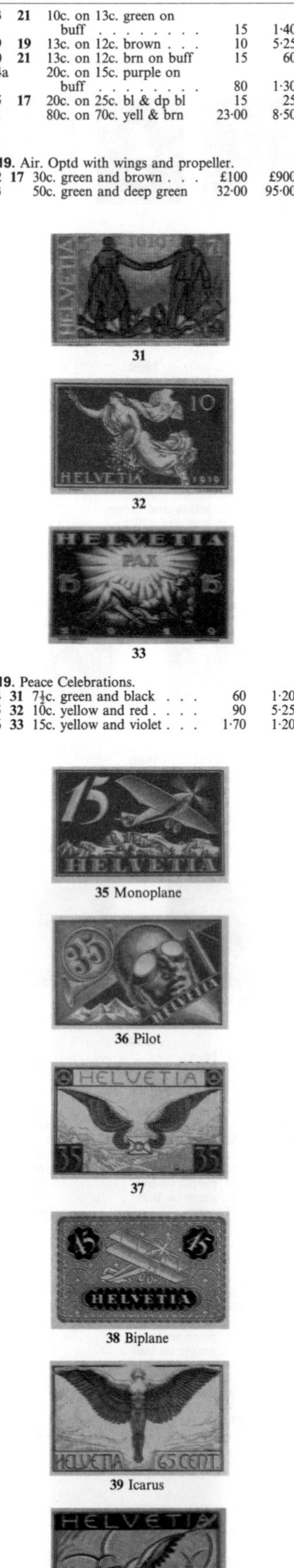

31

32

33

1919. Peace Celebrations.
304 31 7½c. green and black . . . 60 1·20
305 32 10c. yellow and red . . . . 90 5·25
306 33 15c. yellow and violet . . . 1·70 1·20

35 Monoplane

36 Pilot

37

38 Biplane

39 Icarus

40

1923. Air.
316 35 15c. green and red . . . . 2·50 4·50
317a 20c. green and deep green 40 30
318 25c. grey and blue . . . . 7·25 12·00
319 36 35c. cinnamon and brown 16·00 34·00
320a 37 35c. brown and ochre . . 7·25 34·00
321 36 40c. lilac and violet . . . 10·50 34·00
322a 37 40c. blue and green . . . 33·00 37·00
323 38 45c. red and blue . . . . 1·40 4·25
324a 50c. grey and red . . . . 1·70 75
325a 39 65c. blue and deep blue 1·70 4·75
326 75c. orange and purple . . 14·00 42·00
327a 1f. lilac and purple . . . 3·25 1·60
328a 40 2f. chestnut, sepia & brn 11·50 6·00

41

42 Seat of First U.P.U. Congress

1924.
329 41 90c. red, dp green & grn 10·50 35
330 1f.20 red, lake and pink 5·75 1·40
331 1f.50 red, blue & turq . . 25·00 1·50
332a 2f. red, black and grey . . 27·00 3·50

1924. 50th Anniv of U.P.U.
333 – 20c. red 45 90
334 42 30c. blue . . . . 95 4·00
DESIGN: 20c. As T 42 but with different frame.

43 The Mythen

1931.
335 43 3f. brown . . . . 41·00 1·60

44 Symbol of Peace

45 "After the Darkness, Light"

46 Peace and the Air Post

1932. International Disarmament Conference.
338 44 5c. green (postage) 15 15
339 10c. orange 20 10
340 20c. mauve 25 10
341 30c. blue . . . . 2·10 60
342 60c. brown . . . . 14·50 3·00
343 45 1f. grey and blue . . . . 15·00 4·50
344 46 15c. lt green & green (air) 40 1·60
345 20c. pink and red . . . . 1·00 2·20
346 90c. light blue and blue . . 5·75 24·00

47 Louis Favre (engineer)

48 Staubbach Falls

1932. 50th Anniv of St. Gotthard Railway.
347 47 10c. brown 10 15
348 – 20c. red 20 15
349 – 30c. blue . . . . 40 1·10
DESIGNS: 20c. Alfred Escher (President of Railway); 30c. Emil Welti (surveyor).

1934. Landscapes.
350 48 3c. green . . . . 25 1·70
351 – 5c. green 20 10
352 – 10c. mauve 45 10
353 – 15c. orange . . . . 40 1·30
354 – 20c. red 50 10
355 – 25c. brown . . . . 6·50 4·25
356 – 30c. blue . . . . 20·00 45
DESIGNS: 5c. Mt. Pilatus; 10c. Chillon Castle and Dents du Midi; 15c. Grimsel Pass; 20c. St. Gotthard Railway, Biaschina Gorge; 25c. Viamala Gorge; 30c. Rhine Falls, Schaffhausen.
For redrawn designs, see Nos. 368 etc.

1935. Air. Surch.
358 35 10 on 15c. green and red 5·75 32·00
359 46 10 on 15c. light green and green 50 35
360 10 on 20c. pink and red . . 55 1·60
381 39 10 on 65c. blue & deep blue 30 35
361 46 30 on 90c. light blue & blue . . . . 3·00 9·50
362 40 on 20c. pink and red . . 4·00 10·50
363 40 on 90c. light blue & blue . . . . 3·00 10·50

51 Freiburg Cowherd

52 Staubbach Falls

1936. National Defence Fund.
364 51 10c.+5c. violet 35 55
365 20c.+10c. red . . . . . . 65 2·50
366 30c.+10c. blue . . . . . . 3·00 13·00

1936. As T 48 but redrawn with figure of value lower down. Various landscapes.
368A 52 3c. green 15 15
369A – 5c. green 15 10
489 – 5c. brown 25 10
370Ad – 10c. purple 60 15
372A – 10c. brown 10 10
490 – 10c. green 30 10
373A – 15c. orange 30 45
374Ac – 20c. red (Railway) . . . 4·75 15
375A – 20c. red (Lake) 20 10
491 – 20c. brown 30 10
376A – 25c. brown 65 90
492 – 25c. red . . . . 1·80 1·40
377A – 30c. blue . . . . 1·20 15
378A – 35c. green . . . . . . 1·30 1·10
379A – 40c. grey . . . . 7·75 15
494 – 40c. blue . . . . 30·00 30
DESIGNS: 5c. Mt. Pilatus; 10c. Chillon Castle and Dents du Midi; 15c. Grimsel Pass; 20c. (374d) St. Gotthard Railway, Biaschina Gorge; 20c. (Nos. 375, 491) Lake Lugano and Mt. San Salvatore; 25c. (No. 376) Viamala Gorge; 25c. (No. 492) National Park; 30c. Rhine Falls, Schaffhausen; 35c. Mt. Neufalkenstein and Klus; 40c. Mt. Santis and Lake Seealp.

53 Mobile P.O.

1937. For Mobile P.O. Mail.
380 53 10c. yellow and black . . . 25 25

55 International Labour Bureau

1938.
382 55 20c. red and buff 20 15
383 – 30c. blue and light blue . . 30 15
384 – 60c. brown and buff . . . 1·50 1·30
385 – 1f. black and buff . . . . 6·25 10·00
DESIGNS: 30c. Palace of League of Nations; 60c. Inner courtyard of Palace of League of Nations; 1f. International Labour Bureau (different).

1938. Air. Special Flights. Surch **1938 "PRO AERO" 75 75** and bars.
386 38 75c. on 50c. green and red † 4·75

60 William Tell's Chapel

1938. National Fete. Fund for Swiss Subjects Abroad.
387 60 10c.+10c. violet & yellow 40 45

61 First Act of Federal Parliament

1938.
388A 61 3f. brown on blue . . . 10·50 4·00
388C 3f. brown on buff . . . 6·50 30
389A – 5f. blue on blue . . . . 11·00 2·50
389C – 5f. blue on buff . . . . 5·25 30
390B – 10f. green on blue . . . 23·00 90
390C – 10f. green on buff . . . 9·25 1·10
DESIGNS: 5f. "The Assembly at Stans"; 10f. Polling booth.

62 Symbolical of Swiss Culture

64 Crossbow and Floral Branch

1939. National Exhibition, Zurich. Inscr in French (F.), German (G.) or Italian (I.). F.
391 – 10c. violet 30 15
392 62 20c. red . . . . 2·50 30
393 – 30c. blue and buff . . . . 2·75 5·75

G.
391 – 10c. violet 30 10
392 62 20c. red 40 10
393 – 30c. blue and buff . . . . 2·10 1·10

I.
391 – 10c. violet 25 15
392 62 20c. red . . . . 1·50 35
393 – 30c. blue and buff . . . . 1·75 5·00
DESIGNS: 10c. Group symbolic of Swiss Industry and Agriculture; 30c. Piz Rosegg and Tschirva Glacier.

1939. National Exhibition, Zurich. Inscr in French (F.), German (G.) or Italian (I.). F.
394Fa 64 5c. green 70 60
395 Fb 10c. brown . . . . . . 70 1·30
396 Fc 20c. red . . . . 1·25 1·90
397F 30c. blue . . . . 3·50 6·25

G.
394Ga 64 5c. green . . . . 45 1·60
395Ga 10c. brown 40 80
396Ga 20c. red . . . . 95 1·20
397G 30c. blue . . . . 2·75 5·50

I.
394Ia 64 5c. green . . . . 50 2·20
395Ib 10c. brown . . . . . . 70 1·40
396Ia 20c red . . . . 65 2·50
397I 30c. blue . . . . 2·40 7·25

65 Laupen Castle

1939. National Fete. Fund for Destitute Mothers.
398 65 10c.+10c. brn, grey & red 25 40

66 Geneva

1939. 75th Anniv of Geneva (Red Cross) Convention.
399 66 20c. red and buff 30 20
400 30c. blue, grey and red . . 45 1·10

67 "Les Rangiers"

68 "William Tell" (Ferdinand Hodler)

1940. National Fete and Red Cross Fund. Memorial designs inscr "FETE NATIONALE 1940" in German (5c., 20c.), Italian (10c.) and French (30c.).
401 – 5c.+5c. black and green . . 25 90
402 – 10c.+5c. black & orange 25 30
403 – 20c.+5c. black and red . . 2·20 60
404 67 30c.+10c. black and blue 1·30 4·75
DESIGNS—Battle Memorials: 5c. Sempach; 10c. Giornico; 20c. Calven.

1941. Historical Designs.
405 – 50c. blue on green . . . . 4·25 10
406 68 60c. brown on cinnamon 6·25 10
407 – 70c. purple on mauve . . 2·75 45
408 – 80c. black on grey . . . . 1·10 10
408a – 80c. black on mauve . . 2·30 30
409 – 90c. red on pink . . . . 1·10 10
409a – 90c. red on buff . . . . 3·25 95
410 – 1f. green on green . . . . 1·40 10
411 – 1f.20 purple on grey . . . 1·90 10
411a – 1f.20 purple on lilac . . . 3·25 55
412 – 1f.50 blue on buff . . . . 2·00 40
413 – 2f. red on pink . . . . . 2·75 40
413a – 2f. red on cream . . . . 6·00 30
DESIGNS—(Works of art): 50c. "Oath of Union" (James Vibert); 70c. "Kneeling Warrior" (Ferdinand Hodler); 80c. "Dying Ensign" (Hodler); 90c. "Standard Bearer" (Niklaus Deutsch). Portraits: 1f. Col. Louis Pfyffer; 1f.20, George Jenatsch; 1f.50, Lt. Gen. Francois de Reynold; 2f. Col. Joachim Forrer.

69 Ploughing

1941. Agricultural Development Plan.
414 **69** 10c. brown and buff . . . 10 15

70 The Jungfrau

1941. Air. Landscapes.
415 **70** 30c. blue on orange . . . 85 15
415a – 30c. grey on orange . . . 7·25 9·00
416 – 40c. grey on orange . . . 85 15
416a – 40c. blue on orange . . . 36·00 1·50
417 – 50c. green on orange . . 1·10 15
418 – 60c. brown on orange . . 1·50 15
419 – 70c. violet on orange . . 1·20 30
420 – 1f. green on buff . . . . 2·30 35
421 – 2f. red on buff . . . . . 7·25 1·70
422 – 5f. blue on buff . . . . . 24·00 9·25
DESIGNS: 40f. Valais; 50c. Lac Leman; 60c. Alpstein; 70c. Ticino; 1f. Lake Lucerne; 2f. Engadin; 5f. Churfirsten.

1941. Air. Special (Buochs–Payerne) Flights. No. 420 with "PRO AERO 28.V.1941" added.
423 1f. green on buff . . . . . . 5·75 16·00

71 Chemin Creux near Kussnacht

1941. National Fete and 650th Anniv of Swiss Confederation.
424 – 10c.+10c. blue, red & yell 30 50
425 **71** 20c.+10c. scarlet, red and buff 50 70
DESIGN: 10c. Relief map of Lake Lucerne with Arms of Uri, Schwyz and Unterwalden.

72 Arms of Berne, Masons laying Cornerstone and Knight

1941. 750th Anniv of Berne.
426 **72** 10c. multicoloured 10 30

73 "To survive collect salvage"

1942. Salvage Campaign. Inscr in French (F.), German (G.) or Italian (I.). Value and coat of arms in red, tablets in blue. F.
427F **73** 10c. brown 45 30
G.
427G **73** 10c. brown 20 20
I.
427I **73** 10c. brown . . . . 7·50 2·50
INSCRIPTIONS: (G) "Zum Durchhalten/Altstoffe sammeln"; (I) "PER RESISTERE/RACCOGLIETE/LA ROBA VECCHIA".

74 View of Old Geneva

75 Soldiers' Memorial at Forch, near Zurich

1942. National Fete, National Relief Fund and Bimillenary of Geneva.
428 **74** 10c.+10c. black, yellow and red 35 45
429 **75** 20c.+10c. red and yellow 45 85

76

1943. Cent of Swiss Cantonal Postage Stamps.
430 **76** 10c.(4+6) black 10 10

77 Intragna (Ticino)

78 Apollo of Olympia

1943. National Fete and Youth's Vocational Training Fund.
431 **77** 10c.+10c. black, buff and red 35 50
432 – 20c.+10c. red and buff . . 40 80
DESIGN: 20c. Federal Palace, Berne.

1943. Air. Special Flights. 30th Anniv of First Flight across Alps by Oscar Bider. As No. 432, optd **PRO AERO 13.VII.1943** and value.
433 1f. red and buff . . . . . . 2·20 8·00

1944. Olympic Games Jubilee.
434 **78** 10c. black and orange . . 20 45
435 20c. black and red 30 45
436 30c. black and blue . . . . 75 6·75

79 Heiden

1944. National Fete and Red Cross Fund.
437 **79** 5c.+5c. green, buff & red 35 1·50
438 – 10c.+10c. grey, buff and red 35 35
439 – 20c.+10c. red and buff . . 35 55
440 – 30c.+10c. blue, buff and red . . . . 2·40 12·00
DESIGNS: 10c. St. Jacques on the R. Birs; 20c. Castle Ruins, Mesocco; 30c. Basel.

80 Haefeli DH-3 Biplane

81 Symbolical of Faith, Hope and Charity

1944. Air. 25th Anniv of National Air Post.
441 **80** 10c. brown and green . . . 10 20
442 – 20c. red and stone 25 20
443 – 30c. ultramarine and blue 50 65
444 – 1f.50 agate, brown and red 7·25 14·50
AIRCRAFT: 20c. Fokker F.VIIb/3m; 30c. Lockheed 9B Orion; 1f.50, Douglas DC-3.

1945. War Relief Fund.
445 **81** 10c.+10c. green, black and grey 50 30
446 20c.+60c. red, black and grey . . . . 2·50 4·75
MS446a 70 × 110 mm. Imperf. 3f.+7f. blue £180 £170

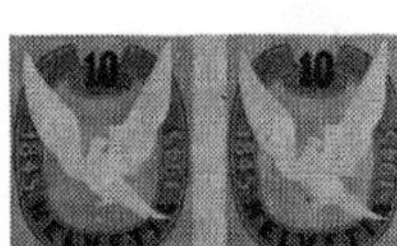

81b "Basel Dove"

1945. Centenary of Basel Cantonal Stamp Issue. Sheet 71 × 63 mm.
MS446b **81b** 10 (c.) green, red and black (sold at 3f.) . . . . . . £120 80·00

82 Trans "Peace to men of good will"

83 Olive Branch

1945. Peace. Inscr "PAX".
447 **82** 5c. green and grey 10 20
448 10c. brown and grey . . . 35 15
449 20c. red and grey 45 15
450 30c. blue and grey . . . . 80 2·30
451 40c. orange and grey . . . 3·00 8·25
452 **83** 50c. red and buff . . . . . 4·25 16·00
453 – 60c. grey and light grey . . 4·75 5·75
454 – 80c. green and buff . . . . 8·75 60·00
455 – 1f. blue and buff . . . . . 11·00 65·00
456 – 2f. brown and buff . . . . 42·00 £130
457 – 3f. green on buff . . . . . 49·00 46·00
458 – 5f. brown on buff £150 £225
459 – 10f. violet on buff . . . . £150 90·00
DESIGNS—As Type **83**: 60c. Keys; 80c. Horn of plenty; 1f. Dove; 2f. Spade and flowers in ploughed field. 38 × 21 mm: 3f. Crocuses; 5f. Clasped hands; 10f. Aged couple.

1945. Red Cross. As T **82**, but red cross and "5+10" in centre of stamp.
460 5c.+10c. green 75 60

85 Silk Weaving

1945. National Fete.
461 **85** 5c.+5c. green and red . . . 90 1·50
462 – 10c.+10c. brown, grey and red 80 40
463 – 20c.+10c. red and buff . . 1·00 45
464 – 30c.+10c. blue, grey and red . . . . 10·50 21·00
DESIGNS: 10, 20c. Jura and Emmental farmhouses; 30c. Timbered house.

86 J. H. Pestalozzi

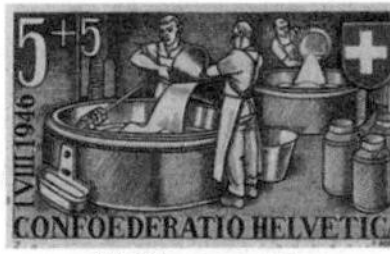

87 Zoglig Instructional Glider

1946. Birth Bicentenary of J. H. Pestalozzi (educational reformer).
465 **86** 10c. purple 20 15

1946. Air. Special (Lausanne, Lucerne, Locarno) Flights.
466 **87** 1f.50 red and grey . . . . 23·00 22·00

88 Cheese-making

89 Chalet in Appenzell

1946. National Fete and Fund for Swiss Citizens Abroad.
467 **88** 5c.+5c. green and red . . . 70 2·00
468 – 10c.+10c. brown, buff and red 65 55
469 **89** 20c.+10c. red and buff . . 85 55
470 – 30c.+10c. blue, grey and red . . . . 5·75 7·25
DESIGNS: 10c. Chalet in Vaud; 30c. Chalet in Engadine.

90 Douglas DC-4 Airliner, Statue of Liberty and St. Peter's Cathedral, Geneva

1947. Air. 1st Geneva–New York "Swissair" Flight.
472 **90** 2f.50 deep blue, blue & red 11·50 15·00

92 Rorschach Station

1947. National Fete. Professional Education of Invalids and Anti-cancer Funds. Inscr "I VIII 1947". Arms in red.
473 – 5c.+5c. green . . . . . . 70 1·90
474 **92** 10c.+10c. black and buff 80 50
475 – 20c.+10c. red and buff . . 1·20 50
476 – 30c.+10c. blue and grey . . 6·00 8·75
DESIGNS: 5c. Platelayers; 20c. Luen-Castiel station; 30c. Fluelen station.

93 "Limmat" (first locomotive in Switzerland)

1947. Centenary of Swiss Federal Railways.
477 **93** 5c. green, yellow and black 25 30
478 – 10c. black and brown . . . 30 15
479 – 20c. red, buff and lake . . 35 15
480 – 30c. blue, grey & light blue 1·40 1·30
DESIGNS: 10c. Class C5/62-10-0 steam locomotive, 1913; 20c. Type Ae8/14 electric locomotive crossing Melide Causeway; 30c. Lorraine Bridge, Berne.

95 Sun of St. Moritz

96 Ice Hockey

1948. 5th Winter Olympic Games.
481 **95** 5c.+5c. brown, yell & grn 50 1·40
482 – 10c.+10c. blue, light blue and brown 55 85
483 **96** 20c.+10c. yellow, black and purple . . . . 85 1·60
484 – 30c.+10c. black, light blue and blue . . . . 2·30 5·00

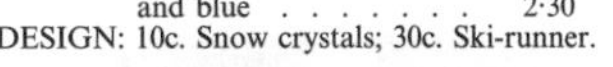

DESIGN: 10c. Snow crystals; 30c. Ski-runner.

97 Johann Rudolf Wettstein

1948. Tercentenary of Treaty of Westphalia and Centenaries of the Neuchatel Revolution and Swiss Federation.
485 **97** 5c. green and deep green 20 30
486 – 10c. black and grey 20 15
487 – 20c. red and pink 30 15
488 – 30c. blue, grey and brown 75 1·10
DESIGNS: 10c. Neuchatel Castle; 20c. Symbol of Helvetia; 30c. Symbol of Federal State.

99 Frontier Guard

1948. National Fete and Anti-Tuberculosis Fund. Coat of arms in red.
495 **99** 5c.+5c. green 55 85
496 – 10c.+10c. slate and grey . . 50 45
497 – 20c.+10c. red and buff . . 50 50
498 – 30c.+10c. blue and grey . . 3·50 4·25
DESIGNS: 10c., 20c., 30c. Typical houses in Fribourg, Valais and Ticino respectively.

1948. National Philatelic Exhibition, Basel ("IMABA"). Sheet 110 × 61 mm. T **97**.
MS498a 10c. purple and gery; 20c. blue and grey (sold at 3f.) . . 75·00 49·00

101 Glider

1949. Air. Special (La Chaux-de-Fonds–St. Gallen–Lugano) Flights.
499 **101** 1f.50 purple and yellow 32·00 34·00

102 Posthorn

1949. Centenary of Federal Post.
500 **102** 5c. yellow, pink and grey . . . 20 30
501 – 20c. yellow, violet and grey 40 20
502 – 30c. yellow, brown & grey 60 5·75
DESIGNS: 20c. Mail coach drawn by five horses; 30c. Postal motor coach and trailer.

103 Main Motif of U.P.U. Monument, Berne

1949. 75th Anniv of U.P.U.
503 **103** 10c. green 20 20
504 – 25c. purple . . . . 55 6·25
505 – 40c. blue . . . . 80 2·30
DESIGNS: 25c. Globe and ribbon; 40c. Globe and pigeons.

104 Postman

1949. National Fete and Youth Fund. T **104** and designs as T **89**, but dated "I. VIII. 1949". Arms in red.
506 **104** 5c.+5c. purple . . . . . 65 1·20
507 – 10c.+10c. green & buff . . 60 55
508 – 20c.+10c. brown & buff 75 60
509 – 40c.+10c. blue & lt blue 4·25 7·00
DESIGNS—Typical houses in: 10c. Basel; 20c. Lucerne; 40c. Prattigau.

106 High-tension Pylons **107** Railway Viaducts over River Sitter, near St. Gall

1949. Landscapes.
510 **106** 3c. black . . . . 3·75 3·75
511 **107** 5c. orange 45 10
512 – 10c. green 30 10
513 – 15c. turquoise 45 15
514a – 20c. purple 75 10
515 – 25c. red 60 10
516 – 30c. green 75 10
517 – 35c. brown . . . . . . 1·70 55
518 – 40c. blue . . . . 1·70 10
519 – 50c. grey . . . . 2·75 10
520 – 60c. green . . . . 7·50 10
521 – 70c. violet . . . . 2·75 20
DESIGNS: 10c. Rack railway, Rochers de Naye; 15c. Rotary snowplough; 20c. Grimsel Reservoir; 25c. Lake Lugano and Melide railway causeway; 30c. Verbois hydro-electric power station; 35c. Alpine road (Val d'Anniviers); 40c. Rhine harbour, Basel; 50c. Suspension railway, Santis; 60c. Railway viaduct, Landwasser; 70c. Survey mark, Finsteraarhorn.

110 First Federal Postage Stamps

111 Putting the Weight

1950. National Fete, Red Cross Fund and Centenary of First Federal Postage Stamps. T **110** and designs, as T **111**, inscr "I. VIII. 1950". Coat of arms in red.
522 **110** 5c.+5c. black 60 65
523 **111** 10c.+10c. green & grey . . 1·10 60
524 – 20c.+10c. green & grey . . 1·10 65
525 – 30c.+10c. mauve & grey 6·25 15·00
526 – 40c.+10c. blue and grey 7·50 8·00
DESIGNS: 20c. Wrestling; 30c. Sprinting; 40c. Rifle-shooting.

112 Arms of Zurich

113 Valaisan Polka

1951. National Fete, Mothers' Fund and 600th Anniv of Zurich. Coat of arms in red.
527 **112** 5c.+5c. black 55 45
528 **113** 10c.+10c. green & grey . . 85 50
529 – 20c.+10c. green & grey . . 1·20 65
530 – 30c.+10c. mauve & grey 6·25 11·00
531 – 40c.+10c. blue and grey 7·75 7·50
DESIGNS—As Type **113**: 20c. Flag-swinging; 30c. "Hornussen" (game); 40c. Blowing alphorn.

1951. National Philatelic Exhibition, Lucerne ("LUNABA"). Sheet 74×54 mm. As No. 529. Imperf.
MS531a 40c. multicoloured (sold at 3f.) £200 £120

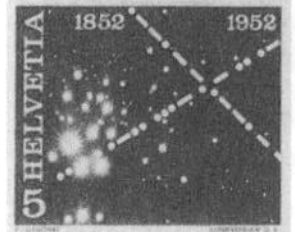

114 "Telegraph" **116** River Doubs

115 Arms of Glarus and Zug

1952. Centenary of Swiss Telecommunications.
532 **114** 5c. orange and yellow . . 40 45
533 – 10c. green and pink . . . 50 10
534 – 20c. mauve and lilac . . . 75 10
535 – 40c. blue and light blue 3·00 2·75
DESIGNS: 10c. "Telephone"; 20c. "Radio"; 40c. "Television".

1952. Pro Patria. Cultural Funds and 600th Anniv of Glarus and Zug joining Confederation.
536 **115** 5c.+5c. red and black . . 50 70
537 **116** 10c.+10c. green and cream 45 40
538 – 20c.+10c. purple & pink 50 40
539 – 30c.+10c. brown & buff 4·25 5·25
540 – 40c.+10c. blue & lt blue 5·00 4·75
DESIGNS—As T **116**: 20c. St. Gotthard Lake; 30c. River Moesa; 40c. Marjelen Lake.

1953. Pro Patria. Emigrants' Fund and 600th Anniv of Berne joining Confederation.
541 5c.+5c. red and black 70 75
542 10c.+10c. green and cream 30 35
543 20c.+10c. purple and pink . . 40 40
544 30c.+10c. brown and buff . 2·75 6·75
545 40c.+10c. blue & light blue 3·75 4·75
DESIGNS—As T **115**: 5c. Arms of Berne (inscr "BERN 1353"). As T **116** (inscr "PRO PATRIA 1953"): 10c. Rapids, R. Reuss; 20c. Lake Sihl; 30c. Aqueduct, Bisse; 40c. Lac Leman.

119 Zurich Airport

1953. Inauguration of Zurich Airport.
546 **119** 40c. blue, grey and red . . 3·50 4·75

120 Alpine Postal Coach and Winter Landscape

1953. For Mobile P.O. Mail.
547 **120** 10c. yellow, green and emerald 20 10
548 – 20c. yellow, red and scarlet 35 10
DESIGN: 10c. Alpine postal coach and summer landscape.

121 Ear of Wheat and Flower **122** Rhine Map and Steering Wheel

1954. Publicity Issue.
549 **121** 10c. multicoloured 65 15
550 – 20c. multicoloured 95 15
551 **122** 25c. green, blue and red 1·60 2·00
552 – 40c. blue, yellow and black . . . . 2·75 1·20
DESIGNS—HORIZ: 10c. Type **121** (Agricultural Exhibition, Lucerne); 20c. Winged spoon (Cooking Exhibition, Berne); 40c. Football and world map (World Football Championship). VERT: 25c. Type **122** (50th anniv of navigation of River Rhine).

123 Opening Bars of "Swiss Hymn"

1954. Pro Patria. Youth Fund and Death Centenary of Father Zwyssig (composer of "Swiss Hymn").
553 **123** 5c.+5c. green 65 75
554 – 10c.+10c. green & turq . . 30 35
555 – 20c.+10c. purple and cream 40 35
556 – 30c.+10c. brown & buff 2·75 6·75
557 – 40c.+10c. deep blue and blue . . . . 5·25 4·75
DESIGNS: 10c. Lake Neuchatel; 20c. Maggia River; 30c. Taubenloch Gorge Waterfall; Schuss River; 40c. Lake Sils.

124 Lausanne Cathedral **125** Alphorn Blower

1955. Publicity Issue. Inscr "1955".
558 **124** 5c. multicoloured 75 20
559 – 10c. multicoloured 75 10
560 **125** 20c. brown and red . . . 1·00 10
561 – 40c. pink, black and blue 1·90 1·20
DESIGNS—HORIZ: 5c. Type **124** (National Philatelic Exhibition, Lausanne); 10c. Vaud girl's hat (Vevey Winegrowers' Festival); 40c. Car steering-wheel (25th International Motor Show, Geneva). VERT: 20c. Type **125** (Alpine Herdsman and Costume Festival, Interlaken).

1955. National Philatelic Exhibition, Lucerne. Sheet 103×52 mm. T **124**. Imperf.
MS561a 10c. and 20c. multicoloured (sold at 2f.) . . . . £150 80·00

126 Federal Institute of Technology, Zurich

1955. Pro Patria. Mountain Population Fund and Centenary of Federal Institute of Technology.
562 **126** 5c.+5c. grey 75 70
563 – 10c.+10c. green and cream 75 35
564 – 20c.+10c. red and pink . . 80 35
565 – 30c.+10c. brown & buff 6·00 4·75
566 – 40c.+10c. blue and light blue . . . . 6·00 4·00
DESIGNS: 10c. Grandfey railway viaduct over River Saane, near Fribourg; 20c. Lake Aegeri; 30c. Lake Grappelensee; 40c. Lake Bienne.

127 "Road Safety" **128** Fokker F.VIIb/3m and Douglas DC-6 Aircraft

1956. Publicity Issue. Inscr "1956".
567 – 5c. yellow, black and green 50 20
568 – 10c. black, green and red 80 10
569 **127** 20c. multicoloured 90 10
570 **128** 40c. blue and red . . . . 3·00 1·00
DESIGNS—HORIZ: 5c. First postal motor coach (50th anniv of postal motor coach service); 10c. Electric train emerging from Simplon Tunnel and Stockalper Palace (50th anniv of opening of Simplon Tunnel).
The 40c. commemorates the 25th anniv of Swissair.

129 Rose, Scissors and Tape-measure **130** Printing Machine's Inking Rollers

1956. Pro Patria. Swiss Women's Fund. T **129** and design as T **116** but inscr "PRO PATRIA 1956".
571 **129** 5c.+5c. green 65 75
572 – 10c.+10c. emerald and green 60 30
573 – 20c.+10c. purple & pink 65 50
574 – 30c.+10c. brown and light brown . . . . 4·25 4·75
575 – 40c.+10c. blue and light blue . . . . 4·25 3·75
DESIGNS: 10c. R. Rhone at St. Maurice; 20c. Katzensee; 30c. R. Rhine at Trin; 40c. Walensee.

1957. Publicity Issue. Inscr "1957".
576 **130** 5c. multicoloured 35 10
577 – 10c. brown, green & turq 2·30 10
578 – 20c. grey and red 70 10
579 – 40c. multicoloured . . . . 2·00 70
DESIGNS: 10c. Electric train crossing bridge over River Ticino (75th anniv of St. Gotthard Railway); 20c. Civil Defence shield and coat of arms ("Civil Defence"); 40c. Munatius Plancus, Basel and Rhine (2000th anniv of Basel).
The 5c. commemorates "Graphic 57" International Exhibition, Lausanne.

131 Shields of Switzerland and the Red Cross **132** "Charity"

1957. Pro Patria. Swiss Red Cross and National Cancer League Funds. Cross in red.
580 **131** 5c.+5c. red and grey . . . 50 60
581 **132** 10c.+10c. purple & grn 50 25
582 20c.+10c. grey and red . . 65 25
583 30c.+10c. blue & brown 3·50 4·00
584 40c.+10c. brown & blue 3·50 3·25

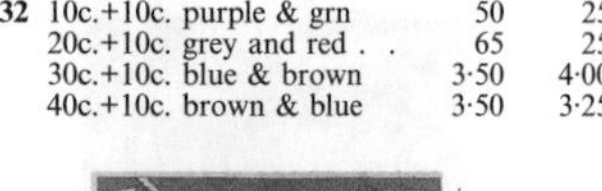
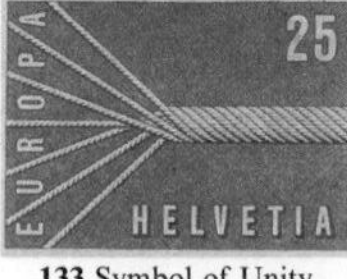

133 Symbol of Unity

1957. Europa.
585 **133** 25c. red 75 20
586 40c. blue . . . . 3·25 45

134 Nyon Castle (2000th anniv of Nyon)

1958. Publicity Issue. Inscr "1958".
587 **134** 5c. violet, buff and green 35 15
588 – 10c. myrtle, red and green 35 10
589 – 20c. red, lilac and vermilion 70 10
590 – 40c. multicoloured . . . . 3·00 95
DESIGNS: 10c. Woman's head with ribbons (Saffa Exhibition, Zurich); 20c. Crossbow (25th anniv as symbol of Swiss manufacture); 40c. Salvation Army bonnet (75th anniv of Salvation Army in Switzerland).

135 "Needy Mother" **136** Fluorite

1958. Pro Patria. For Needy Mothers, T **135** and designs showing minerals, rocks and fossils as T **136**. Inscr "PRO PATRIA 1958".
591 5c.+5c. purple 60 45
592 10c.+10c. yellow, grn & blk 60 25
593 20c.+10c. bistre, red & blk 65 45
594 30c.+10c. purple, brn & blk 3·25 3·50
595 40c.+10c. blue, ultram & blk 3·25 2·50

DESIGNS: 20c. "Lytoceras fimbriatus" ammonite; 30c. Garnet; 40c. Rock crystal.

137 Atomic Symbol

1958. 2nd U.N. Atomic Conference, Geneva.
596 **137** 40c. red, blue and cream . . . 50 25

138 Modern Transport 139 "Swiss Citizens Abroad"

1959. Publicity Issue. Inscr "1959".
597 5c. multicoloured 35 15
598 10c. yellow, grey and green . . 45 10
599 20c. multicoloured 90 10
600 50c. blue, violet and light blue . . . . 1·30 85
DESIGNS: 5c. Type **138** (opening of "The Swiss House of Transport and Communications"); 10c. Lictor's fasces of the Coat of Arms of St. Gall and posthorn (NABAG—National Philatelic Exhibition, St. Gall); 20c. Owl, hare and fish (Protection of Animals); 50c. J. Calvin, Th. de Beze and University building (4th centenary of University of Geneva).

1959. National Philatelic Exhibition, St. Gallen ("NABAG"). Sheet 94 × 57 mm. As No. 598. Imperf.
MS600a 10c. and 20c. multicoloured (sold at 2f.) . . . . 12·00 12·50

1959. Pro Patria. For Swiss Citizens Abroad. T **139** and other designs showing minerals, rocks and fossils as T **136**, and inscr "PRO PATRIA 1959".
601 5c.+5c. red and grey 45 50
602 10c.+10c. multicoloured . . . 70 30
603 20c.+10c. multicoloured . . . 80 35
604 30c.+10c. violet, brn & blk . 2·40 2·10
605 40c.+10c. blue, turquoise and black . . . . 2·40 2·00
DESIGNS: 10c. Agate; 20c. Tourmaline; 30c. Amethyst; 40c. Fossilized giant salamander.

140 "Europa" 142 "Campaign against Cancer"

1959. Europa.
606 **140** 30c. red 65 10
607 50c. blue 75 15

1959. European P.T.T. Conference, Montreux. Optd **REUNION DES PTT D'EUROPE 1959.**
608 **140** 30c. red . . . . 26·00 7·75
609 50c. blue . . . . 26·00 7·75

1960. Publicity Issue. Inscr "1460–1960" (20c.) or "1960" (50c., 75c.).
610 10c. red, light green and green 75 15
611 20c. multicoloured 90 15
612 50c. yellow, ultramarine & blue 90 55
613 75c. red, black and blue . . . 4·00 4·75
DESIGNS: 10c. Type **142** (50th anniv of Swiss National League for Cancer Control); 20c. Charter and sceptre (500th anniv of Basel University); 50c. "Uprooted tree" (World Refugee Year); 75c. Douglas DC-8 jetliner ("Swissair enters the jet age").

143 15th-century Schwyz Cantonal Messenger 143a Lausanne Cathedral

1960. Postal History and "Architectural Monuments" (1st series).
614 – 5c. blue 10 10
615 **143** 10c. green 15 10
616 – 15c. red 10 10
617 – 20c. mauve 30 10
618 **143a** 25c. green 45 10
619p – 30c. red 35 10
620 – 35c. red 90 75
621 – 40c. purple 50 10
622 – 50c. blue 90 10
623 – 60c. red 70 10
624 – 70c. orange . . . . . . 1·20 45
625 – 75c. blue . . . . 1·50 60
626 – 80c. purple 90 10
627 – 90c. green . . . . . . 1·10 10
628 – 1f. orange . . . . . . 1·70 10
629 – 1f.20 red . . . . 1·90 15
632 – 1f.30 brown on lilac . . 1·40 15
630 – 1f.50 green . . . . . . 2·40 25
633 – 1f.70 purple on lilac . . 1·80 15
631 – 2f. blue . . . . 4·00 50
634 – 2f.20 green on green . . 2·40 40
635 – 2f.80 orange on orange . 3·00 35
DESIGNS—HORIZ: 5c. 17th-century Fribourg Cantonal messenger; 15c. 17th-century mule-driver; 20c. 19th-century mounted postman; 1f. Fribourg Town Hall; 1f.20, Basel Gate, Solothurn; 1f.50, Ital Reding's house, Schwyz; 1f.70, 2f., 2f.20, Abbey Church, Einsiedeln. VERT: 30c. Grossmunster, Zurich; 35c., 1f.30, Woodcutters Guildhall, Bienne; 40c. St. Peter's Cathedral, Geneva; 50c. Spalentor (gate), Basel; 60c. Clock Tower, Berne; 70c. Collegiate Church of St. Peter and St. Stephen, Bellinzona; 75c. Kapellbrucke (bridge) and Wasserturm, Lucerne; 80c. St. Gall Cathedral; 90c. Munot Fort, Schaffhausen; 2f.80, as 70c. but redrawn without bell-tower.
See also Nos. 698/713 and 1276.

144 Symbols of Occupational Trades 144a Conference Emblem

1960. Pro Patria. For Swiss Youth. T **144** and other designs showing minerals, rocks and fossils as T **136** and inscr "PRO PATRIA 1960".
636 – 5c.+5c. multicoloured . . 75 60
637 – 10c.+10c. pink, green and black 75 30
638 – 20c.+10c. yellow, purple and black 80 30
639 – 30c.+10c. blue, brown and black . . . . 3·50 2·75
640 **144** 50c.+10c. gold & blue . . 3·25 2·75
DESIGNS: 5c. Smoky quartz; 10c. Orthoclase (feldspar); 20c. Devil's toenail (fossil shell); 30c. Azurite; 50c. Type **144** ("50 Years of National Day Collection").

1960. 50th Anniv of Pro Patria Charity Fund. Sheet 85 × 75 mm. As No. 640. Imperf.
MS641 50c.+10c. gold and blue (block of 4) (sold at 3f.) . . . 29·00 16·00

1960. Europa.
642 **144a** 30c. red 45 10
643 50c. blue 70 20

145 "Aid for Development"

1961. Publicity Issue.
644 **145** 5c. red, blue and grey . . 60 20
645 – 10c. yellow and blue . . . 60 10
646 – 20c. multicoloured . . . . 1·20 20
647 – 50c. red, green and blue . 2·20 75
DESIGNS: 5c. Type **145** ("Aid to countries in process of development"); 10c. Circular emblem ("Hyspa" Exhibition of 20th-century Hygiene, Gymnastics and Sport, Berne); 20c. Hockey stick (World and European Ice Hockey Championships, Geneva and Lausanne); 50c. Map of Switzerland with telephone centres as wiring diagram (inauguration of Swiss fully automatic telephone service).

146 "Cultural Works of Eternity" 147 Doves

1961. Pro Patria. For Swiss Cultural Works, T **146** and other designs showing minerals, rocks and fossils as T **136** and inscr "PRO PATRIA 1961".
648 5c.+5c. blue 45 40
649 10c.+10c. purple, green and black 60 30
650 20c.+10c. red, blue and black 60 30
651 30c.+10c. blue, orange and black . . . . 1·70 2·30
652 50c.+10c. bistre, blue and black . . . . 1·70 2·20
DESIGNS: 10c. Fluorite; 20c. Glarone rabbitfish; 30c. Lazulite; 50c. Fossilized fern.

1961. Europa.
653 **147** 30c. red 40 10
654 50c. blue 50 20

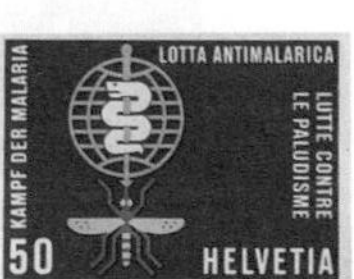

148 St. Matthew 149 W.H.O. Emblem and Mosquito

1961. Wood Carvings from St. Oswald's Church, Zug.
655 **148** 3f. red . . . . 4·00 20
656 – 5f. blue . . . . 6·00 10
657 – 10f. brown . . . . 9·00 45
658 – 20f. red . . . . 17·00 1·90
DESIGNS: 5f. St. Mark; 10f. St. Luke; 20f. St. John.

1962. Publicity Issue.
659 – 5c. multicoloured 70 20
660 – 10c. bistre, purple and green 50 10
661 – 20c. multicoloured 80 15
662 **149** 50c. green, mauve and blue 85 45
DESIGNS: 5c. Electric train (introduction of Trans-Europe Express); 10c. Oarsman (World Rowing Championship, Lucerne); 20c. Jungfraujoch and Monch (50th anniv of Jungfraujoch rack railway station); 50c. Type **149** (malaria eradication).

150 Rousseau 151 Schwyz Gold Ducat

1962. Pro Patria. For Swiss Old People's Homes and Cultural Works.
663 **150** 5c.+5c. blue 15 20
664 – 10c.+10c. blue, black and green 25 25
665 **151** 20c.+10c. yellow, black and red 35 35
666 – 30c.+10c. green, blue and red . . . . 70 1·60
667 – 50c.+10c. violet, black and blue . . . . . . 75 1·40
COINS—As Type **151**: 10c. Obwalden silver-half taler; 30c. Uri batzen; 50c. Nidwalden batzen.

152 Europa "Tree"

1962. Europa.
668 **152** 30c. orange, yellow & brn 60 30
669 50c. blue, green and brown 65 40

153 Campaign Emblem (Freedom from Hunger)

1963. Publicity Issue.
670 – 5c. brown, red and blue 70 20
671 – 10c. red, grey and green 40 10
672 – 20c. lake, red and grey . . 1·50 15
673 **153** 30c. yellow, brown & green . . . . 1·40 1·10
674 – 50c. red, silver and blue 1·00 55
675 – 50c. multicoloured . . . . 1·00 60
DESIGNS: No. 670, Boy scout (50th anniv of Swiss Boy Scout League); 671, Badge (Swiss Alpine Club cent); 672, Luegelkinn Viaduct (50th anniv of Lotschberg Railway); 674, Jubilee Emblem (Red Cross cent); 675, Hotel des Postes, Paris, 1863 (Paris Postal Conference).

1963. International Red Cross Centenary. Sheet 100 × 80 mm. As No. 674. Imperf.
MS675a 50c. multicoloured (block of 4) (sold at 3f.) . . . . 4·50 4·00

154 Dr. Anna Heer (nursing pioneer) 155 Roll of Bandage

1963. Pro Patria. For Swiss Medical and Refugee Aid. T **154** and other designs as T **155** showing Red Cross activities. Inscr "PRO PATRIA 1963".
676 5c.+5c. blue 20 25
677 10c.+10c. red, grey and green 25 15
678 20c.+10c. multicoloured . . . 30 20
679 30c.+10c. multicoloured . . . 90 1·20
680 50c.+10c. red, indigo & blue 1·10 1·20
DESIGNS: 20c. Gift parcel; 30c. Blood plasma; 50c. Red Cross brassard.

156 Glider and Jet Aircraft

1963. Air. 25th Anniv of Swiss "Pro Aero" Foundation. Berne–Locarno or Langenbruck–Berne (helicopter feeder) Special Flights.
681 **156** 2f. multicoloured . . . . 3·00 3·25

157 "Co-operation" 158 Exhibition Emblem

1963. Europa.
682 **157** 50c. brown and blue . . . 55 25

1963. Swiss National Exhibition, Lausanne.
683 **158** 10c. green and olive . . . 20 10
684 20c. red and brown . . . 15 10
685 – 50c. blue, grey and red . . 45 25
686 – 75c. violet, grey and red 55 45
DESIGNS: 50c. "Outlook" (emblem on globe and smaller globe); 75c. "Insight" (emblem on large globe).

159 Great St. Bernard Tunnel

1964. Publicity Issue.
687 5c. blue, red and green . . . 20 15
688 10c. green and blue 25 10
689 20c. multicoloured 50 10
690 50c. multicoloured 85 45
DESIGNS: 5c. Type **159** (Opening of Great St. Bernard Road Tunnel); 10c. Ancient "god of the waters" (Protection of water supplies); 20c. Swiss soldiers of 1864 and 1964 (Centenary of Swiss Association of Non-commissioned Officers); 50c. Standards of Geneva and Swiss Confederation (150th anniv of arrival of Swiss in Geneva).

160 Johann Georg Bodmer (inventor) 161 Europa "Flower"

1964. Pro Patria. For Swiss Mountain Aid and Cultural Funds. T **160** and vert designs of Swiss coins as T **151**. Inscr "PRO PATRIA 1964".
691 5c.+5c. blue 10 15
692 10c.+10c. drab, black & grn 15 15
693 20c.+10c. blue, black & mve 25 20
694 30c.+10c. blue, black & orge 35 55
695 50c.+10c. yellow, brn & bl 70 75
COINS: 10c. Zurich copper; 20c. Basel "doppeldicken"; 30c. Geneva silver thaler; 50c. Berne half gold florin.

1964. Europa.
696 **161** 20c. red 35 10
697 50c. blue 55 20

1964. "Architectural monuments" (2nd series). As T **143a**.
698 5c. mauve 10 10
699 10c. blue 10 10
700 15c. brown 20 10
701 20c. green 25 10
702 30c. red 30 10
703 50c. blue 50 10
704 70c. brown 75 10
705 1f. green . . . . 1·00 10
706 1f.20 red . . . . 1·20 15
707 1f.30 blue . . . . 1·50 55
708 1f.50 green . . . . 1·60 20
709 1f.70 red . . . . 1·90 70
710 2f. orange . . . . 2·10 20
711 2f.20 green . . . . 2·75 55
712 2f.50 green . . . . 2·75 25
713 3f.50 purple . . . . 3·75 30

DESIGNS—HORIZ: 5c. Lenzburg Castle; 10c. Freuler Mansion, Nafels; 15c. Mauritius Church, Appenzell; 20c. Planta House, Samedan; 30c. Town Square, Gais; 50c. Neuchatel Castle and Collegiate Church. VERT: 70c. Lussy "Hochhus", Wolfenschiessen; 1f. Riva San Vitale Church; 1f.20, Payerne Abbey Church; 1f.30, St. Pierre-de Clages Church; 1f.50, Gateway, Porrentruy; 1f.70, Frauenfeld Castle; 2f. Castle Seedorf (Uri); 2f.20, Thomas Tower and Arch, Liestal; 2f.50, St. Oswald's Church, Zug; 3f.50, Benedictine Abbey, Engelberg.

162 Swiss 5r. Stamp of 1854 with "Lozenge" Cancellation

1965. Publicity Issue.
714 – 5c. black, red and blue . . 10 10
715 **162** 10c. brown, blue and green 10 10
716 – 20c. multicoloured 25 10
717 – 50c. red, black and blue 50 35
DESIGNS, etc: 5c. Nurse and patient ("Nursing"); 10c. Type **162** ("NABRA 1965" National Stamp Exhibition, Berne); 20c. WAC Officer (25th anniv of Women's Army Corps); 50c. World telecommunications map (centenary of I.T.U.).

1965. National Philatelic Exhibition, Berrie ("NABARA") Sheet 94 × 61 mm. As T **162**. Imperf.
MS718 10c. orange and green (20r.); 20c. blue and red (40r.) (sold at 3f.) . . . . 1·20 1·30

163 Father T. Florentini

164 Fish-tailed Goose ("Evil")

1965. Pro Patria. For Swiss Abroad and Art Research. Inscr "PRO PATRIA 1965".
719 **163** 5c.+5c. blue 10 10
720 **164** 10c.+10c. multicoloured 10 10
721 – 20c.+10c. multicoloured 25 10
722 – 30c.+10c. brown & blue 40 35
723 – 50c.+10c. blue & brown 55 40
DESIGNS—As Type **164**: (Ceiling paintings in St. Martin's Church, Zillis (Grisons): 20c. One of the magi journeying to Herod; 30c. Fishermen; 50c. The Temptation of Christ.

165 Swiss Emblem and Arms of Cantons

1965. 150th Anniv of Entry of Valais, Neuchatel and Geneva into Confederation.
724 **165** 20c. multicoloured 25 10

166 Matterhorn **167** Europa "Sprig"

1965. Mobile P.O. Issue.
725 **166** 10c. multicoloured 25 10
726 30c. multicoloured 65 60
The 30c. is inscr "CERVIN".

1965. Europa.
727 **167** 50c. green and blue . . . 60 20

168 I.T.U. Emblem and Satellites

1965. I.T.U. Centenary Congress, Montreux. Multicoloured.
728 10c. Type **168** 10 10
729 30c. Symbols of world telecommunications 30 25

169 Figure Skating

1965. World Figure Skating Championships, Davos.
730 **169** 5c. multicoloured 10 10

170 River Kingfisher **171** H. Federer (author)

1966. Publicity Issue. Multicoloured.
731 10c. Type **170** 20 10
732 20c. Mercury's helmet and laurel twig 25 10
733 50c. Phase in nuclear fission and flags 45 20
PUBLICITY EVENTS: 10c. Preservation of natural beauty; 20c. 50th Swiss Industrial Fair, Basel (MUBA); 50c. International Institute for Nuclear Research (CERN).

1966. Pro Patria. For Aid to Mothers. Inscr "PRO PATRIA 1966".
734 **171** 5c.+5c. blue 10 10
735 – 10c.+10c. multicoloured 10 10
736 – 20c.+10c. multicoloured 25 15
737 – 30c.+10c. multicoloured 40 35
738 – 50c.+10c. multicoloured 55 40
DESIGNS—As Type **164**: ("The Flight to Egypt" from ceiling paintings in St. Martin's Church, Zillis (Grisons)): 10c. Joseph's dream; 20c. Joseph on his way; 30c. Virgin and Child; 50c. Angel pointing the way.

172 Society Emblem **173** Europa "Ship"

1966. 50th Anniv of New Helvetic Society for Swiss Abroad.
739 **172** 20c. red and blue 20 10

1966. Europa.
740 **173** 20c. red 25 10
741 50c. blue 50 20

174 Finsteraarhorn

1966. "Swiss Alps".
742 **174** 10c. multicoloured 10 10

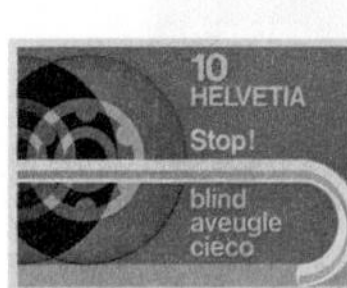

175 White Stick and Motor-car Wheel (Welfare of the Blind) **176** C.E.P.T. Emblem and Cogwheels

1967. Publicity Issue.
743 **175** 10c. multicoloured 10 10
744 – 20c. multicoloured 25 10
DESIGN: 20c. Flags of European Free Trade Area countries (abolition of E.F.T.A. tariffs).

1967. Europa.
745 **176** 30c. blue 30 10

177 Theodor Kocher (surgeon) **178** Cogwheel and Swiss Emblem

1967. Pro Patria. For National Day Collection. Inscr "PRO PATRIA 1967".
746 **177** 5c.+5c. blue 10 10
747 – 10c.+10c. multicoloured 10 10
748 – 20c.+10c. multicoloured 25 10
749 – 30c.+10c. multicoloured 40 35
750 – 50c.+10c. multicoloured 55 40
DESIGNS—As Type **164**: (Ceiling paintings in St. Martin's Church, Zillis (Grisons)): 10c. Annunciation to the Shepherds; 20c. Christ and the woman of Samaria; 30c. Adoration of the Magi; 50c. Joseph seated on throne.

1967. Publicity Issue. Multicoloured.
751 10c. Type **178** 10 10
752 20c. Hour-glass and Sun . . 20 10
753 30c. San Bernadino highway 35 10
754 50c. "OCTI" emblem 50 20
PUBLICITY EVENTS: 10c. 50th anniv of Swiss Week; 20c. 50th anniv of Aged People Foundation; 30c. Opening of San Bernardino road tunnel; 50c. 75th anniv of Central Office for International Railway Transport (OCTI).

179 "Mountains" and Swiss Emblem

1968. Publicity Issue.
755 10c. multicoloured 10 10
756 20c. yellow, brown and blue 25 10
757 30c. blue, ochre and brown 30 10
758 50c. red, turquoise and blue 55 20
DESIGNS AND EVENTS: 10c. T **179** (50th anniv of Swiss Women's Alpine Club); 20c. Europa "key" (Europa); 30c. Staunton rook and chessboard (18th Chess Olympiad, Lugano); 50c. Dispatch "satellites" and aircraft tail-fin (inauguration of new Geneva Air Terminal).

180 "Maius" **181** Protective helmet

1968. Pro Patria. For National Day Collection. Inscr "PRO PATRIA 1968".
759 **180** 10c.+10c. multicoloured 10 10
760 – 20c.+10c. multicoloured 25 15
761 – 30c.+10c. multicoloured 35 10
762 – 50c.+20c. multicoloured 55 50
DESIGNS (Stained-glass panels in the rose window, Lausanne Cathedral): 20c. "Leo"; 30c. "Libra"; 50c. "Pisces" (symbols of the months and signs of the zodiac).

1968. Publicity Issue. Multicoloured.
763 10c. Type **181** 10 10
764 20c. Geneva and Zurich stamps of 1843 . . . . . 25 10
765 30c. Part of Swiss map . . . 30 10
766 50c. "Six Stars" (countries) and anchor 45 25
PUBLICITY EVENTS: 10c. 50th anniv of Swiss Accident Insurance Company; 20c. 125th anniv of Swiss stamps; 30c. 25th anniv of Swiss Territorial Planning Society; 50c. Centenary of Rhine Navigation Act.

182 Guide Camp and Emblem

1969. Publicity Issue. Multicoloured.
767 10c. Type **182** 25 10
768 20c. Pegasus constellation . . 25 10
769 30c. Emblem of Comptoir Suisse 30 10
770 50c. Emblem of Gymnaestrade 45 30
771 2f. Haefeli DH-3 biplane and Douglas DC-8 jetliner . . 2·00 1·40
EVENTS: 10c. 50th anniv of Swiss Girl Guides' Federation; 20c. Opening of first Swiss Planeta-rium, Lucerne; 30c. 50th anniv of Comptoir Suisse, Lausanne; 50c. 5th Gymnaestrada, Basel; 2f. 50th anniv of Swiss Airmail Services.

183 Colonnade **184** "St. Francis of Assisi preaching to the Birds" (Abbey-church, Konigsfelden)

1969. Europa.
772 **183** 30c. multicoloured 35 10
773 50c. multicoloured 50 40

1969. Pro Patria. For National Day Collection. Stained-glass Windows. Multicoloured.
774 10c.+10c. Type **184** 10 10
775 20c.+10c. "The People of Israel drinking" (Berne Cathedral) 25 15
776 30c.+10c. "St. Christopher" (Laufelfingen Church, Basle) 35 20
777 50c.+20c. "Madonna and Child" (St. Jacob's Chapel, Grapplang, Flums) 55 45

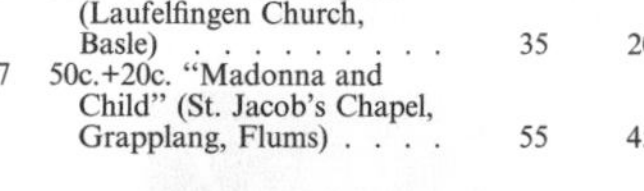

185 Kreuzberge **186** Huldrych Zwingli (Protestant reformer)

1969. Publicity and "Swiss Alps" Issues. Multicoloured.
778 20c. Type **185** 30 10
779 30c. Children crossing road 30 10
780 50c. Hammersmith 50 25
EVENTS: 30c. Road Safety campaign for children; 50c. 50th anniv of I.L.O.

1969. Swiss Celebrities.
781 **186** 10c. violet 10 10
782 – 20c. green 25 10
783 – 30c. red 35 10
784 – 50c. blue 45 35
785 – 80c. brown 80 80
CELEBRITIES: 20c. General Henri Guisan; 30c. Francesco Borromini (architect); 50c. Othmar Schoeck (composer); 80c. Germaine de Stael (writer).

187 Telex Tape **188** "Flaming Sun"

1970. Publicity Issue. Multicoloured.
786 20c. Type **187** 20 10
787 30c. Fireman saving child . . 45 10
788 30c. "Chained wing" emblem 30 10
789 50c. U.N. emblem 50 25
790 80c. New U.P.U. Headquarters 90 95
EVENTS: 20c. 75th anniv of Swiss Telegraphic Agency; 30c. (No. 787), Centenary of Swiss Firemen's Assn; 30c. (No. 788), 50th anniv of "Pro Infirmis" Foundation; 50c. 25th anniv of U.N. Organization; 80c. Inauguration of new U.P.U. headquarters, Berne.

1970. Europa.
791 **188** 30c. red 30 10
792 50c. blue 55 25

1970. Pro Patria. For National Day Collection. Glass paintings by contemporary artists. As T **184** but inscr "1970". Multicoloured.
793 10c.+10c. "Sailor" (G. Casty) 10 15
794 20c.+10c. Architectonic composition (Celestino Piatti) 25 15
795 30c.+10c. "Bull" symbol of Marduk, from "The Four Elements" (Hans Stocker) 35 15
796 50c.+20c. "Man and Woman" (Max Hunziker and Karl Ganz) 55 45

189 Footballer (75th Anniv of Swiss Football Association) **190** Numeral

1970. Publicity and "Swiss Alps" (30c.) Issue. Multicoloured.
797 10c. Type **189** 25 10
798 20c. Census form and pencil (Federal Census) 20 10
799 30c. Piz Palu, Grisons . . . 35 10
800 50c. Conservation Year Emblem (Nature Conservation Year) 45 35

1970. Coil Stamps.
801 **190** 10c. red 10 10
802 20c. green 25 10
803 50c. blue 55 30

191 Female Gymnasts ("Youth and Sport") **193** Europa Chain

1971. Publicity Issue.
804 **191** 10c. multicoloured 20 25
805 – 10c. multicoloured 20 25
806 – 20c. multicoloured 25 10

807 – 30c. multicoloured 30 10
808 – 50c. brown and blue . . . 50 25
809 – 80c. multicoloured 85 65
DESIGNS AND EVENTS: 10c. (No. 805), Male athletes ("Youth and Sport" constitutional amendment); 20c. Stylized rose (child welfare); 30c. "Rayon II" stamp of 1850 and basilisk ("NABA" Philatelic Exhibition, Basel); 50c. "Co-operation" symbol (aid for technical development); 80c. "Intelsat 4" (I.T.U. Space Conference).

1971. Europa.
811 **193** 30c. yellow and mauve . . 30 10
812 50c. yellow and blue . . . 50 20

1971. Pro Patria. For National Day Collection. Contemporary Glass Paintings. As T **184**.
813 10c.+10c. "Religious Abstract", (J. F. Comment) 10 10
814 20c.+10c. "Cockerel", (J. Prahin) 25 15
815 30c.+10c. "Fox", (K. Volk) 35 15
816 50c.+20c. "Christ's Passion" (B. Schorderet) 60 55

194 "Telecommunications Services" (50th anniv of Radio-Suisse)

195 Alexandre Yersin (bacteriologist)

1971. Publicity and "Swiss Alps" (30c.).
817 – 30c. purple, grey & mauve 35 10
818 **194** 40c. multicoloured 40 35
DESIGN: 30c. Les Diablerets, Vaud.

1971. Famous Physicians.
819 **195** 10c. green 10 10
820 – 20c. green 20 10
821 – 30c. red 30 10
822 – 40c. blue 45 45
823 – 80c. purple 80 80
PHYSICIANS: 20c. Auguste Forel (psychiatrist); 30c. Jules Gonin (ophthalmologist); 40c. Robert Koch (German bacteriologist); 80c. Frederick Banting (Canadian physiologist).

196 Warning Triangle and Wrench (75th Annivs of Motoring Organisations)

1972. Publicity Issue.
824 **196** 10c. multicoloured 10 10
825 – 20c. multicoloured 25 10
826 – 30c. orange, red & carmine 30 10
827 – 40c. violet, green and blue 50 30
DESIGNS AND EVENTS: 20c. Signal-box switch table (125th anniv of Swiss Railways); 30c. Stylized radio waves and girl's face (50th anniv of Swiss Broadcasting); 40c. Symbolic tree (50th "Swiss Citizens Abroad" Congress).

197 Swissair Boeing 747-100 Jetliner

198 "Communications"

1972. Air. Pro Aero Foundation and 50th Annivs of North Atlantic and Int Airmail Services.
828 **197** 2f.+1f. multicoloured . . 2·50 1·90

1972. Europa.
829 **198** 30c. multicoloured 30 10
830 40c. multicoloured 45 20

199 Late Stone Age Harpoon Heads

200 Civil Defence Emblem

1972. Pro Patria. For National Day Collection. Archaeological Discoveries (1st series). Mult.
831 10c.+10c. Type **199** 20 15
832 20c.+10c. Bronze water-vessel, c. 570 B.C. 35 15
833 30c.+10c. Gold bust of Marcus Aurelius, 2nd cent A.D. 50 20
834 40c.+20c. Alemannic disc. 7th-cent A.D. 55 65
See also Nos. 869/72, 887/90 and 901/4.

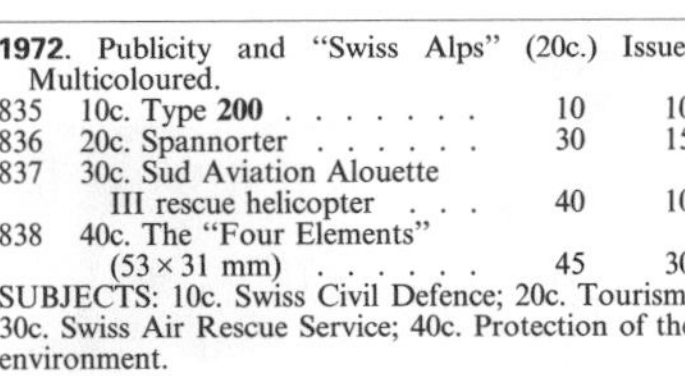

1972. Publicity and "Swiss Alps" (20c.) Issue. Multicoloured.
835 10c. Type **200** 10 10
836 20c. Spannorter 30 15
837 30c. Sud Aviation Alouette III rescue helicopter . . . 40 10
838 40c. The "Four Elements" (53 × 31 mm) 45 30
SUBJECTS: 10c. Swiss Civil Defence; 20c. Tourism; 30c. Swiss Air Rescue Service; 40c. Protection of the environment.

201 Alberto Giacometti (painter)

202 Dish Aerial

1972. Swiss Celebrities.
839 **201** 10c. black and buff . . . 10 10
840 – 20c. black and bistre . . . 25 10
841 – 30c. black and pink . . . 30 10
842 – 40c. black and blue . . . 45 25
843 – 80c. black and purple . . 80 80
PORTRAITS: 20c. Charles Ramuz (novelist); 30c. Le Corbusier (architect); 40c. Albert Einstein (physicist); 80c. Arthur Honegger (composer).

1973. Publicity Issue. Multicoloured.
844 15c. Type **202** 20 20
845 30c. Quill pen 30 10
846 40c. Interpol emblem 45 25
EVENTS: 15c. Construction of Satellite Earth Station, Leuk-Brentjong; 30c. Centenary of Swiss Association of Commercial Employees; 40c. 50th anniv of International Criminal Police Organisation (Interpol).

203 Sottoceneri

204 Toggenburg Inn Sign

1973.
847 **203** 5c. blue and stone . . . 10 10
848 – 10c. green and purple . . 10 10
849 – 15c. blue and orange . . 20 10
850 – 25c. violet and green . . 25 20
851 – 30c. violet and red . . . 30 10
852 – 35c. violet and orange 50 30
853 – 40c. grey and blue . . . 40 10
854 – 50c. green and orange 50 10
855 – 60c. brown and grey . . 65 10
856 – 70c. green and purple . . 75 10
857 – 80c. red and green . . . 85 15
858 – 1f. purple . . . . 1·10 10
859 – 1f.10 blue . . . . 1·20 15
860 – 1f.20 red . . . . 1·30 1·00
861 **204** 1f.30 orange . . . . . . 1·60 25
862 – 1f.50 green . . . . . . 1·70 15
863 – 1f.70 grey . . . . 1·10 40
864 – 1f.80 red . . . . 2·00 20
865 – 2f. blue . . . . 2·20 20
866 – 2f.50 brown . . . . . . 3·25 40
866a – 3f. red . . . . 3·75 70
866b – 3f.50 green . . . . . . 3·00 25
DESIGNS—VERT: 10c. Grisons; 15c. Central Switzerland; 25c. Jura; 30c. Simmental; 35c. Houses, Central Switzerland; 40c. Vaud; 50c. Valais; 60c. Engadine; 70c. Sopraceneri; 80c. Eastern Switzerland. HORIZ: 1f. Rose window, Lausanne Cathedral; 1f.10, Gallus portal, Basel Cathedral; 1f.20, Romanesque capital, St.-Jean-Baptiste Church, Grandson; 1f.50, Medallion, St. Georgen Monastery, Stein am Rhein; 1f.70, Roman Capital, St.-Jean-Baptiste Church, Grandson; 1f.80, Gargoyle, Berne Cathedral; 2f. Oriel, Schaffhausen; 2f.50, Weathercock, St. Ursus Cathedral, Solothurn; 3f. Font, St. Maurice Church, Saanen; 3f.50, Astronomical clock, Berne.

205 Europa "Posthorn"

1973. Europa.
867 **205** 25c. yellow and red . . . 30 25
868 40c. yellow and blue . . . 40 20

1973. Pro Patria. For National Day Collection. Archaeological Discoveries (2nd series). As T **199**, but horiz. Multicoloured.
869 15c.+5c. Rauraric jar 25 25
870 30c.+10c. Head of a Gaul (bronze) 40 15
871 40c.+20c. Almannic "Fish" brooches 65 65
872 60c.+20c. Gold bowl . . . . 1·00 95

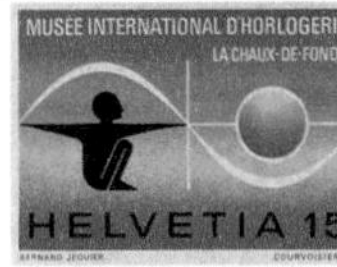

206 Horological Emblem

1973. Publicity Issue. Multicoloured.
873 15c. Type **206** 20 20
874 30c. Skiing emblem 30 10
875 40c. Face of child 40 20
SUBJECTS: 15c. Inaug (1974) of Int Horological Museum, Neuchatel; 30c. World Alpine Skiing Championships, St. Moritz (1974); 40c. "Terre des Hommes" (Child-care organization).

207 Global Hostels

208 Cantonal Messenger (Basel)

1974. Publicity Issue. Multicoloured.
876 15c. Type **207** 15 10
877 30c. Gymnast and hurdlers 30 10
878 40c. Pistol and target 40 25
SUBJECTS: 15c. "50 Years of Swiss Youth Hostels"; 30c. Centenary of Swiss Workmen's Gymnastics and Sports Assn (S.A.T.U.S.); 40c. World Shooting Championships, 1974.

1974. "Internaba 1974" Stamp Exhibition, Basel. Sheet 83 × 73 mm containing T **208** and similer vert designs, showing Cantonal messengers. Multicoloured.
MS879 30c. Type **208**; 30c. Zug; 60c. Uri; 80c. Schwyz (sold at 30f.) 3·75 4·25

209 "Continuity" (Max Bill)

1974. Europa. Swiss Sculptures.
880 **209** 30c. black and red 30 10
881 – 40c. brown, blue and black 45 35
DESIGN: 40c. "Amazone" (Carl Burckhardt).

210 Eugene Borel (first Director of International Bureau, U.P.U.)

211 View of Berne

1974. Centenary of U.P.U.
882 **210** 30c. black and pink . . . 30 15
883 – 40c. black and grey . . . 45 25
884 – 80c. black and green . . . 85 75
DESIGNS: 40c. Heinrich von Stephan (founder of U.P.U.); 80c. Montgomery Blair (U.S. Postmaster-General and initiator of 1863 Paris Postal Conference).

1974. 17th U.P.U. Congress, Lausanne. Mult.
885 30c. Type **211** 30 20
886 30c. View of Lausanne . . . 30 20

1974. Pro Patria. For National Day Collection. Archaeological Discoveries (3rd series). As T **199** but horiz. Multicoloured.
887 15c.+5c. Glass bowl 25 25
888 30c.+10c. Bull's head (bronze) 40 15
889 40c.+20c. Gold brooch 65 60
890 60c.+20c. "Bird" vessel (clay) 95 90

212 "Oath of Allegiance" (sculpture) (W. Witschi)

1974. Publicity Issue.
891 **212** 15c. deep green, green and lilac 20 15
892 – 30c. multicoloured 30 10
893 – 30c. multicoloured 30 10

EVENTS AND COMMEMORATIONS: No. 891, Centenary of Federal Constitution; No. 892, Foundation emblem (Aid for Swiss Sport Foundation); No. 893, Posthorn and "postal transit" arrow (125th anniv of Federal Posts).

213 "Metre" and Krypton Line

214 "The Monch" (F. Hodler)

1975. Publicity Issue.
894 **213** 15c. orange, blue and green 20 25
895 – 30c. brown, purple & yell 30 10
896 – 60c. red, black and blue 60 40
897 – 90c. multicoloured . . . . 1·00 70
DESIGNS AND EVENTS: 15c. Centenary of International Metre Convention; 30c. Heads of women (International Women's Year); 60c. Red Cross flag and barbed-wire (Conference on Humanitarian International Law, Geneva); 90c. Astra airship "Ville de Lucerne", 1910 ("Aviation and Space Travel" Exhibition, Transport and Communications Museum, Lucerne).

1975. Europa. Paintings. Multicoloured.
898 30c. Type **214** 35 15
899 50c. "Still Life with Guitar" (R. Auberjonois) 55 40
900 60c. "L'effeuilleuse" (M. Barraud) 70 50

1975. Pro Patria. Archaeological Discoveries. (4th series). As T **199**. Multicoloured.
901 15c.+10c. Gold brooch, Oron-le-Chatel 25 25
902 30c.+20c. Bronze head of Bacchus, Avenches 45 25
903 50c.+20c. Bronze daggers, Bois-de-Vaux, Lausanne . . 70 80
904 60c.+25c. Glass decanter, Maralto 85 75

215 "Eliminate Obstacles!"

1975. Publicity Issue.
905 **215** 15c. black, green and lilac 20 20
906 – 30c. black, rosine and red 30 10
907 – 50c. brown and bistre . . 60 45
908 – 60c. multicoloured 70 40
DESIGNS: 30c. Organization emblem (Inter-confessional Pastoral Care by Telephone Organization); 50c. European Architectural Heritage Year emblem; 60c. Beat Fischer von Reichenbach (founder) (300th anniv of Fischer postal service).

216 Forest Scene (Federal Forest Laws Cent)

217 Floral Embroidery

1976. Publicity Issue.
909 **216** 20c. multicoloured 20 20
910 – 40c. multicoloured 40 20
911 – 40c. black, orange & pur 40 20
912 – 80c. black and blue . . . 85 75
DESIGNS: No. 910, Fruit and vegetables (campaign to promote nutriments as opposed to alcohol); No. 911, African child (fight against leprosy); No. 912, Early and modern telephones (telephone centenary).

1976. Europa. Handicrafts.
913 **217** 40c. yellow, brown & pink 40 15
914 – 80c. blue, red and stone 80 55
DESIGN: 80c. Decorated pocket watch.

218 Kyburg Castle, Zurich

1976. Pro Patria. Swiss Castles (1st series). Multicoloured.
915 20c.+10c. Type **218** 30 30
916 40c.+20c. Grandson, Vaud 60 25
917 40c.+20c. Murten, Fribourg 60 35
918 80c.+40c. Bellinzona, Ticino 1·40 1·50
See also Nos. 932/5, 955/8 and 977/80.

219 Roe Deer Fawn, Barn Swallow and Frog (World Fed. for Protection of Animals)

1976. Publicity Issue.
919 **219** 20c. black, brown & green . . . 25 25
920 – 40c. black, yellow and red . . . 45 15
921 – 40c. multicoloured 45 15
922 – 80c. red, violet and blue . . . 90 55
DESIGNS: No. 920, "Sun" and inscription ("Save Energy" campaign); No. 921, St. Gotthard mountains (Swiss Alps); No. 922, Skater (World Speed Skating Championships, Davos).

220 Oskar Bider and Bleriot XI

1977. Swiss Aviation Pioneers.
923 **220** 40c. black, mauve and red . . . 45 15
924 – 80c. black, purple and blue 80 60
925 – 100c. black, green & bistre . . . . 1·00 80
926 – 150c. black, brown & grn . . 1·50 1·40
DESIGNS: 80c. Eduard Spelterini and balloon basket; 100c. Armand Dufaux and Dufaux IV biplane; 150c. Walter Mittelholzer and Dornier Do-B Merkur seaplane "Switzerland".

221 Blue Cross (society for care of alcoholics, cent)

1977. Publicity Issues.
927 **221** 20c. blue and brown . . . 20 15
928 – 40c. multicoloured 40 10
929 – 80c. multicoloured 80 55
DESIGNS: 40c. Festival emblem (Vevey vintage festival); 80c. Balloons carrying letters ("Juphilex 1977" youth stamp exhibition, Berne).

222 St. Ursanne

1977. Europa. Landscapes. Multicoloured.
930 40c. Type **222** 40 15
931 80c. Sils-Baselgia 80 60

1977. Pro Patria. Swiss Castles (2nd series). As T **218**. Multicoloured.
932 20c.+10c. Aigle, Vaud . . . 30 30
933 40c.+20c. Pratteln, Basel-Landschaft 55 25
934 70c.+30c. Sargans, St. Gallen . . 90 1·00
935 80c.+40c. Hallwil, Aargau . . 1·10 1·10

223 Factory Worker

1977. Publicity Issue. Multicoloured.
936 20c. Type **223** 20 20
937 40c. Ionic capital 40 15
938 80c. Association emblem and butterfly 85 55
EVENTS: 20c. Centenary of Federal Factories Act; 40c. Protection of cultural monuments; 80c. Swiss Footpaths Association.

224 Sternsingen, Bergun **225** Mailcoach Route Plate, Vaud Canton

1977. Regional Folk Customs.
939 **224** 5c. green 10 10
940 – 10c. red 10 10
941 – 20c. orange 20 10
941b – 25c. brown 40 25
941c – 30c. green 35 15
942 – 35c. green 45 20
943 – 40c. purple 50 10
943c – 45c. blue 65 60
944 – 50c. red 55 10
944b – 60c. brown 80 55
945 – 70c. lilac 80 10
946 – 80c. blue 95 25
947 – 90c. brown . . . . . . 1·00 30
DESIGNS: 10c. Sechselauten, Zurich; 20c. Silvesterklause, Herisau; 25c. Chesstete, Solothurn; 30c. Rollelibutzen, Alstatten; 35c. Gansabhauet, Sursee; 40c. Escalade, Geneva; 45c. Klausjagen, Kussnacht; 50c. Archetringele, Laupen; 60c. Schnabelgeissen, Ottenbach; 70c. Processioni storiche, Mendrisio; 80c. Vogel Gryff, Basel; 90c. Roitschaggata, Lotschental.

1978. Publicity Issue. Multicoloured.
948 20c. Type **225** 25 10
949 40c. View of Lucerne 40 10
950 70c. Title page of book "Melusine" 75 60
951 80c. Stylized camera and lens . 85 60
EVENTS: 20c. "Lemanex '78" National Stamp Exhibition; 40c. 800th anniv of Lucerne; 70c. 500th anniv of Printing at Geneva; 80c. 2nd International Triennial Exhibition of Photography, Fribourg.

226 *La Suisse*, Lake Geneva

1978. "Lemanex 78" National Stamp Exhibtion, Lausanne. Sheet 133 × 149 mm containg T **226** and similar horiz design, showing steamers, with 4 labels. Multicoloured.
MS952 20c. Type **226**; 20c. *Il Verbano*; 40c. *Gotthard*; 40c. *Ville de Neuchatel*; 40c. *Romanshorn*; 40c. *Le Winkeiried*; 70c. *Loetschberg*; 80c. *Waedenswil* (sold at 5f.) . . . . 4·50 4·75

227 Stockalper Palace, Brig **228** Abbe Joseph Bovet (composer)

1978. Europa.
953 **227** 40c. multicoloured 45 10
954 – 80c. blue, brown and black 90 60
DESIGN: 80c. Old Diet Hall, Berne.

1978. Pro Patria. Swiss Castles (3rd series). As T **218**.
955 20c.+10c. Hagenwil, Thurgau . 35 30
956 40c.+20c. Burgdorf, Berne . . 50 20
957 70c.+30c. Tarasp, Graubunden . . . . 1·00 1·10
958 80c.+40c. Chillon, Vaud . . . 1·30 1·30

1978. Celebrities.
959 **228** 20c. green 25 15
960 – 40c. purple 45 10
961 – 70c. grey 75 55
962 – 80c. blue 85 55
DESIGNS: 40c. Henri Dunant (founder of Red Cross); 70c. Carl Gustav Jung (psychiatrist); 80c. Auguste Piccard (physicist).

229 Worker wearing Goggles

1978. Safety at Work. Multicoloured.
963 40c. Type **229** 45 20
964 40c. Worker wearing respirator 45 20
965 40c. Worker wearing safety helmet 45 20

230 Arms of Switzerland and Jura

1978. Creation of Canton of Jura.
966 **230** 40c. red, black and stone . . 45 10

231 Rainer Maria Rilke (writer) **232** Othmar H. Ammann and Verrazano Narrows Bridge

1979. Celebrities.
967 **231** 20c. green 25 15
968 – 40c. red 45 10
969 – 70c. brown 75 55
970 – 80c. blue 85 55
DESIGNS: 40c. Paul Klee (artist); 70c. Herman Hesse (novelist and poet); 80c. Thomas Mann (novelist).

1979. Publicity Issue. Multicoloured.
971 20c. Type **232** 20 15
972 40c. Target and marker . . . 45 10
973 70c. Hot-air balloon "Esperanto" 75 60
974 80c. Aircraft tail fins 85 55
SUBJECTS: 20c. Birth centenary of O. H. Ammann (engineer); 40c. 50th Federal Riflemen's Festival, Lucerne; 70c. World Esperanto Congress, Lucerne; 80c. Basel-Mulhouse Airport.

233 Old Letter Box, Basel **234** Gold Stater

1979. Europa.
975 **233** 40c. multicoloured 45 15
976 – 80c. blue, lt blue & stone . 85 65
DESIGN: 80c. Alpine relay station on the Jungfraujoch.

1979. Pro Patria. Swiss Castles (4th series). As T **218**. Multicoloured.
977 20c.+10c. Oron, Vaud . . . 30 30
978 40c.+20c. Spiez, Berne . . . 50 25
979 70c.+30c. Porrentruy, Jura . . 80 95
980 80c.+40c. Rapperswil, St. Gallen . . . . 1·10 1·20

1979. Publicity Issue. Multicoloured.
981 20c. Type **234** 25 15
982 40c. Child on dove (horiz) . . 45 10
983 70c. Morse key and satellite (horiz) 75 50
984 80c. "Ariane" rocket 85 50
EVENTS: 20c. Centenary of Swiss Numismatic Society; 40c. International Year of the Child; 70c. 50th anniv of Swiss Radio Amateurs; 80c. European Space Agency.

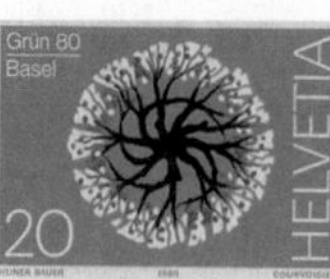

235 Tree in Blossom **236** Johann Konrad Kern (politician)

1980. Publicity Issue. Multicoloured.
985 20c. Type **235** 25 10
986 40c. Carved milk vessel . . . 45 10
987 70c. Winterthur Town Hall . . 70 55
988 80c. Pic-Pic motor car 80 60
SUBJECTS: 20c. Horticultural and Landscape Gardening Exhibition, Basel; 40c. 50th anniv of Arts and Crafts Centre; 70c. Centenary of Society for Swiss Art History; 80c. 50th International Motor Show, Geneva.

1980. Europa.
989 **236** 40c. flesh, black and pink . 45 10
990 – 80c. flesh, black and blue . 85 55
DESIGN: 80c. Gustav Adolf Hasler (communications pioneer).

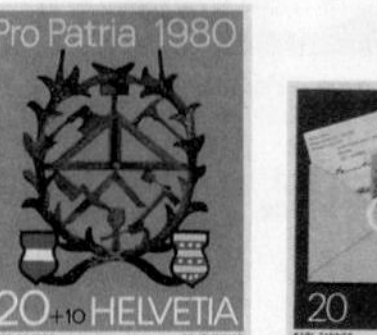

237 Mason and Carpenter **238** Girocheque and Letter Box

1980. Pro Patria. Trade and Craft Signs. Mult.
991 20c.+10c. Type **237** 30 30
992 40c.+20c. Barber 65 20
993 70c.+30c. Hatter . . . . . 1·00 1·20
994 80c.+40c. Baker . . . . . 1·20 1·00

1980. Swiss P.T.T. Services.
995 **238** 20c. multicoloured 25 20
996 – 40c. multicoloured 50 10
997 – 70c. brown, black and lilac 70 50
998 – 80c. multicoloured 80 55
DESIGNS: 40c. Postbus; 70c. Transfer roller (50th anniv of P.T.T. postage stamp printing office); 80c. Flowers and telephone (centenary of telephone in Switzerland).

239 Weather Chart

1980. Publicity Issue. Multicoloured.
999 20c. Type **239** 25 20
1000 40c. Figures and cross . . . 45 25
1001 80c. Motorway sign 90 85
SUBJECTS: 20c. Centenary of Swiss Meteorological Office; 40c. Centenary of Swiss Trades Union Federation; 80c. Opening of St. Gotthard road tunnel.

240 Granary from Kiesen

1981. Publicity Issue. Multicoloured.
1002 20c. Type **240** 25 15
1003 40c. Disabled figures 45 10
1004 70c. "The Parish Clerk" (Albert Anker) (vert) . . 75 65
1005 80c. Theodolite and rod . . 80 55
1006 110c. Tail of DC9-81 . . . 1·10 85
SUBJECTS: 20c. Ballenberg Open-air Museum; 40c. International Year of Disabled Persons; 70c. 150th birth anniv of Albert Anker (artist); 80c. 16th International Federation of Surveyors Congress, Montreux; 110c. 50th anniv of Swissair.

241 Figure leaping from Earth **242** Dancing Couple

1981. 50th Anniv of Swissair.
1007 **241** 2f.+1f. lilac, violet and yellow . . . . 2·40 2·10

1981. Europa. Multicoloured.
1008 40c. Type **242** 45 10
1009 80c. Stone putter 90 60

243 Aarburg Post Office Sign, 1685 **244** Seal of Fribourg

1981. Pro Patria. Postal Signs. Multicoloured.
1010 20c.+10c. Type **243** 35 40
1011 40c.+20c. Mail coach sign of Fribourg Cantonal Post 65 25
1012 70c.+30c. Gordola Post office sign (Ticino Cantonal Post) . . . . . 1·00 1·30
1013 80c.+40c. Splugen post office sign . . . . 1·20 1·10

1981. 500th Anniv of Covenant of Stans.
1014 **244** 40c. red, black and brown 45 15
1015 – 40c. green, black and purple 45 15
1016 – 80c. brown, black and blue 85 60
DESIGNS: 40c. (No. 1015) Seal of Solothurn; 80c. Old Town Hall, Stans.

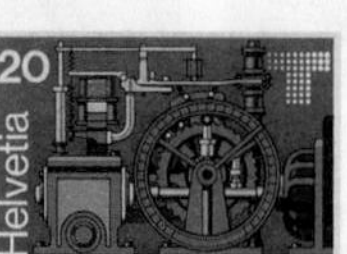

245 Voltage Regulator from Jungfrau Railway's Power Station

1981. Publicity Issue. Multicoloured.
1017 20c. Type **245** 25 15
1018 40c. Crossbow quality seal . . 45 10
1019 70c. Group of youths . . . 75 60
1020 1f.10 Mosaic . . . . 1·20 80

SUBJECTS: 20c. Opening of Technorama of Switzerland, Winterthur (museum of science and technology); 40c. 50th anniv of Organization for Promotion of Swiss Products and Services; 70c. 50th anniv of Swiss Association of Youth Organizations; 1f.10, Restoration of St. Peter's Cathedral, Geneva.

246 Class C4/5 Steam Locomotive

1982. Centenary of St. Gotthard Railway.
1021 **246** 40c. black and purple . . 45 15
1022 – 40c. multicoloured . . . 45 15
DESIGN: No. 1022, Class Re 6/6 electric locomotive.

247 Hoteliers Association Emblem

1982. Publicity Issue. Multicoloured.
1023 20c. Type **247** 25 15
1024 40c. Flag formed by four Fs 45 10
1025 70c. Gas flame encircling emblem 75 55
1026 80c. Lynx and scientific instruments 80 55
1027 110c. Retort . . . . 1·10 80
SUBJECTS: 20c. Centenary of Swiss Hoteliers Association; 40c. 150th anniv of Swiss Gymnastics Association; 70c. 50th anniv of International Gas Union; 80c. 150th anniv of Natural History Museum, Berne; 110c. Centenary of Swiss Society of Chemical Industries.

248 "Swearing Oath of Eternal Fealty, Rutli Meadow" (detail of mural, Heinrich Danioth)

1982. Europa. Multicoloured.
1028 40c. Type **248** 45 20
1029 80c. Treaty of 1291 founding Swiss Confederation 85 55

249 "The Sun", Willisau **250** "Aquarius" and Old Berne

1982. Pro Patria. Inn Signs (1st series). Multicoloured.
1030 20c.+10c. Type **249** 25 30
1031 40c.+20c. "On the Wave", St. Saphorin 65 15
1032 70c.+30c. "The Three Kings", Rheinfelden . . . 85 1·10
1033 80c.+40c. "The Crown", Winterhur . . . . 1·00 95
See also Nos. 1056/9.

1982. Signs of the Zodiac and Landscapes.
1034 **250** 1f. multicoloured . . . 1·00 10
1035 – 1f.10 brown, blue & vio 1·10 10
1036 – 1f.20 green, blue & brn 1·30 20
1036a – 1f.40 multicoloured . . 1·70 1·30
1037 – 1f.50 bl, azure & orge 1·60 20
1038 – 1f.60 multicoloured . . 1·90 85
1039 – 1f.70 cobalt, brn & bl 1·80 15
1040 – 1f.80 brn, grn & dp grn 2·10 1·10
1041 – 2f. cobalt, brown & blue . . . . 2·50 1·80
1042 – 2f. cobalt, brown & blue . . . . 2·10 30
1042a – 2f.50 red, grn & dp grn 2·75 50
1043 – 3f. red, green and black 3·00 30
1044 – 4f. green, violet & purple . . . . 4·25 60
1045 – 4f.50 ochre, blue & brn 4·75 1·20
DESIGNS: 1f.10, "Pisces" and Nax near Sion; 1f.20, "Aries" and the Graustock, Obwalden; 1f.40, "Gemini" and Bischofszell; 1f.50, "Taurus" and Basel Cathedral; 1f.60, "Gemini" and Schonengrund; 1f.70, "Cancer" and Wetterhorn; 1f.80, "Leo" and Areuse Gorge; 2f. (1041), "Virgo" and Aletsch Glacier; 2f. (1042), "Virgo" and Schwarzsee above Zermatt; 2f.50, "Libra" and Fechy; 3f. "Scorpio" and Corippo; 4f. "Sagittarius" and Glarus; 4f.50, "Capricorn" and Schuls.

251 Articulated Tram

1982. Publicity Issue. Multicoloured.
1046 20c. Type **251** 40 15
1047 40c. Salvation Army singer and guitarist 50 10
1048 70c. Dressage rider 75 65
1049 80c. Emblem 80 60
SUBJECTS: 20c. Centenary of Zurich trams; 40c. Centenary of Salvation Army in Switzerland; 70c. World Dressage Championship, Lausanne; 80c. 14th International Water Supply Association Congress, Zurich.

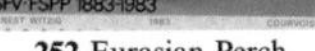

252 Eurasian Perch **253** Jost Burgi's Celestial Globe, 1594

1983. Publicity Issue. Multicoloured.
1050 20c. Type **252** 30 15
1051 40c. University of Zurich . . 45 10
1052 70c. Teleprinter tape forming "JP" 75 65
1053 80c. Micrometer and cycloidal computer drawing 85 55
EVENTS: 20c. Centenary of Swiss Fishing and Pisciculture Federation; 40c. 150th anniv of University of Zurich; 70c. Centenary of Swiss Journalists' Federation; 80c. Centenary of Swiss Machine Manufacturers' Association.

1983. Europa.
1054 **253** 40c. orange, pink and brown 45 15
1055 – 80c. green, blue and black 90 70
DESIGN: 80c. Niklaus Riggenbach's rack and pinion railway, 1871.

1983. Pro Patria. Inn Signs (2nd series). As T **249**. Multicoloured.
1056 20c.+10c. "The Lion", Heimiswil 35 35
1057 40c.+20c. "The Cross", Sachseln 65 20
1058 70c.+30c. "The Jug", Lenzburg Castle . . . . 1·00 1·20
1059 80c.+40c. "The Cavalier", St. George . . . . 1·20 1·10

254 Seal, 1832–48 **255** Gallo-Roman Capital, Martigny

1983. 150th Anniv of Basel-Land Canton.
1060 **254** 40c. multicoloured . . . 45 15

1983. Publicity Issue.
1061 **255** 20c. orange and black 25 15
1062 – 40c. multicoloured . . . 60 10
1063 – 70c. multicoloured . . . 85 70
1064 – 80c. multicoloured . . . 85 55
DESIGNS: 20c. Type **255** (Bimillenary of Octodurus/Martigny); 40c. Bernese shepherd-dog and Schwyz hunting dog (Centenary of Swiss Kennel Club); 70c. Cyclists (Centenary of Swiss Cyclists and Motor Cyclists Federation); 80c. Carrier pigeon and world map (World Communications Year).

256 Pre-stamp Cover, 1839 **257** Bridge

1984. Publicity Issue. Multicoloured.
1065 25c. Type **256** 30 20
1066 50c. Collegiate Church clock and buildings 55 15
1067 80c. Olympic rings and Lausanne . . . . 1·00 65
SUBJECTS: 25c. National Stamp Exhibition, Zurich; 50c. 1100th anniv of Saint-Imier; 80c. Permanent headquarters of International Olympic Committee at Lausanne.

1984. Europa. 25th Anniv of European Posts and Telecommunications Conference.
1068 **257** 50c. purple, red and crimson 60 20
1069 80c. ultramarine, blue and deep blue 95 65

258 Hexagonal Stove from Rosenburg Mansion, Stans **259** Bauschanzli, City Hall and Fraumunster

1984. Pro Patria. Tiled Stoves. Multicoloured.
1070 35c.+15c. Type **258** 50 50
1071 50c.+20c. Winterthur stove (by Hans Heinrich Pfau) Freuler Palace, Nafels . . 70 40
1072 70c.+30c. Box-stove (by Rudolf Stern) from Plaisance, Riaz . . . . . 95 1·10
1073 80c.+40c. Frame-modelled stove (by Leonard Racle) 1·30 1·20

1984. "Naba Zuri 84" National Stamp Exhibition, Zurich. Sheet 145 × 70 mm containing T **259** and similar vert designs forming panorama of Zurich. Multicoloured.
MS1074 50c. Type **259**; 50c. St. Peter's; 50c. Town Hall, Helmhaus and Wasser Church; 50c. Cathedral (sold at 3f.) . . 4·25 4·00

260 Burning Match

1984. Fire Prevention.
1075 **260** 50c. multicoloured . . . 55 15

261 Railway Conductor's Equipment **262** Ernest Ansermet (orchestral conductor)

1985. Publicity Issue. Multicoloured.
1076 35c. Type **261** (cent of Train Staff Association) 65 25
1077 50c. Stone with Latin inscription (2000 years of Rhaeto-Romanic culture) 15 15
1078 70c. Rescue of man (cent of International Lake Geneva Rescue Society) 80 60
1079 80c. Grande Dixence dam (International Large Dams Congress, Lausanne) 95 65

1985. Europa. Music Year. Multicoloured.
1080 50c. Type **262** 65 20
1081 80c. Frank Martin (composer) 90 75

263 Music Box, 1895

1985. Pro Patria. Musical Instruments. Mult.
1082 25c.+10c. Type **263** 50 50
1083 35c.+15c. 18th-century box rattle 65 60
1084 50c.+20c. Emmental necked zither (by Peter Zaugg), 1828 . . . . 80 25
1085 70c.+30c. Drum, 1571 . . . 1·10 1·20
1086 80c.+40c. 20th-century diatonic accordion . . . . 1·30 1·20

264 Baker

1985. Publicity Issue. Multicoloured.
1087 50c. Type **264** (centenary of Swiss Master Bakers' and Confectioners' Federation) 60 15
1088 70c. Cross on abstract background (50th anniv of Swiss Radio International) 80 65
1089 80c. Geometric pattern and emblem (Postal, Telegraph and Telephone International World Congress, Interlaken) . . 85 60

265 Intertwined Ropes

1986. Publicity Issue.
1090 **265** 35c. multicoloured . . . 45 25
1091 – 50c. deep brown, brown and red 35 15
1092 – 80c. orange, green and black 90 65
1093 – 90c. multicoloured . . . 1·00 65
1094 – 1f.10 multicoloured . . . 1·20 1·20
DESIGNS: 35c. Type **265** (50th anniv of Swiss Workers' Relief Organization); 50c. Battle site on 1698 map (600th anniv of Battle of Sempach); 80c. Statuette of Mercury (2000th anniv of Roman Chur); 90c. Gallic head (2000th anniv of Vindonissa); 1f.10, Roman coin of Augustus (2000th anniv of Zurich).

266 Sportsmen **267** Woman's Head

1986. Pro Sport.
1095 **266** 50c.+20c. mult 85 65

1986. Europa. Multicoloured.
1096 50c. Type **267** 55 20
1097 90c. Man's head . . . . . 1·10 75

268 "Bridge in the Sun" (Giovanni Giacometti) **269** Franz Mail Van

1986. Pro Patria. Paintings. Multicoloured.
1098 35c.+15c. Type **268** 60 65
1099 50c.+20c. "The Violet Hat" (Cuno Amiet) 90 25
1100 80c.+40c. "After the Funeral" (Max Buri) . . 1·40 1·40
1101 90c.+40c. "Still Life" (Felix Vallotton) . . . . 1·50 1·30

1986. The Post Past and Present.
1102 **269** 5c. yellow, purple and red 55 15
1103 – 10c. dp grn, grn & orge 50 10
1104 – 20c. orange, brown & bl 20 15
1105 – 25c. dp blue, bl & yell 55 40
1106 – 30c. grey, black & yellow 40 15
1107 – 35c. lake, red and yellow 70 25
1108 – 45c. blue, black & brown 50 30
1109 – 50c. violet, green & pur 55 15
1110 – 60c. orange, yellow & brn 65 30
1111 – 75c. green, dp grn & red 85 70
1112 – 80c. indigo, blue & brn 1·50 50
1113 – 90c. olive, brown & green . . . . 1·70 80
DESIGNS: 10c. Mechanized parcel sorting; 20c. Mule post; 25c. Letter cancelling machine; 30c. Stagecoach; 35c. Post Office counter clerk; 45c. Paddle-steamer "Stadt Luzern", 1830s; 50c. Postman; 60c. Loading mail bags onto airplane; 75c. 17th-century mounted courier; 80c. Town postman, 1900s; 90c. Interior of railway mail sorting carriage.

270 Stylized Doves (International Peace Year)

1986. Publicity Issue. Multicoloured.
1115 35c. Type **270** 45 40
1116 50c. Sun behind snow-covered tree (50th anniv of Swiss Winter Relief Fund) 55 15

1117	80c. Symbols of literature and art (cent of Berne Convention for protection of literary and artistic copyright)	1·00	75
1118	90c. Red Cross, Red Crescent and symbols of aggression (25th Int Red Cross Conference meeting, Geneva)	95	70

271 Mobile Post Office

1987. Publicity Issue. Multicoloured.

1119	35c. Type **271** (50th anniv of mobile post offices) . . .	50	25
1120	50c. Lecturers of the seven faculties (450th anniv of Lausanne University) . .	55	15
1121	80c. Profile, maple leaf and logarithmic spiral (150th anniv of Swiss Engineers' and Architects' Association)	95	65
1122	90c. Boeing 747-300/400 jetliner and electric train (Geneva Airport rail link)	1·20	75
1123	1f.10 Symbolic figure and water (2000th anniv of Baden thermal springs)	1·30	1·20

272 "Scarabaeus" (Bernhard Luginbuhl)

1987. Europa. Sculpture. Multicoloured.

1124	50c. Type **272**	55	20
1125	90c. "Carnival Fountain", Basel (Jean Tinguely) . .	1·20	85

273 Wall Cabinet, 1764

1987. Pro Patria. Rustic Furniture. Multicoloured.

1126	35c.+15c. Type **273**	60	65
1127	50c.+20c. 16th-century chest	80	30
1128	80c.+40c. Cradle, 1782 . . .	1·40	1·50
1129	90c.+40c. Wardrobe, 1698	1·50	1·40

274 Butcher cutting Chops

275 Zug Clock Tower

1987. Publicity Issue. Multicoloured.

1130	35c. Type **274** (centenary of Swiss Master Butchers' Federation)	45	45
1131	50c. Profiles on stamps (50th anniv of Stamp Day) . .	60	20
1132	90c. Cheesemaker breaking up curds (centenary of Swiss Dairying Association)	1·00	70

1987. Bicentenary of Tourism. Multicoloured.

1133	50c. Type **275**	60	15
1134	80c. St. Charles's church, Negrentino, Prugiasco/Blenio valley	90	65
1135	90c. Witches Tower, Sion	1·00	70
1136	1f.40 Jorgenberg Castle, Waltensburg/Vuorz, Surselva	1·60	1·70
MS1137	78 × 102 mm. Nos. 1133/6	4·00	4·00

1987. Flood Victims Relief Fund. No. 1109 surch **7.9.87 +50** and clasped hands.

1138	50c.+50c. violet, grn & pur	1·60	1·00

277 Society Emblem

1988. Publicity Issue. Multicoloured.

1139	25c. Type **277** (cent of Swiss Women's Benevolent Society)	30	25
1140	35c. Brushing woman's hair (centenary of Swiss Master Hairdressers' Association)	40	40
1141	50c. St. Fridolin banner and detail of Aegidius Tschudy's manuscript (600th anniv of Battle of Naefels)	60	15
1142	80c. Map and farming country seen from Beromunster radio tower (European Campaign for Rural Areas)	95	75
1143	90c. Girl playing shawm (50th anniv of Lucerne Int Music Festival)	1·00	70

278 Junkers Ju 52/3m "Auntie Ju" flying past Matterhorn

279 Rudolf von Neuenburg

1988. 50th Anniv of Pro Aero Foundation.

1144	**278** 140c.+60c. mult	2·50	2·50

1988. Pro Patria. Minnesingers. Multicoloured.

1145	35c.+15c. Type **279**	65	70
1146	50c.+20c. Rudolf von Rotenburg	90	40
1147	80c.+40c. Johannes Hadlaub	1·40	1·40
1148	90c.+40c. Hardegger	1·50	1·50

280 Arrows on Map of Europe

281 Snap Link

1988. Europa. Transport and Communications.

1149	**280** 50c. bistre, emerald and green	55	20
1150	– 90c. lilac, green and violet	1·10	70

DESIGN: 90c. Computer circuit on map of Europe.

1988. Publicity Issue. Multicoloured.

1151	35c. Type **281** (50th anniv of Swiss Accident Prevention Office)	45	35
1152	50c. Drilling letters (cent of Swiss Metalworkers' and Watchmakers' Association)	55	20
1153	80c. Triangulation pyramid, theodolite and map (150th anniv of Swiss Federal Office of Topography) . .	95	80
1154	90c. International Red Cross Museum, Geneva (inauguration)	1·10	80

282 "Meta" (Jean Tinguely)

1988. Modern Art.

1155	**282** 90c. multicoloured . . .	2·75	2·10

283 Army Postman

1989. Publicity Issue. Multicoloured.

1156	25c. Type **283** (centenary of Swiss Army postal service)	35	30
1157	35c. Fontaine du Sauvage and Porte au Loup, Delemont (700th anniv of granting of town charter)	45	45
1158	50c. Eye and composite wheel (cent of Public Transport Association) . .	65	20
1159	80c. Class GE 4/4 electric locomotive on viaduct (centenary of Rhaetian Railway)	1·20	95
1160	90c. St. Bernard dog and hospice (2000th anniv of Great St. Bernard Pass)	1·00	70

284 King Friedrich II presenting Berne Town Charter (Bendicht Tschachtlan Chronicle)

285 Hopscotch

1989. Pro Patria. Medieval Chronicles. Mult.

1161	35c.+15c. Type **284**	65	70
1162	50c.+20c. Adrian von Bubenberg watching troops entering Murten (Diebold Schilling's Berne Chronicle)	90	35
1163	80c.+40c. Messenger presenting missive to Council of Zurich (Gerold Edlibach Chronicle) . . .	1·40	1·60
1164	90c.+40c. Schilling presenting Chronicle to Council of Lucerne (Diebold Schilling's Lucerne Chronicle) . . .	1·60	1·60

1989. Europa. Children's Games. Multicoloured.

1165	50c. Type **285**	60	25
1166	90c. Blind-man's buff . . .	1·20	90

286 Bricklayer

287 Testing Device

1989. Occupations.

1168	**286** 2f.75 purple, blk & yell	2·75	1·60
1169	– 2f.80 yellow, brn & bl	3·25	1·30
1170	– 3f. blue, dp brown & brn	3·00	1·30
1171	– 3f.60 orange, brn & pur	3·75	2·40
1173	– 3f.75 deep green, green and light green	3·75	2·75
1174	– 4f. multicoloured	4·00	1·40
1175	– 5f. ultram, stone & bl . .	6·25	1·40
1176	– 5f.50 grey, red and mauve	5·50	3·00

DESIGNS: 2f.80, Cook; 3f. Carpenter; 3f.60, Pharmacist; 3f.75, Fisherman; 4f. Vine grower; 5f. Cheesemaker; 5f.50, Dressmaker.

1989. Publicity Issue. Multicoloured.

1181	35c. Type **287** (cent of Swiss Electrotechnical Association)	45	35
1182	50c. Family on butterfly (50th anniv of Swiss Travel Fund)	55	15
1183	80c. "Wisdom" and "Science" (bronze statues) (centenary of Fribourg University)	95	70
1184	90c. Audio tape (1st anniv of National Sound Archives)	1·00	70
1185	1f.40 Bands of colour forming bridge (centenary of Inter-parliamentary Union)	1·60	1·50

288 Exercises

1989. Pro Sport.

1186	**288** 50c.+20c. mult	1·00	95

289 1882 5c. and 50c. Stamps and Emblem

290 Cats

1990. Publicity Issue. Multicoloured.

1187	25c. Type **289** (centenary of Union of Swiss Philatelic Societies)	35	20
1188	35c. Electric locomotive and electric double-deck railcar (inauguration of Zurich Rapid Transit System)	50	35
1189	50c. Mountain farmer (50th anniv of Assistance for Mountain Communities)	55	15
1190	90c. Ice hockey players (A-series World Ice Hockey Championships, Berne and Fribourg)	1·00	70

1990. Animals. Multicoloured.

1192	10c. Cow	10	10
1193	50c. Type **290**	55	10
1194	70c. Rabbit	80	25
1195	80c. Barn owls	90	25
1196	100c. Horse and foal . . .	1·10	25
1197	110c. Geese	1·20	35
1198	120c. Dog	1·30	65
1199	140c. Sheep	1·60	90
1200	150c. Goats	1·70	90
1201	160c. Turkey	1·80	1·20
1202	170c. Donkey	1·90	90
1203	200c. Chickens	1·90	85

291 Flyswats and Starch Sprinklers Seller

292 Lucerne Post Office

1990. Pro Patria. Street Criers. Engravings by David Herrliberger. Multicoloured.

1205	35c.+15c. Type **291**	65	70
1206	50c.+20c. Clock seller . . .	90	30
1207	80c.+40c. Knife grinder . .	1·40	1·50
1208	90c.+40c. Couple selling pinewood sticks	1·60	1·60

1990. Europa. Post Office Buildings. Mult.

1209	50c. Type **292**	65	20
1210	90c. Geneva Post Office . .	1·00	60

293 Conrad Ferdinand Meyer (writer)

294 Anniversary Emblem and Crosses

1990. Celebrities.

1211	**293** 35c. black and green . .	45	35
1212	– 50c. black and blue . . .	55	15
1213	– 80c. black and yellow . .	85	75
1214	– 90c. black and pink . .	1·00	65

DESIGNS: 50c. Angelika Kauffmann (painter); 80c. Blaise Cendrars (writer); 90c. Frank Buchser (painter).

1990. 700th Anniv (1991) of Swiss Confederation (1st issue).

1215	50c. Type **294**	60	20
1216	90c. Emblem and crosses (different)	1·10	85

See also Nos. 1219/22 and 1224.

295 Geneva Cantonal Post Driver's Brass Badge

1990. "Helvetia Geneve 90" National Stamp Exhibition. Sheet 102 × 78 mm containing T **295** and similar horiz designs. Multicoloured.

MS1217	50c.+25c. Type **295**; 50c.+25c. Place du Bourg-Four, Geneva; 50c.+25c. Rousseau Island, Geneva; 50c.+25c. Geneva 1843 5+5c. stamp on cover . .	4·75	5·00

296 Figures on Jigsaw Pieces

1990. Population Census.

1218	**296** 50c. multicoloured . . .	60	20

297 "700 JAHRE"

298 Alps and City Skyline

1991. 700th Anniv of Swiss Confederation (2nd issue). Multicoloured.
1219 50c. Type **297** 70 40
1220 50c. "700 ONNS" 70 40
1221 50c. "700 ANS" 70 40
1222 50c. "700 ANNI" 70 40
Nos. 1219/22 were issued together, se-tenant. forming a composite design of the Swiss cross in the centre.

1991. 800th Anniv of Berne.
1223 **298** 80c. multicoloured . . . 95 50

299 Federal Palace, Berne, and Capitol, Washington

1991. 700th Anniv of Swiss Confederation (3rd issue). Swiss Emigration to U.S.A.
1224 **299** 160c. multicoloured . . . 1·70 1·00

300 Jettison of "Ariane" Rocket Friction Protection Jacket

301 Abstract

1991. Europa. Europe in Space. Multicoloured.
1225 50c. Type **300** 60 35
1226 90c. Orbit of Halley's Comet, "Giotto" space probe and its trajectory 1·10 85

1991. Pro Patria. Modern Art. Multicoloured.
1227 50c.+20c. Type **301** 80 35
1228 70c.+30c. Artist's monogram 1·10 1·30
1229 80c.+40c. "Labyrinth" . . . 1·40 1·40
1230 90c.+40c. "Man and Beast" 1·50 1·60

302 Stone Bridge, Lavertezzo

1991. Bridges. Multicoloured.
1231 50c. Type **302** 55 15
1232 70c. Wooden Neubrugg, Bremgarten 80 70
1233 80c. Koblenz-Felsenau iron truss railway bridge over River Aar . . . . 1·00 65
1234 90c. Ganter concrete bridge, Simplon Pass . . . . . . 1·00 65

303 P.T.T. Employees

304 Lake Moesola

1991. Centenary of Swiss Postal, Telephone and Telegraph Officials' Union.
1235 **303** 80c. multicoloured . . . 90 50

1991. Mountain Lakes.
1236 **304** 50c. multicoloured . . . 50 10
1237 – 80c. brown, red & purple 85 20
DESIGN: 80c. Fishing boat moored at jetty on Melchsee.
See also No. 1257.

305 Mouth of River Rhine and Caspian Tern

306 Map of Americas and "Santa Maria"

1992. Publicity Issue. Multicoloured.
1238 50c. Type **305** (centenary of Treaty for International Regulation of the Rhine) 55 40
1239 80c. Family (50th anniv of Pro Familia) 85 35
1240 90c. Chemical formula and model of difluorobutane molecule (centenary of International Chemical Nomenclature Conference, Geneva) 90 85

1992. Europa. 500th Anniv of Discovery of America by Columbus. Multicoloured.
1241 50c. Type **306** 60 25
1242 90c. Route map of first voyage and sketch for statue of Columbus (Vincenzo Vela) . . . . . 1·20 80

307 Skier

308 1780s Earthenware Plate, Heimberg

1992. Sierre Int Comics Festival. Mult.
1243 50c. Type **307** 60 25
1244 80c. Mouse-artist drawing strip . . . . 1·00 70
1245 90c. Love-struck man holding bunch of stamp-flowers behind back . . . 1·20 90

1992. Pro Patria. Folk Art. Multicoloured.
1246 50c.+20c. Type **308** 80 40
1247 70c.+30c. Paper cut-out by Johann Jakob Hauswirth 1·20 1·30
1248 80c.+40c. Maplewood cream spoon, Gruyeres . . . . 1·40 1·30
1249 90c.+40c. Carnation from 1780 embroidered saddle cloth, Grisons . . . . . 1·50 1·50

309 Flags and Alps

310 Clowns on Trapeze

1992. Alpine Protection Convention.
1250 **309** 90c. multicoloured . . . 1·00 65

1992. The Circus. Multicoloured.
1251 50c. Type **310** 60 25
1252 70c. Sealion with Auguste the clown 95 70
1253 80c. Chalky the clown and elephant . . . . 1·00 45
1254 90c. Harlequin and horse . . 1·20 85

311 Sport Pictograms

1992. Pro Sport.
1255 **311** 50c.+20c. black & blue 1·30 85

312 Train and Map

313 "A" (first class) Mail

1992. Centenary (1993) of Central Office for International Rail Carriage.
1256 **312** 90c. multicoloured . . . 1·10 85

1993.
1257 – 60c. dp blue, yellow & bl 60 20
1258 **313** 80c. red, orange and scarlet 85 20
DESIGN: 60c. Lake Tanay.

314 Zurich and Geneva 1843 Stamps

315 Paracelsus (after Augustin Hirschvogel) (500th birth anniv)

1993. 150th Anniv of Swiss Postage Stamps. Multicoloured.
1259 60c. Type **314** 70 30
1260 80c. Postal cancellation (stamps for postage) . . . 95 65
1261 100c. Magnifying glass (stamp collecting) . . . . 1·30 80

1993. Publicity Issue.
1262 **315** 60c. brown, grey and blue 70 30
1263 – 80c. multicoloured . . . 1·00 60
1264 – 180c. multicoloured . . . 2·10 2·00
DESIGNS—VERT: 80c. Discus thrower (from Greek vase) (inauguration of Olympic Museum, Lausanne). HORIZ: 180c. Worker's head (cent of International Metalworkers' Federation).

316 "Hohentwiel" (lake steamer) and Flags

317 Interior of Media House, Villeurbanne, France

1993. Lake Constance European Region.
1265 **316** 60c. multicoloured . . . 85 45

1993. Europa. Contemporary Architecture.
1266 **317** 60c. ultramarine, blk & bl 70 25
1267 – 80c. red, black and grey 1·00 80
DESIGN: 80c. House, Breganzona, Ticino.

318 Appenzell Dairyman's Earring

1993. Pro Patria. Folk Art. Multicoloured.
1268 60c.+30c. Type **318** . . . . 1·00 75
1269 60c.+30c. Fluhli enamelled glass bottle, 1738 . . . . 1·00 75
1270 80c.+40c. Driving cows to summer pasture (detail of mural, Sylvestre Pidoux) 1·40 1·50
1271 100c.+40c. Straw hat ornaments . . . . 1·50 1·70

319 "Work No. 095" (Emma Kunz)

320 Kapell Bridge and Water Tower, Lucerne

1993. Paintings by Swiss Women Artists. Mult.
1272 60c. Type **319** 75 35
1273 80c. "Great Singer Lilas Goergens" (Aloise) (33 × 33 mm) . . . . . . 1·00 60
1274 100c. "Under the Rain Cloud" (Meret Oppenheim) (33 × 33 mm) 1·20 90
1275 120c. "Four Spaces with Horizontal Bands" (Sophi Taeuber-Arp) (33 × 33 mm) . . . . . . 1·50 1·50

1993. Kapell Bridge Restoration Fund.
1276 **320** 80c.+20c. carmine and red . . . . 1·70 1·70

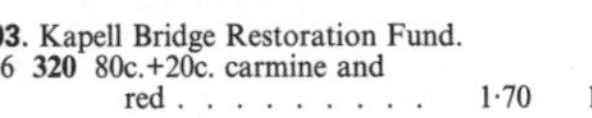

321 Hieroglyphic, Cuneiform and Roman Scripts

1994. "Books and the Press" Exhibition, Geneva. Multicoloured.
1277 60c. Type **321** 70 35
1278 80c. Gothic letterpress script 95 60
1279 100c. Modern electronic fonts . . . . 1·20 1·00

322 Athletes

1994. Publicity Issue. Multicoloured.
1280 60c. Type **322** (50th Anniv of National Sports School, Magglingen) . . . 70 45
1281 80c. Jakob Bernoulli (mathematician) (after Nicolas Bernoulli) and formula and diagram of the law of large numbers (Int Mathematicians' Congress, Zurich) 95 65
1282 100c. Heads, Unisource emblem, globe and flags (collaboration of Swiss, Dutch and Swedish telecommunications companies) . . . . 1·10 85
1283 180c. Radar image, airliner and globe (50th anniv of I.C.A.O.) . . . . 2·10 1·80

323 Footballers

324 "Trieste" (bathyscaphe)

1994. World Cup Football Championship, U.S.A., and Cent (1995) of Swiss Football Association.
1284 **323** 80c. multicoloured . . . 90 55

1994. Europa. Discoveries and Inventions. Vehicles used by Auguste Piccard in Stratospheric and Deep-sea Explorations. Multicoloured.
1285 60c. Type **324** 80 45
1286 100c. "F.N.R.S." (stratosphere balloon) . . 1·70 1·20

325 Neuchatel Weight-driven Clock (Jacques Matthey-Jonais)

326 Symbolic Condom

1994. Pro Patria. Folk Art. Multicoloured.
1287 60c.+30c. Type **325** . . . . 1·00 75
1288 60c.+30c. Embroidered pomegranate on linen . . 1·00 55
1289 80c.+40c. Mould for Krafli pastry . . . . 1·40 1·60
1290 100c.+40c. Paper-bird cradle mobile . . . . 1·60 1·80

1994. Anti-AIDS Campaign.
1291 **326** 60c. multicoloured . . . 85 30

327 Simenon and his Home, Echandens Castle, Lausanne

1994. 5th Death Anniv of Georges Simenon (novelist).
1292 **327** 100c. multicoloured . . . 1·10 75

328 "Swiss Electricity"

1995. Publicity Issue.
1293 **328** 60c. multicoloured . . . 75 30
1294 – 60c. blue and black . . . 75 30
1295 – 80c. multicoloured . . . 1·00 70
1296 – 180c. multicoloured . . . 2·20 1·60
DESIGNS—HORIZ: No. 1293, Type **328** (centenary of Swiss Association of Electricity Producers and Distributors); 1295, "(sda ats)" (centenary of Swiss News Agency); 1296, "ONU UNO" (50th anniv of U.N.O.). VERT: No. 1294, Wrestlers (centenary of Swiss Wrestling Association and National Wrestling and Alpine Herdsmen's Festival, Chur).

329 European Beaver **330** Cream Pail, 1776

1995. Endangered Animals. Multicoloured.
1297 60c. Type **329** 80 30
1298 80c. Map butterfly . . . . 1·10 60
1299 100c. Green tree frog . . . 1·40 90
1300 120c. Little owl . . . . . . 1·70 1·60

1995. Pro Patria. Folk Art. Multicoloured.
1301 60c.+30c. Type **330** . . . . 1·10 55
1302 60c.+30c. Neuchatel straw hat . . . . 1·10 75
1303 80c.+40c. Detail of chest lock, 1580 . . . . 1·40 1·60
1304 100c.+40c. Langnau ceramic sugar bowl . . . . 1·60 1·80

331 Couple and Dove **332** Basel (right-hand part)

1995. Europa. Peace and Freedom.
1305 **331** 60c. blue and cobalt . . 75 45
1306 – 100c. brown and ochre 1·20 90
DESIGN: 100c. Europa with Zeus as bull.

1995. "Basler Taube 1995" Stamp Exhibition, Basel. Sheet 100 × 131 mm. containing T **332** and similar vert designs.
MS1307 60c.+30c. black, violet and blue; 80c+30c. multicoloured; 100c.+50c. black, violet and blue; 100c+50c. black, violet and blue 6·50 6·50
DESIGNS: 80c.+30c. Basel 2½ Dove stamp (150th Anniv of issue); 60c+30c., 100c.+50c. (2) Panorama of Basel by Matthaus Meriam (composite design).

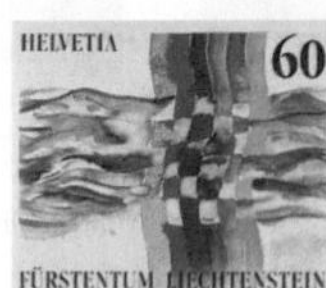

333 Coloured Ribbons woven through River

1995. Switzerland–Liechtenstein Co-operation.
1308 **333** 60c. multicoloured 70 40
No. 1308 was valid for use in both Switzerland and Liechtenstein (see No. 1106 of Liechtenstein).

334 "The Vocation of Andre Carrel" (1925)

1995. Centenary of Motion Pictures. Multicoloured.
1309 60c. Type **334** 85 35
1310 80c. "Anna Goldin – The Last Witch" 95 55
1311 150c. "Pipilotti's Mistakes – Absolution" . . . . . . 1·80 1·50

335 Ear, Eye and Mouth **336** "A" (first class) Mail

1995. "Telecom 95" International Telecommunications Exhibition, Geneva.
1312 **335** 180c. multicoloured . . . 1·90 1·10

1995.
1313 **336** 90c. blue, red and yellow 1·00 35
See also No. 1480.

337 Emblem

1996. Publicity Issue. Multicoloured.
1314 70c. Type **337** (centenary of Touring Club of Switzerland) 80 45
1315 70c. Heart (50th anniv of charity organizations) . . 95 55
1316 90c. Brass band (30th Federal Music Festival, Interlaken) . . . . 1·10 70
1317 90c. Young girls (centenary of Pro Filia (girls' aid society)) . . . . 1·00 70
1318 180c. Jean Piaget (child psychologist, birth centenary) . . . . 2·10 1·80

338 Coloured Ribbons and "Bern 96" Gymnastic Festival Emblem **339** Corinna Bille (writer)

1996. Pro Sport.
1319 **338** 70c.+30c. multicoloured 1·00 1·20

1996. Europa. Famous Women. Multicoloured.
1320 70c. Type **339** 80 45
1321 110c. Iris von Roten-Meyer (feminist writer) . . . . . 1·70 1·00

340 Magdalena Chapel, Wolfenschiessen, and Cross **341** Olympic Rings

1996. Pro Patria. Heritage. Multicoloured.
1322 70c.+35c. Type **340** . . . . 1·10 75
1323 70c.+35c. Underground sawmill and workshop, Col-des-Roches . . . . . 1·10 95
1324 90c.+40c. Baroque baths, Pfafers . . . . 1·50 1·60
1325 110c.+50c. Roman road and milestone, Great St. Bernhard . . . . . . 1·70 1·90

1996. Centenary of Modern Olympic Games.
1326 **341** 180c. multicoloured . . . 2·00 1·70

342 Representation of 1995 "A" Mail Stamp **343** Musical Movement and Mechanical Ring (Isaac-Daniel Piguet)

1996. Guinness World Record for Largest "Living" Postage Stamp represented by Human Beings (arrangement of people to represent stamp design).
1327 **342** 90c. multicoloured . . . 1·50 1·10

1996. Bicentenary of Antoine Favre-Salomon's Invention of the Metal Teeth System for Music Boxes. Multicoloured.
1328 70c. Type **343** 85 40
1329 90c. "Basso-piccolo mandolin" cylinder music box (Eduard Jaccard) . . 1·10 65
1330 110c. Station automaton (Paillard & Co) . . . . . 1·40 1·00
1331 180c. Kalliope disc music box . . . . 2·20 1·90

344 Pattern **345** "The Golden Cow" (Daniel Ammann)

1996. Greetings Stamps. Multicoloured. Self-adhesive.
1332 90c. Type **344** . . . . . . 1·30 1·20
1333 90c. Mottled pattern . . . . 1·30 1·20
1334 90c. Coil pattern . . . . . 1·30 1·20
1335 90c. Flower and leaf pattern 1·30 1·20

1996. Winning Entries in Stamp Design Competition.
1336 **345** 70c. gold and blue . . . 80 50
1337 – 90c. multicoloured . . . 1·10 70
1338 – 110c. multicoloured . . . 1·30 95
1339 – 180c. brown, black and blue . . . . 2·10 2·00
DESIGNS: 90c. "Wake with a Smile" (Max Sprick); 110c. "Leaves" (Elena Emma-Pugliese); 180c. "Dove" (Rene Conscience).

346 Globi delivering Mail **347** Venus of Octodurus

1997. Globi (cartoon character by Robert Lips).
1340 **346** 70c. multicoloured . . . 75 40

1997. Gallo-Roman Works of Art. Multicoloured.
1341 70c. Type **347** (from Forum Claudii Vallensium (now Martigny)) 80 55
1342 90c. Bust of Bacchus (from Augusta Raurica (now Augst)) . . . . 1·10 85
1343 110c. Ceramic fragment showing "Victory" (from Iulio Magus (now Schleitheim)) . . . . . . 1·20 1·10
1344 180c. Mosaic showing female theatrical mask (from Vallon) . . . . . . 2·10 2·10
Each stamp is inscribed with the name of the Foundation bearing responsibility for the preservation of the respective archaeological sites.

348 Class 460 Series 2000 Electric Locomotive

1997. 150th Anniv of Zurich–Barden Railway. Multicoloured.
1345 70c. Type **348** 80 55
1346 90c. Electric "Red Arrow" railcar set, 1935 . . . . . 1·10 90
1347 1f.40 Pullman coach, 1930s 1·60 1·70
1348 1f.70 "Limmat", 1847 (first locomotive in Switzerland) 2·20 2·20

349 Douglas DC-4 "Grand Old Lady" over Globe

1997. 50th Anniv of Swissair's North Atlantic Service.
1349 **349** 180c. multicoloured . . . 2·00 1·70

350 Farmland **351** "Devil and the Goat" (painting by Heinrich Danioth on rock face of Schollenen Gorge)

1997. Publicity Issue. Multicoloured.
1350 70c. Type **350** (centenary of Swiss Farmers' Union) . . 80 55
1351 90c. Street plan (centenary of Swiss Municipalities' Union) . . . . 1·00 85

1997. Europa. Tales and Legends. The Devil's Bridge.
1352 **351** 90c. brown and yellow 95 75

352 St. Valbert's Church, Soubey (Jura) **353** Clouds (Air)

1997. Pro Patria. Heritage and Landscapes. Mult.
1353 70c.+35c. Type **352** . . . . 1·10 90
1354 70c.+35c. Culture mill, Lutzelfluh (Berne) . . . . 1·10 90
1355 90c.+40c. Ittingen Charterhouse (Thurgau) 1·40 1·60
1356 110c.+50c. Casa Patriziale, Russo (Ticino) . . . . . 1·80 1·90

1997. Energy 2000 (energy efficiency programme). The Elements. Multicoloured.
1357 70c. Type **353** 80 55
1358 90c. Burning wood (Fire) . . 1·10 90
1359 110c. Water droplets (Water) . . . . 1·30 1·10
1360 180c. Pile of soil (Earth) . . 2·10 2·10

354 King Rama V and President Adolf Deucher

1997. Centenary of Visit of King Rama V of Siam.
1361 **354** 90c. multicoloured . . . 95 85

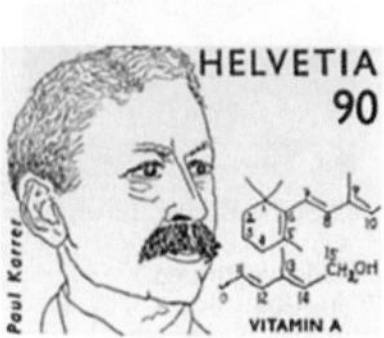

355 Paul Karrer and Molecular Structure of Vitamin A

1997. The Nobel Prize.
1362 **355** 90c. black and grey . . . 1·10 90
1363 – 110c. black and purple 1·30 1·10
DESIGNS: 90c. Type **355** (Chemistry Prize, 1937); 110c. Alfred Nobel (founder of Prize Fund).

356 Woman and Boy (German)

1997. "The Post keeps Us in Touch".
1364 **356** 70c. black, red and blue 95 70
1365 – 70c. black, yellow and blue 95 70
1366 – 70c. black, yellow and green 95 70
1367 – 70c. black, green and red 95 70
DESIGNS: No. 1365, Boy wearing baseball cap with woman (French); 1366, Young couple (Italian); 1367, Girl and man (Romansch).

357 Postal Service Emblem

1998. Separation of Swiss Post and Swisscom (telecommunications).
1368 **357** 90c. black, yellow and red 90 70
1369 – 90c. deep blue, blue and red 90 70
DESIGN: No. 1369, Swisscom emblem.

358 Arrows

1998. Bicentenary of Declaration of Helvetic Republic and 150th Anniv of Swiss Federal State. Multicoloured.
1370 90c. Type **358** 85 85
1371 90c. Face value at bottom right 85 85
1372 90c. Face value at top left 85 85
1373 90c. Face value at top right 85 85

359 Winter Olympics 2006

1998. Swiss Candidacy for Winter Olympic Games.
1374 **359** 90c. multicoloured . . . 1·00 85

360 Elderly Couple

361 "On Top of the Simplon Pass"

1998. Publicity Issues. Multicoloured.
1375 70c. Type **360** (Old Age and Survivor's Insurance) . . 80 60
1376 70c. National Museum, Prangins Castle (centenary of Swiss National Museum, Zurich, and inauguration of Prangins branch) 80 55
1377 90c. Fingerprints (centenary of St. Gallen University) 1·10 75

1998. Paintings by Jean-Frederic Schnyder. Multicoloured.
1378 10c. Type **361** 15 15
1379 20c. "Snowdrift near Neuthal" 25 20
1380 50c. "Franches Montagnes" 55 50
1381 70c. "Two Horses" 80 40
1382 90c. "En Route" 90 25
1383 110c. "Winter Morning by the Alpnachersee" . . . . 1·20 55
1385 140c. "Zug" . . . . 1·60 1·10
1386 170c. "Olive Grove" . . . . 1·70 1·20
1387 180c. "Near Reutigen" . . . 1·90 1·40

362 St. Gall, Rhine Valley

363 Lanterns

1998. Pro Patria. Heritage and Landscapes. Mult.
1390 70c.+35c. Type **362** . . . . 1·10 95
1391 70c.+35c. Round church, Saas Balen . . . . 1·10 95
1392 90c.+40c. Forest, Bodmeren 1·50 1·50
1393 90c.+40c. The old Refuge (museum), St. Gotthard 1·50 1·50
1394 110c.+50c. Smithy, Corcelles 1·80 2·00

1998. Europa. National Festivals. National Day.
1395 **363** 90c. multicoloured . . . 1·00 85

364 In-line Skating

1998. Sports. Multicoloured. Self-adhesive.
1396 70c. Type **364** 60 60
1397 70c. Snow-boarding 60 60
1398 70c. Mountain biking . . . 60 60
1399 70c. Basketball 60 60
1400 70c. Beach volleyball . . . 60 60

365 Bridge 24, Slender West Lake, Yangzhou, China

1998. Lakes. Multicoloured.
1401 20c. Type **365** 55 55
1402 70c. Chillon Castle, Lake Geneva 55 60
MS1403 96 × 70 mm. 90c. Chillion Castle and Bridge 24 (52 × 44 mm) 1·00 1·10

366 Emblem and Face

1998. 50th Anniv of Universal Declaration of Human Rights.
1404 **366** 70c. multicoloured . . . 85 80

367 Christmas Wrapping

1998. Christmas.
1405 **367** 90c. multicoloured . . . 1·00 90

368 Postman with Letter and Posthorn on Globe

1999. 150th Anniv of Swiss Postal Service.
1406 **368** 90c. multicoloured . . . 85 80

369 Little Pingu carrying Parcel

370 Vieux Bois falls in Love at First Sight

1999. Youth Stamps. Pingu (cartoon character). Multicoloured.
1407 70c. Type **369** 85 65
1408 90c. Papa Pingu driving snowmobile . . . . . . 1·10 90

1999. Birth Bicentenary of Rodolphe Topffer (cartoonist). Scenes from "The Love of Monsieur Vieux Boris". Multicoloured. Self-adhesive.
1409 90c. Type **370** 80 85
1410 90c. Vieux Bois declares his love 80 85
1411 90c. Vieux Bois jumps in air with joy, knocking over furniture 80 85
1412 90c. Vieux Bois helping his love over wall 80 85
1413 90c. Wedding of Vieux Bois 80 85

371 "Breitling Orbiter 3"

1999. 1st World Circumnavigation by Balloon, by Bertrand Piccard and Brian Jones.
1414 **371** 90c. multicoloured . . . 1·00 70

372 Envelope Flap

1999. 125th Anniv of Universal Postal Union.
1415 **372** 20c. yellow and black . . 35 35
1416 – 70c. black, red and yellow 95 95
DESIGN—55 × 29 mm: 70c. U.P.U. emblem on card in envelope.
Nos. 1415/16 were issued together, se-tenant, forming a composite design.

373 Jester and Clown

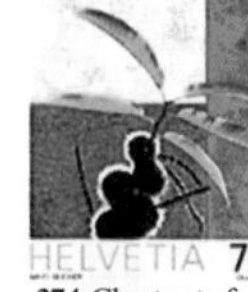
374 Chestnuts from Malcantone

1999. Publicity Issue.
1417 **373** 70c. multicoloured . . . 95 70
1418 – 90c. multicoloured . . . 1·00 90
1419 – 90c. multicoloured . . . 1·00 90
1420 – 1f.10 red and black . . . 1·20 1·10
DESIGNS: No. 1417, Type **373** (50th anniv of SOS Children's Villages); 1418, Sketch of giant puppets (Wine-growers' Festival, Vevey); 1419, Flags of member countries and emblem (50th anniv of Council of Europe); 1420, Red Cross and emblem (50th anniv of Geneva Conventions).

1999. Pro Patria. Heritage and Landscapes. Mult.
1421 70c.+35c. Type **374** . . . . 1·10 95
1422 70c.+35c. La Sarraz Castle 1·10 95
1423 90c.+40c. "Uri" (lake steamer) . . . . 1·50 1·50
1424 110c.+50c. St. Christopher carrying Baby Jesus (detail of fresco, St. Paul's Chapel, Rhazuns) . . . . 1·90 1·90

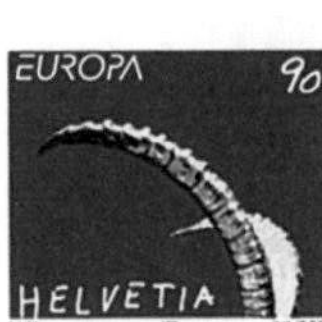
375 Ibex Horns (National Park, Engadine)

376 Roofs of Buildings

1999. Europa. Parks and Gardens.
1425 **375** 90c. black and blue . . . 1·00 80

1999. "naba 2000" National Stamp Exhibition, St. Gallen (1st issue). Sheet 66 × 85 mm containing T **376** and similar vert designs. Multicoloured.
MS1246 20c.+10c. Type **376**; 70c.+30c. Spire of St. Laurenzen's Church; 90c.+30c. Oriel window 2·50 2·50
See also No. **MS**1442.

377 Children holding Pictures

1999. Publicity Issue. Multicoloured.
1427 70c. Type **377** (Children's Rights) 75 55
1428 90c. Carl Lutz (Swiss diplomat in Budapest during Second World War) (24th death anniv) 1·00 75
1429 1f.10 Chemical model of ozone and globe (birth bicentenary of Christian Schönbein (chemist)) . . . 1·20 1·00
1430 180c. "Midday in the Alps" (death centenary of Giovanni Segantini (painter)) . . . . 2·00 1·90

378 Schollenen Gorge Monument, Suvorov and Soldiers

1999. Bicentenary of General Aleksandr Suvorov's Crossing of the Alps. Multicoloured.
1431 70c. Type **378** 70 65
1432 110c. Suvorov vanguard (after engraving by L. Hess) passing Lake Klontal . . . . 1·20 1·10

379 Christmas Bauble

1999. Christmas.
1433 **379** 90c. multicoloured . . . 1·00 80

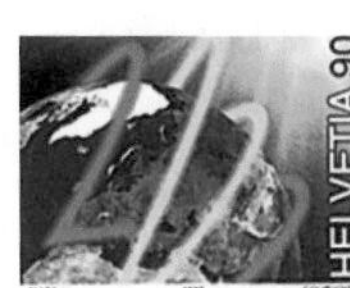
380 "2000" around Globe

1999. Year 2000.
1434 **380** 90c. multicoloured . . . 1·80 1·30

381 Cyclist

382 Alphorn Player

2000. Centenary of International Cycling Union.
1435 **381** 70c. multicoloured . . . 80 70

2000. Snow Storms. Multicoloured.
1436 10c. Type **382** 10 10
1437 20c. Fondue 25 25
1438 30c. Jugs and grapes on tray 40 40
1439 50c. Mountain goat 60 55
1440 60c. Clock 70 70
1441 70c. St. Bernards 80 80
See also No. 1479.

383 "ON I"

384 "frau" and Emblem

2000. "naba 2000" National Stamp Exhibition, St. Gallen (2nd issue). Sheet 65 × 85 mm containing T **383** and similar vert designs. Multicoloured.
MS1442 20c.+10c. Type **383** (right-hand corner; 20c.+10c. "5" (bottom left-hand corner); 70c.+35c. "RAY" (top left-hand corner), 90c.+45c. "Rp" (bottom right-hand corner. . . . . . . 3·25 3·25
The four stamps in **MS**1448 were issued together to form a composite design depicting a modern representation of a 1850 5r. Federal Administration stamp.

2000. Centenary of National Council of Women.
1443 **384** 70c. multicoloured . . . 80 50

385 "Building Europe"

386 Town Square, Nafels

2000. Europa.
1444 **385** 90c. multicoloured . . . 95 95

2000. Pro Patria. "Townscapes 2000" (rejuvenation projects). Multicoloured.
1445 70c.+35c. Type **386** . . . . 1·20 1·10

1446 70c.+35c. Main road, Tengia . . . . 1·20 1·10
1447 90c.+40c. Main road, Brugg 1·60 1·40
1448 90c.+40c. Marketplace, Carouge . . . . 1·60 1·40

387 Payerne Church and Violin

389 Emblem

388 Embroidery

2000. Tourism. Multicoloured (except 1451, blue, turquoise and red).
1449 90c. Willisan farmhouse and horse . . . . 1·10 45
1450 100c. *La Suisse* (lake steamer) and woman looking over Lake Geneva 1·20 70
1451 110c. Kleine Matterhorn glacier and skier . . . . 1·70 1·50
1452 120c. Type **387** . . . . . . 1·40 1·00
1453 130c. St. Saphorin Church and bottle of wine . . . . 1·40 15
1454 180c. National spring and bather, Vals . . . . . . 2·00 1·30
1455 200c. Landscape and walker 2·20 90
1456 220c. Bus and children . . . 2·50 1·90
1457 300c. Stone bridge and mountain bike . . . . . 3·25 65
1459 400c. Airplane fin and man with suitcase . . . . . . 4·50 3·25

2000. St. Gallen Embroidery. Self-adhesive. Imperf.
1460 **388** 5f. cobalt and blue . . . 8·75 8·75
MS1461 158 × 132 mm. No. 1460 × 4 . . . . £110 £110

2000. Population Census.
1462 **389** 70c. multicoloured . . . 80 65

390 "Alien from Outer Space" (Yannick Kehrli)

2000. "Stampin' the Future". Winning Entries in Children's International Painting Competition. Multicoloured. Self-adhesive.
1463 70c. Type **390** 50 65
1464 70c. "Looks below the Sun" (Charlotte Battig) 50 65
1465 70c. "The Perfect World" (Sandra Dobler) 50 65
1466 70c. "My Town" (Stephanie Aerschmann) 50 65

391 Swimming

2000. Olympic Games, Sydney. Multicoloured. Self-adhesive.
1467 90c. Type **391** 95 95
1468 90c. Cycling 95 95
1469 90c. Running 95 95

392 Cathedral and Horsemen

393 Dresden-style Tree Decoration

2000. Stamp Day.
1470 **392** 70c. multicoloured . . . 80 65

2000. Christmas.
1471 **393** 90c. multicoloured . . . 1·20 80

394 Alice Rivaz

2001. Anniversaries.
1472 **394** 70c. multicoloured . . . 80 60
1473 – 90c. multicoloured . . . 1·00 80
1474 – 110c. red, grey and black 1·20 1·30
1475 – 130c. multicoloured . . . 1·40 1·50
DESIGNS—As Type **394**:70c. Type **394** (writer, birth centenary); 110c. "CARITAS" and jigsaw pieces (centenary of Caritas (Christian charity organization)); 130c. Refugees (50th Anniv of United Nations High Commissioner for Refugees). Size 39 × 30 mm: 90c. Airplane (centenary of Aero-Club of Switzerland).

395 Flowers and Envelope

2001. Greetings Stamp.
1476 **395** 90c. multicoloured . . . 95 50

396 Woman's Head

2001. Anniversary and Event. Multicoloured.
1477 70c. Type **396** (re-opening of Vela Museum, Ligornetto) 80 80
1478 90c. Chocolate segment (centenary of Chocosuisse) 1·00 1·00
No. 1478 is impregnated with the scent of chocolate.

2001. Self-adhesive Stamps.
1479 – 70c. mult (as No. 1441) 80 80
1480 **336** 90c. blue, orge & lemon 95 1·00

397 Italian Theatre, La Chaux-de-Fonds

2001. Pro Patria. Cultural Heritage.
1481 70c.+35c. black, orange and red . . . . 1·20 1·20
1482 70c.+35c. black, brown and green . . . . 1·20 1·20
1483 90c.+40c. black, brown and lemon . . . . 1·60 1·60
1484 90c.+40c. multicoloured . . 1·60 1·60
DESIGNS: No. 1482, Hauterive Monastery; 1483, Leuk Castle; 1484, Rorschach Granary.

398 Water

2001. Europa. Water Resources.
1485 **398** 90c. multicoloured . . . 95 95

399 Blue Rainbow Fish

2001. Illustrations from *Rainbow Fish* (book by Martin Pfister). Multicoloured.
1486 70c. Type **399** 65 25
1487 90c. Purple rainbow fish . . 80 50

400 Straits Rhododendron (*Melastoma malabathricum*)

401 "The Birth of Venus"

2001. Switzerland–Singapore Joint Issue. Flowers. Sheet 98 × 68 mm, containing T **400** and similar horiz designs. Multicoloured.
MS1488 70c. Type **400**; 90c. *Saraca cauliflora*; 110c. Edelweiss (*Leontopodium alpinum*); 130c. Gentian (*Gentiana clusii*) . . . 3·75 3·75

2001. Death Centenary of Arnold Bocklin (artist).
1489 **401** 180c. multicoloured . . . 1·70 1·50

402 Buildings (Beat Kehrli)

403 Gablonz-style Christmas Tree Ornament

2001. Stamp Day. Winning entry in stamp design competition.
1490 **402** 70c. multicoloured . . . 65 25

2001. Christmas.
1491 **403** 90c. multicoloured . . . 80 50

404 Ladder, Wall and Stars

2002. Escalade (festival) (celebrating 400th anniv of defeat of Savoyard attack on the city), Geneva.
1492 **404** 70c. multicoloured . . . 65 25

405 "E" and Towers, Biel

2002. "Expo '02" National Exhibition, Biel, Murten, Neuchatel and Yverdon-les-Bains (1st issue). Each featuring "Arteplage" (exhibition platform) of each host town. Multicoloured.
1493 70c. Type **405** 65 25
1494 70c. Reversed "P" and Monolith, Murten 65 25
1495 70c. "O", pebble-shaped construction over water, Neuchatel 65 25
1496 70c. "2" and artificial cloud, Yverdon-les-Bains 65 25
See also No. **MS**1509.

406 RABDe 500 InterCity Tilting Train (ICN)

2002. Centenary of Swiss Federal Railways (SBB) (national railway operator). Multicoloured.
1497 70c. Type **406** 65 25
1498 90c. InterCity 2000 double-deck train 80 50
1499 120c. Railcar, Lucerne–Lenzburg Seetal line . . . 1·10 1·00
1500 130c. 119 Re 460 locomotive 1·20 1·10

407 Facade

2002. Centenary of Federal Parliament Building.
1501 **407** 90c. multicoloured . . . 80 50

408 Augusta A-109-K2 Helicopter and Hawker 800B Air Ambulance

2002. 50th Anniv of Swiss Air Rescue (Rega).
1502 **408** 180c. multicoloured . . . 1·70 1·50

409 Clown

2002. Europa. Circus. Multicoloured.
1503 70c. Type **409** 65 25
1504 90c. Clown (different) . . . 80 50

410 Bruzella, Ticino Canton

2002. Pro Patria. Water Mills Preservation. Water mills. Multicoloured.
1505 70c.+35c. Type **410** 95 50
1506 70c.+35c. Oberdorf, Basel Canton 95 50
1507 90c.+40c. Lussery-Villars, de Vaud Canton . . . . . . 1·20 1·20
1508 90c.+40c. Buren a. d. Aare, Berne Canton . . . . . 1·20 1·20

411 "X"

2002. "Expo '02", 6th National Exhibition, Biel, Murten, Neuchatel and Yverdon-les-Bains (2nd issue). Sheet 95 × 70 mm.
MS1509 **411** 90c. multicoloured 85 85

412 Two Teddies (Switzerland, c. 1950)

413 Emblem

2002. Centenary of the Teddy Bear. Multicoloured. Self-adhesive.
1510 90c. White teddy with pink bow (France, 1925) (26 × 26 mm, round) . . . 80 50
1511 90c. Type **412** 80 50
1512 90c. Teddy with grey-brown bow (Germany, 1904) (22 × 32 mm, oval) . . . 80 50
1513 90c. "Philibert", Swiss Post Teddy (Switzerland, 2002) (26 × 22 mm, rectangle) 80 50
1514 90c. Teddy with grey paws (England, c. 1920) (26 × 26 mm, round) . . . 80 50

2002. Switzerland's Acccesssion to the United Nations.
1515 **413** 90c. multicoloured . . . 80 50

414 Emperor Dragonfly (*Anax imperator*)

2002. Insects. Multicoloured.
1516 10c. Type **414** 10 10
1517 20c. Dark green fritillary (*Mesoacidalia aglaja*) . . 20 10
1518 50c. Alpine longhorn beetle (*Rosalia alpina*) 45 20
1519 100c. Striped bug (*Graphosoma lineatum*) . . 90 50

415 Printing Press (copper engraving, Abraham Bosse)

2002. Swiss Post Stamp Printers, Berne Commemoration.
1520 **415** 70c. multicoloured . . . 65 25

416 Ladybird on Leaf (½-size illustration)

2002. Greeting Stamp. Self-adhesive.
1521 **416** 90c. multicoloured . . . 80 50

417 Quartz

2002. Minerals. Multicoloured.
1522 200c. Type **417** . . . . . . 1·90 1·60
1523 300c. Rutilated quartz . . . 3·00 2·75
1524 400c. Fluorite . . . . 3·75 3·50
1525 500c. Titanite . . . . 4·50 4·25

418 Kingfisher and Jura Water Engineering System (Michele Berri)

419 Bohemian Cardboard Tree Decoration, c. 1900

2002. Stamp Day. Winning Entry in Stamp Design Competition.
1535 **418** 70c. multicoloured . . . 65 25

2002. Christmas.
1536 **419** 90c. multicoloured . . . 80 50

420 Skier

421 "70"

2002. World Alpine Skiing Championship, St. Moritz.
1537 **420** 90c. multicoloured . . . 80 50

2003. Centenary of Swiss National Association of the Blind and Library for the Blind and Visually Impaired.
1538 **421** 70c. orange 65 25
No. 1538 was embossed with 70 in Braille.

422 Hypericum (*Hypericum perforatum*)

424 Contour Lines, Compass and Runner

423 Waterfall

2003. Medicinal Plants. Multicoloured.
1539 70c. Type **422** 65 25
1540 90c. Periwinkle (*Vinca minor*) 80 50
1541 110c. Valerian (*Valeriana officinalis*) . . . . 1·00 60
1542 120c. *Arnica Montana* . . . 1·10 65
1543 130c. Centaury (*Centaurium minus*) . . . . 1·20 70
1544 180c. Mallow (*Malva sylvestris*) . . . . 1·60 1·00
1545 220c. Chamomile (*Matricaria chamomilla*) 2·00 1·80

2003. International Year of Water.
1546 **423** 90c. multicoloured . . . 80 50

2003. World Orienteering Championships, Rapperswil-Jona.
1547 **424** 90c. multicoloured . . . 80 50

425 Horse's Head

2003. Centenary of Marche-Concours (horse show and market), Saignelegier.
1548 **425** 90c. multicoloured . . . 80 50

426 *Alinghi* (yacht)

2003. Switzerland, America's Cup Winners, 2003.
1549 **426** 90c. multicoloured . . . 80 50

427 Eagle

428 Laura

2003. Ticino 2003 International Stamp Exhibition, Locarno. Sheet 96 × 70 mm containing T **427** and similar vert design. Multicoloured.
MS1550 20c. Type **427**; 70c. Gentians 80 80

2003. 20th International Comics Festival, Sierre. Characters created by Tom Tirabosco. Multicoloured.
1551 70c. Type **428** 65 25
1552 70c. Marco 65 25
1553 70c. Louis 65 25
1554 70c. Djema 65 25
MS1555 96 × 70 mm. 90c. Heidi 80 80

429 Innere Wynigen Bridge, Burgdorf, Berne Canton

430 "Don't Forget the Discount Stamp" (Donald Brun)

2003. Historic Bridges and Footbridges. Multicoloured.
1556 70c.+35c. Type **429** . . . . 1·00 1·00
1557 70c.+35c. Salginatobel, Schiers, Grisons . . . . . 1·00 1·00
1558 90c.+40c. Pont St-Jean, Saint Ursanne, Jura Canton . . . . 1·20 1·20
1559 90c.+40c. Reuss, Rottenschwil, Aargau Canton . . . . 1·20 1·20

2003. Europa. Poster Art.
1560 **430** 90c. multicoloured . . . 80 50

431 Diddl and Diddlina

2003. Diddl (cartoon character created by Thomas Goletz). Multicoloured.
1561 70c. Type **431** 65 25
1562 90c. Diddl chasing winged envelopes 80 50

432 Jungfrau-Aletsch-Bietschhorn Region

2003. UNESCO World Heritage Sites. Multicoloured.
1563 90c. Type **432** 80 50
1564 90c. Three Castles, Bellinzona 80 50
1565 90c. Berne Old City 80 50
1566 90c. St. Gall Abbey Precinct 80 50
1567 90c. Mustair Convent . . . 80 50

433 Onion market, Berne

434 Wooden Horseman (Erzgebirge)

2003. Stamp Day. Winning Entry in Stamp Design Competition.
1568 **433** 70c. multicoloured . . . 65 25

2003. Christmas. Regional Tree Decorations. Multicoloured.
1569 70c. Type **434** 65 25
1570 90c. Glass Father Christmas (Thuringa) 80 50

435 Four-leafed Clover

2003. Greetings Stamp.
1571 **435** 90c. multicoloured . . . 80 50

436 Rex Potato Peeler (Alfred Neweczeral, 1947)

2003. Swiss Design Classics. Multicoloured. Self-adhesive gum.
1572 15c. Type **436** 15 10
1587 50c. "Riri" (zip fastener) . . 45 20
1573 85c. Station clock (Hans Hilfiker, 1944) 80 50
1574 100c. Armchair (Heidi Weber (1959) after Le Corbusier (1928) 95 85
1585 100c. "Landi" (chair) (Hans Coray, 1939) 85 75

437 Titeuf and Nadia

438 Centenary Emblem

2004. Titeuf (cartoon created by Philippe Chappuis (Zep)). Multicoloured.
1595 85c. Type **437** (Spring) . . . 75 30
1596 85c. Sitting in refrigerator (Summer) 75 30
1597 85c. Kicking leaves (Autumn) 75 30
1598 85c. With snowman (Winter) 75 30

2004. Centenary of FIFA (Federation Internationale de Football Association).
1599 **438** 1f. multicoloured 85 50

439 Family

2004. Cycling. Sheet 96 × 70 mm containing T **439** and similar horiz design. Multicoloured.
MS1600 1f. × 2, Type **439**; Two cyclists reading map . . . . . 1·70 1·50

440 Past and Present Players

441 Rays

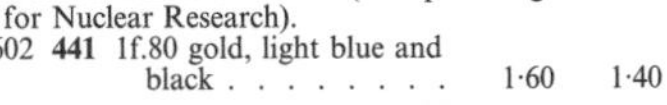

2004. 50th Anniv of UEFA (Union of European Football Associations).
1601 **440** 1f.30 multicoloured . . . 1·10 1·00

2004. 50th Anniv of CERN (European Organization for Nuclear Research).
1602 **441** 1f.80 gold, light blue and black . . . . 1·60 1·40

442 Doorbell and "Helvetia" (Emil Steinberger)

443 Bathing Pavilion, Gorgier

2004. Humour.
1603 **442** 85c. multicoloured . . . 75 30

2004. Pro Patria. Small Buildings Preservation. Multicoloured.
1604 85c.+ 40c. Type **443** . . . . 1·10 55
1605 85c.+ 40c. Granary, Oberramsern . . . . . . 1·10 55
1606 1f.+50c. Seeburg landing stage, Lucerne . . . . . 1·30 1·30
1607 1f.+50c. Ossuary, Gentilino 1·30 1·30

444 Diddl holding Pimboli

2004. Diddl (cartoon character created by Thomas Goletz) (2nd series). Multicoloured.
1608 85c. Type **444** 75 30
1609 1f. Diddl holding flower . . 85 50

445 Olympic Rings, Stadium and Runner

2004. Olympic Games, Athens.
1610 **445** 1f. multicoloured 85 50

446 Sun Lounger and Parasol

2004. Europa. Holidays.
1611 **446** 1f. multicoloured 85 50

447 Zeppelin NT Type Z NO7

2004.
1612 **447** 1f.80 multicoloured . . . 1·60 1·40

448 Boy leapfrogging Pumpkin **449** 1854 10r. Stamp

2004. Suisse Balance (healthy eating campaign).
1613 **448** 85c. multicoloured . . . 75 30

2004. 150th Anniv of Strubeli (dishevelled) Stamps (first stamps showing seated Helvetia ("Mother of the Nation")). Sheet 96 × 70 mm containing T **449** and similar vert design. Multicoloured.
MS1614 85c. × 2, Type **449**; Coin showing Helvetia . . . . . . 1·50 1·30

450 Cat

2004. Swiss Animal Protection (SAP). Multicoloured.
1615 85c. Type **450** 75 30
1616 1f. Hedgehog 85 50
1617 1f.30 Pig . . . . 1·10 1·00

451 Fossil and Mountains

2004. UNESCO World Heritage Site. Mount San Giorgio.
1618 **451** 1f. mauve and black . . 85 50

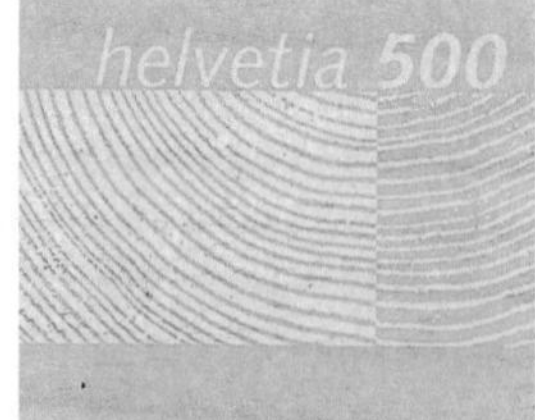

452 Making Cheese

2004. Traditional Food. Cheese. Multicoloured.
1619 1f. Type **452** 85 50
1620 1f. Cheeses and grapes . . . 85 50

453 Wood Grain

2004. Sustainable Wood Production. Self-adhesive.
1621 **453** 5f. ochre . . . . 4·25 3·75
No. 1621 was made from wood veneer which has to be peeled from the backing paper.

454 Hydro Electric Power **455** Star

2004. Stamp Day. Winning Entry in Stamp Design Competition.
1622 **454** 85c. multicoloured . . . 75 30

2004. Christmas. Tree Decorations. Sheet 160 × 56 mm containing T **455** and similar vert designs. Multicoloured.
MS1623 85c. Type **455**; 85c. Church; 1f. Angel; 1f. Horse and rider; 1f. Father Christmas . . . . . . 4·00 3·50

456 Sport

2004. International Year of Sport and Physical Education—2005.
1624 **456** 180c. multicoloured . . . 1·60 1·40

FRANK STAMPS

Issued to charity hospitals for free transmission of their mails.

F 21 **F 49** Deaconess

1911. With control figures at top.
F268 **F 21** 2c. red and green . . . 10 10
F269 3c. red and green . . . 2·40 25
F270 5c. red and green . . . 85 10
F271 10c. red and green . . 1·00 10
F272 15c. red and green . . 20·00 2·75
F273 20c. red and green . . 2·50 40

1935. With or without control figures.
F358A **F 49** 5c. green . . . . . . 4·00 20
F359A – 10c. violet . . . . . 4·00 15
F360A – 20c. red . . . . . . 4·50 25
DESIGNS: 10c. Sister of the Ingenbohl Order; 20c. Henri Dunant (founder of Red Cross).

OFFICIAL STAMPS

1918. Optd **Industrielle Kriegs-wirtschaft**.
O308 **20a** 3c. brown . . . . . . 4·00 24·00
O300 5c. green . . . . 7·75 30·00
O310 7½c. grey . . . . 4·00 18·00
O303 **21** 10c. red on buff . . . . 10·50 37·00
O304 15c. purple on buff . . 10·50 43·00
O313 **17** 20c. yellow and red . . 8·00 42·00
O314 25c. blue and deep blue 8·00 42·00
O315 30c. green and brown 13·50 70·00

1938. Optd with Geneva Cross.
O381A **52** 3c. green 10 25
O382A – 5c. green (No. 369) . . 10 20
O383A – 10c. purple (No. 370) 95 35
O384A – 15c. orange (No. 373) 40 1·20
O385A – 20c. red (No. 375) . . . 45 20
O386A – 25c. brown (No. 376) 45 1·10
O387A – 30c. blue (No. 377) . . 55 55
O388A – 35c. green (No. 378) . . 55 1·20
O389A – 40c. grey (No. 379) . . 55 35
O390 **17** 50c. green and deep green . . . . 95 1·10
O391 60c. brown . . . . . . 1·30 1·80
O392 70c. buff and violet . . 1·30 3·25
O393 80c. buff and grey . . . 1·40 2·30
O395 **41** 90c. red, dp green & green . . . . 1·50 2·75
O394 **17** 1f. green and purple . . 1·50 2·30
O396 **41** 1f.20 red, lake and pink 1·50 3·25
O397 1f.50 red, blue & turquoise . . . . . . 2·50 4·75
O398 – 2f. red, black and grey 3·00 5·25

1942. Optd **Officiel**. (a) Landscape designs of 1936.
O427 **52** 3c. green . . . . 30 1·20
O428 – 5c. green 30 15
O430 – 10c. brown 25 30
O431 – 15c. orange . . . . . . 60 1·20
O432 – 20c. red (Lake) 60 20
O433 – 25c. brown . . . . . . 60 1·75
O434 – 30c. blue . . . . 1·75 60
O435 – 35c. green . . . . . . 1·75 2·00
O436 – 40c. grey . . . . 1·10 45

(b) Historical designs of 1941.
O437 – 50c. blue on green . . . 4·50 3·25
O438 **68** 60c. brown on brown . . 4·75 2·20
O439 – 70c. purple on mauve . . 5·00 6·00
O440 – 80c. black on grey . . . 1·25 1·10
O441 – 90c. red on pink . . . . 1·50 1·00
O442 – 1f. green on green . . . 1·70 1·50
O443 – 1f.20 purple on grey . . 1·90 1·75
O444 – 1f.50 blue on buff . . . 3·25 2·75
O445 – 2f. red on pink . . . . 3·00 3·00

1950. Landscape designs of 1949 optd **Officiel**.
O522 **107** 5c. orange 50 40
O523 – 10c. green 90 40
O524 – 15c. turquoise . . . . . 9·25 11·00
O525 – 20c. purple . . . . . . 2·75 25
O526 – 25c. red . . . . 4·50 6·00
O527 – 30c. green . . . . . . 3·50 1·90
O528 – 35c. brown . . . . . . 4·75 8·25
O529 – 40c. blue . . . . 3·50 1·00
O530 – 50c. grey . . . . 5·75 4·50
O531 – 60c. green . . . . . . 7·50 4·75
O532 – 70c. violet . . . . . . 19·00 16·00

For Swiss stamps overprinted for the use of officials of the League of Nations, International Labour Office and other special U.N. Agencies having their headquarters at Geneva, see sub- section INTERNATIONAL ORGANIZATIONS SITUATED IN SWITZERLAND.

POSTAGE DUE STAMPS

D 10 **D 21** **D 41**

1878.
D 89 **D 10** 1c. blue . . . . . . 2·00 75
D 90 2c. blue . . . . . . 1·40 65
D 98B 3c. blue . . . . . . 8·00 4·50
D 92a 5c. blue . . . . . . † –
D 99B 5c. blue . . . . . . 12·00 4·75
D100B 10c. blue . . . . . £150 2·50
D101A 20c. blue . . . . . £180 1·70
D102A 50c. blue . . . . . £350 7·25
D 96 100c. blue . . . . . £450 5·00
D 97 500c. blue . . . . . £400 8·50
Nos. D89 and D92a have raised backgrounds behind the figure of value.

1883. Numerals in red.
D268 **D 10** 1c. green 15 60
D181C 3c. green . . . . . 7·25 4·75
D269B 5c. green 80 85
D270A 10c. green . . . . . 2·50 1·60
D271B 20c. green . . . . . 2·50 3·00
D204B 50c. green . . . . . 11·00 1·90
D205B 100c. green . . . . 12·00 1·70
D187B 500c. green . . . . £120 12·00
The above were issued in a wide range of shades from pale turquoise to olive between 1883 and 1910. A detailed list of these appears in the Stanley Gibbons Part 8 (Italy and Switzerland) Catalogue.

1910.
D274 **D 21** 1c. green and red . . . 10 15
D275 3c. green and red . . . 10 15
D276 5c. green and red . . . 10 10
D277 10c. green and red . . 10·00 10
D278 15c. green and red . . 50 70
D279 20c. green and red . . 12·00 10
D280 25c. green and red . . 95 40
D281 30c. green and red . . 85 25
D282 50c. green and red . . 1·20 45

1916. Surch.
D299 **D 21** 5 on 3c. red and green 10 20
D300 10 on 1c. red and green . . . . . . 25 5·00
D301 10 on 3c. red and green 25 90
D302 20 on 50c. red & green 70 90

1924.
D329 **D 41** 5c. red and green . . 50 10
D330 10c. red and green . . 2·10 10
D331 15c. red and green . . 1·60 35
D332a 20c. red and green . . 4·25 80
D333 25c. red and green . . 2·10 25
D334 30c. red and green . . 2·10 40
D335 40c. red and green . . 2·75 35
D336 50c. red and green . . 3·25 40

1937. Surch.
D380 **D 41** 5 on 15c. red and green . . . . . . 65 2·75
D381 10 on 30c. red & green 65 95
D382 20 on 50c. red & green 1·20 3·00
D383 40 on 50c. red & green 1·90 7·50

D 54

1938.
D384A **D 54** 5c. red 30 10
D385A 10c. red 45 10
D386A 15c. red . . . . . . 95 2·00
D387A 20c. red 90 10
D388A 25c. red . . . . . . 1·10 1·80
D389A 30c. red . . . . . . 1·20 80
D390A 40c. red . . . . . . 1·20 25
D391A 50c. red . . . . . . 1·60 1·60

POSTCARD STAMPS

P 1 Tourism Emblem

2002. Self-adhesive gum. No value expressed.
P1 **P 1** (1f.30) multicoloured . . . 1·20 50
P2 (1f.80) multicoloured . . . 1·70 85

No. P1 was for use only on postcards sent to countries within Europe and No. P2 to overseas countries. They were not valid for use on other mail or in combination with other stamps.

"PRO JUVENTUTE" CHARITY STAMPS

PREMIUMS. All "Pro Juventute" stamps are sold at an additional premium which goes to Benevolent Societies. Until 1937 these premiums were not shown on the stamps, but were as follows:
2c. for all 3c. franking values; 5c. for all 5, 7½, 10, 15 and 20c. values and 10c. for all 30 and 40c. values.
From 1937, when the premium first appeared on the designs, we show it in the catalogue listing.

C 1 Helvetia and Matterhorn **C 2** Appenzell

1913. Children's Fund.
J1 **C 1** 5c. green . . . . 2·50 4·25

1915. Children's Fund.
J1a **C 2** 5c. green on buff . . . . 2·75 5·50
J2 – 10c. red on buff . . . . . 80·00 55·00
DESIGN: 10c. Girl from Lucerne.

C 4 Berne **C 6** Valais **C 9** Uri

1916. Children's Fund.
J3 – 3c. violet on buff . . . . . 5·75 23·00
J4 **C 4** 5c. green on buff . . . . . 9·25 6·25
J5 – 10c. red on buff . . . . . 39·00 42·00
DESIGNS: 3, 10c. Girls of Freiburg and Vaud.

1917. Children's Fund.
J6 **C 6** 3c. violet on buff . . . . . 4·25 33·00
J7 – 5c. green on buff . . . . . 7·25 4·00
J8 – 10c. red on buff . . . . . 18·00 17·00
DESIGNS: 5c. Man of Unterwalden; 10c. Girl of Ticino.

1918. Children's Fund. Dated "1918".
J9 **C 9** 10c. red, yellow and black on buff . . . . 6·75 11·00
J10 – 15c. multicoloured on buff 9·00 6·50
ARMS: 15c. Geneva.

1919. Children's Fund. As Type **C 9** but dated "1919". Cream paper.
J11 7½c. red, grey and black . . . 2·75 7·75
J12 10c. green, red and black . . 2·75 7·50
J13 15c. red, violet and black . . 3·75 3·75
ARMS: 7½c. Nidwalden; 10c. Vaud; 15c. Obwalden.

1920. Children's Fund. As Type **C 9** but dated "1920". Cream paper.
J14 7½c. red, grey and black . . . 2·75 7·75
J15 10c. blue, red and black . . . 4·50 7·75
J16 15c. red, blue, violet and black . . . . 2·30 3·25
ARMS: 7½c. Schwyz; 10c. Zurich; 15c. Ticino.

1921. Children's Fund. As Type **C 9** but dated "1921". Cream paper.
J17 10c. red, black and green . . 60 1·60
J18 20c. multicoloured . . . . . 2·00 2·00
J19 40c. red and blue . . . . . . 6·75 26·00
ARMS: 10c. Valais; 20c. Berne; 40c. Switzerland.

1922. Children's Fund. As Type **C 9** but dated "1922". Cream paper.
J20 5c. orange, blue and black . . 70 3·75
J21 10c. green and black . . . . 75 1·30
J22 20c. violet, blue and black . . 80 1·30
J23 40c. blue, red and black . . . 8·25 31·00
ARMS: 5c. Zug; 10c. Freiburg; 20c. Lucerne; 40c. Switzerland.

1923. Children's Fund. As Type **C 9** but dated "1923". Cream paper.
J24 5c. orange and black . . . . 40 2·50
J25 10c. multicoloured . . . . . 40 1·10
J26 20c. multicoloured . . . . . 40 1·10
J27 40c. blue, red and black . . . 7·25 24·00
ARMS: 5c. Basel; 10c. Glarus; 20c. Neuchatel; 40c. Switzerland.

1924. Children's Fund. As Type **C 9** but dated "1924". Cream paper.
J28 5c. black and lilac 25 90
J29 10c. red, green and black . . 35 60
J30 20c. black, yellow and red . . 35 55
J31 30c. red, blue and black . . . 1·30 6·25
ARMS: 5c. Appenzell; 10c. Solothurn; 20c. Schaffhausen; 30c. Switzerland.

1925. Children's Fund. As Type **C 9** but dated "1925". Cream paper.
J32 5c. green, black and violet . . 20 75
J33 10c. black and green 25 60
J34 20c. multicoloured 35 60
J35 30c. red, blue and black . . . 1·20 5·25
ARMS: 5c. St. Gall; 10c. Appenzell-Ausser-Rhoden; 20c. Graubunden; 30c. Switzerland.

1926. Children's Fund. As Type C **9** but dated "1926". Cream paper.
J36 5c. multicoloured 20 65
J37 10c. green, black and red . . 20 55
J38 20c. red, black and blue . . . 25 55
J39 30c. blue, red and black . . . 1·10 5·75
ARMS: 5c. Thurgau; 10c. Basel; 20c. Aargau; 30c. Switzerland and Lion of Lucerne.

C **40** Forsaken Orphan

C **42** J. H. Pestalozzi

C **43** J. H. Pestalozzi

1927. Children's Fund. Dated "1927".
J40 C **40** 5c. purple & yell on grey 15 85
J41 – 10c. green & pink on green 15 40
J42 C **42** 20c. red 15 40
J43 C **43** 30c. blue and black . . . 1·00 3·25
DESIGN—As Type C **40**: 40c. Orphan at Pestalozzi School.

C **44** Lausanne

C **47** J. H. Dunant

1928. Children's Fund. Dated "1928".
J44 C **44** 5c. red, purple and black on buff 20 95
J45 – 10c. red, green and black on buff 20 50
J46 – 20c. black, yellow and red on buff 20 50
J47 C **47** 30c. blue and red . . . . 1·10 3·25
DESIGNS—As Type C **44**: 10c. Arms of Winterthur; 20c. Arms of St. Gall.

C **48** Mt. San Salvatore, Lake Lugano

1929. Children's Fund. Dated "1929".
J48 C **48** 5c. red and violet . . . 10 60
J49 – 10c. blue and brown . . 15 35
J50 – 20c. blue and red 20 35
J51 – 30c. blue . . . . 1·00 5·75
DESIGNS: 10c. Mt. Titlis, Lake Engstlen; 20c. Mt. Lyskamm from Riffelberg; 30c. Nicholas de Flue.

C **50** Freiburg

C **51** A. Bitzius—"Jeremias Gotthelf"

1930. Children's Fund. Dated "1930".
J52 C **50** 5c. blue, black and green on buff 15 65
J53 – 10c. multicoloured on buff 15 35
J54 – 20c. multicoloured on buff 20 40
J55 C **51** 30c. blue . . . . 1·10 3·25
ARMS—As Type C **51**: 10c. Altdorf; 20c. Schaffhausen.

C **52** St. Moritz and Silvaplana Lakes

1931. Children's Fund. Dated "1931".
J56 C **52** 5c. green 30 70
J57 – 10c. violet 25 40
J58 – 20c. red 40 40
J59 – 30c. blue . . . . 4·00 8·75
DESIGNS: 10c. The Wetterhorn; 20c. Lac Leman; 30c. Alexandre Vinet.

C **54** Flag swinging

C **56** Vaud

C **59** A. von Haller

1932. Children's Fund. Dated "1932".
J60 C **54** 5c. red and green 50 90
J61 – 10c. orange 60 90
J62 – 20c. red 65 85
J63 – 30c. blue . . . . 1·90 3·75
DESIGNS: 10c. Putting the weight; 20c. Wrestlers; 30c. Eugen Huber.

1933. Children's Fund. Dated "1933".
J64 C **56** 5c. green and buff . . . 30 80
J65 – 10c. violet and buff . . . 30 40
J66 – 20c. scarlet and buff . . 45 50
J67 – 30c. blue . . . . 1·80 4·00
DESIGNS: 10c. Swiss girl from Berne; 20c. Swiss girl from Ticino; 30c. Father Gregoire Girard.

1934. Children's Fund. Dated "1934".
J68 – 5c. green and buff . . . 30 95
J69 – 10c. violet and buff . . . 35 40
J70 – 20c. red and buff 40 45
J71 C **59** 30c. blue . . . . 1·70 4·00
SWISS GIRL DESIGNS—As Type C **56**: 5c. Appenzell; 10c. Valais; 20c. Graubunden.

C **61** Stefano Franscini

C **62** H. G. Nageli

1935. Children's Fund. Dated "1935".
J72 – 5c. green and buff . . . 25 95
J73 – 10c. violet and buff . . . 30 40
J74 – 20c. red and buff 35 65
J75 C **61** 30c. blue . . . . . . 2·00 4·25
SWISS GIRL DESIGNS—As Type C **56**: 5c. Basel; 10c. Lucerne; 20c. Geneva.

1936. Children's Fund.
J76 C **62** 5c. green 30 35
J77 – 10c. purple and buff . . 35 35
J78 – 20c. red and buff 35 70
J79 – 30c. blue and buff . . . 2·75 13·00
SWISS GIRL DESIGNS—As Type C **56**: 10c. Neuchatel; 20c. Schwyz; 30c. Zurich.

C **64** Gen. Henri Dufour

C **66** "Youth"

1937. Children's Fund.
J80 C **64** 5c.+5c. green 10 15
J81 – 10c.+5c. purple 10 15
J82 C **66** 20c.+5c. red, buff and silver 60 30
J83 – 30c.+10c. blue, buff and silver . . . . 95 3·25
DESIGNS: 10c. Nicholas de Flue; 30c. as Type C **66**, but girl's head facing other way.

C **67** Salomon Gessner

C **69** Gen. Herzog

1938. Children's Fund. Dated "1938".
J84 C **67** 5c.+5c. green 20 20
J85 – 10c.+5c. violet & buff . . 20 20
J86 – 20c.+5c. red and buff . . 20 20
J87 – 30c.+10c. blue & buff . . 1·00 2·50
SWISS GIRL DESIGNS—As Type C **56**: 10c. St. Gall; 20c. Uri; 30c. Aargau.

1939. Children's Fund.
J88 C **69** 5c.+5c. green 15 20
J89 – 10c.+5c. violet & buff . . 25 20
J90 – 20c.+5c. red and buff . . 30 45
J91 – 30c.+10c. blue & buff . . 1·30 4·25
SWISS GIRL DESIGNS—As Type C **56**: 10c. Freibourg; 20c. Nidwalden; 30c. Basel.

C **71** Gottfried Keller

C **73** Johann Kasper Lavater

1940. Children's Fund. Dated "1940".
J92 C **71** 5c.+5c. green 15 15
J93 – 10c.+5c. brown & buff 20 15
J94 – 20c.+5c. red and buff . . 30 20
J95 – 30c.+10c. blue & buff . . 1·00 5·25
SWISS GIRL DESIGNS—As Type C **56**: 10c. Thurgau; 20c. Solothurn; 30c. Zug.

1941. Children's Fund. Bicentenary of Birth of Lavater (philosopher) and of Death of Richard (clockmaker). Dated "1941".
J96 C **73** 5c.+5c. green 15 15
J97 – 10c.+5c. brown & buff 20 20
J98 – 20c.+5c. red and buff . . 25 20
J99 – 30c.+10c. blue . . . . . 90 3·50
DESIGNS—As Type C **56**: 10c., 20c. Girls in national costumes of Schaffhausen and Obwalden. As Type C **73**: 30c. Daniel Jean Richard.

C **74** Niklaus Riggenbach (rack railway pioneer)

1942. Children's Fund. Dated "1942".
J100 C **74** 5c.+5c. green 15 20
J101 – 10c.+5c. brn & buff . . 25 25
J102 – 20c.+5c. red and buff . . 25 20
J103 – 30c.+10c. blue . . . . 1·10 3·25
DESIGNS: 10c. and 20c. Girls in national costumes of Appenzell Ausser-Rhoden and Glarus; 30c. Conrad Escher von der Linth (statesman).

C **75** Emanuel von Fellenberg

C **76** Silver Thistle

1943. Death Centenary of Philip Emanuel von Fellenberg (economist).
J104 C **75** 5c.+5c. green 15 20
J105 C **76** 10c.+5c. green, buff and grey 20 25
J106 – 20c.+5c. red, yellow and pink 25 25
J107 – 30c.+10c. blue, light blue and black . . . 1·10 6·00
FLOWERS: As Type C **76**: 20c. "Ladies slipper"; 30c. Gentian.

C **77** Numa Droz

C **78** Ludwig Forrer

1944. Birth Centenary of Droz (statesman).
J108 C **77** 5c.+5c. green 10 15
J109 – 10c.+5c. olive, yellow and green 25 20
J110 – 20c.+5c. red, yellow and grey 35 20
J111 – 30c.+10c. blue, grey and blue . . . . . . 1·00 6·00
DESIGNS: 10c. Edelweiss; 20c. Martagon lily; 30c. "Aquilegia alpina".

1945. Children's Fund. Centenary of Births of Ludwig Forrer (statesman) and Susanna Orelli (social reformer). Dated "1945".
J112 C **78** 5c.+5c. green 20 20
J113 – 10c.+10c. brown . . . 25 15
J114 – 20c.+10c. red, pink and yellow 65 20
J115 – 30c.+10c. blue, mauve and grey . . . . . . 2·30 4·75
DESIGNS: 10c. Susanna Orelli; 20c. Alpine dog rose; 30c. Spring crocus.

C **79** Rudolf Toepffer

C **80** Jacob Burckhardt (historian)

1946. Death Centenary of Rudolf Toepffer (author and painter). Type C **79** and floral designs inscr "PRO JUVENTUTE 1946".
J116 C **79** 5c.+5c. green 20 15
J117 – 10c.+10c. green, grey and orange 40 20
J118 – 20c.+10c. red, grey and yellow 50 25
J119 – 30c.+10c. blue, grey and mauve . . . . . 2·10 4·25
DESIGNS—As Type C **76**: 10c. Narcissus; 20c. Houseleek; 30c. Blue thistle.

1947. Children's Fund. Type C **80** and floral designs inscr "PRO JUVENTUTE 1947".
J120 C **80** 5c.+5c. green 25 15
J121 – 10c.+10c. black, yellow and grey 40 15
J122 – 20c.+10c. brown, orange and grey . . 50 15
J123 – 30c.+10c. blue, pink and grey . . . . . . 1·70 4·25
DESIGNS—As Type C **76**: 10c. Alpine primrose; 20c. Orange lily; 30c. Cyclamen.

C **81** Gen. U. Wille

C **82** Nicholas Wengi

1948. Children's Fund. Type C **81** and floral designs as Type C **76**. Dated "1948".
J124 C **81** 5c.+5c. purple 25 15
J125 – 10c.+10c. green, yellow and grey 50 15
J126 – 20c.+10c. brown, red and buff 50 20
J127 – 40c.+10c. blue, yellow and grey . . . . . . 2·10 4·25
FLOWERS: 10c. Yellow foxglove; 20c. Rust-leaved Alpine rose; 40c. Lily of Paradise.

1949. Children's Fund. Type C **82** and floral designs inscr "PRO JUVENTUTE 1949".
J128 C **82** 5c.+5c. red 30 15
J129 – 10c.+10c. green, grey and yellow 40 20
J130 – 20c.+10c. brown, blue and buff 50 20
J131 – 40c. blue, mauve and yellow . . . . 2·40 3·25
DESIGNS—As Type C **76**: 10c. "Pulsatilla alpina"; 20c. Alpine clematis; 40c. Superb pink.

C **83** General Theophil Sprecher von Bernegg

C **84** Red Admiral Butterfly

1950. Children's Fund. Inscr "PRO JUVENTUTE 1950".
J132 C **83** 5c.+5c. brown 30 20
J133 C **84** 10c.+10c. mult 60 25
J134 – 20c.+10c. black, blue and orange 65 25
J135 – 30c.+10c. brown, grey and mauve . . . . . 4·50 11·50
J136 – 40c.+10c. yellow, brown and blue . . . . . . 4·25 7·00
DESIGNS: 20c. Clifden's nonpareil (moth); 30c. Honey bee; 40c. Moorland clouded yellow (butterfly).

C **85** Johanna Spyri (authoress)

C **86** "Portrait of a Boy" (Anker)

1951. Children's Fund. Type C **85** and various insects as Type C **84**. Inscr "PRO JUVENTUTE 1951".
J137 C **85** 5c.+5c. purple 35 15
J138 – 10c.+10c. blue & grn 45 20
J139 – 20c.+10c. black, cream and mauve 60 20
J140 – 30c.+10c. black, orange and green . . . . . 3·00 7·75
J141 – 40c.+10c. brown, red and blue . . . . . . 3·50 6·25
INSECTS: 10c. Banded agrion (dragonfly); 20c. Scarce swallowtail (butterfly); 30c. Orange-tip (butterfly); 40c. Viennese emperor moth.

1952. Children's Fund. Type C **86** and insects as Type C **84**. Inscr "PRO JUVENTUTE 1952".
J142 C **86** 5c.+5c. red 30 10
J143 – 10c.+10c. orange, black and green 45 20
J144 – 20c.+10c. cream, black and mauve 50 20
J145 – 30c.+10c. blue, black and brown . . . . . 3·25 6·00
J146 – 40c.+10c. buff, brown and blue . . . . . . 3·25 5·00

INSECTS: 10c. Seven-spotted ladybird; 20c. Marbled white (butterfly); 30c. Chalk-hill blue (butterfly); 40c. Oak eggar moth.

1953. Children's Fund. Portraits as Type C **86** and insects as Type C **84**. Inscr "PRO JUVENTUTE 1953".
J147 5c.+5c. red 30 15
J148 10c.+10c. pink, brown and green 40 25
J149 20c.+10c. black, buff and mauve 45 25
J150 30c.+10c. black, red & grn 3·75 5·50
J151 40c.+10c. blue . . . . . . 4·00 4·25
DESIGNS: 5c. "Portrait of a girl" (Anker); 10c. Black arches moth; 20c. Camberwell beauty (butterfly); 30c. "Purpureus kaehleri" (longhorn beetle); 40c. F. Hodler (self-portrait).

1954. Children's Fund. Portrait as Type C **85** and insects as Type C **84**. Inscr "PRO JUVENTUTE 1954".
J152 5c.+5c. brown 30 15
J153 10c.+10c. multicoloured . . 40 20
J154 20c.+10c. multicoloured . . 85 30
J155 30c.+10c. multicoloured . . 4·00 5·00
J156 40c.+10c. multicoloured . . 4·00 4·50
DESIGNS: 5c. Jeremias Gotthelf (novelist) (after Albert Bitzius); 10c. Garden tiger moth; 20c. Buff-tailed bumble bee; 30c. "Ascalaphus libelluloides" (owl-fly); 40c. Swallowtail (butterfly).

1955. Children's Fund. Portrait as Type C **85** and insects as Type C **84**. Inscr "PRO JUVENTUTE 1955".
J157 5c.+5c. purple 30 15
J158 10c.+10c. multicoloured . . 45 20
J159 20c.+10c. multicoloured . . 60 20
J160 30c.+10c. multicoloured . . 3·75 4·00
J161 40c.+10c. black red & blue 3·75 3·75
DESIGNS: 5c. C. Pictet-de-Rochemont; 10c. Peacock (butterfly); 20c. Great horntail; 30c. Yellow tiger moth; 40c. Apollo (butterfly).

1956. Children's Fund. Portrait as Type C **85** and insects as Type C **84**. Inscr "PRO JUVENTUTE 1956".
J162 5c.+5c. purple 30 15
J163 10c.+10c. deep green, red and green 40 15
J164 20c.+10c. multicoloured . . 45 15
J165 30c.+10c. blue, indigo and yellow . . . . 2·40 3·50
J166 40c.+10c. yellow, brn & bl 2·50 3·00
DESIGNS: 5c. Carlo Maderno (architect); 10c. Common burnet (moth); 20c. Lesser purple emperor (butterfly); 30c. Blue ground beetle; 40c. Large white (butterfly).

1957. Children's Fund. Portrait as Type C **85** and insects as Type C **84**. Inscr "PRO JUVENTUTE 1957".
J167 5c.+5c. purple 30 15
J168 10c.+10c. multicoloured . . 40 15
J169 20c.+10c. yellow, brown and mauve 50 15
J170 30c.+10c. emerald, green and purple . . . . 3·25 3·25
J171 40c.+10c. multicoloured . . 3·00 2·10
DESIGNS: 5c. L. Euler (mathematician); 10c. Clouded yellow (butterfly); 20c. Magpie moth; 30c. Rose chafer (beetle); 40c. Rosy underwing (moth).

C **92** Albrecht von Haller (naturalist) C **93** Pansy

1958. Children's Fund. Type C **92** and flowers as Type C **93**. Inscr "PRO JUVENTUTE 1958".
J172 C **92** 5c.+5c. purple 25 15
J173 C **93** 10c.+10c. yellow, brown and green 35 15
J174 – 20c.+10c. mult 50 15
J175 – 30c.+10c. mult . . . . 2·40 2·30
J176 – 40c.+10c. mult . . . . 2·40 2·00
FLOWERS: 20c. Chinese aster; 30c. Morning Glory; 40c. Christmas rose.

1959. Children's Fund. Portrait as Type C **92** and flowers as Type C **93**. Inscr "PRO JUVENTUTE 1959".
J177 5c.+5c. purple 25 15
J178 10c.+10c. multicoloured . . 40 15
J179 20c.+10c. red, green and purple 50 15
J180 30c.+10c. multicoloured . . 2·20 2·00
J181 50c.+10c. multicoloured . . 2·30 2·20
DESIGNS: 5c. Karl Hilty (lawyer); 10c. Marsh marigold; 20c. Poppy; 30c. Nasturtium; 50c. Sweet pea.

1960. Children's Fund. Portrait as Type C **92** and flowers as Type C **93**. Inscr "PRO JUVENTUTE 1960".
J182 5c.+5c. blue 35 10
J183 10c.+10c. yellow, drab and green 35 15
J184 20c.+10c. green, brown and mauve 40 15
J185 30c.+10c. green, blue and brown . . . . 2·20 2·50
J186 50c.+10c. yellow, grn & bl 2·30 2·50
DESIGNS: 5c. Alexandre Calame (painter); 10c. Dandelion; 20c. Phlox; 30c. Larkspur; 50c. Thorn apple.

1961. Children's Fund. Portrait as Type C **92** and flowers as Type C **93**. Inscr "PRO JUVENTUTE 1961".
J187 5c.+5c. blue 15 15
J188 10c.+10c. multicoloured . . 25 15
J189 20c.+10c. multicoloured . . 30 15
J190 30c.+10c. multicoloured . . 1·10 1·80
J191 50c.+10c. multicoloured . . 1·60 1·70
DESIGNS: 5c. J. Furrer (first President of Swiss Confederation); 10c. Sunflower; 20c. Lily-of-the-Valley; 30c. Iris; 50c. Silverweed.

C **97** "Child's World" C **98** Mother and Child

1962. Children's Fund. 50th Anniv of Pro Juventute Foundation. Inscr "1912–1962".
J192 – 5c.+5c. multicoloured 20 15
J193 C **97** 10c.+10c. red & green 25 15
J194 C **98** 20c.+10c. mult 50 30
J195 – 30c.+10c. red, mauve and yellow . . . . . 85 1·80
J196 – 50c.+10c. yellow, brown and blue . . . . . 85 1·70
DESIGNS—As Type C **97**: 5c. Apple blossom; 30c. "Child's World" (child in meadow); 50c. Forsythia.

1963. Children's Fund. Portrait as Type C **86** and flowers as Type C **93**. Inscr "PRO JUVENTUTE 1963".
J197 5c.+5c. blue 10 20
J198a 10c.+10c. multicoloured . . 95 55
J199a 20c.+10c. red, green and carmine 95 55
J200 30c.+10c. multicoloured . . 1·10 1·30
J201 50c.+10c. purple, green and blue . . . . 1·20 1·20
DESIGNS: 5c. "Portrait of a Boy" (Anker); 10c. Oxeye daisy; 20c. Geranium; 30c. Cornflower; 50c. Carnation.

1964. Children's Fund. Portrait as Type C **86** and flowers as Type C **93**. Inscr "PRO JUVENTUTE 1964".
J202 5c.+5c. blue 10 10
J203 10c.+10c. orange, yellow and green 15 10
J204 20c.+10c. red, green and carmine 20 10
J205 30c.+10c. purple, green and brown 45 50
J206 50c.+10c. multicoloured . . 60 50
DESIGNS: 5c. "Portrait of a Girl" (Anker); 10c. Daffodil; 20c. Rose; 30c. Red clover; 50c. White water-lily.

C **101** Western European Hedgehogs C **102** Roe Deer

1965. Children's Fund. Animals. Inscr "PRO JUVENTUTE 1965".
J207 C **101** 5c.+5c. ochre, brown and red 10 10
J208 – 10c.+10c. mult 10 10
J209 – 20c.+10c. blue, brown and chestnut 20 10
J210 – 30c.+10c. blue, black and yellow 45 40
J211 – 50c.+10c. black, brown and blue . . 50 40
ANIMALS: 10c. Alpine marmots; 20c. Red deer; 30c. Eurasian badgers; 50c. Arctic hares.

1966. Children's Fund. Animals. As Type C **101** but inscr "PRO JUVENTUTE 1966". Mult.
J212 5c.+5c. Stoat 10 10
J213 10c.+10c. Eurasian red squirrel 10 10
J214 20c.+10c. Red fox 20 10
J215 30c.+10c. Brown hare . . . 45 40
J216 50c.+10c. Chamois 50 40

1967. Children's Fund. Animals. Inscr "PRO JUVENTUTE 1967". Multicoloured.
J217 10c.+10c. Type C **102** . . . 15 10
J218 20c.+10c. Pine marten . . . 20 10
J219 30c.+10c. Ibex 45 10
J220 50c.+10c. European otter . . 55 50

1968. Children's Fund. Birds. As Type C **102** but inscr "1968". Multicoloured.
J221 10c.+10c. Western capercaillie 20 10
J222 20c.+10c. Northern bullfinch 30 10
J223 30c.+10c. Woodchat shrike 40 25
J224 50c.+20c. Firecrest 70 40

1969. Children's Fund. Birds. As Type C **102**. Inscr "1969". Multicoloured.
J225 10c.+10c. Eurasian goldfinch 20 15
J226 20c.+10c. Golden oriole . . 30 15
J227 30c.+10c. Wallcreeper . . . 45 30
J228 50c.+20c. Jay 70 55

1970. Children's Fund. Birds. As Type C **102**. Inscr "1970". Multicoloured.
J229 10c.+10c. Blue tits 20 10
J230 20c.+10c. Hoopoe 30 15
J231 30c.+10c. Great spotted woodpecker 45 20
J232 50c.+20c. Great crested grebes 65 65

1971. Children's Fund. Birds. As Type C **102**. Inscr "1971". Multicoloured.
J233 10c.+10c. Common redstarts 20 10
J234 20c.+10c. Bluethroats . . . 30 15
J235 30c.+10c. Peregrine falcon 45 15
J236 40c.+20c. Mallards 65 60

C **104** "McGredy's Sunset" Rose C **105** Chestnut

1972. Children's Fund. Roses. Multicoloured.
J237 10c.+10c. Type C **104** . . . 25 15
J238 20c.+10c. "Miracle" 30 15
J239 30c.+10c. "Papa Meilland" 50 25
J240 40c.+20c. "Madame Dimitriu" 80 80
See also Nos. J258/61 and J279/82.

1973. Children's Fund. "Fruits of the Forest". Multicoloured.
J241 15c.+5c. Type C **105** . . . 20 10
J242 30c.+10c. Cherries 40 10
J243 40c.+20c. Blackberries . . . 60 45
J244 60c.+20c. Bilberries 80 95
See also Nos. J245/8, J250/3 and J254/7.

1974. Children's Fund. "Fruits of the Forest". Poisonous Plants. As Type C **105**. Inscr "1974". Multicoloured.
J245 15c.+10c. Daphne 25 10
J246 30c.+20c. Belladonna . . . 45 10
J247 50c.+20c. Laburnum 75 80
J248 60c.+25c. Mistletoe 90 75

1975. Children's Fund. As Type C **105**. Inscr "1975". Multicoloured.
J249 10c.+5c. "Post-Brent" (postman's hamper) . . . 20 15
J250 15c.+10c. Hepatica 25 15
J251 30c.+20c. Rowan 45 10
J252 50c.+20c. Yellow deadnettle 70 75
J253 60c.+25c. Sycamore . . . . 8·00 3·50

1976. Children's Fund. "Fruits of the Forest". As Type C **105**. Inscr "1976". Multicoloured.
J254 20c.+10c. Barberry 30 15
J255 40c.+20c. Black elder . . . 55 20
J256 40c.+20c. Lime 55 20
J257 80c.+40c. Lungwort 85 75

1977. Children's Fund. Roses. As Type C **104**. Inscr "1977". Multicoloured.
J258 20c.+10c. "Rosa foetida bicolor" 30 10
J259 40c.+20c. "Parfum de l'Hay" 55 10
J260 70c.+30c. "R. foetida persiana" . . . . 1·00 1·10
J261 80c.+40c. "R. centifolia muscosa" . . . . 1·10 1·00

C **106** Arms of Aarburg C **107** Letter Balance

1978. Children's Fund. Arms of the Communes (1st series). Multicoloured.
J262 20c.+10c. Type C **106** . . . 25 10
J263 40c.+20c. Gruyeres 55 10
J264 70c.+30c. Castasegna . . . 95 1·00
J265 80c.+40c. Wangen . . . . . 1·00 90
See also Nos. J266/9, J270/3 and J274/7.

1979. Children's Fund. Arms of the Communes (2nd series). As Type C **106**. Multicoloured.
J266 20c.+10c. Cadro 25 10
J267 40c.+20c. Rute 50 10
J268 70c.+30c. Schwamendingen 95 1·10
J269 80c.+40c. Perroy . . . . . 1·00 90

1980. Children's Fund. Arms of the Communes (3rd series). As Type C **106**. Multicoloured.
J270 20c.+10c. Cortaillod 25 10
J271 40c.+20c. Sierre 55 10
J272 70c.+30c. Scuol . . . . . 95 1·10
J273 80c.+40c. Wolfenschiessen 1·10 90

1981. Children's Fund. Arms of the Communes (4th series). As Type C **106**. Multicoloured.
J274 20c.+10c. Uffikon 25 20
J275 40c.+20c. Torre 55 20
J276 70c.+30c. Benken . . . . . 95 1·10
J277 80c.+40c. Preverenges . . . 1·10 95

1982. Children's Fund. Type C **107** and roses as Type C **104**. Multicoloured.
J278 10c.+10c. Type C **107** . . . 20 20
J279 20c.+10c. "La Belle Portugaise" 30 20
J280 40c.+20c. "Hugh Dickson" 55 20
J281 70c.+30c. "Mermaid" . . . 1·00 1·10
J282 80c.+40c. "Madame Caroline" . . . . 1·20 85

C **108** Kitchen Stove, c. 1850 C **109** Heidi and Goat (Johanna Spyri)

1983. Children's Fund. Toys. Multicoloured.
J283 20c.+10c. Type C **108** . . . 30 15
J284 40c.+20c. Rocking horse, 1826 . . . . 60 15
J285 70c.+30c. Doll, c. 1870 . . . 95 1·10
J286 80c.+40c. Steam locomotive, c. 1900 . . . 1·10 1·00

1984. Children's Fund. Characters from Children's Books. Multicoloured.
J287 35c.+15c. Type C **109** . . . 55 50
J288 50c.+20c. Pinocchio and kite (Carlo Collodi) 65 20
J289 70c.+30c. Pippi Long-stocking (Astrid Lindgren) 1·10 1·20
J290 80c.+40c. Max and Moritz on roof (Wilhelm Busch) 1·20 1·10

1985. Children's Fund. Characters from Children's Books. As Type C **109**. Multicoloured.
J291 35c.+15c. Hansel, Gretel and Witch 50 50
J292 50c.+20c. Snow White and the Seven Dwarfs 70 20
J293 80c.+40c. Red Riding Hood and Wolf . . . . 1·10 1·10
J294 90c.+40c. Cinderella and Prince Charming . . . . 1·20 1·20

C **110** Teddy Bear C **111** Girl carrying Pine Branch and Candle

1986. Children's Fund. Toys. Multicoloured.
J295 35c.+15c. Type C **110** . . . 65 60
J296 50c.+20c. Spinning top . . . 75 25
J297 80c.+40c. Steamroller . . . 1·20 1·40
J298 90c.+40c. Doll . . . . . . 1·30 1·20

1987. Children's Fund. Child Development. Pre-school Age. Multicoloured.
J299 25c.+10c. Type C **111** . . . 45 35
J300 35c.+15c. Mother breast-feeding baby 60 65
J301 50c.+20c. Toddler playing with bricks 75 25
J302 80c.+40c. Children playing in sand . . . . 1·20 1·20
J303 90c.+40c. Father with child on his shoulders . . . . . 1·30 1·10

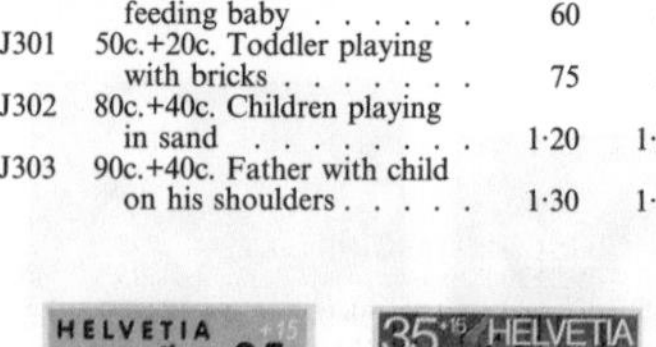

C **112** Learning to Read C **113** Community Work

1988. Children's Fund. Child Development. School Age. Multicoloured.
J304 35c.+15c. Type C **112** . . . 60 65
J305 50c.+20c. Playing triangle 75 25
J306 80c.+40c. Learning arithmetic . . . . 1·30 1·40
J307 90c.+40c. Drawing . . . . 1·40 1·20

1989. Children's Fund. Child Development. Adolescence. Multicoloured.
J308 35c.+15c. Type C **113** . . . 60 65
J309 50c.+20c. Young couple (friendship) 65 30
J310 80c.+40c. Boy at computer screen (vocational training) . . . . 1·30 1·40
J311 90c.+40c. Girl in laboratory (higher education and research) . . . . 1·40 1·20

C **114** Building Model Ship (hobbies) C **115** Ramsons

1990. Child Development. Leisure Activities. Mult.
J312 35c.+15c. Type C **114** . . . 60 60
J313 50c.+20c. Youth group . . . 65 30
J314 80c.+40c. Sport . . . . . . 1·40 1·50
J315 90c.+40c. Music . . . . . . 1·50 1·30

1991. Woodland Flowers. Multicoloured.
J316 50c.+25c. Type C **115** . . . 80 30
J317 70c.+30c. Wood cranesbill 1·10 1·20
J318 80c.+40c. Nettle-leaved bellflower . . . . 1·30 1·10
J319 90c.+40c. Few-leaved hawkweed . . . . 1·40 1·40

C **116** Melchior (wood puppet)

1992. Christmas (J320) and Trees (others). Mult.
J320 50c.+25c. Type C **116** . . . 80 40
J321 50c.+25c. Beech 80 40
J322 70c.+30c. Norway maple . . 1·20 1·30
J323 80c.+40c. Pedunculate oak 1·20 1·20
J324 90c.+40c. Norway spruce . . 1·40 1·30
Nos. J321/4 show silhouette of tree and close-up of its leaves and fruit.

C **117** Christmas Wreath C **118** Candles

1993. Christmas (J325) and Woodland Plants (others). Multicoloured.
J325 60c.+30c. Type C **117** . . . 95 65
J326 60c.+30c. Male fern 95 65
J327 80c.+40c. Guelder rose . . . 1·40 1·30
J328 100c.+50c. "Mnium punctatum" . . . . . . 1·70 1·80

1994. Christmas (J329) and Fungi (others). Mult.
J329 60c.+30c. Type C **118** . . . 95 70
J330 60c.+30c. Wood blewit . . . 95 70
J331 80c.+40c. Red boletus . . . 1·40 1·40
J332 100c.+50c. Shaggy pholiota 1·70 1·70

C **119** Detail of "The Annunciation" (Bartolome Murillo)

1995. Christmas (J333) and Wildlife (others). Mult.
J333 60c.+30c. Type C **119** . . . 95 80
J334 60c.+30c. Brown trout . . . 95 80
J335 80c.+40c. Grey wagtail . . . 1·40 1·50
J336 100c.+50c. Spotted salamander . . . . 1·70 1·80

C **120** Shooting Star and Constellations

1996. Christmas (J337) and Wildlife (others). Mult.
J337 70c.+35c. Type C **120** . . . 1·20 95
J338 70c.+35c. European graylings (fish) . . . . . 1·20 95
J339 90c.+45c. Crayfish . . . . . 1·40 1·40
J340 110c.+55c. European otter 1·80 1·70

C **121** Mistletoe

1997. Christmas (J341) and Wildlife (others). Mult.
J341 70c.+35c. Type C **121** . . . 1·20 1·10
J342 70c.+35c. Three-spined stickleback . . . . 1·20 1·10
J343 90c.+45c. Yellow-bellied toad . . . . 1·40 1·30
J344 110c.+55c. Ruff . . . . . . 1·80 1·60

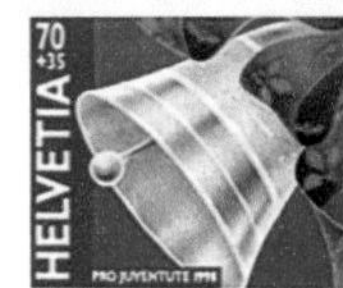

C **122** Christmas Bell

1998. Christmas (J345) and Wildlife (others). Mult.
J345 70c.+35c. Type C **122** . . . 1·20 1·10
J346 70c.+35c. Ramshorn snail 1·20 1·10
J347 90c.+45c. Great crested grebe . . . . 1·50 1·30
J348 110c.+55c. Pike . . . . . . 1·80 1·60

C **123** Children and Snowman (Margaret Strub)

1999. Christmas (J349) and Illustrations from "Nicolo the Clown" (picture book by Verena Pavoni) (others). Multicoloured.
J349 70c.+35c. Type C **123** . . . 1·10 1·00
J350 70c.+35c. Nicolo holding guitar . . . . 1·10 1·00
J351 90c.+45c. Nicolo with his father . . . . 1·40 1·40
J352 110c.+55c. Nicolo with donkey . . . . 1·70 1·70

C **124** Santa Claus C **125** Santa Claus and Cat

2000. Christmas. Illustrations from *Little Albert* (book) by Albert Manser. Multicoloured.
J353 70c.+35c. Type C **124** . . . 1·30 1·20
J354 70c.+35c. Boys sitting on fence and girl . . . . . . 1·30 1·20
J355 90c.+45c. Little Albert with umbrella . . . . 1·60 1·60
J356 90c.+45c. Children sledging 1·60 1·60

2001. Illustrations from Children's Books. Multicoloured.
J357 70c.+35c. Type C **125** (*What's Santa Claus Doing?* (text by Karin von Oldersausen, illustrations by Gabi Fluck)) . . . . . . 1·00 50
J358 70c.+35c. Leopold the leopard in tree (*Leopold and the Sun* by Stephan Brülhart) . . . . 1·00 50
J359 90c.+45c. Bear on scooter (*Honey Bear by S. Brulhart*) . . . . . . 1·25 1·25
J360 90c.+45c. Tom the monkey in tree (*Leopold and the Sun*) . . . . 1·25 1·25

C **126** "Christmas rose"

2002. Roses. Multicoloured.
J361 70c.+35c. Type C **126** . . . 1·00 50
J362 70c.+35c. "Ingrid Bergman" 1·00 50
J363 90c.+45c. "Belle Vaudoise" 1·25 1·25
J364 90c.+45c. "Charmian" . . . 1·25 1·25
J365 130c.+65c. "Fruhlingsgold" 1·80 1·80
No. J361 is impregnated with the fragrance of cinnamon and cloves and Nos. J362/5 with the perfume of roses.

C **127** Playing with Christmas Toys

2003. Children's Rights. The Right to Play. Multicoloured. Self-adhesive gum.
J366 70c.+35c. Type C **127** . . . 1·20 60
J367 85c.+ 35c. Playing shop . . 1·60 1·60
J368 90c.+45c. Skateboarding . . 1·75 1·75
J369 100c.+45c. Playing music . . 2·00 2·00

C **128** Family and Giraffe

2004. Children's Rights. Right to Education. Multicoloured. Self-adhesive gum.
J370 85c.+40c. Type C **128** . . . 1·10 55
J371 85c.+ 40c. Playing cards . . 1·10 55
J372 100c.+50c. Listening to older person read . . . . . . 1·30 1·30
J373 100c.+50c. Teacher and pupils . . . . 1·30 1·30

INTERNATIONAL ORGANIZATIONS SITUATED IN SWITZERLAND

The stamps listed under this heading were issued by the Swiss Post Office primarily for the use of officials of the Organizations named, situated in Geneva.

These stamps could not be legitimately obtained unused before Feburary 1944.

A. LEAGUE OF NATIONS

1922. Optd **SOCIETE DES NATIONS.**
LN 1 **20a** 2½c. bistre on buff . . — 40
LN 2 3c. blue on buff . . . — 4·50
LN 3 5c. orange on buff . . — 2·10
LN 4 5c. grey on buff . . . — 2·10
LN 5 5c. purple on buff . . — 1·20
LN 5a 5c. green on buff . . . — 13·00
LN 6 7½c. green on buff . . — 30
LN 7 **21** 10c. green on buff . . — 35
LN 8 10c. violet on buff . . — 95
LN 9 15c. red on buff . . . — 70
LN10 20c. purple on buff . . — 3·75
LN11 20c. red on buff . . . — 1·50
LN13 25c. red on buff . . . — 75
LN14 25c. brown on buff . . — 9·25
LN15 **17** 30c. green and brown — 7·25
LN16 **21** 30c. blue on buff . . . — 4·25
LN17 **17** 35c. yellow and green — 3·75
LN18 40c. blue . . . . . . — 1·00
LN19 40c. green and mauve — 6·50
LN20a 50c. green & dp green 50 1·30
LN21 60c. brown . . . . . 23·00 80
LN22a 70c. buff and violet . 1·50 35
LN23a 80c. buff and grey . . 1·20 1·70
LN24a **41** 90c. red, dp green & grn . . . . — 3·00
LN25a **17** 1f. green and purple — 3·75
LN26b **41** 1f.20 red, lake and pink . . . . . . 2·50 2·30
LN27a 1f.50 red, bl & turq 2·50 2·50
LN28a 2f. red, black and grey 3·00 3·00
LN29 **22** 3f. red . . . . . . — 1·20
LN29a **43** 3f. brown . . . . . — £100
LN30 – 5f. blue (No. 296) . . — 38·00
LN32 – 10f. mauve (No. 297) — 75·00
LN33 – 10f. green (No. 337) — 85·00

1932. International Disarmament Conference. Optd **SOCIETE DES NATIONS.**
LN34 **44** 5c. green . . . . . . — 10·50
LN35 10c. orange . . . . . — 95
LN36 20c. mauve . . . . . — 95
LN37 30c. blue . . . . . . — 31·00
LN38 60c. brown . . . . . — 9·00
LN39 **45** 1f. grey and blue . . . — 7·50

1934. Landscape designs of 1934 optd **SOCIETE DES NATIONS.**
LN40 **48** 3c. green . . . . . . — 30
LN41 – 5c. green . . . . . . — 40
LN42 – 15c. orange . . . . . — 80
LN43 – 25c. brown . . . . . — 11·00
LN44 – 30c. blue . . . . . . — 95

1937. Landscape designs of 1936 optd **SOCIETE DES NATIONS.**
LN45 A **52** 3c. green 10 20
LN46 A – 5c. green 20 20
LN47Ac – 10c. purple . . . . . — 70
LN49 – 10c. brown 50 45
LN50 A – 15c. orange 30 40
LN51 A – 20c. red (railway) . . — 1·20
LN51Ac – 20c. red (lake) 55 75
LN52 A – 25c. brown 45 65
LN53 A – 30c. blue 45 55
LN54 A – 35c. green 45 65
LN55 A – 40c. grey 75 90

1938. Nos. 382/5 optd **SOCIETE DES NATIONS.**
LN56 **55** 20c. red and buff . . . . — 1·20
LN57 – 30c. blue and light blue — 1·90
LN58 – 60c. brown and buff . . — 3·50
LN59 – 1f. black and buff . . . — 6·00

1938. Nos. 382/5 optd **SERVICE DE LA SOCIETE DES NATIONS** in circle.
LN60 **55** 20c. red and buff . . . . — 1·40
LN61 – 30c. blue and light blue — 2·50
LN62 – 60c. brown and buff . . — 4·50
LN63 – 1f. black and buff . . . — 7·50

1939. Nos. 388c/90c optd **SOCIETE DES NATIONS.**
LN64 **61** 3f. brown on buff . . . 3·00 6·25
LN65 – 5f. blue on buff . . . 5·00 8·50
LN66 – 10f. green on buff . . . 8·00 19·00

1944. Optd **COURRIER DE LA SOCIETE DES NATIONS.** (a) Landscape designs of 1936.
LN67 **52** 3c. green 20 25
LN68 – 5c. green 20 25
LN69 – 10c. brown 20 20
LN70 – 15c. orange 30 30
LN71 – 20c. red (lake) 45 55
LN72 – 25c. brown 55 70
LN73 – 30c. blue 60 75
LN74 – 35c. green . . . . . . 60 1·00
LN75 – 40c. grey . . . . 65 1·30

(b) Historical designs of 1941.
LN76 – 50c. blue on green . . . 1·10 2·00
LN77 **68** 60c. brown on brown . . 1·40 2·40
LN78 – 70c. purple on mauve . . 1·50 2·20
LN79 – 80c. black on grey . . . 1·30 2·00
LN80 – 90c. red on pink . . . . 1·30 2·00
LN81 – 1f. green on green . . . 1·50 2·30
LN82 – 1f.20 purple on grey . . 2·00 3·25
LN83 – 1f.50 blue on buff . . . 2·20 3·75
LN84 – 2f. red on pink . . . . 2·75 4·75

(c) Parliament designs of 1938.
LN85 **61** 3f. brown on buff . . . 4·50 8·75
LN86 – 5f. blue on buff . . . 7·00 12·00
LN87 – 10f. green on buff . . . 12·50 23·00

B. INTERNATIONAL LABOUR OFFICE

Optd **S.d.N. Bureau international du Travail** (Nos. LB1/47).

1923.
LB 1 **20a** 2½c. bistre on buff . . — 20
LB 2 3c. blue on buff . . . — 70
LB 3 5c. orange on buff . . — 35
LB 4 5c. purple on buff . . — 15
LB 5 7½c. green on buff . . — 20
LB 6 **21** 10c. green on buff . . — 30
LB 8 15c. red on buff . . . — 70
LB 9 20c. purple on buff . . — 7·00
LB10 20c. red on buff . . . — 3·00
LB11 25c. red on buff . . . — 65
LB12 25c. brown on buff . . — 1·60
LB13 **17** 30c. green and brown — 31·00
LB14 **21** 30c. blue on buff . . . — 1·10
LB15 **17** 35c. yellow and green — 5·00
LB16 40c. blue . . . . . . — 65
LB17 40c. green and mauve — 7·25
LB18a 50c. green & deep green . . . . 1·20 1·20
LB19 60c. brown . . . . . 90 1·20
LB20a 70c. buff and violet . . 1·20 1·70
LB21 80c. buff and grey . . 6·25 1·00
LB22 **41** 90c. red, dp grn & grn — 2·50
LB23 **17** 1f. green and purple — 1·40
LB24b **38** 1f.20 red, lake and pink . . . . 10·50 2·50
LB25a 1f.50 red, bl & turq . . 2·00 2·00
LB26a 2f. red, black and grey 2·50 3·25
LB27 **22** 3f. red . . . . — 14·00
LB27a **43** 3f. brown . . . . . . — £120
LB28 – 5f. blue (No. 296) . . — 22·00
LB30 – 10f. mauve (No. 297) — 90·00
LB31 – 10f. green (No. 337) — 90·00

1932. International Disarmament Conference.
LB32 **44** 5c. green . . . . — 70
LB33 10c. orange . . . . . — 60
LB34 20c. mauve . . . . . — 85
LB35 30c. blue . . . . . . — 4·25
LB36 60c. brown . . . . . — 4·25
LB37 **45** 1f. grey and blue . . . — 6·00

1937. Landscape design of 1934.
LB38 **48** 3c. green . . . . — 3·00

1937. Landscape designs of 1936.
LB39A **52** 3c. green 20 25
LB40A – 5c. green 20 25
LB41B – 10c. purple . . . . . . — 1·20
LB41e – 10c. brown 30 30
LB42A – 15c. orange 30 25
LB43A – 20c. red (railway) . . . — 1·10
LB43c – 20c. red (lake) 55 75
LB44A – 25c. brown 50 65
LB45A – 30c. blue 50 60
LB46A – 35c. green 50 85
LB47A – 40c. grey 80 90

1938. Nos. 382/5 optd **S.d.N. Bureau international du Travail.**
LB48 **55** 20c. red and buff . . . . — 75
LB49 – 30c. blue and light blue — 1·40
LB50 – 60c. brown and buff . . — 2·75
LB51 – 1f. black and buff . . . — 4·50

1938. Nos. 382/5 optd **SERVICE DU BUREAU INTERNATIONAL DU TRAVAIL** in circle.
LB52 **55** 20c. red and buff . . . . — 2·00
LB53 – 30c. blue and light blue — 1·70
LB54 – 60c. brown and buff . . — 3·75
LB55 – 1f. black and buff . . . — 3·75

1939. Nos. 388c/90c optd **S.d.N. Bureau international du Travail.**
LB56 **61** 3f. brown on buff . . . 3·00 5·50
LB57 – 5f. blue on buff . . . . 4·00 9·75
LB58 – 10f. green on buff . . . 6·75 14·50

1944. Optd **COURRIER DU BUREAU INTERNATIONAL DU TRAVAIL.** (a) Landscape designs of 1936.
LB59 **52** 3c. green 20 20
LB60 – 5c. green 20 25
LB61 – 10c. brown 30 30
LB62 – 15c. orange 40 50
LB63 – 20c. red (lake) 45 60
LB64 – 25c. brown 50 70
LB65 – 30c. blue . . . . 75 1·00
LB66 – 35c. green . . . . . . 80 1·20
LB67 – 40c. grey . . . . 85 1·40

(b) Historical designs of 1941.
LB68 – 50c. blue on green . . . 2·30 3·75
LB69 **68** 60c. brown on brown . . 2·30 3·00
LB70 – 70c. purple on mauve . . 2·75 2·50

LB71 – 80c. black on grey 65 70
LB72 – 90c. red on pink 65 70
LB73 – 1f. green on green 85 75
LB74 – 1f.20 purple on grey 1·00 80
LB75 – 1f.50 blue on buff 1·20 85
LB76 – 2f. red on pink 1·70 1·20

(c) Parliament designs of 1938.
LB77 61 3f. brown on buff 3·75 3·00
LB78 – 5f. blue on buff 5·50 5·00
LB79 – 10f. green on buff 11·50 14·00

1950. Landscape designs of 1949 optd **BUREAU INTERNATIONAL DU TRAVAIL**.
LB80 107 5c. orange 2·75 2·75
LB81 – 10c. green 2·75 4·75
LB82 – 15c. turquoise 3·50 3·00
LB83 – 20c. purple 3·50 5·75
LB84 – 25c. red 3·75 4·50
LB85 – 30c. green 4·00 5·75
LB86 – 35c. brown 4·00 5·00
LB87 – 40c. blue 4·00 5·25
LB88 – 50c. grey 5·50 5·25
LB89 – 60c. green 6·50 7·00
LB90 – 70c. violet 8·00 9·50

LB 4 Miners (bas-relief)

1952. Inscr as in Type LB 4.
LB91 LB 4 5c. purple 10 10
LB92 10c. green 10 10
LB94 – 20c. red 30 25
LB95 – 30c. orange 45 35
LB96 LB 4 40c. blue 1·40 1·20
LB97 50c. blue 20 30
LB98 – 60c. brown 30 25
LB99 – 2f. purple 80 70
DESIGN—HORIZ: 20, 30, 60c., 2f. Globe, flywheel and factory chimney.

1969. Pope Paul's Visit to Geneva. No. LB95 optd **Visite du Pape Paul VI Geneve 10 juin 1969**.
LB100 30c. orange 10 15

LB 6 New Headquarters Building

1974. Inaug of New I.L.O. Headquarters, Geneva.
LB101 LB 6 80c. multicoloured 70 60

LB 7 Man at Lathe

1975.
LB102 LB 7 30c. brown 25 25
LB103 – 60c. blue 45 40
LB104 – 90c. brown, red & grn 70 65
LB105 – 100c. green 80 65
LB106 – 120c. ochre and brown 60 75
DESIGNS: 60c. Woman at drilling machine; 90c. Welder and laboratory assistant; 100c. Surveyor with theodolite; 120c. Apprentice and instructor with slide rule.

LB 8 Keys

1994. 75th Anniv of I.L.O.
LB107 LB 8 180c. multicoloured 1·40 1·60

C. INTERNATIONAL EDUCATION OFFICE

1944. Optd **COURRIER DU BUREAU INTERNATIONAL D'EDUCATION**.
(a) Landscape designs of 1936.
LE1 52 3c. green 20 40
LE2 – 5c. green 50 95
LE3 – 10c. brown 55 1·20
LE4 – 15c. orange 50 1·10
LE5 – 20c. red (lake) 50 1·10
LE6 – 25c. brown 50 1·10
LE7 – 30c. blue 85 1·50
LE8 – 35c. green 75 1·40
LE9 – 40c. grey 95 1·70

(b) Historical designs of 1941.
LE10 – 50c. blue on green 5·25 7·75
LE11 68 60c. brown on brown 5·25 7·75
LE12 – 70c. purple on mauve 5·25 7·75
LE13 – 80c. black on grey 55 1·20
LE14 – 90c. red on pink 65 1·30
LE15 – 1f. green on green 75 1·50
LE16 – 1f.20 purple on grey 95 1·80
LE17 – 1f.50 blue on buff 1·20 3·00
LE18 – 2f. red on pink 1·90 2·75

(c) Parliament designs of 1938.
LE19 61 3f. brown on buff 4·50 12·00
LE20 – 5f. blue on buff 6·75 19·00
LE21 – 10f. green on buff 10·00 27·00

1946. Optd **BIE** vert.
LE22 86 10c. purple 15 25

Optd **BUREAU INTERNATIONAL D'EDUCATION** (Nos. LE23/39).

1948. Landscape designs of 1936.
LE23 5c. brown 1·70 2·00
LE24 10c. green 1·90 2·10
LE25 20c. brown 1·70 2·00
LE26 25c. red 1·70 2·00
LE27 30c. blue 1·90 2·10
LE28 40c. blue 1·70 2·00

1950. Landscape designs of 1949.
LE29 107 5c. orange 70 75
LE30 – 10c. green 90 90
LE31 – 15c. turquoise 90 95
LE32 – 20c. purple 3·00 3·00
LE33 – 25c. red 6·75 8·75
LE34 – 30c. green 6·75 7·75
LE35 – 35c. brown 4·50 6·00
LE36 – 40c. blue 4·75 5·75
LE37 – 50c. grey 5·50 6·00
LE38 – 60c. green 6·50 7·50
LE39 – 70c. violet 7·50 8·75

LE 3 Globe on Books

1958. Inscr as in Type LE 3.
LE40 LE 3 5c. purple 10 10
LE41 10c. green 10 10
LE43 – 20c. red 20 15
LE44 – 30c. orange 30 25
LE45 LE 3 40c. blue 2·20 1·80
LE46 50c. blue 45 35
LE47 – 60c. brown 55 45
LE48 – 2f. purple 1·50 1·30
DESIGN—VERT: 20, 30, 60c., 2f. Pestalozzi Monument, Yverdon.

D. WORLD HEALTH ORGANIZATION

1948. Optd **ORGANISATION MONDIALE DE LA SANTE**. (a) Landscape designs of 1936.
LH1 5c. brown (No. 489) 2·00 1·20
LH2 10c. green (No. 490) 2·50 2·50
LH3 20c. brown (No. 491) 2·30 2·50
LH4 25c. red (No. 492) 2·50 2·75
LH5 40c. blue (No. 494) 3·00 2·40

(b) Landscape designs of 1949.
LH 6 107 5c. orange 70 35
LH 7 – 10c. green 1·40 1·20
LH 8 – 15c. turquoise 1·80 90
LH 9 – 20c. purple 5·25 3·50
LH10 – 25c. red 5·50 5·50
LH11 – 30c. green 2·50 3·25
LH12 – 35c. brown 2·75 4·50
LH13 – 40c. blue 2·50 1·10
LH14 – 50c. grey 3·50 3·75
LH15 – 60c. green 3·50 3·75
LH16 – 70c. violet 5·50 3·25

(c) Historical designs of 1941 (Nos. 408/13).
LH17 80c. black on grey 1·10 1·40
LH18 90c. red on pink 6·25 3·00
LH19 1f. green on green 1·30 1·60
LH20 1f.20 purple on grey 7·75 7·75
LH21 1f.50 blue on buff 17·00 8·50
LH22 2f. red on pink 3·50 2·40

(d) Parliament designs of 1938.
LH23 61 3f. brown on buff 36·00 21·00
LH24 – 5f. blue on buff 7·75 5·50
LH25 – 10f. green on buff 75·00 38·00

LH 2 Staff of Aesculapius

1957.
LH26 LH 2 5c. purple 10 10
LH27 10c. green 10 10
LH29 20c. red 15 15
LH30 30c. orange 25 25
LH31 40c. blue 1·60 1·60
LH32 50c. blue 35 35
LH33 60c. brown 40 40
LH34 2f. purple 1·20 1·20

1962. Malaria Eradication. Optd **ERADICATION DU PALUDISME**.
LH35 LH 2 50c. blue 15 25

LH 4 Staff of Aesculapius

1975.
LH36 LH 4 30c. green, purple and pink 25 25
LH37 60c. yellow, blue and light blue 50 45
LH38 90c. yellow, violet and light violet 75 65
LH39 100c. blue, brown and orange 80 75
LH40 140c. green, turquoise and red 1·20 1·20

LH 5 Staff of Aesculapius

1995.
LH41 LH 5 180c. yellow, brown and red 1·50 1·60

E. INTERNATIONAL REFUGEES ORGANIZATION

Optd **ORGANISATION INTERNATIONALE POUR LES REFUGIES**.

1950. (a) Landscape designs of 1949.
LR1 107 5c. orange 10·00 7·25
LR2 – 10c. green 11·00 8·00
LR3 – 20c. purple 10·00 7·50
LR4 – 25c. red 11·00 8·00
LR5 – 40c. blue 10·50 7·50

(b) Historical designs of 1941 (Nos. 408/13).
LR6 80c. black on grey 10·00 11·50
LR7 1f. green on green 9·50 6·00
LR8 2f. red on pink 9·50 6·00

F. WORLD METEOROLOGICAL ORGANIZATION

LM 1 "The Elements" LM 2 W.M.O. Emblem

1956. Inscr as in Type LM 1.
LM1 LM 1 5c. purple 10 10
LM2 10c. green 10 10
LM4 – 20c. red 15 15
LM5 – 30c. orange 25 25
LM6 LM 1 40c. blue 1·30 1·80
LM7 50c. blue 35 35
LM8 – 60c. brown 40 40
LM9 – 2f. purple 1·40 1·20
DESIGN: 20, 30, 60c., 2f. Weathervane.

1973. Cent of World Meteorological Organization.
LM10 LM 2 30c. red 25 25
LM11 40c. blue 35 35
LM12 – 80c. violet and gold 65 60
LM13 LM 2 1f. brown 80 70
DESIGN: 80c. Emblem and "OMI OMM 1873 1973".

G. UNIVERSAL POSTAL UNION

LP 1 U.P.U. Monument, Berne LP 2 "Letter Post"

1957. Inscr as in Type LP 1.
LP1 LP 1 5c. purple 10 10
LP2 – 10c. green 10 10
LP4 – 20c. red 15 15
LP5 – 30c. orange 25 25
LP6 LP 1 40c. blue 1·30 1·70
LP7 50c. blue 35 35
LP8 – 60c. brown 40 50
LP9 LP 1 2f. purple 1·40 1·70
DESIGN: 10, 20, 30, 60c. Pegasus (sculpture).

1976.
LP10 LP 2 40c. purple, blue and claret 6·00 7·25
LP11 – 80c. multicoloured 60 60
LP12 – 90c. multicoloured 75 75
LP13 – 100c. multicoloured 75 75
LP14 – 120c. multicoloured 1·00 1·00
LP15 – 140c. grey, blue and red 8·25 6·25
DESIGNS: 80c. "Parcel Post"; 90c. "Financial Services"; 100c. Technical co-operation; 120c. Carrier pigeon, international reply coupon and postal money order; 140c. Express Mail Service.
The 120 and 140c. are additionally inscribed "TIMBRE DE SERVICE".

LP 3 Computer, Mail Sacks and Globe

1995.
LP16 LP 3 180c. multicoloured 1·60 1·60

LP 4 Hand reaching for Rainbow

1999. 125th Anniv of Universal Postal Union. Multicoloured.
LP17 20c. Type LP 4 20 20
LP18 70c. Hand holding rainbow 65 65

LP 5 "Q" and Letter

2003.
LP19 LP 5 90c. multicoloured 1·20 1·20

H. UNITED NATIONS

1950. Optd **NATIONS UNIES OFFICE EUROPEEN**. (a) Landscape designs of 1949.
LU 1 107 5c. orange 55 1·30
LU 2 – 10c. green 70 1·10
LU 3 – 15c. turquoise 1·20 1·50
LU 4 – 20c. purple 1·60 2·30
LU 5 – 25c. red 2·50 3·50
LU 6 – 30c. green 2·50 3·50
LU 7 – 35c. brown 5·25 7·25
LU 8 – 40c. blue 3·25 2·75
LU 9 – 50c. grey 4·25 6·25
LU10 – 60c. green 5·00 7·50
LU11 – 70c. violet 5·00 7·25

(b) Historical designs of 1941 (Nos. 408/13).
LU12 80c. black on grey 8·25 6·25
LU13 90c. red on pink 8·25 6·25
LU14 1f. green on green 8·25 6·25
LU15 1f.20 purple on grey 8·25 8·25
LU16 1f.50 blue on buff 8·75 14·00
LU17 2f. red on pink 8·75 10·50

(c) Parliament designs of 1938.
LU18 61 3f. brown on buff 75·00 60·00
LU19 – 5f. blue on buff 75·00 60·00
LU20 – 10f. green on buff £110 95·00

LU 2 LU 4

1955. 10th Anniv of U.N.O.
LU21 LU 2 40c. blue and yellow 1·80 2·10

1955. Nos. LU22/3 and LU27/8 are as Type LU 2 but without dates.
LU22 – 5c. purple 10 10
LU23 – 10c. green 10 10
LU25 LU 4 20c. red 15 15
LU26 30c. orange 25 20
LU27 – 40c. blue 2·20 2·30
LU28 – 50c. blue 40 25
LU29 LU 4 60c. brown 35 35
LU30 2f. purple 90 90

1960. World Refugee Year. Nos. LU25 and LU28 optd **ANNEE MONDIALE DU REFUGIE 1959 1960**.
LU31 20c. red 10 15
LU32 50c. blue 15 25

LU 6 Palace of Nations, Geneva

1960. 15th Anniv of U.N.O.
LU33 LU **6** 5f. blue . . . . . . 2·30 3·00

LU **7**

LU **8** UNCSAT Emblem

1962. Opening of U.N. Philatelic Museum, Geneva.
LU34 LU **7** 10c. green and red . . 10 10
LU35 – 30c. red and blue . . 10 15
LU36 LU **7** 50c. blue and red . . 15 25
LU37 – 60c. brown and green 15 30
DESIGN—HORIZ: 30, 60c. As Type LU **4** but inscr "ONU MUSEE PHILATELIQUE".

1963. U.N. Scientific and Technological Conf, Geneva.
LU38 LU **8** 50c. red and blue . . 25 30
LU39 – 2f. green and purple 60 1·10
DESIGN—HORIZ: 2f. As Type LU **4**, but with emblem.

From 1969 stamps for the Geneva Headquarters were issued by the United Nations (q.v.).

I. INTERNATIONAL TELECOMMUNICATION UNION

LT **1** Transmitting Aerial

LT **2** New H.Q. Building

1958. Inscr as in Type LT **1**.
LT1 LT **1** 5c. purple 10 10
LT2 10c. green 10 10
LT4 – 20c. red 20 15
LT5 – 30c. orange 30 25
LT6 LT **1** 40c. blue . . . . 1·50 1·70
LT7 50c. blue 45 35
LT8 – 60c. brown 55 45
LT9 – 2f. purple . . . . . . 1·80 1·30
DESIGN: 20, 30, 60c., 2f. Receiving aerials.

1973. Inaug of New I.T.U. Headquarters, Geneva.
LT10 LT **2** 80c. black and blue . . 65 60

LT **3** Boeing 747 Jetliner and Ocean Liner

1976. World Telecommunications Network.
LT11 – 40c. blue and red . . 35 30
LT12 LT **3** 90c. violet, blue & yellow 75 65
LT13 – 1f. red, green & yellow 80 80
DESIGNS: 40c. "Sound waves"; 1f. Face and microphone in television screen.

LT **4** Optical Fibre Cables

1988.
LT14 LT **4** 1f.40 multicoloured . . 1·20 1·30

LT **5** Emblem emitting Radio Signals

1994. 100 Years of Radio.
LT15 LT **5** 1f.80 multicoloured . . 1·50 1·60

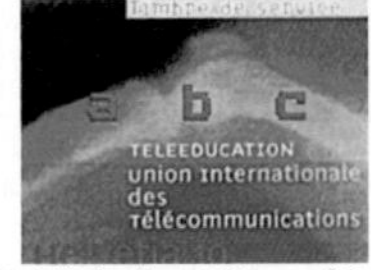

LT **6** "a b c" and X-ray of Bone Joint ("Teleeducation")

1999. Multicoloured.
LT16 10c. Type LT **6** 10 10
LT17 100c. Arrow and X-ray of bone joint ("Telemedicine") 90 90

LT **7** Stylized Face

2003.
LT18 LT **7** 90c. multicoloured . . 1·20 1·20

J. WORLD INTELLECTUAL PROPERTY ORGANIZATION

LV **1** WIPO Seal

1989. Multicoloured.
LV1 40c. Type LV **1** 45 40
LV2 50c. Face and symbolic representation of intellect 60 55
LV3 80c. WIPO building, Geneva 90 85
LV4 100c. Hand pressing buttons, retort and cogwheel (industrial property) . . . 1·20 1·10
LV5 120c. Head, ballet dancer, cello and book (copyright) 1·40 1·30

K. INTERNATIONAL OLYMPIC COMMITTEE

LW **1** Olympic Rings

2000. Olympic Games, Sydney. Self-adhesive.
LW1 LW **1** 20c. multicoloured . . 20 20
LW2 70c. multicoloured . . 60 60

K. INTERNATIONAL OLYMPIC COMMITTEE

LW **2** Olympic Rings, Stadium and Runner

2004. Olympic Games, Athens.
LW3 LW **2** 1f. multicoloured . . 85 50

SYRIA Pt. 6; Pt. 19

A country at the E. end of the Mediterranean Sea, formerly Turkish territory. Occupied by the Allies in 1918 and administered under French Military Occupation. An Arab kingdom was set up in the Aleppo and Damascus area during 1919, but the Emir Faisal came into conflict with the French and was defeated in July 1920. In April 1920, the Mandate was offered to France, becoming effective in September 1923. Separate governments were established for the Territories of Damascus, Aleppo, the Alaouites (including Latakia), Great Lebanon and the Jebel Druze. Syria became a republic in 1934, and the Mandate ended with full Independence in 1942.

In 1958 the United Arab Republic was formed which comprised Egypt and Syria but separate stamps were issued for each territory as they employed different currencies. In 1961 Syria left the U.A.R. and the Syrian Arab Republic was established.

1919. 40 paras = 10 milliemes = 1 piastre.
1920. 100 centimes (or centiemes) = 1 piastre; 100 piastres = 1 Syrian Pound.

A. FRENCH MILITARY OCCUPATION.

1919. Stamps of France surch **T. E. O.** and value in "MILLIEMES" or "PIASTRES".

1 **11** 1m. on 1c. grey £225 £225
2 2m. on 2c. purple £500 £650
3 3m. on 3c. orange £225 £225
4 **15** 4m. on 15c. green 50·00 50·00
5 **18** 5m. on 5c. green 36·00 44·00
6 1p. on 10c. red 46·00 30·00
7 2p. on 25c. blue 27·00 32·00
8 **13** 5p. on 40c. red and blue 36·00 38·00
9 9p. on 50c. brown and lilac 70·00 70·00
10 10p. on 1f. red and yellow 85·00 £100

1919. Nos. 9/13a and 19/23 of French Post Offices in the Turkish Empire ("Blanc", "Mouchon" and "Merson" key-types inscr "LEVANT") optd **T. E. O.** or surch in "MILLIEMES" also.

11 **A** 1m. on 1c. grey 2·75 3·25
12 2m. on 2c. purple 1·90 2·75
13 3m. on 3c. red 3·75 4·00
14 **B** 4m. on 15c. red 1·50 2·50
15 **A** 5m. on 5c. green 1·40 1·30
16 **B** 1p. on 25c. blue 1·00 1·20
17 **C** 2p. on 50c. brown and lilac 1·00 4·25
18 4p. on 1f. red and green 4·00 5·00
19 8p. on 2f. lilac and buff 12·50 12·50
20 20p. on 5f. blue and buff £230 £220
MS17 106 × 16 mm. Nos. 15/16 19·00 50·00

1920. Stamps of France surch **O. M. F. Syrie** and value in "MILLIEMES" or "PIASTRES".

25 **11** 1m. on 1c. grey 1·50 2·25
26 2m. on 2c. purple 2·25 5·00
27 **18** 3m. on 5c. green 3·00 4·25
28 5m. on 10c. red 1·40 3·75
29 **13** 20p. on 5f. blue and buff 70·00 £100

1920. Stamps of France surch **O. M. F. Syrie** and value. (a) Value in "CENTIMES" or "PIASTRES".

31 **11** 25c. on 1c. grey 3·00 2·50
32 50c. on 2c. purple 2·25 2·50
33 75c. on 3c. orange 2·50 4·25
35 **18** 1p. on 5c. green 2·75 30
36 2p. on 10c. red 2·25 2·00
37 2p. on 25c. blue 2·75 35
38 3p. on 25c. blue 2·75 2·75
39 **15** 5p. on 15c. green 3·00 3·25
40 **13** 10p. on 40c. red and blue 4·75 5·50
41 25p. on 50c. brown and lilac 5·50 6·25
42 50p. on 1f. red and yellow 28·00 38·00
44 100p. on 5f. blue and buff 52·00 65·00

(b) Value in "CENTIEMES".

45 **11** 25c. on 1c. grey 1·40 60
46 50c. on 2c. purple 1·30 20
47 75c. on 3c. orange 2·00 4·75

1920. Air. Nos. 35 and 39/40 optd **POSTE PAR AVION** in frame.

57 **18** 1p. on 5c. green £160 55·00
58 **15** 5p. on 15c. green £250 60·00
59 **13** 10p. on 40c. red and blue £350 95·00

1921. Issued at Damascus. Nos. K88/95 of Arab Kingdom surch **O. M. F. Syrie** and value in "CENTIEMES" or "PIASTRES".

60 **K 3** 25c. on 1m. brown 5·50 4·00
61 50c.on $\frac{1}{10}$p green. 5·00 4·25
62 1p.on $\frac{3}{10}$p. yellow 4·25 3·50
63 **K 4** 1p. on 5m. red 11·50 8·50
64a 2p. on 5m. red 7·00 6·75
65 **K 3** 3p. on 1p. blue 9·25 4·00
66 5p. on 2p. green 9·75 16·00
67 10p. on 5p. purple 8·00 10·00
68 25p. on 10p. grey 12·00 22·00

1921. Stamps of France surch **O. M. F. Syrie** and value in "CENTIEMES" or "PIASTRES" (in two lines).

69 **18** 25c. on 5c. green 3·00 1·40
70 50c. on 10c. red 80 15
71 **15** 75c. on 15c. green 85 1·30
72 **18** 1p. on 20c. red 3·00 10
73 **13** 2p. on 40c. red and blue 2·00 10
74 3p. on 60c. violet and blue 3·00 20
75 5p. on 1f. red and yellow 5·25 5·25
76 10p. on 2f. orange and green 8·00 6·75
77 25p. on 5f. blue and buff £110 £120

See also Nos. 81/5.

1921. Air. Nos. 72 and 75/6 optd **POSTE PAR AVION** in frame.

78 **18** 1p. on 20c. red £100 42·00
79 **13** 5p. on 1f. red and yellow £375 £160
80 10p. on 2f. orange and green £350 £160

1921. Stamps of France surch **O.M.F. Syrie** and value in "PIASTRES" in one line.

81 **13** 2p. on 40c. red and blue 2·25 10
82 3p. on 60c. violet and blue 2·25 15
83 5p. on 1f. red and yellow 10·50 7·00
84 10p. on 2f. orange and green 15·50 15·50
85 25p. on 5f. blue and buff 12·00 14·00

1921. Air. Nos. 72 and 75/6 optd **AVION**.

86 **18** 1p. on 20c. red 70·00 32·00
87 **13** 5p. on 1f. red and yellow £130 56·00
88 10p. on 2f. orange and green £160 60·00

1922. Air. Stamps of France surch **Poste par Avion O. M. F. Syrie** and value.

89 **13** 2p. on 40c. red and blue 19·50 50·00
90 3p. on 60c. violet and blue 17·00 46·00
91 5p. on 1f. red and yellow 24·00 50·00
92 10p. on 2f. orange and green 20·00 50·00

1922. Stamps of France surch **O. M. F. Syrie** and value in "CENTIEMES" or "PIASTRES".

93 **11** 10c. on 2c. purple 3·25 4·25
94 **18** 10c. on 5c. orange 2·50 4·50
95 25c. on 5c. orange 1·80 25
96 50c. on 10c. green 3·00 15
96a 1,25p. on 25c. blue 2·75 55
96b 1,50p. on 30c. orange 3·75 1·20
96c **13** 2,50p. on 50c. brn & lilac 3·00 1·90
96d **15** 2,50p. on 50c. blue 3·50 25

B. ARAB KINGDOM.

Prior to the issues listed below, the Kingdom used stamps of Turkey variously overprinted. These are listed in Part 19 (Middle East) of the Stanley Gibbons Catalogue.

K 3 K 4

1920. As Type **K 3** and Type **K 4**.

K88 **K 3** 1m. brown (22 × 17 mm) 30 85
K89 $\frac{1}{10}$ p. green (27 × 21 mm) 75 55
K90 $\frac{3}{10}$ p. yellow (27 × 21 mm) 45 45
K91 **K 4** 5m. red 45 45
K92 **K 3** 1p. blue (27 × 21 mm) 45 25
K93 2p. green (27 × 21 mm) 2·40 95
K94 5p. purple (32 × 35 mm) 3·25 1·60
K95 10p. grey (32 × 35 mm) 3·25 2·30

For 1p. black as Type **K 3**, see Postage Due No. KD96.

1920. Independence Commemoration Optd with Arabic inscription.

K98 **K 4** 5m. red £375 £250

C. FRENCH MANDATED TERRITORY.

Issues for Lebanon and Syria.
Nos. 97/174 are all stamps of France surch.

1923. (a) Surch **Syrie Grand Liban** in two lines and value.

97 **11** 10c. on 2c. purple 25 60
98 **18** 25c. on 5c. orange 1·40 2·50
99 50c. on 10c. green 1·50 75
100 **15** 75c. on 15c. green 2·25 4·25
101 **18** 1p. on 20c. brown 2·75 1·50
102 1,25p. on 25c. blue 2·25 2·00
103 1,50p. on 30c. orange 1·50 3·00
104 1,50p. on 30c. red 1·30 4·00
105 **15** 2,50p. on 50c. blue 1·50 60

(b) Surch **Syrie-Grand Liban** in one line and value.

106 **13** 2p. on 40c. red and blue 2·25 55
107 3p. on 60c. violet and blue 3·50 4·75
108 5p. on 1f. red and yellow 4·25 5·25
109 10p. on 2f. orange & green 14·50 20·00
110 25p. on 5f. blue and buff 48·00 54·00

(c) "Pasteur" issue surch **Syrie Grand Liban** in two lines and value.

111 **30** 50c. on 10c. green 2·25 4·25
112 1,50p. on 30c. red 1·90 4·00
113 2,50p. on 50c. blue 1·20 4·25

1923. Air. Surch **Post par Avion Syrie-Grand Liban** and value.

114 **13** 2p. on 40c. red and blue 46·00 48·00
115 3p. on 60c. violet and blue 32·00 48·00
116 5p. on 1f. red and yellow 50·00 36·00
117 10p. on 2f. orange and green 44·00 48·00

Issues for Syria only.

1924. Surch **SYRIE** and value in two lines. (a) Stamps of 1900–20.

118 **11** 10c. on 2c. purple 1·20 80
119 **18** 25c. on 5c. orange 1·50 65
120 50c. on 10c. green 1·50 80
121 **15** 75c. on 15c. green 3·00 2·25
122 **18** 1p. on 20c. brown 2·00 15
123 1,25p. on 25c. blue 2·75 3·25
124 1,50p. on 30c. orange 3·50 4·50
125 1,50p. on 30c. red 2·50 3·75
127 **13** 2p. on 40c. red and blue 1·40 30
126 **15** 2,50p. on 50c. blue 2·00 80
128 **13** 3p. on 60c. violet and blue 2·75 3·25
129 5p. on 1f. red and yellow 4·50 4·25
130 10p. on 2f. orange and green 6·00 7·00
131 25p. on 5f. blue and yellow 8·75 12·00

(b) "Pasteur issue".

132 **30** 50c. on 10c. green 1·60 2·75
133 1,50p. on 30c. red 2·25 4·75
134 2.50p. on 50c. blue 2·25 3·25

1924. Air. Surch **Poste par Avion Syrie** and value.

135 **13** 2p. on 40c. red and blue 4·00 7·75
136 3p. on 60c. violet and blue 3·50 7·50
137 5p. on 1f. red and yellow 3·00 7·50
138 10p. on 2f. orange & green 2·75 7·75

1924. Olympic Games issue (Nos. 401/4) surch **SYRIE** and value.

139 **31** 50c. on 10c. green and light green 38·00 38·00
140 – 1.25p. on 25c. carmine and red 38·00 38·00
141 – 1.50p. on 30c. red & black 48·00 48·00
142 – 2.50p. on 50c. ultramarine and blue 48·00 48·00

1924. Surch **Syrie** and value in French and Arabic. (a) Issues of 1900–20.

143 **11** 0,p.10 on 2c. red 75 1·60
144 **18** 0,p.25 on 5c. orange 80 2·75
145 0,p.50 on 10c. green 85 4·00
146 **15** 0,p.75 on 15c. green 2·00 4·25
147 **18** 1p. on 20c. brown 1·60 10
148 1,p.25 on 25c. blue 2·75 4·00
149 1p.50 on 30c. red (no comma) 2·50 2·75
150 1,p.50 on 30c. orange 6·00 6·75
151 2p. on 35c. violet 2·50 4·50
152 **13** 2p. on 40c. red and blue 3·25 70
153 2p. on 45c. green and blue 6·75 10·50
154 3p. on 60c. violet and blue 3·00 2·00
155 **15** 3p. on 60c. violet 3·00 5·25
156 4p. on 85c. red 1·70 3·25
157 **13** 5p. on 1f. red and yellow 2·50 4·00
158 10p. on 2f. orange & green 4·25 6·50
159 25p. on 5f. blue and buff 4·50 6·50

(b) "Pasteur" issue.

160 **30** 0,p.50 on 10c. green 70 25
161 0p.75 on 15c. green 3·25 4·75
162 1,p.50 on 30c. red 2·30 4·00
163 2p. on 45c. red 2·75 4·75
164 2p.50 on 50c. blue 1·70 1·30
165 4p. on 75c. blue 2·75 5·00

(c) Olympic Games Issue (Nos. 401/4).

166 **31** 0,p.50 on 10c. green and light green 38·00 38·00
167 – 1p.25 on 25c. carmine and red 38·00 38·00
168 – 1p.50 on 30c. red & black 48·00 48·00
169 – 2p.50 on 50c. ultramarine and blue 48·00 48·00

(d) Ronsard stamp.

170 **35** 4p. on 75c. blue on blue 55 4·75

1924. Air. Surch **Syrie Avion** and new value in French and Arabic.

171 **13** 2p. on 40c. red and blue 3·00 8·75
172 3p. on 60c. violet and blue 4·25 13·50
173 5p. on 1f. red and yellow 2·50 10·50
174 10p. on 2f. orange & green 3·00 12·50

16 Hama

17 Merkab 18 Damascus

1925. Views.

175 **16** 0p.10 violet 10 85
176 **17** 0p.25 black 1·50 1·30
177 – 0p.50 green 65 20
178 – 0p.75 red 1·00 1·70
179 **18** 1p. purple 55 10
180 – 1p.25 green 3·00 3·00
181 – 1p.50 pink 35 35
182 – 2p. brown 2·75 35
183 – 2p.50 blue 2·30 2·25
184 – 3p. brown 1·20 10
185 – 5p. violet 1·00 10
186 – 10p. purple 4·25 1·00
187 – 25p. blue 4·00 5·25

DESIGNS—As Type **17**: 0p.50, Alexandretta; 0p.75, Hama; 1p.25, Latakia; 1p.50, Damascus; 2, 25p. Palmyra (different views); 2p.50, Kalat Yamoun; 3p. Bridge of Daphne; 5, 10p. Aleppo (different views).

1925. Air. Nos. 182 and 184/6 optd **AVION** in French and Arabic.

188 2p. brown 2·30 5·75
189 3p. brown 1·70 5·75
190 5p. violet 1·00 2·75
191 10p. purple 1·60 3·25

1926. Air. Nos. 182 and 184/6 optd with Bleriot XI airplane.

192 2p. brown 3·00 4·00
193 3p. brown 1·00 2·50
194 5p. violet 2·30 3·25
195 10p. purple 2·30 5·50

1926. War Refugees Fund. Nos. 176 etc and 192/5 surch **Secours aux Refugies Afft** and value in French and Arabic.

196 **17** 0p.25 on 0p.25 black (postage) 2·00 5·25
197 – 0p.25 on 0p.50 green 2·50 6·00
198 – 0p.25 on 0p.75 red 80 4·75
199 **18** 0p.50 on 1p. purple 1·80 4·75
200 – 0p.50 on 1p.25 green 2·75 6·25
201 – 0p.50 on 1p.50 pink 1·30 5·50
202 – 0p.75 on 2p. brown 2·50 6·50
203 – 0p.75 on 2p.50 blue 2·50 6·00
204 – 1p. on 3p. brown 1·60 5·25
205 – 1p. on 5p. violet 1·50 4·75
206 – 2p. on 10p. purple 1·60 5·50
207 – 5p. on 25p. blue 1·40 6·50
208 – 1p. on 2p. brown (air) 2·00 6·75
209 – 2p. on 3p. brown 1·50 6·75
210 – 3p. on 5p. violet 1·50 4·00
211 – 5p. on 10p. purple 1·50 6·00

1926. No. 175 etc surch with new value in English and Arabic.

221 05 on 0p.10 violet 10 75
222 1p. on 3p. brown 2·30 90
223 2p. on 1p.25 green 3·25 45
212 3p.50 on 0p.75 red 1·10 3·25
224 4p. on 0p.25 black 2·50 10
215 4p.50 on 0p.75 red 45 10
216 6p. on 2p.50 blue 1·00 1·50
217 7p.50 on 2p.50 blue 1·00 25
218 12p. on 1p.25 green 2·20 3·50
219 15p. on 25p. blue 1·20 10
220 20p. on 1p.25 green 2·75 4·25

1929. Air. Nos. 177 etc, optd with Bleriot XI airplane or surch also in English and Arabic.

225 0p.50 green 50 1·30
226 1p. purple 1·80 2·00
227 2p. on 1p.25 green 3·50 3·50
228 15p. on 25p. blue 3·25 6·00
229 25p. blue 6·00 6·25

1929. Damascus Industrial Exhibition. Nos. 177 etc and various air stamps optd **EXPOSITION INDUSTRIELLE DAMAS 1929** in French and Arabic.

230 0p.50 green (postage) 2·50 3·00
231 1p. purple 2·30 2·75
232 1p.50 pink 2·30 2·75
233 3p. brown 2·30 3·50
234 5p. violet 2·75 2·75
235 10p. purple 3·50 3·50
236 25p. blue 3·00 3·50
237 0p.50 green (No. 225) (air) 3·25 5·75
238 1p. purple (No. 226) 2·75 6·25
239 2p. brown (No. 192) 3·00 3·75
240 3p. brown (No. 193) 2·50 3·50
241 5p. violet (No. 194) 2·30 6·00
242 10p. purple (No. 195) 2·30 4·75
243 25p. blue (No. 229) 2·50 4·75

26 Hama 27 Damascus

1930. Views.

244 **26** 0p.10 mauve 60 3·50
244b 0p.10 purple 10 1·30
245 – 0p.20 blue 30 2·30
245a – 0p.20 red 50 2·25
246 – 0p.25 green 2·50 1·50
246a – 0p.25 violet 2·00 3·25
247 – 0p.50 violet 1·60 10
247a – 0p.75 red 1·60 85
248 – 1p. green 2·75 10
248a – 1p. brown 3·00 10
249 – 1p.50 brown 7·75 3·25
249a – 1p.50 green 10·50 3·50
250 – 2p. violet 3·25 10
251 – 3p. green 3·00 3·25
252 **27** 4p. orange 1·70 10
253 – 4p.50 red 2·75 40
254 – 6p. black 2·30 75
255 – 7p.50 blue 3·00 20
256 – 10p. brown 3·50 45
257 – 15p. green 4·50 85
258 – 25p. purple 2·50 1·80
259 – 50p. brown 50·00 34·00
260 – 100p. red 50·00 55·00

DESIGNS—As Type **26**: 0p.20, Aleppo; 0p.25, Hama (different). As Type **27**: 0p.50, Alexandretta; 0p.75, 4p.50, Homs; 1p., 7p.50, Aleppo (different); 1p.50, 100p. Damascus (different); 2, 10p. Antioch; 3p. Bosra; 5p. Sednaya; 15p. Hama; 25p. St. Simeon; 50p. Palmyra.

28 River Euphrates

1931. Air. Views with Potez 29-4 biplane.

261 – 0p.50 yellow (Homs) 1·30 1·30
261a – 0p.50 brown (Homs) 2·75 2·75
262 – 1p. brown (Damascus) 2·50 1·90
263 **28** 2p. blue 3·25 2·75
264 – 3p. green (Palmyra) 2·00 1·30
265 – 5p. purple (Deir-el-Zor) 1·50 1·20
266 – 10p. blue (Damascus) 1·90 85
267 – 15p. red (Aleppo citadel) 2·30 1·70
268 – 25p. orange (Hama) 4·00 2·75

269 – 50p. black (Zebdani) 5·00 4·75
270 – 100p. mauve (Telebisse) 5·75 3·75

D. REPUBLIC UNDER FRENCH MANDATE.

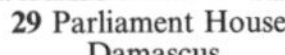

29 Parliament House, Damascus

30 Aboulula el Maari

31 Farman F.190 Airplane over Bloudan

1934. Establishment of Republic.
271 **29** 0p.10 green (postage) 2·00 1·80
272 0p.20 black 1·20 1·60
273 0p.25 red 1·90 1·60
274 0p.50 blue 1·80 2·00
275 0p.75 purple 2·00 1·90
276 **30** 1p. red 3·00 4·00
277 1p.50 green 4·75 4·75
278 2p. brown 5·00 5·00
279 3p. blue 54·00 10·50
280 4p. violet 6·75 5·00
281 4p.50 red 8·50 7·25
282 5p. blue 5·50 6·50
283 6p. brown 5·50 6·00
284 7p.50 blue 8·25 9·25
285 – 10p. brown 11·00 11·00
286 – 15p. blue 12·00 10·00
287 – 25p. red 28·00 36·00
288 – 50p. brown 52·00 56·00
289 – 100p. red 28·00 50·00
DESIGNS—As Type **30**: Nos. 285/7, President Mohammed Ali Bey el-Abed; 288/9, Sultan Saladin.

290 **31** 0p.50 brown (air) 3·00 3·50
291 1p. green 2·75 2·30
292 2p. blue 3·00 3·00
293 3p. red 3·25 5·50
294 5p. purple 5·50 5·75
295 10p. violet 38·00 38·00
296 15p. brown 38·00 30·00
297 25p. blue 55·00 44·00
298 50p. black 55·00 55·00
299 100p. brown 80·00 80·00

1936. Damascus Fair. Optd **1936 FOIRE DE DAMAS** in Arabic and French. (a) Postage stamps of 1930.
300 – 0p.50 violet 3·50 4·50
301 – 1p. brown 3·50 3·50
302 – 2p. violet 2·75 3·00
303 – 3p. green 2·50 2·75
304 **27** 4p. orange 3·50 5·25
305 – 4p.50 red 3·75 5·00
306 – 6p. green 2·75 3·75
307 – 7p. blue 3·00 4·00
308 – 10p. brown 4·50 4·50
(b) Air stamps of 1931.
309 – 0p.50 brown 3·75 7·00
310 – 1p. brown 2·75 2·75
311 **28** 2p. blue 3·25 4·75
312 – 3p. green 3·25 4·75
313 – 5p. purple 3·50 5·50

33 Exhibition Pavilion

1937. Air. Paris International Exhibition.
314 **33** ½p. green 1·70 2·00
315 1p. green 2·75 3·00
316 2p. brown 2·30 2·00
317 3p. red 2·00 2·75
318 5p. orange 3·50 3·00
319 10p. green 5·75 12·00
320 15p. blue 6·75 13·50
321 25p. violet 6·75 13·50

34 Savoia Marchetti S-73 over Aleppo

1937. Air.
322 **34** ½p. violet 10 45
323 – 1p. black 1·10 1·10
324 **34** 2p. green 1·70 1·50
325 – 3p. blue 1·50 1·70
326 **34** 5p. mauve 2·30 90
327 – 10p. brown 1·60 1·10
328 **34** 15p. brown 2·75 1·90
329 – 25p. blue 5·00 6·00
DESIGN: 1, 3, 10, 25p. Potez 62 airplane over Damascus.

1938. Stamps of 1930 surch in English and Arabic.
330 0p.25 on 0p.75 red 10 1·00
331 0p.50 on 1p.50 green 45 65
332 2p. on 7p.50 blue 85 55
333 2p.50 on 4p. orange 90 10
334 5p. on 7p.50 blue 1·40 30
335 10p. on 50p. brown 1·40 1·10
336 10p. on 100p. red 1·30 60

38 CAMS 53H Flying Boat, Maurice Nogues and Flight Route

1938. Air. 10th Anniv of 1st Air Service Flight between France and Syria.
337 **38** 10p. green 2·50 7·00
MS337a 160 × 120 mm. No. 337 in block of four 23·00 37·00

39 Pres. Atasi

41 Palmyra

1938. Unissued stamp surch **12.50** and in Arabic figures.
338 **39** 12p.50 on 10p. blue 2·30 15

1938.
339 **39** 10p. blue 2·50 85
339a 20p. brown 3·00 65

1940.
340 **41** 5p. pink 3·25 65

42 Damascus Museum

45 Deir-el-Zor Bridge

1940.
341 **42** 0p.10 red (postage) 10 65
342 0p.20 blue 10 75
343 0p.25 brown 10 1·30
344 0p.50 blue 10 10
345 – 1p. blue 15 20
346 – 1p.50 brown 35 1·20
347 – 2p.50 green 10 35
348 – 5p. violet 50 10
349 – 7p.50 red 35 45
350 – 50p. purple 3·25 5·25
DESIGNS—As Type **45**: 1p., 1p.50, 2p.50, Hotel de Bloudan; 5p., 7p.50, 50p. Kasr-el-Heir Fortress.

351 **45** 0p.25 black (air) 10 1·50
352 0p.50 blue 10 1·30
353 1p. blue 35 1·70
354 2p. brown 50 1·70
355 5p. green 95 1·80
356 10p. red 1·10 90
357 50p. violet 4·50 5·50

E. SYRIAN REPUBLIC.

46 President Taj Addin el-Husni

47 President Taj Addin el-Husni

1942. National Independence. Inscr "PROCLAMATION DE L'INDEPENDENCE 27 Septembre 1941".
358 **46** 0p.50 green (postage) 3·75 3·75
359 1p.50 brown 3·75 3·75
360 6p. red 3·75 3·75
361 15p. blue 3·75 3·75
362 – 10p. blue (air) 2·50 2·50
363 – 50p. purple 2·50 2·50
MS363a 205 × 138 mm. Nos. 358/63. Imperf £550
DESIGN: 10, 50p. As Type **46**, but President bareheaded and airplane inset.

1942. (a) Postage. Portrait in oval frame.
364 **47** 6p. purple and pink 2·50 2·50
365 15p. blue and light blue 2·50 2·50
(b) Air. Portrait in rectangular frame.
366 10p. green and emerald 4·25 4·25

48 Syria and late President's portrait

49 Pres. Shukri Bey al-Quwatli

1943. Union of Latakia and Jebel Druze with Syria. (a) President bare-headed.
367 **48** 1p. green (postage) 2·00 2·00
368 4p. brown 2·00 2·00
369 8p. violet 2·00 2·00
370 10p. orange 2·00 2·00
371 20p. blue 2·00 2·00
(b) President wearing turban.
372 2p. brown (air) 2·00 2·00
373 10p. purple 2·00 2·00
374 20p. blue 2·00 2·00
375 50p. pink 2·00 2·00

1943. Death of President Taj Addin el-Husni. Nos. 367/75 optd with narrow black border.
376 **48** 1p. green (postage) 2·00 2·00
377 4p. brown 2·00 2·00
378 8p. violet 2·00 2·00
379 10p. orange 2·00 2·00
380 20p. blue 2·00 2·00
381 – 2p. brown (air) 2·00 2·00
382 – 10p. purple 2·00 2·00
383 – 20p. blue 2·00 2·00
384 – 50p. pink 2·00 2·00

1944. Air.
385 **49** 200p. purple 6·00 6·00
386 500p. blue 10·50 10·50

(**50** Trans. "First Congress of Arab Lawyers, Damascus ")

(**51** Trans. "Aboulula-el-Maari. Commemoration of Millenary, 363–1363")

1944. Air. 1st Arab Lawyers' Congress. Optd with T **50**.
387 – 10p. brown (No. 327) 2·20 2·20
388 – 15p. red (No. 267) 2·20 2·20
389 – 25p. orange (No. 268) 2·20 2·20
390 – 100p. mauve (No. 270) 6·50 6·50
391 **49** 200p. purple 10·50 10·50

1945. Millenary of Aboulula-el-Maari (Arab poet and philosopher). Optd with T **51**.
392 – 2p.50 green (No. 347) (postage) 3·25 3·25
393 – 7p.50 red (No. 349) 3·25 3·25
394 – 15p. red (No. 267) (air) 2·20 2·20
395 – 25p. orange (No. 268) 2·20 2·20
396 **49** 500p. blue 22·00 22·00

52 Pres. Shukri Bey al-Quwatli

53 Pres. Shukri Bey al-Quwatli

1945. Resumption of Constitutional Govt.
397 **52** 4p. violet (postage) 35 35
398 6p. blue 35 35
399 10p. red 35 35
400 15p. brown 60 35
401 20p. green 70 50
402 40p. orange 1·30 1·00
403 **53** 5p. green (air) 35 35
404 10p. red 35 35
405 15p. orange 35 35
406 25p. blue 60 35
407 50p. violet 1·00 35
408 100p. brown 2·50 95
409 200p. red 8·75 3·75

(**54**)

(**55**)

1945. Fiscal stamps inscr "TIMBRE FISCAL". (a) Optd with T **54** (No. 411 surch also).
410 25p. brown 4·25 4·25
411 50p. on 75p. brown 4·00 4·00
412 75p. brown 4·75 4·75
413 100p. green 8·75 8·75

(b) Surch as T **55**.
414 12½p. on 15p. green 2·20 2·20
415 25p. on 25s. purple 2·50 2·50
(c) Optd or surch (416) with T **54** and with additional Arabic inscription at top.
416 50p. on 75p. brown 4·25 4·25
417 50p. mauve 2·20 2·20
418 100p. green 3·00 3·00

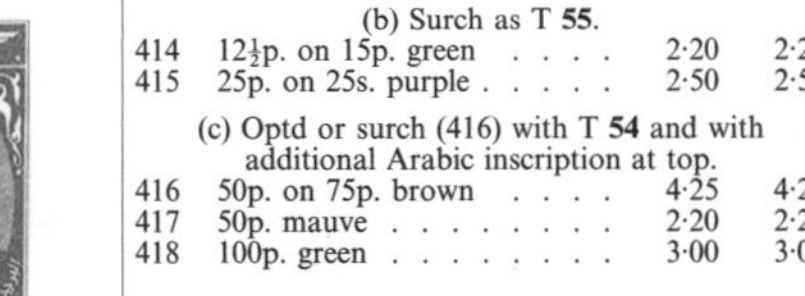

(**56**)

57 Ear of Wheat

58 Pres. Shukri Bey al-Quwatli

60 Arab Horse

1946. Fiscal stamp optd with T **56**.
419 200p. blue 21·00 13·00

1946.
420 **57** 0p.50 orange (postage) 15 10
421 1p. violet 60 15
422 2p.50 grey 70 15
423 5p. green 95 25
424 **58** 7p.50 brown 25 10
425 10p. blue 25 15
426 12p.50 violet 1·10 15
427 – 15p. red 45 15
428 – 20p. violet 70 45
429 – 25p. blue 1·10 45
430 **60** 50p. brown 5·75 95
431 100p. green 12·00 2·20
432a 200p. purple 65·00 6·00
DESIGN—As Type **58**: 15, 20, 25p. Pres. Shukri Bey al-Quwatli bareheaded.

433 – 3p. red (air) 60 15
434 – 5p. green 60 15
435 – 6p. orange 60 15
436 – 10p. grey 45 15
437 – 15p. red 45 15
438 – 25p. blue 50 25
439 – 50p. violet 85 25
440 – 100p. blue 2·00 45
441 – 200p. brown 4·25 1·30
442 – 300p. brown 16·00 2·50
443 – 500p. green 17·00 4·00
DESIGNS—HORIZ: 3, 5, 6p. Flock of sheep; 10, 15, 25p. Kattineh Dam; 50, 100, 200p. Temple ruins, Kanaouat; 300, 500p. Sultan Ibrahim Mosque.

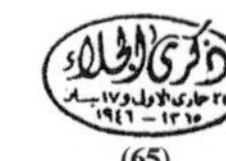

(**65**)

1946. Evacuation of Foreign Troops from Syria. Optd with T **65**.
444 **58** 10p. blue (postage) 60 60
445 12p.50 violet 85 85
446 **60** 50p. brown 2·30 2·30
447 – 25p. blue (No. 438) (air) 2·20 1·30

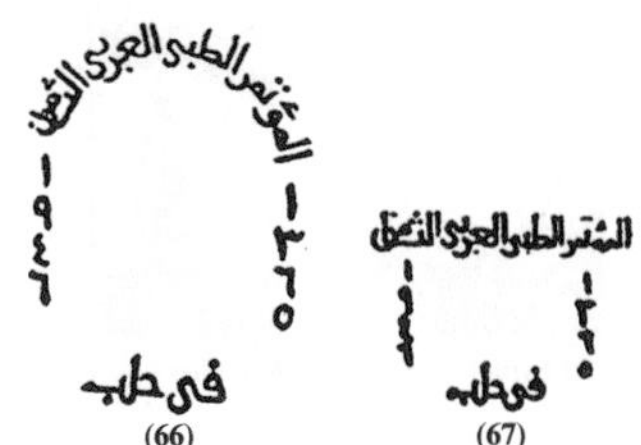

(**66**)

(**67**)

1946. 8th Arab Medical Congress, Aleppo. (a) Postage. Optd with T **66**.
448 25p. blue (No. 429) 1·70 1·50
(b) Air. Optd with T **67**.
449 25p. blue (No. 438) 2·20 1·30
450 50p. violet (No. 439) 2·75 1·70
451 100p. blue (No. 440) 5·25 3·00

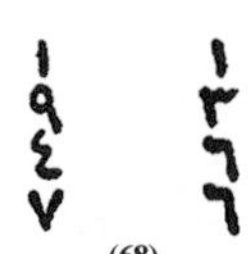

(**68**)

1947. 1st Anniv of Evacuation of Allied Forces. Nos. 444/7 optd as T **68** (= "1947 1366").
452 **58** 10p. blue (postage) 60 15
453 12p.50 violet 85 25
454 **60** 50p. brown 2·30 85
455 – 25p. blue (air) 2·20 1·30

69 Hercules and Lion **70** Mosaic of the Mosque of the Omayades

1947. 1st Arab Archaeological Congress, Damascus.
456 **69** 12p.50 green (postage) . . 85 70
457 **70** 25p. blue . . . . 1·70 1·10
458 – 12p.50 violet (air) . . . . 1·30 70
459 – 50p. brown . . . . 4·25 2·00
MS459a 138 × 188 mm. Nos. 456/9 50·00 50·00
DESIGNS—As T **70**: 12p.50, Window at Kasr El-Heir El-Gharbi; 50p. King Hazael's throne.

71 Courtyard of Azem Palace **72** Congress Symbol

1947. 3rd Arab Engineers' Congress, Damascus. Inscr "3e CONGRES DES INGENIEURS ARABES 1947".
460 **71** 12p.50 purple (postage) . . 70 70
461 – 25p. blue . . . . 1·30 85
462 – 12p.50 green (air) 85 70
463 **72** 50p. violet . . . . 4·00 2·50
MS463a 138 × 188 mm. Nos. 460/3 48·00 48·00
DESIGNS—HORIZ: No. 461, Telephone Exchange Building; 462, Fortress at Kasr El-Heir El-Charqui.

73 Parliament Building **74** Pres. Shukri Bey al-Quwatli

1948. Re-election of Pres. Shukri Bey al-Quwatli.
464 **73** 12p.50 brown and grey (postage) 70 25
465 **74** 25p. mauve . . . . 1·00 70
466 **73** 12p.50 blue and violet (air) 70 35
467 **74** 50p. purple and green . . . 2·75 1·30
MS467a 139 × 186 mm. Nos. 464/7. Imperf £190 £190

75 Syrian Arms **76** Soldier and Flag

1948. Compulsory Military Service.
468 **75** 12p.50 brown and grey (postage) 45 20
469 **76** 25p. multicoloured 85 35
470 **75** 12p.50 blue and light blue (air) 85 45
471 **76** 50p. green, red and black 3·75 1·00
MS471a 137 × 190 mm. Nos. 468/71. Imperf £170 £170

1948. Surch. (a) Postage.
472 – 0p.50 on 0p.75 red (No. 247a) 25 10
472ab **60** 2p.50 on 200p. purple 45 25
472b 10p. on 100p. green . . 60 25
473 25p. on 200p. purple . . 4·25 50

(b) Air.
474 – 2p.50 on 3p. (No. 433) . . 10 10
475 – 2p.50 on 6p. (No. 435) . . 10 10
475a – 2p.50 on 100p. (No. 440) 10 10
476 – 25p. on 200p. (No. 441) . . 50 15
477 – 50p. on 300p. (No. 442) . . 13·00 65
478 – 50p. on 500p. (No. 443) . . 13·00 65

78 Palmyra **79** President Husni el-Zaim and Lockheed Super Constellation over Damascus

1949. 75th Anniv of U.P.U.
479 – 12p.50 violet (postage) . . 2·30 2·30
480 **78** 25p. blue . . . . 4·00 4·00
481 – 12p.50 purple (air) . . . . 8·75 8·75
482 **79** 50p. black . . . . 23·00 16·00
DESIGNS—HORIZ: No. 479, Ain-el-Arous; 481, Globe and mountains.

80 President Husni el-Zaim **81** Pres. Husni el-Zaim and Map

1949. Revolution of 30 March 1949.
483 **80** 25p. blue (postage) . . . . 1·00 70
484 50p. brown (air) . . . . . 4·25 3·00

1949. Presidential Election.
485 **81** 25p. brown & bl (postage) 3·75 2·30
486 50p. green and pink (air) 4·25 3·00
MS486a 125 × 188 mm. Nos. 485/6. Imperf £225 £225

82 Tel-Chehab **83** Damascus

1949.
487 **82** 5p. grey 45 10
488 7p.50 brown 60 15
524 7p.50 green 45 15
489 **83** 12p.50 purple 80 15
490 25p. blue . . . . 1·50 45

84 Syrian Arms **85** G.P.O., Damascus

1950.
491 **84** 0p.50 brown 15 10
492 2p.50 pink 15 15
493 – 10p. violet 45 25
494 – 12p.50 green 85 45
495 **85** 25p. blue . . . . 1·50 25
496 50p. black . . . . 4·75 85
DESIGN—HORIZ: 10, 12p.50, Abous–Damascus road.

86 Port of Latakia

1950. Air.
497 **86** 2p.50 violet 60 15
526 10p. blue . . . . 1·30 15
499 15p. brown . . . . 3·00 25
500 25p. blue . . . . 6·50 45

87 Parliament Building

88 Book and Torch

1951. New Constitution, 1950.
501 **87** 12p.50 black (postage) . . 25 25
502 25p. blue 55 35
503 **88** 12p.50 red (air) 30 15
504 50p. purple . . . . 1·10 65

89 Hama

1952.
505 **89** 0p.50 brown (postage) . . 10 10
506 2p.50 blue 25 10
507 5p. green 25 10
508 10p. red 25 15
509 – 12p.50 black 80 15
510 – 15p. purple . . . . 4·75 25
511 – 25p. blue . . . . 2·30 45
512 – 100p. brown . . . . 8·75 2·30
513 – 2p.50 red (air) 20 10
514 – 5p. green 45 10
515 – 15p. violet 65 15
516 – 25p. blue 85 45
517 – 100p. purple . . . . 6·50 1·00
DESIGNS—Postage: 12p.50 to 100p. Palace of Justice, Damascus. Air: 2p.50 to 15p. Palmyra; 25, 100p. Citadel, Aleppo.

1952. Air. United Nations Social Welfare Seminar, Damascus. Optd **U. N. S. W. S. Damascus 8-20 Dec. 1952** and curved line of Arabic.
518 **86** 10p. blue . . . . 2·30 1·30
519 – 15p. violet (No. 515) . . . 2·30 1·30
520 – 25p. blue (No. 516) . . . . 4·00 1·90
521 – 50p. violet (No. 439) . . . 9·50 2·75

91 Qalaat el Hasn Fortress **92** "Labour"

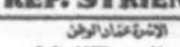

93 "Family" **94** "Communications"

1953.
522 **91** 0p.50 red (postage) 15 10
523 – 2p.50 brown 25 10
525 **91** 12p.50 blue 45 15
527 – 50p. brown (air) . . . . . 2·10 15
DESIGNS: 2p,50, Qalaat el Hasn fortress (different); 50p. G.P.O., Aleppo.

1954.
528 **92** 1p. green (postage) 15 10
529 2½p. red 15 10
530 5p. blue 25 10
531 **93** 7½p. red 35 10
532 10p. black 45 15
533 12½p. violet 45 15
534 – 20p. purple 85 15
535 – 25p. violet . . . . 1·70 60
536 – 50p. green . . . . 4·25 1·00
537 **94** 5p. violet (air) 15 15
538 10p. brown 25 15
539 15p. green 35 15
540 – 30p. brown 45 25
541 – 35p. blue 85 25
542 – 40p. orange . . . . 1·90 45
543 – 50p. purple . . . . 1·50 85
544 – 70p. violet . . . . 4·00 85
DESIGNS—As Type **93**. Postage: 20 to 50p. "Industry". Air: 30 to 70p. Syrian University.

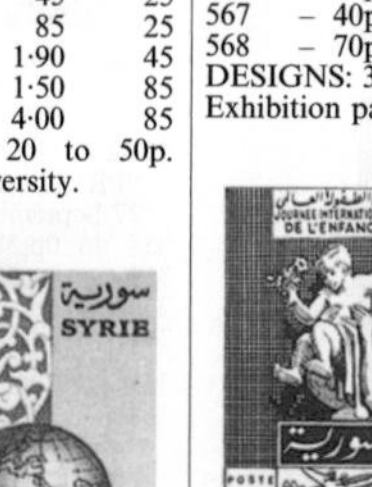

95 Monument to Hejaz Railway **96a**

1954. Air. Damascus Fair. Inscr as in T **95**.
545 **95** 40p. mauve . . . . 1·10 60
546 – 50p. green . . . . 1·50 70
DESIGN—VERT: 50p. Mosque and Syrian flag.

1954. Cotton Festival, Aleppo. Optd **FESTIVAL du COTON. Alep. oct. 1954** and Arab inscription.
547 **93** 10p. black (postage) . . . 80 35
548 – 25p. violet (No. 535) . . . 85 45
549 – 50p. brown (No. 527) (air) 85 55
550 – 100p. purple (No. 517) . . 2·00 1·40

1955. Arab Postal Union.
551 **96a** 12½p. green (postage) . . 60 25
552 25p. violet . . . . 1·10 45
553 5p. brown (air) 35 25

97 **98**

1955. Air. Middle East Rotary Congress.
554 **97** 35p. red . . . . 1·00 70
555 65p. green . . . . 2·20 1·30

1955. Air. 50th Anniv of Rotary International.
556 **98** 25p. violet 70 50
557 75p. blue . . . . 2·30 1·50

99 "Facing the Future" **100** Mother and Child

1955. Air. 9th Anniv of Evacuation of Foreign Troops from Syria.
558 **99** 40p. mauve 60 60
559 – 60p. blue . . . . 1·00 70
DESIGN: 60p. Tank and infantry attack.
See also Nos. 847/9.

1955. Mothers' Day.
560 **100** 25p. red (postage) 60 45
561 35p. violet (air) . . . . . 1·10 85
562 40p. black . . . . 1·70 1·30

101 Lockheed Super Constellation Airliner, Flag and Crowd **102** Syrian Pavilion

1955. Air. Emigrants' Congress.
563 **101** 5p. mauve 60 25
564 – 15p. blue 80 45
DESIGN: 15p. Lockheed Super Constellation over globe.

1955. Air. International Fair, Damascus.
565 **102** 25p.+5p. black 60 60
566 – 35p.+5p. blue 85 85
567 – 40p.+10p. purple . . . . 1·10 1·10
568 – 70p.+10p. green . . . . . 1·70 1·70
DESIGNS: 35, 40p. "Industry and Agriculture"; 70p. Exhibition pavilions and flags.

103 Mother and Baby **104** U.N. Emblem and Torch

1955. Air. International Children's Day.
569 **103** 25p. blue 80 45
570 50p. purple . . . . 1·50 60

1955. 10th Anniv of U.N.O.

571 **104** 7½p. red (postage) 60 45

572 12½p. green . . . . 1·10 65

573 – 15p. blue (air) 85 45

574 – 35p. brown . . . . 1·70 65

DESIGN: 15, 35p. Globe, dove and Scales of Justice.

105 Saracen Gate, Aleppo Citadel

(**106**)

1955. Installation of Aleppo Water Supply from River Euphrates.

575 **105** 7p.50 violet (postage) . . 35 10

576 12p.50 red 50 15

577 30p. blue (air) . . . . . 2·30 1·30

1955. 2nd Arab Postal Union Congress, Cairo. Nos. 551/3 optd with T **106**.

578 12½p. green (postage) 45 35

579 25p. violet . . . . 1·50 60

580 5p. brown (air) 60 15

(**107**) **108** Monument

1956. Visit of King Hussein of Jordan. Nos. 551/3 optd with T **107**.

581 12½p. green (postage) 60 25

582 25p. violet 70 45

583 5p. brown (air) . . . . . . 1·50 60

1956. Air. 10th Anniv of Evacuation of Foreign Troops from Syria.

584 **108** 35p. sepia 70 50

585 – 65p. red . . . . 1·10 70

586 – 75p. grey . . . . 2·20 1·10

DESIGNS: 65p. Winged female figure; 75p. Pres. Shukri Bey al-Quwatli.

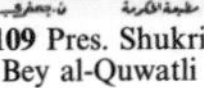

109 Pres. Shukri Bey al-Quwatli **110** Cotton

1956. Air.

587 **109** 100p. black . . . . 1·50 1·10

588 200p. violet . . . . . . 3·00 1·50

589 300p. red . . . . 4·25 3·50

590 500p. green . . . . 8·75 6·50

MS590a 139 × 100 mm. Nos. 587/90. Imperf. Without gum . . . . 75·00 75·00

1956. Aleppo Cotton Festival.

591 **110** 2½p. green 60 60

1956. Air. Nos. 565/8 with premiums obliterated by bars.

592 **102** 25p. black 60 25

593 – 35p. blue 70 45

594 – 40p. purple . . . . 1·50 60

595 – 70p. green . . . . 1·70 1·30

111 Gate of Kasr al-Heir, Palmyra **112** Clay Alphabetical Tablet

1956. Air. 3rd International Fair, Damascus.

596 **111** 15p. brown 60 60

597 – 20p. blue 70 70

598 – 30p. green 95 95

599 – 35p. blue . . . . 1·00 1·00

600 – 50p. purple . . . . 1·30 1·30

MS600a 101 × 136 mm. Nos. 596/600. Imperf. Without gum . . . . 60·00 60·00

DESIGNS: 20p. Cotton mill; 30p. Tractor; 35p. Phoenician galley and cogwheels; 50p. Textiles, carpets and pottery.

1956. Air. International Campaign for Museums.

601 **112** 20p. black . . . . 1·00 60

602 – 30p. red . . . . 1·10 60

603 – 50p. brown . . . . 2·20 1·10

MS603a 139 × 100 mm. Nos. 601/3. Imperf. Without gum . . . . 60·00 60·00

DESIGNS—VERT: 30p. Syrian legionary's helmet. HORIZ: 50p. Lintel of Belshamine Temple, Palmyra.

1956. 11th Anniv of U.N.O. Nos. 571/4 optd **11eme ANNIVERSAIRE de L'ONU** in French and Arabic.

604 **104** 7½p. red (postage) 70 45

605 – 12½p. green 85 60

606 – 15p. blue (air) . . . . . 1·50 70

607 – 35p. brown . . . . 2·75 1·70

114 Oaks and Mosque

1956. Air. Afforestation Day.

608 **114** 10p. brown 45 25

609 40p. green . . . . 1·00 60

115 Azem Palace, Damascus

1957.

610 **115** 12½p. purple 45 15

611 15p. black 60 15

116 "Resistance" **118** Mother and Child

1957. Syrian Defence Force.

612 **116** 5p. mauve 35 15

613 20p. green 60 45

1957. Evacuation of Port Said. Optd **22.12.56 EVACUATION PORT SAID** in French and Arabic.

614 **116** 5p. mauve 35 15

615 20p. green 60 45

1957. Air. Mothers' Day.

616 – 40p. blue 85 80

617 **118** 60p. red . . . . 1·50 1·00

DESIGN: 40p. Mother fondling child.

119 "Sword of Liberty" **120** Freighter "Latakia" and Fair Emblem

1957. Air. 11th Anniv of Evacuation of Foreign Troops from Syria.

618 **119** 10p. brown 15 15

619 – 15p. green 45 25

620 – 25p. violet 60 35

621 – 35p. mauve 85 60

622 **119** 40p. black . . . . 1·40 85

DESIGNS: 15, 35p. Map and woman holding torch; 25p. Pres. Shukri Bey al-Quwatli.

1957. Air. 4th Damascus Fair.

623 **120** 25p. mauve 50 35

624 – 30p. brown 60 45

625 – 35p. blue 85 60

626 – 40p. green . . . . 1·20 70

627 **120** 70p. green . . . . 1·50 1·00

DESIGNS—VERT: 30, 40p. Girls harvesting and cotton picking. HORIZ: 35p. Interior of processing plant.

121 "Cotton" **122** Children at Work and Play

1957. Aleppo Cotton Festival.

628 **121** 12½p. black & grn (postage) 60 25

629 17½p. black & orange (air) 70 45

630 40p. black and blue . . . 1·50 60

1957. International Children's Day.

631 **122** 12½p. green (postage) . . 70 25

632 17½ blue (air) . . . . . . 1·50 60

633 20p. brown . . . . 1·50 60

123 Letter and Post-box

1957. International Correspondence Week.

634 **123** 5p. mauve (postage) . . . 60 30

635 – 5p. green (air) 60 20

DESIGN: 5p. (air) Family writing letters.

(**124**) **125** Scales of Justice, Map and Damascus Silhouette

1957. National Defence Week. Optd with T **124**.

636 **116** 5p. mauve 15 15

637 20p. green 60 25

1957. 3rd Arab Lawyers Union Congress, Damascus.

638 **125** 12½p. green (postage) . . 45 25

639 17½p. red (air) 50 35

640 40p. black . . . . 1·00 60

126 Glider

1957. Air. Gliding Festival.

641 **126** 25p. brown . . . . 1·30 25

642 35p. green . . . . 1·70 45

643 40p. blue . . . . 2·50 85

127 Torch and Map **128** Khaled Ibn el- Walid Mosque, Homs

1957. Afro-Asian Jurists' Congress, Damascus.

644 **127** 20p. brown (postage) . . 60 35

645 30p. green (air) 60 45

646 50p. violet 85 60

1957.

647 **128** 2½p. brown 15 15

UNITED ARAB REPUBLIC

129 Telecommunications Building

1958. Five Year Plan.

648 **129** 25p. blue (postage) . . . 45 25

649 10p. green (air) 45 15

650 – 15p. brown 45 25

DESIGN—VERT: 15p. Telephone, radio tower and telegraph pole.

129a Union of Egypt and Syria

1958. Birth of United Arab Republic.

651 **129a** 12½p. green and yellow (postage) 25 15

652 17½p. brown & blue (air) 35 25

130 "Eternal Flame"

1958. 12th Anniv of Evacuation of Foreign Troops from Syria.

653 **130** 5p. violet & yellow (postage) 60 25

654 15p. red and green . . . 85 60

655 – 35p. black and red (air) 1·50 60

656 – 45p. brown and blue . . . 2·30 85

DESIGN: 35, 45p. Broken chain, dove and olive branch.

131 Scout fixing Tent-peg

1958. Air. 3rd Pan-Arab Scout Jamboree.

657 **131** 35p. brown . . . . 2·50 2·50

658 40p. blue . . . . 3·25 3·25

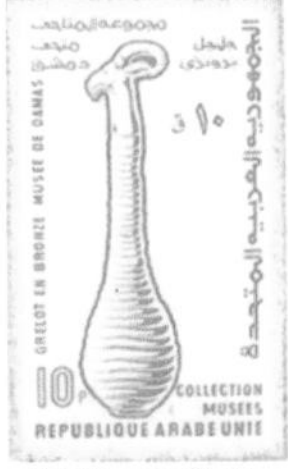

132 Mosque, Chimneys and Cogwheel **133** Bronze Rattle

1958. Air. 5th Int Fair, Damascus. Inscr "1.9.58".

659 – 25p. red 95 70

660 – 30p. green . . . . 1·50 1·00

661 **132** 45p. violet . . . . 1·70 1·30

MS661a 80 × 80 mm. 100p. black, red and green showing UAR flag and Fair Emblem. Imperf . . . £130 £130

DESIGNS—HORIZ: 25p. View of Fair. VERT: 30p. Minaret, vase and emblem.

1958. Ancient Syrian Art.

662 **133** 10p. green 15 15

663 – 15p. brown 25 15

664 – 20p. purple 35 15

665 – 30p. brown 45 15

666 – 40p. grey 50 25

667 – 60p. green 85 45

668 – 75p. blue . . . . 1·30 60

669 – 100p. purple . . . . . . 1·90 1·00

670 – 150p. purple . . . . . . 4·00 1·30

DESIGNS: 15p. Goddess of Spring; 20p. "Lamgi Mari" (statue); 30p. Mithras fighting bull; 40p. Aspasia; 60p. Minerva; 75p. Ancient gourd; 100p. Enamelled vase; 150p. Mosaic from Omayyad Mosque, Damascus.

1958. International Children's Day. Optd **R A U** and Arabic inscription.

670a **122** 12½p. green (postage) . . 65·00 65·00

670b 17½p. blue (air) . . . . 48·00 48·00

670c 20p. brown . . . . . . 48·00 48·00

134 Cotton and Textiles **134a** Hand holding Torch, and Iraqi Flag

1958. Air. Aleppo Cotton Festival.
671 **134** 25p. yellow and brown . . 85 85
672 35p. red and brown . . . 1·30 1·00

1958. Republic of Iraq Commemoration.
673 **134a** 12½p. red 35 25

135 Light Airplane and Children with Model Airplane **137** U.N. Emblem and Charter

136 Damascus

1958. Air. Gliding Festival.
674 **135** 7½p. green . . . . 1·00 60
675 12½p. green . . . . 3·50 2·00

1958. 4th N.E. Regional Conference, Damascus.
676 **136** 12½p. green (postage) . . 50 25
677 17½p. violet (air) 50 45

1958. Air. 10th Anniv of Declaration of Human Rights.
678 **137** 25p. purple 45 35
679 35p. grey 60 45
680 40p. brown 85 60

137a U.A.R. Postal Emblem **137b**

1959. Post Day and Postal Employees' Social Fund.
681 **137a** 20p.+10p. red, black and green 85 85

1959. 1st Anniv of United Arab Republic.
682 **137b** 12½p. red, black and green 20 15

138 Secondary School, Damascus

1959.
683 **138** 12½p. green 25 10

138a "Telecommunications"

1959. Air. Arab Telecommunications Union Commemoration.
684 **138a** 40p. black and green . . 85 50

1959. Second Damascus Conference. No. 684 optd **2nd CONFERANCE DAMASCUS 1-3-1959** in English and Arabic.
685 **138a** 40p. black and green . . 80 50

139a U.A.R. and Yemeni Flags

1959. 1st Anniv of Proclamation of United Arab States (U.A.R. and Yemen).
686 **139a** 12½p. red and green . . 35 25

140 Mother with Children **142**

1959. Arab Mothers' Day.
687 **140** 15p. red 35 25
688 25p. green 50 35

1959. Surch **U.A.R 2½p** and also in Arabic.
689 **92** 2½p. on 1p. green 15 15

1959. Air. 13th Anniv of Evacuation of Foreign Troops from Syria.
690 **142** 15p. green and yellow . . 25 15
691 – 35p. red and grey 60 35
DESIGN: 35p. Broken chain and flame.

143 **144** "Emigration"

1959. Patterns as T **143**.
692 **143** 2½p. violet 10 10
693 – 5p. brown 15 10
694 – 7½p. blue 15 10
695 – 10p. green 20 10
DESIGNS: 5 to 10p. Different styles of ornamental scrollwork.

1959. Air. Emigrants' Congress.
696 **144** 80p. black, red and green 1·30 85

(145) **147**

146 Oil Refinery

1959. Optd as T **145**.
697 **115** 15p. black (postage) . . . 15 15
698 – 50p. green (No. 536) . . . 50 25
690 – 5p. green (No. 635) (air) 15 15
700 – 50p. purple (No. 543) . . 70 35
701 – 70p. violet (No. 544) . . . 1·10 45

1959. Air. Inauguration of Oil Refinery.
702 **146** 50p. red, black and blue 1·70 70

1959. 6th Damascus Fair.
703 **147** 35p. green, violet and grey 85 50
MS703a 80×80 mm. 30p. yellow and green showing Fair Emblem and Globe . . . . 2·20 2·20

148 **149** Child and Factory

1959. Air. Aleppo Cotton Festival.
704 **148** 45p. blue 70 45
705 50p. purple 70 60

1959. Air. Children's Day.
706 **149** 25p. red, blue and lilac . . 50 25

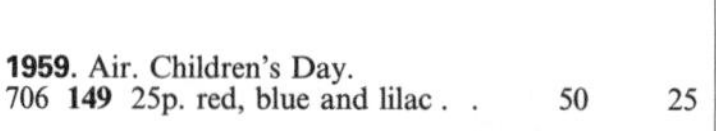

150 Boys' College, Damascus **150a** "Shield against Aggression"

1959.
707 **150** 25p. blue 60 25
708 – 35p. brown 80 35
DESIGN: 35p. Girls' College, Damascus.

1959. Army Day.
709 **150a** 50p. brown 85 45

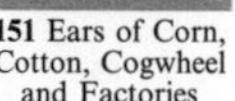

151 Ears of Corn, Cotton, Cogwheel and Factories **152** Mosque and Oaks

1959. Industrial and Agricultural Production Fair, Aleppo.
710 **151** 35p. brown, blue and grey 85 45

1959. Tree Day.
711 **152** 12½p. brown and green . . 25 15

153 A. R. Kawakbi **153a**

1960. 50th Death Anniv of A. R. Kawakbi (writer).
712 **153** 15p. green 35 25

1960. 2nd Anniv of U.A.R.
713 **153a** 12½p. green and red . . 35 25

154 Diesel Train

1960. Latakia–Aleppo Railway Project.
714 **154** 12½p. brown, black & blue . . . . 1·90 85

154a Arab League Centre, Cairo

1960. Inaug of Arab League Centre, Cairo.
715 **154a** 12½p. black and green 35 25

1960. Mothers' Day. Optd **ARAB MOTHERS DAY 1960** in English and Arabic.
716 **140** 15p. red 35 25
717 25p. green 60 35

155a Mother, Child and Map of Palestine

1960. World Refugee Year.
718 **155a** 12½p. red 35 25
719 50p. green 85 60

156 Government Building and Inscription

1960. 14th Anniv of Evacuation of Foreign Troops from Syria.
720 **156** 12½p. multicoloured . . . 50 15

157 Hittin School

1960.
721 **157** 17½p. lilac 50 20

1960. Industrial and Agricultural Production Fair, Aleppo. Optd **1960** and in Arabic.
722 **151** 35p. brown, blue and grey 50 45

159 Mobile Crane and Compasses **(160)**

1960. Air. 7th International Damascus Fair.
723 **159** 50p. black, bistre and red 85 60
MS723a 70×160 mm. 100p. green, blue and brown (Fair emblem containing flags of all nations). Imperf . . . . 3·00 3·00

1960. Air. Aleppo Cotton Festival. Optd with T **160**.
724 **148** 45p. blue 70 45
725 50p. purple 85 60

161 **162** Basketball

1960. Children's Day.
726 **161** 35p. brown and green . . 85 50

1960. Air. Olympic Games.

727 **162** 15p. brown, black and blue 50 15

728 – 20p. brown, black and blue 60 25

729 – 25p. multicoloured . . . 60 25

730 – 40p. violet, pink and black . . . . 1·20 70

DESIGNS: 20p. Swimming; 25p. Fencing (Arab-style); 40p. Horse-jumping.

(163)

164 "UN" and Globe

1960. Tree Day. Optd with T **163**.

731 **152** 12½p. brown and green . . 50 25

1960. Air. 15th Anniv of U.N.O.

732 **164** 35p. red, green and blue 60 35

733 50p. blue, brown and red 85 50

165 Hanano

165a State Emblem

1961. Air. 25th Death Anniv (1960) of Ibrahim Hanano (patriot).

734 **165** 50p. green and brown . . 85 50

1961. 3rd Anniv of U.A.R.

735 **165a** 12½p. violet 35 25

166 St. Simeon's Monastery

167 Raising the Flag

1961.

736 **166** 12½p. blue (postage) . . . 25 15

746 – 200p. blue (air) . . . . . 3·00 1·90

DESIGN—VERT: 200p. Entrance to St. Simeon's Monastery.

1961. Air. 15th Anniv of Evacuation of Foreign Troops from Syria.

737 **167** 40p. green 85 50

168 Eye and Hand "reading" Braille

169 Palestinian and Map

1961. Air. U.N. Campaign for Welfare of Blind.

738 **168** 40p.+10p. black & grn . . 70 60

1961. Air. Palestine Day.

739 **169** 50p. blue and black . . . 85 50

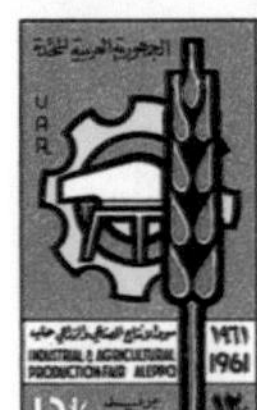

170 Cogwheel and Corn

171 Abou Tammam (796–846)

1961. Industrial and Agricultural Production Fair, Aleppo.

740 **170** 12½p. multicoloured . . . 35 25

1961. Air. Abou Tammam (writer) Commem.

741 **171** 50p. brown 55 25

172 Damascus University, Discus-thrower and Lyre

1961. Air. 5th Universities Youth Festival.

742 **172** 15p. black and red . . . 35 15

743 35p. violet and green . . 1·10 45

MS743a 100 × 63 mm. Nos. 742/3. Imperf . . . . 4·25 4·25

173 Open Window on World

1961. Air. 8th International Damascus Fair.

744 **173** 17½p. violet and green . . 25 15

745 – 50p. violet and black . . 60 35

DESIGN: 50p. U.A.R. Pavilion.

SYRIAN ARAB REPUBLIC

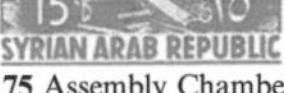

175 Assembly Chamber

176 The Noria, Hama

177 Arch of Triumph, Latakia

178 Arab League Emblem and Headquarters, Cairo

1961. Establishment of Syrian Arab Republic.

747 **175** 15p. red 35 35

748 35p. green 85 45

MS748a 80 × 80 mm. 50p. red, green, black and blue (Syrian flag). Imperf . . . . 3·25 3·25

1961.

749 **176** 2½p. red (postage) . . . 15 15

750 5p. blue 15 15

751 – 7½p. green 30 15

752 – 10p. orange 45 15

753 **177** 12½p. brown 70 10

754 – 12½p. green 50 10

755 – 15p. blue 50 10

756 – 17½p. brown 70 15

757 – 22½p. turquoise 70 15

758 **177** 25p. brown 95 15

759 – 45p. yellow (air) 50 35

760 – 50p. red 70 45

761 – 85p. purple . . . . . . 1·20 50

762 – 100p. purple . . . . . 1·60 60

763 – 200p. green . . . . . . 2·75 1·10

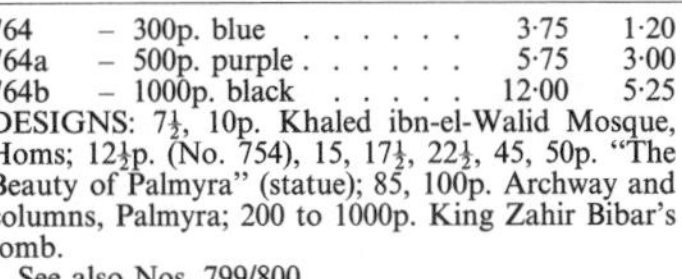

764 – 300p. blue . . . . . . 3·75 1·20

764a – 500p. purple . . . . . 5·75 3·00

764b – 1000p. black . . . . . 12·00 5·25

DESIGNS: 7½, 10p. Khaled ibn-el-Walid Mosque, Homs; 12½p. (No. 754), 15, 17½, 22½, 45, 50p. "The Beauty of Palmyra" (statue); 85, 100p. Archway and columns, Palmyra; 200 to 1000p. King Zahir Bibar's tomb.

See also Nos. 799/800.

1962. Air. Arab League Week.

765 **178** 17½p. turquoise and green 25 15

766 22½p. violet and blue . . 35 35

767 50p. brown and orange 95 60

179 Campaign Emblem

180 Prancing Horse

1962. Air. Malaria Eradication.

768 **179** 12½p. violet, brown & blue 35 25

769 50p. green, brown & yell 85 60

1962. Air. 16th Anniv of Evacuation of Foreign Troops from Syria.

770 **180** 45p. orange and violet . . 50 25

771 – 55p. violet and blue . . . 85 35

DESIGN: 55p. Military commander.

181 Qalb Lozah Church

1962.

772 **181** 17½p. green 45 15

773 35p. green 70 25

182 Martyrs' Memorial, Swaida

183 Jupiter Temple Gate

1962. Syrian Revolution Commemoration.

774 **182** 12½p. brown and drab . . 25 10

775 35p. green and turquoise 60 25

1962.

776 **183** 2½p. turquoise 15 10

777 5p. brown 25 10

778 7½p. brown 35 15

779 10p. purple 25 15

184 Globe, Monument to Hejaz Railway and Handclasp

1962. Air. 9th International Fair, Damascus.

780 **184** 17½p. brown and purple 25 15

781 22½p. mauve and red . . 35 25

782 – 40p. purple and brown . . 45 35

783 – 45p. blue and green . . 85 45

DESIGN: 40, 45p. Fair entrance.

185 Festival Emblem

186 Pres. Kudsi

1962. Air. Aleppo Cotton Festival.

784 **185** 12½p. multicoloured . . . 35 20

785 50p. multicoloured . . . 70 70

See also Nos. 820/1.

1962. Presidential Elections.

786 **186** 12½p. brown and blue (postage) 35 10

787 50p. blue and buff (air) 70 45

187 Zenobia

188 Saadallah el-Jabiri

1962. Air.

788 **187** 45p. violet . . . . 1·30 45

789 50p. red . . . . 1·30 45

790 85p. green . . . . 1·30 60

791 100p. purple . . . . . . 1·50 85

See also Nos. 801/4.

1962. Air. 15th Death Anniv of Saadallah el-Jabiri (revolutionary).

792 **188** 50p. blue 50 35

189 Moharde Woman

190 Ears of Wheat, Hand and Globe

1962. Air. Women in Regional Costumes. Mult.

793 40p. Marje Sultan 50 45

794 45p. Kalamoun 60 45

795 50p. Type **189** 70 50

796 55p. Jabal al-Arab 85 60

797 60p. Afrine 95 60

798 65p. Hauran . . . . 1·30 85

1963. As previous designs but size 20 × 26 mm.

799 – 2½p. violet 15 10

800 – 5p. purple 15 10

801 **187** 7½p. grey 35 10

802 10p. brown 70 10

803 12½p. blue . . . . 1·00 10

804 15p. brown . . . . 1·70 15

DESIGN: Nos. 799/800, "The Beauty of Palmyra" (statue).

1963. Freedom from Hunger.

805 **190** 12½p. black & bl (postage) 25 15

806 – 50p. black and red (air) 50 25

MS806a 90 × 65 mm. Nos. 805/6 2·20 2·20

DESIGN: 50p. Bird feeding young in nest.

191 Faris el-Khouri (politician)

192 S.A.R. Emblem

1963. Air. 17th Anniv of Evacuation of Foreign Troops from Syria.

807 **191** 17½p. brown 35 15

808 **192** 22½p. green and black . . 50 25

193 Eagle

194 Ala el-Ma'ari (bust)

1963. Air. Baathist Revolution Commemoration.

809 **193** 12½p. green 15 15

810 50p. mauve 60 35

1963. Air. 990th Birth Anniv of Ala el-Ma'ari (poet).

811 **194** 50p. violet 60 50

195 Copper Water Jug

1963. Air. 10th International Fair, Damascus.
812 **195** 37½p. multicoloured . . . 50 20
813 50p. multicoloured . . . 60 35

196 Central Bank

1963. Damascus Buildings.
814 – 17½p. violet . . . . . . 1·30 35
815 – 22½p. violet 35 25
816 **196** 25p. brown 25 15
817 – 35p. purple 45 25
BUILDINGS: 17½p. Hejaz Railway Station; 22½p. Mouassat Hospital; 35p. Post Office, Al-Jalaa.

197 "Red Crescent" and Centenary Emblem

198 Child with Ball

1963. Air. Red Cross Centenary. Crescent in red.
818 **197** 15p. black and blue . . . 35 25
819 – 50p. black and green . . 70 45
DESIGN: 50p. "Red Crescent", globe and centenary emblem.

1963. Aleppo Cotton Festival. As T **185** but inscr "POSTAGE" and "1963" in place of "AIRMAIL" and "1962".
820 **185** 17½p. multicoloured . . . 25 15
821 22½p. multicoloured . . . 45 25

1963. Children's Day.
822 **198** 12½p. green and deep green 15 15
823 22½p. green and red . . . 45 20

199 Firas el-Hamadani

200 Flame on Head

1963. Air. Death Millenary of Abou Firas el-Hamadani (poet).
824 **199** 50p. brown and bistre . . 60 50

1963. Air. 15th Anniv of Declaration of Human Rights. Flame in red.
825 **200** 17½p. black and grey . . 15 15
826 22½p. black and green . . 45 15
827 50p. black and violet . . 60 45
MS827a 110 × 70 mm. Nos. 825/7. Imperf . . . . 1·70 1·70

201 Emblem and Flag

1964. Air. 1st Anniv of Baathist Revolution of 8 March 1963. Emblem and flag in red, black and green; inscr in black.
828 **201** 15p. green 15 10
829 17½p. pink 25 15
830 22½p. grey 45 25

202 Ugharit Princess

203 Chahba, Thalassa, Mosaic

1964.
831 **202** 2½p. grey (postage) . . . 10 10
832 5p. brown 10 10
833 7½p. purple 10 10
834 10p. green 10 10
835 12½p. violet 15 15
836 17½p. blue 25 15
837 20p. red 50 15
838 25p. orange 85 20
839 **203** 27½p. red (air) 25 15
840 45p. brown 50 15
841 50p. green 70 15
842 55p. green 70 25
843 60p. blue 85 35

204 Kaaba, Mecca, and Mosque, Damascus

1964. Air. 1st Arab Moslem Wakf Ministers' Conference.
844 **204** 12½p. black and blue . . 15 10
845 22½p. black and purple . . 25 15
846 50p. black and green . . 60 45

1964. Air. 18th Anniv of Evacuation of Foreign Troops from Syria. As T **99** but larger, 38½ × 26 mm. Inscr "1964".
847 **99** 20p. blue 15 15
848 25p. purple 25 25
849 60p. green 60 45

205 Abou al Zahrawi

206 Bronze Chimes

1964. Air. 4th Arab Dental and Oral Surgery Congress, Damascus.
850 **205** 60p. brown 70 50

1964. Air. 11th International Fair, Damascus.
851 **206** 20p. multicoloured . . . 50 15
852 – 25p. multicoloured . . . 60 25
DESIGN: 25p. Fair emblem.

207 Cotton Plant and Symbols

(208)

1964. Air. Aleppo Cotton Festival. No. 854 is optd with T **208**.
853 **207** 25p. multicoloured . . . 40 20
854 25p. multicoloured . . . 40 20

209 Aero Club Emblem

1964. Air. 10th Anniv of Syrian Aero Club.
855 **209** 12½p. black and green . . 25 10
856 17½p. black and red . . . 35 15
857 20p. black and blue . . . 85 15

210 A.P.U. Emblem

211 Book within Hands

1964. Air. 10th Anniv of Arab Postal Union's Permanent Office, Cario.
858 **210** 12½p. black and orange 15 10
859 20p. black and green . . 25 15
860 25p. black and mauve . . 35 15

1964. Air. Burning of Algiers Library.
861 **211** 12½p. black and green . . 15 10
862 17½p. black and red . . . 25 15
863 20p. black and blue . . . 35 15

212 Tennis

1965. Air. Olympic Games, Tokyo. Multicoloured.
864 12½p. Type **212** 15 10
865 17½p. Wrestling 35 15
866 20p. Weightlifting 45 15
MS866a 90 × 57 mm. 100p. Wrestlers and drummer. Imperf . . . . 2·30 2·30

213 Flag, Map and Revolutionaries

1965. 2nd Anniv of Baathist Revolution of 8 March 1963.
867 **213** 12½p. multicoloured . . . 15 10
868 17½p. multicoloured . . . 25 10
869 20p. multicoloured . . . 35 15

214 Rameses II in War Chariot, Abu Simbel

1965. Air. Nubian Monuments Preservation.
870 **214** 22½p. black, blue and green 35 15
871 – 50p. black, green and blue 70 35
DESIGN: 50p. Heads of Rameses II.

215 Weather Instruments and Map

1965. World Meteorological Day.
872 **215** 12½p. black and purple . . 15 10
873 27½p. black and blue . . 35 25

216 Al-Radi

217 Evacuation Symbol

1965. Air. 950th Death Anniv of Al-Sharif al-Radi (writer).
874 **216** 50p. black 70 45

1965. 19th Anniv of Evacuation of Foreign Troops from Syria.
875 **217** 12½p. green and blue . . 15 15
876 27½p. lilac and red . . . 35 15

218 Hippocrates and Avicenna

1965. Air. "Medical Days of the Near and Middle East".
877 **218** 60p. black and green . . 85 60

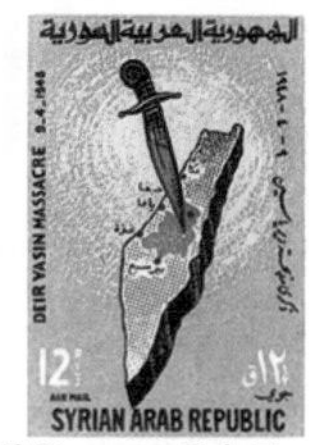
219 Dagger on Deir Yassin, Palestine

1965. Air. Deir Yassin Massacre on 9 April 1948.
878 **219** 12½p. multicoloured . . . 25 10
879 60p. multicoloured . . . 60 35

220 I.T.U. Emblem and Symbols

221 Arab Family, Flags and Map

1965. Air. Centenary of I.T.U.
880 **220** 12½p. multicoloured . . . 25 10
881 27½p. multicoloured . . . 45 15
882 60p. multicoloured . . . 80 50

1965. Palestine Week.
883 **221** 12½p.+5p. multicoloured 25 25
884 25p.+5p. multicoloured 25 25

222 Hands holding Hoe and Pick

223 Welcoming Emigrant

1965. Peasants' Union.
885 **222** 2½p. green 10 10
886 12½p. violet 15 10
887 15p. purple 15 10
The above stamps are inscr "RERUBLIC" for "REPUBLIC".

1965. Air. "Welcome Arab Emigrants".
888 **223** 25p. multicoloured . . . 25 15
889 100p. multicoloured . . . 1·10 70

224 Fair Entrance

226 Cotton Boll and Shuttles

1965. Air. 12th Int Fair, Damascus. Multicoloured.
890 12½p. Type **224** 10 10
891 27½p. Globe and compasses 35 15
892 60p. Syrian brassware 60 45

1965. Air. Aleppo Industrial and Agricultural Production Fair. Optd **INDUSTRIAL & AGRICULTURAL PRODUCTION FAIR-ALEPPO 1965** in English and Arabic.
893 **226** 25p. multicoloured . . . 45 15

1965. Air. Aleppo Cotton Festival.
894 **226** 25p. multicoloured . . . 45 15

227 I.C.Y. Emblem and View of Damascus

1965. Air. International Co-operation Year.
895 **227** 25p. multicoloured . . . 50 15

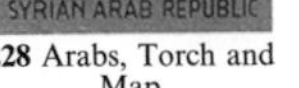
228 Arabs, Torch and Map

229 Industrial Workers

1965. National Revolution Council.
896 **228** 12½p. multicoloured . . . 10 10
897 25p. multicoloured . . . 35 15

1966. Labour Unions.
898 **229** 12½p. blue 10 10
899 15p. red 15 10
900 20p. lilac 25 15
901 25p. brown 35 15

230 Radio Aerial, Globe and Flag

231 Dove-shaped Hand holding Flower

1966. Air. Arab Information Ministers' Conf, Damascus.
902 **230** 25p. multicoloured . . . 25 15
903 60p. multicoloured . . . 60 45

1966. Air. 3rd Anniv of Baathist Revolution of 8 March 1963. Multicoloured.
904 12½p. Type **231** 10 10
905 17½p. Revolutionaries (horiz) 15 10
906 50p. Type **231** . . . . . . 1·10 45

232 Colossi, Abu Simbel

233 Roman Lamp

1966. Air. Nubian Monuments Preservation Week.
907 **232** 25p. blue 35 15
908 60p. grey 70 25

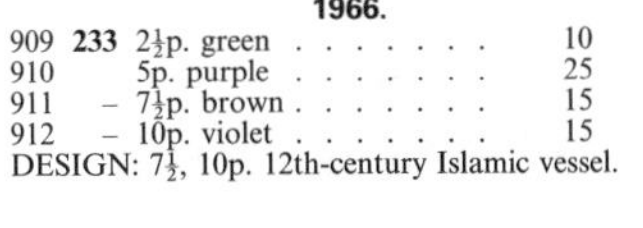
1966.
909 **233** 2½p. green 10 10
910 5p. purple 25 15
911 – 7½p. brown 15 10
912 – 10p. violet 15 10
DESIGN: 7½, 10p. 12th-century Islamic vessel.

234 U.N. Emblem and Headquarters

1966. Air. 20th Anniv of U.N.O.
913 **234** 25p. black and grey . . . 15 15
914 50p. black and green . . . 50 45
MS915 90 × 70 mm. **235** 100p. yellow, blue and black. Imperf 1·70 1·70

236 "Evacuation" (abstract)

1966. 20th Anniv of Evacuation of Foreign Troops from Syria.
916 **236** 12½p. multicoloured . . . 15 10
917 27½p. multicoloured . . . 35 25

237 Workers marching across Globe

1966. Air. Labour Day.
918 **237** 60p. multicoloured . . . 60 45

238 W.H.O. Building

1966. Air. Inauguration of W.H.O. Headquarters, Geneva.
919 **238** 60p. black, blue and yellow 50 25

239 Traffic Signals and Map on Hand

240 Astarte and Tyche (wrongly inscr "ASTRATE")

1966. Air. Traffic Day.
920 **239** 25p. multicoloured . . . 35 15

1966. Air.
921 **240** 50p. brown 50 25
922 60p. grey 85 45

241 Fair Emblem

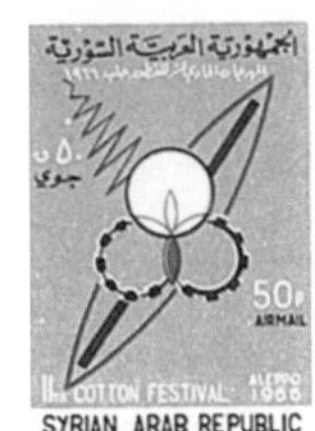
242 Shuttle (stylized)

1966. Air. 13th International Fair, Damascus.
923 **241** 12½p. multicoloured . . . 15 10
924 60p. multicoloured . . . 60 50

1966. Air. Aleppo Cotton Festival.
925 **242** 50p. black, red and grey 60 45

243 Decade Emblem

244 Emir Abd-el-Kader

1966. Air. International Hydrological Decade.
926 **243** 12½p. black, orange & green 15 10
927 60p. black, orange and blue 70 35

1966. Air. Return of Emir Abd-el-Kader's Remains to Algiers.
928 **244** 12½p. black and green . . 35 10
929 50p. brown and green . . 50 35

245 U.N.R.W.A. Emblem

1966. Air. 21st Anniv of U.N. Day and Refugee Week.
930 **245** 12½p.+2½p. black and blue 15 15
931 50p.+5p. black and green 60 60

246 Handclasp and Map

247 Doves and Oil Pipelines

1967. Air. Solidarity Congress, Damascus.
932 **246** 20p. multicoloured . . . 25 15
933 25p. multicoloured . . . 35 15

1967. Air. 4th Anniv of Baathist Revolution of 8 March 1963.
934 **247** 17½p. multicoloured . . . 25 15
935 25p. multicoloured . . . 35 15
936 27½p. multicoloured . . . 50 25

248 Soldier and Citizens with Banner

249 Workers' Monument, Damascus

1967. Air. 21st Anniv of Evacuation of Foreign Troops from Syria.
937 **248** 17½p. green 15 15
938 25p. purple 25 15
939 27½p. blue 35 15

1967. Air. Labour Day.
940 **249** 12½p. turquoise 15 10
941 50p. mauve 60 45

250 Core Bust

251 "African Woman" (vase)

252 Head of a Young Man from Amrith

253 Flags and Fair Entrance

1967.
942 **250** 2½p. green (postage) . . . 10 10
943 5p. red 10 10
944 10p. blue 10 10
945 12½p. brown 15 10
946 **251** 15p. purple 15 15
947 20p. blue 15 15
948 25p. green 25 15
949 27½p. blue 35 15
950 **252** 45p. red (air) 45 25
951 50p. mauve 60 25
952 60p. blue 70 45
953 – 100p. green 85 50
954 – 500p. red . . . . 4·25 3·00
DESIGN—VERT: 100, 500p. Bust of Princess (2nd-century bronze).

1967. Air. 14th International Damascus Fair.
955 **253** 12½p. multicoloured . . . 15 10
956 60p. multicoloured . . . 60 45

254 Statue of Ur-Nina and Tourist Emblem

1967. Air. International Tourist Year.
957 **254** 12½p. purple, black & blue 15 10
958 25p. red, black and blue 15 15
959 27½p. blue, black & lt blue 35 15
MS960 105 × 80 mm. **254** 60p. blue, black and light blue. Imperf . . 95 95

255 Cotton Boll and Cogwheel

257 Ibn el-Naphis (scientist)

1967. Air. Aleppo Cotton Festival.
961 **255** 12½p. black, brown and yellow 15 10
962 60p. black, brown and yellow 60 45

1967. Air. Industrial and Agricultural Production Fair, Aleppo. Optd **INDUSTRIAL & AGRICULTURAL PRODUCTION FAIR ALEPPO 1967** in English and Arabic.
963 **255** 12½p. black, brown & yellow 15 10
964 60p. black, brown & yell 60 45

1967. Air. Sciences Week.
965 **257** 12½p. red and green . . . 10 10
966 27½p. mauve and blue . . 45 15

258 Acclaiming Human Rights

1968. Air. Human Rights Year.
967 **258** 12½p. black, turquoise and blue 15 10
968 60p. black, red and pink 60 50
MS969 105 × 80 mm. 100p. multicoloured (Human Rights emblem and outlines of faces). Imperf . . . . 1·30 1·30

259 Learning to Read

260 "The Arab Revolutionary" (Damascus statue)

1968. Air. Literacy Campaign.
970 **259** 12½p. multicoloured . . . 10 10
971 – 17½p. multicoloured . . . 15 10
972 **259** 25p. multicoloured . . . 35 10
973 – 45p. multicoloured . . . 50 35
DESIGN: 17½, 45p. Flaming torch and open book.

1968. 5th Anniv of Baathist Revolution of 8 March 1963.
974 **260** 12½p. brown, yellow & black 10 10
975 25p. mauve, pink and black 35 15
976 27½p. green, light green and black 35 25

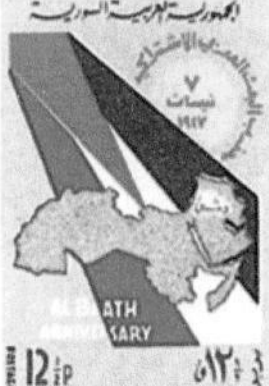

261 Map of North Africa and Arabia

263 Hands holding Spanner, Rifle and Torch

262 Euphrates Dam

1968. 21st Anniv of Baath Arab Socialist Party.
977 **261** 12½p. multicoloured . . . 15 10
978 60p. multicoloured . . . 60 45

1968. Air. Euphrates Dam Project.
979 **262** 12½p. multicoloured . . . 15 10
980 17½p. multicoloured . . . 25 10
981 25p. multicoloured . . . 60 15

1968. "Mobilisation Efforts".
982 **263** 12½p. multicoloured . . . 10 10
983 17½p. multicoloured . . . 15 10
984 25p. multicoloured . . . 35 15

264 Railway Track and Sun

266 Torch, Map and Laurel

265 Oil Pipeline Map

1968. 22nd Anniv of Evacuation of Foreign Troops from Syria.
985 **264** 12½p. multicoloured . . . 60 10
986 27½p. multicoloured . . . 1·50 15

1968. Syrian Oil Exploration.
987 **265** 12½p. blue, green and light green 25 10
988 17½p. blue, brown and pink 60 15

1968. Palestine Day.
989 **266** 12½p. multicoloured . . . 15 10
990 25p. multicoloured . . . 25 15
991 27½p. multicoloured . . . 35 15

267 Refugee Family

1968. Red Crescent Refugees Fund.
992 **267** 12½p.+2½p. black, purple and blue 35 35
993 27½p.+7½p. black, red and violet 35 35

268 Avenzoar (physician) and W.H.O. Emblem

1968. Air. 20th Anniv of W.H.O.
994 **268** 12½p. multicoloured . . . 10 10
995 – 25p. multicoloured . . . 20 10
996 – 60p. multicoloured . . . 55 20
DESIGNS—As Type **268**, but with different portraits of Arab physicians: 25p. Razi; 60p. Jabir.

269 Ear of Corn, Cogwheel and Saracen Gate, Aleppo Citadel

1968. Industrial and Agricultural Production Fair, Aleppo.
997 **269** 12½p. multicoloured . . . 15 10
998 27½p. multicoloured . . . 25 15

270 Emblems of Fair, Agriculture and Industry

271 Gathering Cotton

1968. 15th International Damascus Fair.
999 **270** 12½p. black, green & brown 10 10
1000 – 27½p. multicoloured . . 35 15
1001 **270** 60p. black, orange & blue 60 45
DESIGN—HORIZ: 27½p. Flag, hand with torch and emblems.

1968. Aleppo Cotton Festival.
1002 **271** 12½p. multicoloured . . 10 10
1003 27½p. multicoloured . . 25 15

272 Monastery of St. Simeon the Stylite

273 Oil Derrick

1968. Air. Ancient Monuments (1st series).
1004 **272** 15p. multicoloured . . . 10 10
1005 – 17½p. deep brown, brown and chocolate 15 10
1006 – 22½p. multicoloured . . 15 15
1007 – 45p. multicoloured . . 45 35
1008 – 50p. brown, sepia and blue 50 45
DESIGNS—VERT: 17½p. El Tekkieh Mosque, Damascus; 22½p. Temple columns, Palmyra. HORIZ: 45p. Chapel of St. Paul, Bab Kisan; 50p. Amphitheatre, Bosra.
See also Nos. 1026/30.

1968.
1009 **273** 2½p. green and blue . . 15 10
1010 5p. blue and green . . . 15 10
1011 7½p. blue and green . . 15 10
1012 10p. green and yellow . . 15 10
1013 12½p. red and yellow . . 15 10
1014 15p. brown and bistre 15 15
1015 27½p. brown and orange 35 15

274 Al-Jahez (scientist)

275 Throwing the Hammer

1968. 9th Science Week.
1016 **274** 12½p. black and green 10 10
1017 27½p. black and grey . . 45 25

1968. Air. Olympic Games, Mexico.
1018 **275** 12½p. black, mauve and green 10 10
1019 – 25p. black, red and green 25 15
1020 – 27½p. black, grey and green 35 25
1021 – 60p. multicoloured . . . 50 35
MS1022 105×80 mm. 50p. multicoloured. Imperf . . . . 1·00 1·00
DESIGNS—VERT: 25p. Throwing the discus; 27½p. Running; 60p. Basketball. HORIZ (53×36 mm)—50p. Polo.

276 Aerial View of Airport

1969. Air. Construction of Damascus Int Airport.
1023 **276** 12½p. green, blue & yellow 15 10
1024 17½p. violet, red and green 45 15
1025 60p. black, mauve and yellow . . . . 1·10 35

277 Baal-Shamin Temple, Palmyra

1969. Air. Ancient Monuments (2nd series). Mult.
1026 25p. Type **277** 25 15
1027 45p. Omayyad Mosque, Damascus (vert) 35 25
1028 50p. Amphitheatre, Palmyra 45 35
1029 60p. Khaled ibn el-Walid Mosque, Homs (vert) . . 50 35
1030 100p. St. Simeon's Column, Jebel Samaan 85 70

278 "Sun" and Clenched Fists in Broken Handcuffs

1969. 6th Anniv of Baathist Revolution of 8 March 1963.
1031 **278** 12½p. multicoloured . . 15 10
1032 25p. multicoloured . . . 35 15
1033 27½p. multicoloured . . 35 15

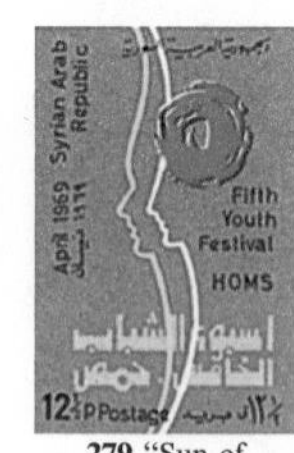

279 "Sun of Freedom"

280 Symbols of Progress

1969. 5th Youth Festival, Homs.
1034 **279** 12½p. red, yellow and blue 10 10
1035 25p. red, yellow and green 25 15

1969. 23rd Anniv of Evacuation of Foreign Troops from Syria.
1036 **280** 12½p. multicoloured . . 10 10
1037 27½p. multicoloured . . 25 15

281 "Workers", Cogwheel and I.L.O. Emblem

1969. Air. 50th Anniv of I.L.O.
1038 **281** 12½p. multicoloured . . 15 10
1039 27½p. multicoloured . . 35 15
MS1040 76×54 mm. 60p. multicoloured 70 70
DESIGN: Larger (54×37 mm)—60p. ILO emblem.

282 Russian Dancers

283 "Fortune" (statue)

1969. Air. 16th Int Damascus Fair. Mult.
1041 12½p. Type **282** 15 10
1042 27½p. Ballet dancers 45 15
1043 45p. Lebanese dancers . . . 50 35
1044 55p. Egyptian dancers . . . 60 35
1045 60p. Bulgarian dancers . . . 85 50

1969. Air. 9th International Archaeological Congress, Damascus. Multicoloured.
1046 17½p. Type **283** 25 10
1047 25p. "Lady from Palmyra" (statue) 35 15
1048 60p. "Motherhood" (statue) 70 25

284 Children dancing

285 Mahatma Gandhi

1969. Air. Children's Day.
1049 **284** 12½p. green, blue and turquoise 15 10
1050 25p. violet, blue and red 25 10
1051 27½p. grey, dp blue & blue 35 15

1969. Birth Centenary of Mahatma Gandhi.
1052 **285** 12½p. brown and buff . . 15 15
1053 27½p. green and yellow 25 15

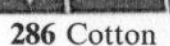

286 Cotton

287 "Arab World" (6th Arab Science Congress)

1969. Aleppo Cotton Festival.
1054 **286** 12½p. multicoloured . . 10 10
1055 17½p. multicoloured . . 15 10
1056 25p. multicoloured . . . 25 15

1969. 10th Science Week.
1057 **287** 12½p. blue and green . . 10 10
1058 – 25p. violet and pink . . 25 25
1059 – 27½p. brown and green 45 45
DESIGNS: 25p. Arab Academy (50th anniv); 27½p. Damascus University (50th anniv of Faculty of Medicine).

288 Cockerel

1969. Air. Damascus Agricultural Museum. Mult.
1060 12½p. Type **288** 15 15
1061 17½p. Cow 25 15
1062 20p. Maize 35 15
1063 50p. Olives 50 25

289 Rising Sun, Hand and Book

1970. 7th Anniv of Baathist Revolution of 8 March 1963.

1064 **289** 17½p. black, brown & blue 10 10
1065 25p. black, blue and red 25 15
1066 27½p. black, brown & green 45 25

290 Map of Arab World, League Emblem and Flag

1970. Silver Jubilee of Arab League.

1067 **290** 12½p. multicoloured . . 10 10
1068 25p. multicoloured . . . 25 15
1069 27½p. multicoloured . . 45 25

291 Dish Aerial and Hand on Book

1970. Air. World Meteorological Day.

1070 **291** 25p. black, yellow & green 50 15
1071 60p. black, yellow & blue 80 50

292 Lenin

1970. Air. Birth Centenary of Lenin.

1072 **292** 15p. brown and red . . 15 10
1073 60p. green and red . . . 70 50

293 Battle of Hattin

1970. 24th Anniv of Evacuation of Foreign Troops from Syria.

1074 **293** 15p. brown and cream 25 15
1075 35p. violet and cream . . 50 25

294 Emblem of Workers' Syndicate

1970. Air. Labour Day.

1076 **294** 15p. brown and green . . 10 10
1077 60p. brown and orange 70 50

295 Young Syrians and Map

1970. Revolution's Youth Union, 1st Youth Week.

1078 **295** 15p. green and brown . . 10 10
1079 25p. brown and ochre 25 25

This issue is inscr "YOUTH'S FIRST WEAK" in error.

296 Refugee Family

1970. World Arab Refugee Week.

1080 **296** 15p. multicoloured . . . 10 10
1081 25p. multicoloured . . . 35 15
1082 35p. multicoloured . . . 35 25

297 Dish Aerial and Open Book

1970. Air. World Telecommunications Day.

1083 **297** 15p. black and lilac . . . 10 10
1084 60p. black and blue . . 70 50

298 New U.P.U. Headquarters Building

1970. Air. New U.P.U. Headquarters Building.

1085 **298** 15p. multicoloured . . . 10 10
1086 60p. multicoloured . . . 45 25

299 "Industry" and Graph

300 Khaled ibn el-Walid

1970.

1087 **299** 2½p. red and brown (postage) 15 10
1088 5p. blue and orange . . 15 15
1089 7½p. grey and purple . . 15 10
1090 10p. brown and light brown 15 10
1091 12½p. red and blue . . . 15 10
1092 15p. mauve and green 15 10
1093 20p. brown and blue . . 15 15
1094 22½p. green and brown 25 15
1095 25p. blue and grey . . . 25 15
1096 27½p. brown and green 25 15
1097 35p. green and red . . . 35 25
1098 **300** 45p. mauve (air) 45 15
1099 50p. green 50 25
1100 60p. brown 70 35
1101 100p. blue 95 35
1102 200p. green . . . . . . 1·70 95
1103 300p. violet . . . . . . 2·50 1·70
1104 500p. grey . . . . 4·25 3·50

301 Medieval Warriors

1970. Air. Folk Tales and Legends.

1105 **301** 5p. multicoloured . . . 15 15
1106 – 10p. multicoloured . . . 15 15
1107 – 15p. multicoloured . . . 15 15
1108 – 20p. multicoloured . . . 25 25
1109 – 60p. multicoloured . . . 60 60

Nos. 1106/9 show horsemen similar to Type **301**.

302 Cotton

1970. Aleppo Agricultural and Industrial Fair. Multicoloured.

1110 5p. Type **302** 15 15
1111 10p. Tomatoes 15 15
1112 15p. Tobacco 15 15
1113 20p. Sugar beet 15 15
1114 35p. Wheat 45 45

303 Mosque in Flames

1970. Air. 1st Anniv of Burning of Al-Aqsa Mosque, Jerusalem.

1115 **303** 15p. multicoloured . . . 15 15
1116 60p. multicoloured . . . 70 35

304 Wood-carving

1970. Air. 17th Damascus Int Fair. Mult.

1117 15p. Type **304** 10 10
1118 20p. Jewellery 15 10
1119 25p. Glass-making 25 15
1120 30p. Copper-engraving . . . 50 25
1121 60p. Shell-work . . . . . . 1·10 45

305 Scout, Encampment and Badge

1970. Pan-Arab Scout Jamboree, Damascus.

1122 **305** 15p. green 35 15

306 Olive Tree and Emblem

1970. World Year of Olive-oil Production.

1123 **306** 15p. multicoloured . . . 15 10
1124 25p. multicoloured . . . 45 15

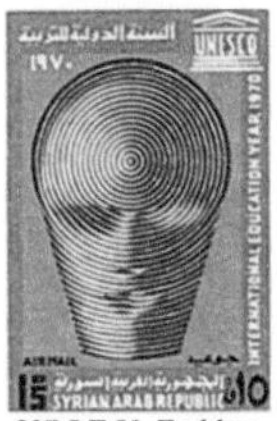

307 I.E.Y. Emblem

1970. Air. International Education Year.

1125 **307** 15p. brown, green & black 10 10
1126 60p. brown, blue & black 70 50

308 U.N. Emblems

309 Protective Shield

1970. Air. 25th Anniv of U.N.O.

1127 **308** 15p. multicoloured . . . 10 10
1128 60p. multicoloured . . . 70 50

1971. 8th Anniv of Baathist Revolution of 8 March 1963.

1129 **309** 15p. blue, yellow & green 10 10
1130 22½p. green, yellow & brown 15 15
1131 27½p. brown, yellow & blue 35 25

310 Girl holding Garland

1971. Air. 25th Anniv of Evacuation of Foreign Troops from Syria.

1132 **310** 15p. multicoloured . . . 15 10
1133 60p. multicoloured . . . 60 35

311 Globe and World Races

1971. Air. Racial Equality Year.

1134 **311** 15p. multicoloured . . . 10 10
1135 60p. multicoloured . . . 60 45

312 Soldier, Worker and Labour Emblems

1971. Labour Day.

1136 **312** 15p. purple, blue & yell 15 15
1137 25p. deep blue, blue and yellow 35 15

313 Hailing Traffic

1971. World Traffic Day.

1138 **313** 15p. red, blue and black 15 10
1139 – 25p. multicoloured . . . 25 15
1140 **313** 45p. red, yellow and black 50 35

DESIGN—VERT: 25p. Traffic signs and signal lights.

314 Cotton, Cogwheel and Factories

1971. Aleppo Agricultural and Industrial Fair.

1141 **314** 15p. black, blue and green 15 10
1142 30p. black, scarlet and red 35 35

315 A.P.U. Emblem

317 Flag and Federation Map

316 Peppers and Fertilizer Plant

1971. 25th Anniv of Sofar Conference and Founding of Arab Postal Union.

1143 **315** 15p. multicoloured . . . 10 10
1144 20p. multicoloured . . . 35 15

1971. 18th Damascus International Fair. Industries. Multicoloured.

1145 5p. Type **316** 10 10
1146 15p. TV set and telephone ("Electronics") 10 10
1147 35p. Oil lamp and dish ("Glassware") 50 35
1148 50p. Part of carpet ("Carpets") 85 50

1971. Arab Federation Referendum.

1149 **317** 15p. green, black and red 15 10

318 Pres. Hafez al-Assad and People's Council Chamber

1971. Air. People's Council and Presidential Election.
1150 **318** 15p. multicoloured . . . 10 10
1151 65p. multicoloured . . . 70 45

319 Pres. Nasser **320** "Telstar" and Dish Aerial

1971. Air. 1st Death Anniv of Pres. Nasser of Egypt.
1152 **319** 15p. brown and green . . 15 10
1153 20p. brown and grey . . 45 15

1971. 25th Anniv of UNESCO.
1154 **320** 15p. multicoloured . . . 15 10
1155 50p. multicoloured . . . 50 35

321 Flaming Torch **322** Quill-pen and Open Book

1971. "Movement of 16 November 1970".
1156 **321** 15p. multicoloured . . . 10 10
1157 20p. multicoloured . . . 25 25

1971. 8th Writers' Congress.
1158 **322** 15p. brown, orange and green 15 10

323 Children with Ball **324** Book Year Emblem

1971. 25th Anniv of UNICEF.
1159 **323** 15p. red, blue and deep blue 15 10
1160 25p. brown, green & blue 35 25

1972. International Book Year.
1161 **324** 15p. violet, blue & brown 15 10
1162 20p. green, light green and brown 35 25

325 Emblems of Reconstruction **326** Baath Party Emblem

1972. 9th Anniv of Baathist Revolution of 8 March 1963.
1163 **325** 15p. violet and green . . 10 10
1164 20p. red and bistre . . . 25 15

1972. 25th Anniv of Baath Party.
1165 **326** 15p. multicoloured . . . 10 10
1166 20p. multicoloured . . . 25 15

327 Eagle, Factory Chimneys and Rifles **328** Flowers and Broken Chain

1972. 1st Anniv of Arab Republics Federation.
1167 **327** 15p. gold, black and red 25 10

1972. 26th Anniv of Evacuation of Foreign Troops from Syria.
1168 **328** 15p. grey and red . . . 15 10
1169 50p. grey and green . . 50 35

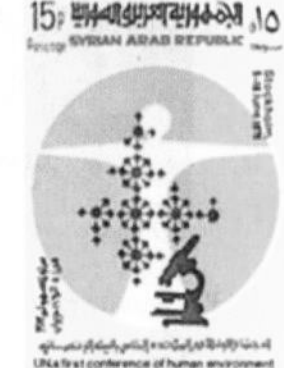

329 Hand with Spanner **331** Environment Emblem

330 Telecommunications Emblem

1972. Labour Day.
1170 **329** 15p. multicoloured . . . 10 10
1171 50p. multicoloured . . . 60 50

1972. Air. World Telecommunications Day.
1172 **330** 15p. multicoloured . . . 15 10
1173 50p. multicoloured . . . 70 25

1972. United Nations Environmental Conservation Conference, Stockholm.
1174 **331** 15p. blue, azure and pink 15 10
1175 50p. purple, orange & yellow 70 35

332 Discus, Football and Swimming

333 Horsemen

1972. Olympic Games, Munich.
1176 **332** 15p. violet, black & bistre 15 10
1177 – 60p. orange, black & blue 50 45
MS1178 100×81 mm. **333** 75p. multicoloured. Imperf . . . . 1·30 1·30
DESIGN: 60p. Running, gymnastics and fencing.

334 Dove and Factory **335** President Hafez al-Assad

1972. Aleppo Agricultural and Industrial Fair.
1179 **334** 15p. multicoloured . . . 15 10
1180 20p. multicoloured . . . 25 15

1972. Air.
1181 **335** 100p. green . . . . . . 1·10 50
1182 500p. brown . . . . . . 5·25 2·20

336 Women's Dance

1972. 19th Damascus International Fair. Mult.
1183 15p. Type **336** 15 10
1184 20p. Tambourine dance . . 15 15
1185 50p. Men's drum dance . . 70 35

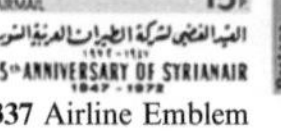

337 Airline Emblem **338** Emblem of Revolution

1972. Air. 25th Anniv of "Syrianair" Airline.
1186 **337** 15p. blue, light blue and black 25 10
1187 50p. blue, grey and black 80 25

1973. 10th Anniv of Baathist Revolution of 8 March 1963.
1188 **338** 15p. green, red and black 10 10
1189 20p. orange, red & black 15 10
1190 25p. blue, red and black 25 15

339 Human Heart

1973. 25th Anniv of W.H.O.
1191 **339** 15p. blue, purple and grey 15 10
1192 20p. blue, purple & brn 50 25

340 Emblems of Agriculture and Industry **341** Globe and Workers

1973. 27th Anniv of Evacuation of Foreign Troops from Syria.
1193 **340** 15p. multicoloured . . . 15 10
1194 20p. multicoloured . . . 15 10

1973. Labour Day.
1195 **341** 15p. black, purple and stone 10 10
1196 50p. black, blue and buff 50 35

342 Family and Emblems **343** Three Heads

1973. 10th Anniv of World Food Programme.
1197 **342** 15p. red and green . . . 15 10
1198 50p. blue and lilac . . . 60 35

1973.

1199 **343** 2½p. green 10 10
1200 5p. orange 10 10
1201 – 7½p. brown 10 10
1202 – 10p. red 10 10
1203 **343** 15p. blue 15 10
1204 – 25p. blue 15 10
1205 – 35p. blue 25 15
1206 – 55p. green 35 15
1207 – 70p. purple 50 25

DESIGNS—HORIZ: 7½, 10, 55p. As Type **343** but with one head above the other two. VERT: 25, 35, 70p. Similar to Type **343**, but with heads in vertical arrangement.

344 Stock

1973. Int Flower Show, Damascus. Mult.
1208 5p. Type **344** 15 15
1209 10p. Gardenia 15 15
1210 15p. Jasmine 15 15
1211 20p. Rose 35 15
1212 25p. Narcissus 35 15

345 Cogs and Flowers

1973. Aleppo Agricultural and Industrial Fair.
1213 **345** 15p. multicoloured . . . 15 10

346 Euphrates Dam

1973. Euphrates Dam Project. Diversion of the River.
1214 **346** 15p. multicoloured . . . 25 15
1215 50p. multicoloured . . . 50 25

347 Deir Ezzor Costume **348** Anniversary Emblem

1973. 20th Damascus International Fair. Costumes. Multicoloured.
1216 5p. Type **347** 15 15
1217 10p. Hassake 15 15
1218 20p. As Sahel 15 15
1219 25p. Zakie 35 15
1220 50p. Sarakeb 50 25

1973. 25th Anniv of Declaration of Human Rights.
1221 **348** 15p. black, red and green 10 10
1222 50p. black, red and blue 45 25

349 Citadel of Ja'abar

1973. "Save the Euphrates Monuments" Campaign. Multicoloured.
1223 10p. Type **349** 15 10
1224 15p. Meskeneh Minaret (vert) 15 10
1225 25p. Psyche, Anab al-Safinah (vert) 25 15

350 W.M.O. Emblem

1973. Centenary of W.M.O.
1226 **350** 70p. multicoloured . . . 50 25

351 Ancient City of Maalula

1973. Arab Emigrants' Congress, Buenos Aires.

1227	**351**	15p. black and blue	15	10
1228	–	50p. black and brown	50	25

DESIGN: 50p. Ruins of Afamia.

352 Soldier and Workers

1973. 3rd Anniv of Revolution of 16 November 1970.

1229	**352**	15p. blue and bistre	10	10
1230		25p. violet and red	25	15

353 Copernicus

1973. 14th Science Week.

1231	**353**	15p. black and gold	25	10
1232	–	25p. black and gold	50	15

DESIGN: 25p. Al-Biruni.

354 National Symbols

355 U.P.U. Monument, Berne

1973. 11th Anniv of Baathist Revolution of 8 March 1963.

1233	**354**	10p. blue and green	15	10
1234		25p. blue and green	15	15

1974. Centenary of U.P.U. Multicoloured.

1235	15p. Type **355**	10	10
1236	20p. Emblem on airmail letter (horiz)	15	10
1237	70p. Type **355**	60	50

356 Postal Institute

1974. Inauguration of Higher Arab Postal Institute, Damascus.

1238	**356**	15p. multicoloured	15	10

357 Sun and Monument

358 Machine Fitter

1974. 28th Anniv of Evacuation of Foreign Troops from Syria.

1239	**357**	15p. multicoloured	10	10
1240		20p. multicoloured	15	10

1974. Labour Day.

1241	**358**	15p. multicoloured	10	10
1242		50p. multicoloured	45	25

359 Abul Fida (historian)

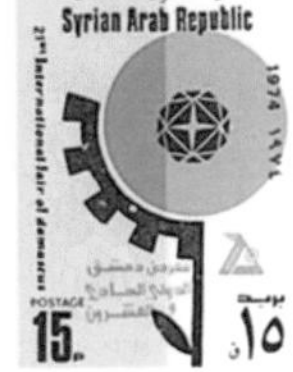

360 Diamond and Part of Cogwheel

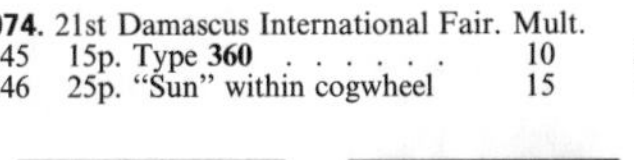

1974. Famous Arabs.

1243	**359**	100p. green	70	45
1244	–	200p. brown	1·60	85

DESIGN: 200p. Al-Farabi (philosopher and encyclopedist).

1974. 21st Damascus International Fair. Mult.

1245	15p. Type **360**	10	10
1246	25p. "Sun" within cogwheel	15	15

361 Figs

362 Flowers within Drop of Blood

1974. Aleppo Agricultural and Industrial Fair. Fruits. Multicoloured.

1247	5p. Type **361**	15	15
1248	15p. Grapes	15	15
1249	20p. Pomegranates	15	15
1250	25p. Cherries	25	15
1251	35p. Rose-hips	45	25

1974. 1st Anniv of October Liberation War. Multicoloured.

1252	15p. Type **362**	25	10
1253	20p. Flower and stars	45	15

363 Knight and Rook

364 Symbolic Figure, Globe and Emblem

1974. 50th Anniv of International Chess Federation.

1254	**363**	15p. blue, lt blue & black	70	15
1255	–	50p. multicoloured	2·30	50

DESIGN: 50p. Knight on chessboard.

1974. World Population Year.

1256	**364**	50p. multicoloured	50	35

365 Ishtup-ilum

366 Oil Rig and Crowd

1974. Statuettes.

1257	**365**	20p. green	15	10
1258	–	55p. brown	35	15
1259	–	70p. blue	60	25

DESIGNS: 55p. Woman with vase; 70p. Ur-nina.

1975. 12th Anniv of Baathist Revolution of 8 March 1963.

1260	**366**	15p. multicoloured	15	10

367 Savings Emblem and Family ("Savings Certificates")

368 Dove Emblem

1975. Savings Campaign.

1261	**367**	15p. black, orange & green	15	10
1262	–	20p. brown, black & orange	25	10

DESIGN: 20p. Family with savings box and letter ("Postal Savings Bank").

1975. 29th Anniv of Evacuation of Foreign Troops from Syria.

1263	**368**	15p. multicoloured	10	10
1264		25p. multicoloured	15	10

369 Worker supporting Cog

370 Camomile

1975. Labour Day.

1265	**369**	15p. multicoloured	10	10
1266		25p. multicoloured	15	10

1975. Int Flower Show, Damascus. Mult.

1267	5p. Type **370**	15	15
1268	10p. Chincherinchi	15	15
1269	15p. Carnations	25	15
1270	20p. Poppy	25	15
1271	25p. Honeysuckle	50	15

371 "Destruction and Reconstruction"

1975. Reoccupation of Qneitra.

1272	**371**	50p. multicoloured	50	35

372 Apples

373 Arabesque Pattern

1975. Aleppo Agricultural and Industrial Fair. Fruits. Multicoloured.

1273	5p. Type **372**	15	15
1274	10p. Quinces	15	15
1275	15p. Apricots	25	15
1276	20p. Mulberries	25	15
1277	25p. Loquats	45	15

1975. 22nd International Damascus Fair.

1278	**373**	15p. multicoloured	10	10
1279		35p. multicoloured	35	15

374 Pres. Hafez al-Assad

1975. 5th Anniv of "Movement of 16 November 1970".

1280	**374**	15p. multicoloured	10	10
1281		50p. multicoloured	50	35

375 Symbolic Woman

376 Bronze "Horse" Lamp

1976. International Women's Year. Multicoloured.

1282	10p. Type **375**	10	10
1283	15p. "Motherhood"	10	10
1284	25p. "Education"	15	15
1285	50p. "Science"	35	25

1976.

1286	–	5p. green	10	10
1287	**376**	10p. green	15	10
1288	–	10p. blue	10	10
1289	–	15p. brown	15	10
1290	**376**	20p. red	15	10
1291		25p. blue	15	10
1292	–	30p. brown	25	15
1293	–	35p. green	25	15
1294	–	40p. orange	25	15
1295	–	50p. blue	45	20
1296	–	55p. mauve	45	15
1297	–	60p. violet	50	15
1298	–	70p. red	50	15
1299	–	75p. orange	50	35
1300	–	80p. green	60	20
1301	–	100p. mauve	85	25
1302	–	200p. blue	1·70	50
1303	–	300p. mauve	2·30	85
1304	–	500p. grey	4·00	2·75
1305	–	1000p. green	7·00	4·25

DESIGNS—VERT: 5p. Wall-painting showing figure of a man; 10p. (No. 1288) Flying goddess with wreath; 30, 35, 40p. Man's head inkstand; 50, 55, 60p. Statue of Nike; 70, 75, 80p. Statue of Hera; 100p. Imdugub-Mari (bird goddess); 200p. Arab astrolabe; 500p. Palmyrean coin of Valabathus; 1000p. Abraxas stone. HORIZ: 15p. Wall-painting showing figures; 300p. Herodian coin from Palmyra.

377 National Theatre, Damascus

1976. 13th Anniv of Baathist Revolution of 8 March 1963.

1306	**377**	25p. green, black & silver	15	15
1307		35p. green, black & silver	25	25

378 Nurse and Emblem

380 Eagle and Stars

379 Syrian 5m. Stamp of 1920

1976. 8th Arab Red Crescent Societies' Conf, Damascus.

1308	**378**	25p. blue, black and red	25	15
1309		100p. violet, black and red	70	50

1976. Arab Post Day.

1310	**379**	25p. multicoloured	25	15
1311		35p. multicoloured	35	25

1976. 30th Anniv of Evacuation of Foreign Troops from Syria.

1312	**380**	25p. multicoloured	25	15
1313		35p. multicoloured	35	25

381 Hand gripping Spanner

382 Cotton Boll

1976. Labour Day.

1314	**381**	25p. blue and black	25	15
1315	–	60p. multicoloured	50	35

DESIGN: 60p. Hand supporting globe.

1976. Aleppo Agricultural and Industrial Fair.

1316	**382**	25p. multicoloured	25	15
1317		35p. multicoloured	35	25

383 Tulips

1976. Int Flower Show, Damascus. Multicoloured.

1318 5p. Type **383** 15 10
1319 15p. Yellow daisies 15 15
1320 20p. Turk's-cap lilies . . . 25 15
1321 25p. Irises 45 15
1322 35p. Honeysuckle 50 25

384 Pottery

1976. Air. 23rd International Damascus Fair. Handicraft Industries. Multicoloured.

1323 10p. Type **384** 15 15
1324 25p. Rug-making 25 25
1325 30p. Metalware 45 45
1326 35p. Wickerware 45 45
1327 100p. Wood-carving 80 80

385 People supporting Olive Branch

1976. Non-aligned Countries Summit Conference, Colombo. Multicoloured.

1328 40p. Type **385** 35 35
1329 60p. Symbolic arrow penetrating "grey curtain" 50 45

386 Football

387 Construction Emblems

1976. 5th Pan-Arab Games. Multicoloured.

1330 5p. Type **386** 15 15
1331 10p. Swimming 45 25
1332 25p. Running 45 25
1333 35p. Basketball 45 25
1334 50p. Throwing the javelin 45 45
MS1335 75 × 56 mm. 100p. Horse-jumping (56 × 36 mm). Imperf 1·90 1·90

1976. 6th Anniv of Movement of 16 November 1970.

1336 **387** 35p. multicoloured . . . 25 15

388 "The Fox and the Crow"

389 Muhammad Kurd-Ali (philosopher)

1976. Fairy Tales. Multicoloured.

1337 10p. Type **388** 15 15
1338 15p. "The Hare and the Tortoise" (horiz) 15 15
1339 20p. "Little Red Riding Hood" 25 25
1340 25p. "The Wolf and the Goats" (horiz) 25 25
1341 35p. "The Wolf and the Lamb" 45 45

1976. Birth Centenary of Muhammad Kurd-Ali.

1342 **389** 25p. multicoloured . . . 25 15

390 Boeing 747SP

1977. Civil Aviation Day.

1343 **390** 35p. multicoloured . . . 85 25

391 Woman hoisting Flag

392 A.P.U. Emblem

1977. 14th Anniv of Baathist Revolution of 8 March 1963.

1344 **391** 35p. multicoloured . . . 45 25

1977. 25th Anniv of Arab Postal Union.

1345 **392** 35p. multicoloured . . . 35 15

393 Mounted Horseman

1977. 31st Anniv of Evacuation of Foreign Troops from Syria.

1346 **393** 100p. multicoloured . . 85 50

394 Industrial Scene and Tools

1977. Labour Day.

1347 **394** 60p. multicoloured . . . 50 45

395 I.C.A.O. Emblem, Boeing 747SP and Globe

1977. 30th Anniv of I.C.A.O.

1348 **395** 100p. multicoloured . . 1·10 85

396 Lemon

397 Mallows

1977. International Agricultural Fair, Aleppo. Mult.

1349 10p. Type **396** 15 15
1350 20p. Lime 20 15
1351 25p. Grapefruit 35 15
1352 35p. Oranges 50 15
1353 60p. Tangerines 65 45

1977. International Flower Show. Multicoloured.

1354 10p. Type **397** 15 10
1355 20p. Cockscomb 25 25
1356 25p. Convolvulus 35 25
1357 35p. Balsam 50 25
1358 60p. Lilac 60 50

398 Young Pioneers and Emblem

1977. Al Baath Pioneers Organization.

1359 **398** 35p. multicoloured . . . 35 25

399 Arabesque Pattern and Coffee Pot

400 Globe and Measures

1977. 24th International Damascus Fair.

1360 **399** 25p. red, blue and black 15 15
1361 60p. brown, green & black 50 45

1977. World Standards Day.

1362 **400** 15p. multicoloured . . . 15 10

401 Microscope, Book and Lyre

1977. 30th Anniv of UNESCO.

1363 **401** 25p. multicoloured . . . 25 10

402 Shield, Surgeon and Crab

403 Archbishop Capucci and Map of Palestine

1977. Fighting Cancer Week.

1364 **402** 100p. multicoloured . . 70 25

1977. 3rd Anniv of Archbishop Capucci's Arrest.

1365 **403** 60p. multicoloured . . . 45 15

404 Blind Man, Eye and Globe

1977. World Blind Week.

1366 **404** 55p. multicoloured . . . 20 15
1367 70p. multicoloured . . . 35 15

405 Dome of the Rock, Jerusalem

1977. Palestinian Welfare.

1368 **405** 5p. multicoloured . . . 15 15
1369 10p. multicoloured . . . 25 15

406 Pres. Hafez al-Assad and Government Palace, Damascus

408 Arrow and Blood Circulation

407 Eurasian Goldfinch

1977. 7th Anniv of Movement of 16 November 1970.

1370 **406** 50p. multicoloured . . . 35 15

1978. Birds. Multicoloured.

1371 10p. Type **407** . . . . . . 1·50 85
1372 20p. Peregrine falcon . . . 1·70 1·00
1373 25p. Feral rock dove . . . 2·20 1·00
1374 35p. Hoopoe . . . . 4·25 1·30
1375 60p. Chukar partridge . . . 5·25 2·40

1978. World Health Day. "Fighting Blood Pressure".

1376 **408** 100p. multicoloured . . 60 25

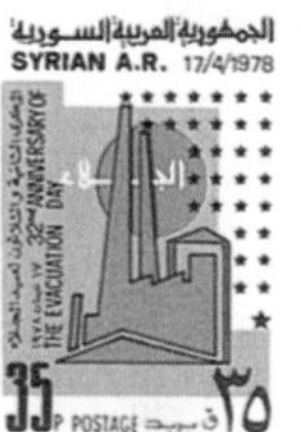
409 Factory, Moon and Stars

410 Geometric Design

1978. 32nd Anniv of Evacuation of Foreign Troops from Syria.

1377 **409** 35p. green, orange & black 25 15

1978. 14th Arab Engineering Conf, Damascus.

1378 **410** 25p. green and black . . 25 10

411 Map of Arab Countries, Flag, Eye and Police

412 Brown Trout

1978. 6th Arab Conference of Police Commanders.

1379 **411** 35p. multicoloured . . . 25 15

1978. Fishes. Multicoloured.

1380 10p. Type **412** 25 15
1381 20p. Seabream 25 15
1382 25p. Grouper 25 15
1383 35p. Striped red mullet . . . 45 25
1384 60p. Wels 50 35

413 President Assad

1978. Air. Re-election of President Hafez al-Assad.

1385 **413** 25p. multicoloured . . . 25 15
1386 35p. multicoloured . . . 35 15
1387 60p. multicoloured . . . 45 15
MS1388 79 × 105 mm. **413** 100p. multicoloured. Imperf 95 95

414 "Lobivia sp." **415** President Hafez al-Assad

1978. International Flower Show, Damascus. Mult.
1389 25p. Type **414** 25 15
1390 30p. "Mamillaria sp." . . . 35 15
1391 35p. "Opuntia sp." 35 15
1392 50p. "Chamaecereus sp." . . 45 25
1393 60p. "Mamillaria sp." (different) 50 45

1978. 8th Anniv of Movement of 16 November 1970.
1394 **415** 60p. multicoloured . . . 45 35

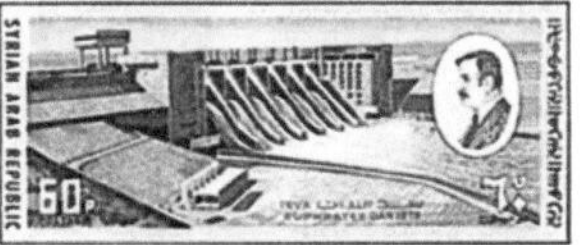

416 Euphrates Dam

1978. Inauguration of Euphrates Dam.
1395 **416** 60p. multicoloured . . . 60 35

417 Fair Emblem **418** Averroes (philosopher)

1979. 25th International Damascus Fair.
1396 **417** 25p. multicoloured . . . 15 10
1397 35p. black, violet and silver 25 15
MS1398 105 × 80 mm. 100p. multicoloured. Imperf 95 95
DESIGN: **MS**1398, Arabesque pattern.

1979. Averroes Commemoration.
1399 **418** 100p. multicoloured . . 1·10 70

419 Standing Figures within Globe **420** Pyramid and Flower

1979. International Year to Combat Racism.
1400 **419** 35p. multicoloured . . . 25 15

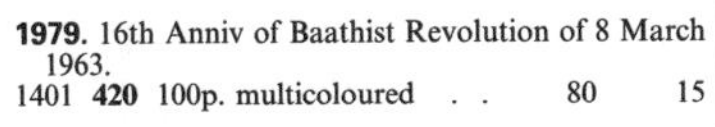

1979. 16th Anniv of Baathist Revolution of 8 March 1963.
1401 **420** 100p. multicoloured . . 80 15

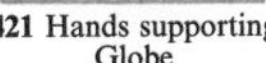

421 Hands supporting Globe **422** Helmet of Homs

1979. 30th Anniv of Declaration of Human Rights.
1402 **421** 60p. multicoloured . . . 45 35

1979. Exhibits from National Museum, Damascus.
1403 – 5p. red 15 10
1404 – 10p. green 25 10
1405 – 15p. mauve 25 15
1406 **422** 20p. green 15 10
1407 – 25p. red 15 10
1408 – 35p. brown 25 15
1409 – 75p. blue 50 25
1410 – 160p. green . . . . . . 1·00 45
1411 – 500p. brown . . . . . . 3·75 1·40

DESIGNS—VERT: 5, 160p. Umayyad window; 10p. Figurine; 15p. Rakka horseman (Abbcid ceramic); 25p. Head of Clipeata (Cleopatra); 35p. Seated statue of Ishtar (Astarte). HORIZ: 75p. Abdul Malik gold coin; 500p. Umar B. Abdul Aziz gold coin.

423 Geometric Design and Flame **424** Ibn Assaker

1979. 33rd Anniv of Evacuation of Foreign Troops from Syria.
1416 **423** 35p. multicoloured . . . 25 15

1979. 900th Anniv of Ibn Assaker (historian and biographer).
1417 **424** 75p. brown, blue & green 50 25

425 Tooth, Emblem and Mosque **426** Welder working on Power Pylon

1979. International Middle East Dental Congress.
1418 **425** 35p. multicoloured . . . 45 15

1979. Labour Day.
1419 **426** 50p. multicoloured . . . 35 25
1420 75p. multicoloured . . . 50 35

427 Girl holding Emblem with Flowers **428** Wright Type A

1979. International Year of the Child. Mult.
1421 10p. Type **427** 15 10
1422 15p. Boy and globe 25 15

1979. 75th Anniv of First Powered Flight. Mult.
1423 50p. Type **428** . . . . . . 1·00 25
1424 75p. Bleriot's plane crossing English Channel . . . . 1·40 45
1425 100p. Lindbergh's "Spirit of St. Louis" . . . . 1·90 50

429 Power Station **430** Flags and Pavilion

1979.
1426 **429** 5p. blue 15 10
1427 10p. mauve 15 10
1428 15p. green 15 10

1979. 26th International Damascus Fair. Mult.
1429 60p. Type **430** 35 15
1430 75p. Lamp post and flags . . . 45 15

431 Running

1979. 8th Mediterranean Games, Split. Mult.
1431 25p. Type **431** 15 15
1432 35p. Swimmer on starting-block 25 15
1433 50p. Football 35 25

432 President Assad with Symbols of Agriculture and Industry

1979. 9th Anniv of Movement of 16 November 1970.
1434 **432** 100p. multicoloured . . 80 25

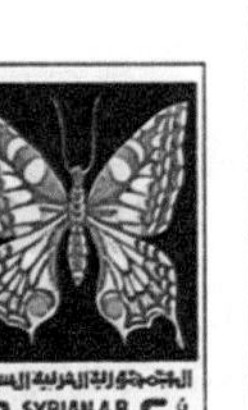

433 Swallowtail **434** Astrolabe

1979. Butterflies. Multicoloured.
1435 20p. Type **433** . . . . . . 1·00 10
1436 25p. Peacock . . . . 1·20 15
1437 30p. White admiral . . . . 1·60 15
1438 35p. Blue morpho . . . . . 1·90 25
1439 50p. Apollo . . . . 2·50 45

1979. International Flower Show, Damascus. Designs similar to T **414** showing various roses.
1440 5p. multicoloured 10 10
1441 10p. multicoloured 15 10
1442 15p. multicoloured 15 10
1443 50p. multicoloured 25 15
1444 75p. multicoloured 50 25
1445 100p. multicoloured 80 35

1980. 2nd International Symposium on History of Arab Science.
1446 **434** 50p. violet 35 15
1447 100p. brown 60 35
1448 1000p. green . . . . . . 6·50 3·75

435 "8" over Buildings **436** Smoker

1980. 17th Anniv of Baathist Revolution of 8 March 1963.
1449 **435** 40p. multicoloured . . . 25 15

1980. World Health Day. Anti-smoking Campaign.
1450 **436** 60p. brown, green & black 50 25
1451 – 100p. multicoloured . . 85 35
DESIGN: 100p. Skull and cigarette.

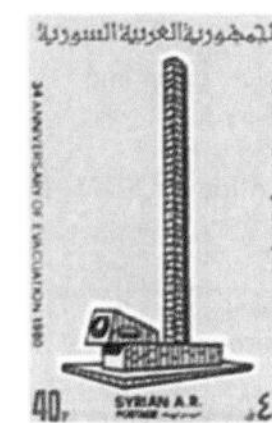

437 Monument

1980. 34th Anniv of Evacuation of Foreign Troops from Syria.
1452 **437** 40p. multicoloured . . . 35 15
1453 60p. multicoloured . . . 45 25

438 Wrestling

1980. Olympic Games, Moscow. Multicoloured.
1454 15p. Type **438** 15 10
1455 25p. Fencing 25 10
1456 35p. Weightlifting 25 15
1457 50p. Judo 35 15
1458 75p. Boxing 50 15
MS1459 105 × 80 mm. 300p. Discus thrower, Games emblem and runner. Imperf . . . . . . 7·00 7·00

439 "Savings"

1980. Savings Certificates.
1460 **439** 25p. violet, red and blue 15 10

440 "Aladdin and the Magic Lamp"

1980. Popular Stories. Multicoloured.
1461 15p. "Sinbad the Sailor" . . 15 10
1462 20p. "Shahrazad and Shahrayar" 35 15
1463 35p. "Ali Baba and the Forty Thieves" 45 15
1464 50p. "Hassan the Clever" . . 50 45
1465 100p. Type **440** 70 60

441 Kaaba and Mosque, Mecca

1980. 1400th Anniv of Hegira.
1466 **441** 35p. multicoloured . . . 35 15

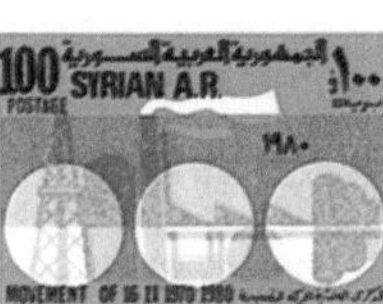

442 Daffodils **443** "Industry"

1980. International Flower Show, Damascus. Mult.
1467 20p. Type **442** 25 25
1468 30p. Dahlias 35 35
1469 40p. Bergamot 45 45
1470 60p. Globe flowers 50 50
1471 100p. Cornflowers 70 70

1980. 10th Anniv of Movement of 16 November 1970.
1472 **443** 100p. multicoloured . . 85 45

444 Construction Worker **445** Children encircling Globe

1980. Labour Day.
1473 **444** 35p. multicoloured . . . 25 15

1980. International Children's Day.
1474 **445** 25p. green, black & yell 25 10

446 Steam-powered Passenger Wagon, 1830 **447** Mother's Arms around Child

1980. Cars. Multicoloured.
1475 25p. Type **446** 35 35
1476 35p. Benz, 1899 . . . . . . 45 45
1477 40p. Rolls-Royce, 1903 . . 45 45
1478 50p. Mercedes, 1906 . . . . 50 50
1479 60p. Austin, 1915 . . . . . 60 60

1980. Mothers' Day. Multicoloured.
1480 40p. Type **447** 35 15
1481 100p. Faces of mother and child 70 45

448 Fair Emblem

1980. 27th International Damascus Fair. Mult.
1482 50p. Type **448** 45 15
1483 100p. As T **448** but with different motif on right 85 45

449 Armed Forces

1980. Army Day.
1484 **449** 50p. multicoloured . . . 1·10 35

450 Arabesque Pattern

451 Geometric Design, Laurel and Hand holding Torch

1981. 18th Anniv of Baathist Revolution of 8 March 1963.
1485 **450** 50p. multicoloured . . . 45 15

1981. 35th Anniv of Evacuation of Foreign Troops from Syria.
1486 **451** 50p. multicoloured . . . 50 15

452 Mosque and Script

1981. History of Arab-Islamic Civilization World Conference, Damascus.
1487 **452** 100p. green, deep green and black 80 45

453 Marching Workers and Emblem

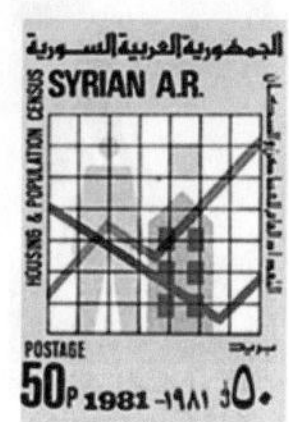
454 Human Figure and House on Graph

1981. May Day.
1488 **453** 100p. multicoloured . . 85 45

1981. Housing and Population Census.
1489 **454** 50p. multicoloured . . . 50 15

455 Family and Savings Emblem

456 Dove and Map on Globe

1981. Savings Certificates.
1490 **455** 50p. black and brown . . 50 15

1981. International Syrian and Palestinian Solidarity Conference, Damascus.
1491 **456** 160p. multicoloured . . 2·20 1·00

457 Avicenna

459 Festival Emblem

458 Glass Lamp

1981. Birth Millenary of Avicenna (philosopher and physician).
1492 **457** 100p. multicoloured . . 85 35

1981. Damascus Museum Exhibits.
1493 **458** 50p. red 60 25
1494 – 180p. multicoloured . . 1·70 85
1495 – 180p. multicoloured . . 1·70 85
DESIGNS: No. 1494, "Grand Mosque, Damascus" (painting); 1495, Hunting scene (tapestry).

1981. Youth Festival.
1496 **459** 60p. multicoloured . . . 50 15

460 Decorative Pattern

461 Palestinians and Dome of the Rock

1981. 28th International Damascus Fair.
1497 **460** 50p. mauve, blue & green 35 15
1498 – 160p. brown, yell & lilac 1·00 50
DESIGN: 160p. Globe encircled by wheat and cogwheel.

1981. Palestinian Solidarity.
1499 **461** 100p. multicoloured . . 85 35

462 F.A.O. Emblem

463 Tobacco Flowers

1981. World Food Day.
1500 **462** 180p. blue, green and black . . . . 1·70 95

1981. International Flower Show, Damascus. Mult.
1501 25p. Type **463** 45 45
1502 40p. Mimosa 85 60
1503 50p. Ixias . . . . 8·75 60
1504 60p. Passion flower 85 60
1505 100p. Dendrobium . . . . 1·00 85

464 Hands releasing Dove and Horseman

1981. 1300th Anniv of Bulgarian State.
1506 **464** 380p. multicoloured . . 2·50 1·00

465 Classroom

1981. International Children's Day.
1507 **465** 180p. black, red & green 1·70 95

466 Reading the Koran and Pres. Assad (½-size illustration)

1981. Koran Reading Competition. Sheet 105 × 80 mm.
MS1508 **466** 500p. multicoloured 8·75 8·75

467 President Assad and Diesel Train

468 Symbols of Development

1981. 11th Anniv of Movement of 16 November 1970.
1509 **467** 60p. blue, black and brown . . . . 1·70 35

1982. 19th Anniv of Baathist Revolution of 8 March 1963.
1510 **468** 50p. grey, red and black 50 15

469 Robert Koch and Microscope

1982. Cent of Discovery of Tubercle Bacillus.
1511 **469** 180p. blue, brown and black . . . . 1·70 70

470 Pattern and Hand holding Rifle

471 Disabled People and Emblem

1982. 36th Anniv of Evacuation of Foreign Troops from Syria.
1512 **470** 70p. red and blue . . . 50 25

1982. International Year of Disabled Persons (1981).
1513 **471** 90p. black, blue and yellow 85 35

472 A.P.U. Emblem

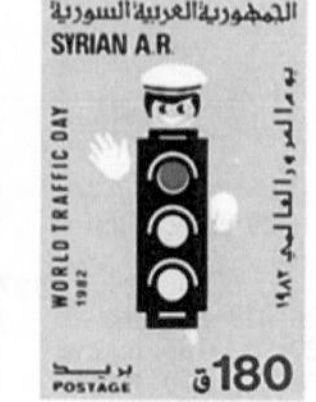
473 Traffic Lights

1982. 30th Anniv of Arab Postal Union.
1514 **472** 60p. red, green and yellow 70 25

1982. World Traffic Day.
1515 **473** 180p. black, red and blue 1·70 70

474 Geometric Pattern

1982. World Telecommunications Day.
1516 **474** 180p. light yellow, brown and yellow . . . . . 1·40 70

475 Oil Rig, Factory Chimneys and Hand holding Torch

476 Mother and Children

1982. Labour Day.
1517 **475** 180p. red, blue and light blue . . . . 1·40 70

1982. Mothers' Day.
1518 **476** 40p. green 25 10
1519 75p. brown 50 25

477 Olives

478 Pres. Assad

1982.
1520 **477** 50p. green 35 15
1521 60p. grey 45 15
1522 – 100p. mauve 60 35
1523 **478** 150p. blue 85 50
1524 – 180p. red . . . . 1·30 60
DESIGN: 100, 180p. Harbour.

479 Footballer

1982. World Cup Football Championship, Spain. Multicoloured.
1525 40p. Type **479** 45 15
1526 60p. Two footballers 60 25
1527 100p. Two footballers (different) . . . . 1·10 85
MS1528 75 × 54 mm. 300p. World Cup emblem. Imperf . . . . . 15·00 15·00

480 Policeman

481 Government Building

1982. Police Day.
1529 **480** 50p. black, red and green 50 15

1982.
1530 **481** 30p. brown 15 10
1531 – 70p. green 50 25
1532 – 200p. red . . . . 1·60 80
DESIGNS—HORIZ: 200p. Ruins. VERT: 70p. Arched wall.

482 Communications Emblem and Map

1982. Arab Telecommunication Day.
1533 **482** 50p. blue, ultramarine and red 50 15

483 Scout pitching Tent

1982. 75th Anniv of Boy Scout Movement.
1534 **483** 160p. green . . . . . . 1·60 70

484 Dish Aerial and World Map

1982. I.T.U. Delegates' Conference, Nairobi.
1535 **484** 180p. blue, ultramarine and red . . . . 1·70 85

485 President Assad

1982. 12th Anniv of Movement of 16 November 1970.
1536 **485** 50p. blue and grey . . . 45 15

486 Water-wheel, Hama

487 Dragonfly

1982.
1537 **486** 5p. brown 10 10
1538 10p. violet 10 10
1539 20p. red 25 10
1540 50p. turquoise 50 15

1982. Insects. Multicoloured.
1541 5p. Type **487** 25 25
1542 10p. Stag beetle 35 35
1543 20p. Seven-spotted ladybird 50 50
1544 40p. Desert locust . . . . . 1·00 1·00
1545 50p. Honey bee . . . . . . 1·10 1·10

488 Honeysuckle

489 Satellites within Dove

1982. Int Flower Show, Damascus. Mult.
1546 50p. Type **488** 50 25
1547 60p. Geranium 70 45

1982. U.N. Conference on Exploration and Peaceful Uses of Outer Space, Vienna.
1548 **489** 50p. multicoloured . . . 50 15

490 Dove on Gun

1982. International Palestine Day.
1549 **490** 50p. multicoloured . . . 85 35

491 Damascus International Airport

1983. 20th Anniv of Baathist Revolution of 8 March 1963.
1550 **491** 60p. multicoloured . . . 1·40 60

492 Communications Emblems

1983. World Communications Year.
1551 **492** 180p. multicoloured . . 1·70 80

493 Figurine

1983.
1552 **493** 380p. brown and green 3·75 1·50

494 Pharmacist

1983. Arab Pharmacists' Day.
1553 **494** 100p. multicoloured . . 1·10 45

495 Liberation Monument, Qneitra

496 Wave within Ship's Wheel

1983. 9th Anniv of Liberation of Qneitra.
1554 **495** 50p. green . . . . 1·00 45
1555 – 100p. brown . . . . . . 2·20 45
DESIGN: 100p. Ruined buildings.

1983. 25th Anniv of I.M.O.
1556 **496** 180p. multicoloured . . 1·90 70

497 Flame on Map

1983. Namibia Day.
1557 **497** 180p. blue, mauve and black . . . . 1·50 70

498 I.S.O. Emblem and Factory

499 Gateway, Bosra

1983. World Standards Day.
1558 **498** 50p. multicoloured . . . 50 25
1559 – 100p. violet, green & black . . . . 1·10 70
DESIGN: 100p. I.S.O. emblem and measuring equipment.

1983. 10th Anniv of World Heritage Agreement.
1560 **499** 60p. brown 60 25

500 Flowers

1983. Int Flower Show, Damascus. Mult.
1561 50p. Type **500** 60 25
1562 60p. Hibiscus 70 50

501 Farmland

502 Factory

1983. World Food Day.
1563 **501** 180p. green, cream and deep green . . . . . 1·70 85

1983.
1564 **502** 50p. green 50 25

503 Statuette

504 Aleppo

1984. International Deir Ez-Zor History and Archaeology Symposium.
1565 **503** 225p. brown . . . . . . 2·50 1·30

1984. International Symposium for the Conservation of Aleppo.
1566 **504** 245p. multicoloured . . 2·50 1·30

505 Alassad Library

1984. 21st Anniv of Baathist Revolution of 8 March 1963.
1567 **505** 60p. multicoloured . . . 85 45

506 Bodies and mourning Woman with Child

1984. Sabra and Shatila (refugee camps in Lebanon) Massacres.
1568 **506** 225p. multicoloured . . 2·30 1·10

507 Mother and Child

509 Swimming

508 Dam, Emblem and Pioneers

1984. Mothers' Day.
1569 **507** 245p. brown and green 2·30 1·30

1984. 9th Regional Festival of Al Baath Pioneers. Multicoloured.
1570 50p. Type **508** 60 45
1571 60p. Pioneers, ruins and emblems 85 50

1984. Olympic Games, Los Angeles. Multicoloured.
1572 30p. Type **509** 45 45
1573 50p. Wrestling 50 50
1574 60p. Running 60 60
1575 70p. Boxing 70 70
1576 90p. Football 95 95
MS1577 77 × 55 mm. 200p. Footballer within football. Imperf 9·50 9·50

510 Flowers

511 Pres. Assad and Text

1984. Int Flower Show, Damascus. Mult.
1578 245p. Type **510** . . . . . 2·50 1·30
1579 285p. Flowers (different) . . 3·00 1·70

1984. 4th Revolutionary Youth Union Congress.
1580 **511** 50p. brown, deep brown and green 50 25
1581 – 60p. multicoloured . . . 50 45
DESIGN—37 × 25 mm: 60p. Pres. Assad and saluting youth.

512 Emblem and Administration Building, Damascus

1984. Arab Postal Union Day.
1582 **512** 60p. multicoloured . . . 50 35

513 Globe, Dish Aerial and Telephone

514 Arabesque Pattern

1984. World Telecommunications Day.
1583 **513** 245p. multicoloured . . 2·50 1·50

1984. 31st International Damascus Fair. Mult.
1584 45p. Type **514** 50 15
1585 100p. Ornate gold decoration . . . . 1·50 60

515 Stylized Aircraft and Emblem

1984. 40th Anniv of I.C.A.O.
1586 **515** 45p. blue and deep blue 60 25
1587 – 245p. blue, ultramarine and deep blue . . . . 2·50 1·50
DESIGN: 245p. Emblem and stylized building.

516 Text, Flag and Pres. Assad

1984. 14th Anniv of Movement of 16 November 1970.
1588 **516** 65p. orange, black and brown 70 85

517 Palmyra Roman Arch and Colonnades

1984. International Tourism Day.
1589 **517** 100p. brown, black and blue . . . . 1·00 50

518 Wooded Landscape

1985. Woodland Conservation.
1590 **518** 45p. multicoloured . . . 70 25

519 University and Students

1985. 26th Anniv (1984) of Aleppo University.
1591 **519** 45p. black, blue and brown 60 25

520 Oil Lamp

1985. 26th Anniv (1984) of Supreme Council of Science.
1592 **520** 65p. green, red and black 85 45

521 Soldier holding Flag

1985. Army Day.
1593 **521** 65p. brown and bistre 85 45

522 Pres. Assad
524 Torch and "22"

523 Flag and Party Emblem

1985. Re-election of President Assad.
1594 **522** 200p. multicoloured . . 2·20 1·50
1595 300p. multicoloured . . 2·75 1·70
1596 500p. multicoloured . . 5·25 2·50
MS1597 140 × 85 mm. Nos. 1594/6. Imperf . . . . 13·00 13·00

1985. 8th Baath Arab Socialist Party Congress.
1598 **523** 50p. multicoloured . . . 60 25

1985. 22nd Anniv of Baathist Revolution of 8 March 1963.
1599 **524** 60p. multicoloured . . . 60 25

525 Tractor and Cow

1985. Aleppo Industrial and Agricultural Fair (1984). Multicoloured.
1600 65p. Type **525** 70 25
1601 150p. Fort and carrots (vert) 1·90 1·00

526 Liberation Movement, Qneitra

1985. 10th Anniv (1984) of Liberation of Qneitra.
1602 **526** 70p. multicoloured . . . 1·50 45

527 Parliament Building

1985. 10th Anniv of Arab Parliamentary Union.
1603 **527** 245p. multicoloured . . 2·75 1·50

528 U.P.U. Emblem and Pigeon with Letter
529 A.P.U. Emblem

1985. World Post Day.
1604 **528** 285p. multicoloured . . 3·75 1·00

1985. 12th Arab Postal Union Conference, Damascus.
1605 **529** 60p. multicoloured . . . 60 45

530 Medal

1985. Labour Day.
1606 **530** 60p. multicoloured . . . 60 45

531 Steam and Diesel Locomotives

1985. 2nd Scientific Symposium.
1607 **531** 60p. blue . . . . 1·50 50

532 Emblem and Child with empty Bowl

1985. U.N. Child Survival Campaign.
1608 **532** 60p. black, green & pink 60 45

533 Pres. Assad and Road

1985. 15th Anniv of Movement of 16 November 1970.
1609 **533** 60p. multicoloured . . . 60 45

534 Emblem and "40"

535 Lily-flowered Tulip

1985. 40th Anniv of U.N.O.
1610 **534** 245p. multicoloured . . 2·30 1·50

1986. Int Flower Show, Damascus (1985). Mult.
1611 30p. Type **535** 45 20
1612 60p. Tulip 85 70

536 Flask

1986. 32nd International Damascus Fair (1985).
1613 **536** 60p. multicoloured . . . 70 45

537 Abd-er-Rahman I

538 Pres. Hafez al-Assad

1986. 1200th Anniv of Abd-er-Rahman I ad Dakhel, Emir of Cordoba.
1614 **537** 60p. brown, cinnamon and light brown . . . 70 45

1988.

1615	**538**	10p. red	10	10
1616		30p. blue	10	10
1616a		50p. lilac	35	15
1617		100p. blue	60	45
1618		150p. brown	85	35
1619		175p. violet	1·00	45
1620		200p. brown	1·20	80
1621		300p. mauve	1·70	1·10
1622		500p. orange	3·00	1·90
1623		550p. pink	3·50	1·40
1624		600p. green	4·25	1·60
1625		1000p. mauve	7·00	4·00
1626		2000p. green	15·00	7·75

For similar design but with full-face portrait, see Nos. 1774/80.

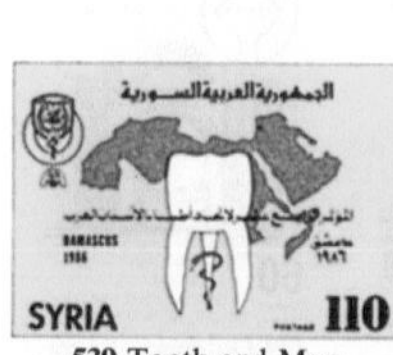
539 Tooth and Map

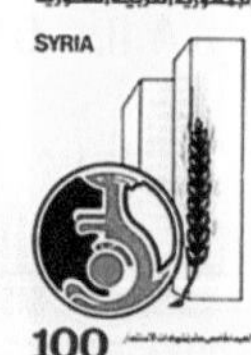
540 Tower Blocks, Ear of Wheat and Kangaroo

1986. 19th Arab Dentists' Union Congress, Damascus.
1627 **539** 110p. multicoloured . . 1·70 1·00

1986. 15th Anniv of Syrian Investment Certificates.
1628 **540** 100p. multicoloured . . 1·30 60

541 Traffic Policewoman, Globe and Traffic Lights

542 Policeman and Building in Laurel Wreath

1986. World Traffic Day.
1629 **541** 330p. multicoloured . . 3·25 1·90

1986. Police Day.
1630 **542** 110p. multicoloured . . 1·00 35

543 Industrial Symbols and Hand Holding Spanner

544 Building

1986. Labour Day.
1631 **543** 330p. red, black and blue 2·75 2·20

1986. 12th Anniv of Liberation of Qneitra.
1632 **544** 110p. multicoloured . . 95 35

545 Pictogram and Ball

546 Mother and Children

1986. World Cup Football Championship, Mexico.
1633 **545** 330p. multicoloured . . 2·50 1·50
1634 370p. multicoloured . . 2·75 1·70
MS1635 105 × 80 mm. 500p. multicoloured (Ball and hemispheres). Imperf . . . . . 5·25 5·25

1986. Mothers' Day.
1636 **546** 100p. multicoloured . . 85 35

547 Pres. Assad and Diesel Train

1986. 23rd Anniv of Baathist Revolution of 8 March 1963.
1637 **547** 110p. multicoloured . . 1·70 85

548 A.P.U. Emblem, Post Office and Box

1986. Arab Post Day.
1638 **548** 110p. multicoloured . . 85 35

549 Fists, Map and Globe

1986. International Palestine Day.
1639 **549** 110p. multicoloured . . 85 35

550 Tulips

1986. Int Flower Show, Damascus. Mult.
1640 10p. Type **550** 15 15
1641 50p. Mauve flowers 45 45
1642 100p. Yellow flowers . . . 1·00 85
1643 110p. Pink flowers . . . . 1·00 85
1644 330p. Yellow flowers (different) . . . . 2·75 1·90

551 Pres. Assad and Tishreen Palace

1986. 16th Anniv of Movement of 16 November 1970.
1645 **551** 110p. multicoloured . . 85 35

552 Rocket and Flags

553 Jug and Star

1986. 1st Anniv of Announcement of Syrian–Soviet Space Flight.
1646 **552** 330p. multicoloured . . 3·00 1·70

1986. 33rd International Damascus Fair.
1647 **553** 110p. multicoloured . . 1·30 85
1648 – 330p. black, green and brown . . . . 3·00 1·70
DESIGN: 330p. Coffee pot.

554 Girls and National Flag

1987. International Children's Art Exhibition.
1649 **554** 330p. multicoloured . . 2·20 1·30

555 U.P.U. Emblem and Airmail Envelope

556 Children in Balloon over Town

1987. World Post Day.
1650 **555** 330p. multicoloured . . 2·20 1·30

1987. International Children's Day.
1651 **556** 330p. multicoloured . . 2·20 1·30

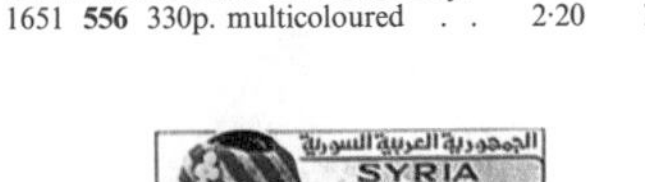
557 Citadel, Aleppo

1987. International Tourism Day.
1652 330p. Type **557** . . . . . 2·30 1·30
1653 370p. Water-wheel, Hama 2·50 1·50

558 Industrial Symbols

1987. 24th Anniv of Baathist Revolution of 8 March 1963.
1654 **558** 100p. multicoloured . . 70 25

559 Doves flying from Globe

560 Party Emblem

1987. International Peace Year.
1655 **559** 370p. multicoloured . . 2·30 1·50

1987. 40th Anniv of Baath Arab Socialist Party.
1656 **560** 100p. multicoloured . . 70 25

561 Stars

1987. 41st Anniv of Evacuation of Foreign Troops from Syria.
1657 **561** 100p. multicoloured . . 70 25

562 Draughtsman

1987. 6th Arab Ministers of Culture Conference.
1658 **562** 330p. blue, green & black . . . . 2·75 1·50

563 Map of Arab Postal Union Members

1987. Arab Post Day.
1659 **563** 110p. multicoloured . . 70 25

564 Couple within Cogwheel

565 Statue

1987. Labour Day.
1660 **564** 330p. multicoloured . . 2·30 1·50

1987. 13th Anniv of Liberation of Qneitra.
1661 **565** 100p. multicoloured . . 70 35

566 Pres. Assad with Children and Nurse

1987. Child Vaccination Campaign.
1662 **566** 100p. multicoloured . . 1·00 60
1663 330p. multicoloured . . 2·50 1·50

567 Dome of the Rock, Battle Scene and Saladin

1987. 800th Anniv of Battle of Hattin.
1664 **567** 110p. multicoloured . . 85 35

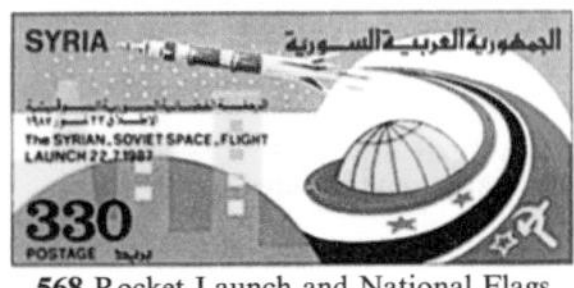
568 Rocket Launch and National Flags

1987. Syrian–Soviet Space Flight. Multicoloured.
1665 330p. Type **568** . . . . . 2·30 1·50
1666 330p. Spacecraft docking with "Mir" space station (37 × 25 mm) . . . . . . 2·30 1·50
1667 330p. Space capsule re-entering Earth's atmosphere and group of cosmonauts (25 × 37 mm) 2·30 1·50
MS1668 150 × 110 mm. 300p. Rocket launch; 300p. Space capsule re-entering atmosphere; 300p. Spacecraft docked with space station; 300p. Stylized Syrian and Soviet cosmonauts. Imperf . . . . 13·00 13·00

569 Flags, Cosmonauts and Pres. Assad

1987. President's Space Conversation with Lt-Col. Mohammed Faris (Syrian cosmonaut).
1669 **569** 500p. multicoloured . . 4·00 1·70

570 Stylized Flowers

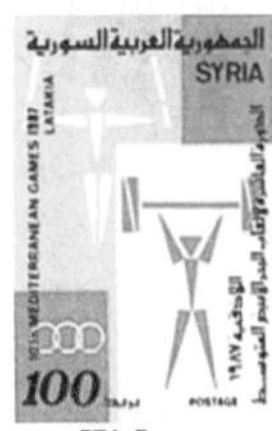
571 Sports Pictograms

1987. 34th International Damascus Fair.
1670 **570** 330p. multicoloured . . 2·20 1·50

1987. 10th Mediterranean Games, Latakia.
1671 **571** 100p. purple and black 60 45
1672 – 110p. multicoloured . . 85 45
1673 – 330p. multicoloured . . 2·20 1·30
1674 – 370p. multicoloured . . 2·50 1·70
MS1675 151 × 112 mm. 300p. × 4, multicoloured . . . . 11·50 11·50
DESIGNS: As Type **571**. HORIZ—110p. Swimming, bird and emblem. VERT—**MS**1671: Gymnastics, weightlifting, tennis and football. 52 × 23 mm—330p. Phoenician galley (Games emblem); 370p. Flags forming "SYRIA".

572 Soldier, Mikoyan Gurevich MiG-21D Fighter, Ship and Tank

573 Trees, Sun and Birds

1987. Army Day.
1676 **572** 100p. multicoloured . . 1·10 45

1987. Tree Day.
1677 **573** 330p. multicoloured . . 2·20 1·30

574 Poppies

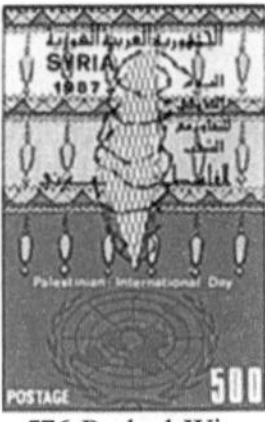
576 Barbed Wire around Map of Israel

575 Pres. Assad acknowledging Applause

1987. International Flower Show, Damascus.
1678 330p. Type **574** . . . . . 2·50 1·00
1679 370p. Mauve flower . . . . 2·75 1·10

1987. 17th Anniv of Corrective Movement of 16 November 1970.
1680 **575** 150p. multicoloured . . 1·00 60

1987. International Palestine Day.
1681 **576** 500p. multicoloured . . 3·75 1·90

577 U.P.U. and U.N. Emblems

1988. World Post Day.
1682 **577** 500p. multicoloured . . 4·00 2·20

578 Bosra Amphitheatre

1988. International Tourism Day. Multicoloured.
1683 500p. Type **578** . . . . . 3·75 1·70
1684 500p. Palmyra ruins . . . . 3·75 1·70

579 Children as Cosmonauts

1988. International Children's Day.
1685 **579** 500p. multicoloured . . 3·75 1·60

580 Hand holding Torch

581 Woman cradling Baby, Children and Adults

1988. 25th Anniv of Baathist Revolution of 8 March 1963.
1686 **580** 150p. multicoloured . . 95 60
MS1687 110 × 81 mm. 500p. No. 1686, map and flag. Imperf 4·25 4·25

1988. Mothers' Day.
1688 **581** 500p. multicoloured . . 3·75 1·70

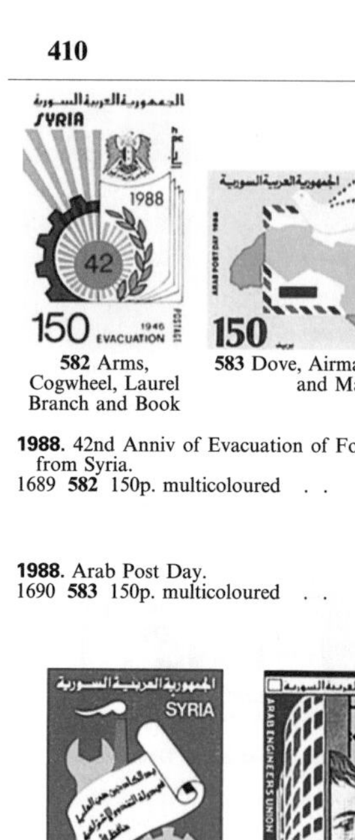

582 Arms, Cogwheel, Laurel Branch and Book

583 Dove, Airmail Envelope and Map

1988. 42nd Anniv of Evacuation of Foreign Troops from Syria.
1689 **582** 150p. multicoloured . . 95 50

1988. Arab Post Day.
1690 **583** 150p. multicoloured . . 95 50

584 Spanner, Chimney, Cogwheel and Scroll

585 Modern Buildings

1988. Labour Day.
1691 **584** 550p. multicoloured . . 3·50 1·70

1988. Arab Engineers' Union.
1692 **585** 150p. multicoloured . . 95 50

586 Lily

1988. Int Flower Show, Damascus. Mult.
1693 550p. Type **586** . . . . . 3·75 1·70
1694 600p. Carnations . . . . . 4·25 2·20

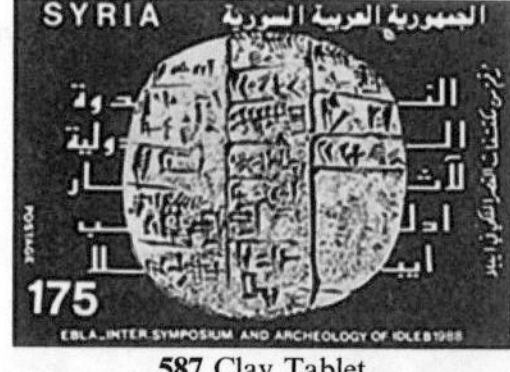

587 Clay Tablet

1988. Int Symposium on Archaeology of Ebla.
1695 **587** 175p. black and brown 1·30 60
1696 – 550p. brown, blue & black . . . . 3·75 1·70
1697 – 600p. multicoloured . . 4·00 1·90
DESIGNS: 550p. King making offering (carving from stone votive basin); 600p. Golden statue of goddess Ishtar.

588 Old City

589 Emblem

1988. Preservation of Sana'a, Yemen.
1698 **588** 550p. multicoloured . . 4·00 1·70

1988. Children's Day.
1699 **589** 600p. black, green and emerald . . . . 4·00 1·90

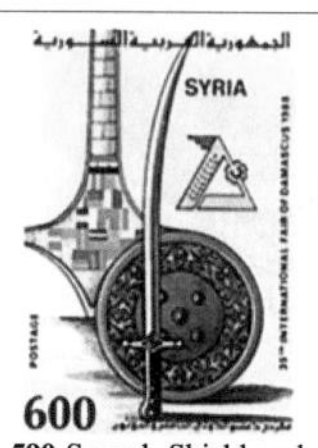

590 Sword, Shield and Emblems

591 Emblem and People

1988. 35th International Damascus Fair.
1700 **590** 600p. multicoloured . . 4·00 1·90

1988. 40th Anniv of W.H.O.
1701 **591** 600p. multicoloured . . 4·00 1·90

592 Emblems and Map

1988. 50th Anniv of Arab Scout Movement.
1702 **592** 150p. mutlicoloured . . 1·50 50

593 Cycling

1988. Olympic Games, Seoul. Multicoloured.
1703 550p. Type **593** . . . . . 4·25 1·70
1704 600p. Football . . . . . . 4·25 1·90
MS1705 80 × 60 mm. 1200p. Emblem and Hodori (mascot). Imperf . . . . 14·00 14·00

594 Old Houses and Modern Flats

1988. Housing. Multicoloured.
1706 150p. Type **594** (Arab Housing Day) . . . . . 1·20 70
1707 175p. House and makeshift shelter (International Year of Shelter for the Homeless (1987)) . . . . 1·30 60
1708 550p. Types of housing (World Housing Day) . . 3·25 1·70
1709 600p. As No. 1707 but inscr for International Day for Housing the Homeless . . 3·50 1·90

595 Euphrates Bridge, Deir el Zor

596 Ear of Wheat and Globe

1988. International Tourism Day. Multicoloured.
1710 550p. Type **595** . . . . . 3·50 1·70
1711 600p. Tetrapylon of Latakia 3·75 1·90
No. 1711 is erroneously inscribed "INTEPNATIONAL".

1988. World Food Day.
1712 **596** 550p. multicoloured . . 3·75 1·60

597 Al-Assad University Hospital

1988. 18th Anniv of Corrective Movement of 16 November 1970.
1713 **597** 150p. multicoloured . . 1·00 50

598 Tree and Flowers

599 Dove with Envelope over Globe

1988. Tree Day.
1714 **598** 600p. multicoloured . . 3·00 1·40

1988. World Post Day.
1715 **599** 600p. multicoloured . . 3·75 1·70

600 Emblem and Doctor within Stethoscope

1989. 10th Anniv of Arab Board for Medical Specializations.
1716 **600** 175p. multicoloured . . 1·10 50

601 Symbols of Agriculture and Industry

1989. 26th Anniv of Baathist Revolution of 8 March 1963.
1717 **601** 150p. multicoloured . . 45 25

602 Pres. Assad and Women

1989. 5th General Congress of Union of Women.
1718 **602** 150p. multicoloured . . 45 25

603 Candle and Books

1989. Arab Teachers' Day.
1719 **603** 175p. multicoloured . . 50 35

604 Nehru

1989. Birth Centenary of Jarwaharlal Nehru (Indian statesman).
1720 **604** 550p. brown & lt brown 1·70 1·00

605 Mother and Children

1989. Mothers' Day.
1721 **605** 550p. multicoloured . . 1·70 1·00

606 Eurasian Goldfinch ("Goldfinch")

1989. Birds. Multicoloured.
1722 600p. Type **606** . . . . . 1·70 1·10
1723 600p. European bee eater ("Bee Eater") . . . . . 1·70 1·10
1724 600p. Turtle dove . . . . . 1·70 1·10

607 State Arms on Map

608 Workers

1989. 43rd Anniv of Evacuation of Foreign Troops from Syria.
1725 **607** 150p. multicoloured . . 45 25

1989. Labour Day.
1726 **608** 850p. green and black 2·40 1·70

609 Snapdragons

610 Girl and Envelope

1989. Int Flower Show, Damascus. Mult.
1727 150p. Type **609** 45 25
1728 150p. "Canaria" 45 25
1729 450p. Cornflowers . . . . 1·30 85
1730 850p. "Clematis sackmani" 2·40 1·70
1731 900p. "Gesneriaceae" . . . 2·50 1·70

1989. Arab Post Day.
1732 **610** 175p. multicoloured . . 50 35

611 Emblem and Map

612 Painted Lady

1989. 13th Arab Teachers' Union General Congress.
1733 **611** 175p. multicoloured . . 50 35

1989. Butterflies. Multicoloured.
1734 550p. Type **612** . . . . . 1·60 1·00
1735 550p. Clouded yellow . . . 1·60 1·00
1736 550p. Large (inscr "small") white . . . . 1·60 1·00

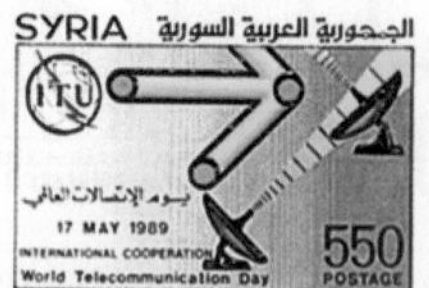

613 Symbols of International Co-operation

1989. World Telecommunications Day.
1737 **613** 550p. multicoloured . . 1·70 1·00

614 Emblem and Map

615 Monument and Al-Baath Pioneers

1989. 17th Arab Lawyers' Union Congress.
1738 **614** 175p. multicoloured . . 50 35

1989. 15th Anniv of Liberation of Qneitra.
1739 **615** 450p. multicoloured . . 1·30 85

616 Globe and Envelopes

1989. World Post Day.
1740 **616** 550p. multicoloured . . 1·70 1·00

617 Parliament Building

1989. Centenary of Interparliamentary Union.
1741 **617** 900p. multicoloured . . 2·50 1·70

618 Emblem and Monument

619 Jaabar Castle, Raqqa

1989. 36th International Damascus Fair.
1742 **618** 450p. multicoloured . . 1·20 50

1989. International Tourism Day. Multicoloured.
1743 550p. Type **619** . . . . . 1·70 1·00
1744 600p. Baal-Shamin Temple, Palmyra . . . . 1·70 1·10

620 Child's View of Intifada

621 Common Carp

1989. Palestinian "Intifada" Movement.
1745 **620** 550p. multicoloured . . 1·40 50

1989. Fishes. Multicoloured.
1746 550p. Type **621** . . . . . 1·40 85
1747 600p. Brown trout . . . . 1·40 85

622 Omayyad Palace, Pres. Assad and Ebla Hotel

1989. 19th Anniv of Corrective Movement of 16 November 1970.
1748 **622** 150p. multicoloured . . 45 25

623 Children of Different Races taking Food from Large Bowl

624 Dove, Globe and Children of Different Races

1990. World Food Day (1989).
1749 **623** 850p. multicoloured . . 2·20 1·10

1990. International Children's Day.
1750 **624** 850p. multicoloured . . 2·20 1·10

625 Flag, Emblem and Ear of Wheat

626 Tree-lined Road

1990. 5th Revolutionary Youth Union Congress.
1751 **625** 150p. multicoloured . . 45 15

1990. 27th Anniv of Baathist Revolution of 8 March 1963.
1752 **626** 600p. multicoloured . . 1·40 50

627 Flag and Arab Fighters

628 Woman carrying Child

1990. 44th Anniv of Evacuation of Foreign Troops from Syria.
1753 **627** 175p. multicoloured . . 45 15

1990. Mothers' Day.
1754 **628** 550p. multicoloured . . 1·40 50

629 Globe and Couple

630 Doctor examining Boy

1990. Labour Day.
1755 **629** 550p. multicoloured . . 1·30 70

1990. World Health Day.
1756 **630** 600p. multicoloured . . 1·30 80

631 Lilies

633 Flag, Tree and City

632 Goalkeeper saving Goal

1990. Int Flower Show, Damascus. Mult.
1757 600p. Type **631** . . . . . 1·30 80
1758 600p. Cyclamen . . . . . . 1·30 80
1759 600p. Marigolds . . . . . 1·30 80
1760 600p. "Viburnum opulus" 1·30 80
1761 600p. Swan river daisies . . 1·30 80

1990. World Cup Football Championship, Italy. Multicoloured.
1762 550p. Type **632** . . . . . 1·30 70
1763 550p. Players marking opponent . . . . 1·30 70
1764 600p. Map of Italy and ball (vert) . . . . 1·30 70
MS1765 74 × 55 mm. 1300p. Floodlit stadium and mascot. Imperf. . 9·50 9·50

1990. 16th Anniv of Liberation of Qneitra.
1766 **633** 550p. multicoloured . . 1·30 70

634 Man and Book

635 Weather Map

1990. International Literacy Year.
1767 **634** 550p. multicoloured . . 1·30 70

1990. World Meteorology Day.
1768 **635** 450p. multicoloured . . 1·00 50

636 Emblem

637 Old and Modern Methods of Ploughing

1990. 37th International Damascus Fair.
1769 **636** 550p. multicoloured . . 1·30 70

1990. United Nations Conference on Least Developed Countries.
1770 **637** 600p. multicoloured . . 1·40 70

638 Boy watering Young Tree

639 Children with Bread and Water in Wheat Field

1990. Tree Day.
1771 **638** 550p. multicoloured . . 1·40 70

1990. World Food Day.
1772 **639** 850p. multicoloured . . 2·20 85

640 Al-Maqdisi and Map

641 Pres. Hafez al-Assad

1990. Death Millenary of Al-Maqdisi (geographer).
1773 **640** 550p. multicoloured . . 1·40 70

1990. (a) As T **538** but with full-face portrait.
1774 50p. lilac 10 10
1775 70p. grey 15 10
1776 100p. blue 15 10
1777 150p. brown ("POSTAGE" in brown) 25 10
1777a 150p. brown ("POSTAGE" in white) 25 10
1778 300p. mauve 50 25
1779 350p. grey 70 35
1780 400p. red 70 35

(b) Type **641**.
1781 175p. multicoloured 35 15
1782 300p. multicoloured 60 15
1783 550p. multicoloured . . . . 1·00 25
1784 600p. multicoloured . . . . 1·40 50

(c) Horiz design with portrait as T **641** within decorative frame.
1786 1000p. multicoloured . . . 2·20 70
1787 1500p. multicoloured . . . 3·00 1·00
1788 2000p. multicoloured . . . 4·25 1·40
1789 2500p. multicoloured . . . 5·25 1·70

642 Pres. Assad with Scouts

1990. 20th Anniv of Corrective Movement of 16 November 1970. Sheet 120 × 95 mm. Imperf.
MS1795 550p. Type **642**; 550p. Pres. Assad and cheering crowd; 550p. Pres. Assad in uniform and Liberation Monument, Qneitra; 550p. Pres. Assad and Euphrates Dam . . . . 5·75 5·75

643 Control Tower, Douglas DC-9-80 Super Eighty Airliner and Emblem

1990. Arab Civil Aviation Day.
1796 **643** 175p. multicoloured . . 50 25

644 Emblem, Open Book, Cogwheel and Ear of Wheat

645 U.P.U. Emblem and Girl posting Letter

1990. 40th Anniv of United Nations Development Programme.
1797 **644** 550p. multicoloured . . 1·30 60

1990. World Post Day.
1798 **645** 550p. multicoloured . . 1·30 60

646 Leapfrog

647 Emblem, Flames and Open Book

1990. World Children's Day.
1799 **646** 550p. multicoloured . . 1·30 80

1990. Arab–Spanish Cultural Symposium.
1800 **647** 550p. multicoloured . . 1·60 85

648 Paths to and away from AIDS

649 Modern Roads and Buildings

1990. World AIDS Day.
1801 **648** 550p. multicoloured . . 1·60 85

1991. 28th Anniv of Baathist Revolution of 8 March 1963.
1802 **649** 150p. multicoloured . . 85 15

650 Lesser Purple Emperor
651 Golden Orioles

1991. Butterflies. Multicoloured.
1803 550p. Type **650** (inscr "Change Ful Great Mars") . . . . 2·20 85
1804 550p. Small tortoiseshell . . 2·20 85
1805 550p. Swallowtail . . . . . 2·20 85

1991. Birds. Multicoloured.
1806 600p. Type **651** . . . . . 1·70 85
1807 600p. House sparrows . . . 1·70 85
1808 600p. European roller . . . 1·70 85

652 Three Generations
653 Statue

1991. Mothers' Day.
1809 **652** 550p. multicoloured . . 1·60 70

1991. 45th Anniv of Evacuation of Foreign Troops from Syria.
1810 **653** 150p. multicoloured . . 45 15

654 Dividers and Spanner
655 Daffodils

1991. Labour Day.
1811 **654** 550p. multicoloured . . 1·60 70

1991. International Flower Show, Damascus. Mult.
1812 550p. Type **655** . . . . . 1·60 70
1813 600p. Bee balm . . . . . . 1·70 70

656 City and Ruins

1991. 17th Anniv of Liberation of Qneitra.
1814 **656** 550p. multicoloured . . 1·60 50

657 Running

1991. 11th Mediterranean Games, Athens. Mult.
1815 550p. Type **657** . . . . . 1·60 70
1816 550p. Football . . . . . . 1·60 70
1817 600p. Show jumping . . . . . 1·70 85
MS1818 80 × 65 mm. 1300p. Dolphins playing water polo. Imperf . . . . 4·00 4·00

658 Hall
660 People encircling Block of Flats

659 Courtyard, Azem Palace, Damascus

1991. 38th International Damascus Fair.
1819 **658** 550p. multicoloured . . 1·70 80

1991. International Tourism Day. Multicoloured.
1820 450p. Type **659** . . . . . 1·30 60
1821 550p. Castle, Arwad Island 1·70 80

1991. Housing Day.
1822 **660** 175p. multicoloured . . 50 25

661 Roller Skating

1991. International Children's Day.
1823 **661** 600p. multicoloured . . 1·70 80

662 Rhazes treating Patient

1991. Science Week.
1824 **662** 550p. multicoloured . . 1·70 80

663 Envelopes and Globe

1991. World Post Day.
1825 **663** 550p. multicoloured . . 1·70 80

664 Globe, Produce and Livestock

1991. World Food Day.
1826 **664** 550p. multicoloured . . 1·70 80

665 Tomb of Unknown Soldier, Damascus

1991.
1827 **665** 600p. multicoloured . . 1·70 80
MS1828 65 × 80 mm. 1000p. Tomb. Imperf . . . . 3·00 3·00

666 Pres. Hafez-al-Assad (½-size illustration)

1991. 21st Anniv of Corrective Movement of 16 November 1970. Sheet 77 × 89 mm.
MS1829 **666** 2500p. multicoloured 7·50 7·50

667 Polluted and Clean Environments
668 Transmission Mast, Globe and Satellite

1991. Environmental Protection.
1830 **667** 175p. multicoloured . . 60 35

1991. International Telecommunications Fair.
1831 **668** 600p. multicoloured . . 1·70 80

669 Leaf and Port

1992. 29th Anniv of Baathist Revolution of 8 March 1963.
1832 **669** 600p. multicoloured . . 1·30 60

670 President Assad

1992. Re-election of President Hafez al-Assad. Multicoloured.
MS1833 Two sheets. (a) 65 × 95 mm. 5000p. Type **670**; (b) 100 × 85 mm. 5000p. Stamp portraits of Pres. Assad as in Type **670** but with state arms and inscriptions in right-hand margin . . . . . . 10·50 10·50

671 Chimneys, Gun-barrel, Ear of Wheat, Dove and Flag

1992. 45th Anniv of Baath Arab Socialist Party.
1834 **671** 850p. multicoloured . . 1·70 85

672 Crane and Mason building Wall

1992. Labour Day.
1835 **672** 900p. black, blue & mauve . . . . 1·40 70

673 Girls at Pedestrian Crossing
674 Girl listening to Mother's Stomach

1992. Road Safety Campaign.
1836 **673** 850p. multicoloured . . 1·70 85

1992. Mothers' Day.
1837 **674** 900p. multicoloured . . 1·90 95

675 Memorial

1992. 46th Anniv of Evacuation of Foreign Troops from Syria.
1838 **675** 900p. multicoloured . . 1·90 95

676 Flax

1992. International Flower Show, Damascus. Mult.
1839 300p. Type **676** 60 25
1840 800p. "Yucca filamentosa" (vert) . . . . 1·70 80
1841 900p. "Zinnia elegans" (vert) . . . . 1·90 95

677 Football

1992. Olympic Games, Barcelona. Multicoloured.
1842 150p. Type **677** 25 15
1843 150p. Running 25 15
1844 450p. Swimming 85 45
1845 750p. Wrestling . . . . . . 1·50 70
MS1846 80 × 125 mm. 5000p. As Nos. 1842/5 but without face values. Imperf . . . . 5·25 5·25

678 Smoker standing in Ashtray
679 Pendant

1992. Anti-smoking Campaign.
1847 **678** 750p. multicoloured . . 1·50 70

1992. 39th International Damascus Fair.
1848 **679** 900p. multicoloured . . 1·70 85

680 Football

1992. 7th Pan-Arab Games, Damascus. Mult.
1849 750p. Type **680** . . . . . 1·50 70
1850 850p. Gymnastics . . . . . 1·70 85
1851 900p. Pole vaulting . . . . 1·90 95

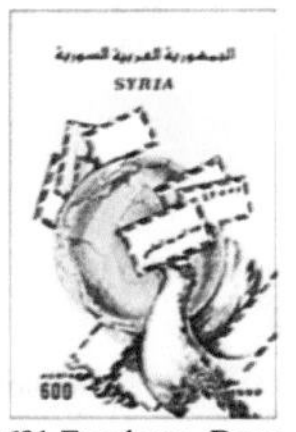

681 Envelopes, Dove and Globe
682 Boy blowing Dandelion Clock

1992. World Post Day.
1852 **681** 600p. multicoloured . . 1·30 60

1992. International Children's Day.
1853 **682** 850p. multicoloured . . 1·70 85

683 Sebtt el-Mardini (astronomer)
684 Table Tennis

1992.
1854 **683** 850p. multicoloured . . 1·70 85

1992. Paralympic Games for Mentally Handicapped, Madrid.
1855 **684** 850p. multicoloured . . 1·70 85

685 People's Square, Damascus
686 Tree

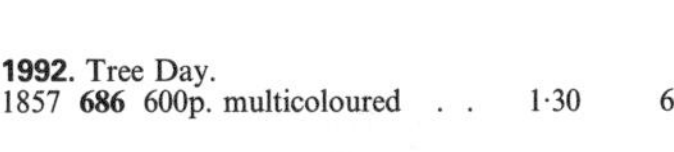
1992. 22nd Anniv of Corrective Movement of 16 November 1970.
1856 **685** 450p. multicoloured . . 95 45

1992. Tree Day.
1857 **686** 600p. multicoloured . . 1·30 60

687 Statue of Pres. Assad, Damascus

1993. 30th Anniv of Baathist Revolution of 8 March 1963.
1858 **687** 1100p. multicoloured . . 1·30 60

688 Common Blue
689 Family

1993. Butterflies. Multicoloured.
1859 1000p. Type **688** . . . . . 1·00 50
1860 1500p. Silver-washed fritillary . . . . 1·50 70
1861 2500p. Blue argus . . . . . 2·50 1·20

1993. Mothers' Day.
1862 **689** 1100p. multicoloured . . 1·30 60

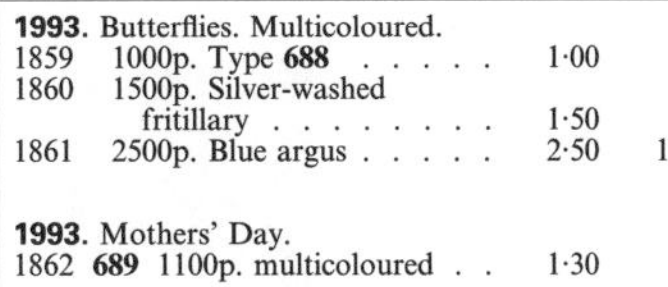

690 Saladin Monument, Damascus

1993. 47th Anniv of Evacuation of Foreign Troops from Syria.
1863 **690** 1100p. multicoloured . . 1·30 60

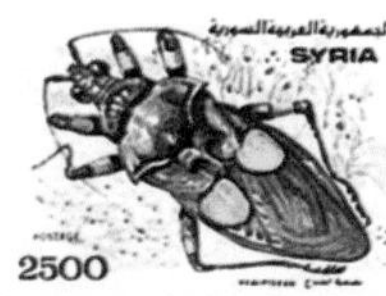

691 Bug

1993.
1864 **691** 2500p. multicoloured . . 2·50 1·20

692 Tractor in Field of Crops

1993. 25th Anniv of Arab Agrarian Union.
1865 **692** 1150p. multicoloured . . 1·30 60

693 Oil Workers

1993. Labour Day.
1866 **693** 1100p. multicoloured . . 1·30 60

694 Eye and Eye-chart

1993. 2nd Pan-Arab Ophthalmology International Council Congress.
1867 **694** 1100p. multicoloured . . 1·30 60

695 Landscapes and Eye
696 "Alcea setosa"

1993. 25th Anniv of National Ophthalmological Association.
1868 **695** 1150p. multicoloured . . 1·30 60

1993. 21st Int Flower Show, Damascus. Mult.
1869 1000p. Type **696** . . . . . 1·10 50
1870 1100p. Primulas . . . . . . 1·30 60
1871 1150p. Gesnerias . . . . . 1·30 60

697 Prism Tomb

1993. International Tourism Day.
1872 **697** 1000p. multicoloured . . 1·30 60

698 Hand posting Letter and Globe

1993. World Post Day.
1873 **698** 1000p. multicoloured . . 1·30 60

699 Boys playing Football
700 Ibn al-Bittar (chemist)

1993. International Children's Day.
1874 **699** 1150p. multicoloured . . 1·30 60

1993. Science Week.
1875 **700** 1150p. multicoloured . . 1·30 60

701 Pres. Assad

1993. 23rd Anniv of Corrective Movement of 16 November 1970. Sheet 76 × 88 mm. Imperf.
MS1876 **701** 2500p. multicoloured 2·00 2·00

702 White Horse

1993. Arab Horses. Multicoloured.
1877 1000p. Type **702** . . . . . 1·10 50
1878 1000p. Horse with white feet 1·10 50
1879 1500p. Black horse . . . . 1·50 70
1880 1500p. White horse with brown mane . . . . . . 1·50 70

703 Orchard in Blossom

1993. Tree Day.
1881 **703** 1100p. multicoloured . . 1·30 60

704 Flags outside Venue

1993. 40th International Damascus Fair.
1882 **704** 1100p. multicoloured . . 1·30 60

705 Basel al-Assad

1994. Basel al-Assad (President's son) Commem.
1883 **705** 2500p. multicoloured . . 2·50 1·30

706 Oranges

1994. 31st Anniv of Baathist Revolution of 8 March 1963. Multicoloured.
1884 1500p. Type **706** . . . . . 1·50 70
1885 1500p. Mandarins . . . . . 1·50 70
1886 1500p. Lemons . . . . . . 1·50 70

707 Flags, Flame, Laurel and Dates

1994. 48th Anniv of Evacuation of Foreign Troops from Syria.
1887 **707** 1800p. multicoloured . . 1·70 85

708 Mechanical Digger loading Truck

1994. Labour Day.
1888 **708** 1700p. multicoloured . . 1·70 85

709 Mother and Child at Different Ages

1994. Mothers' Day.
1889 **709** 1800p. multicoloured . . 1·70 85

710 Emblem, "50" and "75"

1994. 75th Anniv of I.L.O. and 50th Anniv of Philadelphia Declaration (social charter).
1890 **710** 1700p. multicoloured . . 1·50 70

711 Match Scene

1994. World Cup Football Championship, U.S.A. Multicoloured.
1891 1700p. Type **711** . . . . . 1·50 70
1892 1700p. Match scene (different) . . . . 1·50 70
MS1893 80 × 80 mm. 4000p. Match scene (different). Imperf . . . 3·75 3·75

712 Olympic Flag, Greek Temple and "100"

1994. Cent of International Olympic Committee.
1894 **712** 1700p. multicoloured . . 1·30 70

713 Flags, Lanters and Fountain **714** Camomile

1994. 41st International Damascus Fair.
1895 **713** 1800p. multicoloured . . 1·50 70

1994. Int Flower Show, Damascus. Mult.
1896 1800p. Type **714** . . . . . 1·50 70
1897 1800p. Gloxinia . . . . . . 1·50 70
1898 1800p. Mimosa . . . . . . 1·50 70

715 Apollo

1994. Butterflies. Multicoloured.
1899 1700p. Type **715** . . . . . 1·50 70
1900 1700p. Purple emperor (value at right) . . . . . 1·50 70
1901 1700p. Birdwing (value at left) . . . . 1·50 70

716 Symbols and Map

1994. 4th Population Census.
1902 **716** 1000p. multicoloured . . 80 35

717 Al-Kinsi (philosopher)

1994. Science Week.
1903 **717** £S10 multicoloured . . . 85 45

718 Pres. Assad

1994. 24th Anniv of Corrective Movement of 16 November 1970. Sheet 76 × 88 mm. Imperf.
MS1904 **718** £S25 multicoloured 2·20 2·20

719 Airport

1994. 50th Anniv of I.C.A.O.
1905 **719** £S17 multicoloured . . . 1·30 70

720 Al-Marjeh Square **721** Child with Tennis Racquet

1994.
1906 **720** £S50 mauve . . . . . . 4·00 1·90

1994. International Children's Day.
1907 **721** £S10 multicoloured . . . 85 45

722 Girl watching Birds with Envelopes **723** Palmyra Roman Arch

1994. World Post Day.
1908 **722** £S10 multicoloured . . . 85 45

1994. International Tourism Day.
1909 **723** £S17 multicoloured . . . 1·30 70

724 Modern Building

1995. 32nd Anniv of Baathist Revolution of 8 March 1963.
1910 **724** £S18 multicoloured . . . 1·10 80

725 League Emblem and Map **726** Water Pump

1995. 50th Anniv of Arab League.
1911 **725** £S17 multicoloured . . . 1·10 70

1995. World Water Day.
1912 **726** £S17 multicoloured . . . 1·10 70

727 Woman sheltering Figures

1995. Mothers' Day.
1913 **727** £S17 multicoloured . . . 1·10 70

728 Hand holding Tree **729** Family

1995. Tree Day.
1914 **728** 1800p. multicoloured . . 1·10 80

1995. International Year of the Family (1994).
1915 **729** 1700p. multicoloured . . 1·10 70

730 Statue and Flag **731** Honey Bees on Flowers

1995. 49th Anniv of Evacuation of Foreign Troops from Syria.
1916 **730** £S17 multicoloured . . . 1·10 70

1995. 1st Anniv of Arab Apiculturalists Union.
1917 **731** £S17 multicoloured . . . 1·10 70

732 Pres. Assad **733** Welder

1995.
1920 **732** £S10 purple 85 45
1921 £S17 lilac . . . . 1·10 70
1922 £S18 green . . . . . . 1·10 80
1923 £S100 blue . . . . . . 3·00 1·50
1924 £S500 yellow . . . . . 5·25 2·20

1995. Labour Day.
1925 **733** £S10 multicoloured . . . 85 45

734 Anniversary Emblem

1995. 50th Anniv of F.A.O.
1926 **734** £S15 multicoloured . . . 95 60

735 Desert Festival

1995. Tourism Day.
1927 **735** £S18 multicoloured . . . 1·10 80

736 Astilbe **737** Anniversary Emblem on U.N. Headquarters

1995. 23rd Int Flower Show, Damascus. Mult.
1928 £S10 Type **736** 60 60
1929 £S10 Evening primrose . . . 60 60
1930 £S10 Campanula (blue carpet) 60 60

1995. 50th Anniv of U.N.O.
1931 **737** £S18 multicoloured . . . 1·10 80

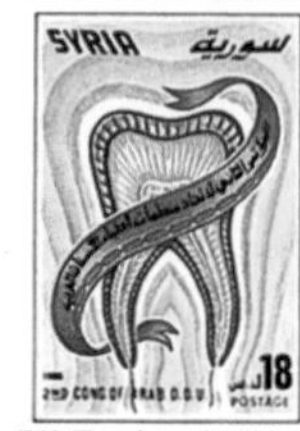

738 Woman holding Globe **740** Tooth and Ribbon

739 Fair Entrance

1995. 4th World Conference on Women, Peking.
1932 **738** £S18 multicoloured . . . 1·10 80

1995. 42nd International Damascus Fair.
1933 **739** £S15 multicoloured . . . 95 60

1995. 2nd Congress of Arab Dentists' Association.
1934 **740** £S18 multicoloured . . . 1·10 80

741 Writing Letters and Air Mail Colours around Globe

1995. World Post Day.
1935 **741** £S15 multicoloured . . . 95 60

742 Children playing on Beach

1995. World Children's Day.
1936 **742** £S18 multicoloured . . . 1·10 80

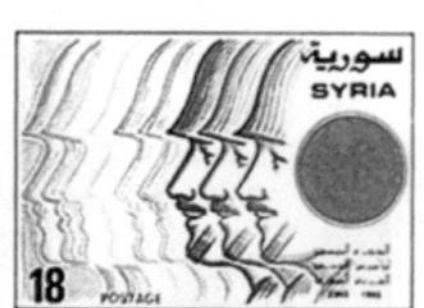

743 Soldiers

1995. 50th Anniv of Syrian Army.
1937 **743** £S18 multicoloured . . . 1·10 80

744 Ahmed ben Maged

1995. 500th Death Anniv of Ahmed ben Maged (cartographer).
1938 **744** £S18 multicoloured . . . 1·10 80

745 Pres. Assad

1995. 25th Anniv of Corrective Movement of 16 November 1970.
1939 **745** £S10 multicoloured . . . 60 45
MS1940 111 × 75 mm. £S50 Pres. Assad and 1975, 1980, 1985 and 1990 stamps. Imperf . . . . . 3·25 3·25

746 Great Tit and Chicks

1995. Birds. Multicoloured.
1941 £S18 Type **746** . . . . . . 1·10 80
1942 £S18 European robin in snow . . . . 1·10 80
1943 £S18 Bluethroat on post . . 1·10 80

747 Pasteur and Laboratory

1995. Death Centenary of Louis Pasteur (chemist).
1944 **747** £S18 multicoloured . . . 1·10 80

748 Olive Tree **749** Pumping Station, Kudairan

1996. Tree Day.
1945 **748** £S17 multicoloured . . . 1·10 70

1996. 33rd Anniv of Baathist Revolution of 8 March 1963.
1946 **749** £S25 multicoloured . . . 1·70 1·10

750 Woman and Horsemen

1996. 50th Anniv of Evacuation of Foreign Troops from Syria.
1947 **750** £S10 multicoloured . . . 60 45
1948 £S25 multicoloured . . . 1·70 1·10
MS1949 80 × 60 mm. **750** £S25 multicoloured. Imperf . . . . 1·70 1·70

751 Woman and Baby

1996. Mothers' Day.
1950 **751** £S10 multicoloured . . . 60 45

752 Textile Factory Workers

1996. Labour Day.
1951 **752** £S15 multicoloured . . . 95 60

753 Memorial

1996. 22nd Anniv of Liberation of Qneitra.
1952 **753** £S10 multicoloured . . . 60 45

754 Map, Palestinian Flag and Arabic Script

1996. 50th Anniv of "Al-Baath" (newspaper).
1953 **754** £S18 multicoloured . . . 1·10 80

755 "Mammilaria erythosperma"

1996. 24th International Flower Show, Damascus. Cacti. Multicoloured.
1954 £S18 Type **755** . . . . . . 1·10 80
1955 £S18 "Notocactus graessnerii" . . . . . . 1·10 80

756 Wrestling

1996. Olympic Games, Atlanta, U.S.A. Mult.
1956 £S17 Type **756** . . . . . . 1·10 70
1957 £S17 Swimming . . . . . . 1·10 70
1958 £S17 Running . . . . . . 1·10 70
MS1959 80 × 59 mm. £S25 Football. Imperf . . . . 1·70 1·70

757 Guglielmo Marconi and Transmitter

1996. Cent (1995) of First Radio Transmissions.
1960 **757** £S17 multicoloured . . . 1·10 70

758 Family protected from burning "AIDS" **759** Fair Emblem, Pattern and Globe

1996. World AIDS Day.
1961 **758** £S17 multicoloured . . . 1·10 70

1996. 43rd International Damascus Fair.
1962 **759** £S17 multicoloured . . . 1·10 70

760 Computer, Emblem and Globe

1996. 5th Anniv of National Information Centre.
1963 **760** £S18 multicoloured . . . 1·10 80

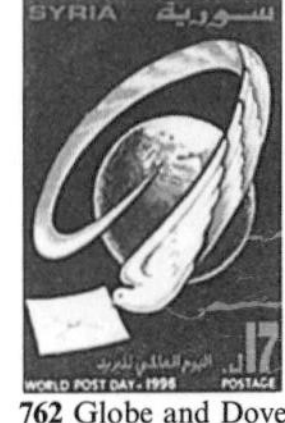

761 Girls playing **762** Globe and Dove with Letter

1996. World Children's Day.
1964 **761** £S10 multicoloured . . . 60 45

1996. World Post Day.
1965 **762** £S17 multicoloured . . . 1·10 70

763 Sons of Musa ibn Shaker

1996. Science Week.
1966 **763** £S10 multicoloured . . . 60 45

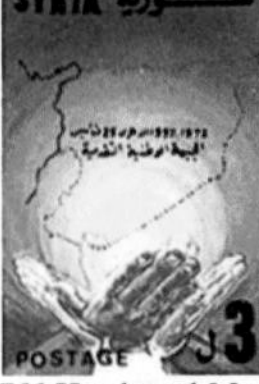

764 Pres. Assad **765** Child sitting on Globe

1996. 26th Anniv of Corrective Movement of 16 November 1970.
1967 **764** £S10 multicoloured . . . 60 45
MS1968 65 × 90 mm. **764** £S50 multicoloured. Imperf . . . . 3·25 3·25

1996. 50th Anniv of U.N.I.C.E.F.
1969 **765** £S17 multicoloured . . . 1·10 70

766 Hands and Map **767** Grain Silos and Wheat

1997. 25th Anniv of National Progressive Front.
1970 **766** £S3 multicoloured . . . 15 10

1997. 34th Anniv of Baathist Revolution of 8 March 1963.
1971 **767** £S15 multicoloured . . . 1·00 70

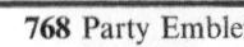
768 Party Emblem **769** Apple Trees

1997. 50th Anniv of Baath Arab Socialist Party.
1972 **768** £S25 multicoloured . . . 1·70 1·10
MS1973 91 × 66 mm. No. 1972. Imperf . . . . 1·70 1·70

1997. Tree Day.
1974 **769** £S10 multicoloured . . . 60 45

770 Mother and Daughter feeding Doves **771** "Beautiful Woman from Palmyra" (relief)

1997. Mothers' Day.
1975 **770** £S15 multicoloured . . . 1·00 70

1997. World Tourism Day (1996).
1976 **771** £S17 multicoloured . . . 1·10 70

772 Grey Mullet

1997. Fishes. Multicoloured.
1977 £S17 Type **772** . . . . . . 1·10 70
1978 £S17 Mediterranean horse mackerel (country inscr at top) . . . . 1·10 70

773 Horsemen

1997. 51st Anniv of Evacuation of Foreign Troops from Syria.
1979 **773** £S15 multicoloured . . . 1·00 70

774 Building Pipeline **775** Library and Books

1997. Labour Day.
1980 **774** £S15 multicoloured . . . 1·00 70

1997. World Book Day.
1981 **775** £S10 multicoloured . . . 60 45

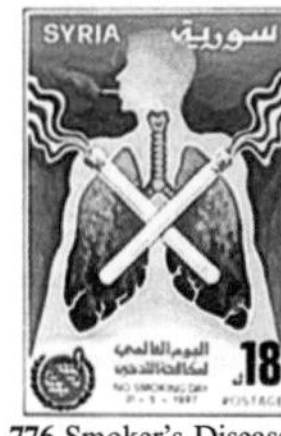

776 Smoker's Diseased Lungs and Cigarettes **777** "Echinoereus purporeus"

1997. World "No Smoking" Day.
1982 **776** £S18 multicoloured . . . 1·10 80

1997. International Flower Show, Damascus. Mult.
1983 £S18 Type **777** . . . . . . 1·10 80
1984 £S18 Irises . . . . 1·10 80

778 Emblem **779** Flags and Monument

1997. 4th Arab Union of Dentists' Associations Congress.
1985 **778** £S10 multicoloured . . . 60 45

1997. 44th International Damascus Fair.
1986 **779** £S17 multicoloured . . . 1·10 70

780 Child reaching for Landmine

1997. International Children's Day.
1987 **780** £S17 multicoloured . . . 1·10 70

781 Post Rider and Dove

1997. World Post Day.
1988 **781** £S17 multicoloured . . . 1·10 70

782 Tourists on Flying Carpet

1997. International Tourism Day.
1989 **782** £S17 multicoloured . . . 1·10 70

783 Jabir ibn Haijan (alchemist)

784 Pres. Assad

1997. Science Week.
1990 **783** £S17 multicoloured . . . 1·10 70

1997. 27th Anniv of Corrective Movement of 16 November 1991. Multicoloured.
1991 £S10 Type **784** 60 45
MS1992 109 × 85 mm. £S50 Portrait as in T **784** with inscriptions arranged beside it. Imperf . . . 3·25 3·25

785 Emblem, Minarets and Banner

1997. 30th Anniv of Organization of the Islamic Conference.
1993 **785** £S10 multicoloured . . . 60 45

786 Sewage Works

1998. 35th Anniv of Baathist Revolution of 8 March 1963.
1994 **786** £S17 multicoloured . . . 1·10 70

787 Mother with Children

1998. Mothers' Day.
1995 **787** £S10 multicoloured . . . 60 45

788 Warrior with Raised Sword

789 Computer and Industrial Sites

1998. 52nd Anniv of Evacuation of Foreign Troops from Syria.
1996 **788** £S10 multicoloured . . . 60 45

1998. Labour Day.
1997 **789** £S18 multicoloured . . . 1·20 80

790 Players challenging for Ball

791 "Bougainvillea glabra"

1998. World Cup Football Championship, France.
1998 **790** £S10 multicoloured . . . 60 45
MS1999 80 × 75 mm. £S25 Match scene. Imperf . . . . 1·70 1·70

1998. International Flower Show, Damascus. Multicoloured.
2000 £S17 Type **791** . . . . . . 1·10 70
2001 £S17 "Hibiscus rosa-sinensis" . . . . 1·10 70

792 Bust of Princess of Banias

793 Mother Teresa

1998. International Tourism Day.
2002 **792** £S17 multicoloured . . . 1·10 70

1998. Death Commemoration of Mother Teresa (founder of Missionaries of Charity).
2003 **793** £S18 multicoloured . . . 1·20 80

794 Post Office

1998. Arab Post Day.
2004 **794** £S10 multicoloured . . . 60 45

795 Cigarette piercing Heart

797 Child on Globe and Dove

796 Doves and World Map

1998. World "No Smoking" Day.
2005 **795** £S15 multicoloured . . . 1·20 80

1998. World Post Day.
2006 **796** £S18 multicoloured . . . 95 60

1998. International Children's Day.
2007 **797** £S18 multicoloured . . . 1·20 80

798 Fish Fountain and Fair Venue

1998. 45th International Damascus Fair.
2008 **798** £S18 multicoloured . . . 1·20 80

799 Pres. Assad and Combat Scenes (½-size illustration)

1998. 25th Anniv of October Offensive against Israel. Sheet 110 × 75 mm.
MS2009 **799** £S25 multicoloured 1·70 1·70

800 Ibn ad-Durainim (mathematician)

1998. Science Week.
2010 **800** £S10 multicoloured . . . 60 45

801 Pres. Assad

1998. 28th Anniv of Corrective Movement of 16 November 1970. Multicoloured.
2011 10p. Type **801** 60 45
MS2012 110 × 75 mm. £S25 Portrait as in T **801** and state flag. Imperf 1·70 1·70

802 Dome of the Rock and Old City

1998. Jerusalem.
2013 **802** £S10 multicoloured . . . 60 45

803 Dromedaries

1998.
2014 **803** £S17 multicoloured . . . 1·10 70

804 Pres. Assad

1999. Re-election of President Hafez al-Assad to Fifth Term.
2015 **804** £S10 multicoloured . . . 60 45
2016 £S17 multicoloured . . . 1·00 70
2017 £S18 multicoloured . . . 1·10 80
MS2018 149 × 119 mm. £S50 multicoloured (Portrait as in T **804** and stamps of 1971, 1978, 1985 and 1992). Imperf 3·25 3·25

805 New Communications Office Building

1990. 36th Baathist Revolution of 8 March 1963. Multicoloured.
2019 £S25 Type **805** . . . . . . 1·60 1·00
MS2020 75 × 110 mm. £S25 Communications Office and statue of Pres. Assad. Imperf 1·60 1·60

806 Fig Tree

807 Mother breast-feeding Baby

1999. Tree Day.
2021 **806** £S17 multicoloured . . . 1·00 70

1999. Mothers' Day.
2022 **807** £S17 multicoloured . . . 1·00 70

808 Woman in Baath Party Colours and Man with Rifle

809 16 November Workers' Further Education Institute

1999. 53rd Anniv of Evacuation of Foreign Troops from Syria.
2023 **808** £S18 multicoloured . . . 1·10 80

1999. Labour Day.
2024 **809** £S10 multicoloured . . . 60 45

810 Crowd with "Human Rights" Banner

1999. 50th Anniv (1998) of Universal Declaration of Human Rights.
2025 **810** £S18 multicoloured . . . 1·10 80

811 Jasmin

1999. International Flower Show, Damascus. Mult.
2026 £S10 Type **811** 60 45
2027 £S10 Acanthus 60 45

812 Show Jumping and Crowd with Lighted Crowns

1999. 10th Friendship Festival, Al Basel.
2028 **812** £S10 multicoloured . . . 60 45

813 Globes and Emblem

1999. 46th International Damascus Fair.
2029 **813** £S15 multicoloured . . . 95 60

814 Patient receiving Treatment and Emblem

815 Postman and Map of Arab States

1999. 7th Arab Union of Dentists' Associations Congress.
2030 **814** £S17 multicoloured . . . 1·00 70

1999. Arab Post Day.
2031 **815** £S10 multicoloured . . . 60 45

816 Abu Hanifah al Deilouri (botanist)

1999. Science Week.
2032 **816** £S17 multicoloured . . . 1·00 70

817 Postal Transport, Emblem and Headquarters, Berne

1999. 125th Anniv of Universal Postal Union.
2033 **817** £S17 multicoloured . . . 1·00 70

818 Ummayed Mosque and Our Lady of Saydnaya Convent, Damascus

1999. 2000 Years of Religious Co-existence.
2034 **818** £S17 multicoloured . . . 1·00 70

819 October 1973 Liberation War Monument and Pres. Assad (statues)

1999. 29th Anniv of Corrective Movement of 16 November 1970. Multicoloured.
2035 £S17 Type **819** . . . . . . 1·00 1·00
2036 £S17 Close-up detail of statue (vert) . . . . . . 1·00 1·00
MS2037 110 × 76 mm. £S25 October 1973 Liberation War Monument and Fountains before statue. Imperf . . . . . 1·50 1·50

820 Children holding Hands around Globe

821 Factories, Corn and Family

1999. International Children's Day.
2038 **820** £S18 multicoloured . . . 1·10 70

2000. 37th Anniv of Baathist Revolution of 8 March 1963.
2039 **821** £S18 multicoloured . . . 1·30 1·30

822 Mother holding Child

824 Rose and Cog

823 Battle Scene (½-size illustration)

2000. Mothers' Day.
2040 **822** £S17 multicoloured . . . 1·20 1·20

2000. 54th Anniv of Evacuation of Foreign Troops from Syria. Sheet 95 × 80 mm.
MS2041 **823** £S25 multicoloured 1·70 1·70

2000. Labour Day.
2042 **824** £S10 multicoloured . . . 70 70

825 Foxy Charaxes

826 Tree and Fruit

2000. Butterflies. Multicoloured.
2043 £S17 Type **825** . . . . . . 1·20 1·20
2044 £S18 Apaturairis . . . . . 1·30 1·30

2000. Tree Day.
2045 **826** £S18 multicoloured . . . 1·30 1·30

827 President Basher Al-Assad

828 Child with Balloons

2000. Election of President Basher Al-Assad.
2046 **827** £S3 multicoloured . . . 15 15
2047 £S10 multicoloured . . . 80 80
2048 £S17 multicoloured . . . 1·30 1·30
2049 £S18 multicoloured . . . 1·40 1·40
MS2050 109 × 75 mm. £S50 President Al-Assad. Imperf . . 4·00 4·00

2000.
2051 **828** £S10 multicoloured . . . 80 80

829 Flags, Exhibition Building and Crowd

2000. 47th International Damascus Fair.
2052 **829** £S15 multicoloured . . . 1·10 1·10

830 U.P.U. Emblem, Envelope and Globe

2000. World Post Day.
2053 **830** £S18 multicoloured . . . 1·40 1·40

831 Map and Emblem

2000. Arab Post Day.
2054 **831** £S18 multicoloured . . . 1·40 1·40

832 Weight Llifting

834 Emblem and Globe

833 Nasir Al-din Altusi (scientist)

2000. Olympic Games, Sydney. Multicoloured.
2055 £S17 Type **832** . . . . . . 1·40 1·40
2056 £S18 Shot-put . . . . . . 1·50 1·50
MS2057 81 × 75 mm. £S25 Javelin 1·90 1·90

2000. Science Week.
2058 **833** £S15 multicoloured . . . 1·10 1·10

2000. 50th Anniv of World Meteorological Organization.
2059 **834** £S10 multicoloured . . . 80 80

835 Cherubs in Rowing Boat and City (mosaic) (½-size illustration)

2000. World Tourism Day. Sheet 111 × 85 mm. Imperf.
MS2060 **835** £S50 multicoloured 4·00 4·00

836 Dam and Emblem

837 Computers

2001. 50th Anniv of Engineer Syndicate. Multicoloured.
2061 £S17 Type **836** . . . . . . 1·30 1·30
MS2062 85 × 95 mm. £S25 As No. 2061 but with design enlarged. Imperf . . . . 1·90 1·90

2001. Al-Marjeh Square. As T **720**.
2063 **720** 100p. light blue-green . . 10 10
2064 £S10 brown red 80 80
2065 £S50 deep blue . . . . 3·50 3·50

2001. 38th Anniv of Baathist Revolution of 8 March 1963.
2066 **837** £S25 multicoloured . . . 1·90 1·90

838 President Hafis al-Assad and Agricultural Painting

2001. 9th Agricultural Congress.
2067 **838** £S25 multicoloured . . . 1·90 1·90

839 Statue of Mother and Baby

840 Horse's Head

2001. Mother's Day.
2068 **839** £S10 multicoloured . . . 80 80

2001. 55th Anniv of Evacuation of Foreign Troops from Syria.
2069 **840** £S25 multicoloured . . . 1·90 1·90

841 Hand, Quill and Emblem

842 Statue of Man holding Spade and Globe

2001. Book and Copyright Day.
2070 **841** £S10 multicoloured . . . 80 80

2001. Labour Day.
2071 **842** £S18 multicoloured . . . 1·40 1·40

843 Weigela

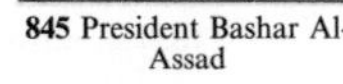
845 President Bashar Al-Assad

844 Ruined Building

2001. International Flower Show, Damascus. Multicoloured.
2072 S£10 Type **843** 80 80
2073 £S10 Mertensia 80 80

2001. 27th Anniv of Liberation of Queneitra.
2074 **844** £S17 multicoloured . . . 1·10 1·10

2001. 1st Anniv of Election of President Bashar Al-Assad.
2075 **845** £S17 multicoloured . . . 1·10 1·10

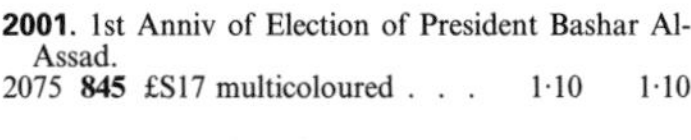

846 People climbing Globe and UNHCR Emblem

2001. 50th Anniv of United Nations High Commissioner for Refugees.
2076 **846** £S17 multicoloured . . . 1·10 1·10

847 Postman and Van

2001. Arab Post Day.
2077 **847** £S18 multicoloured . . . 1·10 1·10

848 Aerial View of Damascus surrounded by Flags

2001. 48th International Damascus Fair.
2078 **848** £S10 multicoloured . . . 80 80

849 Skull, Cigarettes and Ash Tray

2001. World "No Smoking" Day.
2079 **849** £S18 multicoloured . . . 1·40 1·40

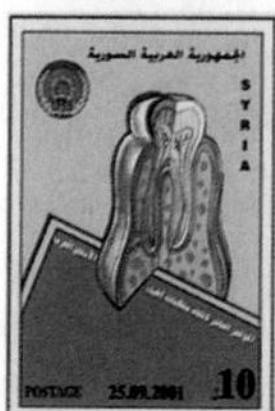
850 Cross Section of Tooth

851 Bust of Princess of Banias

2001. 10th Arab Union of Dentists' Association Congress.
2080 **850** £S10 multicoloured . . . 80 80

2001. World Tourism Day.
2081 **851** £S17 multicoloured . . . 1·10 1·10

852 Globe, Envelope and UPU Emblem

2001. World Post Day.
2082 **852** £S10 multicoloured . . . 80 80

853 Boy

854 Inscribed Scroll

2001. International Children's Day.
2083 **853** £S18 multicoloured . . . 1·40 1·40

2001. Arab Document Day. Multicoloured.
2084 £S10 Type **854** 80 80
MS2085 84 × 110 mm. £S25 As No. 2084 but with design enlarged. Imperf . . . . 1·90 1·90

855 The Citadel, Aleppo

2001. The Aga Khan Award for Architecture Presentation Ceremony, Aleppo. Multicoloured.
2086 £S10 Type **855** 80 80
2087 £S17 The Citadel from below . . . . 1·30 1·30
2088 £S18 As No. 2087 . . . . . 1·40 1·40

856 Planning Commission Building, Damascus

2001. 31st Anniv of Corrective Movement of 16 November 1970.
2089 **856** £S5 multicoloured . . . 35 35
2090 £S15 multicoloured . . . 1·00 1·00

857 Youth Stoning Tank

858 Flowering Tree

2001. Al Aqsa Intifada.
2091 **857** £S17 multicoloured . . . 1·10 1·10

2001. Tree Day.
2092 **858** £S5 multicoloured . . . 35 35

859 Gazelle

861 Mother holding Child

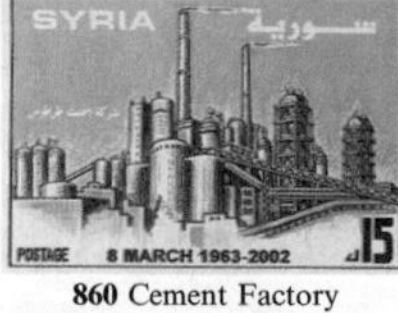
860 Cement Factory

2002.
2093 **859** £S15 multicoloured . . . 1·00 1·00

2002. 39th Anniv of Baathist Revolution of 8 March 1963.
2094 **860** £S15 multicoloured . . . 95 95

2002. Mothers' Day.
2095 **861** £S25 multicoloured . . . 1·60 1·60

862 Party Headquarters

2002. 55th Anniv of Al-Baath Party.
2096 **862** £S15 multicoloured . . . 95 95

863 Map and Emblem

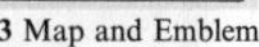
864 UNESCO Emblem

2002. 56th Anniv of Evacuation of Foreign Troops from Syria.
2097 **863** £S15 multicoloured . . . 95 95

2002. Labour Day.
2098 **864** £S10 multicoloured . . . 70 70

865 Players

866 Wallflower

2002. World Cup Football Championships, Japan and South Korea. Multicoloured.
2099 £S5 Type **865** 35 35
2100 £S10 Player chasing ball . . 70 70
MS2101 79 × 65 mm £S25 Player jumping for ball. Imperf . . . 1·30 1·30

2002. International Flower Show, Damascus. Multicoloured.
2102 £S15 Type **866** 95 95
2103 £S17 Narcissus . . . . . . 1·00 1·00

867 Envelopes circling Map of Arab States

2002. Arab Post Day.
2104 **867** £S5 multicoloured . . . 35 35
2105 £S10 multicoloured . . . 70 70

868 Abdul-Rahman Al-Kawakibi

869 Emblem

2002. Death Centenary of Abdul-Rahman Al-Kawakibi (writer).
2106 **868** £S10 multicoloured . . . 70 70

2002. 49th International Damascus Fair. Multicoloured.
2107 £S5 Type **869** 35 35
2108 £S10 Mosaic 70 70

870 Map, Bridge and Train

2002. Centenary of First Syrian Railway.
2109 **870** £S10 multicoloured . . . 70 70

871 Sea Goddess, Shahba (mosaic)

2002. World Tourism Day.
2110 **871** £S10 multicoloured . . . 70 70

872 Protesters and Tank

873 Dove holding Letter

2002. 2nd Anniv of Al Aqsa Intifada. Multicoloured.
2111 £10 Type **872** 70 70
MS2112 64 × 80 mm. £S25 As No. 2111 but with design enlarged. Imperf . . . . 1·30 1·30

2002. World Post Day. Multicoloured.
2113 £S10 Type **873** 70 70
2114 £S10 Envelope and UPU emblem (horiz) 70 70

874 Children

2002. International Children's Day.
2115 **874** £S10 multicoloured . . . 70 70

875 Techrin Thermal Power Plant

2002. 32nd Anniv of Corrective Movement of 16 November 1970.
2116 **875** £S10 multicoloured . . . 70 70

876 Sand Grouse

2002. Birds. Multicoloured.
2117 £S3 Type **876** 20 20
2118 £S5 Francolin 35 35
2119 £S10 Mallard 65 65
2120 £S15 Goose 95 95

877 Pine Tree

878 Anniversary Emblem

2002. Tree Day.
2121 **877** £S10 multicoloured . . . 70 70

2003. Al-Marjeh Square. As T **720**.
2122 **720** 300p. brown 80 80

2003. 40th Anniv of Baathist Revolution of 8 March 1963.
2123 **878** £S15 multicoloured . . . 80 80

879 Stylized Classroom

880 Mother holding Sleeping Child

2003. Teachers' Day.
2124 **879** £S17 multicoloured . . . 85 85

2003. Mothers' Day.
2125 **880** £S32 multicoloured . . . 1·70 1·70

881 Soldier

882 Man and Machine

2003. 57th Anniv of Evacuation of Foreign Troops from Syria.
2126 **881** £S15 multicoloured . . . 80 80

2003. Labour Day.
2127 **882** £S10 multicoloured . . . 1·30 1·30

883 Flower Border (inscr) "Damask rose-violet")

884 Flags and Anniversary Emblem

2003. International Flower Show, Damascus. Multicoloured.
2128 £S10 Type **883** 50 50
2129 £S10 Red flowers (inscr "Anemone") 50 50
2130 £S10 White flowers (inscr "Daisy") 50 50
2131 £S10 Flower border (inscr "Damask rose-gillyflower") 50 50
2132 £S10 Sunflowers 50 50

2003. 50th International Damascus Fair. Multicoloured.
2133 £S32 Type **884** . . . . . . 1·10 65
MS2134 90 × 65 mm. £S50 Jewelled spheres. Imperf . . . . 1·60 1·60

885 Al Hamidieh Souk

2003. World Tourism Day.
2135 **885** £S32 multicoloured . . . 1·70 1·70

886 Flags and Globe

2003. World Post Day.
2136 **886** £S10 multicoloured . . . 50 50

887 Children Playing

2003. International Children's Day.
2137 **887** £S15 multicoloured . . . 80 80

888 Building Facade and Pope John Paul II (⅔-size illustration)

2003. 25th Anniv of the Pontificate of Pope John Paul II.
2138 **888** £S32 multicoloured . . . 1·70 1·70

889 Flower, Map and "33"

890 Binaries, Globe, Figures and Computers

2003. 33rd Anniv of Corrective Movement of 16 November 1970.
2139 **889** £S15 multicoloured . . . 80 80

2003. World Information Technology Summit, Geneva.
2140 **890** £S15 multicoloured . . . 80 80

891 Woodcock (⅔-size illustration)

2003. Birds. Multicoloured.
2141 £S5 Type **891** 35 35
2142 £S10 Lapwing 50 50
2143 £S15 European roller . . . 80 80
2144 £S17 Teal 85 85
2145 £S18 Bustard 90 90

892 Pomegranate

894 Teacher and Pupil

893 Euphrates River Dam (⅔-size illustration)

2003. Tree Day.
2146 **892** £S25 multicoloured . . . 60 40

2004. 41st Anniv of Baathist Revolution of 8 March 1963.
2147 **893** £S10 multicoloured . . . 50 50

2004. Teachers' Day.
2148 **894** £S5 multicoloured . . . 35 35

895 Mother holding Baby

2004. Mothers' Day.
2149 **895** £S15 multicoloured . . . 80 80

896 Map and "58"

2004. 58th Anniv of Evacuation of Foreign Troops from Syria.
2150 **896** £S10 multicoloured . . . 50 50

897 Factory and Cogs

2004. Labour Day.
2151 **897** £S10 multicoloured . . . 50 50

898 Emblem and Players

2004. Centenary of FIFA (Federation Internationale de Football Association). Multicoloured.
2152 £S10 Type **898** 50 50
2153 £S10 Two players and emblem 50 50
MS2154 81 × 66 mm. £S10 Emblem, players and ball. Imperf . . . 90 90

OBLIGATORY TAX STAMPS

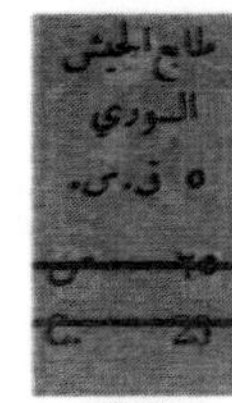
T 57

T 58

T 59

T 60

T 61

1945. Syrian Army Fund. Revenue Stamps surch or optd.
T419 T **57** 5p. on 25p. on 40p. pink . . . . 65·00 3·00
T420 – 5p. on 25p. on 40p. pink . . . . 90·00 7·50
T421 T **58** 5p. on 25p. on 40p. pink . . . . 65·00 1·50
T422 T **59** 5p. blue £100 90
T423 T **60** 5p. blue . . . . 65·00 1·10
T424 – 5p. blue . . . . 80·00 30
T425 T **61** 5p. blue . . . . 80·00 1·00
T426 – 5p. blue . . . . £100 2·00

No. T420 is as Type **57** but with additional overprint as top line of Type **61**.

No. T424 has top line of overprint as Type **59** and other lines as Type **60**.

No. T426 has top line overprinted as Type **61** and other lines as Type **60**.

POSTAGE DUE STAMPS
A. FRENCH MILITARY OCCUPATION

1920. "Mouchon" and "Merson" key-types of French Post Offices in the Turkish Empire (inscr "LEVANT") surch **O. M. F. Syrie Ch. taxe** and value.
D48 B 1p. on 10c. red £190 £190
D49 2p. on 20c. brown £190 £190
D50 3p. on 30c. lilac £190 £190
D51 C 4p. on 40c. red and blue £190 £190

1920. Postage Due stamps of France surch **O. M. F. Syrie** and value.
D60 D **11** 50c. on 10c. brown . . 65 1·20
D52 1p. on 10c. brown . . . 3·00 6·00
D61 1p. on 20c. green . . . 1·20 1·20
D53 2p. on 20c. green . . . 2·30 6·25
D62 2p. on 30c. red . . . . 4·25 6·75
D54 3p. on 30c. red . . . . 2·00 6·00
D63 3p. on 50c. purple . . . 4·25 7·75
D55 4p. on 50c. purple . . . 5·25 13·50
D64 5p. on 1f. purple on yellow . . . . 11·50 16·00

1921. Issued at Damascus. No. KD96 of Arab Kingdom surch **O. M. F. Syrie Chiffre Taxe** and value.
D69 K **3** 50c. on 1p. black . . . . 4·25 9·25
D70 1p. on 1p. black . . . . 2·75 6·75

1921. Issued at Damascus. No. 64a/5 of Syria optd **TAXE**.
D89 K **4** 2p. on 5m. red . . . . . 10·50 13·50
D90 K **3** 3p. on 1p. blue . . . . 27·00 27·00

B. ARAB KINGDOM

1920. As No. K92 but colour changed.
KD96 K **3** 1p. black . . . . . . 1·60 1·50

C. FRENCH MANDATED TERRITORY

1923. Postage Due stamps of France surch **Syrie Grand Liban** and value.
D118 D **11** 50c. on 10c. brown . . 3·50 5·25
D119 1p. on 20c. green . . . 3·75 6·00
D120 2p. on 30c. red . . . 2·50 5·50
D121 3p. on 50c. purple . . 2·25 5·25
D122 5p. on 1f. purple on yellow . . . . . . 6·00 10·00

1924. Postage Due stamps of France surch **SYRIE** and value.
D139 D **11** 50c. on 10c. brown . . 80 4·75
D140 1p. on 20c. green . . . 2·00 4·75
D141 2p. on 30c. red . . . 2·25 5·50
D142 3p. on 50c. purple . . 1·40 5·50
D143 5p. on 1f. purple on yellow . . . . . . 1·90 5·75

1924. Postage Due stamps of France surch **Syrie** and value and also in Arabic.
D175 D **11** 0p.50 on 10c. brown 65 3·50
D176 1p. on 20c. olive . . . 1·60 5·00
D177 2p. on 30c. red . . . . 2·00 4·75
D178 3p. on 50c. purple . . 3·00 5·25
D179 5p. on 1f. red on yellow . . . . . . 3·50 6·75

D 20 Hama

1925.

D192 D **20** 0p.50 brown on yellow 50 1·90
D193 – 1p. purple on pink . . 10 45
D194 – 2p. black on blue . . 1·10 2·25
D195 – 3p. black on red . . . 1·40 1·50
D196 – 5p. black on green . . 1·30 2·50
D197 – 8p. black on blue . . 7·50 9·00
D198 – 15p. black on pink . . 11·50 16·00
DESIGNS—VERT: 1p. Antioch. HORIZ: 2p. Tarsus; 3p. Banias; 5p. Castle; 8p. Ornamental design; 15p. Lion.

E. SYRIAN REPUBLIC

D **221**

1965.

D883 D **221** 2½p. blue 25 15
D884 5p. brown 45 15
D885 10p. green 45 15
D886 17½p. red . . . . . 85 1·00
D887 25p. blue . . . . . 1·30 1·30

TAHITI Pt. 6

The largest of the Society Islands in the S. Pacific Ocean. Later renamed Oceanic Settlements.

100 centimes = 1 franc.

1882. Stamps of French Colonies. "Peace and Commerce" type, surch **25c.**
1 H 25c. on 35c. black on orange £200 £190
3a 25c. on 40c. red on yellow £2750 £3250

1884. Stamps of French Colonies, "Commerce" (perf) and "Peace and Commerce" (imperf) types, surch **TAHITI** and value.
4 J 5c. on 20c. red on green . . . £150 £120
5 10c. on 20c. red on green . . £200 £180
2 H 25c. on 35c. black on orange £3250 £3250
6 25c. on 1f. green £450 £375

1893. Stamps of French Colonies, "Commerce" type, optd **TAHITI**.
7 J 1c. black on blue £500 £450
8 2c. brown on buff £2250 £1700
9 4c. brown on grey £850 £650
10 5c. green on green . . . . . 17·00 27·00
11 10c. black on lilac . . . . . 20·00 35·00
12 15c. blue . . . . 25·00 30·00
13 20c. red on green . . . . . . 48·00 45·00
14 25c. brown £5000 £4500
15 25c. black on pink . . . . . 23·00 32·00
16 35c. black on orange £1500 £1500
17 75c. red on pink . . . . . . 60·00 60·00
18 1f. green . . . . 65·00 60·00

1893. Stamps of French Colonies, "Commerce" type, optd **1893 TAHITI.**
32 J 1c. black on blue £550 £500
33 2c. brown on buff £2500 £1800
34 4c. brown on grey £1000 £900
35 5c. green on green £650 £550
36 10c. black on lilac £200 £200
37 15c. blue . . . . 32·00 22·00
38 20c. red on green . . . . . . 35·00 35·00
39 25c. brown £22000 £20000
40 25c. black on pink . . . . . 35·00 35·00
41 35c. black on orange £1500 £1200
42 75c. red on pink . . . . . . 30·00 35·00
43 1f. green . . . . 35·00 35·00

1903. Stamps of Oceanic Settlements, "Tablet" key-type, surch **TAHITI 10 centimes.**
57 D 10c. on 15c. blue and red . . . 6·00 7·50
58 10c. on 25c. black and red on pink . . . . 5·00 6·00
59 10c. on 40c. red and blue on yellow . . . . 7·00 7·00

1915. Stamps of Oceanic Settlements, "Tablet" key-type, optd **TAHITI** and red cross.
60 D 15c. blue and red £130 £130
61 15c. grey and red . . . . . 25·00 25·00

POSTAGE DUE STAMPS

1893. Postage Due stamps of French Colonies optd **TAHITI.**
D19 U 1c. black £225 £225
D20 2c. black £200 £250
D21 3c. black £225 £275
D22 4c. black £275 £275
D23 5c. black £275 £275
D24 10c. black £275 £275
D25 15c. black £275 £275
D26 20c. black £225 £225
D27 30c. black £275 £275
D28 40c. black £275 £275
D29 60c. black £300 £300
D30 1f. brown £650 £650
D31 2f. brown £650 £650

1893. Postage Due stamps of French Colonies optd **1893 TAHITI.**
D44 U 1c. black £1600 £1600
D45 2c. black £350 £350
D46 3c. black £350 £350
D47 4c. black £350 £350
D48 5c. black £350 £350
D49 10c. black £350 £350
D50 15c. black £350 £350
D51 20c. black £225 £225
D52 30c. black £350 £350
D53 40c. black £350 £350
D54 60c. black £350 £350
D55 1f. brown £350 £350
D56 2f. brown £350 £350
For later issues see **OCEANIC SETTLEMENTS**.

TAJIKISTAN Pt. 10

Formerly a constituent republic of the Soviet Union, Tajikistan became independent in 1991.

1992. 100 kopeks = 1 (Russian) rouble.
1995. 100 tanga = 1 (Tajik) rouble.

1 Hunter (gold relief)

2 Sheikh Muslihiddin Mosque, Khudzand

1992.
1 **1** 50k. multicoloured 15 15

1992.
2 **2** 50k. multicoloured 15 15

3 Traditional Musical Instruments

1992.
3 **3** 35k. multicoloured 15 15

4 Argali

1992.
4 **4** 30k. multicoloured 15 15

3.00
Тоҷикистон
(5)

5.00
1992
1992
Тадж.
(7)

1992. No. 2 surch as T **5**.
5 **2** 5r. on 50k. multicoloured . . 25 25
6 25r. on 50k. multicoloured . . 50 50

1992. No. 3 surch.
7 **3** 15r. on 35k. multicoloured . . 25 25
8 50r. on 35k. multicoloured . . 25 25

1993. No. 6072 of Russia surch as T **7**.
9 **2410** 3r. on 1k. brown 10 10
10 100r. on 1k. brown . . . . 1·75 1·75

60. 00

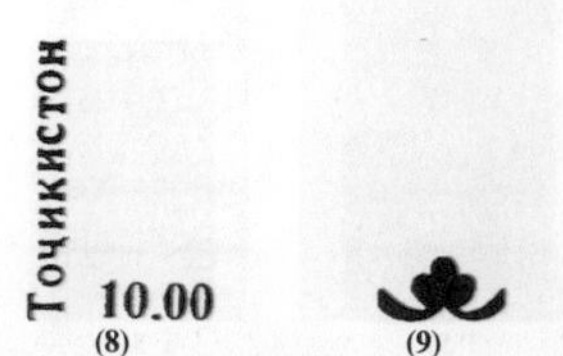

(8) (9)

1993. No. 6073 of Russia surch as T **8**.
11 10r. on 2k. brown 20 20
12 15r. on 2k. brown 50 50

1993. No. 1 surch with T **9**.
13 **1** 60r. on 50k. multicoloured 50 50

10 Mountain Landscape

1993. Multicoloured.
16 1r. Statue of Abuabdullokhi Rudaki, Dushanbe (vert) . . 10 10
17 5r. Type **10** 10 10
18 15r. Mausoleum of Sadriddin Aini (poet), Dushanbe (vert) 10 10
19 20r. State flag and map . . . 10 10
20 25r. Hissar Fort 15 10
21 50r. Aini Opera and Ballet House, Dushanbe 25 15
22 100r. State flag and map (different) 50 30

11 Brown Bear

1993. Mammals. Multicoloured.
23 3r. Type **11** 10 10
24 10r. Red deer 10 10
25 15r. Markhor 15 10
26 25r. Porcupine 25 15
27 100r. Snow leopard . . . . . 1·00 65

12 Geb and Talkhand in Battle

1993. Millenary of "Book of Kings" by Abu-I Kasim Mansur, Firdausi (Persian poet). Multicoloured.
28 5r. Type **12** 10 10
29 20r. Rustam and Sukhrov in combat 25 10
30 30r. Eagle Simurgh brings Zola to his father Som (vert) 35 20
MS31 100 × 81 mm. 50r. Portrait of Firdausi (29 × 44 mm) 55 40

13 Throwing the Hammer

1993. Andrei Abduvaliev's Victory at Olympic Games, Barcelona. Sheet 70 × 70 mm.
MS32 **13** 50r. multicoloured . . . 1·50 1·50

14 Ceiling Decoration

15 Arms

1993.
33 **14** 1r.50 multicoloured 25 15

1994.
34 **15** 10r. multicoloured 10 10
35 15r. multicoloured 10 10
36 35r. multicoloured 10 10
37 50r. multicoloured 10 10
38 100r. multicoloured 10 10
39 160r. multicoloured 15 10
40 500r. mult (23 × 37 mm) . . 40 25
41 1000r. mult (23 × 37 mm) . . 85 55

16 Hamadony (after Vafo Nazarovym)

18 Post Office

МУСОВИҚОТИ ҶАҲОНИИ ВАРЗИШИ САБУК.
Штутгарт 12-22.08.1993.
МЕДАЛИ ТИЛЛО.
(17)

1994. 680th Birth Anniv of Ali Hamadony (Persian mystic).
42 **16** 1000r. multicoloured (inscr in Roman alphabet) . . . 50 35
43 1000r. multicoloured (inscr in Cyrillic) 50 35

1994. Andrei Abduvaliev's Victory at World Athletics Championships, Stuttgart. No. **MS**32 optd with T **17**.
MS44 **13** 50r. multicoloured . . . 1·50 1·50

1994. Historic Monuments. Multicoloured.
45 10r. Statue of Firdausi (vert) 10 10
46 35r. Type **18** 10 10
47 100r. Theatre 10 10
48 160r. Ulum Academy 20 10
49 160r. "Safar" building 20 10

19 Tyrannosaurus

1994. Prehistoric Animals. Multicoloured.
50 500r. Type **19** 30 20
51 500r. Stegosaurus 30 20
52 500r. Anatosaurus 30 20
53 500r. Parasaurolophus 30 20
54 500r. Triceratops 30 20
55 500r. Diatryma 30 20
56 500r. Tyrannosaurus (different) 30 20
57 500r. Spinosaurus 30 20

1995. No. 33 surch **1995** and value.
58 **14** 100r. on 1r.50 mult 10 10
59 600r. on 1r.50 mult 30 15
60 1000r. on 1r.50 mult 50 25
61 5000r. on 1r.50 mult . . . . 1·60 90

21 Gecko ("Alsophylax loricatus")

1995. Lizards. Multicoloured.
62 500r. Type **21** 20 15
63 500r. Sunwatcher ("Phrynocephalus helioscopus") 20 15
64 500r. Toad-headed agama ("Phrynocephalus mystaceus") 20 15
65 500r. Toad agama ("Phrynocephalus sogdianus") 20 15
66 500r. Plate-tailed gecko ("Teratoscincus scineus") . . 20 15
67 500r. Transcaspian desert monitor ("Varanus griseus") 20 15
MS68 80 × 55 mm. 5000r. Schneider's gold Skink ("Eumeces schneiden") . . . . 2·00 2·00

22 National Flag

25 State Arms

23 War Memorial, Dushanbe

1995. Membership of International Organizations. Multicoloured.
69 1000r. Type **22** (Organization for Security and Co-operation in Europe) 45 30
70 1000r. National flag and New York Headquarters (United Nations) (horiz) 45 30
71 1000r. Emblem and national flag (Universal Postal Union) 45 30

1995. 50th Anniv of End of Second World War. Sheet 111 × 76 mm.
MS72 **23** 5000r. multicoloured (gold inscr and rosette in margin) 75 75

1995. "Beijing '95" International Stamp Exhibition, China (73) and "Singapore '95" International Stamp Exhibition (74). Nos. 64 and 67 optd with relevant exhibition emblem.
73 500r. multicoloured 1·25 1·00
74 500r. multicoloured 1·25 1·00

1995.
75 **25** 1r. multicoloured 10 10
76 2r. multicoloured 10 10
77 5r. multicoloured 10 10
78 12r. multicoloured 15 10
79 40r. multicoloured 40 25

26 Bar-headed Goose ("Anser indicus")

1996. Birds. Multicoloured.
80 200r. Type **26** 60 40
81 200r. Indian black-headed gull ("Larus brunnicephalus") 60 40
82 200r. Houbara bustard ("Otis undulata") 60 40
83 200r. Daurian partridge ("Perdix dauricae") 60 40
84 200r. Tibetan sandgrouse ("Syrrhaptes tibetana") 60 40
85 200r. Tibetan snowcock ("Tetraogallus tibetanus") 60 40
MS86 76 × 51 mm. 600r. Ring-necked pheasant ("Phasianus colchicus") 1·75 1·75

27 New York Headquarters

1996. 50th Anniv of UNO. Multicoloured.
87 100r. Type **27** 35 20
MS88 101 × 71 mm. 500r. Close-up view of New York headquarters 1·75 1·75

28 Striped Hyena ("Hyaena hyaena")

1996. "Save the Aral Sea". Sheet 128 × 108 mm containing T **28** and similar horiz designs. Multicoloured.
MS89 100r. Caracal ("Felis caracal"); 100r. Aral trout ("Salmo trutta aralensis"); 100r. Type **28**; 100r. Kaufmann's shovelnose ("Pseudoscaphirhynchus kaufmanni"); 10r. Pike asp ("Aspiolucius esocinus") 2·40 2·40

29 Pallas's Cat

1996. Wild Cats. Multicoloured. (a) With World Wildlife Fund emblem. Pallas's Cat.
90 100r. Type **29** 50 30
91 100r. Close-up 50 30
92 150r. Head 75 50
93 150r. Sitting 75 50

(b) Without W.W.F. emblem.
94 200r. Jungle cat ("Felis chaus") 1·00 75
95 200r. Lynx ("Felis lynx") 1·00 75
MS96 111 × 83 mm. 500r. Pallas's cat 2·50 2·50

30 Diving

31 Kamol Khujandi

1996. Olympic Games, Atlanta, U.S.A. Mult.
97 200r. Type **30** 85 50
98 200r. Football 85 50
99 200r. Throwing the hammer 85 50
100 200r. Judo 85 50
101 200r. Baron Pierre de Coubertin (founder of modern Games) 85 50

1996. Kamol Khujandi (writer) Commemoration.
102 **31** 500r. multicoloured (inscr in Roman letters) 1·60 1·00
103 500r. multicoloured (inscr in Cyrillic letters) 1·60 1·00

32 Emblem

1996. 5th Anniv of Central Asian Postal Union.
104 **32** 100r. multicoloured 1·00 1·00

33 Mt. Krozhenevskoi

1997. Mountains over 7000 m. Multicoloured.
105 100r. Type **33** 45 30
106 100r. Mt. Lenin 45 30
107 100r. Mt. Communism 45 30
MS108 100 × 69 mm. 500r. Mountain climber 2·25 2·25

1997. Nos. 58/61 surch **A 1997**.
109 A (12r.) on 100r. on 1r.50 multicoloured 35 20
110 A (12r.) on 600r. on 1r.50 multicoloured 35 20
111 A (12r.) on 1000r. on 1r.50 multicoloured 35 20
112 A (12r.) on 5000r. on 1r.50 multicoloured 35 20

35 Copper Vessel

36 Woman from Khujand

1998. Crafts. Multicoloured.
113 30r. Type **35** 20 10
114 100r. Cradles 60 40
MS115 64 × 64 mm. 300r. Painted dish. Imperf 1·40 1·40

1998. Traditional Costumes. Multicoloured.
116 100r. Type **36** 40 25
117 100r. Woman from Darvoz carrying pot 40 25
118 150r. Man from Khujand (blue coat) 60 40
119 150r. Man from Darvoz (striped coat) 60 40

37 "Tulipa greigii"

1998. Flowers. Multicoloured.
120 12r. Type **37** 10 10
121 30r. "Crocus korolkowi" 15 10
122 70r. "Iris darwasica" 40 25
123 150r. "Petilium eduardii" 80 50
MS124 68 × 53 mm. 300r. "Juno nicolai" 1·40 1·40

38 "Catocala timur"

1998. Butterflies and Moths. Multicoloured.
125 12r. Type **38** 10 10
126 30r. "Celerio chamyla apocyni" 15 10
127 70r. "Colias sieversi" 40 25
128 150r. Southern swallowtail 80 50
MS129 68 × 53 mm. 300r. "Anthocharis tomyris" 1·40 1·40

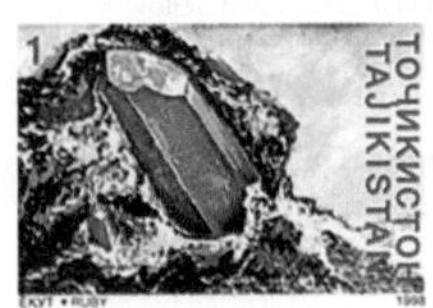

39 Ruby

1998. Minerals. Multicoloured.
130 1r. Type **39** 10 10
131 1r. Sapphire 10 10
132 12r. Tourmaline 10 10
133 12r. Lapis lazuli 10 10
134 150r. Spinel 80 50
135 150r. Amethyst 80 50
MS136 **136** 126 × 85 mm. 350r. Agate 1·60 1·60

40 Ghafurov

1998. Death Commemoration of Bobojon Ghafurov (politician).
137 **40** 12r. multicoloured 10 10
138 150r. multicoloured 80 50

41 Centenary Poster

1999. Birth Bicentenary of Aleksandr Sergeevich Pushkin (poet). Multicoloured.
139 100r. Type **41** 65 40
140 270r. Portrait of Pushkin 1·25 70

42 Diamond Design

43 Key Design

44 Pyramid Design

45 Lion shaped figurine

1999. Carpet Designs. Value expressed by Cyrillic letter.
141 **42** (A) multicoloured 65 40
142 **43** (B) multicoloured 65 40
143 **44** (V) multicoloured 65 40

1999. 1100th Anniv of Samanids State. Multicoloured.
144 30r. Type **45** 20 15
145 50r. Anniversary emblem 35 20
146 100r. Animal-shaped vessel 65 40
147 270r. Clay ornaments 1·25 75
MS148 124 × 105 mm. 500r. Ismoil Somoni (founder) 2·00 2·00

46 Ismoil Somoni

1999. Leaders. Sheet 114 × 77 mm containing T **46** and similar vert designs. Multicoloured.
MS149 100r. Type **46**; 500r. Pres. E. Rahmonov 2·75 2·75

47 *Pleurotus eryngii*

1999. Fungi. Multicoloured.
150 100r. Type **47** 65 40
151 270r. Naked mushroom 1·25 75
MS152 160 × 90 mm. As Nos. 150/1, each × 2 3·75 3·75
MS153 97 × 77 mm. 500r. *Morchella steppicola* 2·00 2·00

TANGANYIKA Pt. 1

Formerly the German colony of German East Africa. After the 1914–18 War it was under British mandate until 1946 and then administered by Britain under United Nations trusteeship until 1961 when it became independent within the British Commonwealth. It had a common postal service with Kenya and Uganda from 1935 to 1961 (for these issues see under Kenya, Uganda and Tanganyika). Renamed Tanzania in 1965.

1915. 16 annas = 1 rupee.
1917. 100 cents = 1 rupee.
1922. 100 cents = 1 shilling.

1915. Stamps of the Indian Expeditionary Forces optd **G. R. POST MAFIA**.
M33 **55** 3p. grey 35·00 80·00
M34 **56** ½a. green 50·00 85·00
M35 **57** 1a. red 55·00 85·00
M36 **59** 2a. lilac 85·00 £140
M37 **61** 2½a. blue £110 £170
M38 **62** 3a. orange £110 £180
M39 **63** 4a. olive £140 £200
M40 **65** 8a. mauve £250 £350
M41 **66** 12a. red £300 £450
M42 **67** 1r. brown and green £350 £475

1916. Stamps of Nyasaland (King George V) optd **N.F.**
N1 ½d. green 1·50 8·00
N2 1d. red 1·50 3·25
N3 3d. purple on yellow 10·00 17·00
N4 4d. black and red on yellow 30·00 40·00
N5 1s. black on green 35·00 45·00

1917. Stamps of Kenya and Uganda (King George V, 1912) optd **G.E.A.**
45 1c. black 15 80
47 3c. green 15 15
48 6c. red 15 10
49 10c. orange 50 60
50 12c. grey 50 2·25
51 15c. blue 80 2·50
52 25c. black and red on yellow 80 3·50
53 50c. black and lilac 80 3·25
54 75c. black on green 1·00 4·50
55 1r. black on green 3·00 7·00

56 2r. red and black on blue . . 11·00 45·00
57 3r. violet and green . . . . . 13·00 80·00
58 4r. red and green on yellow . . 17·00 90·00
59 5r. blue and purple . . . . . 38·00 90·00
60 10r. red and green on green 80·00 £325
61 20r. black and purple on red £190 £400
62 50r. red and green £475 £800

4 Giraffe

5

1922.

74 4 5c. black and purple . . . . 2·25 20
89 5c. black and green . . . . 3·00 1·50
75 10c. black and green . . . . 2·25 85
90 10c. black and yellow . . . 4·25 1·50
76 15c. black and red . . . 2·00 10
77 20c. black and orange . . . 1·75 10
78 25c. black . . . . 5·50 6·50
91 25c. black and blue . . . . 4·00 17·00
79 30c. black and blue . . . . 5·00 5·00
92 30c. black and purple . . . 4·25 13·00
80 40c. black and brown . . . 2·75 4·50
81 50c. black and grey . . . . 2·00 1·50
82 75c. black and yellow . . . 3·25 18·00
83a 5 1s. black and green . . . . 2·50 11·00
84 2s. black and purple . . . . 5·50 15·00
85 3s. black . . . . 16·00 28·00
86a 5s. black and red . . . . . 15·00 75·00
87a 10s. black and blue . . . . 50·00 £100
88a £1 black and orange £160 £300

6

7

1927.

93 6 5c. black and green . . . . 1·75 10
94 10c. black and yellow . . . 2·00 10
95 15c. black and red . . . . 1·75 10
96 20c. black and orange . . 2·75 10
97 25c. black and blue . . . . 3·75 2·00
98 30c. black and purple . . . 2·75 2·50
98a 30c. black and blue . . . . 25·00 30
99 40c. black and brown . . . 2·00 4·50
100 50c. black and grey . . . . 2·50 1·00
101 75c. black and olive . . . 2·00 14·00
102 7 1s. black and green . . . . 4·25 2·75
103 2s. black and purple . . . 19·00 4·50
104 3s. black . . . . 20·00 55·00
105 5s. black and red . . . . . 19·00 17·00
106 10s. black and blue . . . . 55·00 95·00
107 £1 black and orange . . . £150 £275

8 Teacher and Pupils

15 Freedom Torch over Mt. Kilimanjaro

1961. Independence. Inscr "UHURU 1961".

108 8 5c. sepia and green 10 10
109 – 10c. turquoise 10 10
110 – 15c. sepia and blue 10 10
111 – 20c. brown 10 10
112 – 30c. black, green and yellow 10 10
113 – 50c. black and yellow 10 10
114 – 1s. brown, blue and yellow 15 10
115 15 1s.30 multicoloured . . . . 3·00 10
116 – 2s. multicoloured . . . . . 1·00 10
117 – 5s. turquoise and red . . . 1·00 50
118 – 10s. black, purple and blue 15·00 4·75
119 15 20s. multicoloured . . . . 4·00 9·00

DESIGNS—VERT (as Type **8**): 10c. District nurse and child; 15c. Coffee picking; 20c. Harvesting maize; 50c. Serengeti lions. HORIZ (as Type **8**): 30c. Tanganyikan flag. (As Type **15**): 1s. "Maternity" (mother with nurse holding baby); 2s. Dar-es-Salaam waterfront; 5s. Land tillage; 10s. Diamond mine.

19 Pres. Nyerere inaugurating Self-help Project

23 Map of Republic

1962. Inauguration of Republic.

120 19 30c. green 10 10
121 – 50c. multicoloured 10 10
122 – 1s.30 multicoloured 10 10
123 – 2s.50 black, red and blue 30 50

DESIGNS: 50c. Hoisting flag on Mt. Kilimanjaro; 1s.30, Presidential emblem; 2s.50, Independence monument.

1964. United Republic of Tanganyika and Zanzibar Commemoration.

124 23 20c. green and blue 10 10
125 – 30c. blue and sepia 10 10
126 – 1s.30 purple and blue . . . 10 10
127 23 2s.50 purple and blue . . . 80 50

DESIGN: 30c., 1s.30, Torch and spear emblem.

Despite the inscription on the stamps they had no validity in Zanzibar.

OFFICIAL STAMPS

1961. Independence stamps of 1961 optd **OFFICIAL**.

O1 5c. brown and green 10 10
O2 10c. turquoise 10 10
O3 15c. brown and blue 10 10
O4 20c. brown 10 10
O5 30c. black, green and yellow 10 10
O6 50c. black and yellow 10 10
O7 1s. brown, blue and yellow . . 10 10
O8 5s. turquoise and red 75 85

For later issues see **TANZANIA**.

TANZANIA Pt. 1

A republic within the British Commonwealth formerly known as Tanganyika and incorporating Zanzibar.

100 cents = 1 shilling.

NOTE—Stamps inscribed "UGANDA KENYA TANGANYIKA & ZANZIBAR" (or "TANZANIA UGANDA KENYA") will be found listed under Kenya, Uganda and Tanganyika (Tanzania).

For use in Tanzania. Issues to No. 176 were also valid for use in Kenya and Uganda.

25 Hale Hydro-electric Scheme

39 Black-footed Cardinalfish

33 Dar-es-Salaam Harbour

1965.

128 25 5c. blue and orange . . . 10 10
129 – 10c. multicoloured 10 10
130 – 15c. multicoloured 10 10
131 – 20c. sepia, green and blue 10 10
132 – 30c. black and brown . . . 10 10
133 – 40c. multicoloured . . . . 1·00 20
134 – 50c. multicoloured 70 10
135 – 65c. green, brown and blue 2·75 2·50
136 33 1s. multicoloured . . . . . 1·50 10
137 – 1s.30 multicoloured . . . . 6·50 1·50
138 – 2s.50 blue and brown . . . 6·50 1·25
139 – 5s. brown, green and blue 80 20
140 – 10s. yellow, green and blue 1·00 3·50
141 – 20s. multicoloured . . . . 7·00 17·00

DESIGNS—HORIZ (as Type **25**): 10c. Tanzania flag; 20c. Road-building; 50c. Common zebras, Manyara National Park; 65c. Mt. Kilimanjaro. (As Type **33**): 1s.30, Skull of "Zinjanthropus" and excavations, Olduvai Gorge; 2s.50, Fishing; 5s. Sisal industry; 10s. State House, Dar-es-Salaam. VERT (as Type **25**): 15c. National servicemen; 30c. Drum, spear, shield and stool; 40c. Giraffes, Mikumi National Park. (As Type **33**): 20s. Arms of Tanzania.

Z 39 Pres. Nyerere and First Vice-Pres. Karume within Bowl of Flame

1966. 2nd Anniv of United Republic. Mult.

Z142 30c. Type Z **39** 20 45
Z143 50c. Hands supporting Bowl of Flame 20 45
Z144 1s.30 As 50c. 30 45
Z145 2s.50 Type Z **39** . . . . . 40 1·25

Nos. Z142/5 were on sale in Zanzibar only

1967. Fishes. Multicoloured.

142 39 5c. mauve, green and black . . . . 10 2·25
143 – 10c. brown and bistre . . 10 10
144 – 15c. grey, blue and black 10 2·00
145 – 20c. brown and green . . 10 10
146 – 30c. green and black . . 20 10
147 – 40c. yellow, brown & green . . . . 1·00 10
148 – 50c. multicoloured 20 10
149 – 65c. yellow, green & black 2·00 4·50
150 – 70c. multicoloured . . . . 1·00 2·50
151 – 1s. brown, blue and purple 30 10
152 – 1s.30 multicoloured . . . 4·00 10
153a – 1s.50 multicoloured . . . 2·25 10
154 – 2s.50 multicoloured . . . 2·25 3·00
155a – 5s. yellow, black and green . . . . 3·25 10
156a – 10s. multicoloured . . . . 1·00 10
157a – 20s. mutlicoloured . . . . 5·50 15

DESIGNS—As Type **39**: 10c. Sobrinus mud- skipper; 15c. White-spotted puffer; 20c. Thorny seahorse; 30c. Dusky batfish; 40c. Black-spotted sweetlips; 50c. Blue birdwrasse; 65c. Bennett's butterflyfish; 70c. Black-tipped grouper. 42 × 25mm: 1s. Lionfish; 1s.30, Powder-blue surgeonfish; 1s.50, Yellow-finned fusilier; 2s.50, Emperor snapper; 5s. Moorish idol; 10s. Painted triggerfish; 20s. Horned squirrelfish.

53 "Papilio hornimani"

54 "Euphaedra neophron"

1973. (a) As T **53**.

158 53 5c. green, blue and black 60 30
159 – 10c. multicoloured 60 15
160 – 15c. lavender and black . . 60 30
161 – 20c. brown, yellow & black 70 15
162 – 30c. yellow, orange & black 70 10
163 – 40c. multicoloured 70 15
164 – 50c. multicoloured . . . . 1·00 15
165 – 60c. brown, yellow and lake . . . . 1·50 20
166 – 70c. green, orange and black . . . . 1·50 20

(b) As T **54**.

167 54 1s. multicoloured . . . . . 1·50 15
168 – 1s.50 multicoloured . . . . 2·00 45
169 – 2s.50 multicoloured . . . . 2·25 80
170 – 5s. multicoloured . . . . . 2·00 95
171 – 10s. multicoloured . . . . 2·25 6·00
172 – 20s. multicoloured . . . . 2·75 13·00

BUTTERFLIES: 10c. "Colotis ione"; 15c. "Amauris hyalites" (s sp. "makuyuensis"); 20c. "Libythea labdrea (s sp. "laius"); 30c. "Danaus chrysippus"; 40c. "Asterope rosa"; 50c. "Axiocerses styx"; 60c. "Terias hecabe"; 70c. "Acraea insignis"; 1s. "Euphaedra neophron"; 1s.50, "Precis octavia"; 2s.50, "Charaxes eupale"; 5s. "Charaxes pollux"; 10s. "Salamis parhassus"; 20s. "Papilio ophidicephalus".

1975. Nos. 165, 168/9 and 172 surch.

173 80c. on 60c. "Terias hecabe" 2·00 2·00
174 2s. on 1s.50 "Precis octavia" 3·75 6·00
175 3s. on 2s.50 "Charaxes eupale" . . . . 10·00 27·00
176 40s. on 20s. "Papilio ophidicephalus" . . . . . 4·50 12·00

1976. Telecommunications Development. As Nos. 56/9 of Kenya.

177 50c. Microwave tower . . . 10 10
178 1s. Cordless switchboard . . 15 10
179 2s. Telephones 25 30
180 3s. Message switching centre 30 40
MS181 120 × 120 mm. Nos. 177/80 1·10 1·50

1976. Olympic Games, Montreal. As Nos. 61/4 of Kenya.

182 50c. Akii Bua, Ugandan hurdler 10 10
183 1s. Filbert Bayi, Tanzanian runner 15 10
184 2s. Steve Muchoki, Kenyan boxer 25 40
185 3s. Olympic flame and East African flags 30 40
MS186 129 × 154 mm. Nos. 182/5 2·50 1·75

1976. Railway Transport. As Nos. 66/9 of Kenya.

187 50c. Diesel-hydraulic train, Tanzania–Zambia Railway 20 10
188 1s. Nile Bridge, Uganda . . . 25 10
189 2s. Nakuru Station, Kenya 35 30
190 3s. Uganda Railway Class A locomotive, 1896 . . . . . 40 45
MS191 154 × 103 mm. Nos. 187/90 4·00 3·50

1977. Game Fish of East Africa. As Nos. 71/4 of Kenya.

192 50c. Nile perch 20 10
193 1s. Nile mouthbrooder . . . 20 10
194 3s. Sailfish 60 40
195 5s. Black marlin 70 60
MS196 153 × 129 mm. Nos. 192/5 2·75 2·50

1977. Second World Black and African Festival of Arts and Culture. As Nos. 76/9 of Kenya.

197 50c. Maasai manyatta (village), Kenya 15 10
198 1s. "Heartbeat of Africa" (Ugandan dancers) 15 10
199 2s. Makonde sculpture . . . 40 70
200 3s. "Early Man and Technology" (skinning hippopotamus) . . . . . . 45 1·00
MS201 132 × 190 mm. Nos. 197/200 1·10 3·00

1977. 25th Anniv of Safari Rally. As Nos. 81/4 of Kenya. Multicoloured.

202 50c. Rally-car and villagers 15 10
203 1s. Starting line 15 10
204 2s. Car fording river 30 40
205 5s. Car and elephants . . . . 1·00 1·10
MS206 126 × 93 mm. Nos. 202/5 1·40 2·00

1977. Centenary of Ugandan Church. As Nos. 86/9 of Kenya. Multicoloured.

207 50c. Canon Kivebulaya . . . 10 10
208 1s. Modern Namirembe Cathedral 15 10
209 2s. The first Cathedral . . . 30 40
210 5s. Early congregation Kigezi 60 1·40
MS211 126 × 89 mm. Nos. 207/10 1·00 1·75

1977. Endangered Species. As Nos. 96/100 of Kenya. Multicoloured.

212 50c. Pancake tortoise 40 10
213 1s. Nile crocodile 45 10
214 2s. Hunter's hartebeest . . . 1·40 55
215 3s. Red colobus monkey . . 1·50 75
216 5s. Dugong . . . . 1·75 1·00
MS217 127 × 101 mm. Nos. 213/16 4·75 5·50

56 Prince Philip and President Nyerere

1977. Silver Jubilee. Multicoloured.

218 50c. Type **56** 10 10
219 5s. Pres. Nyerere with Queen and Prince Philip 15 25
220 10s. Jubilee emblem and Commonwealth flags . . . 25 40
221 20s. The Crowning 40 60
MS222 128 × 102 mm. Nos. 218/21 75 1·50

57 Improvements in Rural Living Standards

1978. 1st Anniv of Chama Cha Mapinduzi (New Revolutionary Party).

223 57 50c. multicoloured 10 10
224 – 1s. multicoloured 10 10
225 – 3s. multicoloured 25 60
226 – 5s. black, green and yellow 35 1·00
MS227 142 × 106 mm. Nos. 223/6 1·00 1·40

DESIGNS: 1s. Flag-raising ceremony, Zanzibar; 3s. Handing over of TANU headquarters, Dodoma; 5s. Chairman Julius Nyerere.

1978. World Cup Football Championship. As Nos. 122/5 of Kenya. Multicoloured.

228 50c. Joe Kadenge and forwards 10 10
229 1s. Mohamed Chuma and cup presentation 10 10
230 2s. Omari Kidevu and goal mouth scene 30 70
231 3s. Polly Ouma and forwards 40 1·00
MS232 136 × 81 mm. Nos. 228/31 2·25 1·75

1979. 25th Anniv of Coronation. Nos. 218/21 optd **25th ANNIVERSARY CORONATION 2nd JUNE 1953.**

233A 50c. Type **56** 10 10
234A 5s. Pres. Nyerere with Queen and Prince Philip 20 30
235A 10s. Jubilee emblem and Commonwealth flags . . 25 50

236A 20s. The Crowning 40 90
MS237A 128 × 102 mm. Nos. 233A/6A . . . . 75 1·25

60 "Do not Drink and Drive" 61 Lake Manyara Hotel

1978. Road Safety.
238 60 50c. multicoloured 15 10
239 – 1s. multicoloured 20 10
240 – 3s. orange, black and brown 45 70
241 – 5s. multicoloured . . . . . 75 1·40
MS242 92 × 129 mm. Nos. 238/41 1·40 2·00
DESIGNS: 1s. "Show courtesy to young, old and crippled"; 3s. "Observe the Highway Code"; 5s. "Do not drive a faulty vehicle.

1978. Game Lodges. Multicoloured.
243 50c. Type **61** 10 10
244 1s. Lobo Wildlife Lodge . . 10 10
245 3s. Ngorongoro Crater Lodge 20 35
246 5s. Ngorongoro Wildlife Lodge 30 55
247 10s. Mafia Island Lodge . . 40 1·10
248 20s. Mikumi Wildlife Lodge 75 2·75
MS249 118 × 112 mm. Nos. 243/8 5·00 7·50

62 "Racial Suppression"

1978. International Anti-Apartheid Year.
250 62 50c. multicoloured 10 10
251 – 1s. black, green and yellow 10 10
252 – 2s.50 multicoloured 30 75
253 – 5s. multicoloured . . . . . 60 1·40
MS254 127 × 132 mm. Nos. 250/3 1·25 2·75
DESIGNS: 1s. "Racial division"; 2s.50, "Racial harmony"; 5s. "Fall of suppression and rise of freedom".

63 Fokker F.27 Friendship

1978. 75th Anniv of Powered Flight. Mult.
255 50c. Type **63** 20 10
256 1s. De Havilland Dragon Mk 1 on Zanzibar Island, 1930's 25 10
257 2s. Concorde . . . . 1·00 75
258 5s. Wright brothers' Flyer I, 1903 . . . . 1·25 1·25
MS259 133 × 97 mm. Nos. 255/8 2·75 3·50

64 Corporation Emblem

1979. 1st Anniv of Tanzania Posts and Telecommunications Corporation. Mult.
260 50c. Type **64** 10 10
261 5s. Headquarters buildings 50 70
MS262 82 × 97 mm. Nos. 260/1 1·00 1·50

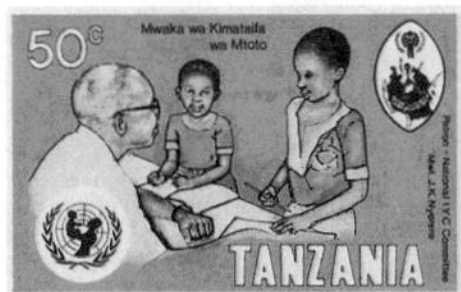

65 Pres. Nyerere (patron of National I.Y.C. Committee) with Children

1979. Int Year of the Child. Mult.
263 50c. Type **65** 10 10
264 1s. Day care centre 15 10
265 2s. "Immunisation" (child being vaccinated) 25 45
266 5s. National I.Y.C. Committee emblem . . . . 40 1·00
MS267 127 × 91 mm. Nos. 263/6 1·25 1·25

1979. Nos. 159 and 166 surch.
268 10c.+30c. multicoloured . . . 2·00 1·50
269 50c. on 70c. green, orange and black . . . . 3·00 2·25
No. 268 was used as a 40c. value.

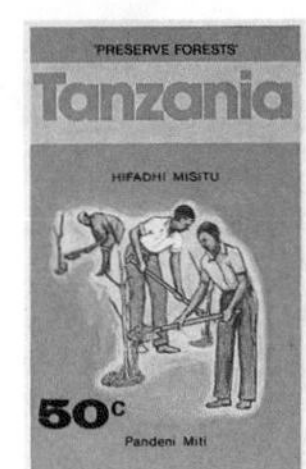

67 Planting Young Trees

1979. Forest Preservation. Multicoloured.
270 50c. Type **67** 15 10
271 1s. Replacing dead trees with saplings 15 10
272 2s. Rainfall cycle 35 50
273 5s. Forest fire warning . . . 60 1·50

68 Mwenge Earth Satellite Station

1979. Inauguration of Mwenge Earth Satellite Station.
274 68 10c. multicoloured 10 10
275 40c. multicoloured 15 10
276 50c. multicoloured 15 10
277 1s. multicoloured 25 20

69 Tabata Dispensary, Dar-es-Salaam

1980. 75th Anniv of Rotary International. Multicoloured.
278 50c. Type **69** 10 10
279 1s. Ngomvu Village water project 10 10
280 5s. Flying Doctor service (plane donation) 35 50
281 20s. Torch and 75th anniversary emblem . . . 60 2·00
MS282 120 × 101 mm. Nos. 278/81 1·00 2·25

70 Zanzibar 1896 2r. Stamp and 1964 25c. Definitive

1980. Death Cent of Sir Rowland Hill. Mult.
283 40c. Type **70** 10 10
284 50c. Tanganyika 1962 Independence 50c. commemorative and man attaching stamp to letter (vert) 10 10
285 10s. Tanganyika 1922 25c. stamp and 1961 1s.30 definitive 35 75
286 20s. Penny Black and Sir Rowland Hill (vert) . . . . 60 1·40
MS287 158 × 120 mm. Nos. 283/6 1·00 2·00

1980. "London 1980" International Stamp Exhibition. Nos. 283/6 optd **'LONDON 1980' PHILATELIC EXHIBITION**.
288 70 40c. multicoloured 10 10
289 – 50c. multicoloured 10 10
290 – 10s. multicoloured 35 75
291 – 20s. multicoloured . . . . 60 1·40
MS292 158 × 120 mm. Nos. 288/91 1·00 2·00

1980. Annual Conference of District 920. Rotary International, Arusha. Nos. 278/81 optd **District 920-55th Annual Conference, Arusha. Tanzania**.
293 69 50c. multicoloured 15 10
294 – 1s. multicoloured 15 10
295 – 5s. multicoloured 30 50
296 – 20s. multicoloured . . . . 75 2·25
MS297 120 × 101 mm. Nos. 293/6 1·25 2·25

73 Conference, Tanzanian Posts and Telecommunications Corporation and U.P.U. Emblems

1980. P.A.P.U. (Pan-African Postal Union) Plenipotentiary Conference, Arusha.
298 73 50c. black and violet . . . 10 10
299 1s. black and blue 10 10
300 5s. black and red 30 80
301 10s. black and green . . . 65 2·00

74 Gidamis Shahanga (marathon) 75 Spring Hare

1980. Olympic Games, Moscow. Multicoloured.
302 50c. Type **74** 10 15
303 1s. Nzael Kyomo (sprints) . . 15 15
304 10s. Zakayo Malekwa (javelin) . . . . 60 1·00
305 20s. William Lyimo (boxing) 1·00 1·75
MS306 172 × 117 mm. Nos. 302/5 1·25 2·25

1980. Wildlife. Multicoloured.
307 10c. Type **75** 10 15
308 20c. Large-spotted genet . . 10 15
309 40c. Banded mongoose . . . 10 10
310 50c. Ratel 10 10
311 75c. Large-toothed rock hyrax 10 15
312 80c. Leopard 30 15
313 1s. Impala 10 10
314 1s.50 Giraffe 30 20
315 2s. Common zebra 30 40
316 3s. Buffalo 30 50
317 5s. Lion 40 65
318 10s. Black rhinoceros . . . . 1·00 1·40
319 20s. African elephant . . . . 1·00 1·60
320 40s. Cheetah . . . . 1·00 3·25
Nos. 313/20 are larger, 40 × 24 mm.

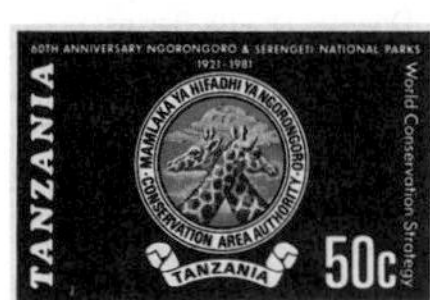

77 Ngorongoro Conservation Area Authority Emblem

1981. 60th Anniv of Ngorongoro and Serengeti National Parks.
321 77 50c. multicoloured 10 10
322 – 1s. black, gold and green 10 10
323 – 5s. multicoloured 30 60
324 – 20s. multicoloured . . . . 80 2·25
DESIGNS: 1s. Tanzania National Parks emblem; 5s. Friends of the Serengeti emblem; 20s. Friends of Ngorongoro emblem.

1981. Royal Wedding. Nos. 220/1 optd **ROYAL WEDDING H.R.H. PRINCE CHARLES 29th JULY 1981**.
325 10s. Jubilee emblem and Commonwealth flags . . . 30 60
326 20s. The Crowning 40 80
MS327 88 × 97 mm. Nos. 325/6 2·00 2·00

79 Mail Runner

1981. Commonwealth Postal Administrations Conference, Arusha. Multicoloured.
328 50c. Type **79** 10 10
329 1s. Letter sorting 10 10
330 5s. Letter Post symbols . . . 30 1·00
331 10s. Flags of Commonwealth nations . . . . 70 2·50
MS332 130 × 100 mm. Nos. 328/31 1·40 3·00

80 Morris Nyunyusa (blind drummer)

1981. International Year of Disabled Persons. Multicoloured.
333 50c. Type **80** 25 10
334 1s. Mgulani Rehabilitation Centre, Dar-es-Salaam . . 30 10
335 5s. Aids for disabled persons 1·00 2·50
336 10s. Disabled children cleaning school compound 1·50 4·00

81 Pres. Mwalimu Julius K. Nyerere

1981. 20th Anniv of Independence. Mult.
337 50c. Type **81** 10 10
338 1s. Electricity plant, Mtoni 10 10
339 3s. Sisal industry 25 90
340 10s. "Universal primary education" . . . . 70 2·50
MS341 120 × 85 mm. Nos. 337/40 1·25 3·00

82 Ostrich 83 Jella Mtaga

1982. Birds. Multicoloured.
342 50c. Type **82** 80 10
343 1s. Secretary bird 85 10
344 5s. Kori bustard . . . . . . 3·00 2·75
345 10s. Saddle-bill stork . . . . 3·75 5·50

1982. World Cup Football Championship, Spain. Multicoloured.
346 50c. Type **83** 30 10
347 1s. Football stadium 35 10
348 10s. Diego Maradona . . . . 3·00 3·00
349 20s. FIFA emblem . . . . . 4·75 5·00
MS350 130 × 100 mm. Nos. 346/9 8·00 8·00

84 "Jade" of Seronera (cheetah) with Cubs

1982. Animal Personalities. Multicoloured.
351 50c. Type **84** 20 10
352 1s. Female golden jackal and cubs 30 10
353 5s. "Fiji" and two sons of "Gombe" (chimpanzees) 50 1·75
354 10s. "Bahati" of Lake Manyara with twins, "Rashidi" and "Ramadhani" (elephants) 1·00 2·75
MS355 120 × 89 mm. Nos. 351/4 1·50 5·00

85 Brick-laying

1982. 75th Anniv of Boy Scout Movement. Multicoloured.
356 50c. Type **85** 15 10
357 1s. Camping 20 10
358 10s. Tracing signs . . . . . 75 1·50
359 20s. Lord Baden-Powell . . . 1·10 2·75
MS360 130 × 100 mm. Nos. 356/9 2·00 4·00

86 Ploughing Field

1982. World Food Day. Multicoloured.
361 50c. Type **86** 10 10
362 1s. Dairy farming 10 10
363 5s. Maize farming 45 60
364 10s. Grain storage . . . . . 75 1·25
MS365 129 × 99 mm. Nos. 361/4 1·25 2·25

87 Immunization

1982. Centenary of Robert Koch's Discovery of Tubercle Bacillus. Multicoloured.

366 50c. Type **87** 15 10
367 1s. Dr. Robert Koch 20 10
368 5s. International Union against TB emblem . . . . 65 1·25
369 10s. World Health Organization emblem . . . 1·25 3·00

88 Letter Post

1982. 5th Anniv of Posts and Telecommunications Corporation. Multicoloured.

370 50c. Type **88** 10 10
371 1s. Training institute 10 10
372 5s. Satellite communications 35 90
373 10s. U.P.U., I.T.U. and T.P.T.C.C. (Tanzania Post and Telecommunications Corporation) emblems . . 60 2·00
MS374 126 × 96 mm. Nos. 370/3 1·50 3·00

89 Pres. Mwalimu Julius Nyerere

1982. Commonwealth Day. Multicoloured.

375 50c. Type **89** 10 10
376 1s. Athletics and boxing . . . 15 10
377 5s. Flags of Commonwealth countries 40 90
378 10s. Pres. Nyerere and members of British Royal Family . . . . 70 1·90
MS379 121 × 100 mm. Nos. 375/8 1·10 2·75

90 Eastern and Southern African Management Institute, Arusha, Tanzania

1983. 25th Anniv of Economic Commission for Africa. Multicoloured.

380 50c. Type **90** 15 10
381 1s. 25th Anniversary inscription and U.N. logo 20 10
382 5s. Mineral collections . . . 2·75 2·75
383 10s. E.C.A. Silver Jubilee logo and O.A.U. flag . . . 2·75 3·50
MS384 132 × 102 mm. Nos. 380/3 5·75 5·75

91 Telephone Cables

1983. World Communications Year. Mult.

385 50c. Type **91** 10 10
386 1s. W.C.Y. logo 10 10
387 5s. Postal service . . . . . . 50 1·50
388 10s. Microwave tower . . . 75 2·50
MS389 102 × 92 mm. Nos. 385/8 1·50 3·75

92 Bagamoyo Boma

1983. Historical Buildings of Tanzania. Multicoloured.

390 1s. Type **92** 10 10
391 1s.50 Beit el Ajaib, Zanzibar 15 25
392 5s. Anglican Cathedral, Zanzibar . . . . 40 1·00
393 10s. Original German Government House and present State House, Dar-es-Salaam . . . . 75 2·00
MS394 130 × 100 mm. Nos. 390/3 1·25 3·00

93 Sheikh Abeid Amani Karume (founder of Afro-Shirazi Party)

1984. 20th Anniv of Zanzibar Revolution. Multicoloured.

395 1s. Type **93** 10 10
396 1s.50 Clove farming 15 25
397 5s. Symbol of Industrial Development . . . . . . 40 1·00
398 10s. New housing schemes . . 75 2·00
MS399 130 × 100 mm. 15s. "Mapinduzi" (ferry) and map 1·25 2·50

94 Boxing

1984. Olympic Games, Los Angeles. Multicoloured.

400 1s. Type **94** 10 10
401 1s.50 Running 15 10
402 5s. Basketball 70 60
403 20s. Football . . . . 1·60 2·25
MS404 130 × 100 mm. Nos. 400/3 2·25 2·75

95 Icarus in Flight

1984. 40th Anniv of I.C.A.O. Mult.

405 1s. Type **95** 10 10
406 1s.50 Douglas DC-10, Boeing 737 aircraft and air traffic controller 15 20
407 5s. Boeing 737 undergoing maintenance . . . . 55 1·25
408 10s. I.C.A.O. badge . . . . . 1·10 2·00
MS409 130 × 100 mm. Nos. 405/8 2·40 3·25

96 Sochi Conical House

1984. Traditional Houses. Multicoloured.

410 1s. Type **96** 10 10
411 1s.50 Isyenga circular type . . 15 20
412 5s. Tembe flatroofed type . . 40 1·25
413 10s. Banda coastal type . . . 70 2·00
MS414 129 × 99 mm. Nos. 410/13 1·50 3·25

97 Production of Cotton Textiles

1985. 5th Anniv of Southern African Development Co-ordination Conference. Multicoloured.

415 1s.50 Type **97** 30 15
416 4s. Diamond mining . . . . 2·00 1·50
417 5s. Map of member countries and means of communication . . . . . 2·00 1·50
418 20s. Flags and signatures of member countries . . . . 2·75 4·00
MS419 110 × 104 mm. Nos. 415/18 8·00 8·00

98 Tortoise

1985. Rare Animals of Zanzibar. Mult.

420 1s. Type **98** 50 10
421 4s. Leopard . . . . 1·25 1·50
422 10s. Civet cat . . . . 1·75 3·75
423 17s.50 Red colobus monkey (vert) . . . . 2·00 5·50
MS424 110 × 93 mm. 15s. Black rhinoceros; 20s. Giant ground pangolin . . . . 1·50 3·50

99 The Queen Mother

1985. Life and Times of Queen Elizabeth the Queen Mother. Multicoloured.

425 20s. Type **99** 10 20
426 20s. Queen Mother waving to crowd 10 20
427 100s. Oval portrait with flowers 30 90
428 100s. Head and shoulders portrait 30 90
MS429 Two sheets, each 125 × 63 mm. (a) Nos. 425 and 427. (b) Nos. 426 and 428 Set of 2 sheets . . . . 80 2·75

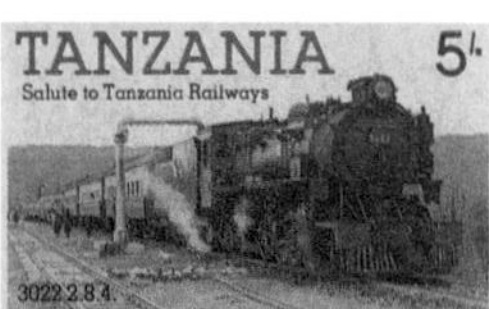

100 Steam Locomotive No. 3022

1985. Tanzanian Railway Steam Locomotives (1st series). Multicoloured.

430 5s. Type **100** 10 20
431 10s. Locomotive No. 3107 . . 15 30
432 20s. Locomotive No. 6004 . . 25 70
433 30s. Locomotive No. 3129 . . 40 1·00
MS434 125 × 93 mm. Nos. 430/3 80 2·75

See also Nos. 445/9.

1985. Olympic Games Gold Medal Winners, Los Angeles. Nos. 400/3 optd.

435 1s. Type **94** (optd **GOLD MEDAL HENRY TILLMAN USA**) 15 10
436 1s.50 Running (optd **GOLD MEDAL USA**) 20 20
437 5s. Basketball (optd **GOLD MEDAL USA**) . . . . . 1·75 1·50
438 20s. Football (optd **GOLD MEDAL FRANCE**) . . . 2·25 4·50
MS439 130 × 100 mm. Nos. 435/8 8·00 10·00

102 Cooking and Water Pots

1985. Pottery. Multicoloured.

440 1s.50 Type **102** 20 10
441 2s. Large pot and frying pot with cover 25 15
442 5s. Trader selling pots . . . 60 35
443 40s. Beer pot . . . . 2·25 5·00
MS444 129 × 98 mm. 30s. Water pots . . . . 4·00 4·00

103 Class 64 Diesel Locomotive

1985. Tanzanian Railway Locomotives (2nd series).

445 **103** 1s.50 multicoloured . . . 50 20
446 – 2s. multicoloured 50 30
447 – 5s. multicoloured 75 75
448 – 10s. multicoloured . . . . 1·00 1·75
449 – 30s. black, brown and red 2·25 3·75
MS450 130 × 100 mm. 15s. black, brown and pink; 20s. black, brown and pink . . . . 9·00 8·00

DESIGNS: 2s. Class 36 diesel locomotive; 5s. DFH1013 diesel shunter; 10s. DE1001 diesel-electric locomotive; 15s. Class 30 steam locomotive; 20s. Class II steam locomotive; 30s. Steam locomotive, Zanzibar, 1906.

104 Young Pioneers

1986. International Youth Year.

451 **104** 1s.50 multicoloured . . . 15 15
452 – 4s. brown, light brown and black 20 50
453 – 10s. multicoloured . . . . 50 1·25
454 – 20s. brown, light brown and black . . . . . . 1·10 2·50
MS455 130 × 100 mm. 30s. brown, light brown and black . . . . 2·25 3·50

DESIGNS: 4s. Child health care; 10s. Uhuru Torch Race; 20s. Young workers and globe; 30s. Young people farming.

105 Rolls-Royce "20/25" (1936)

1986. Centenary of Motoring. Multicoloured.

456 1s.50 Type **105** 10 10
457 5s. Rolls-Royce "Phantom II" (1933) 15 25
458 10s. Rolls-Royce "Phantom I" (1926) 25 60
459 30s. Rolls-Royce "Silver Ghost" (1907) . . . . . . 40 2·25
MS460 125 × 93 mm. Nos. 456/9 80 2·50

106 Rotary Logo and Staunton Queen Chess Piece

1986. World Chess Championships, London and Leningrad.

461 **106** 20s. blue and mauve . . . 35 50
462 – 100s. multicoloured . . . 50 2·50
MS463 124 × 64 mm. Nos. 461/2 1·10 3·25

DESIGN: 100s. Hand moving rook on board.

No. 461 also commemorates Rotary International.

107 Mallard

1986. Birth Bicentenary (1985) of John J. Audubon (ornithologist). Multicoloured.

464 5s. Type **107** 15 35
465 10s. Eider ("American Eider") 25 60
466 20s. Scarlet ibis . . . . . . 30 1·25
467 30s. Roseate spoonbill . . . 40 1·40
MS468 122 × 91 mm. Nos. 464/7 1·00 3·50

108 Pearls

1986. Tanzanian Minerals. Multicoloured.

469 1s.50 Type **108** 80 15
470 2s. Sapphire . . . . 1·10 65
471 5s. Tanzanite . . . . 2·00 1·25
472 40s. Diamonds . . . . 7·25 10·00
MS473 130 × 100 mm. 30s. Rubies 13·00 13·00

110 "Hibiscus calyphyllus"

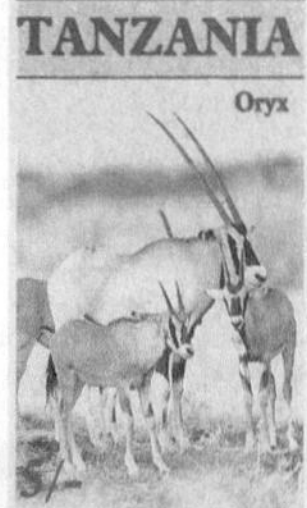

111 Oryx

1986. Flowers of Tanzania. Multicoloured.

474 1s.50 Type **110** 10 10
475 5s. "Aloe graminicola" . . . 15 25
476 10s. "Nersium oleander" . . 20 45
477 30s. "Nymphaea caerulea" 40 2·00
MS478 90 × 119 mm. Nos. 474/7 75 2·50

1986. Endangered Animals of Tanzania. Multicoloured.

479 5s. Type **111** 15 15
480 10s. Giraffe 20 35

481 20s. Rhinoceros 25 85
482 30s. Cheetah . . . . 25 1·40
MS483 91 × 121 mm. Nos. 479/82 75 3·25

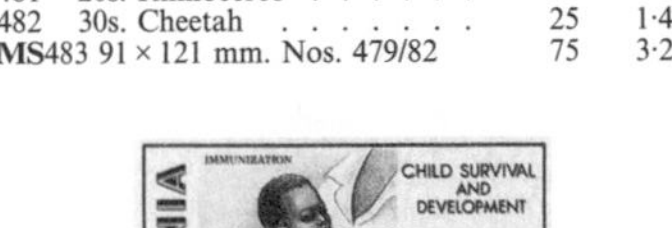
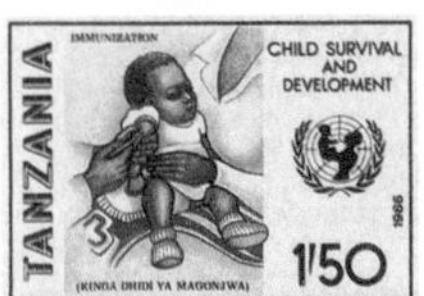

112 Immunization

1986. UNICEF Child Survival Campaign. Multicoloured.
484 1s.50 Type **112** 35 10
485 2s. Growth monitoring . . . 45 15
486 5s. Oral rehydration therapy 80 40
487 40s. Breast-feeding . . . . . 3·50 4·50
MS488 110 × 101 mm. 30s. Healthy baby . . . . 1·00 1·75

113 Angelfish

1986. Marine Life. Multicoloured.
489 1s.50 Type **113** 70 10
490 4s. Parrotfish . . . . 1·50 85
491 10s. Turtle . . . . 2·25 2·75
492 20s. Octopus . . . . 3·50 5·50
MS493 131 × 101 mm. 30s. Corals 2·50 2·50

114 Team Captains shaking Hands

1986. World Cup Football Championship, Mexico. Multicoloured.
494 1s.50 Type **114** 15 10
495 2s. Referee sending player off 15 10
496 10s. Goalkeeper and ball in net . . . . 60 1·00
497 20s. Goalkeeper saving ball 1·00 2·25
MS498 95 × 72 mm. 30s. Winning Argentine team . . . . 1·10 1·25

115 Pres. Nyerere receiving Beyond War Award

1986. International Peace Year. Mult.
499 1s.50 Type **115** 35 10
500 2s. Children of many races 55 20
501 10s. African cosmonaut and rocket launch . . . . . . 1·50 1·75
502 20s. United Nations Headquarters, New York 2·00 3·50
MS503 109 × 86 mm. 30s. International Peace Year symbols 2·75 4·25

116 Mobile Bank Service

1987. 20th Anniv of National Bank of Commerce. Multicoloured.
504 1s.50 Type **116** 30 10
505 2s. National Bank of Commerce Head Office . . 50 20
506 5s. Pres. Mwinyi laying foundation stone 80 90
507 20s. Cotton harvesting . . . 2·00 3·25

117 Parade of Young Party Members

1987. 10th Anniv of Chama Cha Mapinduzi Party and 20th Anniv of Arusha Declaration. Mult.
508 2s. Type **117** 15 10
509 3s. Harvesting coffee 15 10
510 10s. Pres. Nyerere addressing Second Peace Initiative Reunion 20 30
511 30s. Presidents Julius Nyerere and Ali Hassan Mwinyi . . 35 1·25

118 Nungu Nungu Hair Style

121 "Apis mellifera" (bee)

120 Royal Family on Buckingham Palace Balcony after Trooping the Colour

1987. Traditional Hair Styles. Multicoloured.
512 1s.50 Type **118** 30 10
513 2s. Upanga wa jogoo style . . 45 20
514 10s. Morani style . . . . . . 80 1·25
515 20s. Twende kilioni style . . 1·50 2·50
MS516 110 × 99 mm. 30s. Hair plaiting . . . . 2·75 3·50

1987. 60th Birthday (1986) of Queen Elizabeth II. Multicoloured.
517 5s. Type **120** 15 20
518 10s. Queen and Prince Philip at Royal Ascot 20 25
519 40s. Queen Elizabeth II . . . 60 1·50
520 60s. Queen Elizabeth with crowd . . . . 80 2·00
MS521 125 × 90 mm. Nos. 517/20 1·50 3·50

1987. Insects. Multicoloured.
522 1s.50 Type **121** 60 15
523 2s. "Prostephanus truncatus" (grain borer) 80 25
524 10s. "Glossina palpalis" (tsetse fly) . . . . 1·50 2·00
525 20s. "Polistes sp." (wasp) . . 2·25 4·25
MS526 110 × 101 mm. 30s. "Anopheles" sp (mosquito) . . 3·75 5·00

122 Crocodile

1987. Reptiles. Multicoloured.
527 2s. Type **122** 90 25
528 3s. Black-striped grass-snake 95 30
529 10s. Adder . . . . 2·00 1·60
530 20s. Green mamba . . . . . 2·75 3·25
MS531 101 × 101 mm. 30s. Tortoise 1·00 1·00

123 Emblems of Posts/ Telecommunications and Railways

1987. 10th Anniv of Tanzania Communications and Transport Corporations. Multicoloured.
532 2s. Type **123** 75 30
533 8s. Emblems of Air Tanzania and Harbours Authority 1·00 95
MS534 100 × 66 mm. 20s. Methods of transport and communication 2·50 1·75

124 Basketry

1987. Traditional Handicrafts. Multicoloured.
535 2s. Type **124** 15 10
536 3s. Decorated gourds 15 15
537 10s. Stools 30 30
538 20s. Makonde carvings . . . 50 55
MS539 89 × 89 mm. 40s. Makonde carver at work 65 75

1987. 10th Anniv of Tanzania–Zambia Railway (1986). Nos. 445/9 optd **10th Anniversary of TANZANIA ZAMBIA RAILWAY AUTHORITY 1976-1986.**
540 **103** 1s.50 multicoloured . . . 75 30
541 – 2s. multicoloured 80 30
542 – 5s. multicoloured . . . . 1·25 1·25
543 – 10s. multicoloured . . . . 1·75 2·25
544 – 30s. black, brown and red 3·00 6·00

126 Mdako (pebble game)

1988. Traditional Pastimes. Multicoloured.
545 2s. Type **126** 10 10
546 3s. Wrestling 10 10
547 8s. Bull fighting, Zanzibar . . 15 15
548 20s. Bao (board game) . . . 35 35
MS549 100 × 90 mm. 30s. Archery 70 80

127 Plateosaurus

1988. Prehistoric and Modern Animals. Mult.
550 2s. Type **127** 50 65
551 3s. Pteranodon 50 65
552 5s. Apatosaurus ("Brontosaurus") 60 65
553 7s. Lion 60 75
554 8s. Tiger 75 80
555 12s. Orang-utan 75 85
556 20s. Elephant . . . . 1·10 1·50
557 100s. Stegosaurus . . . . . 1·75 3·25

128 Marchers with Party Flag

1988. National Solidarity Walk. Mult.
558 2s.+1s. Type **128** 25 25
559 3s.+1s. Pres. Mwinyi leading Walk 25 25
MS560 121 × 121 mm. 50s.+1s. Pres. Ali Hassan Mwinyi (35 × 25 mm) 75 85

129 Population Symbols on Map

1988. 3rd National Population Census. Mult.
561 2s. Type **129** 10 10
562 3s. Census official at work . . 10 10
563 10s. Community health care 15 15
564 20s. Population growth 1967–88 . . . . 30 30
MS565 96 × 91 mm. 40s. Development of modern Tanzania 65 65

130 Javelin

1988. Olympic Games, Seoul (1st issue). Mult.
566 2s. Type **130** 80 15
567 3s. Hurdling 80 15
568 7s. Long distance running . . 1·40 40
569 12s. Relay racing . . . . . . 1·60 70
MS570 100 × 70 mm. 40s. Badminton . . . . 3·50 1·50

131 Football

132 Goat

1988. Olympic Games, Seoul (2nd issue). Mult.
571 10s. Type **131** 25 10
572 20s. Cycling 60 25
573 50s. Fencing 70 50
574 70s. Volleyball 80 65
MS575 77 × 92 mm. 100s. Gymnastics . . . . 1·50 2·00

1988. Winter Olympic Games, Calgary. As T **131**. Multicoloured.
576 5s. Cross-country skiing . . . 60 20
577 25s. Figure skating . . . . . 1·25 30
578 50s. Downhill skiing . . . . 1·75 80
579 75s. Bobsleighing . . . . . . 2·00 1·50
MS580 77 × 92 mm. 100s. Ice hockey sticks wrapped in Olympic and Canadian colours . . . . . . 2·25 1·25

1988. Domestic Animals. Multicoloured.
581 4s. Type **132** 30 30
582 5s. Rabbit (horiz) 30 30
583 8s. Cows (horiz) 40 40
584 10s. Kitten (horiz) 90 70
585 12s. Pony . . . . 1·40 85
586 20s. Puppy . . . . 1·75 1·25
MS587 102 × 73 mm. 100s. Chicken (horiz) . . . . 1·75 1·75

133 "Love You, Dad" (Pinocchio)

1988. Greetings Stamps. Walt Disney cartoon characters. Multicoloured.
588 4s. Type **133** 20 20
589 5s. "Happy Birthday" (Brer Rabbit and Chip n' Dale) 20 20
590 10s. "Trick or Treat" (Daisy and Donald Duck) 35 20
591 12s. "Be Kind to Animals" (Ferdie and Mordie with Pluto) 40 20
592 15s. "Love" (Daisy and Donald Duck) 50 35
593 20s. "Let's Celebrate" (Mickey Mouse and Goofy) 60 50
594 30s. "Keep in Touch" (Daisy and Donald Duck) 90 80
595 50s. "Love you, Mom" (Minnie Mouse with Ferdie and Mordie) . . . . 1·75 1·75
MS596 Two sheets, each 127 × 101 mm. (a) 150s. "Let's work together" (Goofy dressed as a fireman). (b) 150s. "Have a super Sunday" (Goofy dressed as American footballer) Set of 2 sheets . . . . 4·75 4·50

134 "Charaxes varanes"

135 Independence Torch and Mt. Kilimanjaro

1988. Butterflies. Multicoloured.
597 8s. Type **134** 50 10
598 30s. "Neptis melicerta" . . . 90 30
599 40s. "Mylothris chloris" . . . 1·00 40
600 50s. "Charaxes bohemani" 1·25 50
601 60s. "Myrina silenus" . . . . 1·40 70
602 75s. "Papilio phorcas" . . . . 1·90 90
603 90s. "Cyrestis camillus" . . . 2·25 1·10
604 100s. "Salamis temora" . . . 2·25 1·25
MS605 Two sheets, each 80 × 50 mm. (a) 200s. "Asterope rosa". (b) 250s. "Kallima rumia" Set of 2 sheets . . . . 8·00 6·00

1988. National Monuments. Multicoloured.
606 5s. Type **135** 10 10
607 12s. Arusha Declaration Monument 15 15
608 30s. Askari Monument . . . 30 30
609 60s. Independence Monument 55 60
MS610 100 × 89 mm. 100s. Askari Monument statue . . . . . . 1·25 1·40

136 Eye Clinic

1988. 25th Anniv of Dar-es-Salaam Lions Club. Multicoloured.
611 2s. Type **136** 20 20
612 3s. Family at shallow water well 20 20
613 7s. Rhinoceros and outline map of Tanzania . . . . . 2·50 30
614 12s. Club presenting school desks 30 45
MS615 100 × 65 mm. 40s. Lions International logo . . . . . . 1·00 1·00

137 Loading Patient into Ambulance

1988. 125th Anniv of International Red Cross and Red Crescent. Multicoloured.
616 2s. Type **137** 20 20
617 3s. Mother and baby health clinic 20 20
618 7s. Red Cross flag 40 30
619 12s. Henri Dunant (founder) 45 45
MS620 90 × 90 mm. 40s. Members of Red Cross International Committee, 1863 . . . . . . 1·00 1·00

138 Paradise Whydah **139** Bushbaby

1989. Birds. Multicoloured.
621 20s. Type **138** . . . . 1·00 85
622 20s. Black-collared barbet . . 1·00 85
623 20s. Bateleur . . . . 1·00 85
624 20s. Lilac-breasted roller and African open-bill storks in flight . . . . 1·00 85
625 20s. Red-tufted malachite sunbird and African open-bill stork in flight . . . . 1·00 85
626 20s. Dark chanting goshawk 1·00 85
627 20s. White-fronted bee eater, carmine bee eater and little bee eaters . . . . 1·00 85
628 20s. Narina's trogon and marabou stork in flight . . 1·00 85
629 20s. Grey parrot . . . . . . 1·00 85
630 20s. Hoopoe . . . . 1·00 85
631 20s. Masked lovebird ("Yellow-collared lovebird") . . . . 1·00 85
632 20s. Yellow-billed hornbill . . 1·00 85
633 20s. Hammerkop . . . . . . 1·00 85
634 20s. Violet-crested turaco and flamingos in flight . . . . 1·00 85
635 20s. Malachite kingfisher . . 1·00 85
636 20s. Greater flamingos . . . 1·00 85
637 20s. Yellow-billed storks . . 1·00 85
638 20s. Whale-headed stork ("Shoebill stork") . . . . 1·00 85
639 20s. Saddle-bill stork and blacksmith plover . . . . 1·00 85
640 20s. South African crowned crane . . . . 1·00 85
MS641 Two sheets, each 105 × 75 mm. (a) 350s. Helmeted guineafowl (28 × 42 mm). (b) 350s. Ostrich (28 × 42 mm) Set of 2 sheets . . . . 11·00 6·00
Nos. 622/40 were printed together, se-tenant, forming a composite design of birds at a waterhole.

1989. Fauna and Flora. Multicoloured.
642 5s. Type **139** 15 15
643 10s. Bushbaby holding insect (horiz) 20 20
644 20s. Bushbaby on forked branch 30 30
645 30s. Black cobra on umbrella acacia 60 60
646 45s. Bushbaby at night (horiz) 60 60
647 70s. Red-billed tropic bird and tree ferns . . . . . . 4·00 3·50
648 100s. African tree frog on cocoa tree . . . . 4·00 3·75
649 150s. Black-headed heron and Egyptian papyrus . . . . 7·00 7·50
MS650 Two sheets. (a) 115 × 85 mm. 350s. African palm civet (horiz). (b) 65 × 65 mm. 350s. Pink-backed pelican and baobab Tree (horiz) Set of 2 sheets . . . . 10·00 6·00
Nos. 646, 648/9 and **MS**650 are without the World Wildlife Fund logo.

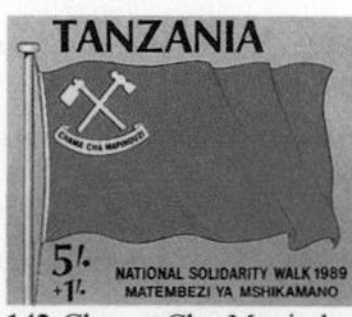

140 Juma Ikangaa (marathon runner) **142** Chama Cha Mapinduzi Party Flag

141 Drums

1989. International Sporting Personalities. Mult.
651 4s. Type **140** 15 15
652 8s.50 Steffi Graf (tennis player) . . . . 1·00 30
653 12s. Yannick Noah (tennis player) 80 40
654 40s. Pele (footballer) 90 65
655 100s. Erhard Keller (speed skater) . . . . 1·00 80
656 125s. Sadanoyama (sumo wrestler) . . . . 1·25 1·00
657 200s. Taino (sumo wrestler) 1·75 1·75
658 250s. T. Nakajima (golfer) . . 5·50 2·75
MS659 Two sheets. (a) 100 × 71 mm. 350s. Joe Louis (boxer). (b) 100 × 76 mm. 350s. I. Aoki (golfer) Set of 2 sheets . . . . 11·00 6·00
The captions on Nos. 658 and **MS**659b are transposed.

1989. Musical Instruments. Multicoloured.
660 2s. Type **141** 75 25
661 3s. Xylophones 75 25
662 10s. Thumbpiano . . . . . 1·25 1·00
663 20s. Fiddles . . . . 1·75 3·50
MS664 91 × 80 mm. 40s. Violins with calebash resonators . . . . . 1·00 1·00

1989. National Solidarity Walk. Mult.
665 5s.+1s. Type **142** 25 25
666 10s.+1s. Marchers with party flag and President Mwinyi 25 25
MS667 122 × 122 mm. 50s.+1s. President Mwinyi (vert) 60 60

143 Class P36 Locomotive, Russia, 1953

1989. Steam Locomotives. Multicoloured.
668 10s. Type **143** 85 35
669 25s. Class 12 streamlined locomotive, Belgium, 1939 95 45
670 60s. Class C62 locomotive, Japan, 1948 . . . . 1·50 1·00
671 75s. Pennsylvania Railroad Class T1 streamlined locomotive, U.S.A., 1942 1·60 1·25
672 80s. Class WP locomotive, India, 1946 . . . . 1·75 1·25
673 90s. East African Railways Class 59 Garratt locomotive No. 5919 . . . 1·75 1·50
674 150s. Class "People" locomotive No. 1206, China . . . . 2·25 2·75
675 200s. Southern Pacific "Daylight" express, U.S.A 2·25 2·75
MS676 Two sheets, each 114 × 85 mm. (a) 350s. Stephenson's "Planet", Great Britain, 1830 (vert). (b) 350s. L.M.S. "Coronation Scot", Great Britain, 1937 (vert) Set of 2 sheets 7·00 8·50

1989. "World Stamp Expo '89" International Stamp Exhibition, Washington. Landmarks of Washington. sheet 78 × 62 mm, containing design as T **201b** of St. Vincent, but vert.
MS677 500s. Union Station . . . 4·00 5·50

144 "Luna 3" Satellite orbiting Moon, 1959

1989. History of Space Exploration and 20th Anniv of First Manned Landing on Moon. Multicoloured.
678 20s. Type **144** 75 40
679 30s. "Gemini 6" and "7", 1965 . . . . 85 45
680 40s. Astronaut Edward White in space, 1965 . . . . . . 95 55
681 60s. Astronaut Aldrin on Moon, 1969 . . . . 1·40 90
682 70s. Aldrin performing experiment, 1969 . . . . . 1·50 1·00
683 100s. "Apollo 15" astronaut and lunar rover, 1971 . . . 1·75 1·40
684 150s. "Apollo 18" and "Soyuz 19" docking in space, 1975 . . . . 2·25 2·25
685 200s. Spacelab, 1983 . . . . 2·40 2·50
MS686 Two sheets, each 110 × 90 mm. (a) 250s. Lunar module "Eagle" and "Apollo 11" emblem. (b) 250s. Projected U.S. space station Set of 2 sheets . . 6·50 7·00

1989. Olympic Medal Winners, Calgary and Seoul. Various stamps optd. (a) Nos. 571/4.
687 10s. Type **131** (optd **Gold-USSR Silver-Brazil Bronze-W. Germany**) 80 40
688 20s. Cycling (optd **Men's Match Sprint, Lutz Hesslich, DDR**) . . . . . 3·00 1·00
689 50s. Fencing (optd **Epee, Schmitt, W. Germany**) . . 2·00 1·60
690 70s. Volleyball (optd **Men's Team, USA**) . . . . 2·75 2·75
MS691 77 × 92 mm. 100s. Gymnastics (optd **Women's Team, Gold — USSR**) . . . . 3·00 3·75

(b) Nos. 576/9.
692 5s. Cross-country skiing (optd **Biathlon, Peter-Roetsch, DDR**) 70 40
693 25s. Figure skating (optd **Pairs, Gordeeva & Grinkov, USSR**) . . . . 1·50 75
694 50s. Downhill skiing (optd **Zurbriggen, Switzerland**) . . 2·25 1·75
695 75s. Bobsleighing (optd **Gold-USSR Silver-DDR Bronze-DDR**) . . . . 2·75 2·50
MS696 77 × 92 mm. 100s. Ice hockey sticks wrapped in Olympic and Canadian colours (optd **Ice Hockey: Gold — USSR**) . . . 7·00 7·00

146 Spotted Tilapia

1989. Reef and Freshwater Fishes of Tanzania. Multicoloured.
697 9s. Type **146** 75 40
698 13s. Painted triggerfish . . . 75 40
699 20s. Powder-blue surgeonfish 1·00 50
700 40s. Red-tailed butterflyfish 1·60 75
701 70s. Red-tailed notho . . . . 2·00 1·25
702 100s. Ansorge's neolebias . . 2·50 1·75
703 150s. Blue panchax . . . . . 2·75 3·00
704 200s. Regal angelfish . . . . 2·75 3·00
MS705 Two sheets, each 112 × 83 mm. (a) 350s. Jewel cichlid (50 × 38 mm). (b) 350s. Dusky batfish (38 × 50 mm) Set of 2 sheets . . . . 12·00 12·00

147 Rural Polling Station

1989. Centenary of Inter-Parliamentary Union.
706 **147** 9s. multicoloured 10 10
707 – 13s. multicoloured 10 10
708 – 80s. multicoloured 40 65
709 – 100s. black, ultram & bl 50 85
MS710 90 × 90 mm. 40s. multicoloured . . . . 70 1·25
DESIGNS: 13s. Parliament Building, Dar-es-Salaam; 40s. Sir William Randal Cremer and Frederic Passy (founders); 80s. Tanzania Parliament in session; 100s. Logo.

148 Logo

1990. 10th Anniv of Pan-African Postal Union.
711 **148** 9s. yellow, green and black 20 15
712 – 13s. multicoloured 20 15
713 – 70s. multicoloured . . . . 1·50 1·10
714 – 100s. multicoloured . . . 2·50 2·25
MS715 90 × 90 mm. 40s. multicoloured . . . . 1·50 2·25
DESIGNS: 13s. Collecting mail from post office box; 40s. Logos of Tanzania Posts and Telecommunications Corporation, P.A.P.U. and U.P.U.; 70s. Taking mail to post office; 100s. Mail transport.

149 Admiral's Flag and "Nina"

1990. 500th Anniv (1992) of Discovery of America by Columbus (50, 60, 75, 200s.) and Modern Scientific Discoveries (others). Multicoloured.
716 9s. Bell XS-1 aircraft (first supersonic flight, 1947) . . 75 50
717 13s. "Trieste" (bathyscaphe) (first dive to depth of 35,000 ft, 1960) 75 50
718 50s. Type **149** . . . . 1·50 90
719 60s. Fleet flag and "Pinta" 1·50 1·10
720 75s. Standard of Castile and Leon and "Santa Maria" 1·50 1·25
721 150s. Transistor technology 1·25 2·00
722 200s. Arms of Columbus and map of First Voyage . . . 2·75 3·00
723 250s. DNA molecule . . . . 2·75 3·00
MS724 Two sheets, each 106 × 78 mm. (a) 350s. Caravels in the Caribbean. (b) 350s. "Voyager II" and Neptune Set of 2 sheets 5·50 7·00

150 Tecopa Pupfish

1990. Extinct Species. Multicoloured.
725 25s. Type **150** . . . . 1·00 60
726 40s. Thylacine . . . . 1·50 1·00
727 50s. Quagga . . . . 1·75 1·10
728 60s. Passenger pigeon . . . . 2·50 1·75
729 75s. Rodriguez saddleback tortoise . . . . 2·25 1·75
730 100s. Toolache wallaby . . . 2·50 2·00
731 150s. Texas red wolf . . . . 2·50 2·50
732 200s. Utah lake sculpin . . . 2·50 2·50
MS733 Two sheets. (a) 102 × 74 mm. 350s. South Island Whekau. (b) 71 × 99 mm. 350s. Hawaii O-o (vert) Set of 2 sheets . . . . . 11·00 11·00

151 Camping

1990. 60th Anniv of Girl Guides Movement in Tanzania. Multicoloured.
734 9s. Type **151** 15 20
735 13s. Guides planting sapling 15 20
736 50s. Guide teaching woman to write 40 65
737 100s. Guide helping at child-care clinic . . . . 65 1·10
MS738 89 × 89 mm. 40s. Guide teaching child to read (vert) . . 1·00 1·25

152 Fishing

1990. 25th Anniv of Union of Tanganyika and Zanzibar. Multicoloured.
739 9s. Type **152** 45 30
740 13s. Vineyard 45 30
741 50s. Cloves . . . . 1·50 1·50
742 100s. Presidents Nyerere and Karume exchanging Union instruments (vert) . . . . 2·50 3·50
MS743 90 × 90 mm. 40s. Arms (vert) 2·25 2·50

153 Footballer **154** Miriam Makeba

1990. World Cup Football Championship, Italy (1st issue). Multicoloured.
744 25s. Type **153** . . . . 1·50 30
745 60s. Player passing ball . . . 2·00 90
746 75s. Player turning . . . . . 2·25 1·25
747 200s. Player kicking ball . . 4·50 5·50
MS748 Two sheets, each 105 × 76 mm. (a) 350s. Two players fighting for possession. (b) 350s. Player kicking ball Set of 2 sheets . . . . 11·00 10·00
See also Nos. 789/92 and 794/7.

1990. Famous Black Entertainers. Mult.
749 9s. Type **154** 15 10
750 13s. Manu Dibango 15 10
751 25s. Fela 20 15
752 70s. Smokey Robinson . . . 1·00 40
753 100s. Gladys Knight . . . . 1·10 55
754 150s. Eddie Murphy . . . . 2·25 2·25
755 200s. Sammy Davis Jnr. . . . 2·50 2·75
756 250s. Stevie Wonder . . . . 2·50 3·00
MS757 Two sheets, each 69 × 88 mm. (a) 350s. Bill Cosby (30 × 39 mm). (b) 350s. Michael Jackson (30 × 39 mm) Set of 2 sheets . . . . 4·25 5·00

155 Ring of People round Party Flag

1990. Solidarity Walk, 1990. Multicoloured.
758 9s.+1s. Type **155** 80 90
759 13s.+1s. President Mwinyi . . 80 90
MS760 90×90 mm. 50s.+1s. Handclasp on map (vert) . . . 1·50 2·00

156 Diesel Train **157** Pope John Paul II

1990. 10th Anniv of Southern African Development Co-ordination Conference. Multicoloured.
761 8s. Type **156** . . . . 1·50 50
762 11s.50 Paper-making plant 25 20
763 25s. Tractor factory and ploughing 30 20
764 100s. Map and national flags 3·50 3·50
MS765 89×89 mm. 50s. Map of Southern Africa . . . . 2·75 3·00

1990. Papal Visit to Tanzania. Multicoloured.
766 10s. Type **157** 20 15
767 15s. Pope in ceremonial robes 25 15
768 20s. Pope giving blessing . . 30 15
769 100s. Papal coat of arms . . 80 1·40
MS770 172×143 mm. 50s. Pope John Paul II (horiz); 50s. St. Joseph's Cathedral, Dar-es-Salaam (horiz); 50s. Christ the King Cathedral, Moshi (horiz); 50s. Saint Theresa's Cathedral, Tabora (horiz); 50s. Cathedral of the Epiphany, Bugando Mwanza (horiz); 50s. St. Mathias Mulumba Kalemba Cathedral, Songea (horiz) . . . . 3·50 3·75

158 Mickey and Minnie Mouse in Herby the Love Bug

1990. Motor Cars from Disney Films. Mult.
771 20s. Type **158** 30 30
772 30s. The Absent-minded Professor's car 35 35
773 45s. Chitty-Chitty Bang-Bang 45 45
774 60s. Mr. Toad's car 65 65
775 75s. Scrooge's limousine . . . 75 75
776 100s. The Shaggy Dog's car 1·00 1·00
777 150s. Donald Duck's nephews cleaning car . . . . 1·60 1·60
778 200s. Fire engine from "Dumbo" . . . . 1·75 1·75
MS779 Two sheets, each 127×112 mm. (a) 350s. The Mickeymobile. (b) 350s. Cruella De Vil and dog wagon from "101 Dalmations" Set of 2 sheets . . 8·50 8·50

159 "St. Mary Magdalen in Penitence" (detail) **160** Klinsmann of West Germany

1990. Paintings by Titian. Multicoloured.
780 5s. Type **159** 10 10
781 10s. "Averoldi Polyptych" (detail) 10 10
782 15s. "Saint Margaret" (detail) 15 15
783 50s. "Venus and Adonis" (detail) 40 40
784 75s. "Venus and the Lutenist" (detail) 55 55
785 100s. "Tarquin and Lucretia" (detail) 70 70
786 125s. "Saint Jerome" (detail) 90 90
787 150s. "Madonna and Child in Glory with Saints" (detail) 1·00 1·00
MS788 Three sheets. (a) 95×110 mm. 300s. "Adoration of the Holy Trinity" (detail). (b) 95×110 mm. 300s. "St. Catherine of Alexandria at Prayer" (detail). (c) 110×95 mm. 300s. "The Supper at Emmaus" (detail) Set of 3 sheets . . . . 9·00 10·00

1990. World Cup Football Championship, Italy (2nd issue). Multicoloured.
789 10s. Type **160** 50 30
790 60s. Serena of Italy 90 60
791 100s. Nicol of Scotland . . . 1·75 1·75
792 300s. Susic of Yugoslavia . . 3·25 4·00
MS793 Two sheets, each 85×95 mm. (a) 400s. Montero of Costa Rica. (b) 400s. Seifo of Belgium Set of 2 sheets . . . . 10·00 10·00

161 Throw-in

1990. World Cup Football Championship, Italy (3rd issue). Multicoloured.
794 9s. Type **161** 60 20
795 13s. Penalty kick 60 20
796 25s. Dribbling 85 25
797 100s. Corner kick . . . . . 3·00 3·50
MS798 82×82 mm. 50s. World Cup and world map . . . . 2·75 3·00

162 Canoe **163** Lesser Masked Weaver

164 Lesser Flamingo

1990. Marine Transport. Multicoloured.
799 9s. Type **162** 20 20
800 13s. Sailing canoe 25 20
801 25s. Dhow 90 25
802 100s. Freighter . . . . 3·50 3·50
MS803 90×90 mm. 40s. Mashua dhow . . . . 2·75 3·25

1990. Birds. Designs as T **163** (5s. to 30s.) or T **164** (40s. to 500s.). Multicoloured.
804 5s. Type **163** 15 40
805 9s. African emerald cuckoo 20 10
806 13s. Little bee eater 30 10
807 15s. Red bishop 30 10
808 20s. Bateleur 40 10
809 25s. Scarlet-chested sunbird 40 10
809a 30s. African wood pigeon 40 15
810 40s. Type **164** 40 15
811 70s. Helmeted guineafowl 45 30
812 100s. Eastern white pelican 55 30
813 170s. Saddle-bill stork . . . 70 85
814 200s. South African crowned crane 80 90
814a 300s. Pied crow . . . . . . 90 1·25
814b 400s. White-headed vulture 1·00 1·60
815 500s. Ostrich . . . . 1·10 1·60
MS816 100×102 mm. 40s. Superb starling; 60s. Lilac-breasted roller 4·00 4·25

165 Athletics

1990. 14th Commonwealth Games, Auckland, New Zealand. Multicoloured.
817 9s. Type **165** 55 20
818 13s. Netball (vert) 80 20
819 25s. Pole vaulting . . . . . 1·25 25
820 100s. Long jumping (vert) . . 2·50 3·00
MS821 100×100 mm. 40s. Boxing (vert) . . . . 1·75 2·50

166 Former German Post Office, Dar-es-Salaam

1991. 150th Anniv of the Penny Black and "Stamp World London 90" International Stamp Exhibition. Multicoloured.
822 50s. Type **166** 75 75
823 50s. "Reichstag" (German mail steamer), 1890 . . . . 75 75
824 75s. Dhows, Zanzibar . . . . 1·10 1·10
825 75s. Cobham's Short S.5 Singapore I flying boat, Mwanza, Lake Victoria, 1928 . . . . 1·10 1·10
826 100s. Air Tanzania Fokker F.27 Friendship over Livingstone's house, Zanzibar . . . . 1·50 1·50
827 100s. Mail train at Moshi station . . . . 1·50 1·50
828 100s. English mail coach, 1840 . . . . 1·50 1·50
829 150s. Stephenson's "Rocket" and mail coach, 1838 . . . 1·90 1·90
830 200s. Imperial Airways Handley Page H.P.42 at Croydon . . . . 2·00 2·00
MS831 Two sheets, each 85×65 mm. (a) 350s. Sir Rowland Hill and Penny Black. (b) 350s. Thurn and Taxis letter of 1860 Set of 2 sheets . . . . 9·00 11·00

167 Petersberg Railway, Konigswinter, Germany

1991. Cog Railways. Multicoloured.
832 8s. Type **167** 50 30
833 25s. "Waumbek" (locomotive), Mt. Washington Railway, U.S.A 70 60
834 50s. Sarajevo–Dubrovnik line, Yugoslavia 85 75
835 100s. Budapest Rack Railway, Hungary . . . . 1·25 1·00
836 150s. Steam locomotive No. 97218, Vordenberg–Eisenerz line, Austria . . . 1·75 1·75
837 200s. Last train on Rimutaka Incline, New Zealand, 1955 1·90 1·90
838 250s. "John Stevens" rack and pinion drive locomotive, U.S.A., 1825 1·90 2·00
839 300s. Mt. Pilatus Rack Railway steam railcar, Switzerland . . . . 2·00 2·00
MS840 Two sheets, each 117×87 mm. (a) 400s. Sylvester Marsh and Presidential excursion train, Mt. Washington Cog Railway, U.S.A., 1869 (51×38 mm). (b) 400s. Steam locomotive, Schneeberg Railway, Austria (51×38 mm) Set of 2 sheets . . . . 8·50 9·00

1991. International Literacy Year (1st issue). As T **226a** of St. Vincent, showing Walt Disney cartoon characters illustrating the Alphabet. Multicoloured.
841/67 1, 2, 3, 5, 10, 15, 18, 20, 25, 30, 35, 40, 45, 50, 55, 60, 75, 80, 90, 100, 120, 125, 145, 150, 160, 175, 200s. Set of 27 . . . . . 14·00 16·00
MS868 Two sheets, each 128×112 mm. (a) 600s. Tiger Lily and Lost Boys. (b) 600s. Mickey Mouse driving miniature railway locomotive (vert) Set of 2 sheets 11·00 12·00
See also Nos. 905/8.

1991. Olympic Games, Barcelona (1st issue). As T **239a** of Sierra Leone. Multicoloured.
869 5s. Archery 40 30
870 10s. Women's gymnastics . . 40 30
871 25s. Boxing 50 30
872 50s. Canoeing 75 55
873 100s. Volleyball . . . . . . 1·40 1·25
874 150s. Men's gymnastics . . . 1·60 1·75
875 200s. 4×100 metres relay . . 2·00 2·25
876 300s. Judo . . . . 2·25 2·50
MS877 Two sheets, each 102×71 mm. (a) 400s. Cycling. (b) 400s. 400 metres men's hurdles Set of 2 sheets . . . . 11·00 11·00
See also Nos. 1309/12 and 1404/11.

167a "Phalaenopsis Lipperose"

1991. "EXPO 90" International Garden and Greenery Exhibition, Osaka. Orchids. Multicoloured.
878 10s. Type **167a** 25 15
879 25s. "Lycoste Aquila" . . . 35 20
880 30s. "Vuylstekeara Cambria Plush" 40 20
881 50s. "Vuylstekeara Monica Burnham" 55 35
882 90s. "Odontocidium Crowborough Plush" . . . 1·00 1·00
883 100s. "Oncidioda Crowborough Chelsea" . . 1·00 1·00
884 250s. "Sophrolaeliocattleya Phena Saturn" . . . . . . 1·75 2·00
885 300s. "Laeliocattleya Lykas" 1·90 2·50
MS886 Two sheets, each 100×69 mm. (a) 400s. "Cymbidium Baldoyle Melbury". (b) 400s. "Cymbidium Tapestry Long Beach" Set of 2 sheets 5·50 6·50

168 Olympic "Sailing" Class Yacht Racing

1991. Record-breaking Sports Events. Mult.
887 5s. Type **168** 40 30
888 20s. Olympic downhill skiing 80 35
889 30s. "Tour de France" cycle race . . . . 2·00 70
890 40s. Le Mans 24-hour endurance motor race . . . 1·75 75
891 75s. Olympic two man bob-sleighing . . . . 2·00 1·10
892 100s. Belgian Grand Prix motor cycle race . . . . . 2·75 1·75
893 250s. Indianapolis 500 motor race . . . . 2·75 3·25
894 300s. Gold Cup power boat championship . . . . . . 2·75 3·50
MS895 Two sheets, each 85×64 mm. (a) 400s. Colorado 500 motor cycle race (vert). (b) 400s. Schneider Trophy air race (vert) Set of 2 sheets . . . . . 9·50 11·00

169 Mickey Mouse as Cowboy

1991. Mickey Mouse in Hollywood. Walt Disney cartoon characters as actors. Mult.
896 5s. Type **169** 30 30
897 10s. Mickey as boxer 30 30
898 15s. Mickey as astronaut . . 30 30
899 20s. Mickey and Minnie as lovers 30 30
900 100s. Mickey as pirate rescuing Minnie . . . . . 1·25 1·25
901 200s. Mickey and Donald Duck as policemen arresting Big Pete . . . . 2·50 2·50
902 350s. Mickey and Donald with Goofy in historical drama . . . . 2·75 2·75
903 450s. Mickey, Donald and Goofy as sailors . . . . . 2·75 2·75
MS904 Two sheets, each 127×96 mm. (a) 600s. Mickey, Minnie and Donald in the mummy's tomb. (b) 600s. Mickey as Canadian Mountie rescuing Minnie from Big Pete Set of 2 sheets . . . . 11·00 11·00

170 Women learning to Read

1991. International Literacy Year (2nd issue). Multicoloured.
905 9s. Type **170** 25 20
906 13s. Teacher with blackboard 30 20
907 25s. Literacy aids 40 25

908 100s. Reading newspaper . . 2·50 3·00
MS909 104 × 73 mm. 50s. Adult education class . . . . 1·50 2·00

171 Ngorongoro Crater

1991. Historical Craters and Caves. Mult.
910 3s. Type **171** . . . . 1·75 1·25
911 5s. Prehistoric rock painting, Kondoa Caves . . . . . . 2·00 1·25
912 9s. Inner crater, Mt. Kilimanjaro . . . . 2·25 1·50
913 12s. Olduvai Gorge . . . . . 3·25 2·25
MS914 91 × 92 mm. 10s. Discarded bottles, Amboni Caves; 10s. Rock paintings, Amboni Caves; 10s. Entrance to Amboni Caves; 10s. Rock formation, Amboni Caves 14·00 10·00

1991. 350th Death Anniv of Rubens. Cartoons for Decius Mus Tapestries. As T **242a** of Sierra Leone. Multicoloured.
915 85s. "Proclamation of the Vision" . . . . 1·75 2·00
916 85s. "Divining of the Entrails" . . . . 1·75 2·00
917 85s. "Dispatch of the Lictors" . . . . 1·75 2·00
918 85s. "Dedication to Death" 1·75 2·00
919 85s. "Victory and Death of Decius Mus" . . . . . . 1·75 2·00
920 85s. "Funeral Rites" . . . . 1·75 2·00
MS921 70 × 100 mm. 500s. "Trophy of War" (detail) (vert) . . . . 9·50 10·00

172 Stegosaurus

1991. Prehistoric Creatures. Multicoloured.
922 10s. Type **172** 25 25
923 15s. Triceratops 25 25
924 25s. Edmontosaurus 40 40
925 30s. Plateosaurus 40 40
926 35s. Diplodocus 45 45
927 100s. Iguanodon . . . . . . 1·40 1·50
928 200s. Silviasaurus . . . . . 2·00 2·50
MS929 90 × 90 mm. 150s. Rhamphorhynchus . . . . . . 2·50 3·00

173 Dairy Farming

1991. 20th Anniv of Tanzania Investment Bank. Multicoloured.
930 10s. Type **173** 25 20
931 13s. Industrial development 30 20
932 25s. Engineering 35 20
933 100s. Tea picking . . . . . 2·00 2·50
MS934 93 × 91 mm. Nos. 930/3 3·00 3·50

174 Pres. Mwinyi leading Walk

1991. National Solidarity Walk. Multicoloured.
935 4s.+1s. Type **174** 75 75
936 30s.+1s. Pres. Mwinyi planting sapling . . . . . 1·50 1·50
MS937 91 × 91 mm. 50s.+1s. Pres. Mwinyi sorting cloves . . . . 2·25 2·75

174a Class 150 Steam Locomotive, 1872 (first locomotive in Japan)

1991. "Phila Nippon '91" International Stamp Exhibition, Tokyo. Japanese Railway Locomotives. Multicoloured.
938 10s. Type **174a** . . . . . . 1·25 65
939 25s. Class 4500 steam locomotive, 1902 . . . . . 1·60 90
940 35s. Class C 62 steam locomotive, 1948 . . . . . 1·75 1·00
941 50s. Mikado steam locomotive . . . . 1·90 1·25
942 75s. Class 6250 steam locomotive, 1915 . . . . . 2·25 1·50
943 100s. Class C 11 steam locomotive, 1932 . . . . . 2·50 1·75
944 200s. Class E 10 steam locomotive, 1948 . . . . . 3·00 3·25
945 300s. Class 8550 steam locomotive, 1899 . . . . . 3·50 4·00
MS946 Four sheets, each 102 × 71 mm. (a) 400s. Series 400 electric train. (b) 400s. Class EH10 electric locomotive, 1954. (c) 400s. Class DD51 diesel-hydraulic locomotive, 1962. (d) 400s. Class EF58 electric locomotive Set of 4 sheets . . . . 12·00 13·00

175 Zebra and Golden-winged Sunbird, Ngorongoro Crater

1991. National Game Parks. Multicoloured.
947 10s. Type **175** . . . . 1·00 70
948 25s. Greater kudu and elephant, Ruaha Park . . . 1·50 1·00
949 30s. Sable antelope and red and yellow barbet, Mikumi Park . . . . 1·50 1·00
950 50s. Leopard and wildebeest, Serengeti Park . . . . . . 1·50 1·25
951 90s. Giraffe and white starred robin, Ngurdoto Park . . 2·75 2·25
952 100s. Eland and Abbot's duiker, Kilimanjaro Park 2·00 1·75
953 250s. Lion and impala, Lake Manyara Park . . . . . . 3·00 3·75
954 300s. Black rhinoceros and ostrich, Tarangire Park . . 4·50 4·50
MS955 Two sheets, each 99 × 68 mm. (a) 400s. Blue-breasted kingfisher and defassa waterbuck, Selous Game Reserve. (b) 400s. Paradise whydah and oryx, Mkomazi Game Reserve Set of 2 sheets . . . . 15·00 13·00

176 "Eronia cleodora"

1991. Butterflies. Multicoloured.
956 10s. Type **176** 55 45
957 15s. "Precis westermanni" . . 70 60
958 35s. "Antanartia delius" . . 1·00 90
959 75s. "Bematistes aganice" . . 1·75 1·60
960 100s. "Kallima jacksoni" . . 1·90 1·75
961 150s. "Apaturopsis cleocharis" . . . . 2·75 2·75
962 200s. "Colotis aurigineus" . . 3·00 3·00
963 300s. "Iolaus crawshayi" . . 3·25 3·50
MS964 Four sheets, each 117 × 76 mm. (a) 400s. "Charaxes zoolina". (b) 400s. "Papilio phorcas". (c) 400s. "Charaxes ethalion". (d) 400s. "Papilio nobilis" Set of 4 sheets . . . . 14·00 15·00

177 Microwave Tower and Dish Aerial

1991. 25th Anniv of Intelsat Satellite System. Multicoloured.
965 10s. Type **177** 50 20
966 25s. Satellite picture of Earth 65 30
967 100s. Mwenge "B" Earth station . . . . 2·00 1·50
968 500s. Mwenge "A" Earth station . . . . 7·00 8·00
MS969 90 × 86 mm. 50s. Satellite links on world map . . . . . . 3·00 3·00

178 Rice Cultivation

1991. 40th Anniv of United Nations Development Programme. Multicoloured (except No. **MS**974).
970 10s. Type **178** 15 10
971 15s. Vocational and Civil Service training 20 10
972 100s. Terrace farming . . . . 1·50 1·60
973 500s. Renovated Arab door (vert) . . . . 5·50 8·00
MS974 90 × 90 mm. 40s. UNDP anniversary emblem (blue and black) . . . . 1·10 1·50

179 Netball

180 "TELECOM 91" Logo

1991. All-Africa Games, Cairo. Mult.
975 10s. Type **179** 50 30
976 15s. Football (horiz) 50 30
977 100s. Tennis . . . . 2·25 1·50
978 200s. Athletics . . . . 2·50 2·75
979 500s. Baseball (horiz) . . . . 6·00 8·00
MS980 80 × 60 mm. 500s. Basketball 9·00 9·00

1991. "TELECOM 91" International Telecommunication Exhibition, Geneva (10, 15s.) and World Telecommunications Day (others). Mult.
981 10s. Type **180** 10 10
982 15s. "TELECOM '91" logo and address on envelope (horiz) 15 10
983 35s. Symbolic telecommunication signals 25 20
984 100s. Symbolic telecommunication signals (horiz) . . . . 70 1·00

181 Japanese Bobtail Cat

1991. Cats. Multicoloured.
985 50s. Type **181** 90 80
986 50s. Cornish rex 90 80
987 50s. Malayan 90 80
988 50s. Tonkinese 90 80
989 50s. Abyssinian 90 80
990 50s. Russian blue 90 80
991 50s. Cymric 90 80
992 50s. Somali 90 80
993 50s. Siamese 90 80
994 50s. Himalayan 90 80
995 50s. Singapura 90 80
996 50s. Manx 90 80
997 50s. Oriental shorthair . . . 90 80
998 50s. Maine coon 90 80
999 50s. Persian 90 80
1000 50s. Birman 90 80

182 Shire Horse

1991. Horses and Ponies. Multicoloured.
1001 50s. Type **182** 85 80
1002 50s. Thoroughbred 85 80
1003 50s. Kladruber 85 80
1004 50s. Appaloosa 85 80
1005 50s. Hanoverian 85 80
1006 50s. Arab 85 80
1007 50s. Breton 85 80
1008 50s. Exmoor 85 80
1009 50s. Connemara 85 80
1010 50s. Lipizzaner 85 80
1011 50s. Shetland 85 80
1012 50s. Percheron 85 80
1013 50s. Pinto 85 80
1014 50s. Orlov 85 80
1015 50s. Palomino 85 80
1016 50s. Welsh cob 85 80

Nos. 1001/16 were printed together, se-tenant, as a sheetlet of 16 with the backgrounds of each horizontal strip of 4 forming a composite design.

183 Yellow Tetra

1991. Aquarium Fish. Multicoloured.
1017 75s. Type **183** 70 70
1018 75s. Five-banded barb . . . 70 70
1019 75s. Simpson platy 70 70
1020 75s. Guppy 70 70
1021 75s. Zebra danio 70 70
1022 75s. Neon tetra 70 70
1023 75s. Siamese fighting fish . . 70 70
1024 75s. Tiger barb 70 70
1025 75s. Two-striped lyretail . . 70 70
1026 75s. Fan-tailed goldfish . . 70 70
1027 75s. Pearl gourami 70 70
1028 75s. Freshwater angelfish . . 70 70
1029 75s. Clown loach 70 70
1030 75s. Red swordtail 70 70
1031 75s. Blue discus 70 70
1032 75s. Rosy barb 70 70

Nos. 1017/32 were printed together, se-tenant, with the backgrounds of each stamp forming a composite design.

184 African Elephant

186 Indian Elephant

185 Budgerigar

1991. African Elephants. Multicoloured.
1033 75s. Type **184** . . . . . . 1·25 1·10
1034 75s. Two elephants fighting 1·25 1·10
1035 75s. Elephant facing forward and tree . . . . 1·25 1·10
1036 75s. Elephant facing left and tree . . . . 1·25 1·10
1037 75s. Cow elephant and calf facing right standing in water . . . . 1·25 1·10
1038 75s. Cow watching over calf in water . . . . 1·25 1·10
1039 75s. Two adults and calf in water . . . . 1·25 1·10
1040 75s. Cow and calf facing left standing in water . . . . 1·25 1·10
1041 75s. Elephant facing right 1·25 1·10
1042 75s. Elephants feeding . . . 1·25 1·10
1043 75s. Elephant feeding . . . 1·25 1·10
1044 75s. Elephant and zebra . . 1·25 1·10
1045 75s. Cow and calf drinking 1·25 1·10
1046 75s. Calf suckling . . . . . 1·25 1·10
1047 75s. Bull elephant . . . . . 1·25 1·10
1048 75s. Cow with small calf . . 1·25 1·10

Nos. 1033/48 were printed together, se-tenant, as a sheetlet of 16 with each horizontal strip of 4 forming a composite design.

1991. Pet Birds. Multicoloured.
1049 75s. Type **185** 90 80
1050 75s. Orange-breasted bunting ("Rainbow Bunting") 90 80
1051 75s. Golden-fronted leafbird 90 80
1052 75s. Black-headed caique . . 90 80
1053 75s. Java sparrow 90 80
1054 75s. Diamond firetail finch 90 80
1055 75s. Peach-faced lovebird . . 90 80
1056 75s. Golden conure 90 80
1057 75s. Military macaw 90 80
1058 75s. Yellow-faced parrotlet 90 80
1059 75s. Sulphur-crested cockatoo 90 80
1060 75s. White-fronted amazon ("Spectacled Amazon Parrot") 90 80
1061 75s. Paradise tanager . . . 90 80
1062 75s. Gouldian finch 90 80
1063 75s. Masked lovebird . . . 90 80
1064 75s. Southern grackle ("Hill Mynah") 90 80

Nos. 1049/64 were printed together, se-tenant, forming a composite design.

1991. Death Centenary (1990) of Vincent van Gogh (artist). As T **215a** of St. Vincent. Multicoloured.
1065 10s. "Peasant Woman Sewing" 70 30
1066 15s. "Head of Peasant Woman with Greenish Lace Cap" 75 35
1067 35s. "Flowering Orchard" 1·25 60
1068 75s. "Portrait of a Girl" . . 2·00 1·00
1069 100s. "Portrait of a Woman with Red Ribbon" . . . 2·25 1·25
1070 150s. "Vase with Flowers" 3·00 3·00
1071 200s. "Houses in Antwerp" 3·25 3·50
1072 400s. "Seated Peasant Woman with White Cap" 6·00 7·50
MS1073 Two sheets, each 127 × 112 mm. (a) 400s. "Bulb Fields" (horiz). (b) 400s. "The Parsonage Garden at Nuenen in the Snow" (horiz). Imperf Set of 2 sheets . . . . 15·00 16·00

1991. Elephants. Multicoloured.
1074 10s. Type **186** 90 50
1075 15s. Indian elephant uprooting tree . . . . . 1·10 65

1076 25s. Indian elephant with calf . . . . 1·40 80
1077 30s. African elephant . . . 1·40 80
1078 35s. Head of African elephant (horiz) . . . . . 1·40 85
1079 100s. African elephant and calf bathing (horiz) . . . 3·00 2·50
1080 200s. Two African elephants (horiz) . . . . 4·50 5·50
MS1081 90 × 90 mm. 400s. Mammoth (horiz) . . . . . . 4·00 4·50

187 Class Em Steam Locomotive, Russia, 1930

1991. Locomotives of the World. Mult.
1082 10s. Type **187** 25 25
1083 15s. "Hikari" express train, Japan, 1964 . . . . . . 35 35
1084 25s. Russian steam locomotive, 1834 (vert) . . 45 45
1085 35s. TGV express train, France, 1979 . . . . . . 55 55
1086 60s. Diesel railcar No. R16-01, France, 1972 . . 80 80
1987 100s. High Speed Train 125, Great Britain, 1972 . . . 1·40 1·40
1088 300s. Russian steam locomotive, 1833 (vert) . . 3·00 3·00
MS1089 91 × 91 mm. French electric locomotive, 1952 (vert) . . . . 1·60 2·00
No. 1088 is inscribed "1837" in error.

1991. Christmas. Walt Disney Christmas Cards. As T **228** of St. Vincent. Multicoloured.
1090 10s. Disney characters in "JOY", 1968 (horiz) . . . 35 20
1091 25s. Mickey, Donald, Pluto and Goofy hanging up stockings, 1981 (horiz) . . 60 40
1092 35s. Characters from Disney film "Robin Hood", 1973 (horiz) 70 45
1093 75s. Mickey looking at Christmas tree, 1967 (horiz) . . . . 1·25 90
1094 100s. Goofy, Mickey, Donald, Chip 'n' Dale on film set, 1969 . . . . . . 1·60 1·25
1095 150s. Mickey on giant bubble, 1976 . . . . . . 2·00 2·00
1096 200s. Clarabelle Cow with electric cow bell, 1935 . . 2·25 2·50
1097 300s. Mickey's nephews with book, 1935 . . . . . . 3·00 3·50
MS1098 Two sheets, each 127 × 102 mm. (a) 500s. Mickey handing out presents, 1935. (b) 500s. Disney cartoon characters, 1968 Set of 2 sheets . . . . . 14·00 14·00

188 Bruce Lee

1992. Entertainers.
1099 75s. × 36 multicoloured Set of 36 . . . . 30·00 27·00
MS1135 Four sheets, each 78 × 108 mm. 500s. × 4 multicoloured (Bruce Lee, Marilyn Monroe, Elvis Presley, Kouyate & Kouyate, each 28 × 42 mm) Set of 4 sheets . . . . 23·00 26·00
Nos. 1099/1134 were issued as four sheetlets each of nine different designs, as Type **188**, depicting Bruce Lee, Marilyn Monroe, Elvis Presley and black entertainers (Scott Joplin, Sammy Davis Jnr, Joan Armatrading, Louis Armstrong, Miriam Makeba, Lionel Ritchie, Whitney Houston, Bob Marley, Tina Turner).

189 Sand Tilefish

1992. Fishes. Multicoloured.
1136 10s. Type **189** 40 40
1137 15s. Five-banded cichlid . . 45 45
1138 25s. Pearly lamprologus . . 60 60
1139 35s. Jewel cichlid 70 70
1140 60s. Two-striped lyretail . . 1·00 1·00
1141 100s. Reef stonefish . . . . 1·50 1·50
1142 300s. Ahl's lyretail . . . . 3·75 4·00
MS1143 90 × 90 mm. 100s. Oarfish 1·60 2·00

190 Chimpanzee in Tree

191 Pope John Paul II in Dominican Republic, 1979

1992. Common Chimpanzee. Multicoloured.
1144 10s. Type **190** 70 50
1145 15s. Feeding 75 55
1146 35s. Two chimpanzees . . . 1·25 85
1147 75s. Adult male with arms folded . . . . 1·75 1·25
1148 100s. Breaking branch . . . 2·00 1·50
1149 150s. Young chimpanzee in tree . . . . 2·75 2·75
1150 200s. Female holding young 3·25 3·50
1151 300s. Chimpanzee sitting in tree . . . . 4·25 4·50
MS1152 Two sheets, each 99 × 68 mm. (a) 400s. Eating termites. (b) 400s. Swinging through trees Set of 2 sheets 7·00 7·00

1992. Papal Visits.
1153/1272 100s. × 120 multicoloured Set of 120 . . . . . 90·00 75·00
DESIGNS: Nos. 1154/1272 Various scenes on Papal visits as Type **191**.

192 Balcony

193 Gogo Costume

1992. Zanzibar Stone Town. Multicoloured.
1273 10s. Type **192** 50 25
1274 20s. Bahlnara Mosque . . . 75 35
1275 30s. High Court Building . . 90 40
1276 200s. National Museum (horiz) . . . . 5·50 6·50
MS1277 91 × 91 mm. 150s. Old Fort (horiz); 300s. Maruhubi ruins (horiz) . . . . 7·00 6·00

1992. Traditional Costumes. Multicoloured.
1278 3s. Type **193** 80 60
1279 5s. Swahili 80 60
1280 9s. Hehe and Makonde . . 1·00 70
1281 12s. Maasai . . . . 1·25 85
MS1282 91 × 91 mm. 40s. Mwarusha 2·75 3·00

194 Melisa and Mike (chimpanzees)

1992. Chimpanzees of the Gombe. Multicoloured.
(a) Horiz designs as T **194**.
1283 10s. Type **194** 70 40
1284 15s. Leakey and David Greybeard 80 50
1285 30s. Fifi terminting . . . . . 1·00 70
1286 35s. Galahad . . . . 1·10 75
MS1287 90 × 90 mm. 100s. Fifi, Flo and Faben . . . . 2·50 2·75

(b) Vert design showing individual chimpanzees.
1288 10s. Leakey 90 90
1289 15s. Fifi 90 90
1290 20s. Faben 90 90
1291 30s. David Greybeard . . . 90 90
1292 35s. Mike 90 90
1293 65s. Galahad 90 90
1294 100s. Melisa . . . . 1·10 1·10
1295 200s. Flo . . . . 1·50 1·50

195 Sorghum Farming, Serena

1992. 25th Anniv of National Bank of Commerce. Multicoloured.
1296 10s. Type **195** 55 15
1297 15s. Samora Avenue branch and computer operator (vert) 60 25
1298 35s. Training centre 85 65
1299 40s. Women dyeing textiles 90 90
MS1300 111 × 117 mm. 30s. Bank head office . . . . 1·25 1·75

196 Giant Spider Conch

197 Basketball

1992. Shells. Multicoloured.
1301 10s. Type **196** 30 30
1302 15s. Bull-mouth helmet . . 35 35
1303 25s. Rugose mitre 50 50
1304 30s. Lettered cone 50 50
1305 35s. True heart cockle . . . 50 50
1306 50s. Ramose murex 60 70
1307 250s. Indian volute . . . . 1·75 3·25
MS1308 91 × 91 mm. 300s. Giant clam . . . . 3·50 4·00

1992. Olympic Games, Barcelona (2nd issue). Multicoloured.
1309 40s. Type **197** 45 30
1310 100s. Billiards 75 60
1311 200s. Table tennis . . . . . 1·25 1·40
1312 400s. Darts . . . . 2·75 3·50
MS1313 90 × 85 mm. 500s. Weightlifting . . . . 3·00 4·25

198 British-designed Radar, Pearl Harbor

1992. 50th Anniv of Japanese Attack on Pearl Harbor. Multicoloured.
1314 75s. Type **198** . . . . . . 1·75 1·40
1315 75s. Winston Churchill . . . 1·75 1·40
1316 75s. Sinking of H.M.S. "Repulse" (battle cruiser) 1·75 1·40
1317 75s. Sinking of H.M.S. "Prince of Wales" (battleship) . . . . 1·75 1·40
1318 75s. Surrender of Singapore 1·75 1·40
1319 75s. Sinking of H.M.S. "Hermes" (aircraft carrier) . . . . 1·75 1·40
1320 75s. Japanese attack on Malayan airfield . . . . 1·75 1·40
1321 75s. Japanese gun crew, Hong Kong . . . . . . 1·75 1·40
1322 75s. Japanese landing craft 1·75 1·40
1323 75s. "Haguro" (Japanese cruiser) . . . . 1·75 1·40

199 French Resistance Monument and Medal

1992. Birth Centenary (1990) of Charles de Gaulle (French statesman). Multicoloured.
1324 25s. Type **199** 50 40
1325 30s. Free French tank on Omaha beach, D-Day . . 50 40
1326 150s. Concorde at Charles de Gaulle Airport . . . . 7·00 6·00
MS1327 115 × 92 mm. 500s. Free French local Cross of Lorraine opt on Petain 1f.50 and De Gaulle label postmarked 25 August 1944 (39 × 51 mm) . . . . 8·50 9·50

200 Scout Bridge, Giraffe and Elephant

1992. 50th Death Anniv (1991) of Lord Baden-Powell (founder of Boy Scout movement). Multicoloured.
1328 10s. Type **200** 80 50
1329 15s. Scouts in boat 80 50
1330 400s. John Glenn's space capsule . . . . 6·00 7·00
MS1331 90 × 117 mm. 500s. Tanzanian scout (39 × 51 mm) 4·25 6·50

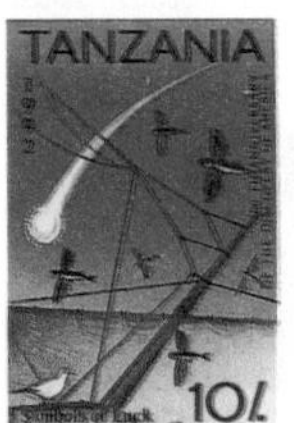

201 Marcella Sembrich as Zerlina in "Don Giovanni"

1992. Death Bicentenary of Mozart.
1332 **201** 10s. black and mauve . . 1·00 40
1333 – 50s. multicoloured . . . 2·50 1·10
1334 – 300s. black and mauve 9·00 9·00
MS1335 115 × 87 mm. 500s. brown, stone and black . . . . 9·00 9·00
DESIGNS—HORIZ: 50s. Planet Jupiter (Symphony No. 41); 300s. Luciano Pavarotti as Idamente in "Idomeneo". VERT (35 × 47 mm): Wolfgang Amadeus Mozart.

1992. "Granada '92" International Stamp Exhibition, Spain. Paintings. As T **250b** of Sierra Leone.
1336 25s. red and black 60 40
1337 35s. multicoloured 70 50
1338 50s. multicoloured 85 60
1339 75s. multicoloured . . . . . 1·25 1·00
1340 100s. black, brown and pink 1·75 1·25
1341 150s. red and black . . . . 2·25 2·25
1342 200s. red and black . . . . 2·50 2·50
1343 300s. multicoloured . . . . 3·00 3·50
MS1344 Two sheets, each 121 × 95 mm. (a) 400s. multicoloured. (b) 400s. multicoloured. Imperf Set of 2 sheets . . . . 8·00 9·00
DESIGNS—HORIZ (49½ × 36 mm): 25s. "A Picador, mounted on a Chulo's Shoulders, spears a Bull" (Goya); 150s. "Another Madness (of Martincho) in the Plaza de Zaragoza" (Goya); 200s. "Recklessness of Martincho in the Plaza de Zaragoza" (Goya). (111 × 86 mm): 400s. (**MS**1344a) "Two Men at Table" (Velasquez); 400s. (**MS**1344b) "Seascape" (Mariana Salvador Maella). VERT: 35s. "Philip IV at Fraga" (Velazquez); 50s. "Head of a Stag" (Velazquez); 75s. "The Cardinal-Infante Ferdinand as a Hunter" (Velazquez); 100s. "The Dream of Reason brings forth Monsters" (Goya); 300s. "Pablo de Valladolid" (Velazquez).

202 Lucky Omens

203 Superb Starling

1992. 500th Anniv of Discovery of America by Columbus. Multicoloured.
1345 10s. Type **202** 20 20
1346 15s. Map and compass . . . 25 25
1347 25s. Look-out in crow's nest 35 35
1348 30s. Amerindians sighting ships (horiz) 40 40
1349 35s. "Pinta" and "Nina" (horiz) 55 45
1350 75s. "Santa Maria" (horiz) 90 80
1351 250s. Wreck of "Santa Maria" . . . . 1·75 2·50
MS1352 93 × 93 mm. 200s. Columbus . . . . 1·75 2·50

1992. Birds. Multicoloured.
1353 5s. Type **203** 55 50
1354 10s. Golden Bishop ("Canary") 65 50
1355 15s. Four-coloured bush shrike 75 55
1356 25s. Grey-headed kingfisher 80 55
1357 30s. River kingfisher (Common Kingfisher") . . 80 55
1358 35s. Yellow-billed oxpecker 80 55
1359 150s. Black-throated honeyguide . . . . 2·50 3·00
MS1360 93 × 92 mm. 300s. European cuckoo (horiz) . . . 2·75 3·50

1992. 15th Death Anniv of Elvis Presley. Nos. 1117/25 optd **15th Anniversary**.
1361 75s. Looking pensive . . . 85 85
1362 75s. Wearing black and yellow striped shirt . . . 85 85
1363 75s. Singing into microphone 85 85
1364 75s. Wearing wide-brimmed hat 85 85
1365 75s. With microphone in right hand 85 85
1366 75s. In Army uniform . . . 85 85
1367 75s. Wearing pink shirt . . 85 85
1368 75s. In yellow shirt 85 85
1369 75s. In jacket and bow tie 85 85

205 Iguanodon

1992. African Dinosaurs. Multicoloured.
1370 100s. Type **205** . . . . . . 1·10 90
1371 100s. Saltasaurus . . . . . 1·10 90
1372 100s. Cetiosaurus . . . . . 1·10 90
1373 100s. Camarasaurus . . . . 1·10 90
1374 100s. Spinosaurus . . . . . 1·10 90
1375 100s. Stegosaurus . . . . . 1·10 90
1376 100s. Allosaurus . . . . . 1·10 90
1377 100s. Ceratosaurus . . . . 1·10 90
1378 100s. Lesothosaurus . . . . 1·10 90
1379 100s. Anchisaurus . . . . . 1·10 90
1380 100s. Ornithomimus . . . . 1·10 90
1381 100s. Baronyx . . . . . . 1·10 90

1382 100s. Pachycephalosaurus . . 1·10 90
1383 100s. Heterodontosaurus . . 1·10 90
1384 100s. Dryosaurus . . . . . 1·10 90
1385 100s. Coelophysis . . . . . 1·10 90
Nos. 1370/85 were printed together, se-tenant, forming a composite design.

206 Spotted Tilapia

1992. Fishes. Multicoloured.
1386 100s. Type **206** 85 85
1387 100s. Butterfly barb 85 85
1388 100s. Blunthead Molino cichlid 85 85
1389 100s. Angel squeaker . . . 85 85
1390 100s. Dickfield's Julie . . . 85 85
1391 100s. Nile mouthbrooder . . 85 85
1392 100s. Blue-finned notho . . . 85 85
1393 100s. Crabro mbuna 85 85
1394 100s. Pearl-scaled lamprologus 85 85
1395 100s. Zebra mbuna 85 85
1396 100s. Marlier's Julie 85 85
1397 100s. Brichard's chalinochromis 85 85
MS1398 Three sheets, each 71 × 55 mm. (a) 500s. Palmqvist's notho. (b) 500s. Electric blue haplochromis. (c) 500s. Short lamprologus Set of 3 sheets . . 11·00 12·00
Nos. 1386/97 were printed together, se-tenant, forming a composite design.

207 Hunting Birds with Catapults

1992. Traditional Hunting. Multicoloured.
1399 20s. Type **207** . . . . . . 1·00 40
1400 70s. Hunting antelope with bow and arrow . . . . . 1·25 65
1401 100s. Hunting antelopes with dogs . . . . 1·75 1·25
1402 150s. Hunting lion with spears and shields . . . . 2·50 3·25
MS1403 100 × 100 mm. 40s. Traditional hunting weapons 2·50 3·00

1992. Olympic Games, Albertville and Barcelona (3rd issue). As T **251a** of Sierra Leone. Multicoloured.
1404 20s. Men's 4000 m pursuit cycling . . . . 1·50 65
1405 40s. Men's double sculls rowing (horiz) 60 20
1406 50s. Water polo (horiz) . . 70 20
1407 70s. Women's single luge (horiz) 80 30
1408 100s. Marathon (horiz) . . 85 50
1409 150s. Women's asymmetrical bars gymnastics (horiz) . . 2·00 2·00
1410 200s. Ice hockey . . . . . 3·25 2·50
1411 400s. Men's rings gymnastics 3·50 4·50
MS1412 Two sheets, each 100 × 71 mm. (a) 500s. Tennis. (b) 500s. Football Set of 2 sheets 12·00 12·00

207a Donald Duck in "Sea Scout", 1939

1992. Mickey's Portrait Gallery. Walt Disney cartoon characters. Multicoloured.
1413 25s. Type **207a** 30 30
1414 25s. Minnie Mouse in "Hawaiian Holiday", 1937 . . . . 30 30
1415 25s. Pluto in "Society Dog Show", 1939 . . . . . 30 30
1416 35s. Donald in "Fire Chief", 1940 . . . . 40 40
1417 50s. Donald in "Truant Officer Donald", 1941 . . 50 50
1418 75s. Goofy in "Clock Cleaners", 1937 . . . . . 60 60
1419 100s. Goofy in "Goofy and Wilbur", 1939 . . . . . 70 70
1420 100s. Mickey Mouse in "Magician Mickey", 1937 70 70
1421 200s. Minnie in "The Nifty Nineties", 1941 . . . . . 1·25 1·25
1422 300s. Mickey and Pluto in "Society Dog Show", 1939 . . . . 1·50 1·50
1423 400s. Pluto and pups in "Pluto's Quin-Puplets", 1937 . . . . 1·60 1·60
1424 500s. Daisy and Donald in "Mr. Duck Steps Out", 1940 . . . . 1·75 1·75
MS1425 Three sheets. (a) 127 × 102 mm. 600s. Goofy in "Forever Goofy". (b) 127 × 102 mm. 600s. Daisy in "Don Donald", 1937. (c) 112 × 104 mm. 600s. Mickey and Minnie in "Brave Little Tailor", 1938 (horiz) Set of 3 sheets . . 9·50 11·00

208 "Couroupita guinensis" **209** Abyssinian Cat

1993. Botanical Gardens of the World. Rio de Janeiro. African Plants. Vert designs as T **208**.
1426/45 70s. × 20 multicoloured Set of 20 . . . . 14·00 16·00
Set of 20 . . . . 13·00 15·00
MS1446 110 × 74 mm. 500s. Avenue of royal palms . . . . 3·25 4·00

1992. Cats. Multicoloured.
1447 20s. Type **209** 55 45
1448 30s. Havana cat 55 45
1449 50s. Persian black cat . . . 65 55
1450 70s. Persian blue cat 75 65
1451 100s. European silver tabby cat . . . . 1·00 85
1452 150s. Persian silver tabby cat . . . . 1·25 1·25
1453 200s. Maine coon cat . . . 1·50 1·50
MS1454 90 × 90 mm. 300s. European cat . . . . 2·75 3·00

209a Baltimore Ohio Tunnel Locomotive No. 5, 1904

1992. "Genova '92" International Stamp Exhibition. Toy Trains manufactured by Lionel. Multicoloured.
1455 10s. Type **209a** 50 25
1456 20s. "Liberty Bell" locomotive No. 385E, 1930 . . . . 60 35
1457 30s. Armoured rail car No. 203, 1917 . . . . . 65 40
1458 50s. Open trolley No. 202, 1910–14 . . . . 90 60
1459 70s. "Macy Special" electric locomotive No. 405 . . . 1·00 70
1460 100s. "Milwaukee Road" bi-polar electric locomotive, 1929 . . . . 1·10 80
1461 200s. New York Central Type S locomotive, 1912 1·50 1·75
1462 300s. Locomotive No. 7, 1914 . . . . 1·75 2·75
MS1463 Two sheets. (a) 91 × 75 mm. 500s. Display model locomotive in clear plastic, 1947. (b) 71 × 89 mm. 500s. Mickey and Minnie Mouse on clockwork handcar, 1936 Set of 2 sheets . . . . 6·00 7·00

210 Count Ferdinand von Zeppelin

1992. Anniversaries and Events. Mult.
1464 30s. Type **210** 50 30
1465 70s. "Santa Maria" 80 80
1466 70s. "Apollo–Soyuz" link-up, 1975 . . . . 80 80
1467 150s. African elephant . . . 1·75 1·25
1468 150s. Child being offered apple . . . . 1·00 1·25
1469 200s. Zebra . . . . 1·10 1·10
1470 200s. Trying on glasses . . 1·10 1·10
1471 300s. Airship "Graf Zeppelin", 1929 . . . . . 1·75 1·75
1472 300s. Christopher Columbus 1·75 1·75
1473 400s. Space shuttle . . . . 2·50 2·50
1474 400s. Wolfgang Amadeus Mozart (vert) . . . . . . 3·25 3·00
MS1475 Five sheets. (a) 110 × 82 mm. 500s. LZ-5 Zeppelin airship. (b) 114 × 81 mm. 500s. Head of Columbus. (c) 110 × 82 mm. 500s. "Voyager 2" space probe. (d) 114 × 81 mm. 500s. African elephant (different). (e) 110 × 68 mm. 500s. Queen of the Night from "The Magic Flute" (vert) Set of 5 sheets . . . . . 15·00 16·00
ANNIVERSARIES AND EVENTS: Nos. 1464, 1471, **MS**1475a, 75th death anniv of Count Ferdinand von Zeppelin; 1465, 1472, **MS**1475b, 500th anniv of discovery of America by Columbus; 1466, 1473, **MS**1475c, International Space Year; 1467, 1469, **MS**1475d, Earth Summit '92, Rio; 1468, International Conference on Nutrition, Rome; 1470, 75th anniv of International Association of Lions Clubs; 1474, **MS**1475e, Death bicentenary of Mozart.

1992. Bicentenary of the Louvre, Paris. Paintings by Jean Chardin. As T **254a** of St Vincent. Multicoloured.
1476 100s. "Young Draughtsman sharpening Pencil" . . . 85 85
1477 100s. "The Buffet" 85 85
1478 100s. "Return from the Market" 85 85
1479 100s. "The Hard-working Mother" 85 85
1480 100s. "Grace" 85 85
1481 100s. "The Copper Water Urn" 85 85
1482 100s. "The House of Cards" 85 85
1483 100s. "Boy with a Top" . . 85 85
MS1484 100 × 70 mm. 500s. "The Ray" (85 × 52 mm) . . . . . 3·50 4·00

211 Carved Head

1992. Makonde Art.
1485 **211** 20s. multicoloured . . . 15 15
1486 – 30s. multicoloured . . . 15 15
1487 – 50s. multicoloured . . . 20 20
1488 – 70s. multicoloured . . . 30 30
1489 – 100s. multicoloured . . . 40 40
1490 – 150s. multicoloured . . . 70 70
1491 – 200s. multicoloured . . . 80 80
MS1492 91 × 91 mm. 350s. multicoloured . . . . 1·75 2·25
DESIGNS: 30s. to 200s. Various carvings.

212 Russian Cycle, 1813

1992. Bicycles of the World. Multicoloured.
1493 20s. Type **212** 20 20
1494 30s. German, 1840 . . . . 20 20
1495 50s. German, 1818 . . . . 30 30
1496 70s. German, 1850 . . . . 30 40
1497 100s. Italian, 1988 . . . . . 35 50
1498 150s. Swedish, 1982 . . . . 50 80
1499 300s. Italian, 1989 . . . . . 70 1·25
MS1500 90 × 90 mm. 350s. British pennyfarthing, 1887 . . . . . 1·00 2·50

213 Seal

1993. Large Sea Creatures. Multicoloured.
1501 20s. Type **213** 65 50
1502 30s. Whale . . . . 1·50 80
1503 70s. Shark . . . . 1·00 1·00
1504 100s. Walrus . . . . 1·25 1·50
MS1505 99 × 91 mm. 500s. Sea turtle 6·00 6·00

214 Boxing **215** "Macrolepiota rhacodes"

1993. Sports. Multicoloured.
1506 20s. Type **214** 15 15
1507 50s. Hockey 75 30
1508 70s. Show jumping 40 40
1509 100s. Marathon running . . 45 45
1510 150s. Football 60 70
1511 200s. Diving 70 90
1512 400s. Basketball . . . . . . 1·75 2·25
MS1513 91 × 91 mm. 300s. High jumping (horiz) . . . . 1·75 2·25

1993. 40th Anniv of Coronation. As T **256a** of St. Vincent.
1514 100s. multicoloured 65 65
1515 150s. multicoloured 85 85
1516 200s. lilac and black . . . . 1·10 1·10
1517 300s. multicoloured . . . . 1·25 1·25
MS1518 102 × 70 mm. 500s. multicoloured . . . . 3·75 3·75
DESIGNS: 100s. Queen Elizabeth II at Coronation (photograph by Cecil Beaton); 150s. Gold salt-cellar; 200s. Prince Philip at Coronation; 300s. Queen Elizabeth II and Prince Andrew. ($28\frac{1}{2} \times 42\frac{1}{2}$ mm): 500s. "Princess Elizabeth opening the New Broadgate, Coventry" (detail) (Dame Laura Knight).

1993. Fungi. Multicoloured.
1519 20s. Type **215** 60 35
1520 40s. "Mycena pura" 80 50
1521 50s. "Chlorophyllum molybdites" 80 50
1522 70s. "Agaricus campestris" 90 60
1523 100s. "Volvariella volvacea" 1·00 70
1524 150s. "Leucoagaricus naucinus" . . . . 1·40 1·25
1525 200s. "Oudemansiella radicata" . . . . 1·60 1·50
1526 300s. "Clitocybe nebularis" 1·75 2·00
MS1527 Two sheets, each 100 × 70 mm. (a) 500s. "Omphalotus olearius". (b) 500s. "Lepista nuda" Set of 2 sheets 6·50 7·50

216 "Geochelone elephantopus" (tortoise) **217** Pancake Tortoise on Rock

1993. Reptiles. Multicoloured.
1528 20s. Type **216** 20 20
1529 50s. "Iguana iguana" . . . 30 30
1530 70s. "Varanus salvator" (lizard) (horiz) 40 40
1531 100s. "Naja oxiana" (cobra) 45 45
1532 150s. "Chamaeleo jacksoni" (horiz) 70 70
1533 200s. "Eunectes murinus" (snake) (horiz) 80 80
1534 250s. "Alligator mississippensis" (horiz) . . 90 90
MS1535 90 × 90 mm. 500s. "Vipera berus" (snake) . . . . 3·00 3·50

1993. Endangered Species. Pancake Tortoise. Multicoloured.
1536 20s. Type **217** 35 35
1537 30s. Drinking 40 40
1538 50s. Under rock 60 60
1539 70s. Tortoise hatching . . . 75 75

218 Elephant

1993. Wildlife.
1540/87 100s. × 48 multicoloured Set of 48 . . . . . . 26·00 27·00
MS1588 Two sheets, each 100 × 71 mm. (a) 500s. Lion cub (horiz). (b) 500s. Elephant calf (horiz) Set of 2 sheets . . . . 7·50 8·50
Nos. 1540/87 were issued together, se-tenant, as four sheetlets each of twelve different vertical designs. The species depicted are, in addition to Type **218**, Gazelle, Hartebeest, Duiker, Genet, Civet, Eastern white pelican, Waterbuck, Blacksmith plover, Lesser pied kingfisher, Black-winged stilt, Bush pig, Brown-hooded kingfisher, Sable antelope, Impala, Buffalo, Leopard, Aardvark, Hippopotamus, Spotted hyena, South African crowned crane, Crocodile, Greater flamingo, Baboon, Potto, Lesser flamingo, Grey-headed kingfisher, Red colobus monkey, Dik-dik, Aardwolf (incorrectly inscribed "ARDWOLF"), Black-backed jackal, Tree pangolin, Serval, Yellow-billed hornbill, Pygmy mongoose, Bat-eared fox, Bushbaby, Egyptian vulture, Ostrich, Greater kudu, Diana monkey, Giraffe, Cheetah, Wildebeest, Chimpanzee, Warthog, Zebra and Rhinoceros.

219 Grant's Zebra galloping

1992. Wild Animals. Multicoloured.
1589 100s. Type **219** 85 85
1590 100s. Grant's zebra standing 85 85
1591 100s. Grant's gazelle doe 85 85
1592 100s. Grant's gazelle buck 85 85
1593 100s. Thomson's gazelle 85 85
1594 100s. White-bearded gnu with calf 85 85
1595 100s. Female cheetah with cubs 85 85
1596 100s. Young cheetah drinking 85 85
1597 100s. Lioness carrying cub in mouth 85 85
1598 100s. Pair of hunting dogs 85 85
1599 100s. Three hunting dogs 85 85
1600 100s. Four hunting dogs 85 85
MS1601 Two sheets, each 106 × 76 mm. (a) 500s. African elephant. (b) 500s. Rhinoceros Set of 2 sheets 10·00 9·00

220 Valentina Tereshkova (first woman in space)

222 Arthur Ashe (tennis)

221 "Iolaus aphnaeoides"

1993. Famous 20th-century Women. Mult.
1602 20s. Type **220** 75 65
1603 40s. Marie Curie (physicist) 1·75 1·00
1604 50s. Indira Gandhi (Prime Minister of India) 1·75 1·00
1605 70s. Wilma Rudolph (Olympic athlete) 1·00 1·00
1606 100s. Margaret Mead (anthropologist) 1·00 1·00
1607 150s. Golda Meir (Prime Minister of Israel) 2·00 1·75
1608 200s. Dr. Elizabeth Blackwell (first female medical doctor) 1·75 1·75
1609 400s. Margaret Thatcher (Prime Minister of Great Britain) 2·75 2·75
MS1610 116 × 80 mm. 500s. Mother Teresa (humanitarian) 3·50 3·50

1993. Butterflies.
1611/54 100s. × 44 multicoloured Set of 44 35·00 30·00
MS1655 Four sheets, each 69 × 58 mm. (a) 500s. "Cymothoe sangaris". (b) 500s. "Precis octavia". (c) 500s. "Charaxes violetta". (d) 500s. "Papilio nobilis" Set of 4 sheets 13·00 13·00

Nos. 1611/54 were printed se-tenant in two sheetlets of 12 (Nos. 1611/34) and one of 20 (Nos. 1635/54). The species depicted, in addition to Type **221**, are "Charaxes eupale", "Danaus formosa", "Antanartia hippomene", "Mylothris sagala", "Charaxes anticlea", "Salamis temora", "Nepheronia argia", "Acraea pseudolycia", "Hypolimnas antevorta", "Colotis hildebrandti", "Acraea bonasia", "Eurema desjardinsi", "Myrina silenus", "Iolaus ismenias", "Charaxes candiope", "Precis artaxia", "Danaus chrysippus", "Axiocerses bambana", "Precis orithya", "Pinacopteryx eriphia", "Iolaus coecolus", "Precis hierta", "Colotis regina", "Euphaedra neophron", "Mylothris poppea", "Aphaneus flavescens", "Eronia leda", "Charaxes zoolina", "Papilio bromius", "Cyrestis camillus", "Hypolycaena buxtoni", "Charaxes achaemenes", "Asterope rosa", "Graphium antheus", "Charaxes acuminatus", "Kallima rumia", "Leptosia alcesta", "Pseudacraea boisduvali", "Iolaus sidus", "Salamis parhassus", "Charaxes protoclea azota", "Charaxes bohemani" and "Papilio ophidicephalus".

1993. Black Sporting Personalities. Multicoloured.
1656 20s. Type **222** 50 40
1657 40s. Michael Jordan (basketball) 60 40
1658 50s. Daley Thompson (decathlon) 60 40
1659 70s. Jackie Robinson (baseball) 50 40
1660 100s. Kareem Abdul-Jabbar (basketball) 80 60
1661 150s. Florence Joyner (athletics) 85 80
1662 200s. Jesse Owens (athletics) 90 1·00
1663 400s. Jack Johnson (boxing) 1·50 1·75
MS1664 72 × 101 mm. 500s. Muhammed Ali (boxing) (horiz) 2·50 2·75

223 Short-finned Mako

1993. Sharks. Multicoloured.
1665 20s. Type **223** 15 15
1666 30s. Lantern shark 20 20
1667 50s. Tiger shark 25 25
1668 70s. African angelshark 35 35
1669 100s. "Pristiophorus cirratus" 45 45
1670 150s. White-tipped reef shark 65 65
1671 200s. Scalloped hammerhead 75 75
MS1672 91 × 91 mm. 350s. Six-gilled shark (vert) 1·75 2·00

224 Alpha Jet

1993. Military Aircraft. Multicoloured.
1673 20s. Type **224** 20 20
1674 30s. Northrop F-5E 20 25
1675 50s. Dassault Mirage 3NG 25 30
1676 70s. MB 339C 35 45
1677 100s. MiG-31 35 50
1678 150s. C-101 Aviojet 40 70
1679 200s. General Dynamics F-16 Fighting Falcon 45 80
MS1680 91 × 91 mm. 500s. EAP fighter (vert) 1·40 2·00

225 Gordon Setter

227 "Ansellia africana"

226 Rhinoceros, Ngorongoro Crater

1993. Dogs. Multicoloured.
1681 20s. Type **225** 20 20
1682 30s. Zwergschnauzer 25 25
1683 50s. Labrador retriever 30 30
1684 70s. Wire fox terrier 45 45
1685 100s. English springer spaniel 50 50
1686 150s. Newfoundlander 70 70
1687 200s. Moscow toy terrier 80 80
MS1688 91 × 91 mm. 350s. Dobermann Pinscher 1·75 2·00

1993. National Parks. Multicoloured.
1689 20s. Type **226** 20 20
1690 50s. Buffalo, Ngurdoto Crater 20 20
1691 70s. Leopard, Kilimanjaro 30 30
1692 100s. Baboon, Gombe 35 35
1693 150s. Lion, Selous 45 45
1694 200s. Giraffe, Mikumi 65 65
1695 250s. Zebra, Serengeti 70 70
MS1696 91 × 91 mm. 500s. Elephant, Lake Manyara (vert) 1·75 2·00

1993. Flowers. Multicoloured.
1697 20s. Type **227** 35 20
1698 30s. "Saintpaulia ionantha" 40 25
1699 40s. "Stapelia semota lutea" 45 30
1700 50s. "Impatiens walleriana" 45 30
1701 60s. "Senecio petraeus" 50 35
1702 70s. "Kalanchoe velutina" 60 40
1703 100s. "Kaempferia brachystemon" 75 60
1704 150s. "Nymphaea colorata" 1·10 1·10
1705 200s. "Thunbergia battiscombei" 1·25 1·25
1706 250s. "Crossandra nilotica" 1·25 1·40
1707 300s. "Spathodea campanulata" 1·40 1·60
1708 350s. "Ruttya fruticosa" 1·40 1·60
MS1709 Two sheets, each 100 × 70 mm. (a) 500s. "Streptocarpus saxorum". (b) 500s. "Glorioso verschurii" Set of 2 sheets 5·25 7·00

228 Norman-Arab

1993. Horses. Multicoloured.
1710 20s. Type **228** 40 30
1711 40s. Nonius 50 40
1712 50s. Boulonnais 50 40
1713 70s. Arab 60 60
1714 100s. Anglo-Arab 70 70
1715 150s. Tarpon 90 1·00
1716 200s. Thoroughbred 1·10 1·40
MS1717 91 × 91 mm. 400s. Anglo-Norman (vert) 1·75 2·00

No. 1716 is inscribed "THOROUGBLED" in error.

229 Berts Warrior

230 Downhill Skiing

1993. Traditional African Costumes. Multicoloured.
1718 20s. Type **229** 10 10
1719 40s. Galla 15 15
1720 50s. Guinean 15 15
1721 70s. Goloff 20 25
1722 100s. Peul 30 30
1723 150s. Abyssinian 45 45
1724 200s. Pahuin 55 55
MS1725 91 × 91 mm. 350s. Zulu 1·10 1·25

1994. Hummel Figurines. As T **251b** of St. Vincent. Multicoloured.
1726 20s. Boy playing accordion 30 25
1727 40s. Girl with guitar and boy with lute 35 30
1728 50s. Boy playing euphonium 35 30
1729 70s. Boy playing mouth organ 40 35
1730 100s. Boy with trumpet on fence 50 45
1731 150s. Boy playing recorder 80 80
1732 200s. Boy with trumpet and bird on feet 90 90
1733 300s. Girl playing banjo 1·25 1·40
1734 350s. Boy carrying double bass on back 1·40 1·60
1735 400s. Girls with banjo and song sheet 1·40 1·60
MS1736 Two sheets, each 70 × 101 mm. (a) 500s. Carol singers. (b) 500s. Angels with trumpets in bell tower Set of 2 sheets 8·00 8·50

1994. Winter Olympic Games, Lillehammer, Norway. Multicoloured.
1737 40s. Type **230** 20 20
1738 50s. Ice hockey 20 20
1739 70s. Speed skating 30 30
1740 100s. Bobsleighing 35 35
1741 120s. Figure skating 40 40
1742 170s. Free style skiing 55 55
1743 250s. Biathlon 75 75
MS1744 93 × 91 mm. 500s Cross-country skiing 1·50 2·00

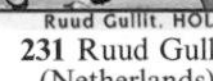

231 Ruud Gullit (Netherlands)

233 African Hawk Eagle

232 Mickey Mouse, Goofy, Pluto and Donald Duck boarding Airliner

1994. World Cup Football Championship, U.S.A. (1st issue). Multicoloured.
1745 20s. Type **231** 40 30
1746 30s. Kevin Sheedy (Ireland) 40 30
1747 50s. Giuseppe Giannini (Italy) 50 40
1748 70s. Julio Cesar (Brazil) 55 45
1749 250s. John Barnes (England) and Grun (Belgium) 1·50 1·50
1750 300s. Chendo (Spain) 1·50 1·50
1751 350s. Frank Rijkaard (Netherlands) 1·60 1·75
1752 400s. Lothar Matthaeus (Germany) 1·60 1·75
MS1753 Two sheets. (a) 76 × 106 mm. 500s. Nicola Berti (Italy). (b) 106 × 76 mm. 500s. Des Walker (England) Set of 2 sheets 7·50 7·50

See also Nos. 1838/45 and 1892/8.

1994. "Hong Kong '94" International Stamp Exhibition. As T **271a** of St. Vincent. Multicoloured.
1754 350s. Blue-barred orange parrotfish and red cap white pearl-scale goldfish at right 1·40 1·40
1755 350s. Regal angelfish and red cap white pearl-scale goldfish at left 1·40 1·40

Nos. 1754/5 were printed together, se-tenant, forming a composite design.

1994. 65th Anniv of Mickey Mouse. Walt Disney Cartoon Characters on World Tour. Mult.
1756 10s. Type **232** 50 25
1757 20s. Daisy Duck and Minnie Mouse dancing, Tonga 60 30
1758 30s. Mickey and Goofy playing bowls, Australia 65 35
1759 40s. Mickey, Donald and Goofy building igloo, Arctic Circle 70 40
1760 50s. Pluto, Goofy, Mickey and Donald on guard at Buckingham Palace, London 70 40
1761 60s. Pluto at Esna Bazaar, Egypt 75 55
1762 70s. Donald being chased by Zsambox herders, Hungary (vert) 75 55
1763 100s. Donald and Daisy on Grand Canal, Venice (vert) 1·00 70
1764 150s. Goofy dancing, Bali (vert) 1·50 1·50
1765 200s. Donald with monks, Thailand (vert) 1·75 1·75
1766 300s. Goofy water skiing at Taj Mahal, India (vert) 2·00 2·50
1767 400s. Mickey, Minnie, Goofy and Donald being carried by Sherpas, Nepal 2·25 2·75
MS1768 Three sheets. (a) 127 × 102 mm. 500s. Mickey at Livingstone's memorial, Ujiji (vert). (b) 127 × 102 mm. 500s. Mickey at Kigoma railway station, Tanzania (vert). (c) 102 × 127 mm. 500s. Mickey climbing Mt. Kilimanjaro (vert) Set of 3 sheets 10·00 11·00

1994. Birds. Multicoloured.
1769 20s. Type **233** 85 85
1770 30s. Whale-headed stork ("Shoe-bill Stork") 85 85
1771 50s. Brown snake eagle ("Harrier Eagle") 1·00 1·00
1772 70s. Black-casqued hornbill ("Casqued Horn-Bill") 1·10 1·10
1773 100s. Crowned cranes 1·10 1·10
1774 150s. Greater flamingos 1·40 1·40
1775 200s. Pair of eastern white pelicans ("Pelicans") (horiz) 1·10 1·10
1776 250s. African jacana and African black crake (horiz) 1·10 1·10
1777 300s. Pair of ostriches (horiz) 1·25 1·25
1778 350s. Pair of helmeted guineafowl (horiz) 1·25 1·25
1779 400s. Malachite kingfisher (horiz) 1·25 1·25
1780 500s. Pair of saddle-bill storks ("Saddle-billed Stork") (horiz) 1·40 1·40

234 Henry Ford and Model "T"

1994. Centenaries of Henry Ford's First Petrol Engine (Nos. 1781 and 1783) and Karl Benz's First Four-wheeled Car (others). Multicoloured.
1781 200s. Type **234** 1·60 1·60
1782 200s. Benz, 1893, and "500 SEL", 1993 1·60 1·60
1783 400s. Ford, 1893, Mustang Cobra and emblem 2·50 2·50
1784 400s. Karl Benz and emblem 2·50 2·50
MS1785 Two sheets, each 106 × 71 mm. (a) 500s. Henry Ford outside first factory. (b) 500s. Benz emblem and bonnet of 1937 "540k" Set of 2 sheets 7·00 8·00

235 Sopwith Pup Biplane

1994. Aviation Anniversaries. Multicoloured.
1786 200s. Type **235** . . . . . . 1·75 1·75
1787 200s. Inflating hot-air balloons . . . . 1·75 1·75
1788 400s. Hawker Siddeley Harrier and design drawing . . . . 2·75 2·75
1789 400s. Jean-Pierre Blanchard and his balloon . . . . . 2·75 2·75
MS1790 Two sheets, each 105 × 71 mm. (a) 500s. Supermarine Spitfire. (b) 500s. Hot-air balloons in flight (vert) Set of 2 sheets . . . . 7·50 7·50
ANNIVERSARIES: Nos. 1786, 1788, 75th anniv of Royal Air Force; Nos. 1787, 1789, Bicentenary of first balloon flight in the U.S.A.

236 Jahazi (sailing canoe) **237** Diatryma

1994. Sailing Ships. Multicoloured.
1791 40s. Type **236** 15 15
1792 50s. Caravel 15 15
1793 70s. Pirate carrack 25 25
1794 100s. Baltic galeass 25 30
1795 170s. Frigate (inscr "Battle-ship") 35 55
1796 200s. British ship of the line (inscr "Frigate") 40 65
1797 250s. Brig 40 75
MS1798 91 × 91 mm. 500s. Clipper 1·25 2·00

1994. Prehistoric Animals. Multicoloured.
1799 40s. Type **237** 60 30
1800 50s. Tyrannosaurus rex . . 60 30
1801 100s. Uintaterius 80 50
1802 120s. Stiracosaurus 90 80
1803 170s. Diplodocus . . . . . 1·25 1·50
1804 250s. Archaeopteryx . . . . 1·40 1·60
1805 300s. Sordes . . . . 1·60 1·90
MS1806 91 × 91 mm. 500s. Dimetrodon . . . . 1·90 2·25
No. 1799 is inscribed "DIATRUMA" in error.

238 Koala Bear with Cub

1994. Endangered Species. Multicoloured.
1807 40s. Type **238** 25 25
1808 70s. Giant panda with cub 40 40
1809 100s. Golden eagles 55 55
1810 120s. African elephant with calf 70 70
1811 250s. Carribean monk seals 90 90
1812 400s. Dolphins . . . . . . 1·00 1·00
1813 500s. Whales . . . . 1·50 1·50
MS1814 90 × 90 mm. 500s. Tiger (vert) . . . . 2·75 2·75

239 Pres. Salmin Amour of Zanzibar **241** Tanzanian Family

240 Lorry at Customs Post

1994. 30th Anniv of Zanzibar Revolution. Multicoloured.
1815 40s. Type **239** 40 10
1816 70s. Amani Karume (first President of Zanzibar) . . 60 20
1817 120s. Harvesting cloves (horiz) . . . . 1·00 1·00
1818 250s. Carved door . . . . . 1·75 2·50
MS1819 91 × 91 mm. 500s. Hands clasped over map . . . . . . 2·00 2·50

1994. 81st/82nd Customs Co-Operation Council Meeting, Arusha. Multicoloured.
1820 20s. Type **240** 65 30
1821 50s. Container ship . . . . 1·10 45
1822 100s. Passengers and airliner 1·75 1·00
1823 150s. Customs and U.P.U. logos . . . . 1·75 2·00
MS1824 99 × 99 mm. 500s. Customs arms (30 × 40 mm) . . . . . . 3·50 3·50

1994. Int Year of the Family. Mult.
1825 40s. Type **241** 20 10
1826 120s. Father playing with children 45 40
1827 170s. Family clinic (horiz) 60 80
1828 250s. Woman harvesting tobacco . . . . 75 1·25
MS1829 91 × 91 mm. 300s. Emblem 1·60 2·00

242 "Trombidium sp."

1994. Arachnids. Multicoloured.
1830 40s. Type **242** 20 20
1831 50s. "Eurypelma sp." . . . 20 20
1832 100s. "Salticus sp." 30 30
1833 120s. "Micrommata rosea" (vert) 35 35
1834 170s. "Araneus sp." (vert) 50 50
1835 250s. "Micrathena sp." (vert) 70 70
1836 300s. "Araneus diadematus" (vert) 80 80
MS1837 92 × 92 mm. 500s. Claw of "Hadogenes" sp (vert) . . . . 1·75 2·00

243 Giuseppe Signori (Italy) **244** Bateleur

1994. World Cup Football Championship, U.S.A. (2nd issue). Multicoloured.
1838 300s. Type **243** . . . . . . 1·00 1·00
1839 300s. Ruud Gullit (Netherlands) . . . . . . 1·00 1·00
1840 300s. Roberto Mancini (Italy) . . . . 1·00 1·00
1841 300s. Marco van Basten (Netherlands) . . . . . . 1·00 1·00
1842 300s. Dennis Bergkamp (Netherlands) . . . . . . 1·00 1·00
1843 300s. Oscar Ruggeri (Argentina) . . . . 1·00 1·00
1844 300s. Frank Rijkaard (Netherlands) . . . . . . 1·00 1·00
1845 300s. Peter Schmeichel (Denmark) . . . . 1·00 1·00
MS1846 100 × 70 mm. 1000s. World Cup trophy . . . . 4·00 4·50
See also Nos. 1892/8.

1994. Birds of Prey. Multicoloured.
1847 40s. Type **244** 50 40
1848 50s. Ornate hawk eagle . . 50 40
1849 100s. Osprey 70 60
1850 120s. Andean condor . . . 70 65
1851 170s. African fish eagle (horiz) 90 90
1852 250s. King vulture . . . . . 1·10 1·25
1853 400s. Peregrine falcon (horiz) . . . . 1·50 1·75
MS1854 90 × 90 mm. 500s. African white-backed vulture . . . . . 2·25 2·50

245 Afghan Hound

1994. Dogs of the World. Multicoloured.
1855/63 120s. × 9 (Type **245**; Basenji; Siberian husky; Irish setter; Norwegian elkhound; Bracco Italiano; Australian cattle dog; German short-haired pointer; Rhodesian ridgeback)
1864/72 120s. × 9 (Alsatian; Japanese chin; Shetland sheepdog; Italian spinone; Great dane; English setter; Welsh corgi; St. Bernard; Irish wolfhound) . . . . . .
1873/81 120s. × 9 (Doberman pinscher; Chihuahua; Bloodhound; Keeshond; Tibetan spaniel; Japanese akita; Tervueren; Chow; Pharaoh hound) . . .
1882/90 120s. × 9 (Alaskan malamute; Scottish cairn terrier; American foxhound; British bulldog; Boston terrier; Borzoi; Shar pei; Saluki; Bernese mountain dog) . . . .
1855/90 Set of 36 . . . . 16·00 17·00
MS1891 Two sheets, each 76 × 106 mm. (a) 1000s. As No. 1856. (b) 1000s. As No. 1868 Set of 2 sheets . . . . 9·00 10·00

246 Players and Flags from Group B

1994. World Cup Football Championship, U.S.A. (3rd issue). Multicoloured.
1892 40s. Type **246** 45 45
1893 50s. Players and flags from Group C 50 50
1894 70s. Players and flags from Group D 60 60
1895 100s. Players and flags from Group E 65 65
1896 170s. Players and flags from Group A 90 90
1897 200s. Players and World Cup . . . . 1·10 1·10
1898 250s. Players and flags from Group F . . . . 1·40 1·40
MS1899 92 × 92 mm. 500s. Player heading ball . . . . 3·25 3·75

247 "Rangaeris amaniensis" **248** "Dicentra spectabilis"

1994. Orchids. Multicoloured.
1900 200s. Type **247** 75 75
1901 200s. "Eulophia macowanii" 75 75
1902 200s. "Cytorchis arcuata" 75 75
1903 200s. "Centrostigma occultans" 75 75
1904 200s. "Cirrhopetalum umbellatum" 75 75
1905 200s. "Ansellia gigantea" . . 75 75
1906 200s. "Angraecum ramosum" 75 75
1907 200s. "Disa englerana" . . . 75 75
1908 200s. "Nervilia stolziana" 75 75
1909 200s. "Satyrium orbiculare" 75 75
1910 200s. "Schizochilus sulphureus" 75 75
1911 200s. "Disa stolzii" 75 75
1912 200s. "Platycornye mediocris" 75 75
1913 200s. "Satyrium breve" . . 75 75
1914 200s. "Eulophia nuttii" . . 75 75
1915 200s. "Disa ornithantha" . . 75 75
MS1916 Two sheets, each 106 × 76 mm. (a) 1000s. "Phaius tankervilliae" (horiz). (b) 1000s. "Eulophia thomsonii" (horiz) Set of 2 sheets . . . . 7·50 8·00

1994. Flowers. Multicoloured.
1917 40s. Type **248** 30 30
1918 100s. "Thunbergia alata" . . 40 45
1919 120s. "Cyrtanthus minimiflorus" 40 50
1920 170s. "Nepenthes hybrida" 45 70
1921 250s. "Allamanda cathartica" 50 80
1922 300s. "Encyclia pentotis" . . 50 85
1923 400s. "Protea lacticolor" . . 55 90
MS1924 91 × 92 mm. 500s. Tradescantia . . . . 1·25 1·75

249 "Limenitis sydyi"

1994. Butterflies. Multicoloured.
1925 120s. Type **249** 70 70
1926 120s. "Agraulis vanillae" . . 70 70
1927 120s. "Danaus chrysippus" 70 70
1928 120s. "Eurytides marcellus" 70 70
1929 120s. "Artopoetes pryeri" 70 70
1930 120s. "Heliconius charitonius" 70 70
1931 120s. "Limenitis weidemeyerii" 70 70
1932 120s. "Phoebis sennae" . . 70 70
1933 120s. "Timelaea albescens" 70 70
1934 120s. "Papilio glaucus" . . 70 70
1935 120s. "Danaus plexippus" 70 70
1936 120s. "Papilio troilus" . . . 70 70
1937 120s. "Hypolimnas antevorta" 70 70
1938 120s. "Cirrochroa imperatrix" 70 70
1939 120s. "Vanessa atalanta" . . 70 70
1940 120s. "Limenitis archippus" 70 70
1941 120s. "Hypolimnas pandarus" 70 70
1942 120s. "Anthocharis belia" 70 70
MS1943 Two sheets, each 101 × 70 mm. (a) 1000s. "Papilio polyxenes". (b) 1000s. "Vanessa cardui" Set of 2 sheets . . . . 8·50 9·00

250 Donald Duck and Goofy with Safari Equipment

1994. Mickey Mouse Safari Club. Walt Disney Cartoon Characters on Safari. Multicoloured.
1944 70s. Type **250** 55 55
1945 70s. Donald and Mickey Mouse with leopard cubs 55 55
1946 100s. Donald photographing antelope 65 65
1947 100s. Donald between elephant's legs 65 65
1948 120s. Mickey with monkeys 70 70
1949 120s. Donald with hippopotamuses 70 70
1950 150s. Goofy carrying equipment 80 80
1951 150s. Mickey, Donald and Goofy sheltering under elephant's ears 80 80
1952 200s. Goofy with zebras . . 90 90
1953 200s. Donald, Goofy and Mickey with lion 90 90
1954 250s. Donald filming monkeys . . . . 1·00 1·00
1955 250s. Giraffe licking Mickey 1·00 1·00
MS1956 Three sheets, each 101 × 121 mm. (a) 1000s. Goofy in tree with camera (vert). (b) 1000s. Donald and Goofy with camera (vert). (c) 1000s. Donald and Mickey with camera (vert) Set of 3 sheets . . . . 11·00 12·00

251 Plan indicating Moon Landing Point

1994. 25th Anniv of First Moon Landing. Multicoloured.
1957 150s. Type **251** 80 80
1958 150s. Photograph showing Sea of Tranquility . . . 80 80
1959 150s. Lunar surface 80 80
1960 150s. Lift-off 80 80
1961 150s. Jettisoning first stage rocket 80 80
1962 150s. Jettisoning second stage rocket 80 80
1963 150s. Lunar module "Eagle" leaving command module 80 80
1964 150s. "Eagle" descending towards lunar surface . . 80 80
1965 150s. Armstrong and Aldrin (astronauts) inside "Eagle" 80 80
1966 150s. "Apollo 11" crew in space suits 80 80
1967 150s. "Eagle" on lunar surface 80 80
1968 150s. Armstrong descending to lunar surface 80 80
1969 150s. Astronaut, "Eagle" and experiment 80 80
1970 150s. Astronaut setting-up equipment 80 80

1971 150s. Reflection in astronaut's visor 80 80
1972 150s. Astronaut and U.S.A. flag 80 80
1973 150s. Astronaut carrying equipment 80 80
1974 150s. "Eagle" blasting off from Moon 80 80
1975 150s. Command module . . 80 80
1976 150s. "Eagle" leaving Moon 80 80
1977 150s. Capsule leaving Moon orbit 80 80
1978 150s. Capsule heading for Earth 80 80
1979 150s. Capsule re-entering Earth's atmosphere . . . 80 80
1980 150s. Capsule in sea 80 80
1981 150s. Recovery crew opening hatch 80 80
1982 150s. Transferring astronauts by helicopter 80 80
1983 150s. Armstrong, Collins and Aldrin (astronauts) after recovery 80 80

252 "Astacus leptodactytus"

1994. Crabs. Multicoloured.
1984 40s. Type **252** 30 30
1985 100s. "Eriocheir sinensis" (vert) 50 50
1986 120s. "Caneer opillo" (vert) 55 55
1987 170s. "Cardisoma quanhumi" 70 70
1988 250s. "Birgus latro" (vert) 85 85
1989 300s. "Menippe mercenaria" 90 90
1990 400s. "Dromia vulgaris" (vert) 95 95
MS1991 92×92 mm. 500s. Coral and crab's claw . . . . 1·60 2·00

1994. Centenary of International Olympic Committee. Gold Medal Winners. As T **285a** of St. Vincent. Multicoloured.
1992 350s. Kristin Otto (Germany) (50 metres freestyle swimming), 1988 1·00 1·00
1993 500s. Carl Lewis (U.S.A.) (various track and field events), 1984 and 1988 . . 1·40 1·40
MS1994 74×104 mm. 1000s. Oksana Baiul (Ukraine) (figure skating), 1994 . . . . 3·00 3·50

1994. 50th Anniv of D-Day (1st issue). As T **284b** of St. Vincent. Multicoloured.
1995 350s. Troops leaving landing craft . . . . 1·50 1·50
1996 600s. Amphibious tank and troops, Omaha Beach . . 2·00 2·00
MS1997 104×74 mm. 1000s. Loading landing craft in England 3·50 4·00
See also Nos. 1998/2016.

253 Supermarine Spitfire over Beaches

1994. 50th Anniv of D-Day (2nd issue). Multicoloured.
1998 200s. Type **253** 85 85
1999 200s. D.U.K.W.s landing on Gold Beach 85 85
2000 200s. Canadian troops landing on Juno Beach . . 85 85
2001 200s. Canadian cyclists disembarking, Juno Beach 85 85
2002 200s. Amphibious Sherman tank on beach 85 85
2003 200s. German gun emplacement 85 85
2004 200s. General Montgomery and British troops on beach 85 85
2005 200s. British engineers with AVRE Churchill tank, Gold Beach 85 85
2006 200s. U.S.S. "Thompson" (destroyer) being refuelled 85 85
2007 200s. H.M.S. "Warspite" (battleship) 85 85
2008 200s. Royal Marines on Juno Beach 85 85
2009 200s. Sherman Mark 1 flail tank leaving landing craft 85 85
2010 200s. General Eisenhower and U.S. troops on Omaha Beach 85 85
2011 200s. North American P-51 Mustang escorting ships 85 85
2012 200s. U.S. coastguard cutter alongside landing craft . . 85 85
2013 200s. U.S. troops in landing craft 85 85
2014 200s. U.S. troops landing on Omaha Beach 85 85

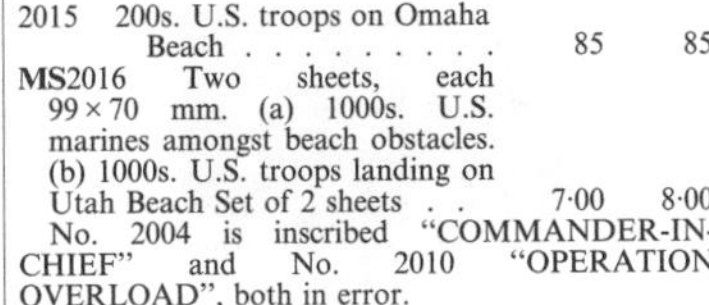

2015 200s. U.S. troops on Omaha Beach 85 85
MS2016 Two sheets, each 99×70 mm. (a) 1000s. U.S. marines amongst beach obstacles. (b) 1000s. U.S. troops landing on Utah Beach Set of 2 sheets . . 7·00 8·00
No. 2004 is inscribed "COMMANDER-IN-CHIEF" and No. 2010 "OPERATION OVERLOAD", both in error.

254 "Deinonychus"

1994. Prehistoric Animals.
2017/48 120s.×32 multicoloured 22·00 23·00
MS2049 80×110 mm. 1000s. multicoloured . . . . 4·50 5·50
DESIGNS—VERT: No. 2018, Styracosaurus; 2019, Anatosaurus; 2020, Plateosaurus; 2021, Iguanodon; 2022, Oviraptor; 2023, Dimorphodons; 2024, Ornithomimus; 2025, Lambeosaurus; 2026, Megalosaurus; 2027, Cetiosaurus; 2028, Hypsilophodon; 2029, Rhamphorynchus; 2030, Scelidosaurus; 2031, Antrodemus; 2032, Dimetrodon; **MS**2049, Brachiosaurus. HORIZ: No. 2033, Brontosaurus; 2034, Albertosaurus; 2035, Parasaurolophus; 2036, Pteranodons; 2037, Stegosaurus; 2038, Tyrannosaurus rex; 2039, Triceratops; 2040, Ornitholestes; 2041, Camarasaurus; 2042, Ankylosaurus; 2043, Trachodon; 2044, Allosaurus; 2045, Corythosaurus; 2046, Struthiomimus; 2047, Camptosaurus; 2048, Heterodontosaurus.
Nos. 2017/32 and 2033/48 respectively were printed together, se-tenant, Nos. 2033/48 forming a composite design.

255 "Hubble" Space Telescope

1994. Space Research. Multicoloured.
2050 40s. Type **255** 30 30
2051 100s. "Mariner" 50 50
2052 120s. "Voyager 2" 55 55
2053 170s. "Work Package-03" 70 70
2054 250s. Orbiting solar observer 85 85
2055 300s. "Magellan" 90 90
2056 400s. "Galilei" 95 95
MS2057 91×91 mm. 500s. "Fobos" 1·90 2·25

It is understood that the following issues were freely available for postal purposes from Tanzanian post offices. Further issues, for which evidence of normal postal use cannot be found, could be obtained from the Philatelic Bureau in Dar-es-Salaam. Such issues will be found in the Appendix.

1995. No. 906 surch **70/-**.
2058 70s. on 13s. Teacher with blackboard . . . . 1·25 55

257 Coconuts

1995. Fruit. Multicoloured.
2059 70s. Type **257** 50 25
2060 100s. Pineapple 65 40
2061 150s. Pawpaw . . . . . . 90 1·00
2062 200s. Tomatoes . . . . . . 1·25 1·40
MS2063 91×91 mm. 500s. Type **257** 3·25 3·50

258 Farmer and Maize Crop

261 *Plumeria rubra acutifolia*

260 Presidents Mwinyi (Tanzania), Moi (Kenya) and Museveni (Uganda)

1995. 50th Anniv of United Nations and Food and Agriculture Organization. Multicoloured designs (except No. **MS**2068).
2064 70s. Type **258** 50 25
2065 100s. Ploughing with ox team (horiz) 65 40
2066 150s. Women in spinning mill (horiz) . . . . . . 90 1·00
2067 200s. Child drawing . . . . 1·25 1·40
MS2068 101×97 mm. 500s. U.N. 50th anniv logo (horiz) (black and blue) . . . . 3·00 3·50

1995. No. 810 surch **100/-**.
2069 100s. on 40s. Lesser flamingo . . . . 1·50 60

1995. 2nd Anniversary of East African Treaty. Multicoloured.
2070 100s. Type **260** 50 15
2071 150s. Map of East Africa and national flags (vert) 1·50 90
2072 180s. Cotton boll (vert) . . 1·00 1·00
2073 200s. Fishermen on Lake Victoria . . . . 1·25 1·50
MS2074 100×102 mm. 500s. Type **260** . . . . 3·00 3·50

1996. Flowers. Multicoloured. (a) Without imprint date.
2075 100s. Type **261** 20 15
2076 140s. *Lilaceae* (different) . . 30 25
2077 180s. *Alamanda* 35 25
2078 200s. *Lilaceae* 40 30
2079 210s. *Zinnia* 40 40
2080 260s. *Malvaviscus penduliflorus* 45 45
2081 300s. *Cannai* 50 50
2082 380s. *Nerium oleander carneum* 65 65
2083 400s. *Hibiscus rosa sinensis* 65 65
2084 600s. *Catharanthus roseus* 90 1·00
2085 700s. *Bougainvillea formosa* 1·00 1·10
2086 750s. *Acalypha* . . . . . . 1·10 1·25
MS2087 88×112 mm. 125s. ×4 in designs of 210, 300, 380 and 700s. (each 31×36 mm) . . . . 1·25 1·50
(b) With 1997 imprint date.
2088 150s. As 140s. 30 25
2088a 500s. As 600s. 60 65
Nos. 2081 and **MS**2087 are inscribed "Carna", both in error.

262 Pineapple

1996. East African Fruit. Multicoloured.
2089 140s. Type **262** 70 40
2090 180s. Orange and limes . . 90 80
2091 200s. Pear and apples . . . 1·25 1·40
2092 300s. Bananas . . . . . . 1·75 1·90
MS2093 92×92 mm. 300s. No. 2092 2·50 2·75

263 Children's Clinic

1996. 25th Anniv of U.N. Volunteers. Mult.
2094 140s. Type **263** . . . . . . 1·00 40
2095 200s. Food distribution . . 1·25 1·00
2096 260s. Clean water supply . . 1·50 1·75
2097 300s. Public education . . . 1·75 1·90
MS2098 95×95 mm. 500s. Refugee camp . . . . 4·00 4·50

264 Couple and Setting Sun

1996. World Aids Day. Multicoloured.
2099 140s. Type **264** . . . . . . 1·00 40
2100 310s. People from various occupations (horiz) . . . 1·75 2·00
2101 370s. Discussion group (horiz) . . . . 2·00 2·25
2102 410s. Orphans with foster mother (horiz) . . . . . 2·25 2·50
MS2103 95×95 mm. 500s. Type **264** 3·50 4·00

265 Game Reserve

1996. 2nd Anniv of Common Market for Eastern and Southern Africa (COMESA). Multicoloured.
2104 140s. Type **265** . . . . . . 1·00 60
2105 180s. Fishermen in canoe . . 1·25 1·00
2106 200s. Container ship at Dar-es-Salaam docks . . . . 1·50 1·50
2107 300s. Goods train on Tazara railway . . . . 2·25 2·50
MS2108 90×90 mm. 500s. Cotton bolls . . . . 4·00 4·50

266 *Bukoba* (ferry) sinking

1997. 1st Anniv of Sinking of *Bukoba* (ferry). Multicoloured.
2109 140s. Type **266** 75 40
2110 350s. Recovering bodies from wreck . . . . 1·60 1·75
2111 370s. Identifying victims . . 1·75 2·00
2112 410s. Religious service for victims . . . . 1·90 2·25
MS2113 90×90 mm. 500s. *Bukoba* (ferry) . . . . 2·75 3·00

267 Mount Kilimanjaro and Animals

1997. Tourist Attractions. Multicoloured.
2114 140s. Type **267** 75 40
2115 310s. Members of the Masai tribe . . . . 1·60 1·75
2116 370s. Old Stone Town, Zanzibar . . . . 1·75 2·00
2117 410s. Buffalo on Ruaha Plains . . . . 1·90 2·25
MS2118 87×87 mm. 500s. Mount Kilimanjaro and elephant . . . 2·75 3·00

268 Red Hornbill

TANZANIA 410/-

269 Mount Kilimanjaro and Elephant

1997. Coastal Birds. Multicoloured.
2119 140s. Type **268** 75 40
2120 350s. Sacred ibis (horiz) . . 1·75 1·75
2121 370s. Gulls (horiz) . . . . . 1·75 2·00
2122 410s. Ring-necked dove (horiz) . . . . 1·90 2·25
MS2123 90×90 mm. 500s. Red hornbill, sacred ibis, gulls and ring-necked dove . . . . . . 2·50 2·75

1997.
2124 **269** 410s. multicoloured . . . 1·75 1·90

1998. Nos. 805/6 and 808 surch **150/-**.
2125 150s. on 9s. African emerald cuckoo . . . . 1·50 1·10
2126 150s. on 13s. Little bee eater 1·50 1·10
2127 150s. on 20s. Bateleur . . . 1·50 1·10

271 Tanzania and P.A.P.U. Flags

1998. 18th Anniv of Pan African Postal Union. Multicoloured.
2128 150s. Type **271** 20 25
2129 250s. P.A.P.U. logo 30 35
2130 400s. Postman making E.M.S. delivery 50 55
2131 500s. Two giraffes 60 65

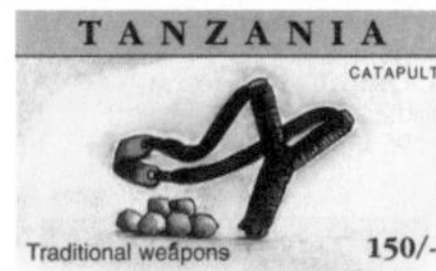

272 Catapult

1998. Traditional Weapons. Multicoloured.
2132 150s. Type **272** 20 25
2133 250s. Cutlass and club 30 35
2134 400s. Rifle and ammunition 50 55
2135 500s. Bow and arrows 60 65

273 Children carrying Banner

1998. Children's Rights in Tanzania. Multicoloured.
2136 150s. Type **273** 20 25
2137 250s. Teacher with children 30 35
2138 400s. Adult with stick and child (vert) 50 55
2139 500s. Child hugging adult (vert) 60 65
MS2140 90 × 90 mm. 500s. As 250s 60 65

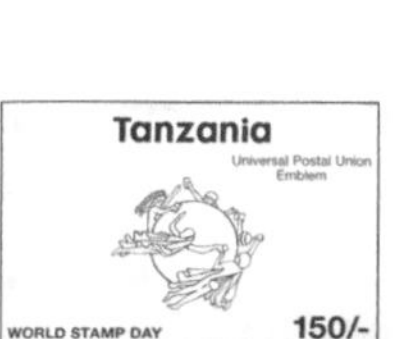

274 U.P.U. Emblem **275** The Dhow Harbour

1998. World Stamp Day. Multicoloured.
2141 150s. Type **274** 20 25
2142 250s. Cancelling mail 30 35
2143 400s. Dove carrying air mail letter 50 55
2144 500s. Woman posting letter 60 65
MS2145 90 × 90 mm. 500s. Woman posting letter, dove and U.P.U. emblem 60 65

1998. Tourist Attractions of Zanzibar. Mult.
2146 100s. Type **275** 10 15
2147 150s. Girl on giant tortoise in countryside 20 25
2148 250s. Children with giant tortoise (horiz) 30 35
2149 300s. Stone Town street 35 40
2150 400s. The Old Fort (horiz) 50 55
2151 500s. Red colobus monkeys (horiz) 60 65
MS2152 70 × 100 mm. 600s. Girl on giant tortoise in Stone Town street 70 75

276 Local Post Office

1999. 5th Anniv of Tanzania Posts Corporation. Multicoloured.
2153 150s. Type **276** 20 25
2154 250s. Post collection van 30 35
2155 350s. Counter services 40 45
2156 400s. Retail facilities 50 55
MS2157 76 × 117 mm. 500s. Headquarters (vert) 60 65

277 Blood Pressure Monitoring

1999. Millennium. Improvement in Living Standards. Multicoloured.
2158 350s. Type **277** 40 45
2159 400s. Children playing 50 55
2160 700s. Maize farming 85 90
2161 750s. Collecting clean water 90 95
MS2162 70 × 101 mm. 1500s. Ostriches (Tourism) (vert) 1·80 1·90

278 Rotary Emblem and "50"

1999. 50th Anniv of Rotary Club of Dar-es-Salaam. Multicoloured.
2163 150s. Type **278** 20 25
2164 250s. Giving child polio plus vaccine (vert) 30 35
2165 350s. Paul Harris (Rotary founder) (vert) 40 45
2166 400s. Women collecting clean drinking water from tap (vert) 50 55
MS2167 70 × 100 mm. 500s. Rotary emblem and "50" (vert) 60 65

279 Mail being loaded onto Aeroplane

1999. 125th Anniv of Universal Postal Union. Multicoloured.
2168 150s. Type **279** 25 20
2169 300s. Children writing letters 50 40
2170 350s. UPU members committee meeting 55 50
2171 400s. Express Mail Service co-ordination 75 85
MS2172 90 × 90 mm. 500s. UPU logo 70 65

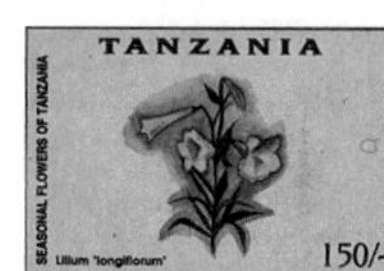

280 *Lilium longiflorum* (cool season)

1999. Seasonal Flowers. Multicoloured.
2173 150s. Type **279** 20 25
2174 250s. *Strelitzia reginae* (summer) 30 35
2175 400s. *Zantedeschia* (cool season) 50 55
2176 500s. Iris apollo (dry season) 60 65
MS2177 97 × 90 mm. 600s. As No. 2175 70 75
No. 2176 is inscribed "Ilis" in error.

281 Taita Falcon

1999. Birds. Multicoloured.
2178 150s. Type **281** 20 25
2179 300s. Banded green sunbird 35 40
2180 400s. Spotted ground thrush 50 55
2181 500s. Fischer's turaco 60 65
MS2182 90 × 90 mm. 600s. Blue swallow 70 75
Nos. 2182and **MS**2183 are inscribed "Taulaco Fisheri" or "atrokaerulea", both in error.

282 Medical Students, Muhimbili University, Tanzania

2000. Universities of East Africa. Multicoloured.
2183 150s. Type **282** 20 25
2184 200s. Students outside Zanzibar University 25 30
2185 600s. Makerere University, Uganda (vert) 70 75
2186 800s. Egerton university, Kenya 95 1·00
MS2187 87 × 87 mm. 500s. Inter University Council for East Africa emblem (84 × 82 mm) 60 65

283 Julius Nyerere in Youth and Old Age

2000. Julius Nyerere (first president of Tanzania, 1962–85) Commemoration. Multicoloured.
2188 200s. Type **283** 25 30
2189 500s. With Edward Sakoine, Prime Minister 60 65
2190 600s. Nyerere (in close-up) (vert) 70 75
2191 800s. Wearing Mgolore, local cloth (vert) 95 1·00
MS2192 90 × 90 mm. 1000s. Nyerere's Mausoleum 1·20 1·30

284 Seronera Wildlife Lodge, Serengeti and Lion

2000. Tourist Attractions of Tanzania. Multicoloured.
2193 400s. Type **284** 50 55
2194 400s. Lake Manyara National Park and elephant 50 55
2195 400s. Ngorongoro Crater, Wildlife Lodge and rhinoceros 50 55
2196 400s. Lobo Wildlife Lodge and giraffes 50 55
2197 400s. Kibo, the central cone of Kilimanjaro, and elephants 50 55
2198 400s. Fish off Mafia Island 50 55
2199 400s. Selous Game Reserve and wild dogs 50 55
2200 400s. Mikumi National Park and elephant 50 55
2201 500s. Seronera Wildlife Lodge, Serengeti and lion 60 65
2202 500s. Lake Manyara National Park and elephant 60 65
2203 500s. Ngorongoro Crater, Wildlife Lodge and rhinoceros 60 65
2204 500s. Lobo Wildlife Lodge and giraffes 60 65
2205 500s. Kibo, the central cone of Kilimanjaro, and elephants 60 65
2206 500s. Fish off Mafia Island 60 65
2207 500s. Selous Game Reserve and wild dogs 60 65
2208 500s. Mikumi National Park and elephant 60 65
2209 600s. Seronera Wildlife Lodge, Serengeti and lion 70 75
2210 600s. Lake Manyara National Park and elephant 70 75
2211 600s. Ngorongoro Crater, Wildlife Lodge and rhinoceros 70 75
2212 600s. Lobo Wildlife Lodge and giraffes 70 75
2213 600s. Kibo, the central cone of Kilimanjaro, and elephants 70 75
2214 600s. Fish off Mafia Island 70 75
2215 600s. Selous Game Reserve and wild dogs 70 75
2216 600s. Mikumi National Park and elephant 70 75
2217 800s. Seronera Wildlife Lodge, Serengeti and lion 95 1·00
2218 800s. Lake Manyara National Park and elephant 95 1·00
2219 800s. Ngorongoro Crater, Wildlife Lodge and rhinoceros 95 1·00
2220 800s. Lobo Wildlife Lodge and giraffes 95 1·00
2221 800s. Kibo, the central cone of Kilimanjaro, and elephants 95 1·00
2222 800s. Fish off Mafia Island 95 1·00
2223 800s. Selous Game Reserve and wild dogs 95 1·00
2224 800s. Mikumi National Park and elephant 95 1·00
MS2225 90 × 90 mm. 1000s. Lion, giraffes, elephant, rhinoceros and Kilimanjaro (vert) 1·20 1·30

285 Children carrying Water Pots on their Heads

2000. Work of World Vision (aid organization) in Tanzania (1st series). Multicoloured.
2226 200s. Type **285** 25 30
2227 600s. Family making bread 70 75
2228 800s. Nurse weighing baby at clinic 95 1·00
2229 1000s. Children reading 1·20 1·30
MS2230 90 × 90 mm. 500s. Boy and girl 60 65

286 Football Match

2000. Olympic Games, Sydney. Multicoloured.
2231 150s. Type **286** 20 25
2232 350s. Basketball game (vert) 40 45
2233 400s. Athletics race (vert) 50 55
2234 800s. Boxing match 95 1·00
MS2235 90 × 90 mm. 500s. Presentation of medals (vert) 60 65

287 Gutting Fish

2000. Zanzibar Millennium. Multicoloured.
2236 150s. Type **287** 20 25
2237 200s. Tortoises, baskets of bread and logo 25 30
2238 400s. Boy and "Kukuza Hadhi ya Elimu na Uchumi Zanzibar" inscription (vert) 50 55
2239 800s. Girl studying and university graduates (vert) 95 1·00
MS2240 90 × 90 mm. 500s. Map and trophy (vert) 60 65

288 Planting Trees

2000. Environmental Protection. Multicoloured.
2241 200s. Type **288** 25 30
2242 400s. Forest stream 50 55
2243 600s. Maintenance of sewage works 70 75
2244 800s. River and forest 95 1·00
MS2245 90 × 90 mm. 1000s. Mt. Kilimanjaro 1·20 1·30

289 Old Man in Deckchair (Retirement) **290** Ruins of the Great Mosque, Kilwa Kisiwani

2000. National Social Security Fund. Multicoloured.
2246 200s. Type **289** 25 30
2247 350s. Factory worker with eye injury (Employment injury) 40 45
2248 600s. Man holding prosthetic leg (Invalidity) 70 75
2249 800s. Mother and baby with nurse (Health insurance) 95 1·00
MS2250 90 × 90 mm. 500s. Pregnant woman (Maternity) 60 65

2000. Old Buildings and Architecture of Tanzania. Multicoloured.
2251 150s. Type **290** 20 25
2252 200s. German Boma (fort), Mikindani, Mtwara 25 30
2253 250s. German Boma, Bagamoyo 30 35
2254 300s. Butiama Museum, Mara 35 40
2255 350s. Chief Government Chemist's Offices 40 45
2256 400s. The Old Post Office, Dar es Salaam 50 55
2257 500s. Dr. Livingstone's Tembe Lodge, Kwihara, Tabora 60 65
2258 600s. Original Governor's Palace and State House, Dar es Salaam (vert) 70 75
2259 700s. Traditional Houses of the Ngoni-Nyamwezi 85 90
2260 800s. Palace of Beit Elajaib, Stonetown, Zanzibar 95 1·00
2261 900s. Tongoni ruins, Tanga 1·10 1·20
2262 1000s. Karimjee Hall, Dar es Salaam 1·20 1·30
MS2263 100 × 100 mm. 1500s. The Old Boma, Mikindani, Southern Tanzania 1·80 1·90

291 Tea Plantation

2000. 40th Anniv of Independence. Multicoloured.
2264 180s. Type **291** 20 25
2265 230s. Tanzania, Uganda and Kenya flags with triple handshake (vert) 30 35
2266 350s. University graduates (vert) 40 45
2267 450s. Lion, leopard, buffalo, rhinoceros, elephant and Mt. Kilimanjaro 55 60
2268 650s. Operating theatre 80 85
2269 950s. Minerals 1·10 1·20
MS2270 92 × 92 mm. 1000s. As 450s. 1·20 1·30

2000. No. 813 surch **200/-**.
2271 200s. on 170s. Saddle-billed stork 25 30

2000. No. 815 surch **800/-**.
2272 800s. on 500s. Ostrich . . . 95 1·00

2000. No. 813 surch **230/-**.
2273 230s. on 170s. Saddle-billed stork 30 35

295 Child Writing

2001. Work of World Vision (aid organization) in Tanzania (2nd series). Multicoloured.
2274 200s. Type **295** 25 30
2275 600s. Children laughing . . 70 75
2276 800s. Child carrying bananas (vert) . . . . . 95 1·00
2277 1000s. Child wearing grey t-shirt (vert) . . . . . 1·20 1·30
MS2277a 90 × 90 mm. 500s. Children lying on grass 60 65

296 Leopard

2001. Endangered Species. Multicoloured.
2278 200s. Type **296** 25 30
2279 400s. Rhinoceros 50 55
2280 600s. Crocodile 70 75
2281 800s. Wild dogs . . . . . . 95 1·00
MS2282 90 × 90 mm. 600s. Cheetah 70 75

297 Child receiving Vaccination

2001. 50th Anniv of United Nations High Commission for Refugees. Multicoloured.
2283 200s. Type **297** 25 30
2284 400s. Refugees in boat on Lake Tanganyika 50 55
2285 600s. Female refugee (vert) 70 75
2286 800s. Refugees with possessions on bike . . . 95 1·00
MS2287 90 × 90 mm. 600s. As No. 2285 . . . . 70 75

298 Dolphins

2001. Rare Species of Zanzibar. Multicoloured.
2288 250s. Type **298** 30 35
2289 300s. Coral plants 35 40
2290 450s. Coral reefs 55 60
2291 800s. Red colobus monkey (vert) . . . . 95 1·00
MS2292 90 × 90 mm. 700s. Colobus monkeys 85 90

299 Children in Class

2001. United Nations Dialogue among Civilisations. Multicoloured.
2293 200s. Type **299** 25 30
2294 400s. People in different dress 50 55
2295 600s. Discussion group . . . 70 75
2296 800s. Couple writing letters 95 1·00
MS2297 90 × 90 mm. 700s. Letter and handshake spanning globe (vert) 85 90

300 Fort Kilwa, Tanzania

2001. Historic Sites of East Africa. Multicoloured.
2298 250s. Type **300** 30 35
2299 300s. Ruins of Maruhubi Palace, Zanzibar 35 40
2300 400s. Old Provincial Office, Nairobi, Kenya (1913) . . 50 55
2301 800s. Mparu Tombs, Hoima, Uganda . . . . . 95 1·00
MS2302 90 × 90 mm. 700s. Map of East Africa with sailing ship 85 90

301 Hippo in River Rufiji, Selous Game Reserve

2001. Scenery of Tanzania. Multicoloured.
2303 200s. Type **301** 25 30
2304 400s. Mangapwani Beach, Zanzibar 50 55
2305 600s. Zebra and Mountains, Mikumi National Park . . 70 75
2306 800s. Balancing stones, Lake Victoria Mwanza (vert) 95 1·00
MS2307 90 × 90 mm. 700s. Giraffes, Ruaha National Park (vert) . . 85 90

302 Makonde Masked Dancer

303 Leopard

2002. Ceremonial Costumes. Multicoloured.
2308 250s. Type **302** 30 35
2309 350s. Mwaka Koga Festival dancers (Zanzibar) . . . 40 45
2310 400s. Lizombe dancer . . . 50 55
2311 450s. Zaramo bridal celebration 55 60
MS2312 90 × 90 mm. 500s. As No. 2306 . . . . 60 65

2002. Animals of the National Parks. Sheet 105 × 150 mm containing T **303** and similar vert designs. Multicoloured.
MS2313 250s. Type **303**; 250s. Elephant; 250s. Rhinoceros; 250s. Lion; 250s. Buffalo . . . . . 1·50 1·60

304 Mount Kilimanjaro

2002. International Year of Mountains. Multicoloured.
2314 250s. Type **304** 30 35
2315 350s. Usambara Mountains 40 45
2316 400s. Uluguru Mountains 50 55
2317 450s. Mwanihara Peak (Udzungwa Mountains) 55 60
MS2318 90 × 90 mm. 500s. As Type **303** 60 65

2002. No. 2077 surch **250/=**.
2319 250s. on 180s. Alamanda . . 30 35

2002. No. 810 surch **250/=**.
2320 250s. on 40s. Lesser flamingo 30 35

307 School Children

308 Raffia Mat Weaving

2002. National Population Census. Multicoloured.
2321 200s. Type **307** 25 30
2322 250s. Group of people (horiz) 30 35
2323 350s. Family (horiz) 40 45
2324 600s. Boy with emblem and statistics (horiz) 70 75

2002. Zanzibar Arts and Crafts. Multicoloured.
2326 200s. Type **308** 25 30
2327 250s. Sewing caps 30 35
2328 350s. Making chair 40 45
2329 400s. Henna tattoos 50 55
MS2330 90 × 90 mm. 800s. Carved wooden door . . . . 95 1·00

309 Ancient City of Kisimkazi, Zanzibar

310 Rhinoceros

2002. Paintings and Archaeology. Multicoloured.
2331 250s. Type **309** 30 35
2332 400s. Remains of Kaole Town, Bagamoyo (horiz) 50 55
2333 450s. Kondoa Irangi rock paintings 55 60
2334 600s. Great Mosque, Kilwa Kisiwani (horiz) 70 75
MS2335 90 × 90 mm. 1000s. As No. 2332 . . . . 1·20 1·30

2003. The Big Five. Multicoloured.
2336 400s. Type **310** 50 55
2337 500s. Elephant 60 65
2338 600s. Lion 70 75
2339 800s. Leopard (vert) . . . . 95 1·00
2340 1000s. Buffalo . . . . . . 1·20 1·30
MS2341 85 × 115 mm. 1500m. The Big Five. Imperf . . . . 1·80 1·90

311 Lions

312 Cotton

2003. Tourism. "The Northern Circuit". Multicoloured.
2342 300s. Type **311** 35 40
2343 350s. Mt. Kilimanjaro . . . 40 45
2344 400s. Zebras 50 55
2345 500s. Elephants 60 65
2346 600s. Leopards 70 75
2347 800s. Rhinoceros . . . . . 95 1·00
MS2348 97 × 75 mm. 1000s. Buffalo 1·20 1·30

2003. Cash Crops. Multicoloured.
2349 250s. Type **312** 30 35
2350 300s. Cashew nuts 35 40
2351 600s. Sisal 70 75
2352 800s. Cloves . . . . 95 1·00
MS2353 99 × 81 mm. 1000s. Tea (horiz) . . . . 1·20 1·30

313 Children Eating

2003. Work of World Vision (aid organization) in Tanzania (3rd series). Multicoloured.
2354 300s. Type **313** 35 40
2355 600s. Children at school . . 70 75
2356 800s. Pumping water into bucket (vert) . . . . . . 95 1·00
2357 1000s. Distributing mosquito nets . . . . 1·20 1·30
MS2358 90 × 90 mm. 500s. Three children in ceremonial robes with microphone 60 65

315 Nyamwezi Dance, Tabora

2003. Traditional Dances of East Africa. Multicoloured.
2364 300s. Type **315** 35 40
2365 500s. Luo dance, Kisumu 60 65
2366 600s. Pemba dance, Zanzibar 70 75
2367 800s. Baganda dance, Kampala . . . . 95 1·00
MS2368 99 × 81 mm. 1000s. Masai dance, Arusha . . . . 1·20 1·30

316 The Old Fort

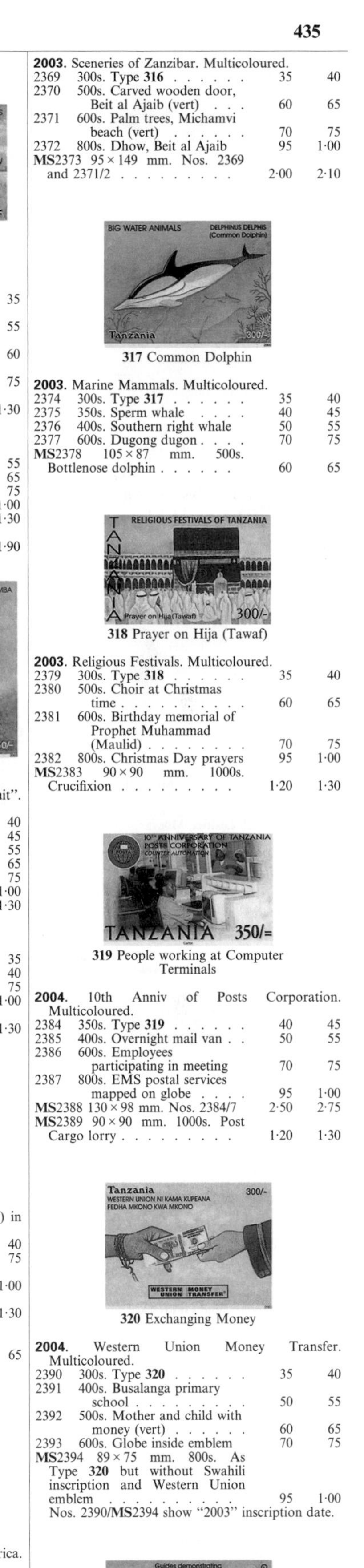

2003. Sceneries of Zanzibar. Multicoloured.
2369 300s. Type **316** 35 40
2370 500s. Carved wooden door, Beit al Ajaib (vert) . . . 60 65
2371 600s. Palm trees, Michamvi beach (vert) 70 75
2372 800s. Dhow, Beit al Ajaib 95 1·00
MS2373 95 × 149 mm. Nos. 2369 and 2371/2 . . . . 2·00 2·10

317 Common Dolphin

2003. Marine Mammals. Multicoloured.
2374 300s. Type **317** 35 40
2375 350s. Sperm whale 40 45
2376 400s. Southern right whale 50 55
2377 600s. Dugong dugon 70 75
MS2378 105 × 87 mm. 500s. Bottlenose dolphin 60 65

318 Prayer on Hija (Tawaf)

2003. Religious Festivals. Multicoloured.
2379 300s. Type **318** 35 40
2380 500s. Choir at Christmas time 60 65
2381 600s. Birthday memorial of Prophet Muhammad (Maulid) 70 75
2382 800s. Christmas Day prayers 95 1·00
MS2383 90 × 90 mm. 1000s. Crucifixion . . . . 1·20 1·30

319 People working at Computer Terminals

2004. 10th Anniv of Posts Corporation. Multicoloured.
2384 350s. Type **319** 40 45
2385 400s. Overnight mail van . . 50 55
2386 600s. Employees participating in meeting 70 75
2387 800s. EMS postal services mapped on globe . . . . 95 1·00
MS2388 130 × 98 mm. Nos. 2384/7 2·50 2·75
MS2389 90 × 90 mm. 1000s. Post Cargo lorry . . . . 1·20 1·30

320 Exchanging Money

2004. Western Union Money Transfer. Multicoloured.
2390 300s. Type **320** 35 40
2391 400s. Busalanga primary school 50 55
2392 500s. Mother and child with money (vert) 60 65
2393 600s. Globe inside emblem 70 75
MS2394 89 × 75 mm. 800s. As Type **320** but without Swahili inscription and Western Union emblem . . . . 95 1·00
Nos. 2390/**MS**2394 show "2003" inscription date.

321 Guides demonstrating Environmentally Friendly Cooker

2004. 75th Anniv of Girl Guides. Multicoloured.
2395 300s. Type **321** 35 40
2396 400s. Camp training 50 55
2397 600s. Bravery training . . . 70 75
2398 800s. Guides assisting at Mother and Child clinic 95 1·00
MS2399 105 × 85 mm. 1000s. As No. 2397 . . . . 1·20 1·30
Nos. 2395/**MS**2399 show "2003" inscription date.

322 Overland Vehicle

2004. 40th Anniv of Tanganyika Christian Refugee Service. Multicoloured.

2400	350s. Type **322**	40	45
2401	600s. Drawing fresh water	70	75
2402	800s. Children in school	95	1·00
2403	1000s. Planting saplings	1·20	1·30
MS2404	85 × 74 mm. 1200s. Combination of designs of Nos. 2400/3 (45 × 35 mm)	1·40	1·50

323 Cheering for Peddle Winners

2003. Dhow Events in Zanzibar. Multicoloured.

2405	350s. Type **323**	40	45
2406	400s. Punting race	50	55
2407	600s. Dhow race	70	75
2408	800s. Sail boat race	95	1·00
MS2409	91 × 90 mm. 1000s. Dhow (vert)	1·20	1·30

324 Removing Water Hyacinth, Mwanza City

2004. 24th Anniv of the Southern African Development Community. Multicoloured.

2410	350s. Type **324**	40	45
2411	500s. Irrigation of maize, Mbayali District, Mbeya	60	65
2412	600s. Paddy fields at Igomelo irrigation scheme	70	75
2413	800s. Installing pipes in new borehole, Mbeya Rural (vert)	95	1·00
MS2414	130 × 100 mm. Nos. 2410/13	2·50	2·75
MS2415	90 × 90 mm. 1000s. Men working in maize fields	1·20	1·30

325 Williamson Diamond Mine, Mwadui

2004. Mining. Multicoloured.

2416	350s. Type **325**	40	45
2417	500s. Semi processed jewels	60	65
2418	600s. Drillers	70	75
2419	800s. Small scale gold miners	95	1·00
MS2420	130 × 100 mm. Nos. 2416/19	2·50	2·75
MS2421	90 × 90 mm. 600s. Unprocessed gemstones	70	75

OFFICIAL STAMPS

1965. Nos. 128 etc, optd **OFFICIAL**.

O 9	**25**	5c. blue and orange	10	1·50
O10	–	10c. multicoloured	10	1·50
O11	–	15c. multicoloured	10	1·50
O12	–	20c. sepia, green and blue	10	1·50
O13	–	30c. black and brown	10	40
O14	–	50c. multicoloured	15	1·50
O15	**33**	1s. multicoloured	30	40
O16	–	5s. brown, green and blue	1·75	8·00

1967. Nos. 142, etc, optd **OFFICIAL**.

O20	5c. mauve, green and black	10	3·00
O21	10c. brown and bistre	10	50
O22	15c. grey, blue and black	10	3·00
O23	20c. brown and green	10	30
O24	30c. green and black	10	30
O36	40c. yellow, brown and green	—	2·50
O25	50c. multicoloured	15	1·60
O26	1s. brown, blue and purple	30	3·00
O27	5s. yellow, black and green	2·50	17·00

1973. Nos. 158 etc, optd **OFFICIAL**.

O40	**53**	5c. green, blue and black	50	3·00
O41	–	10c. multicoloured	65	40
O42	–	20c. brown, yellow & black	80	40
O43	–	40c. multicoloured	1·25	40
O44	–	50c. multicoloured	1·25	40
O45	–	70c. green, orange & black	1·25	75
O46	**54**	1s. multicoloured	1·25	40
O47	–	1s.50 multicoloured	2·50	3·75
O48	–	2s.50 multicoloured	3·00	8·50
O49	–	5s. multicoloured	3·25	12·00

1980. Nos. 307/13 and 315/17 optd **OFFICIAL**.

O54	10c. Type **75**	20	1·50
O55	20c. Large-spotted genet	25	1·00
O56	40c. Banded mongoose	30	1·00
O57	50c. Ratel	30	40
O58	75c. Large-toothed rock hyrax	40	60
O59	80c. Leopard	55	1·50
O60	1s. Impala	55	40
O66	1s.50 Giraffe	4·50	4·00
O61	2s. Common zebra	85	2·75
O62	3s. African buffalo	1·00	3·00
O63	5s. Lion	1·50	4·00

1990. Nos. 804/12 optd **OFFICIAL**.

O70	5s. Type **163**	40	1·75
O71	9s. African emerald cuckoo	50	1·25
O72	13s. Little bee eater	50	1·25
O73	15s. Red bishop	55	1·50
O74	20s. Bateleur	55	1·50
O75	25s. Scarlet-chested sunbird	55	1·50
O76	30s. African wood pigeon	55	1·50
O77	40s. Type **164**	70	1·50
O78	70s. Helmeted guineafowl	1·50	2·25
O79	100s. Eastern white pelican	2·00	2·75

1997. Nos. 2075/6, 2078 and 2081 optd **OFFICIAL**.

O80	100s. *Plumeria rubra acutifolia*	10	15
O81	140s. *Liliaceae*	15	20
O82	200s. *Liliaceae* (different)	25	30
O83	300s. *Canna*	35	40

No. O83 is inscribed "Carna" in error.

POSTAGE DUE STAMPS

The Postage Due stamps of Kenya, Uganda and Tanganyika were used in Tanganyika until 2 January 1967.

D 1

D 2

1967.

D19	**D 1**	5c. red	15	2·75
D20		10c. green	20	2·75
D21		20c. blue	30	3·00
D22		30c. brown	45	3·75
D23		40c. purple	50	5·50
D24		1s. orange	70	6·00

1990.

D30	**D 2**	50c. green	10	50
D31		80c. blue	10	50
D32		1s. brown	10	50
D33		2s. green	10	60
D34		3s. purple	10	60
D35		5s. brown	15	65
D36		10s. brown	25	1·00
D37		20s. brown	40	1·40
D38		40s. blue	10	10
D39		60s. green	10	10
D40		80s. yellow	10	15
D41		100s. blue	10	15

APPENDIX

The following stamps have either been issued in excess of postal needs, or have not been made available to the public in reasonable quantities at face value.

1985.

Life and Times of Queen Elizabeth the Queen Mother. As Nos. 425/8 but embossed on gold foil. 20s. × 2, 100s. × 2.

Tanzanian Railway Locomotives (1st series). As Nos. 430/3 but embossed on gold foil. 5, 10, 20, 30s.

1986.

Caribbean Royal Visit. Optd on previous issues. (a) On Nos. 425/8. 20s. × 2, 100s. × 2. (b) On Nos. 430/3. 5, 10, 20, 30s.

"Ameripex" International Stamp Exhibition, Chicago. Optd on Nos. 425/8. 20s. × 2, 100s. × 2.

1988.

Cent of Statue of Liberty (1986). 1, 2, 3, 4, 5, 6, 7, 8, 10, 12, 15, 18, 20, 25, 30, 35, 40, 45, 50, 60s.

Royal Ruby Wedding. Optd on No. 378. 10s.

125th Anniv of Red Cross. Optd on Nos. 486/7. 5, 40s.

63rd Anniv of Rotary International in Africa. Optd on Nos. 422/3. 10s., 17s.50.

1995.

The Beatles. 100s. × 18.

Hoofed Animals. 70, 100, 150, 180, 200, 260, 380s.

Fauna of Coral Reefs. 70, 100, 150, 180, 200, 260, 380s.

"Singapore '95" International Stamp Exhibition. Trains of the World. 200s. × 18.

Centof Sierra Club. 150s. × 18.

Bats. 70, 100, 150, 180, 200, 260, 380s.

History of Rock and Roll. 250s. × 9.

90th Anniv of Rotary International. 600s.

Winter Olympic Games, Lillehammer, Norway. 300, 400s.

Picasso Paintings. 30, 200, 300s.

450th Death Anniv of Copernicus (astronomer) (1993). 100, 300s.

"Polska'93" International Stamp Exhibition, Poznan. 200, 300s.

95th Birthday of Queen Elizabeth the Queen Mother. 250s. × 4.

Olympic Games, Atlanta, 1996. Olympic History. 200s. × 18.

50th Anniv of End of Second World War in the Pacific. 250s. × 6.

50th Anniv of End of Second World War. 250s. × 8.

Cacti. 70, 100, 150, 180, 200, 260, 380s.

African Reptiles. 200s. × 12.

Predatory Animals. 70, 100, 150, 200, 250, 280, 300s.

50th Anniv of United Nations. 250s. × 3.

50th Anniv of U.N. Food and Agriculture Organization. 250s. × 3.

Cent of Cinema. Biblical Epics. 250s. × 9.

20th Anniv of World Tourism Organization. 100, 300, 400s.

Gerry Garcia (rock musician) Commemoration. 200s.

Frogs. 100, 140, 180, 200, 210, 260, 300s.

Fauna of Kilimanjaro. 100s. × 16, 250s. × 4.

Butterflies. 200s. × 19, 250, 370, 410s.

1996.

Moths and Butterflies. 70, 100, 150, 200, 250, 260, 300s.

Chinese New Year ("Year of the Rat"). 200s. × 4.

Horses. 250s. × 9.

Cats. 100, 150, 200, 250s. × 9, 300s. × 4.

Dogs. 70s, 250s. × 10, 300s. × 4, 600s.

Crocodiles. 100, 150, 200, 250, 260, 300, 380s.

125th Anniv of the Metropolitan Museum, New York. Paintings. 200s. × 18.

Elvis Presley Commemoration. 200s. × 9.

Snakes. 100, 140, 180, 200, 260, 300, 400s.

"China 96", International Stamp Exhibition. Deng Xiaoping. 250s. × 6.

70th Birthday of Queen Elizabeth II. 300s. × 3.

Famous People. 70, 100, 150, 200, 250s. × 6.

Olympic Games, Atlanta. 100, 150, 200, 300s.

Birds. 300s. × 16.

Cent of Radio. Famous People. 70, 100, 150, 200s.

Flowers. 300s. × 16.

Fish. 100, 150, 200s. × 9, 250, 500s.

Mercedes and Ferrari Cars. 250s. × 12.

50th Anniv of UNESCO. 200, 250, 600s.

50th Anniv of UNICEF. 200, 250, 500s.

90th Anniv of Rotary. Nos. 985/1000 and 1589/600 optd **90th ANNIVERSARY OF ROTARY 1905–1995** and emblem. 50s. × 16, 100s. × 12.

International Scout Camp, Thailand and 34th World Scout Conf, Norway. Nos. 1001/16 and 1564/75 optd either **34th WORLD SCOUT CONFERENCE NORWAY JULY 8–12 1996** or **INTERNATIONAL SCOUT CAMP THAILAND MARCH 25–31 1996**, both with Scout emblem. 50s. × 16, 100s. × 12

Fungi. 300s. × 16.

1997.

"Hong Kong 97" International Stamp Exhibition. Portraits of Sun Yat-sen. 300s. × 6.

Horses. 250s. × 12.

Chernobyl's Children. 700s. × 2.

Birds. 140s. × 6, 150, 200, 370s. × 6, 410, 500s.

Flowers. 200s. × 6, 300s. × 6.

175th Anniv of Brothers Grimm's Third Collection of Fairy Tales *Rumpelstiltskin*. 400s. × 3.

Birth Bicent of Hiroshige (Japanese painter). 250s. × 6.

Golden Wedding of Queen Elizabeth and Prince Philip. 370s. × 6.

Return of Hong Kong to China. 1000s. × 5.

Winter Olympic Games, Nagano (1998). 100, 200, 250s. × 4, 500, 600s.

World Cup Football Championship, France (1998). 100, 150, 200, 250s. × 17, 500, 600s.

African Safari. 250s. × 9.

Northern Wilderness (Arctic). 250s. × 9.

Endangered Species. 250s. × 24.

Seven Wonders of the Ancient World. 370s. × 6.

Seven Wonders of the Modern World. 140s. × 6.

Aviation. 100, 150s. × 18, 200, 250s. × 8, 300, 400, 500s.

1998.

Diana, Princess of Wales Commemoration. 150, 250s.

Marine Life. 200s. × 12, 250s. × 18.

Chinese New Year ("Year of the Tiger"). 370s. × 4.

Classic Cars. 370s. × 12.

Aircraft. 300s. × 18.

Exotic Flowers. 250s. × 26.

Endangered Species. 200s. × 12, 370s. × 12.

Eagles. 370s. × 6.

Fauna and Flora. 250, 370s. × 12, 410, 500, 600s.

International Year of the Ocean (1st issue). 150, 200s. × 12, 250, 300s. × 9, 400, 500s.

International Year of the Ocean (2nd issue). 1998 Marine Life overprinted with emblem. 200s. × 12, 250s. × 18.

Fungi and Insects. 140, 150, 200, 250s. × 19, 370, 410, 500, 600s.

Rudolph the Red-nosed Reindeer (cartoon film). 200s. × 12.

25th Death Anniv of Pablo Picasso (painter). 400s. × 2, 500s.

50th Death Anniv of Mahatma Gandhi. 370s.

1st Death Anniv of Diana, Princess of Wales. 600s.

19th World Scout Jamboree, Chile. 600s. × 3.

80th Anniv of Royal Air Force 500s. × 4.

John Denver Commemoration. 370s. × 4.

1999.

Chinese New Year ("Year of the Rabbit"). 4 × 250s.

Marine Life. 200, 250s. × 19, 310, 410s.

Balloons. 370s. × 6.

Tourism booklet. 150s. × 24.

Space. 70, 100, 150, 200, 250, 370s.

Early Flight. 20, 100, 140 s. × 2, 150, 200, 250, 370s. × 7.

Aircraft. 370s. × 6.

Ships of the 19th Century. 370s. × 12.

Endangered Species. 100s. × 20.

Animals. 100, 140, 150, 200, 250, 370s.

Birds of the World. 370s. × 12.

Birds. 370s. × 12.

Flora and Fauna. 100, 140, 150, 200, 250, 370 s. × 13.

Orchids. 200, 250, 370s. × 13.

Dogs of the World. 200s. × 9.

Cats of the World. 100, 140, 150, 200, 250, 370s. × 13.

Cats. 200, 250s. × 9, 370, 410s.

Cats of the East. 500s. × 4.

Prehistoric Animals. 400s. × 6.

50th Anniv of Rotary in Tanzania. 150, 250, 350, 400s.

Queen Mother's Century. 600s. × 4.

APS Stamp Show, Cleveland. Birds of Japan. 250s. × 18.

Fashion Designers. 300s. × 8.

Ballet. 300, 350, 400, 500s.

Hokusai (Japanese artist). 400s. × 6.

Art of India. 500s. × 8.

Military Exploits. 150, 250 s. × 3, 300s. × 3, 350s. × 3, 400s. × 3, 500s. × 3.

Aircraft. 200, 250s. × 9, 300, 400s.

Helicopters. 370s. × 6.

UFOs. 370s. × 12.

Locomotives. 400s. × 6.

History of Trains. 400s. × 12.

Sailing Vessels of the World. 400s. × 12.

Fighting Machines of Second World War. 400s. × 12.

Cars. 400s. × 12.

"China '99". Paintings of Xu Beihong. 15 s. × 10.

"China '99". Macau Returns to China. 300s. × 4.

Underwater Creatures. 150, 250, 300s. × 19, 350, 400, 500s.

Flowers. 150, 250, 350s. × 18, 400, 500s.

Flowers of Africa. 150, 250, 300, 350, 400 s × 13.

Flora and Fauna. 150s. × 2, 250s. × 2, 300s. × 2, 350s. × 2, 400s. × 26, 500s. × 2.

Fungi. 150, 250, 300, 350, 400s. × 13, 500s.

Predators of the Deep. 200, 250, 370s. × 7, 410s.

Prehistoric Animals. 200, 250, 370 s. × 13, 410s.

Sea Birds. 150, 250s. × 16, 300, 350, 400, 500s.

Marine Life. 250s. × 12, 350, 400, 500s.

African Wildlife 300s. × 8.

Central American Rainforest. 350s. × 9.

Butterflies. 400s. × 6.

Cats and Dogs. 400s. × 12.

2000.

Orchids. 200, 250, 370s. × 13

Flowers. 150, 250, 300 × 19, 350, 400, 500s.

Flora and Fauna. 100, 140, 250, 370s. × 13

2002.

Queen Elizabeth the Queen Mother "In Memoriam". 95th Birthday of Queen Elizabeth the Queen Mother (1995 Appendix). Sheet margin inscribed "IN MEMORIAM 1900–2002". 250s. × 4

2004.

Mushrooms. 550s. × 6

Animals. 550s. × 6

Birds. 550s. × 6

Butterflies. 550s. × 6

Orchids. 550s. × 6

TASMANIA Pt. 1

An island south of Australia, one of the States of the Australian Commonwealth, whose stamps it now uses.

12 pence = 1 shilling;
20 shillings = 1 pound.

1

2

1853. Imperf.
3 **1** 1d. blue £4000 £900
11 **2** 4d. orange £2000 £350

3

7

8

1855. Imperf.
28 **3** 1d. red . . . . £100 23·00
34 2d. green . . . . £190 75·00
36 4d. blue . . . . £150 22·00
46 **7** 6d. purple . . . . £200 65·00
41 **8** 1s. orange . . . . £550 75·00

1864. Perf.
82 **3** 1d. red . . . . 45·00 12·00
71 2d. green . . . . £200 60·00
72 4d. blue . . . . £110 18·00
143 **7** 6d. purple . . . . 28·00 13·00
141 **8** 1s. orange . . . . £110 45·00

11

20

1870.
159 **11** ½d. orange . . . . 3·00 2·75
156 1d. red . . . . 4·00 75
157 2d. green . . . . 4·75 75
165 3d. brown . . . . 8·00 4·25
130 4d. blue £750 £425
226 4d. yellow . . . . 12·00 7·00
158 8d. purple . . . . 14·00 5·00
256 9d. blue . . . . 7·00 4·25
131 10d. black . . . . 24·00 27·00
149b 5s. mauve . . . . £180 60·00

1889. Surch **Halfpenny**.
167 **11** 2½d. on 9d. blue . . . . . 9·50 15·00

1889. Surch **d. 2½**.
169 **11** 2½d. on 9d. blue . . . . . 5·00 3·50

1892. Various frames.
216 **20** ½d. orange and mauve . . 1·75 1·00
217 2½d. purple . . . . 2·50 1·50
218 5d. blue and brown . . . . 6·00 2·50
219 6d. violet and black . . . 8·00 3·00
220 10d. lake and green . . . . 9·00 11·00
221 1s. red and green . . . . . 8·00 2·75
222 2s.6d. brown and blue . . 22·00 17·00
223 5s. purple and red . . . . 50·00 19·00
224 10s. mauve and brown . . 95·00 65·00
225 £1 green and yellow . . . £325 £275

22 Lake Marion

23 Mount Wellington

1899.
249 **22** ½d. green . . . . 1·75 50
250 **23** 1d. red . . . . 1·75 20
251b – 2d. violet . . . . 2·75 20
232 – 2½d. blue . . . . 18·00 3·75
246 – 3d. brown . . . . 8·50 4·00
247 – 4d. orange . . . . 13·00 3·75
235 – 5d. blue . . . . 25·00 11·00
236 – 6d. lake . . . . 25·00 20·00

DESIGNS—HORIZ: 2d. Hobart; 3d. Spring River, Port Davey; 5d. Mt. Gould, Lake St. Clair; 6d. Dilston Falls. VERT: 2½d. Tasman's Arch; 4d. Russell Falls.

1904. No. 218 surch **1½d.**
244 **20** 1½d. on 5d. blue and brown . . . . 1·25 80

1912. No. 251b surch **ONE PENNY**.
260 1d. on 2d. violet . . . . . . 1·00 1·00

TCHONGKING (CHUNGKING) Pt. 17

An Indo-Chinese Post Office was opened at Chungking in February 1902 and operated until it closed in December 1922.

1903. 100 centimes = 1 franc.
1919. 100 cents = 1 piastre.

Stamps of Indo-China surch.

1903. "Tablet" key-type surch with value in Chinese and **TCHONGKING**.
1 **D** 1c. black and red on blue . . 4·25 4·50
2 2c. brown and blue on buff 3·25 3·75
3 4c. brown and blue on grey 3·25 3·75
4 5c. green and red . . . . . 3·25 3·50
5 10c. red and blue . . . . . 3·25 4·00
6 15c. grey and red . . . . . 2·75 4·50
7 20c. red and blue on green 3·75 4·25
8 25c. blue and red . . . . . 30·00 45·00
9 25c. black and red on pink 5·00 8·00
10 30c. brown and blue on drab 9·75 12·00
11 40c. red and blue on yellow 42·00 48·00
12 50c. red and blue on pink £170 £170
13 50c. brown and red on blue 95·00 £120
14 75c. brown and red on orange . . . . 45·00 48·00
15 1f. green and red . . . . . 50·00 60·00
16 5f. mauve and blue on lilac 85·00 £100

1906. Surch with value in Chinese and **Tch'ong K'ing**.
17 **8** 1c. green . . . . 2·25 3·50
18 2c. purple on yellow . . . . 2·00 2·75
19 4c. mauve on blue . . . . . 2·50 2·75
20 5c. green . . . . 2·75 2·75
21 10c. pink . . . . 2·75 3·00
22 15c. brown on blue . . . . 7·50 8·00
23 20c. red on green . . . . . 3·25 3·50
24 25c. blue . . . . 4·00 4·25
25 30c. brown on cream . . . 3·75 4·25
26 35c. black on yellow . . . 3·50 3·75
27 40c. black on grey . . . . 6·25 6·50
28 50c. brown on cream . . . 6·25 9·25
29 **D** 75c. brown and red on orange . . . . 35·00 40·00
30 **8** 1f. green . . . . 24·00 32·00
31 2f. brown on yellow . . . . 20·00 32·00
32 **D** 5f. mauve and blue on lilac £100 £110
33 **8** 10f. red on green £110 £120

1908. Native types surch with value in Chinese and **TCHONGKING**.
34 **10** 1c. black and brown . . . . 1·00 75
35 2c. black and brown . . . . 1·10 90
36 4c. black and blue . . . . 1·40 1·60
37 5c. black and green . . . . 2·25 2·00
38 10c. black and red . . . . 1·90 2·50
39 15c. black and violet . . . 2·75 3·50
40 **11** 20c. black and violet . . . 4·00 4·25
41 25c. black and blue . . . . 3·50 3·75
42 30c. black and brown . . . 3·50 4·50
43 35c. black and green . . . . 5·50 7·50
44 40c. black and brown . . . 10·00 16·00
45 50c. black and red . . . . 10·00 11·50
46 **12** 75c. black and orange . . . 9·00 11·50
47 – 1f. black and red . . . . 11·00 15·00
48 – 2f. black and green . . . . 85·00 £100
49 – 5f. black and blue . . . . 35·00 35·00
50 – 10f. black and violet . . . £170 £200

1919. As last, but surch in addition in figures and words.
51 **10** ⅖c. on 1c. black and brown 1·40 30
52 ⅘c. on 2c. black and brown 80 3·00
53 1⅗c. on 4c. black and blue 85 3·00
54 2c. on 5c. black and green 2·50 2·75
55 4c. on 10c. black and red 1·40 1·75
56 6c. on 15c. black and violet 2·75 2·50
57 **11** 8c. on 20c. black and violet 2·25 2·00
58 10c. on 25c. black and blue 3·00 2·25
59 12c. on 30c. black & brown 3·00 95
60 14c. on 35c. black and green 3·50 3·00
61 16c. on 40c. black and brown . . . . 3·50 3·50
62 20c. on 50c. black and red 13·00 12·50
63 **12** 30c. on 75c. black & orange 3·75 4·25
64 – 40c. on 1f. black and red . . 4·25 4·00
65 – 80c. on 2f. black and green 6·25 5·50
66 – 2p. on 5f. black and blue . . 9·00 8·75
67 – 4p. on 10f. black and violet 12·00 11·00

TETE Pt. 9

Formerly using the stamps of Mozambique, this district of Mozambique was permitted to issue its own stamps from 1913 until 1920 when Mozambique stamps were again used.

100 centavos = 1 escudo.

1913. Surch **REPUBLICA TETE** and new value on "Vasco da Gama" issues of (a) Portugese Colonies.
1 ¼c. on 2½r. green . . . . 1·40 1·10
2 ½c. on 5r. red . . . . 1·40 1·10
3 1c. on 10r. purple . . . . . . 1·40 1·10
4 2½c. on 25r. green . . . . . . 1·40 1·10
5 5c. on 50r. blue . . . . 1·40 1·10
6 7½c. on 75r. brown . . . . . . 2·00 1·20
7 10c. on 100r. brown . . . . . 1·40 1·20
8 15c. on 150r. brown . . . . . 1·40 1·20

(b) Macao.
9 ¼c. on ½a. green . . . . 1·40 1·10
10 ½c. on 1a. red . . . . 1·40 1·10
11 1c. on 2a. purple . . . . . . 1·40 1·10
12 2½c. on 4a. green . . . . . . 1·40 1·10
13 5c. on 8a. blue . . . . 1·40 1·10
14 7½c. on 12a. brown . . . . . 2·00 1·20
15 10c. on 16a. brown . . . . . 1·40 1·20
16 15c. on 24a. brown . . . . . 1·40 1·20

(c) Timor.
17 ¼c. on ½c. green . . . . 1·40 1·10
18 ½c. on 1a. red . . . . 1·40 1·10
19 1c. on 2a. purple . . . . . . 1·40 1·10
20 2½c. on 4a. green . . . . . . 1·40 1·10
21 5c. on 8a. blue . . . . 1·40 1·10
22 7½c. on 12a. brown . . . . . 2·00 1·20
23 10c. on 16a. brown . . . . . 1·40 1·20
24 15c. on 24a. brown . . . . . 1·40 1·20

1914. "Ceres" key-type inscr "TETE".
25 **U** ¼c. green 85 55
26 ½c. black 85 55
27 1c. green 85 55
28 1½c. brown 85 55
29 2c. red 85 55
30 2½c. violet 85 55
31 5c. blue 85 55
32 7½c. brown . . . . 1·30 1·20
33 8c. grey . . . . 1·30 1·20
34 10c. red . . . . 1·70 1·20
35 15c. purple . . . . 2·00 1·90
36 20c. green . . . . 2·00 1·90
37 30c. brown on green . . . . 2·00 1·90
38 40c. brown on pink . . . . 2·40 2·10
39 50c. orange on orange . . . 2·75 2·20
40 1e. green on blue . . . . . 3·00 2·50

THAILAND Pt. 21

An independent kingdom in S.E. Asia, previously known as Siam.

1883. 32 solot = 16 atts = 8 peinung (sio) = 4 songpy (sik) = 2 fuang = 1 salung; 4 salungs = 1 tical.
1909. 100 satangs = 1 tical.
1912. 100 satangs = 1 baht.

1 King Chulalongkorn

2

3 King Chulalongkorn

9

1883.
1 **1** 1solot (⅛a.) blue . . . . 6·50 6·50
2 1att red . . . . 8·50 7·50
3 1sio (2a.) red . . . . 16·00 16·00
4 **2** 1sik (4a.) yellow . . . . . . 7·50 8·50
5 **3** 1salung (16a.) orange . . . . 26·00 26·00

1885. Surch. (a) **1 TICAL**.
6 **1** 1t. on 1solot blue £2500 £1700

(b) **1 Tical**.
7 **1** 1t. on 1solot blue £225 £225

1887.
11 **9** 1a. green . . . . 2·10 65
12 2a. green and red . . . . . 3·25 65
13 3a. green and blue . . . . . 7·50 2·50
14 4a. green and brown . . . . 6·50 2·10
15 8a. green and yellow . . . . 6·50 1·70
16 12a. purple and red . . . . 10·50 85
17 24a. purple and blue . . . . 15·00 1·10
18 64a. purple and brown . . . 55·00 16·00

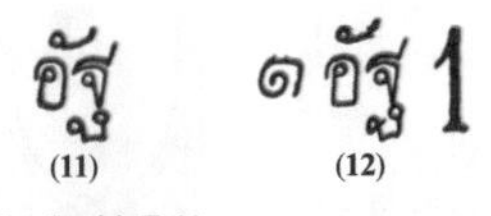
อัฐ (11) ๑ อัฐ 1 (12)

1889. Surch with T **11**.
19 **1** 1a. on 1sio red . . . . 13·00 13·00

1889. (a) Surch as T **12**.
20 **9** 1a. on 2a. green and red . . 2·50 2·10
24 1a. on 3a. green and blue . . 4·25 3·75
26 2a. on 3a. green and blue . . 39·00 32·00

(b) No. 24 further surch as T **12**.
28 **9** 2a. on 1a. on 3a. green & blue £1300 £1100

1 Att.
ราคา ๔ อัฐ (23) ราคา ๑ อัฐ (42)

1892. Surch with T **23**.
32 **9** 4a. on 24a. purple and blue 21·00 17·00

1892. No. 32 further surch **4 atts** in English (with or without full point).
33 **9** 4a. on 24a. purple and blue 6·50 4·25

1892. Surch as T **42**.
63 **9** 1Att. on 12a. purple and red 16·00 3·25
54 1Att. on 12a. purple and red £250 £250
37 1Att. on 64a. purple and brown . . . . 2·10 2·10
46 1Att. on 64a. purple & brown 1·10 85
44 2a. on 64a. purple and brown 85 85
58 3a. on 12a. purple and red 8·50 2·10
60 4a. on 12a. purple and red 10·50 2·10
50 10a. on 24a. purple and blue 5·00 85

49

50

53 Wat Cheng "Temple of Light"

1899.
67 **49** 1a. green . . . . 1·10 45
68 2a. green . . . . 1·10 45
69 2a. red and blue . . . . . 4·25 1·10
70 3a. red and blue . . . . . 2·10 65
71 3a. green . . . . 5·25 3·00
72 4a. red . . . . 5·25 1·30
73 4a. brown and pink . . . . 15·00 1·10
74 6a. red . . . . 60·00 10·00
75 8a. green and orange . . . 25·00 2·50
76 10a. blue . . . . 4·25 1·10
77 12a. purple and red . . . . 12·00 70
78 14a. blue . . . . 13·00 6·50
79 24a. purple and blue . . . . 70·00 6·50
80 28a. brown and blue . . . . 21·00 7·50
81 64a. purple and brown . . . 20·00 6·00

1899.
82 **50** 1a. green . . . . £110 65·00
83 2a. green and red £170 £110
84 3a. red and blue £250 £150
85 4a. black and green £2000 £550
86 10a. pink and green £2000 £750

1905. Surch in English and Siamese.
90 **49** 1a. on 14a. blue . . . . . . 5·25 4·25
91 2a. on 28a. brown and blue 6·50 5·25

1905.
92 **53** 1a. green and yellow . . . 1·10 45
93 2a. grey and violet . . . . 1·10 45
94 2a. green . . . . 4·25 2·50
95 3a. green . . . . 2·10 85
96 3a. grey and violet . . . . 8·50 3·75
97 4a. red and brown . . . . 4·25 45
98 4a. red . . . . 4·25 65
99 5a. red . . . . 4·25 1·10
100 8a. bistre and black . . . 6·50 65
101 9a. blue . . . . 13·00 4·75
102 12a. blue . . . . 8·50 1·50
103 18a. brown . . . . 39·00 10·50
104 24a. brown . . . . 17·00 3·25
105 1t. bistre and blue . . . . 26·00 2·75

54

๒ อัฐ
2 Atts.
(57)

1907. Fiscal stamps optd **Siam. Postage** and new value.
106 **54** 10t. green . . . . £425 65·00
107 20t. green £4750 £250
108 40t. green £3500 £425

1907. Surch **1 att.** and thin line.
109 **9** 1a. on 24a. purple and blue 1·30 65

1908. Surch in English and Siamese as T **57**.
110 **9** 2a. on 24a. purple and blue 1·10 65
111 **53** 4a. on 5a. red . . . . 6·50 2·10
112 **49** 9a. on 10a. blue . . . . . 7·50 2·75

1908. 40th Anniv of Reign of King Chulalongkorn. Optd **Jubilee 1868-1908** in English and Siamese.

113	53	1a. green and yellow	1·10	65
114		3a. green	2·10	1·50
115		4a. on 5a. (No. 111)	3·25	2·10
116		8a. bistre and black	15·00	15·00
117		18a. brown	21·00	13·00

61 Statue of King Chulalongkorn, Bangkok

64 King Chulalongkorn

1908.

118	61	1t. violet and green	21·00	2·10
119		2t. orange and purple	43·00	7·50
120		3t. blue and green	65·00	9·75
121		5t. green and lilac	85·00	17·00
122		10t. red and green	£950	50·00
123		20t. brown and grey	£225	60·00
124		40t. brown and blue	£325	£190

1909. Surch in satangs in English and Siamese.

125	53	2s. on 1a. green & yellow	85	45
127a		2s. on 2a. green	85	45
164		2s. on 2a. grey and violet	4·25	2·10
129		3s. on 3a. green	1·50	1·30
130		3s. on 3a. grey and violet	1·50	45
131		6s. on 4a. red and brown	36·00	32·00
132a		6s. on 4a. red	2·10	65
134		6s. on 5a. red	1·70	1·50
138	49	6s. on 6a. red	1·10	1·10
135	53	12s. on 8a. bistre & black	4·25	65
136		14s. on 9a. blue	6·50	1·10
137		14s. on 12a. blue	13·00	13·00
139	9	14s. on 12a. purple & red	75·00	75·00
140	49	14s. on 14a. blue	9·75	9·75

1910.

141	64	2s. green and orange	1·10	45
142		3s. green	1·10	45
143		6s. red	2·10	45
144		12s. brown and black	6·50	85
145		14s. blue	13·00	1·10
146		28s. brown	24·00	5·25

65 King Vajiravudh

66

1912.

166	65	2s. brown	45	20
167		3s. green	65	30
168		5s. red	1·70	20
149		6s. red	1·30	30
169		10s. brown and black	1·10	20
150		12s. brown and black	1·70	30
151		14s. blue	2·75	65
170		15s. blue	2·50	45
152		28s. brown	10·50	4·75
153	66	1b. brown and blue	13·00	85
154		2b. brown and red	17·00	1·30
155		3b. black and green	19·00	2·10
156		5b. black and violet	30·00	3·25
157		10b. purple and green	£200	34·00
158		20b. brown and blue	£300	39·00

1914. Surch in **Satang** in English and Siamese.

165	64	2s. on 14s. blue	1·70	1·10
159	65	2s. on 14s. blue	1·10	20
160		5s. on 6s. red	2·10	20
161		10s. on 12s. brown & black	2·10	30
162		15s. on 28s. brown	4·25	55

1918. Red Cross Fund. Optd with small cross in circle.

177	65	2s.(+3s.) brown	65	65
178		3s.(+2s.) green	65	65
179		5s.(+5s.) red	2·10	2·10
180		10s.(+5s.) brown and black	2·50	2·50
181		15s.(+5s.) blue	2·50	2·50
182	66	1b.(+25s.) brown & blue	13·00	10·50
183		2b.(+30s.) brown and red	17·00	13·00
184		3b.(+35s.) black and green	26·00	21·00
185		5b.(+40s.) black and violet	£110	75·00
186		10b.(+1b.) purple & green	£250	£190
187		20b.(+1b.) brown & grn	£1300	£1200

1918. Optd **VICTORY** in English and Siamese.

188	65	2s. brown	45	45
189		3s. green	65	65
190		5s. red	1·10	1·10
191		10s. brown and black	1·10	1·10
192		15s. blue	2·10	2·10
193	66	1b. brown and blue	16·00	13·00
194		2b. brown and red	32·00	26·00
195		3b. black and green	75·00	60·00
196		5b. black and violet	£225	£200

1919. Surch in English and Siamese with figures only.

197	65	5s. on 6s. red	1·10	20
198		10s. on 12s. brown & black	2·10	30

(72a) **(72b)**

1920. Scouts' Fund. Various stamps handstamped. (a) With Type **72a**.

199	65	2s.(+3s.) brown	21·00	21·00
200		3s.(+2s.) green	21·00	21·00
201		5s. on 6s. (+5s.) red (No. 160)	32·00	32·00
202		10s. on 12s. (+5s.) brown and black (No. 161)	32·00	32·00
203		15s.(+5s.) blue	65·00	65·00
204	53	1t.(+25s.) bistre and blue	£250	£250

(b) With Type **72b**.

205	65	2s.(+3s.) brown	8·50	8·50
206		3s.(+2s.) green	8·50	8·50
207	73	5s.(+5s.) red on pink	65·00	65·00
208	65	10s. on 12s. (+5s.) brown and black (No. 161)	13·00	13·00
209		15s.(+5s.) blue	13·00	13·00
210	53	1t.(+25s.) bistre and blue	£225	£225

These stamps were sold in aid of the "Wild Tiger" Scouts organization at the premium stated.

73 **(73a)**

1920.

211	73	2s. brown on yellow	65	20
212		3s. green on green	1·10	30
213		3s. brown	85	20
214		5s. red on pink	1·30	20
215		5s. green	15·00	1·90
216		5s. violet on mauve	3·25	20
217		10s. brown and black	2·50	20
218		15s. blue on blue	4·25	20
219		15s. red	24·00	2·50
220		25s. brown	10·50	1·30
221		25s. blue	18·00	1·10
222		50s. black and brown	26·00	75

1920. Scouts' Fund. Optd with T **73a**.

223	73	2s.(+3s.) brown on yellow	6·50	6·50
224		3s.(+2s.) green on green	6·50	6·50
225		5s.(+5s.) red on pink	6·50	6·50
226		10s.(+5s.) brown and black	6·50	6·50
227		15s.(+5s.) blue on blue	10·50	10·50
228		25s.(+25s.) brown	39·00	39·00
229		50s.(+30s.) black & brn	£180	£180

74 "Garuda" Bird

75 Coronation Stone

1925. Air.

230	74	2s. brown on yellow	55	20
231		3s. brown	55	20
239		5s. green	55	20
240		10s. orange and black	55	20
234		15s. red	2·10	55
242		25s. blue	1·10	65
243		50s. black and brown	1·10	75
237		1b. brown and blue	19·00	5·25

1926.

244	75	1t. green and lilac	6·50	1·10
245		2t. red and carmine	15·00	3·25
246		3t. blue and green	32·00	15·00
247		5t. green and violet	39·00	10·50
248		10t. brown and red	£160	13·00
249		20t. brown and blue	£180	43·00

1928. Surch in English and Siamese.

250	73	5s. on 15s. red	2·50	1·60
251	65	10s. on 28s. brown	6·00	55

76 King Prajadhipok

77

1928.

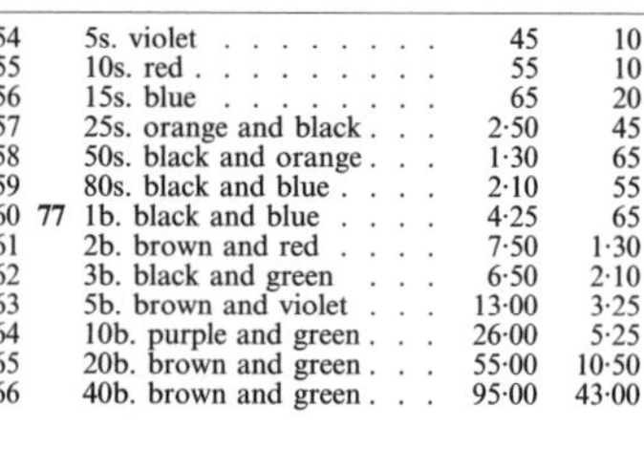

252	76	2s. brown	45	10
253		3s. green	55	20
254		5s. violet	45	10
255		10s. red	55	10
256		15s. blue	65	20
257		25s. orange and black	2·50	45
258		50s. black and orange	1·30	65
259		80s. black and blue	2·10	55
260	77	1b. black and blue	4·25	65
261		2b. brown and red	7·50	1·30
262		3b. black and green	6·50	2·10
263		5b. brown and violet	13·00	3·25
264		10b. purple and green	26·00	5·25
265		20b. brown and green	55·00	10·50
266		40b. brown and green	95·00	43·00

1930. Surch in English and Siamese.

267	64	10s. on 12s. brown & black	4·25	85
268		25s. on 28s. brown	17·00	1·30

79 Kings Prajadhipok and Chao Phya Chakri

81 Chao Phya Chakri (Rama I)

80 Kings Prajadhipok and Chao Phya Chakri

1932. 150th Anniv of Chakri Dynasty and of Bangkok as Capital and Opening of Memorial Bridge over Menam.

269	79	2s. red	85	20
270		3s. green	1·30	45
271		5s. violet	85	20
272	80	10s. black and red	1·30	20
273		15s. black and blue	5·25	65
274		25s. black and mauve	7·50	85
275		50s. black and purple	34·00	1·70
276	81	1b. blue	50·00	10·50

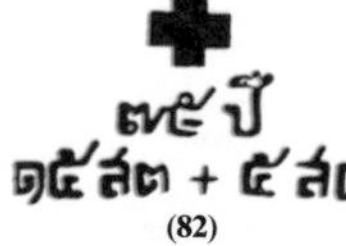

(82)

1939. Red Cross Fund. 75th Anniv of Membership of the International Red Cross. Surch as T **82**.

277	66	5+5s. on 1b. (153)	7·50	7·50
278		10+5s. on 2b. (154)	17·00	17·00
279		15+5s. on 3b. (155)	14·00	14·00

83 National Assembly Hall

1939. 7th Anniv of Constitution and National Day (1st issue).

280	83	2s. brown	2·10	65
281		3s. green	4·25	1·70
282		5s. purple	2·10	10
283		10s. red	8·50	15
284		15s. blue	21·00	65

84 Chakri Palace and "Garuda" Bird

1940. National Day (2nd issue).

285	84	2s. brown	2·10	65
286		3s. green	4·25	1·70
287		5s. purple	3·25	10
288		10s. red	12·00	10
289		15s. blue	26·00	65

85 King Ananda Mahidol

86 Ploughing Rice Field

87 Ban Pa'im Palace, Ayuthia

88 Monument of Democracy, Bangkok

1941.

290	85	2s. brown	65	20
291		3s. green	1·10	65
292		5s. violet	65	20
293		10s. red	65	20
294	86	15s. grey and blue	65	30
295		25s. orange and grey	65	30
296		50s. grey and orange	65	45
297	87	1b. grey and blue	2·50	65
298		2b. grey and red	7·50	1·30
299		3b. grey and green	13·00	3·25
300		5b. red and black	39·00	12·00
301		10b. yellow and green	55·00	34·00

1942. Air. With or without gum.

302	88	2s. brown	2·10	2·10
303		3s. green	21·00	21·00
304		5s. purple	2·10	45
305		10s. red	14·00	65
306		15s. blue	3·25	1·10

89 King Ananda Mahidol

90 Indo-China War Monument, Bangkok

91 Bangkaen Monument and Ears of Rice

1943.

307	89	1b. blue	13·00	1·10

1943.

310	90	3s. green	2·10	85

1943. 10th Anniv of Failure of 1933 Revolt.

311	91	2s. orange	1·70	1·30
312		10s. red	2·50	30

92 King Bhumibol

93

1947.

313	92	5s. violet	45	10
314		10s. red	1·10	10
315		20s. brown	3·00	10
316		50s. green	3·00	10
317		1b. blue and violet	6·50	20
318		2b. green and blue	14·00	85
319		3b. black and red	21·00	1·70
320		5b. red and green	50·00	3·25
321		10b. violet and brown	£180	1·10
322		20b. purple and black	£225	4·25

The baht values are larger, size 21½ × 27 mm.

1947. Coming of Age of King Bhumibol. With gum (10, 50s.) or without gum (others).

323	93	5s. orange	1·10	1·10
324		10s. brown	49·00	48·00
325		10s. green	1·10	1·10
326		20s. blue	4·25	1·10
327		50s. green	8·50	2·10

94 King and Palace

95 King Bhumibol

1950. King's Coronation.

328	94	5s. purple	45	20
329		10s. red	45	20
330		15s. violet	2·10	2·10
331		20s. brown	65	10
332		80s. green	5·25	2·75
333		1b. blue	1·70	20
334		2b. yellow	10·50	85
335		3b. grey	55·00	7·50

1951.

336	95	5s. purple	20	10
337		10s. green	20	10
338		15s. brown	65	10
339		20s. brown	65	10
340		25s. red	20	10
341		50s. green	65	10
342		1b. blue	85	10
343		1b.15 blue	20	10

344 1b.25 red 3·25 20
345 2b. green 3·75 20
346 3b. grey 6·50 30
347 5b. red and blue 26·00 45
348 10b. violet and brown £200 75
349 20b. green and black £180 10·50

96 U.N. Emblem

97 "Garuda" Bird

1951. United Nations Day.
350 **96** 25s. blue 2·50 2·10

1952. Air.
351 **97** 1b.50 purple 3·25 65
352 2b. blue 9·75 1·30
353 3b. grey 13·00 85

1952. United Nations Day. Optd **1952**.
354 **96** 25s. blue 1·70 1·30

1952. 20th Anniv of Constitution. Surch with Vase emblem and **+ 20** in English and Siamese.
355 **76** 80s.+20s. black and blue 14·00 10·50

99 Dancer over Cross

103 Processional Elephant

1953. 60th Anniv of Thai Red Cross Society. Cross in red, figures in blue and red.
356 **99** 25s.+25s. cream & green 4·25 3·25
357 50s.+50s. cream and pink 13·00 10·50
358 1b.+1b. cream and blue 17·00 15·00

1953. United Nations Day. Optd **1953**.
359 **96** 25s. blue 1·10 85

1954. United Nations Day. Optd **1954** vert.
360 **96** 25s. blue 3·25 2·75

1955. Optd **THAILAND** in English and Siamese.
361 **76** 5s. violet 5·25 6·50
362 10s. red 5·25 6·50

1955. Surch.
363 **92** 5s. on 20s. brown 1·30 55
364 10s. on 20s. brown 1·90 55

1955. 400th Birth Anniv of King Naresuan.
365 **103** 25s. red 1·10 10
366 80s. purple 12·00 3·25
367 1b.25 green 32·00 1·10
368 2b. blue 7·50 85
369 3b. brown 21·00 75

1955. Red Cross Fair. Optd **24 98**.
370 **99** 25s.+25s. multicoloured 17·00 10·50
371 50s.+50s. multicoloured 80·00 65·00
372 1b.+1b. red, cream and blue £120 95·00

105 Tao Suranari

106 Equestrian Statue

1955. Tao Suranari Commemoration.
373 **105** 10s. lilac 1·30 30
374 25s. green 85 10
375 1b. brown 21·00 1·70

1955. King Taksin Commemoration.
376 **106** 5s. blue 65 30
377 25s. green 6·75 10
378 1b.25 red 18·00 1·80

1955. U.N. Day. Optd **1955** vert.
379 **96** 25s. blue 3·25 2·75

107 Don Chedi Pagoda

108 Dharmachakra and Sambar

1956.
380 **107** 10s. green 2·10 2·10
381 50s. brown 10·50 85
382 75s. violet 3·25 65
383 1b.50 brown 13·00 1·10

1956. United Nations Day. Optd **1956** vert.
384 **96** 25s. blue 1·10 1·10

1957. 2500th Anniv of Buddhist Era.
385 **108** 5s. brown 45 10
386 10s. purple 45 10
387 15s. green 1·10 85
388 – 20s. orange 1·10 85
389 – 25s. brown 20 10
390 – 50s. mauve 85 25
391 – 1b. brown 1·30 30
392 – 1b.25 blue 17·00 3·50
393 – 2b. purple 3·25 45
DESIGNS: 20s. to 50s. Hand of Peace and Dharmachakra; 1b. to 2b. Nakon Phatom pagoda.

110 U.N. Emblem and Laurel Sprays

111 Gateway to Grand Palace

1957. United Nations Day.
394 **110** 25s. green 55 20
395 25s. brown (1958) 55 20
400 25s. blue (1959) 65 20

1959. 1st South-East Asia Peninsula Games.
396 **111** 10s. orange 20 10
397 – 25s. red 30 10
398 – 1b.25 green 2·00 30
399 – 2b. blue 2·10 55
DESIGNS: 25s. Royal parasols; 1b.25, Bowman; 2b. Wat Arun (temple) and prow of royal barge.

112 Pagoda

113 Wat Arun Temple

1960. World Refugee Year.
401 **112** 50s. brown 20 10
402 2b. green 1·10 65

1960. Leprosy Relief Campaign.
403 **113** 50s. red 20 10
404 2b. blue 1·90 65

114 Indian Elephant

115 S.E.A.T.O. Emblem

1960. 5th World Forestry Congress, Seattle.
405 **114** 25s. green 55 10

1960. S.E.A.T.O. Day.
406 **115** 50s. brown 65 10

116 Siamese Child

117 Letter-writing

1960. Children's Day.
407 **116** 50s. mauve 45 10
408 1b. brown 3·50 65

1960. International Correspondence Week.
409 **117** 50s. mauve 45 10
410 2b. blue 1·90 65

118 U.N. Emblem and Globe

119 King Bhumibol

1960. United Nations Day.
411 **118** 50s. violet 55 20
446 50s. red (1961) 45 20
467 50s. red (1962) 45 20

1961.
422 **119** 5s. purple 10 10
423 10s. green 10 10
424 15s. brown 20 10
425 20s. brown 10 10
426 25s. red 20 10
427 50s. green 20 10
428 80s. orange 1·10 60
429 1b. brown and blue 75 10
430 1b.25 green and red 2·10 75
431 1b.50 green and violet 65 20
432 2b. violet and red 85 10
433 3b. blue and brown 2·10 20
434 4b. black and bistre 2·10 85
435 5b. green and blue 9·75 25
436 10b. black and red 50·00 45
437 20b. blue and green 43·00 2·10
438 25b. blue and green 14·00 1·10
439 40b. black and yellow 43·00 2·50

120 Children in Garden

1961. Children's Day.
440 **120** 20s. blue 45 20
441 2b. violet 2·50 65

121 Pen, Letters and Globe

122 Thai Scout Badge and Saluting Hand

1961. International Correspondence Week.
442 – 25s. myrtle 45 10
443 – 50s. purple 20 10
444 **121** 1b. red 1·30 45
445 2b. blue 1·90 55
DESIGN: 25s., 50s. Pen, and world map on envelope.

1961. 50th Anniv of Thai Scout Movement.
447 **122** 50s. red 20 10
448 – 1b. green 1·10 45
449 – 2b. blue 1·30 55
DESIGNS—VERT: 1b. Scout camp and scout saluting flag; 2b. King Vajiravudh in uniform, and scout, cub and guide marching.

123 Campaign Emblem and Temple

124 Bangkok

1962. Malaria Eradication.
450 **123** 5s. brown 20 10
451 10s. brown 20 10
452 20s. blue 20 10
453 50s. red 20 10
454 – 1b. green 85 15
455 – 1b.50 purple 1·50 55
456 – 2b. blue 1·10 20
457 – 3b. violet 3·25 1·90
DESIGN: 1b. to 3b. Hanuman fighting mosquitoes.

1962. "Century 21" Exhibition, Seattle.
458 **124** 50s. purple 45 10
459 2b. blue 3·75 65

125 Thai Child with Doll

126 Correspondence Symbols

127 Exhibition Emblem

1962. Children's Day.
460 **125** 25s. green 45 20
461 50s. brown 45 10
462 2b. mauve 3·75 65

1962. International Correspondence Week.
463 **126** 25s. violet 45 20
464 50s. red 45 10
465 – 1b. bistre 2·10 45
466 – 2b. green 3·75 55
DESIGN: 1, 2b. Quill pen.

1962. Students' Exhibition, Bangkok.
468 **127** 50s. bistre 65 10

128 Harvesting

1963. Freedom from Hunger.
469 **128** 20s. green 75 20
470 50s. brown 55 10

129 "Temple Guardian"

130 Centenary Emblem

1963. 1st Anniv of Asian–Oceanic Postal Union.
471 **129** 50s. green and brown 55 10

1963. Red Cross Centenary.
472 **130** 50s.+10s. red and grey 20 10
473 – 50s.+10s. red and grey 20 10
DESIGN: No. 473, As Type **130**, but with positions of emblem and inscriptions reversed.

131 G.P.O. Bangkok and (inset) old P.O.

1963. 80th Anniv of Post and Telegraph Department.
474 **131** 50s. green, orange and violet 45 10
475 3b. brown, green and red 4·75 1·20

132 King Bhumibol

133 Children with Dolls

1963.
476 **132** 5s. mauve 10 10
477 10s. green 10 10
478 15s. brown 10 10
479 20s. brown 10 10
480 25s. red 10 10
481 50s. green 10 10
482 75s. lilac 20 10
483 80s. orange 65 35
484 1b. brown and blue 65 20
485 1b.25 bistre and brown 3·25 85
486 1b.50 green and violet 65 45
487 2b. violet and red 45 10
488 3b. blue and brown 1·10 15
489 4b. black and bistre 1·30 20
490 5b. green and blue 7·50 20
491 10b. black and red 13·00 45
492 20b. blue and green 75·00 2·75
493 25b. blue and green 5·25 45
494 40b. black and yellow 75·00 3·50

1963. Children's Day.
505 **133** 50s. red 45 10
506 2b. blue 3·75 55

134 "Garuda" Bird with Scroll in Beak

1963. International Correspondence Week.
507 **134** 50s. purple and turquoise 65 10
508 1b. purple and green 3·25 55
509 – 2b. blue and brown 18·00 65
510 – 3b. green and brown 6·75 1·90
DESIGN: 2b., 3b. Thai women writing letters.

135 U.N. Emblem

137 Mother and Child

136 King Bhumibol

1963. United Nations Day.
511 **135** 50s. blue 45 10

1963. King Bhumibol's 36th Birthday.
512 **136** 1b.50 indigo, yellow & bl 2·10 45
513 5b. blue, yellow & mauve 14·00 2·10

1964. 17th Anniv of U.N.I.C.E.F.
514 **137** 50s. blue 45 10
515 2b. green . . . . 3·50 55

138 "Hand" of Flags, Pigeon and Globe

1964. International Correspondence Week.
516 **138** 50s. mauve and green . . 20 10
517 – 1b. brown and green . . . 3·25 55
518 – 2b. violet and yellow . . 8·25 65
519 – 3b. brown and blue . . . 4·50 1·70
DESIGNS: 1b. Thai girls and map; 2b. Map, pen and pencil; 3b. Hand with quill pen, and globe.

139 Globe and U.N. Emblem

140 King Bhumibol and Queen Sirikit

1964. United Nations Day.
520 **139** 50s. grey 75 10

1965. 15th Royal Wedding Anniv.
521 **140** 2b. multicoloured . . . . 8·50 20
522 5b. multicoloured . . . . 17·00 1·90

141 I.T.U. Emblem and Symbols

1965. I.T.U. Centenary.
523 **141** 1b. green . . . . 3·25 30

142 Goddess, Letters and Globes

1965. International Correspondence Week. Mult.
524 50s. Type **142** 20 10
525 1b. Type **142** . . . . 1·90 45
526 2b. Handclasp, letters and world map . . . . 7·50 45
527 3b. As 2b. . . . . 12·00 2·50

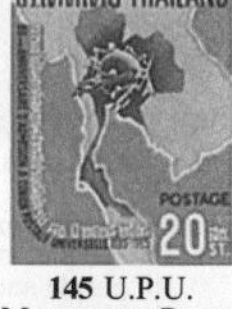

143 Grand Palace, Bangkok

145 U.P.U. Monument, Berne, and Map of Thailand

1965. International Co-operation Year and 20th Anniv of United Nations.
528 **143** 50s. lt blue, yellow & blue 85 10

1965. 80th Anniv of Thailand's Admission to Universal Postal Union.
529 **145** 20s. blue and mauve . . . 20 10
530 50s. black and blue . . . 65 20
531 1b. brown and blue . . . 3·50 55
532 3b. green and brown . . . 7·50 1·70

146 Child and Lotus

1965. Children's Day.
533 **146** 50s. brown and black . . 20 10
534 – 1b. green and black . . . 2·40 65
DESIGN: 1b. Child mounting stairs.

147 Cycling

1966. Publicity for 5th Asian Games, Bangkok.
535 20s. red (Type **147**) 45 10
536 25s. violet (Tennis) 65 20
537 50s. red (Running) 45 10
538 1b. blue (Weightlifting) . . . 1·70 55
539 1b.25 black (Boxing) . . . . 2·50 2·10
540 2b. blue (Swimming) . . . . 5·00 45
541 3b. brown (Basketball) . . . 9·75 3·00
542 5b. purple (Football) . . . . 27·00 9·75
See also Nos. 553/6.

148 Emblem and Fair Buildings

1966. 1st International Trade Fair, Bangkok.
543 **148** 50s. purple 85 45
544 1b. brown . . . . 1·70 65

149 "Reading and Writing"

1966. International Correspondence Week.
545 – 50s. red 20 10
546 – 1b. brown . . . . 1·50 45
547 **149** 2b. violet . . . . 7·50 45
548 3b. green . . . . 4·75 1·60
DESIGN: 50s., 1b. "Map" envelope representing the five continents and pen.

150 U.N. Emblem

151 Pra Buddha Bata (monastery)

1966. United Nations Day.
549 **150** 50s. blue 65 10

1966. 20th Anniv of U.N.E.S.C.O.
550 **151** 50s. green and black . . . 45 10

152 "Goddess of Rice"

1966. International Rice Year.
551 **152** 50s. blue and green . . . 1·10 65
552 3b. red and purple . . . 10·50 3·00

153 Thai Boxing

1966. 5th Asian Games, Bangkok. Each black, red and brown.
553 50s. Type **153** 65 10
554 1b. Takraw (ball game) . . . 2·50 95
555 2b. "Kite fighting" . . . . . 14·00 2·10
556 3b. "Cudgel play" . . . . . 13·00 7·50

154 Chevron Snakehead

1967. Fishes. Multicoloured.
557 1b. Type **154** . . . . 3·25 1·10
558 2b. Short mackerel . . . . . 16·00 1·70
559 3b. Siamese barb . . . . . . 7·50 4·25
560 5b. Siamese fighting fish . . . 9·75 4·75
The 2 and 3b. are size 45×26 mm.

155 Djarmachakra and Globe

1967. Establishment of Buddhist World Fellowship Headquarters in Thailand.
561 **155** 2b. black and yellow . . . 3·50 55

156 Great Indian Hornbill

157 "Vandopsis parishii"

1967. Birds. Multicoloured.
562 20s. Type **156** 45 45
563 25s. Southern grackle ("Talking Myna") 65 65
564 50s. White-rumped shama . . 1·10 20
565 1b. Siamese fireback pheasant ("Diard's Fireback Pheasant") . . . . 2·75 85
566 1b.50 Spotted-necked dove . . 2·75 1·10
567 2b. Sarus crane . . . . . . 14·00 1·10
568 3b. White-throated kingfisher ("White-breasted Kingfisher") . . . . 7·50 5·25
569 5b. Asian open-bill stork ("Open-billed Storks") . . 14·00 5·25

1967. Thai Orchids. Multicoloured.
570 20s. Type **157** 45 30
571 50s. "Ascocentrum curvifolium" 65 20
572 80s. "Rhynchostylis retusa" 1·10 95
573 1b. "Rhynchostylis gigantea" 3·25 85
574 1b.50 "Dendrobium alconeri" 2·10 85
575 2b. "Paphiopedilum callosum" . . . . 12·00 1·10
576 3b. "Dendrobium formosum" 7·50 5·25
577 5b. "Dendrobium primulinum" . . . . . . 12·00 4·25

158 Thai House

1967. Thai Architecture.
578 **158** 50s. violet and blue . . . 1·10 45
579 – 1b.50 chestnut and brown 3·25 1·70
580 – 2b. blue and turquoise . . 13·00 1·70
581 – 3b. brown and yellow . . 8·50 5·75
BUILDINGS: 1b.50, Pagodas; 2b. Temple bell-tower; 3b. Temple.

159 "Sri Suphanahong" (royal barge) and Palace

1967. International Tourist Year.
582 **159** 2b. brown and blue . . . 3·75 85

160 Dove, Globe, People and Letters

1967. International Correspondence Week.
583 **160** 50s. multicoloured 45 15
584 1b. multicoloured . . . . 1·70 45
585 – 2b. black and green . . . 4·25 55
586 – 3b. black and brown . . . 6·50 2·10
DESIGNS: 2, 3b. Handclasp, globe and doves.

161 U.N. Emblem

1967. United Nations Day.
587 **161** 50s. multicoloured 45 10

162 National Flag

1967. 50th Anniv of Thai National Flag.
588 **162** 50s. red, blue & turquoise 45 10
589 2b. red, blue and green 4·75 85

163 Elephant carrying Teak Log

1968. Export Promotion.
590 **163** 2b. brown and red . . . 3·25 45
See also Nos. 630, 655 and 673.

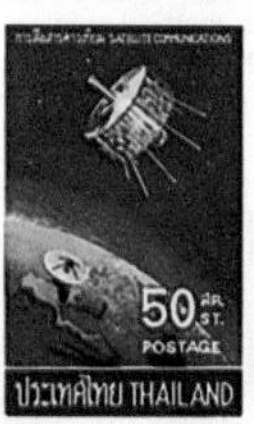

164 Satellite and Thai Tracking Station

1968. "Satellite Communications".
591 **164** 50s. multicoloured 20 10
592 3b. multicoloured . . . . 3·00 1·20

165 "Goddess of the Earth"

1968. International Hydrological Decade.
593 **165** 50s. multicoloured 55 10

166 Snakeskin Gourami

1968. Thai Fishes. Multicoloured.
594 10s. Type **166** 20 10
595 20s. Red-tailed black shark 20 10
596 25s. Thai mahseer 45 20
597 50s. Giant pangasius 65 10
598 80s. Bumblebee catfish 1·70 95
599 1b.25 Rambaia goby 3·25 2·10
600 1b.50 Giant carp 10·50 1·70
601 4b. Clown knifefish 26·00 10·50

167 Blue Peacock

1968. Thai Butterflies. Multicoloured.
602 50s. Type **167** 65 20
603 1b. Golden birdwing 3·75 85
604 3b. Great mormon 12·00 4·25
605 4b. "Papilio palinurus" 16·00 6·50

168 Queen Sirikit

1968. Queen Sirikit's "Third Cycle" Anniversary. Designs showing Queen Sirikit in different Thai costumes.
606 **168** 50s. multicoloured 45 10
607 – 2b. multicoloured 1·70 75
608 – 3b. multicoloured 4·25 2·10
609 – 5b. multicoloured 8·50 2·40

169 W.H.O. Emblem and Medical Equipment

1968. 20th Anniv of W.H.O.
610 **169** 50s. black and green 45 10

170 Globe, Letter and Pen

1968. International Correspondence Week. Mult.
611 50s. Type **170** 20 10
612 1b. Globe on pen nib 85 20
613 2b. Type **170** 2·10 30
614 3b. Globe on pen nib 4·25 1·50

171 U.N. Emblem and Flags

173 King Rama II

172 Human Rights Emblem and Sculpture

1968. United Nations Day.
615 **171** 50s. multicoloured 45 10

1968. 20th Anniv of Human Rights Year.
616 **172** 50s. violet, red and green 55 10

1968. Birth Bicentenary of King Rama II.
617 **173** 50s. yellow and brown 65 10

174 National Assembly Building

1969. First Election Day under New Constitution.
618 **174** 50s. multicoloured 45 10
619 2b. multicoloured 2·75 65

175 I.L.O. Emblem within Cogwheels

1969. 50th Anniv of I.L.O.
620 **175** 50s. blue, black and violet 30 10

176 Ramwong Dance

1969. Thai Classical Dances. Multicoloured.
621 50s. Type **176** 20 10
622 1b. Candle dance 85 45
623 2b. Krathop Mai dance 1·90 30
624 3b. Nohra dance 3·25 1·30

177 "Letters by Post"

1969. International Correspondence Week. Mult.
625 50s. Type **177** 20 10
626 1b. Type **177** 65 20
627 2b. Writing and posting a letter 1·30 30
628 3b. As 2b. 2·10 75

178 Globe in Hand

1969. United Nations Day.
629 **178** 50s. multicoloured 30 10

179 Tin Mine

1969. Export Promotion and 2nd Technical Conf of the International Tin Council, Bangkok.
630 **179** 2b. blue, brown and light blue 2·50 20

180 Loy Krathong Festival

1969. Thai Ceremonies and Festivals. Multicoloured.
631 50s. Type **180** 20 10
632 1b. Marriage ceremony 65 20
633 2b. Khwan ceremony 85 30
634 5b. Songkran festival 3·00 95

181 Breguet 14 Mail Plane

1969. 50th Anniv of Thai Airmail Services.
635 **181** 1b. brown, green and blue 85 20

182 "Phra Rama"

1969. Nang Yai Shadow Theatre. Multicoloured.
636 50s. Type **182** 20 10
637 2b. "Ramasura" 2·10 20
638 3b. "Mekhala" 1·70 75
639 5b. "Ongkhot" 2·40 85

183 "Improvement of Productivity"

1969. Productivity Year.
640 **183** 50s. multicoloured 30 10

184 Thai Temples within I.C.W. Emblem

1970. 19th Triennial Conference of International Council of Women, Bangkok.
641 **184** 50s. black and blue 45 10

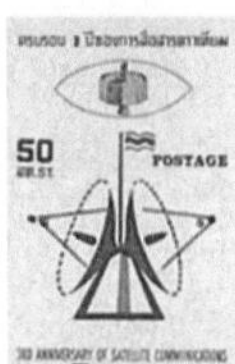

185 Dish Aerials

1970. 3rd Anniv of Thai Satellite Communications.
642 **185** 50s. multicoloured 30 10

186 Households and Data

1970. 7th Population Census.
643 **186** 1b. multicoloured 45 10

187 New Headquarters Building

1970. Inauguration of New U.P.U. Headquarters Building, Berne.
644 **187** 50s. black, green and blue 30 10

188 Khun Ram Kamhang as Teacher

1970. International Education Year.
645 **188** 50s. multicoloured 55 20

189 Swimming Stadium

1970. 6th Asian Games, Bangkok.
646 **189** 50s. lilac, red and yellow 30 10
647 – 1b.50 green, red and blue 75 30
648 – 3b. black, red and bronze 1·10 45
649 – 5b. blue, red and green 2·10 65
STADIUMS: 1b.50, Velodrome; 3b. Subhajala-saya Stadium; 5b. Kittikachorn Indoor Stadium.
See also No. 660.

190 Boy and Girl writing Letter

1970. International Correspondence Week. Mult.
650 50s. Type **190** 20 10
651 1b. Woman writing letter 55 20
652 2b. Women reading letters 1·30 20
653 3b. Man reading letter 1·80 75
See also Nos. 683/6.

191 U.N. Emblem and Royal Palace, Bangkok

194 King Bhumibol lighting Flame

193 The Heroes of Bangrachan

1970. 25th Anniv of United Nations.
654 **191** 50s. multicoloured 65 10

1970. Export Promotion. As T **163**.
655 2b. brown, red and green 1·70 20
DESIGN: 2b. Rubber plantation.

1970. Heroes and Heroines of Thai History.
656 **193** 50s. violet and red 20 10
657 – 1b. purple and violet 45 45
658 – 2b. brown and mauve 2·10 55
659 – 3b. green and blue 1·70 65
DESIGNS: 1b. Heroines Thao Thepkrasatri and Thao Srisunthorn on ramparts; 2b. Queen Suriyothai riding elephant; 3b. Phraya Phichaidaphak and battle scene.

1970. Inaug of 6th Asian Games, Bangkok.
660 **194** 1b. multicoloured 65 10

195 Woman playing So Sam Sai

1970. Classical Thai Musical Instruments. Mult.
661 50s. Type **195** 30 10
662 2b. Khlui phiang-o (flute) 75 20
663 3b. Krachappi (guitar) 1·70 45
664 5b. Thon rammana (drums) 3·25 75

196 Chocolate-point Siamese

1971. Siamese Cats. Multicoloured.
665 50s. Type **196** 20 10
666 1b. Blue-point cat 1·50 45
667 2b. Seal-point cat 2·50 45
668 3b. Pure white cat and kittens 3·75 1·60

197 Pagoda, Nakhon Si Thammarat

1971. Buddhist Holy Places in Thailand. Pagodas.
669 **197** 50s. black, brown and mauve 30 10
670 – 1b. brown, violet and green 55 20
671 – 3b. sepia, brown & orange 1·30 30
672 – 4b. brown, sepia and blue 2·50 1·50
DESIGNS: 1b. Nakhon Phanom; 3b. Nakhon Pathom; 4b. Chiang Mai.

1971. Export Promotion. As T **163**.
673 2b. multicoloured . . . . . 1·30 20
DESIGN: 2b. Corncob and field.

199 Buddha's Birthplace, Lumbini, Nepal

1971. 20th Anniv of World Fellowship of Buddhists.
674 **199** 50s. black and blue . . . 30 10
675 – 1b. black and green . . . 75 30
676 – 2b. black and brown . . . 1·70 45
677 – 3b. black and red . . . . 1·70 85
DESIGNS: 1b. "Place of Enlightenment", Buddha Gaya, Bihar; 2b. "Place of First Sermon", Sarnath, Banaras; 3b. "Place of Final Passing Away", Kusinara.

200 King Bhumibol and Thai People
201 Floating Market, Wat Sai

1971. 25th Anniv of Coronation.
678 **200** 50s. multicoloured 65 10

1971. Visit ASEAN Year.
679 **201** 4b. multicoloured . . . . 1·30 30
ASEAN = Association of South East Asian Nations.

202 King and Queen in Scout Uniform

1971. 60th Anniv of Thai Boy Scout Movement.
680 **202** 50c. black, red and yellow 65 10

1971. "THAILANDPEX 71" National Stamp Exhibition, Bangkok. Optd **4-8 AUGUST 1971 THAILANDPEX'71** in English and Thai and map within "perforations", covering four stamps.
681 **119** 80s. orange . . . . 3·25 2·10
682 **132** 80s. orange . . . . 3·25 2·10
Prices are for blocks of four stamps showing the entire overprint.

1971. International Correspondence Week. As T **190**. Multicoloured.
683 50s. Two girls writing a letter 20 10
684 1b. Two girls reading letters 45 20
685 2b. Women with letter on veranda . . . . 1·10 20
686 3b. Man handing letter to woman . . . . 2·10 75

205 Marble Temple, Bangkok

1971. United Nations Day.
687 **205** 50s. multicoloured 45 10

206 Raising Ducks

1971. Rural Life. Multicoloured.
688 50s. Type **206** 20 10
689 1b. Growing tobacco seedlings 65 30
690 2b. Cooping fish . . . . . . 1·10 20
691 3b. Cleaning rice-seed . . . . 1·90 65

207 Mother and Child

1971. 25th Anniv of U.N.I.C.E.F.
692 **207** 50s. multicoloured 30 10

208 Costumes from Chiang Saen Period (17th-century)

1972. Historical Costumes. Multicoloured.
693 50s. Type **208** 20 10
694 1b. Sukhothai period (13th–14th centuries) 65 20
695 1b.50 Ayudhya period (14th–17th centuries) . . . . . . 1·30 45
696 2b. Bangkok period (18th–19th centuries) . . . . . . 2·10 45

209 Globe and A.O.P.U. Emblem

1972. 10th Anniv of Asian–Oceanic Postal Union.
697 **209** 75s. blue 30 10

210 King Bhumibol

1972.

698	**210**	10s. green	10	10
699		20s. blue	10	10
700		25s. red	10	10
701		50s. green	15	10
702		75s. lilac	10	10
703		1b.25 pink and green . .	45	15
704		2b. violet and red . . .	45	10
705		2b.75 turquoise and purple	45	10
706		3b. blue and brown . .	1·70	15
707		4b. red and blue	65	15
708		5b. brown and violet . .	65	10
709		6b. violet and green . .	1·70	15
710		10b. black and red . . .	95	10
711		20b. green and orange .	2·10	20
898d		40b. violet and brown	3·25	55
712a		50b. green and purple	21·00	95
713		100b. blue and orange	37·00	1·80

211 Two Women, Iko Tribe

1972. Hill Tribes of Thailand. Multicoloured.
714 50s. Type **211** 20 10
715 2b. Musician and children, Musoe tribe 85 20
716 4b. Woman embroidering, Yao tribe . . . . 3·75 2·10
717 5b. Woman with chickens, Maeo tribe . . . . 4·75 55

212 Ruby

1972. Precious Stones.
718 **212** 75s. multicoloured 20 10
719 – 2b. multicoloured . . . . 3·50 55
720 – 4b. black and green . . . 6·50 2·40
721 – 6b. brown, black and red 6·00 2·10
DESIGNS: 2b. Yellow sapphire; 4b. Zircon; 6b. Star sapphire.

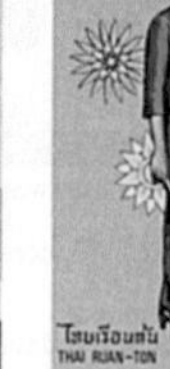

213 Prince Vajiralongkorn
214 Thai Ruan-ton Costume

1972. Prince Vajiralongkorn's 20th Birthday.
722 **213** 75s. multicoloured 45 10

1972. Thai Women's National Costumes. Mult.
723 75s. Type **214** 20 10
724 2b. Thai Chitrlada 45 20
725 4b. Thai Chakri . . . . . . 2·10 1·80
726 5b. Thai Borompimarn . . . 2·75 45
MS727 120 × 160 mm. Nos. 723/6 (sold at 20b.) . . . . 21·00 17·00

215 Rambutan

1972. Thai Fruits. Multicoloured.
728 75s. Type **215** 20 10
729 1b. Mangosteen 85 45
730 3b. Durian . . . . 2·10 75
731 5b. Mango . . . . 7·50 1·30

216 Princess-Mother with Old People

1972. Princess-Mother Sisangwan's 72nd Birthday.
732 **216** 75s. green and orange . . 1·70 20

217 Lod Cave, Phangnga

1972. International Correspondence Week. Mult.
733 75s. Type **217** 20 10
734 1b.25 Kang Kracharn Reservoir, Petchaburi . . 65 45
735 2b.75 Erawan Waterfall, Kanchanaburi . . . . . . 3·50 20
736 3b. Nok-kaw Mountain, Loei 2·50 75

218 Globe on U.N. Emblem
220 Crown Prince Vajiralongkorn

219 Watphrajetubon Vimolmanklaram Rajvaramahaviharn (ancient university)

1972. 25th Anniv of E.C.A.F.E.
737 **218** 75s. multicoloured 30 10

1972. International Book Year.
738 **219** 75s. multicoloured 30 10

1972. Investiture of Crown Prince.
739 **220** 2b. multicoloured 85 20

221 Servicemen and Flag

1973. 25th Anniv of Veterans' Day.
740 **221** 75s. multicoloured 30 10

1973. Red Cross Fair (1972). Nos. 472/3 surch **75+25 2515 1972.**
741 **130** 75s.+25s. on 50s.+10s. 65 55
742 – 75s.+25s. on 50s.+10s. 65 55

223 Emblem, Bank and Coin-box

1973. 60th Anniv of Government Savings Bank.
743 **223** 75s. multicoloured 30 10

224 "Celestial Being" and Emblem

1973. 25th Anniv of W.H.O.
744 **224** 75s. multicoloured 30 10

225 "Nymphaea pubescens"

1973. Lotus Flowers. Multicoloured.
745 75s. Type **225** 20 10
746 1b.50 "Nymphaea pubescens" (different) 65 30
747 2b. "Nelumbo nucifera" . . . 1·90 30
748 4b. "Nelumbo nucifera" (different) . . . . 4·75 1·80

227 King Bhumibol

1973.
749 **227** 5s. purple 20 10
1031 20s. blue 20 10
1031a 25s. red 20 10

1032	50s. green	1·10	10
1032a	75s. violet	20	10
753	5b. brown and violet	3·50	50
754	6b. violet and green	2·10	55
755	10b. brown and red	6·50	65
755a	20b. green and orange	65·00	5·50

228 Silverware

1973. Thai Handicrafts. Multicoloured.

756	75s. Type **228**	20	10
757	2b.75 Lacquerware	85	20
758	4b. Pottery	3·50	1·40
759	5b. Paper umbrellas	3·00	65

229 King Janaka's Procession

1973. "Ramayana" Mural, Temple of Emerald Buddha, Bangkok. Multicoloured.

760	25s. Type **229**	20	10
761	75s. Contest for Sita's hand	20	10
762	1b.50 Monkey prince toppling portico	1·30	1·10
763	2b. Monkey king breaking umbrella	2·10	1·10
764	2b.75 Maleenarj as Court chief	1·50	30
765	3b. Sprinkling holy water	5·25	1·60
766	5b. Tapansura fighting Rama	8·50	4·25
767	6b. Bharata on march	2·10	1·10

230 "Postal Services"

1973. 90th Anniv of Thai Post and Telegraph Department. Multicoloured.

768	75s. Type **230**	20	10
769	2b. "Telecommunication Services"	1·10	45

231 1 Solot Stamp of 1883

1973. "THAIPEX 73" National Stamp Exn.

770	**231** 75s. blue and red	20	10
771	– 1b.25 red and blue	1·10	55
772	– 1b.50 purple and green	2·10	65
773	– 2b. green and orange	2·50	65
MS774	191×97 mm. Nos. 770/3. Imperf (sold at 8b.)	8·50	7·50

DESIGNS: 1b.25, 6s. stamp of 1912; 1b.50, 5s. stamp of 1928; 2b. 3s. stamp of 1941.

232 Interpol Emblem

1973. 50th Anniv of International Criminal Police Organization (Interpol).

775	**232** 75s. multicoloured	30	10

233 "Lilid Pralaw"

1973. Int Correspondence Week. Characters from Thai Literature. Multicoloured.

776	75s. Type **233**	20	10
777	1b.50 "Khun Chang Khun Phan"	85	45
778	2b. "Sang Thong"	2·10	65
779	5b. "Pha Apai Manee"	4·25	95
MS780	166×104 mm. Nos. 776/9 (sold at 15b.)	17·00	16·00

234 Wat Suan Dok Temple, Chiangmai

1973. United Nations Day.

781	**234** 75s. multicoloured	45	10

235 Schomburgk's Deer

1973. Protected Wild Animals. Multicoloured.

782	20s. Type **235**	20	20
783	25s. Kouprey	20	20
784	75r. Common gorals	65	20
785	1b.25 Water buffaloes	65	65
786	1b.50 Javan rhinoceros	2·50	1·70
787	2b. Thamin	7·50	1·70
788	2b.75 Sumatran rhinoceros	3·75	65
789	4b. Mainland serows	4·75	4·25

236 Flame Emblem

1973. 25th Anniv of Declaration of Human Rights.

790	**236** 75s. multicoloured	65	10

238 Children within Flowers

241 "Pha la Phiang Lai"

240 Statue of Krom Luang Songkia Nakarin

1973. Children's Day.

791	**238** 75s. multicoloured	65	10

1974. Red Cross Fair. Nos. 472/3 surch **75+25 1973** in English and Thai.

792	**130** 75s.+25s. on 50s.+10s.	30	30
793	– 75s.+25s. on 50s.+10s.	30	30

1974. 84th Anniv of Siriraj Hospital.

794	**240** 75s. multicoloured	45	10

1974. Thai Classical Dance. Multicoloured.

795	75s. Type **241**	20	10
796	2b.75 "Phra Lak Phlaeng Rit"	1·10	20
797	4b. "Chin Sao Sai"	2·75	1·30
798	5b. "Charot Phra Sumen"	2·75	55

242 World's Largest Teak, Amphur Nam-Pad

1974. 15th Anniv of Arbor Day.

799	**242** 75s. multicoloured	30	10

243 "Increasing Population"

1974. World Population Year.

800	**243** 75s. multicoloured	30	10

244 Royal Chariot

1974. Centenary of National Museum. Mult.

801	75s. Type **244**	20	20
802	2b. Ban Chiang painted pottery vase	85	45
803	2b.75 Avalokitesavara Bodhisattva statue	1·70	30
804	3b. King Mongkut Rama IV	1·90	55

Nos. 802/4 have the face values incorrectly shown as "BATH".

245 "Cassia fistula"

1974. International Correspondence Week. Tropical Plants. Multicoloured.

805	75s. Type **245**	20	10
806	2b.75 "Butea superba"	65	20
807	3b. "Jasminum sambac"	2·50	45
808	4b. "Lagerstroemia speciosa"	1·30	95
MS809	169×100 mm. Nos. 805/8 (sold at 15b.)	15·00	13·00

246 "UPU 100"

1974. Centenary of U.P.U.

810	**246** 75s. multicoloured	30	10

247 Wat Suthat Thepvararam

1974. United Nations Day.

811	**247** 75s. multicoloured	30	10

248 Elephant Round-up

1974. Tourism.

812	**248** 4b. multicoloured	1·70	65

249 "Vanda coerulea"

1974. Thai Orchids (1st series). Multicoloured.

813	75s. Type **249**	20	10
814	2b.75 "Dendrobium aggregatum"	85	20
815	3b. "Dendrobium scabrilingue"	2·40	65
816	4b. "Aerides falcata" var "houlletiana"	1·30	85
MS817	138×105 mm. Nos. 813/16 (sold at 15b.)	21·00	17·00

See also Nos. 847/**MS**851.

250 Boy riding Toy Horse

1974. Children's Day.

818	**250** 75c. multicoloured	65	10

252 Democracy Monument

1975. Democratic Institutions Campaign. Mult.

819	75s. Type **252**	20	10
820	2b. "Rights and Liberties"	75	30
821	2b.75 "Freedom to choose work"	1·60	20
822	5b. Top of monument and text	2·10	65

1975. Red Cross Fair 1974. Nos. 472/3 surch **1974 75+25** in English and Thai.

823	**130** 75s.+25s. on 50s.+10s. red and grey	65	45
824	– 75s.+25s. on 50s.+10s. red and grey	65	45

254 Marbled Cat

1975. Protected Wild Animals (1st series). Mult.

825	20s. Type **254**	20	10
826	75s. Gaur	65	10
827	2b.75 Indian elephant	4·75	65
828	3b. Clouded leopard	3·00	1·30

See Nos. 913/16.

255 White-eyed River Martin

1975. Thailand Birds. Multicoloured.

829	75s. Type **255**	30	10
830	2b. Asiatic paradise fly catcher	1·50	65
831	2b.75 Long-tailed broadbill	1·70	30
832	5b. Sultan tit	3·75	1·10

256 King Bhumibol and Queen Sirikit

1975. Silver Wedding of King Bhumibol and Queen Sirikit. Multicoloured.

833	75s. Type **256**	45	10
834	3b. As Type **256**, but different background	1·30	20

257 "Roundhouse Kick"

1975. Thai Boxing. Multicoloured.

835	75s. Type **257**	30	10
836	2b.75 "Reverse elbow"	1·40	30

837 3b. "Flying knee" . . . . . 1·70 85
838 5b. "Ritual homage" . . . . 5·25 1·30

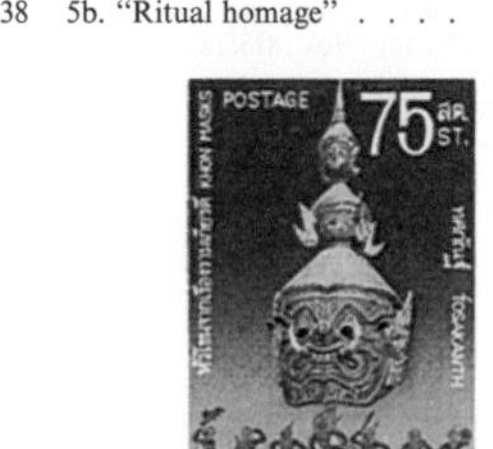
258 Toskanth

1975. Thai Culture. Masks. Multicoloured.
839 75s. Type **258** 30 10
840 2b. Kumbhakarn . . . . . . 1·80 30
841 3b. Rama . . . . 2·40 65
842 4b. Hanuman . . . . 6·50 2·10

259 "Thaipex 75" Emblem

1975. "Thaipex 75" National Stamp Exhibition, Bangkok. Multicoloured.
843 75s. Type **259** 30 10
844 2b.75 Stamp designer 95 20
845 4b. Stamp printing works . . 1·30 85
846 5b. "Stamp collecting" . . . 1·70 45

1975. Thai Orchids (2nd series). As T **249**. Multicoloured.
847 75s. "Dendrobium cruentum" 30 10
848 2b. "Dendrobium parishii" 75 30
849 2b.75 "Vanda teres" . . . . 1·10 30
850 5b. "Vanda denisoniana" . . 2·50 75
MS851 138 × 105 mm. Nos. 847/50 19·00 16·00

260 Green Mussel

1975. Sea Shells. Multicoloured.
852 75s. Type **260** 85 65
853 1b. Great green turban . . . 65 10
854 2b.75 "Oliva mustelina" . . . 2·40 55
855 5b. Money cowrie . . . . . 6·00 1·90

261 Yachting

1975. 8th South-East Asian Peninsula Games, Bangkok (1st issue).
856 **261** 75s. black and blue . . . 20 10
857 – 1b.25 black and mauve 65 30
858 – 1b.50 black and red . . . 1·50 65
859 – 2b. black and green . . . 1·90 65
MS860 118 × 133 mm. Nos. 856/9 16·00 13·00
DESIGNS: 1b.25, Badminton; 1b.50, Volleyball; 2b. Rifle and pistol shooting.
See also Nos. 878/**MS**882.

262 Pataya Beach

1975. International Correspondence Week. Mult.
861 75s. Type **262** 30 10
862 2b. Samila Beach 95 55
863 3b. Prachuap Bay . . . . . 1·90 30
864 5b. Laem Singha Bay . . . . 2·10 75

263 Children within Letters "U N"

1975. United Nations Day.
865 **263** 75s. multicoloured 30 10

264 Early Telegraphs

1975. Centenary of Telegraph Service. Mult.
866 75s. Type **264** 45 20
867 2b.75 Teleprinter and dish aerial 85 20

265 "Sukhrip Khrong Muang"

1975. Thai Ceremonial Barges. Multicoloured.
868 75s. Type **265** 45 10
869 1b. Royal barge "Anekchat Phuchong" . . . . 1·30 45
870 2b. Royal barge "Anantanakarat" . . . . 1·90 55
871 2b.75 "Krabi Ran Ron Rap 2·10 45
872 3b. "Asura Wayuphak" . . . 3·25 85
873 4b. "Asura Paksi" . . . . . 2·50 1·90
874 5b. Royal barge "Sri Suphanahong" . . . . . . 6·00 3·25
875 6b. "Phali Rang Thawip" . . 3·75 2·10

266 King's Cipher and Thai Crown

1975. King Bhumibol's 48th Birthday. Multicoloured.
876 75s. Type **266** 30 10
877 5b. King Bhumibol in uniform . . . . 1·80 45

267 Putting the Shot

1975. 8th South-East Asian Peninsula Games, Bangkok (2nd issue).
878 **267** 1b. black and orange . . . 30 10
879 – 2b. black and green . . . 55 65
880 – 3b. black and yellow . . . 1·30 30
881 – 4b. black and violet . . . 1·70 65
MS882 118 × 130 mm. Nos. 878/81 16·00 13·00
DESIGNS: 2b. Table tennis; 3b. Cycling; 4b. Relay-running.

268 I.W.Y. Emblem on Globe

1975. International Women's Year.
883 **268** 75s. blue, orange and black 30 10

269 Children writing

1976. Children's Day.
884 **269** 75s. multicoloured 65 10

270 "Macrobrachium rosenbergii"

1976. Thai Lobsters and Shrimps. Multicoloured.
885 75s. Type **270** 20 10
886 2b. "Penaeus merguiensis" . . 2·50 65
887 2b.75 "Panulirus ornatus" . . 1·90 20
888 5b. "Penaeus monodon" . . 6·00 1·60

1976. Red Cross Fair 1975. Nos. 472/3 surch **75+25 2518 1975.**
889 **130** 75s.+25s. on 50s.+10s. red and grey 30 30
890 – 75s.+25s. on 50s.+10s. red and grey 30 30

271 Common Gold-backed Woodpecker
272 Ben Chiang Pot

1976. Thailand Birds. Multicoloured.
891 1b. Type **271** 20 10
892 1b.50 Greater green-billed malcoha 45 30
893 3b. Long-billed scimitar babbler . . . . 3·50 1·00
894 4b. Green magpie . . . . . 1·30 50

1976. Ben Chiang Pottery.
895 **272** 1b. multicoloured 20 10
896 – 2b. milticoloured . . . . 3·25 30
897 – 3b. multicoloured . . . . 1·90 20
898 – 4b. multicoloured . . . . 2·10 1·50
DESIGNS: 2b. to 4b. Various items of pottery.

273 Postman of 1883

275 "Drug Addictions"

274 Kinnari

1976. Postmen's Uniforms. Multicoloured.
899 1b. Type **273** 20 10
900 3b. Postman of 1935 . . . . 1·30 20
901 4b. Postman of 1950 . . . . 1·70 1·30
902 5b. Postman of 1974 . . . . 3·25 55

1976. Int Correspondence Week. Deities. Mult.
903 1b. Type **274** . . . . 3·25 75
904 2b. Suphan-Mat-Cha 45 10
905 4b. Garuda 85 20
906 5b. Naga . . . . 1·50 20

1976. United Nations Day.
907 **275** 1b. multicoloured 30 10

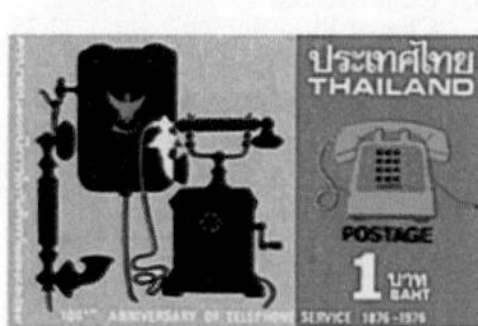
276 Early and Modern Telephones

1976. Telephone Centenary.
908 **276** 1b. multicoloured 30 10

277 Sivalaya

1976. Thai Royal Halls. Multicoloured.
909 1b. Type **277** 20 10
910 2b. Cakri . . . . 4·25 35
911 4b. Mahisra . . . . 1·90 1·10
912 5b. Dusit . . . . 2·10 65

1976. Protected Wild Animals (2nd series). As T **254**. Multicoloured.
913 1b. Bangteng . . . . 2·10 65
914 2b. Malayan tapir . . . . . 2·50 85
915 4b. Sambar 75 20
916 5b. Hog-deer 95 20

278 "From Child to Adult"

1977. Children's Day.
917 **278** 1b. multicoloured 45 10

279 Alsthom Diesel-electric Locomotive No. 4101

1977. 80th Anniv of Thai State Railway. Multicoloured.
918 1b. Type **279** 45 10
919 2b. Davenport diesel locomotive No. 577 . . . 2·00 30
920 4b. Pacific steam locomotive No. 825, Japan . . . . 5·25 3·25
921 5b. George Egestoff's steam locomotive . . . . 8·50 2·40

280 University Building

1977. 60th Anniv of Chulalongkorn University.
922 **280** 1b. multicoloured 55 10

281 Flags of A.O.P.U. Countries

1977. 15th Anniv of Asian–Oceanic Postal Union.
923 **281** 1b. multicoloured 45 10

282 Crippled Ex-Serviceman

1977. Sai-Jai-Thai Foundation Day.
924 **282** 5b. multicoloured 85 15

1977. Red Cross Fair. Nos. 472/3 surch **75+25 2520-1977.**
925 **130** 75s.+25s. on 50s.+10s. red and grey 30 30
926 – 75s.+25s. on 50s.+10s. red and grey 30 30

284 Phra Aphai Mani and Phisua Samut

1977. Puppet Shows. Multicoloured.

927 2b. Type **284** 45 10
928 3b. Rusi and Sutsakhon . . . 1·10 20
929 4b. Nang Vali and Usren . . 65 20
930 5b. Phra Aphai Mani and Nang Laweng's portrait . . 1·10 30

285 Drum Dance

1977. Thai Folk Dances. Multicoloured.

931 2b. Type **285** 30 15
932 3b. Dance of Dip-nets . . . 1·20 15
933 4b. Harvesting dance 45 20
934 5b. Kan dance 65 20

286 1b. Stamp of 1972

1977. "THAIPEX 77" National Stamp Exhibition.

935 **286** 75s. multicoloured 65 10

287 "Pla Bu Thong"

1977. International Correspondence Week. Scenes from Thai Literature. Multicoloured.

936 75s. Type **287** 65 10
937 2b. "Krai Thong" . . . . . 1·10 55
938 5b. "Nang Kaew Na Ma" . . 1·70 20
939 6b. "Pra Rot Mali" . . . . 1·90 45

288 U.N. Building, Bangkok

1977. United Nations Day.

940 **288** 75s. multicoloured 55 10

289 King Bhumibol in Scout Uniform, and Camp Fire

1977. 9th National Scout Jamboree.

941 **289** 75s. multicoloured 85 10

290 Map of A.S.E.A.N. Countries

1977. 10th Anniv of Association of South East Asian Nations.

942 **290** 5b. multicoloured 95 30

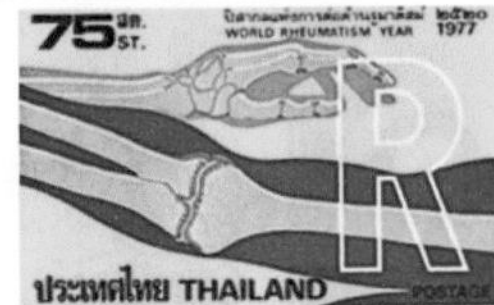

291 Elbow and Wrist Joints

1977. World Rheumatism Year.

943 **291** 75s. multicoloured 45 10

292 Children with Thai Flag

1978. Children's Day.

944 **292** 75s. multicoloured 65 10

293 "Dendrobium heterocarpum"

1978. 9th World Orchid Conference. Mult.

945 75s. Type **293** 65 45
946 1b. "Dendrobium pulchellum" . . . . 1·10 45
947 1b.50 "Doritis pulcherrima var buyssoniana" . . . . 1·50 85
948 2b. "Dendrobium hercoglossum" 45 10
949 2b.75 "Aerides odorata" . . 3·25 10
950 3b. "Trichoglottis fasciata" 45 10
951 5b. "Dendrobium wardianum" 65 20
952 6b. "Dendrobium senile" . . 65 30

294 Agricultural Scenes and Rice Production Graph

1978. Agricultural Census.

953 **294** 75s. multicoloured 20 10

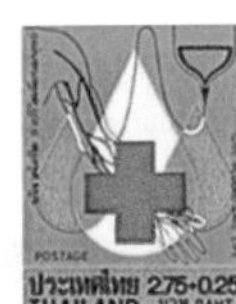

295 Blood Donation and Red Cross

1978. Red Cross.

954 **295** 2b.75+25s. multicoloured 65 65

296 Climbing Perch

1978. Fishes. Multicoloured.

955 1b. Type **296** . . . . 1·30 65
956 2b. Siamese tigerfish 30 10
957 3b. Glass catfish 55 10
958 4b. Esok 85 30

297 "Birth of Prince Siddhartha"

1978. "Buddha's Story" Mural; Puthi Savan Hall, National Museum. Multicoloured.

959 2b. Type **297** 45 20
960 3b. "Prince Siddhartha cuts his hair" . . . . 1·30 45
961 5b. "Buddha descends from Tavatimsa Heaven" . . . 5·25 1·30
962 6b. "Buddha enters Nirvana" 2·50 1·30

298 Bhumibol Dam

1978. Dams. Multicoloured.

963 75s. Type **298** 65 20
964 2b. Sirikit Dam 65 20
965 2b.75 Vajiralongkorn Dam 1·30 20
966 6b. Ubolratana Dam . . . . 1·70 1·10

299 "Idea lynceus"

1978. Butterflies.

967 **299** 2b. black, violet and red 65 30
968 – 3b. multicoloured . . . . 1·10 30
969 – 5b. multicoloured . . . . 3·75 65
970 – 6b. multicoloured . . . . 2·10 1·30

DESIGNS: 3b. Eastern courtier; 5b. "Charaxes durnfordi"; 6b. "Cethosia penthesilea".

300 Phra Chedi Chai Mongkhon, Ayutthaya

301 Mother and Children

1978. International Correspondence Week. Mult.

971 75s. Type **300** 30 20
972 2b. Phra That Hariphunchai, Lamphun 55 20
973 2b.75 Phra Borom That Chaiya, Surat Thani . . . 2·50 20
974 5b. Phra That Choeng Chum, Sakon Nakhon . . . . . 1·10 65

1978. United Nations Day.

975 **301** 75s. multicoloured 45 10

302 Basketball, Hockey and Boxing

1978. 8th Asian Games, Bangkok. Multicoloured.

976 25s. Silhouettes of boxers, footballer and pole-vaulter 20 10
977 2b. Silhouettes of javelin-thrower, weightlifter and runner 30 10
978 3b. Football, shuttlecock, yacht and table-tennis bat and ball 75 20
979 5b. Type **302** . . . . 1·90 65

303 World Map and Different Races holding Hands

1978. International Anti-Apartheid Year.

980 **303** 75s. multicoloured 30 10

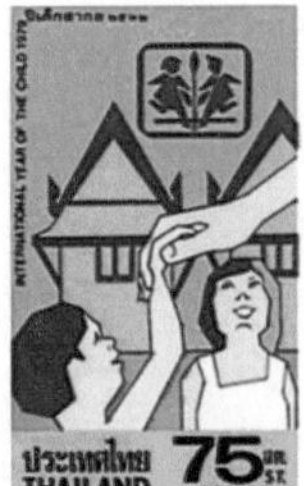

304 Children and S.O.S. Village, Tambol Bangpu

1979. International Year of the Child. Mult.

981 75s. Children painting Thai flag (horiz) 75 20
982 75s. Type **304** 30 10

305 "Matuta lunaris"

1979. Crabs. Multicoloured.

983 2b. Type **305** 65 30
984 2b.75 "Matuta planipes" . . 2·50 30
985 3b. "Portunus pelagicus" . . 1·10 45
986 5b. "Scylla serrata" . . . . 3·25 1·10

306 Eye and Blind People

307 Sugar Apples

1979. Red Cross.

987 **306** 75s.+25s. multicoloured 30 30

1979. Fruits. Multicoloured.

988 1b. Type **307** 85 20
989 2b. Pineapple 65 20
990 5b. Bananas . . . . 2·10 85
991 6b. Longans . . . . 1·70 1·10

308 Planting Sapling

1979. 20th Arbor Day.

992 **308** 75s. multicoloured 25 10

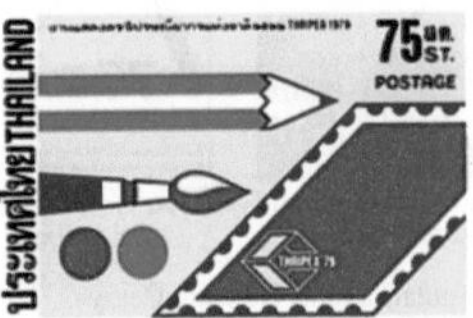

309 Pencil, Brush and Colours

1979. "Thaipex '79" National Stamp Exhibition, Bangkok. Multicoloured.

993 75s. Type **309** 20 10
994 2b. Envelopes 30 15
995 2b.75 Stamp stockbook . . . 75 15
996 5b. Tweezers, stamps and magnifying glass . . . . . 1·90 65

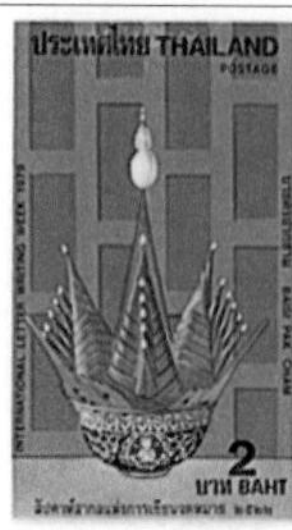
310 Baisi Pak Cham

311 U.N.O. Emblem, Farmer, Cattle and Wheat

1979. International Correspondence Week. Traditional Flower Arrangements. Mult.

997	75s. Kruai upatcha (used at Buddhist ordination ceremony)	20	10
998	2b. Type **310** (used at Braminical ceremonies)	45	15
999	2b.75 Krathong dokmai (for paying respects to elders or superiors)	65	15
1000	5b. Phum dokmai (altar decoration)	1·90	65

1979. United Nations Day.
1001 **311** 75s. multicoloured . . . 25 10

312 "Makutrajakumarn" (frigate)

1979. Ships of the Royal Thai Navy. Mult.

1002	2b. Type **312**	45	20
1003	3b. "Tapi" (frigate)	65	20
1004	5b. "Prabparapak" (missile craft)	3·25	85
1005	6b. T 91 (patrol boat)	3·75	1·10

313 Order of the Rajamitrabhorn

314 Transplanting Rice

1979. Royal Orders and Decorations. Mult.

1006	1b. Type **313**	65	30
1007	1b. Rajamitrabhorn ribbon	65	30
1008	2b. Order of the Royal House of Chakri	65	20
1009	2b. Royal House of Chakri ribbon	65	20
1010	5b. Order of the Nine Gems	1·30	45
1011	5b. Nine Gems ribbon	1·30	45
1012	6b. Knight Grand Cross of the Order of Chula Chom Klao	1·50	65
1013	6b. Chula Chom Klao ribbon	1·50	65

1980. Children's Day. Multicoloured.

1014	75s. Type **314**	30	10
1015	75s. Harvesting rice	30	10

315 Family House and Map of Thailand

316 Golden-fronted Leafbird

1980. Population and Housing Census.
1016 **315** 75s. multicoloured . . . 20 10

1980. 9th Conference of Int Commission for Bird Preservation (Asian Section), Chiang Mai. Mult.

1017	75s. Type **316**	20	10
1018	2b. Chinese yellow tit	30	15
1019	3b. Chestnut-tailed minla	75	20
1020	5b. Scarlet minivet	1·30	65

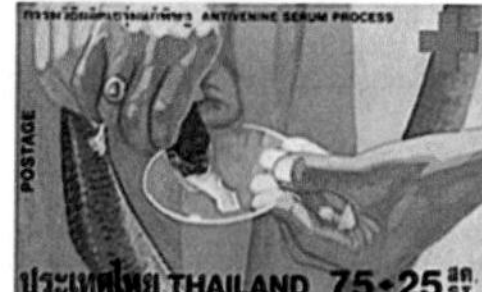
317 Extracting Snake Venom

1980. Red Cross.
1021 **317** 75s.+25s. mult 30 30

318 Smokers and Diagram of Lungs

1980. World Health Day. Anti-smoking Campaign.
1022 **318** 75s. multicoloured . . . 20 10

319 Garuda and Rotary Emblem

1980. 75th Anniv of Rotary International.
1023 **319** 5b. multicoloured . . . 85 15

320 Sai Yok Falls, Kanchanaburi

1980. Waterfalls. Multicoloured.

1024	1b. Type **320**	20	10
1025	2b. Punyaban Falls, Ranong	30	10
1026	5b. Heo Suwat Falls, Nakhon Ratchasima	1·10	45
1027	6b. Siriphum Falls, Chiang Mai	95	65

321 Family and Reverse of F.A.O. Medal

1980. Queen Sirikit's "Fourth Cycle" Anniv (48th Birthday). Multicoloured.

1028	75s. Queen Sirikit (vert)	20	10
1029	5b. Type **321**	85	45
1030	5b. Thai family and obverse of F.A.O. medal	85	45

322 Khao Phanomrung Temple, Buri Ram

1980. Int Correspondence Week. Temples. Mult.

1033	75s. Type **322**	10	10
1034	2b. Prang Ku Temple, Chaiyaphum	30	15
1035	2b.75 Phimai Temple, Nakhon Ratchasima	45	15
1036	5b. Srikhoraphum Temple, Surin	1·10	60

323 Princess Mother

324 Golden Mount Temple, Bangkok

1980. The Princess Mother's 80th Birthday.
1037 **323** 75s. multicoloured . . . 1·10 25

1980. United Nations Day.
1038 **324** 75s. multicoloured . . . 20 10

325 King Bhumibol

326 "King Rama VII signing Constitutional Document"

1980.

1039	**325**	25s. red	55	10
1179		50s. green	1·70	10
1040		75s. violet	10	10
1041		1b. blue	10	10
1040a		1b.25 green	10	10
1180a		1b.50 orange	85	85
1041a		2b. purple and red	3·25	10
1235b		2b. brown	1·30	10
1042a		3b. blue and brown	15	10
1042b		4b. brown and blue	20	10
1043a		5b. brown and lilac	30	10
1044a		6b. lilac and green	45	10
1044b		6b.50 olive and green	45	15
1044c		7b. dp brown & brown	55	10
1044d		7b.50 blue and red	45	20
1044e		8b. green and brown	45	10
1045		8b.50 brown and green	45	20
1045a		9b. brown and blue	45	15
1046		9b.50 green and olive	45	20
1047		10b. green and red	65	10
1048		20b. green and orange	1·10	15
1049		50b. green and lilac	3·25	30
1050		100b. blue and orange	5·25	65

1980. Monument to King Prajadhipok (Rama VII).
1051 **326** 75s. multicoloured . . . 20 10

327 Bowl

1980. Bencharong Ware. Multicoloured.

1052	2b. Type **327**	45	20
1053	2b.75 Covered bowls	45	20
1054	3b. Jar	85	30
1055	5b. Stem-plates	85	55

328 King Vajiravudh

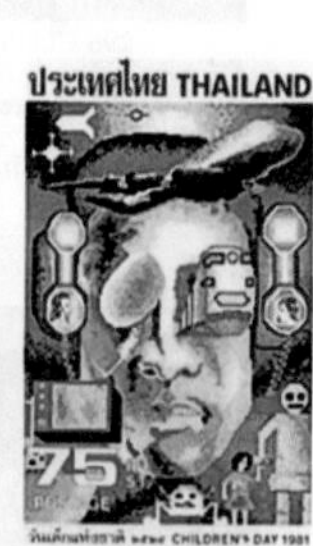
329 "Youth in Electronics Age" (Veth Maichun)

1981. Birth Centenary of King Vajiravudh.
1056 **328** 75s. multicoloured . . . 45 10

1981. Children's Day.
1057 **329** 75s. multicoloured . . . 30 10

330 Mosque, Pattani Province

1981. 1400th Anniv of Hegira.
1058 **330** 5b. multicoloured . . . 1·30 45

331 Palm Leaf Fish Mobile

1981. Int Handicraft Exhibition. Mult.

1059	75s. Type **331**	20	10
1060	75s. Carved teakwood elephant	20	10
1061	2b.75 Basketwork	55	25
1062	2b.75 Thai folk dolls	55	25

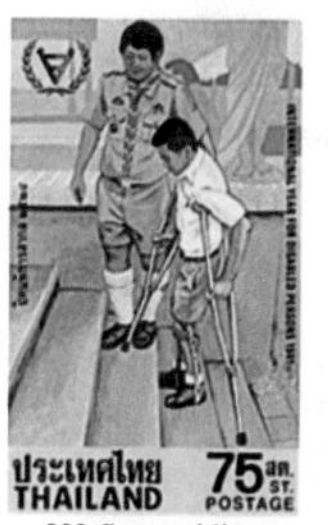
332 Scout aiding Cripple

334 Ongkhot

333 Red Cross Volunteer aiding Refugee

1981. Int Year of Disabled Persons. Mult.

1063	75s. Type **332**	20	10
1064	5b. Disabled person cutting gem-stones	85	30

1981. Red Cross.
1065 **333** 75s.+25s. green and red 65 65

1981. Khon (Thai classical dance) Masks. Mult.

1066	75s. Type **334**	20	10
1067	2b. Maiyarab	30	15
1068	3b. Sukrip	75	20
1069	5b. Indrajit	85	65

336 8a. Stamp, 1899

1981. "Thaipex '81" National Stamp Exn. Mult.

1070	75s. Type **336**	20	10
1071	75s. 28s. stamp, 1910	20	10
1072	2b.75 50s. stamp, 1919	55	30
1073	2b.75 3s. stamp, 1932	55	30

337 Luang Praditphairo

338 Mai Hok-Hian

1981. Birth Centenary of Luang Praditphairo (musician).
1074 **337** 1b.25 multicoloured . . 30 10

1981. International Correspondence Week. Dwarf Trees. Multicoloured.

1075	75s. Type **338**	20	10
1076	2b. Mai Kam-Mao-Lo	30	20
1077	2b.75 Mai Khen	55	15
1078	5b. Mai Khabuan	1·30	65

339 Food Produce

1981. World Food Day.
1079 **339** 75s. multicoloured . . . 25 10

340 Samran Mukhamat Pavilion, Bangkok

1981. United Nations Day.
1080 **340** 1b.25 multicoloured . . 25 10

341 Expressway at Klongtoey

1981. Inaug of First Thai Expressway. Mult.
1081 1b. Type **341** 10 10
1082 5b. Expressway interchange 1·10 35

342 King Cobra

1981. Snakes. Multicoloured.
1083 75s. Type **342** 10 10
1084 2b. Banded krait 65 30
1085 2b.75 Thai cobra 65 15
1086 5b. Malayan pit viper . . . 1·20 55

343 Girl carrying Child **344** Scouts reaching for Peace

1982. Children's Day.
1087 **343** 1b.25 multicoloured . . 25 30

1982. 75th Anniv of Boy Scout Movement.
1088 **344** 1b.25 multicoloured . . 25 10

345 King Buddha Yod-Fa (Rama I)

1982. Bicentenary of Chakri Dynasty and of Bangkok. Multicoloured.
1089 1b. Type **345** 20 10
1090 1b.25 Aerial view of Bangkok 20 10
1091 2b. King Buddha Lert La Naphalai (Rama II) . . . 45 10
1092 3b. King Nang Klao (Rama III) . . . . 1·30 20
1093 4b. King Mongkut (Rama IV) 85 30
1094 5b. King Chulalongkorn (Rama V) . . . . 1·70 65
1095 6b. King Vajiravudh (Rama VI) . . . . 1·70 65
1096 7b. King Prajadhipok (Rama VII) . . . . . . 2·10 1·10
1097 8b. King Ananda Mahidol (Rama VIII) . . . . . . 1·10 65
1098 9b. King Bhumipol Adulyadej (Rama IX) . . 1·10 45
MS1099 Two sheets. (a) 205 × 145 mm. Nos. 1089/98; (b) 195 × 180 mm. Nos. 1089/98 (sold at 130b. pair) . . . . 43·00 34·00

346 Dr. Robert Koch and Cross of Lorraine

1982. Cent of Discovery of Tubercle Bacillus.
1100 **346** 1b.25 multicoloured . . 20 10

347 "Quisqualis indica"

1982. Flowers. Multicoloured.
1101 1b.25 Type **347** 15 10
1102 1b.50 "Murraya paniculata" 25 15
1103 6b.50 "Mesua ferrea" . . . 95 45
1104 7b. "Desmos chinensis" . . 75 30

348 Wat Bowon Sathan Sutthawat

1982. "Bangkok 1983" International Stamp Exhibition (1st issue). Multicoloured.
1105 1b.25 Type **348** 20 10
1106 4b.25 Wat Phra Chetuphon Wimon Mangkhalaram 55 20
1107 6b.50 Wat Mahathat Yuwarat Rangsarit . . . 65 40
1108 7b. Wat Phra Sri Rattana Satsadaram . . . . . . 1·10 30
MS1109 160 × 140 mm. Nos. 1105/8 32·00 26·00
See also Nos. 1133/1135 and 1142/**MS**1146.

349 "Landsat" Satellite **350** Prince Purachatra

1982. 2nd U.N. Conference on the Exploration and Peaceful Uses of Outer Space, Vienna.
1110 **349** 1b.25 multicoloured . . 20 10

1982. Birth Centenary of Prince Purachatra.
1111 **350** 1b.25 multicoloured . . 20 10

351 Covered Jar

1982. International Correspondence Week. Sangalok Pottery. Multicoloured.
1112 1b.25 Type **351** 20 10
1113 3b. Small jar 65 20
1114 4b.25 Celadon plate 45 30
1115 7b. Plate with fish design . . 85 45

352 Loha Prasat, Bangkok

1982. United Nations Day.
1116 **352** 1b.25 multicoloured . . 20 10

353 Chap and Ching

1982. Thai Musical Instruments. Multicoloured.
1117 50s. Type **353** 10 10
1118 1b. Pi nok and pi nai (pipes) 30 10
1119 1b.25 Klong that and taphon (drums) 20 10
1120 1b.50 Khong mong (gong) and krap (wooden sticks) 20 15
1121 6b. Khong wong yai (glockenspiel) . . . . . . 2·10 75
1122 7b. Khong wong lek (glockenspiel) 85 30
1123 8b. Ranat ek (xylophone) 75 30
1124 9b. Ranat thum (xylophone) 75 30

354 Pileated Gibbon **355** Emblem and Flags of Member Countries

1982. National Wild Animal Preservation Day. Monkeys. Multicoloured.
1125 1b.25 Type **354** 20 10
1126 3b. Pigtail macaque . . . . 1·10 15
1127 5b. Slow loris 65 40
1128 7b. Silvered leaf monkey . . 85 45

1982. 15th Anniv of Association of South-East Asian Nations.
1129 **355** 6b.50 multicoloured . . 85 20

356 Child sweeping

1983. Children's Day.
1130 **356** 1b.25 multicoloured . . 20 10

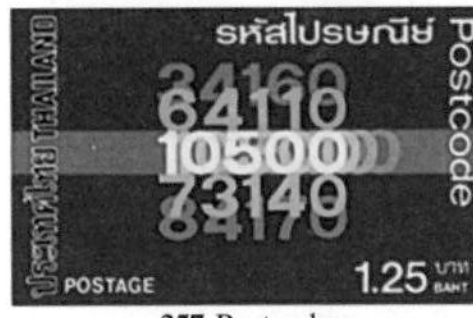

357 Postcodes

1983. 1st Anniv of Postcodes. Multicoloured.
1131 1b.25 Type **357** 25 10
1132 1b.25 Postcoded envelope 25 10

358 Old General Post Office

1983. "Bangkok 1983" International Stamp Exhibition (2nd issue).
1133 **358** 7b. multicoloured . . . 85 15
1134 10b. multicoloured . . . 1·30 25
MS1135 142 × 100 mm. Nos. 1133/4. (sold at 30b.) . . . . 9·75 8·50

359 Junks

1983. 25th Anniv of International Maritime Organization.
1136 **359** 1b.25 multicoloured . . 20 10

360 Civil Servant's Shoulder Strap **362** Prince Sithiporn Kridakara

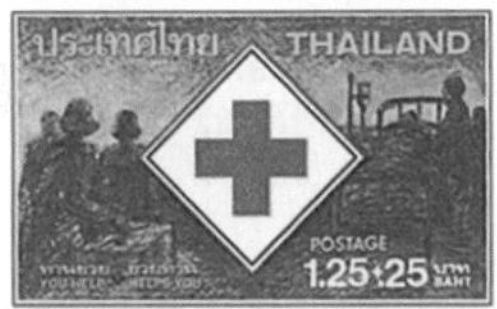

361 Giving and receiving Aid and Red Cross

1983. Civil Servants' Day.
1137 **360** 1b.25 multicoloured . . 20 10

1983. Red Cross.
1138 **361** 1b.25+25s. multicoloured 45 45

1983. Birth Centenary of Prince Sithiporn Kridakara (agriculturalist).
1139 **362** 1b.25 multicoloured . . 20 10

363 Satellite, Map and Dish Aeria

1983. Domestic Satellite Communications System.
1140 **363** 2b. multicoloured . . . 30 10

364 Prince Bhanurangsi **366** Cable Map of A.S.E.A.N. Countries and "Long Lines" (cable ship)

365 Post Box Clearance

1983. Prince Bhanurangsi (founder of Thai postal service) Commemoration.
1141 **364** 1b.25 multicoloured . . 30 10

1983. "Bangkok 1983" International Stamp Exhibition (3rd issue). Multicoloured.
1142 1b.25 Type **365** 10 10
1143 7b.50 Post office counter . . 75 25
1144 8b.50 Mail transportation 55 30
1145 9b.50 Mail delivery 55 30
MS1146 162 × 140 mm. Nos. 1142/5 (sold at 50b.) . . . . 10·50 9·75

1983. Inauguration of Malaysia–Singapore–Thailand Submarine Cable. Multicoloured.
1147 1b.25 Type **366** 10 10
1148 7b. Map of new cable . . . 65 30

367 Flower Coral

1983. Int Correspondence Week. Corals. Mult.
1149 2b. Type **367** 30 10
1150 3b. Lesser valley coral . . . 65 10
1151 4b. Mushroom coral 30 30
1152 7b. Common lettuce coral 95 55

368 Satellite and Submarine Cable Communications Equipment

1983. World Communications Year. Mult.
1153 2b. Type **368** 30 10
1154 3b. Telephone and telegraph service equipment 30 10

369 Fishing for Tuna

1983. United Nations Day.
1155 **369** 1b.25 multicoloured . . 20 10

370 Buddha (sculpture)

1983. 700th Anniv of Thai Alphabet.
1156 **370** 3b. multicoloured . . . 55 15
1157 – 7b. black and brown . . 95 20
1158 – 8b. multicoloured . . . 55 25
1159 – 9b. multicoloured . . . 55 25
DESIGNS—HORIZ: 3b. Sangkhalok pottery; 7b. Thai characters. VERT: 9b. Mahathat Temple.

371 Prince Mahidol of Songkhla

1983. 60th Anniv of Co-operation between Siriraj Hospital and Rockefeller Foundation.
1160 **371** 9b.50 multicoloured . . 85 45

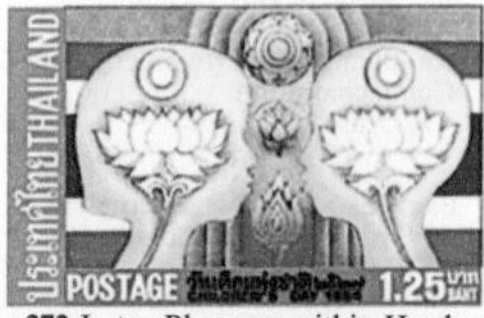

372 Lotus Blossoms within Heads

1984. Children's Day.
1161 **372** 1b.25 multicoloured . . 25 10

373 Running

1984. 17th National Games, Phitsanulok Province. Multicoloured.
1162 1b.25 Type **373** 30 10
1163 3b. Football 20 15

374 Skeletal Joints, Globe and Emblem

1984. 5th South East Asia and Pacific Area League against Rheumatism Congress.
1164 **374** 1b.25 multicoloured . . 30 10

375 Statue of King Naresuan and Modern Armed Forces

376 Royal Institute Emblem in Door Arch

1984. Armed Forces Day.
1165 **375** 1b.25 multicoloured . . 30 10

1984. 50th Anniv of Royal Institute.
1166 **376** 1b.25 multicoloured . . 20 10

1984. Red Cross. No. 954 surch **3.25 + 0.25** in English and Thai.
1167 **295** 3b.25+25s. on 2b.75+25s. mult 85 85

378 King and Queen examining Land Development Project

1984. Royal Initiated Projects. Multicoloured.
1168 1b.25 Type **378** 25 10
1169 1b.25 Improving barren area 25 10
1170 1b.25 Dam, terrace farming and rain-making aircraft 25 10
1171 1b.25 Crops, fish and farm animals 25 10
1172 1b.25 King and Queen of Thailand 25 10

379 Dome Building and University Emblem

1984. 50th Anniv of Thammasat University.
1173 **379** 1b.25 multicoloured . . 20 10

381 A.B.U. Emblem and Map

1984. 20th Anniv of Asia-Pacific Broadcasting Union.
1174 **381** 4b. multicoloured . . . 55 15

382 Chiang Saen Style Buddha

384 "Alocasia indica var. metallica"

1984. Thai Sculptures of Buddhas. Multicoloured.
1175 1b.25 Type **382** 10 10
1176 7b. Sukhothai style 95 35
1177 8b.50 Thong style 45 45
1178 9b.50 Ayutthaya style . . . 45 45

1984. International Correspondence Week. Medicinal Plants. Multicoloured.
1181 1b.50 Type **384** 15 10
1182 2b. "Aloe barbadensis" . . 25 10
1183 4b. "Gynura pseudo-china" 45 20
1184 10b. "Rhoeo spathacea" . . 1·30 65

385 Princess Mother

386 Threshing Rice

1984. 84th Birthday of Princess Mother.
1185 **385** 1b.50 multicoloured . . 15 10

1984. United Nations Day.
1186 **386** 1b.50 multicoloured . . 15 10

387 Bhutan Glory

1984. Butterflies. Multicoloured.
1187 2b. Type **387** 20 10
1188 3b. "Stichophthalma louisa" 20 10
1189 5b. Clipper 45 30
1190 7b. "Stichophthalma godfreyi" 75 30

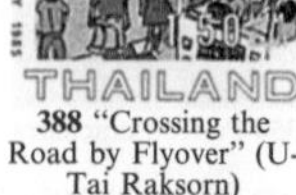

388 "Crossing the Road by Flyover" (U-Tai Raksorn)

390 Monument to Tao-Thep-Krasattri and Tao-Sri-Sundhorn

389 Bangkok Mail Centre

1985. Children's Day. Multicoloured.
1191 1b.50 Type **388** 15 10
1192 1b.50 "Crossing the Road by Flyover" (Sravudh Charoennawee) (horiz) . . 15 10

1985. Inauguration of Bangkok Mail-sorting Centre.
1193 **389** 1b.50 multicoloured . . 15 10

1985. Heroines of Phuket. Bicentennial Ceremony.
1194 **390** 2b. multicoloured . . . 30 10

1985. Red Cross. No. 987 surch **2 + .25 BAHT.**
1195 **306** 2b.+25s. on 75s.+25s. multicoloured 65 65

392 Bank Headquarters, Bangkok, and King Vajiravudh (Rama VI)

1985. 72nd Anniv of Government Savings Bank.
1196 **392** 1b.50 multicoloured . . 15 10

393 Satellite over Thai Buildings

1985. 20th Anniv of International Telecommunications Satellite Organization.
1197 **393** 2b. multicoloured . . . 25 10

394 Douglas DC-6 and DC-8 and Loi-Krathong Festival

1985. 25th Anniv of Thai Airways. Mult.
1198 2b. Type **394** 10 10
1199 7b.50 Douglas DC-10-30 and Thai classical dancing 55 30
1200 8b.50 Airbus Industrie A-300 and Thai buildings 65 35
1201 9b.50 Boeing 747-200 and world landmarks 65 40

395 U.P.U.Emblem

397 Aisvarya Pavilion

396 Pigeon

1985. Centenary of Membership of U.P.U. and I.T.U. Multicoloured.
1202 2b. Type **395** 10 10
1203 10b. I.T.U. Emblem 55 25

1985. National Communications Day.
1204 **396** 2b. blue, red & ultram 20 10

1985. "Thaipex '85" Stamp Exhibition. Multicoloured.
1205 2b. Type **397** 20 10
1206 3b. Varopas Piman Pavilion (horiz) 30 10
1207 7b. Vehas Camrun Pavilion (horiz) 55 25
1208 10b. Vitoon Tassana Tower 65 45
MS1209 155 × 179 mm. Nos. 1205/8 26·00 21·00

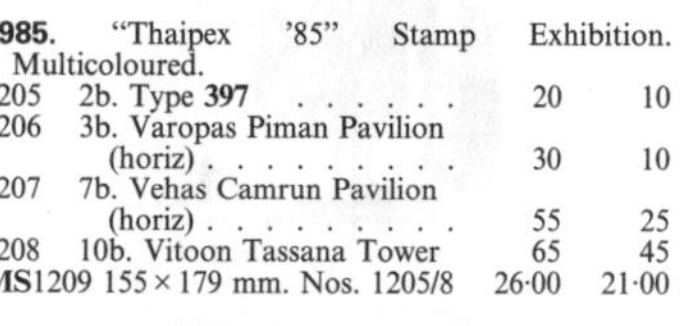

398 King Mongkut, Eclipsed Sun and Telescope

1985. National Science Day.
1210 **398** 2b. multicoloured . . . 25 30

399 Department Seals, 1885 and 1985

1985. Centenary of Royal Thai Survey Department.
1211 **399** 2b. multicoloured . . . 20 10

400 Boxing

1985. 13th South-East Asia Games, Bangkok (1st issue). Multicoloured.

1212	2b. Type **400**	25	10
1213	2b. Putting the shot	25	10
1214	2b. Badminton	25	10
1215	2b. Throwing the javelin	25	10
1216	2b. Weightlifting	25	10
MS1217	186 × 127 Nos. 1212/16 (sold at 20)	13·00	10·50

See also Nos. 1229/**MS**1233.

401 Golden Trumpet

402 Mothers and Children at Clinic

1985. International Correspondence Week. Climbing Plants. Multicoloured.

1218	2b. Type **401**	30	10
1219	3b. "Jasminum auriculatum"	45	10
1220	7b. Passion flower	65	30
1221	10b. Coral-vine	75	45

1985. United Nations Day.
1222 **402** 2b. multicoloured . . . 20 10

403 Prince Dhani Nivat

404 Prince of Jainad

1985. Birth Centenary of Prince Dhani Nivat, Kromamun Bidyalabh Bridhyakorn.
1223 **403** 2b. multicoloured . . . 20 10

1985. Birth Centenary of Rangsit, Prince of Jainad (Minister of Health).
1224 **404** 1b.50 multicoloured . . 15 10

405 Emblem and Buildings

1985. 5th Asian–Pacific Postal Union Congress.

1225	**405**	2b. multicoloured	10	10
1226	–	10b. multicoloured	55	25

DESIGN: 10b. As Type **405** but different buildings.

406 Emblem

1985. International Youth Year.
1227 **406** 2b. multicoloured . . . 55 20

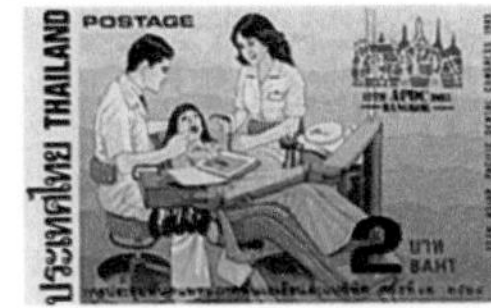
407 Dentist and Nurse tending Patient

1985. 12th Asian–Pacific Dental Congress.
1228 **407** 2b. multicoloured . . . 20 10

408 Volleyball

409 Chevalier de Chaumont presenting Message from Louis XIV to King Narai the Great, 1685

1985. 12th South-East Asia Games, Bangkok (2nd issue). Multicoloured.

1229	1b. Type **408**	20	10
1230	2b. Sepak-takraw (kick-ball)	20	10
1231	3b. Gymnastics	20	10
1232	4b. Bowls	30	20
MS1233	186 × 129 mm. Nos. 1229/32 plus label (sold at 20b.)	13·00	10·50

1985. 300th Anniv of Franco–Thai Relations. Multicoloured.

1234	2b. Type **409**	10	10
1235	8b.50 Siamese emissaries carrying reply from King Narai to Louis XIV (horiz)	65	35

410 Emblem

1986. 3rd Anniv of International and Inauguration of Domestic Express Mail Services.
1236 **410** 2b. multicoloured . . . 15 10

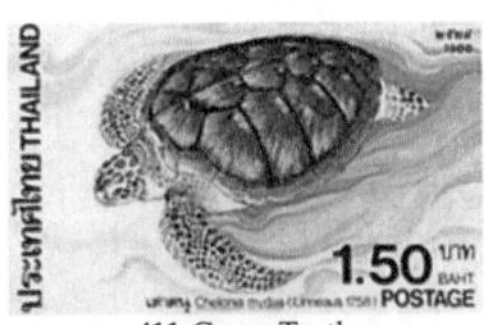
411 Green Turtle

1986. Turtles. Multicoloured.

1237	1b.50 Type **411**	20	10
1238	3b. Hawksbill turtle	45	10
1239	5b. Leatherback turtle	1·30	20
1240	10b. Olive turtle	1·10	30

412 "Family picking Lotus" (Areeya Makarabhundhu)

414 Statue of Sunthon Phu (Sukij Laidej), Amphoe Klaeng

1986. Children's Day.
1241 **412** 2b. multicoloured . . . 20 10

1986. Red Cross. No. 1021 surch. **1986 2 + .25 BAHT** in English and Thai.
1242 **317** 2b.+25s. on 75s.+25s. multicoloured 65 65

1986. Birth Bicentenary of Sunthon Phu (poet).
1243 **414** 2b. multicoloured . . . 20 10

415 Watermelon

1986. Fruit. Multicoloured.

1244	2b. Type **415**	55	10
1245	2b. Malay apple ("Eugenia malaccensis")	55	10
1246	6b. Pomelo ("Citrus maxima")	75	30
1247	6b. Papaya ("Carica papaya")	75	30

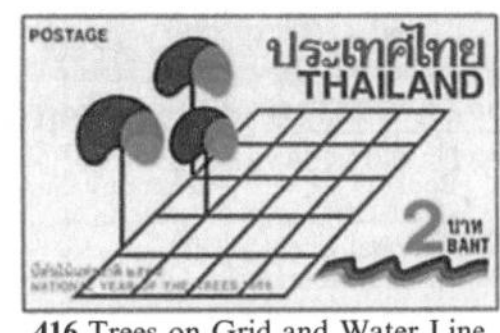
416 Trees on Grid and Water Line

1986. National Tree Year.
1248 **416** 2b. multicoloured . . . 15 10

417 Pigeon flying from Man's Head to Transmission Masts

1986. National Communications Day.
1249 **417** 2b. multicoloured . . . 15 10

418 Chalom

1986. International Correspondence Week. Bamboo Baskets. Multicoloured.

1250	2b. Type **418**	20	10
1251	2b. Krabung	20	10
1252	6b. Kratib	45	15
1253	6b. Kaleb	45	15

1986. No. 1031 surch **1 BAHT**.
1254 **227** 1b. on 20s. blue 10 10

420 Emblem and War Scenes

1986. International Peace Year.
1255 **420** 2b. light blue, blue & red 20 10

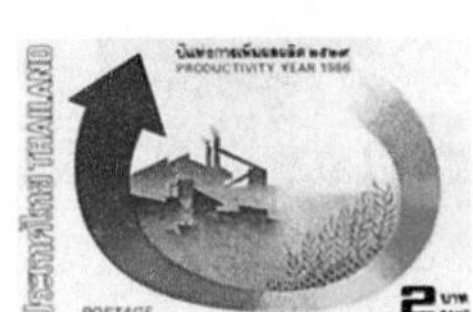
421 Industrial and Agricultural Scenes within Emblem

1986. Productivity Year.
1256 **421** 2b. multicoloured . . . 15 10

422 Scouts saluting and Scout helping Blind Man across Road

1986. 75th Anniv of Thai Scouting. Mult.

1257	2b.+50s. Type **422**	15	15
1258	2b.+50s. Scouting activities	15	15
1259	2b.+50s. King and Queen making presentations to scouts	15	15
1260	2b.+50s. 15th Asia–Pacific Scout Conference, Thailand	15	15

423 Vanda "Varavuth"

1986. 6th ASEAN Orchid Congress, Thailand. Multicoloured.

1261	2b. Type **423**	20	10
1262	3b. Ascocenda "Emma"	20	15
1263	4b. Dendrobium "Sri-Siam" (horiz)	45	30
1264	5b. Dendrobium "Ekapol Panda" (horiz)	45	20
MS1265	116 × 99 mm. Nos. 1261/4	55·00	43·00

424 Chinese Mushroom

1986. Edible Fungi. Multicoloured.

1266	2b. Type **424**	20	10
1267	2b. Oyster fungus ("Pleurotus ostreatus")	20	10
1268	6b. Ear mushroom ("Auricularia polytricha")	55	25
1269	6b. Abalone mushroom ("Pleurotus cystidiosus")	55	25

425 Black Sharkminnow

1986. 60th Anniv of Fisheries Department. Multicoloured.

1270	2b. Type **425**	20	10
1271	2b. Blanc's knifefish ("Notopterus blanci")	20	10
1272	7b. Asian bonytongue ("Scleropages formosus")	45	25
1273	7b. Giant catfish ("Pangasianodon gigas")	45	25

426 Children in Playground

1987. Children's Day. Multicoloured.

1274	2b. Type **426**	30	10
1275	2b. Children in and around swimming pool	30	10

Nos. 1274/5 were printed together, se-tenant, forming a composite design showing "Our School" by Lawan Maneenetr.

427 Northrop F-5 Tiger II and General Dynamics F-16 Fighting Falcon Fighters and Pilot

1987. 72nd Anniv of Royal Thai Air Force.
1276 **427** 2b. multicoloured . . . 30 10

428 King Rama III and Temples

1987. Birth Bicentenary of King Rama III.
1277 **428** 2b. multicoloured . . . 25 10

429 Communications and Transport Systems

1987. 75th Anniv of Ministry of Communications.
1278 **429** 2b. multicoloured . . . 15 10

1987. Red Cross. No. 1065 surch **2 + 0.50 BAHT.**
1279 **333** 2b.+50s. on 75s.+25s. green and red 65 65

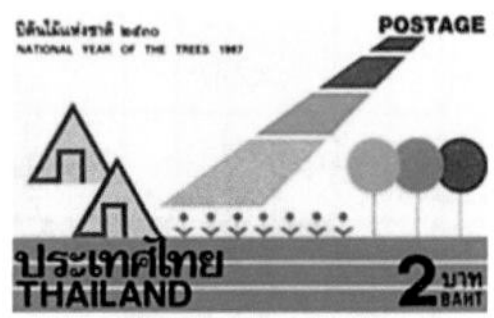
431 Tree-lined Street

1987. National Tree Year.
1280 **431** 2b. multicoloured . . . 15 10

432 Gold Peacock

1987. "Thaipex'87" National Stamp Exhibition. Handicrafts. Multicoloured.
1281 2b. Type **432** 10 10
1282 2b. Gold hand-mirrors . . . 10 10
1283 6b. Gold lustre water urn and finger bowls with trays (horiz) 30 15
1284 6b. Gold swan vase (horiz) 30 15
MS1285 160 × 175 mm. Nos. 1281/4 (sold at 40b.) . . . . 26·00 21·00

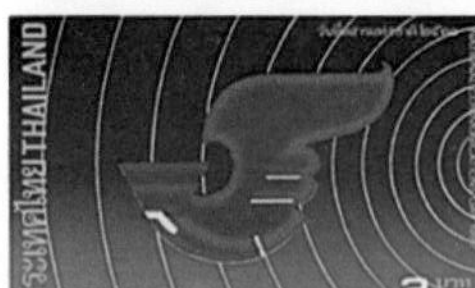
433 Flying Bird and Animal Horn (Somsak Junthavorn)

1987. National Communications Day.
1286 **433** 2b. multicoloured . . . 15 10

434 King Rama IX at Presentation Ceremony, King Rama V and Emblem

1987. Centenary of Chulachomklao Royal Military Academy, Khao Cha-Ngok.
1287 **434** 2b. multicoloured . . . 15 10

435 Spiral Ropes leading to Member Countries' Flags

1987. 20th Anniv of Association of South-East Asian Nations.
1288 **435** 2b. multicoloured . . . 10 10
1289 3b. multicoloured . . . 20 10
1290 4b. multicoloured . . . 20 15
1291 5b. multicoloured . . . 30 15

436 People and Open Book
437 Flower-offering Ceremony, Saraburi

1987. International Literacy Day.
1292 **436** 2b. multicoloured . . . 15 10

1987. Visit Thailand Year.
1293 2b. Type **437** 10 10
1294 3b. Duan Sib Festival (honouring ancestors), Nakhon Si Thammarat 20 10
1295 5b. Bang Fai (rain) Festival, Yasothon 20 15
1296 7b. Loi Krathong, Sukhothai 30 15

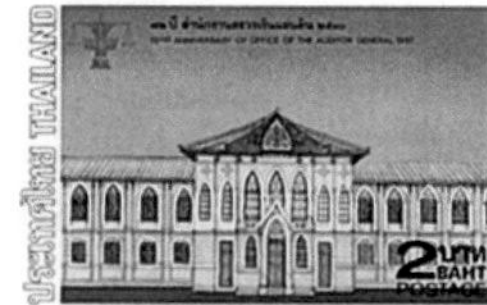
438 Ministry Building

1987. 72nd Anniv of Auditor General's Office.
1297 **438** 2b. multicoloured . . . 15 10

439 Temple of Dawn, "Sri Suphanahong" (royal barge) and Mt Fuji within "100"

1987. Centenary of Japan–Thailand Friendship Treaty.
1298 **439** 2b. multicoloured . . . 20 10

440 Tasselled Garland

1987. International Correspondence Week. Ceremonial Floral Garlands. Multicoloured.
1299 2b. Floral tassle 10 10
1300 3b. Type **440** 20 10
1301 5b. Wrist garland 25 15
1302 7b. Double-ended garland 40 20

1987. No. 1180a surch **2 BAHT.**
1303 **325** 2b. on 1b.50 orange . . 15 10

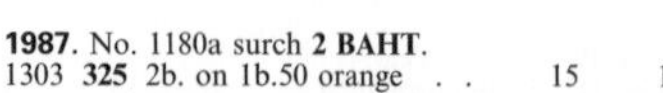

442 Thai Pavilion

1987. Inauguration of Social Education and Cultural Centre.
1304 **442** 2b. multicoloured . . . 15 10

443 King Bhumibol Adulyadej as a Boy

1987. King Bhumibol Adulyadej's 60th Birthday. Multicoloured (except 1320).
1305 2b. Type **443** 20 10
1306 2b. Wedding photograph of King Bhumibol Adulyadej and Queen Sirikit, 1950 20 10
1307 2b. King on throne during Accession ceremony at Paisan Hall, 1950 . . . . 20 10
1308 2b. King as monk on alms round 20 10
1309 2b. Elderly woman greeting King 20 10
1310 2b. King demonstrating to hill tribes how to take medicine 20 10
1311 2b. King and Queen presenting gift bag to wounded serviceman . . . 20 10
1312 2b. King examining new system for small farms . . 20 10
1314 2b. Princess Mother Somdej Phra Sri Nakarindra Boromrajjonnani 55 15
1315 2b. Crown Prince Maha Vajiralongkorn 55 15
1316 2b. Princess Maha Chakri Sirindhorn 55 15
1317 2b. Princess Chulabhorn . . 55 15
1318 2b. King Bhumibol Adulyadej and Queen Sirikit 55 15
1319 2b. King and family (48 × 33 mm) 55 10
1320 100b. gold and blue (King Bhumibol Adulyadej) (48 × 33 mm) . . . . . . 34·00 34·00
MS1313 190 × 144 mm. Nos. 1305/12 (sold at 40b.) . . 17·00 15·00

444 "Teacher's Day" (Nutchaliya Suddhiprasit)
445 Prince Kromamun Bridhyalongkorn (founder)

1988. Children's Day.
1321 **444** 2b. multicoloured . . . 15 10

1988. 72nd Anniv of Thai Co-operatives.
1322 **445** 2b. multicoloured . . . 15 10

446 Society Building

1988. 84th Anniv of Siam Society (for promotion of arts and sciences).
1323 **446** 2b. multicoloured . . . 15 10

447 Phra Phai Luang Monastery

1988. Sukhothai Historical Park. Multicoloured.
1324 2b. Type **447** 10 10
1325 3b. Traphang Thonglang Monastery 20 10
1326 4b. Maha That Monastery 30 20
1327 6b. Thewalai Maha Kaset 45 25

1988. No. 1040a surch **1 BAHT.**
1557 **325** 1b. on 1b.25 green . . . 10 10

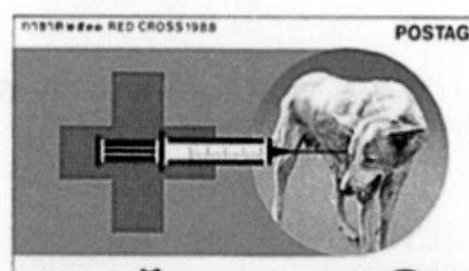
449 Syringe between Red Cross and Dog

1988. Red Cross Anti-rabies Campaign.
1329 **449** 2b. multicoloured . . . 15 10

450 King Rama V (founder)

452 Hand holding Coloured Ribbons

451 Crested Fireback Pheasant

1988. Centenary of Siriraj Hospital.
1330 **450** 5b. multicoloured . . . 1·30 45

1988. Pheasants. Multicoloured.
1331 2b. Type **451** 10 10
1332 3b. Kalij pheasant 20 10
1333 6b. Silver pheasant 45 20
1334 7b. Mrs. Hume's pheasant 55 30

1988. Centenary of International Women's Council.
1335 **452** 2b. multicoloured . . . 15 10

453 King Rama IX in King's Own Bodyguard Uniform

454 King Rama IX in Full Robes

1988.
1631 **453** 25s. brown 10 10
1336 50s. green 10 10
1337 1b. blue 10 10
1753 2b. red 10 10
1339 3b. blue and brown . . . 10 10
1340 4b. red and blue 15 10
1341 5b. brown and lilac . . . 15 10
1342 6b. purple and green . . 20 10
1343 7b. deep brown & brown 20 10
1344 8b. green and brown . . . 20 10
1345 9b. brown and blue . . . 30 10
1346 10b. green and red . . . 35 10
1348 20b. green and orange 65 20
1350 25b. blue and green . . . 75 30
1352 50b. green and lilac . . . 1·50 30
1354 100b. blue and orange 3·00 65

1988. 42nd Anniv of Accession to Throne of King Rama IX. Multicoloured. (a) T **454**.
1356 2b. Type **454** . . . . . . 1·10 10

(b) Royal Regalia. Size 33 × 48 mm (1357) or 48 × 33 mm (others).
1357 2b. Great Crown of Victory 20 10
1358 2b. Sword of Victory and scabbard (horiz) 20 10
1359 2b. Sceptre (horiz) 20 10
1360 2b. Royal Fan and Fly Whisk (horiz) 20 10
1361 2b. Slippers (horiz) 20 10

(c) Thrones.
1362 2b. Atthathit Uthumphon Ratchaat throne (octagonal base) 20 10
1363 2b. Phatthrabit throne (rectangular base) 20 10
1364 2b. Phuttan Kanchanasinghat throne (gold throne on angular steps) 20 10
1365 2b. Butsabokmala Mahachakkraphatphiman throne (ship shape) . . . 20 10
1366 2b. Throne inlaid with mother-of-pearl (blue throne on angular steps) 20 10
1367 2b. Peony design niello throne (circular steps) . . 20 10
MS1368 130 × 172 mm. Nos. 1362/7 (sold at 25b.) . . . . 26·00 21·00

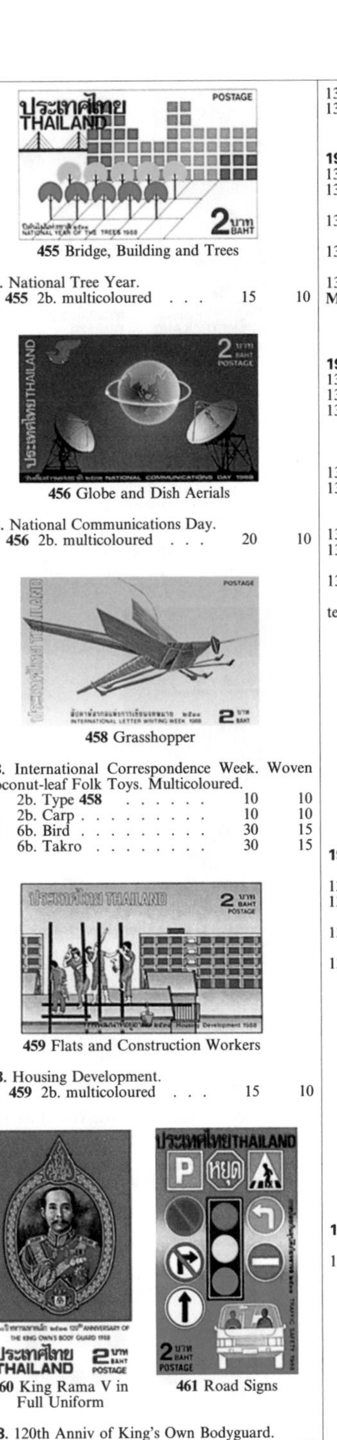

455 Bridge, Building and Trees

1988. National Tree Year.
1369 **455** 2b. multicoloured . . . 15 10

456 Globe and Dish Aerials

1988. National Communications Day.
1370 **456** 2b. multicoloured . . . 20 10

458 Grasshopper

1988. International Correspondence Week. Woven Coconut-leaf Folk Toys. Multicoloured.
1371 2b. Type **458** 10 10
1372 2b. Carp 10 10
1373 6b. Bird 30 15
1374 6b. Takro 30 15

459 Flats and Construction Workers

1988. Housing Development.
1375 **459** 2b. multicoloured . . . 15 10

460 King Rama V in Full Uniform

461 Road Signs

1988. 120th Anniv of King's Own Bodyguard.
1376 **460** 2b. multicoloured . . . 1·70 20

1988. Road Safety Campaign.
1377 **461** 2b. multicoloured . . . 30 20

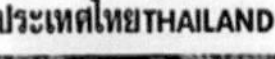

462 "Crotalaria sessiliflora"

464 Knight Grand Commander of Honourable Order of Rama

463 Buddha's Birthplace

1988. New Year. Multicoloured.
1378 1b. Type **462** 15 10
1379 1b. "Uvaria grandiflora" . . 15 10
1380 1b. "Reinwardtia trigyna" 15 10
1381 1b. "Impatiens griffithii" . . 15 10

1988. Buddha Monthon Celebrations. Mult.
1382 2b. Type **463** 10 10
1383 3b. Buddha's place of enlightenment 15 10
1384 4b. Site of Buddha's first sermon 15 15
1385 5b. Buddha's Place of Nirvana 25 15
1386 6b. Statue of Buddha (vert) 40 15
MS1386a 82 × 110 mm. No. 1386 (sold at 15b.) . . . . 7·50 6·50

1988. Insignia of Orders. Multicoloured.
1387 2b. Type **464** 10 10
1388 2b. Close-up of badge . . . 10 10
1389 3b. Knight Grand Cordon (Special Class) of Most Exalted Order of the White Elephant 20 10
1390 3b. Close-up of badge . . . 20 10
1391 5b. Knight Grand Cordon of Most Noble Order of Crown of Thailand . . . 30 15
1392 5b. Close-up of badge . . . 30 15
1393 7b. Close-up of Rarana Varabhorn Order of Merit 45 15
1394 7b. Badge on chain of office 45 15
Stamps of the same value were issued together, se-tenant, each pair forming a composite design.

465 "Floating Market" (Thongbai Siyam)

1989. National Children's Day. Plasticine Paintings by Blind People. Multicoloured.
1395 2b. Type **465** 15 10
1396 2b. "Flying Birds" (Kwanchai Kerd-Daeng) 15 10
1397 2b. "Little Mermaid" (Chalermpol Jiengmai) . . 15 10
1398 2b. "Golden Fish" (Natetip Korsantirak) 15 10

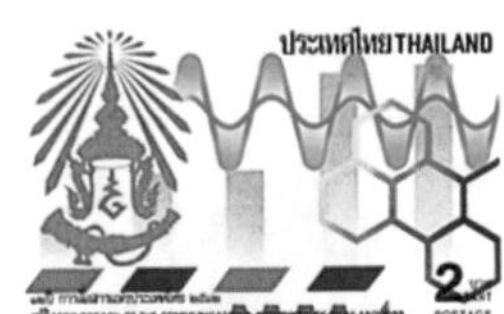

466 Emblem and Symbols of Communication

1989. 12th Anniv of Thai Communications Authority.
1399 **466** 2b. multicoloured . . . 15 10

467 Statue of Kings Rama V and VI and Auditorium

1989. 72nd Anniv of Chulalongkorn University.
1400 **467** 2b. multicoloured . . . 20 10

468 Red Cross Worker

469 Phra Kaeo Monastery

1989. 96th Anniv of Thai Red Cross (1401) and 125th Anniv of Int Red Cross (1402). Mult.
1401 2b. Type **468** 15 10
1402 10b. Red Cross and pillar 55 20

1989. Phra Nakhon Khiri Historical Park. Multicoloured.
1403 2b. Type **469** 10 10
1404 3b. Chatchawan Wiangchai Observatory 25 15
1405 5b. Phra That Chom Phet stupa 45 30
1406 6b. Wetchayan Wichian Phrasat Throne Hall . . . 45 30

470 Lottery Office Building and Profit Recipients

1989. 50th Anniv of Government Lottery Office.
1407 **470** 2b. multicoloured . . . 15 10

471 Campaign Emblem and Figures

472 Gold Nielloware Figures

1989. International Anti-drugs Day.
1408 **471** 2b. multicoloured . . . 15 10

1989. National Arts and Crafts Year. Mult.
1409 2b. Type **472** 10 10
1410 2b. Ceramics 10 10
1411 6b. Ornament inlaid with gemstones (horiz) 30 15
1412 6b. Triangular cushion (horiz) 30 15

473 Thailand Cone

1989. Shells. Multicoloured.
1413 2b. Type **473** 10 10
1414 3b. Thorny oyster 20 10
1415 6b. Great spotted cowrie . . 30 25
1416 10b. Chambered nautilus . . 1·10 65

474 Satellites, Submarine Cable Network and Emblem

1989. 10th Anniv of Asia–Pacific Telecommunity.
1417 **474** 9b. multicoloured . . . 40 20

475 Phya Anuman Rajadhon

1989. Birth Centenary (1988) of Phya Anuman Rajadhon (writer).
1418 **475** 2b. multicoloured . . . 15 10

476 Emblem and School

1989. Centenary of Post and Telecommunications School.
1419 **476** 2b. multicoloured . . . 15 10

477 Communications Symbols

478 Post Box

1989. National Communications Day.
1420 **477** 2b. multicoloured . . . 15 10

1989. "Thaipex '89" National Stamp Exhibition. Post Boxes. Multicoloured.
1421 2b. Type **478** 10 10
1422 3b. Provincial box 15 10
1423 4b. City box 15 15
1424 5b. Imported English box 25 15
1425 6b. West German box sent as gift on introduction of Thai Postal Service . . . 40 15
MS1425a 6b. 127 × 130 mm. Nos. 1421/5 (sold at 30b.) . . . 13·00 10·50

479 Dragonfly

1989. Int Correspondence Week. Mult.
1426 2b. Type **479** 10 10
1427 5b. Dragonfly (different) . . 15 10
1428 6b. Dragonfly (different) . . 15 15
1429 10b. Damselfly 25 15
MS1430 143 × 107 mm. Nos. 1426/9 (sold at 40b.) . . . . 10·50 10·50

480 Means of Transport and Communications

1989. Asia–Pacific Transport and Communications Decade.
1431 **480** 2b. multicoloured . . . 15 10

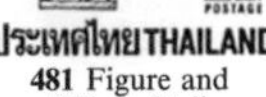

481 Figure and "Thoughts"

482 "Hypericum uralum"

1989. Centenary of Mental Health Care.
1432 **481** 2b. multicoloured . . . 15 10

1989. New Year. Flowers. Multicoloured.
1433 1b. Type **482** 10 10
1434 1b. "Uraria rufescens" . . . 10 10
1435 1b. "Manglietia garrettii" 10 10
1436 1b. "Aeschynanthus macranthus" 10 10
MS1437 85 × 100 mm. Nos. 1433/6 (sold at 14b.) . . . . 1·30 1·30

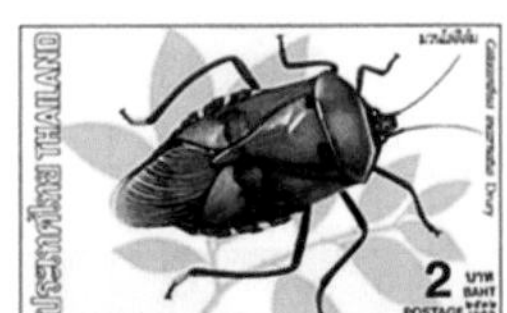

483 "Catacanthus incarnatus" (shieldbug)

1989. Beetles. Multicoloured.
1438 2b. Type **483** 10 15
1439 3b. "Aristobia approximator" 15 10
1440 6b. "Chrysochroa chinensis" 25 15
1441 10b. "Enoplotrupes sharpi" 45 35

484 Medallists on Rostrum

1989. Sports Welfare Fund. Multicoloured.

1442	2b.+1b. Type **484**	10	10
1443	2b.+1b. Nurse attending fallen cyclist	10	10
1444	2b.+1b. Boxing	10	10
1445	2b.+1b. Football	10	10

485 Official, Family and Graph

1990. Population and Housing Census.
1446 **485** 2b. multicoloured . . . 15 10

486 Skipping (Phethai Setharangsi)

1990. National Children's Day. Multicoloured.

1447	2b. Type **486**	15	10
1448	2b. Various sports activities (Chalermpol Wongpim) (vert)	15	10

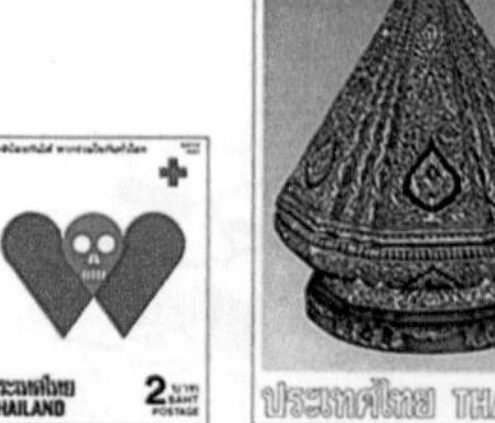
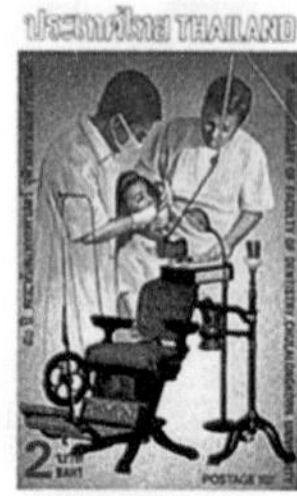
487 Skull splitting Heart
488 Tiap

1990. Red Cross. Anti-AIDS Campaign.
1449 **487** 2b. blue, red and black 15 10

1990. Heritage Conservation Day. Mother-of-Pearl Inlaid Containers. Multicoloured.

1450	2b. Type **488**	10	10
1451	2b. Phan waenfa	10	10
1452	8b. Lung (horiz)	30	25
1453	8b. Chiat klom (horiz)	30	25

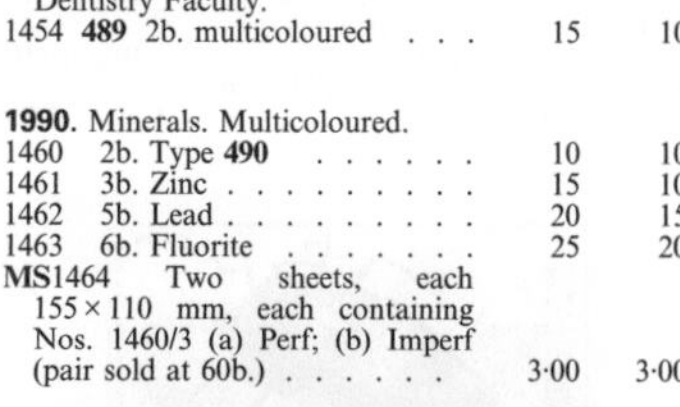
489 Dental Students and Old Chair
490 Tin

1990. 50th Anniv of Chulalongkorn University Dentistry Faculty.
1454 **489** 2b. multicoloured . . . 15 10

1990. Minerals. Multicoloured.

1460	2b. Type **490**	10	10
1461	3b. Zinc	15	10
1462	5b. Lead	20	15
1463	6b. Fluorite	25	20
MS1464	Two sheets, each 155 × 110 mm, each containing Nos. 1460/3 (a) Perf; (b) Imperf (pair sold at 60b.)	3·00	3·00

491 Pigeon

1990. National Communications Day.
1465 **491** 2b. blue, violet and purple . . . 15 10

492 Pigeons and Envelopes

1990. 20th Anniv of Asian–Pacific Postal Training Centre, Bangkok.

1466	**492**	2b. green, blue and black	15	10
1467		8b. blue, green and black	30	20

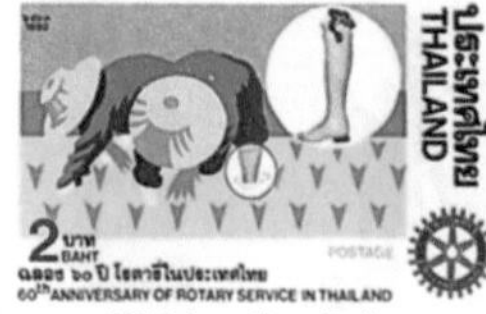
493 Jaipur Foot Project

1990. 60th Anniv of Rotary International in Thailand. Multicoloured.

1468	2b. Type **493**	10	10
1469	3b. Child anti-polio vaccination campaign	15	10
1470	6b. Literacy campaign	20	15
1471	8b. King Chulalongkorn and his engraved cypher (Thai Museum, Nordkapp, Norway)	40	25

494 Account and Staff at Computer Terminals

1990. Centenary of Comptroller-General's Department.
1472 **494** 2b. multicoloured . . . 15 10

495 Flowers in Dish (Cho Muang)

1990. Int Correspondence Week. Mult.

1473	2b. Type **495**	10	10
1474	3b. Flowers on tray (Cha Mongkut)	15	10
1475	5b. Sweetmeats on tray with leaf design (Sane Chan)	20	15
1476	6b. Fruit in bowl (Luk Chup)	40	15
MS1477	Two sheets, each 152 × 127 mm, each containing Nos. 1473/6. (a) Perf; (b) Imperf (pair sold at 60b.)	3·00	3·00

496 Princess Mother with Flower
497 "Cyrtandromoea grandiflora"

1990. 90th Birthday of Princess Mother.
1478 **496** 2b. multicoloured . . . 45 10

1990. New Year. Flowers. Multicoloured.

1479	1b. Type **497**	10	10
1480	1b. "Rhododendron arboreum sp. delavayi"	10	10
1481	1b. "Merremia vitifolia"	10	10
1482	1b. "Afgekia mahidolae"	10	10
MS1483	Two sheets, each 85 × 100 mm, each containing Nos. 1479/82. (a) Perf; (b) Imperf (pair sold at 20b.)	1·70	1·70

498 Wiman Mek Royal Hall

1990. Dusit Palace. Multicoloured.

1484	2b. Type **498**	10	10
1485	3b. Ratcharit Rungrot Royal House	20	10
1486	4b. Aphisek Dusit Royal Hall	20	15
1487	5b. Amphon Sathan Palace	25	15
1488	6b. Udon Phak Royal Hall	30	15
1489	8b. Anantasamakhom Throne Hall	40	25

499 Phrachetuphon Wimolmangkalaram Temple and Supreme Patriarch

1990. Birth Bicentenary of Supreme Patriarch Somdet Phra Maha Samanachao Kromphra Paramanuchitchinorot (formerly Prince Wasukri).
1490 **499** 2b. multicoloured . . . 15 10

500 Judo

1990. Sports Welfare Fund. Multicoloured.

1491	2b.+1b. Type **500**	10	10
1492	2b.+1b. Archery	10	10
1493	2b.+1b. High jumping	10	10
1494	2b.+1b. Windsurfing	10	10

501 Aspects of Petroleum Industry

1990. 12th Anniv of Thai Petroleum Authority.
1495 **501** 2b. multicoloured . . . 15 10

502 Mae Klong Railway Locomotive No. 6

1990. Steam Locomotives. Multicoloured.

1496	2b. Type **502**	10	10
1497	3b. "Sung Noen" locomotive No. 32	20	10
1498	5b. Class C 56 locomotive No. 715, Japan	30	30
1499	6b. Mikado locomotive No. 953, Japan	45	30
MS1500	Two sheets, each 152 × 123 mm, each containing Nos. 1496/9. (a) Perf; (b) Imperf (pair sold at 50b.)	4·25	4·25

503 Luk Khang (tops)

1991. Children's Day. Games. Multicoloured.

1501	2b. Type **503**	10	10
1502	3b. Pid Ta Ti Mo (blindfolded child smashing vase)	10	10
1503	5b. Doen Kala (walking on stones)	20	15
1504	6b. Phong Phang (blind man's buff)	30	15

504 Map, Surveyor and Cartographer
505 Princess (patron) wearing Red Cross Uniform

1991. Land Deeds Project.
1505 **504** 2b. multicoloured . . . 15 10

1991. Red Cross. Princess Maha Chaki Sirindhorn's "Third Cycle" (36th) Birthday.

1506	**505** 2b. multicoloured	55	10
MS1507	Two sheets, each 80 × 105 mm, each containing No. 1506. (a) Perf; (b) Imperf (pair sold at 16b.)	2·50	2·50

506 "Indra's Heavenly Abode"
507 Goddess riding Goat

1991. Heritage Conservation Day. Floral Hanging Decorations. Multicoloured.

1508	2b. Type **506**	10	10
1509	3b. "Celestial Couch"	15	10
1510	4b. "Crystal Ladder"	20	15
1511	5b. "Crocodile"	20	15
MS1512	Two sheets, each 116 × 154 mm, each containing Nos. 1508/11. (a) Perf; (b) Imperf (pair sold at 60b.)	2·50	2·50

1991. Songkran (New Year) Day. Year of the Goat.

1513	**507** 2b. multicoloured	75	30
MS1514	Two sheets, each 80 × 100 mm, each containing No. 1513. (a) Perf; (b) Imperf (pair sold at 16b.)	9·50	9·50

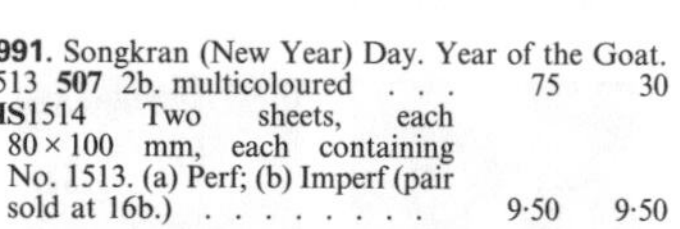
508 Prince Narisranuvattivongs

1991. 44th Death Anniv of Prince Narisranuvattivongs.
1515 **508** 2b. brown, deep brown and yellow . . . 15 10

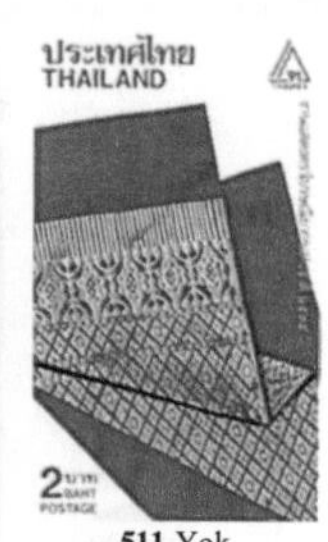
509 Pink Lotus (Sutthiporn Wiset)
511 Yok

510 World Map, Communication Systems and Healthy Tree

1991. Runners-up in International Correspondence Week Competition. Multicoloured.

1516	2b. Type **509**	10	10
1517	3b. Pink lotuses (Mathayom Suksa group, Khonkaen-vityayon School)	15	10

1518 5b. White lotus (Rattanaporn Sukhasem) (horiz) 20 15
1519 6b. Red lotuses (Phanupongs Sayasombat and Kanokwan Cholaphum) (horiz) . . . 20 15

1991. National Communications Day. "Communications and Preservation of the Environment".
1520 **510** 2b. multicoloured . . . 20 10

1991. "Thaipex '91" National Stamp Exhibition. Textile Patterns. Multicoloured.
1521 2b. Type **511** 10 10
1522 4b. Mudmee 15 10
1523 6b. Khit 20 15
1524 8b. Chok 25 25
MS1525 110 × 145 mm. Nos. 1521/4 (sold at 30b.) . . . . 1·10 1·10

512 Workers and Productivity Arrow

1991. International Productivity Congress.
1526 **512** 2b. multicoloured . . . 15 10

513 "Co-operation of Women around the World"

1991. 26th Int Council of Women Triennial.
1527 **513** 2b. multicoloured . . . 15 10

514 Black

1991. International Correspondence Week. Japanese Bantams. Multicoloured.
1528 2b. Type **514** 10 10
1529 3b. Black-tailed buff 20 10
1530 6b. Buff 30 15
1531 8b. White 45 30
MS1532 Two sheets, each 145 × 110 mm, each containing Nos. 1528/31. (a) Perf; (b) Imperf (pair sold at 70b.) . . . . . . 2·50 2·50

515 Silver Coin of King Rama IV and Wat Phra Sri Rattana Satsadaram

1991. World Bank and International Monetary Fund Annual Meetings. Multicoloured.
1533 2b. Type **515** 10 10
1534 4b. Pod Duang money, Wat Mahathat Sukhothai and Wat Aroonrachawararam 15 10
1535 8b. Chieng and Hoi money and Wat Phrathat Doi Suthep 30 20
1536 10b. Funan, Dvaravati and Srivijaya money, Phra Pathom Chedi and Phra Borommathat Chaiya . . 40 25
MS1537 Two sheets, each 145 × 110 mm, each containing Nos. 1533/6. (a) Perf; (b) Imperf (pair sold at 70b.) . . . . . . 2·50 2·50

516 1908 1t. Stamp

518 "Dillenia obovata"

517 Adult and Calves

1991. "Bangkok 1993" International Stamp Exhibition (1st series). Stamps from the 1908 King Chulalongkorn Issue. Multicoloured.
1538 2b. Type **516** 10 10
1539 3b. 2t. stamp 15 10
1540 4b. 3t. stamp 15 10
1541 5b. 5t. stamp 20 15
1542 6b. 10t. stamp 25 15
1543 7b. 20t. stamp 30 15
1544 8b. 40t. stamp 35 25
MS1545 Two sheets, each 80 × 129 mm, each containing No. 1544. (a) Perf; (b) Imperf (pair sold at 30b.) . . . . 2·10 2·10
See also Nos. 1618/**MS**1623, 1666/**MS**1670, 1700/**MS**1704 and **MS**1705.

1991. The Indian Elephant. Multicoloured.
1546 2b. Type **517** 10 10
1547 4b. Elephants pulling log . . 20 15
1548 6b. Adult male resting . . . 25 20
1549 8b. Adults bathing 45 30
MS1550 Two sheets, each 96 × 78 mm, each containing No. 1549. (a) Perf; (b) Imperf (pair sold at 44b.) . . . . 3·50 3·50

1991. New Year. Flowers. Multicoloured.
1551 1b. Type **518** 10 10
1552 1b. "Melastoma sanguineum" 10 10
1553 1b. "Commelina diffusa" . . 10 10
1554 1b. "Plumbago indica" . . . 10 10
MS1555 Two sheets, each 85 × 100 mm, each containing Nos. 1551/4. (a) Perf; (b) Imperf (sold at 20b.) . . . . 1·30 1·30

520 Jogging

522 Prince Mahidol

521 Large Indian Civet

1991. Sports Welfare Fund. Multicoloured.
1558 2b.+1b. Type **520** 10 10
1559 2b.+1b. Cycling 10 10
1560 2b.+1b. Skipping 10 10
1561 2b.+1b. Swimming 10 10

1991. Mammals. Multicoloured.
1562 2b. Type **521** 10 10
1563 3b. Banded linsang 15 10
1564 6b. Asiatic golden cat . . . 20 15
1565 8b. Black giant squirrel . . 30 25
MS1566 Two sheets, each 146 × 110 mm, each containing Nos. 1562/5. (a) Perf; (b) Imperf (pair sold at 60b.) . . . . . . 2·50 2·50

1992. Birth Centenary (1991) of Prince Mahidol of Songkla (pioneer of modern medicine in Thailand).
1567 **522** 2b. brown, gold & yellow 15 10

523 Archaeologists and Dinosaur Skeletons

1992. Centenary of Department of Mineral Resources. Multicoloured.
1568 2b. Type **523** 15 10
1569 2b. Mining excavation . . . 15 10
1570 2b. Extracting natural gas and oil 15 10
1571 2b. Digging artesian wells 15 10

524 Drawing by Nachadong Bunprasoet

1992. Children's Day. "World under the Sea". Children's Drawings. Multicoloured.
1572 2b. Type **524** 10 10
1573 3b. Fishes and seaweed (Varaporn Phadkhan) . . 15 10
1574 5b. Mermaid (Phannipha Ngoenkon) (vert) 15 10

525 Battle Scene (mural, Chan Chittrakon)

1992. 400th Anniv of Duel between King Naresuan the Great of Thailand and Phra Maha Upparacha of Burma.
1575 **525** 2b. multicoloured . . . 15 10

526 "Paphiopedilum bellatulum"

1992. 4th Asia–Pacific Orchid Conf. Mult.
1576 2b. Type **526** 10 10
1577 2b. "Paphiopedilum exul" 10 10
1578 3b. "Paphiopedilum godefroyae" 15 10
1579 3b. "Paphiopedilum concolor" 15 10
1580 6b. "Paphiopedilum niveum" 15 15
1581 6b. "Paphiopedilum villosum" 15 15
1582 10b. "Paphiopedilum parishii" 35 25
1583 10b. "Paphiopedilum sukhahulii" 35 25
MS1584 Four sheets, each 110 × 145 mm. (a) Nos. 1576, 1579/80 and 1582. Perf; (b) As a. but imperf; (c) Nos. 1577/8, 1581 and 1583. Perf; (d) As c. but imperf (4 sheets sold at 120b.) 5·25 5·25

527 Sugar Cane

528 Prince Rabi Badhanasakdi (founder of School of Law)

1992. 21st International Sugar Cane Technologists Society Congress.
1585 **527** 2b. multicoloured . . . 15 10

1992. Centenary of Ministry of Justice. Legal Reformers. Multicoloured.
1586 3b. Type **528** 15 10
1587 5b. King Rama V (reformer of Courts system) 45 15

529 "Innocent" (Kamolporn Tapsuang)

1992. Red Cross.
1588 **529** 2b. multicoloured . . . 15 10

530 Container Ships and Lorry

531 Prince Damrong Rajanubharb (first Minister)

1992. 80th Anniv of Ministry of Transport and Communications. Multicoloured.
1589 2b. Type **530** 10 10
1590 3b. Diesel train and bus . . 15 10
1591 5b. Boeing 747-200 airliner and control tower 15 15
1592 6b. Lorry, satellites and aerials 20 15

1992. Cent of Ministry of the Interior. Mult.
1593 2b. Type **531** 15 10
1594 2b. Polling station 15 10
1595 2b. Emergency services and army 15 10
1596 2b. Child fetching water . . 15 10

532 Royal Ceremony of First Ploughing

1992. Centenary of Ministry of Agriculture and Co-operatives.
1597 **532** 2b. multicoloured . . . 10 10
1598 3b. multicoloured . . . 15 10
1599 4b. multicoloured . . . 20 15
1600 5b. multicoloured . . . 25 15

533 Ministry

535 Demon riding Monkey

534 Western Region

1992. Centenary of Ministry of Education.
1601 **533** 2b. multicoloured . . . 15 10

1992. Thai Heritage Conservation Day. Traditional Carts. Multicoloured.
1602 2b. Type **534** 10 10
1603 3b. Northern region 15 10
1604 5b. North-eastern region . . 20 15
1605 10b. Eastern region 35 25
MS1606 Two sheets, each 145 × 110 mm, each containing Nos. 1602/5. (a) Perf; (b) Imperf (spair sold at 60b.) . . . . . . 2·50 2·50

1992. Songkran (New Year) Day. Year of the Monkey.
1607 **535** 2b. multicoloured . . . 20 10
MS1608 Two sheets, each 80 × 100 mm, each containing No. 1607. (a) Perf; (b) Imperf (pair sold at 16b.) . . . . 2·10 2·10

536 American Brahman and Livestock

1992. 50th Anniv of Department of Livestock Development.
1609 **536** 2b. multicoloured . . . 15 10

537 Birth of Buddha (mural, Wat Angkaeo, Bangkok)
538 Weather Balloon, Dish Aerial, Satellite and Map

1992. Wisakhabucha Day. Multicoloured.
1610 2b. Type **537** 10 10
1611 3b. "Enlightenment of Buddha" (illustration by Phraya Thewaphinimmit from biography) 20 15
1612 5b. Death of Buddha (mural, Wat Kanmatuyaram, Bangkok) 30 25

1992. 50th Anniv of Meteorological Department.
1613 **538** 2b. multicoloured . . . 15 10

539 Bua Tong Field, Mae Hong Son Province
540 1887 64a. stamp

1992. Association of South-East Asian Nations Tourism Year. Multicoloured.
1614 2b. Type **539** 10 10
1615 3b. Klong Larn Waterfall, Kamphaeng Phet Province 15 10
1616 4b. Coral, Chumphon Province 15 10
1617 5b. Khao Ta-Poo, Phangnga Province 20 15

1992. "Bangkok 1993" International Stamp Exhibition (2nd series). Multicoloured.
1618 2b. Type **540** 10 10
1619 3b. 1916 20b. stamp 15 10
1620 5b. 1928 40b. stamp 20 15
1621 7b. 1943 1b. stamp 25 15
1622 8b. 1947 20b. stamp 30 25
MS1623 Two sheets, each 123 × 185 mm, each containing Nos. 1618/22. (a) Perf; (b) Imperf (pair sold at 70b.) . . . . . . 3·50 3·50

541 Prince Chudadhuj Dharadilok
543 Culture and Sports

542 "Communications"

1992. Birth Centenary of Prince Chudadhuj Dharadilok of Bejraburna.
1624 **541** 2b. multicoloured . . . 15 10

1992. National Communications Day.
1625 **542** 2b. multicoloured . . . 15 10

1992. 25th Anniv of Association of South-East Asian Nations. Multicoloured.
1626 2b. Type **543** 10 10
1627 3b. Tourist sites 15 10
1628 5b. Transport and communications 20 10
1629 7b. Agriculture 20 15

544 Sirikit Medical Centre

1992. Inauguration of Sirikit Medical Centre.
1630 **544** 2b. multicoloured . . . 15 10

545 Wedding Ceremony

546 Queen Sirikit and Cipher

1992. 60th Birthday of Queen Sirikit. (a) As T **545**. Multicoloured.
1635 2b. Type **545** 15 10
1636 2b. Royal couple seated at Coronation ceremony . . 15 10
1637 2b. Anointment as Queen 15 10
1638 2b. Seated on chair 15 10
1639 2b. Visiting hospital patient 15 10
1640 2b. Talking to subjects . . . 15 10
MS1641 Two sheets, each 126 × 163 mm, each containing Nos. 1635/40. (a) Perf; (b) Imperf (pair sold at 60b.) . . . . . . 2·50 2·50

(b) Royal Regalia. Enamelled gold objects. As T **546**. Multicoloured.
1642 2b. Bowls on footed tray (betel and areca nut set) 15 10
1643 2b. Kettle 15 10
1644 2b. Water holder within bowl 15 10
1645 2b. Box on footed tray (betel and areca nut set) 15 10
1646 2b. Vase 15 10

(c) Type **546**.
1647 100b. blue and gold . . . . 4·25 4·25

547 Prince Wan Waithayakon
548 Bhirasri

1992. Birth Centenary (1991) of Prince Wan Waithayakon, Krommun Naradhip Bongsprabandh (diplomat).
1648 **547** 2b. multicoloured . . . 15 10

1992. Birth Centenary of Silpa Bhirasri (sculptor).
1649 **548** 2b. multicoloured . . . 15 10

549 "Catalaphyllia jardinei"

1992. Int Correspondence Week. Corals. Mult.
1650 2b. Type **549** 10 10
1651 3b. "Porites lutea" 15 10
1652 6b. "Tubastraea coccinea" 20 15
1653 8b. "Favia pallida" 30 25
MS1654 145 × 110 mm. Nos. 1650/3 (sold at 30b.) . . . . 1·10 1·10

550 "Rhododendron simsii"
551 Figures of Man and Woman

1992. New Year. Flowers. Multicoloured.
1655 1b. Type **550** 10 10
1656 1b. "Cynoglossum lanceolatum" 10 10
1657 1b. "Tithonia diversifolia" 10 10
1658 1b. "Agapetes parishii" . . 10 10
MS1659 Two sheets, each 100 × 85 mm, each containing Nos. 1655/8. (a) Perf; (b) Imperf (pair sold at 20b.) . . . . . . 1·10 1·10

1992. 1st Asian–Pacific Allergy and Immunology Congress, Bangkok.
1660 **551** 2b. multicoloured . . . 15 10

552 Anantasamakhom Throne Hall, National Assembly Building and King Prajadhipok's Monument

1992. 60th Anniv of National Assembly.
1661 **552** 2b. multicoloured . . . 15 10

553 Bank's Emblem and Bang Khun Phrom Palace (old headquarters)

1992. 50th Anniv of Bank of Thailand.
1662 **553** 2b. multicoloured . . . 15 10

554 "River and Life" (Prathinthip Mensin)

1993. Children's Day. Drawings. Mult.
1663 2b. Type **554** 10 10
1664 2b. "Lovely Wild Animals and Beautiful Forest" (Pratsani Thammaprasert) 10 10
1665 2b. "Communications in the Next Decade" (Natchaliya Sutiprasit) 10 10

555 Kendi, Water Dropper and Bottle

1993. "Bangkok 1993" International Stamp Exn (3rd series). Traditional Pottery. Multicoloured.
1666 3b. Type **555** 10 10
1667 6b. Vase and bottles 25 15
1668 7b. Bowls 30 15
1669 8b. Jars 35 20
MS1670 145 × 110 mm. Nos. 1666/9 (sold at 35b.) . . . . 1·40 1·40

556 Anniversary Emblem

1993. Centenary of Thai Teacher Training Institute.
1671 **556** 2b. multicoloured . . . 15 10

557 Agricultural Produce

1993. 50th Anniv of Kasetsart University.
1672 **557** 2b. multicoloured . . . 15 10

558 Buddha preaching (mural, Wat Kanmatuyaram, Bangkok)
559 Queen Sri Bajarindra (first royal patron)

1993. Maghapuja Day.
1673 **558** 2b. multicoloured . . . 15 10

1993. Centenary of Thai Red Cross.
1674 **559** 2b. multicoloured . . . 20 10

560 Clock, Emblem and Attorney General

1993. Centenary of Attorney General's Office.
1675 **560** 2b. multicoloured . . . 15 10

561 Wat Chedi Chet Thaeo

1993. Thai Heritage Conservation Day. Si Satchanalai Historical Park, Sukhothai Province. Mult.
1676 3b. Type **561** 15 10
1677 4b. Wat Chang Lom . . . 15 10
1678 6b. Wat Phra Si Rattanamahathat 20 10
1679 7b. Wat Suan Kaeo Utthayan Noi 25 15
MS1680 145 × 110 mm. Nos. 1676/9 (sold at 25b.) 85 85

562 Demon riding Cock

1993. Songkran (New Year) Day. Year of the Cock.
1681 **562** 2b. multicoloured . . . 10 10
MS1682 Two sheets, each 80 × 100 mm, each containing No. 1681. (a) Perf; (b) Imperf (pair sold at 16b.) 65 65

563 "Marasmius sp."

1993. Fungi. Multicoloured.
1683 2b. Type **563** 10 10
1684 4b. "Coprinus sp." 15 10
1685 6b. "Mycena sp." 20 15
1686 8b. "Cyathus sp." 25 15
MS1687 145 × 110 mm. Nos. 1683/6 (sold at 30b.) . . . . 1·20 1·20

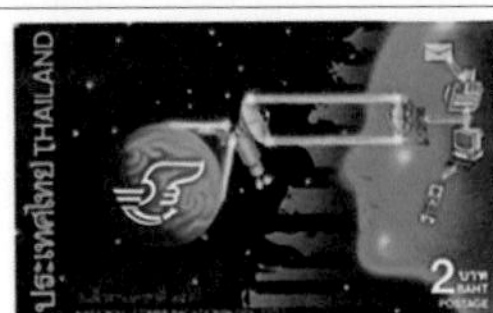
564 "Communications in the Next Decade"

1993. National Communications Day.
1688 **564** 2b. multicoloured . . . 15 10

565 Emblem, Morse Key and Satellite

1993. 110th Anniv of Post and Telegraph Department.
1689 **565** 2b. multicoloured . . . 30 10

566 Monument, Park and Reservoir

1993. Unveiling of Queen Suriyothai's Monument.
1690 **566** 2b. multicoloured . . . 15 10

567 Fawn Ridgeback

1993. International Correspondence Week. The Thai Ridgeback. Multicoloured.
1691 2b. Type **567** 10 10
1692 3b. Black 10 10
1693 5b. Tan 15 10
1694 10b. Grey 40 15
MS1695 145 × 110 mm. Nos. 1691/4 (sold at 30b.) . . . . 1·20 1·20

568 Tangerine **569** Bencharong Cosmetic Jar

1993. Fruits. Multicoloured.
1696 2b. Type **568** 10 10
1697 3b. Bananas 10 10
1698 6b. Star gooseberry 20 15
1699 8b. Marian plum 25 15

1993. "Bangkok 1993" International Stamp Exhibition (4th issue). Multicoloured.
1700 3b. Type **569** 10 10
1701 5b. Bencharong round cosmetic jar 15 10
1702 6b. Lai Nam Thong tall cosmetic jar 15 10
1703 7b. Lai Nam Thong cosmetic jar 20 15
MS1704 110 × 145 mm. Nos. 1700/3 (sold at 30b.) . . . . 1·20 1·20

1993. Bangkok 1993 International Stamp Exhibition (5th issue). Sheet 81 × 100 mm containing No. 1350.
MS1705 **453** 25b. blue and olive 4·00 4·00

570 Emblem and Oil Rigs

1993. 5th Association of South East Asian Nations Council on Petroleum Conference and Exhibition.
1706 **570** 2b. multicoloured . . . 15 10

571 King Prajadhipok **572** "Ipomea cairica"

1993. Birth Centenary of King Prajadhipok (Rama VII).
1707 **571** 2b. brown and gold . . 20 10

1993. New Year. Flowers. Multicoloured.
1708 1b. Type **572** 10 10
1709 1b. "Decaschistia parviflora" 10 10
1710 1b. "Hibiscus tiliaceus" . . 10 10
1711 1b. "Passiflora foetida" . . 10 10
MS1712 100 × 85 mm. Nos. 1708/11 (sold at 10b.) 55 55

1993. No. 1031a surch **1 BAHT**.
1713 **227** 1b. on 25s. red 10 10

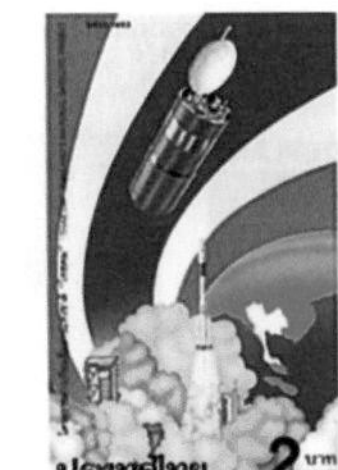
574 "Thaicom-1" Satellite, "Ariane 4" Rocket and Map of Thailand

1993. Launch of "Thaicom-1" (1st Thai communications satellite).
1714 **574** 2b. multicoloured . . . 15 10

575 "Play Land" (Piyathida Chapirom)

1994. Children's Day.
1715 **575** 2b. multicoloured . . . 15 10

576 Hospital Administrative Building

1994. Red Cross. 80th Anniv of Chulalongkorn Hospital.
1716 **576** 2b. multicoloured . . . 10 10

577 Emblem and Book

1994. 60th Anniv of Royal Institute.
1717 **577** 2b. multicoloured . . . 10 10

578 Wat Ratchaburana

1994. Thai Heritage Conservation Day. Phra Nakhon Si Ayutthaya Historical Park. Multicoloured.
1718 2b. Type **578** 10 10
1719 3b. Wat Maha That 10 10
1720 6b. Wat Maheyong 15 10
1721 9b. Wat Phra Si Sanphet . . 30 15
MS1722 145 × 110 mm. Nos. 1718/21 (sold at 25b.) . . . . 1·00 1·00

579 Friendship Bridge

1994. Inauguration of Friendship Bridge (between Thailand and Laos).
1723 **579** 9b. multicoloured . . . 30 15

580 Demon riding Dog

1994. Songkran (New Year) Day. Year of the Dog.
1724 **580** 2b. multicoloured . . . 10 10
1725 Two sheets, each 80 × 100 mm, each containing No. 1724. (a) Perf; (b) Imperf (pair sold at 16b.) . . 65 65

นิทรรศการตราไปรษณียากรไทย - จีน
泰國郵票展覽・北京
(581) (½-size illustration)

1994. Stamp Exhibition, Peking. As No. **MS**1725 but without sheet value and optd in bottom margin with T **581**.
MS1726 Two sheets, each 80 × 100 mm. **580** 2b. multicoloured. (a) Perf; (b) Imperf . . . . 5·50 5·50

582 Football

1994. Centenary of Int Olympic Committee. Mult.
1727 2b. Type **582** 10 10
1728 3b. Running 10 10
1729 5b. Swimming 15 10
1730 6b. Weightlifting 15 10
1731 9b. Boxing 25 20

583 Dome Building

1994. 60th Anniv of Thammasat University.
1732 **583** 2b. multicoloured . . . 10 10

584 "Buddha giving First Sermon" (mural from Wat Thong Thammachat)

1994. Asalhapuja Day.
1733 **584** 2b. multicoloured . . . 10 10

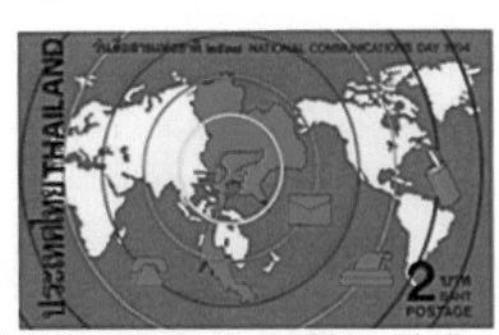
585 Communications orbiting Thailand

1994. National Communications Day.
1734 **585** 2b. multicoloured . . . 10 10

586 "Phricotelphusa limula"

1994. Crabs. Multicoloured.
1735 3b. Type **586** 10 10
1736 5b. "Thaipotamon chulabhorn" 15 15
1737 6b. "Phricotelphusa sirindhorn" 15 15
1738 10b. "Thaiphusa sirikit" . . 30 20
MS1739 145 × 110 mm. Nos. 1735/8 (sold at 30b.) . . . . 1·20 1·20

587 Gold Niello Betel Nut Set

1994. International Correspondence Week. Betel Nut Sets.
1740 2b. Type **587** 10 10
1741 6b. Gold-plated silver niello set 20 10
1742 8b. Silver niello set 30 15
1743 9b. Gold niello set 35 20
MS1744 145 × 110 mm. Nos. 1740/3 (sold at 30b.) . . . . 1·20 1·20

588 Emblem and Workers

1994. 75th Anniv of I.L.O.
1745 **588** 2b. multicoloured . . . 10 10

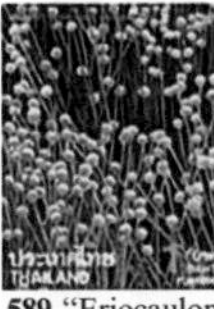
589 "Eriocaulon odoratum"

1994. New Year. Flowers. Multicoloured.
1746 1b. Type **589** 10 10
1747 1b. "Utricularia bifida" . . 10 10
1748 1b. "Utricularia delphinioides" 10 10
1749 1b. "Utricularia minutissima" 10 10
MS1750 85 × 100 mm. Nos. 1746/9 (sold at 10b.) 45 45

590 Making Garland

1994. 60th Anniv of Suan Dusit Teachers' College.
1751 **590** 2b. multicoloured . . . 10 10

591 Chakri Mahaprasart Throne Hall and Kings Chulalongkorn and Bhumibol

1994. 120th Anniv of Council of State.
1754 **591** 2b. stone, blue and green 20 10

592 Emblem and Airplane

1994. 50th Anniv of I.C.A.O.
1755 **592** 2b. multicoloured . . . 10 10

593 Dvaravati Grinding Stone (7–11th century)

1994. 80th Anniv of Pharmacy in Thailand.
1756 2b. Type **593** 10 10
1757 6b. Lopburi grinding stone (11–13th century) 15 10
1758 9b. Bangkok period grinding stone (18–20th century) 25 20

594 Water Polo

1994. 18th South-East Asian Games, Chiang Mai. Multicoloured.
1759 2b.+1b. Type **594** 10 10
1760 2b.+1b. Tennis 10 10
1761 2b.+1b. Hurdling 10 10
1762 2b.+1b. Gymnastics 10 10
MS1763 145 × 110 mm. Nos. 1759/62 (sold at 15b.) 55 55

595 First Bar Building and Kings Vajiravudh and Bhumibol

1995. 80th Anniv of the Bar.
1764 **595** 2b. multicoloured . . . 10 10

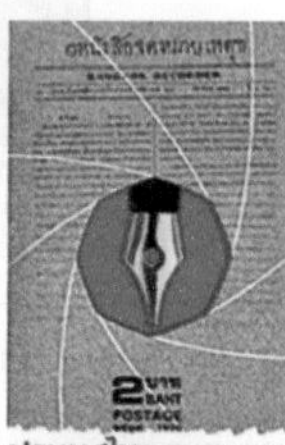

596 "Kites decorate the Summer Sky" (Kontorn Taechoran)
597 Front Page of First Edition and Pen Nib in Camera Shutter

1995. Children's Day. Multicoloured.
1765 2b. Type **596** 10 10
1766 2b. "Trees and Streams" (Yuvadee Samutpong) (horiz) 10 10
1767 2b. "Youths and Religion" (Yutdanai Polyium) (horiz) 10 10

1995. 150th Anniv of "Bangkok Recorder" (newspaper).
1768 **597** 2b. multicoloured . . . 10 10

598 Breguet Biplane and General Dynamics Fighting Falcon Jet Fighter

1995. 80th Anniv of Royal Thai Airforce.
1769 **598** 2b. multicoloured . . . 10 10

599 "Wetchapha"

1995. Red Cross. 40th Anniv of "Wetchapha" (hospital ship).
1770 **599** 2b. multicoloured . . . 10 10

600 Naga Bridge

1995. Thai Heritage Conservation Day. Phimai Historical Park. Multicoloured.
1771 3b. Type **600** 10 10
1772 5b. Brahmin Hall 15 10
1773 6b. Gateway in inner wall 15 10
1774 9b. Main pagoda 25 15
MS1775 145 × 110 mm. Nos. 1771/4 (sold at 30b.) 85 85

601 Administration Hall

1995. 108th Anniv of Ministry of Defence.
1776 **601** 2b. multicoloured . . . 15 10

602 Woman riding Boar

1995. Songkran (New Year) Day.
1777 **602** 2b. multicoloured . . . 10 10
MS1778 Two sheets, each 80 × 100 mm, each containing No. 1777. (a) Perf; (b) Imperf (sold at 16b.) 50 50

603 King Rama V and Saranrom Palace

1995. 120th Anniv of Ministry of Foreign Affairs.
1779 **603** 2b. multicoloured . . . 20 10

604 Emerald Buddha
605 Emblem forming Flower and Globe

1995. Visakhapuja Day. Statues of Buddha. Multicoloured.
1780 2b. Type **604** 10 10
1781 6b. Phra Phuttha Chinnarat 15 10
1782 8b. Phra Phuttha Sihing . . 25 20
1783 9b. Phra Sukhothai Traimit 30 20
MS1784 127 × 151 mm. Nos. 1780/3 (sold at 35b.) . . . . 1·10 1·10

1995. Association of South East Asian Nations Environment Year.
1785 **605** 2b. multicoloured . . . 10 10

606 Emblem

1995. Thailand Information Technology Year.
1786 **606** 2b. multicoloured . . . 10 10

607 Asian Elephants and Young

1995. 20th Anniv of Thailand–China Diplomatic Relations. Multicoloured.
1787 2b. Type **607** 10 10
1788 2b. Asian elephants at river (face value at left) 10 10
MS1789 145 × 110 mm. Nos. 1787/8 (sold at 8b.) 65 65
Nos. 1787/8 were issued together, se-tenant, forming a composite design.

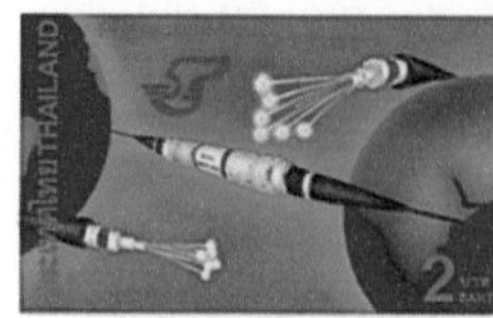

608 Optical Fibre Cables

1995. National Communications Day.
1790 **608** 2b. multicoloured . . . 10 10

609 Khoa Manee
610 Headquarters

1995. "Thaipex'95" National Stamp Exhibition. Cats. Multicoloured.
1791 3b. Type **609** 10 10
1792 6b. Korat 15 15
1793 7b. Sealpoint Siamese . . . 20 15
1794 9b. Burmese 30 20
MS1795 110 × 145 mm. Nos. 1791/4 (sold at 35b.) 95 95

1995. 80th Anniv of Revenue Department.
1796 **610** 2b. multicoloured . . . 10 10

611 Money and Industry

1995. 120th Anniv of National Auditing.
1797 **611** 2b. multicoloured . . . 10 10

612 Khong

1995. International Correspondence Week. Wicker Aquatic Animal Baskets.
1798 2b. Type **612** 10 10
1799 2b. Krachangklom (round basket) 10 10
1800 9b. Sum (open-ended basket) 25 15
1801 9b. Ichu (jar) 25 15
MS1802 110 × 145 mm. Nos. 1798/1801 (sold at 35b.) 95 95

613 Foodstuffs and Anniversary Emblem

1995. 50th Anniv of F.A.O.
1803 **613** 2b. multicoloured . . . 10 10

614 Telescope and Eclipse

1995. Total Solar Eclipse.
1804 **614** 2b. multicoloured . . . 10 10

615 U.N. Building, Thailand

1995. 50th Anniv of U.N.O.
1805 **615** 2b. multicoloured . . . 10 10

616 Tower
617 "Adenium obesum"

1995. "WORLDTECH'95" International Agricultural and Industrial Exhibition, Suranaree. Multicoloured.
1806 2b. Type **616** 10 10
1807 5b. Agriculture 15 10
1808 6b. Modern technology (horiz) 15 10
1809 9b. Reservoirs and coastline (horiz) 25 15

1996. New Year. Flowers. Multicoloured.
1810 2b. Type **617** 10 10
1811 2b. "Bauhinia acuminata" 10 10
1812 2b. "Cananga odorata" . . 10 10
1813 2b. "Thunbergia erecta" . . 10 10
MS1814 100 × 85 mm. Nos. 1810/13 (sold at 15b.) 55 55

618 Vaccinating Cattle

1995. 60th Anniv of Veterinary Science in Thailand.
1815 **618** 2b. multicoloured . . . 10 10

619 Fencing
620 Queen Somdej Phra Sri Patcharin (founder)

1995. 18th South-East Asian Games, Chiang Mai. Multicoloured.
1816 2b.+1b. Type **619** 10 10
1817 2b.+1b. Snooker 10 10
1818 2b.+1b. Diving 10 10
1819 2b.+1b. Pole vaulting . . . 10 10
MS1820 145 × 110 mm. Nos. 1816/19 (sold at 15b.) 55 55
Nos. 1815/18 were issued together, se-tenant, forming a composite design.

1996. Centenary of Siriraj School of Nursing and Midwifery.
1821 **620** 2b. multicoloured . . . 10 10

621 Breguet Biplane and Emblem

1996. National Aviation Day.
1822 **621** 2b. multicoloured . . . 10 10

622 "Visakhapuja Day" (Malinee Sanaewong)

1996. Children's Day. Children's Drawings. Multicoloured.
1823 2b. Type **622** 10 10
1824 2b. "Maghapuja Day" (Thirapon Deephlub) (tree in centre) (vert) 10 10
1825 2b. "Asalhapuja Day" (Voraphat Pankian) (tree at left) (vert) 10 10

623 Handshake and Map of Asia and Europe

1996. Asia–Europe Summit Meeting, Thailand.
1826 **623** 2b. multicoloured . . . 10 10

624 Temiyajataka

1996. Maghapuja Day. Multicoloured.
1827 2b. Type **624** 10 10
1828 6b. Mahajanakajataka . . . 15 10
1829 8b. Suvannasamjataka . . . 20 15
1830 9b. Nemijataka 30 20
MS1831 152 × 127 mm. Nos. 1827/30 (sold at 36b.) . . . . 1·10 1·10

625 Princess Mother and Golden Crematorium

1996. Princess Mother's Cremation.
1832 **625** 2b. multicoloured . . . 20 10

626 Wat Phra Kaeo

1996. Thai Heritage Conservation Day. Kamphaeng Phet Historical Park. Multicoloured.
1833 2b. Type **626** 10 10
1834 3b. Wat Phra Non 10 10
1835 6b. Wat Chang Rop 15 10
1836 9b. Wat Pgra Si Iriyabot . . 30 20
MS1837 145 × 110 mm. Nos. 1833/6 (sold at 28b.) 85 85

627 Buddhist Pagoda, Wat Chiang Man

1996. 700th Anniv of Chiang Mai. Multicoloured.
1838 2b. Type **627** 10 10
1839 6b. Angel sculpture, Wat Chet Yot's Pagoda . . . 15 10
1840 8b. Insignia of Wat Phan Tao monastery 20 15
1841 9b. Sattaphanta 30 20
MS1842 145 × 110 mm. Nos. 1838/41 (sold at 37b.) . . . . 1·10 1·10

628 Rufous-necked Hornbills

629 Angel riding Rat

1996. 2nd International Asian Hornbill Workshop. Multicoloured.
1843 3b. Type **628** 10 10
1844 3b. Long-crested hornbill ("White-crowned Hornbill") 10 10
1845 9b. Blyth's hornbill ("Plain-pouched Hornbill") . . . 25 20
1846 9b. Rhinoceros hornbill . . 25 20
MS1847 110 × 145 mm. Nos. 1843/6 (sold at 35b.) 95 95

1996. Songkran (New Year) Day.
1848 **629** 2b. multicoloured . . . 10 10
MS1849 Two sheets, each 80 × 100 mm, containing No. 1848. (a) Perf; (b) Imperf (sold at 16b.) 50 50
MS1850 Two sheets, each 135 × 160 mm. Nos. 1513, 1607, 1681, 1724, 1777 and 1848. (a) Perf; (b) Imperf (sold at 40b.) 1·30 1·30

630 Royal Ablutions Ceremony

631 King Bhumibol

1996. 50th Anniv of King Bhumibol's Accession to Throne as Rama IX (1st issue). Multicoloured.
(a) Coronation Ceremony. Multicoloured.
1851 3b. Type **630** 10 10
1852 3b. Pouring of the Libation 10 10
1853 3b. Grand Audience 10 10
1854 3b. Royal Progress by land 10 10
1855 3b. Making speech from balcony 10 10
MS1856 Five sheets, each 120 × 110 mm. (a) 3b. Type **630**; (b) 3b. No. 1852; (c) 3b. No. 1853; (d) 3b. No. 1854; (e) 3b. No. 1855 (five sheets sold for 40b.) . . . 1·30 1·30

(b) Royal Regalia. As T **630**.
1857 3b. Betal and areca-nut set 10 10
1858 3b. Water urn 10 10
1859 3b. Gold-enamelled cuspidor and golden spittoon (horiz) 10 10
MS1860 110 × 145 mm. Nos. 1857/9 (sold at 17b.) 65 65

(c) National Development. As T **630** but horiz.
1861 3b. Cultivation of vetiver grass (prevention of soil erosion) 10 10
1862 3b. Chai Pattana aerator (improvement of water quality) 10 10
1863 3b. Airplane (rain-making project) 10 10
1864 3b. Dam (water resources development) 10 10
1865 3b. Sapling (Golden Jubilee Reforestation Campaign) 10 10
MS1866 185 × 122 mm. Nos. 1861/5 plus label (sold at 25b.) 75 75

(d) Type **631**.
1867 100b. multicoloured . . . . 3·75 3·75
See also No. 1885/**MS**1886.

632 Baron Pierre de Coubertin (founder) and Grave

633 King Bhumibol using Short-wave Radio

1996. Centenary of Modern Olympic Games. Multicoloured.
1868 2b. Type **632** 10 10
1869 3b. Lighting Olympic flame at Olympia, Greece . . . 10 10
1870 5b. First modern Games and Olympic flag 15 10
1871 9b. Athlete and medal from 1896 Games 30 20

1996. National Communications Day.
1872 **633** 2b. multicoloured . . . 20 10

634 Tropical Rain Forest

1996. Centenary of Royal Forest Department. Multicoloured.
1873 3b. Type **634** 10 10
1874 6b. Evergreen mountain forest 15 10
1875 7b. Swamp forest 20 15
1876 9b. Mangrove forest 30 20
MS1877 144 × 108 mm. Nos. 1873/6 (sold at 35b.) 95 95

635 "Ramayana"

1996. International Correspondence Week. Thai Novels. Multicoloured.
1878 3b. Type **635** 10 10
1879 3b. Inao and Budsaba in cave ("Inao") 10 10
1880 9b. Lunhap being shown round forest ("Ngao Pa") 25 20
1881 9b. The cursing of Nang Mathanal ("Mathanapatha") . . . 25 20
MS1882 145 × 110 mm. Nos. 1878/81 (sold at 36b.) 95 95

636 Youth Activities

1996. Asia Regional Conference of Rotary International, Thailand.
1883 **636** 2b. multicoloured . . . 10 10

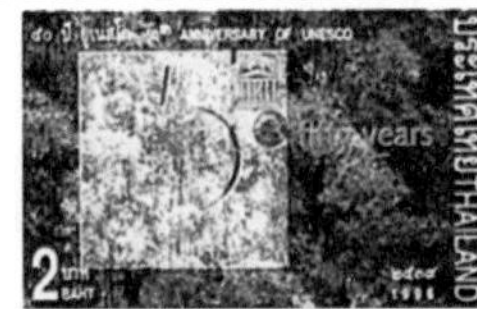
637 Huoy Kha Khang National Park

1996. 50th Anniv of U.N.E.S.C.O.
1884 **637** 2b. multicoloured . . . 10 10

638 "Narai Song Suban H.M. King Rama IX" (new royal barge) (½-size illustration)

1996. 50th Anniv of King Bhumibol's Accession to Throne as Rama IX (2nd issue). Multicoloured.
1885 **638** 9b. multicoloured . . . 25 25
MS1886 170 × 110 mm. No. 1885 (sold at 16b.) 75 75

639 "Limnocharis flava"

640 Indian Whistling Duck ("Dendrocygna javanica")

1996. New Year. Flowers. Multicoloured.
1887 2b. Type **639** 10 10
1888 2b. "Crinum thaianum" (vert) 10 10
1889 2b. "Monochoria hastata" (vert) 10 10
1890 2b. "Nymphoides indicum" 10 10
MS1891 85 × 100 mm. Nos. 1887/90 (sold at 15b.) 55 55

1996. Water Birds. Multicoloured.
1892 3b. Type **640** 10 10
1893 3b. Comb duck ("Sarkidiornis melanotos") (horiz) . . . 10 10
1894 7b. Cotton teal ("Nettapus coromandelianus") (horiz) 20 15
1895 7b. White-winged wood duck ("Cairina scutulata") 20 15
MS1896 153 × 120 mm. Nos. 1892/5 (sold at 33b.) 95 95

641 King Rama IX in Admiral's Uniform

1996.

2005	**641**	50s. green	10	10
1897		2b. red	10	10
2077		2b. red	10	10
2078		4b. red and blue . . .	10	10
1900		5b. red and lilac . . .	15	10
2079		5b. brown and violet	15	10
1901		6b. lilac and green . .	15	10
1902		7b. green and pink . .	20	10
1902a		9b. orange and blue . .	25	10
1903		10b. black and orange	25	10
1903a		12b. blue and green . .	30	15
1903b		15b. green and brown	45	15
1904		20b. red and violet . .	55	15
1905		25b. olive and green . .	65	30
1905a		30b. brown and pink	85	30
1906		50b. green and violet	1·30	45
1907		100b. blue and yellow	2·50	45
1908		200b. purple and mauve	5·25	85
1909		500b. mauve and orange (26 × 31mm)	13·00	2·10

642 Children at Zoo (Ruangchai Khot-Tha)

1996. 50th Anniv of U.N.I.C.E.F.
1910 **642** 2b. multicoloured . . . 10 10

643 Medal, Flag and Boxers

1996. 1st Thai Olympic Gold Medal (won by Somluck Khamsingh for boxing at Atlanta, U.S.A.).
1911 **643** 6b. multicoloured . . . 20 10

644 School, King Rama V and Crown Prince Vajiravudh (Rama VI)

645 "Good Things in my Province" (Natamol Thongsai)

1997. Centenary of Mahavajiravudh School, Songkhla.
1912 **644** 62b. multicoloured . . . 10 10

1997. Children's Day. Children's Drawings. Multicoloured.
1913 2b. Type **645** (dried fish, Samut Prakan) 10 10
1914 2b. "Tourist Sites in my Province", Chanthaburi (Somkiat Thongchomphu) 10 10

646 Old and New Buildings

1997. 20th Anniv of Communications Authority.
1915 **646** 2b. multicoloured . . . 10 10

647 Statue

1997. Unveiling of Statue of Prince Bhanurangsi (founder of postal service) outside Communications Authority, Laksi (Bangkok).
1916 **647** 2b. multicoloured . . . 10 10

648 Building

1997. Laksi Mail Centre. Multicoloured.
1917 2b. Type **648** 10 10
1918 2b. Letter sorting equipment 10 10
Nos. 1917/18 were issued together, se-tenant, forming a composite design.

649 Windsor Palace (University building)

1997. 80th Anniv of Chulalongkorn University. Multicoloured.
1919 2b. Type **649** 10 10
1920 2b. Faculty of Arts building 10 10

650 Early Steam Locomotive

1997. Cent of Thai State Railway. Mult.
1921 3b. Type **650** 10 10
1922 4b. Garratt steam locomotive 15 10
1923 6b. Sulzer diesel-mechanic locomotive 15 15
1924 7b. Hitachi diesel-electric locomotive 20 15
MS1925 Two sheets. (a) 110 × 145 mm. No. 1921; (b) 145 × 110 mm. Nos. 1921/4 (pair sold at 50b.) . . . . 1·50 1·50

651 Rajakarun Museum

1997. Red Cross.
1926 **651** 3b. multicoloured . . . 10 10

652 First Headquarters

1997. 84th Anniv of Government Savings Bank.
1927 **652** 2b. multicoloured . . . 10 10

653 Outer Staircase

1997. Thai Heritage Conservation Day. Phanomrung Historical Park. Multicoloured.
1928 3b. Type **653** 10 10
1929 3b. Pavilion 10 10
1930 7b. Pathway and stairs to Sanctuary 20 15
1931 7b. Naga balustrade and Eastern Gallery central gate 20 15
MS1932 110 × 145 mm. Nos. 1928/31 (sold at 30b.) 85 85

654 Man riding Bull

1997. Songkran (New Year) Day. Year of the Bull.
1933 **654** 2b. multicoloured . . . 10 10
MS1934 Two sheets, each 80 × 100 mm, each containing No. 1933. (a) Perf; (b) Imperf (sold at 16b.) 50 50

655 Pheasant-tailed Jacana

1997. Water Birds. Multicoloured.
1935 3b. Type **655** 10 10
1936 3b. Bronze-winged jacana 10 10
1937 7b. Painted stork 20 15
1938 7b. Black-winged stilt . . . 20 15
MS1939 145 × 110 mm. Nos. 1935/8 (sold at 30b.) 85 85

656 Suthee Aerial and King Bhumibol using Radio

1997. Telecommunications. Multicoloured.
1940 2b. Type **656** 10 10
1941 3b. King using hand-held radio and various radios 10 10
1942 6b. King using computer . . 15 15
1943 9b. King, schoolchildren and "Thaicom" satellite (expanding secondary education to rural areas using satellite technology) 25 20
MS1944 145 × 110 mm. Nos. 1940/3 (sold at 30b.) 85 85

657 First Thai Cinema Advertisement, Equipment and Prince Sanbassatra

1997. Cent of Cinema in Thailand. Mult.
1945 3b. King Prajadhipok filming and King Chulalongkorn's state visit to Europe, 1897 (first film documenting Thai history) 10 10
1946 3b. Type **657** 10 10
1947 7b. Poster for "Double Luck" (first movie with Thai producer) and band outside cinema 20 15
1948 7b. Open-air cinema and poster for "Going Astray" (first Thai sound film) . . 20 15

658 King Ananda Mahidol (Rama VIII) (founder), Building and Operation

1997. 50th Anniv of Faculty of Medicine, Chulalongkorn University.
1949 **658** 2b. multicoloured . . . 10 10

659 Peterhof Palace and King Chulalongkorn

1997. Centenary of Thailand–Russia Diplomatic Relations and State Visit of King Chulalongkorn (Rama V) to Russia.
1950 **659** 2b. multicoloured . . . 10 10

660 Mahosathajataka

1997. Asalhapuja Day. Designs illustrating ten Jataka stories. Multicoloured.
1951 3b. Type **660** 10 10
1952 4b. Bhuridattajataka 15 10
1953 6b. Candakumarajataka . . 15 15
1954 7b. Naradajataka 20 15
MS1955 Five sheets. (a) 152 × 127 mm. Nos. 1951/4; (b) 100 × 80 mm. No. 1951; (c) 100 × 80 mm. No. 1952; (d) 100 × 80 mm. No. 1953; (e) 100 × 80 mm. No. 1954 (set of 5 sold at 66b.) . . . . 2·10 2·10

661 Northern Region

1997. "Thaipex 97" Stamp Exhibition. Traditional Houses. Multicoloured.
1956 2b. Type **661** 10 10
1957 5b. Central region 15 10
1958 6b. North-eastern region . . 15 15
1959 9b. Southern region 25 20
MS1960 125 × 165 mm. Nos. 1956/9 (sold at 32b.) 85 85

662 Cape Blue Water-lily ("Nymphaea capensis")

663 Means of Communications

1997. Greetings booklet stamps. No value indicated. Multicoloured.
1961 (2b.) Type **662** 10 10
1962 (2b.) Indian lotus ("Nymphaea stellata") . . 10 10

1997. National Communications Day.
1963 **663** 2b. multicoloured . . . 10 10

664 Luang Chiang Dao Mountain, Chiang Mai

1997. 30th Anniv of Association of South-East Asian Nations. Tourist Sights. Multicoloured.
1964 2b. Type **664** 10 10
1965 2b. Thi Lo Su Falls, Tak . . 10 10
1966 9b. Thalu Island, Chumphon 25 20
1967 9b. Phromthep Cape, Phuket 25 20

665 "Phuwiangosaurus sirindhornae"

1997. Dinosaurs. Multicoloured.
1968 2b. Type **665** 10 10
1969 3b. "Siamotyrannus isanensis" 10 10
1970 6b. "Siamosaurus suteethorni" 15 15
1971 9b. "Psittacosaurus sattayaraki" 25 20
MS1972 145 × 110 mm. Nos. 1968/71 (sold at 30b.) 85 85

666 King Chulalongkorn

1997. Centenary of Visit to Switzerland of King Chulalongkorn (Rama V).
1973 **666** 2b. multicoloured . . . 10 10

667 Rickshaw and Bicycle Hybrid

1997. International Correspondence Week. Tricycles. Multicoloured.
1974 3b. Type **667** 10 10
1975 3b. Bicycle with attached side-seat and wheel . . . 10 10
1976 9b. Motor tricycle No. 345 25 20

1977 9b. Tuk-tuk (open-sided three-wheel motor) . . . 25 20
MS1978 144 × 110 mm. Nos. 1974/7 (sold at 30b.) 85 85

668 Purple Pacific Drupe

1997. World Post Day. Shells. Multicoloured.
1979 2b. Type **668** 10 10
1980 2b. "Nerita chamaelon" . . 10 10
1981 9b. "Littoraria melanostoma" 25 20
1982 9b. "Cryptospira elegans" 25 20
MS1983 144 × 110 mm. Nos. 1979/82 (sold at 30b.) 85 85

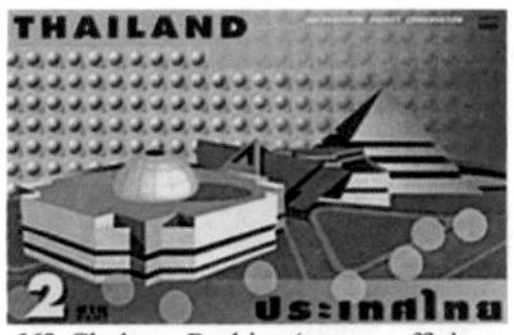

669 Chalerm Prakiat (energy efficient building), Khlong Har

1997. Energy Conservation.
1984 **669** 2b. multicoloured . . . 10 10

670 "Suphannahong" (Royal Barge, 1911) (⅓-size illustration)

1997.
1985 **670** 9b. multicoloured . . . 25 20
MS1986 157 × 95 mm. No. 1985 (sold at 20b.) 65 65

671 "Cassia alata"

1997. New Year. Flowers. Multicoloured.
1987 2b. Type **671** 10 10
1988 2b. "Strophanthus caudatus" 10 10
1989 2b. "Clinacanthus nutans" 10 10
1990 2b. "Acanthus ilicifolius" . . 10 10
MS1991 85 × 100 mm. Nos. 1987/90 (sold at 15b.) 45 45

672 Playing Saxophone and Score of his "Falling Rain"

1997. 70th Birthday of King Bhumibol. Multicoloured.
1992 2b. Type **672** 10 10
1993 2b. At easel and one of his paintings 10 10
1994 2b. Model airplane, "OK" class dinghy and bust and Bhumibol building boat 10 10
1995 2b. Sailing "OK" class dinghy and wearing team blazer with gold medal from South-East Asian Games 10 10
1996 6b. With camera and his photograph of Royal Water Development Project 15 10
1997 7b. Writing and his books "Nai In", "Tito" and "The Story of Mahajanaka" 20 10
1998 9b. Using computer, map from "The Story of Mahajanaka" and his New Year card 25 15

673 "Sport-minded in Maimed Bodies" (Sumonmarl Chaneiam)

674 Dental Tools and Emblem on Tooth

1998. Children's Day. Children's Drawings. Multicoloured.
1999 2b. Type **673** 10 10
2000 2b. "Kite-flying Contest" (Pavinee Rodsawat) . . . 10 10
2001 2b. "Gymnastics" (Kejsarin Nilwong) 10 10
2002 2b. "Windsurf Racing" (Voraphat Phankhian) . . 10 10

1998. 20th Asia Pacific Dental Congress, Bangkok.
2003 **674** 2b. multicoloured . . . 10 10

675 Victory Monument and Military and Civilian Representatives

676 Queen Sirikit (Red Cross president)

1998. 50th Anniv of Veterans' Day.
2004 **675** 2b. multicoloured . . . 10 10

1998. Red Cross.
2015 **676** 2b. multicoloured . . . 10 10

677 Shooting

1998. 13th Asian Games, Bangkok. Multicoloured.
2016 2b.+1b. Type **677** 10 10
2017 3b.+1b. Gymnastics 15 15
2018 4b.+1b. Swimming 15 15
2019 7b.+1b. Windsurfing 20 20

678 Main Tower

1998. Thai Heritage Conservation Day. Phanomrung Historical Park. Multicoloured.
2020 3b. Type **678** 10 10
2021 4b. Minor Tower 15 10
2022 6b. Scripture repository . . 15 10
2023 7b. Lintel depicting Vishnu sleeping in ocean (eastern doorway, Main Tower) 20 15
MS2024 110 × 145 mm. Nos. 2020/3 85 85

679 Woman riding Tiger

1998. Songkran (New Year) Day. Year of the Tiger.
2025 **679** 2b. multicoloured . . . 10 10
MS2026 Two sheets, each 80 × 100 mm, each containing No. 2025. (a) Perf; (b) Imperf (pair sold at 16b.) 50 50

680 Fishing Cat

1998. Wild Cats. Multicoloured.
2027 2b. Type **680** 10 10
2028 4b. Tiger 15 10
2029 6b. Leopard 15 10
2030 8b. Jungle cat 20 15
MS2031 144 × 110 mm. Nos. 2027/30 85 85

681 Airliner and Radar Grid

1998. 50th Anniv of Aerothai (air-traffic control).
2032 **681** 2b. multicoloured . . . 10 10

682 "Vidhurajataka" (Kritsana Moka-siri)

1998. Visakhapuja Day. Prize-winning Drawings of Ten Jataka Stories. Multicoloured.
2033 3b. Type **682** 10 10
2034 4b. "Vessantarajataka: Dana Kanda" (Chuttumrong Chalow-thorn-phises) . . 15 10
2035 6b. "Vessantarajataka: Kumara Kanda" (Surasin Chinna-wong) 15 10
2036 7b. "Vessantarajataka: Sakkapabba Kanda" (Chuttumrong Chalow-thorn-phises) 20 15
MS2037 162 × 120 mm. Nos. 2033/6 (sold at 30b.) 85 85

683 Kiartiwongse and "Phra Ruang" (destroyer)

1998. 75th Death Anniv of Admiral Prince Abhakara Kiartiwongse, Prince of Jumborn.
2038 **683** 2b. multicoloured . . . 10 10

684 Modern Technology (Porntiva Prasert)

1998. "Education Develops People and thus Nation". Under-9 Years Prize-winning Drawings.
2039 **684** 2b. multicoloured . . . 10 10

685 Commemorative Coin and Map and Flags of Europe

1998. Centenary (1997) of First State Visit to Europe of King Chulalongkorn (Rama V).
2040 **685** 6b. multicoloured . . . 15 10
2041 20b. multicoloured . . . 55 30

686 Irrawaddy Dolphin

1998. International Year of the Ocean. Marine Mammals. Multicoloured.
2042 2b. Type **686** 10 10
2043 3b. Bottle-nosed dolphin . . 10 10
2044 6b. Sperm whale 15 10
2045 9b. Dugong 25 15
MS2046 164 × 110 mm. Nos. 2042/5 (sold at 30b.) 85 85

687 Dams

1998. 60th Anniv of Irrigation Engineering.
2047 **687** 2b. multicoloured . . . 10 10

688 Model of Asynchronous Transfer Mode

1998. National Communications Day.
2048 **688** 2b. multicoloured . . . 10 10

689 Faculty Building and Emblems

1998. 50th Anniv of Faculty of Political Science, Chulalongkorn University.
2049 **689** 2b. multicoloured . . . 10 10

690 Correspondence Students

1998. 20th Anniv of Sukhothai Thammathirat Open University.
2050 **690** 2b. multicoloured . . . 10 10

691 Warrior

1998. Chinese Stone Statues. Multicoloured.
2051 2b. Type **691** 10 10
2052 2b. Warrior holding barbed spear 10 10
2053 10b. Warrior holding mace 25 15
2054 10b. Warrior holding spear with jagged blade 25 15
MS2055 110 × 145 mm. Nos. 2051/4 (sold at 35b.) 95 95

692 Archer

1998. "Amazing Thailand" Year. Perforated Hides. Multicoloured.

2056 3b. Type **692** 10 10
2057 3b. Warriors on elephants 10 10
2058 7b. Warrior seizing opponent 20 15
2059 7b. Deity hovering in sky 20 15

693 Kraisara Rajasiha (king lion)

1998. International Correspondence Week. Himavanta Mythical Animals of the Singha (lion) Family. Multicoloured.

2060 2b. Type **693** 10 10
2061 2b. Gajasiha (tusked lions) 10 10
2062 12b. Kesara Singha (hoofed lions) 30 20
2063 12b. Singhas 30 20
MS2064 140 × 99 mm. Nos. 2060/3 (sold at 40b.) 1·10 1·10

694 International Headquarters, Illinois

1998. Thai Presidency of International Association of Lions Clubs.

2065 **694** 2b. multicoloured 10 10

695 "Barleria luplina"

696 Knight Grand Cross (First Class)

1998. New Year. Flowers. Multcoloured.

2066 2b. Type **695** 10 10
2067 2b. Glory lily ("Gloriosa superba") 10 10
2068 2b. "Asclepias curassavica" 10 10
2069 2b. "Sesamum indicum" 10 10
MS2070 99 × 85 mm. Nos. 2066/9 (sold at 15b.) 45 45

1998. Most Admirable Order of the Direkgunabhorn. Multicoloured.

2071 15b. Type **696** 40 25
2072 15b. Close-up of badge 40 25

697 Hockey

1998. 13th Asian Games, Bangkok. Multicoloured.

2073 2b.+1b. Type **697** 10 10
2074 3b.+1b. Wrestling 15 15
2075 4b.+1b. Rowing 15 15
2076 7b.+1b. Show jumping 20 20

698 "Gymkhana" (Khontorn Taechoran)

1999. Children's Day. Children's Paintings. Multicoloured.

2081 2b. Type **698** 10 10
2082 2b. "Swimming" (Sunhapong Phitukburapa) 10 10
2083 2b. "Volleyball" (Vipharat Sae Lim) 10 10
2084 2b. "Sepak Takraw" (three-aside net game) (Phanot Ratanawongkae) 10 10

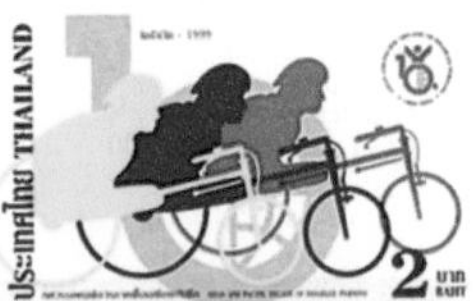
699 Wheel-chair Athletes

1999. Asian and Pacific Decade of Disabled Persons.

2085 **699** 2b. multicoloured 10 10

700 Paddy Sprouts and Workers planting Rice

1999. Rice Cultivation. Multicoloured.

2086 6b. Type **700** 15 10
2087 6b. Workers harvesting rice and ear of paddy 15 10
2088 12b. Paddy-threshing machine 30 20
2089 12b. Golden paddy field and bowl of cooked rice 30 20
MS2090 144 × 110 mm. Nos. 2086/90 (sold at 45b.) 1·20 1·20

701 Birth of Mahajanaka

1999. Maghapuja Day. Showing murals from Wat Tha Sutthawat illustrating the story of Mahajanaka.

2091 3b. Type **701** 10 10
2092 6b. Mani Mekkhala carrying Mahajanaka to Mithila City 15 10
2093 9b. Two mango trees 25 15
2094 15b. Mahajanaka founding educational institute 40 25
MS2095 151 × 127 mm. Nos. 2091/4 (sold at 45b.) 1·20 1·20

702 Queen Somdetch the Queen Grandmother

1999. Red Cross.

2096 **702** 2b. multicoloured 10 10

703 Kite Flying

1999. "BANGKOK 2000" World Youth Stamp Exhibition and 13th Asian International Stamp Exhibition, Bangkok. Children's Games (1st issue). Multicoloured.

2097 2b. Type **703** 10 10
2098 2b. Hoop rolling 10 10
2099 15b. Catching the last one in the line (children passing under arched arms) 40 25
2100 15b. Snatching a baby from Mother Snake 40 25
MS2101 145 × 110 mm. Nos. 2097/2100 (sold at 45b.) 1·20 1·20

See also Nos. 2119/**MS**2123 and 2195/**MS**2199.

704 "Hooks and Squids" Motif

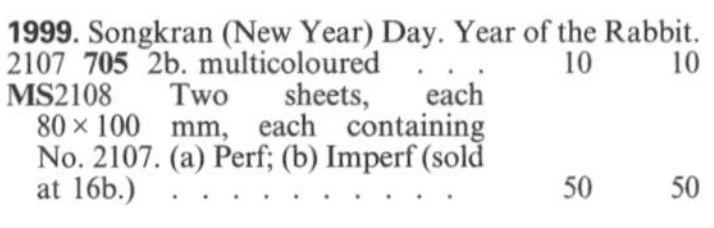
705 Woman riding Rabbit

1999. Thai Heritage Conservation Day. Silk Mudmee Textiles. Multicoloured.

2102 2b. Type **704** 10 10
2103 4b. "Royal Umbrella" motif 15 10
2104 12b. "Naga upholding the Baisi" motif 30 20
2105 15b. "Naga upholding a flower pot" motif 40 25
MS2106 110 × 144 mm. Nos. 2102/5 (sold at 45b.) 1·20 1·20

1999. Songkran (New Year) Day. Year of the Rabbit.

2107 **705** 2b. multicoloured 10 10
MS2108 Two sheets, each 80 × 100 mm, each containing No. 2107. (a) Perf; (b) Imperf (sold at 16b.) 50 50

706 Hands encircling Emblem

1999. Consumer Protection Years, 1998–1999.

2109 **706** 2b. multicoloured 10 10

707 Chitralada Villa, Dusit Palace, Bangkok

1999. Sixth Cycle (72nd Birthday) of King Bhumibol. Royal Palaces (1st issue). Multicoloured.

2110 6b. Type **707** 25 15
2111 6b. Phu Phing Ratchaniwet Palace, Chieng Mai Province (red and green roofs) 25 15
2112 6b. Phu Phan Ratchaniwet Palace, Sakon Nakhon province (with large green lawn) 25 15
2113 6b. Thaksin Ratchaniwet Palace, Narathiwat Province (two-storey building with drive and ornamental trees) 25 15
MS2114 185 × 125 mm. Nos. 2110/13 (sold at 40b.) 1·10 1·10

See also Nos. 2130/**MS**2139, 2146/**MS**2155 and 2161/**MS**2164.

708 Administrative Building and Faculty Emblem

1999. 50th Anniv of Political Science Faculty, Thammasat University.

2115 **708** 3b. multicoloured 10 10

709 Float, Candle Festival, Ubon Ratchathani

1999. 125th Anniv of Universal Postal Union. Multicoloured.

2116 2b. Floating vessel, Light Festival 10 10
2117 15b. Type **709** 80 50

710 King Chulalongkorn and Customs Building

1999. 125th Anniv of the Customs Department.

2118 **710** 6b. multicoloured 35 20

711 Sut Sakhon riding Dragon

1999. "BANGKOK 2000" World Youth Stamp Exhibition and 13th Asian International Stamp Exhibition, Bangkok (2nd issue). Folk Tales. Multicoloured.

2119 2b. Type **711** (Tale of Phra Aphai Mani) 10 10
2120 2b. Rishi transforming tiger cub and cow calf into children (Tale of Honwichai-Khawi) 10 10
2121 15b. Phra Sang climbing out of conch shell (Tale of Sang Thong) 50 30
2122 15b. Khun Chang, Khun Phaen and Nang Phim playing (Tale of Khun Chang and Khun Phaen) 50 30
MS2123 144 × 110 mm. Nos. 2119/22 (sold at 45b.) 2·50 2·50

712 Communication by Eye, Ear, Mouth and Hand

1999. National Communications Day.

2124 **712** 4b. multicoloured 20 15

713 Rabbits

1999. "THAIPEX'99" 13th Thailand Stamp Exhibition, Bangkok. Domestic Rabbits. Multicoloured.

2125 6b. Type **713** 35 20
2126 6b. One golden and one brown rabbit 35 20
2127 12b. One grey and one grey and white rabbit 65 40
2128 12b. Two white rabbits 65 40
MS2129 144 × 110 mm. Nos. 2125/8 (sold at 50b.) 3·50 3·25

714 Prince Mahidol with Bhumibol as Baby

1999. Sixth Cycle (72nd Birthday) of King Bhumibol (2nd issue). Portraits of the King. Multicoloured.

2130 3b. Type **714** 10 10
2131 3b. Princess Mother and her children 10 10
2132 3b. With his brother King Ananda Mahidol 10 10
2133 6b. Bhumibol and King Ananda Mahidol in military uniform 30 20
2134 6b. On wedding day 30 20
2135 6b. Coronation ceremony 30 20
2136 12b. As a monk 65 40
2137 12b. King and Queen with their children 65 40
2138 12b. In royal robes 65 40
MS2139 134 × 214 mm. Nos. 2130/8 (sold at 90b.) 4·75 4·75

715 Older Person with Children

1999. International Year of the Elderly.
2140 **715** 2b. multicoloured 10 10

716 Orchid Tree

718 "Thunbergia laurifolia"

717 In Open-top Car on Returning to School in Switzerland

1999. International Correspondence Week. Flowers. Multicoloured.
2141 2b. Type **716** 10 10
2142 2b. "Bombax ceiba" (red flower) 10 10
2143 12b. "Radermachera ignea" (tubular yellow flowers) 65 40
2144 12b. "Bretschneidera sinensis" (pink bell flowers) 65 40
MS2145 110 × 145 mm. Nos. 2141/4 (sold at 35b.) 1·90 1·90

1999. Sixth Cycle (72nd Birthday) of King Bhumibol (3rd issue). The King and his Subjects. Multicoloured.
2146 3b. Type **717** 10 10
2147 3b. With Buddhist monks 10 10
2148 3b. King and Queen with students 10 10
2149 6b. With soldiers 30 20
2150 6b. With children prostrate at his feet 30 20
2151 6b. With boy on crutches 30 20
2152 12b. Visiting a hilltribe home 65 40
2153 12b. Drawing plan on ground 65 40
2154 12b. Talking to crowds 65 40
MS2155 215 × 135 mm. Nos. 2146/54 (sold at 90b.) 4·75 4·75

1999. New Year. Flowers. Multicoloured.
2156 2b. Type **718** 10 10
2157 2b. "Gmelina arborea" 10 10
2158 2b. "Prunus cerasoides" 10 10
2159 2b. "Fagraea fragans" 10 10
MS2160 99 × 85 mm. Nos. 2156/9 (sold at 15b.) 90 90

719 King Bhumibol

1999. Sixth Cycle (72nd Birthday) of King Bhumibol (4th issue).
2161 **719** 100b. gold and blue 6·00 6·00
2162 100b. silver and blue 6·00 6·00
2163 100b. bronze and blue 6·00 6·00
MS2164 175 × 140 mm. Nos. 2161/3 (sold at 350b.) 22·00 22·00

720 King Bhumibol and Prince Vajiralongkorn

1999. Investiture of Crown Prince Maha Vajiralongkorn.
2165 **720** 3b. multicoloured 20 20

721 Lilies, Thale Noi

2000. Lake of Lilies, Phatthalung Province. Mult.
2166 3b. Type **721** 20 20
2167 3b. Forest and lilies 20 20
2168 3b. Forest, buildings and lilies 20 20
2169 3b. Birds flying over lilies 20 20
2170 3b.15 lily flowers 20 20
2171 3b. Seven lily flowers 20 20
2172 3b. Six lily flowers 20 20
2173 3b. Eight lily flowers and three buds 20 20
2174 3b. Four lily flowers and two buds 20 20
2175 3b. Two lily flowers and eight lily pads 20 20
2176 3b. Two lily flowers 20 20
2177 3b. Three lily flowers 20 20

Nos. 2166/77 were issued together, se-tenant, forming a composite design of the lake.

The stamps are identified by the number of complete flowers shown.

722 Flowers

2000. Kulap Khao Meadow, Chiang Mai Province. Multicoloured.
2178 3b. Type **722** 20 20
2179 3b. Flowers and two peaks 20 20
2180 3b. Flowers, four buds and mountains 20 20
2181 3b. Flowers, three buds and mountains 20 20
2182 3b. Three open flowers 20 20
2183 3b. Open flowers and seven buds 20 20
2184 3b. Open flowers and six buds 20 20
2185 3b. Open flowers and one bud 20 20
2186 3b. One open flower and five buds 20 20
2187 3b. Open flowers and four buds 20 20
2188 3b. Four open flowers 20 20
2189 3b. Four partially open flowers 20 20

Nos. 2178/89 were issued together, se-tenant, forming a composite design of the Kulap Khao meadow.

The stamps are identified by the number of complete flowers and buds shown.

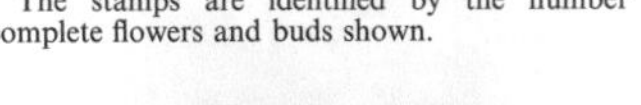

723 Small Dwarf Honey Bee

2000. Bees. Multicoloured.
2190 3b. Type **723** 20 20
2191 3b. Dwarf bee (*Apis florea*) 20 20
2192 3b. Asian honey bee (*Apis cerana*) 20 20
2193 3b. Giant bee (*Apis dorsata*) 20 20
MS2194 Four sheets, each 83 × 54 mm. (a) As Type **723**; (b) As No. 2191; (c) As No. 2192; (d) As No. 2193 2·10 2·10

724 Child being Blessed

2000. "BANGKOK 2000" International Youth Stamp Exhibition and 13th Asian International Stamp Exhibition, Bangkok (3rd issue). Ceremonies. Multicoloured.
2195 2b. Type **724** 10 10
2196 2b. Woman cutting child's hair (Tonsure ceremony) 10 10
2197 15b. Pupils paying respects to teacher 95 60
2198 15b. Boy being carried aloft during ordination of novice 95 60
MS2199 110 × 144 mm. Nos. 2195/8 (sold at 45b.) 2·75 2·75

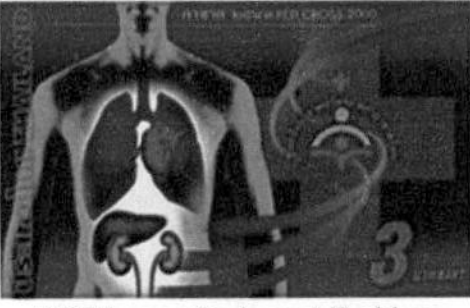

725 Human Body and Emblem

2000. Thai Red Cross Organ Donation Campaign.
2200 **725** 3b. multicoloured 20 10

726 Sukhothai Province

2000. Thai Heritage Conservation. Chok Cloth Designs. Multicoloured.
2201 3b. Type **726** 20 10
2202 6b. Chiang Mai Province 45 30
2203 8b. Uthai Thani Province 65 40
2204 12b. Ratchaburi Province 90 55
MS2205 110 × 145 mm. Nos. 2201/4 (sold at 40b.) 2·50 2·50

727 Angel riding Snake

2000. Songkran (New Year) Day. Year of the Snake.
2206 **727** 2b. multicoloured 10 10
MS2207 Two sheets, each 80 × 100 mm, each containing No. 2206. (a) Perf; (b) Imperf (pair sold at 16b.) 1·00 1·00

728 Engagement Photograph (½-size illustration)

2000. Golden Wedding Anniv of King Bhumibol and Queen Sirikit. Multicoloured.
2208 10b. Type **728** 65 40
2209 10b. Signing marriage register, 1950 65 40
2210 10b. Sitting on thrones during Coronation ceremony 65 40
2211 10b. With family 65 40
2212 10b. King Bhumibol and Queen Sirikit, 2000 65 40

729 Buddha

730 Flowers and Trees, Krachieo

2000. Asalhapuja Day.
2213 **729** 3b. multicoloured 20 20

2000. Krachieo Meadow, Pa Hin Ngam, Chaiyaphum Province. Multicoloured.
2214 3b. Type **730** 20 20
2215 3b. Flowers and sparse trees in distance 20 20
2216 3b. Flowers, two close trees and dense trees in distance 20 20
2217 3b. Flowers, four close trees and dense trees in distance 20 20
2218 3b. Six complete flowers 20 20
2219 3b. Eleven complete flowers 20 20
2220 3b. Seven complete flowers and half a flower at right-hand side 20 20
2221 3b. Six complete flowers and two incomplete flowers at bottom 20 20
2222 3b. Two flowers 20 20
2223 3b. Three flowers close together 20 20
2224 3b. One open and two partially open flowers 20 20
2225 3b. Two complete and three incomplete flowers 20 20

Nos. 2214/25 were issued together, se-tenant, forming a composite design of the meadow.

The stamps are identified by the number of trees or flowers shown.

731 Crown Prince and Rice Seeds Sowing Ceremony

2000. Fourth Cycle (48th Birthday) of Crown Prince Maha Vajiralongkorn.
2226 **731** 2b. multicoloured 10 10
MS2227 125 × 90 mm. No. 2226 (sold at 8b.) 50 50

732 Sun, Emblem, Envelope and Moon

2000. National Communications Day.
2228 **732** 3b. multicoloured 20 10

733 Cabbage Design Tea Set

2000. International Correspondence Week. Rattanakosin Period Tea Sets. Multicoloured.
2229 6b. Type **733** 35 20
2230 6b. Duck and animals in lotus pond design 35 20
2231 12b. Lotus bud design 75 45
2232 12b. Butterflies and bees design 75 45
MS2233 144 × 110 mm. Nos. 2229/32 (sold at 45b.) 2·75 2·75

734 Princess Srinagarindra

2000. Birth Centenary of Princess Srinagarindra the Princess Mother.
2234 **734** 2b. multicoloured 10 10
MS2235 125 × 90 mm. **734** 2b. multicoloured 50 50

735 Glory Bower (*Clerodendrum philippinum*)

736 Flowers

2000. New Year. Flowers. Multicoloured.
2236 2b. Type **735** 10 10
2237 2b. *Capparis micracantha* 10 10
2238 2b. Leopard lily (*Belamcanda chinensis*) 10 10
2239 2b. *Memecylon caeruleum* 10 10
MS2240 85 × 100 mm. Nos. 2236/9 (sold at 15b.) 90 80

2000. Bua Tong Meadow, Mae Hong Son Province. Multicoloured.
2241 3b. Type **736** 20 20
2242 3b. Meadow and trees (top left) 20 20
2243 3b. Meadow 20 20
2244 3b. Meadow and trees (top right) 20 20
2245 3b. Four flowers 20 20
2246 3b. Eleven flowers 20 20
2247 3b. Fifteen flowers 20 20
2248 3b. Twelve flowers 20 20
2249 3b. Three large flowers, two smaller flowers and one dead flower 20 20

2250	3b. Three large flowers	20	20
2251	3b. One large flower	20	20
2252	3b. Five flowers and one dead flower	20	20

Nos. 2241/52 were issued together, se-tenant, forming a composite design.

The stamps are identified by the number of complete flowers shown.

737 Anantanakkharat (Royal Barge, 1914) (½-size illustration)

2000.

2253	**737** 9b. multicoloured	50	30
MS2254	157 × 95 mm. No. 2253 (sold at 15b.)	90	90

738 Moustached Parakeet (*Psittacula alexandri*)

739 King Rama V and First Title Deed

2001. Parrots. Multicoloured.

2255	2b. Type **738**	10	10
2256	5b. Alexandrine parakeet (*Psittacula eupatria*)	30	20
2257	8b. *Psittacula cyanurus*	45	30
2258	10b. Blossom-headed parakeet (*Psittacula roseata*)	60	35
MS2259	110 × 144 mm. Nos. 2255/8 (sold at 35b.)	1·80	1·80

2001. Centenary of Department of Lands.

2260	**739** 5b. multicoloured	30	20

740 Manta Ray

2001. Marine Life. Multicoloured.

2261	3b. Type **740**	20	20
2262	3b. Fishes and jellyfish	20	20
2263	3b. Turtle	20	20
2264	3b. Coral and lionfish	20	20
2265	3b. Black and white fish and coral	20	20
2266	3b. Head of eel and yellow coral	20	20
2267	6b. Fishes and coral(28 × 47 mm)	30	30
2268	6b. Pufferfish and other fishes (28 × 47 mm)	30	30
2269	6b. Yellow and blue fish and coral (45 × 23 mm)	30	30

Nos. 2261/9 were issued together, se-tenant, forming a composite design.

741 Diamond and Ring

2001. Precious Stones. Multicoloured.

2270	3b. Type **741**	20	10
2271	4b. Green sapphire and necklace	30	20
2272	6b. Pearl and necklace	35	20
2273	12b. Blue sapphire and necklace	65	40
MS2274	110 × 144 mm. Nos. 2270/3 (sold at 35b.)	2·10	2·10

742 Women and Orphans

2001. Red Cross. 20th Anniv of Thai Red Cross Children's Homes.

2275	**742** 4b. multicoloured	20	15

743 Gold and Red Brocade

744 Woman riding Snake

2001. Thai Heritage Conservation Day. Showing different brocade designs. Multicoloured.

2276	2b. Type **743**	10	10
2277	3b. Green and gold design	20	15
2278	10b. Orange and gold design	60	25
2279	10b. Pink and gold design	60	25
MS2280	110 × 145 mm. Nos. 2276/9 (sold at 35b.)	2·10	2·10

2001. Songkran (New Year) Day. Year of the Snake.

2281	**744** 2b. multicoloured	10	10
MS2282	Two sheets, each 80 × 100 mm, each containing No. 2281. (a) Perf; (b) Imperf (pair sold at 16b.)	1·00	1·00

745 Buddha

746 Maiyarap, Emerald Buddha Temple

2001. Visakhapuja Day.

2283	**745** 3b. multicoloured	20	15

2001. Demon Statues. Multicoloured.

2284	2b. Type **746**	10	10
2285	5b. Wirunchambang, Emerald Buddha Temple	30	20
2286	10b. Thotsakan, Temple of Dawn	60	35
2287	12b. Sahatsadecha, Temple of Dawn	75	45
MS2288	145 × 110 mm. Nos. 2284/7 (sold at 33b.)	2·10	2·10

747 Prince Purachatra Jayakara (first governor)

2001. 66th Anniv of Rotary International in Thailand.

2289	**747** 3b. multicoloured	20	15

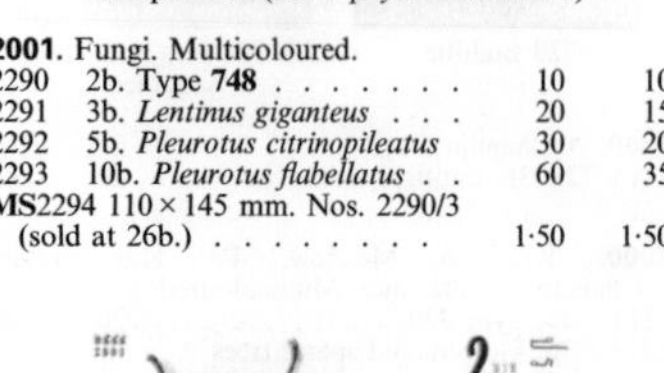

748 Split Gill (*Schizophyllum commune*)

2001. Fungi. Multicoloured.

2290	2b. Type **748**	10	10
2291	3b. *Lentinus giganteus*	20	15
2292	5b. *Pleurotus citrinopileatus*	30	20
2293	10b. *Pleurotus flabellatus*	60	35
MS2294	110 × 145 mm. Nos. 2290/3 (sold at 26b.)	1·50	1·50

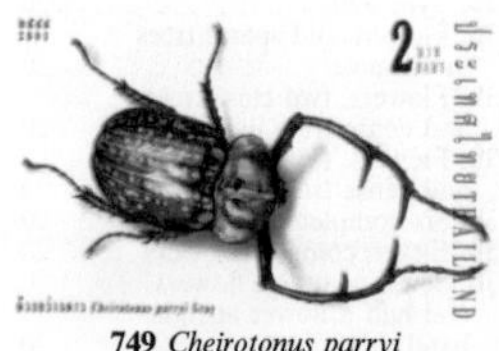

749 *Cheirotonus parryi*

2001. Insects. Multicoloured.

2295	2b. Type **749**	10	10
2296	5b. *Mouhotia batsei*	30	20
2297	6b. *Cladognathus giraffa*	35	30
2298	12b. Violin beetle (*Mormolyce phyllodes*)	65	40
MS2299	145 × 110 mm. Nos. 2295/8 (sold at 34b.)	2·10	2·10

750 Lueng Hang Khoa (Aim-orn Saichumdee)

2001. "THAIPEX '01" National Stamp Exhibition. Domestic Fowl. Winning entries in the 1999 International Letter Writing Week painting competition. Multicoloured.

2300	3b. Type **750**	10	10
2301	4b. Lueng Hang Khoa (Rong Saichumdee)	20	15
2302	6b. Samae Dam (Rong Saichumdee)	35	20
2303	12b. Pradue Hang Dam (Chanthorn Niyomthum)	75	45
MS2304	145 × 110 mm. Nos. 2300/3. Perf or imperf (sold at 33b.)	1·90	1·90

751 "Thai Children in the I.T. Era" (Sriarpha Kamlanglua)

2001. National Communications Day, 2000. Winning Entry in Children's International Letter Writing Week Painting Competition.

2305	**751** 4b. multicoloured	30	20

752 Queen Suriyodaya

2001. Queen Suriyodaya Commemoration.

2306	**752** 3b. multicoloured	30	20
MS2307	90 × 125 mm. No. 2306 (sold at 10b.)	90	90

753 Queen meeting Pres. Jiang Ze Ming and Great Wall of China

2001. Visit by Queen Sirikit to People's Republic of China.

2308	**753** 5b. multicoloured	30	20

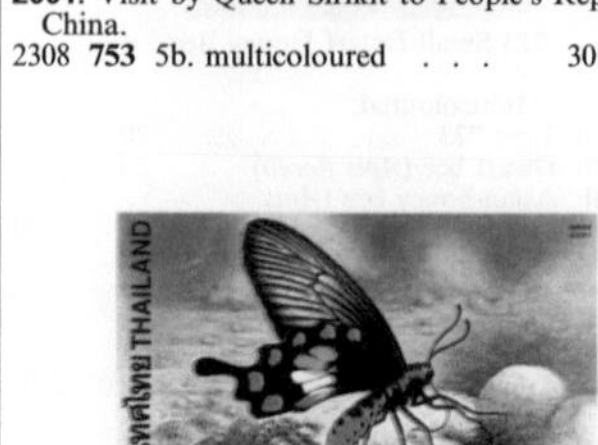

754 *Pachliopta aristolochiae goniopeltis*

2001. Butterflies. Multicoloured.

2309	2b. Type **754**	15	10
2310	4b. *Rhinopalpa polynice*	30	20
2311	10b. *Poritia erycinoides*	65	40
2312	12b. *Spindasis iohita*	75	45
MS2313	145 × 110 mm. Nos. 2309/2312 (sold at 40b.)	2·75	2·75

755 *Piper nigrum*

757 *Pedicularis siamensis*

756 King Chulalongkorn, Academy Buildings and Logo

2001. International Correspondence Week. Plants. Multicoloured.

2314	2b. Type **755**	10	10
2315	3b. *Solanum trilobatum*	20	10
2316	5b. *Boesenbergia rotunda*	30	20
2317	10b. *Ocimum tenuiflorum*	60	35
MS2318	110 × 44 mm. Nos. 2314/17 (sold at 25b.)	1·60	1·60

2001. Centenary of Police Cadet Academy.

2319	**756** 5b. multicoloured	35	20

2001. New Year. Flowers. Multicoloured.

2320	2b. Type **757**	10	10
2321	2b. *Schoutenia glomerata*	10	10
2322	2b. *Gentiana crassa*	10	10
2323	2b. *Colquhounia coccinea*	10	10
MS2324	85 × 100 mm. Nos. 2320/23 (sold at 11b.)	75	75

758 Anekkachat Puchong (Royal Barge, King Rama V) (1/3-size illustration)

2001.

2325	**758** 9b. multicoloured	60	35
MS2326	157 × 95 mm. No. 2325 (sold at 17b.)	1·10	1·10

759 Terminal Building

2002. Foundation Stone Laying Ceremony, Suvarnabhumi Airport Passenger Terminal.

2327	**759** 3b. multicoloured	20	15

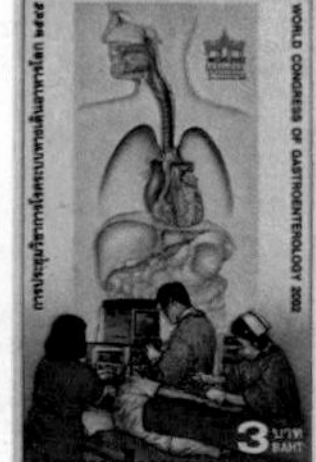

760 Rose

761 Operating Theatre

2002.

2328	**760** 4b. multicoloured	30	20

2002. World Gastroenterology Congress.

2329	**761** 3b. multicoloured	20	15

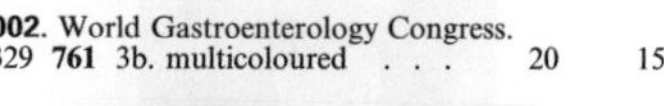

762 Globe, Satellite and Emblem

2002. 25th Anniv of Communications Authority. Multicoloured.

2330	3r. Type **762**	20	15
2331	3r. Envelope and post box	20	15
MS2332	110 × 86 mm. Nos. 2330/1	75	75

Nos. 2330/1 were issued together, se-tenant, forming a composite design.

763 Reclining Buddha

2002. Maghapuja Day.
2333 **763** 3b. multicoloured . . . 20 15

764 Queen Sawang Wadhana Memorial Hospital

2002. Red Cross.
2334 **764** 4b. multicoloured . . . 30 20

765 Headquarters and Emblem

2002. 90th Anniv of Ministry of Transport and Communications.
2335 **765** 3b. multicoloured . . . 20 15

766 Male Puppet

767 Female Angel riding Horse

2002. Heritage Conservation Day. Puppets. Multicoloured.
2336 3b. Type **766** 20 15
2337 3b. Female puppet 20 15
2338 4b. Demon 30 20
2339 15b. Monkey 95 60
MS2340 111 × 145 mm. Nos. 2336/9 (sold at 30b.) . . . . 2·10 2·10

2002. Songkran (New Year) Day. Year of the Horse. Multicoloured.
2341 2b. Type **767** 10 10
MS2342 Two sheets. (a) 80 × 100 mm. No. 2341 Perf or imperf (sold at 8 b.) (b) 137 × 161 mm. 2b. No. 1933; 2b. No. 2025; 2b. No. 2107; 2b. No. 2206; 2b. No. 2281; 2b. No. 2341. Perf or imperf (sold at 14b.) . . . . 1·90 1·90

768 *Betta imbellis*

2002. Fighting Fish. Multicoloured.
2343 3b. Type **768** 20 15
2344 3b. *Betta splendens* (blue) . . 20 15
2345 4b. *Betta splendens* (red) . . 30 20
2346 15b. *Betta splendens* (bi-colour) 90 55
MS2347 144 × 110 mm. Nos. 2343/6 (sold at 30b.) . . . . 2·10 2·10

769 Wat Phra Si Rattanasatsadaram (Temple of the Emerald Buddha)

2002. Tourism. Multicoloured.
2348 3b. Type **769** 10 10
2349 3b. Wat Phra Chetuphon Wimon Mangkhalaram (Wat Pho) 10 10
2350 4b. Wat Arun Ratchawararam (The Temple of Dawn) 15 10
2351 12b. Wat Bechamabophit Dusit Wanaram (The Marble Temple) 35 20
MS2352 144 × 110 mm. Nos. 2348/51 (sold at 27b.) 65 65

770 Crown Prince Maha Vajiralongkorn

2002. 50th Birthday of Crown Prince Maha Vajiralongkorn.
2353 **770** 3b. multicoloured . . . 10 10

771 Figure and Communication Symbols

2002. National Communications Day.
2354 **771** 4b. multicoloured . . . 15 10

772 *Nelumba nucifera*

2002. Water Lilies. Multicoloured.
2355 3b. Type **772** 10 10
2356 3b. *Nymphaea immutablis* . . 10 10
MS2357 110 × 65 mm. Nos. 2355/6 (sold at 9b.) 25 25
Stamps of the same design were issued by Australia.

773 Queen Sirikit

2002. 70th Birthday of Queen Sirikit. Multicoloured.
2358 3b. Type **773** 10 10
2359 3b. "Queen Sirikit" rose . . 10 10
2360 4b. "Queen Sirikit" orchid 15 10
2361 15b. Dona "Queen Sirikit" (shrub) 45 25
MS2362 144 × 109 mm. Nos. 2358/61 (sold at 31b.) 90 90

774 Prince Damrong Rajanubhab and Script

2002. 50th Anniv of National Archives.
2363 **774** 3b. multicoloured . . . 10 10

775 Betel Nut Box

2002. Royal Artefacts from Vimanmek Mansion. Multicoloured.
2364 3b. Type **775** 10 10
2365 3b. Pedestal tray 10 10
2366 4b. Betel nut bowl 10 10
2367 12b. Oblong betel nut box 35 20
MS2368 110 × 145 mm. Nos. 2364/7 (sold at 26b.) 75 75

776 Portrait of Kings Rama V and Rama IX on Ancient Banknote

2002. Centenary of First Thai Banknote.
2369 **776** 5b. multicoloured . . . 15 10
MS2370 162 × 120 mm. No. 2369 (sold at 11b.) 35 35

777 Animal-shaped Coconut Grater

2002. International Letter Writing Week. Thai Kitchenware. Multicoloured.
2371 3b. Type **777** 10 10
2372 3b. Bamboo strainer 10 10
2373 4b. Coconut shell ladles . . 10 10
2374 15b. Earthenware cooking stove 40 25
MS2375 144 × 110 mm. Nos. 2371/4 (sold at 31b.) 65 50

778 Khaochae (rice dish) (Central Region)

2002. Bangkok 2003 International Stamp Exhibition. Thai Food. Showing regional foods. Multicoloured.
2376 3b. Type **778** 10 10
2377 3b. Sato Phat Kung (prawn dish) and Kaenglueang (soup) (southern region) 10 10
2378 4b. Somtam (salad), Kaiyang (chicken dish) and Khaoniao Nueng (rice) (north-eastern region) 10 10
2379 15b. Khaepmu (pork), Namphrik Ong (chilli) and Sai-ua (sausage) (northern region) 40 25
MS2380 110 × 144 mm. Nos. 2376/9 (sold at 30b.) 85 85

779 Dusit Maha Prasat Throne Hall

2002. Palaces. Joint Issue with Sweden. Multicoloured.
2381 4b. Type **779** 10 10
2382 4b. The Royal Palace, Stockholm 10 10
Stamps of the same design were issued by Sweden.

780 *Guaiacum officinale*

2002. New year. Flowers. Multicoloured.
2383 3b. Type **780** 10 10
2384 3b. *Nyctanthes arbor–tristis* 10 10
2385 3b. *Barleria cristata* 10 10
2386 3b. *Thevetia peruviana* . . . 10 10
MS2387 99 × 85 mm Nos. 2383/6 (sold at 16b.) 45 45

781 Young People

2002. 20th (2003) World Scout Jamboree. Multicoloured.
2388 3b. Type **781** 10 10
2389 12b. Beach (Jamboree camp site), Sattahip district . . 35 20

782 Goat

784 "Blue Nile" Rose

783 Pangpond and Dog

2003. Chinese New Year. "Year of the Goat".
2390 **782** 3b. multicoloured . . . 10 10

2003. National Children's Day. Cartoon characters. Multicoloured.
2391 3b. Type **783** 10 10
2392 3b. Pangpond and Hanuman 10 10
2393 3b. Pangpond and Namo . . 10 10
2394 3b. Pangpond and teacher 10 10

2003.
2395 **784** 4b. multicoloured . . . 10 10

785 "Blue Green" (Fau Haribhitak)

2003. Art. Paintings. Multicoloured.
2396 3b. Type **785** 10 10
2397 3b. "Chira Chongkon" (Chamras Kietkong) . . . 10 10
2398 3b. "Moonlight" (Prasong Padmanuja) 10 10
2399 15b. "Lotus Flowers" (Thawee Nandakwang) 45 25

786 Doi Inthanon, Chiang Mai

2003. Bangkok 2003 (2nd issue). Landscapes. Multicoloured.
2400 3b. Type **786** 10 10
2401 3b. Bridge over River Kwai, Kanchanaburi 10 10
2402 3b. Phu Kradung, Loei . . 10 10
2403 15b. Maya bay, Krabi . . . 45 25
MS2404 110 × 145 mm. Nos. 2400/3 (sold at 29b.) 85 85

2003. As T **641**.
2405 **641** 1b. blue 10 10

787 Red Cross Worker carrying Flag

788 Princess Maha Chakri Sirindhorn

2003. Red Cross.
2430 **787** 3b. multicoloured . . . 10 10

2003. Princess Maha Chakri Sirindhorn's 48th Birthday.
2431 **788** 3b. multicoloured . . . 10 10

789 Erawan Suey Nga

2003. Cultural Heritage. Kick Boxing. Designs showing boxing moves. Multicoloured.
2432 3b. Type **789** 10 10
2433 3b. Hak kor aiyara (knee raised) 10 10
2434 3b. Hak nguang aiyara (right leg raised) 10 10
2435 15b. Jarakae fad hang (kick to head) 45 25
MS2436 127 × 152 mm. Nos. 2432/6 (sold at 29b.) 85 85

790 Princess Galyani Vadhana
791 Kings Rama V and VI

2003. Princess Galyani Vadhana's 80th Birthday.
2437 **790** 3b. multicoloured . . . 10 10

2003. Centenary of Inspector General Department.
2438 **791** 3b. multicoloured . . . 10 10

792 King Rama VII (Prajadhipok)

2003. King Prajadhipok Day.
2439 **792** 3b. multicoloured . . . 10 10

793 White-eared Jungle Fowl
794 Buddha holding Bowl

2003. Bantam Fowl. Multicoloured.
2440 3b. Type **793** 10 10
2441 3b. Sugarcane husk coloured 10 10
2442 3b. Black-tailed white . . . 10 10
2443 15b. Dark grey 45 25
MS2444 125 × 90 mm. Nos. 2440/3 (sold at 29b.) 85 85

2003. Asalhapuja Day.
2445 **794** 3b. multicoloured . . . 10 10

795 Circuit Boards, Envelope with Wings and Statue

2003. National Communications Day.
2446 **795** 3b. multicoloured . . . 10 10

796 Thai Post Company Emblem

2003. Inauguration of Thailand Post Company and CAT Telecom Public Company. Multicoloured.
2447 3b. Type **796** 10 10
2448 3b. Communications Authority emblem (24 × 28 mm) 10 10
2449 3b. CAT Telecom emblem 10 10

797 King Rama V (Chulalongkorn)

2003. 150th Birth Anniv of King Chulalongkorn.
2450 **797** 100b. multicoloured . . 3·00 1·80
MS2451 114 × 161 mm. No. 2450 × 4
Perf or imperf . . . . 11·50 11·50

798 House and Family

2003. 50th Anniv of Government Housing Bank.
2452 **798** 3b. multicoloured . . . 10 10

799 *Cassis fistula* (Ratchaphruek)
801 Lychee

800 Basket Maker, Phra Nakhon Si Ayutthaya

2003. National Emblems. Multicoloured.
2453 3b. Type **799** 10 10
2454 3b. Maple leaves, Canada 10 10
MS2455 110 × 85 mm. Nos. 2453/4 (sold at 9b.) 25 25
Stamps of the same design were issued by Canada.

2003. Bangkok 2003 International Stamp Exhibition (3rd issue). Traditional Crafts. Multicoloured.
2456 3b. Type **800** 10 10
2457 3b. Potter, Nakhon Ratchasima 10 10
2458 3b. Leather worker, Nakhon Si Thammarat 10 10
2459 15b. Wood carver, Chiang Mai 45 25
MS2460 110 × 146 mm. Nos. 2456/9.
Perf and imperf (sold at 29b.) 85 85

2003. International Letter Writing Week. Fruits. Multicoloured.
2461 3b. Type **801** 10 10
2462 3b. Roseapple 10 10
2463 3b. Coconut 10 10
2464 15b. Jackfruit 10 10
MS2465 110 × 144 mm. Nos. 2461/4 (sold at 29b.) 85 85

802 Crowd surrounding Democracy Monument

2003. 30th Anniv of Democracy Day (student uprising).
2466 **802** 3b. multicoloured . . . 10 10

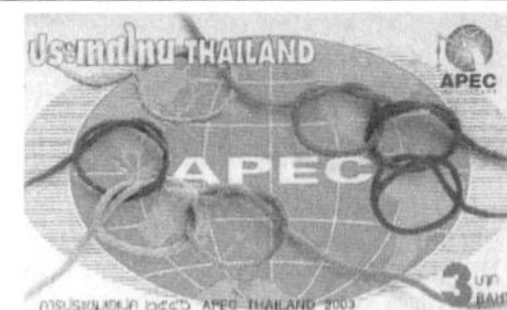

803 Globe and Linked String Loops

2003. Asian Pacific Economic Cooperation Meeting, Thailand.
2467 **803** 3b. multicoloured . . . 10 10

804 *Bougainvillea spectabilis*
805 Flag

2003. New Year. Flowers. Multicoloured.
2468 3b. Type **804** 10 10
2469 3b. *Eucrosia bicolour* 10 10
2470 3b. *Cana xgeneralis* 10 10
2471 3b. *Zinnia violacea* 10 10
MS2472 100 × 85 mm. Nos. 2468/71 (sold at 16b.) 45 45

2003. National Symbols. Multicoloured.
2473 3b. Type **805** 10 10
2474 3b. *Cassis fistula* (Ratchaphruek) 10 10
2475 3b. Pavilion 10 10
2476 3b. Elephant 10 10

806 Thai Elephant

2003. 10th Anniv of Thailand—South Africa Diplomatic Relations. Multicoloured.
2477 3b. Type **806** 10 10
2478 3b. African elephant 10 10
MS2479 92 × 54 mm. No. 2477 10 10

OFFICIAL STAMPS

O **133** (Trans "For Government Service Statistical Research")

1963.
O495 **O 133** 10s. red and pink . . 45 45
O496 20s. red and green . . 45 45
O500 20s. green 45 45
O497 25s. red and blue . . 45 45
O501 25s. blue 45 45
O502 50s. red 45 45
O498 1b. red and grey . . 45 45
O503 1b. grey 45 45
O499 2b. red and bronze . . 45 45
O504 2b. bistre 45 45
The above were used compulsorily by Government Departments between 1 October 1963 and 31 January 1964, to determine the amount of mail sent out by the different departments for the purpose of charging them in the future. They were postmarked in the usual way.

THESSALY Pt. 16

Special stamps issued during the Turkish occupation in the Graeco-Turkish War of 1898.

40 paras = 1 piastre.

20

1898.
M162 **20** 10pa. green . . . . . . 4·25 3·50
M163 20pa. red . . . . . . 4·25 3·50
M164 1pi. blue . . . . 4·25 3·50
M165 2pi. orange . . . . . . 4·25 3·50
M166 5pi. violet . . . . . . 4·25 3·50

THRACE Pt. 3

A portion of Greece to the N. of the Aegean Sea for which stamps were issued by the Allies in 1919 and by the Greek Government in 1920. Now uses Greek stamps.

1919. 100 stotinki = 1 leva.
1920. 100 lepta = 1 drachma.

1920. Stamps of Bulgaria optd **THRACE INTERALLIEE** in two lines.
28 **49** 1s. black 25 30
29 2s. grey 25 30
30 **50** 5s. green 25 30
31 10s. red 25 30
32 15s. violet 30 30
33 – 25s. black and blue (No. 165) 25 30
34 – 1l. brown (No. 168) . . . . 2·75 3·00
35 – 2l. brown (No. 191) . . . . 4·50 4·50
36 – 3l. red (No. 192) . . . . . 7·00 6·75

1920. Stamps of Bulgaria optd **THRACE INTERALLIEE** in one line.
40 **49** 1s. black . . . . 2·40 2·40
41 2s. grey . . . . 2·40 2·40
42 **50** 5s. green 30 30
43 10s. red 30 30
44 15s. violet 60 60
45 – 25s. black and blue (No. 165) 60 60

1920. Stamps of Bulgaria optd **THRACE Interalliee** in two lines vertically.
46 **50** 5s. green 25 25
47 10s. red 25 25
48 15s. violet 25 25
49 50s. brown 30 30

1920. Stamps of Bulgaria optd **THRACE OCCIDENTALE**.
50 **50** 5s. green 25 25
51 10s. red 25 25
52 15s. violet 25 25
53 25s. blue 25 25
54 30s. brown (imperf) 60 60
55 50s. brown 25 25

Διοίκησις
Δυτικῆς
Θράκης
(8)

1920. 1911 stamps of Greece optd with T **8**.
69 **29** 1l. green 25 50
70 **30** 2l. red 25 50
71 **29** 3l. red 25 50
72 **31** 5l. green 25 50
73 **29** 10l. red 25 50
74 **30** 15l. blue 25 50
75 25l. blue 50 75
76 **31** 30l. red . . . . 17·00 27·00
77 **30** 40l. blue . . . . 2·25 3·00
78 **31** 50l. purple . . . . 2·25 3·00
79 **32** 1d. blue . . . . 6·50 9·00
80 2d. red . . . . 15·00 27·00
65 3d. red . . . . 25·00 30·00
66 5d. blue . . . . 13·50 20·00
67 10d. blue . . . . 11·50 13·00
68 – 25d. blue (No. 212) . . . . 29·00 40·00
The opt on the 25d. is in capital letters.

1920. 1916 stamps of Greece, with opt Greece T **38**, optd with T **8**.
81 **29** 1l. green (No. 269) 75 75
82 **30** 2l. red 25 25
83 **29** 10l. red 50 50
84 **30** 20l. purple 50 50
85 **31** 30l. red 70 70
86 **32** 2d. red . . . . 17·00 25·00
87 3d. red . . . . 8·50 15·00
88 5d. blue . . . . 21·00 30·00
89 10d. blue . . . . 15·00 28·00

Διοίκησις
Θράκης
(10)

Ὑπάτη Ἁρμοστεία
Θράκης
5 Λεπτὰ 5
(11)

1920. Issue for E. Thrace. 1911 stamps of Greece optd with T **10**.
93 **29** 1l. green 25 25
94 **30** 2l. red 25 25
95 **29** 3l. red 25 25
96 **31** 5l. green 25 25
97 **29** 10l. red . . . . 50 1·00
98 **30** 20l. lilac . . . . 50 1·00
99 25l. blue . . . . 1·00 1·50
100 40l. blue . . . . 2·40 3·75
101 **31** 50l. purple . . . . 3·75 6·50
102 **32** 1d. blue . . . . 9·00 17·00
103 2d. red . . . . 18·00 26·00
92 – 25d. blue (No. 212) . . . . 40·00 60·00

1920. 1916 stamps of Greece with opt T **38** of Greece, optd with T **10**.
104 **30** 2l. red (No. 270) 25 75
105 **31** 5l. green . . . . 1·40 3·25
106 **30** 20l. purple . . . . 50 1·40
107 **31** 30l. red . . . . 50 1·40
108 **32** 3d. red . . . . 6·00 11·00

109		5d. blue	13·00	23·00
110		10d. blue	23·00	35·00

1920. Occupation of Adrianople. Stamps of Turkey surch as T **11**.

111	**72**	1l. on 5pa. orange	45	60
112	–	5l. on 3pi. blue (No. 965)	45	55
113	–	20l. on 1pi. grn (No. 964)	60	60
114	**69**	25l. on 5pi. on 2pa. blue	70	70
115	**78**	50l. on 5pi. black & grn	4·50	4·50
116	**74**	1d. on 20pa. red	1·75	1·75
117	**30**	2d. on 10pa. on 2pa. olive	1·75	1·75
118	**85**	3d. on 1pi. blue	8·25	8·25
119	**31**	5d. on 20pa. red	8·50	8·50

POSTAGE DUE STAMPS

1919. Postage Due stamps of Bulgaria optd **THRACE INTERALLIEE**. Perf.

D37	D **37**	5s. green	40	40
D38		10s. violet	60	60
D39		50s. blue	2·40	2·40

1920. Postage Due stamps of Bulgaria optd **THRACE OCCIDENTALE**. Imperf or perf (10s.).

D56	D **37**	5s. green	25	25
D57		10s. violet	2·25	2·25
D58		20s. orange	25	25
D59		50s. blue	1·60	1·60

THURN AND TAXIS Pt. 7

The Counts of Thurn and Taxis had a postal monopoly in parts of Germany and issued special stamps.

N. District. 30 silbergroschen = 1 thaler.
S. District. 60 kreuzer = 1 gulden.

NORTHERN DISTRICT

1

1852. Imperf.

1	**1**	¼sgr. black on brown	£160	38·00
2		⅓sgr. black on pink	70·00	£170
4		½sgr. black on green	£425	26·00
5		1sgr. black on blue	£800	£100
8		2sgr. black on pink	£550	23·00
11		3sgr. black on yellow	£550	60·00

1859. Imperf.

12	**1**	¼sgr. red	38·00	47·00
20		¼sgr. black	21·00	47·00
21		⅓sgr. green	30·00	£170
13		½sgr. green	£170	70·00
23		½sgr. orange	65·00	38·00
14		1sgr. blue	£170	32·00
25		1sgr. pink	38·00	21·00
15		2sgr. pink	85·00	60·00
27		2sgr. blue	34·00	70·00
17		3sgr. red	85·00	80·00
29		3sgr. brown	17·00	34·00
18		5sgr. mauve	1·50	£250
19		10sgr. orange	1·70	£550

1865. Rouletted.

31	**1**	¼sgr. black	8·50	£500
32		⅓sgr. green	13·00	£300
33		½sgr. yellow	26·00	38·00
34		1sgr. pink	26·00	26·00
35		2sgr. blue	1·70	80·00
36		3sgr. brown	3·00	34·00

SOUTHERN DISTRICT

3

1852. Imperf.

51	**3**	1k. black on green	£120	30·00
53		3k. black on blue	£350	19·00
57		6k. black on pink	£500	6·75
58		9k. black on yellow	£350	70·00

1859. Imperf.

60	**3**	1k. green	15·00	12·00
62		3k. blue	£350	19·00
68		3k. pink	8·50	26·00
63		6k. pink	£325	41·00
70		6k. blue	8·25	27·00
65		9k. yellow	£350	70·00
73		9k. brown	7·75	25·00
66		15k. purple	1·90	£130
67		30k. orange	1·90	£325

1865. Roul.

74	**3**	1k. green	10·50	16·00
81		3k. pink	1·70	24·00
76		6k. blue	1·90	24·00
77		9k. brown	2·40	27·00

TIBET Pt. 17

Former independent state in the Himalayas, now part of China.

A. CHINESE POST OFFICES

12 pies = 1 anna;
16 annas = 1 Indian rupee.

One Anna

(C 1)

1911. Stamps of China of 1898 surch as Type C **1**.

C 1	**32**	3p. on 1c. brown	3·00	6·00
C 2		½a. on 2c. green	4·00	6·50
C 3		1a. on 4c. red	5·00	6·50
C 4		2a. on 7c. red	5·00	8·00
C 5		2½a. on 10c. blue	5·00	8·00
C 6	**33**	3a. on 16c. green	15·00	14·00
C 7		4a. on 20c. red	14·00	15·00
C 8		6a. on 30c. red	20·00	22·00
C 9		12a. on 50c. green	40·00	35·00
C 10	**34**	1r. on $1 red and pink	£400	£450
C 11		2r. on $2 red and yellow	£750	£900

These stamps were used in Post Offices set up by the Chinese army sent to Tibet in 1910. Following a revolt by the Tibetans these troops were withdrawn during 1912.

B. INDEPENDENT STATE

6⅔ trangka = 1 sang.

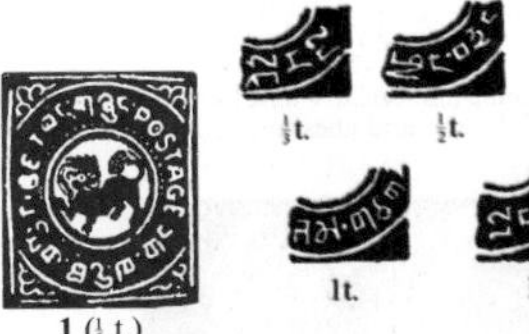

1 (⅙ t.) ⅓t. ½t. ⅔t. 1t. 1s.

1912. Imperf.

1	**1**	⅙t. green	15·00	15·00
2		⅓t. blue	18·00	15·00
3b		½t. purple	18·00	18·00
4		⅔t. red	22·00	18·00
5		1t. red	30·00	40·00
6		1s. green	45·00	45·00

2 (4t.)

1914. Imperf.

7b	**2**	4t. blue	£250	£225
8b		8t. red	£140	£140

In the 8t. the rays from the circles in the corners of the stamp point outwards towards the corner.

3 (1t.) Tibetan Lion ½t. ⅔t. 2t. 4t.

1933. Perf or imperf.

9a	**3**	½t. yellow to orange	9·00	15·00
10b		⅔t. blue	10·00	12·00
11a		1t. red	8·00	8·50
11b		1t. orange	8·00	9·00
12a		2t. red	9·00	8·00
12c		2t. orange	9·50	9·00
13d		4t. green	8·50	5·50

TIERRA DEL FUEGO Pt. 20

An island at the extreme S. of S. America. Stamp issued for use on correspondence to the mainland. Currency is expressed in centigrammes of gold dust.

1 Gold-digger's Pick and Hammer

1891.

1	**1**	10c. red	12·00	

TOBAGO Pt. 1

An island in the British West Indies, north-east of Trinidad. From 1896 to 1913 it used the stamps of Trinidad; from 1913 there were combined issues for Trinidad and Tobago.

12 pence = 1 shilling;
20 shillings = 1 pound.

1

2

1879.

1	**1**	1d. red	90·00	70·00
2		3d. blue	90·00	55·00
3		6d. orange	42·00	60·00
4		1s. green	£400	70·00
5		5s. grey	£700	£650
6		£1 mauve	£4250	

In the above issue only stamps watermarked Crown CC were issued for postal use and our prices are for stamps bearing this watermark. Stamps with watermark Crown CA are fiscals and were never admitted to postal use.

1880. No. 3 divided vertically down the centre and surch with pen and ink.

7	**1**	1d. on half of 6d. orange	£4750	£800

1880. "POSTAGE" added in design.

14	**2**	½d. brown	2·00	13·00
20		½d. green	2·50	1·25
21		1d. red	3·00	1·25
16a		2½d. blue	7·00	1·00
10		4d. green	£180	90·00
22		4d. grey	3·00	2·00
11		6d. buff	£350	£120
23		6d. brown	2·50	5·50
24		1s. yellow	3·00	18·00

1883. Surch in figures and words.

26	**2**	½d. on 2½d. blue	6·00	14·00
30		½d. on 4d. grey	17·00	55·00
27		½d. on 6d. buff	3·25	21·00
28		½d. on 6d. brown	£100	£140
29		1d. on 2½d. blue	70·00	18·00
31		2½d. on 4d. grey	8·00	7·50
13		2½d. on 6d. buff	55·00	55·00

1896. Surch **½d POSTAGE**.

33	**1**	½d. on 4d. lilac and red	65·00	35·00

TOGO Pt. 7; Pt. 1; Pt. 6; Pt. 14

A territory in W. Africa, formerly a German Colony. Divided between France and Gt. Britain in 1919, the British portion being attached to the Gold Coast for administration and using the stamps of that country. In 1956 the French portion became an autonomous republic within the French Union. Full independence was achieved in April 1960.

GERMAN ISSUES

100 pfennig = 1 mark.

1897. Stamps of Germany optd **TOGO**.

G1	**8**	3pf. brown	5·25	7·50
G2		5pf. green	4·50	3·00
G3	**9**	10pf. red	4·50	3·25
G4		20pf. blue	5·25	13·50
G5		25pf. orange	35·00	60·00
G6		50pf. brown	35·00	60·00

1900. "Yacht" key-types inscr "TOGO".

G 7	N	3pf. brown	55	1·00
G21		5pf. green	90	1·25
G 9		10pf. red	23·00	1·80
G10		20pf. blue	1·10	1·60
G11		25pf. black & red on yell	1·10	10·50
G12		30pf. black & orge on buff	1·40	10·50
G13		40pf. black and red	1·10	10·50
G14		50pf. black & pur on buff	1·40	8·00
G15		80pf. black & red on pink	2·75	18·00
G16	O	1m. red	3·00	48·00
G17		2m. blue	5·75	90·00
G18		3m. black	7·50	£160
G19		5m. red and black	£120	£550

ANGLO-FRENCH OCCUPATION

BRITISH ISSUES

1914. Nos. 7/21 (German Colonial Types) optd **TOGO Anglo-French Occupation**.

H 1	N	3pf. brown	£110	95·00
H 2		5pf. green	£100	95·00
H 3		10pf. red	£120	£100
H17		20pf. blue	19·00	12·00
H18		25pf. black & red on yell	25·00	30·00
H19		30pf. blk & orge on buff	19·00	29·00
H 7		40pf. black and red	£225	£250
H 8		50pf. black & pur on buff	£9500	£7500
H 9		80pf. black & red on rose	£225	£275
H10	O	1m. red	£5000	£2500
H11		2m. blue	£8000	£9000
H25		3m. black	†	£45000
H26		5m. lake and black	†	£45000

1914. Nos. 1/2 surch in words.

H27	N	½d on 3pf. brown	35·00	26·00
H28		1d. on 5pf. green	4·25	4·25

1915. Stamps of Gold Coast (King George V) optd **TOGO ANGLO-FRENCH OCCUPATION**.

H34		½d. green	30	1·50
H35		1d. red	30	50
H49		2d. grey	50	70
H50		2½d. blue	50	1·50
H51		3d. purple on yellow	2·25	70
H52		6d. purple	1·75	1·00
H41		1s. black on green	1·75	4·75
H54		2s. purple and blue on blue	4·50	8·50
H55		2s.6d. black and red on blue	4·50	7·00
H44		5s. green and red on yellow	8·00	15·00
H57a		10s. green and red on green	17·00	65·00
H46		20s. purple and black on red	£130	£150

FRENCH ISSUES

1914. Stamps of German Colonies, "Yacht" key-type, optd **Togo Occupation franco-anglaise** or surch also.

1	N	05 on 3pf. brown	50·00	60·00
9		5pf. green	£900	£350
2		10 on 5pf. green	25·00	16·00
10		10pf. red	£1000	£375
3		20pf. blue	55·00	48·00
4		25pf. black & red on yellow	65·00	60·00
5		30pf. black & orge on orange	90·00	90·00
6		40pf. black and red	£450	£400
15		50pf. black & purple on buff	£15000	£10000
7		80pf. black and red on pink	£450	£400
16	O	1m. red		
17		2m. blue	—	£15000
18		3m. black	—	£18000
19		5m. red and black		

1916. Stamps of Dahomey optd **TOGO Occupation franco-anglaise**.

20	**6**	1c. black and violet	15	2·00
21		2c. pink and brown	20	1·60
22		4c. brown and black	20	2·00
23		5c. green and light green	80	2·50
24		10c. pink and orange	20	1·90
25		15c. purple and red	95	1·60
26		20c. brown and grey	85	2·75
27		25c. blue and ultramarine	80	2·75
28		30c. violet and brown	1·25	3·00
29		35c. black and brown	80	3·00
30		40c. orange and black	80	3·00
31		45c. blue and grey	1·00	3·00
32		50c. brown and chocolate	1·25	2·75
33		75c. violet and blue	6·25	9·00
34		1f. black and green	8·50	12·00
35		2f. brown and yellow	11·50	16·00
36		5f. blue and violet	13·50	20·00

FRENCH MANDATE

1921. Stamps of Dahomey optd **TOGO**.

37	**6**	1c. green and grey	20	2·75
38		2c. orange and blue	10	2·25
39		4c. orange and green	20	2·75
40		5c. black and red	20	2·25
41		10c. green and turquoise	20	2·25
42		15c. red and brown	30	2·50
43		20c. orange and green	2·25	3·00
44		25c. orange and grey	1·60	2·00
45		30c. red and carmine	1·75	3·00
46		35c. green and purple	2·50	3·25
47		40c. grey and green	2·50	4·00
48		45c. grey and purple	1·25	4·00
49		50c. blue	2·00	3·00
50		75c. blue and brown	1·25	4·00
51		1f. blue and grey	3·00	4·00
52		2f. red and green	7·00	9·00
53		5f. black and yellow	10·00	12·50

1922. Stamps of 1921 (No. 57 colour changed) surch.

54	**6**	25c. on 15c. red and brown	90	3·00
55		25c. on 2f. red and green	2·00	3·00
56		25c. on 5f. black and orange	2·00	3·00
57		60 on 75c. violet on pink	85	3·25
58		65 on 45c. grey and purple	3·00	3·75
59		85 on 75c. blue and brown	2·50	4·00

5 Coconut Palms

1924.

60	**5**	1c. black and yellow	20	2·75
61		2c. black and red	25	2·00
62		4c. black and blue	1·00	2·50
63		5c. black and orange	30	55
64		10c. black and mauve	10	15
65		15c. black and green	10	55
66	–	20c. black and grey	45	45
67	–	25c. black and green on yellow	45	30
68	–	30c. black and green	35	1·25
69	–	30c. green and olive	75	80
70	–	35c. black and brown	1·90	3·00
71	–	35c. green and turquoise	55	2·75
72	–	40c. black and red	20	50
73	–	45c. black and red	40	1·50
74	–	50c. black and orange on blue	95	2·00
75	–	55c. red and blue	1·50	3·00
76	–	60c. black and purple on pink	2·00	2·75
77	–	60c. red	60	3·00
78	–	65c. brown and lilac	40	60
79	–	75c. black and blue	1·75	1·75
80	–	80c. lilac and blue	1·90	3·25
81	–	85c. brown and orange	1·60	2·75

82 – 90c. pink and red . . . . . 2·50 3·00
83 – 1f. black and purple on blue 2·25 1·50
84 – 1f. blue . . . . 2·50 2·25
85 – 1f. green and lilac . . . . . 3·00 2·50
86 – 1f. orange and red . . . . . 90 2·00
87 – 1f.10 brown and mauve . . . 6·00 3·25
88 – 1f.25 red and mauve . . . . 1·90 2·50
89 – 1f.50 blue . . . . 1·10 2·25
90 – 1f.75 pink and brown . . . . 10·50 3·50
91 – 1f.75 blue and ultramarine 1·75 3·50
92 – 2f. grey and black on blue . . 45 65
93 – 3f. red and green . . . . . . 1·40 2·00
94 – 5f. black and orange on blue 2·00 1·75
95 – 10f. pink and brown . . . . 1·75 2·75
96 – 20f. black and red on yellow 2·25 1·50
DESIGNS: 20c. to 90c. Cocoa trees; 1f. to 20f. Palm trees.

1926. No. 84 surch.
98 1f.25 on 1f. blue . . . . . . 1·60 2·25

1931. "Colonial Exhibition" key-types inscr "TOGO".
99 E 40c. green and black . . . 5·75 7·75
100 F 50c. mauve and black . . . 5·75 7·75
101 G 90c. red and black . . . . 5·00 8·25
102 H 1f.50 blue and black . . . 7·25 8·25

1937. International Exhibition, Paris. As Nos. 168/73 of St.-Pierre et Miquelon.
103 20c. violet . . . . 1·40 3·75
104 30c. green . . . . 2·00 4·00
105 40c. red . . . . 70 4·00
106 50c. brown . . . . 75 4·00
107 90c. red . . . . 80 3·75
108 1f.50 blue . . . . 75 3·25
MS108a 120 × 100 mm. 3f. blue and agate. Imperf. . . . . 3·50 9·00

1938. International Anti-cancer Fund. As T **38** of St. Pierre et Miquelon.
109 1f.75+50c. blue . . . . . . 11·50 26·00

1939. Centenary of Death of R. Caillie. As T **40** of Senegal.
110 90c. orange 30 35
111 2f. violet . . . . 65 2·75
112 2f.25 blue . . . . 60 2·75

1939. New York World's Fair. As T **41** of St. Pierre et Miquelon.
113 1f.25 red . . . . 1·75 3·00
114 2f.25 blue . . . . 30 3·00

1939. 150th Anniv of French Revolution. As T **42** of St. Pierre et Miquelon.
115 45c.+25c. green and black . . 5·00 12·00
116 70c.+30c. brown and black 5·00 12·00
117 90c.+35c. orange and black 5·00 12·00
118 1f.25+1f. red and black . . . 5·00 12·00
119 2f.25+2f. blue and black . . 5·75 12·00

1940. Air. As T **48** of St. Pierre et Miquelon.
120 1f.90 blue . . . . 60 2·75
121 2f.90 red . . . . 50 2·50
122 4f.50 green . . . . 1·10 2·75
123 4f.90 olive . . . . 80 3·00
124 6f.90 orange . . . . 1·10 3·25

8 Pounding Meal **9** Riverside Village

10 Hunting **11** Young Girl

1940.
125 **8** 2c. violet . . . . 10 2·75
126 3c. green . . . . 10 2·75
127 4c. black . . . . 45 2·75
128 5c. red . . . . 70 2·75
129 10c. blue . . . . 70 2·75
130 15c. brown . . . . 35 2·75
131 **9** 20c. plum . . . . 40 1·25
132 25c. blue . . . . 65 2·75
133 30c. black . . . . 15 2·50
134 40c. red . . . . 25 2·75
135 45c. green . . . . 20 2·75
136 50c. brown . . . . 25 3·00
137 60c. violet . . . . 35 2·50
138 **10** 70c. black . . . . 1·25 3·00
139 90c. violet . . . . 1·40 3·25
140 1f. green . . . . 1·90 3·00
141 1f.25 red . . . . 1·00 2·50
142 1f.40 brown . . . . . . 1·90 3·25
143 1f.60 orange . . . . . . 95 2·25
144 2f. blue . . . . 80 1·90
145 **11** 2f.25 blue . . . . 1·75 3·50
146 2f.50 red . . . . 80 1·60
147 3f. violet . . . . 90 2·00
148 5f. red . . . . 1·25 1·60
149 10f. violet . . . . 55 2·50
150 20f. black . . . . 1·00 2·75

1941. National Defence Fund. Surch **SECOURS NATIONAL** and value.
151 +1f. on 50c. (No. 136) . . . 4·25 5·00
152 +2f. on 80c. (No. 80) . . . . 6·25 7·50
153 +2f. on 1f.50 (No. 89) . . . 6·50 7·50
154 +3f. on 2f. (No. 144) . . . . 7·00 7·50

1942. Air. As T **40d** of Senegal.
154a 50f. violet and yellow . . . 1·75 3·25

1944. Nos. 75 and 82 surch **1 fr. 50.**
155 1f.50 on 55c. red and blue . . 85 1·75
156 1f.50 on 90c. pink and red 55 90

1944. No. 139 surch in figures and ornament.
157 **10** 3f.50 on 90c. violet . . . . 1·75 2·25
158 4f. on 90c. violet . . . . . 80 2·50
159 5f. on 90c. violet . . . . . 2·00 3·50
160 5f.50 on 90c. violet . . . . 2·00 3·75
161 10f. on 90c. violet . . . . 2·75 4·00
162 20f. on 90c. violet . . . . 3·00 3·75

18 Oil Extraction Process **19** Archer

20 Postal Runner and Lockheed Constellation

1947.
163 **18** 10c. red (postage) . . . . 15 2·25
164 30c. blue . . . . 15 2·75
165 50c. green . . . . 15 1·50
166 **19** 60c. pink . . . . 15 2·75
167 1f. brown 20 20
168 1f.20 green . . . . 20 3·00
169 – 1f.50 orange . . . . 85 3·00
170 – 2f. bistre . . . . 35 2·00
171 – 2f.50 black . . . . 85 3·75
172 – 3f. blue 95 40
173 – 3f.60 red . . . . 1·00 3·25
174 – 4f. blue 95 25
175 – 5f. brown 95 35
176 – 6f. blue . . . . 1·10 70
177 – 10f. red . . . . 1·25 20
178 – 15f. green . . . . 1·00 45
179 – 20f. green . . . . 1·25 55
180 – 25f. pink 85 65
181 – 40f. blue (air) . . . . . . 8·50 4·00
182 – 50f. mauve and violet . . 3·50 95
183 – 100f. brown and green . . 3·25 1·90
184 **20** 200f. pink . . . . 7·75 9·00
DESIGNS—As Type **18**: VERT: 1f.50 to 2f.50, Women hand-spinning cotton. HORIZ: 3f. to 4f. Drummer and village; 5f. to 10f. Red-fronted gazelles; 15f. to 25f. Trees and village. As Type **20**: 40f. African elephants and Sud Ouest SO.95 Corse II airplane; 50f. Airplane; 100f. Lockheed Constellation.

1949. Air. 75th Anniv of U.P.U. As T **58** of St. Pierre et Miquelon.
185 25f. multicoloured . . . . . 3·00 9·25

1950. Colonial Welfare Fund. As T **59** of St. Pierre et Miquelon.
186 10f.+2f. blue and indigo . . . 3·75 5·25

1952. Centenary of Military Medal. As T **60** of St. Pierre et Miquelon.
187 15f. brown, yellow and green 5·50 5·75

1954. Air. 10th Anniv of Liberation. As T **66** of St. Pierre et Miquelon.
188 15f. violet and blue . . . . . 5·00 2·50

22 Gathering Palm Nuts

23 Roadway through Forest

1954.
189 **22** 8f. purple, lake and violet (postage) . . . . 3·00 2·50
190 15f. brown, grey and blue 3·00 20
191 **23** 500f. blue and green (air) 55·00 50·00

AUTONOMOUS REPUBLIC

24 Goliath Beetle **25** Rural School

1955. Nature Protection.
192 **24** 8f. black and green . . . . 2·25 3·75

1956. Economic and Social Fund Development Fund.
193 **25** 15f. brown and chestnut 1·60 75

26 Togolese Woman and Flag

1957. New National Flag.
194 **26** 15f. brown, red & turquoise 55 35

27 Togolese Woman and "Liberty" releasing Dove

1957. Air. 1st Anniv of Autonomous Republic.
195 **27** 25f. sepia, red and blue . . 60 2·25

28 Konkomba Helmet **29** Kob

30 Torch and Flags

1957. Inscr "REPUBLIQUE AUTONOME DU TOGO".
196 **28** 30c. lilac and red (postage) 10 1·50
197 50c. indigo and blue . . . 10 75
198 1f. lilac and purple . . . 10 1·50
199 2f. brown and green . . . 10 2·75
200 3f. black and green . . . 15 1·60
201 **29** 4f. black and blue . . . . 50 2·50
202 5f. purple and grey . . . 50 60
203 6f. grey and red . . . . . 60 3·00
204 8f. violet and grey . . . 65 3·00
205 10f. brown and green . . 2·25 45
206 – 15f. multicoloured . . . . 2·00 1·25
207 – 20f. multicoloured . . . . 2·50 40
208 – 25f. multicoloured . . . . 2·25 1·00
209 – 40f. multicoloured . . . . 2·50 1·60
210 **30** 50f. multicoloured (air) . . 85 1·10
211 100f. multicoloured . . . . 1·10 1·40
212 200f. multicoloured . . . . 2·50 3·75
213 – 500f. indigo, green and blue . . . . 14·00 9·50
DESIGNS—HORIZ: 15f. to 40f. Teak forest. 48 × 27 mm: 500f. Great egret.
See also Nos. 217/35.

31 "Human Rights" **32** "Bombax"

1958. 10th Anniv of Human Rights Declaration.
214 **31** 20f. red and green 50 35

1959. Tropical Flora.
215 **32** 5f. multicoloured . . . . . 90 1·50
216 – 20f. yellow, green and black . . . . 1·25 1·60
DESIGN—HORIZ: 20f. "Tectona".

1959. As Nos. 196/213 but colours changed and inscr "REPUBLIQUE DU TOGO".
217 **28** 30c. blue & black (postage) 10 2·25
218 50c. green and green . . . 15 2·75
219 1f. purple and green . . . 20 10
220 2f. brown and green . . . 25 10
221 3f. violet and purple . . . 25 75
222 **29** 4f. violet and purple . . . 1·90 1·10
223 5f. brown and green . . . 1·90 85
224 6f. blue and ultramarine 2·00 1·25
225 8f. bistre and green . . . 2·00 1·75
226 10f. brown and violet . . 1·60 85
227 – 15f. multicoloured . . . . 90 1·25
228 – 20f. multicoloured . . . . 1·10 20
229 – 25f. multicoloured . . . . 1·25 1·25
230 – 40f. multicoloured . . . . 1·00 30
231 – 25f. brown, grn & bl (air) 1·10 1·90
232 **30** 50f. multicoloured . . . . 85 1·10
233 100f. multicoloured . . . . 1·10 1·40
234 200f. multicoloured . . . . 2·50 4·00
235 – 500f. sepia, green & purple 12·00 4·50
DESIGN—VERT: 25f. (No. 231) Togo flag and shadow of airliner over Africa.

32a Patient on Stretcher **33** "The Five Continents"

1959. Red Cross Commemoration.
236 **32a** 20f.+5f. red, orge & slate 3·00 2·75
237 – 30f.+5f. red, brown & bl 3·00 3·50
238 – 50f.+10f. red, brn & grn 3·00 3·50
MS238a Three sheets each 78 × 106 mm. Nos. 236/8 in blocks of four. Perf or imperf . . . . 26·00 35·00
DESIGNS: 30f. Mother feeding child; 50f. Nurse superintending blood transfusion.

1959. United Nations Day.
239 **33** 15f. blue and brown . . . 2·00 2·75
240 20f. blue and violet . . . . 2·00 2·75
241 25f. blue and brown . . . 2·25 2·50
242 40f. blue and green . . . . 2·25 2·75
243 60f. blue and red . . . . . 2·50 3·00

34 Skiing **35** "Uprooted Tree"

1960. Olympic Games, California and Rome.
244 **34** 30c. turquoise, red & green 10 65
245 – 50c. purple, red and black 40 2·25
246 – 1f. green, red and black . . 50 2·25
247 – 10f. brown, blue and indigo . . . . 2·50 2·75
248 – 15f. purple and green . . . 2·25 3·00
249 – 20f. chocolate, green & brown . . . . 2·50 3·00
250 – 25f. brown, red and orange 2·75 2·75
DESIGNS—HORIZ: 50c. Ice hockey; 1f. Tobogganing; 10f. Cycling; 25f. Running. VERT: 125f. Throwing the discus; 20f. Boxing.

1960. World Refugee Year.
251 **35** 25f.+5f. green, brown & bl 40 3·25
252 – 45f.+5f. olive, black & bl 40 3·25
DESIGN: 45f. As Type **35** but "TOGO" at foot.

INDEPENDENT REPUBLIC

36 Prime Minister S. Olympio and Flag   **37** Benin Hotel

1960. Independence Commemoration. (a) Postage. Centres multicoloured; backgrounds cream; inscription and frame colours given.
253 **36** 30c. sepia 10 10
254 50c. brown 10 10
255 1f. purple 10 10
256 10f. blue 15 10
257 20f. red 40 15
258 25f. green 50 20

(b) Air.
259 **37** 100f. red, yellow and green 1·60 50
260 200f. multicoloured . . . . 2·75 90
261 – 500f. brown and green . . 9·50 3·25
DESIGN—As Type **37**: VERT: 500f. Palm-nut vulture and map of Togo.

38 Union Jack and Flags

1960. Four-Power "Summit" Conference, Paris. Flags and inscr in red and blue.
262 **38** 50c. buff 10 10
263 – 1f. turquoise 10 10
264 – 20f. grey 35 20
265 – 25f. blue 40 20
DESIGNS—As Type **38** but flags of: 1f. Soviet Union; 20f. France; 25f. U.S.A. The Conference did not take place.

39 Togo Flag   **40** South African Crowned Cranes

1961. Admission of Togo into U.N.O. Flag in red, yellow and green.
266 **39** 30c. red 10 10
267 50c. brown 10 10
268 1f. blue 10 10
269 10f. purple 20 10
270 25f. black 40 15
271 30f. violet 45 20

1961.
272 **40** 1f. multicoloured 50 10
273 10f. multicoloured 70 15
274 25f. multicoloured . . . . 1·10 40
275 30f. multicoloured . . . . 1·25 50

41 Augustino de Souza (statesman)   **42** Daniel Beard (founder of American Boy Scout Movement) and Scout Badge

1961. 1st Anniv of Independence.
276 **41** 50c. black, red and yellow 10 10
277 1f. black, brown and green 10 10
278 10f. black, violet and blue 20 15
279 25f. black, green & salmon 40 10
280 30f. black, blue and mauve 50 20

1961. Boy Scout Movement Commemoration.
281 **42** 50c. lake, green and red . . 10 10
282 – 1f. violet and red 10 10
283 – 10f. black and brown . . . 20 10
284 – 25f. multicoloured 55 15
285 – 30f. red, brown and green 65 20
286 – 100f. mauve and blue . . . 1·60 60
DESIGNS—HORIZ: 1f. Lord Baden-Powell; 10f. Daniel Mensah ("Rover" Scout Chief); 100f. Scout salute. VERT: 25f. Chief Daniel Wilson (Togolese Scout); 30f. Campfire on triangular emblem.

43 Jet Airliner and Motor Launch   **44** UNICEF Emblem

1961. U.N. Economic Commission on Africa. Mult.
287 20f. Type **43** 30 15
288 25f. Electric train and gantry 95 15
289 30f. Excavator and pylons . . 65 30
290 85f. Microscope and atomic symbol . . . . 1·25 50
The designs are superimposed on a map of Africa spread over the four stamps when the 30 and 85f. are mounted below the 20 and 25f.

1961. 15th Anniv of UNICEF.
291 **44** 1f. blue, green and black 10 10
292 – 10f. multicoloured 15 10
293 – 20f. multicoloured 20 10
294 – 25f. multicoloured 45 20
295 – 30f. multicoloured 80 20
296 – 85f. multicoloured . . . . 1·25 60
DESIGNS: 10f. to 85f. Children dancing round the globe. The six stamps, arranged in the following order, form a composite picture: Upper row, 1, 25 and 20f. Lower row, 10, 85 and 30f.

45 Alan Shepard   **47** Togolese Girl

1962. Space Flights Commemoration.
297 **45** 50c. green 10 10
298 – 1f. mauve 15 10
299 **45** 25f. blue 35 20
300 – 30f. violet 50 30
DESIGN: 1, 30f. As Type **45** but portrait of Yuri Gagarin.

1962. Col. Glenn's Space Flight. Surch **100F COL. JOHN H. GLENN U S A VOL ORBITAL 20 FEVRIER 1962.**
301 **45** 100f. on 50c. green . . . . 2·00 2·00

1962. 2nd Anniv of Independence.
303 – 50c. multicoloured 10 10
304 **47** 1f. green and pink 10 10
305 – 5f. multicoloured 20 15
306 **47** 20f. violet and yellow . . . 30 15
307 – 25f. multicoloured 35 15
308 **47** 30f. red and yellow 35 15
DESIGN: 50c., 5, 25f. Independence Monument.

48 Arrows piercing Mosquito

1962. Malaria Eradication.
309 **48** 10f. multicoloured 30 10
310 25f. multicoloured 45 20
311 30f. multicoloured 50 35
312 85f. multicoloured . . . . 1·00 55

49 Presidents Kennedy and Olympio, and Capitol, Washington

1962. Visit of President Olympio to U.S.A.
313 **49** 50c. slate and ochre . . . 10 10
314 1f. slate and blue 10 10
315 2f. slate and red 10 10
316 5f. slate and mauve 10 10
317 25f. slate and lilac 40 15
318 100f. slate and green . . . 1·60 70

50 Stamps of 1897 and Mail-coach

1963. 65th Anniv of Togolese Postal Services.
319 **50** 30c. multicoloured (postage) 10 10
320 – 50c. multicoloured 10 10
321 – 1f. multicoloured 35 10
322 – 10f. multicoloured 45 15
323 – 25f. multicoloured 60 20
324 – 30f. multicoloured 85 40
325 – 100f. multicoloured (air) 2·40 1·00
DESIGNS (Togo stamps of): 50c. 1900 and German imperial yacht "Hohenzollern"; 1f. 1915 and steam mail train; 10f. 1924 and motor-cycle mail carrier; 25f. 1940 and mail-van; 30f. 1947 and Douglas DC-3 airplane; 100f. 1960 and Boeing 707 airplane.

51 Hands reaching for F.A.O. Emblem   **53** Centenary Emblem

52 Lome Port and Togolese Flag

1963. Freedom from Hunger.
326 **51** 50c. multicoloured 10 10
327 1f. multicoloured 10 10
328 25f. multicoloured 60 20
329 30f. multicoloured 85 30

1963. 3rd Anniv of Independence. Flag in red, yellow and green.
330 **52** 50c. black and brown . . . 10 10
331 1f. black and red 15 10
332 25f. black and blue 35 20
333 50f. black and ochre . . . 70 35

1963. Red Cross Centenary. Flag in red, yellow and green; cross red.
334 **53** 25f. blue and black 85 30
335 30f. green and black . . . 1·10 40

54 Broken Shackles and Abraham Lincoln   **55** Flame and U.N. Emblem

1963. Cent of American Slaves' Emancipation. Centre in grey and green.
336 **54** 50c. black & brn (postage) 10 10
337 1f. black and blue 10 10
338 25f. black and red 45 15
339 100f. black and orange (air) . . . . 1·40 60

1963. 15th Anniv of Declaration of Human Rights. Flame in red.
340 **55** 50c. blue and ultramarine 10 10
341 1f. green and black 15 10
342 25f. lilac and blue 40 15
343 85f. gold and blue . . . . 1·10 60

56 Hibiscus   **58** Temple and Isis

1964. Multicoloured.
344 50c. "Odontoglossum grande" (orchid) (postage) 10 10
345 1f. Type **56** 10 10
346 2f. "Papilio dardanus" (butterfly) 35 10
347 3f. "Morpho aega" (butterfly) 55 10
348 4f. "Pandinus imperator" (scorpion) 40 10
349 5f. Tortoise 20 15
350 6f. Strelitzia (flower) 55 15
351 8f. Python 45 15
352 10f. "Bunaea alcinde" (butterfly) 85 15
353 15f. Chameleon . . . . . . 1·25 15
354 20f. Common octopus . . . 1·50 20
355 25f. John Dory (fish) . . . . 1·60 20
356 30f. French angelfish . . . . 2·00 35
357 40f. Pygmy hippopotamus . . 2·00 35
358 45f. African palm civet . . . 3·25 60
359 60f. Bohar reedbuck . . . . 4·50 90
360 85f. Olive baboon . . . . . 5·50 1·00
361 50f. Black-bellied seedcracker (air) . . . . 3·50 50
362 100f. Black and white mannikin . . . . 8·25 90
363 200f. Red-faced lovebird . . 12·00 1·90
364 250f. Grey parrot . . . . . 28·00 4·25
365 500f. Yellow-breasted barbet 38·00 1·10

1964. President Kennedy Memorial Issue. Optd **En Memoire de JOHN F. KENNEDY 1917-1963.** Centre in grey and green.
366 **54** 50c. black & brn (postage) 15 10
367 1f. black and blue 15 10
368 25f. black and red 50 20
369 100f. black and orange (air) . . . . 1·60 80

1964. Nubian Monuments Preservation.
370 **58** 20f. multicoloured 30 10
371 – 25f. mauve and black . . . 35 20
372 – 30f. olive, black and yellow 50 30
DESIGNS: 25f. Head of Rameses II, Abu Simbel; 30f. Temple of Philae.

59 Phosphate Mine, Kpeme

1964. 4th Anniv of Independence.
373 **59** 5f. ochre, bistre and brown 35 10
374 – 25f. lake, brown and violet 35 15
375 – 60f. yellow, olive and green 1·25 50
376 – 85f. blue, slate and violet 1·50 50
DESIGNS: 25f. Mine installations; 60f. Diesel phosphate train; 85f. Loading phosphate onto "Panama Maru" bulk carrier.

60 Togolese breaking Chain   **61** Pres. Grunitzky and "Papilio memnon"

1964. 1st Anniv of African Heads of State Conference, Addis Ababa.
377 **60** 5f. sepia & orange (postage) 15 10
378 25f. sepia and green . . . 35 15
379 85f. sepia and red 95 45
380 100f. sepia & turquoise (air) . . . . 1·25 65

1964. "National Union and Reconciliation".
381 **61** 1f. violet and mauve . . . 20 10
382 – 5f. sepia and ochre 10 10
383 – 25f. violet and blue 45 15
384 **61** 45f. purple and red . . . . 1·75 50
385 – 85f. bronze and green . . . 1·90 60
DESIGNS—President and: 5f. Dove; 25, 85f. Flowers.

62 Football

1964. Olympic Games, Tokyo.
386 **62** 1f. green (postage) 10 10
387 – 5f. blue (Running) 25 15
388 – 25f. red (Throwing the discus) 75 15
389 **62** 45f. turquoise . . . . . . 1·00 40
390 – 100f. brown (Tennis) (air) 1·75 55

1964. French, African and Malagasy Co-operation. As T **60a** of Senegal.
391 25f. brown, bistre and purple 40 20

63 Charles's Hydrogen Balloon, Giffard's Steam-powered Dirigible Airship and Airship LZ-5

1964. Inaug of "Air Togo" (National Airline).
392 **63** 5f. multicoloured (postage) . . . 10 10
393 10f. blue, lake and green . . . 30 10
394 – 25f. ultramarine, orge & blue 50 15
395 – 45f. mauve, green and bl . . . 1·10 35
396 – 100f. multicoloured (air) . . . 1·90 80
DESIGNS: 25, 45f. Farman H.F. III biplane, Lilienthal biplane glider and Boeing 707; 100f. Boeing 707 and Togolese flag.

64 Sun, Globe and Satellites "Ogo" and "Mariner"

1964. International Quiet Sun Years. Sun yellow.
397 **64** 10f. blue and red 15 10
398 – 15f. blue, brown and mauve 20 10
399 – 20f. green and violet . . . 30 10
400 – 25f. purple, green and blue . . . 35 15
401 **64** 45f. blue and green 70 35
402 – 50f. green and red 80 40
SATELLITES: 15, 25f. "Tiros", "Telstar" and orbiting solar observatory; 20, 50f. "Nimbus", "Syncom" and "Relay".

65 Pres. Grunitzky and the Mount of the Beatitudes Church

1965. Israel–Togo Friendship. Inscr "AMITIE ISRAEL–TOGO 1964".
403 – 5f. purple 10 10
404 **65** 20f. blue and purple . . . 20 10
405 – 25f. turquoise and red . . 35 15
406 – 45f. olive, bistre and purple . . 70 35
407 – 85f. turquoise and purple . . 1·10 50
DESIGNS—VERT: 5f. Togolese stamps being printed on Israel press. HORIZ: 25, 85f. Arms of Israel and Togo; 45f. As Type **65** but showing old synagogue, Capernaum.

66 "Syncom 3", Dish Aerial and I.T.U. Emblem

1965. I.T.U. Centenary.
408 **66** 10f. turquoise and green . . . 15 10
409 20f. olive and black . . . 35 15
410 25f. blue and ultramarine . . . 40 15
411 45f. rose and red 70 35
412 50f. green and black . . . 90 45

67 Abraham Lincoln **68** Throwing the Discus

1965. Death Centenary of Lincoln.
413 **67** 1f. purple (postage) 10 10
414 5f. greeen 10 10
415 20f. brown 35 10
416 25f. blue 45 20
417 100f. olive (air) . . . . . 1·60 70

1965. 1st African Games, Brazzaville. Flags in red, yellow and green.
418 **68** 5f. purple (postage) 10 10
419 – 10f. blue 15 10
420 – 15f. brown 35 10
421 – 25f. purple 90 20
422 – 100f. green (air) . . . . . 1·50 65
SPORTS: 10f. Throwing the javelin; 15f. Hand-ball; 25f. Running; 100f. Football.

69 Sir Winston Churchill

1965. Churchill Commemoration.
423 **69** 5f. green (postage) 10 10
424 – 10f. violet and blue 15 10
425 **69** 20f. brown 40 15
426 – 45f. blue 65 35
427 **69** 85f. red (air) . . . . 1·50 65
DESIGNS—HORIZ: 10, 45f. Stalin, Roosevelt and Churchill at Teheran Conference, 1943.

70 Unisphere

1965. New York World's Fair.
428 **70** 5f. plum and blue 15 10
429 – 10f. sepia and green . . . 20 10
430 **70** 25f. myrtle and brown . . 35 20
431 – 50f. myrtle and violet . . . 65 40
432 **70** 85f. brown and red . . . . 1·10 50
DESIGNS: 10f. Native dancers and drummer; 50f. Michelangelo's "Pieta".

71 "Laying Bricks of Peace"

1965. International Co-operation Year.
433 **71** 5f. multicoloured 10 10
434 15f. multicoloured 15 15
435 – 25f. multicoloured 30 15
436 – 40f. multicoloured 60 30
437 – 85f. multicoloured . . . . 1·00 50
DESIGNS: 25, 40f. Hands suppporting globe; 85f. I.C.Y. emblem.

72 Leonov with Camera

1965. Astronauts in Space.
438 **72** 25f. mauve and blue . . . 50 20
439 – 50f. brown and green . . . 90 40
DESIGN: 50f. White with rocket-gun.

73 "ONU" and Doves

1966. 20th Anniv of U.N.O.
440 **73** 5f. brown, yellow and blue (postage) 10 10
441 – 10f. blue, turquoise and orange 20 10
442 – 20f. orange, green and light green 35 15
443 – 25f. blue, turquoise & yell . . 45 20
444 – 100f. ochre, blue and light blue (air) . . . . 1·60 55
DESIGNS: 10f. U.N. Headquarters and emblem; 20f. "ONU" and orchids; 25f. U.N. Headquarters and Adlai Stevenson; 100f. "ONU", fruit and ears of wheat.

74 Pope Paul, Boeing 707 and U.N. Emblem

1966. Pope Paul's Visit to U.N. Organization. Multicoloured.
445 5f. Type **74** (postage) 10 10
446 15f. Pope before microphones at U.N. (vert) 20 10
447 20f. Pope and U.N. Headquarters 35 15
448 30f. As 15f. 45 20
449 45f. Pope before microphones at U.N., and map (air) . . 80 30
450 90f. Type **74** . . . . 1·60 80

75 W.H.O. Building and Roses

1966. Inaug of W.H.O. Headquarters, Geneva. Multicoloured designs showing W.H.O. Building and flower as given.
451 5f. Type **75** (postage) 20 10
452 10f. Alstroemerias 35 10
453 15f. Asters 45 20
454 20f. Freesias 55 35
455 30f. Geraniums 65 35
456 50f. Asters (air) 95 35
457 50f. Type **75** . . . . 1·50 55

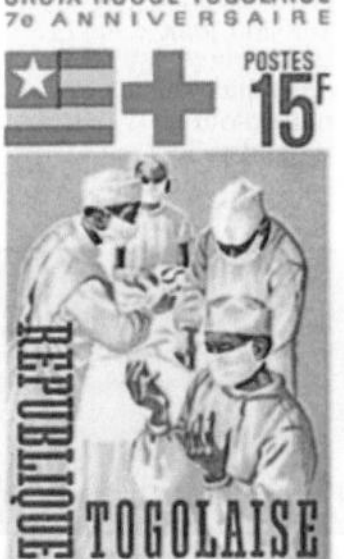

76 Surgical Operation

1966. 7th Anniv of Togolese Red Cross. Mult.
459 5f. Type **76** (postage) 10 10
460 10f. Blood transfusion . . . 15 10
461 15f. Type **76** 30 15
462 30f. Blood transfusion . . . 40 15
463 45f. African man and woman . . 70 45
464 100f. J. H. Dunant (air) . . . 1·75 90

1966. Space Achievements. Nos. 438/9 optd as below or surch also.
465 50f. **(ENVOLEE SURVEYOR 1)** 85 40
466 50f. **(ENVOLEE GEMINI 9)** . . 85 40
467 100f. on 25f. **(ENVOLEE LUNA 9)** . . . . 1·60 70
468 100f. on 25f. **(ENVOLEE VENUS 3)** . . . . 1·60 70

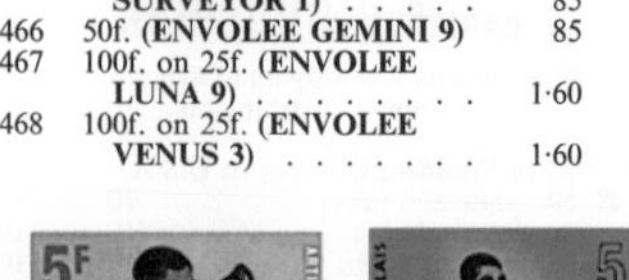

78 Wood-carving **79** Togolese Man

1966. Togolese Arts and Crafts.
469 **78** 5f. brn, yell & bl (postage) . . 10 10
470 – 10f. brown, salmon & green 15 10
471 – 15f. brown, yellow and red . . 30 15
472 – 30f. brown, bistre and violet 55 20
473 – 60f. brown, salmon and blue (air) . . . . 1·40 60
474 **78** 90f. brown, yellow and red . . 1·40 60
DESIGNS: 10, 60f. Basket-making; 15f. Weaving; 30f. Pottery.

1966. Air. Inauguration of Douglas DC-8F Air Services. As T **76a** of Senegal.
475 30f. black, green and yellow . . 65 25

1966. Togolese Costumes and Dances. Mult.
476 5f. Type **79** (postage) 10 10
477 10f. Togolese woman 10 10
478 20f. Female dancer 40 10
479 25f. Male dancer 50 15
480 30f. Dancer in horned helmet . . 65 20
481 45f. Drummer . . . . 1·00 50
482 50f. Female dancer (air) . . . 85 45
483 60f. Dancer in horned helmet . . 1·40 60

80 Footballers and Jules Rimet Cup

1966. World Cup Football Championship, England. Showing football scenes and Jules Rimet Cup.
484 **80** 5f. multicoloured (postage) . . 20 10
485 – 10f. multicoloured 30 10
486 – 20f. multicoloured 50 10
487 – 25f. multicoloured 50 15
488 – 30f. multicoloured 65 20
489 – 45f. multicoloured . . . . 1·00 40
490 – 50f. multicoloured (air) . . 1·00 30
491 – 60f. multicoloured . . . . 1·50 40

81 African Mouthbrooder

1967. Fishes. Multicoloured designs showing fishes with fishing craft in the background.
493 5f. Type **81** (postage) 30 10
494 10f. Golden trevally 50 15
495 15f. Six banded distichodus . . 60 25
496 25f. Jewel cichlid 85 30
497 30f. Type **81** . . . . 1·25 55
498 45f. As 10f. (air) . . . . . . 2·00 70
499 90f. As 15f. . . . . 2·75 1·00

82 African Boy and Greyhound

1967. 20th Anniv (1966) of UNICEF.
500 **82** 5f. multicoloured (postage) . . 20 10
501 – 10f. brown, green & lt grn . . 40 15
502 **82** 15f. black, brown & mauve . . 60 20
503 – 20f. black, ultramarine & blue 75 30
504 **82** 30f. black, blue and olive . . 1·10 35
505 – 45f. bronze, brown and yellow (air) . . . . . . 1·25 40
506 **82** 90c. black, bronze and blue . . 1·75 55
DESIGNS: 10f. Boy and Irish setter; 20f. Girl and doberman; 45f. Girl and miniature poodle.

83 Launching "Diamant" Rocket

1967. French Space Achievements. Multicoloured.
508 5f. Type **83** (postage) 10 10
509 10f. Satellite "A-1" (horiz) 20 10
510 15f. Satellite "FR-1" 30 10
511 20f. Satellite "D-1" (horiz) 40 15
512 25f. As 10f. 50 30
513 40f. As 20f. 70 35
514 50f. Type **83** (air) 95 40
515 90f. As 15f. 1·50 55

84 Bach and Organ

1967. 20th Anniv (1966) of UNESCO.
517 **84** 5f. multicoloured (postage) 10 10
518 – 10f. multicoloured 20 10
519 – 15f. multicoloured 45 20
520 – 20f. multicoloured 55 20
521 – 30f. multicoloured 90 45
522 **84** 45f. multicoloured (air) 1·10 40
523 – 90f. multicoloured 1·60 55
DESIGNS: 10, 90f. Beethoven, violin and clarinet; 15, 30f. Duke Ellington, saxophone, trumpet and drums; 20f. Debussy, grand piano and harp.

85 British Pavilion and Lilies

1967. World Fair, Montreal. Multicoloured.
525 5f. Type **85** (postage) 15 10
526 10f. French Pavilion and roses 30 10
527 30f. "Africa Place" and strelitzia 75 15
528 45f. As 10f. (air) 1·00 35
529 60f. Type **85** 1·10 45
530 90f. As 30f. 1·75 60
531 105f. U.S. Pavilion and daisies 2·25 65

86 "Peace"

1967. Air. Disarmament. Designs showing sections of the "Peace" mural by J. Zanetti at the U.N. Headquarters Building Conference Room.
533 **86** 5f. multicoloured 15 10
534 A 15f. multicoloured 20 10
535 B 30f. multicoloured 40 10
536 **86** 45f. multicoloured 70 35
537 A 60f. multicoloured 1·25 45
538 B 90f. multicoloured 1·60 55

87 Lions Emblem with Supporters

1967. 50th Anniv of Lions International. Mult.
540 10f. Type **87** 20 10
541 20f. Flowers and Lions emblem 35 15
542 30f. Type **87** 45 20
543 45f. As 20f. 1·25 45

88 Bohar Reedbuck

1967. Wildlife.
544 **88** 5f. brown & pur (postage) 10 10
545 – 10f. blue, red and yellow 25 10
546 – 15f. black, lilac and green 45 15
547 – 20f. blue, sepia and yellow 55 25
548 – 25f. brown, yellow and olive 85 35
549 – 30f. blue, violet and yellow 1·75 50
550 – 45f. brown and blue (air) 90 35
551 – 60f. black, brown and green 1·25 50
DESIGNS: 10, 20, 30f. Montagu's harriers (birds of prey); 15f. Common zebra; 25f. Leopard; 45f. Lion; 60f. African elephants.

1967. Air. 5th Anniv of U.A.M.P.T. As T **86a** of Senegal.
552 100f. brown, blue and green 1·60 1·10

89 Stamp Auction and Togo Stamps—1m. (German) of 1900 and 100f. Conference of 1964

1967. 70th Anniv of 1st Togolese Stamps. Mult.
553 5f. Type **89** (postage) 15 10
554 10f. Exhibition and 1d. (British) of 1915 and 50f. I.T.U. of 1965 15 10
555 15f. Stamp shop and 50c. (French) of 1924 40 10
556 20f. Stamp-packet vending machine and 5f. U.N. of 1965 40 10
557 30f. As 15f. 60 30
558 45f. As 10f. 85 40
559 90f. Type **89** (air) 1·50 60
560 105f. Father and son with album and 1f. Kennedy of 1964 1·75 80

89a Currency Tokens

1967. 5th Anniv of West African Monetary Union.
562 **89a** 30f. blue and green 55 30

90 Long Jumping

1967. Olympic Games, Mexico and Grenoble (1968). Multicoloured.
563 5f. Type **90** (postage) 10 10
564 15f. Ski-jumping 20 10
565 30f. Relay runners 55 20
566 45f. Bob-sleighing 90 35
567 60f. As 30f. (air) 1·10 40
568 90f. Type **90** 1·00 55

1967. National Day (29 Sept). Nos. 525/31 optd **JOURNEE NATIONALE DU TOGO 29 SEPTEMBRE 1967.**
570 5f. multicoloured (postage) 35 20
571 10f. multicoloured 35 20
572 30f. multicoloured 1·00 40
573 45f. multicoloured (air) 40 20
574 60f. multicoloured 80 35
575 90f. multicoloured 1·25 45
576 105f. multicoloured 2·25 65

92 "The Gleaners" (Millet) and Benin Phosphate Mine

1968. Paintings and Local Industries.
577 **92** 10f. multicoloured 20 10
578 – 20f. multicoloured 30 10
579 **92** 30f. multicoloured 60 15
580 – 45f. multicoloured 70 20
581 **92** 60f. multicoloured 1·25 45
582 – 90f. multicoloured 1·40 70
DESIGN: 20, 45, 90f. "The Weaver at the Loom" (Van Gogh) and textile plant, Dadia.

93 Brewing Beer

1968. Benin Brewery. Multicoloured.
583 20f. Type **93** 35 10
584 30f. "Drinking at a Bar" (detail from painting by Manet) (vert) 1·00 30
585 45f. Bottling-washing machine and bottle of Benin beer 70 40

94 Decade Emblem and Sunflowers

96 Dr. Adenauer and Europa "Key"

95 Viking Longship and Portuguese Galleon

1968. International Hydrological Decade.
586 **94** 30f. multicoloured (postage) 60 30
587 60f. multicoloured (air) 85 40

1968. Inaug of Lome Port. Multicoloured.
588 5f. Type **95** (postage) 15 10
589 10f. Paddle-steamer "Clermont" and Liner "Athlone Castle" 20 10
590 20f. Quayside, Lome Port 65 20
591 30f. Type **95** 90 35
592 45f. As 10f. (air) 1·10 40
593 90f. Nuclear-powered freighter "Savannah" 2·00 60

1968. Adenauer (German statesman) Commem.
595 **96** 90f. multicoloured 1·60 80

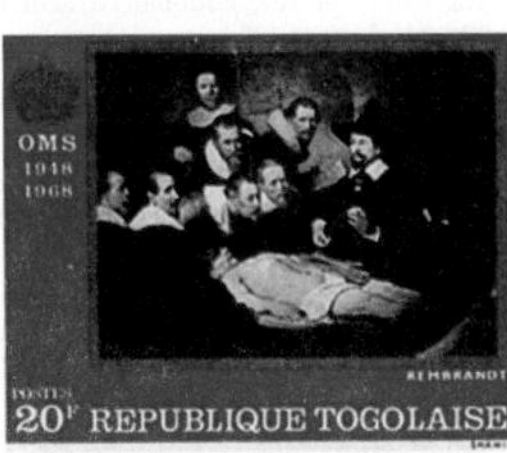

97 "Dr. Turp's Anatomy Lesson" (Rembrandt)

1968. 20th Anniv of World Health Organization. Paintings. Multicoloured.
596 15f. "Expulsion from the Garden of Eden" (Michelangelo) (postage) 30 10
597 20f. Type **97** 40 15
598 30f. "Johann Deyman's Anatomy Lesson" (Rembrandt) 55 20
599 45f. "Christ healing the sick" (Raphael) 85 35
600 60f. As 30f. (air) 85 40
601 90f. As 45f. 1·10 55

98 Wrestling

1968. Olympic Games, Mexico. Multicoloured.
603 15f. Type **98** (postage) 20 15
604 20f. Boxing 45 15
605 30f. Judo 65 20
606 45f. Running 80 35
607 60f. Type **98** (air) 90 40
608 90f. As 45f. 1·25 55

99 "Try Your Luck" **100** Scout and Tent

1968. 2nd Anniv of National Lottery. Mult.
610 30f. Type **99** 55 25
611 45f. Lottery ticket, horse-shoe and cloverleaf 80 30

1968. Air. "Philexafrique" Stamp Exhibition, Abidjan (Ivory Coast, 1969) (1st issue). As T **98a** of Senegal. Multicoloured.
612 100f. "The Letter" (J. A. Franquelin) 2·75 1·90

1968. Togolese Scouts. Multicoloured.
613 5f. Type **100** (postage) 10 10
614 10f. Scoutmaster with cubs 30 10
615 20f. Giving first aid 40 15
616 30f. Scout game 50 20
617 45f. As 10f. 65 35
618 60f. As 20f. (air) 90 45
619 90f. As 30f. 1·25 65
The 10, 20, 45 and 60f. are horiz.

101 "The Adoration of the Shepherds" (Giorgione)

1968. Christmas. Paintings. Multicoloured.
621 15f. Type **101** (postage) 35 10
622 20f. "The Adoration of the Kings" (Brueghel) 45 10
623 30f. "The Adoration" (Botticelli) 55 15
624 45f. "The Adoration" (Durer) 90 35
625 60f. As 20f. (air) 1·00 40
626 90f. As 45f. 1·50 55

102 Martin Luther King

1969. Human Rights Year.
628 **102** 15f. green & brown (postage) 20 10
629 – 20f. violet and turquoise 35 15
630 **102** 30f. blue and red 55 20
631 – 45f. red and olive . . . . 1·10 45
632 – 60f. blue and purple (air) 90 45
633 **102** 90f. brown and green . . 1·25 55
PORTRAITS: 20f. Prof. Rene Cassin (Nobel Peace Prize-winner); 45f. Pope John XXIII; 60f. Robert E. Kennedy.

1969. Air. "Philexafrique" Stamp Exn, Abidjan, Ivory Coast (2nd issue). As T **101a** of Senegal.
635 50f. red, brown and green . . 80 80
DESIGN: 50f. Aledjo Rock and stamp of 1900.

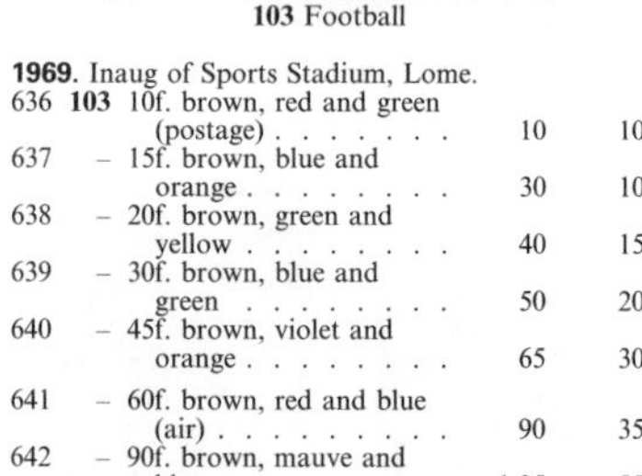

103 Football

1969. Inaug of Sports Stadium, Lome.
636 **103** 10f. brown, red and green (postage) 10 10
637 – 15f. brown, blue and orange 30 10
638 – 20f. brown, green and yellow 40 15
639 – 30f. brown, blue and green 50 20
640 – 45f. brown, violet and orange 65 30
641 – 60f. brown, red and blue (air) 90 35
642 – 90f. brown, mauve and blue . . . . 1·25 55
DESIGNS: 15f. Handball; 20f. Volleyball; 30f. Basketball; 45f. Tennis; 60f. Boxing; 90f. Cycling.

104 Module landing on Moon

1969. 1st Man on the Moon. Multicoloured.
644 1f. Type **104** (postage) . . . 10 10
645 20f. Astronaut and module on Moon 20 10
646 30f. As Type **104** 40 15
647 45f. As 20f. 65 35
648 60f. Astronaut exploring lunar surface (air) 85 40
649 100f. Astronaut gathering Moon rock . . . . 1·40 70

105 "The Last Supper" (Tintoretto)

1969. Religious Paintings. Multicoloured.
651 5f. Type **105** (postage) . . . 15 10
652 10f. "Christ's Vision at Emmaus" (Velazquez) . . 30 10
653 20f. "Pentecost" (El Greco) 50 20
654 30f. "The Annunciation" (Botticelli) 70 20
655 45f. As 10f. . . . . 1·10 45
656 90f. As 20f. (air) . . . . . . 1·90 65

1969. Eisenhower Commem. Nos. 628/33 optd with Eisenhower's silhouette and **EN MEMOIRE DWIGHT D. EISENHOWER 1890-1968**.
658 **102** 15f. green & brown (postage) 25 15
659 – 20f. violet and turquoise 45 15
660 **102** 30f. blue and red 55 20
661 – 45f. red and olive 95 30
662 – 60f. blue and purple (air) 90 45
663 **102** 90f. brown and green . . 1·25 65

107 Bank in Hand and Emblem

1969. 5th Anniv of African Development Bank. Multicoloured.
665 30f. Type **107** (postage) . . . 85 20
666 45f. Diesel locomotive in hand, and emblem . . . . 2·75 75
667 100f. Farmer and cattle in hand, and emblem (air) . . 1·25 55

108 Dunant and Red Cross Workers

1969. 50th Anniv of League of Red Cross Societies. Multicoloured.
668 15f. Type **108** (postage) . . . 35 10
669 20f. Pasteur and help for flood victims 40 10
670 30f. Fleming and flood control 75 20
671 45f. Rontgen and Red Cross post 95 30
672 60f. As 45f. (air) 90 45
673 90f. Type **108** . . . . 1·25 65

109 Weeding Corn

1969. Young Pioneers Agricultural Organization. Multicoloured.
675 1f. Type **109** (postage) . . . 10 10
676 2f. Glidji Agricultural Centre 10 10
677 3f. Founding meeting 10 10
678 4f. Glidji class 15 10
679 5f. Student "pyramid" . . . 15 10
680 7f. Students threshing . . . 15 10
681 8f. Gardening instruction . . 15 10
682 10f. Co-op village 15 10
683 15f. Students gardening . . . 30 15
684 20f. Cattle-breeding 35 15
685 25f. Poultry-farming 45 15
686 30f. Independence parade . . 45 20
687 40f. Boys on high-wire . . . 65 35
688 45f. Tractor and trailer . . . 80 35
689 50f. Co-op village 85 35
690 60f. Tractor-driving tuition 90 45
691 90f. Harvesting manioc (air) 1·10 45
692 100f. Gardening instruction 1·40 55
693 200f. Thinning-out corn . . . 2·25 1·10
694 250f. Drummers marching . . 4·25 1·50
695 500f. Young pioneers marching . . . . 9·50 3·00

111 Books and Map

1969. 12th Anniv of International African Library Development Association.
700 **111** 30f. multicoloured 45 30

1969. Christmas. No. 644/5 and 647/9 optd **JOYEUX NOEL**.
701 1f. Type **104** (postage) . . . 35 20
702 20f. Astronaut and module on Moon . . . . 1·10 45
703 45f. As 20f. . . . . 1·50 1·00
704 60f. Astronaut exploring lunar surface (air) . . . . 1·90 65
705 100f. Astronaut gathering Moon rock . . . . 3·00 1·00

113 George Washington

114 "Ploughing" (Klodt)

1969. "Leaders of World Peace". Multicoloured.
707 15f. Type **113** (postage) . . . 30 10
708 20f. Albert Luthule 35 10
709 30f. Mahatma Gandhi . . . 55 15
710 45f. Simon Boliver 90 20
711 60f. Friedrich Ebert (air) . . 90 35
712 90f. As 30f. . . . . 1·25 50

1970. 50th Anniv of I.L.O. Paintings. Mult.
713 5f. Type **114** (postage) . . . 10 10
714 10f. "Gardening" (Pissarro) 20 10
715 20f. "Harvesting Fruit" (Rivera) 35 10
716 30f. "Seeds of Spring" (Van Gogh) 80 35
717 45f. "Workers of the Fields" (Rivera) 80 35
718 60f. As 30f. (air) . . . . . . 1·00 35
719 90f. As 45f. . . . . 1·50 50

115 Model Coiffures

1970. Togolese Hair-styles. Multicoloured.
721 5f. Type **115** (postage) . . . 15 10
722 10f. As T **115**, but different styles 35 10
723 20f. Fefe style 50 15
724 30f. Danmlongbedji style . . 1·25 20
725 45f. Blom style (air) 90 30
726 90f. Aklui and Danmlongbedji styles . . . 1·60 65
Nos. 723/5 are vert.

116 Togo Stamp and Independence Monument, Lome

1970. 10th Anniv of Independence. Multicoloured.
727 20f. Type **116** (postage) . . . 45 15
728 30f. Pres. Eyademe and Palace 65 20
729 50f. Map, dove and monument (vert) . . . . . 1·10 35
730 60f. Togo stamp and monument (air) 80 40

117 New U.P.U. Headquarters Building

1970. New U.P.U. Headquarters Building.
731 **117** 30f. violet and orange (postage) . . . . 1·00 35
732 50f. red and blue (air) . . 80 35

118 Italy and Uruguay

1970. World Cup Football Championships, Mexico. Multicoloured.
733 5f. Type **118** (postage) . . . 10 10
734 10f. England and Brazil . . . 20 10
735 15f. Russia and Mexico . . . 35 10
736 20f. Germany and Morocco 45 10
737 30f. Rumania and Czechoslovakia 85 20
738 50f. Sweden and Israel (air) 55 30
739 60f. Bulgaria and Peru . . . 65 35
740 90f. Belgium and El Salvador 1·25 50

119 Lenin

1970. Birth Centenary of Lenin. Multicoloured.
742 30f. Type **119** (postage) . . . 1·00 45
743 50f. "Peasant messengers with Lenin" (Serov) (air) . . . 1·10 35

120 British Pavilion

1970. "Expo 70", Osaka, Japan. Multicoloured.
744 2f. Pennants, Sanyo Pavilion (57 × 36 mm) 15 10
745 20f. Type **120** 20 10
746 30f. French Pavilion 45 15
747 50f. Soviet Pavilion 85 30
748 60f. Japanese Pavilion . . . 1·10 45

121 Armstrong, Collins and Aldrin

1970. "Apollo" Moon Flights. Multicoloured.
750 1f. Type **121** (postage) . . . 10 10
751 2f. U.S. flag and moon-rock 10 10
752 20f. Astronaut and module on Moon 35 10
753 30f. Conrad, Gordon and Bean 65 20
754 50f. As 2f. . . . . 1·00 35
755 200f. Lovell, Haise and Swigert ("Apollo 13") (air) 2·50 1·40

1970. Safe Return of "Apollo 13". As Nos. 750/5, but additionally inscr "FELICITATIONS BON RETOUR APOLLO XIII".
757 **121** 1f. multicoloured (postage) 10 10
758 – 2f. multicoloured 10 10
759 – 20f. multicoloured 35 10
760 – 30f. multicoloured 65 20
761 – 50f. multicoloured . . . . 1·00 35
762 – 200f. multicoloured (air) 2·50 1·60

123 "Euchloron megaera"

1970. Butterflies and Moths. Multicoloured.
764 1f. Type **123** (postage) . . . 15 10
765 2f. "Cymothoe sangaris" . . . 30 10
766 30f. "Danaus chrysippus" . . 1·50 35
767 50f. "Morpho sp." . . . . . 2·75 65
768 60f. Type **123** (air) . . . . . 3·00 70
769 90f. "Pseudacraea boisiduvali" . . . . 4·25 95

124 Painting by Velasquez (I.L.O.)

1970. 25th Anniv of U.N.O. Multicoloured.
770 1f. Type **124** (postage) . . . 10 10
771 15f. Painting by Delacroix (F.A.O.) 10 10
772 20f. Painting by Holbein (UNESCO) 20 15
773 30f. Painting of U.N. H.Q., New York 60 15
774 50f. Painting by Renoir (UNICEF 90 35
775 60f. Painting by Van Gogh (U.P.U.) (air) . . . . . . 1·00 35
776 90f. Painting by Carpaccio (W.H.O./O.M.S.) . . . . . 1·50 50

125 "The Nativity" (Botticelli)

1970. Christmas. "Nativity" Paintings by Old Masters. Multicoloured.
778 15f. Type **125** (postage) . . . 15 10
779 20f. Veronese 15 10
780 30f. El Greco 55 15
781 50f. Fra Angelico . . . . . 1·00 30
782 60f. Botticelli (different) (air) 1·25 30
783 90f. Tiepolo . . . . 1·75 45

1971. De Gaulle Commemoration (1st issue). Nos. 708/9 and 711/12 optd **EN MEMOIRE Charles De Gaulle 1890-1970** or surch in addition.
785 30f. multicoloured (postage) 1·10 35
786 30f. on 90f. multicoloured . . 1·10 35
787 150f. on 20f. multicoloured 6·75 1·75
788 200f. on 60f. mult (air) . . . 5·25 2·50

127 De Gaulle and Churchill

1971. De Gaulle Commemoration (2nd issue).
789 **127** 20f. blue & black (postage) 55 15
790 – 30f. red and black 65 20
791 – 40f. green and black . . . 1·00 40
792 – 50f. brown and black . . 1·25 50
793 – 60f. violet and black (air) 2·25 55
794 – 90f. blue and black . . . 3·25 80

DESIGNS: 30f. De Gaulle with Eisenhower; 40f. With Pres. Kennedy; 50f. With Adenauer; 60f. With Pope Paul VI; 90f. General De Gaulle.

128 Shepard and Moon Exploration

1971. Moon Mission of "Apollo 14". Mult.
796 1f. Type **128** (postage) . . . 10 10
797 10f. Mitchell and rock-gathering 15 10
798 30f. Roosa and module approaching Moon 50 15
799 40f. Launch from Moon . . 90 30
800 50f. "Apollo 14" emblem (air) 60 20
801 100f. As 40f. . . . . 1·25 40
802 200f. As 50f. . . . . 2·10 80

129 "The Resurrection" (after Raphael)

131 Sud Aviation Caravelle over Control Tower

130 Cocoa Tree and Pods

1971. Easter. Paintings of "The Resurrection" by various artists. Multicoloured.
804 1f. Type **129** (postage) . . . 15 10
805 30f. Master of Trebon . . . 55 15
806 40f. Type **129** 95 30
807 50f. M. Grunewald (air) . . . 80 30
808 60f. As 30f. . . . . 1·00 40
809 90f. El Greco . . . . 1·50 55

1971. International Cocoa Day. Multicoloured.
811 30f. Type **130** (postage) . . . 55 15
812 40f. Sorting beans 85 20
813 50f. Drying beans . . . . . 1·10 35
814 60f. Agricultural Ministry, Lome (air) 60 30
815 90f. Type **130** . . . . 1·10 50
816 100f. As 40f. . . . . 1·25 60

1971. 10th Anniv of A.S.E.C.N.A. (Aerial Navigation Security Agency).
817 **131** 30f. multicoloured (postage) 90 35
818 100f. multicoloured (air) 1·50 65

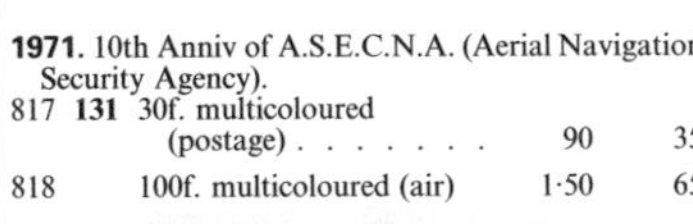

132 Napoleon

1971. 150th Death Anniv of Napoleon. Embossed on gold foil.
819 **132** 1000f. gold . . . . 22·00

133 Great Market, Lome

1971. Tourism. Multicoloured.
821 20f. Type **133** (postage) . . . 35 10
822 30f. Wooden sculpture and protea 55 15
823 40f. Aledjo Gorge and olive baboon 80 20
824 50f. Vale Castle and red-fronted gazelle (air) 65 20
825 60f. Lake Togo and alligator 90 30
826 100f. Furnace, Tokpli, and hippopotamus . . . . . . 1·25 40

134 Gbatchoume Image

1971. Togolese Religions. Multicoloured.
827 20f. Type **134** (postage) . . . 35 15
828 30f. High priest, Temple of Atta Sakuma 50 20
829 40f. "Holy Stone" ceremony 85 30
830 50f. Moslem worshippers, Lome Mosque (air) 55 20
831 60f. Protestants 70 30
832 90f. Catholic ceremony, Djogbegan Monastery . . 95 40

1971. Memorial Issue for "Soyuz 11" Astronauts. Nos. 799/802 optd **EN MEMOIRE DOBROVOLSKY - VOLKOV - PATSAYEV SOYUZ 11** or surch also.
834 40f. multicoloured (postage) 1·00 35
835 90f. on 50f. multicoloured (air) 90 35
836 100f. multicoloured . . . . . 1·10 40
837 200f. multicoloured . . . . . 2·00 65

136 Speed-skating

1971. Winter Games, Sapporo, Japan (1972). Mult.
839 1f. Type **136** (postage) . . . 10 10
840 10f. Slalom skiing 10 10
841 20f. Figure-skating 35 10
842 30f. Bob-sleighing 55 20
843 50f. Ice-hockey . . . . . . 1·10 35
844 200f. Ski-jumping (air) . . . 2·25 95

1971. Air. 10th Anniv of African and Malagasy Posts and Telecommunications Union. As T **141** of Senegal. Multicoloured.
846 100f. U.A.M.P.T. H.Q. and Adjogobo dancers . . . . 1·10 55

137 Togolese Child and Mask

1971. Air. "Children of the World". Embossed on gold foil.
847 **137** 1500f. gold . . . . 15·00

138 Wooden Crocodile

1971. 25th Anniv of UNICEF. Multicoloured.
848 20f. Type **138** (postage) . . . 20 10
849 30f. Toy "Bambi" and butterfly 45 15
850 50f. Toy monkey 80 30
851 50f. Wooden elephant on wheels . . . . 1·00 30
852 60f. Toy turtle (air) 55 20
853 90f. Toy parrot 85 35

139 "Virgin and Child" (Botticelli)

1971. Christmas. "Virgin and Child" Paintings by Old Masters. Multicoloured.
855 10f. Type **139** (postage) . . . 10 10
856 30f. (Maitre de la Vie de Marie) 65 20
857 40f. (Durer) . . . . 1·10 35
858 50f. (Veronese) . . . . 1·40 45
859 60f. (Giorgione) (air) . . . . 1·00 35
860 100f. (Raphael) . . . . . . 1·75 55

140 St. Mark's Basilica, Venice

1972. UNESCO "Save Venice" Campaign. Mult.
862 30f. Type **140** (postage) . . . 90 30
863 40f. Rialto Bridge . . . . . 1·25 40
864 100f. Doge's Palace (air) . . 1·40 65

141 "The Crucifixion" (unknown artist)

1972. Easter. Religious Paintings. Multicoloured.
866 25f. Type **141** (postage) . . . 45 15
867 30f. "The Deposition" (Botticelli) 70 15
868 40f. Type **141** 90 30
869 50f. "The Resurrection" (Thomas de Coloswar) (air) 85 20
870 100f. "The Ascension" (Mantegna) . . . . 1·60 40

142 Heart Emblem and Blacksmith

145 Woman preparing Cassava

143 Hotel de la Paix, Lome

1972. World Heart Month. Multicoloured.
872 30f. Type **142** (postage) . . . 45 15
873 40f. Typist 55 20
874 60f. Javelin-thrower 85 35
875 100f. Type **142** (air) . . . . 1·25 45

1972. O.C.A.M. Summit Conference, Lome. Embossed on gold foil.
877 **143** 1000f. gold, red and green 10·00

1972. Pres. Nixon's Visit to China. Nos. 823/4 optd **VISITE DU PRESIDENT NIXON EN CHINE FEVRIER 1972** and additionally surch (No. 879).
878 300f. on 40f. mult (postage) 4·00 1·90
879 50f. multicoloured (air) . . . 1·00 35

1972. Cassava Industries. Multicoloured.
880 25f. Collecting cassava (horiz) (postage) 45 15
881 40f. Type **145** 65 20
882 60f. Cassava truck and factory (horiz) (air) 90 20
883 80f. Mother with Benin tapioca cake . . . . 1·25 45

146 Video-telephone

148 Basketball

1972. World Telecommunications Day. Mult.
884 40f. Type **146** (postage) 1·00 35
885 100f. "Intelsat 4" and map of Africa (air) 1·50 45

1972. Air. Pres. Nixon's Visit to Russia. No. 743 surch **VISITE DU PRESIDENT NIXON EN RUSSIE MAI 1972** and value.
886 300f. on 50f. multicoloured 5·00 2·75

1972. Olympic Games, Munich. Multicoloured.
887 30f. Type **148** (postage) 50 15
888 40f. Running 65 20
889 50f. Throwing the discus 90 30
890 90f. Gymnastics (air) 65 35
891 200f. Type **148** 1·75 80

149 Pin-tailed Whydah

150 Paul Harris (founder)

1973. Exotic Birds. Multicoloured.
893 25f. Type **149** (postage) 75 25
894 30f. Broad-tailed paradise whydah 1·00 35
895 40f. Yellow-mantled whydah 1·40 55
896 60f. Long-tailed whydah 2·75 90
897 90f. Rose-ringed parakeet (air) 3·75 1·25

1972. Rotary International. Multicoloured.
899 40f. Type **150** (postage) 40 20
900 50f. Rotary and Togo flags 50 30
901 60f. Rotary emblem, map and laurel (air) 65 20
902 90f. As 50f. 90 35
903 100f. Type **150** 1·25 45

151 "Mona Lisa" (L. da Vinci)

1972. Famous Paintings. Multicoloured.
905 25f. Type **151** (postage) 1·10 30
906 40f. "Virgin and Child" (Bellini) 1·25 30
907 60f. "Mystical Marriage of St. Catherine" (Master P.N.'s assistant) (air) 1·00 30
908 80f. "Self-portrait" (L. da Vinci) 1·25 35
909 100f. "St. Marie and Angels" (Botticelli) 1·60 50

1972. 10th Anniv of West African Monetary Union. As T **156** of Senegal.
911 40f. brown, grey and red 55 40

152 Party H.Q. of R.P.T. and Presidents Pompidou and Eyadama

1972. Visit of President Pompidou to Togo. Multicoloured.
912 40f. Type **152** (postage) 1·10 45
913 100f. Party H.Q. rear view and portraits as T **152** (air) 1·75 55

153 Goethe

1972. Air. 140th Death Anniv of Goethe (poet).
914 **153** 100f. multicoloured 1·50 65

154 "The Annunciation" (unknown artist)

1972. Christmas. Religious Paintings. Mult.
915 25f. Type **154** (postage) 35 20
916 30f. "The Nativity" (Master Theodor of Prague) 55 20
917 40f. Type **154** 80 20
918 60f. As 30f. (air) 80 20
919 80f. "The Adoration of the Magi" (unknown artist) 1·00 30
920 100f. "The Flight into Egypt" (Giotto) 1·25 45

155 R. Follereau and Allegory

1973. "World Day of the Leper". (a) Postage. 20th Anniv of Follereau Foundation.
922 **155** 40f. violet and green 1·60 55

(b) Air. Cent of Hansen's Bacillus Discovery.
923 – 100f. blue and red 2·50 85
DESIGN: 100f. Dr. Hansen, microscope and bacillus slide.

156 W.H.O. Emblem

157 "The Crucifixion"

1973. 25th Anniv of W.H.O.
924 **156** 30f. multicoloured 45 15
925 40f. multicoloured 55 20

1973. Easter. Multicoloured.
926 25f. Type **157** (postage) 35 15
927 30f. "The Deposition" 55 20
928 40f. "The Resurrection" 80 20
929 90f. "Christ in Majesty" (air) 1·25 45

158 Astronauts Cernan, Evans and Schmitt

1973. "Apollo 17" Moon Flight. Multicoloured.
931 30f. Type **158** (postage) 80 15
932 40f. Moon rover 1·00 30
933 100f. Discovery of "orange" rock (air) 1·10 40
934 200f. Pres. Kennedy and lift-off 2·25 85

159 Erecting Tent

160 Heliocentric System

1973. International Scout Congress. Nairobi/Addis Ababa. Multicoloured.
936 10f. Type **159** (postage) 20 10
937 20f. Cooking meal (horiz) 45 10
938 30f. Rope-climbing 75 15
939 40f. Type **159** 1·00 20
940 100f. Canoeing (horiz) (air) 1·50 40
941 200f. As 20f. 2·75 85

1973. 500th Birth Anniv of Copernicus. Mult.
943 10f. Type **160** (postage) 15 10
944 20f. Copernicus 30 10
945 30f. "Astronomy" and "Astronautics" 65 15
946 40f. Astrolabe 85 20
947 90f. Type **160** (air) 1·25 35
948 100f. As 20f. 1·40 45

161 Ambulance Team

1973. Togolese Red Cross. Multicoloured.
950 40f. Type **161** (postage) 90 35
951 100f. Dove of peace, sun and map (air) 1·90 65

1973. "Drought Relief". African Solidarity. No. 766 surch **SECHERESSE SOLIDARITE AFRICAINE 100F.**
952 100f. on 30f. multicoloured 1·25 85

163 Classroom

1973. Literacy Campaign. Multicoloured.
953 30f. Type **163** (postage) 35 15
954 40f. African reading book (vert) 85 30
955 90f. Classroom (different) (air) 85 45

1973. African and Malagasy Posts and Telecommunications Union. As T **170** of Senegal.
956 100f. red, yellow and purple 1·10 65

164 Interpol Emblem and H.Q. Paris

165 W.M.O. Emblem in Weather-vane

1973. 50th Anniv of Interpol.
957 **164** 30f. green, brown & yellow 45 15
958 40f. blue, mauve and green 65 20

1973. Centenary of W.M.O.
959 **165** 40f. grn, brn & yell (post) 90 35
960 200f. brown, vio & bl (air) 1·90 85

166 Togo Stamp and Steam and Diesel Locomotives

1973. 75th Anniv of Togolese Postal Services. Mult.
961 25f. Type **166** (postage) 65 20
962 30f. Togo stamp and mail coaches 60 20
963 90f. Togo stamps and mail boats 1·75 45
964 100f. Togo stamps and mail-planes (air) 2·40 80

167 Kennedy and A. Schaerf

168 Flame Emblem and "People"

1973. 10th Death Anniv of Pres. Kennedy.
966 **167** 20f. violet and black on blue (postage) 35 10
967 – 30f. brown and black on brown 50 20
968 – 40f. green & black on green 85 30
969 – 90f. purple and black on mauve (air) 1·60 45
970 – 100f. blue & black on blue 1·60 45
971 – 200f. brown & blk on brown 2·75 80
DESIGNS: 30f. Kennedy and Harold Macmillan; 40f. Kennedy and Konrad Adenauer; 90f. Kennedy and Charles de Gaulle; 100f. Kennedy and Nikita Kruschev; 200f. Kennedy and "Apollo" spacecraft.

1973. Air. 25th Anniv of Declaration of Human Rights.
973 **168** 250f. multicoloured 2·75 1·40

169 "Virgin and Child" (anon)

173 "Girl Before Mirror" (Picasso)

171 Footballers

1973. Christmas. Multicoloured.
974 25f. Type **169** (postage) 50 15
975 30f. "Adoration of the Magi" (Vivarini) 60 20
976 90f. "Virgin and Child" (S. di Pietro) (air) 1·00 35
977 100f. "Adoration of the Magi" (anon) 1·40 40

1974. Lome District Rotary International Convention. Nos. 899, 901 and 903 optd **PREMIERE CONVENTION 210eme DISTRICT FEVRIER 1974 LOME.**
979 **150** 40f. mult (postage) 55 35
980 – 60f. multicoloured (air) 45 20
981 **150** 100f. multicoloured 90 35

1974. World Cup Football Championship, West Germany.
982 **171** 20f. mult (postage) 35 15
983 – 30f. multicoloured 45 15
984 – 40f. multicoloured 55 20
985 – 90f. multicoloured (air) 90 35
986 – 100f. multicoloured 1·00 40
987 – 200f. multicoloured 2·00 70
DESIGNS: Nos. 983/7, similar designs to Type **171**, showing footballers in action.

1974. 10th Anniv of World Food Programme. Nos. 880/1 optd **10e ANNIVERSAIRE DU P. A. M.** or surch also.
989 **145** 40f. multicoloured 55 35
990 – 100f. on 25f. 1·25 80

1974. Picasso Commemoration. Multicoloured.
991 20f. Type **173** (postage) 55 20
992 30f. "The Turkish Shawl" 80 35
993 40f. "Mandoline and Guitar" 1·10 35

994 90f. "The Muse" (air) . . . 1·00 35
995 100f. "Les Demoiselles d'Avignon" . . . 1·25 40
996 200f. "Sitting Nude" . . . 2·50 85

174 Kpeme Village
175 Togolese Postman

1974. Coastal Scenes. Multicoloured.
998 30f. Type **174** (postage) . . 45 20
999 40f. Tropicana tourist village 65 40
1000 90f. Fisherman on Lake Togo (air) . . . 1·00 35
1001 100f. Mouth of Aneche River . . . 1·25 40

1974. Centenary of U.P.U. Multicoloured.
1003 30f. Type **175** (postage) . . 40 20
1004 40f. Postman with cleft carrying-stick . . . 50 30
1005 50f. Type **175** (air) . . . 60 30
1006 100f. As 40f. . . . 1·25 45

176 Map of Member Countries

1974. 15th Anniv of Council of Accord.
1007 **176** 40f. multicoloured . . . 50 30

177 Hauling in Net
178 Earth Station and Probe

1974. Lagoon Fishing. Multicoloured.
1008 30f. Type **177** (postage) . . 45 20
1009 40f. Throwing net . . . 65 30
1010 90f. Fishes in net (air) . . . 1·00 30
1011 100f. Fishing with lines . . 1·25 35
1012 200f. Fishing with basket (vert) . . . 2·75 70

1974. U.S. "Jupiter" Space Mission. Mult.
1014 30f. Type **178** (postage) . . 35 15
1015 40f. Probe transmitting to Earth (horiz) . . . 45 20
1016 100f. Blast-off (air) . . . 95 40
1017 200f. Jupiter probe (horiz) 1·75 70

1974. "Internaba 1974" Stamp Exhibition, Basel. Nos. 884/5 optd **INTERNABA 1974 CENTENARIUM U P U** and emblem.
1019 **146** 40f. mult (postage) . . . 3·50 1·00
1020 – 100f. multicoloured (air) 4·25 1·40

180 "Tympanotomus radula"
181 Groom with Horses

1974. Sea Shells. Multicoloured.
1021 10f. Type **180** (postage) . . 25 20
1022 20f. Giant tun . . . 35 20
1023 30f. Trader cone . . . 55 20
1024 40f. Great ribbed cockle . . 85 20
1025 90f. Ponsonbyi's volute (air) 1·40 40
1026 100f. Iredale's bonnet . . . 1·90 40

1974. Horse-racing. Multicoloured.
1028 30f. Type **181** (postage) . . 45 20
1029 40f. Exercising horses . . . 65 30
1030 90f. Steeple-chaser taking fence (air) . . . 1·00 35
1031 100f. Horses racing . . . 1·50 45

1974. Air. West Germany's Victory in World Cup Football Championship. Nos. 890/1 optd **COUPE DU MONDE DE FOOTBALL MUNICH 1974 VAINQUERS REPUBLIQUE FEDERALE ALLEMAGNE.**
1033 – 90f. multicoloured . . . 90 35
1034 **148** 200f. multicoloured . . . 1·75 80

183 Leopard

1974. Wild Animals. Multicoloured.
1036 20f. Type **183** (postage) . . 50 15
1037 30f. Giraffes . . . 75 20
1038 40f. Two African elephants 1·00 35
1039 90f. Lion and lioness (air) 1·50 45
1040 100f. Black rhinoceros and calf . . . 2·00 45

184 Herd of Cows

1974. Pastoral Economy. Multicoloured.
1042 30f. Type **184** (postage) . . 45 20
1043 40f. Milking . . . 65 30
1044 90f. Cattle at water-hole (air) . . . 85 45
1045 100f. Village cattle-pen . . . 1·10 55

185 Churchill and Frigate H.M.S. "Loch Fada"

1974. Birth Centenary of Sir Winston Churchill. Multicoloured.
1047 30f. Type **185** (postage) . . 50 15
1048 40f. Churchill and Supermarine Spitfires . . 60 20
1049 100f. Type **185** (air) . . . 1·40 35
1050 200f. As 40f. . . . 2·25 80

1975. Opening of Hotel de la Paix, Lome. Optd **Inauguration de la l'hotel Paix 9-1-75.**
1051a **143** 1000f. gold, red and green . . . 9·50

186 "Strelitzia reginae"
189 "Jesus Mocked" (El Greco)

188 Radio Station, Kamina

1975. Flowers of Togo. Multicoloured.
1052 25f. Type **186** (postage) . . 35 15
1053 30f. "Strophanthus sarmentosus" . . . 45 15
1054 40f. "Chlamydocarya macrocarpa" (horiz) . . . 55 20
1055 60f. "Clerodendrum scandens" (horiz) . . . 90 35
1056 100f. "Clerodendrum thosonae" (horiz) (air) . . 1·40 45
1057 200f. "Gloriosa superba" (horiz) . . . 2·50 65

1975. 70th Anniv of Rotary International. Optd **70e ANNIVERSAIRE 23 FEVRIER 1975.**
1059 **150** 40f. mult (postage) . . . 30 25
1060 – 90f. multicoloured (No. 902) (air) . . . 85 35
1061 **150** 100f. multicoloured . . . 1·00 40

1975. Tourism. Multicoloured.
1062 25f. Type **188** . . . 20 10
1063 30f. Benedictine Monastery, Zogbegan . . . 35 20
1064 40f. Causeway, Atchinedji 45 30
1065 60f. Ayome Waterfalls . . . 80 40

1975. Easter. Multicoloured.
1066 25f. Type **189** (postage) . . 20 10
1067 30f. "The Crucifixion" (Master Janoslen) . . . 35 10
1068 40f. "The Descent from the Cross" (Bellini) . . . 55 20
1069 90f. "Pieta" (anon) . . . 95 40
1070 100f. "Christ rising from the Grave" (Master MS) (air) 1·10 35
1071 200f. "The Holy Trinity" (detail) (Durer) . . . 1·90 80

190 Stilt-walking

1975. 15th Anniv of Independence. Mult.
1073 25f. Type **190** (postage) . . 30 10
1074 30f. Dancers . . . 35 15
1075 50f. Independence parade (vert) (air) . . . 40 15
1076 60f. Dancer . . . 60 35

191 Hunting Bush Hare with Club

1975. Hunting. Multicoloured.
1078 30f. Type **191** (postage) . . 45 20
1079 40f. Hunting Eurasian beavers with bow . . . 55 35
1080 90f. Hunting red deer with snare (air) . . . 1·25 45
1081 100f. Hunting wild boar with gun . . . 1·40 55

192 Pounding Palm Nuts

1975. Palm-oil Production. Multicoloured.
1082 30f. Type **192** (postage) . . 35 15
1083 40f. Extracting palm-oil (vert) . . . 40 20
1084 85f. Selling palm-oil (vert) (air) . . . 80 45
1085 100f. Oil-processing plant, Aloknegbe . . . 90 55

193 "Apollo" and "Soyuz" in Docking Procedure

1975. "Apollo–Soyuz" Space Link. Mult.
1087 30f. Type **193** (postage) . . 45 15
1088 50f. "Soyuz" spacecraft (vert) (air) . . . 40 15
1089 60f. Slaton, Brand and Stafford ("Apollo" astronauts) . . . 55 20
1090 90f. Leonov and Kubasov ("Soyuz" cosmonauts) . . 70 30
1091 100f. U.S. and Soviet flags and "Apollo" and "Soyuz" linked . . . 1·10 50
1092 200f. Emblem and globe . . 2·25 65

194 "African Women"

1975. International Women's Year.
1094 **194** 30f. multicoloured . . . 40 15
1095 40f. multicoloured . . . 45 20

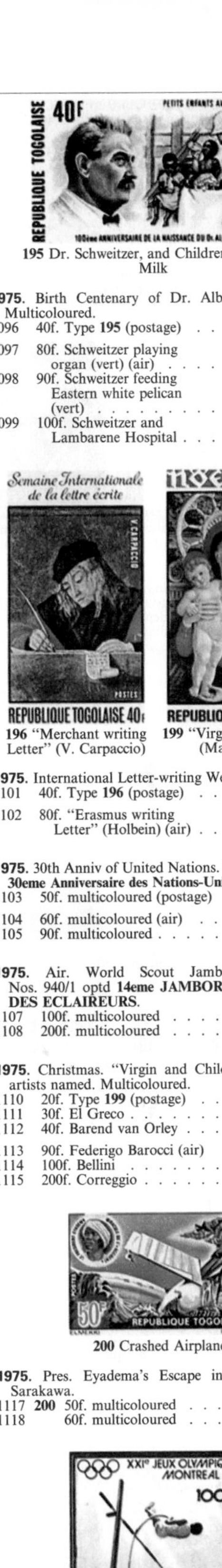

195 Dr. Schweitzer, and Children drinking Milk

1975. Birth Centenary of Dr. Albert Schweitzer. Multicoloured.
1096 40f. Type **195** (postage) . . 55 30
1097 80f. Schweitzer playing organ (vert) (air) . . . 90 30
1098 90f. Schweitzer feeding Eastern white pelican (vert) . . . 1·40 40
1099 100f. Schweitzer and Lambarene Hospital . . . 1·25 35

196 "Merchant writing Letter" (V. Carpaccio)
199 "Virgin and Child" (Mantegna)

1975. International Letter-writing Week. Mult.
1101 40f. Type **196** (postage) . . 55 30
1102 80f. "Erasmus writing Letter" (Holbein) (air) . . 90 35

1975. 30th Anniv of United Nations. Nos. 851/3 optd **30eme Anniversaire des Nations-Unies.**
1103 50f. multicoloured (postage) 55 30
1104 60f. multicoloured (air) . . 50 20
1105 90f. multicoloured . . . 60 30

1975. Air. World Scout Jamboree, Norway. Nos. 940/1 optd **14eme JAMBOREE MONDIAL DES ECLAIREURS.**
1107 100f. multicoloured . . . 95 45
1108 200f. multicoloured . . . 1·75 80

1975. Christmas. "Virgin and Child" paintings by artists named. Multicoloured.
1110 20f. Type **199** (postage) . . 30 20
1111 30f. El Greco . . . 40 20
1112 40f. Barend van Orley . . . 45 20
1113 90f. Federigo Barocci (air) 80 30
1114 100f. Bellini . . . 90 35
1115 200f. Correggio . . . 1·60 55

200 Crashed Airplane

1975. Pres. Eyadema's Escape in Air Crash at Sarakawa.
1117 **200** 50f. multicoloured . . . 7·25 5·00
1118 60f. multicoloured . . . 7·25 5·00

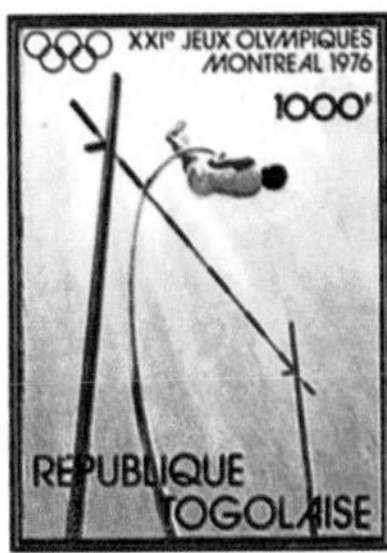

200a Pole Vault

1976. Olympic Games, Montreal. Multicoloured.
1118a 1000f. Type **200a** . . . 10·00
1118b 1000f. Diving . . . 10·00
1118c 1000f. Running . . . 10·00
1118d 1000f. Show-jumping . . . 10·00
1118e 1000f. Cycling . . . 10·00

201 "Frigates forcing the Hudson Passage"

1976. Bicentenary of American Revolution. Mult.

1119 35f. Type **201** (postage) . . 40 20

1120 50f. "George Washington" (G. Stuart) (vert) 55 30

1121 60f. "Surrender of Burgoyne" (Trumbull) (air) 65 20

1122 70f. "Surrender at Trenton" (Trumbull) (vert) 85 30

1123 100f. "Signing of Declaration of Independence" (Trumbull) 90 35

1124 200f. "Washington crossing the Delaware" (E. Leutze) 1·75 60

202 "Salerum" (cable ship) **203** Blind Man and Mosquito

1976. Telephone Centenary. Multicoloured.

1126 25f. Type **202** (postage) . . 30 15

1127 30f. Automatic telephone and tape-recording equipment 40 30

1128 70f. Edison and communications equipment (air) 55 30

1129 105f. Alexander Graham Bell, early and modern telephones 85 40

1976. World Health Day. Multicoloured.

1131 50f. Type **203** (postage) . . 65 30

1132 60f. Eye examination (air) 55 20

204 A.C.P. and C.E.E. Emblems **205** Exhibition Hall

1976. 1st Anniv of A.C.P./C.E.E. Treaty (between Togo and European Common Market). Mult.

1133 10f. Type **204** (postage) . . 15 10

1134 50f. Map of Africa, Europe and Asia 40 30

1135 60f. Type **204** (air) 45 20

1136 70f. As 50f. 55 30

1976. Anniversaries. Multicoloured.

1136a 5f. Type **205** (postage) . . 10 10

1136b 10f. Electricity pylon and flags 15 10

1137 50f. Type **205** 50 30

1138 60f. As 10f. (air) 50 30

The 5f. and 50f. commemorate the 10th anniv of the Marine Exhibition and the 10f. and 60f. the 1st anniv of the Ghana–Togo–Dahomey Electricity Link.

1976. Air. "Interphil '76" International Stamp Exhibition, Philadelphia. Nos. 1121/4 optd **INTERPHIL MAI 29 - JUIN 6**.

1139 60f. multicoloured 40 15

1140 70f. multicoloured 60 20

1141 100f. multicoloured 90 30

1142 200f. multicoloured . . . . 1·40 55

207 Running

1976. Olympic Games, Montreal. Multicoloured.

1144 25f. Type **207** (postage) . . 20 10

1145 30f. Canoeing 35 15

1146 50f. High-jumping 45 20

1147 70f. Sailing (air) 55 20

1148 105f. Motorcycling 85 35

1149 200f. Fencing . . . . 1·60 55

208 "Titan 3" and "Viking" Emblem

1976. "Viking" Space Mission. Multicoloured.

1151 30f. Type **208** (postage) . . 15 10

1152 50f. "Viking" en route between Earth and Mars 40 20

1153 60f. "Viking landing on Mars" (air) 55 20

1154 70f. Nodus Gordii, Mars . . 65 20

1155 100f. "Viking" over Mare Tyrrhenum 85 40

1156 200f. "Viking" landing on Mars (different) . . . . . 1·50 55

209 "Young Routy" **212** Quaid-i-Azam

211 "Adoration of the Shepherds" (Pontormo)

1976. 75th Death Anniv of Toulouse-Lautrec (painter). Multicoloured.

1158 10f. Type **209** (postage) . . 15 10

1159 20f. "Helene Vary" 50 15

1160 35f. "Louis Pascal" 75 15

1161 60f. "Carmen" (air) . . . . 1·00 20

1162 70f. "Maurice at the Somme" . . . . 1·00 30

1163 200f. "Messalina" . . . . . 2·50 60

1976. International Children's Day. Nos. 950/1 optd **Journee Internationale de l'Enfance**.

1165 **161** 40f. mult (postage) . . . 45 15

1166 – 100f. multicoloured (air) 80 45

1976. Christmas. Nativity scenes by artists named. Multicoloured.

1167 25f. Type **211** (postage) . . 35 15

1168 30f. Crivelli 45 15

1169 50f. Pontormo 80 20

1170 70f. Lotto (air) 65 20

1171 105f. Pontormo (different) 1·90 35

1172 200f. Lotto (different) . . . 1·60 55

1976. Birth Centenary of Mohammad Ali Jinnah, "Quaid-i-Azam".

1174 **212** 50f. multicoloured . . . 55 30

1977. Gold Medal Winners, Montreal Olympic Games. Nos. 1146/7 and 1149 optd **CHAMPIONS OLYMPIQUES** with events and countries.

1175 50f. multicoloured (postage) 60 20

1176 70f. multicoloured (air) . . 75 35

1177 200f. multicoloured . . . . 1·75 80

OPTD: 50f. **SAUT EN HAUTEUR POLOGNE**; 70f. **YACHTING - FLYING DUTCHMAN REPUBLIQUE FEDERALE ALLEMAGNE**; 200f. **ESCRIME-FLEURET PAR EQUIPES REPUBLIQUE FEDERALE ALLEMAGNE.**

214 Queen Elizabeth II

1977. Silver Jubilee of Queen Elizabeth II.

1179 **214** 1000f. multicoloured . . 7·75

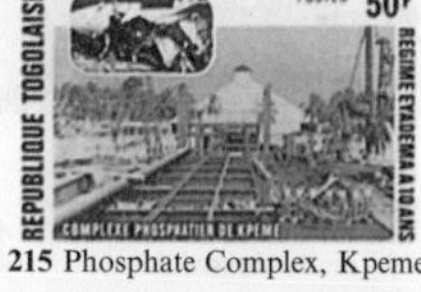

215 Phosphate Complex, Kpeme

1977. 10th Anniv of Eyadema Regime. Mult.

1181 50f. Type **215** (postage) . . 1·25 35

1182 60f. Parliament Building, Lome (air) 55 30

1183 100f. Crowd greeting Pres. Eyadema 80 40

216 Gongophone

1977. Musical Instruments. Multicoloured.

1185 5f. Type **216** (postage) . . . 15 10

1186 10f. Tamtam (vert) 20 10

1187 25f. Dondon 65 15

1188 60f. Atopani (air) 75 20

1189 80f. One-string fiddle (vert) 1·25 30

1190 105f. African flutes (vert) . . 1·75 35

217 Victor Hugo and Guernsey Scene

1977. 175th Birth Anniv of Victor Hugo (writer). Multicoloured.

1192 50f. Victor Hugo as a young man, and residence (postage) 55 15

1193 60f. Type **217** (air) 60 30

218 Beethoven and Birthplace, Bonn

1977. 150th Death Anniv of Ludwig van Beethoven. Multicoloured.

1195 30f. Type **218** (postage) . . 70 15

1196 50f. Beethoven's bust and Heiligenstadt residence . . 75 20

1197 100f. Young Beethoven and grand piano (air) . . . . 1·25 35

1198 200f. Beethoven on death-bed and Trinity Church, Vienna . . . . 2·25 65

219 Benz, 1894

1977. Early Motor Cars. Multicoloured.

1200 35f. Type **219** (postage) . . 65 20

1201 50f. De Dion Bouton, 1903 1·00 30

1202 60f. Cannstatt-Daimler, 1899 (air) 80 20

1203 70f. Sunbeam, 1904 . . . . 90 20

1204 100f. Renault, 1908 . . . . 1·10 35

1205 200f. Rolls-Royce, 1909 . . 1·90 65

220 Lindbergh, Ground Crew and "Spirit of St. Louis"

1977. 50th Anniv of Lindbergh's Transatlantic Flight. Multicoloured.

1207 25f. Type **220** (postage) . . 35 15

1208 50f. Lindbergh before take-off 65 20

1209 60f. Lindbergh with son (air) 50 15

1210 85f. Lindbergh's home, Kent (England) 80 20

1211 90f. "Spirit of St. Louis" over Atlantic 80 30

1212 100f. Concorde over New York City . . . . 1·25 50

1977. 10th Anniv of International French Language Council. Nos. 1192/3 optd **10eme ANNIVERSAIRE DU CONSEIL INTERNATIONAL DE LA LANGUE FRANCAISE.**

1214 **217** 50f. mult (postage) . . . 60 40

1215 60f. multicoloured (air) 55 35

222 Nile Crocodile

1977. Endangered Wildlife. Multicoloured.

1216 5f. African crocodile (postage) 15 15

1217 15f. Type **222** 50 20

1218 60f. Western black-and-white colobus (air) . . . 90 15

1219 90f. Chimpanzee (vert) . . . 1·00 20

1220 100f. Leopard . . . . . . 1·25 30

1221 200f. African manatee . . . 2·25 55

223 Agricultural School, Tove

1977. Agricultural Development. Multicoloured.

1223 50f. Type **223** (postage) . . 50 20

1224 60f. Corn silo (air) 55 15

1225 100f. Hoeing and planting 70 30

1226 200f. Tractor . . . . 1·50 55

224 "Landscape at Sunset" (Rubens)

1977. 400th Birth Anniv of Rubens. Multicoloured.

1228 15f. Type **224** (postage) . . 35 10

1229 35f. "Exchange of the Princesses at Hendaye" 80 15

1230 60f. "Four Negro Heads" (air) 85 15

1231 100f. "Anne of Austria" . . 1·10 40

225 Shuttle after Landing

1977. Space Shuttle. Multicoloured.

1233 20f. Type **225** (postage) . . 20 10

1234 30f. Launching 35 15

1235 50f. Ejecting propellant tanks 55 15

1236 90f. Retrieving a satellite (air) 70 20

1237 100f. Ejecting repaired satellite 85 30

1238 200f. Shuttle landing . . . . 1·50 60

226 Lafayette at 19 (after Le Mire) **227** Lenin and Cruiser "Aurora"

1977. Bicent of Lafayette's Arrival in America.

1240 **226** 25f. brown, yellow and purple (postage) . . . 30 10

1241 – 50f. red, violet and pink 55 15

1242 – 60f. turquoise, green and deep green (air) . . . 50 15

1243 – 105f. blue, light blue and purple 90 35

DESIGNS—HORIZ: 50f. Lafayette at Montpelier; 60f. Lafayette's arrival in New York; 105f. Lafayette with Washington at Valley Forge.

1977. 60th Anniv of Russian Revolution.

1245 **227** 50f. multicoloured . . . 80 30

228 "Madonna and Child" (Lotto) **229** Edward Jenner

1977. Christmas. "Madonna and Child" by artists named. Multicoloured.
1246 20f. Type **228** (postage) . . 20 15
1247 30f. Crivelli 35 15
1248 50f. C. Tura 55 15
1249 90f. Crivelli (different) (air) 65 30
1250 100f. Bellini 90 35
1251 200f. Crivelli (different) . . 1·50 55

1978. World Eradication of Smallpox.
1253 **229** 5f. ochre, black and lilac (postage) 10 10
1254 – 20f. multicoloured . . . 20 10
1255 **229** 50f. ochre, black and green (air) 35 15
1256 – 60f. multicoloured . . . 40 15
DESIGN—HORIZ: 20, 60f. Patients queuing for vaccination.

230 Wright Brothers

1978. 75th Anniv of 1st Flight by Wright Brothers. Multicoloured.
1258 35f. Type **230** (postage) . . 45 20
1259 50f. Wilbur Wright flying Glider No. III 85 35
1260 60f. Orville Wright Flight of 7 min 31 sec (air) . . . . 1·00 40
1261 70f. Wreckage of Wright Type A . . . . 1·10 40
1262 200f. Wright Brothers' cycle workshop, Dearborn, Michigan . . . . . . 1·40 55
1263 300f. Wright Flyer I (1st motorized flight) . . . . 2·00 85

231 "Apollo 8" (10th anniv of first mission) **232** St. John

1978. Anniversaries and Events. Multicoloured.
1265 1000f. Type **231** . . . . . 8·25
1266 1000f. High-jumping (Olympic Games, 1980) 8·25
1267 1000f. Westminster Abbey (25th anniv of Queen Elizabeth II's Coronation) 8·25
1268 1000f. "Duke of Wellington" (150th death anniv of Goya) . . . . . 8·25
1269 1000f. Footballers and Cup (World Cup Football Championship) . . . . . 8·25

1978. The Evangelists. Multicoloured.
1271 5f. Type **232** 10 10
1272 10f. St. Luke 10 10
1273 25f. St. Mark 20 10
1274 30f. St. Mathew 30 10

233 Fishing Harbour

1978. Autonomous Port of Lome. Multicoloured.
1276 25f. Type **233** (postage) . . 45 15
1277 60f. Industrial port (air) . . 80 25
1278 100f. Merchant port . . . . 1·25 40
1279 200f. General view . . . . 1·25 55

234 "Venera 1" Probe **235** Goalkeeper catching Ball

1978. Space Mission—Venus. Multicoloured.
1281 20f. Type **234** (postage) . . 15 10
1282 30f. "Pioneer" (horiz) . . . 20 15
1283 50f. Soviet fuel base and antenna 40 15
1284 90f. "Venera" blast jets (horiz) (air) 40 20
1285 100f. "Venera" antennae . . 55 30
1286 200f. "Pioneer" in orbit . . 1·00 55

1978. World Cup Football Championship, Argentina. Multicoloured.
1288 30f. Type **235** (postage) . . 30 10
1289 50f. Two players with ball 40 15
1290 60f. Heading the ball (air) 60 15
1291 80f. High kick 70 20
1292 200f. Chest stop . . . . . 1·50 55
1293 300f. Player with ball . . . 2·25 85

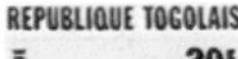

236 Thomas Edison (inventor) **237** "Celerifere" 1818

1978. Centenary of Invention of the Phonograph. Multicoloured.
1295 30f. Type **236** (postage) . . 20 10
1296 50f. Couple dancing to H.M.V. "Victor", phonograph, 1905 . . . . 45 15
1297 60f. Edison's original phonograph (horiz) (air) 40 15
1298 80f. Berliner's first phonograph, 1888 . . . . . . 50 20
1299 200f. Berliner's improved phonograph, 1894 (horiz) 1·25 55
1300 300f. "His Master's Voice" phonograph, c. 1900 (horiz) . . . . 2·00 85

1978. Early Bicycles. Multicoloured.
1302 25f. Type **237** (postage) . . 35 15
1303 50f. First bicycle side-car (vert) 65 20
1304 60f. Bantam bicycle (vert) (air) 55 15
1305 85f. Military folding bicycle 65 20
1306 90f. "La Draisienne" (vert) 90 35
1307 100f. Penny-farthing (vert) 95 40

238 Dunant's Birthplace, Geneva **240** Eiffel Tower

239 "Threshing" (Raoul Dufy)

1978. 150th Birth Anniv of Henri Dunant (founder of Red Cross).
1309 **238** 5f. blue and red (postage) 10 10
1310 – 10f. brown and red . . . 15 10
1311 – 25f. green and red . . . 30 10
1312 – 60f. purple and red (air) 55 20
DESIGNS: 10f. Dunant at 35; 25f. Tending battle casualties, 1864; 60f. Red Cross pavilions, Paris Exhibition, 1867.

1978. Air. "Philexafrique" Stamp Exhibition, Libreville (Gabon), and Int Stamp Fair, Essen, West Germany. As T **237a** of Senegal. Mult.
1314 100f. Jay and Thurn and Taxis ½sgr. stamp of 1854 2·75 2·25
1315 100f. Warthog and Togo 50f. stamp, 1964 . . . . 2·75 2·25

1978. Artists' Anniversaries. Multicoloured.
1316 25f. Type **239** (25th death anniv) (postage) 50 15
1317 50f. "Horsemen on the Seashore" (Gauguin, 75th death anniv) . . . . . . 1·00 15
1318 60f. "Langlois Bridge" (Van Gogh, 125th birth anniv) (air) 60 15
1319 70f. "Sabbath of the Witches" (Goya, 150th death anniv) 75 20
1320 90f. "Christ Among the Doctors" (Durer, 450th death anniv) 85 20
1321 200f. "View of Arco" (Durer) . . . . 1·75 55

1978. Centenary of Paris U.P.U. Congress. Mult.
1323 50f. Type **240** (postage) . . 80 20
1324 60f. Full-rigged ship "Slieve Roe" (air) 85 25
1325 105f. Congress medallion . . 70 30
1326 200f. Steam locomotive, 1870 . . . . 1·60 55

241 "Madonna and Child" (Antonello) **242** H.M.S. "Endeavour" and Route round New Zealand

1978. Christmas. Paintings of the Virgin and Child by artists shown below. Multicoloured.
1328 20f. Type **241** (postage) . . 20 15
1329 30f. Crivelli 35 15
1330 50f. Tura 55 15
1331 90f. Crivelli (different) (air) 65 30
1332 100f. Tura (different) . . . 90 30
1333 200f. Crivelli (different) . . 1·50 55

1979. Death Bicentenary of Captain James Cook. Multicoloured.
1335 25f. Type **242** (postage) . . 80 25
1336 50f. Careening H.M.S. "Endeavour" (horiz) . . . 1·00 35
1337 60f. "Freelove" at Whitby (horiz) (air) . . . . . . 1·25 35
1338 70f. Antarctic voyage of H.M.S. "Resolution" (horiz) . . . . 1·75 60
1339 90f. Capt. Cook . . . . . 2·00 75
1340 200f. Sail plan of H.M.S. "Endeavour" . . . . . . 2·75 1·75

243 Christ entering Jerusalem

1979. Easter. Multicoloured.
1342 30f. Type **243** (postage) . . 20 10
1343 40f. The Last Supper (horiz) 30 15
1344 50f. Descent from the Cross (horiz) 40 15
1345 60f. Resurrection (air) . . . 45 15
1346 100f. Ascension 65 30
1347 200f. Jesus appearing to Mary Magdalene . . . . 1·25 55

244 Statuette of Drummer

1979. Air. "Philexafrique 2" Stamp Exhibition, Libreville. Multicoloured.
1349 60f. Type **244** . . . . . . 1·10 55
1350 100f. Hands with letter . . . 1·60 1·10

245 Einstein Observatory, Potsdam

1979. Birth Centenary of Albert Einstein (physicist).
1351 **245** 35f. red, yellow and black (postage) . . . 20 10
1352 – 50f. green, mauve & black 35 10
1353 – 60f. multicoloured (air) 40 10
1354 – 85f. lilac, brown and black 60 15
1355 – 100f. multicoloured . . . 65 20
1356 – 200f. green, brown & black . . . . 1·40 40
DESIGNS—HORIZ: 50f. Einstein and J. R. Macdonald in Berlin, 1931; 60f. Sight and actuality diagram. VERT: 85f. Einstein playing violin; 100f. Atomic symbol and relativity formula; 200f. Albert Einstein.

246 Children with Flag **247** Planting Sapling

1979. International Year of the Child. Mult.
1358 5f. Type **246** 10 10
1359 10f. Mother with children 10 10
1360 15f. Children's Village symbol on map of Africa (horiz) 15 10
1361 20f. Woman taking children to Children's Village (horiz) 15 10
1362 25f. Children sitting round Fan palm 30 10
1363 30f. Map of Togo showing Children's Villages . . . 35 10

1979. Tree Day.
1365 **247** 50f. green and violet (postage) 50 15
1366 – 60f. brown & green (air) 55 20
DESIGN: 60f. Watering sapling.

248 Sir Rowland Hill **249** Stephenson's "Rocket", 1829

1979. Death Centenary of Sir Rowland Hill. Multicoloured.
1367 20f. Type **248** (postage) . . 15 10
1368 30f. French mail sorting office in the reign of Louis XV (horiz) 20 10
1369 50f. Parisian postbox, 1850 40 15
1370 90f. Bellman collecting letters, 1820 (air) 60 20
1371 100f. "Centre-cycles" used for mail delivery, 1880 (horiz) 65 20
1372 200f. French Post Office railway carriage, 1848 (horiz) . . . . 1·25 40

1979. Railway Locomotives. Multicoloured.
1374 35f. Type **249** (postage) . . 35 10
1375 50f. William Norris's "Austria", 1843 (horiz) 45 15
1376 60f. William Hudson's "General", 1855 (horiz) (air) 55 15
1377 85f. Stephenson locomotive, 1843 (horiz) 75 35
1378 100f. John Jarvis's "De Witt Clinton", 1831 (horiz) . . 85 35
1379 200f. David Joy's "Jenny Lind", 1847 (horiz) . . . 1·75 55

250 Skiing

251 Native praying

1979. Olympic Games, Lake Placid and Moscow. Multicoloured.

1381 20f. Type **250** (postage) . . 15 10

1382 30f. Olympic dinghies . . . 20 15

1383 50f. Throwing the discus . . 40 10

1384 90f. Ski-jumping (air) . . . 65 20

1385 100f. Canoeing 70 20

1386 200f. Gymnastics (rings exercise) . . . . 1·40 40

1979. Togo Religions.

1388 **251** 30f. brown, green and yellow (postage) . . . 20 10

1389 – 50f. blue, brown and red 35 10

1390 – 60f. purple, blue and buff (air) 45 15

1391 – 70f. lilac, orange & green 50 20

DESIGNS—HORIZ: 50f. Catholic priests; 60f. Muslims at prayer; 70f. Protestant preachers.

252 Astronaut on Moon

253 Dish Aerial

1979. 10th Anniv of First Moon Landing. Mult.

1393 35f. Type **252** (postage) . . 30 10

1394 50f. Capsule orbiting Moon 40 10

1395 60f. Armstrong descending to Moon 45 10

1396 70f. Astronaut and flag (air) 50 15

1397 200f. Astronaut performing experiment . . . . . . 1·25 35

1398 300f. Module leaving Moon 2·00 50

1979. 3rd World Telecommunications Exposition, Geneva.

1400 – 50f. light brown, brown and green (postage) . . 35 10

1401 **253** 60f. green, blue and deep blue (air) 50 20

DESIGN—HORIZ: 50f. Television screen.

254 Pres. Eyadema

1979. Air. 10th Anniv of R.P.T. Multicoloured.

1402 1000f. Pres. Eyadema and Party badge . . . . . . 6·75

1403 1000f. Type **254** . . . . . 6·75

255 Holy Family

256 Rotary Emblem

1979. Christmas. Multicoloured.

1404 20f. Type **255** (postage) . . 15 10

1405 30f. Madonna and Child and angels playing musical instruments . . . 20 10

1406 50f. Adoration of the shepherds 40 10

1407 90f. Adoration of the Magi (air) 55 20

1408 100f. Mother presenting Child 70 20

1409 200f. The Flight into Egypt 1·50 40

1980. 75th Anniv of Rotary International. Mult.

1411 25f. Type **256** (postage) . . 15 10

1412 30f. Anniversary emblem . . 30 10

1413 40f. Paul Harris (founder) 35 10

1414 90f. Figure exercising and sun (health) (air) 65 20

1415 100f. Fish and grain (food) 70 20

1416 200f. Family group (humanity) . . . . 1·40 40

257 Shooting (Biathlon)

1980. Winter Olympic Games, Lake Placid. Mult.

1418 50f. Type **257** (postage) . . 50 10

1419 60f. Downhill skiing 40 10

1420 100f. Speed skating (air) . . 70 20

1421 200f. Cross-country skiing 1·40 40

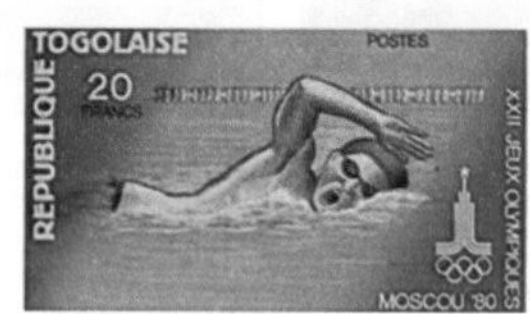

258 Swimming

1980. Olympic Games, Moscow. Multicoloured.

1423 20f. Type **258** (postage) . . 15 10

1424 30f. Gymnastics 20 10

1425 50f. Running 40 10

1426 100f. Fencing (air) 65 20

1427 200f. Pole vaulting . . . . 1·25 45

1428 300f. Hurdles . . . . 2·00 55

259 Truck going to Market

1980. Market Scenes. Multicoloured.

1430 1f. Grinding savo (postage) 10 10

1431 2f. Women preparing meat 10 10

1432 3f. Type **259** 10 10

1433 4f. Unloading produce . . . 10 10

1434 5f. Sugar-cane seller 10 10

1435 6f. Barber doing child's hair 10 10

1436 7f. Vegetable seller 10 10

1437 7f. Mangoes (vert) 10 10

1438 9f. Grain seller 10 10

1439 10f. Fish seller 10 10

1440 15f. Clay pot seller 10 10

1441 20f. Straw baskets 15 10

1442 25f. Lemon and onion seller (vert) 15 10

1443 30f. Straw baskets (different) 20 10

1444 40f. Shore market 30 15

1445 45f. Selling cooked food . . 35 15

1446 50f. Women carrying produce (vert) 35 15

1447 60f. Selling oil 45 15

1448 90f. Linen seller (air) . . . 55 15

1449 100f. Bananas 65 20

1450 200f. Pottery . . . . 1·25 45

1451 250f. Setting-up stalls . . . 1·60 55

1452 500f. Vegetable seller (different) . . . . 3·00 1·10

1453 1000f. Drink seller . . . . 6·00 2·25

See also Nos. D1454/7.

260 Concorde and Map of Africa

1980. 20th Anniv of African Air Safety Organization.

1458 **260** 50f. mult (postage) . . . 55 20

1459 60f. multicoloured (air) 55 25

261 "Christ with Angels" (Mantegna)

263 Radio Waves

1980. Easter. Multicoloured.

1460 30f. Type **261** (postage) . . 30 15

1461 40f. "Christ with Disciples" (Crivelli) 40 15

1462 50f. "Christ borne by His Followers" (Pontormo) 45 15

1463 60f. "The Deposition" (Lotto) (air) 50 10

1464 100f. "The Crucifixion" (El Greco) 70 20

1465 200f. "Christ with Angels" (Crivelli) . . . . 1·40 45

1980. "London 1980" International Stamp Exhibition. No. 1267 optd **Londres 1980**.

1467 1000f. Westminster Abbey 7·25

1980. World Telecommunciations Day.

1469 – 50f. violet and green (postage) 45 10

1470 **263** 60f. pink, brown and blue (air) 50 15

DESIGN—HORIZ: 50f. Satellite.

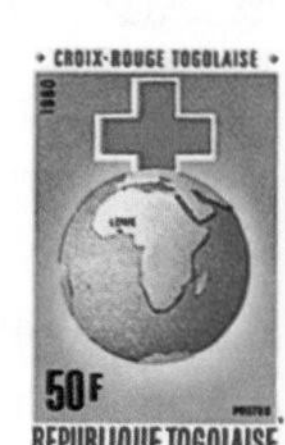

264 Red Cross and Globe

265 Jules Verne

1980. Togo Red Cross. Multicoloured.

1471 50f. Type **264** (postage) . . 55 10

1472 60f. Nurses and patient (air) 45 15

1980. 75th Death Anniv of Jules Verne (writer). Multicoloured.

1473 30f. Type **265** (postage) . . 30 10

1474 50f. "20,000 Leagues under the Sea" 55 10

1475 60f. "From the Earth to the Moon" (air) 40 15

1476 80f. "Around the World in Eighty Days" 55 20

1477 100f. "From the Earth to the Moon" (different) . . 3·50 1·25

1478 200f. "20,000 Leagues under the Sea" (different) . . . 1·75 60

266 "Baroness James de Rothschild"

1980. Birth Bicentenary of Jean Ingres (painter). Multicoloured.

1480 25f. Type **266** (postage) . . 35 10

1481 30f. "Napoleon I on the Imperial Throne" 55 10

1482 40f. "Don Pedro of Toledo putting down the Sword of Henry IV" 50 10

1483 90f. "Jupiter and Thetis" (air) 65 20

1484 100f. "The Countess of Hassonville" 85 20

1485 200f. "Tu Marcellus Eris" . 1·50 35

267 Minnie holding Mirror for Leopard

1980. Walt Disney Characters and Wildlife.

1487 1f. Type **267** 10 10

1488 2f. Goofy cleaning hippo's teeth 10 10

1489 3f. Donald clinging to crocodile 10 10

1490 4f. Donald hanging over cliff edge from rhino's horn 10 10

1491 5f. Goofy riding a water buffalo 10 10

1492 10f. Monkey photographing Mickey 10 10

1493 100f. Doctor Mickey examining giraffe . . . . 1·00 20

1494 300f. Elephant showering Goofy . . . . 2·00 40

1980. 50th Anniv of Pluto. As T **267**.

1496 200f. Pluto in party mood 1·60 40

268 Wreath

1980. Famous Men of the Decade.

1498 **268** 25f. orange and green (postage) 15 10

1499 – 40f. deep green and green 65 20

1500 – 90f. dp blue & blue (air) 60 20

1501 – 100f. lilac and pink . . . 1·10 20

DESIGNS: 40f. Mao Tse Tung; 90f. Pres. Allende; 100f. Pope Paul VI; 200f. Pres. Kenyatta.

269 Tourist Hotel Emblem

270 Human Rights Emblem and Map of Australia

1980. World Tourism Conference, Manila. Mult.

1504 50f. Type **269** 35 10

1505 150f. Conference emblem . . 1·00 35

1980. 30th Anniv of Human Rights Convention.

1506 **270** 30f. violet, purple and black (postage) . . . 30 10

1507 – 50f. green, light green and black 40 10

1508 – 60f. deep blue, blue and black (air) 40 15

1509 – 150f. brown, orange & black . . . . 1·00 35

DESIGNS: 50f. Map of Eurasia; 60f. Map of the Americas; 250f. Map of Africa.

271 Emblem

1980. Air. General Conclave of French-speaking Countries of the American Order of Rosicrucians, Lome.

1511 **271** 60f. multicoloured . . . 50 15

272 Church at Melk, Austria **272a** U.A.P.T. Emblem

1980. Christmas. Multicoloured.
1512 20f. Type **272** (postage) . . 15 10
1513 30f. Tarragona Cathedral, Spain 20 10
1514 50f. Church of St. John the Baptist, Florence 35 10
1515 100f. Cologne Cathedral (air) . . . . 1·75 65
1516 150f. Notre-Dame, Paris . . 1·00 30
1517 200f. Canterbury Cathedral 1·40 35

1980. 5th Anniv of African Posts and Telecommunications Union.
1519 **272a** 100f. multicoloured . . 65 40

273 "February 2nd" Hotel

1981. Inauguration of "February 2nd" Hotel.
1520 **273** 50f. mult (postage) . . . 45 15
1521 60f. multicoloured (air) 45 15

274 "Rembrandt's Father"

1981. Easter. Rembrandt Paintings. Multicoloured.
1522 30f. Type **274** (postage) . . 30 10
1523 40f. "Self-portrait" 35 10
1524 50f. "Rembrandt's Father as an Old Man" 40 10
1525 60f. "Rider on Horseback" 50 15
1526 100f. "Rembrandt's Mother" (air) 70 20
1527 200f. "Man in a Ruff" . . 1·50 45

275 Grey-necked Bald Crow

1981. Birds. Multicoloured.
1529 30f. Type **275** (postage) . . 40 10
1530 40f. Splendid sunbird . . . 50 10
1531 60f. Violet starling 65 15
1532 90f. Red-collard whydah . . 1·10 20
1533 50f. Violet-backed sunbird (air) 65 15
1534 100f. Red bishop . . . . . 1·40 25

276 Dish Aerial

1981. 6th African Postal Union Council Meeting. Multicoloured.
1536 70f. Type **276** 50 15
1537 90f. Telecommunications control room 60 20
1538 105f. Map of Togo and Africa (vert) 70 30

277 Blind Man with Guide Dog

1981. International Year of Disabled People. Mult.
1539 70f. Type **277** (postage) . . 85 30
1540 90f. One-legged carpenter (air) 60 15
1541 200f. Wheelchair basket-ball 1·60 55

278 "Woman with Hat"

1981. Birth Centenary of Pablo Picasso. Mult.
1543 25f. Type **278** (postage) . . 35 10
1544 50f. "She-goat" 45 10
1545 60f. "Violin" 55 15
1546 90f. "Violin and Bottle on Table" (air) 80 20
1547 100f. "Baboon with Young" 90 30
1548 200f. "Mandolin and Clarinet" . . . . 1·90 55

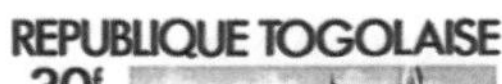

279 Aachen Cathedral, West Germany

1981. World Heritage Convention. Multicoloured.
1550 30f. Type **279** (postage) . . 20 10
1551 40f. Yellowstone National Park, U.S.A. 30 10
1552 50f. Nahanni National Park, Canada 35 10
1553 60f. Cruciform rock churches, Lalibela, Ethiopia 40 15
1554 100f. Old city centre, Cracow, Poland (air) . . 65 20
1555 200f. Goree Island, Senegal 1·25 35

280 "Vostok I" (20th anniv of first Manned Space Flight)

1981. Space Anniversaries. Multicoloured.
1557 25f. Type **280** (postage) . . 15 10
1558 50f. "Freedom 7", first American in space (20th anniv) 35 10
1559 60f. "Lunar Orbiter I" (15th anniv) 40 15
1560 90f. "Soyuz 10" (10th anniv) (air) 60 15
1561 100f. Astronauts on Moon ("Apollo XIV", 10th anniv) 65 20

281 "Adoration of the Magi" **282** Association Emblem and Togo Flag

1981. Christmas. Paintings by Rubens. Mult.
1563 20f. Type **281** (postage) . . 15 10
1564 30f. "Adoration of the Shepherds" 20 10
1565 50f. "Coronation of St. Catherine" 40 10
1566 100f. "Adoration of the Magi" (different) (air) . . 60 20
1567 200f. "Madonna and Child" 1·40 45
1568 300f. "The Madonna giving the Robe to St. Idefonse" 2·25 65

1981. West African Rice Development Association.
1570 **282** 70f. mult (postage) . . . 60 20
1571 105f. multicoloured (air) 65 30

283 Peace Dove and National Flag

1982. 15th Anniv of National Liberation. Mult.
1572 70f. Type **283** (postage) . . 55 20
1573 90f. Pres. Eyadema and citizens (vert) 60 20
1574 105f. Pres. Eyadema and citizens holding hands (vert) (air) 65 35
1575 130f. Hotel complex 90 45

284 Scouts

1982. 75th Anniv of Boy Scout Movement. Mult.
1576 70f. Type **284** (postage) . . 50 15
1577 90f. Signalling (air) 65 20
1578 120f. Constructing a tower 85 30
1579 130f. Scouts with canoe . . 90 50
1580 135f. Scouts and tent . . . 95 35

285 Moses and the Burning Bush **286** Togo and Italy Olympic Stamps

1982. Easter. The Ten Commandments. Mult.
1582 10f. Type **285** (postage) . . 10 10
1583 25f. Jephtha's daughter . . 15 10
1584 30f. St. Vincent Ferrer preaching in Verona . . . 20 10
1585 45f. The denouncing of Noah 30 10
1586 50f. Cain and Abel 35 10
1587 70f. Potiphar's wife . . . 50 20
1588 90f. Isaac blessing Jacob . . 60 35
1589 105f. Susannah and the elders (air) 65 30
1590 120f. Bathsheba 85 35

1982. Air. "Romolymphil" Stamp Exhibition.
1592 **286** 105f. multicoloured . . . 70 30

287 First Stamps of France and Togo

1982. Air. "Philexfrance '82" International Stamp Exhibition.
1593 **287** 90f. multicoloured . . . 65 40

288 Goalkeeper

1982. World Cup Football Championship, Spain. Multicoloured.
1594 25f. Type **288** (postage) . . 15 10
1595 45f. Tackle 35 10
1596 105f. Heading ball (air) . . 65 20
1597 200f. Fighting for possession 1·25 45
1598 300f. Dribble . . . . 2·00 55

289 "Papilio dardanus"

1982. Butterflies. Multicoloured.
1600 15f. Type **289** (postage) . . 20 10
1601 20f. "Belenois calypso" . . 35 10
1602 25f. "Palla decius" 50 10
1603 90f. "Euxanthe eurinome" (air) . . . . 1·60 90
1604 105f. "Mylothris rhodope" 1·75 1·00

290 Infant Jesus

1982. Christmas. Details of Raphael's "Madonna del Baldacchino". Multicoloured.
1606 45f. Type **290** 40 10
1607 70f. Madonna 55 15
1608 105f. Angel 70 20
1609 130f. Angel (different) . . . 1·00 30
1610 150f. Putti . . . . 1·10 35

291 Building, Sokode

1983. Visit of President Mitterrand of France. Mult.
1612 35f. Type **291** (postage) . . 20 10
1613 45f. Children of different races and world map . . 35 15
1614 70f. French and Togolese soldiers (vert) 55 20
1615 90f. President Mitterrand (air) (vert) 70 30
1616 105f. Presidents Mitterrand and Eyadema shaking hands (vert) 80 35
1617 130f. Presidents Mitterrand and Eyadema and crowds 1·00 40

1983. World Cup Football Championship Results. Nos. 1594/8 optd **VAINQUER COUPE DU MONDE FOOTBALL 82 "ITALIE"**.
1618 25f. Type **288** (postage) . . 15 10
1619 45f. Tackle 35 15
1620 105f. Heading ball (air) . . 65 35
1621 200f. Fighting for possession 1·25 55
1622 300f. Dribble . . . . 2·00 80

293 Map of Africa showing W.A.M.U. Members

294 Drummer

1983. 20th Anniv of West African Monetary Union. Multicoloured.

1624	70f. Type **293**	50	15
1625	90f. West African coin	60	20

1983. World Communications Year. Multicoloured.

1626	70f. Type **294** (postage)	55	15
1627	90f. Modern post office and telecommunications system (air)	65	20

295 Boxing

1983. Air. Pre-Olympic Year. Multicoloured.

1628	70f. Type **295**	50	15
1629	90f. Hurdles	60	20
1630	105f. Pole vault	65	20
1631	130f. Sprinting	1·00	30

296 Kondona Dance

1983. Traditional Dances. Multicoloured.

1633	70f. Type **296** (postage)	60	20
1634	90f. Kondona dance (different) (air)	80	20
1635	105f. Toubole dance	90	20
1636	130f. Adjogbo dance	1·10	20

297 Painting by Bellini

1983. Easter. Multicoloured.

1637	35f. Type **297** (postage)	30	10
1638	70f. Raphael (vert)	50	15
1639	90f. Carracci (air)	65	20

298 Catholic Church, Kante

1983. Christmas. Multicoloured.

1641	70f. Type **298** (postage)	50	15
1642	90f. Altar, Dapaong Cathedral (air)	60	20
1643	105f. Protestant church, Dapaong	70	20

299 Wrecked Airplane

1984. 10th Anniv of Sarakawa Assassination Attempt. Multicoloured.

1645	70f. Type **299** (postage)	50	25
1646	90f. Wrecked airplane (different)	60	30
1647	120f. Memorial Hall (air)	85	40
1648	270f. Statue of President Eyadema (vert)	1·90	70

300 Picking Coffee Beans

1984. World Food Programme Day. Multicoloured.

1649	35f. Type **300**	20	10
1650	70f. Harvesting cocoa pods	50	15
1651	90f. Planting rice	65	20

301 Flags, Agriculture and Symbols of Unity Growth

1984. 25th Anniv of Council of Unity.

1653 **301**	70f. multicoloured	50	15
1654	90f. multicoloured	60	20

1984. Air. 19th Universal Postal Union Congress, Hamburg. Nos 1451/2 optd **19E CONGRES UPU HAMBOURG 1984**.

1655	250f. multicoloured	1·60	85
1656	500f. multicoloured	3·25	1·60

303 Tim Thorpe (gold, pentathlon and decathlon, 1912)

304 Thief on right-hand Cross

1984. Air. Olympic Games Medal Winners (1st series). Multicoloured.

1657	500f. Type **303**	4·50	85
1658	500f. Mathias Behr (silver, fencing, 1984)	4·50	85
1659	500f. Fredy Schmidtke (gold, cycling, 1984)	4·50	85
1660	500f. Dietmar Mogenburg (gold, high jumping, 1984)	4·50	85
1661	500f. Sabine Everts (bronze, heptathlon, 1984)	4·50	85
1662	500f. Jesse Owens (gold, 200 m, 1936)	4·50	85
1663	500f. Bob Beamon (gold, long jumping, 1968)	4·50	85
1664	500f. Muhammad Ali (gold, boxing, 1960)	22·00	85

See also Nos. 1825/32.

1984. Easter. Details from stained glass window in Norwich Cathedral. Multicoloured.

1665	70f. Roman guard (postage)	50	15
1666	90f. Mary Magdalene (air)	55	15
1667	120f. The Apostles comforting Mary	80	20
1668	270f. Type **304**	1·60	45
1669	300f. Thief on left-hand Cross	2·00	55

305 Baguida (site of Protectorate Treaty signature, 1884)

1984. Centenary of Proclamation of German Protectorate. Multicoloured.

1671	35f. Type **305**	20	20
1672	35f. Degbenou School, 1893 (horiz)	20	20
1673	35f. Degbenou Catholic Mission, 1893 (horiz)	20	20
1674	35f. Kara suspension bridge, 1911 (horiz)	20	20
1675	35f. Adjido state school (horiz)	20	20
1676	35f. Administration post, Sansane Mango, 1908 (horiz)	20	20
1677	35f. Sokode cotton market, 1910 (horiz)	20	20
1678	45f. Main street, Lome, 1895, and 5m. "Yacht" stamp (horiz)	35	35
1679	45f. Governor's Palace, Lome, 1905 (horiz)	35	35
1680	45f. Drilling police squad, 1905 (horiz)	35	35
1681	45f. Guillaume fountain, Atakpame, 1906	35	35
1682	45f. Constructing Lome–Atakpame railway (horiz)	85	85
1683	45f. Rue de Commerce, Lome, and 10pf. "Yacht" stamp (horiz)	85	85
1684	70f. 20pf. and 2m. "Yacht" stamps, 1900 (horiz)	50	45
1685	70f. Lome wharf, 1903 (horiz)	1·10	1·10
1686	90f. Farming, Sansane Mango, 1908 (horiz)	60	55
1687	90f. Chancellor Otto von Bismark	60	55
1688	90f. Emperor Wilhelm II	60	55
1689	90f. Commissoner J. von Puttkamer, 1891–3	60	55
1690	90f. Consul-General G. Nachtigal, 1884	60	55
1691	90f. Governor A. Koehler, 1895–1902	60	55
1692	90f. Governor W. Horn, 1902–5	60	55
1693	90f. Governor J. G. von Zech, 1905–10	60	55
1694	90f. Governor E. Bruckner, 1911–12	60	55
1695	90f. Governor A. F. von Mecklenberg, 1912–14	60	55
1696	90f. Governor H. G. von Doering, 1914	60	55
1697	120f. Signing of Protectorate Treaty, 1885 (horiz)	90	85
1698	120f. Postmen, 1885	90	85
1699	150f. Children dancing around maps and flags	1·10	95
1700	270f. German gunboat "Mowe", 1884 (horiz)	2·00	1·75
1701	270f. German sail corvette "Sophie", 1884	2·00	1·75
1702	270f. Steam train, Anecho railway, 1905 (horiz)	3·50	2·75
1703	270f. Mallet steam locomotive, Kpalime Railway, 1905 (dated "1907") (horiz)	3·50	2·75
1704	270f. Flags and Presidents of Togo and Germany (horiz)	2·25	1·90

306 High Jumping

1984. Air. Olympic Games, Los Angeles. Mult.

1705	70f. Type **306**	45	25
1706	90f. Cycling	55	20
1707	120f. Football	80	30
1708	250f. Boxing (horiz)	1·60	50
1709	400f. Running (horiz)	2·75	80

307 Donald with Presents and Chip

1984. 50th Anniv of Donald Duck (cartoon character). Multicoloured.

1711	1f. Type **307** (postage)	10	10
1712	2f. Donald and Chip'n'Dale	10	10
1713	3f. Huey, Chip and Dale blowing up balloons	10	10
1714	5f. Donald and Chip holding birthday cake	10	10
1715	10f. Daisy kissing Donald	30	10
1716	15f. Goofy giving Donald his present	40	10
1717	105f. Huey, Dewey and Louie decorating cake (air)	85	15
1718	500f. Huey, Dewey, Louie and Donald with birthday cake	4·50	95
1719	1000f. Huey, Duey and Louie startling Donald	7·50	1·60

308 West African Manatee

1984. Endangered Wildlife. Multicoloured.

1722	45f. Type **308** (postage)	1·50	20
1723	70f. Manatee (close up)	1·25	20
1724	90f. Manatees in water (air)	1·75	35
1725	105f. Manatee with cub	1·75	35

309 Flame and Eleanor Roosevelt

1984. Birth Cent of Eleanor Roosevelt. Mult.

1727	70f. Type **309** (postage)	55	15
1728	90f. Eleanor Roosevelt and Statue of Liberty (air)	65	15

310 Lockheed Constellation, 1944

1984. 40th Anniv of International Civil Aviation Organization. Multicoloured.

1729	70f. Type **310** (postage)	55	30
1730	105f. Boeing 707, 1954 (air)	60	40
1731	200f. Douglas DC-8-61, 1966	1·25	80
1732	500f. Concorde, 1966	3·25	1·75

311 Bristol "400", 1947

1984. Classic Cars. Multicoloured.

1734	1f. Type **311** (postage)	10	10
1735	2f. Frazer Nash "Standard", 1925	10	10
1736	3f. Healey "Silverstone", 1950	10	10
1737	4f. Kissell "Gold Bug Speedstar", 1925	10	10
1738	50f. La Salle 5 litre, 1927	80	15
1739	90f. Minerva 30 h.p., 1921 (air)	70	15
1740	500f. Morgan "Plus 4", 1950	4·25	95
1741	1000f. Napier "40/50 T75 Six", 1921	7·75	2·25

313 "Connestabile Madonna"

1984. Christmas. Paintings by Raphael. Mult.
1744 70f. Type **313** (postage) . . 55 15
1745 290f. "The Cowper Madonna" (air) . . . . . 1·90 65
1746 300f. "The Alba Madonna" 2·00 65
1747 500f. "Madonna of the Curtain" . . . . 3·25 1·10

314 Rack Railway Steam Train, Madeira

1984. Railway Locomotives. Multicoloured.
1749 1f. Type **314** (postage) . . . 10 10
1750 2f. British-built steam locomotive, Egypt 10 10
1751 3f. Garratt steam locomotive, Algeria . . . 10 10
1752 4f. Diesel train, Congo-Ocean Railway 10 10
1753 50f. Italian-built steam locomotive, Libya 40 10
1754 90f. Northern Railway steam locomotive No. 49 (air) 70 15
1755 105f. Mallet steam locomotive, Togo 80 15
1756 500f. Steam locomotive, Rhodesia . . . . 3·75 70
1757 1000f. Beyer-Garratt steam locomotive, East African Railway . . . . 7·50 1·40

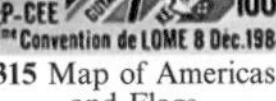

315 Map of Americas and Flags

316 St. Paul

1984. 3rd E.E.C.–African States Convention, Lome. Multicoloured.
1759 100f. Type **315** 80 20
1760 130f. Map of Europe and Africa and flags . . . . . 1·10 30
1761 270f. Map of Asia and Australasia and flags . . 2·00 60
Nos. 1759/61 were printed in se-tenant strips of three, forming a composite design showing map of the world.

1984. The Twelve Apostles. Multicoloured.
1763 1f. Type **316** (postage) . . . 10 10
1764 2f. St. Thomas 10 10
1765 3f. St. Matthew 10 10
1766 4f. St. James, the Less . . . 10 10
1767 5f. St. Simon, the Zealot . . 10 10
1768 70f. St. Thaddeus 85 15
1769 90f. St. Bartholomew (air) 55 15
1770 105f. St. Philip 65 15
1771 200f. St. John . . . . . . 1·25 35
1772 270f. St. James, son of Zebedee . . . . 1·60 45
1773 400f. St. Andrew . . . . . 2·50 80
1774 500f. St. Peter . . . . . . 3·25 90

317 Allez France

1985. Racehorses. Multicoloured.
1776 1f. Type **317** (postage) . . . 10 10
1777 2f. Arkle (vert) 10 10
1778 3f. Tingle Creek (vert) . . . 10 10
1779 4f. Interco 10 10
1780 50f. Dawn Run 95 15
1781 90f. Seattle Slew (vert) (air) 85 20
1782 500f. Nijinsky . . . . . . 4·75 90
1783 1000f. Politician . . . . . . 7·75 2·25

318 Map, Globe and Doves

1985. Air. Peace and Human Rights. Multicoloured.
1785 230f. Type **318** . . . . . . 1·50 55
1786 270f. Palm tree by shore and emblem . . . . 1·75 55
1787 500f. Mining and emblem 3·25 1·10
1788 1000f. Human Rights monument . . . . 6·75 2·50

319 "Christ and the Fisherman"

1985. Easter. Paintings by Raphael. Multicoloured.
1789 70f. "Christ and the Apostles" (postage) . . . 55 15
1790 90f. Type **319** 60 20
1791 135f. "Christ making Benediction" (vert) (air) 1·00 20
1792 150f. "The Entombment" (vert) . . . . 1·10 30
1793 250f. "The Resurrection" (vert) . . . . 1·75 50

320 Profiles and Emblem

1985. 15th Anniv of Cultural and Technical Co-operation Agency.
1795 **320** 70f. multicoloured . . . 50 20
1796 90f. multicoloured . . . 60 30

321 Adifo Dance

1985. Air. Traditional Dances. Multicoloured.
1797 120f. Type **321** 80 30
1798 125f. Whip dance 90 35
1799 290f. Idjombi dance . . . . 1·90 65
1800 500f. Moba dance . . . . . 3·25 95

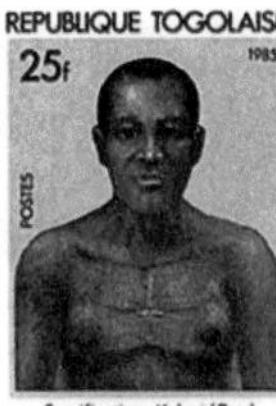

322 Kabye Man

1985. Tribal Markings. Multicoloured.
1801 25f. Type **322** (postage) . . 15 10
1802 70f. Mollah woman 50 20
1803 90f. Moba man (air) 60 20
1804 105f. Kabye woman 80 20
1805 270f. Peda woman . . . . . 1·90 65

323 Woman carrying Basket on Head and Workers on Map

1985. "Philexafrique" Stamp Exhibition, Lome. "Youth and Development". Multicoloured.
1806 200f. Type **323** . . . . . . 1·60 90
1807 200f. Man ploughing field with oxen . . . . 1·60 90

324 Muricate Turrid

1985. Sea Shells. Multicoloured.
1808 70f. Type **324** (postage) . . 95 20
1809 90f. Desjardin's marginalla (air) . . . . 1·00 25
1810 120f. Nifat turrid . . . . . 1·25 25
1811 135f. Rat cowrie . . . . . 1·50 25
1812 270f. Garter cone . . . . . 3·00 60

1985. "Expo '85" World's Fair, Tsukuba, Japan. Nos. 1738 and 1741 optd **EXPOSITION MONDIALE 1985 TSUKUBA, JAPON**.
1814 50f. La Salle 5 litre, 1927 (postage) 85 20
1815 1000f. Napier "40/50 T75 Six", 1921 (air) . . . . . 9·50 2·75

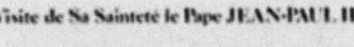

326 Pope giving Blessing

327 Brown Pelican

1985. Air. Visit of Pope John Paul II. Mult.
1817 90f. Pope and children . . . 85 20
1818 130f. Type **326** . . . . . . 1·10 35
1819 500f. Pres. Eyadema greeting Pope . . . . 4·25 2·25

1985. Birth Bicentenary of John J. Audubon (ornithologist). Multicoloured.
1820 120f. Type **327** (postage) . . 1·40 30
1821 270f. Golden eagle . . . . 3·50 70
1822 90f. Bonaparte's gulls (air) 1·10 20
1823 135f. Great-tailed grackle . . 1·75 30
1824 500f. Red-headed woodpecker . . . . . . 7·75 1·50

1985. Air. Olympic Games Medal Winners (2nd series). Nos. 1657/64 optd.
1826 500f. **"ITALIE MEDAILLE D'OR"** . . . . 4·00 85
1827 500f. **"PHILIPPE BOISSE FRANCE MEDAILLE D'OR"** . . . . 4·00 85
1828 500f. **"ROLF GOLZ R.F.A. MEDAILLE D'ARGENT"** . . . . . 4·00 85
1829 500f. **"PATRIK SJOBERG SUEDE MEDAILLE D'ARGENT"** . . . . . 4·00 85
1830 500f. **"GLYNIS NUNN AUSTRALIE MEDAILLE D'OR"** . . 4·00 85
1831 500f. **"KIRK BAPTISTE ETATS UNIS MEDAILLE D'ARGENT"** . . . . . 4·00 85
1832 500f. **"CARL LEWIS ETATS UNIS MEDAILLE D'OR"** . . 4·00 85
1833 500f. **"KEVIN BARRY NLE ZELANDE MEDAILLE D'ARGENT"** . . . . . 4·00 85

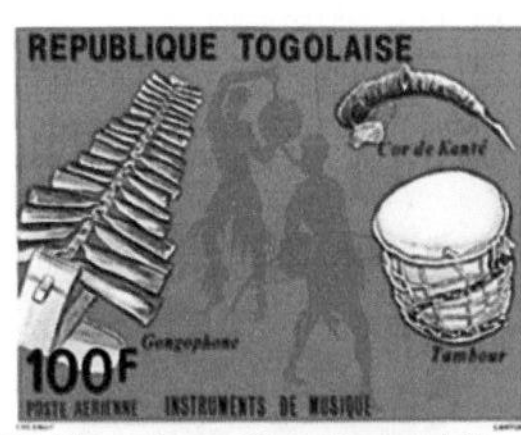

330 Gongophone, Kante Horn and Drum

1985. Air. "Philexafrique" Stamp Exhibition, Lome (2nd issue). Musical Instruments. Mult.
1835 100f. Type **330** . . . . . . 1·40 65
1836 100f. Twin drums, Bassar horn and castanets . . . 1·40 65

331 Open Book, Profile, Hand holding Pencil and Dish Aerial

1985. Air. "Philexafrique" Stamp Exhibition, Lome (3rd issue). "Youth and Development". Multicoloured.
1837 200f. Type **331** . . . . . . 1·90 1·10
1838 200f. Profiles, factory, cogwheel and maize . . . 1·90 1·10

332 Dove, Sun and U.N. Emblem

1985. 40th Anniv of U.N.O. Multicoloured.
1839 90f. Type **332** (postage) . . 60 20
1840 115f. Hands reaching up to Emblem 90 20
1841 150f. Building new bridge on river Kara (air) . . . 1·10 35
1842 250f. Preparing experimental field of millet at Atalote, Keran . . . . 1·60 50
1843 500f. Pres. Eyadema, U.N. Secretary-General, U.N. and national flags . . . . 3·25 85

333 "Madonna of the Rose Garden" (Sandro Botticelli)

335 "The Resurrection" (Andrea Mantegna)

1985. Christmas. Multicoloured.
1844 90f. Type **333** (postage) . . 65 20
1845 115f. "Madonna and Child" (11th-century Byzantine painting) (air) 90 20
1846 150f. "Rest during the flight into Egypt" (Gerard David) . . . . 1·00 30
1847 160f. "African Madonna" (16th-century statue) . . . 1·10 30
1848 250f. "African Madonna" (statue, 1900) . . . . . . 2·00 45

1985. Various stamps optd. (a) Nos. 1739/40 optd **10e ANNIVERSAIRE DE APOLLO-SOYUZ**.
1850 90f. Minerva 30 h.p., 1921 85 30
1851 500f. Morgan "Plus 4", 1950 . . . . 4·75 1·40

(b) Nos. 1752, 1755 and 1757 optd **80e ANNIVERSAIRE du ROTARY INTERNATIONAL**.
1853 4f. Diesel train, Congo-Ocean Railway (postage) 55 35
1854 105f. Mallet steam locomotive, Togo (air) . . 1·10 1·00
1855 1000f. Beyer-Garratt steam locomotive, East African Railway . . . . 11·00 5·75

(c) 150th Anniv of German Railways. Nos. 1753/4 and 1756 optd **150e ANNIVERSAIRE DE CHEMIN FER "LUDWIG"**.
1857 50f. Italian-built steam locomotive, Libya (postage) . . . . 1·00 35
1858 90f. Northern Railway steam locomotive No. 49 (air) . . . . 1·00 50
1859 500f. Steam locomotive, Rhodesia . . . . 6·25 2·75

(d) Nos. 1773/4 optd **"75e ANNIVERSAIRE DE LA MORT DE HENRI DUNANT FONDATEUR DE LA CROIX ROUGE"**.
1861 400f. St. Andrew . . . . . 3·25 1·10
1862 500f. St. Peter . . . . . . 4·00 1·40

(e) Nos. 1780 and 1783 optd **"75e ANNIVERSAIRE DU SCOUTISME FEMININ"**.
1864 50f. Dawn Run 85 20
1865 1000f. Politician . . . . . . 8·25 2·25

1986. Easter. Multicoloured.

1867	25f. Type **335** (postage)	20	10
1868	70f. "Calvary" (Paul Veronese)	55	15
1869	90f. "The Last Supper" (Jacopo Robusti Tintoretto) (horiz) (air)	65	30
1870	200f. "Christ in the Tomb" (Berruguette) (horiz)	1·50	55

336 "Suisie" Space Probe and Kohoutek's Comet

1986. Appearance of Halley's Comet (1st issue). Multicoloured.

1872	70f. Type **336** (postage)	55	15
1873	90f. "Vega I" space probe and people pointing at comet (air)	55	20
1874	150f. Comet and observation equipment	90	30
1875	200f. "Giotto" space probe and comet over town	1·25	40

See also Nos. 1917/20.

337 New York, Statue and Eiffel Tower

338 Cashew Nut

1986. Air. Centenary of Statue of Liberty. Mult.

1877	70f. Type **337**	50	15
1878	90f. Statue, Arc de Triomphe and Brooklyn Bridge	1·25	45
1879	500f. Statue, Pantheon and Empire State Building	3·25	1·10

1986. Fruit. Multicoloured.

1880	70f. Type **338** (postage)	55	15
1881	90f. Pineapple	80	20
1882	120f. Avocado (air)	90	20
1883	135f. Papaw	1·10	20
1884	290f. Mango (vert)	2·25	65

339 Footballers

341 "Ramaria moelleriana"

1986. World Cup Football Championship, Mexico.

1885	**339** 70f. mult (postage)	55	15
1886	– 90f. multicoloured (air)	55	30
1887	– 130f. multicoloured	85	35
1888	– 300f. multicoloured	1·90	70

DESIGNS: 90f. to 300f. Various footballing scenes.

1986. Air. "Ameripex '86" International Stamp Exhibition, Chicago. Nos. 1718/19 optd **AMERIPEX 86**.

1890	500f. Huey, Dewey, Louie and Donald with birthday cake	4·50	1·10
1891	1000f. Huey, Dewey and Louie startling Donald	8·25	2·25

1986. Fungi. Multicoloured.

1893	70f. Type **341**	1·25	50
1894	90f. "Hygrocybe firma"	1·50	70
1895	150f. "Kalchbrennera corallocephala"	2·50	1·25
1896	200f. "Cookeina tricholoma"	3·50	1·75

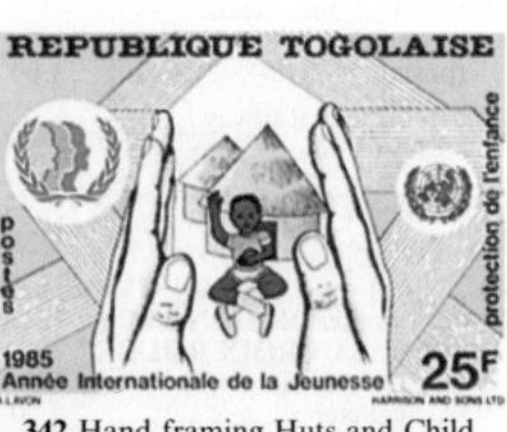

342 Hand framing Huts and Child

1986. International Youth Year (1985). Mult.

1897	25f. Type **342**	30	15
1898	90f. Children feeding birds	1·10	40

343 Wrestlers

344 Miss Sarah Ferguson

1986. Evala Wrestling Contest.

1899	**343** 15f. mult (postage)	15	10
1900	– 20f. multicoloured	30	10
1901	– 70f. multicoloured	65	15
1902	– 90f. multicoloured (air)	40	35

DESIGNS: 20 to 90f. Wrestling scenes.

1986. Wedding of Prince Andrew. Multicoloured.

1903	10f. Type **344** (postage)	55	10
1904	1000f. Prince Andrew (air)	6·75	2·25

1986. World Cup Winners. Nos. 1886/9 optd.

1906	70f. **DEMI-FINALE ARGENTINE 2 BELGIQUE 0** (postage)	55	35
1907	90f. **DEMI-FINALE ALLEMAGNE DE L'OUEST 2 FRANCE 0** (air)	55	20
1908	130f. **3 eme et 4 eme PLACE FRANCE 4 BELGIQUE 2**	85	35
1909	300f. **FINALE ARGENTINE 3 ALLEMAGNE DE L'OUEST 2**	1·90	80

346 Fazao Hotel

1986. Hotels. Multicoloured.

1910	70f. Type **346** (postage)	55	15
1911	90f. Sarakawa Hotel (air)	65	30
1912	120f. The Lake Hotel	90	40

347 Spur-winged Geese

1986. Keran National Park. Multicoloured.

1913	70f. Type **347** (postage)	80	40
1914	90f. Antelope (air)	65	30
1915	100f. African elephant	80	35
1916	130f. Kob	1·00	45

1986. Appearance of Halley's Comet (2nd issue). Nos. 1872/5 optd as T **198a** of Sierra Leone.

1917	**336** 70f. mult (postage)	1·25	35
1918	– 90f. multicoloured (air)	1·00	30
1919	– 150f. multicoloured	1·50	40
1920	– 200f. multicoloured	1·90	70

349 "The Annunciation"

1986. Christmas. Multicoloured.

1922	45f. Type **349** (postage)	45	15
1923	120f. "Nativity" (air)	90	35
1924	130f. "Adoration of the Magi"	1·10	45
1925	200f. "Flight into Egypt"	1·50	65

350 Rainbow and Douglas DC-10

1986. Air. 25th Anniv of Air Afrique.

1927	**350** 90f. multicoloured	75	45

351 Pres. Eyadema and Phosphate Mine

1987. 20th Anniv of National Liberation. Mult.

1928	35f. Type **351** (postage)	20	10
1929	50f. Anie sugar refinery	35	15
1930	70f. Nangbeto Dam	50	20
1931	90f. February 2 Hotel and Posts and Telecommunications building, Lome	60	20
1932	100f. Post and Telecommunications building, Kara (air)	55	15
1933	120f. Peace monument	80	30
1934	130f. Baby being vaccinated	90	35

352 "The Last Supper"

1987. Easter. Paintings from Nadoba Church, Keran. Multicoloured.

1936	90f. Type **352** (postage)	65	30
1937	130f. "Christ on the Cross" (air)	90	30
1938	300f. "The Resurrection"	2·00	65

353 Adenauer speaking in the Bundestag

1987. Air. 20th Death Anniv of Konrad Adenauer (German Chancellor). Multicoloured.

1940	120f. Type **353**	85	30
1941	500f. Adenauer with John F. Kennedy	3·25	1·10

354 Player falling with Ball

1987. World Rugby Football Cup. Multicoloured.

1943	70f. Type **354** (postage)	80	30
1944	130f. Player running with ball (air)	1·25	35
1945	300f. Scrum	2·75	1·25

355 "Adenium obesum"

1987. Flowers. Multicoloured.

1947	70f. Type **355** (postage)	70	20
1948	90f. "Amorphophallus abyssinicus" (vert) (air)	85	30
1949	100f. "Ipomoea mauritiana"	1·00	30
1950	120f. "Salacia togoica" (vert)	1·25	35

356 Wilhelm I Coin and Victory Statue

1987. Air. 750th Anniv of Berlin. Multicoloured.

1951	90f. Type **356**	65	30
1952	150f. Friedrich III coin and Brandenburg Gate	1·00	35
1953	300f. Wilhelm II coin and Place de la Republique	2·00	65

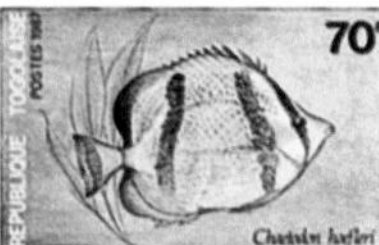

357 Hoefler's Butterflyfish

1987. Fishes. Multicoloured.

1955	70f. Type **357**	1·00	35
1956	90f. Nile pufferfish	1·25	40
1957	120f. Goree spadefish	1·50	60
1958	130f. Dwarf labeo	1·75	60

358 Long Jumping

1987. Olympic Games, Seoul (1988). Mult.

1959	70f. Type **358** (postage)	60	20
1960	90f. Relay race (air)	60	20
1961	200f. Cycling	1·25	45
1962	250f. Javelin throwing	1·60	55

1987. Endangered Wildlife. As Nos. 1722/5 but values changed and size 37 × 24 mm.

1964	60f. Type **308** (postage)	1·00	20
1965	75f. Manatee (close up)	1·10	35
1966	80f. Manatees in water	1·50	35
1967	100f. Manatee with cub (air)	1·75	40

359 Doctor vaccinating Child

1987. "Health for All by Year 2000". Anti-tuberculosis Campaign. Multicoloured.

1968	80f. Type **359** (postage)	55	30
1969	90f. Family under umbrella (vert) (air)	60	30
1970	115f. Faculty of Medicine building, Lome University	80	35

360 "Spring or the Earthly Paradise"

1987. Christmas. Multicoloured.

1971	40f. Type **360** (postage)	35	10
1972	45f. "The Creation of Adam" (Michelangelo)	35	10
1973	105f. "Presentation in the Temple" (vert) (air)	65	20
1974	270f. "The Original Sin" (vert)	1·75	65

361 Men ploughing and Women collecting Water

1988. 10th Anniv of Agricultural Development Fund.

1976	**361** 90f. multicoloured	65	20

363 "The Dance"

1988. 15th Death Anniv of Pablo Picasso (painter). Multicoloured.
1978 45f. Type **363** (postage) . . 45 10
1979 160f. "Portrait of a Young Girl" . . . . 1·50 35
1980 300f. "Gueridon" (air) . . . 2·75 85

364 Cement **365** "Jesus and the Disciples at Emmaus"

1988. Industries. Multicoloured.
1982 125f. Type **364** 85 30
1983 165f. Brewery . . . . 1·10 40
1984 195f. Phosphates . . . . . 1·25 45
1985 200f. Plastics . . . . 1·25 45
1986 300f. Milling (vert) . . . . 2·10 65

1988. Easter. Stained Glass Windows. Mult.
1987 70f. Type **365** (postage) . . 60 15
1988 90f. "Mary at the Foot of the Cross" 80 20
1989 120f. "Crucifixion" (air) . . 85 30
1990 200f. "St. Thomas and Resurrected Jesus" . . . 1·40 45

366 Paris Crowd welcoming Kennedy, 1961 **367** Watchi Chief

1988. 25th Death Anniv of John F. Kennedy (U.S. President). Multicoloured.
1992 125f. Type **366** . . . . . . 1·00 20
1993 155f. Kennedy at Paris Town Hall (vert) . . . . 1·10 20
1994 165f. Kennedy and De Gaulle at Elysee Palace (vert) . . . . 1·25 40
1995 180f. John and Jacqueline Kennedy at Orly Airport 1·40 75

1988. Traditional Tribal Costumes. Multicoloured.
1997 80f. Type **367** 55 20
1998 125f. Watchi woman 85 20
1999 165f. Kotokoli man . . . . 1·10 35
2000 175f. Ewe man . . . . . . 1·10 35

368 Basketball **369** People with Candles

1988. Olympic Games, Seoul. Multicoloured.
2002 70f. Type **368** (postage) . . 50 15
2003 90f. Tennis 60 20
2004 120f. Archery (air) 85 30
2005 200f. Throwing the discus 1·40 45

1988. 40th Anniv of W.H.O. Multicoloured.
2007 80f. Type **369** 55 15
2008 125f. Maps, emblem and "40" 85 20

370 Plaited Style

1988. Hairstyles. Multicoloured.
2009 80f. Type **370** 55 20
2010 125f. Knotted style 85 20
2011 170f. Plaited style with bow 1·00 40
2012 180f. Style with plaits all over head (vert) . . . . . 1·25 40

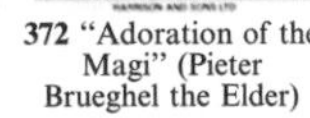

371 Collecting Water (B. Gossner) **372** "Adoration of the Magi" (Pieter Brueghel the Elder)

1988. "Philtogo" National Stamp Exhibition. Designs depicting winning entries of a schools drawing competition. Multicoloured.
2014 10f. Type **371** 10 10
2015 35f. Villagers working on farm (K. Ekoue-Kouvahey) 20 10
2016 70f. Family (A. Abbey) . . 65 15
2017 90f. Village women preparing food (T. D. Lawson) 85 30
2018 120f. Fishermen and boats on shore (A. Tazzar) . . 1·10 30

1988. Christmas. Multicoloured.
2019 80f. Type **372** (postage) . . 55 20
2020 150f. "The Virgin, The Infant Jesus, Saints Jerome and Dominic" (Fra. Filippo Lippi) (air) 1·00 20
2021 175f. "The Madonna, The Infant Jesus, St. Joseph and the Infant St. John the Baptist" (Federico Barocci) . . . . 1·25 35
2022 195f. "The Virgin and Child" (Gentile Bellini) 1·40 45

373 Wreckage of Airplane

1989. 15th Anniv of Sarakawa Assassination Attempt. Multicoloured.
2024 10f. Type **373** 10 10
2025 80f. Tail section (vert) . . . 55 25
2026 125f. Soldiers and wreckage 85 50

374 Anniversary Emblem

1989. 20th Anniv of Benin Electricity Community.
2027 **374** 80f. multicoloured . . . 60 20
2028 125f. multicoloured . . . 95 20

375 Boxing

1989. Prince Emanuel of Liechtenstein Foundation. Multicoloured.
2029 80f. Type **375** 55 20
2030 125f. Long jumping 55 30
2031 165f. Running . . . . . . 1·10 40

376 Table Tennis

1989. Olympic Games, Barcelona (1992). Mult.
2032 80f. Type **376** (postage) . . 65 20
2033 125f. Running (horiz) . . . 90 20
2034 165f. Putting the shot . . . 1·00 35
2035 175f. Basketball . . . . . 1·25 35
2036 380f. High jumping (horiz) (air) . . . . 2·50 55
2037 425f. Boxing (horiz) . . . . 3·00 55

377 Footballers and St. Janvier's Cathedral, Naples

1989. World Cup Football Championship, Italy. Multicoloured.
2039 80f. Type **377** (postage) . . 55 20
2040 125f. Milan Cathedral . . . 85 20
2041 165f. Bevilacqua Palace, Verona . . . . 1·10 35
2042 175f. Baptistry, Florence . . 1·10 35
2043 380f. Madama Palace, Turin (air) . . . . 2·75 55
2044 425f. St. Laurent's Cathedral, Genoa . . . . 2·75 55

378 Bundestag

1989. 40th Anniv of Federal Republic of Germany. Multicoloured.
2046 90f. Type **378** 65 20
2047 125f. Konrad Adenauer (Chancellor, 1949–63) and Theodor Heuss (President, 1949–59) (vert) 95 30
2048 180f. West German flag and emblem . . . . 1·25 40

379 Tractor, Map and Woman at Water-pump

1989. 30th Anniv of Council of Unity.
2049 **379** 75f. multicoloured . . . 55 20

380 Boys learning First Aid

1989. 125th Anniv of International Red Cross. Multicoloured.
2050 90f. Type **380** 50 20
2051 125f. Founding meeting . . 85 35

381 Storming the Bastille **383** People with Banners and Pres. Eyadema

382 Jacques Necker (statesman) and The Three Orders

1989. Bicentenary of French Revolution (1st issue). Multicoloured.
2052 90f. Type **381** 65 20
2053 125f. Oath of the Tennis Court (horiz) . . . . . . 1·00 35
2054 180f. Abolition of Privileges (horiz) . . . . 1·40 45
See also Nos. 2056/9.

1989. Bicentenary of French Revolution (2nd issue). Multicoloured.
2056 90f. Type **382** (postage) . . 65 20
2057 190f. Guy le Chapelier and abolition of seigneurial rights . . . . 1·50 45
2058 425f. Talleyrand-Perigord (statesman) and La Fayette's oath (air) . . . 2·75 55
2059 480f. Paul Barras (revolutionary) and overthrow of Robespierre 3·25 55

1989. 20th Anniv of Kpalime Appeal. Mult.
2061 90f. Type **383** 60 20
2062 125f. Pres. Eyadema addressing gathering . . . 90 35

384 "Apollo II" Launch **386** Emblem

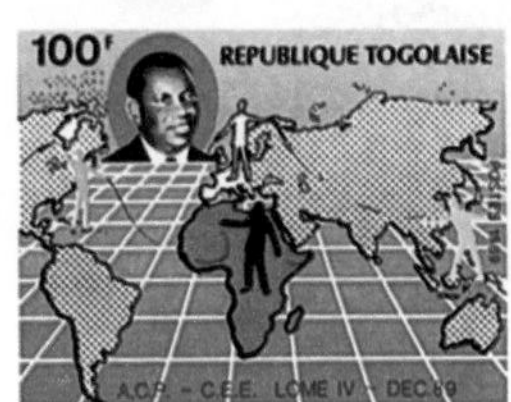

385 Figures on Map (dated "DEC.89")

1989. 20th Anniv of First Manned Landing on Moon. Multicoloured.
2063 40f. Type **384** 30 10
2064 90f. Space capsule in orbit 55 20
2065 150f. Landing capsule . . . 1·10 35
2066 250f. Splashdown . . . . . 1·60 45

1989. 4th Lome Convention (on relations between European Community and African, Caribbean and Pacific countries). Multicoloured.
2068 100f. Type **385** 80 30
2069 100f. As T **385** but dated "15 DEC.89" 80 30

1990. 10th Anniv of Pan-African Postal Union.
2070 **386** 125f. gold, blue & brown 90 30

387 Party Headquarters, Kara

1990. 20th Anniv (1989) of Rally of Togolese People Party. Multicoloured.
2071 45f. Type **387** 35 15
2072 90f. Pres. Eyadema and anniversary emblem . . . 60 20

388 "Myrina silenus" and Scout **389** "Danaus chrysippus"

1990. Scouts, Butterflies and Fungi. Mult.
2073 80f. Type **388** (postage) . . 65 15
2074 90f. "Phlebobus silvaticus" (fungus) 65 15
2075 125f. "Volvariella esculenta" (fungus) 90 20
2076 165f. "Hypolycaena antifaunus" (butterfly) . . 1·10 35
2077 380f. "Termitomyces striatus" (fungus) (air) . . 3·00 55
2078 425f. "Axiocerces harpax" (butterfly) . . . . 3·00 55

1990. Butterflies. Multicoloured.

2080 5f. Type **389** 50 10
2081 10f. "Morpho aega" 50 10
2082 15f. "Papilio demodocus" 50 10
2083 90f. "Papilio dardanus" 1·50 35

390 Emblem **391** Nile Monitor

1990. 9th Convention of Lions Club Internationals District 403, Lome.

2085 **390** 90f. multicoloured 60 35
2086 125f. multicoloured 85 55
2087 165f. multicoloured 1·10 80

1990. Reptiles. Multicoloured.

2088 1f. Type **391** 50 10
2089 25f. Puff adder 75 10
2090 60f. Black-lipped cobra 1·00 15
2091 90f. African rock python 1·25 20

392 Pile of Cowrie Shells **393** Maps, Cogwheel and Arrows

1990. Money Cowrie Shells. Multicoloured.

2092 90f. Type **392** 1·00 20
2093 125f. Cowrie and bead ornament 1·50 25
2094 180f. Headdress with cowries and animal horns 2·00 55

1990. United States–Togo Friendship. Mult.

2095 125f. Type **393** 90 35
2096 180f. Presidents Bush and Eyadema shaking hands (horiz) 1·25 35

394 Cinkasse Post Office

1990. Stamp Day.

2098 **394** 90f. multicoloured 60 35

395 Addressing Crowd, Brazzaville, 1944

1990. 20th Death Anniv of Charles de Gaulle (statesman).

2099 **395** 125f. multicoloured 85 45

396 Thatched Houses

1990. Traditional Housing. Multicoloured.

2100 90f. Type **396** 60 35
2101 125f. Village 85 45
2102 190f. Tamberma house 1·25 65

397 Airport, Airliners and Airline Emblems

1990. New Lome Airport.

2103 **397** 90f. multicoloured 1·00 35

398 Woman carrying Basket on Head (Sikou Dapau)

1990.

2104 **398** 90f. multicoloured 60 35

399 Chimpanzee, Missahoue Kloto

1991. Forests. Multicoloured.

2105 90f. Type **399** 60 35
2106 170f. Jardine's parrot, Aledjo Forest 1·25 75
2107 185f. Grey parrot, Chateau Vial Kloto Forest 1·40 75

400 Dancers

1992. Spirit Dances.

2108 **400** 90f. multicoloured 75 35
2109 – 125f. multicoloured 1·00 55
2110 – 190f. multicoloured 1·50 80

DESIGNS: 125, 190f. Various dances.

401 Royal Python hatching

1992. The Royal Python. Multicoloured.

2111 90f. Type **401** 75 35
2112 125f. Hatchlings emerging from shells 1·00 35
2113 190f. Hatchlings and empty shells 1·50 65
2114 300f. Close-up of hatchling and empty shell 2·25 90

402 Emblem **403** Postal Sorter

1994. 120th Anniv of U.P.U.

2115 **402** 180f. multicoloured 45 20

1994. World Post Day.

2117 **403** 90f. multicoloured 20 10
2118 120f. multicoloured 30 10

404 Footballers

1994. World Cup Football Championship, U.S.A.

2119 **404** 5f. multicoloured 10 10
2120 – 10f. multicoloured 10 10
2121 – 25f. multicoloured 10 10
2122 – 60f. multicoloured 15 10
2123 – 90f. multicoloured 20 10
2124 – 100f. multicoloured 25 10
2125 – 200f. multicoloured 50 20
2126 – 1000f. multicoloured 2·40 95

DESIGNS: 10f. to 1000f. Various footballing scenes.

405 Northern Pike

1995. Fishes. Multicoloured.

2128 10f. Type **405** 10 10
2129 90f. Derbio 35 20
2130 180f. Common carp 75 40

406 "The Resurrection" (detail) (Andrea Mantegna) **407** Hill

1995. Easter. Multicoloured.

2131 90f. Type **406** 20 10
2132 180f. "Calvary" (Paolo Veronese) 45 20
2133 190f. "The Last Supper" (Jacopo Tintoretto) (horiz) 45 20

1995. Birth Bicentenary of Sir Rowland Hill (instigator of postage stamp).

2134 **407** 125f. multicoloured 30 10

408 Secretary Bird **409** Madagascan Belvache

1995. Birds. Multicoloured.

2135 5f. Type **408** 10 10
2136 10f. African paradise flycatcher ("Paradise Flycatcher") 10 10
2137 25f. African spoonbill (horiz) 10 10
2138 60f. Red-cheeked cordon-bleu ("Cordon Bleu") (horiz) 15 10
2139 90f. Orange-breasted sunbird 20 10
2140 100f. Yellow-billed hornbill 25 10
2141 180f. Barn owl (horiz) 45 20
2142 200f. Hoopoe feeding chick (horiz) 50 20
2143 300f. Red-crowned bishop ("Fire-crowned Bishop") 75 30
2144 1000f. Red-throated bee eater 2·40 95

1995. Plants. Multicoloured.

2146 15f. Type **409** 10 10
2147 90f. Marigolds 20 10
2148 125f. Agave (horiz) 30 10

410 Anniversary Emblem **411** Globe and Doves

1995. 50th Anniv of U.N.O. (1st issue).

2149 **410** 180f. multicoloured 45 20

See also Nos. 2150/2.

1995. 50th Anniversaries. Multicoloured. (a) U.N.O. (2nd issue).

2150 25f. Type **411** 10 10
2151 90f. Doves and Headquarters building, New York 20 10
2152 400f. Globe and doves (different) 95 40

Nos. 2150/2 were issued together, se-tenant, forming a composite design.

(b) Food and Agriculture Organization.

2154 45f. Cattle 10 10
2155 125f. Cow 30 10
2156 125f. Mother and child collecting water (horiz) 30 10
2157 200f. Herdsmen 50 20

Nos. 2154/5 and 2157 were issued together, se-tenant, forming a composite design.

412 Montecassino, Italy

1995. 50th Anniv of End of Second World War (1st issue). Victory in Europe. Multicoloured.

2159 45f. Type **412** 10 10
2160 90f. Warsaw in ruins 20 10
2161 125f. Russian tanks in Berlin 30 10
2162 200f. German fighter planes 50 20
2163 200f. American cruiser in north Atlantic 50 20
2164 200f. Capture of Ludendorf Bridge 50 20
2165 200f. Russian "Katyusha" rockets 50 20
2166 500f. United Nations flag 2·50 90

See also Nos. 2191/6.

413 National Flag and Scout Badge **414** Manfred Eigen (Chemistry, 1967)

1995. 18th World Scout Jamboree, Dronten, Netherlands. Multicoloured.

2168 90f. Type **413** 20 10
2169 190f. Saluting scout and camp 45 20
2170 300f. Lord Baden-Powell (founder of Boy Scout Movement) 75 30

1995. Centenary of Nobel Prize Trust Fund. Mult.

2172 200f. Type **414** 50 20
2173 200f. Donald J. Cram (Chemistry, 1987 50 20
2174 200f. Paul J. Flory (Chemistry, 1974) 50 20
2175 200f. Johann Deisenhofer (Chemistry, 1988) 50 20
2176 200f. Percy Williams Bridgman (Physics, 1946) 50 20
2177 200f. Otto Stern (Physics, 1943) 50 20
2178 200f. Arne Tiselius (Chemistry, 1948) 50 20
2179 200f. J. Georg Bednorz (Physics, 1987) 50 20
2180 200f. Albert Claude (Medicine, 1974) 50 20
2181 200f. Elihu Root (Peace, 1912) 50 20
2182 200f. Alfred Fried (Peace, 1911) 50 20
2183 200f. Henri Moissan (Chemistry, 1906) 50 20
2184 200f. Charles Barkla (Physics, 1917) 50 20
2185 200f. Rudolf Eucken (Literature, 1908) 50 20
2186 200f. Carl von Ossietzky (Peace, 1935) 50 20
2187 200f. Sir Edward Appleton (Physics, 1947) 50 20

2188 200f. Camillo Golgi (Medicine, 1906) 50 20
2189 200f. Wilhelm Rontgen (Physics, 1901) 50 20

415 Admiral Isoroko Yamamoto

1995. 50th Anniv of End of Second World War (2nd issue). Victory in the Pacific. Japanese commanders. Multicoloured.
2191 200f. Type **415** 50 20
2192 200f. General Hideki Tojo (Minister of War, 1940–41 and Premier, 1941–44) . . 50 20
2193 200f. Vice-admiral Shigeru Fukudome 50 20
2194 200f. Admiral Shigetaro Shimada 50 20
2195 200f. Rear-admiral Chuichi Nagumo 50 20
2196 200f. General Shizu Ichi Tanaka 50 20

416 Drawing

417 Original and Current Emblems

1995. 95th Birthday of Queen Elizabeth the Queen Mother. Multicoloured.
2198 250f. Type **416** 60 25
2199 250f. Carrying umbrella . . 60 25
2200 250f. Seated at writing table (face value white) 60 25
2201 250f. As young woman . . 60 25
2202 250f. As No. 2200 but face value black 60 25
2203 250f. Cutting cake 60 25
2204 250f. Waving from car . . . 60 25

1995. 90th Anniv of Rotary International.
2206 **417** 1000f. multicoloured . . 2·40 95

418 Woman buying Stamps

1995. World Post Day. Multicoloured.
2208 220f. Type **418** 55 20
2209 315f. Clerk arranging stamps on page 75 30
2210 335f. Sorting office 80 30

419 Nativity

1995. Christmas. Paintings. Multicoloured.
2211 90f. Type **419** 20 10
2212 325f. Adoration of the Wise Men 80 30
2213 340f. Adoration of the shepherds (horiz) 80 30

POSTAGE DUE STAMPS

1921. Postage Due stamps of Dahomy, "figure" key-type, optd **TOGO**.
D54 M 5c. green . . . . 45 3·25
D55 10c. red . . . . 30 3·25
D56 15c. grey . . . . 40 3·50
D57 20c. brown . . . . 2·25 4·25
D58 30c. blue . . . . 1·75 5·00
D59 50c. black . . . . 2·00 3·75
D60 60c. orange . . . . 2·50 4·25
D61 1f. violet . . . . 4·25 8·25

D 8 Cotton Growing

1925. Centres and inscr in black.
D 97 D **8** 2c. blue . . . . 10 2·75
D 98 4c. red . . . . 10 2·75
D 99 5c. greeen . . . . . . 10 2·75
D100 10c. red . . . . 20 3·00
D101 15c. yellow . . . . . . 20 3·00
D102 20c. mauve . . . . . . 1·75 3·00
D103 25c. grey . . . . 1·75 3·25
D104 30c. yellow on blue . . 75 3·00
D105 50c. brown . . . . . . 2·25 3·25
D106 60c. green . . . . . . 1·75 3·00
D107 1f. violet . . . . 1·50 2·75

1927. Surch.
D108 D **8** 2f. on 1f. mauve and red . . . . 2·00 5·50
D109 3f. on 1f. blue and brown . . . . 2·25 6·25

D **12** Native Mask

D **21**

D **31** Konkomba Helmet

1940.
D151 D **12** 5c. black . . . . . . 1·60 2·75
D152 10c. green . . . . . . 1·00 3·00
D153 15c. red . . . . 30 2·75
D154 20c. blue . . . . . . 45 3·00
D155 30c. brown . . . . . 25 3·00
D156 50c. olive . . . . . . 1·10 4·50
D157 60c. violet . . . . . 65 3·00
D158 1f. blue . . . . 1·25 3·50
D159 2f. red . . . . 1·25 3·25
D160 3f. violet . . . . . . 1·75 3·50

1947.
D185 D **21** 10c. blue . . . . . . 10 1·40
D186 30c. red . . . . 10 2·75
D187 50c. green . . . . . . 10 2·75
D188 1f. brown . . . . . . 20 2·75
D189 2f. red . . . . 85 3·00
D190 3f. black . . . . . . 1·10 3·00
D191 4f. blue . . . . 1·10 3·25
D192 5f. brown . . . . . . 80 3·25
D193 10f. orange . . . . . 1·00 3·50
D194 20f. blue . . . . . . 1·40 3·75

1957.
D214 D **31** 1f. violet . . . . . . 1·00 1·75
D215 2f. orange . . . . . 95 2·50
D216 3f. grey . . . . 1·25 2·75
D217 4f. red . . . . 1·25 2·75
D218 5f. blue . . . . 1·25 2·75
D219 10f. green . . . . . . 1·40 3·00
D220 20f. purple . . . . . 1·60 3·25

1959. As Nos. D214/20 but colours changed and inscr "REPUBLIQUE DU TOGO".
D244 D **31** 1f. brown . . . . . . 10 1·10
D245 2f. turquoise . . . . . 10 1·10
D246 3f. orange . . . . . . 10 1·75
D247 4f. blue . . . . 15 1·25
D248 5f. purple . . . . . . 15 2·50
D249 10f. violet . . . . . . 25 2·25
D250 20f. black . . . . . . 35 2·25

D **57** "Cardium costatum"

D **110** Tomatoes

1964. Sea Shells. Multicoloured.
D366 1f. Butterfly cone 20 20
D367 2f. Ermine marginella . . . 20 20
D368 3f. Rat cowrie 20 20
D369 4f. Bubonian conch 30 30
D370 5f. Type D **57** 75 75
D371 10f. "Cancellaria cancellata" . . . . . . 1·00 1·00
D372 15f. African Neptue volute 2·00 2·00
D373 20f. "Tympanotomus radula" . . . . 2·50 2·50

1969. Young Pioneers Agricultural Organization. Multicoloured.
D696 5f. Type D **110** 10 10
D697 10f. Corn on the cob . . . 30 30
D698 19f. Red pepper 40 40
D699 20f. Peanuts 55 55

1980. As T **259**. Multicoloured.
D1454 5f. Women examining produce (vert) 10 10
D1455 10f. Market stall 10 10
D1456 25f. Poultry seller 15 10
D1457 50f. Carvings and ornaments 35 15

APPENDIX

The following stamps have either been issued in excess of postal needs or have not been available to the public in reasonable quantities at face value. Such stamps may later be given full listing if there is evidence of regular postal use.

All embossed on gold foil.

1989.

Prince Emanuel of Liechtenstein Foundation. Air 1500f. × 2.

Bicentenary of French Revolution (2nd issue). Air 1500f.

Scouts, Butterflies and Fungi. Air 1500f.

TOKELAU Pt. 1

Three islands situated north of Samoa. Formerly known as the Union Islands, they were administered as part of the Gilbert and Ellice Islands until transferred to New Zealand in 1925. Administered by Western Samoa (using stamps of Samoa) until they became a dependency of New Zealand in 1949. Adopted name of Tokelau in 1946.

1948. 12 pence = 1 shilling; 20 shillings = 1 pound.
1967. 100 cents or sene = 1 New Zealand dollar.

1 Atafu Village and Map

1a Queen Elizabeth II

1948.
1 **1** ½d. brown and purple 15 50
2 – 1d. red and green 15 30
3 – 2d. green and blue 15 30
DESIGNS: 1d. Nukunonu hut and map; 2d. Fakaofo village and map.

1953. Coronation.
4 **1a** 3d. brown . . . . 1·50 1·50

1956. Surch **ONE SHILLING**.
5 **1** 1s. on ½d. brown and purple 75 1·25

1966. Arms types of New Zealand without value, surch **TOKELAU ISLANDS** and value in sterling.
6 F **6** 6d. blue 25 80
7 8d. green 25 80
8 2s. pink 30 80

1967. Decimal currency. Nos. 1/3 surch.
9 – 1c. on 1d. (No. 2) 20 60
10 – 2c. on 2d. (No. 3) . . . . . 30 1·00
11 **1** 10c. on ½d. (No. 1) . . . . . 70 2·00

1968. Arms types of New Zealand without value, surch **TOKELAU ISLANDS** and value in decimal currency.
12 F **6** 3c. lilac 30 20
13 5c. blue 30 20
14 7c. green 30 20
15 20c. pink 30 30

8 British Protectorate (1877)

8a "The Nativity" (Federico Fiori (Barocci))

1969. History of Tokelau Islands.
16 **8** 5c. blue, yellow and black . . 15 10
17 – 10c. red, yellow and black . . 15 10
18 – 15c. green, yellow and black 20 15
19 – 20c. brown, yellow and black 25 15
DESIGNS: 10c. Annexed to Gilbert and Ellice Islands (1916); 15c. New Zealand Administration (1925); 20c. New Zealand Territory (1948).

1969. Christmas.
20 **8a** 2c. multicoloured 10 15

8b "The Virgin adoring the Child" (Correggio)

1970. Christmas.
21 **8b** 2c. multicoloured 10 20

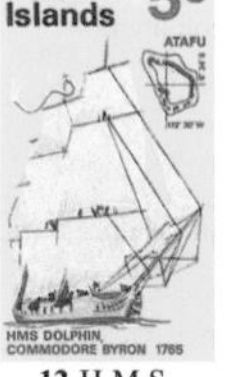
12 H.M.S. "Dolphin", 1765

13 Fan

1970. Discovery of Tokelau Islands. Mult.
22 5c. Type **12** . . . . 1·00 35
23 10c. H.M.S. "Pandora", 1791 1·00 35
24 25c. "General Jackson" (American whaling ship), 1835 (horiz) . . . . 1·75 70

1971. Handicrafts. Multicoloured.
25 1c. Type **13** 15 20
26 2c. Hand-bag 20 30
27 3c. Basket 20 40
28 5c. Hand-bag 20 50
29 10c. Shopping-bag 20 55
30 15c. Hand-bag . . . . 25 1·10
31 20c. Canoe . . . . 25 1·40
32 25c. Fishing hooks . . . . . 25 1·40

14 Windmill Pump

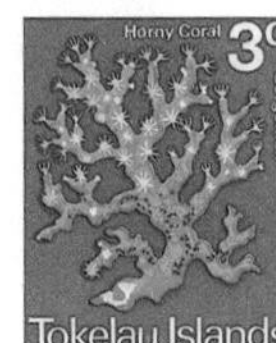
15 Horny Coral

1972. 25th Anniv of South Pacific Commission. Multicoloured.
33 5c. Type **14** 45 70
34 10c. Community well 55 80
35 15c. Pest eradication . . . . 80 1·40
36 20c. Flags of member nations 85 1·40
On No. 35 "PACIFIC" is spelt "PACFIC".

1973. Coral. Multicoloured.
37 3c. Type **15** 50 80
38 5c. Soft coral 50 90
39 15c. Mushroom coral . . . . 75 1·25
40 25c. Staghorn coral . . . . . 80 1·50

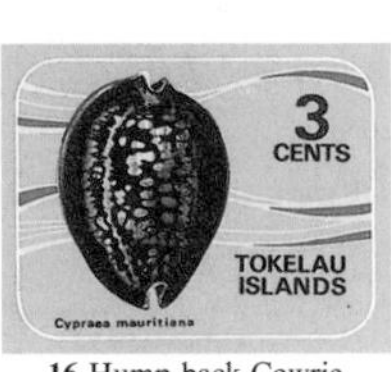
16 Hump-back Cowrie

17 Moorish Idol

1975. "Shells of the Coral Reef". Multicoloured.
41 3c. Type **16** . . . . 60 1·25
42 5c. Tiger cowrie . . . . . . 60 1·25
43 15c. Mole cowrie . . . . . . 75 2·00
44 25c. Eyed cowrie . . . . . . 80 2·25

1975. Fishes. Multicoloured.
45 5c. Type **17** 20 50
46 10c. Long-nosed butterflyfish 20 60
47 15c. Lined butterflyfish 30 80
48 25c. Lionfish ("Red-Fire Fish") 30 90

18 Canoe Building

1976. Multicoloured.
49a 1c. Type **18** 10 15
50 2c. Reef fishing . . . . . . 30 1·90
51a 3c. Weaving preparation . . 10 15
52a 5c. Uma (kitchen) 10 15

53a 9c. Carving (vert) 15 15
54a 20c. Husking coconuts (vert) 15 20
55a 50c. Wash day (vert) 20 20
56a $1 Meal time (vert) 30 30

19 White Tern

20 Westminster Abbey

1977. Birds of Tokelau. Multicoloured.
57 8c. Type **19** 30 40
58 10c. Ruddy turnstone 35 45
59 15c. White-capped noddy 45 70
60 30c. Common noddy 50 90

1978. 25th Anniv of Coronation. Multicoloured.
61 8c. Type **20** 20 20
62 10c. King Edward's Chair 20 20
63 15c. Coronation regalia 30 35
64 30c. Queen Elizabeth II 50 60

21 Canoe Race

1978. Canoe Racing.
65 **21** 8c. multicoloured 20 30
66 – 12c. multicoloured 20 35
67 – 15c. multicoloured 20 40
68 – 30c. multicoloured 30 70
DESIGNS: 12c. to 30c. Different scenes of canoe racing.

22 Rugby

1979. Local Sports. Multicoloured.
69 10c. Type **22** 20 30
70 15c. Cricket 1·00 85
71 20c. Rugby (different) 55 90
72 30c. Cricket (different) 1·00 1·10

23 Surfing

24 Pole Vaulting

1980. Water Sports. Multicoloured.
73 10c. Type **23** 10 15
74 20c. Surfing (different) 15 20
75 30c. Swimming 20 25
76 50c. Swimming (different) 25 35

1981. Sports. Multicoloured.
77 10c. Type **24** 10 10
78 20c. Volleyball 20 20
79 30c. Athletics (different) 25 30
80 50c. Volleyball (different) 30 35

25 Wood Carving

26 Octopus Lure

1982. Handicrafts. Multicoloured.
81 10s. Type **25** 10 20
82 22s. Bow drilling sea shell 10 35
83 34s. Bowl finishing 15 45
84 60s. Basket weaving 25 80

1982. Fishing Methods. Multicoloured.
85 5s. Type **26** 10 10
86 18s. Multiple-hook fishing 20 20
87 23s. Ruvettus fishing 25 25
88 34s. Netting flying fish 25 30
89 63s. Noose fishing 30 40
90 75s. Bonito fishing 40 45

27 Outrigger Canoe

1983. Transport. Multicoloured.
91 5s. Type **27** 10 10
92 18s. Wooden whaleboat 10 15
93 23s. Aluminium whaleboat 10 20
94 34s. "Alia" (fishing catamaran) 15 25
95 63s. "Frysna" (freighter) 25 40
96 75s. Grumman MacKinnon Goose flying boat 30 50

28 Javelin Throwing

1983. Traditional Pastimes. Multicoloured.
97 5s. Type **28** 10 10
98 18s. String game 10 15
99 23s. Fire making 10 20
100 34s. Shell throwing 15 25
101 63s. Hand-ball game 20 40
102 75s. Mass wrestling 25 50

29 Planting and Harvesting

30 Convict Tang ("Manini")

1984. Copra Industry. Multicoloured.
103 48s. Type **29** 30 40
104 48s. Husking and splitting 30 40
105 48s. Drying 30 40
106 48s. Bagging 30 40
107 48s. Shipping 30 40

1984. Fishes. Multicoloured.
108 1s. Type **30** 15 10
109 2s. Flyingfish ("Hahave") 15 10
110 5s. Surge wrasse ("Uloulo") 20 10
111 9s. Unicornfish ("Ume ihu") 20 10
112 23s. Wrasse ("Lafilafi") 40 20
113 34s. Red snapper ("Fagamea") 50 25
114 50s. Yellow-finned tuna ("Kakahi") 70 40
115 75s. Oilfish ("Palu po") 1·00 55
116 $1 Grey shark ("Mokoha") 1·00 70
117 $2 Black marlin ("Hakula") 1·40 1·40

31 "Ficus tinctoria" ("Mati")

1985. Native Trees. Multicoloured.
118 5c. Type **31** 10 10
119 18c. "Morinda citrifolia" ("Nonu") 10 15
120 32c. Breadfruit tree ("Ulu") 15 25
121 48c. "Pandanus tectorius" ("Fala") 25 40
122 60c. "Cordia subcordata" ("Kanava") 30 45
123 75s. Coconut palm ("Niu") 35 55

32 Administration Centre, Atafu

1985. Tokelau Architecture (1st series). Public Buildings. Multicoloured.
124 5c. Type **32** 10 10
125 18c. Administration Centre, Nukunonu 15 15
126 32c. Administration Centre, Fakaofo 15 25
127 48c. Congregational Church, Atafu 20 40
128 60c. Catholic Church, Nukunonu 25 45
129 75c. Congregational Church, Fakaofo 25 55
See also Nos. 130/5.

33 Atafu Hospital

1986. Tokelau Architecture (2nd series). Hospitals and Schools. Multicoloured.
130 5c. Type **33** 10 15
131 18c. St. Joseph's Hospital, Nukunonu 15 15
132 32c. Fenuafala Hospital, Fakaofo 15 30
133 48c. Matauala School, Atafu 20 45
134 60c. Matiti School, Nukunonu 25 60
135 75c. Fenuafala School, Fakaofo 25 90

34 Coconut Crab

1986. Agricultural Livestock. Multicoloured.
136 5c. Type **34** 10 15
137 18c. Pigs 10 15
138 32c. Chickens 20 30
139 48c. Reef hawksbill turtle 25 45
140 60c. Goats 30 55
141 75c. Ducks 35 70

35 "Scaevola taccada" ("Gahu")

1987. Tokelau Flora. Multicoloured.
142 5c. Type **35** 45 50
143 18c. "Hernandia nymphaeifolia" ("Puka") 60 80
144 32c. "Pandanus tectorius" ("Higano") 80 1·10
145 48c. "Gardenia taitensis" ("Tialetiale") 1·00 1·40
146 60c. "Pemphis acidula" ("Gagie") 1·25 1·75
147 75c. "Guettarda speciosa" ("Puapua") 1·40 1·90

36 Javelin Throwing

1987. Tokelau Olympic Sports. Multicoloured.
148 5c. Type **36** 25 30
149 18c. Shot-putting 45 50
150 32c. Long jumping 60 90
151 48c. Hurdling 70 1·10
152 60c. Sprinting 80 1·75
153 75c. Wrestling 1·10 1·90

37 Small Boat Flotilla in Sydney Harbour

1988. Bicentenary of Australian Settlement and "Sydpex '88" National Stamp Exhibition, Sydney. Multicoloured.
154 50c. Type **37** 1·75 2·00
155 50c. Sailing ships and liners 1·75 2·00
156 50c. Sydney skyline and Opera House 1·75 2·00
157 50c. Sydney Harbour Bridge 1·75 2·00
158 50c. Sydney waterfront 1·75 2·00
Nos. 154/8 were printed together, se-tenant, forming a composite aerial view of the re-enactment of First Fleet's arrival.

38 Island Maps and Ministerial Representatives

1988. Political Development. Multicoloured.
159 5c. Type **38** (administration transferred to N.Z. Foreign Affairs Ministry, 1975) 40 50
160 18c. General Fono (island assembly) meeting, 1977 45 55
161 32c. Arms of New Zealand (first visit by New Zealand Prime Minister, 1985) 70 80
162 48c. U.N. logo (first visit by U.N. representative, 1976) 80 1·00
163 60c. Canoe and U.N. logo (first Tokelau delegation to U.N., 1987) 1·00 1·40
164 75c. Secretary and N.Z. flag (first islander appointed as Official Secretary, 1987) 1·50 1·50

39 Three Wise Men in Canoe and Star

1988. Christmas. Designs showing Christmas in Tokelau. Multicoloured.
165 5c. Type **39** 25 35
166 20c. Tokelau Nativity 30 40
167 40c. Flight to Egypt by canoe 55 70
168 60c. Children's presents 60 1·00
169 70c. Christ Child in Tokelauan basket 70 1·10
170 $1 Christmas parade 85 1·40

40 Launching Outrigger Canoe

1989. Food Gathering. Multicoloured.
171 50c. Type **40** 1·75 2·00
172 50c. Paddling canoe away from shore 1·75 2·00
173 50c. Fishing punt and sailing canoe 1·75 2·00
174 50c. Canoe on beach 1·75 2·00
175 50c. Loading coconuts into canoe 1·75 2·00
176 50c. Tokelauans with produce 1·75 2·00
Nos. 171/3 and 174/6 were each printed together, se-tenant, forming composite designs.

41 Basketwork

1990. Women's Handicrafts. Multicoloured.
177 5c. Type **41** 75 65
178 20c. Preparing cloth 1·25 1·10
179 40c. Tokelau fabrics 1·75 1·50
180 60c. Mat weaving 2·25 2·25
181 80c. Weaving palm fronds 3·00 3·25
182 $1 Basket making 3·25 3·50

42 Man with Adze and Wood Blocks

1990. Men's Handicrafts. Multicoloured.
183 50c. Type **42** 1·75 2·00
184 50c. Making fishing boxes 1·75 2·00
185 50c. Fixing handles to fishing boxes 1·75 2·00
186 50c. Two men decorating fishing boxes 1·75 2·00
187 50c. Canoe building (two men) 1·75 2·00
188 50c. Canoe building (three men) 1·75 2·00

43 Swimming

45 Queen Elizabeth II in 1953

44 "Santa Maria"

1992. Olympic Games, Barcelona. Mult.
189 40c. Type **43** 60 60
190 60c. Long jumping 80 90
191 $1 Volleyball . . . . 1·60 1·75
192 $1.80 Running . . . . 2·25 3·25

1992. 500th Anniv of Discovery of America by Columbus. Multicoloured.
193 40c. Type **44** 80 80
194 60c. Christopher Columbus . . 1·10 1·25
195 $1.20 Fleet of Columbus . . . 2·50 2·75
196 $1.80 Columbus landing in the New World . . . . . 3·50 3·75

1993. 40th Anniv of Coronation. Mult.
197 25c. Type **45** 90 90
198 40c. Prince Philip . . . . . 1·25 1·25
199 $1 Queen Elizabeth II in 1993 1·90 2·00
200 $2 Queen Elizabeth II and Prince Philip . . . . . . 3·25 3·50

46 Bristle-thighed Curlew

1993. Birds of Tokelau. Multicoloured.
201 25c. Type **46** 75 75
202 40c. Red-tailed tropic bird . . 1·10 1·10
203 $1 Reef heron . . . . 1·75 1·75
204 $2 Pacific golden plover . . . 2·50 3·25

1994. "Hong Kong '94" International Stamp Exhibition. Multicoloured.
MS205 125 × 100 mm. As Nos. 201/4 (sold at $5) . . . . 5·00 6·00

47 Great Egret ("White Heron")

1994. "Philakorea '94" International Stamp Exhibition, Seoul.
206 **47** $2 multicoloured . . . . . 2·50 3·25
MS207 110 × 76 mm. No. 206 . . 4·00 4·25

48 Model Outrigger Canoe

1994. Handicrafts. Multicoloured.
208 5c. Type **48** 10 10
209 25c. Plaited fan 20 25
210 40c. Plaited baskets 30 35
211 50c. Fishing box 35 40
212 80c. Water bottle 60 65
213 $1 Fishing hook 75 80
214 $2 Coconut gourds . . . . . 1·50 1·60
215 $5 Shell necklace . . . . . . 3·75 4·00

49 Fishing Pigs

1995. Chinese New Year ("Year of the Pig"). Sheet 100 × 75 mm.
MS218 **49** $5 multicoloured . . . 6·50 7·00

1995. "PostX '95" National Stamp Exhibition, Auckland. No. **MS**218 optd with "PostX '95" emblem on sheet margin in red.
MS219 **49** $5 multicoloured . . . 9·50 11·00

50 Pacific Pigeon on Branch

1995. Endangered Species. Pacific Pigeon. Mult.
220 25c. Type **50** 60 65
221 40c. On branch (different) . . 85 90
222 $1 On branch with berries . . 1·40 1·75
223 $2 Chick in nest . . . . . . 2·40 3·25

51 Long Nosed Butterflyfish

52 "Danaus plexippus"

1995. Reef Fishes. Multicoloured.
224 25c. Type **51** 45 55
225 40c. Emperor angelfish . . . 70 75
226 $1 Moorish idol . . . . . . 1·40 1·60
227 $2 Lined butterflyfish . . . . 2·40 3·00
MS228 130 × 90 mm. Lionfish (39 × 34 mm) . . . . 3·25 4·00

1995. "Singapore '95" International Stamp Exhibition. No. **MS**218 optd with exhibition emblem on sheet margin.
MS229 **49** $5 multicoloured . . . 5·50 7·00

1995. Butterflies and Moths. Multicoloured.
230 25c. Type **52** 65 65
231 40c. "Precis villida samoensis" 90 90
232 $1 "Hypolimnas bolina" . . 2·00 2·25
233 $2 "Euploea lewenii" . . . . 3·00 3·50

53 Hawksbill Turtle

1995. Year of the Sea Turtle. Multicoloured.
234 25c. Type **53** 65 65
235 40c. Leatherback turtle . . . 90 90
236 $1 Green turtle . . . . . . 2·00 2·25
237 $2 Loggerhead turtle . . . . 3·00 3·50
MS238 130 × 90 mm. $3 As $2 (50 × 40 mm) . . . . 4·00 5·50

54 Pacific Rat

1996. Chinese New Year ("Year of the Rat"). Sheet 128 × 97 mm.
MS239 **54** $3 multicoloured . . . 4·00 5·00

55 Queen Elizabeth II and Nukunonu

1996. 70th Birthday of Queen Elizabeth II. Each incorporating a different photograph of the Queen. Multicoloured.
240 40c. Type **55** 50 50
241 $1 Atafu at night . . . . . 1·40 1·50
242 $1.25 Atafu . . . . 1·60 1·75
243 $2 Atafu village . . . . . . 2·00 2·50
MS244 64 × 66 mm. $3 Queen Elizabeth II . . . . 3·25 4·00

1996. "CHINA '96" 9th Asian International Stamp Exhibition, Peking. No. **MS**239 optd with exhibition emblem on sheet margin in red.
MS245 128 × 97 mm. $3 Type **54** 4·00 5·50

56 Fraser's Dolphin

1996. Dolphins. Multicoloured.
246 40c. Type **56** . . . . 1·00 1·00
247 $1 Common dolphin . . . . 2·50 2·50
248 $1.25 Striped dolphin . . . . 2·50 2·50
249 $2 Spotted dolphin . . . . . 3·50 3·50

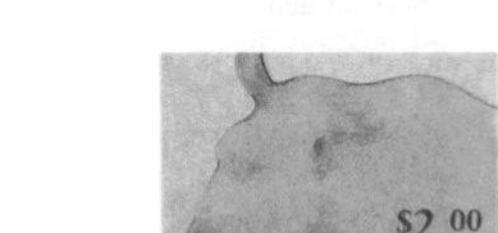

57 Mole Cowrie

1996. Sea Shells. Multicoloured.
250 40c. Type **57** 60 60
251 $1 Humpback cowrie . . . . 1·50 1·50
252 $1.25 Eyed cowrie . . . . . 1·60 1·75
253 $2 Tiger cowrie . . . . . . 2·25 2·75
MS254 123 × 83 mm. $3 Humpback cowrie (different) (50 × 40 mm) 3·50 4·50

1996. "TAIPEI '96" 10th Asian International Stamp Exhibition, Taiwan. No. **MS**239 optd with exhibition emblem on sheet margin.
MS255 128 × 97 mm. $3 Type **54** 3·25 4·00

58 Ox

1997. Chinese New Year ("Year of the Ox"). Sheet 120 × 78 mm.
MS256 **58** $2 multicoloured . . . 2·50 3·25

1997. "HONG KONG '97" International Stamp Exhibition. No. **MS**256 optd with **HONG KONG '97 STAMP EXHIBITION** in gold on sheet margin.
MS257 120 × 78 mm. **58** $2 multicoloured . . . . 3·00 3·50

1997. "Pacific '97" International Stamp Exhibition, San Francisco. No. **MS**256 optd with exhibition emblem on sheet margin.
MS258 120 × 78 mm. **58** $2 multicoloured . . . . 2·25 3·25

59 Humpback Whale

1997. Humpback Whales. Multicoloured.
259 40c. Type **59** 60 55
260 $1 Family of humpback whales . . . . 1·10 1·10
261 $1.25 Humpback whale feeding . . . . 1·40 1·75
262 $2 Humpback whale and calf 2·25 2·75
MS263 135 × 87 mm. Head of humpbacked whale . . . . 2·75 3·25

60 Church by Lagoon

1997. 50th Anniv of South Pacific Commission. Multicoloured.
264 40c. Type **60** 45 45
265 $1 Boy looking across lagoon 90 90
266 $1.25 Bungalow on small island . . . . 1·25 1·50
267 $2 Tokelau from the air . . . 1·90 2·50

61 Gorgonian Coral and Emperor Angelfish

1997. Pacific Year of the Coral Reef. Mult.
268 $1 Type **61** . . . . 1·00 1·25
269 $1 Soft coral . . . . 1·00 1·25
270 $1 Mushroom coral . . . . 1·00 1·25
271 $1 Staghorn coral . . . . . 1·00 1·25
272 $1 Staghorn coral and moorish idols . . . . . . 1·00 1·25
Nos. 268/72 were printed together, se-tenant, with the backgrounds forming a composite design.

1997. "Aupex '97" National Stamp Exhibition, Auckland. No. **MS**263 optd **AUPEX '97, 13–16 NOVEMBER NZ NATIONAL STAMP EXHIBITION** on sheet margin in black.
MS273 135 × 87 mm. $3 Head of humpback whale . . . . . . 2·75 3·50

62 Tiger

62a Carrying Yellow Bouquet

1998. Chinese New Year ("Year of the Tiger"). Sheet 130 × 95 mm.
MS274 **62** $2 multicoloured . . . 1·75 2·50

1998. Diana, Princess of Wales Commemoration. Multicoloured.
275 **62a** $1 Carrying yellow bouquet . . . . 1·00 1·25
MS276 145 × 70 mm. $1 Wearing red polka-dot dress; $1 Wearing matching pink hat and jacket; $1 No. 275; $1 In pink and yellow jacket with flowers (sold at $4+50c. charity premium) . . . 3·50 4·25

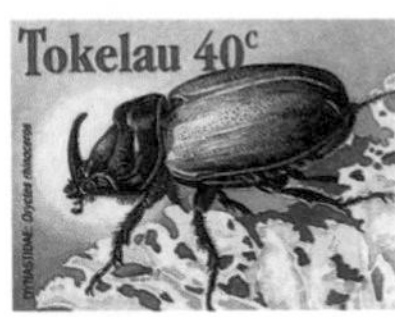

63 1948 ½d. Atafu Village Stamp

1998. 50th Anniv of Tokelau Postage Stamps. Sheet 105 × 80 mm, containing T **63** and similar horiz designs. Multicoloured.
MS277 $1 Type **63**; $1 1948 1d. Nukunono hut stamp; $1 1948 2d. Fakaofo village stamp . . . . 3·00 3·75

64 "Oryctes rhinoceros"

1998. Beetles. Multicoloured.
278 40c. Type **64** 65 65
279 $1 "Tribolium castaneum" . . 1·25 1·25
280 $1.25 "Coccinella repanda" . 1·40 1·40
281 $2 "Amarygmus hydrophiloides" . . . . . 2·00 2·50
MS282 125 × 86 mm. $3 Coccinella repanda (different) . . . . . . 2·50 3·25

65 "Ipomoea pes-caprae"

1998. Tropical Flowers. Multicoloured.
283 40c. Type **65** 40 50
284 $1 "Ipomoea littoralis" . . . 85 95
285 $1.25 "Scaevola taccada" . . 1·00 1·40
286 $2 "Thespesia populnea" . . 1·60 2·25

66 Rabbit

1999. Chinese New Year ("Year of the Rabbit"). Sheet 105 × 70 mm.
MS287 **66** $3 multicoloured . . . 2·25 3·00

67 H.M.S. *Pandora* (frigate)

1999. "Australia '99" International Stamp Exhibition, Melbourne. Sheet 119 × 80 mm.
MS288 **67** $3 multicoloured . . . 2·75 3·25

1999. "iBRA '99" International Stamp Exhibition, Nuremberg. No. **MS**287 optd with the **iBRA** logo on the sheet margin.
MS289 105 × 70 mm. **66** $3 multicoloured . . . . 3·00 3·50

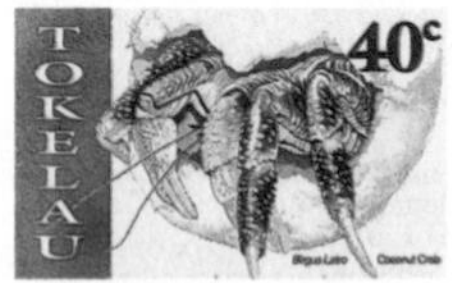

68 Coconut Crab

1999. Pacific Crabs. Multicoloured.
290 40c. Type **68** 40 40
291 $1 Ghost crab 85 85
292 $1.25 Land hermit crab . . . 1·00 1·25
293 $2 Purple hermit crab . . . . 1·60 2·00
MS294 127 × 89 mm. $3 Ghost crab (different) . . . . 3·00 3·50

69 Lift-off **71** Dragon

70 Black-naped Tern Chick and Egg

1999. 30th Anniv of First Manned Landing on Moon. Multicoloured.
295 25c. Type **69** 40 40
296 50c. Rocket stage separation 60 60
297 75c. Aldrin deploying experiment 70 70
298 $1 Planting the flag 85 85
299 $1.25 Separation of command module . . . . 1·00 1·25
300 $2 Recovery of astronauts . . 1·50 2·00
MS301 90 × 65 mm. $3 Lunar module, Earth and Jupiter . . 3·00 3·50

1999. Black-naped Tern. Multicoloured.
302 40c. Type **70** 45 45
303 $1 Black-naped tern perched on pebbles 90 90
304 $1.25 Two black-naped terns 1·10 1·10
305 $2 Two black-naped terns in flight . . . . 1·75 2·00

2000. Chinese New Year ("Year of the Dragon"). Sheet 105 × 70 mm.
MS306 **71** $3 multicoloured . . . 2·25 3·00

2000. "Bangkok 2000" World Youth Stamp Exhibition. No. **MS**306 optd on the margin with **WORLD YOUTH STAMP EXHIBITION BANGKOK 2000** in English and Thai.
MS307 105 × 70 mm. $3 Type **71** 2·25 3·00

72 Nukunonu

2000. "The Stamp Show 2000" International Stamp Exhibition, London. Sheet 105 × 85 mm.
MS308 **72** $6 multicoloured . . . 3·75 4·50

2000. "EXPO 2000" World Stamp Exhibition, Anaheim, U.S.A. No. **MS**301 optd **WORLD STAMP EXPO 2000 7–16 JULY ANAHEIM – U.S.A.** on sheet margin.
MS309 90 × 65 mm. $3 Lunar module, Earth and Jupiter . . 2·50 3·25

73 Queen Elizabeth the Queen Mother

2000. Queen Elizabeth the Queen Mother's 100th Birthday. Multicoloured.
310 40c. Type **73** 55 35
311 $1.20 Queen Mother waving 1·00 1·00
312 $1.80 Wearing diamond earrings and pearl necklace 1·60 1·75
313 $3 Wearing blue hat and tartan scarf . . . . 2·25 2·75

74 *Gehyra oceanica*

2001. Lizards. Multicoloured.
314 40c. Type **74** 70 60
315 $1 *Lepidodactylus lugubris* . . 1·40 1·40
316 $1.25 *Gehyra mutilata* . . . . 1·60 1·75
317 $2 *Emoia cyanura* . . . . . 2·50 2·75

75 Snake

2001. Chinese New Year ("Year of the Snake"). Sheet 105 × 73 mm.
MS318 **75** $3 multicoloured . . . 2·75 3·25

2001. "Hong Kong 2001" Stamp Exhibition. No. **MS**318 optd **HONG KONG 2001** in English and Chinese on the sheet margin.
MS319 105 × 73 mm. $3 Type **75** 2·75 3·25

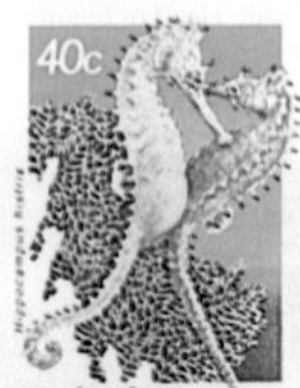

76 Yellow and Orange Seahorses

2001. Seahorses. Multicoloured.
320 40c. Type **76** 40 40
321 $1 Baby seahorses 70 70
322 $1.25 Pink seahorse . . . . . 90 1·00
323 $2 Yellow seahorse . . . . . 1·40 1·75
MS324 104 × 73 mm. $3 No. 320 2·25 2·75

77 Atafu Island

2001. Island Views. Multicoloured.
325 40c. Type **77** 70 60
326 $1 Fakaofo . . . . 1·25 1·25
327 $2 Sunrise over Nukunonu village . . . . 1·90 2·00
328 $2.50 Nukunonu beach . . . 2·00 2·25

78 Princess Elizabeth and Lieutenant Philip Mountbatten, 1947

2002. Golden Jubilee.
329 **78** 40c. brown, red and gold 65 60
330 – $1 multicoloured . . . . . 1·10 1·10
331 – $1.25 black, red and gold 1·40 1·50
332 – $2 multicoloured . . . . . 1·90 2·00
MS333 162 × 95 mm. Nos. 329/2 and $3 multicoloured . . . . . . 7·00 7·00
DESIGNS—HORIZ: $1 Queen Elizabeth in mauve hat; $1.25, Princess Elizabeth holding Prince Charles, 1948; $2 Queen Elizabeth in Poland, 1996. VERT:—(38 × 51 mm): $3 Queen Elizabeth after Annigoni.

79 Horse

2002. Chinese New Year ("Year of the Horse"). Sheet 105 × 70 mm.
MS334 **79** $4 multicoloured . . . 4·00 4·50

2002. "Stampex 2002" Stamp Exhibition, Hong Kong. No. **MS**334 optd **STAMPEX 2002 HONG KONG 22–24 FEBRUARY 2002** in gold on the sheet margin.
MS335 105 × 70 mm. $4 Type **79** 4·00 4·50

80 Pelagic Thresher Sharks

2002. Endangered Species. Pelagic Thresher Shark.
336 **80** 40c. multicoloured 50 40
337 – $1 multicoloured 90 90
338 – $2 multicoloured . . . . . 1·75 1·90
339 – $2.50 multicoloured . . . 1·90 2·00
DESIGNS: $1 to $2.25, Show sharks.

2002. Queen Elizabeth the Queen Mother Commemoration. As T **215** of St. Helena.
340 40c. black, gold and purple 50 40
341 $2 multicoloured . . . . . 2·00 2·25
MS342 145 × 70 mm. $2.50 black and gold; $4 multicoloured . . 8·50 9·00
DESIGNS: 40c. Queen Elizabeth wearing wide-brimmed hat; $2 Queen Mother wearing mauve hat and coat; $2.50, Wearing feathered hat and pearls; $4 Queen Mother smiling. Designs in No. **MS**342 omit the "1900–2002" inscription and the coloured frame.

81 H.M.N.Z.S. *Kaniere* (frigate), 1958–59

2002. Royal New Zealand Navy Ships which have visited Tokelau. Multicoloured.
343 40c. Type **81** 70 60
344 $1 H.M.N.Z.S. *Endeavour* (supply ship), 1990 . . . . 1·40 1·40
345 $2 H.M.N.Z.S. *Wellington* (frigate), 1987, 1988, 1990 2·50 2·50
346 $2.50 H.M.N.Z.S. *Monowai* (survey ship), 1979, 1985, 1994 . . . . 2·75 2·75

82 Ram

2003. Chinese New Year ("Year of the Sheep"). Sheet 105 × 70 mm.
MS347 **82** $4 multicoloured . . . 4·25 4·75

2003. 50th Anniv of Coronation. As T **219** of St. Helena. Multicoloured.
348 $2.50 Queen Elizabeth II with her Maids of Honour . . . 2·50 2·50
349 $4 Queen and Duke of Edinburgh . . . . 3·75 4·00
MS350 95 × 115 mm. $2.50, As No. 348; $4 As No. 349 . . . 4·75 5·00

83 Prince William at Polo Match and at Sighthill Community Education Centre, 2001

2003. 21st Birthday of Prince William of Wales. Multicoloured.
351 $1.50 Type **83** . . . . 1·50 1·50
352 $3 At Tidworth Polo Club, 2002 and at Highgrove, 2000 . . . . 2·75 2·75

2003. "Bangkok 2003" World Philatelic Exhibition. **MS**347 optd **BANGKOK 2003** in English and Thai in gold on the sheet margin.
MS353 105 × 70 mm. $4 Type **82** 3·25 3·75

84 Shoreline with Palm Trees **85** Chinese Character and Monkeys

2003. "Welpex 2003" National Stamp Exhibition, Wellington, New Zealand. Sheet 119 × 80 mm.
MS354 **84** $4 multicoloured . . . 3·50 4·00

2004. Chinese New Year ("Year of the Monkey"). Sheet 105 × 71 mm.
MS355 **85** $4 red, black and gold 3·00 3·25

2004. Hong Kong Stamp Exhibition. No. **MS**355 optd **2004 Hong Kong Stamp Expo** in gold on the sheet margin.
MS356 **85** $4 red, black and gold 3·00 3·25

86 Dawn at Atafu

2004. Scenes. Multicoloured.
357 40c. Type **86** 30 35
358 $1 Fishermen returning to Nukunonu 75 80
359 $2 Early evening at Fakaofo 1·50 1·60
360 $2.50 Beach scene, Atafu . . 1·60 1·70

2004. Commemoration of Visit by Prime Minister of New Zealand. No. **MS**354 optd **NEW ZEALAND PRIME MINISTER'S VISIT AUGUST 2004** in silver with additional rectangular opt on sheet margin.
MS361 **84** $4 multicoloured . . . 3·00 3·25

88 Lesser Frigate Bird

2004. Lesser Frigate Bird. Multicoloured.

362		40c. Type **88**	30	35
363		$1 Birds in flight	75	80
364		$2 Two birds in nest	1·50	1·60
365		$2.50 Juvenile bird	1·60	1·70

89 Rooster

2005. Chinese New Year ("Year of the Rooster"). Sheet 115 × 75 mm.

MS366	**89**	$4 red, black and gold	3·00	3·25

TOLIMA Pt. 20

One of the states of the Granadine Confederation. A department of Colombia from 1886, now uses Colombian stamps.

100 centavos = 1 peso.

1 2 3

1870. On white or coloured paper. Imperf.

6	**1**	5c. black	25·00	20·00
13		10c. black	30·00	18·00

1871. Various frames. Imperf.

14	**2**	5c. brown	75	75
15	**3**	10c. blue	2·00	2·00
16		50c. green	3·00	3·00
17		1p. red	6·00	6·00

6 7 8

9 10 11

1879. Imperf.

18a	**6**	5c. brown	20	20
19	**7**	10c. blue	25	25
20a	**8**	50c. green	25	30
21a	**9**	1p. red	90	1·00

1883. Imperf.

22	**6**	5c. orange	20	20
23	**7**	10c. red	35	35
24	**10**	20c. violet	50	50

1884. Imperf.

25	**11**	1c. grey	10	10
26		2c. red	10	10
27		2½c. orange	10	10
28		5c. brown	10	10
29a		10c. blue	15	15
30		20c. yellow	30	30
31		25c. black	15	15
32		50c. green	20	20
33		1p. red	25	25
34		2p. violet	40	35
35		5p. orange	25	25
36		10p. red	60	60

12 16

1886. Condor's wings touch Arms. Perf.

37	**12**	5c. brown	50	50
38		10c. blue	1·75	1·75
39		50c. green	60	60
40		1p. red	1·25	1·25

1886. Condor's wings do not touch Arms. Perf or imperf.

45	**16**	1c. grey	2·50	2·50
46		2c. red	3·25	3·25
47		2½c. pink	12·00	12·00
48		5c. brown	4·50	4·50
49		10c. blue	6·00	6·00
50		20c. yellow	3·25	3·25
51		25c. black	3·00	3·00
52		50c. green	1·40	1·10
53		1p. red	2·25	2·25
54		2p. violet	4·00	4·00
55		5p. orange	7·50	7·50
56		10p. red	3·50	3·50

20 21

1888. Perf.

67	**20**	1c. blue on red	15	15
68		2c. green on green	15	15
69		5c. red	10	10
70		10c. green	20	25
71		20c. blue on yellow	30	30
65		50c. blue	45	45
72		1p. brown	75	75

1903. Imperf or perf.

85	**21**	4c. black on green	10	10
78		10c. green	10	10
87		20c. orange	20	20
88		50c. black on red	15	15
81		1p. brown	10	10
82		2p. grey	10	10
91		5p. red	10	10
92		10p. black on blue	15	15
92a		10p. black on green	15	15

TONGA Pt. 1

(Or Friendly Is.). A group of islands in the S. Pacific Ocean. An independent Polynesian kingdom formerly under British protection, Tonga became a member of the Commonwealth in June 1970.

1886. 12 pence = 1 shilling;
20 shillings = 1 pound.
1967. 100 seniti = 1 pa'anga.

1 King George I

1886.

1b	**1**	1d. red	10·00	3·25
2b		2d. violet	32·00	2·75
3ab		6d. blue	27·00	2·25
9		6d. orange	16·00	26·00
4ba		1s. green	55·00	3·25

1891. Surch with value in words.

5	**1**	4d. on 1d. red	3·00	11·00
6		8d. on 2d. violet	35·00	90·00

1891. Optd with stars in upper right and lower left corners.

7	**1**	1d. red	45·00	50·00
8		2d. violet	70·00	38·00

5 Arms of Tonga **6** King George I

1892.

10	**5**	1d. red	12·00	19·00
11	**6**	2d. olive	18·00	16·00
12	**5**	4d. brown	48·00	70·00
13	**6**	8d. mauve	55·00	£170
14		1s. brown	80·00	£110

1893. Surch in figures.

15	**5**	½d. on 1d. blue	23·00	27·00
16	**6**	2½d. on 2d. green	14·00	12·00
18		7½d. on 6d. red	24·00	80·00

1893. Surch **FIVE PENCE.**

17	**5**	5d. on 4d. orange	4·00	6·50

1894. Surch vert **SURCHARGE.** and value in words.

21	**5**	½d. on 4d. brown	2·00	7·00
22	**6**	½d. on 1s. brown	2·50	11·00
25		1d. on 2d. blue	48·00	24·00

1894. Surch vert **SURCHARGE.** and value in figures.

26b	**6**	1½d. on 2d. blue	50·00	30·00
27		2½d. on 2d. blue	40·00	48·00
23		2½d. on 8d. mauve	5·00	8·00
24b	**1**	2½d. on 1s. green	15·00	42·00
28b	**6**	7½d. on 2d. blue	60·00	48·00

13 King George II **15** Arms

16 Ovava Tree, Kana-Kubolu

21 View of Haapai

1895. Surch **SURCHARGE** and new value.

29	**13**	½d. on 2½d. red	32·00	32·00
30		1d. on 2½d. red	65·00	40·00
31		7½d. on 2½d. red	55·00	65·00

1895.

32	**13**	1d. green	21·00	26·00
33		2½d. red	20·00	13·00
34b		5d. blue	23·00	50·00
35		7½d. yellow	30·00	48·00

1896. Nos. 26a and 28a surch with typewritten **Half-Penny-** and Tongan inscription.

36Aa	**6**	½d. on 1½d. on 2d. blue	£425	£425
37A		½d. on 7½d. on 2d. blue	85·00	£110

1897.

38a	**15**	½d. blue	70	3·00
55		½d. green	1·00	1·25
39	**16**	1d. black and red	80	80
40a	–	2d. sepia and bistre	15·00	3·50
43b	–	2½d. black and blue	4·50	1·60
78	–	3d. black and green	65	4·25
45	–	4d. green and purple	3·75	4·00
46	–	5d. black and orange	32·00	14·00
79	–	6d. red	3·50	2·25
48	–	7½d. black and green	16·00	23·00
49	–	10d. black and lake	45·00	48·00
50	–	1s. black and brown	14·00	7·50
51a	**21**	2s. black and blue	21·00	29·00
81	–	2s.6d. purple	32·00	23·00
82	–	5s. black and red	16·00	50·00

DESIGNS—VERT (as Type **26**): 2, 2½, 5, 7½, 10d., 1s. King George II. (As Type **16**): 6d. Coral. (As Type **21**): 2s.6d. Red shining parrot. HORIZ (as Type **16**): 3d. Prehistoric trilith at Haamonga; 4d. Breadfruit. (As Type **21**): 5s. Vavau Harbour.

1899. Royal Wedding. Optd **T - L 1 June, 1899.**

54	**16**	1d. black and red	28·00	55·00

26 Queen Salote **29** Queen Salote

1920.

56	**26**	1½d. black	50	3·00
57		2d. purple and violet	9·00	13·00
76		2d. black and purple	7·00	2·75
58		2½d. black and blue	4·75	40·00
59		2½d. blue	2·00	1·00
60		5d. black and orange	3·25	4·75
61		7½d. black and green	1·75	1·75
62		10d. black and lake	2·50	4·75
63		1s. black and brown	1·25	2·50

1923. Nos. 46 and 48/82 surch **TWO PENCE PENI-E-UA.**

64		2d. on 5d. black and orange	1·00	85
65		2d. on 7½d. black and green	20·00	28·00
66		2d. on 10d. black and lake	14·00	50·00
67		2d. on 1s. black and brown	55·00	22·00
68a		2d. on 2s. black and blue	11·00	5·00
69		2d. on 2s.6d. purple	32·00	6·50
70a		2d. on 5s. black and red	3·25	2·50

1938. 20th Anniv of Queen Salote's Accession. Dated "1918–1938" at foot.

71	**29**	1d. black and red	1·00	4·00
72		2d. black and purple	9·50	3·50
73		2½d. black and blue	9·50	3·75

1944. Silver Jubilee of Queen Salote's Accession. Tablet at foot dated "1918–1943".

83	**29**	1d. black and red	15	1·25
84		2d. black and violet	15	1·25
85		3d. black and green	15	1·25
86		6d. black and orange	1·00	2·00
87		1s. black and brown	75	2·00

1949. 75th Anniv of U.P.U. As T **33d/g** of St. Helena.

88		2½d. blue	20	1·00
89		3d. olive	1·60	3·25
90		6d. red	20	50
91		1s. brown	25	50

31 Queen Salote **32** Queen Salote

1950. 50th Birthday of Queen Salote.

92	**31**	1d. red	70	2·25
93	**32**	5d. green	70	2·50
94	–	1s. violet	70	2·75

DESIGN—VERT: 1s. Half-length portrait of Queen.

34 Map **35** Palace, Nuku'alofa

1951. 50th Anniv of Treaty of Friendship with Great Britain.

95	**34**	½d. green	20	2·75
96	**35**	1d. black and red	15	2·75
97	–	2½d. green and brown	30	2·75
98	–	3d. yellow and blue	2·50	3·00
99	–	5d. red and green	1·75	1·00
100	–	1s. orange and violet	1·40	1·25

DESIGNS—HORIZ: 2½d. Beach scene; 5d. Flag and island; 1s. Arms of Tonga and Great Britain. VERT: 3d. H.M.N.Z.S. "Bellona".

40 Royal Palace, Nuku'alofa

1953.

101	**40**	1d. black and brown	10	10
102	–	1½d. blue and green	20	10
103	–	2d. turquoise and black	1·00	20
104	–	3d. blue and green	1·75	20
105	–	3½d. yellow and red	1·00	70
106	–	4d. yellow and red	2·25	10
107	–	5d. blue and brown	60	10
108	–	6d. black and blue	1·00	30
109	–	8d. green and violet	1·50	40
110	–	1s. blue and black	1·00	10
111	–	2s. green and brown	8·00	60
112	–	5s. yellow and lilac	25·00	9·50
113	–	10s. yellow and black	8·00	9·50
114	–	£1 yellow, red and blue	8·00	6·50

DESIGNS—HORIZ: 1½d. Shore fishing with throw-net; 2d. "Hifofua" and "Aoniu" (ketches); 3½d. Map of Tongatapu; 4d. Vava'u Harbour; 5d. Post Office, Nuku'alofa; 6d. Aerodrome, Fua'amotu; 8d. "Matua" (inter-island freighter) at Nuku'alofa Wharf; 2s. Lifuka, Ha'apai; 5s. Mutiny on the "Bounty". VERT: 3d. Swallows' Cave, Vava'u; 1s. Map of Tonga Islands; 10s. Queen Salote; £1 Arms of Tonga.

54 Stamp of 1886

1961. 75th Anniv of Tongan Postal Service.

115	**54**	1d. red and orange	10	10
116	–	2d. blue	1·25	45
117	–	4d. turquoise	20	45
118	–	5d. violet	1·25	45
119	–	1s. brown	1·25	45

DESIGNS: 2d. Whaling ship and whaleboat; 4d. Queen Salote and Post Office, Nuku'alofa; 5d. "Aoniu II" (inter-island freighter); 1s. Douglas DC-4 mail plane over Tongatapu.

1962. Centenary of Emancipation. Stamps of 1953 and No. 117 optd **1862 TAU'ATAINA EMANCIPATION 1962** or surch also.

120		1d. black and brown	10	1·00
121		4d. turquoise (No. 117)	10	90
122		5d. blue and brown	15	90
123		6d. black and blue	20	1·25
124		8d. green and violet	40	1·75
125		1s. blue and black	20	1·00
126		2s. on 3d. blue and green	40	4·00
127		5s. yellow and lilac	5·50	4·00

60 "Protein Foods"

1963. Freedom from Hunger.
128 **60** 11d. blue 50 15

61 Coat of Arms

1963. First Polynesian Gold Coinage Commem. Circular designs backed with paper, inscr overall "TONGA THE FRIENDLY ISLANDS". Imperf.

(a) Postage ¼ koula coin. Diameter 1⅝ in.
129 **61** 1d. red on gold 10 10
130 A 2d. blue on gold 10 10
131 **61** 6d. green on gold 15 15
132 A 9d. purple on gold 15 15
133 **61** 1s.6d. violet on gold . . . 30 30
134 A 2s. green on gold 40 40

(b) Air (i) ½ koula coin. Diameter 2⅛ in.
135 B 10d. red on gold 20 20
136 **61** 2s.4d. green on gold . . . 30 30
137 B 1s.1d. blue on gold 30 30

(ii) 1 koula coin. Diameter 3⅛ in.
138 B 2s.1d. purple on gold . . . 45 45
139 **61** 2s.4d. green on gold . . . 50 50
140 B 2s.9d. violet on gold . . . 50 50
DESIGNS: A, Queen Salote (head); B. Queen Salote (full length).

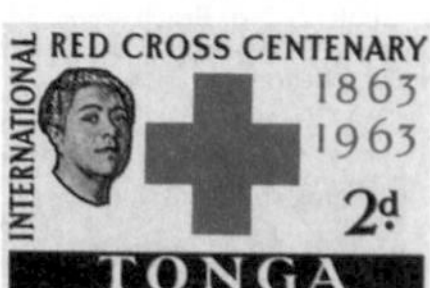

64 Red Cross Emblem

1963. Centenary of Red Cross.
141 **64** 2d. red and black 15 10
142 11d. red and blue . . . . 35 1·50

65 Queen Salote

66 Map of Tongatapu (⅗-size illustration)

1964. Pan-Pacific South-East Asia Women's Assn Meeting, Nuku'alofa. T **65/66** backed with paper inscr overall "TONGA THE FRIENDLY ISLANDS". Imperf.
143 **65** 3d. pink (postage) 15 25
144 9d. blue 20 30
145 2s. green 35 45
146 3s. lilac . . . . 65 1·00

147 **66** 10d. turquoise (air) 20 25
148 1s.2d. black 30 45
149 3s.6d. red . . . . 50 1·00
150 6s.6d. violet . . . . 85 1·75

1965. "Gold Coin" stamps of 1963 surch and with star over old value.
151 **61** 1s.3d. on 1s.6d. (postage) 25 25
152 A 1s.9d. on 9d. 25 25
153 **61** 2s.6d. on 6d. 30 50
154 5s. on 1d. . . . . 16·00 18·00
155 A 5s. on 2d. . . . . 2·75 3·75
156 5s. on 2s. . . . . 70 1·00

157 B 2s.3d. on 10d. (air) 25 40
158 **61** 2s.9d. on 11d. 30 55
159 B 4s.6d. on 2s.1d. . . . . . 13·00 14·00
160 **61** 4s.6d. on 2s.4d. . . . . . 13·00 14·00
161 B 4s.6d. on 2s.9d. . . . . . 7·50 8·50

1966. Centenary of Tupou College and Secondary Education. Nos. 115/16 and 118/19 optd or surch **1866-1966 TUPOU COLLEGE & SECONDARY EDUCATION**.
162 **54** 1d. red and orange (postage) 10 10
163 3d. on 1d. red and orange 10 10
164 – 6d. on 2d. blue 15 10
165 – 1s.2d. on 2d. blue 25 10
166 – 2s. on 2d. blue 45 10
167 – 3s. on 2d. blue 45 15

As above opt but with additional **AIRMAIL** and **CENTENARY**.
168 – 5d. violet (air) 15 10
169 **54** 10d. on 1d. red and brown 15 10
170 – 1s. brown 40 10
171 – 2s.9d. on 2d. blue 50 15
172 – 3s.6d. on 5d. violet 55 15
173 – 4s.6d. on 1s. brown . . . 85 15

1966. Queen Salote Commemoration. Nos. 143/4 and 147/8 optd. **IN MEMORIAM QUEEN SALOTE 1900+1965** (postage) or **1900 1965+** and laurel spray (air) or surch also. Inscr and new figures of value in first colour and obliterating shapes in second colour given.
174 **65** 3d. (silver & blue) (postage) 20 10
175 5d. on 9d. (silver and black) 25 10
176 9d. (silver and black) . . . 40 15
177 1s.7d. on 3d. (silver and blue) . . . . 1·00 80
178 3s.6d. on 9d. (silver & blk) 1·25 1·00
179 6s.6d. on 3d. (silver and blue) . . . . 1·75 2·25

180 **66** 10d. (silver and black) (air) 40 10
181 1s.2d. (black and gold) . . 50 30
182 4s. on 10d. (silver and black) . . . . 1·50 1·10
183 5s.6d. on 1s.2d. (black and gold) . . . . 1·75 2·00
184 10s.6d. on 1s.2d. (gold and black) . . . . 2·25 2·75

1967. Various stamps surch **SENITI** or **Seniti** and value. (a) Postage.
185 1s. on 1d. (No. 101) 10 10
229 2s. on 4d. (No. 106) 10 20
230 3s. on 3d. (No. 104) 10 20
187 3s. on 5d. (No. 107) 10 10
231 4s. on 5d. (No. 107) 10 20
232 5s. on 2d. (No. 108) 10 20
189 5s. on 3½d. (No. 105) . . . 10 10
233 6s. on 6d. (No. 108) 10 20
190 6s. on 8d. (No. 109) 30 10
191 7s. on 1½d. (No. 102) . . . 10 10
192 8s. on 6d. (No. 108) 30 10
235 8s. on 8d. (No. 109) 10 25
193 9s. on 3d. (No. 104) 15 15
236 9s. on 3½d. (No. 105) . . . 20 30
194 10s. on 1s. (No. 110) 15 15
195 11s. on 3d. on 1d. (No. 163) 30 20
238 20s. on 5s. (No. 112) . . . . 1·75 70
196 21s. on 3s. on 2d. (No. 167) 25 35
197 23s. on 1d. (No. 101) . . . 25 35
198 30s. on 2s. (No. 111)* . . . 2·25 2·50
199 30s. on 2s. (No. 111)* . . . 2·50 3·00
200 50s. on 6d. (No. 108) . . . 1·25 1·75
201 60s. on 2d. (No. 103) . . . 1·50 2·00
239 2p. on 2s. (No. 111) . . . . 1·50 3·00
*No. 198 has the surcharged value expressed horizontally; No. 199 has the figures "30" above and below "SENITI".

(b) Air. Surch with **AIRMAIL** added.
240 11s. on 10s. (No. 113) . . . 25 30
241 21s. on 10s. (No. 113) . . . 40 50
242 23s. on 10s. (No. 113) . . . 40 50

74 Coat of Arms (reverse)

1967. Coronation of King Taufa'ahau IV. Circular designs backed with paper inscr overall "TONGA, THE FRIENDLY ISLANDS" etc. Imperf.
202 **74** 1s. orange & bl (b) (post) 10 10
203 A 2s. blue and mauve (c) . . 10 10
204 **74** 4s. green and purple (d) . . 15 10
205 A 15s. turquoise & vio (e) . . 40 25
206 **74** 28s. black and purple (a) 1·00 60
207 A 50s. red and blue (c) . . . 1·75 1·75
208 **74** 1p. blue and red (f) . . . . 2·50 3·00

209 A 7s. red and black (b) (air) 20 10
210 **74** 9s. purple and green (c) . . 30 10
211 A 11s. blue and orange (d) 35 15
212 **74** 21s. black and green (e) . . 65 30
213 A 23s. purple and green (a) 75 45
214 **74** 29s. blue and green (c) . . 1·00 60
215 A 2p. purple and orange (f) 3·50 4·25
DESIGN: A, King Taufa'ahau IV (obverse).

Sizes: (a) Diameter 1½in.; (b) Diameter $1\frac{7}{10}$ in.; (c) Diameter 2in.; (d) Diameter $2\frac{3}{10}$ in.; (e) Diameter $2\frac{7}{10}$ in.; (f) Diameter $2\frac{9}{10}$ in.
The commemorative coins depicted in reverse (Type **74**) are inscribed in various denominations as follows: 1s. "20 SENTIT"; 4s. "PA'ANGA"; 9s. "50 SENITI"; 21s. "TWO PA'ANGA"; 28s. "QUARTER HAU"; 29s. "HALF HAU"; 1p. "HAU".

1967. Arrival of U.S. Peace Corps in Tonga. As Nos. 101/13 but imperf in different colours and surch **The Friendly Islands welcome the United States Peace Corps** and new value (or **S** only).
216 1s. on 1d. black and yellow (postage) 10 10
217 2s. on 2d. blue and red . . . 10 10
218 3s. on 3d. brown and yellow 10 10
219 4s. on 4d. violet and yellow 10 10
220 5s. on 5d. green and yellow 10 10
221 10s. on 1s. red and yellow . . 10 10
222 20s. on 2s. red and blue . . 30 15
223 50s. on 5s. sepia and yellow 2·75 1·25
224 1p. on 10s. yellow . . . . . 70 1·50

225 11s. on 3½d. blue (air) . . . 15 10
226 21s. on 1½d. green 30 20
227 23s. on 3½d. blue 30 20

1968. 50th Birthday of King Taufa'ahua IV. Nos. 202/15 optd **H.M'S BIRTHDAY 4 JULY 1968**.
243 **74** 1s. orange and blue (postage) 10 20
244 A 2s. blue and mauve 20 20
245 **74** 4s. green and purple . . . 30 20
246 A 15s. turquoise and violet 1·00 25
247 **74** 28s. black and purple . . . 1·75 30
248 A 50s. red and blue . . . . . 2·50 1·40
249 **74** 1p. blue and red . . . . . 5·00 4·50

250 A 7s. red and black (air) . . 40 20
251 **74** 9s. purple and green . . . 45 20
252 A 11s. blue and orange . . . 65 20
253 **74** 21s. black and green . . . 1·50 25
254 A 23s. purple and green . . . 1·50 25
255 **74** 29s. blue and green . . . . 1·75 35
256 A 2p. purple and orange . . 8·50 8·50

1968. South Pacific Games Field and Track Trials, Port Moresby, New Guinea. As Nos. 101/13 surch **Friendly Islands Field & Track Trials South Pacific Games Port Moresby 1969** and value.
257 5s. on 5d. green & yell (post) 10 15
258 10s. on 1s. red and yellow . . 10 15
259 15s. on 2s. red and blue . . . 15 20
260 25s. on 2d. blue and red . . 20 25
261 50s. on 1d. black and yellow 35 55
262 75s. on 10s. orange and yellow . . . . 60 1·25

263 6s. on 6d. black & yellow (air) 10 15
264 7s. on 4d. violet and yellow 10 15
265 8s. on 8d. black and yellow 10 15
266 9s. on 1½d. green 10 15
267 11s. on 3d. brown and yellow 15 15
268 21s. on 3½d. blue 20 20
269 38s. on 5s. sepia and yellow 2·25 1·00
270 1p. on 10s. yellow . . . . . 70 1·50

1969. Emergency Provisionals. Various stamps (Nos. 273/6 are imperf and in different colours) surch. (a) Postage.
271 1s. on 1s.2d. blue (No. 165) 1·75 2·75
272 1s. on 2s. on 3d. blue (No. 166) . . . . 1·75 2·75
273 1s. on 6d. blk & yell (No. 108) 60 70
274 2s. on 3½d. blue (No. 105) . . 65 70
275 3s. on 1½d. green (No. 102) 65 70
276 4s. on 8d. blk & yell (No. 109) . . . . 90 1·00

(b) Air. Nos. 171/3 surch.
277 1s. on 2s.9d. on 2d. blue . . 1·75 2·75
278 1s. on 3s.6d. on 5d. violet . . 1·75 2·75
279 1s. on 4s.6d. on 1s. brown . . 1·75 2·75

83 Banana

1969. Coil stamps. Self-adhesive.
280 **83** 1s. red, black and yellow 1·25 1·50
281 2s. green, black and yellow 1·40 1·60
282 3s. violet, black and yellow 1·50 1·75
283 4s. blue, black and yellow 1·60 2·00
284 5s. green, black and yellow 1·75 2·00
See also Nos. 325/9, 413/17, 657/89, O45/9, O82/6 and O169/83.

84 Putting the Shot

1969. 3rd South Pacific Games, Port Moresby. Imperf. Self-adhesive.
285 **84** 1s. black, red & buff (postage) 10 15
286 3s. green, red and buff . . 10 15
287 6s. blue, red and buff . . . 10 15
288 10s. violet, red and buff . . 15 15
289 30s. blue, red and buff . . 30 30

290 – 9s. black, vio & orge (air) 15 15
291 – 11s. black, blue and orange 15 15
292 – 20s. black, green and orange 25 25
293 – 60s. black, red and orange 75 1·25
294 – 1p. black, green and orange . . . . 1·10 2·00
DESIGN: Nos. 290/4, Boxing.

86 Oil Derrick and Map

1969. 1st Oil Search in Tonga. Imperf. Self-adhesive.
295 **86** 3s. multicoloured (postage) 15 15
296 7s. multicoloured 20 20
297 20s. multicoloured 50 50
298 25s. multicoloured 55 50
299 35s. multicoloured 80 80

300 – 9s. multicoloured (air) . . 30 25
301 – 10s. multicoloured 30 25
302 – 24s. multicoloured 60 50
303 – 29s. multicoloured 70 70
304 – 38s. multicoloured 80 80
DESIGN: Nos. 300/4, Oil derrick and island of Tongatapu.

87 Members of the British and Tongan Royal Families

1970. Royal Visit. Imperf. Self-adhesive.
305 **87** 3s. multicoloured (postage) 30 15
306 5s. multicoloured 35 15
307 10s. multicoloured 50 30
308 25s. multicoloured . . . . 1·50 65
309 50s. multicoloured . . . . 2·50 2·00

310 – 7s. multicoloured (air) . . 50 20
311 – 9s. multicoloured 55 30
312 – 24s. multicoloured . . . . 1·50 65
313 – 29s. multicoloured . . . . 1·75 70
314 – 38s. multicoloured . . . . 2·00 90
DESIGN: Nos. 310/14, Queen Elizabeth II and King Taufa'aha Tupou IV.

89 Book, Tongan Rulers and Flag (⅗-size illustration)

1970. Entry into British Commonwealth. Imperf. Self-adhesive.
315 **89** 3s. multicoloured (postage) 20 15
316 7s. multicoloured 30 20
317 15s. multicoloured 55 30
318 25s. multicoloured 70 40
319 50s. multicoloured . . . . 1·25 1·50

320 – 9s. blue, gold and red (air) 20 20
321 – 10s. purple, gold and blue 20 20
322 – 24s. yellow, gold and green 50 30
323 – 29s. blue, gold and red . . 55 30
324 – 38s. yellow, gold and green 70 55
DESIGN—"Star" shaped (size 44×51 mm): Nos. 320/4, Star and King Taufa'ahua Tupou IV.

90 Coconut

1970. Coil stamps. Imperf. Self-adhesive. (a) As T **83** but colours changed.

325 **83** 1s. yellow, purple and black . . . . 65 1·00
326 2s. yellow, blue and black 75 1·00
327 3s. yellow, brown and black . . . . 75 1·00
328 4s. yellow, green and black 75 1·00
329 5s. yellow, red and black 80 1·00

(b) Multicoloured; colour of face values given.

330 **90** 6s. red . . . . 90 1·25
331 7s. purple . . . . 95 1·25
332 8s. violet . . . . 1·10 1·25
333 9s. green . . . . 1·25 1·25
334 10s. orange . . . . 1·25 1·25

91 "Red Cross"

1970. Centenary of British Red Cross. Imperf. Self-adhesive.

335 **91** 3s. red, black and green (postage) 10 20
336 7s. red, black and blue . . 15 20
337 15s. red, black and purple 40 60
338 25s. red, black and blue . . 70 90
339 75s. red, black and brown 4·50 5·00

340 – 9s. red and turquoise (air) 20 20
341 – 10s. red and purple 20 20
342 – 18s. red and green 50 60
343 – 38s. red and blue . . . . . 2·25 2·25
344 – 1p. red and silver . . . . 5·50 7·50

DESIGN—As Type **91**: Nos. 340/4, As Nos. 335/9 but with inscription rearranged and coat of arms omitted.

1971. 5th Death Anniv of Queen Salote. Nos. 174/80, 182/4 with part of old surch obliterated and further surch **1965 1970** and value. On air values the surch includes two laurel leaves.

345 **65** 2s. on 5d. on 9d. (postage) 20 20
346 3s. on 9d. 20 20
347 5s. on 3d. 30 20
348 15s. on 3s.6d. on 9d. . . . 1·00 35
349 25s. on 6s.6d. on 3d. . . . 1·75 80
350 50s. on 1s.7d. on 3d. . . . 2·75 2·00

351 **66** 9s. on 10d. (air) 75 20
352 24s. on 4s. on 10d . . . . 1·75 75
353 29s. on 5s.6d. on 1s.2d. 2·00 1·00
354 38s. on 10s.6d. on 1s.2d. 2·50 1·50

1971. "Philatokyo '71" Stamp Exhibition, Japan. As Nos. 101 etc but imperf with colours changed and surch **PHILATOKYO '71**, emblem and value or **HONOURING JAPANESE POSTAL CENTENARY 1871-1971** (Nos. 357, 362, 364). Nos. 360/4 also surch **AIRMAIL**.

355 3s. on 8d. blk & yell (postage) 10 10
356 7s. on 4d. violet and yellow 15 10
357 15s. on 1s. red and yellow . . 30 20
358 25s. on 1d. black and yellow 40 30
359 75s. on 2s. red and blue . . . 1·75 1·75

360 9s. on 1½d. green (air) . . . 15 10
361 10s. on 4d. violet and yellow 15 10
362 18s. on 1s. red and yellow . . 35 25
363 38s. on 1d. black and yellow 70 50
364 1p. on 2s. red and blue . . . 1·75 2·00

96 Wristwatch

1971. Air. Imperf. Self-adhesive.

365 **96** 14s. multicoloured . . . . 2·25 2·50
365a 17s. multicoloured . . . . 2·50 2·75
366 21s. multicoloured . . . . 2·50 2·75
366a 38s. multicoloured . . . . 3·50 3·75

See also Nos. O65/6a.

97 Pole-vaulter **98** Medal of Merit (reverse)

1971. 4th South Pacific Games, Tahiti. Imperf. Self-adhesive.

367 **97** 3s. multicoloured (postage) 10 10
368 7s. multicoloured 10 10
369 15s. multicoloured 20 20
370 25s. multicoloured 30 35
371 50s. multicoloured 60 90

372 – 9s. multicoloured (air) . . 10 10
373 – 10s. multicoloured 10 10
374 – 24s. multicoloured 30 35
375 – 29s. multicoloured 40 50
376 – 38s. multicoloured 55 70

DESIGN—HORIZ: Nos. 372/6, High-jumper.

1971. Investiture of Royal Tongan Medal of Merit. Multicoloured, colour of medal given. Imperf. Self-adhesive.

377 **98** 3s. gold (postage) 10 10
378 24s. silver 35 25
379 – 38s. brown 60 50

380 – 10s. gold (air) 20 15
381 – 75s. silver . . . . 1·10 1·25
382 **98** 1p. brown . . . . 1·40 1·60

DESIGN—As Type **98**: Nos. 379/81, Obverse of the Medal of Merit.

99 Child

1971. 25th Anniv of UNICEF. Imperf. Self-adhesive.

383 **99** 2s. multicoloured (postage) 10 10
384 4s. multicoloured 10 10
385 8s. multicoloured 10 10
386 16s. multicoloured 25 25
387 30s. multicoloured 45 45

388 – 10s. multicoloured (air) . . 15 15
389 – 15s. multicoloured 25 25
390 – 25s. multicoloured 40 40
391 – 50s. multicoloured . . . . 85 1·00
392 – 1p. multicoloured . . . . 1·75 2·00

DESIGN—VERT (21 × 42 mm): Nos. 388/92, Woman.

100 Map of South Pacific, and "Olovaha"

1972. Merchant Marine Routes. Imperf. Self-adhesive.

393 **100** 2s. multicoloured (postage) 30 40
394 10s. multicoloured 60 30
395 17s. multicoloured 90 30
396 21s. multicoloured . . . . 1·00 40
397 60s. multicoloured . . . . 4·25 3·50

398 – 9s. multicoloured (air) . . 60 30
399 – 12s. multicoloured 75 30
400 – 14s. multicoloured 85 30
401 – 75s. multicoloured . . . . 4·50 4·00
402 – 90s. multicoloured . . . . 4·75 5·50

DESIGN: Nos. 398/402, Map of South Pacific, and "Niuvakai".

101 ¼ Hau Coronation Coin

1972. 5th Anniv of Coronation. Imperf. Self-adhesive.

403 **101** 5s. multicoloured (postage) 10 10
404 7s. multicoloured 10 10
405 10s. multicoloured 15 15
406 17s. multicoloured 30 20
407 60s. multicoloured . . . . 1·00 85

408 – 9s. multicoloured (air) . . 15 15
409 – 12s. multicoloured 20 15
410 – 14s. multicoloured 25 20
411 – 21s. multicoloured 35 20
412 – 75s. multicoloured . . . . 1·25 85

DESIGNS—(47 × 41 mm): Nos. 408/12, As T **101** but with coins above inscription instead of beneath it.

102 Water Melon

1972. Imperf. Self-adhesive. (a) As T **83** but inscription altered omitting "Best in the Pacific", and colours changed.

413 **83** 1s. yellow, red and black 60 30
414 2s. yellow, blue and black 65 30
415 3s. yellow, green and black 70 30
416 4s. yellow, blue and black 70 30
417 5s. yellow, brown and black 70 30

(b) As T **90** but colours changed. Multicoloured. Colour of face value given.

418 **90** 6s. orange 80 35
419 7s. blue 85 35
420 8s. purple 85 35
421 9s. orange 85 35
422 10s. blue 90 35

(c) Type **102**. Multicoloured. Colour of face value given.

423 **102** 15s. blue . . . . 1·75 55
424 20s. orange . . . . 2·00 75
425 25s. brown . . . . 2·25 85
426 40s. orange . . . . 3·50 1·75
427 50s. lemon . . . . 3·50 2·00

1972. Inauguration of Internal Airmail. No. 398 surch **7s NOVEMBER 1972 INAUGURAL Internal Airmail Nuku'alofa – Vava'u**.

428 7s. on 9s. multicoloured . . . 1·00 2·50

104 Hoisting Tongan Flag

1972. Proclamation of Sovereignty over Minerva Reefs. Imperf. Self-adhesive.

429 **104** 5s. multicoloured (postage) 10 10
430 7s. multicoloured 10 10
431 10s. multicoloured 15 15
432 15s. multicoloured 25 20
433 40s. multicoloured 80 55

434 – 9s. multicoloured (air) . . 15 15
435 – 12s. multicoloured 20 15
436 – 14s. multicoloured 25 15
437 – 38s. multicoloured 75 55
438 – 1p. multicoloured . . . . 2·00 2·50

DESIGN—SPHERICAL (52 mm diameter): Nos. 434/8, Proclamation in Govt Gazette.

105 Coins around Bank

1973. Foundation of Bank of Tonga. Imperf. Self-adhesive.

439 **105** 5s. multicoloured (postage) 15 15
440 7s. multicoloured 15 15
441 10s. multicoloured 20 15
442 20s. multicoloured 50 30
443 30s. multicoloured 75 40

444 – 9s. multicoloured (air) . . 25 15
445 – 12s. multicoloured 25 15
446 – 17s. multicoloured 45 20
447 – 50s. multicoloured . . . . 1·50 1·50
448 – 90s. multicoloured . . . . 2·75 3·25

DESIGN—HORIZ (64 × 52 mm): Nos. 444/8, Bank and banknotes.

106 Handshake and Scout in Outrigger Canoe

1973. Silver Jubilee of Scouting in Tonga. Imperf. Self-adhesive.

449 **106** 5s. multicoloured (postage) 20 10
450 7s. multicoloured 30 15
451 15s. multicoloured 95 40
452 21s. multicoloured . . . . 1·25 50
453 50s. multicoloured . . . . 4·50 2·25

454 – 9s. multicoloured (air) . . 50 20
455 – 12s. multicoloured 60 30
456 – 14s. multicoloured 85 50
457 – 17s. multicoloured 95 60
458 – 1p. multicoloured . . . . 10·00 6·50

DESIGN—SQUARE (53 × 53 mm): Nos. 454/8, Scout badge.

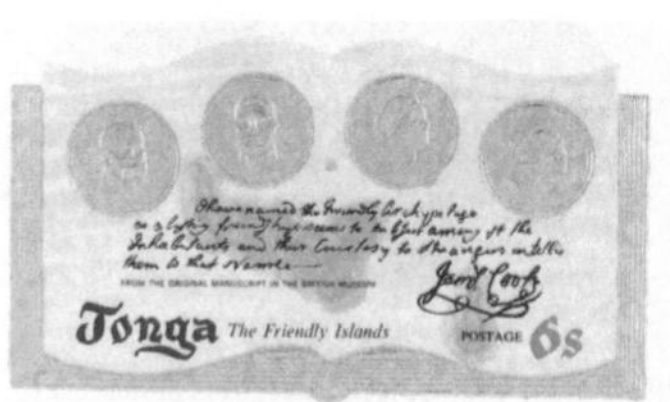

107 Excerpt from Cook's Log-book (⅗-size illustration)

1973. Bicentenary of Capt. Cook's Visit to Tonga. Imperf. Self-adhesive.

459 **107** 6s. multicoloured (postage) 40 30
460 8s. multicoloured 40 35
461 11s. multicoloured 60 40
462 35s. multicoloured . . . . 4·00 2·25
463 40s. multicoloured . . . . 4·00 2·50

464 – 9s. multicoloured (air) . . 70 30
465 – 14s. multicoloured . . . . 1·25 50
466 – 29s. multicoloured . . . . 4·00 2·00
467 – 38s. multicoloured . . . . 4·50 2·50
468 – 75s. multicoloured . . . . 8·50 4·50

DESIGN—VERT: Nos. 464/8, H.M.S. "Resolution".

1973. Commonwealth Games, Christchurch. Various stamps surch **Commonwealth Games CHRISTCHURCH 1974** and No. 474 optd **AIRMAIL** in addition.

469 **97** 5s. on 50s. multicoloured (No. 371) (postage) . . . 15 10
470 – 12s. on 38s. mult (No. 379) 30 15
471 – 14s. on 75s. mult (No. 381) 30 15
472 **98** 20s. on 1p. mult (No. 382) 50 30
473 50s. on 24s. mult (No. 378) 1·00 1·00

474 **97** 7s. on 25s. mult (No. 370) (air) 15 10
475 – 9s. on 38s. mult (No. 376) 20 10
476 – 24s. mult (No. 374) 60 30
477 – 29s. on 9s. mult (No. 374) 70 40
478 – 40s. on 14s. mult (No. 456) 85 90

109 Red Shining Parrot

1974. Air. Imperf. Self-adhesive.
479 **109** 7s. multicoloured 95 65
480 9s. multicoloured . . . . 1·10 75
481 12s. multicoloured . . . . 1·25 75
482 14s. multicoloured . . . . 1·40 75
483 17s. multicoloured . . . . 1·50 1·00
484 29s. multicoloured . . . . 2·50 1·40
485 38s. multicoloured . . . . 3·00 1·50
486 50s. multicoloured . . . . 3·50 5·00
487 75s. multicoloured . . . . 4·75 8·50
For 25s. value in smaller design, 27 × 36 mm, see No. 1284.

110 "Stamped Letter"

1974. Centenary of U.P.U. Imperf. Self-adhesive.
488 **110** 5s. multicoloured (postage) 10 30
489 10s. multicoloured 15 30
490 15s. multicoloured 25 40
491 20s. multicoloured 30 40
492 50s. multicoloured . . . . 1·00 1·60
493 – 14s. multicoloured (air) 25 30
494 – 21s. multicoloured 35 40
495 – 60s. multicoloured . . . . 1·10 1·75
496 – 75s. multicoloured . . . . 1·25 2·25
497 – 1p. multicoloured . . . . 1·50 2·50
DESIGN—HORIZ: Nos. 493/7, Carrier pigeon scattering letters over Tonga.

111 Girl Guides Badges

1974. Tongan Girl Guides. Imperf. Self-adhesive.
498 **111** 5s. multicoloured (postage) 40 30
499 10s. multicoloured 60 30
500 20s. multicoloured . . . . 1·50 65
501 40s. multicoloured . . . . 3·25 1·75
502 60s. multicoloured . . . . 4·00 2·75
503 – 14s. multicoloured (air) 1·00 45
504 – 16s. multicoloured . . . . 1·00 45
505 – 29s. multicoloured . . . . 2·00 1·00
506 – 31s. multicoloured . . . . 2·25 1·25
507 – 75s. multicoloured . . . . 5·50 3·50
DESIGN—VERT: Nos. 503/7, Girl Guide leaders.

112 H.M.S. "Resolution"

1974. Establishment of Royal Marine Institute. Imperf. Self-adhesive.
508 **112** 5s. multicoloured (postage) . . . . 1·25 50
509 10s. multicoloured . . . . 1·40 50
510 25s. multicoloured . . . . 2·75 80
511 50s. multicoloured . . . . 4·00 3·00
512 75s. multicoloured . . . . 5·50 4·50
513 – 9s. multicoloured (air) . . 1·25 30
514 – 14s. multicoloured . . . . 1·75 55
515 – 17s. multicoloured . . . . 2·00 60
516 – 60s. multicoloured . . . . 4·25 3·75
517 – 90s. multicoloured . . . . 6·00 5·50
DESIGN—HORIZ (53 × 47 mm): Nos. 513/17, "James Cook" (bulk carrier).

113 Dateline Hotel, Nuku'alofa

1975. South Pacific Forum and Tourism. Imperf. Self-adhesive.
518 **113** 5s. multicoloured (postage) 10 10
519 10s. multicoloured 10 10
520 15s. multicoloured 20 20
521 30s. multicoloured 45 45
522 1p. multicoloured . . . . 1·60 2·00
523 **113** 9s. multicoloured (air) . . 10 10
524 – 12s. multicoloured 15 15
525 – 14s. multicoloured 20 20
526 – 17s. multicoloured 20 20
527 – 38s. multicoloured 55 65
DESIGNS—(46 × 60 mm): 9, 12, 14s. Beach; 17, 38s. Surf and sea.

114 Boxing

1975. 5th South Pacific Games, Guam. Imperf. Self-adhesive.
528 **114** 5s. multicoloured (postage) 15 20
529 10s. multicoloured 20 20
530 20s. multicoloured 30 35
531 25s. multicoloured 35 50
532 65s. multicoloured . . . . 80 1·75
533 – 9s. multicoloured (air) . . 20 20
534 – 12s. multicoloured 25 20
535 – 14s. multicoloured 25 20
536 – 17s. multicoloured 30 25
537 – 90s. multicoloured . . . . 1·10 2·00
DESIGN—(37 × 43 mm): Nos. 533/7, Throwing the discus.

115 Commemorative Coin

1975. F.A.O. Commemoration. Imperf. Self-adhesive.
538 **115** 5s. multicoloured (postage) 15 10
539 – 20s. multicoloured 35 15
540 – 50s. blue, black and silver 75 35
541 – 1p. blue, black and silver 1·50 1·25
542 – 2p. black and silver . . . 2·50 2·25
543 – 12s. multicoloured (air) 30 15
544 – 14s. multicoloured 30 15
545 – 25s. red, black and silver 45 20
546 – 50s. purple, black & silver 70 50
547 – 1p. black and silver . . . 1·50 1·25
DESIGNS: Nos. 539/47 are as T **52** but showing different coins. Nos. 542 and 544 are horiz, size 75 × 42 mm.

116 Commemorative Coin

1975. Centenary of Tongan Constitution. Mult. Imperf. Self-adhesive.
548 5s. Type **116** (postage) . . . 30 25
549 10s. King George I 40 25
550 20s. King Taufa'ahau IV . . 75 40
551 50s. King George II . . . . 1·50 1·50
552 75s. Tongan arms . . . . . 2·25 2·50
553 9s. King Taufa'ahau IV (air) 40 25
554 12s. Queen Salote 45 30
555 14s. Tongan arms 45 30
556 38s. King Taufa'ahau IV . . 1·00 50
557 1p. Four monarchs . . . . . 2·50 3·00
SIZES: 60 × 40 mm, Nos. 549 and 551; 76 × 76 mm, Nos. 552 and 557; 57 × 56 mm, others.

117 Montreal Logo

1976. 1st Participation in Olympic Games. Imperf. Self-adhesive. (a) Type **117**.
558 5s. red, black & blue (postage) 75 35
559 10s. red, black and green . . 85 35
560 25s. red, black and brown . . 1·75 70
561 35s. red, black and mauve . . 2·25 75
562 70s. red, black and green . . 4·50 3·25

(b) Montreal logo optd on Nos. 500/1, 504 and 507.
563 **111** 12s. on 20s. mult (air) . . 1·50 45
564 – 14s. on 16s. multicoloured 1·50 45
565 – 16s. multicoloured . . . . 1·60 45
566 **111** 38s. on 40s. multicoloured 3·00 60
567 – 75s. multicoloured . . . . 5·50 3·50

118 Signatories of Declaration of Independence

1976. Bicentenary of American Revolution. Imperf. Self-adhesive.
568 **118** 9s. multicoloured (postage) 30 15
569 – 10s. multicoloured 30 15
570 – 15s. multicoloured 45 45
571 – 25s. multicoloured 60 70
572 – 75s. multicoloured . . . . 1·50 2·50
573 – 12s. multicoloured (air) 40 15
574 – 14s. multicoloured 40 20
575 – 17s. multicoloured 50 35
576 – 38s. multicoloured 70 75
577 – 1p. multicoloured . . . . 1·75 3·50
DESIGNS: Nos. 569/77 show the signatories to the Declaration of Independence.

119 Nathaniel Turner and John Thomas (Methodist missionaries)

1976. 150th Anniv of Christianity in Tonga. Imperf. Self-adhesive.
578 **119** 5s. multicoloured (postage) 35 25
579 10s. multicoloured 50 25
580 20s. multicoloured 70 40
581 25s. multicoloured 75 45
582 85s. multicoloured . . . . 2·75 3·75
583 – 9s. multicoloured (air) . . 65 40
584 – 12s. multicoloured 70 45
585 – 14s. multicoloured 80 55
586 – 17s. multicoloured . . . . 1·00 60
587 – 38s. multicoloured . . . . 2·25 1·10
DESIGN: Nos. 583/7 show missionary ship "Triton".

120 Emperor Wilhelm I and King George Tupou I

1976. Centenary of Treaty of Friendship with Germany. Imperf. Self-adhesive.
588 **120** 9s. multicoloured (postage) 20 20
589 15s. multicoloured 30 30
590 22s. multicoloured 40 45
591 50s. multicoloured . . . . 90 1·25
592 73s. multicoloured . . . . 1·40 1·90
593 – 11s. multicoloured (air) 25 25
594 – 17s. multicoloured 40 45
595 – 18s. multicoloured 40 45
596 – 31s. multicoloured 60 80
597 – 39s. multicoloured 70 90
DESIGNS—CIRCULAR (52 mm diameter): Nos. 593/7, Treaty signing.

121 Queen Salote and Coronation Procession

1977. Silver Jubilee. Imperf. Self-adhesive.
598 **121** 11s. mult (postage) . . . 40 30
599 20s. multicoloured 30 30
600 30s. multicoloured 30 30
601 50s. multicoloured 50 65
602 75s. multicoloured 65 85
603 – 15s. multicoloured (air) 30 25
604 – 17s. multicoloured 30 30
605 – 22s. multicoloured . . . . 3·00 1·25
606 – 31s. multicoloured 30 40
607 – 39s. multicoloured 30 40
DESIGN—SQUARE (59 × 59 mm): Nos. 603/7, Queen Elizabeth and King Taufa'ahau.

122 Tongan Coins

1977. 10th Anniv of King's Coronation. Imperf. Self-adhesive.
608 **122** 10s. mult (postage) . . . 20 20
609 15s. multicoloured 25 25
610 25s. multicoloured 35 45
611 50s. multicoloured 75 90
612 75s. multicoloured . . . . 1·00 1·50

613 – 11s. multicoloured (air) 25 20
614 – 17s. multicoloured 30 30
615 – 18s. multicoloured 30 30
616 – 39s. multicoloured 45 60
617 – 1p. multicoloured . . . . 1·50 2·25
DESIGN—OVAL (64 × 46 mm): Nos. 613/17, 1967 Coronation coin.

123 H.M.S. "Resolution"

1977. Bicentenary of Capt. Cook's Last Voyage. Imperf. Self-adhesive.
618 **123** 10s. mult (postage) . . . 1·75 75
619 17s. multicoloured . . . . 2·25 1·10
620 25s. multicoloured . . . . 3·75 2·00
621 30s. multicoloured . . . . 3·75 2·75
622 40s. multicoloured . . . . 4·50 4·50

623 – 15s. multicoloured (air) 1·75 1·25
624 – 22s. multicoloured . . . . 2·75 2·25
625 – 31s. multicoloured . . . . 3·25 2·75
626 – 50s. multicoloured . . . . 4·50 4·50
627 – 1p. multicoloured . . . . 8·00 8·50
DESIGN—52 × 46 mm: Nos. 623/7, Medal and extract from Cook's journal.

124 Humpback Whale

1977. Whale Conservation. Imperf. Self-adhesive.
628 **124** 15s. black, grey and blue (postage) . . . . 3·00 80
629 22s. black, grey and green 3·25 1·25
630 31s. black, grey and orange . . . . 3·75 1·75
631 38s. black, grey and lilac 4·00 2·25
632 64s. black, grey and brown . . . . 6·50 5·50

633 – 11s. multicoloured (air) 3·00 75
634 – 17s. multicoloured . . . . 3·25 90
635 – 18s. multicoloured . . . . 3·25 1·00
636 – 39s. multicoloured . . . . 4·50 2·25
637 – 50s. multicoloured . . . . 5·50 3·25
DESIGN—HEXAGONAL (66 × 51 mm): Nos. 633/7, Sei and fin whales.
For 60s. value as Type **124**, see No. 1282.

1978. Various stamps surch.
638 **115** 15s. on 5s. mult (postage) 1·50 1·75
639 **119** 15s. on 5s. multicoloured 1·50 1·75
640 **117** 15s. on 10s. red, blk & grn . . . . 1·50 1·75
641 **119** 15s. on 10s. multicoloured 1·50 1·75
642 **121** 15s. on 11s. multicoloured 1·50 2·75
643 **114** 15s. on 20s. multicoloured 1·50 1·75
644 – 15s. on 38s. multicoloured (No. O133) . . . . . . 1·50 1·75

645 – 17s. on 9s. multicoloured (No. 533) (air) . . . . 1·75 2·00
646 – 17s. on 9s. mult (No. 583) 1·75 2·00
647 – 17s. on 12s. mult (No. 534) . . . . . . 1·75 2·00
648 – 17s. on 12s. mult (No. 573) . . . . . . 1·75 2·00
649 – 17s. on 18s. mult (No. 595) . . . . . . 1·75 2·00
650 – 17s. on 38s. mult (No. 527) . . . . . . 1·75 2·00
651 – 17s. on 38s. mult (No. 556) . . . . . . 1·75 2·00
652 – 1p. on 35s. mult (No. O151) . . . . 20·00 27·00
653 – 1p. on 38s. mult (No. 576) 8·50 9·00
654 – 1p. on 75s. mult (No. 572) 8·50 9·00
The surcharges on Nos. 638/9 are formed by adding a "1" to the existing face value.

126 Flags of Canada and Tonga

1978. 11th Commonwealth Games, Edmonton. Imperf. Self-adhesive.
655 **126** 10s. blue, red and black (postage) 20 20
656 15s. multicoloured 30 30
657 20s. green, black and red 40 40
658 25s. red, blue and black 45 45
659 45s. black and red . . . . 1·10 1·25

660 – 17s. black and red (air) 40 30
661 – 35s. black, red and blue 70 65
662 – 38s. black, red and green 85 85
663 – 40s. black, red and green 90 90
664 – 65s. black, red and brown 1·60 2·00
DESIGN—LEAF-SHAPED (39 × 40 mm): Nos. 660/4, Maple leaf.

127 King Taufa'ahau Tupou IV

1978. 60th Birthday of King Taufa'ahau Tupou IV. Imperf. Self-adhesive.
665 **127** 2s. black, deep blue and blue (postage) 15 30
666 5s. black, blue and pink 15 30
667 10s. black, blue & mauve 25 25
668 25s. black, blue and grey 55 40
669 75s. black, blue and yellow . . . . 1·40 1·50

670 – 11s. black, bl & yell (air) 25 20
671 – 15s. black, blue and brown 35 25
672 – 17s. black, blue and lilac 40 25
673 – 39s. black, blue and green 80 55
674 – 1p. black, blue and pink 2·00 2·25
DESIGN—STAR SHAPED (44 × 51 mm): Nos. 670/4, Portrait of King.

128 Banana

1978. Coil stamps. Imperf. Self-adhesive.
675 **128** 1s. black and yellow . . 20 50
676 – 2s. blue and yellow . . . 20 50
677 – 3s. brown and yellow . . 30 50
678 – 4s. blue and yellow . . . 30 50
679 – 5s. red and yellow . . . 30 50
680 – 6s. purple, green & brown 40 50
681 – 7s. blue, green and brown 40 50
682 – 8s. red, green and brown 40 50
683 – 9s. mauve, green & brown 40 50
684 – 10s. green and brown . . 40 50
684a – 13s. mauve, green & brown . . . . 9·00 5·00
685 – 15s. green and brown . . 1·25 1·25
686 – 20s. brown and green . . 1·40 1·40
687 – 30s. mauve, brown & green . . . . 1·60 1·60
688 – 50s. black, brown & grn 2·00 2·00
689 – 1p. purple, brown & grn 2·50 3·00
689a – 2p. multicoloured . . . 13·00 14·00
689b – 3p. multicoloured . . . 14·00 15·00
DESIGNS—As Type **128**: 2s. to 5s. Bananas, the number shown coinciding with the face value. 18 × 26 mm: 6s. to 10s. Coconuts. 17 × 30 mm: 13s. to 1p. Pineapple. 55 × 29 mm: 2, 3p. Mixed fruit.
For 10s. value as Type **128** but in smaller size (21 × 9 mm), see No. 1281.

129 Humpback Whale

1978. Endangered Wildlife. Multicoloured. Self-adhesive.
690 15s. Type **129** (postage) . . . 3·50 1·75
691 18s. Insular flying fox . . . . 2·75 1·75
692 25s. Turtle . . . . 2·75 1·75
693 28s. Red shining parrot . . . 6·00 2·25
694 60s. Type **129** . . . . 8·50 6·50

695 17s. Type **129** (air) . . . . . 3·50 1·75
696 22s. As 18s. . . . . 2·75 1·75
697 31s. As 25s. . . . . 2·75 2·00
698 39s. As 28s. . . . . 6·50 3·00
699 45s. As Type **129** . . . . . 7·00 3·50

130 Metrication Symbol

1979. Decade of Progress. Self-adhesive.
700 **130** 5s. multicoloured (postage) 15 30
701 – 11s. multicoloured 60 30
702 – 18s. multicoloured 50 35
703 – 22s. multicoloured 50 30
704 – 50s. multicoloured . . . . 1·75 1·50

705 – 15s. multicoloured (air) 70 30
706 – 17s. multicoloured 70 30
707 – 31s. gold and blue 70 60
708 – 39s. multicoloured 75 65
709 – 1p. multicoloured . . . 3·00 3·50
DESIGNS—VERT (58 × 55 mm): 11, 17s. Map of South Pacific Islands; 22s. New churches; 50, 15s. Air routes; 39s. Government offices; 1p. Communications. TEAR DROP (35 × 52 mm): 18s. Building wall of progress with the assistance of United States Peace Corps. As Type **130**: 31s. Rotary International emblem.

131 Various Envelopes bearing Self-adhesive Stamps

1979. Death Centenary of Sir Rowland Hill and 10th Anniv of Tongan Self-adhesive Stamps. Self-adhesive.
710 **131** 5s. multicoloured (postage) 20 10
711 10s. multicoloured 30 15
712 25s. multicoloured 50 35
713 50s. multicoloured 85 60
714 1p. multicoloured . . . . 1·50 1·25

715 – 15s. multicoloured (air) 40 20
716 – 17s. multicoloured 45 25
717 – 18s. multicoloured 45 25
718 – 31s. multicoloured 60 40
719 – 39s. multicoloured 70 45
DESIGN—MULTI-ANGULAR (53 × 53 mm): 15s. to 39s. Self-adhesive stamps.

132

1979. Air. Coil stamps. Self-adhesive.
720 **132** 5s. black and blue . . . 40 70
721 11s. black and blue . . . 50 70
722 14s. black and violet . . 50 70
723 15s. black and mauve . . 55 70
724 17s. black and mauve . . 55 70
725 18s. black and red . . . 55 50
726 22s. black and red . . . 65 50
726a 29s. black and red . . . 12·00 5·00
727 31s. black and yellow . . 85 1·50
727a 32s. black and brown . . 13·00 5·50
728 39s. black and green . . 1·00 1·00
728a 47s. black and brown . . 13·00 6·50
729 75s. black and green . . 1·50 3·50
730 1p. black and green . . 2·00 4·50

133 Rain Forest, Island of 'Eua

1979. Views as seen through the Lens of a Camera. Self-adhesive.
731 **133** 10s. mult (postage) . . . 30 40
732 18s. multicoloured 30 40
733 31s. multicoloured 50 40
734 50s. multicoloured . . . . 70 1·40
735 60s. multicoloured . . . . 70 2·25

736 – 5s. multicoloured (air) . . 20 30
737 – 15s. multicoloured 30 30
738 – 17s. multicoloured 30 30
739 – 39s. multicoloured 60 60
740 – 75s. multicoloured . . . . 80 2·25
DESIGN: 5s. to 75s. Isle of Kao.

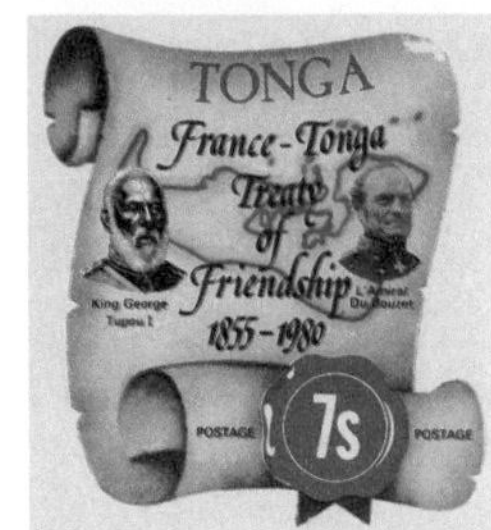

134 King Tupou I, Admiral Du Bouzet and Map of Tonga

1979. 125th Anniv of France–Tonga Treaty of Friendship. Self-adhesive.
741 **134** 7s. multicoloured (postage) 15 15
742 10s. multicoloured 20 20
743 14s. multicoloured 30 30
744 50s. multicoloured . . . . 1·00 1·25
745 75s. multicoloured . . . . 1·50 2·00

746 – 15s. multicoloured (air) 30 30
747 – 17s. multicoloured 35 35
748 – 22s. multicoloured 55 55
749 – 31s. multicoloured 70 90
750 – 39s. multicoloured . . . . 75 1·00
DESIGN: 15s. to 39s. King Tupou II, Napoleon III and "L'Aventure" (French warship).

1980. Olympic Games, Moscow. Nos. 710/19 surch or optd only (Nos. 753 and 755) **1980 OLYMPIC GAMES**, Olympic mascot and symbol.
751 **131** 13s. on 5s. multicoloured (postage) 35 35
752 – 20s. on 10s. multicoloured 55 55
753 – 25s. multicoloured 70 70
754 – 33s. on 50s. multicoloured 85 85
755 – 1p. multicoloured . . . . 3·25 3·50

756 – 9s. on 15s. multicoloured (air) 30 30
757 – 16s. on 17s. multicoloured 50 50
758 – 29s. on 18s. multicoloured 80 80
759 – 32s. on 31s. multicoloured 90 90
760 – 47s. on 39s. multicoloured 1·50 1·75

136 Scout at Campfire

1980. South Pacific Scout Jamboree, Tonga, and 75th Anniv of Rotary International. Self-adhesive.
761 **136** 9s. multicoloured (postage) 30 30
762 13s. multicoloured 40 30
763 15s. multicoloured 40 30
764 30s. multicoloured 75 60
765 – 29s. multicoloured (air) 75 45
766 – 32s. multicoloured 80 45
767 – 47s. multicoloured . . . . 1·10 70
768 – 1p. multicoloured . . . . 2·00 3·75
DESIGN: 29s. to 1p. Scout activities and Rotary emblem.

1980. Various stamps surch.
769 **117** 9s. on 35s. red, black and mauve (postage) 40 50
770 **119** 13s. on 20s. mult 55 80
771 13s. on 25s. mult 55 80
772 – 19s. on 25s. mult (No. 571) . . . . . . 75 1·25
773 **114** 1p. on 65s. mult . . . . 3·00 4·50
773a – 5p. on 25s. mult (No. O214) . . . . 12·00 15·00
773b – 5p. on 2p. mult (No. O215) . . . . 12·00 15·00
774 – 29s. on 14s. mult (No. 585) (air) . . . . 90 1·25
775 – 29s. on 39s. mult (No. 597) . . . . . . 90 1·25
776 – 32s. on 12s. mult (No. 554) . . . . . . 1·10 1·50
777 – 32s. on 14s. mult (No. 574) . . . . . . 1·10 1·50
778 – 47s. on 12s. mult (No. 524) . . . . . . 1·60 2·00
779 – 47s. on 12s. mult (No. 584) . . . . . . 1·60 2·00

138 Red Cross and Tongan Flags, with Map of Tonga

1981. International Year of Disabled Persons. Self-adhesive.
780 **138** 2p. multicoloured (postage) . . . . 2·00 1·25
781 3p. multicoloured . . . . 2·25 1·50
782 – 29s. multicoloured (air) 50 20
783 – 32s. multicoloured 60 25
784 – 47s. multicoloured 70 30
DESIGN: Nos. 782/4, Red Cross flag and map depicting Tongatapu and Eua.

139 Prince Charles and King Taufa'ahau Tupou IV

141 Landing Scene

140 Report of Printing in "Missionary Notices"

1981. Royal Wedding and Centenary of Treaty of Friendship between Tonga and Great Britain. Multicoloured. Self-adhesive.
785 13s. Type **139** 30 30
786 47s. Prince Charles and Lady Diana Spencer 60 30
787 1p.50 Prince Charles and Lady Diana (different) . . 1·00 1·60
788 3p. Prince and Princess of Wales after wedding ceremony . . . . 1·40 2·50

1981. Christmas. 150th Anniv of First Books Printed in Tonga. Multicoloured. Self-adhesive.
789 9s. Type **140** 25 35
790 13s. "Missionary Notice" report (different) 30 40
791 32s. Type in chase . . . . . 85 1·00
792 47s. Bible class . . . . 1·40 1·50

1981. Bicentenary of Maurelle's Discovery of Vava'u. Multicoloured. Self-adhesive.
793 9s. Type **141** 40 40
794 13s. Map of Vava'u 60 50
795 47s. "La Princesa" . . . . . 2·75 1·50
796 1p. "La Princesa" (different) 5·00 6·50
MS797 100 × 78 mm. As No. 796. Imperf . . . . 8·50 13·00
The stamp from No. **MS**797 is as No. 796 but without inscription at foot of design.

142 Battle Scene

1981. 175th Anniv of Capture of "Port au Prince" (ship). Each black and blue. Self-adhesive.
798 29s. Type **142** . . . . 1·25 50
799 32s. Battle scene (different) 1·25 55
800 47s. Map of the Ha'apai Group . . . . 1·75 1·40
801 47s. Native canoes preparing to attack . . . . 1·75 1·40
802 1p. "Port au Prince" . . . . 2·75 2·25

143 Baden-Powell at Brownsea Island, 1907

145 Ball Control

1982. 75th Anniv of Boy Scout Movement and 125th Birth Anniv of Lord Baden-Powell (founder). Multicoloured. Self-adhesive.
803 29s. Type **143** 75 30
804 32s. Baden-Powell on his charger "Black Prince" . . 80 35
805 47s. Baden-Powell at Imperial Jamboree, 1924 . . . . . 1·00 45
806 1p.50 Cover of first "Scouting for Boys" journal . . . . 2·25 1·75
807 2p.50 Newsboy, 1900, and Mafeking Siege 3d. stamp 3·50 4·00

1982. Cyclone Relief. No. 788 optd **CYCLONE RELIEF T$1+50s POSTAGE & RELIEF**.
808 1p.+50s. on 3p. Prince and Princess of Wales after wedding ceremony . . . . 80 2·00

1982. World Cup Football Championship, Spain. Multicoloured. Self-adhesive.
809 32s. Type **145** 75 45
810 47s. Goalkeeping 95 60
811 75s. Heading . . . . 1·40 95
812 1p.50 Shooting . . . . . . 2·50 1·75

146 "Olovaha II" (inter-island freighter)

147 Mail Canoe

1982. Inter-Island Transport. Multicoloured. Self-adhesive.
813 9s. Type **146** 55 15
814 13s. Type **146** 60 25
815 47s. SPIA De Havilland Twin Otter 300 . . . . 1·50 1·00
816 1p. As 47s. . . . . 2·40 3·00

1982. Centenary of Tin Can Mail. Self-adhesive.
817 **147** 13s. multicoloured 15 25
818 – 32s. multicoloured 25 30
819 – 47s. multicoloured 35 35
820 – 2p. black and green . . . 1·40 2·00
MS821 135 × 90 mm. Nos. 817/19. Imperf . . . . 1·25 2·50
MS822 135 × 89 mm. As No. 820 but with gold inscriptions. Imperf 3·00 5·00
DESIGNS: 32s. Mail canoe and ship; 47s. Collecting Tin Can mail; 2p. Map of Niuafo'ou.

148 Decathlon

1982. Commonwealth Games, Brisbane. Mult. Self-adhesive.
823 32s. Type **148** 50 50
824 $1.50 Tongan Police band at opening ceremony (horiz) 4·50 6·50

149 Pupils

1982. Cent of Tonga College. Mult. Self-adhesive.
825 5s. Type **149** (Tongan inscription) . . . . 60 1·25
826 5s. Type **149** (English inscription) . . . . 60 1·25
827 29s. School crest and monument (Tongan inscr) (29 × 22 mm) . . . . . . 2·50 3·00
828 29s. As No. 827 but inscr in English . . . . 2·50 3·00
829 29s. King George Tupou I (founder) and school (Tongan inscr) (29 × 22 mm) . . . . . . 2·50 3·00
830 29s. As No. 829 but inscr in English . . . . 2·50 3·00

1982. Christmas. Nos. 817/9 optd **Christmas Greetings 1982**.
831 13s. Type **147** 25 50
832 32s. Mail boat and ship . . . 60 75
833 47s. Collecting Tin Can mail 70 85

151 H.M.S. "Resolution" and S.S. "Canberra"

1983. Sea and Air Transport. Mult. Self-adhesive.
834 29s. Type **151** . . . . 3·00 1·75
835 32s. Type **151** . . . . 3·00 1·75
836 47s. Montgolfier's balloon and Concorde . . . . . . 4·25 3·00
837 1p.50 As No. 836 . . . . . 6·50 10·00
MS838 120 × 165 mm. 2p.50 "Canberra" (liner) and Concorde 4·00 7·00

152 Globe and Inset of Tonga

1983. Commonwealth Day. Multicoloured. Self-adhesive.
839 29s. Type **152** 35 45
840 32s. Tongan dancers . . . . 6·00 4·25
841 47s. Trawler 50 80
842 1p.50 King Taufa'ahau Tupou IV and flag . . . . 1·75 5·00

153 SPIA De Havilland Twin Otter 300

154 "Intelsat IV" Satellite

1983. Inauguration of Niuafo'ou Airport. Mult. Self-adhesive.
843 32s. Type **153** . . . . 1·00 30
844 47s. Type **153** . . . . 1·10 35
845 1p. SPIA Boeing 707 . . . . 1·75 1·25
846 1p.50 As No. 845 . . . . . 2·75 1·75

1983. World Communications Year. Multicoloured. Self-adhesive.
847 29s. Type **154** 40 20
848 32s. "Intelsat IVA" satellite 50 25
849 75s. "Intelsat V" satellite . . 1·00 70
850 2p. Moon post cover (45 × 32 mm) . . . . . . 1·50 2·00

155 Obverse and Reverse of Pa'anga Banknote

1983. 10th Anniv of Bank of Tonga. Self-adhesive.
851 **155** 1p. multicoloured . . . . 1·25 1·75
852 2p. multicoloured . . . . 2·25 3·00

156 Early Printing Press

157 Yacht off Coast

1983. Printing in Tonga. Multicoloured. Self-adhesive.
853 13s. Type **156** 20 15
854 32s. Arrival of W. Woon . . 40 30
855 1p. Early Tongan print . . . 95 95
856 2p. "The Tonga Chronicle" 1·50 2·00

1983. Christmas. Yachting off Vava'u. Mult. Self-adhesive.
857 29s. Type **157** 60 35
858 32s. View of yacht from cave 60 35
859 1p.50 Anchored yacht . . . 2·00 2·25
860 2p.50 Yacht off coast (different) . . . . 2·75 3·50

158 Abel Tasman and "Zeehan"

1984. Navigators and Explorers of the Pacific (1st series). Self-adhesive.
861 **158** 32s. green and black . . . 1·50 1·50
862 – 47s. violet and black . . . 2·00 2·00
863 – 90s. brown and black . . 3·75 3·75
864 – 1p.50 blue and black . . 5·00 5·00
DESIGNS: 47s. Capt. Samuel Wallis and H.M.S. "Dolphin"; 90s. Capt. William Bligh and H.M.S. "Bounty"; 1p.50, Capt. James Cook and H.M.S. "Resolution".
See also Nos. 896/9.

159 Chaste Mitre

160 Printer checking Newspaper

1984. Marine Life. Multicoloured. Self-adhesive.
865 1s. Type **159** . . . . 40 1·75
866 2s. "Porites sp" . . . . . . 1·00 1·75
867 3s. Red squirrelfish . . . . 1·50 2·00
868 5s. Green map cowrie . . . . 50 1·75
869 6s. "Dardanus megistos" (crab) . . . . 1·50 2·00
870 9s. Variegated shark . . . . 1·50 1·00
871 10s. Bubble cone . . . . . . 1·00 1·75
872 13s. Lionfish . . . . 2·00 1·00
873 15s. Textile or cloth of gold cone . . . . 1·00 2·00
874 20s. White-tailed damselfish 2·50 2·50
875 29s. Princely cone . . . . . 1·75 1·00
876 32s. Powder-blue surgeonfish 3·25 1·00
877 47s. Giant spider conch . . . 3·00 1·60
878 1p. "Millepora dichotama" 10·00 9·50
879 2p. "Birgus latro" (crab) . . 14·00 15·00
880 3p. Rose-branch murex . . . 9·00 16·00
881 5p. Yellow-finned tuna . . . 11·00 19·00
Nos. 865/77 are 25 × 28 mm in size and Nos. 878/81 38 × 23 mm.
For these designs with normal gum but redrawn see Nos. 999/1017a and 1087/95. For similar designs but with face value at foot see Nos. 1218/34 and 1346/7.

1984. 20th Anniv of "Tonga Chronicle" (newspaper). Self-adhesive.
882 **160** 3s. brown and blue . . . 15 20
883 32s. brown and red . . . 60 65

161 U.S.A. Flag and Running

1984. Olympic Games, Los Angeles. Each in black, red and blue. Self-adhesive.
884 29s. Type **161** 25 25
885 47s. Javelin-throwing 30 30
886 1p.50 Shot-putting . . . . . 1·00 1·00
887 3p. Olympic torch . . . . . 1·90 1·90

162 Sir George Airy and Dateline on World Map

1984. Centenary of International Dateline. Mult. Self-adhesive.
888 47s. Type **162** . . . . 1·25 1·00
889 2p. Sir Sandford Fleming and Map of Pacific time zones 4·25 4·50

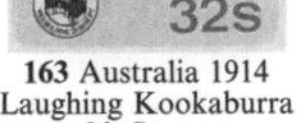

163 Australia 1914 Laughing Kookaburra 6d. Stamp
164 Beach at Sunset ("Silent Night")

1984. "Ausipex" International Stamp Exhibition, Melbourne. Multicoloured. Self-adhesive.
890 32s. Type **163** . . . . 1·50 75
891 1p.50 Tonga 1897 Red shining parrot 2s.6d. . . . 3·25 3·00
MS892 90 × 100 mm. As Nos. 890/1, but without exhibition logo and with "TONGA" and face values in gold. . . . . 4·00 4·00

1984. Christmas. Carols. Mult. Self-adhesive.
893 32s. Type **164** 60 45
894 47s. Hut and palm trees ("Away in a Manger") . . 85 65
895 1p. Sailing boats ("I Saw Three Ships") . . . . . . 1·75 3·50

1985. Navigators and Explorers of the Pacific (2nd series). As T **158**. Self-adhesive.
896 32s. black and blue . . . . . 3·00 1·25
897 47s. black and green . . . . 3·25 1·50
898 90s. black and red . . . . . 7·00 4·00
899 1p.50 black and brown . . . 7·50 6·50
DESIGNS: 32s. Willem Schouten and "Eendracht"; 47s. Jacob Le Maire and "Hoorn"; 90s. Fletcher Christian and "Bounty"; 1p.50, Francisco Maurelle and "La Princessa".

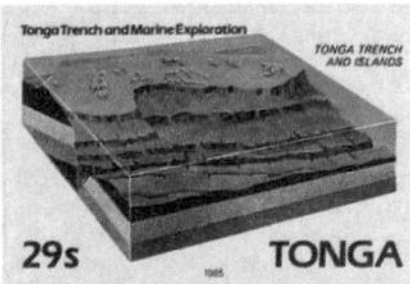

165 Section of Tonga Trench

1985. Geological Survey of the Tonga Trench. Multicoloured. Self-adhesive.
900 29s. Type **165** . . . . 1·25 1·00
901 32s. Diagram of marine seismic survey . . . . . . 1·25 1·00
902 47s. Diagram of aerial oil survey (vert) . . . . 1·50 1·50
903 1p.50 Diagram of sea bed survey (vert) . . . . 4·75 6·00
MS904 100 × 100 mm. 1p.50 Bearded angler (fish) . . . . . 7·50 5·00

166 "Port au Prince" at Gravesend, 1805

1985. 175th Anniv of Will Mariner's Departure for England. Multicoloured. Self-adhesive.
905B 29s. Type **166** 60 50
906B 32s. Capture of "Port au Prince", Tonga, 1806 . . 60 50
907B 47s. Will Mariner on Tongan canoe, 1807 . . . 80 70
908B 1p.50 Mariner boarding brig "Favourite", 1810 2·25 2·75
909B 2p.50 "Cuffnells" in English Channel, 1811 . . . . . 3·50 4·25

167 Quintal (Byron Russell) and Captain Bligh (Charles Laughton)

1985. 50th Anniv of Film "Mutiny on the Bounty". Multicoloured. Self-adhesive.
910 47s. Type **167** . . . . 8·00 8·00
911 47s. Captain Bligh and prisoners . . . . 8·00 8·00
912 47s. Fletcher Christian (Clark Gable) . . . . 8·00 8·00
913 47s. Mutineers threatening Bligh . . . . 8·00 8·00
914 47s. Bligh and Roger Byam (Franchot Tone) in boat 8·00 8·00

168 Lady Elizabeth Bowes-Lyon, 1910
169 Mary and Joseph arriving at Inn

1985. Life and Times of Queen Elizabeth the Queen Mother and 75th Anniv of Girl Guide Movement. Self-adhesive.
915A **168** 32s. black, pink and brown . . . . 1·50 1·25
916A – 47s. black, lilac and brown . . . . 1·75 1·50
917A – 1p.50 black, yellow and brown . . . . 5·00 5·50
918A – 2p.50 multicoloured . . 8·00 9·50
DESIGNS: 47s. Duchess of York at Hadfield Girl Guides' Rally, 1931; 1p.50, Duchess of York in Girl Guide uniform; 2p.50, Queen Mother in 1985 (from photo by Norman Parkinson).

1985. Christmas. Multicoloured. Self-adhesive.
919 32s. Type **169** 55 30
920 42s. The Shepherds 60 40
921 1p.50 The Three Wise Men 2·25 3·00
922 2p.50 The Holy Family . . . 3·25 4·50

170 Comet and Slogan "Maybe Twice in a Lifetime"

1986. Appearance of Halley's Comet. Mult.
923 42s. Type **170** . . . . 3·25 3·25
924 42s. Edmond Halley . . . . 3·25 3·25
925 42s. Solar System . . . . . 3·25 3·25
926 42s. Telescope . . . . 3·25 3·25
927 42s. "Giotto" spacecraft . . 3·25 3·25
928 57s. Type **170** . . . . 3·25 3·25
929 57s. As No. 924 . . . . . . 3·25 3·25
930 57s. As No. 925 . . . . . . 3·25 3·25
931 57s. As No. 926 . . . . . . 3·25 3·25
932 57s. As No. 927 . . . . . . 3·25 3·25
Nos. 923/7 and 928/32 were each printed together, se-tenant, forming composite designs.

1986. Nos. 866/7, 869/70, 872, 874, 879 and 881 surch.
933 4s. on 2s. "Porites sp" . . . 90 2·00
934 4s. on 13s. Lionfish . . . . . 90 2·00
935 42s. on 3s. Red squirrelfish 2·25 1·50
936 42s. on 9s. Variegated shark 2·25 1·50
937 57s. on 6s. "Dardanus megistos" . . . . 2·75 2·00
938 57s. on 20s. White-tailed damselfish . . . . 2·75 2·00
939 2p.50 on 2p. "Birgus latro" 8·50 10·00
940 2p.50 on 5p. Yellow-finned tuna . . . . 8·50 10·00

172 King Taufa'ahau Tupou IV of Tonga

1986. Royal Links with Great Britain and 60th Birthday of Queen Elizabeth II.
941 **172** 57s. multicoloured . . . . 75 1·00
942 – 57s. multicoloured . . . . 75 1·00
943 – 2p.50 brown, black and blue . . . . 3·25 4·00
DESIGNS—HORIZ (as Type **172**): No. 942, Queen Elizabeth II. SQUARE (40 × 40 mm): No. 943, Queen Elizabeth II and King Taufa'ahau Tupou IV, Tonga, 1970.

173 Peace Corps Nurse giving Injection

1986. "Ameripex '86" International Stamp Exhibition, Chicago. 25th Anniv of United States Peace Corps. Multicoloured.
944 57s. Type **173** . . . . 1·25 1·00
945 1p.50 Peace Corps teacher and pupil . . . . 2·25 3·25
MS946 90 × 90 mm. Nos. 944/5, magnifying glass and tweezers 3·00 4·50

174 Hockey

1986. Sporting Events. Multicoloured.
947 42s. Type **174** (World Hockey Cup for Men, London) . . 1·75 1·00
948 57s. Handball (13th Commonwealth Games, Edinburgh) . . . . 1·50 1·00
949 1p. Boxing (13th Commonwealth Games, Edinburgh) . . . . 2·00 2·75
950 2p.50 Football (World Cup Football Championship, Mexico) . . . . 4·75 6·00

175 1886 1d. King George I Definitive

1986. Centenary of First Tonga Stamps. Mult.
951 32s. Type **175** . . . . 1·75 1·10
952 42s. 1897 7½d. King George II inverted centre error . . . . 2·00 1·25
953 57s. 1950 Queen Salote's 50th Birthday 1d. . . . . 2·50 1·40
954 2p.50 1986 Royal Links with Great Britain 2p.50 . . . . 4·25 7·00
MS955 132 × 104 mm. 50s. × 8 Vert designs forming a montage of Tonga stamps . . . . 12·00 12·00

176 Girls wearing Shell Jewellery

1986. Christmas. Multicoloured.
956 32s. Type **176** . . . . 2·25 70
957 42s. Boy with wood carvings (vert) . . . . 2·50 75
958 57s. Children performing traditional dance (vert) . . 2·75 1·10
959 2p. Children in dugout canoe 6·50 10·00

1986. Scout Jamboree, Tongatapu. Nos. 957/8 optd **BOY SCOUT JAMBOREE 5TH-10TH DEC'86**.
960 42s. Boy with wood carvings (vert) . . . . 2·75 2·75
961 57s. Children performing traditional dance (vert) . . 3·25 3·25

178 Dumont D'Urville and "L'Astrolabe"

1987. 150th Anniv of Dumont D'Urville's Second Voyage. Multicoloured.
962 32s. Type **178** . . . . 3·50 1·75
963 42s. Tongan girls (from "Voyage au Pole et dans l'Oceanie") . . . . 3·50 1·75
964 1p. Contemporary chart . . . 8·00 6·00
965 2p.50 Wreck of "L'Astrolabe" . . . . . . 13·00 13·00

179 Noah's Ark

1987. World Wildlife Fund. Sheet 115 × 110 mm containing T **179** and similar vert designs. Multicoloured. P13½.
MS966 42s. Type **179**; 42s. American Bald Eagles; 42s. Giraffes and birds; 42s. Gulls; 42s. Ostriches and elephants; 42s. Elephant; 42s. Lions, zebras, antelopes and giraffes; 42s. Chimpanzees; 42s. Frogs and antelopes; 42s. Lizard and tigers; 42s. Snake and tiger; 42s. "Papilio machaon" (butterfly) 42·00 42·00
The stamps within No. **MS**966 show a composite design of animals entering Noah's Ark.

180 Two Paddlers in Canoe
181 King Taufa'ahau Tupou IV

1987. "Siv'a'alo (Tonga-Fiji-Samoa) Canoe Race. Multicoloured.
967 32s. Type **180** 55 40
968 42s. Five paddlers 65 50
969 57s. Paddlers and canoe bow 80 65
970 1p.50 Two paddlers (different) . . . . 2·10 2·75
MS971 153 × 159 mm. Nos. 967/70 3·50 4·25
The stamps within **MS**971 show a composite design of two canoes racing.

1987. 20th Anniv of Coronation of King Taufa'ahau Tupou IV. Self-adhesive.
972 **181** 1s. black and green . . . 20 60
972d 2s. black and orange . . 2·50 3·25
973 5s. black and mauve . . . 20 60
974 10s. black and lilac . . . 25 60
975 15s. black and red . . . 35 70
976 32s. black and blue . . . 45 80

182 Arms and Tongan Citizens

1987. 125th Anniv of First Parliament.
977 **182** 32s. multicoloured 40 30
978 42s. multicoloured 50 40
979 75s. multicoloured . . . . 90 1·00
980 2p. multicoloured . . . . 2·25 3·00

183 Father Christmas Octopus and Rat with Sack of Presents

1987. Christmas. Cartoons. Multicoloured.
981 42s. Type **183** . . . . 1·00 50
982 57s. Delivering presents by outrigger canoe . . . . . . 1·25 65
983 1p. Delivering presents by motorized tricycle . . . . 2·25 2·50
984 3p. Drinking cocktails . . . 5·50 7·00

184 King Taufa'ahau Tupou IV, "Olovaha II" (inter-island freighter), Oil Rig and Pole Vaulting

1988. 70th Birthday of King Taufa'ahau Tupou IV. Designs each show portrait. Multicoloured.

985 32s. Type **184** . . . . 2·00 80
986 42s. Banknote, coins, Ha'amonga Trilithon and woodcarver . . . . 1·50 80
987 57s. Rowing, communications satellite and Red Cross worker . . . . 1·75 90
988 2p.50 Scout emblem, 1982 47s. Scout stamp and Friendly Islands Airways De Havilland Twin Otter 200/300 aircraft . . . . . 7·50 8·50

See also Nos. 1082/5.

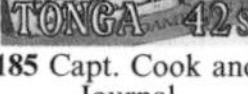

185 Capt. Cook and Journal **186** Athletics

1988. Bicentenary of Australian Settlement. Sheet 115 × 110 mm containing T **185** and similar vert designs. Multicoloured.

MS989 42s. Type **185**; 42s. Ships in Sydney Harbour and Governor Philip; 42s. Australia 1952 2s.6d. aborigine definitive and early settlement; 42s. Burke and Wills (explorers); 42s. Emu, opals and gold prospector's licence; 42s. ANZAC cap badge and soldier; 42s. Cover from first overland mail by Trans Continental; 42s. Ross Smith, England–Australia flown cover and G.B. 1969 1s.9d. commemorative stamp; 42s. Don Bradman and Harold Larwood (cricketers); 42s. World War II campaign medals; 42s. Australia 1978 18c. Flying Doctor Service stamp and sheep station; 42s. Sydney Opera House . . . . . 26·00 27·00

No. **MS**989 exists overprinted on the reverse as described below Nos. 985/8.

1988. Olympic Games, Seoul. Multicoloured.

990 57s. Type **186** 70 65
991 75s. Sailing . . . . 1·10 95
992 2p. Cycling . . . . 6·00 3·75
993 3p. Tennis . . . . 6·50 5·00

187 Traditional Tongan Fale

1988. Music in Tonga. Multicoloured.

994 32s. Type **187** 30 35
995 42s. Church choir 40 45
996 57s. Tonga Police Band outside Royal Palace . . . 1·00 80
997 2p.50 "The Jets" pop group 2·40 3·25

188 Olympic Flame

1988. "Sport Aid '88". Sheet 105 × 75 mm, containing T **188** and design as No. 997. Multicoloured.

MS998 57s. Type **188**; 57s. As No. 997 . . . . 1·40 2·25

1988. Redrawn designs (each showing wider gap between upper and lower lines) as Nos. 865/6, 868/9, 871/6 and 879/81 and new values, all normal gum. Multicoloured.

999 1s. Type **159** . . . . . . 30 1·50
1000 2s. "Porites sp" . . . . . 40 1·75
1001 4s. Lionfish . . . . 2·25 2·25
1002 5s. Green map cowrie . . . 50 1·75
1003 6s. "Dardanus megistos" (crab) . . . . 1·00 2·50
1004 7s. Wandering albatross . . 4·00 2·75
1005 10s. Bubble cone . . . . . 60 1·00
1006 15s. Textile or cloth of gold cone . . . . 60 1·25
1007 20s. White-tailed damselfish 1·00 2·00
1008 32s. Powder-blue surgeonfish . . . . . . 1·00 70
1009 35s. Seahorse . . . . . 3·50 3·00
1010 42s. Lesser frigate bird . . 4·00 70
1011 50s. Princely cone . . . . 4·00 2·00
1012 57s. Brown booby . . . . 4·75 1·00
1013 1p. "Chelonia mydas" (turtle) . . . . 6·00 4·50
1014 1p.50 Humpback whale . . 11·00 7·00
1015 2p. "Birgus latro" (crab) 8·00 8·00
1016 3p. Rose-branch murex . . 2·75 8·00
1017 5p. Yellow-finned tuna . . 13·00 16·00
1017a 10p. Variegated shark . . . 19·00 24·00

Nos. 1013/17 are 41 × 22 mm and No. 1017a 26 × 41.

For smaller designs, 19 × 22 mm, see Nos. 1087/95.

189 Capt. Cook's H.M.S. "Resolution"

1988. Centenary of Tonga–U.S.A. Treaty of Friendship. Multicoloured.

1018 42s. Type **189** 80 70
1019 57s. "Santa Maria" . . . . 1·00 80
1020 2p. Capt. Cook and Christopher Columbus . . 3·25 4·75
MS1021 140 × 115 mm. Nos. 1018/20 4·50 6·50

190 Girl in Hospital Bed

1988. Christmas. 125th Anniv of International Red Cross and 25th Anniv of Tongan Red Cross. Multicoloured.

1022 15s. Type **190** (A) 15 20
1023 15s. Type **190** (B) 15 20
1024 32s. Red Cross nurse reading to young boy (A) 30 35
1025 32s. Red Cross nurse reading to young boy (B) 30 35
1026 42s. Red Cross nurse taking pulse (A) 40 45
1027 42s. Red Cross nurse taking pulse (B) 40 45
1028 57s. Red Cross nurse with sleeping child (A) . . . 55 60
1029 57s. Red Cross nurse with sleeping child (B) . . . 55 60
1030 1p.50 Boy in wheelchair (A) 1·40 2·00
1031 1p.50 Boy in wheelchair (B) 1·40 2·00

Nos. 1022/3, 1024/5, 1026/7, 1028/9 and 1030/1 were printed together, se-tenant, in horizontal pairs throughout the sheets with the first stamp in each pair inscribed "INTERNATIONAL RED CROSS 125TH ANNIVERSARY" (A) and the second "SILVER JUBILEE OF TONGAN RED CROSS" (B).

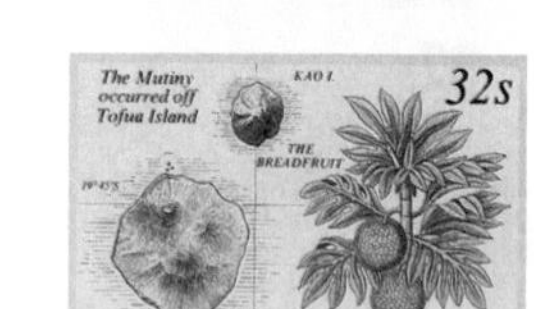

191 Map of Tofua Island and Breadfruit

1989. Bicentenary of Mutiny on the "Bounty". Multicoloured.

1032 32s. Type **191** . . . . . . 2·75 1·75
1033 42s. H.M.S. "Bounty" and chronometer . . . . . . 4·50 2·00
1034 57s. Captain Bligh and "Bounty's" launch cast adrift . . . . 6·00 3·00
MS1035 106 × 80 mm. 2p. Fletcher Christian on H.M.S. "Bounty" (vert); 3p. Bligh cast adrift. . . 10·00 11·00

192 "Hypolimnas bolina"

1989. Butterflies. Multicoloured.

1036 42s. Type **192** . . . . . . 1·00 80
1037 57s. "Jamides bochus" . . . 1·25 90
1038 1p.20 "Melanitis leda" . . . 2·25 2·75
1039 2p.50 "Danaus plexippus" 3·75 5·50

193 Football at Rugby School, 1870

1989. Inauguration of National Sports Stadium and South Pacific Mini Games, Tonga. Designs showing development of rugby, tennis and cricket. Multicoloured.

1040 32s. Type **193** . . . . . . 1·00 1·00
1041 32s. D. Gallaher (All Blacks' captain, 1905) and Springboks rugby match, 1906 . . . . 1·00 1·00
1042 32s. King George V with Cambridge team, 1922, and W. Wakefield (England captain, 1926) 1·00 1·00
1043 32s. E. Crawford (Ireland captain, 1926) and players on cigarette cards . . . . 1·00 1·00
1044 32s. S. Mafi (Tonga captain, 1970s) and modern rugby match . . . . 1·00 1·00
1045 42s. Royal tennis, 1659 . . 1·50 1·50
1046 42s. Major Wingfield and lawn tennis, 1873 . . . . 1·50 1·50
1047 42s. Oxford and Cambridge tennis teams, 1884 . . . . 1·50 1·50
1048 42s. Bunny Ryan, 1910, and players on cigarette cards 1·50 1·50
1049 42s. Boris Becker and modern tennis match . . 1·50 1·50
1050 57s. Cricket match, 1743, and F. Pilch memorial . . 2·25 2·25
1051 57s. W. G. Grace (19th-century cricketer) . . 2·25 2·25
1052 57s. "Boys Own Paper" cricket article, 1909 . . . 2·25 2·25
1053 57s. Australian cricket team, 1909, and players on cigarette cards . . . . . 2·25 2·25
1054 57s. The Ashes urn, and modern cricket match . . 2·25 2·25

194 Short S.30 Modified "G" Class Flying Boat "Aotearoa", 1939 (50th anniv of first flight)

195 CASA C-212 Aviocar landing

1989. Aviation in Tonga. Multicoloured.

1055 42s. Type **194** . . . . . . 2·50 1·10
1056 57s. Chance Vought F4U Corsair, 1943 . . . . . . 3·00 1·50
1057 90s. Boeing 737 at Fua'amotu Airport . . . 5·00 4·50
1058 3p. Montgolfier balloon, Wright Flyer I biplane, Concorde and space shuttle (97 × 26 mm) . . . 13·00 13·00

1989. Christmas. "Flying Home".

1059 **195** 32s. green, brown & orange . . . . 1·75 80
1060 – 42s. green, brown & lt green . . . . 2·00 80
1061 – 57s. green, brown and red . . . . 2·25 90
1062 – 3p. green, brown & mve 7·50 9·00

DESIGNS: 42s. Villagers waving to CASA C-212 Aviocar aircraft; 57s. Outrigger canoe and CASA C-212 Aviocar aircraft; 3p. CASA C-212 Aviocar over headland.

196 Rowland Hill, Mulready Cover and Penny Blacks **198** Boxing

197 1989 U.P.U. Congress Stamps

1989. 20th Universal Postal Union Congress, Washington. Sheet 115 × 110 mm containing T **196** and similar vert designs. Multicoloured.

MS1063 57s. Type **196**; 57s. Early train and steam ship; 57s. Stage coach, Pony Express poster and rider; 57s. French hot-air balloon and flown cover; 57s. Samuel Morse and telegraph key; 57s. Early British mail van and pillar box; 57s. Unloading De Havilland D.H.4.M mail biplane; 57s. "Queen Mary" (liner) and Airship LZ-127 "Graf Zeppelin" flown cover; 57s. Westland Dragonfly helicopter and mail van; 57s. Computer and fax machine; 57s. "Apollo 11" emblem and space cover; 57s. U.P.U. Monument and space shuttle . . . . 30·00 30·00

1989. "World Stamp Expo '89" International Stamp Exhibition, Washington.

1064 **197** 57s. multicoloured . . . 3·00 1·75

1990. 14th Commonwealth Games, Auckland. Mult.

1065 42s. Type **198** 90 70
1066 57s. Archery . . . . 1·50 1·10
1067 1p. Bowls . . . . 2·00 2·50
1068 2p. Swimming . . . . . . 3·50 5·00

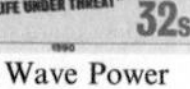

199 Wave Power Installation **201** Departure of Canoe

200 Penny Black

1990. Alternative Sources of Electricity. Mult.

1069 32s. Type **199** . . . . . . 1·00 65
1070 57s. Wind farm . . . . . . 1·50 1·10
1071 1p.20 Experimental solar cell vehicle . . . . 3·00 4·75
MS1072 110 × 90 mm. 2p.50 Planet Earth . . . . 7·00 8·00

1990. 150th Anniv of the Penny Black.

1073 **200** 42s. multicoloured . . . 1·25 1·25
1074 – 42s. multicoloured . . . 1·25 1·25
1075 – 57s. red and black . . . 1·50 1·25
1076 – 1p.50 multicoloured . . 3·50 4·00
1077 – 2p.50 multicoloured . . 5·00 5·50

DESIGNS: 42s. (1074) Great Britain 1840 Twopence Blue; 57s. Tonga 1886 1d.; 1p.50, 1980 South Pacific Scout Jamboree and Rotary 75th anniv 2p. official stamp; 2p.50, 1990 Alternative Sources of Electricity 57s.

1990. Polynesian Voyages of Discovery.

1078 **201** 32s. green 75 65
1079 – 42s. blue . . . . 1·00 80
1080 – 1p.20 brown . . . . . . 2·75 3·00
1081 – 3p. violet . . . . 5·50 8·00

DESIGNS: 42s. Navigating by night; 1p.20, Canoe and sea birds; 3p. Landfall.

1990. Silver Jubilee of King Taufa'ahau Tupou IV. As Nos. 985/8 but inscr "Silver Jubilee of His Majesty King Taufa'ahau Tupou IV. 1965–1990" and with "TONGA" and values in silver.

1082 32s. Type **184** . . . . . . 1·40 75
1083 42s. Banknote, coins Ha'amonga Trilithon and woodcarver . . . . 1·40 75
1084 57s. Rowing, communications satellite and Red Cross worker . . 1·60 85
1085 2p.50 Scout emblem, 1982 47s. Scout stamp and Friendly Islands Airways De Havilland Twin Otter aircraft . . . . 7·00 8·00

1990. As Nos. 1000, 1002, 1003 (value changed), 1005 and 1008 redrawn smaller, 19 × 22 mm. Multicoloured.

1087 2s. "Porites sp." 40 65
1089 5s. Green map cowrie . . . 40 65
1092 10s. Bubble cone 40 65

1093 15s. "Dardanus megistos" (crab) . . . . 2·50 1·00
1095 32s. Powder-blue surgeonfish 65 65

202 Iguana searching for Food

1990. Endangered Species. Banded Iguana. Mult.

1105 32s. Type **202** . . . . . . 1·50 75
1106 42s. Head of male . . . . . 1·75 85
1107 57s. Pair of iguanas during courtship . . . . 2·25 1·25
1108 1p.20 Iguana basking . . . 5·00 6·50

203 Tourism

1990. 40th Anniv of United Nations Development Programme. Multicoloured.

1109 57s. Type **203** . . . . . . 1·25 1·50
1110 57s. Agriculture and Fisheries . . . . 1·25 1·50
1111 3p. Education . . . . . . 6·00 8·00
1112 3p. Healthcare . . . . . . 6·00 8·00

204 Boy **205** Safety at Work

1990. Christmas. Rotary International Interact Project. Multicoloured.

1113 32s. Type **204** 70 40
1114 42s. Young boys 90 55
1115 2p. Girls in western clothes 3·50 4·25
1116 3p. Girls in traditional costumes . . . . 4·50 5·50

1991. Accident Prevention. Multicoloured.

1117 32s. Type **205** (English inscription) 80 80
1118 32s. Safety at home (English inscription) . . 80 80
1119 32s. As No. 1118 (Tongan inscription) 80 80
1120 32s. As Type **205** (incorrectly inscr "Ngauo tokanga") 80 80
1120a 32s. As Type **205** (inscr corrected to "Ngaue tokanga") . . . . 18·00 18·00
1121 42s. Safety in cars (English inscription) . . . . . . 1·25 1·25
1122 42s. Safety on bikes (English inscription) . . 1·25 1·25
1123 42s. As No. 1122 (Tongan inscription) . . . . . . 1·25 1·25
1124 42s. As No. 1121 (Tongan inscription) . . . . . . 1·25 1·25
1125 57s. Safety at sea (English inscription) . . . . . . 1·50 1·50
1126 57s. Safety on the beach (English inscription) . . 1·50 1·50
1127 57s. As No. 1126 (Tongan inscription) . . . . . . 1·50 1·50
1128 57s. As No. 1125 (Tongan inscription) . . . . . . 1·50 1·50

206 Yacht at Dawn

1991. Around the World Yacht Race. Sheet 120 × 103 mm containing T **206** and similar vert designs. Multicoloured.

MS1129 1p. Type **206**; 1p. Yacht in the morning; 1p. Yacht at midday; 1p. Yacht in the evening; 1p. Yacht at night . . . . 6·75 7·50

207 Fishes in the Sea **208** Tonga Temple

1991. Heilala Week. Multicoloured.

1130 42s. Type **207** 70 55
1131 57s. Island and yacht . . . 90 65
1132 2p. Pile of fruit . . . . . . 2·75 3·50
1133 3p. Turtle on beach . . . . 3·50 4·00

1991. Centenary of Church of Latter Day Saints in Tonga. Multicoloured.

1134 42s. Type **208** . . . . . . 1·10 1·10
1135 57s. Temple at night . . . . 1·40 1·40

209 Making T.V. Childcare Programme

1991. Telecommunications in Tonga. Mult.

1136 15s. Type **209** 35 45
1137 15s. T.V. satellite 35 45
1138 15s. Mothers watching programme 35 45
1139 32s. Man on telephone and woman with computer . . 65 75
1140 32s. Telecommunications satellite 65 75
1141 32s. Overseas customer on telephone 65 75
1142 42s. Sinking coaster . . . . 1·10 1·25
1143 42s. Coastguard controller 1·10 1·25
1144 42s. Maritime rescue . . . . 1·10 1·25
1145 57s. Weather satellite above Southern Hemisphere . . 1·25 1·40
1146 57s. Meteorologists collecting data . . . . . 1·25 1·40
1147 57s. T.V. weather map and storm . . . . 1·25 1·40

210 Women's Rowing Eight

1991. "Siu'a'alo" Rowing Festival. Mult.

1148 42s. Type **210** 85 45
1149 57s. Longboat . . . . . . 1·00 55
1150 1p. Outrigger canoe . . . . 2·00 2·00
1151 2p. Stern of fautasi (large canoe) . . . . 3·25 4·25
1152 2p. Bow of fautasi . . . . 3·25 4·25

Nos. 1151/2 were printed together, se-tenant, forming a composite design.

211 Turtles pulling Santa's Sledge

1991. Christmas. Multicoloured.

1153 32s. Type **211** 85 35
1154 42s. Santa Claus on roof of fala (Tongan house) . . . 95 45
1155 57s. Family opening presents 1·10 60
1156 3p.50 Family waving goodbye to Santa . . . . 6·50 8·50

212 "Pangai" (patrol boat) **214** Columbus and Signature

1991. Royal Tongan Defence Force. Mult.

1157 42s. Type **212** . . . . . . 1·00 1·00
1158 42s. Marine in battle dress 1·00 1·00
1159 57s. Tonga Royal Guards 1·25 1·25
1160 57s. Raising the ensign on "Neiafu" (patrol boat) . . 1·25 1·25
1161 2p. "Savea" (patrol boat) (horiz) . . . . 3·00 3·75
1162 2p. King Taufa'ahau Tupou IV inspecting parade (horiz) . . . . 3·00 3·75

1992. No. 1007 surch **1s**.

1163 1s. on 20s. White-tailed damselfish . . . . 65 1·00

1992. 500th Anniv of Discovery of America by Columbus. Sheet 119 × 109 mm containing T **214** and similar vert designs. Multicoloured.

MS1164 57s. Type **214**; 57s. Monastery of Santa Maria de la Chevas; 57s. Obverse and reverse of coin of Ferdinand and Isabella; 57s. Spain commemorative stamps of 1930; 57s. Compass and astrolabe; 57s. Model of "Santa Maria"; 57s. Sketch map and signature; 57s. 15th-century woodcut of Columbus arriving in New World; 57s. Lucayan artefacts and parrot; 57s. Pineapple, bird pendant and Indian nose ring; 57s. Columbus reporting to Spanish Court; 57s. Medal showing Columbus and signature . . . . 24·00 26·00

215 U.S.S. "Arizona" under attack, Pearl Harbor, 1941

1992. 50th Anniv of Outbreak of Pacific War. Multicoloured.

1165 42s. Type **215** . . . . . . 1·60 1·60
1166 42s. Japanese invasion of the Philippines . . . . . 1·60 1·60
1167 42s. U.S. landings in the Gilbert Islands . . . . . 1·60 1·60
1168 42s. Landing on Iwo Jima 1·60 1·60
1169 42s. Admiral Nimitz and Battle of Midway map . . 1·60 1·60
1170 42s. General MacArthur and liberation of Philippines map . . . . 1·60 1·60
1171 42s. Lt-Gen. Holland Smith and map of landings on Saipan and Tinian . . . . 1·60 1·60
1172 42s. Major-Gen. Curtis Lemay and bombing of Japan map . . . . 1·60 1·60
1173 42s. Japanese Mitsubishi A6M Zero-Sen . . . . . 1·60 1·60
1174 42s. Douglas SBD Dauntless 1·60 1·60
1175 42s. Grumman FM-2 Wildcat . . . . 1·60 1·60
1176 42s. Supermarine Seafire Mk III . . . . 1·60 1·60

Nos. 1165/76 were printed togther, se-tenant, forming a composite design.

216 Boxing **217** King Taufa'ahau Taupou IV and Queen Halaevalu

1992. Olympic Games, Barcelona. Mult.

1177 42s. Type **216** 75 50
1178 57s. Diving 95 55
1179 1p.50 Tennis . . . . 4·00 4·25
1180 3p. Cycling . . . . 6·00 6·50

1992. 25th Anniv of the Coronation of King Tupou IV.

1181 **217** 45s. multicoloured . . . 75 45
1182 – 80s. multicoloured . . . 1·50 1·75
1183 – 80s. black and brown . . 1·50 1·75
1184 – 80s. multicoloured . . . 1·50 1·75
1185 – 2p. multicoloured . . . 3·50 4·00

DESIGNS—48 × 35 mm: No. 1182, King Tupou IV and Crown; 1183, Extract from Investiture ceremony; 1184, King Tupou IV and 1967 Coronation 2p. commemorative; 1185, As Type **217** but larger.

Nos. 1181/5 show the King's first name incorrectly spelt as "Tauf'ahau".

1992. No. 1095 surch **45s 45s**.

1186 45s. on 32s. Powder-blue surgeonfish . . . . 4·00 1·50

1992. Nos. 1121/4 surch **60**.

1187 60s. on 42s. Safety in cars (English inscr) . . . . . 3·50 3·50
1188 60s. on 42s. Safety on bikes (English inscr) . . . . . 3·50 3·50
1189 60s. on 42s. As No. 1187 (Tongan inscr) . . . . . 3·50 3·50
1190 60s. on 42s. As No. 1188 (Tongan inscr) . . . . . 3·50 3·50

220 Bats flying Home **222** Tonga Flag and Rotary Emblem (25th anniv of Rotary International in Tonga)

221 Tongan Pearls

1992. Sacred Bats of Kolovai. Multicoloured.

1191 60s. Type **220** . . . . . . 1·60 1·75
1192 60s. Tongan fruit bat . . . 1·60 1·75
1193 60s. Bats alighting on branches . . . . 1·60 1·75
1194 60s. Bats hanging from tree 1·60 1·75
1195 60s. Tongan fruit bat in tree 1·60 1·75

MS1196 96 × 112 mm. 45s. Kula leaving Tonga; 45s. Kula watching Chief's daughter dancing; 2p. Kula between fires and Hina; 2p. Kula leaving Samoa with bats (each 38 × 30 mm) . . . . 8·50 9·50

Nos. 1191/5 were printed together, se-tenant, forming a composite design.

1992. Christmas. Multicoloured.

1197 60s. Type **221** 70 65
1198 80s. Reef fish 90 80
1199 2p. Pacific orchids . . . . . 4·25 5·00
1200 3p. Red shining parrots from Eua . . . . 5·50 7·00

1992. Anniversaries and Events.

1201 **222** 60s. multicoloured . . . 1·00 65
1202 – 80s. multicoloured . . . 1·25 90
1203 – 1p.50 violet, lilac & black . . . . 2·75 3·75
1204 – 3p.50 multicoloured . . 5·50 7·00

DESIGNS: 80s. Pres. Kennedy and Peace Corps emblem (25th anniv of Peace Corps in Tonga); 1p.50, F.A.O. and W.H.O. emblems (International Conference); 3p.50, Globe and Rotary Foundation emblem (75th anniv of Rotary Foundation).

223 Mother and Child **226** Chaste Mitre

224 Anti-smoking and Anti-drugs Symbols with Healthy Food (½-size illustration)

1993. Family Planning.

1205 **223** 15s. black, blue and mauve (English inscr) 40 70
1206 – 15s. black, blue and mauve (Tongan inscr) 40 70
1207 – 45s. black, yellow and green (English inscr) 90 1·00
1208 – 45s. black, yellow and green (Tongan inscr) 90 1·00
1209 – 60s. black, red and yellow (English inscr) 1·90 2·25
1210 – 60s. black, red and yellow (Tongan inscr) 1·90 2·25
1211 – 2p. black, yellow & orange (English inscr) 4·25 4·75
1212 – 2p. black, yellow & orange (Tongan inscr) 4·25 4·75

DESIGNS: 45s. Child on bike; 60s. Girl with cats; 2p. Old man and boy playing chess.

1993. Health and Fitness Campaign. Mult.

1213 60s. Type **224** . . . . . . 1·25 90
1214 80s. Anti-smoking symbol and weight training . . . 1·60 1·10
1215 1p.50 Anti-drugs symbol and water sports . . . . 2·75 3·50
1216 2p.50 Healthy food with cyclist and jogger . . . . 5·00 6·50

1993. Nos. 1001 and 1087 surch.

1217 10s. on 2s. "Porites sp." . . 60·00 15·00
1217a 20s. on 4s. Lionfish £400

1993. As Nos. 867, 872, 875, 877, 999, 1002, 1005, 1007, 1013/16 and 1017a, some with new face values, redrawn as in T **226** with species inscr at foot. Multicoloured.

1218	1s. Type **226**	25	1·00
1219	3s. Red squirrelfish	40	1·50
1220	5s. Green map cowrie	40	1·00
1221a	10s. Bubble cone	40	75
1223a	20s. White-tailed damselfish	60	1·00
1225a	45s. Giant spider conch (as No. 877)	70	70
1227a	60s. Princely cone (as No. 875)	1·00	1·00
1229a	80s. Lionfish (as No. 872)	1·00	1·00
1230	1p. "Chelonia mydas" (turtle)	1·00	1·40
1231	2p. "Birgus latro" (crab)	1·75	3·00
1232	3p. Rose-branch murex	2·50	4·50
1233	5p. Humpback whale (as No. 1014)	5·50	8·00
1234	10p. Variegated shark	23·00	26·00

Nos. 1218/29 are 19 × 22 mm, Nos. 1230/3 are 40 × 28 mm and No. 1234, 28 × 40 mm.

For 1 to 10p. with species inscription at top left, see Nos. 1345/9.

227 Fire Brigade Badge

1993. 25th Annivs of Police Training College and Fire Service. Multicoloured.

1235	45s. Type **227**	1·50	1·75
1236	45s. Police badge and van	1·50	1·75
1237	60s. Police band	1·75	2·00
1238	60s. Fire engine at fire	1·75	2·00
1239	2p. Fire engine at station	4·00	5·00
1240	2p. Policeman and dog handler	4·00	5·00

228 Old Map of Islands

229 King Taufa'ahau Tupou IV and Musical Instruments

1993. 300th Anniv of Abel Tasman's Discovery of Eua. Multicoloured.

1241	30s. Type **228**	80	55
1242	60s. "Heemskirk" and "Zeehaan" at sea	1·25	85
1243	80s. Tongan canoes welcoming ships	1·60	1·25
1244	3p.50 Tasman landing on Eua	6·00	8·00

1993. 75th Birthday of King Taufa'ahau Tupou IV. Multicoloured.

1245	45s. Type **229**	60	45
1246	80s. King Tupou IV and sporting events	1·00	1·40
1247	80s. King Tupou IV and ancient landmarks	1·00	1·40
1248	80s. King Tupou IV and Royal Palace	1·00	1·40
1249	2p. As Type **229** but larger	2·50	3·25

Nos. 1246/9 are larger, 38½ × 51 mm.

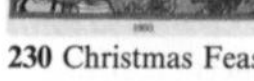

230 Christmas Feast

231 "Land of Sun, Sea and Sand" (Kiley and Peter Moala)

1993. Christmas. Multicoloured.

1250	60s. Type **230**	90	60
1251	80s. Firing home-made cannon	1·25	80
1252	1p.50 Band playing carols	2·50	3·25
1253	3p. Going to church	5·00	6·00

1993. Winners of Children's Painting Competition.

1254 **231**	10s. multicoloured	30	50
1255 –	10s. multicoloured	30	50
1256 –	10s. multicoloured	30	50
1257 –	10s. multicoloured	30	50
1258 –	10s. black and grey	30	50
1259 –	10s. black and grey	30	50
1260 **231**	80s. multicoloured	1·40	1·60
1261 –	80s. multicoloured	1·40	1·60
1262 –	80s. multicoloured	1·40	1·60
1263 –	80s. multicoloured	1·40	1·60
1264 –	80s. multicoloured	1·40	1·60
1265 –	80s. multicoloured	1·40	1·60

DESIGNS: Nos. 1255 and 1261, "Maui, Fisher God of Tonga" (Kiley and Peter Moala); 1256 and 1262, "Traditional Island Transport" (Kiley and Peter Moala); 1257 and 1263, "Young Girl making Kava" (Pulotu Pole'o); 1258 and 1264, "Maui and his Hook" (Salome Tapou); 1259 and 1265, "Communications in the South Pacific" (Fe'ofa'aki Taufa).

232 Boy holding Cockerel

1994. Animal Welfare. Sheet 122 × 100 mm, containing T **232** and similar vert designs. Multicoloured.

MS1266 60s. Type **232**; 60s. Girl with butterfly; 60s. Dog and puppies; 60s. Boy with puppy; 80s. Boy holding puppy; 80s. Girl holding cat . . . 6·00 8·00

233 Tiger Shark

1994. Game Fishing. Multicoloured.

1267	60s. Type **233**	1·10	85
1268	80s. Dolphin (fish)	1·50	1·10
1269	1p.50 Yellow-finned tuna	2·75	3·50
1270	2p.50 Blue marlin	3·50	4·50

234 Hands holding World Cup

1994. World Cup Football Championship, U.S.A. Multicoloured.

1271	80s. Type **234**	1·50	1·50
1272	80s. Player's legs	1·50	1·50
1273	2p. German player (black shorts)	3·25	4·00
1274	2p. American player	3·25	4·00

235 Policewoman

1994. Pan Pacific and South East Asia Women's Association Conference, Tonga. Multicoloured.

1275	45s. Type **235**	1·50	1·50
1276	45s. Woman barrister	1·50	1·50
1277	2p.50 Nurse	4·25	4·75
1278	2p.50 Woman doctor	4·25	4·75

1994. Christmas. No. **MS**1266 optd **MERRY CHRISTMAS** or equivalent in Tongan.

MS1279 60s. Type **232**; 60s. Girl with butterfly; 60s. Dog and puppies; 60s. Boy with puppy; 80s. Boy holding puppy; 80s. Girl holding cat . . . 5·00 6·00

T **236** appears on five of the stamps from the miniature sheet.

The 60s. in the centre of the bottom row (dog and puppies) is overprinted "KILISIMASI FIEFIA".

1994. Visit South Pacific Year '95 (1st issue). No. 1204 surch **VISIT SOUTH PACIFIC YEAR '95 60** and emblem.

1280 60s. on 3p.50 multicoloured . . . 1·25 1·25

See also Nos. 1297/1308.

1994. 25th Anniv of Tongan Self-adhesive Stamps.

(a) Various previous self-adhesive designs, some in smaller size, with new values.

1281 **128**	10s. black and yellow (21 × 9 mm) (postage)	25	40
1282 **124**	60s. black, grey and brown	1·50	2·00
1283 –	60s. multicoloured (as Nos. O214/15)	1·50	2·00
1284 **109**	25s. multicoloured (27 × 36 mm) (air)	1·50	2·00

(b) As Nos. 915/18, but new face value and inscr "SELF-ADHESIVE ANNIVERSARY 1969–1994".

1285 **168**	45s. black, pink and brown	75	85
1286 –	45s. black, lilac and brown (as No. 916)	75	85
1287 –	45s. black, yellow and brown (as No. 917)	1·25	1·50
1288 –	45s. mult (as No. 918)	3·00	4·00

(c) Hologram design, 39 × 29 mm, showing "Tongastar 1" satellite.

1289 – 2p. multicoloured . . . 6·50 7·50

238 Farmer, Produce and Emblem

1995. 50th Anniv of F.A.O.

1290 **238** 5p. multicoloured . . . 11·00 11·00

239 Polynesian Girl with Bicycle on Beach

1995. 25th Anniv of Tonga's Entry into Commonwealth. Children with Bicycles. Mult.

1291	45s. Type **239**	75	55
1292	60s. Children and skyscrapers, Hong Kong	90	60
1293	80s. Boy in African village	1·25	80
1294	2p. Indian boy and palace	2·75	3·75
1295	2p.50 English children and village church	3·25	4·00

240 Three Players running with Ball

242 Soldier on Scrambling Net

1995. World Cup Rugby Championship, South Africa. Two sheets, each 84 × 117 mm, containing T **240** and similar vert designs.

MS1296 (a) 80s. × 2 Type **240**; 80s. × 2 Two players running with ball. (b) 2p. × 2 Player making pass; 2p. × 2 Player receiving pass. Set of 2 sheets . . . 15·00 16·00

The miniature sheets contain two of each design.

1995. Visit South Pacific Year '95 (2nd issue). (a) Nos. 1149/52, but inscr "VISIT SOUTH PACIFIC YEAR '95", optd or surch **WHERE TIME BEGINS** and emblem.

1297	60s. on 57s. Longboat	75	60
1298	80s. on 2p. Stern of fautasi (large canoe)	1·00	1·50
1299	80s. on 2p. Bow of fautasi	1·00	1·50
1300	1p. Outrigger canoe	1·40	1·75

(b) Nos. 1197/1200 inscr either (A) "WHERE TIME BEGINS" or (B) "THE 21st CENTURY STARTS HERE" and surch **WHERE TIME BEGINS 60** and emblem.

1301	60s. on 60s. Type **221** (A)	75	1·00
1302	60s. on 60s. Type **221** (B)	75	1·00
1303	60s. on 80s. Reef fish (A)	75	1·00
1304	60s. on 80s. Reef fish (B)	75	1·00
1305	60s. on 2p. Pacific orchids (A)	75	1·00
1306	60s. on 2p. Pacific orchids (B)	75	1·00
1307	60s. on 3p. Red shining parrots from Eua (A)	75	1·00
1308	60s. on 3p. Red shining parrots from Eua (B)	75	1·00

1995. 50th Anniv of End of Second World War in the Pacific.

1309 **242**	60s. yellow, black & blue	1·25	1·50
1310 –	60s. yellow, black & blue	1·25	1·50
1311 –	60s. yellow, black & blue	1·25	1·50
1312 –	60s. multicoloured	1·25	1·50
1313 –	60s. multicoloured	1·25	1·50
1314 **242**	80s. yellow, black and red	1·25	1·50
1315 –	80s. yellow, black and red	1·25	1·50
1316 –	80s. yellow, black and red	1·25	1·50
1317 –	80s. multicoloured	1·25	1·50
1318 –	80s. multicoloured	1·25	1·50

DESIGNS: Nos. 1310 and 1315, U.S.S. "Nevada" (battleship) with troops in foreground; 1311 and 1316, U.S.S. "West Virginia" (battleship) and rear of landing craft; 1312 and 1317, U.S.S. "Idaho" (battleship) and front of landing craft; 1313 and 1318, Map of South-east Asia and Pacific.

Nos. 1309/18 were printed together, se-tenant, in sheetlets of 10 with the horizontal strips of 5 forming the same composite design.

243 1995 Commonwealth 45s. Stamp and Exhibition Emblem

1995. "Singapore '95" International Stamp Exhibition. Multicoloured.

1319	45s. Type **243**	1·00	1·25
1320	60s. 1995 Commonwealth 60s. stamp and emblem	1·00	1·25

245 Holocaust Victims

1995. 50th Anniv of United Nations and End of Second World War.

1323 **245**	60s. multicoloured	1·00	1·25
1324 –	60s. black and blue	1·00	1·25
1325 –	60s. multicoloured	1·00	1·25
1326 –	80s. multicoloured	1·00	1·25
1327 –	80s. blue and black	1·00	1·25
1328 –	80s. multicoloured	1·00	1·25

DESIGNS—As T **245**: No. 1325, Children of Holocaust survivors with balloons; 1326, Atomic explosion, Hiroshima; 1328, U.S. Space Shuttle. 23 × 35 mm: Nos. 1324 and 1327, U.N. anniversary emblem.

246 "Calanthe triplicata"

249 Running

247 Humpback Whale

1995. Greetings Stamps. Orchids. Inscribed either "MERRY CHRISTMAS" (A) or "A HAPPY 1996" (B). Multicoloured.

1329	20s. Type **246** (A)	50	50
1330	45s. "Spathoglottis plicata" (A)	75	75
1331	45s. As No. 1330 (B)	75	75
1332	60s. "Dendrobium platygastrium" (A)	90	90
1333	60s. As No. 1332 (B)	90	90
1334	80s. "Goodyera rubicunda" (B)	1·25	1·25
1335	2p. "Dendrobium toki" (B)	2·75	3·25
1336	2p.50 "Phaius tankervillae" (A)	3·50	4·00

1996. Endangered Species. Humpback Whale. Multicoloured.

1337	45s. Type **247**	1·40	75
1338	60s. Whale and calf	1·75	80
1339	1p.50 Whale's tail and white-throated storm petrels	3·25	3·75
1340	2p.50 Whale breaking surface	4·75	6·00

248 Rats and Top Left Quarter of Clock Face

1996. Chinese New Year ("Year of the Rat"). Sheets, 127 × 85 mm, containing T **248** and similar horiz designs showing rats and quarter segments of clock face. Multicoloured.

No.	Description		
MS1341	10s. Type **248**; 10s. Top right quarter; 10s. Bottom left quarter; 10s. Bottom right quarter	75	1·00
MS1342	20s. Type **248**; 20s. Top right quarter; 20s. Bottom left quarter; 20s. Bottom right quarter	1·50	1·75
MS1343	45s. Type **248**; 45s. Top right quarter; 45s. Bottom left quarter; 45s. Bottom right quarter	3·00	3·50
MS1344	60s. Type **248**; 60s. Top right quarter; 60s. Bottom left quarter; 60s. Bottom right quarter	4·00	4·50

1996. Multicoloured designs as Nos. 1230/4, but redrawn with species inscriptions at top left.

No.	Description		
1345	1p. "Chelonia mydas" (turtle)	3·25	2·50
1346	2p. "Birgus latro" (crab)	4·75	4·50
1347	3p. Rose branch murex	5·50	6·00
1348	5p. Humpback whale	12·00	12·00
1349	10p. Variegated shark (vert)	20·00	22·00

1996. Centennial Olympic Games, Atlanta. Ancient Greek and Modern Athletes. Multicoloured.

No.	Description		
1350	45s. Type **249**	90	65
1351	80s. Throwing the discus	1·50	1·25
1352	2p. Throwing the javelin	4·00	4·50
1353	3p. Equestrian dressage	5·50	6·50

250 Aspects of Prehistoric Life

1996. 13th Congress of International Union of Prehistoric and Protohistoric Sciences, Forli, Italy. Multicoloured.

No.	Description		
1354	1p. Type **250**	1·75	2·25
1355	1p. Aspects of Egyptian, Greek and Roman civilisations	1·75	2·25

251 "Virgin and Child" (Sassoferrato)

1996. Christmas. Religious Paintings. Mult.

No.	Description		
1356	20s. Type **251**	45	45
1357	60s. "Adoration of the Shepherds" (Murillo)	1·10	75
1358	80s. "Virgin and Child" (Delaroche)	1·40	1·10
1359	3p. "Adoration of the Shepherds" (Champaigne)	4·50	6·00

252 Athletics and Rugby

1996. 50th Anniv of UNICEF Children's Sports. Multicoloured.

No.	Description		
1360	80s. Type **252**	1·60	2·00
1361	80s. Tennis	1·60	2·00
1362	80s. Cycling	1·60	2·00

Nos. 1360/2 were printed together, se-tenant, forming a composite design.

253 Queen Halaevalu Mata'aho and Flag

1996. 70th Birthday of Queen Halaevalu Mata'aho. Multicoloured.

No.	Description		
1363	60s. Type **253**	1·00	65
1364	2p. Queen and obverse (portrait) of commemorative coin	3·25	4·00
1365	2p. Queen and reverse (arms) of commemorative coin	3·25	4·00

254 Globe, the Haamonga and Kao Island

1996. "Towards the Millennium". Multicoloured.

No.	Description		
1366	80s. Type **254**	1·50	1·75
1367	80s. Mount Talau, Royal Palace and satellite	1·50	1·75
1368	2p. Type **254**	3·25	3·75
1369	2p. As No. 1367	3·25	3·75

1997. Chinese New Year ("Year of the Ox"). Sheet 126 × 85 mm, containing horiz designs as T **248**, showing ox and quarter segments of clock face. Multicoloured.

No.	Description		
MS1370	60s. Top left quarter; 60s. Top right quarter; 80s. Bottom left quarter; 2p. Bottom right quarter	5·50	6·50

1997. Nos. 1235/40 surch.

No.	Description		
1371	10s. on 45s. Type **227**	2·75	2·50
1372	10s. on 45s. Police badge and van	2·75	2·50
1373	10s. on 60s. Police band	2·75	2·50
1374	10s. on 60s. Fire engine at fire	2·75	2·50
1375	20s. on 2p. Fire engine at station	3·25	3·00
1376	20s. on 2p. Policeman and dog handler	3·25	3·00

1997. 75th Anniv of Tongan Rugby Union No. **MS**1296 surch (A) **FAKAMANATU TA'U 75 'OE 'AKAPULU 'IUNIONI 'I TONGA** or (B) **"75th ANNIVERSARY TONGA RUGBY FOOTBALL UNION"**.

No.	Description		
MS1377	Two sheets, each 84 × 117 mm. (a) 10s. on 80s. Type **240** (A); 10s. on 80s. Type **240** (B) 10s. on 80s. Two players running with ball (A); 10s. on 80s. Two players running with ball (B). (b) 1p. on 2p. Player making pass (A); 1p. on 2p. Player making pass (B); 1p. on 2p. Player receiving pass (A); 1p. on 2p. Player receiving pass (B) Set of 2 sheets	8·00	8·50

1997. Tongan Medal Winner at Atlanta Olympic Games. Nos. 1350/3 surch **A SILVER FOR TONGA**.

No.	Description		
1378	10s. on 45s. Type **249**	60	80
1379	10s. on 80s. Throwing the discus	60	80
1380	10s. on 2p. Throwing the javelin	60	80
1381	3p. Equestrian dressage	7·50	8·00

258 Captain James Wilson and "Duff" (full-rigged missionary ship)

1997. Birth Bicentenary of King George I and Bicentenary of Christianity in Tonga (1st issue). Multicoloured.

No.	Description		
1382	10s. Type **258**	2·75	2·75
1383	10s. King George Tupou I	85	85
1384	10s. Missionaries landing at Tongatapu	2·75	2·75
1385	10s. Missionaries and Tongans	2·75	2·75
1386	60s. Type **258**	1·50	1·50
1387	60s. As No. 1384	1·50	1·50
1388	60s. As No. 1385	1·50	1·50
1389	80s. Type **258**	1·50	1·50
1390	80s. As No. 1384	1·50	1·50
1391	80s. As No. 1385	1·50	1·50

For 10s. (value as Nos. 1382/5, but smaller, 28 × 18 mm), see Nos. 1405/8.

259 Pacific Swallow

1997. "Pacific '97" International Stamp Exhibition, San Francisco. Sheet 84 × 110 mm.

No.	Description		
MS1392	**259** 2p. multicoloured	3·00	4·00

260 Children and School Building

1997. 50th Anniv of Tonga High School. Mult.

No.	Description		
1393	20s. Type **260**	55	55
1394	60s. Athletic team	1·10	75
1395	80s. School band	1·50	1·00
1396	3p.50 Athletics meeting	4·25	6·50

261 King and Queen of Tonga during Coronation

262 "Lenzites elegans"

1997. King and Queen of Tonga's Golden Wedding and 30th Anniv of the Coronation. Multicoloured. (a) Size 23 × 34 mm.

No.	Description		
1397	10s. Type **261**	1·25	1·25
1398	10s. Moment of Crowning and procession	1·25	1·25
1399	10s. King and Queen of Tonga	1·25	1·25
1400	45s. Royal Crown	1·50	1·50
	(b) Size 50 × 37 mm.		
1401	60s. As T **261**	1·75	1·75
1402	60s. As No. 1398	1·75	1·75
1403	60s. As No. 1399	1·75	1·75
1404	2p. As No. 1400	3·50	4·25

1997. Birth Bicentenary of King George I and Bicentenary of Christianity in Tonga (2nd issue). As Nos. 1382/5, but smaller, 28 × 18 mm.

No.	Description		
1405	10s. Type **258**	80	80
1406	10s. As No. 1384	80	80
1407	10s. As No. 1385	80	80
1408	10s. As No. 1383	50	50

1997. Fungi. Multicoloured. (a) Size 18 × 28 mm.

No.	Description		
1409	10s. Type **262**	1·75	1·75
1410	10s. "Marasmiellus semiustus"	1·75	1·75
1411	10s. "Aseroe rubra"	1·75	1·75
1412	10s. "Podoscypha involuta"	1·75	1·75
1413	10s. "Microporus xanthopus"	1·75	1·75
1414	10s. "Lentinus tuber-regium"	1·75	1·75
	(b) Size 28 × 42 mm.		
1415	20s. Type **262**	1·75	1·75
1416	20s. As No. 1410	1·75	1·75
1417	60s. As No. 1411	2·00	2·00
1418	60s. As No. 1412	2·00	2·00
1419	2p. As No. 1413	3·00	3·00
1420	2p. As No. 1414	3·00	3·00

Nos. 1409/14 were printed together, se-tenant, with the backgrounds forming a composite design.

1998. Diana, Princess of Wales Commemoration. Sheet, 145 × 170 mm, containing vert designs as T **194** of St. Helena. Multicoloured.

No.	Description		
MS1421	10s. Princess Diana, 1992; 80s. Wearing white jacket, 1992; 1p. Wearing black jacket, 1991; 2p.50, Wearing white top, 1993 (sold at 4p.40+50s. charity premium)	4·50	4·75

263 King Taufa'ahua Tupou IV

264 White Tern ("Fairy Tern")

1998. 80th Birthday of King Taufa'ahua Tupou IV.

No.	Description		
1422	**263** 2p.70 multicoloured	5·50	5·50
MS1423	80 × 90 mm. 2p.70, No. 1422 2p.70, No. 276 of Niuafo'ou	6·00	7·00

1998. Chinese New Year ("Year of the Tiger"). Sheet, 126 × 85 mm, containing horiz designs as T **248**, each showing a tiger and quarter segment of clock face. Multicoloured.

No.	Description		
MS1424	55s. Top left quarter; 80s. Top right quarter; 1p. Bottom left quarter; 1p. Bottom right quarter	3·50	4·00

1998. Birds. Multicoloured.

No.	Description		
1425	5s. Type **264**	10	10
1426	10s. Tongan whistler	10	10
1427	15s. Barn owl	10	10
1428	20s. Purple swamphen	10	15
1429	30s. Red-footed booby	15	20
1430	40s. Buff-banded rail ("Banded Rail") (horiz)	20	25
1431	50s. Pacific marsh harrier ("Swamp Harrier") (horiz)	30	35
1432	55s. Blue-crowned lorikeet	30	35
1433	60s. Great frigate bird	35	40
1434	70s. Friendly quail dover ("Friendly Ground Dove") (horiz)	40	45
1435	80s. Red-tailed tropic bird	45	50
1436	1p. Red shining parrot	55	60
1437	2p. Pacific pigeon	1·10	1·20
1438	3p. Pacific golden plover (horiz)	1·70	1·80
1439	5p. Polynesian scrub hen ("Tongan Megapode") (horiz)	2·75	3·00

265 "Chaetodon pelewensis"

1998. International Year of the Ocean. Mult.

No.	Description		
1440	10s. Type **265**	55	75
1441	55s. "Chaetodon lunula"	1·10	1·40
1442	1p. "Chaetodon ephippium"	1·40	2·00

266 Angel (inscr in Tongan)

1998. Christmas. Multicoloured.

No.	Description		
1443	10s. Type **266**	60	40
1444	80s. Angel (inscr in English)	2·25	1·00
1445	1p. Boy with candle (inscr in Tongan)	2·50	1·75
1446	1p.60 Girl holding candle (inscr in English)	3·50	4·50

267 Rabbit and Segment of Flower

1999. Chinese New Year ("Year of the Rabbit"). Sheet 126 × 85 mm, containing horiz designs as T **267**, showing rabbits and segments of flower. Multicoloured.

No.	Description		
MS1447	10s. Three rabbits; 55s. Rabbit eating leaf; 80s. Type **267**; 1p. Rabbit running	2·00	2·50

268 "Heemskerk" (Tasman), 1643

1999. Early Explorers. Multicoloured.

No.	Description		
1448	55s. Type **268**	1·25	60
1449	80s. "L'Astrolabe" (La Perouse), 1788	1·75	1·00
1450	1p. H.M.S. "Bounty" (Bligh), 1789	2·50	2·00
1451	2p.50 H.M.S. "Resolution" (Cook), 1777	3·75	4·25
MS1452	118 × 60 mm. No. 1451	3·75	4·25

269 Neiafu

1999. Scenic Views of Vava'u. Multicoloured.

1453	10s. Type **269**	55	40
1454	55s. Yachts at Port of Refuge	1·00	50
1455	80s. Port of Refuge from the air	1·75	80
1456	1p. Sunset at Neiafu	2·00	1·75
1457	2p.50 Mounu Island	3·50	5·00

270 "Fagraea berteroana"

1999. Fragrant Flowers. Multicoloured.

1458	10s. Type **270**	25	25
1459	80s. "Garcinia pseudoguttfera"	80	65
1460	1p. "Phaleria disperma" (vert)	1·00	1·40
1461	2p.50 "Gardenia taitensis" (vert)	2·40	3·50

271 Crowd and Trilith at Haamonga

1999. New Millennium (1st issue). Multicoloured.

1462	55s. Type **271**	80	1·10
1463	80s. Crowd and doves . . .	1·10	1·40
1464	1p. Tongans watching sunrise	1·25	1·60
1465	2p.50 King Tauf'ahau Tupou IV, dove amd Millennium emblem . . .	1·90	2·25

Nos. 1462/5 were printed together, se-tenant, with the backgrounds forming a composite design.

272 Dove and Heilala (flowers)

2000. New Millennium (2nd issue). Circular designs incorporating a clock face and inscribed "FIRST TO SEE THE MILLENNIUM". Multicoloured.

1466	10s. Type **272**	35	35
1467	1p. Haamonga Arch	1·40	1·40
1468	2p.50 Kalia (traditional canoe)	3·00	3·25
1469	2p.70 Royal Crown	3·00	3·25
MS1470	130 × 90 mm. Nos. 1468/9	6·00	6·50

273 Dragon

2000. Chinese New Year ("Year of the Dragon"). Sheet, 126 × 85 mm, containing T **273** and similar horiz designs. Multicoloured.

MS1471 10s. Type **273**; 55s. Dragon blowing on sphere; 80s. Dragon on hills; 1p. Sea dragon . . . . . 2·50 3·00

274 Queen Elizabeth the Queen Mother

2000. "The Stamp Show 2000" International Stamp Exhibition, London. Queen Elizabeth the Queen Mother's 100th Birthday. Sheet, 106 × 71 mm, containing T **274** and similar vert design. Multicoloured.

MS1472 1p. Type **274**; 2p.50, Queen Salote Tupou III of Tonga . . 3·50 4·00

275 Launch of Proton RU500

276 Siulolo Liku (hurdling)

2000. "EXPO 2000" World Stamp Exhibition, Anaheim, U.S.A. Geostationary Orbital Slot Space Programme. Multicoloured.

1473	10s. Type **275**	35	35
1474	1p. LM3 rocket for "Apstar 1" satellite (horiz)	1·25	1·25
1475	2p.50 "Apstar 1" satellite in orbit (horiz)	2·50	3·25
1476	2p.70 "Gorizont" satellite over Tonga (horiz) . . .	2·50	3·25
MS1477	134 × 80 mm. (trapezium). Nos. 1475/6	5·00	6·00

2000. Olympic Games, Sydney. Multicoloured.

1478	80s. Type **276**	80	1·00
1479	80s. Paea Wolfgramm (boxing)	80	1·00
1480	80s. Olympic Torch passing through Tonga (60 × 45 mm)	80	1·00
1481	80s. Mele Hifo Uhi (discus)	80	1·00
1482	80s. Viliami Toutai (weightlifting)	80	1·00

Nos. 1478/82 were printed together, se-tenant, with a composite series of Australian landmarks running along the bottom of each strip.

277 "Education"

2000. 30th Anniv of Tonga's Membership of the Commonwealth. Multicoloured.

1483	10s. Type **277**	25	25
1484	55s. "The Arts"	60	45
1485	80s. "Health"	85	65
1486	2p.70 "Agriculture"	2·50	3·25

278 Snake

2001. Chinese New Year ("Year of the Snake") and "Hong Kong 2001" Stamp Exhibition. Sheet 125 × 87 mm, containing T **278** and similar horiz designs showing different snakes.

MS1487 10s. multicoloured; 55s. multicoloured; 80s. multicoloured; 1p. multicoloured . . . . . . 3·00 3·25

279 Ma'ulu'ulu Dance

2001. Traditional Tongan Dances. Multicoloured.

1488	10s. Type **279**	30	20
1489	55s. Me'etupaki dance . . .	70	45
1490	80s. Tau'olunga dance . . .	85	65
1491	2p.70 Faha'iula dance . . .	2·50	3·25

280 Fiddler Crab

2001. International Mangrove Environment Day. Multicoloured.

1492	10s. Type **280**	25	25
1493	55s. Spotbill duck ("Black Ducks") and grey mullet (vert)	65	45
1494	80s. Red mangrove and emperor fish (vert) . . .	85	65
1495	1p. Mangrove flowers and reef heron	1·00	1·00
1496	2p.70 Mangrove crab . . .	2·50	3·25
MS1497	165 × 75 mm. Nos. 1492/6	4·50	5·50

281 Fisherman catching Sailfish

2001. Game Fishing in Tonga. Multicoloured.

1498	45s. Type **281**	50	35
1499	80s. Blue marlin and fishing launch	90	65
1500	2p.40 Wahoo	2·50	2·75
1501	2p.60 Dorado	2·75	3·00

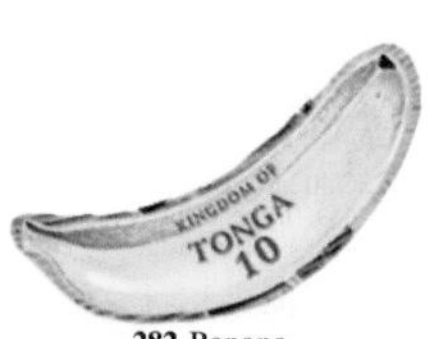

282 Banana

2001. Fruits. Multicoloured. Self-adhesive.

1502	10s. Type **282**	50	70
1503	45s. Coconut	90	1·00
1504	60s. Pineapple	1·00	1·10
1505	80s. Watermelon	1·10	1·25
1506	2p.40 Passion fruit	2·00	2·25

Nos. 1502/6 were printed together, se-tenant, with the surplus self-adhesive paper around each stamp showing a composite design of foliage.

283 *Haliotis ovina* Shell

2001. Shells. Multicoloured.

1507	10s. Type **283**	25	25
1508	80s. *Turbo petholatus* . . .	85	85
1509	1p. *Trochus niloticus*	1·00	1·00
1510	2p.70 *Turbo marmoratus* . .	2·50	3·25

2002. Golden Jubilee. Sheet, 162 × 95 mm, containing designs as T **211** of St. Helena.

MS1511 15s. brownish black, rosine and gold; 90s. multicoloured; 1p.20, grey-black, rosine and gold; 1p.40, multicoloured; 2p.25, multicoloured . . . . 6·00 6·50

DESIGNS—HORIZ: (as Type **211** of St. Helena)—15s. Princess Elizabeth as a young girl; 90s. Queen Elizabeth in yellow outfit; 1p.20, Queen Elizabeth with Prince Charles and Princess Anne; 1p.40, Queen Elizabeth in evening dress. VERT: (38 × 51 mm)—2p.25, Queen Elizabeth after Annigoni.

284 Horses galloping

2002. Chinese New Year ("Year of the Horse"). Sheet 126 × 89 mm, containing T **284** and similar vert designs. Multicoloured.

MS1512 65s. Type **284**; 80s. Palomino and grey horses; 1p. Chestnut horse rearing; 2p.50 Piebald and bay horses . . . . . 5·50 6·00

285 Surfer and Whale

2002. U.N. Year of Eco Tourism. Multicoloured.

1513	5s. Type **285**	30	30
1514	15s. Tongan girl and rocky coastline	30	30
1515	70s. Tropical fish and tourist beach	90	75
1516	1p.40 Island dancer and Haamonga trilith	1·60	1·40
1517	2p.25 Tongan man and canoes at sunset	2·25	2·75

286 Oyster Farm

2002. Development of Tonga Pearl Industry. Multicoloured.

1518	90s. Type **286**	1·00	1·00
1519	1p. Oysters on underwater frame	1·00	1·00
1520	1p.20 Tongan girl and pearls	1·25	1·40
1521	2p.50 Pearls and island scene	2·50	3·00
MS1522	Circular (97 mm diameter). Nos. 1520/1.	3·75	4·25

287 Leaping for Ball

2002. 17th Commonwealth Games, Manchester. Rugby Sevens. Multicoloured.

1523	15s. Type **287**	30	25
1524	30s. Players in a ruck . . .	50	30
1525	90s. Running with ball . . .	1·10	80
1526	4p. Scoring a try	4·00	5·00

288 Woman slitting Pandanus Leaves

289 Red Shining Parrots in Tree Trunk Nest

2002. Weaving. Multicoloured.

1527	30s. Type **288**	40	25
1528	90s. Leaves drying and boy with large baskets	90	70
1529	1p.40 Women weaving baskets	1·40	1·40
1530	2p.50 Girl weaving basket lid	2·50	3·00

2002. 10th Anniv of Eua National Park. Red Shining Parrots. Multicoloured.

1531	45s. Type **289**	75	45
1532	1p. Eating fruit	1·25	1·00
1533	1p.50 Two parrots on branch	1·50	1·75
1534	2p.50 Red shining parrot with wings spread	2·50	3·00

290 Ram

2003. Chinese New Year ("Year of the Sheep"). Sheet 125 × 85 mm, containing **T 290** and similar horiz designs. Multicoloured.
MS1535 65p. Type **290**; 80p. Three ewes; 1p. Three black-faced ewes; 2p.50 Two ewes . . . . 2·75 2·75

291 Queen Elizabeth II in Gold State Coach

2003. 50th Anniv of Coronation.
1536 **291** 90s. blue and gold . . . 50 55
1537 – 1p.20 blue and gold . . 65 70
1538 – 1p.40 blue and gold . . 80 85
1539 – 2p.50 blue and gold . . 1·40 1·50
DESIGNS: 90s. Type **291**; 1p.20 Queen Salote; 1p.40 Queen Salote waving in carriage; 2p.50 Queen Elizabeth.

292 Fishing and Double-Hulled Canoes

2003. Abel Tasman Commemoration. In Search of the Great South Land.
1540 **292** 15s. drab, red and black 10 10
1541 – 75s. drab, red and black 40 45
1542 – 90s. stone, red and black 50 55
1543 – 2p.50 stone, red and black . . . . 1·40 1·50
MS1544 165 × 75 mm. Nos. 1540/3 2·40 2·50
DESIGNS: 15s. Type **292**; 75s. Men rowing ashore with barrels; 90s.Two double-hulled canoes; 2p.50 *Heemskerk* and *Zeehan*.

293 Euakafa Beach

2003. Scenic Beaches. Multicoloured.
1545 15s. Type **293** 10 10
1546 90s. Pangaimotu beach . . . 50 55
1547 1p.40 Fafa beach 80 85
1548 2p.25 Nuku beach . . . . . 1·20 1·30

294 Catholic Church, Neiafu, Vava'u

2003. Christmas. Churches. Multicoloured.
1549 15s. Type **294** 10 10
1550 90s. Wesleyan Church, Uiha, Ha'apai 50 55
1551 1p.40 Cathedral of the Immaculate Conception of Mary 80 85
1552 2p.25 Free Wesleyan Church, Nuku'alofa . . . 1·20 1·30

295 Spider Monkey

2004. Chinese New Year ("Year of the Monkey"). Sheet 95 × 85 mm containing T **295** and similar horiz designs. Multicoloured.
MS1553 60s. Type **295**; 80s. Ring-tailed lemur; 1p. Cotton-top tamarin; 2p.50 White-cheeked gibbon . . . . 2·75 3·00

EXPRESS STAMP

E **1** Short-eared Owl in Flight

1990. Air.
E1 E **1** 10p. black, red and blue 9·50 10·00

OFFICIAL STAMPS

1893. Optd **G.F.B.**
O1 **5** 1d. blue . . . . 11·00 50·00
O2 **6** 2d. blue . . . . 28·00 55·00
O3 **5** 4d. blue . . . . 48·00 £100
O4 **6** 8d. blue . . . . 90·00 £170
O5 1s. blue £110 £200

1893. Nos. O1/5 variously surch.
O 6 **5** ½d. on 1d. blue . . . . . . 19·00 50·00
O 7 **6** 2½d. on 2d. blue . . . . . 25·00 45·00
O 8 **5** 5d. on 4d. blue . . . . . 25·00 45·00
O 9 **6** 7½d. on 8d. blue . . . . . 25·00 80·00
O10 10d. on 1s. blue . . . . . 28·00 85·00

1962. Air. Stamps of 1953 and 1961 optd as Nos. 120/7 but with **OFFICIAL AIRMAIL** in addition.
O11 2d. blue . . . . 14·00 6·00
O12 5d. violet . . . . 15·00 6·50
O13 1s. brown . . . . 10·00 3·75
O14 5s. yellow and lilac . . . . £110 65·00
O15 10s. yellow and black . . . . 45·00 22·00
O16 £1 yellow, red and blue . . . 70·00 35·00

1963. Air. 1st Polynesian Gold Coinage Commemoration. As No. 138 but additionally inscr "OFFICIAL". 1 koula coin. Diameter 3⅝ in. Imperf.
O17 B 15s. black on gold . . . . 8·00 9·00

1965. Air. Surch as Nos. 151/61.
O18 B 30s. on 15s. (No. O17) . . 3·25 4·25

1966. Air. Tupou College and Secondary Education Centenary. No. 117 surch **OFFICIAL AIRMAIL** and new value, with commemoration inscr as Nos. 168/73.
O19 10s. on 4d. green 80 35
O20 20s. on 4d. green . . . . . 1·00 50

1967. Air. No. 112 surch **OFFICIAL AIRMAIL ONE PA'ANGA.**
O21 1p. on 5s. yellow and lilac 7·00 2·50

1967. Air. No. 114 surch **OFFICIAL AIRMAIL** and new value.
O22 40s. on £1 yellow, red & blue 60 75
O23 60s. on £1 yellow, red & blue 80 1·25
O24 1p. on £1 yellow, red and blue . . . . 1·10 2·25
O25 2p. on £1 yellow, red and blue . . . . 1·75 3·00

1967. Air. Arrival of U.S. Peace Corps in Tonga. As No. 114, but imperf and background colour changed, surch as Nos. 216/27 but with **Official Airmail** in addition.
O26 30s. on £1 multicoloured . . 50 30
O27 70s. on £1 multicoloured . . 70 1·25
O28 1p.50 on £1 multicoloured 1·00 2·00

1968. Air. 50th Birthday of King Taufa'ahua IV. No. 207 surch **HIS MAJESTY'S 50th BIRTHDAY OFFICIAL AIRMAIL** and new value.
O29 40s. on 50s. red and blue . . 2·50 70
O30 60s. on 50s. red and blue . . 3·00 1·75
O31 1p. on 50s. red and blue . . 4·00 4·00
O32 2p. on 50s. red and blue . . 7·50 8·00

1968. Air. South Pacific Games Field and Track Trials, Port Moresby, New Guinea. As No. 114 but imperf, background colour changed, surch **Friendly Islands Trials Field & Track South Pacific Games Port Moresby 1969 OFFICIAL AIRMAIL** and value.
O33 20s. on £1 multicoloured . . 20 25
O34 1p. on £1 multicoloured . . 70 1·50

1969. Air. 3rd South Pacific Games, Port Moresby. As Nos. 290/4 surch **OFFICIAL AIRMAIL.**
O35 70s. red, green and turquoise 75 1·60
O36 80s. red, orange and turquoise . . . . 85 1·60

1969. Air. Oil Search. As No. 114 but imperf, background colour changed and optd **1969 OIL SEARCH** and new value.
O37 90s. on £1 multicoloured . . 3·50 5·00
O38 1p.10 on £1 multicoloured 3·50 5·00
No. O37 is additionally optd **OFFICIAL AIRMAIL.**

1969. Air. Royal Visit. As No. 110, but imperf, colour changed, and surch **Royal Visit MARCH 1970 OFFICIAL AIRMAIL** and new value.
O39 75s. on 1s. red and yellow 4·50 4·00
O40 1p. on 1s. red and yellow . . 5·00 4·50
O41 1p.25 on 1s. red and yellow 6·00 6·00

1970. Air. Entry into British Commonwealth. As No. 112, but imperf and surch **Commonwealth Member JUNE 1970 OFFICIAL AIRMAIL** and value.
O42 50s. on 5s. yellow and brown 3·00 1·75
O43 90s. on 5s. yellow and brown 4·00 3·25
O44 1p.50 on 5s. yellow & brown 5·00 5·50

1970. Imperf. Self-adhesive. Colour of "TONGA" given for 6s. to 10s.
O45 **83** 1s. yellow, purple & black 65 1·00
O46 2s. yellow, blue and black 75 1·00
O47 3s. yellow, brown & black 75 1·00
O48 4s. yellow, green and black 75 1·00
O49 5s. yellow, red and black 80 1·00
O50 **90** 6s. blue . . . . 90 1·25
O51 7s. mauve . . . . 95 1·25
O52 8s. gold . . . . 1·10 1·25
O53 9s. red . . . . 1·25 1·25
O54 10s. silver . . . . 1·25 1·25
On the official issues Nos. O45 to O54, the value tablet is black (banana issue) or green (coconut issue). On the postage issues the colour is white.
See also Nos. O82/91.

1970. Air. Centenary of British Red Cross. As No. 102 and 112 but imperf in different colours and surch **Centenary British Red Cross 1870-1970 OFFICIAL AIRMAIL** and value.
O55 30s. on 1½d. green . . . . . 1·75 2·00
O56 80s. on 5s. yellow and brown 5·50 5·00
O57 90s. on 5s. yellow and brown 5·50 5·00

1971. Air. 5th Death Anniv of Queen Salote. As No. 113, but imperf and colour changed surch **OFFICIAL AIRMAIL 1965 IN MEMORIAM 1970** and value.
O58 20s. on 10s. orange . . . . 1·25 80
O59 30s. on 10s. orange . . . . 1·50 1·00
O60 50s. on 10s. orange . . . . 2·75 2·00
O61 2p. on 10s. orange . . . . . 9·00 10·00

1971. Air. Philatokyo '71 Stamp Exhibition, Japan. Nos. O55/7 optd **PHILATOKYO '71** and emblem.
O62 30s. on 5d. green and yellow 90 65
O63 80s. on 5d. green and yellow 1·75 1·75
O64 90s. on 5d. green and yellow 2·00 2·00

1971. Air. As T **96** but inscr "OFFICIAL AIRMAIL".
O65 14s. multicoloured . . . . 2·25 2·50
O65a 17s. multicoloured . . . . 2·50 2·75
O66 21s. multicoloured . . . . 2·50 2·75
O66a 38s. multicoloured . . . . 3·50 3·75

O **13**

1971. Air. 4th South Pacific Games, Tahiti. Imperf. Self-adhesive.
O67 O **13** 50s. multicoloured . . . 60 90
O68 90s. multicoloured . . . 85 1·50
O69 1p.50 multicoloured . . 1·25 1·75

1971. Air. Investiture of Royal Tongan Medal of Merit surch **INVESTITURE 1971 OFFICIAL AIRMAIL.**
O70 **89** 60s. on 3s. multicoloured 80 1·10
O71 80s. on 25s. multicoloured 1·10 1·40
O72 1p.10 on 7s. multicoloured 1·25 1·75

O **15** "UNICEF" and Emblem

1971. Air. 25th Anniv of UNICEF. Imperf. Self-adhesive.
O73 O **15** 70s. multicoloured . . . 1·60 1·75
O74 80s. multicoloured . . . 1·75 2·00
O75 90s. multicoloured . . . 1·90 2·25

1972. Air. Merchant Marine Routes. As T **100** but inscr "OFFICIAL AIRMAIL". Imperf. Self-adhesive.
O76 20s. multicoloured . . . . . 1·25 80
O77 50s. multicoloured . . . . . 2·75 2·50
O78 1p.20 multicoloured . . . . 5·50 7·00
DESIGN: Nos. O76/8, Map of South Pacific and "Aoniu".

1972. Air. 5th Anniv of Coronation. Design similar to T **101**, but inscr "OFFICIAL AIRMAIL".
O79 50s. multicoloured . . . . . 1·00 85
O80 70s. multicoloured . . . . . 1·40 1·25
O81 1p.50 multicoloured . . . . 2·75 3·00
DESIGN—(47 × 57 mm): Nos. O79/81, As Type **101** but with different background.

1972. As Nos. 413/27 but inscr "OFFICIAL POST".
(a) As Nos. 413/17.
O82 **83** 1s. yellow, red and black 30 30
O83 2s. yellow, green and black 35 30
O84 3s. yellow, green and black 40 30
O85 4s. yellow and black . . . 40 30
O86 5s. yellow and black . . . 40 30

(b) As Nos. O50/4 but colours changed. Mult. Colour of "TONGA" given.
O87 **90** 6s. green 45 35
O88 7s. green 55 35
O89 8s. green 55 35
O90 9s. green 55 35
O91 10s. green 60 35

(c) As Nos. 423/7. Multicoloured. Colour of face value given.
O92 **102** 15s. blue . . . . 1·00 55
O93 20s. orange . . . . . . 1·25 75
O94 25s. brown . . . . . . 1·40 85
O95 40s. orange . . . . . . 2·50 1·75
O96 50s. blue . . . . 2·75 2·00

1972. Air. Proclamation of Sovereignty over Minerva Reefs. As T **104**, but inscr "OFFICIAL AIRMAIL".
O97 25s. multicoloured 40 35
O98 75s. multicoloured . . . . . 1·25 1·50
O99 1p.50 multicoloured . . . . 2·50 3·00

1973. Air. Foundation of Bank of Tonga. No. 396 surch **TONGA 1973 ESTABLISHMENT BANK OF TONGA OFFICIAL AIRMAIL**, star and value.
O100 **100** 40s. on 21s. mult . . . 1·50 1·25
O101 85s. on 21s. mult . . . 3·00 3·25
O102 1p.25 on 21s. mult . . . 3·75 6·00

1973. Silver Jubilee of Scouting in Tonga. Nos. O76, O74 and 319 surch or optd.
O103 – 30s. on 20s. mult . . . 10·00 2·75
O104 O **15** 80s. multicoloured . . 25·00 10·00
O105 **89** 1p.40 on 50s. mult . . 35·00 25·00
OVERPRINT AND SURCHARGES: 30s. **SILVER JUBILEE TONGAN SCOUTING 1948-1973**, scout badge and value; 80c. **SILVER JUBILEE 1948-1973** and scout badge; 1p.40, **OFFICIAL AIRMAIL 1948-1973 SILVER JUBILEE TONGAN SCOUTING** and value.

1973. Air. Bicentenary of Capt. Cook's Visit. Design similar to T **107** but inscr "OFFICIAL AIRMAIL".
O106 25s. multicoloured . . . . 3·25 1·50
O107 80s. multicoloured . . . . 8·50 4·50
O108 1p.30 multicoloured . . . . 10·00 7·50
DESIGN—HORIZ (52 × 45 mm): Nos. O106/8, "James Cook" (bulk carrier).

1973. Air. Commonwealth Games, Christchurch. Nos. O67/9 optd **1974 Commonwealth Games Christchurch OFFICIAL AIRMAIL.**
O109 O **13** 50s. multicoloured . . 80 1·10
O110 90s. multicoloured . . 1·40 1·75
O111 1p.50 multicoloured . . 2·00 2·50

O **19** Dove of Peace

1974. Air.
O112 O **19** 7s. green, violet and red 70 30
O113 9s. green, violet & brn 75 35
O114 12s. green, violet & brown 80 85
O115 14s. green, violet & yellow 85 50
O116 17s. multicoloured . . 95 70
O117 29s. multicoloured . . 1·75 1·00
O118 38s. multicoloured . . 2·25 1·25
O119 50s. multicoloured . . 2·75 2·75
O120 75s. multicoloured . . 4·00 4·50

1974. Air. Centenary of U.P.U. As Nos. 488/97 but inscr "OFFICIAL AIRMAIL".
O121 25s. orange, green and black 50 70
O122 35s. yellow, red and black 60 85
O123 70s. orange, blue and black 1·25 2·25
DESIGNS—HORIZ (43 × 40 mm): Nos. O121/3, Letters "UPU".

1974. Air. Tongan Girl Guides. As Nos. 498/507 inscr "OFFICIAL AIRMAIL".
O124 45s. multicoloured . . . . 4·00 2·00
O125 55s. multicoloured . . . . 4·25 2·25
O126 1p. multicoloured . . . . . 7·50 5·50
DESIGNS—OVAL (36 × 52 mm): Nos. O124/6, Lady Baden-Powell.

1974. Air. Establishment of Royal Marine Institute. No. 446 surch **OFFICIAL AIRMAIL 80s** and RMI emblem and No. 451 surch **Establishment Royal Marine Institute Official Airmail TONGA TONGA**, RMI emblem and value.
O127 **106** 30s. on 15s. multicoloured . . . . 2·50 1·75
O128 – 35s. on 15s. multicoloured . . . . 2·75 2·00
O129 – 80s. on 17s. multicoloured . . . . 4·25 4·50

1975. Air. South Pacific Forum and Tourism. As T **113**. Imperf. Self-adhesive.

O130 50s. multicoloured . . . . 1·10 1·00
O131 75s. multicoloured . . . . 1·75 1·50
O132 1p.25 multicoloured . . . . 2·50 2·25
DESIGNS—(49 × 43 mm): 50s. Jungle arch; 75s., 1p.25, Sunset scene.

1975. Air. 5th South Pacific Games. As T **114**. Imperf. Self-adhesive.

O133 38s. multicoloured 55 50
O134 75s. multicoloured . . . . 90 1·60
O135 1p.20 multicoloured . . . . 1·60 3·00
DESIGN—OVAL (51 × 27 mm): Nos. O133/5, Runners on track.

O **21** Tongan Monarchs (⅔-size illustration)

1975. Air. Centenary of Tongan Constitution. Imperf. Self-adhesive.

O136 O **21** 17s. multicoloured . . 75 50
O137 60s. multicoloured . . 1·60 2·00
O138 90s. multicoloured . . 2·25 2·75

1976. Air. First Participation in Olympic Games. As Nos. 558/67 but inscr "OFFICIAL AIRMAIL".

O139 45s. multicoloured . . . . 4·50 1·50
O140 55s. multicoloured . . . . 4·50 1·60
O141 1p. multicoloured . . . . 8·50 8·50
DESIGN—OVAL (36 × 53 mm): Montreal logo.

1976. Air. Bicentenary of American Revolution. As Nos. 568/77 but inscr "OFFICIAL AIRMAIL".

O142 20s. multicoloured 75 50
O143 50s. multicoloured . . . . 1·00 1·50
O144 1p.15 multicoloured . . . . 2·00 3·50

1976. Air. 150th Anniv of Christianity in Tonga.

O145 65s. multicoloured . . . . 2·50 3·00
O146 85s. multicoloured . . . . 2·75 3·75
O147 1p.15 multicoloured . . . . 3·25 4·75
DESIGN—HEXAGONAL (65 × 52 mm): Lifuka Chapel.

1976. Air. Centenary of Treaty of Friendship with Germany.

O148 30s. multicoloured 60 70
O149 60s. multicoloured . . . . 1·40 1·75
O150 1p.25 multicoloured . . . . 2·75 3·50
DESIGN—RECTANGULAR (51 × 47 mm): Text.

1977. Air. Silver Jubilee.

O151 35s. multicoloured 70 40
O152 45s. multicoloured 30 30
O153 1p.10 multicoloured 45 50
DESIGN—57 × 66 mm: Flags of Tonga and the U.K.

1977. Air. 10th Anniv of King's Coronation.

O154 20s. multicoloured 40 45
O155 40s. multicoloured . . . . 80 1·00
O156 80s. multicoloured . . . . 1·75 2·25
DESIGN—SQUARE (50 × 50 mm): 1967 Coronation coin.

1977. Air. Bicent of Capt. Cook's Last Voyage.

O157 20s. multicoloured . . . . 2·75 2·50
O158 55s. on 20s. multicoloured 6·00 6·50
O159 85s. on 20s. multicoloured 8·50 9·00
DESIGN—RECTANGULAR (52 × 46 mm): Text.

1977. Air. Whale Conservation.

O160 45s. multicoloured . . . . 5·50 3·00
O161 65s. multicoloured . . . . 7·50 5·00
O162 85s. multicoloured . . . . 9·00 6·00
DESIGN—HEXAGONAL (66 × 51 mm): Blue whale.

1978. Air. Commonwealth Games, Edmonton.

O163 30s. black, blue and red . . 60 60
O164 60s. black, red and blue . . 1·40 1·75
O165 1p. black, red and blue . . 1·75 2·00
DESIGN—TEAR-DROP (35 × 52 mm): Games emblem.

1978. Air. 60th Birthday of King Taufa'ahau Tupou IV.

O166 26s. black, red and yellow 50 30
O167 85s. black, brown and yellow . . . . 1·40 1·60
O168 90s. black, violet and yellow 1·50 1·60
DESIGN—MEDAL-SHAPED (21 × 45 mm): Portrait of King.

1978. Coil stamps. As Nos. 675/89 but inscr "OFFICIAL POST".

O169 1s. purple and yellow . . . 20 20
O170 2s. brown and yellow . . . 20 20
O171 3s. red and yellow 30 30
O172 4s. brown and yellow . . . 30 30
O173 5s. green and yellow . . . 30 30
O174 6s. brown and green . . . 40 40
O175 7s. black, green and brown 40 40
O176 8s. red, green and brown 40 40
O177 9s. brown and green . . . 40 40
O178 10s. green and brown . . . 40 40
O179 15s. black, brown and green 1·00 1·00
O180 20s. red, brown and green 1·10 1·10
O181 30s. green and brown . . . 1·25 1·50
O182 50s. blue, brown and green 1·50 1·75
O183 1p. violet, brown and green 2·25 2·75

1978. Air. Endangered Wildlife. Multicoloured.

O184 40s. Type **129** . . . . . . 6·50 3·50
O185 50s. Insular flying fox . . . 5·50 3·50
O186 1p.10 Turtle . . . . 7·50 9·00

1979. Air. Decade of Progress. As Nos. 700/9, but inscr "OFFICIAL AIRMAIL".

O187 G 38s. multicoloured . . . 1·25 65
O188 E 74s. multicoloured . . . 1·60 1·75
O189 A 80s. multicoloured . . . 2·50 2·50

1979. Air. Death Centenary of Sir Rowland Hill and 10th Anniv of Tongan Self-adhesive Stamps.

O190 45s. multicoloured 75 60
O191 65s. multicoloured . . . . 1·10 85
O192 80s. multicoloured . . . . 1·25 1·10
DESIGN—HAND SHAPED (45 × 53 mm): 45s. to 80s. Removing self-adhesive stamp from backing paper.

O **22** Blue-crowned Lory (with foliage)

O **23** Blue-crowned Lory (without foliage)

1979. Air. Coil Stamps.

O193 O **22** 5s. multicoloured . . . 60 70
O194 11s. multicoloured . . 65 70
O195 14s. multicoloured . . 65 70
O196 15s. multicoloured . . 70 70
O197 17s. multicoloured . . 70 70
O198 18s. multicoloured . . 70 50
O199 22s. multicoloured . . 80 50
O200 31s. multicoloured . . 90 65
O201 39s. multicoloured . . 1·25 80
O202 75s. multicoloured . . 2·00 3·00
O203 1p. multicoloured . . . 2·50 4·00

1979. Air. Views as seen through the Lens of a Camera.

O204 35s. multicoloured 55 75
O205 45s. multicoloured 65 85
O206 1p. multicoloured . . . . . 1·25 3·00
DESIGN: 35s. to 1p. Niuatoputapu and Tafahi.

1980. Air. 125th Anniv of France–Tonga Friendship Treaty.

O207 40s. multicoloured . . . . 75 1·00
O208 55s. multicoloured . . . . 1·00 1·25
O209 1p.25 multicoloured . . . . 2·00 2·75
DESIGN: 40s. to 1p.25, Establishment of the Principle of Religious Freedom in the Pacific Islands.

1980. Air. Olympic Games, Moscow. Nos. O190/2 surch mascot, **1980 OLYMPIC GAMES**, value and emblem.

O210 26s. on 45s. multicoloured 85 85
O211 40s. on 65s. multicoloured 1·40 1·40
O212 1p.10 on 1p. multicoloured 3·50 3·75

1980. No. O193 redrawn without foliage as Type O **23**.

O213 O **23** 5s. multicoloured . . . £100 80·00

1980. Air. South Pacific Scout Jamboree, Tonga and 75th Anniv of Rotary International.

O214 25s. multicoloured 75 65
O215 2p. multicoloured . . . . . 3·50 6·50
DESIGN: 25s., 2p. Scout camp and Rotary emblem. Nos. O214/15 show maps of Tonga on the reverse.

1980. Air. Nos. O145 surch **T$2**.

O216 2p. on 65s. multicoloured 4·50 6·50

1983. Nos. 834/6 optd **OFFICIAL**.

O217 29s. Type **151** . . . . . . 5·00 5·00
O218 32s. Type **151** . . . . . . 5·00 5·00
O219 47s. Montgolfier's balloon and Concorde . . . . . 10·00 7·50

1984. Nos. 865/79 and 881 optd **OFFICIAL**.

O220 1s. Type **159** . . . . . . 50 1·40
O221 2s. "Porites sp" . . . . . 50 1·40
O222 3s. Red squirrelfish . . . . 50 1·50
O223 5s. Green map cowrie . . . 50 1·25
O224 6s. "Dardanus megistos" . . . 50 1·50
O225 9s. Variegated shark . . . 75 80
O226 10s. Bubble cone . . . . . 80 1·25
O227 13s. Lionfish . . . . 1·25 80
O228 15s. Textile or cloth of gold cone . . . . 1·25 1·75
O229 20s. White-tailed damselfish 1·50 2·00
O230 29s. Princely cone . . . . 1·75 85
O231 32s. Powder-blue surgeonfish . . . . . . 1·75 85
O232 47s. Giant spider conch . . 2·00 90
O233 1p. "Millepora dichotoma" 3·75 3·75
O234 2p. "Birgus latro" . . . . 7·00 7·00
O235 5p. Yellow-finned tuna . . 12·00 13·00

1986. Nos. 933/9 optd **OFFICIAL**.

O236 4s. on 2s. "Porites sp" . . . 90 2·00
O237 4s. on 13s. Lionfish . . . . 90 2·00
O238 42s. on 3s. Red squirrelfish 2·75 2·50
O239 42s. on 9s. Variegated shark 2·75 2·50
O240 57s. on 6s. "Dardanus megistos" . . . . 3·00 2·75
O241 57s. on 20s. White-tailed damselfish . . . . . . 3·00 2·75
O242 2p.50 on 2p. "Birgus latro" 10·00 11·00

1994. Air. 25th Anniv of Tongan Self-adhesive Stamps. Design as No. O192, but inscr "25th ANNIVERSARY OF THE INTRODUCTION OF SELFADHESIVE STAMPS 1969–1994 BERNARD MECHANICK: 1915–80 INVENTOR FREEFORM SELFADHESIVE STAMPS" at centre foot.

O243 80s. multicoloured . . . . 7·00 7·00

O **30** Bubble Cone

1995. Designs as Nos. 1221a, 1223a, 1225a, 1227a and 1229a, but inscr as Type O **30**.

O247 10s. Type O **30** . . . . . 50 1·00
O249 20s. White-tailed dascyllus 75 1·00
O251 45s. Giant spider conch . . 1·00 60
O253 60s. Princely cone . . . . 1·25 75
O255 80s. Lionfish . . . . 1·50 1·00
O256 1p. "Chelonia mydas" (turtle) . . . . 2·00 1·75
O257 2p. "Birgus latro" (crab) . . 3·50 3·75
O258 3p. Rose branch murex . . 4·50 5·00
O259 5p. Humpback whale . . . 8·50 8·50
O260 10p. Variegated shark (vert) 12·00 13·00

TRANSCAUCASIAN FEDERATION
Pt. 10

A Federation of Armenia, Azerbaijan and Georgia, which was absorbed into the U.S.S.R. in 1923.

100 kopeks = 1 rouble.

1 Mt. Ararat and Oilfield

2 Mts. Ararat and Elbruz and Oil-derricks

1923.
1 1 40,000r. purple . . . . 2·00 4·00
2 75,000r. green . . . . 2·00 4·00
3 100,000r. grey . . . . 1·25 2·00
4 150,000r. red . . . . 2·25 1·25
5 2 200,000r. green . . . . 1·25 1·75
6 300,000r. blue . . . . 90 1·75
7 350,000r. brown . . . . . . 90 1·75
8 500,000r. red . . . . 1·75 3·00

1923. Surch **700000 RYb.**
9 1 700,000r. on 40,000r. purple 2·00 4·00
10 700,000r. on 75,000r. green 2·00 4·00

1923. Values in gold kopeks.
11 2 1k. orange . . . . 1·00 1·50
12 2k. green . . . . 1·00 1·50
13 3k. red . . . . 1·00 1·50
14 4k. brown . . . . 1·00 1·50
15 1 5k. purple . . . . 1·00 1·50
16 9k. blue . . . . 1·00 1·50
17 18k. grey . . . . 1·00 1·50

TRANSKEI
Pt. 1

The Republic of Transkei was established on 26 October 1976, as the first of the independent "black homelands" constructed from the territory of the Republic of South Africa.

This independence did not receive international political recognition, but the stamps were accepted as valid on international mail.

Transkei was reincorporated with the Republic of South Africa on 27 April 1994.

100 cents = 1 rand.

1 Lubisi Dam

1976. Transkei Scenes and Occupations. Mult.
1 1c. Type **1** 10 10
2 2c. Soil cultivation 10 10
3 3c. Threshing sorghum . . . 15 10
4a 4c. Transkei matron 15 10
5a 5c. Grinding maize 15 10
6 6c. Cutting "Phormium tenax" 15 10
7 7c. Herd-boy 40 10
8 8c. Felling timber 20 10
9 9c. Agricultural schooling . . 15 15
10a 10c. Tea picking 20 15
11a 15c. Carrying wood 30 15
12a 20c. Weaving industry . . . 35 15
13 25c. Cattle 45 25
14a 30c. Sledge transportation . . 60 45
15 50c. Coat of arms and map 85 50
16 1r. Administration building, Umtata . . . . 50 1·25
17 2r. The Bunga (Parliamentary building), Umtata . . . . 75 2·25

2 K. D. Matanzima

4 "Artemisia afra"

3 Beech 100 King Air of Transkei Airways

1976. Independence. Multicoloured.
18 4c. Type **2** 20 20
19 10c. Flag and mace 45 45
20 15c. K. D. Matanzima, Paramount Chief (different) 55 75
21 20c. Coat of arms 60 80

1977. Transkei Airways' Inaugural Flight. Mult.
22 4c. Type **3** 25 15
23 15c. Beech King Air landing at Matanzima Airport 75 85

1977. Medicinal Plants (1st series). Mult.
24 4c. Type **4** 15 10
25 10c. "Bulbine natalensis" . . . 45 45
26 15c. "Melianthus major" . . . 55 65
27 20c. "Cotyledon orbiculata" 65 90
See also Nos. 88/91.

5 Disc Jockey

6 Blind Basket Weaver

1977. 1st Anniv of Transkei Radio. Mult.
28 4c. Type **5** 15 10
29 15c. Announcer 60 60

1977. Help for the Blind.
30 6 4c. black, lilac and gold . . . 15 10
31 – 15c. black, drab and gold . . 35 35
32 – 20c. black, brown and gold 75 80
DESIGNS: 15c. Hands reading braille; 20c. Blind woman spinning.

7 Men's Carved Pipes

1978. Carved Pipes. Multicoloured.
33 4c. Type **7** 10 10
34 10c. Two men's pipes 15 15
35 15c. Multi-bowled men's pipes 35 55
36 20c. Woman's and witch-doctor's pipes 40 70

8 Angora Goat

9 "Carissa bispinosa"

1978. Weaving Industry. Multicoloured.
37 4c. Type **8** 10 10
38 10c. Spinning mohair 15 15
39 15c. Dyeing mohair 20 25
40 20c. Weaving a mohair rug . . 30 40

1978. Edible Wild Fruits. Multicoloured.
41 4c. Type **9** 15 10
42 10c. "Dovyalis caffra" 20 25
43 15c. "Harpephyllum caffrum" 35 55
44 20c. "Syzygium cordatum" . . 40 70

10 Calipers

12 President K. D. Matanzima

11 Chi Cha Youth

1978. Care of Cripples.
45 10 4c. black, brown and gold 10 10
46 – 10c. black, grey and gold . . 25 25
47 – 15c. black, yellow and gold 40 50
DESIGNS: 10c. Child in wheelchair; 15c. Nurse examining child's leg.

1979. Abakwetha (coming-of-age ceremony of Xhosa males). Multicoloured.
48 4c. Type **11** 10 10
49 10c. Youths in three-month seclusion 20 20
50 15c. Umtshilo dance 35 35
51 20c. Burning of seclusion hut at end of final ceremony . . 45 45

1979. Inaug of Second State President.
52 12 4c. red and gold 15 10
53 15c. green and gold 50 45

13 Windpump

14 Magwa Falls

1979. Water Resources. Multicoloured.
54 4c. Type **13** 15 10
55 10c. Woman ladling water into jar 20 25
56 15c. Indwe River Dam (horiz) 35 55
57 20c. Ncora Dam (horiz) . . . 40 70

1979. Waterfalls. Multicoloured.
58 4c. Type **14** 15 10
59 10c. Bawa Falls 20 25
60 15c. Waterfall Bluff (horiz) . . 35 55
61 20c. Tsitsa Falls (horiz) . . . 40 70

15 Expectant Mother pouring Milk

16 Black Gnat (dry fly)

1979. Child Health. Multicoloured.
62 5c. Type **15** 15 10
63 15c. Mother breast-feeding baby 45 45
64 20c. Immunizing child 60 65

1980. Fishing Flies (1st series). Multicoloured.
65 5c. Type **16** 25 35
66 5c. Zug Bug (nymph) 25 35
67 5c. March Brown (wet fly) . . 25 35
68 5c. Durham Ranger (salmon fly) 25 35
69 5c. Colonel Bates (streamer) 25 35
See also Nos. 83/7, 99/103, 116/20 and 133/7.

17 Rotary Emblem

18 "Encephalartos altensteinii"

1980. 75th Anniv of Rotary International.
70 17 15c. blue and gold 35 30

1980. Cycads. Multicoloured.
71 5c. Type **18** 15 10
72 10c. "Encephalartos princeps" 25 25
73 15c. "Encephalartos villosus" 40 40
74 20c. "Encephalartos friderici-guilielmi" 50 55

19 Red-chested Cuckoo

1980. Birds. Multicoloured.
75 5c. Type **19** 20 10
76 10c. Cape puff-back fly-catcher 45 25
77 15c. South African crowned crane 65 60
78 20c. Spectacled Weaver . . . 70 70

20 Hole in the Wall

1980. Tourism. Multicoloured.
79 5c. Type **20** 15 10
80 10c. Port St. Johns 25 25
81 15c. The Citadel (rock) . . . 40 40
82 20c. The Archway (rock) . . . 50 55

1981. Fishing Flies (2nd series). As T **16**. Mult.
83 10c. Kent's Lightning (streamer) 25 25
84 10c. Wickham's Fancy (dry fly) 25 25
85 10c. Jock Scott (wet fly) . . . 25 25
86 10c. Green Highlander (salmon fly) 25 25
87 10c. Tan Nymph 25 25

1981. Medicinal Plants (2nd series). As T **4**. Mult.
88 5c. "Leonotis leonurus" . . . 15 10
89 15c. "Euphorbia bupleurifolia" 30 30
90 20c. "Pelargonium reniforme" 35 35
91 25c. "Hibiscus trionum" . . . 35 40

21 Eyamakhwenkwe

1981. Xhosa Women's Headdresses. Multicoloured.
92 5c. Type **21** 10 10
93 15c. Eyabafana 20 35
94 20c. Umfazana 25 45
95 25c. Ixhegokazi 30 55
MS96 126 × 91 mm. Nos. 92/5 . . 1·00 1·25

22 State House, Umtata

1981. 5th Anniv of Independence.
97 22 5c. black, brown and green 15 10
98 – 15c. black, brown and green 45 30
DESIGN: 15c. University of Transkei.

1982. Fishing Flies (3rd series). As T **16**. Mult.
99 10c. Blue Charm 30 30
100 10c. Royal Coachman . . . 30 30
101 10c. Light Spruce 30 30
102 10c. Montana Nymph . . . 30 30
103 10c. Butcher 30 30

23 Cub Scout

24 Hippocrates

1982. 75th Anniv of Boy Scout Movement. Mult.
104 8c. Type **23** 15 10
105 10c. Scout planting tree . . . 15 10
106 20c. Scout on raft 25 30
107 25c. Scout with dog 25 30

1982. Celebrities of Medicine (1st series). Mult.
108 15c. Type **24** 20 20
109 20c. Antonie van Leeuwenhoek 25 30
110 25c. William Harvey 30 40
111 30c. Joseph Lister 35 45
See also Nos. 125/8, 160/3, 176/9, 249/52, 273/6, 281/4 and 305/8.

25 City Hall

1982. Centenary of Umtata. Multicoloured.
112 8c. Type **25** 10 10
113 15c. The Bunga 15 15
114 20c. Botha Sigcau Building 20 20
115 25c. Palace of Justice and K. D. Matanzima Building 25 30

1983. Fishing Flies (4th series). As T **16**. Mult.
116 20c. Alexandra 30 30
117 20c. Kent's Marbled Sedge 30 30
118 20c. White Marabou 30 30

119 20c. Mayfly Nymph 30 30
120 20c. Silver Wilkinson 30 30

26 Hotel Complex, Mzamba

1983. Wildcoast Holiday Complex, Mzamba. Mult.
121 10c. Type **26** 15 15
122 20c. Beach scene 25 25
123 25c. Casino 35 35
124 40c. Carousel 50 50

1983. Celebrities of Medicine (2nd series). As T **24**. Multicoloured.
125 10c. Edward Jenner 15 15
126 20c. Gregor Mendel 25 30
127 25c. Louis Pasteur 30 35
128 40c. Florence Nightingale 40 55

27 Lady Frere Post Office

1983. Transkei Post Offices (1st series). Mult.
129 10c. Type **27** 15 15
130 20c. Idutywa 20 30
131 25c. Lusikisiki 20 35
132 40c. Cala 30 55
See also Nos. 156/9.

1984. Fishing Flies (5th series). As T **16**. Mult.
133 20c. Silver Grey 45 45
134 20c. Ginger Quill 45 45
135 20c. Hardy's Favourite 45 45
136 20c. March Brown 45 45
137 20c. Kent's Spectrum Mohawk 45 45

28 Amagqira

1984. Xhosa Culture. Multicoloured.
138 1c. Type **28** 20 10
139 2c. Horseman 20 10
140 3c. Mat making 20 10
141 4c. Xhosa dancers 20 10
142 5c. Shopping with donkeys 20 10
143 6c. Young musicians 30 15
144 7c. Fingo brides 30 20
145 8c. Tasting the beer 30 20
146 9c. Thinning the maize 30 30
147 10c. Dancing demonstration 30 15
148 11c. Water from the river 30 15
148a 12c. Preparing a meal 30 15
148b 14c. Weeding mealies 30 20
149 15c. National sport: stick fighting 20 20
149a 16c. Morning pasture 30 20
150 20c. Abakhwetha dance 30 25
150a 21c. Building of initiation hut 1·50 20
151 25c. Tribesman singing 30 25
152 30c. Jovial matrons 50 35
153 50c. Pipe making 50 60
154 1r. Intonjane 60 1·10
155 2r. Abakhwetha 75 2·00

1984. Transkei Post Offices (2nd series). As T **27**. Multicoloured.
156 11c. Umzimkulu 15 15
157 20c. Mount Fletcher 20 25
158 25c. Qumbu 20 25
159 50c. Umtata 30 50

1984. Celebrities of Medicine (3rd series). As T **24**. Multicoloured.
160 11c. Nicholas of Cusa 15 15
161 25c. William Morton 25 25
162 30c. Wilhelm Rontgen 30 40
163 45c. Karl Landsteiner 40 60

29 Soil Erosion by Overgrazing

1985. Soil Conservation. Multicoloured.
164 11c. Type **29** 15 15
165 25c. Removal of stock and construction of walls as sediment collectors 25 25
166 30c. Regeneration of vegetation 30 40
167 50c. Cattle grazing in lush landscape 40 60

30 Tsitsa Bridge

1985. Bridges. Multicoloured.
168 12c. Type **30** 20 15
169 25c. White Kei Railway Bridge 25 25
170 30c. Mitchell Bridge 35 35
171 50c. Umzimvubu Bridge 55 60

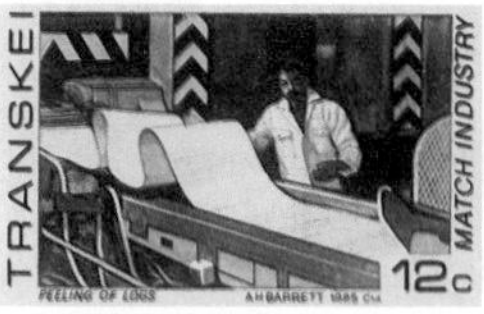

31 Veneer-peeling Machine

1985. Match Industry, Butterworth. Mult.
172 12c. Type **31** 15 15
173 25c. Cutting wood to match-size 20 25
174 30c. Dipping splints in chemical to form match heads 25 35
175 50c. Boxing matches 40 65

1985. Celebrities of Medicine (4th series). As T **24**. Multicoloured.
176 12c. Andreas Vesalius 20 15
177 25c. Marcello Malpighi 30 40
178 30c. Francois Magendie 35 45
179 50c. William Stewart Halsted 50 70

32 Early Street Scene

1986. Historic Port St. Johns. Multicoloured.
180 12c. Type **32** 20 15
181 20c. "Umzimvubu" (coaster) anchored at old jetty 45 45
182 25c. Wagons off-loading maize at jetty 50 50
183 30c. View of town at end of 19th century 50 55
MS184 130 × 94 mm. Nos. 180/3 1·50 1·50

33 "Aloe ferox"

34 First Falls Station, Umtata River

1986. Aloes. Multicoloured.
185 14c. Type **33** 20 15
186 20c. "Aloe arborescens" 30 30
187 25c. "Aloe maculata" 35 35
188 30c. "Aloe ecklonis" 45 45

1986. Hydro-electric Power Stations. Mult.
189 14c. Type **34** 20 15
190 20c. Second Falls, Umtata River 25 25
191 25c. Ncora, Qumanco River 40 40
192 30c. Collywobbles, Mbashe River 50 50

35 Prime Minister George Matanzima

1986. 10th Anniv of Independence. Mult.
193 14c. Type **35** 15 15
194 20c. Technical College, Umtata 25 30
195 25c. University of Transkei, Umtata 30 40
196 30c. Palace of Justice, Umtata 40 50

36 Piper Apache 235 "Ulundi" flying through Clouds

1987. 10th Anniv of Transkei Airways Corporation. Multicoloured.
197 14c. Type **36** 20 15
198 20c. Tail fin of "Ulundi" 30 30
199 25c. Beech 100 King Air 40 40
200 30c. Control tower, K. D. Matanzima Airport 55 60

37 Pondo Girl

38 "Latrodectus indistinctus"

1987. Transkei Beadwork. Multicoloured.
201 16c. Type **37** 15 15
202 20c. Bomvana woman 25 30
203 25c. Xessibe woman 35 40
204 30c. Xhosa man 40 60

1987. Spiders. Multicoloured.
205 16c. Type **38** 20 15
206 20c. "Naephila pilipes" 30 30
207 25c. "Lycosidue sp" 40 40
208 30c. "Argiope nigrovittata" 50 55

39 Common Black Pigs

1987. Domestic Animals. Multicoloured.
209 16c. Type **39** 15 15
210 30c. Goats 20 30
211 40c. Merino sheep 30 50
212 50c. Cattle 45 65

40 "Plocamium corallorhiza"

41 Spinning

1988. Seaweed. Multicoloured.
213 16c. Type **40** 15 15
214 30c. "Gelidium amanzii" 25 30
215 40c. "Ecklonia biruncinata" 30 40
216 50c. "Halimeda cuneata" 40 55

1988. Blanket Factory, Butterworth. Mult.
217 16c. Type **41** 15 15
218 30c. Warping 25 30
219 40c. Weaving 30 40
220 50c. Raising the nap 40 55

42 Map showing Wreck Site

1988. 206th Anniv of Shipwreck of "Grosvenor" (East Indiaman). Multicoloured.
221 16c. Type **42** 40 20
222 30c. "The Wreck of the 'Grosvenor'" (R. Smirke) 50 50
223 40c. Dirk hilt, dividers and coins from wreck 55 55
224 50c. "African Hospitality" (G. Morland) 60 70

43 Small-spotted Cat

1988. Endangered Animals. Multicoloured.
225 16c. Type **43** 60 30
226 30c. Blue duiker 70 60
227 40c. Oribi 85 75
228 50c. Hunting dog 1·25 1·00

44 Class 14 CRB Steam Locomotives

1989. Trains. Multicoloured.
229 16c. Type **44** 20 20
230 30c. Class 14 CRB locomotive and passenger train at Toleni Halt 40 40
231 40c. Double-headed steam train on Great Kei River Bridge (vert) 60 70
232 50c. Double-headed steam train in Kei Valley (vert) 65 80

45 Mat, Baskets and Jar

1989. Basketry. Multicoloured.
233 18c. Type **45** 20 15
234 30c. Basket and jar 30 30
235 40c. Jars and bag 40 50
236 50c. Dish and jars 55 75

46 Chub Mackerel

1989. Seafood. Multicoloured.
237 18c. Type **46** 55 15
238 30c. Squid 70 50
239 40c. Perna or brown mussels 85 70
240 50c. Rock lobster 1·00 1·00

47 Broom Cluster Fig

1989. Trees. Multicoloured.
241 18c. Type **47** 50 20
242 30c. Natal fig 75 55
243 40c. Broad-leaved coral 85 85
244 50c. Cabbage tree 1·10 1·25

48 "Ginkgo koningensis"

49 Aretaeus (discoverer of diabetes)

1990. Plant Fossils. Multicoloured.
245 18c. Type **48** 80 25
246 30c. "Pseudoctenis spatulata" 1·10 80
247 40c. "Rissikia media" 1·25 1·10
248 50c. "Taeniopteris anavolans" 1·40 1·50

1990. Celebrities of Medicine (5th series). Diabetes Research. Multicoloured.
249 18c. Type **49** 70 20
250 30c. Claude Bernard (discovered sugar formation by liver) 1·10 70
251 40c. Oscar Minkowski (discovered pancreas removal caused diabetes) 1·25 90
252 50c. Frederick Banting (discoverer of insulin) 1·40 1·25

50 Diviner dancing to Drum

51 Soldier Lily

1990. Diviners. Multicoloured.

253	21c. Type **50**	60	20
254	35c. Lecturing Imichetywa (novitiates)	90	70
255	40c. Neophyte initiation	1·00	90
256	50c. Diviner's induction ceremony	1·25	1·40

1990. Flowers. Multicoloured.

257	21c. Type **51**	65	20
258	35c. "Disa crassicornis"	90	65
259	40c. Christmas bells	1·00	90
260	50c. Port St. John's creeper	1·25	1·40

52 Pink Ink Plant

53 Common Dolphin

1991. Parasitic Plants. Multicoloured.

261	21c. Type **52**	60	20
262	35c. White harveya	90	70
263	40c. "Alectra sessiliflora"	1·00	1·10
264	50c. "Hydnora africana"	1·25	1·50

1991. Dolphins. Multicoloured.

265	25c. Type **53**	1·00	25
266	40c. Bottle-nosed dolphin	1·40	85
267	50c. Humpbacked dolphin	1·60	1·25
268	60c. Risso's dolphin	1·60	1·60

54 South African Crowned Cranes ("Crowned Cranes")

55 Emil von Behring and Shibasaburo Kitasao (diphtheria)

1991. Endangered Birds. Multicoloured.

269	25c. Type **54**	65	30
270	40c. Cape vulture	1·00	85
271	50c. Wattled crane	1·10	1·10
272	60c. Egyptian vulture	1·25	1·40

1991. Celebrities of Medicine (6th series). Vaccine Development. Multicoloured.

273	25c. Type **55**	90	25
274	40c. Camile Guerin and Albert Calmette (tuberculosis)	1·40	90
275	50c. Jonas Salk (poliomyelitis)	1·60	1·25
276	60c. John Enders (measles)	1·75	1·50

56 "Eulophia speciosa"

57 Thomas Weller (researcher into infectious viruses)

1992. Orchids. Multicoloured.

277	27c. Type **56**	25	20
278	45c. "Satyrium sphaerocarpum"	40	40
279	65c. "Disa scullyi"	60	70
280	85c. "Disa tysonii"	80	1·00

1992. Celebrities of Medicine (7th series). Mult.

281	27c. Type **57**	75	25
282	45c. Ignaz Semmelweis	1·10	80
283	65c. Sir James Simpson	1·50	1·25
284	85c. Rene Laennec	1·75	1·60

58 Red-billed Pintail

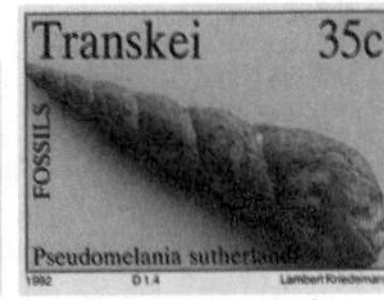

59 "Pseudomelania sutherlandi" (gastropod)

1992. Waterfowl. Multicoloured.

285	35c. Type **58**	60	60
286	35c. Hottentot teal	60	60
287	70c. Maccoa duck	90	90
288	70c. White-backed duck	90	90
289	90c. African black duck	1·10	1·10
290	90c. Egyptian goose	1·10	1·10
291	1r.05 Cape shoveler	1·40	1·40
292	1r.05 Cape teal	1·40	1·40

1992. Marine Fossils. Multicoloured.

293	35c. Type **59**	1·10	35
294	70c. "Gaudryceras denseplicatum" (ammonite)	1·50	1·10
295	90c. "Neithea quinquecostata" (bivalve)	1·60	1·50
296	1r.05 "Pugilina acuticarinatus" (gastropod)	1·75	1·60

60 Papillon

1993. Dogs. Multicoloured.

297	35c. Type **60**	60	30
298	70c. Pekingese	90	90
299	90c. Chihuahua	1·10	1·25
300	1r.05 Dachshund	1·40	1·60

61 Fabrosaurus

1993. Prehistoric Animals. Multicoloured.

301	45c. Type **61**	1·10	40
302	65c. Diictodon	1·50	1·10
303	85c. Chasmatosaurus	1·75	1·60
304	1r.05 Rubidgea	1·75	1·75

62 Sir Alexander Fleming and Howard Florey (discoverer and refiner of penicillin)

63 Laughing Doves

1993. Celebrities of Medicine (8th series). Mult.

305	45c. Type **62**	70	40
306	65c. Alexis Carrel	1·10	1·10
307	85c. James Lind	1·25	1·50
308	1r.05 Santiago Ramon y Cajal	1·40	1·60

1993. Doves. Multicoloured.

309	45c. Type **63**	60	40
310	65c. Tambourine doves	90	90
311	85c. Emerald-spotted wood doves	1·25	1·25
312	1r.05 Namaqua doves	1·50	1·60
MS313	98 × 83 mm. Nos. 309/12	3·75	3·75

64 "Clan Lindsay" (steamer) on Rocks, Mazeppa Bay, 1898

1994. Shipwrecks. Multicoloured.

314	45c. Type **64**	1·25	60
315	65c. "Horizon" (freighter) on rocks near River Mngazi, 1967	1·60	1·25
316	85c. "Oceanos" (pleasure cruiser) sinking near Coffee Bay, 1991	1·90	1·60
317	1r.05 "Forresbank" (freighter) on fire near River Mtakatye, 1958	1·90	1·90

TRANSVAAL Pt. 1

Formerly South African Republic under Boer rule, annexed by Gt. Britain in 1877, restored to the Boers in 1881 and again annexed in 1900 and since 1919 a province of the Union of S. Africa.

12 pence = 1 shilling;
20 shillings = 1 pound.

1

1870. Imperf or roul.

61	1	1d. red	22·00	16·00
22		1d. black	17·00	25·00
53		3d. lilac	45·00	38·00
54a		6d. blue	45·00	38·00
32		1s. green	70·00	38·00

1874. Perf.

38a	1	1d. red	75·00	35·00
171		1d. grey	4·50	1·50
172		3d. black on red	22·00	4·00
173		3d. red	9·00	2·00
173		3d. brown	23·00	3·50
41		6d. blue	£100	45·00
174		1s. green	48·00	3·00

1877. Optd **V. R. TRANSVAAL.** Imperf or roul.

101	1	1d. red	21·00	21·00
102		3d. lilac	70·00	38·00
103		6d. blue	85·00	32·00
113		6d. blue on red	70·00	45·00
104		1s. green	90·00	45·00

1877. Optd **V. R. Transvaal.** Imperf or roul.

116	1	1d. red on blue	48·00	26·00
117		1d. red on orange	17·00	16·00
118		3d. lilac on brown	38·00	24·00
119e		3d. lilac on green	95·00	35·00
149		3d. lilac on blue	42·00	25·00
126		6d. blue on green	70·00	25·00
121		6d. blue on blue	48·00	24·00

9

18

1878. Perf.

133	9	½d. red	21·00	75·00
134a		1d. brown	11·00	3·25
135		3d. red	14·00	4·00
136		4d. olive	19·00	5·00
137		6d. black	10·00	3·75
138		1s. green	£110	35·00
139		2s. blue	£150	70·00

1879. Surch **1 Penny.**

145	9	1d. on 6d. black	38·00	22·00

1882. Surch **EEN PENNY.**

170	9	1d. on 4d. green	12·00	4·25

1885.

175	18	½d. grey	60	10
176b		1d. red	40	10
177		2d. purple	1·75	2·25
178		2d. brown	1·00	10
179		2½d. mauve	2·00	50
180		3d. mauve	2·25	1·00
181		4d. olive	3·50	70
182a		6d. blue	4·75	80
183		1s. green	2·50	50
184		2s.6d. yellow	4·50	2·00
185		5s. grey	6·00	3·25
186		10s. brown	30·00	7·00
187		£5 green	£3250	£180

1885. Surch **HALVE PENNY** vert, reading up or down.

188	1	½d. on 3d. red (No. 173)	4·00	9·50
192	18	½d. on 3d. mauve	3·75	3·75
189	1	½d. on 1s. green (No. 174)	21·00	48·00

1885. Surch with value in words and **Z. A. R.** both vert.

190	9	½d. on 6d. black	50·00	80·00
191		2d. on 6d. black	4·75	10·00

1887. Surch **2d** and thick bar.

194	18	2d. on 3d. mauve	1·50	2·75

1893. Surch **Halve Penny** and bars.

196	18	½d. on 2d. pale brown	85	1·25

1893. Surch in figures and words between bars. (A) in one line, (B) in two.

197	18	1d. on 6d. blue (A)	60	75
198		2½d. on 1s. green (A)	1·00	3·25
199		2½d. on 1s. green (B)	4·00	4·00

29 (Wagon with shafts)

30 (Wagon with pole)

1894.

200	29	½d. grey	60	45
201		1d. red	1·25	10
202		2d. brown	1·25	10
203		6d. blue	2·00	40
204		1s. green	10·00	13·00

1895.

205	30	½d. grey	70	10
206		1d. red	70	10
207		2d. brown	80	10
208		3d. mauve	1·50	55
209		4d. black	2·25	80
210		6d. blue	2·25	70
211		1s. green	2·75	1·25
212		5s. grey	14·00	22·00
212a		10s. brown	14·00	4·50

1895. Surch **Halve Penny** and bar.

213	30	½d. on 1s. green	80	20

1895. Surch **1d.** and thick bar.

214	18	1d. on 2½d. mauve	50	10

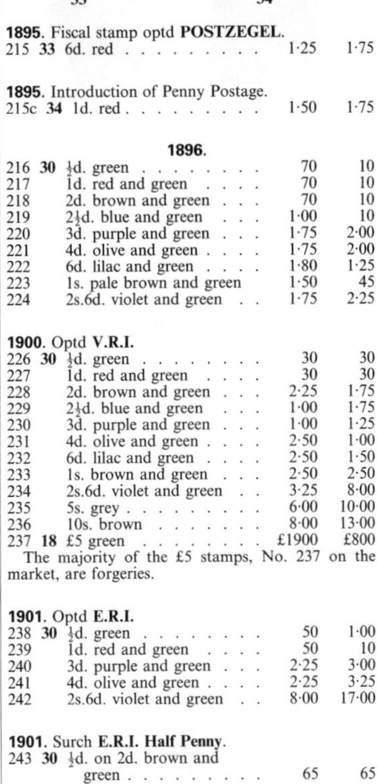

33 34

1895. Fiscal stamp optd **POSTZEGEL.**

215	33	6d. red	1·25	1·75

1895. Introduction of Penny Postage.

215c	34	1d. red	1·50	1·75

1896.

216	30	½d. green	70	10
217		1d. red and green	70	10
218		2d. brown and green	70	10
219		2½d. blue and green	1·00	10
220		3d. purple and green	1·75	2·00
221		4d. olive and green	1·75	2·00
222		6d. lilac and green	1·80	1·25
223		1s. pale brown and green	1·50	45
224		2s.6d. violet and green	1·75	2·25

1900. Optd **V.R.I.**

226	30	½d. green	30	30
227		1d. red and green	30	30
228		2d. brown and green	2·25	1·75
229		2½d. blue and green	1·00	1·75
230		3d. purple and green	1·00	1·25
231		4d. olive and green	2·50	1·00
232		6d. lilac and green	2·50	1·50
233		1s. brown and green	2·50	2·50
234		2s.6d. violet and green	3·25	8·00
235		5s. grey	6·00	10·00
236		10s. brown	8·00	13·00
237	18	£5 green	£1900	£800

The majority of the £5 stamps, No. 237 on the market, are forgeries.

1901. Optd **E.R.I.**

238	30	½d. green	50	1·00
239		1d. red and green	50	10
240		3d. purple and green	2·25	3·00
241		4d. olive and green	2·25	3·25
242		2s.6d. violet and green	8·00	17·00

1901. Surch **E.R.I. Half Penny.**

243	30	½d. on 2d. brown and green	65	65

38

1902.

244	38	½d. black and green	1·50	20
273		½d. green	1·75	10
245		1d. black and red	1·25	15
274		1d. red	1·25	10
246		2d. black and purple	3·25	50
275		2d. purple	3·50	50
247		2½d. black and blue	6·00	1·25
276		2½d. blue	12·00	5·00
264		3d. black and green	3·50	30
265		4d. black and brown	4·75	70
266a		6d. black and orange	3·00	50
251		1s. black and green	11·00	9·00
267		1s. grey and brown	6·50	50
252		2s. black and brown	38·00	40·00
268		2s. grey and yellow	20·00	6·00
253		2s.6d. mauve and black	14·00	10·00
270		5s. black & purple on yellow	19·00	1·50
271		10s. black & purple on red	48·00	2·75
272a		£1 green and violet	£180	16·00

259 £5 brown and violet . . . £1400 £650
Nos. 267, 268 and all values of 2s.6d. and above have the inscription "POSTAGE" on both sides. The rest are inscribed "POSTAGE" at left and "REVENUE" at right.

POSTAGE DUE STAMPS

D 1

1907.
D1 **D 1** ½d. black and green . . . 3·25 1·25
D2 1d. black and red . . . . 4·00 85
D3 2d. brown . . . . . . 4·00 1·25
D4 3d. black and blue . . . 7·50 4·00
D5 5d. black and violet . . . 2·00 12·00
D6 6d. black and brown . . . 4·25 12·00
D7 1s. red and black . . . . 9·00 8·50

TRAVANCORE Pt. 1

A state of south-east India. In 1949 formed part of Travancore-Cochin.

16 cash = 1 chuckram;
28 chuckrams = 1 rupee.

1 Conch or Chank Shell

3 Conch or Chank Shell

1888. Various frames.
9 **3** 4cash pink 30 10
24 – 5cash olive 80 20
34 – 5cash brown . . . . 2·75 20
10 **1** 6cash brown 30 10
4b ½ch. purple 60 25
27 – 10cash pink 40 10
13 – ¾ch. black . . . . 1·50 25
39 – ¾ch. mauve 35 10
14c **1** 1ch. blue 75 10
15 1¼ch. purple 55 55
42 1½ch. red . . . . 2·75 10
16a 2ch. red 60 10
17 – 3ch. violet . . . . 2·75 20
18a **1** 4ch. green . . . . 2·50 35
19 – 7ch. purple . . . . 2·00 50
20 – 14ch. orange . . . . 2·75 2·00

1906. Surch in figures.
21a **1** ¼ on ½ch. purple 50 30
22 ⅜ on ½ch. purple 30 35

1921. Surch in figures.
31 **3** 1c. on 4cash pink 15 20
57 – 1c. on 5cash brown 15 15
58 – 1c. on 5cash purple . . . . . 1·25 20
50 **1** 1c. on 1¼ch. purple 15 50
59 – 2c. on 10cash pink 15 15
51 **1** 2c. on 1¼ch. purple 15 20
32 5c. on 1ch. blue . . . . . . 1·00 10

11 Sri Padmanabha Shrine

13 Maharaja Bala Rama Varma XI

1931. Coronation.
47 **11** 6cash black and green . . . 1·60 1·60
48 – 10cash black and blue . . . 1·25 70
49 **13** 3ch. black and purple . . . 2·75 2·75
DESIGN—As Type **11**: 10cash, State chariot.

16 Maharaja Bala Rama Varma XI and Subramania Shrine

1937. Temple Entry Proclamation.
60 **16** 6cash red . . . . 1·60 1·25
61 – 12cash blue . . . . 2·75 30
62 – 1½ch. green . . . . 1·50 1·50
63 – 3ch. violet . . . . 3·25 2·25
DESIGNS: Portraits of the Maharaja and the temples of Sri Padmanabha (12cash), Mahadeva (1½ch.) and Kanyakumari (3ch.).

17 Lake Ashtamudi

18 Maharaja Bala Rama Varma XI

1939. 27th Birthday of Maharaja.
64 **17** 1ch. green . . . . 4·50 10
65 – 1½ch. red . . . . 3·25 3·50
66 **18** 2ch. orange . . . . 5·50 1·75
67 – 3ch. brown . . . . 6·00 10
68 – 4ch. red . . . . 6·50 40
69 – 7ch. blue . . . . 9·00 17·00
70 – 14ch. green . . . . 7·00 55·00
DESIGNS—As Type **18**: 1½, 3ch. Portraits of Maharaja. As Type **17**: 4ch. Sri Padmanabha Shrine; 7ch. Cape Comorin; 14ch. Pachipari Reservoir.

19 Maharaja and Aruvikara Falls

21 Maharaja Bala Rama Varma XI

1941. 29th Birthday of Maharaja.
71a **19** 6cash violet . . . . 6·50 10
72 – ¾ch. brown . . . . 7·50 20
DESIGN: ¾ch. Maharaja and Marthanda Varma Bridge, Alwaye.

1943. Stamps of 1939 and 1941 surch in figures and capital letters.
73e – 2cash on 1½ch. red (No. 65) 40 25
74a – 4cash on ¾ch. brown (No. 72) . . . . 4·25 30
75a **19** 8cash on 6cash red (as No. 7) . . . . 3·75 10

1946. 34th Birthday of Maharaja.
76a **21** 8cash red . . . . 75 1·60

1946. No. O103 optd **SPECIAL**.
77 **19** 6cash violet . . . . 6·00 2·50

OFFICIAL STAMPS

1911. Optd **On S S**.
O 1 **3** 4cash pink 20 10
O14 – 5cash olive 60 10
O29 – 5cash brown 25 50
O15 **1** 6cash brown 30 10
O54 ½ch. purple 20 10
O18 – 10cash pink 65 10
O39 – ¾ch. black 35 15
O56 – ¾ch. mauve 30 15
O 5 **1** 1ch. blue 65 10
O21 1¼ch. purple 40 10
O59 1½ch. red 40 10
O 6 2ch. red 35 10
O 8 – 3ch. violet 35 10
O10 **1** 4ch. green 55 10
O64 – 7ch. purple . . . . 1·25 30
O65 – 14ch. orange . . . . 1·75 40

1932. Official stamps surch in figures.
O74 – 6c. on 5cash olive . . . . . 1·60 1·40
O75 – 6c. on 5cash brown 20 25
O83 – 12c. on 10cash pink 20 15
O84 **1** 1ch.8ch. on 1¼ch. red 35 25

1939. Optd **SERVICE**.
O 85b **1** 6cash brown 70 30
O 94 – ¾ch. mauve (No. 39) . . 14·00 20
O 96 **17** 1ch. green . . . . . . 1·00 10
O 97b – 1½ch. red (No. 65) . . . 2·00 15
O 95a **1** 1½ch. red . . . . . . 4·50 1·00
O 98 **17** 2ch. orange . . . . . . 2·00 30
O 99 – 3ch. brown (No. 67) . . 1·50 10
O100 – 4ch. red (No. 68) . . . 3·25 85
O101 – 7ch. blue (No. 69) . . . 8·00 35
O102 – 14ch. green (No. 70) . . 14·00 70

1942. Optd **SERVICE**.
O103 **19** 6cash violet 40 50
O104 – ¾ch. brown (No. 72) . . 5·00 10

1942. Nos. 73/5 optd **SERVICE**.
O106a – 2cash on 1½ch. red . . . 50 15
O107a – 4cash on ¾ch. brown . . 2·25 20
O105a **19** 8cash on 6cash red . . 1·25 10

1947. Optd **SERVICE**.
O108 **21** 8cash red . . . . 2·25 70

TRAVANCORE-COCHIN Pt. 1

In 1949 the states of Cochin and Travancore in south-east India were united under the name of the United States of Travancore and Cochin. Now uses stamps of India.

12 pies = 1 anna; 16 annas = 1 rupee.

1949. Stamps of Travancore surch in **PIES** or **ANNAS** in English and native characters.
1e **19** 2p. on 6cash violet 40 20
2d **21** 2p. on 8cash red . . . . . 1·00 30
3e **17** ½a. on 1ch. green 65 40
4a **18** 1a. on 2ch. orange 55 30
5d **11** 2a. on 4ch. brown . . . . . 3·00 55
6a – 3a. on 7ch. blue (No. 69) . . 5·00 3·25
7b – 6a. on 14ch. green (No. 70) 14·00 24·00

1949. No. 106 of Cochin optd **U.S.T.C.**
8 **21** 1a. orange . . . . 5·00 60·00

1950. No. 106 of Cochin optd **T.-C.**
9 **21** 1a. orange . . . . 6·50 55·00

1950. No. 9 surch with new value.
10 **21** 6p. on 1a. orange . . . . . 3·75 48·00
11 9p. on 1a. orange . . . . . 3·50 42·00

5 Conch or Chank Shell

6 Palm Trees

1950.
12 **5** 2p. red . . . . 2·75 3·00
13 **6** 4p. blue . . . . 2·50 15·00

OFFICIAL STAMPS

1949. Stamps of Travancore surch **SERVICE** and value in **PIES** or **ANNAS** in English and native characters.
O 1f **19** 2p. on 6cash (No. 71) . . 40 40
O10e **21** 4p. on 8cash (No. 76a) 30 20
O11b **17** ½a. on 1ch. (No. 64) . . 30 20
O12c **18** 1a. on 2ch. (No. 66) . . 40 20
O 9a – 2a. on 4ch. (No. 68) . . 70 65
O14e – 3a. on 7ch. (No. 69) . . 1·50 1·10
O15 – 6a. on 14ch. (No. 70) . . 1·50 4·00

TRENGGANU Pt. 1

A state of the Federation of Malaya, incorporated in Malaysia in 1963.

100 cents = 1 dollar (Straits or Malayan).

1 Sultan Zain ul ab din

2 Sultan Zain ul ab din

1910.
1 **1** 1c. green . . . . 1·75 1·00
2 2c. brown and purple . . . 1·00 90
3 3c. red . . . . 2·25 2·25
4 4c. orange . . . . 3·50 5·50
5 4c. brown and green . . . . 2·00 3·75
5a 4c. red . . . . 1·25 1·75
6 5c. grey . . . . 1·25 3·50
7 5c. grey and brown . . . . 2·25 2·00
8 8c. blue . . . . 1·25 9·00
9a 10c. purple on yellow . . . 3·25 5·50
10 10c. green and red on yellow 1·25 2·25
11 20c. mauve and purple . . . 3·50 4·25
12 25c. green and purple . . . 8·00 32·00
13 30c. purple and black . . . 6·50 55·00
14 50c. black on green . . . . 4·50 9·00
15 $1 black and red on blue . . 17·00 24·00
16 $3 green and red on green . £160 £350
17 **2** $5 green and purple £170 £475
18 $25 red and green £950 £1800

1917. Surch **RED CROSS 2c.**
19 **1** 2c. on 3c. red . . . . . . 50 7·50
20 2c. on 4c. orange . . . . . 1·50 15·00
21 2c. on 4c. brown and green 3·50 40·00
22 2c. on 8c. blue . . . . . . 1·25 29·00

4 Sultan Suleiman

7 Sultan Ismail

1921. (a) T **4**.
26 **4** 1c. black . . . . 1·75 1·50
27 2c. green . . . . 1·25 2·00
28 3c. green . . . . 2·00 1·00
29 3c. brown . . . . 25·00 14·00
30 4c. red . . . . 1·75 1·25
31 5c. grey and brown . . . . 2·00 5·00
32 5c. purple on yellow . . . . 1·75 1·25
33 6c. orange . . . . 4·00 50
34 8c. grey . . . . 28·00 6·00
35 10c. blue . . . . 2·00 1·00
36 12c. blue . . . . 4·25 4·50
37 20c. purple and orange . . . 2·25 1·50
38 25c. green and purple . . . . 2·25 3·00
39 30c. purple and black . . . . 3·25 3·75
40 35c. red on yellow . . . . . 4·75 8·00
41 50c. green and red . . . . . 8·50 3·25
42 $1 purple and blue on blue . 9·00 3·75
43 $3 green and red on green . . 55·00 £150

(b) Larger type, as T **2**, but portrait of Sultan Suleiman.
25 $5 green and red on yellow . . £120 £300
45 $25 purple and blue £650 £1200
46 $50 green and yellow £1700 £3000
47 $100 green and red £5000 £6000

1922. Optd **MALAYA-BORNEO EXHIBITION.**
48 **4** 2c. green . . . . 4·75 27·00
49 4c. red . . . . 6·50 38·00
50 5c. grey and brown . . . . . 3·25 40·00
51 **1** 10c. green and red on yellow 5·50 32·00
52 20c. mauve and purple . . . 5·50 38·00
53 25c. green and purple . . . . 4·75 35·00
54 30c. purple and black . . . . 5·50 35·00
55 50c. black on green . . . . . 5·50 35·00
56 $1 black and red on blue . . 14·00 70·00
57 $3 green and red on green . . £140 £375
58 **2** $5 green and purple £250 £650

1941. Surch.
59 **4** 2c. on 5c. purple on yellow 6·50 3·50
60 8c. on 10c. blue . . . . . . 7·00 4·00

1948. Silver Wedding. As T **33b/c** of St. Helena.
61 10c. violet . . . . 15 1·75
62 $5 red . . . . 25·00 42·00

1949. 75th Anniv of U.P.U. As T **33d/g** of St. Helena.
63 10c. purple 30 75
64 15c. blue . . . . 1·90 3·00
65 25c. orange . . . . 40 2·25
66 50c. black . . . . 1·00 3·50

1949.
67 **7** 1c. black 15 75
68 2c. orange 20 75
69 3c. green . . . . 1·00 3·25
70 4c. brown 20 60
71 5c. purple . . . . 30 1·75
72 6c. grey . . . . 1·00 60
73 8c. red . . . . 30 2·50
74 8c. green . . . . 65 1·75
75 10c. purple 30 30
76 12c. red . . . . 65 2·75
77 15c. blue . . . . 2·25 30
78 20c. black and green . . . . 2·50 3·75
79 20c. blue 80 40
80 25c. purple and orange . . . 1·75 2·00
81 30c. red and purple . . . . . 1·25 2·25
82 35c. red and purple . . . . . 85 2·25
83 40c. red and purple . . . . . 5·00 15·00
84 50c. black and blue . . . . . 2·00 2·25
85 $1 blue and green . . . . . 7·00 8·00
86 $2 green and red . . . . . 27·00 24·00
87 $3 green and brown . . . . 50·00 55·00

1953. Coronation. As T **33h** of St. Helena.
88 10c. black and purple . . . . 1·25 1·25

1957. As Nos. 92/102 of Kedah but inset portrait of Sultan Ismail.
89 1c. black 10 20
90 2c. red . . . . 1·50 30
91 4c. brown 10 10
92 5c. red 10 10
93 8c. green . . . . 4·00 60
94 10c. brown . . . . 1·00 10
94a 10c. purple . . . . 4·75 30
95 20c. blue . . . . 1·25 1·60
96a 50c. black and blue . . . . . 55 1·60
97 $1 blue and purple . . . . . 6·50 7·00
98 $2 green and red . . . . . . 17·00 7·00
99 $5 brown and green . . . . 17·00 22·00

8 "Vanda hookeriana"

9 Sultan of Trengganu

1965. As Nos. 115/21 of Kedah, but inset portrait of Sultan Ismail as in T **8**.
100 **8** 1c. multicoloured . . . . . 10 2·00
101 – 2c. multicoloured . . . . . 10 2·00
102 – 5c. multicoloured 15 70
103 – 6c. multicoloured . . . . . 15 2·00
104 – 10c. multicoloured 20 25
105 – 15c. multicoloured . . . . . 1·50 10
106 – 20c. multicoloured . . . . . 1·50 1·25
The higher values used in Trengganu were Nos. 20/7 of Malaysia (National Issues).

1970. 25th Anniv of Installation of H.R.H. Tuanku Ismail Nasiruddin Shah as Sultan of Trengganu.
107 **9** 10c. multicoloured . . . . . 1·00 2·25
108 15c. multicoloured . . . . . 60 1·25
109 50c. multicoloured . . . . . 1·00 2·75

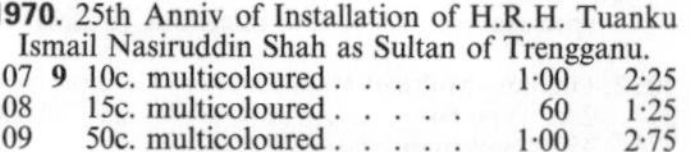

10 "Papilio demoleus"

1971. Butterflies. As Nos. 124/30 of Kedah but with portrait of Sultan Ismail Nasiruddin Shah as in T **10**.

110 – 1c. multicoloured 40 2·50
111 – 2c. multicoloured 80 2·50
112 – 5c. multicoloured 1·00 1·25
113 **10** 6c. multicoloured 1·75 2·75
114 – 10c. multicoloured 1·75 70
115 – 15c. multicoloured 1·75 20
116 – 20c. multicoloured 2·00 1·75

The high values in use with this issue were Nos. 64/71 of Malaysia (National Issues).

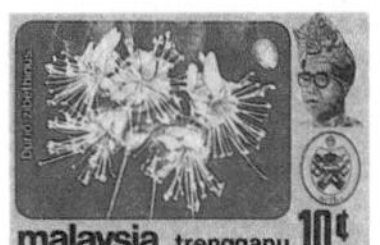

11 "Durio zibethinus"

1979. Flowers. As Nos. 135/41 of Kedah, but with portrait of Sultan Ismail Nasiruddin Shah as in T **11**.

118 1c. "Rafflesia hasseltii" 10 1·25
119 2c. "Pterocarpus indicus" 10 1·25
120 5c. "Largerstoemia speciosa" 10 60
121 10c. Type **11** 15 10
122 15c. "Hibiscus rosa-sinensis" 15 10
123 20c. "Rhododendron scortechinii" 20 10
124 25c. "Etlingera elatior" (inscr "Phaeomeria speciosa") 40 50

12 Sultan Mahmud 13 Rubber

1981. Installation of Sultan Mahmud.

125 **12** 10c. black, blue and gold 35 1·50
126 15c. black, yellow and gold 45 50
127 50c. black, purple and gold 1·00 3·00

1986. As Nos. 152/8 of Kedah but with portrait of Sultan Mahmud and inscr "TERENGGANU" as in T **13**.

135 1c. Coffee 10 10
136 2c. Coconuts 10 10
137 5c. Cocoa 15 10
138 10c. Black pepper 15 10
139 15c. Type **13** 20 10
140 20c. Oil palm 25 15
141 30c. Rice 30 15

14 Sultan Mizan Zainal Abidin and Maziah Palace in 1999

1999. Installation of Sultan Mizan Zainal Abidin as Sultan of Trengganu. Multicoloured.

142 30c. Type **14** 50 25
143 50c. Maziah Palace, 1903 75 50
144 $1 Tengku Tengah Zahara Mosque at night 1·40 2·25

1999. As Nos. 137/8 and 140/1, but with portrait of Sultan Mizan.

147 5c. Cocoa 3·25
148 10c. Black pepper 3·25
150 20c. Oil palm 3·25
151 30c. Rice 80 85

POSTAGE DUE STAMPS

D 1

1937.

D1 **D 1** 1c. red 7·50 55·00
D2 4c. green 9·50 60·00
D3 8c. yellow 55·00 £325
D4 10c. brown £110 95·00

TRIESTE Pt. 8

The Free Territory of Trieste situated on the Adriatic Coast between the frontiers of Italy and Yugoslavia. In 1954, when the Territory was divided between Italy and Yugoslavia, the overprinted issues were superseded by the ordinary issues of these countries in their respective zones.

For stamps of Italy surcharged **1.V.1945. TRIESTE TRST**, five-pointed star and value, see Venezia Giulia Nos. 20/32.

ZONE A

ALLIED MILITARY GOVERNMENT

100 centesimi = 1 lira.

Stamps of Italy variously overprinted **A.M.G. F.T.T.** or **AMG-FTT** (Allied Military Government – Free Territory of Trieste) except where otherwise stated.

1947. Postage stamps of 1945, Nos. 647, etc.

1 25c. blue 20 10
2 50c. violet 20 10
3 1l. green 20 10
4 2l. brown 20 10
5 3l. red 20 10
6 4l. red 20 10
7 5l. blue 20 10
8 6l. violet 20 10
9 8l. green 1·40 85
10 10l. grey 20 10
11 10l. red 5·75 10
12 15l. blue 25 10
13 20l. violet 65 10
14 25l. green 1·75 1·75
15 30l. blue £130 2·75
16 50l. purple 3·00 1·75
17 100l. red (No. 669) 19·00 13·00

1947. Air stamps of 1945, Nos. 670, etc.

18 1l. grey 25 20
19 2l. blue 25 20
20 5l. green 1·10 40
21 10l. red 1·25 40
22 25l. brown 2·25 1·10
23 50l. violet 21·00 2·00
24 100l. green 80·00 3·50
25 300l. mauve 9·00 11·00
26 500l. blue 12·00 10·00
27 1000l. brown £110 85·00

1947. Air. 50th Anniv of Radio (Nos. 688/93).

59 6l. violet 70 70
60 10l. red 70 70
61 20l. orange 5·25 1·40
62 25l. blue 75 70
63 35l. blue 75 70
64 50l. purple 4·50 5·25

1948. Cent of 1848 Revolution (Nos. 706, etc).

65 3l. brown 15 20
66 4l. purple 15 20
67 5l. blue 15 20
68 6l. green 20 20
69 8l. brown 15 20
70 10l. red 15 20
71 12l. green 1·10 70
72 15l. black 6·00 4·00
73 20l. red 7·50 4·50
74 30l. blue 45 1·25
75 50l. violet 3·25 8·50
76 100l. blue 13·50 20·00

1948. Trieste Philatelic Congress stamps of 1945 optd **A.M.G. F.T.T. 1948 TRIESTE** and posthorn.

77 8l. green (postage) 20 20
78 10l. red 20 20
79 30l. blue 1·10 30
80 10l. red (air) 30 20
81 25l. brown 40 55
82 50l. violet 40 55

1948. Rebuilding of Bassano Bridge.

84 **209** 15l. green 85 70

1948. Donizetti.

85 **210** 15l. brown 4·75 70

1949. 25th Biennial Art Exhibition, Venice.

86 **212** 5l. red and flesh 70 20
87 – 15l. green and cream 5·75 3·00
88 – 20l. brown and buff 2·75 1·00
89 – 50l. blue and yellow 7·50 4·75

1949. 27th Milan Fair.

90 **211** 20l. brown 4·25 1·00

1949. 75th Anniv of U.P.U.

91 **213** 50l. blue 2·00 1·75

1949. Centenary of Roman Republic.

92 **214** 100l. brown 28·00 28·00

1949. 1st Trieste Free Election.

93 **218** 20l. red 2·10 1·25

1949. European Recovery Plan.

94 **215** 5l. green 4·50 3·50
95 15l. violet 6·75 6·50
96 20l. brown 6·75 6·50

1949. 2nd World Health Congress, Rome.

97 **219** 20l. violet 7·50 2·75

1949. Giuseppe Mazzini.

98 **216** 20l. black 4·75 1·75

1949. Bicentenary of Vittorio Alfieri.

99 **217** 20l. brown 4·75 1·75

1949. 400th Anniv of Palladio's Basilica at Vicenza.

100 **220** 20l. violet 9·25 6·50

1949. 500th Birth Anniv of Lorenzo de Medici.

101 **221** 20l. blue 4·75 1·75

1949. 13th Bari Fair.

102 **222** 20l. red 4·75 2·25

1949. (a) Postage.

103 **195** 1l. green 15 20
104 – 2l. brown (No. 656) 15 20
105 – 3l. red (No. 657) 15 20
106 **193** 5l. blue 15 20
107 **195** 6l. violet 15 20
108 – 8l. green (No. 661) 9·00 4·75
109 **193** 10l. red 15 20
110 **195** 15l. blue 1·25 20
111 – 20l. purple (No. 665) 65 20
112 **196** 25l. green 18·00 1·75
113 50l. purple 25·00 1·10
114 **197** 100l. red 55·00 4·75

(b) Air.

115 **198** 10l. red 15 10
116 – 25l. brown (No. 676) 25 10
117 **198** 50l. violet 20 10
118 – 100l. green (No. 911) 80 10
119 – 300l. mauve (No. 912) 9·75 3·50
120 – 500l. blue (No. 913) 11·00 7·25
121 – 1000l. purple (No. 914) 16·00 12·00

1949. 150th Anniv of Volta's Discovery of the Electric Cell.

135 **223** 20l. red 2·75 1·75
136 **224** 50l. blue 7·25 6·50

1949. Rebuilding of Holy Trinity Bridge, Florence.

137 **225** 20l. green 2·40 1·40

1949. Death Bimillenary of Catullus (poet).

138 **226** 20l. blue 1·90 1·40

1949. Birth Bicentenary of Domenico Cimarosa (composer).

153 **227** 20l. violet 2·40 1·40

1950. 28th Milan Fair.

154 **228** 20l. brown 2·40 1·00

1950. 32nd Int Automobile Exn, Turin.

155 **229** 20l. violet 90 70

1950. 5th General UNESCO Conference.

156 – 20l. green 1·10 55
157 **230** 55l. blue 7·50 5·50

1950. Holy Year.

158 **231** 20l. violet 1·75 35
159 55l. blue 8·00 4·00

1950. Honouring Gaudenzio Ferrari (painter).

160 **232** 20l. green 1·50 1·25

1950. International Radio Conference.

161 **233** 20l. violet 3·25 3·50
162 55l. blue 12·50 13·00

1950. Death Bicentenary of Ludovico Murator (historian).

163 **234** 20l. brown 2·40 1·00

1950. 900th Death Anniv of D'Arezzo.

164 **235** 20l. green 2·40 1·00

1950. 14th Levant Fair, Bari.

165 **236** 20l. brown 1·60 1·00

1950. 2nd Trieste Fair. Optd **AMG FTT Fiera di Trieste 1950.**

166 **195** 15l. blue 90 1·00
167 – 20l. purple (No. 665) 1·90 35

1950. Wool Industry Pioneers.

168 **237** 20l. blue 80 35

1950. European Tobacco Conf (Nos. 755/7).

169 5l. green and mauve 35 20
170 20l. green and brown 2·25 85
171 55l. brown and blue 14·00 13·00

1950. Bicentenary of Fine Arts Academy.

172 **239** 20l. red and deep brown 1·75 1·00

1950. Birth Centenary of Augusto Righi.

173 **240** 20l. black and buff 2·25 1·00

1950. Provincial Occupations (Nos. 760/78).

176 50c. blue 10 15
177 1l. violet 10 10
178 2l. brown 10 10
179 5l. black 10 10
180 6l. brown 10 10
181 10l. green 10 10
182 12l. green 40 30
183 15l. blue 75 10
184 20l. violet 40 10
185 25l. brown 75 10
186 30l. purple 25 20
187 35l. red 95 65
188 40l. brown 65 30
189 50l. violet 15 10
190 55l. blue 15 30
191 60l. red 2·40 1·60
192 65l. green 15 30
193 100l. brown 1·90 10
194 200l. brown 1·25 2·00

1951. Centenary of 1st Tuscan Stamp.

195 **249** 20l. red and purple 2·25 1·00
196 55l. blue and ultramarine 20·00 21·00

1951. 33rd International Motor Show, Turin.

197 **243** 20l. green 90 1·00

1951. Consecration of Hall of Peace, Rome.

198 **244** 20l. violet 1·10 80

1951. 29th Milan Fair.

199 **245** 20l. brown 1·40 65
200 **246** 55l. blue 1·60 1·40

1951. 10th International Textiles Exn, Turin.

201 **247** 20l. violet 1·10 1·00

1951. 500th Birth Anniv of Columbus.

202 **248** 20l. green 1·60 1·40

1951. International Gymnastic Festival, Florence.

203 **249** 5l. red and brown 3·50 4·00
204 10l. red and green 3·50 4·00
205 15l. red and blue 3·50 4·00

1951. Restoration of Montecassino Abbey.

206 **250** 20l. violet 60 35
207 – 55l. blue (No. 791) 90 50

1951. 3rd Trieste Fair. Optd **AMG-FTT FIERA di TRIESTE 1951** and shield.

208 6l. brown (No. 764) 25 10
209 20l. violet (No. 768) 30 10
210 55l. blue (No. 774) 85 50

1951. 500th Birth Anniv of Perugino.

211 **251** 20l. brown and sepia 55 35

1951. Triennial Art Exhibition, Milan.

212 **252** 20l. black and green 90 1·00
213 – 55l. pink and blue (No. 794) 95 1·00

1951. World Cycling Championship.

214 **253** 25l. black 3·25 1·40

1951. 15th Levant Fair, Bari.

215 **254** 25l. blue 60 35

1951. Birth Centenary of F. P. Michetti.

216 **255** 25l. brown 60 35

1951. Sardinian Stamp Centenary.

217 **256** 10l. black and brown 30 45
218 – 25l. green and red (No. 799) 40 20
219 – 60l. red and blue (No. 800) 80 65

1951. 3rd Industrial and Commercial Census.

220 **257** 10l. green 45 40

1951. 9th National Census.

221 **258** 25l. black 45 20

1951. Forestry Festival.

222 **260** 10l. green and olive 35 20
223 25l. green (No. 807) 55 40

1951. Verdi.

224 – 10l. green and purple (No. 803) 45 20
225 **259** 25l. sepia and brown 40 20
226 – 60l. blue and green (No. 805) 85 85

1952. Bellini.

227 **261** 25l. black 55 35

1952. Caserta Palace.

228 **262** 25l. bistre and green 55 35

1952. 1st International Sports Stamps Exn, Rome.

229 **263** 25l. brown and black 40 35

1952. 30th Milan Fair.

230 **264** 60l. blue 1·10 1·00

1952. Leonardo da Vinci.

231 **265** 25l. orange 15 15
232 – 60l. blue (No. 813) 75 65
233 **265** 80l. red 85 15

1952. Overseas Fair, Naples.

234 **268** 25l. blue 50 35

1952. Modena and Parma Stamp Centenaries.

235 **267** 25l. black and brown 30 15
236 60l. indigo and blue 70 65

1952. Art Exhibition, Venice.

237 **269** 25l. black and cream 55 35

1952. 30th Padua Fair.

238 **270** 25l. red and blue 40 35

1952. 4th Trieste Fair.

239 **271** 25l. green, red and brown 40 35

1952. 16th Levant Fair, Bari.

240 **272** 25l. green 40 35

1952. Savonarola.

241 **273** 25l. violet 40 35

1952. 1st Private Aeronautics Conf, Rome.

242 **274** 60l. blue and ultramarine 90 1·00

1952. Alpine Troops National Exhibition.

243 **275** 25l. black 45 35

1952. Armed Forces Day.
244 **276** 10l. green 10 10
245 **277** 25l. brown & light brown 20 10
246 – 60l. black and blue (No. 827) 50 20

1952. Mission to Ethiopia.
247 **278** 25l. deep brown and brown 60 35

1952. Birth Centenary of Gemito (sculptor).
248 **279** 25l. brown 45 35

1952. Birth Centenary of Mancini (painter).
249 **280** 25l. green 45 35

1952. Centenary of Martyrdom of Belfiore.
250 **281** 25l. blue and black . . . 45 35

1953. Antonello Exhibition, Messina.
251 **282** 25l. red 40 35

1953. 20th "Mille Miglia" Car Race.
252 **283** 25l. violet 40 35

1953. Labour Orders of Merit.
253 **284** 25l. violet 40 35

1953. 300th Birth Anniv of Corelli.
254 **285** 25l. brown 40 35

1953. Coin type.
255 **286** 5l. grey 10 10
256 10l. red 10 10
257 12l. green 10 10
258 13l. purple 10 10
259 20l. brown 10 10
260 25l. violet 10 10
261 35l. red 25 25
262 60l. blue 50 25
263 80l. brown 55 25

1953. 7th Death Centenary of St. Clare.
264 **287** 25l. red and brown . . . 50 35

1953. 5th Trieste Fair. Optd **V FIERA DI TRIESTE AMG FTT 1953**.
265 10l. green (No. 765) 25 20
266 25l. orange (No. 769) 25 20
267 60l. red (No. 775) 30 30

1953. Mountains Festival.
272 **288** 25l. green 60 35

1953. International Agricultural Exn, Rome.
273 **289** 25l. brown 20 10
274 60l. blue 40 30

1953. 4th Anniv of Atlantic Pact.
275 **290** 25l. turquoise and orange 50 35
276 60l. blue and mauve . . . 1·10 1·75

1953. 5th Birth Centenary of Signorelli.
277 **291** 25l. green and brown . . 45 35

1953. 6th Int Microbiological Congress, Rome.
278 **292** 25l. brown and black . . 55 35

1953. Tourist series (Nos. 855/60).
279 10l. brown and sepia 10 10
280 12l. black and blue 10 10
281 20l. brown and orange . . . 10 10
282 25l. green and blue 10 10
283 35l. brown and buff 20 20
284 60l. blue and green 25 20

1954. 25th Anniv of Lateran Treaty.
285 **294** 25l. sepia and brown . . 15 10
286 60l. blue and light blue 35 25

1954. Introduction of Television in Italy.
287 **295** 25l. violet 25 10
288 60l. green 40 30

1954. Encouragement to Taxpayers.
289 **296** 25l. violet 55 20

1954. Milan–Turin Helicopter Mail Flight.
290 **297** 25l. green 50 35

1954. 10th Anniv of Resistance Movement.
291 **298** 25l. black and brown . . 50 35

1954. 6th Trieste Fair. Nos. 282 and 284 of Trieste additionally optd **FIERA DI TRIESTE 1954**.
292 – 25l. green and blue . . . 30 10
293 **293** 60l. blue and green . . . 50 35

1954. Birth Centenary of Catalani.
294 **299** 25l. green 45 35

1954. 7th Birth Centenary of Marco Polo.
295 **300** 25l. brown 20 20
296 60l. green 40 50

1954. 60th Anniv of Italian Touring Club.
297 **301** 25l. green and red 45 30

1954. International Police Congress, Rome.
298 **302** 25l. red 20 10
299 60l. blue 30 25

CONCESSIONAL LETTER POST

1947. Optd **A.M.G. F.T.T.** in two lines.
CL44 – 1l. brn (No. CL649) 15 10
CL45 CL **201** 8l. red . . . . . . 4·00 1·00
CL46 CL **220** 15l. violet . . . . . 25·00 3·50

1949. Optd **AMG-FTT**.
CL122 CL **220** 15l. violet . . . . 1·00 20
CL123 20l. violet . . . . 3·75 20

CONCESSIONAL PARCEL POST

1953.
CP268 CP **288** 40l. orange . . . . 3·50 1·40
CP269 50l. blue . . . . . 3·50 1·40
CP270 75l. brown . . . . 9·75 1·40
CP271 110l. pink . . . . 11·50 1·40
Unused prices are for the complete stamp, used prices for the left half of the stamp.

EXPRESS LETTER STAMPS

1947. Express Letter stamps optd **A.M.G. F.T.T.** in two lines.
E28 – 15l. red (No. E681) . . . 20 20
E29 **200** 25l. orange . . . . 16·00 3·75
E30 30l. violet 40 55
E31 – 60l. red (No. E685) . . . 11·50 6·50

1948. Centenary of 1848 Revolution. Express Letter stamp optd **A.M.G.-F.T.T.**
E83 E **209** 35l. violet . . . . . . 1·25 1·00

1950. Express Letter stamps optd **AMG-FTT** in one line.
E174 E **209** 50l. purple . . . . . 1·75 75
E175 – 60l. red (No. E685) 1·75 85

PARCEL POST STAMPS

Unused prices are for complete stamps, used prices for a half-stamp.

1947. Parcel Post stamps optd **A.M.G. F.T.T.** in two lines on each half of stamp.
P32 P **201** 1l. brown 25 10
P33 2l. blue 25 10
P34 3l. orange 25 10
P35 4l. grey 35 10
P36 5l. purple . . . . . . 1·40 10
P37 10l. violet . . . . . 1·90 10
P38 20l. purple . . . . . 2·75 10
P39 50l. red . . . . 3·75 10
P40 100l. blue . . . . . . 8·00 10
P41 200l. green . . . . . £150 2·00
P42 300l. purple . . . . . 95·00 85
P43 500l. brown . . . . . 50·00 45

1949. Parcel Post stamps optd **AMG-FTT** in one line on each half of stamp.
P139 P **201** 1l. brown . . . . . . 1·10 15
P140 2l. blue 30 10
P141 3l. orange 30 10
P142 4l. grey 30 10
P143 5l. purple 30 10
P144 10l. violet 60 10
P145 20l. purple 60 10
P146 30l. purple 60 10
P147 50l. red 65 10
P148 100l. blue . . . . . . 1·25 10
P149 200l. green . . . . . 12·00 25
P150 300l. purple . . . . . 40·00 30
P151 500l. brown . . . . . 20·00 90
P152 P **928** 1000l. blue . . . . . £120 4·00

POSTAGE DUE STAMPS

1947. Postage Due stamps optd **A.M.G. F.T.T.** in two lines.
D44 D **192** 1l. orange 55 35
D48 D **201** 1l. orange 35 20
D49 2l. green 35 20
D50 3l. red . . . . 75 5·00
D51 4l. brown . . . . . . 3·00 5·50
D45 D **192** 5l. violet . . . . . . 2·50 20
D52 D **201** 5l. violet . . . . . . 65·00 7·25
D53 6l. blue . . . . 13·50 11·50
D54 8l. mauve . . . . . . 19·00 22·00
D46 D **192** 10l. blue . . . . 4·50 20
D55 D **201** 10l. blue . . . . 75·00 5·00
D56 12l. brown . . . . . 16·00 13·00
D47 D **192** 20l. red . . . . 16·00 65
D57 D **201** 20l. purple . . . . . 12·00 1·00
D58 50l. green . . . . . . 1·25 35

1949. Postage Due stamps optd **AMG-FTT** in one line.
D122 D **201** 1l. orange 20 10
D123 2l. green 20 10
D124 3l. red 20 10
D125 5l. violet 45 20
D126 6l. blue 25 20
D127 8l. mauve 25 20
D128 10l. blue 45 20
D129 12l. brown . . . . . 1·10 20
D130 20l. purple . . . . . 2·75 20
D131 25l. red . . . . 4·00 1·00
D132 50l. green . . . . . . 1·60 20
D133 100l. orange . . . . 6·00 20
D134 500l. purple and blue 21·00 11·50

ZONE B
YUGOSLAV MILITARY GOVERNMENT

1948. 100 centesimi = 1 lira.
1949. 100 paras = 1 dinar.

Apart from the definitive issues illustrated below the following are stamps of Yugoslavia (sometimes in new colours), variously overprinted **STT VUJA** or **VUJA-STT** or (Nos. B65 onwards) **STT VUJNA** unless otherwise stated.

B 1 B 2

1948. Labour Day.
B1 B **1** 100l. red and stone (A) . . 6·50 4·50
B2 100l. red and stone (B) . . 7·00 4·50
B3 100l. red and stone (C) . . 6·50 4·50
Inscr in Slovene (A) "I. MAJ 1948 V STO"; Italian (B) "I. MAGGIO 1948 NEL TLT"; or Croat (C) "I. SVIBANJ 1948 U STT".

1948. Red Cross. No. 545 optd and surch.
B3a **131** 2l. on 50p. brown and red . . . . 9·25 8·00

1948. Air. Economic Exhibition, Capodistria.
B4 B **2** 25l. grey 50 40
B5 50l. orange 50 40

B **3** Clasped Hands, Hammer and Sickle

B **4** Fishermen and Flying Boat

B **5** Man with Donkey

B **6** Mediterranean Gull over Chimneys

1949. Labour Day.
B6 B **3** 10l. green 35 25

1949. Air.
B 7 B **4** 1l. turquoise 20 10
B 8 B **5** 2l. brown 20 10
B 9 B **4** 5l. blue 20 10
B10 B **5** 10l. violet . . . . 1·25 40
B11 B **4** 25l. brown . . . . . . 1·40 2·00
B12 B **5** 50l. green . . . . 1·60 1·60
B13 B **6** 100l. brown . . . . . . 3·50 3·00

1949. Partisans issue.
B14 **119** 50p. grey 25 10
B15 1d. green 25 10
B16 **120** 2d. red 25 10
B17 – 3d. red (No. 508) 45 10
B18 **120** 4d. blue 45 10
B19 – 5d. blue (No. 511) . . . 45 10
B20 – 9d. mauve (No. 514) . . 90 80
B21 – 12d. blue (No. 515) . . 2·75 1·25
B22 **119** 16d. blue . . . . 5·25 5·50
B23 – 20d. red (No. 517) . . . 5·50 6·00

1949. 75th Anniv of U.P.U.
B24 – 5d. blue (No. 612) . . . 5·75 6·00
B25 **158** 12d. brown . . . . . 5·75 6·00

1949. Air. Optd **DIN** or surch also.
B26 B **4** 1d. turquoise 15 10
B27 B **5** 2d. brown 15 10
B28 B **4** 5d. blue 20 10
B29 B **5** 10d. violet 40 10
B30 B **4** 15d. on 25l. brown . . . 6·25 7·00
B31 B **5** 20d. on 50l. green . . . . 1·40 3·00
B32 B **6** 30d. on 100l. purple . . . 2·25 3·00

1950. Centenary of Yugoslav Railways.
B33 **116** 2d. green 90 65
B34 – 3d. red (No. 632) . . . . 2·00 65
B35 – 5d. blue (No. 633) . . . 1·75 65
B36 – 10d. orange (No. 633a) 7·75 3·00
MSB36Aa 10d. purple. Perf . . 80·00 90·00
MSB36Ba 10d. purple. Imperf . . 80·00 90·00

B **10** Girl on Donkey

B **11** Workers

1950.
B37 B **10** 50p. grey 20 20
B38 – 1d. red (Cockerel) . . . 20 20
B38a – 1d. brown (Cockerel) 45 20
B39 – 2d. blue (Geese) . . . 20 20
B40 – 3d. brown (Bees) . . . 20 20
B40a – 3d. red (Bees) 60 20
B41 – 5d. green (Oxen) . . . 75 20
B42 – 10d. brown (Turkey) 1·40 80
B43 – 15d. violet (Kids) . . . 9·75 4·00
B44 – 20d. green (Silkworms) 3·25 1·60

1950. May Day.
B45 B **11** 3d. violet 50 35
B46 10d. red 60 45

1950. Red Cross.
B47 **160** 50p. brown and red . . . 70 50

B **12** Worker

B **13** P. P. Vergerio Jr.

1951. May Day.
B48 B **12** 3d. red 75 65
B49 10d. green . . . . . . 1·60 95

1951. Red Cross.
B49a **191** 0d.50 blue and red . . . 9·25 8·25

1951. Festival of Italian Culture.
B50 B **13** 5d. blue 65 65
B51 10d. purple 65 65
B52 20d. brown . . . . . . 65 1·00

1951. Cultural Anniversaries.
B53 **189** 10d. orange 75 80
B54 – 12d. black (As No. 699) 75 80

B **14a** Koper Square

B **15** Cyclists

1952. Air. 75th Anniv of U.P.U.
B54a B **14a** 5d. brown . . . . . 4·00 4·00
B54b – 15d. blue . . . . . 7·25 4·00
B54c – 25d. green . . . . . 6·25 3·50
DESIGNS—VERT: 15d. Lighthouse, Piran. HORIZ: 25d. Hotel, Portoroz.

1952. Physical Culture Propaganda.
B55 B **15** 5d. brown 15 10
B56 – 10d. green 20 10
B57 – 15d. red 20 10
B58 – 28d. blue 55 20
B59 – 50d. red . . . . 1·10 1·00
B60 – 100d. blue . . . . . . 5·75 6·50
DESIGNS: 10d. Footballers; 15d. Rowing four; 28d. Yachting; 50d. Netball players; 100d. Diver.

1952. Marshal Tito's 60th Birthday. As Nos. 727/9 of Yugoslavia additionally inscr "STT VUJA".
B61 **196** 15d. brown . . . . . . 1·60 1·25
B62 **197** 28d. red . . . . 1·50 80
B63 – 50d. green (No. 729) . . 2·10 2·00

1952. Children's Week.
B64 **198** 15d. pink 80 80

1952. 15th Olympic Games, Helsinki. As Nos. 731/6.
B65 **199** 5d. brown on flesh . . . 45 20
B66 – 10d. green on cream . . 45 20
B67 – 15d. violet on mauve . . 45 20
B68 – 28d. brown on buff . . . 95 20
B69 – 50d. brown on yellow . . 5·50 2·00
B70 – 100d. blue on pink . . . 4·50 10·00

1952. Navy Day (Nos. 737/9).
B71 – 15d. purple . . . . . . 1·40 1·10
B72 **200** 28d. brown . . . . . . 1·40 1·10
B73 – 50d. black . . . . . . 2·40 2·40

1952. Red Cross.
B74 **201** 50p. red, grey and black 30 20

1952. 6th Yugoslav Communist Party Congress.
B75 **202** 15d. brown 55 65
B76 15d. turquoise 55 65
B77 15d. brown 55 65
B78 15d. blue 55 65
MSB78b 48 × 70 mm. B **17** 50d. green. Imperf (sold at 85d.) . . 18·00 17·00

B **17** European Anchovy and Starfish

1952. Philatelic Exhibition, Koper.
B78a B 17 15d. brown 1·90 1·25

1953. 10th Death Anniv of Tesla (inventor).
B79 203 15d. red 30 10
B80 30d. blue 70 25

1953. Pictorials of 1950.
B81 1d. grey (No. 705) 4·00 2·50
B86 2d. red (No. 718) 20 20
B82 3d. red (No. 655) 30 20
B87 5d. orange (No. 719) 15 10
B83 10d. green (No. 721) 30 10
B88 15d. red (No. 723) 30 10
B84 30d. blue (No. 712) 3·00 5·25
B85 50d. turquoise (No. 714) 8·50 6·00

1953. United Nations (Nos. 747/9).
B89 204 15d. green 20 15
B90 – 30d. blue 25 15
B91 – 50d. red 65 40

1953. Adriatic Car Rally. As Nos. 750/3.
B92 205 15d. brown and yellow 30 10
B93 – 30d. green and emerald 30 10
B94 – 50d. mauve and orange 30 10
B95 – 70d. deep blue and blue 80 40

1953. Marshal Tito.
B96 206 50d. green 1·60 1·60

1953. 38th Esperanto Congress, Zagreb.
B97 207 15d. grn & turq (postage) 1·00 1·25
B98 300d. green and violet (air) £140 £140

1953. 10th Anniv of Liberation of Istria and Slovene Coast.
B99 209 15d. blue 1·75 1·25

1953. Death Centenary of Radicevic (poet).
B100 210 15d. black 1·10 80

1953. Red Cross.
B101 211 2d. red and bistre 35 15

1953. 10th Anniv of 1st Republican Legislative Assembly. As Nos. 762/4.
B102 212 15d. violet 45 40
B103 – 30d. red 75 40
B104 – 50d. green 75 80

1954. Air. As Nos. 675 etc.
B108 1d. lilac 20 10
B109 2d. green 20 10
B110 3d. purple 20 10
B111 5d. brown 20 10
B112 10d. turquoise 20 10
B113 20d. brown 30 10
B114 30d. blue 30 40
B115 50d. black 50 40
B116 100d. red 1·60 65
B117 200d. violet 2·50 80
B118 500d. orange 12·00 6·00

1954. Animals. As Nos. 765/76.
B119 2d. grey, buff and red 25 20
B120 5d. slate, buff and grey 25 20
B121 10d. brown and green 25 20
B122 15d. brown and blue 30 25
B123 17d. sepia and brown 30 25
B124 25d. yellow, blue and brown 35 25
B125 30d. brown and violet 45 25
B126 35d. black and purple 55 40
B127 50d. brown and green 90 65
B128 65d. black and brown 2·25 2·25
B129 70d. brown and blue 3·25 2·40
B130 100d. black and blue 10·50 9·00

1954. Serbian Insurrection. As Nos. 778/81.
B131 – 15d. multicoloured 40 20
B132 214 30d. multicoloured 40 20
B133 – 50d. multicoloured 40 20
B134 – 70d. multicoloured 65 65

POSTAGE DUE STAMPS

1948. Red Cross. No. D546 surch **VUJA STT** and new value.
BD4 131 2l. on 50p. green and red £100 90·00

1949. On 1946 issue.
BD26 D 126 50p. orange 60 15
BD27 1d. orange 40 15
BD74 1d. brown 15 10
BD28 2d. blue 50 15
BD75 2d. green 15 10
BD29 3d. green 60 15
BD30 5d. violet 70 80
BD76 5d. blue 15 10
BD77 10d. red 10 10
BD78 20d. violet 25 10
BD79 30d. orange 40 20
BD80 50d. blue 3·25 1·10
BD81 100d. purple 3·50 1·60
Nos. BD26/30 optd **STT VUJA** and the rest **STT VUJNA**.

1950. Red Cross. No. D617 optd **VUJA STT**.
BD48 160 50p. purple and red 80 40

BD 12 European Anchovy

1950. Fishes.
BD49 – 50p. brown 55 20
BD50 – 1d. green 1·25 40
BD51 BD 12 2d. blue 1·90 1·25
BD52 3d. blue 1·90 1·25
BD53 5d. purple 4·25 2·75
DESIGN: 50p., 1d. Two meagres.

1951. Red Cross. No. D703 optd **STT VUJA**.
BD54 191 0d.50 green and red 95·00 90·00

The following are optd **STT VUJNA.**

1952. Red Cross. No. D741.
BD82 D 202 50p. red and grey 1·10 65

1953. Red Cross. As No. D762.
BD102 211 2d. red and purple 50 70

TRINIDAD Pt. 1

An island in the West Indies off the coast of Venezuela. Now uses stamps of Trinidad and Tobago.

12 pence = 1 shilling;
20 shillings = 1 pound.

2 Britannia 4 Britannia

1851. Imperf.
2 2 (1d.) purple 13·00 75·00
3 (1d.) blue 13·00 60·00
6 (1d.) grey 45·00 75·00
8 (1d.) red £170 70·00
25 4 4d. lilac £100 £325
28 6d. green – £425
29 1s. blue 95·00 £350

3

1852.
18 3 (1d.) blue £4000 £650
19 (1d.) grey £4000 £400
20 (1d.) red 14·00 £600

1859. Perf.
75 2 (1d.) red 25·00 1·25
70 4 4d. lilac £110 11·00
76 4d. grey £110 70
72c 6d. green 75·00 5·50
63 1s. blue £800 £275
73b 1s. purple £100 4·75
78 1s. yellow £120 3·00

5 10

1869.
113 5 5s. red 55·00 85·00

1879. Surch in words.
98 2 ½d. lilac 12·00 8·00
101 1d. red 30·00 1·25

1882. No. 95 surch **1d** with pen.
104 4 1d. on 6d. green 8·50 5·00

1883.
106 10 ½d. green 4·50 1·25
107 1d. red 10·00 50
108 2½d. blue 12·00 60
110 4d. grey 2·50 60
111 6d. black 3·75 4·25
112 1s. orange 4·25 2·50

11 Britannia

12 Britannia

1896.
114 11 ½d. purple and green 3·25 30
126 ½d. green 65 2·00
115 1d. purple and red 3·50 10
127 1d. black on red 1·25 10
135 1d. red 1·25 10
117 2½d. purple and blue 5·00 20
128 2½d. purple and blue on blue 16·00 25
137 2½d. blue 3·00 15
118 4d. purple and orange 6·50 17·00
129 4d. green and blue on buff 1·75 16·00
138 4d. grey and red on yellow 1·50 8·00
119 5d. purple and mauve 7·00 14·00
120 6d. purple and black 7·50 5·50
140 6d. purple and mauve 7·00 9·50
121 1s. green and brown 7·00 6·50
130 1s. black and blue on yellow 19·00 5·50
142 1s. purple & blue on yellow 10·00 15·00
143 1s. black on green 1·75 1·25
122 12 5s. green and brown 42·00 75·00
131 5s. purple and mauve 48·00 65·00
123 10s. green and blue £160 £300
124 £1 green and red £140 £200

13 Landing of Columbus

14

1898. 400th Anniv of Discovery of Trinidad.
125 13 2d. brown and violet 2·50 1·25

1909. Figures in corners.
146 14 ½d. green 3·75 10
147 – 1d. red 3·75 10
148 – 2½d. blue 13·00 3·25
On the 1d. figures are in lower corners only.

POSTAGE DUE STAMPS

D 1

1885.
D 1 D 1 ½d. black 15·00 45·00
D18 1d. black 1·40 2·25
D19 2d. black 3·00 1·50
D20 3d. black 3·00 3·00
D13 4d. black 12·00 13·00
D14 5d. black 12·00 13·00
D15 6d. black 6·00 10·00
D16 8d. black 12·00 14·00
D17 1s. black 12·00 35·00
For stamps in Type D 1 but with value in cents see under Trinidad and Tobago.

OFFICIAL STAMPS

1894. Optd **O S.**
O1 10 ½d. green 35·00 55·00
O2 1d. red 38·00 60·00
O3 2½d. blue 45·00 90·00
O4 4d. grey 48·00 95·00
O5 6d. black 48·00 95·00
O6 1s. orange 65·00 £130
O7 5 5s. red £160 £475

1909. Optd **OFFICIAL.**
O8 11 ½d. green 1·00 7·00
O9 1d. red 1·00 7·00

1910. Optd **OFFICIAL.**
O10 14 ½d. green 5·00 7·00

TRINIDAD AND TOBAGO Pt. 1

Combined issues for Trinidad and Tobago, administratively one colony. Part of the British Caribbean Federation from 1958 until 31 August 1962, when it became independent within the British Commonwealth.

1913. 12 pence = 1 shilling;
20 shillings = 1 pound.
1935. 100 cents = 1 West Indian dollar.

17

18

1913.
149 17 ½d. green 3·00 10
207 1d. red 60 30
208 1d. brown 60 1·50
209 2d. grey 1·00 1·25
151 2½d. blue 6·50 50
211 3d. blue 3·25 3·00
152a 4d. black and red on yellow 70 6·00
153a 6d. purple and mauve 10·00 4·00
154c 1s. black on green 1·50 3·00
155d 18 5s. purple and mauve 55·00 95·00
156a £1 green and red £130 £190

1915. Optd cross over **21. 10. 15.**
174 17 1d. red 1·50 1·75

1916. Optd **19.10.16.** over cross.
175 17 1d. red 50 2·00

1917. Optd **WAR TAX** in one line (No. 176) or two lines (others).
177 17 ½d. green 10 20
176 1d. red 2·25 2·75
180 1d. red 10 75

1918. Optd **War Tax** in two lines.
187 17 ½d. green 10 1·75
188b 1d. red 10 60

27

28 First Boca

1922.
218 27 ½d. green 50 10
219 1d. brown 50 10
220b 1½d. red 1·75 30
222 2d. grey 50 1·25
223 3d. blue 50 1·25
224 4d. black and red on yellow 3·25 3·25
225 6d. purple and mauve 2·25 25·00
226 6d. green and red on green 1·25 60
227 1s. black on green 5·50 1·75
228 5s. purple and mauve 22·00 38·00
229 £1 green and red £100 £200

1935.
230a 28 1c. blue and green 30 10
231a – 2c. blue and brown 1·00 10
232 – 3c. black and red 1·25 30
233 – 6c. brown and blue 4·25 2·50
234 – 8c. green and orange 3·75 3·50
235 – 12c. black and violet 3·25 1·75
236 – 24c. black and green 3·25 1·50
237 – 48c. green 9·00 15·00
238 – 72c. green and red 29·00 30·00
DESIGNS: 2c. Imperial College of Tropical Agriculture; 3c. Mt. Irvine Bay, Tobago; 6c. Discovery of Lake Asphalt; 8c. Queen's Park, Savannah; 12c. Town Hall, San Fernando; 24c. Govt. House; 48c. Memorial Park; 72c. Blue Basin.

1935. Silver Jubilee. As T **32a** of St. Helena.
239 2c. blue and black 30 75
240 3c. blue and red 30 1·50
241 6c. brown and blue 1·50 2·50
242 24c. grey and purple 6·00 16·00

1937. Coronation. As T **32b** of St. Helena.
243 1c. green 15 60
244 2c. brown 35 15
245 8c. orange 90 2·25

37 First Boca

47 King George VI

1938. Designs as 1935 issue but with portrait of King George VI as in T **37** and without "POSTAGE & REVENUE", and T **47**.
246 37 1c. blue and green 1·00 30
247 – 2c. blue and brown 1·25 20
248 – 3c. black and red 11·00 1·00
248a – 3c. green and purple 30 20
249 – 4c. brown 25·00 1·50
249a – 4c. red 50 1·00
249b – 5c. mauve 50 15
250 – 6c. brown and blue 2·75 80
251 – 8c. green and orange 2·75 1·00
252a – 12c. black and purple 2·75 10
253 – 24c. black and olive 2·50 10
254 – 60c. green and red 8·50 1·50

255 **47** $1.20 green 12·00 1·50
256 $4.80 red 24·00 35·00
NEW DESIGNS: 4c. Memorial Park; 5c. G.P.O. and Treasury; 60c. As No. 238.

1946. Victory. As T **33a** of St. Helena.
257 3c. brown 10 10
258 6c. blue 10 1·50

1948. Silver Wedding. As T **33b/c** of St. Helena.
259 3c. brown 10 10
260 $4.80 red 20·00 26·00

1949. 75th Anniv of U.P.U. As T **33d/g** of St. Helena.
261 5c. purple 35 1·00
262 6c. blue 1·75 1·25
263 12c. violet 40 1·50
264 24c. green 45 1·25

1951. B.W.I. University College. As T **10a/b** of St. Kitts-Nevis.
265 3c. green and brown 20 1·25
266 12c. black and violet 30 1·25

48 First Boca

51 Cipriani Memorial

53 Copper-rumped Hummingbird ("Humming Bird")

1953. Designs as 1938 and 1940 issues but with portrait of Queen Elizabeth in place of King George VI as in T **48** (1c., 2c., 12c.) or facing left (others).
267 **48** 1c. blue and green 20 40
268 – 2c. blue and brown 20 40
269 – 3c. green and purple 20 10
270 – 4c. red 20 40
271 – 5c. mauve 30 30
272 – 6c. brown and blue 50 30
273 – 8c. olive and red 2·25 30
274 – 12c. black and purple 30 10
275 – 24c. black and olive 2·25 30
276 – 60c. green and red 22·00 1·25
277a – $1.20 green 1·25 30
278a – $4.80 red 9·00 14·00

1953. Coronation. As T **33h** of St. Helena.
279 3c. black and green 20 10

1956. No. 268 surch **ONE CENT**.
280 1c. on 2c. blue and brown 1·25 1·75

1958. Inaug of British Caribbean Federation. As T **27a** of St. Kitts-Nevis.
281 5c. green 20 10
282 6c. blue 25 1·50
283 12c. red 25 10

1960.
284 **51** 1c. stone and black 10 20
285 – 2c. blue 10 20
286 – 5c. blue 10 10
287 – 6c. brown 10 1·00
288 – 8c. green 10 1·50
289 – 10c. lilac 10 10
290 – 12c. red 10 1·25
291 – 15c. orange (A) 1·00 50
291a – 15c. orange (B) 6·00 10
292 – 25c. red and blue 80 10
293 – 35c. green and black 3·75 10
294 – 50c. yellow, grey and blue 35 1·00
295 – 60c. red, green and blue 55 30
296 **53** $1.20 multicoloured 15·00 2·75
297 – $4.80 green and blue 22·00 11·00
DESIGNS—HORIZ (as Type **51**): 2c. Queen's Hall; 5c. Whitehall; 6c. Treasury Building; 8c. Governor-General's House; 10c. General Hospital, San Fernando; 12c. Oil refinery; 15c. (A) Crest, (B) Coat of arms; 25c. Scarlet ibis; 35c. Pitch Lake; 50c. Mohammed Jinnah Mosque. VERT (as Type **51**): 60c. Anthurium lilies. (As Type **53**): $4.80, Map of Trinidad and Tobago.

65 Scouts and Gold Wolf Badge

1961. 2nd Caribbean Scout Jamboree. Design multicoloured. Background colours given.
298 **65** 8c. green 15 10
299 25c. blue 15 10

66 "Buccoo Reef" (painting by Carlisle Chang)

1962. Independence.
300 **66** 5c. turquoise 10 10
301 – 8c. grey 40 1·00
302 – 25c. violet 15 10
303 – 35c. multicoloured 2·25 15
304 – 60c. red, black and blue 2·75 3·75
DESIGNS: 8c. Piarco Air Terminal; 25c. Hilton Hotel, Port-of-Spain; 35c. Greater bird of paradise ("Bird of Paradise") and map; 60c. Scarlet ibis and map.

71 "Protein Foods"

1963. Freedom from Hunger.
305 **71** 5c. red 15 10
306 8c. bistre 15 85
307 25c. blue 25 20

72 Jubilee Emblem

1964. Golden Jubilee of Trinidad and Tobago Girl Guides' Association.
308 **72** 6c. yellow, blue and red 10 70
309 25c. yellow, ultram & blue 15 20
310 35c. yellow, blue and green 15 20

73 I.C.Y. Emblem

1965. International Co-operation Year.
311 **73** 35c. brown, green & yellow 65 20

74 Eleanor Roosevelt, Flag and U.N. Emblem

1965. Eleanor Roosevelt Memorial Foundation.
312 **74** 25c. black, red and blue 15 10

75 Parliament Building

1966. Royal Visit. Multicoloured.
313 5c. Type **75** 15 10
314 8c. Map, Royal Yacht "Britannia" and arms 1·25 70
315 25c. Map and flag 1·25 55
316 35c. Flag and panorama 1·25 70

1967. 5th Year of Independence. Nos. 289, 291a and 295 optd **FIFTH YEAR OF INDEPENDENCE 31st AUGUST 1967**.
318 8c. green 10 10
319 10c. lilac 10 10
320 15c. orange 10 10
321 60c. blue, green and red 25 15

80 Musical Instruments

1968. Trinidad Carnival. Multicoloured.
322 5c. Type **80** 10 10
323 10c. Calypso King (vert) 10 10
324 15c. Steel band 10 10
325 25c. Carnival procession 15 10
326 35c. Carnival King (vert) 15 10
327 60c. Carnival Queen (vert) 20 1·00

86 Doctor giving Eye-test

87 Peoples of the World and Emblem

1968. 20th Anniv of World Health Organization.
328 **86** 5c. red, brown and gold 15 10
329 25c. orange, brown and gold 35 15
330 35c. blue, black and gold 40 25

1968. Human Rights Year.
331 **87** 5c. red, black and yellow 10 10
332 10c. blue, black and yellow 15 10
333 25c. green, black and yellow 30 15

88 Cycling

1968. Olympic Games, Mexico. Multicoloured.
334 5c. Type **88** 50 10
335 15c. Weightlifting 20 10
336 25c. Relay-racing 20 10
337 35c. Sprinting 20 10
338 $1.20 Maps of Mexico and Trinidad 1·00 45

93 Cocoa Beans

1969. Multicoloured.
339c 1c. Type **93** 10 20
340 3c. Sugar refinery 10 10
341a 5c. Rufous-vented chachalaca ("Cocrico") 2·00 10
342 6c. Oil refinery 10 10
343 8c. Fertiliser plant 1·50 3·00
344 10c. Green hermit 2·50 10
345 12c. Citrus fruit 15 3·00
346 15c. Arms of Trinidad and Tobago 10 10
347 20c. Flag and outline of Trinidad and Tobago 30 10
348 25c. As 20c. 30 65
349 30c. Chaconia plant 30 10
350 40c. Scarlet ibis 5·50 10
351 50c. Maracas Bay 30 3·50
352 $1 Poui tree 60 15
353 $2.50 Fishing 1·00 4·25
354 $5 Red house 1·00 4·25
Nos. 344/9 and 352 are vert.

108 Captain A. A. Cipriani (labour leader) and Entrance to Woodford Square

1969. 50th Anniv of Int Labour Organization.
355 **108** 6c. black, gold and red 15 25
356 – 15c. black, gold and blue 15 25
DESIGN: 15c. Arms of Industrial Court and entrance to Woodford Square.

110 Cornucopia and Fruit

117 Parliamentary Chamber, Flags and Emblem

114 Space Module landing on Moon

1969. 1st Anniv of C.A.R.I.F.T.A. Mult.
357 6c. Type **110** 10 10
358 10c. Flags of Britain and member nations (horiz) 10 10
359 30c. Map showing C.A.R.I.F.T.A. countries 20 20
360 40c. Boeing 727-100 "Sunjet" in flight (horiz) 40 90

1969. 1st Man on the Moon. Multicoloured.
361 6c. Type **114** 20 10
362 40c. Space module and astronauts on Moon (vert) 30 10
363 $1 Astronauts seen from inside space module 60 35

1969. 15th Commonwealth Parliamentary Association Conference, Port-of-Spain. Mult.
364 10c. Type **117** 10 10
365 15c. J.F. Kennedy College 10 10
366 30c. Parliamentary maces 25 50
367 40c. Cannon and emblem 25 50

121 Congress Emblem

124 "Man in the Moon"

1969. International Congress of the Junior Chamber of Commerce.
368 **121** 6c. black, red and gold 10 10
369 – 30c. gold, lake and blue 25 40
370 – 40c. black, gold and blue 25 40
DESIGNS: (both incorporating the Congress emblem). HORIZ: 30c. Islands at daybreak. VERT: 40c. Palm trees and ruin.

1970. Carnival Winners. Multicoloured.
371 5c. Type **124** 10 10
372 6c. "City beneath the Sea" 10 10
373 15c. "Antelope" God Bambara 15 10
374 30c. "Chanticleer" Pheasant Queen of Malaya 25 10
375 40c. Steel Band of the Year 25 30

129 Statue of Gandhi

131 Symbols of Culture, Science, Arts and Technology

1970. Gandhi Centenary Year (1969). Mult.
376 10c. Type **129** 25 10
377 30c. Head of Gandhi and flag of India (horiz) 45 20

1970. 25th Anniv of U.N.
378 **131** 5c. multicoloured 10 10
379 – 10c. multicoloured 20 10
380 – 20c. multicoloured 20 45
381 – 30c. multicoloured 25 30
DESIGNS AND SIZES: 10c. Children of different races, map and flag (34 × 25 mm); 20c. Noah's Ark, rainbow and dove (34 × 23 mm); 30c. New U.P.U. H.Q. Building ($46 \times 27\frac{1}{2}$ mm).

1970. Inauguration of National Commercial Bank. No. 341 optd **NATIONAL COMMERCIAL BANK ESTABLISHED 1.7.70.**
382 5c. multicoloured 30 10

134 "East Indian Immigrants" (J. Cazabon)

1970. 125th Anniv of San Fernando. Paintings by Cazabon.
383 **134** 3c. multicoloured 10 90
384 – 5c. black, blue and ochre 10 10
385 – 40c. black, blue and ochre 60 20
DESIGNS—HORIZ: 5c. "San Fernando Town Hall"; 40c. "San Fernando Harbour, 1860".

135 "The Adoration of the Shepherds" (detail, School of Seville)

1970. Christmas. Multicoloured.
386 3c. Type **135** 10 10
387 5c. "Madonna and Child with Saints" (detail, Titian) 10 10
388 30c. "The Adoration of the Shepherds" (detail, Le Nain) 15 20
389 40c. "The Virgin and Child, St. John and an Angel" (Morando) 15 10
390 $1 "The Adoration of the Kings" (detail, Veronese) 35 2·50
MS391 114 × 153 mm. Nos. 386/9 1·00 1·25

136 Red Brocket

1971. Trinidad Wildlife. Multicoloured.
392 3c. Type **136** 15 30
393 5c. Collared peccary 20 15
394 6c. Paca 20 50
395 30c. Brazilian agouti . . . 60 3·50
396 40c. Ocelot . . . . 60 2·75

137 A. A. Cipriani

138 "Virgin and Child with St. John" (detail, Bartolommeo)

1971. 9th Anniv of Independence. Mult.
397 5c. Type **137** 10 10
398 30c. Chaconia medal . . . . 30 1·10

1971. Christmas.
399 **138** 3c. multicoloured 15 15
400 – 5c. multicoloured 20 10
401 – 10c. multicoloured 25 10
402 – 15c. multicoloured 30 20
DESIGNS: 5c. Local creche; 10c. "Virgin and Child with Saints Jerome and Dominic" (detail, Lippi); 15c. "Virgin and Child with St. Anne" (detail, Gerolamo dai Libri).

139 Satellite Earth Station, Matura

1971. Satellite Earth Station. Multicoloured.
403 10c. Type **139** 10 10
404 30c. Dish antennae . . . . . 25 1·10
405 40c. Satellite and the Earth 35 1·10
MS406 140 × 76 mm. Nos. 403/5 65 2·25

140 "Morpho peleides x achilleana"

1972. Butterflies. Multicoloured.
407 3c. Type **140** . . . . 75 1·00
408 5c. "Eryphanis polyxena" . . 80 10
409 6c. "Phoebis philea" . . . . 85 1·00
410 10c. "Prepona laertes" . . . 1·00 15
411 20c. "Eurytides telesilaus" . . 1·75 2·25
412 30c. "Eurema proterpia" . . 2·00 2·75

141 "Lady McLeod" (paddle-steamer) and McLeod Stamp

1972. 125th Anniv of First Trinidad Postage Stamp.
413 **141** 5c. multicoloured 25 10
414 – 10c. multicoloured 35 10
415 – 30c. blue, brown and black 70 45
MS416 83 × 140 mm. Nos. 413/15 1·00 1·25
DESIGNS: 10c. Lady McLeod stamp and map; 30c. Lady McLeod and inscription.

142 Trinity Cross

144 "Adoration of the Kings" (detail, Dosso)

143 Bronze Medal, 1964 Relay

1972. 10th Anniv of Independence. Mult.
417 5c. Type **142** 10 10
418 10c. Chaconia Medal 10 10
419 20c. Humming-bird Medal 15 15
420 30c. Medal of Merit 15 20
MS421 93 × 121 mm. Nos. 417/20 60 1·00
See also Nos. 440/4.

1972. Olympic Games, Munich. Multicoloured.
422 10c. Type **143** 15 10
423 20c. Bronze, 1964 200 m . . 25 25
424 30c. Silver, 1952 weightlifting 35 25
425 40c. Silver, 1964 400 m . . 35 25
426 50c. Silver, 1948 weightlifting 35 2·00
MS427 153 × 82 mm. Nos. 422/6 1·75 2·25

1972. Christmas. Multicoloured.
431 3c. Type **144** 10 10
432 5c. "The Holy Family and a Shepherd" (Titian) 10 10
433 30c. As 5c. 70 55
MS434 73 × 99 mm. Nos. 431/3 1·00 1·75

145 E.C.L.A. Building, Chile

1973. Anniversaries. Events described on stamps. Multicoloured.
435 10c. Type **145** 10 10
436 20c. Interpol emblem 45 30
437 30c. W.M.O. emblem 45 30
438 40c. University of the West Indies . . . . 45 1·00
MS439 155 × 92 mm. Nos. 435/8 1·25 1·25

1973. 11th Anniv of Independence. Medals as T **142**. Multicoloured.
440 10c. Trinity Cross 10 10
441 20c. Medal of Merit 20 40
442 30c. Chaconia Medal 20 50
443 40c. Hummingbird Medal . . 30 50
MS444 75 × 122 mm. Nos. 440/3 70 1·25

146 G.P.O., Port-of-Spain

1973. 2nd Commonwealth Conference of Postal Administrations, Trinidad. Multicoloured.
445 30c. Type **146** 20 75
446 40c. Conference Hall, Chaguaramas (wrongly inscr "Chagaramas") . . . 30 75
MS447 115 × 115 mm. Nos. 445/6 60 1·50

147 "Madonna with Child" (Murillo)

1973. Christmas.
448 **147** 5c. multicoloured 10 10
449 $1 multicoloured . . . . 60 1·25
MS450 94 × 88 mm. Nos. 448/9 85 1·40

148 Berne H.Q. within U.P.U. Emblem

1974. Centenary of U.P.U. Multicoloured.
451 40c. Type **148** 30 15
452 50c. Map within emblem . . 30 85
MS453 117 × 104 mm. Nos. 451/2 10·00 20·00

149 "Humming Bird I" (ketch) crossing Atlantic Ocean (1960)

1974. 1st Anniv of World Voyage by H. and K. La Borde. Multicoloured.
454 40c. Type **149** 50 15
455 50c. "Humming Bird II" (ketch) crossing globe . . . 60 1·40
MS456 109 × 84 mm. Nos. 454/5 1·50 4·00

150 "Sex Equality"

1975. International Women's Year.
457 **150** 15c. multicoloured 15 30
458 30c. multicoloured 35 70

151 Common Vampire Bat, Microscope and Syringe

1975. Isolation of Rabies Virus. Multicoloured.
459 25c. Type **151** . . . . 45 1·25
460 30c. Dr. Pawan, instruments and book 55 55

152 Route-map and Tail of Boeing 707

1975. 35th Anniv of British West Indian Airways. Multicoloured.
461 20c. Type **152** 40 80
462 30c. 707 on ground 60 90
463 40c. 707 in flight . . . . . . 70 1·00
MS464 119 × 110 mm. Nos. 461/3 1·50 2·50

153 "From the Land of the Humming Bird"

1975. Carnival. 1974 Prize-winning Costumes. Multicoloured.
465 30c. Type **153** 10 10
466 $1 "The Little Carib" 40 50
MS467 83 × 108 mm. Nos. 465/6 1·10 1·10

154 Angostura Building, Port-of-Spain

1976. 150th Anniv of Angostura Bitters. Mult.
468 5c. Type **154** 10 40
469 35c. Medal, New Orleans, 1885/6 . . . . 20 35
470 45c. Medal, Sydney, 1879 . . 25 40
471 50c. Medal, Brussels, 1897 . . 25 1·40
MS472 119 × 112 mm. Nos. 468/71 65 1·50

1976. West Indian Victory in World Cricket Cup. As T **126** of Barbados.
474 35c. Caribbean map 45 90
475 45c. Prudential Cup 55 90
MS476 80 × 80 mm. Nos. 474/5 1·75 4·00

155 "Columbus sailing Through the Bocas" (Campins)

1976. Paintings, Hotels and Orchids. Mult.
479 5c. Type **155** . . . . 2·50 30
480 6c. Robinson Crusoe Hotel, Tobago . . . . 20 2·75
482 10c. "San Fernando Hill" (J. Cazabon) 20 10
483 12c. "Paphinia cristata" . . . 2·00 4·00
484 15c. Turtle Beach Hotel . . . 50 3·25
485 20c. "East Indians in a Landscape" (J. Cazabon) 70 10
486 25c. Mt. Irvine Hotel 60 10
487 30c. "Caularthron bicornutum" . . . . . . 2·00 2·75
488 35c. "Los Gallos Point" (J. Cazabon) . . . . . . 1·75 10
489 40c. "Miltassia" . . . . . . 3·00 10
490 45c. "Corbeaux Town" (J. Cazabon) . . . . . . 1·00 10
491 50c. "Oncidium ampliatum" 2·25 20
492 70c. Beach facilities, Mt. Irvine Hotel . . . . . . 70 1·25
494 $2.50 "Oncidium papilio" . . 2·25 3·25
495 $5 Trinidad Holiday Inn . . 1·25 7·00
MS497 171 × 100 mm. Nos. 479, 482, 485, 488 and 490 . . . . . . 2·00 1·50
MS498 171 × 88 mm. Nos. 480, 484, 486, 492 and 495 . . . . . . 2·25 7·00
MS499 170 × 90 mm. Nos. 483, 487, 489, 491 and 494 . . . . . . 3·00 5·00

156 Hasely Crawford and Olympic Gold Medal

1977. Hasely Crawford Commemoration.
501 **156** 25c. mulicoloured 30 50
MS502 93 × 70 mm. No. 501 . . 60 1·25

157 Lindbergh's Sikorsky S-38, 1929

1977. 50th Anniv of Airmail Service. Mult.
503 20c. Type **157** 40 20
504 35c. Arrival of Charles and Anne Lindbergh 50 35
505 45c. Boeing 707, c. 1960 . . 60 60
506 50c. Boeing 747-200, 1969 . . 1·00 3·75
MS507 130 × 100 mm. Nos. 503/6 3·00 4·25

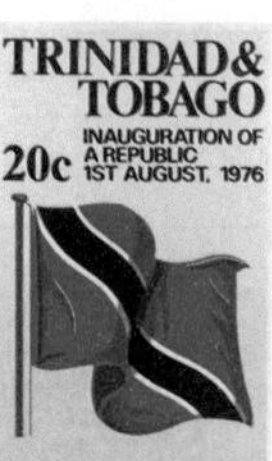

158 National Flag **159** White Poinsettia

1977. Inauguration of Republic. Multicoloured.
508 20c. Type **158** 40 15
509 35c. Coat of arms 60 65
510 45c. Government House 70 85
MS511 125 × 84 mm. Nos. 508/10 1·00 1·50

1977. Christmas. Multicoloured.
512 10c. Type **159** 20 10
513 35c. Type **159** 25 10
514 45c. Red poinsettia 30 30
515 50c. As 45c. . . . . 35 2·50
MS516 112 × 142 mm. Nos. 512/15 1·00 3·50

160 Miss Janelle (Penny) Commissioning with Trophy **162** "Burst of Beauty"

161 Tayra

1978. "Miss Universe 1977" Commemoration. Mult.
517 10c. Type **160** 25 10
518 35c. Portrait 40 60
519 45c. In evening dress 45 75
MS520 186 × 120 mm. Nos. 517/19 1·00 2·00

1978. Wildlife. Multicoloured.
521 15c. Type **161** 20 20
522 25c. Ocelot 30 30
523 40c. Brazilian tree porcupine 50 30
524 70c. Tamandua . . . . . . 65 2·75
MS525 128 × 101 mm. Nos. 521/4 1·50 3·25

1979. Carnival 1978.
526 **162** 5c. multicoloured 10 10
527 – 10c. multicoloured 10 10
528 – 35c. multicoloured 10 10
529 – 45c. multicoloured 10 10
530 – 50c. brown, red and lilac 10 15
531 – $1 multicoloured 20 65
DESIGNS: 10c. Rain worshipper; 35c. "Zodiac"; 45c. Praying mantis; 50c. "Eye of the Hurricane"; $1 Steel orchestra.

163 Day Care **164** Geothermal Exploration

1979. International Year of the Child. Mult.
532 5c. Type **163** 10 10
533 10c. School feeding programme 10 10
534 35c. Dental care 30 15
535 45c. Nursery school 30 20
536 50c. Free bus transport . . . 30 85
537 $1 Medical care . . . . . . 65 2·75
MS538 114 × 132 mm. Nos. 532/7 1·60 2·50

1979. 4th Latin American Geological Congress. Multicoloured.
539 10c. Type **164** 20 10
540 35c. Hydrogeology 35 40
541 45c. Petroleum exploration 40 40
542 70c. Environmental preservation . . . . 55 1·60
MS543 185 × 89 mm. Nos. 539/42 1·50 2·00

165 1879 1d. Stamp and Map of Tobago

1979. Tobago Stamp Centenary.
544 **165** 10c. multicoloured 10 10
545 – 15c. multicoloured 15 10
546 – 35c. multicoloured 20 20
547 – 45c. multicoloured 20 20
548 – 70c. multicoloured . . . . 25 1·50
549 – $1 black, lilac and orange 25 1·75
MS550 165 × 155 mm. Nos. 544/9 1·25 4·00
DESIGNS: 15c. 1879 3d. and 1880 ½d. surcharged on half of 6d; 35c. 1879 6d. and 1886 ½d. surcharged on 6d; 45c. 1879 1s. and 1886 ½d. surcharged on 2½d; 70c. 1879 5s. and Great Britain 1856 1s. with "A14" (Scarborough, Tobago) postmark; $1 1879 £1 and General Post Office, Scarborough, Tobago.

166 1962 60c. Independence Commemorative Stamp and Sir Rowland Hill

1979. Death Cent of Sir Rowland Hill. Mult.
551 25c. Type **166** 30 15
552 45c. 1977 35c. Inauguration of Republic commemorative 35 20
553 $1 1879 Trinidad ½d. surcharge and Tobago, 1880 4d. . . . . 45 1·75
MS554 115 × 125 mm. No. 551/3 1·00 1·75

167 Poui Tree in Churchyard

1980. Centenary of Princes Town. Mult.
555 5c. Type **167** 10 10
556 10c. Princes Town Court House 10 10
557 50c. Locomotive of the Royal Train, 1880 . . . . 60 90
558 $1.50 H.M.S. "Bacchante" (screw corvette) . . . . . 1·00 2·00
MS559 177 × 102 mm. Nos. 555/8 1·60 2·75

1980. Population Census. Nos. 479/80 and 482 optd **1844–1980 POPULATION CENSUS 12th MAY 1980.**
560 5c. Type **155** 20 20
561 6c. Robinson Crusoe Hotel, Tobago 20 80
562 10c. "San Fernando Hill" (J. Cazabon) 20 20

169 Scarlet Ibis (male)

1980. Scarlet Ibis. Multicoloured.
563 50c. Type **169** . . . . 50 1·40
564 50c. Male and female . . . . 50 1·40
565 50c. Hen and nest . . . . . 50 1·40
566 50c. Nest and eggs . . . . . 50 1·40
567 50c. Chick in nest . . . . . 50 1·40

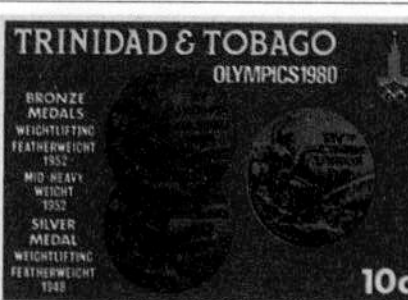

170 Silver and Bronze Medals for Weightlifting, 1948 and 1952

1980. Olympic Games, Moscow.
568 **170** 10c. multicoloured 10 10
569 – 15c. multicoloured 10 10
570 – 70c. multicoloured . . . . 45 1·25
MS571 110 × 149 mm. $2.50 black, silver and red . . . . 2·00 3·50
DESIGNS—HORIZ: 15c. Hasely Crawford (100 metres sprint winner, 1976) and gold medal; 70c. Silver medal for 400 metres and bronze medal for 4 × 400 metres relay, 1964. VERT: $2.50, Olympic Games emblems for Moscow, 1980, Olympia 776 B.C. and Athens, 1896.

171 Charcoal Production

1980. 11th Commonwealth Forestry Conf. Mult.
572 10c. Type **171** 10 10
573 55c. Logging 20 25
574 70c. Teak plantation 30 60
575 $2.50 Watershed management 60 2·25
MS576 135 × 87 mm. Nos. 572/5 1·75 2·75

172 Beryl McBurnie (dance and culture) and Audrey Jeffers (social worker)

1980. Decade for Women (1st issue). Mult.
577 $1 Type **172** 35 55
578 $1 Elizabeth Bourne (judiciary) and Isabella Teshier (government) . . . 35 55
579 $1 Dr. Stella Abidh (public health) and Louise Horne (nutrition) 35 55
See also Nos. 680/2.

173 Netball Stadium

1980. World Netball Tournament.
580 **173** 70c. multicoloured 30 50

174 I.Y.D.P. Emblem, Athlete and Disabled Person

1981. International Year of Disabled Persons.
581 **174** 10c. green, black and red 15 10
582 – 70c. orange, black and red 30 70
583 – $1.50 blue, black and red 40 1·40
584 – $2 flesh, black and red . . 40 1·75
DESIGNS: 70c. I.Y.D.P. emblem and doctor with disabled person; $1.50, Emblem and blind man and woman; $2, Emblem and inscription.

175 "Our Land Must Live"

1981. Environmental Preservation. Mult.
585 10c. Type **175** 15 10
586 55c. "Our seas must live" . . 45 30
587 $3 "Our skies must live" . . 1·60 1·60
MS588 142 × 89 mm. Nos. 555/7 2·50 4·50

176 "Food For Famine"

1981. World Food Day. Multicoloured.
589 10c. Type **176** 10 10
590 15c. "Produce more" (threshing and milling rice) 10 10
591 45c. "Fish for food" (Bigeye) 30 20
592 55c. "Prevent hunger" . . . 35 25
593 $1.50 "Fight malnutrition" . . 85 90
594 $2 "Fish for food" (Small-mouthed grunt) . . . . . 1·10 1·25
MS595 164 × 98 mm. Nos. 589/94 2·75 5·00

177 "First Aid Skills" **178** Pharmacist at Work

1981. President's Award Scheme. Mult.
596 10c. Type **177** 20 10
597 70c. "Motor mechanics" . . 40 45
598 $1 "Expedition" 50 55
599 $2 Presenting an award . . . 60 1·40

1982. Commonwealth Pharmaceutical Conference. Multicoloured.
600 10c. Type **178** 15 10
601 $1 Gerritoute (plant) . . . . 1·75 2·25
602 $2 Rachette (plant) . . . . . 2·75 4·25

179 "Production" **180** Charlotteville

1982. 75th Anniv of Boy Scout Movement. Mult.
603 15c. Type **179** 60 10
604 55c. "Tolerance" . . . . . . 1·50 30
605 $5 "Discipline" . . . . . . 5·50 7·00

1982. 25th Anniv of Tourist Board. Mult.
606 55c. Type **180** 30 25
607 $1 Boating 40 55
608 $3 Fort George . . . . . . 1·25 2·25

181 "Pa Pa Bois"

1982. Folklore. Local Spirits and Demons. Mult.
609 10c. Type **181** 10 10
610 15c. "La Diablesse" 10 10
611 65c. "Lugarhoo", "Phantom" and "Soucouyant" 35 30
612 $5 "Bois de Soleil", "Davens" and "Mamma de l'Eau" . . . . 2·50 3·25
MS613 133 × 100 mm. Nos. 609/12 4·25 6·50

182 Cane Harvesting

1982. Cent of Canefarmers' Association. Mult.
614 30c. Type **182** 30 15
615 70c. Farmers loading bullock cart . . . . 60 1·00
616 $1.50 Cane field in bloom . . 1·10 3·25
MS617 72 × 117 mm. Nos. 614/16 1·40 2·25

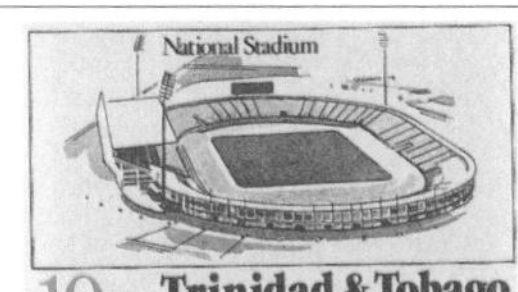

183 National Stadium

1982. 20th Anniv of Independence. Mult.
618 10c. Type **183** 50 10
619 35c. Caroni water treatment plant 60 15
620 50c. Mount Hope Maternity Hospital . . . . 1·50 25
621 $2 National Insurance Board Mall, Tobago . . . . . . 1·75 2·00

184 Commonwealth Flags

1983. Commonwealth Day. Multicoloured.
622 10c. Type **184** 10 10
623 55c. Satellite view of Trinidad and Tobago 25 20
624 $1 "Nodding donkey" oil pump (vert) 40 70
625 $2 Map of Trinidad and Tobago (vert) . . . . . . 85 1·50

185 Lockheed Tristar 500 "Flamingo"

1983. 10th Anniv of CARICOM.
626 **185** 35c. multicoloured . . . . 2·00 2·25

186 V.D.U. Operator

1983. World Communications Year. Mult.
627 15c. Type **186** 20 10
628 55c. Scarborough Post Office, Tobago 30 20
629 $1 Textel building 60 70
630 $3 Morne Blue E.C.M.S. station . . . . 1·10 2·50

187 Financial Complex

1983. Conference of Commonwealth Finance Ministers.
631 **187** $2 multicoloured . . . . 60 1·25

188 King Mackerel

1983. World Food Day. Multicoloured.
632 10c. Type **188** 20 10
633 55c. Four-winged flyingfish 1·00 40
634 70c. Queen or pink conch . . 1·25 1·40
635 $4 Red shrimp . . . . 4·50 7·50

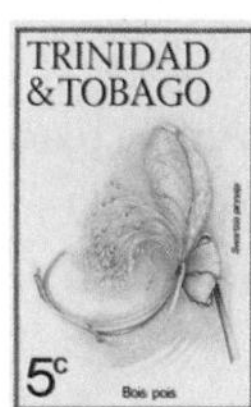

189 Bois Pois

190 Rooks in Staunton and 17th-century Styles

1983. Flowers. Multicoloured.
636A 5c. Type **189** . . . . . . 1·00 2·00
687 10c. Maraval lily 30 30
638A 15c. Star grass . . . . . . 90 1·00
639A 20c. Bois caco 30 55
640A 25c. Strangling fig . . . . 1·10 2·50
641A 30c. "Cassia moschata" . . 50 40
642A 50c. Chalice flower 50 40
643A 65c. Black stick . . . . . 55 1·00
644A 80c. "Columnea scandens" 65 2·00
695 95c. Cat's claw 50 70
696 $1 Bois l'agli 65 30
647A $1.50 "Eustoma exaltatum" 1·25 2·50
648A $2 Chaconia (39 × 29 mm) 1·50 3·00
649A $2.50 "Chrysothemis pulchella" (39 × 29 mm) 1·25 4·00
700 $5 "Centratherum punctatum" (39 × 29 mm) 1·75 2·00
701 $10 Savanna flower (39 × 29 mm) . . . . . . 3·50 4·50

1984. 60th Anniv of Int Chess Federation. Mult.
652 50c. Type **190** . . . . 3·25 50
653 70c. Bishops in Staunton and 12th-century Lewis styles 3·50 2·00
654 $1.50 Queens in Staunton and 13th-century Swedish styles . . . . 4·50 6·00
655 $2 Kings in Staunton and 19th-century Chinese styles 6·00 7·50

191 Swimming

192 Slave Schooner and Shackles

1984. Olympic Games, Los Angeles. Multicoloured.
656 15c. Type **191** 10 10
657 55c. Track and field events 30 20
658 $1.50 Sailing . . . . 1·00 1·75
659 $4 Cycling . . . . 6·50 7·50
MS660 132 × 85 mm. Nos. 656/9 7·50 8·50

1984. 150th Anniv of Abolition of Slavery. Mult.
661 35c. Type **192** . . . . 1·50 40
662 55c. Slave and "Slave Triangle" map . . . . . . 2·50 60
663 $1 "Capitalism and Slavery" (book by Dr. Eric Williams) . . . . 2·50 2·50
664 $2 Toussaint l'Ouverture (Haitian revolutionary) . . 3·25 7·00
MS665 95 × 100 mm. Nos. 661/4 9·00 11·00

193 Children's Band

1984. 125th Anniv of St. Mary's Children's Home. Multicoloured.
666 10c. Type **193** 15 10
667 70c. St. Mary's Children's Home 50 50
668 $3 Group of children . . . . 2·25 4·00

194 Parang Band

1984. Parang Festival. Multicoloured.
669 10c. Type **194** 25 10
670 30c. Music and poinsettia . . 60 15
671 $1 Bandola, bandolin and cuatro (musical instruments) . . . . 1·75 1·25
672 $3 Double bass, fiddle and guitar (musical instruments) 2·75 6·50

195 Capt. A. A. Cipriani and T. U. B. Butler

1985. Labour Day. Labour Leaders.
673 **195** 55c. black and red . . . . 1·60 1·60
674 – 55c. black and yellow . . 1·60 1·60
675 – 55c. black and green . . . 1·60 1·60
DESIGNS: No. 674, C. P. Alexander and Q. O'Connor; 675, A. Cola Rienzi and C. T. W. E. Worrell.

196 "Lady Nelson" (1928)

1985. Ships. Multicoloured.
676 30c. Type **196** 70 25
677 95c. "Lady Drake", (1928) 1·25 1·75
678 $1.50 "Federal Palm" (1961) 1·25 3·00
679 $2 "Federal Maple" (1961) 1·50 3·50

197 Marjorie Padmore (music) and Sybil Atteck (art)

1985. Decade for Women (2nd issue). Mult.
680 $1.50 Type **197** . . . . . . 2·25 2·75
681 $1.50 May Cherrie (medical social worker) and Evelyn Tracey (social worker) . . 2·25 2·75
682 $1.50 Umilta McShine (education) and Jessica Smith-Phillips (public service) . . . . 2·25 2·75

198 Badge of Trinidad and Tobago Cadet Force (75th Anniv)

199 Anne-Marie Javouhey (foundress)

1985. International Youth Year. Multicoloured.
683 10c. Type **198** 45 10
684 65c. Guide badges (75th anniv of Girl Guide movement) . . . . 2·00 2·75
685 95c. Young people of Trinidad . . . . 2·50 3·25

1986. 150th Anniv of Arrival of Sisters of St. Joseph de Cluny. Multicoloured.
702 10c. Type **199** 10 10
703 65c. St. Joseph's Convent, Port-of-Spain . . . . . . 45 1·40
704 95c. Children and statue of Anne-Marie Javouhey . . 65 1·75

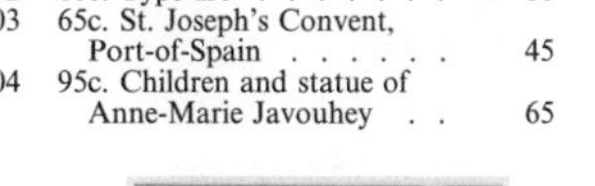

200 Tank Locomotive "Arima"

1986. "Ameripex 86" International Stamp Exhibition, Chicago. Trinidad Railway Locomotives. Multicoloured.
705 65c. Type **200** 25 35
706 95c. Canadian-built steam locomotive No. 22 . . . . 35 60
707 $1.10 Steam tender engine . . 40 1·40
708 $1.50 Saddle tank locomotive 60 2·00
MS709 105 × 80 mm. Nos. 705/8 1·40 3·75

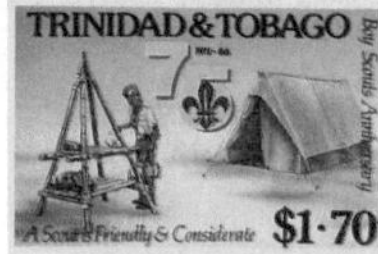

201 Scout Camp

1986. 75th Anniv of Trinidad and Tobago Boy Scouts. Multicoloured.
710 $1.70 Type **201** . . . . . . 1·00 2·00
711 $2 Scouts of 1911 and 1986 1·25 2·25

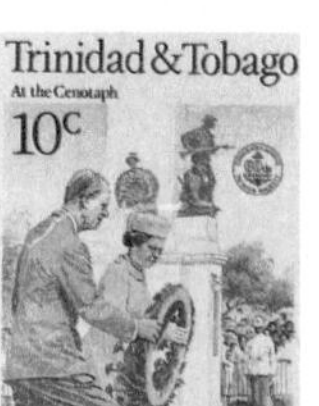

202 Queen and Duke of Edinburgh laying Wreath at War Memorial

203 Eric Williams at Graduation, 1935

1986. 60th Birthday of Queen Elizabeth II. Mult.
712 10c. Type **202** 35 10
713 15c. Queen with Trinidadian dignitaries aboard "Britannia" . . . . 1·00 30
714 30c. With President Ellis Clarke 65 30
715 $5 Receiving bouquet . . . . 3·00 7·00

1986. 75th Birth Anniv of Dr. Eric Williams. Multicoloured.
716 10c. Type **203** 60 10
717 30c. Premier Eric Williams (wearing red tie) 95 30
718 30c. As No. 717 but wearing black and orange tie . . . 95 30
719 95c. Arms of University of West Indies and Dr. Williams as Pro-Chancellor (horiz) . . . . 1·75 1·25
720 $5 Prime Minister Williams and Whitehall (horiz) . . . 2·50 8·00
MS721 105 × 100 mm. Nos. 716/17 and 719/20 . . . . 5·00 9·00

204 "PEACE" Slogan and Outline map of Trinidad and Tobago

205 Miss Giselle La Ronde and BWIA Airliner

1986. International Peace Year. Multicoloured.
722 95c. Type **204** 60 50
723 $3 Peace dove with olive branch . . . . 1·50 3·50

1987. Miss World 1986. Multicoloured.
724 10c. Type **205** . . . . 1·50 20
725 30c. In swimsuit on beach . . 2·25 30
726 95c. Miss Giselle La Ronde 3·75 2·50
727 $1.65 Wearing Miss World sash . . . . 4·75 7·50

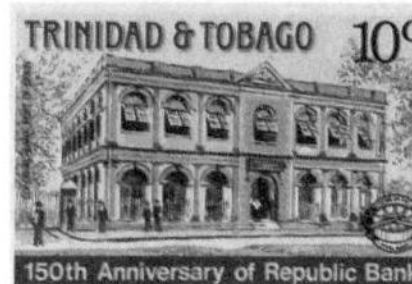

206 Colonial Bank, Port-of-Spain

1987. 150th Anniv of Republic Bank. Mult.
728 10c. Type **206** 10 10
729 65c. Cocoa plantation . . . 1·00 90
730 95c. Oil field . . . . 3·00 2·50
731 $1.10 Belmont Tramway Company tramcar . . . . 3·00 4·00

207 Sergeant in Parade Order and Soldiers in Work Dress and Battle Dress

208 Uriah Butler (labour leader)

207a George John

1988. 25th Anniv of Defence Force. Mult.
732 10c. Type **207** . . . . 1·25 20
733 30c. Women soldiers . . . . 2·50 30
734 $1.10 Defence Force officers 3·50 3·00
735 $1.50 Naval ratings and patrol boat . . . . 4·75 4·50

1988. West Indian Cricket. Showing portrait, cricket equipment and early belt buckle. Mult.
736 30c. Type **207a** . . . . . . 2·00 40
737 65c. Learie Constantine . . . 3·00 1·00
738 95c. Sonny Ramadhin . . . 3·25 1·75
739 $1.50 Gerry Gomez . . . . 3·75 4·00
740 $2.50 Jeffrey Stollmeyer . . . 4·75 7·00

1988. 50th Anniv (1987) of Oilfield Workers Trade Union. Multicoloured.
741 10c. Type **208** 10 10
742 30c. Adrian Rienzi (O.W.T.U. president, 1937–42) 10 10
743 65c. John Rojas (O.W.T.U. president, 1943–62) 15 25
744 $5 George Weekes (O.W.T.U. president, 1962–87) . . . . 1·25 2·50

209 Mary Werges and Santa Rosa Church

1988. Centenary of Borough of Arima. Mult.
745 20c. Type **209** 15 10
746 30c. Governor W. Robinson and Royal Charter 15 10
747 $1.10 Arrival of Governor Robinson at railway station . . . . 2·50 1·75
748 $1.50 Mayor J. F. Wallen and Centenary logo . . . 1·00 2·50

1988. 300th Anniv of Lloyd's of London. As T **152a** of St. Helena. Multicoloured.
749 30c. Queen Mother at topping out of new building, 1984 . . . . . . 1·25 20
750 $1.10 BWIA Lockheed Tristar 500 airliner "Flamingo" (horiz) . . . . 2·50 1·40
751 $1.55 Steel works, Trinidad (horiz) . . . . 1·75 2·00
752 $2 "Atlantic Empress" (tanker) on fire off Tobago, 1979 . . . . 4·25 3·00

210 Colonial Arms of Trinidad & Tobago and 1913 1d. Stamp

1989. Centenary of Union of Trinidad and Tobago. Multicoloured.
753 40c. Type **210** . . . . 1·25 10
754 $1 Pre-1889 Tobago emblem and Tobago 1896 ½d. on 4d. stamp . . . . 2·75 1·00
755 $1.50 Pre-1889 Trinidad emblem and Trinidad 1883 4d. stamp . . . . 3·00 4·00
756 $2.25 Current Arms of Trinidad and Tobago and 1977 45c. Republic commemorative . . . . . 3·50 6·00

211 Blue-throated Piping Guan

1989. Rare Fauna of Trinidad and Tobago. Mult.
757 $1 Type **211** . . . . 3·25 3·50
758 $1 "Phyllodytes auratus" (frog) . . . . 3·25 3·50
759 $1 "Cebus albifrons trinitatis" (monkey) . . . 3·25 3·50
760 $1 Tamandua . . . . 3·25 3·50
761 $1 "Lutra longicaudis" (otter) 3·25 3·50
Nos. 757/61 were printed together, se-tenant, forming a composite background design.

212 Blind Welfare **213** Tenor Pan

1989. Anniveraries. Multicoloured.
762 10c. Type **212** (75th anniv) 90 20
763 40c. Port-of-Spain City Hall (75th anniv) 40 20
764 $1 Guides and Brownies (75th anniv) . . . . 3·00 60
765 $2.25 Red Cross members (50th anniv) . . . . 3·75 2·75

1990. Steel Pans (1st series). Multicoloured.
766 10c. Type **213** 10 10
767 40c. Guitar pans 15 15
768 $1 Cello pans 45 70
769 $2.25 Bass pans . . . . . . 85 2·75
See also Nos. 828/31.

214 "Xeromphalina tenuipes"

1990. "Stamp World London 90" International Stamp Exhibition. Fungi. Multicoloured.
770 10c. Type **214** 35 20
771 40c. "Phallus indusiatus" ("Dictyophora indusiata") 65 25
772 $1 "Leucocoprinus birnbaumii" . . . . 1·25 1·00
773 $2.25 "Crinipellis perniciosa" 2·00 4·00

215 Scarlet Ibis in Immature Plumage

1990. Scarlet Ibis. Multicoloured.
774 40c. Type **215** . . . . 1·50 30
775 80c. Pair in pre-nuptial display . . . . 1·75 1·40
776 $1 Male in breeding plumage 1·75 1·40
777 $2.25 Adult on nest with chick . . . . 2·75 4·25

216 Princess Alice and Administration Building

1990. 40th Anniv of University of West Indies. Multicoloured.
778 40c. Type **216** 60 15
779 80c. Sir Hugh Wooding and Library 80 80
780 $1 Sir Allen Lewis and Faculty of Engineering . . 1·00 1·00
781 $2.25 Sir Shridath Ramphal and Faculty of Medical Sciences . . . . 3·25 6·50

217 Lockheed Lodestar

1990. 50th Anniv of British West Indies Airways. Multicoloured.
782 40c. Type **217** . . . . 1·50 30
783 80c. Vickers Viking 1A . . . 2·00 1·25
784 $1 Vickers Viscount 702 . . . 2·25 1·25
785 $2.25 Boeing 707 . . . . . . 3·25 6·50
MS786 77 × 52 mm. $5 Lockheed L-1011 TriStar 500 . . . . . 4·50 6·50

218 Yellow Oriole **219** "Lygodium volubile"

1990. Birds. Multicoloured.
787 20c. Type **218** 70 50
837 25c. Green-rumped parrotlet 1·75 30
789 40c. Fork-tailed flycatcher . . 80 20
839 50c. Copper-rumped hummingbird 50 20
840 $1 Bananaquit . . . . 2·75 45
841 $2 Violaceous euphonia ("Semp") . . . . 3·25 1·50
793 $2.25 Channel-billed toucan 1·50 2·00
843 $2.50 Bay-headed tanager . . 1·25 2·00
844 $5 Green honeycreeper . . . 1·40 2·75
845 $10 Cattle egret . . . . . . 2·25 4·00
846 $20 Golden-olive woodpecker 4·00 7·50
798 $50 Peregrine falcon . . . . 10·00 15·00

1991. Ferns. Multicoloured.
799 40c. Type **219** 40 15
800 80c. "Blechnum occidentale" 75 70
801 $1 "Gleichenia bifida" . . . 85 85
802 $2.25 "Polypodium lycopodioides" . . . . . . 2·00 3·50

220 Trinidad and Tobago Regiment Anti-aircraft Battery

1991. 50th Anniv of Second World War. Mult.
803 40c. Type **220** . . . . 1·00 30
804 80c. Fairey Barracuda Mk III attacking U-boat . . . . . 1·50 1·00
805 $1 Avro Type 683 Lancaster 1·75 1·00
806 $2.25 H.M.S. "Wye" (frigate) escorting convoy . . . . . 2·75 5·50
MS807 117 × 85 mm. $2.50, Presentation Supermarine Spitfire; $2.50, Presentation Vickers-Armstrong Wellington bomber 8·50 9·50

221 H. E. Rapsey (founder) **222** Baptism (Baptist)

1992. Anniversaries. Multicoloured.
808 40c. Type **221** (centenary of Trinidad Building and Loan Association.) 30 15
809 80c. "Inca clathrata quesneli" (beetle) (Trinidad & Tobago Field Naturalists' Club) . . . . 1·00 1·40
810 $1 Holy Name Convent (centenary) . . . . 1·10 1·60

1992. Religions of Trinidad and Tobago. Mult.
811 40c. Type **222** . . . . 80 1·10
812 40c. Minaret with star and crescent (Islam) . . . . . 80 1·10
813 40c. Logo (Hinduism) . . . . 80 1·10
814 40c. Cross (Christian) . . . . 80 1·10
815 40c. Logo (Baha'i) . . . . . 80 1·10

223 McDonnell Douglas MD-83

1992. Aircraft. Multicoloured.
816 $2.25 Type **223** . . . . . . 2·25 2·75
817 $2.25 Lockheed L-1011 TriStar aircraft . . . . . 2·25 2·50

224 "Trinidad Guardian" Title (75th anniv of newspaper)

1992. Anniversaries. Multicoloured.
818 40c. Type **224** 10 10
819 40c. Nativity scene (Christmas) (vert) 10 10
820 $1 National Museum and Art Gallery (centenary) 35 50
821 $2.25 Cover to St. James Internment Camp, 1942 (50th anniv of Trinidad and Tobago Philatelic Society) . . . . 80 2·25

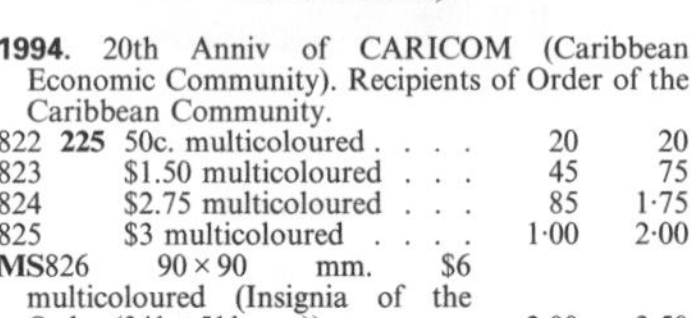

225 Derek Walcott, Sir Shridath Ramphal and William Demas with Caribbean Maps (⅔-size illustration)

1994. 20th Anniv of CARICOM (Caribbean Economic Community). Recipients of Order of the Caribbean Community.
822 **225** 50c. multicoloured 20 20
823 $1.50 multicoloured . . . 45 75
824 $2.75 multicoloured . . . 85 1·75
825 $3 multicoloured . . . . 1·00 2·00
MS826 90 × 90 mm. $6 multicoloured (Insignia of the Order (34½ × 51½ mm)) . . . . 2·00 3·50

226 Aldwyn Roberts Kitchener (bass player)

1994. "Land of Calypso".
827 **226** 50c. multicoloured . . . . 1·75 1·00

227 Quadrophonic Pans

1994. Steel Pans (2nd series). Multicoloured.
828 50c. Type **227** 30 20
829 $1 Tenor base pans 50 30
830 $2.25 Six pans . . . . 1·10 2·00
831 $2.50 Rocket pans . . . . . 1·25 2·00

1994. "Hong Kong '94" International Stamp Exhibition. Nos. 837, 789, 841 and 796 optd **HONG KONG '94** and emblem.
832 25c. Green-rumped parrotlet 30 20
833 40c. Fork-tailed flycatcher . . 35 20
834 $2 Violaceous euphonia . . . 95 1·25
835 $10 Cattle egret . . . . . . 3·25 5·50

228 Trinidad Hilton

230 "Snowballman" (painting, Mahmoud Alladin)

229 Boa Constrictor

1994. Hotels and Lodgings. Multicoloured.
848 $3 Type **228** 90 1·40
849 $3 Sandy Point Village, Tobago 90 1·40
850 $3 Asa Wright Nature Centre and Lodge 90 1·40
851 $3 M.L.'s Bed and Breakfast 90 1·40

1994. Snakes. Multicoloured.
852 50c. Type **229** 20 20
853 $1.25 Vine snake 45 55
854 $2.50 Bushmaster 80 1·25
855 $3 Large coral snake 95 1·40

1995. 50th Anniv of Trinidad Art Society. Mult.
856 50c. Type **230** 40 70
857 50c. "Fishermen" (painting, Sybil Atteck) 40 70
858 50c. Copper sculpture (Ken Morris) 40 70

231 Loggerhead Turtle

1995. Conservation. Multicoloured.
859 $1.25 Type **231** 60 60
860 $2.50 Port-of-Spain Lighthouse (vert) 1·25 1·25
861 $3 "Knowsley" (location of Ministry of Foreign Affairs) 1·00 1·50

232 Brian Lara **234** Wendy Fitzwilliam

233 Red Cross Economy Label on Envelope

1996. Brian Lara (cricketer) Commemoration.
862 **232** 50c. multicoloured 20 10
863 – $1.25 multicoloured 45 35
864 – $2.50 multicoloured 75 1·25
865 – $3 multicoloured 90 1·40
MS866 62 × 75 mm. $3.75 multicoloured; $5.01 multicoloured 4·00 5·00
DESIGNS: $1.25 to $5.01, Cricket scenes.

1996. 50th Anniv of End of Second World War (1995). Multicoloured.
867 50c. Type **233** 35 10
868 $1.25 U.S.S. "Missouri" (battleship), 1944 90 50
869 $2.50 U.S. servicemen playing baseball, 1942 1·10 1·75
870 $3 Fleet Air Arm Fulmar 1 (fighter) 1·40 2·00
MS871 116 × 85 mm. $3 Fleet Air Arm Grumman Mackinnon G-21C Goose flying boat; $3 U.S. Navy airship 2·25 3·25

1997. "HONG KONG '97" International Stamp Exhibition. Sheet 130 × 90 mm, containing design as No. 795. Multicoloured.
MS872 $5 Green honeycreeper 1·50 2·00

1999. Wendy Fitzwilliam ("Miss Universe 1998"). Multicoloured.
873 50c. Type **234** 45 15
874 $1.25 Lying on beach 1·00 40
875 $2.50 In national costume 1·75 2·00
876 $3 In white evening gown 2·00 2·25
MS877 70 × 100 mm. $5 Wearing "Miss Universe" sash 4·50 4·50

235 Bottle of Angostura Bitters

2000. 175th Anniv of Angostura Bitters. Mult. Self-adhesive.
878 75c. Type **235** 25 15
879 $3 Angostura Building inside bottle 1·25 1·50
880 $4.50 Cocktails and Angostura inside bottle (horiz) 1·75 2·25
MS881 120 × 80 mm. Nos. 878/80. Imperf 2·75 3·50

2000. Nos. 789 surch **75c.**
883 75c. on 40c. Fork-tailed flycatcher 3·50 55

237 Maracas Bay

2000. Beaches of Trinidad and Tobago. Mult.
884 75c. Type **237** 40 20
885 $1 Pirate's Bay 50 25
886 $3.75 Pigeon Point 1·50 2·00
887 $5 Toco, North Coast 2·00 2·50

238 Moon over Caroni Landscape

2000. Christmas. Multicoloured.
888 75c. Type **238** 40 20
889 $3.75 Traditional food and drink 1·50 1·50
890 $4.50 Parang singers on beach 1·75 2·00
891 $5.25 Angels playing steel pans 2·25 2·75

239 National Mail Centre

2000. New National Mail Centre. Multicoloured.
892 $3 Type **239** 1·50 1·00
893 $10 Side view of Centre 4·00 4·50

2001. No. 793 surch **75c.**
894 75c. on $2.25 Channel-billed toucan 7·50 3·75

241 Pacca

2001. Endangered Wildlife. Multicoloured.
895 25c. Type **241** 15 10
896 50c. Prehensile-tailed porcupine 20 15
897 75c. Iguana 30 15
898 $1 Leatherback turtle 40 25
899 $2 Golden tegu 60 40
900 $3 Red howler monkey 75 60
901 $4 Weeping capuchin monkey (vert) 1·10 75
902 $5 River otter 1·25 95
903 $10 Ocelot 2·40 2·50
904 $20 Blue-throated piping guan ("Trinidad Piping Guan") (vert) 4·50 5·00

242 Port of Spain Public Library and Carnegie Library, San Fernando

2001. Anniversaries. Multicoloured.
905 75c. Type **242** 50 30
906 75c. National flag and Salvation Army emblem (vert) 50 30
907 $2 William Booth Memorial Hall (vert) 1·25 1·25
908 $3.25 New National Library 1·50 2·00
MS909 Two sheets each 125 × 85 mm. (a) Nos. 905 and 908. (b) Nos. 906/7 3·50 3·75
ANNIVERSARIES: Nos. 905 and 908, 150th anniv of public libraries; 906/7, centenary of Salvation Army in Trinidad and Tobago.

243 National Football Team Logo

2001. FIFA Under 17 World Football Championships. Multicoloured.
910 $2 Type **243** 90 90
911 $3.25 National flag and team slogan 1·50 1·50
912 $4.50 Stryka (team mascot) with national flag 1·75 2·00
913 $5.25 Four new football grounds 2·00 2·25
MS914 110 × 99 mm. Nos. 910/13 5·50 6·50

244 *Pachystachys coccinea*

2001. Flowers. Multicoloured designs.
915 $1 Type **244** 60 25
916 $2.50 *Heliconia psittacorum* 1·40 1·25
917 $3.25 *Brownea latifolia* (horiz) 1·60 1·75
918 $3.75 *Oncidium papilio* 1·75 1·90

245 Congregation and Church inside Wreath

2001. Christmas. Multicoloured.
919 $1 Type **245** 50 25
920 $3.75 Musicians and dancers within Christmas tree 1·50 1·25
921 $4.50 Family and house inside wreath 1·75 1·90
922 $5.25 Church and choir within Christmas tree 1·90 2·25
MS923 118 × 157 mm. Nos. 919/22 5·00 5·50

246 Rufous-breasted Hermit

2002. Hummingbirds. Multicoloured.
924 $1 Type **246** 50 25
925 $2.50 Black-throated mango 1·10 85
926 $3.25 Tufted coquette 1·40 1·50
927 $3.75 White-chested emerald 1·50 1·60

247 Cracker Butterfly

2002. Butterflies. Multicoloured.
928 $1 Type **247** 50 25
929 $3.75 Tiger butterfly 1·60 1·50
930 $4.50 Four continent butterfly 1·75 1·90
931 $5.25 89 butterfly 1·90 2·25

248 Fort Picton

2002. Forts. Multicoloured.
932 $1 Type **248** 50 25
933 $3.75 Fort George 1·50 1·25
934 $4.50 Fort King George 1·60 1·75
935 $5.25 Fort James 1·75 1·90
MS936 152 × 120 mm. Nos. 932/5 4·75 5·00

249 Dr. Eric Williams addressing Public Meeting, Woodford Square, Port of Spain

2002. 40th Anniv of Independence ($1) and Golden Jubilee (others). Showing the 1966 Royal Visit. Multicoloured.
937 $1 Type **249** 50 25
938 $3.75 Queen Elizabeth and Duke of Edinburgh with Dr. Williams and Governor-General 1·50 1·25
939 $4.50 Queen and Duke of Edinburgh with Mayor Taylor, Port of Spain 1·60 1·75
940 $5.25 Queen Elizabeth addressing Parliament 1·75 1·90
MS941 148 × 111 mm. $10 Queen Elizabeth in open car 4·75 5·50

250 Child playing on a Pan **252** Ian Bishop (bowler)

2002. Christmas. Multicoloured.
942 $1 Type **250** 35 25
943 $2.50 Parranderos singers (horiz) 75 65
944 $3.75 Decorated hillside homes (horiz) 1·00 1·25
945 $5.25 Father Christmas in donkey cart 1·50 2·00

2003. Trinidad Cricketers. Multicoloured.
950 $1 Type **252** 40 25
951 $2.50 Deryck Murray (wicket-keeper) 1·00 80
952 $4.50 Augustine Logie (batsman) 1·60 1·75
953 $5.25 Ann John (female cricketer) 1·75 1·90

253 Mountain Immortelle

2003. "Treasures of the Rainforest". Multicoloured. Self-adhesive.
954 $1 Type **253** 35 40
955 $1 Blue-crowned motmot 35 40
956 $1 Red Howler monkey 35 40
957 $1 Butterfly orchid 35 40
958 $1 Channel-billed toucan 35 40
959 $1 Ocelot 35 40
960 $1 Bromeliads 35 40
961 $1 Lineated woodpecker 35 40
962 $1 Tamandua 35 40
963 $1 Emperor butterfly 35 40

254 Children dressed as Flowers

2003. Carnival. Multicoloured.
964 $1 Type **254** 40 25
965 $2.50 Group of minstrels . . 85 70
966 $3.75 Reveller in fly costume (vert) . . . . 1·25 1·25
967 $4.50 Buddha float (vert) . . 1·60 1·75
968 $5.25 Carnival dancers (vert) 1·75 1·90
MS969 90 × 90 mm. No. 968 . . 1·75 2·00

255 President Robinson of Trinidad & Tobago with U.N. Secretary-General Kofi Annan

2003. Inauguration of International Criminal Court. Multicoloured.
970 $1 Type **255** 40 25
971 $2.50 Pres. Robinson with group of international lawyers 85 70
972 $3.75 Pres. Robinson with Ambassador Philippe Kirsch of Canada . . . . 1·25 1·25
973 $4.50 Pres. Robinson with Pres. Ciampi of Italy and Emma Bonino M.E.P. . . . 1·60 1·75
MS974 90 × 90 mm. $6 President Arthur Robinson (vert) . . . . 2·00 2·40

256 Port of Spain Lighthouse

2003. Lighthouses. Multicoloured.
975 $1 Type **256** 40 25
976 $3.75 Chacachacare Lighthouse 90 90
977 $4.50 Port of Spain Lighthouse (different) . . . 1·00 1·25
978 $5.25 Chacachacare Lighthouse (different) . . . 1·25 1·40
MS979 119 × 151 mm. Nos. 975/8 3·50 3·75

257 Boulder Brain Coral

2003. Marine Life. Multicoloured.
980 $1 Type **257** 35 25
981 $2.50 Hawksbill turtle . . . 70 65
982 $3.75 Green moray 85 85
983 $4.50 Creole wrasse . . . . 95 1·00
984 $5.25 Black-spotted sea goddess (sea slug) . . . . 1·10 1·25
MS985 100 × 100 mm. $10 Queen angelfish . . . . 2·50 2·75

258 "Dancing the cocoa"

2003. "Sweet Memories". Multicoloured.
986 $1 Type **258** 30 25
987 $2.50 Dirt oven 70 65
988 $3.75 Washing clothes in river 85 85
989 $4.50 Box-cart racing . . . . 95 1·00
990 $5.25 Pitching marbles . . . 1·10 1·25
MS991 130 × 100 mm. Nos. 986/90 3·50 3·75

259 "View of Port of Spain from Laventille Hill"

2003. Christmas. Paintings by Cazaban. Multicoloured.
992 $1 Type **259** 30 25
993 $2.50 "View of Diego Martin from Fort George" 70 55
994 $3.75 "Corbeaux Town Trinidad" 85 85
995 $4.50 "Rain Clouds over Cedros" . . . . 95 1·00
996 $5.25 "Los Gallos, Icacos Bay" . . . . 1·10 1·25
MS997 150 × 112 mm. $5 "River at St. Ann's"; $6.50 "House in Trinidad" . . . . 1·75 2·00

260 Demonstration ("UNITE AGAINST AIDS")

2003. World AIDS Awareness Day. Multicoloured.
998 $1 Type **260** 35 25
999 $2.50 Despairing man ("STIGMA ISOLATES") 70 55
1000 $3.75 Nurse with girl ("CARE STOPS AIDS") (vert) 85 90
1001 $4.50 Man with family ("FAMILY PROTECTS") (vert) . . . 95 1·10
MS1002 101 × 101 mm. $10 People of Trinidad . . . . 2·40 2·50

261 Aldric Farrel ("The Lord Pretender") **262** Mango

2004. Carnival. Vintage Calypso Singers. Multicoloured.
1003 $1 Type **261** 20 25
1004 $2.50 Roy Lewis ("The Mystic Prowler") 45 50
1005 $3.75 "Lord Kitchener", "The Mighty Sparrow" and "The Roaring Lion" 65 70
1006 $4.50 Rose McArthur Linda Sandy Lewis ("Calypso Rose") 80 85
1007 $5.25 "Nap Hepburne", "Lord Brynner" and "The Mighty Sparrow" . . . . 95 1·00
MS1008 150 × 110 mm. $10 "Calypso Rose" . . . . 1·80 1·90

2004. Fruits. Multicoloured.
1009 $1 Type **262** 20 25
1010 $2.50 Lime 45 50
1011 $3.75 Pineapple 65 70
1012 $4.50 Coconut (horiz) . . . 80 85
1013 $5.25 Orange (horiz) . . . . 95 1·00
MS1014 100 × 100 mm. $10 Guava (horiz) . . . . 1·80 1·90

263 Sprinting **264** Slave Ship

2004. Olympic Games, Athens, Greece. Multicoloured.
1015 $1 Type **263** 20 25
1016 $2.50 Boxing 45 50
1017 $3.75 Taekwondo 65 70
1018 $4.50 Swimming 80 85

2004. Abolition of Slavery. Multicoloured.
1019 $1 Type **264** 20 25
1020 $2.50 Rada community, Belmont 45 50
1021 $3.75 Daaga, Prince of Popo 65 70
1022 $4.50 Slaves singing freedom songs (horiz) 80 85
1023 $5.25 Providence Estate aqueduct, Tobago (horiz) 95 1·00
MS1024 100 × 100 mm. $15 Sandy's escape (horiz) . . . . 2·75 3·00

265 "Lady with Ginger Lillies" **266** "Dame Lorraine"

2004. Christmas. Paintings by Boscoe Holder. Multicoloured.
1025 $1 Type **265** 20 25
1026 $2.50 "View from Maracas Lookout" 45 50
1027 $3.75 "Lady in Peacock Chair" 65 70
1028 $4.50 "Caribbean Beauty in White" (horiz) 80 85
1029 $5.25 "Teteron Bay, Chaguaramas (horiz) . . 95 1·00
MS1030 100 × 100 mm. $10 Detail of "Creole Ladies in Straw Hats" (horiz) . . . . 1·80 1·90

2005. Carnival. Paintings by Hayden Geeawan. Multicoloured.
1031 $1 Type **266** 20 25
1032 $2.50 "Jab Jab" 45 50
1033 $3.25 "Burrokeet" (horiz) . . 60 65
1034 $3.75 "Midnight Robber" . . 65 70
1035 $4.50 "Fancy Indian" . . . 80 85
MS1036 121 × 101 mm. $15 "Fancy Sailor" . . . . 2·75 3·00

OFFICIAL STAMP

1913. Optd **OFFICIAL**.
O14 **17** $\frac{1}{2}$d. green . . . . 1·75 3·50

POSTAGE DUE STAMPS

1947. As Type D **1** of Trinidad but value in cents.
D26a 2c. black . . . . 20 3·75
D27 4c. black . . . . 1·00 3·00
D28a 6c. black . . . . 30 7·50
D29a 8c. black . . . . 35 24·00
D30 10c. black . . . . 1·25 4·50
D31a 12c. black . . . . 40 18·00
D32 16c. black . . . . 2·00 42·00
D33 24c. black . . . . 7·50 8·00

D 2

1969. Size 19 × 24 mm.
D34 **D 2** 2c. green . . . . 15 2·50
D35 4c. red . . . . 25 5·00
D36 6c. brown . . . . 50 4·50
D37 8c. violet . . . . 65 4·75
D38 10c. red . . . . 1·00 5·50
D39 12c. yellow . . . . 80 4·75
D40 16c. green . . . . 1·00 5·50
D41 24c. grey . . . . 1·00 6·00
D42 50c. blue . . . . 1·00 4·50
D43 60c. green . . . . 1·00 4·00

1976. Smaller design, 17 × 21 mm.
D44 **D 2** 2c. green . . . . 20 1·75
D45 4c. red . . . . 25 1·25
D46 6c. brown . . . . 25 1·75
D47 8c. lilac . . . . 30 1·75
D48 10c. red . . . . 30 1·25
D49 12c. orange . . . . 50 1·50

TRIPOLITANIA Pt. 8

One of the provinces into which the Italian colony of Libya was divided.

100 centesimi = 1 lira.

Stamps optd **Tripoli di Barberia**, formerly listed here, will be found under Italian P.O.s in the Levant Nos. 171/81.

Nos. 1/138, except where otherwise described, are Italian stamps, sometimes in new colours, overprinted **TRIPOLITANIA**.

1923. Propagation of the Faith.
1 **66** 20c. orange and green . . . 2·00 6·00
2 30c. orange and red . . . . 2·00 6·00
3 50c. orange and violet . . . 2·00 6·00
4 1l. orange and blue . . . . 2·00 6·00

1923. Fascist March on Rome.
5 **73** 10c. green . . . . 1·40 6·00
6 30c. violet . . . . 1·40 6·00
7 50c. red . . . . 1·40 6·00
8 **74** 1l. blue . . . . 1·40 6·00
9 2l. brown . . . . 1·40 6·00
10 **75** 5l. black and blue . . . . . 1·40 7·50

1924. Manzoni.
11 **77** 10c. black and purple . . . 75 12·00
12 – 15c. black and green . . . . 75 12·00
13 – 30c. black . . . . 75 12·00
14 – 50c. black and brown . . . 75 12·00
15 – 1l. black and blue . . . . . 18·00 90·00
16 – 5l. black and purple £250 £1000

1925. Holy Year.
17 – 20c.+10c. brown & green . . 1·00 4·25
18 **81** 30c.+15c. brown & choc . . 1·00 4·25
19 – 50c.+25c. brown & violet . . 1·00 4·25
20 – 60c.+30c. brown and red . . 1·00 4·25
21 – 1l.+50c. purple and blue . . 1·00 4·25
22 – 5l.+2l.50 purple and red . . 1·00 4·25

1925. Royal Jubilee.
23 **82** 60c. red . . . . 25 2·75
24 1l. blue . . . . 30 2·75
24c 1l.25 blue . . . . 60 9·00

1926. St. Francis of Assisi.
25 **83** 20c. green . . . . 1·00 4·25
26 – 40c. violet . . . . 1·00 4·25
27 – 60c. red . . . . 1·00 4·25
28 – 1l.25 blue . . . . 1·00 4·25
29 – 5l.+2l.50 green . . . . . . 2·00 5·50

1926. As Colonial Propaganda stamps of Somalia, T **21**, but inscr "TRIPOLITANIA".
30 5c.+5c. brown . . . . 20 2·25
31 10c.+5c. green . . . . 20 2·25
32 20c.+5c. green . . . . 20 2·25
33 40c.+5c. red . . . . 20 2·25
34 60c.+5c. orange . . . . . . 20 2·25
35 1l.+5c. blue . . . . 20 2·25

6 Port of Tripoli **9** Palm Tree

1927. 1st Tripoli Trade Fair.
36 **6** 20c.+05c. black and purple 2·00 3·00
37 25c.+05c. black and green . . 2·00 3·00
38 – 40c.+10c. black and brown 2·00 3·00
39 – 60c.+10c. black and brown 2·00 3·00
40 – 75c.+20c. black and red . . . 2·00 3·00
41 – 1l.25+20c. black and blue . . 7·50 9·50
DESIGNS: 40, 60c. Arch of Marcus Aurelius; 75c., 1l.25, View of Tripoli.

1927. 1st National Defence issue.
42 **88** 40+20c. black and brown 1·00 4·25
43 60+30c. brown and red . . 1·00 4·25
44 1l.25+60c. black and blue 1·00 4·25
45 5l.+2l.50 black and green . . 1·50 6·50

1927. Death Centenary of Volta.
46 **91** 20c. violet . . . . 3·00 10·00
47 50c. orange . . . . 3·00 7·00
48 1l.25 blue . . . . 4·00 10·00

1928. 2nd Tripoli Trade Fair.
49 – 30c.+20c. brown & purple . . 1·60 4·25
50 **9** 50c.+20c. brown and green 1·60 4·25
51 – 1l.25+20c. brown and red . . 1·60 4·25
52 – 1l.75+20c. brown and blue 1·60 4·25
53 – 2l.55+50c. sepia & brown . . 2·25 6·00
54 – 5l.+1l. brown and violet . . . 3·00 9·00
DESIGNS: As T **9**: 30c. Tripoli; 1l.25, Camel riders. 38 × 22$\frac{1}{2}$ mm: 1l.75, Arab citadel; 2l.55, Tripoli; 5l. Desert outpost.

1928. 45th Anniv of Italian-African Society. As T **25** of Somalia.
55 20c.+5c. green . . . . 75 3·50
56 30c.+5c. red . . . . 75 3·50
57 50c.+10c. violet . . . . . . 75 3·50
58 1l.25+20c. blue . . . . 75 3·50

1929. 2nd National Defence issue.
59 **89** 30c.+10c. black and red . . 1·40 4·75
60 – 50c.+20c. grey . . . . . . 1·40 4·75
61 – 1l.25+50c. blue & brown . . 1·75 6·00
62 – 5l.+2l. black and olive . . . 1·75 6·00

1929. 3rd Tripoli Trade Fair. Inscr "1929".
63 30c.+20c. black and purple . . 5·00 12·00
64 50c.+20c. black and green . . 5·00 12·00
65 1l.25+20c. black and red . . . 5·00 12·00
66 1l.75+20c. black and blue . . 5·00 12·00
67 2l.55+50c. black and brown 5·00 12·00
68 5l.+1l. black and violet . . . 90·00 £170
DESIGNS—As T **9**: 30c., 1l.25, Different trees; 50c. Dorcas gazelle. 38 × 22$\frac{1}{2}$ mm: 1l.75, Goats; 2l.55, Camel caravan; 5l. Trees.

1929. Abbey of Montecassino.
69 **104** 20c. green . . . . 1·75 4·25
70 – 25c. red . . . . 1·75 4·25
71 – 50c.+10c. red . . . . . . 1·75 8·50
72 – 75c.+15c. brown . . . . . 1·75 8·50
73 **104** 1l.25+25c. purple . . . . 3·25 8·50
74 – 5l.+1l. blue . . . . 3·25 8·50
75 – 10l.+2l. brown . . . . . . 3·25 10·00

1930. 4th Tripoli Trade Fair. Inscr "1930".
76 30c. brown 1·40 4·75
77 50c. violet 1·40 4·75
78 1l.25 blue 1·40 4·75
79 1l.75+20c. red 1·40 7·00
80 2l.55+45c. green 8·00 12·00
81 5l.+1l. orange 8·00 15·00
82 10l.+2l. purple 8·00 17·00
DESIGNS—As T **9**: 30c. Gathering bananas; 50c. Tobacco plant; 1l.25, Venus of Cyrene. 38 × 22½ mm: 5l. Motor and camel transport; 10l. Rome pavilion, at exhibition entrance.

1930. Marriage of Prince Humbert and Princess Marie Jose.
83 **109** 20c. green 45 1·90
84 50c.+10c. red 45 2·50
85 1l.25+25c. red 45 2·75

1930. Ferrucci.
86 **114** 20c. violet (postage) 50 1·60
87 – 25c. green (No. 283) 50 1·60
88 – 50c. black (as No. 284) 50 1·60
89 – 1l.25 blue (No. 285) 50 1·60
90 – 5l.+2l. red (as No. 286) 1·75 2·75
91 **117** 50c. purple (air) 80 2·25
92 1l. blue 80 2·25
93 5l.+2l. red 4·50 10·00

1930. 3rd National Defence issue.
94 **89** 30c.+10c. green and deep green 5·00 15·00
95 – 50c.+10c. violet and green 5·00 15·00
96 – 1l.25+30c. brown and deep brown 5·00 15·00
97 – 5l.+1l.50 green and blue 14·00 42·00

17 Roman Arch

18 Columns of Leptis

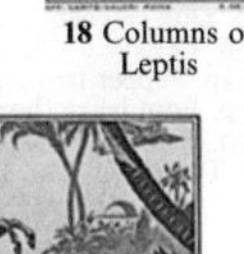

19

1930. 25th Anniv (1929) of Italian Colonial Agricultural Institute.
98 **17** 50c.+20c. brown 1·00 5·00
99 1l.25+20c. blue 1·00 5·00
100 1l.75+20c. green 1·00 5·00
101 2l.55+50c. violet 1·75 5·00
102 5l.+1l. red 1·75 5·00

1930. Virgil.
103 – 15c. grey (postage) 40 1·40
104 – 20c. brown 40 1·40
105 – 25c. green 40 1·10
106 – 30c. brown 40 1·40
107 – 50c. purple 40 1·10
108 – 75c. red 40 1·40
109 – 1l.25 blue 40 1·40
110 – 5l.+1l.50 purple 2·00 7·00
111 – 10l.+2l.50 brown 2·00 7·00
112 **119** 50c. green (air) 1·00 2·25
113 1l. red 1·00 2·25
114 7l.70+1l.30 brown 2·75 10·00
115 9l.+2l. blue 2·75 10·00

1931. Air.
116 **18** 50c. red 20 10
117 60c. red 1·60 6·00
117a 75c. blue 1·60 6·00
118 80c. purple 3·00 6·50
119 **19** 1l. blue 45 10
120 1l.20 brown 6·50 10·00
121 1l.50 red 3·00 6·00
122 5l. green 7·00 7·00

20 Statue of Youth

22 Savoia Marchetti S-55A Flying Boat over Ruins

1931. 5th Tripoli Trade Fair.
123 **20** 10c. black (postage) 2·00 5·00
124 – 25c. green 2·00 5·00
125 – 50c. violet 2·00 5·00
126 – 1l.25 blue 2·00 5·00
127 – 1l.75+25c. red 2·40 7·00
128 – 2l.75+45c. orange 2·40 10·00
129 – 5l.+1l. purple 8·00 17·00
130 – 10l.+2l. brown 30·00 45·00
131 – 50c. blue (air) 2·00 5·00
DESIGNS—As Type **20**: 25c. Arab musician; 50c. (postage) View of Zeughet; 1l.25, Snake charmer; 1l.75, House and windmill; 2l.75, Libyan "Zaptie"; 5l. Arab horseman. As Type E **21**: 10l. Exhibition Pavilion; 50c. (air) Airplane over desert.

1931. St. Antony of Padua.
132 **121** 20c. brown 55 2·50
133 – 25c. green 55 2·50
134 – 30c. black 55 2·50
135 – 50c. purple 55 1·40
136 – 75c. grey 55 2·50
137 – 1l.25 blue 55 2·50
138 – 5l.+2l.50 brown 2·00 11·00

1931. Air. 25th Anniv (1929) of Italian Colonial Agricultural Institute.
139 **22** 50c. blue 1·50 6·00
140 80c. violet 1·50 6·00
141 1l. black 1·50 6·00
142 2l. green 3·00 7·00
143 5l.+2l. red 5·00 15·00

23 Paw-paw Tree

24 Incense Plant

1932. 6th Tripoli Trade Fair. Inscr "1932".
144 **23** 10c. brown (postage) 3·00 6·00
145 – 20c. brown 3·00 6·00
146 – 25c. green 3·00 6·00
147 – 30c. green 3·00 6·00
148 – 50c. violet 3·00 6·00
149 – 75c. red 4·00 10·00
150 – 1l.25 blue 4·00 10·00
151 – 1l.75+25c. brown 18·00 32·00
152 – 5l.+1l. blue 20·00 45·00
153 – 10l.+2l. purple 50·00 90·00
154 – 50c. blue (air) 5·50 12·00
155 – 1l. brown 5·50 12·00
156 – 2l.+1l. black 16·00 45·00
157 – 5l.+2l. red 50·00 90·00
DESIGNS—POSTAGE. VERT: 10c. to 50c. Various trees; 75c. Roman mausoleum at Ghirza; 10l. Dorcas gazelle. HORIZ: 1l.25, Mogadiscio aerodrome; 1l.75, Lioness; 5l. Arab and camel. AIR. HORIZ: 50c., 1l. Marina Fiat MF.5 flying boat over Bedouin camp; 2, 5l. Marina Fiat MF.5 flying boat over Tripoli.

1933. 7th Tripoli Trade Fair. Inscr "1933".
158 – 10c. purple (postage) 24·00 15·00
159 **24** 25c. green 12·00 11·00
160 – 30c. brown 12·00 15·00
161 – 50c. violet 12·00 9·00
162 – 1l.25 blue 22·00 38·00
163 – 5l.+1l. brown 35·00 85·00
164 – 10l.+2l.50 red 35·00 85·00
165 – 50c. green (air) 6·00 12·00
166 – 75c. red 6·00 12·00
167 – 1l. blue 6·00 12·00
168 – 2l.+50c. violet 12·00 24·00
169 – 5l.+1l. brown 15·00 32·00
170 – 10l.+2l.50 black 15·00 32·00
DESIGNS—POSTAGE. VERT: 10c. Ostrich; 50c. Arch of Marcus Aurelius; 1l.25, Golden eagle; 10l. Tripoli and Fascist emblem. HORIZ: 30c. Arab drummer; 5l. Leopard. AIR. HORIZ: 50c., 2l. Seaplane over Tripoli; 75c., 10l. Caproni Ca 101 airplane over Tagiura; 1, 5l. Seaplane leaving Tripoli.

25 Mercury

1933. Airship "Graf Zeppelin".
171 **25** 3l. brown 5·00 35·00
172 – 5l. violet 5·00 35·00
173 – 10l. green 5·00 55·00
174 **25** 12l. blue 5·00 85·00
175 – 15l. red 5·00 70·00
176 – 20l. black 5·00 95·00
DESIGNS: 5, 15l. "Graf Zeppelin" and Arch of Marcus Aurelius; 10, 20l. "Graf Zeppelin" and allegory of "dawn".

26 "Flight"

1933. Air. Balbo Transatlantic Mass Formation Flight.
177 **26** 19l.75 brown and black 10·00 £225
178 44l.75 green and blue 10·00 £225

1934. Air. Rome–Buenos Aires Flight. Optd with Savoia Marchetti S-71 airplane and **1934-XII PRIMO VOLO DIRETTO ROMA = BUENOS-AYRES TRIMOTORE LOMBARDI-MAZZOTTI** or surch also in Italian.
179 **19** 2l. on 5l. brown 1·50 27·00
180 3l. on 5l. green 1·50 27·00
181 5l. brown 1·50 27·00
182 10l. on 5l. red 1·50 27·00

27 Water Carriers

1934. 8th Tripoli Trade Fair.
183 **27** 10c. brown (postage) 2·00 5·00
184 – 20c. red 2·00 5·00
185 – 25c. green 2·00 5·00
186 – 30c. brown 2·00 5·00
187 – 50c. violet 2·00 5·00
188 – 75c. red 2·00 5·00
189 – 1l.25 blue 24·00 38·00
DESIGNS—VERT: 20c. Arab; 25c. Minaret; 50c. Statue of Emperor Claudius. HORIZ: 30c., 1l.25, Moslem shrine; 75c. Ruins of Ghadames.

190 50c. blue (air) 4·50 12·00
191 75c. red 4·50 12·00
192 5l.+1l. green 38·00 95·00
193 10l.+2l. purple 38·00 95·00
194 25l.+3l. brown 42·00 95·00
DESIGNS—HORIZ: 50c., 5l. Marina Fiat MF.5 flying boat off Tripoli; 75c., 10l. Airplane over mosque. VERT: 25l. Caproni Ca 101 airplane and camel.
See also Nos. E195/6.

1934. Air. Oasis Flight. As Nos. 190/4 optd **CIRCUITO DELLE OASI TRIPOLI MAGGIO 1934-XII**.
197 50c. red 4·50 10·00
198 75c. bistre 4·50 10·00
199 5l.+1l. brown 4·50 10·00
200 10l.+2l. blue £140 £200
201 25l.+3l. violet £140 £200
See also Nos. E202/3.

29 Village

1934. 2nd International Colonial Exn, Naples.
204 **29** 5c. brown and green (postage) 1·75 7·50
205 10c. black and brown 1·75 7·50
206 20c. blue and red 1·75 7·50
207 50c. brown and violet 1·75 7·50
208 60c. blue and brown 1·75 7·50
209 1l.25 green and blue 1·75 7·50
210 – 25c. orange and blue (air) 1·75 7·50
211 – 50c. blue and green 1·75 7·50
212 – 75c. orange and brown 1·75 7·50
213 – 80c. green and brown 1·75 7·50
214 – 1l. green and red 1·75 7·50
215 – 2l. brown and blue 1·75 7·50
DESIGNS: 25c. to 75c. Shadow of airplane over desert; 80c. to 2l. Arab camel corps and Caproni Ca 101 airplane.

30

1934. Air. Rome–Mogadiscio Flight.
216 **30** 25c.+10c. green 1·75 5·00
217 50c.+10c. brown 1·75 5·00
218 75c.+15c. red 1·75 5·00
219 80c.+15c. black 1·75 5·00
220 1l.+20c. brown 1·75 5·00
221 2l.+20c. blue 1·75 5·00
222 3l.+25c. violet 14·00 40·00
223 5l.+25c. orange 14·00 40·00
224 10l.+30c. purple 14·00 40·00
225 25l.+2l. green 14·00 40·00

32 Camel Transport

1935. 9th Tripoli Exhibition.
226 – 10c.+10c. brown (post) 50 2·50
227 – 20c.+10c. red 50 2·50
228 – 50c.+10c. violet 50 2·50
229 – 75c.+15c. red 50 2·50
230 – 1l.25+25c. blue 50 2·50
231 – 2l.+50c. green 50 2·50
232 – 25c.+10c. green (air) 70 3·00
233 **32** 50c.+10c. blue 70 3·00
234 – 1l.+25c. blue 70 3·00
235 – 2l.+30c. red 70 3·50
236 – 3l.+1l.50 brown 70 3·75
237 – 10l.+5l. purple 6·00 15·00
DESIGNS—POSTAGE. VERT: 10, 20c. Pomegranate tree; 50c., 2l. Arab flautist; 75c., 1l.25, Arab in burnous. AIR. VERT: 25c., 3l. Watch-tower. HORIZ: 1, 10l. Arab girl and Caproni Ca 101 airplane.

For issue inscr "XII FIERA CAMPIONARIA TRIPOLI" and dated "1938", see Libya Nos. 88/95.

CONCESSIONAL LETTER POST

1931. Optd **TRIPOLITANIA**.
CL123 CL **109** 10c. brown 4·00 5·00

EXPRESS LETTER STAMPS

Express stamps optd **TRIPOLI DI BARBERIA**, formerly listed here, will be found under Italian P.O.s in the Levant Nos. E6/7.

1927. 1st Tripoli Exhibition. Inscr "EXPRES".
E42 1l.25+30c. black and violet 8·00 8·00
E43 2l.50+1l. black and yellow 8·00 8·00
DESIGN—As T **6**: 1l.25, 2l.50, Camels and palm trees.

E **21** War Memorial

1931. 5th Tripoli Trade Fair.
E132 E **21** 1l.25+20c. red 4·50 10·00

1934. Air. 8th Tripoli Trade Fair.
E195 2l.25 black 14·00 38·00
E196 4l.50+1l. blue 14·00 38·00
DESIGN—As T **27**: Nos. E195/6, Caproni Ca 101 airplane over Bedouins in desert.

1934. Air. Oasis Flight. As Nos. E195/6 optd **CIRCUITO DELLE OASI TRIPOLI MAGGIO 1934-XII**.
E202 2l.25 red 4·50 10·00
E203 4l.50+1l. red 4·50 10·00

OFFICIAL STAMP

1934. No. 225 (colour changed) optd **SERVIZIO DI STATO** and Crown.
O226 **30** 25l.+2l. red £1300 £2750

From 1943 to 1951 Tripolitania was under British administration; stamps issued during this period are listed under British Occupation of Italian Colonies. From 1952 it was part of independent Libya.

TRISTAN DA CUNHA Pt. 1

An island in the south Atlantic Ocean west of S. Africa. Following a volcanic eruption the island was evacuated on 10 October 1961, but resettled in 1963.

1952. 12 pence = 1 shilling;
20 shilling = 1 pound.
1961. 100 cents = 1 rand.
1963. Reverted to sterling currency.

1952. Stamps of St. Helena optd **TRISTAN DA CUNHA**.
1 **33** ½d. violet 15 2·50
2 1d. black and green 1·00 1·50
3 1½d. black and red 1·00 1·50
4 2d. black and red 1·00 1·50
5 3d. grey 1·00 1·50
6 4d. blue 4·25 2·50
7 6d. blue 4·25 2·50
8 8d. green 4·25 6·50
9 1s. brown 4·25 2·00
10 2s.6d. purple 20·00 13·00
11 5s. brown 21·00 20·00
12 10s. purple 40·00 30·00

1953. Coronation. As T **33h** of St. Helena.
13 3d. black and green 50 1·25

2 Tristan Crawfish

16 Starfish

1954.
14 **2** ½d. red and brown 10 10
15 – 1d. sepia and green 10 50
16 – 1½d. black and purple 1·75 1·75
17 – 2d. violet and orange 30 20
18 – 2½d. black and red 1·50 60
19 – 3d. blue and olive 60 1·75
20 – 4d. turquoise and blue 60 70
21 – 5d. green and black 60 70
22 – 6d. green and violet 60 75
23 – 9d. lilac and red 60 45
24 – 1s. green and sepia 60 45

25 – 2s.6d. sepia and blue 17·00 8·00
26 – 5s. black and orange 50·00 11·00
27 – 10s. orange and purple 21·00 12·00
DESIGNS—HORIZ: 1d. Carting flax; 2d. Big Beach factory; 2½d. Yellow-nosed albatross (sea birds); 4d. Tristan from S.W.; 5d. Girls on donkeys; 6d. Inaccessible Is. from Tristan; 9d. Nightingale Is; 1s. St. Mary's Church; 2s.6d. Southern elephant seal at Gough Is; 5s. Inaccessible Island rail (bird); 10s. Spinning wheel. VERT: 1½d. Rockhopper penguin; 3d. Island longboat.

1960. Marine Life. Value, fish and inscriptions in black.
28 **16** ½d. orange 15 40
29 – 1d. purple 15 20
30 – 1½d. turquoise 20 70
31 – 2d. green 30 1·00
32 – 2½d. sepia 55 60
33 – 3d. red 1·25 1·25
34 – 4d. olive 1·25 60
35 – 5d. yellow 1·50 60
36 – 6d. blue 1·50 60
37 – 9d. red 1·75 60
38 – 1s. brown 2·25 50
39 – 2s.6d. blue 11·00 12·00
40 – 5s. green 12·00 15·00
41 – 10s. violet 42·00 32·00
FISH: 1d. Concha wrasse; 1½d. Two-spined thornfish; 2d. Atlantic saury; 2½d. Bristle snipefish; 3d. Tristan crawfish; 4d. False jacopever; 5d. Five-fingered morwong; 6d. Long-finned scad; 9d. Christophersen's medusafish; 1s. Blue medusafish; 2s.6d. Snoek; 5s. Blue shark; 10s. Black right whale.

1961. As 1960 issue but values in new currency. Value, fish and inscriptions in black.
42 **16** ½c. orange 10 1·25
43 – 1c. purple (as 1d.) 15 1·25
44 – 1½c. turquoise (as 1½d.) 35 1·25
45 – 2c. sepia (as 2½d.) 65 1·25
46 – 2½c. red (as 3d.) 1·00 1·25
47 – 3c. olive (as 4d.) 1·00 1·25
48 – 4c. yellow (as 5d.) 1·25 1·25
49 – 5c. blue (as 6d.) 1·25 1·25
50 – 7½c. red (as 9d.) 1·25 1·25
51 – 10c. brown (as 1s.) 2·00 1·25
52 – 25c. blue (as 2s.6d.) 8·00 9·00
53 – 50c. green (as 5s.) 18·00 15·00
54 – 1r. violet (as 10s.) 42·00 35·00

1963. Tristan Resettlement. Nos. 176/88 of St. Helena optd **TRISTAN DA CUNHA RESETTLEMENT 1963**.
55 **50** 1d. multicoloured 15 1·00
56 – 1½d. multicoloured 20 70
57 – 2d. red and grey 25 1·00
58 – 3d. multicoloured 30 1·00
59 – 4½d. multicoloured 50 60
60 – 6d. red, sepia and olive 1·50 30
61 – 7d. brown, black and violet 50 30
62 – 10d. purple and blue 50 30
63 – 1s. yellow, green and brown 50 30
64 – 1s.6d. grey, black and blue 4·75 1·00
65 – 2s.6d. red, yellow & turquoise 1·00 45
66 – 5s. yellow, brown and green 6·00 1·00
67 – 10s. red, black and blue 6·00 1·00

1963. Freedom from Hunger. As T **63a** of St. Helena.
68 1s.6d. red 50 30

1964. Cent of Red Cross. As T **63b** of St. Helena.
69 3d. red and black 20 15
70 1s.6d. red and blue 30 20

31 South Atlantic Map

1965.
71 **31** ½d. black and blue 15 15
72 – 1d. black and green 50 15
73 – 1½d. black and blue 50 15
74 – 2d. black and purple 50 15
75 – 3d. black and turquoise 50 15
75a – 4d. black and orange 4·00 4·00
76 – 4½d. black and brown 50 15
77 – 6d. black and green 50 15
78 – 7d. black and red 50 30
79 – 10d. black and brown 50 55
80 – 1s. black and red 50 30
81 – 1s.6d. black and olive 3·50 2·50
82 **31** 2s.6d. black and brown 2·75 2·75
83 – 5s. black and violet 5·00 3·50
84 – 10s. blue and red 1·75 1·25
84a – 10s. black and blue 13·00 9·00
84b – £1 blue and brown 13·00 11·00
DESIGNS—HORIZ: 1d. Flagship of Tristao da Cunha, 1506; 1½d. "Heemstede" (Dutch East Indiaman), 1643; 2d. "Edward" (American whaling ship), 1864; 3d. "Shenandoah" (Confederate warship), 1862; 4d. H.M.S. "Challenger" (survey ship), 1873; 4½d. H.M.S. "Galatea" (screw frigate), 1867; 6d. H.M.S. "Cilicia" (transport), 1942; 7d. Royal Yacht "Britannia"; 10d. H.M.S. "Leopard" (frigate); 1s. "Tjisadane" (liner); 1s.6d. "Tristania" (crayfish trawler); 2s.6d. "Boissevain" (cargo liner); 5s. "Bornholm" (liner); 10s. (No. 84a), "R.S.A." (research vessel). VERT: 10s. (No. 84), £1 Queen Elizabeth II (portrait as in T **31** but larger).

1965. Cent of I.T.U. As T **64a** of St. Helena.
85 3d. red and grey 20 15
86 6d. violet and orange 30 15

1965. I.C.Y. As T **64b** of St. Helena.
87 1d. purple and turquoise 20 15
88 6d. green and lavender 50 25

1966. Churchill Commemoration. As T **64c** of St. Helena.
89 1d. blue 35 40
90 3d. green 1·00 50
91 6d. brown 1·25 65
92 1s.6d. violet 1·40 70

45 H.M.S. "Falmouth" (frigate) at Tristan and Soldier of 1816

1966. 150th Anniv of Tristan Garrison.
93 **45** 3d. multicoloured 15 10
94 6d. multicoloured 15 15
95 1s.6d. multicoloured 20 25
96 2s.6d. multicoloured 25 25

1966. World Cup Football Championship. As T **64d** of St. Helena.
97 3d. multicoloured 20 10
98 2s.6d. multicoloured 50 20

1966. Inauguration of W.H.O. Headquarters, Geneva. As T **64e** of St. Helena.
99 6d. black, green and blue 60 30
100 5s. black, purple and ochre 90 70

1966. 20th Anniv of UNESCO. As T **64f/h** of St. Helena.
101 10d. multicoloured 25 15
102 1s.6d. yellow, violet and olive 35 20
103 2s.6d. black, purple and orange 40 25

46 Calshot Harbour

1967. Opening of Calshot Harbour.
104 **46** 6d. multicoloured 10 10
105 10d. multicoloured 10 10
106 1s.6d. multicoloured 10 15
107 2s.6d. multicoloured 15 20

1967. No. 76 surch **4d** and bars.
108 4d. on 4½d. black and brown 10 10

48 Prince Alfred, First Duke of Edinburgh

1967. Centenary of First Duke of Edinburgh's Visit to Tristan.
109 **48** 3d. multicoloured 10 10
110 6d. multicoloured 10 10
111 1s.6d. multicoloured 10 10
112 2s.6d. multicoloured 15 15

49 Wandering Albatross

1968. Birds. Multicoloured.
113 4d. Type **49** 30 30
114 1s. Wilkins's finch 35 30
115 1s.6d. Tristan thrush 40 55
116 2s.6d. Greater shearwater 60 65

53 Union Jack and Dependency Flag

1968. 30th Anniv of Tristan da Cunha as a Dependency of St. Helena.
117 **53** 6d. multicoloured 10 30
118 – 9d. sepia and blue 10 35
119 **53** 1s.6d. multicoloured 15 40
120 – 2s.6d. red and blue 20 40
DESIGN: 9d. and 2s.6d. St. Helena and Tristan on chart.

55 Frigate

1969. Clipper Ships.
121 **55** 4d. blue 30 40
122 – 1s. red 30 45
123 – 1s.6d. green 35 90
124 – 2s.6d. brown 40 95
DESIGNS: 1s. Full-rigged ship; 1s.6d. Barque; 2s.6d. Full-rigged clipper.

59 Sailing Ship off Tristan da Cunha

1969. United Society for the Propagation of the Gospel. Multicoloured.
125 4d. Type **59** 40 30
126 9d. Islanders going to first gospel service 15 30
127 1s.6d. Landing of the first minister 15 40
128 2s.6d. Procession outside St. Mary's Church 20 40

63 Globe and Red Cross Emblem

1970. Centenary of British Red Cross.
129 **63** 4d. deep green, red and green 10 25
130 9d. bistre, red and green 15 30
131 – 1s.9d. drab, red and blue 25 45
132 – 2s.6d. purple, red and blue 30 55
DESIGN—VERT: Nos. 131/2, "Union Jack" and Red Cross flag.

64 Crawfish and Longboat

1970. Crawfish Industry. Multicoloured.
133 4d. Type **64** 20 30
134 10d. Packing and storing crawfish 25 35
135 1s.6d. Type **64** 40 60
136 2s.6d. As 10d. 40 70

1971. Decimal Currency. Nos. 72, etc surch.
137 **31** ½p. on 1d. black and green 15 15
138 – 1p. on 2d. black and purple 15 15
139 – 1½p. on 4d. black and orange 30 15
140 – 2½p. on 6d. black and green 30 15
141 – 3p. on 7d. black and red 30 15
142 – 4p. on 10d. black and brown 30 20
143 – 5p. on 1s. black and red 30 20
144 – 7½p. on 1s.6d. black & olive 1·50 1·75
145 – 12½p. on 2s.6d. black & brown 1·50 2·50
146 – 15p. on 1½d. black and blue 1·50 3·00
147 – 25p. on 5s. black and violet 1·50 5·50
148 – 50p. on 10s. black and blue (No. 84a) 1·50 11·00

66 "Quest"

1971. 50th Anniv of Shackleton-Rowett Expedition.
149 **66** 1½p. multicoloured 70 30
150 – 4p. brown, green and light green 70 40
151 – 7½p. black, purple and green 70 40
152 – 12½p. multicoloured 75 45
DESIGNS—HORIZ: 4p. Presentation of Scout Troop flag; 7½p. Cachet on pair of 6d. G.B. stamps; 12½p. Shackleton, postmarks and longboat taking mail to the "Quest".

67 H.M.S. "Victory" at Trafalgar and Thomas Swain catching Nelson

1971. Island Families. Multicoloured.
153 1½p. Type **67** 20 40
154 2½p. "Emily of Stonington" (American schooner) (P. W. Green) 20 50
155 4p. "Italia" (barque) (Lavarello and Repetto) 25 60
156 7½p. H.M.S. "Falmouth" (frigate) (William Glass) 30 70
157 12½p. American whaling ship (Rogers and Hagan) 30 85

68 Cow Pudding

1972. Flowering Plants. Multicoloured.
158 ½p. Type **68** 20 15
159 1p. Peak berry 40 15
160 1½p. Sand flower (horiz) 40 20
161 2½p. N.Z. flax (horiz) 40 20
162 3p. Island tree 40 20
163 4p. Bog fern 40 25
164 5p. Dog catcher 2·50 30
165 7½p. Celery 4·25 1·50
166 12½p. Pepper tree 1·25 60
167 25p. Foul berry (horiz) 1·25 1·50
168 50p. Tussock 7·00 2·50
169 £1 Tussac (horiz) 1·75 2·50

69 Launching

1972. Tristan Longboats. Multicoloured.
170 2½p. Type **69** 25 15
171 4p. Under oars 30 15
172 7½p. Coxswain Arthur Repetto (vert) 30 20
173 12½p. Under sail for Nightingale Island (vert) 35 25

1972. Royal Silver Wedding. As T **103** of St. Helena, but with Tristan thrushes and wandering albatrosses in background.
174 2½p. brown 25 30
175 7½p. blue 10 30

71 Church Altar

1973. Golden Jubilee of St. Mary's Church.
176 **71** 25p. multicoloured 40 40

72 H.M.S. "Challenger's" Laboratory

1973. Cent of H.M.S. "Challenger's" Visit. Mult.
177 4p. Type **72** 20 25
178 5p. H.M.S. "Challenger" off Tristan 20 25
179 7½p. "Challenger's" pinnace off Nightingale Is. 20 30
180 12½p. Survey route 30 40
MS181 145 × 96 mm. Nos. 177/80 1·10 2·75

73 Approaching English Port

1973. 10th Anniv of Return to Tristan da Cunha.
182 **73** 4p. brown, yellow and gold 20 25
183 – 5p. multicoloured 20 25
184 – 7½p. multicoloured 20 35
185 – 12½p. multicoloured . . . 30 45
DESIGNS: 5p. Survey party; 7½p. Embarking on "Bornholm"; 12½p. Approaching Tristan.

1973. Royal Wedding. As T **103a** of St. Helena. Multicoloured, background colours given.
186 7½p. blue 15 10
187 12½p. green 15 10

74 Rockhopper Penguin and Egg

1974. Rockhopper Penguins. Multicoloured.
188 2½p. Type **74** . . . . . . 1·50 1·00
189 5p. Rockhopper colony, Inaccessible Island . . . . 2·00 1·40
190 7½p. Penguin fishing . . . . 2·25 1·60
191 25p. Adult and fledgling . . 3·25 2·00

75 Map with Rockhopper Penguin and Wandering Albatross

1974. "The Lonely Island". Sheet 154 × 104 mm.
MS192 **75** 35p. multicoloured . . 3·50 3·50

76 Blenheim Palace

1974. Birth Centenary of Sir Winston Churchill.
193 **76** 7½p. yellow and black . . . 10 10
194 – 25p. black, brown and grey 30 25
MS195 93 × 93 mm. Nos. 193/4 55 1·60
DESIGN: 25p. Churchill with Queen Elizabeth II.

77 "Plocamium fuscorubrum"

1975. Sea Plants.
196 **77** 4p. red, lilac and black . . 15 10
197 – 5p. green, blue and turquoise 15 15
198 – 10p. orange, brown & purple 20 15
199 – 20p. multicoloured 30 25
DESIGNS: 5p. "Ulva lactuca"; 10p. "Epymenia flabellata"; 20p. "Macrocystis pyrifera".

78 Killer Whale

1975. Whales. Multicoloured.
200 2p. Type **78** 75 35
201 3p. Rough-toothed dolphin 75 35
202 5p. Black right whale 90 40
203 20p. Fin whale . . . . 1·60 85

79 ½d. Stamp of 1952

1976. Festival of Stamps, London.
204 **79** 5p. black, violet and lilac 15 15
205 – 9p. black, green and blue 20 15
206 – 25p. multicoloured 30 40
DESIGNS—VERT: 9p. 1953 Coronation stamp. HORIZ: 25p. Mail carrier "Tristania II".

80 Island Cottage

1976. Paintings by Roland Svensson (1st series). Multicoloured.
207 3p. Type **80** 15 15
208 5p. The potato patches (horiz) 15 15
209 10p. Edinburgh from the sea (horiz) 20 20
210 20p. Huts, Nightingale Is. . . 30 35
MS211 125 × 112 mm. Nos. 207/10 1·25 2·00
See also Nos. 234/8 and 272/6.

81 The Royal Standard

1977. Silver Jubilee. Multicoloured.
212 10p. Royal Yacht "Britannia" 15 20
213 15p. Type **81** 15 20
214 25p. Royal family 20 20

82 H.M.S. "Eskimo" (frigate)

1977. Ships' Crests. Multicoloured.
215 5p. Type **82** 15 15
216 10p. H.M.S. "Naiad" (frigate) 20 15
217 15p. H.M.S. "Jaguar" (frigate) 25 25
218 20p. H.M.S. "London" (destroyer) 30 30
MS219 142 × 140 mm. Nos. 215/18 80 1·50

83 Great-winged Petrel

1977. Birds. Multicoloured.
220 1p. Type **83** 15 60
221 2p. White-faced storm petrel 20 90
222 3p. Hall's giant petrel 20 90
223 4p. Soft-plumaged petrel . . 60 1·00
224 5p. Wandering albatross . . 60 1·00
225 10p. Kerguelen petrel . . . . 60 1·00
226 15p. Antarctic tern . . . . . 60 1·00
227 20p. Greater shearwater . . . 1·00 1·00
228 25p. Broad-billed prion . . . 1·00 1·00
229 50p. Antarctic skua . . . . . 1·25 1·00
230 £1 Common diving petrel . . 1·50 1·00
231 £2 Yellow-nosed albatross . . 3·00 1·75
The 3p. to £2 designs are vert.

1978. Nos. 213/14 surch.
232 4p. on 15p. Type **81** . . . . 1·25 3·50
233 7½p. on 25p. Royal family . . 1·25 3·50

1978. Paintings by Roland Svensson (2nd series). As T **80**. Multicoloured.
234 5p. St. Mary's Church . . . 15 15
235 10p. Longboats 15 15
236 15p. A Tristan home 20 25
237 20p. The harbour, 1970 . . . 20 25
MS238 115 × 128 mm. Nos. 234/7 1·10 2·00

85 King's Bull

1978. 25th Anniv of Coronation.
239 **85** 25p. brown, violet and silver 25 30
240 – 25p. multicoloured 25 30
241 – 25p. brown, violet and silver 25 30
DESIGNS: No. 240, Queen Elizabeth II; 241, Tristan crawfish.

86 Sodalite

1978. Local Minerals.
242 3p. Type **86** 25 25
243 5p. Aragonite 30 30
244 10p. Sulphur 45 45
245 20p. Lava containing pyroxene crystal 65 65

87 Two-spined Thornfish

1978. Fishes.
246 **87** 5p. black, brown and green 10 10
247 – 10p. black, brown and green 15 15
248 – 15p. multicoloured 20 20
249 – 20p. multicoloured 30 25
DESIGNS: 10p. Five-fingered morwong; 15p. Concha wrasse; 20p. Tristan jacopever.

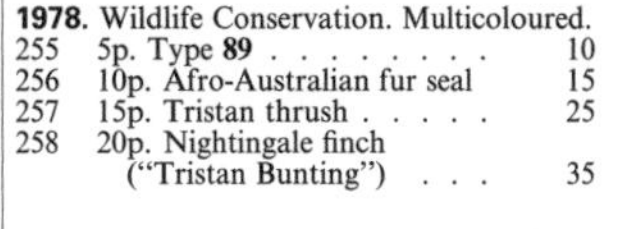

88 R.F.A. "Orangeleaf" (tanker)
89 Southern Elephant Seal

1978. Royal Fleet Auxiliary Vessels. Multicoloured.
250 5p. Type **88** 15 10
251 10p. R.F.A. "Tarbatness" (store carrier) 15 10
252 20p. R.F.A. "Tidereach" (tanker) 20 25
253 25p. R.F.A. "Reliant" (store carrier) 25 30
MS254 136 × 140 mm. Nos. 250/3 65 2·75

1978. Wildlife Conservation. Multicoloured.
255 5p. Type **89** 10 10
256 10p. Afro-Australian fur seal 15 15
257 15p. Tristan thrush 25 20
258 20p. Nightingale finch ("Tristan Bunting") . . . 35 25

90 Tristan Longboat

1978. Visit of "Queen Elizabeth 2". Mult.
259 5p. Type **90** 15 15
260 10p. "Queen Mary" (liner) 15 15
261 15p. "Queen Elizabeth" (liner) 20 25
262 20p. "Queen Elizabeth 2" (liner) 20 25
MS263 148 × 96 mm. 25p. Queen Elizabeth 2 (liner) (131 × 27 mm) 75 1·50

91 1952 "TRISTAN DA CUNHA" overprint on St. Helena 10s. Definitive

1979. Death Centenary of Sir Rowland Hill.
264 **91** 5p. black, lilac and yellow 10 15
265 – 10p. black, red and green 15 20
266 – 25p. multicoloured 30 30
MS267 83 × 103 mm. 50p. black and red 60 70
DESIGNS—HORIZ: 10p. 1954 5s. definitive. VERT: 25p. "TRISTAN DA CUNHA RESETTLEMENT 1963" overprint on St. Helena 3d. definitive; 50p. 1946 1d. 4 Potatoes local label.

92 "The Padre's House"

1979. International Year of the Child. Children's Drawings. Multicoloured.
268 5p. Type **92** 10 10
269 10p. "Houses in the Village" 15 15
270 15p. "St. Mary's Church" . . 15 15
271 20p. "Rockhopper Penguins" 20 25

1980. Paintings by Roland Svensson (3rd series). As T **80**. Multicoloured.
272 5p. "Stoltenhoff Island" (horiz) 10 10
273 10p. "Nightingale from the East" (horiz) 15 20
274 15p. "The Administrator's Abode" 15 25
275 20p. "Ridge where the Goat jump off" 20 30
MS276 126 × 109 mm. Nos. 272/6 70 1·25

93 "Tristania II" (crayfish trawler)
95 "Golden Hind"

94 Queen Elizabeth the Queen Mother at Royal Opera House, 1976

1980. "London 1980" Int Stamp Exhibition. Mult.
277 5p. Type **93** 10 10
278 10p. Mail being unloaded at Calshot Harbour 15 15
279 15p. Tractor transporting mail to Post Office 15 20
280 20p. Ringing the "dong" to summon people to Post Office 20 20
281 25p. Distributing mail . . . 25 25

1980. 80th Birthday of The Queen Mother.
282 **94** 14p. multicoloured 25 25

1980. 400th Anniv of Sir Francis Drake's Circumnavigation of the World. Multicoloured.
283 5p. Type **95** 10 10
284 10p. Drake's route 15 15
285 20p. Sir Francis Drake . . . 20 20
286 25p. Queen Elizabeth I . . . 25 25

96 "Humpty Dumpty"

1980. Christmas. Scenes from Nursery Rhymes. Multicoloured.
287 15p. Type **96** 15 25
288 15p. "Mary had a little Lamb" 15 25
289 15p. "Little Jack Horner" . . 15 25
290 15p. "Hey Diddle Diddle" . . 15 25
291 15p. "London Bridge" . . . 15 25
292 15p. "Old King Cole" . . . 15 25

293 15p. "Sing a Song of Sixpence" 15 25
294 15p. "Tom, Tom the Piper's Son" 15 25
295 15p. "The Owl and the Pussy Cat" 15 25

97 South Atlantic Ocean showing Islands on Mid-Atlantic Ridge

98 Revd. Dodgson as Young Man

1980. 150th Anniv of Royal Geographical Society. Maps. Multicoloured.
296 5p. Type **97** 15 20
297 10p. Tristan da Cunha group (Beauforts Survey, 1806) 15 25
298 15p. Tristan Island (Crawford, 1937–38) 20 30
299 20p. Gough Island (1955–56) 25 40

1981. Centenary of Revd. Edwin Dodgson's Arrival on Tristan da Cunha. Multicoloured.
300 10p. Type **98** 10 15
301 20p. Dodgson and view of Tristan da Cunha (horiz) 20 30
302 30p. Dodgson with people of Tristan da Cunha 25 45
MS303 140 × 134 mm. Nos. 300/2 75 1·40

99 Detail from Captain Denham's Plan, 1853

1981. Early Maps. Multicoloured.
304 5p. Type **99** 15 10
305 14p. Detail from map by A. Dalrymple, 17 March 1781 20 20
306 21p. Detail from Captain Denham's plan, 1853 (different) 25 30
MS307 110 × 70 mm. 35p. Detail from map by J. van Keulen, circa 1700 50 60

100 Wedding Bouquet from Tristan da Cunha

101 Explorer with Rucksack

1981. Royal Wedding. Multicoloured.
308 5p. Type **100** 10 10
309 20p. Investiture of Prince of Wales 15 15
310 50p. Prince Charles and Lady Diana Spencer 45 45

1981. 25th Anniv of Duke of Edinburgh Award Scheme. Multicoloured.
311 5p. Type **101** 10 10
312 10p. Explorer at campsite 10 10
313 20p. Explorer map reading 20 20
314 25p. Duke of Edinburgh 25 25

102 Inaccessible Island Rail on Nest

1981. Inaccessible Island Rail. Multicoloured.
315 10p. Type **102** 20 30
316 10p. Inaccessible Island rail eggs 20 30
317 10p. Rail chicks 20 30
318 10p. Adult rail 20 30

103 Six-gilled Shark

1982. Sharks. Multicoloured.
319 5p. Type **103** 25 10
320 14p. Porbeagle 25 20
321 21p. Blue shark 25 35
322 35p. Golden hammerhead 35 50

104 "Marcella" (barque)

1982. Sailing Ships (1st series). Multicoloured.
323 5p. Type **104** 20 25
324 15p. "Eliza Adams" (full-rigged ship) 20 35
325 30p. "Corinthian" (American whaling ship) 30 45
326 50p. "Samuel and Thomas" (American whaling ship) 40 65
See also Nos. 341/4.

105 Lady Diana Spencer at Windsor, July 1981

106 Lord Baden-Powell

1982. 21st Birthday of Princess of Wales. Mult.
327 5p. Tristan da Cunha coat of arms 10 10
328 15p. Type **105** 25 20
329 30p. Prince and Princess of Wales in wedding portrait 30 40
330 50p. Formal portrait 60 60

1982. 75th Anniv of Boy Scout Movement. Mult.
331 5p. Type **106** 15 15
332 20p. First Scout camp, Brownsea, 1907 20 35
333 50p. Local Scouts on parade (horiz) 45 75
MS334 88 × 104 mm. 50p. Moral of the Acorn and the Oak 75 1·40

1982. Commonwealth Games, Brisbane. Nos. 224 and 228 optd **1ST PARTICIPATION COMMONWEALTH GAMES 1982**.
335 5p. Wandering albatross 15 10
336 25p. Broad-billed prion 40 30

108 Formation of Island

1982. Volcanoes. Multicoloured.
337 5p. Type **108** 15 15
338 15p. Plan showing surface cinder cones and cross-section of volcano showing feeders 25 35
339 25p. Eruption 35 50
340 35p. 1961 Tristan eruption 40 70

1983. Sailing Ships (2nd series). As T **104**. Mult.
341 5p. "Islander" (barque) (vert) 15 15
342 20p. "Roscoe" (full-rigged ship) 25 25
343 35p. "Columbia" (whaling ship) 35 40
344 50p. "Emeline" (schooner) (vert) 50 60

109 Tractor pulling Trailer

1983. Land Transport. Multicoloured.
345 5p. Type **109** 10 15
346 15p. Pack donkeys 15 25
347 30p. Bullock cart 20 40
348 50p. Landrover 30 60

110 Early Chart of South Atlantic

1983. Island History. Multicoloured.
349 1p. Type **110** 30 50
350 3p. Tristao da Cunha's caravel 40 50
351 4p. Notice left by Dutch on first landing, 1643 40 50
352 5p. 17th-century views of the island 40 50
353 10p. British army landing party, 1815 45 50
354 15p. 19th-century view of the settlement 55 70
355 18p. Governor Glass's house 55 70
356 20p. The Revd. W. F. Taylor and Peter Green 65 75
357 25p. "John and Elizabeth" (American whaling ship) 85 75
358 50p. Letters Patent declaring Tristan da Cunha a dependency of St. Helena 1·10 1·50
359 £1 Commissioning of H.M.S. "Atlantic Isle", 1944 1·25 2·50
360 £2 Evacuation, 1961 2·00 4·00

111 "Christ's Charge to St. Peter" (detail)

113 "Agrocybe praecox var. cutefracta"

112 1952 6d. Stamp

1983. 500th Birth Anniv of Raphael.
361 **111** 10p. multicoloured 15 20
362 – 25p. multicoloured 25 35
363 – 40p. multicoloured 45 60
MS364 115 × 90 mm. 50p. multicoloured (horiz) 70 80
On No. **MS**364 the Queen's head has been replaced by the Royal Cypher.
DESIGNS: 25, 40p. Different details of "Christ's Charge to St. Peter" (Raphael).

1984. 150th Anniv of St. Helena as British Colony. Multicoloured.
365 10p. Type **112** 20 35
366 15p. 1952 1s. stamp 25 45
367 25p. 1952 2s.6d. stamp 30 70
368 60p. 1952 10s. stamp 60 1·25

1984. Fungi. Multicoloured.
369 10p. Type **113** 35 70
370 20p. "Laccaria tetraspora" 45 1·00
371 30p. "Agrocybe cylindracea" (horiz) 55 1·10
372 50p. "Sacoscypha coccinea" (horiz) 65 1·40

114 Constellation of "Orion"

115 Sheep-shearing

1984. The Night Sky. Multicoloured.
373 10p. Type **114** 35 80
374 20p. "Scorpius" 40 90
375 25p. "Canis Major" 45 95
376 50p. "Crux" 60 1·10

1984. Tristan Woollens Industry. Multicoloured.
377 9p. Type **115** 15 45
378 17p. Carding wool 20 50
379 29p. Spinning 30 80
380 45p. Knitting 45 90
MS381 120 × 85 mm. As Nos. 377/80, but without white borders around the designs 1·00 3·00

116 "Christmas Dinner-table"

1984. Christmas. Children's Drawings. Mult.
382 10p. Type **116** 20 35
383 20p. "Santa Claus in ox cart" 25 40
384 30p. "Santa Claus in longboat" 30 70
385 50p. "The Nativity" 50 80

117 "H.M.S. 'Julia' Ashore, 1817" (Midshipman C. W. Browne)

118 The Queen Mother at Ascot with Princess Margaret

1985. Shipwrecks (1st series).
386 **117** 10p. blue and light blue 40 80
387 – 25p. brown and green 50 1·40
388 – 35p. brown and yellow 65 1·60
MS389 142 × 101 mm. 60p. multicoloured 75 2·25
DESIGNS—VERT: 25p. Bell from "Mabel Clark", St. Mary's Church. HORIZ: 35p. "Barque 'Glenhuntley' foundering, 1898" (John Hagan); 60p. Map of Tristan da Cunha showing site of shipwrecks.
See also Nos. 411/14 and 426/9.

1985. Life and Times of Queen Elizabeth the Queen Mother. Multicoloured.
390 10p. The Queen Mother and Prince Charles, 1954 20 30
391 20p. Type **118** 30 60
392 30p. Queen Elizabeth the Queen Mother 40 85
393 50p. With Prince Henry at his christening 70 1·25
MS394 91 × 73 mm. 80p. The Queen Mother and the young Princess Anne at Trooping the Colour. 2·75 3·25

119 Jonathan Lambert and "Isles of Refreshment" Flag, 1811

1985. Flags. Multicoloured.
395 10p. Type **119** 60 90
396 15p. 21st Light Dragoons guidon and cannon from Fort Malcolm (1816–17) (vert) 70 1·00
397 25p. White Ensign and H.M.S. "Falmouth" (frigate) offshore, 1816 (vert) 80 1·40
398 60p. Union Jack and Tristan da Cunha (vert) 1·75 2·75

120 Lifeboat heading for Barque "West Riding"

1985. Cent of Loss of Island Lifeboat. Mult.
399 10p. Type **120** 20 60
400 30p. Map of Tristan da Cunha 30 1·00
401 50p. Memorial plaque to lifeboat crew 40 1·50

121 Halley's Comet, 1066, from Bayeux Tapestry

1986. Appearance of Halley's Comet. Mult.
402 10p. Type **121** 30 75
403 20p. Path of Comet . . . . 35 1·25
404 30p. Comet over Inaccessible Island . . . . 40 1·50
405 50p. H.M.S. "Paramour" (pink) and map of South Atlantic . . . . 75 2·00

1986. 60th Birthday of Queen Elizabeth II. As T **145a** of St. Helena. Multicoloured.
406 10p. With Prince Charles, 1950 . . . . 15 35
407 15p. Queen at Trooping the Colour 20 45
408 25p. In robes of Order of the Bath, Westminster Abbey, 1972 . . . . 25 70
409 45p. In Canada, 1977 . . . . 40 1·25
410 65p. At Crown Agents Head Office, London, 1983 . . . 55 1·50

122 " 'Allanshaw' wrecked on East Beach, 1893" (drawing by John Hagan)

1986. Shipwrecks (2nd series).
411 **122** 9p. blue, deep blue and black 30 90
412 – 20p. green, yellow and black . . . . 60 1·50
413 – 40p. blue, violet and black 1·10 2·25
MS414 142 × 80 mm. 65p. brown and black . . . . 1·75 3·50
DESIGNS—VERT: 20p. Church font from wreck of "Edward Vittery", 1881; 40p. Ship's figurehead. HORIZ: 65p. Gaetano Lavarello and Andrea Repetto, survivors from "Ilatia", 1892.

1986. Royal Wedding. As T **146a** of St. Helena. Multicoloured.
415 10p. Prince Andrew and Miss Sarah Ferguson 20 65
416 40p. Prince Andrew piloting helicopter, Digby, Canada, 1985 . . . . 80 1·60

123 Wandering Albatross

124 "Dimorphinoctua cunhaensis" (flightless moth) and Edinburgh

1986. Flora and Fauna of Inaccessible Island. Multicoloured.
417 5p. Type **123** 30 80
418 10p. "Lagenophora nudicaulis" (daisy) 30 90
419 20p. "Cynthia virginiensis" (butterfly) . . . . 50 1·40
420 25p. Wilkins's finch ("Wilkins' Bunting") . . . 55 1·40
421 50p. White-chinned petrel ("Ring-eye") . . . . 70 2·00

1987. Island Flightless Insects and Birds. Mult.
422 10p. Type **124** 25 70
423 25p. "Tristanomyia frustilifera" (fly) and Crater Lake . . . . 35 1·40
424 35p. Inaccessible Island rail ("Flightless Rail") and Inaccessible Island . . . . 65 2·25
425 50p. Gough Island coot ("Gough Island Moorhen") and Gough Island . . . . 80 2·50

125 Castaways from "Blenden Hall" attacking Sea Elephant, 1821

1987. Shipwrecks (3rd series).
426 **125** 11p. black and brown . . 50 1·25
427 – 17p. black and lilac . . . 60 1·60
428 – 45p. black and green . . 80 2·00
MS429 131 × 70 mm. blue, green and light blue . . . . 2·75 3·00

DESIGNS—HORIZ: 17p. Barquentine "Henry A. Paull" stranded at Sandy Point, 1879; 70p. Map of Inaccessible Island showing sites of shipwrecks. VERT: 45p. Gustav Stoltenhoff, 1871, and Stoltenhoff Island.

126 Rockhopper Penguin swimming

1987. Rockhopper Penguins. Multicoloured.
430 10p. Type **126** 85 95
431 20p. Adult with egg . . . . 1·25 1·50
432 30p. Adult with juvenile . . . 1·60 1·90
433 50p. Head of rockhopper penguin . . . . 1·90 2·25

127 Microscope and Published Report

128 Nightingale Finch ("Tristan Bunting")

1987. 50th Anniv of Norwegian Scientific Expedition. Multicoloured.
434 10p. Type **127** . . . . . . 90 1·00
435 20p. Scientists ringing yellow-nosed albatross ("Mollymawk") . . . . . 1·90 2·00
436 30p. Expedition hut, Little Beach Point . . . . 2·25 2·50
437 50p. S.S. "Thorshammer" (whale factory ship) . . . 3·25 3·50

1988. Royal Ruby Wedding. Nos. 406/10 optd **40TH WEDDING ANNIVERSARY.**
438 10p. Princess Elizabeth with Prince Charles, 1950 . . . . 20 25
439 15p. Queen Elizabeth II at Trooping the Colour . . . 25 35
440 25p. In robes of Order of the Bath, Westminster Abbey, 1972 . . . . 35 55
441 45p. In Canada, 1977 . . . . 60 95
442 65p. At Crown Agents Head Office, London, 1983 . . . 75 1·40

1988. Fauna of Nightingale Island. Mult.
443 5p. Type **128** 40 65
444 10p. Tristan thrush (immature) 55 75
445 20p. Yellow-nosed albatross (chick) . . . . 70 1·10
446 25p. Greater shearwater ("Great Shearwater") . . . 70 1·25
447 50p. Elephant seal . . . . . 1·00 2·25

129 Painted Penguin Eggs

1988. Tristan da Cunha Handicrafts. Mult.
448 10p. Type **129** 25 55
449 15p. Moccasins 35 70
450 35p. Knitwear . . . . 75 1·40
451 50p. Model longboat . . . . 1·10 1·75

130 Processing Blubber

1988. 19th-century Whaling. Multicoloured.
452 10p. Type **130** 75 65
453 20p. Harpoon guns 95 85
454 30p. Scrimshaw (carved whale bone) . . . . 1·25 1·00
455 50p. Whaling ships . . . . . 2·00 2·00
MS456 76 × 56 mm. £1 Right whale 3·00 2·75

1988. 300th Anniv of Lloyd's of London. As T **152a** of St. Helena.
457 10p. multicoloured 30 40
458 25p. multicoloured . . . . . 1·10 1·10
459 35p. black and green . . . . 1·50 1·50
460 50p. black and red . . . . . 1·90 1·90
DESIGNS—VERT: 10p. New Lloyd's Building, 1988; 50p. "Kobenhavn" (cadet barque). HORIZ: 25p. "Tristania II" (crayfish trawler); 35p. "St. Helena" (mail ship).

131 "Government House"

1988. Augustus Earle's Paintings, 1824. Mult.
461 1p. Type **131** 30 75
462 3p. "Squall off Tristan" . . . 45 75
463 4p. "Rafting Blubber" . . . 50 75
464 5p. "View near Little Beach" 50 75
465 10p. "Man killing Albatross" 70 75
466 15p. "View on The Summit" 90 1·25
467 20p. "Nightingale Island" . . 1·00 1·40
468 25p. "Earle on Tristan" . . . 1·00 1·60
469 35p. "Solitude–Watching the Horizon" . . . . 1·00 1·75
470 50p. "Northeaster" . . . . . 1·25 2·25
471 £1 "Tristan Village" . . . . 1·75 3·25
472 £2 "Governor Glass at Dinner" . . . . 2·25 4·50

132 Hall's Giant Petrel

133 "Eriosorus cheilanthoides"

1989. Fauna of Gough Island. Multicoloured.
473 5p. Type **132** . . . . 75 1·00
474 10p. Gough Island coot ("Gough Island Moorhen") 85 1·00
475 20p. Gough Island finch ("Gough Bunting") . . . . 1·10 1·40
476 25p. Sooty albatross . . . . 1·25 1·60
477 50p. Amsterdam fur seal . . 1·60 2·50

1989. Ferns. Multicoloured.
478 10p. Type **133** 65 65
479 25p. "Asplenium alvarezense" 1·10 1·10
480 35p. "Elaphoglossum hybridum" . . . . 1·40 1·40
481 50p. "Ophioglossum opacum" . . . . 1·60 1·60

134 Surgeon's Mortar

1989. Nautical Museum Exhibits. Mult.
482 10p. Type **134** 65 65
483 20p. Parts of darting-gun harpoon . . . . 1·10 1·10
484 30p. Ship's compass with binnacle-hood . . . . . . 1·40 1·40
485 60p. Rope-twisting device . . 1·75 1·75

135 Cattle Egret

137 Sea Urchin

136 "Peridroma saucia"

1989. Vagrant Birds. Multicoloured.
486 10p. Type **135** . . . . . . 1·50 1·50
487 25p. Spotted sandpiper . . . 2·25 2·50
488 35p. American purple gallinule ("Purple Gallinule") . . . . 2·50 2·75
489 50p. Barn swallow . . . . . 2·75 3·25

1990. Moths. Multicoloured.
490 10p. Type **136** . . . . . . 90 1·00
491 15p. "Ascalapha odorata" . . 1·25 1·60
492 35p. "Agrius cingulata" . . . 2·00 2·50
493 60p. "Eumorpha labruscae" 2·75 3·25

1990. Echinoderms.
494 **137** 10p. multicoloured . . . 90 1·00
495 – 20p. multicoloured . . . 1·50 2·00
496 – 30p. multicoloured . . . 1·90 2·50
497 – 60p. multicoloured . . . 2·50 3·25
DESIGNS: 20p. to 60p. Different starfish.

1990. 90th Birthday of Queen Elizabeth the Queen Mother. As T **161a** of St. Helena.
498 25p. multicoloured . . . . . 1·25 1·50
499 £1 brown and blue . . . . . 3·25 3·75
DESIGNS—21 × 36 mm: 25p. Queen Mother at the London Coliseum. 29 × 37 mm: £1 Queen Elizabeth broadcasting to women of the Empire, 1939.

1990. Maiden Voyage of "St. Helena II". As T **162** of St. Helena. Multicoloured.
500 10p. "Dunnottar Castle" (liner), 1942 . . . . 1·00 1·00
501 15p. "St. Helena I" (mail ship) at Tristan . . . . . 1·60 1·60
502 35p. Launch of "St. Helena II" (mail ship) . . . . . . 2·25 2·50
503 60p. Duke of York launching "St. Helena II" . . . . . 3·00 3·50
MS504 100 × 100 mm. £1 "St. Helena II" and outline map of Tristan da Cunha . . . . . . 3·75 6·50
No. **MS**504 also contains two imperforate designs of similar stamps from Ascension and St. Helena without face values.

138 H.M.S. "Pyramus" (frigate), 1829

1990. Ships of the Royal Navy (1st series). Mult.
505 10p. Type **138** . . . . . . 1·50 1·25
506 25p. H.M.S. "Penguin" (sloop), 1815 . . . . . . 2·50 2·50
507 35p. H.M.S. "Thalia" (screw corvette), 1886 . . . . . . 2·75 2·75
508 50p. H.M.S. "Sidon" (paddle frigate), 1858 . . . . . . 3·25 3·50
See also Nos. 509/12 and 565/8.

1991. Ships of the Royal Navy (2nd series). As T **138**. Multicoloured.
509 10p. H.M.S. "Milford" (sloop), 1938 . . . . 1·50 1·25
510 25p. H.M.S. "Dublin" (cruiser), 1923 . . . . . . 2·50 2·50
511 35p. H.M.S. "Yarmouth" (cruiser), 1919 . . . . . . 2·75 2·75
512 50p. H.M.S. "Carlisle" (cruiser), 1938 . . . . . . 3·25 3·50

139 "Royal Viking sun" (cruise liner)

1991. Visit of "Royal Viking Sun". Sheet 62 × 47 mm.
MS513 **139** £1 multicoloured . . 5·50 7·50

140 Prince Alfred and H.M.S. "Galatea" (screw frigate), 1867

1991. 70th Birthday of Prince Philip, Duke of Edinburgh.
514 **140** 10p. black, lt blue & blue 1·75 1·75
515 – 25p. black, lt green & green . . . . 2·25 2·50
516 – 30p. black, brown & yellow . . . . 3·00 3·25
517 – 50p. multicoloured . . . 3·50 3·75
DESIGNS: 25p. Prince Philip meeting local inhabitants, 1957; 30p. Prince Philip and Royal Yacht "Britannia", 1957; 50p. Prince Philip and Edinburgh settlement.

141 Pair of Gough Island coots ("Gough Island Moorhens")

1991. Endangered Species. Birds. Mult.
518 8p. Type **141** . . . . 1·75 1·75
519 10p. Gough Island finch ("Gough Bunting") . . . . 1·75 1·75

520 12p. Gough Island coot ("Gough Island Moorhen") on nest . . . . 1·90 1·90
521 15p. Gough Island finch ("Gough Bunting") feeding chicks . . . . 1·90 1·90

1992. 500th Anniv of Discovery of America by Columbus and Re-enactment Voyages. As T **168** of St. Helena. Multicoloured.
522 10p. Map of re-enactment voyages and "Eye of the Wind" (cadet brig) . . . . 1·00 1·50
523 15p. Compass rose and "Soren Larsen" (cadet brigantine) . . . . 1·50 2·00
524 35p. Ships of Columbus . . . 2·50 3·00
525 60p. Columbus and "Santa Maria" . . . . 2·75 3·25

1992. 40th Anniv of Queen Elizabeth II's Accession. As T **168a** of St. Helena. Mult.
526 10p. Tristan from the sea . . 60 60
527 20p. Longboat under sail . . 90 90
528 25p. Aerial view of Edinburgh . . . . 1·00 1·00
529 35p. Three portraits of Queen Elizabeth . . . . 1·25 1·25
530 65p. Queen Elizabeth II . . . 2·25 2·25

142 Coats' Perch

1992. Fishes. Multicoloured.
531 10p. Type **142** 80 90
532 15p. Lined trumpeter . . . . 1·25 1·40
533 35p. Karrer's morid cod . . . 2·25 2·75
534 60p. Long-finned scad . . . 2·75 3·25

143 "Italia" leaving Greenock

1992. Cent of the Wreck of Barque "Italia". Mult.
535 10p. Type **143** . . . . . . 1·00 1·25
536 45p. In mid-Atlantic . . . . 2·50 3·25
537 65p. Driving ashore on Stony Beach . . . . 3·00 3·75
MS538 101 × 75 mm. £1 "Italia" becalmed . . . . 6·00 8·00

144 "Stenoscelis hylastoides"

1993. Insects. Multicoloured.
539 15p. Type **144** . . . . . . 1·25 1·25
540 45p. "Trogloscaptomyza brevilamellata" . . . . . 2·50 2·75
541 60p. "Senilites tristanicola" 3·00 3·50

145 Ampulla and Anointing Spoon

147 "Madonna with Child" (School of Botticelli)

146 "Tristania" and "Frances Repetto" (crayfish trawlers)

1993. 40th Anniv of Coronation.
542 **145** 10p. green and black . . 90 1·00
543 – 15p. mauve and black . . 1·40 1·60
544 – 35p. violet and black . . 1·90 2·50
545 – 60p. blue and black . . . 2·50 3·25
DESIGNS: 15p. Orb; 35p. Imperial State Crown; 60p. St. Edward's Crown.

1993. 30th Anniv of Resettlement of Tristan. Mult.
546 35p. Type **146** . . . . . . 2·25 2·50
547 35p. "Boissevain" (cargo liner) . . . . 2·25 2·50
548 50p. "Bornholm" (liner) and longboat . . . . 2·75 3·50

1993. Christmas. Religious Paintings. Mult.
549 5p. Type **147** 80 80
550 15p. "The Holy Family" (Daniel Gran) . . . . . . 1·75 2·00
551 35p. "The Holy Virgin and Child" (Rubens) . . . . . 2·75 3·25
552 65p. "The Mystical Marriage of St. Catherine with the Holy Child" (Jan van Balen) . . . . 3·50 4·50

148 "Duchess of Atholl" (liner)

1994. Ships. Multicoloured.
553 1p. Type **148** 50 75
554 3p. "Empress of Australia" (liner) 60 90
555 5p. "Anatolia" (freighter) . . 60 90
556 8p. "Viceroy of India" (liner) 70 1·00
557 10p. "Rangitata" (transport) 70 1·00
558 15p. "Caronia" (liner) . . . 80 1·25
559 20p. "Rotterdam" (liner) . . 90 1·25
560 25p. "Leonardo da Vinci" (liner) . . . . 95 1·25
561 35p. "Vistafjord" (liner) . . . 1·25 1·50
562 £1 "World Discoverer" (liner) 2·50 3·00
563 £2 "Astor" (liner) . . . . . 4·50 6·00
564 £5 "St. Helena II" (mail ship) 10·00 12·00

1994. Ships of the Royal Navy (3rd series). As T **138**. Multicoloured.
565 10p. H.M.S. "Nigeria" (cruiser), 1948 . . . . . . 1·25 1·50
566 25p. H.M.S. "Phoebe" (cruiser), 1949 . . . . . . 2·25 2·50
567 35p. H.M.S. "Liverpool" (cruiser), 1949 . . . . . . 2·25 2·50
568 50p. H.M.S. "Magpie" (frigate), 1955 . . . . . . 3·00 3·25

149 Blue Shark

1994. Sharks. Multicoloured.
569 10p. Type **149** . . . . . . 90 1·25
570 45p. Seven-gilled shark . . . 2·50 3·25
571 65p. Short-finned mako . . . 3·25 4·00

150 Pair of Donkeys

1994. Island Livestock (1st series). Multicoloured.
572 10p. Type **150** . . . . . . 1·10 1·25
573 20p. Cattle . . . . 1·40 1·50
574 35p. Ducks and geese . . . . 2·50 3·00
575 60p. Girl bottle-feeding lamb 3·25 4·00
See also Nos. 620/3.

151 Pick-up Truck

1995. Local Transport. Multicoloured.
576 15p. Type **151** . . . . . . 1·10 1·25
577 20p. Sherpa van . . . . . . 1·50 1·50
578 45p. Scooter and Yamaha motorcycle . . . . 2·50 3·00
579 60p. Administrator's Land Rover . . . . 3·00 3·75

1995. 50th Anniv of End of Second World War. As T **182a** of St. Helena. Multicoloured.
580 15p. Sailors training on Lewis guns . . . . 1·25 1·50
581 20p. Tristan Defence Volunteers . . . . 1·50 1·60
582 45p. Wireless and meteorological station . . 2·25 2·75
583 60p. H.M.S. "Birmingham" (cruiser) . . . . 3·00 3·50
MS584 75 × 85 mm. £1 Reverse of 1939–45 War Medal (vert) . . 2·00 2·75

152 Queen Elizabeth the Queen Mother

1995. 95th Birthday of Queen Elizabeth the Queen Mother. Sheet 75 × 103 mm.
MS585 **152** £1.50 multicoloured 7·00 7·50

153 Sub-Antarctic Fur Seal on Rock

1995. Seals. Multicoloured.
586 10p. Type **153** . . . . . . 90 1·25
587 35p. Sub-Antarctic fur seals with pups . . . . 2·00 2·50
588 45p. Southern elephant seal asleep with pups . . . . . 2·50 3·00
589 50p. Southern elephant seals in water . . . . 2·50 3·00

1996. 50th Anniv of United Nations. As T **201a** of St. Helena. Multicoloured.
590 20p. Bedford 4-ton lorry . . 1·25 1·50
591 30p. Saxon armoured personnel carrier . . . . . 1·50 1·75
592 45p. Mi26 heavy lift helicopter . . . . 3·00 3·25
593 50p. R.F.A. "Sir Tristram" (landing ship) . . . . . . 3·00 3·25

1996. 70th Birthday of Queen Elizabeth II. As T **55** of Tokelau, each incorporating a different photograph of the Queen.
594 15p. Tristan from the sea . . 70 1·10
595 20p. Traditional cottage . . . 80 1·40
596 45p. The Residency . . . . . 1·75 2·75
597 60p. The Queen and Prince Philip . . . . 2·25 3·25

154 Old Harbour and "St. Helena I" (mail ship)

1996. Construction of New Harbour. Multicoloured.
598 15p. Type **154** . . . . . . 1·25 1·75
599 20p. Excavator and dump truck (44 × 27 mm) . . . . 1·25 1·75
600 45p. Construction of new mole (44 × 27 mm) . . . . 2·00 2·75
601 60p. New harbour and "St. Helena II" (mail ship) 3·25 4·00

155 Gough Island coot ("Gough Island Moorhen")

156 19th-century Map

1996. Declaration of Gough Island as World Heritage Site. Birds. Multicoloured.
602 15p. Type **155** . . . . . . 85 1·25
603 20p. Wandering albatross . . 95 1·40
604 45p. Sooty albatross . . . . 1·75 2·50
605 60p. Gough Island finch ("Gough Bunting") . . . . 2·25 3·25

1996. Centenary of the Presentation of the Queen Victoria Portrait to Tristan. Multicoloured.
606 20p. Type **156** . . . . . . 1·25 1·25
607 30p. H.M.S. "Magpie" (gunboat) . . . . 1·75 2·00
608 45p. Governor Peter Green 1·90 2·25
609 50p. "Queen Victoria" (H. von Angeli) (detail) . . . . 2·00 2·50

157 Archelon (turtle)

1997. Atlantic Marine Fauna (1st series). Cretaceous Period. Sheet 92 × 100 mm, containing T **157** and similar horiz designs. Multicoloured.
MS610 35p. Type **157**; 35p. Trinacromerum; 35p. Platecarpus; 35p. Clidastes . . . . 4·75 5·50
See also No. **MS**638.

158 Smoke Signals

1997. Visual Communications. Multicoloured.
611 10p. Type **158** 40 75
612 10p. H.M.S. "Eurydice" (frigate) 40 75
613 15p. H.M.S. "Challenger" (survey ship) . . . . 60 1·00
614 15p. Flag hoists . . . . . . 60 1·00
615 20p. Semaphore . . . . . . 70 1·00
616 20p. H.M.S. "Carlisle" (cruiser) . . . . 70 1·00
617 35p. Aldis lamp . . . . . . 80 1·10
618 35p. H.M.S. "Cilicia" (transport) . . . . 80 1·10
Nos. 611/12, 613/14, 615/16 and 617/18 respectively were printed together, se-tenant, forming composite designs.

1997. Return of Hong Kong to China. Sheet 130 × 90 mm, containing designs as No. 605, but with "1997" imprint date.
MS619 60p. Gough Island finch ("Gough Bunting") . . . . . 1·50 2·25

1997. Island Livestock (2nd series). As T **192** of St. Helena. Multicoloured.
620 20p. Chickens 70 90
621 30p. Bull . . . . 90 1·40
622 45p. Sheep . . . . 1·40 2·00
623 50p. Collie dogs . . . . . . 1·75 2·25

1997. Golden Wedding of Queen Elizabeth and Prince Philip. As T **192a** of St. Helena. Mult.
624 15p. Queen Elizabeth 45 80
625 15p. Prince Philip playing polo 45 80
626 20p. Queen Elizabeth with horse 55 90
627 20p. Prince Philip 55 90
628 45p. Queen Elizabeth with Prince Philip in R.A.F. uniform . . . . 1·25 1·60
629 45p. Princess Anne on horseback . . . . 1·25 1·60
MS630 110 × 70 mm. £1.50, Queen Elizabeth and Prince Philip in landau (horiz) . . . . 8·50 9·50
Nos. 624/5, 626/7 and 628/9 respectively were printed together, se-tenant, with the backgrounds forming composite designs.

159 "Hilary" and "Melodie"

1998. 50th Anniv of First Lobster Survey. Lobster Trawlers. Multicoloured.
631 15p. Type **159** 55 80
632 20p. "Tristania II" and "Hekla" 65 90
633 30p. "Pequena" and "Frances Repetto" . . . . 85 1·25
634 45p. "Tristania" and "Gillian Gaggins" . . . . 1·40 1·75
635 50p. "Kelso" and "Edinburgh" . . . . 1·40 1·75
MS636 100 × 80 mm. £1.20, Revd. C. P. Lawrence and lobster . . 4·00 6·00

1998. Diana, Princess of Wales Commemoration. Sheet 145 × 70 mm, containing vert designs as T **149** of St. Helena. Multicoloured.
MS637 35p. Wearing pink jacket, 1993; 35p. Wearing white jacket, 1990; 35p. Laughing, in striped dress, 1991; 35p. Wearing blue and white dress, 1989 (sold at £1.40 + 20p. charity premium) . . . . 3·25 4·00

1998. Atlantic Marine Fauna (2nd series). Miocene Epoch. Sheet 92 × 100 mm, containing horiz designs as T **157**. Multicoloured.
MS638 45p. Carcharodon (shark); 45p. Orycterocetus (sperm whale); 45p. Eurhinodelphis (dolphin); 45p. Hexanchus (shark) and Myliobatis (ray) . . . . 7·00 8·00

160 "Livonia"

1998. Cruise Ships. Multicoloured.
639 15p. Type **160** . . . . . . 1·75 1·75
640 20p. "Professor Molchanov" 1·90 1·90
641 45p. "Explorer" . . . . . . 2·50 2·75
642 60p. "Hanseatic" . . . . . . 2·75 3·00

161 "H. G. Johnson" (barque)

1998. Maritime Heritage (1st series). Mult.
643 15p. Type **161** . . . . . . 1·00 1·50
644 35p. "Theodore" (full-rigged ship) . . . . 1·75 2·25
645 45p. "Hesperides" (full-rigged ship) . . . . 1·90 2·25
646 50p. "Bessfield" (barque) . . 2·00 2·50

1999. Maritime Heritage (2nd series). As T **161**. Multicoloured.
647 20p. "Derwent" (full-rigged ship) . . . . 1·10 1·50
648 30p. "Strathgryfe" (full-rigged ship) . . . . 1·75 2·00
649 50p. "Celestial Empire" (full-rigged ship) . . . . 2·25 2·50
650 60p. "Lamorna" (full-rigged ship) . . . . 2·25 2·50

162 Wandering Albatross Courtship Dance

1999. Endangered Species. Wandering Albatross. Multicoloured.
651 5p. Type **162** 45 70
652 8p. Adult and chick 45 70
653 12p. Adult with spread wings 45 70
654 15p. Two adults in flight . . 45 70

1999. Royal Wedding. As T **197a** of St. Helena. Multicoloured.
655 45p. Photographs of Prince Edward and Miss Sophie Rhys-Jones . . . . 1·25 1·25
656 £1.20 Engagement photograph . . . . 3·00 3·75

1999. "Queen Elizabeth the Queen Mother's Century". As T **199** of St. Helena. Multicoloured (except £1.50).
657 20p. With King George VI and Princess Elizabeth, 1944 . . . . 80 90
658 30p. King George and Queen Elizabeth at Balmoral, 1951 . . . . 1·00 1·10
659 50p. Family group outside Clarence House, 1994 . . . 1·50 1·75
660 60p. Inspecting The Black Watch parade . . . . . . 1·75 2·00
MS661 145 × 70 mm. £1.50, Lady Elizabeth Bowes-Lyon, 1905, and Hurricane squadron, Battle of Britain, 1940 (black) . . . . . 4·00 5·50

163 Winter Sunrise

2000. New Millennium. Multicoloured.
662 20p. Type **163** . . . . . . 1·40 1·40
663 30p. Spring sunrise . . . . . 1·75 1·75
664 50p. Summer sunrise . . . . 2·50 2·50
665 60p. Autumn sunrise . . . . 2·75 2·75

164 King Manuel I of Portugal

2000. Monarchs connected with Tristan da Cunha. Multicoloured (except 1p. and 5p.).
666 1p. Type **164** (black, stone and brown) 10 10
667 3p. Frederick Henry, Prince of Orange 10 10
668 5p. Empress Maria Theresa of Austria (green, stone and black) 10 10
669 8p. King George III 15 20
670 10p. King George IV 20 25
671 15p. King William IV 30 35
672 20p. Queen Victoria 40 45
673 25p. King Edward VII . . . 50 55
674 35p. King George V 70 75
675 £1 King Edward VIII . . . . 2·00 2·10
676 £2 King George VI . . . . . 4·00 4·25
677 £5 Queen Elizabeth II . . . 10·00 10·50

165 Longboat under Oars

2000. "The Stamp Show 2000" International Stamp Exhibition. Visit of *Cutty Sark* (clipper), 1876 Multicoloured.
678 15p. Type **165** 85 85
679 45p. Longboat under sail . . 1·75 2·00
680 50p. *Cutty Sark* at sea . . . 2·75 2·75
681 60p. *Cutty Sark* on display at Greenwich . . . . 2·75 2·75
MS682 102 × 65 mm. £1.50, "Cutty Sark" off Tristan da Cunha . . 6·00 7·50

2000. 18th Birthday of Prince William. As T **48** of South Georgia and South Sandwich Islands. Multicoloured.
683 45p. Prince Charles with sons, 1985 . . . . 1·60 2·00
684 45p. Prince William in 1995 1·60 2·00
685 45p. Prince William in 1999 (horiz) . . . . 1·60 2·00
686 45p. Prince William in overcoat and scarf (horiz) 1·60 2·00
MS687 175 × 95 mm. 45p. With Shetland pony, 1995 (horiz) and Nos. 683/6. . . . . 8·50 8·50

166 *Agulhas* (South African Antarctic research ship)

2000. Helicopters and Ships. Multicoloured.
688 10p. Type **166** 75 85
689 10p. S.A. 330J Puma helicopter, 1999 . . . . . 75 85
690 15p. H.M.S. *London* (destroyer) . . . . 85 1·10
691 15p. Westland Wessex HAS1 helicopter, 1964 . . . . . 85 1·10
692 20p. H.M.S. *Endurance II* (ice patrol ship) . . . . 95 1·25
693 20p. Westland Lynx HAS3 helicopter, 1996 . . . . . 95 1·25
694 50p. U.S.S. *Spiegel Grove* (landing ship) . . . . . . 1·40 1·75
695 50p. Sikorsky UH-19F helicopter, 1963 . . . . . 1·40 1·75
Nos. 688/9, 690/1, 692/3 and 694/5 were each printed together, se-tenant, with the backgrounds forming composite designs.

167 Winston Churchill as Home Secretary and Siege of Sidney Street, 1911

2000. Centenary of Sir Winston Churchill's Election to Parliament. Multicoloured.
696 20p. Type **167** . . . . . . 1·50 1·25
697 30p. As Chancellor of the Exchequer, 1925, and with Pres. Roosevelt at signing of Atlantic Treaty, 1941 . . 1·75 1·75
698 50p. Showing Victory sign and making V.E. Day broadcast, 1945 . . . . . 2·25 2·25
699 60p. In retirement and greeting Queen Elizabeth II at 10 Downing Street, 1955 2·25 2·25

168 Inaccessible Island Rail

2001. "HONG KONG 2001" Stamp Exhibition. Sheet 150 × 90 mm, containing T **168** and similar horiz design showing island bird. Multicoloured.
MS700 30p. Type **168**; 45p. Black-faced spoonbill . . . . 4·25 4·25

169 Letter from Tristan da Cunha, 1846

2001. Death Centenary of Queen Victoria. Mult.
701 15p. Type **169** 65 70
702 20p. Prince Alfred, Duke of Edinburgh (vert) 75 80
703 30p. H.M.S. *Galatea* (screw frigate) . . . . 1·00 1·10
704 35p. Queen Victoria (vert) . . 1·00 1·25
705 50p. Charles Dickens (vert) . 1·40 1·75
706 60p. Longboats re-supplying warship . . . . 1·50 1·75
MS707 104 × 80 mm. £1.50, Queen Victoria outside St. Paul's during Diamond Jubilee celebrations 4·00 6·00

170 Longboat under Sail

2001. Tristan Longboats. Multicoloured.
708 30p. Type **170** 70 75
709 30p. Two longboats at sea (face value at bottom right) 70 75
710 30p. Two longboats at sea (face value at bottom left) 70 75
711 30p. Longboat with multicoloured mainsail near island 70 75
712 30p. Longboat with blue and white striped sail near island 70 75
713 30p. Longboat with white mainsail near island . . . 70 75
714 30p. Longboat with blue mainsail near island . . . 70 75
715 30p. Longboat in harbour . . 70 75

2001. Hurricane Relief. Nos. 688/95 optd **HURRICANE RELIEF 2001**. Multicoloured.
716 10p. Type **166** 80 95
717 10p. S.A. 330J Puma helicopter, 1999 . . . . . 80 95
718 15p. H.M.S. *London* (destroyer) . . . . 1·10 1·25
719 15p. Westland Wessex HAS1 helicopter, 1964 . . . . . 1·10 1·25
720 20p. H.M.S. *Endurance II* (ice patrol ship) . . . . 1·25 1·40
721 20p. Westland Lynx HAS3 helicopter, 1996 . . . . . 1·25 1·40
722 50p. U.S.S. *Spiegel Grove* (landing ship) . . . . . . 1·75 2·00
723 50p. Sikorsky UH-19F helicopter, 1963 . . . . . 1·75 2·00

172 Head of White-chinned Petrel ("Spectacled Petrel")

2001. Birdlife World Bird Festival (1st series). White-chinned Petrel. Sheet 175 × 80 mm, containing T **172** and similar multicoloured designs.
MS724 35p. Type **172**; 35p. Petrel in front of cliffs (*vert*); 35p. Petrel, descending to sea (*vert*); 35p. Petrel flying; 35p. Petrel chick 8·00 8·50
See also Nos. 770/**MS**774.

173 H.M.S. *Julia* (sloop), 1817

2001. Royal Navy Connections with Tristan da Cunha. Multicoloured.
725 20p. Type **173** 75 80
726 20p. H.M.S. *Penguin* (sloop), 1815 . . . . 75 80
727 35p. H.M.S. *Beagle* (screw sloop), 1901 . . . . . . 1·10 1·25
728 35p. H.M.S. *Puma* (frigate), 1962 . . . . 1·10 1·25
729 60p. H.M.S. *Monmouth* (frigate), 1997 . . . . . 1·60 1·75
730 60p. H.M.S. *Somerset* (frigate), 1999 . . . . . . 1·60 1·75

174 Procession at St. Mary's Anglican Church

2001. 150th Anniv of Arrival of First U.S.P.G. Missionary on Tristan da Cunha. Multicoloured (except No. 731).
731 35p. Type **174** (brown, black and yellow) . . . . 1·50 1·75
732 35p. St. Joseph's Catholic Church . . . . 1·50 1·75
733 60p. Altar, St. Mary's Church (vert) . . . . 2·25 2·50
734 60p. Stained glass, St. Joseph's Church (vert) 2·25 2·50

175 1952 Overprints on St. Helena 3d., 4d., 1s. and 2s.6d.

2002. 50th Anniv of First Stamp Issue. Mult (except 60p.).
735 15p. Type **175** . . . . 90 1·00
736 20p. 1952 6d., 8d., 5s. and 10s. overprinted stamps . . 1·00 1·00
737 50p. 1952 ½d., 1d., 1½d. and 2d. overprinted stamps . . 2·25 2·50
738 60p. Buying stamps, 1952 (black, sepia and bistre) . . 2·25 2·50
MS739 146 × 90 mm. 45p. × 4 As Nos. 735/8, but each inscr "Tristan da Cunha" in mock manuscript 6·50 7·00

2002. Golden Jubilee. As T **211** of St. Helena.
740 15p. black, red and gold . . 85 90
741 30p. multicoloured . . . . . 1·40 1·50
742 45p. multicoloured . . . . . 1·90 2·00
743 50p. multicoloured . . . . . 2·00 2·25
MS744 162 × 95 mm. Nos. 740/3 and 60p. multicoloured . . . . . . 7·00 7·50
DESIGNS—HORIZ: 15p. Princess Elizabeth, 1947; 30p. Queen Elizabeth in evening dress, Buckingham Palace, 1991; 45p. Queen Elizabeth in multicoloured turban; 50p. Queen Elizabeth at Newmarket, 1997. VERT: (38 × 51 mm)—50p. Queen Elizabeth after Annigoni.
DESIGNS as Nos. 740/3 in No. **MS**744 omit the gold frame around each stamp and the "Golden Jubilee 1952-2002" inscription.

176 Pelagic Armourhead (fish)

2002. Extension of Fishing Industry to New Species. Multicoloured.
745 20p. Type **176** 70 75
746 35p. Yellowtail . . . . . . 1·10 1·25
747 50p. Splendid alfonsino . . . 1·50 1·75
MS748 140 × 75 mm. 60p. *San Liberatore* (stern trawler) and Nos. 745/7 . . . . 4·00 5·00

2002. Queen Elizabeth the Queen Mother Commemoration. As T **215** of St. Helena.
749 20p. black, gold and purple 80 70
750 £1.50 multicoloured . . . . 4·50 5·00
MS751 145 × 70 mm. 75p. black and gold; 75p. multicoloured . . . 5·00 6·00
DESIGNS: 20p. Queen Elizabeth visiting a shipyard, 1942; 75p. black and gold (No. **MS**751) Duchess of York with Princess Margaret, 1930; 75p. multicoloured (No. **MS**751) Queen Mother at Cheltenham Races; £1.50, Queen Mother on her birthday, 1995.
Designs in No. **MS**751 omit the "1900–2002" inscription and the coloured frame.

177 Gray's Beaked Whale

2002. Marine Mammals. Multicoloured.
752 30p. Type **177** . . . . 1·50 1·50
753 30p. Dusky dolphin . . . . 1·50 1·50
754 30p. False killer whale . . . 1·50 1·50
755 30p. Long-finned pilot whale 1·50 1·50
756 30p. Sperm whale . . . . . 1·50 1·50
757 30p. Shepherd's beaked whale 1·50 1·50
MS758 81 × 92 mm. £2 Humpback whale . . . . 7·50 8·50
Nos. 752/7 were printed together, se-tenant, forming a composite design.

178 Captain Denham and Officers of H.M.S. *Herald* (survey ship)

2002. 150th Anniv of Survey by H.M.S. *Herald*. Multicoloured (except 20p.).
759 20p. Type **178** (ochre and agate) 70 75
760 35p. H.M.S. *Herald* in Bay of Biscay . . . . 1·10 1·25
761 50p. H.M.S. *Herald* off Tristan da Cunha, 1852 . . 1·50 1·75
762 60p. H.M.S. *Herald* and H.M.S. *Torch* (paddle steamer) at sunset . . . . 1·60 1·90

179 Great Barrier Reef, Australia (longest reef)

2003. World Geographical Records. Multicoloured.
763 30p. Type **179** . . . . 90 1·00
764 30p. Greenland (biggest island) . . . . 90 1·00
765 30p. Sahara (biggest desert) 90 1·00
766 30p. River Amazon (longest river) . . . . 90 1·00
767 30p. Mt Everest (highest mountain) . . . . 90 1·00
768 30p. Edinburgh, Tristan da Cunha (most remote inhabited island) . . . . 90 1·00
MS769 90 × 68 mm £2 Closer view of Edinburgh . . . . 6·50 7·50

180 Atlantic Yellow-nosed Albatross (pair)

2003. BirdLife International (2nd series). Atlantic Yellow-nosed Albatross. Multicoloured.
770 15p. Type **180** 60 60
771 30p. Albatross on nest (vert) 1·00 1·00
772 45p. Albatross in flight (vert) 1·40 1·50
773 50p. Two albatrosses in flight 1·50 1·60
MS774 175 × 80 mm. Nos. 770/3 and £1 Pair in flight . . . . 6·75 7·50

2003. 50th Anniv of Coronation. As T **21** of St. Helena. Multicoloured.
775 20p. Queen Elizabeth II with Royal family 70 70
776 £1.50 Archbishop and bishops paying homage to Queen . . . . 4·25 4·50
MS777 95 × 115 mm. 75p. As 20p.; 75p. As £1.50 . . . . 4·25 4·50

2003. As T **220** of St. Helena.
778 £2.80 black, mauve and cream . . . . 6·00 6·50

2003. 21st Birthday of Prince William of Wales. As T **55** of South Georgia and South Sandwich Islands. Multicoloured.
779 50p. Prince William at Sighthill Community Education Centre, 2001 and playing polo, 2002 . . 1·50 1·60
780 50p. In Scotland, 2001 and on Raleigh International Expedition, 2000 . . . . . 1·50 1·60

181 Corporal William Glass arriving on HMS *Falmouth* (1816)

2003. 150th Death Anniv of William Glass (founding settler of Tristan). Multicoloured.
781 30p. Type **181** 90 95
782 30p. Corporal Glass with other Royal Artillerymen 90 95
783 30p. William Glass and family remaining on Tristan (1817) 90 95
784 30p. William Glass and family 90 95
785 30p. Governor William Glass conducting marriage of eldest daughter Mary (1833) 90 95
786 30p. Governor William Glass as old man (1853) 90 95
Nos. 781/6 were printed together, se-tenant, with a small se-tenant label describing the stamp design at the foot of each stamp.

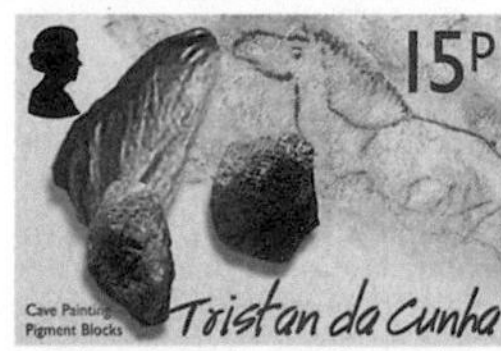

182 RFA *Tideflow*

2003. Royal Navy Connections with Tristan da Cunha (2nd series). Multicoloured.
787 20p. Type **182** 65 70
788 20p. RFA *Tidespring* (tanker) 65 70
789 35p. RFA *Gold Rover* (tanker) . . . . 1·10 1·25
790 35p. RFA *Diligence* (repair ship) . . . . 1·10 1·25
791 60p. RFA *Wave Chief* . . . 1·75 1·90
792 60p. Royal Yacht *Britannia* 1·75 1·90
Nos. 791/2 have no white margins and form a composite background design.

183 Pigment Blocks and Cave Painting

2004. History of Writing. Multicoloured.
793 15p. Type **183** 55 55
794 20p. Clay tablet 65 65
795 35p. Egyptian writing palette 1·10 1·25
796 45p. Goose quill pen . . . . 1·40 1·50
797 50p. Fountain pen . . . . . 1·50 1·60
798 60p. Ballpoint pen . . . . . 1·60 1·75
MS799 100 × 90 mm. £1.50 Word processing . . . . 4·25 4·50

184 Subantarctic Fur Seal

2004. Endangered Species. Subantarctic Fur Seal. Multicoloured.
800 35p. Type **184** 70 75
801 35p. Seal swimming 70 75
802 35p. Two seals 70 75
803 35p. Seal on rocks 70 75

185 Flag 186 Nelson's Quadrant

2004. New Island Flag. Self-adhesive.
804 **185** 30p. multicoloured . . . 60 65

2004. Merchant Ships. As T **227** of St. Helena. Multicoloured.
805 20p. RMS *Dunnottar Castle* 40 45
806 20p. RMS *Caronia* 40 45
807 35p. MV *Edinburgh* 70 75
808 35p. SA *Agulhas* 70 75
809 60p. MV *Hanseatic* . . . . . 1·20 1·30
810 60p. MV *Explorer* . . . . . 1·20 1·30

2005. Bicentenary of the Battle of Trafalgar. Multicoloured.
811 15p. Type **186** 30 35
812 20p. HMS *Royal Sovereign* breaks the line (horiz) . . . 40 45
813 25p. Thomas Swain helping wounded Lord Nelson (horiz) 50 55
814 35p. HMS *Victory* breaks the line (horiz) 70 75
815 50p. Lord Nelson . . . . . 1·00 1·10
816 60p. HMS *Victory* . . . . . 1·20 1·30
MS817 120 × 79 mm. 75p. Captain Sir Thomas Hardy; 75p. HMS *Victory* firing signal shot . . . 1·50 1·60

187 Rockhopper Penguins

2005. Islands (1st series). Tristan da Cunha. Multicoloured.
818 50p. Type **187** . . . . 1·00 1·10
819 50p. Southern elephant seals 1·00 1·10
820 50p. Tristan rock lobster . . 1·00 1·10
821 50p. Crowberry . . . . . . 1·00 1·10
822 50p. Island settlement and volcano . . . . 1·00 1·10
See also Nos. 823/7.

2005. Islands (2nd series). Gough Island. As T **187**. Multicoloured.
823 50p. Gough moorhen . . . . 1·00 1·10
824 50p. Subantarctic fur seal . . 1·00 1·10
825 50p. Bluefish . . . . 1·00 1·10
826 50p. Gough tree fern . . . . 1·00 1·10
827 50p. South African weather station . . . . 1·00 1·10

POSTAGE DUE STAMPS

1957. As Type D **1** of Barbados.
D1 1d. red . . . . 1·75 12·00
D2 2d. yellow . . . . 2·50 4·75
D3 3d. green . . . . 2·50 5·50
D4 4d. blue . . . . 4·50 7·00
D5 5d. lake . . . . 2·50 23·00

D 2 D 3 Outline Map of Tristan da Cunha

1976.
D11 D **2** 1p. purple 10 30
D12 2p. green 10 30
D13 4p. violet 15 35
D14 5p. blue 15 40
D15 10p. brown 15 45

1986.
D16 D **3** 1p. brown & light brown 10 60
D17 2p. brown and orange 10 60
D18 5p. brown and red . . . 15 60
D19 7p. black and violet . . 15 60
D20 10p. black and blue . . 20 60
D21 25p. black and green . . 45 1·10

TRUCIAL STATES Pt. 1

Seven Arab shaikhdoms on the Persian Gulf and Gulf of Oman, in treaty relations with Great Britain. The following stamps were issued at the British Postal Agency at Dubai until it closed on 14 June 1963.

Individual issues were later made by Abu Dhabi, Ajman, Dubai, Fujeira, Ras al Khaima, Sharjah and Umm al Qiwain.

100 naye paise = 1 rupee.

1 Palms 2 Dhow

1961.
1 **1** 5n.p. green . . . . 1·25 10
2 15n.p. brown 50 30
3 20n.p. blue . . . . 1·25 10
4 30n.p. orange 50 10
5 40n.p. violet 50 10
6 50n.p. bistre 50 10
7 75n.p. grey 60 10
8 **2** 1r. green . . . . 5·50 3·25
9 2r. black . . . . 5·50 21·00
10 5r. red . . . . 7·00 23·00
11 10r. blue . . . . 12·00 23·00

TUNISIA Pt. 6; Pt. 14

Formerly a French Protectorate in N. Africa, Tunisia became an independent kingdom in 1956 and a republic in 1957.

1888. 100 centimes = 1 franc.
1959. 1000 milliemes = 1 dinar.

1 2

1888. Arms on plain background.
1 **1** 1c. black on blue . . . . . . 1·75 2·25
2 2c. brown on buff 75 75
3 5c. green on green . . . . . 12·50 12·50
4 15c. blue on blue . . . . . . 35·00 4·75
5 25c. black on pink . . . . . 80·00 20·00
6 40c. red on yellow . . . . . 48·00 32·00
7 75c. pink on pink . . . . . . 60·00 75·00
8 5f. mauve on lilac £375 £250

1888. Arms on shaded background.
9 **2** 1c. black on blue 30 15
10 2c. brown on buff 30 15
22 5c. green . . . . 4·25 10
12 10c. black on lilac . . . . . 9·25 15
23 10c. red . . . . 3·75 10
14 15c. blue . . . . 60·00 35
24 15c. grey . . . . 6·00 15
15 20c. red on green . . . . . 18·00 35
16 25c. black on pink . . . . . 20·00 45
25 25c. blue . . . . 17·00 20
26 35c. brown . . . . 50·00 95
17 40c. red on yellow . . . . . 10·00 25
18 75c. pink on pink . . . . . £130 55·00
19 75c. violet on yellow . . . . 20·00 2·25
20 1f. green . . . . 20·00 4·25
27 2f. lilac £110 £110
21 5f. mauve on lilac . . . . . £160 60·00

1902. Surch **25** and bars.
28 **2** 25 on 15c. blue . . . . . . 2·50 2·00

4 Mosque at Kairouan 6 Ruins of Hadrian's Aqueduct

5 Agriculture 7 Carthaginian Galley

1906.
30 **4** 1c. black on yellow 10 10
31 2c. brown 10 10
32 3c. red . . . . 10 1·00
33 5c. green on green 15 10
34 **5** 10c. red 25 10
35 15c. violet . . . . 1·50 15
36 20c. brown 15 10
37 25c. blue . . . . 1·40 20
38 **6** 35c. brown and green . . . . 10·00 85
39 40c. red and brown . . . . . 4·75 60
40 75c. red and purple 50 45
41 **7** 1f. brown and red . . . . . 1·75 60
42 2f. green and brown . . . . 5·75 1·75
43 5f. blue and violet . . . . . 15·00 5·00
See also Nos. 72/8, 105 and 107/13.

1908. Surch.
44 **2** 10 on 15c. grey 55 25
45 35 on 1f. green . . . . . . 2·00 2·75
46 40 on 2f. lilac . . . . 3·25 7·25
47 75 on 5f. mauve on lilac . . 2·25 7·00

1911. Surch in figures and bar.
48 **5** 10 on 15c. violet 3·25 20
60 15c. on 10c. red 1·50 10
79 20c. on 15c. violet 1·75 15

1915. Red Cross Fund. Optd with red cross.
49 **5** 15c. violet 60 45

1916. Red Cross Fund. Optd with red cross and bars.
50 **4** 5c. green on green 45 2·25

1916. Prisoners-of-War Fund. Surch with red cross and **10c.**
51 **5** 10c. on 15c. brown on blue 1·25 2·25
52 10c. on 20c. brown on yellow 1·75 3·00
53 10c. on 25c. blue on green 1·90 4·25
54 **6** 10c. on 35c. violet and green 4·00 8·25
55 10c. on 40c. black and brown 2·50 4·50
56 10c. on 75c. green and red 4·25 12·50
57 **7** 10c. on 1f. green and red 5·25 5·75
58 10c. on 2f. blue and brown 80·00 £100
59 10c. on 5f. red and violet £100 £110

1918. Prisoners-of-War Fund. Surch **15c** and red cross.
61 **5** 15c. on 20c. black on green 1·75 3·50
62 15c. on 25c. blue 1·75 3·50
63 **6** 15c. on 35c. red and olive 2·75 5·00
64 15c. on 40c. blue and brown 2·75 6·00
65 15c. on 75c. black and red 7·00 11·00
66 **7** 15c. on 1f. violet and red 13·50 32·00
67 15c. on 2f. red and brown 75·00 85·00
68 15c. on 5f. black and violet £120 £130

1919. Air. Optd **Poste Aerienne** and wings or surch **30c** and bars also.
69 **6** 30c. on 35c. brown and green 1·60 2·00
70 30c. blue and olive 30 1·10

1920. New values and colours changed.
72 **4** 5c. orange 10 20
73 **5** 10c. green 20 20
74 25c. violet 20 10
75 **6** 30c. violet and purple 1·60 80
76 **5** 30c. red 1·60 2·25
77 50c. blue 1·50 60
78 **6** 60c. violet and green 1·25 85

18 Ruin at Dougga

1922.
80 **18** 10c. green 15 20
81 30c. red 1·90 1·90
82 50c. blue 75 40
See also Nos. 104 and 106.

1923. War Wounded Fund. Surch **AFFt**, medal and new value.
83 **4** 0c. on 1c. blue 40 2·50
84 0c. on 2c. brown 30 3·00
85 1c. on 3c. green 80 3·00
86 2c. on 5c. mauve 80 2·75
87 **18** 3c. on 10c. mauve on blue 90 2·50
88 **5** 5c. on 15c. green 1·50 3·00
89 5c. on 20c. blue on red 2·50 4·50
90 5c. on 25c. mauve on blue 3·50 4·50
91 **18** 5c. on 30c. orange 2·50 4·50
92 **6** 5c. on 35c. mauve and blue 3·00 4·25
93 5c. on 40c. brown and blue 3·00 3·50
94 **18** 10c. on 50c. black on blue 3·00 3·75
95 **6** 10c. on 60c. blue and brown 3·00 3·25
96 10c. on 75c. green & mauve 3·75 6·75
97 **7** 25c. on 1f. mauve and lake 4·75 6·75
98 25c. on 2f. red and blue 15·00 27·00
99 25c. on 5f. brown and green 40·00 80·00

1923. Surch.
100 **4** 10 on 5c. green on green 1·00 1·50
101 **5** 20 on 15c. violet 2·00 2·00
102 30 on 20c. brown 10 25
103 50 on 25c. blue 1·25 10

1923. New values and colours.
104 **18** 10c. pink 30 10
105 **5** 15c. brown on orange 60 10
106 **18** 30c. mauve 10 10
107 **5** 40c. black on pink 65 65
108 40c. green 10 10
109 **6** 60c. carmine and red 1·50 2·25
110 75c. scarlet and red 1·00 85
111 **7** 1f. light blue and blue 35 20
112 2f. red and green on pink 2·00 2·25
113 5f. green and lilac 2·00 2·75

1925. Parcel Post stamps surch **PROTECTION DE L'ENFANCE POSTES** and value in figures.
114 **P 8** 1c. on 5c. red and brown on rose 10 1·40
115 2c. on 10c. blue and brown on yellow 10 1·25
116 3c. on 20c. red and purple on mauve 75 3·25
117 5c. on 25c. red and green on green 55 3·25
118 5c. on 40c. green and red on yellow 1·00 3·00
119 10c. on 50c. green and violet on mauve 1·75 4·50
120 10c. on 75c. brown and green on green 1·90 3·75
121 25c. on 1f. green and blue on blue 1·60 3·75
122 25c. on 2f. purple and red on rose 2·50 8·75
123 25c. on 5f. brown and red on green 23·00 55·00

21 Arab Woman
22 Grand Mosque, Tunis 
23 Mosque, Place Halfaouine, Tunis 

24 Amphitheatre, El Djem

1926.
124 **21** 1c. red 10 50
125 2c. green 10 55
126 3c. blue 10 1·60
127 5c. green 25 10
128 10c. mauve 1·25 15
129 **22** 15c. lilac 30 10
130 20c. red 10 15
131 25c. green 70 15
131a 25c. mauve 1·10 20
132 30c. mauve 15 15
133 30c. green 95 15
134 40c. brown 20 20
134a 45c. green 2·00 3·25
135 **23** 50c. black 1·00 10
135a 50c. blue 1·40 10
135b 50c. green 60 20
135c 60c. red 15 25
135d 65c. blue 2·25 20
135e 70c. red 20 45
136 75c. red 2·00 15
136a 75c. mauve 1·40 10
137 80c. blue 75 1·75
137a 80c. brown 30 75
138 90c. red 15 10
138a 90c. blue 13·00 14·00
139 1f. purple 25 10
139a 1f. red 10 10
140 **24** 1f.05 pink and blue 35 1·00
141 1f.25 blue and light blue 65 1·25
141a 1f.25 red 1·90 2·75
141b 1f.30 violet and blue 70 70
141c 1f.40 purple 3·00 3·00
142 1f.50 blue and light blue 1·25 1·40
142a 1f.50 orange and red 1·25 60
143 2f. brown and red 50 20
143a 2f. red 40 15
143b 2f.25 blue 70 2·25
143c 2f.50 green 60 45
144 3f. orange and blue 1·25 20
144a 3f. violet 30 15
145 5f. green and red on green 1·50 80
145a 5f. brown 1·50 3·00
146 10f. grey and red on blue 6·25 3·50
146a 10f. pink 2·00 2·75
146b 20f. red and mauve on pink 2·00 55
For similar designs see Nos. 172/91, 220/31 and 257/286.

1927. Surch **1f 50**.
147 **24** 1f.50 on 1f.25 blue and ultramarine 30 95

1927. Air. Optd **Poste Aerienne** and airplane or surch in figures and bars also.
148 **7** 1f. light blue and blue 1·00 1·40
152 **24** 1f.30 mauve and orange 1·75 1·60
169 1f.50 on 1f.30 mve & orge 1·90 40
170 1f.50 on 1f.80 red and green 2·25 40
171 1f.50 on 2f.55 brn & mve 3·50 1·00
149 **6** 1f.75 on 75c. scarlet and red 1·25 2·00
150 **7** 1f.75 on 5f. green and lilac 2·75 4·00
153 **24** 1f.80 red and green 2·00 3·75
151 **7** 2f. red and green on pink 3·00 2·50
154 **24** 2f.55 brown and mauve 1·40 2·50

26 First Tunis–Chad Motor Service

1928. Child Welfare.
155 **26** 40c.+40c. brown 1·10 3·00
156 50c.+50c. purple 65 3·25
157 75c.+75c. blue 60 3·00
158 1f.+1f. red 1·50 3·50
159 1f.50+1f.50 blue 1·10 3·25
160 2f.+2f. green 70 3·50
161 5f.+5f. brown 1·10 3·50

1928. Surch.
162 **4** 3c. on 5c. orange 10 1·40
163 **5** 10c. on 15c. brown on orange 15 20
164 **18** 25c. on 30c. mauve 15 20
165 **23** 40c. on 80c. blue 15 1·00
166 **22** 50c. on 40c. brown 4·00 20
167 **23** 50c. on 75c. red 15 60

1929. Precancelled **AFFRANCHts POSTES** and surch **10**.
168 **22** 10 on 30c. mauve 1·25 3·00

28  **29**  **30**

31

1931.
172 **28** 1c. blue 10 1·40
173 2c. brown 10 1·25
174 3c. black 15 2·25
175 5c. green 10 95
176 10c. red 10 95
177 **29** 15c. purple 70 70
178 20c. brown 10 15
179 25c. red 10 15
180 30c. green 20 15
181 40c. orange 10 15
182 **30** 50c. blue 20 10
183 75c. yellow 1·10 45
184 90c. red 1·00 1·40
185 1f. olive 40 20
186 **31** 1f.50 blue 15 25
187 2f. brown 1·10 20
188 3f. green 10·50 13·00
189 5f. red 23·00 22·00
190 10f. black 38·00 29·00
191 20f. brown 32·00 40·00

1937. Surch.
191a **23** 25c. on 65c. blue 10 10
192 0.65 on 50c. blue 95 10
193 65 on 50c. blue 1·60 10
193b 1FR on 90c. blue 1·40 15
193c **24** 1F. on 1f.25 red 30 2·25
193d 1F. on 1f.40 purple 20 80
193e 1F. on 2f.25 blue 15 65
194 1f.75 on 1f.50 blue and light blue 3·25 85

1938. 50th Anniv of Tunisian Postal Service. Surch **1888 1938** and value.
196 **28** 1c.+1c. blue 2·25 4·00
197 2c.+2c. brown 2·00 3·75
198 3c.+3c. black 1·50 3·75
199 5c.+5c. green 2·25 3·75
200 10c.+10c. red 2·25 3·75
201 **29** 15c.+15c. purple 2·00 3·75
202 20c.+20c. brown 2·25 4·00
203 25c.+25c. red 1·75 3·75
204 30c.+30c. green 1·75 3·75
205 40c.+40c. orange 1·75 3·75
206 **30** 50c.+50c. blue 2·25 3·75
207 75c.+75c. yellow 1·75 3·75
208 90c.+90c. red 1·75 3·75
209 1f.+1f. olive 1·60 4·00
210 **31** 1f.50+1f. blue 2·25 3·75
211 2f.+1f.50 brown 2·50 4·50
212 3f.+2f. green 2·25 5·50
213 5f.+3f. red 9·75 29·00
214 10f.+5f. black 22·00 50·00
215 20f.+10f. brown 75·00 75·00

1941. National Relief. Surch **SECOURS NATIONAL 1941** and value.
216 **22** 1f. on 45c. green 1·25 4·75
217 **24** 1f.30 on 1f.25 red 1·50 4·75
218 1f.50 on 1f.40 purple 1·60 4·25
219 2f. on 2f.25 blue 1·25 4·75

1941. As stamps of 1926 but without monogram "RF".
220 **22** 30c. red 40 3·25
221 **23** 1f.20 grey 15 80
222 1f.50 brown 25 20
223 **24** 2f.40 pink and red 1·10 2·75
224 2f.50 light blue and blue 20 30
225 3f. violet 1·25 2·50
226 4f. blue and black 85 1·25
227 4f.50 brown and green 1·40 1·50
228 5f. black 15 15
229 10f. violet and purple 20 15
230 15f. red 5·00 6·00
231 20f. red and lilac 3·25 3·50

41a "Victory"
42 Allied Soldiers 

1943.
232 **41a** 1f.50 red 85 40

1943. Charity. Tunisian Liberation.
233 **42** 1f.50+8f.50 red 15 1·25

43 Mosque and Olive Trees
44 Sidi Mahrez Mosque 

45 Ramparts of Sfax

1944.
234 **43** 30c. yellow 20 2·75
235 40c. brown 25 2·50
236 60c. orange 25 1·25
237 70c. red 25 2·25
238 80c. green 35 2·50
239 90c. violet 25 2·50
240 1f. red 25 15
241 1f.50 blue 20 15
242 2f.40 red 25 2·75
243 2f.50 brown 25 20
244 3f. violet 25 25
245 4f. blue 40 25
246 4f.50 green 35 30
247 5f. grey 25 15
248 6f. brown 20 30
249 10f. lake 25 50
250 15f. brown 30 70
251 20f. lilac 40 70
Nos. 234/41 are smaller, $15\frac{1}{2} \times 19$ mm.

1944. Forces Welfare Fund. Surch **+ 48 frcs pour nos Combattants**.
252 **43** 2f.+48f. red ($21\frac{1}{4} \times 26\frac{1}{2}$ mm) 65 3·25

1945. Forces Welfare Fund. Surch **POUR NOS COMBATTANTS** and value.
253 **44** 1f.50+8f.50 brown 95 3·00
254 **45** 3f.+12f. green 1·10 3·25
255 – 4f.+21f. brown 1·00 3·00
256 – 10f.+40f. red 80 3·25
DESIGNS—HORIZ: 4f. Camel patrol at Fort Saint; 10f. Mosque at Sidi-bou-Said.

1945. New values and colours.
257 **23** 10c. brown 10 50
258 30c. olive 10 45
259 40c. red 15 15
260 50c. turquoise 10 15
261 60c. blue 15 25
262 80c. green 15 95
263 1f.20 brown 20 2·25
264 1f.50 lilac 15 15
265 2f. green 10 15
267 **24** 2f.40 red 50 3·00
268 **23** 2f.50 brown 1·50 20
269 **24** 3f. brown 10 10
270 **23** 3f. red 15 15
271 **24** 4f. blue 1·90 1·40
272 **23** 4f. violet 1·40 15
273 **24** 4f. violet 1·75 55
273a **23** 4f. orange 95 25
274 4f.50 blue 90 20
275 **24** 5f. green 60 20
275a **23** 5f. blue 65 30
275b 5f. green 25 10
276 **24** 6f. blue 1·25 65
277 6f. red 1·50 85
278 **23** 6f. red 20 15
279 **24** 10f. orange 80 35
280 10f. blue 1·25 30
281 15f. mauve 50 20
281a **23** 15f. red 1·00 15
282 **24** 20f. green 25 10
283 25f. violet 1·25 75
284 25f. orange 75 50
285 50f. red 45 25
286 100f. red 65 35

1945. Anti-tuberculosis Fund. Type of France optd **TUNISIE**.
287 **222** 2f.+1f. orange 15 1·50

1945. Postal Employees' War Victims' Fund. Type of France optd **TUNISIE**.
288 **223** 4f.+6f. brown 1·25 2·75

1945. Stamp Day. Type of France (Louis XI) optd **TUNISIE**.
289 **228** 2f.+3f. green 20 1·90

1945. War Veterans' Fund. Surch **ANCIENS COMBATTANTS R F** and value.
290 **21** 4f.+6f. on 10c. blue 1·00 2·50
291 **23** 10f.+30f. on 80c. green 1·40 2·75

49 Legionary

1946. Welfare Fund for French Troops in Indo-China.
292 **49** 20f.+30f. black, red and green . . . . 1·60 3·50

1946. Red Cross Fund. Surch with cross **1946** and new values.
293 **23** 80c.+50c. green . . . . . 35 3·00
294 1f.50+1f.50 lilac . . . . . 50 3·00
295 2f.+2f. green . . . . . . 45 2·75
296 **24** 2f.40+2f. red . . . . . . 80 3·25
297 4f.+4f. blue . . . . 90 3·50

1946. Stamp Day. La Varane Type of France optd **TUNISIE**.
298 **241** 3f.+2f. blue . . . . . . 35 1·90

1947. Stamp Day. Louvois Type of France optd **TUNISIE**.
299 **253** 4f.50+5f.50 brown . . . . 1·75 3·00

1947. Naval Charities. Type of France surch **TUNISIE** and new value.
300 **234** 10+15 on 2f.+3f. blue . . 1·00 3·25

1947. Welfare Fund. Surch **SOLIDARITE 1947 +40 F.**
301 **24** 10f.+40f. black . . . . . 3·00 3·00

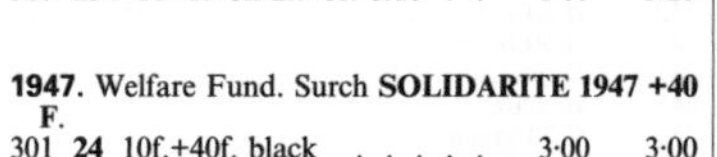

53 Arabesque Ornamentation from Great Mosque at Kairouan

54 Neptune

1947.
302 **53** 3f. green and turquoise . . . 85 1·25
303 4f. red and purple . . . . 3·00 1·90
304 **54** 5f. black and green . . . 70 1·10
305 **53** 6f. red and brown . . . 55 10
306 **54** 10f. black and brown . . 40 20
306a **53** 10f. violet . . . . 1·75 10
306b 12f. brown . . . . 2·00 1·60
306c 12f. orange and brown . . 1·50 15
306d 15f. red and brown . . . 2·00 2·25
307 **54** 18f. blue and green . . . 1·40 3·00
307a 25f. turquoise and blue . 2·25 20
307b **53** 30f. blue and deep blue . 1·60 65

55 Feeding a Fledgling

57 Triumphal Arch, Sbeitla

1947. Infant Welfare Fund.
308 **55** 4f.50+5f.50 green . . . . . 50 1·90
309 6f.+9f. blue . . . . 45 1·90
310 8f.+17f. red . . . . 20 2·00
311 10f.+40f. violet . . . . . 45 2·00

1948. Stamp Day. Type of France (Arago) optd **TUNISIE**.
312 **253** 6f.+4f. red . . . . 1·25 3·50

1948. Anti-tuberculosis Fund. Surch **AIDEZ LES TUBERCULEUX +10f.**
313 **53** 4f.+10f. orange and green 25 3·00

1948. Army Welfare Fund.
315 **57** 10f.+40f. green and bistre 1·25 3·50
316 18f.+42f. dp blue & blue 1·25 3·50

1949. Stamp Day. Type of France (Choiseul), optd **TUNISIE**.
317 **278** 15f.+5f. black . . . . . 2·25 2·75

58 Child in Cot

1949. Child Welfare Fund.
318 **58** 25f.+50f. green . . . . . 3·25 4·25

59 Oued Mellegue Barrage

1949. Tunisian Development.
319 **59** 15f. black 65 60

60 Bird from Antique Mosaic

61 Globe, Mounted Postman and Sud Est Languedoc Airliner

1949. Air.
320 **60** 100f. brown and green . . 1·90 1·40
321 200f. black and blue (A) 2·75 1·50
322 200f. black and blue (B) . . 4·50 3·75

In A the Arabic inscription is in two lines and in B it is in one line.

1949. 75th Anniv of U.P.U.
323 **61** 5f. green on blue (postage) 1·40 3·25
324 15f. brown on blue . . . . 1·90 3·50
325 15f. blue on blue (air) . . . 1·00 1·75

1949. Free French Association Fund. Surch Lorraine Cross and **FFL +15F.**
326 **54** 10f.+15f. red and blue . . 1·60 2·25

1950. Stamp Day. Type of France (Postman) optd **TUNISIE**.
327 **292** 12f.+3f. green . . . . . 2·00 3·25

62 "Tunisia Thanks France"

63 Old Soldier

1950. Franco–Tunisian Relief Fund.
328 **62** 15f.+35f. red . . . . . . 2·00 3·75
329 25f.+45f. blue . . . . . . 2·00 3·75

1950. Veterans' Relief Fund.
330 **63** 25f.+25f. blue . . . . . . 3·25 4·25

64 Horse (bas-relief)

65 Hermes of Berbera

1950. (a) Size 21½ × 17½ mm.
331 **64** 10c. blue . . . . 15 1·75
332 50c. brown . . . . 10 2·25
333 1f. violet 15 30
334 2f. grey 75 15
335 3f. brown 55 30
336 4f. orange . . . . 1·00 1·25
337 5f. green 95 10
338 8f. blue . . . . 1·25 50
340 12f. red 75 20
341 15f. red 30 25
342 15f. blue . . . . 2·40 25

(b) Size 22½ × 18¼ mm.
343 **64** 15f. red . . . . 2·40 1·60
344 15f. blue . . . . 2·00 1·75
345 30f. blue . . . . 3·00 50

1950.
346 **65** 15f. red . . . . 1·50 2·50
347 25f. blue 45 15
348 50f. green 95 25

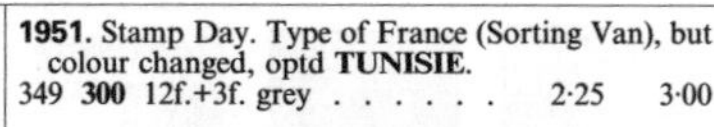

1951. Stamp Day. Type of France (Sorting Van), but colour changed, optd **TUNISIE**.
349 **300** 12f.+3f. grey . . . . . . 2·25 3·00

66 Sleeping Child

1951. Child Welfare Fund.
350 **66** 30f.+15f. blue . . . . . . 3·00 3·00

67 Gammarth National Cemetery

68 Panel from Great Mosque at Kairouan

1951. War Orphans' Fund.
351 **67** 30f.+10f. blue . . . . . . 1·75 2·25

1952. Stamp Day. Type of France (Mail Coach), optd **TUNISIE**.
352 **319** 12f.+3f. violet . . . . . 2·00 2·50

1952. Army Welfare Fund. Inscr "OEUVRES SOCIALES DE L'ARMEE".
353 – 15f.+1f. indigo and blue (postage) . . . . 1·75 1·60
354 **68** 50f.+10f. green and black (air) . . . . 4·25 4·75

DESIGN: 15f. Ornamental stucco, Bardo Palace.

69 Schoolboys clasping Hands

70 Charles Nicolle

1952. Holiday Camp Fund.
355 **69** 30f.+10f. green . . . . . 2·75 3·00

1952. Golden Jubilee of Tunisian Medical Sciences Society.
356 **70** 15f. brown . . . . 45 1·25
357 30f. blue . . . . 1·10 1·75

1952. Centenary of Military Medal. Type of France surch **Tunisie +5F.**
358 **327** 15f.+5f. green . . . . . 95 4·00

1953. Stamp Day. Type of France (Count D'Argenson), optd **TUNISIE**.
359 **334** 12f.+3f. red . . . . . . 50 3·50

71 Tower and Flags

72 Tozeur Mosque

1953. 1st International Fair, Tunis.
360 **71** 8f. brown and deep brown 50 2·75
361 12f. green and emerald . . 40 3·25
362 15f. indigo and blue . . . 30 1·50
363 18f. deep violet and violet 35 3·25
364 30f. red and carmine . . . 55 3·25

1953. Air.
365 – 100f. blue, turquoise & green . . . . 4·25 2·50
366 – 200f. sepia, purple & brown . . . . 5·50 3·25
367 – 500f. brown and blue . . . 21·00 22·00
368 **72** 1000f. green . . . . 25·00 50·00

DESIGNS: 100, 200f. Monastir; 500f. View of Korbous.

For similar stamps but without "R F" see Nos. 423/6.

1954. Stamp Day. Type of France (Lavallette), optd **TUNISIE**.
369 **346** 12f.+3f. blue . . . . . . 2·00 3·25

73 Courtyard, Sousse

74 Sidi Bou Maklouf Mosque, Le Kef

1954.
370 **73** 50c. green . . . . 10 2·25
371 1f. red 10 20
372 – 2f. purple 30 30
373 – 4f. turquoise . . . . . . 1·75 35
374 – 5f. violet . . . . 1·60 20
375 – 8f. brown . . . . 1·00 70
376 – 10f. green . . . . 2·25 1·10
377 – 12f. brown . . . . 2·00 40
378 – 15f. blue (18 × 22 mm) . . 2·75 1·10
386 – 15f. blue (17 × 21½ mm) . . 1·00 10
379 **74** 18f. brown . . . . 3·00 3·25
380 – 20f. blue . . . . 2·25 25
381 – 25f. blue . . . . 2·50 30
382 – 30f. purple . . . . 1·90 2·75
383 – 40f. green . . . . 2·25 1·60
384 – 50f. lilac . . . . 2·75 20
385 – 75f. red . . . . 5·50 4·75

DESIGNS—As Type **73**: 2, 4f. Takrouna ramparts; 5, 8f. Dwellings and Mosque, Tatahouine; 10, 12f. Cave dwellings, Matmata; 15f. Street, Sidi-bou-said. As Type **74**: 20, 25f. Genoese Fort, Tabarka; 30, 40f. Bab-el-Khadra Gate, Tunis; 50, 75f. Four-storey dwellings, Medenine.

For similar stamps but without "R F" see Nos. 406/22.

76 Bey of Tunisia

76a Paris Balloon Post, 1870

1954.
387 **76** 8f. deep blue and blue . . 2·25 3·25
388 12f. indigo and blue . . . 2·25 2·75
389 15f. red and carmine . . . 2·25 3·00
390 18f. deep brown and brown 2·25 2·75
391 30f. deep green and green 2·50 3·75

1955. Stamp Day.
392 **76a** 12f.+3f. brown . . . . . 3·25 1·40

77

1955. 50th Anniv of "L'Essor" (Tunisian Amateur Dramatic Society).
393 **77** 15f. blue, red and orange 2·50 2·75

78 Tunisian Buildings and Rotary Emblem

79 Bey of Tunisia

1955. 50th Anniv of Rotary International.
394 **78** 12f. deep brown and brown 35 3·00
395 15f. brown and grey . . . 35 3·00
396 18f. lilac and violet . . . 30 3·25
397 25f. deep blue and blue . . 35 3·25
398 30f. indigo and blue . . . 60 3·50

1955.
399 **79** 15f. blue . . . . 2·00 10

80 "Embroidery"

81 Bey of Tunisia

80a Francis of Taxis

1955. 3rd International Fair, Tunis.
400 **80** 5f. lake 1·50 2·75
401 12f. blue 1·40 2·75
402 – 15f. green 1·75 2·50
403 – 18f. red 1·75 3·00
404 – 20f. violet 2·00 3·25
405 – 30f. purple 75 2·00
DESIGNS: 15, 18f. "Pottery"; 20, 30f. "Jasmin sellers".

1956. Nos. 365/6 and 368/86 re-engraved without "R F".
406 50c. green (postage) 10 95
407 1f. red 10 10
408 2f. purple 15 20
409 4f. blue 15 20
410 5f. violet 15 15
411 8f. brown 15 30
412 10f. green 15 10
413 12f. brown 15 20
414 15f. blue (18 × 22 mm) 2·50 2·00
415 15f. blue (17 × 21½ mm) 15 15
416 18f. brown 15 35
417 20f. blue 25 15
418 25f. blue 1·40 10
419 30f. purple 45 15
420 40f. green 45 25
421 50f. lilac 2·00 25
422 75f. red 65 65
423 100f. blue, turquoise and green (air) 2·50 30
424 200f. sepia, purple and brown 3·50 1·60
425 500f. brown and blue 8·00 9·00
426 1000f. green 12·50 16·00

1956. Stamp Day.
427 **80a** 12f.+3f. green 1·90 1·90

INDEPENDENT KINGDOM

1956. Autonomous Government.
428 **81** 5f. blue 35 35
429 – 12f. purple 35 35
430 **81** 15f. red 35 35
431 – 18f. grey 45 35
432 **81** 20f. green 45 35
433 – 30f. brown 90 40
DESIGN: 12, 18, 30f. Tunisian girl releasing dove.

82 Farhat Hached
83 Market Scene

1956. Labour Day.
434 **82** 15f. lake 30 30
435 30f. blue 35 35

1956. Tunisian Products.
436 – 12f. violet, purple & mauve 60 20
437 – 15f. green, brown and blue 60 20
438 – 18f. blue 90 35
439 – 20f. brown 90 35
440 **83** 25f. brown 1·25 55
441 30f. blue 1·40 55
DESIGNS—VERT: 12f. Bunch of grapes; 15f. Sprig of olives; 18f. Harvesting; 20f. Man with basket containing wedding offering.

84 Pres. Habib Bourguiba
85 Pres. Bourguiba and Agricultural Workers

1957. 1st Anniv of Independence.
442 **84** 5f. blue 20 20
443 **85** 12f. pink 20 20
444 **84** 20f. blue 30 20
445 **85** 25f. green 35 20
446 **84** 30f. brown 40 30
447 **85** 50f. red 80 50

86 Dove and Handclasp

1957. 5th International Confederation of Free Trade Unions Congress.
448 **86** 18f. purple 35 35
449 – 20f. red 40 40
450 **86** 25f. green 40 40
451 – 30f. blue 45 45
DESIGN—VERT: 20, 30f. Handclasp and Labour Exchange.

INDEPENDENT REPUBLIC

(87)

1957. Tunisian Army Fortnight. No. 417 optd with T **87**.
452 20f.+10f. blue 55 55

88 Tunisian Soldiers and Flag

1957. Proclamation of Republic.
453 **88** 20f. red 16·00 16·00
454 25f. violet 16·00 16·00
455 30f. brown 16·00 16·00

1957. 5th International Fair, Tunis. As No. 404 but additionally inscr "5e FOIRE INTERNATIONALE" and Arabic inscriptions at sides, surch **+ 10F**.
456 20f.+10f. violet 45 45

90 Pres Bourguiba on Ile de la Galite
91 Tunisian Emblems and Map

1958. 6th Anniv of Exile of Pres. Bourguiba.
457 **90** 20f. blue and brown 55 35
458 25f. blue and violet 55 35

1958. 2nd Anniv of Independence.
459 **91** 20f. green and brown 35 15
460 – 25f. brown and blue 35 15
461 – 30f. brown, deep brown and red 45 20
DESIGNS: 25f. Mother and child; 30f. Clenched fist holding Tunisian flag.
For 20f. brown and blue see No. 464.

92 Andreas Vesalius (scientist) and A. ibn Khaldoun
93 Planting Olives

1958. Brussels International Exhibition.
462 **92** 30f. green and bistre 45 20

1958. Labour Day.
463 **93** 20f. multicoloured 45 45

1958. 3rd Anniv of Return of Pres. Bourguiba. As T **91** but with inscr altered.
464 **91** 20f. brown and blue 40 20

94
95 Pres. Bourguiba

1958. 1st Anniv of Proclamation of Tunisian Republic.
465 **94** 5f. purple and bistre 45 20
466 10f. deep green & lt green 45 20
467 15f. brown and orange 45 20
468 20f. violet, olive and yellow 45 20
469 25f. purple 45 20

1958. Pres. Bourguiba's 55th Birthday.
470 **95** 20f. purple and violet 35 20

96 Fishermen with Catch
97 UNESCO Headquarters, Paris

1958. 6th International Fair.
471 **96** 25f. purple, red and green 70 35

1958. Inaug of UNESCO Building.
472 **97** 25f. myrtle 60 35

98 "Shedding the veil"
99 Hand holding plant

1959. Emancipation of Tunisian Women.
473 **98** 20m. turquoise 45 30

1959. 25th Anniv of Neo-Destour (Nationalist Party) and Victory Congress.
474 **99** 5m. red, brown and purple 30 10
475 – 10m. multicoloured 35 15
476 – 20m. blue 40 20
477 – 30m. blue, turquoise & brown 65 40
DESIGNS—VERT: 10m. Tunisians with flaming torch and flag on shield; 20m. Pres. Bourguiba in exile at Borj le Boeuf, 1954. HORIZ: 30m. Pres. Bourguiba and Borj le Boeuf, 1934.

100 "Tunisia"

1959. 3rd Anniv of Independence.
478 **100** 50m. multicoloured 65 35

101 Tunisian Horseman
102 "Freedom"

1959. Designs as T **101**.
479 ½m. brown, green and emerald 35 10
480 1m. bistre and blue 10 10
481 2m. brown, yellow and blue 15 10
482 3m. myrtle 10 10
483 4m. brown 30 15
484 5m. myrtle 20 10
485 6m. violet 20 15
486 8m. purple 65 30
487 10m. red, green and bistre 20 10
487a 12m. violet and bistre 65 20
488 15m. blue 60 10
489 16m. green 30 20
490 20m. turquoise 1·00 30
491 20m. purple, olive and myrtle 2·25 30
492 25m. blue, brown & turquoise 30 20
493 30m. brown, green & turq 45 10
494 40m. green 1·60 20
495 45m. green 70 30
496 50m. multicoloured 90 20
497 60m. brown and green 1·25 35
498 70m. multicoloured 1·40 50
499 75m. brown 1·25 55
500 90m. brown, green and blue 1·60 55
501 95m. multicoloured 1·90 1·00
502 100m. multicoloured 2·00 90
503 200m. red, bistre and blue 5·00 2·50
504 ½d. brown 16·00 6·75
505 1d. ochre and green 25·00 13·50
DESIGNS—VERT: ½m. Ain Draham; 2m. Camel-driver; 3m. Saddler's shop; 5m. Type **101**; 6m. Weavers; 8m. Gafsa; 10m. Woman holding pomegranates; 12m. Turner; 20m. (No. 491), Gabes; 40m. Kairouan; 70m. Carpet weaver; 75m. Nabeul vase; 95m. Olive-gatherer; ½d. Sbeitla. HORIZ: 1m. Kairouan environs; 4m. Medenine; 15m. Monastir; 16m. Tunis; 20m. (No. 490), Room in Arab house, Sidi-Bou-Said; 25m. Sfax; 30m. Aqueduct, Medjerda Valley; 45m. Bizerta; 50m. Djerba; 60m. Le Jerid; 90m. Le Kef; 100m. Sidi-bou-Said highway; 200m. Old port of Sfax; 1d. Beja ploughman.

1959. Africa Freedom Day.
506 **102** 40m. brown and blue 50 35

103 Postman
104 Clenched Hands

1959. Stamp Day.
507 **103** 20m.+5m. brown & orge 45 45

1959. U.N. Day.
508 **104** 80m. brown, blue & purple 65 45

105
106 Dancer and Coin

1959. Red Crescent Day.
509 **105** 10m.+5m. multicoloured 35 35

1959. 1st Anniv of Tunisian Central Bank.
510 **106** 50m. black and blue 50 50

107 "Uprooted Tree"
108 Camel Rider telephoning

1960. World Refugee Year. Inscr "ANNEE MONDIALE DES REFUGIES 1959–1960".
511 **107** 20m. blue 40 20
512 – 40m. black and purple 50 35
DESIGN—HORIZ: 40m. Doves.

1960. Stamp Day.
513 **108** 60m.+5m. orange, blue and olive 80 80

109 Pres. Bourguiba signing Promulgation
110 Fair Emblems

1960. Promulgation of Constitution.
514 **109** 20m. red, brown and green 40 35

1960. 5th Sousse National Fair.
515 **110** 100m. black and green 65 45

111 President Bourguiba
112 Jamboree Emblems

1960.
516 **111** 20m. black 20 10
517 30m. black, red and blue 35 10
518 40m. black, red and green 45 20

1960. 4th Arab Scout Jamboree, Tunis.
519 **112** 10m. turquoise 35 35
520 – 25m. purple, red and green 40 35
521 – 30m. lake, violet and green 60 35

522 – 40m. black, blue and red 65 40
523 – 60m. violet, purple & sepia . . . . 1·25 55
DESIGNS: 25m. Saluting hand with scouts as fingers; 30m. Camp bugler; 40m. Scout peacock badge; 60m. Scout by camp fire.

113 Cyclist in Stadium
114

1960. Olympic Games.
524 **113** 5m. brown and olive . . . 30 25
525 – 10m. purple, green & blue 35 30
526 – 15m. carmine and red . . 35 30
527 – 25m. slate and blue . . . 45 40
528 – 50m. blue and green . . . 85 65
DESIGNS: 10m. Flowers composed of Olympic rings; 15m. Girl with racquet; 25m. Runner; 50m. Handball player.

1960. 5th World Forestry Congress, Seattle.
529 **114** 8m. lake, green and blue 35 15
530 – 15m. green 40 20
531 – 25m. red, green and violet 65 30
532 – 50m. turquoise, brown & green . . . . 1·10 50
DESIGNS: 15m. Removing bark from tree; 25m. Tree within leaf; 50m. Diamond pattern featuring palm.

115 U.N. Emblem and People's Arms
116 Dove of Peace

1960. U.N. Day.
533 **115** 40m. blue, red and black 65 45

1961. 5th Anniv of Independence.
534 **116** 20m. blue, bistre & purple 30 20
535 30m. brown, violet & blue 35 20
536 40m. ultramarine, blue & green 55 40
537 – 75m. blue, mauve and olive 80 45
DESIGN: 75m. Globe and Arms of Tunisia.

117 Tunisian Animals and Map of Africa
118 Stamps and Magnifier

1961. Africa Day and 3rd Anniv of Accra Conference. Inscr "JOURNEE DE L'AFRIQUE 15.4.1961".
538 **117** 40m. green, brown and bistre 35 20
539 – 60m. black, brown & turquoise 40 30
540 – 100m. violet, emerald and grey 70 45
541 – 200m. brown and orange 1·40 1·00
DESIGNS (all showing outline of Africa): 50m. Profiles of Negress and Arab woman; 100m. Masks and "Africa Day" in Arabic; 200m. Clasped hands.

1961. Stamp Day. Inscr "JOURNEE DU TIMBRE 1961". Multicoloured.
542 12m.+4m. Kerkennah dancer and costume of stamps (vert) 45 45
543 15m.+5m. Mobile postal delivery (vert) 60 60
544 20m.+6m. Type **118** 65 65
545 50m.+5m. Postman in shirt depicting stamps (vert) . . 80 80

119 "Celebration"
120 Dag Hammarskjoeld

1961. National Day.
546 **119** 25m. brown, red and violet 45 15
547 – 50m. brown, choc & grn 45 20
548 – 95m. mauve, brown & blue 65 40
DESIGNS: 50m. Family celebrating in street; 95m. Girl astride crescent moon.

1961. U.N. Day.
549 **120** 40m. blue 60 35

121 Arms of Tunisia
122 Mosquito in Web

1962. 10th Anniv of Independence Campaign. Arms in red, yellow, blue and black.
550 **121** 1m. yellow and black . . . 10 10
551 2m. pink and black . . . 15 15
552 3m. blue and black . . . 15 15
553 6m. grey and black . . . 20 20

1962. Malaria Eradication. Inscr "LE MONDE UNI CONTRE LE PALUDISME".
554 **122** 20m. brown 45 30
555 – 30m. brown, green & chocolate 45 30
556 – 40m. red, green and brown 80 35
DESIGNS—VERT: 30m. "Horseman" attacking mosquito; 40m. Hands destroying mosquito.

123 African

1962. Africa Day. Inscr "JOURNEE DE L'AFRIQUE 1962".
557 **123** 50m. brown and buff . . 55 35
558 – 10m. multicoloured . . . 80 45
DESIGN: 100m. Symbolic figure clasping "Africa".

124 Dancer
125 Rejoicing Tunisians

1962. May Day. Inscr "FETE DU TRAVAIL 1962".
559 **124** 40m. multicoloured . . . 40 20
560 – 60m. brown 45 30
DESIGN: 60m. Worker with pneumatic drill.

1962. National Day.
561 **125** 20m. black and salmon 50 35

126 Gabes Costume
127 U.N. Emblem and Tunisian Flag

1962. Republic Festival. Regional Costumes. Mult.
562 5m. Type **126** 55 20
563 10m. Mahdia 65 35
564 15m. Kairouan 90 45
565 20m. Hammamet . . . . . . 1·10 55
566 25m. Djerba . . . . 1·25 55
567 30m. As 10m. . . . . 1·25 65
568 40m. As 20m. . . . . 1·40 65
569 50m. Type **126** . . . . . . 1·40 85
570 55m. Ksar Hellal . . . . . 2·50 1·00
571 60m. Tunis . . . . 3·00 1·40

1962. U.N. Day.
572 **127** 20m. red, black and grey 35 30
573 – 30m. multicoloured . . . 40 30
574 – 40m. blue, black & brown 65 35
DESIGNS—HORIZ: 30m. "Plant" with three leaves and globe. VERT: 40m. Globe and dove.

128 A. Q. Chabbi (poet)
129 Pres. Bourguiba

1962. Aboul Qasim Chabbi Commemoration.
575 **128** 15m. violet 35 20

1962.
576 **129** 20m. blue 15 15
577 30m. red 15 10
578 40m. green 20 15

130 Hached Telephone Exchange
131 Runners

1962. Modernization of Telephone System.
579 **130** 5m. multicoloured 30 20
580 – 10m. multicoloured . . . 35 20
581 – 15m. multicoloured . . . 50 35
582 – 50m. flesh, brown & black 80 50
583 – 100m. blue, purple & black . . . . 2·00 90
584 – 200m. multicoloured . . . 2·75 1·40
DESIGNS: 10m. Carthage Telephone Exchange; 15m. Aerial equipment; 50m. Telephone switchboard operators; 100m. Telephone equipment as human figure; 200m. Belvedere Telephone Exchange.

1963. 13th International Military Sports Council Cross-country Championships.
585 **131** 30m. brown, green & black 60 45

132 Dove with Wheatear and Globe
133 Centenary Emblem

1963. Freedom from Hunger.
586 **132** 20m. blue and brown . . 30 20
587 – 40m. purple and brown 40 20
DESIGN: 40m. Child taking nourishment.

1963. Red Cross Centenary.
588 **133** 20m. red, grey and brown 45 20

1963. U.N. Day. Nos. 542/5 optd **1963 O.N.U.** in English and Arabic.
589 12m.+4m. multicoloured . . 30 30
590 15m.+5m. multicoloured . . 35 35
591 20m.+6m. multicoloured . . 40 40
592 50m.+5m. multicoloured . . 65 65

135 "Miss World"
136 "Out of Reach"

1963. 15th Anniv of Declaration of Human Rights.
593 **135** 30m. brown and green . . 45 30

1964. Nubian Monuments Preservation.
594 **136** 50m. ochre, brown & blue 45 30

137 "Unsettled Forecast"
138 Mohamed Ali (trade union leader)

1964. World Meteorological Day.
595 **137** 40m. mauve, blue & brown 45 20

1964. 70th Birth Anniv of Mohamed Ali.
596 **138** 50m. purple 45 35

139 Africa within Flower
140 Pres. Bourguiba

1964. 1st Anniv of Addis Ababa Conference of the Organization of African Unity.
597 **139** 60m. multicoloured . . . 50 30

1964. National Day.
598 **140** 20m. blue 15 10
599 30m. brown 20 10

141 "Bizerte" ("ship")
142 Fulvous Babbler

1964. Neo-Destour Congress, Bizerta.
600 **141** 50m. green and black . . 40 30

1965. Air. Tunisian Birds. Multicoloured.
601 25m. Type **142** . . . . . . 1·50 50
602 55m. Great grey strike . . . 2·25 75
603 55m. Cream-coloured courser 2·50 95
604 100m. Chaffinch . . . . . . 3·00 1·10
605 150m. Greater flamingoes . . 5·25 2·40
606 200m. Barbary partridge . . 8·00 2·75
607 300m. European roller . . . 12·50 5·25
608 500m. Houbara bustard . . . 18·00 6·25
SIZES—As Type **142**: 55m. (both). Others, 23 × 32½ mm.

143 Early Telegraphist and Aerial Mast
144 Carthaginian Coin

1965. I.T.U. Centenary.
609 **143** 55m. blue and black . . . 50 30

1965. Festival of Popular Arts, Carthage.
610 **144** 5m. purple and green . . 15 10
611 10m. purple and yellow 30 20
612 75m. purple and blue . . 65 20

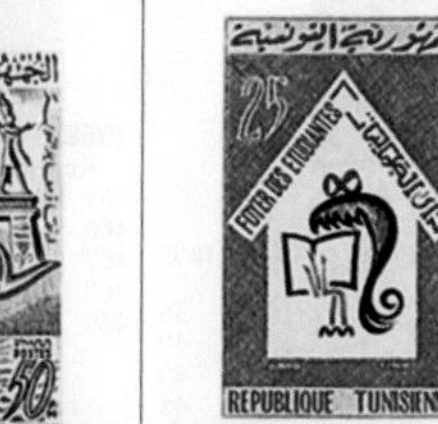

145 Girl reading Book

146 Joined Hooks

1965. Opening of Students' Home, Tunis.
613 **145** 25m. blue, black and red 30 20
614 40m. black, blue and red 40 20
615 50m. red, black and blue 45 30

1965. International Co-operation Year.
617 **146** 40m. blue, purple & black 45 25

147 Women bathing
149 Independence

148 Pres. Bourguiba and Hands

1966. Mineral Springs. Inscr "EAUX MINERALES".
618 **147** 10m. red, ochre and grey 30 20
619 – 20m. multicoloured . . . 40 30
620 – 30m. red, blue and yellow 45 35
621 – 100m. olive, yellow & blue 1·10 55
DESIGNS: 20m. Man pouring water; 30m. Woman pouring water; 100m. Mountain and fronds of tree.

1966. 10th Anniv of Independence.
622 **148** 5m. lilac and blue 15 10
623 10m. green and blue . . . 20 15
624 **149** 25m. multicoloured . . . 20 15
625 – 40m. multicoloured . . . 55 20
626 – 60m. multicoloured . . . 80 35
DESIGNS—As Type **149**—HORIZ: 40m. "Development". VERT: 60m. "Promotion of Culture" ("man" draped in books, palette, musical instruments, etc).

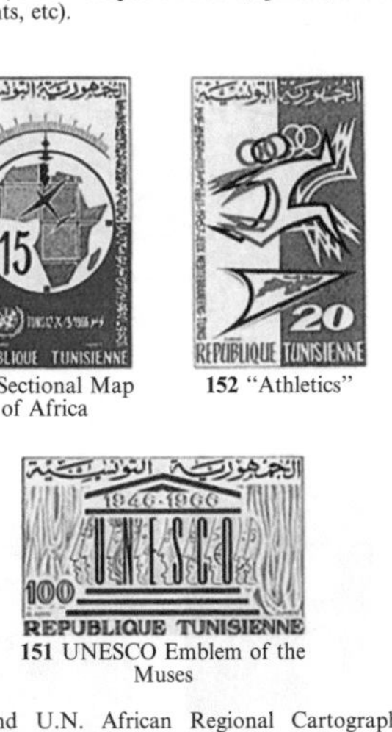

150 Sectional Map of Africa
152 "Athletics"

151 UNESCO Emblem of the Muses

1966. 2nd U.N. African Regional Cartographic Conference, Tunisia.
627 **150** 15m. multicoloured . . . 30 20
628 35m. multicoloured . . . 35 20
629 40m. multicoloured . . . 50 35

1966. 20th Anniv of UNESCO.
631 **151** 100m. brown and black 85 35

1967. Publicity for Mediterranean Games (September, 1967).
632 **152** 20m. brown, blue and red 20 15
633 30m. black and blue . . . 40 30

153 Gabes Costume and Fair Emblem
154 Emblems of Civilization

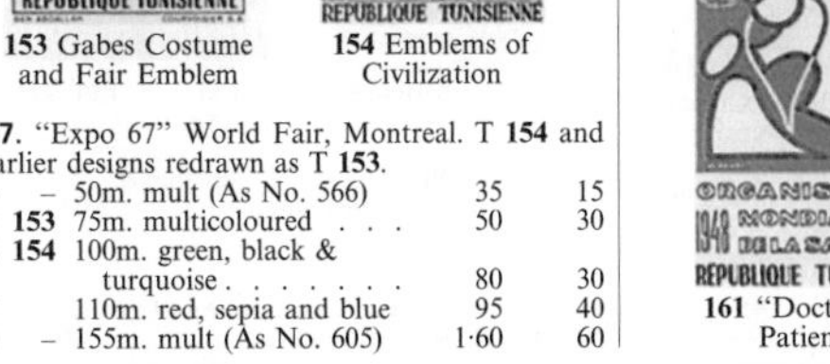

1967. "Expo 67" World Fair, Montreal. T **154** and earlier designs redrawn as T **153**.
634 – 50m. mult (As No. 566) 35 15
635 **153** 75m. multicoloured . . . 50 30
636 **154** 100m. green, black & turquoise 80 30
637 110m. red, sepia and blue 95 40
638 – 155m. mult (As No. 605) 1·60 60

155 Tunisian Pavilion, Pres. Bourguiba and Map

1967. "National Day at World Fair, Montreal".
639 **155** 65m. purple and red . . . 40 35
640 – 105m. brown, red and blue 50 35
641 – 120m. blue 60 40
642 – 200m. black, red & purple 1·25 50
DESIGNS: 105m. As Type **155**, but with profile bust of Pres. Bourguiba. Tunisian pavilion (different view) with: 120m. Silhouette and 200m. Bust of Pres. Bourguiba.

156 "Tunisia" holding Clover
158 Bas-relief from Statue of Apollo

157 Tennis Club

1967. 10th Anniv of Republic. Multicoloured.
643 25m. Type **156** 20 15
644 40m. Woman releasing doves (vert) 35 15

1967. Mediterranean Games, Tunis.
645 **157** 5m. red and green 20 20
646 – 10m. multicoloured . . . 20 15
647 – 15m. black 35 20
648 – 35m. turquoise, purple & black 45 20
649 – 75m. green, violet and red 80 40
DESIGNS—VERT: 10m. "Spring Triumphs" (squared panel). HORIZ: 15m. Olympic swimming pool; 35m. Sports Palace; 75m. Olympic stadium.

1967. Tunisian History. Punic period.
650 **158** 15m. red, black and green 30 20
651 – 20m. flesh, red and blue 35 20
652 – 25m. brown and olive . . 45 20
653 – 30m. red and grey 45 20
654 – 40m. lemon, yellow & purple 50 20
655 – 60m. multicoloured . . . 75 30
DESIGNS: 20m. Sea horseman (Kerkouane medallion); 25m. Hannibal (bronze bust); 30m. "The Sacrifice" (votive stele); 40m. Hamilcar (coin); 60m. Glass funeral pendant mask.

159 "Human Rights"
160 "Electronic Man"

1968. Human Rights Year.
656 **159** 25m. red 40 35
657 60m. blue 45 20

1968. Electronics in Postal Service.
658 **160** 25m. blue, brown & purple 35 30
659 40m. black, brown & green 35 30
660 60m. purple, slate and blue 45 35

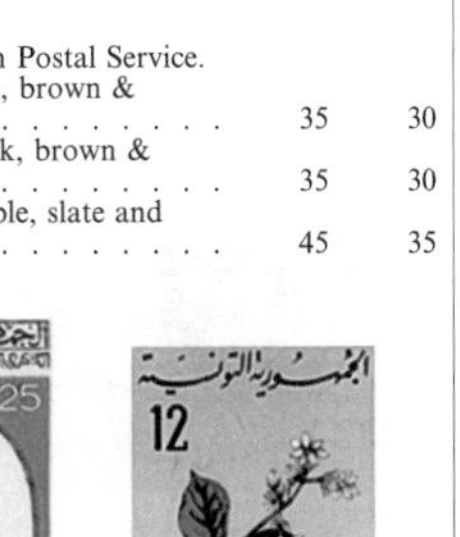

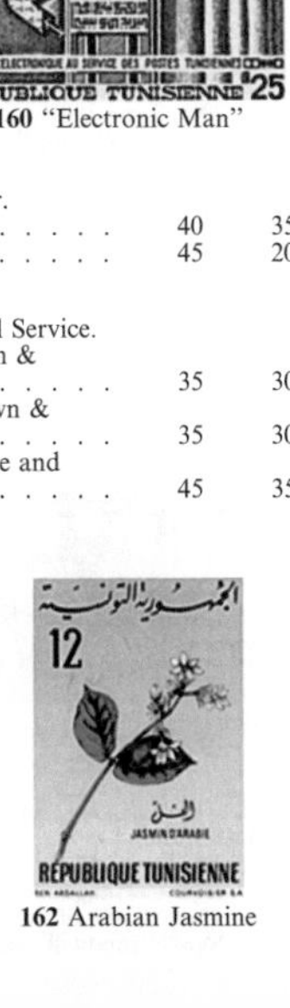

161 "Doctor and Patient"
162 Arabian Jasmine

1968. 20th Anniv of W.H.O.
661 **161** 25m. green and turquoise 40 35
662 60m. red and lake 45 35

1968. Tunisian Flowers. Multicoloured.
663 5m. Flax 20 15
664 6m. Indian shot 20 15
665 10m. Pomegranate 30 15
666 12m. Type **162** 30 15
667 15m. Raponticum 35 15
668 20m. Geranium 40 20
669 25m. Madonna lily 40 30
670 40m. Almond 60 30
671 50m. Capers 80 45
672 60m. Ariana rose . . . . . 1·25 70
673 100m. Jasmine . . . . 1·90 1·10

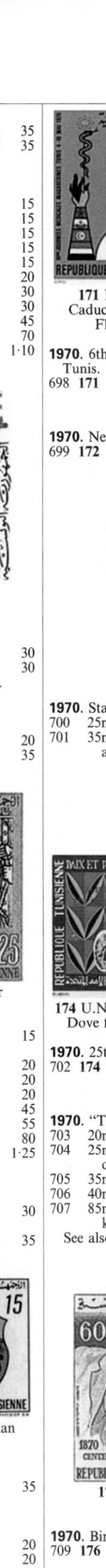

163 Globe on "Sunflower"
164 Flautist

1968. Red Crescent Day.
674 **163** 15m. red, green and blue 35 30
675 – 25m. red and purple . . . 40 30
DESIGN: 25m. Red crescent on wings of dove.

1968. Stamp Day.
676 **164** 20m. multicoloured . . . 35 20
677 50m. multicoloured . . . 40 35

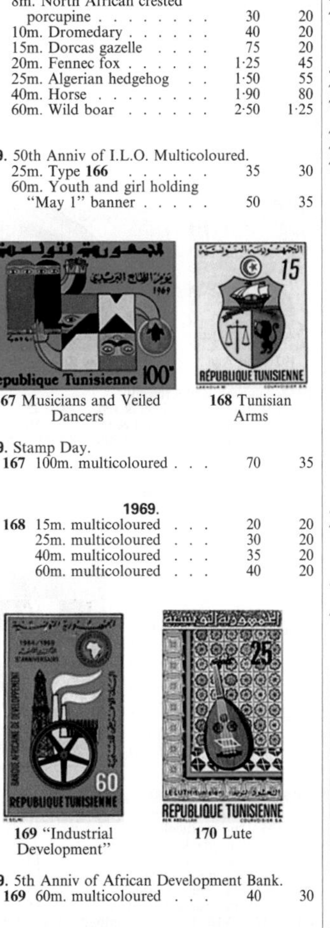

165 Golden Jackal
166 Worker

1968. Fauna. Multicoloured.
678 5m. Type **165** 20 15
679 8m. North African crested porcupine 30 20
680 10m. Dromedary 40 20
681 15m. Dorcas gazelle 75 20
682 20m. Fennec fox . . . . . 1·25 45
683 25m. Algerian hedgehog . . 1·50 55
684 40m. Horse . . . . 1·90 80
685 60m. Wild boar . . . . . . 2·50 1·25

1969. 50th Anniv of I.L.O. Multicoloured.
686 25m. Type **166** 35 30
687 60m. Youth and girl holding "May 1" banner 50 35

167 Musicians and Veiled Dancers
168 Tunisian Arms

1969. Stamp Day.
688 **167** 100m. multicoloured . . . 70 35

1969.
689 **168** 15m. multicoloured . . . 20 20
690 25m. multicoloured . . . 30 20
691 40m. multicoloured . . . 35 20
692 60m. multicoloured . . . 40 20

169 "Industrial Development"
170 Lute

1969. 5th Anniv of African Development Bank.
693 **169** 60m. multicoloured . . . 40 30

1970. Musical Instruments. Multicoloured.
694 25m. Type **170** 45 35
695 50m. Zither 55 35
696 70m. Rehab 80 35
697 90m. Naghrat (drums) . . . 1·00 35
Nos. 695 and 697 are horiz, size 33 × 22 mm.

171 Nurse, Caduceus and Flags
172 New U.P.U. Headquarters Building

1970. 6th North-African Maghreb Medical Seminar, Tunis.
698 **171** 25m. multicoloured . . . 35 20

1970. New U.P.U. Headquarters Building, Berne.
699 **172** 25m. brown and red . . . 40 20

173 Mounted Postman

1970. Stamp Day. Multicoloured.
700 25m. Type **173** 20 20
701 35m. "Postmen of yesterday and today" (23 × 38 mm) 35 20

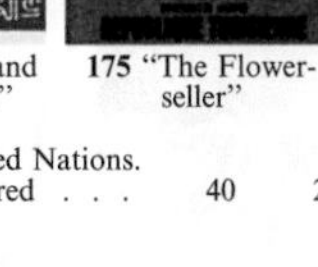

174 U.N. Emblem, "N" and Dove forming "O.N.U."
175 "The Flower-seller"

1970. 25th Anniv of United Nations.
702 **174** 40m. multicoloured . . . 40 20

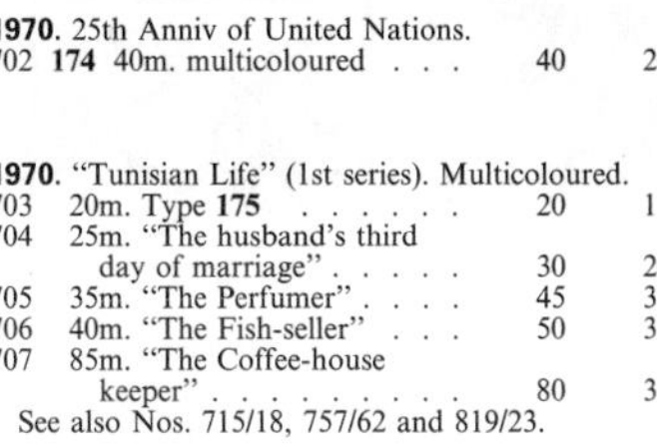

1970. "Tunisian Life" (1st series). Multicoloured.
703 20m. Type **175** 20 15
704 25m. "The husband's third day of marriage" 30 20
705 35m. "The Perfumer" 45 35
706 40m. "The Fish-seller" . . . 50 35
707 85m. "The Coffee-house keeper" 80 35
See also Nos. 715/18, 757/62 and 819/23.

176 Lenin
177 Dish Aerial and Flags

1970. Birth Centenary of Lenin.
709 **176** 60m. lake . . . . 1·25 35

1971. Maghreban Posts and Telecommunciations Co-ordination.
710 **177** 25m. multicoloured . . . 40 35

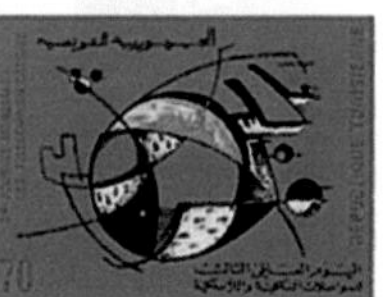

178 U.N. Building and Symbol
179 Globe and Satellites

1971. Racial Equality Year.
711 **178** 80m. multicoloured . . . 45 30

1971. World Telecommunications Day.
712 **179** 70m. multicoloured . . . 40 20

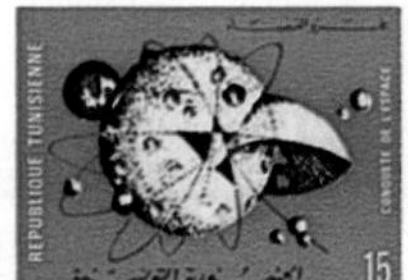

180 Moon, Earth and Satellites

1971. "Conquest of Space".
713 **180** 15m. black and blue . . . 35 20
714 – 90m. black and red . . . 60 30
DESIGN: 90m. Space allegory.

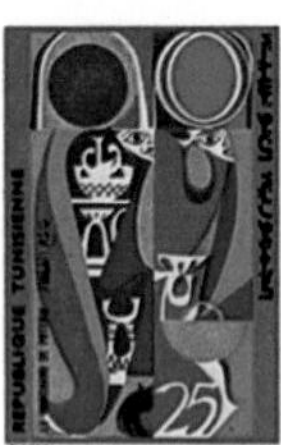

181 "The Pottery Dealer" 182 Pres. Bourguiba

1971. "Tunisian Life" (2nd series). Multicoloured.
715 25m. Type **181** 35 20
716 30m. "The Esparto dealer" 35 20
717 40m. "The Poulterer" 45 20
718 50m. "The Dyer" 55 30

1971. 8th P.S.D. Destourian Socialist Party Congress, Tunis. Multicoloured.
720 25m. Type **182** 20 20
721 30m. Bourguiba in bed, 1938 (horiz) 20 20
722 50m. Bourguiba acclaimed . . 35 30
723 80m. Bourguiba—"Builder of the Nation" (horiz) 45 30
SIZES: 30m., 80m. $13\frac{1}{2} \times 14$; 50m. As Type **182**.

183 Shah Mohammed Riza Pahlavi and Achaemenidian Effigy 184 Pimento

1971. 2500th Anniv of Persian Empire. Mult.
724 25m. Type **183** 30 20
725 50m. "King Bahram-Gur hunting" (14th-century) . . 35 20
726 100m. "Coronation of Louhrasap" (Persian 11th-century miniature) . . 60 30

1971. "Flowers, Fruits and Folklore". Mult.
728 1m. Type **184** 10 10
729 2m. Mint 20 15
730 5m. Pear 35 20
731 25m. Laurel rose 40 30
732 60m. Quince 80 20
733 100m. Grapefruit . . . . . 1·50 35
Each design includes a scene from Tunisian folklore.

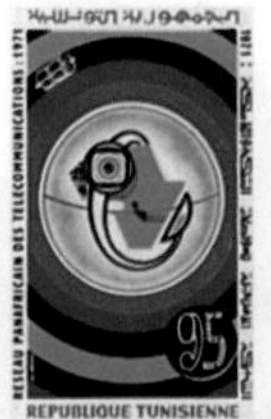
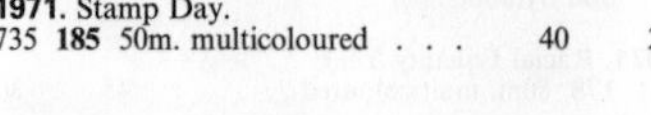

185 "The Musicians of Kerkena" 186 Telephone

1971. Stamp Day.
735 **185** 50m. multicoloured . . . 40 20

1971. Pan-African Telecommunications Network.
736 **186** 95m. multicoloured . . . 50 45

187 UNICEF Emblem 189 Olive-tree Emblem

188 Rialto Bridge, Venice

1971. 25th Anniv of UNICEF.
737 **187** 110m. multicoloured . . . 50 35

1971. UNESCO "Save Venice" Campaign. Multicoloured.
738 25m. Gondolier (vert) 35 20
739 30m. De Medici and Palace (vert) 40 20
740 50m. Prow of gondola (vert) 45 35
741 80m. Type **188** 80 35

1972. World Olive-oil Year.
742 **189** 60m. multicoloured . . . 40 20

190 Tunisian reading Book 191 Heart Emblem

1972. International Book Year.
743 **190** 90m. multicoloured . . . 50 40

1972. World Health Day. Multicoloured.
744 25m. Type **191** 35 20
745 60m. Heart within "hour-glass" 55 35

192 "Old Age" 193 "Only One Earth"

1972. Tunisian Red Crescent.
746 **192** 10m.+10m. violet & red 35 30
747 – 75m.+10m. brown & red 50 35
DESIGN: 75m. Mother and Child ("Child Care").

1972. U.N. Environmental Conservation Conf, Stockholm.
748 **193** 60m. green and brown . . 50 20

194 Hurdling 195 Chessboard

1972. Olympic Games, Munich.
749 – 5m. multicoloured 10 10
750 **194** 15m. multicoloured . . . 15 10
751 – 20m. black, green and gold 15 10
752 – 25m. multicoloured . . . 15 15
753 – 60m. multicoloured . . . 35 20
754 – 80m. multicoloured . . . 45 30
DESIGNS—VERT: 5m. Handball; 20m. Athletes saluting. HORIZ: 25m. Football; 60m. Swimming; 80m. Running.

1972. 20th Chess Olympiad, Skopje, Yugoslavia.
756 **195** 60m. multicoloured . . . 1·25 55

196 "The Fisherman"

1972. "Tunisian Life" (3rd series). Multicoloured.
757 5m. Type **196** 20 15
758 10m. "The Basket-maker" . . 20 15
759 25m. "The Musician" 30 15
760 50m. "The Berber Bride" . . 55 20
761 60m. "The Flower-seller" . . 80 20
762 80m. "The Mystic" . . . . . 1·10 40

197 New P.T.T. H.Q., Tunis

1972. Stamp Day.
764 **197** 25m. multicoloured . . . 30 20

198 Dome of the Rock, Jerusalem

1973. Dome of the Rock Commemoration.
765 **198** 25m. multicoloured . . . 40 30

199 Globe and Beribboned Pen

1973. 9th Writers' Congress and 11th Poetry Festival. Multicoloured.
766 25m. Type **199** 20 20
767 60m. Lyre emblem 35 20

200 Heads of Family 201 Figures "10" and Bird feeding Young

1973. Family Planning. Multicoloured.
768 20m. Type **200** 20 20
769 25m. Family profiles and bird 35 30

1973. 10th Anniv of World Food Programme. Multicoloured.
770 25m. Type **201** 60 20
771 60m. Symbolic "10" 60 20

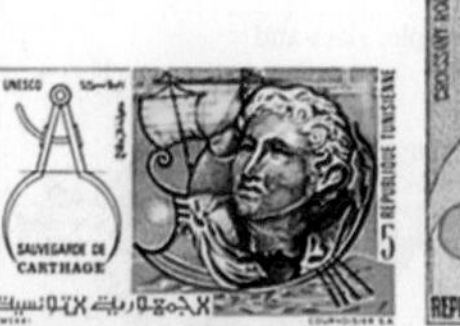

202 Sculptured Roman Head 203 Red Crescent Nurse

1973. UNESCO "Save Carthage" Campaign. Multicoloured.
772 5m. Type **202** 30 20
773 25m. Carthagian mosaics . . 45 35
774 30m. "Cycle of mosaics" . . 45 35
775 40m. "Goodwill" stele (vert) 60 35
776 60m. Preacher's hand (from Korba statue) 70 35
777 75m. "Malga" (17th-century potsherd) (vert) 85 40

1973. Tunisian Red Crescent.
779 **203** 25m.+10m. multicoloured 45 35
780 – 60m.+10m. red and grey 65 35
DESIGN—HORIZ: 60m. Arms of blood donors.

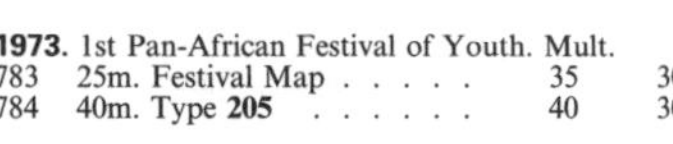

204 "World Telecommunications" 205 Smiling Youth

1973. 5th World Telecommunications Day. Mult.
781 60m. Type **204** 35 20
782 75m. "The Universe" 40 20

1973. 1st Pan-African Festival of Youth. Mult.
783 25m. Festival Map 35 30
784 40m. Type **205** 40 30

206 Scout Badge

1973. International Scouting.
785 **206** 25m. multicoloured . . . 35 30

207 "Rover" in Car

1973. 2nd Pan-Arab Rover Rally.
786 **207** 60m. multicoloured . . . 40 35

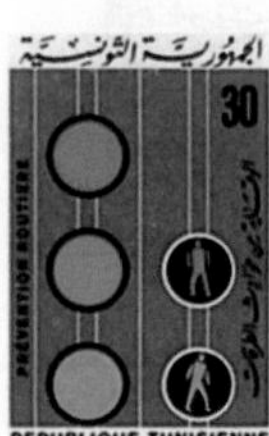

208 Traffic Lights 209 Winged Camel

1973. Road Safety. Multicoloured.
787 25m. Motorway junction (horiz) 35 30
788 30m. Type **208** 40 30

1973. Stamp Day. Multicoloured.
789 10m. Peacock ("collectors pride") (horiz) 35 20
790 65m. Type **209** 40 35

210 Copernicus 211 O.A.U. Emblems within Arms

1973. 500th Birth Anniv of Copernicus.
791 **210** 60m. multicoloured . . . 1·25 35

1973. 10th Anniv of Organization of African Unity.
792 **211** 25m. multicoloured . . . 40 20

212 Interpol Emblem and Handclasp
213 Flower Offering

1973. 50th Anniv of International Criminal Police Organization (Interpol).
793 **212** 65m. multicoloured . . . 45 35

1973. 25th Anniv of Declaration of Human Rights.
794 **213** 60m. multicoloured . . . 55 35

214 W.M.O. H.Q., Geneva

1973. W.M.O. Centenary. Multicoloured.
795 25m. Type **214** 40 20
796 60m. Earth and emblems . . 45 30

215 President Bourguiba, 1934
216 Scientist using Microscope

1974. 40th Anniv of Neo-Destour Party.
797 **215** 15m. purple, red and black 20 20
798 – 25m. brown, orange & black 20 20
799 – 60m. blue, red and black 30 20
800 – 75m. brown, mauve & black 35 20
801 – 100m. green, orange & black 45 35
DESIGNS: Nos. 798/801, Various portraits of Pres. Bourguiba (founder), similar to Type **215**.

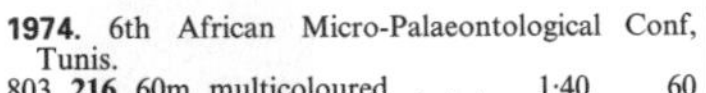

1974. 6th African Micro-Palaeontological Conf, Tunis.
803 **216** 60m. multicoloured . . . 1·40 60

217 "Blood Donation"
218 Telephonist holding Globe

1974. Tunisian Red Crescent. Multicoloured.
804 25m.+10m. Type **217** . . . 35 35
805 75m.+10m. "Blood Transfusion" 45 45

1974. Inauguration of International Automatic Telephone Service. Multicoloured.
806 15m. Type **218** 20 20
807 60m. Telephone dial 45 35

219 Population Emblems

1974. World Population Year.
808 **219** 110m. multicoloured . . . 55 35

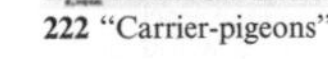
220 Pres. Bourguiba and Emblem
222 "Carrier-pigeons"

221 Aircraft crossing Globe

1974. Destourian Socialist Party Congress.
809 **220** 25m. blue, turquoise & black 20 20
810 – 60m. red, yellow and black 30 25
811 – 200m. purple, green & black 90 50
DESIGNS—HORIZ: 60m. Pres. Bourguiba and sunflower; 200m. Pres. Bourguiba and sunflower.

1974. 25th Anniv of Tunisian Aviation.
813 **221** 60m. multicoloured . . . 45 35

1974. Centenary of U.P.U. Multicoloured.
814 25m. Type **222** 35 25
815 60m. Handclasp 45 30

223 Bardo Palace as "Ballot Box"
224 Postman with Parcels on Head

1974. Legislative and Presidential Elections.
816 **223** 25m. blue, green and black 35 30
817 – 100m. black and orange 50 35
DESIGN: 100m. Pres. Bourguiba on poll card.

1974. Stamp Day.
818 **224** 75m. multicoloured . . . 45 20

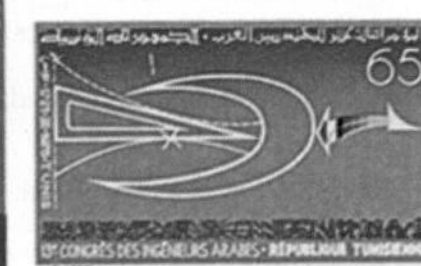

225 "The Water-carrier"
226 Stylized Bird

1975. "Scenes from Tunisian Life" (4th series). Multicoloured.
819 5m. Type **225** 15 15
820 15m. "The Scent Sprinkler" 20 20
821 25m. "The Washer-women" 20 20
822 60m. "The Potter" 35 20
823 110m. "The Fruit-seller" . . 85 50

1975. 13th Arab Engineers' Union Conference, Tunis. Multicoloured.
825 25m. Skyscraper and scaffolding (vert) 20 20
826 65m. Type **226** 75 30

227 Gold Coffee-pot and Tray

1975. Handicrafts. Multicoloured.
827 10m. Type **227** 20 20
828 15m. Horseman and saddlery (embroidery) 20 20
829 25m. Still life (painting) . . . 30 20
830 30m. Bird-cage (fine-crafts) (vert) 35 20
831 40m. Silver head-dress (jewellery) (vert) 35 20
832 60m. Textile patterns 55 30

228 Man and Scales
229 "Telecommunications"

1975. Tunisian Red Crescent Campaign against Malnutrition.
833 **228** 50m.+10m. mult 40 35

1975. 7th World Telecommunications Day.
834 **229** 50m. multicoloured . . . 30 20

230 Allegory of Victory
231 Tunisian Woman

1975. 20th Anniv of "Victory" (Return of Bourguiba). Multicoloured.
835 25m. Type **230** 20 20
836 65m. Return of President Bourguiba (horiz) 35 20

1975. International Women's Year.
837 **231** 110m. multicoloured . . . 55 30

232 Children on Road Crossing

1975. Road Safety Campaign.
838 **232** 25m. multicoloured . . . 20 20

233 Djerba

1975. "Tunisia, Yesterday and Today" (1st series). Multicoloured.
839 10m. Type **233** 20 20
840 15m. Tunis 20 20
841 20m. Monastir 20 20
842 65m. Sousse 45 30
843 500m. Tozeur . . . . 3·75 35
844 1d. Kairouan . . . . 6·25 2·50
See also Nos. 864/7.

234 Figures representing Sport
235 Bouquet of Flowers

1975. 7th Mediterranean Games, Algiers. Mult.
845 25m. Type **234** 20 20
846 50m. "Ship of sport" (horiz) 35 20

1975. Stamp Day.
847 **235** 100m. multicoloured . . . 45 20

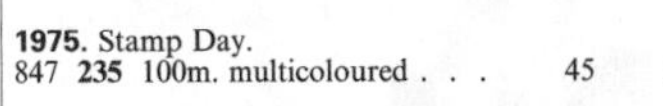

236 College Building

1975. Centenary of Sadiki College.
848 **236** 25m. multicoloured . . . 30 20

237 "Duck"
238 Early and Modern Telephones

1976. Tunisian Mosaics. Multicoloured.
849 5m. Type **237** 30 20
850 10m. Fish 30 20
851 25m. Lioness (40 × 27 mm) 55 45
852 60m. Gorgon (40 × 27 mm) 60 45
853 75m. Circus spectators (27 × 40 mm) 65 45
854 100m. Virgil (27 × 40 mm) . . 1·25 45

1976. Telephone Centenary.
856 **238** 150m. multicoloured . . . 55 30

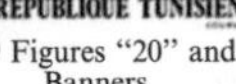

239 Figures "20" and Banners
240 Blind Man with Stick

1976. 20th Anniv of Independence. Mult.
857 40m. Type **239** 20 20
858 100m. Figures "20" and flag emblem 40 20
859 150m. Floral allegory of "Tunisia" 60 30

1976. World Health Day.
861 **240** 100m. black and red . . . 45 20

241 Blood Donation
242 "Urban Development"

1976. Tunisian Red Crescent.
862 **241** 40m.+10m. mult 40 30

1976. "Habitat" Human Settlements Conference, Vancouver.
863 **242** 40m. multicoloured . . . 30 20

243 Henna Tradition

1976. "Tunisia, Yesterday and Today" (2nd series). Multicoloured.
864 40m. Type **243** 20 20
865 50m. Diving for sponges . . 55 20
866 65m. Weaving 35 20
867 110m. Pottery 50 35

244 "Spirit of 1776" (Willard)

1976. Bicentenary of American Revolution.
868 **244** 200m. multicoloured . . . 1·40 65

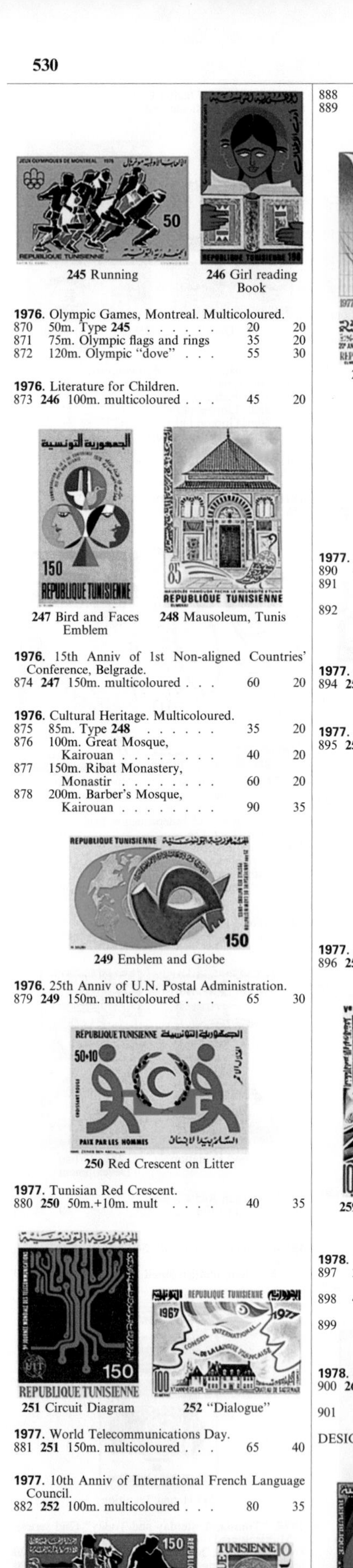

245 Running

246 Girl reading Book

1976. Olympic Games, Montreal. Multicoloured.

870	50m. Type **245**	20	20
871	75m. Olympic flags and rings	35	20
872	120m. Olympic "dove"	55	30

1976. Literature for Children.

873 **246**	100m. multicoloured	45	20

247 Bird and Faces Emblem

248 Mausoleum, Tunis

1976. 15th Anniv of 1st Non-aligned Countries' Conference, Belgrade.

874 **247**	150m. multicoloured	60	20

1976. Cultural Heritage. Multicoloured.

875	85m. Type **248**	35	20
876	100m. Great Mosque, Kairouan	40	20
877	150m. Ribat Monastery, Monastir	60	20
878	200m. Barber's Mosque, Kairouan	90	35

249 Emblem and Globe

1976. 25th Anniv of U.N. Postal Administration.

879 **249**	150m. multicoloured	65	30

250 Red Crescent on Litter

1977. Tunisian Red Crescent.

880 **250**	50m.+10m. mult	40	35

251 Circuit Diagram

252 "Dialogue"

1977. World Telecommunications Day.

881 **251**	150m. multicoloured	65	40

1977. 10th Anniv of International French Language Council.

882 **252**	100m. multicoloured	80	35

253 Footballers

254 Gold Coin

1977. 1st World Junior Football Tournament.

883 **253**	150m. multicoloured	90	45

1977. Cultural Patrimony. Multicoloured.

884	10m. Type **254**	10	10
885	15m. 13th-century stele	15	15
886	20m. 17th-century illuminated manuscript	20	15
887	30m. Glass painting	35	20
888	40m. Ceramic pot decor	40	20
889	50m. Gate, Sidi-Bou-Said	45	20

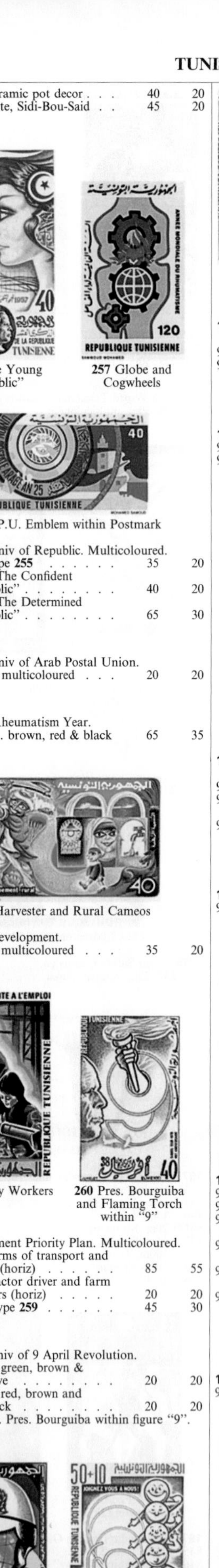

255 "The Young Republic"

257 Globe and Cogwheels

256 A.P.U. Emblem within Postmark

1977. 20th Anniv of Republic. Multicoloured.

890	40m. Type **255**	35	20
891	100m. "The Confident Republic"	40	20
892	150m. "The Determined Republic"	65	30

1977. 25th Anniv of Arab Postal Union.

894 **256**	40m. multicoloured	20	20

1977. World Rheumatism Year.

895 **257**	120m. brown, red & black	65	35

258 Harvester and Rural Cameos

1977. Rural Development.

896 **258**	40m. multicoloured	35	20

259 Factory Workers

260 Pres. Bourguiba and Flaming Torch within "9"

1978. Employment Priority Plan. Multicoloured.

897	20m. Forms of transport and driver (horiz)	85	55
898	40m. Tractor driver and farm workers (horiz)	20	20
899	100m. Type **259**	45	30

1978. 40th Anniv of 9 April Revolution.

900 **260**	40m. green, brown & olive	20	20
901 –	60m. red, brown and black	20	20

DESIGN: 60m. Pres. Bourguiba within figure "9".

261 Policeman in Safety Helmet

262 "Blood Donors"

1978. 6th African Regional Interpol Conference.

902 **261**	150m. multicoloured	80	35

1978. Tunisian Red Crescent.

903 **262**	50m.+10m. mult	45	30

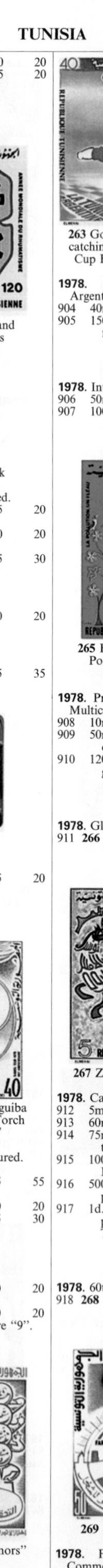

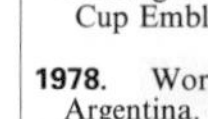

263 Goalkeeper catching World Cup Emblem

264 Hammer and Chisel chipping away Apartheid

1978. World Cup Football Championship, Argentina. Multicoloured.

904	40m. Type **263**	30	20
905	150m. Footballer, map and flags	85	35

1978. International Anti-Apartheid Year. Mult.

906	50m. Type **264**	20	20
907	100m. Black and white doves	45	30

265 Flora, Fauna and Polluting Factory

266 Crane removing Smallpox from Globe

1978. Protection of Nature and the Environment. Multicoloured.

908	10m. Type **265**	15	15
909	50m. "Pollution of the oceans"	40	20
910	120m. "Making the deserts green"	95	20

1978. Global Eradication of Smallpox.

911 **266**	150m. multicoloured	65	35

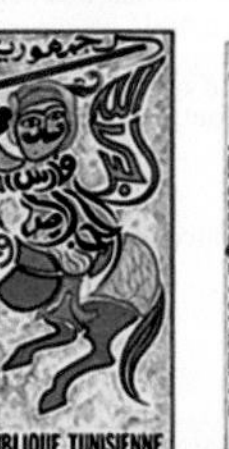

267 Zlass Horseman

268 Lenin Banner

1978. Calligraphy, Art and Traditions. Mult.

912	5m. Type **267**	10	10
913	60m. Djerba wedding	30	15
914	75m. Women potters from the Mogods	40	15
915	100m. Dove over cupolas of Marabout Sidi Mahrez	45	20
916	500m. Opening of the ploughing season, Jenduba	3·25	1·00
917	1d. Man on swing between palm trees (Spring Festival, Tozeur)	5·50	2·25

1978. 60th Anniv of Russian Revolution.

918 **268**	150m. multicoloured	1·10	45

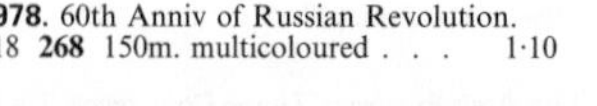

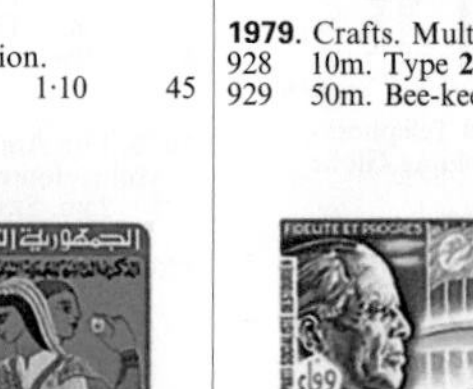

269 Farhat Hached

270 Family Group

1978. Farhat Hached (Trade Union leader). Commemoration.

919 **269**	50m. multicoloured	35	10

1978. 10th Anniv of Tunisian Family Planning Association.

920 **270**	50m. multicoloured	40	20

271 "The Sun"

273 Hand holding Bird

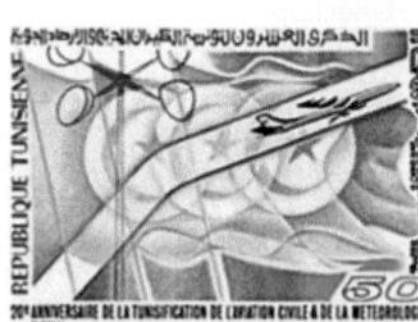

272 Boeing 747 and Flags

1978. Solar Energy.

921 **271**	100m. multicoloured	60	20

1978. 20th Anniv of Tunisian Civil Aeronautics and Meteorology.

922 **272**	50m. multicoloured	30	20

1979. Tunisian Red Crescent.

923 **273**	50m.+10m. mult	40	30

274 Pres. Bourguiba

275 Sun, Yacht and Golfer

1979. 20th Anniv of Constitution.

924 **274**	50m. brown, yellow & black	20	20

1979. Inauguration of El Kantaoui Port.

925 **275**	150m. multicoloured	65	30

276 Korbous

277 Bow-net Making

1979. Tunisian Landscapes. Multicoloured.

926	50m. Type **276**	15	10
927	100m. Mides	35	15

1979. Crafts. Multicoloured.

928	10m. Type **277**	15	10
929	50m. Bee-keeping	35	10

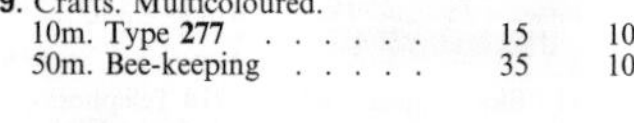

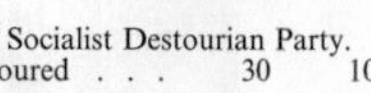

278 Pres. Bourguiba and "10"

279 Dish Aerial and Satellite

1979. 10th Congress of Socialist Destourian Party.

930 **278**	50m. multicoloured	30	10

1979. 3rd World Telecommunications Exhibition, Geneva.

931 **279**	150m. multicoloured	65	35

280 World Map, Koran and Symbols of Arab Achievements   **281** Children crossing Road

1979. The Arabs.
932 **280** 50m. multicoloured . . . 20 15

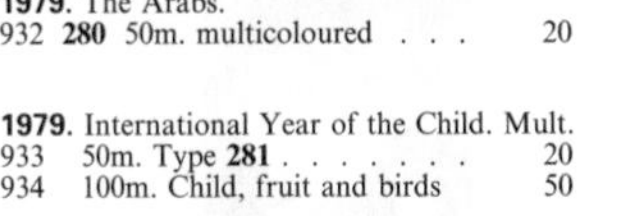

1979. International Year of the Child. Mult.
933 50m. Type **281** 20 15
934 100m. Child, fruit and birds 50 20

282 Dove and Olive Tree   **283** Symbolic Figure

1979. 2nd World Olive-oil Year.
935 **282** 150m. multicoloured . . . 80 35

1979. 20th Anniv of Central Bank of Tunisia.
936 **283** 50m. multicolourd 20 20

284 Children and Jujube Tree

1979. Animals and Plants. Multicoloured.
937 20m. Type **284** 20 10
938 30m. Common peafowl . . . 40 25
939 70m. Goat 65 20
940 85m. Girl and date palm . . 70 20

285 Coded Letter

1980. Introduction of Postal Coding.
941 **285** 50m. multicoloured . . . 30 20

286 Smoker

1980. World Health Day. Anti-smoking Campaign.
942 **286** 150m. multicoloured . . . 65 30

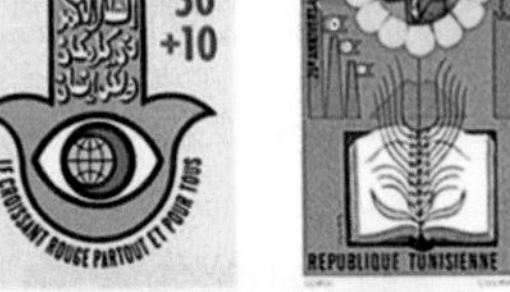

287 Red Crescent and Globe forming an Eye   **288** President Bourguiba, Flower and Open Book

1980. Tunisian Red Crescent.
943 **287** 50m.+10m. mult 40 30

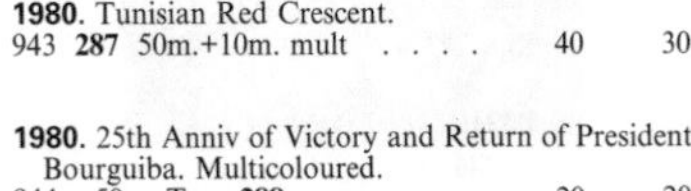

1980. 25th Anniv of Victory and Return of President Bourguiba. Multicoloured.
944 50m. Type **288** 20 20
945 100m. Pres. Bourguiba, dove and mosque 85 35

289 Gymnast as Butterfly   **290** Tools

1980. Turin Gymnastic Games.
946 **289** 100m. multicoloured . . . 45 20

1980. Handicrafts. Multicoloured.
947 30m. Type **290** 30 20
948 75m. Woman embroidering 40 20

291 Ibn Khaldoun (philosopher)   **292** Avicenna

1980. Ibn Khaldoun Commemoration.
949 **291** 50m. multicoloured . . . 20 20

1980. Birth Millenary of Avicenna (philosopher).
950 **292** 100m. sepia and brown 65 35

293 Al-Biruni and Scientific Diagram

1980. The Arabs' Contribution to Science.
951 **293** 50m. multicoloured . . . 35 20

294 Yachts at Sidi Bou Said

1980. Sidi Bou Said.
952 **294** 100m. multicoloured . . . 65 35

295 "Tourists"

1980. World Tourism Conference, Manila.
953 **295** 150m. multicoloured . . . 55 20

296 "Wedding at Djerba"

1980. Yahia (painter) Commemoration.
954 **296** 50m. multicoloured . . . 40 30

297 Aircraft over Tozeur   **299** Spider's Web

298 "Eye"

1980. Opening of Tozeur International Airport.
955 **297** 85m. multicoloured . . . 35 20

1980. 7th Afro-Asian Congress on Ophthalmology.
956 **298** 100m. multicoloured . . . 55 35

1980. 1400th Anniv of Hegira. Multicoloured.
957 50m. Type **299** 20 20
958 80m. Minarets 35 20

300 Face as Camera

1980. Carthage Cinematographic Days.
959 **300** 100m. multicoloured . . . 45 30

301 "Ophrys scolopax scolopax"

1980. Flora and Fauna. Multicoloured.
960 20m. Type **301** 20 20
961 25m. "Cyclamen europaeum" 20 20
962 50m. Mouflon 20 20
963 100m. Golden eagle 90 40

302 Kairouan Mosque

1980. Conservation of Kairouan.
964 **302** 85m. multicoloured . . . 35 20

303 H. von Stephan   **304** Hands holding Bottle containing Blood Drop

1981. 150th Birth Anniv of Heinrich von Stephan (founder of U.P.U.).
965 **303** 150m. multicoloured . . . 65 35

1981. 20th Anniv of Tunisian Blood Donors Association.
966 **304** 75m. multicoloured . . . 65 45

305 Flags and Pres. Bourguiba

1981. 25th Anniv of Independence. Multicoloured.
967 50m. Type **305** 20 20
968 60m. Stork and ribbons forming "25" 35 20
969 85m. Stylized birds 55 35
970 120m. Victory riding a winged horse 55 35

306 Flower and Pres. Bourguiba

1981. Special Congress of Destourian Socialist Party. Multicoloured.
972 50m. Type **306** 20 15
973 75m. Arrows forming flower 35 20

307 Mosque, Mahdia and Galley

1981. Tourism. Multicoloured.
974 50m. Type **307** 20 20
975 85m. Djerid bride passing Great Mosque of Tozeur (vert) 35 30
976 100m. Needle rocks, Tabarka 45 30

308 Stylized Peacock hatching Egg

1981. Red Crescent.
977 **308** 50m.+10m. mult 35 35

309 I.T.U. and W.H.O. Emblems and Ribbons forming Caduceus   **310** Flowers and Youths

1981. World Telecommunications Day.
978 **309** 150m. multicoloured . . . 60 30

1981. Youth Festival.
979 **310** 100m. multicoloured . . . 45 20

311 Kemal Ataturk   **312** Skifa Khala, Mahdia

1981. Birth Centenary of Kemal Ataturk.
980 **311** 150m. multicoloured . . . 65 35

1981. Tunisian Monuments.
981 **312** 150m. multicoloured . . . 65 35

313 Cheikh Mohamed Tahar ben Achour and Minaret

1981. Cheikh Mohamed Tahar ben Achour (scholar and teacher) Commemoration.
982 **313** 200m. multicoloured . . . 1·00 45

314 Rejoicing Woman

315 Tree with Broken Branch

1981. 25th Anniv of Personal Status Code. Multicoloured.
983 50m. Type **314** 20 20
984 100m. Dove and head of woman 40 30

1981. International Year of Disabled People.
985 **315** 250m. multicoloured . . . 1·00 65

316 Stylized Figure and Ka'aba, Mecca

317 Food Sources

1981. Pilgrimage to Mecca.
986 **316** 50m. multicoloured . . . 30 20

1981. World Food Day.
987 **317** 200m. multicoloured . . . 90 50

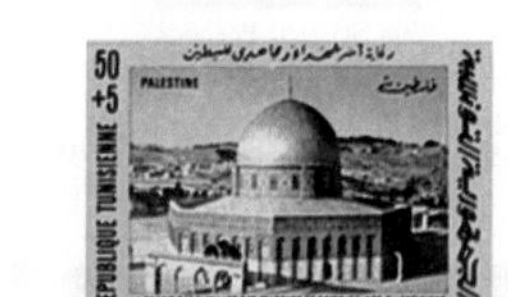
318 Dome of the Rock

1981. Palestinian Welfare.
988 **318** 50m.+5m. mult 35 20
989 150m.+5m. mult 60 35
990 200m.+5m. mult 90 50

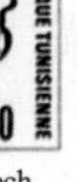
319 Mnaguech (earring)

321 Chemist (detail from 13th-century manuscript)

320 Ship passing under Bridge

1981. Jewellery. Multicoloured.
991 150m. Type **319** 60 30
992 180m. Mahfdha (pendant) (horiz) 70 35
993 200m. Essalta (hairnet) . . . 90 40

1981. Bizerta Drawbridge.
994 **320** 230m. multicoloured . . . 80 40

1982. Arab Pharmacists' Union.
995 **321** 80m. multicoloured . . . 55 35

322 Ring of People around Red Crescent

1982. Red Crescent.
996 **322** 80m.+10m. mult 40 30

323 "Ocean Research"

324 "Productive Family"

1982. International Symposium "Ocean Venture", Tunis.
997 **323** 150m. multicoloured . . . 80 45

1982. The Productive Family.
998 **324** 80m. multicoloured . . . 35 20

325 Pres. Bourguiba and Woman's Head

326 Scout within "50"

1982. 25th Anniv of Republic.
999 **325** 80m. blue and black . . 30 20
1000 – 100m. multicoloured . . 40 30
1001 – 200m. multicoloured . . 65 35
DESIGNS: 100m. President and woman with "XXV" headband; 200m. President and woman with "25" in hair.

1982. 75th Anniv of Scout Movement and 50th Anniv of Tunisian Scout Movement. Multicoloured.
1003 80m. Type **326** 35 20
1004 200m. Scout camp (vert) . . 65 20

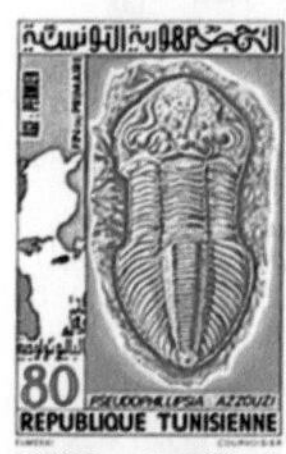
327 "Pseudophillipsia azzouzi"

328 Tunisian Woman

1982. Fossils. Multicoloured.
1005 80m. Type **327** 45 35
1006 200m. "Mediterraneo-trigonia cherahilensis" . . 1·40 65
1007 280m. "Numidiopleura enigmatica" (fish) (horiz) 2·50 1·40
1008 300m. "Micreschara tunisiensis" . . . . 2·00 1·40
1009 500m. "Mantelliceras pervinquieri" . . . . . 3·75 2·00
1010 1000m. "Elephas africanavus" (horiz) . . . 6·25 3·00

1982. 30th Anniv of Arab Postal Union.
1011 **328** 80m. multicoloured . . . 40 20

329 I.T.U. Emblem

330 Tunisian Buildings and Congress Centre

1982. I.T.U. Delegates' Conference, Nairobi.
1012 **329** 200m. multicoloured . . 65 45

1982. "Tunisia Land of Congresses".
1013 **330** 200m. multicoloured . . 65 30

331 "Feeding the World"

332 Tahar Haddad

1982. World Food Day.
1014 **331** 200m. multicoloured . . 65 30

1982. Tahar Haddad (social reformer) Commem.
1015 **332** 200m. brown 80 35

333 Microscope

334 Figure dancing in Rain

1982. Cent of Discovery of Tubercle Bacillus.
1016 **333** 100m. multicoloured . . 55 30

1982. Stories and Songs from Tunisia. Multicoloured.
1017 20m. Type **334** 15 15
1018 30m. Woman with broom 15 15
1019 70m. Boy and fisherman . . 20 15
1020 80m. Chicken (horiz) . . . 30 20
1021 100m. Woman admiring herself in mirror (horiz) 40 20
1022 120m. Two girls 45 30

335 Clasped Hands and Palestine Flag

1982. Palestinian Solidarity Day.
1023 **335** 80m. multicoloured . . . 30 20

336 Farhat Hached

337 Bourguiba Sidi Saad Dam

1982. 30th Death Anniv of Farhat Hached.
1024 **336** 80m. red 35 20

1982. Inauguration of Bourguiba Sidi Saad Dam.
1025 **337** 80m. multicoloured . . . 45 20

338 Environment Emblem on Blackboard

339 Giving Blood

1982. Opening of Environment Training Work School.
1026 **338** 80m. multicoloured . . . 35 15

1983. Red Crescent.
1027 **339** 80m.+10m. mult 50 30

340 "Communications"

1983. World Communications Year.
1028 **340** 200m. multicoloured . . 55 30

341 Dove and Map of Africa

1983. 20th Anniv of Organization of African Unity.
1029 **341** 230m. blue and deep blue 65 40

342 Customs Officer, Globes and Suitcases

1983. 20th Anniv of Customs Co-operation Council.
1030 **342** 100m. multicoloured . . 35 20

343 Aly Ben Ayed

344 Carved Face, El Mekta

1983. Aly Ben Ayed (actor) Commemoration.
1031 **343** 80m. red, black and deep red 30 30

1983. Pre-historic Artefacts. Multicoloured.
1032 15m. Type **344** 20 20
1033 20m. Neolithic necklace, Kef el Agab (horiz) 30 20
1034 30m. Neolithic grindstone, Redeyef (horiz) 30 20
1035 40m. Animal petroglyph, Gafsa 35 20
1036 80m. Dolmen, Mactar (horiz) 40 30
1037 100m. Bi-face flint, El Mekta 55 30

345 Dove, Barbed Wire and Dome of the Rock

1983. Palestinian Welfare.
1038 **345** 80m.+5m. mult 40 40

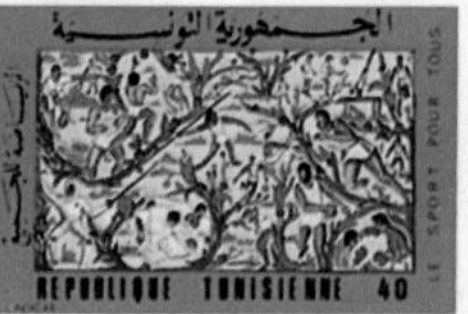
346 Sporting Activities

1983. Sport for All.
1039 **346** 40m. multicoloured . . . 15 10

347 Tunisian with Flag and "Destour" (French freighter)

1983. 20th Anniv of Evacuation of Foreign Troops.
1040 **347** 80m. multicoloured . . . 30 20

348 Fishing Boats and Fishes

1983. World Fishing Day.
1041 **348** 200m. multicoloured . . 1·00 25

349 "The Weaver" (Hedi Khayachi)

1983. Hedi Khayachi (painter) Commem.
1042 **349** 80m. multicoloured . . . 45 35

350 Saluting the Flag **351** Air Hostess and Airliner

1983. Salute to the Flag.
1043 **350** 100m. multicoloured . . 35 20

1983. 25th Anniv of Tunisian Civil Aviation and Meteorology.
1044 **351** 150m. multicoloured . . 55 20

352 Pres. Bourguiba and Archway **353** Map of Africa

1984. 50th Anniv of Neo-Destour Party. Mult.
1045 40m. Type **352** 15 10
1046 70m. Bourguiba and torch 20 10
1047 80m. Bourguiba and flag . . 30 15
1048 150m. Bourguiba and wall 50 30
1049 200m. Bourguiba and dove (horiz) 60 35
1050 230m. Pres. Bourguiba (horiz) 70 45

1984. 4th School of Molecular Biology.
1052 **353** 100m. multicoloured . . 55 30

354 First Aid

1984. Red Crescent.
1053 **354** 80m.+10m. mult 40 30

355 Ibn el Jazzar **356** "Co-operation"

1984. Ibn el Jazzar (doctor) Commem.
1054 **355** 80m. multicoloured . . . 40 30

1984. Economic Co-operation among Developing Countries.
1055 **356** 230m. multicoloured . . 80 35

357 Witch, Maiden and Coquette

1984. Stories and Songs from Tunisia. Mult.
1056 20m. Type **357** 10 10
1057 80m. Puppet, hands and mouse 30 20
1058 100m. Boy and horse (vert) 35 15

358 Family facing the Future

1984. 20th Anniv of Tunisian Education and Family Organization.
1059 **358** 80m. multicoloured . . . 30 20

359 Medina, Tunis **360** Aboul Qasim Chabbi

1984. National Heritage Protection.
1060 **359** 100m. multicoloured . . 35 30

1984. 50th Death Anniv of Aboul Qasim Chabbi (poet).
1061 **360** 100m. sepia, light brown and brown 35 20

361 Emblem, Stylized Bird and Airplane

1984. 40th Anniv of International Civil Aviation Organization.
1062 **361** 200m. multicoloured . . 65 20

362 Band and Singers

1984. Sahara Festival.
1063 **362** 20m. multicoloured . . . 45 20

363 Telephonist, Satellite and Dish Aerial

1984. 20th Anniv of "Intelsat" Communication Satellite.
1064 **363** 100m. multicoloured . . 35 15

364 "Mediterranean Countryside"

1984. Jilani Abdulwahelb (artist) Commem.
1065 **364** 100m. multicoloured . . 55 35

365 Profile and Exterior of House **366** Crescents and Stars within Circle

1985. "Expo 85" World's Fair, Tsukuba.
1066 **365** 200m. multicoloured . . 65 35

1985. Red Crescent.
1067 **366** 100m.+10m. mult . . . 35 30

367 Hands reaching from Sea and Flames **368** Pres. Bourguiba on Horseback

1985. 3rd Civil Protection Week.
1068 **367** 100m. multicoloured . . 30 15

1985. 30th Anniv of Independence. Mult.
1069 75m. Type **368** 20 10
1070 100m. Pres. Bourguiba in boat and crowd on quay (horiz) 30 10
1071 200m. Pres. Bourguiba in sombrero 55 20
1072 230m. Pres. Bourguiba waving to crowd from balcony (horiz) 60 20

369 Pres. Bourguiba and Ancient Sculpture

1985. Tunisian Day at "Expo '85" World's Fair, Tsukuba.
1074 **369** 250m. multicoloured . . 80 30

370 Images within Film **372** Heart as Dove and I.Y.Y. Emblem

371 Dark Clouds, Sun and Flowers

1985. International Amateur Film Festival, Kelibia.
1075 **370** 250m. multicoloured . . 1·50 1·10

1985. Stories and Songs from Tunisia. Multicoloured.
1076 25m. Type **371** 10 10
1077 50m. Man's profile and hand holding women . . 15 10
1078 100m. Man and cooking pot over fire 35 15

1985. International Youth Year.
1079 **372** 250m. multicoloured . . 80 30

373 "The Perfumiers Hall"

1985. Painting by Hedi Larnaout.
1080 **373** 100m. multicoloured . . 45 20

374 Matmata Wedding Dress **375** Stylized People and U.N. Emblem

1985. Wedding Dresses (1st series). Mult.
1081 20m. Type **374** 10 10
1082 50m. Moknine dress 15 10
1083 100m. Tunis dress 35 15
See also Nos. 1099/1101.

1985. 40th Anniv of U.N.O.
1084 **375** 250m. multicoloured . . 80 30

376 Harvest (Makthar stele)

1985. Food Self-sufficiency.
1085 **376** 100m. multicoloured . . 35 20

377 Emblem illuminating Globe and Flags **378** Aziza Othmana

1985. 40th Anniv of Arab League.
1086 **377** 100m. multicoloured . . 30 15

1985. Aziza Othmana (founder of hospitals) Commemoration.
1087 **378** 100m. brown, green and red 45 20

379 Surveying Instruments and Books forming Face **380** Dove and Pres. Bourguiba

1985. Centenary of Land Law.
1088 **379** 100m. multicoloured . . 30 10

1986. 30th Anniv of Independence.
1089 **380** 100m. multicoloured . . 30 10
1090 – 120m. black, blue and deep blue 35 15
1091 – 280m. blue, violet and black 80 35
1092 – 300m. multicoloured . . 85 40
DESIGNS—HORIZ: 120m. Rocket; 280m. Horse and rider. VERT: 300m. Balloons.

381 Hulusi Behcet (dermatologist) **382** Map and Red Crescent

1986. 3rd Mediterranean Rheumatology Days, Tunis, and Ninth International Society of Geographical Ophthalmology Congress, Monastir. Multicoloured.
1094 300m. Type **381** . . . . . 1·25 35
1095 380m. Behcet and sun and eye emblems . . . . . . 1·60 45

1986. World Red Crescent and Red Cross Day.
1096 **382** 120m.+10m. mult . . . 40 30

383 Pres. Bourguiba, Symbols and "12"

1986. 12th Destourian Socialist Party Congress, Tunis. Multicoloured.
1097 120m. Type **383** 30 10
1098 300m. Flaming torch, Pres. Bourguiba and "12" . . . 85 30

384 Homt Souk Dress **385** Hassen Husni Abdulwaheb

1986. Wedding Dresses (2nd series). Mult.
1099 40m. Type **384** 10 10
1100 280m. Mahdia dress 80 30
1101 300m. Nabeul dress 90 35

1986. Hassen Husni Abdulwaheb (historian) Commemoration.
1102 **385** 160m. red 55 20

386 Reconstructed View of Carthage

1986. 2800th Anniv of Foundation of Carthage.
1103 **386** 2d. purple . . . . 6·75 2·50

387 Arrow Head, El Borma, 3000 B.C. **388** "Bedouins"

1986. Prehistoric Artefacts. Multicoloured.
1104 10m. Type **387** 20 20
1105 20m. Tomb, Sejnane, 1000 B.C. 20 20
1106 50m. Bas-relief, Zaghouan, 1000 B.C. (horiz) 35 20
1107 120m. Neolithic vase, Kesra (horiz) 55 20
1108 160m. Painting of Phoenician ship, Kef el Blida, 800 B.C. (horiz) . . 65 20
1109 250m. 7th-century decorated pottery, Sejnane . . . . . 1·40 35

1986. Painting by Ammar Farhat.
1110 **388** 250m. multicoloured . . 1·25 35

389 Doves and Globe

1986. International Peace Year.
1111 **389** 300m. multicoloured . . 85 35

390 Emblem **391** Computer Terminal

1986. 40th Anniv of F.A.O.
1112 **390** 280m. multicoloured . . 80 30

1986. Introduction of Computers into Education.
1113 **391** 2d. multicoloured . . . 6·75 2·50

392 Mother and Child **393** Mountain Gazelle (Chambi National Park)

1986. Child Survival.
1114 **392** 120m. multicoloured . . 35 10

1986. National Parks. Multicoloured.
1115 60m. Type **393** 15 10
1116 120m. Addax (Bou Hedma National Park) 30 10
1117 350m. Monk seal (Zembra and Zembretta National Park) 85 30
1118 380m. Greylag goose (Ichkeul National Park) 1·25 40

394 Pres. Bourguiba and Arms

1987. Centenary of Monastir Municipality.
1119 **394** 120m. multicoloured . . 35 15

395 Radiation and Red Crescent Symbols in Face

1987. Radiation Protection and Red Crescent.
1120 **395** 150m.+10m. mult . . . 55 45

396 Samuel Morse (inventor) and Morse Key

1987. 150th Anniv of Morse Telegraph.
1121 **396** 500m. multicoloured . . 1·40 55

397 Pres. Bourguiba and Woman's Head

1987. 30th Anniv of Republic. Designs each show Pres. Bourguiba and a different woman's head.
1122 **397** 150m. mve, brn and yell 35 25
1123 – 250m. brown, red & yell 55 25
1124 – 350m. blue, brn & grn 80 20
1125 – 500m. multicoloured . . 1·10 35

398 Hand injecting Baby in Globe and Dove holding Syringe **399** "The Road"

1987. Universal Vaccination for Everyone by 1990. 40th Anniv of United Nations Children's Fund.
1127 **398** 250m. multicoloured . . 65 45

1987. 25th Death Anniv of Azouz Ben Rais (painter).
1128 **399** 250m. multicoloured . . 90 45

400 Couple's Faces in House

1987. Arab Housing Day.
1129 **400** 150m. multicoloured . . 40 30

401 Dove carrying Parcel **402** Ibn Mandhour

1987. 30th Anniv of Consultative Postal Studies Council. Multicoloured.
1130 150m. Type **401** 35 10
1131 350m. Postman and electronically sorted letters 80 30

1987. 675th Death Anniv of Ibn Mandhour (lexicographer).
1132 **402** 250m. purple 80 45

403 Bunches of Grapes **404** Player with Ball

1987. International Vine Year.
1133 **403** 250m. multicoloured . . 80 35

1987. 6th African Nations Volleyball Championship, Tunis.
1134 **404** 350m. multicoloured . . 1·10 45

405 Players and Ball **406** Tunis Institute and Adrien Loir (first director)

1987. African Basketball Championships.
1135 **405** 350m. multicoloured . . 1·40 45

1987. Centenary of Pasteur Institute, Paris.
1136 **406** 250m. green, brown and black 80 35

407 Midoun **408** Narcissi

1987. Costumes. Multicoloured.
1137 20m. Type **407** 10 10
1138 30m. Tozeur 10 10
1139 150m. Sfax 40 15

1987. Flowers. Multicoloured.
1140 30m. Type **408** 10 10
1141 150m. Gladioli 40 15
1142 400m. Iris . . . . 1·00 35
1143 500m. Tulips . . . . 1·50 55

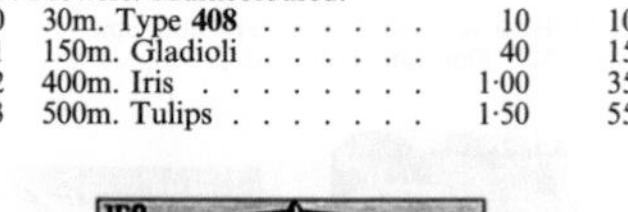

409 Hand holding Scales of Justice

1988. Declaration of 7 November 1987. Mult.
1144 150m. Type **409** (Justice for all) 35 20
1145 200m. Girl with party badges as flowers in hair (Multi-party system) (vert) 45 20
1146 350m. Girl in cornfield wearing coat of arms (International co-operation and friendship) 80 35
1147 370m. Maghreb states emblem (vert) 90 35

410 Couple

1988. Youth and Change. Multicoloured.
1149 75m. Type **410** 20 15
1150 150m. Young people 35 15

411 Crowd with Banners

1988. 50th Anniv of Martyrs' Day.
1151 **411** 150m. orange and brown 35 15
1152 – 500m. multicoloured . . 1·40 40
DESIGN: 500m. Martyrs monument.

412 Roses and Banners

1988. 125th Anniv of Red Cross.
1153 **412** 150m.+10m. mult . . . 45 35

413 Hand saving drowning Country

1988. 1st Democratic Constitutional Assembly Congress.
1154 **413** 150m. multicoloured . . 35 15

414 Sportsmen

1988. Olympic Games, Seoul. Multicoloured.
1155 150m. Type **414** 40 20
1156 430m. Sportsman (different) 1·00 45

415 Beit Hussein Sari and Eye

416 "7" and Flowers

1988. Restoration of Sana'a, Yemen.
1157 **415** 200m. multicoloured . . 45 20

1988. 1st Anniv of Presidency of Zine el Abidine.
1158 **416** 150m. multicoloured . . 35 15

417 "Amilcar Beach, 1942"

1988. 70th Birth Anniv of Amara Debbeche (painter).
1159 **417** 100m. multicoloured . . 35 20

418 Boeing 747 and Globe forming "40"

419 Man holding Book

1988. 40th Anniv of Tunis Air.
1160 **418** 500m. multicoloured . . 1·50 70

1988. 40th Anniv of Declaration of Human Rights.
1161 **419** 370m. black 85 45

420 Tweezers and Magnifying Glasses forming "100"

1988. Cent of First Tunisian Postage Stamps.
1162 **420** 150m. multicoloured . . 55 30

421 18th-century Door, Rue du Tresor

422 Ali Douagi

1988. Tunis Doorways and Fountains. Mult.
1163 50m. Type **421** 10 10
1164 70m. 19th-century door, Rue el Mbazaa 15 10
1165 100m. 15th-16th century door, Rue des Fabricants de Tamis 20 10
1166 150m. 19th-century door, Rue Bach Hamba 30 15
1167 370m. 16th-17th century door, Rue el Ariane . . . 70 30
1168 400m. Fountain, Manouba, 1793 . . . . 80 35

1989. 40th Death Anniv of Ali Douagi (writer).
1169 **422** 1d. blue . . . . 2·50 65

423 Stretcher Bearers

424 Crippled Person and Healthy Girl

1989. Red Crescent.
1170 **423** 150m.+10m. mult . . . 40 30

1989. National Day for Disabled People.
1171 **424** 150m. multicoloured . . 45 20

425 Children using Computer and Microscope

1989. Knowledge Day.
1172 **425** 180m. multicoloured . . 40 20

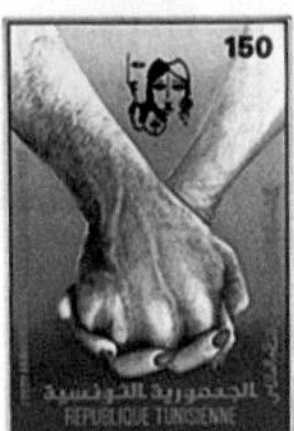

426 Clasped Hands

1989. 20th Anniv of Tunisian Family Planning Association.
1173 **426** 150m. multicoloured . . 35 15

427 Family

1989. Family Welfare.
1174 **427** 150m. multicoloured . . 35 15

428 Tortoise

1989. Endangered Animals. Multicoloured.
1175 250m. Type **428** 65 35
1176 350m. Oryx . . . . 1·00 45

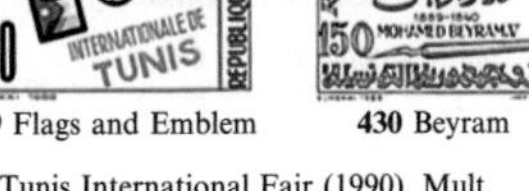

429 Flags and Emblem

430 Beyram

1989. Tunis International Fair (1990). Mult.
1177 150m. Type **429** 35 15
1178 370m. Fair Pavilion 80 35

1989. Death Centenary of Mohamed Beyram (writer).
1179 **430** 150m. purple and black 35 15

431 Actors wearing Comedy Masks

432 Monument, Tunis

1989. Carthage Theatre Festival.
1180 **431** 300m. multicoloured . . 65 35

1989. 2nd Anniv of Declaration of 7 November 1987.
1181 **432** 150m. multicoloured . . 35 20

433 Nehru

434 Members' Flags

1989. Birth Centenary of Jawaharlal Nehru (Indian statesman).
1182 **433** 300m. brown 65 35

1990. Maghreb Union Presidential Summit.
1183 **434** 200m. multicoloured . . 45 30

435 Museum and Sculptures

1990. Centenary of Bardo Museum.
1184 **435** 300m. multicoloured . . 80 45

436 Ceramic Tiles, Vases and Crockery

1990. Arts and Crafts. Multicoloured.
1185 75m. Type **436** 15 10
1186 100m. Copper pots and grinder 20 15

437 Ram and Ewes

1990. Ram Museum. Multicoloured.
1187 400m. Type **437** 90 35
1188 450m. Ram's head . . . . 1·25 45

438 Houses within Crescent

440 Child's Drawing

439 Olympic Rings and Athlete

1990. Red Crescent.
1190 **438** 150m.+10m. mult . . . 35 20

1990. Tunisian Olympic Movement.
1191 **439** 150m. multicoloured . . 35 15

1990. The Child and the Environment.
1192 **440** 150m. multicoloured . . 35 15

441 Sbiba Horseman

442 Dougga

1990. Costumes. Multicoloured.
1193 150m. Type **441** 45 35
1194 500m. Bou Omrane man . . 1·40 65

1990. Tourism.
1195 **442** 300m. multicoloured . . 65 35

443 Adults learning to Read and Write

1990. International Literacy Year.
1196 **443** 120m. multicoloured . . 30 15

444 Figures, Tree and Fishes in Water

445 Fireworks and Date

1990. Water.
1197 **444** 150m. multicoloured . . 45 30

1990. 3rd Anniv of Declaration of 7 November 1987. Multicoloured.
1198 150m. Type **445** 35 15
1199 150m. Clock tower 35 15

446 Kheireddine et Tounsi

447 Red Deer

1990. Death Centenary of Kheireddine et Tounsi (political reformer).
1200 **446** 150m. green 45 20

1990. Flora and Fauna. Multicoloured.
1201 150m. Type **447** 35 15
1202 200m. Thistle 45 15

1203 300m. Water buffalo 65 20
1204 600m. Orchid . . . . 1·40 55

448 Members' Flags forming Stars

449 Montazah Tabarka

1991. 2nd Anniv of Maghreb Union.
1205 **448** 180m. multicoloured . . 45 20

1991. Tourism.
1206 **449** 450m. multicoloured . . 1·00 45

450 Doves and Emblem

451 Common Seabream

1991. Red Crescent. Help for War Victims.
1207 **450** 180m.+10m. mult . . . 45 35

1991. Fishes. Multicoloured.
1208 180m. Type **451** 65 30
1209 350m. Striped red mullet . . 1·25 55
1210 450m. Atlantic mackerel . . 1·60 65
1211 550m. Common pandora . . 2·00 1·00

452 Vase of Flowers (Taieb Khlif)

1991. Children's Rights.
1212 **452** 450m. multicoloured . . 1·25 35

453 "Plein-Sud" (anon.)

1991.
1213 **453** 400m. multicoloured . . 90 35

454 Bracelets and Ring

455 Date and Profile of Woman

1991. Jewellery. Multicoloured.
1214 120m. Type **454** 30 15
1215 180m. Headdress and necklace (vert) 40 15
1216 220m. Headdress, earrings and collar (vert) 45 20
1217 730m. Key-ring (vert) . . . 2·25 80

1991. 4th Anniv of Declaration of 7 November 1987.
1218 **455** 180m. multicoloured . . 45 20

456 Sorting Office

1991. Tunis-Carthage Sorting Office.
1219 **456** 80m. blue, red and green 20 10

457 Dove and Globe

458 Bayram Ettounsi

1991. World Human Rights Day.
1220 **457** 450m. blue . . . . . . 1·25 35

1991. 31st Death Anniv of Bayram Ettounsi.
1221 **458** 200m. blue 45 15

459 Emblem on Microchip

460 G.P.O.

1992. "Expo '92" World's Fair, Seville.
1222 **459** 180m. multicoloured . . 45 20

1992. Centenary of General Post Office, Tunis.
1223 **460** 180m. brown 45 20
1224 – 450m. brown . . . . . 1·25 35
DESIGN—VERT: 450m. Different view of G.P.O.

461 "When the Subconscious Awakes" (Moncef ben Amor)

1992.
1225 **461** 500m. multicoloured . . 1·40 45

462 Running

463 European Bee Eater

1992. Olympic Games, Barcelona. Multicoloured.
1226 180m. Type **462** 65 30
1227 450m. Judo (vert) . . . . . 1·60 55

1992. Birds. Multicoloured.
1228 100m. Type **463** 55 20
1229 180m. Eurasian goldfinch 80 40
1230 200m. European serin . . . 1·10 40
1231 500m. Western greenfinch 2·50 95

464 President and Children

465 Women and Open Book

1992. United Nations Convention on Rights of the Child.
1233 **464** 180m. multicoloured . . 45 30

1992. African Regional Human Rights Conference, Tunis.
1234 **465** 480m. multicoloured . . 1·50 65

466 Ribbon forming "7"

467 "Acacia tortilis"

1992. 5th Anniv of Declaration of 7 November 1987. Multicoloured.
1235 180m. Type **466** 45 20
1236 730m. President with people and doves . . . . 2·10 90

1992. National Tree Day.
1237 **467** 180m. multicoloured . . 45 30

468 Stylized Figure and Emblems

1992. International Nutrition Conference, Rome.
1238 **468** 450m. multicoloured . . 1·50 55

469 Chemesse

470 "Billy Goat between Two Bushes" (El Jem)

1992. Traditional Costumes. Multicoloured.
1239 100m. Type **469** 30 20
1240 350m. Hanifites 85 45

1992. Mosaics. Multicoloured.
1241 100m. Type **470** 30 15
1242 180m. "Wild Duck" (El Jem) 75 35
1243 350m. "Racehorse" (Sidi Abdallah) . . . . 1·25 45
1244 450m. "Gazelle in the Grass" (El Jem) . . . . . 1·40 70

471 Wolf

1992. Flora and Fauna. Multicoloured.
1245 20m. Type **471** 10 10
1246 60m. "Hoya carnosa" (plant) (vert) 10 10

472 Line Graph on World Map

1993. United Nations World Conference on Human Rights, Vienna.
1247 **472** 450m. multicoloured . . 1·40 60

473 Publicity Poster inside Open Brief-case

474 "Relaxing on the Patio" (Ali Guermassi)

1993. Arab-African Fair, Tunis.
1248 **473** 450m. multicoloured . . 1·25 30

1993.
1249 **474** 450m. multicoloured . . 1·25 30

475 Conference Emblem

476 Blood Transfusion

1993. Constitutional Democratic Assembly Party Conference.
1250 **475** 180m. red and black . . 50 15

1993. Red Crescent. "Dignity for All".
1251 **476** 120m.+30m. mult . . . 60 35

477 Louis Pasteur and Charles Nicolle (former director)

1993. Centenary of Pasteur Institute, Tunis.
1252 **477** 450m. multicoloured . . 1·40 60

478 "7"

479 Carpet

1993. 6th Anniv of Declaration of 7 November 1987. Multicoloured.
1253 180m. Type **478** 50 15
1254 450m. "7"s and waves . . . 1·25 50

1993. Kairouan Carpets.
1255 **479** 100m. multicoloured . . 15 10
1256 – 120m. multicoloured . . 15 10
1257 – 180m. multicoloured . . 50 15
1258 – 350m. multicoloured . . 1·10 60
DESIGNS: 120m. to 350m. Different carpets.

480 Boy with Guitar (Donia Haik)

481 Ballot Box, Hands and Map

1993. School Cultural Activities. Children's drawings. Multicoloured.
1259 180m. Type **480** 50 15
1260 180m. Painting and reading (Anissa Chatbouri) (horiz) 50 15

1994. Presidential and Legislative Elections.
1261 **481** 180m. multicoloured . . 50 15

482 Players, Trophy and Mascot

1994. African Nations Cup Football Championship. Multicoloured.

1262 180m. Type **482** 50 15
1263 350m. Trophy, goalkeeper making save and mascot 1·00 25
1264 450m. Map of Africa, Olympic Rings, player, trophy and mascot . . . 1·25 60

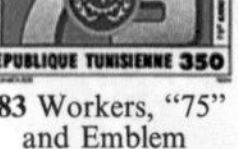

483 Workers, "75" and Emblem **484** Family within House

1994. 75th Anniv of I.L.O.
1265 **483** 350m. multicoloured . . 1·10 25

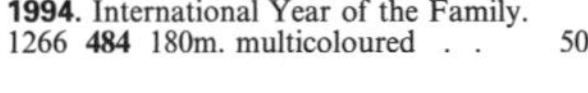

1994. International Year of the Family.
1266 **484** 180m. multicoloured . . 50 15

485 President Ben Ali **486** Blackthorn

1994. Re-election of President Zine el Abidine Ben Ali.
1267 **485** 180m. multicoloured . . 50 15
1268 350m. multicoloured . . 1·00 75

1994. Plants. Multicoloured.
1270 50m. Type **486** 10 10
1271 100m. "Xeranthemum inapertum" 15 10
1272 200m. "Orchis simia" . . . 60 15
1273 1d. "Scilla peruviana" . . . 2·75 1·50

487 Dove and Emblem

1994. 30th Organization of African Unity Summit Meeting, Tunis.
1274 **487** 480m. multicoloured . . 1·40 60

488 Torch with Map as Flame and Centenary Emblem

1994. Centenary of International Olympic Committee.
1275 **488** 450m. multicoloured . . 1·50 60

489 Pencil and Postal and Tourism Motifs

1994. "Philakorea 1994" International Stamp Exhibition, Seoul.
1276 **489** 450m. multicoloured . . 1·50 60

490 Clouded Yellow

1994. Butterflies. Multicoloured.
1277 100m. Type **490** 15 10
1278 180m. Red admiral 50 15
1279 300m. Scarce swallowtail (vert) 75 20
1280 350m. African monarch . . 1·00 50
1281 450m. Painted lady (vert) . . 1·25 60
1282 500m. Swallowtail (vert) . . 1·50 60

491 President Ben Ali and Anniversary Emblem **492** Boxers and Globe

1994. 7th Anniv of Declaration of 7 November 1987. Multicoloured.
1283 350m. Type **491** . . . . . 1·00 25
1284 730m. "7", fireworks and state crest (vert) . . . . . 1·90 50

1994. 41st Military Boxing Championships, Tunis.
1285 **492** 450m. multicoloured . . 1·40 60

493 Tailfins **494** Greylag Geese

1994. 50th Anniv of I.C.A.O.
1286 **493** 450m. multicoloured . . 1·00 30

1994. Wildlife. Multicoloured.
1287 180m. Type **494** 25 15
1288 350m. Tufted duck and European pochard (horiz) 75 25
1289 500m. Water buffaloes . . . 1·10 60
1290 1000m. European otters (horiz) . . . . 2·10 1·25

495 "Composition" (Ridha Bettaieb)

1994.
1291 **495** 500m. multicoloured . . 1·10 35

496 "50", Map and Emblem **497** Oil Lamp

1995. 50th Anniv of League of Arab States.
1292 **496** 180m. multicoloured . . 25 15

1995. Glassware. Multicoloured.
1293 450m. Type **497** 60 30
1294 730m. Oil lamp with handle 95 50

498 Chebbi

1995. 60th Death Anniv (1994) of Aboulkacem Chebbi (poet).
1295 **498** 180m. multicoloured . . 25 15

499 Earring

1995. 4th World Conference on Women, Peking.
1296 **499** 180m. multicoloured . . 25 15

500 Farming

1995. 50th Anniv of F.A.O.
1297 **500** 350m. multicoloured . . 45 25

501 U.N. Workers and Anniversary Emblem over World Map

1995. 50th Anniv of U.N.O.
1298 **501** 350m. multicoloured . . 45 25

502 Crops

1995. Anti-desertification Campaign.
1299 **502** 180m. multicoloured . . 25 15

503 President Ben Ali visiting Village **504** Hannibal (Carthaginian general)

1995. 8th Anniv of Declaration of 7 November 1987. Multicoloured.
1300 180m. Type **503** 25 15
1301 350m. President Ben Ali meeting children 45 25

1995.
1302 **504** 180m. purple 25 15

505 Human Rights Award

1995. World Human Rights Day.
1304 **505** 350m. multicoloured . . 45 25

506 Bird carrying Olive Branch and People crossing Road

1995. Safety of Pedestrians.
1305 **506** 350m. multicoloured . . 45 25

507 "Ophrys lapethica" **508** Modern and Traditional Work

1995. Flora and Fauna. Multicoloured.
1306 50m. Type **507** 10 10
1307 180m. Dorcas gazelle . . . 25 15
1308 300m. "Scupellaria cypria" 40 20
1309 350m. Houbara bustard . . 45 25

1996. 50th Anniv of Tunisian General Workers' Union.
1310 **508** 440m. multicoloured . . 55 30

509 Man's Jebba, Khamri **510** "March 20 1996 1956"

1996. National Traditional Costume Day. Mult.
1311 170m. Type **509** 20 10
1312 200m. Woman's embroidered kaftan, Hammamet 25 15

1996. 40th Anniv of Independence. Multicoloured.
1313 200m. Type **510** 25 15
1314 390m. "20", "40", dove and rainbow 50 25

511 "Hannana" (Noureddine Khayachi)

1996.
1315 **511** 810m. multicoloured . . 1·00 50

512 Seven-spotted Ladybirds

1996. Insects. Multicoloured.
1316 200m. Type **512** 25 15
1317 810m. Honey bee . . . . . 1·00 50

513 Mascot **514** Magnifying Glass on "Stamp"

1996. World Environment Day.
1318 **513** 390m. multicoloured . . 50 25

1996. "Capex'96" International Stamp Exhibition, Toronto, Canada.
1319 **514** 200m. multicoloured . . 25 15

515 Flags over Stadium **516** Woman's Hands holding Dove

1996. Centenary of Olympic Games and Olympic Games, Atlanta. Multicoloured.
1320 20m. Type **515** 10 10
1321 200m. Runner, fireworks and "100" (vert) 25 15
1322 390m. Mosaic of ancient Greek wrestlers 50 25

1996. 40th Anniv of Code of Personal Status.
1323 **516** 200m. multicoloured . . 25 15

517 Ramparts of Sousse **518** Hammer breaking Chain on Anvil

1996. Ancient Buildings. Multicoloured.
1324 20m. Type **517** 10 10
1325 200m. Numide de Dougga mausoleum (vert) 25 15
1326 390m. Arch of Trajan, Makthar 50 25

1996. International Year against Poverty.
1327 **518** 390m. multicoloured . . 50 25

519 Candles on "7" and Map

1996. 9th Anniv of Declaration of 7 November 1987. Multicoloured.
1328 200m. Type **519** 25 15
1329 390m. Girl with doves . . . 50 25

520 Camels outside Traditional Dwellings

1996. National Saharan Tourism Day. Mult.
1330 200m. Type **520** 25 15
1331 200m. Traditional pattern 25 15
Nos. 1330/1 were issued together, se-tenant, forming a composite design.

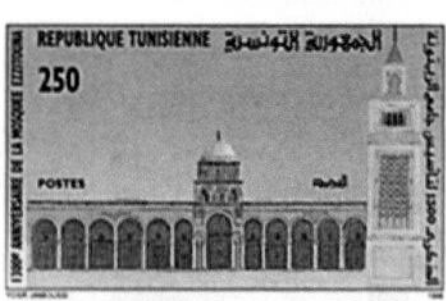

521 Facade

1996. 1300th Anniv of Ezzitouna Mosque.
1332 **521** 250m. multicoloured . . 25 15

522 Campaign Symbols **523** United Nations Emblem, Trophy and Open Book

1996. National Solidarity Day. Multicoloured.
1333 500m. Type **522** 55 30
1334 500m. Jigsaw showing public services 55 30

1996. World Human Rights Day.
1335 **523** 500m. multicoloured . . 55 30

524 Schoolchildren

1996. 50th Anniv of UNICEF.
1336 **524** 810m. multicoloured . . 85 45

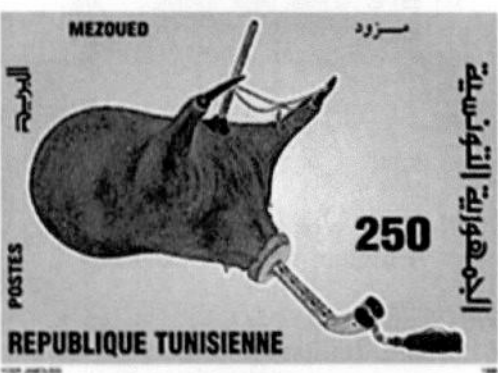

525 Mezoued (bagpipes)

1996. Musical Instruments. Multicoloured.
1337 250m. Type **525** 25 15
1338 300m. Gombri (stringed instrument) 30 15
1339 350m. Tabla (drum) 35 20
1340 500m. Tar tounsi (tambourine) 55 30

1997. As Nos. 1337/40 but smaller, 38 × 24 mm, and face values changed.
1341 20m. As No. 1339 . . . . . 10 10
1342 30m. Type **525** 10 10
1343 50m. As No. 1338 . . . . . 10 10
1344 100m. As No. 1340 . . . . 10 10

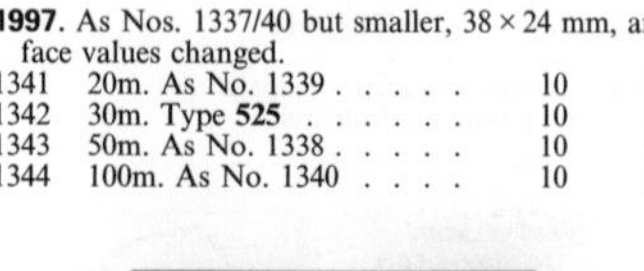

526 Writing Implements and Open Book

1997. World Book and Authors' Rights Day.
1345 **526** 1d. multicoloured . . . 1·00 50

527 Mediterranean Blue Mussels

1997. Molluscs. Multicoloured.
1346 50m. Type **527** 10 10
1347 70m. Clams 10 10
1348 350m. Common octopus . . 35 20
1349 500m. Common cuttlefish 55 30

528 San Francisco–Oakland Bay Bridge **529** Tennis Player and Runner

1997. "Pacific 97" International Stamp Exhibition, San Francisco.
1350 **528** 250m. multicoloured . . 25 15

1997. Mediterranean Games, Bari, Italy.
1351 **529** 350m. multicoloured . . 35 20

530 Emblems **531** State Arms

1997. Tunis, Cultural Capital.
1352 **530** 250m. multicoloured . . 25 15

1997. 40th Anniv of Republic. Multicoloured.
1353 130m. Type **531** 15 10
1354 500m. Airplane and flowers (horiz) 55 30

532 African Spiny-tailed Lizard

1997. Reptiles. Multicoloured.
1355 100m. Type **532** 10 10
1356 350m. Chameleon (vert) . . 40 20
1357 500m. Desert monitor . . . 55 30

533 Ariana Rose

1997.
1358 **533** 350m. multicoloured . . 40 20

534 Pres. Ben Ali with Elderly Woman

1997. World Day for Protection of the Elderly.
1359 **534** 250m. multicoloured . . 25 15

535 "Autumn" (Ammar Farhat)

1997. Art. Multicoloured.
1360 250m. Type **535** 25 15
1361 250m. "In Cafe Maure" (Farhat) 25 15
1362 250m. "Old Man" (Farhat) 25 15
1363 250m. "Fisher of Men" (sculpture, Hedi Selmi) . . 25 15
1364 500m. "Cafe des Nattes" (Sidi Bou Said) (horiz) . . 55 30
1365 500m. "Lesson" (Yahia Turki) (horiz) 55 30
1366 1000m. "Hand-spinner" (Farhat) . . . . 1·10 55

536 Pres. Ben Ali with Child, Flag and Doves forming "7"

1997. 10th Anniv of Declaration of 7 November 1987.
1367 – 250m. violet and gold . . 25 15
1368 **536** 500m. multicoloured . . 50 25
DESIGN—VERT: 250m. "7", globe and laurel leaves.

537 Sandrose (mineral)

1997.
1369 **537** 250m. multicoloured . . 25 15

538 Scales, Emblem and World Map

1997. International Day of Human Rights.
1370 **538** 500m. multicoloured . . 50 25

539 Arab

1997. Horses. Multicoloured.
1371 50m. Type **539** 10 10
1372 70m. Barbary 10 10
1373 250m. Arab-Barbary (vert) 25 15
1374 500m. Head of Arab (vert) 50 25

540 Memorial and Flowers

1998. 40th Anniv of Bombing of Sakiet Sidi Youssef.
1375 **540** 250m. multicoloured . . 25 15

541 Children and Flowers

1998. 5th School Health Week.
1376 **541** 250m. multicoloured . . 25 15

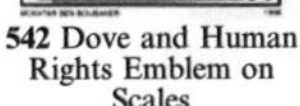

542 Dove and Human Rights Emblem on Scales
543 Monument

1998. Centenary of Tunisian Bar.
1377 **542** 250m. multicoloured . . 25 15

1998. Martyrs' Day. Multicoloured.
1378 250m. Type **543** 25 15
1379 520m. Roses and "9" . . . 55 30

544 Okba Ibn Nafaa Mosque, Kairouan

1998.
1380 **544** 500m. multicoloured . . 50 25

545 National Team

1998. World Cup Football Championship, France. Multicoloured.
1381 250m. Type **545** 25 15
1382 500m. Player, ball and trophy (vert) 50 25

546 Crab

1998. Marine Life. Multicoloured.
1383 110m. Type **546** 10 10
1384 250m. King prawn 25 15
1385 1000m. Lobster . . . . . . 1·00 50

547 Dove, Flag and Torch Bearers

1998. Constitutional Democratic Assembly Party Congress. Multicoloured.
1386 250m. Type **547** 25 15
1387 250m. President Ben Ali, flag, torch bearers and banners (horiz) 25 15

548 Isaac ibn Soleimane, Ahmed ibn el Jazzar and Constantin the African (physicians)

1998. 36th International History of Medicine Congress.
1388 **548** 500m. multicoloured . . 50 25

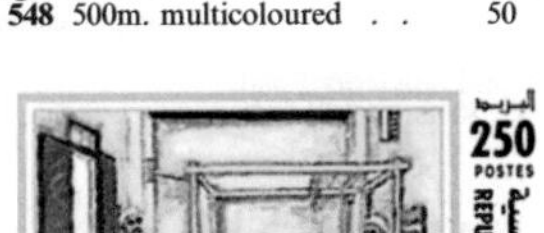

549 "Weaver" (Ali Guermassi)

1998. Paintings. Multicoloured.
1389 250m. Type **549** 25 15
1390 250m. "Musician" (Noureddine Khayachi) (vert) 25 15
1391 500m. "Still Life" (Ali Khouja) (vert) 50 25

550 Bank and Anniversary Emblem
551 Symbols of Industry and Agriculture

1998. 40th Anniv of Central Bank of Tunisia.
1392 **550** 250m. multicoloured . . 25 15

1998. 11th Anniv of Declaration of 7 November 1987.
1393 **551** 250m. multicoloured . . 25 15

552 "Tunisia" in Arabic and Anniversary Emblem

1998. 50th Anniv of Universal Declaration of Human Rights.
1394 **552** 250m. multicoloured . . 25 15

553 Ibn Rushd
554 Saliha (singer)

1998. 800th Death Anniv of Ibn Rushd (Averroes) (philosopher and physician).
1395 **553** 500m. multicoloured . . 50 25

1998. Musicians. Multicoloured.
1396 250m. Type **554** 25 15
1397 250m. Kaddour Srarfi (composer and violinist) (horiz) 25 15
1398 500m. Ali Riahi (singer and composer) 50 25

555 Mountain Gazelles

1998. Boukornine National Park. Multicoloured.
1399 70m. Type **555** 10 10
1400 110m. Brown hare 10 10
1401 250m. Bonelli's eagles . . . 25 15
1402 500m. Persian cyclamen . . 50 25

556 Orange Tree

1999. Trees. Multicoloured.
1403 250m. Type **556** 25 15
1404 250m. Date palm (vert) . . 25 15
1405 500m. Olive tree 50 20

557 Thuburbo Majus
558 "L'Intemporel" (Moncef ben Amor)

1999. Archaeological Sites. Multicoloured.
1406 50m. Type **557** 10 10
1407 250m. Baths at Bulla Regia (horiz) 25 15
1408 500m. Zaghouan aqueduct (horiz) 50 20

1999. Paintings. Multicoloured.
1409 250m. Type **558** 25 15
1410 250m. "Betrothal" (Ali Guermassi) 25 15
1411 250m. "Pottery" (Ammar Farhat) 25 15
1412 250m. "Hat and Fan Seller" (Yahia Turki) 25 15

559 Arms, Columns and Legislative Chamber

1999. 40th Anniv of Constitution.
1413 **559** 250m. multicoloured . . 25 15

560 Acacia

1999. Flowers. Multicoloured.
1414 70m. Type **560** 10 10
1415 250m. Bougainvillea ("Bougainvillea spectabilis") 25 15
1416 250m. Common poppy ("Papaver rhoeas") . . . 25 15
1417 500m. Carnation 50 25

561 Stamps, Globe as Eye and Emblem

1999. "Philexfrance 99" International Stamp Exhibition, Paris.
1419 **561** 500m. multicoloured . . 50 25

562 Haddad and Women

1999. Birth Centenary of Tahar Haddad.
1420 **562** 500m. multicoloured . . 50 25

563 Loggerhead Turtle

1999. Marine Life. Multicoloured.
1421 250m. Type **563** 25 15
1422 500m. Grouper 50 25

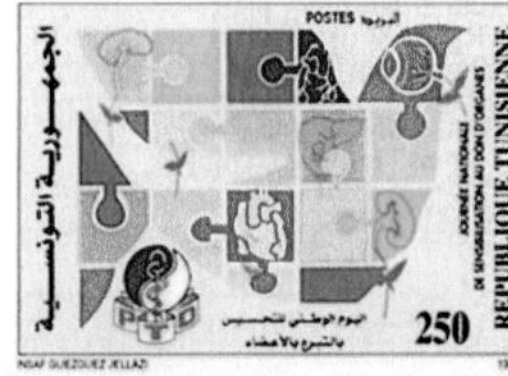

564 Body Parts as Jigsaw Puzzle of Dove

1999. National Organ Donation Awareness Day.
1423 **564** 250m. multicoloured . . 25 15

565 U.P.U. Emblem
566 Ballot Box, Ear of Wheat and Sailing Boat

1999. 125th Anniv of Universal Postal Union.
1424 **565** 500m. multicoloured . . 50 25

1999. Presidential and Legislative Elections.
1425 **566** 500m. multicoloured . . 50 25

567 Tamarisk
568 Computer, Pencil and rising Sun

1999. Flora and Fauna. Multicoloured.
1426 250m. Type **567** 25 15
1427 500m. Dromedary 50 25

1999. 12th Anniv of Declaration of 7th November 1987.
1428 **568** 250m. multicoloured . . 25 15

569 Emblem and Scales of Justice
570 Ahmed Ibn Abi Dhiaf

1999. World Human Rights Day.
1429 **569** 250m. multicoloured . . 25 15

1999. Death Anniversaries. Multicoloured.
1430 250m. Type **570** (125th anniv) 25 15
1431 250m. Abdelaziz Thaalbi (55th anniv) 25 15
1432 500m. Khemaies Tarnane (35th anniv) (horiz) . . . 50 25

571 "2000" and 20th-Century Symbols

1999. New Millennium.
1433 **571** 250m. multicoloured . . 25 15

572 17th-Century Ceramic Dish, Tunis

2000. Archaeological Sites and Artefacts. Mult.
1434 100m. Type **572** 10 10
1435 110m. 9th-century plate, Raqqada (triangular) . . 10 10
1436 250m. Water Temple, Zaghouan (35 × 35 mm) 20 10
1437 500m. "Ulysses and the Sirens" (mosaic), Dougga (35 × 35 mm) 45 25

573 *Carthage* (car ferry)

2000.
1438 **573** 500m. multicoloured . . 45 25

574 Archway and Palm Tree

2000. "EXPO 2000" World's Fair, Hanover, Germany.
1439 **574** 1000m. multicoloured . . 95 50

575 Carob Tree

2000. Trees. Multicoloured.
1440 50m. Type **575** 10 10
1441 100m. Apricot 10 10
1442 250m. Avocado (vert) . . . 25 10
1443 400m. Apple 35 15

576 Emblem
577 Emblem and Sydney Opera House

2000. Mediterranean Games, Tunis (1st series).
1444 **576** 500m. multicoloured . . 45 20
See also Nos. 1473/4.

2000. Olympic Games, Sydney.
1445 **577** 500m. multicoloured . . 45 20

578 Freesias
579 Dove, Sun and Symbols

2000. Flowers. Multicoloured.
1446 110m. Type **578** 10 10
1447 200m. Chrysanthemums . . 20 10
1448 250m. Rose "Golden Times" 25 10
1449 250m. Vase of flowers (33 × 49 mm) 25 10
1450 500m. Rose "Calibra" . . . 45 20

2000. 13th Anniv of Declaration of 7 November 1987.
1451 **579** 250m. multicoloured . . 25 10

580 "Still life" (Hedi Khayachi)

2000. Paintings. Multicoloured.
1452 100m. Type **580** 10 10
1453 250m. "Landscape" (Abdelaziz Berraies) . . . 25 10
1454 250m. "The Sharpener" (Ali Guermassi) 25 10
1455 400m. "The Seller of Dates and Milk" (Yahia Turki) (vert) 35 15

581 Monument
583 Imam Sahnoun

582 *Neverita josephinia*

2000. International Year of Human Rights.
1456 **581** 500m. multicoloured . . 45 20

2000. Shells. Multicoloured.
1457 50m. Type **582** 10 10
1458 250m. Trunculus murex (*Phyllonotus trunculus*) . . 25 10
1459 250m. *Columbella rustica* . . 25 10
1460 1d. *Arca noe* 95 45

2000. Personalities. Multicoloured.
1461 250m. Type **583** 25 10
1462 250m. Ibn Arafa 25 10
1463 250m. Ali Belhaouane . . . 25 10
1464 1d. Mohamed Jamoussi (musician) 95 45

584 Map and Flags

2001. Tunisia's Presidency of NATO. Security Council.
1465 **584** 250m. multicoloured . . 25 10

585 Globe, Clasped Hands and Dove
586 Symbols of Communications

2001. World Solidarity Fund.
1466 **585** 500m. multicoloured . . 50 25

2001. Digital Culture Year.
1467 **586** 250m. multicoloured . . 25 10

587 Flag, Father and Child

2001. Mohamed Dohra Commemoration.
1468 **587** 600m. multicoloured . . 60 30

588 Tunis Town Hall

2001. Tourism. Multicoloured.
1469 250m. Type **588** 25 10
1470 250m. Ghighis (Roman ruins), Djerba Island . . . 25 10
1471 250m. 19th-century tile, Tunis (vert) 25 10
1472 500m. "The Needles", Tabarka (vert) 50 25

589 Emblem, Stadium and Running Track

2001. Mediterranean Games, Tunis (2nd series). Multicoloured.
1473 250m. Type **589** 15 10
1474 500m. Runners and gold medal 50 25

590 "Sidi Bou Said" (Pierre Boucherle)

2001. Paintings. Multicoloured.
1475 250m. Type **590** 25 10
1476 250m. "Still Life" (Pierre Boucherle) 25 10
1477 250m. "Dream" (Aly Ben Salem) (vert) 25 10
1478 500m. "Traditional Outdoor Marriage" (Aly Ben Salem) 50 25

591 Stylized Faces and Arrows

2001. United Nations Year of Dialogue among Civilizations.
1479 **591** 500m. multicoloured . . 50 25

592 Emblem and Symbols of Employment

2001. National Employment Fund.
1480 **592** 250m. multicoloured . . 20 10

593 Anniversary Medal

2001. 14th Anniv of Declaration of 7th November.
1481 **593** 250m. multicoloured . . 25 10

594 Marbled White Butterfly

2001. Butterflies and Moth. Multicoloured.
1482 250m. Type **594** 25 10
1483 250m. Butterfly (inscr "Ariane") 25 10
1484 250m. Butterfly (inscr "Pacha a deux queues") 25 10
1485 500m. Moth (inscr "Grand paan de nuit") 40 20
MS1486 137 × 126 mm. 250m. × 2, Nos. 1482/3; 500m. × 2, Nos. 1484/5. Imperf . . . . . 1·30 1·30

595 Crossbill
596 Scales of Justice and Globe

2001. Birds. Multicoloured.
1487 250m. Type **595** 25 10
1488 500m. Great tit 40 20
1489 600m. Jay 50 25
1490 600m. Stork 50 25
MS1491 120 × 131 mm. 300m. No. 1487; 500m. No. 1488; 600m. × 2, No. 1489/90 . . . . . . 1·20 1·20

2001. International Human Rights Day.
1492 **596** 250m. multicoloured . .

597 Ibrahim Ibn Al Aghlab

2001. Personalities. Multicoloured.
1493 250m. Type **597** 25 10
1494 250m. Ibn Rachiq Al Kairaouani 25 10
1495 350m. Abdelaziz Laroui . . 30 15
1496 650m. Assad Ibn Al Fourat 55 25

598 Modern Script

2001. Calligraphy. Multicoloured.
1497 350m. Type **598** 30 15
1498 350m. Ancient script (vert) 30 15

599 Tower, El Kef Kasbah

600 Rabbit (*Oryctolagus cuniculus*)

2002. Archaeological Sites. Multicoloured.
1499 250m. Type **599** 25 10
1500 390m. Amphitheatre, Oudhna (horiz) 30 15
1501 600m. Hall, Baron d'Erlanger Palace 50 25
1502 600m. Figures, Virgil Mosaic 50 25

2002. Fauna of Zembra and Zembretta National Park. Multicoloured.
1503 250m. Type **600** 20 10
1504 250m. Mouflon sheep (*Ovis musimon*) 20 10
1505 600m. Audouin's Gull (*Larus audouinii*) 50 25
1506 600m. Peregrine Falcon (*Falco peregrinus brookei*) 50 25
MS1507 127×131 mm. 400 m. ×2, Nos. 1503/4; 600 m. ×2, Nos. 1505/6 . . . . 1·75 1·75

601 Slender-horned Gazelle (*Gazella leptoceros*)

2002. Tourism. Multicoloured.
1508 250m. Type **601** 20 10
1509 390m. Sahara 30 15
1510 600m. Horseman 50 25
1511 600m. Tamghza 50 25
MS1512 141×140 mm. 400m. ×2, Nos. 1508/9; 600m. ×2, Nos. 1510/11. Imperf . . . . . 1·75 1·75

602 Player, Ball and Trophy

603 Sheikh Mohamed Senoussi

2002. World Cup Football Championships, Japan and South Korea. Multicoloured.
1513 390m. Type **602** 30 15
1514 600m. Trophy and ball . . . 50 25
MS1515 116×116 mm. 500m. No. 1513; 1d. No. 1514 . . . . 1·30 1·30

2002. Personalities. Multicoloured.
1516 100m. Type **603** 10 10
1517 250m. Mosbah Jarbou . . . 20 10
1518 250m. Mohamed Daghbaji 20 10
1519 1d.100 Abou Al Hassen . . 95 45

604 Wheelchair Racer

2002. World Disabled Athletics Championship, Villeneuve d'Ascq. Multicoloured.
1520 100m. Type **604** 10 10
1521 700m. Discus thrower (vert) 60 30

605 Conference Emblem and Animals

2002. 27th World Veterinary Conference, Tunis.
1522 **605** 600m. multicoloured . . 50 25

606 Club Emblem

2002. 20th Anniv of CIGV (international travellers club).
1523 **606** 600m. multicoloured . . 50 25

607 Dove and Couple holding Torch

608 Farhat Hached

2002. 15th Anniv of Declaration of 7th November.
1524 **607** 390m. multicoloured . . 35 15

2002. 50th Death Anniv of Farhat Hached (founder of General Union of Tunisian Workers).
1525 **608** 390m. multicoloured . . 35 15

609 Scales and Globe

610 "Wedding" (Habib Bouabana)

2002. International Human Rights Day.
1526 **609** 390m. multicoloured . . 35 15

2002. Art. Multicoloured.
1527 250m. Type **610** 20 10
1528 250m. Folk Art (Ammar Farhat) 20 10
1529 250m. "Gazelles in Clearing" (Aly Ben Salem) (horiz) 20 10
1530 900m. "Still Life" (Pierre Boucherle) 80 40

611 Spinner

2003. Mosaics. Multicoloured.
1531 390m. Type **611** 35 20
1532 600m. Inscr "Africa" . . . 55 30

612 Young Scouts

2003. 70th Anniv of Tunisian Scouting. Multicoloured.
1533 250m. Type **612** 20 10
1534 600m. Adult scouts (vert) . . 55 30

613 Open Book

2003. National Book Year.
1535 **613** 390m. multicoloured . . 35 20

614 "Washerwomen" (Yahia Turki)

2003. Yahia Turki (artist) Commemoration.
1536 **614** 1d. multicoloured . . . 90 45

615 Horse and Buildings, Farhat Hached, Rades

2003. Parks. Multicoloured.
1537 200m. Type **615** 20 10
1538 250m. Animal park, Friguia 20 10
1539 390m. La Marsa park . . . 35 20
1540 1d. Ennahli park 90 45

616 Air Balloons, Ruins and Coastal Development

617 Emblems

2003. National Tourism Day.
1541 **616** 600m. multicoloured . . 55 30

2003. Constitutional Rally.
1542 **617** 250m. multicoloured . . 20 10

618 Habib Bourguiba

619 Oryx dammah

2003. Birth Centenary of Habib Bourguiba (president, 1957—1987).
1543 **618** 390m. multicoloured . . 35 20

2003. Flora and Fauna. Multicoloured.
1544 50m. Type **619** 10 10
1545 50m. Nyanthes sambac . . 10 10
1546 100m. Ram 10 10
1547 100m. Myrtle communis . . 10 10
1548 100m. Rosa canina (36×36 mm) 10 10
1549 200m. Ostrich (Struthio camelus) 20 10
1550 200m. No. 1548 . . . . . . 20 10
1551 250m. No. 1545 (36×36 mm) 20 10
1552 250m. No. 1546 (36×36 mm) 20 10
1553 390m. No. 1549 (36×36 mm) 35 20

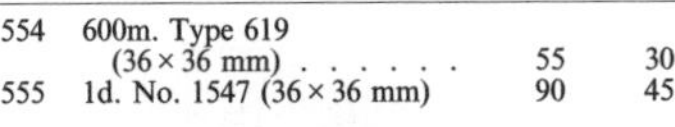

1554 600m. Type 619 (36×36 mm) 55 30
1555 1d. No. 1547 (36×36 mm) 90 45

620 Stylized Figures and Flag

621 "5+5" and Participants Flags

2003. 16th Anniv of Declaration of 7th November.
1556 **620** 250m. multicoloured . . 20 10

2003. First 5+5 Summit, Tunis.
1557 **621** 600m. multicoloured . . 55 30

622 Figures surrounding Globe

624 Map of Africa, Stylized Players and Trophy

623 Machmoum El Fell

2003. 55th Anniv of Universal Declaration of Human Rights.
1558 **622** 350m. multicoloured . . 30 15

2003. Silverwork. Multicoloured.
1559 600m. Type **623** 55 30
1560 600m. Khelel brooch . . . 55 30
MS1561 120×81 mm. Nos. 1559/60 1·00 1·00

2004. African Nations Football Championship. Multicoloured.
1562 250m. Type **624** 20 10
1563 600m. Map as figure holding trophy 55 30

625 Flag and People holding Torch

626 Conference Emblem

2004. 70th Anniv of Ksar Helal Congress.
1564 **625** 250m. multicoloured . . 20 10

2004. League of Arab States Summit Conference, Tunis.
1565 **626** 600m. multicoloured . . 55 30

627 Brazier

2004. Copper Handicrafts. Multicoloured.
1566 50m. Type **627** 10 10
1567 100m. Water jug 10 10
1568 150m. Jug and bowl 10 10
1569 200m. Jug 20 10
1570 250m. Amphora 20 10
1571 250m. Bucket 20 10
1572 300m. No. 1571 . . . . . . 25 15
1573 600m. Type 627 . . . . . . 55 30
1574 700m. No. 1570 . . . . . . 60 30
1575 1d. No. 1568 . . . . 90 45

628 Husseinite Era Gold Coin (1767)

2004. Early Currency. Multicoloured.
1576 250m. Type **628** 20 10
1577 250m. Islamic era gold dinar (706) 20 10
1578 600m. Punic era gold coin (310 BC) 50 30
1579 600m. Punic era silver coin (300 BC) 55 30
1580 1d. Banknote (1847) (67 × 30 mm) 90 45

629 Anniversary Emblem

2004. 40th Anniv of African Development Bank.
1581 **629** 700m. multicoloured . . 60 30

630 Garden Rake, Teeth as Flowers and Watering Can (A. El Mediouni)

2004. Children's Drawings.
1582 **630** 250m. multicoloured . . 20 10

631 Ballot Envelopes and Ballot Box

2004. Presidential and Legislative Elections.
1583 **631** 250m. multicoloured . . 20 10

632 Clock Tower and Computer Operators

2004. 17th Anniv of Declaration of 7th November.
1584 **632** 250m. multicoloured . . 20 10

633 El Abidine Mosque, Carthage

2004.
1585 **633** 250m. multicoloured . . 20 10

PARCEL POST STAMPS

P 8 Mail Carrier

P 25 Date Gathering

1906.
P44 **P 8** 5c. purple and green . . . 60 15
P45 10c. pink and red . . . 15 55
P46 20c. red and brown . . . 1·60 20
P47 25c. brown and blue . . . 2·00 20
P48 40c. red and grey . . . . 2·25 70
P49 50c. violet and brown . . 2·50 15
P50 75c. blue and brown . . . 3·75 20
P51 1f. red and brown . . . . 2·50 10
P52 2f. blue and red . . . . . 6·00 30
P53 5f. brown and violet . . . 4·50 75

1926.
P147 **P 25** 5c. blue and brown . . 15 20
P148 10c. mauve and red . . 35 40
P149 20c. black and green . . 1·40 15
P150 25c. black and brown 55 45
P151 40c. green and red . . 1·00 1·25
P152 50c. black and violet 1·25 55
P153 60c. red and brown . . 1·40 1·40
P154 75c. green and lilac . . 1·75 45
P155 80c. brown and red . . 2·25 25
P156 1f. pink and blue . . . 2·00 20
P157 2f. red and mauve . . . 1·75 20
P158 4f. black and red . . . 2·25 20
P159 5f. violet and brown . . 1·90 15
P160 10f. grn & red on grn 1·75 35
P161 20f. vio & grn on pink 11·50 1·75

POSTAGE DUE STAMPS

D 3

D 20 Carthaginian Statue

D 86 Agricultural Produce

1901.
D28 **D 3** 1c. black 15 15
D29 2c. orange 10 15
D30 5c. blue 10 10
D31 10c. brown 15 10
D32 20c. green . . . . 2·75 20
D33 30c. red . . . . 2·50 20
D34 50c. lake . . . . 1·00 30
D35 1f. olive . . . . 1·00 1·25
D36 2f. red on green . . . . 2·25 2·50
D37 5f. black on yellow . . . 40·00 48·00

1914. Surch **2 FRANCS**.
D49 **D 3** 2f. on 5f. black on yell 85 30

1923.
D100 **D 20** 1c. black . . . . . . 10 2·50
D101 2c. black on yellow . . 10 95
D102 5c. purple . . . . . . 10 2·00
D103 10c. blue . . . . . . 20 2·25
D104 20c. orange on yellow 20 20
D105 30c. brown 35 20
D106 50c. red . . . . 90 1·00
D107 60c. mauve . . . . . 1·25 25
D108 80c. brown . . . . . . 15 2·50
D109 90c. red 20 65
D110 1f. green 15 20
D111 2f. green 65 90
D112 3f. violet on pink . . . 1·50 2·50
D113 5f. violet 50 50

1945.
D287 **D 20** 10c. green . . . . . 10 2·75
D288 50c. violet . . . . . . 10 2·75
D289 2f. pink 15 60
D290 4f. blue . . . . 25 2·25
D291 10f. mauve . . . . . 40 2·00
D292 20f. brown . . . . . . 1·50 80
D293 30f. blue . . . . . . 2·75 2·75
Nos. D293 is inscribed "TIMBRE TAXE".

1957.
D448 **D 86** 1f. green 20 20
D449 2f. brown 20 20
D450 3f. green 40 40
D451 4f. blue 45 45
D452 5f. mauve 45 45
D453 10f. red 45 45
D454 20f. sepia . . . . . . 1·75 1·75
D455 30f. blue . . . . . . 1·90 1·90

1960. Inscr "REPUBLIQUE TUNISIENNE" and new currency.
D534 **D 86** 1m. green 10 10
D535 2m. brown 10 10
D536 3m. green 15 15
D537 4m. blue 15 15
D538 5m. violet 20 20
D539 10m. red 40 40
D540 20m. brown 60 60
D541 30m. blue 70 70
D542 40m. brown 15 15
D543 100m. green 40 30

TURKEY Pt. 16

Formerly an empire, this country is now a republic, the greater part of its territory lying in Asia Minor.

1863. 40 paras = 1 piastre or grush.
1942. 100 paras = 1 kurus.
1947. 100 kurus = 1 lira.

For designs as Types **1**, **2**, **9**, **15**, **21**, **23**, **25**, **28** and **30** but in black or brown, see Postage Due stamps.

1

2

1863. Imperf.
1 **1** 20pa. black on yellow . . . . 60·00 12·50
2 1pi. black on purple . . . . 85·00 30·00
3 2pi. black on blue . . . . . 85·00 35·00
4 5pi. black on red . . . . . . £150 55·00

1865. Perf.
11 **2** 10pa. green . . . . 5·25 38·00
64 10pa. mauve 40 45
35a 10pa. brown . . . . 85·00 2·10
12 20pa. yellow . . . . 2·10 3·25
65 20pa. green 40 70
94 20pa. grey . . . . 1·50 3·00
13 1pi. lilac . . . . 3·75 4·00
66 1pi. yellow . . . . 40 1·25
14 2pi. blue . . . . 2·00 2·25
95 2pi. red to brown 60 70
15 5pi. red . . . . 2·25 3·75
46 5pi. blue . . . . 50 7·50
39c 5pi. grey . . . . 22·00 23·00
16 25pi. orange £300 £300
48 25pi. red . . . . 28·00 75·00

1876. Surch with value in figures and **Pres**.
77 **2** ¼pre. on 10pa. mauve . . . . 1·40 3·50
78 ½pre. on 20pa. green . . . . 4·75 6·50
79 1¼pre. on 50pa. red . . . . . 40 1·25
80 2pre. on 2pi. brown . . . . . 22·00 9·75
81 5pre. on 5pi. blue . . . . . 2·50 42·00

9

15

1876.
89 **9** 5pa. black and yellow . . . 90 1·25
96 5pa. lilac £150 £150
109 5pa. black . . . . 65 1·10
113 5pa. green and yellow . . . 1·10 3·75
82 10pa. black and mauve . . 95 1·90
90 10pa. black and green . . 1·40 1·25
97 10pa. green . . . . 75 1·10
83 20pa. purple and green . . 42·00 8·00
91 20pa. black and pink . . . 45 80
103 20pa. pink 65 75
84 50pa. blue and yellow . . . 40 3·25
92 1pi. black and grey (A) . . 19·00 4·25
93 1pi. black and blue (B) . . 75·00 3·25
99 1pi. blue 75 95
85 2pi. black and flesh 40 95
126a 2pi. yellow . . . . 1·90 3·75
110 2pi. orange and blue . . . 65 1·10
114 2pi. mauve and grey . . . 75 75
86 5pi. pink and blue . . . . 1·60 5·00
115 5pi. brown . . . . 2·75 7·00
111 5pi. green . . . . 1·90 3·75
87 25pi. purple and mauve . . 9·50 38·00
107 25pi. black £225 £225
112 25pi. brown . . . . 15·00 60·00
116 25pi. red and yellow . . . 18·00 50·00

1892. Various frames.
141 **15** 10pa. green 70 70
142a 20pa. red 50 30
143 1pi. blue . . . . 1·50 30
144 2pi. brown 75 30
145 5pi. purple . . . . 1·50 4·00

1897. Surch **5 5 Cinq Paras**.
160 **15** 5pa. on 10pa. green . . . 1·75 25

21

22

23

1901. For Internal Mail.
167 **21** 5pa. violet 35 20
168 10pa. green 35 20
169 20pa. red 35 20
170 1pi. blue 35 20
171 2pi. orange 35 20
203 5pi. mauve . . . . 2·25 60
173 25pi. brown . . . . 5·00 1·25
174 50pi. brown . . . . 22·00 3·00

1901. For Foreign Mail.
175 **22** 5pa. brown 80 30
176 10pa. green 35 30
177 20pa. mauve 35 30
178 1pi. blue 80 30
179 2pi. blue . . . . 1·50 50
180 5pi. brown . . . . 1·50 50
181 25pi. green . . . . 60·00 22·00
182 50pi. yellow . . . . £130 65·00

1905.
212 **23** 5pa. brown 40 30
213 10pa. green 40 30
214 20pa. pink 40 30
215 1pi. blue 40 30
216 2pi. blue 45 30
217 2½pi. purple . . . . 1·00 30
218 5pi. brown . . . . 1·25 65
219 10pi. orange . . . . 1·10 65
220 25pi. green . . . . 7·50 4·50
221 50pi. purple . . . . 38·00 13·00

(24)

Type **24** is the Turkish letter "B" which stands for Behie = discount.

1906. Optd with T **24**.
230 **23** 10pa. green . . . . 2·25 95
231 20pa. pink . . . . 2·25 95
232 1pi. blue . . . . 2·25 95
233 2pi. blue . . . . 7·50 3·00

25

27

28

1908.
234 **25** 5pa. brown 70 30
235 10pa. green . . . . 1·50 30
236 20pa. red . . . . 26·00 30
237 1pi. blue . . . . 8·00 30
238 2pi. black . . . . 6·00 30
239 2½pi. brown . . . . 2·10 30
240 5pi. purple . . . . 20·00 55
241 10pi. red . . . . 60·00 1·40
242 25pi. green . . . . 8·00 3·50
243 50pi. brown . . . . 45·00 32·00

1908. Optd as T **24** but smaller.
252 **25** 10pa. green . . . . 4·25 2·25
253 20pa. red . . . . 5·00 2·75
254 1pi. blue . . . . 9·00 3·00
255 2pi. black . . . . 23·00 7·75

1908. Granting of Constitution.
256 **27** 5pa. brown 30 55
257 10pa. green 30 55
258 20pa. red . . . . 1·25 70
259 1pi. blue . . . . 1·25 80
260 2pi. black . . . . 9·75 13·00

1909.
271 **28** 2pa. green 40 35
261 5pa. brown 40 30
262 10pa. green 40 30
263 20pa. red 40 30
264 1pi. blue . . . . 1·00 30
265 2pi. black . . . . 1·10 30
266 2½pi. brown . . . . 48·00 15·00
267 5pi. purple 80 85
268 10pi. red . . . . 22·00 65
269 25pi. green . . . . £275 75·00
270 50pi. brown . . . . 65·00 75·00

1909. Optd as T **24** but smaller.
289 **28** 10pa. green . . . . 1·60 50
290 20pa. red . . . . 1·60 50
291 1pi. blue . . . . 3·25 1·75
292 2pi. black . . . . 48·00 19·00

1910. No. 261 surch **2** and Turkish inscr.
296 **28** 2pa. on 5pa. brown . . . 30 20

30 G.P.O., Constantinople

31 Mosque of Selim

1913.
333 **30** 2pa. green 35 25
334 5pa. bistre 35 25
335 10pa. green 35 25
336 20pa. pink 35 25
337 1pi. blue 35 25
338 2pi. grey 35 25
339 5pi. purple . . . . 2·25 30
340 10pi. red . . . . 4·50 90
341 25pi. green . . . . 15·00 20·00
342 50pi. brown . . . . 55·00 75·00

1913. Optd as T **24** but smaller.

343	**30**	10pa. green	30	30
344		20pa. pink	30	30
345		1pi. blue	40	55
346		2pi. grey	9·50	4·50

1913. Recapture of Adrianople.

353	**31**	10pa. green	65	30
963		20pa. red	1·60	1·25
355		40pa. blue	1·60	1·25

For Type **31** surcharged, see Postage Due stamps.

32 Obelisk of Theodosius

34 Leander's Tower

1914.

499	**32**	2pa. purple	15	15
500	–	4pa. brown	15	15
501	**34**	5pa. purple	20	20
961		5pa. brown	40	15
502	–	6pa. blue	20	20
503	–	10pa. green	20	20
504	–	20pa. red	35	25
505	–	1pi. blue	30	25
964	–	1pi. green	2·10	20
506	–	1½pi. grey and red	35	20
507	–	1¾pi. brown and grey	35	20
508	–	2pi. black and green	1·25	50
509	–	2½pi. green and orange	45	20
965	–	3pi. blue	45	20
510	–	5pi. lilac	1·90	90
966	–	5pi. grey	21·00	30
511	–	10pi. brown	3·75	40
967	–	10pi. lilac	3·25	25
512	–	25pi. green	48·00	3·50
968	–	25pi. purple	2·25	1·25
513	–	50pi. pink	3·50	2·00
969	–	50pi. brown	3·00	6·00
514	–	100pi. blue	55·00	18·00
515	–	200pi. black and green	£275	£275

DESIGNS—VERT: 4pa. Column of Constantine; 6pa. Seven Towers Castle, Yedikule. HORIZ: 10pa. Lighthouse-Garden, Constantinople; 20pa. Castle of Europe; 1pi. Mosque of Sultan Ahmed; 1½pi. Monument to Martyrs of Liberty; 1¾, 3pi. Fountains of Suleiman; 2pi. Cruiser "Hamidiye"; 2½, 5 (966) pi. Candilli, Bosphorus; 5pi. (510) Former Ministry of War; 10pi. Sweet Waters of Europe; 25pi. Suleiman Mosque; 50pi. Bosphorus at Rumeli Hisar; 100pi. Sultan Ahmed's Fountain; 200pi. Sultan Mohamed V. SIZES—As Type **32**: 4, 6pa; 31½ × 20 mm: 10pa. to 1pi; 26 × 21 mm: 1½pi. to 2½ pi; 38 × 24 mm: 5pi. to 50pi; 40 × 25½ mm: 100, 200pi.

1914. Stamps of 1914 optd with small star.

516	10pa. green	55	60
517	20pa. red	7·25	60
518	1pi. blue	1·25	60
519	1¾pi. brown and grey	90	1·25
520	2pi. black and green	35·00	1·90

(49)

1914. 7th Anniv of Constitution No. 506 surch with T **49**.

521	1pi. on 1½pi. grey and red	1·25	1·50

(50)

1914. Abrogation of the Capitulations. Nos. 501/11 optd with T **50**.

524	5pa. purple	1·25	50
526	10pa. green	2·00	50
527	20pa. red	2·00	50
528	1pi. blue	4·75	1·25
530	2pi. black and green	7·25	1·25
532	5pi. lilac	18·00	2·50
533	10pi. brown	£110	35·00

(51)

1915. Nos. 514/15 surch as T **51**.

534	10pi. on 100pi. blue	32·00	19·00
535	25pi. on 200pi. black & green	11·50	6·00

(53) ("1331" = 1915)

1915. Various issues optd with T **53**. I. On postage stamps. (a) 1892 and 1897 issues.

536	**15**	5pa. on 10pa. green	45	20
537		10pa. green	45	20
538		2pi. brown	45	20
539		5pi. purple	1·90	20

(b) 1901 issues. (i) For Internal mail.

540	**21**	5pa. violet	45	20
541		10pa. green	75	20
542		20pa. red	75	20
543		1pi. blue	75	20
544		2pi. orange	1·90	20
545		5pi. mauve	1·00	50
546		25pi. brown	5·75	1·00

(ii) For Foreign mail.

547	**22**	5pa. brown	45	20
548		1pi. blue	2·10	20
549		2pi. blue	1·10	20
550		5pi. brown	7·75	50
551		25pi. green	30·00	10·50

(c) 1905 and 1906 issues.

552	**23**	5pa. buff	45	20
553b		10pa. green	45	20
561		10pa. green (230)	75	20
554a		20pa. pink	45	20
555a		1pi. blue	1·00	20
556b		2pi. grey	1·50	20
562		2pi. grey (233)	2·10	20
557		2½pi. purple	1·50	20
558a		5pi. brown	50	20
559		10pi. orange	7·75	20
560		25pi. green	55·00	2·10

(d) 1908 issues.

563	**25**	5pa. brown		
564		2pi. black	60·00	22·00
569a		2pi. black (255)	7·75	75
565		2½pi. brown	1·50	20
566a		5pi. purple	60·00	16·00
567		10pi. red	7·75	3·00
568		25pi. green	20·00	3·00

(e) 1909 issues.

570	**28**	5pa. brown	45	20
572		20pa. red	45	20
579		20pa. red (290)	75	20
573		1pi. blue	75	20
581		1pi. blue (291)	75	20
574		2pi. black	75	20
582		2pi. black (292)	1·00	20
575		2½pi. brown	38·00	12·00
576		5pi. purple	45	20
577		10pi. red	5·00	20
578		25pi. green	£1200	£650

(f) 1913 issues.

583	**30**	5pa. bistre	45	20
584		10pa. green	45	20
591		10pa. green (343)	45	20
585		20pa. pink	45	20
592		20pa. pink (344)	45	20
586		1pi. blue	45	20
593		1pi. blue (345)	1·10	20
587		2pi. grey	1·00	20
594		2pi. grey (346)	3·75	1·00
588		5pi. purple	1·10	20
589		10pi. red	5·75	50
590		25pi. green	16·00	4·50

II. On printed matter stamps (for use as postage stamps). (a) 1894 issue.

595	**15**	10pa. green	11·50	20
596		2pi. brown	50	75

(b) 1901 issues.

597	**21**	5pa. violet	50	20
600	**22**	10pa. green	1·50	75
598	**21**	20pa. red	1·50	75
599		5pi. mauve	11·50	3·75

(c) 1905 issues.

601b	**23**	5pa. buff	45	20
602		2pi. grey	7·75	3·00
603		5pi. brown	5·75	45

(d) 1908 issues.

604	**25**	2pi. black	£750	£300
605a		5pi. purple	4·50	75

(e) 1909 issues.

606	**28**	5pa. brown	45	20
608		5pi. purple	45·00	16·00

(54) (56)

1915. Various issues optd with T **54** (star varies). I. On postage stamps. (a) 1892 issue, also surch with T **56**.

630	**15**	10pa. on 20pa. red	60	20

(b) 1901 issues.

631	**21**	1pi. blue	45	20
632a		5pi. mauve	5·00	75

(c) 1905 and 1906 issues, Nos. 633 and 636 also surch with T **56**.

609a	**23**	10pa. green	45	45
611b		10pa. green (230)	25·00	4·50
633		10pa. on 20pa. pink	45	25
636		10pa. on 20pa. pink (231)	45	45
634		1pi. blue	5·75	75
637		1pi. blue (232)	45	45
610		10pi. orange	9·00	45

(d) 1908 issues.

612	**25**	10pa. green	90	45
614a		10pa. green (252)	£180	£110
638		20pa. red		
640a		20pa. red (253)	60	45
641		1pi. blue (254)	60	45
613		5pi. purple	35·00	4·50
639		10pi. red	£375	£160

(e) 1909 issues.

616	**28**	10pa. green	45	45
620		10pa. green (289)	45	45
643		20pa. red	45	45
647		20pa. red (290)	1·00	45
645		1pi. blue	45	45
649		1pi. blue (291)	1·50	45
619		5pi. purple	4·75	45
646		10pi. red	£130	75·00

(f) 1913 issues.

623	**30**	10pa. green	60	60
625		10pa. green (343)	60	60
650		20pa. pink	45	35
653		20pa. pink (344)	60	35
624		1pi. blue	60	35
652		10pi. red	16·00	10·00

(g) 1916 Postal Jubilee issue.

654	**60**	10pa. red	60	45
655		20pa. blue	60	45
656		1pi. black and violet	65	45
657		5pi. black and brown	65	45

II. On printed matter stamps (for use as postage stamps). (a) 1894 issue, also surch with T **56**.

658	**15**	10pa. on 20pa. red	45	25

(b) 1901 issue.

659	**22**	5pi. brown	5·75	75

(c) 1908 issue.

626	**25**	10pa. green	£275	£140
627		5pi. purple	35·00	4·75

(d) 1909 issue.

629	**28**	10pa. green	45	45

(57) ("1332" = 1916) (58) (59)

1916. Various issues optd with T **57**, some also surch in piastres as T **58**. I. On postage stamps. (a) 1892 and 1897 issues.

660	**15**	5pa. on 10pa. green (160)	45	45
661		10pa. green	45	40
662		20pa. red	45	40
663		1pi. blue	38·00	38·00
664		2pi. brown	4·00	1·10
665		5pi. purple	38·00	38·00

(b) 1901 issues. (i) Internal mail.

666	**21**	5pa. violet	38·00	38·00
667		10pa. green	1·10	1·00
668		20pa. red	45	45
669		1pi. blue	60	45
670		2pi. orange	1·10	45
671a		10pi. on 25pi. brown	3·75	1·00
672		10pi. on 50pi. brown	5·75	2·10
673a		25pi. brown	5·75	1·10
674		50pi. brown	7·75	1·10

(ii) Foreign mail.

675	**22**	5pa. brown	45	20
676		10pa. green	75	20
677		20pa. mauve	45	20
678		1pi. blue	60	20
679		2pi. blue	3·75	60
680		5pi. on 25pi. green	38·00	38·00
681		10pi. on 25pi. green	38·00	38·00
682		25pi. green	38·00	38·00

(c) 1905 and 1906 issues.

683	**23**	5pa. buff	45	45
692a		10pa. green (230)	75	60
684		20pa. pink	45	45
693		20pa. pink (231)	75	60
685a		1pi. blue	45	45
694a		1pi. blue (232)	75	45
686a		2pi. grey	75	75
687		2½pi. purple	5·75	1·10
688		10pi. on 25pi. green	5·75	1·10
689		10pi. on 50pi. purple	5·75	1·10
690		25pi. green	5·75	1·00
691		50pi. purple	3·75	75

(d) 1908 issues.

701	**25**	2pi. black (255)	38·00	38·00
695		2½pi. brown	38·00	38·00
696		10pi. on 25pi. green	13·00	7·75
697a		10pi. on 50pi. brown	38·00	38·00
698		25pi. on 50pi. brown	38·00	38·00
699		25pi. green	5·75	75
700		50pi. brown	38·00	38·00

(e) 1908 Constitution issue.

702	**27**	5pa. brown	38·00	38·00

(f) 1909 issues.

703	**28**	5pa. brown	50	2·40
704		10pa. green	38·00	38·00
705		20pa. red	38·00	38·00
707		1pi. blue	80	50
711		1pi. blue (291)	38·00	38·00
708		2pi. black	2·10	1·10
712		2pi. black (292)	38·00	38·00
709		2½pi. brown	38·00	38·00
710		5pi. purple	38·00	38·00

(g) 1913 issues.

713	**30**	5pa. bistre	45	45
714		20pa. pink	1·10	45
715		1pi. blue	1·10	45
720		1pi. blue (345)	80	80
716		2pi. grey	2·10	80
717		10pi. on 50pi. brown	7·75	2·10
718		25pi. green	4·50	1·50
719		50pi. brown	10·50	2·10

(h) 1913 Adrianople issue.

721	**31**	10pa. green	50	30
722		20pa. red	80	40
723		40pa. blue	1·90	70

(i) 1914 Constitution issue with further surch.

724		60pa. on 1pi.on 1½pi. grey and red	2·50	75

(j) 1916 Postal Jubilee issues.

725	**60**	5pi. black and brown	1·50	1·00

II. On printed matter stamps (for use as postage stamps). (a) 1894 issues.

726	**15**	5pa. on 10pa. green	45	45
727		10pa. green	75	20
728		20pa. red	40	20
729		5pi. purple	38·00	38·00

(b) 1901 issues. (i) Internal mail.

730	**21**	5pa. violet	26·00	38·00
731		10pa. green	26·00	38·00
732		20pa. red	50	45
733		1pi. blue	50	45
734		2pi. orange	80	45

(ii) Foreign mail.

735	**22**	5pa. brown	15	10
736		10pa. green	25	10
737		20pa. mauve	20	10
738		1pi. blue	35	15

(c) 1905 issue.

739	**23**	5pa. buff	45	45
740		10pa. green	38·00	19·00
741		20pa. pink	38·00	19·00
742a		1pi. blue	1·10	45

(d) 1908 issue.

743a	**25**	5pa. brown	38·00	38·00

(e) 1909 issue.

744	**28**	5pa. brown	38·00	38·00

III. On 1913 Adrianople postage due issues (for use as postage stamps).

745	**31**	10 on 2pa. on 10pa. green	42·00	38·00
746		20 on 5pa. on 20pa. red	42·00	38·00
747		40 on 10pa. on 40pa. blue	42·00	38·00

1916. Occupation of Sinai Peninsula. Optd with T **59**.

749	**21**	5pa. violet	60	30
750		10pa. green	65	30
751	**28**	20pa. red	1·60	35
752		1pi. blue	3·00	60
753	**30**	5pi. purple	9·50	1·50

60 Old G.P.O., Constantinople

(61)

1916. Jubilee of Constantinople City Post.

754	**60**	5pa. green	1·10	15
755		10pa. red	1·10	15
756		20pa. blue	1·10	15
757		1pi. black and violet	1·10	15
758		5pi. black and brown	14·50	85

1916. National Fete. Optd with T **61**.

759	**15**	10pa. green	1·25	1·50
760b	**23**	20pa. red	2·25	75
761a		1pi. blue	7·00	1·90
762b		2pi. grey	8·25	1·00
763		2½pi. purple	14·00	1·10

62 Dolmabahce Palace

63 Sentry

64 Sultan Mohamed V

1916.

764	**62**	10pi. violet	18·00	2·40
765		10pi. green on grey	7·25	2·40
766		10pi. brown	11·00	65
767	**63**	25pi. red on buff	1·90	65
768	**64**	50pi. red	3·50	2·10
769		50pi. green on yellow	2·00	10·00
770		50pi. blue	1·10	1·00

65 Off to the Front

(66)

1917. Charity.

771	**65**	10pa. purple	80	30

1917. Various issues optd with T **66** or surch in addition. A. On postage stamp issue of 1865.

782	**2**	10pa. mauve	32·00	32·00
772a		20pa. yellow	32·00	32·00
783		20pa. green	32·00	32·00
785		20pa. grey	32·00	32·00
773b		1pi. lilac	32·00	32·00
784		1pi. yellow	32·00	32·00
774		2pi. blue	32·00	32·00
780		2pi. red to brown	32·00	32·00
775		5pi. red	32·00	32·00
778		5pi. blue	32·00	32·00
779		25pi. red	32·00	32·00

B. On surcharged postage stamp issue of 1876.

787 **2** ¼pre. on 10pa. mauve . . . 32·00 32·00
788 ½pre. on 20pa. green . . . . 32·00 32·00
789 1¼pre. on 50pa. red . . . . 32·00 32·00

C. On postage stamp issue of 1876.

790 **9** 5pa. black and yellow . . . 32·00 32·00
791 5pa. black 50 50
792 10pa. black and green . . . 32·00 32·00
793 10pa. green . . . . 32·00 32·00
794 50pa. black and yellow . . . 32·00 32·00
795 2pi. black and flesh . . . . 32·00 32·00
796 2pi. ochre . . . . 32·00 32·00
797 2pi. orange and blue . . . . 1·25 25
798 5pi. brown . . . . 32·00 32·00
799 5pi. green . . . . 32·00 32·00
801 25pi. purple and mauve . . 32·00 32·00
802 25pi. brown . . . . 32·00 32·00

D. On postage stamp issue of 1892.

803 **15** 20pa. purple 75 75
804 2pi. brown . . . . 1·50 1·00

E. On postage stamp issue of 1901.

805 **21** 5pa. violet . . . . 23·00 23·00
806 10pa. green . . . . 2·25 2·25
807 20pa. red 50 50
808 1pi. blue 50 50
809 2pi. orange . . . . 1·50 3·00
810 5pi. mauve . . . . 23·00 23·00
811 10pi. on 50pi. brown . . . 23·00 23·00
812 25pi. brown . . . . 3·00 2·25

F. On postage stamp issue of 1901.

813 **22** 5pa. brown . . . . 1·50 1·90
814 20pa. mauve 50 50
815 1pi. blue . . . . 1·25 1·25
816 2pi. blue . . . . 3·00 3·00
817 5pi. brown . . . . 23·00 23·00
818 10pi. on 50pi. yellow . . . £110 £110
819 25pi. green . . . . 55·00 23·00

G. On postage stamp issues of 1905 and 1906.

820 **23** 5pa. buff 45 45
821 10pa. green . . . . 23·00 23·00
830 10pa. green (No. 230) . . . 1·00 1·25
822 20pa. pink 45 45
831 20pa. pink (No. 231) . . . 45 45
823 1pi. blue 45 45
832 1pi. blue (No. 232) 45 45
824 2pi. grey . . . . 3·00 3·00
833 2pi. grey (No. 233) . . . . 23·00 23·00
825 2½pi. purple . . . . 3·00 3·00
826 5pi. brown . . . . 23·00 23·00
827 10pi. orange . . . . 23·00 23·00
828 10pi. on 50pi. purple . . . 23·00 23·00
829 25pi. green . . . . 23·00 23·00

H. On postage stamp issues of 1908.

834a **25** 5pa. brown . . . . 2·25 2·25
835 10pa. green 50 50
840 10pa. green (No. 252) . . 60·00 60·00
841 1pi. blue (No. 254) . . . 23·00 23·00
836 2pi. black . . . . 23·00 23·00
842 2pi. black (No. 255) . . . 23·00 23·00
837a 2½pi. brown . . . . 2·25 2·25
838 10pi. on 50pi. brown . . . 23·00 23·00
839 25pi. green . . . . 23·00 23·00

I. On Constitution issue of 1908.

843 **27** 5pa. brown . . . . 1·25 1·25

J. On postage stamp issues of 1909.

844 **28** 5pa. brown 50 50
846 10pa. green 50 50
854 10pa. green (No. 289) . . 60·00 60·00
847 20pa. red 50 50
849 1pi. blue 50 50
856 1pi. blue (No. 291) . . . 13·00 13·00
850 2pi. black . . . . 2·25 2·25
857 2pi. black (No. 292) . . . 12·00 12·00
851 2½pi. brown . . . . 23·00 23·00
852a 5pi. purple . . . . 23·00 23·00
853 10pi. red . . . . 23·00 23·00

K. On postage stamp issues of 1913.

858 **30** 5pa. bistre . . . . 75 1·25
859 10pa. green . . . . 23·00 23·00
865 10pa. green (No. 343) . . . 1·00 1·00
860 20pa. pink . . . . 1·00 1·00
861 1pi. blue . . . . 1·00 1·00
866 1pi. blue (No. 345) . . . 2·10 2·10
862 2pi. grey . . . . 2·10 2·10
867 2pi. grey (No. 346) . . . . 23·00 23·00
863 5pi. purple . . . . 23·00 23·00
864 10pi. red . . . . 23·00 23·00

L. On Adrianople Commem stamps of 1913.

868 **31** 10pa. green . . . . 1·50 1·50
869 40pa. blue . . . . 2·10 2·10

M. On Constitution Commem of 1914 with additional surch in Turkish.

870 60pa. on 1pi. on 1½pi. grey and red (No. 521) . . . . 1·00 1·00

N. On postage stamp issues of 1916.

871 **63** 25pi. red on buff . . . . . 3·00 3·00
872 **64** 50pi. red . . . . 12·00 12·00
873 50pi. green on yellow . . . 10·00 10·00
874 50pi. blue . . . . 23·00 23·00

O. On stamps of Eastern Roumelia of 1881 (T **9** of Turkey, but inscr "ROUMELIE ORIENTALE" at left).

876 5pa. lilac . . . . 23·00 23·00
877 10pa. green . . . . 23·00 23·00
875 20pa. black and red . . . . 23·00 23·00
878 20pa. red . . . . 23·00 23·00

P. On printed matter stamps of 1893 optd with Type N **16**.

879 **15** 20pa. red (No. N 156a) . . 2·50 2·50
880 1pi. blue (No. N 157) . . . 45 65

Q. On printed matter stamps of 1901 optd with Type N **23**.

881 **21** 5pa. violet (No. N183) . . 1·50 1·50
882 10pa. green (No. N184) . . 15·00 12·50
883 20pa. red (No. N185) . . . 1·00 45
884 1pi. blue (No. N186) . . . 2·10 2·10
885 **21** 2pi. orange (No. N187) . . 1·50 1·90
886 5pi. mauve (No. N188) . . 23·00 23·00

R. On printed matter stamps of 1901 optd with Type N **23**.

887 **22** 5pa. brown (No. N189) . . 2·50 2·50
888 10pa. green (No. N190) . . 2·50 2·50
889 20pa. mauve (No. N191) . 2·50 2·50
890 2pi. blue (No. N193) . . . 30·00 30·00

S. On printed matter stamps of 1905 optd with Type N **23**.

891d **23** 5pa. brown (No. N222) . . 45 45
892 10pa. green (No. N223) . . 1·00 1·25
893 20pa. pink (No. N224) . . 45 45
894 1pi. blue (No. N225) . . 45 45
895 2pi. grey (No. N226) . . 23·00 23·00
896 5pi. brown (No. N227) . . 23·00 23·00

T. On printed matter stamp of 1908 optd with Type N **27**.

897 **25** 5pa. brown (No. N244) . . 23·00 23·00

U. On postage due stamps of 1865.

898 D **4** 20pa. brown . . . . . . 30·00 30·00
899 1pi. brown . . . . 30·00 30·00
900 2pi. brown . . . . 30·00 30·00
901 5pi. brown . . . . 30·00 30·00
902 25pi. brown . . . . 30·00 30·00

V. On postage due stamps of 1888.

904 **9** 1pi. black (D118) . . . . 30·00 30·00
905 2pi. black (D119) . . . . . 30·00 30·00

W. On postage due stamps of 1892.

906 **15** 20pa. black (D146) . . . . 1·00 1·25
907 1pi. black (D148) . . . . 1·00 1·25
908 2pi. black (D149) . . . . . 1·00 1·25

X. On Adrianople commemoration issue of 1913 (postage due stamps surch in Arabic further surch).

909 **31** 10 on 2pa. on 10pa. green (D356) 60 60
910 20 on 5pa. on 20pa. red (D357) 60 60
911 40 on 10pa. on 40pa. blue (D358) . . . . 1·00 1·00
912 40 on 20pa. on 40pa. blue (D359) . . . . 2·10 2·50

The overprints on printed matter and postage due stamps were surcharged for ordinary postage.

67 In the Trenches

69 Howitzer at Sedd el Bahr

1917. Surch variously in Turkish.

913 **67** 5pa. on 1pi. red 50 45
915 **65** 10pa. on 20pa. red . . . . 1·75 45
914 **69** 5pi. on 2pa. blue . . . . . 7·50 70

72 Mosque at Ortakoy

73 Lighthouse, Achir Kapu

74 Martyrs' Column

77 Seraglio Point

75 Map of Gallipoli

76 Map of Gallipoli

1917.

916 **69** 2pa. violet 55 20
917 **72** 5pa. orange 55 20
918 **73** 10pa. green 55 20
919 **74** 20pa. red 55 20
920 **75** 1pi. blue . . . . 1·10 20
921 **76** 50pa. blue . . . . 1·25 70
921b **77** 2pi. blue and brown . . . 1·50 25
922 – 5pi. brown and blue . . . 14·00 1·00

DESIGNS—As T **77**. 5pi. Pyramids.

1918. Surch **5 Piastres 5** and in Turkish.

923 **69** 5pi. on 2pa. blue . . . . . 7·50 80

1918. No. 913 with additional surch.

924 **67** 2pa. on 5pa. on 1pi. red . . 80 70

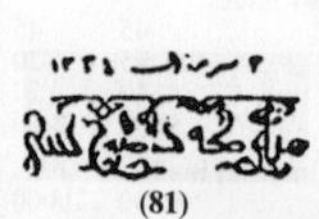
(**81**)

84 Wells at Beersheba

85 Sentry at Beersheba

87 Turkish Column in Sinai

1918. Armistice. Optd as T **81**.

925 **84** 20pa. purple 20 25
926 **75** 1pi. blue . . . . 4·00 4·00
927 **85** 1pi. blue . . . . 75·00 75·00
937 D **51** 1pi. blue (No. D518) . . 75·00 75·00
928 **76** 50pa. blue 25 30
929 **77** 2pi. blue and brown . . 25 30
930 – 2½pi. green and orange (No. 509) . . . . . . 75·00 80·00
931 – 5pi. brown and blue (No. 922) 25 25
932 **62** 10pi. green on grey . . . 3·00 3·00
933 **63** 25pi. red on buff . . . . 3·00 3·00
934 **87** 25pi. blue . . . . 75·00 75·00
935 – 50pi. pink (No. 513) . . 75·00 75·00
936 **64** 50pi. green on yellow . . 4·00 4·00

1918. Stamp of 1909 optd with Sultan's toughra and surch in Turkish.

938 **28** 5pa. on 2pa. green 75 75

86 Dome of the Rock, Jerusalem

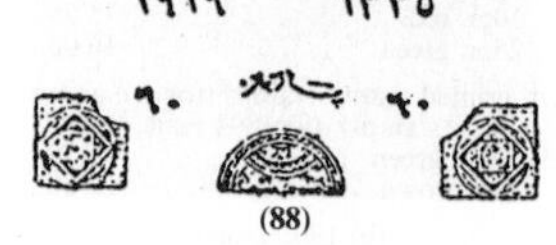
(**88**)

1919. Accession of Sultan Mohamed VI. Optd with date as in T **88** and ornaments or inscription.

939 **84** 20pa. purple . . . . . . 1·75 1·75
940 **85** 1pi. blue . . . . 2·50 10·50
941 **86** 60pa. on 10pa. green . . 1·10 4·50
942 **87** 25pi. blue . . . . 5·00 23·00

The illustrations Type **85** (optd with date and inscription at foot) and **86** (surch with T **88**) illustrate Nos. 940/1. Nos. 939 and 942 are overprinted with the date and the central motif only at bottom of Type **88**.

(**89**) (**91**)

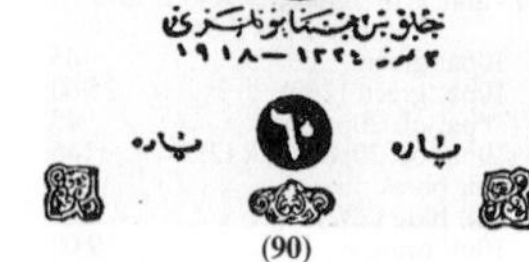
(**90**)

1919. 1st Anniv of Sultan's Accession. Optd or surch as T **89**, **90** or **91**.

943 **69** 2pa. violet . . . . . . 55 2·10
944 **72** 5pa. orange 25 35
945 **28** 5pa. on 2pa. green . . . 25 35
946 **30** 10pa. on 2pa. green . . 25 35
960a D **49** 10pa. on 5pa. brown . . 13·50 13·00
947 **73** 10pa. green 55 60
948 **74** 20pa. red 25 35
960b D **50** 20pa. red . . . . 13·50 13·00
949 **75** 1pi. blue 40 75
960c D **51** 1pi. blue . . . . 13·50 13·00
950 **76** 60pa. on 50pa. blue . . 80 75
951 **77** 60pa. on 2pi. blue and brown 25 35
952 2pi. blue and brown . . 35 35
960d D **52** 2pi. blue . . . . 13·50 13·00
952a – 2½pi. green and orange (No. 509) . . . . . 13·50 13·00
953 – 5pi. brown and blue (No. 922) 25 35
954 **62** 10pi. brown . . . . . . 1·10 1·00
955 **84** 10pi. on 20pa. purple . . 35 35
956 **63** 25pi. red and buff . . . 1·25 1·25
957 **85** 35pi. on 1pi. blue . . . 2·00 1·25
958 **64** 50pi. green on yellow . . 2·25 2·10
958a 50pi. red . . . . 12·50 12·50
959 **86** 100pi. on 60pa. on 10pa. green . . . . . 3·25 3·00
960 **87** 250pi. on 25pi. blue . . 3·25 3·00

Types **84** and **87** illustrate Nos. 955 and 960.

1921. Surch in figures and words and in Turkish characters.

970 **65** 30pa. on 10pa. purple . . . 55 35
971 – 60pa. on 10pa. green (No. 503) 55 35
972 **67** 4½pi. on 1pi. red . . . . . 1·25 40
973 – 7½ on 3pi. blue (No. 965) . . 8·50 85

Numerous fiscal and other stamps were surcharged or overprinted by the Turkish Nationalist Government at Angora during 1921, but as they are not often met with by general collectors we omit them. A full listing will be found in Part 16 (Central Asia) of the Stanley Gibbons catalogue. Nos. A79/90 and A119/24 were the only definitive issue of the Angora Government at this period.

A **24** National Pact

A **25** Parliament House, Sivas

1921.

A79 A **24** 10pa. purple 20 10
A80 – 20pa. green 25 10
A81 – 1pi. blue 45 15
A82 – 2pi. purple . . . . . . 1·75 15
A83 – 5pi. blue . . . . 1·40 15
A84 – 10pi. brown . . . . . . 3·75 25
A85 – 25pi. red . . . . 9·25 15
A86 A **25** 50pi. blue (A) 45 45
A87 50pi. blue (B) 40 85
A88 – 100pi. violet . . . . . 60·00 2·75
A89 – 200pi. violet . . . . . £170 35·00
A90 – 500pi. green . . . . . 90·00 17·00

DESIGNS—HORIZ: 20pa. Izmir Harbour; 1pi. Mosque, Adrianople; 10pi. Legendary grey wolf, Boz Kurt; 25pi. Castle Adana; 200pi. Map of Anatolia. VERT: 2pi. Mosque, Konya; 5pi. Soldier taking oath; 100pi. Mosque, Ourfa; 500pi. Declaration of faith from Koran.

Type (B) of the 50pi. as illustrated. In Type (A) the inscription at the top is similar to that of Type A **30** and the figures in the value tablets are above instead of below the Turkish inscription.

A **30** First Parliament House, Angora

1922.

A119 A **30** 5pa. mauve 25 30
A120 10pa. green 65 35
A121 20pa. red 90 55
A122 1pi. orange . . . . . 5·25 85
A123 2pi. brown . . . . . 10·00 3·00
A124 3pi. red . . . . 1·00 35

(**94a**)

1923. Izmir (Smyrna) Economic Congress. Nos. 918 and A80/4 optd with T **94a**.

973b **73** 10pa. green . . . . . . 3·00 2·10
973c – 20pa. green . . . . . . 3·00 3·25
973d – 1pi. blue . . . . 5·75 4·50
973e – 2pi. purple . . . . . . 5·75 6·75
973f – 5pi. blue . . . . 8·50 10·00
973g – 10pi. brown . . . . . . 13·00 18·00

95

96 Kemal Ataturk and Sakarya Bridge

1923.

974 95 10pa. grey 15 10
975 20pa. yellow 15 10
976 1pi. mauve 15 10
977 1½pi. green 15 10
978 2pi. green . . . . 1·00 10
979 3pi. brown 45 10
980 3½pi. brown . . . . . . 1·25 30
1001 4½pi. red 65 10
1002 5pi. violet . . . . 1·60 10
1003 7½pi. blue . . . . 1·60 10
1004 10pi. grey . . . . 4·75 1·10
1012a 10pi. blue . . . . 50·00 70
986 95 11½pi. pink . . . . . . 1·75 40
1006 15pi. brown . . . . . . 4·75 1·10
988 18¾pi. green . . . . . . 2·75 65
989 22½pi. orange . . . . . 4·00 85
990 25pi. brown . . . . . . 15·00 80
991 50pi. grey . . . . 45·00 1·10
992 100pi. purple . . . . . . £150 1·90
993 500pi. green . . . . . . £325 80·00

1924. Treaty of Lausanne.
1013 96 1½pi. green 85 60
1014 3pi. violet . . . . 1·25 60
1015 4½pi. pink . . . . 1·75 1·75
1016 5pi. brown . . . . 2·10 2·50
1017 7½pi. blue . . . . 1·75 1·75
1018 50pi. orange . . . . . . 12·50 11·50
1019 100pi. purple . . . . . . 42·00 19·00
1020 200pi. olive . . . . 60·00 25·00

97 Legendary Blacksmith and Grey Wolf, Boz Kurt

98 Gorge and River Sakarya

99 Fortress of Ankara

100 Kemal Ataturk

1926.

1021 97 10pa. grey 10 10
1022 20pa. orange 10 10
1023 1gr. red 15 10
1024 98 2gr. green . . . . 1·25 45
1025 2½gr. black . . . . . . 1·75 10
1026 3gr. red . . . . 2·10 10
1027 99 5gr. violet . . . . 3·25 10
1028 6gr. red 90 10
1029 10gr. blue . . . . 8·75 10
1030 15gr. orange . . . . . . 10·50 10
1031 100 25gr. black and green . . 11·50 25
1032 50gr. black and red . . . 14·50 30
1033 100gr. black and olive 30·00 85
1034 200gr. black and brown 75·00 65

(101 "1927 Izmir Exhibition")

(102 "Izmir, 9 Sept, 1928")

1927. Izmir (Smyrna) Exhibition. Optd with T **101**.
1035 97 1gr. red 20 10
1036 98 2gr. green 25 15
1037 2½gr. black 85 45
1038 3gr. red . . . . 1·10 45
1039 99 5gr. violet . . . . 2·40 45
1040 6gr. red 85 10
1041 10gr. blue . . . . 2·25 1·25
1042 15gr. orange . . . . . . 3·50 1·50
1043 100 25gr. black and green . . 11·50 5·00
1044 50gr. black and red . . . 23·00 15·00
1045 100gr. black and olive 42·00 38·00

1928. 2nd Izmir Exhibition. T **97/9** optd with T **102** and T **100** optd **928** and 2 lines of Turkish.
1053 97 10pa. grey 15 10
1054 20pa. orange 15 10
1055 1gr. red 50 10
1056 98 2gr. green 65 45
1057 2½gr. black 65 45
1058 3gr. red 65 45
1059 99 5gr. violet . . . . 80 1·10
1060 6gr. red 50 10
1061 10gr. blue . . . . 2·25 75
1062 15gr. orange . . . . . . 2·40 45
1063 100 25gr. black and green . . 8·75 7·50
1064 50gr. black and red . . . 11·00 7·50
1065 100gr. black and olive 25·00 17·00
1066 200gr. black and brown 35·00 17·00

1929. Surch with value in "Paradir" or "Kurustur".
1067 97 20par. on 1gr. red 35 15
1068 99 2½kur. on 5gr. violet . . . 50 25
1069 6kur. on 10gr. blue . . . 5·00 45

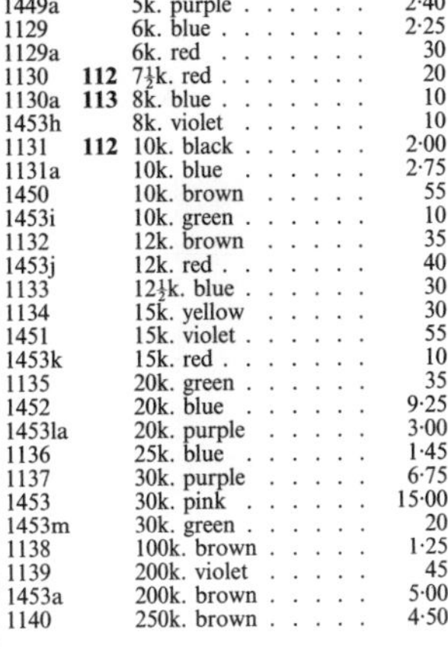
106 Bridge over Kizil-Irmak

107 Gorge and River Sakarya

1929. T **106/7** and 1926 stamps but inscr "TURKIYE CUMHURIYETI".
1076 97 10pa. green 10 10
1077 106 20pa. violet 10 10
1078 1k. green 25 35
1079 97 1½k. green 30 25
1070 106 2k. black . . . . 3·25 30
1080 2k. violet . . . . 2·40 45
1081 2½k. green . . . . 1·50 45
1072 3k. purple . . . . 3·00 35
1082 3k. red . . . . 15·00 45
1083 97 4k. red . . . . 6·75 15
1084 99 5k. purple . . . . 9·50 15
1085 97 6k. blue . . . . 6·00 15
1086 107 7½k. red 20 15
1088 99 12½k. blue 35 15
1089 15k. orange 45 15
1090 107 17½k. black 50 55
1091 99 20k. brown . . . . 35·00 60
1092 107 25k. brown 60 40
1093 99 30k. brown . . . . 1·25 40
1094 107 40k. purple . . . . 1·25 40
1075 100 50k. black and red . . . 38·00 2·00

109

112 Kemal Ataturk

113

1930.

1095 109 50k. black and red . . . 2·50 35
1096 100k. black and olive . . 2·50 45
1097 200k. black and green 2·50 95
1098 500k. black and brown 17·00 4·75

1930. Opening of Ankara–Sivas Railway. Surch **Sivas D. Y. 30ag. 930** and value.
1099 97 10pa. on 10pa. green . . 15 10
1100 106 10pa. on 20pa. violet . . 20 25
1101 20pa. on 1k. green . . . 35 25
1102 97 1k. on 1½k. green . . . 25 10
1103 106 1½k. on 2k. violet . . . 45 45
1104 2k. on 2½k. green . . . 1·10 65
1105 2½k. on 3k. red 85 65
1106 97 3k. on 4k. red 85 35
1107 99 4k. on 5k. purple 85 35
1108 97 5k. on 6k. blue . . . . 1·60 60
1109 107 6k. on 7½k. red 25 35
1110 99 7½k. on 12½k. blue . . . 55 35
1111 12½k. on 15k. orange . . 40 35
1112 107 15k. on 17½k. black . . 2·25 1·25
1113 99 17½k. on 20k. brown . . 1·90 80
1114 107 20k. on 25k. brown . . 3·00 95
1115 99 25k. on 30k. brown . . 1·90 1·90
1116 107 30k. on 40k. purple . . . 3·00 1·90
1117 109 40k. on 50k. black and red . . . . 6·00 1·90
1118 50k. on 100k. black and green . . . . 42·00 3·25
1119 100k. on 200k. black and green . . . . 55·00 6·00
1120 250k. on 500k. black and brown . . . . 45·00 4·75

1931. Surch **1 Kurus**.
1121 97 1k. on 1½k. green . . . . 2·10 15

1931.

1122 112 10pa. green 10 10
1444 10pa. brown 10 10
1444a 10pa. red 10 10
1123 20pa. orange 10 10
1445 20pa. green 10 10
1453b 20pa. yellow 10 10
1123a 30pa. violet 10 10
1124 113 1k. green 10 10
1453c 1k. orange 10 10
1124a 112 1½k. lilac 10 10
1125 113 2k. violet 10 15
1125a 2k. green 15 10
1447 2k. mauve 10 10
1447a 2k. yellow 45 10
1453d 2k. pink 10 10
1126 112 2½k. green 15 10
1126a 113 3k. brown 10 10
1448 3k. orange 10 10
1448a 3k. blue 20 10
1127 4k. black 90 10
1453f 4k. green 10 10
1128 5k. red 15 10
1128a 5k. black 55 10
1453g 5k. blue . . . . 1·60 10
1449a 5k. purple . . . . . . 2·40 10
1129 6k. blue . . . . 2·25 10
1129a 6k. red 30 10
1130 112 7½k. red 20 10
1130a 113 8k. blue 10 10
1453h 8k. violet 10 10
1131 112 10k. black . . . . 2·00 10
1131a 10k. blue . . . . 2·75 15
1450 10k. brown 55 10
1453i 10k. green 10 10
1132 12k. brown 35 10
1453j 12k. red 40 10
1133 12½k. blue 30 10
1134 15k. yellow 30 10
1451 15k. violet 55 10
1453k 15k. red 10 10
1135 20k. green 35 10
1452 20k. blue . . . . 9·25 10
1453la 20k. purple . . . . . . 3·00 10
1136 25k. blue . . . . 1·45 10
1137 30k. purple . . . . . . 6·75 10
1453 30k. pink . . . . 15·00 10
1453m 30k. green 20 10
1138 100k. brown . . . . . . 1·25 15
1139 200k. violet 45 15
1453a 200k. brown . . . . . . 5·00 35
1140 250k. brown . . . . . . 4·50 10

114 Tree with Roots in Six Balkan Capitals

115 "Rebirth of Turkey"

1931. 2nd Balkan Conference.
1141 114 2½k. green 10 10
1142 4k. red 15 10
1143 6k. blue 15 10
1144 7½k. red 20 10
1145 12k. orange 20 10
1146 12½k. blue 30 10
1147 30k. violet 45 10
1148 50k. brown 75 10
1149 100k. purple . . . . . . 1·10 10

1933. 10th Anniv of Turkish Republic.
1150 115 1½k. green 50 15
1151 2k. bistre 50 15
1152 – 3k. red 50 35
1153 – 6k. blue 50 25
1154 115 12½k. blue 90 65
1155 25k. brown . . . . . . 2·00 1·25
1156 – 50k. brown . . . . . . 4·50 1·50
DESIGNS—HORIZ: 3, 6, 50k. Wheat, cogwheels, factory, "X" and Kemal Ataturk.

1934. Air. Optd **1934** and airplane or surch also.
1157 107 7½k. lake 10 15
1158 99 12½k. on 15k. orange . . 10 15
1159 107 20k. on 25k. brown . . . 10 20
1160 25k. brown 10 30
1161 40k. purple 35 50

1934. Izmir International Fair. Optd **Izmir 9 Eylul 934 Sergisi** or surch also.
1162 97 10pa. green 20 10
1163 1k. on 1½k. green . . . 25 10
1164 107 2k. on 25k. brown . . . 40 15
1165 5k. on 7½k. red . . . . 4·00 2·10
1166 6k. on 17½k. black . . . 2·00 85
1167 99 12½k. blue . . . . 4·00 2·50
1168 15k. on 20k. brown . . 35·00 20·00
1169 107 20k. on 25k. brown . . 26·00 15·00
1170 109 50k. on 100k. black and green . . . . 48·00 15·00

119 Alliance Badge

120 Mrs. C. Chapman Catt

1935. 12th Congress of the International Women's Alliance, Istanbul.
1171 119 20pa.+20pa. bistre . . . 35 40
1172 – 1k.+1k. red 40 40
1173 – 2k.+2k. blue 50 75
1174 – 2½k.+2½k. green 50 75
1175 – 4k.+4k. blue . . . . . . 1·00 1·40
1176 – 5k.+5k. purple . . . . . 1·50 2·00
1177 – 7½k.+7½k. red . . . . . 2·25 3·00
1178 120 10k.+10k. orange . . . . 2·25 3·00
1179 – 12½k.+12½k. blue . . . . 4·25 5·75
1180 – 15k.+15k. violet . . . . 5·25 7·00
1181 – 20k.+20k. red . . . . . 8·75 12·00
1182 – 25k.+25k. green . . . . 11·00 15·00
1183 – 30k.+30k. blue . . . . . 55·00 70·00
1184 – 50k.+50k. green £110 £140
1185 – 100k.+100k. red . . . . 75·00 £100

DESIGNS: 1k. Woman teacher; 2k. Woman farmer; 2½k. Typist; 4k. Woman pilot and policewoman; 5k. Women voters; 7½k. Yildiz Palace, Istanbul; 12½k. Jane Addams; 15k. Grazia Deledda; 20k. Selma Lagerlof; 25k. Bertha von Suttner; 30k. Sigrid Undset; 50k. Mme. Curie-Sklodowska; 100k. Kemal Ataturk.

1936. Remilitarization of Dardanelles. Surch **BOGAZLAR MUKAVELESININ IMZASI 20/7/1936** and value in figures.
1186 107 4k. on 17½k. black . . . 50 50
1187 5k. on 25k. brown . . . 55 50
1188 100 6k. on 50k. black and red 35 30
1189 109 10k. on 100k. black and olive 95 40
1190 20k. on 200k. black and green . . . . 3·25 50
1191 50k. on 500k. black and brown . . . . 3·25 95

122 Stag

124 Arms of Turkey, Greece, Rumania and Yugoslavia

1937. 2nd Turkish Historical Congress.
1192 122 3k. violet 30 65
1193 – 6k. blue 40 70
1194 122 7½k. red 60 30
1195 – 12½k. blue . . . . 1·90 1·60
DESIGN: 6, 12½k. Bust of Ataturk.

1937. Balkan Entente.
1196 124 8k. red . . . . 6·25 2·10
1197 12½k. blue . . . . 8·00 3·25

1938. Air. Surch **1937** with airplane above and value.
1198 107 4½k. on 7½k. lake . . . 25 70
1199 99 9k. on 15k. orange . . . 15·00 15·00
1200 107 35k. on 40k. purple . . . 2·40 3·25

127 Fig Tree

129 Railway Bridge

1938. Izmir International Fair.
1201 – 10pa. brown 20 10
1202 – 30pa. violet 25 15
1203 127 2½k. green 45 45
1204 – 3k. orange 35 15
1205 – 5k. green 85 35
1206 – 6k. brown . . . . 2·25 1·40
1207 – 7½k. red . . . . 2·25 1·10
1208 – 8k. red . . . . 2·25 75
1209 – 12k. purple . . . . . . 2·50 1·40
1210 – 12½k. blue . . . . 7·50 5·25
DESIGNS—HORIZ: 10pa. An Izmir boulevard; 30pa. Izmir Fair; 6k. Woman gathering grapes. VERT: 3k. Clock Tower, Hukunet Square; 5k. Olive branch; 7½k. Woman gathering grapes; 8k. Izmir Harbour; 12k. Equestrian statue of Ataturk; 12½k. Ataturk.

1938. 15th Anniv of Proclamation of Turkish Republic.
1211 – 2½k. green 30 15
1212 – 3k. red 20 15
1213 – 6k. bistre 45 20
1214 129 7½k. red . . . . 1·00 60
1215 – 8k. purple . . . . 2·40 3·50
1216 – 12½k. blue . . . . 85 2·00
DESIGNS—HORIZ: 2½k. Military display; 3k. Aerial view of Kayseri; 8k. Scout buglers. VERT: 6k. Ataturk driving a tractor; 12½k. Ataturk.

130 Kemal Ataturk teaching Alphabet

1938. 10th Anniv of Introduction of Latin Alphabet into Turkey.
1217 130 2½k. green 25 25
1218 3k. orange 20 25
1219 6k. purple 25 35
1220 7½k. red 35 50
1221 8k. red 90 65
1222 12½k. blue . . . . 80 1·75

1938. Death of Kemal Ataturk. Mourning Issue. Optd **21-11-1938** and bar.
1223 113 3k. brown 10 25
1224 5k. red 10 25
1225 6k. blue 15 70
1226 112 7½k. red 10 25
1227 113 8k. blue 85 90
1228 112 12½k. blue . . . . 1·75 2·75

133 Presidents Inonu and Roosevelt and Map of North America

1939. 150th Anniv of U.S. Constitution.
1229 – 2½k. green, red and blue 20 20
1230 **133** 3k. brown and blue . . . 20 20
1231 – 6k. violet, red and blue 20 20
1232 – 7½k. red and blue . . . 30 15
1233 **133** 8k. purple and blue . . . 45 45
1234 – 12½k. ultramarine & blue 1·25 95
DESIGNS—VERT: 2½, 6k. Turkish and U.S. flags. HORIZ: 7½, 12½k. Ataturk and George Washington.

1939. Cession of Hatay to Turkey. Surch **Hatayin Anavatana Kavusmasi 23/7/1939** and new values.
1235 **107** 3k. on 25k. brown . . . 25 30
1236 **109** 6k. on 200k. black and green 15 25
1237 **107** 7½k. on 25k. brown . . 35 55
1238 **109** 12k. on 100k. (1096) . . 35 30
1239 12½k. on 200k. (1097) . . 60 55
1240 17½k. on 500k. (1098) . . 1·25 1·10

135 Railway Bridge over River Firat

136 Kemal Ataturk

1939. Opening of Ankara–Erzurum Railway.
1241 **135** 3k. red . . . . 1·25 2·40
1242 – 6k. brown . . . . 1·25 4·25
1243 – 7½k. red . . . . 1·60 4·50
1244 – 12½k. blue . . . . 2·75 7·00
DESIGNS—VERT: 6k. Steam locomotive. HORIZ: 7½k. Railway in Firat gorge; 12½k. Tunnel entrance at Atma-Bogazi.

1939. 1st Death Anniv of Kemal Ataturk.
1245 – 2½k. green 15 20
1246 – 3k. blue 20 25
1247 – 5k. brown 25 25
1248 **136** 6k. brown 25 25
1249 – 7½k. red 95 40
1250 – 8k. olive 30 65
1251 – 12½k. blue 40 65
1252 – 17½k. red . . . . 1·25 1·00
MS1252a 90 × 119 mm. 100k. indigo 20·00 25·00
DESIGN: 2½k. Ataturk's residence; 3k. to 17½k. Portraits of Kemal Ataturk as Type **136**.

1940. Balkan Entente. As T **103** of Yugoslavia, but with the torch and Arms of Turkey, Greece, Rumania and Yugoslavia rearranged.
1253 8k. blue 85 45
1254 10k. blue . . . . 1·75 30

137 Namik Kemal

139 Map and Census Figures

1940. Birth Centenary of Namik Kemal (poet).
1255 **137** 6k. brown 30 30
1256 8k. olive . . . . 1·10 90
1257 12k. red . . . . 1·10 1·10
1258 12½k. blue . . . . 2·10 1·25

1940. Izmir International Fair. Surch **IZMIR ENTERNASYONAL FUARI 1940** and value.
1259 **109** 6k. on 200k. black and green 25 25
1260 10k. on 200k. black and green 25 25
1261 12k. on 500k. black and brown 30 30

1940. National Census.
1262 **139** 10pa. green 15 10
1263 3k. orange 25 20
1264 6k. red 45 35
1265 10k. blue 80 60

140 Hurdling

1940. 11th Balkan Games.
1266 – 3k. olive . . . . 65 1·75
1267 – 6k. red . . . . 2·75 3·25
1268 **140** 8k. brown . . . . 1·10 1·10
1269 – 10k. blue . . . . 2·00 85
DESIGNS—VERT: 3k. Running; 6k. Pole vaulting; 10k. Throwing the discus.

141 Postmen of 1840 and 1940

1940. Centenary of First Adhesive Postage Stamps.
1270 – 3k. green 15 10
1271 **141** 6k. red 30 25
1272 – 10k. blue 60 60
1273 – 12k. brown 75 55
DESIGNS—HORIZ: 3k. Mail carriers on horseback. VERT: 10k. Early paddle-steamer and modern mail launch; 12k. G.P.O., Istanbul.

142 Exhibition Building

1941. Izmir International Fair.
1274 – 30pa. green 15 10
1275 **142** 3k. grey 10 10
1276 – 6k. red 10 10
1277 – 10k. blue 10 10
1278 – 12k. purple 15 15
1279 – 17½k. brown 65 30
DESIGNS—HORIZ: 30pa. Freighter "Etrusk" in Izmir harbour; 6, 17½k. Exhibition pavilions; 12k. Girl in field. VERT: 10k. Equestrian statue.

143 Barbarossa's Corsair Fleet

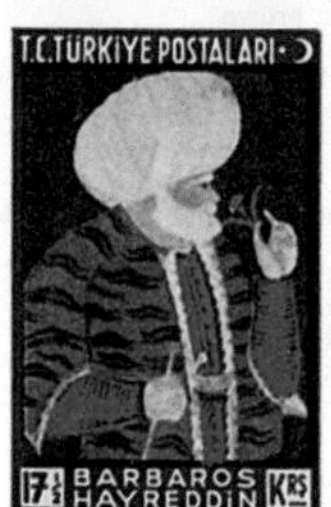

144 Barbarossa

1941. 400th Death Anniv of Barbarossa (Khair-ed-Din).
1280 – 20pa. violet 10 10
1281 **143** 3k. blue 35 25
1282 6k. red 55 60
1283 10k. blue 65 60
1284 12k. brown 80 60
1285 **144** 17½k. multicoloured . . 95 1·10
DESIGN—24 × 37 mm: 20pa. Barbarossa's tomb.

1941. Air. Surch with airplane and new value.
1286 **107** 4½k. on 25k. brown . . . 1·60 1·25
1287 **109** 9k. on 200k. black & grn 4·00 7·25
1288 35k. on 500k. blk & brn 2·50 4·00

146 Pres. Inonu

147

1942.
1289 **146** 0.25k. bistre 10 10
1290 0.50k. green 10 10
1291 1k. grey 10 10
1292 1½k. mauve 10 10
1293 2k. green 10 10
1294 4k. brown 10 15
1295 4½k. black 10 10
1296 5k. blue 10 10
1297 6k. red 10 10
1298 6¾k. blue 20 15
1299 9k. violet 35 15
1300 10k. blue 10 10
1301 13½k. purple 10 10
1302 16k. green 10 10
1303 17½k. red 10 10
1304 20k. purple 15 20
1305 27½k. orange 15 20
1306 37k. brown 10 15
1307 50k. violet . . . . . . 20 1·10
1308 100k. brown . . . . . . 1·10 1·10
1309 **147** 200k. brown . . . . . . 4·25 1·00

148 Ankara

150 Pres. Inonu

149 Tile-decorating

1943. Inscr "TURKIYE POSTALARI" between two crescents and stars.
1310 **148** 0.25k. yellow 10 10
1311 – 0.50k. green 20 10
1312 – 1k. olive 10 10
1313 – 1½k. violet 10 10
1314 – 2k. green 15 10
1315 – 4k. red 65 15
1316 – 4½k. black 65 30
1317 **149** 5k. blue 35 15
1318 – 6k. red 10 10
1319 – 6¾k. blue 10 10
1320 – 10k. blue 10 10
1321 – 13½k. mauve 15 10
1322 – 16k. green 85 15
1323 – 17½k. brown 30 10
1324 – 20k. brown 35 10
1325 – 27½k. orange 40 30
1326 – 37k. brown 30 10
1327 – 50k. purple . . . . . . 2·50 15
1328 – 100k. olive . . . . . . 3·75 75
1329 **150** 200k. brown . . . . . . 3·75 65
MS1329a 90 × 120 mm. **150** 200k. sepia . . . . 12·00 15·00
DESIGNS—VERT: 0.50k. Mohair goats; 2k. Oranges; 4k. Merino sheep; 4½k. Steam train entering tunnel; 6k. Statue of Kemal Ataturk, Ankara, 6¾, 10k. Full face portrait of Pres. Inonu; 17½k. Republic Monument, Istanbul; 20k. National Defence Monument, Ankara; 27½k. P.O., Istanbul; 37k. Monument at Afyon; 100k. Ataturk and Inonu. HORIZ: 1k. Antioch; 1½k. Ankara Reservoir; 13½k. National Assembly building; 16k. View of Arnavutkoy; 50k. People's House, Ankara.

152 Fair Entrance

1943. Izmir International Fair.
1330 – 4½k. grey 10 10
1331 **152** 6k. red 10 10
1332 – 6¾k. blue 10 10
1333 **152** 10k. blue 20 10
1334 – 13½k. brown 35 25
1335 – 27½k. grey 45 35
DESIGNS—VERT: 4½, 13½k. Girl eating grapes. HORIZ: 6¾, 27½k. Fair Pavilion.

153 Marching Athletes

154 Soldier guarding Flag

1943. 20th Anniv of Republic.
1336 **153** 4½k. olive 35 40
1337 **154** 6k. red 10 10
1338 – 6¾k. blue 30 10
1339 – 10k. blue 10 10
1340 – 13½k. olive 20 15
1341 – 27½k. brown 20 25
DESIGNS—HORIZ: 6¾k. Railway bridge over River Firat; 10k. Hospital; 13½k. Ankara. VERT: 27½k. President Inonu.

155 Filling Census Form

157 Pres. Inonu

1945. National Census.
1342 **155** 4½k. olive 25 10
1343 9k. violet 30 10
1344 10k. blue 30 30
1345 18k. red . . . . 1·25 65
MS1345a 90 × 120 mm. **155** 1l. purple. Imperf . . . . 20·00 8·50

1945. Surch 4½ **KURUS**.
1346 4½k. on 6¾k. blue (No. 1319) 15 10

1946.
1347 **157** 0.25k. red 10 10
1348 1k. green 15 10
1349 1½k. purple 15 10
1350 9k. violet 40 10
1351 10k. blue 40 10
1352 50k. brown . . . . . . 3·25 10

158 U.S.S. "Missouri"

159 Sower

1946. Visit of U.S. Battleship "Missouri" to Istanbul.
1353 **158** 9k. violet 10 10
1354 10k. blue 15 10
1355 27½k. grey 20 10

1946. Agrarian Reform.
1356 **159** 9k. violet 10 10
1357 10k. blue 10 10
1358 18k. olive 20 10
1359 27½k. orange 35 25

160 Dove of Peace

161 Monument at Afyon

1947. Izmir International Fair.
1360 **160** 15k. purple and violet 10 10
1361 20k. blue and deep blue 10 10
1362 30k. brown and black . . 20 10
1363 1l. olive and green . . . 60 10

1947. 25th Anniv of Battle of Dumlupinar.
1364 **161** 10k. brown & lt brown 15 10
1365 – 15k. violet and grey . . 15 10
1366 – 20k. blue and grey . . . 20 10
1367 **161** 30k. green and grey . . 35 10
1368 – 60k. green and bistre . . 55 25
1369 – 1l. green and grey . . . 1·10 65
DESIGN: 15, 60k. Ismet Inonu; 20k., 1l. Kemal Ataturk.

163 Istanbul, Grapes and Ribbon

1947. International Vintners' Congress.
1370 **163** 15k. purple 10 10
1371 20k. blue 10 10
1372 60k. brown 20 10

164 Steam Express Train

165 Pres. Inonu

1947. International Railway Congress, Istanbul.
1373 **164** 15k. purple 15 10
1374 20k. blue 20 10
1375 60k. olive 40 15

1948.
1376 **165** 0.25k. red 10 10
1377 1k. black 10 10
1378 2k. purple 10 10
1379 3k. orange 10 10
1380 4k. green 10 10
1381 5k. blue 10 10
1382 10k. brown 10 10
1383 12k. red 50 30
1384 15k. violet 15 10
1385 20k. blue 25 10
1386 30k. brown 1·25 30
1387 60k. black 2·50 35
1388 1l. olive 5·00 1·10
1389 2l. brown 19·00 4·25
1390 5l. purple 12·00 17·00
The lira values are larger.

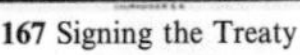

167 Signing the Treaty

168 Statue of Kemal Ataturk

1948. 25th Anniv of Treaty of Lausanne.
1391 **167** 15k. purple 10 10
1392 – 20k. blue 15 10
1393 – 40k. green 25 10
1394 **167** 1l. brown 35 25
DESIGN: 20, 40k. Lausanne Palace.

1948. 25th Anniv of Proclamation of Republic.
1395 **168** 15k. violet 10 10
1396 20k. blue 15 10
1397 40k. green 20 10
1398 1l. brown 55 25

170 Douglas DC-6 over Izmir

1949. Air.
1399 **170** 5k. violet and lilac 20 10
1400 – 20k. brown and lilac 15 10
1401 – 30k. green and grey 50 10
1402 **170** 40k. blue and light blue 85 15
1403 – 50k. brown and mauve 60 10
1404 – 1l. green and blue 1·90 25
AIRCRAFT: 20, 50k. Vickers Viking 1B; 30k., 1l. Light monoplane.

172 Wrestlers

1949. 5th European Wrestling Championships. Designs depicting wrestling holds and inscr as in T **172**.
1405 – 15k. mauve (vert) 40 20
1406 – 20k. blue (vert) 1·00 35
1407 **172** 30k. brown 40 30
1408 – 60k. green (horiz) 95 65

173 Galley

1949. Navy Day.
1409 **173** 5k. violet 15 10
1410 – 10k. brown 20 10
1411 – 15k. red 20 10
1412 – 20k. blue 25 10
1413 – 30k. slate 40 15
1414 – 40k. olive 60 25
DESIGNS—HORIZ: 15k. Cruiser "Hamidiye"; 20k. Submarine "Sakarya"; 30k. Battlecruiser "Yavuz". VERT: 10k. Ship of the line "Mahmudiye"; 40k. Statue of Barbarossa.

175 Exhibition Building

1949. Istanbul Fair.
1415 **175** 15k. brown 10 10
1416 20k. blue 10 10
1417 30k. olive 20 10

176 U.P.U. Monument, Berne

1949. 75th Anniv of U.P.U.
1418 – 15k. violet 10 10
1419 – 20k. blue 10 10
1420 **176** 30k. red 10 10
1421 40k. green 20 10
DESIGN: 15, 20k. as Type **176** but vert.

177 Sud Est Languedoc over Bogazia

1950. Air.
1422 **177** 2l.50 green and blue 7·50 4·50

178 Youth, Istanbul and Ankara

180 Voting

1950. 2nd World Youth Union Meeting.
1423 **178** 15k. violet 10 10
1424 20k. blue 15 10

1950. General Election.
1425 **180** 15k. brown 10 10
1426 20k. blue 10 10
1427 – 30k. blue and green 20 10
DESIGNS—HORIZ: 30k. Kemal Ataturk and map of Turkey.

181 Hazel Nut

182 Map and Statistics

1950. Izmir Fair.
1428 **181** 8k. green and yellow 25 15
1429 – 12k. mauve 35 20
1430 – 15k. brown 45 20
1431 – 20k. blue and light blue 55 25
1432 – 30k. brown 70 35
DESIGN: 12k. Acorns; 15k. Cotton; 20k. Fair symbol; 30k. Tobacco.

1950. National Census.
1433 **182** 15k. brown 10 10
1434 20k. blue 15 10

183 Hezarfen Celebi's "Bird Flight" and Tower

184 Farabi (philosopher)

1950. Air. International Civil Aviation Congress, Istanbul.
1435 **183** 20k. blue and green 10 10
1436 – 40k. blue and brown 10 10
1437 – 60k. blue and violet 40 10
DESIGNS—VERT: 40k. Biplane over Taurus Mountains. HORIZ: 60k. Douglas DC-3 airplane over Istanbul.

1950. 1000th Death Anniv of Farabi.
1438 **184** 15k. multicoloured 25 10
1439 20k. multicoloured 50 20
1440 60k. multicoloured 95 40
1441 1l. multicoloured 1·40 75

185 Mithat Pasha and Deposit Bank

1950. 3rd Co-operative Congress, Istanbul.
1442 **185** 15k. violet 45 25
1443 – 20k. blue 45 25
DESIGN: 20k. Agricultural Bank.

1951. Air. Industrial Congress, Ankara. Nos. 1399, 1401 and 1403 optd **SANAYI KONGRESI 9-NISAN-1951**.
1454 **170** 5k. violet and lilac 20 10
1455 – 30k. green and grey 40 15
1456 – 50k. brown and mauve 55 35

187 "Iskendrun" (liner)

1951. 25th Anniv of Coastal Trading Rights.
1457 – 15k. blue 30 10
1458 **187** 20k. blue 30 10
1459 – 30k. grey 55 10
1460 – 1l. green 65 40
DESIGNS—HORIZ: 15k. Tug "Hora" and liner "Providence"; 30k. Diver and launch. VERT: 1l. Lighthouse.

188 Mosque of Sultan Ahmed

189 Count Carton de Wiart

1951. 40th Interparliamentary Conference, Istanbul.
1461 **188** 15k. green 10 10
1462 – 20k. blue 10 10
1463 **189** 30k. brown 20 10
1464 – 60k. purple 40 40
DESIGNS—As Type **188**: 20k. Dolmabahce Palace; 60k. Rumeli Tower.

190 F.A.O. Emblem and Silo **191** A. H. Tarhan

1952. U.N. Economic Conf, Ankara. Inscr "Ankara 1951".
1465 **190** 15k. green 15 10
1466 – 20k. violet 15 10
1467 – 30k. blue 35 20
1468 – 60k. red 70 30
MS1468a 132 × 110 mm. Nos. 1465/8. Imperf 55·00 38·00
DESIGNS: 20k. Int Bank emblem and hydro-electric station; 30k. U.N. emblem and New York headquarters; 60k. Ankara University.

1952. Birth Centenary of Tarhan (writer).
1469 **191** 15k. purple 15 10
1470 20k. blue 15 10
1471 30k. brown 35 20
1472 60k. green 70 30

192 Bergama

193 Kemal Ataturk

1952. Views. Imperf or perf.
1473 **192** 1k. orange 10 10
1474 – 2k. green 10 10
1475 – 3k. brown 10 10
1476 – 4k. green 10 10
1477 – 5k. brown 10 10
1478 **193** 10k. brown 15 10
1479 12k. red 20 20
1480 15k. violet (medallion) 20 10
1481 20k. blue (medallion) 35 10
1482 – 30k. green 30 10
1483 – 40k. blue 1·60 10
1484 – 50k. green 35 10
1485 – 75k. black 1·50 10
1486 – 1l. violet 35 10
1487 – 2l. blue 1·25 10
1488 – 5l. brown 14·00 4·25
DESIGNS—VERT: 2k. Ruins at Milas; 3k. Karatay Gate, Konya; 4k. Trees on Kozak Plateau; 5k. Urgup; 30k. Emirsultan Mosque, Bursa; 40k. Yenicami (New Mosque), Istanbul. HORIZ: 50k. Waterfall, Tarsus; 75k. Rocks at Urgup; 1l. Dolmabahce Palace, Istanbul; 2l. Pavilion, Istanbul; 5l. Interior of Istanbul Museum.

1952. Surch **0.50 Kurus**.
1489 **192** 0.50k. on 1k. orange 20 15

196 Congress Building

197 Turkish Sentry

1952. 8th Int Mechanics Congress, Istanbul.
1490 **196** 15k. violet 25 10
1491 20k. blue 25 15
1492 60k. brown 55 25

1952. Turkish Participation in Korean War.
1493 **197** 15k. slate 20 10
1494 – 20k. blue 20 10
1495 – 30k. brown 25 15
1496 – 60k. red and green 70 35
DESIGNS: 20k. Turkish soldier and flag; 30k. Soldier and Korean child reading comic paper; 60k. Soldiers planting Turkish flag.

198 Doves, Hand and Red Crescent

199 Bas-relief on Monument

1952. 75th Anniv of Red Crescent Society.
1497 **198** 15k. red and green 20 10
1498 – 20k. red and blue 30 15
DESIGN: 20k. Red Crescent flag.

1952. 75th Anniv of Battle of Erzurum.
1499 **199** 15k. violet 15 10
1500 – 20k. blue 20 15
1501 – 40k. grey 45 20
DESIGNS—HORIZ: 20k. Azizye Monument, Erzurum; 40k. View of Erzurum.

200 Pigeon carrying Newspaper

202 Sultan Mohammed II (after Gentile Bellini)

201 Rumeli Fort

1952.

1502 **200** 0.50k. green 10 10
1503 0.50k. violet 10 10
1503a 0.50k. orange 10 10
1503b 0.50k. brown 10 10

1953. 500th Anniv of Fall of Constantinople.
1504 **201** 5k. blue and ultramarine 50 20
1505 – 8k. grey 85 20
1506 – 10k. blue 55 20
1507 – 12k. purple 65 20
1508 – 15k. brown 65 10
1509 – 20k. red 65 10
1510 – 30k. green . . . . 1·40 55
1511 – 40k. violet . . . . . . 2·40 60
1512 – 60k. brown . . . . . . 1·40 85
1513 – 1l. green . . . . 4·00 1·10
1514 – 2l. multicoloured . . . . 7·50 3·75
1515 **202** 2½l. lt brn, yell & brn . . 5·50 3·75
MS1515a 100 × 125 mm. No. 1515. Imperf . . . . 45·00 25·00
DESIGNS—As Type **201**: HORIZ: 8k. Turkish army at Edirne; 10k. Horsemen and fleet; 12k. Landing of Turkish Army; 15k. Topkapi ramparts; 40k. Sultan Mohammed II and Patriarch Yenadios; 60k.15th-century map of Constantinople; 1l. Mausoleum of Mohammed II. VERT: 20k. Turkish army entering Constantinople; 30k. Sultan Mohammed II Mosque. As Type **202**: 2l. Sultan Mohammed II (after miniature by Sinan).

203 Odeon Theatre, Ephesus

1953. Views of Ephesus. Inscr "EFES". Multicoloured centres.
1516 **203** 12k. green 15 10
1517 – 15k. violet 10 10
1518 – 20k. slate 20 10
1519 – 40k. turquoise 35 20
1520 – 60k. blue 60 20
1521 – 1l. red . . . . 2·10 1·00
DESIGNS: 15k. St. John's Church and Acropolis; 20k. Statue of Blessed Virgin, Panaya Kapulu; 40k. Council Church ruins; 60k. Grotto of the Seven Sleepers; 1l. House of the Blessed Virgin, Panaya Kapulu.

204 Pres. Bayar, Mithat Pasha, Dr. Delitsch and Ankara Bank

1953. 5th International Public Credit Congress.
1522 **204** 15k. brown 20 10
1523 – 20k. turquoise 30 15
DESIGN: 20k. Pres. Bayar, Mithat Pasha and Ankara University.

205 Berdan Barrage

1953. 30th Anniv of Republic.
1524 – 10k. bistre 10 10
1525 **205** 15k. slate 10 10
1526 – 20k. red 10 10
1527 – 30k. olive 65 35
1528 – 35k. blue 20 15
1529 – 55k. lilac 25 30
DESIGNS—HORIZ: 10k. Combine-harvester; 20k. Soldiers on parade; 30k. Diesel train; 35k. Yesilkoy airport. VERT: 55k. Kemal Ataturk.

206 Kemal Ataturk and Mausoleum

1953. Transfer of Ashes of Kemal Ataturk to Mausoleum.
1530 **206** 15k. black 10 10
1531 20k. purple 15 10

207 Map of World and Compass

1954. 5th Anniv of N.A.T.O.
1532 **207** 15k. brown 40 25
1533 – 20k. blue 40 25
1534 – 40k. green . . . . 5·25 2·00
DESIGNS: 20k. Globe and stars; 40k. Allegory of growth of N.A.T.O.

208 "Industry, Agriculture and Construction" **209** Flying Exercise

1954. 5th Anniv of Council of Europe.
1535 **208** 10k. brown . . . . . . 3·00 1·25
1536 – 15k. green . . . . 1·60 35
1537 – 20k. blue . . . . 1·60 35
1538 **208** 30k. violet . . . . . . 6·00 2·50
DESIGN: 15, 20k. Flag and figure of "Peace and Justice".

1954. 47th Conference of International Aeronautical Federation. Inscr "20.IX.1954".
1539 **209** 20k. black 10 10
1540 – 35k. lilac 10 10
1541 – 45k. blue 20 10
DESIGNS: 35k. Baron Delagrange and glider; 45k. Ataturk and formation of De Havilland Tiger Moth biplanes.

(209a)

1954. 1st Anniv of Reorganisation of Turkish Posts. Sheet 122 × 132 mm. T **209a** and similar vert designs.
MS1541a 20k. turquoise (telephone receivers); 30k. ultramarine (telegraph pole); 1l. purple (T **209a**) . . . . 8·00 5·50

210 Z. Gokalp **211** Yesilkoy Airport

1954. 30th Death Anniv of Gokalp (sociologist).
1542 **210** 15k. violet 10 10
1543 20k. green 20 10
1544 30k. red 30 15

1954. Air.
1545 **211** 5k. blue and brown . . . 65 10
1546 – 20k. blue and brown . . 30 10
1547 – 35k. blue and green . . 50 10
1548 **211** 40k. blue and red . . . 50 10
1549 – 45k. blue and violet . . 1·00 10
1550 – 55k. blue and black . . 3·25 20
DESIGNS: 20, 45k. Frontal view of Yesilkoy Airport; 35, 55k. Ankara Airport.

212 Kemal Ataturk **213** Relief Map of the Dardanelles

1955.
1551 **212** 15k. red 10 10
1552 20k. blue 15 10
1553 40k. slate 20 10
1554 50k. green 25 10
1555 75k. brown 60 10

1955. 40th Anniv of Battle of Canakkale (Dardanelles).
1556 **213** 15k. green 10 10
1557 – 20k. brown 10 10
1558 – 30k. blue 20 10
1559 – 60k. drab 45 20
DESIGNS—VERT: 20k. Gunner Seyid loading gun; 60k. Ataturk in uniform. HORIZ: 30k. Minelayer "Nusret".

214 "Reconstruction" **215** Lilies

1955. Town Planning Congress.
1560 **214** 15k. grey 10 10
1561 20k. blue 15 10
1562 50k. brown 20 10
1563 1l. violet 45 10

1955. Spring Flower Festival. Inscr "ISTANBUL 1955".
1564 – 10k. red and green . . . 25 10
1565 – 15k. yellow and green . . 25 10
1566 – 20k. red and green . . . 35 10
1567 **215** 50k. green and yellow . . 90 25
FLOWERS: 10k. Carnations; 15k. Tulips; 20k. Roses.

216 First-aid Centre

1955. 18th Congress of International Documentation Office of Military Medicine.
1568 **216** 20k. red and grey . . . 10 10
1569 – 30k. green and light green 10 10
DESIGN: 30k. Gulhane Military Hospital, Ankara.

217 Footballers

1955. Int Military Football Championships.
1570 **217** 15k. blue 20 10
1571 – 20k. red 35 10
1572 – 1l. green 75 30
DESIGNS—VERT: 20k. Footballers' badge. HORIZ: 1l. Championship plaque.

218 Police Monument, Ankara

1955. International Police Commission Meeting, Istanbul.
1573 **218** 15k. green and turquoise 15 10
1574 – 20k. violet and lilac . . 15 10
1575 – 30k. black and grey . . 20 10
1576 – 45k. brown & light brown 15 10
DESIGNS: 20k. Dolmabahce Palace, Istanbul; 30k. Police College, Ankara; 45k. Police Martyrs' Monument, Istanbul.

219 Radio Mast **220** Istanbul University

1955. Cent of Telecommunications in Turkey.
1577 – 15k. olive 10 10
1578 **219** 20k. red 10 10
1579 – 45k. brown 15 10
1580 **219** 60k. blue 25 15
DESIGNS—HORIZ: 15, 45k. Telegraph table and pole.

1955. 10th Meeting of Governors of Int Reconstruction and Development Bank and Int Monetary Fund.
1581 – 15k. orange 10 10
1582 **220** 20k. red 15 10
1583 – 60k. purple 20 10
1584 – 1l. blue 35 20
DESIGNS: 15k. Faculty of Letters, Istanbul; 60k. Hilton Hotel; 1l. Kiz Kulesi.

221 Ruins, Istanbul **222**

1955. 10th International Congress of Byzantine Research.
1585 **221** 15k. green and blue . . 15 10
1586 – 20k. red and orange . . 15 10
1587 – 30k. brown and pink . . 20 10
1588 – 75k. blue and lilac . . . 35 10
DESIGNS—VERT: 20k. Obelisk and Sultan Ahmed Mosque; 75k. Map of Istanbul in 1422. HORIZ: 30k. Church of St. Sophia.

1955. 10th International Road Planning Congress.
1589 – 20k. mauve 10 10
1590 **222** 30k. green 15 10
1591 – 55k. blue 25 10
DESIGNS: 20k. Congress emblem; 55k. Bridges.

223 Population Pictograph

1955. National Census.
1592 **223** 15k. grey and red . . . 15 10
1593 20k. lilac and red . . . 15 10
1594 30k. blue and red . . . 15 10
1595 60k. green and red . . . 30 10

224 Santa Claus Church, Demre **225** Kemal Ataturk

1955. Tourism.
1596 – 18k. green and blue . . 20 10
1597 – 20k. brown and blue . . 20 10
1598 – 30k. brown and green . . 20 10
1599 – 45k. green and brown . . 55 35
1600 – 50k. brown and green . . 25 10
1601 **224** 65k. black and red . . . 30 10
DESIGNS—VERT: 18k. Waterfall near Antalya; 45k. Theatre doorway ruins, Side; 50k. Countryside, Antalya. HORIZ: 20k. Alanya; 30k. Amphitheatre, Aspendos.

1955.
1602 **225** 0.50k. pink 10 10
1603 1k. yellow 10 10
1604 2k. blue 10 10
1605 3k. red 10 10
1606 5k. brown 10 10
1606a 6k. green 10 10
1607 10k. green 10 10
1607a 18k. purple 15 10
1608 20k. blue 10 10
1609 25k. olive 15 10
1610 30k. violet 15 10
1611 40k. brown 20 10
1612 75k. slate 45 15

226 Mausoleum of Hudavent Hatum **227** Zubeyde

1956. 25th Anniv of Turkish Historical Association.
1613 **226** 40k. deep blue and blue 15 10

1956. Mothers' Day.
1614 **227** 20k. brown & buff (perf) 10 10
1615 20k. olive and green (imperf) 30 25

228 Shah of Iran and Queen Soraya **229** Kemal Ataturk

1956. Visit of Shah of Iran to Turkey.
1616 **228** 100k. green and light green (perf) 35 25
1617 100k. red and green (imperf) . . . . 3·25 2·00

1956.
1618 **229** ½k. green 10 10
1619 1k. orange 10 10
1620 3k. green 10 10
1621 5k. violet 10 10
1622 6k. mauve 10 10
1623 10k. purple 10 10
1624 12k. brown 10 10
1625 15k. blue 10 10
1626 18k. pink 10 10
1627 20k. brown 10 10
1628 25k. green 10 10
1629 30k. slate 10 10
1630 40k. olive 10 10
1631 50k. orange 15 10
1632 60k. blue 30 10
1633 70k. turquoise 60 10
1634 75k. brown 50 10
See also Nos. 1659/78.

230 Erenkoy Sanatorium
231

1956. Turkish Post Office Health Service.
1635 **230** 50k. turquoise and pink 20 10

1956. 25th Izmir International Fair.
1636 **231** 45k. green (postage) . . 10 10
1637 25k. brown (air) 10 10

Sheet 103 × 52 mm.
MS1637a 50k. red (cement works); 50k. ultramarine (harbour project) (horiz). Imperf . . . . 1·75 1·25

232 Serpent in Bottle
233 Medical Clinic, Kayseri

1956. International Anti-Alcoholism Congress.
1638 **232** 25k. multicoloured . . . 10 10

1956. 750th Anniv of Medical Clinic, Kayseri.
1639 **233** 60k. violet and yellow 10 10

234 Sariyar Barrage

235 Wrestling

1956. Inauguration of Sariyar Dam.
1640 **234** 20k. red 10 10
1641 20k. blue 10 10

1956. Olympic Games. Inscr as in T **235**.
1642 **235** 40k. sepia on green . . . 15 10
1643 – 65k. red on grey 20 10
DESIGN: 65k. Another wrestling match.

236 Mehmet Akif Ersoy

237 Vase of Troy

1956. 20th Death Anniv of Ersoy (poet).
1644 **236** 20k. brown and green . . 10 10
1645 20k. red and grey . . . 10 10
1646 20k. violet and pink . . 10 10
Each stamp is inscribed with a different line of verse from the Turkish National Anthem composed by Ersoy.

1956. Troy Commemoration. Inscr "TRUVA (TROIA)".
1647 – 15k. green . . . . 1·00 75
1648 **237** 20k. purple 50 60
1649 – 30k. brown . . . . . . 1·10 1·00
DESIGNS—HORIZ: 15k. Troy Amphitheatre; 30k. Trojan Horse.

238 Mobile X-ray Unit
239 Pres. Heuss

1957. T.B. Relief Campaign.
1650 **238** 25k. red and drab . . . 10 10

1957. Visit of President of West Germany.
1651 **239** 40k. brown and yellow (postage) 10 10
1652 40k. purple and pink (air) 10 10

240 View of Bergama

1957. Bergama Fair.
1653 **240** 30k. brown 10 10
1654 – 40k. green 10 10
DESIGN: 40k. Folk-dancing.

241

1957. Turkish-American Friendship.
1655 **241** 25k. violet 10 10
1656 40k. blue 10 10

242 Osman Hamdi Bey (founder)

243 Kemal Ataturk

1957. 75th Anniv of Fine Arts Academy, Istanbul.
1657 **242** 20k. drab, buff and black 10 10
1658 – 30k. grey, green & lt grn 10 10
DESIGN—HORIZ: 30k. Hittite relic of Alacahoyuk; Inscr "GUZEL SANATLAR AKADEMISI 75. YIL".

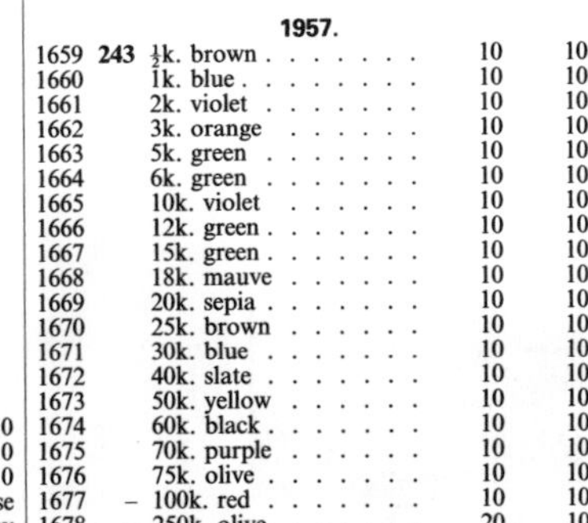

1957.
1659 **243** ½k. brown 10 10
1660 1k. blue 10 10
1661 2k. violet 10 10
1662 3k. orange 10 10
1663 5k. green 10 10
1664 6k. green 10 10
1665 10k. violet 10 10
1666 12k. green 10 10
1667 15k. green 10 10
1668 18k. mauve 10 10
1669 20k. sepia 10 10
1670 25k. brown 10 10
1671 30k. blue 10 10
1672 40k. slate 10 10
1673 50k. yellow 10 10
1674 60k. black 10 10
1675 70k. purple 10 10
1676 75k. olive 10 10
1677 – 100k. red 10 10
1678 – 250k. olive 20 10
Nos. 1677/8 are larger, 21 × 29 mm.

244 Mohammed Zahir Shah
245 Amasya Medical Centre

1957. Visit of Mohammed Zahir Shah of Afghanistan.
1679 **244** 45k. red and orange (postage) 10 10
1680 25k. deep green and green (air) 10 10

1957. 11th Congress of World Medical Association.
1681 **245** 25k. red and yellow . . 10 10
1682 – 65k. blue and yellow . . 10 10
DESIGN—HORIZ: 65k. Sultan Mohammed School, 1557.

246 Sultan Mohammed II Mosque

1957. 400th Anniv of the Suleiman Mosque, Istanbul.
1683 **246** 20k. green 10 10
1684 – 1l. brown 10 10
DESIGN—VERT: 1l. Mimar Koca Sinan (architect).

1957. 2nd Philatelic Exhibition, Istanbul. Surch **50 Kurus ISTANBUL Filatelik II. Sergisi 1957.**
1685 50k. on 2l. blue (No. 1487) 10 10

248 Forestry Map of Turkey

1957. Centenary of Forestry Teaching.
1686 **248** 20k. green and brown . . 10 10
1687 – 25k. green and blue . . 10 10
DESIGN—VERT: 25k. Planting fir-tree.

249 Fuzuli (poet)
250 Franklin

1957. Fuzuli Year.
1688 **249** 50k. multicoloured . . . 15 10

1957. 250th Birth Anniv of Benjamin Franklin.
1689 **250** 65k. purple 10 10
1690 65k. blue 10 10

251 Mevlana's Tomb, Konya

252 Adana

251a

1957. 750th Birth Anniv of Mevlana (poet).
1691 **251** 50k. violet, blue and green 10 10
1692 – 100k. deep blue and blue 10 10
MS1692a 54 × 102 mm. **251a** 100k. multicoloured. Imperf . . . . 1·75 1·10
DESIGN—HORIZ: 100k. Konya Museum.

1958. Turkish Towns. As T **252**. (a) 26 × 21 mm.
1693 5k. brown (Adana) 10 10
1694 5k. mauve (Adapazari) . . . 10 10
1695 5k. red (Adiyaman) 10 10
1696 5k. brown (Afyon) 10 10
1697 5k. green (Amasya) 10 10
1698 5k. blue (Ankara) 10 10
1699 5k. green (Antakya) 10 10
1700 5k. green (Antalya) 10 10
1701 5k. lilac (Artvin) 10 10
1702 5k. orange (Aydin) 10 10
1703 5k. violet (Balikesir) . . . 10 10
1704 5k. green (Bilecik) 10 10
1705 5k. purple (Bingol) 10 10
1706 5k. blue (Bitlis) 10 10
1707 5k. purple (Bolu) 10 10
1708 5k. brown (Burdur) 10 10
1709 5k. green (Bursa) 10 10
1710 5k. blue (Canakkale) . . . 10 10
1711 5k. violet (Cankiri) 10 10
1712 5k. blue (Corum) 10 10
1713 5k. blue (Denizli) 10 10
1714 5k. orange (Diyrbakir) . . . 10 10
1715 5k. violet (Edirne) 10 10
1716 5k. green (Elazig) 10 10
1717 5k. blue (Erzincan) 10 10
1718 5k. orange (Erzurum) . . . 10 10
1719 5k. green (Eskisehur) . . . 10 10
1720 5k. green (Gaziantep) . . . 10 10
1721 5k. blue (Giresun) 10 10
1722 5k. blue (Gumusane) . . . 10 10
1723 5k. purple (Hakkari) 10 10
1724 5k. mauve (Isparta) 10 10
1725 5k. blue (Istanbul) 10 10
1726 5k. blue (Izmir) 10 10
1727 5k. blue (Izmit) 10 10
1728 5k. violet (Karakose) . . . 10 10
1729 5k. green (Kars) 10 10
1730 5k. mauve (Kastamonu) . . 10 10
1731 5k. green (Kayseri) 10 10
1732 5k. brown (Kirklareli) . . . 10 10
1733 5k. orange (Kirsehir) . . . 10 10
1734 5k. blue (Konya) 10 10
1735 5k. violet (Kutahya) 10 10
1736 5k. brown (Malatya) 10 10
1737 5k. green (Manisa) 10 10
1738 5k. purple (Maras) 10 10
1739 5k. red (Mardin) 10 10
1740 5k. green (Mersin) 10 10
1741 5k. green (Mugla) 10 10
1742 5k. green (Mus) 10 10
1743 5k. green (Nevsehir) 10 10
1744 5k. red (Nigde) 10 10
1745 5k. blue (Ordu) 10 10
1746 5k. violet (Rize) 10 10
1747 5k. purple (Samsun) 10 10
1748 5k. brown (Siirt) 10 10
1749 5k. blue (Sinop) 10 10
1750 5k. green (Sivas) 10 10
1751 5k. blue (Tekirdag) 10 10
1752 5k. red (Tokat) 10 10
1753 5k. blue (Trabzon) 10 10
1754 5k. orange (Tunceli) 10 10
1755 5k. brown (Urfa) 10 10
1756 5k. green (Usak) 10 10
1757 5k. red (Van) 10 10
1758 5k. mauve (Yozgat) 10 10
1759 5k. blue (Zonguldak) . . . 10 10

(b) 32½ × 22 mm.
1760 20k. brown (Adana) 10 10
1761 20k. mauve (Adapazari) . . 10 10
1762 20k. red (Adiyaman) 10 10
1763 20k. brown (Afyon) 10 10
1764 20k. green (Amasya) 10 10
1765 20k. blue (Ankara) 10 10
1766 20k. blue (Antakya) 10 10
1767 20k. green (Antalya) 10 10
1768 20k. blue (Artvin) 10 10
1769 20k. orange (Aydin) 10 10
1770 20k. purple (Balikesir) . . . 10 10
1771 20k. green (Bilecik) 10 10
1772 20k. grey (Bingol) 10 10
1773 20k. violet (Bitlis) 10 10
1774 20k. purple (Bolu) 10 10
1775 20k. brown (Burdur) 10 10
1776 20k. green (Bursa) 10 10
1777 20k. blue (Canakkale) . . . 10 10
1778 20k. purple (Cankiri) . . . 10 10
1779 20k. grey (Corum) 10 10
1780 20k. blue (Denizli) 10 10
1781 20k. red (Diyrbakir) 10 10
1782 20k. grey (Edirne) 10 10
1783 20k. green (Elazig) 10 10
1784 20k. blue (Erzincan) 10 10
1785 20k. orange (Erzurum) . . . 10 10
1786 20k. green (Eskisehur) . . . 10 10
1787 20k. green (Gaziantep) . . . 10 10
1788 20k. blue (Giresun) 10 10
1789 20k. blue (Gumusane) . . . 10 10
1790 20k. purple (Hakkari) . . . 10 10
1791 20k. mauve (Isparta) 10 10
1792 20k. blue (Istanbul) 10 10
1793 20k. blue (Izmir) 10 10
1794 20k. green (Izmit) 10 10
1795 20k. violet (Karakose) . . . 10 10
1796 20k. green (Kars) 10 10
1797 20k. mauve (Kastamonu) . . 10 10
1798 20k. green (Kayseri) 10 10
1799 20k. brown (Kirklareli) . . . 10 10
1800 20k. brown (Kirsehir) . . . 10 10
1801 20k. blue (Konya) 10 10
1802 20k. violet (Kutahya) . . . 10 10
1803 20k. brown (Malatya) . . . 10 10
1804 20k. green (Manisa) 10 10
1805 20k. purple (Maras) 10 10
1806 20k. red (Mardin) 10 10
1807 20k. green (Mersin) 10 10
1808 20k. green (Mugla) 10 10
1809 20k. green (Mus) 10 10
1810 20k. green (Nevsehir) . . . 10 10
1811 20k. red (Nigde) 10 10

1812 20k. blue (Ordu) 10 10
1813 20k. violet (Rize) 10 10
1814 20k. purple (Samsun) . . . 10 10
1815 20k. brown (Siirt) 10 10
1816 20k. blue (Sinop) 10 10
1817 20k. green (Sivas) 10 10
1818 20k. blue (Tekirdag) 10 10
1819 20k. red (Tokat) 10 10
1820 20k. blue (Trabzon) 10 10
1821 20k. red (Tunceli) 10 10
1822 20k. brown (Urfa) 10 10
1823 20k. grey (Usak) 10 10
1824 20k. red (Van) 10 10
1825 20k. red (Yozgat) 10 10
1826 20k. blue (Zonguldak) . . . 10 10

253 254 Hierapolis at Pamukkale

1958. 75th Anniv of the Institute of Economics and Commerce, Ankara.
1827 **253** 20k. orange, blue & bistre 10 10
1828 25k. blue, orange & bistre 10 10

1958. Pamukkale Tourist Publicity. Inscr "PAMUKKALE".
1829 **254** 20k. brown 10 10
1830 – 25k. blue 10 10
DESIGN—HORIZ: 25k. Travertins (rocks) near Denizli.

255 Katib Celebi 256 Letters

1958. 300th Death Anniv of Katib Celebi (author).
1831 **255** 50k.+10k. black 10 10

1958. International Correspondence Week.
1832 **256** 20k. orange and black 10 10

257 Symbol of Industry 258 Symbol of "Europa"

1958. Industrial Fair, Istanbul.
1833 **257** 40k. black and blue . . 10 10

1958. Europa.
1834 **258** 25k. lilac and violet . . 10 10
1835 40k. blue and ultramarine 10 10

259 Bulldozer 260 Flame of Remembrance

1958. 35th Anniv of Republic.
1836 **259** 15k.+5k. orange 10 10
1837 – 20k.+5k. brown 10 10
1838 – 25k.+5k. green 10 10
DESIGNS—VERT: 20k. Portrait of Kemal Ataturk. HORIZ: 25k. Army tanks and Republic F-84G Thunderjets.

1958. 20th Death Anniv of Kemal Ataturk.
1839 **260** 25k. red 10 10
1840 – 75k. green 10 10
DESIGN: 75k. Sword, sprig and bust of Kemal Ataturk.

261 262 Blackboard

1959. 25th Anniv of Faculty of Agriculture, Ankara University.
1841 **261** 25k. yellow and violet 10 10

1959. 75th Anniv of Boys' High School, Istanbul.
1842 **262** 75k. black and yellow . . 10 10

263 Eagle 265 "Karadeniz" (liner)

264 Theatre, Ankara

1959. Air. Birds.
1843 – 40k. purple and mauve 25 10
1844 – 65k. myrtle and turquoise 30 10
1845 – 85k. blue and black . . 35 10
1846 **263** 105k. bistre and yellow 45 10
1847 – 125k. lilac and violet . . 65 10
1848 – 155k. green and yellow 75 15
1849 – 195k. blue and black . . 85 20
1850 – 245k. brown and orange 95 20
BIRDS (in flight)—HORIZ: 40k. Barn swallows; 65k. Cranes; 85k. Gulls. VERT: 125k. House martin; 155k. Demoiselle crane; 195k. Gulls; 245k. Turtle dove.

1959. Centenary of Turkish Theatre.
1851 **264** 20k. brown and green . . 10 10
1852 – 25k. green and orange 10 10
DESIGN: 25k. Portrait of Sinasi and masks.

1959.
1853 – 1k. blue 10 10
1854 **265** 5k. blue 15 10
1855 – 10k. blue 10 10
1856 – 15k. brown 25 10
1857 – 20k. green 10 10
1858 – 25k. lilac 10 10
1859a – 30k. purple 20 10
1860 – 40k. blue 25 10
1861 – 45k. violet 30 10
1862 – 55k. brown 30 10
1863 – 60k. green 40 10
1864 – 75k. olive . . . . . . 1·60 10
1865 – 90k. blue . . . . 3·50 10
1866 – 100k. grey . . . . . . 5·25 10
1867 – 120k. purple . . . . . 1·60 10
1868 – 150k. orange . . . . . 1·60 10
1869 – 200k. green . . . . . 2·25 10
1870 – 250k. brown . . . . . 2·25 10
1871 – 500k. blue . . . . . . 3·50 10
DESIGNS—HORIZ: 1k. Vickers Viscount 700 airliner; 10k. Grain silo; 15k. Steel works; 20k. Euphrates Bridge; 25k. Zonguldak Harbour; 30k. Oil refinery; 40k. Rumeli Hisari Fortress; 45k. Sugar factory; 55k. Coal mine; 150k. Combine-harvester. VERT: 60k. Telegraph pole; 75k. Railway; 90k. Crane loading "Kars" (container ship); 100k. Cement factory; 120k. Coast road; 200k. Electric transformer; 250, 500k. Portrait of Ataturk.

1959. Postage Due Stamps surch **20 = 20** for ordinary postage.
1872 **D 121** 20k. on 20pa. brown 10 10
1873 20k. on 2k. violet . . 10 10
1874 20k. on 3k. violet . . 10 10
1875 20k. on 5k. green . . 10 10
1876 20k. on 12k. red . . . 10 10

267 Northern Hemisphere and Stars

1959. 10th Anniv of N.A.T.O.
1877 **267** 105k. red 10 10
1878 195k. green 10 10

268 Amphitheatre, Aspendos 270 Basketball Players

1959. Aspendos Festival.
1879 **268** 20k. violet and bistre . . 10 10
1880 20k. brown and green . . 10 10

1959. 10th Anniv of Council of Europe. Surch **X. YIL** in circle of stars and **105 AVRUPA KONSEYI**.
1881 **259** 105k. on 15k.+5k. orange 10 10

1959. 11th European and Mediterranean Basketball Championships, Istanbul.
1882 **270** 25k. red and blue . . . 10 10

271 Marine Symbols 272 Goreme

1959. 50th Anniv of Turkish Merchant Marine College.
1883 **271** 30k. multicoloured . . . 10 10
1884 – 40k. multicoloured . . . 10 10
DESIGN: 40k. As 30k. but seahorse in place of anchor symbol.

1959. Tourist Publicity.
1885 **272** 105k.+10k. orange and violet 10 10

273 Mounted Warrior

1959. 888th Anniv of Battle of Malazgirt.
1886 **273** 2½l. purple and blue . . 15 10

274 Istanbul

1959. 15th International T.B. Conf, Istanbul.
1887 **274** 105k.+10k. blue and red 15 10

275 Ornamental Pattern 276 Kemal Ataturk

1959. 1st International Congress of Turkish Arts.
1888 **275** 30k. red and black . . . 10 10
1889 – 40k. blue, black and ochre 10 10
1890 – 75k. blue, yellow and red 10 10
DESIGNS—HORIZ: 40k. Sultan Mohammed II Mosque in silhouette. VERT: 75k. Circular ornament.

1959.
1891 **276** 500k. blue 65 20
MS1891a 53 × 74 mm. **276** 500k. red. Imperf . . . . 1·00 1·00

277 Faculty Building 278 Crossed Sabres

1959. Centenary of Turkish Political Science Faculty.
1892 **277** 40k. brown and green . . 10 10
1893 40k. blue and brown . . 10 10
1894 – 1l. ochre and violet . . . 10 10
DESIGN—VERT: 1l. "S.B.F." emblem of Faculty.

1960. 125th Anniv of Territorial War College.
1895 **278** 30k. red and yellow . . 10 10
1896 – 40k. yellow, brown & red 10 10
DESIGN: 40k. Bayonet in bowl of fire.

279 "Uprooted Tree" and Globe

1960. World Refugee Year.
1897 **279** 90k. black and turquoise 10 10
1898 – 105k. black and yellow 10 10
DESIGN: 105k. "Uprooted Tree" and houses representing refugee camp.

280 Mental Home, Manisa 281 Carnations

1960. Manisa Fair. Inscr "MANISA MESIR BAYRAMI".
1899 **280** 40k.+5k. violet & mve 10 10
1900 40k.+5k. green & blue 10 10
1901 – 90k.+5k. purple & mve 10 10
1902 – 105k.+10k. mult 10 10
DESIGNS—VERT: 90k. Sultan Mosque, Manisa; 30½ × 42½ mm: 105k. Merkez Muslihittin Efendi (portrait).

1960. Spring Flowers Festival, Istanbul. Inscr "1960". Flowers in natural colours. Colours of inscriptions and backgrounds given.
1903 **281** 30k. red and yellow . . 10 10
1904 – 40k. green and grey . . 10 10
1905 – 75k. red and blue . . 20 10
1906 – 105k. green and pink . . 30 20
FLOWERS: 40k. Jasmine; 75k. Rose; 105k. Tulips.

282 Map of Cyprus

1960. Proclamation of Cyprus Republic. Inscr "KIBRIS CUMHURIYETI".
1907 – 40k. mauve and blue . . 10 10
1908 **282** 105k. yellow, blue & grn 10 10
DESIGN: 40k. Town Centre, Nicosia.

283 Globe

1960. 16th Women's Int Council Meeting.
1909 **283** 30k. yellow and lilac . . 10 10
1910 – 75k. drab and blue . . 10 10
DESIGN: 75k. Women, "W.I.C." emblem and nest.

283a Football 285 "Population"

1960. Olympic Games.
1911 30k. green (Type **283a**) . . . 10 10
1912 30k. black (Basketball) . . . 10 10
1913 30k. blue (Wrestling) . . . 10 10
1914 30k. purple (Hurdling) . . . 10 10
1915 30k. brown (Show jumping) 10 10
MS1915a 215 × 160 mm. Nos. 1911/15 . . . . 8·50

1960. Europa. As T **144a** of Switzerland but size 32½ × 22½ mm.
1916 75k. turquoise and green . . 25 10
1917 105k. light and deep blue . . 35 20

1960. National Census.
1918 – 30k.+5k. red and blue 10 10
1919 **285** 50k.+5k. blue & turq . . 10 10

DESIGN—HORIZ: 30k. Graph showing outlines of human faces.

286 "Justice" **287** Agah Efendi and Front Page of Newspaper "Turcamani Ahval"

1960. Trial of Ex-Government Officials.
1920 – 40k. bistre and violet . . 10 10
1921 – 105k. red and green . . 10 10
1922 **286** 195k. red and green . . 10 10
DESIGNS—HORIZ: 40k. Badge of Turkish Army; 105k. Trial scene.

1960. Turkish Press Centenary.
1923 **287** 40k. purple and blue . . 10 10
1924 60k. purple and ochre 10 10

288 U.N. Headquarters and Emblem

1960. 15th Anniv of U.N.O.
1925 – 90k. ultramarine and blue 10 10
1926 **288** 105k. brown and green 10 10
DESIGN—VERT: 90k. U.N. emblem, "XV" and hand holding torch.

289 Revolutionaries

1960. Revolution of 27 May 1960.
1927 **289** 10k. grey and black . . 10 10
1928 – 30k. violet 10 10
1929 – 40k. red and black . . . 10 10
1930 – 105k. multicoloured . . 10 10
DESIGNS—HORIZ: 30k. Kemal Ataturk and hand with torch; 105k. Soldiers and wounded youth. VERT: 40k. Prancing horse breaking chain.

290 Faculty Building

1960. 25th Anniv of History and Geography Faculty.
1931 **290** 30k. black and green . . . 10 10
1932 – 40k. black and buff . . . 10 10
1933 – 60k. olive, buff and green 10 10
DESIGNS—HORIZ: 40k. Sun disc, cuneiform writing and map of Turkey. VERT: 60k. Ataturk's statue.

291 "Communications and Transport" **292**

1961. 9th Central Treaty Organization Ministers' Meeting, Ankara.
1934 **291** 30k. black and violet . . 10 10
1935 – 40k. black and green . . 10 10
1936 – 75k. black and blue . . 10 10
DESIGNS: 40k. Road and rail construction, telephone and telegraph; 75k. Parliament building, Ankara.

1961. 1st Anniv of 27 May Revolution.
1937 **292** 30k. multicoloured . . . 10 10
1938 – 40k. green, cream & black 10 10
1939 – 60k. red, green and deep green 10 10
DESIGNS—HORIZ: 40k. Boz Kurt and warriors. VERT: 60k. "Progress".

293 North American F100 Jet and Rocket

1961. 50th Anniv of Turkish Air Force.
1940 – 38k. orange, lake & black 10 10
1941 **293** 40k. violet and red . . . 10 10
1942 – 75k. buff, grey and black 10 15
DESIGNS—HORIZ: 30k. Rockets. VERT: 75k. Ataturk, eagle and North American Super Sabre jets.

294 Old Observatory

1961. 50th Anniv of Kandilli Observatory, Istanbul.
1943 **294** 10k.+5k. turquoise and green 10 10
1944 – 30k.+5k. violet and black 10 10
1945 – 40k.+5k. brown and sepia 10 10
1946 – 75k.+5k. olive and green 10 10
DESIGNS—HORIZ: 30k. Observatory emblem; 75k. Observatory building. VERT: 40k. F. Gokmen.

295 Kemal Ataturk **295a**

1961.
1947 **295a** 1k. brown 10 10
1948 5k. blue 10 10
1949 **295** 10k. mauve 85 10
1950 **295a** 10k. sepia 85 10
1951 30k. green . . . . . . 1·75 10
1952 10l. violet (22 × 32 mm) 13·00 10

296 Doves

1961. Europa.
1960 **296** 30k. blue 10 10
1961 40k. grey 10 10
1962 75k. red 30 10

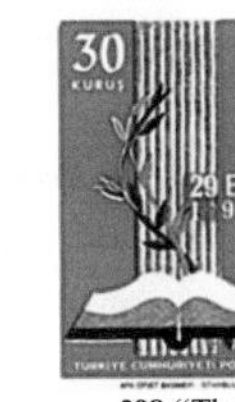

297 Tulip and Cogwheel **298** "The Constitution"

1961. Centenary of Professional and Technical Schools.
1963 **297** 30k. pink, silver and slate 10 10
1964 – 75k. red, black and blue 10 10
DESIGN—HORIZ: 75k. Inscr "100 Yili 1861–1961" and tulip and cogwheel emblem.

1961. Opening of Turkish Parliament.
1965 **298** 30k. black, bistre and red 10 10
1966 75k. black, green and blue 10 10

299 Insecticide-sprayers ("Malaria Eradication") **300** N.A.T.O. and Anniversary Emblem

1961. 15th Anniv of UNICEF.
1967 **299** 10k.+5k. turquoise . . . 10 10
1968 – 30k.+5k. violet 10 10
1969 – 75k.+5k. brown 10 10
DESIGNS—HORIZ: 30k. Mother and child ("Child Welfare"). VERT: 75k. Mother giving pasteurized milk to children ("Education on Nourishment").

1962. 10th Anniv of Turkish Admission to N.A.T.O.
1970 – 75k. black, silver and blue 10 10
1971 **300** 105k. black, silver and red 10 10
DESIGN—VERT: 75k. Peace dove over N.A.T.O. and Anniv emblems.

301 Mosquito on Map of Turkey **302** "Strelitzia reginae"

1962. Malaria Eradication.
1972 **301** 30k.+5k. brown 10 10
1973 75k.+5k. mauve & blk 10 10

1962. Flowers. Multicoloured.
1974 30k.+10k. "Poinsettia pulcherrima" 15 10
1975 40k.+10k. Type **302** 20 10
1976 75k.+10k. "Nymphea alba" 20 10

303 Scouts in Camp **304** Soldier (Victory Monument, Ankara)

1962. 50th Anniv of Turkish Scout Movement.
1977 **303** 30k. red, black and green 10 10
1978 – 60k. red, black and lilac 15 10
1979 – 105k. red, black & brown 20 10
DESIGNS: 60k. Two scouts with flag; 105k. Wolf Cub and Brownie.

1962. 40th Anniv of Battle of Dumlupinar.
1980 **304** 30k. green 10 10
1981 – 40k. brown and black . . 10 10
1982 – 75k. grey 10 10
DESIGNS—HORIZ: 40k. Ox-cart carrying ammunition. (Victory Monument, Ankara). VERT: 75k. Kemal Ataturk.

305 Europa "Tree" **306** Shrine of the Virgin Mary

1962. Europa.
1983 **305** 75k. sepia and green . . 15 10
1984 105k. sepia and red . . . 15 10
1985 195k. sepia and blue . . 20 10

1962. Tourist Issue. Multicoloured.
1986 30k. Type **306** 10 10
1987 40k. Interior 10 10
1988 75k. Exterior 15 10
1989 105k. Statue of the Virgin 10 10
DESIGNS: The 40 and 75k. show horiz views of the Virgin Mary's house at Ephesus.

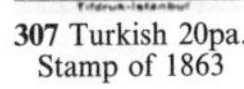

307 Turkish 20pa. Stamp of 1863 **308** Julian's Column, Ankara

1963. Stamp Centenary.
1990 **307** 10k. black, yellow & brn 10 10
1991 – 30k. black, pink and violet 10 10
1992 – 40k. black, blue & turq 10 10
1993 – 75k. black, pink & brown 10 10
DESIGNS—Turkish stamps of 1863: 30k. (1pi.); 40k. (2pi.); 75k. (5pi.).

1963.
1994 **308** 1k. green and olive . . . 10 10
1995 1k. violet 10 10
1996 – 5k. sepia and brown . . 15 10
1997 – 10k. mauve and green 20 10
1998 – 30k. black and violet . . 45 10
1999 – 50k. green, brown & yell 70 10
2000 – 60k. grey . . . . 1·75 10
2001 – 100k. brown 70 10
2002 – 150k. green . . . . . . 6·75 10
DESIGNS—HORIZ: 5k. Ethnographic Museum; 10k. Citadel; 30k. Educational Establishment, Gazi; 50k. Ataturk's Mausoleum; 60k. Presidential Palace, Ankara; 100k. Ataturk's house; 150k. National Museum, Ankara.

309 "Clinging to the World" **310** Wheat and Census Graph

1963. Freedom from Hunger.
2010 **309** 30k. deep blue and blue 10 10
2011 – 40k. deep brown & brown 10 10
2012 – 75k. deep green and green 10 10
DESIGNS: 40k. Sowers; 75k. Emblem and Globe within hands.

1963. Agricultural Census. Unissued stamps with "KASIM 1960" obliterated with bars. Inscr "UMUMI ZIRAAT SAYIMI".
2013 **310** 40k.+5k. multicoloured 10 10
2014 – 60k.+5k. multicoloured 10 10
DESIGN—HORIZ: 60k. Wheat and chart.

311 Atomic Symbol on Map **312** Ucserefili Mosque

1963. 1st Anniv of Opening of Turkish Nuclear Research Centre.
2015 **311** 50k. brown & deep brown 10 10
2016 – 60k. multicoloured . . . 10 10
2017 – 100k. blue & ultramarine 10 10
DESIGNS: 60k. Various symbols; 100k. Emblem of Turkish Atomic Energy Commission.

1963. 600th Anniv of Conquest of Edirne.
2018 **312** 10k. green, ultramarine and blue 10 10
2019 – 30k. blue and red . . . 10 10
2020 – 60k. multicoloured . . . 15 10
2021 – 100k. multicoloured . . 20 10
DESIGNS—HORIZ: 30k. Meric Bridge; 60k. Kum Kasri (building). VERT: 100k. Sultan Amurat I.

313 Soldier and Sun

1963. 600th Anniv of Turkish Army.
2022 **313** 50k. black, red and blue 10 10
2023 100k. black, red & bistre 10 10

314 Globe and Emblems **315** Mithat Pasha (founder)

1963. Red Cross Centenary. Multicoloured.
2024 50k.+10k. Type **314** 10 10
2025 60k.+10k. "Flowers" emblem (vert) 10 10
2026 100k.+10k. Three emblems on flags 10 10

1963. Centenary of Turkish Agricultural Bank.
2027 – 30k. brown, green and yellow 10 10
2028 – 50k. blue and lilac . . . 10 10
2029 **315** 60k. green and black . . 10 10
DESIGNS—HORIZ: 30k. Ploughing and irrigation; 50k. Agricultural Bank, Ankara.

316 Exhibition Hall, Istanbul, and 5pi. stamp of 1863

1963. "Istanbul '63" International Stamp Exn.
2030 **316** 10k. salmon, black and yellow 10 10
2031 – 50k. green, red and black 10 10
2032 – 60k. sepia, black and blue 10 10
2033 – 100k. violet and purple 10 10
2034 – 130k. brown, orge & yell 10 10
DESIGNS: 50k. Sultan Ahmed's Mosque, Obelisk and 3pi. on 2pa. Nationalist Government (Angora) stamp of 1920; 60k. Istanbul skyline and 10pi. (Angora) stamp of 1922; 100k. Rumeli Fort and 6k. stamp of 1929/30; 130k. Ankara Fort and 12½k. air stamp of 1934.

1963. International Philatelic Exhibition, Istanbul ("F.I.P. GUNU"). Miniature sheets (88 × 116 mm) comprising reproductions of T **1**.
MS2034a 10k. yellow, brown and black (20pa.); 50k. lilac, pink and black (1pi.); 60k. green, blue and black (2pi.); 130k. brown, pink and black (5pi.) . . . . 1·25 1·25

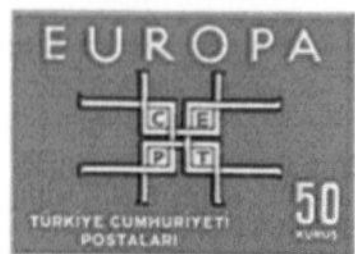

317 "Co-operation"

1963. Europa.
2035 **317** 50k. orange, black and red 10 10
2036 130k. blue, black & green 15 10

318 Ataturk and Old Parliament House

319 Kemal Ataturk

1963. 40th Anniv of Turkish Republic. Multicoloured.
2037 30k. Type **318** 10 10
2038 50k. Ataturk and flag . . . 10 10
2039 60k. Ataturk and new Parliament House 15 10

1963. 25th Death Anniv of Kemal Ataturk.
2040 **319** 50k. multicoloured . . . 15 10
2041 60k. multicoloured . . . 15 10

320 R.S. Dag (painter)

321 N.A.T.O. Emblem and "XV"

1964. Cultural Celebrities.
2042 – 1k. black and red . . . 10 10
2043 – 5k. black and green . . 10 10
2044 **320** 10k. black and brown . . 15 10
2045 – 50k. black and blue . . 55 10
2046 – 60k. black and grey . . 65 10
2047 – 100k. ultramarine & blue 85 10
2048 – 130k. black and green 2·40 00
PORTRAITS: 1k. H. R. Gurpinar (romanticist, birth cent); 5k. J. H. Izmirli (savant, 20th death anniv); 10k. Type **320** (20th death anniv); 50k. R. Z. M. Ekrem (writer, 50th death anniv); 60k. A. M. Pasa (commander, 125th birth anniv); 100k. A. Rasim (writer, birth cent); 130k. S. Zeki (mathematician, birth cent).

1964. 15th Anniv of N.A.T.O.
2049 **321** 50k. red, violet & turq 15 10
2050 – 130k. black and red . . 20 10
DESIGN: 130k. N.A.T.O. emblem and laurel sprig.

322 "Europa" holding Torch

1964. 15th Anniv of Council of Europe.
2051 **322** 50k. blue, brown & yell 10 10
2052 – 130k. orange, ultramarine and blue 15 10
DESIGN: 130k. Torch and circlet of stars.

323 Haga Mosque, Istanbul

324 Kars Castle

1964. Tourist Issue.
2053 **323** 50k. green and olive . . 10 10
2054 – 50k. red and purple . . 10 10
2055 – 50k. violet and blue . . 10 10
2056 – 60k. green, black & pur 10 10
2057 – 60k. brown and sepia . . 10 10
DESIGNS—HORIZ: No. 2054 Temple of Zeus, Silifke; 2055 Amasra. VERT: No. 2056 Mersin; 2057 Augustus' Temple, Ankara.

1964. 900th Anniv of Conquest of Kars.
2058 **324** 50k. black and lilac . . . 10 10
2059 – 130k. multicoloured . . 15 10
DESIGN: 130k. Alpaslan warrior.

325 Europa "Flower"

326 Grazing Cattle

1964. Europa.
2060 **325** 50k. blue, grey and orange 30 10
2061 130k. purple, green & bl 45 20

1964. Animal Protection Fund. Multicoloured.
2062 10k.+5k. Type **326** 10 10
2063 30k.+5k. Horned sheep . . 10 10
2064 50k.+5k. Horses 15 10
2065 60k.+5k. Three horned sheep 20 10
2066 100k.+5k. Dairy cows . . . 35 10
The 30k. and 60k. are vert.

327 Running

328 Mustafa Resit

1964. Olympic Games, Tokyo.
2067 **327** 10k.+5k. black, red and brown 15 10
2068 – 50k.+5k. black, red and olive 15 10
2069 – 60k.+5k. black, red and blue 15 10
2070 – 100k.+5k. black, red and violet 30 10
DESIGNS—VERT: 50k. Torch-bearer; 60k. Wrestling; 100k. Throwing the discus.

1964. 125th Anniv of Reformation Decrees. Multicoloured.
2071 50k. Mustafa Resit and the pashas (horiz 48 × 32 mm) 20 10
2072 60k. Type **328** 20 10
2073 100k. As 50k. 25 10

329 Kemal Ataturk

330 Glider

1964.
2074 **329** 1k. green 10 10
2075 5k. blue 10 10
2076 10k. blue 45 10
2077 25k. green 85 10
2078 30k. purple . . . . . . 1·10 10
2079 50k. brown . . . . . . 1·75 10
2080 150k. orange . . . . . 5·00 10

1965. 40th Anniv of Turkish Civil Aviation League. Multicoloured.
2081 60k. Parachutist (vert) . . . 10 10
2082 90k. Type **330** 10 10
2083 130k. Ataturk and squadron of aircraft (vert) 10 10

331 CENTO Emblem

1965. Completion of CENTO Telecommunications Projects. Multicoloured.
2084 30k. Type **331** 10 10
2085 50k. Aerial mast (vert) . . . 10 10
2086 75k. Hand pressing button (inaugural ceremony) . . 10 10

332 Monument and Soldiers

1965. 50th Anniv of Battle of the Dardanelles. Multicoloured.
2087 50k.+10k. Wreath and map 10 10
2088 90k.+10k. Type **332** 10 10
2089 130k.+10k. Dardanelles Monument and flag (vert) 10 10

333 Beach at Ordu

1965. Tourism. Multicoloured.
2090 30k. Type **333** 10 10
2091 50k. Manavgat Falls 10 10
2092 60k. Istanbul 10 10
2093 100k. Urfa 10 10
2094 130k. Alanya 10 10

334 I.T.U. Emblem and Symbols

1965. I.T.U. Centenary.
2095 **334** 50k. multicoloured . . . 10 10
2096 130k. multicoloured . . 10 10

335 I.C.Y. Emblem

1965. International Co-operation Year.
2097 **335** 100k. red, green and salmon 10 10
2098 130k. violet, green and grey 15 10

336 "Co-operation"

337 R. N. Guntekin

1965. 1st Anniv of Regional Development Co-operation Pact. Multicoloured.
2099 50k. Type **336** 10 10
2100 75k. Globe and flags of Turkey, Iran and Pakistan 10 10

1965. Cultural Celebrities.
2101 **337** 1k. black and red . . . 10 10
2102 – 5k. black and blue . . . 10 10
2103 – 10k. black and ochre . . 15 10
2104 – 25k. black and brown . . 20 10
2105 – 30k. black and grey . . 35 10
2106 – 50k. black and yellow . . 55 10
2107 – 60k. black and purple . . 50 10
2108 – 150k. black and green 80 10
2109 – 220k. black and brown 55 10
PORTRAITS: 5k. Dr. B. O Akalin; 10k. T. Fikret; 25k. T. Cemil; 30k. Ahmet Vefik Pasa; 50k. O. Seyfettin; 60k. K. Mimaroglu; 150k. H. Z. Usakligil; 220k. Y. K. Beyatli.

338 Kemal Ataturk and Signature

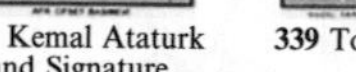
339 Tobacco Plant

1965.
2110 **338** 1k. black and mauve . . 10 10
2111 5k. black and green . . 15 10
2112 10k. black and blue . . 20 10
2113 50k. black and gold . . 20 10
2114 150k. black and silver . . 65 10
See also Nos. 2170/4.

1965. 2nd International Tobacco Congress. Mult.
2115 30k.+5k. Type **339** 10 10
2116 50k.+5k. Leander's Tower and tobacco leaves (horiz) 10 10
2117 100k.+5k. Tobacco leaf . . 10 10

340 Europa "Sprig"

1965. Europa.
2118 **340** 50k. green, blue and grey 40 15
2119 130k. green, blk & ochre 55 30

341 Civilians supporting Map

1965. National Census. Inscr "GENEL NUFUS SAYIMI".
2120 **341** 10k. multicoloured . . . 10 10
2121 – 50k. light green, green and black 10 10
2122 – 100k. black, blue & orge 15 10
DESIGNS—HORIZ: 50k. Year "1965". VERT: 100k. Human eye and figure.

342 Ankara Castle and Airliner

1965. "Ankara '65" National Stamp Exn. Inscr "I. MILLI PUL SERGISI".
2123 **342** 10k. red, yellow and violet 10 10
2124 – 30k. multicoloured . . . 10 10
2125 – 50k. blue, red and olive 10 10
2126 – 100k. multicoloured . . 15 10
MS2127 50 × 95 mm. 150k. multicoloured . . . . 1·25 1·10
DESIGNS—HORIZ: 30k. Archer; 50k. Horseman; 100k. Three thematic "stamps" and medal. VERT: 150k. Hands holding stamp album.

343 Training-ship "Savarona"

344 Halide E. Adivar

1965. Turkish Naval Society Congress.
2128 **343** 50k. brown and blue . . 25 10
2129 – 60k. indigo and blue . . 30 10
2130 – 100k. brown and blue . . 45 10
2131 – 130k. purple and blue . . 55 15
2132 – 220k. black and blue . . 90 20
DESIGNS: 60k. Submarine "Piri Reis"; 100k. Destroyer "Alpaslan"; 130k. Destroyer "Gelibolu"; 220k. Destroyer "Gemlik".

1966. Cultural Celebrities.
2133 – 25k. brown and grey . . 40 10
2134 – 30k. brown and mauve 15 10
2135 **344** 50k. black and blue . . 15 10
2136 – 60k. brown and green . . 40 10
2137 – 130k. black and blue . . 90 10
PORTRAITS: 25k. H. S. Arel; 30k. K. Akdik; 60k. Abdurrahman Seref; 130k. Naima.

345 Roof Panel, Green Mausoleum, Burs

346 Volleyball

1966. Turkish Faience. Multicoloured.
2138 50k. Type **345** 25 10
2139 60k. "Spring Flowers", Sultan Mausoleum, Istanbul 90 50
2140 130k. 16th-cent tile, Iznik 60 25

1966. Int Military Volleyball Championships.
2141 **346** 50k. multicoloured . . . 10 10

347 Bodrum

348 Golden Pitcher

1966. Tourism. Multicoloured.
2142 10k. Type **347** 10 10
2143 30k. Kusadasi 15 10
2144 50k. Anadoluhisari (horiz) 10 10
2145 90k. Marmaris 10 10
2146 100k. Izmir (horiz) 10 10

1966. Ancient Works of Art. Multicoloured.
2147 30k.+5k. Ivory eagle and rabbit (horiz) 10 10
2148 50k.+5k. Deity in basalt . . 10 10
2149 60k.+5k. Bronze bull . . 15 10
2150 90k.+5k. Type **348** 20 15

349 View of Dam

1966. Inaug of Keban Dam. Multicoloured.
2151 50k. Type **349** 10 10
2152 60k. Keban valley and bridge 10 10

350 King Faisal

1966. Visit of King of Saudi Arabia.
2153 **350** 100k. deep red and red 15 10

351 "Stamp" and "Postmark"

352

1966. "Balkanfila" Stamp Exhibition, Istanbul. Multicoloured.
2154 50k. Type **351** 10 10
2155 60k. Stamp "flower" 10 10
2156 75k. "Stamps" in form of display frames 10 10
MS2157 75 × 50 mm. **352** 100k. chestnut, blue and yellow. Imperf 1·10 85

353 Sultan Suleiman on Horseback

354 Europa "Ship"

1966. 400th Death Anniv of Sultan Suleiman. Multicoloured.
2158 60k. Type **353** 25 15
2159 90k. Mausoleum, Istanbul 50 20
2160 130k. Sultan Suleiman (profile) 75 45

1966. Europa.
2161 **354** 50k. ultramarine, bl & blk 25 15
2162 130k. purple, lilac & black 50 20

355 Grand Hotel Ephesus, Izmir

1966. 33rd International Fairs Union Congress, Izmir. Multicoloured.
2163 50k.+5k. Type **355** 10 10
2164 60k.+5k. Konak Square, Izmir (vert) 10 10
2165 130k.+5k. Izmir Fair . . . 10 10

356 "Education, Science and Culture"

1966. 20th Anniv of UNESCO.
2166 **356** 130k. chestnut, yellow and brown 10 10

357 University of Technology

358 Ataturk (equestrian statue)

1966. 10th Anniv of Middle East University of Technology. Multicoloured.
2167 50k. Type **357** 10 10
2168 100k. Atomic symbol . . . 10 10
2169 130k. Symbols of the sciences 15 10

1966. As Nos. 2110/14.
2170 **338** 25k. black and green . . 10 10
2171 30k. black and pink . . 15 10
2172 50k. black and violet . . 50 10
2173 90k. black and brown . . 70 10
2174 100k. black and drab . . 80 10

1966. Greetings Card Stamp.
2175 **358** 10k. black and yellow . . 10 10
See also Nos. 2218/9, 2257/8, 2303 and 2418.

359 De Havilland Dragon Rapide

360 A. Mithat (author)

1967. Air. Aircraft.
2176 **359** 10k. black and pink . . 20 15
2177 – 60k. red, black and green 15 10
2178 – 130k. red, black and blue 35 10
2179 – 220k. red, sepia and ochre 45 10
2180 – 270k. red, blue and salmon 50 10
DESIGNS: 60k. Fokker F27 Friendship; 130k. Douglas DC-9-30; 220k. Douglas DC-3; 270k. Vickers Viscount 700.

1967. Cultural Celebrities.
2181 **360** 1k. black and green . . 10 10
2182 – 5k. black and ochre . . 15 10
2183 – 50k. black and violet . . 35 10
2184 – 100k. black and yellow 85 10
2185 – 150k. black and yellow 1·75 10
PORTRAITS: 5k. T. Reis (naval commander); 50k. S. Mehmet (statesman); 100k. Nedim (philosopher); 150k. O. Hamdi (painter).

361 Karogoz and Hacivat (puppets)

1967. International Tourist Year. Multicoloured.
2186 50k. Type **361** 30 10
2187 60k. Sword and shield game 35 15
2188 90k. Military Band 45 30
2189 100k. Karagoz (puppet) (vert) 70 35

362 "Vaccination"

363 Fallow Deer

1967. 250th Anniv of 1st Smallpox Vaccination, Edirne.
2190 **362** 100k. multicoloured . . 15 10

1967. Game Animals. Multicoloured.
2191 50k. Type **363** 20 10
2192 60k. Wild goat 20 10
2193 100k. Brown bear 30 10
2194 130k. Wild boar 40 15

364 Emblem and Footballers 365 Cogwheels

1967. 20th Int Junior Football Tournament. Mult.
2195 50k. Type **364** 30 10
2196 130k. Footballers and emblem 45 15

1967. Europa.
2197 **365** 100k.+10k. mult 30 10
2198 130k.+10k. mult 50 35

366 Kemal Ataturk

367 Road Junction on Map

1967.
2199 **366** 10k. black and green . . 85 10
2200 50k. black and pink . . 1·25 10

1967. Opening of "E 5" Motorway. Mult.
2201 60k.+5k. Type **367** 15 10
2202 130k.+5k. Motorway map and emblem (vert) 30 15

368 Sivas Hospital

1967. 750th Anniv of Sivas Hospital.
2203 **368** 50k. multicoloured . . . 15 10

369 Selim Tarcan and Olympic Rings

1967. 1st Turkish Olympic Competitions, Istanbul. Multicoloured.
2204 50k. Type **369** 10 10
2205 60k. Pierre de Coubertin and Olympic Rings . . . 10 10

370 St. John's Church, Ephesus

371 Common Kestrel

1967. Pope Paul VI's Visit to Virgin Mary's House, Ephesus. Multicoloured.
2206 130k. Interior of Virgin Mary's House, Ephesus 10 10
2207 220k. Type **370** 15 10

1967. Air. Birds.
2208 **371** 10k. brown and salmon 50 15
2209 – 60k. brown and yellow 40 10
2210 – 130k. purple and blue . . 90 10
2211 – 220k. sepia and green . . 95 10
2212 – 270k. brown and lilac . . 1·50 15
DESIGNS: 60k. Imperial eagle; 130k. Pallid harrier; 220k. Northern sparrow hawk; 270k. Common buzzard.

372 Exhibition Emblem

1967. International Ceramics Exn, Istanbul.
2213 **372** 50k. multicoloured . . . 10 10

373 Emblem and Istanbul Skyline

1967. Congress of International Large Dams Commission, Istanbul.
2214 **373** 130k. blue and drab . . 10 10

374 "Stamps" and Map

1967. "Izmir '67" Stamp Exhibition. Mult.
2215 50k. Type **374** 10 10
2216 60k. "Stamps" and grapes 15 10
MS2217 100 × 52 mm. Nos. 2215/16 1·25 1·10

1967. Greetings Card Stamps. As T **358**.
2218 10k. black and green . . . 10 10
2219 10k. black and red 10 10
DESIGNS: Equestrian statues of Ataturk at: No. 2218 Samsun; No. 2219 Izmir.

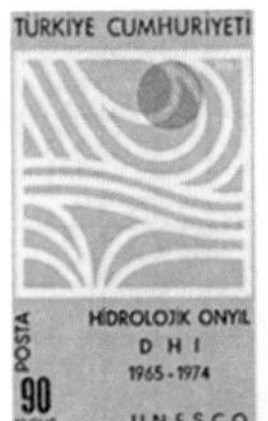

375 Decade Emblem

376 Girl with Angora Cat

1967. International Hydrological Decade.
2220 **375** 90k. yellow, black & grn 15 10
2221 130k. yellow, black & lilac 20 10

1967. 125th Anniv of Turkish Veterinary Medical Service. Multicoloured.
2222 50k. Type **376** 15 10
2223 60k. Horse 20 10

377 Human Rights Emblem — **378** Kemal Ataturk

1968. Human Rights Year.
2224 **377** 50k. multicoloured . . . 15 10
2225 130k. multicoloured . . 20 10

1968.
2226 **378** 1k. blue and light blue 10 10
2227 5k. green and light green 15 10
2228 50k. brown and yellow 1·10 10
2229 200k. brown and pink 2·75 10

379 "The Investiture"

1968. Turkish Book Miniatures. Multicoloured.
2230 50k. Type **379** 40 10
2231 60k. "Suleiman the Magnificent receiving an ambassador" (vert) . . . 50 15
2232 90k. "The Sultan's Archery Practice" 70 35
2233 100k. "The Musicians" . . 80 40

380 Scales of Justice

1968. Turkish Courts Centenary. Multicoloured.
(a) Supreme Court.
2234 50k. Type **380** 15 10
2235 60k. Ahmet Cevdet Pasha (president) and scroll . . 20 10
(b) Court of Appeal.
2236 50k. Book 15 10
2237 60k. Mithat Pasha (first president) and scroll . . . 80 40
MS2236 79 × 109 mm. 130k. Symbolic dove 85 75

381 W.H.O. Emblem

1968. 20th Anniv of W.H.O.
2238 **381** 130k.+10k. yellow, black and blue 15 10

382 Europa "Key"

1968. Europa.
2239 **382** 100k. yellow, red and blue 55 25
2240 130k. yellow, red & green . . . . 1·10 35

383 Etem Pasha and Dr. Marko

1968. Turkish Red Crescent Fund. Multicoloured.
2241 50k.+10k. Type **383** 20 10
2242 60k.+10k. Omer Pasha and Dr. Abdullah 25 15
2243 100k.+10k. Kemal Ataturk and Dr. Refik Saydam in front of Red Crescent Headquarters (vert) . . . 30 20

384 "Kismet" — **385** "Protection against Usury" (after Koseoglu)

1968. Sadun Boro's World Voyage in Ketch "Kismet".
2244 **384** 50k. multicoloured . . . 35 10

1968. Centenary of Pawnbroking Office, Istanbul.
2245 **385** 50k. multicoloured . . . 20 10

386 Battle of Sakarya and Obverse of Medal

1968. Independence Medal. Multicoloured.
2246 50k. Type **386** 10 10
2247 130k. National Anthem and reverse of medal 20 10

387 Old and New Emblems within "100"

1968. Centenary of Galatasaray High School. Multicoloured.
2248 50k. Type **387** 10 10
2249 60k. Gulbaba offering flowers to Bayazet II . . 20 10
2250 100k. Kemal Ataturk and School Building 30 10

388 President De Gaulle — **389** Kemal Ataturk

1968. President De Gaulle's Visit to Turkey.
2251 **388** 130k. multicoloured . . 20 10

1968. 30th Death Anniv of Kemal Ataturk.
2252 **389** 30k. black and yellow . . 15 10
2253 – 50k. black and green . . 15 10
2254 – 60k. black and turquoise 45 10
2255 – 100k. black, green and bistre 35 10
2256 – 250k. multicoloured . . . 50 15
DESIGNS: 50k. Ataturk's Cenotaph; 60k. Ataturk at railway carriage window. (32½ × 43 mm): 100k. Ataturk's portrait and "address to youth"; 250k. Ataturk in military uniform.

1968. Greetings Card Stamps. As T **358** but dated "1968".
2257 10k. black and mauve . . . 10 10
2258 10k. black and blue 10 10
DESIGNS: Equestrian statues of Ataturk at: No. 2257 Antakya; No. 2258 Zonguldak.

390 Ince Minara Mosque, Konya — **391** Dove and N.A.T.O. Emblem

1968. Historic Buildings.
2259 **390** 1k. sepia and brown . . 10 10
2260 – 10k. maroon and purple 10 10
2261 – 50k. green and grey . . 20 10
2262 – 100k. green & light green 75 10
2263 – 200k. blue and light blue 40 10
DESIGNS: 10k. Doner Kumbet (tomb), Kayseri; 50k. Karatay University, Konya; 100k. Ortakoy Mosque, Istanbul; 200k. Ulu Mosque, Divrigi.

1969. 20th Anniv of N.A.T.O.
2264 **391** 50k.+10k. black, blue and green 10 10
2265 – 130k.+10k. gold, blue and deep blue 25 15
DESIGN: 130k. Stars around globe and N.A.T.O. emblem.

392 "Education"

1969. Turkish Economy.
2266 **392** 1k. black and red . . . 10 10
2267 1k. black and green . . . 10 10
2268 1k. black and violet . . 10 10
2269 1k. black and brown . . 10 10
2270 1k. black and grey . . . 10 10
2271 – 50k. brown and ochre 30 10
2272 – 90k. black and olive . . 50 10
2273 – 100k. red and black . . 25 10
2274 – 180k. violet and orange 1·40 10
DESIGNS: 50k. Farm workers and tractor ("Agriculture"); 90k. Ladle, factory and cogwheel ("Industry"); 100k. Road sign and graph ("Highways"); 180k. Derricks ("Oil Industry").

393 I.L.O. Emblem

1969. 50th Anniv of I.L.O.
2275 **393** 130k. red and black . . 10 10

394 "Hafsa Sultan" (unknown artist)

1969. Hafsa Sultan (medical pioneer) Commem.
2276 **394** 60k. multicoloured . . . 15 15

395 Colonnade

1969. Europa.
2277 **395** 100k. multicoloured . . 20 10
2278 130k. multicoloured . . 25 20

396 Kemal Ataturk in 1919 — **397** Symbolic Map of Istanbul

1969. 50th Anniv of Kemal Ataturk's Landing at Samsun. Multicoloured.
2279 50k. Type **396** 15 10
2280 60k. Cargo liner "Bandirma" (horiz) . . . 25 15

1969. 22nd Int Chambers of Commerce Congress, Istanbul.
2281 **397** 130k. multicoloured . . 10 10

398 "Suleiman the Great holding Audience" (16th-cent Turkish miniature) — **399** Kemal Ataturk in Civilian Dress

1969. 5th Anniv of Regional Co-operation for Development Pact Miniatures. Multicoloured.
2282 50k. Type **398** 20 10
2283 80k. "Kneeling Servant" (17th-cent Persian) . . . 30 15
2284 130k. "Lady on Balcony" (18th-cent Mogul–Pakistan) 40 20

1969. 50th Anniv of Erzurum Congress.
2285 **399** 50k. black and violet . . 10 10
2286 – 60k. black and green . . 15 10
DESIGN—HORIZ: 60k. Ataturk's statue, Erzurum.

401 Red Cross Societies' Emblems

1969. 21st International Red Cross Conf, Istanbul.
2291 **401** 100k.+10k. red, blue and ultramarine 10 10
2292 – 130k.+10k. mult 20 10
DESIGN: 130k. Conference emblem and silhouette of Istanbul.

402 Congress Hall

1969. 50th Anniv of Sivas Congress.
2293 **402** 50k. purple, black and red 10 10
2294 – 60k. olive, black & yellow 15 10
DESIGN: 60k. Congress delegates.

403 Halay Scarf Dance

1969. Turkish Folk-dances. Multicoloured.
2295 30k. Bar dancers 10 10
2296 50k. Caydacira "candle" dance 20 10
2297 60k. Type **403** 25 10
2298 100k. Kilic-Kalkan sword dance 35 10
2299 130k. Zeybek dance (vert) 40 15

404 Bleriot XI "Prince Celaladdin"

1969. 55th Anniv of First Turkish Airmail Service.
2300 **404** 60k. deep blue and blue 10 10
2301 – 75k. black and bistre . . 10 10
DESIGN: 75k. 1914 First Flight cover.

405 "Kutadgu Bilig"

1969. 900th Anniv of "Kutadgu Bilig" (political manual) Compilation.
2302 **405** 130k. brown, gold and bistre 10 10

1969. Greetings Card Stamp. As T **358**.
2303 10k. brown and green . . . 10 10
DESIGN: 10k. Equestrian statue of Ataturk at Bursa.

406 "Ataturk's Arrival" (S. Tuna)

1969. 50th Anniv of Kemal Ataturk's Arrival in Ankara. Multicoloured.
2304 50k. Type **406** 40 20
2305 60k. Ataturk's motorcade 40 25

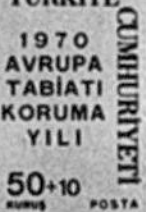

407 "Erosion Control"

1970. Nature Conservation Year. Multicoloured.
2306 50k.+10k. Type **407** 15 10
2307 60k.+10k. "Protection of Flora" 10 10
2308 130k.+10k. "Protection of Wildlife" 30 15

408 Bosphorus Bridge (model) (½-size illustration)

1970. Commencement of Work on Bosphorus Bridge. Multicoloured.
2309 60k. Type **408** 25 10
2310 130k. Symbolic bridge linking Europe and Asia 45 20

409 Ataturk and Signature **410** Education Year Emblem

1970.
2311 **409** 1k. brown and red . . . 10 10
2312 50k. green and olive . . 20 10

1970. International Education Year.
2313 **410** 130k. blue, purple & mve 10 10

411 Turkish Pavilion Emblem **412** Kemal Ataturk

1970. World Fair "Expo '70", Osaka, Japan. Multicoloured.
2314 50k. Type **411** 10 10
2315 100k. Turkish pavilion and Expo emblem 15 10

1970.
2316 **412** 5k. black and silver . . . 10 10
2317 30k. black and bistre . . 25 10
2318 50k. black and pink . . 30 10
2319 75k. black and lilac . . . 45 10
2320 100k. black and blue . . 50 10

413 Opening Ceremony

1970. 50th Anniv of Turkish National Assembly. Multicoloured.
2321 50k. Type **413** 10 10
2322 60k. First Assembly in session 10 10

414 Emblem of Cartography Directorate

1970. "75 Years of Turkish Cartography". Multicoloured.
2323 50k. Type **414** 10 10
2324 60k. Dornier Do-28 airplane and contour map 15 10
2325 100k. Survey equipment . . 10 10
2326 130k. Lt.-Gen. Mehmet Sevki Pasha and relief map of Turkey 15 10
Nos. 2324 and 2326 are larger, size 48 × 33 mm.

415 "Flaming Sun"

1970. Europa.
2327 **415** 100k. red, orange & black 25 10
2328 130k. green, orange & blk 45 25

416 New U.P.U. Headquarters Building

1970. New U.P.U. Headquarters Building, Berne.
2329 **416** 60k. black, blue & lt blue 10 10
2330 130k. black, green and light green 15 10

417 "Roe-deer" (Seker Ahmet Pasha) **418** "Turkish Folklore"

1970. Turkish Paintings. Multicoloured.
2331 250k. Type **417** 25 15
2332 250k. "Lady with Mimosa" (Osman Hamdi) 25 15
See also Nos. 2349/50, 2364/5, 2396/7, 2416/17 and 2443/4.

1970. "Ankara 70" National Stamp Exhibition. Multicoloured.
2333 10k. "Tree" of stamps and open album (vert) 10 10
2334 50k. Type **418** 10 10
2335 60k. Ataturk statue and "stamps" 15 10
MS2336 79 × 109 mm. 130k. Symbolic dove 85 75

419 Fethiye (Turkey)

1970. 6th Anniv of Regional Co-operation for Development. Multicoloured.
2337 60k. Type **419** 10 10
2338 80k. Seeyo-Se-Pol Bridge, Isfahan (Iran) 10 10
2339 130k. Saiful Malook Lake (Pakistan) 10 10
No. 2338 is larger 41 × 26 mm.

420 Tomb of Haci Bektas Veli

1970. 700th Death Anniv of Haci Bektas Veli (mystic). Multicoloured.
2340 30k. Type **420** 10 10
2341 100k. Sultan Balim's tomb (vert) 25 10
2342 180k. Haci Bektas Veli (vert) 35 10
No. 2342 is larger, size 32 × 49 mm.

421 Symbolic "Fencer" and Globe

1970. World Fencing Championships.
2343 **421** 90k.+10k. black, blue and light blue 10 10
2344 – 130k.+10k. orange, green, black and blue 15 10
DESIGN: 130k. Modern fencer, folk-dancer and globe.

422 I.S.O. Emblem

1970. 8th International Standardization Organization General Assembly, Ankara.
2345 **422** 110k. red, gold and black 10 10
2346 150k. blue, gold and black 10 10

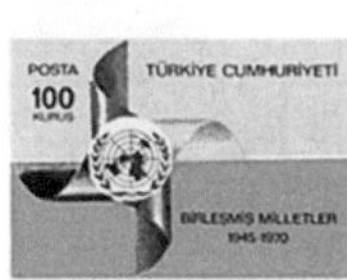

423 U.N. Emblem within Windmill

1970. 25th Anniv of United Nations. Mult.
2347 100k. Type **423** 10 10
2348 220k. World's people supporting U.N. (vert) . . 15 10

1970. Turkish Paintings. As T **417**. Mult.
2349 250k. "Fevzi Cakmak" (Avni Lifij) (vert) 35 10
2350 250k. "Fishing-boats" (Nazmi Ziya) (75 × 33 mm) 30 10

424 Turkish Troops Advancing

1971. 50th Anniv of First Battle of Inonu.
2351 **424** 100k. multicoloured . . 20 10
See also No. 2368.

425 Kemal Ataturk **429** Hands enclosing "Four Races"

428 "Turkish Village" (A. Sekur)

1971.
2352 **425** 5k. blue and grey . . . 10 10
2353 25k. red and grey . . . 30 10
2354 – 25k. brown and pink . . 10 10
2355 **425** 100k. violet and grey . . 50 10
2356 – 100k. green and flesh . . 50 10
2357 – 250k. blue and drab . . 95 10
2358 **425** 400k. green and bistre 2·10 10
DESIGNS: Nos. 2354, 2356 and 2357, Portraits similar to Type **425** but larger, 21 × 26 mm, and with face value at bottom right.

1971. Turkish Paintings. Multicoloured.
2364 250k. Type **428** 25 10
2365 250k. "Yildiz Palace Garden" (A. R. Bicakcilar) 25 10
See also Nos. 2396/7, 2416/17 and 2443/4.

1971. Racial Equality Year.
2366 **429** 100k. multicoloured . . 10 10
2367 250k. multicoloured . . 10 10

1971. 50th Anniv of Second Battle of Inonu. Design similar to T **424**. Multicoloured.
2368 100k. Turkish machine-gunners 20 10

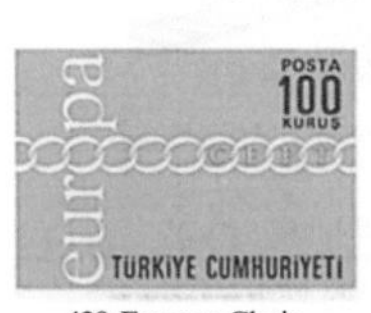

430 Europa Chain **431** Pres. C. Gursel

1971. Europa.
2369 **430** 100k. violet, yellow & bl 55 25
2370 150k. green, red & orange 70 40

1971. 11th Anniv of 27 May 1960 Revolution.
2371 **431** 100k. multicoloured . . 15 10

432 Lockhead Super Starfighter **433** "Care of Children"

1971. Air. "60 Years of Turkish Aviation". Multicoloured.
2372 110k. Type **432** 35 10
2373 200k. Victory Monument, Afyon and aircraft . . . 50 10
2374 250k. Air Force emblem and jet fighters (horiz) 55 10
2375 325k. Lockheed Super Starfighters and pilot . . 95 15
2376 400k. Bleriot XI airplane of 1911 (horiz) 80 15
2377 475k. Hezarfen Celebi's "bird flight" from Galata Tower (horiz) . . . . . . 1·10 20

1971. 50th Anniv of Children's Protection Society.
2378 **433** 50k.+10k. red, pur & blk 10 10
2379 – 100k.+15k. mult 10 10
2380 – 110k.+15k. mult 10 10
DESIGNS—VERT: 100k. Child standing on protective hand. HORIZ: 110k. Mother and child.

434 Selimiye Mosque, Edirne

1971. 7th Anniv of Regional Co-operation for Development Pact. Mosques. Multicoloured.
2381 100k. Type **434** 10 10
2382 150k. Chalharbagh Mosque School (Iran) 10 10
2383 200k. Badshahi Mosque (Pakistan) (horiz) 15 10

435 Alpaslan (Seljuk leader) and Cavalry

1971. 900th Anniv of Battle of Malazgirt.
2384 **435** 100k. multicoloured . . 20 10
2385 – 250k. red, yellow & black 35 15
DESIGN: 250k. Seljuk mounted archer.

436 Officer and Troop Column

1971. 50th Anniv of Battle of Sakarya.
2386 **436** 100k. multicoloured . . 20 10

437 Diesel Train and Map (Turkey–Iran Line)

1971. International Rail Links.
2387 – 100k. multicoloured . . 20 10
2388 – 110k. violet and blue . . 20 10
2389 **437** 250k. multicoloured . . 40 10
DESIGNS: 100k. Diesel train crossing bridge (Turkey–Bulgaria line); 110k. Train ferry, "Orhan Atliman", Lake Van (Turkey–Iran line).

438 Football

1971. Mediterranean Games, Izmir.
2390 **438** 100k. black, violet & blue 15 10
2391 – 200k. multicoloured . . 15 10
MS2392 50×95 mm. 250k. multicoloured. Imperf 75 65
DESIGNS—Vert: 200k. "Athlete and stadium"; 250k. "Athlete putting the shot, and map".

439 Tomb of Cyrus the Great

1971. 2500th Anniv of Persian Empire.
2393 **439** 25k. multicoloured . . . 10 10
2394 – 100k. multicoloured . . 15 10
2395 – 150k. brown and drab . . 25 10
DESIGNS—VERT: 100k. Persian mosaic of woman. HORIZ: 150k. Kemal Ataturk and Riza Shah Pahlavi.

1971. Turkish Paintings. As T **428**. Mult.
2396 250k. "Sultan Mohammed I and Entourage" 25 15
2397 250k. "Cinili Kosk Palace" 25 15

441 UNICEF Emblem **442** Yunus Emre

1971. 25th Anniv of UNICEF.
2404 **441** 100k.+10k. mult 10 10
2405 250k.+15k. mult 10 10

1971. 650th Death Anniv of Yunus Emre (folk-poet).
2406 **442** 100k. multicoloured . . 10 10

443 First Turkish Map of the World (1072) and Book Year Emblem

1972. International Book Year.
2407 **443** 100k. multicoloured . . 30 10

444 Doves and N.A.T.O. Emblem **445** Human Heart

1972. 20th Anniv of Turkey's Membership of N.A.T.O.
2408 **444** 100k. black, grey & green 30 15
2409 250k. black, grey and blue 60 20

1972. World Health Day.
2410 **445** 250k.+25k. red, black and grey 10 10

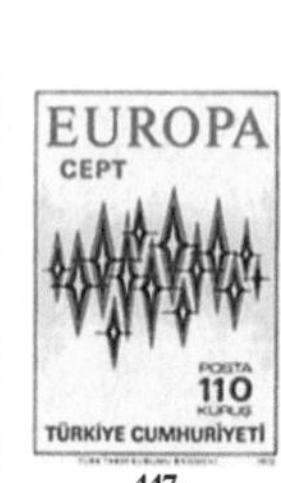

447 "Communications" **448** "Fisherman" (G. Dareli)

1972. Europa.
2414 **447** 110k. multicoloured . . 90 30
2415 250k. multicoloured . . 1·40 40

1972. Turkish Paintings. As T **428**. Multicoloured.
2416 250k. "Gebze" (Osman Hamdi) 25 15
2417 250k. "Forest" (S. A. Pasa) 25 15

1972. As T **358**.
2418 25k. black and brown . . . 10 10
DESIGN: 25k. Equestrian statue of Ataturk at Ankara.

1972. Regional Co-operation for Development. Multicoloured.
2419 100k. Type **448** 40 15
2420 125k. "Will and Power" (Chughtai) 45 20
2421 150k. "Iranian Woman" (Behzad) 70 35

449 Olympic Rings

1972. Olympic Games, Munich.
2422 **449** 100k.+15k. mult 15 10
2423 – 110k.+25k. mult 10 10
2424 – 250k.+25k. mult 15 15
DESIGNS: 110k. "Athletes"; 250k. "Stadium".

450 Ataturk at Observation Post

1972. 50th Anniv of Turkish War of Liberation. Multicoloured. (a) The Great Offensive.
2425 100k. Type **450** 20 10
2426 110k. Artillery 25 10

(b) Commander-in-Chief's Offensive.
2427 100k. Hand-to-hand fighting 25 10

(c) Entry into Izmir.
2428 100k. Commanders in open car 25 10

451 "Diagnosis and Cure" **452** Kemal Ataturk

1972. Fight against Cancer.
2429 **451** 100k. red, black and blue 10 10

1972. Various sizes.
2430 **452** 5k. light blue on blue 10 10
2430a 25k. orange on orange 10 10
2431 100k. lake on buff . . 55 10
2431a 100k. light grey on grey 15 10
2431b 100k. olive on green . . 20 10
2432 110k. blue on blue . . 50 10
2432a 125k. green and grey 60 10
2433 150k. brown on buff 50 10
2433a 150k. green on green 15 10
2434 175k. purple on yellow 75 10
2434a 200k. red on buff . . . 60 10
2434b 200k. brown on buff 20 10
2435 250k. lilac on pink . . 40 10
2435a 400k. turquoise on blue 25 10
2436 500k. violet on pink . . 1·00 10
2437 500k. blue on blue . . 45 10
2438 10l. mauve on pink . . 90 10

453 U.I.C. Emblem **454** University Emblem

1972. 50th Anniv of International Railway Union.
2439 **453** 100k. brown, buff & grn 10 10

1973. Bicent of Technical University, Istanbul.
2440 **454** 100k.+25k. mult 10 10

455 Europa "Posthorn" **456** Helmet and Sword

1973. Europa.
2441 **455** 110k. multicoloured . . 50 30
2442 250k. multicoloured . . 1·10 50

1973. Turkish Painters. As T **428**. Multicoloured.
2443 250k. "Old Almshouses, Istanbul" (Ahmet Ziya Akbulut) (horiz) 25 15
2444 250k. "Flowers in Vase" (Suleyman Seyyit) (vert) 25 15

1973. Land Forces' Day.
2445 **456** 90k. green, brown & grey 10 10
2446 – 100k. green, brown and light green 10 10
DESIGN: 100k. As Type **456**, but wreath enclosing design.

457 Carved Head, Tomb of Antiochus I (Turkey) **458** Peace Dove and "50"

1973. Regional Co-operation for Development. Multicoloured.
2447 100k. Type **457** 10 10
2448 150k. Statue, Lut excavations (Iran) 15 10
2449 200k. Street in Moenjodaro (Pakistan) 20 10

1973. 50th Anniv of Lausanne Peace Treaty.
2450 **458** 100k.+25k. mult 10 10

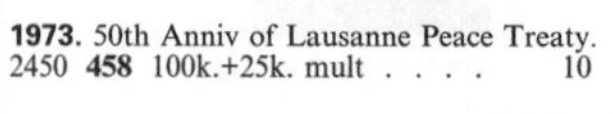

459 Minelayer "Nusret II" **460** "Al-Biruni" (from 16th-century miniature)

1973. Bicentenary of Turkish Navy. Mult.
2451 5k. Type **459** 10 10
2452 25k. Destroyer "Istanbul" 15 10
2453 100k. Motor torpedo-boat "Simsek" 30 10
2454 250k. Cadet brig "Nurud-i-Futuh" (48×32 mm) . . 90 20

1973. Millenary of Abu Reihan al-Biruni.
2455 **460** 250k. multicoloured . . 10 10

461 "Equal Opportunity" **463** "Balkanfila" Emblem

1973. Centenary of Darussafaka High School.
2456 **461** 100k. multicoloured . . 10 10

1973. "Balkanfila IV" Stamp Exhibition, Izmir (1st issue).
2458 **463** 100k. multicoloured . . 10 10
See also Nos. 2462/3.

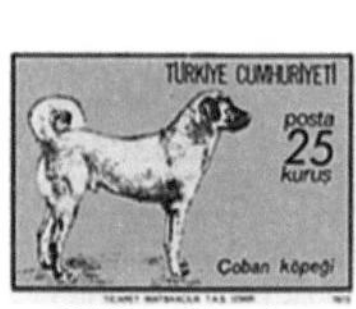

464 Sivas Sheepdog **465** Kemal Ataturk

1973. Animals.
2459 **464** 25k. blue, yellow & black 10 10
2460 – 100k. yellow, black & bl 20 10
DESIGN: 100k. Angora cat.

1973. 35th Death Anniv of Kemal Ataturk.
2461 **465** 100k. brown and drab 10 10

466 Bosphorus and "Stamps" **467** "Flower" Emblem

1973. "Balkanfila IV" Stamp Exhibition (2nd issue). Multicoloured.
2462 110k. Type **466** 10 10
2463 250k. "Balkanfila" in decorative script 15 10

1973. 50th Anniv of Republic.
2464 **467** 100k. red, violet and blue 10 10
2465 – 250k. multicoloured . . 15 10
2466 – 475k. yellow and blue . . 20 10
MS2467 79×110 mm. 500k. multicoloured . . . . 1·60 1·40
DESIGNS: As T **467**—250k. "Hands" supporting "50"; 475k. Cogwheel and ears of corn. 32×49 mm. 500k. Kemal Ataturk.

468 Bosphorus Bridge **469** Bosphorus Bridge and UNICEF Emblem

1973. Opening of Bosphorus Bridge, Istanbul. Multicoloured.
2468 100k. Type **468** 10 10
2469 150k. View of Bosphorus and bridge 20 10

1973. UNICEF Ceremony. Children of Europe and Asia linked by Bosphorus Bridge.
2470 **469** 200k. multicoloured . . 25 10

470 Mevlana Celaleddin **471** Cotton

1973. 700th Death Anniv of Mevlana Celaleddin (poet and mystic).
2471 – 100k. green, blue & black 15 10
2472 **470** 250k. multicoloured . . 25 10
DESIGN: 100k. Tomb and dancing dervishes.

1973. Export Products.
2473 **471** 75k. grey, blue and black 15 10
2474 – 90k. bistre, blue and black 20 10
2475 – 100k. black, blue & green 25 10
2476 – 250k. multicoloured . . 1·75 10
2477 – 325k. yellow, blue & blk 50 10
2478 – 475k. black, blue & brn 45 10
DESIGNS: 90k. Grapes; 100k. Figs; 250k. Citrus fruits; 325k. Tobacco; 475k. Hazelnuts.

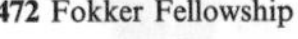

472 Fokker Fellowship **473** President Inonu

1973. Air. Multicoloured.
2479 110k. Type **472** 25 10
2480 250k. Douglas DC-10 . . . 55 10

1973. President Inonu's Death.
2481 **473** 100k. brown and buff . . 10 10

474 "Statue of a King" (Hittite era) **475** Doctor and Patient

1974. Europa. Sculptures. Multicoloured.
2482 110k. Type **474** . . . . . . 1·25 50
2483 250k. "Statuette of a Child" (c. 2000 B.C.) . . . . . . 2·10 80

1974. 75th Anniv of Sisli Paediatrics Hospital.
2484 **475** 110k. black, grey and blue 10 10

476 Silver and Gold Idol **477** Population Year Emblem

1974. Archaeological Treasures. Multicoloured.
2485 125k. Type **476** 10 10
2486 175k. Painted jar (horiz) . . 10 10
2487 200k. Bulls (statuettes) (horiz) 15 10
2488 250k. Jug 20 10

1974. World Population Year.
2489 **477** 250k.+25k. mult 15 10

479 Turkish Carpet

1974. Regional Co-operation for Development. Multicoloured.
2496 100k. Type **479** 45 25
2497 150k. Iranian carpet 80 40
2498 200k. Pakistani carpet . . . 1·25 50

480 Dove and Map of Cyprus

1974. Turkish Intervention in Cyprus.
2499 **480** 250k. multicoloured . . 15 10

481 "Getting to Grips" **482** Dove with Letter

1974. World Free-style Wrestling Championships, Ankara. Multicoloured.
2500 90k. Type **481** 10 10
2501 100k. "Throw" (vert) . . . 15 10
2502 250k. "Lock" 20 10

1974. Centenary of Universal Postal Union.
2503 **482** 110k. gold, dp blue & bl 10 10
2504 – 200k. brown and green 10 10
2505 – 250k. multicoloured . . 15 10
DESIGNS: 200k. Dove; 250k. Arrows encircling globe.

483 Open Book (Law Reform)

1974. Works and Reforms of Ataturk (1st series).
2506 **483** 50k. black and blue . . 10 10
2507 – 150k. multicoloured . . 15 10
2508 – 400k. multicoloured . . 15 10
DESIGNS—VERT: 150k. "Tree" ("National Economy"); 400k. Students facing sun ("Reform of Education").
See also Nos. 2543/5, 2566/8, 2597/9, 2639/41 and 2670/2.

484 Marconi **485** Arrows (3rd Five Year Development Programme)

1974. Birth Centenary of Marconi (radio pioneer).
2509 **484** 250k.+25k. black, brown and red 15 10

1974. "Turkish Development".
2510 **485** 25k. black and brown . . 10 10
2511 – 100k. grey and brown 15 10
DESIGNS—HORIZ: 100k. Map of Turkey within cogwheel (industrialization).

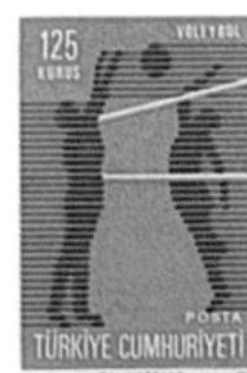
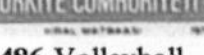

486 Volleyball **487** Dr. Albert Schweitzer

1974. Ball Games.
2512 **486** 125k. black and blue . . 20 10
2513 – 175k. black and orange 20 10
2514 – 250k. black and green 30 10
DESIGNS: 175k. Basketball; 250k. Football.

1975. Birth Centenary of Dr. Albert Schweitzer.
2515 **487** 250k.+50k. mult 15 10

488 Automatic Telex Network

1975. Posts and Telecommunications.
2516 **488** 5k. black and yellow . . 10 10
2517 – 50k. green and orange 10 10
2518 – 100k. black and blue . . 15 10
DESIGNS: 50k. Postal cheques; 100k. Radio link.

489 "Going to the Classroom" (I. Sivga) **490** Karacaoglan Monument (H. Gezer), Mut

1975. Children's Drawings. Multicoloured.
2519 25k. Type **489** 10 10
2520 50k. "View from a Village" (H. Dogru) 10 10
2521 100k. "Folklore" (B. Aktan) 10 10

1975. Karacaoglan (musician) Commem.
2522 **490** 110k. mauve, green & brn 10 10

491 "Orange-gathering in Hatay" (C. Tollu)

1975. Europa. Paintings. Multicoloured.
2523 110k. Type **491** 65 55
2524 250k. "The Yoruks" (T. Zaim) . . . . 1·10 95

492 Turkish Porcelain Vase **493** Namibia located on Map of Africa

1975. Regional Co-operation for Development. Traditional Crafts. Multicoloured.
2525 110k. Type **492** 40 30
2526 200k. Ceramic plate (Iran) (horiz) 80 40
2527 250k. Camel-skin vase (Pakistan) . . . . 1·25 60

1975. Namibia Day.
2528 **493** 250k.+50k. mult 10 10

494 Horon Folk-dancers

1975. Turkish Folk Dances. Multicoloured.
2529 100k. Type **494** 20 15
2530 125k. Kasik 25 15
2531 175k. Bengi 30 15
2532 250k. Kasap 40 15
2533 325k. Kafkas (vert) 55 25

495 "Oguz Khan slaying Dragon" **498** Two Women and Symbol (Women's Participation in Public Life)

497 Turbot

1975. Tales of Dede Korkut. Multicoloured.
2534 90k. Type **495** 10 10
2535 175k. Tale of Duha Koca Oglu Deli Dumrul Hikayesi (horiz) 10 10
2536 200k. "Pillaging the Home of Salur Kazan" 10 10

1975. Fishes. Multicoloured.
2538 75k. Type **497** 60 55
2539 90k. Common carp 80 55
2540 175k. Brown trout . . . . 1·40 75
2541 250k. Red mullet . . . . . 2·10 80
2542 475k. Gilthead seabream . . 2·75 95

1975. Works and Reforms of Ataturk (2nd series).
2543 **498** 100k. red, black and stone 10 10
2544 – 110k. multicoloured . . 10 10
2545 – 250k. multicoloured . . 15 10
DESIGNS—VERT: 110k. Symbol and inscription (Nationalization of Insurance Companies). HORIZ: 250k. Arrows (Orientation of the Fine Arts).

499 Z. Gokalp **500** Ceramic Plate

1976. Birth Cent of Ziya Gokalp (philosopher).
2546 **499** 200k.+25k. mult 10 10

1976. Europa. Multicoloured.
2547 200k. Type **500** . . . . . . 1·10 90
2548 400k. Dessert jug . . . . . 2·25 1·75

501 Silhouette of Istanbul

1976. 7th Islamic Conference, Istanbul.
2549 **501** 500k. multicoloured . . 15 10

502 "Lunch in Field" (S. Yucel)

1976. "Samsun '76" Youth Stamp Exn. Mult.
2550 50k. Type **502** 10 10
2551 200k. "Boats on the Bosphorus" (E. Kosemen) (vert) 10 10
2552 400k. "Winter View" (R. Cetinkaya) 15 10

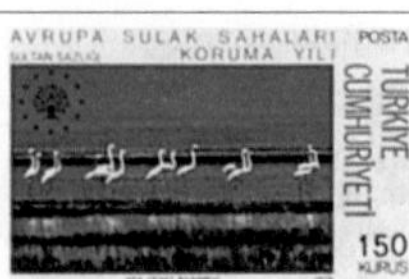
503 Sultan Marshes

1976. European Wetlands Conservation Year. Turkish Landscapes. Multicoloured.
2553 150k. Type **503** 20 10
2554 200k. Lake Manyas 20 10
2555 250k. Lake Borabey 30 10
2556 400k. Manavgat waterfalls 30 10

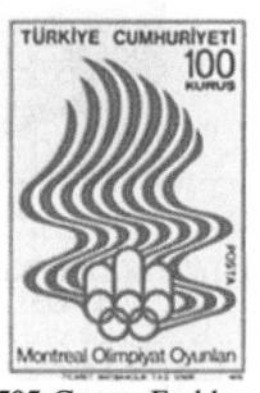
504 "Hodja with Liver" **505** Games Emblem and Flame

1976. Nasreddin Hodja (humourist) Commem. "The Liver and the Kite". Multicoloured.
2557 150k. Type **504** 10 10
2558 250k. "Friend offers recipe" 10 10
2559 600k. "Kite takes liver, leaving recipe" 15 10

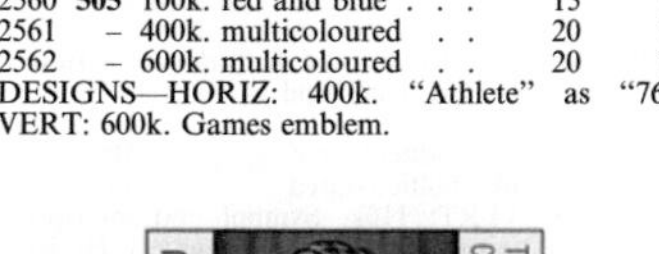

1976. Olympic Games, Montreal.
2560 **505** 100k. red and blue . . . 15 10
2561 – 400k. multicoloured . . 20 10
2562 – 600k. multicoloured . . 20 10
DESIGNS—HORIZ: 400k. "Athlete" as "76". VERT: 600k. Games emblem.

506 Kemal Ataturk (Turkey)

1976. Regional Co-operation for Development. Heads of State. Multicoloured.
2563 100k. Type **506** 10 10
2564 200k. Riza Shah Pahlavi (Iran) 10 10
2565 250k. Mohammed Ali Jinnah (Pakistan) 15 10

507 Peace Dove and Sword (Army Reform) **508** White Spoonbill

1976. Works and Reforms of Ataturk (3rd series).
2566 **507** 100k. black and red . . 10 10
2567 – 200k. multicoloured . . 10 10
2568 – 400k. multicoloured . . 15 10
DESIGNS: 200k. Words, books and listeners (Ataturk's speeches); 400k. Peace doves and globe ("Peace throughout the World").

1976. Turkish Birds. Multicoloured.
2569 100k.+25k. Type **508** . . . 30 15
2570 150k.+25k. European roller 40 20
2571 200k.+25k. Greater flamingo 60 25
2572 400k.+25k. Waldrapp (horiz) . . . . 1·00 1·25

509 "Hora" (oil exploration ship) **510** Musical Symbols

1977.
2573 **509** 400k. multicoloured . . 20 10

1977. 150th Anniv of Presidential Symphony Orchestra.
2574 **510** 200k. multicoloured . . 10 10

511 Kemal Ataturk in "100"

1977. Centenary of Parliament.
2575 **511** 200k. black and red . . 10 10
2576 – 400k. black and brown 15 10
DESIGN: 400k. Hand placing ballot-paper in box.

512 Pamukkale

1977. Europa. Landscapes. Multicoloured.
2577 200k. Type **512** . . . . . . 1·00 90
2578 400k. Zelve . . . . 2·00 1·25

513 Edict of Karamanoglu Mehmet Bey and "Ongun" Bird

1977. 700th Anniv of Official Turkish Language.
2579 **513** 200k.+25k. black and green 10 10

514 Head-shaped Vase, Turkey

1977. Regional Co-operation for Development. Pottery. Multicoloured.
2580 100k. Type **514** 20 10
2581 255k. Earthenware pot (Iran) 35 10
2582 675k. Model bullock cart (Pakistan) 80 15
MS2583 107 × 78 mm. Nos. 2580/2 2·25 1·10

515 Stylized Sailing Yacht **522** "Globe" and Emblem

1977. European Finn Class Sailing Championships.
2584 **515** 150k. black, blue and light blue 10 10
2585 – 200k. blue and deep blue 20 10
2586 – 250k. black and blue . . 25 10
DESIGNS—HORIZ: 200k. VERT: 250k. Both showing stylized sailing yachts.

1977. Surch **10 KURUS**.
2592 **409** 10k. on 1k. brn & red 10 10

1977. 10th World Energy Conference.
2593 **522** 100k.+25k. black, brown and pink 10 10
2594 – 600k.+50k. red, black and blue 10 10
DESIGN: 600k. Similar design showing a "globe" and emblem.

523 Kemal Ataturk **524** "Head and Book" (Rationalism)

1977. Size 20½ × 22½ mm.
2595 **523** 200k. blue on light blue 25 10
2596 250k. turquoise on blue 30 10
See also Nos. 2619/25.

1977. Works and Reform of Ataturk (4th series). Multicoloured.
2597 100k. Type **524** 10 10
2598 200k. Words by Ataturk (National Sovereignty) . . 10 10
2599 400k. Symbol (Leadership for Liberation of Nations) 15 10

525 Allama Muhammad Iqbal **526** Overturned Car

1977. Birth Centenary of Allama Muhammad Iqbal (Pakistani poet).
2600 **525** 400k. multicoloured . . 15 10

1977. Road Safety.
2601 **526** 50k. black, blue and red 10 10
2602 – 150k. black, grey and red 10 10
2603 – 250k. black, brown & red 15 10
2604 – 500k. black, grey and red 25 10
2605 – 800k. deep green, green and red 35 10
2606 – 10l. green, red and black 45 10
DESIGNS—VERT: 150k. Arrow crossing white lines and pool of blood; 500k. "Children crossing" sign; 800k. "No overtaking" sign; 10l. Footprints in road and on pedestrian crossing. HORIZ: 250k. Tractor pulling trailer loaded with people.

527 Lighted Match and Trees **531** Riza Shah Pahlavi of Iran

530 Ishakpasa Palace, Dogubeyazit

1977. Forest Conservation.
2607 **527** 50k. black, red and green 10 10
2608 – 250k. black, green & grey 20 10
DESIGN: 250k. "Tree germination".
See also No. 2699.

1978. Europa. Multicoloured.
2616 2½l. Type **530** . . . . 1·00 60
2617 5l. Anamur Castle . . . . . 1·75 1·25

1978. Birth Centenary of Riza Shah Pahlavi of Iran.
2618 **531** 5l. multicoloured 10 10

1978. As Type **523** but larger, 19 × 25 mm.
2619 10k. brown 10 10
2620 50k. grey 10 10
2621 1l. red 10 10
2622 2½l. lilac 10 10
2623 5l. blue 15 10
2624 25l. blue and light blue . . 50 10
2625 50l. orange and light orange 90 10

532 Athletics

1978. "Gymnasiade '78" World School Games.
2626 **532** 1l.+50k. deep green and green 10 10
2627 – 2½l.+50k. blue & orge . . 15 10
2628 – 5l.+50k. blue and pink 15 15
2629 – 8l.+50k. blue and green 25 15
DESIGNS: 2½l. Gymnastics; 5l. Table tennis; 8l. Swimming.

533 Salmon Rose

1978. Regional Co-operation for Development. Multicoloured.
2630 2½l. Type **533** 15 15
2631 3½l. Pink roses 25 15
2632 8l. Red roses 35 20

534 Anti-Apartheid Year Emblem **535** View of Ankara

1978. International Anti-Apartheid Year.
2633 **534** 10l. multicoloured . . . 15 10

1978. Turkish–Libyan Friendship. Multicoloured.
2634 2½l. Type **535** 10 10
2635 5l. View of Tripoli 15 10

536 Ribbon and Chain

1978. 25th Anniv of European Convention on Human Rights.
2636 **536** 2½l.+50k. blue, green and black 20 10
2637 – 5l.+50k. red, blue and black 25 15
DESIGN: 5l. Ribbon and flower.

537 Mosque and Bridge

1978. "Edirne 78" Youth Philatelic Exhibition. Sheet 72 × 52 mm. Imperf.
MS2638 **537** 15l. blue, black and red 1·00 1·00

538 Independence Medal

1978. Works and Reforms of Ataturk (5th series).
2639 **538** 2½l. multicoloured . . . 10 10
2640 – 3½l. red and black . . . 10 10
2641 – 5l. multicoloured 15 10
DESIGNS—HORIZ: 3½l. Talking heads (Language reform). VERT: 5l. "ABC" in Arabic and Roman scripts (Adoption of Latin alphabet).

539 Bosphorus Waterside Residence of Koprulu Huseyin Pasa, Istanbul (1699)

1978. Traditional Turkish Houses. Multicoloured.
2642 1l. Type **539** 10 10
2643 2½l. Residence of Saatci Ali Efendi, Izmit, 1774 . . . 25 10
2644 3½l. House of Bey, Kula (vert) 35 15
2645 5l. House of Bahaeddin Aga, Milas (vert) 65 15
2646 8l. House of Safranbolu . . 90 20

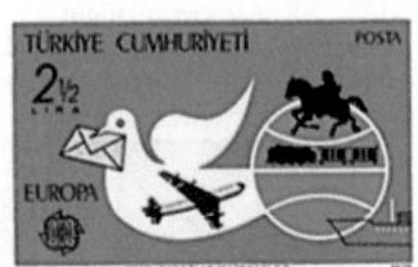

541 Children with Globe as Balloon
542 Mail Transport

1979. International Year of the Child.
2649 – 2½l.+50k. black, gold and red 10 10
2650 **541** 5l.+50k. multicoloured 10 10
2651 – 8l.+50k. multicoloured 15 10
DESIGNS: 2½l. Children embracing beneath hearts; 8l. Adult and child balancing globe.

1979. Europa.
2652 **542** 2½l. black, green and blue 30 10
2653 – 5l. orange and black . . 30 15
2654 – 7½l. black and blue . . . 65 20
DESIGNS: 5l. Telex keyboard, morse key and telegraph poles; 7½l. Telephone dial and dish aerial.

543 Kemal Ataturk
544 "Turkish Harvest" (Namik Ismail)

1979.
2655 **543** 50k. green 10 10
2656 1l. green and light green 10 10
2657 2½l. lilac 15 10
2657a 2½l. blue 10 10
2748 2½l. orange 20 10
2658 5l. blue and light blue 15 10
2659 7½l. brown 25 10
2659a 7½l. red 25 10
2660 10l. mauve 35 10
2661a 10l. mauve (22 × 22 mm) 15 10
2661 20l. grey 40 10

1979. Regional Co-operation for Development. Paintings. Multicoloured.
2662 5l. Type **544** 15 10
2663 7½l. "Iranian Goldsmith" (Kamal el Molk) 15 10
2664 10l. "Pakistan Village Scene" (Ustad Baksh) . . 25 10

545 Colemanite
546 Highway forming Figure 8

1979. 10th World Mining Congress. Mult.
2665 5l. Type **545** 10 10
2666 7½l. Chromite 15 10
2667 10l. Antimonite 20 10
2668 15l. Sulphur 55 10

1979. 8th European Communications Ministers' Symposium.
2669 **546** 5l. multicoloured 10 10

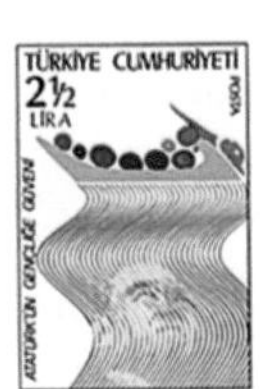

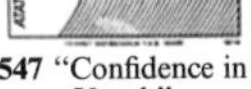

547 "Confidence in Youth"
548 Poppy ("Papaver somniferum")

1979. Works and Reforms of Ataturk (6th series).
2670 **547** 2½l. multicoloured . . . 10 10
2671 – 3½l. multicoloured . . . 10 10
2672 – 5l. black and orange . . 15 10
DESIGNS—HORIZ: 3½l. "Secularism". VERT: 5l. "National Oath".

1979. Flowers (1st series). Multicoloured.
2673 5l. Type **548** 15 10
2674 7½l. Oleander ("Nerium oleander") 15 10
2675 10l. Late spider orchid ("Ophrys holosericea") . . 15 20
2676 15l. Mandrake ("Mandragora autumnalis") 25 15
See also Nos. 2705/8.

1979. "Ankara 79" Stamp Exhibition. Sheet 122 × 57 mm.
MS2677 No. 2658 × 8 . . . . . 1·25 1·10

549 Ibrahim Muteferrika (first printer) and Presses

1979. 250th Anniv of Turkish Printing.
2678 **549** 10l. multicoloured . . . 15 10

550 Black Partridge
551 Olives, Leaves and Globe in Oil-drop

1979. Wildlife Conservation. Multicoloured.
2679 5l.+1l. Type **550** 25 15
2680 5l.+1l. Great bustard . . . 25 15
2681 5l.+1l. Demoiselle crane . . 25 15
2682 5l.+1l. Goitred gazelle . . . 25 15
2683 5l.+1l. Mouflon 25 15
Nos. 2679/83 were issued together, se-tenant, forming a composite design.

1979. 2nd World Olive-oil Year.
2684 **551** 5l. multicoloured 10 10
2685 – 10l. yellow and green . . 15 10
DESIGN: 10l. Globe in oil drop.

553 Uskudarli Hoca Ali Riza (artist)

1980. Europa. Multicoloured.
2692 7½l. Type **553** 25 25
2693 10l. Ali Sami Boyar (artist) 45 35
2694 20l. Dr. Hulusi Behcet (skin specialist) 65 45

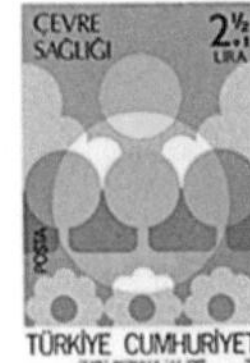

554 Flowers and Trees
555 Lighted Match and Trees

1980. Environmental Protection. Multicoloured.
2695 2½l.+1l. Type **554** 10 10
2696 7½l.+1l. Sun and water . . . 10 10
2697 15l.+1l. Factory polluting atmosphere 15 10
2698 20l.+1l. Flower surrounded by oil 20 10

1980. Forest Conservation.
2699 **555** 50k. green, red and brown 10 10
See also No. 2607.

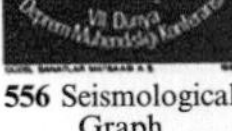

556 Seismological Graph
557 Games Emblem and Pictograms

1980. 7th World Conference on Earthquake Engineering.
2700 – 7½l. brown, blue & orange 10 10
2701 **556** 20l. black, orange & blue 15 10
DESIGN: 7½l. Pictorial representation of earthquake within globe.

1980. 1st Islamic Games, Izmir. Multicoloured.
2702 7½l. Type **557** 10 10
2703 20l. As No. 2702 but with different sports around emblem 20 10

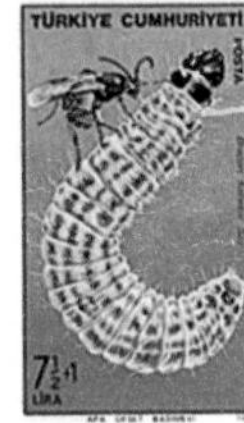

558 Ornamental Window
559 "Bracon hebetor" and Larva of Dark Arches Moth

1980. 1400th Anniv of Hegira.
2704 **558** 20l. multicoloured . . . 20 10

1980. Flowers (2nd series). As T **548**. Mult.
2705 2½l. Manisa tulip ("Tulipa hayatii") 10 10
2706 7½l. Ephesian bellflower ("Campanula ephesia") 15 10
2707 15l. Crocus ("Crocus ancyrensis") 25 15
2708 20l. Anatolian orchid ("Orchis anatolica") . . . 40 20

1980. Useful Insects (1st series). Multicoloured.
2709 2½l.+1l. "Rodolia cardinalis" (ladybird) and cottony cushion scale 20 10
2710 7½l.+1l. Type **559** 20 10
2711 15l.+1l. Caterpillar-hunter and larva of gypsy moth 30 15
2712 20l.+1l. "Deraeocoris rutilus" (leaf bug) 35 20
See also Nos. 2763/6.

560 Kemal Ataturk
561 Ibn Sina Teaching

1980.
2713 **560** 7½l. brown and pink . . 30 10
2714 10l. brown & lt brown 20 10
2719a 15l. blue 45 10
2715 20l. violet and mauve 30 10
2719b 20l. orange 25 10
2716 30l. grey and light grey 40 10
2717 50l. red and yellow . . 65 10
2719c 65l. green 90 10
2718 75l. green and lt green 1·25 10
2719d 90l. mauve . . . . . . 1·50 10
2719 100l. blue and light blue . . . . 1·40 10

1980. Birth Millenary of Ibn Sina (Avicenna) (philosopher and physician). Multicoloured.
2720 7½l. Type **561** 20 10
2721 20l. Ibn Sina (vert) 35 15

562 Ataturk and Figures "100"
563 Disabled Person in Wheelchair

1981. "Balkanfila VIII" Stamp Exhibition, Ankara.
2722 **562** 10l. red and black . . . 20 10

1981. International Year of Disabled Persons.
2723 **563** 10l.+2½l. multicoloured 15 10
2724 20l.+2½l. multicoloured 25 15

564 Sultan Mohammed the Conqueror
565 Gaziantep

1981. 500th Death Anniv of Mohammed the Conqueror.
2725 **564** 10l. multicoloured . . . 20 10
2726 20l. multicoloured . . . 35 10

1981. Folk Dances and Europa (35, 70l.). Multicoloured.
2727 ½l. Type **565** 15 10
2728 10l. Balikesir 20 15
2729 15l. Kahramanmaras . . . 30 15
2730 35l. Antalya . . . . 1·10 50
2731 70l. Burdur . . . . 1·75 70

566 Ataturk in 1919 (S.G. 2279)
568 Carpet

1981. Birth Centenary of Kemal Ataturk. Previous stamps showing Ataturk. Multicoloured.
2732 **566** 2½l. multicoloured . . . 15 10
2733 – 7½l. black and brown . . 15 10
2734 – 10l. multicoloured . . . 20 15
2735 – 20l. blue, red and black 30 20
2736 – 25l. black, red and orange 40 20
2737 – 35l. multicoloured . . . 60 30
MS2738 120 × 120 mm. As No. 2732; 37½l. As No. 2733; 50l. As No. 2734; 100l. As No. 2735; 125l. As No. 2736; 175l. As No. 2737 7·50 7·00
DESIGNS: 7½l. Ataturk in civilian dress (S.G. No. 2285); 10l. Ataturk and old Parliament House (S.G. No. 2037); 20l. Ataturk teaching Latin alphabet (S.G. No. 1222); 25l. Remilitarization of Dardanelles surcharged stamp (S.G. No. 1188); 35l. Ataturk in evening dress (from miniature sheet).

1981. Various stamps surch **10 LIRA**.
2739 – 10l. on 60k. red, black and green (No. 2177) 45 10
2740 **452** 10l. on 110k. blue on blue 45 10
2741 10l. on 400k. turquoise on blue 45 10
2742 – 10l. on 800k. green, turq & red (No. 2605) . . . 45 10

1981. 2nd International Congress of Turkish Folklore. Multicoloured.
2743 7½l. Type **568** 10 10
2744 10l. Embroidery 15 10
2745 15l. Drum and "zurna" . . 20 10
2746 20l. Embroidered napkin . . 25 15
2747 30l. Rug 30 15

569 Ataturk (SG 1185)

1981. "Balkanfila VIII" Stamp Exhibition, Ankara (2nd issue). Sheet 104 × 82 mm containing T **569** and similar vert designs.
MS2749 50l. red, blue and black; 50l. indigo, red and black (Tree (SG No. 1146)) . . . . 1·90 1·50

570 Ataturk Centenary and E.P.S. Emblem

1981. 5th European Physical Society General Congress.
2750 **570** 10l. multicoloured . . . 25 15
2751 30l. multicoloured . . . 45 15

571 F.A.O. Emblem

1981. World Food Day.
2752 **571** 10l. multicoloured . . . 20 15
2753 30l. multicoloured . . . 40 15

572 Olive Branch and Constitution on Map of Turkey

1981. Inauguration of Constituent Assembly.
2754 **572** 10l. multicoloured . . . 30 15
2755 30l. multicoloured . . . 55 15

574 Kemal Ataturk

575 Green Tiger Beetle

1981.
2762 **574** 2½l. red on grey 40 10

1981. Useful Insects (2nd series). Multicoloured.
2763 10l.+2½l. Type **575** 30 15
2764 20l.+2½l. "Syrphus vitripennis" (hover fly) . . 45 25
2765 30l.+2½l. "Ascalaphus macaronius" (owl-fly) . . 40 25
2766 40l.+2½l. "Empusa fasciata" 70 35

576 Students and Silhouette of Ataturk
577 Sun
578 Kemal Ataturk

1981. Literacy Campaign.
2767 **576** 2½l. orange and blue . . 35 10

1982. Energy Conservation.
2768 **577** 10l. yellow, blue & green 20 10

1982.
2769 **578** 1l. green 10 10
2770 – 2½l. lilac 10 10
2771 – 5l. blue 15 10
2772 – 10l. red 30 10
2773 – 35l. brown 50 10
DESIGNS: 2½ to 35l. Different portraits of Ataturk.

579 "Magnolias"
580 Dr. Tevfik Saglam

1982. Birth Centenary of Ibrahim Calli (painter). Multicoloured.
2774 10l. Type **579** 20 10
2775 20l. "Fishermen" (horiz) . . 40 15
2776 30l. "Sewing Woman" . . . 55 20

1982. Centenary of Discovery of Tubercle Bacillus. Multicoloured.
2777 10l.+2½l. Type **580** 15 10
2778 30l.+2½l. Dr. Robert Koch 30 25

581 Sultanhan Caravanserai

1982. Europa. Sheet 78 × 80 mm containing T **581** and similar square design. Multicoloured.
MS2779 30l. × 2, Type **581**; 70l. × 2, Map of silk route . . . . . . 1·75 1·50
The two values form a composite design.

582 Kul Tigin Monument
584 Demirkazik

583 Tanker and Emblem

1982. 1250th Anniv of Kul Tigin Monument. Multicoloured.
2780 10l. Type **582** 15 15
2781 30l. Head of Kul Tigin . . . 30 15

1982. Inauguration of Pendik Shipyard.
2782 **583** 30l. multicoloured . . . 35 15

1982. Anatolian Mountains. Multicoloured.
2783 7½l. Agri Dagi 20 10
2784 10l. Buzul Dagi (horiz) . . . 25 10
2785 15l. Type **584** 30 15
2786 20l. Erciyes (horiz) 50 15
2787 30l. Kackar Dagi 65 25
2788 35l. Uludag (horiz) 80 25

585 Colorado Potato Beetle

1982. Insect Pests (1st series). Multicoloured.
2789 10l.+2½l. "Eurydema spectabile" (shield-bug) 30 20
2790 15l.+2½l. Olive fruit-fly . . . 45 20
2791 20l.+2½l. "Klapperichicen viridissima" (cicada) . . . 50 25
2792 20l.+2½l. Type **585** 70 35
2793 35l.+2½l. "Rhynchites auratus" (weevil) 80 35
See also Nos. 2830/4.

586 Open Book and Figures

1982. Centenary of Beyazit State Library.
2794 **586** 30l. multicoloured . . . 35 15

1982. "Antalya 82" Youth Philatelic Ehibition. Sheet 75 × 61 mm.
MS2795 No. 2713 × 4 . . . . . 60 25

587 Drum

1982. Musical Instruments. Multicoloured.
2796 7½l. Type **587** 25 15
2797 10l. Lute ("Baglama") . . . 35 20
2798 15l. Horn ("Zurna") (horiz) 45 20
2799 20l. Stringed instrument ("Kemence") (horiz) . . . 60 20
2800 30l. Flute ("Mey") . . . . 1·10 25

588 Temple of Artemis, Sart

1982. Ancient Cities.
2801 **588** 30l. multicoloured . . . 35 20

589 Family on Map

1983. Family Planning and Mother and Child Health. Multicoloured.
2802 10l. Type **589** 20 10
2803 35l. Mother and child . . . 25 15

590 Council Emblem

1983. 30th Anniv of Customs Co-operation Council.
2804 **590** 45l. multicoloured . . . 45 15

591 People, Ballot Box and Constitution

1983. 1982 Constitution. Multicoloured.
2805 10l. Type **591** 15 10
2806 30l. Constitution, scales and olive branch 25 15

592 Richard Wagner

1983. Death Cent of Richard Wagner (composer).
2807 **592** 30l.+5l. multicoloured 30 20

593 Hamdi Bey

1983. 38th Death Anniv of Hamdi Bey (telegraphist).
2808 **593** 35l. multicoloured . . . 30 20

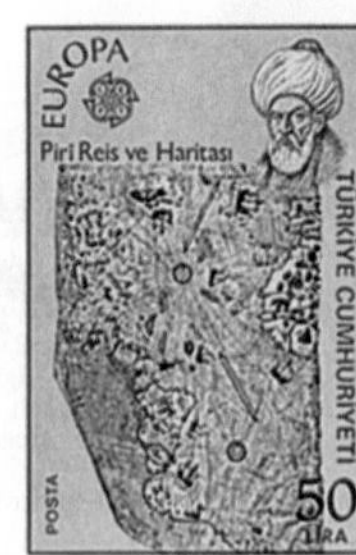

594 Piri Reis (geographer) and Map

1983. Europa. Multicoloured.
2809 50l. Type **594** . . . . 4·00 5·00
2810 100l. Ulugh Bey (Central Asian ruler) and observatory . . . . . . 8·00 7·50

595 Olive Branch and Athletes

1983. Youth Week.
2811 **595** 15l. multicoloured . . . 20 15

596 Junkers Ju 52/3m and Boeing 727

1983. 50th Anniv of Turkish State Airline. Multicoloured.
2812 50l. Type **596** 55 20
2813 70l. Airport at night 65 25
No. 2812 is wrongly inscribed "F-13".

597 Hellenic Statue of Eros
598 Oludeniz

1983. 18th Council of Europe Art Exhibition, Istanbul. Multicoloured.
2814 15l. Type **597** 35 15
2815 35l. Hittite carving of two-headed duck (horiz) . . . 60 20
2816 50l. Ottoman zinc flask and jug 85 15
2817 70l. Busts of Marcus Aurelius and his wife Faustina (horiz) . . . . . 1·10 25

1983. Coastal Protection. Multicoloured.
2818 10l. Type **598** 25 15
2819 25l. Olimpos 45 15
2820 35l. Kekova 65 20

1983. Nos. 2655 and 2699 surch **5 LIRA**.
2821 **543** 5l. on 50k. green 20 10
2822 **555** 5l. on 50k. green, red and brown 20 10

600 Dove carrying Letter
601 Kemal Ataturk

1983. World Communications Year. Mult.
2823 15l. Type **600** 25 10
2824 50l. Telephone pole and telephone wires (horiz) . . 35 10
2825 70l. Telephone dial and letter within ornamental design 45 20
See also **MS**2835.

1983.
2826 **601** 15l. blue and light blue 20 10
2827 50l. blue and green . . . 65 10
2828 100l. blue and orange . . 1·50 10

602 Topkapi Serail, Istanbul

1983. Aga Khan Award for Architecture.
2829 **602** 50l. yellow, black & green 60 20

1983. Insect Pests (2nd series). As T **585**. Multicoloured.
2830 15l.+5l. Sun pest 20 20
2831 25l.+5l. "Phyllobius nigrofasciatus" (weevil) 35 20
2832 35l.+5l. "Cercopsis intermedia" (froghopper) 40 25
2833 50l.+10l. Striped bug . . . 60 25
2834 75l.+10l. "Capnodis miliaris" 75 40

1983. "Izmir 83" National Stamp Exhibition. Sheet 76 × 78 mm.
MS2835 No. 2826 × 5 plus label 1·40 1·25

603 Map and Flag of Turkey

1983. 60th Anniv of Republic.
2836 **603** 15l. multicoloured . . . 25 15
2837 50l. multicoloured . . . 45 20

605 Temple of Aphrodite, Aphrodisias

1983. Ancient Cities.
2838 **605** 50l. multicoloured . . . 35 15

607 St. Sophia's from Sultan Ahmed Mosque, Istanbul

608 Police Badge and Ribbon protecting Citizens

1984. UNESCO International Campaign for Istanbul and Goreme. Multicoloured.
2850 25l. Type **607** 20 15
2851 35l. Rock dwellings and chapels, Goreme 35 15
2852 50l. Suleymaniye district, Istanbul 45 25

1984. Turkish Police Organization.
2853 **608** 15l. multicoloured . . . 20 15

609 Bridge

610 Kaftan (16th-century)

1984. Europa. 25th Anniv of C.E.P.T.
2854 **609** 50l. multicoloured . . . 1·25 1·75
2855 100l. multicoloured . . . 3·75 2·40

1984. Topkapi Museum (1st series). Mult.
2856 20l.+5l. Type **610** 40 25
2857 70l.+15l. Ceremonial ewer 90 50
2858 90l.+20l. Gold inlaid and jewelled swords . . . . . 1·25 55
2859 100l.+25l. Kaaba lock . . . 1·40 70
See also Nos. 2892/5, 2925/8 and 2967/70.

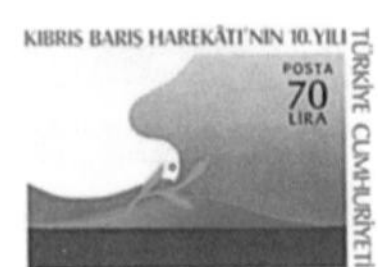
611 Mete Khan and Flag of Great Hun Empire

1984. Turkic States (1st series). Multicoloured.
2860 10l. Type **611** 30 20
2861 20l. Panu and flag of Western Hun Empire . . 55 25
2862 50l. Attila and flag of European Hun Empire . . 1·40 30
2863 70l. Aksunvar and flag of Ak Hun Empire . . . . 2·00 35
See also Nos. 2896/9, 2930/3 and 2971/4.

612 Peace Dove

1984. 10th Anniv of Turkish Forces in Cyprus.
2864 **612** 70l. multicoloured . . . 70 20

613 Olympic Colours

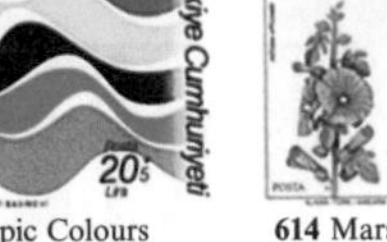
614 Marsh Mallow

1984. Olympic Games, Los Angeles. Mult.
2865 20l.+5l. Type **613** 30 25
2866 70l.+15l. Medallion of wrestler (vert) 90 30
2867 100l.+20l. Stylized athlete 1·50 45

1984. Wild Flowers. Multicoloured.
2868 5l. "Narcissus tazetta" . . 15 10
2868a 10l. Type **614** 15 10
2869 20l. Common poppy . . . 15 10
2870 70l. "Cyclamen pseudoibericum" 75 10
2870a 100l. False chamomile . . 1·25 10
2871 200l. Snowdrops . . . . . 1·50 10
2872 300l. "Tulipa sintenesii" . . 2·25 10

615 Soldier and Flag

616 Liquidamber

1984. Armed Forces Day.
2873 **615** 20l. multicoloured . . . 20 10
2874 – 50l. multicoloured . . . 40 10
2875 – 70l. red, blue and black 70 15
2876 – 90l. multicoloured . . . 95 20
DESIGNS: 50l. Olive branch as sword hilt; 70l. Emblem, soldier and flag; 90l. Soldier, olive branch and map.

1984. Forest Resources. Multicoloured.
2877 10l. Type **616** 25 20
2878 20l. Oriental spruce 40 25
2879 70l. Oriental beech . . . . 1·10 25
2880 90l. Cedar of Lebanon . . . 1·75 50

617 Pres. Inonu

618 Detail of 13th-century Seljukian Carpet

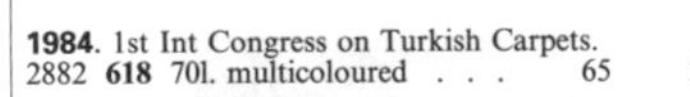

1984. Birth Cent of Ismet Inonu (Prime Minister 1923–37 and 1962–65; President 1938–50).
2881 **617** 20l. multicoloured . . . 35 20

1984. 1st Int Congress on Turkish Carpets.
2882 **618** 70l. multicoloured . . . 65 20

619 Great Mosque and University, Harran

1984. Ancient Cities.
2883 **619** 70l. multicoloured . . . 1·10 20

620 Women and Ballot Box

1984. 50th Anniv of Turkish Women's Suffrage.
2884 **620** 20l. multicoloured . . . 25 10

621 "Icarus" (Hans Herni)

1984. 40th Anniv of I.C.A.O.
2885 **621** 100l. multicoloured . . . 1·00 20

622 1951 Interparliamentary Conference 15k. Stamp

1985. "Istanbul '87" International Stamp Exhibition. Sheet 116×82 mm containing T **622** and similar design.
MS2886 70l. ×4, multicoloured 1·75 1·50

623 Glider and Parachutist

1985. 60th Anniv of Turkish Aviation League. Multicoloured.
2887 10l. Type **623** 20 10
2888 20l. Cameron Viva 77 hot-air balloon (vert) 30 15

624 Globe and Satellite

625 Score and Ulvi Cemal Erkin (composer)

1985. 20th Anniv of International Telecommunications Satellite Organization.
2889 **624** 100l. multicoloured . . . 90 20

1985. Europa. Music Year. Multicoloured.
2890 100l. Type **625** . . . . . . 2·75 1·50
2891 200l. Score and Mithat Fenmen (composer and pianist) . . . . 4·00 2·40

1985. Topkapi Museum (2nd series). As T **610**. Multicoloured.
2892 10l.+5l. Plate decorated with peacock 25 15
2893 20l.+10l. Jug and cup . . . 35 15
2894 100l.+15l. Porcelain ewer and bowl . . . . 1·50 40
2895 120l.+20l. Chinese porcelain plate . . . . 1·75 50

1985. Turkic States (2nd series). As T **611**. Multicoloured.
2896 10l. Bilge Kagan and flag of Gokturk Empire 20 15
2897 20l. Bayan Kagan and flag of Avar Empire 30 15
2898 70l. Hazar Kagan and flag of Hazar Empire . . . . 1·60 20
2899 100l. Kutlug Kul Bilge Kagan and flag of Uygur Empire . . . . 1·90 35

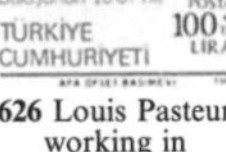
626 Louis Pasteur working in Laboratory

627 I.Y.Y. Emblem within Globe and Profiles

1985. Centenary of Discovery of Anti-rabies Vaccine.
2900 **626** 100l.+15l. mult . . . . 1·40 25

1985. International Youth Year. Multicoloured.
2901 100l. Type **627** . . . . . . 1·00 15
2902 120l. Globe and I.Y.Y. Emblem . . . . 1·25 15

628 Postman and Couple Dancing

629 Aynalikavak Palace

1985. Introduction of Post Codes.
2903 **628** 10l. black, yellow & brn 15 10
2904 20l. black, yellow and red 25 10
2905 20l. black, yellow & green 25 10
2906 20l. black, yellow and blue 25 10
2907 70l. blue, yellow & purple 90 10
2908 100l. black, yellow and grey . . . . 1·25 10

1985. National Palaces Symposium. Multicoloured.
2909 20l. Type **629** 25 10
2910 100l. Beylerbeyi Palace . . . 1·25 15

630 U.N. Emblem, Headquarters and Flags in "40"

1985. 40th Anniv of U.N.O.
2911 **630** 100l. multicoloured . . . 1·25 15

631 Alanya

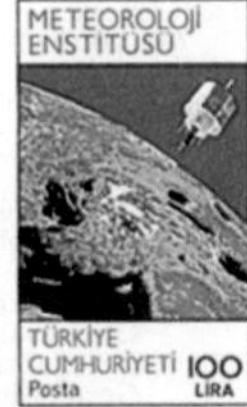
632 Satellite and Infra-red Picture of Earth's Surface

1985. Ancient Cities.
2912 **631** 100l. multicoloured . . . 1·25 15

1985. 60th Anniv of Meteorological Institute.
2913 **632** 100l. multicoloured . . . 1·25 15

633 Emblem

634 Kemal Ataturk

1985. Centenary of Isik Lyceum, Istanbul.
2914 **633** 20l. gold, blue and red 25 10

1985.
2915 **634** 10l. blue and cobalt . . 15 10
2916 20l. brown and lilac . . 20 10
2917 100l. purple and lilac . . 90 10

635 Girl and Flower

1986. International 23rd April Children's Festival, Ankara. Multicoloured.
2918 20l. Type **635** 20 15
2919 100l. Family 85 25
2920 120l. Balloon seller . . . . 2·25 35

636 Boy drawing in Smoke from Chimney

637 Trophy

1986. Europa. Multicoloured.
2921 100l. Type **636** . . . . . . 1·50 90
2922 200l. Plaster on dead half of leaf (vert) . . . . 2·25 1·50

1986. Ataturk International Peace Prize. Multicoloured.
2923 20l. Type **637** 20 15
2924 100l. Front view of trophy 1·10 25

1986. Topkapi Museum (3rd series). As T **610**. Multicoloured.
2925 20l.+5l. Censer 20 10
2926 100l.+10l. Jade and jewelled tankard 70 20
2927 120l.+15l. Dagger and sheath . . . . 1·10 25
2928 200l.+30l. Willow buckler 1·50 35

638 "Abdulhamit"

639 Wrestlers oiling Themselves

1986. Centenary of Turkish Submarine Fleet.
2929 **638** 20l. multicoloured . . . 40 15

1986. Turkic States (3rd series). As T **611**. Multicoloured.
2930 10l. Bilge Kul Kadir Khan and flag of Kara Khanids Empire 15 10
2931 20l. Alp Tekin and flag of Ghaznavids Empire . . . 30 15
2932 100l. Seljuk and flag of Great Seljuk Empire . . . 1·25 15
2933 120l. Muhammed Harezmsah and flag of Harezmsah State . . . . 1·60 20

1986. Kirkpinar Wrestling. Multicoloured.
2934 10l. Type **639** 15 15
2935 20l. Opening ceremony . . . 25 25
2936 100l. Wrestlers . . . . . . 1·40 35

640 Chateau de la Muette, Paris (headquarters)

1986. 25th Anniv of Organization for Economic Co-operation and Development.
2937 **640** 100l. multicoloured . . . 60 20

641 Benz "Einspur" Tricar, 1886

1986. Centenary of Motor Car. Multicoloured.
2938 10l. Type **641** 20 20
2939 20l. Rolls-Royce "Silver Ghost", 1906 . . . . 40 20
2940 100l. Mercedes touring car, 1928 . . . . 1·50 60
2941 200l. Impression of speeding car . . . . 3·25 60

642 "Arrangement with Tulips" (Feyhaman Duran)

643 Celal Bayar

1986. Artists' Birth Centenaries. Multicoloured.
2942 100l. Type **642** 95 20
2943 120l. "Landscape with Fountain" (Huseyin Avni Lifij) (horiz) . . . . . . 1·10 25

1986. Celal Bayar (Prime Minister 1937–39; President 1950–60) Commemoration.
2944 **643** 20l. brown, gold and mauve 15 15
2945 – 100l. green, gold and mauve . . . . 1·10 15
DESIGN: 100l. Profile of Celal Bayar.

645 Kubad-Abad

1986. Ancient Cities.
2950 **645** 100l. multicoloured . . . 90 20

646 N.A.T.O. Emblem and Dove with Olive Branch

1986. 32nd N.A.T.O. Assembly, Istanbul.
2951 **646** 100l.+20l. mult . . . . 1·10 20

647 Ersoy and National Flag

648 Driver wearing Seat Belt

1986. 50th Death Anniv of Mehmet Akif Ersoy (composer of national anthem).
2952 **647** 20l. multicoloured . . . 25 20

1987. Road Safety.
2953 **648** 10l. violet, red and blue 10 10
2954 – 20l. red, blue and brown 15 10
2955 – 150l. brown, red & green 65 10
DESIGNS: 20l. Smashed drinking glass and road; 150l. Broken speed limit sign and road.

649 Spurge Hawk Moth

1987. Moths and Butterflies. Multicoloured.
2956 10l. Type **649** 40 25
2957 20l. Red admiral 80 35
2958 100l. Jersey tiger moth . . . 2·75 1·10
2959 120l. Clouded yellow . . . 3·50 1·90

650 Modern Housing and Emblem

651 Casting

1987. International Year of Shelter for the Homeless.
2960 **650** 200l. multicoloured . . . 90 20

1987. 50th Anniv of Turkish Iron and Steel Works. Multicoloured.
2961 50l. Type **651** 20 10
2962 200l. Karabuk Works . . . 75 15

652 Map of Turkey and Grand National Assembly Building, Ankara

1987. "Sovereignty belongs to the People".
2963 **652** 50l. multicoloured . . . 35 15

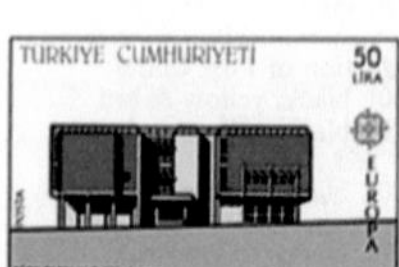

653 Turkish History Institution, Ankara (Turgut Cansever and Ertur Yener)

1987. Europa. Architecture. Multicoloured.
2964 50l. Type **653** 60 55
2965 200l. Social Insurance Institution, Zeyrek (Sedad Hakki Eldem) . . . . . . 1·90 1·00

654 Olympic Rings as Flames

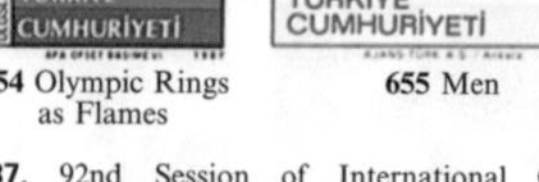

655 Men

1987. 92nd Session of International Olympic Committee, Istanbul.
2966 **654** 200l. multicoloured . . . 1·10 30

1987. Topkapi Museum (4th series). As T **610**. Multicoloured.
2967 20l.+5l. Crystals and jewelled ewer 20 20
2968 50l.+10l. Emerald, gold and diamond ceiling pendant (horiz) 35 25
2969 200l.+15l. Sherbet jug . . . 1·00 50
2970 250l.+30l. Crystal, gold and jewelled writing drawer (horiz) . . . . 1·40 70

1987. Turkic States (4th series). As T **611**. Multicoloured.
2971 10l. Batu Khan and flag of Golden Horde State . . . 25 25
2972 20l. Timur (Tamerlane) and flag of Great Timur Empire 35 25
2973 50l. Babur Shah and flag of Mughal Empire 85 35
2974 200l. Osman Bey and flag of Ottoman Empire . . . . 3·75 1·00

1987. Paintings from Mehmet Siyah Kalem's "Album of the Conqueror". Multicoloured.
2975 10l. Type **655** 20 30
2976 20l. Donkey rider and attendants (horiz) 25 50
2977 50l. Man whipping fallen horse (horiz) 65 55
2978 200l. Demon . . . . 2·40 1·00

656 Cancer Cells and Pipette holding Drug

1987. 15th International Chemotherapy Congress, Istanbul.
2979 **656** 200l.+25l. mult 55 25

657 Ihlamur Pavilion

1987. Royal Pavilions (1st series). Multicoloured.
2980 50l. Type **657** 25 25
2981 200l. Kucuksu Pavilion . . 95 40
See also Nos. 3019/20.

658 Suleiman receiving Barbarossa (miniature)

659 Cemal Gursel 1960—66

1987. Suleiman the Magnificent. Multicoloured.
2982 30l. Suleiman 20 30
2983 50l. Suleiman's tougra (horiz) 25 30
2984 200l. Type **658** . . . . . . 1·40 50
2985 270l. Sculpture of Suleiman from U.S. House of Representatives and inscribed scroll . . . . . 2·10 90

1987. Turkish Presidents. Sheet 111 × 143 mm containing T **659** and similar vert designs, each sepia, vermilion and gold.
MS2986 50l. Type **659**; 50l. Cevdet Sunay, 1966–73; 50l. Fahri S. Koruturk, 1973–80; 50l. Kenan Evren (current President); 50l. Ismet Inonu, 1938–50; 50l. Celal Bayar, 1950–60; 100l. Kemal Ataturk, 1923–38 (29 × 39 mm) 1·00 1·00

660 Sinan and Selimiye Mosque, Edrine

661 Means of Transport

1988. 400th Death Anniv of Mimar Sinan (architect). Multicoloured.
2987 50l. Type **660** 15 10
2988 200l. Suleiman Mosque . . 50 25

1988. Europa. Transport and Communications. Multicoloured.
2989 200l. Type **661** 65 60
2990 600l. Electric impulses forming globe between telephone and computer terminal (horiz) . . . . . 2·10 1·25

662 Syringes between Healthy and Sick Children

1988. Health. Multicoloured.
2991 50l. Type **662** 15 10
2992 200l. Capsules forming cross on bottle (vert) 25 10
2993 300l. Heart in cogwheel and heart-shaped worker . . . 40 10
2994 600l. Organs for transplant on open hands (vert) . . 1·00 10

663 American Standard Steam Locomotive, 1850s

1988. Locomotives. Each agate, light brown and brown.
2995 50l. Type **663** 80 25
2996 100l. Saronno side-tank locomotive No. 3328, 1897 . . . . 1·40 35
2997 200l. Henschel Krupp steam locomotive No. 46020, 1933 . . . . 2·10 40
2998 300l. Type E 43001 electric locomotive, 1987 . . . 2·75 70
2999 600l. MTE-Tulomsas diesel locomotive, 1984 . . . . 4·75 90

664 Articulated Lorry

1988. 21st International Road Transport Union World Congress, Istanbul.
3000 **664** 200l.+25l. mult 45 15

665 Scales and Map

1988. 120th Anniv of Court of Cassation (appeal court).
3001 **665** 50l. multicoloured . . . 25 20

666 Fatih Sultan Mohamed Bridge, Bosphorus

1988. Completion of Bridges. Multicoloured.
3002 200l. Type **666** . . . . . . 1·00 45
3003 300l. Seto Great road and rail Bridge, Japan . . . . 1·50 60

667 Telephone Dial and Wires over Villages

1988. Completion of Telephone Network to Every Village.
3004 **667** 100l. multicoloured . . . 30 10

669 Running **670** Weightlifting

1988. Olympic Games, Seoul. Multicoloured.
3005 100l. Type **669** 25 25
3006 200l. Archery 35 25
3007 400l. Weightlifting 75 35
3008 600l. Football (vert) . . . . 1·25 55

1988. Naim Suleymanoglu, Olympic and World Heavyweight Record Holder for Weightlifting.
3009 **670** 1000l. multicoloured . . 3·50 1·25

671 Lush Scene in Hands surrounded by Barren Earth **672** General Dynamics F-16 Fighters and Cogwheel

1988. European Campaign for Rural Areas. Multicoloured.
3010 100l.+25l. Type **671** 20 15
3011 400l.+50l. Rural scene in eye 70 25

1988. Turkish Aerospace Industries. Mult.
3012 50l. Type **672** 15 15
3013 200l. Birds forming jet fighter (horiz) 55 25

673 "Gonepteryx cleopatra"

1988. Butterflies. Multicoloured.
3014 100l. Type **673** (wrongly inscr "G. rhamni") . . . 1·10 1·75
3015 200l. Hermit . . . . 2·00 1·75
3016 400l. Eastern festoon . . . 3·50 2·10
3017 600l. Camberwell beauty . . 5·25 3·00
MS3018 122 × 79 mm. Nos. 3014/17 1·25 1·25

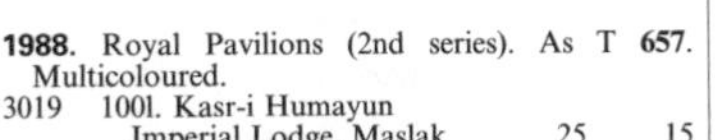

1988. Royal Pavilions (2nd series). As T **657**. Multicoloured.
3019 100l. Kasr-i Humayun Imperial Lodge, Maslak 25 15
3020 400l. Sale Pavilion, Yildiz 1·00 30

674 Ataturk

1988. 50th Death Anniv of Kemal Ataturk (President, 1923–38). Sheet 105 × 70 mm.
MS3021 **674** 400l. chestnut and violet 50 50

675 Large-leaved Lime

1988. Medicinal Plants. Multicoloured.
3022 150l. Type **675** 20 15
3023 300l. Common mallow . . . 40 15
3024 600l. Henbane 70 20
3025 900l. Deadly nightshade . . 1·10 25

676 Seated Goddess with Child (clay statuette)

1989. Archaeology (1st series). Multicoloured.
3026 150l. Type **676** 40 20
3027 300l. Lead figurine of god and goddess 80 25
3028 600l. Clay human-shaped vase . . . . 1·25 35
3029 1000l. Hittite ivory figurine of mountain god . . . . 2·25 40
See also Nos. 3062/5, 3104/7 and 3134/7.

1989. Nos. 2826, 2915 and 2916 surch.
3030 **601** 50l. on 15l. blue and light blue 25 10
3031 **634** 75l. on 10l. blue and cobalt 30 10
3032 150l. on 20l. brown and lilac 50 10

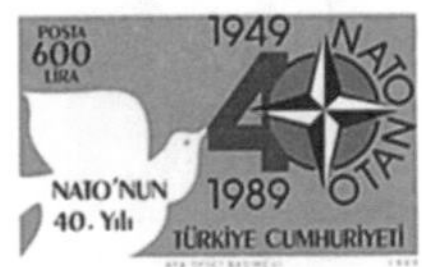

678 Dove and Emblem

1989. 40th Anniv of N.A.T.O.
3033 **678** 600l. ultram, blue & red 65 30

679 Silkworm Moth Larva on Leaf **680** Leap-frog

1989. Silk Industry. Multicoloured.
3034 150l.+50l. Type **679** 25 25
3035 600l.+100l. Silkworm moth cocoon and lengths of cloth 80 45

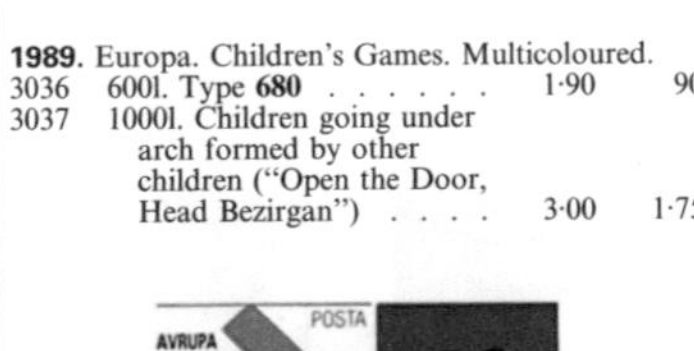

1989. Europa. Children's Games. Multicoloured.
3036 600l. Type **680** . . . . . . 1·90 90
3037 1000l. Children going under arch formed by other children ("Open the Door, Head Bezirgan") . . . . 3·00 1·75

681 Arrow and Anniversary Emblem

1989. 40th Anniv of Council of Europe.
3038 **681** 600l.+100l. mult 65 30

683 Paddle-steamer "Sahilbent" **684** Birds

1989. Steamers. Multicoloured.
3045 150l. Type **683** . . . . . . 1·40 45
3046 300l. "Ragbet" (paddle-steamer) . . . . 2·10 70
3047 600l. "Tari" (freighter) . . . 3·00 1·10
3048 1000l. "Guzelhisar" (ferry) 5·25 1·75

1989. Bicentenary of French Revolution.
3049 **684** 600l. multicoloured . . . 95 30

685 Kemal Ataturk **687** Camera

1989.
3050 **685** 2000l. blue and grey . . 1·25 10
3051 5000l. brown and grey 2·10 10
See also Nos. 3093/4, 3144 and 3199/3200.

1989. No. 2916 surch **LIRA 500**.
3052 **634** 500l. on 20l. brown and lilac 35 10

1989. 150th Anniv of Photography. Mult.
3053 175l. Type **687** 20 15
3054 700l. Coloured lens shutter 75 25

688 "Manzara" (Hikmet Onat) **689** Nehru

1989. State Exhibition of Paintings and Sculpture. Multicoloured.
3055 200l. Type **688** 20 15
3056 700l. "Sari Saz" (Bedri Rahmi Eyuboglu) 60 25
3057 1000l. "Kadin" (sculpture, Zuhtu Muridoglu) . . . . 1·10 30

1989. Birth Centenary of Jawaharlal Nehru (Indian statesman).
3058 **689** 700l. multicoloured . . . 65 25

690 Loggerhead Turtle **691** Turkish Memorial

1989. Sea Turtles. Multicoloured.
3059 700l. Type **690** . . . . . . 1·40 55
3060 1000l. Common green turtle 2·75 1·25
MS3061 82 × 78 mm. Nos. 3059/60 1·40 1·40

1990. Archaeology (2nd series). As T **676**. Multicoloured.
3062 100l. Ivory statuette of goddess (vert) 15 15
3063 200l. Clay ram's head and antelope's head twin ceremonial vessel 25 25
3064 500l. Gold goddess pendant (vert) 65 25
3065 700l. Ivory statuette of lion 1·10 40

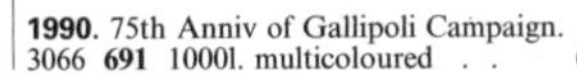

1990. 75th Anniv of Gallipoli Campaign.
3066 **691** 1000l. multicoloured . . 65 25

692 Turkish Garden (left half)

1990. International Garden and Greenery Exposition, Osaka. Multicoloured.
3067 1000l. Type **692** 50 15
3068 1000l. Right half of garden 50 15
Nos. 3067/8 were issued together, se-tenant, forming a composite design.

1990. Various stamps surch.
3069 – 50l. on 5l. mult (No. 2868) 45 10
3070 **648** 100l. on 10l. red, violet & bl 90 10
3071 150l. on 10l. red, violet & bl 90 10
3072 – 200l. on 70l. mult (No. 2870) . . . . . 1·75 10
3073 – 300l. on 20l. red, blue and brown (No. 2954) 1·25 10
3074 – 300l. on 70l. mult (No. 2870) . . . . . 1·25 10
3075 – 1500l. on 20l. mult (No. 2869) . . . . . 4·25 10

694 "70" and Ataturk **695** Antalya

1990. 70th Anniv of Establishment of Nationalist Provisional Government.
3076 **694** 300l. multicoloured . . . 30 15

1990. European Tourism Year. Multicoloured.
3077 300l.+50l. Type **695** 15 15
3078 1000l.+100l. Istanbul . . . 45 30

696 Ankara Post Office **697** Map and Dove as Open Book

1990. Europa. Post Office Buildings. Mult.
3079 700l. Type **696** 90 90
3080 1000l. Istanbul Post Office (horiz) . . . . 1·75 1·75

1990. European Supreme Courts' Conference, Ankara.
3081 **697** 1000l. blue, dp blue & red 90 25

698 Fire Salamander

1990. World Environment Day. Multicoloured.
3082 300l. Type **698** 25 20
3083 500l. Banded newt 45 25
3084 1000l. Fire-bellied toads . . 70 35
3085 1500l. Common tree frog (vert) . . . . 1·25 40

699 "Ertugrul" (frigate) and Turkish and Japanese Women **701** Smoker's Body shattering

1990. Centenary of First Turkish Envoy to Japan.
3086 **699** 1000l. multicoloured . . 1·10 25

1990. Anti-addiction Campaign. Multicoloured.
3087 300l. on 50l. Type **701** . . . 20 20
3088 1000l. on 100l. Addict injecting drug into skeletal arm (horiz) 65 35

702 "Self-portrait"

703 Emblem, Pen, Open Book and Globe

1990. Death Centenary of Vincent van Gogh (painter). Multicoloured.
3089 300l. Type **702** 70 35
3090 700l. "Boats in Saintes Maries" (horiz) . . . . . 1·50 40
3091 1000l. "Sunflowers" . . . . 1·75 60
3092 1500l. "Road with Cypress" 2·25 75

1990. As T **685** but inscription redrawn and dated "1990".
3093 **685** 500l. green and grey . . 50 10
3094 1000l. mauve and grey 70 10

1990. International Literacy Year.
3095 **703** 300l. multicoloured . . . 50 15

704 "Portrait" (Nurullah Berk)

705 Tatar Courier and Modern Postal Transport

1990. State Exhibition of Painting and Sculpture. Multicoloured.
3096 300l. Type **704** 20 10
3097 700l. "Derya Kuzulari" (Cevat Dereli) 55 15
3098 1000l. "Artist's Mother" (bust) (Nijad Sirel) . . . 80 25

1990. 150th Anniv of Ministry of Posts and Telecommunications. Multicoloured.
3099 200l. Type **705** 20 10
3100 250l. Computer terminal and Morse key 15 10
3101 400l. Manual and digital telephone exchanges . . . 20 10
3102 1500l. Telegraph wires, dish aerial and satellite . . . . 1·00 10
MS3103 108 × 78 mm. Nos. 3099/3102 . . . . 1·00 1·00

1991. Archaeology (3rd series). As T **676**. Multicoloured.
3104 300l. Clay figurine of woman (vert) 20 15
3105 500l. Bronze sistrum (vert) 35 15
3106 1000l. Clay kettle on stand (vert) 65 20
3107 1500l. Clay ceremonial vessel (vert) . . . . . . 1·40 25

707 Lake Abant

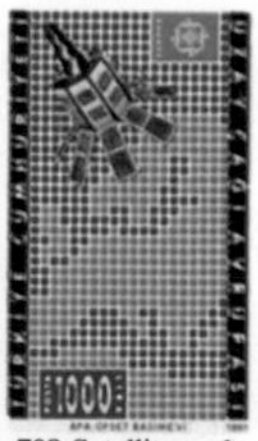

708 Satellite and Map of Europe

1991. Lakes. Multicoloured.
3110 250l. Type **707** 20 10
3111 500l. Lake Egirdir 25 10
3112 1500l. Lake Van 95 20

1991. Europa. Europe in Space. Multicoloured.
3113 1000l. Type **708** 85 45
3114 1500l. Satellite and map of Europe (different) . . . . 1·40 55

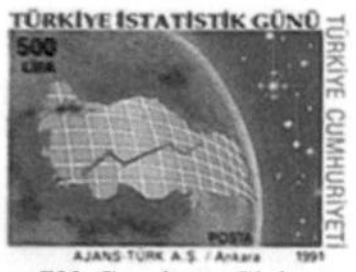

709 Graph on Globe

1991. National Statistics Day.
3115 **709** 500l. multicoloured . . . 25 10

710 Cable Ship, Map, Cable and Telephone Handset

711 Emblem

1991. Eastern Mediterranean Fibre Optic Cable System (EMOS-1).
3116 **710** 500l. multicoloured . . . 25 10

1991. European Transport Ministers' Conference, Antalya.
3117 **711** 500l. multicoloured . . . 30 15

712 Emre

713 Harpsichord, Score and Mozart

1991. "Yunus Emre (13th-century poet) Year of Love". Multicoloured.
3118 500l.+100l. Type **712** . . . 25 10
3119 1500l.+100l. Globe, and Emre as tree 90 20

1991. Death Bicentenary of Wolfgang Amadeus Mozart (composer).
3120 **713** 1500l.+100l. mult . . . 70 40

714 "Abdulcanbaz" (Turhan Selcuk)

715 13th-century Seljukian Wall Plaque

1991. Caricature. Multicoloured.
3121 500l. "Amcabey" (Cemal Nadir Guler) (horiz) . . . 35 10
3122 1000l. Type **714** 70 25

1991. Turkish Ceramics. Multicoloured.
3123 500l. Type **715** 25 15
3124 1500l. Late 16th-century Ottoman wall plaque . . 80 30

716 Emblem

717 Dam, Water and Sun

1991. Turkish Grand National Assembly's Protection of Human Rights International Symposium, Ankara.
3125 **716** 500l. multicoloured . . . 25 10

1991. South-eastern Anatolia Project (hydro-electric power and irrigation development).
3126 **717** 500l. multicoloured . . . 25 10

718 Keloglan and Genie with Tray of Food

719 Sand Boa

1991. "Keloglan" (fairy tale). Multicoloured.
3127 500l. Type **718** 25 10
3128 1000l. Keloglan and dinner guests 45 15
3129 1500l. Keloglan ploughing 90 20

1991. World Environment Day. Snakes. Mult.
3130 250l. Type **719** 90 95
3131 500l. Four-lined snake . . . 1·50 1·90
3132 1000l. Ottoman viper . . . 3·00 2·00
3133 1500l. Caucasus viper . . . 4·25 3·50

1992. Archaeology (4th series). As T **676**. Multicoloured.
3134 300l. Clay statuette of Mother Goddess (vert) . . 15 15
3135 500l. Bronze statuette (vert) 20 15
3136 1000l. Hittite clay vase (vert) 60 20
3137 1500l. Urartian lion (vert) 85 25

721 Emblem and People

722 Balloons

1992. 30th Anniv of Supreme Court.
3140 **721** 500l.+100l. mult 20 15

1992. Europa. 500th Anniv of Discovery of America by Columbus.
3141 – 1500l. blue and red . . . 80 50
3142 **722** 2000l. multicoloured . . 1·25 75
DESIGN—HORIZ: 1500l. Stylized caravel.

723 Immigrant Ship

1992. 500th Anniv of Jewish Immigration.
3143 **723** 1500l. multicoloured . . 55 20

724 Kemal Ataturk

1992.
3144 – 250l. orange, ochre and gold 15 10
3145 **724** 10000l. blue, grey & gold 2·75 10
DESIGN: 250l. Portrait of Ataturk as in Type **685**.

725 Court Emblem

726 Congress Emblem

1992. 130th Anniv of Court of Accounts.
3146 **725** 500l. multicoloured . . . 20 10

1992. 3rd Turkish Economy Congress, Izmir.
3147 **726** 1500l. multicoloured . . 55 20

727 Northern Lapwing

728 Ears of Grain, Cogwheel and Hands

1992. World Environment Day. Birds. Mult.
3148 500l. Type **727** 25 20
3149 1000l. Golden oriole 50 30
3150 1500l. Common shelduck . . 90 45
3151 2000l. White-throated kingfisher (vert) . . . . . 1·00 60

1992. Black Sea Economic Co-operation Conference, Istanbul.
3152 **728** 1500l. multicoloured . . 45 20

729 Doves forming Olympic Flame

730 Soldiers and Old Woman

1992. Olympic Games, Barcelona. Multicoloured.
3153 500l. Type **729** 15 20
3154 1000l. Boxing 25 30
3155 1500l. Weightlifting 60 35
3156 2000l. Wrestling . . . . . . 1·00 60

1992. Legend of Anatolia. Multicoloured.
3157 500l. Type **730** 15 10
3158 1000l. Old woman filling trough with buttermilk . . 25 15
3159 1500l. Soldiers drinking from trough 30 25

731 Bride and Mother-in-law Dolls from Merkez Kapikaya

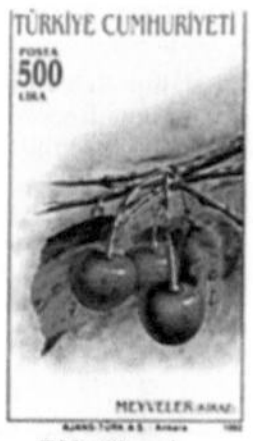

732 Cherries

1992. Traditional Crafts. Multicoloured.
3160 500l. Knitted flowers from Icel-Namrun (horiz) . . . 15 10
3161 1000l. Type **731** 25 15
3162 3000l. Woven saddlebag from Hakkari (horiz) . . 90 25

1992. Fruit (1st series). Multicoloured.
3163 500l. Type **732** 15 10
3164 1000l. Apricots 25 20
3165 3000l. Grapes 85 25
3166 5000l. Apples . . . . 1·50 35
See also Nos. 3176/9.

734 Mountaineering

735 Sait Faik Abasiyanik

1992. 26th Anniv of Turkish Mountaineering Federation (3169) and 80th Anniv of Turkish Scout Movement (3170). Multicoloured.
3169 1000l.+200l. Type **734** . . . 25 20
3170 3000l.+200l. Scouts watering sapling (horiz) 80 35

1992. Anniversaries. No value expressed.
3171 **735** (T) blue, indigo and red 30 10
3172 – (T) blue, orange and violet 30 10
3173 – (M) blue, green & orange 85 10
3174 – (M) blue, red and indigo 85 10
3175 – (M) blue, red and green 85 10

DESIGNS: No. 3171, Type **935** (writer, 86th birth anniv); 3172, Fikret Mualla Saygi (painter, 25th death anniv); 3173, Muhsin Ertugrul (actor and producer, birth centenary); 3174, Cevat Sakir Kabaagaeli (writer, 19th death anniv); 3175, Asik Veysel Satiroglu (poet, 98th birth anniv).

Nos. 3171/2 were intended for greeting cards and Nos. 3173/5 for inland letters.

1993. Fruit (2nd series). As T **732**. Multicoloured.

3176 500l. Bananas 20 20
3177 1000l. Oranges 25 20
3178 3000l. Pears 90 20
3179 5000l. Pomegranates . . . . 1·50 30

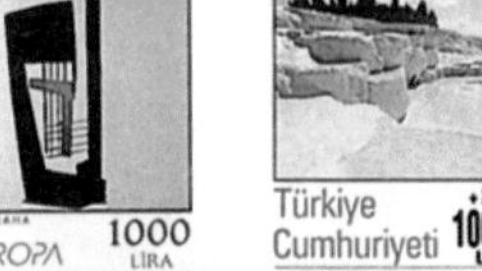

736 Sculpture (Hadi Bara)   **737** Terraces

1993. Europa. Contemporary Art. Multicoloured.

3180 1000l. Type **736** 45 55
3181 3000l. Carved figure (Zuhtu Muridoglu) . . . . 1·40 75

1993. Campaign for the Preservation of Pamukkale. Multicoloured.

3182 1000l.+200l. Type **737** . . . 20 20
3183 3000l.+500l. Close-up of terrace 75 30

738 Buildings and Emblem   **739** Rize

1993. Economic Co-operation Organization Conference, Istanbul.

3184 **738** 2500l. ultramarine, blue and gold 50 20

1993. Traditional Houses (1st series). Multicoloured.

3185 1000l. Type **739** 20 15
3186 2500l. Rize (different) (horiz) 45 20
3187 3000l. Trabzon 55 25
3188 5000l. Black Sea houses (horiz) 95 45

See also Nos. 3222/5, 3256/9, 3283/6 and 3318/21.

740 Mausoleum

1993. 900th Birth Anniv of Hoca Ahmet Yesevi (philosopher).

3189 **740** 3000l. gold, blue & lt blue 45 15

741 Haci Arif Bey

1993. Death Anniversaries. No value expressed. Each brown and red.

3190 (T) Type **741** (composer, 109th) 45 10
3191 (T) Neyzen Tevfik Kolayli (singer, 40th) 45 10
3192 (M) Orhan Veli Kanik (poet, 43rd) 70 10
3193 (M) Cahit Sitki Taranci (poet, 27th) 70 10
3194 (M) Munir Nurettin Seluk (composer, 12th) 70 10

Nos. 3190/1 were intended for greetings cards and Nos. 3192/4 for inland letters.

742 Emblem

1993. Istanbul's Bid to host Summer Olympic Games in Year 2000.

3195 **742** 2500l. multicoloured . . 65 10

1993. As T **685** but inscription redrawn and dated "1993".

3199 **685** 5000l. violet and gold . . 1·25 10
3200 20000l. mauve and gold 5·00 10

744 Amphora on Sea-bed

1993. Mediterranean Treaty. Multicoloured.

3201 1000l. Type **744** 20 20
3202 3000l. Dolphin 80 30

745 Emblem

1993. U.N. Natural Disaster Relief Day.

3203 **745** 3000l.+500l. mult . . . 65 30

746 Prayer Mat   **747** Laurel Wreath, Torch and Silhouette of Kemal Ataturk

1993. Handicrafts. Multicoloured.

3204 1000l. Type **746** 15 10
3205 2500l. Silver earrings . . . 20 15
3206 5000l. Crocheted purse . . . 70 20

1993. 70th Anniv of Republic.

3207 **747** 1000l. multicoloured . . 20 15

748 Man in Gas Mask and Fire

1993. Civil Defence.

3208 **748** 1000l. multicoloured . . 20 15

749 Satellite, Globe and Map   **750** Ears of Corn

1994. "Turksat" Communications Satellite. Multicoloured.

3209 1500l. Type **749** 10 10
3210 5000l. Satellite and map showing satellite's "foot-print" 40 10

1994. 40th Anniv of Water Supply Company.

3211 **750** 1500l. multicoloured . . 25 15

751 Ezogelin Corbasi   **752** Marie Curie

1994. Traditional Dishes. Multicoloured.

3212 1000l. Type **751** 15 15
3213 1500l. Karisik dolma . . . 20 15
3214 3500l. Shish kebabs . . . 25 25
3215 5000l. Baklava 60 25

1994. Europa. Discoveries. Multicoloured.

3216 1500l. Type **752** (discoverer of radium) 30 35
3217 5000l. Albert Einstein and equation (formulator of Theory of Relativity) (horiz) 95 50

754 Faselis, Antalya

1994. Environment Day. Multicoloured.

3220 6000l. Type **754** 55 15
3221 8500l. Gocek, Mugla (vert) 80 20

755 Bursa

1994. Traditional Houses (2nd series). Multicoloured.

3222 2500l. Type **755** 20 15
3223 3500l. Uskudar 25 20
3224 6000l. Anadolu Hisari . . . 60 25
3225 8500l. Edirne 85 25

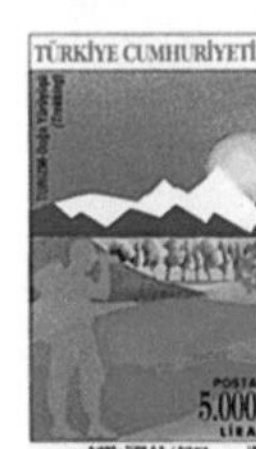

756 Trekking in Mountains   **757** Centenary Emblem over City

1994. Tourism. Multicoloured.

3226 5000l. Type **756** 40 20
3227 10000l. White-water rafting (horiz) 90 30

1994. Centenary of International Olympic Committee.

3228 **757** 12500l.+500l. mult . . . 1·00 30

758 "2001"

1994. Seven Year Plan.

3229 **758** 2500l. multicoloured . . 20 15

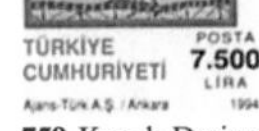

759 Kusak Design   **760** Kemal Ataturk

1994. Embroidery. Multicoloured.

3230 7500l. Type **759** 65 20
3231 12500l. Paalik design (horiz) 1·00 25

1994.

3232 **760** 50000l. violet, mve & red 2·00 10

761 Common Morel   **762** "Platanus orientalis"

1994. Fungi. Multicoloured.

3233 2500l. Type **761** 20 25
3234 5000l. "Agaricus bernardii" 35 25
3235 7500l. Saffron milk cap . . 60 35
3236 12500l. Parasol mushroom 1·25 55

1994. Trees. Multicoloured.

3237 7500l.+500l. Type **762** . . . 75 30
3238 12500l.+1000l. "Cupressus sempervirens" (vert) . . . 1·10 50

763 Silver Jug   **765** Starry Sky

1994. Traditional Crafts. Multicoloured.

3239 2500l. Type **763** 35 25
3240 5000l. Silver censer 40 25
3241 7500l. Necklace (horiz) . . . 60 40
3242 12500l. Gold brooch (half horse and half fish) (horiz) . . . . 1·10 55

1995. Centenary of Motion Pictures.

3245 **765** 15000l. blue and red . . 95 10

766 Women

1995. Nevruz Festival.

3246 **766** 3500l. multicoloured . . 25 15

767 "Ballad of Manas" (Kirghiz epic, millenary)

1995. Anniversaries.

3247 **767** 3500l.+500l. brown, yellow and red 20 15
3248 – 3500l.+500l. mult . . . 20 15

DESIGN—VERT: No. 3248, Abay Kunanbay and books (Kazakh philosopher and politician, 150th birth anniv).

768 Anniversary Emblem   **769** Carnations

1995. 75th Anniv of National Assembly.

3249 **768** 3500l.+500l. black, red and blue 20 10

1995. Europa. Peace and Freedom. Multicoloured.

3250 3500l. Type **769** 25 30
3251 15000l. Leaves 95 50

771 Beysehir Coast

1995. World Environment Day. National Parks. Multicoloured.

3253 5000l. Type **771** 15 15
3254 15000l. Yedigoller 60 15
3255 25000l. Ilgaz mountains . . 1·10 25

1995. Traditional Houses (3rd series). As T **755**. Multicoloured.

3256 5000l. Izmir (vert) 20 25
3257 10000l. Kula (vert) 35 35
3258 15000l. Mugla 70 50
3259 20000l. Birgi . . . . 1·10 55

772 Delegates, Flags and Globe

1995. 1st Muslim Parliamentary Members Congress, Islamabad.
3260 **772** 5000l. multicoloured . . 20 15

773 Painting of Townscape (left detail)

1995. "Istanbul 96" International Stamp Exhibition. Multicoloured.
3261 7000l. Type **773** 30 15
3262 7000l. Aerial photo of bay (left detail) 30 15
3263 25000l. Painting of townscape (right detail) 1·40 20
3264 25000l. Aerial photo of bay (right detail) . . . . . . 1·40 20
Nos. 3261/4 were issued together, se-tenant, forming two composite designs.

774 Spirit embracing Earth

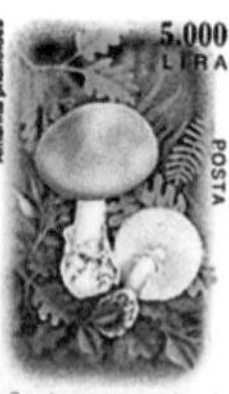

776 Death Cap

1995. 50th Anniversaries. Multicoloured.
3265 15000l. Type **774** (UNESCO) 60 35
3266 30000l. Anniversary emblem (U.N.O.) . . . . 1·40 50

1995. Fungi. Multicoloured.
3268 5000l. Type **776** 15 15
3269 10000l. "Lepiota helveola" 30 20
3270 20000l. Beefsteak morel . . 80 30
3271 30000l. "Amanita gemmata" 1·60 35

777 Living in Harmony

1996. Aid for Bosnia and Herzegovina.
3272 **777** 10000l.+2500l. mult . . 35 15

778 Rainbow, Flower, Sun and Hearts

1996. Children's Rights. Multicoloured.
3273 6000l. Type **778** 20 15
3274 10000l. Child drawing "A" 30 25

779 Honey Bee on Flower

1996. "Istanbul '96" International Stamp Exhibition (2nd issue). Sheet 118 × 78 mm containing T **779** and similar horiz designs. Multicoloured.
MS3275 5000l. Type **779**; 10000l. Anatolian karabash (dog); 15000l. Black cockerel; 30000l. Trout 1·00 1·00

780 Nene Hatun (revolutionary)

1996. Europa. Famous Women. Multicoloured.
3276 10000l. Type **780** . . . . . 55 3·50
3277 40000l. Halide Edip Adivar (writer and politician) . . 2·00 5·00

781 Kemal Ataturk

782 Istanbul

1996.
3278 **781** 50000l. brown and pink 95 10
3279 – 100000l. blue and orange 2·40 10
DESIGN: 100000l. Ataturk (different).

1996. "HABITAT II" Second United Nations Conference on Human Settlements, Istanbul.
3280 **782** 50000l. multicoloured . . 95 30

783 Player with Ball

1996. European Football Championship, England. Multicoloured.
3281 15000l. Type **783** 45 35
3282 50000l. Football composed of participating countries' flags (horiz) . . . . . . 1·25 50

1996. Traditional Houses (4th series). As T **755**. Multicoloured.
3283 10000l. Kayseri 20 20
3284 15000l. Konya 30 25
3285 25000l. Ankara (vert) . . . 50 35
3286 50000l. Konya (vert) . . . . 1·40 45

784 Archery

1996. Centenary of Modern Olympic Games and "Istanbul '96" International Stamp Exhibition (3rd issue). Sheet 118 × 78 mm containing T **784** and similar horiz designs. Multicoloured.
MS3287 10000l. Type **784**; 15000l. Wrestling; 25000l. Weightlifting; 50000l. Hurdling . . . . . . 2·40 2·40

1996. Various stamps surch. (a) Postcard Rate. Surch **T** and emblem.
3292 – T (10000l.) on 250l. orange, brown and gold (No. 3144) . . . 30 10
3293 **685** T (10000l.) on 2000l. blue and grey 30 10
(b) Domestic Letter Rate. Nos. 3099 and 3101/2 surch **M**.
3294 **705** M (15000l.) on 200l. multicoloured 80 10
3295 – M (15000l.) on 400l. multicoloured 80 10
3296 – M (15000l.) on 1500l. multicoloured 80 10

788 Printing Works and Association Emblem

1996. 50th Anniv of Journalists' Association.
3297 **788** 15000l. multicoloured . . 30 15

789 Airplane

1996. "Istanbul '96" Stamp Exhibition. Sheet 118 × 78 mm containing T **789** and similar horiz designs. Multicoloured.
MS3298 Type **789**; 50000l. Helicopter and liner superstructure; 75000l. Railway locomotive; 100000l. Coach and liner hull . . . . 6·50 6·50

790 Cogwheels on Sphere and Globe

1996. Year of Small and Medium Businesses.
3299 **790** 15000l. multicoloured . . 35 20

791 Emblem

1996. 50th Anniv of Ankara University.
3300 **791** 15000l.+2500l. mult . . 35 20

792 Amasya Bayezit Public Library

1996. Historical Buildings. Multicoloured.
3301 10000l. Type **792** (500th anniv) 20 15
3302 15000l. Divrigi Mosque and Hospital 30 20

794 "50" and Sword impaled in Crab

795 Mohammed Ali Jinnah (first Governor-General)

1997. 50th Anniv of National Cancer Research and Prevention Association.
3304 **794** 25000l.+5000l. mult . . 40 20

1997. 50th Anniv of Independence of Pakistan.
3305 **795** 25000l.+5000l. mult . . 40 20

796 Head

1997. Turkish Van Cat. Sheet 115 × 76 mm containing T **796** and similar horiz designs. Multicoloured.
MS3306 25000l. Hindquarters; 50000l. Hind legs; 75000l. Fore legs; 150000l. Type **796** . . . . 2·80 2·80
The stamps form a composite design of the cat.

797 Cicgdem's Dreams (Cahit Ucuk)

1997. Europa. Tales and Legends. Multicoloured.
3307 25000l. Type **797** 40 25
3308 70000l. Bird of Zumrud-u Anka . . . . 1·10 45

798 Alphabet and Statue of Mehmet Bey

799 "Ophrys tenthredinifera"

1997. Language Festival, Bayrami.
3309 **798** 25000l. multicoloured . . 30 20

1997. Orchids. Multicoloured.
3310 25000l. Type **799** 25 10
3311 70000l. Bee orchid 90 10

800 Erosion of Mountain Region

1997. Environment Day.
3312 **800** 35000l. multicoloured . . 45 20

801 Tulip and "XX5"

802 Urfa

1997. 25th Anniv of Istanbul Festival.
3313 **801** 15000l. blue, black & red 20 20
3314 25000l. mauve, blk & grn 30 20
3315 70000l. green, black & mve 85 20
3316 75000l. violet, black & bl 90 25
3317 100000l. turq, blk & pink 1·25 25

1997. Traditional Houses (5th series). Multicoloured.
3318 25000l. Type **802** 25 25
3319 40000l. Mardin (horiz) . . . 45 25
3320 80000l. Diyarbakir (horiz) 95 35
3321 100000l. Kemaliye . . . . . 1·25 45

804 Madonna Lily

805 Glider

1997. Plants. Multicoloured.
3324 40000l. Type **804** 35 10
3325 100000l. Poinsettia . . . . 1·25 10

1997. 1st International Aerial Sports Meeting. Multicoloured.
3326 40000l. Type **805** 50 25
3327 40000l. Hang-glider 50 25
3328 100000l. Hot-air balloon . . 1·40 35
3329 100000l. Kemal Ataturk at aerobatics display . . . . 1·40 35

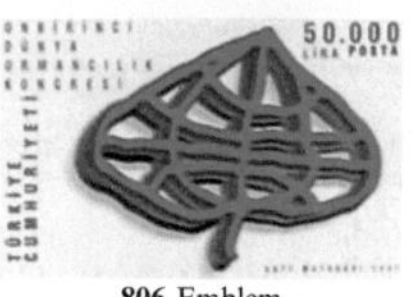

806 Emblem

1997. International Forestry Congress, Ankara.
3330 **806** 50000l. multicoloured . . 60 10

807 Gymnast

808 Canakkale

1997. 15th European Gymnastics Congress.
3331 **807** 100000l. multicoloured 1·10 50

1997. Traditional Women's Headdresses (1st series). Multicoloured.
3332 50000l. Type **808** 55 20
3333 50000l. Gaziantep 55 20
3334 100000l. Bursa . . . . . . 1·10 25
3335 100000l. Isparta . . . . . . 1·10 25
See also Nos. 3363/6, 3402/5, 3425/8 and 3455/8.

809 Alpine Skiing

1998. Winter Olympic Games, Nagano, Japan. Multicoloured.
3336 125000l. Type **809** 65 20
3337 125000l. Downhill skier . . 65 20
Nos. 3336/7 were issued together, se-tenant, forming a composite design.

810 "With Great Respect to the Mehmetcik" Statue, Gallipoli

812 "Tulipa armena"

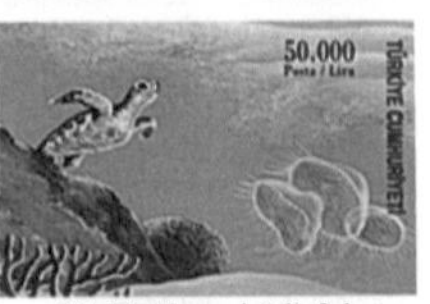
811 Turtle and Jellyfish

1998. War Memorials. Multicoloured.
3338 125000l. Type **810** 55 20
3339 125000l. "Mother with Children", National War Memorial, Wellington, New Zealand 55 20

1998. International Year of the Ocean. Sheet 123 × 76 mm containing T **811** and similar horiz designs. Multicoloured.
MS3340 50000l. Type **811**; 75000l. Shoal of fish and octopus; 125000l. Crab and coral on ocean floor; 125000l. Angelfish and starfish 4·00 4·00

1998. International Tulip Festival, Bursa. Mult.
3341 50000l. "Tulipa sylvestris" 40 10
3342 75000l. Type **812** 75 10
3343 100000l. "Tulipa armena" (purple) . . . . 1·10 10
3344 125000l. "Tulipa saxatilis" 1·40 10

813 Ataturk and Parliament Building

1998. Europa. National Festivals. Multicoloured.
3345 100000l. Type **813** (Republic Day) 80 35
3346 150000l. Ataturk with children (Children's Festival) . . . . 1·25 60

814 Two Owls

1998. World Environment Day. Sheet 108 × 72 mm containing T **814** and similar square designs. Multicoloured.
MS3347 150000l. Type **814**; 150000l. Owl flying and owl on stone 1·10 1·10

816 Ballroom dancing

817 Kemel Ataturk

1998. Contemporary Culture. Each red, black and yellow.
3353 75000l. Type **816** 45 10
3354 100000l. Cello player (vert) 55 10
3355 150000l. Ballet dancer (vert) 1·10 15

1998.
3356 **817** 150000l. brown & mve 95 10
3357 175000l. brown and blue 1·40 10
3358 250000l. mauve & brn 1·75 10
3359 500000l. blue and brown 3·50 15

818 State Flag

1998. 75th Anniv of Republic. Each red and black.
3360 175000l. Type **818** 85 25
3361 275000l. Silhouette of Ataturk and flag . . . . 1·40 25
MS3362 Two sheets, each 128 × 83 mm. (a) No. 3360; (b) No. 3361 . . . . 1·20 1·20

1998. Traditional Women's Headdresses (2nd series). As T **808**. Multicoloured.
3363 75000l. Ankara 35 15
3364 75000l. Afyon 35 15
3365 175000l. Mugla 80 20
3366 175000l. Mus 80 20

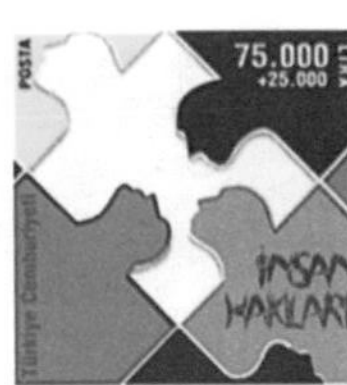
819 Jigsaw Pieces

1998. 50th Anniv of Universal Declaration of Human Rights. Multicoloured.
3367 75000l.+25000l. Type **819** 40 25
3368 175000l.+25000l. Heart and human figures 85 45

820 Academy

1998. Centenary of Military Health Academy, Gata.
3369 **820** 75000l.+10000l. multicoloured 40 25

821 Feza Gursey (physicist, 6th anniv)

1998. Death Anniversaries. Value expressed by letter.
3370 **821** (T) orange, purple and brown 35 10
3371 – (T) violet and purple . . 35 10
3372 – (T) emerald, green and purple 35 10
3373 – (M) blue, violet and purple 80 10
3374 – (M) light purple, deep purple and purple . . 80 10
DESIGNS: No. 3371, Haldun Taner (writer, 12th anniv); 3372, Vasfi Riza Zobu (actor, 6th anniv); 3373, Ihap Hulusi Gorey (graphic designer, 12th anniv); 3374, Bedia Muvahhit (actress, 5th anniv).
Nos. 3370/2 were intended for greetings cards and Nos. 3373/4 for inland letters.

822 Ataturk and Monument (Tankut Oktem)

1999. Centenary of Kemal Ataturk's Entry into Military Academy.
3375 **822** 75000l.+5000l. mult . . 35 25

823 Anniversary Emblem

1999. 50th Anniv of North Atlantic Treaty Organization.
3376 **823** 200000l. blue, red and black 95 25

824 Council Ministers

1999. 700th Anniv of Foundation of Ottoman Empire. Multicoloured.
3377 175000l. Type **824** 75 25
3378 175000l. Horseman visiting Sultan 75 25
3379 175000l. Sultan on horseback and janissaries 75 25
MS3380 Two sheets. (a) 80 × 119 mm. 200000l. "Passing of Yildirim Bayezid Han through the Crusaders in Nigbolu" (Omer Faruk Atabek); (b) 119 × 80 mm. 200000l. "Life at the Ottomon Court" (Sebahat Kircak) . . . 40 40

825 Anniversary Emblem

826 Koprulu Canyon National Park

1999. 50th Anniv of Council of Europe.
3381 **825** 175000l.+10000l. mult 90 90

1999. Europa. Parks and Gardens. Multicoloured.
3382 175000l. Type **826** 80 45
3383 200000l. Kackarlar National Park (horiz) 95 60

828 Marbled Duck

1999. World Environment Day. Birds. Two sheets, each 108 × 72 mm containing square designs as T **828**. Multicoloured.
MS3386 Two sheets (a) 100000l. Type **828**; 200000l. Kruper's nuthatch ("Sitta krueperi"); (b) 100000l. Little bustard ("Tetrax tetrax"); 200000l. Spur-winged plover ("Hoplopterus spinosus") 60 60

829 Kemel Ataturk

1999. 80th Anniv of Erzurum and Sivas Congresses. Sheet 122 × 77 mm containing T **829** and similar horiz designs. Multicoloured.
MS3387 100000l. Type **829**; 100000l. Ataturk and Congress members seated; 200000l. Congress venue; 200000l. Ataturk outside building 60 60

830 "Degisim" (sculpture, Remzi Savas)

831 Temple of Zeus, Aizonoi

1999. Contemporary Art. Multicoloured.
3388 250000l. Type **830** 95 50
3389 250000l. "Anadolu'nun Gizemi" (painting, Zafer Gencaydin) 95 50

1999. World Tourism Day. Multicoloured.
3390 125000l. Type **831** 55 25
3391 125000l. Mosaic, Antakya Archaeological Museum (horiz) 55 25
3392 225000l. Yacht, Bodrum . . 1·10 50
3393 225000l. Golf course, Belek, Antalya . . . . 1·10 50

832 Cubuk-1 Dam, Ankara

833 Kemal Ataturk

1999. Dams. Multicoloured.
3394 225000l. Type **832** 95 55
3395 250000l. Ataturk Dam and hydro-electric power plant, River Euphrates . . 1·00 60

1999.
3396 **833** 225000l. mauve & green 90 10
3397 250000l. lilac and brown 1·00 10
3398 500000l. green & mauve 1·75 10
3399 1000000l. red and blue 3·50 10

834 Hands cradling Rubble and Daisies

1999. Thanks for Overseas Aid to Earthquake Victims. Multicoloured.
3400 225000l. Type **834** 70 35
3401 250000l. Rubble, rescue teams and handshake (horiz) 80 40

1999. Traditional Women's Headdresses (3rd series). As T **808**. Multicoloured.
3402 150000l. Manisa, Yunt Dagi 50 25
3403 150000l. Nigde 50 25
3404 250000l. Amasya, Merzifon 75 25
3405 250000l. Antalya 75 25

835 Sarapsa Fort, Alanya

1999. The Silk Road. Multicoloured.
3406 1500001. Type **835** 45 25
3407 2500001. Obruk Fort, Kanya 70 35

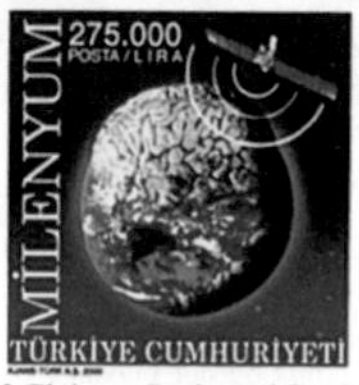

836 Globe as Brain and Satellite

2000. Millennium. Multicoloured.
3408 2750001. Type **836** 70 35
3409 3000001. Mediterranean monk seal 75 40

837 *Bug* (paddle-steamer)

2000. Ships. Multicoloured.
3410 1250001. Type **837** 70 35
3411 1500001. *Gulcemal* (liner) . . 75 40
3412 2750001. *Nusret* (paddle-steamer) 95 50
3413 3000001. *Bandirma* (cargo liner) . . . . 1·00 50

839 Flowers and Turkish Emblem

840 "Building Europe"

2000. 80th Anniv of Turkish National Assembly. Multicoloured.
3418 2750001. Type **839** 60 30
3419 3000001. Turkish emblem as flowers (horiz) 75 40

2000. Europa.
3420 **840** 3000001. multicoloured 60 40

841 Church, Mosque and Synagogue

2000. Tourism. Multicoloured.
3421 2750001.+1000001. Type **841** 60 55
3422 3000001.+1000001. Folk dancing 75 60

842 Imperial Eagle "Aquila heliaca"

2000. World Environment Day. Birds. Two sheets, each 109 × 70 mm containing T **842** and similar square designs. Multicoloured.
MS3423 (a) 2750001. Type **842**; 2750001. Green woodpeckers ("Picus viridis"). (b) 2750001. White-headed ducks ("Oxyura leucocephala"); 2750001. Avocet ("Recurvirostra avosetta") . . 75 75

843 Woman Weaving

2000. Nomads of the High Plateaux. Sheet 106 × 79 mm containing T **843** and similar horiz designs. Multicoloured.
MS3424 3000001. Type **843**; 3000001. Women cooking; 3000001. Women washing clothes; 3000001. Women outside tent with cattle 90 90

2000. Traditional Women's Headdresses (4th series). As T **808**. Multicoloured.
3425 2750001. Corum 60 35
3426 2750001. Trabzon 60 35
3427 2750001. Tunceli 60 35
3428 2750001. Izmir 60 35

844 Mausoleum, Ahlat

845 General Yakup Sevki Subasi

2000. Mausolea and Memorial. Multicoloured.
3429 1500001.+2500001. Type **844** 40 20
3430 2000001.+2500001. Memorial, Tunceli (horiz) 50 25
3431 2750001.+2500001. Domed mausoleum, Skopje, Macedonia 55 30
3432 3000001.+2500001. Mausoleum, Azerbaijan 65 35

2000. Military Leaders. Multicoloured.
3433 1000001. Type **845** 20 10
3434 2000001. General Musa Kazim Karabekir 45 20
3435 2750001. Marshal Mustafa Fevzi Cakmak 55 30
3436 3000001. General Cevat Cobanli 60 35

846 Gymnastics

2000. Olympic Games, Sydney. Multicoloured.
3437 1250001. Type **846** 30 10
3438 1500001. Swimming 35 15
3439 2750001. High jump 55 30
3440 3000001. Archery 60 30

847 *Crocus chrysanthus*

850 Globe, Satellite and Rocket

848 Arslan Baba

2000. Crocuses. Multicoloured.
3441 2500001. Type **847** 45 10
3442 2750001. *Crocus olivieri* . . . 45 10
3443 3000001. *Crocus biflorus* . . 50 10
3444 12500001. *Crocus sativus* . . 2·10 25

2000. Historic Buildings. Multicoloured.
3445 2000001. Type **848** 20 10
3446 2750001. Karasac Ana 30 10
3447 3000001. Hoca Ahmet Yesevi 30 10

2001. Launch of Turksat 2A Satellite.
3450 **850** 2000001. multicoloured 20 10

851 Afyon

852 Dudenbasi Waterfalls

2001. Women's Regional Costumes (1st series). Multicoloured.
3451 2000001. Type **851** 20 10
3452 2000001. Balikesir 20 10
3453 3250001. Kars 35 10
3454 3250001. Tokat 35 10
See also Nos. 3494/7.

2001. Traditional Women's Headdresses (5th series). As T **808**. Multicoloured.
3455 2000001. Mersin-Silifke . . . 20 10
3456 2500001. Sivas 25 10
3457 4250001. Aydin 45 10
3458 4500001. Hakkari 45 10

2001. Europa. Water Resources. Multicoloured.
3459 4500001. Type **852** 45 10
3460 5000001. Yerkopru Falls . . 50 10

853 Captain Mehmet Fethi Bey (pilot) and Muaret-I-Milliye

2001. 87th Anniv of First Istanbul–Cairo Flights by Turkish Crews. Multicoloured.
3461 2500001. Type **853** 25 10
3462 3000001. First Lieutenant Sadik Bey (navigator) and Muaret-I-Miliye 30 10
3463 4500001. First Lieutenant Nuri Bey (pilot) and Prince Celaleddin 45 10
3464 5000001. Captain Ismail Hakki Bey (navigator) and Prince Celaleddin . . 50 10

854 Ataturk and Turkish Flag

856 Myrtle (*Myrtus communis*)

855 Fieldfare ("Turdis pilaris")

2001. 120th Birth Anniv of Kemal Ataturk (President, 1923–38). Multicoloured.
3465 3000001. Type **854** 30 10
3466 4500001. Ataturk and building (horiz) 45 10

2001. World Environment Day. Birds. Two sheets, 109 × 73 mm containing square designs as T **855**. Multicoloured.
MS3467 Two sheets (a) 3000001. Type **855**; 3000001. Goldfinch ("Carduelis carduelis"). (b) 4500001. European bee eater ("Merops apiaster"); 4500001. Hoopoe ("Upupa epops") . . 1·20 1·20

2001. Plants. Multicoloured.
3468 2500001. Type **856** 25 10
3469 3000001. Yarrow (*Achillea millefolium*) 30 10
3470 4500001. St. John's Wort (*Hypericum perforatum*) 45 10
3471 5000001. Moyes rose (*Rosa moyesii*) 50 10
3472 17500001. Whitethorn (*Crataegus oxyacantha*) 1·75 30

857 Mare and Foal

2001. Horses. Multicoloured.
3473 3000001. Type **857** 30 10
3474 4500001. Horses galloping 45 10
3475 4500001. Heads of three horses 45 10
3476 5000001. Horse (vert) . . . 50 10

858 *Resitpasa*

2001. Merchant Ships. Multicoloured.
3477 2500001. Type **858** 25 10
3478 3000001. *Gulnihal* 30 10
3479 3000001. *Mithatpasa* 30 10
3480 5000001. *Aydin* 50 10

859 Obverse and Reverse of 1 Lira Coin, 1937

2001. Coins. Multicoloured.
3481 3000001.+2500001. Type **859** 35 15
3482 3000001.+2500001. Obverse and reverse of 100 Kurus coin, 1934 . . . . 35 10
3483 4500001.+2500001. Obverse and reverse of Sultan Mehmet II gold coin, 1451 . . . . 50 20
3484 5000001.+2500001. Obverse and reverse of Sultan Meliksah gold coin, 467 50 25

860 Sultan Tekes's Tomb, Turkmenistan

2001. Buildings.
3485 **860** 3000001. green and black 30 10
3486 – 3000001. red, yellow and black 30 10
3487 – 4500001. red, lilac and black 45 10
3488 – 5000001. blue and black 50 10
DESIGNS: No. 3486, Sirvansahlar Palace; 3487, Timur's Tomb, Samarkand; 3488, Yildirim Beyazit's Tomb.

861 Ashab-I Keff (13th-century)

2001. Caravanserais (inns) along the Silk Road. Multicoloured.
3489 3000001. + 2500001. Type **861** 55 20
3490 5000001. + 2500001. Horozlu (13th-century) 75 30

863 N.A.T.O. Emblem on "50"

2002. 50th Anniv of Turkey's Membership of North Atlantic Treaty Organization.
3492 **863** 4000001. + 2500001. multicoloured 65 25

864 People Celebrating in Garden

865 Clown

2002. Sultan Nevruz Festival.
3493 **864** 4000001. multicoloured 40 10

2002. Women's Regional Costumes (2nd series). As T **851**. Multicoloured.
3494 3500001. Kastamonu 35 15
3495 4000001. Canakkale 40 10
3496 5000001. Amasya-Ilisu . . . 50 10
3497 6000001. Elazig 60 10

2002. Europa. Circus.
3498 **865** 5000001. multicoloured 50 10

866 Referee and Footballers

2002. World Cup Football Championship, Japan and South Korea (1st issue). Multicoloured.
3499 400000l. Type **866** 40 10
3500 600000l. World cup, football and player 60 10
See also Nos. 3508/9.

867 Muzaffer Sarisozen (musician)

2002. Personalities.
3501 **867** 100000l. red, brown and black 10 10
3502 – 400000l. blue, indigo and black 40 10
3503 – 500000l. brown, deep brown and black . . . 50 10
3504 – 600000l. lilac, purple and black 60 10
3505 – 2500000l. green, olive and black . . . . . . 2·25 35
DESIGNS: 400000l. Arif Nihat Asya (teacher, writer and politician); 500000l. Vedat Tek (architect); 600000l. Hilmi Ziya Ulken (philosopher); 2500000l. Ibrahim Calli (artist).

868 Anatolian Leopard (*Panthera pardus tulliana*)

2002. World Environment Day. Sheet 109 × 80 mm, containing T **868** and similar horiz designs. Multicoloured.
MS3506 400000l. Type **868**; 400000l. Eurasian lynx (*Lynx lynx*); 400000l. Tiger (*Panthera tigris*); 400000l. Caracal (*Felis caracal*) 1·60 1·60

869 Painted Top Shell and Edible Cockle

2002. Shells. Sheet 103 × 78 mm, containing T **869** and similar horiz designs. Multicoloured.
MS3507 400000l. Type **869**; 500000l. *Netted nassa*; 600000l. Common northern whelk; 750000l. Common periwinkle . . . . 2·25 2·25

870 Footballers

2002. World Cup Football Championship, Japan and South Korea (2nd issue). Multicoloured.
3508 400000l. Type **870** 40 10
3509 700000l. Turkish team (third place play-off winners) . . 70 10

871 Steam Locomotive

2002. Railways. Multicoloured.
3510 500000l.+25000l. Type **871** 75 10
3511 700000l.+25000l. Modern locomotive 95 15

872 Violin

2002. Musical Instruments. Multicoloured.
3512 450000l. Type **872** 45 10
3513 700000l. Double bass . . . 70 10

873 *Ege*

2002. Merchant Ships. Multicoloured.
3514 450000l. Type **873** 45 10
3515 500000l. *Ayvalik* 50 10
3516 700000l. *Marakaz* 70 10
3517 700000l. *Karadeniz* 70 10

874 Pasha Gazi Kasim Mosque, Pecs

2002. Cultural Heritage. Sheet 105 × 65 mm, containing T **874** and similar square designs. Multicoloured.
MS3518 450l. Type **874**; 700l. Rakoczi Mansion, Tekirdag
Stamps of a similar design were issued by Hungary. 15 15

876 Eagle and Flags

2003. Centenary of Besiktas Gymnastic Club. Multicoloured.
3524 500000l. Type **876** 45 10
3525 700000l. Eagle, stars, badge and stadium 60 10
3526 750000l. Badge and footballers 65 10
3527 1000000l. Emblem 90 15

877 Face, Minarets and Mountains **878** Siege of Constantinople

2003. Europa. Poster Art. Multicoloured.
3528 500000l. Type **877** 45 10
3529 700000l. Trees and children (theatre poster) 60 10

2003. 550th Anniv of Conquest of Istanbul (Constantinople). Multicoloured.
3530 500000l. Type **878** 45 10
3531 500000l. Sultan Mehmet II 45 10
3532 700000l. Sultan's robe . . . 60 10
3533 1500000l. Sultan Mehmet II (different) . . . . 1·30 20

879 Gazelle (*Gazella subgutturosa*)

2003. World Environment Day. Sheet 111 × 78 mm containing T **879** and similar horiz designs. Multicoloured.
MS3534 500000l. × 4, Type **879**; Red deer (*Cervus elephus*); Roe deer (*Capreolus capreolus*); Fallow deer (*Cervus dama*) . . . . 1·80 25

880 Western Zodiac **881** Quince Flowers

2003.
3535 **880** 500000l. multicoloured 45 10

2003. Women's Regional Costumes (3rd series). As T **851**. Multicoloured.
3536 500000l. Gaziantep 45 10
3537 500000l. Sivas 45 10
3538 700000l. Erzincan 60 10
3539 700000l. Ankara-Beyazari 60 10

2003. Flowering Trees. Multicoloured.
3540 500000l. Type **881** 45 10
3541 700000l. Wild cherry 60 10
3542 750000l. Plum 65 10
3543 1000000l. Pomegranate . . . 90 15
3544 3000000l. Orange . . . . . 2·75 40

883 Tram

2003. Rail Transport. Multicoloured.
3549 600000l.+50000l. Type **883** 55 25
3550 800000l.+50000l. Subway train 75 35

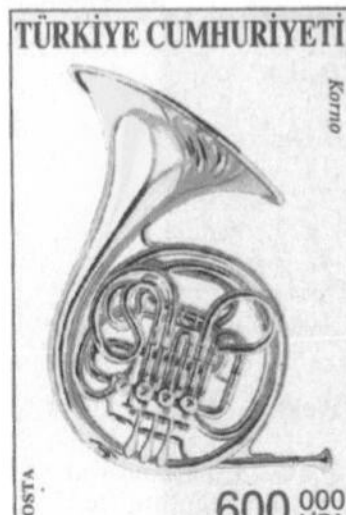

884 Horn

2003. Brass Instruments. Multicoloured.
3551 600000l. Type **884** 55 10
3552 800000l. Trumpet 70 10

886 Kemal Ataturk (first president) and National Flag

2003. 80th Anniv of Republic. Multicoloured.
3554 600000l. Type **886** 55 10
3555 600000l. Kemal Ataturk and cavalry 55 10

887 *Karadeniz*

2003. Ships. Frigates. Multicoloured.
3556 600000l. Type **887** 55 10
3557 600000l. *Gediz* 55 10
3558 700000l. *Salihreis* 60 10
3559 700000l. *Kocatepe* 60 10

888 Mithat Pasha, Bank Facade and Farmers

2003. 140th Anniv of Ziraat Bank.
3560 **888** 600000l. multicoloured 55 10

889 Villa, Trabzon **890** Ibrahim Erzurumlu

2003. Cultural Heritage. Multicoloured.
3561 600000l. Type **889** 55 10
3562 700000l. Museum, Adapazan 60 10
3563 800000l. House, Saloniki . . 70 10
3564 1000000l. Museum, Ankara 90 15

2003. 300th Birth Anniv of Ibrahim Hakki Erzurumlu (writer and mystic).
3565 **890** 600000l.+50000l. multicoloured 55 25

OBLIGATORY TAX STAMPS

T 101 Nurse bandaging Patient **T 102** Biplane

1926. Red Crescent.
T1035 – 1g. red, yellow & blk 25 15
T1036 **T 101** 2½g. multicoloured 35 15
T1037 – 5g. multicoloured . . 50 20
T1038 – 10g. multicoloured 85 60
DESIGNS—VERT: 1g. Red crescent and decorative archway; 5g. Refugees. HORIZ: 10g. Stretcher bearers.

1926. Aviation Fund.
T1039 **T 102** 20pa. brown & green 35 20
T1040 1g. green and stone 35 20
T1041 5g. violet and green 1·00 25
T1042 5g. red and green . . 19·00 2·50
The 5g. stamps are 40 × 29 mm.

T 103 Biplane over Ankara ٢٠ پاره (T 104)

1927. Aviation Fund.
T1043 **T 102** 20pa. red and green 10 10
T1044 1g. green and ochre 20 10
T1045 **T 103** 2g. brown and green 35 10
T1046 2½g. red and green 1·40 55
T1047 5g. blue and buff . . 30 10
T1048 10g. blue and pink 1·40 50
T1049 15g. green and yellow . . . . . . 1·40 40
T1050 20g. brown and ochre . . . . . . 2·10 90
T1051 50g. blue & light blue . . . . 6·75 1·90
T1052 100g. red and blue 48·00 35·00
The 20pa. and 1g. are 25 × 15 mm.

1927. Red Crescent No. T1035 and charity labels surch with Type T **104** or similar types.
T1053 20pa. on 1g. red, yell & blk . . . . 2·50 30
T1054 20pa. on 1g. brown . . . 1·25 30
T1055 20pa. on 2½g. lilac . . . . 1·25 30
DESIGNS: 26 × 21 mm. No. T1054 Hospital ship. No. T1055 Nurse tending patient.
No. T1053 has an extra line of Turkish characters in the surcharge.

T 105 Red Crescent on Map of Turkey **T 106** Cherubs holding Star

1928. Red Crescent. Various frames. Crescent in red.
T1067 **T 105** ¼pi. brown 15 10
T1068 1pi. purple 15 10
T1069 2½pi. orange 15 10
T1070 5pi. brown 55 15
T1071 10pi. green 55 20

T1072 20pi. blue 90 20
T1073 50pi. purple . . . . 3·00 15
See also Nos. T1171/4 and T1198/1212.

1928. Child Welfare.
T1074 T **106** 1g. olive and red . . 20 10
T1075 2½g. brown and red 20 10
T1076 5g. green and red . . 60 15
T1077 25g. black and red 1·90 45
See also Nos. T1160/1 and T1165/6.

1930. Aviation Fund. Nos. T1039, T1043, T1045 and T1049 surch.
T1099 T **102** Bir (1)k. on 20pa. brown and green 29·00 10·50
T1100 Bir (1)k. on 20pa. red and green . . 20 25
T1101 T **103** Yuz (100)pa. on 2g. brown and green 20 25
T1102 T **102** 5k. on 20pa. red and green 20 25
T1103 Bes (5)k. on 20pa. red and green . . 2·25 60
T1104 T **103** On (10)k. on 2g. brown and green 90 35
T1105 Elli (50)k. on 2g. brown and green 3·50 1·50
T1106 Bir (1)l. on 2g. brown and green 11·00 4·00
T1107 Bes (5)l. on 15g. green and yellow £600

T **114** Biplane over Ankara
T **118** Biplane

1931. Aviation Fund.
T1141 T **114** 20pa. black 30 10
See also Nos. T1154/6.

1932. Child Welfare. No. T1074 surch.
T1150 T **106** 20pa. on 1g. olive and red 45 20
T1153 3k. on 1g. olive and red . . . . 1·25 40

1932. Aviation Fund. As Type T **114** but larger, 22 × 30 mm, and with sky shaded.
T1154 1k. purple 20 10
T1155 5k. red 45 20
T1156 10k. green 80 20

1932. Red Crescent. Nos. T1067, T1069 and T1071 surch.
T1157 T **105** 1k. on 2½pi. orange 30 15
T1158 5k. on ½pi. brown . . 65 20
T1159 5k. on 10pi. green 1·00 40

1933. Child Welfare. As Type T **106** but inscr "IZMIR HIMAYEI ETFAL CEMIYETI".
T1160 1k. violet and red 40 35
T1161 5k. brown and red . . . . 1·90 60

1933. Aviation Fund.
T1162 T **118** On (10)pa. green . . 25 10
T1163 Bir (1)k. red 45 15
T1164 Bes (5)k. lilac . . . 60 15

1934. Child Welfare. As Type T **106** but inscr "Turkiye Himayeietfal Cemiyeti".
T1165 20pa. purple and red . . . 40 10
T1166 15k. green and red . . . . 1·60 40

T **119** Red Crescent and Map of Turkey

1934. Inscr "TURKIYE HILALIAHMER CEMIYETI" (different frame on 5k.).
T1171 T **119** ¼k. blue and red . . 20 10
T1172 1k. brown and red 40 10
T1173 2½k. brown and red 50 25
T1174 5k. green and red . . 90 35
See also Nos. T1198/1212.

1936. Child Welfare. Nos. T1074/5 and T1165 optd **P.Y.S.** or surch also.
T1186 T **106** 20pa. purple and red 2·10 65
T1187 1g. olive and red . . 50 35
T1188 3k. on 2½g. brn & red . . . . 2·10 65

1937. Red Crescent. As Types T **105** and T **119** but inscr "TURKIYE KIZILAY CEMIYETI". Various frames.
T1204 ¼k. blue and red 50 15
T1199 1k. mauve and red 35 15
T1200 2½k. orange and red 55 25
T1201 5k. green and red . . . . 1·10 25
T1209 5k. brown and red 60 15
T1202 10k. green and red . . . . 1·10 50
T1203 20k. black and red . . . . 2·10 60
T1211 50k. purple and red . . . 12·00 35
T1212 1l. blue and red . . . . . 48·00 2·10

1938. Child Welfare. No. T1075 surch. (a) Value in figures and words above **P. Y. S.**
T1213 T **106** 20pa. on 2½g. brown and red . . . . . 1·10 40
T1214 1k. on 2½g. brown and red . . . . . 1·10 40

(b) **P. Y. S.** above value in figures and words.
T1215 T **106** 20pa. on 2½g. brown and red . . . . . 1·90 75
T1216 1k. on 2½g. brown and red . . . . . 1·90 70

(c) **1 kurus**.
T1217 T **106** 1k. on 2½g. brown and red . . . . . 1·90 40

T **138** Laughing Child
T **139** Nurse and Baby

1940. Child Welfare. Star in red.
T1259 T **138** 20pa. green 15 10
T1260 1k. lilac 25 10
T1261 T **139** 1k. blue 20 15
T1262 2½k. mauve 70 25
T1263 T **138** 3k. black 25 10
T1264 T **139** 5k. lilac 20 10
T1265 10k. green 50 10
T1266 T **138** 15k. blue . . . . . 1·00 30
T1267 T **139** 25k. olive . . . . . 3·75 50
T1268 50k. olive . . . . . 4·50 60

T **145** Soldier and Map of Turkey
T **151** Child eating

1941. National Defence.
T1289 T **145** 1k. violet 20 10
T1290 2k. blue . . . . . . 3·00 10
T1291 3k. brown . . . . . 4·25 40
T1292 4k. mauve . . . . . 1·60 15
T1293 5k. pink . . . . . . 7·00 2·10
T1294 10k. blue . . . . . 20·00 12·00

1943. Child Welfare. Inscr "SEFKAT PULLARI 1943".
T1330 T **151** 0.50k. violet and red 15 10
T1331 0.50k. green and red 15 10
T1332 – 1k. blue and red . . 15 10
T1333 – 3k. red and orange 35 15
T1334 – 15k. black, buff and red 75 25
T1335 – 100k. blue and red 1·40 50
MST1336 140 × 118 mm. Nos. T1330/5 . . . . 3·25 5·00
DESIGNS—VERT: 1k. Nurse with baby; 15k. Baby and emblem; 100k. President Inonu and child. HORIZ: 3k. Nurse and child.

T **152** Child Welfare Emblem
T **155** Pres. Inonu and Victim

1943. Child Welfare. Star in red.
T1337 T **152** 20pa. blue 15 10
T1338 – 1k. green 15 10
T1339 – 3k. brown 15 10
T1340 – 5k. orange . . . . . 1·60 15
T1341 – 5k. brown . . . . . 1·90 15
T1342 – 10k. red 85 10
T1343 – 15k. lilac . . . . . 1·75 10
T1344 – 25k. violet . . . . . 1·90 15
T1345 – 50k. blue . . . . . 2·75 20
T1346 – 100k. green . . . . 4·50 25
DESIGNS—VERT: 1k. Hospital; 3k. Nurse and children; 5k. Baby in cot; 10k. Nurse bathing baby; 15k. Nurse helping child to drink; 50k. Child. HORIZ: 25k. Baby with bottle; 100k. Hospital.

1944. Red Crescent. Inscr "TURKIYE KIZILAY CEMIYETI".
T1347 – 20pa. brown, flesh, red and blue . . . 25 10
T1348 T **155** 1k. olive, yellow, green and red . . 25 15
T1349 – 2½k. blue and red . . 45 15
T1350 – 5k. blue and red . . 1·90 25
T1351 – 10k. blue, green and red . . . . 1·90 25
T1352 – 50k. green, black and red . . . . 5·50 35
T1353 – 1l. yellow, black and red . . . . 10·50 70

DESIGNS—VERT: 20pa. Nurse tending dreaming patient; 5k. Soldier and nurse; 10k. Feeding victims; 50k. Wounded soldiers on raft; 1l. Nurse within red crescent. HORIZ: 2½k. Stretcher bearers and hospital ship.

T **156** Nurse helping Child to Drink
T **159** Nurse tucking Baby in Cot

1945. Child Welfare. Star in red.
T1354 – 1k. lilac 15 10
T1355 – 2½k. blue 35 15
T1356 T **156** 5k. green 40 35
T1357 – 10k. brown . . . . 2·25 60
T1358 – 250k. black . . . . 23·00 3·00
T1359 – 500k. violet . . . . 38·00 2·75
DESIGNS—VERT (21 × 20 mm): 1k. Nurse carrying baby; 2½k. Nurse holding child; 10k. Child sucking thumb. HORIZ (28 × 22 mm): 250, 500k. Emblem.

1946. 25th Anniv of Child Welfare Organization.
T1360 T **159** 20pa. brown and red 10 10
T1361 – 1k. blue and red . . 10 10
T1362 – 2½k. red 30 10
T1363 – 5k. brown and red 50 15
T1364 – 15k. purple and red 75 25
T1365 – 25k. green and red 1·25 40
T1366 – 50k. green and red 1·90 40
T1367 – 150k. brown and red 5·00 40
MST1368 80 × 105 mm. 250k. blue, pink and red . . . . 12·00 11·00
DESIGNS: 1k. Mother and baby; 2½k. Nurse holding child above head; 5k. Doctor examining baby; 15k. Nurse feeding baby; 25k. Nurse bathing baby; 50k. Nurse weighing baby; 150k. Nurse, and child in cot; 250k. Pres Inonu and child.

T **160** Pres. Inonu and Victim
T **169** Nurse and Children playing

1946. Red Crescent. As Nos. T1347/8, T1350 and T1353 and new design inscr "TURKIYE KIZILAY DERNEGI".
T1369 – 20pa. yellow, grey, blue and red . . . 15 10
T1532 – 20pa. brown, yellow, violet and red . . 20 10
T1370 T **155** 1k. multicoloured . . 4·75 70
T1371 T **160** 1k. brown, blue and red 25 15
T1533 – 1k. green, blk & red 20 10
T1372 – 5k. blue and red . . 40 15
T1373 – 20k. red, blue & pur 1·25 75
T1374 – 1l. black, yell & red 5·50 2·75
T1375 – 250k. black, green and red . . . . 11·00 1·10
T1376 – 5l. black, pink and red . . . . 16·00 1·40
T1377 – 10l. blue and red . . 27·00 20·00
DESIGNS—VERT: 20pa. As No. T1347; 1k. (T1533), As No. T1352; 5k. As No. T1350; 1l. As No. T1353; 5l. Nurse tending patient; 10l. Soldier, red crescent and figure symbolizing Victory. HORIZ: 20k. Ankara Hospital; 250k. Nurse helping injured soldier.

1948. Child Welfare. Star in red.
T1399 T **169** 20pa. blue 15 10
T1400 – 20pa. mauve 15 10
T1401 – 1k. green 15 10
T1402 – 3k. purple 30 10
T1403 – 15k. grey 60 10
T1404 – 30k. orange . . . . 1·10 1·10
T1405 – 150k. green . . . . 5·75 45
T1406 – 300k. red . . . . . 11·50 3·50
DESIGNS—VERT: 20pa. (No. 1400) Nurse and children walking; 1k. Nurse feeding two children; 3k. Nurse with three children; 15k. Parents and two children; 150k. Nurse holding baby; 300k. Heads of nurse and child. HORIZ: 30k. Father handing baby to nurse.

T **177** Ruins and Tent
T **179** "Grief"

1949. Red Crescent.
T1422 T **177** 5k. black, red & pur 55 25
T1423 10k. purple, red and flesh 55 25

1950. Red Crescent. Crescent in red.
T1425 T **179** ¼k. blue . . . . . . 1·40 10
T1426 1k. blue 15 10
T1427 2k. mauve 25 15
T1428 2½k. orange 25 65
T1429 3k. green 30 65
T1430 4k. drab 40 15
T1431 5k. blue 65 10
T1432 10k. pink . . . . . 3·00 25
T1433 25k. brown . . . . 4·50 25
T1434 – 50k. blue . . . . . 4·50 1·25
T1435 – 100k. green . . . . 8·00 1·25
DESIGN: 50, 100k. Plant with broken stem.

1952. (a) Red Crescent. Nos. T1427 and T1429/30 surch.
T1489 T **179** 20pa. on 2k. mauve and red 80 25
T1490 20pa. on 3k. green and red 30 15
T1491 20pa. on 4k. drab and red 45 15

(b) Child Welfare. Nos. T1355, T1362 and T1339 surch.
T1492 – 1k. on 2½k. blue and red 75 20
T1493 – 1k. on 2½k. red 30 10
T1494 – 1k. on 3k. brown and red 40 15

T **208** Nurse and Baby
T **211** Globe and Flag

1954. Child Welfare. Inscr "SEFKAT PULLARI 1954".
T1534 – 20pa. yellow & orange 15 10
T1535 – 20pa. green and red 15 10
T1536 T **208** 1k. blue and red . . 20 10
DESIGN: Nos. 1534/5, Nurse with two children.
See also Nos. T1569 and T1573/4.

1954. Red Crescent.
T1545 T **211** 1k. multicoloured . . 20 10
T1546 – 5k. red, grey and green 20 10
T1547 – 10k. grey, green and red 35 10
DESIGNS: 5k. Nurse with wings on cloud; 10k. Arm and hand.
See also Nos. T1652, T1656/8, T1838 and T1840/3.

T **212** Florence Nightingale
T **215** Children Kissing

1954. Red Crescent. Centenary of Florence Nightingale's Arrival at Scutari.
T1551 T **212** 20k. green, brown and red 25 10
T1552 – 30k. brown, black and red 30 10
T1553 – 50k. stone, black and red 30 10
DESIGNS: 30k. Florence Nightingale (three-quarter face); 50k. Selimiye Barracks.

1955. Child Welfare. Inscr "SEFKAT PULLARI 1955". Star in red.
T1564 T **215** 20pa. blue 10 10
T1565 20pa. brown 10 10
T1566 1k. purple 10 10
T1567 3k. bistre 10 10
T1568 5k. orange 10 10
T1569 T **208** 10k. green 50 10
T1570 – 15k. blue 30 25
T1571 – 25k. lake 40 25
T1572 – 50k. green 80 45
T1573 T **208** 2½l. brown . . . . . £170 70·00
T1574 10l. violet £550 £190
DESIGN: 15 to 50k. Nurse carrying baby.

1955. Red Crescent. Nos. T1373 and T1435 surch.
T1575 20pa. on 20k. red, blue and purple 15 10
T1576 20pa. on 100k. green and red 15 10

T **219** Nurse
T **227** Woman and Children

1955. Red Crescent. Congress of International Council of Nurses.
T1578 T 219 10k. brown, red and black 25 15
T1579 – 15k. green, red and black 30 15
T1580 – 100k. blue and red 1·25 60
DESIGNS—HORIZ: 15k. Nurses marching. VERT: 100k. Emblem, Red Cross and Red Crescent flags and nurses.

1956. Child Welfare. Star in red.
T1614 T 227 20pa. salmon 15 10
T1615 20pa. olive 15 10
T1616 1k. blue 20 10
T1617 1k. violet 20 10
T1618 3k. brown 75 25
T1619 – 10k. red 1·50 75
T1620 – 25k. green 2·10 75
T1621 – 50k. blue 3·50 80
T1622 – 2½l. lilac 7·00 2·10
T1623 – 5l. brown 14·00 5·00
T1624 – 10l. green 27·00 7·50
DESIGNS: 10k. to 50k. Flag and building; 2½l. to 10l. Mother and baby.

1956. Red Crescent. No. T1545 surch.
T1625 T 211 20pa. on 1k. mult 10 10
T1626 2.5k. on 1k. mult 10 10

1956. Child Welfare. Nos. 1399/1406 optd **IV. DUNYA Cocuk Gunu 1 Ekim 1956.** Nos. 1644/6 surch, also.
T1639 T 169 20pa. red and blue 4·50 4·50
T1640 – 20pa. mauve and red 4·50 4·50
T1641 – 1k. green and red 4·50 4·50
T1642 – 3k. purple and red 4·50 4·50
T1643 – 15k. grey and red 4·50 4·50
T1644 – 25k. on 30k. orange and red 4·50 4·50
T1645 – 100k. on 150k. green and red 4·50 4·50
T1646 – 250k. on 300k. deep red and red 4·50 4·50

1957. Red Crescent. As No. T1373 but inscr "TURKIYE KIZILAY CEMIYETI", new design and as Nos. T1545/6. Crescent in red.
T1651 – ¼k. drab and brown 10 10
T1652 T 211 1k. black, bis & green 10 10
T1653 – 2½k. green & dp green 15 10
T1655 – 20k. red, brown and blue 1·75 15
T1656 T 211 25k. grey, black and green 1·50 25
T1657 50k. blue and green 2·40 25
T1658 100k. violet, black and green 4·50 25
DESIGNS—VERT: ¼, 2½k. Flower being watered. HORIZ: 20k. Ankara hospital.

T 239 Two Babies

T 246 Nurse and Child

1957. Child Welfare.
T1659 T 239 20pa. green and red 10 10
T1660 20pa. pink and red 10 10
T1661 1k. blue and red 10 10
T1662 3k. orange and red 30 15
T1683 T 246 100k. brown and red 40 10
T1684 150k. green and red 40 10
T1685 250k. violet and red 75 10

T 254 Florence Nightingale

T 255 Child's Head and Butterfly

1958. Florence Nightingale Foundation. Crescent in red.
T1829 T 254 1l. green 20 10
T1830 1½l. grey 20 10
T1831 2½l. blue 20 10

1958. Child Welfare. Butterflies. Multicoloured.
T1832 20k. Type T 255 30 25
T1833 25k. Brimstone 35 35
T1834 50k. Little tiger blue (horiz) 70 45
T1835 75k. Green-veined white (horiz) 95 70
T1836 150k. Peacock 1·40 90

1958. Red Crescent. As Nos. T1651/3, T1546 and T1656/8 but colours changed. Crescent in red.
T1837 – ¼k. lilac 25 10
T1838 T 211 1k. black, brown and green 30 10
T1839 – 2½k. grey and red 50 10
T1840 – 5k. red, brown and green 90 10
T1841 T 211 25k. black, green and brown 3·75 25
T1842 50k. purple, black and green 4·50 25
T1843 100k. drab, black and green 7·00 45

OFFICIAL STAMPS

O 160 O 241 O 284

1947.
O1360 O 160 10pa. brown 10 10
O1361 1k. green 10 10
O1362 2k. purple 10 10
O1363 3k. orange 10 10
O1364 5k. turquoise 25·00 10
O1365 10k. brown 6·25 10
O1366 15k. violet 90 10
O1367 20k. blue 1·25 10
O1368 30k. olive 1·25 10
O1369 50k. blue 1·25 10
O1370 1l. green 1·90 10
O1371 2l. red 2·50 90

1951. Postage stamps optd **RESMI** between bars with star and crescent above.
O1458 165 0.25k. red 15 10
O1454 5k. blue 15 10
O1461 10k. brown 15 10
O1462 15k. violet 15 10
O1456 20k. blue 25 10
O1469 30k. brown 3·50 10
O1470 60k. black 3·75 15

1955. Postage stamps optd **RESMI** between wavy bars with star and crescent above or surch also.
O1568 165 0.25k. red 10 10
O1587 ½k. on 1k. black 10 10
O1569 1k. black 10 10
O1570 2k. purple 15 10
O1593 2k. on 4k. green 10 10
O1571 3k. orange 15 10
O1594 3k. on 4k. green 10 10
O1572 4k. green 15 10
O1573 5k. on 15k. violet 15 10
O1581 5k. blue 25 10
O1595 10k. on 12k. red 10 10
O1574 10k. on 15k. violet 15 10
O1575 15k. violet 15 10
O1576 20k. blue 25 10
O1585 30k. brown 15 10
O1577 40k. on 1l. olive 30 10
O1590 75k. on 1l. olive 20 10
O1578 75k. on 2l. brown 35 10
O1579 75k. on 5l. purple 8·50 10·00

1957.
O1655 O 241 5k. blue 10 10
O1843 5k. red 15 10
O1656 10k. brown 10 10
O1844 10k. olive 15 10
O1657 15k. violet 10 10
O1845 15k. red 10 10
O1658 20k. red 10 10
O1846 20k. violet 10 10
O1659 30k. olive 10 10
O1660 40k. purple 10 10
O1847 40k. blue 10 10
O1661 50k. grey 10 10
O1662 60k. green 10 10
O1848 60k. orange 25 10
O1663 75k. orange 10 10
O1849 75k. grey 25 10
O1664 100k. green 15 10
O1850 100k. violet 30 10
O1665 200k. lake 15 10
O1851 200k. brown 70 10

1960.
O1916 O 284 1k. orange 10 10
O1917 5k. red 10 10
O1918 10k. green 65 10
O1919 30k. brown 15 10
O1920 60k. green 25 10
O1921 1l. purple 45 10
O1922 1½l. blue 35 10
O1923 2½l. violet 75 10
O1924 5l. blue 3·50 10

O 303 O 320

1962.
O1977 O 303 1k. brown 10 10
O1978 5k. green 10 10
O1979 10k. brown 10 10
O1980 15k. blue 15 10
O1981 25k. red 35 10
O1982 30k. blue 20 10

1963. Surch.
O2003 O 303 50k. on 30k. blue 15 10
O2004 O 284 100k. on 60k. green 20 10

1963.
O2042 O 320 1k. green 10 10
O2043 5k. brown 10 10
O2044 10k. green 10 10
O2045 50k. red 15 10
O2046 100k. blue 25 10

O 329 O 344

1964.
O2074 O 329 1k. grey 10 10
O2075 5k. blue 10 10
O2076 10k. yellow 10 10
O2077 30k. red 25 10
O2078 50k. green 25 10
O2079 60k. brown 60 10
O2080 80k. turquoise 1·40 10
O2081 130k. blue 1·40 10
O2082 200k. purple 2·75 10

1965.
O2133 O 344 1k. green 10 10
O2134 10k. blue 10 10
O2135 50k. orange 20 10

O 358 Usak Carpet

O 372 Doves Emblem

O 383

1966. Turkish Carpets.
O2175 O 358 1k. orange 10 10
O2176 – 50k. green 10 10
O2177 – 100k. red 25 10
O2178 – 150k. blue 35 10
O2179 – 200k. bistre 40 10
O2180 – 500k. lilac 95 10
DESIGNS (Carpets of): 50k. Bergama; 100k. Ladik; 150k. Selcuk; 200k. Nomad; 500k. Anatolia.

1967.
O2213 O 372 1k. blue & light blue 10 10
O2214 50k. blue and orange 15 10
O2215 100k. blue & mauve 25 10

1968.
O2241 O 383 50k. brown and green 15 10
O2242 150k. black & orange 40 10
O2243 500k. brown and blue 60 10

O 400 O 427 O 440

1969.
O2287 O 400 1k. red and green 10 10
O2288 10k. blue and green 10 10
O2289 50k. brown and green 10 10
O2290 100k. mauve & green 20 10

1971.
O2359 O 427 5k. blue and brown 10 10
O2360 10k. red and blue 10 10
O2361 30k. violet & orange 10 10
O2362 50k. brown and blue 10 10
O2363 75k. green and buff 15 10

1971. Face-value and border colour given first.
O2398 O 440 5k. blue and grey 10 10
O2399 25k. green and brown 10 10
O2400 100k. brown & green 15 10
O2401 200k. brown & ochre 15 10
O2402 250k. purple & violet 15 10
O2403 500k. blue & light blue 40 10

O 446 O 462 O 478 Trellis Motif

1972.
O2411 O 446 5k. blue and brown 10 10
O2412 100k. green & brown 10 10
O2413 200k. red and brown 15 10

1973.
O2457 O 462 100k. blue and cream 10 10

1974.
O2490 O 478 10k. brown on pink 10 10
O2491 25k. purple on blue 10 10
O2492 50k. red on mauve 10 10
O2493 150k. brown on grn 15 10
O2494 250k. red on pink 25 10
O2495 500k. brown on yell 50 10

O 496 O 528 O 529

1975.
O2537 O 496 100k. red and blue 10 10

1977. Surch.
O2587 O 320 5k. on 1k. green 10 10
O2588 O 329 5k. on 1k. grey 10 10
O2589 O 344 5k. on 1k. green 10 10
O2590 O 358 5k. on 1k. orange 10 10
O2591 O 372 5k. on 1k. blue and light blue 10 10

1977.
O2609 O 528 250k. green and blue 10 10

1978.
O2610 O 529 50k. pink and red 10 10
O2611 2½l. buff and brown 10 10
O2612 4½l. lilac and green 15 10
O2613 5l. blue and violet 15 10
O2614 10l. light green and green 50 10
O2615 25l. yellow and red 95 10

O 540 O 552 O 573

1979.
O2647 O 540 50k. deep orange and orange 10 10
O2648 2½l. blue & light blue 10 10

1979.
O2686 O 552 50k. violet and pink 10 10
O2687 1l. red and green 10 10
O2688 2½l. mauve and light mauve 10 10
O2689 5l. purple and blue 10 10
O2690 7½l. blue and lilac 15 10
O2691 10l. blue and buff 20 10
O2692 35l. purple and silver 65 10
O2693 50l. blue and pink 1·00 10

1981.
O2756 O 573 5l. red and yellow 1·85 10
O2757 10l. red and pink 1·90 10
O2758 35l. mauve and grey 2·50 10
O2759 50l. blue and pink 3·75 10
O2760 75l. emerald & green 5·00 10
O2761 100l. blue & lt blue 5·75 10

O 606 O 644 O 720

1983.
O2839 O 606 5l. blue and yellow 35 10
O2840 15l. blue and yellow 40 10
O2841 20l. blue and grey 30 10
O2842 50l. blue & light blue 1·90 10
O2843 65l. blue and mauve 2·40 10
O2844 70l. blue and pink 60 10
O2845 90l. blue and brown 2·00 10
O2846 90l. blue & light blue 2·10 10
O2847 100l. blue and green 1·60 10
O2848 125l. blue and green 3·50 10
O2849 230l. blue and orange 2·50 10

1986.
O2946 O 644 5l. blue and yellow 10 10
O2947 10l. blue and pink 15 10
O2948 20l. blue and grey 20 10
O2949 50l. blue & light blue 30 10
O2950 100l. blue and green 1·25 10
O2951 300l. blue and lilac 1·90 10

1989. Various stamps surch.
O3039 O 644 500l. on 10l. blue and pink 1·00 10
O3040 O 606 500l. on 15l. blue and yellow 1·00 10
O3041 O 644 500l. on 20l. blue and grey 1·00 10
O3042 O 606 1000l. on 70l. blue and pink 2·00 10
O3043 1000l. on 90l. blue and brown 2·00 10
O3044 1250l. on 230l. blue and orange 3·00 10

1991. Nos. O2843 and O2846 surch.
O3108 **O 606** 100l. on 65l. blue and mauve . . . 20 10
O3109 250l. on 90l. blue and light blue . . 60 10

1992.
O3138 **O 720** 3000l. deep brown and brown . . . 1·10 10
O3139 5000l. green & lt grn 1·90 10

O 733  O 743  O 753

1992.
O3167 **O 733** 1000l. blue and green 20 10
O3168 10000l. green & blue 2·00 10

1993.
O3196 **O 743** 1000l. green & brown 35 10
O3197 1500l. green & brown 70 10
O3198 5000l. brown & green . . . . . . 2·10 10

1994.
O3218 **O 753** 2500l. dp mve & mve 20 10
O3219 25000l. brn & stone 2·50 10

O 764  O 770  O 775

1995.
O3243 **O 764** 3500l. violet and light violet 50 10
O3244 17500l. green and light green . . . . 2·00 10

1995.
O3252 **O 770** 50000l. green and olive . . . . . . 1·90 10

1995.
O3267 **O 775** 5000l. red and orange 25 10

O 785  O 793  O 803

1996.
O3288 **O 785** 15000l. red and blue 30 10
O3289 – 20000l. violet and green 40 10
O3290 – 50000l. green and violet . . . . . . 1·10 10
O3291 – 100000l. blue and red . . . . 2·10 10
DESIGNS: 20000l. Hearts forming pattern; 50000l. Leaves forming pattern; 100000l. Ornate scroll pattern.

1997.
O3303 **O 793** 25000l. blue and mauve 35 10

1997.
O3322 **O 803** 40000l. violet and red 35 10
O3323 – 250000l. green and red . . . . 3·00 10
DESIGN: 250000l. Diamond-shaped pattern.

O 815  O 827  O 838

1998.
O3348 **O 815** 40000l. light blue and blue 25 10
O3349 – 75000l. lilac and orange 45 10
O3350 – 100000l. purple . . . 50 10
O3351 – 200000l. green and brown . . . . . 1·10 10
O3352 – 500000l. green and brown . . . . . 2·25 10
DESIGNS: 75000l. Pattern forming St. Andrew's cross with fleur-de-lis finials; 100000l. Diamond-shaped pattern; 200000l. Pattern with central circle; 500000l. Pattern forming five crosses.

1999.
O3384 **O 827** R (75000l.) lilac and blue 70 10
O3385 – RT (275000l.) grey and pink . . . . 1·90 10
DESIGN: No. O3385, Pattern of flowers.
No. O3384 was for use on Official letters and No. O3385 for use on Official registered letters.

2000.
O3414 **O 838** 50000l. pink and blue 15 10
O3415 – 75000l. grey and brown 20 10
O3416 – 500000l. blue and brown . . . . . 1·10 10
O3417 – 1250000l. buff and blue . . . . . 2·50 10
DESIGNS: 75000l. Squares and triangles; 500000l. Clover leaf pattern; 1250000l. Fleur de Lys pattern.

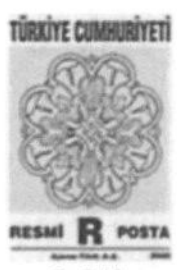

O 849  O 862  O 875

2000.
O3448 **O 849** R yellow and blue 50 15
O3449 RT blue and ultramarine . . . 50 15
No. O3448 was for use on Official letters and No. O3449 for use on Official registered letters.

2001.
O3491 **O 862** R yellow and blue 50 15
No. O3491 was for use on Official letters.

2002.
O3519 **O 875** 50000l. blue and red 15 10
O3520 – 100000l. yellow and green 30 10
O3521 – 250000l. blue and red 55 15
O3522 – 500000l. orange and blue . . . . . . 1·00 30
O3523 – 1500000l. yellow, light green and green . . . . . . 2·75 1·60
DESIGNS: 100000l. Pattern of curved lines; 250000l. Pattern of leaves; 500000l. Pattern with diamond shape in centre; 1500000l. Oval shaped pattern.

O 882  O 885

2003.
O3545 **O 882** 500000l. red and blue 45 10
O3546 – 750000l. blue and buff 65 10
O3547 – 1000000l. green and blue 90 15
O3548 – 3000000l. buff and blue . . . . . . 2·75 40
DESIGNS: 750000l. Cross-shaped pattern; 1000000l. Diamond-shaped pattern; 3000000l. Pattern of four holly leaves.

2003.
O3553 **O 885** mauve and pink . . 50 25

POSTAGE DUE STAMPS

D 2  D 4

1863. Imperf.
D 7 **D 2** 20pa. black on brown . . 90·00 32·00
D 8 1pi. black on brown . . £110 38·00
D 9 2pi. black on brown . . £450 £110
D10 5pi. black on brown . . £325 £130

1865.
D18 **D 4** 20pa. brown . . . . 1·40 3·75
D19 1pi. brown . . . . 1·40 3·25
D74 2pi. brown . . . . 7·50 11·00
D70 5pi. brown . . . . 3·75 16·00
D76 25pi. brown . . . . 32·00 £100

1888. As T 9.
D117 **9** 20pa. black . . . . 3·25 10·00
D118 1pi. black . . . . 3·25 10·00
D119 2pi. black . . . . 3·25 10·00

1892. As T 15.
D146 **15** 20pa. black . . . . 4·50 4·00
D147 20pa. black on red . . . . . 1·50 12·00
D148 1pi. black . . . . 15·00 4·75
D149 2pi. black . . . . 12·00 4·75

1901. As T 21.
D195 **21** 10pa. black on red . . . 2·50 3·75
D196 20pa. black on red . . . 2·10 6·00
D197 1pi. black on red . . . . 1·75 6·50
D198 2pi. black on red . . . . 1·25 7·75

1905. As T 23.
D228 **23** 1pi. black on red . . . . 1·40 3·75
D229 2pi. black on red . . . . 2·75 11·50

1908. As T 25.
D250 **25** 1pi. black on red . . . . 60·00 4·50
D251 2pi. black on red . . . . 4·25 35·00

1909. As T 28.
D288 **28** 1pi. black on red . . . . 12·50 65·00
D287 2pi. black on red . . . . 75·00 £130

1913. As T 30.
D347 **30** 2pa. black on red 45 65
D348 5pa. black on red 45 65
D349 10pa. black on red . . . 45 65
D350 20pa. black on red . . . 45 65
D351 1pi. black on red . . . . 1·50 5·00
D352 2pi. black on red . . . . 7·75 18·00

1913. Adrianople Issue surch.
D356 **31** 2pa. on 10pa. green . . . 2·50 1·25
D357 5pa. on 20pa. red . . . 2·50 1·25
D358 10pa. on 40pa. blue . . . 7·50 2·50
D359 20pa. on 40pa. blue . . . 17·00 12·00

D 49  D 50

D 51  D 52

1914.
D516 **D 49** 5pa. brown . . . . . . 40 11·00
D517 **D 50** 20pa. red . . . . . . 40 11·00
D518 **D 51** 1pi. blue . . . . . . 70 11·00
D519 **D 52** 2pi. blue . . . . . . 70 11·00

AD 26  D 101 Bridge over Kizil-Irmak

1921.
AD91 **AD 26** 20pa. green . . . . 30 1·00
AD92 1pi. green . . . . . 35 1·40
AD93 2pi. brown . . . . 80 2·75
AD94 3pi. red . . . . . 1·60 6·00
AD95 5pi. blue . . . . . 2·75 7·00

1926.
D1035 **D 101** 20pa. orange . . . 1·10 1·00
D1036 1gr. red . . . . . 1·25 1·40
D1037 2gr. green . . . . . 1·75 1·75
D1038 3gr. purple . . . . 2·50 3·00
D1039 5gr. violet . . . . . 5·50 5·00

D 121

1936.
D1186 **D 121** 20pa. brown 10 10
D1187 2k. blue 10 10
D1188 3k. violet 10 10
D1189 5k. green 10 15
D1190 12k. red 10 30

PRINTED MATTER STAMPS

1879. Optd **IMPRIMES** in scroll.
N88 **9** 10pa. black and mauve . . £120 £100

(N 14)

1891. Stamps of 1876 optd with Type N 14.
N132 **9** 10pa. green . . . . 42·00 12·50
N134 20pa. pink . . . . 70·00 20·00
N136 1pi. blue . . . . £130 90·00
N138 2pi. yellow £350 £250
N139 5pi. brown £550 £375

1892. Stamps of 1892 optd with Type N 14.
N150 **15** 10pa. green . . . . £250 65·00
N151 20pa. red £475 £130
N152 1pi. blue . . . . 75·00 90·00
N153 2pi. brown . . . . £120 90·00
N154 5pi. purple £1300 £1200

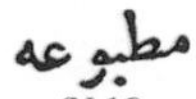

(N 16) 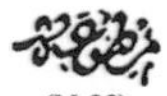 (N 23) 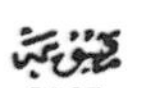 (N 27)

1894. Stamps of 1892 optd with Type N 16.
N161 **15** 5pa. on 10pa. grn (160) 1·75 40
N155 10pa. green . . . . . . 70 1·50
N156a 20pa. red . . . . . . 1·90 1·25
N157 1pi. blue . . . . . . 1·90 1·25
N158 2pi. brown . . . . . . 21·00 7·75
N159 5pi. purple . . . . . . 65·00 48·00

1901. Stamps of 1901 optd with Type N 23.
N183 **21** 5pa. violet . . . . 6·50 1·50
N184 10pa. green . . . . . . 22·00 1·40
N185 20pa. red . . . . . . 4·75 1·00
N186 1pi. blue . . . . . . 12·50 1·50
N187 2pi. orange . . . . . . 45·00 3·00
N188 5pi. mauve . . . . . . 90·00 22·00

1901. Stamps of 1901 optd with Type N 23.
N189 **22** 5pa. brown 45 65
N190 10pa. green . . . . . . 2·25 4·50
N191 20pa. mauve . . . . . . 20·00 5·00
N192 1pi. blue . . . . . . 35·00 17·00
N193 2pi. blue . . . . . . 90·00 26·00
N194 5pi. brown . . . . . . £200 65·00

1905. Stamps of 1905 optd with Type N 23.
N222 **23** 5pa. brown 90 55
N223 10pa. green . . . . . . 20·00 1·75
N224 20pa. pink 90 60
N225 1pi. blue 90 60
N226 2pi. blue . . . . . . 48·00 8·50
N227 5pi. brown . . . . . . £120 13·00

1908. Stamps of 1908 optd with Type N 27.
N244 **25** 5pa. brown . . . . . . 10·00 35
N245 10pa. green . . . . . . 12·00 35
N246 20pa. red . . . . . . 12·00 35
N247 1pi. blue . . . . . . 65·00 1·50
N248 2pi. black . . . . . . £100 3·75
N249 5pi. purple . . . . . . £130 10·00

1909. Stamps of 1909 optd with Type N 27.
N276 **28** 5pa. brown . . . . . . 2·50 90
N277 10pa. green . . . . . . 5·00 2·25
N278 20pa. red . . . . . . 42·00 2·50
N279 1pi. blue . . . . . . 75·00 8·50
N280 2pi. black . . . . . . £190 48·00
N281 5pi. purple . . . . . . £350 75·00

1911. New value of 1909 issue.
N332 **28** 2pa. olive 90 90

1920. No. 500 surch.
N961 5 on 4pa. brown 90 50

TURKMENISTAN Pt. 10

Formerly a constituent republic of the Soviet Union, Turkmenistan became independent on 27 October 1991.

1992. 100 kopeks = 1 rouble.
1994. 100 tenge = 1 manat.

1 19th-century Gold and Jewelled Bib  **2** Asiatic Wild Ass

1992. Treasure in National Museum.
1 **1** 50k. multicoloured 10 10
See also No. 4.

1992. Animals of Central Asia. Multicoloured.
2 20k. Type **2** 10 10
3 40k. Cobra (vert) 10 10

3 President Saparmyrat Niyazov and Reverse of National Flag

1992. History and Culture.
4 10r. Type **1** 35 20
5 10r. Girl in traditional dress and Kopet-Daga Mountains 35 20
6 10r. Mollanepes Drama Theatre, Ashkhabad 35 20
7 10r. Akhaltekin horseman (vert) 35 20
8 15r. Arms (vert) 50 30
9 25r. Type **3** 75 50
MS10 111 × 79 mm. 10r. Map of Turkmenistan. Imperf . . . . 1·50 1·50
For similar design to Type **3** but with flag reversed, see No. 12.

4 Traditional Musical Instruments

1992.
11 **4** 35k. multicoloured 15 10

5 National Flag and President Saparmyrat Niyazov

1992. 1st Anniv of Independence.
12 **5** 25r. multicoloured . . . . . 1·00 65
For similar design but with flag reversed, see No 9.

6 Carpet

1992.
13 **6** 1r. multicoloured 15 10

1992. Nos. 7/8 optd with horse's head.
14 10r. multicoloured 25 15
15 15r. multicoloured 60 40

8 Weightlifting

1993. Olympic Games, Barcelona. Multicoloured.
16 1r. Type **8** 10 10
17 3r. Show jumping 25 15
18 5r. Wrestling 40 30
19 10r. Canoeing . . . . 1·00 60
20 15r. National Olympic emblem 1·50 80
MS21 108 × 82 mm. 15r. Flags and sports pictograms. Imperf . . . 1·50 1·50

9 Presidents William Clinton and Niyazov

1993. Visit of President Saparmyrat Niyazov to United States of America. Type **9** with different dates. Multicoloured.
22 **9** 100r. Dated "21.03.93" . . . 45 30
23 100r. Dated "22.03.93" . . . 45 30
24 100r. Dated "23.03.93" . . . 45 30
25 100r. Dated "24.03.93" . . . 45 30
26 100r. Dated "25.03.93" . . . 45 30

1993. Nos. 16/20 surch.
27 10r. on 3r. Show jumping . . 10 10
28 15r. on 5r. Wrestling 25 15
29 15r. on 10r. Canoeing 40 30
30 25r. on 1r. Type **8** . . . . . 1·00 60
31 50r. on 15r. National Olympic emblem . . . . 1·50 80

11 Seal on Ice

1993. The Caspian Seal. Multicoloured.
32 15r. Type **11** 10 10
33 25r. Seal on sandy beach . . . 15 10
34 50r. Seal on pebble beach . . 25 15
35 100r. Adult with young . . . 50 35
36 150r. Seal swimming . . . . . 1·00 75
37 500r. Seal on sandy beach (different) . . . . 2·75 1·75
Nos. 33 and 37 were issued together, se-tenant, forming a composite design.

12 Sulphur Spring, Cheleken

1994. 115th Anniv of Nobel Partnership to Exploit Black Sea Oil. Multicoloured.
38 1m. Type **12** 20 10
39 1m.50 "Turkmen" (oil tanker) 30 20
40 2m. Drilling in Cheleken . . . 40 30
41 3m. Nobel brothers and Petr Bilderling (partners) (vert) 65 40
MS42 93 × 68 mm. 5m. Statue and oil derricks . . . . 1·25 1·25

13 Repetek Institute

1994. Repetek Nature Reserve. Multicoloured.
43 3m. Type **13** 15 10
44 5m. Dromedaries in Repetek Desert 20 15
45 5m. Saw-scaled viper 20 15
46 10m. Transcaspian desert monitor 45 30
47 20m. Tortoise 95 75
MS48 86 × 69 mm. 10m. *Haloxylon amodendron* 60 60

14 National Olympic Committee Emblem

1994. Centenary of International Olympic Committee.
49 **14** 11m.25 multicoloured . . . 70 50
MS50 106 × 76 mm. **14** 20m. multicoloured . . . . 1·40 1·40

15 Aral Trout (*Salmo trutta aralensis*)

1996. "Save the Aral Sea". Sheet 128 × 108 mm containing T **15** and similar horiz designs. Multicoloured.
MS51 100m. Caracal (*Felis caracal*); 100m. Type **15**; 100m. Striped hyena; (*Hyaena hyaena*); 100m. Kaufmann's shovelnose (*Pseudoscaphirhynchus Kaufmann*); 100m. Pike asp (*Aspiolucius esocinus*) . . . . 2·50 2·50

16 Diesel Train

1996. 5th Anniv of Independence. Multicoloured.
52 100m. Type **16** (inauguration of Turkmenistan–Iran railway) 15 10
53 100m. Turkmenistan highlighted on globe (vert) 15 10
54 300m. Presidents Rafsanjani of Iran, Niyazov of Turkmenistan and Demirel of Turkey (opening of Turkmenistan–Iran–Turkey gas pipeline) 45 30
55 300m. Saparmyrat International Airport, Ashgabat (vert) 45 30
56 500m. Boutros Boutros-Ghali (United Nations Secretary General) and President Saparmyrat Niyazov (vert) 75 50
57 1000m. National flag and arms 1·40 1·00

17 Judo

1997. Olympic Games, Atlanta, U.S.A. Mult.
58 100m. Type **17** 25 15
59 300m. Athletics 80 60
60 300m. Greco-Roman wrestling 80 60
61 300m. Boxing 80 60
62 500m. Shooting . . . . 1·25 90
MS63 86 × 105 mm. 1000m. Olympic torch . . . . 2·50 2·50

18 Woman in Red Dress and Blue Shawl

19 American Kestrel

1999. National Costumes. Multicoloured.
64 500m. Type **18** 20 10
65 1000m. Woman in red dress 35 25
66 1200m. Woman in pink dress 40 30
67 2500m. Woman in red dress and embroidered shawl . . 90 65
68 3000m. Woman in green dress 1·25 90

1999. Birds of Prey. Multicoloured.
69 1000m. Type **19** 40 30
70 1000m. Peregrine falcon "Falco peregrinus" facing left 40 30
71 1000m. Peregrine falcon facing right 40 30
72 2500m. Common kestrel on branch . . . . 1·00 75
73 3000m. Peregrine falcon on branch . . . . 1·40 1·10
Nos. 69/73 were issued together, se-tenant, with the backgrounds forming a composite design.

TURKS ISLANDS Pt. 1

A group of islands in the Br. W. Indies, S.E. of the Bahamas, now grouped with the Caicos Islands and using the stamps of Turks and Caicos Islands. A dependency of Jamaica until August 1962, when it became a Crown Colony.

12 pence = 1 shilling.

1

1867.
55 **1** 1d. brown . . . . 70·00 30·00
63 1d. red . . . . 3·00 3·00
2 6d. black . . . . 95·00 £120
59 6d. brown . . . . 3·00 3·50
3 1s. blue . . . . 90·00 60·00
6 1s. lilac £5000 £2000
60 1s. brown . . . . 4·50 3·25
52 1s. green £160 £120

1881. Surch with large figures.
17 **1** ½ on 1d. red . . . . 50·00 £110
8 ½ on 6d. black . . . . 70·00 £100
9 ½ on 1s. blue . . . . 95·00 £160
19 ½ on 1s. lilac . . . . 90·00 £170
34 2½ on 1d. red £650
28 2½ on 6d. black £150 £300
36 2½ on 1s. lilac £550 £700
38 2½ on 1s. blue £750
47 4 on 1d. red £750 £475
43 4 on 6d. black . . . . 75·00 £100
45 4 on 1s. lilac £400 £550

31

34

1881.
70 **31** ½d. green . . . . 2·75 2·00
56 2½d. brown . . . . 22·00 11·00
65 2½d. blue . . . . 3·00 2·75
50 4d. blue . . . . £130 60·00
57 4d. grey . . . . 19·00 2·75
71 4d. purple and blue . . . . 11·00 14·00
72 **34** 5d. olive and red . . . . . 4·75 14·00

1889. Surch **One Penny.**
61 **31** 1d. on 2½d. brown . . . . 8·00 10·00

1893. Surch **½d.** and bar.
68 **31** ½d. on 4d. grey £140 £170

TURKS AND CAICOS ISLANDS Pt. 1

(See TURKS ISLANDS)

1900. 12 pence = 1 shilling; 20 shillings = 1 pound.
1969. 100 cents = 1 dollar.

35 Badge of the Islands

36

1900.
110 **35** ½d. green . . . . 5·00 15
102 1d. red . . . . 3·50 75
103 2d. brown . . . . 1·00 1·25
104a 2½d. blue . . . . 1·75 1·00
112 3d. purple on yellow . . . 2·25 6·00
105 4d. orange . . . . 3·75 7·00
106 6d. mauve . . . . 2·50 6·50
107 1s. brown . . . . 3·25 18·00
108 **36** 2s. purple . . . . 40·00 55·00
109 3s. red . . . . 55·00 75·00

37 Turk's-head Cactus

38

1909.
115 **37** ¼d. mauve . . . . 1·75 1·00
116 ¼d. red 60 40
162 ¼d. black . . . . 80 1·00
117 **38** ½d. green 75 40
118 1d. red . . . . 1·25 40
119 2d. grey . . . . 2·75 1·40
120 2½d. blue . . . . 3·25 3·75
121 3d. purple on yellow . . . 2·50 2·00
122 4d. red on yellow . . . . 3·25 7·00
123 6d. purple . . . . 7·00 6·00
124 1s. black on green . . . . 7·00 8·50
125 2s. red and green . . . . . 32·00 48·00
126 3s. black on red . . . . . 32·00 40·00

39

1913.
129 **39** ½d. green . . . . 50 1·75
130a 1d. red . . . . 1·10 2·00
131 2d. grey . . . . 2·25 3·50
132 2½d. blue . . . . 2·25 3·00
133d 3d. purple on yellow . . . 2·25 8·50
134a 4d. red on yellow . . . . 1·60 7·50
135 5d. green . . . . 6·50 22·00
136 6d. purple . . . . 2·50 3·50
137 1s. orange . . . . 1·50 5·00
138 2s. red on green . . . . . 7·50 26·00
139 3s. black on red . . . . . 15·00 26·00

1917. Optd **WAR TAX** in one line.
143 **39** 1d. red . . . . 10 1·25
144 3d. purple on yellow . . . 60 1·75

1918. Optd **WAR TAX** in two lines.
150 **39** 1d. red . . . . 10 1·00
148 3d. purple on yellow . . . 10 2·25

44 45

1922. Inscr "POSTAGE".
163 **44** ½d. green . . . . 2·00 3·00
164 1d. brown . . . . 50 3·25
165 1½d. red . . . . 6·50 15·00
166 3d. grey . . . . 50 5·00
167 2½d. purple on yellow . . . 50 1·75
168 3d. blue . . . . 50 5·00
169 4d. red on yellow . . . . 1·25 16·00
170 5d. green . . . . 85 22·00
171 6d. purple . . . . 70 5·50
172 1s. orange . . . . 80 18·00
173 2s. red on green . . . . 2·00 9·00
175 3s. black on red . . . . 5·00 27·00

1928. Inscr "POSTAGE & REVENUE".
176 **45** ½d. green 75 50
177 1d. brown 75 70
178 1½d. red . . . . 75 3·25
179 2d. grey 75 50
180 2½d. purple on yellow . . . 75 5·00
181 3d. blue . . . . 75 6·50
182 6d. purple . . . . 75 7·50
183 1s. orange . . . . 3·75 7·50
184 2s. red on green . . . . 6·00 35·00
185 5s. green on yellow . . . 11·00 35·00
186 10s. purple on blue . . . . 50·00 £100

1935. Silver Jubilee. As T **32a** of St. Helena.
187 ½d. black and green 30 75
188 3d. brown and blue . . . . 2·75 4·50
189 6d. blue and green . . . . . 1·75 4·75
190 1s. grey and purple . . . . . 1·75 3·25

1937. Coronation. As T **32b/c** of St. Helena.
191 ½d. green 10 10
192 2d. grey 65 50
193 3d. blue 65 50

46 Raking Salt **47** Salt Industry

1938.
194 **46** ½d. black 20 10
195a ½d. green . . . . 1·50 70
196 1d. brown 75 10
197 1½d. red 75 15
198 2d. grey . . . . 1·00 30
199a 2½d. orange . . . . 2·25 1·75
200 3d. blue 70 30
201 6d. mauve . . . . 16·00 2·25
201a 6d. sepia 50 20
202 1s. bistre . . . . 4·75 9·00
202a 1s. olive 50 20
203a **47** 2s. red . . . . 17·00 18·00
204a 5s. green . . . . 35·00 22·00
205 10s. violet . . . . 12·00 7·50

1946. Victory. As T **33a** of St. Helena.
206 2d. grey 10 10
207 3d. blue 15 10

1948. Silver Wedding. As T **33b/c** of St. Helena.
208 1d. brown 15 10
209 10s. violet . . . . 8·00 11·00

50 Badge of the Islands

51 Blue Ensign bearing Dependency Badge

1948. Centenary of Dependency's Separation from the Bahamas.
210 **50** ½d. green . . . . 1·25 15
211 2d. red . . . . 1·25 15
212 **51** 3d. blue . . . . 1·75 15
213 – 6d. violet . . . . 1·00 30
214 – 2s. black and blue . . . . 1·25 1·00
215 – 5s. black and green . . . 1·50 4·25
216 – 10s. black and brown . . . 1·50 4·25
DESIGNS—HORIZ: 6d. Map of Turks and Caicos Is; 2, 5, 10s. Queen Victoria and King George VI.

1949. 75th Anniv of U.P.U. As T **33d/g** of St. Helena.
217 2½d. orange . . . . 20 1·60
218 3d. blue . . . . 2·00 60
219 6d. brown 20 75
220 1s. olive 20 35

65 Bulk Salt Loading

66 Dependency's Badge

1950.
221 **65** ½d. green 85 40
222 – 1d. brown 80 75
223 – 1½d. red . . . . 1·25 55
224 – 2d. orange . . . . 1·00 40
225 – 2½d. olive . . . . 1·25 50
226 – 3d. blue 60 40
227 – 4d. black and pink . . . . 2·75 70
228 – 6d. black and blue . . . . 2·00 50
229 – 1s. black and turquoise . . 1·00 40
230 – 1s.6d. black and red . . . 8·50 3·25
231 – 2s. green and blue . . . . 3·00 4·50
232 – 5s. blue and black . . . 18·00 8·50
233 **66** 10s. black and violet . . . 18·00 18·00
DESIGNS—As Type **65**: 1d. Salt Cay; 1½d. Caicos mail; 2d. Grand Turk; 2½d. Diving for sponges; 3d. South Creek; 4d. Map; 6d. Grand Turk Light; 1s. Government House; 1s.6d. Cockburn Harbour; 2s. Govt Offices; 5s. Loading salt.

1953. Coronation. As T **33h** of St. Helena.
234 2d. black and orange . . . . 30 1·25

1955. As 1950 but with portrait of Queen Elizabeth II.
235 5d. black and green 60 70
236 8d. black and brown . . . . 2·50 70
DESIGNS—HORIZ—As Type **65**: 5d. M.V. "Kirksons"; 8d. Greater flamingos in flight.

69 Queen Elizabeth II (after Annigoni)

70 Bonefish

1957.
237 **69** 1d. blue and red 30 20
238 **70** 1½d. grey and orange . . . 15 30
239 – 2d. brown and olive . . . 15 15
240 – 2½d. red and green 20 15
241 – 3d. turquoise and purple 20 15
242 – 4d. lake and black . . . 1·25 15
243 – 5d. green and brown . . . 1·25 40
244 – 6d. red and blue . . . . 2·00 55
245 – 8d. red and black . . . . 3·25 20
246 – 1s. blue and black . . . . 1·25 10
247 – 1s.6d. sepia and blue . . . 12·00 1·50
248 – 2s. blue and brown . . . . 12·00 2·50
249 – 5s. black and red . . . . 5·50 2·00
250 – 10s. black and purple . . . 14·00 8·00
DESIGNS—As Type **70**: 2d. Red grouper; 2½d. Spiny lobster; 3d. Albacore; 4d. Mutton snapper; 5d. Permit; 6d. Queen or pink conch; 8d. Greater flamingoes; 1s. Spanish mackeral; 1s.6d. Salt Cay; 2s. "Uakon" (Caicos sloop); 5s. Cable Office. As Type **84**: 10s. Dependency's badge.

83 Map of the Turks and Caicos Is.

1959. New Constitution.
251 **83** 6d. olive and orange . . . 50 70
252 8d. violet and orange . . . 50 40

84 Brown Pelican

1960.
253 **84** £1 brown and red . . . . 40·00 16·00

1963. Freedom from Hunger. As T **63a** of St. Helena.
254 8d. red 30 15

1963. Cent of Red Cross. As T **63b** of St. Helena.
255 2d. red and black 15 50
256 8d. red and blue 30 50

1964. 400th Birth Anniv of Shakespeare. As T **45a** of St. Lucia.
257 8d. green 30 10

1965. Cent of I.T.U. As T **64a** of St. Helena.
258 1d. red and brown 10 10
259 2s. green and blue 20 20

1965. I.C.Y. As T **64b** of St. Helena.
260 1d. purple and turquoise . . 10 15
261 8d. green and blue 20 15

1966. Churchill Commemoration. As T **64c** of St. Helena.
262 1d. blue 10 10
263 2d. green 20 10
264 8d. brown 35 10
265 1s.6d. violet . . . . 50 1·00

1966. Royal Visit. As T **48a** of St. Kitts-Nevis.
266 8d. black and blue 40 10
267 1s.6d. black and mauve . . . 60 20

86 Andrew Symmer and Royal Warrant

1966. Bicent of "Ties with Britain".
268 – 1d. blue and orange . . . 10 10
269 **86** 8d. red, blue and yellow . . 20 15
270 – 1s.6d. multicoloured . . . 25 20
DESIGNS: 1d. Andrew Symmer going ashore; 1s.6d. Arms and Royal Cypher.

1966. 20th Anniv of UNESCO. As T **64f/h** of St. Helena.
271 1d. multicoloured 10 10
272 8d. yellow, violet and olive 20 10
273 1s.6d. black, purple and orange 30 40

88 Turk's-head Cactus

1967.
274 **88** 1d. yellow, red and violet 10 10
275 – 1½d. brown and yellow . . 1·00 10
276 – 2d. grey and yellow 20 10
277 – 3d. agate and green . . . 20 10
278 – 4d. mauve, black & turq 2·00 10
279 – 6d. brown and blue 40 10
280 – 8d. yellow, turquoise & blue 40 10
281 – 1s. purple and turquoise 20 10
282 – 1s.6d. yellow, brown & blue 50 20
283 – 2s. multicoloured . . . . 60 1·75
284 – 3s. mauve and blue 55 40
285 – 5s. ochre, blue and light blue . . . . 1·25 2·75
286 – 10s. multicoloured . . . . 1·75 3·00
287 – £1 blue, silver and red . . 3·00 6·50
DESIGNS—HORIZ: 1½d. Boat-building; 4d. Conch industry; 1s. Fishing; 2s. Crawfish industry; 3s. Maps of Turks and Caicos Islands and West Indies; 5s. Fishing industry; 10s. Arms of Turks and Caicos Islands. VERT: 2d. Donkey; 3d. Sisal industry; 6d. Salt industry; 8d. Skin-diving; 1s.6d. Water-skiing; £1 Queen Elizabeth II.

102 Turks Islands 1d. Stamp of 1867

1967. Stamp Centenary.
288 **102** 1d. black and mauve . . 15 10
289 – 6d. black and grey . . . 25 15
290 – 1s. black and blue 25 15
DESIGNS: 6d. Queen Elizabeth "stamp" and Turks Islands 6d. stamp of 1867; 1s. Turks Islands 1s. of 1867.

104 Human Rights Emblem and Charter

1968. Human Rights Year.
291 **104** 1d. multicoloured 10 10
292 8d. multicoloured 15 15
293 1s.6d. multicoloured . . . 15 15

105 Dr. Martin Luther King and "Freedom March"

1968. Martin Luther King. Commem.
294 **105** 2d. brown and blue . . . 10 10
295 8d. brown and lake . . . 15 15
296 1s.6d. brown and violet 15 15

1969. Decimal Currency. Nos. 274/87 surch, and new value in old design (¼c.).
297 ¼c. multicoloured (as No. 286) 10 10
298 1c. on 1d. yellow, red & violet 10 10
299 2c. on 2d. grey and yellow 10 10
300 3c. on 3d. agate and green 10 10
301 4c. on 4d. mauve, blk & turq . . . . 1·50 10
302 5c. on 6d. brown and blue 10 10
303 7c. on 8d. yellow, turq & bl 10 10
304 8c. on 1½d. brown and yellow 10 10
305 10c. on 1s. purple & turquoise 20 10
306 15c. on 1s.6d. yell, brn & bl 25 10
307 20c. on 2s. multicoloured . . 30 25
308 30c. on 3s. mauve and blue 55 35
309 50c. on 5s. ochre, blue & lt bl . . . . 1·25 45
310 $1 on 10s. multicoloured . . 2·50 1·00
311a $2 on £1 blue, silver and red 2·00 3·25

107 "The Nativity with John the Baptist"

109 Coat of Arms

1969. Christmas. Scenes from 16th-century "Book of Hours". Multicoloured.
312 1c. Type **107** 10 10
313 3c. "The Flight into Egypt" 10 10
314 15c. Type **107** 15 10
315 30c. As 3c. 25 20

1970. New Constitution.
316 **109** 7c. multicoloured 20 25
317 35c. multicoloured 35 25
For similar $10 design but without commemorative inscription, see No. 946.

110 "Christ bearing the Cross"

1970. Easter. Details from the "Small Engraved Passion" by Durer.
318 **110** 5c. grey and blue 10 10
319 – 7c. grey and red 10 10
320 – 50c. grey and brown . . . 50 90
DESIGNS: 7c. "Christ on the Cross" ; 50c. "The Lamentation of Christ".

113 Dickens and Scene from "Oliver Twist"

1970. Death Cent of Charles Dickens.
321 **113** 1c. black & blue on yellow 10 50
322 – 3c. black and blue on flesh 10 40
323 – 15c. black & blue on flesh 20 20
324 – 30c. black & drab on blue 40 40

DESIGNS (showing Dickens and scene): 3c. "A Christmas Carol"; 15c. "Pickwick Papers"; 30c. "The Old Curiosity Shop".

114 Ambulance, 1870

1970. Cent of British Red Cross. Mult.
325 1c. Type **114** 10 20
326 5c. Ambulance, 1970 . . . . 20 10
327 15c. Type **114** 40 15
328 30c. As 5c. 50 20

115 Duke of Albemarle and Coat-of-Arms

1970. Tercentenary of Issue of Letters Patent. Multicoloured.
329 1c. Type **115** 10 30
330 8c. Arms of Charles II and Elizabeth II 20 40
331 10c. Type **115** 20 15
332 35c. As 8c. 40 75

116 Boat-building

1971. Designs as Nos. 274/87 but values in decimal currency as T **116**.
333 **88** 1c. yellow, red and violet 10 10
334 – 2c. grey and yellow (as No. 276) 10 10
335 – 3c. agate and green (as No. 277) 15 10
336 – 4c. mauve, black and turquoise (as No. 278) 1·25 10
337 – 5c. brown and blue (as No. 279) 40 10
338 – 7c. yellow, turquoise and blue (as No. 280) . . . 30 10
339 **116** 8c. brown and yellow . . 1·25 10
340 – 10c. purple and turquoise (as No. 281) 75 10
341 – 15c. yellow, brown and blue (as No. 282) . . . 1·00 65
342 – 20c. mult (as No. 283) . . 1·50 3·25
343 – 30c. purple and blue (as No. 284) . . . . 2·00 1·25
344 – 50c. ochre, blue and light blue (as No. 285) . . . 3·00 2·00
345 – $1 mult (as No. 286) . . . 3·00 3·00
346 – $2 blue, silver and red (as No. 287) . . . . 4·00 8·00

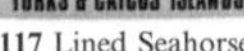

117 Lined Seahorse

119 The Wilton Diptych (Left Wing)

118 Pirate Sloop

1971. Tourist Development. Multicoloured.
347 1c. Type **117** 10 10
348 3c. Queen or pink conch shell 15 10
349 15c. Oystercatcher (horiz) . . 50 20
350 30c. Sailfish ("Blue marlin") (horiz) 35 25

1971. Pirates. Multicoloured.
351 2c. Type **118** 10 10
352 3c. Pirate treasure 10 10
353 15c. Marooned sailor 45 15
354 30c. Buccaneers 70 45

1971. Christmas. Multicoloured.
355 2c. Type **119** 10 10
356 2c. The Wilton Diptych (Right Wing) 10 10
357 8c. Type **119** 10 10
358 8c. As No. 356 . . . . . . 10 10
359 15c. Type **119** 20 10
360 15c. As No. 356 . . . . . . 20 10

120 Cape Kennedy Launching Area

1972. 10th Anniv of Colonel Glenn's Splashdown. Multicoloured.
361 5c. Type **120** 10 10
362 10c. "Friendship 7" space capsule 10 10
363 15c. Map of Islands and splashdown 15 10
364 20c. N.A.S.A. space medal (vert) 15 10

121 "Christ before Pilate" (Rembrandt)

122 Christopher Columbus

1972. Easter.
365 **121** 2c. black and lilac 10 10
366 – 15c. black and pink . . . 20 10
367 – 30c. black and yellow . . 30 15
DESIGNS—HORIZ: 15c. "The Three Crosses" (Rembrandt). VERT: 30c. "The Descent from the Cross" (Rembrandt).

1972. Discoverers and Explorers. Mult.
368 ¼c. Type **122** 20 75
369 8c. Sir Richard Grenville (horiz) . . . . 1·00 30
370 10c. Capt. John Smith . . . 1·00 10
371 30c. Juan Ponce de Leon (horiz) . . . . 1·75 90

1972. Royal Silver Wedding. As T **103** of St. Helena, but with Turk's-head cactus and spiny lobster in background.
372 10c. blue 15 10
373 20c. green 15 10

124 Treasure Hunting, c. 1700

126 Sooty Tern

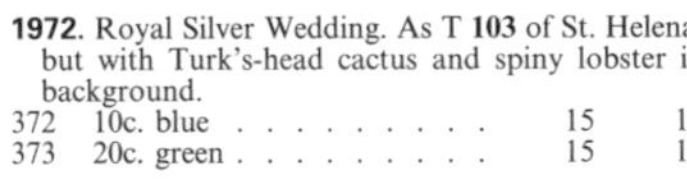

125 Arms of Jamaica and Turks and Caicos Islands

1973. Treasure.
374 **124** 3c. multicoloured 10 10
375 – 5c. purple, silver and black 10 10
376 – 10c. purple, silver & black 20 10
377 – 30c. multicoloured . . . 60 30
MS378 127 × 108 mm. Nos. 374/7 1·10 2·25
DESIGNS: 5c. Silver Bank medallion (obverse); 10c. Silver Bank medallion (reverse); 30c. Treasure hunting, 1973.

1973. Centenary of Annexation by Jamaica.
379 **125** 15c. multicoloured 25 10
380 35c. multicoloured 45 20

1973.
381 ¼c. Type **126** 10 40
382 1c. Magnificent frigate bird 30 60
383 2c. Common noddy 30 60
384 3c. Blue-grey gnatcatcher . . 85 50
385 4c. Little blue heron . . . . 35 1·50
386 5c. Catbird 30 30
387 7c. Black-whiskered vireo . . 4·50 30
388 8c. Osprey . . . . 5·00 3·25
389 10c. Greater flamingo . . . . 70 1·25
390 15c. Brown pelican . . . . . 1·25 50
459 20c. Parula warbler . . . . . 1·50 75
392 30c. Northern mockingbird 1·75 90
461 50c. Ruby-throated hummingbird . . . . . . 1·50 2·25
462 $1 Bananaquit . . . . 2·50 2·75
463 $2 Cedar waxwing . . . . . 6·00 4·50
464 $5 Painted bunting . . . . . 1·75 2·25

127 Bermuda Sloop

1973. Vessels. Multicoloured.
396 2c. Type **127** . . . . 15 1·00
397 5c. H.M.S. "Blanche" (screw sloop) 20 10
398 8c. "Grand Turk" (American privateer) and "Hinchinbrook II" (British packet), 1813 . . . . . . 25 1·00
399 10c. H.M.S. "Endymion" (frigate), 1790 . . . . . . 25 15
400 15c. "Medina" (paddle-steamer) 25 80
401 20c. H.M.S. "Daring" (brig), 1804 . . . . 30 1·25
MS402 198 × 101 mm. Nos. 296/401 1·25 3·00

1973. Royal Wedding. As T **103a** of St. Helena.
403 12c. blue 10 10
404 18c. blue 10 10

128 Duho (stool)

1974. Lucayan Remains. Multicoloured.
405 6c. Type **128** 10 10
406 10c. Broken wood bowl . . . 15 10
407 12c. Greenstone axe 15 10
408 18c. Wood bowl 15 10
409 35c. Fragment of duho . . . 20 20
MS410 240 × 90 mm. Nos. 405/9 1·10 1·75

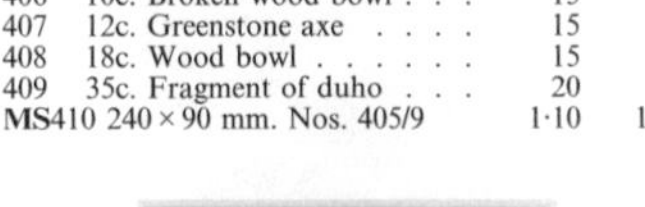

129 G.P.O., Grand Turk

1974. Centenary of U.P.U. Multicoloured.
426 4c. Type **129** 10 10
427 12c. Sloop and island map 20 10
428 18c. "U.P.U." and globe . . 20 10
429 55c. Posthorn and emblem 35 35

130 Churchill and Roosevelt

1974. Birth Cent of Sir Winston Churchill. Mult.
430 12c. Type **130** 15 15
431 18c. Churchill and vapour-trails 15 15
MS432 85 × 85 mm. Nos. 430/1 40 45

131 Spanish Captain circa 1492

132 Ancient Windmill Salt Cay

1975. Military Uniforms. Multicoloured.
433 5c. Type **131** 10 10
434 20c. Officer, Royal Artillery, 1783 . . . . 20 15
435 25c. Officer, 67th Foot, 1798 25 15
436 35c. Private, 1st West India Regiment, 1833 . . . . . 35 25
MS437 145 × 88 mm. Nos. 433/6 1·00 2·00

1975. Salt-raking Industry. Multicoloured.
438 6c. Type **132** 15 10
439 10c. Salt pans drying in sun (horiz) 15 10
440 20c. Salt-raking (horiz) . . . 25 25
441 25c. Unprocessed salt heaps 30 30

133 Star Coral

1975. Island Coral. Multicoloured.
442 6c. Type **133** 15 10
443 10c. Elkhorn coral 20 10
444 20c. Brain coral 35 15
445 25c. Staghorn coral 40 20

134 American Schooner

136 "The Virgin and Child with Flowers" (C. Dolci)

135 1s.6d. Royal Visit Stamp of 1966

1976. Bicent of American Revolution. Mult.
446 6c. Type **134** 25 15
447 20c. British ship of the line 30 20
448 25c. American privateer "Grand Turk" 30 25
449 55c. British ketch 40 65
MS450 95 × 151 mm. Nos. 446/9 1·00 4·00

1976. 10th Anniv of Royal Visit. Mult.
466 20c. Type **135** 30 30
467 25c. 8d. Royal Visit stamp 40 30

1976. Christmas. Multicoloured.
468 6c. Type **136** 10 10
469 10c. "Virgin and Child" with St. John and an Angel" (Studio of Botticelli) . . . 10 10
470 20c. "Adoration of the Magi" (Master of Paraiso) 30 15
471 25c. "Adoration of the Magi" (French miniature) 30 20

137 Balcony Scene, Buckingham Palace

139 "Flight of the Holy Family" (Rubens)

138 Col. Glenn's "Mercury" Capsule

1977. Silver Jubilee. Multicoloured.
472 6c. Queen presenting O.B.E. to E. T. Wood 10 10
473 25c. Queen with regalia . . . 15 20
474 55c. Type **137** 30 45
MS475 120 × 97 mm. $5 Queen Elizabeth II . . . . 1·00 80

1977. 25th Anniv of U.S. Tracking Station. Multicoloured.
476 1c. Type **138** 10 10
477 3c. Moon buggy "Rover" (vert) 10 10
478 6c. Tracking Station, Grand Turk 10 10
479 20c. Moon landing craft (vert) 15 15

480 25c. Col. Glenn's rocket launch (vert) 20 20
481 50c. "Telstar 1" satellite . . . 30 40

1977. Christmas. 400th Birth Anniv of Rubens. Multicoloured.
482 ½c. Type **139** 10 10
483 ½c. "Adoration of the Magi" (1634) 10 10
484 1c. "Adoration of the Magi" (1624) 10 10
485 6c. "Virgin within Garland" 10 10
486 20c. "Madonna and Child Adored by Angels" 15 10
487 $2 "Adoration of the Magi" (1618) . . . . 1·25 1·25
MS488 100 × 81 mm. $1 detail of 20c. . . . . 1·00 1·40

140 Map of Passage

1978. Turks Islands Passage. Multicoloured.
489A 6c. Type **140** 15 20
490A 20c. Caicos sloop passing Grand Turk Lighthouse 45 75
491A 25c. Motor cruiser 45 85
492A 55c. "Jamaica Planter" (freighter) . . . . 95 2·25
MS493A 136 × 88 mm. Nos. 489A/92A . . . . 1·10 2·75

141 "Queen Victoria" (Sir George Hayter) **142** Ampulla and Anointing Spoon

1978. 25th Anniv of Coronation. Multicoloured.
(a) Monarchs in Coronation robes.
494 6c. Type **141** 10 10
495 10c. "King Edward VII" (Sir Samuel Fildes) 10 10
496 25c. King George V 20 10
497 $2 King George VI 50 70
MS498 161 × 113 mm. $2.50 Queen Elizabeth II 75 75
(b) Coronation regalia. Self-adhesive.
499 15c. Type **142** 15 30
500 25c. St. Edward's Crown . . 15 30
501 $2 Queen Elizabeth II in Coronation robes . . . . 1·00 2·50

143 Wilbur Wright and Wright Type A

1978. 75th Anniv of Powered Flight. Mult.
502 1c. Type **143** 10 10
503 6c. Wright brothers and Cessna 337 Super Skymaster 10 10
504 10c. Orville Wright and Lockheed L.188 Electra . . 10 10
505 15c. Wilbur Wright and Douglas C-47 Skytrain . . 15 15
506 35c. Wilbur Wright and Britten Norman Islander 35 35
507 $2 Wilbur Wright and Wright Type A . . . . 1·00 2·00
MS508 111 × 84 mm. $1 Orville Wright and Wright glider No. III 60 1·60
No. 502 is inscr "FLYER III" in error.

144 Hurdling

1978. 11th Commonwealth Games, Edmonton. Multicoloured.
509 6c. Type **144** 10 10
510 20c. Weightlifting 15 15
511 55c. Boxing 20 30
512 $2 Cycling . . . . 50 1·25
MS513 105 × 79 mm. $1 Sprinting 55 1·50

145 Indigo Hamlet

1978. Fishes. Multicoloured.
514A 1c. Type **145** 15 50
515A 2c. Tobacco fish 75 50
516A 3c. Bar jack 50 30
517A 4c. Porkfish 75 50
518A 5c. Spanish grunt 50 40
519A 7c. Yellow-tailed snapper 1·00 1·25
520A 8c. Four-eyed butterflyfish 1·00 15
521A 10c. Yellow-finned grouper 50 15
522A 15c. Beau Gregory . . . . 1·50 30
523A 20c. Queen angelfish . . . 50 30
524A 30c. Hogfish . . . . 1·75 40
525A 50c. Royal gramma ("Fairy basslet") . . . . 1·00 65
526A $1 Fin-spot wrasse . . . . 1·50 1·60
527A $2 Stoplight parrotfish . . 1·50 2·50
528A $5 Queen triggerfish . . . . 1·50 6·50
Some values exist both with or without imprint date at foot.

146 "Madonna of the Siskin"

1978. Christmas. Paintings by Durer. Mult.
529 6c. Type **146** 15 10
530 20c. "The Virgin and Child with St. Anne" 20 15
531 35c. "Paumgartner Nativity" (horiz) 35 15
532 $2 "Praying Hands" . . . 85 1·40
MS533 137 × 124 mm. $1 "Adoration of The Magi" (horiz) 2·25 3·25

147 Osprey

1979. Endangered Wildlife. Multicoloured.
534 6c. Type **147** 75 20
535 20c. Green turtle 65 20
536 25c. Queen or pink conch . . 75 25
537 55c. Rough-toothed dolphin 90 50
538 $1 Humpback whale . . . . 2·00 2·50
MS539 117 × 85 mm. $2 Iguana 2·50 4·25

148 "The Beloved" (painting by D. G. Rossetti)

1979. International Year of the Child. Multicoloured.
540 6c. Type **148** 10 10
541 25c. "Tahitian Girl" (P. Gauguin) 15 10
542 55c. "Calmady Children" (Sir Thomas Lawrence) 25 20
543 $1 "Mother and Daughter" (detail, P. Gauguin) . . . 45 45
MS544 112 × 85 mm. $2 "Marchesa Elena Grimalda" (A. van Dyck) 55 1·50

149 "Medina" (paddle-steamer) and Handstamped Cover

150 Cuneiform Script

1979. Death Centenary of Sir Rowland Hill.
(a) As T **149**. Multicoloured.
545 6c. Type **149** 10 10
546 20c. Sir Rowland Hill and map of Caribbean 15 15
547 45c. "Orinoco I" (mail paddle-steamer) and cover bearing Penny Black stamp 20 20
548 75c. "Shannon" (screw steamer) and letter to Grand Turk 30 30
549 $1 "Trent I" (paddle-steamer) and map of Caribbean . . 35 35
550 $2 Turks Islands 1867 and Turks and Caicos Islands 1900 1d. stamps . . . . . 3·50 4·00
MS551 170 × 113 mm. As No. 550 70 1·50
(b) As T **150**. Self-adhesive.
552 **150** 5c. black and green . . . 10 10
553 – 5c. black and green . . . 10 10
554 – 5c. black and green . . . 10 10
555 – 15c. black and blue . . . 20 20
556 – 15c. black and blue . . . 20 20
557 – 15c. black and blue . . . 20 20
558 – 25c. black and blue . . . 30 30
559 – 25c. black and blue . . . 60 45
560 – 25c. black and blue . . . 30 30
561 – 40c. black and red 45 45
562 – 40c. black and red 45 45
563 – 40c. black and red 45 45
564 – $1 black and yellow . . . 70 1·25
DESIGNS—HORIZ: No. 533, Egyptian papyrus; No. 554, Chinese paper; No. 555, Greek runner; No. 556, Roman post horse; No. 557, Roman post ship; No. 558, Pigeon post; No. 559, Railway post; No. 560, Packet paddle-steamer; No. 561, Balloon post; No. 562, First airmail; No. 563, Supersonic airmail. VERT: No. 564, Original stamp press.

1979. "Brasiliana 79" International Stamp Exhibition, Rio de Janeiro. No. MS551 optd **BRASILIAN 79**.
MS565 170 × 113 mm. $2 Turks Islands 1867 and Turks and Caicos Islands 1900 1d. stamps 65 1·50

152 "St. Nicholas", Prikra, Ukraine **153** Pluto and Starfish

1979. Christmas. Religious Art. Multicoloured.
566 1c. Type **152** 10 10
567 3c. "Emperor Otto II with Symbols of Empire" (Master of the Registrum Gregorii) 10 10
568 6c. "Portrait of St. John" (Book of Lindisfarne) . . . 10 10
569 15c. "Adoration of the Majestas Domini" (prayer book of Otto II) 10 10
570 20c. "Christ attended by Angels" (Book of Kells) . . 15 15
571 25c. "St. John the Evangelist" (Gospels of St. Medard of Soissons), Charlemagne 20 15
572 65c. "Christ Pantocrator", Trocany, Ukraine 30 35
573 $1 "Portrait of St. John" (Canterbury Codex Aureus) 45 60
MS574 106 × 133 mm. $2 "Portrait of St. Matthew" (Book of Lindisfarne) . . . . 70 1·50

1979. International Year of the Child. Walt Disney cartoon characters. At the Seaside. Multicoloured.
575 ¼c. Type **153** 10 10
576 ½c. Minnie Mouse in summer outfit 10 10
577 1c. Mickey Mouse underwater 10 10
578 2c. Goofy and turtle 10 10
579 3c. Donald Duck and dolphin 10 10
580 4c. Mickey Mouse fishing . . 10 10
581 5c. Goofy surfing 10 10
582 25c. Pluto and crab 45 20
583 $1 Daisy water-skiing . . . . 75 2·25
MS584 126 × 96 mm. $1.50 Goofy after water-skiing accident . . 1·00 1·60

154 "Christina's World" (painting by Andrew Wyeth)

1979. Works of Art. Multicoloured.
585 6c. Type **154** 10 10
586 10c. Ivory leopards, Benin (19th-cent) 10 10
587 20c. "The Kiss" (painting by Gustav Klimt) (vert) . . . 15 15
588 25c. "Portrait of a Lady" (painting by R. van der Weyden) (vert) 15 15
589 80c. Bull's head harp, Sumer, c. 2600 B.C. (vert) 20 30
590 $1 "The Wave" (painting by Hokusai) 25 50
MS591 110 × 140 mm. $2 "Holy Family" (painting by Rembrant) (vert) . . . . 70 1·25

155 Pied-billed Grebe

1980. Birds. Multicoloured.
592 20c. Type **155** 70 55
593 25c. Ovenbirds at nest . . . 75 55
594 35c. Hen harrier . . . . . . 1·00 60
595 55c. Yellow-bellied sapsucker 1·25 65
596 $1 Blue-winged teal . . . . . 1·50 3·00
MS597 107 × 81 mm. $2 Glossy ibis . . . . 2·75 2·25

156 Stamp, Magnifying Glass and Perforation Gauge

1980. "London 1980" Int Stamp Exhibition. Mult.
598 **156** 25c. black and yellow . . 15 15
599 – 40c. black and green . . 15 25
MS600 76 × 97 mm. $2 red, black and blue . . . . 70 1·10
DESIGN: 40c. Tweezers, stamp and perforation gauge; $2 Earls Court Exhibition Centre.

157 Atlantic Trumpet Triton

1980. Shells. Multicoloured.
601 14c. Type **157** 15 20
602 20c. Measled cowrie 15 25
603 30c. True tulip 20 35
604 45c. Lion's-paw scallop . . . 25 45
605 55c. Sunrise tellin 30 55
606 70c. Crown cone 35 70

158 Queen Elizabeth the Queen Mother

1980. 80th Birthday of The Queen Mother.
607 **158** 80c. multicoloured . . . . 50 1·40
MS608 57 × 80 mm. **158** $1.50 multicoloured . . . . 80 2·00

159 Doctor examining Child and Lions International Emblem

1980. "Serving the Community". Mult.
609 10c. Type **159** 15 10
610 15c. Students receiving scholarships and Kiwanis International emblem . . . 20 10
611 45c. Teacher with students and Soroptimist emblem 40 35
612 $1 Lobster trawler and Rotary International emblem 75 80
MS613 101 × 74 mm. $2 School receiving funds and Rotary International emblem . . . . 1·00 2·00
No. MS613 also commemorates the 75th anniv of Rotary International.

1980. Christmas. Scenes from Walt Disney's "Pinocchio". As T **153**. Multicoloured.

614 ¼c. Scene from "Pinocchio" 10 10
615 ½c. As puppet 10 10
616 1c. Pinocchio changed into a boy 10 10
617 2c. Captured by fox 10 10
618 3c. Pinocchio and puppeteer 10 10
619 4c. Pinocchio and bird's nest nose 10 10
620 5c. Pinocchio eating 10 10
621 75c. Pinocchio with ass ears 1·00 90
622 $1 Pinocchio underwater . . 1·25 1·00
MS623 127 × 102 mm. $2 Pinocchio dancing (vert) . . . . 2·50 2·50

160 Martin Luther King Jr

1980. Human Rights. Personalities. Mult.

624 20c. Type **160** 15 10
625 30c. John F. Kennedy . . . 30 25
626 45c. Roberto Clemente (baseball player) 45 35
627 70c. Sir Frank Worrel (cricketer) . . . . 2·00 1·50
628 $1 Harriet Tubman . . . . . 1·10 1·50
MS629 103 × 80 mm. $2 Marcus Garvey . . . . 1·10 1·25

161 Yachts

1980. South Caicos Regatta. Multicoloured.

630 6c. Type **161** 10 10
631 15c. Trophy and yachts . . . 15 15
632 35c. Spectators watching speedboat race 25 20
633 $1 Caicos sloops 60 65
MS634 113 × 85 mm. $2 Queen Elizabeth II and map of South Caicos (vert) . . . . 80 1·75

162 Night Queen Cactus

163 "Woman with Fan"

1981. Flowering Cacti. Multicoloured.

635 25c. Type **162** 20 25
636 35c. Ripsaw cactus 25 35
637 55c. Royal strawberry cactus 30 60
638 80c. Caicos cactus . . . . . 40 1·00
MS639 72 × 68 mm. $2 Turks head cactus . . . . 1·00 2·00

1981. 50th Anniv of Walt Disney's Pluto (cartoon character). As T **153**. Multicoloured.

640 10c. Pluto listening to queen or pink conch shell 10 10
641 75c. Pluto on raft and porpoise 50 90
MS642 127 × 101 mm. $1.50 Pluto in scene from film "Simple Things" 1·00 2·25

1981. Easter. Walt Disney Cartoon Characters. As T **153**. Multicoloured.

643 10c. Donald Duck and Louie 20 20
644 25c. Goofy and Donald Duck 25 40
645 60c. Chip and Dale . . . . . 30 1·00
646 80c. Scrooge McDuck and Huey . . . . 35 1·40
MS647 126 × 101 mm. $4 Chip (or Dale) . . . . 4·00 3·50

1981. Birth Centenary of Picasso. Mult.

648 20c. Type **163** 15 15
649 45c. "Woman with Pears" . . 20 15
650 80c. "The Accordionist" . . 30 40
651 $1 "The Aficionado" 45 60
MS652 102 × 127 mm. $2 "Girl with a Mandolin" . . . . 1·00 1·00

164 Kensington Palace **165** Lady Diana Spencer

1981. Royal Wedding. Multicoloured.

653 35c. Prince Charles and Lady Diana Spencer 15 10
654 65c. Type **164** 20 20
655 90c. Prince Charles as Colonel of the Welsh Guards 25 30
MS656 90 × 82 mm. $2 Glass Coach 50 55

1981. Royal Wedding. Multicoloured. Self-adhesive.

657 20c. Type **165** 25 30
658 $1 Prince Charles 35 70
659 $2 Prince Charles and Lady Diana Spencer . . . . . . 1·10 2·25

166 Marine Biology Observation

1981. Diving. Multicoloured.

660 15c. Type **166** 20 15
661 40c. Underwater photography 35 35
662 75c. Wreck diving 60 70
663 $1 Diving with dolphins . . . 80 1·00
MS664 91 × 75 mm. $2 Diving flag 1·75 2·25

1981. Christmas. As T **153** showing scenes from Walt Disney's cartoon film "Uncle Remus".

665 ¼c. multicoloured 10 10
666 ½c. multicoloured 10 10
667 1c. multicoloured 10 10
668 2c. multicoloured 10 10
669 3c. multicoloured 10 10
670 4c. multicoloured 10 10
671 5c. multicoloured 10 10
672 75c. multicoloured . . . . . 1·00 80
673 $1 multicoloured . . . . . . 1·25 1·00
MS674 128 × 103 mm. multicoloured 1·75 2·25

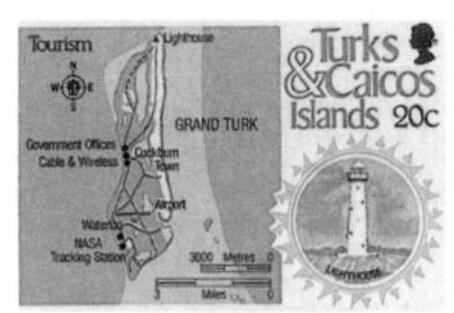

167 Map of Grand Turk, and Lighthouse

1981. Tourism. Multicoloured.

675 20c. Type **167** 60 50
676 20c. Map of Salt Cay, and "industrial archaeology" 60 50
677 20c. Map of South Caicos, and "island flying" 60 50
678 20c. Map of East Caicos, and "beach combing" 60 50
679 20c. Map of Central Grand Caicos, and cave exploring 60 50
680 20c. Map of North Caicos and camping and hiking 60 50
681 20c. Map of North Caicos, Parrot Cay, Dellis Cay, Fort George Cay, Pine Cay and Water Cay, and "environmental studies" . . 60 50
682 20c. Map of Providenciales, and scuba diving 60 50
683 20c. Map of West Caicos, and "cruising and bird sanctuary" 60 50
684 20c. Turks and Caicos Islands flag 60 50

168 "Junonia evarete" **169** Flag Salute on Queen's Birthday

1982. Butterflies. Multicoloured.

685 20c. Type **168** 30 30
686 35c. "Strymon maesites" . . 45 55
687 65c. "Agraulis vanillae" . . . 70 1·25
688 $1 "Eurema dina" . . . . . 1·00 2·00
MS689 72 × 56 mm. $2 "Anaea intermedia" . . . . 2·50 3·75

1982. 75th Anniv of Boy Scout Movement. Multicoloured.

690 40c. Type **169** 50 50
691 50c. Raft building 60 60
692 75c. Sea scout cricket match 1·10 1·60
693 $1 Nature study . . . . . . 1·50 1·75
MS694 100 × 70 mm. $2 Lord Baden-Powell and scout salute 1·50 3·00

170 Footballer **171** Washington crossing the Delaware and Phillis Wheatley (poetess)

1982. World Cup Football Championship, Spain.

695 **170** 10c. multicoloured 15 15
696 – 25c. multicoloured 20 20
697 – 45c. multicoloured 25 25
698 – $1 multicoloured 80 80
MS699 117 × 83 mm. $2 multicoloured . . . . 1·25 2·00

DESIGNS: 25c. to $2, Various footballers.

1982. 250th Birth Anniv of George Washington and Birth Centenary of Franklin D. Roosevelt.

700 20c. Type **171** 20 30
701 35c. George Washington and Benjamin Banneker (surveyor) 30 45
702 65c. Franklin D. Roosevelt meeting George Washington Carver (agricultural researcher) . . 35 80
703 80c. Roosevelt as stamp collector . . . . 45 1·00
MS704 100 × 70 mm. $2 Roosevelt with stamp showing profile of Washington . . . . 1·00 2·50

172 "Second Thoughts" **173** Princess of Wales

1982. Norman Rockwell (painter) Commemoration. Multicoloured.

705 8c. Type **172** 15 10
706 15c. "The Proper Gratuity" 20 20
707 20c. "Doctor's Office" (inscr "Before the Shot") 25 30
708 25c. "Bottom of the Sixth" (inscr "The Three Umpires") 25 30

1982. 21st Birthday of Princess of Wales. Multicoloured.

713 8c. Sandringham 15 35
714 35c. Prince and Princess of Wales . . . . 55 1·00
709 55c. As 8c. 35 45
710 70c. As 35c. 60 55
711 $1 Type **173** 90 80
715 $1.10 Type **173** . . . . . . 80 2·00
MS712 102 × 76 mm. $2 Princess Diana (different) . . . . 1·50 1·75

174 Cessna 337 Super Skymaster over Caicos Cays

1982. Aircraft. Multicoloured.

716 8c. Type **174** 15 15
717 15c. Lockheed JetStar II over Grand Turk 20 25
718 65c. Sikorsky S.58 helicopter over South Caicos 65 80
719 $1.10 Cessna 182 Skylan over Providenciales . . . . . 1·10 1·25
MS720 99 × 69 mm. $2 Boeing 727-200 over Turks and Caicos Islands . . . . 2·00 2·50

1982. Christmas. Scenes from Walt Disney's Cartoon film "Mickey's Christmas Carol". As T **153**. Multicoloured.

721 1c. Donald Duck, Mickey Mouse and Scrooge . . . 10 10
722 1c. Goofy (Marley's ghost) and Scrooge 10 10
723 2c. Jiminy Cricket and Scrooge 10 10
724 2c. Huey, Dewey and Louie 10 10
725 3c. Daisy Duck and youthful Scrooge 10 10
726 3c. Giant and Scrooge . . . 10 10
727 4c. Two bad wolves, a wise pig and a reformed Scrooge 10 10
728 65c. Donald Duck and Scrooge . . . . 1·00 75
729 $1.10 Mortie and Scrooge . . 1·60 1·25
MS730 126 × 101 mm. $2 Mickey and Minnie Mouse with Mortie 2·75 2·50

175 West Caicos Mule-drawn Wagon

1983. Trams and Locomotives. Multicoloured.

731 15c. Type **175** 20 25
732 55c. West Caicos steam locomotive 65 70
733 90c. East Caicos mule-drawn sisal train . . . . 90 1·00
734 $1.60 East Caicos steam locomotive . . . . 1·75 1·90
MS735 99 × 69 mm. $2.50 Steam sisal train . . . . 2·25 2·25

176 Policewoman on Traffic Duty

1983. Commonwealth Day. Multicoloured.

736 1c. Type **176** 85 50
737 8c. Stylized sun and weather vane 30 20
738 65c. Yacht . . . . 85 1·00
739 $1 Cricket . . . . 2·00 2·00

177 "St. John and the Virgin Mary" (detail) **179** First Hydrogen Balloon "The Globe", 1783

178 Minke Whale

1983. Easter. Designs showing details from the "Mond Crucifixion" by Raphael. Multicoloured.

740 35c. Type **177** 20 25
741 50c. "Two Women" 30 35
742 95c. "Angel with two jars" 40 60
743 $1.10 "Angel with one jar" 60 80
MS744 100 × 130 mm. $2.50 "Christ on the Cross" . . . . 2·00 2·00

1983. Whales. Multicoloured.

745 50c. Type **178** . . . . 2·00 2·00
746 65c. Black right whale . . . 2·25 2·25
747 70c. Killer whale . . . . . 2·50 2·50
748 95c. Sperm whale . . . . . 2·75 2·75
749 $1.10 Cuvier's beaked whale 3·00 3·00
750 $2 Blue whale . . . . 5·00 5·00
751 $2.20 Humpback whale . . . 5·50 5·50
752 $3 Long-finned pilot whale 6·25 6·25
MS753 112 × 82 mm. $3 Fin whale 7·00 5·00

1983. Bicentenary of Manned Flight. Mult.

754 25c. Type **179** 20 25
755 35c. "Friendship 7" 25 35
756 70c. First hot air balloon "Le Martial", 1783 . . . . . 40 70
757 95c. Space shuttle "Columbia" 55 90
MS758 112 × 76 mm. $2 Montgolfier balloon and space shuttle . . . 1·25 2·00

180 Fiddler Pig

1983. Christmas. Walt Disney Cartoon Characters. Multicoloured.

759 1c. Type **180** 10 10
760 1c. Fifer Pig 10 10
761 2c. Practical Pig 10 10
762 2c. Pluto 10 10
763 3c. Goofy 10 10
764 3c. Mickey Mouse 10 10
765 35c. Gyro Gearloose 70 35
766 50c. Ludwig von Drake . . . 1·00 60
767 $1.10 Huey, Dewey and Louie . . . . 1·40 1·25
MS768 127 × 102 mm. $2.50 Mickey and Minnie Mouse with Huey, Dewey and Louie . . . . . . 3·25 4·00

181 Bermudan Sloop

1983. Ships. Multicoloured.

769 4c. Arawak dug-out canoe 1·00 2·75
770 5c. "Santa Maria" . . . . 1·00 2·75
771 8c. British and Spanish ships in battle . . . . 2·25 2·75
772 10c. Type **181** . . . . . . 2·25 1·50
773a 20c. U.S. privateer "Grand Turk" . . . . 50 2·25
774a 25c. H.M.S. "Boreas" (frigate) . . . . 60 2·25
775 30c. H.M.S. "Endymion" (frigate) attacking French ship, 1790s . . . . 3·00 1·50
776a 35c. "Caesar" (barque) . . . 60 2·75
777a 50c. "Grapeshot" (American schooner) . . . . 60 2·25
778a 65c. H.M.S. "Invincible" (battle cruiser) . . . . . 2·50 3·50
779a 95c. H.M.S. "Magicienne" (cruiser) . . . . 2·50 3·50
780 $1.10 H.M.S. "Durban" (cruiser) . . . . 6·00 3·75
781a $2 "Sentinel" (cable ship) 2·50 6·50
782 $3 H.M.S. "Minerva" (frigate) . . . . 7·50 7·50
783 $5 Caicos sloop . . . . . . 7·50 13·00

182 Pres. Kennedy and Signing of Civil Rights Legislation

1983. 20th Death Anniv of J. F. Kennedy (U.S. President).

784 **182** 20c. multicoloured 20 15
785 $1 multicoloured . . . . 50 1·25

183 Clarabelle Cow Diving

1984. Olympic Games, Los Angeles. Mult. A. Inscr "1984 LOS ANGELES".

786A 1c. Type **183** 10 10
787A 1c. Donald Duck in 500 m kayak race 10 10
788A 2c. Huey, Dewey and Louie in 1000m kayak race . . 10 10
789A 2c. Mickey Mouse in single kayak 10 10
790A 3c. Donald Duck highboard diving 10 10
791A 3c. Minnie Mouse in kayak slalom 10 10
792A 25c. Mickey Mouse freestyle swimming 70 45
793A 75c. Donald Duck playing water-polo . . . . 2·00 2·00
794A $1 Uncle Scrooge and Donald Duck yachting 2·00 2·00
MS795A 117 × 90 mm. $2 Pluto platform diving . . . . 4·00 4·50

B. Inscr "1984 OLYMPICS LOS ANGELES" and Olympic emblem.

786B 1c. Type **183** 10 10
787B 1c. Donald Duck in 500 m kayak race 10 10
788B 2c. Huey, Dewey and Louie in 1000m kayak race . . 10 10
789B 2c. Mickey Mouse in single kayak 10 10
790B 3c. Donald Duck highboard diving 10 10
791B 3c. Minnie Mouse in kayak slalom 10 10
792B 25c. Mickey Mouse freestyle swimming 70 45
793B 75c. Donald Duck playing water-polo . . . . 2·00 2·00
794B $1 Uncle Scrooge and Donald Duck yachting 2·00 2·00
MS795B 117 × 90 mm. $2 Pluto platform diving . . . . 4·00 6·00

184 "Cadillac V-16", 1933

1984. Classic Cars and 125th Anniv of first Commercial Oil Well. Multicoloured.

796 4c. Type **184** 30 10
797 8c. Rolls-Royce "Phanton III", 1937 . . . . 40 15
798 10c. Saab "99", 1969 . . . . 40 15
799 25c. Maserati "Bora", 1973 90 40
800 40c. Datsun "260Z", 1970 . . 1·25 65
801 55c. Porsche "917", 1971 . . 1·40 80
802 80c. Lincoln "Continental", 1939 . . . . 1·50 90
803 $1 Triumph "TR3A", 1957 1·60 1·25
MS804 70 × 100 mm. $2 Daimler, 1886 . . . . 2·00 2·50

185 "Rest during the Flight to Egypt, with St. Francis"

1984. Easter. 450th Death Anniv of Correggio (painter). Multicoloured.

805 15c. Type **185** 20 15
806 40c. "St. Luke and St. Ambrose" 45 40
807 60c. "Diana and her Chariot" 65 65
808 95c. "The Deposition of Christ" 80 80
MS809 100 × 79 mm. $2 "The Nativity with Saints Elizabeth and John the Younger" (horiz) . . 1·25 2·50

1984. Universal Postal Union Congress, Hamburg. Nos. 748/9 optd **19TH UPU CONGRESS, HAMBURG, WEST GERMANY. 1874–1984** and emblem. Multicoloured.

810 95c. Sperm whale . . . . . 2·50 3·00
811 $1.10 Goosebeak whale . . . 2·50 3·00
MS812 112 × 82 mm. $3 Fin whale 4·25 4·25

187 "The Adventure of the Second Stain"

1984. 125th Birth Anniv of Sir Arthur Conan Doyle (author). Multicoloured.

813 25c. Type **187** . . . . 2·75 1·50
814 45c. "The Adventure of the Final Problem" . . . . . 3·50 2·25
815 70c. "The Adventure of the Empty House" . . . . . . 5·50 3·50
816 85c. "The Adventure of the Greek Interpreter" . . . . 6·50 4·00
MS817 100 × 70 mm. $2 Sir Arthur Conan Doyle . . . . 11·00 11·00

188 Orange Clownfish **190** Magnolia Warbler

189 Donald Duck cutting down Christmas Tree

1984. "Ausipex" International Stamp Exhibition, Melbourne. 175th Birth Anniv of Charles Darwin. Multicoloured.

818 5c. Type **188** 60 50
819 35c. Monitor lizard . . . . . 2·25 1·75
820 50c. Rainbow lory . . . . . 3·50 3·25
821 $1.10 Koalas . . . . 3·75 4·25
MS822 100 × 70 mm. $2 Eastern grey kangaroo . . . . 2·50 4·50

1984. Christmas. Walt Disney Cartoon Characters. Designs showing scenes form "Toy Tinkers". Multicoloured.

823 20c. Type **189** 85 45
824 35c. Donald Duck and Chip n' Dale playing with train set . . . . 1·10 75
825 50c. Donald Duck and Chip n' Dale playing with catapult . . . . 1·60 1·10
826 75c. Donald Duck, Chip n' Dale and Christmas tree 2·25 1·75
827 $1.10 Donald Duck, toy soldier and Chip 'n' Dale 2·50 2·50
MS828 126 × 102 mm. $2 Donald Duck as Father Christmas . . 3·25 4·00

1985. Birth Bicentenary of John J. Audubon (ornithologist). Multicoloured.

829 25c. Type **190** . . . . 2·00 75
830 45c. Short-eared owl . . . . 3·00 1·50
831 70c. Mourning dove and eggs 3·50 2·75
832 85c. Caribbean martin . . . 3·50 3·00
MS833 100 × 70 mm. $2 Oystercatcher and chicks . . . 4·50 4·50

191 Leonardo da Vinci and Illustration of Glider Wing (15th century)

1985. 40th Anniv of International Civil Aviation Organization. Pioneers. Multicoloured.

834 8c. Type **191** 65 40
835 25c. Sir Alliott Verdon Roe and Avro (Canada) CF-102 jetliner (1949) . . . . . 1·75 55
836 65c. Robert H. Goddard and first liquid fuel rocket (1926) . . . . 2·50 1·75
837 $1 Igor Sikorsky and Vought-Sikorsky VS-300 helicopter prototype (1939) . . . . . 6·00 4·25
MS838 100 × 70 mm. $2 Amelia Earhart's Lockheed 10E Electra (1937) . . . . 2·75 3·25

192 Benjamin Franklin and Marquis de Lafayette

1985. Centenary of Statue of Liberty's Arrival in New York. Multicoloured.

839 20c. Type **192** 80 50
840 30c. Frederic Bartholdi (designer) and Gustave Eiffel (engineer) . . . . . 1·10 80
841 65c. "Isere" (French screw warship) arriving in New York with statue, 1885 . . 2·50 1·75
842 $1.10 United States fund raisers Louis Agassiz, Charles Sumner, H. W. Longfellow and Joseph Pulitzer . . . . 2·50 2·00
MS843 99 × 69 mm. $2 Dedication ceremony, 1886 . . . . 3·00 3·50

193 Sir Edward Hawke and H.M.S. "Royal George" (ship of the line), 1782

1985. Salute to Royal Navy. Multicoloured.

844 20c. Type **193** . . . . . . 2·50 1·90
845 30c. Lord Nelson and H.M.S. "Victory" (ship of the line), 1805 . . . . 3·00 2·25
846 65c. Admiral Sir George Cockburn and H.M.S. "Albion" (ship of the line), 1802 . . . . 4·00 3·25
847 95c. Admiral Sir David Beatty and H.M.S. "Indefatigable" (battle cruiser), 1916 . . . . . . 5·00 4·75
MS848 99 × 69 mm. $2 18th-century sailor and cannon (vert) . . . 3·25 4·00

194 Mark Twain riding on Halley's Comet

1985. International Youth Year. Birth Annivs of Mark Twain (150th) and Jakob Grimm (Bicentenary). Multicoloured.

849 25c. Type **194** . . . . 1·25 55
850 35c. "Grand Turk" (Mississippi river steamer) 2·00 70
851 50c. Hansel and Gretel and gingerbread house (vert) . . 2·25 1·50
852 95c. Rumpelstiltskin (vert) . . 3·00 2·75
MS853 99 × 68 mm. $2 Mark Twain and the Brothers Grimm . . . 3·50 5·00

195 The Queen Mother outside Clarence House **196** King George II and Score of "Zadok the Priest" (1727)

1985. Life and Times of Queen Elizabeth the Queen Mother. Multicoloured.

854 30c. Type **195** 70 45
855 50c. Visiting Biggin Hill airfield (horiz) . . . . . . 2·25 1·00
856 $1.10 80th birthday portrait 2·25 2·50
MS857 56 × 85 mm. $2 With Prince Charles at Garter ceremony, Windsor Castle, 1968 . . . . 2·00 3·00

1985. 300th Birth Anniv of George Frederick Handel (composer).

858 **196** 4c. multicoloured 65 50
859 – 10c. multicoloured . . . . 1·00 50
860 – 50c. multicoloured . . . . 2·50 2·50
861 – $1.10 multicoloured . . . 3·00 5·50
MS862 101 × 76 mm. $2 black, purple-blue . . . . 5·00 7·50

DESIGNS: 10c. Queen Caroline and score of "Funeral Anthem" (1737); 50c. King George I and score of "Water Music" (1714); $1.10, Queen Anne and score of "Or la Tromba" from "Rinaldo" (1711); $2 George Frederick Handel.

1985. 300th Birth Anniv of Johann Sebastian Bach (composer). As T **189a** of Sierra Leone. Mult.

863 15c. Bassoon . . . . 1·00 40
864 40c. Natural horn . . . . . 1·50 85
865 60c. Viola d'amore . . . . . 2·00 1·25
866 95c. Clavichord . . . . . . 2·25 2·25
MS867 102 × 76 mm. $2 Johann Sebastian Bach . . . . 4·00 4·00

197 Harley-Davidson Dual Cylinder (1915) on Middle Caicos

1985. Centenary of the Motor Cycle. Mult.

868 8c. Type **197** 85 30
869 25c. Triumph "Thunderbird" (1950) on Grand Turk 1·75 70
870 55c. BMW "K100RS" (1985) on North Caicos 2·75 1·75
871 $1.20 Honda "1100 Shadow" (1985) on South Caicos 3·75 7·00
MS872 100 × 77 mm. $2 Daimler single track (1885) (vert) 4·50 4·50

198 Pirates in Prison

1985. 30th Anniv of Disneyland, U.S.A. Designs showing scenes from "Pirates of the Caribbean" exhibition. Multicoloured.

873 1c. Type **198** 10 10
874 1c. The fate of Captain William Kidd 10 10
875 2c. Bartholomew Roberts 10 10
876 2c. Two buccaneers 10 10
877 3c. Privateers looting 10 10
878 3c. Auction of captives 10 10
879 35c. Singing pirates 1·50 80
880 75c. Edward Teach—"Blackbeard" 3·00 3·25
881 $1.10 Sir Henry Morgan 3·50 4·00
MS882 123 × 86 mm. $2.50 Mary Read and Anne Bonney 5·00 4·50

199 Brownies from China, Turks and Caicos and Papua New Guinea

1985. 75th Anniv of Girl Guide Movement and 35th Anniv of Grand Turk Company. Multicoloured.

883 10c. Type **199** 75 40
884 40c. Brownies from Surinam, Turks and Caicos and Korea 1·75 1·25
885 70c. Guides from Australia, Turks and Caicos and Canada 2·50 3·00
886 80c. Guides from West Germany, Turks and Caicos and Israel 2·75 3·00
MS887 107 × 76 mm. $2 75th anniv emblem 3·00 3·50

200 Iguana and Log

1986. Turks and Caicos Ground Iguana. Multicoloured.

888 8c. Type **200** 2·25 1·25
889 10c. Iguana on beach 2·25 1·25
890 20c. Iguana at nest 3·50 2·50
891 35c. Iguana eating flowers 6·50 4·50
MS892 105 × 76 mm. $2 Map showing habitat 13·00 14·00

201 Duke and Duchess of York after Wedding

202 "Prophecy of Birth of Christ to King Achaz"

1986. Royal Wedding. Multicoloured.

893 35c. Type **201** 1·50 55
894 65c. Miss Sarah Ferguson in wedding carriage 2·50 1·40
895 $1.10 Duke and Duchess of York on Palace balcony after wedding 3·00 2·75
MS896 85 × 85 mm. $2 Duke and Duchess leaving Westminster Abbey 4·25 4·50

1987. Christmas. Illuminated illustrations by Giorgio Clovio from "Farnese Book of Hours". Multicoloured.

897 35c. Type **202** 1·25 85
898 50c. "The Annunciation" 1·75 1·75
899 65c. "The Circumcision" 2·25 2·25
900 95c. "Adoration of the Kings" 3·25 4·00
MS901 76 × 106 mm. $2 "The Nativity" 4·75 6·00

203 H.M.S. "Victoria" (ship of the line), 1859, and Victoria Cross

1987. 150th Anniv of Accession of Queen Victoria. Multicoloured.

902 8c. Type **203** 1·75 1·00
903 35c. "Victoria" (paddle-steamer) and gold sovereign 3·00 2·25
904 55c. Royal Yacht "Victoria and Albert I" and 1840 Penny Black stamp 3·25 2·75
905 95c. Royal Yacht "Victoria and Albert II" and Victoria Public Library 4·50 5·00
MS906 129 × 76 mm. $2 "Victoria" (barque) 6·00 7·00

1987. Bicentenary of U.S. Constitution. As T **210a** of Sierra Leone. Multicoloured.

907 10c. State Seal, New Jersey 25 35
908 35c. 18th-century family going to church ("Freedom of Worship") (vert) 75 75
909 65c. U.S. Supreme Court, Judicial Branch, Washington (vert) 1·40 1·75
910 80c. John Adams (statesman) (vert) 1·60 2·50
MS911 105 × 75 mm. $2 George Mason (Virginia delegate) (vert) 1·75 4·00

204 "Santa Maria"

1988. 500th Anniv (1992) of Discovery of America by Columbus (1st issue). Multicoloured.

912 4c. Type **204** 45 30
913 25c. Columbus meeting Tainos Indians 95 60
914 70c. "Santa Maria" anchored off Indian village 2·75 3·25
915 $1 Columbus in field of grain 2·75 3·25
MS916 105 × 76 mm. $2 "Santa Maria", "Pinta" and "Nina" 3·50 4·50

See also Nos. 947/51, 1028/36, 1072/80 and 1166/76.

205 Arawak Artifact and Scouts in Cave, Middle Caicos

207 Football

1988. World Scout Jamboree, Australia. Mult.

917 8c. Type **205** 20 15
918 35c. "Santa Maria" scouts and Hawks Nest Island (horiz) 55 55
919 65c. Scouts diving to wreck of galleon 95 1·25
920 95c. Visiting ruins of 19th-century sisal plantation (horiz) 1·40 1·75
MS921 118 × 82 mm. $2 Splashdown of John Glenn's "Mercury" capsule, 1962 3·75 5·00

No. **MS**921 is inscribed "Sight" in error.

1988. Royal Ruby Wedding. Nos. 772, 774 and 781 optd **40TH WEDDING ANNIVERSARY H.M. QUEEN ELIZABETH II H.R.H. THE DUKE OF EDINBURGH.**

922 10c. Type **181** 75 50
923 25c. H.M.S. "Boreas" (frigate) 1·25 55
924 $2 "Sentinel" (cable ship) 4·00 4·50

1988. Olympic Games, Seoul. Multicoloured.

925 8c. Type **207** 45 15
926 30c. Yachting 80 50
927 70c. Cycling 5·00 2·00
928 $1 Athletics 1·75 2·25
MS929 102 × 71 mm. $2 Swimming 2·75 3·75

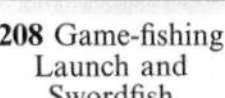

208 Game-fishing Launch and Swordfish

210 Coat of Arms

209 Princess Alexandra and Government House

1988. Billfish Tournament. Multicoloured.

930 8c. Type **208** 55 30
931 10c. Competitors with swordfish catch 55 30
932 70c. Game-fishing launch 2·25 3·00
933 $1 Atlantic blue marlin 2·75 3·50
MS934 119 × 85 mm. $2 Stylized sailfish 4·00 5·00

1988. Christmas. 500th Birth Anniv of Titian (artist). As T **183a** of St. Vincent, inscr "CHRISTMAS 1988" and with royal cypher at top right. Multicoloured.

935 15c. "Madonna and Child with Saint Catherine" 40 30
936 25c. "Madonna with a Rabbit" 50 40
937 35c. "Virgin and Child with Saints" 60 50
938 40c. "The Gypsy Madonna" 70 60
939 50c. "The Holy Family and a Shepherd" 80 70
940 65c. "Madonna and Child" 95 85
941 $3 "Madonna and Child with Saints" 4·25 6·00
MS942 Two sheets, each 110 × 95 mm. (a) $2 "Adoration of the Magi" (detail). (b) $2 "The Annunciation" (detail) Set of 2 sheets 6·00 7·50

1988. Visit of Princess Alexandra. Mult.

943 70c. Type **209** 2·50 1·50
944 $1.40 Princess Alexandra and map of islands 7·50 4·50
MS945 92 × 72 mm. $2 Princess Alexandra (vert) 11·00 10·00

1988.

946 **210** $10 multicoloured 11·00 13·00

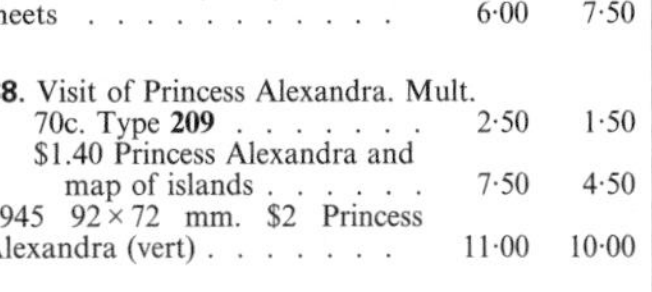

210a Cutting Tree Bark for Canoe

1989. 500th Anniv (1992) of Discovery of America by Columbus (2nd issue). Pre-Columbian Carib Society. Multicoloured.

947 10c. Type **210a** 15 15
948 50c. Body painting 80 80
949 65c. Religious ceremony 95 1·10
950 $1 Canoeing (vert) 1·50 1·75
MS951 87 × 70 mm. $2 Cave pictograph (horiz) 3·50 5·00

1989. "World Stamp Expo '89" International Stamp Exhibition, Washington (1st issue). Sheet 77 × 62 mm containing horiz design as T **201b** of St. Vincent. Multicoloured.

MS952 $1.50 Lincoln Memorial 2·50 3·50

210b Andrew Jackson and Railway Locomotive "DeWitt Clinton"

1989. "World Stamp Expo '89" International Stamp Exhibition, Washington. Bicentenary of the U.S. Presidency. Multicoloured.

953 50c. Type **210b** 1·10 1·10
954 50c. Martin van Buren, Moses Walker and early baseball game 1·10 1·10
955 50c. William H. Harrison and campaign parade 1·10 1·10
956 50c. John Tyler, Davy Crockett and the Alamo, Texas 1·10 1·10
957 50c. James K. Polk, California gold miner and first U.S. postage stamp 1·10 1·10
958 50c. Zachary Taylor and Battle of Buena Vista, 1846 1·10 1·10
959 50c. Rutherford B. Hayes and end of Confederate Reconstruction 1·10 1·10
960 50c. James A. Garfield and Battle of Shiloh 1·10 1·10
961 50c. Chester A. Arthur and opening of Brooklyn Bridge, 1883 1·10 1·10
962 50c. Grover Cleveland, Columbian Exposition, Chicago, 1893, and commemorative stamp 1·10 1·10
963 50c. Benjamin Harrison, Pan-American Union Building and map of Americas 1·10 1·10
964 50c. William McKinley and Rough Rider Monument 1·10 1·10
965 50c. Hebert Hoover, Sonya Heine (skater) and Ralph Metcalf (athlete) 1·10 1·10
966 50c. Franklin D. Roosevelt with dog and in wheelchair 1·10 1·10
967 50c. Statue of Washington by Frazer and New York World's Fair, 1939 1·10 1·10
968 50c. Harry S. Truman, Veterans Memorial Building, San Francisco, and U.N. emblem 1·10 1·10
969 50c. Dwight D. Eisenhower and U.S. troops landing in Normandy, 1944 1·10 1·10
970 50c. John F. Kennedy and "Apollo 11" astronauts on Moon, 1969 1·10 1·10

1989. Christmas. Paintings by Bellini. As T **204a** of St. Vincent. Multicoloured.

971 15c. "Madonna and Child" 80 50
972 25c. "The Madonna of the Shrubs" 90 50
973 35c. "The Virgin and Child" 1·00 60
974 40c. "The Virgin and Child with a Greek Inscription" 1·10 70
975 50c. "The Madonna of the Meadow" 1·25 80
976 65c. "The Madonna of the Pear" 2·25 2·25
977 70c. "The Virgin and Child" (different) 2·50 2·50
978 $1 "Madonna and Child" (different) 3·50 3·75
MS979 Two sheets, each 96 × 72 mm. (a) $2 "The Virgin and Child enthroned". (b) $2 "The Madonna with John the Baptist and another Saint" Set of 2 sheets 11·00 13·00

211 Lift-off "Apollo 11"

212 "Zephyranthes rosea"

1990. 20th Anniv of First Manned Landing on Moon. Multicoloured.

980 50c. Type **211** 1·10 1·25
981 50c. Lunar module "Eagle" on Moon 1·10 1·25
982 50c. Aldrin gathering dust sample 1·10 1·25
983 50c. Neil Armstrong with camera 1·10 1·25
984 50c. "Eagle" re-united with command module "Columbia" 1·10 1·25

Nos. 980/4 were printed together, se-tenant, with Nos. 981/3 forming a composite design.

1990. Island Flowers. Multicoloured.

985 8c. Type **212** 30 20
986 10c. "Sophora tomentosa" 30 20
987 15c. "Coccoloba uvifera" 40 25
988 20c. "Encyclia gracilis" 40 30
989 25c. "Tillandsia streptophylla" 50 35
990a 30c. "Maurandella antirrhiniflora" 70 60
991 35c. "Tillandsia balbisiana" 60 50
992a 50c. "Encyclia rufa" 1·00 1·00
993a 65c. "Aechmea lingulata" 1·25 1·25
994 80c. "Asclepias curassavica" 1·40 1·50
995 $1 "Caesalpinia bahamensis" 1·50 1·60
996 $1.10 "Capparis cynophallophora" 2·00 2·75
997 $1.25 "Stachytarpheta jamaicensis" 2·50 3·00
998 $2 "Cassia biflora" 3·00 4·00
999 $5 "Clusia rosea" 7·00 9·00
1000 $10 "Opuntia bahamana" 14·00 17·00

213 Queen Parrotfish

1990. Fishes. Multicoloured.
1001 8c. Type **213** 25 20
1002 10c. Queen triggerfish . . . 25 20
1003 25c. Sergeant major 60 45
1004 40c. Spotted goatfish . . . 85 75
1005 50c. Neon goby . . . . . . 1·00 85
1006 75c. Nassau grouper . . . . 1·50 1·50
1007 80c. Yellow-headed jawfish 1·75 2·00
1008 $1 Blue tang . . . . 1·75 2·00
MS1009 Two sheets, each 115 × 80 mm. (a) $2 Butter hamlet. (b) $2 Queen angelfish Set of 2 sheets . . . . 13·00 14·00

214 Yellow-billed Cuckoo

1990. Birds (1st series). Multicoloured.
1010 10c. Type **214** . . . . . . 1·10 60
1011 15c. White-tailed tropic bird 1·50 60
1012 20c. Kirtland's warbler . . . 2·25 85
1013 30c. Yellow-crowned night heron . . . . 2·25 85
1014 50c. Black-billed whistling duck ("West Indian tree duck") . . . . 2·50 1·10
1015 80c. Yellow-bellied sapsucker . . . . 3·25 2·50
1016 $1 American kestrel . . . . 3·25 2·50
1017 $1.40 Northern mockingbird 3·75 4·00
MS1018 Two sheets, each 104 × 78 mm. (a) $2 Yellow warbler. (b) $2 Osprey Set of 2 sheets . . . . 18·00 18·00
See also Nos. 1050/8.

215 "Anartia jatrophae"

216 Penny "Rainbow Trial" in Blue

215a Rock Beauty

1990. Butterflies (1st series). Multicoloured.
1019 15c. Type **215** 80 45
1020 25c. "Phoebis sennae" (horiz) . . . . 1·00 60
1021 35c. "Euptoieta hegesia" (horiz) . . . . 1·25 75
1022 40c. "Hylephila phylaeus" (horiz) . . . . 1·40 80
1023 50c. "Eurema chamberlaini" (horiz) . . . . 1·40 1·00
1024 60c. "Brephidium exilis" . . 1·60 1·40
1025 90c. "Papilio aristodemus" (horiz) . . . . 2·75 3·00
1026 $1 "Marpesia eleuchea" . . 2·75 3·00
MS1027 Two sheets, each 106 × 76 mm. (a) $2 "Hemiargus thomast" (horiz). (b) $2 "Danaus gilippus (horiz) Set of 2 sheets 11·00 12·00
See also Nos. 1081/9.

1990. 500th Anniv (1992) of Discovery of America by Columbus (3rd issue). New World Natural History–Fishes. Multicoloured.
1028 10c. Type **215a** 50 30
1029 15c. Coney 60 40
1030 25c. Red hind 85 60
1031 50c. Banded butterflyfish . . 1·40 1·25
1032 60c. French angelfish . . . 1·75 1·50
1033 75c. Black-barred soldierfish 1·90 1·90
1034 90c. Stoplight parrotfish . . 2·00 2·25
1035 $1 French grunt . . . . . 2·25 2·40
MS1036 Two sheets, each 109 × 75 mm. (a) $2 Blue chromis. (b) $2 Grey angelfish Set of 2 sheets . . . . 9·00 10·00

1990. 150th Anniv of the Penny Black.
1037 **216** 25c. blue . . . . 1·50 60
1038 – 75c. brown . . . . . . 3·00 2·50
1039 – $1 blue . . . . 3·75 3·25
MS1040 144 × 111 mm. $2 black 5·00 6·00
DESIGNS: 75c. 1d. red-brown colour trial of December, 1840; $1 2d. blue of 1840; $2 Penny black.

217 Pillar Box No. 1, 1855

218 Queen Elizabeth the Queen Mother

1990. "Stamp World London 90" Int Stamp Exhibition. British Pillar Boxes.
1041 **217** 35c. brown and grey . . 1·25 65
1042 – 50c. blue and grey . . . 1·60 1·10
1043 – $1.25 blue and grey . . 3·50 4·00
MS1044 143 × 111 mm. $2 red and black . . . . 6·00 6·50
DESIGNS: 50c. Penfold box, 1866; $1.25, Air mail box, 1935; $2 "k" type box, 1979.

1990. 90th Birthday of Queen Elizabeth the Queen Mother.
1045 **218** 10c. multicoloured . . . 35 15
1046 – 25c. multicoloured . . . 75 50
1047 – 75c. multicoloured . . . 1·40 1·60
1048 – $1.25 multicoloured . . 2·00 2·50
MS1049 70 × 73 mm. $2 multicoloured . . . . 4·00 5·00
DESIGNS: 25, 75c., $2, Recent photographs of the Queen Mother.

219 Stripe-headed Tanager

1990. Birds (2nd series). Multicoloured.
1050 8c. Type **219** 90 55
1051 10c. Black-whiskered vireo (horiz) 90 55
1052 25c. Blue-grey gnatcatcher (horiz) . . . . 1·50 60
1053 40c. Lesser scaup (horiz) . . 2·00 1·00
1054 50c. Bahama pintail (horiz) 2·00 1·10
1055 75c. Black-necked stilt (horiz) . . . . 2·50 2·50
1056 80c. Oystercatcher . . . . . 2·50 2·75
1057 $1 Louisiana heron (horiz) 3·00 3·25
MS1058 Two sheets, each 98 × 69 mm. (a) $2 American coot (horiz). (b) $2 Bahama woodstar (horiz) Set of 2 sheets . . . . 7·50 8·50

220 "Triumph of Christ over Sin and Death" (detail, Rubens)

221 Canoeing

1990. Christmas. 350th Death Anniv of Rubens. Multicoloured.
1059 10c. Type **220** 50 20
1060 35c. "St. Theresa Praying" (detail) . . . . 1·00 45
1061 45c. "St. Theresa Praying" (different detail) . . . . . 1·10 60
1062 50c. "Triumph of Christ over Sin and Death" (different detail) . . . . . 1·25 65
1063 65c. "St. Theresa Praying" (different detail) . . . . . 1·75 1·10
1064 75c. "Triumph of Christ over Sin and Death" (different detail) . . . . . 2·00 1·40
1065 $1.25 "St. Theresa Praying" (different detail) . . . . . 2·50 3·75
MS1066 Two sheets, each 70 × 100 mm. (a) $2 "Triumph of Christ over Sin and Death" (different detail). (b) $2 "St. Theresa Praying" (different detail) Set of 2 sheets . . . . 11·00 12·00

1991. Olympic Games, Barcelona (1992). Mult.
1067 10c. Type **221** 35 25
1068 25c. 100 metre sprint . . . 70 50
1069 75c. Pole vaulting . . . . . 1·60 1·60
1070 $1.25 Javelin . . . . 2·25 3·00
MS1071 109 × 70 mm. $2 Basketball 6·50 6·50

1991. 500th Anniv (1992) of Discovery of America by Columbus (4th issue). History of Exploration. As T **220a** of St. Vincent. Multicoloured.
1072 5c. Henry Hudson in Hudson's Bay , 1611 . . 85 55
1073 10c. Roald Amundsen's airship N.1 "Norge", 1926 85 55
1074 15c. Amundsen's "Gjoa" in the Northwest Passage, 1906 . . . . 1·40 70
1075 50c. Submarine U.S.S. "Nautilus" under North Pole, 1958 . . . . 1·75 70
1076 75c. Robert Scott's "Terra Nova", 1911 . . . . . . 3·00 1·25
1077 $1 Byrd and Bennett's Fokker F.VIIa/3m "Josephine Ford" aircraft over North Pole, 1926 . . 3·25 2·00
1078 $1.25 Lincoln Ellsworth's Northrop Gamma "Polar Star" on trans-Antarctic flight, 1935 . . . . 3·50 3·50
1079 $1.50 Capt. James Cook in the Antarctic, 1772–75 . . 4·50 5·00
MS1080 Two sheets, each 116 × 76 mm. (a) "Santa Maria" (vert). (b) $2 Bow of "Nina" (vert) Set of 2 sheets . . . . 9·00 10·00

222 "Anartia jatrophae"

1991. Butterflies (2nd series). Multicoloured.
1081 5c. Type **222** 35 40
1082 25c. "Historis osius" 80 50
1083 35c. "Agraulis vanillae" . . 90 65
1084 45c. "Junonia evarete" . . . 1·10 90
1085 55c. "Dryas julia" . . . . . 1·25 1·25
1086 65c. "Siproeta stelenes" . . 1·60 1·60
1087 70c. "Appias drusilla" . . . 1·75 1·75
1088 $1 "Ascia monuste" . . . . 1·90 2·00
MS1089 Two sheets, each 114 × 72 mm. (a) $2 "Phoebis philea". (b) "Pseudolycaena marsyas" Set of 2 sheets . . . 10·00 11·00

223 Protohydrochoerus

1991. Extinct Species of Fauna. Mult.
1090 5c. Type **223** 70 60
1091 10c. Phororhacos 70 60
1092 15c. Prothylacynus 85 60
1093 50c. Borhyaena . . . . . . 2·00 1·10
1094 75c. Smilodon . . . . . . 2·50 1·60
1095 $1 Thoatherium . . . . . 2·75 2·00
1096 $1.25 Cuvieronius . . . . . 3·00 3·25
1097 $1.50 Toxodon . . . . . . 3·00 3·50
MS1098 Two sheets, each 79 × 59 mm. (a) $2 Astrapotherium. (b) $2 Mesosaurus Set of 2 sheets . . 11·00 12·00

1991. 65th Birthday of Queen Elizabeth II. As T **220b** of St. Vincent. Multicoloured.
1099 25c. Queen and Prince Philip at St. Paul's Cathedral, 1988 . . . . . 65 45
1100 35c. Queen and Prince Philip 80 60
1101 65c. Queen and Prince Philip at Garter Ceremony, 1988 . . . . . 1·40 1·40
1102 80c. Queen at Windsor, May 1988 . . . . 1·75 2·00
MS1103 68 × 90 mm. $2 Separate photographs of Queen and Prince Philip . . . . 4·00 5·00

224 "Pluteus chrysophlebius"

1991. Fungi. Multicoloured.
1104 10c. Type **224** 40 30
1105 15c. "Leucopaxillus gracillimus 55 30
1106 20c. "Marasmius haematocephalus" 65 40
1107 35c. "Collybia subpruinosa" 85 45
1108 50c. "Marasmius atrorubens" (vert) . . . . 1·25 75
1109 65c. "Leucocoprinus birnbaumii" (vert) . . . . 1·50 1·25
1110 $1.10 "Trogia cantharelloides" (vert) . . 2·00 2·50
1111 $1.25 "Boletellus cubensis" (vert) . . . . 2·00 2·75
MS1112 Two sheets, each 85 × 59 mm. (a) $2 "Pynrhoglossum pyrrhum" (vert). (b) $2 "Gerronema cirtinum" Set of 2 sheets . . . . 10·00 11·00

1991. 10th Wedding Anniv of the Prince and Princess of Wales. As T **220b** of St. Vincent. Multicoloured.
1113 10c. Prince and Princess of Wales, 1987 . . . . . . 80 25
1114 45c. Separate photographs of Prince, Princess and sons . . . . 2·50 90
1115 50c. Prince Henry in fire engine and Prince William applauding . . . . 3·50 1·50
1116 $1 Princess Diana in Derbyshire, 1990, and Prince Charles . . . . . 3·25 3·00
MS1117 68 × 90 mm. $2 Prince, Princess and Family, Majorca, 1990 . . . . 5·50 6·00

1991. Death Centenary (1990) of Vincent van Gogh (artist). As T **215a** of St. Vincent. Multicoloured.
1118 15c. "Weaver with Spinning Wheel" . . . . 1·00 60
1119 25c. "Head of a Young Peasant with Pipe" (vert) 1·25 60
1120 35c. "Old Cemetery Tower at Nuenen" (vert) . . . . 1·40 60
1121 45c. "Cottage at Nightfall" 1·50 70
1122 50c. "Still Life with Open Bible" . . . . 1·50 75
1123 65c. "Lane, Jardin du Luxembourg" . . . . . 2·25 1·60
1124 80c. "Pont du Carrousel and Louvre, Paris" . . . . . 2·75 3·25
1125 $1 "Vase with Poppies, Cornflowers, Peonies and Chrysanthemums" (vert) 3·00 3·25
MS1126 Two sheets, each 117 × 80 mm. (a) $2 "Ploughed Field" (horiz). (b) $2 "Entrance to the Public Park" (horiz). Imperf Set of 2 sheets . . . . 10·00 11·00

225 Series "8550" Steam Locomotive, 1899

1991. "Phila Nippon '91" International Stamp Exhibition, Tokyo. Japanese Steam Locomotives. Multicoloured.
1127 8c. Type **225** 70 60
1128 10c. Class C57, 1937 . . . . 70 50
1129 45c. Series 4110, 1913 . . . 1·50 70
1130 50c. Class C55, 1935 . . . . 1·50 70
1131 65c. Series 6250, 1915 . . . 2·00 1·40
1132 80c. Class E10, 1948 . . . . 2·25 2·25
1133 $1 Series 4500, 1902 . . . . 2·25 2·50
1134 $1.25 Class C11, 1932 . . . 2·50 3·50
MS1135 Two sheets, each 112 × 80 mm. (a) $2 Class C58, 1938. (b) $2 Class C62, 1948 Set of 2 sheets . . . . 9·00 9·00

1991. Christmas. Religious Paintings by Gerard David. As T **241a** of St. Vincent. Multicoloured.
1136 8c. "Adoration of the Shepherds" (detail) . . . 55 20
1137 15c. "Virgin and Child Enthroned with Two Angels" 75 25
1138 35c. "The Annunciation" (outer wings) . . . . . . 1·25 50
1139 45c. "The Rest on the Flight to Egypt" (different) . . . 1·40 75
1140 50c. "The Rest on the Flight to Egypt" (different) . . . 1·40 90
1141 65c. "Virgin and Child with Angels" . . . . 2·00 1·25
1142 80c. "Adoration of the Shepherds" . . . . 2·50 2·75
1143 $1.25 "Perussis Altarpiece" (detail) . . . . 3·00 3·75
MS1144 Two sheets, each 102 × 127 mm. (a) $2 "The Nativity". (b) $2 "Adoration of the Kings" Set of 2 sheets . . 8·00 9·00

1992. 40th Anniv of Queen Elizabeth II's Accession. As T **229a** of St. Vincent. Multicoloured.
1145 10c. Garden overlooking sea 65 40
1146 20c. Jetty . . . . 1·00 55
1147 25c. Small bay . . . . . . 1·25 60
1148 35c. Island road . . . . . 1·40 75
1149 50c. Grand Turk . . . . . 1·75 1·10
1150 65c. Beach . . . . 2·00 1·60
1151 80c. Marina . . . . 2·25 2·25
1152 $1.10 Grand Turk (different) 2·50 2·75
MS1153 Two sheets, each 75 × 97 mm. (a) $2 Beach (different). (b) $2 Foreshore, Grand Turk Set of 2 sheets . . 11·00 12·00

1992. "Granada '92" Int Stamp Exn, Spain. Religious Paintings. As T **250b** of Sierra Leone. Mult.
1154 8c. "St. Monica" (Luis Tristan) 70 20
1155 20c. "The Vision of Ezekiel: The Resurrection of the Flesh" (detail) (Francisco Collantes) . . . . 1·00 30

1156 45c. "The Vision of Ezekiel: The Resurrection of the Flesh" (different detail) (Collantes) . . . . 1·50 65
1157 50c. "The Martyrdom of St. Phillip" (Jose de Ribera) . . . . 1·50 65
1158 65c. "St. John the Evangelist" (Juan Ribalta) 2·00 1·25
1159 80c. "Archimedes" (De Ribera) . . . . 2·25 2·50
1160 $1 "St. John the Baptist in the Desert" (De Ribera) 2·50 2·75
1161 $1.25 "The Martyrdom of St. Phillip" (detail) (De Ribera) . . . . 2·75 3·25
MS1162 Two sheets, each 95 × 120 mm. (a) $2 "The Baptism of Christ" (Juan Fernández Navarrete). (b) $2 "Battle at EL Sotillo" (Francisco Zurbarán). Imperf Set of 2 sheets . . . . 11·00 12·00

226 Boy Scout on Duty at New York World's Fair, 1964

1992. 17th World Scout Jamboree, Korea. Multicoloured.
1163 $1 Type **226** . . . . 2·75 3·00
1164 $1 Lord Baden-Powell (vert) 2·75 3·00
MS1165 117 × 89 mm. $2 Silver Buffalo award . . . . 6·50 7·00

227 "Nina" and Commemorative Coin

1992. 500th Anniv of Discovery of America by Columbus (5th issue). Multicoloured.
1166 10c. Type **227** 85 55
1167 15c. Departure from Palos 1·00 55
1168 20c. Coat of arms of Columbus . . . . 1·00 65
1169 25c. Ships of Columbus . . 1·50 65
1170 30c. "Pinta" . . . . 1·50 65
1171 35c. Landfall in the New World . . . . 1·50 70
1172 50c. Christopher Columbus 1·75 1·00
1173 65c. "Santa Maria" . . . . 2·00 1·25
1174 80c. Erecting commemorative cross . . 2·00 2·25
1175 $1.10 Columbus meeting Amerindian . . . . . . 2·25 2·75
MS1176 Two sheets, each 70 × 100 mm. (a) $2 Coins showing ships of Columbus. (b) $2 Coins showing landing in the New World Set of 2 sheets . . . . 11·00 11·00

1992. Christmas. Religious Paintings. As T **241a** of St. Vincent. Multicoloured.
1177 8c. "Nativity" (detail) (Simon Bening) 70 15
1178 15c. "Circumcision" (detail) (Bening) . . . . 1·00 30
1179 35c. "Flight to Egypt" (detail) (Bening) . . . . . 1·60 60
1180 50c. "Massacre of the Innocents" (detail) (Bening) . . . . 1·75 80
1181 65c. "The Annunciation" (Dieric Bouts) . . . . . 2·00 1·25
1182 80c. "The Visitation" (Bouts) . . . . 2·50 2·75
1183 $1.10 "Adoration of the Angels" (Bouts) . . . . . 2·75 3·00
1184 $1.25 "Adoration of the Wise Men" (Bouts) . . . 2·75 3·25
MS1185 Two sheets, each 77 × 102 mm. (a) $2 "The Virgin seated with the Child" (detail) (Bouts). (b) $2 "The Virgin and Child" (detail) (Bouts) Set of 2 sheets . . . . 11·00 12·00

228 American Astronaut repairing Satellite

1993. Anniversaries and Events. Mult.
1186 25c. Type **228** . . . . . . 2·00 60
1187 50c. Dead and flourishing trees . . . . 2·25 90
1188 65c. Food and World map 2·75 1·60
1189 80c. Polluted and clean seas 3·25 3·00
1190 $1 Lions Club emblem . . . 3·25 3·00
1191 $1.25 Projected orbiting quarantine modules . . . 3·75 4·00
MS1192 Two sheets, each 107 × 80 mm. (a) $2 Projected orbital Martian vehicle. (b) $2 Industrialised town and clean beach Set of 2 sheets . . . . . 13·00 14·00
ANNIVERSARIES AND EVENTS: Nos. 1186, 1191, MS1192a, International Space Year; 1187, 1189, MS1192b, Earth Summit '92, Rio; 1188, International Conference on Nutrition, Rome; 1190, 75th anniv of International Association of Lions Clubs.

1993. Visit of the Duke of Edinburgh. Nos. 1100/1 optd **Royal Visit HRH Duke of Edinburgh 20th March 1993**.
1193 35c. Queen and Prince Philip . . . . 2·00 1·00
1194 65c. Queen and Prince Philip at Garter Ceremony, 1988 . . . . . 2·75 1·75
MS1195 68 × 90 mm. $2 Separate photographs of Queen and Prince Philip . . . . 5·50 5·50

1993. 40th Anniv of Coronation. As T **256a** of St. Vincent.
1196 15c. multicoloured 65 75
1197 50c. multicoloured . . . . . 1·10 1·40
1198 $1 green and black . . . . 1·60 1·75
1199 $1.25 multicoloured . . . . 1·60 1·75
MS1200 70 × 100 mm. $2 multicoloured . . . . 5·50 6·00
DESIGNS: 15c. Communion Chalice and Plate; 50c. Queen Elizabeth II at Coronation (photograph by Cecil Beaton); $1 Queen Elizabeth during Coronation ceremony; $1.25, Queen Elizabeth and Prince Philip. (28½ × 42½ mm.)—$2 "Queen Elizabeth II" (detail).

230 Omphalosaurus

1993. Prehistoric Animals. Multicoloured.
1201 8c. Type **230** 30 30
1202 15c. Coelophysis 40 30
1203 20c. Triceratops 45 30
1204 35c. Dilophosaurus 65 50
1205 50c. Pterodactylus 80 65
1206 65c. Elasmosaurus . . . . . 1·10 1·00
1207 80c. Stegosaurus . . . . . . 1·25 1·40
1208 $1.25 Euoplocephalus . . . 1·60 2·25
MS1209 Two sheets, each 100 × 70 mm. (a) $2 As 20c. (b) $2 As 35c. Set of 2 sheets . . . . 10·00 11·00

1993. Christmas. Religious Paintings. As T **256b** of St. Vincent. Black, yellow and red (Nos. 1210/12, 1217) or multicoloured (others).
1210 8c. "Mary, Queen of the Angels" (detail) (Durer) 60 20
1211 20c. "Mary, Queen of the Angels" (different detail) (Durer) 90 30
1212 35c. "Mary, Queen of the Angels" (different detail) (Durer) . . . . 1·25 50
1213 50c. "Virgin and Child with St. John the Baptist" (Raphael) . . . . 1·60 70
1214 65c. "The Canagiani Holy Family" (detail) (Raphael) 2·00 1·25
1215 80c. "The Holy Family with the Lamb" (detail) (Raphael) . . . . 2·25 2·25
1216 $1 "Virgin and Child with St. John the Baptist" (different detail) (Raphael) 2·75 2·75
1217 $1.25 "Mary, Queen of the Angels" (different detail) (Durer) . . . . 3·00 3·50
MS1218 Two sheets, each 102 × 127 mm. (a) $2 "Mary, Queen of the Angels" (different detail) (Durer). (b) $2 "The Canagiani Holy Family" (different detail) (Raphael) (horiz) Set of 2 sheets . . . . 8·00 9·00

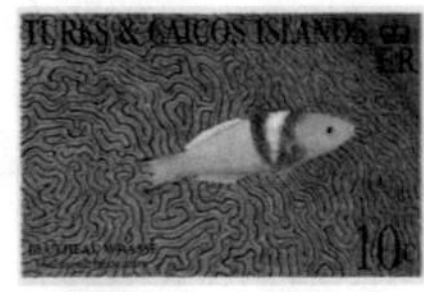

231 Blue-headed Wrasse

1993. Fishes. Multicoloured.
1219 10c. Type **231** 30 20
1220 20c. Honeycomb cowfish . . 50 40
1221 25c. Glass-eyed snapper . . 50 40
1222 35c. Spotted drum 65 50
1223 50c. Jolt-headed porgy . . . 90 70
1224 65c. Small-mouthed grunt 1·10 1·00
1225 80c. Candy basslet ("Peppermint bass") . . . 1·25 1·50
1226 $1.10 Indigo hamlet . . . . 1·75 2·25
MS1227 Two sheets, each 106 × 75 mm. (a) $2 Bonnethead. (b) $2 Atlantic sharp-nosed shark Set of 2 sheets . . . . 7·50 8·50
The captions on No. MS1227 have been transposed in error.

232 Killdeer Plover ("Killdeer")

1993. Birds. Multicoloured.
1228 10c. Type **232** . . . . . . 1·00 75
1229 15c. Yellow-crowned night heron (vert) . . . . . . 1·40 75
1230 35c. Northern mockingbird 2·00 75
1231 50c. Eastern kingbird (vert) 2·25 1·00
1232 65c. Magnolia warbler . . . 2·75 1·50
1233 80c. Cedar waxwing (vert) 3·00 3·00
1234 $1.10 Ruby-throated hummingbird . . . . . . 3·00 3·00
1235 $1.25 Painted bunting (vert) 3·25 3·50
MS1236 Two sheets, each 100 × 70 mm. (a) $2 Ruddy duck. (b) $2 American kestrel (vert) Set of 2 sheets . . . . 13·00 13·00

233 Sergio Goycoechea (Argentina)

1994. World Cup Football Championship, U.S.A. Multicoloured.
1237 8c. Type **233** 40 20
1238 10c. Bodo Illgner (Germany) 40 20
1239 50c. Nico Claesen (Belgium), Bossis and Amoros (France) . . . . 1·50 70
1240 65c. German players celebrating . . . . 1·75 1·10
1241 80c. Cameroun players celebrating . . . . 2·00 2·00
1242 $1 Cuciuffo (Argentina), Santin and Francescoli (Uruguay) . . . . 2·00 2·25
1243 $1.10 Hugo Sanchez (Mexico) . . . . 2·00 2·50
MS1244 Two sheets, each 100 × 70 mm. (a) $2 The Silverdome, Michigan. (b) $2 Michel Platini (France) (vert) Set of 2 sheets . . . . 6·50 7·50
No. 1237 is inscribed "Segio" and No. 1238 "Bado", both in error.

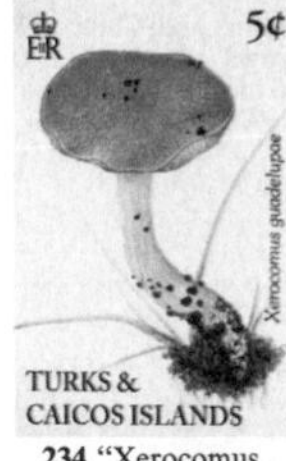

234 "Xerocomus guadelupae"

1994. Fungi. Multicoloured.
1245 5c. Type **234** 30 30
1246 10c. "Volvariella volvacea" 30 30
1247 35c. "Hygrocybe atrosquamosa" (horiz) . . 65 50
1248 50c. "Pleurotus ostreatus" (horiz) 90 65
1249 65c. "Marasmius pallescens" (horiz) . . . . 1·25 1·00
1250 80c. "Coprinus plicatilis" . . 1·40 1·50
1251 $1.10 "Bolbitius vitellinus" (horiz) . . . . 1·60 1·90
1252 $1.50 "Pyrrhoglossum lilaceipes" . . . . 2·00 2·50
MS1253 Two sheets, each 102 × 72 mm. (a) $2 "Russula cremeolilacina". (b) $2 "Lentinus edodes" (horiz) Set of 2 sheets 8·00 8·00

235 "The Annunciation"

1994. Christmas. Illustrations from 15th-century French Book of Hours. Multicoloured.
1254 25c. Type **235** . . . . . . 1·10 35
1255 50c. "The Visitation" . . . 1·90 75
1256 65c. "Annunciation to the Shepherds" . . . . 2·25 1·25
1257 80c. "The Nativity" . . . . 2·50 2·50
1258 $1 "Flight into Egypt" . . . 2·75 2·75
MS1259 63 × 86 mm. $2 "The Adoration of the Magi" . . . 5·00 6·00

236 "Dryas julia"

1994. Butterflies. Multicoloured.
1260 15c. Type **236** 40 35
1261 20c. "Urbanus proteus" . . 45 40
1262 25c. "Colobura dirce" . . . 50 40
1263 50c. "Papilio homerus" . . 90 65
1264 65c. "Chiodes catillus" . . . 1·25 1·00
1265 80c. "Eurytides zonaria" . . 1·50 1·75
1266 $1 "Hypolymnas misippus" 1·60 1·75
1267 $1.25 "Phoebis avellaneda" 1·75 2·00
MS1268 Two sheets, each 100 × 70 mm. (a) $2 "Eurema adamst". (b) $2 "Morpho peleides" Set of 2 sheets . . . 6·50 7·00

237 General Montgomery and British Troops landing on Juno Beach

1994. 50th Anniv of D-Day. Multicoloured.
1269 10c. Type **237** 30 30
1270 15c. Admiral Ramsay and British commandos at Sword Beach 45 35
1271 35c. Gun crew on H.M.S. "Belfast" (cruiser) 65 45
1272 50c. Montgomery and Eisenhower with Air Chief Marshal Tedder 90 65
1273 65c. General Eisenhower and men of U.S. 101st Airborne Division . . . . 1·25 1·00
1274 80c. Lt-Gen. Bradley and U.S. troops landing on Omaha Beach . . . . . . 1·40 1·50
1275 $1.10 Arrival of U.S. reinforcements . . . . . 1·60 1·75
1276 $1.25 Eisenhower at briefing 1·75 1·90
MS1277 Two sheets, each 100 × 70 mm. (a) $2 Landing craft and barrage balloon. (b) $2 Eisenhower and Montgomery Set of 2 sheets . . . . 6·50 7·00

238 "Cattleya deckeri"

1995. Orchids. Multicoloured.
1278 8c. Type **238** 50 20
1279 20c. "Epidendrum carpophorum" 70 30
1280 25c. "Epidendrum ciliare" 70 35
1281 50c. "Encyclia phoenicea" 95 70
1282 65c. "Bletia patula" . . . . 1·25 1·10
1283 80c. "Brassia caudata" . . . 1·40 1·50
1284 $1 "Brassavola nodosa" . . 1·60 1·60
1285 $1.25 "Bletia purpurea" . . 1·90 2·25
MS1286 Two sheets, each 100 × 70 mm. (a) $2 "Vanilla planifolia". (b) $2 "Ionopsis utricularioides" Set of 2 sheets 7·50 8·00

1995. 25th Anniv of First Manned Moon Landing. As T **284a** of St. Vincent. Multicoloured.
1287 10c. "Apollo 11" 30 30
1288 20c. Moon landing simulation 45 35
1289 25c. "Astronauts on the Moon" (detail) (Kovales) 50 35
1290 35c. First human foot on Moon 65 45
1291 50c. Astronaut Aldrin conducting solar wind experiment 90 65
1292 65c. Astronauts planting U.S.A. flag . . . . 1·25 1·00
1293 80c. Space module "Columbia" over lunar surface . . . . 1·40 1·50
1294 $1.10 "Apollo 11" after splashdown . . . . 1·60 1·90
MS1295 Two sheets, each 104 × 84 mm. (a) $2 Sample of Moon rock. (b) $2 "Apollo 11" lift-off, Cape Canaveral (vert) Set of 2 sheets . . . . 7·00 7·50

239 Elasmosaurus

1995. Jurassic Marine Reptiles. Multicoloured.
1296 35c. Type **239** 65 65
1297 35c. Plesiosaurus 65 65
1298 35c. Ichthyosaurus 65 65
1299 35c. Archelon 65 65
1300 35c. Askeptosaurus 65 65
1301 35c. Macroplata 65 65
1302 35c. Ceresiosaurus 65 65
1303 35c. Liopleurodon 65 65
1304 35c. Henodus 65 65
1305 35c. Muraenosaurus 65 65
1306 35c. Placodus 65 65
1307 35c. Kronosaurus 65 65
Nos. 1296/1307 were printed together, se-tenant, forming a composite design.
No. 1303 is inscribed "Lipoleurodon" in error.

240 Fencing

1995. Centenary of Int Olympic Committee. Mult.
1308 8c. Type **240** 40 30
1309 10c. Speed skating 40 30
1310 15c. Diving 60 30
1311 20c. Cycling 2·25 85
1312 25c. Ice hockey 2·25 85
1313 35c. Figure skating 1·25 70
1314 50c. Football 1·50 90
1315 65c. Bobsleighing 1·50 1·25
1316 80c. Supergiant slalom 1·50 1·60
1317 $1.25 Show jumping 2·50 3·00
MS1318 Two sheets, each 89 × 110 mm. (a) $2 Downhill skiing. (b) $2 Gymnastics Set of 2 sheets 6·50 7·50
Both miniature sheets are incorrectly dated "1984–1994" on the margin.

241 Cat and Kitten

242 Belted Kingfisher

1995. Cats. Multicoloured.
1319 15c. Type **241** 90 50
1320 20c. Tabby on branch 95 50
1321 35c. Cat and ladybird 1·40 50
1322 50c. Black and white cat 1·75 75
1323 65c. Red cat with flower in paw 2·00 1·25
1324 80c. White cat on pink pillow 2·25 1·75
1325 $1 Siamese with flower in paws 2·25 2·25
1326 $1.25 Cats preening 2·50 3·00
MS1327 Two sheets, each 106 × 76 mm. (a) $2 Kitten and ladybirds. (b) $2 Kittens asleep Set of 2 sheets 8·50 8·50

1995. Birds. Multicoloured.
1328 10c. Type **242** 50 50
1329 15c. Clapper rail 60 50
1330 20c. American redstart 70 50
1331 25c. Roseate tern 80 50
1332 35c. American purple gallinule ("Purple Gallinule") 90 55
1333 45c. Ruddy turnstone 1·00 70
1334 50c. Barn owl 1·50 90
1335 60c. Brown booby 1·25 90
1336 80c. Great blue heron 1·50 1·25
1337 $1 Antillean nighthawk 2·00 2·00
1338 $1.25 Thick-billed vireo 2·25 2·25
1339 $1.40 Greater flamingo ("American Flamingo") 2·50 3·00
1340 $2 Wilson's plover 3·50 4·00
1341 $5 Blue-winged teal 8·00 9·00
1342 $10 Pair of reddish egrets (50 × 28 mm) 15·00 16·00

1995. 95th Birthday of Queen Elizabeth the Queen Mother. As T **299a** of St. Vincent.
1344 50c. brown, light brown and black 1·75 1·75
1345 50c. multicoloured 1·75 1·75
1346 50c. multicoloured 1·75 1·75
1347 50c. multicoloured 1·75 1·75
MS1348 102 × 127 mm. $2 multicoloured 5·50 5·50
DESIGNS: No. 1344, Queen Elizabeth the Queen Mother (pastel drawing); 1345, Wearing tiara; 1346, At desk (oil painting); 1347, Wearing blue dress; **MS**1348, wearing pale blue dress and hat.

1995. 50th Anniv of End of Second World War in Europe. As T **296a** of St. Vincent. Multicoloured.
1349 10c. Churchill, Roosevelt and Stalin at Yalta Conference 50 50
1350 15c. Liberated Allied prisoners of war 50 50
1351 20c. Meeting of American and Soviet soldiers at River Elbe 55 50
1352 25c. Pres. Roosevelt's funeral cortege 55 35
1353 60c. U.S. bugler sounding cease-fire 1·10 1·10
1354 80c. U.S. sailor kissing nurse, New York 1·50 1·75
1355 $1 Nuremburg Trials 1·75 2·00
MS1356 104 × 74 mm. $2 Fireworks over Allied capital 3·00 3·75

243 William James Scuba, 1825

1995. "Singapore '95" International Stamp Exhibition. Deep Sea Diving. Multicoloured.
1357 60c. Type **243** 1·25 1·25
1358 60c. Rouquayrol apparatus, 1864 1·25 1·25
1359 60c. Fluess oxygen-rebreathing apparatus, 1878 1·25 1·25
1360 60c. Armoured diving suit, 1900 1·25 1·25
1361 60c. Diving on the "Lusitania" in Peress armoured diving suit, 1935 1·25 1·25
1362 60c. Cousteau Gagnan aqualung, 1943 1·25 1·25
1363 60c. Underwater camera, 1955 1·25 1·25
1364 60c. Sylvia Earle's record dive, 1979 1·25 1·25
1365 60c. Spider propeller-driven rigid suit, 1984 1·25 1·25
MS1366 Two sheets, each 107 × 77 mm. (a) $2 Helmet diver, 1935. (b) $2 Jacques-Yves Cousteau (aqualung pioneer) Set of 2 sheets 6·00 6·50

1995. Christmas. Religious Paintings by Piero di Cosimo. As T **281a** of Sierra Leone. Mult.
1367 20c. "Madonna and Child with St. Giovannino" 90 50
1368 25c. "Adoration of the Child" 90 50
1369 60c. "Madonna and Child with St. Giovannino, St. Margherita and Angel" 2·00 1·25
1370 $1 "Madonna and Child with Angel" 2·25 2·75
MS1371 76 × 106 mm. $2 "Madonna and Child with Angels and Saints" (detail) 5·50 6·00

244 Daisies and Female Symbol ("Rights of Women and Children")

1996. 50th Anniv of the United Nations. Multicoloured.
1372 15c. Type **244** 30 25
1373 60c. Peace dove escaping from prison 80 80
1374 80c. Symbolic candles ("Human Rights") 1·10 1·50
1375 $1 People on open book 1·40 1·75
MS1376 107 × 78 mm. $2 National flags forming "50" 3·25 4·25

245 Farmer on Tractor

1996. 50th Anniv of Food and Agriculture Organization. Sheet 111 × 80 mm.
MS1377 **245** $2 multicoloured 2·40 3·00

1996. 70th Birthday of Queen Elizabeth II. As T **323a** of St. Vincent. Multicoloured.
1378 80c. As Type **323a** of St. Vincent 1·25 1·40
1379 80c. In blue coat and hat 1·25 1·40
1380 80c. At Trooping the Colour 1·25 1·40
MS1381 125 × 104 mm. $2 In yellow dress and hat 3·75 4·00

246 Glaucus, God of Divers, 2500 B.C.

1996. "China '96" Asian International Philatelic Exhibition, Beijing. Underwater Exploration (1st series). Multicoloured.
1382 55c. Type **246** 1·25 1·25
1383 55c. Alexander the Great, 332 B.C. 1·25 1·25
1384 55c. Salvage diver, 1430 1·25 1·25
1385 55c. Borelli's rebreathing device, 1680 1·25 1·25
1386 55c. Edmund Halley's diving bell, 1690 1·25 1·25
1387 55c. John Lethbridge's diving machine, 1715 1·25 1·25
1388 55c. Klingert's diving apparatus, 1789 1·25 1·25
1389 55c. Drieberg's triton, 1808 1·25 1·25
1390 55c. Seibe's diving helmet, 1819 1·25 1·25
MS1391 Two sheets, each 102 × 77 mm. (a) $2 12th-century Arab diver. (b) $2 Caribbean pearl diver, 1498 Set of 2 sheets 7·00 8·00
See also Nos. 1392/1401 and 1460/9.

1996. "Capex '96" World Stamp Exhibition, Toronto. Underwater Exploration (2nd series). As T **246**. Multicoloured.
1392 60c. Jim Jarrat exploring "Lusitania", 1935 1·00 1·00
1393 60c. Cousteau's first use of scuba gear for exploration, 1952 1·00 1·00
1394 60c. Discovery of oldest shipwreck, 1959 1·00 1·00
1395 60c. Raising of the "Vasa", 1961 1·00 1·00
1396 60c. Mel Fisher discovering "Atocha", 1971 1·00 1·00
1397 60c. Barry Clifford discovering "Whydah", 1984 1·00 1·00
1398 60c. Argo robot over the "Bismarck", 1989 1·00 1·00
1399 60c. Discovery of "Land Tortoise" in Lake George, New York, 1991 1·00 1·00
1400 60c. Nuclear submarine recovering artefacts from Roman shipwreck, 1994 1·00 1·00
MS1401 Two sheets, each 102 × 77 mm. (a) $2 Diver investigates the "Edmund Fitzgerald". (b) $2 Alvin exploring the "Titanic" Set of 2 sheets 5·50 7·00

247 Show Jumping

1996. Olympic Games, Atlanta. Sports on Medals. Multicoloured.
1402 55c. Type **247** 90 1·00
1403 55c. Cycling 90 1·00
1404 55c. Fencing 90 1·00
1405 55c. Gymnastics 90 1·00
1406 55c. Pole vaulting 90 1·00
1407 55c. Sprinting 90 1·00
1408 55c. Swimming 90 1·00
1409 55c. Diving 90 1·00
1410 55c. Hurdling 90 1·00
1411 55c. Long-distance running 90 1·00

248 James McCartney (First Chief Minister)

249 Space Dog

1996. 20th Anniv of Ministerial Government.
1412 **248** 60c. multicoloured 70 75

1996. Working Dogs. Multicoloured.
1413 25c. Type **249** 55 55
1414 25c. Greyhound 55 55
1415 25c. St. Bernard 55 55
1416 25c. Dog with medals 55 55
1417 25c. Retriever 55 55
1418 25c. Dog with bone 55 55
1419 25c. "Hearing ear" dog 55 55
1420 25c. Husky 55 55
1421 25c. Police alsatian 55 55
1422 25c. Guard dog 55 55
1423 25c. Boxer 55 55
1424 25c. Sniffer dog 55 55
MS1425 Two sheets, each 106 × 76 mm. (a) $2 Labrador guide dog. (b) $2 Border sheep dog Set of 2 sheets 7·50 7·50

250 Winnie the Pooh asleep in Chair

1996. Christmas. "Winnie the Pooh". Mult.
1426 15c. Type **250** 70 40
1427 20c. Piglet holding star decoration 70 40
1428 35c. Tigger carrying presents 90 55
1429 50c. Pooh, Tigger and Piglet singing carols 1·25 80
1430 60c. Winnie and Rabbit 1·40 1·10
1431 80c. Tigger and Roo 2·00 1·75
1432 $1 Santa Pooh filling stockings 2·25 2·25
1433 $1.25 Christopher Robin and Winnie the Pooh 2·50 3·00
MS1434 Two sheets. (a) 124 × 98 mm. $2 Piglet decorating biscuits. (b) 98 × 124 mm. $2.60, Piglet placing star on tree Set of 2 sheets 9·50 9·50

251 Giant Milkweed

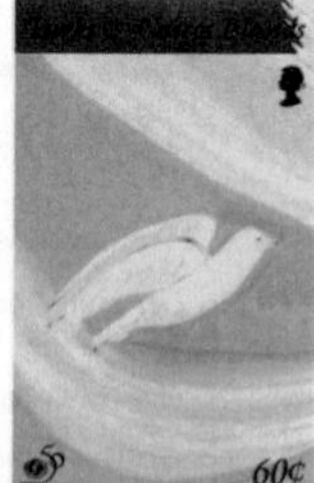

253 White Dove (face value at right)

252 Canterbury Cathedral Tower

1997. Flowers. Multicoloured.
1435 20c. Type **251** 55 65
1436 20c. Geiger tree 55 65
1437 20c. Passion flower 55 65
1438 20c. Hibiscus 55 65
1439 60c. Yellow elder 80 90
1440 60c. Prickly poppy 80 90
1441 60c. Frangipani 80 90
1442 60c. Seaside mahoe 80 90
MS1443 Two sheets, each 105 × 76 mm. (a) $2 Firecracker. (b) $2 Chain of love Set of 2 sheets 5·50 6·50

1997. 50th Anniv of UNESCO. Two sheets, each 127 × 102 mm, containing T **252** and similar horiz design. Multicoloured.
MS1444 (a) $2 Type **252**; (b) $2 High Altar, Canterbury Cathedral Set of 2 sheets 5·50 6·50
The miniature sheets of No. **MS**1444 are inscribed "CATHREDRAL" in error.

1997. 50th Anniv of UNICEF. Multicoloured.
1445 60c. Type **253** 1·40 1·75
1446 60c. White dove (with face value at left) 1·40 1·75
1447 60c. Three children 1·40 1·75
1448 60c. Two children with pets 1·40 1·75

1997. Golden Wedding of Queen Elizabeth and Prince Philip. As T **347a** of St. Vincent. Multicoloured.
1449 60c. Queen Elizabeth II 1·50 1·50
1450 60c. Royal coat of arms 1·50 1·50
1451 60c. Queen Elizabeth and Prince Philip in carriage 1·50 1·50
1452 60c. Queen Elizabeth and Prince Philip on royal visit 1·50 1·50
1453 60c. Windsor Castle 1·50 1·50

1454 60c. Prince Philip . . . . . 1·50 1·50
MS1455 100 × 70 mm. $2 Princess Elizabeth and Duke of Edinburgh on wedding day . . . . . . 4·75 5·50

1997. "Pacific '97" International Stamp Exhibition, San Francisco. Death Centenary of Heinrich von Stephan (founder of the U.P.U.). As T **347c** of St. Vincent.
1456 50c. mauve 75 85
1457 50c. brown 75 85
1458 50c. blue 75 85
MS1459 80 × 117 mm. $2 mauve and black . . . . 2·75 3·50
DESIGNS: No. 1456, British mail coach, 1700s; 1457, Von Stephan and Mercury; 1458, Space Shuttle; MS1459, Von Stephan and Ancient Greek messenger.

1997. "STAMPSHOW '97" 111th Annual A.P.S. Convention, Milwaukee. Underwater Exploration (3rd series). As T **246**. Multicoloured.
1460 20c. Edgerton underwater camera, 1954 . . . . 50 60
1461 20c. Conshelf habitat, 1963 50 60
1462 20c. "Sealab II", 1965 . . . 50 60
1463 20c. Research habitat Tektite, 1970 . . . . . . 50 60
1464 20c. Galapagos volcanic rift, 1974 . . . . 50 60
1465 20c. Epaulard robot survey craft, 1979 . . . . 50 60
1466 20c. Underwater sealife, 1995 . . . . 50 60
1467 20c. One-man research vessel, 1996 . . . . . . 50 60
1468 20c. Okhotsk Tower, Japan, 1996 . . . . 50 60
MS1469 Two sheets, each 72 × 103 mm. (a) $2 Coelacanth. (b) John Williamson making underwater movie Set of 2 sheets 6·00 7·00

254 "Adoration of an Angel" (detail) (Studio of Fra Angelico)

1997. Christmas. Religious Paintings. Mult.
1470 15c. Type **254** 35 25
1471 20c. "Scenes from the life of St. John the Baptist" (detail) (Master of Saint Severin) 40 30
1472 35c. "Archangel Gabriel" (Masolino de Panicale) . . 65 45
1473 50c. "Jeremiah with two Angels" (detail) (Gherardo Starnina) . . . 85 65
1474 60c. "Jeremiah with Two Angels" (different detail) (Starnina) 95 75
1475 80c. "The Annunciation" (detail) (Giovanni di Palo di Grazia) . . . . 1·25 1·40
1476 $1 "The Annunciation" (detail) (Carlo di Braccesco) . . . . 1·40 1·50
1477 $1.25 "The Nativity" (detail) (Benvenuto di Giovanni Guasta) . . . . 1·75 2·50
MS1478 Two sheets. (a) 130 × 105 mm. $2 "The Journey of the Magi" (detail) (Benozzo Gozzoli). (b) 105 × 130 mm. $2 "The Wilton Diptych" (right panel) (anon) Set of 2 sheets 6·00 7·00

255 Black-finned Snapper

1998. Endangered Species. International Year of the Reef. Fishes. Multicoloured.
1479 25c. Type **255** 45 50
1480 25c. Dog snapper 45 50
1481 25c. Cubera snapper 45 50
1482 25c. Mahogany snapper . . 45 50

256 Spotted Flamingo Tongue (John Petrak)

1998. 1st World Open Underwater Photographic Competition Prizewinners (1997). Multicoloured.
1483 20c. Type **256** 40 35
1484 50c. Feather duster (Dave Bothwell) 80 75
1485 60c. Squirrel fish (Waldermar Seifert) . . . 95 90
1486 80c. Queen angelfish (Ralph Oberlander) . . . . . . 1·25 1·40
1487 $1 Barracuda (Steve Rosenburg) . . . . 1·50 1·60
1488 $1.25 Royal gramma ("Fairy Basslet") (John Petrak) . . . . 1·90 2·25
MS1489 Two sheets, each 148 × 85 mm. (a) $2 Spotted Cleaning Shrimp (Micheal Boyer). (b) $2 Rough File Clam (Steve Rosenburg) Set of 2 sheets . . 6·00 7·00

257 Bird and Logo

258 University Arms on Banner (50th anniv of University of West Indies)

1998. International Year of the Ocean. Multicoloured.
1490 50c. Type **257** . . . . . . 80 1·00
1491 50c. Stylized crab . . . . . 80 1·00
1492 50c. Fish . . . . 80 1·00
1493 50c. Logo in cloverleaf . . . 80 1·00
MS1494 102 × 71 mm. $2 Queen and globe logo . . . . 3·00 3·50

1998. Anniversaries and Events. Multicoloured.
1495 20c. Type **258** 40 35
1496 60c. Global logo (UNESCO World Solar Energy Programme Summit) . . . 1·00 1·00
1497 80c. Flame (50th anniv of Universal Declaration of Human Rights) . . . . . 1·25 1·50
1498 $1 John Glenn (astronaut) (second space flight) . . . 1·75 2·00
MS1499 100 × 72 mm. $2 Space shuttle (John Glen's second space flight) . . . . 3·00 3·50

259 S.E. 5A Aircraft

1998. 80th Anniv of Royal Air Force. Multicoloured.
1500 20c. Type **259** . . . . . . 1·00 40
1501 50c. Sopwith Camel . . . . 1·50 85
1502 60c. Supermarine Spitfire . . 1·60 1·25
1503 80c. Avro Lancaster . . . . 2·00 2·00
1504 $1 Panavia Tornado . . . . 2·25 2·25
1505 $1.25 Hawker Hurricane . . 2·50 3·00
MS1506 Two sheets, each 100 × 80 mm. (a) $2 Hawker Siddley Harrier. (b) $2 Avro Vulcan Set of 2 sheets . . . . 8·50 8·50

260 Diana, Princess of Wales

261 "Magi's Visit"

1998. 1st Death Anniv of Diana, Princess of Wales.
1507 **260** 60c. multicoloured . . . 1·50 1·25

1998. Christmas. Paintings by Thomasita Fessler. Multicoloured.
1508 50c. Type **261** . . . . . . 1·10 1·25
1509 50c. "Flight into Egypt" . . 1·10 1·25
1510 50c. "Wedding Feast" . . . 1·10 1·25
1511 50c. "Maria" . . . . 1·10 1·25
1512 50c. "Annunciation and Visitation" (57 × 46 mm) 1·10 1·25
1513 50c. "Nativity" (57 × 46 mm) . . . . . . 1·10 1·25
MS1514 105 × 103 mm. $2 "Queen of Mothers" . . . . 3·25 3·75

262 Flamingos

1999. Marine Life. Multicoloured.
1515 20c. Type **262** 60 60
1516 20c. Sailing dinghies 60 60
1517 20c. Seagulls and lighthouse 60 60
1518 20c. House on beach . . . 60 60
1519 20c. Yellowtail snapper and pillar coral 60 60
1520 20c. Yellowtail snapper and elliptical star coral 60 60
1521 20c. Porkfish 60 60
1522 20c. Spotted eagle ray . . . 60 60
1523 20c. Large ivory coral . . . 60 60
1524 20c. Shy hamlet and mustard hill coral 60 60
1525 20c. Blue crust coral 60 60
1526 20c. Fused staghorn coral 60 60
1527 20c. Queen angelfish and massive starlet coral . . . 60 60
1528 20c. Pinnate spiny sea fan 60 60
1529 20c. Knobby star coral . . . 60 60
1530 20c. Lowridge cactus coral 60 60
1531 20c. Orange telesto coral . . 60 60
1532 20c. Spanish hogfish and knobby ten-ray star coral 60 60
1533 20c. Clown wrasse and boulder brain coral . . . 60 60
1534 20c. Rainbow parrotfish and regal sea fan 60 60
1535 20c. Bluestriped grunt and great star coral 60 60
1536 20c. Blue tang and stinging coral 60 60
1537 20c. Lavender thin finger coral 60 60
1538 20c. Juvenile French grunt and brilliant sea fingers 60 60
MS1539 Two sheets, each 100 × 70 mm. (a) $2 Elkhorn coral. (b) Sea fan Set of 2 sheets . . 8·00 9·00
Nos. 1515/38 were printed together, se-tenant, with the backgrounds forming a composite design.
No. 1520 is inscribed "ELIPITICAL STAR CORAL" in error.

263 Prince Edward and Miss Sophie Rhys-Jones

265 Peacock Flounder (M. Lynn)

264 Lady Elizabeth Bowes-Lyon, 1907

1999. Royal Wedding. Multicoloured.
1540 60c. Type **263** . . . . . . 1·40 1·40
1541 60c. Prince Edward . . . . 1·40 1·40
1542 60c. Miss Sophie Rhys-Jones 1·40 1·40
1543 60c. Prince Edward and Miss Sophie Rhys-Jones (different) . . . . 1·40 1·40
MS1544 Two sheets, each 75 × 60 mm. (a) $2 Prince Edward and Miss Sophie Rhys Jones in front of buliding. (b) $2 Prince Edward and Miss Sophie Rhys-Jones in front of tree Set of 2 sheets . . . . 7·00 8·00

1999. Queen Elizabeth the Queen Mother's 99th Birthday. Multicoloured.
1545 50c. Type **264** . . . . . . 1·10 1·10
1546 50c. Lady Elizabeth Bowes-Lyon, 1919 . . . . . . 1·10 1·10
1547 50c. On wedding day, 1923 1·10 1·10
1548 50c. With Princesses Elizabeth and Margaret, 1936 . . . . 1·10 1·10
1549 50c. King George VI and Queen Elizabeth during Second World War . . . 1·10 1·10
1550 50c. Queen Elizabeth the Queen Mother, 1958 . . . 1·10 1·10
1551 50c. Wearing blue outfit, 1960 . . . . 1·10 1·10
1552 50c. Wearing floral dress, 1970 . . . . 1·10 1·10
1553 50c. With Princes Charles and William, 1983 . . . . 1·10 1·10
1554 50c. Queen Mother, 1999 . . 1·10 1·10
No. 1549 is inscribed "GEORGE IV" in error.

1999. Winning Entries from 2nd World Open Underwater Photographic Competition. Mult.
1555 10c. Type **265** (inscr "Painted Tunicates (S. Genkins)" in error) 40 40
1555b 10c. Painted Tunicates (S. Genkins) 40 40
1556 20c. Peacock flounder (S. Genkins) (inscr "Peacock Flounder (M. Lynn)" in error) . . 60 60
1556b 20c. Type **265** 60 60
1557 50c. Squat anemone shrimps (M. Boyer) . . 1·25 80
1558 60c. Juvenile drum (N. Army) . . . . 1·40 1·10
1559 80c. Batwing coral crab (R. Jarnutowski) . . . . 1·60 1·60
1560 $1 Moon jellyfish (R. Kaufman) . . . . . 1·75 1·90
MS1561 Two sheets, each 85 × 68 mm. (a) $2 Christmas Tree Worms (B. Joubert) (48½ × 36 mm). (b) $2 Longhorn Nudibranch (Trina Lochlear) (48½ × 36 mm) Set of 2 sheets 8·00 9·00

266 Constellations over Earth and "2000"

1999. New Millennium. Multicoloured.
1562 20c. Type **266** 80 40
1563 50c. Big Ben, London (30 × 47 mm) . . . . . . 1·50 1·25
1564 50c. Flamingo, Turks and Caicos Islands (30 × 47 mm) . . . . . . 1·50 1·25
1565 50c. Empire State Building, New York (30 × 47 mm) 1·50 1·25
1566 50c. Roman Coliseum, Rome (30 × 47 mm) . . . 1·50 1·25
1567 50c. Dome of the Rock, Jerusalem (30 × 47 mm) 1·50 1·25
1568 50c. Eiffel Tower, Paris (30 × 47 mm) . . . . . . 1·50 1·25
1569 $1 As 20c. . . . . 2·00 2·25
MS1570 Two sheets, each 106 × 86 mm. (a) $2 Part of globe and Turks and Caicos Islands flag (30 × 47 mm). (b) $2 Part of globe and Turks and Caicos Islands coat of arms (30 × 47 mm). Set of 2 sheets . . . . 10·00 11·00

267 "The Mystic Marriage of Saint Catherine" (Anthony Van Dyck)

1999. Christmas. Multicoloured.
1571 20c. Type **267** 75 35
1572 50c. "Rest on the Flight into Egypt" . . . . 1·50 75
1573 $2 "Holy Family with Saints John and Elizabeth" . . . 4·50 5·00
MS1574 102 × 122 mm. $2 "The Madonna of the Rosary" . . . 5·00 5·50
No. 1571 is inscribed "Marrige" in error.

268 *Pholiota squarroides*

2000. Fungi. Multicoloured.
1575 50c. Type **268** . . . . . . 1·25 1·40
1576 50c. *Psilocybe squmosa* . . 1·25 1·40
1577 50c. *Spathularia velutipes* 1·25 1·40
1578 50c. *Russula* . . . . 1·25 1·40
1579 50c. *Clitocybe clavipes* . . . 1·25 1·40

1580 50c. *Boletus frostii* 1·25 1·40
MS1581 Two sheets, each 108×71 mm. (a) $2 *Strobilurus conigenoides* (horiz). (b) $2 *Stereum ostrea* (horiz) Set of 2 sheets 7·50 8·00
Nos. 1575/80 were printed together, se-tenant, with the background forming a composite design.

2000. Olympic Games, Sydney. As T **396b** of St. Vincent. Multicoloured.
1582 50c. Johan Oxenstierna (Swedish swimmer), 1932 1·25 1·40
1583 50c. Javelin 1·25 1·40
1584 50c. Aztec Stadium, Mexico City, 1968, and Mexican flag 1·25 1·40
1585 50c. Ancient Greek long-distance running 1·25 1·40

269 Bush Turkey ("Scrub Turkey")

2000. Caribbean Birds. Multicoloured.
1586 50c. Type **269** 1·25 1·40
1587 50c. Glaucous-winged gull ("Sickle Bill Gull") 1·25 1·40
1588 50c. Black-capped chickadee ("Chickadee") 1·25 1·40
1589 60c. Cattle egret ("Egret") 1·25 1·40
1590 60c. Royal tern ("Tern") 1·25 1·40
1591 60c. Osprey 1·25 1·40
1592 60c. Great blue heron 1·25 1·40
1593 60c. Brown pelican ("Pelican") 1·25 1·40
1594 60c. Bahama pintail 1·25 1·40
MS1595 Two sheets, each 95×82 mm. (a) $2 Greater flamingo ("Flamingo"). (b) $2 Hyacinth macaw ("Macaw") Set of 2 sheets 8·00 8·50

270 Airedale Terriers

2000. Cats and Dogs of the World. Multicoloured.
1596 60c. Type **270** 1·40 1·50
1597 60c. Beagle 1·40 1·50
1598 60c. Dalmatian 1·40 1·50
1599 60c. Chow chow 1·40 1·50
1600 60c. Chihuahua 1·40 1·50
1601 60c. Pug 1·40 1·50
1602 80c. Egyptian mau 1·50 1·60
1603 80c. Manx 1·50 1·60
1604 80c. Burmese 1·50 1·60
1605 80c. Korat 1·50 1·60
1606 80c. Maine coon 1·50 1·60
1607 80c. American shorthair 1·50 1·60
MS1608 Two sheets, each 95×82 mm. (a) $2 Collie. (b) Devon rex Set of 2 sheets 8·50 9·50

271 Sir Winston Churchill

2000. 60th Anniv of the Battle of Britain. Multicoloured (except No. MS1625a).
1609 50c. Type **271** 1·10 1·25
1610 50c. Barrage balloon 1·10 1·25
1611 50c. Heinkel He-III/Casa 2 IIIE (fighter) 1·10 1·25
1612 50c. Saying goodbye to young evacuee 1·10 1·25
1613 50c. Hawker Hurricane (fighter) 1·10 1·25
1614 50c. Dr. Jocelyn Peakins (clergyman) in Home Guard 1·10 1·25
1615 50c. R.A.F. squadron scramble 1·10 1·25
1616 50c. Members of Royal Observer Corps watching sky 1·10 1·25
1617 50c. James "Ginger" Lacey 1·10 1·25
1618 50c. Douglas Bader 1·10 1·25
1619 50c. Edgar "Cobber" Kain 1·10 1·25
1620 50c. Air Vice-Marshal Keith Park (commander, No. 11 Group) 1·10 1·25
1621 50c. James "Johnny" Johnson 1·10 1·25
1622 50c. Adolph "Sailor" Malan 1·10 1·25
1623 50c. Alan "Al" Deere 1·10 1·25
1624 50c. Air Vice-Marshal, Trafford Leigh-Mallory (commander, No. 12 Group) 1·10 1·25
MS1625 Two sheets. (a) 86×136 mm. $2 Child evacuees (pink, grey and black). (b) 118×85 mm. $2 Winston Churchill, Union Jack and pilots Set of 2 sheets 8·50 8·50

272 Giant Swallowtail

2000. Caribbean Butterflies. Multicoloured.
1626 50c. Type **272** 1·10 1·25
1627 50c. Common morpho 1·10 1·25
1628 50c. Tiger pierid 1·10 1·25
1629 50c. Banded king shoemaker 1·10 1·25
1630 50c. Figure-of-eight butterfly 1·10 1·25
1631 50c. Polydamas swallowtail 1·10 1·25
1632 50c. Clorinde 1·10 1·25
1633 50c. Blue night butterfly 1·10 1·25
1634 50c. Small lace-wing 1·10 1·25
1635 50c. Mosaic 1·10 1·25
1636 50c. Monarch 1·10 1·25
1637 50c. Grecian shoemaker 1·10 1·25
MS1638 Two sheets, each 68×98 mm. (a) $2 Orange-barred sulphur. (b) $2 White peacock Set of 2 sheets 8·50 8·50
Nos. 1626/31 and 1632/37 were each printed together, se-tenant, with the backgrounds forming composite designs.

273 *Neptune* (sailing packet)

2001. Sailing Ships of the World. Multicoloured.
1639 60c. Type **273** 1·10 1·25
1640 60c. American clipper (vert) 1·10 1·25
1641 60c. U.S.C.G. *Eagle* (cadet barque) 1·10 1·25
1642 60c. *Gloria* (Colombian cadet ship) 1·10 1·25
1643 60c. Viking longship 1·10 1·25
1644 60c. *Henri Grace a Dieu* (English galleon) 1·10 1·25
1645 60c. *Golden Hind* (Drake) 1·10 1·25
1646 60c. H.M.S. *Endeavour* (Cook) 1·10 1·25
1647 60c. *Anglo-Norman* (British barque) 1·10 1·25
1648 60c. *Libertad* (Argentine full-rigged cadet ship) 1·10 1·25
1649 60c. Northern European cog 1·10 1·25
1650 60c. 16th-century carrack 1·10 1·25
1651 60c. *Mayflower* (Pilgrim Fathers) 1·10 1·25
1652 60c. *Queen Anne's Revenge* (Blackbeard) 1·10 1·25
1653 60c. *Holkar* (British barque) 1·10 1·25
1654 60c. *Amerigo Vespucci* (Italian cadet ship) 1·10 1·25
MS1655 Two sheets, each 48×67 mm. (a) $2 U.S.S. Constitution (frigate) (vert). (b) $2 Danmark (full-rigged Danish cadet ship) (vert) Set of 2 sheets 7·50 8·00
No 1642 is inscribed "Columbia" and 1648 "Liberated", both in error.

274 Beluga

2001. Whales and Dolphins. Multicoloured.
1656 50c. Type **274** 1·10 1·25
1657 50c. Dwarf sperm whale 1·10 1·25
1658 50c. Killer whale, swimming underwater 1·10 1·25
1659 50c. Shortfin pilot whale 1·10 1·25
1660 50c. Bowhead whale 1·10 1·25
1661 50c. Two killer whales 1·10 1·25
1662 50c. Pygmy sperm whale 1·10 1·25
1663 50c. Right whale 1·10 1·25
1664 50c. Sperm whale with calf 1·10 1·25
1665 50c. California grey whale 1·10 1·25
1666 50c. Narwhal 1·10 1·25
1667 50c. Killer whale leaping 1·10 1·25
1668 50c. Bryde's whale 1·10 1·25
1669 50c. Two belugas 1·10 1·25
1670 50c. Sperm whale 1·10 1·25
1671 50c. Three pilot whales 1·10 1·25
MS1672 Two sheets, each 92×69 mm. (a) $2 Humpback whale and calf. (b) $2 Cuviers beacked whale Set of 2 sheets 7·50 8·00

274a Woman on beach

2001. United Nations Women's Human Rights Campaign. Multicoloured.
1673 90c. Type **274a** 1·40 1·40
1674 $1 "Caribbean Woman II" 1·60 1·60

2001. Death Centenary of Queen Victoria. As T **425** of St. Vincent. Multicoloured.
1675 60c. Queen Victoria in old age, wearing white cap 1·10 1·25
1676 60c. As a girl in evening dress 1·10 1·25
1677 60c. Bare-headed 1·10 1·25
1678 60c. Wearing diadem 1·10 1·25
1679 60c. Holding fan 1·10 1·25
1680 60c. In Coronation robes (after Franz Winterhalter) 1·10 1·25
1681 60c. In carriage 1·10 1·25
1682 60c. As Empress of India 1·10 1·25
MS1683 Two sheets, each 82×113 mm. (a) $2 Queen Victoria carrying umbrella. (b) $2 Wearing white hat and veil Set of 2 sheets 7·50 8·00

2001. 75th Birthday of Queen Elizabeth II. As T **428** of St. Vincent. Multicoloured.
1684 60c. Queen Elizabeth wearing purple hat and coat 1·10 1·25
1685 60c. Wearing tiara and evening dress 1·10 1·25
1686 60c. In green hat and coat 1·10 1·25
1687 60c. Wearing diadem and ruby necklace 1·10 1·25
1688 60c. In red hat and coat 1·10 1·25
1689 60c. Wearing tiara and veil 1·10 1·25
MS1690 78×140 mm. $2 Queen Elizabeth robes of the Order of the Bath 3·75 4·00

275 "Rikaku II as a Fisherman" (Hirosada)

276 *Dismorphia cubana*

2001. "Philanippon '01" International Stamp Exhibition, Tokyo. Japanese Art. Multicoloured.
1691 60c. Type **275** 1·10 1·25
1692 60c. "Autumn Moon in Mirror" (Suzuki Harunobu) 1·10 1·25
1693 60c. "Musical Party" (Hishikawa Morunobu) 1·10 1·25
1694 60c. "Kannon and Four Farmers" (H. Gatto) 1·10 1·25
1695 60c. "Rain in Fifth Month" (I. Kunisada) 1·10 1·25
1696 60c. "The Lives of Women" (Utagawa Kuniyoshi) 1·10 1·25

2001. Butterflies. Multicoloured.
1697 10c. Type **276** 10 15
1698 15c. *Parides gundalachianus* (vert) 15 20
1699 20c. *Graphium androcles* 20 25
1700 25c. Eastern black swallowtail 25 30
1701 35c. *Papilio velvois* (vert) 35 40
1702 45c. Schaus swallowtail (vert) 50 55
1703 50c. Pipevine swallowtail (vert) 55 60
1704 60c. *Euploea Mniszechii* (vert) 65 70
1705 80c. *Papilio caiguanabus* (vert) 85 90
1706 $1 *Graphium encelades* (vert) 1·10 1·20
1707 $1.25 *Calisto zangis* 1·30 1·40
1708 $1.40 Eastern tiger swallowtail 1·50 1·60
1709 $2 *Graphium milon* (vert) 2·10 2·20
1710 $5 Palamedes swallowtail 5·25 5·50
1711 $10 Zebra swallowtail 10·50 11·00
No. 1704 is inscribed "MNISZECKI", in error

277 Crossing Place Trail Monument, Middle Caicos

279 Duchess of York, 1923

278 Sooty Tern

2002. Golden Jubilee. Multicoloured (except Nos. 1718/19).
1712 25c. Type **277** 25 30
1713 25c. Wades Green Plantation, North Caicos 25 30
1714 25c. Underwater scenery, Grand Turk 25 30
1715 25c. St. Thomas Anglican Church, Grand Turk 25 30
1716 25c. Ripsaw Band, Grand Turk 25 30
1717 25c. Basket weaving 25 30
1718 60c. Princess Mary with cannon, Grand Turk, 1960 (black and gold) 65 70
1719 60c. Queen Elizabeth on South Caicos, 1966 (black, gold and blue) 65 70
1720 60c. Princess Alexandra on Providenciales, 1988 65 70
1721 60c. Duke of Edinburgh on Grand Turk, 1998 65 70
1722 60c. Prince Andrew and aquarium, Grand Turk, 2000 65 70
1723 80c. Salt gathering, Salt Cay 85 90
1724 80c. Space capsule, Grand Turk 85 90
1725 80c. Legislative Council Chamber, Grand Turk 85 90
1726 80c. Map of Turks and Caicos Islands 85 90
1727 80c. National Museum, Grand Turk 85 90

2002. 20th World Scout Jamboree, Thailand. As T **116** of St. Kitts. Multicoloured.
1728 80c. Scout wood-working 85 90
1729 80c. Rifle shooting 85 90
1730 80c. Swinging over river 85 90
1731 80c. Scouts in tent at night 85 90
MS1732 107×127 mm. $2 Disabled scouts playing football 2·10 2·20

2002. International Year of Mountains. As T **115** of St. Kitts, but vert. Multicoloured.
1733 80c. Devil's Peak, South Africa 85 90
1734 80c. Drakensburg Mountains, South Africa 85 90
1735 80c. Mont Blanc, France 85 90
1736 80c. Roan Mountain, Tennessee, U.S.A. 85 90
1737 80c. Mount Sefton, New Zealand 85 90
1738 80c. Mount Cook, New Zealand 85 90
MS1739 107×127 mm. $2 North-west Highlands, Scotland 2·10 2·20

2002. U.N. Year of Eco Tourism. As T **449** of St. Vincent. Multicoloured.
1740 60c. Humpback whale and lighthouse 65 70
1741 60c. Yacht 65 70
1742 60c. Two yachts racing 65 70
1743 60c. Queen angelfish 65 70
1744 60c. Manta and tropical fish 65 70
1745 60c. Turtle with boy wearing snorkle 65 70
MS1746 98×70 mm. $2 "Jojo" (Bottlenose Dolphin) (85×28 mm) 2·10 2·20
Nos. 1740/5 were printed together, se-tenant, forming a composite design.

2002. "United We Stand". Support for Victims of 11 September 2001 Terrorist Attacks. As T **114** of St. Kitts. Multicoloured.
1747 50c. U.S. and Turks and Caicos flags with Statue of Liberty's torch 55 60

2002. Birds and Insects. Multicoloured.
1748 60c. Type **278** 65 70
1749 60c. Magnificent frigatebird 65 70
1750 60c. American white pelican 65 70
1751 60c. Northern shoveler 65 70
1752 60c. Northern oriole ("Baltimore Oriole") 65 70
1753 60c. Roseate spoonbill 65 70
1754 60c. Hawk moth 65 70
1755 60c. Burnet moth 65 70
1756 60c. Mammoth wasp 65 70
1757 60c. Branch-boring beetle 65 70
1758 60c. Flower mantid on leaf 65 70

1759 60c. Flower mantid on tree trunk 65 70
MS1760 Two sheets, each 95×93 mm. (a) $2 Greater flamingo (vert). (b) $2 Tiphiid wasp Set of 2 sheets . . . . . 4·25 4·50
Nos. 1748/53 (birds) and 1754/9 (insects) were each printed together, se-tenant, with the backgrounds forming composite designs.
No. 1753 is inscribed "ROSTATE" in error.

2002. Queen Elizabeth the Queen Mother Commemoration. Multicoloured.
1761 80c. Type **279** 85 90
1762 80c. Queen Elizabeth the Queen Mother on Remembrance Day . . . 85 90

280 Charles Lindbergh as a Young Man

2002. 75th Anniv of First Solo Transatlantic Flight. Multicoloured.
1763 60c. Type **280** 65 70
1764 60c. Lindbergh with *Spirit of St. Louis* 65 70
1765 60c. *Spirit of St. Louis* . . . 65 70
1766 60c. *Spirit of St. Louis* taking off from Roosevelt Field 65 70
1767 60c. *Spirit of St. Louis* above Atlantic 65 70
1768 60c. Lindbergh in Paris . . 65 70

281 John Kennedy as a Young Man

282 "Madonna and Child" (Giovanni Bellini)

2002. Pres John Kennedy Commemoration. Multicoloured, centre colours given.
1769 **281** 60c. brown 65 70
1770 – 60c. mauve 65 70
1771 – 60c. grey 65 70
1772 – 60c. blue 65 70
1773 – 60c. violet 65 70
1774 – 60c. bistre 65 70
DESIGNS: Nos. 1770/4, Showing different portraits.

2002. Christmas. Religious Paintings. Mult.
1775 20c. Type **281** 20 25
1776 25c. "Adoration of the Magi" (Antonio Correggio) (horiz) 25 30
1777 60c. "Transfiguration of Christ" (Bellini) 65 70
1778 80c. "Polyptych of St. Vincent Ferrer," (Bellini) 85 90
1779 $1 "Miraculous Mass" (Simone Martini) . . . . 1·10 1·20
MS1780 90×125 $2 "Christ in Heaven with Four Saints" (Domenico Ghirlandaio) (horiz) 2·10 2·20
No. 1776 is inscribed "ADORATIO" in error.

2003. Japanese Art. As T **467** of St. Vincent. Multicoloured.
1781 25c. "Nagata no Taro Nagamune" (detail) (Utagawa Kuniyoshi) . . 25 30
1782 35c. "Ichikawa Danjuro VII" (Utagawa Kunisada) 35 40
1783 60c. "Nagata no Taro Nagamune" (different detail) (Utagawa Kuniyoshi) 65 70
1784 $1 "Nagata no Taro Nagamune" (different detail) (Utagawa Kuniyoshi) . . . . 1·10 1·20
MS1785 150×150 mm. 80c. Kabuki theatre actor (looking forwards); 80c. Actor with sword in mouth; 80c. Actor holding sword; 80c. Actor with red and yellow quilt 3·50 3·75
MS1786 85×115 mm. $2 "Two Women by a River" (Hashimoto Chikanobu) . . . . 2·10 2·20
Stamps from No. **MS**1785 all show details from "Scroll of Actors" by Toyohara Chikanobu et al.

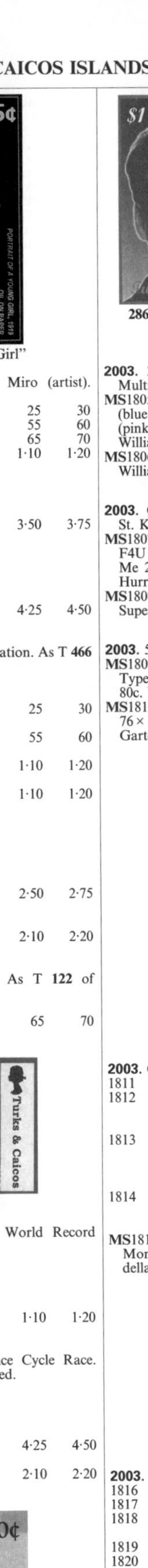

283 "Portrait of a Young Girl"

2003. 20th Death Anniv of Joan Miro (artist). Multicoloured.
1787 25c. Type **283** 25 30
1788 50c. "Table with Glove" . . 55 60
1789 60c. "Self-portrait, 1917" . . 65 70
1790 $1 "The Farmer's Wife" . . 1·10 1·20
MS1791 200×135 mm. 80c. "Portrait of Ramon Sunyer"; 80c. "Self Portrait, 1919"; 80c. "Portrait of a Spanish Dancer"; 80c. "Portrait of Joana Obrador" 3·50 3·75
MS1792 Two sheets. (a) 83×104 mm. $2 "Flowers and Butterfly". Imperf. (b) 104×83 mm. $2 "Still Life of the Coffee Grinder". Imperf Set of 2 sheets . . . . 4·25 4·50

2003. Rembrandt (artist) Commemoration. As T **466** of St. Vincent. Multicoloured.
1793 25c. "Portrait of a Young Man resting his Chin on his Hand" 25 30
1794 50c. "A Woman at an Open Door" 55 60
1795 $1 "The Return of the Prodigal Son" . . . . . 1·10 1·20
1796 $1 "Portrait of an Elderly Man" . . . . 1·10 1·20
MS1797 185×182 mm. 60c. "Nicolaas van Bambeeck"; 60c. "Agatha Bas, Wife of Nicolaas van Bambeeck"; 60c. "Portrait of a Man holding his Hat"; 60c. "Saskia in a Red Hat" (all 35×47 mm) . . . . 2·50 2·75
MS1798 96×128 mm. $2 "Christ driving the Money-changers from the Temple" . . . . 2·10 2·20

2003. 30th Anniv of CARICOM. As T **122** of St. Kitts. Multicoloured.
1799 60c. Union Jack, flamingo and emblem 65 70

284 Tanya Streeter

2003. Tanya Streeter's Freediving World Record (2002). Multicoloured.
MS1800 98×179 mm. 20c. Type **284**; 20c. Tanya Streeter and practice dive; 20c. At seashore; 20c. With map of Turks and Caicos; 20c. Descending dive rope 1·10 1·20

2003. Centenary of Tour de France Cycle Race. As T **127** of St. Kitts. Multicoloured.
MS1801 160×100 mm. $1 Eddy Merckx (1974); $1 Bernard Thevenet (1975); $1 Lucien van Impe (1976); $1 Bernard Thevenet (1977) . . . . 4·25 4·50
MS1802 100×70 mm. $2 Bernard Hinault (1979) . . . . 2·10 2·20

285 Teddy Bear in Military Uniform

2003. Centenary of the Teddy Bear. German Teddy Bears. Multicoloured.
MS1803 184×129 mm. 50c. Type **285**; 50c. Teddy bear wearing blue dress, apron and headscarf; 50c. Musician bear carrying violin; 50c. Marching teddy bear wearing sword . . . . 2·10 2·20
MS1804 70×96 mm. $2 Beer mug with teddy bear pattern . . . . 2·10 2·20

286 Prince William

287 Queen Elizabeth II wearing Imperial State Crown

2003. 21st Birthday of Prince William of Wales. Multicoloured.
MS1805 167×118 mm. $1 Type **286** (blue background); $1 Type **286** (pink background); $1 Prince William (head and shoulders) 3·25 3·50
MS1806 76×101 mm. $2 Prince William . . . . 2·10 2·20

2003. Centenary of Powered Flight. As T **126** of St. Kitts. Multicoloured.
MS1807 116×136 mm. 60c. Vought F4U Corsair; 60c. Messerschmitt Me 262; 60c. A6M; 60c. Hawker Hurricane . . . . 2·50 2·75
MS1808 101×76 mm. $2 Supermarine Spitfire Mk IX . . 2·10 2·20

2003. 50th Anniv of Coronation. Multicoloured.
MS1809 147×91 mm. 80c. Type **287**; 80c. Wearing lilac dress; 80c. Wearing diadem . . . . . 2·50 2·75
MS1810 Two sheets, each 76×101 mm. (a) $2 Queen in Garter robes. (b) $5 In profile 7·50 7·75

288 "Madonna of the Harpies" (detail, Andrea del Sarto)

2003. Christmas. Multicoloured.
1811 25c. Type **288** 25 30
1812 60c. "Madonna and Child with St. Giovannino" (detail, del Sarto) 65 70
1813 80c. "Madonna and Child with St. Giuseppe and St. Pietro Martre" (detail, del Sarto) 85 90
1814 $1 "Madonna and Child with the Angels" (detail, del Sarto) . . . . . . 1·10 1·20
MS1815 81×115 mm. $2 Montefeltro Altarpiece (Piero della Francesca) . . . . 2·10 2·20

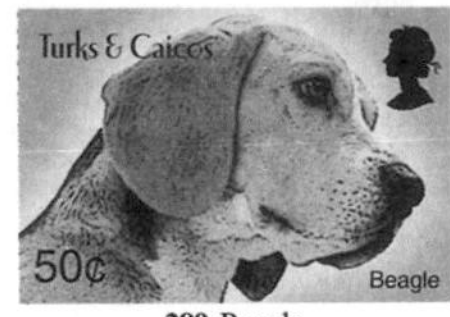

289 Beagle

2003. Dogs and Cats. Multicoloured.
1816 50c. Type **289** 55 60
1817 50c. Persian 55 60
1818 60c. Sabueso Espagnol (dog) (vert) 65 70
1819 60c. Cymric (cat) 65 70
1820 80c. Basset hound (vert) . . 85 90
1821 80c. Maine coon (cat) (vert) 85 90
1822 $1 Jack Russell terrier (vert) 1·10 1·20
1823 $1 Tiffany (cat) . . . . . . 1·10 1·20
MS1824 Two sheets. (a) 96×66 mm. $2 Dachshund. (b) 66×96 mm. $2 Kurile Island Bobtail (cat) (vert) 4·25 4·50

290 *Papilio thersites*

2003. Butterflies. Multicoloured.
1825 50c. Type **290** 55 60
1826 60c. *Papilio andraemon* . . . 65 70
1827 80c. *Papilio pelaus* 85 90
1828 $1 *Consul hippona* . . . . . 1·10 1·20
MS1829 96×66 mm. $2 *Papilio pelaus* . . . . 2·10 2·20

291 *Laelia anceps*

2003. Orchids. Multicoloured.
1830 50c. Type **291** 55 60
1831 60c. *Laelia briegeri* 65 70
1832 80c. *Laelia fidelensis* 85 90
1833 $1 *Laelia cinnabarina* . . . 1·10 1·20
MS1834 96×66 mm. $2 *Laelia rubescens* . . . . 2·10 2·20

TUSCANY Pt. 8

Formerly an independent duchy in C. Italy, now part of Italy.

1851. 60 quattrini = 20 soldi = 12 crazie = 1 Tuscan lira.
1859. 1 Tuscan lira = 1 Italian lira.

1 Arms of Tuscany

5 Arms of Savoy

1851. Imperf.
1 **1** 1q. black on blue £5000 £950
2 1q. black on grey £4750 £900
24 1q. black £600 £550
4 1s. orange on blue £8000 £1000
5 1s. orange on grey £6000 £950
25 1s. buff £18000 £2750
6 2s. red on blue £20000 £3000
7 1c. red on blue £3750 £110
9 1c. red on grey . . . . . . £3750 48·00
26 1c. red £4500 £250
10 2c. blue on blue £3750 £110
11 2c. blue on grey . . . . . . £1800 55·00
28 2c. blue . . . . £1000 50·00
13 4c. green on blue £4000 £140
14 4c. green on grey . . . . . £3000 60·00
30 4c. green . . . . £4250 85·00
16 6c. blue on blue £4000 £110
17 6c. blue on grey . . . . . . £5000 80·00
31 6c. blue . . . . £5000 95·00
20 9c. purple on blue £8000 £190
22 9c. purple on grey . . . . . £8000 90·00
33 9c. brown £16000 £2750
23 60c. red on blue £36000 £18000

1860. Imperf.
36 **5** 1c. purple £1100 £400
40 5c. green £5000 £150
43 10c. brown . . . . £1100 18·00
45 20c. blue . . . . £4250 80·00
48 40c. red £6000 £120
50 80c. red £14000 £600
51 3l. buff £100000 £40000

NEWSPAPER STAMP TAX

N 3

1854.
N1 **N 3** 2s. black . . . . 32·00

TUVA Pt. 10

A province lying between the Sajan and Tannu Ola range. Formerly known as North Mongolia and Tannu, Tuva was incorporated into the U.S.S.R. on 11 October 1944.

PRICES. The prices quoted in the used column are for stamps cancelled to order where these occur. Postally used copies are worth considerably more.

1926. 100 kopeks = 1 rouble.
1934. 100 kopeks = 1 tugrik.
1936. 100 kopeks = 1 aksha.

1 Wheel of Eternity

1926.
1 **1** 1k. red . . . . 1·25 1·10
2 2k. blue . . . . 1·25 1·10

3 5k. orange 1·25 1·10
4 8k. green 1·50 1·25
5 10k. violet 1·50 1·25
6 30k. brown 1·75 1·25
7 50k. black 1·75 1·25
8 1r. turquoise 2·50 2·25
9 3r. red 5·00 4·50
10 5r. blue 8·00 6·00
The rouble values are larger, 22½ × 30 mm.

1927. Surch **TOUVA POSTAGE** and value.
11 **1** 8k. on 50k. black 6·50 5·50
12 14k. on 1r. turquoise 7·50 5·50
13 18k. on 3r. red 10·00 9·00
14 28k. on 5r. blue 14·00 9·50

4 Tuvan Woman

5 Map of Tuva

6 Mongolian Sheep and Tents

7 Fording a River

8 Reindeer (⅔-size illustration)

1927.
15 **4** 1k. brown, red and black 60 35
16 – 2k. brown, green and violet 90 45
17 – 3k. green, yellow and black 1·40 50
18 – 4k. brown and blue 60 35
19 – 5k. blue, black and orange 60 35
20 **5** 8k. sepia, blue and red 70 55
21 – 10k. red, black and green 4·50 75
22 – 14k. orange and blue 8·00 3·25
23 **6** 18k. brown and blue 8·00 3·50
24 – 28k. sepia and green 6·00 2·25
25 **7** 40k. green and red 4·00 2·00
26 – 50k. brown, black and green 3·00 1·75
27 – 70k. bistre and red 5·00 2·75
28 **8** 1r. violet and brown 8·00 5·50
DESIGNS—As Type **4**: 2k. Red deer; 3k. Common goral; 4k. Mongolian tent; 5k. Tuvan man. As Type **5**: 10k. Archers; 14k. Camel caravan. As Type **6**: 28k. Landscape. As Type **7**: 50k. Girl carpet-weaver; 70k. Horseman.

1932. Stamps of 1927 surch **ТЬВА POSTA** and value (10k. optd only).
29 **7** 1k. on 40k. green and red 5·50 6·50
30 – 2k. on 50k. brown, black and green 6·00 5·50
31 – 3k. on 70k. bistre and red 6·00 5·50
32 **5** 5k. on 8k. sepia, blue and red 7·50 5·50
33 – 10k. red, black and green 7·50 7·50
34 – 15k. on 14k. orange and blue 7·50 7·00

1932. Stamps of 1927 surch.
35 **5** 10k. on 8k. brown £150
36 – 15k. on 14k. orange and blue £250
37 **6** 35k. on 18k. brown and blue 60·00 60·00
38 – 35k. on 28k. sepia and green 70·00 70·00

1933. Fiscal stamps (20 × 39 mm) surch **Posta** and value. (a) Numerals 6¾ mm tall.
39 15k. on 6k. yellow £120 £100
40 35k. on 15k. brown £475 £400

(b) Numerals 5¼ mm tall.
41 15k. on 6k. yellow £150 £140
42 35k. on 15k. brown £500 £450

12 Mounted Hunter

13 Interior of Tent

14 Yak

1934. Perf or imperf.
43 **12** 1k. orange 1·00 40
44 – 2k. green 1·00 75
45 **13** 3k. red 1·00 75
46 – 4k. purple 2·50 1·50
47 **14** 5k. blue 2·50 1·50
48 – 10k. brown 2·50 1·50
49 – 15k. lake 2·50 1·50
50 – 20k. black 3·00 2·00
DESIGNS—As Type **12**: 2k. Hunter. As Type **13**: 4k. Tractor. As Type **14**: 10k. Camel caravan; 15k. Lassoing reindeer; 20k. Corsac fox-hunting.

15 Kalinin K-5 over Yaks

16 Western Capercaillie

1934. Air.
51 **15** 1k. red 1·00 75
52 – 5k. green 1·00 75
53 **16** 10k. brown 4·00 85
54 – 15k. red 2·00 75
55 – 25k. purple 2·00 75
56 **15** 50k. green 2·00 75
57 – 75k. red 2·00 75
58 **15** 1t. blue 2·00 1·25
59 – 2t. blue (55 × 28 mm) 3·00 2·25
DESIGNS—As Type **15**: 5, 15k. Tupolev ANT-25 over camels. As Type **16**: 25k. Junkers F-13 with skis over argali; 75k. Junkers F-13 over ox-cart; 2t. Tupolev ANT-9 over roe deer.
The 2t. also comes larger, 61 × 31 mm.

1935. No. 49 surch.
60 20k. on 15k. lake 85·00

18 Map of Tuva

19 Rocky Outcrop

1935. Landscapes.
61 **18** 1k. orange 90 75
62 – 3k. green 90 75
63 – 5k. red 1·10 75
64 – 10k. violet 1·10 75
65 **19** 15k. green 1·25 95
66 – 25k. blue 1·25 95
67 – 50k. sepia 1·25 1·00
DESIGNS—As Type **18**: 3, 5, 10k. Views of River Yenisei. As Type **19**: 25k. Bei-kem rapids; 50k. Mounted hunter.

20 Eurasian Badger

21 Corsac Fox

22 Elk

1935. Animals.
68 **20** 1k. orange 1·10 85
69 – 3k. green 1·10 85
70 – 5k. mauve 1·10 90
71 **21** 10k. red 1·10 90
72 – 25k. red 1·50 1·00
73 – 50k. blue 1·50 1·00
74 **22** 1t. violet 1·50 1·00
75 – 2t. blue 1·50 1·00
76 – 3t. brown 1·50 1·10
77 – 5t. blue 1·50 1·25
DESIGNS—As Type **20**—VERT: 3k. Eurasian red squirrel. HORIZ: 5k. Sable. As Type **21**: 25k. European otter; 50k. Lynx. LARGER (61 × 31 mm): 2t. Yak; 3k. Bactrian camel. As Type **22**: 5t. Brown bear.
See also No. 115.

23 Arms of Republic

24 Wrestlers

25 Herdsman

26 Sports Meeting

27 Partisans

1936. 15th Anniv of Independence. (a) Postage.
78 **23** 1k. green 1·25 55
79 – 2k. sepia 1·25 55
80 – 3k. blue 1·75 60
81 **24** 4k. red 2·00 60
82 – 5k. purple 3·25 50
83 **24** 6k. green 3·00 50
84 – 8k. purple 3·00 55
85 – 10k. red 3·50 50
86 – 12k. agate 4·00 75
87 – 15k. green 5·00 55
88 – 20k. blue 5·00 75
89 **25** 25k. red 5·00 55
90 – 30k. purple 15·00 1·00
91 **25** 35k. red 5·00 55
92 – 40k. sepia 5·00 55
93 – 50k. blue 5·00 55
94 **26** 70k. plum 5·00 1·10
95 – 80k. green 5·00 1·10
96 **27** 1a. red 6·00 1·10
97 2a. red 5·75 1·10
98 – 3a. blue 5·75 1·10
99 – 5a. agate 5·75 1·10
DESIGNS—As Type **23**: 2k. President Gyrmittazi; 3k. Camel and driver. As Type **24**: 5, 8k. Archers; 10, 15k. Fishermen; 12, 20k. Brown bear hunt. As Type **25**: 30k. Bactrian camel and steam goods train; 40, 50k. Horse-racing. As Type **26**: 8k., 5a. 1921 war scene; 3a. Confiscation of cattle.
See also Nos. 116 and 118/19.

28 Yak Transport

29 Horseman and Airship

30 Seaplane over Waves

(b) Air.
100 **28** 5k. blue and flesh 2·00 75
101 – 10k. purple and brown 3·00 80
102 **28** 15k. agate and grey 3·00 80
103 **29** 25k. purple and cream 4·00 90
104 – 50k. red and cream 4·00 1·10
105 **29** 75k. green and yellow 4·00 1·10
106 **30** 1a. green and turquoise 4·00 1·25
107 2a. red and cream 5·00 1·25
108 3a. sepia and flesh 5·00 2·00
DESIGNS—As Type **28**: 10k. Horse-drawn reaper. As Type **29**: 50k. Feast of the women.
See also No. 117.

1938. Various stamps surch with large numerals and old values obliterated.
109 5k. on 2a. red (No. 97)
110 5k. on 2a. red and cream (No. 107)
111 10k. on 1t. blue (No. 58)
112 20k. on 50k. sepia (No. 67)
113 30k. on 2a. red and cream (No. 107)
114 30k. on 3a. sepia and flesh (No. 108)
See also Nos. 120/1.

1938. Previous types with designs modified and colours changed.
115 5k. green (No. 70) £100
116 10k. blue (No. 85) £100
117 15k. brown (No. 102) £100
118 20k. red (No. 88) £225
119 30k. purple (as No. 95) . . . £100
In Nos. 116/19 the dates have been removed and in No. 117 "AIR MAIL" also.

1939. Nos. 58 and 67 surch with small thick numerals and old values obliterated.
120 1k. on 1t. blue . . . .
121 20k. on 50k. sepia . . . . .
See also Nos. 122/3.

1940. Various stamps surch.
122 10k. on 1t. blue (No. 58) . .
123 20k. on 50k. sepia (No. 67)
124 20k. on 50k. blue (No. 73)
125 20k. on 50k. blue (No. 93)
126 20k. on 50k. red and cream (No. 104) . . . .
127 20k. on 75k. green and yellow (No. 105) . . . . .
128 20k. on 80k. green (No. 95)

1942. Nos. 98/9 surch.
129 25k. on 3a. blue . . . . . .
130 25k. on 5a. agate . . . . . .

34 Tuvan Woman

1942. 21st Anniv of Independence. Imperf.
131 **34** 25k. blue £225
132 – 25k. blue £225
133 – 25k. blue £225
DESIGNS: No. 132 Agricultural Exhibition building; No. 133 Government building.

35 Coat of Arms

36 Government Building

1943. 22nd Anniv of Independence. With or without gum.
134 **35** 25k. blue . . . . 30·00
135 25k. black . . . . 40·00
136 25k. green . . . . 80·00
137 **36** 50k. green . . . . 80·00

TUVALU Pt. 1

Formerly known as the Ellice Islands and sharing a joint administration with the Gilbert group. On 1 January 1976 the two island groups separated and the Ellice Is. were renamed Tuvalu.

100 cents = $1 Australian.

1 Tuvaluan and Gilbertese

1976. Separation. Multicoloured.
1 4c. Type **1** 35 80
2 10c. Map of the islands (vert) 50 1·00
3 35c. Gilbert and Ellice canoes 70 1·50

1976. Nos. 173/87 of Gilbert and Ellice Islands optd **TUVALU.**
14 1c. Cutting toddy 30 30
20 2c. Lagoon fishing 30 40
21 3c. Cleaning pandanus leaves 30 40
22 4c. Casting nets 30 45
5 5c. Gilbertese canoe 50 60
15 6c. De-husking coconuts . . . 30 30
6 8c. Weaving pandanus fronds 30 60
7 10c. Weaving a basket 30 65
16 15c. Tiger shark . . . . . . 1·00 40
23 20c. Beating a rolled pandanus leaf 30 60
24 25c. Loading copra 30 60
25 35c. Fishing at night 70 70
17 50c. Local handicrafts 30 50
18 $1 Weaving coconut screen . . 35 60
19 $2 Coat of arms 50 60

3 50c. Coin and Octopus

4 Niulakita and Seven-ridged Leathery Turtle

1976. New Coinage. Multicoloured.
26 5c. Type **3** 25 15
27 10c. Red-eyed crab 35 20
28 15c. Flying fish 45 25
29 35c. Green turtle 60 50

1976. Multicoloured.
58 1c. Type **4** 50 15
59 2c. Nukulaelae and sleeping mat 20 25
60 4c. Nui and taro (vegetable) 20 15
61 5c. Nanumanga and grass skirt 25 15
62 6c. Nukufetau and coconut crab 20 35
63 8c. Funafuti and banana tree 20 25
64 10c. Map of Tuvalu 20 20
37 15c. Niutao and flying fish . . 75 20
38 20c. Vaitupu and maneapa (meeting hall) 35 40
66 25c. Nanumea and fish-hook 80 20
67 30c. Fatele (local dancing) . . 30 20
40 35c. Te Ano (game) 35 20
68 40c. Screw pine 30 15
41 50c. Canoe pole fishing . . . 35 20
42 $1 Reef fishing by flare . . . 35 20
43 $2 Living house 35 20
69 $5 M.V. "Nivanga" . . . . . 1·00 2·25

5 Title Page of New Testament

1976. Christmas. Multicoloured.
45 5c. Type **5** 20 25
46 20c. Lotolelei Church 20 25
47 25c. Kelupi Church 20 25
48 30c. Mataloa o Tuvala Church 25 25
49 35c. Palataise o Keliso Church 25 25

6 The Queen and Duke of Edinburgh after Coronation

1977. Silver Jubilee. Multicoloured.
50 15c. Type **6** 15 10
51 35c. Prince Philip carried ashore at Vaitupu 20 15
52 50c. The Queen and attendants 30 20
MS53 98 × 144 mm. Nos. 50/2 . . 1·00 1·00

7 "Health"

1977. 30th Anniv of South Pacific Commission. Multicoloured.
54 5c. Type **7** 15 20
55 20c. "Education" 15 20
56 30c. "Fruit-growing" 15 20
57 35c. Map of S.P.C. area . . . 20 25

8 Scout Promise

1977. 50th Anniv of Scouting in the Central Pacific. Multicoloured.
73 5c. Type **8** 15 20
74 20c. Canoeing 15 20
75 30c. Scout shelter 20 25
76 35c. Lord Baden-Powell . . . 20 25

9 Hurricane Beach (Expedition photo)

1977. Royal Society Expeditions, 1896–97.
77 **9** 5c. multicoloured 15 15
78 – 20c. black and blue 15 20
79 – 30c. black and blue 20 20
80 – 35c. multicoloured 20 20
DESIGNS—VERT: 20c. Boring apparatus on H.M.S. "Porpoise"; 30c. Dredging chart. HORIZ: 35c. Charles Darwin and H.M.S. "Beagle".

10 Pacific Pigeon

13 White Frangipani

11 "Lawedua" (inter-island coaster)

1978. Wild Birds. Multicoloured.
81 8c. Type **10** 35 25
82 20c. Reef heron 40 40
83 30c. White tern ("Fairy Tern") 45 50
84 40c. Lesser frigate bird 45 55

1978. Ships. Multicoloured.
85 8c. Type **11** 15 15
86 20c. "Wallacia" (tug) 15 15
87 30c. "Cenpac Rounder" (freighter) 20 20
88 40c. "Pacific Explorer" (freighter) 20 20

1978. 25th Anniv of Coronation. As Nos. 422/5 of Montserrat. Multicoloured.
89 8c. Canterbury Cathedral . . . 10 10
90 30c. Salisbury Cathedral . . . 10 10
91 40c. Wells Cathedral 10 10
92 $1 Hereford Cathedral 30 30
MS93 137 × 108 mm. Nos. 89/92 45 70

1978. Independence. Nos. 63/4, 37/8, 67/40 and 68 optd **INDEPENDENCE 1ST OCTOBER 1978.**
94 8c. Funafuti and banana tree 10 10
95 10c. Map of Tuvalu 10 10
96 15c. Niutao and four-winged flyingfish 10 10
97 20c. Vaitupu and maneapa (house) 10 10
98 30c. Fatele (local dancing) . . 15 15
99 35c. Te Ano (game) 15 15
100 40c. Screw pine 15 15

1978. Wild Flowers. Multicoloured.
101 8c. Type **13** 10 10
102 20c. Susana 10 10
103 30c. Tiale 15 15
104 40c. Inato 20 25

14 Squirrelfish

1979. Fishes (1st series). Multicoloured.
105 1c. Type **14** 10 10
106 2c. Band-tailed goatfish . . 10 10
107 4c. Regal angelfish 10 10
108 5c. Melon butterflyfish . . . 10 10
109 6c. Semi-circle angelfish . . 10 10
110 8c. Blue-striped snapper . . 10 10
111 10c. Clown anemonefish . . 15 10
112 15c. Chevron butterflyfish 20 10
113 20c. Yellow-edged lyretail ("Fairy cod") 25 15
114 25c. Clown triggerfish . . . 25 20
115 30c. Long-nosed butterflyfish 25 10
116 35c. Yellow-finned tuna . . 30 15
117 40c. Spotted eagle ray . . . 30 10
117b 45c. Black-tipped grouper 1·50 2·25
118 50c. Hammerhead 30 20
119 70c. Lionfish (vert) 30 30
120 $1 Painted triggerfish (vert) 30 30
121 $2 Copper-banded butterflyfish ("Beaked coralfish") (vert) 50 30
122 $5 Tiger shark (vert) . . . 70 35
See also Nos. 770/81.

15 "Explorer of the Pacific"

1979. Death Bicent of Capt. James Cook. Mult.
123 8c. Type **15** 15 20
124 30c. "A new island is discovered" 15 20
125 40c. "Transit of Venus, Tahiti, 3 June, 1769" . . . 15 20
126 $1 Cook's death 15 30

16 Grumman Mackinnon Goose Flying Boat and Nukulaelae Island

1979. Internal Air Service. Multicoloured.
127 8c. Type **16** 15 15
128 20c. Goose and Vaitupu . . 15 15
129 30c. Goose and Nui 20 20
130 40c. Goose and Funafuti . . 25 30

17 Sir Rowland Hill, 1976 4c. Separation Commemorative and London's First Pillar Box, 1855

1979. Death Cent of Sir Rowland Hill. Mult.
131 30c. Type **17** 15 15
132 40c. Sir Rowland Hill, 1976 10c. Separation commemorative and Penny Black 15 15
133 $1 Sir Rowland Hill, 1976 35c. Separation commemorative and mail coach 25 30
MS134 148 × 140 mm. Nos. 131/3 70 1·25

18 Child's Face

1979. International Year of the Child.
135 **18** 8c. multicoloured 10 10
136 – 20c. multicoloured 10 10
137 – 30c. multicoloured 10 15
138 – 40c. multicoloured 15 25
DESIGN: 20c. to 40c. Children's faces.

19 Eyed Cowrie

1980. Cowrie Shells. Multicoloured.
139 8c. Type **19** 10 10
140 20c. Jester cowrie 10 10
141 30c. Closely-related carnelian cowrie 15 15
142 40c. Golden cowrie 25 20

20 Philatelic Bureau, Funafuti, and 1976 8c. Definitive

1980. "London 1980" Int Stamp Exhibition. Mult.
143 10c. Type **20** 10 10
144 20c. Nukulaelae postmark and 1976 2c. definitive . . 15 15
145 30c. Fleet Post Office, U.S. Navy, airmail cover, 1943 15 20
146 $1 Map and arms of Tuvalu 35 40
MS147 160 × 136 mm. Nos. 143/6 65 1·10

21 Queen Elizabeth the Queen Mother at Royal Variety Performance, 1978

1980. 80th Birthday of The Queen Mother.
148 **21** 15c. multicoloured 25 20

22 "Aethaloessa calidalis"

1980. Moths. Multicoloured.
149 8c. Type **22** 10 10
150 20c. "Parotis suralis" 15 10
151 30c. "Dudua aprobola" . . . 20 15
152 40c. "Decadarchis simulans" 20 15

23 Air Pacific De Havilland Heron 2

1980. Aviation Commemorations. Mult.
153 8c. Type **23** 10 10
154 20c. Hawker Siddeley H.S.748 . . . . 15 10
155 30c. Short S.25 Sunderland flying boat 15 15
156 40c. Orville Wright and Wright Flyer III 20 15
COMMEMORATIONS: 8c. 1st regular air service to Tuvalu, 1964; 20c. Air service to Tuvalu; 30c. Wartime R.N.Z.A.F. flying boat service to Funafuti, 1945; 40c. Wright Brothers' 1st flight, 17 December, 1903.

1981. No. 118 surch **45 CENTS**.
157 45c. on 50c. Hammerhead . . 25 40

25 "Hypolimnas bolina" (male)

27 U.P.U. Emblem

26 "Elizabeth" (brig), 1809

1981. Butterflies. Multicoloured.
158 8c. Type **25** 15 10
159 20c. "Hypolimnas bolina" (female) 20 15
160 30c. "Hypolimnas bolina" (female) (different) 20 20
161 40c. "Precis villida" (male) 25 20

1981. Ships (1st series). Multicoloured.
162 10c. Type **26** 15 15
163 25c. "Rebecca" (brigantine), 1819 . . . . 15 20
164 35c. "Independence II" (whaling ship), 1821 . . . 20 25
165 40c. H.M.S. "Basilisk" (paddle-sloop), 1872 . . . 25 30
166 45c. H.M.S. "Royalist" (screw-corvette), 1890 . . . 30 35
167 50c. "Olivebank" (barque), 1920 . . . . 30 35
See also Nos. 235/40, 377/80, 442/5, 809/12 and 832/6.

1981. Royal Wedding. Royal Yachts. As T **14a/b** of St. Kitts. Multicoloured.
168 10c. "Carolina" 10 15
169 10c. Prince Charles and Lady Diana Spencer 35 50
170 45c. "Victoria and Albert III" 10 15
171 45c. As No. 169 . . . . . . 40 65
172 $2 "Britannia" 25 50
173 $2 As No. 169 . . . . 75 1·50
MS174 120 × 109 mm. $1.50, As No. 169 . . . . 50 75

1981. U.P.U. Membership.
177 **27** 70c. blue 20 30
178 $1 brown 30 45
MS179 86 × 71 mm. Nos. 177/8 70 2·25

28 Map of Funafuti, and Anchor

1982. Amatuku Maritime School. Mult.
180 10c. Type **28** 10 10
181 25c. Motor launch 20 20
182 35c. School buildings and jetty 25 30
183 45c. School flag and freighter 30 35

29 Caroline of Brandenburg-Ansbach, Princess of Wales, 1714

1982. 21st Birthday of Princess of Wales. Multicoloured.
184 10c. Type **29** 10 10
185 45c. Coat of arms of Caroline of Brandenburg-Ansbach 10 10
186 $1.50 Diana, Princess of Wales 50 30

1982. Tonga Cyclone Relief. Nos. 170/1 optd **TONGA CYCLONE RELIEF 1982 +20c**.
187 45c.+20c. "Victoria and Albert III" 10 30
188 45c.+20c. Prince Charles and Lady Diana Spencer . . . 30 1·10

1982. Birth of Prince William of Wales. Nos. 184/6 optd **ROYAL BABY**.
189 10c. Type **29** 10 10
190 45c. Coat of arms of Caroline of Brandenburg-Ansbach 10 10
191 $1.50 Diana, Princess of Wales 30 30

31 Tuvalu and World Scout Badge

1982. 75th Anniv of Boy Scout Movement. Multicoloured.
192 10c. Type **31** 15 15
193 25c. Campfire 25 40
194 35c. Parade 30 45
195 45c. Boy scout 40 55

32 Tuvalu Crest and Duke of Edinburgh's Standard

1982. Royal Visit. Multicoloured.
196 25c. Type **32** 15 20
197 45c. Tuvalu flag and Queen's Royal Standard 25 30
198 50c. Portrait of Queen Elizabeth II 25 30
MS199 104 × 85 mm. Nos. 196/8 60 1·75

33 Fisherman's Hat and Equipment

1983. Handicrafts. Multicoloured.
200 1c. Type **33** 15 10
201 2c. Cowrie shell handbags 15 10
202 5c. Wedding and baby food baskets 15 10
203 10c. Model canoe 15 10
203a 15c. Ladies' sun hats . . . . 2·25 2·00
204 20c. Palm climbing rope and platform with toddy pot 15 20
205 25c. Pandanus baskets . . . 15 20
205a 30c. Basket tray and coconut stand . . . . . 2·00 1·40
206 35c. Pandanus pillows and shell necklaces 25 30
207 40c. Round baskets and fans 20 35
208 45c. Reef sandals and fish trap 20 40
209 50c. Rat trap (vert) 20 45
209a 60c. Fisherman's waterproof boxes (vert) . . . . . . 2·25 1·40
210 $1 Pump drill and adze (vert) 20 45
211 $2 Fisherman's hat and canoe bailers (vert) . . . 30 55
212 $5 Fishing rod, lures and scoop nets (vert) 60 75

34 "Te Tautai" (trawler)

1983. Commonwealth Day. Multicoloured.
213 20c. Type **34** 15 15
214 35c. Traditional dancing, Motufoua School 15 25
215 45c. Satellite view of Pacific 20 30
216 50c. "Morning Star" (container ship) 25 40

35 "Pantala flavescens"

1983. Dragonflies. Multicoloured.
217 10c. Type **35** 15 10
218 35c. "Anax guttatus" 20 35
219 40c. "Tholymis tillarga" . . . 20 40
220 50c. "Diplacodes bipunctata" 25 50

36 Brigade Members Racing

1983. Centenary of Boys' Brigade. Mult.
221 10c. Type **36** 10 10
222 35c. B.B. members in outrigger canoe 20 30
223 $1 On parade . . . . 50 1·00

1983. No. 210 surch **60c**.
224 60c. on $1 Pump drill and adze 70 70

38 Montgolfier Balloon, 1783

1983. Bicentenary of Manned Flight. Mult.
225 25c. Type **38** 20 20
226 35c. Grumman Mackinnon Turbo Goose (horiz) . . . 20 25
227 45c. Beech 200 Super King Air (horiz) 25 30
228 50c. "Double Eagle II" balloon 25 35
MS229 114 × 145 mm. Nos. 225/8 70 1·00

39 Early Communications

1983. World Communications Year. Mult.
230 25c. Type **39** 15 15
231 35c. Radio operator 20 20
232 45c. Modern teleprinter . . . 20 20
233 50c. Funafuti transmitting station 25 25

1984. No. 208 surch **30c**.
234 30c. on 45c. Reef sandals and fish trap 35 40

1984. Ships (2nd series). As T **26**. Mult.
235 10c. "Titus" (freighter), 1897 25 15
236 20c. "Malaita" (freighter), 1905 . . . . 25 15
237 25c. "Aymeric" (freighter), 1906 . . . . 25 15
238 35c. "Anshun" (freighter), 1965 . . . . 30 25
239 45c. "Beaverbank" (freighter), 1970 . . . . 30 30
240 50c. "Benjamin Bowring" (freighter), 1981 . . . . . 30 30

41 Southern Pacific Railroad Class GS-4

1984. Leaders of the World. Railway Locomotives (1st series). As T **41**. The first in each pair shows technical drawings and the second the locomotive at work.
241 1c. multicoloured 10 10
242 1c. multicoloured 10 10
243 15c. multicoloured 20 25
244 15c. multicoloured 20 25
245 40c. multicoloured 25 30
246 40c. multicoloured 25 30
247 60c. multicoloured 35 40
248 60c. multicoloured 35 40
DESIGNS: Nos. 241/2, Southern Pacific Railroad Class GS-4, U.S.A. (1941); 243/4, New South Wales Govt Class AD 60, Australia (1952); 245/6, New South Wales Govt Class C38, Australia (1943); 247/8, Class "Achilles" "Lord of the Isles", Great Britain (1892).
See also Nos. 253/68, 273/80, 313/20 and 348/55.

42 "Ipomoea pes-caprae"

1984. Beach Flowers. Multicoloured.
249 25c. Type **42** 25 25
250 45c. "Ipomoea macrantha" 40 40
251 50c. "Triumfetta procumbens" 45 45
252 60c. "Portulaca quadrifida" 50 50

1984. Leaders of the World. Railway Locomotives (2nd series). As T **41**. The first design in each pair shows technical drawings and the second the locomotive at work.
253 10c. multicoloured 10 10
254 10c. multicoloured 10 10
255 15c. multicoloured 10 15
256 15c. multicoloured 10 15
257 20c. multicoloured 10 15
258 20c. multicoloured 10 15
259 25c. multicoloured 10 15
260 25c. multicoloured 10 15
261 40c. multicoloured 10 20
262 40c. multicoloured 10 20
263 50c. multicoloured 10 20

264 50c. multicoloured 10 20
265 60c. multicoloured 10 20
266 60c. multicoloured 10 20
267 $1 multicoloured 15 25
268 $1 multicoloured 15 25

DESIGNS: Nos. 253/4, Illinois Central Railroad "Casey Jones" type locomotive No. 382, U.S.A. (1896); 255/6, Erie Railroad Triplex type, U.S.A. (1914); 257/8, Class 370 Advanced Passenger Train, Great Britain (1981); 259/60, LMS Class 4F, Great Britain (1924); 261/2, GWR Class "Tornado Rover", Great Britain (1888); 263/4, Class 73 electric locomotive "Broadlands", Great Britain (1967); 265/6, "Locomotion", Great Britain (1825); 267/8, Class C57, Japan (1937).

43 Exhibition Emblem

1984. "Ausipex" International Stamp Exhibition, Melbourne. Multicoloured.

269 60c. Type **43** 20 30
270 60c. Arms of Tuvalu 20 30
271 60c. Tuvalu flag 20 30
272 60c. Royal Exhibition Building, Melbourne . . . 20 30

1984. Leaders of the World. Railway Locomotives (3rd series). As T **41**. The first in each pair shows technical drawings and the second the locomotive at work.

273 1c. multicoloured 10 10
274 1c. multicoloured 10 10
275 15c. multicoloured 15 20
276 15c. multicoloured 15 20
277 30c. multicoloured 20 25
278 30c. multicoloured 20 25
279 $1 multicoloured 40 65
280 $1 multicoloured 40 65

DESIGNS: Nos. 273/4, Class 9700, Japan (1897); 275/6, Paris-Lyon-Mediterranee Class 231C/K, France (1909); 277/8, Class 640, Italy (1907); 279/80, Paris-Orleans Class 4500, France (1906).

44 A. Shrewsbury

1984. Leaders of the World. Cricketers. As T **44**. The first in each pair shows the cricketer in action and the second a head portrait.

281 5c. multicoloured 15 40
282 5c. multicoloured 15 40
283 30c. multicoloured 25 45
284 30c. multicoloured 25 45
285 50c. multicoloured 25 45
286 50c. multicoloured 25 45
287 60c. multicoloured 30 45
288 60c. multicoloured 30 45

DESIGNS: 281/2, A. Shrewsbury; 283/4, H. Verity; 285/6, E. H. Hendren; 287/8, J. Briggs.

45 Trees and Stars

1984. Christmas. Children's Drawings. Mult.

289 15c. Type **45** 10 10
290 40c. Fishing from outrigger canoes 20 20
291 50c. Three Wise Men bearing gifts 25 25
292 60c. The Holy Family . . . 35 35

46 Morris Minor

1984. Leaders of the World. Automobiles (1st series). As T **46**. The first in each pair shows technical drawings and the second paintings.

293 1c. black, brown and yellow 10 10
294 1c. multicoloured 10 10
295 15c. black, pink and lilac . . 10 15
296 15c. multicoloured 10 15
297 50c. black, brown and mauve 20 20
298 50c. multicoloured 20 20
299 $1 black, green and blue . . 30 40
300 $1 multicoloured 30 40

DESIGNS: Nos. 293/4, "Morris Minor"; 295/6, Studebaker "Avanti"; 297/8, Chevrolet "International Six"; 299/300, Allard "J2".

See also Nos. 321/8, 356/71, 421/32 and 446/69.

47 Common Flicker

1985. Leaders of the World. Birth Bicentenary of John J. Audubon (ornithologist). Multicoloured.

301 1c. Type **47** 10 10
302 1c. Say's phoebe 10 10
303 25c. Townsend's warbler . . 20 30
304 25c. Bohemian waxwing . . . 20 30
305 50c. Prothonotary warbler . . 20 50
306 50c. Worm-eating warbler . . 20 50
307 70c. Broad-winged hawk . . 30 65
308 70c. Hen harrier 30 65

48 Black-naped Tern

1985. Birds and their Eggs. Multicoloured.

309 15c. Type **48** 60 20
310 40c. White-capped noddy . . 1·10 50
311 50c. White-tailed tropicbird 1·10 60
312 60c. Sooty tern . . . . . . 1·25 70

1985. Leaders of the World. Railway Locomotives (4th series). As T **41**. The first in each pair shows technical drawings and the second the locomotive at work.

313 5c. multicoloured 10 10
314 5c. multicoloured 10 10
315 10c. multicoloured 10 10
316 10c. multicoloured 10 10
317 30c. multicoloured 30 35
318 30c. multicoloured 30 35
319 $1 multicoloured 50 80
320 $1 multicoloured 50 80

DESIGNS: Nos. 313/14, GWR "Churchward 28XX", Great Britain (1905); 315/16, Class KF No. 605, China (1935); 317/18, Class 99.77 No. 99773, Germany (1952); 319/20, Pearson type, Great Britain (1853).

1985. Leaders of the World. Automobiles (2nd series). As T **46**. The first in each pair shows technical drawings and the second paintings.

321 1c. black, green and deep green 10 10
322 1c. multicoloured 10 10
323 20c. black, pink and red . . 15 20
324 20c. multicoloured 15 20
325 50c. black, blue and violet . . 20 30
326 50c. multicoloured 20 30
327 70c. black, pink and brown 20 35
328 70c. multicoloured 20 35

DESIGNS: No. 321/2, Rickenbacker (1923); 323/4, Detroit-Electric two door brougham (1914); 325/6, Packard "Clipper" (1941); 327/8, Audi "Quattro" (1982).

49 Curtiss P-40N Warhawk

1985. World War II Aircraft. Multicoloured.

329 15c. Type **49** . . . . 2·00 1·00
330 40c. Consolidated B-24 Liberator . . . . 2·50 1·75
331 50c. Lockhead PV-1 Ventura 2·50 2·00
332 60c. Douglas C-54 . . . . . 2·50 2·25
MS333 110 × 108 mm. Nos. 329/32 5·00 4·00

50 Queen Elizabeth the Queen Mother

51 Guide playing Guitar

1985. Leaders of the World. Life and Times of Queen Elizabeth the Queen Mother. Various portraits.

334 **50** 5c. multicoloured 10 20
335 – 5c. multicoloured 10 20
336 – 30c. multicoloured 10 20
337 – 30c. multicoloured 10 20
338 – 60c. multicoloured 15 25
339 – 60c. multicoloured 15 25
340 – $1 multicoloured 15 40
341 – $1 multicoloured 15 40
MS342 85 × 114 mm. $1.20 multicoloured; $1.20 multicoloured . . . . 60 1·50

Each value issued in pairs showing a floral pattern across the bottom of the portraits which stops short of the left-hand edge on the first stamp and of the right-hand edge on the second.

1985. 75th Anniv of Girl Guide Movement. Multicoloured.

343 15c. Type **51** 15 20
344 40c. Building camp-fire . . . 40 45
345 50c. Patrol leader with Guide flag 50 55
346 60c. Guide saluting 60 65
MS347 141 × 77 mm. Nos. 343/6 1·50 2·00

1985. Leaders of the World. Railway Locomotives (5th series). As T **41**. The first in each pair shows technical drawings and the second the locomotive at work.

348 10c. multicoloured 10 15
349 10c. multicoloured 10 15
350 40c. multicoloured 20 30
351 40c. multicoloured 20 30
352 65c. multicoloured 25 40
353 65c. multicoloured 25 40
354 $1 multicoloured 30 55
355 $1 multicoloured 30 55

DESIGNS: Nos. 348/49, 'LNER "Green Arrow", Great Britain (1936); 350/1, Conrail Class SD-50 diesel locomotive No. 6729, U.S.A. (1982); 352/3, "Flying Hamburger", Germany (1932); 354/5, Class 1070, Japan (1925. Dated "1908" in error).

1985. Leaders of the World. Automobiles (3rd series). As T **46**. The first in each pair shows technical drawings and the second paintings.

356 5c. black, grey and mauve . . 10 15
357 5c. multicoloured 10 15
358 10c. black, pink and red . . 10 20
359 10c. multicoloured 10 20
360 15c. black, brown and red . . 10 20
361 15c. multicoloured 10 20
362 35c. black, red and blue . . . 15 30
363 35c. multicoloured 15 30
364 40c. black, light green & green 15 30
365 40c. multicoloured 15 30
366 55c. black, stone and green 15 30
367 55c. multicoloured 15 30
368 $1 black, deep brown & brown 25 40
369 $1 multicoloured 25 40
370 $1.50 black, pink and red . . 30 45
371 $1.50 multicoloured 30 45

DESIGNS: Nos. 356/7, Cord "L-29" (1929); 358/9, Horch "670 V-12" (1932); 360/1, Lanchester (1901); 362/3, Citroen "2 CV" (1950); 364/5, MGA (1957); 366/7, Ferrari "250 GTO" (1962); 368/9, Ford "V-8" (1932); 370/1, Aston Martin "Lagonda" (1977).

52 Stalk-eyed Ghost Crab

1986. Crabs. Multicoloured.

372 15c. Type **52** 80 90
373 40c. Red and white painted crab . . . . 1·00 1·25
374 50c. Red-spotted crab . . . . 1·00 1·75
375 60c. Red hermit crab . . . . 1·00 2·00

53 Chess Knight on Board and Flags of U.S. and U.S.S.R. (World Chess Championships)

1986. International Events. Sheet 148 × 127 mm, containing T **53** and similar vert design. Multicoloured.

MS376 $3 Type **53**; $3 Emblem (80th anniv of Rotary) . . . . . . 5·50 8·00

1986. Ships (3rd series). Missionary Vessels. As T **26**. Multicoloured.

377 15c. "Messenger of Peace" (schooner) 70 70
378 40c. "John Wesley" (brig) . . 85 1·00
379 50c. "Duff" (full-rigged ship) 85 1·25
380 60c. "Triton" (brigantine) . . 85 1·75

1986. 60th Birthday of Queen Elizabeth II. As T **167** of British Virgin Islands. Mult.

381 10c. Queen wearing ceremonial cloak, New Zealand, 1977 . . . . . . 15 15
382 90c. Before visit to France, 1957 . . . . 30 35
383 $1.50 Queen in 1982 . . . . 45 80
384 $3 In Canberra, 1982 (vert) 60 1·50
MS385 85 × 115 mm. $4 Queen carring bouquet . . . . 3·00 6·00

54 Peace Dove carrying Wreath and Rainbow

1986. 25th Anniv of United States Peace Corps.

386 **54** 50c. multicoloured . . . . 80 1·00

55 Island and Flags of Tuvalu and U.S.A.

56 South Korean Player

1986. "Ameripex" Int Stamp Exhibition, Chicago.

387 **55** 60c. multicoloured . . . . 85 1·00

1986. World Cup Football Championship, Mexico. Multicoloured.

388 1c. Type **56** 10 10
389 5c. French player 10 10
390 10c. West German captain with World Cup trophy, 1974 . . . . 10 10
391 40c. Italian player 50 50
392 60c. World Cup final, 1974 (59 × 39 mm) 65 65
393 $1 Canadian team (59 × 39 mm) . . . . . . 80 1·00
394 $2 Northern Irish team (59 × 39 mm) . . . . . . 1·25 2·00
395 $3 English team (59 × 39 mm) 1·75 3·00
MS396 Two sheets, each 85 × 114 mm. (a) $1.50 As No. 393; (b) $2.50 As No. 394 Set of 2 sheets . . . . 4·25 7·00

1986. Royal Wedding (1st issue). As T **164a** of St. Lucia. Multicoloured.

397 60c. Prince Andrew and Miss Sarah Ferguson 25 45
398 60c. Prince Andrew with prize-winning bull 25 45
399 $1 Prince Andrew at horse trials (horiz) 30 70
400 $1 Miss Sarah Ferguson and Princess Diana (horiz) . . 30 70
MS401 85 × 115 mm. $6 Duke and Duchess of York after wedding (horiz) . . . . 1·75 5·00

See also Nos. 433/6.

57 Mourning Gecko

1986. Lizards. Multicoloured.

402 15c. Type **57** 55 55
403 40c. Oceanic stump-toed gecko . . . . 1·00 1·00
404 50c. Azure-tailed skink . . . 1·25 1·50
405 60c. Moth skink . . . . . . 1·50 2·00

1986. "Stampex '86" Stamp Exhibition, Adelaide. No. 386 optd **STAMPEX 86 ADELAIDE** and kangaroo.

406 **54** 50c. multicoloured 55 65

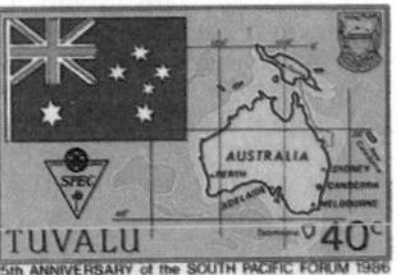

59 Map and Flag of Australia

1986. 15th Anniv of South Pacific Forum. Maps and national flags. Multicoloured.

407 40c. Type **59** 70 70
408 40c. Cook Islands 70 70
409 40c. Micronesia 70 70
410 40c. Fiji 70 70
411 40c. Kiribati 70 70
412 40c. Western Samoa 70 70
413 40c. Nauru 70 70
414 40c. Vanuatu 70 70
415 40c. New Zealand 70 70
416 40c. Tuvalu 70 70
417 40c. Tonga 70 70
418 40c. Solomon Islands 70 70

419 40c. Papua New Guinea . . 70 70
420 40c. Niue 70 70

1986. Automobiles (4th series). As T **46**. The first in each pair show technical drawings and the second paintings.
421 15c. multicoloured 15 15
422 15c. multicoloured 15 15
423 40c. multicoloured 20 25
424 40c. multicoloured 20 25
425 50c. multicoloured 20 30
426 50c. multicoloured 20 30
427 60c. multicoloured 20 35
428 60c. multicoloured 20 35
429 90c. multicoloured 25 35
430 90c. multicoloured 25 35
431 $1.50 multicoloured 30 45
432 $1.50 multicoloured 30 45
DESIGNS: Nos. 421/2, Copper "500" (1953); 423/4, Rover "2000" (1964); 425/6, Ruxton (1930); 427/8, Jowett "Jupiter" (1950); 429/30, Cobra "Daytona Coupe" (1964); 431/2, Packard Model F "Old Pacific" (1903).

1986. Royal Wedding (2nd issue). Nos. 397/400 optd **Congratulations to T.R.H. The Duke & Duchess of York**.
433 60c. Prince Andrew and Miss Sarah Ferguson . . . . . 1·00 1·50
434 60c. Prince Andrew with prize-winning bull . . . . 1·00 1·50
435 $1 Prince Andrew at horse trials (horiz) . . . . 1·60 1·75
436 $1 Miss Sarah Ferguson and Princess Diana (horiz) . . 1·60 1·75

60 Sea Star

1986. Coral Reef Life (1st series). Mult.
437 15c. Type **60** 85 85
438 40c. Pencil urchin . . . . . 1·60 1·90
439 50c. Fragile coral . . . . . 1·75 2·00
440 60c. Pink coral . . . . 2·00 2·25
See also Nos. 498/501, 558/62 and 822/6.

1986. Centenary of Statue of Liberty. Vert views of Statue as T **121a** of Montserrat in separate miniature sheets. Multicoloured.
MS441 Nine sheets, each 85 × 115 mm. $1.25; $1.50; $1.80; $2; $2.25; $2.50; $3; $3.25; $3.50 Set of 9 sheets . . . . 6·00 9·00

1987. Ships (4th series). Missionary Steamers. As T **26**. Multicoloured.
442 15c. "Southern Cross IV" . . 1·10 1·10
443 40c. "John Williams VI" . . 2·25 2·50
444 50c. "John Williams IV" . . 2·50 2·75
445 60c. M.S. "Southern Cross" . . 2·50 2·75

1987. Automobiles (5th series). As T **46**. The first in each pair shows technical drawings and the second paintings.
446 1c. multicoloured 10 10
447 1c. multicoloured 10 10
448 2c. multicoloured 10 10
449 2c. multicoloured 10 10
450 5c. multicoloured 10 10
451 5c. multicoloured 10 10
452 10c. multicoloured 15 20
453 10c. multicoloured 15 20
454 20c. multicoloured 20 25
455 20c. multicoloured 20 25
456 30c. multicoloured 25 30
457 30c. multicoloured 25 30
458 40c. multicoloured 30 35
459 40c. multicoloured 30 35
460 50c. multicoloured 30 40
461 50c. multicoloured 30 40
462 60c. multicoloured 30 40
463 60c. multicoloured 30 40
464 70c. multicoloured 30 45
465 70c. multicoloured 30 45
466 75c. multicoloured 30 45
467 75c. multicoloured 30 45
468 $1 multicoloured 40 70
469 $1 multicoloured 40 70
MS470 100 × 85 mm. Nos. 468/9 2·25 6·50
DESIGNS: Nos. 446/7, Talbot-Lago (1938); 448/9, Du Pont "Model G" (1930); 450/1, Riley "RM" (1950); 452/3, Chevrolet "Baby Grand" (1915); 454/5, Shelby "Mustang GT 500 KR" (1968); 456/7, Ferrari "212 Export Barchetta" (1952); 458/9, Peerless "Model 48-Six" (1912); 460/1, Sunbeam "Alpine" (1954); 462/3, Matra-Ford "MS 80" (1969); 464/5, Squire 1½ Litre (1934); 466/7, Talbot "105" (1931); 468/9, Plymouth "Model Q" (1928).

61 "Nephrolepis saligna"

62 Floral Arrangement

1987. Ferns. Multicoloured.
471 15c. Type **61** 50 65
472 40c. "Asplenium nidus" . . . 80 1·00
473 50c. "Microsorum scolopendria" . . . . . . 95 1·25
474 60c. "Pteris tripartita" . . . 1·10 1·50
MS475 62 × 62 mm. $1.50 "Psilotum nuclum" . . . . 2·25 2·50

1987. Flowers and "Fous". Designs showing either floral arrangements or "fous" (women's headdresses). Multicoloured.
476 15c. Type **62** 25 35
477 15c. "Fou" 25 35
478 40c. "Fou" 55 75
479 40c. Floral arrangement . . . 55 75
480 50c. Floral arrangement . . . 65 80
481 50c. "Fou" 65 80
482 60c. "Fou" 75 90
483 60c. Floral arrangement . . . 75 90

63 Queen Victoria, 1897 (photo by Downey)

1987. Royal Ruby Wedding and 150th Anniv of Queen Victoria's Accession.
484 **63** 40c. brown, black and green 70 55
485 – 60c. purple, black and green 85 75
486 – 80c. brown, black and blue 1·10 1·40
487 – $1 brown, black and purple 1·40 1·60
488 – $2 multicoloured . . . . . 2·00 2·75
MS489 86 × 101 mm. $3 black . . 2·50 4·00
DESIGNS: 60c. Wedding of Princess Elizabeth and Duke of Edinburgh, 1947; 80c. Queen, Duke of Edinburgh and Prince Charles, 1950; $1 Queen with Princess Anne, 1950; $2 Queen Elizabeth II, 1970; $3 Queen and Prince Charles at Princess Anne's christening, 1950.

64 Coconut Crab

1987. Crustaceans. Multicoloured.
490 40c. Type **64** . . . . 1·00 1·25
491 50c. Painted crayfish . . . . 1·25 1·50
492 60c. Ocean crayfish . . . . . 1·40 1·75

65 Aborigine and Ayers Rock

1987. World Scout Jamboree, Australia, and Bicent of Australian Settlement. Multicoloured.
493 40c. Type **65** 30 45
494 60c. Capt. Cook and H.M.S. "Endeavour" 70 90
495 $1 Scout saluting and Scout Park entrance 70 95
496 $1.50 Koala and kangaroo 80 1·25
MS497 115 × 85 mm. $2.50 Lord and Lady Baden Powell . . . . . 2·00 3·25

1988. Coral Reef Life (2nd series). As T **60**. Multicoloured.
498 15c. Spanish dancer 85 85
499 40c. Hard corals . . . . . . 1·00 1·40
500 50c. Feather stars . . . . . 1·00 1·60
501 60c. Staghorn corals . . . . 1·00 1·60

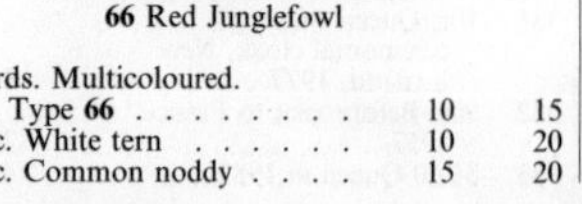

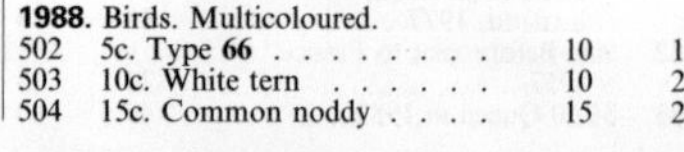

66 Red Junglefowl

1988. Birds. Multicoloured.
502 5c. Type **66** 10 15
503 10c. White tern 10 20
504 15c. Common noddy 15 20
505 20c. Phoenix petrel 20 40
506 25c. Pacific golden plover . . 20 45
507 30c. Crested tern 25 45
508 35c. Sooty tern 25 50
509 40c. Bristle-thighed curlew . . 25 40
510 45c. Bar-tailed godwit ("Eastern Bar-tailed Godwit") 25 45
511 50c. Eastern reef heron . . . 25 50
512 55c. Great frigate bird ("Greater Frigate-bird") . . 30 70
513 60c. Red-footed booby . . . 30 75
514 70c. Rufous-necked sandpiper ("Red-necked Stint") . . . 30 1·00
515 $1 Long-tailed koel ("New Zealand Long-tailed Cuckoo") . . . . 30 1·50
516 $2 Red-tailed tropic bird . . 35 3·00
517 $5 Buff-banded rail ("Banded Rail") . . . . 65 6·00

67 Henri Dunant (founder)

69 "Ganoderma applanatum"

68 H.M.S. "Endeavour"

1988. 125th Anniv of International Red Cross.
518 **67** 15c. red and brown 10 20
519 – 40c. red and blue 20 40
520 – 50c. red and green 25 50
521 – 60c. red and purple 35 70
MS522 96 × 66 mm. $1.50 red and green . . . . 90 2·50
DESIGNS: 40c. Junior Red Cross members on parade; 50c. Red Cross worker with boy in wheelchair; 60c. First aid training; $1.50, Lecture.

1988. Voyages of Captain Cook. Multicoloured.
523 20c. Type **68** 70 80
524 40c. Stern of H.M.S. "Endeavour" . . . . . 80 1·10
525 50c. Cook preparing to land at Tahiti (vert) . . . . . . 90 1·25
526 60c. Maori chief (vert) . . . 90 1·40
527 80c. H.M.S. "Resolution" and Hawaiian canoe . . . 90 1·75
528 $1 "Captain Cook" (after Nathaniel Dance) (vert) . . 1·10 1·90
MS529 115 × 85 mm. $2.50 H.M.S. "Resolution" in Antarctic . . . 6·00 8·00

1988. Fungi (1st series). Multicoloured.
530 40c. Type **69** . . . . 80 1·40
531 50c. "Pseudoepicoccum cocos" (brown leaf spot) 90 1·50
532 60c. "Rigidoporus lineatus" ("Rigidoporus zonalis") . . 1·00 1·75
533 90c. "Rigidoporus microporus" . . . . 1·10 2·00
See also Nos. 554/7.

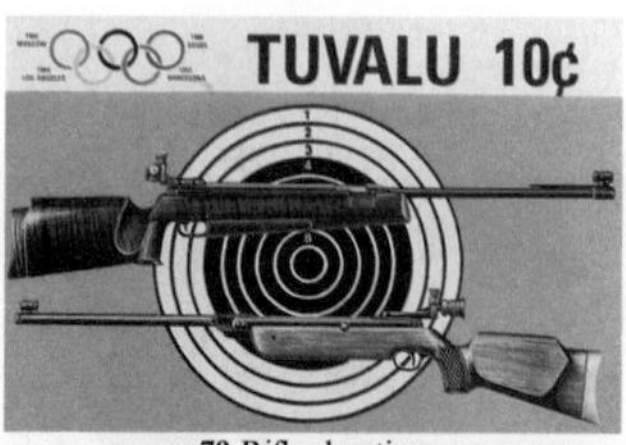

70 Rifle-shooting

1988. Olympic Games, Seoul. Multicoloured.
534 10c. Type **70** 35 65
535 20c. Judo 45 70
536 40c. Canoeing 70 90
537 60c. Swimming . . . . . . 90 1·25
538 80c. Sailing . . . . 1·10 1·75
539 $1 Gymnastics . . . . 1·40 1·75

71 Queen Elizabeth II in Ceremonial Canoe

1988. 10th Anniv of Independence.
540 **71** 60c. multicoloured 60 70
541 – 90c. multicoloured . . . . 90 1·10
542 – $1 multicoloured (horiz) . . 1·00 1·40
543 – $1.20 multicoloured . . . 1·25 1·75
MS544 Designs as Nos. 540/3 in separate miniature sheets, each 85 × 85 mm. Set of 4 sheets . . 3·50 5·00
DESIGNS: 90c. to $1.20, Scenes from Royal Visit of 1982.

72 Virgin Mary

1988. Christmas. Multicoloured.
545 15c. Type **72** 55 55
546 40c. Christ Child 90 80
547 60c. Joseph . . . . 1·10 1·75
MS548 73 × 99 mm. $1.50 Angel 1·75 2·50

73 Dancing Skirt and Dancer

1989. Traditional Dancing Skirts. Designs showing skirts and dancer silhouettes.
549 **73** 40c. multicoloured 70 90
550 – 50c. multicoloured . . . . 80 1·00
551 – 60c. multicoloured . . . . 90 1·25
552 – 90c. multicoloured . . . . 1·40 1·75
MS553 110 × 75 mm. $1.50 multicoloured (dancer) (vert) 3·75 5·00

1989. Fungi (2nd series). As T **69**. Multicoloured.
554 40c. "Trametes marianna" ("Trametes muelleri") . . . 1·75 1·75
555 50c. "Pestalotiopsis palmarum" (grey leaf spot) 1·90 1·90
556 60c. "Trametes cingulata" . . 2·00 2·00
557 90c. "Schizophyllum commune" . . . . 2·75 2·75

1989. Coral Reef Life (3rd series). As T **60**. Multicoloured.
558 40c. Pennant coralfish . . . 1·75 1·75
559 50c. Orange-finned anemonefish . . . . 2·00 2·00
560 60c. Narrow-banned batfish 2·25 2·25
561 90c. Thread-finned butterflyfish . . . . 2·75 2·75
MS562 110 × 85 mm. Nos. 558/61 8·00 9·00

74 "Nivaga II"

1989. Delivery of "Nivaga II" (new inter-island ship). Sheet 116 × 85 mm.
MS563 **74** $1.50 multicoloured 4·00 5·50

75 Trumpet Triton Shell

76 "Cocus nucifera"

1989. Christmas. Multicoloured.
564 40c. Type **75** 85 85
565 50c. Posy of flowers . . . . 1·00 1·00

566 60c. Germinating coconut . . 1·25 1·25
567 90c. Jewellery . . . . 2·25 2·75

1990. Tropical Trees. Multicoloured.
568 15c. Type **76** 80 80
569 30c. "Rhizophora samoensis" 1·25 1·25
570 40c. "Messerschmidia argentea" . . . . 1·40 1·40
571 50c. "Pandanus tectorius" . . 1·60 1·75
572 60c. "Hernandia nymphaeifolia" . . . . . 1·75 1·90
573 90c. "Pisonia grandis" . . . 2·25 2·75

77 Penny Black with "Stamp World London 90" Emblem

1990. 150th Anniv of the Penny Black, and "Stamp World London 90" International Stamp Exhibition.
574 **77** 15c. multicoloured . . . . 1·50 1·50
575 40c. multicoloured . . . . 2·75 2·75
576 90c. multicoloured . . . . 4·50 5·00
MS577 115 × 85 mm. **77** $2 multicoloured . . . . 8·00 9·50

78 Japanese Camouflaged Freighter

1990. Second World War Ships (1st series). Multicoloured.
578 15c. Type **78** . . . . 1·25 1·25
579 30c. U.S.S. "Unimack" (seaplane tender) . . . . . 1·75 1·75
580 40c. "Amagiri" (Japanese destroyer) . . . . 1·90 1·90
581 50c. U.S.S. "Platte" (attack transport) . . . . 2·00 2·00
582 60c. Japanese "Shumushu" Class escort . . . . 2·25 2·25
583 90c. U.S.S. "Independence" (aircraft carrier) . . . . . 3·00 3·00
See also Nos. 613/16.

79 "Erythrina fusca"

81 Mary and Joseph travelling to Bethlehem

80 Land Resources Survey

1990. Flowers. Multicoloured.
584 15c. Type **79** 30 50
585 30c. "Capparis cordifolia" . . 50 70
586 40c. "Portulaca pilosa" . . . 60 80
587 50c. "Cordia subcordata" . . 75 90
588 60c. "Scaevola taccada" . . . 80 1·00
589 90c. "Suriana maritima" . . 1·25 2·00

1990. 40th Anniv of United Nations Development Programme. Multicoloured.
590 40c. Type **80** 80 80
591 60c. Satellite earth station . . 1·50 1·50
592 $1.20 "Te Tautai" (trawler) 3·25 4·25

1990. Christmas. Multicoloured.
593 15c. Type **81** 55 55
594 40c. The Nativity . . . . . 1·00 1·00
595 60c. Shepherds with flock . . 1·50 1·50
596 90c. Wise Men bearing gifts 2·00 2·50

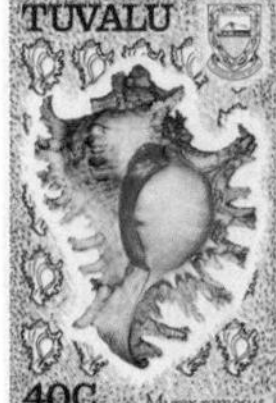

82 Ramose Murex **84** Green Turtle

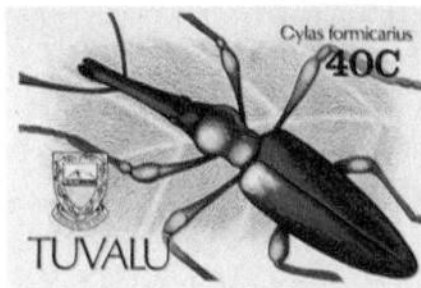

83 "Cylas formicarius" (beetle)

1991. Sea Shells. Multicoloured.
597 40c. Type **82** . . . . 1·50 1·50
598 50c. Marble cone . . . . . . 1·60 1·60
599 60c. Commercial trochus . . 1·75 1·75
600 $1.50 Green map cowrie . . 3·50 4·00

1991. Insects. Multicoloured.
601 40c. Type **83** . . . . 2·25 1·60
602 50c. "Heliothis armiger" (moth) . . . . 2·50 1·75
603 60c. "Spodoptera litura" (moth) . . . . 2·75 2·00
604 $1.50 "Agrius convolvuli" (moth) . . . . 7·00 8·50

1991. Endangered Marine Life. Multicoloured.
605 40c. Type **84** . . . . 1·75 1·25
606 50c. Humpback whale . . . 2·25 1·50
607 60c. Hawksbill turtle . . . . 2·25 1·60
608 $1.50 Sperm whale . . . . . 5·00 6·50

85 Football **87** Traditional Dancers

86 U.S.S. "Tennessee" (battleship)

1991. 9th South Pacific Games. Multicoloured.
609 40c. Type **85** . . . . 1·75 1·25
610 50c. Volleyball . . . . 2·25 1·75
611 60c. Lawn tennis . . . . . . 3·50 2·50
612 $1.50 Cricket . . . . 8·50 8·50

1991. Second World War Ships (2nd series). Multicoloured.
613 40c. Type **86** . . . . 2·75 2·00
614 50c. "Haguro" (Japanese cruiser) . . . . 3·00 2·00
615 60c. H.M.N.Z.S. "Achilles" (cruiser) . . . . 3·25 2·50
616 $1.50 U.S.S. "North Carolina" (battleship) . . . 6·50 9·00

1991. Christmas. Multicoloured.
617 40c. Type **87** . . . . 1·75 1·25
618 50c. Solo dancer . . . . . . 2·00 1·50
619 60c. Dancers in green costumes . . . . 2·50 1·75
620 $1.50 Dancers in multicoloured costumes . . 5·00 7·00

88 Southern Fish Constellation

1992. Pacific Star Constellations. Mult.
621 40c. Type **88** . . . . 2·00 1·75
622 50c. Scorpion . . . . 2·25 1·75
623 60c. Archer . . . . 2·75 2·25
624 $1.50 Southern Cross . . . . 6·00 7·00

89 King George VI and Cargo Liner

1992. Cent of British Occupation of Tuvalu. Mult.
625 40c. Type **89** . . . . 2·25 2·00
626 50c. King George V and freighter with barges at wharf . . . . 2·50 2·00
627 60c. King Edward VII and freighter . . . . 2·75 2·25
628 $1.50 Queen Victoria and warship . . . . 5·00 6·50

90 Columbus with King Ferdinand and Queen Isabella of Spain

1992. 500th Anniv of Discovery of America by Columbus.
629 **90** 40c. blue and black 70 80
630 – 50c. purple and black . . . 80 90
631 – 60c. green and black . . . 90 1·10
632 – $1.50 purple and black . . 2·25 3·50
DESIGNS: 50c. Columbus and Polynesians; 60c. Columbus and South American Indians; $1.50, Columbus and North American Indians.

91 Blue-spotted Butterflyfish

1992. Fishes. Multicoloured.
633 15c. Type **91** 40 40
634 20c. Bridled parrotfish . . . 45 40
635 25c. Clown surgeonfish . . . 45 50
636 30c. Moon wrasse 55 50
637 35c. Harlequin filefish 60 50
638 40c. Bird wrasse 70 50
639 45c. Black-finned pigfish . . 75 50
640 50c. Blue damselfish 80 60
641 60c. Hump-headed wrasse . . 90 70
642 70c. Ornate butterflyfish (vert) . . . . 1·00 1·25
643 90c. Saddle butterflyfish (vert) 1·25 1·50
644 $1 Vagabond butterflyfish (vert) . . . . 1·40 1·60
645 $2 Pennant coralfish (vert) . . 2·25 3·00
646 $3 Moorish idol (vert) . . . 3·00 4·00

92 Discus Throwing **95** Fishermen and Angel

93 Blue Coral

1992. Olympic Games, Barcelona. Mult.
647 40c. Type **92** . . . . 1·25 1·00
648 50c. Javelin throwing . . . . 1·50 1·25
649 60c. Shotput . . . . 1·75 1·50
650 $1.50 Competitor's foot . . . 3·25 4·50
MS651 100 × 71 mm. $2 Olympic stadium, Barcelona . . . . . 4·25 5·00

1992. Endangered Species. Blue Coral.
652 **93** 10c. multicoloured . . . . 1·00 1·00
653 – 25c. multicoloured . . . . 2·00 2·00
654 – 30c. multicoloured . . . . 2·00 2·00
655 – 35c. multicoloured . . . . 2·25 2·25
DESIGNS: 25c. to 35c. Different coral formations.

1992. "Kuala Lumpur '92" International Philatelic Exhibition. Nos. 636, 638 and 640/1 optd **KL92 KUALA LUMPUR '92** and emblem.
656 30c. Moon wrasse . . . . . 1·60 1·60
657 40c. Bird wrasse . . . . . . 1·75 1·75
658 50c. Blue damselfish . . . . 2·00 2·00
659 60c. Hump-headed wrasse . . 2·00 2·00

1992. Christmas. Multicoloured.
660 40c. Type **95** 90 70
661 50c. Fishing canoes following star . . . . 1·00 80
662 60c. Nativity scene . . . . . 1·25 1·00
663 $1.50 Christmas gifts . . . . 2·25 3·25

96 "Calophyllum inophyllum"

1993. Flowers. Multicoloured.
664 40c. Type **96** 30 35
665 50c. "Hibiscus tiliaceus" . . 35 40
666 60c. "Lantana camara" . . . 40 45
667 $1.50 "Plumeria rubra" . . . 1·10 1·25

97 Japanese Nakajima B5N "Kate" Bombers attacking Island

1993. 50th Anniv of War in the Pacific. Mult.
668 40c. Type **97** 30 35
669 50c. Japanese anti-aircraft gun (vert) 35 40
670 60c. American troops storming beach 40 45
671 $1.50 Map of Funafuti Atoll (vert) . . . . 1·10 1·25

98 "Cepora perimale"

1993. "Indopex '93" International Stamp Exhibition", Surabaya, Indonesia. Sheet 81 × 111 mm.
MS672 **98** $1.50 multicoloured 1·10 1·25

99 Fluted Giant Clam

1993. Marine Life. Multicoloured.
673 40c. Type **99** 30 35
674 50c. Anemone crab 35 40
675 60c. Octopus 40 45
676 $1.50 Green turtle . . . . . 1·10 1·25

100 Queen Elizabeth II and Prince Philip in Land Rover

1993. 40th Anniv of Coronation.
677 **100** 40c. multicoloured 30 35
678 – 50c. multicoloured 35 40
679 – 60c. multicoloured 40 45
680 – $1.50 multicoloured . . . 1·10 1·25
MS681 88 × 88 mm. $2 green, yellow and black . . . . 1·50 1·60
DESIGNS: 50c. Queen Elizabeth drinking kava; 60c. Queen Elizabeth with parasol; $1.50, Ceremonial welcome; $2 Crowning of Queen Elizabeth II, 1953.

1993. "Taipei '93" International Stamp Exhibition, Taiwan. Sheet, 85 × 85 mm, containing multicoloured design as T **98**.
MS682 $1.50, "Geoffroyi godart" (vert) . . . . 1·10 1·25

1993. "Bangkok 1993" International Stamp Exhibition, Thailand. Sheet, 86 × 86 mm, containing horiz design as T **98**.
MS683 $1.50 "Paradisea staudinger" 1·10 1·25

101 Hermit Crab and Shells on Beach

102 Virgin and Child with Christmas Tree

1993. Environmental Protection. Mult.

684	40c. Type **101**	30	35
685	50c. Conch shell and starfish	35	40
686	60c. Crab, seaweed and shells	40	45
687	$1.50 Herring gull and human footprint on beach	1·10	1·25
MS688	126 × 80 mm. Nos. 684/7	2·10	2·50

1993. Christmas. Multicoloured.

689	40c. Type **102**	30	35
690	50c. Candle	35	40
691	60c. Angel	40	45
692	$1.50 Decorated palm tree	1·10	1·25

1994. "Hong Kong '94" International Stamp Exhibition. Sheet 85 × 85 mm containing multicoloured design as T 98.

MS693	$2 "Danaus plexippus" (vert)	1·50	1·60

103 Beach

1994. Island Scenery. Multicoloured.

694	40c. Type **103**	30	35
695	50c. Lagoon	35	40
696	60c. Distant island	40	45
697	$1.50 Launch and outrigger canoes on beach	1·10	1·25

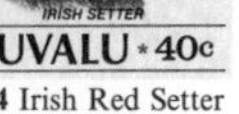

104 Irish Red Setter

105 World Cup, Australian Player and Sydney Opera House

1994. Chinese New Year ("Year of the Dog"). Multicoloured.

698	40c. Type **104**	30	35
699	50c. Golden retriever	35	40
700	60c. West Highland terrier	40	45
701	$1.50 German shepherd	1·10	1·25

1994. World Cup Football Championship, U.S.A. Multicoloured.

702	40c. Type **105**	30	35
703	50c. English player and Big Ben, London	35	40
704	60c. Argentinian player and House of Assembly, Buenos Aires	40	45
705	$1.50 German player and Brandenburg Gate, Berlin	1·10	1·25
MS706	105 × 99 mm. $2 American player and Statue of Liberty, New York	1·50	1·60

106 Giant Button Top

107 Pekingese and Logo

1994. Sea Snails. Multicoloured.

707	40c. Type **106**	30	35
708	50c. Tapestry turban	35	40
709	60c. "Planaxis savignyi"	40	45
710	$1.50 Green-lined paper bubble	1·10	1·25

1994. "Philakorea '94" International Stamp Exhibition, Seoul. Sheet 106 × 72 mm.

MS711	**107** $1.50 multicoloured	1·10	1·25

1994. "Singpex '94" Stamp Exhibition. Nos. 502/3 and 509/10 optd **SINGPEX '94 AUG 31-SEP 5 SINGAPORE** and emblem.

712	5c. Type **66**	10	10
713	10c. White tern	10	10
714	40c. Bristle-thighed curlew	30	35
715	45c. Bar-tailed godwit	30	35

109 "Saturn V" Launch

1994. 25th Anniv of First Manned Moon Landing. Multicoloured.

716	40c. Type **109**	30	35
717	50c. "Apollo 11" capsule	35	40
718	60c. Neil Armstrong and American flag	40	45
719	$1.50 Capsule re-entry	1·10	1·25

110 Boys swimming with Log

1994. Christmas. Local Customs. Multicoloured.

720	40c. Type **110**	30	35
721	50c. Fishermen landing catch	35	40
722	60c. Christmas dinner	40	45
723	$1.50 Traditional dancers	1·10	1·25

111 Pig asleep

1995. Chinese New Year ("Year of the Pig"). Multicoloured.

724	40c. Type **111**	30	35
725	50c. Two pigs and vegetation	35	40
726	60c. Three pigs	40	45
727	$1.50 Sow suckling piglets	1·10	1·25

112 Emblem and Man with Produce in Wheelbarrow

1995. 50th Anniv of F.A.O. Multicoloured.

728	40c. Type **112**	30	35
729	50c. Man holding basket of food	35	40
730	60c. Woman slicing produce	40	45
731	$1.50 Woman mixing food	1·10	1·25

113 Beach and Lagoon

1995. Visit South Pacific Year. Multicoloured.

732	40c. Type **113**	30	35
733	50c. Catamaran	35	40
734	60c. Traditional hut	40	45
735	$1.50 Village on beach	1·10	1·25

114 "Dendrobium comptonii"

1995. Pacific Coastal Orchids. Multicoloured.

736	40c. Type **114**	30	35
737	50c. "Dendrobium involutum"	35	40
738	60c. "Dendrobium rarum"	40	45
739	$1.50 "Grammatophyllum scriptum"	1·10	1·25

115 Japanese Soldier and Maps of Tuvalu and Japan

1995. 50th Anniv of End of Second World War. Multicoloured.

740	40c. Type **115**	30	35
741	50c. American soldier and beach landing	35	40
742	60c. American marine and tree	40	45
743	$1.50 American soldier and atomic explosion	1·10	1·25

116 Tuvalu Dancer

1995. "JAKARTA '95" Stamp Exhibition, Indonesia. Sheet 85 × 85 mm.

MS744	**116** $1 multicoloured	75	80

117 "Phalaenopsis amabilis"

118 Tuvaluans in Outrigger Canoes

1995. "Singapore '95" International Stamp Exhibition. Sheet 85 × 85 mm.

MS745	**117** $1 multicoloured	75	80

1995. 50th Anniv of United Nations. Sheet 83 × 70 mm, containing T **118** and similar vert design. Multicoloured.

MS746	$1 Type **118**; $1 U.N. headquarters, New York	75	80

119 "Silent Night" and Aerial View of Airfield

1995. Christmas. Christmas Carols. Multicoloured.

747	40c. Type **119**	30	35
748	50c. "O Come all ye Faithful" and choir boys	35	40
749	60c. "The First Nowell" and choir girls	40	45
750	$1.50 "Hark the Herald Angels sing" and angel	1·10	1·25

120 1976 Separation 4 c. Stamp

1996. 20th Anniv of Separation from Gilbert Islands and of First Tuvalu Postage Stamps. Sheet 108 × 82 mm, containing T **120** and similar horiz designs showing values from 1976 Separation issue.

MS751	40c. Type **120**; 60c. 1976 10c. stamp; $1 1976 35c. stamp	1·50	1·60

121 Rat with Jar

1996. Chinese New Year ("Year of the Rat"). Sheet 130 × 87 mm containing T **121** and similar vert design. Multicoloured.

MS752	50c. Type **121**; 50c. Rat drinking from jar	70	75

1996. "HONGPEX '96" International Stamp Exhibition. Sheet as No. **MS**752, but additionally inscr with "HONGPEX '96" emblem on sheet margin.

MS753	50c. Type **121**; 50c. Rat drinking from jar	1·40	1·75

1996. "indonesia 96" International Youth Stamp Exhibition, Bandung. No. **MS**744 optd **indonesia 96**.

MS754	85 × 85 mm. 116 $1 multicoloured	1·60	1·90

1996. "CHINA '96" 9th Asian International Stamp Exhibition, Peking. Sheet as No. **MS**752, but additionally inscr with "CHINA '96" emblem and puppet holding envelope on sheet margin.

MS755	50c. Type **121**; 50c. Rat drinking from jar	1·40	1·75

123 Volleyball

1996. Olympic Games, Atlanta. Multicoloured.

756	40c. Type **123**	30	35
757	50c. Swimming	35	40
758	60c. Weightlifting	40	45
759	$1.50 Boxing	1·10	1·25

1996. "TAIPEI '96" 10th Asian International Stamp Exhibition, Taiwan. No. 639 surch **$1.00 TAIPEI '96 21-27 OCTOBER** and emblem.

760	$1 on 45c. Black-finned pigfish	70	75

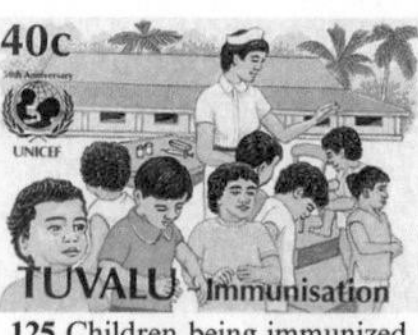

125 Children being immunized

1996. 50th Anniv of UNICEF. Multicoloured.

761	40c. Type **125**	30	35
762	50c. Teacher and children	35	40
763	60c. Domestic water tanks and child	40	45
764	$1.50 Children in hydroponic greenhouse	1·10	1·25

126 Wise Men following Star

1996. Christmas. Multicoloured.

765	40c. Type **126**	30	35
766	50c. Shepherds and star	35	40
767	60c. Wise men presenting gifts	40	45
768	$1.50 The Nativity	1·10	1·25

1997. Fishes (2nd series). As T **14**. Multicoloured.

770	25c. Sehel's grey mullet	20	25
771	30c. Leatherback	25	30
772	40c. Hump-backed snapper ("Paddletail")	35	40
773	45c. Long-nosed emperor	40	45
774	50c. Blue-spined unicornfish	40	45
775	55c. Oblique-banded snapper	45	50
776	60c. Twin-spotted snapper ("Red bass")	50	55
777	70c. Rusty jobfish	60	65
778	90c. Leopard flounder	75	80
779	$1 Ruby snapper	85	90
780	$2 Yellow-striped snapper	1·70	1·80
781	$3 Black jack	2·50	2·75

128 White Pekin Ducks

1997. "Pacific '97" International Stamp Exhibition, San Francisco. Ducks. Multicoloured.
782 40c. Type **128** 30 35
783 50c. Muscovy ducks 35 40
784 60c. Pacific black ducks . . . 40 45
785 $1.50 Mandarin ducks . . . 1·10 1·25

129 Korat King Cat

1997. Cats. Multicoloured.
786 40c. Type **129** 30 35
787 50c. Long-haired ginger kitten 35 40
788 60c. Shaded cameo 40 45
789 $1.50 Maine coon . . . . . 1·10 1·25

1997. Return of Hong Kong to China. Sheet, 130 × 90 mm, containing design as No. 780.
MS790 $2 Yellow-striped snapper 1·40 1·50

1997. Golden Wedding of Queen Elizabeth and Prince Philip. As T **87** of Kiribati. Multicoloured.
791 40c. Queen Elizabeth and Prince Philip in Land Rover 30 35
792 40c. Queen Elizabeth 30 35
793 50c. Queen Elizabeth accepting ceremonial gift 35 40
794 50c. Prince Philip 35 40
795 60c. Three portraits of Queen Elizabeth 40 45
796 60c. Queen Elizabeth and Prince Philip leaving Philatelic Bureau 40 45
MS797 110 × 70 mm. $2 Queen Elizabeth and Prince Philip in landau (horiz) . . . . 1·50 1·60

Nos. 791/2, 793/4 and 795/6 respectively were printed together, se-tenant, with the backgrounds forming composite designs.

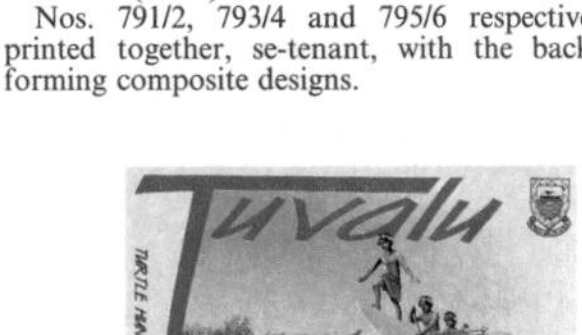

130 Turtle Hunting

1997. Christmas. Multicoloured.
798 40c. Type **130** 30 35
799 50c. Pole fishing 35 40
800 60c. Canoe racing 40 45
801 $1.50 Traditional dancing . . 1·10 1·25

131 Tiger

1998. Chinese New Year ("Year of the Tiger"). Sheet 110 × 69 mm.
MS802 **131** $1.40 multicoloured 1·20 1·30

1998. Diana, Princess of Wales Commemoration. Sheet, 145 × 70 mm, containing vert designs as T **91** of Kiribati. Multicoloured.
MS803 80c. Wearing pearl drop earrings, 1990; 80c. Wearing black evening dress, 1995; 80c. Wearing tiara, 1992; 80c. Wearing beige coat (sold at $3.20 + 20c. charity premium) . . . . 2·75 3·00

1998. 80th Anniv of the Royal Air Force. As T **270** of Samoa. Multicoloured.
804 40c. Hawker Woodcock . . . 35 40
805 50c. Vickers Victoria 40 45
806 60c. Bristol Brigand 50 55
807 $1.50 De Havilland D.H.C.1 Chipmunk . . . . 1·30 1·40
MS808 110 × 77 mm. $1 Sopwith Pup; $1 Armstrong Whitworth F.K.8; $1 North American Harvard; $1 Vultee Vengeance 3·25 3·50

132 "Los Reyes" and "Santiago" (Alvare Mendana)

1998. Ships (5th series). Multicoloured.
809 40c. Type **132** 35 40
810 50c. "Morning Star II" (missionary schooner) . . . 40 45
811 60c. "The Light" (missionary brigantine) 50 55
812 $1.50 New Zealand missionary schooner . . . 1·30 1·40

133 Bottlenose Dolphin

1998. Dolphins and Porpoises. Multicoloured.
813 40c. Type **133** 35 40
814 50c. Dall's porpoise 40 45
815 60c. Harbour porpoise . . . 50 55
816 $1.50 Common dolphin . . . 1·30 1·40

134 Bikenibeu Paeniu, Teacher and Class

1998. 20th Anniv of Independence. Prime Ministers of Tuvalu. Multicoloured.
817 40c. Type **134** 35 40
818 60c. Kamuta Latasi and diagram of communications network 50 55
819 90c. Sir Tomasi Puapua and emblem of Trust Fund . . 75 80
820 $1.50 Sir Toaripi Lauti and emblem of Maritime School . . . . 1·30 1·40
MS821 115 × 81 mm. Nos. 817/20 2·75 3·00

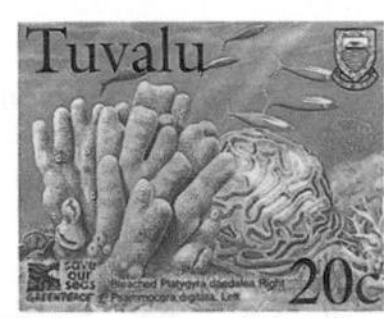

135 "Psammocra digitata" and Bleached "Platygyra daedalea"

1998. Coral Reef Life (4th series). Multicoloured.
822 20c. Type **135** 15 20
823 30c. Bleached "Acropora robusta" 25 30
824 50c. Bleached "Acropora hyacinthus" 40 45
825 $1 Bleached "Acropora danai" and "Montastrea curta" 85 90
MS826 74 × 54 mm. $1.50, Bleached "Seriatopora" and Bleached "Stylophora" . . . . 1·30 1·40

136 Mary and Joseph travelling to Bethlehem

1998. Christmas. Multicoloured.
827 40c. Type **136** 35 40
828 50c. Shepherds and angel . . 40 45
829 60c. The Nativity 50 55
830 $1.50 Visit of Wise Men . . 1·30 1·40

137 Rabbit playing Pipa and Chinese Lantern

1999. Chinese New Year ("Year of the Rabbit"). Sheet 115 × 75 mm.
MS831 **137** $2 multicoloured . . 1·70 1·80

138 "Heemskerk" (Tasman), 1642

1999. "Australia '99" World Stamp Exhibition, Melbourne. Ships (6th series). Multicoloured.
832 40c. Type **138** 35 40
833 50c. H.M.S. "Endeavour" (Cook), 1769 . . . . . . 40 45
834 90c. "Sophia Jane" (paddle-steamer), 1831 . . . . . . 75 80
835 $1.50 "Chusan I" (screw steamer), 1852 . . . . . . 1·30 1·40
MS836 135 × 75 mm. $2 H.M.S. "Supply" (brig), 1788 . . . . 1·70 1·80

1999. Kosovo Relief Campaign. Nos. 505, 508, 512 and 515 optd **Kosovo Relief Fund**.
837 20c. Phoenix petrel 15 20
838 35c. Sooty tern 30 35
839 55c. Great frigate bird . . . 45 50
840 $1 Long-tailed koel 85 90

1999. 30th Anniv of the First Manned Landing on Moon. As T **94a** of St. Kitts. Multicoloured.
841 40c. Lift-off 35 40
842 60c. Lander approaches Moon 50 55
843 90c. Lander leaving Moon . . 75 80
844 $1.50 Crew recovery . . . . 1·30 1·40
MS845 90 × 80 mm. $2 Earth as seen from Moon (circular, 40 mm diameter). . . . . 1·70 1·80

1999. "Queen Elizabeth the Queen Mother's Century". As T **199** of St. Helena. Multicoloured.
846 40c. King George VI and Queen Elizabeth inspecting bomb damage, 1940 . . . 35 40
847 60c. Queen Elizabeth with her daughters, 1951 . . . . . 50 55
848 90c. With Princes William and Harry, 1995 . . . . . 75 80
849 $1.50 Inspecting the Queen's Dragoon Guards . . . . . 1·30 1·40
MS850 145 × 70 mm. $2 Lady Elizabeth Bowes-Lyon aged 6, and Yuri Gagarin (first cosmonaut) 1·70 1·80

140 "Solandra maxima" (flower)

1999. Flowers. Multicoloured.
851 90c. Type **140** 75 80
852 90c. "Cistus" sp. 75 80
853 90c. "Pandorea jasminoides" 75 80
854 90c. "Grewia caffra" 75 80
855 90c. "Mandevilla x amabilis" 75 80
856 90c. "Punica granatum" (open flowers) 75 80
857 90c. "Cassytha filiformis" . . 75 80
858 90c. "Wollastonia biflora" . . 75 80
859 90c. "Portulacacae lueta" (without local inscr) . . . 75 80
860 90c. "Portulacacae lueta" (also inscr "TAMOLOC") 75 80
861 90c. "Vigna marina" 75 80
862 90c. "Punica granatum" (closed flowers) 75 80
MS863 97 × 104 mm. $3 "Cassia surattensis" (vert) . . . . . . 2·50 2·75

No. **MS**863 is inscribed "SCRAMBLED EGGES" in error.

Nos. 851/6 and 857/62 were each printed together, se-tenant, with the backgrounds forming composite designs.

141 Lady of Peace

1999. New Millennium. Allegories of Peace. Mult.
864 90c. Type **141** 75 80
865 90c. Olive branch 75 80
866 90c. Dove 75 80
867 90c. Lion 75 80
868 90c. Lamb 75 80
869 90c. Cherub with bouquet ("War crowning Peace") 75 80
870 90c. As Type **142**, but with white frame 75 80
MS871 94 × 75 mm. $2 Sunrise and "2000" (46 × 28 mm). . . . . 1·70 1·80

Nos. 864/9 were printed together, se-tenant, forming a composite design.

142 Sand Tiger Shark showing Teeth

2000. Endangered Species. Sand Tiger Shark. Mult.
872 10c. Type **142** 10 15
873 30c. Sand tiger shark swimming 25 30
874 50c. Sand tiger shark over seaweed 40 45
875 60c. Group of sand tiger sharks 50 55
MS876 207 × 135 mm. As Nos. 872/5, but without WWF pander emblem . . . . 1·20 1·40

143 Chevron Butterflyfish

2000. Marine Life. Multicoloured.
877 90c. Type **143** 75 80
878 90c. Mandarin fish 75 80
879 90c. Bicoloured angelfish . . 75 80
880 90c. Copper-banded butterflyfish 75 80
881 90c. Clown anemonefish . . 75 80
882 90c. Lemon-peel angelfish . . 75 80
883 90c. Manta ray 75 80
884 90c. White shark 75 80
885 90c. Hammerhead shark . . 75 80
886 90c. Tiger shark 75 80
887 90c. Great barracuda 75 80
888 90c. Leatherback turtle . . . 75 80
889 90c. Common tern 75 80
890 90c. Red-billed tropic bird ("White-tailed Tropicbird") 75 80
891 90c. Emperor snapper . . . 75 80
892 90c. Clown triggerfish 75 80
893 90c. Pennant coralfish ("Longfin Bannerfish") . . 75 80
894 90c. Harlequin tuskfish . . . 75 80
895 90c. Wilson's storm petrel . . 75 80
896 90c. Common dolphin . . . 75 80
897 90c. Yellow seahorse ("Spotted Seahorse") . . . 75 80
898 90c. Threeband demoiselle . . 75 80
899 90c. Coral hind 75 80
900 90c. Palette surgeonfish . . . 75 80
901 90c. Great frigatebird 75 80
902 90c. Brown booby 75 80
903 90c. Dugong 75 80
904 90c. Red knot 75 80
905 90c. Common starfish 75 80
906 90c. Hawksbill turtle 75 80
907 90c. Whale shark 75 80
908 90c. Six-blotched hind ("Sixspot Grouper") . . . 75 80
909 90c. Blue-streaked cleaner wrasse 75 80
910 90c. Lemon shark 75 80
911 90c. Spotted boxfish ("Spotted Trunkfish") . . 75 80
912 90c. Forceps butterflyfish ("Long-nosed Butterflyfish") 75 80
MS913 Three sheets, each 103 × 73 mm. (a) $3 Pygmy parrotfish. (b) $3 Picasso triggerfish. (c) $3 Sailfish Set of 3 sheets . . . . 7·50 7·75

Nos. 877/82, 883/8, 889/94, 895/900, 901/6 and 907/12 were each printed together, se-tenant, with the backgrounds forming composite designs.

144 Glasswing Butterfly

2000. South Pacific Butterflies. Multicoloured.
914 90c. Type **144** 75 80
915 90c. Leftwing butterfly . . . 75 80
916 90c. Moth butterfly 75 80
917 90c. Blue triangle 75 80
918 90c. Beak butterfly 75 80
919 90c. Plane butterfly 75 80
920 90c. Birdwing (vert) 75 80
921 90c. Tailed emperor (vert) . . 75 80
922 90c. Orchard shallowtail (vert) 75 80
923 90c. Union jack (vert) . . . 75 80
924 90c. Long-tailed blue (vert) 75 80
925 90c. Common jezebel (vert) 75 80
926 90c. Caper white (vert) . . . 75 80
927 90c. Common Indian crow (vert) 75 80
928 90c. Eastern flat (vert) . . . 75 80
929 90c. Cairns birdwing (vert) 75 80
930 90c. Monarch (vert) 65 70
931 90c. Meadow argus (vert) . . 65 70
MS932 Two sheets, each 70 × 100 mm. (a) $3 Great egg-fly (vert). (b) $3 Palmfly Set of 2 sheets . . . . 5·00 5·25

Nos. 914/19, 920/5 and 926/31 were each printed together, se-tenant, with the backgrounds forming composite designs.

145 Pekin Robin ("Red-Billed Leiothrix")

146 Oriental Shorthair

2000. South Pacific Birds. Multicoloured.

933 90c. Type **145** 75 80
934 90c. Grey shrike-thrush . . . 75 80
935 90c. Great frigatebird 75 80
936 90c. River kingfisher ("Common Kingfisher") . . 75 80
937 90c. Chestnut-breasted mannikin ("Chestnut-breasted Finch") 75 80
938 90c. White tern 75 80
939 90c. Rainbow lorikeet . . . 75 80
940 90c. White-throated tree creeper 75 80
941 90c. White-tailed kingfisher 75 80
942 90c. Golden whistler 75 80
943 90c. Grey plover ("Black-bellied Plover") 75 80
944 90c. Australian stone-curlew ("Beach Thick-knee") . . . 75 80
945 90c. White-collared kingfisher 75 80
946 90c. Peale's petrel ("Scaled Petrel") 75 80
947 90c. Blue wren ("Superb Blue Wren") 75 80
948 90c. Osprey 75 80
949 90c. Great cormorant 75 80
950 90c. Peregrine falcon 75 80
MS951 Two sheets. (a) 100 × 70 mm. $3 Broad-billed prion (horiz). (b) 70 × 100 mm $3 Morepork Set of 2 sheets . . . . 5·00 5·25

Nos. 933/8, 939/44 and 945/50 were each printed together, se-tenant, with the backgrounds forming composite designs.

No. 945 is inscribed "Kingisher" in error.

2000. Cats and Dogs. Multicoloured.

952 90c. Type **146** 75 80
953 90c. Balinese 75 80
954 90c. Somali 75 80
955 90c. Chinchilla Persian . . . 75 80
956 90c. Tonkinese 75 80
957 90c. Japanese bobtail 75 80
958 90c. Oriental shorthair (head) 75 80
959 90c. Balinese (head) 75 80
960 90c. Somali (head) 75 80
961 90c. Chinchilla Persian (head) 75 80
962 90c. Tonkinese (head) 75 80
963 90c. Japanese bobtail (head) 75 80
964 90c. Fox terrier (horiz) . . . 75 80
965 90c. Collie (horiz) 75 80
966 90c. Boston terrier (horiz) . . 75 80
967 90c. Welsh corgie (horiz) . . 75 80
968 90c. Pointer (horiz) 75 80
969 90c. Dalmatian (horiz) . . . 75 80
970 90c. Dalmatian (head) . . . 75 80
971 90c. Boston terrier (head) . . 75 80
972 90c. Fox terrier (head) . . . 75 80
973 90c. Pointer (head) 75 80
974 90c. Welsh corgi (head) . . . 75 80
975 90c. Collie (head) 75 80
MS976 Two sheets. (a) 96 × 70 mm. $3 Oriental shorthair. (b) 70 × 96 mm. $3 Scottish terrier (horiz) Set of 2 sheets . . . . 5·00 5·25

147 Common Noddy ("Brown Noddy")

2000. Fauna. Multicoloured.

977 90c. Type **147** 75 80
978 90c. Great frigatebird 75 80
979 90c. Emperor angelfish . . . 75 80
980 90c. Common dolphin . . . 75 80
981 90c. Hermit crab 75 80
982 90c. Threadfin butterflyfish 75 80
983 90c. Red-footed booby . . . 75 80
984 90c. Red-tailed tropicbird . . 75 80
985 90c. Grey plover ("Black-bellied Plover") 75 80
986 90c. Common tern 75 80
987 90c. Ruddy turnstone 75 80
988 90c. Sanderling 75 80
MS989 70 × 93 mm. $3 Great frigatebird (vert) . . . . 2·50 2·75

Nos. 977/82 and 983/8 were each printed together, se-tenant, with the backgrounds forming composite designs.

148 Green Dragon

2001. Chinese New Year ("Years of the Dragon and Snake"). Multicoloured.

990 40c. Type **148** 35 40
991 60c. Green snake with orange markings 50 55
992 90c. Orange snake with green markings 75 80
993 $1.05 Blue dragon 90 95

149 Anglo Specialist Rescue Unit

2001. Fire Service. Multicoloured.

994 60c. Type **149** 50 55
995 90c. Anglo 4800 water/foam tender 75 80
996 $1.50 Bronto 33-2T1 combined telescopic ladder/ hydraulic platform . . . . 1·30 1·40
997 $2 Anglo 450 LRX water tenders . . . . 1·70 1·80
MS998 105 × 55 mm. $3 Wormald "Arrestor" ARFFV in gateway to Motufoua Secondary School 2·50 2·75

Nos. 994/7 also commemorate the first anniv of the fire tragedy at Motufoua Secondary School.

150 Tuvaluan Boy with Japanese Family

2001. "Philanippon '01" International Stamp Exhibition, Tokyo. 13th Asian-Pacific Children's Convention, Fukuoka. Sheet 94 × 80 mm.

MS999 **150** $3 multicoloured . . 2·50 2·75

2001. 101st Birthday of Queen Elizabeth the Queen Mother. Nos. 846/9 optd or surch **101 birthday**.

1000 60c. Queen Elizabeth with her daughters, 1951 . . . 50 55
1001 90c. With Princes William and Harry, 1995 . . . . 75 80
1002 $1.50 Inspecting the Queen's Dragoon Guards . . . . 1·30 1·40
1003 $2 on 40c. King George VI and Queen Elizabeth inspecting bomb damage, 1940 . . . . 1·70 1·80
MS1004 145 × 70 mm. $5 on $2 Lady Elizabeth Bowes-Lyon aged 6, and Yuri Gagarin (first cosmonaut) 4·25 4·50

152 Tuvaluan Girl

2001. Inauguration of .tv Corporation (Internet Service Provider). Each featuring satellite dish and web address. Multicoloured.

1005 40c. Type **152** 35 40
1006 60c. Local dancers 50 55
1007 90c. Tuvaluan man blowing conch shell 75 80
1008 $1.50 Young child with flower garland around head . . . . 1·30 1·40
MS1009 85 × 50 mm. $2 Satellite dishes and web address . . . . 1·70 1·80

153 Mosquito

2001. Insects. Multicoloured.

1010 25c. Type **153** 20 25
1011 30c. Giant African snail . . 25 30
1012 40c. Cockroach 35 40
1013 45c. Stick insect 40 45
1014 50c. Green stink bug . . . 40 45
1015 55c. Dragonfly 45 50
1016 60c. Caterpillar of monarch butterfly 50 55
1017 70c. Coconut beetle 60 65
1018 90c. Honey bee 75 80
1019 $1 Monarch butterfly . . . 85 90
1020 $2 Common eggfly butterfly 1·70 1·80
1021 $3 Painted lady butterfly . . 2·50 2·75

2002. "United We Stand". Support for Victims of 11 September 2001 Terrorist Attacks. As T **445** of St. Vincent.

1022 $2 multicoloured (blue background) . . . . . . 1·70 1·80
1023 $2 multicoloured (yellow background) . . . . . . 1·70 1·80

154 The Paulownia Court

2002. Japanese Art. "The Tale of Genji" (Murasaki Shikibu). Multicoloured.

1024 40c. Type **154** 35 40
1025 40c. The Broom Tree . . . 35 40
1026 40c. The Shell of the Locust 35 40
1027 40c. Evening Faces 35 40
1028 40c. Lavender 35 40
1029 40c. The Safflower 35 40
1030 60c. The Festival of the Cherry Blossoms 50 55
1031 60c. Heartvine 50 55
1032 60c. The Sacred Tree . . . 50 55
1033 60c. The Orange Blossoms 50 55
1034 60c. Suma 50 55
1035 60c. Akashi 50 55
1036 90c. The Wormwood Patch 75 80
1037 90c. The Gate House . . . 75 80
1038 90c. A Picture Contest . . . 75 80
1039 90c. The Wind in the Pines 75 80
1040 90c. A Rack of Cloud . . . 75 80
1041 90c. The Morning Glory . . 75 80
MS1042 Three sheets, each 93 × 124 mm. (a) $4 An Autumn Excursion (chapter 7). (b) $4 Channel Buoys (chapter 14). (c) $4 The Maiden (chapter 21). Imperf Set of 3 sheets . . . . 10·00 10·50

Nos. 1024/9 (chapters 1/6), 1030/5 (chapters 8/13) and 1036/41 (chapters 15/20).

155 Young Hospital Patient in Wheelchair

2002. UNICEF. Rights of the Child. Multicoloured.

1043 40c. Type **155** 35 40
1044 60c. Children by roadside 50 55
1045 90c. Nauti Primary School, Funafuti 75 80
1046 $1.50 Mother and baby . . 1·30 1·40
MS1047 110 × 80 mm. $1 Taulosa Karl; $1 Simalua Jacinta Enele (Tuvalu representatives at UN special session on children) . . 1·70 1·80

2002. Golden Jubilee. As T **110** of St. Kitts. Multicoloured.

1048 $1.50 Princes William and Harry as young boys . . 1·30 1·40
1049 $1.50 Queen Elizabeth at garden party . . . . . . 1·30 1·40
1050 $1.50 Queen Elizabeth with Prince Philip wearing robes of Order of the Bath . . . . 1·30 1·40
1051 $1.50 Queen Elizabeth in red hat and coat . . . . 1·30 1·40
MS1052 76 × 108 mm. $4 Queen Elizabeth on horseback for Trooping the Colour . . . . . 3·25 3·50

2002. World Cup Football Championship, Japan and Korea. As T **113** of St. Kitts. Multicoloured.

1053 90c. Tom Finney (England) 75 80
1054 90c. Publicity poster, Germany, 1974 . . . . . 75 80
1055 90c. Portuguese player . . . 75 80
1056 90c. Uruguayan player . . . 75 80
1057 90c. Suwon Stadium, Korea (56 × 42 mm) 75 80
MS1058 64 × 86 mm. $4 Johann Cruyff (Holland) . . . . . . 3·25 3·50

No. **MS**1058 is inscribed "JOHAN CRUFF" in error.

156 Duchess of York, 1923

2002. Queen Elizabeth the Queen Mother Commemoration. Each multicoloured ($1.50) or black and lilac (others).

1059 60c. Type **156** 50 55
1060 60c. Duchess of York, 1923 (different) (face value at left) 50 55
1061 90c. Queen Mother at Sandringham, 1992 (29 × 25 mm) 75 80
1062 90c. Queen Mother accepting posy from child, 1989 (29 × 25 mm) 75 80
1063 90c. Queen Mother with teddy bear, Queen Charlotte's Hospital, 1989 (29 × 25 mm) 75 80
1064 90c. Queen Mother with family, Didcot, 1989 (29 × 25 mm) 75 80
1065 $1.50 Queen Mother at Tower Hamlets Memorial Garden, 2001 (40 × 30 mm) . . . . . . 1·30 1·40
MS1066 Two sheets, each 65 × 101 mm. (a) $2 Lady Elizabeth Bowes-Lyon with her brother David; $2 Queen Mother in old age. (b) $2 Queen Elizabeth smelling rose, 1950s; $2 Queen Mother, 1971(each 26 × 40 mm). Set of 2 sheets . . . . 6·75 7·00

157 Citizen of the World Badge

2002. 20th World Scout Jamboree, Thailand. Multicoloured.

1067 $1.50 Type **157** . . . . . . 1·30 1·40
1068 $1.50 First Aid badge . . . 1·30 1·40
1069 $1.50 Personal Fitness badge 1·30 1·40
1070 $1.50 Environmental Science badge . . . . 1·30 1·40
MS1071 66 × 85 mm. $5 Lord Baden-Powell (vert) . . . . . 4·25 4·50

158 Mt Fitzroy, Argentina

2002. International Year of Mountains. Muticoloured.

1072 $1.50 Type **158** . . . . . 1·30 1·40
1073 $1.50 Mt Foraker, U.S.A. 1·30 1·40
1074 $1.50 Mt Fujiyama, Japan 1·30 1·40
1075 $1.50 Mt Makalu, Nepal . . 1·30 1·40
MS1076 63 × 84 mm. $4 Mt Godwin-Austen (K2), Kashmir (vert) . . . . 3·25 3·50

No. 1072 is inscribed "CHILE" in error.

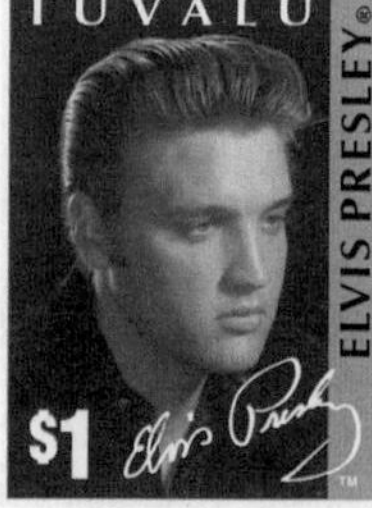

159 Elvis Presley

2002. 25th Death Anniv of Elvis Presley.

1077 **159** $1 multicoloured 85 90

160 Palomino Horse **161** Ram in Bushes

2003. End of Chinese "Year of the Horse". Multicoloured.
1078 40c. Type **160** 35 40
1079 60c. White Arab horse . . . 50 55
1080 90c. Wild horse 75 80
1081 $2 Chestnut horse . . . . . 1·70 1·80
MS1082 75 × 75 mm. $1.50 Seahorse; $1.50 Group of seahorses . . . 2·50 2·75

2003. Chinese New Year ("Year of the Ram"). Multicoloured.
1083 75c. Type **161** 65 70
1084 75c. Side view of ram's head 65 70
1085 75c. Front view of ram's head 65 70

162 Diana, Princess of Wales

2003. 5th Death Anniv of Diana, Princess of Wales. Multicoloured.
1086 $1 Type **162** 85 90
1087 $1 Princess Diana wearing emerald necklace 85 90
1088 $1 Wearing blue evening dress 85 90
1089 $1 Wearing turquoise scarf 85 90
1090 $1 Wearing pink blouse . . 85 90
1091 $1 Wearing lace dress . . . 85 90
MS1092 90 × 105 mm. $4 Princess Diana and rose . . . . 3·25 3·50

163 John F. Kennedy in Solomon Islands, 1943

2003. Life and Times of President John F. Kennedy. Two sheets containing T **163** and similar vert designs.
MS1093 127 × 142 mm. $1.75 Type **163** (green and black); $1.75 As Commander of USS *PT109* (motor torpedo boat) (deep brown, brown and black); $1.75 Receiving Medal for Gallantry, 1941 (deep blue, deep blue and black); $1.75 On crutches in Senate Campaign, 1952 (lilac and black) . . . . 6·00 6·25
MS1094 70 × 77 mm. $4 With father and brothers (lavender, violet and black) . . . . 3·25 3·50

164 Orville Wright, Dayton, Ohio, 1903

2003. Centenary of Powered Flight. Sheets containing T **164** and similar horiz designs. Multicoloured.
MS1095 178 × 96 mm. $1.75 Type **164**; $1.75 Wilbur Wright with King Alphonso of Spain, Pau, France, 1909; $1.75 Wright Type A biplane, Le Mans, France, 1908; $1.75 Voisin "Boxkite", France, 1907 . . . . 6·00 6·25
MS1096 178 × 96 mm. $1.75 Gabriel Voisin's motor boat powered glider, France, 1905; $1.75 Trajan Vuia in *Vuia No. 1*, France, 1906; $1.75 Santos-Dumont's biplane 14 bis, France, 1906; $1.75 Wright Type A biplane, Virginia, 1908 6·00 6·25
MS1097 Two sheets, each 95 × 65 mm. (a) $4 Wright Type A biplane, Virginia, 1908. (b) $4 Curtiss *June Bug*, 1908 Set of s two sheets . . . . 6·50 6·75

165 Princess Elizabeth **166** Prince William as Schoolboy

2003. 50th Anniv of Coronation. Multicoloured.
MS1098 155 × 93 mm. $2 Type **165**; $2 Queen wearing diadem; $2 Queen wearing yellow hat and coat . . . . 5·00 5·25
MS1099 76 × 106 mm. $4 Queen Elizabeth II . . . . 3·25 3·50

2003. 21st Birthday of Prince William of Wales. Multicoloured.
MS1100 156 × 86 mm. $1.50 Type **166**; $1.50 Wearing blue shirt; $1.50 Wearing polo helmet 3·50 3·75
MS1101 76 × 105 mm. $4 Prince William . . . . 3·25 3·75

167 V16 Sport Phaeton (1931)

2003. Centenary of General Motors Cadillac. Multicoloured.
MS1102 126 × 176 mm. $1.50 Type **167**; $1.50 Eldorado Convertible (1959); $1.50 Seville Elegante (1979); $1.50 Seville Elegante (1983) . . . . 5·00 5·25
MS1103 89 × 125 mm. $4 Cadillac 3·25 3·50

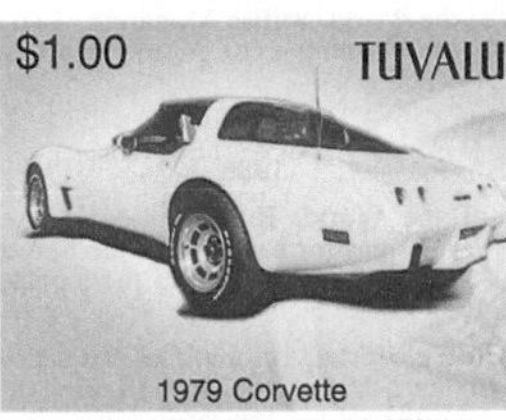

168 Yellow Corvette (1979)

2003. 50th Anniv of General Motors Chevrolet Corvette. Multicoloured.
MS1104 126 × 146 mm. $1 Type **168**; $1 Red Corvette (1979); $1 Silver Corvette (1979); $1 Corvette (1980) . . . . 3·25 3·50
MS1105 126 × 90 mm. $4 Corvette (1990) . . . . 3·25 3·50

2003. Centenary of Tour de France Cycle Race. As T **127** of St. Kitts. Multicoloured.
MS1106 158 × 98 mm. $1 Gastone Nencini (1960); $1 Jacques Anquetil (1961); $1 Jacques Anquetil (1962); $1 Jacques Anquetil (1963) . . . . 3·25 3·50
MS1107 98 × 68 mm. $4 Jan Janssen (1968) . . . . 3·25 3·50

169 Blue-grey Gnatcatcher

2003. Birds, Butterflies, Flowers and Orchids. Multicoloured.
MS1108 115 × 115 mm. $1.25 Type **169**; $1.25 White-eyed vireo; $1.25 Clapper rail; $1.25 Sandhill crane . . . . 4·00 4·25
MS1109 135 × 115 mm. $1.25 Malachite; $1.25 White hairstreak; $1.25 Giantswallowtail; $1.25 Bahamian swallowtail . . . 4·00 4·25
MS1110 91 × 135 mm. $1.25 *Rhododendron yakushimanum*; $1.25 *Tulipa* "Golden Artist"; $1.25 *Lilium*"Golden Splendor"; $1.25 *Anthurium andraeanum* (all vert) . . . . 4·00 4·25
MS1111 107 × 116 mm. $1.25 *Dimerandra emarginata*; $1.25 *Oncidium lanceanum*; $1.25 *Isochilus linearis*; $1.25 *Oeceoclades maculate* (all vert) 4·00 4·25
MS1112 Four sheets. (a) 95 × 65 mm. $3 Grasshopper sparrow. (b) 65 × 95 mm. $3 Polydamas swallowtail. Imperf. (c) 65 × 95 mm. $3 *Rosa* "Candy Bianca". Imperf. (d) 95 × 65 mm. $3 *Oncidium ampliatum* Set of 4 sheets . . . . 9·75 10·00

170 "Monkey and Old Tree"

2004. Chinese New Year ("Year of the Monkey"). Paintings by Chang Dai-Chien.Multicoloured.
MS1113 1175 × 106 mm. 75c. × 4 Type **170** . . . . 2·40 2·50
MS1114 66 × 96 mm. $1.50 "Two Monkeys" . . . . 1·20 1·30

171 "100th Year of Baseball", 1939

2004. 25th Death Anniv of Norman Rockwell (artist) (2003). Designs showing covers for Saturday Evening Post. Multicoloured.
MS1115 146 × 178 mm. $1.25 Type **171**; $1.25 "The Locker Room (The Rookie)", 1957; $1.25 "The Dugout", 1948; $1.25 "Game Called because of Rain", 1949 . . . . 4·00 4·25
MS1116 91 × 98 mm. $3 "New Kids in the Neighborhood", 1967 (detail) (horiz) . . . . 2·40 2·50

172 "Les Seins Aux Fleurs Rouges"

2004. Death Centenary of Paul Gauguin (artist). Multicoloured.
1117 50c. Type **172** 40 45
1118 60c. "Famille Tahitienne" 50 55
1119 $1 "Tahitiennes Sur La Plage" 80 85
1120 $2 "Jeune Fille a L'Eventail" . . . . 1·60 1·70
MS1121 129 × 154 mm. $1 "Nafea Faa Ipoipo"; $1 "Le Cheval Blanc"; $1 "Pape Moe"; $1 "Contes Barbares" . . . . . . 3·25 3·50
MS1122 93 × 73 mm. $4 "Femmes de Tahiti". Imperf . . . . 3·25 3·50

173 "Philadelphia and Elizabeth Wharton" (Anthony Van Dyck)

2004. 300th Anniv of St. Petersburg. "Treasures of the Hermitage". Multicoloured.
1123 50c. Type **173** 40 45
1124 80c. "A Glass of Lemonade" (Gerard Terboch) 65 70
1125 $1 "A Mistress and Her Servant" (Pieter De Hooch) 80 85
1126 $1.20 "Portrait of a Man and His Three Sons" (Bartholomaeus Bruyn the Elder) . . . . 1·00 1·10
MS1127 80 × 68 mm. $4 "The Milkmaid's Family" (Louis Le Nain). Imperf . . . . 3·25 3·50

174 "Seated Woman, 1945"

2004. 30th Death Anniv (2003) of Pablo Picasso (artist). Multicoloured.
MS1128 131 × 166 mm. $1.50 Type **174**; $1.50 "Woman in Armchair, 1949"; $1.50 "Bust of Francoise, 1946"; $1.50 "Head of a Woman, 1046" . . . . . . 5·00 5·25
MS1129 97 × 70 mm. $4 "Franoise Gilot with Paloma and Claude, 1951". Imperf . . . . 3·25 3·50

175 Girl Reading Speech

2004. AIDS Awareness. Multicoloured.
1130 60c. Type **175** 50 55
1131 90c. School girl and panellists at table 75 80
1132 $1.50 Kilogatasi drama group . . . . 1·20 1·30
1133 $2 Panellists at table . . . . 1·60 1·70
MS1134 110 × 80 mm. $3 Group discussion . . . . 2·40 2·50

176 Chen Shui-bian (Pres. of Republic of China)

2004. Inauguration of Chen Shui-bian, Pres. of the Republic of China. Sheet 110 × 80 mm containing T **176** and similar vert design. Multicoloured.
MS1135 $2 Type **176**; $2 Honourable Saufatu Sopoanga (Prime Minister of Tuvalu) . . 3·25 3·50

OFFICIAL STAMPS

1981. Nos. 105/22 optd **OFFICIAL**.

O 1	**14**	1c. multicoloured	10	10
O 2	–	2c. multicoloured	10	10
O 3	–	4c. multicoloured	10	10
O 4	–	5c. multicoloured	10	10
O 5	–	6c. multicoloured	10	10
O 6	–	8c. multicoloured	10	10
O 7	–	10c. multicoloured	15	15
O 8	–	15c. multicoloured	15	15
O 9	–	20c. multicoloured	20	20
O10a	–	25c. multicoloured	25	25
O11	–	30c. multicoloured	20	20
O12	–	35c. multicoloured	20	20
O13	–	40c. multicoloured	20	20
O14	–	45c. multicoloured	25	25
O15	–	50c. multicoloured	30	30
O16	–	70c. multicoloured	40	40
O17	–	$1 multicoloured	40	40
O18a	–	$2 multicoloured	75	75
O19	–	$5 multicoloured	1·00	75

1983. Nos. 202/3a, 205/12, 224 and 234 optd **OFFICIAL**.

O20	5c. Wedding and baby food baskets	10	40
O21	10c. Hand-carved model of canoe	10	40
O22	15c. Ladies' sun hats	15	70
O23	25c. Pandanus baskets	25	60
O24	30c. on 45c. Reef sandals and fish trap	50	70
O25	30c. Basket tray and coconut stand	30	70
O26	35c. Pandanus pillows and shell necklaces	40	75
O27	40c. Round baskets and fans	45	75
O28	45c. Reef sandals and fish trap	45	75
O29	50c. Rat trap	50	75
O30	60c. on $1 Pump drill and adze	75	75
O31	60c. Fisherman's waterproof boxes	60	1·00
O32	$1 Pump drill and adze	75	1·00
O33	$2 Fisherman's hat and canoe bailers	1·00	1·00
O34	$5 Fishing rod, lures and scoop nets	1·75	2·50

1989. Nos. 502/17 optd **OFFICIAL**.

O35	5c. Type **66**	30	55
O36	10c. White tern	30	55
O37	15c. Common noddy	45	55
O38	20c. Phoenix petrel	45	55
O39	25c. Pacific golden plover	50	75
O40	30c. Crested tern	50	75
O41	35c. Sooty tern	55	80
O42	40c. Bristle-thighed curlew	55	80
O43	45c. Bar-tailed godwit	65	85
O44	50c. Reef heron	70	90
O45	55c. Great frigate bird	70	90
O46	60c. Red-footed booby	70	90
O47	70c. Rufous-necked sandpiper	80	1·00
O48	$1 Long-tailed koel	1·10	1·10
O49	$2 Red-tailed tropic bird	2·00	1·90
O50	$5 Buff-banded rail	4·25	4·50

POSTAGE DUE STAMPS

D 1 Tuvalu Crest

1981.

D 1	D 1	1c. black and purple	10	10
D 2		2c. black and blue	10	10
D 3		5c. black and brown	10	10
D13		10c. black and green	10	10
D14		20c. black and brown	15	20
D 6		30c. black and orange	15	30
D 7		40c. black and blue	15	40
D 8		50c. black and green	20	45
D 9		$1 black and mauve	30	80

Some values exist with or without the imprint date at foot.

APPENDIX

The following stamps for individual islands of Tuvalu have either been issued in excess of postal needs, or have not been made available to the public in reasonable quantities at face value.

FUNAFUTI

1984.

Leaders of the World. Railway Locomotives (1st series). Two designs for each value, the first showing technical drawings and the second the locomotive at work. 15, 20, 30, 40, 50, 60c. each × 2.

Leaders of the World. Automobiles (1st series). Two designs for each value, the first showing technical drawings and the second the car in action. 1, 10, 40c., $1 each × 2.

Leaders of the World. Railway Locomotives (2nd series). Two designs for each value, the first showing technical drawings and the second the locomotive at work. 5, 15, 25, 35, 40, 55, 60c., $1 each × 2.

1985.

Leaders of the World. Automobiles (2nd series). Two designs for each value, the first showing technical drawings and the second the car in action. 1, 30, 55, 60c. each × 2.

Leaders of the World. Railway Locomotives (3rd series). Two designs for each value, the first showing technical drawings and the second the locomotive at work. 5, 15, 35, 40, 50c., $1 each × 2.

Leaders of the World. Life and Times of Queen Elizabeth the Queen Mother. Two designs for each value, showing different portraits. 5, 25, 80c., $1.05 each × 2.

1986.

60th Birthday of Queen Elizabeth II. 10, 50c., $1.50, $3.50.

Royal Wedding (1st issue). 60c., $1 each × 2.

Royal Wedding (2nd issue). Previous Royal Wedding stamps optd **Congratulations T.R.H. The Duke & Duchess of York**. 60c., $1 each × 2.

Railway Locomotives (4th series). Two designs for each value, the first showing technical drawings and the second the locomotive at work. 20, 40, 60c., $1.50 each × 2.

1987.

Automobiles (3rd series). Two designs for each value, the first showing technical drawings and the second the car in action. 10, 20, 40, 60, 75, 80c., $1.50 each × 2.

Royal Ruby Wedding. 20, 50, 75c., $1.20, $1.75.

1988.

Olympic Games, Seoul. 10, 20, 40, 50, 80, 90c.

NANUMAGA

1984.

Leaders of the World. Automobiles (1st series). Two designs for each value, the first showing technical drawings and the second the car in action. 5, 10, 25, 30, 40c., $1 each × 2.

Leaders of the World. British Monarchs. Two designs for each value, forming a composite picture. 10, 20, 30, 40, 50c., $1 each × 2.

Leaders of the World. Automobiles (2nd series). Two designs for each value, the first showing technical drawings and the second the car in action. 5, 10, 50c., $1 each × 2.

1985.

Leaders of the World. Railway Locomotives. Two designs for each value, the first showing technical drawings and the second the locomotive at work. 10, 25, 50, 60c. each × 2.

Leaders of the World. Flowers. 25, 30, 40, 50c. each × 2.

Leaders of the World. Automobiles (3rd series). Two designs for each value, the first showing technical drawings and the second the car in action. 10, 25, 75c., $1 each × 2.

Leaders of the World. Life and Times of Queen Elizabeth the Queen Mother. Two designs for each value, showing different portraits. 15, 55, 65, 90c. each × 2.

1986.

60th Birthday of Queen Elizabeth II. 5c., $1, $1.75, $2.50.

World Cup Football Championship, Mexico. 1, 2, 5, 5, 10, 20, 35, 50, 60, 75c., $1, $2, $4.

Royal Wedding (1st issue). 60c., $1 each × 2.

Royal Wedding (2nd issue). Previous Royal Wedding stamps optd as for Funafuti. 60c., $1 each × 2.

1987.

Automobiles (4th series). Two designs for each value, the first showing technical drawings and the second the car in action. 5, 10, 15, 20, 25, 40, 60c., $1 each × 2.

Royal Ruby Wedding. 15, 35, 60c., $1.50, $1.75.

NANUMEA

1984.

Leaders of the World. Railway Locomotives (1st series). Two designs for each value, the first showing technical drawings and the second the locomotive at work. 15, 20, 30, 40, 50, 60c. each × 2.

Leaders of the World. Famous Cricketers. Two designs for each value, the first showing a portrait and the second the cricketer in action. 1, 10, 40c., $1 each × 2.

1985.

Leaders of the World. Automobiles (1st series). Two designs for each value, the first showing technical drawings and the second the car in action. 5, 40, 50, 60c. each × 2.

Leaders of the World. Railway Locomotives (2nd series). Two designs for each value, the first showing technical drawings and the second the locomotive at work. 1, 35, 50, 60c. each × 2.

Leaders of the World. Automobiles (2nd series). Two designs for each value, the first showing technical drawings and the second the car in action. 15, 20, 50, 60c. each × 2.

Leaders of the World. Cats. 5, 30, 50c., $1 each × 2.

Leaders of the World. Life and Times of Queen Elizabeth the Queen Mother. Two designs for each value, showing different portraits. 5, 30, 75c., $1.05 each × 2.

1986.

60th Birthday of Queen Elizabeth II. 10, 80c., $1.75, $3.

World Cup Football Championship, Mexico. 1, 2, 5, 10, 25, 40, 50, 75, 90c., $1, $2.50, $4.

Royal Wedding (1st issue). 60c., $1 each × 2.

Royal Wedding (2nd issue). Previous Royal Wedding stamps optd as for Funafuti. 60c., $1 each × 2.

Automobiles (3rd series). Two designs for each value, the first showing technical drawings and the second the car in action. 10, 20, 35, 50, 75c., $2 each × 2.

1987.

Royal Ruby Wedding. 40, 60, 80c., $1, $2.

NIUTAO

1984.

Leaders of the World. Automobiles (1st series). Two designs for each value, the first showing technical drawings and the second the car in action. 15, 30, 40, 50c. each × 2.

Leaders of the World. Railway Locomotives (1st series). Two designs for each value, the first showing technical drawings and the second the locomotive at work. 5, 10, 20, 40, 50c., $1 each × 2.

1985.

Leaders of the World. Famous Cricketers. Two designs for each value, the first showing a portrait and the second the cricketer in action. 1, 15, 50c., $1 each × 2.

Leaders of the World. Birth Bicent of John J. Audubon (ornithologist). Birds. 5, 15, 25c., $1 each × 2.

Leaders of the World. Automobiles (2nd series). Two designs for each value, the first showing technical drawings and the second the car in action. 20, 25, 40, 60c. each × 2.

Leaders of the World. Railway Locomotives (2nd series). Two designs for each value, the first showing technical drawings and the second the locomotive at work. 10, 30, 45, 60, 75c., $1.20 each × 2.

Leaders of the World. Life and Times of Queen Elizabeth the Queen Mother. Two designs for each value, showing different portraits. 15, 35, 70, 95c. each × 2.

1986.

60th Birthday of Queen Elizabeth II. 5, 60c., $1.50, $3.50.

Royal Wedding (1st series). 60c., $1 each × 2.

Royal Wedding (2nd series). Previous Royal Wedding stamps optd as for Funafuti. 60c., $1 each × 2.

1987.

Royal Ruby Wedding. 60th Birthday of Queen Elizabeth II issue of 1986 optd **40th WEDDING ANNIVERSARY OF H.M. QUEEN ELIZABETH II**. 5, 60c., $1.50, $3.50.

NUI

1984.

Leaders of the World. Railway Locomotives (1st series). Two designs for each value, the first showing technical drawings and the second the locomotive at work. 15, 25, 30, 50c. each × 2.

Leaders of the World. British Monarchs. Two designs for each value, forming a composite picture. 1, 5, 15, 40, 50c., $1 each × 2.

1985.

Leaders of the World. Railway Locomotives (2nd series). Two designs for each value, the first showing technical drawings and the second the locomotive at work. 5, 15, 25c., $1 each × 2.

Leaders of the World. Automobiles (1st series). Two designs for each value, the first showing technical drawings and the second the car in action. 25, 30, 40, 50c. each × 2.

Leaders of the World. Famous Cricketers. Two designs for each value, the first showing a portrait and the second the cricketer in action. 1, 40, 60, 70c. each × 2.

Leaders of the World. Life and Times of Queen Elizabeth the Queen Mother. Two designs for each value, showing different portraits. 5, 50, 75, 85c. each × 2.

Leaders of the World. Automobiles (2nd series). Two designs for each value, the first showing technical drawings and the second the car in action. 5, 15, 40, 60, 90c., $1.10 each × 2.

1986.

60th Birthday of Queen Elizabeth II. 10, 80c., $1.75, $3.

Royal Wedding (1st issue). 60c., $1 each × 2.

Royal Wedding (2nd issue). Previous Royal Wedding stamps optd as for Funafuti. 60c., $1 each × 2.

1987.

Railway Locomotives (3rd series). Two designs for each value, the first showing technical drawings and the second the locomotive at work. 10, 25, 35, 40, 60, 75c., $1, $1.25 each × 2.

Royal Ruby Wedding. 20, 50, 75c., $1.20, $1.75.

1988.

Railway Locomotives (4th series). Two designs for each value, the first showing technical drawings and the second the locomotive at work. 5, 10, 20, 25, 40, 50, 60, 75c. each × 2.

NUKUFETAU

1984.

Leaders of the World. Automobiles (1st series). Two designs for each value, the first showing technical drawings and the second the car in action. 10, 25, 30, 50, 60c. each × 2.

Leaders of the World. British Monarchs. Two designs for each value, forming a composite picture. 1, 10, 30, 50, 60c., $1 each × 2.

1985.

Leaders of the World. Famous Cricketers. Two designs for each value, the first showing a portrait and the second the cricketer in action. 1, 10, 55c., $1 each × 2.

Leaders of the World. Railway Locomotives (1st series). Two designs for each value, the first showing technical drawings and the second the locomotive at work. 1, 10, 60, 70c. each × 2.

Leaders of the World. Automobiles (2nd series). Two designs for each value, the first showing technical drawings and the second the car in action. 5, 10, 15, 20, 50, 60, 75c., $1.50 each × 2.

Leaders of the World. Life and Times of Queen Elizabeth the Queen Mother. Two designs for each value, showing different portraits. 10, 45, 65c., $1 each × 2.

1986.

Leaders of the World. Railway Locomotives (2nd series). Two designs for each value, the first showing technical drawings and the second the locomotive at work. 20, 40, 60c., $1.50 each × 2.

60th Birthday of Queen Elizabeth II. 5, 40c., $2, $4.

Royal Wedding (1st issue). 60c., $1 each × 2.

Royal Wedding (2nd issue). Previous Royal Wedding stamps optd as for Funafuti. 60c., $1 each × 2.

1987.

Railway Locomotives (3rd series). Two designs for each value, the first showing technical drawings and the second the locomotive at work. 5, 10, 15, 25, 30, 50, 60c., $1 each × 2.

Royal Ruby Wedding. 60th Birthday of Queen Elizabeth II issue of 1986 optd as for Niutao. 5, 40c., $2, $4.

NUKULAELAE

1984.

Leaders of the World. Railway Locomotives (1st series). Two designs for each value, the first showing technical drawings and the second the locomotive at work. 5, 15, 40c., $1 each × 2.

Leaders of the World. Famous Cricketers. Two designs for each value, the first showing a portrait and the second the cricketer in action. 5, 15, 30c., $1 each × 2.

Leaders of the World. Railway Locomotives (2nd series). Two designs for each value, the first showing technical drawings and the second the locomotive at work. 5, 20, 40c., $1 each × 2.

1985.

Leaders of the World. Automobiles (1st series). Two designs for each value, the first showing technical drawings and the second the car in action. 5, 35, 50, 70c. each × 2.

Leaders of the World. Dogs. 5, 20, 50, 70c. each × 2.

Leaders of the World. Railway Locomotives (3rd series). Two designs for each value, the first showing technical drawings and the second the locomotive at work. 10, 25, 50c., $1 each × 2.

Leaders of the World. Automobiles (2nd series). Two designs for each value, the first showing technical drawings and the second the car in action. 10, 25, 35, 50, 75c., $1 each × 2.

Leaders of the World. Life and Times of Queen Elizabeth the Queen Mother. Two designs for each value, showing different portraits. 5, 25, 85c., $1 each × 2.

1986.

60th Birthday of Queen Elizabeth II. 10c., $1, $1.50, $3.

Railway Locomotives (4th series). Two designs for each value, the first showing technical drawings and the second the locomotive at work. 10, 15, 25, 40, 50, 80c., $1, $1.50 each × 2.

Royal Wedding (1st issue). 60c., $1 each × 2.

Royal Wedding (2nd issue). Previous Royal Wedding stamps optd as for Funafuti. 60c., $1 each × 2.

1987.

Royal Ruby Wedding. 15, 35, 60c., $1.50, $1.75.

VAITUPU

1984.

Leaders of the World. Automobiles (1st series). Two designs for each value, the first showing technical drawings and the second the car in action. 15, 25, 30, 50c. each × 2.

Leaders of the World. British Monarchs. Two designs for each value, forming a composite picture. 1, 5, 15, 40, 50c., $1 each × 2.

Leaders of the World. Automobiles (2nd series). Two designs for each value, the first showing technical drawings and the second the car in action. 5, 15, 25, 30, 40, 50, 60c. $1 each × 2.

1985.

Leaders of the World. Railway Locomotives (1st series). Two designs for each value, the first showing technical drawings and the second the locomotive at work. 10, 25, 50, 60c. each × 2.

Leaders of the World. Butterflies. 5, 15, 50, 75c. each × 2.

Leaders of the World. Automobiles (3rd series). Two designs for each value, the first showing technical drawings and the second the car in action. 15, 30, 40, 60c. each × 2.

Leaders of the World. Life and Times of Queen Elizabeth the Queen Mother. Two designs for each value, showing different portraits. 15, 40, 65, 90c. each × 2.

1986.

Leaders of the World. Railway Locomotives (2nd series). Two designs for each value, the first showing technical drawings and the second the locomotives at work. 5, 25, 80c., $1 each × 2.

60th Birthday of Queen Elizabeth II. 5, 60c., $2, $3.50.

Royal Wedding (1st issue). 60c., $1 each × 2.

Royal Wedding (2nd issue). Previous Royal Wedding stamps optd as for Funafuti. 60c., $1 each × 2.

1987.

Railway Locomotives (3rd series). Two designs for each value, the first showing technical drawings and the second the locomotive at work. 10, 15, 25, 35, 45, 65, 85c., $1 each × 2.

Royal Ruby Wedding. 60th Birthday of Queen Elizabeth II issue of 1986 optd as for Niutao. 5, 60c., $2, $3.50.

UBANGI-SHARI Pt. 6

Formerly part of the French Congo. Ubangi-Shari became a separate colony in 1904 (although stamps of the French Congo continued to be used until 1915). From 1915 to 1922 it shared a postal administration with Chad.

From 1936 to 1958 Ubangi-Shari was part of French Equatorial Africa. In December 1958 it became the autonomous state of the Central African Republic.

100 centimes = 1 franc.

A. UBANGI-SHARI-CHAD

1915. Stamps of Middle Congo optd **OUBANGUI-CHARI-TCHAD.**

1	1	1c. green and brown	20	3·00
2		2c. violet and brown	25	3·00
3		4c. blue and brown	35	3·25
4		5c. green and blue	1·10	2·75
19		5c. yellow and blue	3·00	3·25
5		10c. red and blue	1·40	80
20		10c. green and turquoise	2·75	3·25
5a		15c. purple and pink	3·75	4·00
6		20c. brown and blue	1·90	5·75
7	2	25c. blue and green	3·00	3·00
21		25c. green and black	2·50	3·00
8		30c. red and green	2·75	3·25
22		30c. red	2·50	3·25
9		35c. brown and blue	5·75	10·50
10		40c. green and brown	5·75	13·00
11		45c. violet and orange	6·00	13·00
12		50c. green and orange	5·00	14·50
23		50c. blue and green	2·50	3·50
13		75c. brown and blue	14·00	24·00
14	3	1f. green and violet	10·00	22·00
15		2f. violet and green	17·00	23·00
16		5f. blue and pink	55·00	60·00

1916. No. 5 surch **5c** and cross.

18		10c.+5c. red and blue	2·25	3·50

B. UBANGI-SHARI

1922. Stamps of Middle Congo, new colours, optd **OUBANGUI-CHARI.**

24	1	1c. violet and green	35	2·75
25		2c. green and pink	40	3·00
26		4c. brown and purple	1·75	3·50
27		5c. blue and pink	1·90	3·50
28		10c. green and turquoise	3·75	4·25
29		15c. pink and blue	4·00	4·75
30		20c. brown and pink	8·00	14·00
31		25c. violet and pink	4·50	10·50
32		30c. red	3·25	7·25
33		35c. violet and green	6·50	13·00
34		40c. blue and mauve	5·50	11·50
35		45c. brown and mauve	5·50	11·00
36		50c. blue and light blue	3·25	5·50
37		60 on 75c. violet on pink	4·25	7·75
38		75c. brown and pink	5·50	13·50
39	3	1f. green and blue	7·75	14·00
40		2f. green and pink	7·75	20·00
41		5f. green and brown	15·00	14·00

1924. Stamps of 1922 and similar stamps additionally optd **AFRIQUE EQUATORIALE FRANCAISE.**

42	1	1c. violet and green	10	2·50
43		2c. green and pink	10	3·00
44		4c. brown and chocolate	10	2·75
44c		4c. brown	1·40	4·00
45		5c. blue and pink	30	2·50
46		10c. green and turquoise	85	3·00
47		10c. red and blue	65	2·00
48		15c. pink and blue	55	3·50
49		20c. brown and pink	2·25	2·50
50	2	25c. violet and pink	1·75	95
51		30c. red	1·00	2·50
52		30c. brown and pink	50	1·10
53		30c. olive and green	2·50	2·25
54		35c. violet and green	30	2·50
55		40c. blue and mauve	1·40	2·00
56		45c. brown and mauve	1·90	3·00
57		50c. blue and light blue	1·75	2·00
58		50c. grey and blue	2·25	80
59		60 on 75c. violet on pink	1·10	2·25
60		65c. brown and blue	3·75	4·25
61		75c. brown and pink	2·50	3·50
62		75c. blue and light blue	2·00	2·50
63		75c. purple and brown	3·50	4·00
64		90c. pink and red	1·25	15·00
65a	3	1f. green and blue	35	1·25
66		1f.10 brown and blue	3·50	6·00
67		1f.25 mauve and green	7·00	11·00
68		1f.50 ultramarine and blue	7·25	19·00
69		1f.75 brown and orange	9·50	12·00
70		2f. green and pink	3·00	3·00
71		3f. mauve on pink	6·50	12·00
72		5f. green and brown	5·25	5·00

1925. As last but new colours and surch.

73	3	65 on 1f. violet and brown	1·10	3·00
74		85 on 1f. violet and brown	80	4·00
75		90 on 75c. pink and red	2·75	2·75
76		1f.25 on 1f. blue & ultram	1·00	1·40
77		1f.50 on 1f. ultramarine & bl	3·00	2·75
78		3f. on 5f. brown and red	3·75	6·50
79		10f. on 5f. red and mauve	12·00	27·00
80		20f. on 5f. mauve and grey	30·00	42·00

1931. "International Colonial Exhibition" key-types inscr "OUBANGUI-CHARI".

103	E	40c. green	5·50	11·00
104	F	50c. mauve	4·50	3·50
105	G	90c. red	3·50	11·50
106	H	1f.50 blue	5·75	5·50

POSTAGE DUE STAMPS

1928. Postage Due type of France optd **OUBANGUI-CHARI A. E. F.**

D81	D 11	5c. blue	40	3·25
D82		10c. brown	55	3·25
D83		20c. olive	75	2·75
D84		25c. red	65	3·25
D85		30c. red	70	4·25
D86		45c. green	1·00	3·25
D87		50c. purple	80	5·00
D88		60c. brown on cream	90	4·75
D89		1f. red on cream	1·25	5·50
D90		2f. red	1·25	7·75
D91		3f. violet	1·25	7·75

D 12 Mobaye D 13 E. Gentil

1930.

D 92	D 12	5c. olive and blue	25	2·25
D 93		10c. brown and red	25	3·25
D 94		20c. brown and green	60	3·50
D 95		25c. brown and blue	2·00	3·50
D 96		30c. green and brown	2·00	5·00
D 97		45c. olive and green	2·75	7·00
D 98		50c. brown and mauve	4·75	13·50
D 99		60c. black and violet	6·00	14·50
D100	D 13	1f. black and brown	2·50	6·25
D101		2f. brown and mauve	2·00	10·00
D102		3f. brown and red	2·25	14·50

UGANDA Pt. 1

A Br. Protectorate in Central Africa until it attained independence within the British Commonwealth in 1962. From 1903 to 1962 used the stamps listed under "Kenya, Uganda and Tanganyika".

1895. 200 cowries = 1 rupee.
1896. 16 annas = 1 rupee.
1962. 100 cents = 1 shilling.

U G 20 — 2

V.96.R 25 Uganda — 3

1895. Typewritten in black.

17	2	5(c.) black	£1600	£950
18		10(c.) black	£1600	£1000
19		15(c.) black	£1000	£1000
20		20(c.) black	£1600	£650
21		25(c.) black	£950	£950
6		30(c.) black	£1400	£1400
7		40(c.) black	£2750	£1200
8		50(c.) black	£1200	£1000
9		60(c.) black	£1700	£1700

1895. Typewritten in violet.

35	2	5(c.) violet	£500	£500
36		10(c.) violet	£475	£475
37		15(c.) violet	£600	£425
38		20(c.) violet	£375	£275
39		25(c.) violet	£750	£750
40		30(c.) violet	£1000	£750
41		40(c.) violet	£900	£900
42		50(c.) violet	£850	£900
43		100(c.) violet	£2500	£2500

1896. Typewritten in violet.

44	3	5(c.) violet	£475	£500
45		10(c.) violet	£425	£400
46		15(c.) violet	£475	£500
47		20(c.) violet	£275	£200
48		25(c.) violet	£450	
49		30(c.) violet	£500	£650
50		40(c.) violet	£550	£650
51		50(c.) violet	£600	£650
52		60(c.) violet	£1500	
53		100(c.) violet	£1400	£1500

4

8

1896.

55	4	1a. black	19·00	24·00
56		2a. black	25·00	29·00
57		3a. black	27·00	32·00
58		4a. black	26·00	30·00
59		8a. black	29·00	32·00
60		1r. black	75·00	95·00
61		5r. black	£225	£350

1896. Optd with large **L.**

70	4	1a. black	£190	£160
71		2a. black	95·00	£110
72		3a. black	£250	£275
73		4a. black	£100	£150
74		8a. black	£190	£225
75		1r. black	£375	£425
76		5r. black	£14000	£14000

1898.

84a	8	1a. red	2·00	1·00
86		2a. brown	3·00	7·00
87a		3a. grey	12·00	13·00
88		4a. green	5·50	6·50
89		8a. green	7·50	24·00

Larger type with lions at either side of portrait.

90	–	1r. blue	40·00	42·00
91	–	5r. brown	70·00	£100

1902. Stamps of British East Africa optd **UGANDA.**

92	11	½a. green	2·00	1·40
93		2½a. blue	2·75	3·00

11 Ripon Falls and Speke Memorial

1962. Centenary of Speke's Discovery of Source of Nile.

95	11	30c. black and red	15	20
96		50c. black and violet	15	10
97		1s.30 black and green	30	20
98		2s.50 black and blue	1·60	1·90

12 Murchison Falls 14 Mulago Hospital

1962. Independence.

99	12	5c. green	10	10
100	–	10c. brown	10	10
101	–	15c. black, red and green	10	10
102	–	20c. plum and buff	10	10
103	–	30c. blue	10	10
104	–	50c. black and turquoise	10	10
105	14	1s. sepia, red and turquoise	15	10
106	–	1s.30 orange and violet	20	10
107	–	2s. black, red and blue	40	50
108	–	5s. red and deep green	4·00	1·00
109	–	10s. slate and brown	2·00	2·50
110	–	20s. brown and blue	2·50	15·00

DESIGNS—As Type **12**: 10c. Tobacco growing; 15c. Coffee growing; 20c. Ankole cattle; 30c. Cotton; 50c. Mountains of the Moon. As Type **14**: 1s.30, Cathedrals and mosque; 2s. Makerere College; 5s. Copper mining; 10s. Cement industry; 20s. Parliament Buildings.

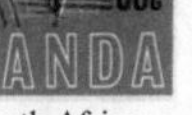

15 South African Crowned Crane

16 Black BeeEater

18 Ruwenzori Turaco

1965. International Trade Fair, Kampala.

111	15	30c. multicoloured	10	10
112		1s.30 multicoloured	20	10

1965. Birds.

113	16	5c. multicoloured	10	10
114	–	10c. brown, black and blue	10	10
115	–	15c. yellow and brown	20	10
116	–	20c. multicoloured	20	10
117	–	30c. black and brown	1·50	10
118	–	40c. multicoloured	1·00	1·75
119	–	50c. blue and violet	25	10
120	–	65c. red, black and grey	2·50	2·75
121	18	1s. multicoloured	50	10
122	–	1s.30 brown, black & yell	5·50	30
123	–	2s.50 multicoloured	4·25	65
124	–	5s. multicoloured	7·00	4·00
125	–	10s. multicoloured	11·00	11·00
126	–	20s. multicoloured	21·00	38·00

DESIGNS—HORIZ (as Type **16**): 10c. African jacana; 30c. Sacred ibis; 65c. Red-crowned bishop. (As Type **18**): 2s.50, Great blue turaco; 10s. Black-collared lovebird. 20s. South African crowned crane ("Crowned Crane"). VERT (as Type **16**): 15c. Orange weaver; 20c. Narina's trogon ("Narina Trogon"); 40c. Blue-breasted kingfisher; 50c. Whale-headed stork. (As Type **18**): 1s.30, African fish eagle; 5s. Lilac-breasted roller.

19 Carved Screen

1967. 13th Commonwealth Parliamentary Association Conference. Multicoloured.

127		30c. Type **19**	10	10
128		50c. Arms of Uganda	10	10
129		1s.30 Parliamentary Building	10	10
130		2s.50 Conference Chamber	15	1·75

20 "Cordia abyssinica"

21 "Acacia drepanolobium"

1969. Flowers.

131a	20	5c. brown, green & yellow	40	10
132	–	10c. multicoloured	10	10
133	–	15c. multicoloured	40	10
134	–	20c. violet, olive and green	15	10
135	–	30c. multicoloured	20	10
136	–	40c. violet, green and grey	20	10
137	–	50c. multicoloured	20	10
138	–	60c. multicoloured	45	2·00
139	–	70c. multicoloured	25	30
140	21	1s. multicoloured	20	10
141	–	1s.50 multicoloured	25	10
142a	–	2s.50 multicoloured	1·25	10
143a	–	5s. multicoloured	1·75	10
144a	–	10s. multicoloured	3·75	10
145	–	20s. multicoloured	1·00	5·00

DESIGNS—As Type **20**: 10c. "Grewia similis"; 15c. "Cassia didymobotrya"; 20c. "Coleus barbatus"; 30c. "Ochna ovata"; 40c. "Ipomoea spathulata"; 50c. "Spathodea nilotica"; 60c. "Oncoba spinosa"; 70c. "Carissa edulis". As Type **21**: 1s.50, "Clerodendrum myricoides"; 2s.50, "Acanthus arboreus"; 5s. "Kigelia aethiopium"; 10s. "Erythrina abyssinica"; 20s. "Monodora myristica".

1975. Nos. 140, 142a and 145 surch.

146		2s. on 1s. multicoloured	2·00	1·50
147		3s. on 2s.50 multicoloured	18·00	40·00
148		40s. on 20s. multicoloured	4·00	3·50

23 Millet

24 Maize

1975. Ugandan Crops.
149 23 10c. black, green and brown 10 10
150 – 20c. multicoloured 10 10
151 – 30c. multicoloured 10 10
152 – 40c. multicoloured 10 10
153 – 50c. multicoloured 10 10
154 – 70c. black, green & turq 10 15
155 – 80c. multicoloured 10 15
156 24 1s. multicoloured 10 10
157 – 2s. multicoloured 30 30
158 – 3s. multicoloured 50 45
159 – 5s. multicoloured 50 75
160 – 10s. multicoloured . . . . 50 1·25
161 – 20s. green, black and purple . . . . 70 2·50
162 – 40s. green, blue and orange 1·10 4·50
DESIGNS—As Type **23**: 20c. Sugar; 30c. Tobacco; 40c. Onions; 50c. Tomatoes; 70c. Tea; 80c. Bananas. As Type **24**: 2s. Pineapples; 3s. Coffee; 5s. Oranges; 10s. Groundnuts; 20s. Cotton; 40s. Runner beans.
Face value colours: 5s. green; 10s. brown; 20s. mauve; 40s. orange.
For these values with colours changed, see Nos. 220/3.

1976. Telecommunications Development. As Nos. 56/60 of Kenya.
163 50c. Microwave tower . . . 10 10
164 1s. Cordless switchboard . . 10 10
165 2s. Telephone 20 25
166 3s. Message Switching Centre 30 45
MS167 120 × 120 mm. Nos. 163/6 90 1·25

1976. Olympic Games, Montreal. As Nos. 61/5 of Kenya.
168 50c. Akii Bua, hurdler . . . 10 10
169 1s. Filbert Bayi, runner . . . 10 10
170 2s. Steve Muchoki, boxer . . 30 30
171 3s. East African flags 40 45
MS172 129 × 154 mm. Nos. 168/71 4·00 5·00

1976. Railway Transport. As Nos. 66/70 of Kenya.
173 50c. Diesel-hydraulic train, Tanzania–Zambia railway 15 10
174 1s. Nile Bridge, Uganda . . . 15 10
175 2s. Nakuru Station, Kenya 50 45
176 3s. Uganda Railway Class A locomotive, 1896 . . . . . 55 55
MS177 154 × 103 mm. Nos. 173/6 2·25 2·50

1977. Game Fish of East Africa. As Nos. 71/5 of Kenya. Multicoloured.
178 50c. Nile perch 15 10
179 1s. Nile mouthbrooder . . . 20 10
180 3s. Sailfish 60 40
181 5s. Black marlin 80 60
MS182 153 × 129 mm. Nos. 178/81 3·25 2·00

1977. Second World Black and African Festival of Arts and Culture. As Nos. 76/80 of Kenya. Multicoloured.
183 50c. Maasai manyatta (village), Kenya 10 10
184 1s. "Heartbeat of Africa" (Ugandan dancers) 10 10
185 2s. Makonde sculpture, Tanzania 25 55
186 3s. "Early man and technology" (skinning hippopotamus) 35 85
MS187 132 × 109 mm. Nos. 183/6 1·25 2·25

1977. 25th Anniv of Safari Rally. As Nos. 81/5 of Kenya. Multicoloured.
188 50c. Rally-car and villagers 10 10
189 1s. Starting-line 10 10
190 2s. Car fording river 25 35
191 5s. Car and elephants . . . . 80 1·00
MS192 126 × 93 mm. Nos. 188/91 1·50 2·50

1977. Centenary of Ugandan Church. As Nos. 86/90 of Kenya. Multicoloured.
193 50c. Canon Kivebulaya . . . 10 10
194 1s. Modern Namirembe Cathedral 10 10
195 2s. Old Namirembe Cathedral 20 40
196 5s. Early congregation, Kigezi 45 1·10
MS197 126 × 89 mm. Nos. 193/6 1·00 1·75

1977. Design as No. 155 surch **80c**.
198 80c. on 60c. multicoloured . . 30 20

1977. Endangered Species. As Nos. 96/101 of Kenya. Multicoloured.
199 50c. Pancake tortoise 30 10
200 1s. Nile crocodile 45 10
201 2s. Hunter's hartebeest . . . 1·25 40
202 3s. Red colobus monkey . . 1·50 75
203 5s. Dugong . . . . 1·50 1·00
MS204 127 × 101 mm. Nos. 200/3 4·50 4·00

1978. World Cup Football Championship, Argentina (1st issue). As Nos. 122/6 of Kenya. Multicoloured.
205 50c. Joe Kadenge and forwards 15 10
206 1s. Mohamed Chuma and cup presentation 15 10
207 2s. Omari Kidevu and goalmouth scene 30 45
208 5s. Polly Ouma and forwards 50 1·25
MS209 136 × 81 mm. Nos. 205/8 2·00 2·75

26 Shot Putting

1978. Commonwealth Games, Edmonton. Multicoloured.
210 50c. Type **26** 10 10
211 1s. Long jumping 15 10
212 2s. Running 20 40
213 5s. Boxing . . . . 40 1·10
MS214 114 × 85 mm. Nos. 210/13 1·25 3·00

1978. World Cup Football Championship, Argentina (2nd issue). As Nos. 205/8, but additionally inscr "WORLD CUP 1978".
215 50c. Polly Ouma and forwards 15 10
216 2s. Omari Kidevu and goalmouth scene 30 10
217 5s. Joe Kadenge and forwards . . . . 60 1·00
218 10s. Mohamed Chuma and cup presentation . . . . . 90 2·00
MS219 140 × 87 mm. Nos. 215/18 2·00 2·75

1978. As Nos. 159/62, but colours changed.
220 5s. mult (face value in blue) 50 70
221 10s. mult (face value in mauve) 50 85
222 20s. mult (face value in brown) 55 85
223 40s. mult (face value in red) 65 1·10

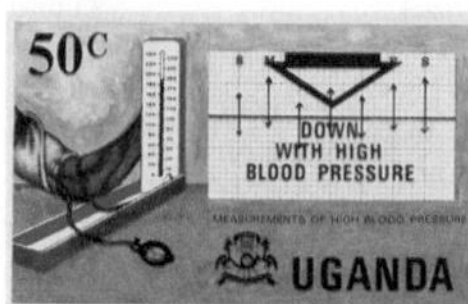

27 Measurements of High Blood Pressure

1978. "Down with High Blood Pressure". Multicoloured.
224 50c. Type **27** 15 10
225 1s. Hypertension and the heart 15 10
226 2s. Fundus of the eye in hypertension 40 45
227 5s. Kidney and high blood pressure . . . . 75 1·40
MS228 180 × 115 mm. Nos. 224/7 1·25 2·75

28 Off Loading Cattle

1978. 75th Anniv of Powered Flight. Multicoloured.
229 1s. Type **28** 15 10
230 1s.50 "Domestic services" (passengers boarding Britten Norman Islander) 25 15
231 2s.70 Export of Uganda coffee 25 35
232 10s. "Time machines in the air" (Wright Flyer III and Concorde) . . . . 75 1·50
MS233 166 × 110 mm. Nos. 299/32 1·75 2·75

29 Queen Elizabeth II leaving Owen Falls Dam

1979. 25th Anniv of Coronation (1978). Multicoloured.
234 1s. Type **29** 15 10
235 1s.50 Regalia 15 10
236 2s.70 Coronation ceremony 30 20
237 10s. Royal family on balcony of Buckingham Palace . . 50 1·25
MS238 150 × 102 mm. Nos. 234/7 1·40 1·25

30 Dr. Joseph Kiwanuka (first Ugandan bishop)

1979. Centenary of Catholic Church in Uganda. Multicoloured.
239 1s. Type **30** 10 10
240 1s.50 Lubaga Cathedral . . . 10 10
241 2s.70 Ugandan pilgrimage to Rome, Holy Year, 1975 . . 15 25
242 10s. Friar Lourdel-Mapeera (early missionary) 50 80
MS243 128 × 91 mm. Nos. 239/42 1·00 2·00

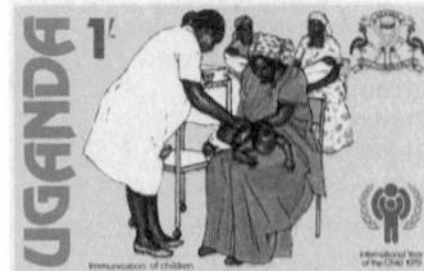

31 Immunization of Children

1979. International Year of the Child. Multicoloured.
244 1s. Type **31** 10 10
245 1s.50 Handicapped children at play 15 20
246 2s.70 Ugandan I.Y.C. emblem 15 35
247 10s. Children in class . . . . 40 1·10
MS248 136 × 113 mm. Nos. 244/7 1·10 2·00

1979. Liberation. Optd **UGANDA LIBERATED 1979**. (a) Nos. 149/62.
249 23 10c. black, green and brown 10 10
250 – 20c. multicoloured 10 10
251 – 30c. multicoloured 10 10
252 – 40c. multicoloured 10 10
253 – 50c. multicoloured 10 10
254 – 70c. black, green & turq 10 10
255 – 80c. multicoloured 10 10
256 24 1s. multicoloured 15 15
257 – 2s. multicoloured 20 25
258 – 3s. multicoloured 35 40
259 – 5s. multicoloured 55 60
260 – 10s. multicoloured . . . . 80 1·25
261 – 20s. green, black and purple . . . . 1·00 2·40
262 – 40s. green, black and orange . . . . 1·50 4·75

(b) Nos. 210/13.
263 50c. Type **26** 10 10
264 1s. Long jumping 15 20
265 2s. Running 25 30
266 5s. Boxing 60 65

(c) Nos. 207, 215, 217/18.
267 50c. Polly Ouma and forwards 10 10
268 2s. Omari Kidevu and goalmouth scene 20 30
269 5s. Joe Kadenge and forwards 55 65
270 10s. Mohamed Chuma and cup presentation . . . . . 1·00 1·40

(d) Nos. 220/3.
271 5s. multicoloured 55 60
272 10s. multicoloured . . . . . 60 1·25
273 20s. multicoloured . . . . . 60 2·40
274 40s. multicoloured . . . . . 75 4·75

(e) Nos. 229/32.
275 1s. Type **28** 35 20
276 1s.50 "Domestic services" . . 45 25
277 2s.70 Export of Uganda coffee 55 55
278 10s. "Time machines in the air" . . . . 2·00 2·50

(f) Nos. 234/7.
279 1s. Type **29** 10 20
280 1s.50 Regalia 15 20
281 2s.70 Coronation ceremony 20 40
282 10s. Royal family on balcony of Buckingham Palace . . 85 1·75
MS283 150 × 102 mm. Nos. 234/6 and 15s. as No. 237 . . . . 1·50 3·25

(g) Nos. 239/42.
284 1s. Type **30** 10 20
285 1s.50 Lubaga Cathedral . . . 15 25
286 2s.70 Ugandan pilgrimage to Rome, Holy Year, 1975 . . 30 50
287 10s. Friar Lourdel-Mapeera (early missionary) . . . . 90 1·75
MS288 128 × 91 mm. Nos. 239/42 1·75 2·75

(h) Nos. 244/8.
289 1s. Type **31** 20 20
290 1s.50 Handicapped children at play 25 25
291 2s.70 Ugandan I.Y.C. emblem 50 60
292 10s. Children in class . . . . 1·40 1·75
MS293 136 × 113 mm. Nos. 289/92 2·25 3·50

35 Radio Wave Symbol

1979. 50th Anniv of International Consultative Radio Committee and International Telecom-munications Union.
294 35 1s. multicoloured 10 10
295 1s.50 multicoloured 15 10
296 2s.70 multicoloured 15 35
297 10s. multicoloured . . . . 40 1·10

36 20s. Definitive Stamp of 1965 and Sir Rowland Hill

1979. Death Cent of Sir Rowland Hill. Mult.
298 1s. Type **36** 10 10
299 1s.50 1967 13th Commonwealth Parliamentary Association Conference 50c. commemorative 15 10
300 2s.70 1962 Independence 20s. commemorative 15 30
301 10s. Uganda Protectorate 1898 1a. . . . . 40 1·25
MS302 154 × 98 mm. Nos. 298/301 65 1·50

37 Impala

38 Lions with Cub

1979. Wildlife.
303A 10c. Type **37** 10 20
304A 20c. Large-spotted genet . . 10 20
305A 30c. Thomson's gazelle . . 10 20
306A 50c. Lesser bushbaby . . . 10 10
307A 80c. Hunting dog 10 10
308A 1s. Type **38** 10 10
309A 1s.50 Gorilla 40 10
310B 2s. Common zebra 35 20
311A 2s.70 Leopard with cub . . 35 20
312A 3s.50 Black rhinoceros . . . 50 55
313A 5s. Waterbuck 25 55
314A 10s. African buffalo . . . . 30 1·00
315A 20s. Hippopotamus . . . . 65 2·00
316A 40s. African elephant . . . 1·00 3·50
SIZES—As Type **37**: 10c. to 80c. As Type **38**: 1s. to 40s.
See also Nos. 433/9.

1980. "London 1980" International Stamp Exhibition. Nos. 298/301 optd **LONDON 1980**.
317 36 1s. multicoloured 15 10
318 – 1s.50 multicoloured 20 10
319 – 2s.70 multicoloured 35 25
320 – 10s. multicoloured 80 80
MS321 154 × 99 mm. Nos. 317/20 1·40 1·75

40 Rotary Emblem

1980. 75th Anniv of Rotary International. Multicoloured.
322 1s. Type **40** 10 10
323 20s. Paul P. Harris (founder) with wheel-barrow containing "Rotary projects" (horiz) . . . . . 1·25 2·00
MS324 100 × 76 mm. Nos. 322/3. Imperf . . . . 1·75 2·50

41 Football

1980. Olympic Games, Moscow. Multicoloured.
325 1s. Type **41** 10 10
326 2s. Relay 10 10
327 10s. Hurdles 45 75
328 20s. Boxing . . . . 75 2·00
MS329 118 × 90 mm. 2s.70, 3s., 5s., 25s. As Nos. 325/8 . . . . . . 1·25 2·25

1981. Olympic Medal Winners. Nos. 325/8 optd.
330 41 1s. multicoloured 10 10
331 – 2s. multicoloured 15 15
332 – 10s. multicoloured 55 80
333 – 20s. multicoloured . . . . 85 2·25
MS334 118 × 90 mm. 2s.70, 3s. 5s., 25s. As Nos. 330/3 . . . . . . 1·00 2·50

OVERPRINTS: 1s. **FOOTBALL GOLD MEDALISTS, C.S.S.R.**; 2s. **RELAY GOLD MEDALIST U.S.S.R.**; 10s. **HURDLES 110m. GOLD MEDALIST THOMAS MUNKLET, D.D.R.**; 20s. **BOXING WELTERWEIGHT SILVER MEDALIST JOHN MUGABI, UGANDA.**

43 "Christ in the Storm on the Sea of Galilee" (painting, Rembrandt) (½-size illustration)

1980. Christmas. Sheet 79 × 101 mm. Imperf.
MS335 **43** 25s. multicoloured . . 4·25 4·75

44 Heinrich von Stephan and U.P.U. Emblem

1981. 150th Birth Anniv of Heinrich von Stephan (founder of U.P.U.). Multicoloured.
336 1s. Type **44** 10 10
337 2s. U.P.U. Headquarters 15 15
338 2s.70 Air mail, 1935 40 20
339 10s. Mail transport by train, 1927 1·10 80
MS340 112 × 95 mm. Nos. 336/9 2·25 1·90

45 Tower of London

1981. Royal Wedding. Multicoloured. (a) Previously unissued stamps surch.
341e 10s. on 1s. Prince Charles and Lady Diana Spencer 15 20
342e 50s. on 5s. Type **45** 20 30
343e 200s. on 20s. Prince Charles at Balmoral 45 80
MS344 95 × 80 mm. 250s. on 25s. Royal Mews 3·00 5·50

(b) Stamps reissued with new face values.
345 10s. As No. 341 10 15
346 50s. Type **45** 15 20
347 200s. As No. 343 30 40
MS348 95 × 80 mm. 250s. As No. MS344 50 65

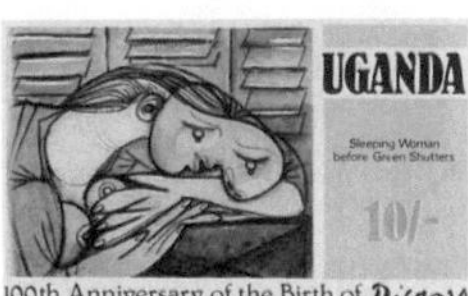

48 "Sleeping Woman before Green Shutters"

1981. Birth Centenary of Picasso. Mult.
349 10s. Type **48** 10 10
350 20s. "Bullfight" 20 20
351 30s. "Detail of a Nude asleep in a Landscape" 25 30
352 200s. "Interior with a Girl Drawing" 1·10 3·25
MS353 120 × 146 mm. 250s. "Minotaure" (112 × 139 mm). Imperf 2·25 4·00

49 Deaf People using Sign Language

1981. Int Year of Disabled Persons. Mult.
354 1s. Type **49** 10 10
355 10s. Disabled teacher in classroom 15 10
356 50s. Teacher and disabled children 70 50
357 200s. Blind person with guide dog 1·40 2·00
MS358 122 × 93 mm. Nos. 354/7 3·00 4·00

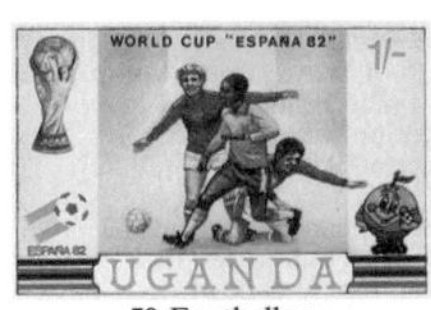

50 Footballers

1981. World Cup Football Championship, Spain (1982).
359 **50** 1s. multicoloured 10 10
360 – 10s. multicoloured 15 10
361 – 50s. multicoloured 70 50
362 – 200s. multicoloured 2·00 2·00
MS363 116 × 77 mm. 250s. multicoloured 3·00 3·00
DESIGNS: Nos. 360/63, various football scenes.

51 Mpoma Satellite Earth Station

1982. "Peaceful Use of Outer Space". Multicoloured.
364 5s. Type **51** 25 15
365 10s. "Pioneer II" (satellite) 35 35
366 50s. Space Shuttle 1·00 2·00
367 100s. "Voyager 2" (satellite) 1·50 4·00
MS368 118 × 89 mm. 150s. Space Shuttle (different) 3·75 2·00

52 Dr. Robert Koch **54** Yellow-billed Hornbill ("Hornbill")

1982. Centenary of Robert Koch's Discovery of Tubercle Bacillus. Multicoloured.
369 1s. Type **52** 30 10
370 10s. Microscope 90 40
371 50s. Ugandans receiving vaccinations 2·25 2·50
372 100s. Tubercle virus 3·50 4·25
MS373 85 × 64 mm. 150s. Medical College classroom scence (horiz) 4·50 2·00

1982. 21st Birthday of Princess of Wales. Nos. 345/7 optd **21st BIRTHDAY HRH Princess of Wales JULY 1 1982.**
374 10s. Prince Charles and Lady Diana Spencer 20 10
375 50s. Type **45** 50 40
376 200s. Prince Charles at Balmoral 1·00 1·00
MS377 95 × 82 mm. 250s. Royal Mews 2·00 2·00

1982. Birds. Multicoloured.
378 1s. Type **54** 15 10
379 20s. Superb starling 60 35
380 50s. Bateleur ("Bateleur Eagle") 1·25 1·75
381 100s. Saddle-bill stork 2·00 2·50
MS382 115 × 85 mm. 200s. Laughing dove 7·00 9·00

55 Scout Band

1982. 75th Anniv of Boy Scout Movement. Multicoloured.
383 5s. Type **55** 40 10
384 20s. Scout receiving Bata Shoe trophy 1·10 45
385 50s. Scouts with wheelchair patient 1·75 2·25
386 100s. First aid instruction 2·25 3·50
MS387 112 × 85 mm. 150s. Lord Baden-Powell 2·50 3·00

56 Swearing-in of Roosevelt

1982. 250th Birth Anniv of George Washington and Birth Centenary of Franklin D. Roosevelt. Multicoloured.
388 50s. Type **56** 30 30
389 200s. Swearing-in of Washington 75 1·25
MS390 100 × 69 mm. 150s. Washington at Mt Vernon 1·00 1·25
MS391 100 × 70 mm. 150s. Roosevelt at Hyde Park Mansion 1·00 1·25

57 Italy v. West Germany

1982. World Cup Football Championship Winners. Multicoloured.
392 10s. Type **57** 30 25
393 200s. Victorious Italian team 1·50 3·50
MS394 97 × 117 mm. 250s. Espana '82 emblem with Spanish and Italian flags 1·50 2·00

58 Dancers

1983. Commonwealth Day. Cultural Art. Multicoloured.
395 5s. Type **58** 10 10
396 20s. Traditional currency 15 20
397 50s. Homestead 35 55
398 100s. Drums 70 1·10

59 "St. George and the Dragon" (Raphael)

1983. 500th Birth Anniv of Raphael (painter). Multicoloured.
399 5s. Type **59** 10 10
400 20s. "St. George and the Dragon" (different) 25 20
401 50s. "Crossing the Red Sea" (detail) 50 60
402 200s. "The Expulsion of Heliodorus" (detail) 90 3·00
MS403 126 × 101 mm. 250s. "The Meeting of Pope Leo the Great and Attila the Hun" (detail) 1·40 1·40

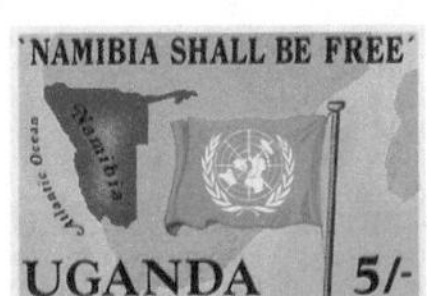

60 Map showing Namibia and U.N. Flag

1983. Commemorations. Multicoloured.
404 5s. Type **60** 10 10
405 200s. 7th Non-aligned Summit Conference logo 60 2·50

61 Elephants in Grassland

1983. Endangered Species (1st series). Mult.
406 5s. Elephants in "Elephants' Graveyard" 1·50 50
407 10s. Type **61** 1·75 50
408 30s. Elephants at waterhole 3·75 2·50
409 70s. Elephants having dust bath 6·00 7·00
MS410 87 × 64 mm. 300s. Grevy's zebra drinking (vert) 6·50 3·25
See also No. 642 for the 10s. redrawn and Nos. 988/91 for these designs with different face values.

1983. Centenary of Boys' Brigade. Nos. 383/6 optd **BOYS BRIGADE CENTENARY 1883-1983** or surch also.
411 5s. Type **55** 10 10
412 20s. Scout receiving Bata Shoe trophy 15 15
413 50s. Scouts with wheelchair patient 20 30
414 400s. on 100s. First aid instruction 1·50 3·00
MS415 112 × 85 mm. 150s. Lord Baden-Powell 70 1·25

63 Mpoma Satellite Earth Station

1983. World Communications Year. Mult.
416 20s. Type **63** 25 15
417 50s. Railroad computer and operator 55 85
418 70s. Cameraman filming lions 60 1·50
419 100s. Aircraft cockpit 70 2·00
MS420 128 × 103 mm. 300s. Communications satellite 1·00 1·75

1983. Nos. 303, 305/9 and 313 surch.
421 100s. on 10c. Type **37** 85 60
422 135s. on 1s. Type **38** 1·00 80
423 175s. on 30c. Thomson's gazelle 1·25 1·25
424 200s. on 50c. Lesser bushbaby 1·25 1·40
425 400s. on 80c. Hunting dog 2·25 3·00
426 700s. on 5s. Waterbuck 3·50 6·00
427 1000s. on 1s.50 Gorilla 6·50 10·00

65 The Nativity

1983. Christmas. Multicoloured.
428 10s. Type **65** 10 10
429 50s. Shepherds and Angels 20 30
430 175s. Flight into Egypt 60 1·25
431 400s. Angels blowing trumpets 1·00 2·75
MS432 85 × 57 mm. 300s. The Three Kings 1·40 1·75

1983. As Nos. 308/12 and 315/16, but with face values in revalued currency.
433 100s. Type **38** 90 35
434 135s. Gorilla 1·25 50
435 175s. Common zebra 1·40 80
436 200s. Leopard with cub 1·75 90
437 400s. Black rhinoceros 3·00 3·25
438 700s. African elephant 5·00 6·50
439 1000s. Hippopotamus 8·00 8·50

66 Ploughing with Oxen

1984. World Food Day. Multicoloured.
440 10s. Type **66** 15 10
441 300s. Harvesting bananas 2·75 5·50

67 Ruth Kyalisiima, Sportsman of the Year 1983

1984. Olympic Games, Los Angeles. Mult.
442 5s. Type **67** 10 10
443 115s. Javelin-throwing 65 1·00
444 155s. Wrestling 70 1·40
445 175s. Rowing 70 1·60
MS446 108 × 79 mm. 500s. Fund-raising walk (vert) 1·00 1·25

68 Entebbe Airport

1984. 40th Anniv of I.C.A.O. Mult.
447 5s. Type **68** 15 10
448 115s. Loading cargo plane 1·50 1·75
449 155s. Uganda police helicopter 2·50 2·75
450 175s. East African Civil Flying School, Soroti 2·75 3·25
MS451 100 × 70 mm. 250s. Balloon race 2·00 1·75

69 "Charaxes druceanus"

1984. Butterflies. Multicoloured.
452 5s. Type **69** 30 10
453 115s. "Papilio lormieri" 2·50 2·00
454 155s. "Druryia antimachus" 3·00 2·50
455 175s. "Salamis temora" 4·25 3·25
MS456 127 × 90 mm. 250s. "Colotis protomedia" 4·50 2·50

70 Blue-finned notho

1985. Lake Fishes. Multicoloured.
457 5s. Type **70** 30 40
458 10s. Semutundu 40 40
459 50s. Grey bichir 75 30
460 100s. Walking catfish 85 30
461 135s. Elephant-snout fish 1·25 1·00
462 175s. Lake Victoria squeaker 1·25 1·60
463 205s. Brown's haplochromis 1·25 2·00
464 400s. Nile perch 1·25 2·25
465 700s. African lungfish 1·25 2·75
466 1000s. Radcliffe's barb 1·25 3·00
467 2500s. Electric catfish 1·50 3·75

71 The Last Supper

1985. Easter. Multicoloured.
468 5s. Type **71** 10 10
469 115s. Christ showing the nail marks to Thomas 1·40 1·40
470 155s. The raising of the Cross 1·60 2·25
471 175s. Pentecost 1·90 2·75
MS472 99 × 70 mm. 250s. The last prayer in the Garden 80 1·25

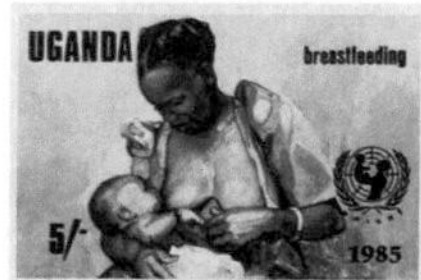

72 Breast Feeding

1985. UNICEF Child Survival Campaign. Multicoloured.
473 5s. Type **72** 10 10
474 115s. Growth monitoring 1·75 1·75
475 155s. Immunization 2·25 2·50
476 175s. Oral re-hydration therapy 2·50 3·00
MS477 77 × 55 mm. 500s. Pregnant woman preparing nourishing food 4·25 5·00

73 Queen Elizabeth the Queen Mother

74 Sedge Warbler

1985. Life and Times of Queen Elizabeth the Queen Mother and Decade for Women. Multicoloured.
478 **73** 1000s. Type **73** 1·40 2·10
MS479 57 × 81 mm. 1500s. The Queen Mother inspecting Kings African Rifles, Kampala 2·25 3·50

1985. Birth Bicentenary of John J. Audubon (ornithologist) (1st issue). Multicoloured.
480 115s. Type **74** 2·00 1·50
481 155s. Cattle egret 2·25 1·75
482 175s. Crested lark 2·50 2·25
483 500s. Tufted duck 3·25 4·50
MS484 99 × 69 mm. 1000s. Twany owl 11·00 11·00
See also Nos. 494/8.

1985. Olympic Gold Medal Winners, Los Angeles. Nos. 442/5 optd or surch also.
485 5s. Type **67** (optd **GOLD MEDALIST BENITA BROWN-FITZGERALD USA**) 10 10
486 115s. Javelin-throwing (optd **GOLD MEDALIST ARTO HAERKOENEN FINLAND**) 60 30
487 155s. Wrestling (optd **GOLD MEDALIST ATSUJI MIYAHARA JAPAN**) 70 40
488 1000s. on 175s. Rowing (surch **GOLD MEDALIST WEST GERMANY**) 2·75 2·00
MS489 108 × 79 mm. 1200s. on 500s. Fund rasing walk (surch **MEN'S HURDLES EDWIN MOSES USA**) 2·25 2·50
On No. **MS**489 only the new value appears on the stamp the remainder of the surcharge is on the sheet margin.

76 Women carrying National Women's Day Banner

77 Man beneath Tree laden with Produce (F.A.O.)

76a Rock Ptarmigan

1985. Decade for Women. Multicoloured.
490 5s. Type **76** 10 10
491 115s. Girl Guides (horiz) 1·75 2·00
492 155s. Mother Teresa (Nobel Peace Prize winner, 1979) 3·00 3·25
MS493 85 × 59 mm. 1500s. As 115s. 4·00 4·00
No. 491 and **MS**493 also commemorates the 75th anniversary of Girl Guide movement.

1985. Birth Bicentenary of John J. Audubon (ornithologist) (2nd issue). Multicoloured.
494 5s. Type **76a** 55 10
495 155s. Sage grouse 2·00 1·75
496 175s. Lesser yellowlegs 2·00 2·25
497 500s. Brown-headed cowbird 3·25 4·50
MS498 72 × 102 mm. 1000s. Whooping crane 9·50 9·50

1986. 40th Anniv of U.N.O.
499 **77** 10s. multicoloured 10 10
500 – 180s. multicoloured 40 30
501 – 200s. blue, brown and green 40 35
502 – 250s. blue, black and red 40 40
503 – 2000s. multicoloured 1·25 5·00
MS504 69 × 69 mm. 2500s. multicoloured 1·75 2·75
DESIGNS—HORIZ: 180s. Soldier of U.N. Peace-keeping Force; 250s. Hands releasing peace dove. VERT: 200s. U.N. emblem; 2000s. Flags of U.N. and Uganda; 2500s. U.N. Building, New York, and Flags of member nations.

78 Goalkeeper catching Ball

1986. World Cup Football Championship, Mexico. Multicoloured.
505 10s. Type **78** 10 10
506 180s. Player with ball 85 55
507 250s. Two players competing for ball 1·00 65
508 2500s. Player running with ball 5·50 6·00
MS509 87 × 66 mm. 3000s. Player kicking ball (vert) 4·75 3·50

1986. Liberation by National Resistance Army. Nos. 462, 464/7 and **MS**493 optd **NRA LIBERATION 1986**.
510 175s. Lake Victoria squeaker 70 70
511 400s. Nile perch 1·25 1·25
512 700s. African lungfish 1·75 2·50
513 1000s. Radcliffe's barb 2·00 3·00
514 2500s. Electric catfish 3·00 6·00
MS514a 85 × 59 mm. 1500s. Girl Guides 5·00 2·50

1986. Appearance of Halley's Comet (1st issue). As T **191b** of Sierre Leone. Multicoloured.
515 50s. Tycho Brahe and Arecibo Radio Telescope, Puerto Rico 20 10
516 100s. Recovery of astronaut John Glenn from sea, 1962 35 15
517 140s. "The Star in the East" (painting by Giotto) 50 30
518 2500s. Death of Davy Crockett at the Alamo, 1835 3·75 6·00
MS519 102 × 70 mm. 3000s. Halley's Comet over Uganda 6·50 6·00
See also Nos. 544/8.

80 Niagara Falls

81 "Gloria" (Colombia)

1986. "Ameripex '86" International Stamp Exn, Chicago. American Landmarks. Mult.
520 50s. Type **80** 15 10
521 100s. Jefferson Memorial, Washington D.C. 25 15
522 250s. Liberty Bell, Philadelphia 50 35
523 1000s. The Alamo, San Antonio, Texas 1·25 2·25
524 2500s. George Washington Bridge, New York–New Jersey 1·75 5·00
MS525 87 × 64 mm. 3000s. Grand Canyon 2·00 3·25

1986. 60th Birthday of Queen Elizabeth II. As T **191c** of Sierre Leone.
526 100s. black and yellow 60 15
527 140s. multicoloured 60 20
528 2500s. multicoloured 3·25 4·25
MS529 120 × 85 mm. 3000s. black and brown 4·00 4·00
DESIGNS: 100s. Princess Elizabeth at London Zoo; 140s. Queen Elizabeth at race meeting, 1970; 2500s. With Prince Philip at Sandringham, 1982; 3000s. Engagement photograph, 1947.

1986. Centenary of Statue of Liberty. Cadet Sailing Ships. Multicoloured.
530 50s. Type **81** 60 20
531 100s. "Mircea" (Rumania) 95 30
532 140s. "Sagres II" (Portugal) (horiz) 1·60 1·00
533 2500s. "Gazela Primiero" (U.S.A.) (horiz) 7·00 11·00
MS534 113 × 82 mm. 3000s. Statue of Liberty 3·25 3·50
No. 533 is inscribed "Primero" in error.

1986. Royal Wedding. As T **192c** of Sierre Leone. Multicoloured.
535 50s. Prince Andrew and Miss Sarah Ferguson (horiz) 10 10
536 140s. Prince Andrew with Princess Anne at shooting match (horiz) 20 20
537 2500s. Prince Andrew and Miss Sarah Ferguson at Ascot (horiz) 2·75 4·00
MS538 88 × 88 mm. 3000s. Prince Andrew and Miss Sarah Ferguson (different) 3·00 3·25

1986. World Cup Football Championship Winners, Mexico. Nos. 505/8 optd **WINNERS Argentina 3 W.Germany 2** or surch also.
539 50s. on 10s. Type **78** 10 10
540 180s. Player with ball 25 25
541 250s. Two players competing for ball 35 35
542 2500s. Player running with ball 2·75 4·50
MS543 87 × 66 mm. 3000s. Player kicking ball (vert) 4·75 3·25

1986. Appearance of Halley's Comet (2nd issue). Nos. 515/18 optd as T **198a** of Sierre Leone.
544 50s. Tycho Brahe and Arecibo Radio Telescope, Puerto Rico 20 15
545 100s. Recovery of astronaut John Glenn from sea, 1962 35 20
546 140s. "The Star in the East" (painting by Giotto) 55 40
547 2500s. Death of Davy Crockett at the Alamo, 1835 5·50 7·50
MS548 102 × 70 mm. 3000s. Halley's Comet over Uganda 5·50 5·00

83 St. Kizito

1986. Christian Martyrs of Uganda. Mult.
549 50s. Type **83** 15 10
550 150s. St. Kizito instructing converts 30 25
551 200s. Martyrdom of Bishop James Hannington, 1885 40 30
552 1000s. Burning of Bugandan Christians, 1886 1·60 3·25
MS553 89 × 59 mm. 1500s. King Mwanga of Buganda passing sentence on Christians 1·50 2·25

84 "Madonna of the Cherries" (Titian)

1986. Christmas. Religious Paintings. Mult.
554 50s. Type **84** 25 15
555 150s. "Madonna and Child" (Durer) (vert) 60 30
556 200s. "Assumption of the Virgin" (Titian) (vert) 70 40
557 2500s. "Praying Hands" (Durer) (vert) 5·50 8·50
MS558 Two sheets, each 102 × 76 mm. (a) 3000s. "Presentation of the Virgin in the Temple" (Titian). (b) 3000s. "Adoration of the Magi" (Durer) Set of 2 sheets 8·00 9·00

85 Red-billed Fire Finch and Glory Lily

1987. Flora and Fauna. Multicoloured.
559 2s. Type **85** 55 55
560 5s. African pygmy kingfisher and nandi flame 70 70
561 10s. Scarlet-chested sunbird and crown of thorns 85 70
562 25s. White rhinoceros and yellow-billed oxpecker 1·50 1·00
563 35s. Lion and elephant grass 1·00 1·10
564 45s. Cheetahs and doum palm 1·25 1·50
565 50s. Red-cheeked cordon-bleu and desert rose 2·00 2·00
566 100s. Giant eland and acacia 2·25 3·50
MS567 Two sheets, each 98 × 67 mm. (a) 150s. Carmine bee eaters and sausage tree. (b) 150s. Cattle egret and zebras Set of 2 sheets 7·00 8·00

86 Tremml's "Eagle" (longest man-powered flight), 1987

1987. Milestones of Transportation. Mult.
568 2s. Type **86** 20 50
569 3s. Junkers W.33 "Bremen" (first east-west transatlantic flight), 1928 20 50
570 5s. Lockheed Vega 5 "Winnie Mae" (Post's first solo round-the-world flight), 1933 30 60
571 10s. "Voyager" (first non-stop round-the-world flight), 1986 40 60
572 15s. Chanute biplane glider, 1896 70 80
573 25s. Airship N.1 "Norge" and polar bear (first transpolar flight), 1926 1·00 1·00
574 35s. Curtiss Golden Flyer biplane and U.S.S. "Pennsylvania" (battleship) (first take-off and landing from ship), 1911 1·40 1·25
575 45s. Shepard and "Freedom 7" spacecraft (first American in space), 1961 1·60 1·50
576 100s. Concorde (first supersonic passenger flight), 1976 5·50 5·50

87 Olympic Torch-bearer

1987. Olympic Games, Seoul (1988) (1st issue). Multicoloured.
577 5s. Type **87** 10 10
578 10s. Swimming 20 25
579 50s. Cycling . . . . 1·00 1·25
580 100s. Gymnastics . . . . . . 2·00 2·50
MS581 100 × 775 mm. 150s. Boxing 3·00 4·00
See also Nos. 628/32.

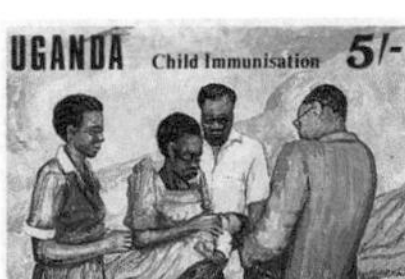

88 Child Immunization

1987. 25th Anniv of Independence.
582 **88** 5s. multicoloured 15 10
583 – 10s. multicoloured 30 25
584 – 25s. multicoloured 70 70
585 – 50s. multicoloured . . . . 1·25 1·50
MS586 90 × 70 mm. 100s. black, red and yellow . . . . 2·00 2·75
DESIGNS: 10s. Mulago Hospital, Kampala; 25s. Independence Mounument, Kampala City Park; 50s. High Court, Kampala; 100s. Stylized head of crested crane, "25" and Ugandan flag.

89 Eastern Golden-backed Weaver ("Golden-backed Weaver")

90 Hippocrates (physician) and Surgeons performing Operation

1987. Birds of Uganda. Multicoloured.
587 5s. Type **89** . . . . 1·00 80
588 10s. Hoopoe . . . . 2·00 1·25
589 15s. Red-throated bee eater . . 2·25 1·25
590 25s. Lilac-breasted roller . . 2·75 1·60
591 35s. African pygmy goose ("Pygmy Goose") . . . . 2·75 1·75
592 45s. Scarlet-chested sunbird 3·00 2·75
593 50s. South African crowned crane ("Crowned Crane") 3·00 2·75
594 100s. Long-tailed fiscal ("Long-tailed Fiscal Shrike") . . . . 4·75 5·50
MS595 Two sheets, each 80 × 60 mm. (a) 150s. African fish eagle. (B) 150s. Barn owl Set of 2 sheets . . . . 7·00 8·50

1987. Great Scientific Discoveries. Mult.
596 5s. Type **90** 60 30
597 25s. Einstein and deep space (Theory of Relativity) . . . 2·50 1·75
598 35s. Isaac Newton and diagram from "Opticks" (Theory of Colour and Light) . . . . 2·75 2·50
599 45s. Karl Benz and early Benz and modern Mercedes car . . . . 3·25 3·00
MS600 97 × 70 mm. 150s. "Challenger" (space shuttle) (vert) 3·75 4·00

91 Scout with Stamp Album and Uganda Stamps

1987. World Scout Jamboree, Australia. Multicoloured.
601 5s. Type **91** 20 10
602 25s. Scouts planting tree . . 70 70
603 35s. Canoeing, Lake Victoria 1·25 85
604 45s. Hiking . . . . 1·75 1·10
MS605 95 × 65 mm. 150s. Jamboree and Uganda scout emblems . . 3·00 4·00

92 "The Annunciation"

1987. Christmas. Scenes from French diptych, c. 1250. Multicoloured.
606 5s. Type **92** 10 10
607 10s. "The Nativity" 20 25
608 50s. "Flight into Egypt" . . 1·00 1·25
609 100s. "The Adoration of the Magi" . . . . 2·00 2·50

93 Class 12 Light Shunter Locomotive

94 Columbite-Tantalite

1988. Locomotives of East Africa Railways. Multicoloured.
611 5s. Type **93** 60 35
612 10s. Class 92 diesel-electric 70 45
613 15s. Steam locomotive No. 2506 . . . . 90 60
614 25s. Class 11 tank locomotive 1·25 85
615 35s. Class 24 steam locomotive . . . . 1·50 1·10
616 45s. Class 21 steam locomotive . . . . 1·75 1·40
617 50s. Class 59 Garratt steam locomotive, 1955 . . . . . 2·00 1·60
618 100s. Class 87 diesel-electric locomotive . . . . 3·00 2·40
MS619 Two sheets, each 100 × 74 mm. (a) 150s. Class 31 steam locomotive. (b) 150s. Class 59 Garratt steam locomotive Set of 2 sheets . . . . 8·00 7·50

1988. Minerals. Multicoloured.
620 1s. Type **94** 15 15
621 2s. Galena 20 20
622 5s. Malachite 35 35
623 10s. Cassiterite 55 55
624 35s. Ferberite . . . . 1·50 1·50
625 50s. Emerald . . . . 2·00 2·00
626 100s. Monazite . . . . . . 3·00 3·00
627 150s. Microcline . . . . . . 4·00 4·00

95 Hurdling

1988. Olympic Games, Seoul (2nd issue). Mult.
628 5s. Type **95** 10 10
629 25s. High jumping 40 50
630 35s. Javelin throwing 45 55
631 45s. Long jumping 55 70
MS632 85 × 114 mm. 150s. Olympic medals . . . . 1·00 1·50

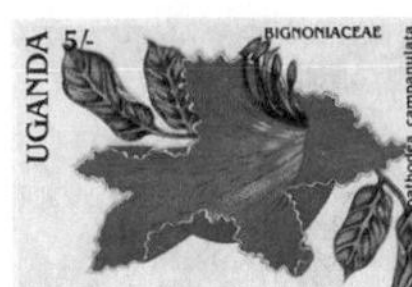

96 "Spathodea campanulata"

1988. Flowers. Multicoloured.
633 5s. Type **96** 15 15
634 10s. "Gloriosa simplex" . . . 15 15
635 20s. "Thevetica peruviana" (vert) 20 20
636 25s. "Hibiscus schizopetalus" 20 25
637 35s. "Aframomum sceptrum" 20 30
638 45s. "Adenium obesum" . . 20 35
639 50s. "Kigelia africana" (vert) 25 40
640 100s. "Clappertonia ficifolia" 35 75
MS641 Two sheets, each 109 × 79 mm. (a) 150s. "Costus spectabilis". (b) 150s. "Canarina abyssinica" (vert) Set of 2 sheets 2·00 2·75

97 Elephants in Grassland (Type **61** redrawn)

1988. Endangered Species (2nd series).
642 **97** 10s. multicoloured . . . . 70·00 4·00

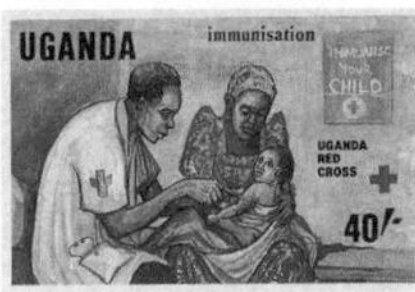

98 Red Cross Worker vaccinating Baby

1988. 125th Anniv of International Red Cross.
643 **98** 10s. red, yellow and black 25 15
644 – 40s. multicoloured 70 70
645 – 70s. multicoloured . . . . 1·50 2·00
646 – 90s. multicoloured . . . . 2·00 2·25
MS647 110 × 78 mm. 150s. multicoloured . . . . 1·00 1·60
DESIGNS—HORIZ: 10s. "AIDS" with test tube as "I"; 70s. Distributing food to refugees; 90s. Red Cross volunteers with accident victim. VERT: Henri Dunant (founder).

1988. 500th Birth Anniv of Titian (artist). As T **183a** of St. Vincent. Multicoloured.
648 10s. "Portrait of a Lady" . . 15 15
649 20s. "Portrait of a Man" . . 20 20
650 40s. "Isabella d'Este" 35 35
651 50s. "Vincenzo Mosti" . . . 45 45
652 70s. "Pope Paul III Farnese" 50 60
653 90s. "Violante" 60 75
654 100s. "Titian's Daughter Lavinia" 70 85
655 250s. "Dr. Parma" . . . . . 1·40 1·90
MS656 Two sheets, each 110 × 95 mm. (a) 350s. "The Speech of Alfonso D'Avalos" (detail). (b) 350s. "Cain and Abel" (detail) Set of 2 sheets . . . . 6·50 7·50

99 Giraffes, Kidepo Valley National Park

1988. National Parks of Uganda. Mult.
657 10s. Type **99** . . . . 1·50 30
658 25s. Zebras, Lake Mburo National Park . . . . . . 1·75 30
659 100s. African buffalo, Murchison Falls National Park . . . . 2·25 2·50
660 250s. Eastern white pelicans, Queen Elizabeth National Park . . . . 7·00 7·00
MS661 97 × 68 mm. 350s. Roan antelopes, Lake Mburo National Park . . . . 2·50 2·75

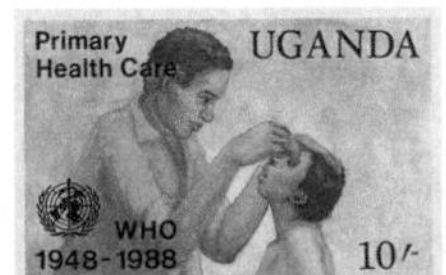

100 Doctor examining Child's Eyes

1988. 40th Anniv of W.H.O. Multicoloured.
662 10s. Type **100** 20 15
663 25s. Mental health therapist with patient 40 30
664 45s. Surgeon performing operation 60 60
665 100s. Dentist treating girl . . 1·25 1·50
666 200s. Doctor examining child 2·00 2·50
MS667 107 × 88 mm. 350s. Delegates approving Declaration of Alma-Ata, 1978 . . . . 2·50 3·50

1988. Christmas. "Santa's Helpers". As T **219a** of Sierre Leone showing Walt Disney cartoon characters. Multicoloured.
668 50s. Father Christmas with list . . . . 1·25 1·00
669 50s. Goofy carrying presents 1·25 1·00
670 50s. Mickey Mouse on toy train . . . . 1·25 1·00
671 50s. Reindeer at window . . 1·25 1·00
672 50s. Donald Duck's nephew with building blocks . . . 1·25 1·00
673 50s. Donald Duck holding sack . . . . 1·25 1·00
674 50s. Chip n' Dale on conveyor belt . . . . . . 1·25 1·00
675 50s. Donald Duck's nephew operating conveyor belt . . 1·25 1·00
MS676 Two sheets, each 127 × 102 mm. (a) 350s. Mickey Mouse loading sack of toys on sleigh (horiz). (b) 350s. Mickey Mouse and Chip n'Dale grooming reindeer. Set of 2 sheets . . . 7·50 8·50
Nos. 668/75 were printed together, se-tenant, as a composite design.

1989. Olympic Gold Medal Winners, Seoul. Nos. 628/31 optd or surch.
677 5s. Type **95** (optd **110 M HURDLES R. KINGDOM USA**) . . . 10 10
678 25s. High jumping (optd **HIGH JUMP G. AVDEENKO USSR**) 20 25
679 35s. Javelin throwing (optd **JAVELIN T. KORJUS FINLAND**) 25 30
680 300s. on 45s. Long jumping (optd **LONG JUMP C. LEWIS USA**) . . . . . 2·50 3·00
MS681 85 × 114 mm. 350s. on 150s. Olympic medals with medal table optd on sheet margin . . . . 3·00 4·00

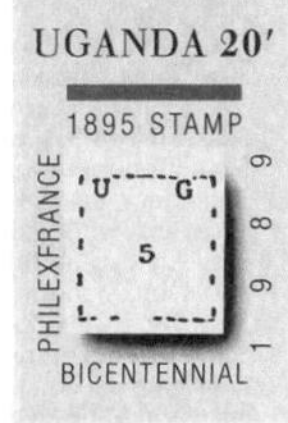

102 Goalkeeper with Ball

103 1895 5 Cowries Stamp

1989. World Cup Football Championship, Italy (1990) (1st issue). Multicoloured.
682 10s. Type **102** 25 15
683 25s. Player kicking ball (horiz) 55 40
684 75s. Heading ball towards net (horiz) . . . . 1·25 1·10
685 200s. Tackling . . . . 2·25 2·75
MS686 118 × 87 mm. 300s. Football and World Cup trophy (horiz) 2·50 3·25
See also Nos. 849/53.

1989. Japanese Art. Paintings by Hokusai. As T **188a** of St. Vincent. Multicoloured.
687 10s. "Fuji and the Great Wave off Kanagawa" . . . 30 30
688 15s. "Fuji from Lake Suwa" 40 35
689 20s. "Fuji from Kajikazawa" 40 35
690 60s. "Fuji from Shichirigahama" . . . . . 1·25 85
691 90s. "Fuji from Ejiri in Sunshu" . . . . 1·50 1·10
692 120s. "Fuji above Lightning" 1·75 1·25
693 200s. "Fuji from Lower Meguro in Edo" . . . . . 2·50 2·00
694 250s. "Fuji from Edo" . . . 2·75 2·25
MS695 Two sheets, each 102 × 76 mm. (a) 500s. "The Red Fuji from the Foot". (b) 500s. "Fuji from Umezawa" Set of 2 sheets . . . . 9·00 9·00

1989. "Philexfrance 89" International Stamp Exhibition, Paris.
696 **103** 20s. black, red and brown 60 35
697 – 70s. black, green and blue 1·50 1·00
698 – 100s. black, violet & pink 1·75 1·50
699 – 250s. black, yell & lt yell 2·50 3·00
MS700 176 × 131 mm. Nos. 696/9 (sold at 500s.) . . . . 6·50 8·00
DESIGNS: 70s. 1895 10 on 50 cowries stamp; 100s. 1896 25 cowries stamp; 250s. 1896 1 rupee stamp.

104 Scout advising on Immunization

1989. 2nd All African Scout Jamboree, Uganda, and 75th Anniv of Uganda Scout Movement. Multicoloured.
701 10s. Type **104** 30 15
702 70s. Poultry keeping . . . . 1·10 1·00
703 90s. Scout on crutches leading family to immunization centre . . . 1·50 2·00
704 100s. Scouts making bricks 1·50 2·00
MS705 99 × 67 mm. 500s. Ugandan Scout logo (vert) . . . . . . 3·25 4·50

105 "Suillus granulatus"

106 Saddle-bill Stork

1989. Fungi. Multicoloured.
706 10s. Type **105** 40 30
707 15s. "Omphalotus olearius" 55 40
708 45s. "Oudemansiella radicata" . . . . 1·25 1·00
709 50s. "Clitocybe nebularis" . . 1·25 1·10
710 60s. "Macrolepiota rhacodes" 1·40 1·25
711 75s. "Lepista nuda" . . . . 1·60 1·40
712 150s. "Suillus luteus" . . . . 2·75 3·00

713 200s. "Agaricus campestris" 3·00 3·25
MS714 Two sheets, each 100 × 68 mm. (a) 350s. "Bolbitius vitellinus" (b) 350s. "Schizophyllum commune" Set of 2 sheets 12·00 11·00

1989. Wildlife at Waterhole. Multicoloured.
715 30s. Type **106** 75 75
716 30s. Eastern white pelican 75 75
717 30s. Marabou stork 75 75
718 30s. Egyptian vulture 75 75
719 30s. Bateleur 75 75
720 30s. African elephant 75 75
721 30s. Giraffe 75 75
722 30s. Goliath heron 75 75
723 30s. Black rhinoceros 75 75
724 30s. Common zebra and oribi 75 75
725 30s. African fish eagle 75 75
726 30s. Hippopotamus 75 75
727 30s. Black-backed jackal and eastern white pelican 75 75
728 30s. African buffalo 75 75
729 30s. Olive baboon 75 75
730 30s. Bohar reedbuck 75 75
731 30s. Lesser flamingo and serval 75 75
732 30s. Whale-headed stork ("Shoebill Stork") 75 75
733 30s. South African crowned crane 75 75
734 30s. Impala 75 75
MS735 Two sheets, each 99 × 68 mm. (a) 500s. Lion. (b) 500s. Long-crested eagle Set of 2 sheets 6·50 8·00

Nos. 715/34 were printed together, se-tenant, forming a composite design showing wildlife at a waterhole.

107 Rocket on Launch Pad

1989. 20th Anniv of First Manned Landing on Moon. Multicoloured.
736 10s. Type **107** 35 20
737 20s. Lunar module "Eagle" on Moon 50 30
738 30s. "Apollo 11" command module 60 40
739 50s. "Eagle" landing on Moon 90 60
740 70s. Astronaut Aldrin on Moon 1·40 85
741 250s. Neil Armstrong alighting from "Eagle" (vert) 4·00 2·50
742 300s. "Eagle" over Moon 4·00 2·75
743 350s. Astronaut Aldrin on Moon (vert) 4·00 3·00
MS744 Two sheets, each 77 × 104 mm. (a) 500s. "Saturn" rocket (vert). (b) 500s. "Apollo 11" capsule on parachutes (vert) Set of 2 sheets 7·50 9·00

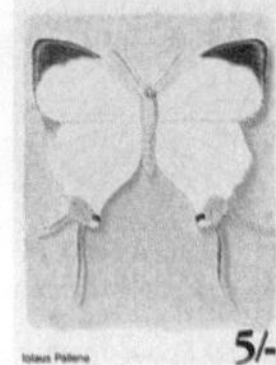

108 "Aphniolaus pallene"

1989. Butterflies. T **108** and similar vert designs showing "UGANDA" in black. Multicoloured.
745 5s. Type **108** 30 20
746 10s. "Hewitsonia boisduvali" 40 25
747 20s. "Euxanthe wakefieldi" 60 30
748 30s. "Papilio echerioides" 70 30
749 40s. "Acraea semivitrea" 75 40
750 50s. "Colotis antevippe" 75 40
751 70s. "Acraea perenna" 90 70
752 90s. "Charaxes cynthia" 90 70
753 100s. "Euphaedra neophron" 90 70
754 150s. "Cymothoe beckeri" 1·25 1·00
755 200s. "Vanessula milca" 1·25 1·25
756 400s. "Mimacraea marshalli" 1·50 2·50
757 500s. "Axiocerses amanga" 1·50 2·75
758 1000s. "Precis hierta" 2·00 4·50

For these, and similar designs showing "UGANDA" in blue, see Nos. 864/80.

109 John Hanning Speke and Map of Lake Victoria

1989. Exploration of Africa. Multicoloured.
760 10s. Type **109** 65 35
761 25s. Sir Richard Burton and map of Lake Tanganyika 85 50
762 40s. Richard Lander and Bakota bronze 90 65
763 90s. Rene Caillie and mosque, Timbuktu 1·50 1·00
764 125s. Sir Samuel Baker and dorcas gazelle 1·60 1·75
765 150s. Pharaoh Necho and ancient Phoenician merchant ship 1·75 1·90
766 250s. Vasco da Gama and 15th-century caravel 2·75 3·00
767 300s. Sir Henry Morton Stanley and "Lady Alice" (sectional boat) 3·00 3·25
MS768 Two sheets, each 73 × 103 mm. (a) 500s. Dr. David Livingstone and steam launch "Ma Robert" (b) 500s. Mary Kingsley and map of Ogooue River Set of 2 sheets 8·50 9·50

110 Logo (25th anniv of African Development Bank)

1989. Anniversaries. Multicoloured.
769 10s. Type **110** 25 15
770 20s. Arrows and dish aerials (World Telecommunication Day) 25 20
771 75s. Two portraits of Nehru (birth centenary) 2·25 1·50
772 90s. Pan Am Boeing 314A flying boat "Dixie Clipper" (50th anniv of first scheduled trans-Atlantic airmail flight) 2·25 1·50
773 100s. George Stephenson and "Locomotion", 1825 (175th anniv of first practical steam locomotive) 2·50 1·75
774 150s. Concorde cockpit (20th anniv of first test flight) 3·75 3·25
775 250s. "Wapen von Hamburg" and "Leopoldus Primus" (galleons) (800th anniv of Port of Hamburg) 3·50 4·00
776 300s. Concorde and cockpit interior (20th anniv of first test flight) 4·25 4·25
MS777 Two sheets (a) 91 × 87 mm. 500s. Revolutionary with musket and Bastille, Paris (bicentenary of French Revolution). (b) 110 × 82 mm. 500s. Emperor Frederick I Barbarossa and Hamburg charter (800th anniv of Port of Hamburg) Set of 2 sheets 8·50 9·50

111 "Aerangis kotschyana"

112 "Thevetia peruviana"

1989. Orchids. Multicoloured.
778 10s. Type **111** 25 25
779 15s. "Angraecum infundibulare" 30 30
780 45s. "Cyrtorchis chailluana" 70 70
781 50s. "Aerangis rhodosticta" 75 75
782 100s. "Eulophia speciosa" 1·50 1·50
783 200s. "Calanthe sylvatica" 2·25 2·25
784 250s. "Vanilla imperialis" 2·40 2·40
785 350s. "Polystachya vulcanica" 2·75 2·75
MS786 Two sheets each 110 × 82 mm. (a) 500s. "Ansellia africana". (b) 500s. "Ancistrochilus rothschildianus" Set of 2 sheets 10·00 10·00

1989. Christmas. Paintings by Fra Angelico. As T **204a** of St. Vincent. Multicoloured.
787 10s. "Madonna and Child" 15 10
788 20s. "Adoration of the Magi" 20 15
789 40s. "Virgin and Child enthroned with Saints" 40 30
790 75s. "The Annunciation" 70 60
791 100s. "Virgin and Child" (detail, "St. Peter Martyr" triptych) 85 75
792 150s. "Virgin and Child enthroned with Saints" (different) 1·25 1·50
793 250s. "Virgin and Child enthroned" 1·75 2·25
794 350s. "Virgin and Child" (from Annalena altarpiece) 2·00 3·25
MS795 Two sheets, each 72 × 96 mm. (a) 500s. "Virgin and Child" (from Bosco ai Frati altarpiece). (b) 500s. "Madonna and Child with Twelve Angels" Set of 2 sheets 5·00 6·00

1990. "Expo '90" International Garden and Greenery Exhibition, Osaka (1st issue). Flowering Trees. Multicoloured.
796 10s. Type **112** 15 15
797 20s. "Acanthus eminens" 20 20
798 90s. "Gnidia glauca" 50 50
799 150s. "Oncoba spinosa" 70 70
800 175s. "Hibiscus rosa-sinensis" 75 75
801 400s. "Jacaranda mimosifolia" 1·25 1·75
802 500s. "Erythrina abyssinica" 1·40 1·90
803 700s. "Bauhinia purpurea" 1·60 2·25
MS804 Two sheets, each 93 × 85 mm. (a) 1000s. "Delonix regia". (b) 1000s. "Cassia didymobotrya" Set of 2 sheets 10·00 11·00

See also Nos. 820/8.

1990. 50th Anniv of Second World War. As T **206a** of St. Vincent. Multicoloured.
805 5s. Allied penetration of German West Wall, 1944 25 25
806 10s. Flags of the Allies, VE Day, 1945 35 35
807 20s. Capture of Okinawa, 1945 45 45
808 75s. Appointment of Gen. De Gaulle to command all Free French forces, 1944 70 60
809 100s. Invasion of Saipan, 1944 85 75
810 150s. Airborne landing, Operation Market Garden, 1944 1·50 1·40
811 200s. MacArthur's return to Philippines, 1944 1·60 1·50
812 300s. "Shoho" (Japanese aircraft carrier) under attack, Coral Sea, 1942 1·75 1·75
813 350s. First Battle of El Alamein, 1942 1·90 1·90
814 500s. Naval Battle of Guadalcanal, 1942 2·25 2·50
MS815 112 × 83 mm. 1000s. Battle of Britain, 1940 (vert) 3·75 4·50

1990. 90th Birthday of Queen Elizabeth the Queen Mother. As T **208a** of St. Vincent.
816 250s. black, mauve and blue 1·40 1·50
817 250s. black, mauve and blue 1·40 1·50
818 250s. black, mauve and blue 1·40 1·50
MS819 90 × 75 mm. 1000s. multicoloured 3·25 3·50

DESIGNS: No. 816, Queen Elizabeth with corgi; Nos. 817, MS819, Queen Elizabeth wearing feathered hat; No. 818, Queen Elizabeth at wartime inspection.

1990. "EXPO 90". International Garden and Greenery Exhibition, Osaka (2nd issue). Nos. 778/85 optd **EXPO '90** and emblem.
820 10s. Type **111** 70 40
821 15s. "Angraecum infundibulare" 70 40
822 45s. "Cyrtorchis chailluana" 1·10 45
823 50s. "Aerangis rhodosticta" 1·10 45
824 100s. "Eulophia speciosa" 1·75 80
825 200s. "Calanthe sylvatica" 2·50 2·50
826 250s. "Vanilla imperialis" 2·75 3·25
827 350s. "Polystachya vulcanica" 3·00 4·00
MS828 Two sheets, each 110 × 82 mm. (a) 500s. "Ansellia africana" (b) 500s. "Ancistrochilus rothschildianus" Set of 2 sheets 8·50 9·50

The overprint on No. MS828 occurs on the sheet margin and includes an additional inscription.

114 P.A.P.U. Emblem

1990. 10th Anniv of Pan-African Postal Union.
829 **114** 80s. multicoloured 1·00 70
MS830 97 × 67 mm. 750s. black and blue 3·50 4·50

DESIGN: 750s. Clasped hands.

115 Unissued G. B. "V R" Penny Black

1990. 150th Anniv of the Penny Black.
831 **115** 25s. multicoloured 50 15
832 – 50s. red, black and green 70 25
833 – 100s. multicoloured 1·00 45
834 – 150s. multicoloured 1·50 1·10
835 – 200s. multicoloured 1·75 1·25
836 – 300s. multicoloured 2·00 1·75
837 – 500s. multicoloured 2·25 2·75
838 – 600s. multicoloured 2·25 3·00
MS839 Two sheets (a) 107 × 77 mm. 1000s. multicoloured. (b) 119 × 85 mm. 1000s. black and red Set of 2 sheets 8·00 9·00

DESIGNS: 50s. Canada 1858–59 3d. Beaver; 100s. Baden 1851 9k. on green error; 150s. Basel 1845 2½r. Dove; 200s. U.S.A. 1918 24c. Inverted "Jenny" error; 300s. Western Australia 1854 1d. Black Swan; 500s. Uganda 1895 20c. "narrow" typewritten stamp; 600s. G.B. Twopenny blue; 1000s. (No. MS839a), Uganda 1895 20c. "wide" typewritten stamp; 1000s. (No. MS839b), Sir Rowland Hill.

No. MS839 also commemorates "Stamp World London 90" International Stamp Exhibition.

116 African Jacana

1990. Wild Birds of Uganda. Multicoloured.
840 10s. Type **116** 60 35
841 15s. Southern ground hornbill 60 35
842 45s. Kori bustard (vert) 85 50
843 50s. Secretary bird 85 50
844 100s. Egyptian geese 1·25 85
845 300s. Goliath heron (vert) 2·25 2·75
846 500s. Ostrich with chicks (vert) 2·75 3·50
847 650s. Saddle-bill stork (vert) 3·00 4·00
MS848 Two sheets, each 98 × 69 mm. (a) 1000s. Lesser flamingo (vert). (b) 1000s. Vulturine guineafowl (vert) Set of 2 sheets 9·50 10·00

117 Roger Milla of Cameroon

1990. World Cup Football Championship, Italy (2nd issue). Multicoloured.
849 50s. Type **117** 35 25
850 100s. Ramzy of Egypt 55 45
851 250s. David O'Leary of Ireland 1·50 1·25
852 600s. Littbarsky of West Germany 2·00 2·50
MS853 Two sheets, each 75 × 90 mm. (a) 1000s. Ali McCoist of Scotland. (b) 1000s. Ekstrom of Sweden Set of 2 sheets 8·00 9·00

118 Mickey and Minnie Mouse at Breakfast

1990. Health and Safety Campaign. Designs showing Walt Disney cartoon characters. Multicoloured.
854 10s. Type **118** 30 10
855 20s. Donald Duck's nephews doing kerb drill 40 15
856 50s. Donald and Mickey stopping Big Pete smoking 70 35
857 90s. Mickey stopping Donald choking 1·25 40
858 100s. Mickey and Goofy using seat belts 1·40 45
859 250s. Mickey and Minnie dancing 2·25 2·25
860 500s. Donald Duck's fitness class 3·25 4·00
861 600s. Mickey's nephews showing lights at night 3·50 4·50
MS862 Two sheets, each 135 × 115 mm. (a) 1000s. Mickey weighing nephew (vert). (b) 1000s. Mickey and Pluto walking (vert) Set of 2 sheets 9·50 10·00

1990. As Nos. 746/55 and new values, showing butterflies, as T **108** with "UGANDA" in blue. Multicoloured.
864A 10s. "Hewitsonia boisduvali" 30 15
865A 20s. "Euxanthe wakefieldi" 40 20
866A 30s. "Papilio echerioides" 40 20
867A 40s. "Acraea semivitrea" 40 20
868B 50s. "Colotis antevippe" 50 30
869A 70s. "Acraea perenna" 50 30
870A 90s. "Charaxes cynthia" 60 30
871A 100s. "Euphaedra neophron" 60 40
872A 150s. "Cymothoe beckeri" 60 40
873B 200s. "Vanessula milca" 85 60
874B 400s. "Mimacraea marshalli" 1·25 1·25
875B 500s. "Axiocerses amanga" 1·25 1·25
876B 1000s. "Precis hierta" 2·50 2·75
877B 2000s. "Precis hierta" 3·25 5·50
878A 3000s. "Euphaedra eusemoides" 6·00 8·50
879A 4000s. "Acraea natalica" 6·50 10·00
880A 5000s. "Euphaedra themis" 6·50 11·00

1990. Christmas. 350th Death Anniv of Rubens. As T **242a** of Sierra Leone, but inscr "CHRISTMAS 1990". Multicoloured.
881 10s. "Baptism of Christ" (detail) (vert) 10 10
882 20s. "St. Gregory the Great and other Saints" (detail) (vert) 15 10
883 100s. "Saints Nereus, Domitilla and Achilleus" (detail) (vert) 65 35
884 150s. "St. Gregory the Great and other Saints" (different detail) (vert) 90 60
885 300s. "Saint Augustine" (detail) (vert) . . . . . . 1·50 1·75
886 400s. "St. Gregory the Great and other Saints" (different detail) (vert) . . . . 1·60 1·90
887 500s. "Baptism of Christ" (different detail) (vert) . . 1·75 2·00
888 600s. "St. Gregory the Great and other Saints" (different detail) (vert) . . . . 1·90 2·75
MS889 Two sheets, each 110×71 mm. (a) 1000s. "The Triumph of Faith" (detail). (b) 1000s. "The Victory of Eucharistic Truth over Heresy" (detail). Set of 2 sheets . . . . 9·00 11·00

119 Census Emblem

1990. National Population and Housing Census. Multicoloured.
890 20s. Type **119** 30 30
MS891 105×73 mm. 1000s. Symbolic people and dwellings 4·50 5·00

120 Damselfly

1991. Fauna of Uganda's Wetlands. Mult.
892 70s. Type **120** 85 75
893 70s. Purple swamphen ("Gallinule") 85 75
894 70s. Sitatunga 85 75
895 70s. Western reef heron ("Purple heron") 85 75
896 70s. Bushpig 85 75
897 70s. Vervet monkey 85 75
898 70s. Long reed frog 85 75
899 70s. Malachite kingfisher . . 85 75
900 70s. Marsh mongoose 85 75
901 70s. Painted reed frog 85 75
902 70s. African jacana 85 75
903 70s. Charaxes butterfly . . . 85 75
904 70s. Nile crocodile 85 75
905 70s. Herald snake 85 75
906 70s. Dragonfly 85 75
907 70s. Lungfish 85 75
MS908 118×78 mm. 1000s. Nile monitor (horiz) . . . . 6·50 7·50
Nos. 892/907 were printed together, se-tenant, forming a composite design.

121 Slug Haplochromis

1991. Fishes of Uganda. Multicoloured.
909 10s. Type **121** 10 10
910 20s. Palmquist's notho . . . 15 15
911 40s. Silver distichodus . . . 20 20
912 90s. Sauvege's haplochromis 40 40
913 100s. Blue calliurum 45 45
914 350s. Johnston's haplochromis . . . . 1·10 1·25
915 600s. Colour-tailed haplochromis . . . . . . 2·25 2·50
916 800s. Jewel cichlid . . . . . 2·50 3·00
MS917 Two sheets, each 100×74 mm. (a) 1000s. Haplochromis. (b) 1000s. Striped panchax Set of 2 sheets . . . . 13·00 14·00

1991. Olympic Games, Barcelona (1992). As T **239a** of Sierra Leone. Multicoloured.
918 20s. Women's 100 metres hurdles 40 20
919 40s. Long jump 55 20
920 125s. Table tennis . . . . . 1·25 1·00
921 250s. Football . . . . 1·75 1·75
922 500s. Men's 800 metres . . . 2·25 3·25
MS923 Two sheets, each 110×71 mm. (a) 1200s. Opening Ceremony at Seoul Games (horiz). (b) 1200s. Women's 4×100 metres relay (horiz) Set of 2 sheets . . 10·00 12·00

122 South African Railways Class 15f Steam Locomotive, 1938–48

1991. African Railway Locomotives. Mult.
924 10s. Type **122** 80 30
925 20s. Rhodesian Railways 12th Class steam locomotive, 1900s . . . . 1·00 45
926 80s. Class "Tribal" steam locomotive, Tanzam Railway, 1951–56 . . . . 2·00 80
927 200s. Steam locomotive, Egypt, 1905 . . . . 2·75 1·50
928 300s. Mikado steam locomotive, Sudan, 1930 2·75 2·25
929 400s. East African Railways Class 59 Garratt steam locomotive, 1955 . . . . . 3·00 2·75
930 500s. East African Railways Mallet steam locomotive, 1900 . . . . 3·00 2·75
931 1000s. Type 5 F 1 electric locomotive, South Africa, 1970 . . . . 3·25 3·75
MS932 Four sheets, each 100×70 mm. (a) 1200s. Atlantic steam locomotive, Egypt, 1900s. (b) 1200s. Rhodesian Railways 12th Class steam locomotive, 1930. (c) 1200s. Benguela Railway Class 11 steam locomotive, Angola, 1920. (d) 1200s. Natal Govt Mallet steam locomotive, 1905–19 Set of 4 sheets . . . . 16·00 17·00
No. 924 is incorrectly captioned as a Rhodesia Railways 10th Class locomotive.

123 Lord Baden-Powell and Scout Emblem

1991. World Scout Jamboree, Mount Sorak, Korea.
933 **123** 20s. multicoloured 60 30
934 – 80s. multicoloured 95 65
935 – 100s. multicoloured . . . 1·10 75
936 – 150s. black and green . . 1·60 1·00
937 – 300s. multicoloured . . . 2·25 1·90
938 – 400s. multicoloured . . . 2·25 2·25
939 – 500s. multicoloured . . . 2·50 2·25
940 – 1000s. multicoloured . . . 3·25 4·00
MS941 Two sheets. (a) 76×115 mm. 1200s. black and stone. (b) 115×76 mm. 1200s. black and blue Set of 2 sheets . . . . . 12·00 12·00
DESIGNS: 80s. Scouts and Uganda 1982 100s. anniversary stamp; 100s. Scout encampment, New York World's Fair, 1939; 150s. Cover and illustration from "Scouting for Boys"; 300s. Cooking on campfire; 400s. Aldrin and Armstrong on Moon; 500s. Scout salutes; 1000s. Statue to the Unknown Scout, Gillwell Park; 1200s. (**MS**941a) Jamboree emblem; 1200s. (**MS**941b) Lord Baden-Powell, W. Boyce and Revd. L. Hadley.

1991. "Phila Nippon '91" International Stamp Exhibition, Tokyo. As T **221** of St. Vincent showing Walt Disney cartoon characters and Japanese traditions. Multicoloured.
942 10s. Uncle Scrooge celebrating Ga-No-Iwai . . 20 20
943 20s. Mickey Mouse removing shoes 30 20
944 70s. Goofy leading cart-horse 70 50
945 80s. Daisy Duck and Minnie Mouse exchanging gifts . . 80 60
946 300s. Minnie kneeling at doorway . . . . 2·00 2·00
947 400s. Donald Duck and Mickey taking a hot volcanic sand bath . . . . 2·25 2·25
948 500s. Clarabelle Cow burning incense . . . . 2·25 2·25
949 1000s. Mickey and Minnie writing New Year cards . . 3·00 3·50
MS950 Two sheets, each 127×112 mm. (a) 1200s. Mickey conducting (vert). (b) 1200s. Mickey in public bath (vert) Set of 2 sheets . . . . 12·00 12·00

1991. Death Cent (1990) of Vincent van Gogh (artist). As T **215a** of St. Vincent. Multicoloured.
951 10s. "Snowy Landscape with Arles" 40 30
952 20s. "Peasant Woman binding Sheaves" (vert) . . 50 30
953 60s. "The Drinkers" 80 50
954 80s. "View of Auvers" . . . 95 65
955 200s. "Mourning Man" (vert) 2·00 1·25
956 400s. "Still Life: Vase with Roses" . . . . 2·50 2·25
957 800s. "The Raising of Lazarus" . . . . 3·50 4·00
958 1000s. "The Good Samaritan" (vert) . . . . 3·50 4·00
MS959 Two sheets, each 102×76 mm. (a) 1200s. "First Steps" (95×71 mm). (b) 1200s. "Village Street and Steps in Auvers" (95×71 mm). Imperf Set of 2 sheets . . . . 13·00 14·00

1991. 65th Birthday of Queen Elizabeth II. As T **220b** of St. Vincent. Multicoloured.
960 70s. Queen and Prince Charles after polo match 1·50 45
961 90s. Queen at Balmoral, 1976 1·50 55
962 500s. Queen with Princess Margaret, August 1980 . . 3·00 2·25
963 600s. Queen and Queen Mother leaving St. George's Chapel, Windsor . . . . 3·25 2·75
MS964 68×90 mm. 1200s. Separate photographs of Queen and Prince Philip . . . . 4·50 4·50

1991. 10th Wedding Anniv of Prince and Princess of Wales. As T **220b** of St. Vincent. Multicoloured.
965 20s. Prince and Princess of Wales in July 1986 . . . . 70 15
966 100s. Separate photographs of Prince, Princess and sons . . . . 1·75 50
967 200s. Prince Henry and Prince William . . . . . . 1·90 1·00
968 1000s. Separate photographs of Prince and Princess in 1988 . . . . 7·00 6·50
MS969 68×90 mm. 1200s. Princess William and Henry on Majorca and Prince and Princess of Wales in Cameroun . . . . 6·50 5·50

124 General Charles de Gaulle **125** "Volvariella bingensis"

1991. Birth Centenary (1990) of Charles de Gaulle (French statesman). Multicoloured.
970 20s. Type **124** 25 20
971 70s. Liberation of Paris, 1944 55 45
972 90s. De Gaulle with King George VI, 1940 . . . . . 65 55
973 100s. Reviewing Free French troops, 1940 (horiz) . . . 70 60
974 200s. Broadcasting to France, 1940 (horiz) . . . . 1·25 1·00
975 500s. De Gaulle in Normandy, 1944 (horiz) . . 2·00 2·00
976 600s. De Gaulle at Albert Hall, 1940 (horiz) . . . . 2·00 2·25
977 1000s. Inauguration as President, 1959 . . . . . 3·00 3·50
MS978 Two sheets. (a) 104×76 mm. 1200s. De Gaulle entering Paris, 1944. (b) 107×76 mm. 1200s. De Gaulle with Eisenhower, 1942 (horiz) Set of 2 sheets . . . . 9·50 10·00

1991. Fungi. Multicoloured.
979 20s. Type **125** 40 30
980 70s. "Agrocybe broadwayi" 70 55
981 90s. "Camarophyllus olidus" 80 65
982 140s. "Marasmius arborescens" . . . . . . 1·25 1·10
983 180s. "Marasmiellus subcinereus" . . . . 1·40 1·40
984 200s. "Agaricus campestris" 1·40 1·40
985 500s. "Chlorophyllum molybdites" . . . . 2·50 2·50
986 1000s. "Agaricus bingensis" 4·00 4·50
MS987 Two sheets, each 96×65 mm. (a) 1200s. "Leucocoprinus cepaestipes" (horiz). (b) 1200s. "Laccaria ohiensis" ("Laccaria lateritia") (horiz) Set of 2 sheets . . . . 9·00 9·50

1991. Endangered Species (3rd series). As Nos. 406/9, but with changed face values, and additional horiz designs as T **61**. Multicoloured.
988 100s. Elephants in "Elephants' Graveyard" . . 75 45
989 140s. Type **61** 95 75
990 200s. Elephants at waterhole 1·50 1·25
991 600s. Elephants having dust bath . . . . 3·00 4·25
MS992 Two sheets, each 102×74 mm. (a) 1200s. Giraffe. (b) 1200s. Rhinoceros and red-billed oxpecker Set of 2 sheets 17·00 17·00

126 "Anigozanthos manglesii"

1991. Botanical Gardens of the World. Mult.
993/1032 90s.×20, 100s.×20 . . Set of 40 . . . . 18·00 20·00
MS1033 Two sheets, each 110×75 mm. (a) 1400s. The Pagoda, Kew. (b) 1400s. Temple of the Winds, Melbourne Set of 2 sheets . . . . 13·00 14·00
Nos. 993/1032 were issued together, se-tenant, as two sheetlets of 20 containing designs as Type **126**. The 90 s values show "Anigozanthos manglesii", "Banksia grandis", "Clianthus formosus", "Gossypium sturtianum", "Callistemon lanceolatus", "Saintpaulia ionantha", "Calodendrum capense", "Aloe ferox x arborescens", "Bolusanthus speciousus", "Lithops schwantesii", "Protea repens", "Plumbago capensis", "Clerodendrum thomsoniae", "Thunbergia alata", "Schotia latifolia", "Epacris impressa", "Acacia pycnantha", "Telopea speciosissima", "Wahlenbergia gloriosa", "Eucalyptus globulus" from Melbourne, and the 100s. "Cypripedium calceolus", "Rhododendron thomsonii", "Ginkgo biloba", "Magnolia campbellii", "Wisteria sinensis", "Clerodendrum ugandense", "Eulophia horsfallii", "Aerangis rhodosticta", "Abelmoschus moschatus", "Gloriosa superba", "Carissa edulis", "Ochna kirkii", "Canarina abyssinica", "Nymphaea caerulea", "Ceropegia succulenta", "Strelitzia reginae", "Strongylodon macrobotrys", "Victoria amazonica", "Orchis militaris" and "Sophora microphylla" from Kew.

1991. Nos. 573, 597 and 614 surch **20/-**.
1034 20s. on 25s. Airship N.1 "Norge" and polar bear (first transpolar flight), 1926 . . . .
1035 20s. on 25s. Einstein and deep space (Theory of Relativity) . . . .
1035a 20s. on 25s. Tank locomotive No. 126 . .

1991. Christmas. Paintings by Piero della Francesca. As T **248a** of Sierra Leone. Multicoloured.
1036 20s. "Madonna with Child and Angels" 50 20
1037 50s. "The Baptism of Christ" 75 20
1038 80s. "Polyptych of Mercy" 1·00 40
1039 100s. "Polyptych of Mercy" (detail) . . . . 1·00 40
1040 200s. "The Annunciation" from "The Legend of the True Cross" . . . . . . 1·75 80
1041 500s. "Pregnant Madonna" 2·75 2·50
1042 1000s. "The Annunciation" from "Polyptych of St. Anthony" . . . . . . 4·00 4·50
1043 1500s. "The Nativity" . . . 5·00 7·50
MS1044 Two sheets, each 102×127 mm. (a) 1800s. "The Brera Altarpiece". (b) 1800s. "Madonna and Child" from "Polyptych of St. Anthony" Set of 2 sheets . . . . 13·00 14·00

128 Boy Scout Monument, New York, and Ernest Thompson (first Chief Scout of U.S.A.)

1992. Anniversaries and Events. Multicoloured.
1045 20s. Type **128** 80 30
1046 50s. Treehouse design and Daniel Beard (vert) . . . 85 40
1047 400s. Lilienthal's signature and "Flugzeug Nr. 8" . . 1·50 1·75
1048 500s. Demonstator demolishing Berlin Wall 1·60 2·25
1049 700s. "The Magic Flute" . . 6·00 6·00
MS1050 Two sheets. (a) 114×85 mm. 1200s. Class VL8 electric locomotive leaving tunnel. (b) 117×89 mm. 1500s. Ugandan Boy Scout badge Set of 2 sheets 10·00 11·00
ANNIVERSARIES AND EVENTS: Nos. 1045/6, **MS**1050b, 50th death anniv of Lord Baden-Powell and World Scout Jamboree, Korea; No. 1047, Centenary of Otto Lilienthal's first gliding experiments; No. 1048, Bicentenary of Brandenburg Gate, Berlin; No. 1049, Death bicentenary of Mozart; **MS**1050a, Centenary of Trans-Siberian Railway.

129 U.S.S. "Vestal" (repair ship) under Attack

1992. 50th Anniv of Japanese Attack on Pearl Harbor. Multicoloured.

1051 200s. Type **129** 1·25 1·10
1052 200s. Japanese Mitsubishi A6M Zero-Sen 1·25 1·10
1053 200s. U.S.S. "Arizona" (battleship) on fire 1·25 1·10
1054 200s. U.S.S. "Nevada" (battleship) passing burning ships 1·25 1·10
1055 200s. Japanese Aichi D3A "Val" bomber attacking 1·25 1·10
1056 200s. Douglas SBD Dauntless bombers attacking "Hiryu" (carrier) at Midway 1·25 1·10
1057 200s. Japanese Mitsubishi A6M Zero-Sen aircraft attacking Midway Island 1·25 1·10
1058 200s. U.S. Marine Brewster F2A Buffalo (fighter) defending Midway 1·25 1·10
1059 200s. American Grumman F6F Hellcat aircraft and carrier 1·25 1·10
1060 200s. U.S.S. "Yorktown" (carrier) torpedoed 1·25 1·10

130 Three Modern Hot Air Balloons

1992. 120th Anniv (1990) of Paris Balloon Post. Multicoloured.

1061 200s. Type **130** 1·25 1·10
1062 200s. Sport balloons and top of "Double Eagle II" 1·25 1·10
1063 200s. Pro Juventute balloon and top of Branson's "Virgin Otsuka Pacific Flyer" 1·25 1·10
1064 200s. Blanchard and Jeffries' balloon 1·25 1·10
1065 200s. Nadar's "Le Geant" and centre of "Double Eagle II" 1·25 1·10
1066 200s. Branson's "Virgin Otsuka Pacific Flyer" 1·25 1·10
1067 200s. Montgolfier balloon 1·25 1·10
1068 200s. "Double Eagle II" basket and Paris balloon of 1870 1·25 1·10
1069 200s. Henri Giffard's balloon "Le Grand Ballon Captif" 1·25 1·10

Nos. 1061/9 were printed together, se-tenant, forming a composite design.

1992. Mickey's World Tour. As T **250a** of Sierra Leone showing Walt Disney cartoon characters in different countries. Multicoloured.

1070 20s. Mickey Mouse and Goofy on African safari (horiz) 50 20
1071 50s. Mickey charming Pluto's tail, India (horiz) 70 20
1072 80s. Minnie Mouse, Donald and Daisy Duck as Caribbean calypso band (horiz) 1·00 25
1073 200s. Goofy pulling Donald and Daisy in rickshaw, China (horiz) 1·60 60
1074 500s. Mickey and Minnie on camel, Egypt (horiz) 2·25 1·75
1075 800s. Donald and Pete sumo wrestling, Japan (horiz) 2·50 2·75
1076 1000s. Goofy bullfighting, Spain (horiz) 2·50 2·75
1077 1500s. Mickey playing football, Italy (horiz) 3·00 4·00
MS1078 Two sheets, each 83 × 104 mm. (a) 2000s. Mickey as Cossack dancer, Russia. (b) 2000s. Daisy as Wagnerian diva, Germany Set of 2 sheets 12·00 13·00

1992. 40th Anniv of Queen Elizabeth II's Accession. As T **220b** of St. Vincent. Multicoloured.

1079 100s. Lake Victoria 80 25
1080 200s. Lake and mountains 1·25 60
1081 500s. Lakeside fields 2·50 2·25
1082 1000s. River Nile 3·75 4·25
MS1083 Two sheets, each 74 × 97 mm. (a) 1800s. Waterfalls. (b) 1800s. Owen Falls Dam Set of 2 sheets 12·00 11·00

1992. Prehistoric Animals. As T **250c** of Sierra Leone. Multicoloured.

1084 50s. Kentrosaurus 50 30
1085 200s. Iguanodon 1·00 80
1086 250s. Hypsilophodon 1·10 90
1087 300s. Brachiosaurus 1·25 1·10
1088 400s. Peloneustes 1·40 1·40
1089 500s. Pteranodon 1·50 1·50
1090 800s. Tetralophodon 2·00 2·50
1091 1000s. Megalosaurus 2·00 2·50
MS1092 Two sheets, each 100 × 70 mm. (a) 2000s. As 250s. (b) 2000s. As 1000s. Set of 2 sheets 14·00 13·00

131 "The Entry into Jerusalem" (detail) (Giotto)

132 Adungu

1992. Easter. Religious Paintings. Mult.

1093 50s. Type **131** 65 15
1094 100s. "Pilate and the Watch" (Psalter of Robert de Lisle) 85 20
1095 200s. "The Kiss of Judas" (detail) (Giotto) 1·25 55
1096 250s. "Christ washing the Feet of the Disciples" (Vita Christi manuscript) 1·40 75
1097 300s. "Christ seized in the Garden" (Melissende Psalter) 1·50 85
1098 500s. "Doubting Thomas" (Vita Christi manuscript) 2·25 1·75
1099 1000s. "The Marys at the Tomb" (detail) (anon) 3·75 4·25
1100 2000s. "The Ascension" (Florentine manuscript) 5·50 7·50
MS1101 Two sheets, each 72 × 102 mm. (a) 2500s. "The Piercing of Christ's Side" (detail) (Limoges enamel). (b) 2500s. "Agony at Gethsemane" (detail) (Limoges enamel) Set of 2 sheets 13·00 14·00

1992. Traditional Musical Instruments. Mult.

1102 50s. Type **132** 50 20
1103 100s. Endingidi 65 35
1104 200s. Akogo 90 60
1105 250s. Nanga 95 70
1106 300s. Engoma 1·10 1·10
1107 400s. Amakondere 1·25 1·40
1108 500s. Akakyenkye 1·50 1·60
1109 1000s. Ennanga 2·75 4·00

133 Map of Known World, 1486

1992. 500th Anniv of Discovery of America by Columbus and "World Columbian Stamp Expo '92" Exhibition, Chicago. Multicoloured.

1110 50s. Type **133** 20 20
1111 100s. Map of Africa, 1508 30 30
1112 150s. Map of West Indies, 1500 50 50
1113 200s. "Nina" and astrolabe 60 60
1114 600s. "Pinta" and quadrant 1·50 1·50
1115 800s. Sand glass 1·60 1·60
1116 900s. 15th-century compass 1·75 1·75
1117 2000s. Map of World, 1492 3·50 3·50
MS1118 Two sheets, each 95 × 75 mm. (a) 2500s. Sections of globe, 1492. (b) 2500s. Europe and Africa from map by Henricus Martellus, 1490 (vert) Set of 2 sheets 9·25 10·00

1992. Hummel Figurines. As T **215b** of St. Vincent. Multicoloured.

1119 50s. Girl with washing 30 20
1120 200s. Girl scrubbing floor 70 50
1121 250s. Girl sweeping floor 80 60
1122 300s. Girl with baby 90 70
1123 600s. Boy mountaineer 2·00 2·00
1124 900s. Girl knitting 2·50 2·75
1125 1000s. Boy on stool 2·75 3·00
1126 1500s. Boy with telescope 3·00 3·50
MS1127 Two sheets, each 97 × 122 mm. (a) 500s. As No. 1119; 500s. As No. 1120; 500s. As No. 1121; 500s. As No. 1122. (b) 500s. As No. 1124; 500s. As No. 1123; 500s. As No. 1125; 500s. As No. 1126 Set of 2 sheets 9·50 11·00

134 Spotted Hyena

1992. Wildlife. Multicoloured.

1128 50s. Type **134** 35 15
1129 100s. Impala 45 25
1130 200s. Giant forest hog 65 35
1131 250s. Pangolin 75 55
1132 300s. Golden monkey 85 60
1133 800s. Serval 2·25 2·50
1134 1000s. Small-spotted genet ("Bush genet") 2·25 2·75
1135 3000s. Waterbuck 5·50 7·50
MS1136 Two sheets, each 100 × 70 mm. (a) 2500s. Gorilla. (b) 2500s. Hippopotamus Set of 2 sheets 9·00 10·00

1992. Olympic Games, Barcelona. As T **250d** of Sierra Leone. Multicoloured.

1137 50s. Men's javelin 30 20
1138 100s. Men's high jump (horiz) 40 30
1139 200s. Fencing (pentathlon) 60 45
1140 250s. Men's volleyball 65 60
1141 300s. Women's platform diving 70 60
1142 500s. Men's team cycling 4·00 2·25
1143 1000s. Women's tennis 4·25 4·50
1144 2000s. Boxing (horiz) 5·00 7·50
MS1145 Two sheets, each 100 × 70 mm. (a) 2500s. Men's basketball. (b) 2500s. Baseball Set of 2 sheets 15·00 15·00

135 Red-headed Falcon

136 Goofy in "Hawaiian Holiday", 1937

1992. Birds. Multicoloured.

1146 20s. Type **135** 35 20
1147 30s. Yellow-billed hornbill 40 20
1148 50s. Purple heron 40 20
1149 100s. Regal sunbird 50 20
1150 150s. White-browed robin chat 60 25
1151 200s. Shining-blue kingfisher 70 30
1152 250s. Great blue turaco 80 40
1153 300s. African emerald cuckoo 90 60
1154 500s. Abyssinian roller 1·25 1·00
1155 800s. South African crowned crane 1·75 1·75
1156 1000s. Doherty's bush shrike 2·00 2·25
1157 2000s. Splendid glossy starling 3·25 4·00
1158 3000s. Little bee eater 4·50 6·50
1159 4000s. Red-faced lovebird ("Red-headed Lovebird") 6·00 8·00

1992. Postage Stamp Mega Event, New York. Sheet 100 × 70 mm. containing vert design as T **240a** of St. Vincent. Multicoloured.

MS1160 2500s. United Nations Headquarters 3·75 4·25

1992. 60th Anniv of Goofy. Multicoloured.

1162 50s. Type **136** 30 20
1163 100s. Riding pennyfarthing cycle, 1941 40 20
1164 200s. Goofy and Mickey Mouse as firemen, 1935 60 35
1165 250s. Skiing, 1941 (horiz) 65 40
1166 300s. One man band, 1937 (horiz) 70 60
1167 1000s. Asleep against boat, 1938 (horiz) 2·25 2·50
1168 1500s. Ancient Olympic champion, 1942 3·25 3·75
1169 2000s. Pole vaulting, 1942 3·50 3·75
MS1170 Two sheets. (a) 105 × 115 mm. 3000s. Goofy and Wilbur the grasshopper, 1939 (horiz). (b) 92 × 116 mm. 3000s. Wyatt Goofy and Goofy today Set of 2 sheets 12·00 12·00

137 "The Annunciation" (Zurbaran)

1992. Christmas. Religious Paintings by Francisco Zurbaran. Multicoloured.

1171 50s. Type **137** 40 15
1172 200s. "The Annunciation" (different) 85 35
1173 250s. "The Virgin of the Immaculate Conception" 90 45
1174 300s. "The Virgin of the Immaculate Conception" (detail) 1·10 50
1175 800s. "Holy Family with Saints Anne, Joachim and John the Baptist" 2·75 3·00
1176 900s. "Holy Family with Saints Anne, Joachim and John the Baptist" (detail) 3·00 3·25
1177 1000s. "Adoration of the Magi" 3·00 3·25
1178 2000s. "Adoration of the Magi" (detail) 4·25 6·00
MS1179 Two sheets, each 76 × 102 mm. (a) 2500s. "The Virgin of the Immaculate Conception (different). (b) 2500s. "The Virgin of the Immaculate Conception" (different) Set of 2 sheets 13·00 14·00

138 Man cleaning Granary

1992. Anniversaries and Events. Multicoloured.

1180 50s. Type **138** 20 15
1181 200s. Mother breast feeding 55 40
1182 250s. Mother feeding baby 60 50
1183 300s. Boy collecting water from pump 60 75
1184 300s. "Voyager 2" passing Jupiter 2·25 1·25
1185 800s. Mother and baby 1·50 2·25
1186 800s. Impala 1·50 2·25
1187 1000s. Mountain zebra 3·25 3·50
1188 1000s. Count Ferdinand von Zeppelin and airship 3·25 3·50
1189 2000s. "Voyager 2" passing Neptune 7·50 7·50
1190 3000s. Count Ferdinand von Zeppelin and Clement-Bayard airship "Fleurus" 8·00 9·00
MS1191 Four sheets, each 115 × 85 mm. (a) 2500s. "Voyager 2" and Jupiter. (b) 2500s. Warthog. (c) 2500s. Count Ferdinand von Zeppelin with Robert Brothers and Colin Hullin balloon. (d) 2500s. Doctor inoculating boy Set of 4 sheets 21·00 22·00

ANNIVERSARIES AND EVENTS: Nos. 1180/3, 1185, United Nations World Health Organization Projects; Nos. 1184, 1189, **MS**1191a, International Space Year; Nos. 1186/7, **MS**1191b, Earth Summit '92, Rio; Nos. 1188, 1190, **MS**1191c, 75th death anniv of Count Ferdinand von Zeppelin (airship pioneer); **MS**1191d, 75th anniv of International Association of Lions Clubs.

139 Hands releasing Dove with Lubaga and Kampala Catholic Cathedrals

1993. Visit of Pope John Paul II. Mult.

1192 50s. Type **139** 50 10
1193 200s. Pope and Kampala Cathedral 90 30
1194 250s. Pope and Catholic worshipper 1·00 45
1195 300s. Ugandan bishops and Pope 1·10 60
1196 800s. Pope John Paul II waving 2·50 2·50
1197 900s. Pope and Kampala Cathedral (different) 2·50 2·50
1198 1000s. Pope, national flag and Kampala Cathedral 2·50 2·50
1199 2000s. Pope and national flag 4·00 4·50
MS1200 Two sheets, each 100 × 70 mm. (a) 3000s. Pope on aircraft steps (vert). (b) 3000s. Pope delivering blessing (vert) Set of 2 sheets 13·00 13·00

1993. Bicentenary of the Louvre, Paris. Paintings by Rembrandt. As T **254a** of St. Vincent. Multicoloured.

1201 500s. "Self Portrait at Easel" 1·10 1·10
1202 500s. "Birds of Paradise" 1·10 1·10
1203 500s. "The Carcass of Beef" 1·10 1·10
1204 500s. "The Supper at Emmaus" 1·10 1·10
1205 500s. "Hendrickje Stoffels" 1·10 1·10
1206 500s. "The Artist's Son, Titus" 1·10 1·10
1207 500s. "The Holy Family" (left detail) 1·10 1·10
1208 500s. "The Holy Family" (right detail) 1·10 1·10
MS1209 100 × 70 mm. 2500s. "The philosopher in Meditation" (89 × 57 mm) 4·50 5·00

140 Afghan Hound

1993. Dogs of the World. Multicoloured.
1210 50s. Type **140** 90 30
1211 100s. Newfoundland . . . . 1·25 30
1212 200s. Siberian huskies . . . 1·75 50
1213 250s. Briard . . . . 1·75 65
1214 300s. Saluki . . . . 1·75 85
1215 800s. Labrador guide-dog (vert) . . . . 3·25 3·25
1216 1000s. Greyhound . . . . . 3·50 3·50
1217 1500s. Pointer . . . . . . 4·00 4·75
MS1218 Two sheets, each 103 × 80 mm. (a) 2500s. Cape hunting dog. (b) 2500s. Norwegian elkhound pup Set of 2 sheets 17·00 17·00

1993. 40th Anniv of Coronation. As T **256a** of St. Vincent. Multicoloured.
1219 50s. Queen Elizabeth II at Coronation (photograph by Cecil Beaton) 30 35
1220 200s. Orb and Sceptre . . . 50 60
1221 500s. Queen Elizabeth during Coronation . . . 90 1·10
1222 1500s. Queen Elizabeth II and Princess Margaret . . 2·25 2·50
MS1223 69 × 100 mm. 2500s. "The Crown" (detail) (Grace Wheatley) ($28\frac{1}{2} \times 42\frac{1}{2}$ mm) . . . . 5·00 5·00

1993. Asian International Stamp Exhibitions. As T **263** of St. Vincent, but vert. Multicoloured.
(a) "Indopex '93", Surabaya, Indonesia. Javanese Wayang Puppets
1224 600s. Bupati karma, Prince of Wangga . . . . 1·25 1·50
1225 600s. Rahwana . . . . . . 1·25 1·50
1226 600s. Sondjeng Sandjata . . 1·25 1·50
1227 600s. Raden Damar Wulan 1·25 1·50
1228 600s. Unidentified puppet 1·25 1·50
1229 600s. Hanaman . . . . . . 1·25 1·50
MS1230 135 × 105 mm. 2500s. Candi Mendut Temple, Java . . . . 6·00 7·00

(b) "Taipei '93", Taiwan. Funerary Pottery Figures
1231 600s. Tomb guardian god in green armour . . . . . . 1·25 1·50
1232 600s. Civil official and shrine . . . . 1·25 1·50
1233 600s. Tomb guardian god in green and gold armour . . 1·25 1·50
1234 600s. Civil official in red robe . . . . 1·25 1·50
1235 600s. Chimera (tomb guardian) . . . . 1·25 1·50
1236 600s. Civil official in red and green robe . . . . . 1·25 1·50
MS1237 135 × 105 mm. 2500s. Statue of the Sacred Mother, Taiyuan . . . . 6·00 7·00

(c) "Bangkok '93", Thailand. Sculptured Figures
1238 600s. Standing Buddha in gilded red sandstone, 13th–15th century . . . . 1·25 1·50
1239 600s. Crowned Buddha in bronze, 13th century . . . 1·25 1·50
1240 600s. Thepanom in stone, 15th century . . . . . . 1·25 1·50
1241 600s. Crowned Buddha in bronze, 12th century . . . 1·25 1·50
1242 600s. Avalokitesvara in bronze, 9th century . . . 1·25 1·50
1243 600s. Lop Buri standing Buddha in bronze, 13th century . . . . 1·25 1·50
MS1244 135 × 105 mm. 2500s. Buddha, Wat Mahathat . . . 6·00 7·00

141 Gutierrez (Uruguay) and Voeller (Germany)

142 York Minster, England

1993. World Cup Football Championship, U.S.A. (1994) (1st issue). Multicoloured.
1245 50s. Type **141** 60 15
1246 200s. Tomas Brolin (Sweden) . . . . 1·25 40
1247 250s. Gary Lineker (England) . . . . 1·50 45
1248 300s. Munoz and Butragueno (Spain) . . . 1·50 65
1249 800s. Carlos Valderrama (Colombia) . . . . 2·75 3·00
1250 900s. Diego Maradona (Argentina) . . . . 2·75 3·00
1251 1000s. Pedro Troglio (Argentina) . . . . 2·75 3·00
1252 2000s. Enzo Scifo (Belgium) 4·00 5·50
MS1253 Two sheets, each 103 × 72 mm. (a) 2500s. Brazilians celebrating. (b) 2500s. De Napoli (Italy) and Skuhravy (Czechoslovakia) (horiz) Set of 2 sheets . . . . 13·00 14·00
See also Nos. 1322/8.

1993. Cathedrals of the World. Multicoloured.
1254 50s. Type **142** 40 15
1255 100s. Notre Dame, Paris . . 55 20
1256 200s. Little Metropolis, Athens 85 40
1257 250s. St. Patrick's, New York 90 45
1258 300s. Ulm, Germany . . . 95 50
1259 800s. St. Basil's, Moscow . . 2·50 2·75
1260 1000s. Roskilde, Denmark 2·50 2·75
1261 2000s. Seville, Spain . . . . 4·00 5·50
MS1262 Two sheets, each 70 × 100 mm. (a) 2500s. Namirembe, Uganda. (b) 2500s. St. Peter's, Vatican City Set of 2 sheets . . . . 10·00 11·00

1993. Christmas. Religious Paintings. As T **265a** of St. Vincent. Black, yellow and red (Nos. 1263, 1265, 1267, 1270 and **MS**1271a) or multicoloured (others).
1263 50s. "Virgin with Carthusian Monks" (detail) (Durer) 50 10
1264 100s. "Sacred Family" (detail) (Raphael) 75 10
1265 200s. "Virgin with Carthusian Monks" (different detail) (Durer) 1·10 30
1266 250s. "The Virgin of the Rose" (Raphael) . . . . 1·25 35
1267 300s. "Virgin with Carthusian Monks" (different detail) (Durer) 1·25 40
1268 800s. "Sacred Family" (different detail) (Raphael) 2·75 3·00
1269 1000s. "Virgin with Beardless Joseph" (Raphael) . . . . 2·75 3·00
1270 2000s. "Virgin with Carthusian Monks" (different detail) (Durer) 4·25 6·00
MS1271 Two sheets, each 102 × 127 mm. (a) 2500s. "Virgin with Carthusian Monks" (different detail) (Dürer). (b) 2500s. "Sacred Family" (different detail) (Raphael) Set of 2 sheets . . . 13·00 13·00
Nos. **MS**1271 is inscribed "Canthusian Monks" in error.

143 Mickey Mouse asleep on Stegosaurus

1993. Prehistoric Animals and Walt Disney Cartoon Characters. Multicoloured.
1272 50s. Type **143** 55 20
1273 100s. Minnie Mouse on pteranodon 65 20
1274 200s. Mickey being licked by mamenchisaurus 90 40
1275 250s. Mickey doing cave painting . . . . 1·00 45
1276 300s. Mickey wind-surfing on dinosaur . . . . . . 1·10 60
1277 500s. Mickey and Donald Duck sliding on diplodocus . . . . 1·75 1·40
1278 800s. Mamenchisaurus carrying Mickey . . . . 2·50 3·00
1279 1000s. Pluto on triceratops 2·50 3·00
MS1280 Two sheets, each 128 × 102 mm. (a) 2500s. Mickey and Minnie. (b) 2500s. Mickey feeding tyrannosaurus rex Set of 2 sheets . . . . 11·00 12·00
No. 1273 is inscribed "PTERANDOM" and No. 1278 "MAMENSHISAURUS", both in error.

144 "Woman in Yellow" (Picasso)

145 Passion Fruit

1993. Anniversaries and Events. Multicoloured.
1281 100s. Type **144** 40 15
1282 200s. Head of cow and syringe 50 30
1283 250s. "Gertrude Stein" (Picasso) 60 35
1284 500s. Early telescope . . . . 2·25 1·50
1285 800s. "Creation" (S. Witkiewicz after J. Glogowski) . . . . . . 2·00 2·50
1286 1000s. Modern telescope . . 3·25 3·50
1287 1000s. "For the Right to Work" (A. Strumillo) . . 2·25 3·50
MS1288 Three sheets. (a) 75 × 105 mm. 2500s. "Woman by a Window" (detail) (Picasso). (b) 105 × 75 mm. 2500s. Copernicus. (c) 105 × 75 mm. 2500s. "Temptation of Saint Antony I" (detail) (S. Witkiewicz) (horiz) Set of 3 sheets . . . . 13·00 14·00
ANNIVERSARIES AND EVENTS: Nos. 1281, 1283, **MS**1288a, 20th death anniv of Picasso (artist); No. 1282, Pan African Rinderpest Campaign; Nos. 1284, 1286, **MS**1288b, 450th death anniv of Copernicus (astronomer); Nos. 1285, 1287, 1288c, "Polska '93" International Stamp Exhibition, Poznan.

1994. Fruits and Crops. Multicoloured.
1289 50s. Type **145** 45 10
1290 100s. Sunflower 55 10
1291 150s. Bananas 70 25
1292 200s. Runner beans 80 30
1293 250s. Pineapple 85 55
1294 300s. Jackfruit 95 70
1295 500s. Sorghum . . . . . . 1·75 1·75
1296 800s. Maize . . . . 2·50 3·25
MS1297 Two sheets, each 101 × 71 mm. (a) 2000s. Sesame. (b) 2000s. Coffee (horiz) Set of 2 sheets . . . . 8·50 9·00

146 Ford Model "A", 1903

1994. Centenaries of Henry Ford's First Petrol Engine (Nos. 1298/1301, **MS**1306a) and Karl Benz's First Four-wheeled Car (others). Multicoloured.
1298 700s. Type **146** . . . . . . 1·25 1·50
1299 700s. Ford Model "T" snowmobile, 1932 . . . . 1·25 1·50
1300 700s. Ford "Mustang" . . . 1·25 1·50
1301 700s. Lotus-Ford racing car, 1965 . . . . 1·25 1·50
1302 800s. Mercedes-Benz "S600" coupe, 1994 . . . . . . 1·25 1·50
1303 800s. Mercedes-Benz "W196" racing car, 1955 1·25 1·50
1304 800s. Mercedes-Benz "W125" road speed record car, 1938 . . . . 1·25 1·50
1305 800s. Benz "Viktoria", 1893 1·25 1·50
MS1306 Two sheets, each 85 × 85 mm. (a) 2500s. Henry Ford (vert). (b) 2500s. Karl Benz (vert) Set of 2 sheets . . . . 9·00 10·00

1994. "Hong Kong '94" International Stamp Exhibition (1st issue). As T **271a** of St. Vincent. Multicoloured.
1307 500s. Hong Kong 1988 60c. Catholic Cathedral stamp and religious shrines, Repulse Bay . . . . . . 80 1·00
1308 500s. Uganda 1993 2500s. Namirembe Cathedral stamp and religious shrines, Repulse Bay (different) . . . . 80 1·00
Nos. 1307/8 were printed together, se-tenant, forming a composite design.

1994. "Hong Kong '94" International Stamp Exhibition (2nd issue). Ching Dynasty Snuff Boxes. As T **271b** of St. Vincent, but vert. Multicoloured.
1309 200s. Glass box with pavilion design 50 60
1310 200s. Porcelain box with quail design 50 60
1311 200s. Porcelain box with floral design 50 60
1312 200s. Porcelain box with openwork design 50 60
1313 200s. Agate box with carved Lion-dogs 50 60
1314 200s. Agate box with man on donkey design 50 60
Captions for Nos. 1310/11 are transposed.

147 Meteorological Weather Station

1994. World Meteorological Day. Multicoloured.
1315 50s. Type **147** 60 15
1316 200s. Weather observatory at training school, Entebbe (vert) . . . . . 1·40 55
1317 250s. Satellite link . . . . . 1·40 60
1318 300s. Recording temperatures . . . . . . 1·60 90
1319 400s. Automatic weather station (vert) . . . . . 1·75 1·75
1320 800s. Crops damaged by hailstones . . . . 2·75 4·00
MS1321 105 × 75 mm. 2500s. Barograph . . . . 7·00 8·00

1994. World Cup Football Championship, U.S.A. (2nd issue). As T **268** of Sierra Leone. Multicoloured.
1322 500s. Georges Grun (Belgium) . . . . 1·50 1·50
1323 500s. Oscar Ruggeri (Argentina) . . . . 1·50 1·50
1324 500s. Frank Rijkaard (Netherlands) . . . . . . 1·50 1·50
1325 500s. Magid "Tyson" Musisi (Uganda) . . . . 1·50 1·50
1326 500s. Ronald Koeman (Netherlands) . . . . . . 1·50 1·50
1327 500s. Igor Shalimov (Russia) 1·50 1·50
MS1328 Two sheets, each 70 × 100 mm. (a) 2500s. Ruud Gullit (Netherlands). (b) 2500s. Player and R.F.K. Stadium, Washington D.C. Set of 2 sheets 10·00 11·00

No. 1326 is inscribed "DONALD KOEMAN" in error.

148 Milking Cow

1994. 50th Anniv of Heifer Project International.
1329 **148** 100s. multicoloured . . . 1·00 60

149 "Lobobunaea goodii"

150 Wooden Stool

1994. Moths. Multicoloured.
1330 100s. Type **149** 35 20
1331 200s. "Bunaeopsis hersilia" 65 40
1332 300s. "Rufoglanis rosea" . . 80 60
1333 350s. "Acherontia atropos" 85 75
1334 400s. "Rohaniella pygmaea" 95 95
1335 450s. "Euchloron megaera" 1·00 1·25
1336 500s. "Epiphora rectifascia" 1·10 1·25
1337 1000s. "Polyphychus coryndoni" . . . . 1·90 2·50
MS1338 Two sheets, each 117 × 88 mm. (a) 2500s. As Type **149**. (b) 2500s. "Lobobunaea goodii" (wings folded) Set of 2 sheets . . . . 9·50 10·00

1994. Crafts. Multicoloured.
1339 100s. Type **150** 25 10
1340 200s. Wood and banana fibre chair 45 30
1341 250s. Raffia and palm leaves basket 50 35
1342 300s. Wool tapestry showing tree planting 55 45
1343 450s. Wool tapestry showing hair grooming 85 90
1344 500s. Wood sculpture of a drummer . . . . 95 1·10
1345 800s. Gourds . . . . 1·75 2·25
1346 1000s. Bark cloth handbag 2·00 2·50
MS1347 Two sheets, each 100 × 70 mm. (a) 2500s. Raffia baskets. (b) 2500s. Papyrus hats Set of 2 sheets . . . . 9·50 10·00

151 Turkish Angora Cat and Blue Mosque

1994. Cats. Multicoloured.
1348 50s. Type **151** 55 25
1349 100s. Japanese bobtail and Mt. Fuji 70 25
1350 200s. Norwegian forest cat and windmill, Holland . . 90 40
1351 300s. Egyptian mau and pyramids (vert) . . . . . 1·10 75
1352 450s. Rex and Stonehenge, England (vert) . . . . . 1·50 1·50
1353 500s. Chartreux and Eiffel Tower, France . . . . . 1·60 1·60
1354 1000s. Burmese and Shwe Dagon Pagoda (vert) . . 2·75 3·00
1355 1500s. Maine coon and Pemaquid Point Lighthouse (vert) . . . . 3·50 4·25
MS1356 Two sheets, each 100 × 76 mm. (a) 2500s. Russian blue. (b) 2500s. Manx Set of 2 sheets . . . . 12·00 12·00

152 Child carrying Building Block

1994. 75th Anniv of I.L.O.
1357 **152** 350s. multicoloured . . . 1·50 1·50

1994. 25th Anniv of First Manned Moon Landing. Astronauts. As Nos. 1977/89 of Antigua. Multicoloured.

1358 50s. Alan Shepard Jnr . . . 80 80
1359 100s. M. Scott Carpenter . . 90 90
1360 200s. Virgil Grissom . . . . 1·25 1·25
1361 300s. L. Gordon Cooper Jnr 1·40 1·40
1362 400s. Walter Schirra Jnr . . 1·60 1·60
1363 500s. Donald Slayton . . . 1·60 1·60
1364 600s. John Glenn Jnr . . . 1·60 1·60
MS1365 88 × 91 mm. 3000s. "Apollo 11" anniversary emblem 7·00 7·50

1994. Centenary of International Olympic Committee. Gold Medal Winners. As T **285a** of St. Vincent. Multicoloured.

1366 350s. John Akii-Bua (Uganda) (400 metres hurdles), 1972 (horiz) . . 60 45
1367 900s. Heike Herkel (Germany) (high jump), 1992 (horiz) . . . . . . 1·25 1·75
MS1368 107 × 76 mm. 2500s. Aleski Urmanov (Russia) (figure skating), 1994 . . . . 5·00 5·50

1994. 50th Anniv of D-Day. As T **284b** of St. Vincent. Multicoloured.

1369 300s. Mulberry Harbour pier 50 40
1370 1000s. Mulberry Harbour floating bridge . . . . . 1·50 2·00
MS1371 105 × 76 mm. 2500s. Aerial view of Mulberry Harbour . . 4·75 5·50

1994. "Philakorea '94" International Stamp Exhibition, Seoul. As T **286a** of St. Vincent, but vert. Multicoloured.

1372 100s. Sari Pagoda, Paekyangsa 10 10
1373 350s. Ch'omsongdae 50 60
1374 1000s. Pulguksa Temple . . 1·40 2·00
MS1375 76 × 106 mm. 2500s. Bronze mural, Pagoda Park, Seoul . . 3·00 3·50

153 Ugandan family

1994. International Year of the Family.

1376 **153** 100s. multicoloured . . . 40 20

154 Baby Simba

1994. "The Lion King". Characters from Walt Disney's cartoon film. Multicoloured.

1377 100s. Type **154** 30 30
1378 100s. Mufasa, Simba and Sarabi 30 30
1379 100s. Young Simba and Nala 30 30
1380 100s. Timon 30 30
1381 100s. Rafiki 30 30
1382 100s. Pumbaa 30 30
1383 100s. The Hyenas 30 30
1384 100s. Scar 30 30
1385 100s. Zazu 30 30
1386 200s. Rafiki and Mufasa . . 35 35
1387 200s. Rafiki holding Simba with Mufasa and Sarabi 35 35
1388 200s. Rafiki holding Simba aloft 35 35
1389 200s. Scar and Zazu 35 35
1390 200s. Rafiki having vision 35 35
1391 200s. Simba and Scar . . . 35 35
1392 200s. Simba and Nala . . . 35 35
1393 200s. Simba with mane of leaves 35 35
1394 200s. Simba, Nala and Zazu 35 35
1395 250s. Scar and Simba . . . 40 40
1396 250s. Mufasa rescues Simba 40 40
1397 250s. Scar killing Mufasa . . 40 40
1398 250s. Simba falling off cliff 40 40
1399 250s. Timon, Pumbaa and Simba at pool 40 40
1400 250s. Simba, Timon and Pumbaa 40 40
1401 250s. Rafiki with staff . . . 40 40
1402 250s. Simba and Nala . . . 40 40
1403 250s. Simba looking into pool 40 40
MS1404 Three sheets. (a) 127 × 94 mm. 2500s. Jungle animals. (b) 127 × 102 mm. 2500s. Simba and Timon on branch. (c) 127 × 94 mm. 2500s. Simba with parents and Rafiki (vert) Set of 3 sheets . . . . 13·00 14·00

1994. Centenary (1992) of Sierra Club (environmental protection society). Endangered Species. As T **276a** of Sierra Leone. Multicoloured. (a) Vert designs.

1405 100s. Chimpanzee with arms folded 60 55
1406 200s. Head of chimpanzee 80 80
1407 250s. Head of African wild dog 80 80
1408 300s. Head of cheetah . . . 80 90
1409 500s. Geleda baboon . . . 90 1·00
1410 600s. Geleda baboon from back . . . . 1·00 1·10
1411 800s. Head of Grevy's zebra 1·10 1·25
1412 1000s. Geleda baboon sitting on rock . . . . 1·25 1·40

(b) Horiz designs.

1413 200s. Pair of cheetahs . . . 80 90
1414 250s. Cheetah cubs 80 90
1415 300s. African wild dog at rest . . . . 90 1·00
1416 500s. Head of African wild dog . . . . 1·00 1·10
1417 600s. Grevy's zebra . . . . 1·10 1·25
1418 800s. Chimpanzee lying down . . . . 1·25 1·40
1419 1000s. Grevy's zebra feeding 1·40 1·50

155 Terminal Building, Entebbe International Airport

1994. 50th Anniv of I.C.A.O. Mult.

1420 100s. Type **155** 90 20
1421 250s. Control tower, Entebbe International Airport . . . . 1·60 1·10

156 Game Poachers **157** "Adoration of the Christ Child" (Filippino Lippi)

1994. Ecology. Multicoloured.

1422 100s. Type **156** 50 10
1423 250s. Villagers at rubbish dump 90 45
1424 350s. Fishermen . . . . . . 1·25 1·25
1425 500s. Deforestation . . . . 1·90 2·25

1994. Christmas. Religious Paintings. Multicoloured.

1426 100s. Type **157** 30 10
1427 200s. "The Holy Family rests on the Flight into Egypt" (Annibale Carracci) 50 30
1428 300s. "Madonna with Christ Child and St. John" (Piero di Cosimo) 70 40
1429 350s. "The Conestabile Madonna" (Raphael) . . 80 65
1430 450s. "Madonna and Child with Angels" (after Antonio Rossellino) . . . 90 1·00
1431 500s. "Madonna and Child with St. John" (Raphael) 1·00 1·00
1432 900s. "Madonna and Child" (Luca Signorelli) . . . . 2·00 2·50
1433 1000s. "Madonna with the Child Jesus, St. John and an Angel" (pseudo Pier Francesco Fiorentino) . . 2·00 2·50
MS1434 Two sheets, each 115 × 95 mm. (a) 2500s. "The Madonna of the Magnificat" (detail) (Sandro Botticelli). (b) 2500s. "Adoration of the Magi" (detail) (Fra Angelico and Filippo Lippi) Set of 2 sheets . . . . 9·00 10·00

No. 1426 is inscribed "Fillipino" in error.

158 "Self-portrait" (Tintoretto)

1995. 400th Death Anniv (1994) of Jacopo Tintoretto (painter). Multicoloured.

1435 100s. Type **158** 25 10
1436 300s. "A Philosopher" . . . 65 45
1437 400s. "The Creation of the Animals" (detail) (horiz) 80 80
1438 450s. "The Feast of Belshazzar" (detail) (horiz) 85 85
1439 500s. "The Raising of the Brazen Serpent" 95 95
1440 1000s. "Elijah fed by the Angel" . . . . 1·90 2·50
MS1441 Two sheets. (a) 114 × 124 mm. 2000s. "Moses striking Water from a Rock" (detail). (b) 124 × 114 mm. 200s. "Finding of Moses" (detail) Set of 2 sheets . . . . 8·00 9·00

159 White-faced Whistling Duck ("White-faced Tree-duck")

1995. Waterfowl and Wetland Birds of Uganda. Multicoloured.

1442 200s. Type **159** 65 65
1443 200s. Common shoveler ("European Shoveler") . . 65 65
1444 200s. Hartlaub's duck . . . 65 65
1445 200s. Verreaux's eagle owl ("Milky Eagle-owl") . . . 65 65
1446 200s. Pied avocet ("Avocet") 65 65
1447 200s. African fish eagle . . 65 65
1448 200s. Spectacled weaver . . 65 65
1449 200s. Black-headed gonolek 65 65
1450 200s. Great crested grebe . . 65 65
1451 200s. Red-knobbed coot . . 65 65
1452 200s. Woodland kingfisher 65 65
1453 200s. Pintail 65 65
1454 200s. Squacco heron 65 65
1455 200s. Purple swamphen ("Purple Gallinule") . . . 65 65
1456 200s. African darter 65 65
1457 200s. African jacana 65 65
MS1458 Two sheets, each 106 × 76 mm. (a) 2500s. African pygmy goose. (b) 2500s. Fulvous whistling duck ("Fulvous Tree-duck") Set of 2 sheets . . . . 8·50 9·50

Nos. 1442/57 were printed together, se-tenant, forming a composite design.

1995. 18th World Scout Jamboree, Netherlands. Nos. 701/4 optd or surch **18th World Scout Jamboree Mondial, Holland, August 1995**.

1459 100s. Scouts making bricks 20 10
1460 450s. on 70s. Poultry keeping 85 55
1461 800s. on 90s. Scout on crutches leading family to immunization centre . . . 1·40 1·60
1462 1500s. on 10s. Type **104** . . 2·25 2·75
MS1463 115 × 76 mm. 2500s. on 1200s. Lord Baden-Powell, W. Boyce and Revd. L. Hadley 4·00 4·75

1995. 50th Anniv of End of Second World War in Europe. As T **296a** of St. Vincent. Multicoloured.

1464 500s. Soviet artillery in action . . . . 1·10 1·10
1465 500s. Soviet tanks on the Moltke Bridge . . . . . 1·10 1·10
1466 500s. Kaiser Wilhelm Memorial Church, Berlin 1·10 1·10
1467 500s. Soviet tanks and Brandenburg Gate . . . 1·10 1·10
1468 500s. U.S. Boeing B-17 Flying Fortress . . . . . 1·10 1·10
1469 500s. Soviet tanks enter Berlin . . . . 1·10 1·10
1470 500s. Ruins of the Chancellery . . . . 1·10 1·10
1471 500s. The Reichstag on fire 1·10 1·10
MS1472 104 × 74 mm. 2500s. Hoisting the Soviet flag on the Reichstag (57 × 42½ mm) . . . 4·75 5·00

161 Dove, Child, Dish Aerial, Food and Emblem **161a** Woman peeling Maize

1995. 50th Anniv of United Nations. Multicoloured.

1473 450s. Type **161** 55 45
1474 1000s. Hands releasing bird and insects . . . . . . 1·50 2·25
MS1475 100 × 70 mm. 2000s. Child's hand holding adult's finger (horiz) 2·50 3·25

1995. 50th Anniv of F.A.O. Multicoloured.

1476 350s. Type **161a** 55 75
1477 500s. Woman and child with maize 65 85
1478 1000s. Woman and baby with maize . . . . 80 1·10
MS1479 100 × 70 mm. 2000s. Child and head of cow . . . . . . 2·50 3·25

Nos. 1476/8 were printed together, se-tenant, forming a composite design.

1995. 90th Anniv of Rotary International. As T **299** of St. Vincent, but vert. Multicoloured.

1480 2000s. Paul Harris (founder) and logo . . . . 2·00 2·75
MS1481 70 × 100 mm. 2000s. National flag and logo . . . . 2·25 3·00

1995. 95th Birthday of Queen Elizabeth the Queen Mother. As T **299a** of St. Vincent. Multicoloured.

1482 500s. brown, light brown and black . . . . 1·90 1·90
1483 500s. multicoloured . . . . 1·90 1·90
1484 500s. multicoloured . . . . 1·90 1·90
1485 500s. multicoloured . . . . 1·90 1·90
MS1486 102 × 127 mm. 2500s. multicoloured . . . . 5·50 5·50

DESIGNS: No. 1482, Queen Elizabeth the Queen Mother (pastel drawing); 1483, With bouquet of flowers; 1484, At desk (oil painting); 1485, Wearing turquoise-blue dress; **MS**1466, Wearing pale blue dress.

162 Australian Flag in Form of "VJ"

1995. 50th Anniv of End of Second World War in the Pacific. Designs showing national flags as "VJ".

1487 **162** 600s. red, violet and black . . . . 1·25 1·25
1488 – 600s. red, violet and black . . . . 1·25 1·25
1489 – 600s. red, violet and black . . . . 1·25 1·25
1490 – 600s. multicoloured . . . 1·25 1·25
1491 – 600s. red, orange and black . . . . 1·25 1·25
1492 – 600s. red and black . . . . 1·25 1·25
MS1493 108 × 76 mm. 2500s. multicoloured . . . . 5·00 5·50

DESIGNS: No. 1488, Great Britain; 1489, New Zealand; 1490, United States of America; 1491, People's Republic of China; 1492, Canada; **MS**1493, American soldier and Flag.

163 Velociraptor

1995. Prehistoric Animals. Multicoloured.

1494 150s. Type **163** 85 65
1495 200s. Head of psittacosaurus 85 65
1496 300s. Archaeopteryx (vert) 1·00 1·00
1497 300s. Quetzalcoatlus and volcano (vert) . . . . . . 1·00 1·00
1498 300s. Pteranodon and volcano (vert) . . . . . . 1·00 1·00
1499 300s. Brachiosaurus (vert) 1·00 1·00
1500 300s. Tsintaosaur (vert) . . 1·00 1·00
1501 300s. Allosaur (vert) . . . . 1·00 1·00
1502 300s. Tyrannosaurus (vert) 1·00 1·00
1503 300s. Apatosaur (vert) . . . 1·00 1·00
1504 300s. Giant dragonfly (vert) 1·00 1·00
1505 300s. Dimorphodon (vert) 1·00 1·00
1506 300s. Triceratops (vert) . . . 1·00 1·00
1507 300s. Compsognathus (vert) 1·00 1·00
1508 350s. Head of dilophosaurus 1·10 1·10
1509 400s. Kentrosaurus . . . . 1·25 1·25
1510 500s. Stegosaurus . . . . . 1·40 1·40
1511 1500s. Pterodaustro . . . . 2·50 3·00
MS1512 Two sheets, each 106 × 75 mm. (a) 2000s. Head of parasaurolophus. (b) 2000s. Head of shunosaurus Set of 2 sheets 7·50 8·00

Nos. 1496/1507 were printed together, se-tenant, forming a composite design.

No. 1502 is inscribed "Tyranosaur" and No. 1506 "Tricreatops", both in error.

164 Rough-scaled Bush Viper **165** Bell's Hinged Tortoise

1995. Reptiles. Multicoloured.

1513 50s. Type **164** 10 10
1514 100s. Pygmy python . . . 10 10
1515 150s. Three-horned chameleon 10 15
1516 200s. African rock python 15 20
1516a 300s. Armadillo girdled lizard 25 30
1517 350s. Nile monitor 25 30
1518 400s. Savannah monitor . . 30 35
1519 450s. Bush viper 35 40
1520 500s. Nile crocodile 40 45
1520a 600s. Spotted sandveld lizard 45 50
1521 700s. Type **165** 55 60
1521a 700s. Bell's hinged tortoise 55 60
1522 900s. Rhinoceros viper . . 70 75
1523 1000s. Gabon viper 75 80
1524 2000s. Spitting cobra . . . 1·50 1·60
1525 3000s. Leopard tortoise . . 2·25 2·40
1526 4000s. Puff adder . . . . 3·00 3·25

1527 5000s. Common house gecko . . . . 3·75 4·00
1528 6000s. Dwarf chameleon 4·50 4·75
1529 10000s. Boomslang (snake) 7·75 8·00
SIZES—21 × 21 mm: 50, 100, 150, 200, 350, 400, 450, 500s.; 18 × 20 mm: 300, 600, 700s. (No. 1521a); 38½ × 24½ mm: 700s. (No. 1521), 900s. to 10000s.

166 Nsambya Church

1995. Local Anniversaries. Multicoloured.
1530 150s. Type **166** 45 20
1531 450s. Namilyango College 90 70
1532 500s. Figures with symbolic wheel 95 75
1533 1000s. Volunteers with food sacks . . . . 1·75 2·50
ANNIVERSARIES: Nos. 1530/1, Centenary of Mill Hill Missionaries in Uganda; 1532, Centenary of International Co-operative Alliance; 1533, 25th anniv of U.N. volunteers.

167 Bwindi Forest

1995. Landscapes. Multicoloured.
1534 50s. Type **167** 25 20
1535 100s. Karamoja 30 20
1536 450s. Sunset, Lake Mburo National Park 80 70
1537 500s. Sunset, Gulu District 85 75
1538 900s. Mist, Kabale District 1·50 2·00
1539 1000s. Ruwenzori Mountains . . . . 1·60 2·00

1995. Waterfalls. As T **167**. Multicoloured.
1540 50s. Sipi Falls (vert) 25 20
1541 100s. Murchison Falls . . . 30 20
1542 450s. Bujagali Falls 80 70
1543 500s. The Two Falls at Murchison 85 75
1544 900s. Falls, Ruwenzori Mountains (vert) . . . . 1·50 2·00
1545 1000s. Falls, Ruwenzori Mountains (different) (vert) . . . . 1·60 2·00

168 Peter Rono (1500 m), 1988

1995. Olympic Games, Atlanta (1996). Multicoloured.
1546 50s. Type **168** 20 10
1547 350s. Reiner Klimke (dressage), 1984 . . . . . 90 40
1548 450s. German team (cycling time trials), 1988 . . . . 1·75 70
1549 500s. Grace Birungi (athlete) 90 70
1550 900s. Francis Ogola (athlete) 1·40 1·75
1551 1000s. Nyakana Godfrey (boxer) . . . . 1·50 1·75
MS1552 Two sheets, each 106 × 76 mm. (a) 2500s. Sebastian Coe (1500 metres), 1980 and 1984. (b) 2500s. Rolf Dannenberg (discus), 1984 (vert) Set of 2 sheets 7·00 8·00

169 Common Peafowl ("Peafowl")

1995. Domestic Animals. Multicoloured.
1553 200s. Type **169** 55 55
1554 200s. Pouter pigeon 55 55
1555 200s. Feral rock dove ("Rock Doves") 55 55
1556 200s. Mallard ("Rouen Duck") 55 55
1557 200s. Guineafowl 55 55
1558 200s. Donkey 55 55
1559 200s. Shetland ponies . . . 55 55
1560 200s. Palomino horse . . . 55 55
1561 200s. Pigs 55 55
1562 200s. Border collie 55 55
1563 200s. Merino sheep 55 55
1564 200s. Milch goat 55 55
1565 200s. Black dutch rabbit . . 55 55
1566 200s. Lop rabbit 55 55
1567 200s. Somali cat 55 55
1568 200s. Asian cat 55 55
MS1569 Two sheets, each 106 × 76 mm. (a) 2500s. Saddle-bred horses. (b) 2500s. Oxen Set of 2 sheets . . . . 8·50 8·50
Nos. 1553/68 were printed together, se-tenant, forming a composite design.

170 Scouts putting Child on Scales

171 Hermann Staudinger (1953 Chemistry)

1995. Uganda Boy Scouts in the Community. Multicoloured.
1570 150s. Type **170** 50 20
1571 350s. Scouts carrying children 85 45
1572 450s. Checking health cards (horiz) 95 70
1573 800s. Holding child for immunization (horiz) . . 1·75 2·00
1574 1000s. Weighing child before immunization . . . . . . 1·90 2·25

1995. Centenary of Nobel Prize Trust Fund. Multicoloured.
1575 300s. Type **171** 75 75
1576 300s. Fritz Haber (1918 Chemistry) 75 75
1577 300s. Bert Sakmann (1991 Medicine) 75 75
1578 300s. Adolf Windaus (1926 Chemistry) 75 75
1579 300s. Wilhelm Wien (1911 Physics) 75 75
1580 300s. Ernest Hemingway (1954 Literature) 75 75
1581 300s. Richard Willstatter (1915 Chemistry) 75 75
1582 300s. Stanley Cohen (1986 Medicine) 75 75
1583 300s. Hans Jensen (1963 Physics) 75 75
1584 300s. Otto Warburg (1931 Medicine) 75 75
1585 300s. Heinrich Wieland (1927 Chemistry) 75 75
1586 300s. Albrecht Kossel (1910 Medicine) 75 75
1587 300s. Hideki Yukawa (1949 Physics) 75 75
1588 300s. F. W. de Klerk (1993 Peace) 75 75
1589 300s. Nelson Mandela (1993 Peace) 75 75
1590 300s. Odysseus Elytis (1979 Literature) 75 75
1591 300s. Ferdinand Buisson (1927 Peace) 75 75
1592 300s. Lev Landau (1962 Physics) 75 75
1593 300s. Halldor Laxness (1955 Literature) 75 75
1594 300s. Wole Soyinka (1986 Literature) 75 75
1595 300s. Desmond Tutu (1984 Peace) 75 75
1596 300s. Susumu Tonegawa (1987 Medicine) 75 75
1597 300s. Louis de Broglie (1929 Physics) 75 75
1598 300s. George Seferis (1963 Literature) 75 75
MS1599 Two sheets, each 105 × 76 mm. (a) 2000s. Nelley Sachs (1966 Literature). (b) 2000s. Werner Forssmann (1956 Medicine) Set of 2 sheets . . . 8·00 8·50
Nos. 1575/86 and 1587/98 respectively were printed together, se-tenant, forming composite designs.

1995. Christmas. Religious Paintings. As T **281a** of Sierra Leone. Multicoloured.
1600 150s. "The Virgin and Child" (Holbein the Younger) 40 20
1601 350s. "Madonna" (Procaccini) 70 35
1602 500s. "The Virgin and Child" (Pisanello) 95 50
1603 1000s. "Madonna and Child" (Crivelli) . . . . . 1·75 2·00
1604 1500s. "The Nativity of the Virgin" (Le Nain) . . . . 2·25 3·00
MS1605 Two sheets, each 102 × 127 mm. (a) 2500s. "Madonna and Child" (detail) (Bellini). (b) 2500s. "The Holy Family" (detail) (Andrea del Sarto) Set of 2 sheets . . . . . 8·50 8·50

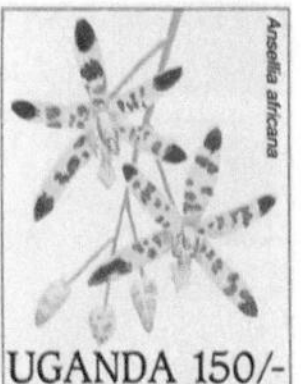

172 "Ansellia africana"

1995. Orchids. Multicoloured.
1606 150s. Type **172** 60 40
1607 350s. "Aerangis iuteoalba" 75 75
1608 350s. "Satyrium sacculatum" 75 75
1609 350s. "Bolusiella maudiae" 75 75
1610 350s. "Habenaria attenuata" 75 75
1611 350s. "Cyrtorchis arcuata" 75 75
1612 350s. "Eulophia angolensis" 75 75
1613 350s. "Tridactyle bicaudata" 75 75
1614 350s. "Eulophia horsfallii" 75 75
1615 350s. "Diaphananthe fragrantissima" 75 75
1616 450s. "Satyricum crassicaule" 85 85
1617 500s. "Polystachya cultriformis" 90 90
1618 800s. "Disa erubescens" . . 1·40 1·60
MS1619 Two sheets, each 66 × 76 mm. (a) 2500s. "Rangaeris amaniensis". (b) 2500s. "Diaphananthe pulchella" Set of 2 sheets . . . . 8·50 9·00

173 Rat and Purple Grapes

1996. Chinese New Year ("Year of the Rat"). Multicoloured.
1620 350s. Type **173** 50 55
1621 350s. Rat and radishes . . . 50 55
1622 350s. Rat eating corn . . . 50 55
1623 350s. Rat eating cucumber 50 55
MS1624 100 × 74 mm. Nos. 1620/3 1·25 1·60
MS1625 106 × 76 mm. 2000s. Rat and green grapes . . . . . . 2·50 3·00

174 Wild Dog and Pup

1996. Wildlife of Uganda. Multicoloured. (a) Horiz designs.
1626 150s. Type **174** 50 35
1627 200s. African fish eagle . . 55 40
1628 250s. Hippopotamus 55 40
1629 350s. Leopard 55 50
1630 400s. Lion 55 60
1631 450s. Lioness 60 65
1632 500s. Meerkats 60 65
1633 550s. Pair of black rhinoceroses 85 85

(b) Vert designs.
1634 150s. Gorilla 50 35
1635 200s. Cheetah 50 40
1636 250s. African elephant . . . 70 45
1637 350s. Thomson's gazelle . . 55 50
1638 400s. Crowned crane . . . 70 60
1639 450s. Saddlebill 70 70
1640 500s. Vulture 70 70
1641 550s. Zebra 70 80
MS1642 Two sheets. (a) 72 × 102 mm. 200s. Grey heron (horiz). (b) 102 × 72 mm. 2000s. Giraffe Set of 2 sheets . . . . 6·00 7·00

175 Mickey Mouse and Goofy on Platform at Calais

1996. Mickey's Orient Express. Walt Disney Cartoon Characters. Multicoloured.
1643 50s. Type **175** 35 30
1644 100s. Mickey and Goofy at Athens 45 30
1645 150s. Mickey showing Donald Duck his Pullman ticket 60 30
1646 200s. Daisy and Donald Duck in Pullman car . . 75 30
1647 250s. Mickey and Minnie Mouse in dining car . . . 80 40
1648 300s. Goofy as guard assisting Mickey and Minnie 90 50
1649 600s. Mickey and Donald preparing for bed . . . . 1·75 2·00
1650 700s. Mickey and Minnie at Orient Express accident, Frankfurt, 1901 . . . . . 1·90 2·25
1651 800s. Mickey and Goofy building snowman and Orient Express in snowdrift, 1929 . . . . . 2·00 2·25
1652 900s. Disney characters filming "Murder on the Orient Express" . . . . . 2·25 2·50
MS1653 Two sheets, each 132 × 106 mm. (a) 2500s. Donald driving Orient Express. (b) 2500s. Mickey, Minnie and Goofy on Observation platform Set of 2 sheets . . . . 9·50 11·00

176 "Autumn Pond"

178 "Coprinus disseminatus"

177 Tomb Mural, Xi'an (½-size illustration)

1996. "CHINA '96" 9th Asian International Stamp Exhibition, Peking. Paintings by Qi Baishi. Multicoloured.
1654 50s. Type **176** 30 20
1655 100s. "Partridge and Smartweed" 40 20
1656 150s. "Begonias and Mynah" 50 30
1657 200s. "Chrysanthemums, Cocks and Hens" 50 30
1658 250s. "Crabs" 50 30
1659 300s. "Wisterias and Bee" 65 60
1660 350s. "Smartweed and Ink-drawn Butterflies" 70 70
1661 400s. "Lotus and Mandarin Ducks" 75 75
1662 450s. "Lichees and Locust" 85 85
1663 500s. "Millet and Praying Mantis" 90 90
MS1664 135 × 114 mm. 800s. "Morning Glories and Locust" (50 × 38 mm); 800s. "Shrimps" (50 × 38 mm) . . . . 6·00 6·50
The painting titles on 150s. and 200s. are transposed in error, with "CHRYSANTHEMUMS" shown as "RYSANTHEMUMS".

1996. "CHINA '96" 9th Asian International Stamp Exhibition, Peking (2nd issue). Sheet 140 × 90 mm.
MS1664a **177** 500s. multicoloured 2·00 2·00

1996. African Fungi. Multicoloured.
1665 150s. Type **178** 50 50
1666 300s. "Coprinus radians" . . 60 60
1667 350s. "Hygrophorus coccineus" 60 60
1668 400s. "Marasmius siccus" 70 70
1669 450s. "Cortinarius collinitus" 80 80
1670 500s. "Cortinarius cinnabarinus" 80 80
1671 550s. "Coltricia cinnamomea" 85 90
1672 1000s. "Mutinus elegans" 1·50 1·75
MS1673 Two sheets, each 110 × 80 mm. (a) 2500s. "Inocybe sororia". (b) 2500s. "Flammulina velutipes" Set of 2 sheets . . . 6·50 7·00

179 "Catopsilia philea"

1996. Butterflies. Multicoloured.
1674 50s. Type **179** 45 50
1675 100s. "Dione vanillae" . . . 45 50
1676 150s. "Metamorpha dido" 55 60
1677 200s. "Papilio sesostris" . . 60 65
1678 250s. "Papilio neophilus" . . 60 65
1679 300s. "Papilio thoas" . . . 60 65
1680 350s. "Diorina periander" 65 70
1681 400s. "Morpho cipris" . . . 65 70
1682 450s. "Catonephele numilia" 70 75
1683 500s. "Heliconius doris" . . 70 75
1684 550s. "Prepona antimache" 70 75
1685 600s. "Eunica alcmena" . . 75 80
MS1686 Two sheets, each 100 × 70 mm. (a) 2500s. "Caligo martia" (b) 2500s. "Heliconius doris" (different) Set of 2 sheets 6·50 7·00

1996. 70th Birthday of Queen Elizabeth II. As T **323a** of St. Vincent. Different photographs. Multicoloured.
1687 500s. Queen Elizabeth II . . 1·40 1·40
1688 500s. In evening dress . . . 1·40 1·40
1689 500s. Wearing red coat and hat . . . . 1·40 1·40
MS1690 125 × 103 mm. 2000s. Queen Elizabeth II . . . . . . 4·50 4·50

179a Asian Children

1996. 50th Anniv of UNICEF. Multicoloured.
1691 450s. Type **179a** . . . . . 90 1·00
1692 500s. South American children . . . . 1·00 1·10
1693 550s. Boy holding pencil . . 1·10 1·25
MS1694 74 × 104 mm. 2000s. African mother and child . . . 2·75 3·50

179b Darien National Park, Panama

1996. 50th Anniv of UNESCO. Multicoloured.
1695 450s. Type **179b** . . . . . 1·00 1·10
1696 500s. Los Glaciares National Park, Argentina . . . . . 1·10 1·25
1697 550s. Tubbatha Reef Marine Park, Philippines . . . . 1·25 1·40
MS1698 104 × 74 mm. 2500s. Ruwenzori Mountains National Park, Uganda . . . . 4·00 4·50
No. **MS**1698 is inscribed "RWENZORI" in error.

180 Statue of Menorah, Knesset

1996. 3000th Anniv of Jerusalem. T **180** and similar vert designs. Multicoloured.
MS1699 114 × 95 mm. 300s. Type **180**, 500s. Jerusalem Theatre. 1000s. Israel Museum 3·50 3·50
MS1700 104 × 74 mm. 2000s. Grotto of the Nativity . . . . 3·50 3·50

1996. Centenary of Radio. Entertainers. As T **326** of St. Vincent. Multicoloured.
1701 200s. Ella Fitzgerald 35 20
1702 300s. Bob Hope 70 40
1703 500s. Nat "King" Cole . . . 80 70
1704 800s. George Burns and Gracie Allen . . . . 1·25 1·50
MS1705 74 × 104 mm. 2000s. Jimmy Durante . . . . 3·00 3·25

181 Electric Locomotive, 1968 (Japan)

1996. Railway Locomotives. Multicoloured.
1706 450s. Type **181** 90 90
1707 450s. Stephenson's "Rocket", 1829 . . . . . 90 90
1708 450s. William Norris's "Austria", 1843 . . . . . 90 90
1709 450s. Early American steam locomotive 90 90
1710 450s. Steam locomotive, 1947 (India) 90 90
1711 450s. Class 103 electric locomotive (Germany) . . 90 90
1712 550s. GWR steam locomotive "Lady of Lynn" (England) 90 90
1713 550s. Steam locomotive, 1930 (China) 90 90
1714 550s. Meyer-Kitson steam locomotive (Chile) 90 90
1715 550s. Union Pacific "Centennial" diesel locomotive No. 6900 (U.S.A.) 90 90
1716 550s. Type 581 diesel locomotive (Japan) . . . 90 90
1717 550s. Class 120 electric locomotive (Germany) . . 90 90
MS1718 Two sheets, each 106 × 76 mm. (a) 2500s. Type 99 steam locomotive (Germany); (b) 2500s. LNER Class A4 steam locomotive "Mallard", Great Britain Set of 2 sheets . . . . 7·50 8·00

182 Postal and Telecommunications Corporation Emblem

1996. Centenary of Postal Services. Multicoloured.
1719 150s. Type **182** 25 20
1720 450s. Loading postbus . . . 1·25 1·25
1721 500s. Modern postal transportation . . . . . 1·50 1·50
1722 550s. 1896 25c. violet and 1r. black stamps . . . . . 1·50 1·75

183 Two American River Steamers and 1904 Games, St. Louis

1996. Olympic Games, Atlanta (1st issue). Multicoloured.
1723 350s. Type **183** 80 45
1724 450s. George Finnegan (U.S.A.) (boxing), 1904 85 65
1725 500s. Chariot racing 95 85
1726 800s. John Flanagan (U.S.A.) (hammer), 1904 (vert) . . . . 1·40 1·75
See also Nos. 1764/81.

184 Mango **185** Traditional Costumes from Western Uganda

1996. Fruit. Multicoloured.
1727 150s. Type **184** 35 20
1728 350s. Orange 75 50
1729 450s. Pawpaw 85 75
1730 500s. Avocado 90 85
1731 550s. Watermelon (horiz) . . 1·00 1·10

1996. Christmas. Religious Paintings. As T **337** of St. Vincent. Multicoloured.
1732 150s. "Annunciation" (Lorenzo di Credi) . . . 40 20
1733 350s. "Madonna of the Loggia" (detail) (Botticelli) 80 40
1734 400s. "Virgin in Glory with Child and Angels" (Lorenzetti) 85 60
1735 450s. "Adoration of the Child" (Lippi) 90 80
1736 500s. "Madonna of the Loggia" (Botticelli) . . . 1·00 1·00
1737 550s. "The Strength" (Botticelli) . . . . 1·10 1·50
MS1738 Two sheets, each 106 × 76 mm. (a) 2500s. "Holy Allegory" (Bellini) (horiz); (b) 2500s. "The Virgin on the Throne with Child and the Saints" (ghirlandaio) (horiz) Set of 2 sheets . . . . 7·50 8·00

1996. 20th Anniv of "Rocky" (film). Sheet 143 × 182 mm, containing vert design as T **338** of St. Vincent. Multicoloured.
MS1739 800s. × 3 Sylvester Stallone in "Rocky III" . . . . 4·00 5·00

1997. Traditional Costumes. Multicoloured.
1740 150s. Type **185** 40 20
1741 300s. Acholi headdress . . . 75 80
1742 300s. Alur headdress 75 80
1743 300s. Bwola dance headdress 75 80
1744 300s. Madi headdress . . . 75 80
1745 300s. Karimojong headdress with plume 75 80
1746 300s. Karimojong headdress with two feathers 75 80
1747 350s. Karimojong women 80 65
1748 450s. Ganda traditional dress (horiz) 90 90
1749 500s. Acholi traditional dress (horiz) 95 95

186 Ox

1997. Chinese New Year ("Year of the Ox"). Multicoloured.
1750 350s. Type **186** 65 75
1751 350s. Cow suckling calf . . 65 75
1752 350s. Cow and calf lying down 65 75
1753 350s. Ox lying down 65 75
MS1754 111 × 83 mm. Nos. 1750/3 2·40 2·75
MS1755 76 × 106 mm. 1500s. Young calf (vert) . . . . 2·40 2·75

187 Giraffe running

1997. Endangered Species. Rothschild's Giraffe. Multicoloured.
1756 300s. Type **187** 80 80
1757 300s. Two adult giraffes . . 80 80
1758 300s. Head of giraffe . . . 80 80
1759 300s. Giraffe with calf . . . 80 80
MS1760 75 × 109 mm. 2500s. Head of giraffe (different) (horiz) . . 5·00 5·00

188 "The Constitution" on Open Book

1997. Promulgation of New Constitution (8 Oct 1995). Multicoloured.
1761 150s. Type **188** 40 20
1762 350s. "The Constitution" on scroll 75 50
1763 550s. "THE CONSTITUTION" on closed book (vert) . . . . 1·25 1·50

189 Kitel Son (Japan) (marathon), 1936 **190** "Red Plum Blossom and Daffodil"

1997. Olympic Games, Atlanta (2nd issue). Previous Gold Medal Winners. Multicoloured.
1764 150s. Type **189** 50 60
1765 150s. Bob Hayes (U.S.A.) (100 m), 1964 . . . . . . 50 60
1766 200s. Walter Davis (U.S.A.) (high jump), 1952 . . . . 55 65
1767 200s. Rod Milburn (110 m hurdles), 1972 . . 55 65
1768 250s. Matthes (swimming), 1968 . . . . 60 70
1769 250s. Filbert Bayi (Tanzania) (athletics), 1976 . . . . 60 70
1770 300s. Akii Bua (Uganda) (400 m hurdles), 1972 . . 65 75
1771 300s. H. Kipchoge Keino (Kenya) (steeplechase), 1972 . . . . 65 75
1772 350s. Nordwig (Germany) (pole vault), 1972 . . . . 70 80
1773 350s. Ron Ray (U.S.A.) (athletics), 1976 . . . . . 70 80
1774 400s. Wilma Rudolph (U.S.A.) (100 m relay), 1960 . . . . 75 85
1775 400s. Joe Frazer (U.S.A.) (boxing), 1976 . . . . . 75 85
1776 450s. Abebe Bikila (Ethiopia) (marathon), 1964 . . . . 80 90
1777 450s. Carl Lewis (U.S.A.) (100 m), 1984 . . . . . . 80 90
1778 500s. Edwin Moses (U.S.A.) (400 m hurdles), 1984 . . 85 95
1779 500s. Gisela Mauermayer (Germany) (discus), 1936 85 95
1780 550s. Rady Williams (U.S.A.) (long jump), 1972 . . . . 90 1·00
1781 550s. Dietmar Mogenburg (Germany) (high jump), 1984 . . . . 90 1·00

Nos. 1764, 1766, 1768, 1770, 1772, 1774, 1776, 1778 and 1780 and 1765, 1767, 1769, 1771, 1773, 1775, 1777, 1779 and 1781 respectively were printed together, se-tenant, with the backgrounds forming composite designs.

No. 1769 is incorrectly inscribed "Eiilbert" and is dated "1976"; Filbert Bayi did not participate in the 1976 Games. No. 1779 is incorrectly inscribed "Mauemayer" and wrongly identifies the event as the shotput.

1997. "HONG KONG '97" International Stamp Exhibition. Paintings by Wu Changshuo. Mult.
1782 50s. Type **190** 30 40
1783 100s. "Peony" 40 45
1784 150s. "Rosaceae" 50 55
1785 200s. "Pomegranate" . . . 55 60
1786 250s. "Peach, Peony and Plum Blossom" 55 60
1787 300s. "Calyx Canthus" . . . 60 65
1788 350s. "Chrysanthemum" . . 60 65
1789 400s. "Calabash" 65 70
1790 450s. "Chrysanthemum" (different) 70 75
1791 500s. "Cypress Tree" . . . 70 75
MS1792 137 × 105 mm. 550s. "Litchi" (50 × 37 mm); 1000s. "Water Lily" (50 × 37 mm). . . 2·50 3·00

191 Woody

1997. Disney's "Toy Story" (cartoon film). Multicoloured.
1793 100s. Type **191** 55 55
1794 100s. Buzz Lightyear . . . 55 55
1795 100s. Bo Peep 55 55
1796 100s. Hamm 55 55
1797 100s. Slinky 55 55

1798 100s. Rex 55 55
1799 150s. Woody on bed (horiz) 65 65
1800 150s. Woody at microphone (horiz) 65 65
1801 150s. Bo Peep (horiz) . . . 65 65
1802 150s. Buzz Lightyear (horiz) 65 65
1803 150s. Slinky and Rex (horiz) 65 65
1804 150s. Woody hiding (horiz) 65 65
1805 150s. "Halt! Who goes there" (horiz) 65 65
1806 150s. Rex, Slinky and Buzz Lightyear (horiz) 65 65
1807 150s. "You're just an action figure!" (horiz) 65 65
1808 200s. "I'm the only sheriff in these parts" (horiz) . . . 65 65
1809 200s. Green toy soldiers (horiz) 65 65
1810 200s. Woody and Buzz (horiz) 65 65
1811 200s. Woody pointing (horiz) 65 65
1812 200s. Buzz Lightyear (horiz) 65 65
1813 200s. Green aliens (horiz) 65 65
1814 200s. "This is an intergalactic emergency" (horiz) 65 65
1815 200s. Buzz and Woody argue (horiz) 65 65
1816 200s. Buzz and Woody in buggy (horiz) 65 65
MS1817 Three sheets, each 133 × 108 mm. (a) 133 × 108 mm. 2000s. Woody; (b) 108 × 133 mm. 2000s. Buzz Lightyear, Rex and other toys; (c) 2000s. Buzz Lightyear Set of 3 sheets . . . 15·00 15·00

192 "Pioneer 10"

1997. Space Exploration. Multicoloured.
1818 250s. Type **192** 70 75
1819 250s. "Voyager 1" 70 75
1820 250s. "Viking Orbiter" . . . 70 75
1821 250s. "Pioneer – Venus 1" 70 75
1822 250s. "Mariner 9" 70 75
1823 250s. "Galileo" Entry Probe 70 75
1824 250s. "Mariner 10" 70 75
1825 250s. "Voyager 2" 70 75
1826 300s. "Sputnik 1" 70 75
1827 300s. "Apollo" spacecraft 70 75
1828 300s. "Soyuz" spacecraft . . 70 75
1829 300s. "Intelsat 1" 70 75
1830 300s. Manned manoeuvring Unit 70 75
1831 300s. "Skylab" 70 75
1832 300s. "Telstar 1" 70 75
1833 300s. Hubble Telescope . . 70 75
MS1834 Two sheets, each 103 × 73 mm. (a) 2000s. Space Shuttle *Challenger* (35 × 61 mm). (b) 2000s. "Viking Lander" on Mars (61 × 35 mm) Set of 2 sheets 7·00 7·50
Nos. 1818/25 and 1826/33 respectively were printed together, se-tenant, with the backgrounds forming composite designs.

193 Deng Xiaoping and Port

1997. Deng Xiaoping (Chinese statesman) Commemoration.
1835 **193** 500s. multicoloured . . . 85 85
1836 550s. multicoloured . . . 90 90
1837 1000s. multicoloured . . . 1·75 2·25
MS1838 100 × 70 mm. 200s. multicoloured (Deng Xiaoping and Shenzhen) . . . . 3·25 3·75

194 Water Hyacinth and Pebbles **195** Men's Slalom

1997. Environmental Protection. Multicoloured.
1839 500s. Water hyacinth and Lake Victoria (inscr at top left) 85 85
1840 500s. Water hyacinth and Lake Victoria (inscr at top right) 85 85
1841 500s. Type **194** 85 85
1842 500s. Larger clump of water hyacinth and pebbles . . 85 85
1843 550s. Buffalo 85 85
1844 550s. Uganda kob 85 85
1845 550s. Vulturine guineafowl ("Guinea Fowl") 85 85
1846 550s. Marabou stork . . . 85 85
MS1847 106 × 76 mm. 2500s. Gorilla 4·50 4·50
Nos. 1839/42 and 1843/6 respectively were printed together, se-tenant, with the backgrounds forming composite designs.
No. 1845 is inscribed "GUINEA FOWEL" and No. 1846 "MALIBU STORK", both in error.

1997. 10th Anniv of Chernobyl Nuclear Disaster. As T **347** of St. Vincent.
1848 500s. As Type **347** of St. Vincent . . . . 1·00 1·00
1849 700s. As No. 1848 but inscribed "CHABAD'S CHILDREN OF CHERNOBYL" at foot 1·25 1·25

1997. 50th Death Anniv of Paul Harris (founder of Rotary International). As T **347a** of St. Vincent. Multicoloured.
1850 1000s. Paul Harris and child drinking . . . . 1·75 2·25
MS1851 78 × 107 mm. 2500s. The first Rotarians . . . . 2·50 3·25

1997. Golden Wedding of Queen Elizabeth and Prince Philip. As T **347b** of St. Vincent. Multicoloured.
1852 200s. Queen Elizabeth II . . 1·10 1·25
1853 200s. Royal coat of arms . . 1·10 1·25
1854 200s. Queen Elizabeth and Prince Philip at reception 1·10 1·25
1855 200s. Queen Elizabeth and Prince Philip on royal visit . . . . 1·10 1·25
1856 200s. Buckingham Palace . . 1·10 1·25
1857 200s. Prince Philip in military uniform . . . . 1·10 1·25
MS1858 100 × 70 mm. 2000s. Princess Elizabeth in wedding dress . . . . 3·00 3·50

1997. "Pacific '97" International Stamp Exhibition, San Francisco. Death Centenary of Heinrich von Stephan (founder of the U.P.U.). As T **347c** of St. Vincent.
1859 800s. blue . . . . 1·10 1·25
1860 800s. brown . . . . 1·10 1·25
1861 800s. green . . . . 1·10 1·25
MS1862 82 × 119 mm. 2500s. deep blue and blue . . . . 3·00 3·50
DESIGNS: No. 1859, Chinese post boat; 1860, Von Stephan and Mercury; 1861, Russian post cart; **MS**1862, Von Stephan and French postman on stilts.

1997. Winter Olympic Games, Nagano, Japan (1998). Multicoloured.
1863 350s. Type **195** 50 35
1864 450s. Two-man bobsled . . 60 45
1865 500s. Ski jumping (horiz) . . 70 75
1866 500s. Giant slalom (horiz) 70 75
1867 500s. Cross-country skiing (horiz) 70 75
1868 500s. Ice hockey (horiz) . . 70 75
1869 500s. Pairs figure skating (man) (horiz) 70 75
1870 500s. Pairs figure skating (woman) (horiz) 70 75
1871 800s. Women's slalom (horiz) . . . . 1·10 1·25
1872 2000s. Men's speed skating (horiz) . . . . 2·25 3·00
MS1873 Two sheets, each 103 × 72 mm. (a) 2500s. Downhill skiing (horiz). (b) 2500s. Women's figure skating (horiz) Set of 2 sheets . . . . 6·50 7·50
Nos. 1865/70 were printed together, se-tenant, with the backgrounds forming a composite design.

196 Main Building, Makerere University

1997. 75th Anniv of Makerere University. Multicoloured.
1874 150s. Type **196** 40 20
1875 450s. East African School of Librarianship building (vert) 80 80
1876 500s. Buyana Stock Farm, Makerere University . . . 90 90
1877 550s. Ceramic dish from School of Architecture and Fine Arts . . . . . 1·00 1·25

1997. World Cup Football Championship, France (1998). As T **351a** of St. Vincent. Multicoloured (except Nos. 1878, 1880, 1883 and 1886).
1878 200s. Fritz Walter, Germany (brown) 50 25
1879 250s. Paulo Rossi (horiz) . . 50 50
1880 250s. Mario Kempes (black) (horiz) 50 50
1881 250s. Gerd Muller (horiz) 50 50
1882 250s. Grzegorz Lato (horiz) 50 50
1883 250s. Joseph Gaetjens (black) (horiz) 50 50
1884 250s. Eusebio Ferreica da Silva (horiz) 50 50
1885 250s. Salvatore Schillaci (horiz) 50 50
1886 250s. Leonidas da Silva (black) (horiz) 50 50

1887 250s. Gary Lineker (horiz) 50 50
1888 250s. Argentine and West German player chasing ball (horiz) 50 50
1889 250s. Azteca Stadium (horiz) 50 50
1890 250s. Maradona holding World Cup (horiz) . . . 50 50
1891 250s. Argentine and West German players with goalkeeper (horiz) 50 50
1892 250s. West German player tackling Argentine player (horiz) 50 50
1893 250s. Ball in back of net (horiz) 50 50
1894 250s. Argentine team (horiz) 50 50
1895 250s. Players competing to head ball (horiz) 50 50
1896 300s. Daniel Pasarella, Argentina 55 45
1897 450s. Dino Zoff, Italy . . . 70 70
1898 500s. Bobby Moore, England 80 80
1899 550s. Franz Beckenbaur, West Germany 85 90
1900 600s. Diego Maradona, Argentina . . . . 90 1·10
MS1901 Two sheets. (a) 102 × 127 mm. 2000s. Celebrating West German players, 1990 (horiz). (b) 127 × 102 mm. 2000s. Bobby Moore, 1966 (horiz) Set of 2 sheets . . . . 7·00 7·50
No. 1883 is inscribed "ADEMIR" in error.

197 Mahatma Gandhi

1997. 50th Death Anniv of Mahatma Gandhi (1998) (1st issue).
1902 **197** 600s. brown and black 1·10 1·25
1903 – 700s. brown and black 1·25 1·40
MS1904 73 × 103 mm. 1000s. multicoloured . . . . 2·25 2·25
DESIGNS: 700s., 1000s. Different portait.
See also Nos. 2021/2.

198 "Cupid and Dolphin" (Andrea del Verrocchio)

1997. Christmas. Paintings and Sculptures. Multicoloured.
1905 200s. Type **198** 50 20
1906 300s. "The Fall of the Rebel Angels" (Pieter Brueghel the Elder) 70 30
1907 400s. "The Immaculate Conception" (Bartolome Murillo) 85 50
1908 500s. "Music-making Angel" (Rosso Fiorentino) . . . 90 80
1909 600s. "Cupid and Psyche" (Adolphe-William Bouguereau) . . . . . . 1·00 1·25
1910 700s. "Cupid and Psyche" (Antonio Canova) . . . . 1·25 1·50
MS1911 Two sheets, each 105 × 96 mm. (a) 2500s. Mary and Angels (detail, "The Assumption of the Virgin") (El Greco) (horiz). (b) 2500s. Angel holding baby (detail, "The Assumption of the Virgin") (El Greco) (horiz) Set of 2 sheets . . . . 7·50 8·50

199 Diana, Princess of Wales

1997. Diana, Princess of Wales Commemoration.
1912 **199** 600s. multicoloured . . . 1·25 1·40

200 Tiger

1998. Chinese New Year ("Year of the Tiger"). Multicoloured.
1913 350s. Type **200** 55 60
1914 350s. Tiger leaping 55 60
1915 350s. Tiger resting 55 60
1916 350s. Tiger yawning 55 60
MS1917 106 × 76 mm. 1500s. Tiger 2·00 2·25

201 Mountain Gorilla **202** Namugongo Martyrs Shrine, Kampala

1998. 18th Anniv of Pan African Postal Union.
1918 **201** 300s.+150s. mult . . . . 1·10 1·50

1998. Tourist Attractions. Multicoloured.
1919 300s. Type **202** 40 30
1920 400s. Kasubi Tombs, Kampala (horiz) 60 40
1921 500s. Tourist launch in Kazinga Channel, Queen Elizabeth Park (horiz) . . 80 70
1922 600s. Elephant, Queen Elizabeth Park (horiz) . . 1·25 1·25
1923 700s. Bujagali Falls, River Nile at Jinja (horiz) . . . 1·40 1·50

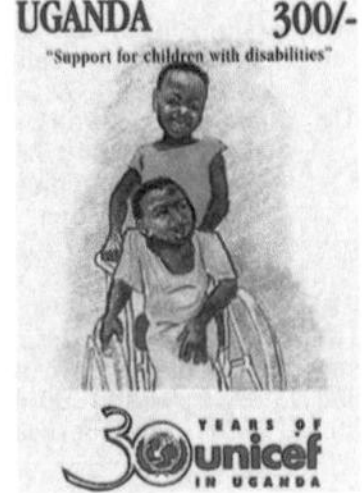

203 Mother Teresa, 1928 **204** Child in Wheelchair

1998. Mother Teresa Commemoration. Mult.
1924 300s. Type **203** 60 60
1925 300s. Holding child (56 × 42 mm) 60 60
1926 300s. Mother Teresa at United Nations, 1975 (56 × 42 mm) 60 60
1927 300s. Facing left 60 60
1928 300s. Full face portrait . . . 60 60
1929 300s. With children (56 × 42 mm) 60 60
1930 300s. Mother Teresa rescuing child (56 × 42 mm) 60 60
1931 300s. Smiling 60 60
MS1932 95 × 81 mm. 2000s. Mother Teresa with Diana, Princess of Wales (50 × 37 mm) . . . . . 4·25 4·25

1998. 30th Anniv of UNICEF. Multicoloured.
1933 300s. Type **204** 55 30
1934 400s. Child receiving oral vaccination against polio 70 55
1935 600s. Children outside toilet 1·10 1·25
1936 700s. Children in class . . . 1·25 1·40

205 Pteranodon

1998. Prehistoric Animals. Multicoloured.
1937 300s. Type **205** 55 30
1938 400s. Diplodocus 65 45
1939 500s. Lambeosaurus 80 60
1940 600s. Centrosaurus 85 95
1941 600s. Cetiosaurus (vert) . . 85 95
1942 600s. Brontosaurus (vert) . . 85 95
1943 600s. Brachiosaurus (vert) 85 95
1944 600s. Deinonychus (vert) . . 85 95
1945 600s. Dimetrodon (vert) . . 85 95
1946 600s. Megalosaurus (vert) 85 95
1947 700s. Parasaurolophus . . . 95 1·10
MS1948 Two sheets, each 73 × 103 mm. (a) 2500s. Tyrannosaurus rex (42 × 56 mm). (b) 2500s. Iguanodon (42 × 56 mm) Set of 2 sheets . . 8·50 9·50

Nos. 1941/6 were printed together, se-tenant, with the backgrounds forming a composite design.

206 Rita Dove

1998. UNESCO. World Literacy Campaign. 20th-century Afro-American Writers. Multicoloured.
1949 300s. Type **206** 90 90
1950 300s. Mari Evans 90 90
1951 300s. Sterling A. Brown . . 90 90
1952 300s. June Jordan 90 90
1953 300s. Stephen Henderson . . 90 90
1954 300s. Zora Neale Hurston 90 90

207 Mickey Mouse and Monster

1998. 70th Birthday of Mickey Mouse. Scenes from cartoon film "Runaway Brain". Multicoloured.
1955 400s. Type **207** 90 90
1956 400s. Mickey and Pluto with newspaper 90 90
1957 400s. Mickey and Pluto in front of television 90 90
1958 400s. Mickey and Minnie fleeing 90 90
1959 400s. Mickey on television screen 90 90
1960 400s. Monster and hostage Minnie Mouse clinging to skyscraper 90 90
1961 400s. Mickey Mouse throwing lasso 90 90
1962 400s. Mickey circling Monster on lasso 90 90
1963 400s. Mickey and Minnie on rope 90 90
MS1964 Two sheets, each 127 × 102 mm. (a) 3000s. Mickey and Minnie hugging on roof. (b) 3000s. Mickey and Minnie on liferaft (vert). Set of 2 sheets 11·00 11·00

1998. "Israel 98" International Stamp Exhibition, Tel-Aviv. Nos. **MS**1699/1700 optd with **98** and logo and each further optd "**ISRAEL 98 - WORLD STAMP EXHIBITION TEL-AVIV 13-21 MAY 1998**" on margin.
MS1965 114 × 95 mm. 300s. Type **180**; 500s. Jerusalem Theatre; 1000s. Israel Museum 3·25 3·25
MS1966 104 × 74 mm. 2000s. Grotto of the Nativity . . . . 3·25 3·25

209 "Santa Maria" (Columbus)

1998. Ships of the World. Multicoloured.
1967 1000s. Type **209** . . . . . 1·40 1·60
1968 1000s. "Mayflower" (Pilgrim Fathers) . . . . 1·40 1·60
1969 1000s. Barque . . . . . . 1·40 1·60
1970 1000s. Fishing schooner . . 1·40 1·60
1971 1000s. Chesapeake oyster boat . . . . 1·40 1·60
1972 1000s. Java Sea schooner . . 1·40 1·60
MS1973 Two sheets, each 100 × 70 mm. (a) 3000s. Thames barge (27 × 41 mm); (b) 3000s. Felucca (41 × 27 mm) Set of 2 sheets . . . . 8·00 8·50

210 Grumman F4F Wildcat (U.S.A.)

1998. Aircraft. Multicoloured.
1974 500s. Type **210** 75 75
1975 500s. Mitsubishi A6M Zero-Sen (Japan) 75 75
1976 500s. Supermarine Seafire ("Spitfire") (Great Britain) 75 75
1977 500s. Hawker Siddeley Harrier (Great Britain) . . 75 75
1978 500s. S3A Viking (U.S.A.) 75 75
1979 500s. Corsair (U.S.A.) . . . 75 75
1980 600s. Dornier Do-X (flying boat) (1929) 75 75
1981 600s. German Zucker mail rocket (1930) 75 75
1982 600s. North American X-15 rocket plane (1959) . . . 75 75
1983 600s. Goddard's rocket (1930s) 75 75
1984 600s. Wright Brothers' "Flyer I" (1903) 75 75
1985 600s. 16 0R Sikorsky (first helicopter) (1939) 75 75
MS1986 Two sheets. (a) 85 × 110 mm. 2500s. P-40 Tomahawk (U.S.A.) (1940). (b) 110 × 85 mm. 2500s. SH-346 Seabat recovery helicopter (U.S.A.) Set of 2 sheets . . . . 7·50 7·50
Nos. 1974/9 and 1980/5 respectively were printed together, se-tenant, forming composite designs.

211 "Onosma" sp.

213 Diana, Princess of Wales

212 Bohemian Waxwing

1998. Flowers of the Mediterranean. Multicoloured.
1987 300s. Type **211** 55 55
1988 300s. "Rhododendron luteum" 55 55
1989 300s. "Paeonia mascula" . . 55 55
1990 300s. "Geranium macrorrhizum" 55 55
1991 300s. "Cyclamen graecum" 55 55
1992 300s. "Lilium rhodopaedum" 55 55
1993 300s. "Narcissus pseudonarcissus" 55 55
1994 300s. "Paeonia rhodia" . . 55 55
1995 300s. "Aquilegia amaliae" 55 55
1996 600s. "Paeonia peregrina" (horiz) 75 75
1997 600s. "Muscari comutatum" (horiz) 75 75
1998 600s. "Sternbergia" sp. (horiz) 75 75
1999 600s. "Dianthus" sp. (horiz) 75 75
2000 600s. "Verbascum" sp. (horiz) 75 75
2001 600s. "Aubrieta gracilis" (horiz) 75 75
2002 600s. "Galanthus nivalis" (horiz) 75 75
2003 600s. "Campanula incurva" (horiz) 75 75
2004 600s. "Crocus sieberi" (horiz) 75 75
MS2005 Two sheets. (a) 70 × 100 mm. 2000s. "Paeonia parnassica" (b) 100 × 70 mm. 2000s. "Pancratium maritimum" Set of 2 sheets . . . . 6·50 7·00

1998. Christmas. Birds. Multicoloured.
2006 300s. Type **212** 55 30
2007 400s. House sparrow . . . 65 40
2008 500s. Black-capped chickadee 75 50
2009 600s. Northern bullfinch ("Eurasian Bullfinch") . . 85 80
2010 700s. Painted bunting . . . 95 95
2011 1000s. Common cardinal ("Northern Cardinal") . . 1·40 1·75
MS2012 Two sheets, each 70 × 97 mm. (a) 2500s. Winter wren (vert). (b) 2500s. Red-winged blackbird (vert) Set of 2 sheets 7·50 7·50
No. **MS**2012a is inscribed "Winter Wreu" in error.

1998. 25th Death Anniv of Pablo Picasso (painter). As T **373** of St. Vincent. Multicoloured.
2013 500s. "Woman Reading" (vert) 75 75
2014 600s. "Portrait of Dora Maar" (vert) 85 90
2015 700s. "Les Demoiselles d'Avignon" . . . . 1·00 1·25
MS2016 127 × 101 mm. 2500s. "Night Fishing at Antibes" (vert) 3·25 3·50
No. 2015 is inscribed "Des Moiselles D'Avignon" in error.

1998. 19th World Scout Jamboree, Chile. As T **373b** of St. Vincent. Multicoloured (except **MS**2020).
2017 700s. Cub Scouts greeting President Eisenhower, 1956 . . . . 85 95
2018 700s. Scout with "Uncle Dan" Beard, 1940 . . . . 85 95
2019 700s. Vice-President Hubert Humphrey as Scout leader, 1934 . . . . . . 85 95
MS2020 70 × 100 mm. 2000s. Scout with pet beaver (purple, grey & brown) . . . . 3·00 3·25

1998. 50th Death Anniv of Mahatma Gandhi (2nd issue). As T **373c** of St. Vincent.
2021 600s. multicoloured . . . . 3·50 3·00
MS2022 98 × 58 mm. 2500s. brown, mauve and black . . . . . . 4·50 4·75
DESIGN—HORIZ: 600s. Gandhi as a young man. VERT: 2500s. Gandhi in Bombay law office.

1998. 1st Death Anniv of Diana, Princess of Wales.
2023 **213** 700s. multicoloured . . . 1·40 1·60

214 Rabbit

1999. Chinese New Year ("Year of the Rabbit"). Multicoloured.
2024 350s. White rabbit 75 80
2025 350s. Rabbit with carrot . . 75 80
2026 350s. Brown and white rabbit 75 80
2027 350s. Type **214** 75 80
MS2028 106 × 76 mm. 1500s. Rabbit 2·75 3·25

215 Post Office Emblem and Slogan

1999. Uganda Post Limited Commemoration.
2029 **215** 300s. multicoloured . . . 1·25 55

216 Iru Hairstyle

1999. Hairstyles. Multicoloured.
2030 300s. Type **216** 60 30
2031 500s. Enshunju hairstyle . . 85 75
2032 550s. Elemungole hairstyle 90 1·10
2033 600s. Lango hairstyle . . . 1·00 1·25
2034 700s. Ekikuura hairstyle . . 1·10 1·40

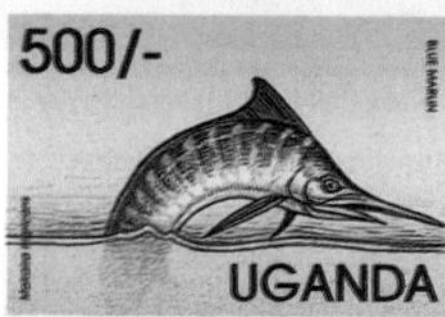

217 Blue Marlin

1999. International Year of the Ocean. Multicoloured.
2035 500s. Type **217** 85 85
2036 500s. Arctic tern 85 85
2037 500s. Common dolphin . . 85 85
2038 500s. Blacktip shark 85 85
2039 500s. Manta ray 85 85
2040 500s. Blackedge moray . . . 85 85
2041 500s. Loggerhead turtle . . 85 85
2042 500s. Sail-finned tang . . . 85 85
2043 500s. Two-spotted octopus 85 85
2044 500s. Atlantic wolffish . . . 85 85
2045 500s. Equal sea star 85 85
2046 500s. Purple sea urchin . . 85 85
2047 500s. Mountain crab 85 85
MS2048 Two sheets, each 110 × 85 mm. (a) 2500s. Sea nettle jellyfish. (b) 2500s. "Decatopecten striatus" (scallop) Set of 2 sheets 7·50 8·00
Nos. 2035/43 and Nos. 2044/7 respectively were printed together, se-tenant, with the backgrounds forming a composite design.
No. 2036 is inscribed "ARTIC TERN" in error.

218 Cows feeding (income generation)

1999. International Year of the Elderly. Mult.
2049 300s. Type **218** 60 30
2050 500s. Elderly man reading with child 85 75
2051 600s. Playing board game 95 1·10
2052 700s. Food distribution . . 1·10 1·40

219 L'Hoest's Monkey

220 Saturn V Rocket Launch

1999. Primates. Multicoloured.
2053 300s. Type **219** 60 30
2054 400s. Diademed monkey ("Sykes/Blue Monkey") 70 40
2055 500s. Patas monkey 85 70
2056 600s. Red-tailed monkey . . 95 1·00
2057 700s. Eastern black and white colobus . . . . . . 1·10 1·25
2058 1000s. Mountain gorilla . . 1·40 1·75
MS2059 73 × 54 mm. 2500s. Olive baboon (35 × 26 mm) . . . . . 4·25 4·75

1999. 150th Death Anniv of Katsushika Hokusai (Japanese artist). As T **384b** of St. Lucia. Multicoloured.
2060 700s. "Dragon flying over Mount Fuji" (detail) . . . 1·10 1·10
2061 700s. "Famous Poses from the Kabuki Theatre" (one woman) . . . . 1·10 1·10
2062 700s. "Kitsune No Yomeiri" 1·10 1·10
2063 700s. "Dragon flying over Mount Fuji" (complete picture) . . . . 1·10 1·10
2064 700s. "Famous Poses from the Kabuki Theatre" (man and woman) . . . . 1·10 1·10
2065 700s. "Girl holding Cloth" 1·10 1·10
MS2066 100 × 70 mm. 3000s. "Japanese Spaniel" . . . . . 4·75 5·00
No. 2065 is inscribed "GIRL HOLDING CLOTHE" in error.

1999. "Queen Elizabeth the Queen Mother's Century". As T **386a** of St. Vincent.
2067 1200s. multicoloured . . . . 1·75 1·90
2068 1200s. black and gold . . . 1·75 1·90
2069 1200s. black and gold . . . 1·75 1·90
2070 1200s. multicoloured . . . . 1·75 1·90
MS2071 152 × 155 mm. 3000s. multicoloured . . . . 6·00 6·00
DESIGNS: No. 2067, Duchess of York wearing evening cape; 2068, Wedding of Duke and Duchess of York, 1923; 2069, Formal portrait of Queen Mother; 2070, Queen Mother at evening reception; **MS**2071, Queen Mother visiting Cambridge, 1961.
No. **MS**2071 also shows the Royal Arms embossed in gold.

1999. 30th Anniv of First Manned Landing on Moon. Multicoloured.
2072 600s. Type **220** . . . . . . 90 1·00
2073 600s. Command and service module "Columbia" . . . 90 1·00
2074 600s. Edwin E. Aldrin descending ladder . . . . 90 1·00
2075 600s. Saturn V rocket on launch pad . . . . 90 1·00
2076 600s. Lunar module "Eagle" 90 1·00
2077 600s. Edwin E. Aldrin on Moon surface . . . . . . 90 1·00
2078 700s. Mercury mission "Freedom 7", 1961 . . . 1·00 1·10
2079 700s. "Gemini 4", 1965 . . 1·00 1·10
2080 700s. "Apollo 11" command and service module "Columbia" . . . . . . 1·00 1·10
2081 700s. "Vostok 1", 1961 . . 1·00 1·10
2082 700s. Saturn V rocket . . . 1·00 1·10
2083 700s. "Apollo 11" lunar module "Eagle" . . . . . 1·00 1·10
MS2084 Two sheets, each 76 × 106 mm. (a) 3000s. Edwin E. Aldrin with scientific experiment. (b) 3000s. "Apollo 11" command module re-entering Earth's atmosphere . . 8·50 9·00
Nos. 2078/83 were each printed together, se-tenant, with the backgrounds forming a composite design.

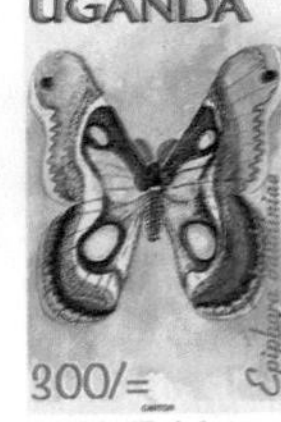

221 African Penduline Tit ("Penduline Tit") **222** "Epiphora bauhiniae" (moth)

1999. Birds of Uganda. Multicoloured.

2085 300s. Type **221** 60 45
2086 500s. Grey-headed kingfisher 70 75
2087 500s. Green-headed sunbird 70 75
2088 500s. Speckled pigeon . . . 70 75
2089 500s. Grey parrot 70 75
2090 500s. Barn owl 70 75
2091 500s. South African crowned crane ("Grey Crowned Crane") 70 75
2092 500s. Whale-headed stork ("Shoebill") 70 75
2093 500s. Black heron 70 75
2094 600s. Scarlet-chested sunbird 75 80
2095 600s. Lesser honeyguide . . 75 80
2096 600s. African palm swift . . 75 80
2097 600s. Swamp flycatcher . . 75 80
2098 600s. Lizard buzzard . . . 75 80
2099 600s. Osprey 75 80
2100 600s. Cardinal woodpecker 75 80
2101 600s. Pearl-spotted owlet . . 75 80
2102 700s. Speke's weaver ("Fox's Weaver") 85 95
2103 700s. Chin spot puff-backed flycatcher ("Chin-spot Flycatcher") 85 95
2104 700s. Blue swallow 85 95
2105 700s. Purple-breasted sunbird 85 95
2106 700s. Comb duck ("Knob-billed Duck") 85 95
2107 700s. Red-collared whydah ("Red-collared Widowbird") 85 95
2108 700s. Ruwenzori turaco . . 85 95
2109 700s. African cuckoo hawk 85 95
2110 1000s. Yellow-fronted tinkerbird . . . . 1·40 1·50
2111 1200s. Zebra waxbill . . . . 1·50 1·75
2112 1800s. Sooty chat ("Sooty Anteater Chat") . . . . 2·25 2·75
MS2113 Two sheets, each 76 × 106 mm. (a) 3000s. Four-banded sandgrouse. (b) 3000s. Paradise whydah Set of 2 sheets 8·50 9·00

Nos. 2086/93, 2094/2101 and 2102/9 were each printed together, se-tenant, with the backgrounds forming composite designs.

Nos. 2100/1 are inscribed "Cardinal Woopecker" or "Glaucidium periatum", both in error.

2000. Moths. Multicoloured.

2114 300s. Type **222** 20 25
2115 400s. "Phylloxiphia formosa" (horiz) 25 30
2116 500s. "Bunaea alcinoe" . . 30 35
2117 600s. "Euchloron megaera" (horiz) 35 40
2118 700s. "Argema mimosae" 45 50
2119 1800s. "Denephila nerii" (horiz) . . . . 1·10 1·20
MS2120 75 × 52 mm. 3000s. "Lobobunaea angasana" (horiz) 1·90 2·00

223 Postman with Women and Child **224** *Eulophia paivenna*

2000. 125th Anniv of the Universal Postal Union. Multicoloured.

2121 600s. Type **223** 35 40
2122 700s. American mother and child reading letter by post box 45 50
2123 1200s. Mail coach 75 80

2000. Orchids. Multicoloured.

2124 600s. Type **224** 35 40
2125 600s. *Ansellia gigantea* . . . 35 40
2126 600s. *Anglaecopsis gracillima* 35 40
2127 600s. *Bonatea steudneri* . . . 35 40
2128 600s. *Bulbophyllum falcatum* 35 40
2129 600s. *Aerangis citrata* . . . 35 40
2130 600s. *Eulophiella Elisabethae* 35 40
2131 600s. *Aerangis rhodosticta* 35 40
2132 600s. *Angraecum scottianum* 35 40
2133 600s. *Angraecum eichcerianum* 35 40
2134 600s. *Angraecum leonis* . . . 35 40
2135 600s. *Arpophyllum giganteum* 35 40
2136 600s. *Bulbophyllum barbigerum* 35 40
2137 600s. *Angeraelum giryamae* 35 40
2138 600s. *Aeraungis ellisii* . . . 35 40
2139 600s. *Disa uniflora* 35 40
2140 600s. *Eulophia alta* 35 40
2141 600s. *Ancistrochilus stylosa* 35 40
2142 700s. *Eulophia orthoplectra* 45 50
2143 700s. *Cirrhopetalum umbellatum* 45 50
2144 700s. *Eulophiella rolfei* . . . 45 50
2145 700s. *Eulophia porphyroglossa* 45 50
2146 700s. *Eulophia petersii* . . . 45 50
2147 700s. *Cyrtorchis arcuata* . . 45 50
2148 700s. *Eurychone rothschildiana* 45 50
2149 700s. *Eulophia quartiniana* 45 50
2150 700s. *Eulophia stenophylia* (single flower) 45 50
2151 700s. *Grammangis ellisii* . . 45 50
2152 700s. *Eulophia stenophylia* (several flowers) 45 50
2153 700s. *Oeoniella polystachys* 45 50
2154 700s. *Cymbidiella humblotii* 45 50
2155 700s. *Polystachya bella* . . . 45 50
2156 700s. *Vanilla polycepis* . . . 45 50
2157 700s. *Eulophiella roemplerana* 45 50
2158 700s. *Habenaria englerana* 45 50
2159 700s. *Ansella frallana* . . . 45 50
MS2160 Four sheets, each 95 × 65 mm. (a) 3000s. *Cymbidiella rhodochila* (horiz). (b) 3000s. *Calanthe corymbosa* (horiz). (c) 3000s. *Ancistrochilus rothschildianus* (horiz). (d) 3000s. *Polystachya tayloriana* (horiz) Set of 4 sheets . . . . 7·50 7·75

Nos. 2124/32, 2133/41, 2142/50 and 2151/9 were each printed together, se-tenant, with the backgrounds forming composite designs.

225 Short-tailed Admiral

2000. "The Stamp Show 2000" International Stamp Exhibition, London. Butterflies. Multicoloured.

2161 300s. Type **225** 20 25
2162 400s. Guineafowl 25 30
2163 500s. *Charaxes anticlea* . . 30 35
2164 500s. *Epitola posthumus* . . 30 35
2165 500s. Beautiful monarch . . 30 35
2166 500s. Blue-banded nymph 30 35
2167 500s. *Euxanthe crossleyi* . . 30 35
2168 500s. African map butterfly 30 35
2169 500s. Western blue charaxes 30 35
2170 500s. Noble butterfly . . . 30 35
2171 600s. Green-veined charaxes 35 40
2172 600s. Ansorge's leaf butterfly 35 40
2173 600s. Crawshay's sapphire blue 35 40
2174 600s. *Palla ussheri* 35 40
2175 600s. Friar 35 40
2176 600s. Blood-red cymothoe 35 40
2177 600s. Mocker swallowtail . . 35 40
2178 600s. Green charaxes ("Charaxes eupale") . . . 35 40
2179 700s. *Acraea pseudolycia* . . 45 50
2180 700s. *Colotis protomedia* ("Veined Yellow") 45 50
2181 700s. Buxton's hairstreak . . 45 50
2182 700s. *Iolaus isomenias* . . . 45 50
2183 700s. Veined swallowtail . . 45 50
2184 700s. Fig-tree blue 45 50
2185 700s. Scarlet tip 45 50
2186 700s. Gaudy commodore ("Precis octavia") 45 50
2187 1200s. Club-tailed charaxes 75 80
2188 1800s. *Cymothoe egesta* . . 1·10 1·20
MS2189 Two sheets, each 63 × 69 mm. (a) 3000s. African monarch. (b) 3000s. Kigezi swordtail Set of 2 sheets . . . 3·75 4·00

Nos. 2163/70, 2171/8 and 2179/86 were each printed together, se-tenant, with the backgrounds forming composite designs.

No. 2165 is inscribed "Danasus formosa", No. 2169 "Western Blue Caraxes" and No. 2183 "Graphium lionidas", all in error.

225a King Philip II of France, 1180–1223

2000. Monarchs of the Millennium.

2190 **225a** 900s. grey, brown and bistre 55 60
2191 – 900s. grey, brown and bistre 55 60
2192 – 900s. grey, brown and bistre 55 60
2193 – 900s. purple, brown and bistre 55 60
2194 – 900s. multicoloured . . 55 60
2195 – 900s. multicoloured . . 55 60
2196 – 900s. grey, brown and bistre 55 60
2197 – 900s. grey, brown and bistre 55 60
2198 – 900s. grey, brown and bistre 55 60
MS2199 Two sheets. (a) 117 × 137 mm. 3000s. multicoloured. (b) 116 × 136 mm. 3000s. multicoloured Set of 2 sheets . . . . 3·75 4·00

DESIGNS: No. 2191, King Richard I of England, 1189–99; 2192, King William I of England, 1066–87; 2193, Tsar Boris III of Bulgaria, 1918–43; 2194, Emperor Charles V of Holy Roman Empire, 1519–58; 2195, Emperor Pedro II of Brazil, 1831–89; 2196, Empress Elizabeth of Austria, 1854–98; 2197, Emperor Francis Joseph of Austria, 1848–1916; 2198, King Frederik of Bohemia, 1619–20; **MS**2199a, King Mutesa I of Buganda; No. **MS**2199b, King Cwa II of Kabaleega.

No. 2198 is inscribed "FREDRICH" in error.

225b Pope Agapitus II, 946–55

2000. Popes of the Millennium. Multicoloured (except **MS**2206).

2200 900s. Type **225b** 55 60
2201 900s. Alexander II, 1061–73 55 60
2202 900s. Anastasius IV, 1153–54 . . . . 55 60
2203 900s. Benedict VIII, 1012–24 55 60
2204 900s. Benedict VII, 974–83 55 60
2205 900s. Callistus, 1119–24 . . 55 60
MS2206 116 × 137 mm. 3000s. Celestine III, (grey, brown and buff) . . . . 1·90 2·00

225c Bow of Merchant Ship (opening of Japan to foreign trade, 1853)

2000. New Millennium. People and Events of Nineteenth Century (1850–1900). Multicoloured.

2207 300s. Type **225c** 20 25
2208 300s. First elevator, 1854 . . 20 25
2209 300s. Ladle of molten steel (Bessemer Process, 1854) 20 25
2210 300s. Florence Nightingale (founder of nursing, 1854) 20 25
2211 300s. Louis Pasteur (French chemist, discovered bacteriology, 1856) . . . 20 25
2212 300s. Oil gusher (first oil well, 1859) 20 25
2213 300s. Charles Darwin (*The Origin of Species*, 1859) 20 25
2214 300s. Gregor Mendel (law of heredity, 1866) 20 25
2215 300s. Alfred Nobel (invention of dynamite, 1867) 20 25
2216 300s. Modern freighter in Canal (opening of Suez Canal, 1869) 20 25
2217 300s. Early telephone (invented 1876) 20 25
2218 300s. Light bulb (invention of electric light, 1879) . . 20 25
2219 300s. Clocks (World's time zones established, 1884) 20 25
2220 300s. Electric motor (invented 1888) 20 25
2221 300s. Cinema projector (first motion pictures, 1895) . . 20 25
2222 300s. *Monitor* and *Merrimack* (ironclad warships) (American Civil War, 1861–65) (59 × 39 mm) 20 25
2223 300s. Olympic Torch and Rings (revival of Games, 1896) 20 25

226 Education in the Millennium

2000. Anniversaries and Events. Multicoloured.

2224 300s. Type **226** 55 30
2225 500s. Controlled and open borders (6th anniv of Comesa Treaty) 80 50
2226 600s. Flags of member countries (50th anniv of Commonwealth) . . . . 1·25 1·25
2227 600s. Aspects of the River Nile in the Millennium . . 1·25 1·25
2228 700s. Non-traditional exports in the Millennium 1·25 1·25
2229 1200s. World map (50th anniv of Commonwealth) 1·75 1·90
2230 1400s. People and exports crossing border (6th anniv of Comesa Treaty) . . . 1·90 2·25
2231 1800s. Tourism in the Millennium . . . . 2·50 3·00

227 Kenya Railways Class A 60 Steam Locomotive

2000. African Railway Locomotives. Multicoloured.

2232 300s. Type **227** 20 25
2233 400s. Mozambique Railways Baldwin type 25 30
2234 600s. Uganda Railways Class 73 diesel locomotive 35 40
2235 700s. South Africa Railways Baby Garratt type 45 50
2236 700s. Uganda Railways Class 36 diesel locomotive (from back) 45 50
2237 700s. Rhodesian Railways 12th Class 45 50
2238 700s. Rhodesian Railways Garratt type 45 50
2239 700s. Uganda Railways Class 62 diesel locomotive 45 50
2240 700s. South African Railways Beyer-Garratt type 45 50
2241 700s. Sudan Railways oil-burning locomotive . . . 45 50
2242 700s. Nigerian Railways coal train 45 50
2243 700s. South Africa Railways steam locomotive 45 50
2244 700s. Uganda Railways Class 36 diesel locomotive (from front) 45 50
2245 700s. South African Railways Class 19D . . . 45 50
2246 700s. Algeria Railways Garratt type 45 50
2247 700s. Cameroon Railways locomotive No. 194 . . . 45 50
2248 700s. South Africa Railways electric freight locomotive 45 50
2249 700s. Rhodesian Railways Class 14A 45 50
2250 700s. Egyptian Railways British-built locomotive 45 50
2251 700s. Uganda Railways Class 73 diesel locomotive 45 50
2252 1200s. Uganda Railways Class 82 diesel locomotive 75 80
2253 1400s. East Africa Railways Beyer-Garratt type . . . 85 90
2254 1800s. Rhodesian Railways Beyer-Garratt type . . . 1·10 1·20
2255 2000s. East African Railways Garratt type . . 1·20 1·30
MS2256 Three sheets, each 106 × 76 mm. (a) 3500s. East Africa Railways steam locomotive (56 × 42 mm). (b) 3500s. Angola, Benguala Railway No. 402 (56 × 42 mm). (c) 3500s. Mozambique Railways Alco type (56 × 42 mm) Set of 2 sheets . . 6·50 6·75

No. 2237 also shows part of the inscription for No. 2236 in error.

228 "The Nativity" (Drateru Oliver)

2000. Christmas. Young People's Paintings. Mult.

2257 300s. Type **228** 60 30
2258 400s. "Baby Jesus and Donkey" (Brenda Tumwebaze) (horiz) . . . 70 35
2259 500s. "Angels" (Joseph Mukiibi) 85 45
2260 600s. "Holy Family in Stable" (Paul Serunjogi) (horiz) 95 50
2261 700s. "Holy Family with Oxon" (Edward Maswere) (horiz) . . . . 1·10 60
2262 1200s. "Children worshipping baby Jesus" (Ndeba Harriet) (horiz) 1·75 2·25

2263	1800s. "Madonna and Child with Shepherd" (Jude Kasagga)	2·50	3·00
MS2264	Two sheets, each 85 × 110 mm. (a) 3000s. "King with Gift and Christmas Tree" (Nicole Kwiringira). (b) 3000s. "Adoration of the Shepherds" (Michael Tinkamanyire) Set of 2 sheets	9·50	11·00

229 Snake

2001. Chinese New Year ("Year of the Snake") and "Hong Kong 2001" Stamp Exhibition. Showing different snakes. Multicoloured.

2265	600s. Type **229**	1·00	1·10
2266	600s. Snake coiled around man	1·00	1·10
2267	600s. Snakes showing fangs	1·00	1·10
2268	600s. Snake on branch	1·00	1·10
MS2269	115 × 75 mm. 2500s. Cobra	4·50	5·00

230 Bongo

2001. Endangered Wildlife. Multicoloured.

2270	600s. Type **230**	1·25	1·25
2271	600s. Black rhinoceros	1·25	1·25
2272	600s. Leopard (vert)	1·25	1·25
MS2273	Two sheets. (a) 110 × 85 mm. 3000s. Mountain gorillas. (b) 85 × 110 mm. 3000s. Parrot (vert) Set of 2 sheets	11·00	11·00

231 Holy Family

233 Anemometer

232 East African School of Library and Information Science, Makerere

2001. 2000th Birth Anniv of Jesus Christ. Multicoloured.

2274	300s. Type **231**	55	30
2275	700s. Madonna and child	1·10	1·10
2276	1200s. The Nativity (horiz)	1·75	2·25

2001. East African Universities. Multicoloured.

2277	300s. Type **232**	55	30
2278	400s. Nairobi University	65	35
2279	1200s. Nkrumah Hall, University of Dar-es-Salaam	1·75	2·25
2280	1800s. Makerere, Kenyata and Open Universities (vert)	2·50	3·00

2001. 50th Anniv (2000) of World Meteorological Organization. Multicoloured.

2281	300s. Type **233**	75	30
2282	2000s. Tropical sun recorder (horiz)	2·75	3·50

234 Working in the Fields

2001. 50th Anniv of United Nations High Commissioner for Refugees. Economic Development. Multicoloured.

2283	300s. Type **234**	55	30
2284	600s. Community building project	95	50
2285	1200s. Carpentry class	1·75	2·00
2286	1800s. New water supply	2·50	3·00

235 "Segawa Kikunojo and Ichikawa Danjuro as Samurai" (Kiyonobu II)

2001. "Philanippon '01" International Stamp Exhibition, Tokyo. Japanese Woodcuts. Multicoloured.

2287	600s. Type **235**	35	40
2288	700s. "Tchimura Kamezo as Warrior" (Kiyohiro)	45	50
2289	1000s. "Ichikawa Danjuro as Shirobei Tadanobu" (Kiyomitsu)	60	65
2290	1200s. "Actor Arashi Sangoro" (Shunsho)	75	80
2291	1400s. "Matsumoto Koshiro IV as Juro Sukenari" (Kiyonaga)	85	90
2292	2000s. "Pheasant on Pine Branch" (Kiyomasu II)	1·20	1·30
MS2293	68 × 105 mm 3500s. Depicts "Tale of Ise" (Eishi)	2·10	2·20

236 Blue and Cream Shorthair

2001. Cats and Dogs. Multicoloured.

2294	400s. Tabby British shorthair (vert)	25	30
2295	600s. Type **236**	35	40
2296	600s. Manx	35	40
2297	600s. Angora	35	40
2298	600s. Red and white British shorthair	35	40
2299	600s. Turkish cat	35	40
2300	600s. Egyptian mau	35	40
2301	700s. Rottweiler	45	50
2302	700s. Flat-coated retriever	45	50
2303	700s. Samoyed	45	50
2304	700s. Poodle	45	50
2305	700s. Maltese	45	50
2306	700s. Irish terrier	45	50
2307	900s. Turkish cat (vert)	55	60
2308	1100s. German shepherd (vert)	70	75
2309	1200s. Irish setter (vert)	75	80
2310	1300s. English sheepdog	80	85
2311	1300s. German shepherd	80	85
2312	1300s. Great Dane	80	85
2313	1300s. Boston terrier	80	85
2314	1300s. Bull terrier	80	85
2315	1300s. Australian terrier	80	85
2316	1400s. Red tabby shorthair	85	90
2317	1400s. Japanese bobtail	85	90
2318	1400s. Siamese	85	90
2319	1400s. Tabby Persian	85	90
2320	1400s. Black and white Persian	85	90
2321	1400s. Russian blue	85	90
MS2322	Four sheets. (a) 106 × 76 mm. 3500s. American calico shorthair (vert). (b) 76 × 106 mm. 3500s. Blue-eyed british shorthair (vert). (c) 106 × 76 mm. 3500s. Bloodhound (vert). (d) 106 × 76 mm. 3500s. Pointer Set of 4 sheets	8·75	9·00

2001. Death Centenary of Queen Victoria. As T **101** of St. Kitts. Multicoloured.

2323	1000s. Queen Victoria wearing brown	60	65
2324	1000s. Queen Victoria in white bonnet	60	65
2325	1000s. Wearing feathered hat	60	65
2326	1000s. In evening dress	60	65
2327	1000s. Queen Victoria wearing choker with pendant	60	65
2328	1000s. In black dress, looking down	60	65
MS2329	107 × 83 mm. 3500s. Queen Victoria in furred hat	2·10	2·20

2001. 75th Death Anniv of Claude-Oscar Monet (French painter). As T **103** of St. Kitts. Multicoloured.

2330	1200s. "Storm, Belle-Ile Coast"	75	80
2331	1200s. "Manneporte, Etretat"	75	80
2332	1200s. "Rocks at Low Tide, Pourville"	75	80
2333	1200s. "Wild Sea"	75	80
MS2334	137 × 109 mm. 3500s. "Sunflowers" (vert)	2·10	2·20

2001. 75th Birthday of Queen Elizabeth II. As T **104** of St. Kitts. Multicoloured.

2335	1000s. Princess Elizabeth as a baby, 1926	60	65
2336	1000s. Princess Elizabeth aged 5, 1931	60	65

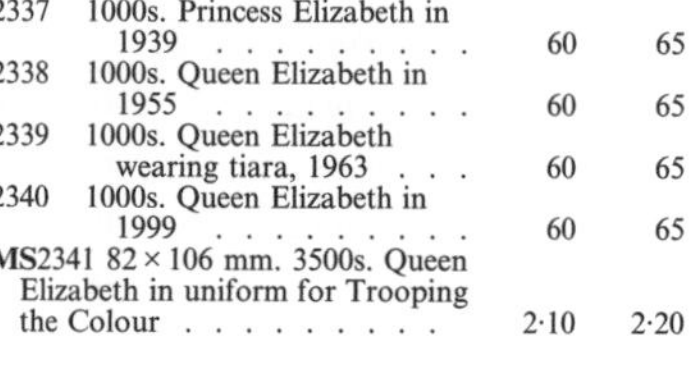

2337	1000s. Princess Elizabeth in 1939	60	65
2338	1000s. Queen Elizabeth in 1955	60	65
2339	1000s. Queen Elizabeth wearing tiara, 1963	60	65
2340	1000s. Queen Elizabeth in 1999	60	65
MS2341	82 × 106 mm. 3500s. Queen Elizabeth in uniform for Trooping the Colour	2·10	2·20

237 "Woman combing her Hair" (Toulouse-Lautrec)

2001. Death Centenary of Henri de Toulouse-Lautrec (French painter). Multicoloured.

2342	1500s. Type **237**	95	1·00
2343	1500s. "The Toilette"	95	1·00
2344	1500s. "English Girl at the Star Inn, Le Havre"	95	1·00
MS2345	74 × 109 mm. 3500s. "Aristide Bruant"	2·10	2·20

2001. Centenary of Royal Navy Submarine Service. As T **107** of St. Kitts. Multicoloured.

2346	1000s. H.M.S. *Tribune* (submarine) (vert)	60	65
2347	1000s. H.M.S. *Royal Oak* (battleship, launched 1914) (vert)	60	65
2348	1000s. H.M.S. *Invincible* (aircraft carrier) (vert)	60	65
2349	1000s. H.M.S. *Dreadnought* (nuclear submarine) (vert)	60	65
2350	1000s. H.M.S. *Ark Royal* (aircraft carrier, launched 1950) (vert)	60	65
2351	1000s. H.M.S. *Cardiff* (destroyer) (vert)	60	65
MS2352	70 × 57 mm. 3500s. H.M.S. Triad (submarine)	2·10	2·20

238 Carrying Ebola Victim on Stretcher

2001. U.N. Year of Dialogue among Civilizations (3000s.) and International Year of Volunteers (others). Multicoloured.

2353	300s. Type **238**	55	30
2354	700s. Blood donor session	1·10	65
2355	2000s. Provision of clean water	2·50	3·00
2356	3000s. Children encircling Globe (vert)	3·50	4·00

239 *Amanita excelsa*

2001. Fungi. Multicoloured.

2357	300s. Type **239**	55	30
2358	500s. *Coprinus cinereus*	80	55
2359	600s. *Scleroderma aurantium*	90	80
2360	700s. *Armillaria mellea*	1·10	1·10
2361	1200s. *Leopiota procera*	1·75	2·00
2362	2000s. *Flammulina velutipes*	2·75	3·25
MS2363	Two sheets, each 100 × 70 mm. (a) 3000s. *Amanita phalloides*. (b) 3000s. *Amanita fulva* Set of 2 sheets	10·00	11·00

240 Long Drums

242 White Horse

241 Namugongo Shrine, Uganda

2001. Christmas. Musical Instruments. Mult.

2364	400s. Type **240**	50	25
2365	800s. Animal horn trumpets (horiz)	90	65
2366	1000s. Bugisu clay drum	1·10	85
2367	1200s. Musical bows	1·40	1·40
2368	1400s. Pan pipes	1·60	1·75
2369	2000s. Two-man xylophone (horiz)	2·25	2·75
MS2370	Two sheets. (a) 85 × 110 mm. 3500s. Eight-stringed giant bow harp. (b) 110 × 85 mm. 3500s. Nativity (horiz) Set of 2 sheets	9·00	10·00

2002. Historical Sites of East Africa. Multicoloured.

2371	400s. Type **241**	25	30
2372	800s. Maruhubi Palace ruins, Zanzibar	50	55
2373	1200s. Kings' Burial Grounds, Mparo, Hoima	75	80
2374	1400s. Old Law Courts, Mombasa (vert)	85	90

2002. Chinese New Year ("Year of the Horse"). Multicoloured.

2375	1200s. Type **242**	75	80
2376	1200s. Piebald horse	75	80
2377	1200s. Dun horse	75	80
MS2378	75 × 105 mm. 3000s. Rearing horse	1·90	2·00

2002. Golden Jubilee. As T **110** of St. Kitts. Multicoloured.

2379	1500s. Young Queen Elizabeth looking to her left	95	1·00
2380	1500s. Queen Elizabeth in striped hat	95	1·00
2381	1500s. Queen Elizabeth in evening dress	95	1·00
2382	1500s. As No. 2379, but Queen Elizabeth looking to her right	95	1·00
MS2383	76 × 108 mm. 3500s. Queen Elizabeth wearing straw hat	2·10	2·20

2002. "United We Stand". Support for Victims of 11 September 2001 Terrorist Attacks. As T **179** of St. Kitts, but showing Ugandan flag.

2384	1500s. multicoloured	95	1·00

2002. International Year of Mountains. As T **115** of St. Kitts. Multicoloured.

2385	2000s. Mount Tateyama, Japan	1·20	1·30
2386	2000s. Mount Nikko Semdjoda-Hara, Japan	1·20	1·30
2387	2000s. Mount Hodaka, Japan	1·20	1·30
MS2388	70 × 55 mm. 3500s. Mount Fuji, Japan	2·10	2·20

2002. 20th World Scout Jamboree, Thailand. As T **116** of St. Kitts. Multicoloured.

2389	1400s. Scout from 1930s in forest	85	90
2390	1400s. Scout from 1930s saluting	85	90
2391	1400s. Two scouts with packs	85	90
2392	1400s. International Scouts symbol	85	90
MS2393	60 × 78 mm. 3500s. Lord Baden-Powell (vert)	2·10	2·20

243 Two Women with Symbol and Makerere University

2002. 8th International Interdisciplinary Congress on Women, Kampala. Multicoloured.

2394	400s. Type **243**	25	30
2395	1200s. Arms of Makerere University (vert)	75	80

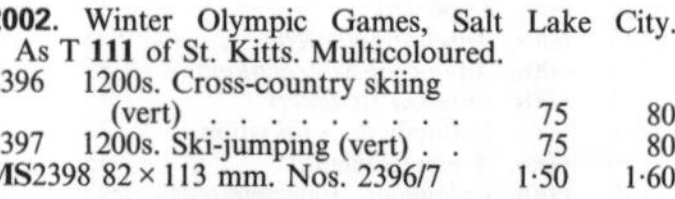

2002. Winter Olympic Games, Salt Lake City. As T **111** of St. Kitts. Multicoloured.

2396	1200s. Cross-country skiing (vert)	75	80
2397	1200s. Ski-jumping (vert)	75	80
MS2398	82 × 113 mm. Nos. 2396/7	1·50	1·60

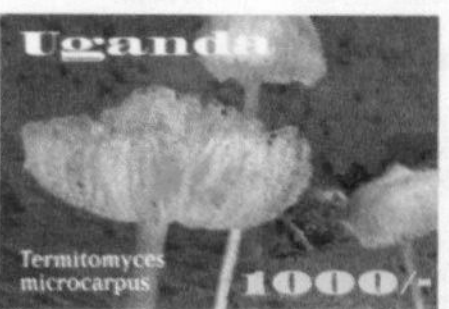

244 *Termitomyces microcarpus* (fungus)

2002. Flora and Fauna. Multicoloured.

2399 400s. White rhinoceros (vert) 25 30
2400 800s. *Macrotermes subhyalinus* (insect) (vert) 50 55
2401 1000s. Type **244** 60 65
2402 1000s. *Agaricus trisulphuratus* 60 65
2403 1000s. *Macrolepiota zeyheri* 60 65
2404 1000s. *Lentinus stupeus* . . . 60 65
2405 1000s. *Lentinus sajor-caju* . . 60 65
2406 1000s. *Lentinus velutinus* . . 60 65
2407 1000s. *Nudaurelia cytherea* (caterpillar) 60 65
2408 1000s. *Locusta migratoria* (locust) 60 65
2409 1000s. *Anacridium aegyptium* (grasshopper) 60 65
2410 1000s. *Sternotomis bohemanni* (longhorn beetle) 60 65
2411 1000s. *Papilio dardanus* (butterfly) 60 65
2412 1000s. *Mantis polyspilota* (mantid) 60 65
2413 1200s. Uganda kob 75 80
2414 1200s. Hartebeest 75 80
2415 1200s. Topi 75 80
2416 1200s. Olive baboon 75 80
2417 1200s. Lion 75 80
2418 1200s. Common warthog . . . 75 80
2419 1200s. *Canarina eminii* . . . 75 80
2420 1200s. *Vigna unguiculata* . . 75 80
2421 1200s. *Gardenia ternifolia* . . 75 80
2422 1200s. *Canavalia rosea* . . . 75 80
2423 1200s. *Hibiscus calyphyllus* 75 80
2424 1200s. *Nymphaea lotus* . . . 75 80
2425 1200s. *Gloriosa superba* (flower) (vert) 75 80
2426 1400s. *Cyptotrama asprata* (fungus) (vert) 85 90
MS2427 Four sheets, each 95 × 70 mm. (a) 4000s. *Podoscypha parvula* (fungus). (b) 4000s. *Glossina austeni* (tsetse fly). (c) 4000s. Waterbuck (vert). (d) 4000s. *Abutilon grandiflorum* (flower) Set of 4 sheets . . . . 10·00 10·50

Nos. 2401/6 (fungi), 240712 (insects), 2423/28 (mammals) and 2419/24 (flowers) were each printed together, se-tenant, with the backgrounds forming composite designs.

245 Cetiosaurus

246 President John Kennedy

2002. Prehistoric Animals. Multicoloured.

2428 600s. Type **245** 35 40
2429 600s. Brontosaurus 35 40
2430 600s. Brachiosaurus 35 40
2431 600s. Deinonychus 35 40
2432 600s. Dimetrodon 35 40
2433 600s. Megalosaurus 35 40

2002. Famous People of the Late 20th Century. Six miniature sheets containing T **246** and similar vert designs. Multicoloured (except No. **MS**2434/5).

(a) Life and Times of President John F. Kennedy. Two sheets containing portraits as T **246**.

MS2434 117 × 97 mm. 1200s. Type **246**; 1200s. In profile; 1200s. Facing right, speaking; 1200s. Smiling, facing forwards (all green and black) . . . . 3·00 3·25
MS2435 125 × 97 mm. 1400s. Wearing white jacket (brown and black); 1400s.Wearing brown jacket and white tie (light brown and black); 1400s. Wearing brown jacket and dark tie (brown and black); 1400s. Wearing brown jacket and dark tie (light brown and black) . . . . 3·50 3·75

(b) President Ronald Reagan. Two sheets, each containing four different portraits.

MS2436 138 × 115 mm. 1200s. Smiling with mouth open; 1200s. Looking down; 1200s. S[illegible]g with mouth closed; 1200s. Facing forwards . . . . 3·00 3·25
MS2437 120 × 95 mm. 1400s. Wearing red necktie (facing right); 1400s. Wearing grey sweater; 1400s. Close up of face; 1400s. Wearing red tie (facing forwards) 3·50 3·75

(c) 5th Death Anniv of Diana, Princess of Wales.

MS2438 125 × 150 mm. 1200s. Wearing red dress with white collar; 1200s. Wearing white jacket; 1200s. Wearing red and white jacket and hat; 1200s. Wearing evening dress and necklace . . . . 3·00 3·25
MS2439 140 × 115 mm. 2000s. Wearing white blouse; 2000s. Wearing lace blouse; 2000s. Wearing headscarf on visit to Middle East; 2000s. Wearing tiara and white jacket . . . . 4·75 5·00

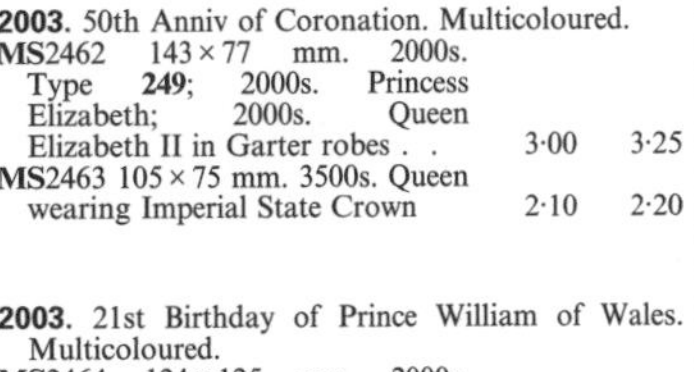

247 Ram (laying down)

248 Princess Katrina-Sarah Ssangalyambogo and Bulange Building

2003. Chinese New Year ("Year of the Ram"). Sheet, 107 × 120 mm, containing T **247** and similar vert designs. Multicoloured.

MS2440 1000s. Type **247**; 1000s. Ram on hilltop; 1000s. Ram and six rams heads; 1000s. Six rams; 1000s. Ram (looking backwards); 1000s. Ram climbing mountain 3·75 4·00

2003. Paintings by Rembrandt. As T **466** of St. Vincent. Multicoloured.

2441 400s. "Jacob Blessing the Sons of Joseph" (detail) 25 30
2442 1000s. "A Young Woman in Profile with Fan" 60 65
2443 1200s. "The Apostle Peter (Kneeling)" 80 85
2444 1400s. "The Painter Hendrick Martensz Sorgh" 85 90
MS2445 185 × 175 mm. 1400s. "Portrait of Margaretha de Geer"; 1400s. "Portrait of a White Haired Man"; 1400s. "Portrait of Nicolaes Ruts"; 1400s. "Portrait of Catrina Hooghsaet" . . . . 3·50 3·75
MS2446 138 × 135 mm. 5000s. "Joseph accused by Potiphar's Wife" (detail) . . . . 3·00 3·25

2003. 20th Death Anniv of Joan Miro (artist). As T **282** of Turks and Caicos Islands. Multicoloured.

2447 400s. "Group of Personages in the Forest" (horiz) . . 25 30
2448 800s. "Nocturne" (horiz) . . 50 55
2449 1200s. "The Smile of a Tear" (horiz) 80 85
2450 1400s. "Personage before the Sun" (horiz) 85 90
MS2451 132 × 175 mm. 1400s. "Man's Head III"; 1400s. "Catalan Peasant by Moonlight"; 1400s. "Woman in the Night"; 1400s. "Seated Woman" . . . 3·50 3·75
MS2452 Two sheets, each 102 × 82 mm. (a) 3500s. "Self Portrait II". Imperf. (b) 3500s. "Woman with Three Hairs, Birds, and Constellations". Imperf Set of 2 sheets . . . .

2003. Japanese Art. As T **467** of St. Vincent. Multicoloured.

2453 400s. "Beauty arranging her Hair" (Keisai Eisen) . . . 25 30
2454 1000s. "Geishas" (detail) (Kitagawa Tsukimaro) . . 60 65
2455 1200s. "True Beauties" (Toyohara Chikanobu) . . 75 80
2456 1400s. "Geishas" (different detail) (Kitagawa Tsukimaro) 85 90
MS2457 150 × 148 mm. 1200s. "Scene in a Villa" (detail of two women and urn) (Toyohara Kunichika); 1200s. "Scene in a Villa" (detail of two women behind screen) (Toyohara Kunichika); 1200s. "Visiting a Flower Garden" (detail of two women in garden) (Utagawa Kunisada); 1200s. "Visiting a Flower Garden" (detail of woman picking flowers) (Utagawa Kunisada) . . . . 3·25 3·50
MS2458 90 × 152 mm. 5000s. "Woman and Children" (detail) (Chikakazu) . . . . 3·00 3·25

2003. 2nd Birthday of Princess Katrina-Sarah Ssangalyambogo of Buganda. Multicoloured.

2459 400s. Type **248** 25 30
2460 1200s. Princess and Twekobe Palace, Mengo (vert) 80 85
2461 1400s. Princess and royal drum (vert) 85 90

249 Princess Elizabeth as Baby

250 Prince William

2003. 50th Anniv of Coronation. Multicoloured.

MS2462 143 × 77 mm. 2000s. Type **249**; 2000s. Princess Elizabeth; 2000s. Queen Elizabeth II in Garter robes . . 3·00 3·25
MS2463 105 × 75 mm. 3500s. Queen wearing Imperial State Crown 2·10 2·20

2003. 21st Birthday of Prince William of Wales. Multicoloured.

MS2464 124 × 125 mm. 2000s. Type **250**; 2000s. Prince William as boy holding presents; 2000s. As teenager . . . . 3·75 4·00
MS2465 105 × 76 mm. 5000s. Prince William as adult . . . . 3·00 3·25

251 Seville Elegante (1979)

2003. Centenary of General Motors Cadillac. Multicoloured.

MS2466 118 × 167 mm. 1200s. Type **251**; 1200s. Eldorado Touring Coupe (1998); 2000s. Escalade (2002); 2000s. Seville Elegante (1983) . . . . . . 3·75 4·00
MS2467 89 × 126 mm. 3500s. Eldorado . . . . 2·10 2·20

252 Corvette (1970)

2003. 50th Anniv of General Motors Chevrolet Corvette. Multicoloured.

MS2468 145 × 125 mm. 1400s. Type **252**; 1400s. Corvette (1972); 1400s. Collector Edition Corvette (1982); 1400s. Corvette (1977) 3·25 3·50
MS2469 125 × 90 mm. 3500s. Collector Edition Corvette (1982) 2·10 2·20

253 Endogoro Dance

254 Women holding Meeting ("Promote Gender Equity and Empower Women")

2003. Cultural Dances and Dresses of East Africa. Multicoloured.

2470 400s. Type **253** 25 60
2471 800s. Karimojong dancers 50 55
2472 1400s. Dance from Teso . . 85 90
MS2473 70 × 105 mm. 1200s. Kiga; 1200s. Acholi; 1200s. Karimojong; 1200s. Ganda . . . . 2·40 2·50

2003. United Nations Millennium Development Goals. Multicoloured.

2474 400s. Type **254** 25 30
2475 400s. Men pushing bicycle for pregnant woman ("Improve Maternal Health") 25 30
2476 600s. Women fetching water ("Ensure Environmental Sustainability") 35 40
2477 1000s. Woman feeding children ("Reduce Child Mortality") 60 65
2478 1200s. Couple and storage hut ("Eradicate Extreme Poverty and Hunger") . . 75 80
2479 1200s. Family outside house ("Combat HIV/AIDS, Malaria and other diseases") 75 80
2480 1400s. Teacher and schoolchildren ("Achieve Universal Primary Education") 85 90
2481 2000s. Emblem ("Develop a Global Partnership for Development") . . . . . 1·20 1·30

255 Mary and Joseph

2003. Christmas. Multicoloured.

2482 300s. Type **255** 20 25
2483 400s. Angels and Shepherds 25 30
2484 1200s. Nativity 75 80
2485 1400s. Three Wise Men . . 85 90
MS2486 105 × 70 mm. 3000s. Nativity (different) . . . . . . 1·90 2·00

256 Outline of Africa, Boy and Basket of Food

2004. International Food Policy Research Institute. Conference on Sustainable Food and Nutrition, Kampala. Multicoloured.

2487 400s. Type **256** 25 30
2488 1400s. As No. 2487 but showing girl . . . . . . 8·85 9·00

257 Adult making Child carry Baby and Bundle of Sticks

2004. Kids In Need. Prevention of Child Labour. Multicoloured.

2489 400s. Type **257** 25 30
2490 2000s. Speaker and people around blackboard . . . 1·20 1·30

258 Child laughing

2004. Straight Talk Foundation. Adolescent Health. Multicoloured.

2491 400s. Type **258** 25 30
2492 1200s. Boy reading paper . . 75 80

259 "Celebrate Rotary 100 Years"

2004. Centenary of Rotary International. Multicoloured.

2493 400s. Type **259** 25 30
2494 1200s. Rotary international emblem (vert) 75 80

POSTAGE DUE STAMPS

The Postage Due stamps of Kenya, Uganda and Tanganyika were used in Uganda until 2 January 1967.

D 1

D 3 Lion

1967.

D 7 D 1 5c. red . . . . 15 2·50
D 8 10c. green . . . . 15 2·50
D 9 20c. blue . . . . 25 3·00
D10 30c. brown . . . . 35 4·00

D11		40c. purple	55	4·50
D17		1s. orange	1·75	11·00

These stamps exist in limited quantities overprinted **UGANDA LIBERATED 1979**.

1979. Liberation. As Nos. D7/11 and D17 optd **LIBERATED 1979**.

D18	D 1	5c. red	15	40
D19		10c. green	15	40
D20		20c. blue	20	40
D21		30c. brown	20	60
D22		40c. purple	20	60
D23		1s. orange	20	60

1985. Animals.

D24	D 3	5s. black and turquoise	15	60
D25	–	10s. black and lilac . . .	15	60
D26	–	20s. black and orange . .	30	75
D27	–	40s. black and lilac . . .	80	1·10
D28	–	50s. black and blue . . .	80	1·10
D29	–	100s. black and mauve	1·40	1·75

DESIGNS: 10s. African buffalo; 20s. Kob; 40s. African elephant; 50s. Common zebra; 100s. Black rhinoceros.

UKRAINE Pt. 10

A district of S.W. Russia, which issued stamps during its temporary independence after the Russian Revolution. In 1923 it became a constituent republic of the U.S.S.R.

In 1991 it became an independent republic.

1918. 100 shahiv = 1 hryvna (grivna);
2 hriven = 1 rouble;
1992. 100 kopeks = 1 rouble.
1992. Karbovanets (coupon currency).
1996. 100 kopiykas = 1 hyrvna.

(L 6)

(L 8)

1918. Arms types of Russia optd with Trident device in various types according to the district. Imperf or perf.

L 51 **22** 1k. orange 10 10
L 52 2k. green 10 10
L 53 3k. red 10 10
L 54 **23** 4k. red 10 10
L 55 **22** 5k. red 10 10
L138 7k. blue 10 10
L 57 **23** 10k. blue 10 10
L 58 **22** 10k. on 7k. blue 15 10
L159 **9** 14k. red and blue 15 20
L 60 15k. blue and purple . . 10 10
L 61 **14** 20k. red and blue 10 10
L 62 **9** 20k. on 14k. red and blue 10 10
L145 25k. mauve and green . . 10 25
L 64 35k. green and purple . . 10 10
L 65 **14** 50k. green and purple . . 10 10
L 66 **9** 70k. orange and brown 10 10
L 47 **15** 1r. orange and brown . . 15 15
L 72 **11** 3r.50 grey and black . . 10·00 16·00
L212 3r.50 green and brown 20 20
L 49 **20** 5r. blue and green . . . 40 60
L 73 **11** 7r. yellow and black . . . 7·00 10·00
L 14 7r. pink and green . . . 90 2·00
L 36 **20** 10r. grey, red and yellow 5·50 6·50

1 Trident (from Arms of Grand Duke Vladimir the Great)

2 Peasant

3 Ceres

4 Trident

5

1918. Without inscription on back. Imperf.

1 **1** 10s. brown 20 50
2 **2** 20s. brown 20 50
3 **3** 30s. blue 20 50
4 **4** 40s. green 20 50
5 **5** 50s. red 20 50

1918. With trident and four lines of inscription on back.

6 **1** 10s. brown . . . . 2·50 5·00
7 **2** 20s. brown . . . . 2·50 5·00
8 **3** 30s. blue . . . . 2·50 5·00
9 **4** 40d. green . . . . 2·50 5·00
10 **5** 50s. red . . . . 2·50 5·00

6a Trident

6b Parliament Building

Stamps of the above and similar designs were prepared for use but never used.

7 Spectre of Famine

8 T. G. Shevchenko (Ukrainian poet)

1923. Charity.

12 **7** 10+10k. blue and black . . . 1·00 2·25
13 **8** 20+20k. brown and orange 1·00 2·25
14 – 90+30k. black and bistre . . 2·00 4·50
15 – 150+50k. red and black . . 4·00 6·00

DESIGNS—VERT: 90k. "Death" and peasant; 150k. "Ukraine" (woman) distributing bread.

11 Cossack Chief with Musician and Standard Bearer

12 Galician Emigrant Couple

1992. 500th Anniv (1990) of Ukraine Cossacks.
20 **11** 15k. multicoloured 15 10

1992. Centenary (1991) of Ukrainian Emigration to Canada.
21 **12** 15k. multicoloured 15 10

13 Mykola Lysenko and Score from "Taras Bulba"

1992. 150th Birth Anniv of Mykola Lysenko (composer).
22 **13** 1r. brown, red and bistre . . 10 10

14 Mykola Kostomarov, Quill Pen and Scroll

15 Ceres

1992. 175th Birth Anniv of Mykola Kostomarov (historian).
23 **14** 20k. brown and light brown 10 10

1992.

46 **15** 50k. blue 10 10
47 70k. brown 10 10
48 1r. green 10 10
49 2r. violet 10 10
50 5r. blue 10 10
51 10r. red 15 10
52 20r. green 30 20
53 50r. brown 75 50

16 Rhythmic Gymnastics

17 State Flag and Trident Symbol

1992. Olympic Games, Barcelona. Multicoloured.
54 3r. Type **16** 10 10
55 4r. Pole vaulting 10 10
56 5r. Type **16** 10 10

1992. 1st Anniv of Regained Independence.
57 **17** 2r. multicoloured 10 10

18 Three Cranes on Globe

1992. World Congress of Ukrainians, Kyiv.
58 **18** 2r. multicoloured 10 10

19 Folk Musicians

1992. 25th Anniv of Ukraine Philatelic Federation and First Stamp Exibition, Ivano—Frankivsk. Sheet 93 × 73 mm.
MS59 **19** 2r. multicoloured . . . 15 15

20 U.P.U. Emblem and Hand writing

1992. Correspondence Week.
60 **20** 5r. multicoloured 10 10

21 Congress Emblem

1992. World Congress of Ukrainian Jurists, Kyiv.
61 **21** 15r. multicoloured 15 10

22 Embroidery

1992. Ukraine Folk Art.
62 **22** 0.50k. black and orange . . 10 10

23 Arms of Austria and Ukraine with Traditional Costumes of Galicia and Bukovina

1992. Ukrainians in Austria.
63 **23** 5k. multicoloured 15 10

24 Students and Academy, 1632 (after I. Shyrsky)

1992. 360th Anniv of Mogilyanska's Academy, Kyiv.
64 **24** 1k.50 black, blue and brown 10 10

25 Runner and Olympic Medals

1992. Ukrain Medal Winners at Olympic Games, Barcelona. Sheet 90 × 70 mm.
MS65 **25** 10k. multicoloured . . 1·60 1·60

26 Lviv Arms

27 Cardinal Slipyj

1993. Regional Arms.
66 **26** 3k. blue, deep blue and gold 10 10
67 – 5k. lake, gold and red . . . 20 15
DESIGN: 5k. Kyiv.

1993. Birth Centenary (1992) of Cardinal Josyf Slipyj.
68 **27** 15k. multicoloured 45 30

28 Hansa Brandenburg C-I

1993. 75th Anniv of First Vienna–Cracow–Lviv–Kyiv Flight.
69 **28** 35k. black, blue and mauve 30 20
70 – 50k. multicoloured 40 30
DESIGN: 50k. Airbus Industrie A300.

29 Candles and Traditional Foods

1993. Easter.
71 **29** 15k. multicoloured 40 30

30 "Country Wedding in Lower Austria" (Ferdinand Georg Waldmuller)

31 National Famine Monument, Kyiv

1993. 45th Anniv of Declaration of Human Rights.
72 **30** 5k. multicoloured 30 20

1993. 60th Anniv of Famine Deaths.
73 **31** 75k. brown 10 10

32 1918 10sh. Stamp

1993. Stamp Day. 75th Anniv of First Ukrainian Postage Stamps.
74 **32** 100k. blue and brown . . . 15 10

33 Kyiv

34 Mowing

1993. 50th Anniv of Liberation of Kyiv.
75 **33** 75k. multicoloured 15 10

1993. Agricultural Scenes.
76 **34** 50k. green 10 10
77 – 100k. blue 10 10
78 – 150k. red 10 10
79 – 200k. orange 10 10
80 – 300k. purple 10 10
81 – 500k. brown 20 15
DESIGNS: 100k. Laden bullock carts; 150, 300k. Shepherd and flock; 200, 500k. Women cutting corn.

35 Madonna and Child (Albrecht Durer)

36 St. Ahapit

1994. Ukrainian Health Fund.
82 **35** 150k.+20k. black, gold and red 10 10

1994. St. Ahapit (medieval doctor).
83 **36** 200k. black and red 10 10

37 Dog's-tooth Violet ("Erythronium denscanis")

38 Laden Bullock Carts

1994. Red Book of Ukraine. Multicoloured.
84 200k. Type **37** 15 10
85 200k. Lady's slipper ("Cypripedium calceolus") 15 10

1994. Agricultural Scenes. Value expressed by Cyrillic letter.
86 – A (5000k.) red 25 15
87 **38** V (10000k.) blue 75 50
DESIGN: A, Shepherd and flock.
The Cyrillic "V" on No. 87 resembles a "B".

39 Women cutting Corn

40 Cutting Hay

1994. Agricultural Scenes. Value expressed by Cyrillic letter.
88 **39** B (100k.) brown 10 10
89 **40** G (250k.) green 10 10

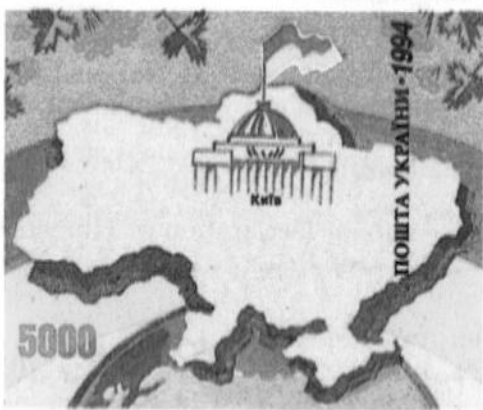
41 Parliament Building and Map

1994. Independence Day. Sheet 68 × 90 mm. Imperf.
MS90 **41** 5000k. multicoloured 20 20

42 Kyiv University

1994. 160th Anniv of Kyiv University. Multicoloured.
91 10000k. Type **42** 40 30
MS92 100 × 80 mm. 25000k. Kyiv University (different) (40 × 28 mm) 1·10 1·10

43 Map and Airplanes (Liberation of Ukraine)

1994. 50th Anniv of Liberation. Multicoloured.
93 500k. Map and rocket launchers (Russia) 10 10
94 500k. Type **43** 10 10
95 500k. Map, tank and soldiers (Byelorussia) 10 10

44 Ploughing

45 Fishing

1994. Agricultural Scenes. Value expressed by Cyrillic letter.
96 **44** D (100k.) mauve 10 10
97 **45** Zh (5300k.) blue 30 10

46 Bee-Keeping

47 Potter at Wheel

1994. Agricultural Scenes. Value expressed by Cyrillic letter.
98 **46** Ye (1800k.) brown 15 10
99 **47** E (17000k.) red 95 40

48 Ceramics and Map

49 Reader and Arms

1994. 100th Anniv of Excavation of Tripillya.
100 **48** 4000k. multicoloured . . . 10 10

1994. 500th Anniv of First Book printed in Ukrainian Language, "Book of Hours" by Sh. Fiol.
101 **49** 4000k. multicoloured . . . 10 10

50 Repin and Study of Soldier

1994. 150th Birth Anniv of Ilya Repin (painter).
102 **50** 4000k. multicoloured . . . 10 10

51 Sofiyivka Park and Statue

1994. Bicent of Sofiyivka Nature Park, Uman.
103 **51** 5000k. multicoloured . . . 10 10

52 Uzhhorod Castle

1995. 1100th Anniv of Uzhhorod.
104 **52** 5000k. multicoloured . . . 10 10

53 Ivan Franko (writer)

54 Peregrine Falcon

1995. Personalities. Multicoloured.
105 3000k. Type **53** 10 10
106 3000k. Ivan Pulyui (physicist) (vert) 10 10
107 3000k. Lesya Ukrainka (writer) 10 10

1995. Red Book of Ukraine. Birds. Multicoloured.
108 5000k. Type **54** 35 25
109 10000k. Common crane . . . 75 50

55 Rylskyi

56 Doves, Bell Tower and River

1995. Birth Centenary of Maksym Rylskyi (writer).
110 **55** 50000k. multicoloured . . 45 30

1995. 50th Anniv of End of Second World War.
111 **56** 100000k. multicoloured . . 75 60

57 Figures around Globe on Map of Ukraine

1995. 70th Anniv of Artek International Children's Holiday Camps, Crimea.
112 **57** 5000k. multicoloured . . . 10 10

58 Ivan Kotlyarevski and Scene from "Eneida" (poem)

1995. Writers. Multicoloured.
113 1000k. Type **58** 10 10
114 3000k. Taras Shevchenko and cover of "Kobzar" 10 10

59 Siege of Theodosia

1995. 17th-century Hetmans. Petro Konashevich-Sahaidachnyi.
115 **59** 30000k. multicoloured . . 25 15

60 Lugansk

1995. Regional Arms.
116 **60** 10000k. multicoloured . . 10 10

61 Bell Tower of Domition Church, National Museum and Dominican Cathedral

1995. National Stamp Exhibition, Lviv.
117 **61** 50000k.+5000k. mult . . . 35 20

62 St. Elias's Church, Subotov, and Battle Scene

1995. 17th-century Hetmans. Bohdan Khimelnytskyi.
118 **62** 40000k. multicoloured . . 25 15

63 St. Michael's Cathedral, Kyiv

1995. 17th-century Hetmans. Ivan Mazepa.
119 **63** 30000k. multicoloured . . 25 15

64 Part of Rainbow and White Stork

65 Girl carrying Water Pails

1995. European Nature Conservation Year.
120 **64** 50000k. multicoloured . . 35 20

1995. Regional Arms. As T **60**.
121 10000k. multicoloured . . . 10 10
DESIGN: 10000k. Chernihiv.

1995. International Children's Day.
122 **65** 50000k. multicoloured . . 35 20

66 Anniversary Emblem

67 Hrushevskyi

1995. 50th Anniv of U.N.O.
123 **66** 50000k. blue, violet and black 35 20

1995. 60th Death Anniv (1994) of Mykhailo Hrushevskyi (first President).
124 **67** 50000k. multicoloured . . 35 20

68 Karpenko-Karyi

69 Shafaryk

1995. 150th Birth Anniv of Ivan Karpenko-Karyi (dramatist).
125 **68** 50000k. multicoloured . . 35 20

1995. Birth Bicentenary of Pavel Shafaryk (historian and philologist).
126 **69** 30000k. green 25 15

70 Trolleybus

71 Tramcar

72 Bus

1995. Transport. Value expressed by Cyrillic letter.
127 **70** I (1000k.) blue 35 20
128 **71** K (2000k.) green 50 30
129 **72** Z (3000k.) pink 75 50

73 Oksana Bayul (gold, ice-skating)

1996. Ukrainian Medal Winners at Winter Olympic Games, Lillehammer. Sheet 90×70 mm containing T **73** and similar vert designs. Multicoloured.
MS130 40000k. Valentia Tserbe (bronze, biathlon); 50000k. Type **73** 90 75

74 Research Aids  **75** Krymskyi

1996. 150th Anniv of Observatory, Taras Shevchenko University, Kyiv. Multicoloured.
131 20000k. Type **74** 15 10
132 30000k. Telescope 25 15
133 50000k. Sun over observatory buildings 40 30

1996. 125th Birth Anniv of Ahatanhel Krymskyi (writer).
134 **75** 20000k. brown and ochre 15 10

76 Kozlovskyi  **77** Animals

1996. 3rd Death Anniv of Ivan Kozlovskyi (tenor).
135 **76** 20000k. multicoloured . . 15 10

1996. Centenary of Kharkiv Zoo.
136 **77** 20000k. olive, green and blue 15 10

78 Dovshenko and Birthplace

1996. Birth Centenary of Oleksandr Dovshenko (film producer and set designer).
137 **78** 4000k. multicoloured . . . 10 10

79 Lighted Candle within Tower  **80** Vasyl Fedorovych, Volodymyr Levkovich and Levko Platonovych Symyrenko

1996. 10th Anniv of Chernobyl Nuclear Disaster.
138 **79** 20000k. multicoloured . . 15 10

1996. Symyrenko Family.
139 **80** 20000k. multicoloured . . 15 10
Vasil was a sugar refiner; Volodimir and Levko fruit growers and researchers.

81 Stefanik

1996. 60th Death Anniv of Vasyl Stefanyk (writer and politician).
140 **81** 20000k. multicoloured . . 15 10

82 Miklukho-Maklai

1996. 150th Birth Anniv of Mikola Mikolaiovich Miklukho-Maklai (explorer and philologist).
141 **82** 40000k. multicoloured . . 30 20

83 Wrestling

1996. Olympic Games, Atlanta, U.S.A. Mult.
142 20000k. Type **83** 15 10
143 40000k. Handball 30 20
MS144 40×70 mm. 100000k. Gymnast 80 80

84 "100" and Ancient Greek Athletes  **85** Trident Emblem and "V" in National Colours

1996. Centenary of Modern Olympic Games.
145 **84** 40000k. bistre, turquoise and blue 30 20

1996. 5th Anniv of Independence.
146 **85** 20000k. multicoloured . . 15 10

86 "Sich-1"  **87** Series OD Steam Locomotive

1996. 1st Ukrainian Satellite.
147 **86** 20000k. multicoloured . . 15 10

1996. Railway Locomotives. Multicoloured.
148 20000k. Type **87** 30 20
149 40000k. Class 2TE-116 diesel locomotive 65 45

88 Antonov  **89** Piddubnyi

1996. 90th Birth Anniv of Oieh Antonov (aircraft designer). Multicoloured.
150 20000k. Type **88** 20 15
151 20000k. Antonov An-2 biplane 20 15
152 40000k. Antonov An-124 airliner 40 25
153 40000k. Antonov An-225 piggybacking airplane . . . 40 25

1996. 125th Birth Anniv of Ivan Piddubnyi (weightlifting world champion).
154 **89** 40k. multicoloured 30 20

90 Academician Vernadskyi Antarctic Station  **91** Eidelwiess

1996. 1st Ukrainian Antarctic Expedition.
155 **90** 20k. multicoloured 20 15

1996. Protected Flowers. Multicoloured.
156 20k. Type **91** 20 10
157 40k. "Narcissus anqustifolius" 30 20

92 Emblem  **93** Kosenko

1996. 50th Anniv of UNESCO.
158 **92** 20k. multicoloured 15 10

1996. Birth Centenary of W. S. Kosenko (composer).
159 **93** 20k. multicoloured 15 10

94 St. Sophia Cathedral, Kyiv

1996. Churches. Multicoloured.
160 20k. Type **94** 15 10
161 20k. St. Elias's Church, Subotov 15 10
162 20k. St. George's Church, Drogobych 15 10
163 20k. Trinity Cathedral, Novomoskovsk 15 10

95 Mohyla

1996. 400th Birth Anniv of Petro Mohyla (Metropolitan of Kyiv).
164 **95** 20k. black and brown . . . 15 10

96 Mother and Child within Emblem

1996. 50th Anniv of UNICEF.
165 **96** 20k. multicoloured 15 10

97 Lynx

1997. Protected Animals. Multicoloured.
166 20k. Type **97** 15 10
167 20k. Brown bear 15 10

98 Cathedral of the Holy Cross, Poltava

1997. Religious Buildings. Multicoloured.
168 20k. Type **98** 15 10
169 20k. St. George's Cathedral, Lviv 15 10
170 20k. St. Mary's Church, Sythtsi 15 10

99 Kyiv and Schek

1997. Europa. Tails and Legends. The Founders of Kyvi. Sheet 100×80 mm containing T **99** and similar vert designs. Each green, yellow and brown.
MS171 40k. Type **99**; 40k. Khoryv and their sister Lybid 75 75

100 Taras Shevchenko Monument, Stamps and Exhibition Hall

1997. 4th National Stamp Exhibition, Cherkasy.
172 **100** 10k. multicoloured . . . 10 10

101 Kondratyuk and Diagram of Space Orbit

1997. Birth Centenary of Yury Kondratyuk (space pioneer).
173 **101** 20k. multicoloured . . . 15 10

102 Arms, Map on Open Book and Assembly Building

1997. 1st Anniv of Constitution.
174 **102** 20k. multicoloured . . . 15 10

103 Fire, Fern and Couple  **104** Princess Olga (regent of Kyiv, 945–55)

1997. Midsummer Festival of Ivana Kupala.
175 **103** 20k. multicoloured . . . 15 10

1997. Famous Women. Multicoloured.
176 40k. Type **104** 30 20
177 40k. Roxolana (wife of Sultan Suleiman II of Turkey) 30 20

105 Taras Shevchenko Monument, Buenos Aires

1997. Centenary of First Ukranian Emigration to Argentina.
178 **105** 20k. multicoloured . . . 15 10

106 For Military Service for Ukraine

108 Kruschenlnytska

107 Dmytro Vyshnevetskyi Baida

1997. Orders and Medals.
179 **106** 20k. multicoloured . . . 10 10
180 – 20k. multicoloured . . . 10 10
181 – 30k. grey, red and blue 20 15
182 – 40k. multicoloured . . . 25 20
183 – 60k. multicoloured . . . 35 25
MS184 100 × 80 mm. 60k. × 2, each slate, crimson and blue 90 90
DESIGNS: No. 180, For Meritorious Service; 181, For Valour; 182, Order of Bohdan Khemelnytskyi; 183, For Special Contributions. 34 × 43 mm—No. **MS**184, Order of Prince Yaroslav medal (profile in centre); badge (helmet in centre).

1997. Hetmans. Multicoloured.
185 20k. Type **107** 15 10
186 20k. Stockholm, Pylyp Orlik and Thessalonika 15 10

1997. 125th Birth Anniv of Solomiya Kruschenlnytska (opera singer).
187 **108** 20k. multicoloured . . . 15 10

109 Antonov An-74 TK-200

1997. Aircraft. Multicoloured.
188 20k. Type **109** 15 10
189 40k. Antonov An-38-100 . . 30 20

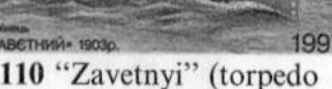

110 "Zavetnyi" (torpedo boat), 1903

111 "Columbia" (space shuttle) and Flags

1997. Ships. Multicoloured.
190 20k. Type **110** 15 10
191 40k. "Akademik Sergei Korolov" (research ship), 1970 . . . . 30 20

1997. Ukraine–U.S.A. Space Flight.
192 **111** 40k. multicoloured . . . 40 30

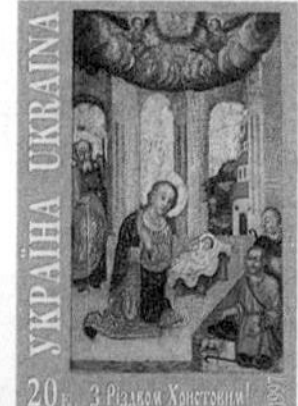

112 Krichevskyi

113 "Nativity" (icon)

1997. 125th Birth Anniv of Vasyl Krichevskyi (painter and architect).
193 **112** 10k. stone, brown & black 10 10

1997. Christmas.
194 **113** 20k. multicoloured . . . 15 10

114 Painted Rooster, Dnipropetrovsk

1997. Folk Art. Multicoloured. Buff margins.
195 20k. Type **114** 15 10
196 20k. Fur-trimmed waistcoat, Chernivtsi 15 10
197 40k. Ceramic ram, Poltava 25 20
198 40k. Wooden plate, Ivano-Frankivsk 25 20
MS199 115 × 149 mm. As Nos. 195/8 but with white margins, each × 2. 1·50 1·50

115 Skovoroda

116 Arms of Zakarpattskaya Oblast

1997. 275th Birth Anniv of Grigorii Skovoroda (philosopher).
200 **115** 60k. multicoloured . . . 40 30

1997. Regional Arms.
201 **116** 20k. multicoloured . . . 10 10

117 Skylark

1997. Animals. Sheet 114 × 121 mm containing T **117** and similar vert designs. Multicoloured.
MS202 20k. Type **117**; 20k. Black stork; 20k. Garden dormouse; 40k. White-tailed eagle; 40k. Long-eared hedgehog; 40k. Wild boar . . . . 1·50 1·50

118 Sosyura

119 Figure Skating

1998. Birth Centenary of Volodimyr Sosyura (poet).
203 **118** 20k. blue, black and brown 10 10

1998. Winter Olympic Games, Nagano, Japan. Multicoloured.
204 20k. Type **119** 10 10
205 20k. Biathlon 10 10

120 City Walls

1998. 2500th Anniv of Bilhorod-Dnistrovskyi.
206 **120** 20k. multicoloured . . . 10 10

121 "Hetman Sagaidachnyi" (frigate)

1998.
207 **121** 30k. multicoloured . . . 25 20

122 1 Million Karbovanets Coin showing Bohdan Khmelnytskyi

123 Festival of Ivana Kupala

1998. Coins.
208 **122** 30k. black, green & purple 20 15
209 – 30k. black, green & purple 20 15
210 – 60k. brown, green and purple 30 25
211 – 60k. brown, green and purple 35 25
212 – 1h. brown, green & purple 60 40
213 – 1h. black, green and purple 60 40
DESIGNS: No. 209, 10 hryven coin showing Petro Mohila; 210, 500 hryven coin showing Virgin Mary; 211, 200 hryven coin showing Taras Shevchenko; 212, Gold coin of Vladymyr Svyatoslavich; 213, Silver coin of Vladymyr Svyatoslavich.

1998. Europa. National Festivals.
214 **123** 40k. multicoloured . . . 30 20

124 Red Deer

1998. Centenary of New Askaniya National Park. Sheet 100 × 800 mm containing T **124** and similar horiz designs. Multicoloured.
MS215 40k. Type **124**; 60k. Wild horses 70 70

125 "Empress Maria Theresa" (J. E. Liotard)

1998. Paintings. Multicoloured.
216 20k. Type **125** 15 10
217 20k. "Man playing Cello" (G. Honthorst) 15 10
218 40k. "Madonna and Child" (icon) 25 20
MS219 93 × 73 mm. 1r.20 "Madonna and Child" 75 75

126 University Campus

1998. Centenary of Kyvi Technical University (1st issue). Sheet 113 × 80 mm.
MS220 **126** 1h. multicoloured . . 55 55
See also Nos. 232/6.

127 Askold and Dir

1998. 1st Rulers of Kyiv.
221 **127** 3h. purple and bistre . . 95 85

128 Armoured Rider and Swordsman

1998. 350th Anniv of Start of Campaign for Independence. Each brown, green and purple.
222 30k. Type **128** 15 10
223 30k. Warriors with staves and swordsman 15 10
224 40k. Stavesman, swordsman and archer 20 15
225 40k. Group of archers . . . 20 15
226 60k. Rider 30 20
227 2h. Hetman Bohdan Khmelnytskyi 65 65
Nos. 222/7 were issued together, se-tenant, forming a composite design.

129 Crown of Prince Danylo Galitsky

1998. 1100th Anniv of the Town of Halich.
228 **129** 20k. multicoloured . . . 10 10

130 Anna Yaroslavna

1998. Anna Yaroslavna (daughter of King Yaroslav of Kyiv and wife of King Henri I of France).
229 **130** 40k. multicoloured . . . 20 15

131 Lisyansky

1998. 225th Birth Anniv of Yurii Fyodorovich Lisyansky (first Ukrainian to circumnavigate world).
230 **131** 40k. multicoloured . . . 20 15

132 Natalia Uzhvii

1998. Birth Centenary of Natalia Uzhvii (actress).
231 **132** 40k. brown and gold . . 20 15

133 V. L. Kyrpychov (first Director)

1998. Centenary of Kyiv Technical University. Multicoloured.
232 10k. Type **133** 10 10
233 20k. E. Paton (metallurgist) and bridge in Kyiv 20 15
234 20k. Stefan Timoshenko (materials scientist) and formula 20 15
235 30k. Igor Sikorsky (aircraft designer) and test flight in Kyiv 30 20
236 40k. Sergei Korolev (space scientist) and spacecraft . . 40 25

134 Emblem and Posthorn on "Stamp"

135 Monk Nestor (early chronicler)

1998. World Post Day.
237 **134** 10k. multicoloured . . . 10 10

1998. Millenary of Book Production in Ukraine.
238 **135** 20k. multicoloured . . . 10 10

136 Cathedral of the Transfiguration, Chernigov

1998. Cathedrals. Multicoloured.
239 20k. Type **136** 10 10
240 20k. Pokrovsky Cathedral, Kharkov 10 10

137 Red-breasted Geese

1998. Endangered Species. The Red-breasted Goose. Multicoloured.
241 20k. Type **137** 10 10
242 30k. Goose 15 10
243 40k. Goose with chicks . . . 20 15
244 60k. Geese with chicks . . . 30 20
MS245 290 × 120 mm. Nos. 241/4, each × 2 . . . . 1·25 1·25

138 Battle of Chyhyryn, Doroshenko and Volokolamsk

1998. Hetmans. Petro Doroshenko.
246 **138** 20k. multicoloured . . . 10 10

139 Antonov An-140

1998. Aircraft. Multicoloured.
247 20k. Type **139** 10 10
248 40k. Antonov An-70 . . . . 20 15

140 Hrinchenko and his Dictionary

1998. 135th Birth Anniv of B. Hrinchenko (philologist).
249 **140** 20k. multicoloured . . . 10 10

141 Folk Icon

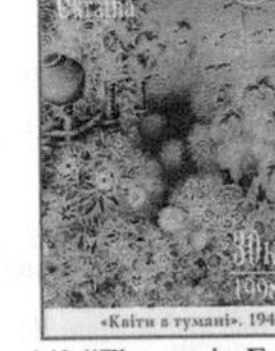
143 "Flowers in Fog"

142 Map of Australia and Waratah

1998. Christmas.
250 **141** 30k. multicoloured . . . 10 10

1998. 50th Anniv of Ukrainians in Australia.
251 **142** 40k. multicoloured . . . 15 10

1998. 50th Anniv of Universal Declaration of Human Rights. Paintings by Kateryna Bilokur. Multicoloured.
252 30k. Type **143** 10 10
253 50k. "Bouquet of Flowers" 20 15

144 Meteorites striking Earth

1998. Illinetsk Meteorite Impact Site.
254 **144** 40k. multicoloured . . . 20 10

145 Paradzhanov

1999. 75th Birth Anniv of Sergei Paradzhanov (film director).
255 **145** 40k. multicoloured . . . 20 15

146 Ivasyuk

1999. 50th Birth Anniv of Volodymyr Ivasyuk (composer).
256 **146** 30k. multicoloured . . . 10 10

147 Quiver

1999. Scythian Gold. Multicoloured.
257 20k. Type **147** 10 10
258 40k. Statuette of boar 15 10
259 50k. Statuette of young elk 15 10
260 1h. Pectoral 30 20

148 Girls in Central Ukrainian National Costume

149 Lake and Carpathian Mountains

1999. Spring.
261 **148** 30k. multicoloured . . . 10 10

1999. Europa. Parks and Gardens. Synievyr Lake National Park. Multicoloured.
262 50k. Type **149** 10 10
263 1h. Lake and European grayling 25 15
Nos. 262/3 were issued together, se-tenant, forming a composite design.

150 Mirny

1999. 150th Birth Anniv of Panas Mirny (writer).
264 **150** 40k. multicoloured . . . 10 10

151 Balzac

1999. Birth Bicentenary of Honore de Balzac (writer).
265 **151** 40k. black, gold and red 10 10

152 Anniversary Emblem and Headquarters, Strasbourg

1999. 50th Anniv of Council of Europe.
266 **152** 40k. multicoloured . . . 10 10

153 Pushkin

1999. Birth Bicentenary of Aleksandr Sergyevich Pushkin (poet).
267 **153** 40k. multicoloured . . . 10 10

154 Baidak

1999. Traditional Warships. Multicoloured.
268 30k. Type **154** 10 10
269 30k. Chaika 10 10

155 Great Prince Yaroslav

1999. 800th Anniv of Accession of Prince Yaroslav (the Wise). Sheet 104 × 84 mm.
MS270 **155** 1h.20 multicoloured 60 60

156 St. George on Horseback (15th- century icon)

1999. Centenary of National Art Museum, Kyiv. Multicoloured.
271 30k. Type **156** 10 10
272 60k. "The Girl in the Red Hat" (O. O. Murashko) . . 15 10

157 Heraldic Lion (emblem of Lviv) and Armoured Knight

1999. 800th Anniv of Galitsian-Volynian State.
273 **157** 50k. multicoloured . . . 10 10

158 Honey Bee on Flower

159 Monument, Berne

1999. Bee-keeping.
274 **158** 30k. multicoloured . . . 10 10

1999. 125th Anniv of Universal Postal Union.
275 **159** 30k. multicoloured . . . 10 10

160 Crest and Scroll

161 Order of Princess Olga

1999. 1100th Anniv of Poltava.
276 **160** 30k. multicoloured . . . 10 10

1999. Order and Medals. Multicoloured.
277 30k. Type **161** 10 10
MS278 100 × 80 mm. 2h.50 For Service to the State (34 × 49 mm); 2h.50 Order of the Golden star (34 × 49 mm) . . . . 2·40 2·40

162 Madonna and child (icon)

164 Bank Emblem

163 Red Deer (Stuzhitsya Regional Landscape Park)

1999. International year of The Elderly. Sheet115 × 90 mm.
MS279 **162** 1h.20+10k. multicoloured 30 30

1999. Animals of the East Carpathian Mountains. Multicoloured.
280 1h.40 Type **163** 35 25
281 1h.40 Wild cat (Bieszczadzki National Park) 35 25

1999. 160th Anniv of National Bank.
282 **164** 3h. multicoloured 75 50
MS283 112 × 120 mm. **164** 5h. multicoloured . . . . 1·20 1·20

165 Vyhovskyi and Battle of Konotop

1999. Hetmans. Ivan Vyhovskyi.
284 **165** 30k. multicoloured . . . 10 10

166 Three Wise Men

1999. Christmas. Multicoloured.
285 30k. Type **166** 10 10
286 60k. Nativity 15 10

168 Space Rocket and Car on Moon (Ivan Kovalevskyi)

1999. Winning Entries in Children's Stamp Design Competition. Multicoloured.
287 10k. Type **168** 10 10
288 10k. Elephant wearing space helmet (Ivan Chuev) . . . 10 10
289 10k. Aliens and space ship (Dmitro Verzhbyikyi) . . . 10 10

169 Russian Desman

1999. Endangered Species. Multicoloured.
290 40k. Type **169** 10 10
291 40k. Stag beetle (*Lucanus cervus*) 10 10
292 60k. Griffon vulture 15 10

170 Angel and Church, Kyiv

171 Boot-lace Fungus

1999. St. Andriya Pervozvannoho Commemoration.
293 **170** 60k. multicoloured . . . 15 10

1999. Fungi. Multicoloured.
294 30k. Type **171** 10 10
295 30k. Velvet-footed pax (*Paxillus atrotomentosus*) 10 10
296 30k. Oyster mushroom (*Pleurotus ostreatus*) . . . 10 10
297 30k. Chanterelle (*Cantharellus cibarius*) 10 10
298 30k. Field mushroom (*Agaricus campestris*) . . . 10 10

172 KRAZ-65032 Lorry

1999. Motor Vehicles. Multicoloured.
299 30k. Type **172** 10 10
300 30k. Tavriya car 10 10

173 Girl wearing New Year's Costume

1999. New Year.
301 **173** 50k. multicoloured . . . 10 10

174 Ships, Polubotok and St. Petersburg

1999. Hetmans. Pavel Polubotok.
302 **174** 30k. multicoloured . . . 10 10

175 "Pea Wild"

1999. Paintings by Mariya Primachenko. Mult.
303 30k. Type **175** 10 10
304 30k. "Wild Boar" 10 10

176 Gulebichibna

178 Our Lady Oranta (mosaic), Sophia Cathedral, Kyiv

177 Deer and Wild Cat

1999. 425th Birth Anniv (2000) of Galshka Gulebichibna.
305 **176** 30k. multicoloured . . . 10 10

1999. Nature Reserves. Sheet 112 × 122 mm containing T **177** and similar horiz designs. Multicoloured.
MS306 10k. Type **177** (Karpatskyi Reserve); 30k. Owl ox and wolf (Poliskyi Reserve); 40k. Eagle catching fish (Kanivskyi Reserve); 60k. Deer and warthog (Trakhtemiriv Reserve); 1h. Goat and duck (Askaniya-Nova Reserve); 1h. Birds beside lake (Karadeazhskyi Reserve) . . . 85 85

2000. Birth Bimillenary of Jesus Christ. Sheet 151 × 101 mm containing T **178** and similar vert designs. Multicoloured.
MS307 80k. Type **178**; 80k. Jesus Christ (fresco, Spaso-Preobrazhenskoi Church, Polotsk, Belarus); 80k. Our Lady Volodimirska (icon, National Tretyakov Gallery, Moscow) 50 50

179 Moscow Bridge, 1976

2000. Bridges in Kyiv. Multicoloured.
308 10k. Type **179** 10 10
309 30k. Ye. O. Paton Bridge, 1953 . . . . 10 10
310 40k. Pedestrian bridge, 1957 10 10
311 60k. Metro bridge, 1965 . . . 15 10

180 National Theatre, Kyiv

2000. Theatres. Sheet 92 × 135mm containing T **180** and similar horiz designs. Multicoloured.
MS312 40k. Type **180**; 40k. State Theatre, Odessa; 40k. Mykoy Lysenka Theatre, Kharkov; 40k. Ivan Franka Theatre, Lviv . . 40 40

181 Medieval Monk

2000. Peresoonytske Gospel (16th-century Ukranian translation). Sheet 121 × 85 mm.
MS313 **181** 1h.50 multicoloured 35 35

182 Petrusenko

183 Churai

2000. Birth Centenary of Oksana Petrusenko (singer). Multicoloured.
314 **182** 30k. multicoloured . . . 10 10

2000. Marusia Churai (songwriter) Commemoration.
315 **183** 40k. multicoloured . . . 10 10

184 Cossack Forces attacking Derbent Fortress, Danylo Apostol and Church

2000. Hetmans. Multicoloured.
316 30k. Type **184** 10 10
317 30k. Kozacha Dibrova (Cossack council), Ivan Samoilovych and Tobol'sk 10 10

185 Globe and Emblem

186 "Building Europe"

2000. 50th Anniv of World Meteorological Organization.
318 **185** 30k. multicoloured . . . 10 10

2000. Europa.
319 **186** 3h. multicoloured . . . . 1·40 1·40

187 Podillia Region

2000. Easter. Sheet 103 × 137 containing T **187** and similar horiz designs showing traditional egg decorations. Multicoloured.
MS320 30k. Type **187**; 30k. Chernihiv region; 30k. Kyiv; 30k. Odeska region: 70k. Hutsulschyna redion; 70k. Volynska region 80 80

188 Woman with Letter and Austria 1850 2k. Stamp

2000. "WIPA 2000" International Stamp Exhibition, Vienna. Sheet 160 × 46 mm containing T **188** and similar horiz designs. Multicoloured.
MS321 80k. Type **188**; 80k. Man writing letter and Great Britain Penny Black 40 40

189 Sunflower, Map and Emblem (Donetsk)

2000. Regions. Multicoloured.
322 30k. Type **189** 10 10
323 30k. Statue, map and churches (Kyiv) 10 10

190 Buildings and Emblem

2000. National Stamp Exhibition, Donetsk.
324 **190** 30k. multicoloured . . . 10 10

191 Buildings

192 High Jump

2000. 900th Anniv of Ostroh.
325 **191** 30k. multicoloured . . . 10 10

2000. Olympic Games, Sydney. Multicoloured.
326 30k. Type **192** 10 10
327 30k. Boxing 10 10
328 70k. Sailing 20 10
329 1h. Rhythmic gymnastics . . 25 10

193 Prokopovych

2000. 150th Death Anniv of Petro Prokopovych (beekeeper).
330 **193** 30k. multicoloured . . . 10 10

194 *St. Paul* (ship of the line)

195 "Leafy Plants with Flowers–1950s Series"

2000. Ships. Multicoloured.
331 40k. Type **194** 10 10
332 70k. *St. Nicholas* (frigate) . . 20 10

2000. Paintings by Tetiana Pata. Multicoloured.
333 40k. Type **195** 10 10
334 40k. "Viburnum Berries and Bird" 10 10

196 Tower and Arms

197 Women harvesting

2000. 900th Anniv of Dubno.
335 **196** 30k. multicoloured . . . 10 10

2000. Harvest Festival.
336 **197** 30k. multicoloured . . . 10 10

198 Presidential Flag

2000. Official Presidential Symbols. Multicoloured.
337 60k. Type **198** 15 10
338 60k. Mace 15 10
339 60k. Seal 15 10
340 60k. Chain of office 15 10

199 Elk, Map and Arms

2000. Regions. Volynska.
341 **199** 30k. multicoloured . . . 10 10

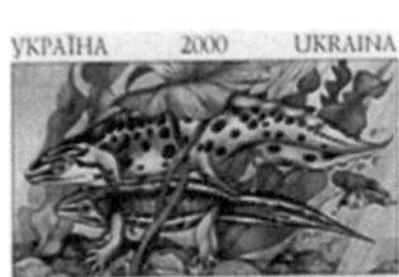

200 Kyiv General Post Office, Anniversary Emblem and Figures

2000. 225th Anniv of Kyiv General Post Office.
342 **200** 30k. blue, green and silver 10 10

201 Common Newts (*Triturus vulgaris*)

2000. Endangered Amphibians. Multicoloured.
343 30k. Type **201** 10 10
344 70k. European fire salamander (*Salamandra salamandra*) 20 10

202 Drogobych

2000. 250th Birth Anniv of Yuri Drogobych (Kotermack) (first Ukrainian Doctor and author of the first book printed in Slav).
345 **202** 30k. multicoloured . . . 10 10

203 Mount Breskul **204** Marigolds

2000. Carpathian National Park. Sheet 90 × 60 mm containing T **203** and similar vert designs. Multicoloured.
MS346 80k. Type **203**; 80k. Mount Hoberla 40 40

2000. Flora. Sheet 130 × 150 mm containing T **204** and similar vert designs. Multicoloured.
MS347 30k. Type **204**; 30k. Camomile; 30k. Hollyhocks; 30k. Poppies; 30k. Periwinkle; 30k. Cornflower; 30k. Morning glory; 30k. Martagon lily; 30k. Peony; 30k. Bluebells 70 70

205 Grapes, Map and Lastivske Hnizdo Castle

2000. Regions. Crimea.
348 **205** 30k. multicoloured . . . 10 10

206 Young Boy and Witch

2000. Animated Children's Folk Tales. Multicoloured.
349 30k. Type **206** 10 10
350 30k. Elderly couple and duck ("Crooked Duck") 10 10
351 30k. Cat and rooster 10 10

207 Bridge joining Globes and Father Frost carrying Tree

2000. New Year.
352 **207** 30k. multicoloured . . . 10 10

208 St. Onufius Church, Lviv **209** Prince Volodymyr the Great

2000. Churches. Multicoloured.
353 30k. Type **208** 10 10
354 30k. Church of Christ's Birth, Velyke 10 10
355 70k. Church of the Resurrection, Sumy 10 10

2000. 2000 Years of Christianity. Sheet 78 × 96 mm.
MS356 **209** 2h. multicoloured . . 45 45

210 Dymytryi Rostovskyi and Icons

2001. 350th Birth Anniv of Dymytryi Rostovskyi.
357 **210** 75k. multicoloured . . . 20 20

211 Basket of Roses and Two Doves

2001. St. Valentine's Day.
358 **211** 30k. multicoloured . . . 10 10

212 Danylo Romanovich and Flag

2001. 800th Birth Anniv of Prince Danylo Romanovich (ruler of Galicia and Volhynia (now in Poland and the Ukraine)). Sheet 86 × 106 mm.
MS359 **212** 3k. multicoloured . . 80 80

213 Turkish Prison, Yuryi Khmelnytskyi and Kamianets-Podilskyi Fortifications

2001. Hetmans. Multicoloured.
360 30k. Type **213** 10 10
361 50k. Ukraine and Polish armies, portrait and Mykhailo Khanenko relinquishing power to Ivan Samoilovych 15 15

214 1877 and Modern Telephones

2001. 125th Anniv of the Telephone.
362 **214** 70k. multicoloured . . . 10 10

215 Girl with Yellow Hair (Alyna Nochvaj)

2001. Children's Paintings. Multicoloured.
363 10k. Type **215** 10 10
364 30k. Landscape (Olyia Pynych) 10 10
365 40k. Shopping (Dasha Chemberzhi) 15 15

216 Mallow Flowers **217** Fox throwing Fish from Sled (Sister Fox and Brother Wolf)

2001. Multicoloured.
366 5k. Periwinkle 10 10
367 B (10k.) Type **216** 10 10
367a 10k. As Type **216** 10 10
368 D (30k.) Carnation 10 10
368a 30k. Carnation 10 10
368b 30k. Carnation 10 10
369 45k. Cornflower 10 10
369a 45k. Cornflower 10 10
370 65k. Sweetpea 15 15
371 E (71k.) Sunflower 20 20
371a E (71k.) Sunflower 20 20
372 C (80k.) Lilac 20 20
372a C (80k.) Lilac 20 20
373 Zh. (2h.66) Viburnum berries 70 70
373a Zh. (2h.66) Viburnum berries 70 70
374 € (3h.65) Wheat 95 95
374a € (3h.65) Wheat 95 95
375 P (10h.84) Trident . . . . 2·75 2·75
375a P (10h.84) Trident . . . . 2·75 2·75

2001. Folktales. Multicoloured.
382 30k. Type **217** 10 10
383 30k. Animals inside glove (Glove) 10 10
384 30k. Wolf with food and drink (Sirko) 10 10

218 *Twelve Apostles* (barque)

2001. Sailing Ships. Multicoloured.
385 20k. Type **218** 10 10
386 30k. *Three Saints* (barque) . . 10 10
See also Nos. 428/9 and 282/3.

219 Pebbles and Fish **221** Bee collecting Pollen

220 Holy Trinity enclosed in Flower Wreath

2001. Europa. Water Resources.
387 1h. Type **219** 25 25
388 1h. Pebbles, fish and medusa (56 × 40 mm) 25 25
Nos. 387/8 were issued together, se-tenant, forming a composite design.

2001. Holy Trinity.
389 **220** 30k. multicoloured . . . 10 10

2001. Beekeeping. Sheet 185 × 144 mm containing T **221** and similar vert designs. Multicoloured.
MS390 50k. Type **221**; 50k. Honey and honey products; 50k. Worker bee on honeycomb; 50k. Queen; 50k. Hive; 50k. Drone 60 60

222 Uspensky Cathedral

2001. 950th Anniv of Kiec Pechersk Lavra (monastery). Sheet 112 × 113 mm.
MS391 **222** 1h.50 multicoloured 40 40

223 Pope John Paul II

2001. Visit of Pope John Paul II.
392 **223** 3h. multicoloured 80 80

224 Decorated Box, Flask, Map and Arms

2001. Regions. Zakarpatska.
393 **224** 30k. multicoloured . . . 10 10

225 Virgin and Child

2001. Khaneko Museum of Art, Kiev. Sheet 130 × 78 mm containing T **225** and similar multicoloured designs.
MS394 20k. Type **225**; 30k. John the Baptist; 50k. St. Sergius and St. Bacchus (56 × 40 mm) . . . 25 25

226 Red Kite (*Milvus milvus*)

2001. Endangered Species. Multicoloured.
395 1h. Type **226** 25 25
396 1h. Jerboa (*Scirtopoda telum*) 25 25

227 Dmitro Bortnjansky

2001. 250th Birth Anniv of Dmitro Bortnjansky (composer).
397 **227** 20k. multicoloured . . . 10 10

228 Player and Ball

2001. Ukrainian Football.
398 **228** 50k. multicoloured . . . 15 15

229 Ukrainian Flag held by Members of Parliament

2001. 10th Anniv of Independence. Sheet 95 × 80 mm.
MS399 **229** 3h. multicoloured . . 80 80

230 Tractor, Map and Arms

2001. Regions. Kharkov.
400 **230** 30k. multicoloured . . . 10 10

231 Church, Map and Arms

2001. Regions. Chernigov.
401 **231** 30k. multicoloured . . . 10 10

232 Church, Map, Arms and Sunflowers

2001. Regions. Kirovograd.
402 **232** 30k. multicoloured . . . 10 10

233 Messenger with Horn and Dnipropetrovsk

2001. 7th National Philatelic Exhibition, Dnipropetrovsk.
403 **233** 30k. multicoloured . . . 10 10

234 Children encircling Globe

2001. United Nations Year of Dialogue among Civilizations.
404 **234** 70k. multicoloured . . . 20 20

235 Seahorses

2001. Fauna of the Black Sea. Sheet 115 × 90 mm containing T **235** and similar horiz design. Multicoloured.
MS405 30k. Type **235**; 70k. Dolphins 25 25

236 Children wearing Fancy Dress

2001. Christmas.
406 **236** 30k. multicoloured . . . 10 10

237 St. Nikolas and Child

2001. St. Nikolas.
407 **237** 30k. multicoloured . . . 10 10

238 Decorated Tree and Children

2001. New Year.
408 **238** 30k. multicoloured . . . 10 10

239 Taras Chevtchenko

2001. Poets. Multicoloured.
409 40k. Type **239** 10 10
410 40k. Akakii Tsereteli 10 10
Nos. 399/400 were issued together, se-tenant, forming a composite design. Stamps of the same design were issued by Georgia.

240 Women wearing Traditional Costumes from Kiev

2001. Traditional Costumes (1st series). Multicoloured.
411 20k. Type **240** 10 10
412 20k. Musicians and woman, Chernigov 10 10
413 20k. Woman, child, bishop and clergy, Poltava 10 10
414 50k. Couple wearing coats, Kiev 15 15
415 50k. Couple and child, Chernigov 15 15
416 50k. Two girls, Poltava . . . 15 15
MS417 100 × 140 mm. Nos. 411/6 75 75
See also Nos. 467/**MS**473 and 518/**MS**524.

241 Chorna Rada (red council), Ivan Bryukhovetsky and Death by Mob

2002. Hetmans. Multicoloured.
418 40k. Type **241** 10 10
419 40k. Election, Demiyan Mnogogreshnyi and Tobolsk, Siberia 10 10
420 40k. Moscow, Pavlo Teterya and stealing the war chest 10 10

242 Scythian Horseman

2002. History of Ukraine. (1st series).
421 **242** 40k. brown, blue and black 10 10
422 – 40k. brown, green and black 10 10
423 – 40k. brown, green and black 10 10
424 – 40k. brown, blue and black 10 10
DESIGNS: Type **242**; Warrior wearing armour; Young warrior and horseman; Horsewoman.
See also Nos. 478/81.

243 Zhanna Pintusevitsch (runner)

2002. Ukrainian Sportswomen. Multicoloured.
425 40k. Type **243** (100 metre gold medal, World Athletics Championship, 2001) 10 10
426 40k. Jana Klotschkowa (swimmer) (2 gold and 2 silver medals, Olympic Games, 2000) 10 10

244 War Memorial, Rye field and Arms

2002. Regions. Kiev.
427 **244** 40k. multicoloured . . . 10 10

2002. Sailing Ships. As T **218**. Multicoloured.
428 40k. *Sizopol* (frigate) 10 10
429 40k. *Perseus* (brig) 10 10

245 15k. Ukraine Stamp of 1992

2002. 10th Anniv of First Modern Ukraine Stamp.
430 **245** 40k. multicoloured . . . 10 10

246 Leonid Glibov

2002. 175th Birth Anniv of Leonid Glibov (writer).
431 **246** 40k. multicoloured . . . 10 10

247 Knights and Chessboard

2002. 16th World Chess Championships, Moscow.
432 **247** 3h.50 multicoloured . . . 90 90

248 Tiger

2002. Europa. Circus. Sheet 106 × 71 mm containing T **248** and similar multicoloured design.
MS433 1h.75 × 2, Type **248**; Lion (vert) 90 90

249 Hands holding Wreath

2002. Palm Sunday.
434 **249** 40k. multicoloured . . . 10 10

250 Leopard Snake

2002. Endangered Species. The Leopard Snake (*Elaphe situla*). Multicoloured.
435 40k. Type **250** 10 10
436 70k. Two snakes entwined . . 20 20
437 80k. Snake, branch and flowers 20 20
438 2h.50 Head, coils and beetle 65 65
Nos. 435/8 were issued together, forming a composite design.

251 Opera House, Donetsk

2002. Ukrainian Opera Houses. Sheet 108 × 80 mm. T **251** and similar horiz designs. Multicoloured.
MS439 1h.25 × 2, Type **251**; Opera house, Dnepropetrovsk 65 65

252 Mary and Jesus (statue), Coastal Landscape and Arms

2002. Regions. Lugansk.
440 **252** 40k. multicoloured . . . 10 10

253 Shag (*Phalacrocorax aristotelis*)

2002. Endangered Species. Multicoloured.
441 70k. Type **253** 20 20
442 70k. Harbour porpoise (*Phocoena phocoena*) . . . 20 20

254 Mikola Leontovich

2002. 125th Birth Anniv of Mikola Leontovich (composer).
443 **254** 40k. multicoloured . . . 10 10

255 Decorated Eggs, Buildings and Arms

2002. Regions. Chernovtsy.
444 **255** 40k. multicoloured . . . 10 10

255a Oyster Catcher (*Haematopus ostralegos*)

2002. Black Sea Nature Reserve. Sheet 96 × 100 mm containing T **255a** and similar multicoloured designs.
MS445 50k. × 5 Type **255**; Slender-billed gull (*Larus genei*); Iris pumila (22 × 26 mm); Western curlew (*Numenius arquata*) (26 × 22 mm); Kentish plover (*Charadrius Alexandrinus*) (26 × 22 mm) 65 65

256 Fox and Kolobok (bun) (Kolobok)

2002. Folktales. Multicoloured.
446 40k. Type **256** 10 10
447 40k. Cat and porridge (Pan Kotski) 10 10
448 40k. Couple and chicken (Kurochka Raba) 10 10

257 Flowers (1963)

2002. Hanna Sobachko-Shostak (folk artist) Commemoration. Multicoloured.
449 45k. Type **257** 10 10
450 45k. Vase of flowers (1964) 10 10
451 45k. Flowers (different) (1964) 10 10

258 Yury Kondra

2002. Space Pioneers (1st series). Multicoloured.
452 40k. Type **258** 10 10
453 45k. Mikhail Jangel 10 10
454 50k. Nikolai Kibalchich . . . 15 15
455 70k. Sergei Korlev 15 15
See also Nos. 488/91.

259 Caspian Seal (*Phoca caspica*)

2002. Endangered Species. Marine Animals. Multicoloured.
456 75k. Type **259** 15 15
457 75k. *Huso huso ponticus* (fish) 15 15
Stamps of the same design were issued by Kazakhstan.

260 Monument, Sea, Lighthouse and Arms

2002. Regions. Odessa.
458 **260** 45k. multicoloured . . . 10 10

261 Monument, Arms and Old Town Walls

2002. Millenary of Khotin.
459 **261** 40k. multicoloured . . . 10 10

262 Exhibition Emblem

2002. Odesafil 2002 Philatelic Exhibition.
460 **262** 45k. multicoloured . . . 10 10

263 Monument, Lake and Arms

2002. Regions. Cherkassy.
461 **263** 45k. multicoloured . . . 10 10

264 Church, Landscape and Arms

2002. Regions. Sumy.
462 **264** 45k. multicoloured . . . 10 10

265 "Askoldova Mogila"

2002. Paintings of Kiev (1st series). Taras Shevchenko (artist and poet) Commemoration.
463 45k. Type **265** 10 10
464 75k. "Kiev" 15 15
465 80k. "Saint Aleksandr Castle, Kiev" 20 20
See also Nos. 500/3.

266 Father Christmas carrying Tree

2002. New Year.
466 **266** 45k. multicoloured . . . 10 10

2002. Traditional Costumes (2nd series). As T **240**. Multicoloured.
467 45k. Family, Vinnitsa 10 10
468 45k. Old man, women and child, Vinnitsa 10 10
469 45k. Young women dancing, Cherkassy 10 10
470 45k. Couple carrying pails, Cherkassy 10 10
471 45k. Bishop and family, Ternopol 10 10
472 45k. Women, child and young man, Ternopol . . . 10 10
MS473 100 × 140 mm. Nos. 467/72 60 60

267 Goat on Bridge (Koza-Dereza)

2003. Folktales. Multicoloured.
474 45k. Type **267** 10 10
475 45k. Couple and bull (Straw Bull) 10 10
476 45k. Fox and crane (Fox and Crane) 10 10
Nos. 474/6 were issued together, se-tenant, forming a composite design.

268 Speed Skater

2003.
477 **268** 65k. multicoloured . . . 15 15

2003. History of Ukraine (2nd series). As T **242**.
478 45k. brown, blue and black 10 10
479 45k. purple, bistre and black 10 10
480 45k. purple, bistre and black 10 10
481 45k. brown, blue and black 10 10
DESIGNS: No. 478 4th-century warrior; 479 5th-century bowman; 480 6th-century warrior with axe and shield; 481 6th-century spear thrower.

2003. Ships. T **218**. Multicoloured.
482 1h. *Grozny* (paddle steamer) 25 25
483 1h. *Odessa* (paddle steamer) 25 25

269 Mikola Arkas

2003. 150th Birth Anniv of Mikola Arkas (composer).
484 **269** 45k. multicoloured . . . 10 10

270 Kingfisher (*Alcedo atthis*)

2003. Javorivsky National Park. Sheet 130 × 92 mm containing T **270** and similar multicoloured designs.
MS485 1h. Type **270**; 1h.50 Emperor moth (*Eudia pavonia*) (33 × 45 mm); 1h. *Cypripedium calceolus* (36 × 41 mm) 80 80

271 Mary holding Crane ("May it be to me as you have said")

2003. Europa. Poster Art. Multicoloured.
486 1h.75 Type **271** 40 40
487 1h.75 Angel holding atomic symbol ("You are highly favoured, the Lord is with you") 40 40
Nos. 486/7 were issued together, se-tenant forming a composite design.

272 Oleksandr Zasiadko

2003. Space Pioneers (2nd series).Multicoloured.
488 45k. Type **272** 10 10
489 65k. Kostiantyn Konstantynov 15 15
490 70k. Valetyn Hlushko 15 15
491 80k. Volodymyr Chelomei . . 20 20

273 Heart enclosing Figure

2003. Ukrainian Red Cross.
492 **273** 45k. gold, vermilion and black 10 10

274 Rocket, Bridge and Arms

2003. Regions. Dnipropetrovsk.
493 **274** 45k. multicoloured . . . 10 10

275 Lion supporting Shield, Buildings and Arms

2003. Regions. Lviv.
494 **275** 45k. multicoloured . . . 10 10

276 Crowd, Kirill Rozumovsky and Ruin

2003. Hetmans. Multicoloured.
495 45k. Type **276** 10 10
496 45k. Farm workers, Ivan Skoropadsky and his inauguration 10 10

277 Volodymyr Monomakh

2003. Volodymyr Monomakh (prince of Kyiv, 1113–25) Commemoration. Sheet 100 × 80 mm.
MS497 **277** 3h.50 multicoloured 80 80

278 Northern Eagle Owl (*Bubo bubo*)

279 Oleksandr Myshuha

2003. Owls. Sheet 135 × 131 mm containing T **278** and similar vert designs. Multicoloured.
MS498 45k × 12, Type **278**; Ural owl (*Strix uralensis*); Tawny owl (*Strix aluco*); Great grey owl (*Strix nebulosa*); Eurasian pygmy owl (*Glaucidium passerinum*); Tengmalm's owl (*Aegolius funereus*); Eurasian scops owl (*Otus scops*); Little owl (*Athene noctua*); Barn owl (*Tyto alba*); Long-eared owl (*Asio otus*); Short-eared owl (*Asio flammeus*); Hawk owl (*Surnia ulula*) 1·20 1·20

2003. 150th Birth Anniv of Oleksandr Myshuha (singer).
499 **279** 45k. multicoloured 10 10

2003. Paintings of Kiev (2nd series). As T **265**. Multicoloured.
500 45k. "Podil from Schekavytsia" (Mykhailo Sazhyn) 10 10
501 45k. "Ruins of St. Irene's Monastery" (Mykhailo Sazhyn) 10 10
502 45k. "Old Town from Yaroslaviv Val" (Vasyl Timm) 10 10
503 45k. "The Cathedral of the Assumption" (Vasyl Timm) 10 10

280 Flowers surrounding Church (Makovii)

282 Maniava

281 Borys Hmyria

2003. Holidays. Multicoloured.
504 45k. Type **280** 10 10
505 45k. Church and fruit (Spas) 10 10

2003. Birth Centenary of Borys Romanovych Hmyria (singer).
506 **281** 45k. multicoloured 10 10

2003. Monasteries. Sheet 116 × 85 mm containing T **282** and similar vert design. Multicoloured.
MS507 1h.25 × 2, Type **282**; Carpathian 60 60

283 Yachts and Mosque

2003. 2500th Anniv of Yevpatoria.
508 **283** 45k. multicoloured 10 10

284 Danish Coin and "Arrival of Scandinavian Seamen" (detail)

2003. Ancient Trade Route along Gulf of Finland and Dnieper River, Ukraine. Multicoloured.
509 80k. Type **284** 20 20
510 80k. 11th-century silver coin and Viking ship 20 20
Stamps of the same design were issued by Estonia.

285 Horse and Rider (statue), Walls and Arms

2003. Regions. Khmelnytstk.
511 **285** 45k. multicoloured 10 10

286 Sunflowers, Ships and Arms

2003. Regions. Mykolaiv.
512 **286** 45k. multicoloured 10 10

287 Statue, Power Station Dam and Arms

2003. Regions. Zaporizhia.
513 **287** 45k. multicoloured 10 10

288 Hryhorii Kvitka-Osnovianenko

2003. 225th Birth Anniv of Hryhorii Kvitka-Osnovianenko (writer).
514 **288** 45k. multicoloured 10 10

289 Cross surrounding Starving Woman

2003. 70th Anniv of 1932–33 Famine.
515 **289** 45k. multicoloured 10 10

290 The Nativity

291 Snow-covered House, Tree and Father Christmas

2003. Christmas.
516 **290** 45k. multicoloured 10 10

2003. New Year.
517 **291** 45k. multicoloured 10 10

2003. Traditional Costumes (3rd series). As T **240**. Multicoloured.
518 45k. Two women, Kharkia 10 10
519 45k. Child, woman and musician, Kharkia 10 10
520 45k. Young couple and matchmaker, Sumy 10 10
521 45k. Girl preparing for marriage, Sumy 10 10
522 45k. Woman, two men, child and toboggan, Donetsk 10 10
523 45k. Harvesting corn, Donetsk 10 10
MS524 100 × 140 mm. Nos. 518/23 60 60

UMM AL QIWAIN Pt. 19

One of the Trucial States in the Persian Gulf. In July 1971 formed the United Arab Emirates with five other Gulf Shaikdoms.

1964. 100 naye paise = 1 rupee.
1967. 100 dirhams = 1 riyal.

1 Shaikh Ahmed bin Rashid al Moalla and Mountain Gazelles

1964. Multicoloured. (a) Size as T **1**.
1 1n.p. Type **1** 20 20
2 2n.p. Snake 20 20
3 3n.p. Striped hyena 20 20
4 4n.p. Clown triggerfish 20 20
5 5n.p. Lionfish 20 20
6 10n.p. Diamond fingerfish 20 20
7 15n.p. Palace 20 20
8 20n.p. Town buildings 20 20
9 30n.p. Tower 30 20

(b) Size $42\frac{1}{2} \times 27$ mm.
10 40n.p. Type **1** 30 20
11 50n.p. Snake 45 30
12 50n.p. Striped hyena 60 40
13 1r. Clown triggerfish 80 50
14 1r.50 Lionfish 1·00 60
15 2r. Diamond fingerfish 1·40 1·20

(c) Size $53\frac{1}{2} \times 33\frac{1}{2}$ mm.
16 3r. Palace 2·40 2·00
17 5r. Town buildings 4·50 3·00
18 10r. Tower 6·75 5·50

2 Discus Thrower and Stadium

1964. Olympic Games, Tokyo. Multicoloured.
19 50n.p. Type **2** 30 10
20 1r. Main stadium 80 20
21 1r.50 Swimming pool 1·20 40
22 2r. Main stadium 1·50 50
23 3r. Komazawa gymnasium 2·30 80
24 4r. Stadium entrance 3·00 1·00
25 5r. Type **2** 3·50 1·30

3 Cortege leaving White House

1965. Pres. Kennedy Commemoration. Each black and gold on coloured paper as given below.
26 **3** 10n.p. blue 10 10
27 – 15n.p. stone 10 10
28 – 50n.p. stone 30 10
29 – 1r. pink 60 20
30 – 2r. stone 1·00 30
31 – 3r. lilac 1·80 60
32 – 5r. blue 3·00 80
33 – 7r.50 buff 4·50 1·50
MS33a 115 × 70 mm. Nos. 32/3 but colours changed 9·75 7·25
DESIGNS—As T **3** (Funeral scenes): 15n.p. Coffin-bearers; 50n.p. Hearse; 1r. Presidents Eisenhower and Truman; 2r. Foreign dignitaries. 33 × 51 mm: 3r. Mrs. Kennedy and family at grave; 5r. Last salute; 7r.50, Pres. Kennedy.

1965. Air. Designs similar to Nos. 1/9 but inscr "AIR MAIL". Multicoloured. (a) Size $43 \times 26\frac{1}{2}$ mm.
34 15n.p. Type **1** 30 10
35 25n.p. Snake 50 10
36 35n.p. Striped hyena 50 10
37 50n.p. Clown triggerfish 80 10
38 75n.p. Lionfish 1·00 10
39 1r. Diamond fingerfish 1·30 20

(b) Size 53 × 34 mm.
40 2r. Palace 2·20 40
41 3r. Town buildings 3·25 70
42 5r. Tower 4·00 1·30

4 Tribute to Ruler (reverse of 10n.p. piece)

1965. Arabian Gulf Area Monetary Conf. Circular designs on silver foil, backed with paper inscr overall "Walsall Security Paper" in English and Arabic. Imperf. (a) Diameter 43 mm.
43 **4** 10n.p. purple and black 10 10
44 – 25n.p. blue and green 3·00 3·00

(b) Diameter $55\frac{1}{2}$ mm.
45 **4** 1r. red and violet 80 80
46 – 2r. green and orange 1·70 1·70

(c) Diameter 64 mm.
47 **4** 3r. blue and mauve 2·40 2·40
48 – 5r. purple and blue 3·50 3·50
SILVER PIECES: Nos. 44, 46, 48 each show the obverse side (Shaikh Ahmed).

5 "Penny Black" and Egyptian 5p. Stamp of 1866

1966. Centenary Stamp Exhibition, Cairo.
49 **5** 3n.p. multicoloured 10 10
50 – 5n.p. multicoloured 10 10
51 – 7n.p. multicoloured 15 10
52 – 10n.p. multicoloured 15 10
53 – 15n.p. multicoloured 15 10
54 – 25n.p. multicoloured 20 15
55 – 50n.p. multicoloured 50 15
56 – 75n.p. multicoloured 70 20
57 – 1r. multicoloured 1·00 30
58 – 2r. multicoloured 2·00 70
MS58a 110 × 70 mm. 5r. multicoloured 4·00 2·00
DESIGNS: As Type **5** with Egyptian 5p. stamp: 7n.p. Brazil 30r. "Bull's-eye" of 1843; 15n.p. Mauritius "Post Office" One Penny of 1847; 50n.p. Belgium 10c. "Epaulettes" of 1849; 1r. New South Wales One Penny and Victoria One Penny of 1850. As Type **5**, but with Egyptian "Pyramid and Star" watermark of 1866: 5n.p. Basel $2\frac{1}{2}$r. "Dove" of 1845, Geneva 5c.+5c. "Double Eagle" and Zurich 4r. "Numeral" of 1843; 10n.p. U.S. St. Louis "Bears" 5c., Baltimore 5c. and New York 5c. "Postmasters" stamps of 1845; 25n.p. France 20c. "Ceres" of 1849; 75n.p. Bavaria 1k. of 1850; 2r. Spain 6c. of 1850; 5r. Egyptian 5p. stamp of 1866.

6 Sir Winston Churchill with Lord Alanbrooke and Field Marshal Montgomery

1966. Churchill Commemoration. Multicoloured designs each including Churchill.
59 3n.p. Type **6** 10 10
60 4n.p. With Roosevelt and Stalin at Yalta 10 10
61 5n.p. In garden at No. 10 Downing Street, London 10 10
62 10n.p. With Eisenhower 10 10
63 15n.p. With Lady Churchill in car 10 10
64 50n.p. Painting in Morocco 30 10
65 75n.p. Walking – on holiday 40 10
66 1r. Funeral cortege 50 20
67 3r. Lying-in-state, Westminster Hall 1·50 30
68 5r. Churchill giving "Victory" sign 3·00 1·00
MS69 100 × 100 mm. Nos. 67/8 6·75 6·75

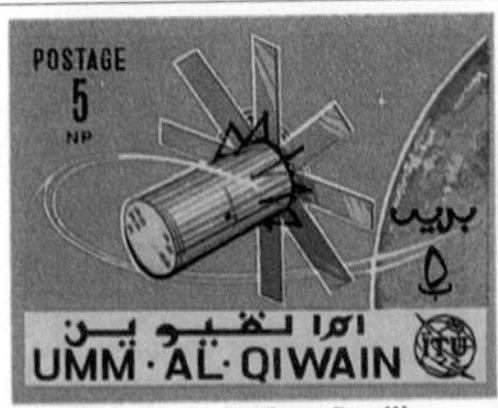

7 Communications Satellite

1966. Centenary (1965) of I.T.U. Communications Satellites. Multicoloured.

70	5n.p. Type **7**	10	10
71	10n.p. "Tiros"	20	10
72	25n.p. "Telstar"	30	10
73	50n.p. "Ariel"	50	20
74	75n.p. "Ranger"	70	30
75	1r. "Alouette"	1·70	30
76	2r. "Vanguard 1"	1·70	50
77	3r. "Explorer 10"	1·90	70
78	5r. "Early Bird"	3·00	1·30
MS79	120 × 79 mm. Nos. 75/6	5·00	2·40

NEW CURRENCY SURCHARGES. In 1967 various issues appeared surcharged in dirhams and riyals. The 1964 definitives, 1965 air stamps and officials with this surcharge are listed as there is evidence of their postal use. Nos. 19/33 and 49/68 also exist with these surcharges.

1967. Various issues with currency names changed by overprinting. (i) Nos. 1/18 (1964 Definitives).

80	1d. on 1n.p.	10	10
81	2d. on 2n.p.	10	10
82	3d. on 3n.p.	10	10
83	4d. on 4n.p.	10	10
84	5d. on 5n.p.	10	10
85	10d. on 10n.p.	10	10
86	15d. on 15n.p.	2·00	80
87	20d. on 20n.p.	2·00	80
88	30d. on 30n.p.	2·00	80
89	40d. on 40n.p.	30	20
90	50d. on 50n.p.	40	20
91	70d. on 70n.p.	60	20
92	1r. on 1r.	70	30
93	1r.50 on 1r.50	1·20	50
94	2r. on 2r.	1·50	60
95	3r. on 3r.	5·50	2·00
96	5r. on 5r.	7·25	3·25
97	10r. on 10r.	11·00	5·00

(ii) Nos. 34/42 (Airmails).

98	15d. on 15n.p.	20	10
99	25d. on 25n.p.	20	10
100	35d. on 35n.p.	50	20
101	50d. on 50n.p.	70	30
102	75d. on 75n.p.	1·20	50
103	1r. on 1r.	1·50	60
104	2r. on 2r.	3·25	1·40
105	3r. on 3r.	5·50	2·20
106	5r. on 5r.	8·75	3·50

9 Blue-spotted Boxfish

1967. Fish of the Arabian Gulf. Multicoloured. (a) Postage. (i) Size 46 × 21 mm.

116	1d. Type **9**	10	10
117	2d. Parrotfish	10	10
118	3d. Striped sweetlips	10	10
119	4d. Black-wedged butterflyfish	10	10
120	5d. Japanese bonyhead	10	10
121	10d. Reticulate damselfish	20	10
122	15d. Picasso triggerfish	20	10
123	20d. Undulate triggerfish	30	10
124	30d. Black-saddled pufferfish	30	10

(ii) Size 56 × 26 mm.

125	40d. Type **9**	40	10
126	50d. As 2d.	50	20
127	70d. As 3d.	60	20
128	1r. As 4d.	70	20
129	1r.50 As 5d.	1·10	30
130	2r. As 10d.	1·30	40
131	3r. As 15d. (No. 122)	1·80	60
132	5r. As 20d.	3·00	1·00
133	10r. As 30d.	5·00	2·20

(b) Air. Size 70 × 35 mm.

134	15d. Type **9**	20	10
135	25d. As 2d.	30	10
136	35d. As 3d.	40	20
137	50d. As 4d.	50	20
138	75d. As 5d.	60	20
139	1r. As 10d.	70	20
140	2r. As 15d. (No. 122)	1·30	40
141	3r. As 20d.	1·80	60
142	5r. As 30d.	3·00	1·00

OFFICIAL STAMPS

1965. Designs similar to Nos. 1/9, additionally inscr "ON STATE'S SERVICE". Multicoloured. (a) Postage. Size $42\frac{1}{2}$ × 27 mm.

O49	25n.p. Type **1**	30	10
O50	40n.p. Snake	40	10
O51	50n.p. Striped hyena	60	20
O52	75n.p. Clown triggerfish	90	20
O53	1r. Lionfish	1·10	30

(b) Air. (i) Size $42\frac{1}{2}$ × 27 mm.

O54	75n.p. Diamond fingerfish	90	20

(ii) Size 53 × 34 mm.

O55	2r. Palace	2·20	70
O56	3r. Town buildings	3·25	1·00
O57	5r. Tower	4·50	1·50

1967. Nos. O49/57 with currency names changed by overprinting.

O107	25d. on 25n.p. (postage)	30	20
O108	40d. on 40n.p.	40	20
O109	50d. on 50n.p.	60	40
O110	75d. on 75n.p.	70	50
O111	1r. on 1r.	90	60
O112	75d. on 75d. (air)	70	50
O113	2r. on 2r.	2·00	1·50
O114	3r. on 3r.	2·40	1·50
O115	5r. on 5r.	4·00	2·40

For later issues see **UNITED ARAB EMIRATES**.

APPENDIX

The following stamps have either been issued in excess of postal needs or have not been available to the public in reasonable quantities at face value. Such stamps may later be given full listing if there is evidence of regular postal use.

1967.

Self-portraits of Famous Painters. Postage 10, 15, 25, 50, 75d., 1, 1r.50; Air 1r.25, 2, 2r.50, 3, 5r.

Dogs. Postage 15, 25, 50, 75d., 1r.; Air 1r.25, 2r.50, 4r.

"Expo 67" World Fair, Montreal. Famous Paintings. 25, 50, 75d., 1, 1r.50, 2, 3r.

1968.

Falcons. Postage 15, 25, 50, 75d., 1r.; Air 1r.50, 3, 5r.

Winter Olympic Games, Grenoble. Postage 10, 25, 75d., 1r.; Air 1r.50, 2, 3, 5r.

Famous Paintings. Postage 25, 50, 75d., 1, 1r.50, 2r.50; Air 1, 2, 3, 4, 5r.

Olympic Games, Mexico (1st issue). Optd on (a) 1964 Tokyo Olympic Games Issue. Postage 1r.50, 2, 4, 5r. (b) 1968 Winter Olympic Games issue. Air 1r.50, 2, 5r.

Robert Kennedy Memorial. Optd on 1965 Pres. Kennedy issue. Postage 3, 5, 7r.50.

Olympic Games, Mexico (2nd issue). Postage 10, 25, 50d., 1, 2r.; Air 2r.50, 3, 4, 5r.

Still Life Paintings. Postage 25, 50d., 1, 1r.50, 2r.; Air 1r.25, 2r.50, 3, 3r.50, 5r.

Mexico Olympic Medal Winners. Optd on Olympic Games, Mexico issue. Postage 10, 25, 50d., 1, 2r.; Air 2r.50, 3, 4, 5r.

Aviation History. Aircraft. Postage 25, 50d., 1, 1r.50, 2r.; Air 1r.25, 2r.50, 3, 5r.

1969.

"Apollo 8" Moon Orbit. Optd on 1968 Aviation History issue. Postage 25, 50d., 1, 1r.50, 2r.; Air 1r.25, 2r.50, 3, 5r.

Horses (1st series). Postage 25, 50, 75d., 1, 2r.; Air 1r.50, 2r.50, 4, 5r.

Olympic Games, Munich, 1972 (1st issue). Optd on 1968 Olympic Games, Mexico issue. Postage 10, 25, 50d., 1, 2r.; Air 2r.50, 3, 4, 5r.

Winter Olympic Games, Sapporo 1972 (1st issue). Optd on 1968 Winter Olympics Grenoble issue. Postage 10, 25, 75d., 1r.; Air 1r.50, 2, 3, 5r.

Veteran and Vintage Cars. Postage 15d. × 8, 25d. × 8, 50d. × 8, 75d. × 8; Air 1r. × 8, 2r. × 8.

Famous Films. Postage 10, 15, 25, 50, 75d., 1r.; Air 1r.50, 2r.50, 3, 4, 5r.

"Apollo 12" Moon Landing. 10, 20, 30, 50, 75d., 1r.

1970.

"Apollo 13" Astronauts. 10, 30, 50d.

"Expo 70" World Fair, Osaka, Japan. 5, 10, 20, 40d., 1, 1r.25.

150th Anniv of British Landing on Trucial Coast. Uniforms. 10, 20, 30, 50, 75d., 1r.

1971.

Animals. Postage 10, 15, 20, 25d.; Air 5r.

Winter Olympic Games, Saporro, 1972 (2nd issue). Postage 5, 10, 15, 20, 25d.; Air 50, 75d., 1, 3, 5r.

Olympic Games, Munich, 1972 (2nd issue). Postage 5, 10, 15, 20, 25d.; Air 50, 75d., 1, 3, 5r.

1972.

Durer's Religious Paintings. Postage 5, 10, 15, 20, 25d.; Air 3r.

Horses (2nd series). Postage 10, 15, 20, 25d.; Air 50d., 3r.

Locomotives (plastic surfaced). Postage 5, 10, 20, 40, 50d.; Air 6r.

Winter Olympic Games, Sapporo, 1972 (3rd issue) (plastic surfaced). Postage 5, 10, 20, 40, 50d.; Air 6r.

Easter, Religious Paintings. Postage 5, 10, 20, 50d.; Air 1, 3r.

Kennedy Brothers Memorial. Postage 5, 10, 15, 20d.; Air 1, 3r.

Winston Churchill Memorial. Postage 5, 10, 15, 20d.; Air 3r.

Arab Rulers. Postage 5d. × 6, 10d. × 6, 15d. × 6, 20d. × 6; Air 3r. × 6.

13th World Jamboree, 1971 (plastic surfaced). Postage 5, 10, 20, 40, 50d.; Air 6r.

Fish. Postage 5, 10, 20, 40, 50d.; Air 6r.

International Airlines. Postage 5, 10, 15, 20, 25d.; Air 50d.

"Apollo 15" Moon Mission. Postage 5, 10, 15, 20, 25d.; Air 50, 75d., 1, 3, 5r.

Olympic Games, Munich, 1972 (3rd issue) (plastic surfaced). Postage 5, 10, 20, 40, 50d.; Air 6r.

2500th Anniv of Founding of Persian Empire. Postage 10, 20, 30, 40, 50, 60d.; Air 1r.

Portraits of Charles de Gaulle. 5, 10, 15, 20, 25d.

Paintings of Napoleon. Postage 5, 10, 15, 20, 25d.; Air 5r.

Butterflies. Postage 5, 10, 15, 20, 25d.; Air 3r.

Penguins. Postage 5, 10, 15, 20d.; Air 50d., 4r.

Cars. Postage 5, 10, 15, 20, 25d.; Air 3r.

Masks (1st series). Postage 5, 10, 15, 20, 25d.; Air 50d., 1, 3r.

Dogs and Cats. Postage 5, 5, 10, 10, 15, 15, 20, 20, 25, 25d.; Air 5, 5r.

Roses. Postage 10, 15, 20, 25d.; Air 50d., 5r.

Marine Fauna. Postage 5, 10, 15, 20, 25, 50d.; Air 1, 3r.

Masks (2nd series). Postage 5, 10, 15, 20, 25d.; Air 50d., 1, 3r.

Navigators. Postage 5, 10, 15, 20, 25, 50d.; Air 1, 3r.

Exotic Birds (1st series). Horiz and vert designs. Air 1r. × 16.

Exotic Birds (2nd series). Horiz designs. Air 1r. × 16.

In common with the other states of the United Arab Emirates the Umm al Qiwain stamp contract was terminated on 1 August 1972 and any further new issues released after that date were unauthorized.

UNITED ARAB EMIRATES Pt. 19

Following the withdrawal of British forces from the Gulf and the ending of the Anglo-Trucial States treaties six of the states, Abu Dhabi, Ajman, Dubai, Fujeira, Sharjah and Umm al Qiwain, formed an independent union on 2 December 1971. The seventh state, Ras al Khaima, joined during February 1972. Each emirate continued to use its own stamps, pending the introduction of a unified currency. A Union Postal administration came into being on 1 August 1972 and the first stamps appeared on 1 January 1973.

For Abu Dhabi stamps optd U.A.E., etc, see under that heading.

100 fils = 1 dirham.

1 U.A.E. Flag and Map of Gulf

1973. Multicoloured. (a) Size 42 × 25 mm.

1	5f. Type **1**	10	10
2	10f. Type **1**	15	10
3	15f. Eagle emblem	45	10
4	35f. As 15f.	50	10

(b) Size 46 × 30 mm.

5	65f. Almaqta Bridge, Abu Dhabi	1·00	25
6	75f. Khor Fakkan, Sharjah	1·30	25
7	1d. Clock Tower, Dubai	1·50	45
8	$1\frac{1}{4}$d. Buthnah Fort, Fujeira	4·25	2·20
9	2d. Alfalaj Fort, Umm al Qiwain	44·00	8·75
10	3d. Khor Khwair, Ras al Khaima	8·75	6·50
11	5d. Ruler's Palace, Ajman	10·50	6·50
12	10d. President Shaikh Zaid	22·00	13·00

2 Youth and Girl within Shield

1973. National Youth Festival. Multicoloured.

13	10f. Type **2**	6·00	35
14	1d.25 Allegory of Youth	15·00	8·75

3 Traffic Lights and Road Sign

1973. Traffic Week. Multicoloured.

15	35f. Type **3**	3·00	1·50
16	75f. Pedestrian-crossing (horiz)	6·00	2·75
17	1d.25 Traffic policeman	10·50	4·00

4 "Three Races of the World"

1973. 25th Anniv of Declaration of Human Rights.

18	**4**	35f. black, yellow and blue	1·70	70
19		65f. black, yellow and red	4·00	1·30
20		$1\frac{1}{4}$d. black, yellow and green	6·50	3·50

5 U.P.U. Emblem

1974. Centenary of Universal Postal Union.

21	**5**	25f. multicoloured	1·70	85
22		60f. multicoloured	2·50	1·30
23		$1\frac{1}{4}$d. multicoloured	5·25	4·25

6 Medical Equipment (Health Service)

1974. Third National Day.

24	**6**	10f. red, brown and lilac	1·00	25
25	–	35f. gold, green and blue	2·10	85
26	–	65f. brown, sepia and blue	2·75	1·30
27	–	$1\frac{1}{4}$d. multicoloured	6·00	3·50

DESIGNS—49 × 30 mm: 35f. Children reading (Education); 65f. Tools and buildings (Construction); $1\frac{1}{4}$d. U.A.E. flag with emblems of U.N. and Arab League.

7 Arab Couple with Candle and Book

1974. International Literacy Day.

28	**7**	35f. multicoloured	2·40	50
29	–	65f. black, blue and brown	2·75	1·00
30	–	1d.25 black, blue and brown	5·25	2·10

DESIGN—VERT: 65f., 1f.25, Arab couple with book.

8 Oil De-gassing Installation

1975. 9th Arab Oil Conference. Multicoloured.

31	25f. Type **8**	1·20	45
32	50f. "Al Ittiad" (offshore oil drilling platform)	2·50	80

33		100f. Underwater storage tank	6·50	1·90
34		125f. Marine oil production platform	8·75	2·20
MS35		168 × 122 mm. Nos. 31/4	26·00	17·00

9 Station and Dish Aerial

1975. Inauguration of Jabal Ali Satellite Earth Station. Multicoloured.

36		15f. Type **9**	1·00	35
37		35f. Satellite beaming information to Earth	2·30	50
38		65f. As 35f.	4·00	85
39		2d. Type **9**	7·75	4·00

10 "Snapshots" within Eagle Emblem

11 Symbols of Learning

1975. Fourth National Day. Multicoloured.

40		10f. Type **10**	60	15
41		35f. Shaikh Mohamed bin Hamad al Sharqi of Fujeira	1·70	85
42		60f. Shaikh Rashid bin Humaid al Naimi of Ajman	2·50	1·70
43		80f. Shaikh Ahmed bin Rashid al Moalla of Umm al Qiwain	3·50	2·20
44		90f. Shaikh Sultan bin Mohammed al Qasimi of Sharjah	4·00	2·20
45		1d. Shaikh Saqr bin Mohammed al Qasimi of Ras al Khaima	4·25	2·50
46		1d.40 Shaikh Rashid bin Said of Dubai	6·00	3·50
47		5d. Shaikh Zaid bin Sultan al Nahayyan of Abu Dhabi, President of U.A.E	26·00	13·00

1976. Arab Literacy Day. Multicoloured.

48		15f. Type **11**	45	25
49		50f. Arabs seeking enlightenment	1·70	60
50		3d. As 50f.	8·75	5·75

1976. No. 6 surch **50** in English and Arabic.

50a		50f. on 75f. multicoloured	44·00	10·50

12 Man and Road Signs

13 Headphones

1976. Traffic Week. Multicoloured.

51		15f. Type **12**	1·50	80
52		80f. Example of dangerous driving and road signals (horiz)	7·00	3·75
53		140f. Children on road crossing (horiz)	13·00	7·00

1976. International Telecommunications Day.

54	13	50f. multicoloured	1·00	45
55		80f. multicoloured	2·40	85
56		2d. multicoloured	5·25	2·50

14 U.A.E. Crest

15 President Shaikh Zaid

1976.

57	14	5f. red	10	10
58		10f. brown	15	15
59		15f. pink	15	15
60		35f. brown	45	15
61		50f. violet	85	45
62		60f. bistre	1·00	45
63		80f. green	1·30	45
64		90f. blue	1·70	50
65		1d. blue	2·20	60
66		140f. green	2·20	95
67		250f. violet	4·25	1·40
68		2d. grey	4·25	1·60
69		5d. blue	9·50	4·25
70		10d. mauve	17·00	10·50

1976. Fifth National Day.

71	15	15f. multicoloured	2·50	45
72		140f. multicoloured	8·75	3·50

16 Falcon's Head and Gulf

17 Mohammed Ali Jinnah (Quaid-i-Azam)

1976. International Falconry Congress, Abu Dhabi.

73	16	80f. multicoloured	2·30	1·30
74		2d. multicoloured	5·75	2·50

1976. Birth Centenary of Mohammed Ali Jinnah (founder of Pakistan).

75	17	50f. multicoloured	4·00	1·00
76		80f. multicoloured	5·75	2·20

19 A.P.U. Emblem

20 U.A.E. Crest

1977. 25th Anniv of Arab Postal Union.

78	19	50f. multicoloured	3·00	1·00
79		80f. multicoloured	4·75	1·90

1977.

80	20	5f. red and black	25	25
81		10f. brown and black	25	25
82		15f. pink and black	45	35
83		35f. brown and black	80	25
84		50f. mauve and black	1·20	35
85		60f. bistre and black	2·10	70
86		80f. green and black	2·10	45
87		90f. blue and black	2·40	25
88		1d. blue and black	3·25	50
89		1d.40 green and black	4·25	1·40
90		1d.50 violet and black	5·25	1·50
91		2d. grey and black	6·50	2·10
92		5d. blue and black	16·00	5·25
93		10d. purple and black	26·00	10·50

21 Arab Scholar and Emblems

1977. International Literacy Day.

94	21	50f. multicoloured	2·30	1·00
95		3d. multicoloured	8·75	5·25

22 Armoured Cars

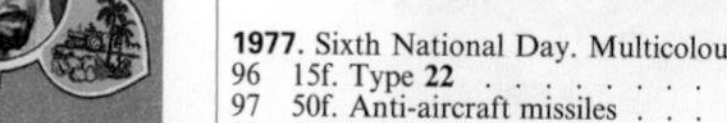

1977. Sixth National Day. Multicoloured.

96		15f. Type **22**		
97		50f. Anti-aircraft missiles		
98		150f. Soldiers marching		
		Set of 3	£500	

Nos. 96/8 were withdrawn from sale on day of issue as the date in Arabic was wrongly inscribed backwards.

23 Posthorn Dhow

24 Koran on Map of World

1979. 2nd Gulf Postal Organization Conf, Dubai.

99	23	50f. multicoloured	95	60
100		5d. multicoloured	6·00	4·75

1980. The Arabs.

101	24	50f. multicoloured	70	45
102		1d.40 multicoloured	1·70	1·20
103		3d. multicoloured	3·75	2·50

25 Dassault Mirage III Jet Fighters and Sud Aviation Alouette III Helicopter

1980. Ninth National Day.

104	25	15f. multicoloured	45	25
105		50f. multicoloured	1·30	45
106		80f. multicoloured	1·70	1·00
107		150f. multicoloured	2·50	1·70
MS108		120 × 85 mm. **25** 3d. multicoloured	10·50	10·50

26 Family on Graph

27 Mosque and Kaaba, Mecca

1980. Population Census.

109	26	15f. blue and pink	60	25
110	–	80f. brown and grey	1·90	85
111	–	90f. brown and buff	2·30	1·00
112	26	2d. blue and cobalt	5·75	4·75

DESIGN: 80, 90f. Figure standing in doorway.

1980. 1400th Anniv of Hejira.

113	27	15f. multicoloured	45	15
114		80f. multicoloured	1·30	60
115		90f. multicoloured	1·50	85
116		140f. multicoloured	3·75	2·30
MS117		90 × 120 mm. **27** 2d. multicoloured (36 × 57 mm)	8·75	8·75

28 Figures supporting O.P.E.C. Emblem

29 Policeman helping Child across Road

1980. 20th Anniv of Organization of Petroleum Exporting Countries. Multicoloured.

118		50f. Type **28**	80	45
119		80f. Type **28**	1·40	70
120		90f. O.P.E.C. emblem and globe	1·70	95
121		140f. As No. 120	3·00	2·30
MS122		120 × 90 mm. 3d. As No. 120 (68 × 52 mm)	11·50	11·50

1981. Traffic Week. Multicoloured.

123		15f. Type **29**	60	15
124		50f. Policeman and traffic signs (21 × 31 mm)	1·30	60
125		80f. Type **29**	1·90	1·00
126		5d. As No. 124	7·00	5·75

30 Symbols of Industry

1981. Tenth National Day.

127	30	25f. blue and black	85	35
128	–	150f. multicoloured	3·00	1·40
129	–	2d. red, green and black	4·25	2·50

DESIGNS: 150f. Soldiers; 2d. Flag and U.N. and U.A.E emblems.

31 Helping the Disabled (pictogram) and I.Y.D.P. Emblem

32 U.A.E. Crest

1981. Int Year of Disabled Persons. Mult.

130		25f. Type **31**	60	25
131		45f. Disabled person in wheelchair (pictogram) (vert)	1·30	60
132		150f. As No. 131	4·00	1·70
133		2d. Type **31**	4·75	2·50

1982. Multicoloured. Background colour given.

(a) Size 17 × 21 mm.

134	32	5f. pink	15	10
135		10f. green	15	10
136		15f. violet	15	10
137		25f. brown	25	10
138		35f. brown	35	15
139		50f. blue	3·00	1·50
140		75f. yellow	85	50
141		100f. grey	1·00	70
142		110f. green	1·00	70
143		125f. mauve	1·30	95
144		150f. blue	1·70	1·10
145		175f. blue	1·90	1·00

(b) Size 23 × 27 mm.

146	32	2d. green	2·20	1·30
147		250f. pink	2·75	1·30
148		3d. blue	2·50	1·70
149		5d. yellow	4·25	2·20
150		10d. brown	7·75	4·25
151		20d. silver	15·00	9·50
151c		50d. purple	44·00	22·00

33 Flags of Competing Countries and Emblem

1982. 6th Arab Gulf Football Championships. Multicoloured.

152		25f. Type **33**	60	45
153		75f. American bald eagle holding ball over stadium (vert)	1·90	1·20
154		125f. Footballers (vert)	2·50	2·10
155		3d. As No. 153	6·00	4·75

34 Figure breaking Gun

1982. 2nd U.N. Disarmament Conference.

156	34	25f. multicoloured	45	15
157		75f. multicoloured	1·30	85
158		125f. multicoloured	2·20	1·70
159		150f. multicoloured	2·50	2·20

35 National Emblems

1982. 11th National Day. Multicoloured.

160		25f. Type **35**	45	25
161		75f. Dove and flag (vert)	1·40	85
162		125f. As 75f.	2·30	1·50
163		150f. Type **35**	2·50	2·20

36 Arab writing

37 W.C.Y. Emblem

1983. Arab Literacy Day.

No.	Type	Description	Unused	Used
164	–	25f. multicoloured	26·00	50·00
165	36	35f. brown, violet and black	1·00	60
166	–	75f. yellow, black & mauve	26·00	44·00
167	36	3d. brown, yellow and black	7·75	3·50

DESIGN: 25, 75f. Koran and lamp.

1983. World Communications Year.

No.	Type	Description	Unused	Used
168	37	25f. multicoloured	85	15
169		150f. multicoloured	2·50	1·30
170		2d. multicoloured	3·00	1·70
171		3d. multicoloured	4·25	2·50

38 Satellite Orbit within "20"

1984. 20th Anniv of International Telecommunications Satellite Consortium.

No.	Type	Description	Unused	Used
172	38	2d. blue, purple & deep blue	4·00	3·50
173		2½d. blue, purple and green	5·75	5·25

39 Shaikh Hamad bin Mohamed al Sharqi and Buthnah Fort, Fujeira

1984. 13th National Day. Multicoloured.

No.	Type	Description	Unused	Used
174		1d. Type **39**	2·30	1·30
175		1d. Shaikh Rashid bin Ahmed al Moalla and Alfalaj Fort, Umm al Qiwain	2·30	1·30
176		1d. Shaikh Humaid bin Rashid al Naimi and Palace, Ajman	2·30	1·30
177		1d. Shaikh Saqr bin Mohammed al-Qasimi and harbour, Ras al Khaima	2·30	1·30
178		1d. Shaikh Zaid bin Sultan al Nahayyan and refinery, Abu Dhabi	2·30	1·30
179		1d. Shaikh Sultan bin Mohammed al Qasimi, oil well and mosque, Sharjah	2·30	1·30
180		1d. Shaikh Rashid bin Said and building, Dubai	2·30	1·30

40 Pictograms of Refuse Collection

41 Globe and Knights

1985. Tidy Week.

No.	Type	Description	Unused	Used
181	40	5d. orange and black	7·75	6·50

1985. World Junior Chess Championship, Sharjah.

No.	Type	Description	Unused	Used
182	41	2d. multicoloured	4·00	2·20
183		250f. multicoloured	5·75	3·50

42 Map and Hand holding Flag

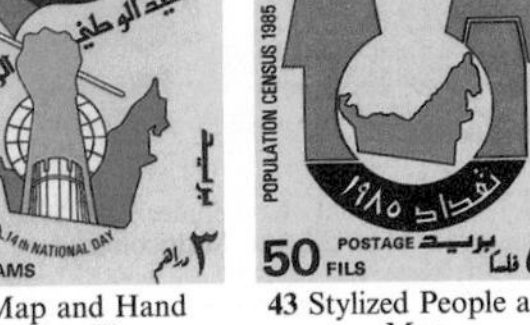

43 Stylized People and Map

1985. 14th National Day.

No.	Type	Description	Unused	Used
184	42	50f. multicoloured	50	45
185		3d. multicoloured	4·00	2·20

1985. Population Census.

No.	Type	Description	Unused	Used
186	43	50f. multicoloured	70	45
187		1d. multicoloured	1·70	85
188		3d. multicoloured	4·25	2·20

44 Profiles looking at Sapling

45 Emblem

1985. International Youth Year. Multicoloured.

No.	Type	Description	Unused	Used
189		50f. Type **44**	60	60
190		175f. Open book, flame and people between hemispheres (horiz)	95	95
191		2d. Youth carrying globe on back	1·70	1·70

1986. Arabic Woman and Family Day.

No.	Type	Description	Unused	Used
192	45	1d. multicoloured	65	40
193		3d. multicoloured	1·70	1·30

46 Globe, Map and Posthorn

47 Sakar Falcon

1986. 1st Anniv of General Postal Authority. Multicoloured.

No.	Type	Description	Unused	Used
194		50f. Type **46**	50	45
195		1d. Banner around globe (vert)	1·10	60
196		2d. As No. 195	2·20	1·70
197		250f. Type **46**	2·50	2·30

1986.

No.	Type	Description	Unused	Used
198	47	50f. gold, blue and green	60	60
199		75f. gold, blue and mauve	95	95
200		125f. gold, blue and grey	1·70	1·70

48 Container Ship in Dock

49 Dawn, Satellite, Emblem and Dish Aerials

1986. 10th Anniv of United Arab Shipping Company. Multicoloured.

No.	Type	Description	Unused	Used
201		2d. Type **48**	3·25	1·90
202		3d. Container ship at sea (vert)	4·00	3·00

1986. 10th Anniv of Emirates Telecommunications Corporation.

No.	Type	Description	Unused	Used
203		250f. Type **49**	2·75	1·90
204		3d. As Type **49** but with sun behind emblem	3·50	2·50

50 Emblem, Boeing 737 Airliner and Camel Rider

1986. 1st Anniv of Emirates Airlines. Multicoloured.

No.	Type	Description	Unused	Used
205		50f. Type **50**	95	70
206		175f. Boeing 737, emblem and national colours	3·25	3·00

51 Emblem and Member States' Crests

1986. 7th Supreme Council Session of Gulf Co-operation Council, Abu Dhabi.

No.	Type	Description	Unused	Used
207		50f. Type **51**	60	45
208		1d.75 Emblem beneath tree	2·30	1·90
209		3d. As No. 208	3·75	3·75

The face value of No. 208 is wrongly shown as "1.75 FILS".

52 Dubai Trade Centre

1986. 27th Chess Olympiad, Dubai. Mult.

No.	Type	Description	Unused	Used
210		50f. Type **52**	85	60
211		2d. Chess players (miniature from King Alfonso X's "Book of Chess, Dice and Tablings") (horiz)	4·00	3·25
212		250f. Chess players (miniature) (different) (horiz)	4·75	4·00
MS213		154×90 mm. Nos. 210/12. Perf or imperf	11·50	11·50

53 Dhow, Oil Rig, Tower Block and Sun's Rays

1986. 15th National Day. Multicoloured.

No.	Type	Description	Unused	Used
214		50f. Type **53**	80	35
215		1d. Type **53**	1·50	70
216		175f. Flag and hands holding Arabic "15" (vert)	2·50	1·90
217		2d. As No. 216	3·00	2·50

54 Emblem

1986. Arab Police Day.

No.	Type	Description	Unused	Used
218	54	50f. multicoloured	85	60
219		1d. multicoloured	1·70	1·50

55 Emblem on Landscape

56 Boeing 737 Airliner and Map

1987. Municipalities and Environment Week.

No.	Type	Description	Unused	Used
220	55	50f. multicoloured	95	70
221		1d. multicoloured	1·70	1·50

1987. 1st Anniv of United Arab Emirates Flight Information Region.

No.	Type	Description	Unused	Used
222	56	200f. multicoloured	2·50	2·50
223		250f. multicoloured	3·25	3·25

57 Flower in Droplet

58 University Emblem

1987. "Save Energy". Multicoloured.

No.	Type	Description	Unused	Used
224		50f. Type **57**	60	60
225		2d. Globe as sun over oil derrick	6·50	6·50

1987. 10th Anniv of U.A.E. University.

No.	Type	Description	Unused	Used
226	58	1d. multicoloured	1·00	1·00
227		3d. multicoloured	3·00	3·00

59 Oil Rig

1987. 25th Anniv of First Crude Oil Shipment from Abu Dhabi.

No.	Type	Description	Unused	Used
228	59	50f. multicoloured	60	60
229	–	1d. light blue, black and blue	1·10	1·10
230	–	175f. grey, black and blue	2·20	1·90
231	–	2d. multicoloured	2·50	2·50

DESIGNS—VERT: 1d. Aerial view of drilling platform; 175f. Rig workers with drill head. HORIZ: 2d. Oil tanker at sea.

60 Trees and Dates in Arched Window

61 Graph and Woman holding Baby

1987. Arab Palm Tree and Dates Day. Multicoloured.

No.	Type	Description	Unused	Used
232		50f. Type **60**	60	35
233		1d. Trees and fruit	1·10	70

1987. U.N.I.C.E.F Child Survival Campaign.

No.	Type	Description	Unused	Used
234	61	50f. multicoloured	45	35
235	–	1d. blue, black and pink	85	70
236	–	175f. black, green & emer	1·60	1·30
237	–	2d. multicoloured	1·90	1·60

DESIGNS—VERT: 1d. Vaccinating baby; 175f. Oral rehydration therapy. HORIZ: 2d. Mother breastfeeding.

62 Emblem on Man's Head and Globe

63 Salim bin Ali al-Owais

1987. International Year of Shelter for the Homeless.

No.	Type	Description	Unused	Used
238	62	2d. multicoloured	2·30	2·10
239		250f. multicoloured	3·00	2·50

1987. Birth Centenary of Salim bin Ali al-Owais (poet).

No.	Type	Description	Unused	Used
240	63	1d. multicoloured	1·50	1·50
241		2d. multicoloured	3·25	3·25

64 Lockheed TriStar 500 and Terminal Building

1987. 6th Anniv of Abu Dhabi Int Airport. Mult.

No.	Type	Description	Unused	Used
242		50f. Type **64**	60	60
243		50f. Reception area	60	60

244 100f. Lockheed TriStar 500 over air traffic control centre 1·70 1·70
245 100f. Lockheed TriStar 500 and Boeing 737 at gangways 1·70 1·70

65 Writing in Sand, Black-lip Pearl Oyster and Pearls

1988. National Arts Festival.
246 **65** 50f. multicoloured 80 80
247 250f. multicoloured 3·00 3·00

66 Fisherman on Shore (Layla Mohammed Khalfan)

1988. Children's Paintings. Multicoloured.
248 50f. Type **66** 60 35
249 1d. Woman and flowers (Zeinab Nasir Mohammed) (vert) 1·00 85
250 1d.75 Flowers with girls' faces (Fatma Ali Abdullah) (vert) 1·70 1·50
251 2d. Teddy bear, cat and girls playing (Saaly Mohammed Jowda) 1·90 1·70

67 Masked Youth

68 Emblem and Urban and Desert Scenes

1988. Palestinian "Intifida" Movement.
252 **67** 2d. multicoloured 2·20 1·30
253 250f. multicoloured 2·50 1·60

1988. National Banking Anniversaries. Mult.
254 50f. Type **68** (20th anniv of National Bank of Abu Dhabi) 1·30 1·30
255 50f. Emblem (25th anniv of National Bank of Dubai Ltd) 1·30 1·30

69 Map, Fork-lift Truck and Container Lorry

70 Swimming

1988. 16th Anniv of Port Rashid. Multicoloured.
256 50f. Type **69** 45 45
257 1d. Container ship and view of port 85 85
258 175f. Ro-ro ferry and small boats at anchorages 1·70 1·70
259 2d. Container ship at dockside 2·10 2·10

1988. Olympic Games, Seoul. Multicoloured.
260 2d. Type **70** 1·90 1·90
261 250f. Cycling 2·40 2·40

71 Vase

1988. 1st Anniv of Ras al Khaimah National Museum. Multicoloured.
262 50f. Type **71** 45 35
263 3d. Gold ornament (horiz) 2·50 2·20

72 Emblem

1988. 18th Arab Scouts Conference, Abu Dhabi.
264 **72** 1d. multicoloured 1·30 70

73 Dahlia

1989. 10th Tree Day. Multicoloured.
265 50f. Ghaf tree 45 35
266 100f. Palm tree 85 70
267 250f. Type **73** 2·20 1·70

74 Airport

1989. 10th Anniv of Sharjah International Airport.
268 **74** 50f. multicoloured 60 60
269 100f. multicoloured 1·30 1·30

75 Short S.23 Flying Boat

1989. 80th Anniv of Gulf Postal Services. Multicoloured.
270 50f. Type **75** 85 85
271 3d. "Bombala" (freighter) 4·25 4·25

76 Newspaper

1989. 20th Anniv of "Al-Ittihad" (newspaper). Multicoloured.
272 50f. Type **76** 50 50
273 1d. Newspaper offices 1·00 1·00

77 Emblem and Map

1989. 5th Anniv of Gulf Investment Corporation.
274 **77** 50f. multicoloured 45 45
275 2d. multicoloured 1·70 1·70

78 Offering Leaf to Child

1989. International Volunteer Day. U.A.E. Red Crescent Society. Multicoloured.
276 2d. Type **78** 1·70 1·70
277 250f. Crippled child in open hands (vert) 2·10 2·10

79 Bank Emblem and Buildings

80 Compass and Dhow

1989. 20th Anniv of Commercial Bank of Dubai. Multicoloured.
278 50f. Type **79** 50 50
279 1d. Bank building 1·00 1·00

1989. Bin Majid (15th-century navigator) Heritage Revival. Multicoloured.
280 1d. Type **80** 95 95
281 3d. Dhow (vert) 2·75 2·75

81 Festival Sites

82 Saker Falcon

1990. 3rd National Arts Festival, Al-Ain.
282 **81** 50f. multicoloured 35 50
283 1d. multicoloured 1·00 1·00

1990. Multicoloured, background colour given. (a) Size 18 × 23 mm.
284 **82** 5f. blue 15 15
285 20f. mauve 15 15
286 25f. pink 15 15
287 50f. brown 35 15
288 100f. bistre 70 45
288a 125f. yellow 2·10 1·10
288b 125f. bistre 40 35
289 150f. green 1·10 60
290 175f. green 1·30 70
290a 25d. pink 7·25 6·00
290b 50d. orange 14·50 11·50

(b) Size 21 × 26 mm.
291 **82** 2d. lilac 1·50 85
292 250f. blue 1·90 1·00
292a 275f. red 3·50 1·70
292b 275f. blue 80 65
293 3d. pink 2·30 1·30
293a 325f. grey 3·75 2·30
293b 325f. pink 1·10 90
293c 375f. white 5·00 3·50
293d 375f. orange 1·10 90
293e 4d. turquoise 3·50 1·75
293f 4d. grey 1·20 1·10
294 5d. orange 3·75 2·20
294a 6d. rose 6·50 3·25
294b 6d. white 1·80 1·50
295 10d. yellow 7·50 4·25
296 20d. green 15·00 8·75
297 50d. green 39·00 22·00

83 Children and Leaves

84 Leaning Tower of Pisa, Flag and U.A.E. Mascot

1990. Children's Culture Festival.
301 **83** 50f. multicoloured 45 45
302 250f. multicoloured 1·90 1·90

1990. World Cup Football Championship, Italy. Multicoloured.
303 50f. Type **84** 50 50
304 1d. Desert, flag and mascot (vert) 1·00 1·00
305 2d. Mascot on ball (vert) 1·90 1·90
306 250f. Flags around mascot 2·40 2·40
MS307 82 × 60 mm. 3d. Mascot and world map (vert) 4·00 4·00

85 Projects and Buildings

1990. 25th Anniv of Dubai Chamber of Commerce and Industry. Multicoloured.
308 **85** 50f. multicoloured 45 45
309 1d. multicoloured 80 80

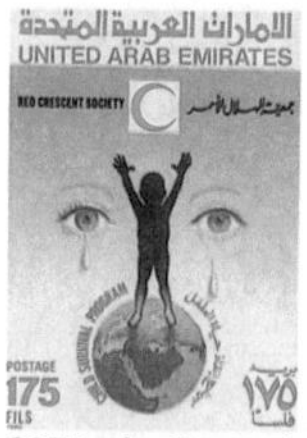

86 Weeping Eyes and Child on Globe

87 Periwinkle ("Catharanthus roseus")

1990. Child Survival Programme. Multicoloured.
310 175f. Type **86** 1·20 1·20
311 2d. Emaciated child and newspapers 1·40 1·40

1990. Flowers. Multicoloured.
312 50f. "Centavrea pseudo sinaica" 70 70
313 50f. Ushar bush ("Calotropis procera") 70 70
314 50f. "Argyrolobeum roseum" 70 70
315 50f. "Lamranthus roseus" 70 70
316 50f. "Hibiscus rosa sinensis" 70 70
317 50f. "Nerium oleander" 70 70
318 50f. Type **87** 70 70
319 50f. "Bougainvillaea glabra" (wrongly inscr "Bogainvillea") 70 70
MS320 Two sheets, each 90 × 120 mm. (a) Nos. 312/15; (b) Nos. 316/19 6·00 6·00

88 O.P.E.C. Emblem and Flame

89 Industrial Pollution and Dead Animals

1990. 30th Anniv of Organization of Petroleum Exporting Countries. Multicoloured.
321 50f. Emblem, flames, hands and oil rigs 60 35
322 1d. Type **88** 1·10 80
323 175f. Emblem and droplet 1·70 1·30

1990. "Our Planet Our Health". Multicoloured.
324 50f. Type **89** 35 35
325 3d. Industrial and vehicle pollution covering globe 2·30 2·30

90 Grand Mosque, Abu Dhabi

91 U.A.E. Crest and Graph

1990. Mosques. Multicoloured.
326 1d. Type **90** 70 70
327 2d. Al-Jumeirah Mosque, Dubai (vert) 1·50 1·50

1990. 10th Anniv of Central Bank. Mult.
328 50f. Type **91** 45 45
329 175f. Banknotes and building (horiz) 1·70 1·70

92 Tree

93 Globes and Buildings

1990. International Conference on High-salinity Tolerant Plants, Al-Ain. Multicoloured.
330 50f. Type **92** 50 50
331 250f. Trees along shoreline 1·70 1·70

1991. Abu Dhabi International Fair.
332 **93** 50f. multicoloured 50 35
333 2d. multicoloured 1·70 1·50

94 Emblem

1991. World Telecommunications Day. "Telecommunications and Safety of Human Life".
334 **94** 2d. multicoloured . . . . 1·90 1·50
335 3d. multicoloured . . . . 2·75 2·30

95 Shaikh Saqr Mosque, Ras al Khaimah

1991. Mosques. Multicoloured.
336 1d. Type **95** 70 70
337 2d. King Faisal Mosque, Sharjah . . . . 1·60 1·60
See also Nos. 371/2 and 411/12.

96 "Native Games" (Robba Mohamed Sofian)

1991. Children's Paintings. Multicoloured.
338 50f. Type **96** 45 35
339 1d. "National Day" (Yasmin Mohamed al-Rahim) . . . 85 70
340 175f. "Blind Man's Buff" (Amal Ibrahim Mohamed) 1·60 1·30
341 250f. "Native Dance" (Amina Ali Hassan) . . . . 1·90 1·70

97 Yellow-banded Angelfish

1991. Fishes. Multicoloured.
342 50f. Type **97** 50 50
343 50f. Hump-backed snapper 50 50
344 50f. Golden trevally 50 50
345 50f. Two-banded seabream ("Porgy") 50 50
346 1d. Yellow-finned seabream ("Black Bream") 70 70
347 1d. Three-banded grunt . . . 70 70
348 1d. Convict ("Greasy") grouper 70 70
349 1d. Rabbitfish 70 70
MS350 121 × 152 mm. Nos. 342/9 5·25 5·25

98 Shaikh Rashid and Abu Dhabi Airport

99 Fire Fighting

1991. 1st Death Anniv of Shaikh Rashid bin Said al-Maktoum (ruler of Dubai). Multicoloured.
351 50f. Type **98** 45 35
352 1d. Shaikh Rashid and modern and old buildings (horiz) 85 70
353 175f. Shaikh Rashid and seafront hotels . . . . . . 1·40 1·40
354 2d. Jebel Ali container port, Shaikh Rashid and dish aerial (horiz) . . . . . . 1·50 1·50

1991. Civil Defence Day.
355 **99** 50f. multicoloured 50 50
356 1d. multicoloured . . . . 1·10 1·10

100 Panavia Tornado F Mk 3 Jet Fighter over Dubai Airport

101 Flags and Emblem

1991. Int Aerospace Exhibition, Dubai. Mult.
357 175f. Type **100** . . . . . . 1·30 1·30
358 2d. View of under-side of Panavia Tornado over Dubai airport . . . . . . 1·50 1·50

1991. 10th Anniv of Gulf Co-operation Council.
359 **101** 50f. multicoloured 35 35
360 3d. multicoloured . . . . 2·30 2·30

102 Shaikh Zaid bin Sultan al Nahayyan of Abu Dhabi (President of U.A.E.)

1991. 20th National Day. Multicoloured.
361 75f. Type **102** 80 80
362 75f. Shaikh Humaid bin Rashid al Naimi of Ajman and fort (to right of stamp) with cannon 80 80
363 75f. Shaikh Maktoum bin Rashid al-Maktoum of Dubai and fort (to left of stamp) with cannon . . . 80 80
364 75f. Shaikh Hamad bin Mohamed al Sharqi of Fujeira and fort on hillock 80 80
365 75f. Shaikh Saqr bin Mohamed al-Qasimi of Ras al Khaima and fort (tower and tree in foreground) . . 80 80
366 75f. Shaikh Sultan bin Mohamed al Qasimi of Sharjah and fort (to left of stamp with Arabs in doorway) 80 80
367 75f. Shaikh Rashid bin Ahmed al Moalla of Umm al Qiwain and fort (to right of stamp with trees growing over walls) 80 80
MS368 70 × 90 mm. 3d. Shaikh Zaid of Abu Dhabi and parade of army and tanks. Imperf . . . . . . 3·75 3·75

103 Derrick

104 Fort Jahili, Al Ain

1992. 20th Anniv of Abu Dhabi National Oil Company.
369 **103** 175f. multicoloured . . . 80 80
370 250f. multicoloured . . . 1·10 1·10

1992. Mosques. As T **95**. Multicoloured.
371 50f. Shaikh Rashid bin Humaid al Naimi Mosque, Ajman 50 50
372 1d. Shaikh Ahmed bin Rashid al Moalla Mosque, Umm al Qiwain . . . . . 1·00 1·00

1992. "Expo '92" World's Fair, Seville.
373 **104** 2d. multicoloured . . . . 1·50 1·50
374 250f. multicoloured . . . . 44·00 44·00

105 Emblem and Family

1992. Deaf Child Week. Multicoloured.
375 1d. Type **105** . . . . 1·00 70
376 3d. Hearing aid in ear . . . 2·50 2·30

106 Aerial View of Port

1992. 20th Anniv of Zayed Sea Port, Abu Dhabi. Multicoloured.
377 50f. Type **106** 35 35
378 1d. Cranes on dockside . . . 70 70
379 175f. Loading container ship 1·30 1·30
380 2d. Map showing routes from port . . . . 1·70 1·70

107 Yachting

108 Football Match (Najla Saif Mohamed Harib)

1992. Olympic Games, Barcelona. Multicoloured.
381 50f. Type **107** 35 35
382 1d. Running 70 70
383 175f. Swimming . . . . . . 1·40 1·40
384 250f. Cycling . . . . 1·90 1·90
MS385 60 × 90 mm. 3d. Show jumping . . . . 2·50 2·50

1992. Children's Paintings. Multicoloured.
386 50f. Type **108** 35 35
387 1d. Children in park (Anoud Adnan Ali Mohamed) . . 70 70
388 2d. Family at playground (Ahlam Ibrahim Ahmed) 1·50 1·50
389 250f. Children playing amongst trees (Dallal Ali Salih) . . . . 1·90 1·90

109 Bank Building

110 Tambourah

1992. 15th Anniv of Emirates Bank International.
390 **109** 50f. multicoloured 35 35
391 – 175f. gold, brown and red 1·30 1·30
DESIGN—33 × 40 mm: 175f. Bank emblem.

1992. Musical Instruments. Multicoloured.
392 50f. Type **110** 45 45
393 50f. Oud (stringed instrument) 45 45
394 50f. Rababah (stringed instrument with bow) . . . 45 45
395 1d. Mizmar (wind instrument) and shindo (drum) (horiz) 80 80
396 1d. Marwas and duff (hand-held drums) (horiz) 80 80
397 1d. Tabel (drum) and hibban (bagpipe) (horiz) 80 80
MS398 Two sheets. (a) 75 × 95 mm. Nos. 392/4; (b) 95 × 75 mm. Nos. 395/7 . . . . 4·25 4·25

111 Emblem

1992. 13th Supreme Council Session of Gulf Co-operation Council, Abu Dhabi.
399 **111** 50f. multicoloured 35 35
400 2d. multicoloured . . . . 1·60 1·60

112 Camel Race

1992. The Dromedary. Multicoloured.
401 50f. Type **112** 35 35
402 1d. Camel riders and mother with young (vert) 80 80
403 175f. Camels at well and mother with young . . . . 1·40 1·40
404 2d. Camels (vert) . . . . . . 1·60 1·60

113 Golf

114 Club Building

1993. Tourism. Multicoloured.
405 50f. Type **113** 50 50
406 1d. Fishing (vert) 80 80
407 2d. Sailing . . . . 1·60 1·60
408 250f. Sight-seeing by car . . 1·90 1·90

1993. Dubai Creek Golf and Yacht Club. Mult.
409 2d. Type **114** . . . . 1·60 1·60
410 250f. Club building and sea shore . . . . 1·90 1·90

1993. Mosques. As T **95**. Multicoloured.
411 50f. Thabit bin Khalid Mosque, Fujeira 50 50
412 1d. Sharq al Morabbah Mosque, Al-Ain . . . . . 1·00 1·00

115 National Crest and Sports

1993. National Youth Festival. Multicoloured.
413 50f. Type **115** 45 45
414 3d. National crest and sciences . . . . 2·75 2·75

116 Textile Cone

1993. Sea Shells. Multicoloured.
415 25f. Type **116** 25 25
416 50f. Atlantic pearl oyster . . 35 35
417 100f. Woodcock murex . . . 80 80
418 150f. "Natica pulicaris" . . . 1·10 1·10
419 175f. Giant spider conch . . 1·30 1·30
420 200f. "Cardita bicolor" . . . 1·60 1·60
421 250f. Gray's cowrie . . . . 1·90 1·90
422 300f. "Cymatium trilineatum" 2·30 2·30

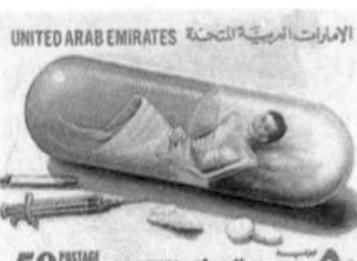
117 Addict within Capsule

1993. Anti-drugs Campaign. Multicoloured.
423 50f. Type **117** 50 50
424 1d. Family on skull, globe and drugs (vert) 85 85

118 Commercial Buildings

119 Aerial View of Port

1993. 25th Anniv of Abu Dhabi National Bank. Multicoloured.
425 50f. Type **118** 35 35
426 1d. Bank emblem 80 80
427 175f. Bank building and emblem . . . . 1·40 1·40
428 2d. Commercial buildings within shield . . . . 1·60 1·60

1993. Dubai Ports Authority. Multicoloured.
429 50f. Type **119** 35 35
430 1d. Cranes loading containers 80 80
431 2d. Aerial view of port (different) . . . . 1·60 1·60
432 250f. Arrowed routes on globe . . . . 1·90 1·90

120 Soldiers on Parade (Mouza Musabah al-Mazroui)

1993. National Day. Children's Paintings. Multicoloured.
433 50f. Type **120** 35 35
434 1d. Woman and children (Shreen Naeem Hassan Radwan) (vert) 80 80
435 175f. Flag and dhow (Samiha Mohamad Sultan) . . . . 1·50 1·50
436 2d. Decorations and fireworks (Omer Abdulla Rabia Thani) . . . . . . 1·70 1·70

121 Hili Tomb

1993. Archaeological Finds from Al-Ain. Multicoloured.
437 50f. Type **121** 35 35
438 1d. Hili decorative tile . . . 80 80
439 175f. Qattarah figure . . . . 1·40 1·40
440 250f. Hili bowl . . . . 2·30 2·30

122 Horse rearing

1994. Arab Horses. Multicoloured.
441 50f. Type **122** 35 35
442 1d. Grey (horiz) 80 80
443 175f. Bay with white blaze . . 1·40 1·40
444 250f. Piebald (horiz) . . . . 2·30 2·30

123 Children with Flags and Balloons

1994. 10th Children's Festival, Sharjah. Children's Paintings. Multicoloured.
445 50f. Type **123** 50 50
446 1d. Children in forest . . . . 1·00 1·00
447 175f. Children with balloons and child painting . . . . 1·70 1·70
448 2d. Children in garden . . . 1·90 1·90

124 Dubai, Map and Emblems

125 Holy Kaaba and Globe

1994. 10th Arab Towns Organization Congress, Dubai. Multicoloured.
449 50f. Type **124** 35 35
450 1d. Different view of Dubai, map and emblems (horiz) 80 80

1994. Pilgrimage to Mecca. Multicoloured.
451 50f. Type **125** 50 50
452 2d. Crowds around Holy Kaaba . . . . 2·10 2·10

126 Homes (Arab Housing Day)

127 Covered Vessel

1994. Anniversaries and Events. Multicoloured.
453 1d. Type **126** 85 85
454 1d. Children playing and couple (International Year of the Family) (horiz) . . . 85 85
455 1d. National Olympic Committee emblem, rings and sports (cent of Int Olympic Committee) (horiz) 85 85
456 1d. Paper, pen-nib and dove (10th anniv of Emirates Writers' Association) . . . 85 85

1994. Archaeological Finds from Al-Qusais, Dubai. Multicoloured.
457 50f. Type **127** 45 45
458 1d. Jug (horiz) 85 85
459 175f. Jug (different) (horiz) 1·50 1·50
460 250f. Bowl (horiz) . . . . . 2·20 2·20

128 Arabian Leopard

1994. Environmental Protection. The Cat Family. Multicoloured.
461 50f. Type **128** 45 45
462 1d. Gordon's wildcat 85 85
463 2d. Caracal . . . . 1·70 1·70
464 250f. Sandcat . . . . 2·50 2·50

129 Little Green Bee Eaters

1994. Birds. Multicoloured.
465 50f. Type **129** 45 45
466 175f. White-collared kingfishers . . . . 1·40 1·40
467 2d. Crab plovers . . . . . . 1·70 1·70
468 250f. Indian rollers . . . . . 2·50 2·50
MS469 90 × 60 mm. 3d. Greater flamingos (29 × 40 mm) . . . . 2·75 2·75

130 Championship Emblem

131 Horse's Head

1994. 12th Arab Gulf Football Championship, Abu Dhabi. Multicoloured.
470 50f. Type **130** 35 35
471 3d. Match scene (horiz) . . . 2·30 2·30

1995. Archaeological Finds from Mulaiha, Sharjah. Multicoloured.
472 50f. Type **131** 35 35
473 175f. Coin . . . . 1·40 1·40
474 2d. Ancient writing on leather 1·60 1·60
475 250f. Stone tablet (horiz) . . 1·70 1·70

132 Al-Naashat

1995. National Dances. Multicoloured.
476 50f. Type **132** 35 35
477 175f. Al-Ayaalah . . . . . . 1·40 1·40
478 2d. Al-Shahhoh . . . . . . 1·60 1·60

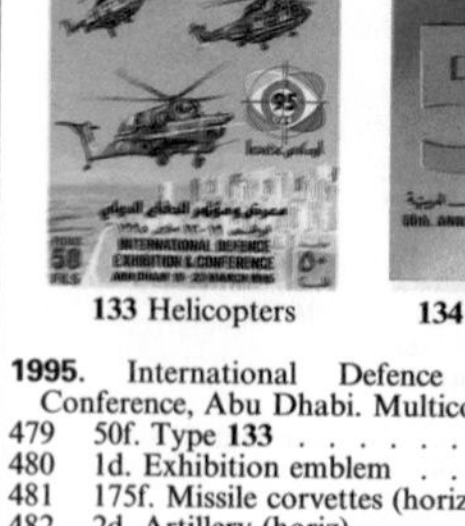

133 Helicopters

134 Arab League

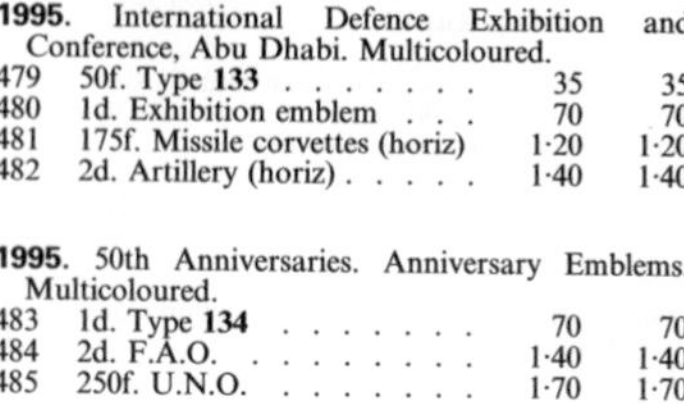

1995. International Defence Exhibition and Conference, Abu Dhabi. Multicoloured.
479 50f. Type **133** 35 35
480 1d. Exhibition emblem . . . 70 70
481 175f. Missile corvettes (horiz) 1·20 1·20
482 2d. Artillery (horiz) . . . . . 1·40 1·40

1995. 50th Anniversaries. Anniversary Emblems. Multicoloured.
483 1d. Type **134** 70 70
484 2d. F.A.O. . . . . 1·40 1·40
485 250f. U.N.O. . . . . 1·70 1·70

135 Symbols of Postal Services

1995. 10th Anniv of General Postal Authority.
486 **135** 50f. multicoloured 45 45

136 Exhibition Emblem

1995. 1st Gulf Co-operation Council Stamp Exhibition, Abu Dhabi.
487 **136** 50f. multicoloured 45 45

137 Bowling Hoop

138 Lesser Kestrel

1995. National Games. Multicoloured.
488 50f. Type **137** 25 25
489 175f. Swinging 95 95
490 2d. Sticks in stone square game . . . . 1·00 1·00
491 250f. Stone game . . . . . . 1·30 1·30

1995. Birds. Multicoloured.
492 50f. Type **138** 35 35
493 175f. Socotra cormorant . . 1·30 1·30
494 2d. Cream-coloured courser 1·50 1·50
495 250f. Hoopoe . . . . 1·70 1·70

139 Figures and Tower Block

1995. Population and Housing Census. Mult.
496 50f. Type **139** 25 25
497 250f. City and stylized family 1·30 1·30

140 "Folklore Show" (Ibtisam Mussa)

1995. National Day. Children's Paintings. Multicoloured.
498 50f. Type **140** . . . . 25 2·50
499 175f. "Children dancing" (Shimaa Mohamed Abdullah Khoury) 95 95
500 2d. "Children holding balloons" (Khoula Ibrahim) . . . . 1·00 1·00
501 250f. "Car festival" (Fatima Jumaa) . . . . 1·30 1·30

141 Dugongs

1996. Environmental Protection. Sea Mammals. Multicoloured.
502 50f. Type **141** 25 25
503 2d. Common dolphins . . . 1·10 1·10
504 3d. Humpback whales . . . 1·70 1·70
MS505 90 × 70 mm. Nos. 502/4 3·00 3·00

142 Competitor

143 Earthenware Urn (Bathna-Fujaira)

1996. Hobie Cat 16 World Championships. Mult.
506 50f. Type **142** 25 25
507 3d. Hobie 1b catamaran and building . . . . 1·70 1·70

1996. Archaeological Finds. Multicoloured.
508 50f. Type **143** 25 25
509 175f. Earthenware pot with handles (Bidya-Fujaira) . . 95 95
510 250f. Bronze bangle (Qidfa-Fujaira) . . . . 1·50 1·50
511 3d. Bronze ring (Dibba-Fujaira) (horiz) . . . . . 1·70 1·70

144 Shooting

1996. Olympic Games, Atlanta. Multicoloured.
512 50f. Type **144** 25 25
513 1d. Cycling (vert) 50 50
514 250f. Running (vert) . . . . 1·40 1·40
515 350f. Swimming . . . . . . 1·70 1·70

145 Emblem

146 Emblem, Landmarks and Players

1996. 21st Anniv of Women's Union. Multicoloured.
516 50f. Type **145** 25 25
517 3d. Woman's hands and emblem (horiz) . . . . . . 1·70 1·70

1996. 11th Asian Football Cup Championship. Multicoloured.
518 1d. Type **146** 60 60
519 250f. Player with ball . . . . 1·60 1·60

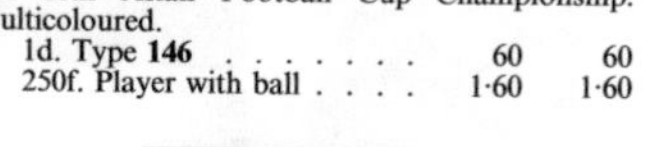

147 "Drug" Snake crushing weeping Globe

1996. Anti-drugs Campaign. Multicoloured.
520 50f. Type **147** 50 50
521 3d. Healthy man and drug-wrecked skull . . . . . . 1·40 1·40

148 Shaikh Said and House

1996. Centenary of Shaikh Said al Maktoum House (museum). Multicoloured.
522 50f. Type **148** 25 25
523 250f. Shaikh Said and close-up view of House . . . . 1·40 1·40
524 350f. House at sunset . . . . 1·90 1·90

149 Chestnut-bellied Sandgrouse

150 Head forming Waterfall (Abdullah Muhammed Abdullah al-Sharhan)

1996. Birds. Multicoloured.
525 50f. Type **149** 15 15
526 150f. Striated scops owl . . . 85 85
527 250f. Grey hypocolius . . . 1·30 1·30
528 3d. White-throated robin . . 1·70 1·70
529 350f. Sooty falcon . . . . . 1·90 1·90

1996. Children's Paintings. Multicoloured.
530 50f. Type **150** 15 15
531 1d. Dhows (Hamda Muhammed Abdullah) (horiz) 50 50
532 250f. Flowers (Hind Muhammed bin Dhahi) . . 1·30 1·30
533 350f. Girl and tent (Lin Atta Yaghi) . . . . 1·70 1·70

151 Emirates Rulers

152 U.A.E. Crest

153 Shaikh and Trees

1996. 25th National Day. Multicoloured.
534 50f. Type **151** 25 25
535 1d. Emirates crest and flag 45 45
536 150f. Type **151** 70 70
537 3d. As No. 535 . . . . . . 1·40 1·40
MS538 70 × 90 mm. 5d. Score of national anthem. Imperf . . . 2·75 2·75

1996. 30th Anniv of Accession of Shaikh Zaid ibn Sultan al Nahayyan of Abu Dhabi and 25th Anniv of United Arab Emirates. (a) Type **152**.
539 **152** 50f. multicoloured 25 25
540 1d. multicoloured 60 60

(b) As T **153**. Multicoloured.
541 50f. Type **153** 25 25
542 1d. Shaikh and dates 50 50
543 250f. Type **153** . . . . . . 1·40 1·40
544 350f. As No. 542 . . . . . . 1·70 1·70
MS545 90 × 70 mm. 5d. Shaikh on horseback. Imperf . . . . . . 2·75 2·75

154 Loew's Blue

1997. Butterflies. Multicoloured.
546 50f. Type **154** 25 25
547 1d. Swallowtail 70 70
548 150f. Blue argus . . . . . . 1·00 1·00
549 250f. African monarch . . . 1·90 1·90

155 Festival Poster

1997. Shopping Festival, Dubai. Multicoloured.
550 50f. Type **155** 25 25
551 250f. Emblem (vert) . . . . 1·20 1·20

156 Helicopter lifting Vehicle

157 Sky and Anniversary Emblem

1997. International Defence Exhibition and Conference, Abu Dhabi. Multicoloured.
552 50f. Type **156** 25 25
553 1d. Exhibition emblem . . . 45 45
554 250f. Weapons demonstration 1·20 1·20
555 350f. Frigates and submarine 1·70 1·70

1997. 20th Anniv of Emirates Bank Group. Multicoloured.
556 50f. Type **157** 25 25
557 1d. Anniversary emblem . . 60 60

158 "TEND" and Emblem

160 Stamps and Magnifying Glass

159 Silver Coins spilling from Pot

1997. Technological, Education and National Development. Multicoloured.
559 50f. Type **158** 25 25
560 250f. Emblem . . . . 1·20 1·20

1997. Sharjah Heritage. Multicoloured.
561 50f. Type **159** 25 25
562 3d. Courtyard and minarets 1·60 1·60

1997. Emirates Philatelic Association. Multicoloured.
563 50f. Type **160** 25 25
564 250f. Magnifying glass, tweezers and "river" of stamps (horiz) . . . . . . 1·30 1·30

161 Cats and Kittens

1997. Children's Paintings. Multicoloured.
565 50f. Type **161** 25 25
566 1d. Fashion parade 50 50
567 250f. Group of children (vert) 1·40 1·40
568 3d. Abstract . . . . 1·70 1·70

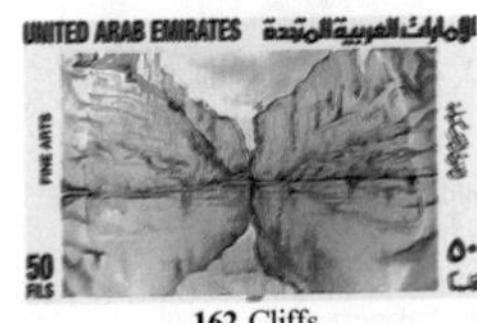

162 Cliffs

1997. Fine Arts. Multicoloured.
569 50f. Type **162** 35 35
570 50f. Still-life (vert) 35 35
571 50f. Modern painting in blues and yellows 35 35
572 50f. Couple (vert) 35 35
573 50f. Waterfall and rocks . . 35 35
574 50f. Coral hind (fish) (vert) 35 35
MS575 149 × 105 mm. 5d. Architecture. Imperf . . . . . 3·00 3·00

163 Jet Fighter over Airport

1997. International Aerospace Exhibition, Dubai. Multicoloured.
576 250f. Type **163** 75 75
577 3d. Buildings, airplane and oil rig 85 85

164 Park

1997. 26th National Day. Environmental Protection. Multicoloured.
578 50f. Type **164** 25 25
579 1d. Mountains and forest . . 50 50
580 150f. Mountains and river . . 80 80
581 250f. Landscaped road verge 1·50 1·50

165 Emblems and Venue

167 Laser Dinghies

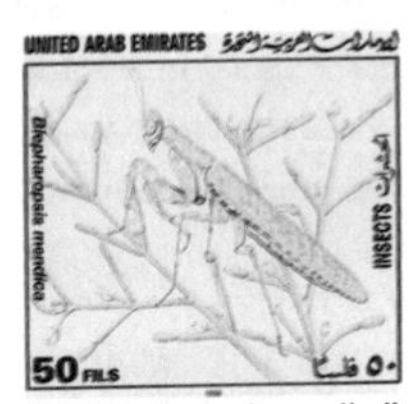

166 "Blepharopsis mendica" (praying mantis)

1997. 3rd Afro–Arab Trade Fair, Sharjah. Mult.
582 150f. Type **165** 85 85
583 350f. Organization of African Unity and Arab League emblems' handclasp over Fair emblem (horiz) . . . 1·00 1·00

1998. Insects. Multicoloured.
584 50f. Type **166** 25 25
585 150f. "Galeodes" sp. (spider) 80 80
586 250f. "Crocothemis arythraea" (darter) . . . . 1·40 1·40
587 350f. "Xylocopa aestuans" (carpenter bee) . . . . . . 1·90 1·90

1998. World Sailing Championships, Dubai. Multicoloured.
588 50f. Type **167** 25 25
589 1d. Racing yachts (horiz) . . 50 50
590 250f. High-performance 2-man dinghies (horiz) . . . 1·40 1·40
591 3d. Catamarans . . . . . . 1·70 1·70

168 Military Personnel

1998. Triple International Defence Exhibition and Conference, Abu Dhabi. Multicoloured.
592 50f. Type **168** 35 35
593 1d. Exhibition emblem and city (vert) 60 60
594 150f. Radar equipment (vert) 95 95
595 350f. Rocket launcher and communications equipment (vert) . . . . 2·30 2·30

169 Emblem and City Landmarks

170 Oryx on Hillside

1998. Sharjah, Arab Cultural Capital. Multicoloured.
596 50f. Type **169** 25 25
597 3d. Emblem and tower . . . 1·70 1·70

1998. Protection of the Environment. Multicoloured.
598 1d. Type **170** 50 50
599 350f. Palm tree and sun . . . 1·90 1·90

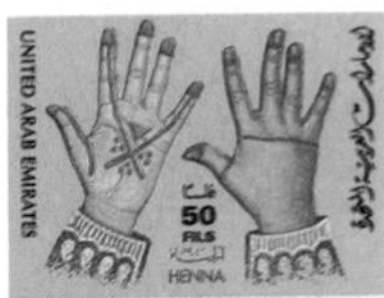

171 Decorated Hands

1998. Henna.
600 **171** 50f. multicoloured 25 25
601 – 1d. multicoloured 50 50
602 – 150f. multicoloured . . . 80 80
603 – 2d. multicoloured . . . . 1·10 1·10
604 – 250f. multicoloured . . . 1·40 1·40
605 – 3d. multicoloured . . . . 1·70 1·70
DESIGNS: 1d. to 3d. Different hand decorations.

172 Underwater Scene (Rashid al Shayaa)

1998. Paintings. Multicoloured.
606 50f. Type **172** 25 25
607 1d. Woman and cradle (Nadia Othman al Baroot) 50 50
608 250f. Village scene (Mahmoud Hassan) (vert) 1·30 1·30
609 350f. Rural still life (Shaikha Saeed) . . . . 1·90 1·90

173 Mountain Road

1998. 27th National Day. Tourism. Multicoloured.
610 50f. Type **173** 25 25
611 350f. Dubai Harbour . . . . 1·90 1·90

174 "Indigofera arabica"

1998. Wild Flowers. Multicoloured.
612 25f. Type **174** 10 10
613 50f. "Centaureum pulchellum" 25 25
614 75f. "Lavandula citriodora" 35 35
615 1d. "Taverniera glabra" . . . 50 50
616 150f. "Convolvulus deserti" 80 80
617 2d. "Capparis spinosa" . . . 1·00 1·00
618 250f. "Rumex vesicrius" . . 1·40 1·40
619 3d. "Anagallis arvensis" . . 1·70 1·70
620 350f. "Tribulus arabicus" . . 1·90 1·90
621 5d. "Reichardia tinitana" . . 2·75 2·75

175 "Anthia duodecimguttata" (ground beetle)

177 U.P.U. Emblem

176 Emblem

1999. Insects and Arachnids. Multicoloured.
622 50f. Type **175** 35 35
623 150f. Oleander hawk moth 95 95
624 250f. "Acorypha glaucopsis" 1·70 1·70
625 350f. "Androctonus crassicauda" . . . . 2·30 2·30

1999. International Monuments Day. Multicoloured.
626 150f. Type **176** 80 80
627 250f. Al Faheidi fort, Dubai 1·40 1·40

1999. 125th Anniv of Universal Postal Union. Mult.
628 50f. Type **177** 95 95
629 350f. U.P.U. emblem and "125" . . . . 2·30 2·30
MS630 90 × 70 mm. 5d. Hemispheres, UPU emblem and "125". Imperf . . . . 3·25 3·25

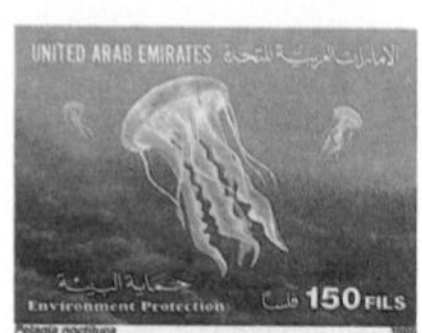

178 Jellyfish

1999. Protection of the Environment. Multicoloured.
631 50f. Feather star 25 25
632 150f. Type **178** 95 95
633 250f. Spanish dancer . . . . 1·70 1·70
634 3d. Sponge . . . . 1·90 1·90

179 Woman braiding

180 Championship Emblem

1999. Crafts. Multicoloured.
635 50f. Type **179** 25 25
636 1d. Braided trousers 60 60
637 250f. Weaving palm leaves 1·70 1·70
638 350f. Woven palm leaf products . . . . 2·30 2·30

1999. 14th World Tenpin Bowling Championship, Abu Dhabi. Multicoloured.
639 50f. Type **180** 35 35
640 250f. Competitor . . . . . . 1·70 1·70

181 Couple outside House

1999. Children's Paintings. Multicoloured.
641 50f. Type **181** 25 25
642 1d. Pattern 60 60
643 150f. Underwater scene . . . 95 95
644 250f. Family having picnic 1·70 1·70

182 "2000" and Dove

184 Conference Emblem

183 Dubai Port

1999. Year 2000.
645 **182** 50f. black and silver . . . 25 25
646 – 250f. blue and gold . . . 1·70 1·70
DESIGN: 250f. "2000" and dove (different).

2000. Centenary of Dubai Ports and Customs. Multicoloured.
647 50f. Type **183** 35 35
648 3d. Dubai Customs House . . 2·30 2·30

2000. Int Conference on Desertification, Dubai.
649 **184** 250f. multicoloured . . . 1·90 1·90

185 River

2000. Environmental Protection. Multicoloured.
650 50f. Type **185** 35 35
651 250f. Beach . . . . 1·70 1·70

186 Swimming

2000. Olympic Games, Sydney. Multicoloured.
652 50f. Type **186** 45 45
653 2d. Athletics . . . . 1·70 1·70
654 350f. Shooting . . . . 3·00 3·00

187 Ribbon and Award

188 Map of United Arab Emirates and Barometer

2000. International Holy Koran Award. Mult.
655 50f. Type **187** 45 45
656 250f. Pres. Shaikh Zaid ibn Sultan al Nahayyan (recipient of award) . . . . 2·20 2·20

2000. 50th Anniv of World Meteorological Organization. Multicoloured.
657 50f. Type **188** 45 45
658 250f. Old map of Gulf region and sun dial . . . . 2·20 2·20

189 Airplanes

2000. Expansion of Dubai International Airport.
659 **189** 50f. multicoloured 45 45
660 350f. multicoloured . . . 3·00 3·00

190 White Crescent forming Smile

2001. Development and Environment.
661 **190** 50f. green 45 45
662 – 2d.50 green and deep green . . . . 1·90 1·90
663 – 3d. green, light green and deep green . . . . . . 2·30 2·30
664 – 3d.50 light green, green and deep green . . . . 2·75 2·75
DESIGNS: 250f. White flower casting shadow; 3d. Heart-shaped leaf; 350f. Heart-shaped world map.

191 "Dubai Millennium" (race horse)

2001. "Dubai Millennium", Dubai World Cup Horse Race Winner. Multicoloured.
665 3d. Type **191** . . . . 2·40 2·40
666 350f. In paddock . . . . . . 2·75 2·75

192 Calligraph

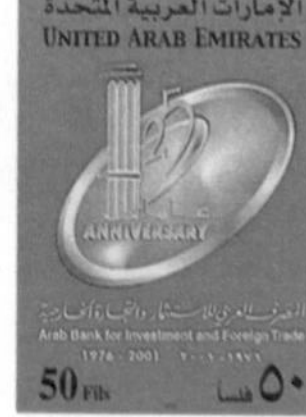

193 Anniversary Emblem and Plate

2001. Sultan Bin Ali Al Owais (poet) Commemoration. Multicoloured.
667 50f. Type **192** 50 50
668 1d. Sultan bin Ali Al Owais 1·00 1·00

2001. 25th Anniv of Arab Investment and Foreign Trade Bank. Multicoloured.
669 50f. Type **193** 45 45
670 1d. Emblem and ribbon . . . 95 95

194 Al Shahoof

2001. Traditional Craft. Multicoloured.
671 50f. Type **194** 45 45
672 250f. Al Bagarah . . . . . . 2·10 2·10
673 3d. Al Sam'aa . . . . 2·40 2·40
674 350f. Al Jahboot . . . . . . 3·00 3·00

195 Three birds ("Changing")

2001. Emirates Post. Multicoloured.
675 50f. Type **195** 50 50
676 250f. Corporate emblem ("Growing") . . . . 2·50 2·50
677 3d. Emblem ("Achieving") 3·00 3·00

196 Stylized Stamp

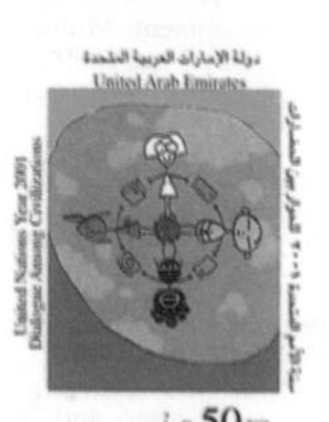

197 Children encircling Globe

2001. 7th GCC (Arab Gulf States Co-operation Council) Stamp Exhibition, Dubai.
678 **196** 50f. vermilion, green and black 60 60

2001. United Nations Year of Dialogue among Civilizations. Multicoloured.
679 50f. Type **197** 50 50
680 250f. Leaves . . . . 2·50 2·50

198 Mosque

2001. Children's Paintings. Multicoloured.
681 1d. Type **198** 85 85
682 250f. Boat building . . . . . 2·20 2·20
683 3d. Man pouring coffee (vert) 2·50 2·50
684 350f. Falconry . . . . 3·00 3·00

199 Emblem, Fighter Plane and Ship

200 Conference Emblem

2001. 25th Anniv of Unification of Armed Forces.
685 **199** 1d. multicoloured . . . . 1·10 1·10

2002. International Conference on Water Resources, Dubai.
686 **200** 50f. multicoloured 60 60

201 Emblem

203 "1"

202 Saluki and Sand Storm

2002. 25th Anniv of United Arab Emirates University. Multicoloured.
687 50f. Type **201** 50 50
688 1d. As No. 687 . . . . . . 1·00 1·00

2002. Hunting Dogs. Saluki. Multicoloured.
689 50f. Type **202** 50 50
690 150f. Facing left . . . . . . 1·60 1·60
691 250f. Five hounds . . . . . 2·50 2·50
692 3d. Facing right . . . . . . 3·25 3·25

2002. 1st Anniv of UAE Postal Corporation.
693 **203** 50f. blue 50 50
MS694 81 × 120 mm. 3d. multicoloured (45 × 120 mm) 6·00 6·00
DESIGN: 3d. Corporation emblem and "1".

204 Open Book

2002. Rashid Bin Al Suwadi (Al Khadhar) (poet) Commemoration. Multicoloured.
695 50f. Type **204** 70 70
696 250f. Al Khadhar . . . . . 3·50 3·50

205 Sun, Antelope's Head and Yacht

2002. Children's Paintings. Multicoloured.
697 50f. Type **205** 45 45
698 1d. Figures with raised arms 80 80
699 2d. Globe with arms . . . . 1·60 1·60
700 250f. Fish . . . . 1·90 1·90
701 3d. Child holding heart . . . 2·40 2·40
702 350f. Stick children . . . . . 2·75 2·75
703 5d. Arabic script . . . . . . 4·00 4·00

206 Sand Dunes and Emblem

2002. Sheikh Hamdan Bin Rashid Al Maktoum Award for Medical Science. Multicoloured.

704	50f. Type **206**	45	45
705	250f. Emblem and map of UAE	2·30	2·30

207 Ajman

208 View of Earth from Space

2002. 31st National Day. Showing landmarks of Emirate named. Multicoloured.

706	50f. Type **207**	35	35
707	50f. Sharjah	35	35
708	50f. Dubai	35	35
709	50f. Abu Dhabi	35	35
710	50f. Ras Al-Khaimah	35	35
711	50f. Fujairah	35	35
712	50f. Umm al Quwain	35	35
MS713	175 × 117 mm. Nos. 706/12. (Imperf)	3·50	3·50

2003. Thuraya Telecommunications Satellite.

714 **208**	25f. multicoloured	25	25
715	250f. multicoloured	1·70	1·70

209 Pottery Jar with Geometric Designs

2003. Al Ain National Museum. Multicoloured.

716	50f. Type **209**	30	30
717	275f. Pottery vase with animal designs	1·90	1·80
718	4d. Iron Age bronze axe	2·75	3·00
719	6d. Soap stone mortar	3·25	3·00

210 Buildings and Emblem

2003. 40th Anniv of National Bank of Dubai.

720 **210**	50f. multicoloured	30	25
721	4d. multicoloured	2·50	2·75
722	6d. multicoloured	3·25	3·00

211 Arabian Leopard

2003. Animals. Multicoloured.

723	50f. Type **211**	30	30
724	50f. Blanford's fox	30	30
725	50f. Caracal	30	30
726	50f. Cheetah	30	30
727	50f. Gordon's wild cat	30	30
728	50f. Striped hyena	30	30
729	50f. Jackal	30	30
730	50f. White-tailed mongoose	30	30
731	50f. Ruppell's fox	30	30
732	50f. Sand cat	30	30
733	50f. Small spotted genet	30	30
734	50f. Arabian wolf	30	30

212 Dirham, Al Walid Bin Abdul Malik Caliphate

2003. Arab Coins. Multicoloured.

735	50f. Type **212**	30	30
736	125f. Dirham, Abdul Malik Bin Marwan caliphate	95	1·10
737	275f. Dinar showing Al Mustansir Billah Al Fatimi	1·90	1·80
738	375f. Dinar, Abdul Malik Bin Marwan caliphate	2·30	2·20
MS739	106 × 73 mm. 5d. Dirham, Muhammed Al Ameen caliphate. Imperf	2·40	2·20

213 Sheikh Zayed Bin Sultan Al Nahyan and Camel

2003. 37th Anniv of Accession of Sheikh Zayed Bin Sultan Al Nahyan, President of United Arab Emirates. Multicoloured.

740	50f. Type **213**	30	30
741	175f. Sheikh and high-rise buildings	1·00	95

214 Championship Emblem

2003. FIFA World Youth Football Championships, United Arab Emirates 2003.

742 **214**	375f. multicoloured	2·20	2·20

215 Emirates Towers, Dubai

2003. IMF and World Bank Group Meetings, Dubai. Dubai 2003 Expo. Multicoloured.

743	50f. Type **215**	30	30
744	175f. Falcon	1·10	95
745	275f. Domes (horiz)	1·90	1·80
746	375f. Traditional boat	2·20	2·20
MS747	118 × 74 mm. 5d. Emblem. Imperf	2·50	2·50

216 Archway with Zakharaf (design)

2003. Peace Message. Multicoloured.

748	50f. Type **216**	30	30
749	225f. Traditional house with barjeel (wind tower)	1·50	1·40
750	275f. Traditional merchant's house with decorative columns	2·50	2·40
751	325f. Abras (traditional boats)	2·75	2·50

217 Al Areesh (palm frond) House

2003. Traditional Houses. Multicoloured.

752	50f. Type **217**	25	25
753	175f. Al Teen (mud)	1·20	1·10
754	275f. Al Saf (pebbles)	1·90	1·80
755	325f. Al Shaar (tent)	2·75	2·50

218 Peregrine Falcon

2003. Falcons. Multicoloured.

756	50f. Type **218**	30	30
757	125f. Gyr-peregrine	65	60
758	275f. Gyrfalcon	1·50	1·40
759	375f. Saker	1·70	1·60

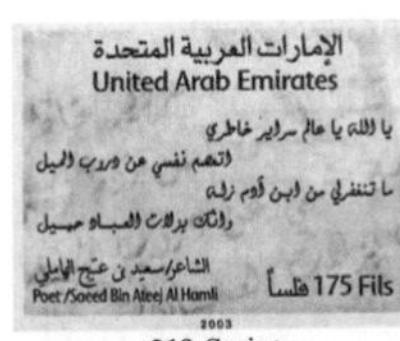

219 Script

2003. Saeed Bin Ateej al Hamli (poet) Commemoration. Multicoloured.

760	125f. Type **219**	95	1·10
761	175f. Script (different)	1·10	95

220 Mohammed Bin Saeed Bin Ghubash

221 Clasped Hands enclosed in Heart

2004. 35th Death Anniv of Mohammed Bin Saeed Bin Ghubash (scholar). Multicoloured.

762	50f. Type **220**	35	35
763	175f. Books	1·10	95

2004. 4th Family Meeting. Multicoloured.

764	3d.75 Type **221**	1·20	95
765	4d. Clasped hands (different)	1·10	90

222 Emblem

2004. Centenary of FIFA (Federation Internationale de Football Association).

766 **222**	375f. multicoloured	1·00	80

223 Decorated Pot

2004. Handicrafts. Multicoloured.

767	50f. Type **223**	15	10
768	125f. Flowers (painting)	35	30
769	275f. Twig collage	80	65
770	5d. Plaque	1·40	1·10

224 Running

2004. Olympic Games, Athens 2004. Multicoloured.

771	50f. Type **224**	15	10
772	125f. Shooting	35	30
773	275f. Swimming	80	65
774	375f. Runner holding Olympic torch	1·10	90

225 Black Fin-less Porpoise

2004. Endangered Species. Multicoloured.

775	50f. Type **225**	15	10
776	175f. Serranidae	45	30
777	275f. Whale shark	80	65
778	375f. Dugongidae	1·10	90

226 Removing Mine

227 Sheikh Bin Mohammed Al Qassimi

2004. Mine Clearance in South Lebanon. Multicoloured.

779	275f. Type **226**	80	65
780	375f. Detector, map, flags and wounded (horiz)	1·10	90

2004.

781 **227**	50f. multicoloured	15	10
782	125f. multicoloured	35	30
783	275f. multicoloured	80	65
784	4d. multicoloured	1·10	90

UNITED NATIONS Pt. 22; Pt. 8; Pt. 2

A. NEW YORK HEADQUARTERS

For use on mail posted at the Post Office at U.N. Headquarters, New York.

NOTE: Similar designs, but in different colours and values in Swiss Francs (F.S.) are issues of the Geneva office. Those with face values in Austrian Schillings are issues of the Vienna office. These are listed after the New York issues.

100 cents = 1 dollar.

1 "Peoples of the World"

3 U.N. Emblem

1951.

1 **1**	1c. mauve	10	15
2 –	$1\frac{1}{2}$c. green	10	15
3 **3**	2c. violet	10	15
4 –	3c. blue and purple	10	15
5 –	5c. blue	10	15
6 **1**	10c. brown	10	15
7 –	15c. blue and violet	10	20
8 –	20c. brown	30	30
9 –	25c. blue and black	30	30
10 –	50c. blue	2·30	2·00
11 **3**	$1 red	1·20	85

DESIGNS—VERT: $1\frac{1}{2}$, 50c. U.N. Headquarters, New York; 5c. Clasped hands. HORIZ: 3, 15, 25c. U.N. flag; 20c. Hemispheres and U.N. emblem.

A **7** Seagull and Airplane

1951. Air.

A12 A **7**	6c. red	10	10
A13	10c. green	10	10
A14 –	15c. blue	10	10
A15 –	25c. black	10	10

DESIGN: 15, 25c. Swallows and U.N. emblem.

7 Veterans' War Memorial Building, San Francisco

1952. 7th Anniv of Signing of U.N. Charter.
12 **7** 5c. blue 15 15

8 "Flame of Freedom"

1952. Human Rights Day.
13 **8** 3c. green 10 10
14 5c. blue 15 15

9 Homeless Family

1953. Protection for Refugees.
15 **9** 3c. brown 10 10
16 5c. blue 20 20

10 "Universal Postal Union"

1953. Universal Postal Union.
17 **10** 3c. sepia 15 20
18 5c. blue 40 40

11 Gearwheels and U.N. Emblem

12 "Flame of Freedom"

1953. Technical Assistance for Underdeveloped Areas.
19 **11** 3c. grey 10 15
20 5c. green 20 20

1953. Human Rights Day.
21 **12** 3c. blue 15 10
22 5c. red 70 30

13 F.A.O. Symbol

14 U.N. Emblem and Anvil

1954. Food and Agriculture Organization.
23 **13** 3c. yellow and green 25 15
24 8c. yellow and blue 60 35

NOTE. In the following issues the majority of the values unillustrated have the commemorative inscription or initials in another language.

1954. International Labour Organization.
25 **14** 3c. brown 15 15
26 8c. mauve 90 45

15 U.N. European Office, Geneva

16 Mother and Child

1954. United Nations Day.
27 **15** 3c. violet . . . . 1·60 85
28 8c. red 20 15

1954. Human Rights Day.
29 **16** 3c. orange . . . . 5·50 1·60
30 8c. green 15 20

17 "Flight"

1955. International Civil Aviation Organization.
31 **17** 3c. blue . . . . 1·30 50
32 8c. red 50 80

18 UNESCO Symbol

1955. U.N. Educational, Scientific and Cultural Organization.
33 **18** 3c. mauve 10 15
34 8c. blue 15 15

19 U.N. Charter

20 "Flame of Freedom"

19a (½-size illustration)

1955. 10th Anniv of U.N.
35 **19** 3c. red 70 40
36 4c. green 25 10
37 8c. black 15 20
MS38 **19a** 83 × 100 mm. Nos. 35/7. Imperf . . . . 50·00 10·00

1955. Human Rights Day.
39 **20** 3c. blue 10 15
40 8c. green 20 20

21 "Telecommunication"

22 Staff of Aesculapius

1956. International Telecommunication Union.
41 **21** 3c. blue 10 15
42 8c. red 20 25

1956. World Health Organization.
43 **22** 3c. blue 10 15
44 8c. brown 20 25

23 General Assembly

1956. United Nations Day.
45 **23** 3c. slate 10 10
46 8c. olive 10 10

24 "Flame of Freedom"

25 Weather Balloon

1956. Human Rights Day.
47 **24** 3c. purple 10 10
48 8c. blue 10 10

1957. World Meteorological Organization.
49 **25** 3c. blue 10 10
50 8c. red 10 10

26 U.N.E.F. Badge

A 26 "Flight"

1957. United Nations Emergency Force.
51 **26** 3c. blue 05 10
52 8c. red 10 05

1957. Air.
A51 A **26** 4c. brown 15 15
A52 5c. red 15 15
A53 – 7c. blue 15 15

DESIGNS—HORIZ: 7c. U.N. flag and Douglas DC-8-60 airplane.

On the 5c. value inscriptions are redrawn larger than those on Type A **26**.

27 U.N. Emblem over Globe

28 "Flames of Freedom"

1957. U.N. Security Council.
55 **27** 3c. brown 10 10
56 8c. green 10 10

1957. Human Rights Day.
57 **28** 3c. brown 10 10
58 8c. black 10 10

29 Atomic Symbol

30 Central Hall, Westminster (site of first General Assembly)

1958. International Atomic Energy Agency.
59 **29** 3c. olive 10 10
60 8c. blue 15 10

1958. U.N. General Assembly Buildings.
61 **30** 3c. blue 10 10
62 8c. purple 10 10

See also Nos. 69/70, 77/8 and 123/4.

31 U.N. Seal

32 Cogwheels

1958.
63 **31** 4c. orange 10 10
64 8c. blue 10 10

1958. Economic and Social Council.
65 **32** 4c. turquoise 10 10
66 8c. red 15 10

33 Hands holding Globe

1958. Human Rights Day.
67 **33** 4c. green 10 10
68 8c. brown 15 10

34 New York City Building, Flushing Meadows (1946–50)

35 Emblems of U.N. Industry and Agriculture

1959. U.N. General Assembly Buildings.
69 **34** 4c. mauve 10 10
70 8c. turquoise 10 10

1959. U.N. Economic Commission for Europe.
71 **35** 4c. blue 10 10
72 8c. red 25 15

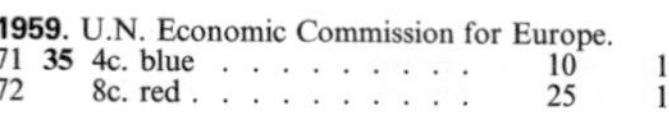

36 "The Age of Bronze" (Rodin)

37 "Protection for Refugees"

1959. U.N. Trusteeship Council.
73 **36** 4c. red 10 10
74 8c. green 25 15

1959. World Refugee Year.
75 **37** 4c. red and bistre 10 10
76 8c. blue and bistre 15 10

38 Palais de Chaillot, Paris (1948, 1951)

1960. U.N. General Assembly Buildings.
77 **38** 4c. blue and purple 10 10
78 8c. brown and green 25 10

39 Steel Girder and Map

1960. U.N. Economic Commission for Asia and the Far East ("ECAFE").
79 **39** 4c. purple, buff and turquoise 10 10
80 8c. green, pink and blue . . 20 15

40 Tree and Emblems 41 U.N. Headquarters and Emblem

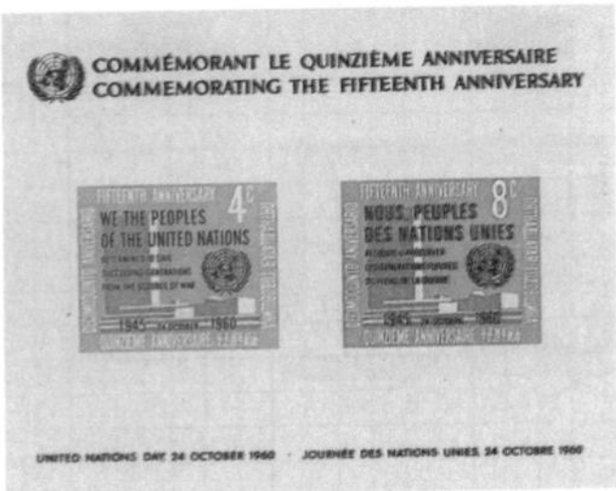

41a (½-size illustration)

1960. 5th World Forestry Congress, Seattle.
81 **40** 4c. multicoloured 10 05
82 8c. multicoloured 05 10

1960. 15th Anniv of U.N.
83 **41** 4c. blue 10 05
84 8c. black 20 05
MS85 **41a** 92 × 70 mm. Nos. 83/4. Imperf 60 50

42 Double Block and Hook 43 Scales of Justice

1960. International Bank for Reconstruction and Development ("World Bank").
86 **42** 4c. multicoloured 10 05
87 8c. multicoloured 15 05

1961. International Court of Justice.
88 **43** 4c. black, brown and yellow 15 05
89 8c. black, green and yellow 15 05

44 I.M.F. Emblem

1961. International Monetary Fund.
90 **44** 4c. blue 20 15
91 7c. brown and yellow . . . 20 10

45 "Peace" 53 Globe and Weather Vane

52 Flags

1961.
92 **45** 1c. multicoloured 10 05
93 – 2c. multicoloured 15 15
94 – 3c. multicoloured 10 05
95 – 5c. red 10 05
96 – 7c. brown, black and blue 20 15
97 – 10c. black, green and blue 25 15
98 – 11c. gold, light blue and blue 20 05
99 **52** 30c. multicoloured 35 30
100 **53** 50c. multicoloured 95 40

DESIGNS—HORIZ: 32 × 23 mm: 2c. Map of the World; 10c. Three figures on globe ("Races United"). 30½ × 23½ mm: 3c. U.N. Flag. 36½ × 23½ mm: 5c. Hands supporting "UN" and globe. 37½ × 22½ mm: 11c. U.N. emblem across globe. VERT—21 × 26 mm: 7c. U.N. emblem as flowering plant.
For 1c. in same design, but smaller, see No. 146 and for 5c. multicoloured see No. 165.

54 Cogwheel and Map of S. America 55 Africa Hall, Addis Ababa

1961. Economic Commission for Latin America.
101 **54** 4c. red, olive and blue . . 10 10
102 11c. purple, red and green 20 15

1961. Economic Commission for Africa.
103 **55** 4c. multicoloured 10 10
104 11c. multicoloured 15 10

56 Bird feeding Young 57 "Housing and Community Facilities"

1961. 15th Anniv of UNICEF.
105 **56** 3c. multicoloured 10 05
106 4c. multicoloured 10 05
107 13c. multicoloured 15 10

1962. U.N. Housing and Related Community Facilities Programme.
108 **57** 4c. multicoloured 15 10
109 7c. multicoloured 15 10

58 Mosquito and W.H.O. Emblem 59 U.N. Flag at Half-mast

1962. Malaria Eradication.
110 **58** 4c. multicoloured 10 10
111 11c. multicoloured 25 10

1962. Dag Hammarskjold (U.N. Secretary-General, 1953–61) Memorial Issue.
112 **59** 5c. indigo, blue and black 10 10
113 15c. blue, grey and black 20 20

60 Congo on World Map 61 "Peace in Space"

1962. U.N. Congo Operation.
114 **60** 4c. multicoloured 15 10
115 11c. multicoloured 15 10

1962. U.N. Committee on Peaceful Uses of Outer Space.
116 **61** 4c. blue 10 05
117 11c. mauve 25 10

62 Conference Emblem 63 Wheat

1963. Science and Technology Conf, Geneva.
118 **62** 5c. multicoloured 10 10
119 11c. multicoloured 25 10

1963. Freedom from Hunger.
120 **63** 5c. yellow, green and orange 10 05
121 11c. yellow, red and orange 25 10

A 65 "Flight" 64 "Bridge" over Map of West New Guinea

1963. Air. Multicoloured.
A122 6c. "Space" 35 30
A123 8c. Type A **65** 10 05
A124 13c. "Bird" 20 15
A125 15c. "Birds in Flight" . . . 10 10
A126 25c. Douglas DC-8 and airmail envelope 20 10
SIZES—HORIZ: 6c. As Type A **65**; 13, 25c. 30½ × 23 mm. VERT: 15c. 23 × 30½ mm.

1963. United Nations Temporary Executive Authority (UNTEA) in West New Guinea.
122 **64** 25c. green, blue and drab 40 25

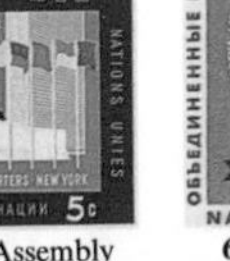
65 General Assembly Building and Flags 66 "Flame of Freedom"

1963. U.N. General Assembly Buildings.
123 **65** 5c. multicoloured 10 10
124 11c. multicoloured 20 15

1963. 15th Anniv of Declaration of Human Rights.
125 **66** 5c. multicoloured 10 10
126 11c. multicoloured 20 15

67 Ships at Sea

1964. Inter-Governmental Maritime Consultative Organization (I.M.C.O.).
127 **67** 5c. multicoloured 15 15
128 11c. multicoloured 30 25

68 "Trade and Development"

1964. U.N. Trade and Development Conf, Geneva.
129 **68** 5c. yellow, black and red 15 15
130 11c. yellow, black and bistre 15 15

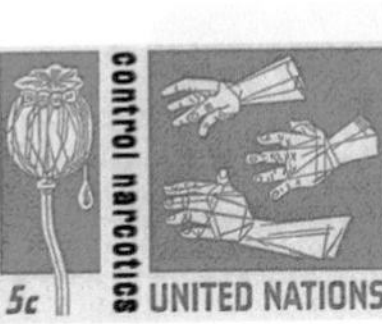

69 Opium Poppy and Reaching Hands 70 Atomic Explosion and Padlock

1964. Narcotics Control.
131 **69** 5c. red and black 15 15
132 11c. green and black . . . 50 35

1964. Cessation of Nuclear Testing.
133 **70** 5c. sepia and brown . . . 15 15

71 "Teaching" 72 Key, Globe and "Graph"

1964. "Education for Progress".
134 **71** 4c. multicoloured 15 15
135 5c. multicoloured 15 20
136 11c. multicoloured 15 15

1965. U.N. Special Fund.
137 **72** 5c. multicoloured 15 15
138 11c. multicoloured 15 20

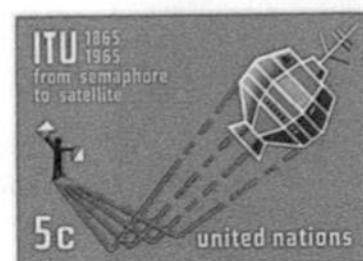
73 Cyprus "Leaves" and U.N. Emblem 74 "From Semaphore to Satellite"

1965. Peace-keeping Force in Cyprus.
139 **73** 5c. olive, black and orange 10 15
140 11c. green, black & lt green 15 15

1965. I.T.U. Centenary.
141 **74** 5c. multicoloured 15 10
142 11c. multicoloured 25 20

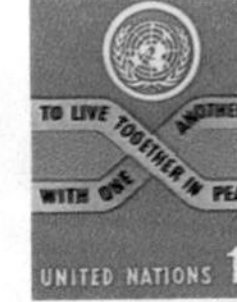
75 I.C.Y. Emblem 76 "Peace"

75a (½-size illustration)

1965. 20th Anniv of United Nations and International Co-operation Year.
143 **75** 5c. blue 25 15
144 15c. mauve 25 30
MS145 **75a** 92 × 70 mm. Nos. 143/4 40 30

1965.
146 **76** 1c. multicoloured 10 10
147 – 15c. multicoloured 25 10
148 – 20c. multicoloured 30 15
149 – 25c. ultramarine and blue 45 15
150 – $1 blue and turquoise . . . 2·00 1·30
DESIGNS—24½ × 30 mm: 15c. Opening words, U.N. Charter. 22 × 32 mm: 20c. U.N. emblem and Headquarters. 24 × 24 mm: 25c. U.N. emblem. 33 × 23 mm: $1 U.N. emblem encircled.

81 "Expanding Population" 82 Globe and Flags

1965. Population Trends and Development.
151 **81** 4c. multicoloured 10 10
152 5c. multicoloured 10 10
153 11c. multicoloured 20 20

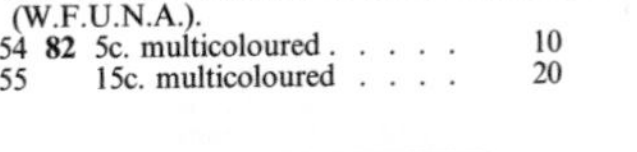

1966. World Federation of United Nations Assns. (W.F.U.N.A.).
154 **82** 5c. multicoloured 10 10
155 15c. multicoloured 20 20

83 W.H.O. Building

1966. Inaug of W.H.O. Headquarters, Geneva.
156 **83** 5c. multicoloured 10 10
157 11c. multicoloured 20 20

84 Coffee

1966. International Coffee Agreement of 1962.
158 **84** 5c. multicoloured 10 10
159 11c. multicoloured 20 20

85 Military Observer

86 Children in Closed Railway Wagon

1966. U.N. Military Observers.
160 **85** 15c. multicoloured 25 25

1966. 20th Anniv of UNICEF. Multicoloured.
161 4c. Type **86** 10 10
162 5c. Children in locomotive and tender 20 10
163 11c. Children in open railway wagon 40 20

89 U.N. Headquarters and World Map

91 "UN" and Emblem

1967.
164 **89** $1\frac{1}{2}$c. multicoloured 10 10
165 – 5c. multicoloured 15 10
166 – 6c. multicoloured 15 10
167 **91** 13c. blue, gold and black 25 15
DESIGNS—HORIZ: 5c. As No. 95. 23 × 34 mm: 6c. Aerial view of U.N. Headquarters.

92 "Progress through Development"

93 U.N. Emblem and Fireworks

1967. U.N. Development Programme.
168 **92** 5c. multicoloured 10 10
169 11c. multicoloured 20 10

1967. New Independent Nations Commem.
170 **93** 5c. multicoloured 10 10
171 11c. multicoloured 20 15

94 "Peace"

99 Baggage Labels

1967. "Expo 67", World Fair, Montreal.
172 **94** 4c. brown and red 10 10
173 – 5c. brown and blue 10 10
174 – 8c. multicoloured 15 10
175 – 10c. brown and green . . . 15 10
176 – 15c. chestnut and brown 20 25
DESIGNS—VERT: 5c. "Justice"; 10c. "Fraternity"; 15c. "Truth". HORIZ (32 × $23\frac{1}{2}$ mm): 8c. Facade of U.N. Pavilion.
The above stamps are expressed in Canadian currency and were valid for postage only from the U.N. Pavilion at the World Fair.

1967. International Tourist Year.
177 **99** 5c. multicoloured 20 10
178 15c. multicoloured 65 20

100 "Towards Disarmament"

101 "The Kiss of Peace" (part of Chagall's stained glass window)

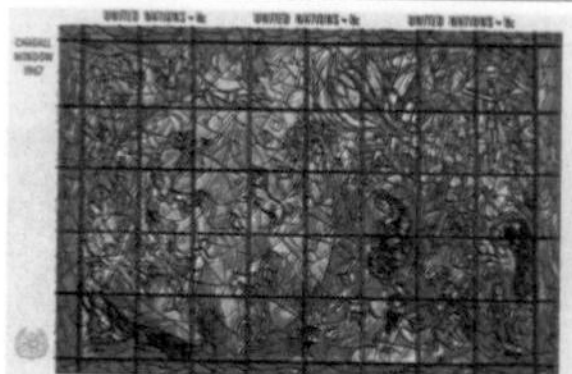
102 ($\frac{1}{2}$-size illustration)

1967. Disarmament Campaign.
179 **100** 6c. multicoloured 10 10
180 13c. multicoloured 20 15

1967. United Nations Art (1st issue). Chagall's Memorial Window in U.N. Secretariat Building.
181 **101** 6c. multicoloured 15 15
MS182 **102** 123 × 81 mm. 6c. × 6. multicoloured 50 40
The miniature sheet is divisible into six 6c. stamps size 41 × 46mm, 24 × 46mm, $41\frac{1}{2}$ × $33\frac{1}{2}$mm, 29 × $33\frac{1}{2}$ mm and $41\frac{1}{2}$ × 47 mm.
See also Nos. 185/6, 201/2, 203/4, 236/7 and 251/2.

103 Globe and Diagram of U.N. Organs

104 Starcke's Statue

1968. U.N. Secretariat.
183 **103** 6c. multicoloured 15 15
184 13c. multicoloured 20 15

1968. United Nations Art (2nd issue). Henrik Starcke's Statue in U.N. Trusteeship Council Chamber.
185 **104** 6c. multicoloured 15 15
186 75c. multicoloured . . . . 1·20 75

105 Industrial Skyline

1968. U.N. Industrial Development Organization (U.N.I.D.O.).
187 **105** 6c. multicoloured 15 15
188 13c. multicoloured 15 15

A 106 "Winged Envelopes"

A 107 Aircraft and U.N. Emblem

1968. Air.
A189 A **106** 10c. multicoloured . . 15 15
A190 A **107** 20c. multicoloured . . 25 15

106 Radar Scanner

1968. World Weather Watch.
189 **106** 6c. multicoloured 15 10
190 20c. multicoloured 30 20

107 Human Rights Emblem

108 Textbooks

1968. Human Rights Year.
191 **107** 6c. gold, ultramarine & bl 15 15
192 13c. gold, red and pink 20 15

1969. United Nations Institute for Training and Research (U.N.I.T.A.R.).
193 **108** 6c. multicoloured 15 10
194 13c. multicoloured 20 15
In the 13c. the name and value panel is at foot of stamp.

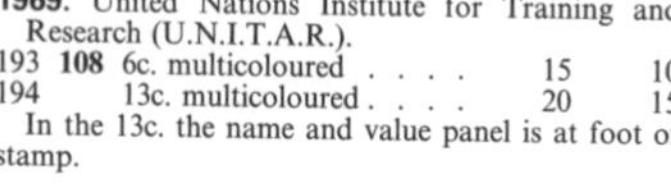

109 U.N. Building, Santiago

1969. U.N. Building, Santiago, Chile.
195 **109** 6c. blue, light blue & green 15 15
196 15c. purple, red and buff 20 15

110 "Peace Through International Law"

1969. 20th Anniv of Session of U.N. Int Law Commission.
197 **110** 6c. multicoloured 15 15
198 13c. multicoloured 20 15

111 "Labour and Development"

1969. 50th Anniv of I.L.O.
199 **111** 6c. multicoloured 15 15
200 20c. multicoloured 15 15

112 "Ostrich"

114 Peace Bell

1969. United Nations Art (3rd issue). 3rd-century A.D. Tunisian Mosaic, Delegates' North Lounge. Multicoloured.
201 6c. Type **112** 15 15
202 13c. "Ring-necked Pheasant" 15 15

1970. United Nations Art (4th issue). Japanese Peace Bell.
203 **114** 6c. multicoloured 15 15
204 25c. multicoloured 30 20

115 River, Power Lines and Map

1970. Lower Mekong Basin Development Project.
205 **115** 6c. multicoloured 15 15
206 13c. multicoloured 15 15

116 "Fight Cancer"

1970. 10th Int Cancer Congress, Houston, Texas.
207 **116** 6c. black and blue 15 15
208 13c. black and olive . . . 15 15

117 Laurel Branch

120 Scales and Olive-branch

119 ($\frac{1}{2}$-size illustration)

1970. 25th Anniv of United Nations.
209 **117** 6c. multicoloured 15 15
210 13c. multicoloured 15 15
211 – 25c. gold, light blue & blue 30 25
MS212 96 × 78 mm. **119** Nos. 209/11. Imperf 55 50
DESIGN—VERT: 25c. U.N. emblem.
On No. 210 the inscription is in French.

1970. "Peace, Justice and Progress" (Aims of the United Nations).
213 **120** 6c. multicoloured 15 15
214 13c. multicoloured 15 15

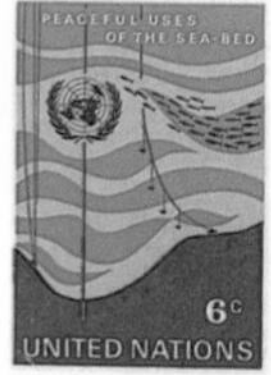

121 U.N. Emblem on Sea-bed

122 "Refugees" (sculpture, Kaare Nygaard)

1971. Peaceful Uses of the Sea-bed.
215 **121** 6c. multicoloured 10 10

1971. U.N. Work with Refugees.
216 **122** 6c. black, yellow & brown 15 15
217 13c. black, turq & blue 15 15

123 Wheatsheaf on Globe

124 New U.P.U. H.Q. Building

1971. World Food Programme.
218 **123** 13c. multicoloured 15 15

1971. Opening of New U.P.U. Headquarters Building, Berne.
219 **124** 20c. multicoloured 20 20

125 Four-leafed Clover

127 U.N. H.Q., New York

1971. Racial Equality Year. Multicoloured.
220 8c. Type **125** 15 15
221 13c. Linked globes (horiz) . . 15 15

1971. Multicoloured.
222 8c. Type **127** 15 15
223 60c. U.N. emblem and flags 65 60
224 95c. "Letter changing Hands" 1·10 90

130 "Maia" (Picasso)

131 "X" over Atomic Explosion

1971. U.N. International Schools.
225 **130** 8c. multicoloured 15 15
226 21c. multicoloured 25 15

1972. Non-proliferation of Nuclear Weapons.
227 **131** 8c. blue, black and pink 10 10

132 "Proportions of Man" (Leonardo da Vinci)

A 134 Birds in Flight

1972. World Health Day.
228 **132** 15c. multicoloured 20 15

1972. Air.
A229 – 9c. multicoloured . . 15 15
A230 A **134** 11c. multicoloured . . 15 15
A231 – 17c. orange, yellow and red 25 15
A232 – 21c. multicoloured . . 35 20
DESIGNS—23 × 31 mm: 9c. "Contemporary Flight". 38 × 23 mm: 17c. Clouds. 33 × 23 mm: 21c. "U.N." jetstream.

137 Environmental Emblem

138 Europe "Flower"

1972. U.N. Environmental Conservation Conf, Stockholm.
233 **137** 8c. multicoloured 15 15
234 15c. multicoloured 20 15

1972. Economic Commission for Europe (E.C.E.).
235 **138** 21c. multicoloured 35 25

139 "World United" (detail, Sert mural, Geneva)

140 Laurel and Broken Sword

1972. United Nations Art (5th issue).
236 **139** 8c. brown, gold & lt brown 15 15
237 15c. brown, gold and green 25 15

1973. Disarmament Decade.
238 **140** 8c. multicoloured 15 15
239 15c. multicoloured 30 25

141 Skull on Poppy

142 Emblems within Honeycomb

1973. "Stop Drug Abuse" Campaign.
240 **141** 8c. multicoloured 15 15
241 15c. multicoloured 30 25

1973. U.N. Volunteers Programme.
242 **142** 8c. multicoloured 15 15
243 21c. multicoloured 30 25

143 Namibia on Map of Africa

1973. U.N. Resolution on Namibia (South West Africa).
244 **143** 8c. multicoloured 15 15
245 15c. multicoloured 30 25

144 Human Rights Flame

1973. 25th Anniv of Declaration of Human Rights.
246 **144** 8c. multicoloured 15 15
247 21c. multicoloured 30 20

145 H.Q. Building

1973. Inauguration of New I.L.O. Headquarters Building, Geneva.
248 **145** 10c. multicoloured 15 15
249 21c. multicoloured 30 20

146 Globe within Posthorn

1974. Centenary of U.P.U.
250 **146** 10c. multicoloured 20 15

147 "Children's Choir" (mural detail, C. Portinari)

1974. United Nations Art (6th issue). Brazilian Peace Mural, Delegates' Lobby.
251 **147** 10c. multicoloured 15 15
252 18c. multicoloured 35 25

148 Peace Dove

1974.
253 **148** 2c. blue and ultramarine 15 15
254 – 10c. multicoloured 15 15
255 – 18c. multicoloured 25 15
DESIGNS—VERT: 10c. U.N. Headquarters, New York; 18c. Globe over U.N. emblem and flags.

A 151 Globe and Jet Aircraft

154 Young Children with Globe

1974. Air. Multicoloured.
A256 13c. Type A **151** 20 15
A257 18c. "Channels of Communication" (38 × 23 mm) 25 15
A258 26c. Dove in flight and U.N. Headquarters . . . 40 30

1974. World Population Year.
259 **154** 10c. multicoloured 15 15
260 18c. multicoloured 35 20

155 Ship and Fish

156 Satellite, Globe and Symbols

1974. U.N. Conference on "Law of the Sea".
261 **155** 10c. multicoloured 15 15
262 26c. multicoloured 50 20

1975. Peaceful Uses of Outer Space.
263 **156** 10c. multicoloured 15 15
264 26c. multicoloured 35 25

157 "Sex Equality"

158 "The Hope of Mankind"

159 (½-size illustration)

1975. International Women's Year.
265 **157** 10c. multicoloured 15 15
266 18c. multicoloured 35 20

1975. 30th Anniv of U.N.O.
267 **158** 10c. multicoloured 15 15
268 26c. multicoloured 40 25
MS269 88 × 70 mm. **159** Nos. 267/8. Imperf 65 50

160 Cupped Hand

161 Wild Rose and Barbed Wire

1975. "Namibia—United Nations Direct Responsibility".
270 **160** 10c. multicoloured 15 15
271 18c. multicoloured 30 15

1975. U.N. Peace-keeping Operations.
272 **161** 13c. blue 20 15
273 26c. mauve 40 35

162 "Bird of Peace"

166 Linked Ribbons

1976. Multicoloured.
274 3c. Type **162** 15 15
275 4c. "Gathering of Peoples" (39 × 23 mm) 15 15
276 30c. U.N. flag (23 × 39 mm) 40 25
277 50c. "Universal Peace" (Dove and rainbow) (23 × 39 mm) 75 50

1976. World Federation of U.N. Associations.
278 **166** 13c. multicoloured 15 15
279 26c. multicoloured 30 25

167 Globe and Crate

168 Houses bordering Globe

1976. U.N. Conf on Trade and Development.
280 **167** 13c. multicoloured 15 15
281 31c. multicoloured 35 25

1976. U.N. Conf on Human Settlements.
282 **168** 13c. multicoloured 15 15
283 25c. multicoloured 35 25

169 Magnifying Glass and Emblem

170 Stylized Ear of Wheat

1976. 25th Anniv of U.N. Postal Administration.
284 **169** 13c. multicoloured 15 15
285 31c. multicoloured . . . . 1·20 1·00

1976. World Food Council.
286 **170** 13c. multicoloured 20 15

171 U.N. Emblem

173 Rain Drops and Funnel

172 W.I.P.O. Headquarters Building

1976.
287 **171** 9c. multicoloured 15 15

1977. World Intellectual Property Organization Headquarters.
288 **172** 13c. multicoloured 15 15
289 31c. multicoloured 40 25

1977. United Nations Water Conference.
290 **173** 13c. multicoloured 15 15
291 25c. multicoloured 40 25

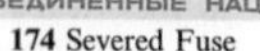

174 Severed Fuse

175 Winged Airmail Letter

1977. Security Council.
292 **174** 13c. multicoloured 15 15
293 31c. multicoloured 40 25

1977. Air. Multicoloured.
A294 25c. Type **175** 40 25
A295 31c. Globe and airplane (horiz) 45 35

177 "Combat Racism"

178 Atomic Symbol and Produce

1977. Campaign Against Racial Discrimination.
296 **177** 13c. black and yellow . . 15 15
297 25c. black and red 35 25

1977. Peaceful Uses of Atomic Energy.
298 **178** 13c. multicoloured 15 15
299 18c. multicoloured 30 20

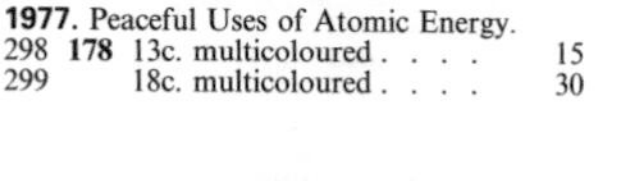

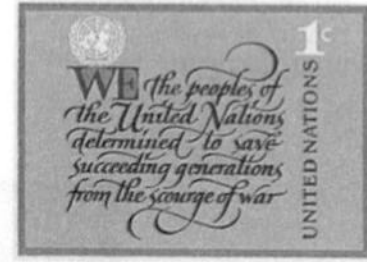

179 U.N. Charter

1978. Multicoloured.
300 1c. Type **179** 15 15
301 25c. Knotted flags 30 25
302 $1 Multi-racial group 95 85

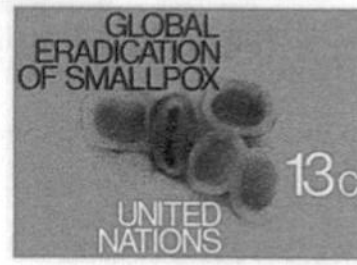

182 Smallpox Bacilli

1978. Global Eradication of Smallpox.
303 **182** 13c. black and red 15 15
304 31c. black and blue . . . 40 30

183 Broken Manacle

184 Clouds within Ribbon

1978. "Namibia: Liberation, Justice, Co-operation".
305 **183** 13c. multicoloured 15 15
306 18c. multicoloured 25 15

1978. International Civil Aviation Organization—Safety in the Air.
307 **184** 13c. multicoloured 15 15
308 25c. multicoloured 35 25

185 General Assembly

1978. General Assembly.
309 **185** 13c. multicoloured 25 15
310 18c. multicoloured 30 20

186 Hemispheres within Cogwheels

187 Hand holding Olive Branch

1978. Technical Co-operation among Developing Countries.
311 **186** 13c. multicoloured 15 15
312 31c. multicoloured 40 30

1979. Multicoloured.
313 5c. Type **187** 15 15
314 14c. Multiple "tree" 15 15
315 15c. Globe and peace dove 25 20
316 20c. Doves crossing globe . . 25 20

191 Fire and Flood

1979. U.N. Disaster Relief Co-ordinator.
317 **191** 15c. multicoloured 20 15
318 20c. multicoloured 30 25

192 Child's Drawing

193 Olive Branch and Map of Namibia

1979. International Year of the Child.
319 **192** 15c. multicoloured 15 15
320 31c. multicoloured 40 25

1979. "For a Free and Independent Namibia".
321 **193** 15c. multicoloured 15 15
322 31c. multicoloured 35 25

194 Sword and Scales of Justice

195 Graph

1979. International Court of Justice.
323 **194** 15c. olive, green and black 15 15
324 20c. blue, lt blue & black 35 25

1980. New International Economic Order. Multicoloured.
325 15c. Type **195** 15 15
326 31c. Key 40 35

197 Doves

1980. U.N. Decade for Women.
327 **197** 15c. multicoloured 15 15
328 20c. multicoloured 25 20

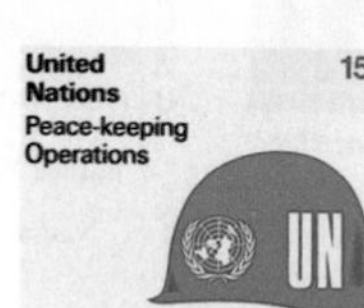

198 Helmet

1980. Peace-keeping Operations.
329 **198** 15c. blue and black . . . 20 15
330 – 31c. multicoloured 40 30
DESIGN: 31c. "Peace-keeping".

200 "35" composed of Flags

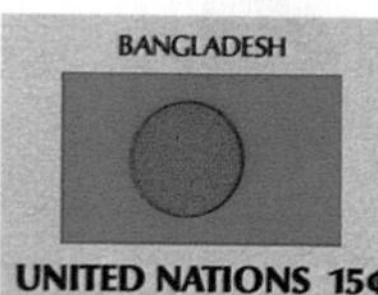

203 Flag of Bangladesh

202 (½-size illustration)

1980. 35th Anniv of United Nations. Mult.
331 15c. Type **200** 15 15
332 31c. Stylized flower 35 25
MS333 92 × 73 mm. **202** Nos. 331/2. Imperf 60 60

1980. Flags of Member Nations (1st series). Multicoloured.
334 15c. Type **203** 15 15
335 15c. Guinea 15 15
336 15c. Mali 15 15
337 15c. Surinam 15 15
338 15c. Cameroun 15 15
339 15c. Hungary 15 15
340 15c. Madagascar 15 15
341 15c. Rwanda 15 15
342 15c. El Salvador 15 15
343 15c. France 15 15
344 15c. Venezuela 15 15
345 15c. Yugoslavia 15 15
346 15c. Fiji 15 15
347 15c. Luxembourg 15 15
348 15c. Turkey 15 15
349 15c. Vietnam 15 15
See also Nos. 359/74, 383/98, 408/23, 434/9, 458/74, 486/501, 508/23, 537/52, 563/78, 710/17, 744/51, 785/92 and 849/56.

204 Various Emblems forming Bunch of Flowers

1980. Economic and Social Council. Mult.
350 15c. Type **204** 25 20
351 20c. Economic and social emblems 35 25

206 Text and U.N. Emblem

207 Jigsaw

1981. Inalienable Rights of the Palestinian People.
352 **206** 15c. multicoloured 20 20

1981. International Year of Disabled Persons.
353 **207** 20c. multicoloured 25 15
354 – 35c. black and orange . . 45 30
DESIGN: 35c. Disabled person.

209 "Sebastocrator Kaloyan and his Wife Desislava" (13th-cent Bulgarian fresco)

210 Sun and Sea

1981. Art.
355 **209** 20c. multicoloured 25 20
356 31c. multicoloured 40 40

1981. New and Renewable Sources of Energy.
357 **210** 20c. multicoloured 25 20
358 – 40c. gold and blue 45 40
DESIGN: 40c. U.N. energy conference emblem.

1981. Flags of Member Nations (2nd series). As T **203**. Multicoloured.
359 20c. Djibouti 20 15
360 20c. Sri Lanka 20 15
361 20c. Bolivia 20 15
362 20c. Equatorial Guinea . . . 20 15
363 20c. Malta 20 15
364 20c. Czechoslovakia 20 15
365 20c. Thailand 20 15
366 20c. Trinidad and Tobago . . 20 15
367 20c. Ukrainian S.S.R. 20 15
368 20c. Kuwait 20 15
369 20c. Sudan 20 15
370 20c. Egypt 20 15
371 20c. United States 20 15
372 20c. Singapore 20 15
373 20c. Panama 20 15
374 20c. Costa Rica 20 15

212 Grafted Plant

214 "Respect for Human Rights"

1981. 10th Anniv of U.N. Volunteers Programme. Multicoloured.
375 18c. Type **212** 30 20
376 28c. "10" enclosing symbols of services 55 40

1982. Multicoloured.
377 17c. Type **214** 25 15
378 28c. "Granting of Independence to Colonial Countries and Peoples" . . 40 25
379 40c. "Second Disarmament Decade" 65 45

217 Hand holding Seedling

219 Olive Branch and U.N. Emblem

1982. Human Environment. Multicoloured.
380 20c. Type **217** 20 20
381 40c. Symbols of the environment 65 50

1982. Second United Nations Conference on Exploration and Peaceful Uses of Outer Space.
382 **219** 20c. ultramarine, blue and green 40 25

1982. Flags of Member Nations (3rd series). As T **203**. Multicoloured.
383 20c. Austria 20 15
384 20c. Malaysia 20 15
385 20c. Seychelles 20 15
386 20c. Ireland 20 15
387 20c. Mozambique 20 15
388 20c. Albania 20 15
389 20c. Dominica 20 15
390 20c. Solomon Islands 20 15
391 20c. Philippines 20 15
392 20c. Swaziland 20 15
393 20c. Nicaragua 20 15
394 20c. Burma 20 15
395 20c. Cape Verde 20 15
396 20c. Guyana 20 15
397 20c. Belgium 20 15
398 20c. Nigeria 20 15

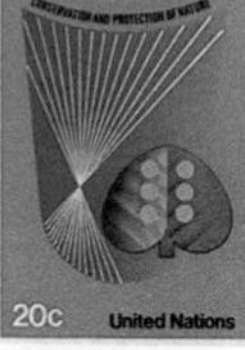

220 Tree (flora)

222 Interlocking Arrows

1982. Conservation and Protection of Nature. Multicoloured.
399 20c. Type **220** 30 25
400 28c. Butterfly (insects) . . . 50 40

1983. World Communications Year. Mult.
401 20c. Type **222** 40 20
402 40c. Cable network 60 50

224 Ship and Buoy **226** Giving Food

1983. Safety at Sea: International Maritime Organization. Multicoloured.
403 20c. Type **224** 35 20
404 37c. Stylized liner 50 40

1983. World Food Programme.
405 **226** 20c. red 30 25

227 Coins and Cogwheels **229** "Window Right"

1983. Trade and Development. Multicoloured.
406 20c. Type **227** 25 20
407 28c. Emblems of trade . . . 55 45

1983. Flags of Member Nations (4th series). As T **203**. Multicoloured.
408 20c. United Kingdom 25 15
409 20c. Barbados 25 15
410 20c. Nepal 25 15
411 20c. Israel 25 15
412 20c. Malawi 25 15
413 20c. Byelorussian S.S.R. . . . 25 15
414 20c. Jamaica 25 15
415 20c. Kenya 25 15
416 20c. China 25 15
417 20c. Peru 25 15
418 20c. Bulgaria 25 15
419 20c. Canada 25 15
420 20c. Somalia 25 15
421 20c. Senegal 25 15
422 20c. Brazil 25 15
423 20c. Sweden 25 15

1983. 35th Anniv of Declaration of Human Rights. Multicoloured.
424 20c. Type **229** 25 20
425 40c. "Treaty with Nature" . . 60 50

231 World Population

1984. International Conference on Population, Mexico.
426 **231** 20c. multicoloured 25 20
427 40c. multicoloured 60 45

232 Fertilizing Crops

1984. World Food Day. Multicoloured.
428 20c. Type **232** 25 20
429 40c. Planting rice 50 45

234 Grand Canyon, U.S.A **236** Mother with Baby

1984. World Heritage—U.N. Educational, Scientific and Cultural Organization. Multicoloured.
430 20c. Type **234** 20 15
431 50c. Polonnaruwa, Sri Lanka 60 55

1984. Future for Refugees.
432 **236** 20c. brown and black . . 35 25
433 – 50c. black and blue . . . 85 65
DESIGN: 50c. Mother with child.

1984. Flags of Member Nations (5th series). As T **203**. Multicoloured.
434 20c. Burundi 45 30
435 20c. Pakistan 45 30
436 20c. Benin 45 30
437 20c. Italy 45 30
438 20c. Poland 45 30
439 20c. Papua New Guinea . . 45 30
440 20c. Uruguay 45 30
441 20c. Chile 45 30
442 20c. Paraguay 45 30
443 20c. Bhutan 45 30
444 20c. Central African Republic 45 30
445 20c. Australia 45 30
446 20c. Tanzania 45 30
447 20c. United Arab Emirates 45 30
448 20c. Ecuador 45 30
449 20c. Bahamas 45 30

238 Emblem and Figures linking Arms **239** Turin Centre Emblem

1984. International Youth Year.
450 **238** 20c. multicoloured 40 25
451 35c. multicoloured . . . . 1·10 85

1985. 20th Anniv of Turin Centre of International Labour Organization.
452 **239** 23c. blue 50 35

240 Farming and Mediums of Communication

1985. 10th Anniv of United Nations University, Tokyo.
453 **240** 50c. multicoloured . . . . 1·10 80

241 People of Various Nations

1985. Multicoloured.
454 22c. Type **241** 30 25
455 $3 Paintbrush and emblem 3·25 2·00

243 "Snow Scene" (Andrew Wyeth)

245 (½-size illustration)

1985. 40th Anniv of U.N.O. Multicoloured.
456 22c. Type **243** 40 25
457 45c. "Harvest Scene" (Andrew Wyeth) . . . . . 1·10 65
MS458 76 × 82 mm. **245** Nos. 456/7. Imperf . . . . 1·50 1·25

1985. Flags of Member Nations (6th series). As T **203**. Multicoloured.
459 22c. Grenada 45 40
460 22c. Federal Republic of Germany 45 40
461 22c. Saudi Arabia 45 40
462 22c. Mexico 45 40
463 22c. Liberia 45 40
464 22c. Mauritius 45 40
465 22c. Chad 45 40
466 22c. Dominican Republic . . 45 40
467 22c. Oman 45 40
468 22c. Ghana 45 40
469 22c. Sierra Leone 45 40
470 22c. Finland 45 40
471 22c. Uganda 45 40
472 22c. St. Thomas and Prince Islands 45 40
473 22c. U.S.S.R. 45 40
474 22c. India 45 40

246 Woman feeding Child **248** "Africa in Crisis"

1985. UNICEF Child Survival Campaign. Multicoloured.
475 32c. Type **246** 30 25
476 33c. Mother breast-feeding child 55 45

1986. Africa in Crisis.
477 **248** 22c. multicoloured 40 35

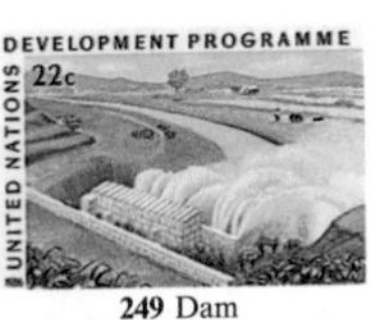

249 Dam

1986. Development Programme. Water Resources. Multicoloured.
478 22c. Type **249** . . . . 1·30 80
479 22c. Working in the fields . . 1·30 80
480 22c. Girls at waterhole . . . 1·30 80
481 22c. Women at well . . . . 1·30 80
Nos. 478/81 were printed together, se-tenant, forming a composite design.

253 Magnifying Glass and Stamp

1986. Philately: The International Hobby.
482 **253** 22c. lilac and blue 35 20
483 – 44c. brown and green . . 75 55
DESIGN: 44c. Engraver.

255 Peace Doves

1986. International Peace Year.
484 **255** 22c. multicoloured 45 30
485 – 33c. multicoloured . . . . 1·30 1·00
DESIGN: 33c. Words for "Peace" around U.N. emblem.

1986. Flags of Member Nations (7th series). As T **203**. Multicoloured.
486 22c. New Zealand 50 35
487 22c. Laos 50 35
488 22c. Burkina Faso 50 35
489 22c. Gambia 50 35
490 22c. Maldives 50 35
491 22c. Ethiopia 50 35
492 22c. Jordan 50 35
493 22c. Zambia 50 35
494 22c. Iceland 50 35
495 22c. Antigua and Barbuda . . 50 35
496 22c. Angola 50 35
497 22c. Botswana 50 35
498 22c. Rumania 50 35
499 22c. Togo 50 35
500 22c. Mauritania 50 35
501 22c. Colombia 50 35

257 (½-size illustration)

1986. 40th Anniv of World Federation of United Nations Associations. Sheets 120 × 65 mm. Multicoloured.
MS502 **257** 22c. Woman and children (Edna Hibel); 33c. Clasped hands (Slavador Dali); 39c. Kites, people planting and oxen (Don Kingman); 44c. Refugees (Chaim Gross) . . . 3·50 2·25

258 Trygve Lie (after Harald Dal)

1987. 9th Death Anniv of Trygve Lie (first U.N. Secretary-General).
503 **258** 22c. multicoloured 75 60

259 Men with Surveying Equipment and Blueprints

1987. International Year of Shelter for the Homeless.
504 **259** 22c. deep brown, brown and black 35 20
505 – 44c. multicoloured . . . . 1·10 80
DESIGN: 44c. Cutting bamboo.

261 Construction Workers

1987. Anti-drugs Campaign. Multicoloured.
506 22c. Type **261** 55 40
507 33c. University graduates . . 1·10 80

1987. Flags of Member Nations (8th series). As T **203**. Multicoloured.
508 22c. Comoros 50 40
509 22c. People's Democratic Republic of Yemen 50 40
510 22c. Mongolia 50 40
511 22c. Vanuatu 50 40
512 22c. Japan 50 40
513 22c. Gabon 50 40
514 22c. Zimbabwe 50 40
515 22c. Iraq 50 40
516 22c. Argentina 50 40
517 22c. Congo 50 40
518 22c. Niger 50 40
519 22c. St. Lucia 50 40
520 22c. Bahrain 50 40
521 22c. Haiti 50 40
522 22c. Afghanistan 50 40
523 22c. Greece 50 40

263 Family and U.N. Building, New York **265** Measles

1987. United Nations Day. Multicoloured.
524 22c. Type **263** 35 25
525 39c. Dancers 60 50

1987. "Immunize Every Child". Multicoloured.
526 22c. Type **265** . . . . 1·00 45
527 44c. Tetanus . . . . 1·50 1·00

267 Wheat as U.N. Emblem

1988. "For a Better World".
528 **267** 3c. yellow, brown and black 30 15

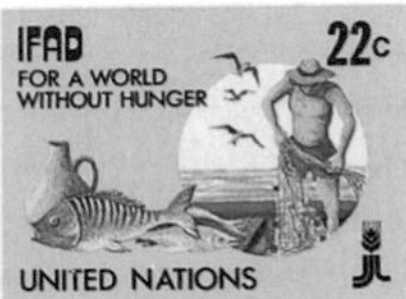

268 Fisherman

1988. International Fund for Agricultural Development "For a World Without Hunger" Campaign. Multicoloured.

529	22c. Type **268**	40	30
530	33c. Farmers ploughing with oxen	85	65

270 Tropical Rain Forest Canopy

272 Teacher at Blackboard

1988. "Survival of the Forests". Multicoloured.

531	25c. Type **270**	1·80	80
532	44c. Tropical rain forest floor	2·30	1·30

Nos. 531/2 were printed together, se-tenant, forming a composite design.

1988. International Volunteer Day. Mult.

533	25c. Type **272**	40	30
534	50c. Teaching basketry (horiz)	95	80

274 Cycling

276 Flame

277 (⅓-size illustration)

1988. "Health in Sports". Multicoloured.

535	25c. Type **274**	60	35
536	38c. Marathon (horiz)	1·10	85

1988. Flags of Member Nations (9th series). As T **203**. Multicoloured.

537	25c. Spain	50	35
538	25c. St. Vincent and Grenadines	50	35
539	25c. Ivory Coast	50	35
540	25c. Lebanon	50	35
541	25c. Yemen	50	35
542	25c. Cuba	50	35
543	25c. Denmark	50	35
544	25c. Libya	50	35
545	25c. Qatar	50	35
546	25c. Zaire	50	35
547	25c. Norway	50	35
548	25c. German Democratic Republic	50	35
549	25c. Iran	50	35
550	25c. Tunisia	50	35
551	25c. Samoa	50	35
552	25c. Belize	50	35

1988. 40th Anniv of Declaration of Human Rights.

553	**276** 25c. multicoloured	50	25
MS554	120×79 mm. **277** $1 multicoloured	1·50	1·10

278 Electricity Production

280 "Blue Helmet" Soldier

1989. World Bank. Multicoloured.

555	25c. Type **278**	65	35
556	45c. Planting rice	1·30	80

1989. Award of Nobel Peace Prize to United Nations Peace-keeping Forces.

557	**280** 25c. multicoloured	40	30

281 U.N. Headquarters, New York

1989.

558	**281** 45c. multicoloured	60	45

282 Satellite Image of Storm over Chesapeake Bay Area

284 Band

1989. 25th Anniv of World Weather Watch. Multicoloured.

559	25c. Type **282**	65	40
560	36c. Typhoon Abby approaching China	1·50	1·30

1989. 10th Anniv of United Nations Vienna International Centre. Multicoloured.

561	25c. Type **284**	2·10	40
562	90c. Mountain and butterfly as tree	2·50	1·40

1989. Flags of Member Nations (10th series). As T **203**. Multicoloured.

563	25c. Indonesia	55	45
564	25c. Lesotho	55	45
565	25c. Guatemala	55	45
566	25c. Netherlands	55	45
567	25c. Algeria	55	45
568	25c. Brunei	55	45
569	25c. St. Kitts and Nevis	55	45
570	25c. United Nations	55	45
571	25c. Honduras	55	45
572	25c. Kampuchea	55	45
573	25c. Guinea-Bissau	55	45
574	25c. Cyprus	55	45
575	25c. South Africa	55	45
576	25c. Portugal	55	45
577	25c. Morocco	55	45
578	25c. Syria	55	45

286 "Table of Universal Brotherhood" (Jose Clemente Orozco) (Article 1)

1989. Declaration of Human Rights (1st series). Multicoloured.

579	25c. Type **286**	35	25
580	45c. "Composition II" (V. Kandinsky) (Article 2)	75	65

See also Nos. 592/3, 609/10, 626/7 and 637/8.

288 Port Activities

1990. International Trade Centre.

581	**288** 25c. multicoloured	1·30	1·00

289 "AIDS"

1990. Anti-AIDS Campaign. Multicoloured.

582	25c. Type **289**	40	30
583	40c. Group at risk	1·30	80

291 Madagascar Periwinkle

1990. Medicinal Plants. Multicoloured.

584	25c. Type **291**	65	50
585	90c. American ginseng	1·70	1·20

293 Ribbons forming "45"

295 (⅓-size illustration)

1990. 45th Anniv of U.N.O. Multicoloured.

586	25c. Type **293**	65	55
587	45c. "45" and U.N. Emblem	2·30	1·20
MS588	100×73 mm. **295** Nos. 586/7	5·50	3·00

296 Youth waylaying Elderly Man

1990. Crime Prevention. Multicoloured.

590	25c. Type **296**	95	55
591	36c. Burglars leaving burning building	2·10	1·00

1990. Universal Declaration of Human Rights (2nd series). As T **286**. Multicoloured.

592	25c. Sarcophagus of Plotinus (detail) (Article 7)	40	25
593	45c. "Combined Chambers of High Court of Appeal" (Charles Paul Renouard, from "The Dreyfus Case") (Article 8)	75	60

300/303 Alpine Lake and Wildlife (½-size illustration)

1991. Economic Commission for Europe. "For a Better Environment".

594	**300** 30c. multicoloured	95	70
595	**301** 30c. multicoloured	95	70
596	**302** 30c. multicoloured	95	70
597	**303** 30c. multicoloured	95	70

Nos. 594/7 were printed together, se-tenant, forming the composite design illustrated.

304 Desert

306 U.N. Building

1991. 1st Anniv of Namibian Independence. Multicoloured.

598	30c. Type **304**	85	50
599	50c. Open grassland	1·50	1·20

1991.

600	**306** $2 blue	2·50	1·60

307 Children around Globe (Nicole Delia Legnani)

1991. 30th Anniv (1989) of U.N. Declaration on the Rights of the Child and 1990 World Summit on Children, New York. Children's Drawings. Multicoloured.

601	30c. Type **307**	1·10	80
602	70c. Dove, rainbow and houses (Alissa Duffy)	2·75	1·80

309 Bubbles of Toxin approaching City

1991. Banning of Chemical Weapons. Mult.

603	30c. Type **309**	1·50	1·10
604	90c. Hand pushing back barrels of toxins	2·75	1·70

311 U.N. Flag

1991. Multicoloured.

605	30c. Type **311**	75	45
606	50c. "The Golden Rule" (mosaic, Norman Rockwell) (vert)	1·30	80

313 1951 1c. Stamp

1991. 40th Anniv of United Nations Postal Administration.

607	**313** 30c. red on cream	95	70
608	– 40c. purple on cream	1·60	1·00

DESIGN: 40c. 1951 2c. stamp.

1991. Declaration of Human Rights (3rd series). As T **286**. Multicoloured.

609	30c. "The Last of England" (Ford Maddox Brown) (Article 13)	50	35
610	50c. "The Emigration to the East" (Tito Salas) (Article 14)	1·10	80

317 Uluru National Park, Australia

319/20 Sea Life (½-size illustration)

1992. 20th Anniv of UNESCO World Heritage Convention. Multicoloured.

611	30c. Type **317**	60	45
612	50c. Great Wall of China	1·10	80

1992. "Clean Oceans".

613	**319** 29c. multicoloured	45	45
614	**320** 29c. multicoloured	45	45

Nos. 613/14 were issued together, se-tenant, forming the composite design illustrated.

321/324 Planet Earth (½-size illustration)

1992. 2nd U.N. Conference on Environment and Development, Rio de Janeiro.
615 **321** 29c. multicoloured 75 45
616 **322** 29c. multicoloured 75 45
617 **323** 29c. multicoloured 75 45
618 **324** 29c. multicoloured 75 45
Nos. 615/18 were issued together, se-tenant, forming the composite design illustrated.

325/326 "Mission Planet Earth" (⅔-size illustration)

1992. International Space Year. Roul.
619 **325** 29c. multicoloured . . . . 2·75 2·30
620 **326** 29c. multicoloured . . . . 2·75 2·30
Nos. 619/20 were issued together, se-tenant, forming the composite design illustrated.

327 Winged Man with V.D.U.

1992. Commission on Science and Technology for Development. Multicoloured.
621 29c. Type **327** 40 35
622 50c. Man sitting in crocodile's mouth 70 55

329 Aerial View of Building

1992. United Nations University, Tokyo. Mult.
623 4c. Type **329** 15 15
624 40c. Front elevation of building 60 45

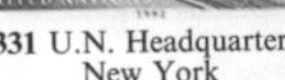
331 U.N. Headquarters, New York

334 Family Life

1992.
625 **331** 29c. multicoloured 75 60

1992. Universal Declaration of Human Rights (4th series). As T **286**. Multicoloured.
626 29c. "Lady writing a letter with her Maid" (Johannes Vermeer) (Article 19) . . . 75 60
627 50c. "The Meeting"(Ester Almqvist) (Article 20) . . . 95 95

1993. "Ageing: Dignity and Participation". 10th Anniv (1992) of International Plan of Action on Ageing. Multicoloured.
628 29c. Type **334** 85 60
629 52c. Health and nutrition . . 1·50 1·10

336 Queensland Hairy-nosed Wombat

1993. Endangered Species (1st series). Multicoloured.
630 29c. Type **336** 45 40
631 29c. Whooping crane ("Grus americana") 45 40
632 29c. Giant clams ("Tridacnidae") 45 40
633 29c. Sable antelope ("Hippotragus niger") . . 45 40
See also Nos. 649/52, 667/70, 694/7, 720/3, 755/8, 803/6, 819/22, 841/4 and 875/8.

340 "United Nations"

1993.
634 **340** 5c. multicoloured 60 40

341 Personal Environment

1993. 45th Anniv of W.H.O. Multicoloured.
635 29c. Type **341** 95 65
636 50c. Family environment . . 1·10 80

1993. Declaration of Human Rights (5th series). As T **286**. Multicoloured.
637 29c. "Shocking Corn" (Thomas Hart Benton) (Article 25) 75 50
638 35c. "The Library" (Jacob Lawrence) (Article 26) . . 1·10 80

345/348 Peace (½-size illustration)

1993. International Peace Day. Roul.
639 **345** 29c. multicoloured . . . . 1·70 1·20
640 **346** 29c. multicoloured . . . . 1·70 1·20
641 **347** 29c. multicoloured . . . . 1·70 1·20
642 **348** 29c. multicoloured . . . . 1·70 1·20
Nos. 639/42 were issued together, se-tenant, forming the composite design illustrated.

349 Chameleon

1993. The Environment—Climate. Mult.
643 29c. Type **349** 70 60
644 29c. Storm 40 60
645 29c. Antelopes fleeing from flood 70 60
646 29c. Lesser bird of paradise 40 60
Nos. 643/6 were issued together, se-tenant, forming a composite design.

353 Equality across Generations

1994. Int Year of the Family. Mult.
647 29c. Type **353** . . . . 1·10 80
648 45c. Poor family . . . . . . 1·70 1·20

1994. Endangered Species (2nd series). As T **336**. Multicoloured.
649 29c. Chimpanzees ("Pan troglodytes") 50 40
650 29c. St. Lucia amazon ("Amazona versicolor") . . 50 40
651 29c. American crocodile ("Crocodylus acutus") . . 50 40
652 29c. Addra gazelles ("Gazelle dama") 50 40

359 "Dove of Peace" (mosaic)

362 Refugee crossing Bridge of Hands

1994.
653 **359** 10c. multicoloured 15 15
654 – 19c. multicoloured 55 30
655 – $1 brown . . . . 2·10 1·60
DESIGNS: 19c. "Sleeping Child" (stained-glass window after drawing by Stanislaw Wyspianski); $1 "Mourning Owl" (Vanessa Isitt).

1994. United Nations High Commissioner for Refugees.
656 **362** 50c. multicoloured . . . . 1·10 80

363/366 Shattered Globe and "Warning" (⅔-size illustration)

1994. International Decade for Natural Disaster Reduction.
657 **363** 29c. multicoloured . . . . 1·50 1·00
658 **364** 29c. multicoloured . . . . 1·50 1·00
659 **365** 29c. multicoloured . . . . 1·50 1·00
660 **366** 29c. multicoloured . . . . 1·50 1·00
Nos. 657/60 were issued together, se-tenant, forming the composite design illustrated.

367 Children Playing (health and family planning)

1994. International Population and Development Conference, Cairo. Multicoloured.
661 29c. Type **367** 65 45
662 52c. Family unit (demographic changes) . . 1·10 80

369 Map and Looped Ribbon

371 Anniversary Emblem

1994. 30th Anniv of United Nations Conference on Trade and Development. Multicoloured.
663 29c. Type **369** 45 40
664 50c. Map and coiled ribbon 80 55

1995. 50th Anniv of U.N.O. (1st issue).
665 **371** 32c. multicoloured . . . . 1·10 70
See also Nos. 673/4 and 679/90.

372 "Social Summit 1995"

1995. World Summit for Social Development, Copenhagen.
666 **372** 50c. multicoloured 95 80

1995. Endangered Species (3rd series). As T **336**. Multicoloured.
667 32c. Giant armadillo ("Priodontes maximus") . . 55 45
668 32c. American bald eagle ("Haliaeetus leucocephalus") 55 45
669 32c. Fijian banded iguana ("Brachylophus fasciatus") 55 45
670 32c. Giant panda ("Ailuropoda melanoleuca") 55 45

377 Man looking out to Sea

1995. "Youth: Our Future". 10th Anniv of International Youth Year. Multicoloured.
671 32c. Type **377** 85 35
672 55c. Family cycling . . . . . 1·20 65

379 Signing U.N. Charter

381 (½-size illustration)

1995. 50th Anniv of U.N.O. (2nd issue).
673 **379** 32c. black 55 35
674 – 50c. purple 85 55
MS675 92 × 70 mm. **381** Nos. 673/4. Imperf . . . . 2·00 1·75
DESIGN: 50c. Veterans' Memorial Hall and Opera House, San Francisco (venue for signing of Charter).

382 Mother and Child

1995. 4th World Conference on Women, Peking.
676 32c. Type **382** 65 30
677 40c. Harpist and cranes . . . 95 40

384 U.N. Headquarters, New York

1995.
678 **384** 20c. multicoloured 30 15

385/387 (½-size illustration)

388/390 (½-size illustration)

391/393 (½-size illustration)

394/396 (½-size illustration)

1995. 50th Anniv of U.N.O. (3rd issue).

679 **385** 32c. multicoloured . . . . 1·10 65
680 **386** 32c. multicoloured . . . . 1·10 65
681 **387** 32c. multicoloured . . . . 1·10 65
682 **388** 32c. multicoloured . . . . 1·10 65
683 **389** 32c. multicoloured . . . . 1·10 65
684 **390** 32c. multicoloured . . . . 1·10 65
685 **391** 32c. multicoloured . . . . 1·10 65
686 **392** 32c. multicoloured . . . . 1·10 65
687 **393** 32c. multicoloured . . . . 1·10 65
688 **394** 32c. multicoloured . . . . 1·10 65
689 **395** 32c. multicoloured . . . . 1·10 65
690 **396** 32c. multicoloured . . . . 1·10 65

Nos. 679/81 and 682/4 form the left and right halves respectively of a composite design, and Nos. 685/7 and 688/90 another composite design.

397 Rainbow and Faces within "Sun"

398 Mural

1996. 50th Anniv of World Federation of United Nations Associations.

691 **397** 32c. multicoloured 40 25

1996. Murals by Fernand Leger in General Assembly, U.N. Headquarters. Multicoloured.

692 32c. Type **398** 40 25
693 60c. Mural (different) 85 60

1996. Endangered Species (4th series). As T **336**. Multicoloured.

694 32c. "Masdevallia veitchiana" 65 50
695 32c. Saguaro ("Carnegiea gigantea") 65 50
696 32c. West Australian pitcher plant ("Cephalotus follicularis") 65 50
697 32c. "Encephalartos horridus" 65 50

404 Deer under Tree

1996. "Habitat II" Second United Nations Conference on Human Settlements, Istanbul, Turkey. Multicoloured.

698 32c. Type **404** 70 45
699 32c. City and countryside . . 70 45
700 32c. Walking in city park . . 70 45
701 32c. City and village 70 45
702 32c. Village and parrot . . . 70 45

Nos. 698/702 were issued together, se-tenant, forming a composite design.

409 Basketball

411 (⅓-size illustration)

1996. Sport and the Environment. Multicoloured.

703 32c. Type **409** 85 60
704 50c. Volleyball . . . . 1·20 1·20
MS705 88 × 78 mm. **411** Nos. 703/4 1·60 1·25

412 Two Birds

1996. "A Plea for Peace". Winners of China Youth Design Competition. Multicoloured.

706 32c. Type **412** 55 35
707 60c. Peace dove . . . . . . 1·10 40

414 "Yeh-Shen" (Chinese tale)

416 Cherry Tree

1996. 50th Anniv of UNICEF. Children's Stories.

708 32c. Type **414** 55 40
709 60c. "The Ugly Duckling" (Hans Christian Andersen) 1·30 1·00

1997. Flags of Member Nations (11th series). As T **203**. Multicoloured.

710 32c. Liechtenstein 55 40
711 32c. Republic of Korea . . . 55 40
712 32c. Kazakhstan 55 40
713 32c. Latvia 55 40
714 32c. Tajikistan 55 40
715 32c. Georgia 55 40
716 32c. Armenia 55 40
717 32c. Namibia 55 40

1997. Multicoloured.

718 8c. Type **416** 35 25
719 55c. Rose "Peace" (horiz) . . 1·10 55

1997. Endangered Species (5th series). As T **336**. Multicoloured.

720 32c. African elephant ("Loxodonta africana") . . 55 40
721 32c. Major Mitchell's cockatoo ("Cacatua leadbeateri") 55 40
722 32c. Black-footed ferret ("Mustela nigripes") . . . 55 40
723 32c. Puma ("Felis concolor") 55 40

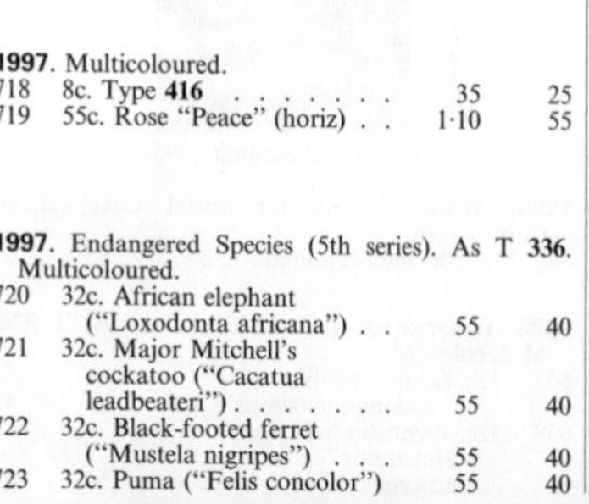

422/425 Ocean Scene (⅔-size illustration)

426 (⅓-size illustration)

1997. "Earth Summit + 5". 5th Anniv of United Nations Conference on Environment and Development.

724 **422** 32c. multicoloured 95 65
725 **423** 32c. multicoloured 95 65
726 **424** 32c. multicoloured 95 65
727 **425** 32c. multicoloured 95 65
MS728 Two sheets, each 90 × 75 mm. (a) **426** $1 multicoloured. Imperf; (b) No. MS728a optd for "Pacific 97" in bottom margin . . . . 10·00 10·00

Nos. 724/7 were issued together, se-tenant, forming the composite design illustrated.

427 Clipper

432 1986 22c. Philately Stamp

1997. 50th Anniversaries of Economic Commission for Europe and Economic and Social Commission for Asia and the Pacific. Multicoloured.

729 32c. Type **427** 55 25
730 32c. Sail/steam ship 55 25
731 32c. Liner 55 25
732 32c. Hovercraft 55 25
733 32c. Hydrofoil 55 25

Nos. 729/33 were issued together, se-tenant, forming a composite design.

1997. "Tribute to Philately". Multicoloured.

734 32c. Type **432** 70 55
735 50c. 1986 44c. Philately stamp . . . . 1·20 70

434 Kneeling Warrior

1997. 25th Anniv of World Heritage Convention. Terracotta Warriors from Emperor Qin Shi Huang's Tomb, Xian, China. Multicoloured.

736 8c. Type **434** 25 25
737 8c. Ranks of armoured warriors 25 25
738 8c. Head 25 25
739 8c. Group in wrap-over tunics 25 25
740 8c. Head and shoulders . . . 25 25
741 8c. Group in armour 25 25
742 32c. Type **434** 60 25
743 60c. As No. 737 . . . . . . 1·10 65

1998. Flags of Member Nations (12th series). As T **203**.

744 32c. blue, grey and black . . 65 40
745 32c. multicoloured 65 40
746 32c. multicoloured 65 40
747 32c. multicoloured 65 40
748 32c. multicoloured 65 40
749 32c. red, grey and black . . . 65 40
750 32c. multicoloured 65 40
751 32c. black, blue and grey . . 65 40

FLAGS: No. 744, Micronesia; 745, Slovakia; 746, Democratic People's Republic of Korea; 747, Azerbaijan; 748, Uzbekistan; 749, Monaco; 750, Czech Republic; 751, Estonia.

440 Boy holding Dove

1998. Multicoloured.

752 1c. Type **440** 15 15
753 2c. Birds 15 15
754 21c. Dancing around U.N. emblem 40 15

1998. Endangered Species (6th series). As T **366**. Multicoloured.

755 32c. Lesser bushbaby ("Galago senegalensis") . . 55 25
756 32c. Hawaiian goose ("Branta sandvicensis") 55 25
757 32c. Golden birdwing ("Troides aeacus") 55 25
758 32c. Sun bear ("Helarctos malayanus") 55 25

447 Turtles

1998. International Year of the Ocean. Multicoloured.

759 32c. Type **447** 55 25
760 32c. Rays 55 40
761 32c. Sunfishes 55 40
762 32c. Head of whale 55 40
763 32c. Dugongs 55 40
764 32c. Striped fishes 55 40
765 32c. Dolphin (fish) and orca 55 40
766 32c. Jellyfish and seahorse . . 55 40
767 32c. Sealions, seahorse and fishes 55 40
768 32c. Dolphins, octopus and diver's head 55 40
769 32c. Submersible 55 40
770 32c. Sharks 55 40

448 Jaguar

449 (½-size illustration)

1998. Rainforest Preservation.

771 **448** 32c. multicoloured 55 40
MS772 82 × 70 mm. **449** $2 multicoloured . . . . 2·75 1·75

450 Soldier holding Binoculars

1998. 50 Years of United Nations Peacekeeping. Multicoloured.

773 33c. Type **450** 70 45
774 40c. Soldiers sitting on tank 75 30

452 Man carrying Flag

1998. 50th Anniv of Universal Declaration of Human Rights. Multicoloured.

775 32c. Type **452** 65 35
776 55c. Walking pens . . . . . 1·10 60

454 Blue and White Vase (Mirror Room)

1998. World Heritage Site. Schonbrunn Palace, Vienna. Multicoloured.

777 11c. Type **454** 35 30
778 11c. Detail of wall hanging (Johann Wenzl Bergl) . . . 35 30
779 11c. Porcelain stove 35 30
780 15c. Palace facade (horiz) . . 40 40
781 15c. Great Palm House (horiz) 40 40
782 15c. Gloriette (horiz) 40 40
783 33c. As No. 782 . . . . . . 65 40
784 60c. As No. 778 . . . . . . 1·00 45

1999. Flags of Member Nations (13th series). As T **203**. Multicoloured.

785 33c. Lithuania 60 35
786 33c. San Marino 60 35
787 33c. Turkmenistan 60 35
788 33c. Marshall Islands 60 35
789 33c. Moldova 60 35
790 33c. Kyrgyzstan 60 35
791 33c. Bosnia and Herzegovina 60 35
792 33c. Eritrea 60 35

460 Man putting Banner of Flags around Globe

1999. Multicoloured.

793 33c. Type **460** 55 25
794 $5 Roses . . . . 7·25 2·50

462 Tasmanian Wilderness

1999. World Heritage Sites in Australia. Mult.

795 5c. Type **462** 15 15
796 5c. Wet Tropics, Queensland 15 15
797 5c. Great Barrier Reef . . . 15 15
798 15c. Uluru-Kata Tjuta National Park 25 25
799 15c. Kakadu National Park 25 25
800 15c. Willandra Lakes Region 25 25
801 33c. As No. 800 . . . . . . 70 60
802 60c. As No. 796 . . . . . . 1·00 1·20

1999. Endangered Species (7th series). As T **336**. Multicoloured.

803 33c. Tiger ("Panthera tigris") 55 15
804 33c. Secretary bird ("Sagittarius serpentarius") 55 15
805 33c. Green tree python ("Chondropython viridis") 55 15
806 33c. Long-tailed chinchilla ("Chinchilla lanigera") . . 55 15

472/473 International Planetary Exploration (½-size illustration)

474 (½-size illustration)

1999. 3rd Conference on Exploration and Peaceful Uses of Outer Space, Vienna.

807 **472** 33c. multicoloured 80 45
808 **473** 33c. multicoloured 80 45
MS809 90 × 75 mm. **474** $2 multicoloured . . . . 2·50 2·50

Nos. 807/8 were issued together, se-tenant, forming the composite design illustrated.

475/478 19th-century Mail Transport (½-size illustration)

1999. 125th Anniv of Universal Postal Union.

810 **475** 33c. multicoloured 55 25
811 **476** 33c. multicoloured 55 25
812 **477** 33c. multicoloured 55 25
813 **478** 33c. multicoloured 55 25

Nos. 810/13 were issued together, se-tenant, forming the composite design illustrated.

479 U.N. Headquarters, New York

483 Glory Window (Gabrielle Loire), Chapel of Thanksgiving, Dallas

480 (½-size illustration)

481 Couple with Books

1999. "In Memoriam: Fallen in the Cause of Peace".

814 **479** 37c. multicoloured . . . . 1·70 1·40
MS815 90 × 75 mm. **480** $1 multicoloured . . . . 1·25 1·25

1999. Education: Keystone to the 21st Century. Multicoloured.

816 33c. Type **481** 55 25
817 60c. Heart and open book . . 1·10 45

2000. International Year of Thanksgiving.

818 **483** 33c. multicoloured 75 60

2000. Endangered Species (8th series). As T **336**. Mult.

819 33c. Brown bear (*Ursus arctos*) 55 25
820 33c. Black-bellied bustard (*Lissotis melanogaster*) . . 55 25
821 33c. Chinese crocodile lizard (*Shinisaurus crocodilurus*) 55 25
822 33c. Pygmy chimpanzee (*Pan paniscis*) 55 25

488 "Crawling Toward the Millennium" (Sam Yeates)

2000. "Our World 2000" International Art Exhibition, New York. Entries in Millennium Painting Competition. Multicoloured.

823 33c. Type **488** 55 25
824 60c. "Crossing" (Masakazu Takahata) (vert) . . . . . 1·10 45

2000. "Anahiem 2000" International Stamp Exhibition, California. No. **MS**809 optd **WORLD STAMP EXPO 2000 ANAHEIM, CALIFORNIA U.S.A. 7 – 16 JULY 2000** in the margin.

MS825 90 × 75 mm. **474** $2 multicoloured . . . . 1·50 1·50

491 Auditorium, General Assembly Building, 1956

2000. 55th Anniv of the United Nations and 50th Anniv of Opening of U.N. Headquarters, New York.

826 **491** 33c. blue, green and ochre 55 25
827 – 55c. blue, green and ochre 95 45
MS828 67 × 86 mm. Nos. 826/7 1·50 1·50

DESIGN: 55c. Headquarters, 1951.

493 Globe, Sun and Olympic Rings (Mateja Prunk)

2000. Winning Entry in "International Flag of Peace" Children's Design Competition.

829 **493** 33c. multicoloured 55 25

494 Workers in Rice Field

495 (⅓-size illustration)

2000. "The United Nations in the 21st Century". Sheet 141 × 161 containing T **494** and similar horiz designs, forming the overall design T **495**. Multicoloured.

MS830 33c. Type **494**; 33c. Loading Machinery and supplies; 33c. Posting votes; 33. Mother holding child receiving vaccination; 33c. Sack of grain and women using water pump. 33c. Men building house . . . . 2·75 2·75

496 Granada

2000. World Heritage Sites in Spain. Multicoloured.

831 5c. Type **496** 15 15
832 5c. Cliff-top Houses, Cuence 15 15
833 5c. Roman Aqueduct, Segovia 15 15
834 15c. Archaeological Site, Merida 25 25
835 15c. Toledo 25 25
836 15c. Guell Park, Barcelona 25 25
837 33c. As No. 831 . . . . . . 55 25
838 60c. As No. 834 . . . . . . 1·10 45

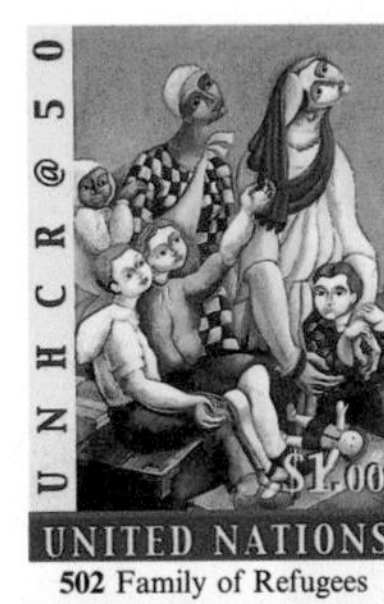

502 Family of Refugees

503 (½-size illustration)

2000. 50th Anniv of United Nations High Commissioner for Refugees.

839 **502** 33c. multicoloured 55 25
MS840 121 × 82 mm. **503** $1 multicoloured . . . . 1·20 1·20

2001. Endangered Species (9th series). As T **336**. Multicoloured.

841 34c. Spotted phalanger (*Phalanger maculatus*) . . . 55 25
842 34c. Resplendent quetzal (*Pharomachrus mocinno*) . . 55 25
843 34c. Gila monster (*Heloderma suspectum*) 55 25
844 34c. Eastern black and white colobus (*Colobus guereza*) 55 25

508 Landscape and Silhouette (Jose Zaragoza)

2001. United Nations International Year of Volunteers. Multicoloured.

845 34c. Type **508** 55 25
846 80c. Piano keys, hands and music score (John Terry) 1·30 65

510 Sunflower

2001. Multicoloured.
847 7c. Type **510** 15 15
848 34c. Rose 55 25

2001. Flags of Member Nations (14th series). As T **203**. Multicoloured.
849 34c. Slovenia 55 25
850 34c. Palau 55 25
851 34c. Tonga 55 25
852 34c. Croatia 55 25
853 34c. Macedonia 55 25
854 34c. Kiribati 55 25
855 34c. Andorra 55 25
856 34c. Nauru 55 25

512 Pagoda, Kyoto

2001. World Heritage Sites in Japan. Multicoloured.
857 5c. Type **512** 15 15
858 5c. Imperial Palace, Nara . . 15 15
859 5c. Himeji Castle 15 15
860 20c. Shirakawa-go and Gokayama Villages 35 30
861 20c. Itsukushima Shinto Shrine 35 30
862 20c. Temple, Nikko 35 30
863 34c. As No. 857 . . . . . . 55 25
864 70c. As No. 860 . . . . . . 1·20 55

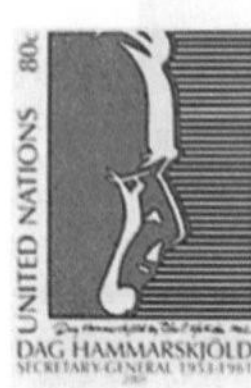

518 Hammarskjold

519 "Stamps" and Ribbons

2001. 40th Death Anniv of Dag Hammarskjold (United Nations Secretary General, 1953–61).
865 **518** 80c. blue . . . . 1·30 65

2001. 50th Anniv of United Nations Postal Administration.
866 **519** 34c. multicoloured 55 25
867 – 80c. multicoloured . . . . 1·30 65
MS868 102 × 102 mm. $1 × 2, cobalt and blue . . . . 2·80 2·80
DESIGNS: 80c. Presents; $1 Emblem.

522 Landscape, Butterfly and Goose

2001. Climate Change. Multicoloured.
869 34c. Type **522** 55 25
870 34c. Penguin and tomato plant 55 25
871 34c. Palm tree and solar panel 55 25
872 34c. Hand planting sapling 55 25
Nos. 869/72 were issued together, se-tenant, forming a composite design.

526 United Nations Flag

2001. Kofi Annan, Winner of Nobel Peace Prize, 2001.
873 **526** 34c. multicoloured 55 25

527 Children carrying Stamps

2002.
874 **527** 80c. multicoloured . . . . 1·10 40

2002. Endangered Species (10th series). As T **336**. Multicoloured.
875 34c. Hoffmann's two-toed sloth (*Choloepus hoffmanni*) 50 25
876 34c. American bighorn (*Ovis canadensis*) 50 25
877 34c. Cheetah (*Acinonyx jubatus*) 50 25
878 34c. San Esteban Island chuckwalla (*Sauromalus varius*) 50 25

532 Wooden Mask, Dili

2002. East Timor Independence. Multicoloured.
879 34c. Type **532** 45 20
880 57c. Traditional wooden door panels 70 30

534 Khan-Tengri, Kyrgyzstan

2002. International Year of Mountains. Multicoloured.
881 34c. Type **534** 45 20
882 34c. Kilimanjaro, Tanzania 45 20
883 80c. Mt. Foraker, U.S.A . . 1·00 40
884 80c. Paine Grande, Chile . . 1·00 40

538 Sun, Earth and Planets

2002. World Summit on Sustainable Development, Johannesburg. Multicoloured.
885 37c. Type **538** 45 20
886 37c. Women's profile 45 20
887 60c. Yacht 75 30
888 60c. Figures wearing fashionable dress 75 30

542 Duomo di Sant'Andrea, Amalfi Coast

2002. World Heritage Sites in Italy. Multicoloured.
889 5c. Type **542** 10 10
890 5c. View across Islands, Aeolian Islands 10 10
891 5c. Del Moro Fountain, Rome 10 10
892 15c. Santa Maria del Fiore, Florence 20 20
893 15c. Leaning Tower, Pisa . . 20 20
894 15c. The Forum, Pompeii . . 20 20
895 37c. As No. 892 . . . . . . 45 20
896 70c. As No. 889 . . . . . . 85 35

548 AIDS Symbol on U.N. Secretariat Building, New York

549 (½-size illustration)

2002. AIDS Awareness Campaign. Multicoloured.
897 70c. Type **548** 85 35
MS898 80 × 80 mm. 37c.+6c. **549** 60 25
The premium was for AIDS charities.

550 Artefacts (½-size illustration)

2003. Indigenous Art. Sheet 121 × 97 mm. Multicoloured.
MS899 37c. Paracas (detail), Peru; 37c. Sinu pendant, Colombia; 37c. Hicholi embroidery, Mexico; 37c. Rigpaktsa back ornament, Brazil; 37c. Woollen textile, Santiago, Chile; 37c. Huari hat, Bolivia 2·40 2·40

551 Interlocking Hands and "peace"

2003.
900 **551** 23c. multicoloured 25 10

552 United Nations Emblem

2003.
901 **552** 37c. gold and blue 40 15

553 Bi-plane Propeller

2003. Centenary of Powered Flight. Multicoloured.
902 23c. Type **553** 25 10
903 70c. As No. 902 . . . . . . 75 30
Nos. 902/3 were issued in tê-bêe pairs forming a composite design of a propeller.

554 United Nations Headquarters, New York

2003. Greetings from the United Nations.
904 **554** 70c. multicoloured 75 30

555 Great Hornbill

2003. 30th Anniv of Convention on International Trade in Endangered Species (CITES). Multicoloured.
905 37c. Type **555** 40 15
906 37c. Scarlet ibis 40 15
907 37c. Knob-billed goose . . . 40 15
908 37c. White-faced whistling duck 40 15

559 Animals and Freshwater

2003. International Year of Freshwater. Multicoloured.
909 23c. Type **559** 25 10
910 37c. Decay 40 15
Nos. 909/10 were issued together, se-tenant, forming a composite design.

561 Yosemite National Park

2003. World Heritage Sites in USA. Showing USA National Parks. Multicoloured.
911 10c. Type **561** 10 10
912 10c. Smoky Mountains . . . 10 10
913 10c. Olympic National Park 10 10
914 20c. Hawaii Volcanoes . . . 20 10
915 20c. Everglades 20 10
916 20c. Yellowstone National Park 20 10
917 37c. As No. 911 . . . . . . 40 15
918 60c. As No. 914 . . . . . . 65 25
Nos. 911/18 have blue bands at top and bottom edges.

567 Ralph Bunche

568 Flag at Half-mast

2003. Ralph Bunche (politician) Commemoration.
919 **567** 37c. multicoloured 40 15

2003. In Memoriam. Support for United Nations Staff Killed or Injured in Terrorist Attacks.
920 **568** 60c. multicoloured 65 25

B. GENEVA HEADQUARTERS

For use on mail posted at the United Nations Geneva Headquarters. Before 1969 the Swiss PTT issued stamps for use at the Palais des Nations; these are listed at the end of Switzerland.

100 centimes = 1 Swiss franc.

NOTE: References to numbers and types in this section. other than to those with a "G" prefix are to the United Nations (New York Office) listing. Designs adapted for the Geneva issue are inscribed in French and have face values in francs.

G **4** Palais des Nations, Geneva

G **5** Palais des Nations, Geneva

1969. Existing United Nations (New York) designs adapted with new colours and values in Swiss francs (F.S.). 30 and 40c. new designs. Multicoloured unless otherwise stated.
G 1 – 5c. (As No. 164) 10 10
G 2 – 10c. (As No. 94) 10 10
G 3 – 20c. (As No. 97) 20 10
G 4 G **4** 30c. multicoloured . . . 25 15
G 5 G **5** 40c. multicoloured . . . 30 25
G 6 – 50c. (As No. 147, but scroll inscr in French) 40 25
G 7 – 60c. gold, red and brown (As No. 98) 40 25
G 8 – 70c. red, gold and black (As No. 167) 50 35
G 9 – 75c. (As No. A125) . . . 50 45
G10 – 80c. (As No. 148) . . . 55 45
G11 **52** 90c. (Inscr in French) . . 65 50
G12 – 1f. deep green and green (As No. 149) 75 40
G13 **53** 2f. multicoloured . . . . 1·50 1·20
G14 **104** 3f. multicoloured . . . . 2·40 2·10
G15 **3** 10f. blue . . . . 7·75 7·25

1971. Peaceful Uses of the Sea-bed.
G16 **121** 30c. multicoloured . . . 35 35

1971. United Nations Work with Refugees.
G17 **122** 50c. black, orange and red 55 55

1971. World Food Programme.
G18 **123** 50c. multicoloured . . . 55 55

1971. Opening of New Universal Postal Union Headquarters Building, Berne.
G19 **124** 75c. multicoloured . . . 85 85

1971. Racial Equality Year. Designs as Nos. 220/1, with background colours changed.
G20 30c. Type **125** 40 35
G21 50c. Linked globes (horiz) 40 35

1971. U.N. International Schools.
G22 **130** 1f.10 multicoloured . . . 85 75

1972. Non-proliferation of Nuclear Weapons.
G23 **131** 40c. multicoloured . . . 65 65

1972. World Health Day.
G24 **132** 80c. multicoloured . . . 75 75

1972. United Nations Environmental Conservation Conference, Stockholm.
G25 **137** 40c. multicoloured . . . 45 45
G26 80c. multicoloured . . . 70 70

1972. Economic Commission for Europe (ECE).
G27 **138** 1f.10 multicoloured . . . 1·30 1·30

1972. United Nations Art.
G28 **139** 40c. multicoloured . . . 45 45
G29 80c. multicoloured . . . 80 80

1973. Disarmament Decade.
G30 **140** 60c. multicoloured . . . 50 50
G31 1f.10 multicoloured . . . 85 85

1973. "No Drugs" Campaign.
G32 **141** 60c. multicoloured . . . 60 60

1973. U.N. Volunteers Programme.
G33 **142** 80c. multicoloured . . . 70 70

1973. "Namibia" (South West Africa).
G34 **143** 60c. multicoloured . . . 60 60

1973. 25th Anniv of Declaration of Human Rights.
G35 **144** 40c. multicoloured . . . 30 30
G36 80c. multicoloured . . . 70 70

1973. Inauguration of New I.L.O. Headquarters, Geneva.
G37 **145** 60c. multicoloured . . . 40 40
G38 80c. multicoloured . . . 90 90

1973. Centenary of Universal Postal Union.
G39 **146** 30c. multicoloured . . . 25 25
G40 60c. multicoloured . . . 50 50

1974. Brazilian Peace Mural.
G41 **147** 60c. multicoloured . . . 55 55
G42 1f. multicoloured 80 80

1974. World Population Year.
G43 **154** 60c. multicoloured . . . 70 70
G44 80c. multicoloured . . . 75 75

1974. U.N. Conference on "Law of the Sea".
G45 **155** 1f.30 multicoloured . . . 1·20 1·20

1975. Peaceful Uses of Outer Space.
G46 **156** 60c. multicoloured . . . 50 50
G47 90c. multicoloured . . . 90 90

1975. International Women's Year.
G48 **157** 60c. multicoloured . . . 55 55
G49 90c. multicoloured . . . 80 80

1975. 30th Anniv of U.N.O.
G50 **158** 60c. multicoloured . . . 45 45
G51 90c. multicoloured . . . 70 70
MSG52 92 × 70 mm. Nos. G50/1. Imperf . . . . 1·10 1·10

1975. "Namibia—U.N. Direct Responsibility".
G53 **160** 50c. multicoloured . . . 45 45
G54 1f.30 multicoloured . . . 85 85

1975. U.N. Peace Keeping Operations.
G55 **161** 60c. blue 80 80
G56 70c. violet 65 65

1976. World Federation of U.N. Associations.
G57 **166** 90c. multicoloured . . . 75 75

1976. U.N. Conf on Trade and Development.
G58 **167** 1f.10 multicoloured . . . 95 95

1976. U.N. Conf on Human Settlements.
G59 **168** 40c. multicoloured . . . 35 35
G60 1f.50 multicoloured . . . 1·20 1·20

G **46** U.N. Emblem within Posthorn
G **49** Rain Drop and Globe

1976. 25th Anniv of U.N. Postal Administration.
G61 G **46** 80c. multicoloured . . . 2·25 2·00
G62 1f.10 multicoloured . . 2·25 2·10

1976. World Food Council Publicity.
G63 **170** 70c. multicoloured . . . 55 55

1977. World Intellectual Property Organization Publicity.
G64 **172** 80c. multicoloured . . . 70 70

1977. U.N. Water Conference.
G65 G **49** 80c. multicoloured . . . 70 70
G66 1f.10 multicoloured . . 90 90

G **50** Protective Hands

1977. Security Council Commemoration.
G67 G **50** 80c. multicoloured . . . 70 70
G68 1f.10 multicoloured . . 90 90

G **51** "Intertwining of Races"

1977. "Combat Racism".
G69 G **51** 40c. multicoloured . . . 30 30
G70 1f.10 multicoloured . . 90 90

G **52** Atoms and Laurel Leaf
G **53** Tree and Birds

1977. "Peaceful Uses for Atomic Energy".
G71 G **52** 80c. multicoloured . . . 70 70
G72 1f.10 multicoloured . . 90 90

1978.
G73 G **53** 35c. multicoloured . . . 30 30

G **54** Smallpox Bacilli and Globe
G **56** Aircraft Flightpaths

1978. Global Eradication of Smallpox.
G74 G **54** 80c. multicoloured . . . 70 70
G75 1f.10 multicoloured . . 90 90

1978. "Namibia: Liberation, Justice, Co-operation".
G76 **183** 80c. multicoloured . . . 70 70

1978. International Civil Aviation Organization—Safety in the Air.
G77 G **56** 70c. multicoloured . . . 55 55
G78 80c. multicoloured . . . 65 65

G **57** Globe, Flags and General Assembly Interior

1978. General Assembly.
G79 G **57** 70c. multicoloured . . . 55 55
G80 1f.10 multicoloured . . 90 90

1978. Technical Co-operation among Developing Countries.
G81 **186** 80c. multicoloured . . . 80 80

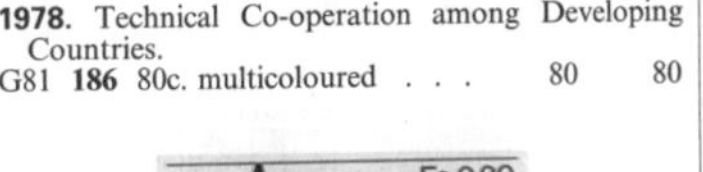
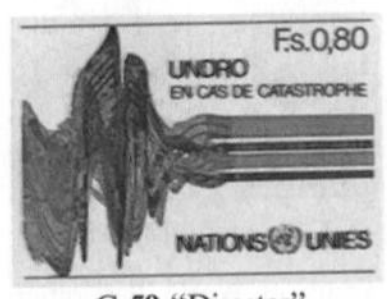

G **59** "Disaster"

1979. United Nations Disaster Relief Co-ordinator.
G82 G **59** 80c. multicoloured . . . 65 65
G83 1f.50 multicoloured . . 1·40 1·40

G **60** Children and Rainbow
G **62** Int Court of Justice and Scales

1979. International Year of the Child.
G84 G **60** 80c. multicoloured . . . 75 75
G85 1f.10 multicoloured . . 1·10 1·10

1979. "For a Free and Independent Namibia".
G86 **193** 1f.10 multicoloured . . . 1·00 1·00

1979. International Court of Justice.
G87 G **62** 80c. multicoloured . . . 70 70
G88 1f.10 multicoloured . . 95 95

G **63** Key symbolizing Unity of Action
G **64** Emblem

1980. New International Economic Order.
G89 G **63** 80c. multicoloured . . . 70 70

1980. U.N. Decade for Women.
G90 G **64** 40c. multicoloured . . . 30 30
G91 70c. multicoloured . . . 50 50

1980. Peace Keeping Operations.
G92 **198** 1f.10 blue and green . . 95 95

1980. 35th Anniv of United Nations.
G93 – 40c. black and blue . . . 35 35
G94 **200** 70c. multicoloured . . . 60 60
MSG95 92 × 73 mm. Nos. G93/4. Imperf 90 90
DESIGN: 40c. Dove and "35".

1980. Economic and Social Council.
G96 **204** 40c. multicoloured . . . 35 35
G97 – 70c. blue, red and black 60 60
DESIGN: 70c. Human figures ascending graph.

1981. Inalienable Rights of the Palestinian People.
G98 **206** 80c. multicoloured . . . 70 70

G **71** Disabled Person
G **77** "Anti-apartheid"

1981. International Year of Disabled Persons.
G99 G **71** 40c. black and blue . . 40 40
G100 – 1f.50 black and red . . 1·30 1·30
DESIGN: 1f.50, Knot pattern.

1981. Art.
G101 **209** 80c. multicoloured . . . 70 70

1981. New and Renewable Sources of Energy.
G102 **210** 1f.10 multicoloured . . 95 95

1981. 10th Anniv of U.N. Volunteers Programme. Multicoloured.
G103 40c. Type **212** 35 35
G104 70c. Emblems of science, agriculture and industry 60 60

1982. Multicoloured.
G105 30c. Type G **77** 30 30
G106 1f. Flags 85 85

1982. Human Environment. Multicoloured.
G107 40c. Leaves 35 35
G108 1f.20 Type **217** . . . . . 1·10 1·10

1982. Second United Nations Conference on Exploration and Peaceful Uses of Outer Space.
G109 **219** 80c. violet, pink & green 70 70
G110 – 1f. multicoloured . . . 80 80
DESIGN: 1f. Satellite and emblems.

G **83** Bird
G **85** Cable Network

1982. Conservation and Protection of Nature. Multicoloured.
G111 40c. Type G **83** 35 35
G112 1f.50 Snake (reptiles) . . . 1·30 1·30

1983. World Communications Year.
G113 G **85** 1f.20 multicoloured . . 1·10 1·10

1983. Safety at Sea: International Maritime Organization. Multicoloured.
G114 40c. Type **224** 35 35
G115 80c. Radar screen within lifebelt 80 80

1983. World Food Programme.
G116 **226** 1f.50 blue . . . . . . 1·40 1·40

1983. Trade and Development. Multicoloured.
G117 80c. Type **227** 75 75
G118 1f.10 Exports . . . . . . 1·00 1·00

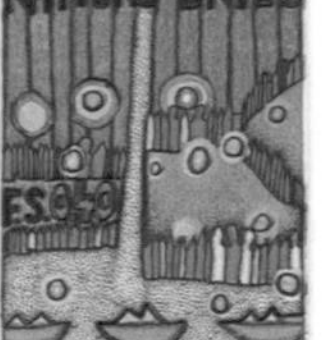

G **91** "Homo Humus Humanitas"
G **93** World Housing

1983. 35th Anniv of Universal Declaration of Human Rights. Multicoloured.
G119 40c. Type G **91** 50 50
G120 1f.20 "Droit de Creer" . . 1·20 1·20

1984. International Conference on Population, Mexico City.
G121 G **93** 1f.20 multicoloured . . 1·10 1·10

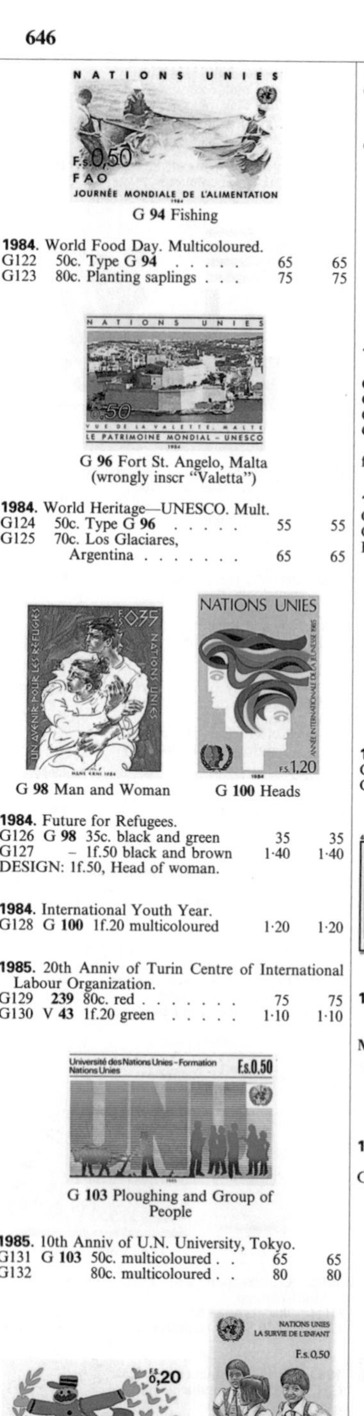

G **94** Fishing

1984. World Food Day. Multicoloured.
G122 50c. Type G **94** 65 65
G123 80c. Planting saplings . . . 75 75

G **96** Fort St. Angelo, Malta (wrongly inscr "Valetta")

1984. World Heritage—UNESCO. Mult.
G124 50c. Type G **96** 55 55
G125 70c. Los Glaciares, Argentina 65 65

G **98** Man and Woman G **100** Heads

1984. Future for Refugees.
G126 G **98** 35c. black and green 35 35
G127 – 1f.50 black and brown 1·40 1·40
DESIGN: 1f.50, Head of woman.

1984. International Youth Year.
G128 G **100** 1f.20 multicoloured 1·20 1·20

1985. 20th Anniv of Turin Centre of International Labour Organization.
G129 **239** 80c. red 75 75
G130 V **43** 1f.20 green . . . . . 1·10 1·10

G **103** Ploughing and Group of People

1985. 10th Anniv of U.N. University, Tokyo.
G131 G **103** 50c. multicoloured . . 65 65
G132 80c. multicoloured . . 80 80

G **104** Postman G **108** Children

1985.
G133 G **104** 20c. multicoloured . . 20 20
G134 – 1f.20 blue and black 95 95
DESIGN: 1f.20, Doves.

1985. 40th Anniv of United Nations Organization. Multicoloured.
G135 50c. Type **243** 50 50
G136 70c. "Harvest Scene" (Andrew Wyeth) 65 65
MSG137 76 × 81 mm. Nos. G135/6. Imperf . . . . 1·80 1·80

1985. UNICEF. Child Survival Campaign. Multicoloured.
G138 50c. Type G **108** 40 40
G139 1f.20 Child drinking . . . 1·30 1·30

G **110** Children raising Empty Bowls to weeping Mother G **111** Herring Gulls

1986. Africa in Crisis.
G140 G **110** 1f.40 multicoloured 1·50 1·50

1986.
G141 G **111** 5c. multicoloured . . 15 15

G **112** Tents in Clearing

1986. Development Programme. Timber Production. Multicoloured.
G142 35c. Type G **112** . . . . . 2·50 2·30
G143 35c. Felling tree . . . . . 2·50 2·30
G144 35c. Logs on lorries . . . . 2·50 2·30
G145 35c. Girls with sapling . . 2·50 2·30
Nos. G142/5 were printed together, se-tenant, forming a composite design.

1986. Philately: The International Hobby.
G146 **253** 50c. green and red . . . 55 55
G147 – 80c. black and orange 95 95
DESIGN: 80c. United Nations stamps (as Type V **56**).

G **118** Ribbon forming Dove

1986. International Peace Year. Multicoloured.
G148 45c. Type G **118** 55 55
G149 1f.40 "Paix" and olive branch . . . . 1·50 1·60

G120 (½-size illustration)

1986. 40th Anniv of World Federation of United Nations associations. Sheet 120 × 65 mm. Multicoloured.
MSG150 G**120** 35c. Birds (Benigno Gomez); 45c. Circle and prisms (Alexander Calder); 50c. "Eye" (Joan Miro); 70c. Done and musical instruments (Ole Hamann) 6·25 7·50

1987. 9th Death Anniv of Trygve Lie (first U.N. Secretary-General).
G151 **258** 1f.40 multicoloured . . 1·50 1·50

G **122** Abstract

1987. Multicoloured.
G152 90c. Type G **122** 90 90
G153 1f.40 Armillary Sphere, Geneva Centre (30 × 30 mm) . . . . . . 1·40 1·40

G **124** Mixing Cement and Carrying Bricks

1987. International Year of Shelter for the Homeless.
G154 G **124** 50c. green and black 60 60
G155 – 90c. blue, turquoise and black . . 1·10 1·10
DESIGN: 90c. Fitting windows and painting.

G **126** Mother and Baby

1987. Anti-drugs Campaign. Multicoloured.
G156 80c. Type G **126** . . . . . 1·10 1·10
G157 1f.20 Workers in paddy field . . . . 1·60 1·60

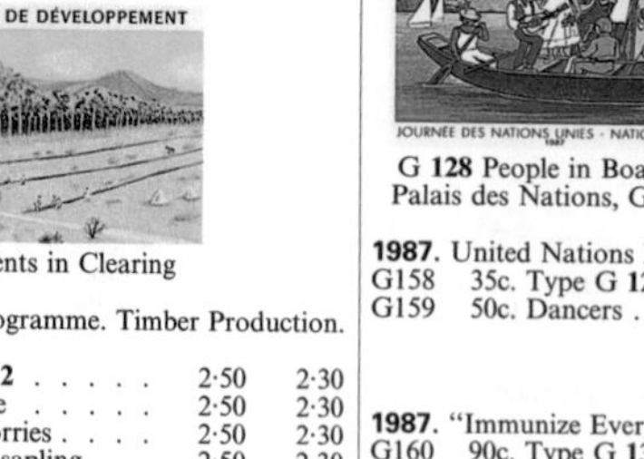

G **128** People in Boat and Palais des Nations, Geneva G **130** Whooping Cough

1987. United Nations Day. Multicoloured.
G158 35c. Type G **128** 45 45
G159 50c. Dancers 75 75

1987. "Immunize Every Child". Multicoloured.
G160 90c. Type G **130** . . . . . 1·00 1·00
G161 1f.70 Tuberculosis . . . . 1·90 1·90

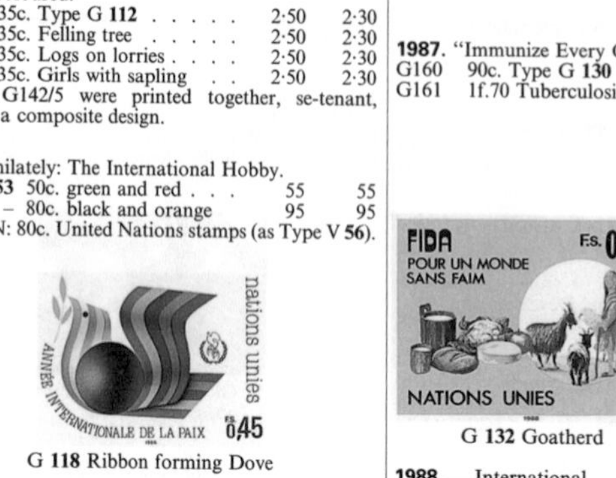

G **132** Goatherd G **134** People

1988. International Fund for Agricultural Development "For a World Without Hunger" Campaign. Multicoloured.
G162 35c. Type G **132** 55 55
G163 1f.40 Women and baskets of fruit . . . . 1·50 1·50

1988.
G164 G **134** 50c. multicoloured . . 50 50

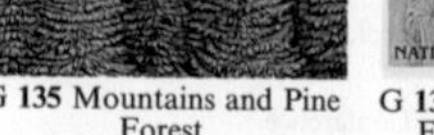

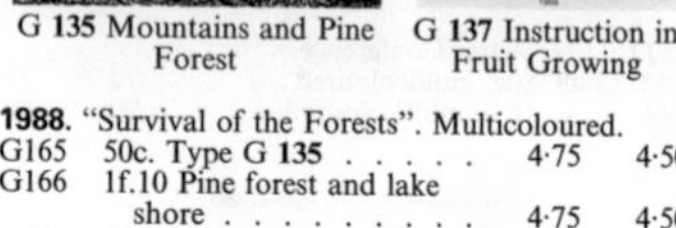

G **135** Mountains and Pine Forest G **137** Instruction in Fruit Growing

1988. "Survival of the Forests". Multicoloured.
G165 50c. Type G **135** . . . . . 4·75 4·50
G166 1f.10 Pine forest and lake shore . . . . 4·75 4·50
Nos. G165/6 were printed together, se-tenant, forming a composite design.

1988. International Volunteer Day. Mult.
G167 80c. Type G **137** 80 80
G168 90c. Teaching animal husbandary (horiz) . . . 95 95

G **139** Football G **142** Communications

1988. "Health in Sports". Multicoloured.
G169 50f. Type G **139** 55 55
G170 1f.40 Swimming . . . . . 1·60 1·60

1988. 40th Anniv of Declaration of Human Rights.
G171 **276** 90c. multicoloured . . . 1·00 1·00
MSG172 120 × 79 mm. 2f. multicoloured . . . . 1·60 1·80

1989. World Bank. Multicoloured.
G173 80c. Type G **142** 85 85
G174 1f.40 Industry . . . . 1·50 1·50

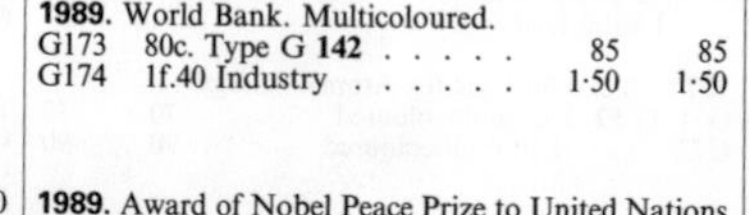

1989. Award of Nobel Peace Prize to United Nations Peace-keeping Forces.
G175 **280** 90c. multicoloured . . . 1·10 1·10

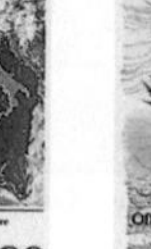

G **145** Cold Arctic Air over Europe G **147** Tree and Birds

1989. 25th Anniv of World Weather Watch.
G176 90c. Type G **145** . . . . . 1·00 1·00
G177 1f.10 Surface temperatures of Kattegat . . . . . . 1·30 1·30

1989. 10th Anniv of United Nations Vienna International Centre.
G178 50c. Type G **147** 75 75
G179 2f. Woman and flower . . 2·10 2·10

G **149** "Young Mother sewing" (Mary Cassatt) (Article 3)

1989. Universal Declaration of Human Rights (1st series). Multicoloured.
G180 35f. Type G **149** 80 80
G181 80f. "Runaway Slave" (Albert Mangones) (Article 4) . . . . 1·80 1·80
See also Nos. G193/4, G209/10, G224/5 and G234/5.

1990. International Trade Centre.
G182 **288** 1f.50 multicoloured . . 1·80 1·80

G **152** Palais des Nations G **155** Frangipani

1990.
G183 G **152** 5f. multicoloured . . 5·00 5·00

1990. Anti-AIDS Campaign. Multicoloured.
G184 50c. Type **289** 65 65
G185 80c. "Man" (Leonardo da Vinci) . . . . 1·10 1·10

1990. Medicinal Plants. Multicoloured.
G186 90c. Type G **155** . . . . . 1·00 1·00
G187 1f.40 "Cinchona officinalis" 1·60 1·60

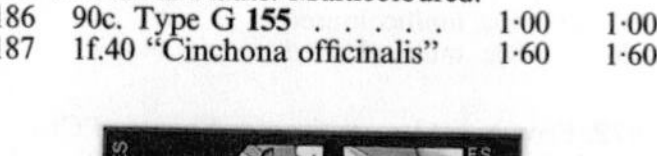

G **157** Projects forming "45"

1990. 45th Anniv of U.N.O. Multicoloured.
G188 90c. Type G **157** . . . . . 1·10 1·10
G189 1f.10 Dove and "45" . . . 1·50 1·50
MSG190 100 × 73 mm. Nos. G188/9 3·25 3·25

G **159** Men making Deal over Painting

1990. Crime Prevention. Multicoloured.
G191 50c. Type G **159** 65 65
G192 2f. Man spilling waste from cart . . . . 2·50 2·50

1990. Universal Declaration of Human Rights (2nd series). As Type G **149**.
G193 35c. multicoloured . . . . 1·20 1·20
G194 90c. black and flesh . . . . 3·00 3·00
DESIGNS: 35c. "Prison Courtyard" (Vincent van Gogh) (Article 9); 90c. "Katho's Son Redeems the Evil Doer from Execution" (Albrecht Durer) (Article 10).

G **163/166** Lake (½-size illustration)

1991. Economic Commission for Europe. "For a Better Environment".

G195	G **163** 90c. multicoloured . .	2·00	2·00
G196	G **164** 90c. multicoloured . .	2·00	2·00
G197	G **165** 90c. multicoloured . .	2·00	2·00
G198	G **166** 90c. multicoloured . .	2·00	2·00

Nos. G195/8 were issued together, se-tenant, forming the composite design illustrated.

G **167** Mountains

G **169** Papers and Ballot Box

1991. 1st Anniv of Namibian Independence. Multicoloured.

G199	70c. Type G **167**	85	75
G200	90c. Baobab	1·00	95

1991. Multicoloured.

G201	80c. Type G **169**	90	90
G202	1f.50 U.N. emblem	1·70	1·70

G **171** Baby in Open Hands (Ryuta Nakajima)

1991. 30th Anniv (1989) of U.N. Declaration of the Rights of the Child and 1990 World Summit on Children, New York. Children's Drawings. Multicoloured.

G203	80c. Type G **171**	1·00	1·00
G204	1f.10 Children playing amongst flowers (David Popper)	1·20	1·20

G **173** Bubble of Toxin, City and Drums

1991. Banning of Chemical Weapons. Mult.

G205	80c. Type G **173**	95	95
G206	1f.40 Hand pushing back gas mask	1·50	1·50

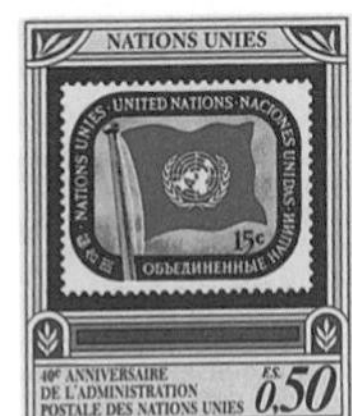

G **175** U.N. (New York) 1951 15c. Stamp

1991. 40th Anniv of United Nations Postal Administration.

G207	G **175** 50c. blue and lilac on cream	60	60
G208	– 1f.60 blue on cream	1·90	1·90

DESIGN: 1f.60, U.N. (New York) 1951 50c. stamp.

1991. Declaration of Human Rights (3rd series). As Type G **149**. Multicoloured.

G209	50c. "Early Morning in Ro, 1925" (Paul Klee) (Article 15)	1·70	1·70
G210	90c. "The Marriage of Arnolfini" (Jan van Eyck) (Article 16) . . .	3·25	3·25

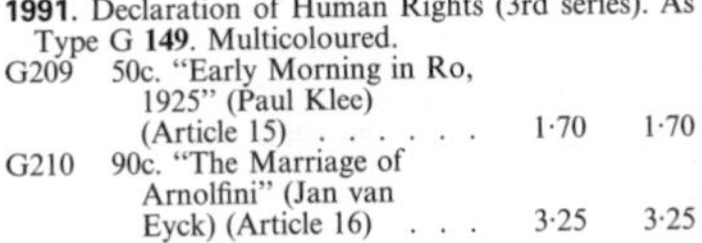

G **179** Sagarmatha National Park, Nepal

G **181** U.N. Headquarters, New York

1992. 20th Anniv of UNESCO World Heritage Convention. Multicoloured.

G211	50c. Type G **179**	60	60
G212	1f.10 Stonehenge, United Kingdom	1·70	1·70

1992.

G213	G **181** 3f. multicoloured . .	3·00	3·00

G **182/183** Sea Life (½-size illustration)

1992. "Clean Oceans".

G214	G **182** 80c. multicoloured . .	1·40	1·40
G215	G **183** 80c. multicoloured . .	1·40	1·40

Nos. G214/15 were issued together, se-tenant, forming the composite design illustrated.

G **184/187** Planet Earth (½-size illustration)

1992. 2nd U.N. Conference on Environment and Development, Rio de Janeiro.

G216	G **184** 75c. multicoloured . .	1·10	1·10
G217	G **185** 75c. multicoloured . .	1·10	1·10
G218	G **186** 75c. multicoloured . .	1·10	1·10
G219	G **187** 75c. multicoloured . .	1·10	1·10

Nos. G216/19 were issued together, se-tenant, forming the composite design illustrated.

G **188/189** "Mission Planet Earth" (⅔-size illustration)

1992. International Space Year. Roul.

G220	G **188** 1f.10 multicoloured	1·60	1·60
G221	G **189** 1f.10 multicoloured	1·60	1·60

Nos. G220/1 were issued together, se-tenant, forming the composite design illustrated.

G **190** Women in Science and Technology

G **194** Voluntary Work

1992. Commission on Science and Technology for Development. Multicoloured.

G222	90c. Type G **190**	1·10	1·10
G223	1f.60 Graduate using V.D.U.	1·90	1·90

1992. Universal Declaration of Human Rights (4th series). As Type G **149**. Multicoloured.

G224	50c. "The Oath of the Tennis Court" (Jacques Louis David) (Article 21)	1·70	1·70
G225	90c. "Rocking Chair I" (Henry Moore) (Article 22)	3·25	3·25

1993. "Ageing: Dignity and Participation". 10th Anniv (1992) of International Plan of Action on Ageing. Multicoloured.

G226	50c. Type G **194**	60	60
G227	1f.60 Security of employment	1·80	1·80

G **196** Gorilla

1993. Endangered Species (1st series). Multicoloured.

G228	80c. Type G **196**	90	90
G229	80c. Peregrine falcon ("Falco peregrinus") . .	90	90
G230	80c. Amazon manatee ("Tricheous inunguis")	90	90
G231	80c. Snow leopard ("Panthera uncia") . . .	90	90

See also Nos. G246/9, G264/7, G290/3, G308/11, G333/6, G372/5, G389/92, G409/12 and G433/6.

G **200** Neighbourhood and Community Environment

1993. 45th Anniv of W.H.O. Multicoloured.

G232	60c. Type G **200**	75	75
G233	1f. Urban environment . .	1·20	1·20

1993. Declaration of Human Rights (5th series). As Type G **149**. Multicoloured.

G234	50c. "Three Musicians" (Pablo Picasso) (Article 27)	1·40	1·40
G235	90c. "Voice of Space" (Rene Magritte) (Article 28)	2·75	2·75

G **204/207** Peace (½-size illustration)

1993. International Peace Day. Roul.

G236	G **204** 60c. multicoloured . .	95	95
G237	G **205** 60c. multicoloured . .	95	95
G238	G **206** 60c. multicoloured . .	95	95
G239	G **207** 60c. multicoloured . .	95	95

Nos. G236/9 were issued together, se-tenant, forming the composite design illustrated.

G **208** Polar Bears

1993. The Environment—Climate. Multicoloured.

G240	1f.10 Type G **208**	1·60	1·60
G241	1f.10 Whale in melting ice	1·60	1·60
G242	1f.10 Elephant seal	1·60	1·60
G243	1f.10 Adelie penguins . . .	1·60	1·60

Nos. G240/3 were issued together, se-tenant, forming a composite design.

G **212** Father calling Child

G **218** Hand delivering Refugee to New Country

1994. International Year of the Family. Mult.

G244	80c. Type G **212**	85	85
G245	1f. Three generations . . .	1·20	1·60

1994. Endangered Species (2nd series). As Type G **196.** Multicoloured.

G246	80c. Mexican prairie dogs ("Cynomys mexicanus")	90	90
G247	80c. Jabiru ("Jabiru mycteria")	90	90
G248	80c. Blue whale ("Balaenoptera musculus")	90	90
G249	80c. Golden lion tamarin ("Leontopithecus rosalia")	90	90

1994. U.N. High Commissioner for Refugees.

G250	G **218** 1f.20 multicoloured	1·50	1·50

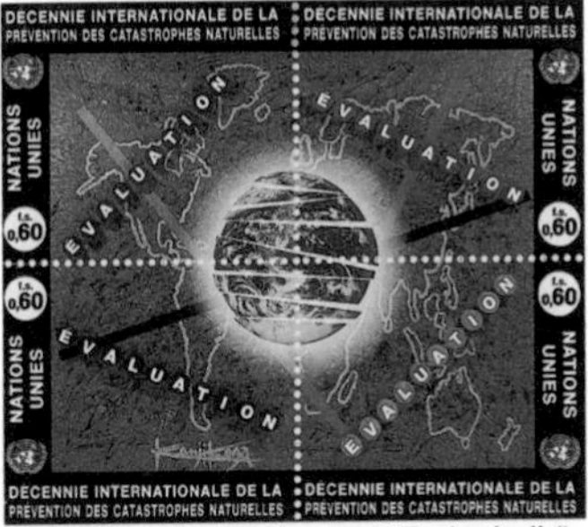

G **219/222** Shattered Globe and "Evaluation" (⅔-size illustration)

1994. International Decade for Natural Disaster Reduction.

G251	G **219** 60c. multicoloured . .	1·00	1·00
G252	G **220** 60c. multicoloured . .	1·00	1·00
G253	G **221** 60c. multicoloured . .	1·00	1·00
G254	G **222** 60c. multicoloured . .	1·00	1·00

Nos. G251/4 were issued together, se-tenant, forming the composite design illustrated.

G **223** Mobilization of Resources in Developing Countries

1994. International Population and Development Conference, Cairo. Multicoloured.

G255	60c. Type G **223**	65	65
G256	80c. Internal migration of population	85	85

G **225** Palais des Nations, Geneva

1994. Multicoloured.

G257	60c. Type G **225**	70	70
G258	80c. "Creation of the World" (detail of tapestry, Oili Maki) . . .	95	95
G259	1f.80 Palais des Nations . .	1·90	1·90

G **228** Map and Linked Ribbons

1994. 30th Anniv of United Nations Conference on Trade and Development.

G260	80c. Type G **228**	1·00	1·00
G261	1f. Map and ribbons . . .	1·20	1·20

1995. 50th Anniv of U.N.O. (1st issue).

G262	**371** 80c. multicoloured . . .	95	95

See also Nos. G270/1 and G275/86.

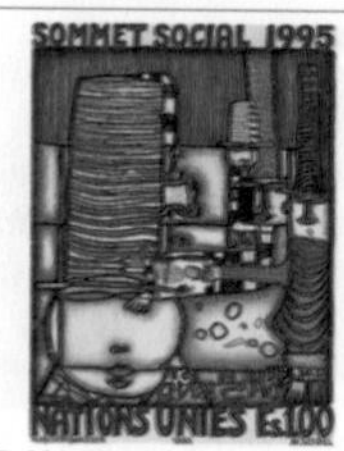

G **231** "Social Summit 1995"

1995. World Summit for Social Development, Copenhagen.
G263 G **231** 1f. multicoloured . . 1·40 1·40

1995. Endangered Species (3rd series). As Type G **196**. Multicoloured.
G264 80c. Crowned lemur ("Lemur coronatus") . . 90 95
G265 80c. Giant scops owl ("Otus gurneyi") 90 95
G266 80c. Painted frog ("Atelopus varius zeteki") 90 95
G267 80c. American wood bison ("Bison bison athabascae") 90 95

G **236** Field in Summer

1995. "Youth: Our Future". 10th Anniv of International Youth Year. Multicoloured.
G268 80c. Type G **236** 95 95
G269 1f. Field in winter . . . . 1·20 1·20

1995. 50th Anniv of U.N.O. (2nd issue).
G270 **379** 60c. purple 75 75
G271 – 1f.80 green . . . . . . 1·90 1·90
MSG272 92 × 70 mm. Nos. G270/1. Imperf . . . . 2·75 2·75
DESIGN: 1f.80, Veteran's Memorial Hall and Opera House, San Francisco (venue for signing of Charter).

G **240** Woman and Cranes G **254** Catching Fish

1995. 4th World Conference on Women, Peking. Multicoloured.
G273 60c. Type G **240** 80 80
G274 1f. Women worshipping (30 × 49 mm) . . . . . . 1·20 1·20

1995. 50th Anniv of U.N.O. (3rd issue).
G275 **385** 30c. multicoloured . . . 40 40
G276 **386** 30c. multicoloured . . . 40 40
G277 **387** 30c. multicoloured . . . 40 40
G278 **388** 30c. multicoloured . . . 40 40
G279 **389** 30c. multicoloured . . . 40 40
G280 **390** 30c. multicoloured . . . 40 40
G281 **391** 30c. multicoloured . . . 40 40
G282 **392** 30c. multicoloured . . . 40 40
G283 **393** 30c. multicoloured . . . 40 40
G284 **394** 30c. multicoloured . . . 40 40
G285 **395** 30c. multicoloured . . . 40 40
G286 **396** 30c. multicoloured . . . 40 40
Nos. G275/80 and G281/6 respectively were issued together, se-tenant, forming two composite designs.

1996. 50th Anniv of World Federation of United Nations Associations.
G287 G **254** 80c. multicoloured . . 1·10 1·10

G **255** "Galloping Horse treading on a Flying Swallow" (Chinese bronze sculpture, Han Dynasty)

1996. Multicoloured.
G288 40c. Type G **255** 40 45
G289 70c. Palais des Nations, Geneva 75 85

1996. Endangered Species (4th series). As Type G **196**. Multicoloured.
G290 80c. "Paphiopedilum delenatii" 85 85
G291 80c. "Pachypodium baronii" 85 85
G292 80c. Yellow amaryllis ("Sternbergia lutea") . . 85 85
G293 80c. Cobra plant ("Darlingtonia californica") 85 85

G **261** Family on Verandah of House

1996. "Habitat II" Second United Nations Conference on Human Settlements, Istanbul, Turkey. Multicoloured.
G294 70c. Type G **261** 85 85
G295 70c. Women in traditional dress in gardens . . . . 1·10 1·10
G296 70c. Produce seller and city 1·10 1·10
G297 70c. Boys playing on riverside . . . . 1·10 1·10
G298 70c. Elderly couple reading newspaper . . . . 1·10 1·10
Nos. G294/8 were issued together, se-tenant, forming a composite design.

G **266** Cycling G **268** Birds in Treetop

1996. Sport and the Environment. Multicoloured.
G299 70c. Type G **266** 75 75
G300 1f.10 Running (horiz) . . . 1·30 1·30
MSG301 88 × 78 mm. Nos. G299/300 . . . . 1·60 1·60

1996. "A Plea for Peace". Winning Entries in China Youth Design Competition. Multicoloured.
G302 90c. Type G **268** 95 95
G303 1f.10 Flowers growing from bomb . . . . 1·30 1·30

G **270** "The Sun and the Moon" (South American legend)

1996. 50th Anniv of UNICEF. Multicoloured.
G304 70c. Type G **270** 80 80
G305 1f.80 "Ananse" (African spider tale) . . . . . . 1·70 1·70

G **272** U.N. Flag

1997.
G306 10c. Type G **272** 15 15
G307 1f.10 "Building Palais des Nations" (detail of fresco, Massimo Campigli) . . . . 1·10 1·10

1997. Endangered Species (5th series). As Type G **196**. Multicoloured.
G308 80f. Polar bear ("Ursus maritimus") 85 85
G309 80f. Blue crowned pigeon ("Goura cristata") . . . 85 85
G310 80f. Marine iguana ("Amblyrhynchus cristatus") 85 85
G311 80f. Guanaco ("Lama guanicoe") 85 85

G **278/281** Sunrise over Mountains (¾-size illustration)

1997. "Earth Summit + 5". 5th Anniv of United Nations Conference on Environment and Development.
G312 G **278** 45f. multicoloured . . 60 60
G313 G **279** 45f. multicoloured . . 60 60
G314 G **280** 45f. multicoloured . . 60 60
G315 G **281** 45f. multicoloured . . 60 60
MSG316 90 × 75 mm. 1f.10 Motifs as Nos. G312/15. Imperf . . . 1·25 1·25
Nos. G312/15 were issued together, se-tenant, forming the composite design illustrated.

G **282** Fokker F.7 Trimotor and Airship

1997. 50th Anniversaries of Economic Commission for Europe and Economic and Social Commission for Asia and the Pacific. Multicoloured.
G317 70f. Type G **282** . . . . . 1·00 1·00
G318 70f. Lockheed Constellation and Boeing 314 flying boat . . . . 1·00 1·00
G319 70f. De Havilland D.H.106 Comet and Boeing 747 jetliners . . . . 1·00 1·00
G320 70f. Ilyushin and Boeing 747 jetliners . . . . . 1·00 1·00
G321 70f. Concorde Supersonic jetliner . . . . 1·00 1·00
Nos. 317/21 were issued together, se-tenant, forming a composite design.

1997. "Tribute to Philately". Multicoloured.
G322 70c. Type G **432** 85 85
G323 1f.10 1986 80c. philately stamp (as Type V **227**) 1·20 1·20

1997. 25th Anniv of World Heritage Convention. Terracotta Warriors from Emperor Qin Shi Huang's Tomb, Xian, China. Multicoloured.
G324 10c. As Type **434** 35 35
G325 10c. As No. 737 . . . . . 55 55
G326 10c. As No. 738 . . . . . 25 25
G327 10c. As No. 739 . . . . . 25 25
G328 10c. As No. 740 . . . . . 25 25
G329 10c. As No. 741 . . . . . 25 25
G330 45c. As No. 738 . . . . . 50 50
G331 70c. As No. 739 . . . . . 70 70

G **295** Palais des Nations, Geneva

1998.
G332 G **295** 2f. multicoloured . . 2·10 2·10

1998. Endangered Species (6th series). As Type G **196**. Multicoloured.
G333 80c. Tibetan stump-tailed macaques ("Macaca thibetana") 85 85
G334 80c. Greater flamingoes ("Phoenicopterus ruber") 85 85
G335 80c. Queen Alexandra's birdwings ("Ornithoptera alexandrae") 85 85
G336 80c. Fallow deer ("Cervus dama") 85 85

G **300** Bull Seal

1998. International Year of the Ocean. Multicoloured.
G337 45c. Type G **300** 50 50
G338 45c. Polar bears 50 50
G339 45c. Polar bear, musk oxen, king penguins and seal on ice 50 50
G340 45c. Diver 50 50
G341 45c. Seals 50 50
G342 45c. Narwhal 50 50
G343 45c. Fishes and shark . . . 50 50
G344 45c. Shark's tail, seal and horned puffin 50 50
G345 45c. Fishes and gentoo penguin's back 50 50
G346 45c. Fish and jellyfishes . . 50 50
G347 45c. Seal, gentoo penguin and squid 50 50
G348 45c. gentoo penguin hunting fishes 50 50

G **301** Orang-utan with Young

1998. Rainforest Preservation.
G349 G **301** 70c. multicoloured . . 85 85
MSG350 82 × 70 mm. G **301** 3f. multicoloured . . . . 3·00 3·00

G **302** Soldier with Children

1998. 50 Years of United Nations Peacekeeping. Multicoloured.
G351 70c. Type G **302** 75 75
G352 90c. Soldier holding baby 1·00 1·00

G **304** Birds

1998. 50th Anniv of Universal Declaration of Human Rights. Multicoloured.
G353 90c. Type G **304** . . . . . 1·00 1·00
G354 1f.80 Hand releasing birds 2·00 2·00

1998. World Heritage Site. Schonbrunn Palace, Vienna. Multicoloured.
G355 10c. As No. 780 . . . . . 50 55
G356 10c. As No. 781 . . . . . 60 60
G357 10c. As No. 782 . . . . . 30 30
G358 30c. As Type **454** 40 45
G359 30c. As No. 778 . . . . . 40 45
G360 30c. As No. 779 . . . . . 40 45
G361 70c. As No. 781 . . . . . 60 60
G362 1f.10 As Type **454** . . . . 1·20 1·30

G **312** Palais Wilson, Geneva

1999. Headquarters of United Nations High Commissioner for Human Rights.
G363 G **312** 1f.70 red . . . . . . 1·90 1·90

1999. World Heritage Sites in Australia. Mult.
G364 10c. As Type **462** 25 25
G365 10c. As No. 796 . . . . . 20 20
G366 10c. As No. 797 . . . . . 20 20
G367 20c. As No. 798 . . . . . 30 30
G368 20c. As No. 799 . . . . . 30 30
G369 20c. As No. 800 . . . . . 30 30
G370 90c. As No. 801 . . . . . 1·10 1·10
G371 1f.10 As No. 802 . . . . . 1·30 1·30

1999. Endangered Species (7th series). As Type G **196**. Multicoloured.
G372 90c. Asiatic wild ass ("Equus hemionus") . . 95 95
G373 90c. Hyacinth macaw ("Anodorhynchus hyacinthinus") 95 95
G374 90c. Jamaican boa ("Epicrates subflavus") 95 95
G375 90c. Bennett's tree kangaroo ("Dendrolagus bennettianus") 95 95

G 323/324 Satellite-aided Agriculture (½-size illustration)

1999. 3rd Conference on Exploration and Peaceful Uses of Outer Space, Vienna.
G376 G **323** 45c. multicoloured . . 60 60
G377 G **324** 45c. multicoloured . . 60 60
MSG378 90 × 75 mm. 2f. Combined design as Nos. G376/7 (71 × 29 mm) . . . . 1·90 1·90
MSG379 90 × 75 mm. 2f. As No. **MS**G378 but additionally inscr "PHILEXFRANCE 99 LE MONDIAL DU TIMBRE PARIS 2 AU 11 JUILLET 1999" in bottom margin . . . . 2·00 2·00
Nos. G376/7 were issued together, se-tenant, forming the composite design illustrated.

G 325/328 Early 20th-century Mail Transport (½-size illustration)

1999. 125th Anniv of Universal Postal Union.
G380 G **325** 70c. multicoloured . . 85 85
G381 G **326** 70c. multicoloured . . 85 85
G382 G **327** 70c. multicoloured . . 85 85
G383 G **328** 70c. multicoloured . . 85 85
Nos. G380/3 were issued together, se-tenant, forming the composite design illustrated.

G 329 Palais des Nations, Geneva

1999. "In Memoriam: Fallen in the Cause of Peace".
G384 G **329** 1f.10 multicoloured 1·30 1·30
MSG385 90 × 75 mm. 2f. multicoloured . . . . 2·10 2·10

G 331 Couple on Globe

1999. Education: Keystone to the 21st Century.
G386 90c. Type G **331** . . . . . 1·00 1·00
G387 1f.80 "Environment" . . . 2·10 2·10

2000. International Year of Thanksgiving. Mult.
G388 90c. As Type **483** . . . . 1·30 1·30

2000. Endangered Species (8th series). As Type G **196**. Multicoloured.
G389 90c. Hippopotamus (*Hippopotamus amphibius*) 1·40 1·40
G390 90c. Coscoroba swan (*Coscoroba coscoroba*) . . 1·40 1·40
G391 90c. Emerald monitor (*Varanus prasinus*) . . . 1·40 1·40
G392 90c. Sea otter (*Enhydra lutris*) . . . . 1·40 1·40

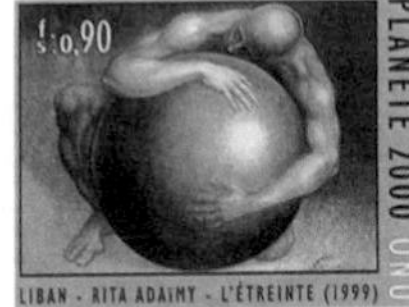

G 338 "The Embrace" (Rita Adaimy)

2000. "Our World 2000" International Art Exhibition, New York. Entries in Millennium Painting Competition. Multicoloured.
G393 90c. Type G **338** . . . . . 1·30 1·30
G394 1f.10 "Living Single" (Richard Kimanthi) (vert) 1·30 1·30

G 340 Corner Stone Dedication, 1949

2000. 55th Anniv of the United Nations and 50th Anniv of Opening of U.N. Headquarters, New York.
G395 G **340** 90c. red, blue and ochre . . . . . . 1·20 1·20
G396 – 1f.40 red, blue and ochre . . . . . . 1·50 1·50
MSG397 67x86 mm. Nos. G395/6 2·70 2·70
DESIGN: 1f.40, Window cleaner, Secretariat Building, 1951.

G 342 Two Women

G 343 (½-size illustration)

2000. "The United Nations of the 21st century". Sheet 141 × 165 mm containing Type G **342** and similar horiz designs, forming the overall design Type G **343**. Multicoloured.
MSG398 50c. Type G **342**; 50c. Man carrying bricks on head; 50c. Soldier and villagers; 50c. Dam and doves; 50c. Men digging; 50c. Men damming irrigation channel 2·75 2·75

2000. World Heritage Sites in Spain. Multicoloured.
G399 10c. As Type **496** 25 25
G400 10c. As No. 832 . . . . . 25 25
G401 10c. As No. 833 . . . . . 25 25
G402 20c. As No. 834 . . . . . 25 25
G403 20c. As No. 835 . . . . . 25 25
G404 20c. As No. 836 . . . . . 25 25
G405 1f. As No. 837 . . . . . . 1·10 1·10
G406 1f.20 As No. 838 . . . . . 1·20 1·20

G 350 Family of Refugees

2000. 50th Anniv of United Nations High Commissioner for Refugees.
G407 G **350** 80c. multicoloured . . 1·10 1·10
MSG408 121 × 82 mm. 1f.80 multicoloured . . . . 1·75 1·75

2001. Endangered Species (9th series). As Type G **196**. Multicoloured.
G409 90c. Lynx (*Felis lynx canadensis*) . . . . . . 1·10 1·10
G410 90c. Green peafowl (*Pavo muticus*) . . . . 1·10 1·10
G411 90c. Galapagos tortoise (*Geochelone elephantopus*) 1·10 1·10
G412 90c. Lemur (*Lepilemur* sp.) 1·10 1·10

G 356 Hands forming Heart (Ernest Pignon-Ernest)

2001. United Nations International Year of Volunteers. Multicoloured.
G413 90c. Type G **356** . . . . . 1·10 1·10
G414 1f.30 Women's head and white dove (Paul Siche) 1·20 1·20

2001. World Heritage Sites in Japan. Multicoloured.
G415 10c. As Type **512** 20 20
G416 10c. As No. 858 . . . . . 20 20
G417 10c. As No. 859 . . . . . 20 20
G418 30c. As No. 860 . . . . . 40 40
G419 30c. As No. 861 . . . . . 40 40
G420 30c. As No. 862 . . . . . 40 40
G421 1f.10 As No. 858 . . . . . 1·20 1·20
G422 1f.30 As No. 861 . . . . . 1·00 1·60

2001. 40th Death Anniv of Dag Hammarskjold (United Nations Secretary General, 1953–61).
G423 **518** 2f. red . . . . 1·30 1·30

G 365 Postman and "Stamps"

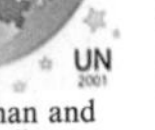

G 368 Flowers and Coastline

2001. 50th Anniv of United Nations Postal Administration.
G424 G **365** 90c. multicoloured . . 95 95
G425 – 1f.30 multicoloured 1·40 1·40
MS426 102 × 102 mm. 1f.30, 1f.80 cobalt and carmine . . . . . 3·00 3·00
DESIGNS: G425, Trumpets and "Stamps"; **MS**426, Emblem.

2001. Climate Change. Multicoloured.
G427 90c. Type G **368** 95 95
G428 90c. Wind-powered generators and brick making 95 95
G429 90c. Power station inside glass dome 95 95
G430 90c. Couple sitting beside lake 95 95
Nos. G427/30 were issued together, se-tenant, forming a composite design.

2001. Kofi Annan, Winner of Nobel Peace Prize, 2001.
G431 **526** 90c. multicoloured . . . 95 95

G 373 Armillary Sphere, Ariana Park

2002.
G432 G **373** 1f.30 multicoloured 1·00 1·00

2002. Endangered Species (10th series). As Type G **196**. Multicoloured.
G433 90c. Bald uakari (*Cacajao calvus*) 95 95
G434 90c. Ratel (*Mellivora capensis*) 95 95
G435 90c. Pallas's cat (*Otocolobus manul*) 95 95
G436 90c. Savannah monitor (*Varanus exanthematicus*) 95 95

2002. East Timor Independence. As T **532**. Multicoloured.
G437 90c. Wooden statue 75 75
G438 1f.30 Carved wooden container . . . . 1·10 1·10

2002. International Year of Mountains. As T **534**. Multicoloured.
G439 70c. Type Weisshorn, Switzerland 55 55
G440 70c. Mount Fuji, Japan . . 55 55
G441 1f.20 Vinson Massif, Antarctica 95 95
G442 1f.20 Kamet, India 95 95

G 384 Sun, Water, Birds and Flowers

2002. World Summit on Sustainable Development, Johannesburg. Multicoloured.
G443 90c. Type G **384** 75 75
G444 90c. Figure's wearing fashionable dress 75 75
G445 1f.80 Women's profile . . . 1·50 1·50
G446 1f.80 Yacht . . . . 1·50 1·50

2002. World Heritage Sites in Italy. As T **542**. Multicoloured.
G447 10c. Duomo di Sant'Andrea, Amalfi Coast 10 10
G448 10c. View across Islands, Aeolian Islands 10 10
G449 10c. Del Moro Fountain, Rome 10 10
G450 20c. Santa Maria del Fiore, Florence 20 20
G451 20c. Leaning Tower, Pisa 20 20
G452 20c. The Forum, Pompeii 20 20
G453 90c. As No. G451 . . . . 80 80
G454 1f.30 As No. G448 . . . . 1·20 1·20

2002. AIDS Awareness Campaign. As T **548**.
G455 1f.30 AIDS Symbol on UN Secretariat Building, New York . . . . 1·20 1·20
MSG456 80 × 80 mm. 90c.+30c. AIDS symbol on UN Secretariat Building, New York at night 1·20 1·20
The premium was for AIDS charities.

G 396 Doves

2002.
G457 G **396** 3f. multicoloured . . 2·75 2·75

2003. Indigenous Art. Sheet 121 × 97 mm. As T **550**. Multicoloured.
MSG458 90c. Inca poncho, Peru; 90c. Bahia statue, Brazil; 90c. Blanket, Ecuador; 90c. Mayan stone sculpture, Xunantunich, Belize; 90c. Embroidered fabric, Guatemala; 90c. Colima terracotta sculpture, Mexico . . . . . . 4·75 4·75

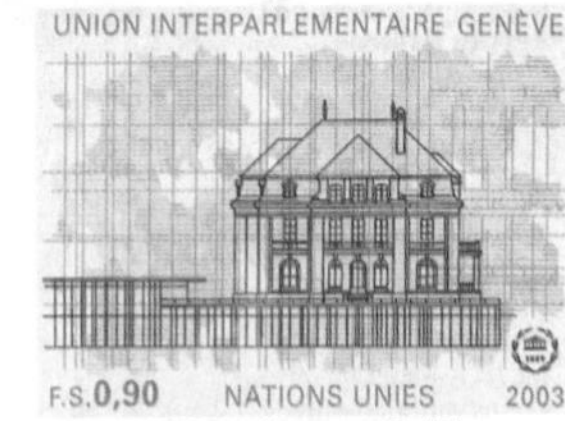

G 398 Headquarters Building

2003. Inauguration of New Inter-Parliamentary Union Headquarters, Geneva.
G459 G **398** 90c. multicoloured . . 80 80

2003. 30th Anniv of Convention on International Trade in Endangered Species (CITES). As T **555**. Multicoloured.
G460 90c. Red-breasted goose (*Branta ruficollis*) 80 80
G461 90c. Bald ibis (*Geronticus calvus*) 80 80
G462 90c. Fulvous whistling duck (*Dendrocygna bicolour*) 80 80
G463 90c. Channel-billed toucan (*Ramphastos vitellinus*) 80 80

2003. International Year of Freshwater. As T **559**. Multicoloured.
G464 70c. Autumnal trees and stream 60 60
G465 1f.30 Depleted lake . . . . 1·10 1·10
Nos. G464/5 were issued together, se-tenant, forming a composite design.

2003. World Heritage Sites in USA. As T **561**. Showing USA National Parks. Multicoloured.
G466 10c. Yosemite National Park 10 10
G467 10c. Smoky Mountains . . 10 10
G468 10c. Olympic National Park 10 10
G469 30c. Hawaii Volcanoes . . 25 25
G470 30c. Everglades 25 25
G471 30c. Yellowstone National Park 25 25
G472 90c. As G470 . . . . 80 80
G473 1f.30 As G471 . . . . . . 1·10 1·10
Nos. G466/73 have chestnut bands top and bottom.

2003. Ralph Bunche (politician) Commemoration. As T **567**. Multicoloured.
G474 1f.80 Ralph Bunche . . . . 1·60 1·60

2003. In Memoriam. Support for United Nations Staff Killed or Injured in Terrorist Attacks. As T **568**. Multicoloured.
G475 85c. Flag at half-mast . . . 75 75

C. VIENNA HEADQUARTERS.

For use on mail posted at the United Nations Vienna International Centre and by the International Atomic Energy Agency.

1979. 100 groschen = 1 schilling.
2002. 100 cents = 1 euro.

NOTE. Reference to numbers and types in this section, other than those with a "V" prefix, are to the United Nations (New York or Geneva) Headquarters listing. Designs adapted for the Vienna issues are inscribed in Austrian and have face values in schillings.

V **4** Donaupark Complex

1979. Some designs adapted from issues of New York or Geneva Headquarters. Multicoloured.
V1 50g. Type G **53** 10 10
V2 1s. As No. 94 . . . . 10 10
V3 2s.50 Type **162** 30 30
V3a 3s. "... for a better world" 35 35
V4 4s. Type V **4** 35 35
V5 5s. Type A **134** 45 40
V6 6s. Aerial view of Donaupark (vert) 55 50
V7 10s. As Type **52**, but without frame 90 85

1980. New International Economic Order.
V8 **195** 4s. multicoloured . . . . 1·10 1·10

V **9** Dove and World Map

1980. U.N. Decade for Women.
V 9 V **9** 4s. multicoloured 40 40
V10 6s. multicoloured 60 60

V **10** "Peace-keeping"

V **11** Dove and "35"

1980. Peace-keeping Operations.
V11 V **10** 6s. multicoloured . . . 70 70

1980. 35th Anniv of U.N.O.
V12 V **11** 4s. black and red . . . 40 40
V13 – 6s. multicoloured . . . 60 60
MSV14 92 × 73 mm. Nos. V12/13. Imperf . . . . 1·25 1·10
DESIGN: 6s. Stylized flower.

V **13** Economic and Social Emblems

1980. Economic and Social Council. Multicoloured.
V15 V **13** 4s. multicoloured . . . 40 40
V16 – 6s. green, red and black 60 60
DESIGN: 6s. Figures ascending graph.

1981. "Inalienable Rights of the Palestinian People".
V17 **206** 4s. multicoloured 40 40

1981. International Year of Disabled Persons.
V18 **207** 4s. multicoloured 40 40
V19 – 6s. orange and black . . 60 60
DESIGN: 6s. Knot pattern.

1981. Art.
V20 **209** 6s. multicoloured 65 65

V **19** U.N. Energy Conference Emblem

1981. New and Renewable Sources of Energy.
V21 V **19** 7s.50 gold and mauve 85 85

V **20** Symbols of Services

1981. 10th Anniv of U.N. Volunteers Programme. Multicoloured.
V22 5s. Type V **20** 50 50
V23 7s. Emblems of science, agriculture and industry 75 75

V **22** Symbols of the Environment

V **24** Satellite and Emblems

1982. Human Environment. Multicoloured.
V24 5s. Type V **22** 50 50
V25 7s. Leaves 75 75

1982. Second United Nations Conference on Exploration and Peaceful Uses of Outer Space.
V26 V **24** 5s. multicoloured . . . 55 55

V **25** Fish

V **28** Radar Screen within Lifebelt

1982. Conservation and Protection of Nature. Multicoloured.
V27 5s. Type V **25** 45 45
V28 7s. Elephant (mammals) . . 80 80

1983. World Communications Year.
V29 **222** 4s. multicoloured 40 40

1983. Safety at Sea: International Maritime Organization. Multicoloured.
V30 4s. Type V **28** 40 40
V31 6s. Stylized liner 60 60

1983. World Food Programme.
V32 **226** 5s. green 50 45
V33 7s. brown 70 70

V **31** Exports

V **33** "Die Zweite Haut"

1983. Trade and Development. Multicoloured.
V34 5s. Type V **31** 45 45
V35 8s.50 Emblems of trade . . . 90 90

1983. 35th Anniv of Declaration of Human Rights. Multicoloured.
V36 5s. Type V **33** 80 80
V37 7s. "Recht auf Traume" . . 1·10 1·10

V **35** World Agriculture

1984. International Conference on Population, Mexico City.
V38 V **35** 7s. multicoloured . . . 80 80

V **36** Irrigation

1984. World Food Day. Multicoloured.
V39 4s.50 Type V **36** 45 45
V40 6s. Combine harvesters . . . 65 65

V **38** Serengeti National Park, Tanzania

V **40** Woman with Child

1984. World Heritage—UNESCO. Mult.
V41 3s.50 Type V **38** 35 35
V42 15s. Schibam, Yemen . . . . 1·50 1·50

1984. Future for Refugees.
V43 V **40** 4s.50 black and brown 50 50
V44 – 8s.50 black and yellow 90 90
DESIGN: 8s.50, Woman.

V **42** Stylized Figures

V **43** U Thant Pavilion

1984. International Youth Year.
V45 V **42** 3s.50 multicoloured . . 35 35
V46 6s.50 multicoloured . . 75 75

1985. 20th Anniv of Turin Centre of International Labour Organization.
V47 V **43** 7s.50 violet 85 85

V **44** Rural Scene and Researcher with Microscope

1985. 10th Anniv of United Nations University, Tokyo.
V48 V **44** 8s.50 multicoloured . . 1·00 1·00

V **45** "Boat"

V **49** Oral Immunization

1985. Multicoloured.
V49 4s.50 Type V **45** 50 45
V50 15s. Sheltering under U.N. umbrella . . . . 1·60 1·40

1985. 40th Anniv of United Nations Organization. Multicoloured.
V51 6s.50 Type **243** 70 70
V52 8s.50 "Harvest Scene" (Andrew Wyeth) 90 90
MSV52 8s.50 76 × 82 mm. Nos. V51/2. Imperf . . . . 1·75 1·60

1985. UNICEF. Child Survival Campaign. Multicoloured.
V54 4s. Type V **49** 60 60
V55 6s. Mother and baby 85 85

V **51** "Africa in Crisis"

V **52** Growing Crops

1986. "Africa in Crisis".
V56 V **51** 8s. multicoloured . . . 1·00 1·00

1986. Development Programme. Village Scene. Multicoloured.
V57 4s.50 Type V **52** 75 75
V58 4s.50 Villagers with livestock 75 75
V59 4s.50 Woodwork instructor 75 75
V60 4s.50 Nutrition instructor . . 75 75
Nos. V57/60 were issued together, se-tenant, forming a composite design.

V **56** United Nations Stamps

1986. Philately: The International Hobby.
V61 V **56** 3s.50 blue and brown 55 55
V62 – 6s.50 blue and red . . . 90 90
DESIGN: 6s.50, Engraver.

V **58** Olive Branch and Rainbow

1986. International Peace Year. Multicoloured.
V63 5s. Type V **58** 70 70
V64 6s. Doves on U.N. emblem 85 85

V **60** (⅓-size illustration)

1986. 40th Anniv of World Federation of United Nations Associations Sheet 120 × 65 mm. Multicoloured.
MSV65 V **60** 4s. Horse's head (Elisabeth von Janota-Bzowski; 5s. Horse rider carved from rock face (Ernst Fuchs); 6s. Abstract (Victor Vassrely); 7s. Couple (Wofgang Hutter) . . . . 3·50 3·25

1986. 9th Death Anniv of Trygve Lie (first U.N. Secretary-General).
V66 **259** 8s. multicoloured . . . . 1·20 1·20

V **62** Family looking at New Houses

1987. International Year of Shelter for the Homeless.
V67 V **62** 4s. orange, blk & yell 60 60
V68 – 9s.50 orange and black 1·30 1·30
DESIGN: 9s.50, Family entering door of new house.

V **64** Footballers

1987. Anti-drugs Campaign. Multicoloured.
V69 5s. Type V **64** 70 70
V70 8s. Family . . . . 1·20 1·20

V **66** U.N. Centre, Vienna

1987. Multicoloured.
V71 2s. Type V **66** 25 25
V72 17s. Wreath of olive leaves and doves around globe 2·10 1·80

V **68** Dancers and Vienna Headquarters
V **70** Poliomyelitis

1987. United Nations Day. Multicoloured.
V73 5s. Type V **68** 65 65
V74 6s. Dancers 75 75

1987. "Immunize Every Child". Multicoloured.
V75 4s. Type V **70** 60 60
V76 9s.50 Diphtheria . . . . . . 1·40 1·40

V **72** Woman planting

1987. International Fund for Agricultural Development "For a World without Hunger" Campaign. Multicoloured.
V77 4s. Type V **72** 60 60
V78 6s. Women and foodstuffs 85 85

V **74** Hills and Forest in Autumn
V **76** Testing Blood Pressure

1988. "Survival of the Forests". Multicoloured.
V79 4s. Type V **74** . . . . . . 2·75 2·75
V80 5s. Forest in autumn . . . . 3·00 3·00
Nos. V79/80 were issued together, se-tenant, forming a composite design.

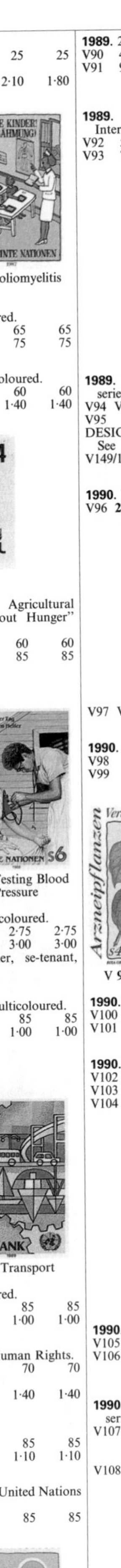

1988. International Volunteer Day. Multicoloured.
V81 6s. Type V **76** 85 85
V82 7s.50 Building houses (horiz) 1·00 1·00

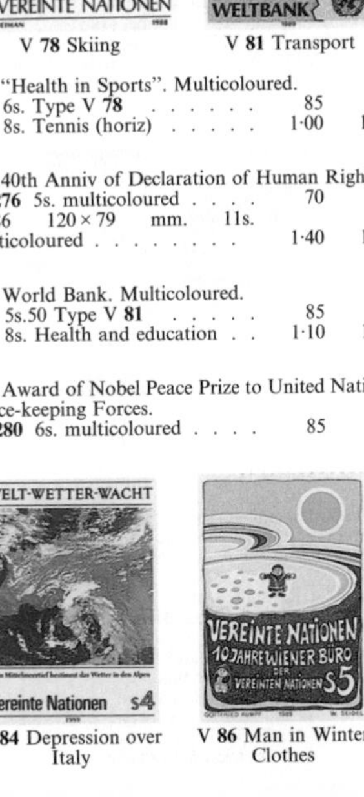

V **78** Skiing
V **81** Transport

1988. "Health in Sports". Multicoloured.
V83 6s. Type V **78** 85 85
V84 8s. Tennis (horiz) . . . . . 1·00 1·00

1988. 40th Anniv of Declaration of Human Rights.
V85 **276** 5s. multicoloured 70 70
MSV86 120 × 79 mm. 11s. multicoloured . . . . 1·40 1·40

1989. World Bank. Multicoloured.
V87 5s.50 Type V **81** 85 85
V88 8s. Health and education . . 1·10 1·10

1989. Award of Nobel Peace Prize to United Nations Peace-keeping Forces.
V89 **280** 6s. multicoloured 85 85

V **84** Depression over Italy
V **86** Man in Winter Clothes

1989. 25th Anniv of World Weather Watch.
V90 4s. Type V **84** 60 60
V91 9s.50 Short-range rainfall forecast for Tokyo . . . . 1·30 1·30

1989. 10th Anniv of United Nations Vienna International Centre. Multicoloured.
V92 5s. Type V **86** 70 70
V93 7s.50 Abstract . . . . 1·10 1·10

V **88** "Prisoners" (Kathe Kollwitz) (Article 5)

1989. Universal Declaration of Human Rights (1st series).
V94 V **88** 4s. black 45 45
V95 – 6s. multicoloured . . . 70 70
DESIGN: 6s. "Jurisprudence" (Raphael) (Article 6).
See also Nos. V107/8, V122/3, V138/9 and V149/150.

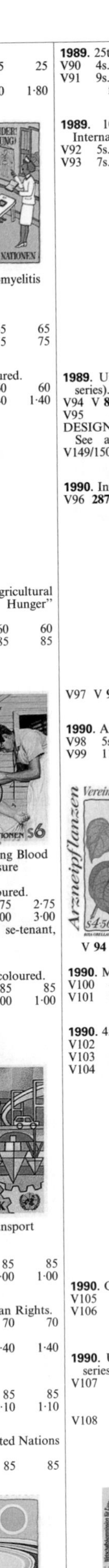

1990. International Trade Centre.
V96 **287** 12s. multicoloured . . . 1·60 1·60

V **91** "Earth" (painting by Kurt Regschek in I.A.E.A. Building)

1990.
V97 V **91** 1s.50 multicoloured . . 20 20

1990. Anti-AIDS Campaign. Multicoloured.
V98 5s. Type **289** 70 70
V99 11s. Attacking infected blood 1·50 1·50

V **94** Annatto
V **96** "45"

1990. Medicinal Plants. Multicoloured.
V100 4s.50 Type V **94** 60 60
V101 9s.50 Cundeamor . . . . . 1·30 1·30

1990. 45th Anniv of U.N.O. Multicoloured.
V102 7s. Type V **96** 95 95
V103 9s. "45" (different) . . . . 1·20 1·20
V104 100 × 73 mm. Nos. V 102/3 1·90 1·90

V **98** Men fighting

1990. Crime Prevention. Multicoloured.
V105 6s. Type V **98** 85 85
V106 8s. Masked man damaging painting . . . . 1·10 1·10

1990. Universal Declaration of Human Rights (2nd series). As Type V **88**. Multicoloured.
V107 4s.50 "Before the Judge" (Sandor Bihari) (Article 11) 95 55
V108 7s. "Young Man greeted by Woman writing Poem" (Suzuki Harunobu) (Article 12) . . . . . . 1·00 80

V **102/105** Mediterranean Coastline and Wildlife (½-size illustration)

1991. Economic Commission for Europe. "For a Better Environment".
V109 V **102** 5s. multicoloured . . 65 65
V110 V **103** 5s. multicoloured . . 65 65
V111 V **104** 5s. multicoloured . . 65 80
V112 V **105** 5s. multicoloured . . 65 65
Nos. V109/12 were issued together, se-tenant, forming the composite design illustrated.

V **106** Scrubland
V **108** Different Races

1991. 1st Anniv of Namibian Independence. Multicoloured.
V113 6s. Type V **106** 85 85
V114 9s.50 Sand dune . . . . . 1·30 1·30

1991.
V115 V **108** 20s. multicoloured . . 2·50 2·50

V **109** Boy and Girl (Anna Harmer)

1991. 30th Anniv (1989) of U.N. Declaration of the Rights of the Child and 1990 World Summit on Children, New York. Children's Drawings. Multicoloured.
V116 7s. Type V **109** 95 95
V117 9s. Child's world (Emiko Takegawa) . . . . 1·30 1·30

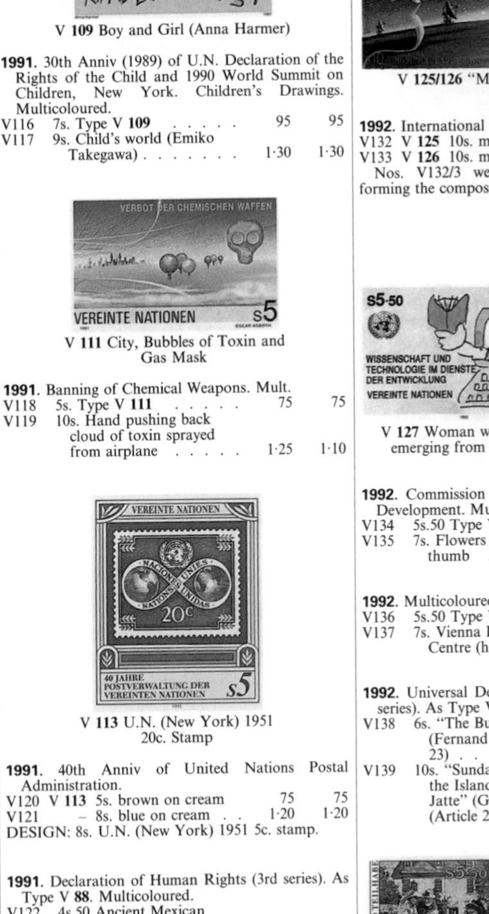

V **111** City, Bubbles of Toxin and Gas Mask

1991. Banning of Chemical Weapons. Mult.
V118 5s. Type V **111** 75 75
V119 10s. Hand pushing back cloud of toxin sprayed from airplane . . . . . 1·25 1·10

V **113** U.N. (New York) 1951 20c. Stamp

1991. 40th Anniv of United Nations Postal Administration.
V120 V **113** 5s. brown on cream 75 75
V121 – 8s. blue on cream . . 1·20 1·20
DESIGN: 8s. U.N. (New York) 1951 5c. stamp.

1991. Declaration of Human Rights (3rd series). As Type V **88**. Multicoloured.
V122 4s.50 Ancient Mexican pottery (Article 17) . . . 60 60
V123 7s. "Windows, 1912" (Robert Delaunay) (Article 18) 90 90

V **117** Iguacu National Park, Brazil

V **119/120** Sea Life (½-size illustration)

1992. 20th Anniv of UNESCO. World Heritage Convention. Multicoloured.
V124 5s. Type V **117** 80 80
V125 9s. Abu Simbel, Egypt . . . 1·40 1·40

1992. "Clean Oceans".
V126 V **119** 7s. multicoloured . . 95 90
V127 V **120** 7s. multicoloured . . 1·10 90
Nos. V126/7 were issued together, se-tenant, forming the composite design illustrated.

V **121/124** Planet Earth (½-size illustration)

1992. 2nd U.N. Conference on Environment and Development, Rio de Janeiro.
V128 V **121** 5s.50 multicoloured 70 70
V129 V **122** 5s.50 multicoloured 70 70
V130 V **123** 5s.50 multicoloured 70 70
V131 V **124** 5s.50 multicoloured 70 70
Nos. V128/131 were issued together, se-tenant, forming the composite design illustrated.

V **125/126** "Mission Planet Earth" (⅔-size illustration)

1992. International Space Year. Roul.
V132 V **125** 10s. multicoloured . . 1·40 1·40
V133 V **126** 10s. multicoloured . . 1·40 1·40
Nos. V132/3 were printed together, se-tenant, forming the composite design illustrated.

V **127** Woman with Book emerging from V.D.U.
V **129** Woman's Profile, Birds, Butterfly and Rose

1992. Commission on Science and Technology for Development. Multicoloured.
V134 5s.50 Type V **127** 80 75
V135 7s. Flowers growing from thumb . . . . 1·00 1·00

1992. Multicoloured.
V136 5s.50 Type V **129** 75 70
V137 7s. Vienna International Centre (horiz) 95 90

1992. Universal Declaration of Human Rights (4th series). As Type V **88**. Multicoloured.
V138 6s. "The Builders" (Fernand Leger) (Article 23) 85 85
V139 10s. "Sunday Afternoon on the Island of La Grande Jatte" (Georges Seurat) (Article 24) . . . . . . 1·40 1·40

V **133** Housing and Environment
V **135** Grevy's Zebra

1993. "Ageing: Dignity and Participation". 10th Anniv (1992) of International Plan of Action on Ageing. Multicoloured.
V140 5s.50 Type V **133** 90 80
V141 7s. Education . . . . 1·00 95

1993. Endangered Species (1st series). Multicoloured.
V142 7s. Type V **135** 85 85
V143 7s. Humboldt penguin ("Spheniscus humboldti") 85 85
V144 7s. Desert monitor ("Varanus griseus") . . . 85 85
V145 7s. Wolf ("Canis lupus") . . 85 85
See also Nos. V161/4, V179/82, V205/8, V223/6, V249/52, V288/91, V304/7, V324/7 and V353/6.

V 139 Globe, Doves and U.N. Emblem

V 140 Regional and National Environment

1993.
V146 V **139** 13s. multicoloured . . 1·90 1·80

1993. 45th Anniv of W.H.O. Multicoloured.
V147 6s. Type V **140** 90 85
V148 10s. Continental and global environment . . . . . . 1·40 1·40

1993. Declaration of Human Rights (5th series). As Type V **88**. Multicoloured.
V149 5s. "Lower Austrian Peasants' Wedding" (Ferdinand Waldmuller) (Article 29) 70 70
V150 6s. "Outback" (Sally Morgan) (Article 30) . . 85 85

V **144/147** Peace (½-size illustration)

1993. International Peace Day. Roul.
V151 V **144** 5s.50 multicoloured 70 70
V152 V **145** 5s.50 multicoloured 70 70
V153 V **146** 5s.50 multicoloured 70 70
V154 V **147** 5s.50 multicoloured 70 70
Nos V151/4 were issued together, se-tenant, forming the composite design illustrated.

V **148** Monkeys

1993. The Environment—Climate. Multicoloured.
V155 7s. Type V **148** 90 90
V156 7s. Eastern bluebird and factory chimneys 90 90
V157 7s. Volcano, smokestacks and tree stumps 90 90
V158 7s. Great horned owl in desert 90 90
Nos. V155/8 were issued together, se-tenant, forming a composite design.

V **152** Family holding Hands

1994. International Year of the Family. Mult.
V159 5s.50 Type V **152** 90 90
V160 8s. Family at work . . . . 1·30 1·30

1994. Endangered Species (2nd series). As Type V **135**. Multicoloured.
V161 7s. Ocelot ("Felis pardalis") 85 85
V162 7s. White-crested white eye ("Zosterups albogularis") 85 85
V163 7s. Mediterranean monk seals ("Monachus monachus") 85 85
V164 7s. Indian elephant ("Elephas maximus") . . 85 85

V **158** Tree and Doves

V **161** Hands ready to help Refugees

1994. Multicoloured.
V165 50g. Type V **158** 15 15
V166 4s. Herring gulls 60 60
V167 30s. Globe and dove . . . 4·00 4·00

1994. United Nations High Commissioner for Refugees.
V168 V **161** 12s. multicoloured . . 1·80 1·80

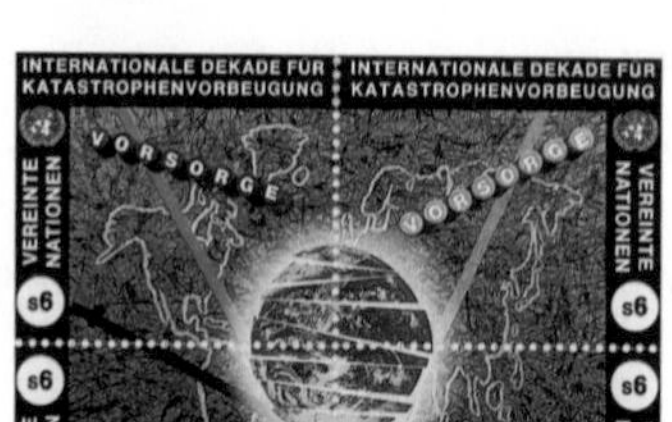

V **162/165** Shattered Globe and "Preparation" (⅔-size illustration)

1994. International Decade for Natural Disaster Reduction.
V169 V **162** 6s. multicoloured . . 85 75
V170 V **163** 6s. multicoloured . . 85 75
V171 V **164** 6s. multicoloured . . 85 75
V172 V **165** 6s. multicoloured . . 75 75
Nos. V169/72 were issued together, se-tenant, forming the composite design illustrated.

V **166** Enhancing Role of Women

1994. International Population and Development Conference, Cairo. Multicoloured.
V173 5s.50 Type V **166** 85 90
V174 7s. Relationship of population and environment . . . . . . 1·00 1·10

V **168** Map and Crossed Ribbons

1994. 30th Anniv of United Nations Conference on Trade and Development. Multicoloured.
V175 6s. Type V **168** 85 90
V176 7s. Map and ribbons forming star . . . . . . 1·00 1·10

1995. 50th Anniv of U.N.O. (1st issue).
V177 **371** 7s. multicoloured . . . 1·00 1·10
See also Nos. V185/6 and V190/201.

V **171** "Social Summit 1995"

1995. World Summit for Social Development, Copenhagen.
V178 V **171** 14s. multicoloured . . 2·40 2·75

1995. Endangered Species (3rd series). As Type V **135**. Multicoloured.
V179 7s. Black rhinoceros ("Diceros bicornis") . . . 80 85
V180 7s. Golden conure ("Aratinga guarouba") 80 85
V181 7s. Variegated langur ("Pygathrix nemaeus") 80 85
V182 7s. Arabian oryx ("Oryx leucoryx") 80 85

V **176** Village in Winter

1995. "Youth: Our Future". 10th Anniv of International Youth Year. Multicoloured.
V183 6s. Type V **176** 85 90
V184 7s. Wheat stacks in field . . 1·00 1·10

1995. 50th Anniv of U.N.O. (2nd issue).
V185 **379** 7s. green . . . . 1·00 1·10
V186 – 10s. black . . . . 1·50 1·70
MSV187 92 × 70 mm. Nos. V185/6. Imperf . . . . 1·75 1·75
DESIGN: 10s. Veterans' Memorial Hall and Opera House, San Francisco (venue for signing of U.N. Charter).

V **180** Women in Jungle

V **194** Jester holding Dove

1995. 4th World Conference on Women, Peking. Multicoloured.
V188 5s.50 Type V **180** 85 90
V189 6s. Woman reading book (28 × 48 mm) 85 95

1995. 50th Anniv of U.N.O. (3rd issue).
V190 **385** 3s. multicoloured . . . 40 45
V191 **386** 3s. multicoloured . . . 40 45
V192 **387** 3s. multicoloured . . . 40 45
V193 **388** 3s. multicoloured . . . 40 45
V194 **389** 3s. multicoloured . . . 40 45
V195 **390** 3s. multicoloured . . . 40 45
V196 **391** 3s. multicoloured . . . 40 45
V197 **392** 3s. multicoloured . . . 40 45
V198 **393** 3s. multicoloured . . . 40 45
V199 **394** 3s. multicoloured . . . 40 45
V200 **395** 3s. multicoloured . . . 40 45
V201 **396** 3s. multicoloured . . . 40 40
Nos. V190/5 and V196/201 respectively were issued together, se-tenant, forming two composite designs.

1996. 50th Anniv of World Federation of United Nations Associations. Multicoloured.
V202 V **194** 7s. multicoloured . . 1·00 1·10

V **195** U.N. Flag

V **201** Family with Agricultural Products

1996. Multicoloured.
V203 1s. Type V **195** 20 20
V204 10s. Abstract painting (Karl Korab) . . . . 1·40 1·50

1996. Endangered Species (4th series). As Type V **135**. Multicoloured.
V205 7s. Venus slipper orchid ("Cypripedium calceolus") 80 85
V206 7s. "Aztekium ritteri" . . 80 85
V207 7s. "Euphorbia cremersii" 80 85
V208 7s. "Dracula bella" 80 85

1996. "Habitat II" Second U.N. Conf on Human Settlements, Istanbul, Turkey. Mult.
V209 6s. Type V **201** 75 80
V210 6s. Women with sacks of grain 75 80
V211 6s. Woman and city 75 80
V212 6s. Ploughing with oxen . . 75 80
V213 6s. Villlage and elephant . . 75 80
Nos. V209/13 were issued together, se-tenant, forming a composite design.

V **206** Gymnastics

1996. Sport and the Environment. Multicoloured.
V214 6s. Type V **206** . . . . . 90 1·00
V215 7s. Hurdling . . . . 1·10 1·20
MSV216 88 × 78 mm. Nos. V214/15 1·90 1·90

V **208** Dove and Butterflies

1996. "A Plea for Peace". Winners of China Youth Design Competition. Multicoloured.
V217 7s. Type V **208** . . . . . 1·10 1·20
V218 10s. Children and flowers in dove . . . . 1·40 1·50

V **210** "Hansel and Gretel" (Brothers Grimm)

V **212** Red Phoenix

1996. 50th Anniv of UNICEF. Children's Stories.
V219 5s.50 Type V **210** 75 85
V220 8s. "How Maui Stole Fire from the Gods" (Pacific Islands myth) . . . . . 1·00 1·10

1997. Details of "Phoenixes flying Down" by Sagenji Yoshida. Multicoloured.
V221 5s. Type V **212** 70 75
V222 6s. Green phoenix 85 90

1997. Endangered Species (5th series). As Type V **135**. Multicoloured.
V223 7s. Barbary ape ("Macaca sylvanus") 80 85
V224 7s. Stanley crane ("Anthropoides paradisea") 80 85
V225 7s. Przewalski's horse ("Equus przewalskii") . . 80 85
V226 7s. Giant anteater ("Myrmecophaga tridactyla") 80 85

V **218/221** River Scene (⅔-size illustration)

1997. "Earth Summit + 5". 5th Anniv of United Nations Conference on Environment and Development.
V227 V **218** 3s.50 multicoloured 45 35
V228 V **219** 3s.50 multicoloured 45 35
V229 V **220** 3s.50 multicoloured 45 35
V230 V **221** 3s.50 multicoloured 45 65
MSV230 V **231** 90 × 75 mm. 11s. Motifs as Nos. V227/30. Imperf 1·75 1·60
Nos. V227/30 were issued together, se-tenant, forming the composite design illustrated.

V **222** Stephenson's Locomotive "Rocket" and Darraque Motor Car (1901)

V **227** 1986 3s.50 Philately Stamp

1997. 50th Anniversaries of Economic Commission for Europe and Economic and Social Commission for Asia and the Pacific. Multicoloured.
V232 7s. Type V **222** 85 85
V233 7s. Russian steam locomotive and American streetcar 85 85
V234 7s. Diesel train and British double-decker bus . . . 85 85
V235 7s. Diesel locomotive and articulated trailer lorry 85 85
V236 7s. High speed electric train and electric-powered car 85 85

Nos. V232/6 were issued together, se-tenant, forming a composite design.

1997. "Tribute to Philately". Multicoloured.
V237 6s.50 Type V **227** 55 65
V238 7s. 1986 6s.50 Philately stamp 55 65

1997. 25th Anniv of World Heritage Convention. Terracotta Warriors from Emperor Qin Shi Huang's Tomb, Xian, China. Multicoloured.
V239 1s. As Type **434** 40 45
V240 1s. As No. 737 . . . . . . 55 60
V241 1s. As No. 738 . . . . . . 25 30
V242 1s. As No. 739 . . . . . . 25 30
V243 1s. As No. 740 . . . . . . 25 30
V244 1s. As No. 741 . . . . . . 25 30
V245 3s. As No. 740 . . . . . . 35 35
V246 6s. As No. 741 . . . . . . 55 60

V **235** Japanese Peace Bell, Vienna

1998. Multicoloured.
V247 6s.50 Type V **235** 85 95
V248 9s. Underground train passing Vienna Centre . . 1·30 1·40

1998. Endangered Species (6th series). As Type V **135**. Multicoloured.
V249 7s. Green turtle ("Chelonia mydas") 80 85
V250 7s. Burrowing owl ("Speotyto cunicularia") 80 85
V251 7s. Raja Brooke's birdwing ("Trogonoptera brookiana") 80 85
V252 7s. Lesser panda ("Ailurus fulgens") 80 85

V **241** Shark

1998. International Year of the Ocean. Multicoloured.
V253 3s.50 Type V **241** 55 60
V254 3s.50 Diver and submersible 55 60
V255 3s.50 Diver and dolphins 55 60
V256 3s.50 School of fishes above diver and submersible . . 55 60
V257 3s.50 Sealions 55 60
V258 3s.50 Diver and underwater camera 55 60
V259 3s.50 Angelfishes 55 60
V260 3s.50 Fishes and diver . . . 55 60
V261 3s.50 Turtle 55 60
V262 3s.50 Butterflyfishes 55 60
V263 3s.50 Anemonefish, other fishes and starfish 55 60
V264 3s.50 Starfish and butterflyfishes 55 60

V **242** Ocelot

1998. Rainforest Preservation.
V265 V **242** 6s.50 multicoloured 1·00 1·10
MSV266 82 × 70 mm. 22s. multicoloured . . . . 3·00 3·00

V **243** Soldier distributing Supplies

1998. 50 Years of United Nations Peacekeeping. Multicoloured.
V267 4s. Type V **243** 55 65
V268 7s.50 Voters . . . . 1·10 1·30

V **245** Open Head

V **253** "Volcanic Landscape" (detail, Peter Pongratz)

1998. 50th Anniv of Universal Declaration of Human Rights. Multicoloured.
V269 4s.50 Type V **245** 75 85
V270 7s. Cogwheels . . . . . . 1·10 1·00

1998. World Heritage Site. Schonbrunn Palace, Vienna. Multicoloured.
V271 1s. As Type **454** 60 55
V272 1s. As No. 778 . . . . . . 70 80
V273 1s. As No. 779 . . . . . . 30 35
V274 2s. As No. 780 . . . . . . 30 35
V275 2s. As No. 781 . . . . . . 30 35
V276 2s. As No. 782 . . . . . . 35 35
V277 3s.50 As No. 780 . . . . . 80 80
V278 7s. As No. 779 . . . . . . 2·10 2·10

1999.
V279 V **253** 8s. multicoloured . . 1·20 1·40

1999. World Heritage Sites in Australia. Mult.
V280 1s. As Type **462** 40 45
V281 1s. As No. 796 . . . . . . 55 60
V282 1s. As No. 797 . . . . . . 20 20
V283 2s. As No. 798 . . . . . . 25 30
V284 2s. As No. 799 . . . . . . 25 30
V285 2s. As No. 800 . . . . . . 30 35
V286 4s.50 As No. 801 . . . . . 45 55
V287 6s.50 As No. 802 . . . . . 75 70

1999. Endangered Species (7th series). As Type V **135**. Multicoloured.
V288 7s. Orang-utan ("Pongo pygmaeus") 80 85
V289 7s. Dalmatian pelican ("Pelecanus crispus") . . 80 85
V290 7s. Yellow anaconda ("Eunectes notaeus") . . 80 85
V291 7s. Caracal ("Caracal caracal") 80 85

V **264/265** Global Weather Forecasting (½-size illustration)

1999. Third Conference on Exploration and Peaceful Uses of Outer Space, Vienna.
V292 V **264** 3s.50 multicoloured 55 60
V293 V **265** 3s.50 multicoloured 55 60
MSV293 V **294** 90 × 75 mm. 13s. Combined design as Nos. V292/3 (71 × 29 mm) . . . . 1·75 1·75

Nos. V292/3 were issued together, se-tenant, forming the composite design illustrated.

V **266/269** Modern Communications (½-size illustration)

1999. 125th Anniv of Universal Postal Union.
V295 V **266** 33c. multicoloured . . 95 1·00
V296 V **267** 33c. multicoloured . . 95 1·00
V297 V **268** 33c. multicoloured . . 95 1·00
V298 V **269** 33c. multicoloured . . 95 1·00

Nos. V295/8 were issued together, se-tenant, forming the composite design illustrated.

V **270** U.N. Centre, Vienna

1999. "In Memoriam: Fallen in the Cause of Peace".
V299 V **270** 6s.50 multicoloured 1·10 1·20
MSV300 90 × 75 mm. 14s. multicoloured . . . . 1·40 1·40

V **272** Couple leaping over Open Book

1999. Education: Keystone to the 21st Century.
V301 7s. Type V **272** . . . . . 1·00 1·10
V302 13s. Group of readers . . . 2·00 2·20

DENOMINATION. From Nos. V303 to V346, United Nations Vienna Centre stamps are denominated both in Austrian schillings and in euros. As no cash for the latter was in circulation the catalogue uses the schilling value.

2000. International Year of Thanksgiving.
V303 **483** 7s. multicoloured . . . 95 1·00

2000. Endangered Species (8th series). As Type V **135**. Multicoloured.
V304 7s. Leopard (*Panthera pardus*) 80 85
V305 7s. White spoonbill (*Platalea leucorodia*) . . . 80 85
V306 7s. Chilean guemal (*Hippocamelus bisulcus*) 80 85
V307 7s. Killer whale (*Orcinus orca*) 80 85

V **279** "Tomorrow's Dream" (Voltaire Perez)

2000. "Our World 2000" International Art Exhibition, New York. Entries in Millennium Painting Competition. Multicoloured.
V308 7s. Type V **279** . . . . . 95 1·00
V309 8s. "Remembrance" (Dimitris Nalbandis) . . 1·10 1·20

V **281** Dome of General Assembly Hall, 1951

2000. 55th Anniv of the United Nations and 50th Anniv of Opening of U.N. Headquarters, New York.
V310 V **281** 7s. green, yellow and ochre . . . . . . 95 1·00
V311 – 9s. green, yellow and ochre . . . . . . 1·00 1·10
MSV312 67 × 86 mm. Nos. V310/11 1·50 1·50

DESIGN: 9s. Ceremony to mark completion of steel framework of Secretariat Building, 1949.

V **283** Agriculture

V **284** (½-size illustration)

2000. "The United Nations in the 21st Century" Sheet 141 × 165 mm containing Type V **283** and similar horiz designs, forming the overall design Type V **284**. Multicoloured.
MSV313 3s.50 Type V **283**; 3s.50 Soldiers with children; 3s.50 Women working; 3s.50 Soldiers using landmine detectors; 3s.50 detectors; 3s.50 Scientist in laboratory; 3s.50 Disabled athletes 2·00 2·00

2000. World Heritage Sites in Spain. Multicoloured.
V314 1s. As Type **496** 40 40
V315 1s. As No. 832 . . . . . . 45 50
V316 1s. As No. 833 . . . . . . 20 20
V317 2s. As No. 834 . . . . . . 25 30
V318 2s. As No. 835 . . . . . . 25 30
V319 2s. As No. 836 . . . . . . 30 35
V320 4s.50 As No. 837 . . . . . 65 65
V321 6s.50 As No. 838 . . . . . 80 80

V **291** Family of Refugees

2000. 50th Anniv of United Nations Commissioner for Refugees.
V322 V **291** 7s. multicoloured . . 1·00 1·10
MSV323 121 × 82 mm. 25s. multicoloured . . . . 2·25 2·25

2001. Endangered Species (9th series). As Type V **135**. Multicoloured.
V324 7s. Spectacled bear (*Tremarctos ornatus*) . . 80 85
V325 7s. Laysan duck (*Anas laysanensis*) 80 85
V326 7s. Aardwolf (*Proteles cristatus*) 80 85
V327 7s. Silver langur (*Trachypithecus cristatus*) 80 85

V **297** Couple (Nguyen Thanh Chuong)

2001. United Nations International Year of Volunteers. Multicoloured.
V328 10s. Type V **297** . . . . . 1·30 1·40
V329 12s. Hands and heart (Ikko Tanaka) . . . . 1·25 1·40

2001. World Heritage Sites in Japan.
V330 1s. As Type **512** 45 50
V331 1s. As No. 858 . . . . . . 15 15
V332 1s. As No. 859 . . . . . . 15 15
V333 2s. As No. 860 . . . . . . 25 25
V334 2s. As No. 861 . . . . . . 25 25
V335 2s. As No. 862 . . . . . . 25 30
V336 7s. As No. 859 . . . . . . 65 70
V337 15s. As No. 862 . . . . . 1·30 1·40

2001. 40th Death Anniv of Dag Hammarskjold (United Nations Secretary General, 1953–61).
V338 **518** 7s. green 85 90

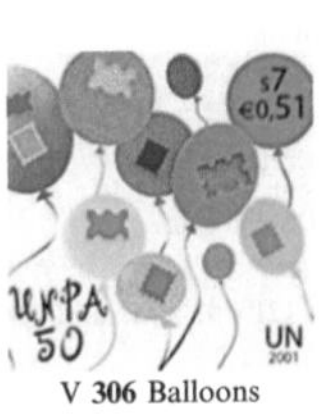

V **306** Balloons

V **309** Futuristic Electric Car and Solar Panels

2001. 50th Anniv of Untied Nations Postal Administration.
V339 V **306** 7s. multicoloured . . 65 40
V340 – 8s. multicoloured . . 75 45
MSV341 102 × 102 mm. 21s. × 2 cobalt and green . . . . 3·75 3·75

DESIGNS: V340, Cake; **MS**V341, Emblem.

2001. Climate Change. Multicoloured.
V342 7s. Type V **309** . . . . . . 90 1·00
V343 7s. Airship, cyclists and horse rider . . . . 90 1·00
V344 7s. Couple walking, balloon and coastline . . . . . . 90 1·00
V345 7s. Train and traffic signs in glass dome . . . . 90 1·00

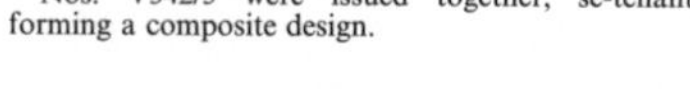

Nos. V342/5 were issued together, se-tenant, forming a composite design.

2001. Kofi Annan, Winner of Nobel Peace Prize, 2001.

V346	**526**	7s. multicoloured	1·00	1·10

V **314** Semmering Railway

2002. Multicoloured.

V347	7c. Type V **314**	15	15
V348	51c. Pferdeschwemme, Salzburg	80	85
V349	58c. Aggstein Ruin	90	1·00
V350	73c. Hallstatt	1·10	90
V351	87c. Melk Abbey	1·60	95
V352	€2.03 Kapitelschwemme, Salzburg	1·90	1·90

2002. Endangered Species (10th series). As Type V **135**. Multicoloured.

V353	51c. Siamang gibbon (*Hylobates syndactylus*)	80	85
V354	51c. Jackass penguin (*Spheniscus demersus*)	80	85
V355	51c. Banded linsang (*Prionodon linsang*)	80	85
V356	51c. Sonoran green toad (*Bufo retiformis*)	80	85

2002. East Timor Independence. As T **532**. Multioloured.

V357	51c. Carved deer horn container	75	75
V358	€1.09 Weaving loom	1·50	1·50

2002. International Year of Mountains. As T **534**. Multocoloured.

V359	22c. Mt. Cook, New Zealand	30	30
V360	22c. Mt. Robson, Canada	30	30
V361	51c. Rakaposhi, Pakistan	75	75
V362	51c. Sagarmatha, Nepal	75	75

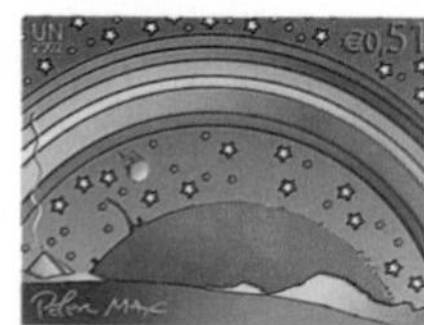

V **330** Rainbow

2002. World Summit on Sustainable Development, Johannesburg. Multicoloured.

V363	51c. Type V **330**	75	75
V364	51c. Women's profiles	75	75
V365	58c. Figures wearing fashionable dress	80	80
V366	58c. Wave and doves	80	80

2002. World Heritage Sites in Italy. As T **542**. Multicoloured.

V367	7c. Duomo di Sant'Andrea, Amalfi Coast	10	10
V368	7c. View across Islands, Aeolian Islands	10	10
V369	7c. Del Moro Fountain, Rome	10	10
V370	15c. Santa Maria del Fiore, Florence	25	25
V371	15c. Leaning Tower, Pisa	25	25
V372	15c. The Forum, Pompeii	25	25
V373	51c. As No. 372	75	75
V374	58c. As No. 369	80	80

2002. AIDS Awareness Campaign. As T **549**. Multicoloured.

V375	€1.53 AIDS Symbol on UN Secretariat Building, New York	2·10	2·10
MSV376	80×80 mm. 51c.+25c. AIDS Symbol on UN Secretariat Building, New York at night	1·10	1·10

The premium was for AIDS charities.

2003. Indigenous Art. Sheet 121×97 mm. As T **550**. Multicoloured.

MSV377	51c. Mola, Panama; 51c. Mochican vessel, Peru; 51c. Tarabuco cloth, Bolivia; 51c. Masks, Cuba; 51c. Aztec headdress, Mexico; 51c. Bird-shaped staff head, Colombia	4·25	4·25

V **343** Kunsthistorisches Museum, Vienna

2003. Architecture. Multicoloured.

V378	25c. Type V **343**	30	30
V379	€1 Belevedere Palace, Vienna	1·40	1·40

2003. 30th Anniv of Convention on International Trade in Endangered Species (CITES). As T **555**. Multicoloured.

V380	51c. Baikal teal (*Anas Formosa*)	70	70
V381	51c. Hagedash ibis (*Bostrychia hagedash*)	70	70
V382	51c. Toco toucan (*Ramphostos toco*)	70	70
V383	51c. Egyptian goose (*Alopochen aegyptiacus*)	70	70

2003. International Year of Freshwater. As T **559**. Multicoloured.

V384	55c. Snow scene with bridge	70	70
V385	75c. Snow scene with horse	1·00	1·00

Nos. V384/5 were issued together, se-tenant, forming a composite design.

V **351** Schloss Eggenberg, Graz

2003.

V386	V **351**	4c. multicoloured	10	10

2003. World Heritage Sites in USA. As T **561**. Showing USA National Parks. Multicoloured.

V387	15c. Yosemite National Park	20	20
V388	15c. Smoky Mountains	20	20
V389	15c. Olympic National Park	20	20
V390	20c. Hawaii Volcanoes	25	25
V391	20c. Everglades	25	25
V392	20c. Yellowstone National Park	25	25
V393	55c. As No. V389	70	70
V394	75c. As No. V391	1·00	1·00

V387/94 have olive bands at top and bottom edges.

2003. Ralph Bunche (politician) Commemoration. As T **567**. Multicoloured.

V395	€2.10 Ralph Bunche	2·75	2·75

2003. In Memoriam. Support for United Nations Staff Killed or Injured in Terrorist Attacks. As T **568**. Multicoloured.

V396	€2.10 Flag at half-mast	2·75	2·75

E. EAST TIMOR

UNITED NATIONS TRANSITIONAL ADMINISTRATION IN EAST TIMOR

100 cents = 1 dollar.

Following negotiations between Portugal and Indonesia a referendum was conducted on 30 August 1999 with the majority voting for independence for East Timor. On the 20 September 1999 the first United Nations peace keeping troops arrived in East Timor and the Indonesian troops began to withdraw. By October the United Nations had established the International Force for East Timor (I.N.T.E.R.F.E.T.). On the 19 October 1999 the Indonesian Consultative Assembly confirmed the establishment and on the 25 October 1999 the United Nations voted to replace I.N.T.E.R.F.E.T. with a force to help with the establishment of a United Nations Transitional Administration of East Timor (U.N.T.A.E.T.). The East Timor National Council (E.T.N.C.), which was formed to help with policy recommendations, held it's first meeting on 11 December 1999.

1 Man with Arms Raised

2000. (a) Inscr "Dom.".

1	**1**	(21c.) multicoloured	25	25

(b) Inscr "Int.".

2	**1**	($1.05) multicoloured	1·30	1·30

No. 1 was for use on Domestic mail and No. 2 was for use on International mail.

F. Kosovo

United Nations Interim Administration Mission

The following stamps were issued by the United Nations Interim Administration Mission (U.N.M.I.K.) and the Post & Telecommunications of Kosovo for postal purposes in Kosovo. They were for local use only for the first two months with international use commencing in May 2000.

K **1** Orpheus (mosaic, 5–6th century, Podujeve)

K **2** Bird

2000. Artefacts. Multicoloured.

K1	20pf. Type K **1**	10	10
K2	30pf. "Dardanian idol", 3500 B.C.	20	20
K3	50pf. Obverse and reverse of 4th-century B.C. silver coin, Damastion	30	30
K4	1m. Mother Teresa (statue, Prizren)	65	65
K5	2m. Map of Kosovo showing various sites	1·25	1·25

2001. Art. Multicoloured designs.

K 6	20pf. Type K **2**	10	10
K 7	30pf. Musician	20	20
K 8	50pf. Butterfly and pear (horiz)	30	30
K 9	1m. Children and stars	65	65
K10	2m. Handprints surrounding globe	1·25	1·25

Nos. K6/10 have the face values shown in deutsche Marks and euros.

UNITED STATES OF AMERICA

Pt. 22

A Federal Republic in N. America, consisting of 50 states and one federal district.

100 cents = 1 dollar.

PRICES. On the issues before 1890 the gum is rarely complete and the unused prices quoted are for stamps with part original gum.

1 Franklin (after drawings by James B. Longacre)

2 Washington (after painting by Stuart)

1847. Imperf.

1	**1**	5c. brown	£4000	£400
2	**2**	10c. black	£16000	£1100

The 5c. blue and 10c. orange, both imperf, come from miniature sheets isssued in 1947 to commemorate the Centenary Philatelic Exhibition, New York.

3 Franklin (after bust by Caffieri)

4 Washington (after bust by Houdon)

5 Jefferson

6 Washington

7 Washington

8 Washington

9 Franklin (after bust by Caffieri)

10 Washington (after Trumbull painting)

1851. Imperf.

11	**3**	1c. blue	£250	75·00
13a	**4**	3c. red	£225	7·50
14	**5**	5c. brown	£10000	£500
16	**6**	10c. green	£1200	£140
19	**7**	12c. black	£3000	£190

1857. Perf.

26	**3**	1c. blue	£110	28·00
28	**4**	3c. red	45·00	4·00
33	**5**	5c. brown	£375	£160
39	**6**	10c. green	£150	45·00
40c	**7**	12c. black	£250	£100

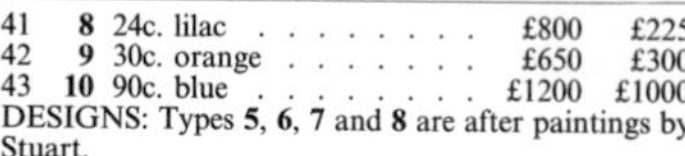

41	**8**	24c. lilac	£800	£225
42	**9**	30c. orange	£650	£300
43	**10**	90c. blue	£1200	£1000

DESIGNS: Types **5**, **6**, **7** and **8** are after paintings by Stuart.

11 Franklin

12 Washington

13 Jefferson

14 Washington

15 Washington

16 Washington

17 Franklin

18 Washington

19 Andrew Jackson (after miniature by J. W. Dodge)

20 Lincoln (from a photograph)

1861.

60b	**11**	1c. blue	80·00	26·00
69	**19**	2c. black	£300	30·00
62	**12**	3c. red	45·00	2·30
63	**13**	5c. yellow	£10000	£325
72		5c. brown	£325	90·00
64	**14**	10c. green	£400	25·00
65	**15**	12c. black	£325	49·00
73	**20**	15c. black	£1100	95·00
66c	**16**	24c. blue	£4500	£375
74		24c. lilac	£600	80·00
74b		24c. grey	£600	80·00
67	**17**	30c. orange	£900	90·00
68a	**18**	90c. blue	£1500	£275

21 Franklin (after Houdon bust)

22 Post Rider

23 Baldwin Steam Locomotive

24 Washington (after Stuart)

25 Shield and Eagle

26 Paddle-steamer "Adriatic" (after C. Parsons)

27 Landing of Columbus (after Vanderlyn)

28 Declaration of Independence (after Trumbull)

30 Lincoln (from a photograph)

1869.

114	**21**	1c. brown	£400	85·00
115	**22**	2c. brown	£300	40·00
116	**23**	3c. blue	£130	8·75
117	**24**	6c. blue	£950	95·00
118	**25**	10c. orange	£650	80·00
119	**26**	12c. green	£650	75·00
121	**27**	15c. blue and brown	£1100	£150
122	**28**	24c. purple and green	£3500	£550
123	**25**	30c. red and blue	£2750	£325
124	**30**	90c. black and red	£6500	£1500

31 Franklin

32 Jackson

33 Washington

34 Lincoln

35 Stanton

36 Jefferson

37 Henry Clay

38 Daniel Webster

39 General Winfield Scott

40 Alexander Hamilton

41 Commodore Perry

42 General Zachary Taylor (from a daguerreotype)

1870.

207	31	1c. blue	40·00	50
148	32	2c. brown	90·00	4·25
185		2c. red	70·00	2·30
208	33	3c. green	43·00	55
219		3c. red	40·00	37·00
161	34	6c. red	£200	6·25
151	35	7c. red	£475	49·00
210	36	10c. brown	70·00	3·25
153	37	12c. purple	£800	70·00
191	38	15c. orange	£190	16·00
155	39	24c. violet	£800	65·00
192	40	30c. black	£325	35·00
222		30c. brown	£275	60·00
193	41	90c. red	£1400	£140
223		90c. violet	£600	£130

1875.

181	42	5c. blue	£160	11·00

43 Garfield (from a photograph)

44 Washington (after bust by Houdon)

45 Jackson (after bust by Powers)

46 Franklin

47 Franklin

1882.

217	46	1c. blue	55·00	1·00
213	44	2c. brown	25·00	40
218		2c. green	19·00	40
214	45	4c. green	£150	10·00
220		4c. red	£100	12·00
211	43	5c. brown	£150	6·00
221		5c. blue	£120	7·75

1890. No triangles in upper corners.

224	47	1c. blue (Franklin)	20·00	40
225a	–	2c. red (Washington)	16·00	35
226	–	3c. violet (Jackson)	50·00	4·00
227	–	4c. sepia (Lincoln)	50·00	2·00
228	–	5c. brown (Grant)	50·00	1·60
229	–	6c. red (Garfield)	50·00	13·50
230	–	8c. purple (Sherman)	49·00	6·25
231	–	10c. green (Webster)	£100	2·00
232	–	15c. blue (Clay)	£140	14·50
233	–	30c. black (Jefferson)	£225	20·00
234	–	90c. orange (Perry)	£375	70·00

58 Columbus in Sight of Land

83 Jefferson

1893. Columbian Exposition, Chicago.

235	58	1c. blue	16·00	25
236	–	2c. purple	14·50	30
237	–	3c. green	46·00	10·00
238	–	4c. blue	70·00	5·75
239	–	5c. brown	70·00	5·75
240	–	6c. violet	65·00	15·00
241	–	8c. red	60·00	7·75
242	–	10c. sepia	£100	5·50
243	–	15c. green	£190	48·00
244	–	30c. orange	£250	55·00
245	–	50c. slate	£450	£110
246	–	$1 red	£1200	£375
247	–	$2 lake	£1300	£450
248	–	$3 green	£1900	£850
249	–	$4 red	£2500	£950
250	–	$5 black	£2750	£1200

DESIGNS: 2c. Landing of Columbus; 3c. "Santa Maria", flagship of Columbus; 4c. Fleet of Columbus; 5c. Columbus soliciting aid of Isabella; 6c. Columbus welcomed at Barcelona, Ferdinand (left) and Balboa (right); 8c. Columbus restored to favour; 10c. Columbus presenting natives; 15c. Columbus announcing his discovery; 30c. Columbus at La Rabida; 50c. Recall of Columbus; $1 Isabella pledging her jewels; $2 Columbus in chains; $3 Columbus describing his third voyage; $4 Isabella and Columbus; $5 Columbus, America and Liberty.

1894. Triangles in upper corners as T **83**. Same portraits as issue of 1890, except dollar values.

267	–	1c. blue	4·25	30
283	–	1c. green	7·75	35
270	–	2c. red	4·50	30
271	–	3c. violet	27·00	1·20
285	–	4c. brown	24·00	95
273	–	5c. brown	27·00	1·50
286	–	5c. blue	22·00	85
274	–	6c. brown	65·00	3·75
287a	–	6c. purple	21·00	3·25
275	–	8c. brown	47·00	95
276	–	10c. green	65·00	1·20
289	–	10c. brown	80·00	1·90
277	–	15c. blue	£200	7·25
290	–	15c. green	£110	7·00
278	83	50c. orange	£250	11·50
279	–	$1 black (Perry)	£425	48·00
281a	–	$2 blue (Madison)	£500	£140
282	–	$5 green (Marshall)	£1800	£350

88 Father Marquette on the Mississippi

97 "City of Alpena" (Great Lakes steamer)

1898. Trans-Mississippi Exposition, Omaha.

291	88	1c. green	24·00	4·00
292	–	2c. red	20·00	1·00
293	–	4c. orange	£120	16·00
294	–	5c. blue	£120	12·50
295	–	8c. purple	£140	27·00
296	–	10c. violet	£170	16·00
297	–	50c. green	£450	£120
298	–	$1 black	£1200	£350
299	–	$2 brown	£1900	£650

DESIGNS: 2c. Farming in the West; 4c. Indian hunting American bison; 5c. Fremont on Rocky Mountains; 8c. Troops guarding emigrant train; 10c. Hardships of emigration; 50c. Western mining prospector; $1 Western cattle in storm; $2 Eads Bridge over Mississippi at St. Louis and paddle-steamer "Grey Eagle".

1901. Pan-American Exhibition, Buffalo. Inscr "COMMEMORATIVE SERIES, 1901."

300	97	1c. black and green	17·00	2·00
301	–	2c. black and red	14·50	60
302	–	4c. black and brown	60·00	9·25
303	–	5c. black and blue	48·00	9·75
304	–	8c. black and brown	75·00	33·00
305	–	10c. black and brown	£120	16·00

DESIGNS: 2c. "Empire State Express"; 4c. Automobile; 5c. Railway bridge below Niagara Falls; 8c. Canal locks at Sault Sainte Marie; 10c. "Saint Paul" (liner).

103 Franklin

104 Washington

105 Jackson

106 Grant

107 Lincoln

108 Garfield

109 Martha Washington

110 Webster

111 Harrison

112 Clay

113 Jefferson

114 Farragut

115 Madison

116 Marshall

1902. Inscr "SERIES 1902". 1, 4 and 5c. perf or imperf.

306	103	1c. green	6·50	20
307	104	2c. red	9·75	20
308a	105	3c. violet	33·00	1·40
309a	106	4c. brown	38·00	75
310	107	5c. blue	43·00	95
311	108	6c. lake	49·00	1·70
312	109	8c. violet	32·00	1·40
313	110	10c. brown	48·00	1·20
314	111	13c. purple	32·00	5·00
315	112	15c. olive	£110	3·50
316	113	50c. orange	£325	16·00
317	114	$1 black	£550	40·00
485	115	$2 blue	£275	28·00
486	116	$5 green	£250	28·00

117 Washington (after Stuart)

118 Robert R. Livingston (after Stuart)

1903. Perf or imperf.

326	117	2c. red	4·00	25

1904. International Exposition, St. Louis, and Louisiana Purchase. Inscr "COMMEMORATIVE SERIES OF 1904".

330	118	1c. green	26·00	3·00
331	–	2c. red	20·00	1·10
332	–	3c. violet	65·00	21·00
333	–	5c. blue	80·00	12·50
334	–	10c. brown	£150	22·00

DESIGNS: 2c. Thomas Jefferson; 3c. James Monroe (after Vanderlyn); 5c. William McKinley; 10c. Map of Louisiana Purchase.

123 Capt. John Smith, Pocahontas and Powhatan (after painting)

1907. Jamestown Exposition.

335	123	1c. green	21·00	2·50
336	–	2c. red	27·00	2·40
337	–	5c. blue	£120	16·00

DESIGN: 2c. Founding of Jamestown, 1607; 5c. Princess Pocahontas.

126 Franklin

127

128

1908. 1 to 5c. perf or imperf.

338	126	1c. green	5·50	20
505	128	1c. green	25	25
339	127	2c. red	5·75	20
506	128	2c. red	25	20
537		3c. violet	1·70	30
510		4c. brown	10·00	25
503		5c. blue	3·75	75
513		6c. orange	10·50	1·40
514		7c. black	24·00	85
344		8c. green	33·00	1·70
345		10c. yellow	55·00	1·10
346		13c. green	35·00	14·50
347		15c. blue	50·00	4·25
348		50c. violet	£250	14·00
349		$1 black	£400	55·00

DESIGNS: Types **127** and **128**, Washington (after Houdon bust).

129 Lincoln (detail of statue by Saint Gaudens in Grant Park, Chicago)

1909. Birth Centenary of Abraham Lincoln. Perf or imperf.

374	129	2c. red	4·75	1·10

130 Wm. H. Seward

131 "Clermont" and "Half Moon" on Hudson River

1909. Alaska–Yukon–Pacific Exposition. Perf or imperf.

377	130	2c. red	6·00	1·30

1909. Hudson–Fulton Celebration. Perf or imperf.

379	131	2c. red	8·75	2·75

133 Franklin (after Caffieri bust)

138 Franklin (after Caffieri bust)

1912.

515	133	8c. olive	10·50	90
516		9c. pink	11·50	1·50
517		10c. yellow	14·00	20
518		11c. green	7·75	2·50
519		12c. brown	7·75	55
520		13c. green	9·25	4·50
521		15c. grey	30·00	75
522		20c. blue	41·00	25
523		30c. orange	34·00	90
524		50c. lilac	60·00	70
525		$1 black	55·00	1·30
526	138	$2 black and orange	£650	£130
527		$2 black and red	£170	23·00
528		$5 black and green	£225	25·00

134 Balboa

135 Panama Canal (after model of Pedro Miguel Locks)

1913. Panama–Pacific Exposition. Inscr "SAN FRANCISCO 1915".

423	134	1c. green	13·50	1·20
424	135	2c. red	15·00	45
425	–	5c. blue	60·00	4·25
426	–	10c. yellow	£110	17·00

DESIGNS: 5c. Golden Gate, San Francisco; 10c. Discovery of San Francisco Bay (after painting by Mathew).

A 139 Curtiss JN-4 "Jenny"

139 Liberty and Allies' Flags

1918. Air.

A546	A 139	6c. orange	7·75	2·50
A547		16c. green	90·00	28·00
A548		24c. blue and red	95·00	36·00

1919. Victory.

546	139	3c. violet	6·00	2·50

140 The "Mayflower"

1920. Tercentenary of Landing of Pilgrim Fathers. Inscr as in T **140**.

556	140	1c. green	3·25	2·30
557	–	2c. red	5·00	1·40
558	–	5c. blue	33·00	11·00

DESIGNS: 2c. Landing of the Pilgrims (after drawing by White); 5c. Signing the Compact.

144 Franklin

157 Indian Chief

158 Statue of Liberty

159 Golden Gate

165 America

176 Wilson

1922. Perf or imperf (1, 1½, 2c.).

559	–	½c. brown (Hale)	20	20
632	**144**	1c. green	15	15
612	–	1½c. brown (Harding)	20	15
634	–	2c. red (Washington)	10	15
636a	–	3c. violet (Lincoln)	20	15
637	–	4c. brown (Martha Washington)	1·50	15
608	–	5c. blue (T. Roosevelt)	1·40	30
639	–	6c. orange (Garfield)	1·40	15
640	–	7c. black (McKinley)	1·40	15
641	–	8c. green (Grant)	1·40	15
642	–	9c. pink (Jefferson)	1·40	15
610	–	10c. orange (Monroe)	2·20	25
571a	–	11c. blue (Hayes)	1·00	30
571b	–	11c. green (Hayes)	1·00	40
693	–	12c. violet (Cleveland)	3·75	20
694	–	13c. green (B. Harrison)	1·30	20
695	**157**	14c. blue	2·50	40
696	**158**	15c. grey	6·00	20
697	**176**	17c. black	3·25	20
698	**159**	20c. red	7·00	20
699	–	25c. green (Niagara)	7·25	20
700	–	30c. brown (American bison)	11·00	20
701	–	50c. lilac (Arlington Amphitheatre and Unknown Soldier's Tomb)	30·00	20
579	–	$1 brown (Lincoln Memorial)	38·00	35
580	–	$2 blue (Capitol, Washington)	90·00	8·50
581	**165**	$5 blue and red	£140	12·00

The 25c. to $2 are horiz designs as T **159**, the remainder vert as T **144**.

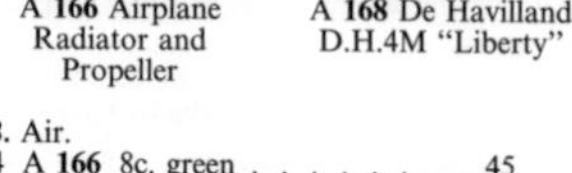
A **166** Airplane Radiator and Propeller
A **168** De Havilland D.H.4M "Liberty"

1923. Air.

A614	A **166**	8c. green	45	20
A615	–	16c. blue	65·00	23·00
A616	A **168**	24c. red	70·00	24·00

DESIGN: 16c. Air mail service insignia.

166 Harding

167 "Nieu Nederland" (emigrant ship)

1923. President Harding Memorial.

614	**166**	2c. black	50	10

1924. Huguenot–Walloon Tercentenary.

618	**167**	1c. green	2·10	2·75
619	–	2c. red	5·00	1·90
620	–	5c. blue	19·00	11·00

DESIGNS: 2c. Landing at Fort Orange; 5c. Ribault Memorial, Mayport, Florida.

170 Washington at Cambridge

173 Sloop "Restaurationen"

1925. 150th Anniv of Battle of Lexington and Concord.

621	**170**	1c. green	2·00	2·30
622	–	2c. red	3·75	3·50
623	–	5c. blue	17·00	10·00

DESIGNS: 2c. Battle of Lexington-Concord; 5c. Statue of "Minute Man".

1925. Norse-American Centennial. Dated "1825 1925".

624	**173**	2c. black and red	2·75	2·40
625	–	5c. black and blue	10·00	9·25

DESIGN: 5c. "Raven" (replica Viking longship).

A **177** De Havilland D.H.4M Biplanes and Relief Map of U.S.A.

1926. Air.

A628	A **177**	10c. blue	2·20	35
A629		15c. brown	4·75	2·75
A630		20c. green	6·00	1·60

177 Liberty Bell

1926. 150th Anniv of Independence and Sesquicentennial Exhibition.

628	**177**	2c. red	2·75	45

178 Ericsson Memorial (J. E. Fraser) in Washington, D.C.

179 Alexander Hamilton's Battery (after painting by E. F. Ward)

1926. John Ericsson Commemoration.

629	**178**	5c. violet	5·50	3·50

1926. 150th Anniv of Battle of White Plains.

644	**179**	2c. red	1·30	1·50

A **180** "Spirit of St. Louis"

1927. Air. Lindbergh's Transatlantic Flight.

A646	A **180**	10c. blue	75	85

181 Green Mountain Boy

182 Surrender of Gen. Burgoyne (after painting by Trumbull)

1927. 150th Anniv of Independence of Vermont and Battle of Bennington.

646	**181**	2c. red	1·00	80

1927. 150th Anniv of Burgoyne Campaign.

647	**182**	2c. red	2·40	1·90

183 Washington at Valley Forge (after engraving by J. C. McRae)

A **184** Air Beacon, Sherman Hill, Rocky Mountains

1928. 150th Anniv of Valley Forge.

648	**183**	2c. red	60	40

1928. Air.

A649	A **184**	5c. blue and red	2·75	3·00

1928. 150th Anniv of Discovery of Hawaii. Optd **HAWAII 1778 - 1928.**

649	2c. red (No. 634)	4·00	4·00
650	5c. blue (No. 608)	8·25	10·50

1928. 150th Anniv of Battle of Monmouth. Optd **MOLLY PITCHER.**

651	2c. red (No. 634)	70	70

186 Wright Flyer I

1928. Civil Aeronautics Conference and 25th Anniv of Wright Brothers' First Flight.

652	**186**	2c. red	75	75
653	–	5c. blue	4·00	3·00

DESIGN: 5c. Globe and Ryan B-5 Brougham biplane.

188 George Rogers Clark at Vincennes (from painting by F. C. Yohn)

1929. 150th Anniv of Surrender of Fort Sackville.

654	**188**	2c. black and red	40	50

1929. Stamps of 1922 optd. (a) **Kans.**

655	**144**	1c. green	2·00	1·70
656	**166**	1½c. brown	3·00	2·00
657	–	2c. red	3·50	90
658	–	3c. violet	16·00	10·00
659	–	4c. brown	14·50	6·50
660	–	5c. blue	10·00	6·75
661	–	6c. orange	21·00	12·50
662	–	7c. black	22·00	17·00
663	–	8c. olive	70·00	50·00
664	–	9c. red	11·00	8·50
665	–	10c. yellow	17·00	9·00

(b) **Nebr.**

666	**144**	1c. green	2·75	1·50
667	**166**	1½c. brown	2·75	1·80
668	–	2c. red	2·75	1·30
669	–	3c. violet	10·50	7·50
670	–	4c. brown	16·00	10·50
671	–	5c. blue	15·00	10·50
672	–	6c. orange	34·00	16·00
673	–	7c. black	19·00	12·50
674	–	8c. olive	28·00	17·00
675	–	9c. red	33·00	18·00
676	–	10c. yellow	95·00	15·00

191 Edison's Original Lamp

192 Maj.-Gen. Sullivan

1929. 50th Anniv of Edison's First Electric Lamp.

678	**191**	2c. red	45	20

1929. 150th Anniv of Maj.-Gen. Sullivan's Western Campaign.

680	**192**	2c. red	50	40

193 Gen. Wayne Memorial in Fallen Timbers Park, by E. W. Laville

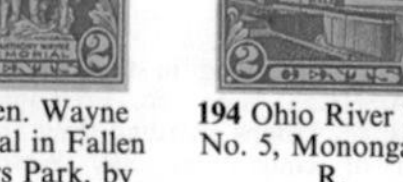
194 Ohio River Lock No. 5, Monongahela R.

1929. 135th Anniv of Battle of Fallen Timbers.

681	**193**	2c. red	65	65

1929. Completion of Ohio River Canalization.

682	**194**	2c. red	40	45

A **195** Air Mail Pilot's Badge

1930. Air.

A684	A **195**	5c. violet	65	85
A685		6c. orange	15	15
A686		8c. green	55	15

195 Seal of the Colony
196 Governor and Indian

1930. Massachusetts Bay Colony Tercentenary.

683	**195**	2c. red	40	40

1930. 250th Anniv of Original Settlement near Charleston.

684	**196**	2c. red	1·00	1·10

A **197** Over the Atlantic

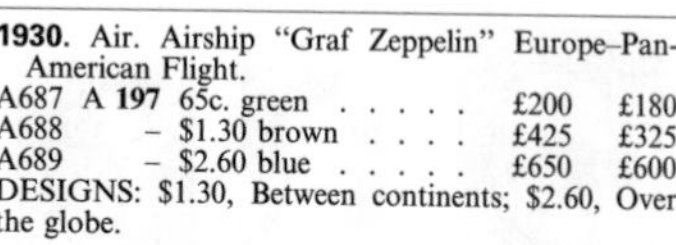
1930. Air. Airship "Graf Zeppelin" Europe–Pan-American Flight.

A687	A **197**	65c. green	£200	£180
A688	–	$1.30 brown	£425	£325
A689	–	$2.60 blue	£650	£600

DESIGNS: $1.30, Between continents; $2.60, Over the globe.

197 Harding

199 George Washington (after statue by F. Vittor in Braddock, Pa.)

1930.

685	**197**	1½c. brown	30	10
686	–	4c. brown	80	10

DESIGN: 4c. Taft.

1930. 175th Anniv of Battle of Braddock's Field.

689	**199**	2c. red	80	90

200 Gen. Wilhelm von Steuben (from medallion by Karl Dautert)

201 Gen. Casimir Pulaski (from etching by H. B. Hall)

1930. Birth Bicentenary of Gen. von Steuben.

690	**200**	2c. red	30	45

1931. 150th Death Anniv of Gen. Pulaski.

691	**201**	2c. red	15	15

202 Red Cross Nurse (from poster "The World's Greatest Mother")

203 Rochambeau, Washington, De Grasse (Washington, after painting by Trumbull, others from old engravings)

1931. 50th Anniv of American Red Cross Society.

702	**202**	2c. black and red	15	15

1931. 150th Anniv of Surrender of Cornwallis at Yorktown.

703	**203**	2c. black and red	20	25

204 George Washington

205 George Washington

1932. Birth Bicentenary of George Washington. Portraits dated "1732 1932".

704	**204**	½c. sepia	10	15
705	**205**	1c. green	15	15
706	–	1½c. brown	20	15
707	–	2c. red	10	15
708	–	3c. violet	40	20
709	–	4c. brown	15	15
710	–	5c. blue	95	20
711	–	6c. orange	2·10	20
712	–	7c. black	15	20
713	–	8c. olive	1·90	70
714	–	9c. red	1·50	25
715	–	10c. yellow	7·00	20

For 3c. as No. 707, see No. 720.

216 Skiing

217 Tree-planting

1932. Winter Olympic Games, Lake Placid.

716	**216**	2c. red	25	20

1932. 60th Anniv of Establishment of Arbor Day.

717	**217**	2c. red	10	15

218 Sprinter

219 Discus Thrower

221 Wm. Penn

1932. Summer Olympic Games, Los Angeles.
718 **218** 3c. violet . . . . 1·00 15
719 **219** 5c. blue . . . . 1·60 25

1932. As No. 707, but without date.
720 3c. violet 15 15

1932. 250th Anniv of Penn's Arrival in America.
723 **221** 3c. violet 15 20

222 Webster

223 Gen. Oglethorpe

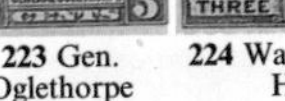

224 Washington's H.Q.

1932. 150th Birth Anniv of Daniel Webster.
724 **222** 3c. violet 20 20

1933. Bicentenary of Founding of Georgia.
725 **223** 3c. violet 15 20

1933. 150th Anniv of Proclamation of Peace after War of Independence.
726 **224** 3c. violet 15 15

225 Fort Dearborn (after painting by Dwight Benton)

226 Federal Building

1933. "Centenary of Progress" International Exhibition, Chicago.
727 **225** 1c. green 15 15
728 **226** 3c. violet 15 15

227 Agriculture, Commerce and Industry

1933. National Recovery Act.
729 **227** 3c. violet 10 15

A **230** Chicago Federal Building, "Graf Zeppelin" and Friedrichshafen Hangar

1933. Air. "Graf Zeppelin" Chicago Flight.
A732 A **230** 50c. green . . . . . 60·00 50·00

230 Routes of various Admiral Byrd Flights

1933. Byrd Antarctic Expedition.
752 **230** 3c. blue 35 50

231 Gen. Kosciuszko (from statue in Lafayette Park, Washington)

233 The "Ark" and the "Dove" (from drawing by E. Tunis)

1933. 150th Anniv of Naturalization of Kosciuszko.
733 **231** 5c. blue 30 25

1934. Maryland Tercentenary.
735 **233** 3c. red 10 15

234 "Portrait of my Mother" by Whistler

1934. Mothers' Day. Perf or imperf.
736 **234** 3c. violet 10 15

235 Nicolet's Landing at Green Bay (after painting by E. W. Deming)

1934. Tercentenary of Wisconsin.
738 **235** 3c. violet 10 15

236 "El Capitan", Yosemite

237 Grand Canyon

1934. National Parks.
739 **236** 1c. green 10 15
740 **237** 2c. red 10 15
741 – 3c. violet 10 15
742 – 4c. brown 20 30
743 – 5c. blue 40 45
744 – 6c. blue 70 80
745 – 7c. black 40 70
746 – 8c. green . . . . 1·10 1·10
747 – 9c. red . . . . 1·00 50
748 – 10c. grey . . . . 2·00 70
DESIGNS—VERT: 5c. "Old Faithful" geyser, Yellowstone; 8c. Great White Throne, Zion; 10c. Mount le Conte, Smoky Mountain. HORIZ: 3c. Mirror Lake, Mt. Rainier; 4c. Cliff dwellings, Mesa Verde; 6c. Crater Lake and Wizard Is; 7c. Great Head, Acadia; 9c. Mt. Rockwell and Two Medicine Lake Glacier.

248 The Charter Oak

1935. Connecticut Tercentenary.
771 **248** 3c. purple 10 10

249 Exhibition Grounds, Point Loma and San Diego Bay

1935. California Pacific Int Exn, San Diego.
772 **249** 3c. violet 10 10

250 Boulder Dam, Nevada

251 Seal of Michigan

1935. Dedication of Boulder Dam.
773 **250** 3c. violet 10 10

1935. Michigan Centenary.
774 **251** 3c. violet 10 10

A **253** Martin M-130 Flying Boat

1935. Air. Trans-Pacific Air Mail.
A775 – 20c. green 10 10
A776 A **253** 25c. blue 10 10
A777 – 50c. red . . . . . . 9·00 4·50
Nos. A775 and A777 are as Type A **253** but without the date.

252 S. Houston, S. F. Austin, and the Alamo

253 Roger Williams (from statue in Roger Williams Park, Providence, R. I.)

1936. Centenary of Declaration of Texan Independence.
775 **252** 3c. violet 10 10

1936. Rhode Island Tercentenary.
776 **253** 3c. violet 10 10

255 First Settlement, Old State House and Capitol

1936. Centenary of Arkansas.
778 **255** 3c. violet 10 10

256 Map of Old Oregon Territory

257 Susan B. Anthony (detail from statue by Adelaide Johnson in Capitol)

1936. Centenary of Oregon.
779 **256** 3c. violet 10 10

1936. 16th Anniv of Women's Suffrage.
780 **257** 3c. purple 10 10

258 Washington and Greene, Mt. Vernon in background

263 Jones, Barry and Battle of Flamborough Head

1936. Army and Navy Heroes. (a) Army.
781 **258** 1c. green 10 10
782 – 2c. red 10 10
783 – 3c. purple 10 10
784 – 4c. blue 15 20
785 – 5c. blue 30 20
DESIGNS: 2c. Jackson, Scott and the Hermitage; 3c. Sherman, Grant and Sheridan; 4c. Lee, Jackson and Stratford Hall; 5c. West Point Military Acadamy.

(b) Navy.
786 **263** 1c. green 10 10
787 – 2c. red 10 10
788 – 3c. purple 10 10
789 – 4c. blue 15 20
790 – 5c. blue 30 20
DESIGNS: 2c. Decatur, MacDonough and U.S.S. "United States" (frigate); 3c. Farragut, Porter and U.S.S. "Hartford" (steam frigate); 4c. Sampson, Dewey and Schley; 5c. Seal of Naval Academy and cadets.

268 Cutler, Putnam and Map of N. W. Territory

1937. 150th Anniv of Enactment of North West Territory Ordinance.
791 **268** 3c. violet 10 10

269 Virginia Dare

1937. 350th Birth Anniv of Virginia Dare.
792 **269** 5c. blue 15 20

271 Signing the Constitution (after painting by J. B. Stearns)

1937. 150th Anniv of U.S. Constitution.
794 **271** 3c. mauve 10 10

272 Statue to Kamehameha I, Honolulu

273 Mt. McKinley, Alaska

274 Fortaleza Castle, Puerto Rico

275 Charlotte Amalie (St. Thomas), Virgin Islands

1937. Territorial Issue.
795 **272** 3c. violet 10 15
796 **273** 3c. violet 10 10
797 **274** 3c. violet 10 10
798 **275** 3c. mauve 10 10

276 Benjamin Franklin

A **308** American Bald Eagle and Shield

1938. Presidential Series.
799 **276** ½c. orange 10 10
800 – 1c. green 10 10
801 – 1½c. brown 10 10
802 – 2c. red 10 10
803 – 3c. violet 10 10
804 – 4c. purple 50 10
805 – 4½c. grey 10 15
806 – 5c. blue 10 10
807 – 6c. red 20 10
808 – 7c. brown 20 10
809 – 8c. green 25 10
810 – 9c. pink 40 10
811 – 10c. red 25 10
812 – 11c. blue 50 10
813 – 12c. mauve 70 10
814 – 13c. green . . . . 1·00 15
815 – 14c. blue 65 10
816 – 15c. slate 35 10
817 – 16c. black 65 40
818 – 17c. red 65 10
819 – 18c. purple . . . . 1·20 10
820 – 19c. mauve . . . . 1·00 55
821 – 20c. green 50 10
822 – 21c. blue 90 20
823 – 22c. red 70 55
824 – 24c. black . . . . 2·75 25
825 – 25c. mauve 50 10
826 – 30c. blue . . . . 3·00 10
827 – 50c. lilac . . . . 4·00 10
828 – $1 black and purple . . . 5·00 15
830 – $2 black and green . . . 15·00 4·00
831 – $5 black and red . . . . 70·00 4·25

DESIGNS: 1c. Washington; 1½c. Martha Washington; 2c. John Adams; 3c. Jefferson; 4c. Madison; 4½c. White House; 5c. James Monroe; 6c. John Quincy Adams; 7c. Jackson; 8c. Martin van Buren; 9c. Wm. Henry Harrison; 10c. John Tyler; 11c. James K. Polk; 12c. Zachary Taylor; 13c. Millard Fillmore; 14c. Franklin Pierce; 15c. James Buchanan; 16c. Lincoln; 17c. Johnson; 18c. Grant; 19c. Rutherford B. Hayes; 20c. James A. Garfield; 21c. Chester A. Arthur; 22c. Grover Cleveland; 24c. Benjamin Harrison; 25c. William McKinley; 30c. Theodore Roosevelt; 50c. Taft; $1 Woodrow Wilson; $2 Harding; $5 Coolidge.

1938. Air.
A845 A **308** 6c. red and blue . . . 15 10

308 Colonial Court House

1938. 150th Anniv of Ratification of U.S. Constitution.
845 **308** 3c. violet 15 10

309 Landing of the Swedes and Finns from "Calmare Nyckel" (after S. Arthurs)

310 Colonization of the West (from statue by G. Borglum at Marietta, Ohio)

1938. Tercentenary of Scandinavian Settlement in America.
846 **309** 3c. mauve 10 10

1938. North West Territory Sesquicentennial.
847 **310** 3c. violet 10 10

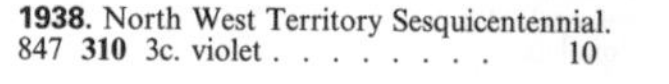

311 Old Capitol Building, Iowa

312 Tower of the Sun

1938. Iowa Territory Centennial.
848 **311** 3c. violet 10 10

1939. Golden Gate Int Exn, San Francisco.
849 **312** 3c. purple 10 10

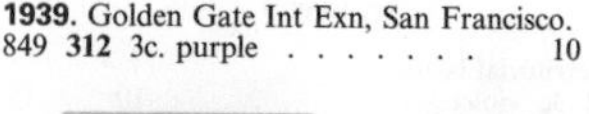

313 Trylon and Perisphere

314 Inauguration of Washington

1939. New York World's Fair.
850 **313** 3c. violet 10 10

1939. 150th Anniv of Election of Washington as First President.
851 **314** 3c. purple 20 10

A **315** Winged Globe

1939. Air.
A852 A **315** 30c. blue . . . . . . 1·00 15

315 Baseball

1939. Baseball Centenary.
852 **315** 3c. violet 45 10

316 T. Roosevelt, Goethals and "Andrea F. Luckenbach" (freighter) in Gaillard Cut

317 Stephen Daye Press (from sketch by G. F. Trenholm)

1939. 25th Anniv of Opening of Panama Canal.
853 **316** 3c. purple 15 10

1939. Tercent of Printing in Colonial America.
854 **317** 3c. violet 10 15

318 Washington, Montana, N. and S. Dakota

319 Washington Irving

324 Henry W. Longfellow

329 Horace Mann

334 John James Audubon

339 Stephen Collins Foster

344 Gilbert Charles Stuart

349 Eli Whitney

1939. 50th Anniv of Statehood of Washington, Montana and N. and S. Dakota.
855 **318** 3c. mauve 10 10

1940. Famous Americans. (a) Authors.
856 **319** 1c. green 10 10
857 – 2c. red 10 10
858 – 3c. purple 10 10
859 – 5c. blue 15 20
860 – 10c. brown . . . . 90 1·20
PORTRAITS: 2c. J. Fenimore Cooper; 3c. Ralph Waldo Emerson; 5c. Louisa May Alcott; 10c. Samuel L. Clemens ("Mark Twain").

(b) Poets.
861 **324** 1c. green 10 10
862 – 2c. red 10 10
863 – 3c. purple 10 10
864 – 5c. blue 20 25
865 – 10c. brown . . . . 95 1·70
PORTRAITS: 2c. John Greenleaf Whittier; 3c. James Russell Lowell; 5c. Walt Whitman; 10c. James Whitcomb Riley.

(c) Educationalists.
866 **329** 1c. green 10 10
867 – 2c. red 10 15
868 – 3c. purple 10 10
869 – 5c. blue 20 25
870 – 10c. brown . . . . 85 1·30
PORTRAITS: 2c. Mark Hopkins; 3c. Charles W. Eliot; 5c. Frances E. Willard; 10c. Booker T. Washington.

(d) Scientists.
871 **334** 1c. green 10 10
872 – 2c. red 10 10
873 – 3c. purple 10 10
874 – 5c. blue 15 20
875 – 10c. brown . . . . 70 1·10
PORTRAITS: 2c. Dr. Crawford W. Long; 3c. Luther Burbank; 5c. Dr. Walter Reed; 10c. Jane Addams.

(e) Composers.
876 **339** 1c. green 10 10
877 – 2c. red 10 10
878 – 3c. purple 10 10
879 – 5c. blue 20 25
880 – 10c. brown . . . . 2·50 1·30
PORTRAITS: 2c. John Philip Sousa; 3c. Victor Herbert; 5c. Edward A. MacDowell; 10c. Ethelbert Nevin.

(f) Artists.
881 **344** 1c. green 10 10
882 – 2c. red 10 10
883 – 3c. purple 10 10
884 – 5c. blue 25 20
885 – 10c. brown . . . . 1·20 1·50
PORTRAITS: 2c. James A. McNeill Whistler; 3c. Augustus Saint-Gaudens; 5c. Daniel Chester French; 10c. Frederic Remington.

(g) Inventors.
886 **349** 1c. green 10 10
887 – 2c. red 10 10
888 – 3c. purple 15 10
889 – 5c. blue 75 40
890 – 10c. brown . . . . 8·00 2·40
PORTRAITS: 2c. Samuel F. B. Morse; 3c. Cyrus Hall McCormick; 5c. Elias Howe; 10c. Alexander Graham Bell.

354 "Pony Express"

355 "The Three Graces" (after Botticelli's "Spring")

1940. 80th Anniv of Inauguration of Pony Express.
891 **354** 3c. red 15 20

1940. 50th Anniv of Pan-American Union.
892 **355** 3c. mauve 15 15

356 State Capitol, Boise

357 Wyoming State Seal

1940. 50th Anniv of Idaho.
893 **356** 3c. violet 10 10

1940. 50th Anniv of Wyoming.
894 **357** 3c. purple 10 10

358 Coronado and His Captains (after painting by Gerald Cassidy)

360 Anti-aircraft Gun

1940. 400th Anniv of Coronado Expedition.
895 **358** 3c. violet 10 10

1940. National Defence.
896 – 1c. green 10 10
897 **360** 2c. red 10 10
898 – 3c. violet 10 15
DESIGNS: 1c. Statue of Liberty; 3c. Hand holding torch.

362 Emancipation Monument (from statue by Thomas Ball, Lincoln Park, Washington)

363 State Capitol Building, Montpelier

1940. 75th Anniv of Abolition of Slavery.
899 **362** 3c. violet 10 15

1941. 150th Anniv of Vermont.
900 **363** 3c. violet 10 10

A **364** Mail Plane

1941. Air.
A901 A **364** 6c. red 10 15
A902 8c. green 10 10
A903 10c. violet 45 25
A904 15c. red 10 10
A905 20c. green 10 10
A906 30c. blue 15 20
A907 50c. orange 15 20

364 Daniel Boone and Companions viewing Kentucky (from mural by Gilbert White in State Capitol, Frankfort)

365 Symbolical of Victory

1942. 150th Anniv of Kentucky.
901 **364** 3c. violet 15 10

1942. Independence Day.
902 **365** 3c. violet 10 10

366 Lincoln and Sun Yat-sen

367 Allegory of Victory

1942. Chinese War Effort.
903 **366** 5c. blue 30 20

1943. Allied Nations.
904 **367** 2c. red 10 10

368 Liberty holding Torch of Freedom and Enlightenment

369 Flag of Poland

1943. Four Freedoms.
905 **368** 1c. green 10 10

1943. Flags of Oppressed Nations. Frames in violet, flags in national colours.
906 5c. Type **369** 25 20
907 5c. Czechoslovakia 25 20
908 5c. Norway 15 20
909 5c. Luxembourg 15 20
910 5c. Netherlands 15 20
911 5c. Belgium 15 20
912 5c. France 15 20
913 5c. Greece 30 40
914 5c. Yugoslavia 15 25
915 5c. Albania 15 25
916 5c. Austria 15 20
917 5c. Denmark 15 20
918 5c. Korea 15 30

382 "Golden Spike Ceremony" (mural, John McQuarrie)

1944. 75th Anniv of First Transcontinental Railway.
919 **382** 3c. violet 10 10

383 Paddle-steamer "Savannah"

1944. 125th Anniv of Transatlantic Crossing of "Savannah."
920 **383** 3c. violet 10 10

384 "What Hath God Wrought"

1944. Centenary of First Telegraph Message.
921 **384** 3c. mauve 10 10

385 View of Corregidor

1944. Defence of Corregidor.
922 **385** 3c. violet 10 10

386 Open-air Cinema

1944. 50th Anniv of Motion Pictures.
923 **386** 3c. violet 20 15

387 Gates of St. Augustine, State Seal and Capitol

1945. Centenary of Statehood of Florida.
924 **387** 3c. purple 10 10

388 "Toward United Nations"

1945. San Francisco Conference.
925 **388** 5c. blue 10 10

389 Franklin D. Roosevelt and Hyde Park

393 Raising U.S.A. Flag at Iwo Jima

1945. Pres. Roosevelt Commemoration. Inscr "1882 1945".
926 **389** 1c. green 10 10
927 – 2c. red 15 10
928 – 3c. violet 15 10
929 – 5c. blue 15 10
DESIGNS: 2c. "Little White House", Warm Springs, Georgia; 3c. "White House", Washington; 5c. Western Hemisphere and Four Freedoms.

1945. U.S. Marines.
930 **393** 3c. green 15 15

394 U.S. Troops marching through Paris

1945. U.S. Army.
931 **394** 3c. olive 15 10

395 U.S. Sailors

1945. U.S. Navy.
932 **395** 3c. blue 15 10

396 "Arthur Middleton" (supply ship) and Coastguard Landing Craft)

397 Alfred E. Smith

1945. U.S. Coastguard.
933 **396** 3c. green 15 10

1945. Alfred E. Smith (Governor of New York) Commemoration.
934 **397** 3c. violet 15 10

398 Flags of U.S.A. and Texas

1945. Centenary of Texas Statehood.
935 **398** 3c. blue 15 10

399 "Liberty" type Freighter unloading Cargo

400 Honourable Discharge Emblem

1946. U.S. Mercantile Marine.
936 **399** 3c. green 15 10

1946. Honourable Discharged Veterans of Second World War.
937 **400** 3c. violet 15 10

401 Andrew Jackson, John Sevier and Tennessee State Capitol

1946. 150th Anniv of Tennessee Statehood.
938 **401** 3c. violet 15 10

402 Iowa State Flag and Map

1946. Centenary of Iowa Statehood.
939 **402** 3c. blue 15 10

403 Smithsonian Institution

1946. Centenary of Smithsonian Institution.
940 **403** 3c. purple 15 10

A 404 Douglas DC-4

1946. Air.
A941 A **404** 5c. red 15 10

404 Entry into Santa Fe (after painting by Kenneth M. Chapman)

405 Thomas A. Edison

1946. Centenary of Entry of Stephen Watts Kearny Expedition into Santa Fe.
941 **404** 3c. purple 15 10

1947. Birth Cent of Thomas Edison (scientist).
942 **405** 3c. violet 15 10

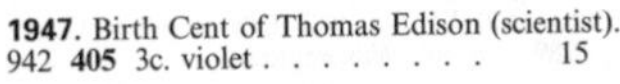

A 406 Douglas DC-4

406 Joseph Pulitzer (from portrait by J. S. Sargent)

1947. Air.
A943 A **406** 5c. red 15 10
A944 6c. red 15 10

1947. Birth Centenary of Joseph Pulitzer (journalist and newspaper publisher).
943 **406** 3c. violet 15 10

407 Washington, Franklin and Evolution of Postal Transport

1947. U.S. Postage Stamp Centenary.
944 **407** 3c. blue 25 10

409 "The Doctor" (after painting by Sir Luke Fildes)

1947. Medical Profession.
946 **409** 3c. purple 15 10

410 Pioneer Caravan

1947. Centenary of Utah.
947 **410** 3c. violet 15 10

A 411 Pan-American Union Building, Washington

1947. Air.
A948 A **411** 10c. black 15 10
A949 – 15c. green 15 10
A950 – 25c. blue 15 10
DESIGNS: 15c. Statue of Liberty and New York City; 25c. San Francisco–Oakland Bay Suspension Bridge.

411 U.S.S. "Constitution"

412 Great Blue Heron and Map of Florida

1947. 150th Anniv of Launching of Frigate U.S.S. "Constitution" ("Old Ironsides").
948 **411** 3c. green 25 15

1947. Dedication of Everglades National Park, Florida.
949 **412** 3c. green 30 15

413 George Washington Carver

414 Sutter's Mill, Coloma

1948. 5th Death Anniv of George Washington Carver (scientist).
950 **413** 3c. violet 15 10

1948. Cent of Discovery of Gold in California.
951 **414** 3c. violet 15 10

415 Gov. Winthrop Sargent, Map and Seal of Mississippi Territory (from portrait by Gilbert Stuart)

1948. 150th Anniv of Mississippi Territory.
952 **415** 3c. purple 15 10

416 Four Chaplains and Liner "Dorchester"

1948. 5th Death Anniv of George Fox, Clark Poling, John Washington and Alexander Goode (who gave up life-jackets).
953 **416** 3c. black 15 10

417 Scroll and State Capitol, Madison

1948. Centenary of Statehood of Wisconsin.
954 **417** 3c. violet 15 10

418 Pioneer and Covered Wagon

1948. Centenary of Swedish Pioneers in Middle West.
955 **418** 5c. blue 15 10

419 Elizabeth Stanton, Carrie C. Catt, and Lucretia Mott

A 420 Map of New York, Ring and Planes (from Poster by G. A. Lorimer)

1948. Progress of American Women.
956 **419** 3c. violet 15 10

1948. Air. Golden Anniv of New York City Council.
A957 A **420** 5c. red 15 15

420 William Allen White

421 Niagara Railway Suspension Bridge (from print by H. Peters)

1948. Honouring W. A. White (editor and author).
957 **420** 3c. purple 15 10

1948. Centenary of Friendship between United States and Canada.
958 **421** 3c. blue 15 15

422 Francis Scott Key

1948. Honouring F. S. Key (author of "Star Spangled Banner").
959 **422** 3c. red 15 15

423 Boy and Girl Students

1948. Salute to Youth.
960 **423** 3c. blue 15 15

424 John McLoughlin, Jason Lee and Covered Wagon

425 Harlan Fiske Stone

1948. Oregon Territory Centennial.
961 **424** 3c. red 15 15

1948. Honouring Chief Justice H. F. Stone.
962 **425** 3c. purple 15 15

426 Palomar Mountain Observatory

427 Clara Barton and Cross

1948. Dedication of Palomar Observatory.
963 **426** 3c. blue 15 15

1948. Honouring Clara Barton (founder of American Red Cross).
964 **427** 3c. red 15 15

428 Light Brahma Rooster

1948. Centenary of American Poultry Industry.
965 **428** 3c. brown 15 15

429 Star and Palm Branch

430 Fort Kearny and Pioneers (Pioneer group from sculpture on Nebraska State Capitol)

1948. Honouring Bereaved Mothers.
966 **429** 3c. yellow 15 10

1948. Centenary of Fort Kearny, Nebraska.
967 **430** 3c. violet 15 10

431 Peter Stuyvesant and Fire Engines (from painting in Library of Congress)

1948. Tercentenary of Volunteer Firemen.
968 **431** 3c. red 15 10

432 Indian Seals and Map of Oklahoma

1948. Centenary of Five Civilized Indian Tribes of Oklahoma.
969 **432** 3c. brown 15 10

433 Statue of Capt. William Owen "Bucky" O'Neill, Prescott, Arizona (S. H. Borglum)

1948. 50th Anniv of Organization of Rough Riders.
970 **433** 3c. purple 15 10

434 Juliette Gordon Low

435 Will Rogers

1948. Honouring Juliette Gordon Low (founder of U.S.A. Girl Scouts).
971 **434** 3c. green 15 10

1948. Honouring Will Rogers (political commentator).
972 **435** 3c. purple 15 10

436 Rocket Testing

437 Moina Michael and Poppies

1948. Centenary of Fort Bliss.
973 **436** 3c. red 15 15

1948. Honouring Moina Michael (founder of Memorial Poppy).
974 **437** 3c. red 15 10

438 Abraham Lincoln (from statue by D. C. French at Lincoln, Neb.)

439 Torch and Emblem

1948. 85th Anniv of Gettysburg Address.
975 **438** 3c. blue 20 10

1948. Centenary of American Turners' Society.
976 **439** 3c. red 20 10

440 Joel Chandler Harris

441 Pioneer and Red River Ox Cart

1948. Birth Centenary of J. C. Harris (author).
977 **440** 3c. purple 15 10

1949. Cent of Territorial Status of Minnesota.
978 **441** 3c. green 15 10

442 Washington, Lee and University Building

1949. Bicentenary of Washington and Lee University, Lexington, Virginia.
979 **442** 3c. blue 15 10

443 Puerto Rican, Cogwheel and Ballot Box

1949. 1st Gubernatorial Election in Puerto Rico.
980 **443** 3c. green 15 10

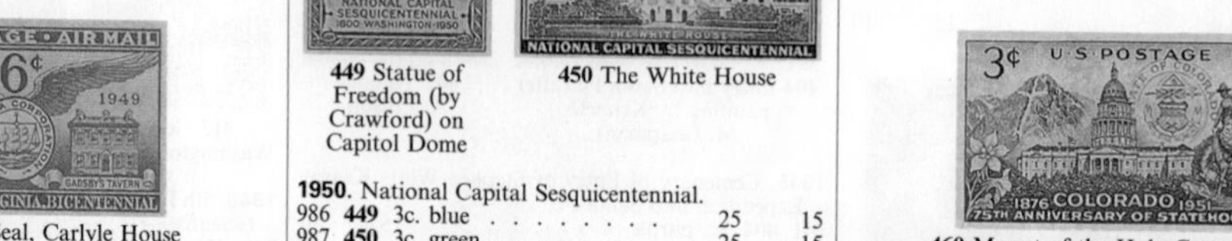

A **444** Wings, Seal, Carlyle House and Gadsby's Tavern

1949. Air. Bicentenary of Alexandria, Virginia.
A981 A **444** 6c. red 15 10

444 Map, "Het Vergulde Vsanker" (sailing barge) and Shield

1949. Tercentenary of Annapolis, Maryland.
981 **444** 3c. green 20 10

445 Young and Old Soldiers

446 Edgar Allan Poe

1949. Final National Encampment of the Grand Army of the Republic.
982 **445** 3c. red 15 10
For similar stamp see No. 995.

1949. Death Centenary of Edgar Allan Poe (poet and author).
983 **446** 3c. purple 25 10

A **447** U.P.U Monument, Berne and P.O. Department, Washington

1949. Air. 75th Anniv of U.P.U.
A984 A **447** 10c. violet 15 10
A985 – 15c. blue 15 10
A986 – 25c. red 15 10
DESIGNS: 15c. Globe and birds; 25c. Globe and Boeing 377 Stratocruiser.

A **450** Wright Brothers and Wright Flyer I

1949. Air. 46th Anniv of Wright Brothers' First Flight.
A987 A **450** 6c. purple 15 10

447 Symbolic of Investments

448 Samuel Gompers

1950. 75th Anniv of American Bankers' Assn.
984 **447** 3c. green 15 10

1950. Birth Centenary of Samuel Gompers (labour leader).
985 **448** 3c. purple 15 10

449 Statue of Freedom (by Crawford) on Capitol Dome

450 The White House

1950. National Capital Sesquicentennial.
986 **449** 3c. blue 25 15
987 **450** 3c. green 25 15
988 – 3c. violet 20 10
989 – 3c. purple 15 10
DESIGNS—HORIZ: No. 988, U.S. Supreme Court building; 989, Capitol, Washington.

453 Casey Jones, Locomotive No. 382 and "Rocket" Diesel Train

1950. Honouring Railway Engineers.
990 **453** 3c. purple 20 10

454 Kansas City in 1850 and 1950

1950. Centenary of Kansas City.
991 **454** 3c. violet 15 10

455 Scouts and Badge

1950. American Boy Scouts.
992 **455** 3c. brown 20 10

456 First Capitol and W. H. Harrison

1950. Sesquicentennial of Indiana.
993 **456** 3c. blue 20 10

457 Pioneers

1950. Centenary of California.
994 **457** 3c. yellow 15 10

1951. Final Reunion of United Confederate Veterans. As T **445**, but initials at left and in hat badge changed to "UCV".
995 **445** 3c. grey 15 10

458 Log Cabin

1951. Centenary of Nevada.
996 **458** 3c. olive 15 10

459 Cadillac Disembarking

1951. 250th Anniv of Landing of Cadillac at Detroit.
997 **459** 3c. blue 15 10

460 Mount of the Holy Cross, State Seal and Capitol

1951. 75th Anniv of Colorado.
998 **460** 3c. violet 15 10

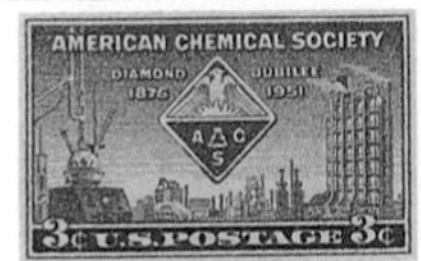

461 Emblem and Chemical Plant

1951. 75th Anniv of American Chemical Society.
999 **461** 3c. purple 20 10

462 Washington at Brooklyn

1951. 175th Anniv of Battle of Brooklyn.
1000 **462** 3c. violet 15 10

463 Betsy Ross and Flag

1952. Birth Bicentenary of Betsy Ross (maker of First American flag).
1001 **463** 3c. red 15 10

464 Emblem and Young Club Members

1952. 50th Anniv of 4-H Clubs.
1002 **464** 3c. green 15 10

465 Horse-drawn "Pioneer" Coach, "Tom Thumb" (1829) and Diesel Locomotive

1952. 125th Anniv of Baltimore and Ohio Railway.
1003 **465** 3c. blue 20 10

466 Cars of 1902 and 1952

467 "Torch of Freedom"

1952. 50th Anniv of American Automobile Assn.
1004 **466** 3c. blue 20 10

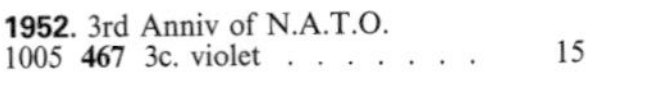

1952. 3rd Anniv of N.A.T.O.
1005 **467** 3c. violet 15 10

A **467** Diamond Head, Oahu, Honolulu

1952. Air.
A1005 A **467** 80c. purple . . . . 5·00 1·10

468 Grand Coulee Dam

1952. 50th Anniv of Columbia Basin Reclamation.
1006 **468** 3c. green 15 10

469 Lafayette and Flags

1952. 175th Anniv of Lafayette's Arrival in America.
1007 **469** 3c. blue 20 10

470 Mt. Rushmore National Memorial

471 Bridges in 1852 and 1952

1952. 25th Anniv of Mt. Rushmore National Memorial.
1008 **470** 3c. green 15 10

1952. Centenary of American Society of Civil Engineers.
1009 **471** 3c. blue 15 10

472 Women in Uniform

1952. Women's Services Commemoration.
1010 **472** 3c. blue 15 10

473 Gutenberg and Elector of Mainz (after Edward Laning)

1952. 500th Anniv of Printing of First Book from Movable Type.
1011 **473** 3c. violet 15 10

474 Newspaperboy and Torch of Free Enterprise

1952. Newspaperboys Commemoration.
1012 **474** 3c. violet 15 10

475 Red Cross and Globe

1952. International Red Cross.
1013 **475** 3c. blue and red 20 10

476 Guardsman and Amphibious Landing

1953. National Guard.
1014 **476** 3c. blue 15 10

477 Map and Seal of Ohio

1953. 150th Anniv of Ohio.
1015 **477** 3c. sepia 20 10

478 Seal of Washington Territory and Settlers

1953. Centenary of Washington Territory.
1016 **478** 3c. green 15 10

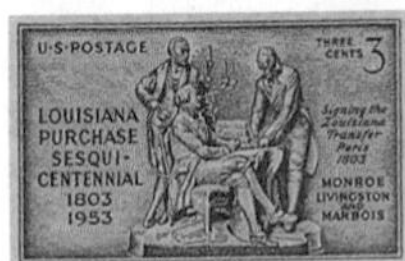

479 Monroe, Livingston and Marbois signing Transfer (from sculpture plaque by Karl Bitter)

1953. 150th Anniv of Louisiana Purchase.
1017 **479** 3c. purple 20 10

A **480** Wright Flyer I and Boeing 377 Stratocruiser

1953. Air. 50th Anniv of Aviation.
A1018 A **480** 6c. red 15 10

480 Commodore Perry and U.S.S. "Susquehanna" and "Mississippi" (paddle-gunboats) in Tokyo Bay

1953. Centenary of Opening of Japan to Foreign Trade.
1018 **480** 5c. turquoise 30 15

481 "Wisdom", "Justice and Divine Inspiration" and "Truth"

1953. 75th Anniv of American Bar Association.
1019 **481** 3c. violet 15 10

482 "Sagamore Hill"

1953. Opening of Theodore Roosevelt's Home.
1020 **482** 3c. green 15 10

483 Young Farmer and Landscape

1953. 25th Anniv of "Future Farmers of America".
1021 **483** 3c. blue 15 10

484 Truck and Distant City

1953. 50th Anniv of Trucking Industry.
1022 **484** 3c. violet 15 10

485 Gen. Patton and Tanks in Action

1953. Gen. George Patton and U.S. Armoured Forces.
1023 **485** 3c. violet 15 10

486 New York in 1653 and 1953

1953. Tercent of Foundation of New York City.
1024 **486** 3c. purple 20 10

487 Pioneer Family

1953. Centenary of Gadsden Purchase.
1025 **487** 3c. chestnut 15 10

488 Low Memorial Library

1954. Bicentenary of Columbia University.
1026 **488** 3c. blue 15 10

490 Washington (after Stuart)

492 Mount Vernon

501 Statue of Liberty

516 "The Sower" and Mitchell Pass (from statue on Capitol, Lincoln, Neb)

1954. Liberty Issue.

1027	–	½c. red	15	10
1028	**490**	1c. green	15	10
1029	–	1¼c. turquoise	15	10
1030	**492**	1½c. lake	15	10
1031	–	2c. red	15	10
1032	–	2½c. blue	15	10
1033	**501**	3c. violet	15	10
1034	–	4c. mauve	15	10
1035	–	4½c. green	15	10
1036	–	5c. blue	15	10
1037	–	6c. red	20	10
1038	–	7c. red	20	10
1039	**501**	8c. red and blue	25	10
1040	–	8c. red and blue	20	10
1041	–	8c. brown	20	10
1042	–	9c. purple	30	10
1043	–	10c. red	25	10
1044	–	11c. blue and red	20	10
1045	–	12c. red	35	10
1046	–	15c. red	65	10
1047	–	20c. blue	45	10
1059	–	25c. turquoise	50	20
1049	–	30c. black	1·10	10
1050	–	40c. lake	1·70	10
1051	–	50c. violet	1·50	10
1052	–	$1 violet	4·50	10
1053	–	$5 black	70·00	6·25

DESIGNS—As Type **490**: ½c. Benjamin Franklin; 2c. Jefferson; 4c. Lincoln; 5c. Monroe; 6c. Theodore Roosevelt; 7c. Woodrow Wilson; 8c. (No. 1040), As Type **501** but torch flame below "P"; 8c. (No. 1041), Gen. John J. Pershing; 11c. As No. 1040; 12c. Benjamin Harrison; 15c. John Jay; 25c. Paul Revere; 30c. Robert E. Lee; 40c. John Marshall; 50c. Susan B. Anthony; $1 Patrick Henry; $5 Alexander Hamilton. As Type **492**—VERT: 2½c. Bunker Hill Monument and Massachusetts flag. HORIZ: 1¼c. Palace of the Governors, Santa Fe; 4½c. The Hermitage; 9c. The Alamo; 10c. Independence Hall; 20c. Monticello, Thomas Jefferson's home.

1954. Centenary of Nebraska Territory.
1062 **516** 3c. violet 15 10

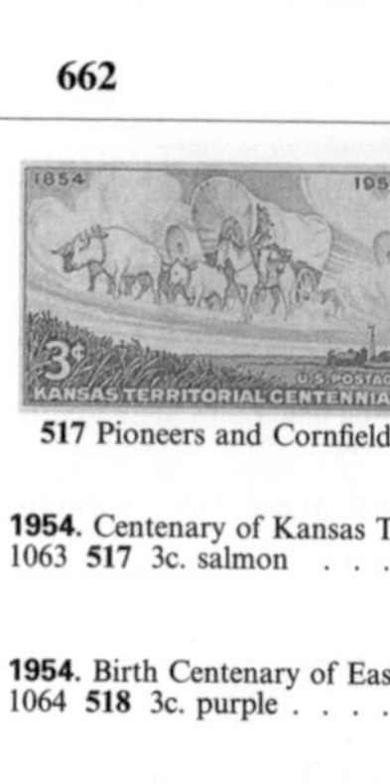
517 Pioneers and Cornfield

518 George Eastman

1954. Centenary of Kansas Territory.
1063 **517** 3c. salmon 15 10

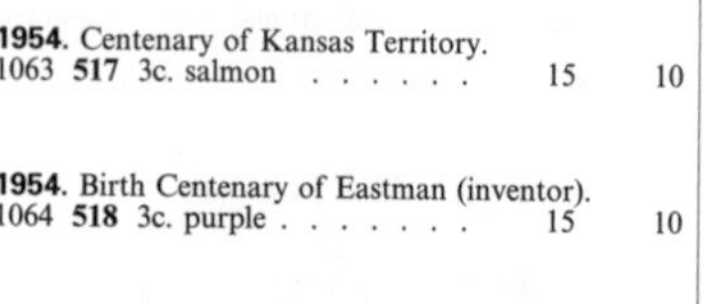

1954. Birth Centenary of Eastman (inventor).
1064 **518** 3c. purple 15 10

519 Landing on Riverbank, Missouri

A 520 American Bald Eagle in Flight

1954. 150th Anniv of Lewis and Clark Expedition.
1065 **519** 3c. purple 15 10

1954. Air.
A1066 A **520** 4c. blue 15 10
A1067 5c. red 25 10

520 "Peale in his Museum" (self-portrait)

521 Open Book and Symbols of Subjects taught

1955. 150th Anniv of Pennsylvania Academy of Fine Arts.
1066 **520** 3c. purple 15 10

1955. Centenary of First Land-Grant Colleges.
1067 **521** 3c. green 15 10

522 Torch, Globe and Rotary Emblem

1955. 50th Anniv of Rotary International.
1068 **522** 8c. blue 15 10

523 Marine, Coastguard, Soldier, Sailor and Airman

1955. Armed Forces Reserve.
1069 **523** 3c. purple 15 10

524 "The Old Man of the Mountains"

525 The Great Lakes and "Altadoc" (freighter)

1955. 150th Anniv of Discovery of "The Old Man of the Mountains" (New Hampshire landmark).
1070 **524** 3c. turquoise 20 10

1955. Soo Locks Centenary.
1071 **525** 3c. blue 15 10

526

1955. "Atoms for Peace".
1072 **526** 3c. blue 20 10

527 Plan of Fort, Ethan Allen and Artillery

528 Mellon (after Edward Birley)

1955. Bicentenary of Fort Ticonderoga.
1073 **527** 3c. brown 20 10

1955. Birth Centenary of Andrew W. Mellon (philanthropist).
1074 **528** 3c. red 20 10

529 Benjamin Franklin (after painting by Benjamin West)

530 Log Cabin

1956. 250th Birth Anniv of Franklin.
1075 **529** 3c. red 15 10

1956. Birth Centenary of Booker T. Washington.
1076 **530** 3c. blue 15 10

532 New York Coliseum and Columbus Monument

1956. 5th International Philatelic Exn, New York.
1078 **532** 3c. violet 15 10

533 Pronghorns

536 H. W. Wiley

1956. Wild Life Conservation.
1079 **533** 3c. purple 15 10
1080 – 3c. sepia 15 10
1081 – 3c. green 20 10
DESIGNS: No. 1080, Common Turkey; 1081, Chinook "king" salmon.

1956. 50th Anniv of Pure Food and Drug Laws.
1082 **536** 3c. green 20 10

537 Wheatland

538 Mosaic by L. M. Winter, A.F.L.-C.I.O. Headquarters

1956. Home of James Buchanan.
1083 **537** 3c. sepia 20 10

1956. Labour Day.
1084 **538** 3c. blue 20 10

539 Nassau Hall (contemporary engraving by Dawkins)

540 Devils Tower

1956. Bicentenary of Nassau Hall.
1085 **539** 3c. black on orange . . 20 10

1956. 50th Anniv of Devils Tower National Monument.
1086 **540** 3c. violet 15 10

541 "The Key to World Peace"

1956. Children's Friendship.
1087 **541** 3c. blue 15 10

542 Alexander Hamilton and Federal Hall, New York

543 Women, Children and Shield

1957. Birth Bicentenary of Alexander Hamilton.
1088 **542** 3c. red 15 10

1957. Infantile Paralysis Relief Campaign.
1089 **543** 3c. mauve 15 10

544 Survey Flag and Coastguard Vessels "Pathfinder", "Explorer" and "Surveyor"

1957. 150th Anniv of Coast and Geodetic Survey.
1090 **544** 3c. blue 15 10

545 Ancient and Modern Capitals

546 Eagle and Ladle

1957. Cent of American Institute of Architects.
1091 **545** 3c. mauve 15 10

1957. Centenary of American Steel Industry.
1092 **546** 3c. blue 15 10

547 Festival Emblem and Aircraft Carrier U.S.S. "Forrestal"

1957. Jamestown Festival and Int Naval Review.
1093 **547** 3c. green 15 10

548 Arrow piercing Atomic Symbol

1957. 50th Anniv of Oklahoma Statehood.
1094 **548** 3c. blue 15 10

549 Teacher with Pupils

1957. Teachers of America Commemoration.
1095 **549** 3c. red 15 10

550 U.S. Flag

1957. Flag Issue.
1096 **550** 4c. red and blue 20 15

A 551 Boeing B-52 Stratofortress and Lockheed F-104 Starfighters

551 "Virginia of Sagadahock" (shallop) and Arms of Maine

1957. Air. 50th Anniv of U.S. Air Force.
A1097 A **551** 6c. blue 15 10

1957. 350th Anniv of American Shipbuilding.
1097 **551** 3c. violet 15 10

552 Pres. Magsaysay of the Philippines (medallion)

553 Marquis de Lafayette (portrait by Court in Versailles Museum)

1953. Pres. Magsaysay Commemoration.
1098 **552** 8c. ochre, blue and red 25 10

1957. Birth Bicentenary of Marquis de Lafayette.
1099 **553** 3c. red 15 10

554 Whooping Cranes

555 "Religious Freedom"

1957. Wild Life Conservation.
1100 **554** 3c. blue, orange and green 15 10

1957. Tercentenary of Flushing Remonstrance.
1101 **555** 3c. black 15 10

556 "Abundance"

557 U.S. Pavilion

1958. Gardening and Horticulture Commem.
1102 **556** 3c. green 15 10

1958. Brussels International Exhibition.
1103 **557** 3c. purple 15 10

558 James Monroe (portrait by Stuart)

1958. Birth Bicentenary of Pres. James Monroe.
1104 **558** 3c. violet 15 10

559 Lake in Minnesota

1958. Centenary of Minnesota Statehood.
1105 **559** 3c. green 15 10

560 Sun's Surface and Hands (after Michelangelo's "The Creation of Adam")

1958. I.G.Y.
1106 **560** 3c. red and black 15 10

561 Gunston Hall (after drawing by Rene Clarke)

562 Mackinac Bridge

1958. Bicentenary of Gunston Hall, Virginia (home of George Mason, patriot).
1107 **561** 3c. green 15 10

1958. Mackinac Bridge Commemoration.
1108 **562** 3c. turquoise 15 10

563 Simon Bolivar (after painting by Ricardo Arcevedo-Bernal)

A **564** Silhouette of Jet Airliner

1958. Bolivar Commemoration.
1109 **563** 4c. ochre 15 10
1110 8c. brown, blue and red 15 15

See also Nos. 1116/17, 1124/5, 1135/6, 1146/7. 1158/9, 1164/5, 1167/8 and 1173/4.

1958. Air.
A1111 A **564** 7c. blue 20 15
A1112 7c. red 25 10

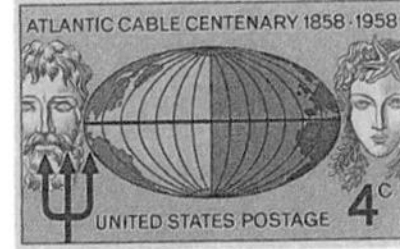

564 Globe, Neptune and Mermaid

1958. Centenary of Inaug of Atlantic Cable.
1111 **564** 4c. purple 15 10

565 Abraham Lincoln (from painting by G. Healy)

570 Hand with Quill Pen and Printing Press

1958. 150th Birth Anniv of Lincoln.
1112 **565** 1c. green 15 10
1113 – 3c. red 20 10
1114 – 4c. brown 25 10
1115 – 4c. blue 25 10

DESIGNS: No. 1113, Bust of Lincoln; 1114, Addressing Electorate; 1115, Lincoln Statue, Washington.

1958. Lajos Kossuth Commemoration. Medallion portrait as T **563**.
1116 4c. green 15 10
1117 8c. brown, blue and red . . 25 15

1958. Freedom of the Press.
1118 **570** 4c. black 15 10

571 Mail Coach under Attack

572 Noah Webster (engraving by G. Parker after painting by James Herring)

1958. Overland Mail Centenary.
1119 **571** 4c. red 15 10

1958. Birth Bicentenary of Noah Webster (lexicographer).
1120 **572** 4c. red 15 10

573 Forest Pines

574 British Forces occupying Fort Duquesne (from etching by T. B. Smith)

1958. Forest Conservation.
1121 **573** 4c. yellow, green & brown 15 10

1958. Bicentenary of Fort Duquesne.
1122 **574** 4c. blue 15 10

A **575** Stars on Alaskan Map

1959. Air. Alaska Statehood.
A1123 A **575** 7c. blue 15 10

575 Covered Wagon and Mt. Hood

577 N.A.T.O. Emblem

1959. Centenary of Oregon Statehood.
1123 **575** 4c. green 20 10

1959. San Martin Commemoration. Medallion portrait as T **563**.
1124 4c. blue 15 10
1125 8c. ochre, red and blue . . . 25 20

1959. 10th Anniv of N.A.T.O.
1126 **577** 4c. blue 20 10

578 Peary with Dog-team and Submarine U.S.S. "Nautilus"

1959. Arctic Explorations by Robert Peary (50th anniv of reaching North Pole) and U.S.S. "Nautilus".
1127 **578** 4c. blue 15 10

579

1959. World Peace through World Trade.
1128 **579** 8c. red 25 15

580 Discovery of Silver at Mt. Davidson, Nevada (from a print)

1959. Cent of Discovery of Silver in Nevada.
1129 **580** 4c. black 15 10

581 Maple Leaf linked with American Eagle

1959. Opening of St. Lawrence Seaway.
1130 **581** 4c. blue and red 15 10

582 New U.S. Flag (with 49 stars)

1959. Inauguration of New United States Flag.
1131 **582** 4c. red, blue and orange 15 10

A **583** John Wise's Balloon "Jupiter"

A **584** Hawaiian Warrior, Map and Star

1959. Air. Centenary of Balloon "Jupiter's" Mail-carrying Flight.
A1132 A **583** 7c. red and blue . . 15 10

1959. Air. Hawaii Statehood.
A1133 A **584** 7c. red 20 10

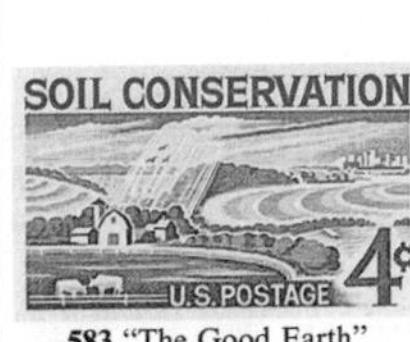

583 "The Good Earth"

584 Oil Derrick

1959. Soil Conservation.
1132 **583** 4c. green, brown and blue 15 10

1959. Centenary of First Oil-well at Titusville, Pennsylvania.
1133 **584** 4c. brown 25 10

A **585** Runner with Olympic Torch

585 "Happy Children with Healthy Teeth"

1959. Air. 3rd Pan-American Games, Chicago.
A1134 A **585** 10c. red and blue . . 20 10

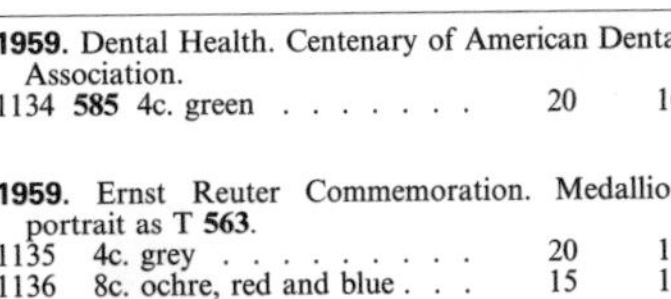

1959. Dental Health. Centenary of American Dental Association.
1134 **585** 4c. green 20 10

1959. Ernst Reuter Commemoration. Medallion portrait as T **563**.
1135 4c. grey 20 10
1136 8c. ochre, red and blue . . . 15 15

A **588** Statue of Liberty

587 Dr. E. McDowell (from painting)

1959. Air.
A1137 – 10c. black and green 15 10
A1138 – 13c. black and red 20 10
A1139 A **588** 15c. black & orge (A) 20 10
A1140 15c. black & orge (B) 20 10
A1141 – 25c. black and brown 20 10

DESIGNS: 10, 13c. Liberty Bell; 15c. Statue has double frame-line (A) or single frame-line (B); 25c. Abraham Lincoln.

1959. 150th Anniv of First Recorded Successful Abdominal Operation.
1137 **587** 4c. purple 15 10

588

1960. "American Credo" series.
1138 **588** 4c. red and blue 20 10
1139 – 4c. green and bistre . . . 20 10
1140 – 4c. red and grey 25 10
1141 – 4c. blue and red 25 10
1142 – 4c. green and purple . . 20 10
1143 – 4c. brown and green . . 20 10

INSCRIPTIONS: No. 1139, "Fear to do ill, and you need fear Nought else" (Franklin); 1140, "I have sworn … Hostility against every form of TYRANNY over the mind of man" (Jefferson); 1141, "And this be our Motto in GOD is our TRUST" (Francis Scott Key); 1142, "Those who Deny freedom to others Deserve it not for Themselves" (Lincoln); 1143, "Give me LIBERTY or give me DEATH" (P. Henry).

594 Scout Saluting

595 Olympic Rings and Snow Crystal

1960. 50th Anniv of American Boy Scout Movement.
1144 **594** 4c. ochre, red and blue 15 10

1960. Winter Olympic Games.
1145 **595** 4c. blue 15 10

1960. Thomas Masaryk Commemoration. Medallion portrait as T **563**.
1146 4c. blue 15 10
1147 8c. ochre, red and blue . . . 25 15

597 "Towards the Light"

1960. World Refuge Year.
1148 **597** 4c. black 20 15

598 "Irrigation"

599 S.E.A.T.O. Emblem

1960. Water Conservation Campaign.
1149 **598** 4c. green, brown and blue 15 10

1960. S.E.A.T.O. Conference.
1150 **599** 4c. blue 15 10

600 Mother and Child

601 New U.S. Flag (with 50 stars)

1960. American Womanhood Commemoration.
1151 **600** 4c. violet 15 10

1960. New United States Flag (50 stars).
1152 **601** 4c. red and blue 15 10

602 Pony Express

1960. Centenary of Pony Express.
1153 **602** 4c. brown 15 10

603 Cripple operating Press

604 Congress Seal

1960. Employment of the Handicapped Campaign.
1154 **603** 4c. blue 15 10

1960. 5th World Forestry Congress, Seattle.
1155 **604** 4c. green 15 10

605 Dolores Bell (Mexico)

606 Washington Monument and Cherry Blossom

1960. 150th Anniv of Mexican Independence.
1156 **605** 4c. red and green 15 10

1960. Centenary of U.S.–Japan Treaty.
1157 **606** 4c. red and turquoise . . 15 10

1960. Jan Paderewski Commemoration. Medallion portrait as T **563**.
1158 4c. blue 15 10
1159 8c. ochre, red and blue . . . 25 15

608 Robert A. Taft

609 Steering Wheel, Motor Transport and Globes

1960. Robert A. Taft Memorial Issue.
1160 **608** 4c. violet 15 10

1960. "Wheels of Freedom" (Motor Industry).
1161 **609** 4c. blue 15 10

610 Boy

611 New P.O. Building

1960. Cent of Boys' Clubs of America Movement.
1162 **610** 4c. red, black and indigo 15 10

1960. Inauguration of 1st U.S. Automated P.O., Providence, Rhode Island.
1163 **611** 4c. blue and red 15 10

1960. Marshal Mannerheim Commem. Medallion portrait as T **563**.
1164 4c. blue 15 10
1165 8c. ochre, red and blue . . . 25 20

613 Camp Fire Girls Emblem

615 George

1960. 50th Anniv of Camp Fire Girls Movement.
1166 **613** 4c. red and blue 15 10

1960. Garibaldi Commem. Medallion portrait as T **563**.
1167 4c. green 15 10
1168 8c. ochre, red and blue . . . 20 20

1960. Senator Walter F. George Memorial Issue.
1169 **615** 4c. violet 15 10

616 Andrew Carnegie

617 Dulles

1960. Andrew Carnegie.
1170 **616** 4c. red 15 10

1960. John Foster Dulles Memorial Issue.
1171 **617** 4c. violet 15 10

618 "Echo I" Communications Satellite

1960. "Communications for Peace".
1172 **618** 4c. violet 20 10

1961. Mahatma Gandhi Commemoration. Medallion portrait as T **563**.
1173 4c. red on orange 15 10
1174 8c. ochre, red and blue . . . 25 20

620 Trail Boss and Prairie

621 Horace Greeley (from steel engraving by A. H. Ritchie)

1961. Range Conservation.
1175 **620** 4c. black, orange and blue 15 10

1961. Horace Greeley (editor).
1176 **621** 4c. violet 15 10

622 Sea Coast Gun

1961. Civil War Centennial. Battles.
1177 **622** 4c. green 30 10
1178 – 4c. black on pink . . . 25 10
1179 – 5c. indigo and blue . . . 25 10
1180 – 5c. black and red 25 15
1181 – 5c. black and blue . . . 40 10
DESIGNS—HORIZ: No. 1178, Rifleman (Shiloh); 1179, Armed combat (Gettysburg); 1180, Artillery crew (Wilderness). VERT: No. 1181, Soldier and rifles (Appomattox).

627 Sunflower and Pioneers

1961. Centenary of Kansas Statehood.
1182 **627** 4c. red, green and brown on yellow 15 10

628 Senator G. W. Norris

1961. Birth Centenary of George W. Norris.
1183 **628** 4c. green 15 10

629 Curtiss A-1 Seaplane, 1911 (Navy's first plane)

1961. 50th Anniv of U.S. Naval Aviation.
1184 **629** 4c. blue 15 10

630 "Balanced Judgement"

631 "The Smoke Signal" (after Remington)

1961. 150th Anniv of Workmen's Compensation Law.
1185 **630** 4c. blue 15 10

1961. Birth Centenary of Frederic Remington (painter).
1186 **631** 4c. multicoloured 15 10

632 Dr. Sun Yat-sen

633 Basketball

1961. 50th Anniv of Republic of China.
1187 **632** 4c. blue 20 10

1961. Birth Centenary of Dr. James A. Naismith (inventor of basketball).
1188 **633** 4c. brown 20 10

634 Nurse lighting Candle of Dedication

635 Ship Rock, New Mexico

1961. Nursing.
1189 **634** 4c. multicoloured 20 10

1962. 50th Anniv of Statehood of New Mexico.
1190 **635** 4c. lake, ochre & turq 15 10

636 Saguaro Cactus and Flowers

637 "U.S. Man in Space"

1962. 50th Anniv of Arizona Statehood.
1191 **636** 4c. blue, green and red 15 10

1962. Project Mercury. Colonel John Glenn's Space Flight.
1192 **637** 4c. blue and yellow . . . 15 10

638 U.S. and Campaign Emblems

1962. Malaria Eradication.
1193 **638** 4c. ochre and blue . . . 15 10

639 C. E. Hughes

640 Space Needle and Monorail

1962. Birth Centenary of Chief Justice Hughes.
1194 **639** 4c. black on buff 15 10

1962. "Century 21" Exn ("World's Fair"), Seattle.
1195 **640** 4c. blue and red 15 10

641 Mississippi Sternwheel Steamer

1962. 150th Anniv of Lousiana Statehood.
1196 **641** 4c. myrtle, red and blue 15 10

642 Settlers' Homestead

1962. Centenary of Homestead Act.
1197 **642** 4c. grey 15 10

643 Girl Scout and Flag

1962. 50th Anniv of U.S. Girl Scouts.
1198 **643** 4c. red 15 10

644 Senator McMahon and Atomic Symbol

1962. Brien McMahon.
1199 **644** 4c. violet 15 10

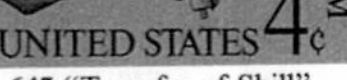

645 "Transfer of Skill" 646 Sam Rayburn

1962. 25th Anniv of National Apprenticeship Act.
1200 **645** 4c. black on olive . . . 15 10

1962. Sam Rayburn (Speaker of House of Representatives) Commemoration.
1201 **646** 4c. brown and blue . . . 15 10

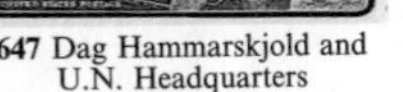

647 Dag Hammarskjold and U.N. Headquarters 648 Christmas Laurel Wreath

1962. Hammarskjold.
1202 **647** 4c. brown, yellow & black 15 10
1203 4c. brown, yellow & black 15 15

No. 1203 has the yellow colour inverted and comes from a special printing made after a few examples had been discovered.

1962. Christmas.
1204 **648** 4c. green and red 15 10

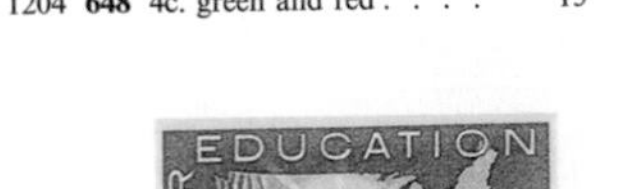

649 "Lamp of Learning" and Map

1962. Higher Education.
1205 **649** 4c. black and green . . . 15 10

651 Washington (after Houdon) A 652 Capitol, Washington, and Douglas DC-8

1962.
1206 – 1c. green 15 10
1207 **651** 5c. blue 15 10
DESIGN: 1c. Andrew Jackson.

1962. Air.
A1210 A **652** 8c. red 15 10

652 "Breezing Up" (after Winslow Homer) 653 U.S. Flag and White House

1962. Winslow Homer.
1210 **652** 4c. multicoloured 15 10

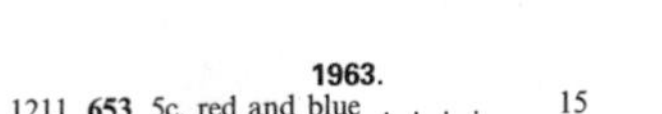

1963.
1211 **653** 5c. red and blue 15 10

654 Charter and Quill

1963. 300th Anniv of Carolina Charter.
1212 **654** 5c. sepia and red 25 10

A **655** P. M. G. Montgomery Blair, Letters and Globe (after portrait by Thomas Sully) 655 "Food for Peace"

1963. Air. Centenary of Paris Postal Conferences.
A1213 A **655** 15c. purple, bl & red 15 10

1963. Freedom from Hunger.
1213 **655** 5c. brown, green and red 15 10

656 Map and State Capitol, Charleston A 657 American Bald Eagle

1963. Centenary of West Virginia Statehood.
1214 **656** 5c. red, black and green 15 10

1963. Air.
A1215 A **657** 6c. red 15 10

657 Broken Link A 658 Amelia Earhart and Lockheed "Electra"

1963. Centenary of Emancipation Proclamation.
1215 **657** 5c. black, blue and red 15 10

1963. Air. Amelia Earhart Commemoration.
A1216 A **658** 8c. purple and red 15 10

658 Torch of Progress 659 Cordell Hull

1963. "Alliance for Progress".
1216 **658** 5c. green and blue . . . 15 10

1963. Cordell Hull Commemoration.
1217 **659** 5c. turquoise 20 10

660 Eleanor Roosevelt

1963. Eleanor Roosevelt Commemoration.
1218 **660** 5c. violet 20 10

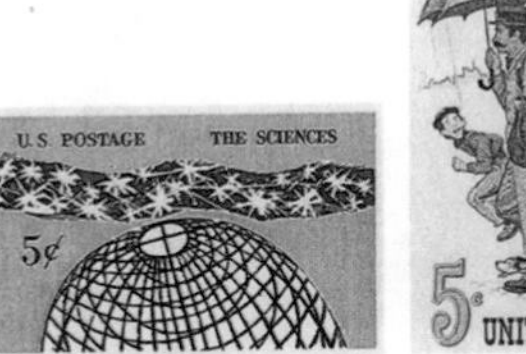

661 "The Sciences" 662 City Mail Postman

1963. Centenary of National Academy of Science.
1219 **661** 5c. black, red and blue 15 10

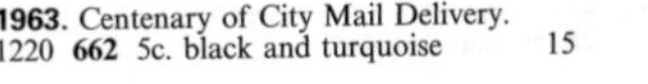

1963. Centenary of City Mail Delivery.
1220 **662** 5c. black and turquoise 15 10

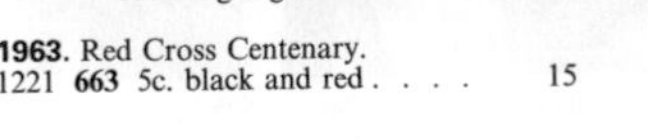

663 Red Cross Flag and S.S. "Morning Light" 664 Christmas Tree

1963. Red Cross Centenary.
1221 **663** 5c. black and red 15 10

1963. Christmas.
1222 **664** 5c. black, blue and red 15 10

665 "Columbia Jays" (print) (actually Collie's Magpie-jays) 666 Sam Houston (from lithograph by F. Davignon)

1963. John James Audubon Commemoration.
1223 **665** 5c. multicoloured 20 10
See also No. A1304.

1964. Sam Houston Commemoration.
1224 **666** 5c. black 15 10

667 "Jerked Down"

1964. Birth Centenary of C. M. Russell (artist).
1225 **667** 5c. multicoloured 15 10

668 Mall with Unisphere and "The Rocket Thrower" (after De Lue) 669 John Muir (naturalist) and Forest

1964. New York World's Fair.
1226 **668** 5c. turquoise 15 15

1964. John Muir Commemoration.
1227 **669** 5c. brown, emerald & green 15 10

670 Pres. Kennedy and "Eternal Flame" 671 Philip Carteret at Elizabethtown (1664) (after painting in Union County Courthouse)

1964. President Kennedy Memorial Issue.
1228 **670** 5c. blue on grey 25 10

1964. Tercentenary of New Jersey.
1229 **671** 5c. blue 20 10

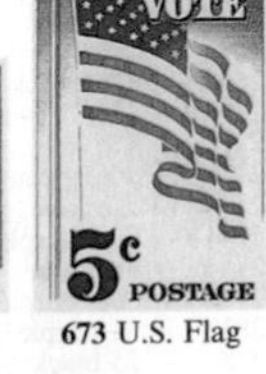

672 Virginia City in 19th Century 673 U.S. Flag

1964. Centenary of Nevada Statehood.
1230 **672** 5c. multicoloured 15 10

1964. "Register and Vote" Campaign.
1231 **673** 5c. red and blue 15 10

674 Shakespeare 675 Drs. William and Charles Mayo (after J. E. Fraser)

1964. 400th Birth Anniv of William Shakespeare.
1232 **674** 5c. sepia on buff 20 10

1964. Mayo Brothers (founders of Mayo Clinic) Commemoration.
1233 **675** 5c. green 20 10

A **676** R. H. Goddard, "Atlas" Rocket and Launching Tower

1964. Air. Robert H. Goddard Commem.
A1234 A **676** 8c. blue, red & yellow 15 10

676 Lute, Horn and Music Score

1964. American Music.
1234 **676** 5c. black, red and blue on light blue 15 10

677 Sampler

1964. "Homemakers" Commemoration.
1235 **677** 5c. multicoloured 15 10

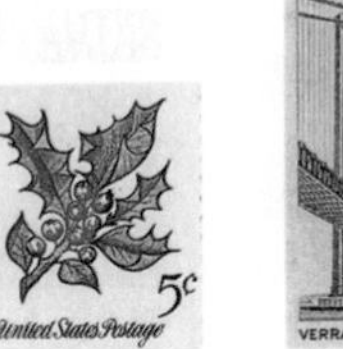
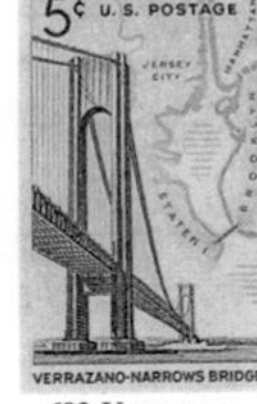

678 Holly 682 Verrazano-Narrows Bridge

1964. Christmas. Each red, green and black.
1236 5c. Type **678** 20 15
1237 5c. Mistletoe 20 15
1238 5c. Poinsettia 20 15
1239 5c. Pine cone 20 15

1964. Opening of Verrazano-Narrows Bridge, New York.
1240 **682** 5c. green 15 10

683 "Abstract Art" (from lithograph by S. Davis)

1964. "To the Fine Arts".
1241 **683** 5c. red, black and blue 15 10

684 Radio Waves

685 General Jackson leading Troops into Battle

1964. Amateur Radio.
1242 **684** 5c. purple 20 10

1965. 150th Anniv of Battle of New Orleans.
1243 **685** 5c. red, blue and black 20 10

686 Discus-thrower (Washington statue)

687 Microscope and Stethoscope

1965. Centenary of Sokol Physical Fitness Organization in the U.S.A.
1244 **686** 5c. blue and lake 15 10

1965. Crusade Against Cancer.
1245 **687** 5c. black, violet and red 15 10

688 Sir Winston Churchill (from photo by Karsh)

1965. Churchill Commemoration.
1246 **688** 5c. black 15 10

689 Procession of Barons, and King John's Crown

1965. 750th Anniv of Magna Carta.
1247 **689** 5c. black, yellow & violet 15 10

690 I.C.Y. Emblem

691 "One hundred years of service"

1965. International Co-operation Year.
1248 **690** 5c. black and blue . . . 15 10

1965. Centenary of Salvation Army.
1249 **691** 5c. black, red and blue 15 10

692 Dante

693 Herbert Hoover

1965. 700th Anniv of Dante's Birth.
1250 **692** 5c. red on flesh 15 10

1965. Hoover Commemoration.
1251 **693** 5c. red 15 10

694 Robert Fulton (after Houdon) and "Clermont"

695 Spanish Knight and Banners

1965. Birth Bicent of Robert Fulton (inventor).
1252 **694** 5c. black and blue . . . 15 10

1965. 400th Anniv of Florida Settlement.
1253 **695** 5c. black, red and yellow 15 10

696 Traffic Signal

697 Elizabeth Clarke Copley (from "The Copley Family" by John S. Copley)

1965. Traffic Safety.
1254 **696** 5c. red, black and green 15 10

1965. John Singleton Copley.
1255 **697** 5c. brown, drab and black 15 10

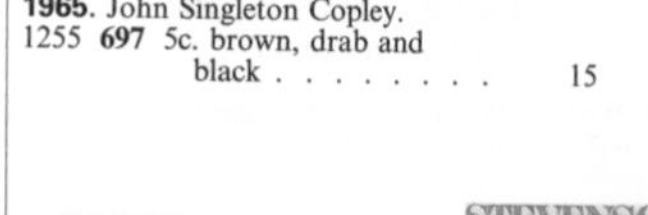

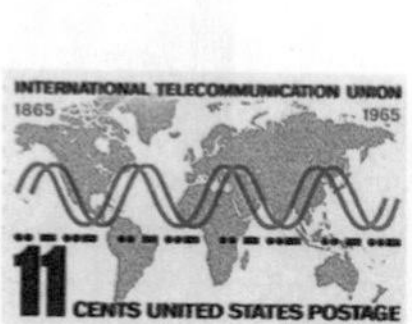

698 Radio "Waves" on World Map (based on Galt projection)

699 Adlai Stevenson (from photo by P. Halsman)

1965. Centenary of I.T.U.
1256 **698** 11c. red, black and brown 30 20

1965. Stevenson Commemoration.
1257 **699** 5c. multicoloured 15 10

700 Archangel Gabriel (weathervane) (after painting by L. Chabot)

705 Lincoln (after photo by M. Brady)

1965. Christmas.
1258 **700** 5c. green, ochre and red 15 10

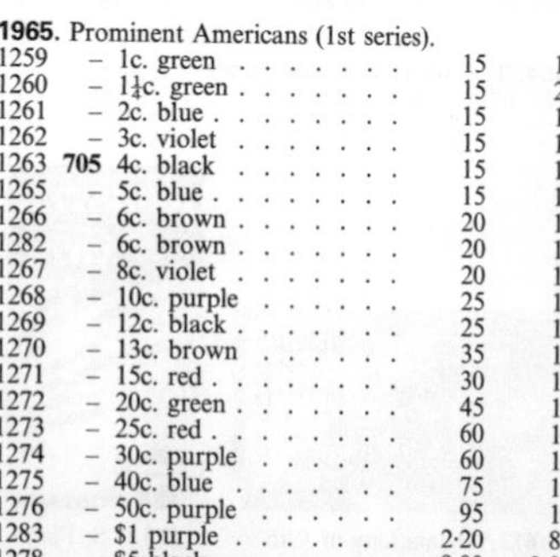

1965. Prominent Americans (1st series).

1259	–	1c. green	15	10
1260	–	1¼c. green	15	20
1261	–	2c. blue	15	10
1262	–	3c. violet	15	10
1263	**705**	4c. black	15	10
1265	–	5c. blue	15	10
1266	–	6c. brown	20	10
1282	–	6c. brown	20	10
1267	–	8c. violet	20	10
1268	–	10c. purple	25	10
1269	–	12c. black	25	10
1270	–	13c. brown	35	10
1271	–	15c. red	30	10
1272	–	20c. green	45	10
1273	–	25c. red	60	10
1274	–	30c. purple	60	10
1275	–	40c. blue	75	10
1276	–	50c. purple	95	10
1283	–	$1 purple	2·20	80
1278	–	$5 black	9·00	2·20

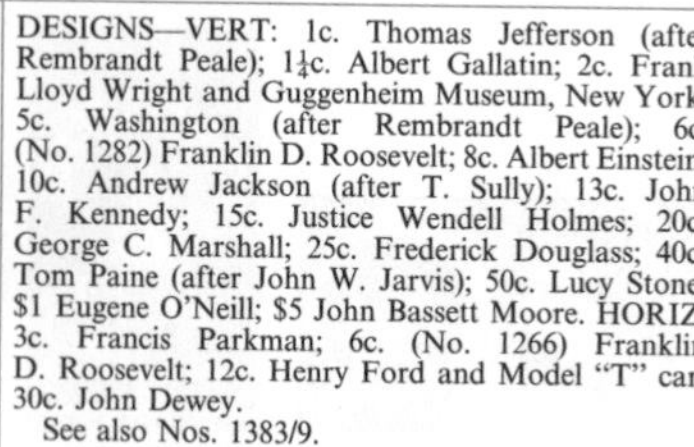

DESIGNS—VERT: 1c. Thomas Jefferson (after Rembrandt Peale); 1¼c. Albert Gallatin; 2c. Frank Lloyd Wright and Guggenheim Museum, New York; 5c. Washington (after Rembrandt Peale); 6c. (No. 1282) Franklin D. Roosevelt; 8c. Albert Einstein; 10c. Andrew Jackson (after T. Sully); 13c. John F. Kennedy; 15c. Justice Wendell Holmes; 20c. George C. Marshall; 25c. Frederick Douglass; 40c. Tom Paine (after John W. Jarvis); 50c. Lucy Stone; $1 Eugene O'Neill; $5 John Bassett Moore. HORIZ: 3c. Francis Parkman; 6c. (No. 1266) Franklin D. Roosevelt; 12c. Henry Ford and Model "T" car; 30c. John Dewey.

See also Nos. 1383/9.

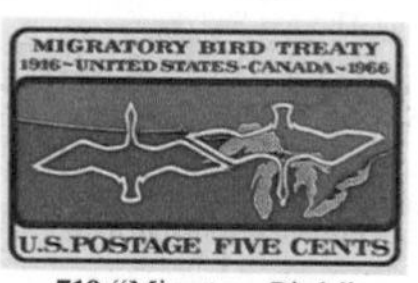

719 "Migratory Birds"

1966. 50th Anniv of Migratory Bird Treaty.
1286 **719** 5c. red, blue and black 15 10

720 Dog

721 Seal, Emblem and Map

1966. Humane Treatment of Animals.
1287 **720** 5c. black and brown . . 15 10

1966. 150th Anniv of Indiana Statehood.
1288 **721** 5c. blue, brown & yellow 15 10

722 Lou Jacobs (clown)

723 SIPEX "Letter"

1966. The American Circus.
1289 **722** 5c. multicoloured 20 10

1966. 6th Int Philatelic Exn, Washington (SIPEX).
1290 **723** 5c. multicoloured 15 10

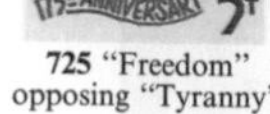

725 "Freedom" opposing "Tyranny"

726 Polish Eagle

1966. 175th Anniv of Bill of Rights.
1292 **725** 5c. red, indigo and blue 15 10

1966. Polish Millennium.
1293 **726** 5c. red 15 10

727 N.P.S. Emblem

728 Marines Past and Present

1966. 50th Anniv of National Park Service.
1294 **727** 5c. black, green & yellow 15 10

1966. 50th Anniv of Marine Corps Reserve.
1295 **728** 5c. multicoloured 15 10

729 Women of 1891 and 1966

730 Johnny Appleseed and Apple

1966. 75th Anniv of General Federation of Women's Clubs.
1296 **729** 5c. black, pink and blue 15 10

1966. Johnny Appleseed.
1297 **730** 5c. black, red and green 15 10

731 Jefferson Memorial, Washington

732 Map of Great River Road

1966. "Beautification of America" Campaign.
1298 **731** 5c. black, green and pink 15 10

1966. Opening of Great River Road.
1299 **732** 5c. red, yellow and blue 15 10

733 Statue of Liberty and U.S. Flag (after photo by B. Noble)

734 "Madonna and Child" (after Memling)

1966. 25th Anniv of U.S. Savings Bond Programme and Tribute to U.S. Servicemen.
1300 **733** 5c. multicoloured 15 10

1966. Christmas.
1301 **734** 5c. multicoloured 15 10

735 "The Boating Party" (after Mary Cassatt)

A 736 Tlingit Totem, Southern Alaska

1966. Mary Cassatt.
1302 **735** 5c. multicoloured 15 10

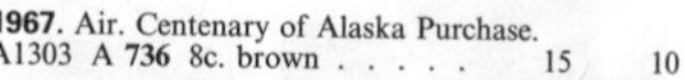

1967. Air. Centenary of Alaska Purchase.
A1303 A **736** 8c. brown 15 10

736 Recruiting Poster

A 737 "Columbia Jays" by Audubon

1967. Centenary of National Grange (farmers' organization).
1303 **736** 5c. multicoloured 15 10

1967. Air.
A1304 A **737** 20c. multicoloured 15 10

See also No. 1223.

737 Canadian Landscape

1967. Canadian Centennial.
1304 **737** 5c. multicoloured 15 10

738 Canal Barge

1967. 150th Anniv of Erie Canal.
1305 **738** 5c. multicoloured 15 10

739 Peace Dove Emblem

1967. "Search for Peace" (Lions Int essay theme).
1306 **739** 5c. black, red and blue 15 10

740 H. D. Thoreau 742 Radio Tower and "Waves"

741 Hereford Bull

1967. 150th Birth Anniv of Henry Thoreau (writer).
1307 **740** 5c. black, red and green 15 10

1967. Centenary of Nebraska Statehood.
1308 **741** 5c. multicoloured 15 10

1967. "Voice of America". 25th Anniv of Radio Branch of United States Information Agency.
1309 **742** 5c. black, red and blue 15 10

743 Davy Crockett and Pine

1967. Davy Crockett Commemoration.
1310 **743** 5c. black, green & yellow 15 10

744 Astronaut in Space 746 "Planned City"

1967. U.S. Space Achievements. Multicoloured.
1311 5c. Type **744** 30 15
1312 5c. "Gemini 4" over Earth 30 20
Nos. 1311/12 were issued together se-tenant, forming a composite design.

1967. Urban Planning.
1313 **746** 5c. ultramarine, black & blue 15 10

747 Arms of Finland 748 "The Biglin Brothers racing" (Eakins)

1967. 50th Anniv of Finnish Independence.
1314 **747** 5c. blue 15 10

1967. Thomas Eakins.
1315 **748** 5c. multicoloured 15 10

749 "Madonna and Child with Angels" (Memling) 750 Magnolia

1967. Christmas.
1316 **749** 5c. multicoloured 15 10

1967. 150th Anniv of Mississippi Statehood.
1317 **750** 5c. brown, green and turquoise 15 10

A 751 "Fifty Stars" 751 U.S. Flag and The White House

1968. Air.
A1318 A **751** 10c. red 15 10

1968. Flag Issue.
1318 **751** 6c. multicoloured 20 10
1320 8c. multicoloured 20 10

752 Homestead and Cornfield 753 Map of the Americas

1968. 150th Anniv of Illinois Statehood.
1323 **752** 6c. multicoloured 20 10

1968. "HemisFair '68" Exn, San Antonio.
1324 **753** 6c. blue, pink and white 20 10

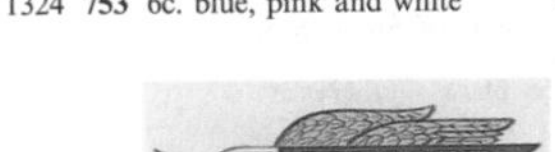

754 Eagle with Pennant (after late 19th-century wood carving)

1968. "Airlift".
1325 **754** $1 brown, blue and buff 2·20 1·90
No. 1325 was issued primarily for a special reduced-rate parcels service to forces personnel overseas and in Alaska, Hawaii and Puerto Rico.

755 Boys and Girls 756 Policeman with Small Boy

A 756 Curtiss JN-4 "Jenny"

1968. Youth Programme of Elks Benevolent Society.
1326 **755** 6c. blue and red 20 10

1968. Air. 50th Anniv of Scheduled Airmail Services.
A1327 A **756** 10c. black, red & blue 25 20

1968. "Law and Order".
1328 **756** 6c. blue, red and black 20 10

757 Eagle Weathervane 758 Fort Moultrie, 1776

1968. "Register and Vote".
1329 **757** 6c. yellow, orange & black 20 10

1968. Historic Flags.
1330 **758** 6c. blue 30 25
1331 – 6c. red and blue 20 25
1332 – 6c. green and blue . . . 20 25
1333 – 6c. red and blue 20 25
1334 – 6c. blue, yellow and red 20 25
1335 – 6c. red and blue 20 25
1336 – 6c. blue, red and green 20 25
1337 – 6c. red and blue 20 25
1338 – 6c. blue, red and yellow 20 25
1339 – 6c. red, yellow and blue 20 25
FLAGS: No. 1331, U.S. (Fort McHenry), 1795–1818; 1332, Washington's Cruisers, 1775; 1333, Bennington, 1777; 1334, Rhode Island, 1775; 1335, First Stars and Stripes, 1777; 1336, Bunker Hill, 1775; 1337, Grand Union, 1776; 1338, Philadelphia Light Horse, 1775; 1339, First Navy Jack, 1775.

768 Walt Disney (after portrait by P. E. Wenzel) 769 Father Jacques Marquette (explorer) with Jolliet and Indians Canoeing

1968. Walt Disney Commemoration.
1340 **768** 6c. multicoloured 35 10

1968. Marquette Commemoration.
1341 **769** 6c. multicoloured 20 10

770 Rifle, Tomahawk, Powder-horn and Knife

1968. Daniel Boone Commemoration.
1342 **770** 6c. multicoloured 20 10

771 Ship's Wheel and River Tanker

1968. Arkansas River Navigation Project.
1343 **771** 6c. black, blue & lt blue 20 10

772 "Leif Erikson" (statue by Stirling Calder, Reykjavik, Iceland) 773 Pioneers racing to Cherokee Strip

1968. Leif Erikson Commemoration.
1344 **772** 6c. sepia and brown . . 20 10

1968. 75th Anniv of Opening of Cherokee Strip to Settlers.
1345 **773** 6c. brown 20 10

774 "Battle of Bunker's Hill (detail) (after John Trumbull) 775 Wood Ducks

1968. John Trumbull.
1346 **774** 6c. multicoloured 20 10

1968. Waterfowl Conservation.
1347 **775** 6c. multicoloured 20 10

776 "The Annunciation" (Jan van Eyck) 777 "Chief Joseph" (after C. Hall)

1968. Christmas.
1348 **776** 6c. multicoloured 20 10

1968. "The American Indian".
1349 **777** 6c. multicoloured 20 10

A 778 "U.S.A." and Jet Aircraft

1968. Air.
A1350 A **778** 20c. red, blue & blk 45 15
A1351 21c. blue, red & blk 40 15

778 Capitol and Flowers ("Cities")

1969. "Beautification of America" Campaign.
1352 **778** 6c. multicoloured 40 15
1353 – 6c. multicoloured 40 15
1354 – 6c. multicoloured 40 15
1355 – 6c. multicoloured 40 15
DESIGNS: No. 1353, Potomac River and flowers ("Parks"); 1354, Motorway and flowers ("Highways"); 1355, Road and trees ("Streets").

782 "Eagle" (U.S. Seal) 783 "July Fourth"

1969. 50th Anniv of American Legion.
1356 **782** 6c. black, blue and red . . . 20 10

1969. Grandma Moses (Mrs. A. M. R. Moses).
1357 **783** 6c. multicoloured 20 10

784 Earth and Moon's Surface (from an astronaut's photograph)

785 W. C. Handy (statue, Memphis)

1969. Moon Flight of "Apollo 8".
1358 **784** 6c. ochre, blue and black 20 10

1969. Handy (composer) Commemoration.
1359 **785** 6c. mauve, blue and violet 20 10

786 Belfry, Carmel Mission

787 Powell exploring Colorado River

1969. Bicentenary of California.
1360 **786** 6c. multicoloured 20 10

1969. John Wesley Powell (geologist). Centenary of Colorado River Exploration.
1361 **787** 6c. multicoloured 20 10

788 Camellia and Common Flicker

1969. 150th Anniv of Alabama Statehood.
1362 **788** 6c. multicoloured 20 10

791 Ocotillo

1969. 11th International Botanical Congress, Seattle. Multicoloured.
1363 6c. Douglas fir 40 15
1364 6c. Lady's slipper 40 15
1365 6c. Type **791** 40 15
1366 6c. Franklinia 40 15

A **793** Astronaut setting foot on Moon

1969. Air. 1st Man on the Moon.
A1367 A **793** 10c. multicoloured 25 15

793 Daniel Webster and Dartmouth Hall

794 Striker

1969. 150th Anniv of Dartmouth College Legal Case.
1368 **793** 6c. green 20 10

1969. Centenary of Professional Baseball.
1369 **794** 6c. multicoloured 85 10

795 Footballer and Coach

1969. Centenary of Intercollegiate Football.
1370 **795** 6c. green and red 40 10

796 Dwight D. Eisenhower (from photograph by B. Noble)

1969. Eisenhower Commemoration.
1371 **796** 6c. black, blue and lake 20 10

797 "Winter Sunday in Norway, Maine" (unknown artist)

1969. Christmas.
1372 **797** 6c. multicoloured 20 10

798 Rehabilitated Child

800 "Old Models" (William Harnett)

1969. Rehabilitation of the Handicapped.
1373 **798** 6c. multicoloured 20 10
No. 1373 also commemorates the 50th anniv of the National Society for Crippled Children and Adults.

1969. William M. Harnett.
1376 **800** 6c. multicoloured 20 10

804 Prehistoric Creatures (from mural by R. Zallinger in Yale's Peabody Museum)

1970. Natural History. Centenary of American Natural History Museum. Multicoloured.
1377 6c. American bald eagle . . 20 15
1378 6c. African elephant herd . . 20 15
1379 6c. Haida ceremonial canoe 20 15
1380 6c. Type **804** 20 15

805 "The Lighthouse at Two Lights" (painting by Edward Hopper in Metropolitan Museum of Art, New York

1970. Maine Statehood Sesquicentennial.
1381 **805** 6c. multicoloured 20 10

806 American Bison

1970. Wildlife Conservation.
1382 **806** 6c. black on brown . . . 20 10

807 Dwight D. Eisenhower

809 Benjamin Franklin

1970. Prominent Americans (2nd series).
1383 **807** 6c. blue 20 10
1384 **809** 7c. blue 20 10
1392 **807** 8c. maroon 20 10
1390 8c. black, blue and red 20 10
1386 – 14c. black 25 15
1387 – 16c. brown 30 15
1388 – 18c. violet 40 15
1389 – 21c. green 40 10
DESIGNS: VERT: 14c. F. H. La Guardia; 16c. Ernest T. Pyle; 18c. Dr. Elizabeth Blackwell; 21c. Amadeo P. Giannini (after painting by J. Kozlowski).

822 Edgar Lee Masters

823 Suffragettes, 1920, and Woman operating Voting Machine

1970. Edgar Lee Masters (poet) Commem.
1401 **822** 6c. black and bistre . . . 20 10

1970. 50th Anniv of Women's Suffrage.
1402 **823** 6c. blue 20 10

824 Symbols of South Carolina

1970. 300th Anniv of South Carolina.
1403 **824** 6c. multicoloured 20 10

825 Stone Mountain Memorial

1970. Dedication of Stone Mountain Confederate Memorial.
1404 **825** 6c. black 20 10

826 Fort Snelling and Keel Boat

1970. 150th Anniv of Fort Snelling, Minnesota.
1405 **826** 6c. multicoloured 20 10

828 City Park

1970. Prevention of Pollution.
1406 6c. Wheat 20 15
1407 6c. Type **828** 20 15
1408 6c. Blue-gilled sunfish . . . 20 15
1409 6c. Western gull 20 15

832 Toy Steam Locomotive (after drawing by C. Hemming)

1970. Christmas. Multicoloured.
1410 6c. "The Nativity" (L. Lotto) (vert) 20 10
1411 6c. Type **832** 30 15
1412 6c. Toy horse on wheels . . 30 15
1413 6c. Mechanized tricycle . . 30 15
1414 6c. Doll's pram 30 15
Nos. 1412/14 are taken from "Golden Age of Toys" by Fondin and Remise.

836 "U.N." and Emblem

1970. 25th Anniv of U.N.O.
1415 **836** 6c. red, blue and black 20 10

837 "Mayflower" and Pilgrims

838 Disabled American Veterans Emblem

1970. 350th Anniv of Landing of the Pilgrim Fathers in America.
1416 **837** 6c. multicoloured 20 10

1970. 50th Anniv of Disabled American Veterans Organization, and Armed Forces Commemoration.
1417 **838** 6c. multicoloured 20 15
1418 – 6c. black, blue and red 20 15
DESIGN: No. 1418, Inscriptions—"Prisoners of War", "Missing and Killed in Action".

840 Ewe and Lamb

841 General Douglas MacArthur

1970. 450th Anniv of Introduction of Sheep into North America.
1419 **840** 6c. multicoloured 20 10

1971. 91st Birth Anniv of General Douglas MacArthur.
1420 **841** 6c. black, blue and red 20 10

842 "Giving Blood Saves Lives"

1971. Salute to Blood Donors.
1421 **842** 6c. deep blue, red & blue 20 10

A **844** Jet Aircraft

A **845** Winged Letter

1971. Air.
A1422 – 9c. red 20 20
A1423 A **844** 11c. red 20 10
A1424 A **845** 13c. red 20 10
DESIGN—HORIZ: 9c. Delta-wing plane.

846 "Settlers and Indians" (after mural "Independence and the Opening of the West" by Thomas H. Benton)

1971. 150th Anniv of Missouri Statehood.
1427 **846** 8c. multicoloured 20 10

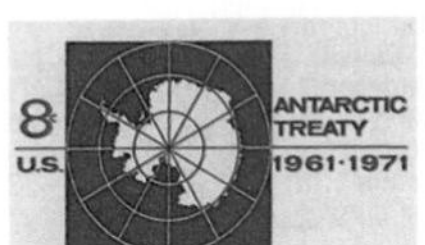
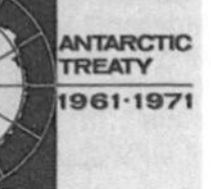
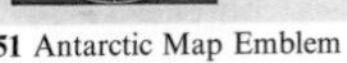

847 Rainbow Trout

1971. Wildlife Conservation. Multicoloured.
1428 8c. Type **847** 20 15
1429 8c. Alligator 20 15
1430 8c. Polar bear and cubs . . 20 15
1431 8c. California condor . . . 20 15

851 Antarctic Map Emblem **852** Postal Service Emblem

1971. 10th Anniv of Antarctic Treaty.
1432 **851** 8c. blue and red 20 10

1971. Reorganization of U.S. Post Office as U.S. Postal Service.
1433 **852** 8c. multicoloured 20 10

853 Bicentennial Emblem A **854** Head of Statue of Liberty

1971. American Revolution Bicent. Bicentennial Commisssion Emblem.
1434 **853** 8c. multicoloured 20 10

1971. Air.
A1435 A **854** 17c. blue, red & grn 40 20

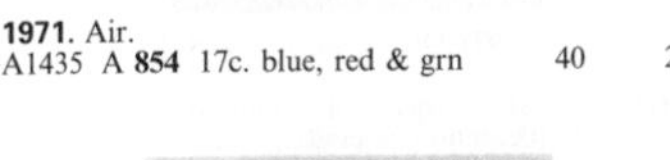

855 "The Wake of the Ferry" (John Sloan)

1971. Birth Centenary of John Sloan (artist).
1436 **855** 8c. multicoloured 20 10

856 Landing Module on Moon **858** Emily Dickinson

1971. Decade of U.S. Space Achievements. Mult.
1437 8c. Type **856** 20 15
1438 8c. Astronauts in lunar rover 20 15

Nos. 1437/8 were issued together, se-tenant, forming a composite design.

1971. 85th Death Anniv of Emily Dickinson (poet).
1439 **858** 8c. multicoloured on green 20 10

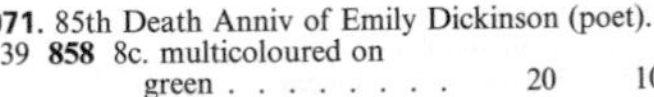

859 Watch-tower, El Morro, San Juan **860** Drug Victim

1971. 450th Anniv of San Juan, Puerto Rico.
1440 **859** 8c. multicoloured 20 10

1971. Drug Abuse Prevention Week.
1441 **860** 8c. black, lt blue & blue 20 10

861 Hands reaching to "CARE" **866** "Adoration of the Shepherds" (Giorgione)

862 Decatur House, Washington D.C.

1971. 25th Anniv of "CARE" (Co-operative for American Relief Everywhere).
1442 **861** 8c. multicoloured 20 10

1971. Historic Preservation.
1443 **862** 8c. black & flesh on cream 20 15
1444 – 8c. black & flesh on cream 20 15
1445 – 8c. black & flesh on cream 20 15
1446 – 8c. black & flesh on cream 20 10

DESIGNS: No. 1444, Whaling ship "Charles W. Morgan", Mystic, Conn; 1445, San Francisco cable car; 1446, San Xavier del Bac Mission, Tucson, Arizona.

1971. Christmas. Multicoloured.
1447 8c. Type **866** 20 10
1448 8c. "Partridge in a Pear Tree" 20 10

868 Sidney Lanier **869** Peace Corps Poster (D. Battle)

1972. 90th Death Anniv (1971) of Sidney Lanier (poet).
1449 **868** 8c. black, brown and blue 20 10

1972. Peace Corps.
1450 **869** 8c. red, light blue & blue 20 10

870/873 Cape Hatteras National Seashore

875 "Old Faithful", Yellowstone Park A **877** Statue and Temple, City of Refuge, Hawaii

1972. Centenary of National Parks.
1451 **870** 2c. multicoloured (postage) 10 10
1452 **871** 2c. multicoloured . . 10 10
1453 **872** 2c. multicoloured . . 10 10
1454 **873** 2c. multicoloured . . 10 10
1455 – 6c. multicoloured . . 20 10
1456 **875** 8c. multicoloured . . 20 10
1457 – 15c. multicoloured 25 25
A1458 A **877** 11c. mult (air) . . . 20 15

DESIGNS—HORIZ (As Type A **877**): 6c. Theatre at night, Wolf Trap Farm, Virginia; 15c. Mt. McKinley, Alaska.

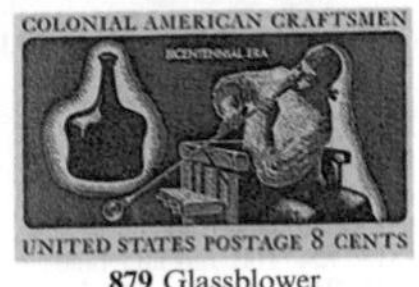

878 American Family **879** Glassblower

1972. Family Planning.
1459 **878** 8c. multicoloured 20 10

1972. Bicentenary of American Revolution. American Colonial Craftsmen.
1460 **879** 8c. brown on yellow . . 20 20
1461 – 8c. brown on yellow . . 20 20
1462 – 8c. brown on yellow . . 20 20
1463 – 8c. brown on yellow . . 20 20

DESIGNS: No. 1461, Silversmith; 1462, Wigmaker; 1463, Hatter.

883 Cycling

1972. Olympic Games, Munich and Sapporo, Japan. Multicoloured.
1464 6c. Type **883** (postage) . . 20 10
1465 8c. Bobsleighing 20 10
1466 15c. Running 35 25
A1467 11c. Skiing (air) 25 20

887 Classroom Blackboard

1972. 75th Anniv of Parent Teacher Association.
1468 **887** 8c. black and yellow . . 20 10

888 Northern Fur Seals

1972. Wildlife Conservation. Multicoloured.
1469 8c. Type **888** 20 15
1470 8c. Common cardinal (bird) 20 15
1471 8c. Brown pelicans 20 15
1472 8c. American bighorn . . . 20 15

892 19th-century Country Post Office and Store

1972. Centenary of Mail Order Business.
1473 **892** 8c. multicoloured 20 10

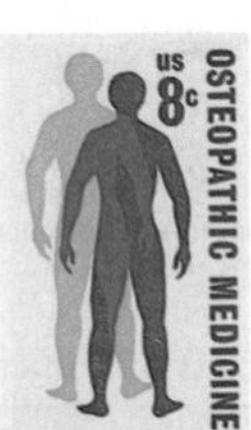

893 "Quest for Health" **894** "Tom Sawyer" (N. Rockwell)

1972. 75th Anniv of American Osteopaths.
1474 **893** 8c. multicoloured 20 10

1972. "The Adventures of Tom Sawyer" by Mark Twain.
1475 **894** 8c. multicoloured 20 10

895 "Angels" (detail, "Mary, Queen of Heaven" by Master of the St. Lucy Legend) **897** Pharmaceutical Equipment

1972. Christmas. Multicoloured.
1476 8c. Type **895** 20 10
1477 8c. Santa Claus 20 10

1972. 120th Anniv of American Pharmaceutical Association.
1478 **897** 8c. multicoloured 25 10

898 Five Cent Stamp of 1847 under Magnifier

1972. 125th Anniv of 1st U.S. Stamp, and Stamp Collecting Promotion.
1479 **898** 8c. brown, black & green 20 10

899 "LOVE"

1973. Greetings Stamp.
1480 **899** 8c. red, green and blue 20 10

900 Pamphleteers with Press

1973. American Revolution Bicentennial. Colonial Communications.
1481 **900** 8c. green, blue and red 20 10
1482 – 8c. black, red and blue 20 10
1483 – 8c. multicoloured 20 10
1484 – 8c. multicoloured 20 10

DESIGNS: No. 1482, Posting a broadside; 1483, Post-rider; 1484, Drummer.

904 George Gershwin (composer) and Scene from "Porgy and Bess" **908** Nicolas Copernicus (after 18th-cent engraving)

1973. American Arts Commemoration. Mult.
1485 8c. Type **904** 20 10
1486 8c. Robinson Jeffers (poet) and people of Carmel . . 20 10
1487 8c. Henry Tanner (painter) and palette 20 10
1488 8c. Willa Cather (novelist) and pioneer family . . . 20 10

1973. 500th Birth Anniv of Copernicus (astronomer).
1489 **908** 8c. black and yellow . . 20 10

909 Counter Clerk
919 Harry S. Truman

1973. Postal Service Employees. Multicoloured.
1490 8c. Type **909** 20 15
1491 8c. Collecting mail 20 15
1492 8c. Sorting on conveyor belt 20 15
1493 8c. Sorting parcels 20 15
1494 8c. Cancelling letters 20 15
1495 8c. Sorting letters by hand 20 15
1496 8c. Coding desks 20 15
1497 8c. Loading mail-van . . . 20 15
1498 8c. City postman 20 15
1499 8c. Rural postman 20 15

1973. Pres. Harry Truman Commemoration.
1500 **919** 8c. black, red and blue 20 10

920/923 Boston Tea Party (½-size illustration)

1973. American Revolution Bicentennial. The Boston Tea Party.
1501 **920** 8c. multicoloured 20 15
1502 **921** 8c. multicoloured 20 15
1503 **922** 8c. multicoloured 20 15
1504 **923** 8c. multicoloured 20 15

924 Marconi's Spark Coil and Gap (1901)

1973. Progress in Electronics. Multicoloured.
1505 6c. Type **924** (postage) . . 20 10
1506 8c. Modern transistor circuit 25 15
1507 15c. Early microphone and radio speaker, radio and T.V. camera tubes . . . 25 25
A1508 11c. DeForest audions (1915) (air) 20 15

928 Lyndon B. Johnson (from painting by Elizabeth Shoumatoff)
929 Angus and Longhorn Cattle (painting by F. C. Murphy)

1973. Pres. Lyndon B. Johnson Commem.
1509 **928** 8c. multicoloured 20 10

1973. "Rural America" Centenaries.
1510 8c. Type **929** 20 10
1511 10c. Institute marquee . . . 20 10
1512 10c. Steam train crossing wheatfield 20 10
CENTENARIES: No. 1510, Introduction of Aberdeen Angus cattle into United States; 1511, Foundation of Chautauqua Institution (adult education organization); 1512, Introduction of hard winter wheat into Kansas.

932 "Small Cowper Madonna" (Raphael)
933 Christmas Tree in Needlepoint

1973. Christmas.
1513 **932** 8c. multicoloured 20 10
1514 **933** 8c. multicoloured 20 10

934 U.S. Flags of 1777 and 1973
935 Jefferson Memorial

936 "Mail Transport" (from poster by R. McDougall)
937 Liberty Bell

1973.
1519 **937** 6.3c. red 20 10
1515 **934** 10c. red and blue 20 10
1516 **935** 10c. blue 20 10
1517 **936** 10c. multicoloured . . . 25 10

A **938** Statue of Liberty

1974. Air.
A1521 A **938** 18c. black, red & bl 35 35
A1522 – 26c. black, bl & red 45 15
DESIGN: 26c. Mt. Rushmore National Memorial.

940 "VFW" and Emblem
941 Robert Frost

1974. 75th Anniv of Veterans of Foreign Wars Organization.
1523 **940** 10c. red and blue 20 10

1974. Birth Centenary of Robert Frost (poet).
1524 **941** 10c. black 20 10

942 "Cosmic Jumper" and "Smiling Sage" ("Preserve the Environment" theme)

1974. "Expo 74" World Fair, Spokane.
1525 **942** 10c. multicoloured . . . 20 10

943 Horse-racing

1974. Centenary of Kentucky Derby.
1526 **943** 10c. multicoloured . . . 20 10

944 "Skylab" in Orbit

1974. "Skylab" Space Project.
1527 **944** 10c. multicoloured . . . 20 10

945 "Michelangelo" (detail from "School of Athens" by Raphael)

1974. Centenary of U.P.U. Multicoloured.
1528 10c. Type **945** 20 20
1529 10c. "Five Feminine Virtues" (Hokusai) . . . 20 20
1530 10c. "Old Scraps" (J. F. Peto) 20 20
1531 10c. "The Lovely Reader" (J. Liotard) 20 20
1532 10c. "The Lady Writing Letter" (G. Terborch) . . 20 20
1533 10c. "Inkwell and Quill" (detail from "Young Boy with Top" by J. Chardin) 20 20
1534 10c. "Mrs. John Douglas" (T. Gainsborough) . . . 20 20
1535 10c. "Don Antonio Noriega" (F. Goya) . . . 20 20

955 Amethyst
957 Covered Wagon at Fort Harrod

1974. Mineral Heritage. Multicoloured.
1536 10c. Petrified wood 20 15
1537 10c. Tourmaline 20 15
1538 10c. Type **955** 20 15
1539 10c. Rhodochrosite 20 15

1974. Bicentenary of Fort Harrod, First Settlement in Kentucky.
1540 **957** 10c. multicoloured . . . 20 10

959 "We ask but for peace ..." (First Continental Congress)
962 Slogan, Molecules and Petrol Drops

1974. American Revolution Bicentennial. First Continental Congress.
1541 – 10c. blue and red 20 15
1542 **959** 10c. grey, blue and red 20 15
1543 – 10c. grey, red and blue 20 15
1544 – 10c. red and blue 20 15
DESIGNS: No. 1541, Carpenters' Hall, Philadelphia; 1543, "Deriving their just powers ..." (Declaration of Independence); 1544, Independence Hall, Philadelphia.

1974. Energy Conservation.
1545 **962** 10c. multicoloured . . . 20 10

963 "The Headless Horseman"
964 Child clasping Hand

1974. Washington Irving's "Legend of Sleepy Hollow".
1546 **963** 10c. multicoloured . . . 20 10

1974. Help for Retarded Children.
1547 **964** 10c. lake and brown . . 20 10

966 "The Road — Winter" (from a Currier and Ives print, drawn by O. Knirsch)

1974. Christmas. Multicoloured.
1548 10c. "Angel" (detail, Perussis altarpiece) (vert) 20 10
1549 10c. Type **966** 20 15
1550 10c. Dove weathervane, Mount Vernon 20 20
No. 1550 has self-adhesive gum.

968 "Benjamin West" (self-portrait)
969 "Pioneer" Spacecraft passing Jupiter

1975. Benjamin West (painter) Commem.
1551 **968** 10c. multicoloured . . . 20 10

1975. U.S. Unmanned Space Missions. Mult.
1552 10c. Type **969** 20 10
1553 10c. "Mariner 10", Venus and Mercury 20 10

971 Overlapping Circles

1975. Collective Bargaining in Labour Relations.
1554 **971** 10c. multicoloured . . . 20 10

972 Sybil Ludington on Horseback

1975. American Revolution Bicent. Contributors to the Cause.
1555 **972** 8c. multicoloured 20 10
1556 – 10c. multicoloured . . . 20 10
1557 – 10c. multicoloured . . . 20 10
1558 – 18c. multicoloured . . . 30 20
DESIGNS: No. 1556, Salem Poor loading musket; 1557, Haym Salomon writing in ledger; 1558, Peter Francisco carrying cannon.

976 "Lexington" (from painting "Birth of Liberty" by H. Sandham)
977 Paul Laurence Dunbar (poet)

1975. American Revolution Bicentennial. Battles of Lexington and Concord.
1559 **976** 10c. multicoloured . . . 20 10

1975. Dunbar Commemoration.

1560	**977**	10c. multicoloured . . .	20	15

978 D. W. Griffith (film producer)

1975. Griffith Commemoration.

1561	**978**	10c. multicoloured . . .	20	10

979 "Bunker Hill, 1775", (John Trumbull)

980 Marine with Musket

1975. Bicentenary of American Revolution. Battle of Bunker Hill.

1562	**979**	10c. multicoloured . . .	20	10

1975. American Revolution Bicentennial. U.S. Military Services. Multicoloured.

1563	10c. Type **980**	20	15
1564	10c. Militiaman with musket	20	15
1565	10c. Soldier with flintlock	20	15
1566	10c. Sailor with grappling-iron	20	15

984 Docking Manoeuvre

1975. "Apollo–Soyuz" Space Test Project. Mult.

1567	10c. Type **984**	20	15
1568	10c. Spacecraft docked . . .	20	15

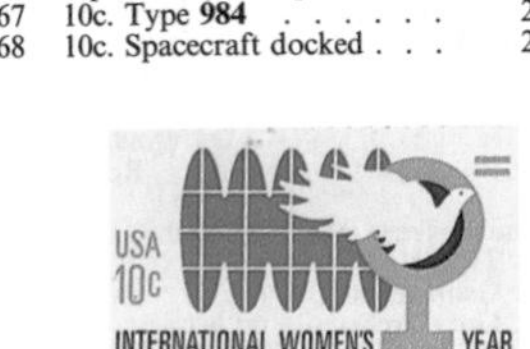

986 "Worldwide Equality"

1975. International Women's Year.

1569	**986**	10c. multicoloured . . .	20	15

987 Stagecoach and Modern Lorry

1975. Bicentenary of Postal Services. Mult.

1571	10c. Type **987**	20	10
1572	10c. Early steam and modern diesel locomotives	20	15
1573	10c. Curtiss JN-4 "Jenny" and Boeing 747-100 jetliner	20	15
1574	10c. Telecommunications satellite	20	15

991 Law Book, Gavel and Globe

1975. "World Peace through Law".

1575	**991**	10c. brown, blue & green	20	15

992 Coins and Engine-turned Motif

1975. "Banking and Commerce".

1576	**992**	10c. multicoloured . . .	20	10
1577	–	10c. multicoloured . . .	20	15

DESIGN: No. 1577, As Type **992**, but design reversed with different coins.

994 "Madonna and Child" (Ghirlandaio)

995 "Christmas Card" (from early design by Louis Prang)

1975. Christmas.

1578	**994**	(10c.) multicoloured . .	20	15
1579	**995**	(10c.) multicoloured . .	20	10

Nos. 1578/9 were each sold at 10c. Because of an imminent increase in the postage rates the two designs were issued without face values.

1002 Early Printing Press

1020 Flag over Independence Hall

1975.

1580	–	1c. deep blue on grey	15	10
1581	–	2c. red on cream . . .	15	10
1582	–	3c. olive on green . .	15	10
1597b	–	3.1c. lake on yellow	15	15
1598	–	3.5c. lilac on yellow	15	20
1582a	–	4c. red on cream . . .	15	10
1599	–	7.7c. brown on yellow	20	20
1600	–	7.9c. red on yellow . .	20	20
1601	–	8.4c. blue on yellow	20	20
1583	–	9c. green on grey . .	30	10
1584	–	9c. green	60	45
1585	–	10c. purple on grey	20	10
1585a	**1002**	11c. orange on grey	20	10
1585b	–	12c. brown on cream	25	10
1586	–	13c. brown on cream	30	10
1595	–	13c. multicoloured . .	25	10
1596	–	15c. blue, red and black	35	10
1605	–	16c. blue	30	10
1589	–	24c. red on blue . . .	45	10
1589a	–	28c. brown on blue . .	55	10
1590	–	29c. blue on light blue	55	30
1591	–	30c. green on turquoise	55	15
1592	–	50c. black, red & brn	90	15
1593	–	$1 multicoloured . . .	2·00	25
1594	–	$2 multicoloured . . .	3·75	60
1594a	–	$5 multicoloured . . .	9·00	1·90

DESIGNS: 1c. Inkwell and quill; 2c. Speaker's stand; 3c. Ballot box; 3.1c. Guitar; 3.5c. Weaver violins; 4c. Books, spectacles and bookmark; 7.7c. Saxhorns; 7.9c. Drum; 8.4c. Grand piano; 9c. (both) Dome of Capitol; 10c. "Contemplation of Justice" (statue, J. E. Fraser); 12c. Statue of Liberty torch; 13c. (No. 1586) Liberty Bell; 13c. (No. 1595) Eagle and shield; 15c. Fort McHenry flag; 16c. Statue of Liberty; 24c. Old North Church, Boston; 28c. Fort Nisqually, Washington; 29c. Sandy Hook Lighthouse, N.J.; 30c. Morris Township School; 50c. Iron "Betty" lamp; $1 Rush lamp and candle holder; $2 Kerosene lamp; $5 Railway conductor's lantern.

1975.

1606	**1020**	13c. red and blue . . .	25	15
1606c	–	13c. red and blue . . .	30	20

DESIGN: No. 1606c, Flag over Capitol, Washington.

1021 Drummer Boy (after A. M. Willard)

1024 Boeing 737 Jetliner

1976. American Revolution Bicentennial. "The Spirit of '76". Multicoloured.

1607	13c. Type **1021**	20	15
1608	13c. Old drummer	20	15
1609	13c. Fifer	20	15

Nos. 1607/9 were issued together, se-tenant, forming a composite design.

1976. Air.

A1610	**1024**	25c. black, blue & red	55	15
A1611	–	31c. black, blue & red	60	15

DESIGN: 31c. As 25c. but with background of U.S. flag.

1026 "Interphil 76"

1976. "Interphil 76" International Stamp Exhibition, Philadelphia.

1612	**1026**	13c. red and blue . . .	25	10

1027 Delaware Flag

1976. Bicentenary of American Revolution. State Flags. Multicoloured.

1613	13c. Type **1027**	25	30
1614	13c. Pennsylvania	25	30
1615	13c. New Jersey	25	30
1616	13c. Georgia	25	30
1617	13c. Connecticut	25	30
1618	13c. Massachusetts	25	30
1619	13c. Maryland	25	30
1620	13c. South Carolina	25	30
1621	13c. New Hampshire . . .	25	30
1622	13c. Virginia	25	30
1623	13c. New York	25	30
1624	13c. North Carolina	25	30
1625	13c. Rhode Island	25	30
1626	13c. Vermont	25	30
1627	13c. Kentucky	25	30
1628	13c. Tennessee	25	30
1629	13c. Ohio	25	30
1630	13c. Louisiana	25	30
1631	13c. Indiana	25	30
1632	13c. Mississippi	25	30
1633	13c. Illinois	25	30
1634	13c. Alabama	25	30
1635	13c. Maine	25	30
1636	13c. Missouri	25	30
1637	13c. Arkansas	25	30
1638	13c. Michigan	25	30
1639	13c. Florida	25	30
1640	13c. Texas	25	30
1641	13c. Iowa	25	30
1642	13c. Wisconsin	25	30
1643	13c. California	25	30
1644	13c. Minnesota	25	30
1645	13c. Oregon	25	30
1646	13c. Kansas	25	30
1647	13c. West Virginia	25	30
1648	13c. Nevada	25	30
1649	13c. Nebraska	25	30
1650	13c. Colorado	25	30
1651	13c. North Dakota	25	30
1652	13c. South Dakota	25	30
1653	13c. Montana	25	30
1654	13c. Washington	25	30
1655	13c. Idaho	25	30
1656	13c. Wyoming	25	30
1657	13c. Utah	25	30
1658	13c. Oklahoma	25	30
1659	13c. New Mexico	25	30
1660	13c. Arizona	25	30
1661	13c. Alaska	25	30
1662	13c. Hawaii	25	30

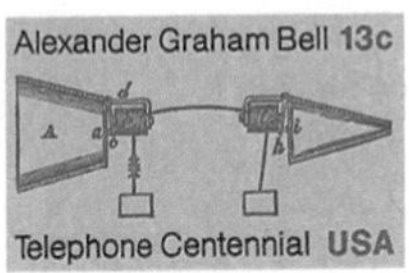

1028 Bell's Telephone

1976. Telephone Centenary.

1663	**1028**	13c. violet, black and red on brown	25	10

1029 Stout Air Pullman and Laird Swallow Biplane

1976. Commercial Aviation.

1664	**1029**	13c. multicoloured . . .	25	10

1030 Laboratory Equipment

1976. Centenary of American Chemical Society.

1665	**1030**	13c. multicoloured . . .	25	10

1035 Benjamin Franklin and 1776 Map of North America

1040 Diving

1036/1039 "Signing the Declaration of Independence" (John Turnbull) (½-size illustration)

1976. American Revolution Bicentennial.

1667	**1035**	13c. multicoloured . . .	25	10

1976. American Revolution Bicentennial.

1668	**1036**	13c. multicoloured . . .	40	15
1669	**1037**	13c. multicoloured . . .	40	15
1670	**1038**	13c. multicoloured . . .	40	15
1671	**1039**	13c. multicoloured . . .	40	15

Nos. 1668/71 were issued together, se-tenant, forming the composite design illustrated.

1976. Olympic Games, Innsbruck and Montreal. Multicoloured.

1672	13c. Type **1040**	30	15
1673	13c. Skiing	30	15
1674	13c. Running	30	15
1675	13c. Skating	30	15

1044 Clara Maass

1045 A. S. Ochs

1976. Birth Centenary of Clara Maass (martyr to yellow fever).

1676	**1044**	13c. multicoloured . . .	30	15

1976. Adolph S. Ochs (publisher of "New York Times") Commemoration.

1677	**1045**	13c. black	25	10

1046 "Winter Pastime" (N. Currier)

1976. Christmas.

1678	13c. Type **1046**	25	10
1679	13c. "Nativity" (John S. Copley)	25	10

1048 "Washington at Princeton" (Peale)

1050 Zia Pot

1049 Early Gramophone

1977. American Revolution Bicentennial.

1680	**1048**	13c. multicoloured . . .	25	10

1977. Centenary of Sound Recording.

1681	**1049**	13c. multicoloured . . .	25	10

1977. American Folk Art. Pueblo Art.

1682	13c. Type **1050**	25	15
1683	13c. San Ildefonso pot . . .	25	15

1684 13c. Hopi pot 25 15
1685 13c. Acoma pot 25 15

1054 "Spirit of St. Louis"

1977. 50th Anniv of Lindbergh's Transatlantic Flight.
1686 **1054** 13c. multicoloured . . . 25 10

1055 Columbine and Rocky Mountains

1056 American Swallowtail

1977. Centenary (1976) of Colorado Statehood.
1687 **1055** 13c. multicoloured . . . 25 10

1977. Butterflies. Multicoloured.
1688 13c. Type **1056** 25 15
1689 13c. Checkerspot 25 15
1690 13c. Dogface 25 15
1691 13c. Falcate orange-tip . . . 25 15

1060 Marquis de Lafayette

1977. American Revolution Bicent. Bicentenary of Lafayette's Landing on Coast of South Carolina.
1692 **1060** 13c. black, blue and red 25 10

1061 Seamstress

1977. American Revolution Bicentenary. "Skilled Hands for Independence". Multicoloured.
1693 13c. Type **1061** 25 15
1694 13c. Blacksmith 25 15
1695 13c. Wheelwright 25 15
1696 13c. Leatherworker 25 15

1065 Peace Bridge and Dove

1977. 50th Anniv of Opening of Peace Bridge.
1697 **1065** 13c. blue 25 10

1066 "Herkimer at Oriskany" (F. Yohn)

1977. American Revolution Bicent. Bicentenary of Battle of Oriskany.
1698 **1066** 13c. multicoloured . . . 25 10

1067 Farmhouses, El Pueblo

1977. Bicentenary of First Civil Settlement in Alta California.
1699 **1067** 13c. multicoloured . . . 25 10

1068 Members of the Continental Congress

1977. Bicentenary of Drafting of the Articles of Constitution.
1700 **1068** 13c. brown and red . . 25 10

1069 "Vitaphone" Projector and Sound Equipment

1977. 50th Anniv of Talking Pictures.
1701 **1069** 13c. multicoloured . . . 25 10

1070 "Surrender of Burgoyne at Saratoga" (J. Trumbull)

1977. American Revolution Bicent. Surrender of General Burgoyne.
1702 **1070** 13c. multicoloured . . . 25 10

1071 "Conservation"

1073 Washington at Valley Forge (after Leyendecker)

1977. Energy Conservation and Development.
1703 **1071** 13c. multicoloured . . . 25 15
1704 – 13c. multicoloured . . . 25 15
DESIGN: No. 1704, "Development".

1977. Christmas.
1705 **1073** 13c. multicoloured . . . 25 10
1706 – 13c. multicoloured . . . 25 10
DESIGN: No. 1706, Rural mailbox.

1075 Carl Sandburg

1076 Indian Head Penny

1978. Birth Centenary of Carl Sandburg (poet and biographer).
1707 **1075** 13c. black and brown 25 10

1978.
1708 **1076** 13c. brown & blue on buff 25 10

1077 Captain James Cook (after Nathaniel Dance)

1079 Harriet Tubman and Slaves

1978. Bicentenary of Capt. Cook's Visits to Hawaii and Alaska.
1709 **1077** 13c. blue 25 15
1710 – 13c. green 25 15
DESIGN—HORIZ: No. 1710, H.M.S. "Resolution" and H.M.S. "Discovery" at Hawaii (after John Webber).

1978. Black Heritage. Harriet Tubman (organizer of slave "underground railway").
1711 **1079** 13c. multicoloured . . . 30 10

1082 Quilt Design

1978. American Folk Art. Quilts.
1712 – 13c. brown and grey . . 25 15
1713 – 13c. red and grey . . . 25 15
1714 **1082** 13c. multicoloured . . . 25 15
1715 – 13c. multicoloured . . . 25 15
DESIGNS: No. 1712, Chequered; 1713, Dotted; 1715, Striped.

1084 Ballet

1978. American Dance.
1716 **1084** 13c. blue, mauve & black 25 15
1717 – 13c. orange, red & black 25 15
1718 – 13c. green, yellow & black 25 15
1719 – 13c. blue, ultram & black 25 15
DESIGNS: No. 1717, Theatre; 1718, Folk dance; 1719, Modern.

1088 "Louis XVI and Benjamin Franklin" (statuette, C. G. Sauvage)

1089 Dr. Papanicolaou

1978. Bicentenary of French Alliance.
1720 **1088** 13c. black, blue and red 25 10

1978. Dr. George Papanicolaou (developer of Pap (cancer detection) test) Commemoration.
1721 **1089** 13c. brown 25 10

1090 American Eagle

1091 Jimmie Rodgers

1978. No value expressed.
1722 **1090** (15c.) orange 30 10
For "B" stamp see No. 1843, for "C" stamp Nos. 1909/10 and for "D" stamp Nos. 2137/8.

1978. Performing Arts and Artists. Jimmie Rodgers, "Father of Country Music".
1725 **1091** 13c. multicoloured . . . 25 10

1093 Camera and Accessories

1094 George M. Cohan

1978. Photography.
1727 **1093** 15c. multicoloured . . . 35 10

1978. Performing Arts. Birth Centenary of George M. Cohan (actor and playwright).
1728 **1094** 15c. multicoloured . . . 45 10

1095 "Red Masterpiece" and "Medallion" Roses

1096 "Viking 1" Lander scooping Soil from Mars

1978. Roses.
1729 **1095** 15c. red, orange & grn 30 10

1978. 2nd Anniv of "Viking 1" Landing on Mars.
1730 **1096** 15c. multicoloured . . . 35 10

1097 Great Grey Owl

1101 Wright Brothers and Wright Flyer I

1978. Wildlife Conservation. American Owls. Mult.
1731 15c. Type **1097** 30 15
1732 15c. Saw-whet owl 30 15
1733 15c. Barred owl 30 15
1734 15c. Great horned owl . . . 30 15

1978. Air. 75th Anniv of First Powered Flight. Multicoloured.
A1735 31c. Type **1101** 60 15
A1736 31c. Wright Flyer I and Wright Brothers (in bowler hats) 60 15

1103 White Pine

1107 "Madonna and Child with Cherubim" (Andrea della Robbia)

1978. American Trees. Multicoloured.
1737 15c. Type **1103** 25 15
1738 15c. Giant sequoia 25 15
1739 15c. Grey birch 25 15
1740 15c. White oak 25 15

1978. Christmas. Multicoloured.
1741 15c. Type **1107** 30 10
1742 15c. Child on rocking horse 30 10

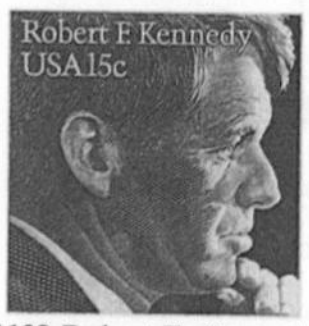

1109 Robert F. Kennedy

1110 Martin Luther King

1979. Robert F. Kennedy Commemoration.
1743 **1109** 15c. blue 30 10

1979. Black Heritage. Martin Luther King (Civil Rights leader).
1744 **1110** 15c. multicoloured . . . 35 10

1111 Children of Different Races

1112 John Steinbeck

1979. International Year of the Child.
1745 **1111** 15c. red 30 10

1979. Literary Arts. John Steinbeck (novelist).
1746 **1112** 15c. blue 30 10

1113 Einstein

1114 Chanute and Glider

1979. Birth Cent of Albert Einstein (physicist).
1747 **1113** 15c. brown 30 10

1979. Air. Aviation Pioneers. Octave Chanute. Multicoloured.
A1748 21c. Type **1114** 55 30
A1749 21c. Chanute and glider (different) 55 30

1116 Coffee Pot

1120 Virginia Rotunda (Thomas Jefferson)

1979. American Folk Art. Pennsylvania Toleware. Multicoloured.
1750 15c. Type **1116** 25 15
1751 15c. Tea caddy 25 15
1752 15c. Sugar bowl with lid . . 25 15
1753 15c. Coffee pot with gooseneck spout 25 15

1979. American Architecture. Each black and red.
1754 15c. Type **1120** 35 15
1755 15c. Baltimore Cathedral (Benjamin Latrobe) . . . 35 15
1756 15c. Boston State House (Charles Bulfinch) 35 15
1757 15c. Philadelphia Exchange (William Strickland) . . . 35 15

1124 Persistent Trillium

1128 Guide Dog

1979. Endangered Flora. Multicoloured.
1758 15c. Type **1124** 35 15
1759 15c. Hawaiian wild broadbean 35 15
1760 15c. Contra costa wallflower 35 15
1761 15c. Antioch dunes evening primrose 35 15

1979. 50th Anniv of First U.S. Guide Dog Programme.
1762 **1128** 15c. multicoloured . . . 30 10

1129 Child with Medal

1130 Throwing the Javelin (Decathlon)

1979. Special Olympic Games for the Handicapped.
1763 **1129** 15c. multicoloured . . . 30 10

1979. Olympic Games, Moscow (1980). Mult.
1764 10c. Type **1130** (postage) 25 20
1765 15c. Running (horiz) . . . 20 15
1766 15c. Swimming (horiz) . . 25 20
1767 15c. Rowing (horiz) . . . 25 20
1768 15c. Show jumping (horiz) 25 20
A1769 31c. High jumping (horiz) (air) 55 35

1136 John Paul Jones (after Peale)

1137 "Rest on the Flight to Egypt" (G. David)

1979. American Revolution Bicentennial. John Paul Jones (naval commander).
1770 **1136** 15c. multicoloured . . . 30 10

1979. Christmas. Multicoloured.
1771 15c. Type **1137** 30 10
1772 15c. Santa Claus tree ornament 30 10

1139 Will Rogers

1140 Vietnam Service Medal Ribbon

1979. Performing Arts and Artists. Will Rogers (cowboy philosopher).
1773 **1139** 15c. multicoloured . . . 30 10

1979. Vietnam Veterans.
1774 **1140** 15c. multicoloured . . . 35 10

1141 Wiley Post

1143 W. C. Fields

1979. Air. Aviation Pioneers. Wiley Post. Mult.
A1775 25c. Type **1141** . . . . . 1·00 40
A1776 25c. Wiley Post and Lockheed Vega "Winnie Mae" . . . . 1·00 40

1980. Performing Arts and Artists. W. C. Fields (comedian).
1777 **1143** 15c. multicoloured . . . 35 10

1144 Speed Skating

1148 Robertson Windmill, Williamsburg, Va.

1980. Winter Olympic Games, Lake Placid. Mult.
1778 15c. Type **1144** 35 20
1779 15c. Downhill skiing 35 20
1780 15c. Ski jumping 35 20
1781 15c. Ice hockey 35 20

1980. Windmills.
1782 **1148** 15c. brown on yellow 35 10
1783 – 15c. brown on yellow 35 10
1784 – 15c. brown on yellow 35 10
1785 – 15c. brown on yellow 35 10
1786 – 15c. brown on yellow 35 10
DESIGNS: No. 1783, Replica of old windmill, Portsmouth, R.I.; 1784, Cape Cod windmill, Eastham, Mass.; 1785, Dutch mill, Fabyan Park Forest Preserve, Ill.; 1786, Southwestern windmill, Texas.

1153 Benjamin Banneker

1980. Black Heritage. Benjamin Banneker (astronomer and mathematician).
1787 **1153** 15c. multicoloured . . . 35 10

1154 Photograph and Envelope

1157 "P.S. Write Soon"

1980. National Letter Writing Week.
1788 **1154** 15c. multicoloured . . . 35 15
1789 **1157** 15c. multicoloured (purple background) 35 15
1790 – 15c. multicoloured . . . 35 15
1791 **1157** 15c. multicoloured (green background) 35 15
1792 – 15c. multicoloured . . . 35 15
1793 **1157** 15c. blue, black and red 35 15
DESIGNS—As T **1154**: No. 1790, Flowers and envelope; 1792, Capitol and envelope.

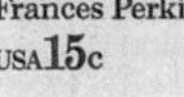

1158 Frances Perkins

1159 Dolley Madison (after Stuart)

1980. Frances Perkins (first woman Cabinet member) Commemoration.
1794 **1158** 15c. blue 30 10

1980.
1795 **1159** 15c. dp brown & brown 30 10

1160 Emily Bissell

1161 Helen Keller and Anne Sullivan

1980. Emily Bissell (crusader against tuberculosis) Commemoration.
1796 **1160** 15c. black and red . . . 30 10

1980. Birth Centenary of Helen Keller.
1797 **1161** 15c. multicoloured . . . 30 10

1162 Veterans Administration Emblem

1163 Statue of Gen. Galvez, Mobile

1980. 50th Anniv of Veterans Administration.
1798 **1162** 15c. red and blue . . . 30 10

1980. General Bernardo de Galvez (leader of Spanish forces in Louisiana during American Revolution) Commemoration.
1799 **1163** 15c. multicoloured . . . 30 10

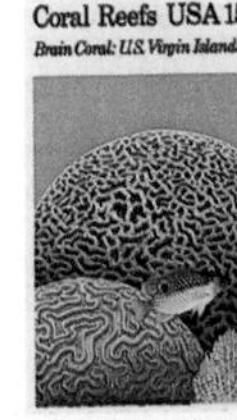

1164 Brain Corals

1168 American Bald Eagle

1980. Coral Reefs. Multicoloured.
1800 15c. Type **1164** 30 15
1801 15c. Elkhorn coral 30 15
1802 15c. Chalice coral 30 15
1803 15c. Finger coral 30 15

1980. Organized Labour.
1804 **1168** 15c. multicoloured . . . 30 10

1169 Edith Wharton

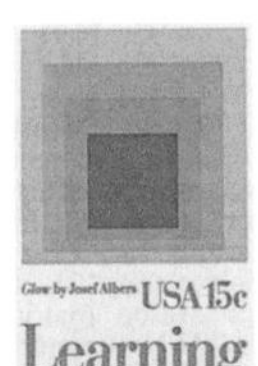

1170 "Homage to the Square: Glow" (J. Albers)

1980. Literary Arts. Edith Wharton (novelist).
1805 **1169** 15c. violet 35 10

1980. American Education.
1806 **1170** 15c. multicoloured . . . 40 10

1171 Heiltsuk, Bella Bella

1980. American Folk Art, Indian Masks. Mult.
1807 15c. Type **1171** 35 15
1808 15c. Chilkat Tlingit 35 15
1809 15c. Tlingit 35 15
1810 15c. Bella Coola 35 15

1175 Smithsonian Institution, Washington (James Renwick)

1179 Philip Mazzei

1980. American Architecture.
1811 **1175** 15c. black and red . . . 25 15
1812 – 15c. black and red . . . 25 15
1813 – 15c. black and red . . . 25 15
1814 – 15c. black and red . . . 25 15
DESIGNS: No. 1812, Trinity Church, Boston (Henry Hobson Richardson); 1813, Penn Academy, Philadelphia (Frank Furness); 1814, Lyndhurst, Tarrytown, New York (Alexander Jackson Davis).

1980. Air. 250th Birth Anniv of Philip Mazzei (patriot).
A1815 **1179** 40c. multicoloured . . 80 15

1180 "Madonna and Child" (Epiphany Window, Washington Cathedral)

1181 Antique Toys

1980. Christmas.
1816 **1180** 15c. multicoloured . . . 30 10
1817 **1181** 15c. multicoloured . . . 35 10

1191 Sequoyah (Cherokee scholar) (after C. B. Wilson)

1203 Blanche Stuart Scott and Curtiss Golden Flyer

1980. Great Americans. With "c" after face value.
1818 – 1c. black 15 10
1819 – 2c. black 15 10
1820 – 3c. green 15 10
1821 – 4c. violet 15 10

1822 – 5c. red 15 10
1823 – 10c. blue 20 10
1824 – 13c. red 30 10
1825 – 17c. green 30 15
1826 – 18c. blue 30 15
1827 **1191** 19c. brown 30 15
1828 – 20c. purple 40 15
1829 – 20c. green 45 15
1830 – 20c. black 45 10
1831 – 30c. green 55 10
1832 – 35c. black 70 15
1833 – 37c. blue 70 15
1834 – 40c. green 80 15

DESIGNS: 1c. Dorothea Dix (social pioneer); 2c. Igor Stravinsky (composer); 3c. Henry Clay (politician); 4c. Carl Schurz (reformer); 5c. Pearl Buck (author) (after F. Elliot); 10c. Richard Russell (politician); 13c. Crazy Horse (Sioux chief) (after K. Ziolkowski); 17c. Rachel Carson (scientist); 18c. George Mason (patriot); 20c. (No. 1828), Ralph Bunche (U.N. Secretariat member); 20c. (No. 1829), Thomas H. Gallaudet (educator of the deaf); 20c. (No. 1830), Pres. Harry S. Truman; 30c. Frank C. Laubach (literacy educator); 35c. Charles R. Drew (surgeon); 37c. Robert Millikan (physicist); 40c. Lillian M. Gilbreth (engineer).

For similar designs without "c", see Nos. 2108/36.

1980. Air. Aviation Pioneers. Multicoloured.
A1839 28c. Type **1203** 65 15
A1840 35c. Glenn Curtiss and Curtiss "June Bug" . . 85 20

1205 Everett Dirksen

1206 Whitney Moore Young

1981. Senator Everett Dirksen Commemoration.
1841 **1205** 15c. grey 30 10

1981. Black Heritage. Whitney Moore Young (civil rights leader).
1842 **1206** 15c. multicoloured . . . 30 10

1981. Non-denominational "B" stamp. As T **1090**.
1843 (18c.) lilac 35 10

1207 Rose

1981. Flowers. Multicoloured.
1846 18c. Type **1207** 40 15
1847 18c. Camellia 40 15
1848 18c. Dahlia 40 15
1849 18c. Lily 40 15

1211 ". . . for amber waves of grain"

1212 Stars

1981.
1851 **1212** 6c. blue and red 70 30
1850 **1211** 18c. brown, red and blue 40 20
1852 – 18c. lilac, red and blue 65 25
1853 – 18c. brown, blue and red 40 10

DESIGNS—As T **1211**: No. 1852, "... for purple mountain majesties"; 1853, "... from sea to shining sea".

1215 Nurse and Child

1216 Money Box

1981. Centenary of American Red Cross.
1854 **1215** 18c. multicoloured . . . 40 10

1981. 150th Anniv of First Savings and Loans Association.
1855 **1216** 18c. multicoloured . . . 40 15

1217 American Bighorn

1238 Detroit Electric Auto, 1917

1981. Wildlife.
1856 **1217** 18c. brown 80 20
1857 – 18c. brown 80 20
1858 – 18c. brown 80 20
1859 – 18c. brown 80 20
1860 – 18c. brown 80 20
1861 – 18c. brown 80 20
1862 – 18c. brown 80 20
1863 – 18c. brown 80 20
1864 – 18c. brown 80 20
1865 – 18c. brown 80 20

DESIGNS: No. 1857, Puma; 1858, Common seal; 1859, American bison; 1860, Brown bear; 1861, Polar bear; 1862, Red deer; 1863, Elk; 1864, White-tailed deer; 1865, Pronghorn.

1981. Transport. With "c" after face value.
1866 – 1c. violet 15 10
1867 – 2c. black 15 10
1868 – 3c. green 15 10
1869 – 4c. brown 15 10
1870 – 5c. green 15 10
1871 – 5.2c. red 20 15
1872 – 5.9c. blue 20 20
1873 – 7.4c. brown 20 20
1874 – 9.3c. red 25 20
1875 – 10.9c. mauve 30 20
1876 – 11c. red 25 20
1877 **1238** 17c. blue 40 20
1878 – 18c. brown 40 15
1879 – 20c. red 40 10

DESIGNS: 1c. Omnibus, 1880s; 2c. Steam locomotive, 1870s; 3c. Railway handcar, 1880s; 4c. Concord stagecoach, 1890s; 5c. Pope motor-cycle, 1913; 5.2c. Sleigh, 1880s; 5.9c. Bicycle, 1870s; 7.4c. Baby buggy, 1880s; 9.3c. Mail wagon, 1880s; 10.9c. Hansom cab, 1890s; 11c. Railway caboose, 1890s; 18c. Surrey, 1890s; 20c. Amoskeag fire pumper, 1860s.

For similar designs without "c", see Nos. 2150/74 and 2477/82.

1247 Exploring the Moon ("Apollo" mission)

1255 Joseph Wharton (founder of Wharton School)

1981. Space Achievements.
1886 **1247** 18c. multicoloured . . . 35 20
1887 – 18c. multicoloured . . . 35 20
1888 – 18c. multicoloured . . . 35 20
1889 – 18c. multicoloured . . . 35 20
1890 – 18c. multicoloured . . . 35 20
1891 – 18c. multicoloured . . . 35 20
1892 – 18c. multicoloured . . . 35 20
1893 – 18c. multicoloured . . . 35 20

DESIGNS: No. 1887, Space Shuttle loosing boosters; 1888, Space Shuttle performing experiment; 1889, Understanding the Sun ("Skylab"); 1890, Probing the Planets ("Pioneer II"); 1891, Space Shuttle launch; 1892, Space Shuttle landing; 1893, Comprehending the Universe (space telescope).

Nos. 1886/93 were issued together in se-tenant blocks of eight, each block forming a composite design.

1981. Cent of Professional Management Education.
1894 **1255** 18c. blue and black . . 40 10

1256 Great Blue Heron

1260 Disabled Man using Microscope

1981. Wildlife Habitats.
1895 **1256** 18c. multicoloured . . . 40 15
1896 – 18c. multicoloured . . . 40 15
1897 – 18c. multicoloured . . . 40 15
1898 – 18c. multicoloured . . . 40 15

DESIGNS: No. 1896, American badger; 1897, Brown bear; 1898, Ruffed grouse.

1981. International Year of Disabled Persons.
1899 **1260** 18c. multicoloured . . . 40 10

1261 Edna St. Vincent Millay

1262 "Alcoholism. You can beat it!"

1981. Edna St. Vincent Millay (poet) Commem.
1900 **1261** 18c. multicoloured . . . 40 10

1981. Anti-alcoholism Campaign.
1901 **1262** 18c. blue and black . . 50 10

1263 New York University Library (Stanford White)

1267 Bobby Jones (golfer)

1981. American Architecture (3rd series).
1902 **1263** 18c. black and brown 45 15
1903 – 18c. black and brown 45 15
1904 – 18c. black and brown 45 15
1905 – 18c. black and brown 45 15

DESIGNS: No. 1903, Biltmore House, Asheville, North Carolina (Richard Morris Hunt); 1904, Palace of Arts, San Francisco (Bernard Maybeck); 1905, Bank, Owatonna, Minnesota (Louis Sullivan).

1981. American Sports Personalities.
1906 **1267** 18c. green . . . . . . 1·10 10
1907 – 18c. red 55 10

DESIGN: No. 1907, Babe Zaharias (golfer and athlete).

1269 "Coming through the Rye"

1981. Frederic Remington (sculptor) Commem.
1908 **1269** 18c. brown, green and light brown 40 10

1981. Non-denominational "C" stamp. As T **1090** but inscribed "Domestic Mail".
1909 (20c.) brown (19 × 22 mm) 45 15
1910 (20c.) brown (15 × 18½ mm) 50 15

1271 James Hoban and White House

1981. 150th Death Anniv of James Hoban (architect).
1912 **1271** 18c. multicoloured . . . 40 15
1913 20c. multicoloured . . . 40 10

1272 Map of Yorktown Peninsula

1274 "Madonna and Child" (Botticelli)

1981. Bicentenary of Battles of Yorktown and Virginia Capes. Multicoloured.
1914 18c. Type **1272** 35 15
1915 18c. French ships blocking Chesapeake Bay 35 15

1981. Christmas. No value expressed. Mult.
1916 (20c.) Type **1274** 40 10
1917 (20c.) Teddy bear on sleigh 40 10

1276 John Hanson

1277 Barrel Cactus

1981. John Hanson (American revolutionary leader) Commemoration.
1918 **1276** 20c. multicoloured . . . 40 10

1981. Desert Plants. Multicoloured.
1919 20c. Type **1277** 40 15
1920 20c. Agave (horiz) 40 15
1921 20c. Saguaro 40 15
1922 20c. Beavertail cactus (horiz) 40 15

1281 Flag over Supreme Court

1282 American Bighorn

1981.
1923c **1281** 20c. black, red and blue 40 10

1982.
1926 **1282** 20c. blue 40 10

1283 Franklin D. Roosevelt

1982. Birth Centenary of President Franklin D. Roosevelt.
1927 **1283** 20c. blue 40 10

1284 Flowers spelling "Love"

1285 George Washington

1982. Greetings Stamp.
1928 **1284** 20c. multicoloured . . . 80 15

1982. 250th Birth Anniv of George Washington.
1929 **1285** 20c. multicoloured . . . 40 10

1286 Common Flicker (inscr "Yellow-hammer") and Camellia (Alabama)

1287 Stripes in National Colours

1982. State Birds and Flowers. Multicoloured.
1930 20c. Type **1286** 45 40
1931 20c. Willow grouse (inscr "Ptarmigan") and forget-me-not (Alaska) 45 40
1932 20c. Cactus wren and saguaro cactus blossom (Arizona) 45 40
1933 20c. Northern mockingbird and apple blossom (Arkansas) 45 40
1934 20c. California quail and California poppy (California) 45 40
1935 20c. Lark bunting and Rocky Mountain columbine (Colorado) . . 45 40
1936 20c. American robin and mountain laurel (Connecticut) 45 40

1937 20c. Blue hen chicken and peach blossom (Delaware) 45 40
1938 20c. Northern mockingbird and orange blossom (Florida) 45 40
1939 20c. Brown thrasher and Cherokee rose (Georgia) 45 40
1940 20c. Hawaiian goose and hibiscus (Hawaii) 45 40
1941 20c. Mountain bluebird and syringa (Idaho) 45 40
1942 20c. Common cardinal and violet (Illinois) 45 40
1943 20c. Common cardinal and peony (Indiana) 45 40
1944 20c. American (inscr "Eastern") goldfinch and wild rose (Iowa) 45 40
1945 20c. Western meadowlark and sunflower (Kansas) 45 40
1946 20c. Common cardinal and goldenrod (Kentucky) . . 45 40
1947 20c. Brown pelican and magnolia (Louisiana) . . 45 40
1948 20c. Black-capped chickadee, white pine cone and tassel (Maine) 45 40
1949 20c. Northern (inscr "Baltimore") oriole and black-eyed susan (Maryland) 45 40
1950 20c. Black-capped chickadee and mayflower (Massachusetts) 45 40
1951 20c. American robin and apple blossom (Michigan) 45 40
1952 20c. Great northern diver (inscr "Common Loon") and showy lady slipper (Minnesota) 45 40
1953 20c. Northern mockingbird and magnolia (Mississippi) 45 40
1954 20c. Eastern bluebird and red hawthorn (Missouri) 45 40
1955 20c. Western meadowlark and bitterroot (Montana) 45 40
1956 20c. Western meadowlark and goldenrod (Nebraska) 45 40
1957 20c. Mountain bluebird and sagebrush (Nevada) . . . 45 40
1958 20c. Purple finch and lilac (New Hampshire) 45 40
1959 20c. American goldfinch and violet (New Jersey) . . . 45 40
1960 20c. Road-runner and yucca flower (New Mexico) . . 45 40
1961 20c. Eastern bluebird and rose (New York) 45 40
1962 20c. Common cardinal and flowering dogwood (North Carolina) 45 40
1963 20c. Western meadowlark, and wild prairie rose (North Dakota) 45 40
1964 20c. Common cardinal and red carnation (Ohio) . . . 45 40
1965 20c. Scissor-tailed flycatcher and mistletoe (Oklahoma) 45 40
1966 20c. Western meadowlark and Oregon grape (Oregon) 45 40
1967 20c. Ruffed grouse and mountain laurel (Pennsylvania) 45 40
1968 20c. Rhode Island red and violet (Rhode Island) . . 45 40
1969 20c. Carolina wren and Carolina jessamine (South Carolina) 45 40
1970 20c. Common pheasant ("Ring-necked Pheasant") and pasque flower (South Dakota) 45 40
1971 20c. Northern mockingbird and iris (Tennessee) . . . 45 40
1972 20c. Northern mockingbird and bluebonnet (Texas) 45 40
1973 20c. California gull and sego lily (Utah) 45 40
1974 20c. Hermit thrush and red clover (Vermont) 45 40
1975 20c. Common cardinal and flowering dogwood (Virginia) 45 40
1976 20c. American goldfinch and rhododendron (Washington) 45 40
1977 20c. Common cardinal ("Cardinal") and "Rhododendron maximum" (West Virginia) 45 40
1978 20c. American robin and wood violet (Wisconsin) 45 40
1979 20c. Western meadowlark and Indian paint bush (Wyoming) 45 40

1982. Bicent of U.S.A.–Netherlands Diplomatic Relations.
1980 **1287** 20c. red, blue and black 40 10

1288 Library of Congress

1289 Garment Tag

1982. Library of Congress.
1981 **1288** 20c. black and red . . . 40 10

1982. Consumer Education.
1982 **1289** 20c. blue 75 25

1290 Solar Energy

1294 Frontispiece from "Ragged Dick"

1982. Knoxville World's Fair.
1983 **1290** 20c. multicoloured . . . 45 15
1984 – 20c. multicoloured . . . 45 15
1985 – 20c. blue, light blue and black 45 15
1986 – 20c. blue, black and brown 45 15
DESIGNS: No. 1984, Synthetic fuels; 1985, Breeder reactor; 1986, Fossil fuels.

1982. 150th Birth Anniv of Horatio Alger (novelist).
1987 **1294** 20c. black and red on buff 40 10

1295 Family Group

1296 John, Ethel and Lionel Barrymore

1982. Ageing Together.
1988 **1295** 20c. red 40 10

1982. Performing Arts and Artists. The Barrymores (theatrical family).
1989 **1296** 20c. multicoloured . . . 45 10

1297 Dr. Mary Walker

1298 Maple Leaf and Rose

1982. Dr. Mary Walker (army surgeon) Commem.
1990 **1297** 20c. multicoloured . . . 40 10

1982. 50th Anniv of International Peace Garden (on U.S.A.–Canada border).
1991 **1298** 20c. multicoloured . . . 40 10

1299 Typographic Design

1300 Jackie Robinson

1982. America's Libraries.
1992 **1299** 20c. red and black . . . 40 10

1982. Black Heritage. Jackie Robinson (baseball player).
1993 **1300** 20c. multicoloured . . . 1·60 20

1301 Touro Synagogue

1982. Touro Synagogue, Newport, Rhode Island.
1994 **1301** 20c. multicoloured . . . 45 10

1302 Open Air Theatre

1982. Wolf Trap Farm Park, Vienna, Virginia.
1995 **1302** 20c. multicoloured . . . 40 10

1303 Fallingwater, Mill Run, Pennsylvania (Frank Lloyd Wright)

1982. American Architecture.
1996 **1303** 20c. black and brown 60 20
1997 – 20c. black and brown 60 20
1998 – 20c. black and brown 60 20
1999 – 20c. black and brown 60 20
DESIGNS: No. 1997, Illinois Institute of Technology, Chicago (Mies van der Rohe); 1998, Gropius House, Lincoln, Massachusetts (Walter Gropius); 1999, Dulles Airport, Washington D.C. (Eero Saarinen).

1307 St. Francis and Doves

1982. 800th Birth Anniv of St. Francis of Assisi.
2000 **1307** 20c. multicoloured . . . 40 10

1308 Ponce de Leon and Map of Florida

1309 "Madonna and Child" (Tiepolo)

1982. Ponce de Leon (explorer) Commemoration.
2001 **1308** 20c. multicoloured . . . 45 10

1982. Christmas. Multicoloured.
2002 20c. Type **1309** 40 10
2003 20c. Building a snowman (horiz) 60 20
2004 20c. Sledging (horiz) 60 20
2005 20c. Decorating a Christmas tree (horiz) 60 20
2006 20c. Skating (horiz) 60 20

1314 Puppy and Kitten

1316 Industrial Complex

1982.
2007 **1314** 13c. multicoloured . . . 30 10

1983. Science and Industry.
2015 **1316** 20c. multicoloured . . . 40 10

1317 Benjamin Franklin and Great Seal of Sweden

1983. Bicentenary of Sweden–U.S.A. Treaty of Amity and Commerce.
2016 **1317** 20c. indigo, brown and black 25 10

1319/1320 Hot Air Ballooning

1983. Bicentenary of Manned Flight. Mult.
2017 20c. "Intrepid", 1861 (vert) 40 20
2018 20c. Type **1319** 40 20
2019 20c. Type **1320** 40 20
2020 20c. Stratosphere balloon "Explorer II", 1935 (vert) 40 20

1322 C.C.C. Workers repairing Trail

1983. 50th Anniv of Civilian Conservation Corps.
2021 **1322** 20c. multicoloured . . . 40 10

1323 Shot Putting

1327 Joseph Priestley (after G. Stuart)

1983. Air. Olympic Games, Los Angeles (1984) (1st issue). Multicoloured.
A2022 40c. Type **1323** 90 30
A2023 40c. Gymnastics 90 30
A2024 40c. Swimming 90 30
A2025 40c. Weightlifting 90 30
See also Nos. A2034/7, 2040/3, A2058/61 and 2079/82.

1983. 250th Birth Anniv of Joseph Priestley (discoverer of oxygen).
2026 **1327** 20c. multicoloured . . . 40 10

1328 Reaching Hands

1983. Voluntary Work.
2027 **1328** 20c. black and red . . . 50 15

1329 "Concord"

1983. 300th Anniv of First German Settlers in America.
2028 **1329** 20c. brown 45 15

1330 Joggers and Electrocardiograph Trace

1983. Physical Fitness.
2029 **1330** 20c. multicoloured . . . 50 15

1331 Brooklyn Bridge, New York

1983. Centenary of Brooklyn Bridge.
2030 **1331** 20c. blue 45 15

1332 Norris Hydro-electric Dam

1983. 50th Anniv of Tennessee Valley Authority.
2031 **1332** 20c. multicoloured . . . 40 10

1333 Army, Air Force and Navy Medals of Honour

1334 Scott Joplin

1983. Medal of Honour.
2032 **1333** 20c. multicoloured . . . 40 15

1983. Black Heritage. Scott Joplin (ragtime composer).
2033 **1334** 20c. multicoloured . . . 70 15

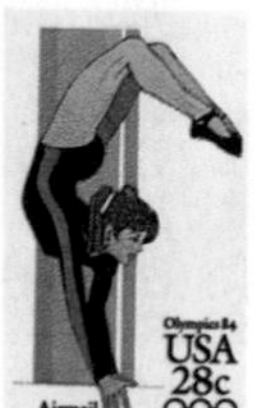

1335 Gymnastics

1339 Babe Ruth

1983. Air. Olympic Games, Los Angeles (1984) (2nd issue). Multicoloured.

A2034	28c. Type **1335**	80	30
A2035	28c. Hurdling	80	30
A2036	28c. Basketball	80	30
A2037	28c. Football	80	30

1983. American Sports Personalities. Babe Ruth (baseball player).
2038 **1339** 20c. blue . . . . 1·90 15

1340 Hawthorne (after C. G. Thompson)

1341 Discus

1983. Literary Arts. Nathaniel Hawthorne (writer).
2039 **1340** 20c. multicoloured . . . 40 10

1983. Olympic Games, Los Angeles (1984) (3rd issue). Multicoloured.

2040	13c. Type **1341**	40	20
2041	13c. High jump	40	20
2042	13c. Archery	40	20
2043	13c. Boxing	40	20

1345 American Bald Eagle and Moon

1983.
2044 **1345** $9.35 multicoloured . . 20·00 11·50

1346 Signing the Treaty of Paris (after Benjamin West)

1347 Text in Early and Modern Type

1983. Bicentenary of Treaty of Paris.
2045 **1346** 20c. multicoloured . . . 40 10

1983. Centenary of Civil Service.
2046 **1347** 20c. stone, red and black 45 10

1348 Part of Proscenium and Modern Facade

1983. Centenary of Metropolitan Opera, New York.
2047 **1348** 20c. yellow and purple 40 10

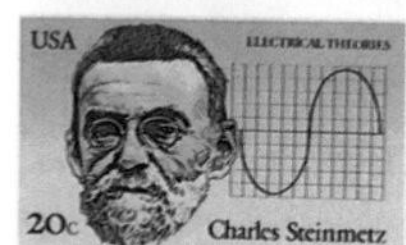

1349 Charles Steinmetz and Graph

1983. American Inventors.

2048	**1349**	20c. pink and black . .	50	20
2049	–	20c. pink and black . .	50	20
2050	–	20c. pink and black . .	50	20
2051	–	20c. pink and black . .	50	20

DESIGNS: No. 2049, Edwin Armstrong and frequency modulator; 2050, Nikola Tesla and induction motor; 2051, Philo T. Farnsworth and television camera.

1353 "John Mason" Streetcar, New York City, 1832

1983. Streetcars. Multicoloured.

2052	20c. Type **1353**	40	20
2053	20c. Electric streetcar, Montgomery, Alabama, 1886	40	20
2054	20c. "Bobtail" horsecar, Sulphur Rock, Arkansas, 1926	40	20
2055	20c. St. Charles streetcar, New Orleans, 1923 . . .	40	20

1357 "Madonna and Child" (Raphael)

1358 Santa Claus

1983. Christmas.
2056 **1357** 20c. multicoloured . . . 40 10
2057 **1358** 20c. multicoloured . . . 40 15

1359 Fencing

1983. Air. Olympic Games, Los Angeles (1984) (4th issue). Multicoloured.

A2058	35c. Type **1359**	90	35
A2059	35c. Cycling	90	45
A2060	35c. Volleyball	90	35
A2061	35c. Pole vault	90	35

1363 Martin Luther

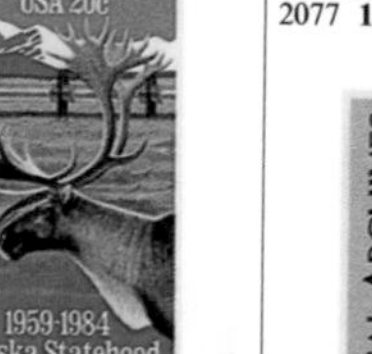

1364 Reindeer and Pipeline

1983. 500th Birth Anniv of Martin Luther.
2062 **1363** 20c. multicoloured . . . 40 10

1984. 25th Anniv of Alaska Statehood.
2063 **1364** 20c. multicoloured . . . 40 10

1365 Ice Dancing

1369 Column and "$" Sign

1984. Winter Olympic Games, Sarajevo. Mult.

2064	20c. Type **1365**	60	20
2065	20c. Downhill skiing	60	20
2066	20c. Cross-country skiing . .	60	20
2067	20c. Ice hockey	60	20

1984. 50th Anniv of Federal Deposit Insurance Corporation.
2068 **1369** 20c. multicoloured . . . 40 10

1370 "Love"

1371 Carter G. Woodson

1984. Greetings Stamp.
2069 **1370** 20c. multicoloured . . . 40 15

1984. Black Heritage. Carter G. Woodson (historian).
2070 **1371** 20c. multicoloured . . . 40 10

1372 Hand holding Plant

1373 Coin and "$" Sign

1984. 50th Anniv of Soil and Water Conservation Movement.
2071 **1372** 20c. multicoloured . . . 40 10

1984. 50th Anniv of Credit Union Act.
2072 **1373** 20c. multicoloured . . . 40 10

1374 Wild Pink

1984. Orchids. Multicoloured.

2073	20c. Type **1374**	50	20
2074	20c. Yellow lady's slipper	50	20
2075	20c. Spreading pogonia . .	50	20
2076	20c. Pacific calypso	50	20

1378 Eastern Polynesian Canoe and Pacific Golden Plover

1984. 25th Anniv of Hawaii Statehood.
2077 **1378** 20c. multicoloured . . . 55 10

1379 Silhouettes of Lincoln and Washington

1380 Diving

1984. 50th Anniv of National Archives.
2078 **1379** 20c. black, olive and red 45 10

1984. Olympic Games, Los Angeles (5th issue). Multicoloured.

2079	20c. Type **1380**	75	20
2080	20c. Long jump	75	20
2081	20c. Wrestling	75	20
2082	20c. Canoeing	75	20

1384 Bayou Wildlife

1984. Louisiana World Exposition, New Orleans.
2083 **1384** 20c. multicoloured . . . 40 10

1385 Laboratory Equipment

1984. Health Research.
2084 **1385** 20c. multicoloured . . . 45 10

1386 Fairbanks in Film Roles

1387 Jim Thorpe

1984. Performing Arts and Artists. Douglas Fairbanks (film actor).
2085 **1386** 20c. multicoloured . . . 50 10

1984. American Sports Personalities. Jim Thorpe (athlete, footballer and baseball player).
2086 **1387** 20c. brown 45 10

1388 John McCormack

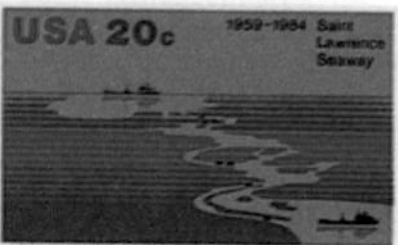

1389 St. Lawrence Seaway

1984. Performing Arts and Artists. John McCormack (singer).
2087 **1388** 20c. multicoloured . . . 45 10

1984. 25th Anniv of St. Lawrence Seaway.
2088 **1389** 20c. multicoloured . . . 40 10

1390 "Mallards dropping In" (Jay Norwood Darling)

1984. 50th Anniv of Migratory Bird Hunting and Conservation Stamp Act.
2089 **1390** 20c. blue 60 10

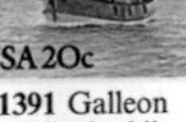

1391 Galleon "Elizabeth"

1392 Melville (after J. O. Eaton)

1984. Explorers. 400th Anniv of First Raleigh Expedition to Roanoke Island, North Carolina.
2090 **1391** 20c. multicoloured . . . 40 10

1984. Literary Arts. Herman Melville (novelist).
2091 **1392** 20c. green 40 10

1393 Horace Moses

1394 Smokey Bear and American Black Bear Cub clinging to burnt Tree

1984. Horace Moses (founder of Junior Achievement (training organization) Commem.
2092 **1393** 20c. orange and black 50 10

1984. Smokey Bear (symbol of forest fire prevention campaign).
2093 **1394** 20c. multicoloured . . . 45 10

1395 Clemente and Flag of Puerto Rico

1396 Beagle and Boston Terrier

1984. American Sports Personalities. Roberto Clemente (baseball player).
2094 **1395** 20c. multicoloured . . . 2·00 25

1984. Centenary of American Kennel Club. Mult.
2095 20c. Type **1396** 60 20
2096 20c. Chesapeake Bay retriever and cocker spaniel 60 20
2097 20c. Alaskan malamute and collie 60 20
2098 20c. Black and tan coonhound and American foxhound 60 20

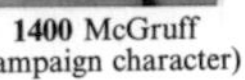

1400 McGruff (campaign character)

1401 "Family Unity"

1984. National Crime Prevention Month.
2099 **1400** 20c. multicoloured . . . 40 10

1984. National Stamp Collecting Month.
2100 **1401** 20c. black, red and blue 60 10

1402 Eleanor Roosevelt

1403 Abraham Lincoln reading to his Son, Tad

1984. Eleanor Roosevelt Commemoration.
2101 **1402** 20c. blue 40 10

1984. "Nation of Readers".
2102 **1403** 20c. brown and red . . 45 10

1404 "Madonna and Child (Fra Filippo Lippi)

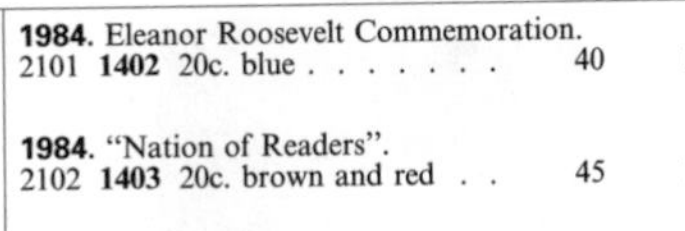

1406 Uniformed Group and Flag

1984. Christmas.
2103 20c. Type **1404** 40 10
2104 20c. Santa Claus 40 10

1984. Hispanic Americans.
2105 **1406** 20c. multicoloured . . . 40 10

1407 Memorial (Maya Ying Lin)

1984. Vietnam Veterans Memorial, Washington, D.C.
2106 **1407** 20c. black, green and deep green 55 10

1408 Kern

1409 Margaret Mitchell (writer)

1985. Performing Arts and Artists. Birth Centenary of Jerome Kern (composer).
2107 **1408** 22c. multicoloured . . . 45 10

1985. Great Americans. Without "c" after face value.
2108 **1409** 1c. brown 15 10
2109 – 2c. blue 15 10
2110 – 3c. blue 15 10
2111 – 4c. blue 15 10
2112 – 5c. green 15 10
2113 – 6c. red 20 15
2114 – 7c. red 20 10
2115 – 8c. brown 20 15
2116 – 9c. green 20 15
2117 – 10c. red 30 10
2118 – 11c. blue 20 10
2119 – 14c. green 30 10
2120 – 14c. red 25 10
2121 – 15c. purple 35 10
2122 – 17c. green 40 10
2123 – 21c. purple 45 15
2124 – 22c. blue 45 10
2125 – 23c. violet 45 15
2126 – 25c. blue 50 15
2127 – 28c. green 50 25
2128 – 39c. mauve 75 15
2129 – 45c. blue 85 20
2130a – 50c. brown 70 30
2131 – 56c. red . . . . . . 1·00 30
2132 – 65c. blue . . . . . . 1·10 25
2133 – $1 green . . . . . . 3·00 25
2134a – $1 blue . . . . . . 1·80 25
2135 – $2 violet . . . . . . 3·75 50
2136 – $5 brown . . . . . . 9·25 1·50

DESIGNS: 2c. Mary Lyon (educator); 3c. Paul Dudley White (cardiologist); 4c. Father Flanagan (founder of Boys Town); 5c. Hugo L. Black (Supreme Court Justice); 6c. Walter Lippmann (journalist); 7c. Abraham Baldwin (politician); 8c. General Henry Knox; 9c. Sylvanus Thayer (military educator) (after R. Weir); 10c. Red Cloud (Oglala Sioux chief); 11c. Alden Partridge (educationist); 14c. (No. 2119) Sinclair Lewis (writer) (after S. Melik); 14c. (No. 2120) Julia Ward Howe (author of "Battle Hymn of the Republic") (after J. Elliott); 15c. Buffalo Bill Cody (showman); 17c. Belva Ann Lockwood (women's rights campaigner); 21c. Chester Carlson (inventor of photocopying); 22c. J. J. Audubon (ornithologist); 23c. Mary Cassatt (artist); 25c. Jack London (writer); 28c. Sitting Bull (Hunkpapa Sioux chief); 39c. Grenville Clark (peace activist); 45c. Dr. Harvey Cushing (neurosurgeon); 50c. Admiral Chester W. Nimitz; 56c. John Harvard (philanthropist) (after D. C. French); 65c. Gen. Henry Harley "Hap" Arnold; $1 (No. 2133) Bernard Revel (scholar); $1 (No. 2134) Johns Hopkins (philanthropist); $2 William Jennings Bryan (politician); $5 Bret Harte (writer).

1985. Non-denominational "D" stamp. As T **1090** but inscribed "Domestic Mail".
2137 (22c.) green (18 × 21 mm) . . 55 10
2138 (22c.) green (15 × 18 mm) . . 70 15

1438 Alfred V. Verville and Verville-Sperry R-3

1985. Air. Aviation Pioneers.
A2142 33c. Type **1438** 70 15
A2143 39c. Lawrence and Elmer Sperry and Curtiss F flying boat 70 15

1440 Loading Mail into "China Clipper"

1441 Mary McLeod Bethune

1985. Air. 50th Anniv of Martin M-130 Flying Boat, First Transpacific Airmail Flight.
A2144 **1440** 44c. multicoloured . . 80 25

1985. Black Heritage. Mary McLeod Bethune (social activist).
2145 **1441** 22c. multicoloured . . . 45 10

1442 Lesser Scaup ("Broadbill") Decoy, 1890 (Ben Holmes)

1446 Omnibus, 1880s

1985. American Folk Art. Duck Decoys. Mult.
2146 22c. Type **1442** . . . . . . 1·40 20
2147 22c. Mallard decoy, 1900 (Percy Grant) . . . . . . 1·40 20
2148 22c. Canvasback decoy, 1929 (Bob McGraw) . . . 1·40 20
2149 22c. Redhead decoy, 1925 (Keyes Chadwick) . . . . 1·40 20

1985. Transport. Without "c" after face value.
2150 **1446** 1c. violet 15 10
2151 – 2c. black 20 10
2152 – 3c. purple 15 10
2153 – 3.4c. green 15 10
2154 – 4.9c. black 15 15
2155 – 5c. black 15 15
2156 – 5.3 black 15 15
2157 – 5.5c. red 15 15
2158 – 6c. brown 20 15
2159 – 7.1c. red 20 20
2160 – 7.6c. brown 20 15
2161 – 8.3c. green 20 20
2162 – 8.4c. purple 20 10
2163 – 8.5c. green 20 20
2163a – 10c. blue 20 15
2164 – 10.1c. grey 20 20
2165 – 11c. black 25 20
2166 – 12c. blue 35 20
2167 – 12.5c. green 25 20
2167b – 13c. black 25 30
2168 – 13.2c. green 25 20
2169 – 14c. blue 25 20
2170 – 15c. violet 30 20
2170b – 16.7c. red 30 20
2171 – 17c. blue 45 20
2172 – 17.5c. violet 40 20
2172b – 20c. purple 40 20
2172c – 20.5c. red 55 25
2172d – 21c. green 45 20
2173 – 24.1c. blue 55 30
2174 – 25c. brown 50 15

DESIGNS: 2c. Steam locomotive, 1870s; 3c. Conestoga wagon, 1800s; 3.4c. School bus, 1920s; 4.9c. Buckboard, 1880s; 5c. Milk wagon, 1900s; 5.3c. Lift, 1900s; 5.5c. Star Route truck, 1910s; 6c. Tricycle, 1880s; 7.1c. Tractor, 1920s; 7.6c. Carreta, 1770s; 8.3c. "McKean" ambulance, 1860s; 8.4c. Wheelchair, 1920s; 8.5c. Tow truck, 1920s; 10c. Canal barge, 1880s; 10.1c. Oil wagon, 1890s; 11c. Stutz "Bearcat", 1933; 12c. Stanley "Steamer", 1909; 12.5c. Pushcart, 1880s; 13c. Police patrol wagon, 1880s; 13.2c. Coal wagon, 1870s; 14c. Iceboat, 1880s; 15c. Tug, 1900s; 16.7c. Popcorn wagon, 1902; 17c. Dog sledge, 1920s; 17.5c. Marmon "Wasp", 1911; 20c. Cable car, 1880s; 20.5c. Ahrens-Fox fire engine, 1900s; 21c. Railway mail van, 1920s; 24.1c. Pope tandem, 1890s; 25c. Bread wagon, 1880s.

The 5.3, 7.6, 8.4, 13, 13.2, 16.7, 21 and 24.1c. were only issued with precancelled inscription of the type of service in red and the 20.5c. in black. Prices in the unused column are for stamps with full gum.

1471 Ice Skating, Skiing and Emblem

1472 Flag over Capitol, Washington

1985. Winter Special Olympic Games, Park City, Utah.
2175 **1471** 22c. multicoloured . . . 45 10

1985.
2176 **1472** 22c. black, red and blue 50 10
2178 – 22c. black, red and blue 50 10
DESIGN—40 × 22 mm: No. 2178, Flag over Capitol, Washington, and inscription "Of the People By the People For the People".

1474 Frilled Dogwinkle

1479 Coloured Lines and "Love"

1985. Sea Shells.
2179 **1474** 22c. red and black . . . 35 10
2180 – 22c. red, purple and black 35 10
2181 – 22c. red and black . . . 35 10
2182 – 22c. purple and black 35 10
2183 – 22c. red, purple and black 35 10
DESIGNS: No. 2180, Reticulated cowrie helmet; 2181, New England neptune; 2182, Calico scallop; 2183, Lightning whelk.

1985. Greetings Stamp.
2184 **1479** 22c. multicoloured . . . 45 10

1480 American Bald Eagle and Moon

1985.
2185 **1480** $10.75 multicoloured 20·00 9·25

1481 Electricity Pole and Rural Landscape

1985. 50th Anniv of Rural Electrification Administration.
2186 **1481** 22c. multicoloured . . . 45 10

1482 1c. Franklin Stamp, 1870

1483 Abigail Adams

1985. "Ameripex 86" International Stamp Exhibition, Chicago.
2187 **1482** 22c. multicoloured . . . 45 10

1985. Abigail Adams (wife of Pres. John Adams and writer) Commemoration.
2188 **1483** 22c. multicoloured . . . 45 15

1484 Bartholdi (after J. Frappa) and Statue of Liberty)

1985. Frederic Auguste Bartholdi (sculptor of Statue of Liberty) Commemoration.
2189 **1484** 22c. multicoloured . . . 45 10

1485 Troops in Mountain Pass

1985. Korean War Veterans.
2190 **1485** 22c. green and red . . . 55 10

1486 Disabled and Needy People

1985. 50th Anniv of Social Security Act.
2191 **1486** 22c. blue and deep blue 45 10

1487 Junipero Serra and Mission San Gabriel

1985. Air. Death Bicentenary (1984) of Father Junipero Serra (missionary).
A2192 **1487** 44c. multicoloured . . 95 20

1488 "Battle of the Marne" (Harvey Dunn)

1985. World War I Veterans.
2193 **1488** 22c. green and red . . . 45 10

1489 Quarter Horse

1493 Alphabet, Spectacles, Quill and Apple

1985. Horses. Multicoloured.
2194 22c. Type **1489** 90 55
2195 22c. Morgan horse 90 55
2196 22c. Saddlebred horse . . . 90 55
2197 22c. Appaloosa 90 55

1985. Public Education.
2198 **1493** 22c. multicoloured . . . 90 10

1494 Y.M.C.A. Youth Camping (centenary)

1985. International Youth Year. Multicoloured.
2199 22c. Type **1494** 70 20
2200 22c. Boy Scouts of America (75th anniv) 70 20
2201 22c. Big Brothers and Big Sisters 70 20
2202 22c. Camp Fire Inc. (75th anniv) 70 20

1498 Hungry Faces **1499** Envelopes

1985. "Help End Hunger".
2203 **1498** 22c. multicoloured . . . 45 10

1985.
2204 **1499** 21.1c. multicoloured 45 30
No. 2204 exists both with and without precancel "ZIP + 4".

1500 "Genoa Madonna" (Luca della Robbia)

1502 George Washington (after Stuart) and Washington Monument

1985. Christmas.
2205 **1500** 22c. multicoloured . . . 45 10
2206 – 22c. red, green and black 45 10
DESIGN—HORIZ: No. 2206, Poinsettias.

1985.
2207 **1502** 18c. multicoloured . . . 50 25
No. 2207 exists both with and without precancel "PRESORTED FIRST-CLASS".

1503 Old State House, Little Rock

1986. 150th Anniv of Arkansas State.
2208 **1503** 22c. multicoloured . . . 45 10

1504 Sheet of Stamps, Handstamp and Magnifying Glass

1508 Puppy

1986. "Ameripex 86" International Stamp Exhibition, Chicago. Stamp Collecting. Mult.
2209 22c. Type **1504** 45 20
2210 22c. Boy holding stamp in tweezers 45 20
2211 22c. Mounted stamps and 3c. U.S. stamp under glass 45 20
2212 22c. "Ameripex" miniature sheet on cover and handstamp 45 20

1986. Greetings Stamp.
2213 **1508** 22c. multicoloured . . . 45 10

1509 Sojourner Truth

1510 Texan Flag and Santa Anna's Spur

1986. Black Heritage. Sojourner Truth (human rights activist).
2214 **1509** 22c. multicoloured . . . 50 10

1986. 150th Anniv of Battle of San Jacinto.
2215 **1510** 22c. red, blue and black 45 10

1511 Muskellunge

1986. Fishes. Multicoloured.
2216 22c. Type **1511** . . . . . . 1·10 20
2217 22c. Atlantic cod . . . . . 1·10 20
2218 22c. Large-mouthed black bass . . . . 1·10 20
2219 22c. Blue-finned tuna . . . 1·10 20
2220 22c. Bullhead catfish . . . . 1·10 20

1516 Modern Hospital **1517** Ellington

1986. Public Hospitals. 250th Anniv of Bellevue Hospital Centre, New York.
2221 **1516** 22c. multicoloured . . . 45 10

1986. Performing Arts and Artists. Duke Ellington (jazz musician).
2222 **1517** 22c. multicoloured . . . 45 10

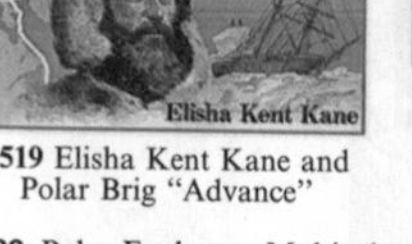

1519 Elisha Kent Kane and Polar Brig "Advance"

1523 Head of Statue

1986. Polar Explorers. Multicoloured.
2224 22c. Type **1519** 85 20
2225 22c. Adolphus W. Greely . . 85 20
2226 22c. Vilhjalmur Stefansson 85 20
2227 22c. Robert E. Peary and Matthew Henson 85 20

1986. Centenary of Statue of Liberty.
2228 **1523** 22c. blue and red . . . 45 10

1524 Blanket Design **1525** Blanket Design

1526 Blanket Design **1527** Blanket Design

1986. American Folk Art. Navajo Blankets.
2229 **1524** 22c. multicoloured . . . 70 15
2230 **1525** 22c. multicoloured . . . 70 15
2231 **1526** 22c. multicoloured . . . 70 15
2232 **1527** 22c. multicoloured . . . 70 15

1528 T. S. Eliot

1529 Highlander Figure (tobacconist)

1986. Literary Arts. Thomas Stearns Eliot (poet).
2233 **1528** 22c. red 45 10

1986. American Folk Art. Carved Wooden Figures. Multicoloured.
2234 22c. Type **1529** 60 15
2235 22c. Ship's figurehead . . . 60 15
2236 22c. Nautical figure (nautical instrument maker) 60 15
2237 22c. Indian (cigar store) . . 60 15

1533 "Madonna" (Il Perugino)

1535 White Pine and Lake Huron

1986. Christmas. Multicoloured.
2238 22c. Type **1533** 45 10
2239 22c. Winter village 45 10

1987. 150th Anniv of Michigan Statehood.
2240 **1535** 22c. multicoloured . . . 45 10

1536 Stylized Runner **1537** Heart

1986. 10th Pan-American Games, Indianapolis.
2241 **1536** 22c. multicoloured . . . 45 10

1987. Greetings Stamp.
2242 **1537** 22c. multicoloured . . . 45 10

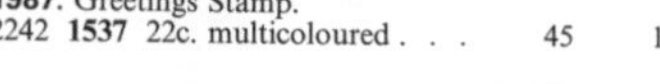

1538 Du Sable

1539 Caruso as Duke of Mantua in "Rigoletto"

1987. Black Heritage. Jean Baptiste Pointe du Sable (founder of Chicago).
2243 **1538** 22c. multicoloured . . . 45 10

1987. Performing Arts and Artists. Enrico Caruso (operatic tenor).
2244 **1539** 22c. multicoloured . . . 45 10

1540 Badges

1987. 75th Anniv of Girl Scouts of America.
2245 **1540** 22c. multicoloured . . . 45 10

1541 "Congratulations!"

1987. Greetings Stamps. Multicoloured.
2246 22c. Type **1541** 70 30
2247 22c. "Get Well!" (18 × 33 mm) 70 30
2248 22c. "Thank You!" (18 × 33 mm) 70 30
2249 22c. "Love You, Dad!" . . 70 30
2250 22c. "Best Wishes!" (18 × 21 mm) 70 30
2251 22c. "Happy Birthday!" (18 × 21 mm) 70 30
2252 22c. "Love You, Mother!" 70 30
2253 22c. "Keep in Touch!" (18 × 21 mm) 70 30

1549 Ethnic Faces

1550 Flag and Fireworks

1987. Centenary of United Way Volunteer Organization.
2254 **1549** 22c. multicoloured . . . 45 10

1987.
2255 **1550** 22c. multicoloured . . . 45 10

1551 Barn Swallows

1552 State Seal

1987. "Capex '87" International Stamp Exhibition, Toronto. North American Wildlife. Multicoloured.
2256 22c. Type **1551** 85 30
2257 22c. Monarch butterflies on field thistle 85 30
2258 22c. Bighorn sheep 85 30
2259 22c. Broad-tailed hummingbird on Colorado columbine . . . 85 30
2260 22c. Rabbit and red clover 85 30
2261 22c. Osprey 85 30
2262 22c. Mountain lion 85 30
2263 22c. Luna moth on trumpet honeysuckle 85 30
2264 22c. Mule deer 85 30
2265 22c. Grey squirrel on red oak 85 30
2266 22c. Armadillo and Texas prickly pear 85 30
2267 22c. Eastern chipmunk and European white birch . . 85 30
2268 22c. Moose 85 30
2269 22c. Black bear 85 30
2270 22c. Tiger swallowtail butterflies on orange milkweed 85 30
2271 22c. Northern bobwhite ("Bobwhite") and purple coneflower 85 30
2272 22c. Ringtail and Cape marigold 85 30
2273 22c. Red-winged blackbird on common cattail . . . 85 30
2274 22c. American lobster . . . 85 30
2275 22c. Black-tailed hare and beavertail 85 30
2276 22c. Scarlet tanager and American basswood . . . 85 30
2277 22c. Woodchuck and dandelion 85 30
2278 22c. Roseate spoonbill and red mangrove 85 30
2279 22c. American bald eagle . . 85 30
2280 22c. Alaskan brown bear . . 85 30
2281 22c. Iiwi on "Ohia lehua" 85 30
2282 22c. Badger 85 30
2283 22c. Pronghorns 85 30
2284 22c. River otter 85 30
2285 22c. Ladybird on rose . . . 85 30
2286 22c. Beaver, maple and quaking aspen 85 30
2287 22c. White-tailed deer . . . 85 30
2288 22c. Blue jays on Table Mountain pine 85 30
2289 22c. Pikas 85 30
2290 22c. Bison 85 30
2291 22c. Snowy egret 85 30
2292 22c. Grey wolf 85 30
2293 22c. Mountain goat 85 30
2294 22c. Deer mouse 85 30
2295 22c. Black-tailed prairie dog 85 30
2296 22c. Box turtle and Virginia creeper 85 30
2297 22c. Wolverine 85 30
2298 22c. American elk 85 30
2299 22c. California sea-lion . . . 85 30
2300 22c. Northern mockingbird on royal poinciana . . . 85 30
2301 22c. Racoon 85 30
2302 22c. Bobcat 85 30
2303 22c. Black-footed ferret . . 85 30
2304 22c. Canada goose 85 30
2305 22c. Red fox and red maple 85 30

1987. Bicentenary of Delaware Statehood.
2306 **1552** 22c. multicoloured . . . 60 10

1553 Arabesque from Door, Dar Batha Palace, Fez

1554 Faulkner (after M. L. Goldsborough)

1987. Bicentenary of Diplomatic Relations with Morocco.
2307 **1553** 22c. red and black . . . 45 10

1987. Literary Arts. 25th Death Anniv of William Faulkner (novelist).
2308 **1554** 22c. green 40 10

1555 Squash Blossoms (Ruth Maxwell)

1556 Floral Design (Mary McPeek)

1557 Floral Design (Leslie Saari)

1558 Dogwood Blossoms (Trenna Ruffner)

1987. American Folk Art. Lacemaking.
2309 **1555** 22c. white, blue and ultramarine 65 15
2310 **1556** 22c. white, blue and ultramarine 65 15
2311 **1557** 22c. white, blue and ultramarine 65 15
2312 **1558** 22c. white, blue and ultramarine 65 15

1559 Independence Hall

1987. Bicentenary of Pennsylvania Statehood.
2313 **1559** 22c. multicoloured . . . 65 10

1560 "The Bicentennial ..."

1987. Bicentenary of United States Constitution (1st issue). Multicoloured.
2314 22c. Type **1560** 65 15
2315 22c. "We the people ..." . . 65 15
2316 22c. "Establish justice ..." 65 15
2317 22c. "And secure ..." . . . 65 15
2318 22c. "Do ordain ..." 65 15
See also No. 2320.

1565 Farmer with Basket of Produce

1566 First Page of Constitution and Hand holding Quill Pen

1987. Bicentenary of New Jersey Statehood.
2319 **1565** 22c. mullticoloured . . 60 10

1987. Bicentenary of United States Constitution (2nd issue).
2320 **1566** 22c. multicoloured . . . 55 15

1567 Ledger Page and Pen Nib

1568 "Stourbridge Lion", 1829

1987. Centenary of American Institute of Certified Public Accountants.
2321 **1567** 22c. multicoloured . . . 2·40 25

1987. Steam Railway Locomotives. Multicoloured.
2322 22c. Type **1568** 70 20
2323 22c. "Best Friend of Charleston", 1830 . . . . 70 20
2324 22c. "John Bull", 1831 . . . 70 20
2325 22c. "Brother Jonathan", 1832 . . . . 70 20
2326 22c. "Gowan and Marx", 1839 . . . . 70 20

1573 "A Gentleman in Adoration before the Madonna" (detail, Giovanni Battista Moroni)

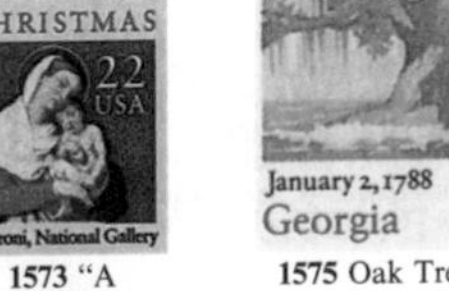

1575 Oak Tree

1987. Christmas. Multicoloured.
2327 22c. Type **1573** 45 10
2328 22c. Baubles on tree (horiz) 45 10

1988. Bicentenary of Georgia Statehood.
2329 **1575** 22c. multicoloured . . . 60 10

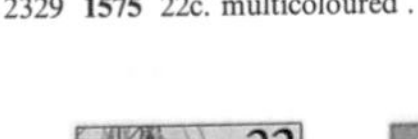

1576 "Charles W. Morgan" (whaling ship) and Mystic Town

1577 Slalom

1988. Bicentenary of Connecticut Statehood.
2330 **1576** 22c. multicoloured . . . 60 10

1988. Winter Olympic Games, Calgary.
2331 **1577** 22c. multicoloured . . . 45 10

1578 Koala and American Bald Eagle

1579 Johnson and Music Score

1988. Bicentenary of Australian Settlement.
2332 **1578** 22c. multicoloured . . . 45 10

1988. Black Heritage. James Weldon Johnson (writer, lyricist and diplomat).
2333 **1579** 22c. multicoloured . . . 45 10

1580 Siamese and Exotic Shorthair Cats

1584 "A Southwest View of the Statehouse, Boston" (S. Hill)

1988. Cats. Multicoloured.
2334 22c. Type **1580** 60 20
2335 22c. Abyssinian and Himalayan cats 60 20
2336 22c. Maine coon and Burmese cats 60 20
2337 22c. American shorthair and Persian cats 60 20

1988. Bicentenary of Massachusetts Statehood.
2338 **1584** 22c. blue, black and red 60 10

1585 St. Anne's Church, "Clarence Crockett" (yacht) and Statehouse, Annapolis

1586 Rockne

1988. Bicentenary of Maryland Statehood.
2339 **1585** 22c. multicoloured . . . 60 10

1988. American Sports Personalities. Birth Centenary of Knute Rockne (football player and coach).
2340 **1586** 22c. multicoloured . . . 50 10

1587 Earth

1588 Map, Settlers, Indians, "Calmare Nyckel" and "Fagel Grip"

1988. No value expressed.
2341 **1587** (25c.) multicoloured . . 55 10

1988. Air. 350th Anniv of Founding of New Sweden (settlement in America).
A2345 **1588** 44c. multicoloured . . 1·10 45

1589 Common Pheasant

1590 Flag and Clouds

1988.
2346 **1589** 25c. multicoloured . . . 65 10

1988.
2347 **1590** 25c. multicoloured . . . 50 10

1591 "Aerodrome No. 5" and Langley

1593 Flag over Half Dome, Yosemite National Park

1988. Air. Aviation Pioneers. Samuel Pierpont Langley.
A2348 **1591** 45c. multicoloured . . 95 20

1988.
2352 **1593** 25c. blue, red and green 55 10

1594 Palmetto Trees and Sea Grass

1595 Rose-breasted Grosbeak on Dogwood

1988. Bicentenary of South Carolina Statehood.
2353 **1594** 25c. multicoloured . . . 60 10

1988. Multicoloured.
2354 25c. Type **1595** 50 10
2355 25c. Saw-whet owl on Eastern hemlock 50 10

1597 Ouimet

1598 Old Man of the Mountain

1988. American Sports Personalities. 75th Anniv of Francis Ouimet's Open Golf Championship Victory.
2356 **1597** 25c. multicoloured . . . 75 10

1988. Bicentenary of New Hampshire Statehood.
2357 **1598** 25c. multicoloured . . . 35 10

1599 Sikorsky and Vought Sikorsky VS-300 Helicopter Prototype

1600 Carriage and Capitol Building, Williamsburg

1988. Air. Aviation Pioneers. Igor Sikorsky.
A2358 **1599** 36c. multicoloured . . 70 25

1988. Bicentenary of Virginia Statehood.
2359 **1600** 25c. multicoloured . . . 60 10

1601 Rose

1602 Trinity Church, Wall Street and Federal Hall, New York City

1988. Greetings Stamp.
2360 **1601** 25c. multicoloured . . . 50 10

1988. Bicentenary of New York Statehood.
2361 **1602** 25c. multicoloured . . . 60 10

1603 Roses

1604 Gymnast

1988. Greetings Stamp.
2362 **1603** 45c. multicoloured . . . 85 20

1988. Olympic Games, Seoul.
2363 **1604** 25c. multicoloured . . . 50 10

1605 Locomobile, 1928

1610 Honey Bee on Clover

1988. Classic Cars. Multicoloured.
2364 25c. Type **1605** . . . . . 1·10 35
2365 25c. Pierce-Arrow, 1929 . . 1·10 35
2366 25c. Cord, 1931 . . . . . 1·10 35
2367 25c. Packard, 1932 . . . . 1·10 35
2368 25c. Duesenberg, 1935 . . . 1·10 35

1988.
2369 **1610** 25c. multicoloured . . . 55 10

1611 Nathaniel Palmer (after Samuel Waldo) and "Hero"

1615 Buck (Gustav Dentzel)

1988. Antarctic Explorers. Multicoloured.
2370 25c. Type **1611** 80 20
2371 25c. Charles Wilkes (after Samuel Bell Waugh) and "Polar Star" 80 20
2372 25c. Richard E. Byrd and Ford Trimotor "Floyd Bennett" 80 20
2373 25c. Lincoln Ellsworth and Northrop Gamma "Polar Star" 80 20

1988. American Folk Art. Carousel Animals. Mult.
2374 25c. Type **1615** 85 20
2375 25c. Armoured horse (Daniel C. Muller) . . . 85 20
2376 25c. Camel (Charles Looff) 85 20
2377 25c. Goat (Charles Looff) 85 20

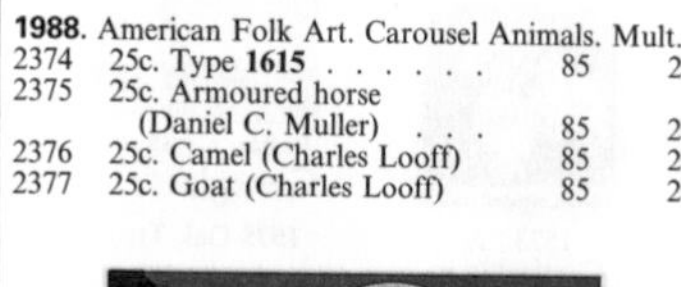

1619 American Bald Eagle and Moon

1988.
2378 **1619** $8.75 multicoloured . . 16·00 7·50

1620 "Madonna and Child" (detail, Sandro Botticelli)

1622 "Happy Birthday"

1988. Christmas.
2379 25c. Type **1620** 50 10
2380 25c. "White Christmas" (horiz) 55 10

1988. Greetings Stamps. Multicoloured.
2381 25c. Type **1622** 85 25
2382 25c. "Thinking of you" . . 85 25
2383 25c. "Love you" 85 25
2384 25c. "Best Wishes" 85 25

1626 "C.M. Russell and Friends" (Charles M. Russell)

1627 A. Philip Randolph

1989. Centenary of Montana Statehood.
2385 **1626** 25c. multicoloured . . . 60 15

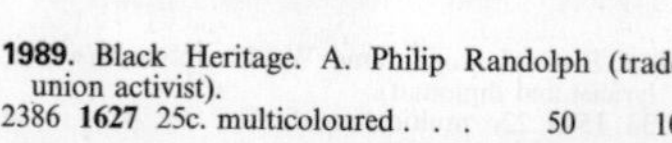

1989. Black Heritage. A. Philip Randolph (trade union activist).
2386 **1627** 25c. multicoloured . . . 50 10

1628 Grain Elevator and Buckboard

1629 Mt. Rainer and Canoe on Reflection Lake

1989. Centenary of North Dakota Statehood.
2387 **1628** 25c. multicoloured . . . 55 15

1989. Centenary of Washington Statehood.
2388 **1629** 25c. multicoloured . . . 55 10

1630 "Experiment", 1788–90

1989. Paddle-steamers. Multicoloured.
2389 25c. Type **1630** 70 15
2390 25c. "Phoenix", 1809 . . . 70 15
2391 25c. "New Orleans", 1812 70 15
2392 25c. "Washington", 1816 . . 70 15
2393 25c. "Walk in the Water", 1818 . . . . 70 15

1635 Cancelled 1869 90c. Lincoln Stamp

1636 Toscanini

1989. "World Stamp Expo'89" International Stamp Exhibition, Washington D.C.
2394 **1635** 25c. red, black & brown 50 10

1989. Performing Arts and Artists. Arturo Toscanini (conductor).
2395 **1636** 25c. multicoloured . . . 55 10

1637 "Car of History" Clock (Carlo Franzoni)

1638 Eagle and Shield over Vice-President's Chair

1989. Bicentenary of House of Representatives.
2396 **1637** 25c. multicoloured . . . 55 10

1989. Bicentenary of Senate.
2397 **1638** 25c. multicoloured . . . 55 10

1639 George Washington (statue, J. Q. A. Ward)

1640 Pasque Flowers, Pioneer Woman and House

1989. Bicentenary of Executive Branch.
2398 **1639** 25c. multicoloured . . . 60 15

1989. Centenary of South Dakota Statehood.
2399 **1640** 25c. multicoloured . . . 50 10

1641 Gehrig

1643 Hemingway

1642 Liberty, Equality and Fraternity

1989. American Sports Personalities. Lou Gehrig (baseball player).
2400 **1641** 25c. multicoloured . . . 85 10

1989. Air. Bicentenary of French Revolution.
A2401 **1642** 45c. multicoloured . . 90 25

1989. Literary Arts. Ernest Hemingway (novelist).
2402 **1643** 25c. multicoloured . . . 55 10

1644 Astronauts planting Flag on Moon

1645 Dogwood Blossoms

1989. 20th Anniv of First Manned Moon Landing.
2403 **1644** $2.40 multicoloured . . 5·00 2·40

1989. Bicentenary of North Carolina Statehood.
2404 **1645** 25c. multicoloured . . . 60 10

1646 Letter Carriers

1647 Eagle and Flag as Shield

1989. Centenary of National Association of Letter Carriers.
2405 **1646** 25c. multicoloured . . . 50 10

1989. Bicentenary of Bill of Rights.
2406 **1647** 25c. black, red and blue 70 15

1648 Tyrannosaurus Rex

1652 Mimbres Ritual Figure

1989. Prehistoric Animals. Multicoloured.
2407 25c. Type **1648** 85 35
2408 25c. Pteranodon 85 35
2409 25c. Stegosaurus 85 35
2410 25c. Brontosaurus 85 35

1989. America. Pre-Columbian Carvings. Mult.
2411 25c. Type **1652** (postage) 50 15
A2412 45c. Calusa "Key Marco cat" (air) 90 25

1654 "Dream of St. Catherine of Alexandria" (detail, Ludovico Carracci)

1656 Eagle and Shield

1989. Christmas. Multicoloured.
2413 25c. Type **1654** 50 10
2415 25c. Gifts on sleigh (horiz) 55 10

1989. Self-adhesive. Imperf.
2416 **1656** 25c. multicoloured . . . 60 15

1658 Western Stagecoach

1663 Hypersonic Airliner

1989. 20th U.P.U. Congress, Washington D.C. (1st issue). Classic Mail Transport. Multicoloured.
2418 25c. Type **1658** 75 25
2419 25c. "Chesapeake" (Mississippi river steamer) 75 25
2420 25c. Curtiss JN-4 "Jenny" biplane 75 25
2421 25c. Motor car 75 25
See also Nos. A2423/6.

1989. Air. 20th Universal Postal Union Congress, Washington D.C. (2nd issue). Mail Transport of the Future. Multicoloured.
A2423 45c. Type **1663** 95 35
A2424 45c. Hovercar 95 35
A2425 45c. Rover vehicle delivering mail to space colony 95 35
A2426 45c. Space shuttle delivering mail to space station 95 35

1668 Mountain Bluebird

1669 Lovebirds

1990. Centenary of Idaho Statehood.
2428 **1668** 25c. multicoloured . . . 45 10

1990. Greetings Stamp.
2429 **1669** 25c. multicoloured . . . 45 10

1670 Ida Wells

1671 John Marshall

1990. Black Heritage. Ida B. Wells (civil rights activist).
2431 **1670** 25c. multicoloured . . . 65 15

1990. Bicentenary of Supreme Court.
2432 **1671** 25c. multicoloured . . . 60 10

1672 Beach Umbrella

1674 Luis Munoz Marin

1990.
2433 **1672** 15c. multicoloured . . . 35 20

1990. Great Americans. (a) Ordinary Gum.
2435 **1674** 5c. red 25 15
2437 – 20c. red 30 15
2439 – 29c. blue 50 20
2440 – 29c. black 50 15
2442 – 32c. brown 60 25
2443 – 32c. green 60 50
2444 – 32c. red 60 50
2445 – 32c. blue 60 50
2448 – 35c. black 55 20
2450 – 40c. blue 65 25
2452 – 46c. red 80 60
2454 – 52c. lilac . . . . . . 1·00 20
2456 – 55c. green 85 45
2458 – 75c. red . . . . 1·10 30
2460a – 78c. violet . . . . . . 1·20 80

(b) Self-adhesive Gum.
2464 – 55c. black . . . . 00 1·00
2466 – 77c. blue . . . . 1·30 90

DESIGNS: 20c. Virginia Agpar; 29c. (No. 2439) Earl Warren; 29c. (No. 2440) Thomas Jefferson (President, 1801–09); 32c. (No. 2442) Milton S. Hershey; 32c. (No. 2443) Cal Farley; 32c. (No. 2444) Henry Luce; 32c. (No. 2445) Lila and DeWitt Wallace (after Paul Calle); 35c. Dennis Chavez; 40c. Lt-Gen. Claire Chennault; 46c. Ruth Benedict; 52c. Hubert Humphrey (Vice-president, 1965–69); 55c. (No. 2456) Dr. Alice Hamilton; 55c. (No. 2464) Justin Morrill; 75c. Wendell Wilkie; 77c. Mary Breckinridge; 78c. Alice Paul.

1710 "High Mountain Meadows" (Conrad Schwiering)

1990. Centenary of Wyoming Statehood.
2471 **1710** 25c. multicoloured . . . 55 10

1711 Judy Garland ("The Wizard of Oz")

1715 Marianne Moore

1990. Classic Films. Multicoloured.
2472 25c. Type **1711** . . . . . . 1·20 35
2473 25c. Clark Gable and Vivien Leigh ("Gone with the Wind") . . . . 1·20 35
2474 25c. Gary Cooper ("Beau Geste") . . . . 1·20 35
2475 25c. John Wayne ("Stagecoach") . . . . . 1·20 35

1990. Literary Arts. Marianne Moore (poet).
2476 **1715** 25c. multicoloured . . . 45 10

1717 Circus Wagon, 1900s ("05")

1755 Admiralty Head, Nugent Sound

1990. Transport.
2477 – 4c. purple 15 15
2478 **1717** 5c. red 15 15
2484 – 5c. red 15 15
2485 – 5c. brown 15 15
2487 – 5c. red 15 15
2486 – 10c. green 20 20
2479 – 20c. green 30 20
2480 – 23c. blue 35 20
2481 – 32c. blue 50 20
2482 – $1 blue and red . . . . 1·40 35

DESIGNS: 4c. Richard Dudgeon steam carriage, 1866; 5c. (Nos. 2485, 2487) Birch bark canoe, 1800s; 5c. (No. 2484) Circus wagon 1900s ("5c."); 10c. Tractor trailer, 1930s; 20c. Mt. Washington Cog Railway, 1870s; 23c. Lunch wagon, 1890s; 32c. Ferryboat, 1900s; $1 Benoist Type XIV flying boat.

1990. Lighthouses. Multicoloured.
2516 25c. Type **1755** 80 20
2517 25c. Cape Hatteras 80 20
2518 25c. West Quoddy Head . . 65 20
2519 25c. American Shoals . . . 80 20
2520 25c. Sandy Hook, New York Harbour 80 20

1760 Stars and Stripes

1761 Slater Mill

1990. Self-adhesive. Imperf.
2521 **1760** 25c. red and blue . . . 60 55

1990. Bicentenary of Rhode Island Statehood.
2522 **1761** 25c. multicoloured . . . 60 10

1763 Bobcat

1990. Wildlife.
2523 **1763** $2 multicoloured . . . 2·50 50

1769 Jesse Owens

1990. American Olympic Medal Winners. Mult.
2530 25c. Type **1769** 70 20
2531 25c. Ray Ewry 70 20
2532 25c. Hazel Wightman . . . 70 20
2533 25c. Eddie Eagan 70 20
2534 25c. Helene Madison . . . 70 20

1774 Assiniboine

1990. American Folk Art. Indian Headdresses. Multicoloured.
2535 25c. Type **1774** 60 30
2536 25c. Cheyenne 60 30
2537 25c. Comanche 60 30
2538 25c. Flathead 60 30
2539 25c. Shoshone 60 30

1779 Micronesian Outrigger Canoe and Flag

1990. 4th Anniv of Ratification of Marshall Islands and Micronesia Compacts of Free Association. Multicoloured.
2540 25c. Type **1779** 55 20
2541 25c. Marshallese stick chart, outrigger canoe and flag 55 20

1781 Killer Whales

1990. Marine Mammals. Multicoloured.
2542 25c. Type **1781** 70 20
2543 25c. Northern sea lions . . 70 20
2544 25c. Sea otter 70 20
2545 25c. Common dolphin . . . 70 20

1785 Grand Canyon

1990. America. Natural World. Multicoloured.
2546 25c. Type **1785** (postage) 55 15
A2547 45c. Tropical island coastline (air) . . . . . 1·00 20

1787 Eisenhower and Soldiers

1788 "Madonna and Child" (Antonello da Messina)

1990. Birth Cent of Dwight David Eisenhower (President, 1953–61).
2548 **1787** 25c. multicoloured . . . 60 15

1990. Christmas. Multicoloured.
2549 25c. Type **1788** 50 15
2551 25c. Christmas tree 50 15

1790 Tulip

1791

1991. No value expressed.
2552 **1790** (29c.) multicoloured . . 65 15

1991. No value expressed. Make-up rate stamp.
2556 **1791** (4c.) red and brown . . 15 10

1792 Stars and Stripes

1991. No value expressed. Self-adhesive. Imperf.
2557 **1792** (29c.) red, blue and black 70 35

1794 Federal Palace, Berne, and Capitol, Washington

1795 Farm

1991. 700th Anniv of Swiss Confederation.
2559 **1794** 50c. multicoloured . . . 1·10 30

1991. Bicentenary of Vermont Statehood.
2560 **1795** 29c. multicoloured . . . 65 15

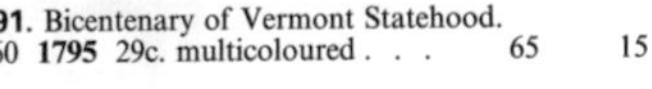

1796 Fawn

1797 Flag over Mt. Rushmore

1991.
2561 **1796** 19c. multicoloured . . . 40 10

1991.
2562 **1797** 29c. red, brown & black 55 15

1798 Tulip

1799 Wood Duck

1991.
2564 **1798** 29c. multicoloured . . . 55 20

1991. (a) Inscriptions in black.
2565 **1799** 29c. multicoloured . . . 60 15

(b) Inscriptions in red.
2567 **1799** 29c. multicoloured . . . 65 15

1800 Flag and Olympic Rings

1801 Quimby and Bleriot XI Airplane

1991.
2569 **1800** 29c. multicoloured . . . 55 15

1991. Air. Aviation Pioneers. Harriet Quimby (first American woman pilot).
A2570 **1801** 50c. multicoloured . . 95 30

1802 American Bald Eagle   **1803** Heart-shaped Globe

1991. 50th Anniv of "E Series" Defence Bonds.
2571 **1802** 29c. multicoloured . . . 55 15

1991. Greetings Stamps. Multicoloured.
2572 29c. Type **1803** 55 15
2574 52c. Fischer's lovebirds (21 × 35 mm) . . . . . . 1·10 15

1805 Hot-air Balloon   **1806** Piper and Piper J-3 Cub

1991.
2575 **1805** 19c. multicoloured . . . 40 20

1991. Air. Aviation Pioneers. William Piper.
A2576 **1806** 40c. multicoloured . . 85 25

1807 Saroyan   **1808** Flags on Parade

1991. Literary Arts. 10th Death Anniv of William Saroyan (dramatist and novelist).
2578 **1807** 29c. multicoloured . . . 55 15

1991. 125th Anniv of Memorial Day.
2579 **1808** 29c. multicoloured . . . 55 15

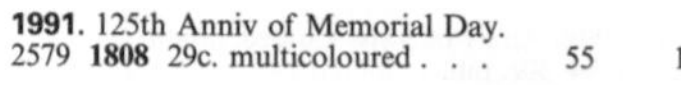

1809 Royal Wulff   **1814** Porter and Score

1991. Fishing Flies. Multicoloured.
2580 29c. Type **1809** . . . . . . 1·10 20
2581 29c. Jock Scott . . . . . . 1·10 20
2582 29c. Apte tarpon fly . . . . 1·10 20
2583 29c. Lefty's deceiver . . . . 1·10 20
2584 29c. Muddler minnow . . . 1·10 20

1991. Performing Arts and Artists. Birth Centenary of Cole Porter (composer).
2585 **1814** 29c. multicoloured . . . 65 15

1815 American Bald Eagle

1991. U.S. Olympic Festival.
2586 **1815** $9.95 multicoloured . . 17·00 7·25

1816 U.S.S. "Glacier" (ice-breaker) near Palmer Station   **1817** American Kestrel

1991. Air. 30th Anniv of Antarctic Treaty.
A2587 **1816** 50c. multicoloured . . 95 30

1991. Birds. Multicoloured.
2588 1c. Type **1817** 15 10
2589 3c. Eastern bluebird 15 15
2590 30c. Common cardinal ("Cardinal") 50 20

For Nos. 2588/9 and 2c. but with face value expressed as "1c" etc see No. 3023 etc.

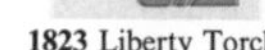

1823 Liberty Torch   **1824** South-West Asia Service Medal

1991. Self-adhesive. Imperf.
2591 **1823** 29c. green, gold & black 65 30

1991. Operations Desert Shield and Desert Storm (liberation of Kuwait).
2592 **1824** 29c. multicoloured . . . 55 15

1825 American Bald Eagle

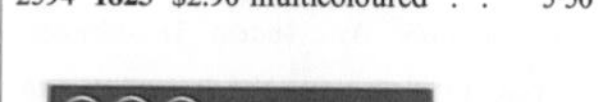

1991.
2594 **1825** $2.90 multicoloured . . 5·50 2·50

1826 Pole Vaulting   **1831** Rowing Boat

1991. Olympic Games, Barcelona (1992). Mult.
2595 29c. Type **1826** 60 20
2596 29c. Throwing the discus . . 60 20
2597 29c. Running 60 20
2598 29c. Throwing the javelin 60 20
2599 29c. Hurdling 35 15

1991.
2600 **1831** 19c. multicoloured . . . 25 10

1832 Coins and Banknotes   **1833** Shot at Goal

1991. Cent Convention of American Numismatic Association.
2603 **1832** 29c. multicoloured . . . 65 15

1991. Centenary of Basketball.
2604 **1833** 29c. multicoloured . . . 65 15

1834 Stan Laurel and Oliver Hardy

1991.
2605 **1834** 29c. black, violet and red . . . . 1·00 20
2606 – 29c. black, red and violet 50 20
2607 – 29c. black, violet and red 50 20
2608 – 29c. black, violet and red 50 20
2609 – 29c. black, red and violet 70 20

DESIGNS: No. 2606, Edgar Bergen and Charlie McCarthy; 2607, Jack Benny; 2608, Fanny Brice; 2609, Bud Abbott and Lou Costello.

1839 American Bald Eagle

1991.
2610 **1839** $14 multicoloured . . . 23·00 13·00

1840 Burma Road Convoy

1991. 50th Anniv of America's Entry into Second World War. Multicoloured.
2611 29c. Type **1840** 65 60
2612 29c. America's first peacetime draft 65 60
2613 29c. Lend-Lease Act 65 60
2614 29c. Roosevelt and Churchill (Atlantic Charter) 65 60
2615 29c. Munitions factory . . . 65 60
2616 29c. Sinking of "Reuben James" (destroyer) . . . 65 60
2617 29c. Gas mask (Civil Defence) 65 60
2618 29c. Delivery of "Patrick Henry" (first "Liberty" freighter) 65 60
2619 29c. U.S.S. "West Virginia" and U.S.S. "Tennessee" ablaze, Pearl Harbor . . 65 60
2620 29c. US Declaration of War on Japan 65 60

1850 Pennsylvania Avenue, 1903   **1851** Matzeliger

1991. Bicentenary of District of Columbia.
2621 **1850** 29c. multicoloured . . . 55 15

1991. Black Heritage. Jan Ernst Matzeliger (inventor of shoe lasting machine).
2622 **1851** 29c. multicoloured . . . 55 15

1852 Flag   **1853** Postal Service Emblem and Olympic Rings

1991.
2623 **1852** 23c. blue, red and black 30 15

1991.
2624 **1853** $1 multicoloured . . . 1·60 60

1854 "Mariner 10" and Mercury

1991. Space Exploration. Multicoloured.
2625 29c. Type **1854** 60 25
2626 29c. Venus and "Mariner 2" 60 25
2627 29c. Earth and "Landsat" 60 25
2628 29c. Moon and Lunar Orbiter 60 25
2629 29c. "Viking" Orbiter and Mars 60 25
2630 29c. Jupiter and "Pioneer 11" 60 25
2631 29c. "Voyager 2" and Saturn 60 25
2632 29c. Uranus and "Voyager 2" 60 25
2633 29c. Neptune and "Voyager 2" 60 25
2634 29c. Pluto 60 25

1864 Early Explorers from Asia   **1865** "Madonna and Child with Donor" (detail, Antoniazzo Romano)

1991. Air. America. Voyages of Discovery.
A2635 **1864** 50c. multicoloured . . 95 35

1991. Christmas. No value expressed. Mult.
2636 (29c.) Type **1865** 55 15
2637 (29c.) Santa Claus in chimney (horiz) 65 15
2639 (29c.) Santa Claus checking list (horiz) 60 20
2640 (29c.) Santa Clause leaving by chimney (horiz) 60 20
2642 (29c.) Santa Claus on sleigh (horiz) 60 20

1871 Eagle and Shield   **1872** Ice Hockey

1991. Inscr "Bulk Rate USA".
2644 **1871** (10c.) multicoloured . . 20 15

For design T **1871** but inscribed "USA Bulk Rate" see Nos. 2800/1.

1992. Winter Olympic Games, Albertville. Mult.
2645 29c. Type **1872** 50 20
2646 29c. Figure skating 50 20
2647 29c. Speed skating 50 20
2648 29c. Skiing 50 20
2649 29c. Two-man bobsleigh . . 50 20

1877 1869 15c. Columbus Stamp   **1878** Du Bois

1992. "World Columbian Stamp Expo'92", Chicago.
2650 **1877** 29c. multicoloured . . . 55 15

1992. Black Heritage. William Edward Burghardt Du Bois (founder of Niagara Movement (precursor of National Association for Advancement of Colored People)).
2651 **1878** 29c. multicoloured . . . 65 15

1879 Heart in Envelope   **1880** Catcher and Baserunner

1992. Greetings Stamp.
2652 **1879** 29c. multicoloured . . . 55 15

1992. Addition of Baseball to Olympic Games.
2653 **1880** 29c. multicoloured . . . 85 15

1881 Flag over White House   **1882** Seeking Queen Isabella's Support

1992. Bicentenary of White House.
2654 **1881** 29c. red and blue . . . 50 15

1992. 500th Anniv of Discovery of America by Columbus. Multicoloured.
2655 29c. Type **1882** 60 20
2656 29c. Crossing the Atlantic . 60 20
2657 29c. Approaching land . . . 60 20
2658 29c. Coming ashore 60 20

1886 Exchange Facade and Trading Floor

1893 Russian Cosmonaut and Space Shuttle

1992. Bicentenary of New York Stock Exchange.
2659 **1886** 29c. green, black and red 55 15

1992. International Space Year. Multicoloured.
2661 29c. Type **1893** 65 20
2662 29c. American astronaut and "Mir" space station . . . 65 20
2663 29c. "Apollo" and "Vostok" spacecraft and Sputnik . . 65 20
2664 29c. "Soyuz", "Mercury" and "Gemini" spacecraft 65 20

1897 Army Lorry using New Highway

1898 My Old Kentucky Home State Park, Bardstown

1992. 50th Anniv of Alaska Highway.
2665 **1897** 29c. multicoloured . . . 55 15

1992. Bicentenary of Kentucky Statehood.
2666 **1898** 29c. multicoloured . . . 55 15

1899 Football

1904 Ruby-throated Hummingbird

1992. Olympic Games, Barcelona. Multicoloured.
2667 29c. Type **1899** 60 30
2668 29c. Gymnastics 60 30
2669 29c. Volleyball 60 30
2670 29c. Boxing 60 30
2671 29c. Swimming 60 30

1992. Hummingbirds. Multicoloured.
2672 29c. Type **1904** 65 20
2673 29c. Broad-billed hummingbird 65 20
2674 29c. Costa's hummingbird 65 20
2675 29c. Rufous hummingbird 65 20
2676 29c. Calliope hummingbird 65 20

1909 Flag in "USA"

1910 Indian Paintbrush

1992. Presorted First Class stamp.
2678 **1909** 23c. multicoloured . . . 45 20

1992. Wild Flowers. Multicoloured.
2680 29c. Type **1910** 55 30
2681 29c. Fragrant water lily . . 55 30
2682 29c. Meadow beauty 55 30
2683 29c. Jack-in-the-pulpit . . . 55 30
2684 29c. California poppy . . . 55 30
2685 29c. Large-flowered trillium 55 30
2686 29c. Tickseed 55 30
2687 29c. Shooting star 55 30
2688 29c. Stream violet 55 30
2689 29c. Bluets 55 30
2690 29c. Herb Robert 55 30
2691 29c. Marsh marigold . . . 55 30
2692 29c. Sweet white violet . . 55 30
2693 29c. Claret cup cactus . . . 55 30
2694 29c. White mountain avens 55 30
2695 29c. Sessile bellwort 55 30
2696 29c. Blue flag 55 30
2697 29c. Harlequin lupine . . . 55 30
2698 29c. Twinflower 55 30
2699 29c. Common sunflower . . 55 30
2700 29c. Sego lily 55 30
2701 29c. Virginia bluebells . . . 55 30
2702 29c. Ohi'a lehua 55 30
2703 29c. Rosebud orchid 55 30
2704 29c. Showy evening primrose 55 30
2705 29c. Fringed gentian 55 30
2706 29c. Yellow lady's slipper 55 30
2707 29c. Passionflower 55 30
2708 29c. Bunchberry 55 30
2709 29c. Pasqueflower 55 30
2710 29c. Round-lobed hepatica 55 30
2711 29c. Wild columbine 55 30
2712 29c. Fireweed 55 30
2713 29c. Indian pond lily . . . 55 30
2714 29c. Turk's cap lily 55 30
2715 29c. Dutchman's breeches 55 30
2716 29c. Trumpet honeysuckle 55 30
2717 29c. Jacob's ladder 55 30
2718 29c. Plains prickly pear . . 55 30
2719 29c. Moss campion 55 30
2720 29c. Bearberry 55 30
2721 29c. Mexican hat 55 30
2722 29c. Harebell 55 30
2723 29c. Desert five spot . . . 55 30
2724 29c. Smooth Solomon's seal 55 30
2725 29c. Red maids 55 30
2726 29c. Yellow skunk cabbage 55 30
2727 29c. Rue anemone 55 30
2728 29c. Standing cypress . . . 55 30
2729 29c. Wild flax 55 30

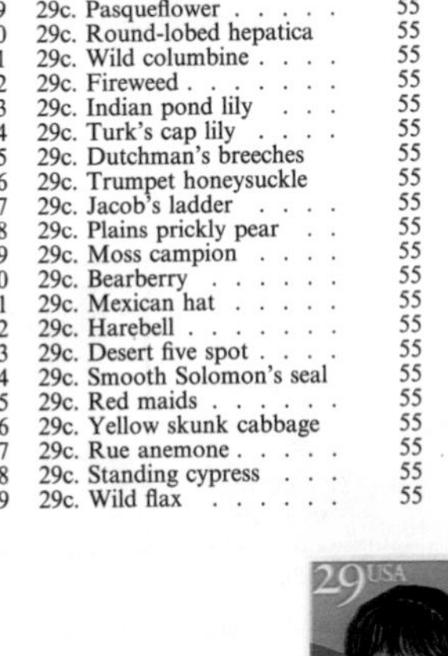

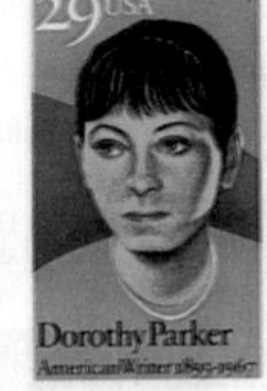

1911 Doolittle Raid on Tokyo

1921 Dorothy Parker

1992. United States Participation in Second World War. Multicoloured.
2730 29c. Type **1911** 65 50
2731 29c. Ration stamps 65 50
2732 29c. Douglas SBD-3 Dauntless on aircraft carrier (Battle of Coral Sea) 65 50
2733 29c. Japanese occupation of Corregidor 65 50
2734 29c. Japanese invasion of Aleutian Islands 65 50
2735 29c. Allies decipher enemy codes 65 50
2736 29c. U.S.S. "Yorktown" ablaze (Battle of Midway) 65 50
2737 29c. Woman engaged in war effort 65 50
2738 29c. Marines landing at Guadalcanal 65 50
2739 29c. Allied tanks in North Africa 65 50

1992. Literary Arts. Dorothy Parker (short story writer, poet and critic).
2740 **1921** 29c. multicoloured . . . 55 15

1922 Von Karman and Rocket

1923 Flag and "I pledge allegiance ..."

1992. Theodore von Karman (space pioneer).
2741 **1922** 29c. multicoloured . . . 55 15

1992. Centenary of Pledge of Allegiance.
2742 **1923** 29c. mult (value in blk) 55 15
2743 29c. mult (value in red) 65 25

1924 Azurite

1928 Eagle and Shield

1992. Minerals. Multicoloured.
2744 29c. Type **1924** 65 15
2745 29c. Copper 65 20
2746 29c. Variscite 65 20
2747 29c. Wulfenite 65 20

1992. Self-adhesive. Imperf.
2748 **1928** 29c. mult (inscr in red) 65 20
2749 29c. mult (inscr in grn) 65 20
2750 29c. mult (inscr in brn) 65 20

1929 Spanish Galleon, Map and Cabrillo

1930 Giraffe

1992. 450th Anniv of Discovery of California by Juan Rodriguez Cabrillo.
2751 **1929** 29c. multicoloured . . . 55 15

1992. Wild Animals. Multicoloured.
2752 29c. Type **1930** 50 20
2753 29c. Giant panda 50 20
2754 29c. Greater flamingo ("Flamingo") 50 20
2755 29c. King penguins 50 20
2756 29c. White Bengal tiger . . 50 20

1935 "Madonna and Child with Saints" (Giovanni Bellini)

1940 Pumpkinseed

1992. Christmas. Multicoloured.
2757 29c. Type **1935** 55 15
2758 29c. Wheeled racing horse (horiz) 65 15
2759 29c. Toy steam locomotive (horiz) 65 20
2760 29c. Toy steam engine (horiz) 65 20
2761 29c. Toy steamer (horiz) . . 65 20
No. 2759 also comes imperf and self-adhesive.

1992.
2767 **1940** 45c. multicoloured . . . 70 20

1941 Rooster

1992. New Year.
2768 **1941** 29c. multicoloured . . . 65 15

1942 Elvis Presley

1943 Spacecraft and Ringed-planet

1993. Elvis Presley (rock singer and actor).
2769 **1942** 29c. multicoloured . . . 70 20
For similar design but inscr "ELVIS PRESLEY" see Type **1987**.

1993. Space Fantasy. Multicoloured.
2770 29c. Type **1943** 55 20
2771 29c. Space capsules 55 20
2772 29c. Astronauts 55 20
2773 29c. Spaceship 55 20
2774 29c. Spacecraft and planet 55 20

1948 Julian

1949 Route Map

1993. Black Heritage. Percy Lavon Julian (research chemist).
2775 **1948** 29c. multicoloured . . . 55 15

1993. 150th Anniv of Oregon Trail.
2776 **1949** 29c. multicoloured . . . 55 15

1950 Athletes

1951 Princess Grace

1993. World University Games, Buffalo.
2777 **1950** 29c. multicoloured . . . 55 15

1993. 10th Death Anniv of Princess Grace of Monaco (former Grace Kelly).
2778 **1951** 29c. blue 75 15

1952 "Oklahoma"

1993. Broadway Musicals. Multicoloured. (a) No frame. Size 36 × 28 mm.
2779 29c. Type **1952** 55 15

(b) With frame. Size 35 × 27 mm.
2780 29c. "Show Boat" 65 20
2781 29c. "Porgy and Bess" . . . 65 20
2782 29c. Type **1952** 65 20
2783 29c. "My Fair Lady" . . . 65 20

1956 Clown

1993. Bicentenary of First Circus Performance in America. Multicoloured.
2784 29c. Type **1956** 65 20
2785 29c. Ringmaster 65 20
2786 29c. Trapeze artiste 65 20
2787 29c. Elephant 65 20

1960 Pioneers racing to Cherokee Strip

1961 Acheson

1993. Centenary of Cherokee Strip Land Run.
2789 **1960** 29c. multicoloured . . . 55 15

1993. Birth Centenary of Dean Acheson (Secretary of State, 1949–53).
2790 **1961** 29c. green 55 15

1962 Steeplechase

1966 Hyacinths

1993. Equestrian Sports. Multicoloured.
2791 29c. Type **1962** 65 20
2792 29c. Thoroughbred racing 65 20
2793 29c. Harness racing 65 20
2794 29c. Polo 65 20

1993. Garden Flowers. Multicoloured.
2795 29c. Type **1966** 55 20
2796 29c. Daffodils 55 20
2797 29c. Tulips 55 20
2798 29c. Irises 55 20
2799 29c. Lilac 55 20

1971 Eagle and Shield

1972 Atlantic Convoy

1993. Coil stamps. Inscr "USA Bulk Rate". Multicoloured, colours of eagle given.

2800 **1971** (10c.) yellow and brown . . 20 15
2801 (10c.) gold and brown . . 20 15

No. 2802 exists with both ordinary gum and self-adhesive gum.

For design as Type **1971** but inscr "Bulk Rate USA" see No. 2644.

1993. United States Participation in Second World War. Multicoloured.

2803 29c. Type **1972** 65 50
2804 29c. Treating the wounded . . 65 50
2805 29c. Allied attack on Sicily . . 65 50
2806 29c. Consolidated B-24 Liberators bombing Ploesti refineries 65 50
2807 29c. G.I.s with mail from home 65 50
2808 29c. Allied invasion of Italy . . 65 50
2809 29c. War Savings stamps and bonds 65 50
2810 29c. Willie and Joe (cartoon characters) 65 50
2811 29c. Gold Star emblem . . . 65 50
2812 29c. Marine assault on Tarawa, Gilbert Islands . . 65 50

1982 Futuristic Space Shuttle

1993.

2813 **1982** $2.90 multicoloured . . 5·00 2·10

1983 Hank Williams

1993. Country Music. Multicoloured. (a) No frame.

2815 29c. Type **1983** 70 35
2816 29c. Patsy Cline 70 45
2817 29c. Carter Family 70 45
2818 29c. Bob Wills 70 45

(b) With frame.

2819 29c. Type **1983** 70 20
2820 29c. Carter Family 70 20
2821 29c. Patsy Cline 70 20
2822 29c. Bob Wills 70 20

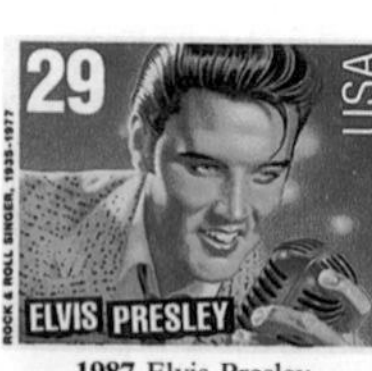

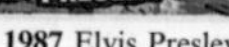

1987 Elvis Presley

1994 Louis

1993. Rock and Rhythm and Blues Music. Mult. (a) No frame.

2823 29c. Type **1987** 70 30
2824 29c. Buddy Holly 70 30
2825 29c. Ritchie Valens 70 30
2826 29c. Bill Haley 70 30
2827 29c. Dinah Washington . . 70 30
2828 29c. Otis Redding 70 30
2829 29c. Clyde McPhatter . . . 70 30

(b) With frame.

2830 29c. Type **1987** 70 20
2831 29c. Bill Haley 70 20
2832 29c. Clyde McPhatter . . . 70 20
2833 29c. Ritchie Valens 70 20
2834 29c. Otis Redding 70 20
2835 29c. Buddy Holly 70 20
2836 29c. Dinah Washington . . 70 20

1993. Joe Louis (boxer).

2837 **1994** 29c. multicoloured . . . . 1·75 15

1995 Red Squirrel

1996 Benjamin Franklin, Liberty Hall, Philadelphia, Post Rider and Printing Press

1993. Self-adhesive. Imperf.

2838 **1995** 29c. multicoloured . . . 65 20

1993. Inauguration of National Postal Museum, Washington. Multicoloured.

2839 29c. Type **1996** 65 20
2840 29c. Pony Express rider, Civil War soldier and stagecoach 65 20
2841 29c. Curtiss JN-4 "Jenny" biplane, pilot, railway mail/baggage car and mail truck 65 20
2842 29c. Gold rush miner's letter and stamps 65 20

2000 Red Rose

2001 Mother signing "I Love You"

1993. Self-adhesive. (a) Pink rose. Imperf (29c.) or roul (32c.).

2843 **2000** 29c. multicoloured . . . 60 15
3047 32c. multicoloured . . . 45 10

(b) Yellow rose. Roul.

3266 **2000** 32c. multicoloured . . . 70 25

1993. Deaf Communication. Multicoloured.

2845 29c. Type **2001** 55 20
2846 29c. "I Love You" in sign language 55 20

2003 African Violet

1993.

2847 **2003** 29c. multicoloured . . . 65 15

2004 "Madonna and Child in a Landscape" (Giovanni Battista Cima de Conegliano)

2005 Snowman

1993. Christmas. (a) Type **2004**.

2848 29c. multicoloured 55 15

(b) As T **2005**. Multicoloured. Perf or imperf (self-adhesive).

2849 29c. Type **2005** 55 20
2850 29c. Toy soldier 55 20
2851 29c. Jack-in-the-box 55 20
2852 29c. Reindeer 55 20

All designs come in more than one version, which differ slightly in size.

2009 "Rebecca of Sunnybrook Farm" (Kate Douglas Wiggin)

1993. Classic Children's Books. Multicoloured.

2863 29c. Type **2009** 50 20
2864 29c. "Little House on the Prairie" (Laura Ingalls Wilder) 50 20
2865 29c. "The Adventures of Huckleberry Finn" (Mark Twain) 50 20
2866 29c. "Little Women" (Louisa May Alcott) . . . 50 20

2013 Latte Stones and Flag

2014 Pine Cone

1993. 15th Anniv of Commonwealth of Northern Mariana Islands.

2867 **2013** 29c. multicoloured . . . 55 15

1993. Self-adhesive. Imperf.

2868 **2014** 29c. red, green and black 65 20

2015 Caravels off Puerto Rico

2016 Red Ribbon

1993. 500th Anniv of Columbus's Landing at Puerto Rico.

2869 **2015** 29c. multicoloured . . . 55 15

1993. World AIDS Day.

2870 **2016** 29c. red and black . . . 55 15

2017 Skiing

2022 Murrow

1994. Winter Olympic Games. Lillehammer. Mult.

2872 29c. Type **2017** 55 40
2873 29c. Luge 55 40
2874 29c. Ice dancing 55 40
2875 29c. Cross-country skiing . . 55 40
2876 29c. Ice hockey 55 40

1994. 29th Death Anniv of Edward Murrow (radio and television journalist).

2877 **2022** 29c. brown 55 15

2023 Heart-shaped Sun

2024 Davis

1994. Greetings Stamp. Self-adhesive. Imperf.

2878 **2023** 29c. multicoloured . . . 65 25

1994. Black Heritage. Dr. Allison Davis (educationist).

2879 **2024** 29c. sepia and brown 55 25

2025 American Bald Eagle

2026 Pekingese

1994. Self-adhesive. Imperf.

2880 **2025** 29c. multicoloured . . . 65 25

1994. New Year.

2881 **2026** 29c. multicoloured . . . 95 25

2027 Dove on Heart-shaped Bouquet of Roses

2029 Troopers on Western Frontier

1994. Greetings Stamps. Multicoloured.

2882 29c. Type **2027** (16 × 24½ mm) 35 15
2883 29c. Type **2027** (18 × 27 mm) 60 15
2884 52c. Doves on flower arrangement . . . . . . 1·00 50

1994. "Buffalo Soldiers" (U.S. Army black regiments).

2885 **2029** 29c. multicoloured . . . 55 15

2030 Rudolph Valentino

2040 Lilies

1994. Silent Screen Stars.

2886 **2030** 29c. black, violet and red 50 40
2887 – 29c. black, violet and red 50 40
2888 – 29c. black, red and violet . . . . 1·10 40
2889 – 29c. black, red and violet 50 40
2890 – 29c. black, violet and red 50 40
2891 – 29c. black, red and violet 50 40
2892 – 29c. black, violet and red 50 40
2893 – 29c. black, violet and red 50 40
2894 – 29c. black, red and violet 50 40
2895 – 29c. black, red and violet 50 40

DESIGNS: No. 2887, Clara Bow; 2888, Charlie Chaplin; 2889, Lon Chaney; 2890, John Gilbert; 2891, Zasu Pitts; 2892, Harold Lloyd; 2893, Keystone Cops; 2894, Theda Bara; 2895, Buster Keaton.

1994. Garden Flowers. Multicoloured.

2896 29c. Type **2040** 50 25
2897 29c. Zinnias 50 25
2898 29c. Gladioli 50 25
2899 29c. Marigolds 50 25
2900 29c. Roses . . . . 1·20 40

2045 Surrender at Saratoga (after John Trumbull)

2046 U.S.A. Player kicking Ball

1994.

2901 **2045** $1 blue . . . . 2·25 1·25

1994. World Cup Football Championship, U.S.A. Multicoloured.

2902 29c. Type **2046** 65 25
2903 40c. Controlling the ball . . 75 40
2904 50c. Heading the ball . . . 95 55

2050 Liberating New Guinea

2060 Statue of Liberty

1994. United States Participation in Second World War. Multicoloured.

2906 29c. Type **2050** 65 85
2907 29c. P-51 escorting B-17 bombers 65 85
2908 29c. Normandy Landings . . 65 85
2909 29c. Glider and paratroops . 65 85
2910 29c. Submarine crew 65 85
2911 29c. Liberating Rome . . . 65 85
2912 29c. Troops clearing Saipan bunkers 65 85
2913 29c. Red Ball Express truck 65 85
2914 29c. U.S.S. "Pennsylvania" (battleship) (Battle of Leyte Gulf) 65 85
2915 29c. Battle of the Bulge . . 65 85

1994. Self-adhesive. Imperf.

2918 **2060** 29c. multicoloured . . . 65 20
3273 32c. multicoloured . . . 75 30

2061 "Triple Self-portrait"

1994. Birth Centenary of Norman Rockwell (illustrator).
2919 **2061** 29c. multicoloured . . . 60 15

2063 Astronauts planting Flag on Moon

1994. 25th Anniv of First Manned Moon Landing.
2921 **2063** $9.95 multicoloured . . 17·00 18·00

2065 William Hudson's "General", 1855

1994. Locomotives. Multicoloured.
2923 29c. Type **2065** 60 25
2924 29c. Walter McQueen's "Jupiter", 1868 . . . . . 60 25
2925 29c. Wilson Eddy's No. 242, 1874 . . . . 60 25
2926 29c. Theodore Ely's No. 10, 1881 . . . . 60 25
2927 29c. William Buchanan's No. 999, 1893 . . . . . 60 25

2070 Meany

2072 Al Jolson

2071 Presidents Washington and Jackson

1994. Birth Centenary of George Meany (trades unionist).
2928 **2070** 29c. blue 55 15

1994.
2929 **2071** $5 green . . . . 7·50 3·00

1994. Popular Music. Multicoloured.
2930 29c. Type **2072** 75 65
2931 29c. Bing Crosby 75 65
2932 29c. Ethel Waters 75 65
2933 29c. Nat "King" Cole . . . 75 65
2934 29c. Ethel Merman 75 65

2077 "Male Type (eastern seaboard)"

2078 Bessie Smith

1994. Literary Arts. Birth Centenary of James Thurber (writer and cartoonist).
2935 **2077** 29c. multicoloured . . . 55 15

1994. Jazz and Blues Music. Multicoloured.
2936 29c. Type **2078** 85 50
2937 29c. Muddy Waters 85 50
2938 29c. Billie Holiday 85 50
2939 29c. Robert Johnson 85 50
2940 29c. Jimmy Rushing 85 50
2941 29c. "Ma" Rainey 85 50
2942 29c. Mildred Bailey 85 50
2943 29c. Howlin' Wolf 85 50

2086/9 Sea Life ($\frac{1}{2}$-size illustration)

1994. Wonders of the Seas.
2944 **2086** 29c. multicoloured . . . 50 25
2945 **2087** 29c. multicoloured . . . 50 25
2946 **2088** 29c. multicoloured . . . 50 25
2947 **2089** 29c. multicoloured . . . 50 25
Nos. 2944/7 were issued together, se-tenant, forming the composite design illustrated.

2090 Black-necked Crane

2092 Home on the Range

1994. Cranes. Multicoloured.
2948 29c. Type **2090** 65 25
2949 29c. Whooping crane . . . 65 25

1994. Legends of the West. Multicoloured.
2950 29c. Type **2092** 65 70
2951 29c. Buffalo Bill (William Cody) 65 70
2952 29c. Jim Bridger 65 70
2953 29c. Annie Oakley 65 70
2954 29c. Native American culture 65 70
2955 29c. Chief Joseph 65 70
2956 29c. Bill Pickett 65 70
2957 29c. Bat Masterson 65 70
2958 29c. John Fremont 65 70
2959 29c. Wyatt Earp 65 70
2960 29c. Nellie Cashman 65 70
2961 29c. Charles Goodnight . . . 65 70
2962 29c. Geronimo 65 70
2963 29c. Kit Carson 65 70
2964 29c. Wild Bill Hickok . . . 65 70
2965 29c. Western wildlife 65 70
2966 29c. Jim Beckwourth . . . 65 70
2967 29c. Bill Tilghman 65 70
2968 29c. Sacagawea 65 70
2969 29c. Overland mail 65 70
Each stamp is inscribed on the back, under the gum, with a brief history of the subject depicted.

2097 "Virgin and Child" (Elisabetta Sirani)

2100 Common Cardinal

1994. Christmas. Multicoloured. (a) Perf.
2970 29c. Type **2097** 55 15
2972 29c. Stocking 55 15

(b) Self-adhesive. Imperf.
2973 29c. Santa Claus 65 30
2974 29c. Type **2100** 65 40
Nos. 2972/3 are as Type **2097** in size.

2102 Dove with Olive Branch

2103 Old Glory

1994. Make-up Rate stamp. No value expressed.
2976 **2102** (3c.) blue, brn & red . . 20 20

1994. With service indicator. (a) Nonprofit Presort. Green background.
2978 **2103** (5c.) multicoloured . . 25 40

(b) Postcard rate. Yellow background.
2979 **2103** (20c.) mult (black "G") 30 25
2980 (20c.) mult (red "G") 45 30

(c) First-Class Presort. Blue background.
2981 **2103** (25c.) multicoloured . . 55 50

2104 Old Glory

2106 Boar

1994. No value expressed. Perf (Nos. 2982, 2984); perf or imperf (self-adhesive) (No. 2986).
2982 **2104** (32c.) mult (red "G") 65 25
2984 (32c.) mult (blue "G") 75 40
2986 (32c.) mult (black "G") 80 25

1994. New Year.
2991 **2106** 29c. multicoloured . . . 65 50

2107 Cherub (detail from "Sistine Madonna" by Raphael)

2108 Alligator

1995. Greetings Stamp. No value expressed. (a) Size 20 × 26 mm.
2992 **2107** (32c.) multicoloured . . 60 20

(b) Size 18 × 22 mm. Self-adhesive. Imperf.
2993 **2107** (32c.) multicoloured . . 70 15
For Type **2107** but with face value "32", see No. 3035.

1995. 150th Anniv of Florida Statehood.
2994 **2108** 32c. multicoloured . . . 65 25

2109 Butte

2110 Front of Motor Car

1995. Non-profit Organizations Stamp. Ordinary or self-adhesive gum.
2995 **2109** (5c.) orange, blue and yellow 15 25

1995. Bulk Rate Stamp. Ordinary or self-adhesive gum.
2997 **2110** (10c.) vermilion, black and red 20 25

2111 Motor Car Tail Fin

2112 Juke Box

2113 Flag over Field

1995. Presorted First Class Postcard Stamp. Ordinary or self-adhesive gum.
2999 **2111** (15c.) multicoloured . . 30 30

1995. Presorted First Class Stamp. Ordinary or self-adhesive gum.
3003 **2112** (25c.) multicoloured . . 50 50

1995. Self-adhesive. Imperf.
3007 **2113** 32c. multicoloured . . . 70 40

2115 Flag over Porch

2116 Globe in Bath (Christy Millard)

1995. Perf or imperf (self-adhesive).
3008 **2115** 32c. multicoloured . . . 60 40

1995. 25th Anniv of Earth Day. Multicoloured.
3017 32c. Type **2116** 65 30
3018 32c. Solar energy (Jennifer Michalove) 65 30
3019 32c. Youth planting tree (Brian Hailes) 65 30
3020 32c. Family cleaning up beach (Melody Kiper) . . 65 25

2119 Nixon

2120 Bessie Coleman

1995. 1st Death Anniv of Richard Nixon (President, 1968–74).
3021 **2119** 32c. multicoloured . . . 60 25

1995. Black Heritage. Bessie Coleman (aviator).
3022 **2120** 32c. black and red . . . 60 25

1995. Birds. Value expressed as "1c" etc. Mult.
3023 1c. As T **1817** 15 10
3024 2c. Red-headed woodpecker 15 20
3025 3c. As No. 2589 . . . . . 15 15
No. 3023 also comes self-adhesive.

2125 Cherub

1995. Greetings Stamps. Details from "Sistine Madonna" by Raphael. Ordinary gum (Nos. 3035/6) or self-adhesive (Nos. 3038/9). Perf (Nos. 3035/6, 3038) or imperf (No. 3039).
3035 **2107** 32c. multicoloured ($19\frac{1}{2} \times 27$ mm) . . . 60 25
3038 32c. multicoloured ($18\frac{1}{2} \times 22$ mm) . . . 60 30
3036 **2125** 55c. multicoloured ($27 \times 20\frac{1}{2}$ mm) . . . 1·00 50
3039 55c. multicoloured ($21\frac{1}{2} \times 19$ mm) . . . 1·00 55

2126 Golf

1995. Sports. Multicoloured.
3040 32c. Type **2126** 70 45
3041 32c. Volleyball 70 45
3042 32c. Baseball 70 45
3043 32c. Bowls 70 45
3044 32c. Tennis 70 45

2131 Flag and Identification Tags

2132 Marilyn Monroe

1995. Memorial Day.
3045 **2131** 32c. multicoloured . . . 60 30

1995. Legends of Hollywood.
3046 **2132** 32c. multicoloured . . . 85 40

2133 Blue Jay

2134 Horseman carrying Flag

1995. Ordinary or self-adhesive gum.
3048 **2133** 20c. multicoloured . . . 45 15

1995. 150th Anniv of Texas Statehood.
3051 **2134** 32c. multicoloured . . . 70 25

2135 Split Rock, Lake Superior

2140 "Challenger" (space shuttle)

1995. Great Lakes Lighthouses. Multicoloured.
3052 32c. Type **2135** 65 30
3053 32c. St. Joseph, Lake Michigan 65 30
3054 32c. Spectacle Reef, Lake Huron 65 30
3055 32c. Marblehead, Lake Erie 65 30
3056 32c. Thirty Mile Point, Lake Ontario 65 30

1995.
3057 **2140** $3 multicoloured . . . 5·00 2·00

2141 Emblem

2142 U.S.S. "Monitor" and C.S.S. "Virginia" (ironclads) in Battle

1995. 50th Anniv of U.N.O.
3058 **2141** 32c. blue 60 30

1995. 130th Anniv of End of American Civil War. Multicoloured.
3059 32c. Type **2142** 75 75
3060 32c. Gen. Robert E. Lee (Confederate) 75 75
3061 32c. Clara Barton (Union nurse) 75 75
3062 32c. Gen. Ulysses Grant (Union) 75 75
3063 32c. Battle of Shiloh 75 75
3064 32c. Jefferson Davis (Confederate President) 75 75
3065 32c. Vice-Admiral David Farragut (Union) 75 75
3066 32c. Frederick Douglass (journalist and diplomat) 75 75
3067 32c. Rear-Admiral Raphael Semmes (Confederate) . . 75 75
3068 32c. Abraham Lincoln (U.S. President, 1861–65) . . . 75 75
3069 32c. Harriet Tubman (black rights campaigner) 75 75
3070 32c. Brig.-Gen. Stand Watie (Confederate) 75 75
3071 32c. Gen. Joseph Johnston (Confederate) 75 75
3072 32c. Major-Gen. Winfield Hancock (Union) 75 75
3073 32c. Mary Chesnut (Confederate diarist) . . . 75 75
3074 32c. Battle of Chancellorsville 75 75
3075 32c. Major-Gen. William Sherman (Union) 75 75
3076 32c. Phoebe Pember (Confederate nurse) . . . 75 75
3077 32c. Lt.-Gen. Thomas "Stonewall" Jackson (Confederate) 75 75
3078 32c. Battle of Gettysburg . . 75 75
Each stamp is inscribed on the back, under the gum, with a brief history of the subject depicted.

2147 Peaches

1995. Multicoloured. Ordinary or self-adhesive gum.
3079 32c. Type **2147** 65 20
3080 32c. Pear 65 20

2149 King Horse, 1910 (Stein and Goldstein)

2150 Indian Pony, 1905 (Daniel Muller)

2151 Armoured Horse, 1912 (Stein and Goldstein)

2152 Lillie Belle, 1917 (C. W. Parker Co)

1995. Carousel Horses.
3085 **2149** 32c. multicoloured . . . 75 25
3086 **2150** 32c. multicoloured . . . 75 25
3087 **2151** 32c. multicoloured . . . 75 25
3088 **2152** 32c. multicoloured . . . 75 25

2153 Launch of Space Shuttle "Endeavour"

1995.
3089 **2153** $10.75 multicoloured 17·00 8·25

2154 1913 and 1976 Women's Rights Marches

1995. 75th Anniv of Ratification of 19th Amendment (giving women the right to vote).
3090 **2154** 32c. multicoloured . . . 60 25

2155 Coleman Hawkins

1995. Jazz Musicians. Multicoloured. (a) With value in white.
3091 32c. Louis Armstrong . . . 85 50

(b) With value in black.
3092 32c. Type **2155** 85 80
3093 32c. Louis Armstrong . . . 85 80
3094 32c. James Johnson 85 80
3095 32c. Jelly Roll Morton . . . 85 80
3096 32c. Charlie Parker 85 80
3097 32c. Eubie Blake 85 80
3098 32c. Charles Mingus 85 80
3099 32c. Thelonious Monk . . . 85 80
3100 32c. John Coltrane 85 80
3101 32c. Erroll Garner 85 80

2165 Marines raising Flag on Iwo Jima

2175 Asters

1995. United States Participation in Second World War. Multicoloured.
3102 32c. Type **2165** 70 70
3103 32c. Liberation of Manila 70 70
3104 32c. Troops advancing on Okinawa 70 70
3105 32c. Bridge across River Elbe 70 70
3106 32c. Liberation of concentration camp survivors 70 70
3107 32c. German Surrender at Reims 70 70
3108 32c. Refugees 70 70
3109 32c. President Truman announcing Japanese surrender 70 70
3110 32c. News of victory reaches America 70 70
3111 32c. Honouring returned service personnel 70 70

1995. Garden Flowers. Multicoloured.
3112 32c. Type **2175** 65 30
3113 32c. Chrysanthemums . . . 65 30
3114 32c. Dahlias 65 30
3115 32c. Hydrangea 65 30
3116 32c. Rudbeckias 65 30

2180 Rickenbacker

2181 Racoon Butterflyfish, Soldierfish, Shell and Palau Flag

1995. Aviation Pioneers. Eddie Rickenbacker (fighter pilot).
3117 **2180** 60c. multicoloured . . . 1·10 40

1995. 1st Anniv of Independence of Palau.
3118 **2181** 32c. multicoloured . . . 60 25

2182 Santa Claus on Rooftop

2186 The Yellow Kid

1995. Christmas (1st issue). Victorian Designs from writing tablet (T **2182**) or postcards (others). Ordinary or self-adhesive gum.
3119 32c. Type **2182** 60 25
3120 32c. Boy holding jumping jack 60 25
3121 32c. Boy holding tree . . . 60 25
3122 32c. Santa Claus making toy sleigh 60 25
See also Nos. 3153/7.

1995. Centenary of Comic Strips. Multicoloured.
3131 32c. Type **2186** 65 70
3132 32c. Katzenjammer Kids . . 65 70
3133 32c. Little Nemo in Slumberland 65 70
3134 32c. Bringing Up Father . . 65 70
3135 32c. Krazy Kat 65 70
3136 32c. Rube Goldberg's Inventions 65 70
3137 32c. Toonerville Folks . . . 65 70
3138 32c. Gasoline Alley 65 70
3139 32c. Barney Google 65 70
3140 32c. Little Orphan Annie . . 65 70
3141 32c. Popeye 65 70
3142 32c. Blondie 65 70
3143 32c. Dick Tracy 65 70
3144 32c. Alley Oop 65 70
3145 32c. Nancy 65 70
3146 32c. Flash Gordon 65 70
3147 32c. Li'l Abner 65 70
3148 32c. Terry and the Pirates 65 70
3149 32c. Prince Valiant 65 70
3150 32c. Brenda Starr, Reporter 65 70
Each stamp is inscribed on the back, under the gum, with a brief history of the subject depicted.

2187 "Swift" (racing sloop) and Academy Chapel

1995. 150th Anniv of Naval Academy, Annapolis.
3151 **2187** 32c. multicoloured . . . 60 25

2188 Williams and Streetcars

1995. Literary Arts. Tennessee Williams (dramatist).
3152 **2188** 32c. multicoloured . . . 60 25

2189 "Enthroned Madonna and Child" (Giotto)

2190 Midnight Angel (after Ellen Clapsaddle)

2191 Children Sledding

2192 Polk

1995. Christmas (2nd issue). (a) Ordinary gum. Perf.
3153 **2189** 32c. multicoloured . . . 60 25

(b) Self-adhesive. Roul (No. 3137) or imperf (No. 3187).
3155 **2190** 32c. multicoloured . . . 75 25
3157 **2191** 32c. multicoloured . . . 75 40

1995. Birth Bicentenary of James K. Polk (President, 1844–49).
3158 **2192** 32c. brown 60 20

2193 Columbia Battery-powered Car, 1898

2198 Delicate Arch, Arches National Park

1996. Veteran Cars. Multicoloured.
3159 32c. Type **2193** 60 65
3160 32c. Winton Car, 1899 . . . 60 65
3161 32c. White Steam-powered Car, 1901 . . . . . . 60 65
3162 32c. Duryea Car, 1893 . . . 60 65
3163 32c. Haynes Car, 1894 . . . 60 65

1996. Centenary of Utah Statehood.
3164 **2198** 32c. multicoloured . . . 65 25

2199 Crocus

2204 Just

1996. Garden Flowers. Multicoloured.
3165 32c. Type **2199** 65 30
3166 32c. Winter aconites 65 30
3167 32c. Pansies 65 30
3168 32c. Snowdrops 65 30
3169 32c. Anemones 65 30

1996. Black Heritage. Ernest Just (marine biologist).
3170 **2204** 32c. multicoloured . . . 65 25

2205 The Castle (first Smithsonian building)

1996. 150th Anniv of Smithsonian Institution.
3171 **2205** 32c. multicoloured . . . 55 25

2206 Rat

1996. New Year.
3172 **2206** 32c. multicoloured . . . 65 25

2207 Frederic Ives (halftone process)

2211 Face, Map and Compass

1996. Pioneers of Communication. Multicoloured.
3173 32c. Type **2207** 60 40
3174 32c. William Dickson (motion pictures) 60 40
3175 32c. Eadweard Muybridge (photography) 60 40
3176 32c. Ottmar Mergenthaler (linotype) 60 40

1996. 50th Anniv of Fulbright Scholarships (international educational exchange programme).
3177 **2211** 32c. multicoloured . . . 55 25

2212 Jacqueline Cochran

2213 Mountains

1996. Aviation Pioneers. Jacqueline Cochran (first woman to fly faster than speed of sound).
3178 **2212** 50c. multicoloured . . . 90 50

1996. Non-profit Organizations. No value expressed. Ordinary or self-adhesive gum.
3179 **2213** (5c.) multicoloured . . 15 25

2214 Runners **2215** Decathlon

1996. 100th Boston Marathon.
3183 **2214** 32c. multicoloured . . . 55 25

1996. Olympic Games, Atlanta. Multicoloured.
3184 32c. Type **2215** 65 65
3185 32c. Men's canoeing 65 65
3186 32c. Women's running . . . 65 65
3187 32c. Women's diving . . . 65 65
3188 32c. Men's cycling 65 65
3189 32c. Freestyle wrestling . . 65 65
3190 32c. Women's gymnastics 65 65
3191 32c. Women's sailboarding 65 65
3192 32c. Men's putting the shot 65 65
3193 32c. Women's football . . . 65 65
3194 32c. Beach volleyball . . . 65 65
3195 32c. Men's rowing 65 65
3196 32c. Men's sprinting 65 65
3197 32c. Women's swimming . . 65 65
3198 32c. Women's softball . . . 65 65
3199 32c. Men's hurdling 65 65
3200 32c. Men's swimming . . . 65 65
3201 32c. Men's gymnastics . . . 65 65
3202 32c. Show jumping 65 65
3203 32c. Men's basketball . . . 65 65

2216 "Red Poppy" **2217** State Capitol, Nashville

1996. 10th Death Anniv of Georgia O'Keeffe (painter).
3204 **2216** 32c. multicoloured . . . 60 25

1996. Bicentenary of Tennessee. Ordinary or self-adhesive gum.
3205 **2217** 32c. multicoloured . . . 60 30

2218 Fancy Dance **2223** Mastodon

1996. Traditional Amerindian Dances.
3207 32c. Type **2218** 65 40
3208 32c. Butterfly dance 65 40
3209 32c. Traditional dance . . . 65 40
3210 32c. Raven dance 65 40
3211 32c. Hoop dance 65 40

1996. Prehistoric Animals.
3212 32c. Type **2223** 65 40
3213 32c. Sabre-tooth tiger . . . 65 40
3214 32c. Eohippus 65 40
3215 32c. Woolly mammoth . . . 65 40

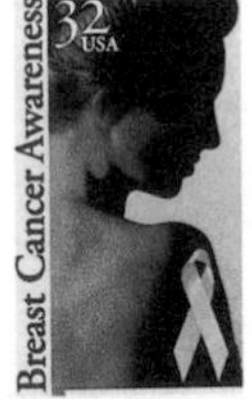

2227 Woman and Ribbon **2228** James Dean

1996. Breast Cancer Awareness Campaign.
3216 **2227** 32c. multicoloured . . . 75 25

1996. Legends of Hollywood.
3217 **2228** 32c. multicoloured . . . 75 30

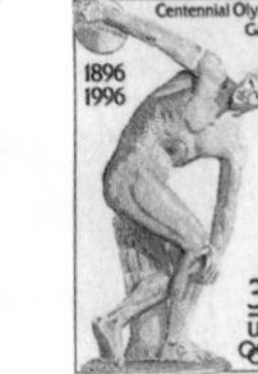

2229 Mighty Casey **2233** "The Discus Thrower" (Miron)

1996. Folk Heroes. Multicoloured.
3218 32c. Type **2229** 65 50
3219 32c. Paul Bunyan 65 50
3220 32c. John Henry 65 50
3221 32c. Pecos Bill 65 50

1996. Centenary of Modern Olympic Games.
3222 **2233** 32c. brown 65 25

2234 "Young Corn" (Grant Wood) **2235** Early Postal Carrier and Horse-drawn Mail Wagon

1996. 150th Anniv of Iowa Statehood. Ordinary or self-adhesive gum.
3223 **2234** 32c. multicoloured . . . 60 30

1996. Centenary of Free Rural Postal Deliveries.
3225 **2235** 32c. multicoloured . . . 60 25

2236 "Robert E. Lee"

1996. 19th-century Paddle-steamers. Self-adhesive.
3226 32c. Type **2236** 65 40
3227 32c. "Sylvan Dell" 65 40
3228 32c. "Far West" 65 40
3229 32c. "Rebecca Everingham" 65 40
3230 32c. "Bailey Gatzert" . . . 65 40

2241 Count Basie

1996. Big Band Leaders (Nos. 3231/4) and Songwriters (Nos. 3235/8). Multicoloured.
3231 32c. Type **2241** 75 40
3232 32c. Tommy and Jimmy Dorsey 75 40
3233 32c. Glenn Miller 75 40
3234 32c. Benny Goodman . . . 75 40
3235 32c. Harold Arlen 75 40
3236 32c. Johnny Mercer 75 40
3237 32c. Dorothy Fields 75 40
3238 32c. Hoagy Carmichael . . 75 40

2249 Fitzgerald

1996. Birth Centenary of Francis Scott Fitzgerald (writer).
3239 **2249** 23c. multicoloured . . . 45 25

2250 Black-footed Ferret

1996. Endangered Species. Multicoloured.
3240 32c. Type **2250** 65 65
3241 32c. Thick-billed parrot . . 65 65
3242 32c. Hawaiian monk seal . . 65 65
3243 32c. American crocodile . . 65 65
3244 32c. Ocelot 65 65
3245 32c. Schaus swallowtail . . 65 65
3246 32c. Wyoming toad 65 65
3247 32c. Brown pelican 65 65
3248 32c. California condor . . . 65 65
3249 32c. Gila trout 65 65
3250 32c. San Francisco garter snake 65 65
3251 32c. Woodland caribou . . 65 65
3252 32c. Florida panther 65 65
3253 32c. Piping plover 65 65
3254 32c. Florida manatee . . . 65 65

2251 Circuit Boards covering Brain

1996. Computer Technology. 50th Anniv of ENIAC (Army computer system).
3255 **2251** 32c. multicoloured . . . 55 30

2252 Family at Fireside **2256** Ice Skaters

1996. Christmas (1st issue). Multicoloured. Ordinary or self-adhesive gum (Nos. 3256/9), self-adhesive (No. 3264).
3256 32c. Type **2252** 65 25
3257 32c. Decorating Christmas tree 65 25
3258 32c. Santa Claus in chimney and child sleeping 65 25
3259 32c. Mother and child carrying gifts 65 25
3264 32c. Type **2256** 70 40
See also No. 3268.

2257 Lighted Candles **2258** Madonna and Child (detail from "Adoration of the Shepherds", Paolo de Matteis)

1996. Festival of Hanukkah. Self-adhesive.
3265 **2257** 32c. multicoloured . . . 60 25
3693 33c. multicoloured . . . 55 25

1996. Christmas (2nd issue). Ordinary or self-adhesive gum.
3268 **2258** 32c. multicoloured . . . 55 25

2260 Ox **2261** Davis on Inspection Tour in France, 1944

1997. New Year.
3271 **2260** 32c. multicoloured . . . 65 40

1997. Black Heritage. Brigadier-General Benjamin Davis. Self-adhesive.
3272 **2261** 32c. blk, lt grey & grey 65 30

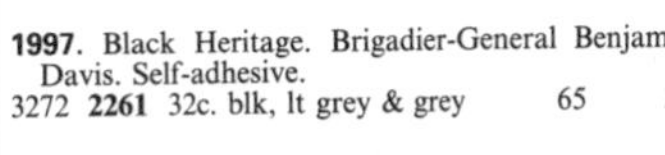
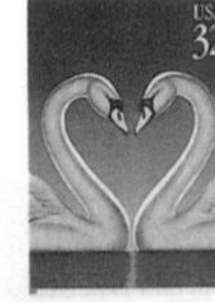

2262 Mute Swans

1997. Greetings Stamps. Mult. Self-adhesive.
3274 32c. Type **2262** 70 30
3275 55c. Mute swans (horiz) . . 95 60

2264 Adult and Child with Book **2265** Beetle, Moth and Lava on Citron

1997. Helping Children Learn. Self-adhesive.
3276 **2264** 32c. multicoloured . . . 70 30

1997. 350th Birth Anniv of Maria Sibylla Merian (painter). Self-adhesive. (a) Size $18\frac{1}{2} \times 24\frac{1}{2}$ mm. Multicoloured.
3277 32c. Type **2265** 70 65
3278 32c. Cockroaches on flowering pineapple . . . 70 30

(b) Size $19\frac{1}{2} \times 27\frac{1}{2}$ mm.
3279 32c. Type **2265** 65 30
3280 32c. As No. 3278 . . . . . 65 30

2267 U.S. Mail Coach

1997. "Pacific 97" International Stamp Exhibition, San Francisco.
3281 **2267** 32c. red 65 55
3282 – 32c. blue 65 55
DESIGN: No. 3282, "Richard S. Ely" (clipper).

2269 Wilder (after Michael Deas)

1997. Literary Arts. Birth Centenary of Thornton Wilder (novelist, playwright and essayist).
3283 **2269** 32c. multicoloured . . . 60 25

2270 Holocaust Survivors and Wallenberg

1997. Raoul Wallenberg (Swedish diplomat) Commemoration.
3284 **2270** 32c. multicoloured . . . 60 30

2271 Ceratosaurus

1997. Prehistoric Animals. Multicoloured.
3285 32c. Type **2271** 65 70
3286 32c. Camptosaurus ($38\frac{1}{2} \times 30$mm) 65 70
3287 32c. Camarasaurus ($38\frac{1}{2} \times 30$ mm) 65 70
3288 32c. Brachiosaurus (30×38 mm) 65 70
3289 32c. Stegosaurus ($38\frac{1}{2} \times 30$ mm) 65 70
3290 32c. Allosaurus ($38\frac{1}{2} \times 30$ mm) 65 70
3291 32c. Goniopholis 65 70
3292 32c. Opisthias 65 70
3293 32c. Parasaurolophus . . . 65 70
3294 32c. Edmontonia ($38\frac{1}{2} \times 30$ mm) 65 70
3295 32c. Einiosaurus ($38\frac{1}{2} \times 30$ mm) 65 70
3296 32c. Daspletosaurus ($30 \times 38\frac{1}{2}$ mm) 65 70
3297 32c. Corythosaurus ($38\frac{1}{2} \times 30$ mm) 65 70
3298 32c. Ornithomimus ($38\frac{1}{2} \times 30$ mm) 65 70
3299 32c. Palaeosaniwa 65 70
Nos. 3285/99 were issued together, se-tenant, forming two composite designs.

2272 Bugs Bunny

2274 Map of Europe and General George Marshall

1997. Bugs Bunny (cartoon character). Self-adhesive.
3300 **2272** 32c. multicoloured . . . 60 30

1997. 50th Anniv of European Recovery Program ("Marshall Plan").
3303 **2274** 32c. multicoloured . . . 60 25

2275 North American P-51 Mustang Fighter

1997. American Aircraft. Multicoloured.
3304 32c. Type **2275** 60 65
3305 32c. Wright Model B biplane 60 65
3306 32c. Piper J-3 Cub light airplane 60 65
3307 32c. Lockheed Vega 60 65
3308 32c. Northrop Alpha . . . 60 65
3309 32c. Martin B-10 bomber 60 65
3310 32c. Vought Corsair fighter 60 65
3311 32c. Boeing B-47 Stratojet 60 65
3312 32c. Gee Bee 60 65
3313 32c. Beech Staggerwing . . 60 65
3314 32c. Boeing B-17 Flying Fortress bomber 60 65
3315 32c. Stearman PT-13 biplane 60 65
3316 32c. Lockheed Constellation 60 65
3317 32c. Lockheed P-38 Lightning fighter 60 65
3318 32c. Boeing P-26 "Peashooter" fighter . . . 60 65
3319 32c. Ford Trimotor "Tin Goose" 60 65
3320 32c. Douglas DC-3 . . . . 60 65
3321 32c. Boeing 314 Clipper flying boat 60 65
3322 32c. Curtiss JN-4 "Jenny" trainer 60 65
3323 32c. Grumman F4F Wildcat fighter 60 65

Each stamp is inscribed on the back, under the gum, with a description of the airplane depicted.

2276 Bear Bryant

1997. Football Coaches. Multicoloured. (a) With red line above coach's name.
3324 32c. Type **2276** 65 50
3325 32c. Pop Warner 65 50
3326 32c. Vince Lombardi . . . 65 50
3327 32c. George Halas 65 50

(b) Without red line.
3328 32c. Type **2276** 65 80
3329 32c. As No. 3325 . . . . . 65 80
3330 32c. As No. 3326 . . . . . 65 80
3331 32c. As No. 3327 . . . . . 65 80

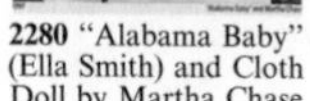
2280 "Alabama Baby" (Ella Smith) and Cloth Doll by Martha Chase

2281 Humphrey Bogart

1997. American Dolls. Multicoloured.
3332 32c. Type **2280** 75 65
3333 32c. "The Columbian Doll" (Emma Adams and Marietta Adams Ratta) 75 65
3334 32c. "Raggedy Ann" (John Gruelle) 75 65
3335 32c. Cloth doll by Martha Chase 75 65
3336 32c. "American Child" (Dwees Cochran) 75 65
3337 32c. "Baby Coos" 75 65
3338 32c. Plains Indian doll . . . 75 65
3339 32c. Moulded doll by Izannah Walker 75 65
3340 32c. "Babyland Rag" . . . 75 65
3341 32c. "Scootles" (Rose O'Neill) 75 65
3342 32c. Doll with papier-mache head, cloth body and leather arms by Ludwig Greiner 75 65
3343 32c. "Betsy McCall" 75 65
3344 32c. "Skippy" 75 65
3345 32c. "Maggie Mix-up" . . . 75 65
3346 32c. Wooden moveable dolls by Albert Schoenut . . . 75 65

1997. Legends of Hollywood.
3347 **2281** 32c. multicoloured . . . 65 30

2282 Flag and Bandsmen

2283 Lily Pons as Rosina in "The Barber of Seville" and as Lucia in "Lucia di Lammermoor"

1997. Centenary of "The Stars and Stripes Forever" by John Philip Sousa.
3348 **2282** 32c. multicoloured . . . 60 15

1997. Opera Singers. Multicoloured.
3349 32c. Type **2283** 75 50
3350 32c. Richard Tucker as the Duke in "Rigoletto" and in "Carmen" 75 50
3351 32c. Lawrence Tibbet as the Toreador in "Carmen" . . 75 50
3352 32c. Rosa Ponselle in "Norma" 75 50

2287 Leopold Stokowski (Philadelphia Symphony Orchestra)

2295 Varela

1997. Classical Conductors (Nos. 3353/6) and Composers (Nos. 3357/60). Multicoloured.
3353 32c. Type **2287** 75 50
3354 32c. Arthur Fiedler (Boston Pops Orchestra) 75 50
3355 32c. George Szell (Cleveland Orchestra) 75 50
3356 32c. Eugene Ormandy (Philadelphia Symphony Orchestra) 75 50
3357 32c. Samuel Barber 75 50
3358 32c. Ferde Grofe 75 50
3359 32c. Charles Ives 75 50
3360 32c. Louis Moreau Gottschalk 75 50

1997. Father Felix Varela (social reformer).
3361 **2295** 32c. violet 55 50

2296 U.S.A.F. Thunderbirds flying in Formation

1997. 50th Anniv of United States Air Force.
3362 **2296** 32c. multicoloured . . . 55 30

2297 Lon Chaney as The Phantom of the Opera

1997. Movie Monsters. Multicoloured.
3363 32c. Type **2297** 65 50
3364 32c. Bela Lugosi as Dracula 65 50
3365 32c. Boris Karloff in "Frankenstein" 65 50
3366 32c. Boris Karloff as The Mummy 65 50
3367 32c. Lon Chaney Jr. as The Wolf Man 65 50

2302 Bell XS-1 Rocket Airplane

1997. 50th Anniv of First Supersonic Flight (by Charles Yeager). Self-adhesive.
3368 **2302** 32c. multicoloured . . . 60 30

2303 Uniformed Women

1997. Women in Military Service.
3369 **2303** 32c. multicoloured . . . 60 30

2304 Family

1997. Kwanzaa Festival. Self-adhesive.
3370 **2304** 32c. multicoloured . . . 60 25
3694 33c. multicoloured . . . 55 25

2305 "Madonna and Child with Saints and Angels" (Sano di Pietro)

2306 Holly

1997. Christmas (1st issue). Self-adhesive.
3371 **2305** 32c. multicoloured . . . 60 25

1997. Christmas (2nd issue). Self-adhesive.
3372 **2306** 32c. multicoloured . . . 60 25

2308 Tiger

2309 Skier

1998. New Year.
3374 **2308** 32c. multicoloured . . . 65 30

1998. Alpine Skiing.
3375 **2309** 32c. multicoloured . . . 65 30

2310 Madam Walker

1998. Black Heritage. Madam C. J. Walker (designer of cosmetics for black women). Self-adhesive.
3376 **2310** 32c. brown, grey and black 65 30

2311 Model T Ford

2312 Charlie Chaplin as the Little Tramp

1998. The Twentieth Century (1st series). (a) The 1900s. Red (No. 3389) or multicoloured (others).
3377 32c. Type **2311** 55 65
3378 32c. President Theodore Roosevelt 55 65
3379 32c. Film frame from "The Great Train Robbery", 1903 . . . . 55 65
3380 32c. Box of Crayola crayons, 1903 . . . . . 55 65
3381 32c. Children with ice cream cones, St. Louis World's Fair, 1904 . . . . 55 65
3382 32c. Advertisement for "unfailing" elixir (Pure Food and Drugs Act, 1904) 55 65
3383 32c. Wright Brothers' Flyer I (first powered flight, Kitty Hawk, 1903) . . . 55 65

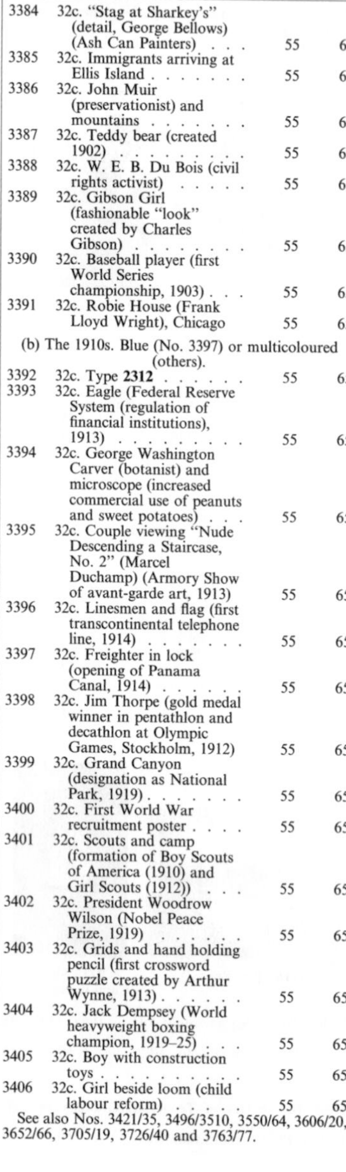
3384 32c. "Stag at Sharkey's" (detail, George Bellows) (Ash Can Painters) . . . 55 65
3385 32c. Immigrants arriving at Ellis Island 55 65
3386 32c. John Muir (preservationist) and mountains 55 65
3387 32c. Teddy bear (created 1902) 55 65
3388 32c. W. E. B. Du Bois (civil rights activist) 55 65
3389 32c. Gibson Girl (fashionable "look" created by Charles Gibson) 55 65
3390 32c. Baseball player (first World Series championship, 1903) . . . 55 65
3391 32c. Robie House (Frank Lloyd Wright), Chicago 55 65

(b) The 1910s. Blue (No. 3397) or multicoloured (others).
3392 32c. Type **2312** 55 65
3393 32c. Eagle (Federal Reserve System (regulation of financial institutions), 1913) 55 65
3394 32c. George Washington Carver (botanist) and microscope (increased commercial use of peanuts and sweet potatoes) . . . 55 65
3395 32c. Couple viewing "Nude Descending a Staircase, No. 2" (Marcel Duchamp) (Armory Show of avant-garde art, 1913) 55 65
3396 32c. Linesmen and flag (first transcontinental telephone line, 1914) 55 65
3397 32c. Freighter in lock (opening of Panama Canal, 1914) 55 65
3398 32c. Jim Thorpe (gold medal winner in pentathlon and decathlon at Olympic Games, Stockholm, 1912) 55 65
3399 32c. Grand Canyon (designation as National Park, 1919) 55 65
3400 32c. First World War recruitment poster 55 65
3401 32c. Scouts and camp (formation of Boy Scouts of America (1910) and Girl Scouts (1912)) . . . 55 65
3402 32c. President Woodrow Wilson (Nobel Peace Prize, 1919) 55 65
3403 32c. Grids and hand holding pencil (first crossword puzzle created by Arthur Wynne, 1913) 55 65
3404 32c. Jack Dempsey (World heavyweight boxing champion, 1919–25) . . . 55 65
3405 32c. Boy with construction toys 55 65
3406 32c. Girl beside loom (child labour reform) 55 65

See also Nos. 3421/35, 3496/3510, 3550/64, 3606/20, 3652/66, 3705/19, 3726/40 and 3763/77.

2313 U.S.S. "Maine"

1998. Centenary of Sinking of the "Maine" (battleship) (cause of Spanish–American War).
3407 **2313** 32c. black and red . . . 65 30

2314 Southern Magnolia

2319 "Black Cascade, 13 Verticals"

1998. Flowers and Fruits. Self-adhesive.
3408 32c. Type **2314** 60 40
3409 32c. Blue paloverde 60 40
3410 32c. Yellow poplar 60 40
3411 32c. Prairie crab apple . . . 60 40
3412 32c. Pacific dogwood 60 40

1998. Birth Centenary of Alexander Calder (sculptor).
3413 **2319** 32c. black, grey and red 65 40
3414 – 32c. multicoloured . . . 65 40
3415 – 32c. black, grey and red 65 40
3416 – 32c. multicoloured . . . 65 40
3417 – 32c. black, red and grey 65 40

DESIGNS: No. 3414, "Untitled"; 3415, "Rearing Stallion"; 3416, "Portrait of a Young Man"; 3417, "Un Effet du Japonais".

2324 Dancers in Traditional Costumes

2325 Sylvester and Tweety

1998. Cinco de Mayo Festival. Self-adhesive.
3418 **2324** 32c. multicoloured . . . 65 25
3594 33c. multicoloured . . . 55 25

1998. Sylvester and Tweety (cartoon characters). Self-adhesive.
3419 **2325** 32c. multicoloured . . . 55 15

2326 Babe Ruth (baseball player)

2327 Wisconsin

1998. The Twentieth Century (2nd series). The 1920s. Brown (Nos. 3432/3) or mult (others).
3421 32c. Type **2326** 55 65
3422 32c. The Gatsby style ("The Great Gatsby" by F. Scott Fitzgerald, 1925) 55 65
3423 32c. Federal agents pouring away wine (after Ben Shahn) (prohibition) . . . 55 65
3424 32c. Electric model steam train 55 65
3425 32c. Woman voter (19th Amendment, 1920) . . . 55 65
3426 32c. Dinner plate and cutlery (Emily Post's writings on etiquette) . . 55 65
3427 32c. Margaret Mead (anthropologist) 55 65
3428 32c. Flapper doing the Charleston (after John Held jr.) 55 65
3429 32c. Radio 55 65
3430 32c. Chrysler Building, New York (Art Deco style) . . 55 65
3431 32c. Jazz trombonists . . . 55 65
3432 32c. Notre Dame's Four Horsemen (college football players) 55 65
3433 32c. Charles Lindbergh and "Spirit of St. Louis" (first non-stop solo trans-Atlantic flight) 55 65
3434 32c. "Automat" (detail, Edward Hopper) (American Realism) . . . 55 65
3435 32c. Torn banknote (Stock Market crash, 1929) . . . 55 65

1998. 150th Anniv of Wisconsin Statehood.
3436 **2327** 32c. multicoloured . . . 55 45

2328 Diner

2329 Wetlands

1998. Presorted First-Class Mail coil stamp. Ordinary or self-adhesive gum.
3437 **2328** (25c.) multicoloured . . 40 50

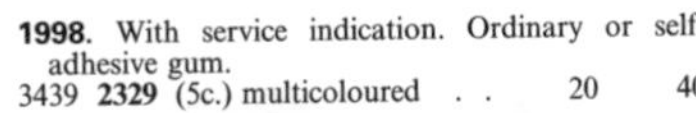
1998. With service indication. Ordinary or self-adhesive gum.
3439 **2329** (5c.) multicoloured . . 20 40

2331 Family watching Douglas C-54 Transport

1998. 50th Anniv of Berlin Airlift (relief during Soviet blockade).
3443 **2331** 32c. multicoloured . . . 60 25

2332 Leadbelly

1998. Folk Music. Multicoloured.
3444 32c. Type **2332** 65 25
3445 32c. Woody Guthrie 65 50
3446 32c. Sonny Terry 65 50
3447 32c. Josh White 65 50

2336 Mission of San Miguel

1998. 400th Anniv of Spanish Settlement at San Gabriel.
3448 **2336** 32c. multicoloured . . . 55 30

2337 Mahalia Jackson

1998. Gospel Music. Multicoloured.
3449 32c. Type **2337** 65 50
3450 32c. Roberta Martin 65 50
3451 32c. Clara Ward 65 50
3452 32c. Sister Rosetta 65 50

2341 Benet

2342 Woman

1998. Literary Arts. Birth Centenary of Stephen Vincent Benet (poet).
3453 **2341** 32c. multicoloured . . . 55 15

1998. Breast Cancer Awareness Campaign. Inscr "First Class". Self-adhesive.
3454 **2342** (32c.+8c.) mult 65 60

2343 Antillean Euphonia

2347 Common Pheasant ("Ringed-necked Pheasant")

1998. Tropical Birds. Multicoloured.
3455 32c. Type **2343** 65 50
3456 32c. Green-throated carib 65 50
3457 32c. Crested honeycreeper 65 50
3458 32c. Cardinal honeyeater . . 65 40

1998. Self-adhesive.
3459 **2347** 20c. multicoloured . . . 35 40

2348 Alfred Hitchcock (director)

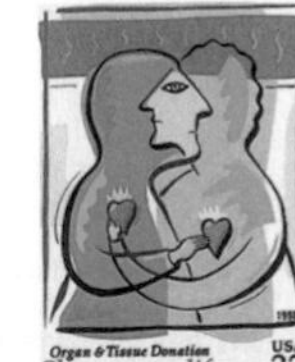

2349 Couple swapping Hearts

1998. Legends of Hollywood.
3465 **2348** 32c. black and silver . . 65 25
No. 3465 includes a cut-out of Hitchcock's trademark caricature above his right shoulder.

1998. Organ and Tissue Donation Campaign. Self-adhesive.
3466 **2349** 32c. multicoloured . . . 60 25

2350 Red Fox

2351 Bicycle Handlebars

1998. Self-adhesive.
3467 **2350** $1 multicoloured . . . 1·40 50

1998. Ordinary or self-adhesive gum.
3468 **2351** (10c.) black, grn & vio 25 25

2352 Dog

1998. "Bright Eyes". Multicoloured. Self-adhesive.
3470 32c. Type **2352** 60 25
3471 32c. Cat 60 50
3472 32c. Hamster 60 50
3473 32c. Goldfish 60 50
3474 32c. Parakeet 60 50

2357 Gold Prospectors

1998. Centenary of Klondike Gold Rush.
3475 **2357** 32c. multicoloured . . . 60 45

2358 "Portrait of Richard Mather" (John Foster)

2359 Pres. Franklin D. Roosevelt making Radio Broadcast

1998. American Art. Multicoloured.
3476 32c. Type **2358** 60 65
3477 32c. "Mrs. Elizabeth Freake and Baby Mary" (The Freake Limner) 60 65
3478 32c. "Girl in Red Dress with Cat and Dog" (Ammi Phillips) 60 65
3479 32c. "Rubens Peale with Geranium" (Rembrandt Peale) 60 65
3480 32c. "Long-billed Curlew, Numenius longrostris" (John James Audubon) 60 65
3481 32c. "Boatmen on the Missouri" (George Caleb Bingham) 60 65
3482 32c. "Kindred Spirits" (Asher B. Durand) . . . 60 65
3483 32c. "Westwood Children" (Joshua Johnson) 60 65
3484 32c. "Music and Literature" (William Harnett) 60 65
3485 32c. "Fog Warning" (Winslow Homer) 60 65
3486 32c. "White Cloud, Head Chief of the Iowas" (George Catlin) 60 65
3487 32c. "Cliffs of Green River" (Thomas Moran) 60 65
3488 32c. "Last of the Buffalo" (Albert Bierstadt) 60 65
3489 32c. "Niagara" (Frederic Edwin Church) 60 65
3490 32c. "Breakfast in Bed" (Mary Cassatt) 60 65
3491 32c. "Nighthawks" (Edward Hopper) 60 65
3492 32c. "American Gothic" (Grant Wood) 60 65
3493 32c. "Two against the White" (Charles Sheeler) 60 65
3494 32c. "Mahoning" (Franz Kline) 60 65
3495 32c. "No. 12" (Mark Rothko) 60 65

1998. The Twentieth Century (3rd series). The 1930s. Blue (No. 3497) or multicoloured (others).
3496 32c. Type **2359** 55 65
3497 32c. Empire State Building (completed 1931) 55 65
3498 32c. Front cover of "Life" magazine's first issue, 1936 . . . . 55 65
3499 32c. Eleanor Roosevelt (First Lady) and child . . 55 65
3500 32c. New Deal economic recovery plan 55 65
3501 32c. Superman (first comic book super hero, 1938) 55 65

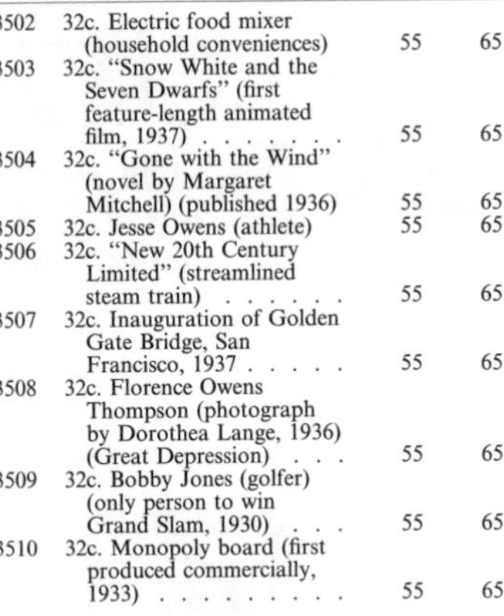
3502 32c. Electric food mixer (household conveniences) 55 65
3503 32c. "Snow White and the Seven Dwarfs" (first feature-length animated film, 1937) 55 65
3504 32c. "Gone with the Wind" (novel by Margaret Mitchell) (published 1936) 55 65
3505 32c. Jesse Owens (athlete) 55 65
3506 32c. "New 20th Century Limited" (streamlined steam train) 55 65
3507 32c. Inauguration of Golden Gate Bridge, San Francisco, 1937 . . . . . 55 65
3508 32c. Florence Owens Thompson (photograph by Dorothea Lange, 1936) (Great Depression) . . . 55 65
3509 32c. Bobby Jones (golfer) (only person to win Grand Slam, 1930) . . . 55 65
3510 32c. Monopoly board (first produced commercially, 1933) 55 65

2360 Ballerina

2361 City Domes and Vehicle

1998. 50th Anniv of New York City Ballet.
3511 **2360** 32c. multicoloured . . . 60 25

1998. Future of Space Travel. Multicoloured.
3512 32c. Type **2361** 60 40
3513 32c. Capsule preparing to land 60 40
3514 32c. Space pioneer on rock 60 40
3515 32c. Capsule taking off and pioneer with vehicle . . . 60 40
3516 32c. Dome and bridge over canyon 60 40
Nos. 3512/16 were issued together, se-tenant, forming a composite design.

2366 Flower and Bee

1998. "Giving and Sharing". Self-adhesive.
3517 **2366** 32c. multicoloured . . . 60 30

2367 "Florentine Madonna and Child" (sculpture, anon)

2368 Evergreen Wreath

1998. Christmas. Multicoloured. Self-adhesive.
(a) Size $19\frac{1}{2} \times 26\frac{1}{2}$ mm.
3518 32c. Type **2367** 60 25
3519 32c. Type **2368** 60 50
3520 32c. Victorian wreath . . . 60 50
3521 32c. Chilli wreath 60 50
3522 32c. Tropical wreath 60 50
(b) Size 17×22 mm.
3523 32c. Type **2368** 65 50
3524 32c. As No. 3520 . . . . . 65 50
3525 32c. As No. 3521 . . . . . 65 50
3526 32c. As No. 3522 . . . . . 65 50

2372 Uncle Sam's Hat

2373 Rooster Weathervane

1998. First-Class Rate stamps. No value expressed. Ordinary or self-adhesive gum.
3527 **2372** (33c.) multicoloured . . 60 25

1998. No value expressed. Make-up Rate stamps.
3533 **2373** (1c.) multicoloured (blue imprint date) ($21 \times 17\frac{3}{4}$ mm) . . . 20 15
3534 (1c.) multicoloured (black imprint date) ($21 \times 18\frac{1}{4}$ mm) . . . 20 20

2374 Uncle Sam

2375 Space Shuttle landing

1998. Self-adhesive.
3535 **2374** 22c. multicoloured . . . 40 30

1998. Multicoloured. Self-adhesive.
3538 $3.20 Type **2375** . . . . . 5·25 1·20
3539 $11.75 Space shuttle on transport plane . . . . . 20·00 10·00

2377 Eagle and Shield

2378 Rabbit

1998. Presorted coil stamp. Ordinary or self-adhesive gum.
3540 **2377** (10c.) multicoloured . . 20 25

1999. Chinese New Year.
3545 **2378** 33c. multicoloured . . . 60 50

2379 Malcolm X

2380 Heart of Pink Roses

1999. Black Heritage. Malcolm X (el-Hajj Malik el-Shabazz) (black nationalist leader). Self-adhesive.
3546 **2379** 33c. green, grey and black 65 25

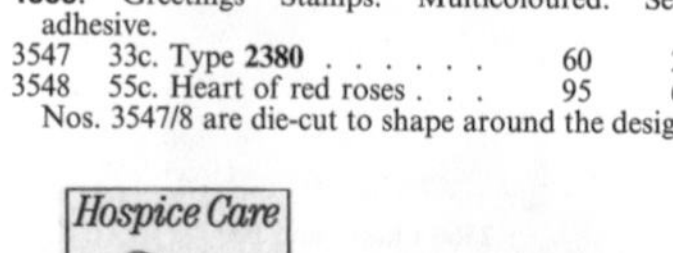

1999. Greetings Stamps. Multicoloured. Self-adhesive.
3547 33c. Type **2380** 60 25
3548 55c. Heart of red roses . . . 95 65
Nos. 3547/8 are die-cut to shape around the design.

2382 Butterfly and Hospice

2383 Uncle Sam and Soldiers (World War II)

1999. Hospice Care. Self-adhesive.
3549 **2382** 33c. multicoloured . . . 60 25

1999. The Twentieth Century (4th series). The 1940s. Brown (No. 3560) or mult (others).
3550 33c. Type **2383** 55 65
3551 33c. Penicillin (development of antibiotics) 55 65
3552 33c. Jackie Robinson (baseball player) 55 65
3553 33c. President Harry Truman 55 65
3554 33c. Women's War Effort poster ("We Can Do It") 55 65
3555 33c. Filming of television programme 55 65
3556 33c. Couple jitterbugging . . 55 65
3557 33c. Jackson Pollock at work (Abstract Expressionism) 55 65
3558 33c. Soldier studying (Servicemen's Readjustment Act (GI Bill), 1944) 55 65
3559 33c. Big Band music 55 65
3560 33c. United Nations building, New York (International Style of architecture) 55 65
3561 33c. Postwar baby boom (front cover of "The Saturday Evening Post", 2 November 1946) 55 65
3562 33c. Slinky (coiled wire toy) 55 65
3563 33c. Poster for Broadway production of "A Streetcar Named Desire" (Tennessee Williams), 1947 . . . . 55 65
3564 33c. Scene from Orson Welles's "Citizen Kane" (film), 1941 . . . . 55 65
A brief description of the subject is printed under the gum on the back of each stamp.

2384 Flag and Skyscrapers

2385 Irish Immigration Ship

1999. Ordinary or self-adhesive gum.
3565 **2384** 33c. multicoloured . . . 55 25

1999. Irish Immigration.
3570 **2385** 33c. multicoloured . . . 55 40

2386 Alfred Lunt and Lynn Fontanne (actors)

1999. Preforming Arts and Artists.
3571 **2386** 33c. multicoloured . . . 55 40

2387 Arctic Hare

2392 Flag and Alphabet on Board

1999. Arctic Animals. Multicoloured.
3572 33c. Type **2387** 60 40
3573 33c. Arctic fox 60 40
3574 33c. Snowy owl 60 40
3575 33c. Polar bear 60 40
3576 33c. Grey wolf 60 40

1999. Automatic Teller Machine stamp.
3577 **2392** 33c. multicoloured . . . 60 40

2395 Blueberries

2399 Daffy Duck

1999. Berries. Self-adhesive. Multicoloured.
3579 33c. Type **2395** 55 50
3580 33c. Raspberries 55 50
3581 33c. Strawberries 55 50
3582 33c. Blackberries 55 50

1999. Daffy Duck (cartoon character). Self-adhesive.
3591 **2399** 33c. multicoloured . . . 55 40

2400 Ayn Rand

2401 Bird-of-Paradise Flower

1999. Literary Arts. Ayn Rand (novelist).
3593 **2400** 33c. multicoloured . . . 55 25

1999. Tropical Flowers. Self-adhesive. Mult.
3595 33c. Type **2401** 55 65
3596 33c. Royal poinciana . . . 55 65
3597 33c. Gloriosa lily 55 65
3598 33c. Chinese hibiscus . . . 55 65

A **2405** Rio Grande

2410 "Franklinia alatamaha" (after William Bartram)

1999. Air. Self-adhesive. Multicoloured.
A3599 40c. Type A **2405** . . . 65 60
A3600 48c. Niagara Falls . . . 90 70
A3601 60c. Grand Canyon . . . 1·00 85
A3602 60c. Acadia National Park, Maine 80 20
A3603 70c. Nine-mile Piaine, Nebrasska 90 20
A3600a 80c. Mt. Mckinley, Alaska . . . . 1·10 25

1999. 300th Birth Anniv of John and 260th Birth Anniv of William Bartram (botanists). Self-adhesive.
3605 **2410** 33c. multicoloured . . . 55 30

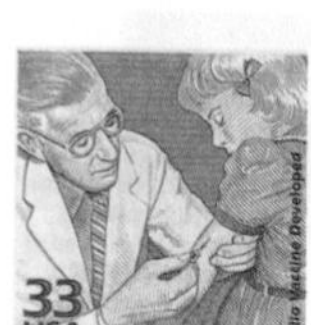
2411 Polio Vaccination

2412 Male Gender Sign

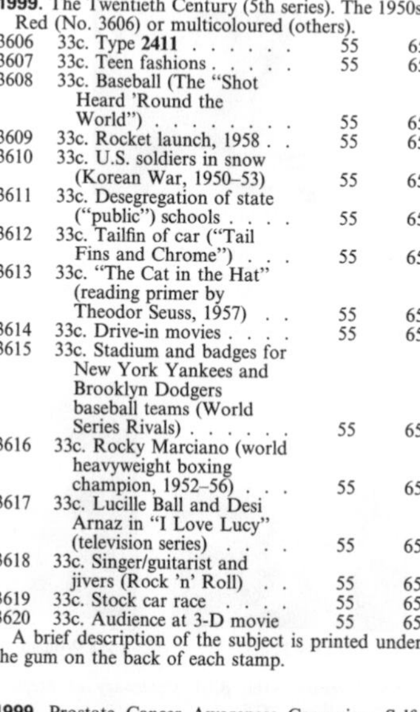

1999. The Twentieth Century (5th series). The 1950s. Red (No. 3606) or multicoloured (others).
3606 33c. Type **2411** 55 65
3607 33c. Teen fashions 55 65
3608 33c. Baseball (The "Shot Heard 'Round the World") 55 65
3609 33c. Rocket launch, 1958 . . 55 65
3610 33c. U.S. soldiers in snow (Korean War, 1950–53) 55 65
3611 33c. Desegregation of state ("public") schools 55 65
3612 33c. Tailfin of car ("Tail Fins and Chrome") . . . 55 65
3613 33c. "The Cat in the Hat" (reading primer by Theodor Seuss, 1957) . . 55 65
3614 33c. Drive-in movies 55 65
3615 33c. Stadium and badges for New York Yankees and Brooklyn Dodgers baseball teams (World Series Rivals) 55 65
3616 33c. Rocky Marciano (world heavyweight boxing champion, 1952–56) . . . 55 65
3617 33c. Lucille Ball and Desi Arnaz in "I Love Lucy" (television series) 55 65
3618 33c. Singer/guitarist and jivers (Rock 'n' Roll) . . 55 65
3619 33c. Stock car race 55 65
3620 33c. Audience at 3-D movie 55 65
A brief description of the subject is printed under the gum on the back of each stamp.

1999. Prostate Cancer Awareness Campaign. Self-adhesive.
3621 **2412** 33c. multicoloured . . . 55 30

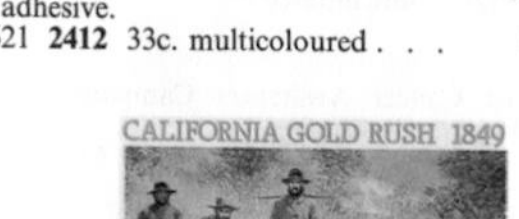
2413 Prospectors

1999. 150th Anniv of California Gold Rush.
3622 **2413** 33c. multicoloured . . . 55 30

2414 Long-horned Cowfish, Black-tailed Damselfish, Cleaner Shrimp and Flame Hawkfish

2415 Copper-band Butterflyfish, Mushroom Polyps and Blue Starfish

2416 Powder-blue Surgeonfish and Long-spined Sea Urchin

2417 Clown Anemonefish and Red Hermit Crab

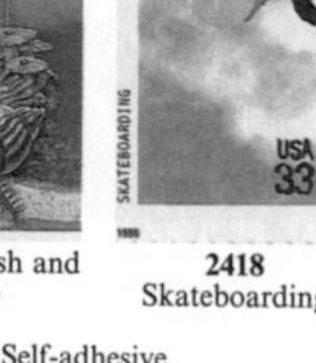
2418 Skateboarding

1999. Aquarium Fishes. Self-adhesive.
3623 **2414** 33c. multicoloured . . . 55 65
3624 **2415** 33c. multicoloured . . . 55 65
3625 **2416** 33c. multicoloured . . . 55 65
3626 **2417** 33c. multicoloured . . . 55 40
Nos. 3623/6 were issued together, se-tenant, forming a composite design.

1999. "Xtreme" Sports. Self-adhesive. Mult.
3627 33c. Type **2418** 60 40
3628 33c. BMX biking 60 40
3629 33c. Snowboarding 60 40
3630 33c. Inline skating 60 40

2422 Free-blown Glass

2426 James Cagney

1999. American Glass. Multicoloured.
3631 33c. Type **2422** 55 40
3632 33c. Mould-blown glass . . 55 65
3633 33c. Pressed glass 55 40
3634 33c. Art glass 55 40

1999. Legends of Hollywood.
3635 **2426** 33c. multicoloured . . . 60 65

2427 Mitchell and SPAD XVI Biplane

2428 Rose

1999. 120th Birth Anniv of Billy Mitchell (aviation pioneer). Self-adhesive.
3636 **2427** 55c. multicoloured . . . 95 80

1999. Self-adhesive.
3637 **2428** 33c. multicoloured . . . 55 25

2429 Flag

1999. "Honoring Those Who Served". Self-adhesive.
3638 **2429** 33c. red, blue and black 55 25

2430 Stars

1999. 125th Anniv of Universal Postal Union.
3639 **2430** 45c. blue and red . . . 75 60

2431 "Daylight"

1999. Trains. Multicoloured.
3640 33c. Type **2431** 55 40
3641 33c. "20th Century Limited" 55 40
3642 33c. "Super Chief" 55 40
3643 33c. "Congressional" . . . 55 40
3644 33c. "Hiawatha" 55 40
Details of the trains are printed under the gum on the back of each stamp.

2436 Olmsted (after John Singer Sargent) and Central Park, New York

1999. 77th Birth Anniv of Frederick Law Olmsted (landscaper).
3645 **2436** 33c. multicoloured . . . 55 25

2437 Max Steiner

1999. Hollywood Composers. Multicoloured.
3646 33c. Type **2437** 75 65
3647 33c. Dimitri Tiomkin . . . 75 65
3648 33c. Bernard Herrmann . . 75 65
3649 33c. Franz Waxman 75 65
3650 33c. Alfred Newman 75 65
3651 33c. Erich Wolfgang Korngold 75 65

2443 Martin Luther King (Civil Rights leader)

1999. The Twentieth Century (6th series). The 1960s. Black (No. 3654) or mult (others).
3652 33c. Type **2443** 55 65
3653 33c. Bird on guitar neck (Woodstock Music Festival, 1969) 55 65
3654 33c. Footprint (first manned moon landing, 1969) . . . 55 65
3655 33c. Members of Green Bay Packers football team . . 55 65
3656 33c. Starship "Enterprise" (television series "Star Trek") 55 65
3657 33c. Peace Corps volunteers 55 65
3658 33c. Troops disembarking from helicopter (Vietnam War) 55 65
3659 33c. Ford Mustang sportscar 55 65
3660 33c. Barbie doll 55 65
3661 33c. Integrated circuit . . . 55 65
3662 33c. Lasers 55 65
3663 33c. Ticket to football match (Super Bowl I) . . 55 65
3664 33c. Peace symbol 55 65
3665 33c. Roger Maris (baseball player) 55 65
3666 33c. Yellow submarine (The Beatles pop group) . . . 55 65

A brief description of the subject is printed under the gum on the back of each stamp.

2444 Ira and George Gershwin

1999. Broadway Songwriters. Multicoloured.
3667 33c. Type **2444** 75 65
3668 33c. Alan Jay Lerner and Frederick Loewe 75 65
3669 33c. Lorenz Hart 75 65
3670 33c. Richard Rodgers and Oscar Hammerstein II . . 75 65
3671 33c. Meredith Willson . . . 75 65
3672 33c. Frank Loesser 75 65

2450 Black Widow

1999. Insects and Spiders. Multicoloured.
3673 33c. Type **2450** 55 65
3674 33c. Elderberry longhorn . . 55 65
3675 33c. Ladybird ("Lady beetle") 55 65
3676 33c. Yellow garden spider 55 65
3677 33c. Dogbane beetle 55 65
3678 33c. Flower fly 55 65
3679 33c. Assassin bug 55 65
3680 33c. Ebony jewelwing . . . 55 65
3681 33c. Velvet ant 55 65
3682 33c. Monarch (caterpillar) 55 65
3683 33c. Monarch (butterfly) . . 55 65
3684 33c. Eastern Hercules beetle 55 65
3685 33c. Bombadier beetle . . . 55 65
3686 33c. Dung beetle 55 65
3687 33c. Spotted water beetle . . 55 65
3688 33c. True katydid 55 65
3689 33c. Spiny-backed spider . . 55 65
3690 33c. Periodical cicada . . . 55 65
3691 33c. Scorpionfly 55 65
3692 33c. Jumping spider 55 65

Descriptions of the subject are printed under the gum on the back of each stamp.

2451 Dove with Laurel

1999. 50th Anniv of North Atlantic Treaty Organization.
3695 **2451** 33c. multicoloured . . . 55 25

2452 "Madonna and Child" (Bartolomeo Vivarini) **2453** Stag

1999. Christmas. Self-adhesive. (a) Size 20 × 27 mm.
3696 **2452** 33c. multicoloured . . . 55 40

(b) Size 27 × 20½ mm.
3697 **2452** 33c. gold and red . . . 55 25
3698 33c. gold and blue . . . 55 25
3699 33c. gold and violet . . 55 25
3700 33c. gold and green . . 55 50

(c) Size 21½ × 19½ mm.
3701 **2453** 33c. gold and red . . . 65 15
3702 33c. gold and blue . . . 65 15
3703 33c. gold and violet . . 65 40
3704 33c. gold and green . . 65 40

2454 Hands holding Globe (first Earth Day, 1970) **2455** New Year Baby

1999. The Twentieth Century (7th series). The 1970s. Blue (Nos. 3712, 3714) or multicoloured (others).
3705 33c. Type **2454** 55 65
3706 33c. Scene from "All in the Family" (television series) 55 65
3707 33c. Big Bird (character from children's television series "Sesame Street") . . 55 65
3708 33c. Disco dancers 55 65
3709 33c. American football helmet (winning of four Super Bowls by Pittsburgh Steelers) . . . 55 65
3710 33c. Statue of Liberty and fireworks (bicentenary of United States, 1976) . . . 55 65
3711 33c. Secretariat (racehorse) (winner of Triple Crown, 1973) 55 65
3712 33c. Video cassette recorder 55 65
3713 33c. "Pioneer 10" (launch of Jupiter space probe, 1972) 55 65
3714 33c. Emblem of Women's Rights Movement 55 65
3715 33c. 1970s fashion 55 65
3716 33c. Cameraman filming American football match (television series "Monday Night Football") 55 65
3717 33c. "Smiley face" badges 55 65
3718 33c. Girl gazing at Boeing jumbo jet 55 65
3719 33c. Scan of skull ("Medical imaging") 55 65

A brief description of the subject is printed under the gum on the back of each stamp.

1999. Year 2000. Self-adhesive.
3720 **2455** 33c. multicoloured . . . 65 40

2456 Dragon

2000. New Year.
3725 **2456** 33c. multicoloured . . . 55 25

2457 Space Shuttle "Columbia" **2458** Patricia Harris

2000. The Twentieth Century (8th series). The 1980s. Multicoloured.
3726 33c. Type **2457** 55 65
3727 33c. Poster for "Cats" (stage musical) 55 65
3728 33c. San Francisco 49ers (American football team) 55 65
3729 33c. Welcome in Washington for homecoming of hostages held in siege of U.S. Embassy, Teheran 55 65
3730 33c. Figure skater 55 65
3731 33c. Dish aerials (cable TV) 55 65
3732 33c. Vietnam Veterans Memorial 55 65
3733 33c. Compact disc 55 65
3734 33c. Cabbage Patch doll . . 55 65
3735 33c. Opening shot of "The Cosby Show" (television comedy series) 55 65
3736 33c. Fall of the Berlin Wall 55 65
3737 33c. Children playing video game 55 65
3738 33c. "E.T." the Extra-Terrestrial (film) 55 65
3739 33c. Personal computer . . . 55 65
3740 33c. Hip-hop culture 55 65

A brief description of the subject is printed under the gum on the back of each stamp.

2000. Black Heritage. Patricia Roberts Harris (diplomat). Self-adhesive.
3741 **2458** 33c. multicoloured . . . 55 25

2459 S-Class Submarine

2000. Centenary of United States Navy Submarine Fleet. Multicoloured.
3743 22c. Type **2459** 35 15
3744 33c. Los Angeles Class . . . 55 65
3745 55c. Ohio Class 85 40
3746 60c. U.S.S. *Holland I*, 1900 95 45
3747 $3.20 Gato Class (77 × 22 mm) . . . . . . 4·75 6·50

2466 "Silent Music I"

2467 "Royal Tide I"

2468 "Black Chord"

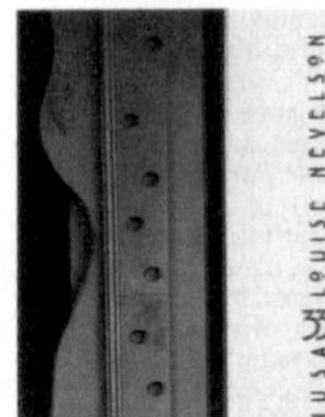

2469 "Nightsphere-Light"

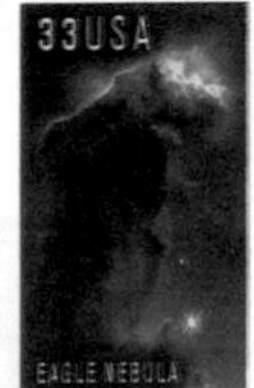

2470 "Dawn's Wedding Chapel I" **2471** Eagle Nebula

2000. Birth Centenary of Louise Nevelson (sculptress).
3749 **2466** 33c. multicoloured . . . 55 65
3750 **2467** 33c. multicoloured . . . 55 65
3751 **2468** 33c. multicoloured . . . 55 65
3752 **2469** 33c. multicoloured . . . 55 65
3753 **2470** 33c. multicoloured . . . 55 65

2000. 10th Anniv of Hubble Space Telescope. Mult.
3754 33c. Type **2471** 55 40
3755 33c. Ring Nebula 55 40
3756 33c. Lagoon Nebula 55 40
3757 33c. Egg Nebula 55 40
3758 33c. Galaxy NGC 1316 . . 55 40

A brief description of the subject is printed under the gum on the back of each stamp.

2476 Sunuitao Peak, Ofu Island and Alia (fishing catamaran)

2000. Centenary of Samoa's Status as an Unorganized United States Territory.
3759 **2476** 33c. multicoloured . . . 55 15

2477 Main Reading Room, Thomas Jefferson Building, Library of Congress **2478** Road Runner and Wile E. Coyote

2000. Bicentenary of Library of Congress, Washington, D.C.
3760 **2477** 33c. multicoloured . . . 55 40

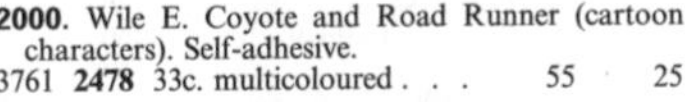

2000. Wile E. Coyote and Road Runner (cartoon characters). Self-adhesive.
3761 **2478** 33c. multicoloured . . . 55 25

2479 Baseball and Newspaper Headline

2000. The Twentieth Century (9th series). The 1990s. Multicoloured.
3763 33c. Type **2479** 55 65
3764 33c. Soldier and Chinook helicopters (Iraqi invasion of Kuwait, 1990) 55 65
3765 33c. Set from *Seinfeld* (television comedy show) 55 65
3766 33c. Snowboarder (increased popularity in extreme sports) 55 65
3767 33c. Child writing (improvement in quality of education) 55 65
3768 33c. Hand and butterfly (computer generated art) 55 65
3769 33c. Peregrine falcon (recovery of endangered species) 55 65
3770 33c. Space shuttle *Discovery* (John Glenn's (first American to orbit Earth) return to space, 1998) . . 55 65

3771 33c. Olympic gold medal (30th anniv of special Olympics, 1998) 55 65
3772 33c. Man using virtual reality game 55 65
3773 33c. Tyrannosaurus rex (*Jurassic Park* (film), 1993) 55 65
3774 33c. Poster for *Titanic* (film), 1997 . . . . 55 65
3775 33c. Increase in popularity of off-road vehicles . . . 55 65
3776 33c. Computer keyboard (introduction of the Internet and the World Wide Web) 55 65
3777 33c. Man using mobile phone (increase in use of cellular phones) 55 65

A brief description of the subject is printed under the gum on the back of each stamp.

2480 John L. Hines and 4th Division Insignia (Distinguished Service Cross and Medal)

2000. Distinguished Soldiers. Multicoloured.
3778 33c. Type **2480** 60 40
3779 33c. Omar N. Bradley and First Army Insignia (Army Chief of Staffs) . . 60 40
3780 33c. Alvin C. York and 82nd Division Insignia (Medal of Honor) 60 40
3781 33c. Audie L. Murphy and 3rd Infantry Division Insignia (Medal of Honor) 60 40

2484 Athletes

2000. Summer Sports. Lilac Bloomsday Run, Washington.
3782 **2484** 33c. multicoloured . . . 55 30

2485 Stylized Man and Woman

2486 Basketball

2000. Adoption Awareness. Self-adhesive.
3783 **2485** 33c. multicoloured . . . 55 25

2000. Youth Team Sports.
3784 33c. Type **2486** 60 40
3785 33c. American football . . . 60 40
3786 33c. Soccer 60 40
3787 33c. Baseball 60 40

2490 Sons of Liberty Flag, 1775

2491 Blackberries

2000. History of the American Flag.
3788 **2490** 33c. red and black . . . 55 65
3789 – 33c. multicoloured . . . 55 65
3790 – 33c. red and black . . . 55 65
3791 – 33c. red, blue and black 55 65
3792 – 33c. red, blue and black 55 65
3793 – 33c. red and black . . . 55 65
3794 – 33c. red, blue and black 55 65
3795 – 33c. red, blue and black 55 65
3796 – 33c. red, blue and black 55 65
3797 – 33c. blue, red and black 55 65
3798 – 33c. red, blue and black 55 65
3799 – 33c. red, blue and black 55 65
3800 – 33c. red, blue and black 55 65
3801 – 33c. red, blue and black 55 65
3802 – 33c. red, blue and black 55 65
3803 – 33c. red, blue and black 55 65
3804 – 33c. red, blue and black 55 65
3805 – 33c. red, blue and black 55 65
3806 – 33c. red, blue and black 55 65
3807 – 33c. red, blue and black 55 65

DESIGNS: No. 3789, New England flag, 1775; 3790, Forster flag, 1775; 3791, Continental Colors, 1776; 3792, Francis Hopkinson flag, 1777; 3793, Brandywine flag, 1777; 3794, John Paul Jones flag, 1779; 3795, Pierre L'Enfant flag, 1783; 3796, Indian Peace flag, 1803; 3797, Easton flag, 1814; 3798, Star-Spangled Banner, 1814; 3799, Bennington flag, 1820; 3800, Great Star flag, 1837; 3801, 29-Star flag, 1847; 3802, Fort Sumter flag, 1861; 3803, Centennial flag, 1876; 3804, 38-Star flag, 1877; 3805, Peace flag, 1891; 3806, 48-Star flag, 1912; 3807, 50-Star flag, 1960.

A brief history of the subject is printed under the gum on the back of each stamp.

2000. Berries. Self-adhesive. Multicoloured.
3808 33c. Type **2491** 55 15
3809 33c. Raspberries 55 15
3810 33c. Blueberries 55 15
3811 33c. Strawberries 55 25

2495 Jackie Robinson

2000. Legends of Baseball. Self-adhesive. Mult.
3812 33c. Type **2495** 55 65
3813 33c. Eddie Collins 55 65
3814 33c. Christy Mathewson . . 55 65
3815 33c. Ty Cobb 55 65
3816 33c. George Sisler 55 65
3817 33c. Rogers Hornsby . . . 55 65
3818 33c. Mickey Cochrane . . . 55 65
3819 33c. Babe Ruth 55 65
3820 33c. Walter Johnson 55 65
3821 33c. Roberto Clemente . . . 55 65
3822 33c. Lefty Grove 55 65
3823 33c. Tris Speaker 55 65
3824 33c. Cy Young 55 65
3825 33c. Jimmie Foxx 55 65
3826 33c. Pie Traynor 55 65
3827 33c. Satchel Paige 55 65
3828 33c. Honus Wagner 55 65
3829 33c. Josh Gibson 55 65
3830 33c. Dizzy Dean 55 65
3831 33c. Lou Gehrig 55 65

2501 "Astronauts" (Zachary Canter)

2507 Joseph W. Stillwell

2000. "Stampin' the Future". Winning Entries in Children's International Painting Competition. Self-adhesive. Multicoloured.
3833 33c. Type **2501** 55 40
3834 33c. "Children" (Sarah Lipsey) 55 40
3835 33c. "Rocket" (Morgan Hill) 55 40
3836 33c. "Dog" (Ashley Young) 55 40

2000. Great Americans. (a) Ordinary gum.
3837 **2507** 10c. black and red . . . 20 25
3838 – 33c. black and red . . . 55 15

(b) Self-adhesive.
3839 – 76c. black and red . . . . 1·10 65
3840 – 83c. black and red . . . . 1·20 75

DESIGNS: 33c. Claude Pepper; 76c. Hattie W. Caraway; Edna Ferber.

2538 Coastline

2539 Edward G. Robinson

2000. 150th Anniv of Californian Statehood.
3870 **2538** 33c. multicoloured . . . 55 40

2000. Legends of Hollywood.
3871 **2539** 33c. multicoloured . . . 55 40

2540 Fanfin Anglerfish

2000. Deep Sea Creatures. Multicoloured.
3872 33c. Type **2540** 55 15
3873 33c. Sea cucumber 55 15
3874 33c. Fangtooth 55 15
3875 33c. Amphipod 55 40
3876 33c. Medusa 55 40

2545 Wolfe

2000. Birth Centenary of Thomas Wolfe (writer).
3877 **2545** 33c. multicoloured . . . 55 25

2546 North Facade

2547 Lion Statue, New York Public Library

2000. Bicentenary of The White House as President's Residence. Self-adhesive.
3878 **2546** 33c. multicoloured . . . 55 25

2000. Presorted coil stamp. Self-adhesive or oridinary gum.
3879 **2547** (10c.) multicoloured . . 20 25

2548 Farm and Flag

2000. Ordinary or self-adhesive gum.
3880 **2548** (34c.) multicoloured . . 55 50

2549 Statue of Liberty

2550 Statue of Liberty

2000. First-Class Rate stamps. (a) Ordinary or self-adhesive gum.
3883 **2549** (34c.) multicoloured . . 55 80

(b) Self-adhesive gum.
3885 **2550** (34c.) multicoloured . . 55 65

2551 Lily

2552 Freesia

2553 Lily

2554 Orchid

2555 Statue of Liberty

2556 Statue of Liberty

2000. Flowers. Self-adhesive.
3886 **2551** (34c.) multicoloured . . 55 50
3887 **2552** (34c.) multicoloured . . 55 50
3888 **2553** (34c.) multicoloured . . 55 50
3889 **2554** (34c.) multicoloured . . 55 50

2001. (a) Ordinary or Self-adhesive gum.
3894 **2555** 34c. multicoloured . . . 55 80

(b) Self-adhesive.
3895 **2556** 34c. multicoloured . . . 55 50

2557 Red Rose and "LOVE"

2558 Snake

2001. Greeting Stamps. First-Class Rate stamp. Self-adhesive.
3897 **2557** (34c.) multicoloured . . 55 65

2001. New Year.
3898 **2558** 34c. multicoloured . . . 55 25

2559 Roy Wilkins

2560 Capitol, Washington

2001. Black Heritage. Roy Wilkins (civil rights pioneer). Self-adhesive.
3899 **2559** 34c. blue and black . . 55 25

2001. Self-adhesive.
3900 $3.50 Type **2560** . . . . . 5·50 5·00
3901 $12.25 Washington Monument . . . . 18·00 16·00

Nos. 3900/1 each incorporate an additional hidden inscription "PRIORITY MAIL" (No. 3900) or "EXPRESS MAIL" (No. 3901) visible only under a special decoder.

No. 3900 was intended mainly for Priority mail and No. 3901 for Express Mail Service but they could be used on other mail as well.

2562 "First in the Fight, Always Faithful" (recruitment poster, James Montgomery Flagg)

2563 Farm and Flag

2001. American Illustrators. Black (No. 3918) or multicoloured (others). Self-adhesive.
3902 34c. Type **2562** 55 65
3903 34c. "Interlude (The Lute Players)" (mural, Maxfield Parrish) 55 65
3904 34c. Couple dancing (advertisement, Joseph Christian Leyendecker) . . 55 65
3905 34c. Man sawing ice (advertisement, Robert Fawcett) 55 65
3906 34c. Couple in car (advertisement, Coles Philips) 55 65
3907 34c. Woman combing hair ("How I Make a Picture") (Al Parker) 55 65
3908 34c. Br'er Rabbit (Arthur Burdett Frost) 55 65
3909 34c. "An Attack on a Galleon" (illustration, Howard Pyle) 55 65
3910 34c. Kewpies (Rose O'Neill) 55 65
3911 34c. Steam boat (magazine cover illustration, Dean Cornwell) 55 65
3912 34c. "Galahad's Departure" (detail of mural, Edwin Austin Abbey) 55 65
3913 34c. "The First Lesson" (magazine cover illustration, Jessie Willcox Smith) 55 65
3914 34c. Woman holding artist's palette (magazine cover illustration, Neysa McMein) 55 65
3915 34c. "Back Home for Keeps" (advertisement, Jon Whitcomb) 55 65
3916 34c. "Something for Supper" (Harvey Dunn) 55 65
3917 34c. "A Dash for the Timber" (Frederic Remington) 55 65
3918 34c. Scene from *Moby Dick* (book illustration, Rockwell Kent) 55 65
3919 34c. "Captain Bill Bones" (book illustration, Newell Convers Wyeth) 55 65
3920 34c. Doctor and child (magazine cover illustration, Norman Rockwell) 55 65
3921 34c. "The Girl He Left Behind" (John Held Jr.) 55 65

A brief biography of the artist is printed on the backing paper on the back of each stamp.

2001. Ordinary or Self-adhesive gum.
3922 **2563** 34c. multicoloured . . . 55 50

2564 Lily **2565** Freesia **2566** Lily

2567 Orchid

2001. Flowers. Self-adhesive.

3930	**2564**	34c. multicoloured	55	50
3931	**2565**	34c. multicoloured	55	65
3932	**2566**	34c. multicoloured	85	65
3933	**2567**	34c. multicoloured	35	65

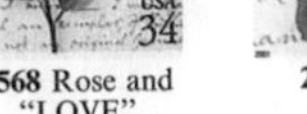

2568 Rose and "LOVE" **2569** Rose and "LOVE"

2001. Greetings Stamps. Self-adhesive.

3938	**2568**	34c. multicoloured	55	15
3939	**2569**	55c. multicoloured	55	15
3940		57c. multicoloured	85	65

2570 George Washington **2571** Bison

2001. Self-adhesive.

3941	**2570**	20c. red	35	65
3942		23c. green	1·10	35

3942 also comes with ordinary gum.

2001. Self-adhesive.

3951	**2571**	21c. multicoloured	35	65
3961		57c. multicoloured	85	65

2572 Art Deco Eagle **2573** Apple

2001. Self-adhesive.

3960	**2572**	55c. multicoloured	85	15

2001. Fruit. Self-adhesive.

3965	34c. Type **2573**	55	15
3966	34c. Orange	55	15

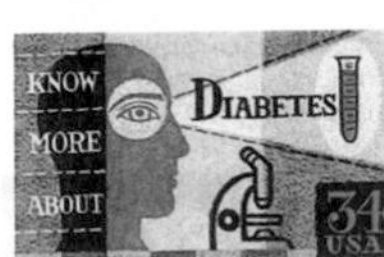

2576 Head, Test-tube and Microscope

2001. Diabetes Awareness Campaign. Self-adhesive.

3969	**2576**	34c. multicoloured	55	30

2577 Obverse of Medals and Alfred Nobel (founder)

2001. Centenary of Nobel Prizes.

3970	**2577**	34c. yell, lt brn & brn	55	80

2578 1c. Stamp with Inverted Centre

2581 Exposition Emblem

2001. Centenary of Pan-American Exposition.

3971	**2578**	1c. black and green	30	15
3972	–	2c. black and red	30	15
3973	–	4c. black and brown	30	15
3974	**2581**	80c. red and blue	85	30

DESIGNS: No. 3972, 2c. stamp with inverted centre; 3973, 4c. stamp with inverted centre.

2583 Great Plains Prairie (½-size illustration)

2001. Nature of America. (3rd series). Sheet 233 × 172 mm. Forming the overall design T **2583**. Multicoloured. Self-adhesive.

MS3975 34c. Canada geese and Pronghorn deer; 34c. Bison, burrowing owls and buffalo grass; 34c. Bison, wild alfalfa and prairie dogs (horiz); 34c. Black-tailed prairie dog; 34c. Painted lady butterfly, coneflower and wild rose (horiz); 34c., Camel cricket and western meadow lark; 34c. Badger and buffalo grass; 34c. Eastern short-horned lizard and plains pocket gopher; 34c. Plains spadefoot and dung beetle (horiz); 34c. Two-striped grasshopper and Ord's kangaroo rat . . . 4·50 1·40

The back of the sheet has a description of the plains prairie and a key to the flora and fauna in the design.

2584 Snoopy as World War I Flying Ace (Charles M. Schultz)

2001. "Peanuts" (comic strip). Self-adhesive.

3976	**2584**	34c. multicoloured	45	15

2585 Flag **2586** Kahlo

2001. "Honoring Veterans". Self-adhesive.

3977	**2585**	34c. multicoloured	45	15

2001. Frida Kahlo (artist) Commemoration.

3978	**2586**	34c. multicoloured	45	15

2587 Ebbets Field, Brooklyn **2588** Atlas (statue), Rockefeller Centre, New York City

2001. Baseball Fields. Multicoloured. Self-adhesive.

3979	34c. Type **2587**	45	15
3980	34c. Tiger Stadium, Detroit	45	15
3981	34c. Crosley Field, Cincinnati	45	15
3982	34c. Yankee Stadium, New York City	45	15
3983	34c. Polo Grounds, New York City	45	15
3984	34c. Forbes Field, Pittsburgh	45	15
3985	34c. Fenway Park, Boston	45	15
3986	34c. Comiskey Park, Chicago	45	15
3987	34c. Shibe Park, Philadelphia	45	15
3988	34c. Wrigley Field, Chicago	45	15

A brief description of the stadium is included on the backing paper of each stamp.

2001. Presorted coil stamp. Multicoloured. Self-adhesive.

3989	**2588**	(10c.) multicoloured	15	10

2589 Leonard Bernstein (composer) **2590** Car

2001.

3990	**2589**	34c. black	45	15

2001. Presorted First-Class Card coil stamp. Self-adhesive.

3991	**2590**	(15c.) multicoloured	20	10

2591 Lucille Ball **2592** Diamond in Square

2593 Lone Star

2594 Sunshine and Shadow

2595 Double Ninepatch

2001. Legends of Hollywood. Self-adhesive.

3992	**2591**	34c. multicoloured	45	15

2001. Amish Quilts. Self-adhesive.

3993	**2592**	34c. multicoloured	45	15
3994	**2593**	34c. multicoloured	45	15
3995	**2594**	34c. multicoloured	45	15
3996	**2595**	34c. multicoloured	45	15

2596 Venus Flytrap **2600** Calligraphy

2001. Carnivorous Plants. Multicoloured. Self-adhesive.

3997	34c. Type **2596**	45	15
3998	34c. Yellow trumpet	45	15
3999	34c. Cobra lily	45	15
4000	34c.25 99 English sundew	45	15

2001. Eid al-Fitr and Eid al-Adha (Islamic festivals). Self-adhesive.

4001	**2600**	34c. gold, blue and brown	45	15

2601 Fermi **2602** Porky Pig delivering Letter

2001. Birth Centenary of Enrico Fermi (nuclear physicist).

4002	**2601**	34c. multicoloured	45	15

2001. Porky Pig (cartoon character). Self-adhesive.

4003	**2603**	34c. multicoloured	45	15
MS4004		87 × 130 mm. No. 4003	60	25

2603 "Virgin and Child" (Lorenzo Costa) **2604** Santa Claus with Armful of Presents

2001. Christmas. (1st issue). Self-adhesive gum.

4005	**2603**	34c. multicoloured	45	15

2001. Christmas (2nd issue). Mulicoloured. Self-adhesive. (a) Size18 × 25 mm.

4006	34c. Type **2604**	45	15
4007	34c. Wearing blue outfit	45	15
4008	34c. Wearing red outfit with fur collar	45	15
4009	34c. Wearing holly wreath	45	15
	(b) Size18 × 21 mm.		
4010	34c. As T **2640**	45	15
4011	34c. As No. 4007	45	15
4012	34c. As No. 4008	45	15
4013	34c. As No. 4009	45	15

2608 Madison

2001. 250th Birth Anniv of James Madison (fourth president of United States).

4018	**2608**	34c. green and black	45	15

2609 Cornucopia **2610** Flag

2001. Thanksgiving Festival. Self-adhesive.

4019	**2609**	34c. multicoloured	45	15

2001. Hanukkah and Kawanzaa Festivals. As Nos. 3265 and 3370 but with face values changed. Self-adhesive.

4020	**2257**	34c. multicoloured	45	15
4021	**2304**	34c. multicoloured	45	15

See also Nos. 3693/4.

2001. "United We Stand". Self-adhesive.

4022	**2610**	34c. multicoloured	45	15

2611 Snowboarding

2002. Winter Sports. Multicoloured. Self-adhesive.

4030	34c. Type **2611**	35	10
4031	34c. Ice hockey	35	10
4032	34c. Figure skating	35	10
4033	34c. Ski jumping	35	10

2615 Man and Boy

2002. Mentoring a Child. Self-adhesive.
4034 **2615** 34c. multicoloured . . . 35 10

2616 Langston Hughes

2002. 25th Anniv of Black Heritage Stamps. Langston Hughes (writer) Self-adhesive.
4035 **2616** 34c. multicoloured . . . 35 10

2617 "HAPPY BIRTHDAY"

2002. Greetings Stamp. Self-adhesive.
4036 **2617** 34c. multicoloured . . . 35 10

2618 Horse

2002. New Year. Year of the Horse. Self-adhesive.
4037 **2618** 34c. multicoloured . . . 35 10

2619 Academy Arms

2002. Centenary of West Point Military Academy. Self-adhesive.
4038 **2619** 34c. multicoloured . . . 35 10

2620 Alabama

2002. Greetings from America. Multicoloured. Self-adhesive.
4039 34c. Type **2620** 35 10
4040 34c. Alaska 35 10
4041 34c. Arizona 35 10
4042 34c. Arkansas 35 10
4043 34c. California 35 10
4044 34c. Colorado 35 10
4045 34c. Connecticut 35 10
4046 34c. Delaware 35 10
4047 34c. Florida 35 10
4048 34c. Georgia 35 10
4049 34c. Hawaii 35 10
4050 34c. Idaho 35 10
4051 34c. Illinois 35 10
4052 34c. Indiana 35 10
4053 34c. Iowa 35 10
4054 34c. Kansas 35 10
4055 34c. Kentucky 35 10
4056 34c. Louisiana 35 10
4057 34c. Maine 35 10
4058 34c. Maryland 35 10
4059 34c. Massachusetts 35 10
4060 34c. Michigan 35 10
4061 34c. Minnesota 35 10
4062 34c. Mississippi 35 10
4063 34c. Missouri 35 10
4064 34c. Montana 35 10
4065 34c. Nebraska 35 10
4066 34c. Nevada 35 10
4067 34c. New Hampshire . . . 35 10
4068 34c. New Jersey 35 10
4069 34c. New Mexico 35 10
4070 34c. New York 35 10
4071 34c. North Carolina 35 10

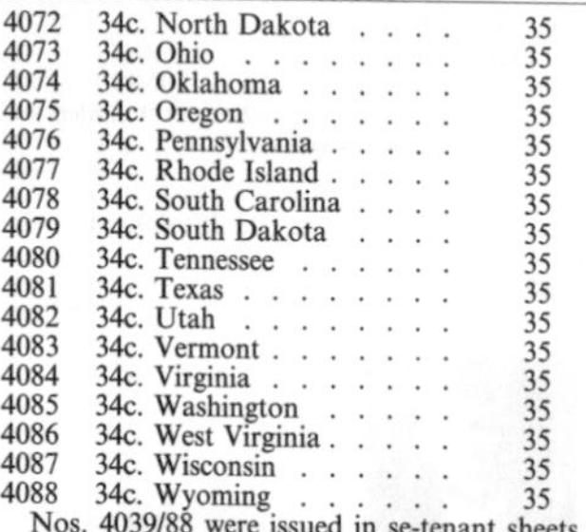
4072 34c. North Dakota 35 10
4073 34c. Ohio 35 10
4074 34c. Oklahoma 35 10
4075 34c. Oregon 35 10
4076 34c. Pennsylvania 35 10
4077 34c. Rhode Island 35 10
4078 34c. South Carolina . . . 35 10
4079 34c. South Dakota 35 10
4080 34c. Tennessee 35 10
4081 34c. Texas 35 10
4082 34c. Utah 35 10
4083 34c. Vermont 35 10
4084 34c. Virginia 35 10
4085 34c. Washington 35 10
4086 34c. West Virginia 35 10
4087 34c. Wisconsin 35 10
4088 34c. Wyoming 35 10

Nos. 4039/88 were issued in se-tenant sheets of 50 stamps, with list of bird, flower, tree, capital and statehood printed on the backing paper of each stamp.

2621 Longleaf Pine Forest (⅓-size illustration)

2001. Nature of America (4th series). Sheet 233 × 172 mm forming the overall design T **2621**. Multicoloured. Self-adhesive.
MS4089 34c. Bachman's sparrow; 34c. Northern bobwhites; 34c. Fox squirrel and red-bellied woodpecker; 34c. Grey fox (horiz); 34c. Brown-headed nuthatch; 34c. Broad-headed skink; 34c. Rosebud orchid; 34c. Grass-pink orchid (horiz); 34c. Eastern towhee; 34c. Sweetbay and pine woods treefrog 3·50 3·50

The backing paper of the sheet has a description of the pine of forest and a key to the flora and fauna in the design.

2622 Toleware Coffee Pot

2623 Star

2002. Arts and Crafts. Multicoloured.
4090 1c. Tiffany lamp 10 10
4091 5c. Type **2622** 10 10
4092 10c. Early American clock 10 10

2002. Make-up Rate Stamps. Ordinary or Self-adhesive gum.
4100 **2623** 3c. red, ultramarine and black 10 10

2624 Fire-fighters raising Flag

2625 Mail Van

2002. Heroes of America. Self-adhesive.
4110 **2624** (34c.+11c.) multicoloured 50 15

The premium was for assistance to families of those killed or disabled in the line of duty on September 11th. The face value became 37c.+8c. on 30 June 2002.

2002. Antique Toys. Multicoloured. Self-adhesive.
4111 (37c.) Type **2625** 40 10
4112 (37c.) Steam locomotive . . 40 10
4113 (37c.) Taxi 40 10
4114 (37c.) Fire pump 40 10

2629 Flag

2630 Flag

2002. First Class Stamps. Ordinary or Self-adhesive gum.
4115 **2629** (37c.) multicoloured . . 40 10

2002. Self-adhesive gum.
4123 **2630** 37c. multicoloured . . . 40 10

2631 Senator Daniel Webster (c. 1850, A. S. Southworth and J. J. Hawes)

2632 Louisiana and Scarlet Tanagers

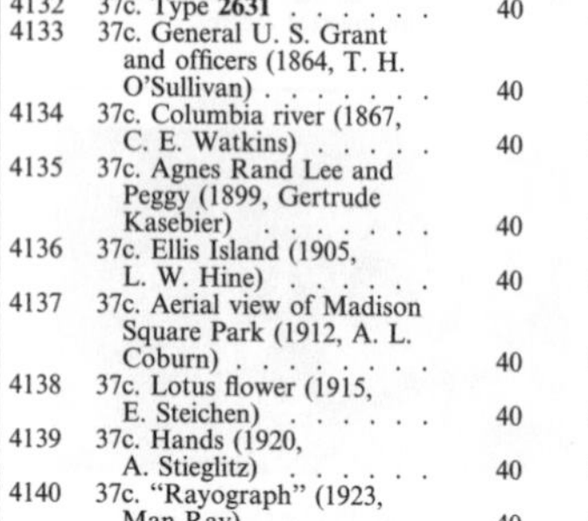

2002. American Photographers. Showing works by photographers. Each black. Self-adhesive.
4132 37c. Type **2631** 40 10
4133 37c. General U. S. Grant and officers (1864, T. H. O'Sullivan) 40 10
4134 37c. Columbia river (1867, C. E. Watkins) 40 10
4135 37c. Agnes Rand Lee and Peggy (1899, Gertrude Kasebier) 40 10
4136 37c. Ellis Island (1905, L. W. Hine) 40 10
4137 37c. Aerial view of Madison Square Park (1912, A. L. Coburn) 40 10
4138 37c. Lotus flower (1915, E. Steichen) 40 10
4139 37c. Hands (1920, A. Stieglitz) 40 10
4140 37c. "Rayograph" (1923, Man Ray) 40 10
4141 37c. "Two shells" (1927, E. Weston) 40 10
4142 37c. Woman with corsage (1931, J. VanDerZee) . . 40 10
4143 37c. Man in vehicle (1935, Dorothea Lange) 40 10
4144 37c. Sharecropper's kitchen (1936, W. Evans) 40 10
4145 37c. Soldiers (1944, W. E. Smith) 40 10
4146 37c. Church steeple (1946, P. Strand) 40 10
4147 37c. Sand dunes (1948, A. Adams) 40 10
4148 37c. Ida C. Pabst (1958, Imogen Cunningham) . . 40 10
4149 37c. New York skyline (A. Kertesz) 40 10
4150 37c. Woman walking (1965, G. Winogrand) 40 10
4151 37c. Snow scene (1971, M. White) 40 10

Nos. 4132/51 were issued in se-tenant sheetlets of 20 stamps. The backing paper of the sheet has a description of the photograph and a short biography of the photographer.

2002. John James Audubon Commemoration. Self-adhesive.
4152 **2632** 37c. multicoloured . . . 40 10

2633 Harry Houdini (escape artist)

2634 Eagle (detail, woven coverlet)

2002. Self-adhesive.
4153 **2633** 37c. multicoloured . . . 40 10

No. 4153 incorporates an additional hidden design of chains across the figure visible only under a special decoder.

2002. Self-adhesive.
4154 **2634** 60c. multicoloured . . . 65 20

2002. Antique Toys. As Nos. 4111/14, but with value expressed. Self-adhesive.
4155 37c. multicoloured 40 10
4156 37c. multicoloured 40 10
4157 37c. multicoloured 40 10
4158 37c. multicoloured 40 10

2635 Jefferson Memorial

2002. Self-adhesive.
4163 **2635** $3.85 multicoloured . . 4·00 1·20
4164 **2560** $13.65 multicoloured 15·00 4·50

Nos. 4163/4 each incorporate additional hidden designs, Jefferson's signature at lower left (No. 4164) or Union flag at top right (No. 4165) visible only under a special decoder.

No. 4163 was intended mainly for Priority mail and No. 4164 for Express Mail Service but they could be used on other mail as well.

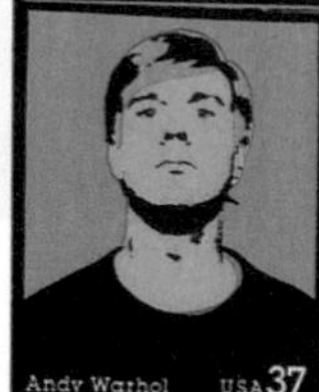

2636 Andy Warhol

2002. Andy Warhol (artist) Commemoration. Self-adhesive.
4165 **2636** 37c. multicoloured . . . 40 10

2637 Teddy Bear

2638 Teddy Bear

2639 Teddy Bear

2640 Teddy Bear

2002. Centenary of the Teddy Bear. Self-adhesive.
4166 **2637** 37c. multicoloured . . . 40 10
4167 **2638** 37c. multicoloured . . . 40 10
4168 **2639** 37c. multicoloured . . . 40 10
4169 **2640** 37c. multicoloured . . . 40 10

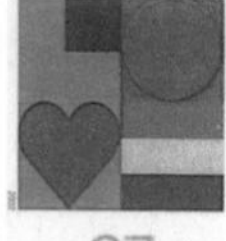

2641 Heart and Circle

2643 Ogden Nash

2002. Multicoloured. Self-adhesive.
4170 37c. Type **2641** 40 10
4171 60c. Circle and heart . . . 65 20

2002. Birth Centenary of Frederick Ogden Nash (writer). Self-adhesive.
4172 **2643** 37c. multicoloured . . . 40 10

2644 Duke Kahanamoku (swimmer and surfer)

2002. Duke Paoa Kahanamoku Commemoration. Self-adhesive.
4173 **2644** 37c. multicoloured . . . 40 10

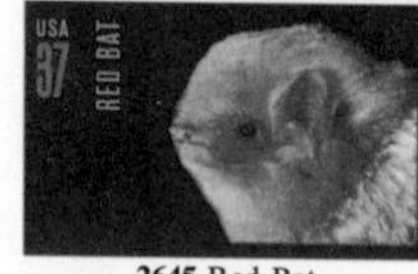

2645 Red Bat

2002. National Stamp Collecting Month. Bats. Multicoloured. Self-adhesive.
4174 37c. Type **2645** 40 10
4175 37c. Leaf-nosed bat 40 10
4176 37c. Pallid bat 40 10
4177 37c. Spotted bat 40 10

2649 Nellie Bly

2002. Women Journalists. Multicoloured. Self-adhesive.
4178 37c. Type **2649** 40 10
4179 37c. Ida M. Tarbell 40 10
4180 37c. Ethel L. Payne 40 10

4181 37c. Marguerite Higgins . . 40 10

2653 Irving Berlin (composer)

2002. Self-adhesive.
4182 **2653** 37c. multicoloured . . . 40 10

2654 Kitten

2002. Animal Population Control Campaign. Multicoloured. Self-adhesive.
4183 37c. Type **2654** 40 10
4184 37c. Puppy 40 10

2656 "Virgin and Child" (Jan Gossaert)

2657 Cary Grant (actor)

2002. Christmas. (1st issue). Self-adhesive.
4185 **2656** 37c. multicoloured . . . 40 10
See also No. 4323.

2002. Hanukkah, Kwanzaa and Eid Festivals. As Nos. 3265, 3370 and 4001 but with face values changed.
4186 **2257** 37c. multicoloured . . . 40 10
4187 **2304** 37c. multicoloured . . . 40 10
4188 **2600** 37c. gold, blue and brown 40 10

2002. Self-adhesive.
4189 **2657** 37c. multicoloured . . . 40 10

2659 Sea Coast

2659a 1851 Hawaiian 2 cent Postage Stamp

2002. Non-profit Organisations. Ordinary or self-adhesive gum.
4190 **2659** (5c.) multicoloured . . 10 10

2002. Hawaiian Missionary Stamps. Sheet 147 × 157 mm containing T **2659**a and similar vert designs. Multicoloured.
MS4193 37c. Type **2659**a; 37c. 1851 5 cent stamp; 37c. 1851 13 cent stamp; 37c. 1852 13 cent stamp 1·60 1·60

2002. Greetings stamp. As No. 4036 but with face value changed. Self-adhesive.
4194 **2617** 37c. multicoloured . . . 40 10

2660 Snowman wearing Check Scarf

2664 Thurgood Marshall

2002. Christmas Holiday Snowmen. Multicoloured. Self-adhesive. (a) 19 × 27 mm.
4245 37c. Type **2660** 40 10
4246 37c. Snowman wearing tartan scarf 40 10
4247 37c. Snowman wearing top hat 40 10
4248 37c. Snowman with pipe . . 40 10

(b) Size 18 × 21 mm.
4249 37c. As No. 4245 . . . . . 40 10
4250 37c. As No. 4246 . . . . . 40 10
4251 37c. As No. 4247 . . . . . 40 10
4252 37c. As No. 4248 . . . . . 40 10

2003. Black Heritage. Thurgood Marshall (first black Supreme Court judge). Self-adhesive.
4261 **2664** 37c. black 40 10

2665 Goat

2003. New Year. Year of the Goat. Self-adhesive.
4262 **2665** 37c. multicoloured . . . 40 10

2666 Zora Neale Hurston

2003. Zora Neale Hurston (writer) Commemoration. Self-adhesive.
4263 **2666** 37c. multicoloured . . . 40 10

2667 Man wearing Medal

2669 Wisdom (Rockefeller Centre, New York)

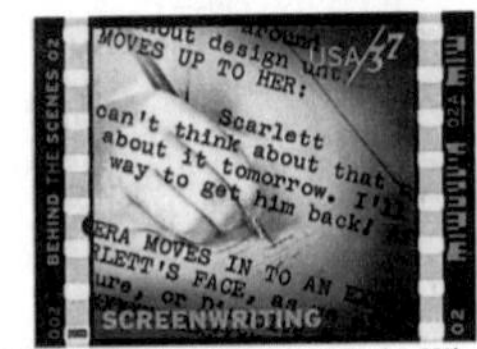

2668 Script for "Gone with the Wind" (film)

2002. Special Olympics Programme (disabled sports). Self-adhesive.
4264 **2667** 80c. multicoloured . . . 85 25

2003. American Film Making. Multicoloured. Self-adhesive.
4265 37c. Type **2668** (screenwriting) 40 10
4266 37c. Perry Ferguson and scenery design (art direction) 40 10
4267 37c. John Cassavetes (directing) 40 10
4268 37c. Camera and cameraman (cinematography) 40 10
4269 37c. Edith Head and dress design (costume design) 40 10
4270 37c. Hands, scissors and film (film editing) 40 10
4271 37c. Musical notation and hand holding pencil (music) 40 10
4272 37c. Model of E.T. (film character) (special effects) 40 10
4273 37c. Boris Karloff as Frankenstein (make up) 40 10
4274 37c. Hand and sound mixing board 40 10
The backing paper of the sheet has a brief description of the stamp.

2003. Self-adhesive.
4275 **2669** $1 multicoloured . . . 1·10 35

2670 Farm in Landscape

2671 Brown Pelican

2003. Bicentenary of Ohio State. Self-adhesive.
4276 **2670** 37c. multicoloured . . . 40 10

2003. Centenary of Pelican Island Wildlife Refuge, Florida. Self-adhesive.
4277 **2671** 37c. multicoloured . . . 40 10
A brief description of the Wildlife Refuge is printed on the back of the stamp.

2672 Uncle Sam riding Penny-farthing Bicycle

2673 Cesar Chavez

2003. "Old Glory". Multicoloured. Self-adhesive.
4278 37c. Type **2672** 40 10
4279 37c. Benjamin Harrison presidential campaign badge 40 10
4280 37c. Silk bookmark (c.1893) 40 10
4281 37c. Modern fan showing flag 40 10
4282 37c. Woman holding flag (statue) (19th-century) . . 40 10

2003. 10th Death Anniv of Cesar Chavez (workers rights activist). Self-adhesive.
4283 **2673** 37c. multicoloured . . . 40 10

2674 Robert Livingston and Francois de Barbe-Marbois shaking Hands and James Monroe Signing Treaty

2676 Purple Heart (military medal)

2675 Wright Flyer

2003. Bicentenary of Treaty purchasing Louisiana Territory from France. Self-adhesive.
4284 **2674** 37c. multicoloured . . . 40 10

2003. Centenary of Powered Flight. Self-adhesive.
4285 **2675** 37c. multicoloured . . . 40 10
MS4286 130 × 87 mm. No. 4235 40 40

2003.
4287 **2676** 37c. multicoloured . . . 40 10

2677 Audrey Hepburn

2678 Hillsboro Inlet, Florida

2003. Legends of Hollywood. Self-adhesive.
4289 **2677** 37c. multicoloured . . . 40 10

2003. South Eastern Lighthouses. Multicoloured. Self-adhesive.
4290 37c. Type **2678** 40 10
4291 37c. Old Cape Henry, Virginia 40 10
4292 37c. Cape Lookout, North Carolina 40 10
4293 37c. Morris Island, South Carolina 40 10
4294 37c. Tybee Island, Georgia 40 10

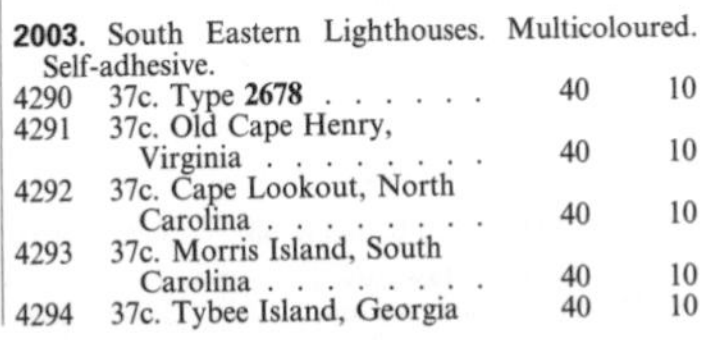

2683 Eagle

2684 Raven

2685 Arctic Tundra (½-size illustration)

2003. Pre-sorted First Class Mail Coil Stamps. Self-adhesive.
4295 **2683** 25c. buff and blue . . . 30 10
4296 25c. blue and buff . . . 30 10
4297 25c. buff and emerald 30 10
4298 25c. slate and buff . . . 30 10
4299 25c. blue and buff . . . 30 10
4300 25c. blue and buff . . . 30 10
4301 25c. buff and vermilion 30 10
4302 25c. emerald and buff 30 10
4303 25c. buff and slate . . . 30 10
4304 25c. vermilion and buff 30 10

2003. Nature of America (5th series). Sheet 233 × 172 mm containing T **2684** and forming the overall design T **2685**. Multicoloured. Self-adhesive.
MS4305 37c. Type **2684**; 37c. Bison; 37c. Caribou (horiz); 37c. Gyrfalcon (horiz); 37c. Grey wolf; 37c. Grizzly bear (horiz); 37c. Arctic ground squirrel; 37c. Singing vole (horiz); 37 c.Willow ptarmigan (horiz); 37c. Arctic grayling (horiz) . . . . . . 4·00 4·00
The backing paper of the sheet has a description of the tundra and a key to the flora and fauna in the design.

2686 Korean War Veterans' Memorial, Washington, DC

2003. 50th Anniv of End of Korean War. Self-adhesive.
4306 **2686** 37c. black, blue and vermilion 40 10

2687 "Young Mother"

2691 Bronko Nagurski

2003. Mary Cassatt (artist) Commemoration. Multicoloured. Self-adhesive.
4307 37c. Type **2687** 40 10
4308 37c. "Children playing on Beach" 40 10
4309 37c. "On Balcony" 40 10
4310 37c. "Child in Straw Hat" 40 10

2003. Early Football Players. Multicoloured. Self-adhesive.
4311 37c. Type **2691** 40 10
4312 37c. Walter Camp 40 10
4313 37c. Ernie Nevers 40 10
4314 37c. Red Grange 40 10

2695 Roy Acuff

2003. Birth Centenary of Roy Acuff (singer). Self-adhesive.

4315	**2695**	37c. black, scarlet and lemon	40	10

2696 Images of Washington, DC

2003. Washington, District of Columbia. Self-adhesive.

4314	**2696**	37c. multicoloured	40	10

2697 Scarlet King Snake

2003. Reptiles. Multicoloured. Self-adhesive.

4317	37c. Type **2697**	40	10
4318	37c. Blue-spotted salamander	40	10
4319	37c. Reticulate collared lizard	40	10
4320	37c. Ornate chorus frog	40	10
4321	37c. Ornate box turtle	40	10

2702 Crying Child

2003. Family Violence Campaign. Self-adhesive.

4322	**2702**	(45c.) multicoloured	50	15

2003. "Virgin and Child" (Jan Gossaert) (2nd issue). Self-adhesive.

4323	**2656**	37c. multicoloured	40	10

2703 Deer and Panpipes

2707 Snowy Egret

2003. Christmas. Music Makers. Self-adhesive.

4324	37c. Type **2703**	40	10
4325	37c. Father Christmas and drum	40	10
4326	37c. Father Christmas and trumpet	40	10
4327	37c. Deer and horn	40	10

(b) Size 18 × 21 mm.

4332	37c. As Type **2703**	40	10
4333	37c. As No. 4325	40	10
4334	37c. As No. 4236	40	10
4335	37c. As No. 4237	40	10

2003. Self-adhesive.

4336	**2707**	37c. multicoloured	40	10

CERTIFIED MAIL

C 524 Postman

1955.

C1070	**C 524**	15c. red	45	30

NEWSPAPER STAMPS

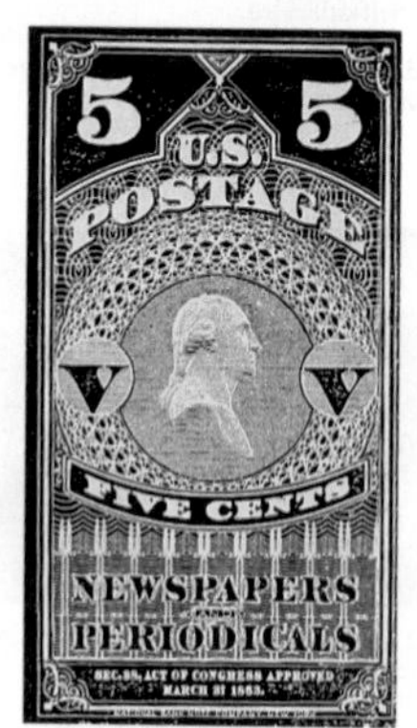

N 21 Washington (½-size illustration)

1865. 5c. with coloured or white border.

N78	**N 21**	5c. blue	£175
N80	–	10c. green	£130
N81	–	25c. red	£140

DESIGNS: 10c. Franklin; 20c. Lincoln.

N 42 "Freedom" **N 87** "Freedom"

1875. Different Frames.

N252	**N 42**	1c. black	15·00	5·00
N291	**N 87**	1c. black	4·00	4·00
N228	**N 42**	2c. black	14·00	3·75
N292	**N 87**	2c. black	4·25	3·25
N229	**N 42**	3c. black	17·00	4·75
N230		4c. black	17·00	4·75
N293	**N 87**	5c. black	6·75	5·00
N231	**N 42**	6c. black	28·00	10·00
N232		8c. black	28·00	10·00
N185		9c. black	£160	55·00
N233		10c. black	26·00	10·00
N294	**N 87**	10c. black	4·25	3·25
N253	A	12c. red	38·00	13·50
N254		24c. red	40·00	13·50
N295		25c. red	8·25	10·00
N255		36c. red	65·00	20·00
N256		48c. red	£110	30·00
N296		50c. red	10·00	12·50
N191		60c. red	£100	43·00
N258		72c. red	£140	47·00
N240		84c. red	£225	£110
N241		96c. red	£160	80·00
N242	–	$1.92 brown	£120	70·00
N297	–	$2 red	13·50	20·00
N243	–	$3 red	£110	70·00
N298	–	$5 blue	23·00	27·00
N244	–	$6 blue	£170	£110
N245	–	$9 orange	£140	75·00
N299	–	$10 green	23·00	27·00
N246	–	$12 green	£200	95·00
N300	–	$20 black	25·00	28·00
N247	–	$24 purple	£220	£120
N248	–	$36 red	£275	£130
N249	–	$48 brown	£350	£180
N301	–	$50 red	33·00	28·00
N250	–	$60 violet	£325	£180
N302	–	$100 violet	37·00	33·00

DESIGNS: A, Astraea or "Justice"; $1.92, Ceres; $2, $3 "Victory"; $5, $6 Clio; $9 Minerva; $10, $12 Vesta; $20, $24 "Peace"; $36, $50 "Commerce"; $48 Hebe; $60, $100 Minnehaha.

OFFICIAL STAMPS

For list of stamps used on correspondence from individual Government Departments, between 1873 and 1879, see the Stanley Gibbons Part 22 (U.S.A.) Catalogue.

O 1315 Eagle **O 1438** **O 1588**

1983.

O2008	**O 1315**	1c. blue, red & blk	10	20
O2009		4c. blue, red & blk	15	20
O2010		13c. blue, red & blk	25	65
O2011		14c. blue, red & blk	25	35
O2012		17c. blue, red & blk	30	75
O2015		20c. blue, red & blk	85	1·10
O2016		22c. blue, red & blk	45	1·20
O2013		$1 blue, red & blk	1·30	2·30
O2014		$5 blue, red & blk	10·50	13·00

1985. No value expressed. (a) Inscr "Postal Card Rate D".

O2140	**O 1438**	(14c.) bl, red & blk	3·25	3·25

(b) Inscr "Domestic Letter Rate D"

O2141	–	(22c.) blue, red and black	3·00	2·00

1988. No value expressed.

O2344	**O 1588**	(25c.) bl, blk & red	75	1·00

O 1592 **O 1793** **O 2001**

1988.

O2348	**O 1592**	1c. blue, black & red	10	10
O2349		4c. blue, black & red	10	15
O2350		15c. blue, blk & red	35	25
O2352		19c. blue, blk & red	30	40
O2353		20c. blue, blk & red	45	35
O2351		23c. blue, blk & red	40	35
O2354		25c. blue, blk & red	45	55
O2355		29c. blue, blk & red	55	85

1991. Value expressed as "F".

O2558	**O 1793**	(29c.) blue, blk & red	1·10	55

1993.

O2844	**O 2001**	1c. blue, blk & red	10	10
O2845		10c. blue, blk & red	10	20
O2846		20c. blue, blk & red	25	35
O2847		23c. blue, blk & red	25	35
O2849		32c. blue, blk & red	35	25
O2850		33c. blue, blk & red	35	40
O2851		34c. blue, blk & red	35	35
O2852		37c. blue, blk & red	40	40
O2848		$1 blue, blk & red	1·60	1·50

No. O2844 has the face value expressed as "1c." The line above the face value consists of "USA" and the year date repeated several times.

1994. Value expressed as "G".

O2990	**O 1793**	(32c.) blue, blk & red	35	40

PARCEL POST STAMPS

P 134 Post Office Clerk

1912.

P423	**P 134**	1c. red	3·00	80
P424	–	2c. red	3·50	60
P425	–	3c. red	12·00	4·00
P426	–	4c. red	20·00	1·60
P427	–	5c. red	29·00	1·20
P428	–	10c. red	38·00	1·40
P429	–	15c. red	48·00	6·50
P430	–	20c. red	80·00	13·50
P431	–	25c. red	70·00	3·50
P432	–	50c. red	£150	24·00
P433	–	75c. red	50·00	19·00
P434	–	$1 red	£190	19·00

DESIGNS: 2c. City carrier; 3c. Railway postal clerk; 4c. Rural carrier; 5c. Steam mail train; 10c. "Kronprinz Wilhelm" (liner) and mail tender; 15c. Automobile service; 20c. Wright Type A biplane carrying mail; 25c. Manufacturing (Pullman works); 50c. Dairying; 75c. Harvesting; $1 Fruit growing.

PARCEL POST POSTAGE DUE STAMPS

PD 134

1912.

PD423	**PD 134**	1c. green	7·25	3·00
PD424		2c. green	55·00	12·50
PD425		5c. green	10·00	3·50
PD426		10c. green	£120	32·00
PD427		25c. green	70·00	3·25

POSTAGE DUE STAMPS

D 43 **D 87**

1879.

D207	**D 43**	1c. brown	36·00	4·75
D222		2c. brown	40·00	3·25
D209		3c. brown	32·00	2·50
D224		5c. brown	£225	14·50
D225		10c. brown	£200	10·50
D226		30c. brown	£120	26·00
D213		50c. brown	£275	50·00

1891.

D235	**D 43**	1c. red	20·00	80
D236		2c. red	23·00	60
D237		3c. red	41·00	6·25
D238		5c. red	50·00	6·25
D239		10c. red	75·00	13·50
D240		30c. red	£275	£110
D241		50c. red	£300	£110

1894.

D529	**D 87**	½c. red	70	15
D530		1c. red	7·50	60
D531		2c. red	8·50	70
D532		3c. red	7·25	15
D533		5c. red	7·25	15
D534		10c. red	11·50	15
D535a		30c. red	60·00	20
D536		50c. red	85·00	20

D 201 **D 202** **D 581**

1931.

D702	**D 201**	½c. red	60	10
D703		1c. red	15	10
D704		2c. red	15	10
D705		3c. red	15	10
D706		5c. red	25	10
D707		10c. red	90	10
D708		30c. red	6·50	20
D709		50c. red	7·50	15
D699a	**D 202**	$1 red	20·00	15
D700a		$5 red	29·00	15

1959. Centres in black.

D1130	**D 581**	½c. red	1·10	90
D1131		1c. red	15	10
D1132		2c. red	15	10
D1133		3c. red	15	10
D1134		4c. red	15	10
D1135		5c. red	15	10
D1136		6c. red	15	10
D1137		7c. red	15	10
D1138		8c. red	15	10
D1139		10c. red	15	10
D1140		11c. red	25	15
D1141		13c. red	25	15
D1142		17c. red	25	25
D1143		30c. red	50	10
D1144		50c. red	85	10
D1145		$1 red	1·90	10
D1146		$5 red	7·75	15

In the dollar values the numerals are double-lined and vertical.

REGISTERED LETTER STAMP

R 133 American Bald Eagle

1911.

R404	**R 133**	10c. blue	80·00	3·75

SPECIAL DELIVERY AIR STAMPS

AE 247 Great Seal of U.S.A.

1934.

AE750	**AE 247**	16c. blue	55	60
AE751		16c. blue and red	30	15

SPECIAL DELIVERY STAMPS

E 46 Messenger Running

1885. Inscr "AT A SPECIAL DELIVERY OFFICE".

E217	**E 46**	10c. blue	£190	28·00

1888. Inscr "AT ANY POST OFFICE".

E283	**E 46**	10c. blue	£200	6·25
E251		10c. orange	£120	12·50

E 117 Messenger on Bicycle

1917.

E529	**E 117**	10c. blue	14·00	90

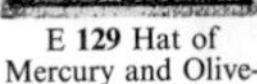
E 129 Hat of Mercury and Olive-branch

E 143 Delivery by Motor Cycle

1908.
E374 E 129 10c. green . . . . . 44·00 26·00

1922.
E648 E 143 10c. blue 50 10
E648a 10c. violet 50 15
E649 13c. blue 35 10
E650 15c. orange 60 45
E651 17c. yellow . . . . . 2·75 2·20

E 144 Delivery by Van

1925.
E652 E 144 20c. black . . . . . 1·50 20

E 520 Delivery by Hand

1954.
E1066 E 520 20c. blue 55 10
E1067 30c. lake 60 10

E 799 Arrows

1969.
E1374 E 799 45c. red and blue . . 1·20 20
E1375 60c. blue and red . . 1·20 15

SPECIAL HANDLING STAMPS

SH 173

1925.
SH624 SH 173 10c. green . . . . 1·10 65
SH625 15c. green . . . . 1·10 60
SH626 20c. green . . . . 1·75 1·20
SH628 25c. green . . . . 17·00 6·50

UNITED STATES POSTAL AGENCY IN SHANGHAI Pt. 17

These stamps were valid for use on mail despatched from the U.S. Postal Agency in Shanghai to addresses in the United States. This agency was closed on 31 December 1922.

100 cents = 1 dollar (Chinese).

1919. United States stamps of 1908–12 surch **SHANGHAI CHINA** and new value.
1 128 2c. on 1c. green . . . . . 19·00 21·00
17 2Cts. on 1c. green . . . . 90·00 85·00
2 4c. on 2c. pink . . . . . 19·00 21·00
18 4Cts. on 2c. red . . . . . 80·00 75·00
3 6c. on 3c. violet . . . . . 38·00 50·00
4 8c. on 4c. brown . . . . . 40·00 50·00
5 10c. on 5c. blue . . . . . 48·00 50·00
6 12c. on 6c. orange . . . . 60·00 70·00
7 14c. on 7c. black . . . . . 65·00 85·00
8 133 16c. on 8c. olive . . . . 42·00 45·00
9 18c. on 9c. orange . . . . 45·00 55·00
10 20c. on 10c. yellow . . . . 42·00 45·00
11a 24c. on 12c. red . . . . . 50·00 55·00
12 30c. on 15c. grey . . . . . 60·00 90·00
13 40c. on 20c. blue . . . . . 90·00 £140
14 60c. on 30c. red . . . . . 85·00 £120
15 $1 on 50c. lilac £350 £425
16 $2 on $1 black £300 £350

UPPER SENEGAL AND NIGER Pt. 6

A French Colony in W. Africa, E. of Senegal, formerly called Senegambia and Niger, and became part of French Sudan in 1920.

100 centimes = 1 franc.

1906. "Faidherbe", "Palms" and "Balay" key-types inscr "HT-SENEGAL-NIGER" in blue (10, 40c., 5f.) or red (others).
35 I 1c. grey 55 75
36 2c. brown . . . . 60 1·25
37 4c. brown on blue . . . . . 2·25 2·25
38 5c. green . . . . 4·00 2·00
39 10c. red . . . . 5·25 80
40 15c. violet . . . . 4·25 5·50
41 J 20c. black on blue . . . . . 1·75 3·50
42 25c. blue . . . . 9·00 2·50
43 30c. brown on pink . . . . 3·50 10·00
44 35c. black on yellow . . . . 1·40 1·75
45 40c. red on blue . . . . . 5·25 10·00
46 45c. brown on green . . . . 7·00 10·50
47 50c. violet . . . . 5·75 7·50
48 75c. green on orange . . . . 6·25 12·00
49 K 1f. black on blue . . . . . 15·00 25·00
50 2f. blue on red . . . . . . 35·00 48·00
51 5f. red on yellow . . . . . 70·00 80·00

7 Touareg

1914.
59 7 1c. violet and purple . . . . 10 2·50
60 2c. purple and grey . . . . . 10 1·60
61 4c. blue and black . . . . . 1·50 1·75
62 5c. green and light green . . 10 1·25
63 10c. carmine and red . . . . 55 3·00
64 15c. yellow and brown . . . 75 3·00
65 20c. black and purple . . . . 2·25 3·50
66 25c. blue and ultramarine . . 85 2·75
67 30c. chocolate and brown . . 2·00 3·25
68 35c. violet and red . . . . . 2·00 3·75
69 40c. red and grey . . . . . 1·75 3·25
70 45c. brown and blue . . . . 1·50 3·25
71 50c. green and black . . . . 2·50 3·25
72 75c. brown and yellow . . . 2·00 3·50
73 1f. purple and brown . . . . 3·75 5·50
74 2f. blue and green . . . . . 2·00 5·00
75 5f. black and violet . . . . . 15·00 12·00

1915. Red Cross. Surch **5c** and red cross.
76 7 10c.+5c. carmine and red . . 2·25 2·75

POSTAGE DUE STAMPS

1906. "Natives" key-type inscr "HT-SENEGAL-NIGER".
D52 L 5c. green and red . . . . . 1·60 1·40
D53 10c. purple and blue . . . 3·50 3·25
D54 15c. blue and red on blue . 4·75 6·25
D55 20c. black & red on yellow . 5·50 6·00
D56 50c. violet and red . . . . 21·00 17·00
D57 60c. black and red on buff . 14·00 21·00
D58 1f. black and red on flesh . 32·00 35·00

1915. "Figures" key-type inscr "HT. SENEGAL-NIGER".
D77 M 5c. green . . . . 1·10 2·75
D78 10c. red . . . . 1·25 2·75
D79 15c. grey . . . . 1·25 3·00
D80 20c. brown . . . . 1·10 3·00
D81 30c. blue . . . . 2·00 4·50
D82 50c. black . . . . 2·00 4·00
D83 60c. orange . . . . 5·50 8·50
D84 1f. violet . . . . 3·25 7·00

For later issues see **FRENCH SUDAN**.

UPPER SILESIA Pt. 7

Stamps issued during a plebiscite held in 1921 to decide the future of the district. After the plebiscite it was divided between Germany and Poland.

100 pfenning = 1 mark.

1

9 Coal-mine in Silesia

1920.
1 1 2½pf. grey 35 45
2 3pf. brown 45 85
3 5pf. green 15 35
4 10pf. brown . . . . 45 1·10
5 15pf. violet 15 45
6 20pf. blue 15 45
7 50pf. purple . . . . 4·75 7·25
8 1m. pink . . . . 4·75 10·50
9 5m. orange . . . . 4·25 10·50

1920. Surch.
10 1 5pf. on 15pf. violet . . . . . 17·00 55·00
12 5pf. on 20pf. blue . . . . . 65 2·10
14 10pf. on 20pf. blue . . . . . 65 1·70
17 50pf. on 5m. orange . . . . 15·00 47·00

1920.
19 9 2½pf. grey 25 45
20 3pf. purple 35 45
21 5pf. green 25 45
22 10pf. red 25 45
23 15pf. violet 25 45
24 20pf. blue . . . . 35 1·10
25 25pf. brown 25 45
26 30pf. yellow 25 45
27 40pf. green . . . . 35 1·10

Same design, but larger.
28 9 50pf. grey 25 45
29 60pf. blue . . . . 35 1·30
30 75pf. green 85 65
31 80pf. purple 65 65
32 1m. mauve 65 45
33 2m. brown 50 45
34 3m. violet 65 45
35 5m. orange . . . . 2·30 3·00

1921. Optd **Plebiscite 20 mars 1921.**
36 9 10pf. red . . . . 3·75 8·50
37 15pf. violet . . . . 3·75 8·50
38 20pf. blue . . . . 5·50 13·00
39 25pf. brown . . . . 12·00 26·00
40 30pf. yellow . . . . 10·50 19·00
41 40pf. green . . . . 10·50 19·00
42 50pf. grey . . . . 10·50 26·00
43 60pf. blue . . . . 13·00 23·00
44 75pf. green . . . . 13·00 26·00
45 80pf. purple . . . . 21·00 34·00
46 1m. mauve . . . . 23·00 65·00

1922. Type **9** in new colours and surch.
47 9 4m. on 60pf. green . . . . . 75 1·70
48 10m. on 75pf. red . . . . . 85 2·50
49 20m. on 80pf. orange . . . . 6·25 14·00

OFFICIAL STAMPS

1920. Stamps of Germany optd **C.I.H.S.** within a circle. (a) Stamps of 1902 and 1916.
O 1 24 2pf. grey . . . . — £1000
O 2 2½pf. grey £1900 £650
O 3 10 3pf. brown . . . . — £700
O 4 5pf. green £1000 £500
O 5 24 7½pf. orange £1900 £850
O 6 10 10pf. red £700 £300
O 7 24 15pf. violet £700 £250
O 8 10 20pf. blue £700 £300
O 9 25pf. black & red on yell — £1000
O10 30pf. blk & orge on pink £1200 £275
O11 24 35pf. brown £1200 £250
O12 10 40pf. black and red . . . £750 £250
O13 50pf. black & pur on pink £750 £250
O14 60pf. purple £1200 £250
O15 75pf. black and green . . £700 £250
O16 80pf. black and red on red — £1000
O17 12 1m. red £1900 £650
O18 13 2m. blue . . . . 22·00 30·00

(b) War Charity. Nos. 105/6.
O19 10 10+5pf. red . . . .
O20 24 15+5pf. violet . . . . . .

(c) National Assembly at Weimar. Nos. 107/10.
O21 26 10pf. red £1300 £850
O22 27 15pf. blue and brown . . 00 £850
O23 28 25pf. red and green . . . 00 £1000
O24 30pf. red and purple . . . £1300 £950

1920. Official stamps of Germany optd **C.G.H.S.** (a) As Types O 31 and O 32 (with figures "21").
O25 5pf. green 35 60
O26 10pf. red 35 60
O27 15pf. brown 35 60
O28 20pf. blue 35 60
O29 30pf. orange on buff 35 60
O30 50pf. violet on buff . . . . 45 1·70
O31 1m. red on buff . . . . . . 5·00 8·50

(b) As Types O 31 and O 32 but without figures.
O32 5pf. green . . . . 1·30 2·50
O33 10pf. red 15 60
O34 15pf. purple 15 60
O35 20pf. blue 15 60
O36 30pf. orange on buff 15 60
O37 40pf. red 15 60
O38 50pf. violet on buff 15 60
O39 60pf. brown 15 60
O40 1m. red on buff 15 60
O41 1m.25 blue on yellow . . . 15 60
O43 2m. blue 25 60
O44 5m. brown on yellow 25 60

UPPER VOLTA Pt. 6; Pt. 14

Formerly part of Upper Senegal and Niger, Upper Volta was created a separate colony in 1919. In 1932 it was divided among French Sudan, Ivory Coast and Niger but was reconstituted as a separate territory in 1947 from when it used the stamps of French West Africa.

In 1958 it became an autonomous republic within the French Community and attained full independence in 1960.

In 1984 the name of the state was changed to Burkina Faso.

100 centimes = 1 franc.

1920. Stamps of Upper Senegal and Niger optd **HAUTE-VOLTA**.
1 7 1c. violet and purple . . . . 20 2·25
2 2c. purple and grey . . . . . 10 2·50
3 4c. blue and black . . . . . 10 2·50
4 5c. green and light green . . 90 3·25
18 5c. chocolate and brown . . 40 2·25
5 10c. carmine and red . . . 60 3·25
19 10c. green and light green . 15 2·50
20 10c. blue and mauve . . . . 30 3·00
6 15c. yellow and brown . . . 50 3·25
7 20c. black and purple . . . 75 3·75
8 25c. blue and ultramarine . . 2·75 3·75
21 25c. green and black . . . . 50 2·75
9 30c. chocolate and brown . . 3·00 4·50
22 30c. carmine and red . . . 45 3·50
23 30c. red and violet . . . . 50 3·50
23a 30c. turquoise and green . . 2·00 3·75
10 35c. violet and red . . . . 1·25 3·75
11 40c. red and grey . . . . . 55 3·25
12 45c. brown and blue . . . . 55 3·25
13 50c. green and black . . . . 50 7·75
24 50c. blue and ultramarine . 80 3·00
25 50c. blue and orange . . . 25 2·75
26 60c. red . . . . 20 2·50
26a 65c. blue and brown . . . . 2·50 4·00
14 75c. brown and yellow . . . 1·75 4·50
15 1f. purple and brown . . . 80 4·00
16 2f. blue and green . . . . . 1·90 4·00
17 5f. black and violet . . . . 2·00 7·50

1922. Surch in figures and bars.
27 7 0,01 on 15c. yellow & brown 1·75 4·00
28 0,02 on 15c. yellow & brown 70 4·00
29 0,05 on 15c. yellow & brown 30 4·00
30 25c. on 2f. blue and green . 1·50 4·00
31 25c. on 5f. black and violet . 1·50 3·75
32 60 on 75c. violet on pink . . 55 2·75
33 65 on 45c. brown and blue . 1·50 3·75
34 85 on 45c. brown and yellow . . . . 2·00 4·25
35 90c. on 75c. pink and red . 1·25 4·75
36 1f.25 on 1f. lt blue & blue . 65 4·00
37 1f.50 on 1f. ultram & bl . . 1·25 4·25
37a 3f. on 5f. brown and pink . 2·00 6·50
38 10f. on 5f. pink and green . 14·50 24·00
39 20f. on 5f. violet and brown . 15·00 38·00

3 Hausa Man

5 Hausa Warrior

1928.
40 3 1c. blue and green . . . . . 35 2·25
41 2c. brown and mauve . . . . 15 3·00
42 4c. black and yellow . . . . 15 2·75
43 5c. indigo and blue . . . . . 65 2·75
44 10c. blue and pink . . . . . 1·25 3·75
45 15c. brown and blue . . . . 1·75 4·50
46 20c. brown and green . . . . 1·10 4·25
47 – 25c. brown and yellow . . . 1·40 2·75
48 – 30c. deep green and green . . 1·60 3·75
49 – 40c. black and pink . . . . 2·25 3·25
50 – 45c. brown and blue . . . . 2·00 4·50
51 – 50c. black and green . . . . 2·00 2·00
52 – 65c. indigo and blue . . . . 2·50 5·25
53 – 75c. black and mauve . . . . 2·75 4·25
54 – 90c. red and mauve . . . . 2·50 4·25
55 5 1f. brown and green . . . . 2·75 4·75
56 1f.10 blue and mauve . . . . 3·25 4·75
57 1f.50 blue . . . . 3·00 6·50
58 2f. black and blue . . . . . 4·00 7·75
59 3f. brown and yellow . . . . 4·00 9·00
60 5f. brown and mauve . . . . 4·50 9·00
61 10f. black and green . . . . 12·00 29·00
62 20f. black and pink . . . . . 22·00 42·00
DESIGN—VERT: 25c. to 90c. Hausa woman.

1931. "Colonial Exhibition" key-types inscr "HAUTE-VOLTA".
63 E 40c. green and black . . . . 4·00 7·50
64 F 50c. mauve and black . . . 3·75 7·25
65 G 90c. red and black . . . . . 1·50 7·25
66 B 1f.50 blue and black . . . . 1·50 10·00

6 President Coulibaly

7 Antelope Mask

1959. 1st Anniv of Republic.
67 6 25f. purple and black 40 20

1960. Animal Masks.
68 7 30c. violet and red 10 10
69 40c. purple and ochre 10 10
70 50c. olive and turquoise . . . 10 10
71 – 1f. black, brown and red . . 10 10
72 – 2f. multicoloured 10 10
73 – 4f. black, violet and blue . . 20 10
74 – 5f. red, brown and bistre . . 20 10
75 – 6f. purple and turquoise . . . 20 20
76 – 8f. brown and red 20 20
77 – 10f. purple and green 20 20
78 – 15f. blue, brown and red . . 40 20
79 – 20f. green and blue 40 30
80 – 25f. purple, green and blue . 50 30
81 – 30f. black, brown & turquoise 70 30
82 – 40f. black, red and blue . . . 80 40
83 – 50f. brown, green and mauve 1·00 40
84 – 60f. blue and brown . . . . 1·25 65

85 – 85f. blue and turquoise . . . 2·00 1·00
MASKS: 1f. to 4f. Wart-hog; 5f. to 8f. Monkey; 10f. to 20f. Buffalo; 25f. Antelope; 30f. to 50f. Elephant; 60f., 85f. Secretary bird.

8 President Yameogo

8a C.C.T.A. Emblem

1960.
86 **8** 25f. purple and grey 40 20

1960. 10th Anniv of African Technical Co-operation Commission.
87 **8a** 25f. indigo and blue 50 40

8b Conseil de l'Entente Emblem

1960. 1st Anniv of Conseil de l'Entente.
88 **8b** 25f. multicoloured 50 30

9

1960. Proclamation of Independence.
89 **9** 25f. brown, red and black . . 55 40

10 Holste Broussard Airplane and Map

1961. Air.
90 **10** 100f. blue, green and red . . 1·90 80
91 – 200f. brown, red and green 4·75 1·40
92 – 500f. multicoloured . . . . 11·00 5·00
DESIGNS: 200f. Scene at Ouagadougou Airport; 500f. Aerial view of Champs Elysees, Ouagadougou.

11 W.M.O. Emblem, Sun and Meteorological Instruments

1961. 1st World Meteorological Day.
93 **11** 25f. red, blue and black . . 55 35

12 Arms of Republic

1961. Independence Festival.
94 **12** 25f. multicoloured 45 30

1962. Air. "Air Afrique" Airline. As T **47a** of Senegal.
95 25f. mauve, green and purple 55 30

13 W.M.O. Emblem, Weather Station and Crops

1962. World Meteorological Day.
96 **13** 25f. blue, green and black 55 40

1962. Malaria Eradication. As T **47b** of Senegal.
97 25f.+5f. red 70 70

14 Nurse and Hospital

1962. Establishment of Red Cross in Upper Volta.
98 **14** 25f. brown, blue and red . . 60 40

15 African Buffalo at Water-hole

1962. Hunting and Tourism.
99 **15** 5f. green, blue and sepia 35 20
100 – 10f. green, yellow & brown 45 35
101 – 15f. green, yellow & brown 1·10 60
102 – 25f. green, blue and mauve 1·10 60
103 – 50f. green, blue and mauve 1·60 1·40
104 – 85f. green, blue and brown 3·75 2·40
DESIGNS—VERT: 15f. Waterbuck; 85f. Kob. HORIZ: 10f. Lion and lioness; 25f. Arly Camp; 50f. Diapaga Camp.

15a Football

1962. Abidjan Games, 1961. Multicoloured.
105 20f. Type **15a** 45 30
106 25f. Cycling 65 35
107 85f. Boating . . . . 1·40 70

1962. 1st Anniv of Union of African and Malagasy States. As T **47c** of Senegal.
108 30f. multicoloured . . . . . . 1·10 75

16 Flag and U.N. Emblem

1962. Air. 2nd Anniv of Admission to U.N.
109 **16** 50f. multicoloured 65 35
110 100f. multicoloured . . . . 1·40 65

17 G.P.O., Ouagadougou

1962. Air. Opening of Ouagadougou P.O.
111 **17** 100f. multicoloured . . . . 1·40 60

1963. Freedom from Hunger. As T **47d** of Senegal.
112 25f.+5f. blue, brn & myrtle 70 70

18 Rainfall Map

19 Basketball

1963. World Meteorological Day.
113 **18** 70c. multicoloured 85 55

1963. Dakar Games. Centres in black and red.
114 **19** 20f. violet 35 20
115 – 25f. ochre (Discus) 45 20
116 – 50f. blue (Judo) 90 40

20 "Argyreia nervosa"

1963. Flowers. Multicoloured.
117 50c. "Hibiscus rosa-sinensis" 10 10
118 1f. "Oldenlandia grandiflora" 10 10
119 1f.50 "Portulaca grandiflora" 10 10
120 2f. "Nicotiana tabacum" . . 10 10
121 4f. "Ipomaea stolonifera" . . 15 10
122 5f. "Striga senegalensis" . . . 15 10
123 6f. "Vigna" 20 10
124 8f. "Lepidagathis heudelotiana" 30 20
125 10f. "Euphorbia splendens" 30 15
126 15f. "Hippeastrum equestre" 40 30
127 25f. Type **20** 55 30
128 30f. "Quisqualis indica" . . . 70 35
129 40f. "Nymphea lotus" . . . 1·25 50
130 50f. "Plumeria alba" . . . . 1·40 55
131 60f. "Crotalaria retusa" . . . 1·75 80
132 85f. "Hibiscus esculentus" . . 2·40 1·10
The 50c. to 10f. are vert.

21 Douglas DC-8 in Flight

1963. Air. 1st Jet-flight, Ouagadougou–Paris.
133 **21** 200f. multicoloured . . . . 4·25 1·25

1963. Air. African and Malagasy Posts and Telecommunications Union. As T **5a** of Rwanda.
134 85f. multicoloured . . . . . 1·25 60

22 Centenary Emblem and Globe

24 "Declaration universelle. . ."

1963. Red Cross Centenary.
135 **22** 25f. multicoloured 90 65

1963. Air. 1st Anniv of "Air Afrique". Surch **AIR AFRIQUE 19-11-63 50F**.
136 **21** 50f. on 200f. multicoloured 1·10 65

1963. 15th Anniv of Declaration of Human Rights.
137 **24** 25f. multicoloured 60 40

25 "Europafrique"

26 "Telecommunications"

1964. Air. "Europafrique".
138 **25** 50f. multicoloured . . . . 1·25 70

1964. Admission of Upper Volta to I.T.U.
139 **26** 25f. multicoloured 45 30

27 Rameses II, Abu Simbel

1964. Air. Nubian Monuments Preservation.
140 **27** 25f. purple and green . . . 65 45
141 100f. brown and blue . . . 2·25 1·75

28 Barograph, Landscape and W.M.O. Emblem

1964. World Meteorological Day.
142 **28** 50f. mauve, blue and green 85 55

29 Dove and Letters

1964. 1st Anniv of Admission to U.P.U.
143 **29** 25f. sepia and blue 45 30
144 – 60f. sepia and orange . . . 90 65
DESIGN: 60f. Jet airliner and letters.

30 Head of Athlete (bronze)

31 Symbols of Solar Research

1964. Air. Olympic Games, Tokyo.
145 **30** 15f. green, red and sepia 35 15
146 – 25f. green, red and sepia 50 20
147 – 85f. green, red and brown 1·10 70
148 – 100f. chocolate, red & brn 1·60 85
DESIGNS: 25f. Seated athlete (bronze); 85f. "Victorious athlete" (bronze); 100f. Venus de Milo.

1964. International Quiet Sun Years.
149 **31** 30f. red, ochre and green 60 40

32 Grey Woodpecker

33 President Kennedy

1964. Air.
150 **32** 250f. multicoloured . . . . 13·00 4·50

1964. French, African and Malagasy Co-operation. As T **60a** of Senegal.
151 70f. brown, red and blue . . 1·00 55

1964. Air. Pres. Kennedy Commemoration.
152 **33** 100f. multicoloured . . . . 1·60 1·10

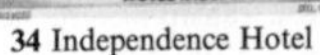

34 Independence Hotel **35** Pygmy Sunbird

1964. Opening of Independence Hotel, Ouagadougou.
153 **34** 25f. multicoloured . . . . 1·75 65

1965. Birds. Multicoloured.
154 10f. Type **35** (postage) . . . 1·25 40
155 15f. Olive-bellied sunbird . . 1·40 60
156 20f. Splendid sunbird . . . . 2·50 80
157 500f. Abyssinian roller (27 × 48 mm) (air) . . . . 28·00 8·75

36 Sun and Emblems

1965. Air. World Meterological Day.
158 **36** 50f. multicoloured 85 35

37 Grand Cascade, Banfora

1965. Banfora Waterfalls.
159 – 5f. brown, blue and green 15 10
160 **37** 25f. blue, green and red . . 55 20
DESIGN—VERT: 5f. Comoe Cascade.

38 Hughes Telegraph and Modern Telephone

1965. Air. I.T.U. Centenary.
161 **38** 100f. red, green & turquoise . . . . 1·90 85

39 I.C.Y. Emblem

1965. Air. International Co-operation Year.
162 **39** 25f. multicoloured 45 20
163 100f. multicoloured . . . . 1·25 50

40 Football, Boots and Net **42** "Early Bird" Satellite in Orbit

41 Sacred Alligator of Sabou

1965. 1st African Games, Brazzaville.
164 **40** 15f. green, red and purple 30 20
165 – 25f. purple, orange and blue 40 25
166 – 70f. red and green . . . . 1·00 55
DESIGNS: 25f. Boxing gloves and ring; 70f. Tennis racquets, ball and net.

1965. Air. Fauna.
167 **41** 60f. green, turquoise & brn 2·25 65
168 – 85f. brown, bistre and green . . . . 2·75 85
DESIGN—VERT: 85f. Lion.

1965. Air. Space Telecommuncations.
169 **42** 30f. red, brown and blue 55 30

43 Lincoln **45** Dromedary

44 President Yameogo

1965. Death Centenary of Abraham Lincoln.
170 **43** 50f. multicoloured 65 40

1965. Pres. Yameogo.
171 **44** 25f. multicoloured 45 20

1966. Insects and Fauna. Multicoloured.
172 1f. "Nemopistha imperatrix" (vert) 10 10
173 2f. Python (vert) 10 10
174 3f. "Sphodromantis lineola" 10 10
175 4f. "Staurocleis magnifica occidentalis" 15 10
176 5f. Warthog (vert) 20 10
177 6f. "Pandinus imperator" . . 20 10
178 8f. Savanna monkey (vert) . . 35 15
179 10f. Type **45** 35 20
180 15f. Leopard (vert) 65 25
181 20f. African buffalo 90 30
182 25f. Pygmy hippopotamus (vert) . . . . 1·00 35
183 30f. Agama (lizard) 70 35
184 45f. Viper (vert) . . . . . 1·40 40
185 50f. Chameleon (vert) . . . . 1·75 55
186 60f. "Ugada limbata" (vert) 2·25 80
187 85f. African elephant . . . . 2·40 1·00
The 1, 3, 4, 6 and 60f. are insects, the remainder are fauna.

46 Communications Satellite **47** Ritual Mask

1966. Air. World Meteorological Day.
188 **46** 50f. black, lake and blue 55 30

1966. World Festival of Negro Arts, Dakar. Multicoloured.
189 20f. Type **47** 40 15
190 25f. Plumed head-dress . . . 45 20
191 60f. Dancer . . . . 1·10 40

48 Bobo-Dioulasso Mosque

1966. Religious Buildings. Multicoloured.
192 25f. Type **48** 45 30
193 25f. Po Church 45 30

49 Satellite "FR 1" and Ouagadougou Tracking Station

1966. Air. Inauguration of Ouagadougou Tracking Station.
194 **49** 250f. lake, brown and blue 4·00 1·90

50 W.H.O. Building

1966. Air. Inauguration of W.H.O. Headquarters, Geneva.
195 **50** 100f. black, blue and yellow . . . . 1·60 70

51 Nurse and Red Cross on Globe **52** Scouts by Campfire

1966. Red Cross.
196 **51** 25f. multicoloured 55 30

1966. Scouting.
197 **52** 10f. multicoloured 35 15
198 – 15f. black, brown and buff 35 15
DESIGN: 15f. Scouts on cliff.

53 Inoculating Cattle

1966. Prevention of Cattle Plague Campaign.
199 **53** 25f. black, yellow and blue 85 45

1966. Air. Inauguration of DC-8F Air Services. As T **76a** of Senegal.
200 25f. olive, black and brown 55 35

54 Ploughing with Donkey

1966. Rural Education (25f.) and 3rd Anniv of Kamboince Centre (30f.). Multicoloured.
201 25f. Type **54** 40 20
202 30f. "Rotation of crops", Kamboince Centre 45 20

55 Sir Winston Churchill

1966. Air. Churchill Commemoration.
203 **55** 100f. green and red . . . . 1·60 65

56 Pope Paul and Dove over U.N. General Assembly Building

1966. Air. Pope Paul's Peace Appeal before U.N.
204 **56** 100f. violet and blue . . . 1·60 65

57 UNESCO Emblem

1966. 20th Anniv of UNESCO and UNICEF.
205 **57** 50f. red, blue and black . . 65 40
206 – 50f. violet, purple and red 65 40
DESIGN: No. 206, UNICEF emblem and child-care theme.

58 Arms of Upper Volta **59** Man and Woman holding Emblems

1967.
207 **58** 30f. multicoloured 55 15

1967. Europafrique.
208 **59** 60f. multicoloured 90 40

60 Acclaiming Lions Emblem

1967. Air. 50th Anniv of Lions International.
209 **60** 100f. ultramarine, bl & brn 1·60 65

61 W.M.O. Emblem and Landscape **62** "Diamant" Rocket

1967. Air. World Meteorological Day.
210 **61** 50f. green, turquoise & blue 85 40

1967. Air. French Space Achievements.
211 **62** 5f. green, orange and blue 15 10
212 – 20f. lilac, purple and blue 40 15
213 – 30f. green, blue and red . . 55 20
214 – 100f. green, violet & purple 1·40 60
DESIGNS—HORIZ: 20f. "FR-1" satellite; 100f. "D1-D" satellite. VERT: 30f. "D1-C" satellite.

63 Dr. Schweitzer and Organ Pipes

1967. Air. 2nd Death Anniv of Dr Albert Schweitzer.
215 **63** 250f. black and purple . . 4·00 1·90

64 Scout waving Hat

1967. World Scout Jamboree, Idaho. Mult.
216 5f. Type **64** (postage) 35 10
217 20f. Scouts' handclasp . . . 80 45
218 100f. Jamboree emblem and world map (48 × 27 mm) (air) . . . . 1·40 65

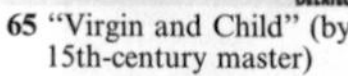

65 "Virgin and Child" (by 15th-century master)
67 Postman on Cycle

66 Bank Book and Coins

1967. Air. Religious Paintings. Multicoloured.
219 30f. Type **65** 50 30
220 50f. "The Deposition of Christ" (Dirk Bouts) . . . 85 40
221 100f. "Christ giving Blessing" (Bellini) . . . . 1·40 80
222 250f. "The Evangelists" (Jordaens) . . . . 4·00 1·90
See also Nos. 237/40.

1967. National Savings Bank.
223 **66** 30f. green, brown & orange 45 20

1967. Air. 5th Anniv of U.A.M.P.T. As T **86a** of Senegal.
224 100f. green, lake and blue . . 1·40 55

1967. Stamp Day.
225 **67** 30f. brown, green and blue 65 45

1967. 5th Anniv of West African Monetary Union. As T **89a** of Togo.
226 30f. violet and blue 30 15

68 Les Deux Alpes
69 Human Rights Emblem

1967. Winter Olympic Games, Grenoble (1968).
227 – 15f. green, blue and brown 40 30
228 **68** 50f. blue and green 70 40
229 – 100f. green, blue and red 1·60 1·00
DESIGNS—HORIZ: 15f. St. Nizier-du-Moucherotte; 100f. Cable-car, Villard-de-Lans.

1968. Human Rights Year.
230 **69** 20f. red, gold and blue . . 40 15
231 30f. red, gold and green . . 45 20

70 Student and School

1968. National School of Administration.
232 **70** 30f. blue, turquoise & brn 45 20

71 Sud Aviation Caravelle "Ouagadougou"

1968. Air.
233 **71** 500f. black, blue and purple . . . . 9·00 4·50

72 W.M.O. Emblem, Sun and Cloud-burst

1968. Air. World Meteorological Day.
234 **72** 50f. blue, red and green . . 85 35

73 Human Figures and W.H.O. Emblem

1968. 20th Anniv of W.H.O.
235 **73** 30f. indigo, red and blue 45 20
236 50f. blue, brown and green 65 35

1968. Air. Paintings. Old Masters in the Louvre. As T **65**. Multicoloured.
237 20f. "Still Life" (Gauguin) (36 × 50 mm) 35 30
238 60f. "Anne of Cleves" (Holbein the Younger) (36 × 50 mm) 65 50
239 90f. "The Pawnbroker and His Wife" (Quentin Metsys) (38 × 40 mm) . . . 1·00 70
240 200f. "The Cart" (Le Nain) (50 × 37 mm) . . . . . . 2·40 1·60

74 "Europafrique"

1968. Air. "Europafrique".
241 **74** 50f. red, black and ochre 70 35

75 Telephone Exchange

1968. Inauguration of Automatic Telephone Exchange, Bobo-Dioulasso.
242 **75** 30f. multicoloured 55 30

76 Colima Acrobat with Bells

1968. Air. Olympic Games, Mexico.
243 **76** 10f. brown, yellow and red 35 20
244 – 30f. blue, red and green . . 50 30
245 – 60f. lake, brown and blue 1·10 45
246 – 100f. lake, blue and green 1·40 70
DESIGNS—VERT: 30f. Pelota-player (Veracruz); 60f. Javelin-thrower (Colima). HORIZ: 100f. Athlete with cape (Jalisco).
The designs represent early Mexican statuary.

77 Weaving

1968. Handicrafts.
247 – 5f. black, purple and brown (postage) 20 10
248 **77** 30f. brown, orange and mauve 50 20
249 – 100f. purple, red and yellow (air) . . . . . 1·40 65
250 – 150f. black, blue & brown 2·25 1·00
DESIGNS—As Type **77**: 5f. Metal-work; 48 × 27 mm: 100f. Pottery; 150f. Basket-making.

1968. Air. "Philexafrique" Stamp Exhibition, Abidjan (Ivory Coast, 1969) (1st issue). As T **98a** of Senegal. Multicoloured.
251 100f. "Too Late" or "The Letter" (A. Cambon) . . . 2·50 2·25
See also No. 256.

78 Mahatma Gandhi
79 "Grain for the World"

1968. Air. "Workers for Peace".
252 **78** 100f. black, yellow & green 1·40 80
253 – 100f. black, light green and green . . . . 1·40 80
DESIGNS: No. 253, Albert Luthuli.

1969. World Food Programme.
255 **79** 30f. purple, slate and blue 45 20

1969. Air. "Philexafrique" Stamp Exn, Abidjan (Ivory Coast) (2nd issue). As T **101a** of Senegal. Multicoloured.
256 50f. Dancers of Tengrela and stamp of 1928 . . . . . . 2·50 2·25

80 Loom and I.L.O. Emblem

1969. 50th Anniv of I.L.O.
257 **80** 30f. blue, lake and green 50 30

81 Cattle and Labourer

1969. Air. World Meteorological Day.
258 **81** 100f. brown, blue and green . . . . 2·50 1·40

82 "Lions" Emblem within Eye

1969. Air. 12th Congress of 403 District, Lions International, Ouagadougou.
259 **82** 250f. multicoloured . . . . 2·75 1·40

83 Blood Donor

1969. 50th Anniv of League of Red Cross Societies.
260 **83** 30f. black, red and blue . . 60 40

84 Nile Pike

1969. Fishes.
261 – 20f. buff, brown and blue (postage) . . . . 1·10 55
262 – 25f. purple, brown and blue . . . . 1·10 55
263 **84** 30f. black and olive . . . 1·60 85
264 – 55f. olive, yellow and green 2·00 1·10
265 – 85f. blue, mauve and brown . . . . 3·75 2·40
266 – 100f. blue, yell & pur (air) 2·25 1·50
267 – 150f. blue, black and red 3·75 1·90
DESIGNS: 20f. Gudgeon tetra; 25f. Poll's tetra; 55f. Half-striped characin; 85f. Sharp-toothed tetra. 48 × 27 mm: 100f. Roman's tetra; 150f. Arnoult's squeaker.

85 Astronaut and Moon

1969. Air. Moon Flight of "Apollo 8". Embossed on gold foil.
268 **85** 1,000f. gold . . . . 18·00

1969. Air. 1st Man on the Moon. No. 214 optd **L'HOMME SUR LA LUNE JUILLET 1969** and "Apollo 11" emblem.
269 100f. green, violet and purple 3·25 3·25

87 "Bonaparte crossing the Great St. Bernard" (J. L. David)

1969. Air. Birth Bicent of Napoleon Bonaparte. Multicoloured.
270 50f. Type **87** . . . . 1·60 80
271 150f. "First Presentation of the Legion of Honour" (Debret) . . . . 5·00 2·00
272 250f. "Napoleon before Madrid" (C. Vernet) . . . 6·75 3·25

1969. 5th Anniv of African Development Bank.
273 30f. brown, emerald and green 35 15

88 Millet
89 Stylized Tree

1969. Agricultural Produce.
274 **88** 15f. brown, green and yellow (postage) 45 20
275 – 30f. blue and mauve . . . 55 35
276 – 100f. brown and violet (air) 1·40 40
277 – 200f. green and red . . . . 2·50 80
DESIGNS: 30f. Cotton. LARGER—48 × 27mm: 100f. Ground-nuts; 200f. Rice.

1969. Air. Europafrique.
278 **89** 100f. multicoloured 90 55

1969. 10th Anniv of Aerial Navigation Security Agency for Africa and Madagascar (A.S.E.C.N.A.). As T **112** of Senegal.
279 100f. brown . . . . 1·25 75

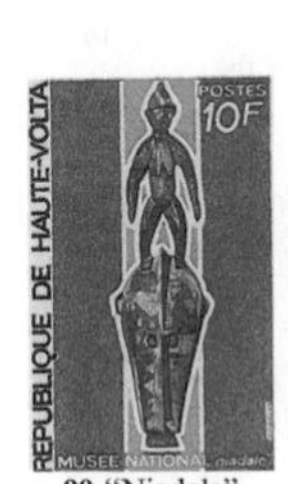

90 "Niadale" **91** Lenin

1970. Figurines and Masks in National Museum.
280 **90** 10f. brown, orange and red 20 10
281 – 30f. brown, blue and violet 40 20
282 – 45f. brown, blue and green 70 30
283 – 80f. brown, purple, & violet . . . . 1·25 60
DESIGNS: 30f. "Niaga"; 45f. "Iliu bara"; 80f. "Karan Weeba".

1970. Air. Birth Centenary of Lenin.
284 **91** 20f. brown and ochre . . . 35 20
285 – 100f. red, blue and green 1·25 80
DESIGN—HORIZ: 100f. "Lenin addressing workers" (A. Serov).

92 African Huts and City Buildings **93** Cauris Dancers

1970. Linked Cities' Day.
286 **92** 30f. brown, blue and red 50 30

1970. Upper Volta Dances. Multicoloured.
287 5f. Mask of Nebwa Gnomo dance (horiz) 20 15
288 8f. Type **93** 30 15
289 20f. Gourmantches dancers 40 15
290 30f. Larlle dancers (horiz) . . 50 20

94 "Pupils", Sun and Emblem of Education Year

1970. Int Education Year. Multicoloured.
291 40f. Type **94** 40 20
292 90f. Visual aids and emblem 95 45

95 New U.P.U. Headquarters Building, U.P.U. Monument and Abraham Lincoln

1970. New U.P.U. Headquarters Building.
293 **95** 30f. grey, red and brown 50 20
294 60f. purple, green & brown 85 35

96 Footballers and Cup

1970. Air. World Cup Football Championship, Mexico.
295 **96** 40f. lake, green and brown 45 30
296 – 100f. brown, purple & green . . . . 1·10 55
DESIGN: 100f. Goalkeeper saving ball, Globe and footballers.

97 Franklin D. Roosevelt **98** Naval Construction

1970. Air. 25th Anniv of Roosevelt's Death.
297 **97** 10f. brown, black and green 20 20
298 – 200f. red, violet and grey 1·60 80
DESIGN—HORIZ: 200f. Roosevelt with his stamp collection.

1970. Hanover Fair.
299 **98** 15f. multicoloured 70 35
300 – 45f. green, blue and black 60 35
301 – 80f. purple, brown & black 1·40 50
DESIGNS: 45f. Test-tubes and retorts ("Chemistry"); 80f. Power transmission lines and pylons ("Electrotechniques").

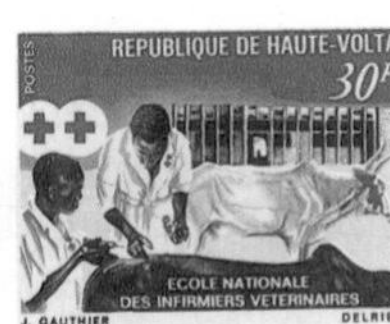

99 Inoculating Cattle

1970. National Veterinary School.
302 **99** 30f. multicoloured 55 35

100 "Manchurian Cranes and Seashore" and Expo Monorail Coach **101** Nurse attending Patient

1970. Air. World Fair "EXPO 70" Osaka, Japan.
303 50f. Type **100** . . . . 1·40 60
304 150f. "Geisha", rocket and satellite . . . . 1·40 80

1970. Upper Volta Red Cross.
305 **101** 30f. brown, red and green 60 35

102 "Nurse and Child" (F. Hals) **103** U.N. Emblem and Dove

1970. "Europafrique". Multicoloured.
306 25f. Type **102** 50 20
307 30f. "Courtyard in Delft" (Hoogh) 60 35
308 150f. "Christina of Denmark" (Holbein) . . . 2·25 90
309 250f. "Hofburg Courtyard, Innsbruck" (Durer) . . . . 4·00 1·40

1970. Air. 25th Anniv of U.N.O.
310 **103** 60f. ultramarine, bl & grn 65 30
311 – 250f. violet, brown & grn 2·75 1·10
DESIGNS—HORIZ: 250f. U.N. emblem and two doves.

104 Front of Car

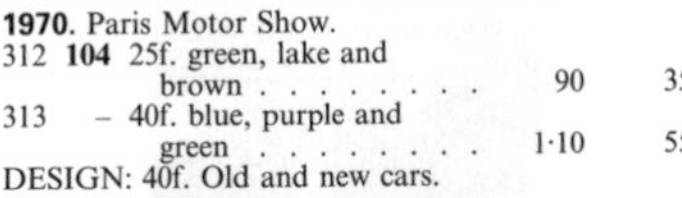

1970. Paris Motor Show.
312 **104** 25f. green, lake and brown 90 35
313 – 40f. blue, purple and green . . . . 1·10 55
DESIGN: 40f. Old and new cars.

105 "Holy Family"

1970. Christmas.
314 **105** 300f. silver . . . . 6·75
315 1000f. gold . . . . 18·00

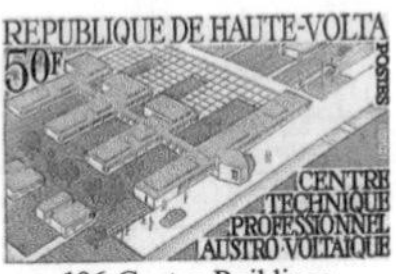

106 Centre Buildings

1970. Inauguration of Austro-Voltaic Centre.
316 **106** 50f. orange, green and red 55 30

107 Arms and Stork

1970. 10th Anniv of Independence.
317 **107** 30f. multicoloured (postage) 45 20
318 – 500f. blk, red & gold (air) 5·50
DESIGN—27 × 37 mm: 500f. Family and flag.
No. 318 is embossed on gold foil.

108 U.N. "Key" and Split Globe

1970. 10th Anniv of U.N. Declaration on Colonies.
319 **108** 40f. red, blue and brown 60 35
320 – 50f. multicoloured 55 30
DESIGN: 50f. Two maps of Africa showing former colonies.

109 Pres. Nasser **111** Heads of Different Races

110 Beingolo Hunting Horn

1971. Air. Pres. Nasser Commemoration.
321 **109** 100f. multicoloured . . . 90 40

1971. Musical Instruments.
322 **110** 5f. brown, red and blue 20 15
323 – 15f. brown, red and green 35 20
324 – 20f. red, grey and blue . . 65 20
325 – 25f. drab, green and red 80 40
INSTRUMENTS—VERT: 15f. Mossi "guitar"; 20f. Gurunssi "flutes". HORIZ: 25f. Lunga "drum".

1971. Racial Equality Year.
326 **111** 50f. brown, red & turq . . 55 30

112 "The Purple Herons" (Egypt, 1354)

1971. Air. Muslim Miniatures. Multicoloured.
327 100f. Type **112** . . . . . . 1·40 60
328 250f. Page from the Koran (Egypt, c. 1368–88) (vert) 2·75 1·25

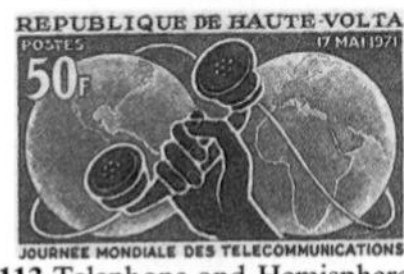

113 Telephone and Hemispheres

1971. World Telecommunications Day.
329 **113** 50f. violet, grey and brown 60 30

114 Olympic Rings and Events

1971. Air. "Pre-Olympic Year".
330 **114** 150f. red, violet and blue 2·25 1·10

115 Cutting Cane and Sugar Factory, Banfora **117** Scout and Pagodas

116 "Gonimbrasia hecate"

1971. Local Industries. Multicoloured.
331 10f. Type **115** 20 10
332 35f. Cotton-plant and textiles ("Voltex" project) 35 20

1971. Butterflies. Multicoloured.
333 1f. Type **116** 10 10
334 2f. "Hamanumida daedalus" 10 10
335 3f. "Ophideres materna" . . 20 10
336 5f. "Danaus chrysippus" . . 45 20
337 40f. "Hypolimnas misippus" 2·25 1·10
338 45f. "Danaus petiverana" . . 3·25 1·40

1971. Air. 13th World Scout Jamboree, Asagari (Japan).
339 **117** 45f. multicoloured 65 35

118 Actor with Fan **119** African with Seed-packet

1971. "Philatokyo" Stamp Exn, Tokyo. Mult.
340 25f. Type **118** 35 20
341 40f. Actor within mask . . . 50 25

1971. National Seed-protection Campaign. Multicoloured.
342 35f. Grading seeds (horiz) . . 40 20
343 75f. Type **119** 60 30
344 100f. Harvesting crops (horiz) 60 35

1971. 10th Anniv of Volta Red Cross. Surch **Xe ANNIVERSAIRE** and new value.
345 **101** 100f. on 30f. brown, red and purple . . . . . . 1·25 65

121 Teacher and Class

122 Soldier and Tractors

1971. "Women's Access to Education". Multicoloured.
346 35f. Type **121** 45 20
347 50f. Family learning alphabet 60 35

1971. Dakiri Project. Military Aid for Agriculture. Multicoloured.
348 15f. Type **122** 45 15
349 40f. Soldiers harvesting (horiz) 65 40

123 General De Gaulle and Map

1971. Air. De Gaulle Commemoration.
350 **123** 40f. multicoloured 55 55
351 – 500f. gold and green . . . 10·50 9·50
DESIGN—VERT (30 × 40 mm): 500f. De Gaulle.
No. 351 is embossed on gold foil.

1971. Air. 10th Anniv of African and Malagasy Posts and Telecommunications Union. As No. 432 of Rwanda. Multicoloured.
352 100f. U.A.M.P.T. H.Q. and Mossi dancer . . . . . . 1·10 50

124 "Simulium damnosum" and Preventive Measures

1971. Regional Anti-onchocerciasis Campaign.
353 **124** 40f. multicoloured 55 35

125 Pres. Lamizana

126 Children acclaiming Emblem

1971.
354 **125** 35f. multicoloured 30 20

1971. 25th Anniv of UNICEF.
355 **126** 45f. multicoloured 50 35

127 Peulh Straw Hut

1971. Traditional Housing (1st series). Mult.
356 10f. Type **127** 15 10
357 20f. Gourounsi house 30 15
358 35f. Mossi huts 45 30
See also Nos. 370/2.

128 Town Halls of Bobo-Dioulasso and Chalons-sur-Marne, France

1971. "Twin Cities" Co-operation.
359 **128** 40f. multicoloured 65 40

129 Ice-hockey

130 Running

1972. Air. Winter Olympic Games, Sapporo, Japan.
360 **129** 150f. purple, blue and red 1·90 1·00

1972. Air. UNESCO "Save Venice" Campaign. As T **145** of Senegal. Multicoloured.
361 100f. "La Musica" (P. Longhi) (vert) . . . . 1·90 1·00
362 150f. "Panorama da Ponte della Marina" (detail, Caffi) (horiz) . . . . . . 2·75 1·25

1972. Air. Olympic Games, Munich.
363 **130** 65f. brown, blue and green 60 45
364 – 200f. brown and blue . . 1·90 1·25
DESIGN: 200f. Throwing the discus.

131 Louis Armstrong

1972. Famous Negro Musicians. Multicoloured.
366 45f. Type **131** (postage) . . . 1·25 65
367 500f. Jimmy Smith (air) . . . 6·75 4·50

132 Globe and Emblems

1972. World Red Cross Day.
368 **132** 40f. multicoloured (postage) 55 40
369 100f. multicoloured (air) 1·10 45

133 Bobo House

134 Hair Style

1972. Traditional Housing (2nd series). Mult.
370 45f. Type **133** 55 30
371 50f. Dagari house 65 35
372 90f. Interior of Bango house (horiz) . . . . 1·25 50

1972. Upper Volta Hair Styles.
373 **134** 25f. multicoloured 35 15
374 – 35f. multicoloured 50 20
375 – 75f. multicoloured . . . . 1·10 45
DESIGNS: 35, 75f. Similar hair styles.

135 "Teaching"

1972. 2nd National Development Plan.
376 **135** 10f. mauve, green and turquoise (postage) . . 10 10
377 – 15f. brown, orange & green 20 15
378 – 20f. brown, green and blue 30 15
379 – 35f. brown, blue and green 50 20
380 – 40f. brown, green & purple 55 30
381 – 85f. black, red & blue (air) 70 50
DESIGNS: 15f. Doctor and patient ("Health"); 20f. Factory and silos ("Industry"); 35f. Cattle ("Cattle-raising"); 40f. Rice-planting ("Agriculture"); 85f. Road-making machine ("Infrastructure").

1972. 10th Anniv of West African Monetary Union. As T **156** of Senegal.
382 40f. grey, blue and mauve . . 45 20

136 Lottery Building

1972. 5th Anniv of National Lottery.
383 **136** 35f. multicoloured 50 20

137 Presidents Pompidou and Lamizana

1972. Air. Visit of Pres. Pompidou to Upper Volta.
384 **137** 40f. multicoloured . . . . 1·60 1·60
385 – 250f. multicoloured . . . 6·00 6·00
DESIGN: 250f. As T **137** but frame differs and portraits are embossed on gold.

138 Mary Peters (pentathlon)

1972. Air. Gold Medal-winners, Olympic Games, Munich. Multicoloured.
386 40f. Type **138** 35 15
387 65f. Ragno-Lonzi (fencing) 55 20
388 85f. Touritcheva (gymnastics) 80 30
389 200f. Maury (sailing) . . . . 1·60 65
390 300f. Meyfarth (high-jumping) . . . . 2·75 1·10

139 Donkeys

1972. Animals. Multicoloured.
392 5f. Type **139** 10 10
393 10f. Spur-winged geese . . . 55 20
394 30f. Goat 55 20
395 50f. Bull 80 30
396 65f. Dromedaries . . . . . . 1·10 40

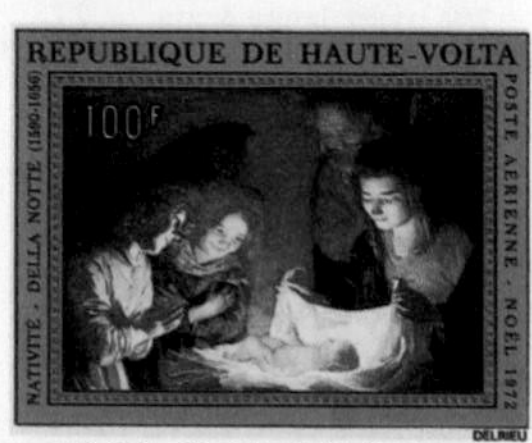

140 "The Nativity" (Della Notte)

1972. Air. Christmas. Religious Paintings. Multicoloured.
397 100f. Type **140** . . . . . . 1·10 65
398 200f. "The Adoration of the Magi" (Durer) . . . . . . 2·25 1·60

141 Mossi Hair-style and Village

1973. Air.
399 **141** 5f. multicoloured 10 10
400 40f. multicoloured 55 20

1973. 25th Anniv of W.H.O. No. 353 surch **O. M. S. 25 Anniversaire 45F.**
401 **124** 45f. on 40f. multicoloured 50 30

1973. 12th Anniv of African and Malagasy Posts and Telecommunications Union. As T **170** of Senegal.
402 100f. purple, red and yellow 1·00 55

1974. 15th Anniv of Council of Accord. As T **176** of Togo.
403 40f. multicoloured 30 20

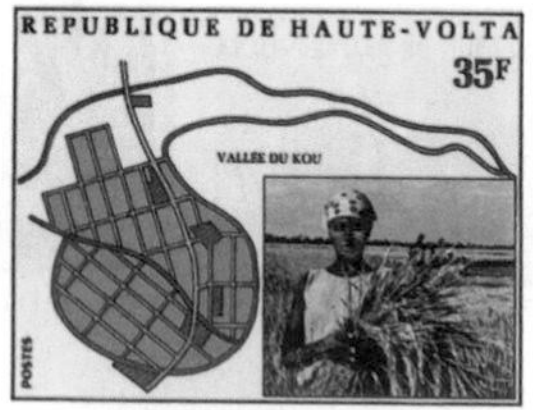

143 Map and Harvester

1974. Kou Valley Project.
404 **143** 35f. multicoloured 55 35

144 Woman, Globe and I.W.Y. Emblem

1975. International Women's Year.
405 **144** 65f. multicoloured 65 45

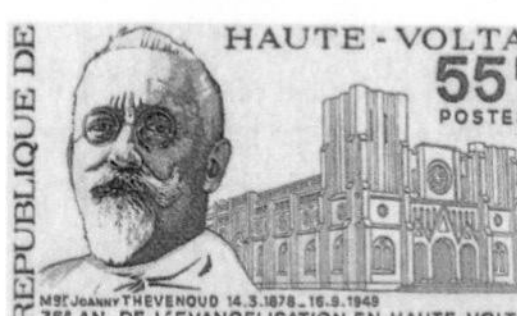

145 Mgr. Joanny Thevenoud and Cathedral

1975. 75th Anniv of Evangelization of Upper Volta.
406 **145** 55f. black, brown & green 65 35
407 – 65f. black, brown & green 80 45
DESIGN: 65f. Father Guillaume Templier and Cathedral.

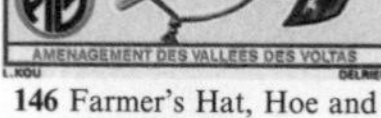

146 Farmer's Hat, Hoe and Emblem

147 Diseased People

1975. Development of the Volta Valleys.
408 **146** 15f. multicoloured 15 10
409 50f. multicoloured 50 25

1976. Campaign against Onchocerciasis (roundworm).
410 **147** 75f. mauve, orange & grn 85 35
411 250f. sepia, orange & brn 2·50 1·10

148 Globe and Emblem

1976. Non-aligned Countries' Summit Conference, Colombo, Sri Lanka. Multicoloured.
412 55f. Type **148** 45 20
413 100f. Globe, dove and emblem 90 50

149 Washington at Trenton

1976. "Interphil '76" International Stamp Exhibition, Philadelphia. Multicoloured.
414 60f. Type **149** (postage) . . . 55 15
415 90f. Seat of Government, Pennsylvania 80 20
416 100f. Siege of Yorktown (air) 80 30
417 200f. Battle of Cape St. Vincent . . . . 1·60 60
418 300f. Peter Francisco's act of bravery . . . . 2·40 80

150 U.P.U. and U.N. Emblems

1976. 25th Anniv of U.N. Postal Administration.
420 **150** 200f. blue, bronze and red 1·60 90

151 Tenkodogo Commune

152 Bronze Statuette

1977. Arms. Multicoloured.
421 10f. Type **151** 15 10
422 20f. Ouagadougou 20 10
423 55f. Type **151** 55 20
424 100f. As 20f. 70 35

1977.
425 **152** 55f. multicoloured 45 20
426 – 65f. multicoloured 45 20
DESIGN: 65f. Bronze statuette of woman with bowl.

153 Samo Granary

154 Gouin Basket

1977. Millet Granaries. Multicoloured.
427 5f. Type **153** 10 10
428 35f. Boromo 30 20
429 45f. Banfora 45 20
430 55f. Mossi 55 30

1977. Local Handicrafts. Baskets and Bags. Multicoloured.
431 30f. Type **154** 20 15
432 40f. Bissa 40 20
433 60f. Lobi 60 25
434 70f. Mossi 65 30

155 "Crinum ornatum"

156 General De Gaulle

1977. Fruits and Flowers. Multicoloured.
435 2f. "Cordia myxa" 10 10
436 3f. "Opilia celtidifolia" . . . 15 10
437 15f. Type **155** 20 10
438 25f. "Haemanthus multiflorus" 20 10
439 50f. "Hannoa undulata" . . 10 10
440 90f. "Cochlospermum planchonii" . . . . 1·00 40
441 125f. "Clitoria ternatea" . . 1·10 50
442 150f. "Cassia alata" . . . . 1·40 90
443 175f. "Nauclea latifolia" (horiz) . . . . 1·60 1·00
444 300f. "Bombax costatum" (horiz) . . . . 2·50 1·40
445 400f. "Eulophia cucullata" 4·25 1·40

1977. Personalities. Multicoloured.
446 100f. Type **156** . . . . . . 1·60 50
447 200f. King Baudouin . . . . 1·60 50

157 Queen Elizabeth II

1977. Silver Jubilee of Queen Elizabeth II. Multicoloured.
448 200f. Type **157** . . . . . . 1·60 50
449 300f. Queen Elizabeth II taking salute at Trooping the Colour . . . . 2·25 60

158 Cars on "Road" of Banknotes

1977. 10th Anniv of National Lottery.
451 **158** 55f. multicoloured 55 40

159 Selma Lagerlof and Bean Geese

1977. Nobel Prize Winners. Multicoloured.
452 55f. Type **159** (Literature, 1909) 80 25
453 65f. Guglielmo Marconi and early transmitter (Physics, 1909) 45 20
454 125f. Bertrand Russell, laurel, book and dove (Literature, 1950) 95 30
455 200f. Dr. L. C. Pauling, formula and atomic explosion (Chemistry, 1954) . . . . 1·40 50
456 300f. Robert Koch, slide and X-ray plate (Medicine, 1905) . . . . 2·40 70

160 "The Three Graces"

1977. 400th Birth Anniv of Rubens.
458 55f. "Heads of Four Negroes" (horiz) 40 10
459 65f. Type **160** 50 15
460 85f. "Bathsheba at the Fountain" 50 20
461 150f. "The Drunken Silenus" 1·25 45
462 200f. "The Story of Maria de Medici" (detail) . . . 1·60 55
463 300f. "The Story of Maria de Medici" (different detail) 2·50 70

161 Lenin

1977. 60th Anniv of Russian Revolution. Multicoloured.
465 10f. Type **161** 15 10
466 85f. Lenin Monument and Kremlin 65 40
467 200f. Lenin with children (horiz) . . . . 1·90 1·10
468 500f. Lenin and Pres. Brezhnev (horiz) . . . . . 4·50 2·25

162 Stadium and Brazil 5cr.80 Stamp of 1950

1978. World Cup Football Championship, Argentina. Multicoloured.
469 55f. Type **162** 35 10
470 65f. Brazil 1969 Pele stamp 45 15
471 125f. G.B. 1966 England winners stamp 90 30
472 200f. Chile 1962 World Cup stamp . . . . 1·40 45
473 300f. Switzerland 1954 World Cup stamp . . . . 2·00 65

163 Jean Mermoz

1978. Aviation History. Multicoloured.
475 65f. Type **163** 60 20
476 75f. Anthony Fokker 65 30
477 85f. Wiley Post 75 35
478 90f. Otto Lilienthal (vert) . . 85 35
479 100f. Concorde . . . . . . 1·10 40

164 "Crateva religiosa"

165 Microwave Antennae

1978. Trees of Upper Volta. Multicoloured.
481 55f. Type **164** 55 35
482 75f. "Ficus sp." 65 45

1978. World Telecommunications Day.
483 **165** 65f. multicoloured 55 40

166 Bobo Fetish Portals

1978. Sacred Objects. Multicoloured.
484 55f. Type **166** 55 30
485 65f. Mossi fetish 65 40

167 U.P.U. Emblem over Globe

1978. Air. Centenary of Paris Postal Congress.
486 **167** 350f. multicoloured . . . 2·75 1·60

168 Capt. Cook and H.M.S. "Endeavour"

1978. 250th Birth Anniv of Captain James Cook. Multicoloured.
487 65f. Type **168** . . . . 1·00 40
488 85f. Death of Captain Cook 55 15
489 250f. Cook and navigation instruments . . . . 1·60 55
490 350f. Cook and H.M.S. "Resolution" . . . . . . 3·50 2·25

169 Yuri Gagarin and Spacecraft

1978. "Conquest of Space". Multicoloured.
491 50f. Type **169** 40 20
492 60f. Jules Verne, "Apollo 11" badge and Neil Armstrong in space-suit . . . . 2·75 90
493 100f. Montgolfier medallion and balloon, Bleriot XI and Concorde 85 40

170 I.A.Y. Emblem

1978. Air. Anti-Apartheid Year.
494 **170** 100f. multicoloured . . . 80 45

1978. 25th Anniv of Coronation of Queen Elizabeth II. Nos. 448/9 optd **ANNIVERSAIRE DU COURONNEMENT 1953-1978.**
495 **157** 200f. multicoloured . . . 1·40 90
496 – 300f. multicoloured . . . 2·25 1·40

1978. Air. "Philexafrique" Stamp Exhibition, Libreville (Gabon), and Int Stamp Fair, Essen, West Germany (1st series). As T **237a** of Senegal. Multicoloured.
498 100f. River kingfisher and Hanover 1850 1ggr. stamp 2·00 1·40
499 100f. Hippopotamus and 1964 250f. Grey woodpecker stamp . . . . 2·00 1·40
See also Nos. 518/19.

172 "Trent Castle"

1978. 450th Death Anniv of Albrecht Durer. Multicoloured.
500 65f. Type **172** 55 15
501 150f. "Virgin and Child" (vert) . . . . 1·10 35
502 250f. "Saints George and Eustace" (vert) . . . . . . 1·90 60
503 350f. "H. Holzschuher" (vert) 2·75 90

173 Horus

174 Jules Verne

1978. Air. UNESCO Campaign: "Save the Philae Temples". Multicoloured.
504 200f. Type **173** . . . . . . 1·40 65
505 300f. Stylized falcon . . . . 2·00 1·00

1978. 150th Birth Anniv of Jules Verne (author).
506 **174** 20f. purple, blue and green . . . . 1·60 90

175 Human Rights Flame

1978. 30th Anniv of Declaration of Human Rights.
507 **175** 55f. multicoloured 50 30

1979. World Cup Football Championship Winners. Nos. 469/73 optd.
508 **162** 55f. multicoloured 45 25
509 – 65f. multicoloured 50 30
510 – 125f. multicoloured . . . 95 55
511 – 200f. multicoloured . . . 1·40 85
512 – 300f. multicoloured . . . 2·10 1·10

OPTS.: 55f. **VAINQUEURS 1950 URUGUAY 1978 ARGENTINE;** 65f. **VAINQUEURS 1970 BRESIL 1978 ARGENTINE;** 125f. **VAINQUEURS 1966 GRANDE BRETAGNE 1978 ARGENTINE;** 200f. **VAINQUEURS 1962 BRESIL 1978 ARGENTINE;** 300f. **VAINQUEURS 1954 ALLEMAGNE (RFA) 1978 ARGENTINE.**

177 Radio Station

1979. 10th Anniv of Posts and Telecommunications Organization. Multicoloured.
514 55f. Type **177** 40 20
515 65f. Loading mail aboard Beech A100 King Air monoplane 50 30

178 Children listening to Story

1979. International Year of the Child.
516 **178** 75f. multicoloured 85 45

179 Wave Pattern and Human Figures

1979. World Telecommunications Day.
517 **179** 70f. multicoloured 55 35

180 Basket Weaving and Upper Volta 50c. Stamp of 1963

1979. "Philexafrique" Exhibition, Libreville, Gabon (2nd series). Multicoloured.
518 100f. Type **180** . . . . . . 1·60 1·40
519 100f. Concorde, van, shouting man and U.P.U. emblem 1·60 1·40

181 Volta Squeaker

1979. Freshwater Fish. Multicoloured.
520 20f. Type **181** 50 25
521 50f. Como tetra . . . . . . 1·40 75
522 85f. Airbreathing catfish . . . 2·00 1·00

182 Class 241-P Steam Locomotive, France

1979. Death Centenary of Sir Rowland Hill. Multicoloured.
523 65f. Type **182** 55 20
524 165f. Class 215 diesel locomotive, Germany . . . 1·25 50
525 200f. Class "Warship" diesel locomotive, Great Britain 1·40 60
526 300f. French TGV express train . . . . 2·40 90

183 Kob

1979. Endangered Animals. Multicoloured.
528 30f. Type **183** 20 10
529 40f. Roan antelope 35 10
530 60f. Caracal 65 10
531 100f. African elephant . . . 1·00 35
532 175f. Hartebeest . . . . . . 1·60 45
533 250f. Leopard . . . . 2·50 55

184 Teacher and Class

1979. World Literacy Day. Multicoloured.
534 55f. Farmer reading book (vert) 45 35
535 250f. Type **184** . . . . . . 2·00 1·25

185 Telecommunications

1979. 3rd World Telecommunications Exhibition, Geneva.
536 **185** 200f. multicoloured . . . 1·40 70

186 King Vulture

1979. Protected Birds. Multicoloured.
537 5f. Type **186** 45 10
538 10f. Hoopoe 45 15
539 15f. Ruppell's griffon 55 20
540 25f. Intermediate egret . . . 75 25
541 35f. Ostrich . . . . 1·25 30
542 45f. Crowned crane . . . . . 1·50 35
543 125f. Cassin's hawk eagle . . 3·25 1·40

187 Airport

1979. 20th Anniv of A.S.E.C.N.A. (Air Navigation Security Agency).
544 **187** 65f. multicoloured 60 40

188 Headquarters Building

1979. Opening of West African Savings Bank Building, Dakar, Senegal.
545 **188** 55f. multicoloured 50 30

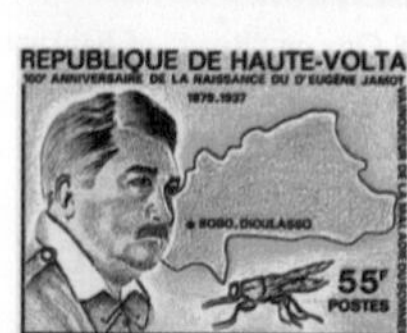

189 Jamot, Map and Tsetse Fly

1979. Birth Centenary of Eugene Jamot (discoverer of cure for sleeping sickness).
546 **189** 55f. multicoloured 85 45

190 Stamp under Magnifying Glass

1980. Stamp Day.
547 **190** 55f. multicoloured 50 25

191 Electric Locomotives

1980. 25th Anniv of World Locomotive Speed Record.
548 **191** 75f. multicoloured . . . . 1·40 45
549 100f. multicoloured . . . 2·10 65

192 Pope John Paul II

1980. Papal Visit. Multicoloured.
550 55f. Pres. Lamizana, Pope and Cardinal Pau Zoungrana (horiz) 85 35
551 100f. Type **192** . . . . . . 1·40 85

193 Telephone

194 Mountains and Statue

1980. World Telecommunications Day.
552 **193** 50f. multicoloured 40 20

1980. Solar Energy. Multicoloured.
553 65f. Sun and Earth 50 20
554 100f. Type **194** 80 40

195 Downhill Skiing (L. Stock)

1980. Winter Olympic Games Winners. Mult.
555 65f. Type **195** 45 15
556 100f. Women's downhill skiing (A. Moser-Proell) . . 65 20
557 200f. Figure skating (A. Poetzsch) . . . . . . 1·40 35
558 350f. Slalom (I. Stenmark) (vert) . . . . 2·25 60

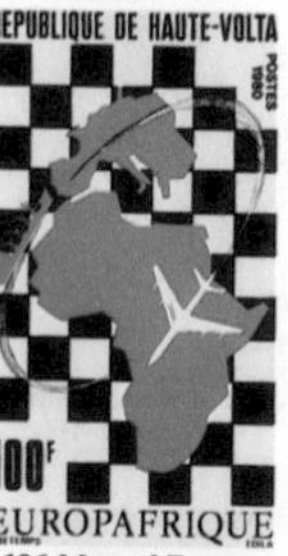

196 Map of Europe and Africa

197 Hand pushing back Sand Dune

1980. Europafrique.
560 **196** 100f. red, black and green 90 45

1980. Operation "Green Sahara". Multicoloured.
561 50f. Type **197** 50 20
562 55f. Hands planting saplings 60 35

198 Cyclists

1980. Air. Olympic Games, Moscow. Cycling.
563 **198** 65f. multicoloured 55 15
564 – 150f. multicoloured (vert) 1·10 40
565 – 250f. multicoloured . . . 1·90 55
566 – 350f. multicoloured . . . 2·75 90

DESIGNS: 150f. to 350f. Different cyclists.

199 Installation of Chief

1980. National History. Multicoloured.

568	30f. Type **199**	35	15
569	55f. Moro Naba, Emperor of Mossis	55	30
570	65f. Princess Guimbe Ouattara (vert)	60	30

200 Gourounsi Mask　**201** Tractor, Cattle and Grain (Agriculture)

1980. World Tourism Conference, Manila.

571 **200**	65f. multicoloured	55	30

1980. 5th Anniv of West African Economic Council. Multicoloured.

572	55f. Type **201**	35	15
573	65f. "Communications"	90	35
574	75f. Dam and highway	45	30
575	100f. "Industry"	1·40	50

1980. Air. Olympic Winners. Nos. 563/6 optd.

576 **198**	65f. multicoloured	30	25
577 –	150f. multicoloured	75	50
578 –	250f. multicoloured	1·25	90
579 –	350f. multicoloured	1·60	1·00

OVERPRINTS: 65f. **SOUKHOROUCHENKOV (URSS)**; 150f. **HESSLICH (RDA)**; 250f. **LANG (POL)**; 350f. **DILL-BUNDI (SUISSE)**.

203 Coat of Arms and Map

1980. 20th Anniv of Independence.

581 **203**	500f. multicoloured	4·25	2·50

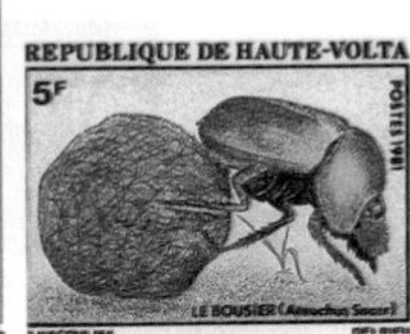

204 "Sistine Madonna" (detail)　**205** "Scarabaeus sacer"

1980. Christmas. Multicoloured.

582	60f. Type **204**	45	15
583	150f. "Virgin de l'Impannata"	1·10	40
584	250f. "Alba Madonna"	1·75	55

1980. 5th Anniv of African Post and Telecommunications. As T **272a** of Togo.

585	55f. multicoloured	50	30

1981. Insects. Multicoloured.

586	5f. Type **205**	10	10
587	10f. "Gryllus campestris"	10	10
588	15f. Termites	15	10
589	20f. "Mantis religiosa" (vert)	25	10
590	55f. "Nyctaon pyri"	75	25
591	65f. "Locusta migratorius" (vert)	85	35

206 Bobo Mask, Hounde　**207** College Emblem

1981. Masks. Multicoloured.

592	45f. Type **206**	40	15
593	55f. Bwa mask	45	20
594	85f. Kouroumba mask	60	35
595	105f. Gourounsi mask	80	40

1981. 25th Anniv of Notre-Dame College, Kologh'naba.

596 **207**	55f. multicoloured	45	20

208 Von Stephan and U.P.U. Emblem

1981. 150th Birth Anniv of Heinrich von Stephan (founder of U.P.U.).

597 **208**	65f. multicoloured	60	35

209 Ribbons forming Caduceus, I.T.U. and W.H.O. Emblems　**210** Series ZE Diesel-electric Train

1981. World Telecommunications Day.

598 **209**	90f. multicoloured	60	35

1981. Abidjan–Niger Railway. Multicoloured.

599	25f. Type **210**	50	15
600	30f. "La Gazelle" express train	90	25
601	40f. "Le Belier" express train	1·10	60

211 Group of Trees

1981. Tree Month.

602 **211**	70f. multicoloured	70	40

212 Nurse and Doctor with Medical Equipment　**213** Handicapped Sculptor

1981. 25th Anniv of Upper Volta Red Cross.

603 **212**	70f. multicoloured	60	40

1981. International Year of Disabled People.

604 **213**	70f. multicoloured	60	35

214 Koudougou

1981. Landscapes. Multicoloured.

605	35f. Type **214**	30	15
606	45f. Toma	40	20
607	85f. Volta Noire	65	30

215 Agricultural Scenes within Map

1981. World Food Day.

608 **215**	90f. multicoloured	70	45

216 Topi

1981. Wildlife Protection. Multicoloured.

609	5f. Type **216**	10	10
610	15f. Waterbuck	15	15
611	40f. Roan antelopes	35	20
612	60f. Dorcas gazelle	60	35
613	70f. African elephant	1·00	55

217 Campaign Emblem　**219** Donkey

218 Papaya

1981. Anti-Apartheid Campaign.

614 **217**	90f. red	60	35

1981. Fruit and Vegetables. Multicoloured.

615	20f. Type **218**	15	10
616	35f. Fruit and vegetables	30	15
617	75f. Mangoes (vert)	50	30
618	90f. Melons	60	35

1981. Stock Breeding. Multicoloured.

619	10f. Type **219**	10	10
620	25f. Pig	20	10
621	70f. Cow	55	20
622	90f. Helmeted guineafowl (vert)	80	40
623	250f. Rabbit	1·75	90

220 Women carrying Rice　**221** Father and Son

1981. 10th Anniv of West African Rice Development Association.

625 **220**	90f. multicoloured	90	45

1982. 20th Anniv of World Food Programme.

626 **221**	50f. multicoloured	40	15

222 Morhonaba Palace, Ouagadougou

1982. Traditional Houses. Multicoloured.

627	30f. Type **222**	20	10
628	70f. Bobo (horiz)	50	20
629	100f. Gourounsi (horiz)	70	30
630	200f. Peulh (horiz)	1·40	60
631	250f. Dagari (horiz)	1·60	65

223 Hexagonal Pattern

1982. World Telecommunications Day.

632 **223**	90f. multicoloured	85	40

224 Symbols of National Life　**225** Passing Ball

1982. National Life.

633 **224**	90f. multicoloured	60	30

1982. Air. World Cup Football Championship, Spain. Multicoloured.

634	70f. Type **225**	50	15
635	90f. Tackle	60	30
636	150f. Running with ball	1·10	40
637	300f. Receiving ball	2·00	85

226 Water Lily　**227** Symbols of Communication on Map of Africa

1982. Flowers. Multicoloured.

639	25f. Type **226**	15	10
640	40f. Kapoka	35	10
641	70f. Frangipani	60	35
642	90f. "Cochlospermum planchonii"	80	45
643	100f. Cotton	90	45

1982. African Post and Telecommunications Union.

644 **227**	70f. multicoloured	45	15
645	90f. multicoloured	65	35

228 Children holding Torch

1982. 25th Anniv of Cultural Aid Fund.

646 **228**	70f. multicoloured	50	30

229 Hairstyle

1983.

647 **229**	90f. multicoloured	65	30
648	120f. multicoloured	90	35
649	170f. multicoloured	1·25	50

230 Audience watching Film

1983. 8th Film Festival, Ouagadougou. Mult.

650	90f. Type **230**	85	55
651	500f. Dumarou Ganda	4·25	2·50

231 Joseph Montgolfier and First Demonstration of Hot-air Balloon, 1783

1983. Bicentenary of Manned Flight. Mult.
652 15f. Type **231** (postage) . . . 10 10
653 25f. Jean-Francois Pilatre de Rozier and first manned flight, 1783 . . . . 15 10
654 70f. Jacques Charles and hydrogen balloon "The Globe", 1783 . . . . . . 50 10
655 90f. John Jeffries and first Channel crossing, 1785 . . 65 20
656 100f. Wilhelmine Reichardt and ascent on a horse, 1798 (air) 85 30
657 250f. Salomon Andree and Spitzbergen–Expedition, 1897 . . . . 1·60 55

232 Campaign Emblem and River **233** Man reading Letter

1983. International Drinking Water Decade. Mult.
659 60f. Type **232** 45 20
660 70f. Woman carrying water 55 35

1983. World Communications Year. Multicoloured.
661 30f. Type **233** 20 15
662 35f. Type **233** 30 15
663 45f. Canoe and Boeing 727 airliner 40 20
664 90f. Woman on telephone . . 65 35

234 Space Shuttle "Challenger"

1983. Air. World Events. Multicoloured.
665 90f. Type **234** 60 20
666 120f. World Cup football final 85 30
667 300f. World Cup football final (different) . . . . . 1·90 60
668 450f. Royal wedding . . . . 2·50 85

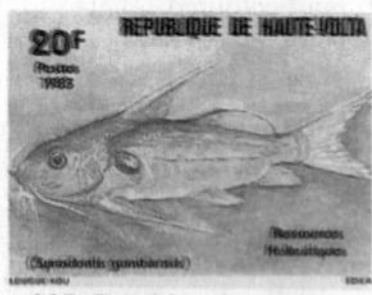

235 Gambian Squeaker

1983. Fishery Resources. Multicoloured.
670 20f. Type **235** 30 20
671 30f. Gunther's krib 75 45
672 40f. Line fishing (vert) . . . 75 45
673 50f. Net fishing 85 55
674 75f. Trap fishing . . . . . . 1·25 85

236 Soling Class Yacht

1983. Air. Pre-Olympic Year. Multicoloured.
675 90f. Type **236** 65 20
676 120f. Type 470 yacht . . . . 1·00 30
677 300f. Windsurfing . . . . . 2·25 60
678 400f. Windsurfing (different) 2·75 85

237 Planting a Sapling

1983. Campaign for Control of the Desert. Multicoloured.
680 10f. Type **237** 15 10
681 50f. Plantation 40 10
682 100f. Control of forest fires 90 35
683 150f. Woman cooking . . . 1·40 60
684 200f. Control of timber trade (vert) . . . . 1·60 90

238 Arms of Upper Volta

1983. 25th Anniv of Republic. Multicoloured.
685 90f. Type **238** 55 30
686 500f. Family with flag . . . 3·25 1·40

239 "Self-portrait" (Picasso)

1983. Celebrities' Anniversaries. Multicoloured.
687 120f. Type **239** . . . . . 1·40 35
688 185f. "Self-portrait with a Palette" (Manet (1832–1883)) . . . . 1·40 45
689 300f. Fresco detail (Raphael (1483–1520)) (horiz) . . . 2·25 60
690 350f. Fresco detail (Raphael) (different) (horiz) . . . 2·50 85
691 500f. J. W. Goethe (1749–1832) (portrait by Georg Oswald) . . . . 3·50 1·10

240 "Adoration of the Shepherds"

1983. Air. Christmas. Multicoloured.
692 120f. Type **240** 85 30
693 350f. "Virgin of the Garland" 2·40 65
694 500f. "Adoration of the Magi" . . . . 3·00 1·00

242 Handball

1984. Air. Olympic Games, Los Angeles. Multicoloured.
695 90f. Type **242** 55 20
696 120f. Volleyball 80 30
697 150f. Handball (horiz) . . . 1·10 35
698 250f. Basketball (horiz) . . . 1·60 50
699 300f. Football (horiz) . . . . 2·00 65

243 Greater Flamingo

1984. Air. Birds. Multicoloured.
701 90f. Type **243** . . . . 1·25 45
702 185f. Kori bustard (vert) . . 2·00 1·10
703 200f. Red-billed oxpecker (vert) . . . . 2·40 1·10
704 300f. Southern ground hornbill . . . . 3·25 1·75

244 Pres. Houari Boumedienne of Algeria

1984. Air. Celebrities. Multicoloured.
705 5f. Type **244** 10 10
706 125f. Gottlieb Daimler (automobile designer) and car 90 30
707 250f. Louis Bleriot (aviator) and Bleriot XI airplane . . 1·60 50
708 300f. Pres. Abraham Lincoln of U.S.A. and White House . . . . 2·25 55
709 400f. Henry Dunant (founder of Red Cross), red cross and battle of Solferino . . 2·75 70
710 450f. Auguste Piccard and bathyscape "Trieste" . . . 3·00 1·40
711 500f. Robert Baden-Powell (founder of Boy Scout movement) and scouts . . 3·25 95
712 600f. Anatole Karpov, 1978 world chess champion . . 3·75 1·10

245 Seedling and Clasped Hands within Circle of Flags **246** "Polystictus leoninus"

1984. 25th Anniv of Council of Unity.
714 **245** 90f. multicoloured 65 30
715 100f. multicoloured . . . 80 35

1984. Fungi and Flowers. Multicoloured.
716 25f. Type **246** (postage) . . . 40 20
717 185f. "Pterocarpus lucens" 1·60 60
718 200f. "Phlebopus colossus sudanicus" . . . . 3·25 1·25
719 250f. "Cosmos suplhureus" 2·25 85
720 300f. "Trametes versicolour" (air) . . . . 4·50 1·40
721 400f. "Ganoderma lucidum" 5·50 1·75

247 Cheetah with Cubs

1984. Protected Animals. Multicoloured.
723 15f. Type **247** (postage) . . . 10 10
724 35f. Two cheetahs 30 10
725 90f. Cheetah 65 20
726 120f. Cheetah with cubs (different) 90 35
727 300f. Baboons (air) . . . . . 2·25 55
728 400f. Marabou stork and African white-backed vulture . . . . 3·50 80

248 CC 2400 Diesel Locomotive and Lumber Train

1984. Transport. Multicoloured. (a) Locomotives.
730 40f. Type **248** 40 10
731 100f. Steam locomotive No. 1806 . . . . 1·00 20
732 145f. Steam locomotive "Livingstone" . . . . . . 1·90 40
733 450f. Class C51 steam locomotive, Japan . . . . 5·00 1·00

(b) Ships.
734 20f. "Maiden Queen" 15 10
735 60f. "Scawfell" 50 15
736 120f. "Harbinger" . . . . . 1·00 35
737 400f. "True Briton" . . . . 3·25 1·25

For later issues see **BURKINA FASO**.

OFFICIAL STAMPS

O **18** African Elephant

1963.
O112 O **18** 1f. sepia and brown . . 10 10
O113 5f. sepia and green . . 15 15
O114 10f. sepia and violet 20 20
O115 15f. sepia and orange 25 25
O116 25f. sepia and purple 35 35
O117 50f. sepia and green 65 65
O118 60f. sepia and red . . 75 75
O119 85f. sepia and myrtle 1·25 1·25
O120 100f. sepia and blue 1·50 1·50
O121 200f. sepia and mauve 2·75 2·75

POSTAGE DUE STAMPS

1920. Postage Due stamps of Upper Senegal and Niger, "Figures" Key-type, optd **HAUTE-VOLTA**.
D18 M 5c. green . . . . 15 3·25
D19 10c. red . . . . 15 3·25
D20 15c. grey . . . . 15 3·25
D21 20c. brown . . . . . . 25 3·75
D22 30c. blue . . . . 40 4·25
D23 50c. black . . . . . . 35 4·25
D24 60c. orange . . . . . . 40 4·25
D25 1f. violet . . . . 50 4·75

1927. Surch.
D40 M 2f. on 1f. mauve . . . . . 1·25 8·75
D41 3f. on 1f. brown . . . . . 1·75 9·75

1928. "Figures" key-type inscr "HAUTE-VOLTA".
D63 M 5c. green 35 75
D64 10c. red 35 75
D65 15c. grey 50 95
D66 20c. brown 50 95
D67 30c. blue . . . . 65 1·25
D68 50c. black . . . . . . 1·75 3·00
D69 60c. orange . . . . . . 2·25 4·00
D70 1f. violet . . . . 3·50 6·50
D71 2f. purple . . . . 6·75 10·00
D72 3f. brown . . . . 7·50 11·00

D **13** Red-fronted Gazelle

1962. Figures of value in black.
D 95 D **13** 1f. blue 10 10
D 96 2f. orange 10 10
D 97 5f. blue 15 15
D 98 10f. purple 30 30
D 99 20f. green 55 55
D100 50f. red . . . . 1·40 1·40

APPENDIX

The following stamps have either been issued in excess of postal needs or have not been available to the public in reasonable quantities at face value. Such stamps may later be given full listing if there is evidence of regular postal use.

1973.

Gold Medal Winners, Munich Olympic Games (2nd series). Air 50, 60, 90, 150, 350f.

Christmas 1972. Paintings of the Madonna and Child. Air 50, 75, 100, 125, 150f.

Moon Mission of "Apollo 17". Air 50, 65, 100, 150, 200f.

Gold Medal Winners, Munich Olympic Games (3rd series). Air 35, 45, 75, 250, 400f.

Exploration of the Moon. Air 50, 65, 100, 150, 200f.

Wild Animals. Air 100, 150, 200, 250, 500f.

10th Anniv of Organization of African Unity. Air 45f.

Europafrique. European Paintings. Air 50, 65, 100, 150, 200f.

Historic Railway Locomotives, French Railway Museum, Mulhouse. Air 10, 40, 50, 150, 250f.

Upper Volta Boy Scouts. Postage 20f.; Air 40, 75, 150, 200f.

Pan-African Drought Relief. Surch on values of 1973 Europafrique issue. Air 100f. on 65f., 200f. on 150f.

10th Death Anniv of President John Kennedy. Rockets. Postage 5, 10, 30f.; Air 200, 300f.

50th Anniv of International Police Organization (Interpol). 50, 65, 70, 150f.

Tourism. Postage 35, 40f.; Air 100f.

Religious Buildings. Postage 35, 40f.; Air 200f.

Folk-dancers. Postage 35, 40f.; Air 100, 225f.

Famous Men. 5, 10, 20, 25, 30, 50, 60, 75, 100, 175, 200, 250f.

1974.

World Cup Football Championship, Munich (1st issue). Postage 5, 40f.; Air 75, 100, 250f.

Pres. De Gaulle Commemoration. Postage 35, 40, 60f.; Air 300f.

World Cup Football Championship (2nd issue). Postage 10, 20, 50f.; Air 150, 300f.

Centenary of Universal Postal Union. Postage 35, 40, 85f.; Air 100, 200, 300f.

World Cup Football Championship (3rd issue). Previous Finals. Postage 10, 25, 50f.; Air 150, 200, 250f.

Centenary of Berne Convention. 1974 U.P.U. issue optd. Postage 35, 40, 85f., Air 100, 200, 300f.

Bouquets of Flowers. Postage 5, 10, 30, 50f.; Air 300f.

1975.

Birth Centenary of Sir Winston Churchill. 50, 75, 100, 125, 300f.

Bicentenary of American Revolution (1st issue). 35, 40, 75, 100, 200, 300f.

Railway Locomotives. Postage 15, 25, 50f.; Air 100, 200f.

Vintage and Veteran Cars. Postage 10, 30, 35f.; Air 150, 200f.

Bicent of American Revolution (2nd issue). Postage 30, 40, 50f.; Air 200, 300f.

Birth Cent of Dr Albert Schweitzer. Postage 5, 15f.; Air 150, 175, 200f.

"Apollo–Soyuz" Joint Space Test Project. Postage 40, 50f.; Air 100, 200, 300f.

Paintings by Picasso. Postage 50, 60, 90f.; Air 150, 350f.

"Expo '75" Exhibition, Okinawa, Japan. Postage 15, 25, 45, 50, 60f.; Air 150f.

Winter Olympic Games, Innsbruck. Postage 35, 45, 85f.; Air 100, 200f.

1976.

Olympic Games, Montreal (1st issue). "Pre-Olympic Year" (1975). Postage 40, 50, 100f.; Air 125, 150f.

Olympic Games, Montreal (2nd issue). Postage 30, 55, 75f.; Air 150, 200f.

Zeppelin Airships. Postage 10, 40, 50f.; Air 100, 200, 300f.

"Viking" Space Flight. Postage 30, 55, 75f.; Air 200, 300f.

1977.

Olympic Games Medal Winners, 1976 Olympic Games issue optd. Postage 30, 55, 75f.; Air 150, 200f.

1983.

Bicentenary of Manned Flight. Air 1500f.

UPPER YAFA — Pt. 19

A Sultanate of South Arabia, formerly part of the Western Aden Protectorate. Independent from September to December 1967 and then part of the People's Democratic Republic of Yemen.

1000 fils = 1 dinar.

1 Flag and Map

1967.

UY 1 1 5f. mult (postage) 20 20
UY 2 10f. multicoloured 20 20
UY 3 20f. multicoloured 25 25
UY 4 25f. multicoloured 30 25
UY 5 40f. multicoloured 50 30
UY 6 50f. multicoloured 65 40
UY 7 – 75f. multicoloured (air) 80 65
UY 8 – 100f. multicoloured . . . 1·10 75
UY 9 – 250f. multicoloured . . . 2·50 2·50
UY10 – 500f. multicoloured . . . 3·25 4·50

DESIGNS: UY7/10, Arms of Sultanate.

APPENDIX

The following stamps have either been issued in excess of postal needs or have not been available to the public in reasonable quantities at face value. Such stamps may later be given full listing if there is evidence of regular postal use.

1967.

Olympic Games, Mexico (1968). Postage 15, 25, 50, 75f.; Air 150f.

Sculptures. Postage 10, 30, 60, 75f.; Air 150f.

Paintings from the Louvre. Postage 50f.; Air 100, 150, 200, 250f.

World Cup Football Championship, England (1966). Postage 5, 10, 50f.; Air 100f.

Paintings by Old Masters. Postage 10, 15, 20, 25, 30, 40, 50, 60, 75f.; Air 150f.

Human Rights Year and 5th Death Anniv of J. F. Kennedy. Postage 5, 10, 50, 75f.; Air 125f.

Persian Miniatures. 10, 20, 30, 40, 50f.

Ballet Paintings. 20, 30, 40, 50, 60f.

Portraits by Old Masters. Postage 25, 50, 75f.; Air 100, 125, 150, 175, 200, 225, 250f.

Winter Olympic Games, Grenoble (1968). 1967 World Cup issue optd. Postage 5f. × 2, 10f. × 2, 50f. × 2; Air 100f. × 2.

20th Anniv of UNICEF. Paintings. Postage 50, 75f.; Air 100, 125, 250f.

Flower Paintings. Postage 5, 10, 50f.; Air 100, 150f.

URUGUAY — Pt. 20

A republic in S. America, bordering on the Atlantic Ocean, independent since 1828.

1856. 120 centavos = 1 real.
1859. 1000 milesimos = 100 centesimos = 1 peso.

1

1856. Imperf.
1 1 60c. blue £190
2 80c. green £170
3 1r. red £150

3

4

1858. Imperf.
5 3 120c. blue £130 £120
6 180c. green . . . . 38·00 55·00
7 240c. red . . . . 38·00 £225

1859. Imperf.
15 4 60c. purple . . . . 15·00 13·50
16 80c. yellow . . . . £130 25·00
17 100c. red . . . . 38·00 29·00
18 120c. blue . . . . 25·00 9·50
12 180c. green . . . . 9·50 11·50
13 240c. red . . . . 35·00 35·00

6 8 9

1864. Imperf.
20a 6 6c. red . . . . 5·75 3·75
21 8c. green . . . . 9·75 9·75
22 10c. yellow . . . . 13·50 9·25
23 12c. blue . . . . 5·75 4·50

1866. Surch in figures. Imperf.
24 6 5c. on 12c. blue . . . . . 9·50 19·00
25 10c. on 8c. green . . . . . 9·50 25·00
26 15c. on 10c. yellow . . . . 11·50 29·00
27a 20c. on 6c. red . . . . . . 13·50 29·00

1866. Imperf.
28 8 1c. black . . . . 95 1·50
29 9 5c. blue . . . . 1·50 85
30 10c. green . . . . 5·50 2·25
31 15c. yellow . . . . 9·25 3·75
32 20c. red . . . . 11·00 3·75

1866. Perf.
37 8 1c. black . . . . 2·25 2·25
33 9 5c. blue . . . . 2·00 35

34 10c. green . . . . 3·75 35
35 15c. yellow . . . . 2·00 1·40
36 20c. red . . . . 4·50 1·10

10

11

1877. Roul. Various frames.
42 10 1c. brown 25 20
43 11 5c. green 30 15
44 10 10c. red 40 15
45 20c. bistre 60 25
46 50c. black . . . . 3·00 1·10
47 1p. blue . . . . 17·00 5·50

15 J. Suarez

16

1881. Perf.
60a 15 7c. blue 75 90

1882.
62 16 1c. green 40 40
63 – 2c. red 35 35

The central device on the 2c. shows a mountain.

18 Arms

20 Gen. Maximo Santos

21 General Artigas

26

1883.
66 18 1c. green 50 30
67 2c. red 60 40
68 20 5c. blue 75 60
69 21 10c. brown . . . . 1·10 75

1883. Optd **1883 Provisorio**. Roul.
75 11 5c. green 50 40

1884. Optd **PROVISORIO 1884** or surch **1 CENTESIMO** also.
76 10 1c. on 10c. red 15 15
77 – 2c. red (No. 63) 50 50

1884.
79 26 5c. blue . . . . 1·00 50

28

29

31 Gen. Artigas

32 M. Santos 33 34

1884. Roul.
100 28 1c. green 20 20
83a 1c. grey 40 30
101 29 2c. red 20 25
85a 28 5c. blue . . . . 1·00 15
86 5c. lilac 25 10
87 31 7c. brown 95 60
103 7c. orange 60 40
88 32 10c. brown 20 20
89 33 20c. mauve 75 30
105 20c. brown 75 40
90 34 25c. lilac . . . . 1·40 50
106 25c. red . . . . 1·10 60

35

36

1887. Roul.
99 35 10c. mauve 70 40

1888. Roul.
104 36 10c. violet 25 25

1889. Optd **Provisorio**. Roul.
114 28 5c. lilac 15 15

38 39

40

41 42

43

44 Figure of Justice

45 Mercury

46

1889. Perf.
115 38 1c. green 40 20
116 39 2c. red 20 25
117 40 5c. blue 20 15
118 41 7c. brown 60 25
119 42 10c. green . . . . 1·50 25
120 43 20c. orange . . . . 1·10 30
121 44 20c. brown . . . . 2·00 40
122 45 50c. blue . . . . 3·50 1·10
123 46 1p. violet . . . . 8·50 2·00

See also Nos. 142/52, 220, 222 224 and 236/7.

1891. Optd **Provisorio 1891**. Roul.
133 28 5c. lilac 10 10

1892. Optd **Provisorio 1892** or surch also in words.
135 28 1c. green 40 40
137 43 1c. on 20c. orange 15 10
136 41 5c. on 7c. brown 15 30

50

51

52

53

54

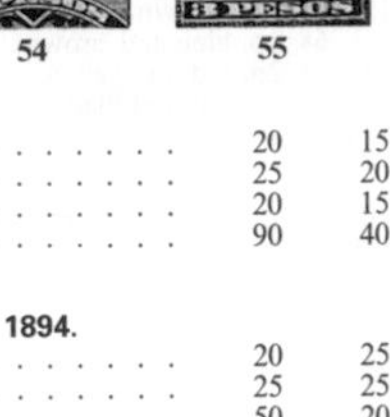
55

1892. Perf.
138 50 1c. green 20 15
139 51 2c. red 25 20
140 52 5c. blue 20 15
141 53 10c. orange 90 40

1894.
142 38 1c. blue 20 25
143 39 2c. brown 25 25
144 40 5c. red 50 20
145 41 7c. green . . . . 2·75 1·10
146 42 10c. orange . . . . 1·50 30
147 43 20c. brown . . . . 2·75 75
148 44 25c. red . . . . 3·50 1·50
149 45 50c. purple . . . . 6·25 2·25
150 46 1p. blue . . . . 11·00 3·00
151 54 2p. red . . . . 11·50 7·00
152 55 3p. purple . . . . 11·50 7·00

56 Gaucho

57 Solis Theatre

58 Steam Locomotive

59 Bull's Head

60 Ceres

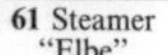
61 Steamer "Elbe"

62 Amazon

63 Mercury

64

65 Montevideo Fortress

66 Montevideo Cathedral

1895.

153	**56**	1c. bistre	20	20
154	**57**	2c. blue	20	20
155	**58**	5c. red	4·00	20
156	**59**	7c. green	3·75	1·00
157	**60**	10c. brown	85	30
158	**61**	20c. black and green	7·00	55
159	**62**	25c. black and brown	2·75	60
160	**63**	50c. black and blue	3·50	1·50
161	**64**	1p. black and brown	5·50	2·00
162	**65**	2p. green and violet	11·50	7·75
163	**66**	3p. blue and red	11·50	6·25

For further stamps in these types, see Nos. 183/93 and 221.

67 J. Suarez

68 J. Suarez Monument

72

1896. Unveiling of President Joaquin Suarez Monument.

177	**67**	1c. black and red	20	15
178	**68**	5c. black and blue	25	20
179	–	10c. black and lake	45	25

DESIGN: 10c. Larger stamp showing whole Suarez Monument.

1897. Optd **PROVISORIO 1897**.

180	**67**	1c. black and red	30	30
181	**68**	5c. black and blue	40	30
182	–	10c. black and lake	50	50

1897.

183	**56**	1c. blue	20	15
184	**57**	2c. purple	30	20
185	**58**	5c. green	3·50	15
186	**59**	7c. orange	1·75	60
187	**72**	10c. red	85	35
188	**61**	20c. black and mauve	6·50	40
189	**62**	25c. blue and red	1·50	35
190	**63**	50c. brown and green	2·75	70
191	**64**	1p. blue and brown	4·50	1·40
192	**65**	2p. red and yellow	4·50	65
193	**66**	3p. red and lilac	4·25	1·10

See also No. 223.

1897. End of Civil War. Optd with palm leaf and **PAZ 1897**.

197	**56**	1c. blue	40	30
198	**57**	2c. purple	55	55
199	**58**	5c. green	3·25	2·50
200	**72**	10c. red	1·40	1·40

1898. Surch **PROVISIONAL ½ CENTESIMO**.

209	**38**	½c. on 1c. blue	15	15
210	**56**	½c. on 1c. bistre	15	15
211	**67**	½c. on 1c. black and red	15	15
212	**57**	½c. on 2c. blue	15	15
213	**68**	½c. on 5c. black and blue	20	15
214	**59**	½c. on 7c. green	20	15

75 Liberty

76 Monument to Gen. Artigas

1898.

215	**75**	5m. red	20	20
216		5m. violet	25	25

1899.

217	**76**	5m. blue	25	15
218		5m. orange	25	15
220	**39**	2c. orange	20	20
221a	**58**	5c. blue	2·75	15
222	**41**	7c. red	2·25	1·10
223	**72**	10c. purple	30	25
224	**43**	20c. blue	1·10	20

1900. No. 182 surch **1900 5 CENTESIMOS** and bar.

229		5c. on 10c. black and lake	25	15

78

79

80

81

82

1900.

230	**78**	1c. green	30	15
231a	**79**	2c. red	10	15
232b	**80**	5c. blue	60	15
233	**81**	7c. brown	85	30
234	**82**	10c. lilac	45	20
236	**45**	50c. red	3·50	35
237	**46**	1p. green	11·00	75

85 General Artigas

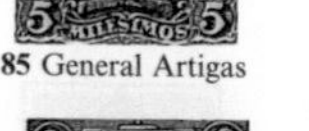
86

87

88

89

90

91

1904.

251	**85**	5m. yellow	30	15
252	**86**	1c. green	50	15
253a	**87**	2c. orange	20	15
254b	**88**	5c. blue	40	10
255	**89**	10c. lilac	40	20
256	**90**	20c. green	1·40	40
257	**91**	25c. bistre	1·50	40

1904. End of the Civil War. Optd **Paz-1904**.

258	**86**	1c. green	35	30
259	**87**	2c. orange	40	35
260	**88**	5c. blue	1·00	50

95

96

1906.

268	**95**	5c. blue	50	15

1906.

269	**96**	5c. blue	20	10
270		7c. brown	40	25
271		50c. red	2·25	40

98 Cruiser "Montevideo" and Cadet Ship "Diez-y-Ocho de Julio"

1908. 83rd Anniv of Revolt of the "Immortal 33" under Levalleja. Roul.

279	**98**	1c. green and red	1·25	85
280		2c. green	1·25	85
281		5c. green and orange	1·25	85

99 Montevideo Port

1909. Opening of the Port of Montevideo.

282	**99**	2c. black and brown	1·75	80
283		5c. black and red	1·75	80

1909. Surch **Provisorio** and value.

284	**82**	8c. on 10c. violet	40	30
285	**44**	23c. on 25c. brown	75	30

103 Centaur

1910. Centenary of 1810 Argentine Revolution.

286	**103**	2c. red	30	20
287		5c. blue	30	20

1910. Surch **PROVISORIO 5 MILESIMOS** (or **CENTESIMOS) 1910**.

294	**78**	5m. on 1c. green	10	20
295	**45**	5c. on 50c. red	15	30
296	**96**	5c. on 50c. red	40	30

107 Artigas

108

1910.

297	**107**	5m. purple	15	10
298		1c. green	15	10
299		2c. red	20	10
324		2c. pink	25	10
319		4c. yellow	30	10
300		5c. blue	20	10
301		8c. black	40	15
327		8c. blue	25	10
302		20c. brown	70	20
303	**108**	23c. blue	4·00	50
330		50c. orange	9·00	90
331		1p. red	9·00	1·25

109

114 Liberty offering Peace to Uruguay

1911. 1st Pan-American Postal Congress.

306	**109**	5c. black and red	35	25

1911. Centenary of Battle of Las Piedras. Surch **ARTIGAS**, value and **1811-1911**.

314	**81**	2c. on 7c. brown	35	25
315		5c. on 7c. brown	35	20

1913. Centenary of 1813 Conference. Optd **CENTENARIO DE LAS INSTRUCCIONES DEL AÑO XIII**.

332	**107**	2c. brown	30	40
333		4c. yellow	30	40
334		5c. blue	30	40

1918. Promulgation of New Constitution.

347	**114**	2c. brown and green	35	25
348		5c. blue and brown	35	25

115 Montevideo Harbour

116 Statue of Liberty, New York

118 J. E. Rodo

1919.

349	**115**	5m. grey and violet	20	10
350		1c. grey and green	25	10
351		2c. grey and red	25	10
352		4c. grey and orange	60	10
353		5c. grey and blue	70	10
354		8c. brown and blue	85	20
355		20c. grey and brown	3·00	35
356		23c. brown and green	4·25	70
357		50c. blue and brown	4·75	3·25
358		1p. blue and red	11·50	2·75

1919. Peace Commemoration.

359	**116**	2c. brown and red	20	10
360		4c. brown and orange	30	10
361		5c. brown and blue	35	10
362		8c. blue and brown	50	20
363		20c. black and bistre	1·40	40
364		23c. black and green	2·00	70

1920. Honouring J. E. Rodo (writer).

372	**118**	2c. black and lake	35	45
373		4c. blue and orange	40	30
374		5c. brown and blue	50	35

1921. Air. Optd with airplane and **CORREO AEREO**.

377	**44**	25c. brown	2·10	1·50

120 Mercury

122 Damaso A. Larranaga

1921.

378	**120**	5m. mauve	30	10
410		5m. black	20	10
380		1c. green	30	10
411		1c. mauve	25	10
411a		1c. violet	25	10
412		2c. orange	35	10
412a		2c. red	40	10
384		3c. green	40	20
385		4c. yellow	25	10
386		5c. blue	25	10
413		5c. brown	40	10
414		8c. red	55	50
388		12c. blue	1·10	50
389		36c. olive	4·50	1·50

1921. 150th Birth Anniv of D. A. Larranaga.

390	**122**	5c. slate	75	55

127 Artigas Monument

128 Southern Lapwing

1923. Unveiling of Monument to Artigas.

418	**127**	2c. brown and red	30	10
419		5c. brown and violet	30	10
420		12c. brown and blue	40	20

1923. Various sizes.

450	**128**	5m. grey	35	20
422		1c. yellow	25	30
451		1c. pink	60	30
477		1c. purple	1·10	40
528		1c. violet	25	40
423		2c. mauve	25	30
529		2c. red	25	40
453		3c. green	80	30
454		5c. blue	60	20
455		8c. red	80	30
456		10c. green	60	20
457		12c. blue	90	30
458		15c. mauve	80	30
459		20c. brown	1·50	30
429		36c. green	4·00	1·50
460		36c. red	6·50	1·25
430		50c. orange	7·50	2·10
461		50c. olive	7·50	1·75
431		1p. red	30·00	17·00
462		1p. buff	11·00	4·00
432		2p. green	30·00	17·00
463		2p. lilac	27·00	12·00

130 131 Biplane

1923. Centenary of Battle of Sarandi.

No.	Type	Description	Unused	Used
433	130	2c. green	35	25
434		5c. red	35	25
435		12c. blue	35	25

1924. Air.

No.	Type	Description	Unused	Used
436	131	6c. blue	75	85
437		10c. red	1·10	1·25
438		20c. green	2·00	2·00

134 "Victory" of Samothrace

1924. Uruguayan Football Victory in Olympic Games.

No.	Type	Description	Unused	Used
464	134	2c. red	8·50	6·25
465		5c. purple	8·50	6·25
466		12c. blue	8·50	6·25

135 Landing of Lavalleja

1925. Centenary of Rising against Brazilian Rule.

No.	Type	Description	Unused	Used
467	135	2c. grey and red	60	70
468		5c. grey and mauve	60	70
469		12c. grey and blue	60	70

136 Parliament House

1925. Inauguration of Parliament House.

No.	Type	Description	Unused	Used
470	136	5c. black and violet	60	40
471		12c. black and blue	60	40

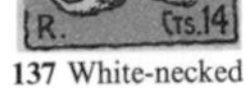

137 White-necked Heron 138 Gen. F. Rivera

139 Gaucho Cavalryman at Rincon

1925. Air. Centenary of Assembly of Florida.

(a) Inscr "MONTEVIDEO".

No.	Type	Description	Unused	Used
472	137	14c. black and blue	15·00	7·75

(b) Inscr "FLORIDA".

No.	Type	Description	Unused	Used
473	137	14c. black and blue	15·00	7·75

1925. Centenary of Battle of Rincon.

No.	Type	Description	Unused	Used
474	138	5c. pink (postage)	40	30
475	139	45c. green (air)	—	4·50

140 Battle of Sarandi

1925. Centenary of Battle of Sarandi.

No.	Type	Description	Unused	Used
482	140	2c. green	60	55
483		5c. mauve	60	55
484		12c. blue	75	60

141 Albatross 145 New G.P.O., Montevideo

1926. Air. Imperf.

No.	Type	Description	Unused	Used
495	141	6c. blue	70	70
496		10c. red	95	95
497		20c. green	1·40	1·40
498		25c. violet	1·40	1·40

See also Nos. 569/80.

1927. Philatelic Exhibition, Montevideo. Imperf.

No.	Type	Description	Unused	Used
534	145	2c. green	2·00	2·00
535		5c. red	2·00	2·00
536		8c. blue	2·00	2·00

1928. Opening of San Carlos–Rocha Railway. Surch **Inauguracion Ferrocarril SAN CARLOS a ROCHA 14/1/928** and value.

No.	Type	Description	Unused	Used
537	128	2c. on 12c. blue	2·25	2·25
538		5c. on 12c. blue	2·25	2·25
539		10c. on 12c. blue	2·25	2·25
540		15c. on 12c. blue	2·25	2·25

147 Gen. F. Rivera (after M. Bucasso)

1928. Centenary of Conquest of Las Misiones.

No.	Type	Description	Unused	Used
541	147	5c. red	30	15

148 Artigas 149 Artigas Statue, Paysandu

1928.

No.	Type	Description	Unused	Used
542	148	5m. black	10	10
762		5m. brown	10	10
868		5m. orange	10	10
543		1c. violet	10	10
544		1c. purple	10	10
869		1c. blue	10	10
687		15m. black	25	15
545		2c. green	10	10
764		2c. brown	10	10
870		2c. red	10	10
546		3c. bistre	20	10
871		3c. green	10	10
548		5c. red	15	10
549		5c. olive	15	10
766		5c. blue	15	10
767		5c. turquoise	30	10
872		5c. violet	10	10
550		7c. red	15	10
551		8c. blue	20	10
552		8c. brown	20	10
553		10c. orange	30	15
768		12c. blue	30	10
556		15c. blue	45	10
557		17c. violet	40	15
558		20c. brown	55	15
757		20c. buff	70	35
770		20c. red	40	30
771		20c. violet	35	10
560		24c. red	70	40
561		24c. yellow	40	35
562		36c. olive	70	40
563		50c. grey	1·75	95
564		50c. black	2·25	85
772		50c. sepia	1·10	45
566		1p. green	4·00	1·50
567	149	2p. brown and blue	5·00	2·75
568		3p. black and red	6·25	6·25

1928. Air. Re-issue of T **141**. Perf.

No.	Type	Description	Unused	Used
634	141	4c. brown	1·50	1·50
569		10c. green	75	70
570		20c. orange	1·10	85
571		30c. blue	1·10	85
572		38c. green	1·75	1·50
573		40c. yellow	2·10	2·00
574		50c. violet	2·25	2·25
575		76c. orange	4·25	4·25
576		1p. red	3·50	3·50
577		1p.14 blue	10·00	8·75
578		1p.52 yellow	15·00	15·00
579		1p.90 violet	18·00	17·00
580		3p.80 red	50·00	45·00

150 Goal Posts 151 General Garzon

1928. Uruguayan Football Victories in 1924 and 1928 Olympic Games.

No.	Type	Description	Unused	Used
581	150	2c. purple	4·50	3·75
582		5c. red	4·50	3·75
583		8c. blue	4·50	3·75

1928. Unveiling of Monument to Gen. Garzon. Imperf.

No.	Type	Description	Unused	Used
584	151	2c. red	75	75
585		5c. green	75	75
586		8c. blue	75	75

154 Artigas 156 Pegasus

1929.

No.	Type	Description	Unused	Used
759	154	1p. brown	3·00	1·40
596		2p. green	5·00	2·75
597		2p. red	11·00	7·75
760		2p. blue	5·75	5·50
598		3p. blue	7·00	5·00
761		3p. black	8·75	7·00
600		4p. violet	11·00	8·50
601		4p. green	11·00	7·75
602		5p. red	13·50	11·00
603		5p. orange	11·00	7·75
604		10p. blue	38·00	35·00
605		10p. red	38·00	35·00

1929. Air. Size 34½ × 23½ mm.

No.	Type	Description	Unused	Used
617	156	1c. mauve	25	25
659		1c. blue	25	25
618		2c. yellow	25	25
660		2c. olive	25	25
619		4c. blue	45	40
661		4c. lake	45	40
620		6c. violet	25	40
662		6c. brown	25	40
621		8c. orange	1·10	1·10
663		8c. grey	1·25	1·10
664		8c. green	35	30
622		16c. blue	1·10	75
665		16c. red	1·10	1·10
623		24c. purple	95	95
666		24c. violet	1·25	1·10
624		30c. brown	1·10	1·10
667		30c. green	60	30
625		40c. brown	2·00	2·00
668		40c. orange	2·00	1·75
626		60c. blue	1·75	1·25
669		60c. green	3·00	2·25
670		60c. red	95	60
627		80c. blue	3·00	3·00
671		80c. green	5·00	4·00
628		90c. blue	3·00	2·10
672		90c. olive	5·00	4·00
629		1p. red	2·25	2·00
630		1p.20 olive	7·00	7·00
673		1p.20 red	11·00	9·25
631		1p.50 purple	7·00	5·50
674		1p.50 sepia	3·75	3·50
632		3p. red	11·50	11·00
675		3p. blue	7·75	7·75
633		4p.50 black	20·00	18·00
676		4p.50 lilac	14·00	12·50
677		10p. blue	7·00	5·50

For stamps as Type **156**, but smaller, see Nos. 725/44.

157 Rio Negro Railway Bridge 159 "Peace"

1930. Independence Centenary.

No.	Type	Description	Unused	Used
639	157	5m. black	55	15
640	–	1c. sepia	20	15
641	159	2c. lake	20	15
642	–	3c. green	25	20
643	–	5c. blue	25	20
644	–	8c. red	35	20
645	–	10c. violet	25	35
646	–	15c. green	30	25
647	–	20c. blue	2·00	70
648	–	24c. lake	60	30
649	–	50c. red	4·00	1·75
650	–	1p. black	3·00	1·50
651	–	2p. blue	7·00	4·50
652	–	3p. red	10·00	7·00
653	–	4p. orange	11·50	8·50
654	–	5p. lilac	17·00	10·00

DESIGNS—HORIZ: 1c. Gaucho horse-breaker; 5c. Head of Liberty and Uruguayan flag; 10c. "Artigas", from picture by Blanes; 15c. Seascape; 20c. Montevideo harbour, 1830; 24c. Head of Liberty and Arms of Uruguay; 50c. Montevideo Harbour, 1930. VERT: 3c. Montevideo; 8c. Allegorical figure with torch; 1p. to 5p. Artigas Monument.

161 163 J. Zorrilla de San Martin

1930. Fund for Old People.

No.	Type	Description	Unused	Used
655	161	1c.+1c. violet	20	15
656		2c.+2c. green	25	25
657		5c.+5c. red	30	30
658		8c.+8c. blue	30	30

1932.

No.	Type	Description	Unused	Used
679	163	1½c. purple	20	10
680		3c. green	30	10
681		7c. blue	35	10
682		12c. blue	30	35
683		1p. brown	9·25	6·25

1932. Surch.

No.	Type	Description	Unused	Used
684	161	1½c. on 2c.+2c. green	25	15

167 J. Zorrilla de San Martin 168 Flag of the Race

1933. Various portraits.

No.	Type	Description	Unused	Used
689	–	15m. red (Lavalleja)	15	10
690	–	3c. green (Rivera)	10	10
691	167	7c. grey	15	10

1933. 441st Anniv of Columbus' Departure from Palos.

No.	Type	Description	Unused	Used
692	168	3c. green	15	20
693		5c. pink	20	25
694		7c. blue	20	20
695		8c. red	60	30
696		12c. blue	25	25
697		17c. violet	75	40
698		20c. brown	1·50	95
699		24c. bistre	2·00	95
700		36c. red	2·25	1·10
701		50c. brown	2·75	1·40
702		1p. brown	7·75	3·50

169 Sower

1933. Opening of the 3rd National Assembly.

No.	Type	Description	Unused	Used
703	169	3c. green	20	15
704		5c. violet	35	25
705		7c. blue	30	20
706		8c. red	40	40
707		12c. blue	75	45

170 Map and Albatross

1933. 7th Pan-American Conference, Montevideo.

No.	Type	Description	Unused	Used
708	170	3c. green, brown and black	1·10	1·10
709		7c. blue, black and brown	60	45
710		12c. blue, red and grey	95	75
711		17c. red, blue and grey	2·10	2·10
712		20c. yellow, green and blue	2·25	2·25
713		36c. red, yellow and black	3·00	3·00

1934. Air. Closure of the 7th Pan-American Conference. Optd **SERVICIO POSTAL AEREO 1-1-34** in circle.

No.	Type	Description	Unused	Used
714	170	17c. red, blue and grey	7·75	6·25
715		36c. red, yellow and black	7·25	6·25

172

1934. 1st Anniv of Third Republic.
716 **172** 3c. green 25 35
717 7c. red 25 35
718 12c. blue 60 30
719 17c. brown and pink 75 70
720 20c. yellow and grey 95 75
721 36c. violet and green 95 95
722 50c. grey and blue 2·50 2·00
723 1p. red and mauve 6·25 4·00

1935. Air. As T **156**, but size 31½ × 21½ mm.
725 15c. yellow 95 75
726 22c. red 60 50
727 30c. purple 95 75
728 37c. purple 50 40
729 40c. red 75 50
730 47c. red 1·50 1·40
731 50c. blue 50 50
732 52c. blue 1·50 1·40
733 57c. blue 75 70
734 62c. green 70 50
735 87c. green 2·10 1·75
736 1p. olive 1·40 85
737 1p.12 brown 1·40 85
738 1p.20 brown 4·50 3·75
739 1p.27 brown 4·50 3·75
740 1p.62 red 3·00 3·00
741 2p. lake 5·00 4·50
742 2p.12 grey 5·00 4·50
743 3p. blue 4·50 4·50
744 5p. orange 16·00 16·00

173 Friendship of Uruguay and Brazil
174 Florencio Sanchez

1935. Visit of President Vargas of Brazil.
747 **173** 5m. brown 50 30
748 15m. black 25 25
749 3c. green 30 25
750 7c. orange 35 20
751 12c. blue 50 50
752 50c. brown 2·00 1·50

1935. 25th Death Anniv of F. Sanchez (dramatist).
753 **174** 3c. green 15 10
754 7c. brown 20 10
755 12c. blue 55 35

176 Rio Negro Dam
178 Artigas

1937.
780 **176** 1c. violet (postage) 30 10
781 10c. blue 20 10
782 15c. red 75 50
783 1p. brown 3·00 1·10
793 8c. green (air) 35 35
794 20c. green 75 50
785 35c. brown 2·10 2·00
786 62c. green 25 20
787 68c. orange 60 40
788 68c. brown 50 20
789 75c. violet 2·10 60
790 1p. red 75 55
791 1p.38 red 7·00 6·25
792 3p. blue 3·75 75

1939. (a) Plain background.
806 **178** 5m. orange 10 10
807 1c. blue 10 10
808 2c. violet 10 10
809 5c. brown 15 10
810 8c. red 20 10
811 10c. green 35 10
812 15c. blue 40 30
813 1p. brown 1·25 30
1008 1p. purple 1·25 30
814 2p. lilac 3·00 1·25
815 4p. orange 3·75 1·50
816 5p. red 5·25 2·50
Nos. 806/12 are size 16 × 19 mm. No. 1008 is 18 × 22 mm. and Nos. 813/6 are 24 × 29½ mm.

(b) Lined background. (i) Size 17 × 22 mm.
835 **178** 5m. orange 10 10
848 5m. black 10 10
849 5m. blue 10 10
836 1c. blue 10 10
837 1c. purple 10 10
838 2c. violet 10 10
839 2c. orange 15 10
840a 2c. brown 10 10
1152 2c. grey 10 10
841 3c. green 15 10
842 5c. brown 15 10
843b 7c. blue 10 10
844 8c. red 25 10
845 10c. green 15 10
851 10c. brown 25 10
852 12c. blue 25 10
853 20c. mauve 70 15
846 50c. bistre 3·00 60
847 50c. green 2·10 75
1153 50c. brown 10 10

(ii) Size 23½ × 29½ mm.
1024 **178** 2p. brown 3·50 1·50

180 Airplane over "La Carreta" (sculpture, Jose Bellini)

1939. Air.
817 **180** 20c. blue 30 25
818 20c. violet 20 25
820 35c. red 25 20
821 50c. orange 25 20
822 75c. pink 30 15
823 1p. blue 85 10
824 1p.38 violet 1·50 60
825 1p.38 orange 1·40 1·25
826a 2p. blue 2·25 45
827 5p. lilac 3·00 60
828 5p. green 3·75 1·50
829 10p. red 23·00 15·00

181 Congress of Montevideo

1939. 50th Anniv of 1st International Juridical Congress, Montevideo.
830 **181** 1c. red 20 10
831 2c. green 25 20
832 5c. red 25 20
833 12c. blue 30 35
834 50c. violet 1·10 75

183 Juan Manuel Blanes (artist)
185 Francisco Acuna de Figueroa

1941. 40th Death Anniv of Blanes.
855 **183** 5m. brown 20 10
856 1c. brown 20 10
857 2c. green 20 10
858 5c. red 50 10
859 12c. blue 60 45
860 50c. violet 2·75 2·10

1942. 80th Death Anniv of Figueroa (author of words of National Anthem).
863 **185** 1c. brown 15 15
864 2c. green 15 15
865 5c. red 30 15
866 12c. blue 60 40
867 50c. violet 1·75 1·50

1943. Surch **Valor $ 0.005.**
873 **178** 5m. on 1c. blue

187
189 Clio

1943.
874 **187** 1c. on 2c. brown 10 10
875 2c. on 2c. brown 15 10

1943. Centenary of Historical and Geographical Institute. Montevideo.
878 **189** 5m. violet 20 10
879 1c. blue 20 10
880 2c. red 35 15
881 5c. brown 35 20

191
192 Emblems of Y.M.C.A.

1944. 75th Anniv of Founding of Swiss Colony.
889 **191** 1c. on 3c. green 10 10
890 5c. on 7c. brown 20 10
891 10c. on 12c. blue 40 25

1944. Centenary of Young Men's Christian Assn.
892 **192** 5c. blue 10 10

1944. Air. Air stamps of 1935, Nos. 730, etc, surch.
893 40c. on 47c. red 25 40
894 40c. on 57c. blue 30 25
895 74c. on 1p.12 brown 30 25
896 79c. on 87c. green 1·10 75
897 79c. on 1p.27 brown 1·50 1·25
898 1p.20 on 1p.62 red 85 60
899 1p.43 on 2p.12 grey 1·10 75

194 Legislative Palace

1945. Air.
900 **194** 2p. blue 1·75 70

195 Book
198 Statue

1945. Birth Centenary of Jose Pedro Varela (writer).
901 **195** 5m. green 15 10
902 – 1c. brown (Varela) 15 10
903 – 2c. red (Statue) 15 10
904a **198** 5c. blue 15 10
Nos. 902/3 are vert.

205 Eduardo Acevedo (statesman)
200 Jose Pedro Varela (writer)

1945.
905 – 5m. violet 10 10
911 – 1c. brown 10 10
912 **205** 2c. purple 10 10
945 – 3c. green 10 10
906 **200** 5c. red 15 10
907 – 10c. blue 25 15
946 – 20c. brown and green 55 30
PORTRAITS: 5m. Santiago Vazquez (statesman); 1c. Sylvestre Blanco (statesman); 3c. Bruno Mauricio de Zabala (founder of Montevideo); 10c. Jose Ellauri (President, 1873–75); 20c. Col. Luis de Larrobla (first Postmaster).

206 Full-rigged Ship "La Eolo"

1945. Air.
913 **206** 8c. green 2·50 45

1945. Air. Victory. Surch with figure as "Victory of Samothrace", **1945** and new value. No. 908 optd **VICTORIA** also.
914 **180** 14c. on 50c. orange 35 30
915 23c. on 50c. orange 40 35
916 23c. on 1p.38 orange 50 40
908 **156** 44c. on 75c. brown 70 40
917 **180** 1p. on 1p. 38 orange 2·00 1·10

1946. Inaug of Rio Negro Hydro-electric Power Plant. Optd **INAUGURACION DICIEMBRE, 1945.** No. 918 also surch **CORREO 20 CENTS.**
918 **176** 20c. on 68c. brown (postage) 80 35
919 62c. green (air) 50 45

1946. As T **187.** (a) Postage. Optd **CORREOS** and Caduceus.
920 **187** 5m. orange 10 10
921 2c. brown 10 10
922 3c. green 10 10
923 5c. blue 10 10
924 10c. brown 15 10
925 20c. green 50 15
926 50c. brown 1·10 60
927 3p. red 4·25 2·25

(b) Air. Optd **SERVICIO AEREO** and an airplane.
928 **187** 8c. red 10 10
929 50c. brown 40 25
930 1p. blue 50 30
931 2p. olive 2·25 1·10
932 3p. red 2·25 1·10
933 5p. red 4·50 3·00

217 Douglas DC-4
215 National Airport

1947. Air.
947 **217** 3c. brown 10 10
948 8c. red 15 10
949 10c. black 10 10
950 10c. red 10 10
951 14c. blue 25 15
952 15c. brown 15 10
953 20c. purple 15 15
954 21c. lilac 20 15
955 23c. green 25 20
956 27c. green 20 10
957 31c. brown 30 15
958 36c. blue 20 10
959 36c. black 20 15
960 50c. turquoise 35 25
961 50c. blue 25 10
962 62c. blue 40 25
963 65c. red 40 25
964 84c. orange 55 40
941 **215** 1p. brown and red 95 20
965 **217** 1p.08 plum 65 45
966 2p. blue 1·10 40
942 **215** 3p. brown and blue 1·75 95
967 **217** 3p. orange 1·25 50
943 **215** 5p. brown and green 3·75 2·00
968 **217** 5p. green 2·50 1·10
969 5p. grey 1·50 75
944 **215** 10p. brown and purple 4·00 3·00
970 **217** 10p. green 6·25 3·50

1947. As T **187** but surch in figures above shield and wavy lines.
976 2c. on 5c. blue 10 10
977 3c. on 5c. blue 10 10

219 "Ariel"
221 Bas-reliefs

1948. Unveiling of Monument to J. E. Rodo (writer).
978 **219** 1c. brown and olive 10 10
979 – 2c. brown and violet 10 10
980 **221** 3c. brown and green 15 10
981 5c. brown and mauve 20 10
982 10c. brown and red 20 10
983 12c. brown and blue 25 15
984 **219** 20c. brown and purple 55 35
985 – 50c. brown and red 1·50 70
DESIGN: 2, 50c. Bust of J. E. Rodo.
The 5c. and 12c. are as Type **221** but inscr "UN GRAN AMOR ES EL ALMA MISMA DE QUIEN AMA".

1948. Air. As T **187**, optd **AVIACION** and airplane.
986 12c. blue 20 10
987 24c. green 35 15
988 36c. grey 50 25

223 Paysandu
225 River Santa Lucia Railway Bridge

1948. Industrial and Agricultural Exhibitions, Paysandu.
989 **223** 3c. green 15 10
990 – 7c. blue 20 10
DESIGN—HORIZ: 7c. Livestock, sower and arms of Paysandu.

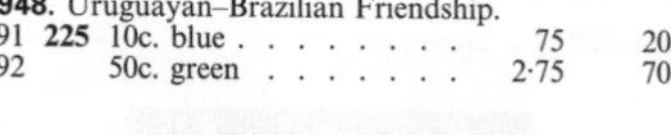

1948. Uruguayan–Brazilian Friendship.
991 **225** 10c. blue 75 20
992 50c. green 2·75 70

226 Ploughing

1949. 4th American Labour Conference.
993 **226** 3c. green 15 10
994 – 7c. blue 20 10
DESIGN—HORIZ: 7c. Horseman herding cattle.

227 Medical Faculty

1949. Air. Centenary of Montevideo University.
995 – 15c. red 10 10
996 **227** 27c. brown 15 10
997 – 31c. blue 25 10
998 – 36c. green 30 10
DESIGNS: 15c. Architectural faculty; 31c. Engineering faculty; 36c. View of University.

228 Cannon and Buildings

229 Kicking Football

1950. Bicentenary of Cordon (district of Montevideo).
1003 **228** 1c. mauve 10 10
1004 3c. green 10 10
1005 7c. blue 15 10

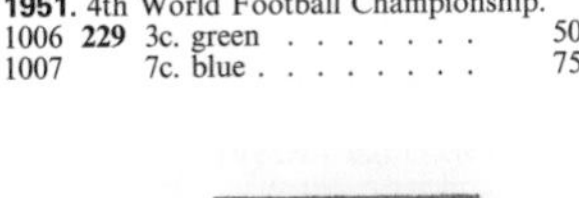

1951. 4th World Football Championship.
1006 **229** 3c. green 50 15
1007 7c. blue 75 35

230 Gen. Artigas

231 Emigration from Eastern Provinces

1952. Death Cent of Artigas. Dated "1950".
1009 **230** 5m. blue 10 10
1010 – 1c. black and blue . . . 10 10
1011 – 2c. brown and violet . . 10 10
1012 **231** 3c. sepia and green . . . 10 10
1013 – 5c. black and orange . . 15 10
1014 **231** 7c. black and olive . . . 15 10
1015 – 8c. black and red 25 10
1016 – 10c. red, blue and brown 25 10
1017 – 14c. blue 30 10
1018 – 20c. red, blue and yellow 45 20
1019 – 50c. olive and brown . . 80 35
1020 – 1p. olive and blue . . . 1·75 70
DESIGNS (all show Artigas except 10c. and 20c.)—As Type **230**: 1c. at Las Huerfanas; 2c. at Battle of Las Piedras; 5c. in Cerrito; 14c. at Ciudadela; 20c. Arms; 50c. in Paraguay; 1p. Bust. As Type **231**: 7c. Dictating instructions; 8c. in Congress; 10c. Flag.

232 Boeing 377 Stratocruiser over Mail Coach

234 Franklin D. Roosevelt

1952. 75th Anniv of U.P.U. (1949).
1021 **232** 3c. green 10 10
1022 7c. black 15 10
1023 12c. blue 20 10

1953. 5th Postal Congress of the Americas and Spain.
1025 **234** 3c. green 10 10
1026 7c. blue 15 10
1027 12c. brown 25 15

235 Ceibo (National Flower)

236 Ombu Tree

237 Parliament House

239 Exhibition Entrance

1954.
1028 **235** 5m. multicoloured . . . 10 10
1029 – 1c. black and red 10 10
1030 **236** 2c. green and brown . . 10 10
1031 – 3c. multicoloured 10 10
1032 **237** 5c. brown and lilac . . . 10 10
1033 – 7c. green and brown . . 10 10
1034 – 8c. blue and red 20 10
1035 **236** 10c. green and orange 20 10
1036 – 12c. sepia and blue . . . 15 10
1037 – 14c. black and purple . . 20 10
1038 **235** 20c. multicoloured . . . 25 10
1039 – 50c. multicoloured . . . 55 20
1040 **237** 1p. brown and red . . . 95 30
1041 – 2p. sepia and red . . . . 2·00 80
1042 – 3p. green and lilac . . . 2·10 60
1043 – 4p. blue and brown . . . 5·50 2·50
1044 **236** 5p. green and blue . . . 5·00 2·00
DESIGNS—As T **235**: 3c., 50c. Passion flower. As T **236**—HORIZ: 1c., 14c. Gaucho breaking-in horse. VERT: 7c., 3p. Montevideo Citadel. As T **237**—VERT: 8c., 4p. Isla de Lobos lighthouse and southern sealions. HORIZ: 12c., 2p. Outer Gateway of Montevideo, 1836.

1956. 1st National Production Exhibition.
1050 **239** 3c. green (postage) . . . 10 10
1051 7c. blue 10 10
1052 – 20c. blue (air) 30 20
1053 – 31c. green 35 30
1054 – 36c. red 60 35
DESIGN—HORIZ: Nos. 1052/4, Exhibition symbol and two airliners.

241 Uruguay's First Stamp and "Diligencia"

1956. Air. Centenary of First Uruguay Stamps. Stamp in blue.
1055 **241** 20c. green and yellow . . 35 20
1056 31c. brown and blue . . 40 25
1057 36c. red and pink . . . 50 35

242 Pres. Jose Batlle y Ordonez

248 High Diver

1956. Birth Centenary of Jose Batlle y Ordonez (President, 1903–07 and 1911–15).
1058 **242** 3c. red (postage) 10 10
1059 – 7c. sepia 10 10
1060 – 10c. mauve (air) 10 10
1061 **242** 20c. slate 15 10
1062 – 31c. brown 20 15
1063 – 36c. green 30 20
PORTRAIT OF PRESIDENT—VERT: 7c. Wearing overcoat; 10c. Similar to Type **242**; 36c. Profile, facing right. HORIZ: 31c. Seated at desk.

1957. Surch **5** or **10 Cts.**
1071 **242** 5c. on 3c. red 10 10
1072 – 10c. on 7c. sepia (No. 1059) 10 10

1958. 14th S. American Swimming Championships, Montevideo. Inscr as in T **248**.
1073 **248** 5c. green 15 10
1074 – 10c. blue 35 15
DESIGN—HORIZ: 10c. Diving.

249 Dr. E. Acevedo

250 Flags

1958. Birth Centenary of Dr. Eduardo Acevedo (lawyer).
1075 **249** 5c. black and green . . . 10 10
1076 10c. black and blue . . . 15 10

1958. Air. Day of the Americas.
1077 **250** 23c. black and blue . . . 15 15
1078 34c. black and green . . 20 15
1079 44c. black and mauve . . 35 20

251 Baygorria Dam

252 "Flame of Freedom"

1958. Inauguration of Baygorria Hydro-electric Power Station.
1080 **251** 5c. black and green . . . 10 10
1081 10c. black and brown . . 10 10
1082 – 1p. black and blue . . . 40 15
1083 – 2p. black and mauve . . 60 35
DESIGN: 1, 2p. Aerial view of dam.

1958. Air. 10th Anniv of Declaration of Human Rights.
1084 **252** 23c. black and blue . . . 15 10
1085 34c. black and green . . 20 15
1086 44c. black and red . . . 35 25

1958. Nos. 1028, 1031 and 1033 surch with Caduceus and value.
1087 5c. on 3c. multicoloured . . 10 10
1088 10c. on 7c. green and brown 10 10
1089 20c. on 5m. multicoloured 15 10

254 Statue on Capt. Boiso Lanza Monument

1959. Air. Centres in black.
1090 **254** 3c. brown 10 10
1091 8c. mauve 10 10
1092 38c. black 10 10
1093 50c. yellow 15 10
1094 60c. violet 15 10
1095 90c. olive 20 15
1096 1p. blue 30 15
1097 2p. orange 70 50
1098 3p. green 85 50
1099 5p. purple . . . . 1·10 85
1100 10p. red . . . . 3·75 2·50
See also Type **266**.

255 Santos-Dumont and his Biplane "14 bis"

1959. Air. Santos-Dumont Commemoration.
1101 **255** 31c. multicoloured . . . 15 15
1102 36c. multicoloured . . . 15 15

257 "Tourism in Uruguay"

258 Gabriela Mistral (poet)

1959. Air. Tourist Publicity and 50th Anniv of Punta del Este.
1103 **257** 10c. blue and ochre . . . 10 10
1104 – 38c. buff and green . . . 15 10
1105 – 60c. buff and violet . . . 25 15
1106 **257** 90c. green and red . . . 30 20
1107 – 1p.05 buff and blue . . . 35 25
DESIGN: 38, 60c., 1p.05, Beach and compass.

1959. 2nd Death Anniv of Gabriela Mistral.
1108 **258** 5c. green 10 10
1109 10c. blue 10 10
1110 20c. red 15 10

259 Dr. Vaz Ferreira

260 Emblem of Y.M.C.A.

1959. Honouring Dr. Carlos Vaz Ferreira (philosopher).
1111 **259** 5c. black and blue . . . 10 10
1112 10c. black and ochre . . 10 10
1113 20c. black and red . . . 10 10
1114 50c. black and violet . . 25 10
1115 1p. black and green . . 40 20

1959. Air. 50th Anniv of Y.M.C.A. in Uruguay.
1116 **260** 38c. black, grey and green 25 25
1117 50c. black, grey and blue 30 20
1118 60c. black, grey and red 35 35

261 Boy and Dam

262 Artigas and Washington

1959. National Recovery.
1119 **261** 5c.+10c. green and orange (postage) . . . 10 10
1120 10c.+10c. blue & orange 10 10
1121 1p.+10c. violet & orange 40 30
1122 38c.+10c. brown and orange (air) 20 20
1123 60c.+10c. green & orge 30 30

1960. Air. Visit of President Eisenhower.
1124 **262** 38c. black and red . . . 15 15
1125 50c. black and blue . . . 20 15
1126 60c. black and green . . 25 15

1960. Air. Surch with caduceus and **20 c.**
1128 **217** 20c. on 27c. green . . . 10 10

265 Martinez

266 Statue on Lanza Monument

1960. Birth Centenary of Dr. Martin C. Martinez.
1129 **265** 3c. black and purple . . 10 10
1130 5c. black and violet . . 10 10
1131 10c. black and blue . . . 10 10
1132 20c. black and brown . . 10 10
1133 1p. black and grey . . . 25 10
1134 2p. black and orange . . 55 15
1135 3p. black and olive . . . 85 30
1136 4p. black and brown . . 1·10 65
1137 5p. black and red . . . 1·25 70

1960. Air.
1138 **266** 3c. black and lilac . . . 10 10
1139 20c. black and red . . . 10 10
1140 38c. black and blue . . . 10 10
1141 50c. black and buff . . . 10 10
1142 60c. black and green . . 15 10
1143 90c. black and red . . . 25 15
1144 1p. black and grey . . . 30 15
1145 2p. black and green . . 45 25
1146 3p. black and purple . . 40 20
1147 5p. black and salmon . . 60 40
1148 10p. black and yellow . . 1·10 65
1149 20p. black and blue . . 2·50 1·25

267 Refugees 268 Scene of Revolution

1960. World Refugee Year.
1150 – 10c. black & bl (postage) 10 10
1151 267 60c. black and mauve (air) 20 20
DESIGN: 10c. "Uprooted tree".

1960. 150th Anniv of Argentine May Revolution.
1154 268 5c. black & blue (postage) 10 10
1155 10c. brown and blue 10 10
1156 38c. olive and blue (air) 15 10
1157 59c. red and blue 15 15
1158 60c. violet and blue 25 15

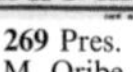
269 Pres. M. Oribe 270 Pres. Gronchi

1961. 104th Death Anniv of Manuel Oribe (President, 1835–38).
1159 269 10c. black and blue 10 10
1160 20c. black and brown 10 10
1161 40c. black and green 15 10

1961. Air. Visit of President of Italy.
1162 270 90c. multicoloured 25 20
1163 1p.20 multicoloured 30 25
1164 1p.40 multicoloured 35 30

271 Carrasco Airport Building

1961. Air. Carrasco National Airport.
1165 271 1p. grey and violet 20 20
1166 2p. grey and olive 45 10
1167 3p. grey and yellow 35 35
1168 4p. grey and purple 55 20
1169 5p. grey and turquoise 60 30
1170 10p. grey and blue 1·10 45
1171 20p. grey and red 2·00 1·25

272 "Charging Horsmen" (by C. M. Herrera)

1961. 150th Anniv of 28 February Revolution.
1172 272 20c. black and blue 15 10
1173 40c. black and green 25 10

273 Welfare, Justice and Education

1961. Latin-American Economic Commission Conference, Punta del Este. (a) Postage. Centres in bistre.
1174 273 2c. violet 10 10
1175 5c. orange 10 10
1176 10c. red 10 10
1177 20c. green 10 10
1178 50c. lilac 10 10
1179 1p. blue 25 15
1180 2p. yellow 55 35
1181 3p. grey 55 35
1182 4p. blue 85 45
1183 5p. brown 95 60

(b) Air. Centres in black.
1184 273 20c. orange 10 10
1185 45c. green 15 10
1186 50c. purple 15 10
1187 90c. violet 20 15
1188 1p. red 25 20
1189 1p.40 lilac 35 25
1190 2p. ochre 20 25
1191 3p. blue 30 35
1192 4p. yellow 40 50
1193 5p. blue 55 40
1194 10p. green 1·10 70
1195 20p. mauve 2·00 1·50

274 Gen. Rivera 275 Symbols of Swiss Settlers

1962. Honouring Gen. Fructuoso Rivera (1st President, 1830–35).
1196 274 10c. black and red 10 10
1197 20c. black and ochre 10 10
1198 40c. black and green 15 10

1962. Centenary of First Swiss Settlers.
1199 275 10c. red, black and blue (postage) 10 10
1200 20c. red, black and green 10 10
1201 – 90c. black, red and orange (air) 20 20
1202 – 1p.40 black, red and blue 30 30
DESIGN—HORIZ: 90c., 1p.40, Wheatsheaf, harvester and Swiss flag.

276 B. P. Berro 277 Red-crested Cardinal

1962. Bernardo Prudencio Berro (President, 1860–64).
1203 276 10c. black and blue 10 10
1204 20c. black and brown 10 10

1962. Birds.
1205 – 2c. brown, pink and black (postage) 25 10
1206 – 50c. brown and black 75 15
1207 – 1p. brown and black 1·00 40
1208 – 2p. black, brown and grey 1·50 75
1209 277 20c. red, black and grey (air) 25 15
1210 – 45c. red, blue and black 45 15
1211 – 90c. brown, black and red 1·10 15
1212 – 1p. blue, black and brown 75 25
1213 – 1p.20 multicoloured 1·50 25
1214 – 1p.40 brown, black and blue 2·25 45
1215 – 2p. yellow, black & brown 1·50 45
1216 – 3p. black, yellow & brown 2·25 70
1217 – 5p. black, blue and green 4·00 1·00
1218 – 10p. multicoloured 7·00 2·10
1219 – 20p. orange, black and grey 15·00 7·25
BIRDS—HORIZ: 2c. Rufous-bellied thrush; 45c. Diademed tanager; 50c. Rufous hornero; 1p. (1207), Chalk-browed mockingbird; 1p. (1212), Shiny-headed cowbird; 1p.20, Great kiskadee; 2p. (1208), Rufous-collared sparrow; 2p. (1215), Yellow cardinal; 3p. Hooded siskin; 5p. Sayaca tanager; 10p. Blue and yellow tanager; 20p. Scarlet-headed blackbird. VERT: 90c. Vermilion flycatcher; 1p.40, Fork-tailed flycatcher.

Nos. 1208, 1210, 1212 and 1215 have no frame; Nos. 1206 and 1214 have a thin frame line; the others are as Type 277.

278 D. A. Larranaga

1963. 85th Death Anniv of Damaso Antonio Larranaga (founder of National Library).
1220 278 20c. sepia and turquoise 20 20
1221 40c. sepia and drab 20 20

279 U.P.A.E. Emblem

1963. 50th Anniv of Postal Union of the Americas and Spain.
1222 279 20c. blue & black (postage) 10 10
1223 45c. green and black (air) 10 10
1224 90c. red and black 20 15

280 Campaign Emblem 281 Anchors

1963. Freedom from Hunger.
1225 280 10c. yell & grn (postage) 10 10
1226 20c. yellow and brown 10 10
1227 90c. yellow and red (air) 20 15
1228 1p.40 yellow and violet 25 20

1963. World Voyage of "Alferez Campora".
1229 281 10c. vio & orge (postage) 10 10
1230 20c. grey and red 10 10
1231 – 90c. green & orange (air) 30 10
1232 – 1p.40 blue and yellow 40 25
DESIGN: 90c., 1p.40, Sailing ship "Alferez Campora".

282 Large Intestine Congress Emblem

1963. 1st Uruguayan Proctological Congress, Punta del Este.
1233 282 10c. red, black and green 10 10
1234 20c. red, black and ochre 10 10

283 Centenary Emblem

1964. Red Cross Centenary.
1235 283 20c. red and blue 10 10
1236 40c. red and grey 15 10

284 L. A. de Herrera

1964. 5th Death Anniv of Luis A. de Herrera (statesman).
1237 284 20c. black, green and blue 10 10
1238 40c. black, lt blue & blue 10 10
1239 80c. black, yellow & blue 15 10
1240 1p. black, lilac and blue 15 10
1241 2p. black, slate and blue 25 20

285 Pres. De Gaulle

1964. Air. Visit of President of France. Multicoloured.
1242 1p.50 Type 285 40 15
1243 2p.40 Flags of France and Uruguay 50 40

286 Reliefs from Abu Simbel

1964. Nubian Monuments Preservation. Multicoloured.
1244 20c. Type 286 (postage) 10 10
1245 1p.30 Sphinx, Sebua (air) 30 15
1246 2p. Rameses II, Abu Simbel 65 30
Nos. 1245/6 are vert.

292 Arms 288 Pres. Kennedy

1965. Air.
1261 292 20p. multicoloured 1·25 70
1248 – 50p. blue, yellow and grey 3·75 3·00
DESIGN—HORIZ (38 × 27 mm) 50p. National flag.

1965. Pres. Kennedy Commemoration. Frame and laurel in gold.
1249 288 20c. blk & grn (postage) 10 10
1250 40c. black and brown 10 10
1251 1p.50 black and lilac (air) 20 10
1252 2p.40 black and blue 30 15

289 "Tete-beche" Pair of Uruguayan 8c. Stamps of 1864

290 6c. "Arms-type" of 1964

1965. 1st River Plate Stamp Exn, Montevideo. (a) Postage. T 289.
1253 40c. green and black 10 10

(b) Air. As T 290 showing Arms-type stamps of 1864 (values in brackets).
1254 1p. black and blue (12c.) 10 10
1255 1p. black and orange (T 290) 10 10
1256 1p. black and green (8c.) 10 10
1257 1p. black and bistre (10c.) 10 10
1258 1p. black and red (6c.) 10 10
Nos. 1254/8 were issued together in sheets of 10 (5 × 2), each design arranged in a vertical pair with "URUGUAY" either at top or bottom.

291 B. Nardone

1965. 1st Death Anniv of Benito Nardone (statesman).
1259 291 20c. black and green 10 10
1260 – 40c. black and green 10 10
DESIGN—VERT: 40c. Portrait as Type 291, but Nardone with microphone.

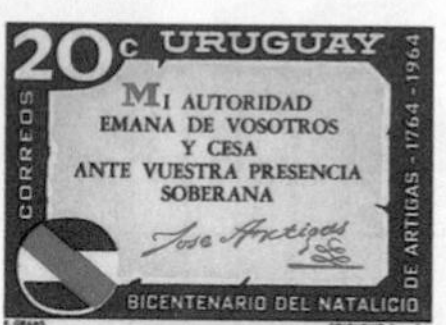

293 Part of Artigas' Speech before the 1813 Congress

1965. Birth Bicent (1964) of Gen. Jose Artigas.
1262 293 20c. red, blue and yellow (postage) 10 10
1263 – 40c. olive, black and blue 10 10
1264 – 80c. multicoloured 10 10
1265 – 1p. multicoloured (air) 10 10

1266 – 1p.50 multicoloured . . 15 15
1267 **293** 2p.40 multicoloured . . 25 20
DESIGNS—HORIZ: 40c. Bust of Artigas; 80c. Artigas and his army flag; 1p.50, Bust, flag and exodus of his followers to Argentina. VERT: 1p. Artigas' statue.

295 Football

1965. Olympic Games, Tokyo (1964).
1269 **295** 20c. orange, black and green (postage) . . . 10 10
1270 – 40c. olive, black & brown 10 10
1271 – 80c. red, black and drab 10 10
1272 – 1p. green, black and blue 10 10
1273 – 1p. grey, black & red (air) 10 10
1274 – 1p.50 blue, black & grn 15 15
1275 – 2p. blue, black and red 15 15
1276 – 2p.40 orange, black & bl 20 15
1277 – 3p. yellow, black and lilac 25 20
1278 – 20p. pink, blue & indigo 70 50
DESIGNS: 40c. Basketball; 80c. Cycling; 1p. (No. 1272) Swimming; 1p. (No. 1273) Boxing; 1p.50, Running; 2p. Fencing; 2p.40, Sculling; 3p. Pistol-shooting; 20p. Olympic "Rings".

1965. Surch with caduceus and value.
1280 **178** 10c. on 7c. blue 10 10

1966. 50th Anniv of Uruguay Architects' Assn. Surch **CINCUENTENARIO Sociedad Arquitectos del Uruguay** and value.
1281 **261** 4c. on 5c.+10c. green and orange 10 10

298 I.T.U. Emblem and Satellite

1966. Air. Centenary of I.T.U.
1282 **298** 1p. deep blue, red & blue 15 10

299 Sir Winston Churchill

1966. Churchill Commemoration.
1283 **299** 40c. brown, red and blue (postage) 10 10
1284 – 2p. brn, red & gold (air) 20 10
DESIGN—VERT: 2p. Churchill-full-face portrait and signed quotation.

300 Arms and View of Rio de Janeiro

1966. 400th Anniv of Rio de Janeiro.
1285 **300** 40c. grn & brn (postage) 10 10
1286 80c. red and brown (air) 10 10

301 I.C.Y. Emblem

1966. Air. I.C.Y.
1287 **301** 1p. black and green . . 15 10

302 Army Engineer

304 Pres. Shazar

1966. 50th Anniv of Army Engineers.
1288 **302** 20c. multicoloured . . . 15 10

1966. Air. Visit of President of Israel.
1291 **304** 7p. multicoloured . . . 40 30

305 Crested Screamer

306 Jules Rimet Cup, Ball and Globe

1966. Air.
1292 **305** 100p. multicoloured . . 8·00 2·40

1966. Air. World Cup Football Championship.
1293 **306** 10p. yellow and violet 50 30

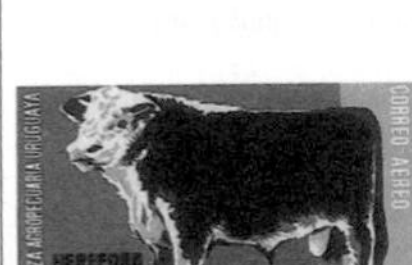

307 Hereford Bull

308 L. Batlle Berres (1947–51 and 1955–56)

1966. Air. Cattle-breeding.
1294 **307** 4p. brown, chest & sepia 15 10
1295 – 6p. black, green & turq 25 10
1296 – 10p. mauve, green & turq 35 20
1297 – 15p. black, red and orange 30 30
1298 – 20p. brown, yell & grey 50 40
1299 – 30p. brown and yellow 75 55
1300 – 50p. brown, grey & green . . . . 1·25 85
DESIGNS (Cattle breeds): 6p. Dutch; 10p. Shorthorn; 15p. Aberdeen Angus; 20p. Norman; 30p. Jersey; 50p. Charolais.

1966. Former Uruguayan Presidents.
1301 **308** 20c. black and red . . . 10 10
1302 – 20c. black and blue . . 10 10
1303 – 20c. brown and blue . . 10 10
PRESIDENTS: No. 1302, Daniel Fernandez Crespo (1963–64); 1303, Dr. Washington Beltran (1965–66).

309 Gutenberg Press

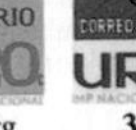
310 Capt. Boiso Lanza

1966. 50th Anniv of State Printing Works.
1304 **309** 20c. sepia, green & brown 10 10

1966. Air. Honouring Boiso Lanza (pioneer military aviator).
1305 **310** 25c. black, blue & ultram 75 55

311 Fireman

313 General J. A. Lavalleja

1966. 50th Anniv of Firemen's Corps.
1306 **311** 20c. black and red . . . 25 15

1966. 2nd River Plate Stamp Exn, Montevideo.
(a) Postage. No. 1253 optd **Segunda Muestra y Jornadas Rioplatenses**, etc.
1307 **187** 40c. green and black . . 10 10

(b) Air. Nos. 1254/8 optd **CENTENARIO DEL SELLO ESCUDITO RESELLADO**, etc.
1308 1p. blue 10 10
1309 1p. orange 10 10
1310 1p. green 10 10
1311 1p. bistre 10 10
1312 1p. red 10 10
Nos. 1308/12 commemorate the centenary of Uruguay's first surcharged stamps.

1966. Heroes of War of Independence.
1313 **313** 20c. brown, red and blue 10 10
1314 – 20c. blue, black and grey 10 10
1315 – 20c. black and blue . . . 10 10
DESIGNS—VERT: No. 1314, Gen. L. Gomez. HORIZ: 1315, Gen. A. Saravia on horseback.

1966. Air. 40th Anniv of Uruguayan Philatelic Club. No. 1036 surch **40 ANIVERSARIO Club Filatelico del Uruguay $ 1.00 aereo**.
1316 1p. on 12p. sepia and blue 10 10

315 Dante

316 Sunflower

1966. Air. 700th Birth Anniv (1965) of Dante (writer).
1317 **315** 50c. brown and sepia . . 10 10

1967. 20th Anniv of Young Farmers' Movement.
1318 **316** 40c. sepia, yellow & brn 10 10

317 Planetarium

1967. 10th Anniv of Montevideo Planetarium.
1319 **317** 40c. blk & mve (postage) 15 10
1320 – 5p. black and blue (air) 35 15
DESIGN: 5p. Planetarium projector.

318 Pres. Makarios

319 Dr. Schweitzer

1967. Air. Visit of President of Cyprus.
1321 **318** 6p.60 black and mauve 20 15

1967. Air. Schweitzer Commemoration.
1322 **319** 6p. multicoloured . . . 20 15

320 Corriedale Ram

322 Church, San Carlos

321 Uruguayan Flag and Globe

1967. Air. Uruguayan Sheep-breeding.
1323 **320** 3p. black, bistre and red 10 10
1324 – 4p. black, bistre and green 15 10
1325 – 5p. black, bistre and blue 20 10
1326 – 10p. black, bistre & yellow 35 30
DESIGNS (sheep breeds): 4p. "Ideal"; 5p. Romney Marsh; 10p. Australian merino.

1967. Air. Heads of State Meeting, Punta del Este.
1327 **321** 10p. gold, blue and black 25 20

1967. Bicentenary of San Carlos.
1328 **322** 40c. black, red and blue 10 10

323 E. Acevedo (lawyer and statesman)

325 Ansina

324 "Numeral" Stamps of 1866

1967. Eduardo Acevedo Commemoration.
1329 **323** 20c. brown and green . . 10 10
1330 40c. green and orange 10 10

1967. Air. Centenary of "Numeral" Stamps of 1866.
1331 **324** 3p. blue, green and black 20 10
1332 – 6p. ochre, red and black 35 15
DESIGN: 6p. As T **324**, but depicting 15c. and 20c. stamps of 1866.

1967. Air. Honouring Ansina (servant of Gen. Artigas).
1334 **325** 2p. red, blue and black 10 10

326 Douglas DC-4 over Runway

327 Making Basket

1967. Air. 30th Anniv of PLUNA Airline.
1335 **326** 10p. multicoloured . . . 35 25

1967. Air. World Basketball Championships, Montevideo. Multicoloured.
1336 5p. Type **327** 20 10
1337 5p. Running 20 10
1338 5p. Holding 20 10
1339 5p. Pivot 20 10
1340 5p. Dribbling 20 10

1967. Air. Nos. 1210 and 1223 surch with new value in figures only.
1343 – 5p.90 on 45c. red, bl & blk 55 20
1344 **279** 5p.90 on 45c. green & blk 20 15

330 "Don Quixote and Sancho Panza" (after Denry Torres)

1967. Air. 420th Birth Anniv of Cervantes (writer).
1345 **330** 8p. brown and bistre . . 25 15

331 Arms of Carmelo

332 J. E. Rodo

1967. 150th Anniv of Founding of Carmelo.
1346 **331** 40c. deep blue, ochre and blue 10 10

1967. 50th Death Anniv of Jose E. Rodo (writer). Multicoloured.
1347 1p. Type **332** 10 10
1348 2p. Portrait and sculpture 10 10
The 2p. is horiz.

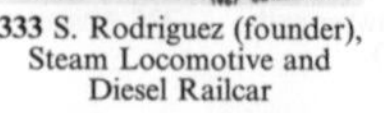

333 S. Rodriguez (founder), Steam Locomotive and Diesel Railcar

334 Child and Map of Americas

1967. Centenary of 1st National Railway in Uruguay.
1349 **333** 2p. brown and ochre . . 30 10

1967. 40th Anniv of Inter-American Children's Institute.
1350 **334** 1p. red and violet . . . 15 10

1967. No. 1033 surch **1.00 PESO** and caduceus.
1351 1p. on 7c. green and brown 10 10

336 Primitive Club

337 Level Crossing and Traffic Sign

1967. Air. Archaeological Discoveries. Each black and grey.
1352 15p. Type **336** 10 10
1353 20p. Lance-head 20 10
1354 30p. Axe-head 45 15
1355 50p. Sculptured "bird of El Polonio" 60 25
1356 75p. Cooking pot 60 40
1357 100p. Sculptured "bird" of Balizas (horiz) 85 35
1358 150p. Bolas . . . . 1·10 40
1359 200p. Arrow-heads . . . . 1·50 85

1967. Air. Pan American Highways Congress.
1360 **337** 4p. black, yellow and red 30 10

338 Lions Emblem and Map

339 Boy Scout

1967. Air. 50th Anniv of Lions International.
1361 **338** 5p. violet, yellow & green 15 10

1968. Air. Lord Baden-Powell Commemoration.
1362 **339** 9p. brown and orange 15 10

340 Cocoi Heron

341 Sun, Transport and U.N. Emblem

1968. Birds.
1363 – 1p. brown and buff . . . 1·10 25
1364 **340** 2p. black and green . . 1·40 25
1365 – 3p. purple, black & orge 1·50 25
1366 – 4p. black and brown . . 3·50 55
1367 – 4p. black and orange . . 3·50 55
1368 – 5p. black, yellow & brown . . . . 4·00 75
1369 – 10p. violet and black . . 7·00 1·25
BIRDS—VERT: 1p. Great horned owl; 4p. (No. 1367), Black-tailed stilt. HORIZ: 3p. Brown-hooded gull; 4p. (No. 1366), White-faced whistling duck; 5p. Wattled jacana; 10p. Snowy egret.

1968. Air. International Tourist Year (1967).
1370 **341** 10p. multicoloured . . . 65 15

342 Presidents of Uruguay and Brazil, and Concord Bridge

343 Footballer

1968. Opening of Concord Bridge between Uruguay and Brazil.
1371 **342** 6p. brown 15 10

1968. Penarol Club's Victory in Intercontinental Soccer Championships.
1372 **343** 1p. black and lemon . . 15 10

344 St. John Bosco

1968. 75th Anniv of "Don Bosco Workshops".
1373 **344** 2p. black and brown . . 10 10

345 Octopus

1968. Air. Uruguayan Marine Fauna.
1374 **345** 15p. black, blue and turquoise 45 15
1375 – 20p. brown, blue & green 40 15
1376 – 25p. multicoloured . . . 45 20
1377 – 30p. black, green and blue 50 25
1378 – 50p. salmon, blue and green 95 40
DESIGNS—HORIZ: 20p. River Plate pejerrey; 25p. Dorado. VERT: 30p. Spotted sorubim; 50p. Short-finned squid.

346 Sailors' Monument, Montevideo

1968. 150th Anniv of Uruguayan Navy.
1379 **346** 2p. black and green (postage) 10 10
1380 – 6p. black and green . . 10 10
1381 – 12p. black and blue . . 50 15
1382 – 4p. black, red & blue (air) 10 10
1383 – 6p. multicoloured . . . 10 10
1384 – 10p. red, yellow and blue 15 10
1385 – 20p. black and blue . . 90 15
DESIGNS—HORIZ: 4p. Tailplane (Naval Air Force); 6p. (No. 1383), Naval Arms; 12p. Screw gunboat "Suarez"; 20p. Artigas's privateer "Isabel". VERT: 6p. (No. 1380), Buoy and lighthouse; 10p. Mast-head and signal flags.

347 President Gestido

1968. 1st Death Anniv of President Oscar D. Gestido.
1386 **347** 6p. brown, red and blue 10 10

348 Sculling

1969. Air. Olympic Games, Mexico.
1387 **348** 30p. black, brown & blue 30 20
1388 – 50p. black, brown & yell 45 30
1389 – 100p. black, brown & grn 75 50
DESIGNS: 50p. Running; 100p. Football.

349 Cogwheel, Ear of Wheat and Two Heads

1969. 25th Anniv of Uruguay Trades University.
1390 **349** 2p. black and red . . . 10 10

350 Cycling

1969. World Cycling Championships, Montevideo (1968).
1391 **350** 6p. blue, orange and green (postage) . . . 20 10
1392 – 20p. multicoloured (air) 30 15
DESIGN—VERT: 20p. Cyclist and globe.

351 EFIMEX "Stamp" on Easel

1969. Air. "EFIMEX" Stamp Exhibition, Mexico City (1968).
1393 **351** 20p. red, green and blue 20 15

353 Gymnasts and Emblem

354 Pres. Baltasar Brum

1969. 75th Anniv of "L'Avenir" Gymnastics Club.
1395 **353** 6p. black and red . . . 15 10

1969. 36th Death Anniv of Baltasar Brum (President, 1919–23).
1396 **354** 6p. black and red . . . 15 10

356 Sun and Fair Emblem (½-size illustration)

1969. 2nd World Industrial Fair, Montevideo.
1399 **356** 2p. multicoloured . . . 15 10

357 Emblem, Quill and Book

358 Modern Diesel Locomotive

1969. Air. 10th Latin-American Notaries' Congress, Montevideo.
1400 **357** 30p. black, orange & grn 35 25

1969. Centenary of Uruguayan Railways.
1401 **358** 6p. black, red and blue 40 25
1402 – 6p. black, red and blue 40 25
DESIGN: No. 1402 Steam locomotive and diesel train.

360 Automobile Club Badge

362 I.L.O. Emblem

361 Belloni and "Combat" (monument). (½-size illustration)

1969. Air. 50th Anniv of Uruguay Automobile Club.
1404 **360** 10p. blue and red . . . 15 10

1969. 4th Death Anniv of Jose Belloni (sculptor).
1405 **361** 6p. green, black and gold 10 10

1969. Air. 50th Anniv of I.L.O.
1406 **362** 30p. turquoise and black 30 20

363 Training Centre Emblem

364 Exhibition Emblem

1969. 25th Anniv (1967) of Reserve Officers' Training Centre.
1407 **363** 1p. lemon and blue . . . 10 10
1408 – 2p. brown and blue . . . 15 10
DESIGN: 2p. Reservist in uniform and civilian dress.

1969. Air. "ABUEXPO 69" Philatelic Exhibition, Sao Paulo, Brazil.
1409 **364** 20p. yellow, blue & green 25 10

365 Rotary Emblem and Hemispheres

366 Dr. Morquio and Child

1969. Air. South American Regional Rotary Conference, and 50th Anniv of Rotary Club, Montevideo.
1410 **365** 20p. gold, ultram & blue 40 10

1969. Air. Birth Cent (1967) of Dr. Luis Morquio (pediatrician).
1411 **366** 20p. brown and red . . 20 10

1969. Air. New Year. No. 1345 surch **FELIZ ANO 1970 6.00 PESOS**.
1412 **330** 6p. on 8p. brown & bis 10 10

368 Pres. Tomas Berreta

369 Mahatma Gandhi

1969. 22nd Death Anniv of Dr. Tomas Berreta (President, 1947).
1413 **368** 6p. red and black . . . 15 10

1970. Air. Birth Cent (1969) of Mahatma Gandhi.
1414 **369** 100p. brown, ochre & blue 85 85

370 Teju Lizard

371 Dr. E. C. Ciganda

1970. Air. Fauna.
1415 – 20p. black, green & pur 95 25
1416 **370** 30p. black, green & yell 40 20
1417 – 50p. black, brown & yell 40 35
1418 – 100p. brown, bistre and orange 60 55
1419 – 150p. brown and green 95 80
1420 – 200p. black, brown & red . . . . 1·25 1·25
1421 – 250p. black, blue and grey . . . . 1·50 1·50

DESIGNS—VERT: 20p. Greater rhea. HORIZ: 50p. Capybara; 100p. Mulita armadillo; 150p. Puma; 200p. Coypu; 250p. South American fur seal.

1970. Air. Birth Centenary of Evaristo C. Ciganda (pioneer of teachers' pensions law).
1422 **371** 6p. brown and green . . 10 10

372 Garibaldi

373 Bank Emblem

1970. Air. Centenary of Garibaldi's Participation in Defence of Uruguay against Brazil and Argentina.
1423 **372** 20p. mauve and pink . . 15 10

1970. 11th Inter-American Development Bank Governors' Meeting, Punta del Este.
1424 **373** 10p. blue and gold . . . 15 10

374 Stylized Tree

375 Footballer and Emblem

1970. 2nd National Forestry Exhibition.
1425 **374** 2p. black, green and red 10 10

1970. Air. World Cup Football Championship, Mexico.
1426 **375** 50p. multicoloured . . . 55 30

376 Artigas' House, Sauce

1970. 120th Death Anniv of Artigas.
1427 **376** 15p. black, blue and red 15 10

377 "U.N."

1970. Air. 25th Anniv of United Nations.
1428 **377** 32p. blue, gold and light blue 25 15

378 Sun, Sea and Map

1970. Tourist Publicity.
1429 **378** 5p. blue 10 10

379 Eisenhower and U.S. Flag

1970. Air. 1st Death Anniv of Dwight D. Eisenhower (American soldier and statesman).
1430 **379** 30p. blue, red and grey 30 15

380 First Man on the Moon

1970. Air. 1st Anniv of Moon Landing from "Apollo 11".
1431 **380** 200p. multicoloured . . 1·50 1·50

381 Mt. Fuji

1970. "EXPO 70" World Fair, Osaka, Japan. Each with EXPO emblem and arms of Uruguay.
1432 **381** 25p. blue, green & yellow 25 15
1433 – 25p. blue, orange & green 25 15
1434 – 25p. blue, yellow & violet 25 15
1435 – 25p. blue, violet & orange 25 15
DESIGNS: No. 1433, Geishas; 1434, Tower of the Sun; 1435, Youth totem.

382 Flag of 1825

1970. Air. 145th Anniv of Revolt of the "Immortal 33" under Levalleja.
1436 **382** 500p. black, red and blue 3·50 3·50

383 Rheumatology Congress Emblem

1970. Air. 5th Pan-American Rheumatology Congress, Punta del Este.
1437 **383** 30p. deep blue, blue and yellow 30 15

384 Street Scene

1970. 290th Anniv of Colonia del Sacramento (1st European settlement in Uruguay).
1439 **384** 5p. multicoloured . . . 10 10

385 "Mother and Son" (statue, E. Prati)

386 Flags of Member Countries

1970. "Homage to Mothers".
1440 **385** 10p. black and green . . 15 10

1970. Air. 10th Anniv of Founding of Latin-American Association for Free Trade by the Montevideo Treaty.
1441 **386** 22p. multicoloured . . . 30 15

387 "Stamp" Emblem

389 Dr. Alfonso Espinola

388 "Playing Ring-o-Roses" (Ana Gaye)

1970. "URUEXPO 70" Stamp Exn, Montevideo.
1442 **387** 15p. violet, blue & brown 15 10

1970. International Education Year. Children's Drawings. Multicoloured.
1443 10p. Type **388** 20 15
1444 10p. "Two Girls" (Andrea Burcatovsky) (vert) . . . 20 15
1445 10p. "Boy at Desk" (Humberto Abel Garcia) (vert) 20 15
1446 10p. "Spaceman" (Aquiles Vaxelaire) 20 15

1971. 125th Birth Anniv (1970) of Dr. Alfonso Espinola (physician and philanthropist).
1447 **389** 5p. black and orange . . 15 10

391 "Stamps" and Poster (½-size illustration)

1971. "EFU 71" Stamp Exn, Montevideo.
1449 **391** 15p. multicoloured . . . 20 10

392 5c. Coin of 1840 (obverse)

1971. Numismatics Day.
1450 **392** 25p. black, brown & blue 40 30
1451 – 25p. black, brown & blue 40 30
DESIGN: No. 1451, Reverse of coin showing "Sun" emblem.

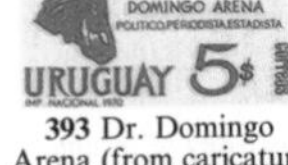

393 Dr. Domingo Arena (from caricature by A. Sifredi)

395 Dr. Jose Arias

394 Opening Bars of Anthem

1971. Birth Centenary (1970) of Arena (lawyer and statesman).
1452 **393** 5p. lake 10 10

1971. National Anthem Commemoration.
1453 **394** 15p. black, blue and gold 40 25

1971. 1st Death Anniv of Dr Jose Arias (statesman).
1454 **395** 5p. brown 15 10

396 "Yellow Fever" (J. M. Blanes)

1971. Air. 70th Death Anniv of Juan Blanes (artist).
1455 **396** 50p. multicoloured . . . 30 30

397 Eduardo Fabini

1971. 21st Death Anniv of Eduardo Fabini (composer).
1456 **397** 5p. black and red . . . 40 10

398 "Two Races"

1971. Air. Racial Equality Year.
1457 **398** 27p. black, pink and gold 30 15

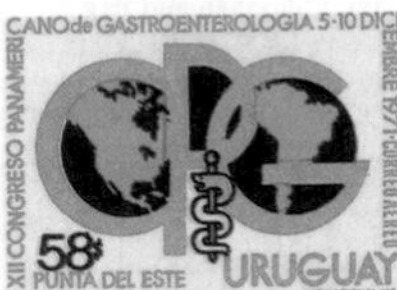

399 Congress Emblem

1971. Air. 12th Pan-American Gastro-enterological Congress, Punta del Este.
1458 **399** 58p. orange, black & grn 55 35

400 J. E. Rodo and U.P.A.E. Emblem

1971. Birth Centenary of Jose E. Rodo (writer and first delegate to U.P.A.E).
1459 **400** 15p. black and blue . . 20 15

401 Old Water-cart and Tap

1971. Centenary of Montevideo's Water Supply.
1460 **401** 5p. multicoloured . . . 15 10

402 Sheep and Roll of Cloth

1971. Wool Production.
1461 **402** 5p. green, grey & lt green 10 10
1462 – 15p. grey, violet and blue 20 10
DESIGN: 15p. Sheep, and loading bales of cloth.

403 Dr. Jose Elorza and Sheep

1971. 12th Death Anniv of Dr. Jose Elorza (sheep-breeder).
1463 **403** 5p. black, green and blue 15 10

404 Creole Horse

1971. Uruguayan Horse-breeding.
1464 **404** 5p. black, blue and orange 20 10

405 Bull, Sheep and Ears of Corn

1971. Cent of Uruguayan Rural Association.
1465 **405** 20p. multicoloured . . . 30 15

406 Police Emblem

1971. Honouring Police Heroes.
1466 **406** 10p. blue, black and grey 25 10
1467 – 20p. multicoloured . . . 45 15
DESIGN: 20p. Policeman and flag.

407 1896 10 Peso Banknote (obverse)

1971. 75th Anniv of Uruguayan State Bank.
1468 **407** 25p. green, black and gold 30 25
1469 – 25p. green, black and gold 30 25
DESIGN: No. 1469 Reverse of banknote showing rural scene.

408 Labourer and Arms

1971. 150th Anniv of Town of Durazno.
1470 **408** 20p. multicoloured . . . 25 10

409 Shield and Laurel (½-size illustration)

1971. Uruguay's Victory in Liberators' Cup Football Championships.
1471 **409** 10p. gold, red and blue 20 10

411 Voter and Ballot-box

1971. General Election.
1473 **411** 10p. black and blue . . 10 10
1474 – 20p. black and blue . . 25 15
DESIGN—HORIZ: 20p. Voters in line.

412 C.I.M.E. Emblem and Globe

1971. Air. 20th Anniv of Inter-Governmental Committee for European Migration (C.I.M.E.).
1475 **412** 30p. multicoloured . . . 35 25

413 Exhibition Emblem and Map of Uruguay
414 Juan Lindolfo Cuestas (1897–1903)

1971. "EXPO LITORAL" Industrial Exhibition, Paysandu.
1476 **413** 20p. purple and blue . . 35 15

1971. Uruguayan Presidents. Each brown and blue.
1477 10p. Type **414** 10 10
1478 10p. J. Herrara y Obes (1890–94) 10 10
1479 10p. Claudio Williman (1907–11) 10 10
1480 10p. Jose Serrato (1923–27) 10 10
1481 10p. Andres Martinez Trueba (1951–55) 10 10

415 Llama Emblem
417 Olympic Symbols

1971. Air. "EXFILIMA" Stamp Exn, Lima, Peru.
1482 **415** 37p. multicoloured . . . 35 30

1972. Air. Olympic Games, Munich (1st issue).
1484 **417** 50p. black, red and yellow 20 10
1485 – 100p. multicoloured . . 40 30
1486 – 500p. grey, red and blue 1·10 1·10
DESIGNS: 100p. Athlete and torch; 500p. Discus-thrower.
See also Nos. 1493/4.

418 Chemical Jar
419 Bartolome Hidalgo

1972. Air. 50th Anniv of Discovery of Insulin.
1487 **418** 27p. multicoloured . . . 20 10

1972. 150th Death Anniv (1973) of Bartolome Hidalgo (Gaucho poet).
1488 **419** 5p. black, red and brown 20 10

420 "Flagship"
421 "Face" on Beethoven Score

1972. Air. American Stamp Day.
1489 **420** 37p. multicoloured . . . 25 15

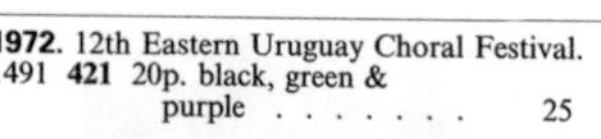
1972. 12th Eastern Uruguay Choral Festival.
1491 **421** 20p. black, green & purple 25 10

422 Dove supporting Wounded Bird (after Maria Mullin)
424 Columbus Monument, Colon

423 Footballer and 1928 Gold Medal

1972. Dionisio Diaz (9 year-old hero) Commemoration.
1492 **422** 10p. multicoloured . . . 15 10

1972. Air. Olympic Games, Munich. Mult.
1493 100p. Type **423** 40 30
1494 300p. Olympic flag (vert) . . 70 75

1972. Centenary of Colon (suburb of Montevideo).
1495 **424** 20p. black, blue and red 10 10

1972. Uruguay's Victory in Intercontinental Football Cup Championships. No. 1471 surch **COPA INTER CONTINENTAL 1971**, football cup and **50**.
1496 **409** 50p. on 10p. gold, red and blue 35 30

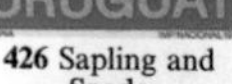
426 Sapling and Spade
428 U.N.C.T.A.D. Emblem

427 Cross of Remembrance

1972. Tree Planting Campaign.
1497 **426** 20p. black, myrtle & grn 15 10

1972. Air. 2nd Death Anniv of Dan Mitrione (U.S. police instructor assassinated by terrorists in Uruguay).
1498 **427** 37p. violet and gold . . 15 10

1972. Air. 3rd United Nations Conference on Trade and Development (U.N.C.T.A.D.), Santiago, Chile.
1499 **428** 30p. multicoloured . . . 15 10

429 Brazilian "Bull's-Eye" Stamp of 1843

1972. Air. "EXFILBRA 72" Stamp Exhibition, Rio de Janeiro.
1500 **429** 50p. multicoloured . . . 20 10

430 Compass Rose and Map of South America
431 "Birds' Nests in Tree"

1972. Air. Campaign for Extension of Territorial Waters to 200 Mile Limit.
1501 **430** 37p. multicoloured . . . 15 10

1972. National Building Project for Communal Dwellings.
1502 **431** 10p. multicoloured . . . 10 10

432 Amethyst

1972. Uruguayan Mineralogy. Rocks and Gems.
1503 **432** 5p. multicoloured . . . 15 10
1504 – 9p. multicoloured . . . 20 10
1505 – 15p. green, brown & blk 35 15
DESIGNS: 9p. Agate; 15p. Chalcedony.

433 "The Three Holy Kings" (R. Barradas)

1972. Air. Christmas.
1506 **433** 20p. multicoloured . . . 20 15

435 Infantry Uniform of 1830
436 Red Cross over Map

1972. Military Uniforms. Multicoloured.
1509 10p. Type **435** 15 10
1510 20p. Artigas cavalry regiment uniform 30 15

1972. 75th Anniv of Uruguayan Red Cross.
1511 **436** 30p. multicoloured . . . 30 10

438 Open Book
439 General Jose Artigas

1972. 25th Anniv of Full Civil Rights for Uruguayan Women.
1513 **438** 10p. gold, blue & lt blue 10 10

1972.

1514	**439**	5p. yellow	10	10
1515		10p. brown	10	10
1516		15p. green	10	10
1517		20p. lilac	10	10
1518		30p. blue	20	10
1519		40p. orange	20	10
1520		50p. red	15	10
1521		75p. green	25	15
1522		100p. green	30	15
1523		150p. brown	15	25
1524		200p. blue	25	30
1525		250p. violet	30	35
1526		500p. grey	60	75
1527		1000p. blue	1·10	1·10

440 Cup and Ear of Wheat on Map
441 E. Fernandez and J. P. Varela (founders)

1973. 30th Anniv of Inter-American Institute for Agricultural Sciences.
1531 **440** 30p. black, yellow and red 15 10

1973. Centenary (1968) of Friends of Popular Education Society.
1532 **441** 10p. black, green & brn 10 10

442 Columbus and Map

1973. American Tourist Year.
1533 **442** 50p. purple 20 15

443 Carlos Ramirez

1973. Eminent Uruguayan Jurists. Each black, brown and bistre.
1534 10p. Type **443** 10 10
1535 10p. Justino Jimenez de Arechaga 10 10
1536 10p. Juan Ramirez 10 10
1537 10p. Justino E. Jimenez de Arechaga 10 10

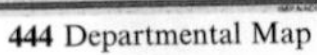

444 Departmental Map

447 Priest, Indians and Soriano Church

446 Francisco de los Santos and Artigas

1973. Uruguayan Departments.
1538 **444** 20p. multicoloured . . . 30 15
See also No. 1844.

1973. Francisco de los Santos (courier) Commem.
1540 **446** 20p. emerald, black and green 20 10

1973. Villa Santo Domingo Soriano (first Spanish Settlement in Uruguay) Commemoration.
1541 **447** 20p. black, violet and blue 15 10

448 "SOYP" and Fish

1973. Inauguration of 1st Fishery Station of Oceanographic and Fishery Service (S.O.Y.P.).
1542 **448** 100p. multicoloured . . 35 15

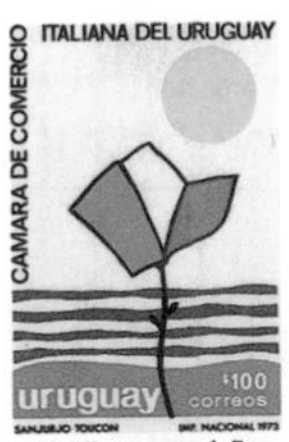

449 Flower and Sun

451 Luis A. de Herrera

1973. Italian Chamber of Commerce in Uruguay.
1543 **449** 100p. multicoloured . . 25 15

1973. Birth Centenary of Luis A. de Herrera (conservative leader).
1545 **451** 50p. brown, sepia & grey 20 10

452 Festival Emblem

1973. "Festival of Nations", Montevideo.
1546 **452** 50p. multicoloured . . . 20 10

453 Artery and Heart within "Arm"

454 "Madonna (R. Barradas)

1973. 3rd Pan-American Voluntary Blood Donors' Congress.
1547 **453** 50p. black, red and pink 20 10

1973. Christmas.
1548 **454** 50p. black, yellow & grn 15 10

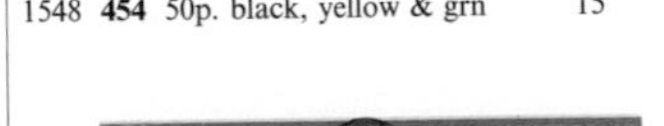

455 Copernicus (½-size illustration)

1973. 500th Birth Anniv of Nicholas Copernicus (astronomer).
1549 **455** 50p. multicoloured . . . 15 10

456 Hands in Prayer, and Andes

457 O.E.A. Emblem and Map

1973. Rescue of Survivors from Andes Air-crash.
1550 **456** 50p. green, blue and black 15 10
1551 – 75p. multicoloured . . . 20 15
DESIGN: 75p. Flower with broken stem, and Christ of the Andes statue.

1974. 25th Anniv of Organization of American States (O.E.A.).
1552 **457** 250p. multicoloured . . 40 50

458 Games' Emblem

1974. 1st International Scout Games, Montevideo.
1553 **458** 250p. multicoloured . . 40 50

459 Hector Sedes and Motor-car

462 "The Three Gauchos"

1974. Hector Sedes (motor-racing driver) Commemoration.
1554 **459** 50p. brown, black & grn 15 10

1974. Centenary of Antonio Lussich's Poem "Los Tres Gauchos".
1560 **462** 50p. multicoloured . . . 15 10

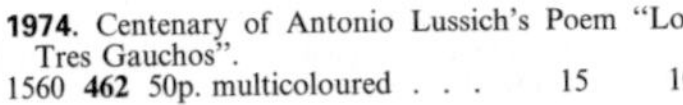

463 Rifle, Target and Swiss Flag

1974. Centenary of Swiss Rifle Club, Nueva Helvecia.
1561 **463** 100p. multicoloured . . 30 15

464 Compass Rose on Map

465 Emblem and Stadium

1974. Military Geographical Service.
1562 **464** 50p. black, emerald & grn 15 10

1974. World Cup Football Championship, Munich. Multicoloured.
1563 50p. Type **465** 15 10
1564 75p. Emblem and footballer (horiz) 20 15
1565 1000p. Emblem and footballer (different) (horiz) . . . . 11·00 7·50

466 Old and New School Buildings, and Founders

1974. Centenary of Osimani-Llerena Technical School, Salto.
1566 **466** 75p. black and brown . . 20 15

467 Carlos Gardel

468 "Ball and Net"

1974. 39th Death Anniv of Carlos Gardel (singer).
1567 **467** 100p. multicoloured . . 35 15

1974. 1st Women's World Cup Volleyball Championships.
1568 **468** 200p. purple, yellow & blk 45 25

469 "Protect Your Heart"

470 Vidal and Statue

1974. Uruguayan "Pro Cardias" Heart Foundation.
1569 **469** 75p. red, yellow and green 20 15

1974. Bicentenary (1973) of Founding of San Jose by Eusebio Vidal.
1570 **470** 75p. blue and light blue 15 10
No. 1570 is incorrectly inscr "1873–1973".

471 Artigas Monument

472 W.P.Y. Emblem

1974. Dedication of Artigas Monument, Buenos Aires, Argentine Republic.
1571 **471** 75p. multicoloured . . . 15 10

1974. Air. World Population Year.
1572 **472** 500p. red, black and grey 55 70

473 Montevideo Citadel Gateway and Emblem

474 Mast and Radio Waves

1974. Air. Events of 1974.
1573 **473** 200p. multicoloured . . 55 40
1574 300p. multicoloured . . 70 60

1974. 50th Anniv of Broadcasting in Uruguay.
1575 **474** 100p. multicoloured . . 20 10

475 "Sheet of Stamps" and "URUEXPO 74" Emblem

1974. 10th Anniv of "Circulo Filatelico" Journal of Montevideo Stamp Club.
1576 **475** 100p. blue, red and black 20 10

476 Envelopes and Emblem

1974. Centenary of Universal Postal Union.
1577 **476** 100p. multicoloured . . 10 10
1578 – 200p. black, gold and lilac 20 10
DESIGN—VERT: 200p. U.P.U. emblem on envelope, laurel and globe.

477 Mexican Official Stamp of 1884 and Arms

1974. Air. "EXFILMEX" Interamerican Philatelic Exhibition, Mexico City.
1579 **477** 200p. multicoloured . . 20 10

478 Artigas Monument

1974. Dedication of Artigas Monument. Ventura Hill, Minas.
1580 **478** 100p. multicoloured . . 10 10

479 Early Map of Montevideo

1974. 250th Anniv of Montevideo's Fortifications.
1581 **479** 300p. brown, red & green 50 20

480 Naval Vessel in Dry-dock and Badge

1974. Centenary of Montevideo Naval Arsenal.
1582 **480** 200p. multicoloured . . 40 30

481 Balloon

1974. History of Aviation. Multicoloured.
1583 100p. Type **481** 25 15
1584 100p. Farman H.F.III biplanes 25 15
1585 100p. Castaibert's Morane Saulnier Type I 25 15
1586 100p. Bleriot XI 25 15
1587 150p. Military and civil pilots' "wings" 35 20
1588 150p. Nieuport 17 biplane 35 20
1589 150p. Breguet Bidon biplane 35 20
1590 150p. Caproni Ca 5 biplane 35 20

482 Pan de Azucar Mountain and Cross

1974. Centenary of Pan de Azucar (town).
1591 **482** 150p. multicoloured . . 25 20

483 Adoration of the Kings

1974. Christmas. Multicoloured.
1592 100p. Type **483** (postage) . . 10 10
1593 150p. Kings with Gifts . . . 15 10
1594 240p. Kings following the Star (air) 20 15

484 Rowers, Fireworks and Nike of Samothrace Statue

1975. Centenary of Montevideo Rowing Club.
1596 **484** 150p. multicoloured . . 15 10

485 "Treaty of Purificacion, 1817" (J. Zorrilla de San Martin)

1975. Recognition of Artigas Government by Great Britain in Treaty of Purificacion, 1817.
1597 **485** 100p. multicoloured . . 10 10

486 Spanish 6c. Stamp of 1850, and National Colours

1975. Air. "ESPANA 75" Stamp Exhibition, Madrid.
1598 **486** 400p. multicoloured . . 35 20

487 Rose

1975. Bicentenary of Rosario.
1600 **487** 150p. multicoloured . . 20 10

488 "The Oath of the Thirty-three" (J. M. Blanes)

1975. 150th Anniv of 1825 Liberation Movement.
1601 **488** 150p. multicoloured . . 20 10

489 Michelangelo's Motif for Floor of Capitol, Rome

1975. Air. 500th Birth Anniv of Michelangelo.
1602 **489** 1p. multicoloured . . . 60 50

490 Columbus and Caravel

492 Emblem of Montreal Olympics (1976) and World Cup Football Championship (Argentina, 1978)

491 Sun and 4p.50 Air Stamp of 1929

1975. Spanish–American Stamp Day.
1603 **490** 1p. multicoloured . . . 1·00 60

1975. Air. Uruguayan Stamp Day.
1604 **491** 1p. black, yellow and grey . . . . 2·50 1·40

1975. Air. "Exfilmo-Espamer 75" Stamp Exhibition, Montevideo. Multicoloured.
1605 1p. Type **492** 40 60
1606 1p. "Independence" (U.S. and Uruguayan flags) . . 40 60
1607 1p. Emblems of U.P.U. and Spanish-American Postal Union 40 60

493 Jose Artigas and J. Francisco de Larrobla

1975. 150th Anniv of Independence.
1608 **493** 50c. multicoloured . . . 40 35

494 Col. L. Oliveira and Fortress

1975. 150th Anniv of Capture of Santa Teresa Fortress.
1609 **494** 10c. multicoloured . . . 20 10

495 Battle Scene from Painting by D. Hequet

1975. 150th Anniv of Battle of Rincon.
1610 **495** 15c. black and gold . . . 20 10
See also Nos. 1620/1.

496 Florencio Sanchez

1975. Birth Cent of Florencio Sanchez (dramatist). Multicoloured.
1611 20c. Type **496** 30 10
1612 20c. "En Familia" 30 10
1613 20c. "Barranca Abajo" . . 30 10
1614 20c. "Mi Hijo el Doctor" 30 10
1615 20c. "Camilita" 30 10
Nos. 1612/15 show scenes from plays and are horiz 38 × 26 mm.

1975. Surch in revalued currency.
1616 **439** 10c. on 20p. lilac 10 10
1617 15c. on 40p. orange . . 10 10
1618 50c. on 50p. red 35 20
1619 1p. on 1000p. blue . . . 40 40

1975. 150th Anniv of Artigas' Exile and Battle of Sarandi. As T **495**. Multicoloured.
1620 15c. Artigas' house, Ibiray (Paraguay) 20 10
1621 25c. Battle scene 40 20

498 Maria E. Vaz Ferreira (poetess)

1975. Birth Centenaries.
1622 **498** 15c. black, yellow & pur 20 10
1623 – 15c. black, orange & pur 20 10
DESIGN: No. 1623, Julio Herrera y Reissig (poet).

499 "Virgin and Child" (stained-glass window)

500 Colonel L. Latorre

1975. Christmas. Multicoloured.
1624 20c. Type **499** 35 15
1625 30c. "Virgin and Child" (different) 50 30
1626 60c. "Fireworks" (horiz) . . 40 40

1975. 59th Death Anniv of Col. Lorenzo Latorre (President, 1876–80).
1627 **500** 15c. multicoloured . . . 15 10

501 "Ariel", Stars and Book

1976. 75th Anniv of Publication of "Ariel" by Jose Rodo.
1628 **501** 15c. multicoloured . . . 15 10

502 "Oncidium bifolium" (orchid)

1976. Air. Multicoloured.
1629 50c. Type **502** 45 20
1630 50c. Geoffroy's cat 45 20

503 "Water Sports"

504 Telephone Receiver

1976. 23rd South American Swimming, Diving and Water-polo Championships, Maldonado.
1631 **503** 30c. multicoloured . . . 20 15

1976. Telephone Centenary.
1632 **504** 83c. multicoloured . . . 30 25

505 Dornier Wal Flying Boat "Plus Ultra"

506 Dornier Wal Flying Boat and Airliner rising around Hour-glass

1976. 50th Anniv of "Plus Ultra" Spain–South America Flight.
1633 **505** 63c. multicoloured . . . 60 25

1976. 50th Anniv of Lufthansa Airline.
1634 **506** 83c. multicoloured . . . 55 35

507 Louis Braille and word "Braille"

1976. 150th Anniv of Braille System for the Blind.
1635 **507** 60c. black and brown . . 40 25

508 Signing of Declaration of Independence

1976. Bicentenary of American Revolution.
1636 **508** 1p.50 multicoloured . . 1·25 95

509 "Candombe" (Pedro Figari)

1976. 150th Anniv of Abolition of Slavery.
1637 **509** 30c. multicoloured . . . 15 10

510 Rivera Monument

511 Southern Lapwing

1976. Dedication of General Rivera Monument.
1638 **510** 5p. on 10p. multicoloured . . . . 2·00 95

1976.
1639 **511** 1c. violet 20 10
1640 – 5c. green 10 10
1641 – 15c. red 15 10
1642 – 20c. black 10 10
1643 – 30c. grey 15 10
1644 – 45c. blue 10 10
1645 – 50c. green 25 10
1646 – 1p. brown 45 10
1646b – 1p. yellow 25 10
1647 – 1p.75 green 35 10
1648 – 1p.95 grey 40 10
1649 – 2p. green 90 70
1649a – 2p. mauve 35 10
1650 – 2p.65 violet 45 15
1651 – 5p. blue . . . . 2·00 2·00
1651a – 10p. brown . . . . . . 3·25 2·00

DESIGNS—VERT: 5c. Passion flower; 15c. National flower; 20c. Indian lance-head; 30c. Indian statue; 45c., 1p. (No. 1646b), 1p.75, 1p.95, 2p. (both), 2p.65, 5, 10p., Artigas; 1p. (No. 1646), "At Dawn" (J. M. Blanes). HORIZ: 50c. "Branding Cattle" (J. M. Blanes).

513 Office Building and Reverse of First Uruguayan Coin of 1840

1976. 150th Anniv of State Accounting Office.
1652 **513** 30c. black, brown & blue 25 15

514 Hand-pump within Flames

516 Championship Emblem

515 Uruguay 60c. Stamp of 1856 and "Commemorative Postmark"

1976. Centenary of Fire Service.
1653 **514** 20c. black and red . . . 15 10

1976. 50th Anniv of Uruguay Philatelic Club.
1654 **515** 30c. red, blue and bistre 15 10

1976. 5th World Universities' Football Championships, Montevideo.
1655 **516** 83c. multicoloured . . . 40 20

517 Human Eye and Spectrum

1976. Prevention of Blindness.
1656 **517** 20c. multicoloured . . . 25 10

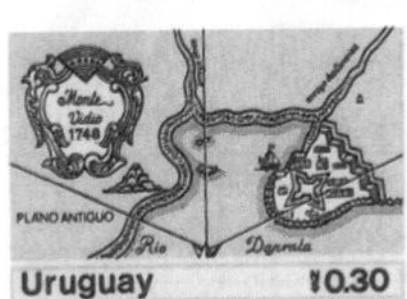

518 Map of Montevideo

1976. 250th Anniv of Montevideo. Multicoloured.
1657 30c. Type **518** 15 10
1658 45c. Montevideo panorama. 1842 . . . . 20 10
1659 70c. First settlers, 1726 . . . 35 15
1660 80c. Montevideo coin (vert) 40 20
1661 1p.15 Montevideo's first arms (vert) 55 30

519 "VARIG" Emblem

1977. 50th Anniv of VARIG Airline.
1662 **519** 80c. multicoloured . . . 50 40

520 Artigas Mausoleum

1977. Mausoleum of General Jose Artigas.
1663 **520** 45c. multicoloured . . . 30 10

521 Arch on Map

1977. Cent of Salesian Education in Uruguay.
1664 **521** 45c. multicoloured . . . 30 10

522 Globe and Emblems

1977. Air. 150th Anniv of Uruguayan Postal Services.
1665 **522** 8p. multicoloured . . . 2·75 2·50

523 Children

524 "Windmills"

1977. 50th Anniv of Inter-American Children's Institute.
1667 **523** 45c. multicoloured . . . 30 10

1977. Hispanidad Day.
1668 **524** 70c. red, yellow and black 35 15

525 Sun on "Stamp" and Stripes of Uruguayan Flag

1977. Stamp Day.
1669 **525** 45c. multicoloured . . . 20 10

527 Globe and Aircraft

1977. 30th Anniv of International Civil Aviation Organization.
1670 **527** 45c. mutlicoloured . . . 15 10

528 "The Holy Family"

1977. Christmas.
1671 **528** 45c. multicoloured . . . 15 10
1672 – 70c. red, yellow and black 20 10

DESIGN—HORIZ: (45 × 26 mm): 70c. "Santa Claus".

529 Arms, Map and Products

530 Postman clearing Mail-box

1977. Rio Negro Department.
1673 **529** 45c. multicoloured . . . 15 10

1977. 150th Anniv of National Mail Service. Multicoloured.
1674 50c. Type **530** 15 10
1675 50c. Loading mail-van . . . 15 10
1676 50c. Post Office counter, Montevideo G.P.O . . . 15 10
1677 50c. Post-boxes area 15 10
1678 50c. Sorting mail 15 10
1679 50c. Postal sorters 15 10
1680 50c. Postmen sorting "walks" 15 10
1681 50c. Postman on rounds . . 15 10
1682 50c. Postmen on motor-scooters 15 10
1683 50c. Postal counter, Carrasco Airport 15 10

531 Edison's First "Phonograph"

1977. Centenary of Sound Recording.
1684 **531** 50c. purple and yellow 15 10

532 "R" and Spectrum

1977. World Rheumatism Year.
1685 **532** 50c. multicoloured . . . 15 10

533 Emblem, Diploma, Sword and Flag

1978. 50th Anniv of Military College.
1686 **533** 50c. multicoloured . . . 15 10

534 Arms and Map

537 "Wandering Angels" (detail)

1978. Department of Artigas.
1687 **534** 45c. multicoloured . . . 40 20

1978. Air. "Riccione" and "Europhil 78" Stamp Exhibitions, Italy and Urphila Stamp Exhibition, Uruguay. Optd **EUROPA 1978 ITALIA Riccione 78 urphila '78**.
1689 **522** 8p. multicoloured . . . 3·00 2·50

1978. National Artists. Luis A. Solari. Multicoloured.

1690 1p.50 Type **537** 30 20

1691 1p.50 "Wandering Angels" (horiz 38 × 30 mm) 30 20

1692 1p.50 "Wandering Angels" (detail) 30 20

538 Bernardo O'Higgins

1978. Birth Bicentenary of Bernardo O'Higgins (national hero of Chile).

1693 **538** 1p. multicoloured 25 10

539 Telephone Dials and "Antel" Emblem

1978. Telephone Automation.

1694 **539** 50c. multicoloured 10 10

540 San Martin and Army of the Andes Monument (J. M. Ferrari)

541 Spanish Tiles

1978. Birth Bicentenary of General Jose de San Martin.

1695 **540** 1p. multicoloured 25 10

1978. Hispanidad.

1696 **541** 1p. blue, yellow and black 25 10

542 Corners of "Stamps"

1978. Stamp Day.

1697 **542** 50c. multicoloured 10 10

543 Boeing 727 in Flight

545 Flag Monument, Montevideo

544 Angel blowing Trumpet

1978. PLUNA Airline Inaugural Boeing 727 Flight.

1698 **543** 50c. multicoloured 15 10

1978. Christmas.

1699 **544** 50c. green, orange & black 10 10

1700 1p. blue, red and black 20 10

1978. Homage to the National Flag.

1701 **545** 1p. multicoloured 25 10

546 Horacio Quiroga

547 Arms and Map of Paysandu

1978. Birth Centenary of Horacio Quiroga (playwright).

1702 **546** 1p. black, yellow and red 25 10

1979. Department of Paysandu.

1703 **547** 45c. multicoloured 10 10

548 Olympic Rings and Ciudadela

1979. Olympic Games, Moscow (1980) and Winter Olympics, Lake Placid (1980). Multicoloured.

1704 5p. Type **548** 90 85

1705 7p. Lake Placid emblem 1·10 1·25

See also Nos. 1728/9.

549 Arms and Map of Salto

1979. Department of Salto.

1706 **549** 45c. multicoloured 10 10

550 Artilleryman, 1830

551 Arms and Map of Maldonado

1979. Uruguayan Military Uniforms. Mult.

1707 5p. Type **550** 85 85

1708 5p. Sapper, 1837 85 85

1979. Department of Maldonado.

1709 **551** 45c. multicoloured 10 10

552 Salto Grande Dam

1979. Salto Grande Dam.

1710 **552** 2p. multicoloured 50 15

553 Centenary Symbol and Branch

1979. Centenary of Crandon Uruguayan–American High School.

1711 **553** 1p. blue and violet 20 10

554 Kites

1979. International Year of the Child (1st issue).

1712 **554** 2p. multicoloured 35 15

See also Nos. 1715, 1718 amd 1720.

555 Arms and Map of Cerro Largo

1979. Department of Cerro Largo.

1713 **555** 45c. multicoloured 10 10

556 Arms and Map of Trienta y Tres

1979. Department of Trienta y Tres.

1714 **556** 50c. multicoloured 10 10

557 Cinderella

1979. International Year of the Child (2nd issue).

1715 **557** 2p. multicoloured 35 20

558 National Coat of Arms

1979. 150th Anniv of First National Coat of Arms.

1716 **558** 8p. multicoloured 1·10 1·10

559 U.P.U. Emblem and Arrow

1979. 18th U.P.U. Congress, Rio de Janeiro.

1717 **559** 5p. multicoloured 85 50

560 "Chico Carlo" (Juana de Ibarbourou)

561 Drawing by J. M. Torres-Garcia

1979. International Year of the Child (3rd issue).

1718 **560** 1p. multicoloured 20 10

1979. 31st Death Anniv of Joaquin Torres-Garcia (artist).

1719 **561** 10p. yellow and black 1·40 1·25

562 Madonna and Child

1979. Christmas and International Year of the Child (4th issue).

1720 **562** 10p. multicoloured 1·40 1·25

563 Arms and Map of Durazno

1979. Department of Durazno.

1721 **563** 50c. multicoloured 15 10

564 Dish Aerial and Sun

1979. 3rd World Telecommunications Exposition, Geneva.

1722 **564** 10p. black, yellow & lav 95 80

565 Caravel

1979. Hispanidad Day.

1723 **565** 10p. multicoloured 1·75 85

566 10c. Coin of 1877

1979. Centenary of 1st Silver Coinage. Multicoloured.

1724 **566** 10c. silver, black & green 10 10

1725 – 20c. silver, black & green 10 10

1726 – 50c. silver, black and blue 10 10

1727 – 1p. silver, black and blue 20 10

DESIGNS: 20c. 1877 20c. coin; 50c. 1877 50c. coin; 1p. 1877 1p. coin.

1980. Events. Multicoloured.

1728 3p. Type **548** 60 25

1729 3p. As No. 1705 60 25

1730 5p. Olympic rings 90 40

1731 5p. "Uruguay 79" stamp exhibition emblem 90 40

1732 7p. Chessboard and rook (23rd Chess Olympiad, Buenos Aires, 1978) 1·25 55

1733 7p. Detail from Greek vase (Olympic Games) 1·25 55

1734 10p. Detail from Greek vase (different) 1·75 80

568 Thomas Edison and Lamp

1980. Centenary of Electric Light.

1736 **568** 2p. multicoloured 40 20

569 Arms of Colonia **571** Association Emblem

1980. Colonia.
1737 **569** 50c. multicoloured . . . 15 10

1980. 50th Anniv of Uruguayan Printers' Association.
1739 **571** 1p. yellow, mauve & blue 20 15

572 Geometric Design **573** Zorilla de San Martin and Page of "La Leyenda Patria"

1980. Stamp Day.
1740 **572** 1p. multicoloured . . . 20 10

1980. "La Leyenda Patria".
1741 **573** 1p. multicoloured . . . 20 10

574 Boeing 747-200C Cargo Airplane

1980. Inauguration of Lufthansa Cargo Container Service.
1742 **574** 2p. multicoloured . . . 40 20

575 Conference Emblem and Flags

1980. 8th World Hereford Conference, Punta del Este, and Livestock Exhibition, Prado, Montevideo.
1743 **575** 2p. multicoloured . . . 40 20

576 Lions Emblem and Map of South America

1980. 9th Latin-American Lions Forum.
1744 **576** 1p. multicoloured . . . 20 10

579 Rotary Emblem and Globe **580** Hand stubbing out Cigarette

1980. 75th Anniv of Rotary International.
1747 **579** 5p. multicoloured . . . 85 70

1980. World Health Day. Anti-smoking Campaign.
1748 **580** 1p. pink, black and green 20 10

581 Jose Artigas **582** Angel blowing Trumpet

1980.

1749	**581**	10c. blue	10	10
1750		20c. orange	10	10
1751		50c. red	10	10
1752		60c. yellow	10	10
1753		1p. grey	15	15
1754		2p. brown	35	15
1755		3p. green	55	30
1756		4p. blue	65	40
1757		5p. green	30	10
1757a		6p. orange	10	10
1758		7p. purple	95	70
1759		10p. blue	50	25
1760		12p. black	20	10
1761		15p.50 green	25	15
1762		20p. purple	1·00	85
1763		30p. brown	1·25	1·25
1764		50p. blue	2·00	2·00

1980. Christmas.
1765 **582** 2p. multicoloured . . . 30 15

583 Title Page of Constitution

1980. 150th Anniv of Constitution.
1766 **583** 4p. blue and gold . . . 70 35

584 Montevideo Football Stadium **585** Conquistador

1980. Gold Cup Football Championship, Montevideo.
1767 **584** 5p. multicoloured . . . 50 35
1768 – 5p. yellow, black and red 50 35
1769 – 10p. multicoloured . . . 1·10 1·10
DESIGNS—As T **584**. No. 1768, Gold cup. 25 × 79 mm: No. 1769, Mascot and flags of participating countries.

1981. Hispanidad Day.
1771 **585** 2p. multicoloured . . . 35 15

586 U.P.U. Emblem **587** Alexander von Humboldt

1981. Centenary of U.P.U. Membership.
1772 **586** 2p. multicoloured . . . 35 15

1981. 122nd Death Anniv of Alexander von Humboldt (naturalist).
1773 **587** 2p. multicoloured . . . 40 15

588 Trophy and Open Book

1981. International Education Exhibition and Congress, Montevideo.
1774 **588** 2p. green, black and lilac 35 15

589 Flags and Trophy **590** Musical Notes over Map of the Americas

1981. Uruguayan Victory in Gold Cup Football Championship.
1775 **589** 2p. multicoloured . . . 40 15
1776 5p. multicoloured . . . 60 35

1981. 40th Anniv of Inter-american Institute of Musicology.
1777 **590** 2p. multicoloured . . . 40 15

591 Boeing 707

1981. Inaugural Flight to Madrid of Pluna Airline.
1778 **591** 2p. multicoloured . . . 40 15
1779 5p. multicoloured . . . 60 40
1780 10p. multicoloured . . . 1·25 70
Nos 1778/80 are inscribed "BOEING 737".

592 Cavalryman of Gen. Manuel Oribe, 1843

1981. Army Day. Multicoloured.
1781 2p. Type **592** 40 15
1782 2p. Infantry of Montevideo, 1843 . . . . 40 15

593 Conference Emblem on Suitcase

1981. World Tourism Conference, Manila (1980).
1783 **593** 2p. multicoloured . . . 35 15

594 Peace Dove and Atomic Emblem **596** Arms and Map of Rocha

1981. 25th Anniv of National Atomic Energy Commission.
1784 **594** 2p. multicoloured . . . 35 15

595 Footballer

1981. Europe–South America Football Cup.
1785 **595** 2p. multicoloured . . . 40 15

1981. Department of Rocha.
1786 **596** 2p. multicoloured . . . 40 15

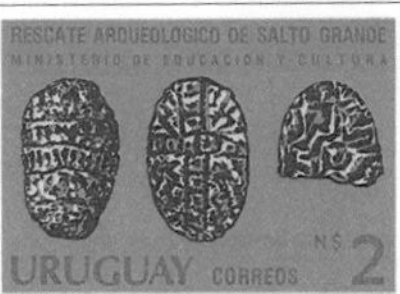

597 Carved Stone Tablets

1981. Salto Grande Archaeological Rescue Excavations.
1787 **597** 2p. multicoloured . . . 40 15

598 Artigas Monument, Minas **599** A.N.C.A.P. Anniversary Emblem

1981. 10th Lavalleja Week.
1788 **598** 4p. multicoloured . . . 70 35

1981. 50th Anniv of National Administration for Combustible Fuels, Alcohol and Portland Cement.
1789 **599** 2p. multicoloured . . . 35 15

600 I.Y.D.P. Emblem

1981. International Year of Disabled Persons.
1790 **600** 2p. deep blue, red and blue 35 15

601 Sun Disc

1981. Senior Level Meeting on Environmental Law, Montevideo.
1791 **601** 5p. multicoloured . . . 60 35

602 Hands holding Knife and Fork

1981. World Food Day.
1792 **602** 2p. multicoloured . . . 40 15

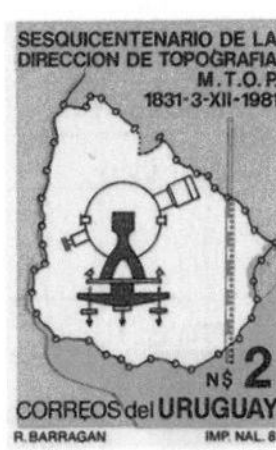

603 Theodolite and Measuring Rod on Map of Uruguay

1981. 150th Anniv of Topographic Survey.
1793 **603** 2p. multicoloured . . . 40 15

604 Bank of Uruguay

1981. 85th Anniv of Bank of Uruguay.
1794 **604** 2p. multicoloured . . . 40 15

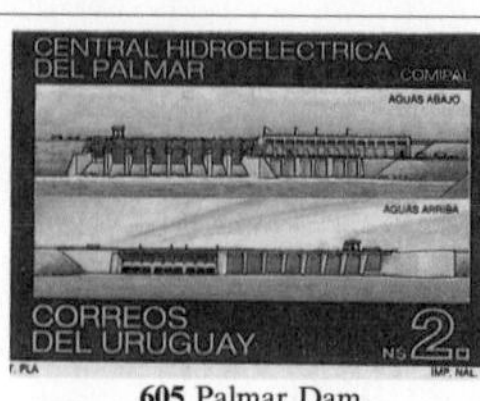

605 Palmar Dam

1981. Palmar Central Hydro-electric Project.
1795 **605** 2p. multicoloured . . . 40 15

606 Father Christmas 607 Joaquin Suarez

1981. Christmas.
1796 **606** 2p. multicoloured . . . 40 15

1982. Birth Bicentenary of Joaquin Suarez.
1797 **607** 5p. multicoloured . . . 60 35

608 Lockheed Super Constellation and Route Map

1982. 25th Anniv of 1st Germany–Uruguay Lufthansa Flight. Multicoloured.
1798 3p. Type **608** 50 30
1799 7p. Boeing 747-200 and route map 90 70

609 American Air Forces Co-operation Emblem
610 Private, Florida Battalion, 1865

1982. 22nd American Air Forces' Commanders Conference.
1800 **609** 10p. multicoloured . . . 1·25 80

1982. Army Day. Multicoloured.
1801 3p. Type **610** 55 20
1802 3p. Captain of Artillery, 1872 . . . . 55 20

611 Face and Satellite in Outer Space
612 Pinocchio

1982. Peaceful Uses of Outer Space Conference, Vienna.
1803 **611** 3p. multicoloured . . . 75 40

1982. Centenary of Publication of Carlo Collodi's "Pinocchio".
1804 **612** 2p. multicoloured . . . 40 15

613 Arms of Flores

1982. Department of Flores.
1805 **613** 2p. multicoloured . . . 40 15

614 Zorrilla de San Martin

1982. 50th Death Anniv of Juan Zorrilla de San Martin (writer).
1806 **614** 3p. multicoloured . . . 60 35

615 Cadet Schooner "Capitan Miranda" (after J. Rivera)

1982. 165th Anniv of Navy.
1807 **615** 3p. multicoloured . . . 1·50 30

616 Figures reading Book 617 Scales of Justice

1982. National Literacy Campaign.
1808 **616** 3p. blue, deep blue and yellow 25 10

1982. Stamp Day.
1809 **617** 3p. green 30 15
1810 – 3p. red 30 15
DESIGN: No. 1810, Volcano.

618 Star, Family and Symbols of Economic Progress

1982. Christmas.
1811 **618** 3p. multicoloured . . . 30 15

619 Fabini

1983. Birth Centenary of Edouardo Fabini (composer).
1812 **619** 3p. deep brown & brown 30 15

620 2nd Cavalry Regiment, 1885 621 "Santa Maria" on Globe

1983. Army Day. Multicoloured.
1813 3p. Type **620** 40 15
1814 3p. Military College, 1885 . . . . 40 15

1983. Visit of King and Queen of Spain. Multicoloured.
1815 3p. Type **621** . . . . . . 2·00 30
1816 7p. Royal couple and Uruguayan and Spanish flags (44 × 31 mm) 80 40

622 Headquarters Building 623 Exhibition Emblem

1983. Inauguration of Postal Union of the Americas and Spain H.Q., Montevideo.
1817 **622** 3p. black, blue and brown 30 15

1983. "Brasiliana 83" International Stamp Exhibition, Rio de Janeiro.
1818 **623** 3p. multicoloured . . . 30 15

624 Space Shuttle "Columbia"

1983. 1st Flight of Space Shuttle "Columbia".
1819 **624** 7p. multicoloured . . . 65 30

625 "Delin 1900" Car

1983. 1st Imported Car.
1820 **625** 3p. blue and black . . . 30 15

626 Goethe and Scene from "Faust"

1983. 150th Death Anniv (1982) of Johann Wolfgang von Goethe (writer).
1821 **626** 7p. blue and black . . . 65 30

627 "Moonlit Landscape" 628 Statue of Lavelleja

1983. 6th Death Anniv of Jose Cuneo (artist).
1822 **627** 3p. multicoloured . . . 30 15

1983. Bicentenary of Minas City.
1823 **628** 3p. multicoloured . . . 30 15

629 W.C.Y. Emblem

1983. World Communications Year.
1824 **629** 3p. multicoloured . . . 20 10

630 Garibaldi

1983. Death Centenary (1982) of Guiseppe Garibaldi (Italian revolutionary).
1825 **630** 7p. multicoloured . . . 50 30

631 "Graf Zeppelin"

1983. Zeppelin Flight over Montevideo (1934).
1826 **631** 7p. black, blue and mauve 90 35

632 Footballers, World Cup and Italian Team Badge

1983. Italy's Victory in World Cup Football Championship (1982).
1827 **632** 7p. multicoloured . . . 65 30

633 Virgin, Child and Star

1983. Christmas.
1828 **633** 4p.50 multicoloured . . 25 10

634 "50" on Telephone Dial

1984. 50th Anniv of Automatic Telephone Dialling.
1829 **634** 4p.50 multicoloured . . 25 10

635 Leandro Gomez

636 Emblem, Map, Flag and Tanker

1984. General Leandro Gomez Commemoration.
1830 **635** 4p.50 blue, light blue and black 25 10

1984. 25th Anniv (1983) of International Maritime Organization.
1831 **636** 4p.50 multicoloured . . 50 15

637 Flags and Emblem

638 Map of Uruguay and Bank Emblem

1984. American Women's Day.
1832 **637** 4p.50 multicoloured . . 25 10

1984. 25th Annual Meeting of Governors of International Development Bank, Punta del Este.
1833 **638** 10p. blue, gold and black 55 20

639 Simon Bolivar

1984. Birth Bicentenary (1983) of Simon Bolivar.
1834 **639** 4p.50 lt brown & brown 25 10

640 Club Emblem and Radio Waves

1984. 50th Anniv (1983) of Uruguay Radio Club.
1835 **640** 7p. multicoloured . . . 40 20

641 Monument

1984. 1930 World Cup Football Championship Monument.
1836 **641** 4p.50 multicoloured . . 25 10

642 National Emblem within "200"

1984. Bicentenary (1983) of San Jose de Mayo.
1837 **642** 4p.50 multicoloured . . 25 10

643 Emblem

1984. 50th Anniv of Tourist Organization.
1838 **643** 4p.50 gold, violet and blue 25 10

644 Artillery Uniform, 1895

645 Artigas on Horseback

1984. Army Day. Multicoloured.
1839 4p.50 Type **644** 25 15
1840 4p.50 2nd Battalion Cazadores uniform, 1894 25 15

1984.
1841 **645** 4p.50 black and blue . . 25 15
1842 8p.50 brown and blue . . 45 25

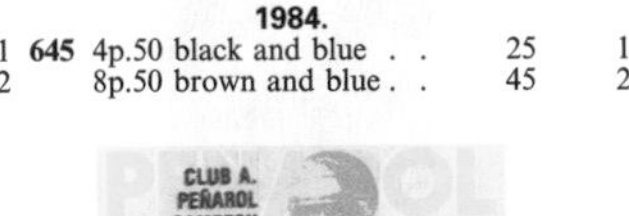

646 Trophy

1984. Penarol Athletic Club. Winners of European–South American Football Cup, 1982.
1843 **646** 4p.50 black, yellow and deep yellow 25 10

1984. Uruguayan Departments.
1844 **444** 4p.50 multicoloured . . 25 10

647 Child holding Flower and "50 AÑOS"

1984. 50th Anniv of Children's Council.
1845 **647** 4p.50 multicoloured . . 25 10

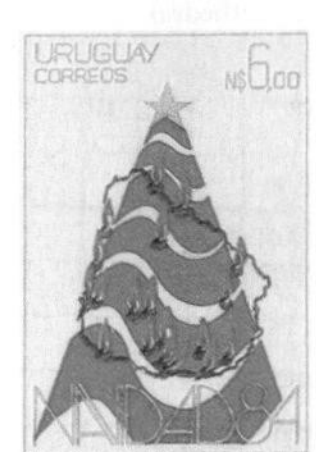

648 Christmas Tree with Candles

649 Pelota Player and Flags

1984. Christmas.
1846 **648** 6p. multicoloured . . . 30 10

1985. 1st Junior Pelota World Championship.
1847 **649** 4p.50 multicoloured . . 25 10

650 Bruno Mauricio de Zabala

652 Carlos Gardel

651 Emblems of Los Angeles and Sarajevo Games and Olympic Rings

1985. 300th Birth Anniv (1983) of Don Bruno Mauricio de Zabala (Governor of Buenos Aires and founder of Montevideo).
1848 **650** 4p.50 multicoloured . . 25 10

1985. 90th Anniv of International Olympic Committee.
1849 **651** 12p. multicoloured . . . 45 25

1985. 50th Death Anniv of Carlos Gardel (entertainer).
1850 **652** 6p. grey, blue and brown 25 10

653 Emblem and Flags of Member States

1985. 25th Anniv of American Air Forces' Co-operation System.
1851 **653** 12p. multicoloured . . . 20 10

654 Icarus

1985. 40th Anniv of I.C.A.O.
1852 **654** 4p.50 deep blue, green and blue 10 10

655 Stylized Factory and "50"

1985. 50th Anniv of FUNSA Tyre Factory.
1853 **655** 6p. multicoloured . . . 10 10

656 Cross and Clasped Hands

1985. Centenary of Catholic Workers Circle.
1854 **656** 6p. multicoloured . . . 10 10

657 I.Y.Y. Emblem

1985. International Youth Year.
1855 **657** 12p. red and black . . . 20 10

658 Peace Dove and Sun

1985. "Return to Democracy".
1856 **658** 20p. blue, yellow and violet 30 15

659 Books forming "8"

661 Map and Arms

660 Emblem

1985. 8th International Book Exhibition.
1857 **659** 20p. multicoloured . . . 30 15

1985. Centenary of Military School.
1858 **660** 10p. multicoloured . . . 20 10

1985. Centenary of Flores Department.
1859 **661** 6p. multicoloured . . . 10 10

662 Father Christmas

1985. Christmas.
1860 **662** 10p. multicoloured . . . 20 10
1861 22p. multicoloured . . . 35 20

663 Monument to Isabel the Catholic

1985. Hispanidad Day.
1862 **663** 12p. black, red and brown 15 10

664 Emblem and Meeting Logo

1986. 3rd Inter-American Agriculture Co-operation Institute Meeting.
1863 **664** 12p. yellow, red and black 20 10

665 Emblem and Flag

1986. World Post Day.
1864 **665** 15p.50 multicoloured . . 25 10

666 Map and Symbolic House

1986. 6th Population and 4th Housing Census (1985).
1865 **666** 10p. black, blue and yellow 20 10

667 Emblem

1986. 50th Anniv (1985) of Conaprole Milk and Cattle Co-operative.
1866 **667** 10p. gold, blue and light blue 20 10

668 U.N. Emblem and Population Diagram

1986. 40th Anniv (1985) of U.N.O.
1867 **668** 20p. multicoloured . . . 30 15

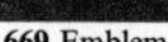

669 Emblem **670** Manuel Oribe

1986. 50th Anniv (1985) of National Brokers and Auctioneers Association.
1868 **669** 10p. black, deep blue and blue 15 10

1986. Liberation Heroes.

1869	**670**	1p. green (postage) . .	10	10
1870		2p. red	10	10
1871	A	3p. blue	10	10
1872		5p. blue	10	10
1872a	**670**	5p. blue	10	10
1873		7p. brown	10	10
1874	B	10p. mauve	10	10
1875	C	10p. green	10	10
1875a	**670**	10p. green	10	10
1876		15p. blue	10	10
1877	B	17p. blue	15	10
1877a	**670**	20p. brown	15	10
1877b	A	25p. orange	10	10
1878	B	26p. brown	10	10
1879	C	30p. orange	20	15
1879a	A	30p. blue	10	10
1879b	B	45p. red	25	20
1880	C	50p. ochre	30	20
1880a	A	50p. mauve	30	20
1881	C	60p. grey	40	40
1881a	A	60p. orange	10	20
1881b	B	60p. mauve	10	10
1881c		75p. red	10	10
1881d		90p. red	10	10
1882	C	100p. red	60	75
1882a		100p. brown	30	30
1882b		150p. green	35	35
1883		200p. green	1·25	1·10
1883a		300p. blue	60	60
1883b		500p. red	1·25	1·25
1883c		1000p. red	2·00	2·00
1884	B	22p. violet (air) . . .	15	10

DESIGNS: A, Lavalleja; B, Jose Fructuoso Rivera; C, Jose Gervasio Artigas.

671 Mosaic in National Colours

1986. Italian Chamber of Commerce in Uruguay.
1885 **671** 20p. multicoloured . . . 20 10

672 Armenian Flag and Monument **673** Emblem and Footballer

1986. 71st Anniv of Armenian Genocide.
1886 **672** 10p. black, red and blue 10 10

1986. World Cup Football Championship, Mexico.
1887 **673** 20p. multicoloured . . . 20 15

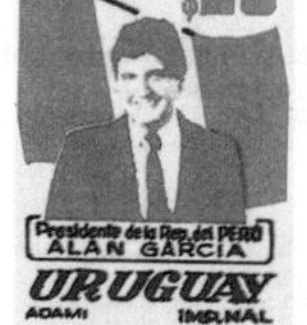

674 Newspaper Page **675** Alan Garcia

1986. Centenary of "El Dia".
1888 **674** 10p. gold, black and red 10 10

1986. Visit of President of Peru.
1889 **675** 20p. brown, red and blue 15 15

676 Map, Gen. Sucre and Simon Bolivar **677** Jose Sarney

1986. Visit of Pres. Jaime Lusinchi of Venezuela.
1890 **676** 20p. multicoloured . . . 15 15

1986. Visit of President of Brazil.
1891 **677** 20p. multicoloured . . . 15 15

678 Michelini

1986. 10th Death Anniv of Zelmar Michelini (senator).
1892 **678** 10p. blue and red . . . 10 10

679 Menorah and "50"

1986. 50th Anniv of B'nai B'rith in Uruguay.
1893 **679** 10p. brown, gold and red 10 10

680 Handshake across "GATT"

1986. General Agreement on Tariffs and Trade Assembly, Punta del Este.
1894 **680** 10p. multicoloured . . . 10 10

681 Dr. Raul Alfonsin

1986. Visit of President of Argentina.
1895 **681** 20p. orange, black & blue 15 15

682 Fishes in Sea

1986. Quality Exports. Multicoloured.
1896 20p. Type **682** 30 15
1897 20p. Lambs 15 15

683 Flags and Dr. Blanco

1986. Visit of Dr. Salvador Jorge Blanco, President of Dominican Republic.
1898 **683** 20p. multicoloured . . . 15 15

684 Dr. Pertini

1986. Visit of Dr. Sandro Pertini, President of Italy.
1899 **684** 20p. yellow and green . . 15 15

685 Douglas DC-10 and DC-3 Aircraft and Flags

1986. 40th Anniv of First Scheduled Spain-Uruguay Flight.
1900 **685** 20p. multicoloured . . . 45 15

686 Statue of Sts. Philip and John and Montevideo Cathedral

1987. Hispanidad Day.
1901 **686** 10p. red and black . . . 10 10

687 Emblem

1987. 50th Anniv (1986) of Juventus Catholic Cultural Organization.
1902 **687** 10p. yellow, black and blue 10 10

688 Ruiz

1987. 10th Death Anniv (1986) of Hector Gutierrez Ruiz (Chamber of Deputies member).
1903 **688** 10p. brown and red . . 10 10

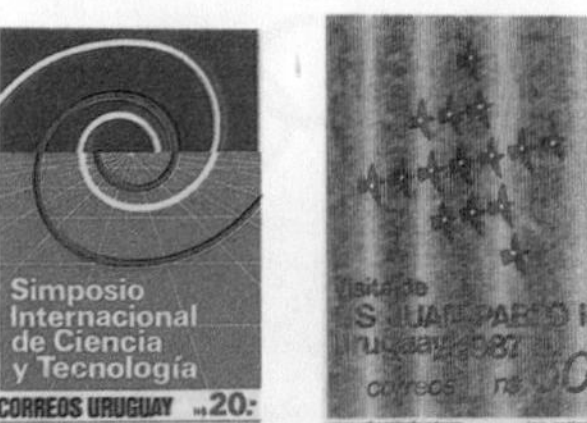

689 Emblem **690** "Arrowhead" of Flying Doves

1987. International Science and Technology Symposium, Montevideo and Punta del Este (1986).
1904 **689** 20p. multicoloured . . . 15 15

1987. Visit of Pope John Paul II.
1905 **690** 50p. orange and grey . . 35 45

691 Dr. Arias and Emblem **692** "70" and Menorah

1987. Birth Centenary of Dr. Jose F. Arias (founder of Uruguay Trades University).
1906 **691** 10p. multicoloured . . . 10 10

1987. 70th Anniv of Uruguayan Jewish Community.
1907 **692** 10p. blue, orange & black 10 10

693 De Havilland Dragon Fly

1987. 50th Anniv (1986) of Pluna National Airline. Multicoloured.
1908 10p. Type **693** 10 10
1909 20p. Douglas DC-3 . . . . 15 10
1910 25p. Vickers Viscount 810 15 15
1911 30p. Boeing 707 . . . . . . 20 15

694 Artigas Antarctic Base

1987.
1912 **694** 20p. multicoloured . . . 15 15

695 Sun, Symbolic House and "75"

1987. 75th Anniv of Uruguayan Mortgage Bank.
1913 **695** 26p. multicoloured . . . 20 15

696 Dairy Products **697** "Holy Family"

1987. Uruguayan Quality Exports. Multicoloured.
1914 51p. Type **696** 35 20
1915 51p. Map and cattle 35 20

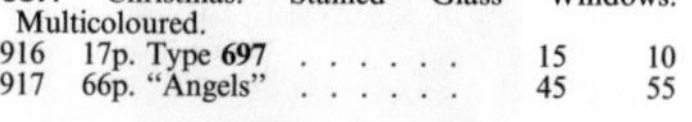

1987. Christmas. Stained Glass Windows. Multicoloured.
1916 17p. Type **697** 15 10
1917 66p. "Angels" 45 55

698 Pres. Duarte **699** Airplane and Globe forming "60"

1988. Visit of Pres. Jose Napoleon Duarte of El Salvador.
1918 **698** 20p. blue and yellow . . 15 15

1988. 60th Anniv (1987) of VARIG (airline).
1919 **699** 66p. blue, yellow & black 45 50

700 Emblem and Globe

1988. International Peace Year (1986).
1920 **700** 10p. multicoloured . . . 10 10

701 Flags and Beret

702 Farman "Shorthorn" within Airplane Wing

1988. 75th Anniv (1987) of Basque Immigration.
1921 **701** 66p. multicoloured . . . 45 45

1988. 75th Anniv of Air Force.
1922 **702** 17p. multicoloured . . . 20 10

703 Lantern and "75"

1988. 75th Anniv (1987) of UTE (hydro-electric dam programme).
1923 **703** 17p. multicoloured . . . 15 10
1924 – 17p. black, blue and green 15 10
1925 – 51p. black and blue . . 35 20
1926 – 51p. black, blue and red 35 20
1927 – 66p. blue, black & yellow 45 25
DESIGNS: No. 1924, Baygorria Dam; 1925, Dr. Gabriel Terra Dam; 1926, Constitucion Dam; 1927, Map showing dam sites on River Negro.

704 Flag and Globe

1988. 75th Anniv (1986) of Postal Union of the Americas and Spain.
1928 **704** 66p. multicoloured . . . 45 45

705 Menorah in "40"

1988. 40th Anniv of Israel.
1929 **705** 66p. blue and black . . 45 45

706 Airmail Envelope and Postman

1988. "Post, Messenger of Peace".
1930 **706** 66p. multicoloured . . . 45 45

707 Emblem on Map

709 Col. Pablo Banales (founder)

708 Matos Rodriguez

1988. 60th Anniv of Inter-American Institute for the Child.
1931 **707** 30p. lt green, green & blk 20 15

1988. Gerardo H. Matos Rodriguez (composer) Commemoration.
1932 **708** 17p. black and violet . . 15 10
1933 – 51p. brown on lt brown 35 20
DESIGN: 51p. Matos Rodriguez and score of "La Cumparsita".

1988. Centenary (1987) of Fire Service. Mult.
1934 17p. Type **709** 15 10
1935 26p. Fireman, 1900 . . . . 20 15
1936 34p. Emblem (horiz) 20 15
1937 51p. Merryweather fire engine, 1907 (horiz) . . . 35 20
1938 66p. 8-man hand pump, 1888 (horiz) 45 25
1939 100p. Magirus mechanical ladder, 1921 (44 × 25 mm) 70 40

710 Route Map and "Capitan Miranda"

1988. 1st World Voyage of "Capitan Miranda".
1940 **710** 30p. multicoloured . . . 90 30

711 Citrus Fruits

1988. Exports. Multicoloured.
1941 30p. Type **711** 20 15
1942 45p. Rice 35 20
1943 55p. Shoes 40 20
1944 55p. Clothes 40 20

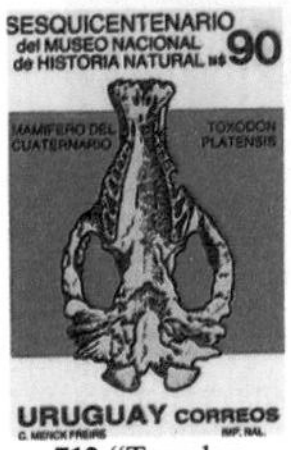

712 "Toxodon platensis" (mammal bone)

713 Bird posting Letter

1988. 150th Anniv of National Natural History Museum, Montevideo.
1945 – 30p. brown, yellow & blk 50 20
1946 **712** 90p. brown, blue & black 65 60
DESIGN: 30p. "Usnea densirostra" (moss).

1988. Postal Officers' Day. Unissued stamp surch.
1947 **713** 30p. on 10p.+5p. yellow, black and blue 10 10

714 Abstract

1988. 150th Anniv (1986) of Battle of Carpinteria.
1948 **714** 30p. multicoloured . . . 10 10

715 Virgin and Child

716 "Self-portrait" (Joaquin Torres Garcia)

1988. Christmas.
1949 **715** 115p. multicoloured . . 55 55

1988. Uruguayan Painters. Multicoloured.
1950 115p. Type **716** 50 50
1951 115p. Poster for Pedro Figari exhibition, Montevideo 50 50
1952 115p. "Squares and Rectangles LXXVIII" (Jose P. Costigliolo) . . . 50 50
1953 115p. "Manolita Pina, 1920" (Joaquin Torres Garcia) 50 50

717 "Santa Maria"

1989. Hispanidad Day.
1954 **717** 90p. multicoloured . . . 75 45
1955 115p. multicoloured . . 90 55

718 Emblem

1989. Cent of Armenian Organization Hnchakian.
1956 **718** 210p. blue, yellow and red 40 35

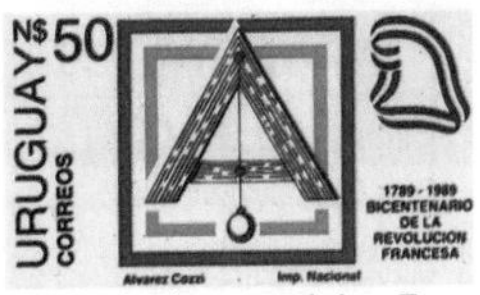

719 Plumb Line suspended on Frame

1989. Bicentenary of French Revolution. Each black, red and blue.
1957 50p. Type **719** 10 10
1958 50p. Tree of Liberty 10 10
1959 210p. Eye in centre of sunburst 40 35
1960 210p. "Liberty", "Equality", "Fraternity" around phrygian cap 40 35

720 Map

1989. "Use the Post Code". Each black and red.
1961 50p. Type **720** 10 10
1962 210p. Map showing numbered zones (vert) . . 40 35

721 Map, Cow, Factory and Baby

722 "Tiradentes"

1989. 3rd Pan-American Milk Congress.
1963 **721** 170p. deep blue and blue 30 25

1989. Birth Bicentenary of Joaquin Jose da Silver Xavier.
1964 **722** 170p. multicoloured . . 30 25

723 Emblem and Flag

1989. Interparliamentary Union Centenary Conference, London.
1965 **723** 210p. red, blue and black 40 35

724 F.A.O. Emblem, Map and Fruit Slices

1989. 8th Intergovernmental Group on Citrus Fruits Meeting.
1966 **724** 180p. multicoloured . . 30 25

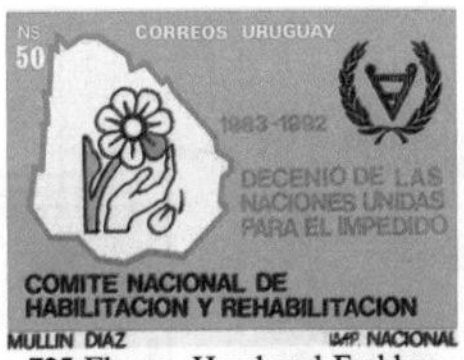

725 Flower, Hand and Emblem

1989. U.N. Decade for Disabled People. Mult.
1967 50p. Type **725** 10 10
1968 210p. Disabled people and emblem 40 35

726 Nacurutu Artefact

727 Virgin of the Thirty Three

1989. America. Pre-Columbian Culture.
1969 **726** 60p. multicoloured . . . 10 10
1970 180p. multicoloured . . 30 25

1989. Christmas. Multicoloured.
1971 70p. Type **727** 10 10
1972 210p. "Adoration of the Animals" (Barradas) (horiz) 15 15

728 Old and Modern Buildings

1989. Bicentenary of Pando.
1973 **728** 60p. multicoloured . . . 10 10

729 Hospital Building

1990. Bicentenary of Charity Hospital.
1974 **729** 60p. flesh, black & brown 10 10

730 Map and Arms of Soriano

731 Luisa Luisi

1990. Departments. Multicoloured.

1975	70p. Type **730**	10	10
1976	70p. Florida (vert)	10	10
1977	90p. San Jose (vert)	10	10
1978	90p. Canelones	10	10
1979	90p. Lavalleja (vert)	10	10
1980	90p. Rivera	10	10

1990. Writers. Multicoloured.

1981	60p. Type **731**	10	10
1982	60p. Javier de Viana	10	10
1983	75p. J. Zorilla de San Martin	10	10
1984	75p. Dekmira Agustini . . .	10	10
1985	170p. Julio Casal	45	45
1986	170p. Alfonsina Storni . . .	45	45
1987	210p. Juana de Ibarbourou	55	55
1988	210p. Carlos Roxlo	55	55

732 Mercedes Church

733 Ear of Wheat and Tractor

1990. Bicentenary of Mercedes.
1989 **732** 70p. multicoloured . . . 10 10

1990. 10th Anniv of International Agricultural Fund.
1990 **733** 210p. multicoloured . . 55 55

734 Glass and Smashed Car

1990. Road Safety. Multicoloured.

1991	70p. Type **734**	70	70
1992	70p. Traffic waiting at red light	70	70
1993	70p. Road signs	70	70
1994	70p. Children crossing road at green light	70	70

735 Sculpture of Artigas 736 Woman

1990. Artigas Day.
1995 **735** 60p. blue and red . . . 10 10

1990. International Women's Day.
1996 **736** 70p. multicoloured . . . 10 10

737 Gonzalo Ramirez

738 Microphone and Radio Mast

1990. Centenary of 1st International Juridical Congress, Montevideo.

1997	**737** 60p. black, yellow & mve	55	55
1998	– 60p. black, blue & mauve	55	55
1999	– 60p. multicoloured . . .	55	55
2000	– 60p. multicoloured . . .	55	55

DESIGNS: No. 1998, Ildefonso Garcia; 1999, Flags and left half of 50th anniversary memorial; 2000, Flags and right half of memorial.

1990. The Media. Multicoloured.

2001	70p. Type **738**	70	70
2002	70p. Newpaper vendor . . .	70	70
2003	70p. Television screen, camera and aerial	70	70
2004	70p. Books and type	70	70

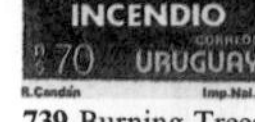

739 Burning Trees

741 "Nativity" (Juan B. Maino)

740 American Deer

1990. Fire Prevention.
2005 **739** 70p. black, yellow and red 70 70

1990. America. The Natural World. Mult.

2006	120p. Type **740**	10	10
2007	360p. "Peltophorum dubium" (vert)	85	85

1990. Christmas.

2008	**741** 170p. multicoloured . .	40	40
2009	830p. multicoloured . .	2·00	2·00

742 Carlos Federico Saez

1990. Artists. Multicoloured.

2010	90p. Type **742**	10	10
2011	90p. Pedro Blanes Viale . .	10	10
2012	210p. Edmundo Prati . . .	55	55
2013	210p. Jose L. Zorrilla de San Martin	55	55

743 Mechanical Digger

1991. 75th Anniv of Army Engineers Division.
2014 **743** 170p. multicoloured . . 40 40

744 Drum and Masks

1991. Carnival.
2015 **744** 170p. multicoloured . . 40 40

745 Campaign Emblem

1991. Campaign against AIDS.

2016	**745** 170p. multicoloured . .	40	40
2017	830p. multicoloured . .	2·00	2·00

746 Anniversary Emblem

1991. Centenary of Organization of American States.
2018 **746** 830p. yellow, blue & blk 2·00 2·00

747 Textiles

1991. Uruguayan Quality Exports. Multicoloured.

2019	120p. Type **747**	10	10
2020	120p. Clothes (vert)	10	10
2021	400p. Semi-precious stones and granite	55	60

748 Flint Axe and Stone Monument

1991. Education. Multicoloured.

2022	120p. Type **748**	10	10
2023	120p. Wheel and pyramids	10	10
2024	330p. Printing press and diagram of planetary orbits	45	45
2025	330p. Space probe and computer diagram	45	45

749 Sword piercing Crab

1991. Anti-cancer Day.
2026 **749** 360p. red and black . . 45 45

750 College Arms 751 College Building

1991. Centenary of Holy Family College.
2027 **750** 360p. multicoloured . . 45 45

1991. Centenary of Immaculate Heart of Mary College.
2028 **751** 1370p. multicoloured . . 1·60 1·60

752 Emblem

1991. 7th Pan-American Maccabiah Games.
2029 **752** 1490p. multicoloured . . 1·75 1·75

753 World Map and Dornier Wal Flying Boat "Plus Ultra"

1991. "Espamer '91" Spain–Latin America Stamp Exhibition, Buenos Aires.
2030 **753** 1510p. multicoloured . . 2·00 2·00

754 "Oath of the Constitution" (P. Blanes Viale)

1991. 1830 Constitution.
2031 **754** 360p. multicoloured . . 45 45

755 Gateway, Sacramento

756 "William Tell" (statue) and Flags

1991.

2032	**755** 360p. brown and yellow	45	45
2033	– 540p. grey and blue . .	65	65
2034	**755** 600p. brown, yellow & blk	55	55
2035	– 825p. grey, blue and black	1·10	1·10
2036	– 1510p. brown and green	2·00	2·00
2037	– 2500p. brown, grn & blk	2·50	2·50

DESIGNS: 540, 825p. First locomotive in Uruguay, 1869; 1510, 2500p. Horse tram.

For 800p. as Type **755** see No. 2103.

1991. 700th Anniv of Swiss Confederation.
2038 **756** 1510p. multicoloured . . 2·50 2·50

757 Yacht

758 Emblem

1991. Whitbread Regatta.

2040 **757** 1510p. multicoloured . . 1·75 1·75

1991. 50th Anniv of Uruguayan Society of Actors.

2041 **758** 450p. black and red . . 50 50

759 Camera and Photograph

1991. 150th Anniv of First Photograph in Rio de la Plata.

2042 **759** 1370p. multicoloured . . 1·50 1·50

760 Anniversary Emblem

1991. 25th Anniv of CREA (livestock organization).

2043 **760** 450p. multicoloured . . 50 50

761 Margarita Xirgu

1991. 22nd Death Anniv of Margarita Xirgu (actress).

2044 **761** 360p. brown, light brown and yellow 40 40

762 "General Rivera" (gunboat)

1991. Centre for Study of Naval and Maritime History. Multicoloured.

2045 450p. Type **762** 45 45

2046 450p. "Salto" (coastguard patrol boat) 45 45

2047 1570p. "Uruguay" (cruiser) 1·60 1·60

2048 1570p. "Pte. Oribe" (tanker) 1·60 1·60

763 "Rio de la Plata, 1602" (woodcut)

1991. America. Voyages of Discovery.

2049 **763** 450p. brown and yellow 50 50

2050 – 1740p. green and brown 1·90 1·90

DESIGN—HORIZ: 1740p. Amerigo Vespucci.

764 "The Tree is the Fountain of Life"

1991. World Food Day.

2051 **764** 1740p. multicoloured . . 1·75 1·75

765 "The Table" (Zoma Baitler)

1991.

2052 **765** 360p. multicoloured . . 40 40

766 Gladiator, 1902

1991. Old Cars. Multicoloured.

2053 360p. Type **766** 40 40

2054 1370p. E.M.F., 1909 . . . . 1·50 1·50

2055 1490p. Renault, 1912 . . . 1·50 1·50

2056 1510p. Clement-Bayard, 1903 (vert) . . . . 1·75 1·75

767 Emblem

768 Club Badge and Trophy

1991. 60th General Assembly of Interpol, Punta del Este.

2057 **767** 1740p. multicoloured . . 1·75 1·75

1991. National Football Club, Winners of World Cup Football Cup, 1988, and the Toyota Cup. Multicoloured.

2058 450p. Type **768** 50 50

2059 450p. Trophies on football pitch (horiz) 50 50

769 School and Pupils

1991. Centenary of Maria Auxiliadora Institute.

2060 **769** 450p. blue, black and red 50 50

770 "LATU"

1991. 25th Anniv of Uruguay Technological Laboratory.

2061 **770** 1570p. blue and deep blue . . . . 1·50 1·50

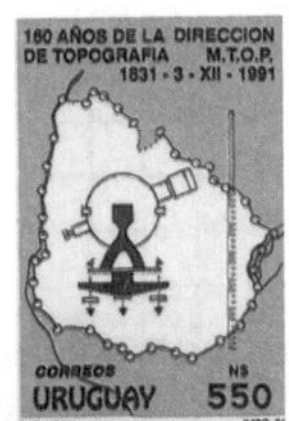

771 Emblem and Couple

772 Theodolite and Measuring Rod on Map of Uruguay

1991. World AIDS Day.

2062 **771** 550p. black, yellow & bl 55 55

2063 2040p. black, lilac & grn 2·00 2·00

1991. 160th Anniv of Topographic Survey.

2064 **772** 550p. multicoloured . . 55 55

773 Angel

1991. Christmas. Multicoloured.

2065 550p. Type **773** 55 55

2066 2040p. "Adoration of the Angels" . . . . 1·90 1·90

774 Anibal Troilo

1992. Musicians.

2067 **774** 450p. black, mauve & bl 40 40

2068 – 450p. black, orange & red 40 40

2069 – 450p. black, light green and green 40 40

2070 – 450p. black, blue & mve 40 40

DESIGNS: No. 2068, Francisco Canaro; 2069, Pintin Castellanos; 2070, Juan de Dios Filiberto.

775 Worker and Factory Building

1992. Quality Exports.

2071 **775** 120p. multicoloured . . 15 15

776 Pres. Aylwin

777 Trophy

1992. Visit of President Patricio Aylwin of Chile.

2072 **776** 550p. multicoloured . . 50 50

1992. Penarol F.C., Three-times World Club Football Champions.

2073 **777** 600p. black and yellow 55 55

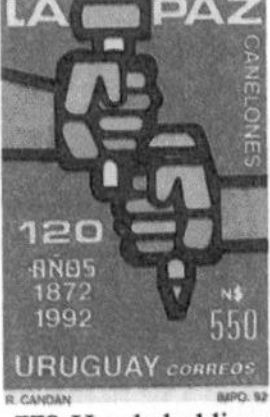

778 Hands holding Hammer and Chisel

779 No Smoking Emblem

1992. 120th Anniv of La Paz.

2075 **778** 550p. multicoloured . . 50 50

1992. World No Smoking Day.

2076 **779** 2500p. red, black & brn 2·00 2·00

780 Heart and Emblems

1992. World Health Day. "Health in Rhythm with the Heart".

2077 **780** 2500p. ultramarine, blue and red . . . . 2·10 2·10

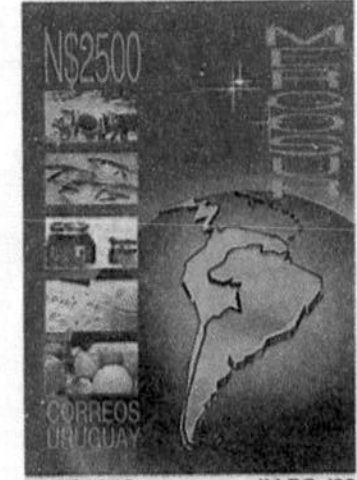

781 Map of South America and Food Products

1992. Mercosur (South American economic organization).

2078 **781** 2500p. multicoloured . . 2·10 2·10

782 Stamp

1992. "Olymphilex 92" International Olympic Stamps Exhibition, Barcelona.

2079 **782** 2900p. multicoloured . . 2·25 2·25

783 Emblems

1992. 22nd Latin American–Caribbean Regional Conference of Food and Agricultural Organization.

2080 **783** 2500p. multicoloured . . 1·75 1·75

784 Children with Basket of Food

1992. International Nutrition Conference, Rome.

2081 **784** 2900p. multicoloured . . 2·10 2·10

785 Vallejo

1992. Birth Centenary of Cesar Vallejo (painter and poet).

2082 **785** 2500p. brown & lt brown . . . . 1·75 1·75

786 Monument and Route Map

787 Ruins of Sacramento and Lighthouse

1992. Centenary of Christopher Columbus Monument, Durazno.

2083 **786** 700p. black, blue & green 50 50

1992. 500th Anniv of Discovery of America by Columbus.

2084 **787** 700p. multicoloured . . 50 50

788 Caravel 789 Emblem

1992. America. 500th Anniv of Discovery of America by Columbus. Multicoloured.
2085 700p. Type **788** 50 50
2086 2900p. Globe showing Americas and old map (horiz) . . . . 2·10 2·10

1992. Centenary of Christopher Columbus Philanthropic Society.
2087 **789** 700p. black, mauve and magenta 50 50

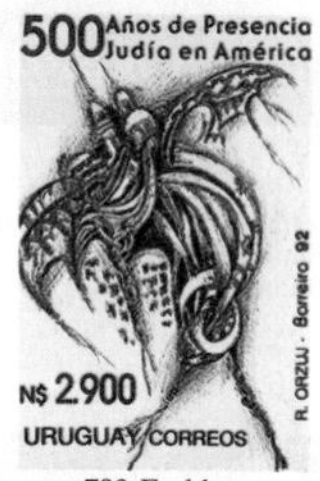

790 Emblem

1992. 500th Anniv of Presence of Jews in America.
2088 **790** 2900p. multicoloured . . 2·10 2·10

791 Arms

1992. 50th Anniv of Jose Pedro Varela Teachers' College.
2089 **791** 700p. multicoloured . . 50 50

792 Cambadu Building 793 Emblem

1992. Centenary of Chamber of Wholesale and Retail Traders.
2090 **792** 700p. grey, black and red 50 50

1992. 50th Anniv of Lebanon Club of Uruguay.
2091 **793** 2900p. multicoloured . . 2·10 2·10

794 Nativity 796 Immigrant

795 Map and Emblem

1992. Christmas. Multicoloured.
2092 800p. Type **794** 55 55
2093 3200p. Star . . . . 2·10 2·10

1992. 22nd Latin American and Carribean Lions Clubs Forum.
2094 **795** 2700p. multicoloured . . 1·75 1·75

1992. Immigrants Day.
2095 **796** 800p. green and black 55 55

797 Oribe 799 Anniversary Emblem

798 Anniversary Emblem

1992. Birth Bicentenary of Manuel Oribe (Liberation hero). Multicoloured.
2096 800p. Type **797** 55 55
2097 800p. Oribe (founder) and Eastern University (horiz) 55 55

1992. 90th Anniv of Pan-American Health Organization.
2098 **798** 3200p. multicoloured . . 2·10 2·10

1992. 50th Anniv of Jose H. Molaguero S.A.
2099 **799** 800p. brown and stone 55 55

800 Satellite and Map

1992. 70th Anniv of ANDEBU (association of broadcasting stations).
2100 **800** 2700p. multicoloured . . 1·75 1·75

801 Emblem and Shanty Town

1992. 30th Anniv of Caritas Uruguaya.
2101 **801** 3200p. multicoloured . . 2·00 2·00

802 Gonzalez Pecotche (founder) and Emblem

1992. 60th Anniv of Logosofia.
2102 **802** 800p. yellow and blue . . 55 55

1993. Size 35 × 24 mm.
2103 **755** 800p. olive and green . . 30 15

Currency Reform
1 (new) peso = 1000 (old) pesos.

803 Wilson Ferreira Aldunate 804 Post Car

1993.
2104 **803** 80c. red, black and grey 30 15

1993.
2105 **804** 1p. blue and yellow . . . 40 20

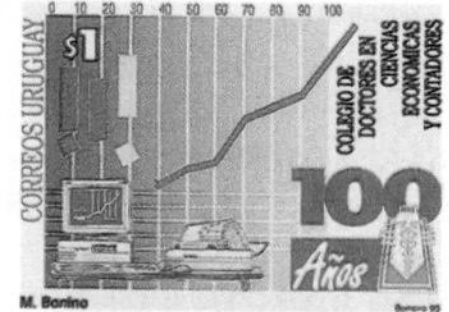

805 Graph and Personal Computer

1993. Centenary of Economic Sciences and Accountancy College.
2106 **805** 1p. multicoloured . . . 40 20

807 Magirus Deutz Fire Engine, 1958 808 Earth

1993. 50th Anniv of National Fire Service.
2108 **807** 1p. multicoloured . . . 40 20

1993. 15th Congress of Postal Union of the Americas, Spain and Portugal.
2109 **808** 3p.50 multicoloured . . 1·25 60

809 Schooner and Pedro Campbell (first Navy General)

1993. 175th Anniv (1992) of Uruguayan Navy.
2110 **809** 1p. multicoloured . . . 20 10

810 Emblem

1993. 25th Anniv of International University Circles.
2111 **810** 1p. multicoloured . . . 20 10

811 Hupmobile, 1910

1993. 75th Anniv of Uruguay Automobile Club.
2112 **811** 3p.50 multicoloured . . 70 35

813 Bird 814 Armadillo

1993. No value expressed.
2114 **813** (1p.20) blue and azure 25 15
2115 (1p.40) emerald and green 30 15
2147 (1p.60) red and pink . . 35 20
2148 (1p.80) brown and pink 30 15
2186 (2p.) grey 35 20
2207 (2p.30) violet 35 20
These were sold at the current inland letter rate.

1993.
2116 **814** 1p.20 brown and green 25 15

815 Village and Soldier

1993. Uruguayan Battalion of Peace-keeping Force in Cambodia.
2117 **815** 1p. multicoloured . . . 20 10

816 Dish Aerials and Studio

1993. 30th Anniv of National Television Channel 5.
2118 **816** 1p.20 multicoloured . . 25 15

817 "The Tree of Life" (detail, Pablo Serrano)

1993. 60th Anniv of Anda.
2119 **817** 1p.20 multicoloured . . 25 15

818 Arms and Officers

1993. 50th Anniv of Juan Carlos Gomez Folle National Police School.
2120 **818** 1p.20 multicoloured . . 25 15

819 Graphics

1993. 75th Anniv of "Diario El Pais" (newspaper).
2121 **819** 1p.20 multicoloured . . 25 15

820 Broad-nosed Caiman

1993. America. Endangered Animals. Multicoloured.
2122 1p.20 Type **820** 25 15
2123 3p.50 Burrowing owl (vert) 3·50 3·50

821 Power Lines supplying Illuminated Building

1993. 14th Latin American Conference on Rural Electrification.
2124 **821** 3p.50 multicoloured . . 70 35

822 Emblem 823 Red-legged Seriema

1993. 150th Anniv of B'nai B'rith (Jewish cultural and social organization).
2125 **822** 3p.70 multicoloured . . 75 40

1993. Natural World.
2126 **823** 20c. brown and pink . . 50 20
2127 – 30c. yellow and violet . . 65 25
2128 – 50c. brown and pink . . 15 15
DESIGNS—VERT: 30c. Saffron-cowled blackbird. HORIZ: 50c. Two-toed anteater.

825 Crucifix, Mother Francisca and Nuns with Sick People

826 Amerindian

1993. Beatification of Mother Francisca Rubatto.
2130 **825** 1p.20 multicoloured . . 25 15

1993. International Year of Indigenous Peoples.
2131 **826** 3p.50 multicoloured . . 70 35

827 Emblem on Map

1993. 75th Anniv of Montevideo Rotary Club.
2132 **827** 3p.50 blue and gold . . 70 35

829 Phoenician Cargo Ship (carving)

1993. 50th Anniv of Independence of Lebanon.
2134 **829** 3p.70 brown, deep brown and green . . . 75 40

830 Haedo

831 Ribbon

1993. Eduardo Victor Haedo.
2135 **830** 1p.20 multicoloured . . 25 15

1993. Anti-AIDS Campaign.
2136 **831** 1p.40 multicoloured . . 30 15

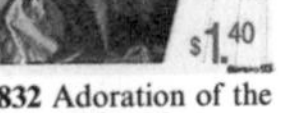

832 Adoration of the Wise Men

833 Adult with Chick and Eggs

1993. Christmas. Multicoloured.
2137 1p.40 Type **832** 30 15
2138 4p. Adoration of the Shepherds 80 40

1993. The Greater Rhea. Multicoloured.
2139 20c. Type **833** 25 25
2140 20c. Adults sitting and standing 25 25
2141 50c. Close-up of head . . . 65 40
2142 50c. Adults feeding 65 40

834 Child's view of life (Alejandro Cuende)

835 Emblem

1994. Children's Rights Day.
2143 **834** 1p.40 multicoloured . . 30 15

1994. National Postal Directorate.
2144 **835** 1p.40 blue and yellow . . 30 15

836 Torch Carrier

1994. 5th World Sports Congress, Punta del Este.
2145 **836** 4p. multicoloured . . . 80 40

837 Frigate

1994. 17th Inter-American Naval Conference.
2146 **837** 3p.70 multicoloured . . 75 40

838 Emblem

839 Sheep

1994. 7th Iberian–American Youth Organization Conference.
2149 **838** 3p.90 multicoloured . . 70 35

1994. 4th International Merino Sheep Conference.
2150 **839** 4p.30 multicoloured . . 75 40

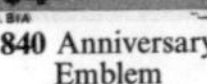

840 Anniversary Emblem

844 Dove flying from Ballot Box

843 Estable

1994. 75th Anniv of I.L.O.
2151 **840** 4p.30 multicoloured . . 75 40

1994. Birth Centenary of Clemente Estable (biologist).
2154 **843** 1p.60 green and black 30 15

1994. 75th Anniv of Electoral Court.
2155 **844** 1p.60 multicoloured . . 30 15

845 Hand pulling Worm from Dog's Mouth

1994. National Commission on Eradication of Tapeworms.
2156 **845** 1p.60 multicoloured . . 30 15

847 First Co-operative Headquarters, Rochdale, England

1994. 150th Anniv of Co-operative Movement.
2158 **847** 4p.30 multicoloured . . 75 40

848 National Flags on Plugs

1994. 30th Anniv of Commission for Regional Integration of Electricity.
2159 **848** 1p.60 multicoloured . . 30 15

849 Astronaut standing on Moon

1994. 25th Anniv of First Manned Moon Landing.
2160 **849** 3p. multicoloured . . . 55 30

850 Family

1994. International Year of the Family.
2161 **850** 4p.80 multicoloured . . 85 45

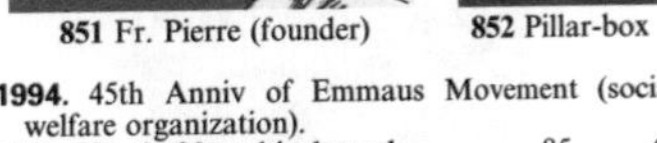

851 Fr. Pierre (founder)

852 Pillar-box

1994. 45th Anniv of Emmaus Movement (social welfare organization).
2162 **851** 4p.80 multicoloured . . 85 45

1994. 150th Anniv of Neighbourhood Pillar Boxes.
2163 **852** 50c. yellow and green . . 10 10
2164 1p. yellow and brown . . 15 10
2165 1p.80 yellow and blue . . 30 15
2166 2p.60 yellow and brown 40 20
2168 7p.50 yellow and violet 1·10 55

853 "The Man of Lugano"

1994. 50th Death Anniv of Goffredo Sommavilla (painter).
2169 **853** 4p.80 multicoloured . . 85 45

854 Swimmer

856 Saravia

855 Fernandez and Pupils with National Flag

1994. Centenary of International Olympic Committee.
2170 **854** 4p.80 multicoloured . . 85 45

1994. 125th Anniv of Elbio Fernandez School.
2171 **855** 1p.80 multicoloured . . 30 15

1994. 90th Death Anniv of Gen. Aparicio Saravia.
2172 **856** 1p.80 blue, turquoise and deep blue 30 15

857 Statuette

858 Town Plan

1994. 65th Anniv of General Association of Uruguayan Writers.
2173 **857** 1p.80 multicoloured . . 30 15

1994. 6th Latin American Town Planning Congress.
2174 **858** 4p.80 multicoloured . . 85 45

860 Mail Coach

1994. America. Postal Transport. Multicoloured.
2176 1p.80 Type **860** 30 15
2177 4p.80 "Eolo" (paddle-steamer) 85 45

861 Plan

1994. 1st International Seminar on Provision of Roads in Uruguay, Punte del Este.
2178 **861** 2p. multicoloured . . . 35 20

863 Computer Terminal and Reporter

1994. 50th Anniv of Uruguay Press Association.
2180 **863** 2p. multicoloured . . . 35 20

864 Statuette

1994. 50th Anniv of Uruguay Marketing Association.
2181 **864** 2p. multicoloured . . . 35 20

866 Dove over Latin America

1994. 25th Anniv of Latin American Movement "Long Live the People".
2183 **866** 4p.30 multicoloured . . 75 40

867 Draw Balls

1994. 55th Anniv of Lottery.
2184 **867** 2p. multicoloured . . . 35 20

868 Footballers  **869** Tree

1994. 85th Anniv of Young Men's Christian Association.
2185 **868** 2p. multicoloured . . . 35 20

1994. Christmas. Multicoloured.
2187 2p. Type **869** 35 20
2188 5p.50 Star over village . . . 1·00 50

870 Emblem and Venue

1994. 4th Assembly of Latin American and Caribbean Organization of Higher Fiscal Entities, Montevideo.
2189 **870** 5p.50 multicoloured . . 1·00 50

871 Cross and Crescent on Globe

1994. 75th Anniv of International Federation of Red Cross and Red Crescent Societies.
2190 **871** 5p. multicoloured . . . 90 45

872 Chuy Post Office

1995.
2191 **872** 20c. green 10 10
2192 10p. brown . . . . . . 1·50 75
2195 10p. mauve and black 1·10 55

873 CANT 18 Flying Boat

1995. 70th Anniv of Naval Aviation.
2198 **873** 2p. multicoloured . . . 30 15

874 Swimming Park

1995. 20th Anniv of World Tourism Organization. Multicoloured.
2199 5p. Type **874** 75 40
2200 5p. Deer and greater rhea 75 40
2201 5p. Ranch 75 40
2202 5p. Beach resort 75 40

875 Lifeboat

1995. 17th World Lifeguards' Conference.
2203 **875** 5p. multicoloured . . . 75 40

876 Globe and Emblem forming "90"

1995. 90th Anniv of Rotary International.
2204 **876** 5p. ultramarine, blue and gold 75 40

877 Anniversary Emblem and Airplane

1995. 50th Anniv of International Civil Aviation Organization.
2205 **877** 5p. ultramarine, orange and blue 75 40

878 Mascagni and Set from "Cavalleria Rusticana" (opera)

1995. 50th Death Anniv of Piero Mascagni (composer).
2206 **878** 5p. multicoloured . . . 75 40

879 Cimarron

1995.
2208 **879** 2p.30 multicoloured . . 35 20

881 Paysandu Players  **882** Orange incorporating Globe

1995. America Cup Football Championship, Uruguay. Multicoloured.
2210 2p.30 Type **881** 35 20
2211 2p.30 Rivera players 35 20
2212 2p.30 Ball in net 35 20
2213 2p.30 Montevideo players 35 20
2214 2p.30 Maldonado players 35 20
Nos. 2210/14 were issued together, se-tenant, forming a composite design of a match.

1995. 50th Anniv of F.A.O.
2215 **882** 5p.50 multicoloured . . 80 40

883 U.N. Soldier and Detail of World Map

1995. Participation in United Nations Peace-keeping Forces.
2216 **883** 2p.30 multicoloured . . 35 20

884 Italian National Colours on Map of Italy

1995. Visit of President Scalfaro of Italy.
2217 **884** 5p.50 multicoloured . . 80 40

885 People walking Hand in Hand towards Gateway  **887** Postal Symbol

1995. Latin American Integration Day.
2218 **885** 5p. multicoloured . . . 75 40

1995. No Value Expressed.
2220 **887** (2p.60) yellow & green 40 20
2221 (2p.90) yellow and blue 40 20
2222 (3p.20) pink and red . . 45 25
2223 (3p.50) brown & purple 50 25

888 Carlos Gardel (entertainer)

1995.
2226 **888** 5p.50 multicoloured . . 80 40

889 "Notocactus roseinflorus"  **890** Varela

1995. Flowers. Multicoloured.
2227 3p. Type **889** 45 25
2228 3p. "Verbena chamaedryfolia" 45 25
2229 3p. "Bauhinia candicans" 45 25
2230 3p. "Tillandsia aeranthos" 45 25
2231 3p. "Eichhornia crassipes" 45 25

1995. 150th Birth Anniv of Jose Verela (educationalist).
2232 **890** 2p.60 multicoloured . . 40 20

891 Monument  **892** "Dicksonia sellowiana"

1995. Holocaust Monument, Pueblo Judio.
2233 **891** 6p. multicoloured . . . 90 45

1995. America. Environmental Protection. Multicoloured.
2234 3p. Type **892** 45 25
2235 6p. Maned wolf (horiz) . . 90 45

894 Anniversary Emblem over Globe

1995. 50th Anniv of U.N.O.
2237 **894** 6p. multicoloured . . . 90 45

895 Beyer Peacock, 1876

1995. Steam Railway Locomotives. Multicoloured.
2238 3p. Type **895** 45 25
2239 3p. Criollo, 1895 . . . . . 45 25
2240 3p. Beyer Peacock, 1910 . . 45 25

896 Brigantine (privateer of Artigas)

1995. 178th Anniv of Naval Service. Multicoloured.
2241 3p. Type **896** 45 25
2242 3p. "Montevideo" (training frigate) 45 25
2243 3p. "Pte. Rivera" (tanker) 45 25

897 Crib  **900** Rosa Luna (dancer)

898 Lumiere Brothers and Film Reel

1995. Christmas. Multicoloured.
2244 2p.90 Type **897** 45 25
2245 6p.50 Beam of light and rose window 95 50

1995. Centenary of Motion Pictures.
2246 **898** 6p. violet, deep mauve and mauve 90 45

1996. Carnival. Multicoloured.
2248 2p.90 Type **900** 45 25
2249 2p.90 Santiago Luz (clarinettist) 45 25
2250 2p.90 Pepino (clown) . . . 45 25

901 Cantegril Country Club

1996. Golf. Multicoloured.
2251 2p.90 Type **901** 45 25
2252 2p.90 Cerro Golf Club . . . 45 25
2253 2p.90 Fay Crocker and trophy 45 25
2254 2p.90 Lago Golf Club . . . 45 25
2255 2p.90 Uruguay Golf Club 45 25

902 Solis Theatre

1996. Montevideo, Latin American Cultural Capital.
2256 **902** 2p.90 multicoloured . . 45 25

904 Zitarrosa

1996. 60th Birth Anniv of Alfredo Zitarrosa (musician).
2258 **904** 3p. multicoloured . . . 45 25

906 Skeletons

1996. Archaeological Congress.
2260 **906** 3p.20 multicoloured . . 45 25

907 "Glyptodon claripes"

1996. Prehistoric Animals. Multicoloured.
2261 3p.20 Type **907** 45 25
2262 3p.20 "Macrauchenia patachonica" 45 25
2263 3p.20 "Toxodon platensis" 45 25
2264 3p.20 "Glossotherium robostum" 45 25
2265 3p.20 "Titanosaurus" . . . 45 25

908 People-Houses

1996. Population and Housing Censuses.
2266 **908** 3p.20 multicoloured . . 45 25

909 Dion-Buton Double-deck Bus, 1912

1996. Old Vehicles. Multicoloured.
2267 3p.20 Type **909** 45 25
2268 3p.20 Ford Model "A" patrol car, 1928 . . . . . 45 25
2269 3p.20 Raleigh bicycle, 1940 45 25
2270 3p.20 Magirus fire-engine, 1926 . . . . 45 25
2271 3p.20 Hotchkiss ambulance, 1917 . . . . 45 25

911 Children and Globe holding Hands (Soraya Campanella)

1996. "Care for Our Planet: Everyone's Mission".
2273 **911** 3p.20 multicoloured . . 45 25

912 New Postal Administration Emblem

914 "Nuestra Senora de la Encina" (caravel), 1726

1996. Postal Emblems.
2273a **912** 5p. yellow and blue . . 60 30
2274 7p. yellow and blue . . 1·00 50

1996. Sailing Ships. Multicoloured.
2276 3p.20 Type **914** 45 25
2277 3p.20 "San Francisco" (ship of the line), 1729 . . . . 45 25
2278 3p.20 Etienne Moreau's fleet, 1720 . . . . . . 45 25
2279 3p.20 "Atrevida" (corvette), 1789–94 . . . . 45 25
2280 3p.20 "Nuestra Senora de la Luz" (brig), 1752 . . . . 45 25

915 "Flores Landscape" (Carmelo de Arzadun)

1996.
2281 **915** 3p.50 multicoloured . . 50 25

916 Old Jewish Quarter

1996. 80th Anniv of Jewish Community in Uruguay.
2282 **916** 7p.50 red, yellow and purple . . . . 1·10 55

917 Dr. Victor Bertullo (veterinary researcher)

1996. Scientists. Multicoloured.
2283 3p.50 Type **917** 50 25
2284 3p.50 Tomas Beno Hirschfeld (chemical engineer) (horiz) 50 25
2285 3p.50 Enrique Legrand (astronomer and physicist) 50 25
2286 3p.50 Dr. Miguel C. Rubino (veterinary researcher) (horiz) 50 25

919 Aristotle (philosopher)

1996. Scientists. Multicoloured.
2288 7p.50 Type **919** . . . . . 1·10 55
2289 7p.50 Sir Isaac Newton (mathematician) . . . . . 1·10 55
2290 7p.50 Albert Einstein (physicist) . . . . 1·10 55

920 500 Peso Note

1996. Centenary of Republica Oriental Bank. Mult.
2291 3p.50 Type **920** 50 25
2292 3p.50 Ten peso note 50 25

921 Narbona Chapel

1996. National Heritage Day. Multicoloured.
2293 3p.50 Type **921** 50 25
2294 3p.50 Map of Gorriti Island showing sites of Spanish fortifications 50 25

922 "125" and Emblem

1996. 125th Anniv of Uruguay Rural Association.
2295 **922** 3p.50 multicoloured . . 50 25

924 Angel Rodriguez (South American boxing champion, 1917)

1996. Sports Personalities. Multicoloured.
2297 3p.50 Type **924** 50 25
2298 3p.50 Leandro Noli (winner of first Uruguayan cycling race, 1939) 50 25
2299 3p.50 Eduardo G. Risso (Olympic rowing medallist, 1948) 50 25
2300 3p.50 Estrella Puente (South American javelin champion, 1949) 50 25
2301 3p.50 Oscar Moglia (Olympic basketball medallist, 1956) 50 25

925 Gaucho

1996. America. Traditional Costumes. Multicoloured.
2302 3p.50 Type **925** 50 25
2303 3p.50 Countrywoman . . . 50 25

927 Satellite

1996. 3rd Space Conference of the Americas.
2305 **927** 3p.50 multicoloured . . 50 25

928 "Football Match" (Julio Suarez)

1996. Centenary of Comics. Museum of Humour and Anecdotes, Minas.
2306 **928** 4p. multicoloured . . . 60 30

929 Institute Building

1996. Centenary of Hygiene Institute.
2307 **929** 4p. multicoloured . . . 60 30

930 De Azara

1996. 175th Death Anniv of Felix de Azara (naturalist).
2308 **930** 4p. multicoloured . . . 60 30

931 Angels blowing Trumpets over Globe

1996. Centenary of Seventh Day Adventist Church in Uruguay.
2309 **931** 3p.50 multicoloured . . 50 25

932 Hands fingering Frets and Lyre (National Folklore Festival, Durazno)

1997. Festivals. Multicoloured. Self-adhesive and imperf (2315) or ordinary (others) gum.
2310 4p. Type **932** 50 25
2311 4p. Man smoking cigar (Festival of Gaucho Traditions, Tacuarembo) (vert) 50 25
2312 5p. Stage (Beer Week, Paysandu) 60 30
2313 5p. Ruben Lena and bridge over river (Olimar River Festival, Treinta y Tres) (vert) 60 30
2314 5p. Guitar and horseman (Minas y Abril Festival, Lavelleja) 60 30
2315 5p. Man mounted on blindfolded horse tied to post (Criolla Parque Roosevelt, Canelones) . . 60 30

933 Naked Mushroom ("Tricholoma nudum")

1997. Fungi. Multicoloured.
2316 4p. Type **933** 50 25
2317 4p. Yellow stainer ("Agaricus xanthodermus") 50 25
2318 4p. "Russula sardonia" . . 50 25
2319 4p. Girl hugging dog and "Microsporum canis" . . 50 25
2320 4p. "Polyporus versicolor" 50 25

934 Black-finned Pearlfish

1997. Fishes. Multicoloured. Self-adhesive. Imperf.
2321 4p. Type **934** 45 25
2322 4p. Uruguayan pearlfish ("Cynolebia viarius") . . 45 25

935 Buceo

1997. Yachting Harbours. Multicoloured. Self-adhesive. Imperf.
2323 4p. Type **935** 50 25
2324 4p. Colonia 50 25
2325 4p. Punta del Este 50 25
2326 4p. Santiago Vazquez . . . 50 25

936 Artigas and Lancer

1997. Bicentenary of Artigas's Lancers (Presidential escort).
2327 **936** 4p. multicoloured . . . 50 25

937 Cadet

1997. 50th Anniv of General Artigas Military Academy.
2328 **937** 4p. multicoloured . . . 50 25

938 Ambulance

1997. 18th Anniv of United Coronary Mobile (first mobile medical emergency unit in the world). Self-adhesive. Imperf.
2329 **938** 5p. multicoloured . . . 60 30

939 Toy holding Box

940 Anchorena, 1920

1997. 50th Anniv (1996) of UNICEF. Self-adhesive. Imperf.
2330 **939** 5p. multicoloured . . . 60 30

1997. Lighthouses. Mult. Self-adhesive. Imperf.
2331 5p. Type **940** 60 30
2332 5p. Farallon, 1870 . . . . . 60 30
2333 5p. Jose Ignacio, 1877 . . . 60 30
2334 5p. Santa Maria, 1874 . . . 60 30
2335 5p. Vigia, 18th-century . . . 60 30

941 "Devincenzia gallinali"

1997. Prehistoric Animals. Multicoloured. Self-adhesive. Imperf.
2336 5p. Type **941** 60 30
2337 5p. "Smilodon populator" 60 30
2338 5p. "Mesosaurus tenuidens" 60 30
2339 5p. "Doedicurus clavicaudatus" 60 30
2340 5p. "Artigasia magna" . . . 60 30

942 Melo Cathedral

1997. Dioceses. Multicoloured.
2341 5p. Type **942** 60 30
2342 5p. Monsignor Mariano Soler (first archbishop of Archdiocese of Montevideo) 60 30
2343 5p. Monsignor Jacinto Vera (first bishop of Archdiocese of Montevideo) 60 30
2344 5p. Salto Cathedral 60 30

943 Boy admiring Stamps in Album

1997. Youth Philately. Multicoloured.
2345 1p. Type **943** 10 10
2346 1p. Winking boy with tweezers and magnifying glass 10 10
2347 2p. Boy thinking "MMMM... FILATELIA?" 25 15
2348 2p. Boy thinking of stamps 25 15
2349 2p. Boy rejecting friend's offer of football game . . 25 15

944 Black Skimmers

1997. "Pacific 97" International Stamp Exhibition, San Francisco, U.S.A.
2350 **944** 10p. multicoloured . . . 1·25 65

945 Theatre

1997. 85th Anniv of Teatro Maccio, San Jose.
2351 **945** 5p. black, red and stone 60 30

946 Toy Steam Train

1997. 70th Anniv of Inter-American Institute for the Child.
2352 **946** 5p. multicoloured . . . 60 30

947 Fola and Boy beside Bed (Geoffrey Foladori)

1997. Comic Strip Characters. Multicoloured.
2353 5p. Type **947** 60 30
2354 5p. Peloduro running for goal (Julio Suarez) . . . 60 30

948 Sun, Birds and Waves

1997. 90th Anniv of Punta del Este.
2355 **948** 5p. multicoloured . . . 60 30

949 Street

1997. World Heritage Site. Colonia del Sacramento.
2356 **949** 5p. multicoloured . . . 60 30

950 Baldwin Steam Locomotive, 1889

1997. Centenary of General Artigas Central Station, Montevideo. Multicoloured.
2357 4p.+1p. Type **950** 60 30
2358 4p.+1p. Hudswell Clarke steam locomotive, 1895 60 30
2359 4p.+1p. Station facade and Luis Andreoni 60 30
2360 4p.+1p. Hawthorn Leslie steam locomotive, 1914 60 30
2361 4p.+1p. General Electric diesel shunting locomotive, 1954 . . . . 60 30

951 Wailing Wall (Jerusalem) and Theodor Herzl (founder)

1997. Centenary of Zionist Congress, Basel.
2362 **951** 5p. multicoloured . . . 60 30

952 Woman giving Letter to Postman

953 Postal Symbol

1997. Collection at Sender's Address Service. Self-adhesive. Imperf.
2363 **952** 15p. multicoloured . . 1·75 90
2363a 20p. multicoloured . . 2·25 1·10
2364 – 25p. green, yell & blk 1·00 1·50
2364a – 32p. green, yell & blk 3·50 1·75
2364b – 80p. green, yell & blk 9·00 4·50
DESIGNS: Nos. 2364/64b Black-chested buzzard eagle (*Geranoaetus melanoleucus*).

1997. No Value Expressed.
2365 **953** (4p.) yellow and brown 50 25
2367 (–) blue 60 30
2368 (–) blue and violet . . . 60 30
2369 (–) green and grey . . . 60 30

954 "Creole Willow" (Dante Picarelli)

955 Clock Tower

1997. Centenary of Discovery of Acetylsalycylic Acid (aspirin) by Dr. Felix Hoffman.
2371 **954** 6p. multicoloured . . . 75 35

1997. 1st National Administration of Posts.
2372 **955** 6p. blue and black . . . 75 35

956 Arms and Map

1997. Department of Salto.
2373 **956** 6p. multicoloured . . . 75 35

957 Felix Mendelssohn-Bartholdy and Score

1997. Composers' Death Anniversaries. Multicoloured.
2374 6p. Type **957** (150th anniv) 75 35
2375 6p. Johannes Brahms and score (centenary) 75 35

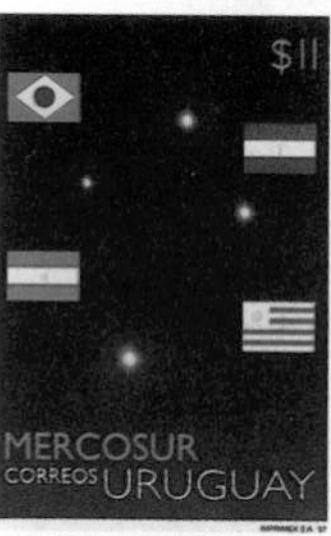

958 Antler and Lucas Kraglievich (palaeontologist)

1997. 160th Anniv of National Natural History Museum, Montevideo. Multicoloured.
2376 6p. Type **958** 75 35
2377 6p. Plant and Jose Arechavaleta (botanist) 75 35
2378 6p. Left-eyed flounder and Garibaldi Devincenzi (zoologist) 75 35
2379 6p. Flint axe head and Antonio Tadei (archaeologist) 75 35

959 Members' Flags and Southern Cross

960 Von Stephan (after Anton Weber)

1997. Mercosur (South American Common Market).
2380 **959** 11p. mult (6th anniv) . . 1·40 70

1997. Death Centenary of Heinrich von Stephan (founder of Universal Postal Union).
2382 **960** 11p. multicoloured . . . 1·40 70

962 Postwoman

1997. America. Postal Delivery. Multicoloured.
2384 6p. Type **962** 75 35
2385 11p. Woman receiving letters from postman . . . 1·40 70

963 Base and Gentoo Penguin

1997. Artigas Scientific Base, Antarctica.
2386 **963** 6p. multicoloured . . . 75 35

964 River Scene

1997. 70th Death Anniv (1998) of Domingo Laporte (artist).
2387 **964** 6p. multicoloured . . . 75 35

965 Building

1997. 80th Anniv of Casa de Galicia.
2388 **965** 6p. multicoloured . . . 75 35

966 Arme 2 Biplane "Montevideo"

1997. 3rd International Aeronautical and Space History Congress.
2389 **966** 6p. multicoloured . . . 75 35

967 Map, Painting Materials and Legislative Palace Tower

971 Three Kings

969 "General Artigas" (gunboat)

1997. 1st Interparliamentary Mercosur Paintings Biennale, Montevideo.
2390 **967** 11p. multicoloured . . . 1·40 70

1997. 180th Anniv of Navy.
2392 **969** 6p. multicoloured . . . 75 35

1997. Christmas. Multicoloured.
2394 6p. Type **971** 75 35
2395 11p. Madonna and Child . . 1·40 70

972 Adesio Lambardo and Bronze Medal (Olympic Games, Helsinki, 1952)

1997. Sportsmen. Multicoloured.
2396 6p. Type **972** 75 35
2397 6p. Guillermo Douglas (single sculls) and bronze medal (Olympic Games, Rome, 1932) 75 35
2398 6p. Obdulio Varela (footballer) and World Cup Trophy (Uruguay, 1950 World Cup champion) 75 35
2399 6p. Atilio Francois (cyclist) and silver medal (World Cycling Championships, Paris, 1947) 75 35
2400 6p. Juan Lopez Testa (South American 100 metres champion, Buenos Aires, 1947) 75 35

973 Silhouette and Personal Computer

1997. "Mevifil '97" First International Exhibition of Philatelic Audio-Visual and Computer Systems.
2401 **973** 11p. multicoloured . . . 1·40 70

974 Land Rover

1997. "INDEPEX 97" International Stamp Exhbition, New Delhi. Transport Anniversaries. Multicoloured.
2402 6p. Type **974** (50th anniv) 75 35
2403 6p. Henry Ford (50th death anniv) and motor car . . 75 35
2404 6p. Robert Bosch (centenary of electric motor) 75 35
2405 6p. Rudolf Diesel (centenary of diesel engine) 75 35

975 Academy Flag and Officer

1997. 90th Anniv of Naval Academy.
2406 **975** 6p. multicoloured . . . 75 35

976 Courthouse

1997. 90th Anniv of Uruguay Supreme Court.
2407 **976** 6p. multicoloured . . . 75 35

977 Postal Transport and Stone Relief

1997. 170th Anniv of Uruguay Post Office.
2408 **977** 6p. multicoloured . . . 75 35

978 Houses and Dr. Gallinal (founder)

1997. 30th Anniv of Movement for the Eradication of Insanitary Rural Housing.
2409 **978** 6p. multicoloured . . . 75 35

979 Preparing Materials

1997. Construction. Multicoloured.
2410 6p. Type **979** 75 35
2411 6p. Planning 75 35
2412 6p. Construction in progress 75 35
Nos. 2410/12 were issued together, se-tenant, forming a composite design.

981 Princess Diana with African Boy

982 Constructivist Painting

1998. Death Commemoration of Diana, Princess of Wales. Multicoloured.
2414 2p.+1p. Type **981** 30 15
2415 2p.+1p. Wearing protective mask 30 15

1998. Birth Centenary (1997) of Hector Ragni (artist).
2417 **982** 6p. multicoloured . . . 65 35

983 Naval Station, Montevideo

1998. 220th Anniv (1996) of Establishment of First Spanish Naval Station in America.
2418 **983** 6p. multicoloured . . . 65 35

984 Cartoon by Oscar Abmn

1998. Cartoonists. Multicoloured.
2419 6p. Type **984** 65 35
2420 6p. Cartoon by Emilio Cortinas 65 35

985 Ferreira

1998. 10th Death Anniv of Wilson Ferreira Aldunate (politician).
2421 **985** 6p. multicoloured . . . 65 35

986 Butia Palm

1998. Trees. Multicoloured.
2422 6p. Type **986** 65 35
2423 6p. Butia palms by stream 65 35
2424 6p. Ombu grove 65 35
2425 6p. Ombu ("Phytolacca dioica"), leaf and fruit . . 65 35

987 "Testudinites sellowi"

1998. Prehistoric Animals. Fossilised remains found in Uruguay. Multicoloured.
2426 6p. Type **987** 65 35
2427 6p. "Proborhyaena gigantea" 65 35
2428 6p. "Propachyrucos schiaffinos" 65 35
2429 6p. "Stegomastodon platensis" 65 35

988 "Sabbath" (Nelson Romero)

1998. 50th Anniv of State of Israel.
2430 **988** 12p. multicoloured . . . 1·25 70

989 Map of Americas and Sun

1998. 50th Anniv of Organization of American States.
2431 **989** 12p. blue, yellow & silver 1·25 70

990 Athlete

1998. 61st World Congress of Sports Journalism.
2432 **990** 6p. multicoloured . . . 65 35

991 Farmhouses

1998. 50th Anniv of Land Settlement Institute.
2433 **991** 6p. multicoloured . . . 65 35

992 Common Caracara

1998. Birds. Multicoloured.
2434 6p. Type **992** 65 35
2435 6p. Black-necked swan ("Cygnus melancoryphus") 65 35
2436 6p. Roseate spoonbill ("Platalea ajaja") 65 35
2437 6p. Buff-necked ibis ("Theristicus caudatus") 65 35

995 Demonstration outside Parliament, 1983

1998. Labour Day.
2440 **995** 6p. brown and black . . 65 35

996 Electric Tramcar, 1906

1998. 50th Anniv of Circle for Studies on Public Transport. Trams of Montevideo. Multicoloured.
2441 6p. Type **996** 65 35
2442 6p. German Transatlantica tramcar, 1907 . . . . . . 65 35
2443 6p. German Transatlantica tramcar, 1908 . . . . . . 65 35
2444 6p. Transatlantica double-deck tramcar, 1916 . . . 65 35

997 Pampas Cat

1998. Big Cats. Multicoloured.
2445 6p. Type **997** 65 35
2446 6p. Ocelot ("Felis pardalis") 65 35
2447 6p. Tree-ocelot ("Felis wiedii") 65 35
2448 6p. Jaguar ("Panthera onca") 65 35

998 "Sirius" (schooner)

1998. Ships. Multicoloured.
2449 6p. Type **998** 65 35
2450 6p. "18 de Julio" (sail/steam gunboat) 65 35
2451 6p. "Maldonado" (transport paddle-steamer) 65 35
2452 6p. "Instituto de Pesca No. 1" (fishery research vessel) 65 35

999 Chapel, Orphans Lime-quarry, Colonia

1998. Mercosur. Jesuit Missions.
2453 **999** 12p. multicoloured . . . 1·25 70

1000 Monument (Juan Ferrari)

1998. 125th Anniv of Monument to the Peace of 6 April 1872.
2454 **1000** 6p. multicoloured . . . 65 35

1001 Headquarters and Obus 155 mm. M114 A-2 Gun

1998. Centenary of Fifth Artillery Batallion.
2455 **1001** 6p. multicoloured . . . 65 35

1002 Imperial Moth

1998. Moths. Multicoloured.
2456 6p. Type **1002** 65 35
2457 6p. *Protoparce lucetius* . . 65 35

1003 Artigas Monument

1004 Lomba and Porcupine

1998. Centenary of First Artigas Monument, San Jose.
2458 **1003** 6p. multicoloured . . . 65 35

1998. 80th Birth Anniv of Dr. Mauricio Lopez Lomba (doctor and philanthropist).
2459 **1004** 6p. multicoloured . . . 65 35

1005 Conservatory Emblem

1006 Jose Fernandez Vergara (founder)

1998. Centenary of Falleri-Balzo Music Conservatory, Montevideo.
2460 **1005** 6p. multicoloured . . . 65 35

1998. 95th Anniv of Pueblo Vergara (town).
2461 **1006** 6p. multicoloured . . . 65 35

1008 Institution Building

1009 *La Princesa* (frigate) and Emblem

1998. 145th Anniv of Spanish Association of Primary Mutual Assistance (medical organization).
2463 **1008** 6p. multicoloured . . . 65 35

1998. "Espamer'98" Iberian–Latin American Stamp Exhibition, Buenos Aires. 230th Anniv of First Montevideo–La Coruna Maritime Mail Service.
2464 **1009** 12p. multicoloured . . 1·25 65

1010 Students with Banners

1998. 15th Anniv of School and University Students' Demonstration, Montevideo.
2465 **1010** 6p. brown and black . . 65 35

1011 Junkers J52

1998. "IBEROAMERICANA'98" Iberian–American Stamp Exhibition, Maia, Portugal. Aircraft. Mult.
2466 6p. Type **1011** 65 35
2467 6p. SPAD VII 65 35
2468 6p. Ansaldo SVA-10 . . . . 65 35
2469 6p. Neybar 65 35

1012 Allende

1998. 25th Death Anniv of Salvador Allende (Chilean President, 1970–73).
2470 **1012** 12p. multicoloured . . 1·25 65

1013 Fabregat (teacher and writer)

1998. 50th Anniv of Enrique Rodriguez Fabregat's Participation in United Nations Conciliation Commission.
2471 **1013** 6p. multicoloured . . . 65 35

1014 Microphone, Emblem and Station Headquarters, Montevideo and Emblem

1998. 70th Anniv of Radio Carve.
2472 **1014** 6p. multicoloured . . . 65 35

1015 Julia Guarino (architect)

1998. America. Famous Women. Multicoloured.
2473 6p. Type **1015** 65 35
2474 12p. Paulina Luisi (doctor) 1·25 65

1016 Universal Postal Union Emblem and Stars

1998. World Post Day. "ILSAPEX '98" International Stamp Exhibition, Johannesburg, South Africa.
2475 **1016** 12p. multicoloured . . 1·25 65

1017 Emblem and Equipment

1998. 50th Anniv of Association of Pharmacies.
2476 **1017** 6p. multicoloured . . . 65 35

1018 Globe and Postal Services

1998. Small Packets Service. Self-adhesive.
2477 **1018** 25p. multicoloured . . 2·75 1·40

1019 Lancia Fire Engine, 1930

1998. "Italia 98" International Stamp Exhibition, Milan, Italy. Motor Vehicles. Multicoloured.
2478 6p. Type **1019** 65 35
2479 6p. Maserati "San Remo", 1946 . . . . 65 35
2480 6p. Alfa Romeo trolleybus, 1954 . . . . 65 35
2481 6p. Fiat "500" Topolino, 1936 . . . . 65 35

1020 Hector Maria Artola (musician) and Score

1021 "Play in order to help" (Melissa Migliozzi)

1998. Personalities. Multicoloured.
2482 6p. Type **1020** 65 35
2483 6p. Serafin J. Garcia (writer) 65 35
2484 6p. Nerses Ounanian (sculptor) (horiz) 65 35

1998. "Juvenalia'98" Youth Exhibition, Montevideo. Winning Entry in Children's Stamp Design Competition.
2485 **1021** 6p. multicoloured . . . 65 35

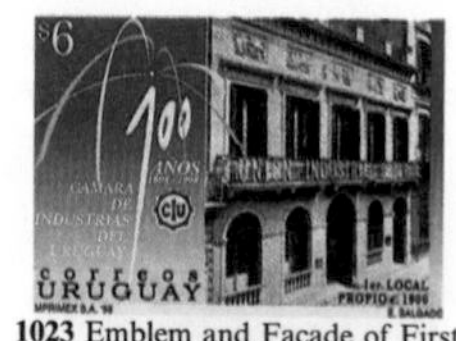
1023 Emblem and Facade of First Premises

1998. Centenary of Chamber of Industries.
2487 **1023** 6p. multicoloured . . . 65 35

1024 Emblem and Artigas Monument, Montevideo

1998. 16th Triennial Congress of Expenditure Controller Boards.
2488 **1024** 12p. silver and blue . . 1·25 65

1025 Pink *Oxalis pudica*

1998. Flowers. Multicoloured. Self-adhesive.
2489 1p. Type **1025** 10 10
2490 4p. White *Oxalis pudica* . . 45 25
2491 6p. *Eugenia uniflora* 65 35
2492 7p. *Eugenia uniflora* 75 40
2493 9p. *Eugenia uniflora* . . . . 1·00 50
2494 10p. *Aechmea recurvata* . . 1·10 55
2495 14p. *Acca sellowiana* . . . 1·40 70
2498 50p. *Acca sellowiana* . . . . 5·50 3·50
See also Nos. 2726/8.

1026 "St. Peter's Tears" (detail, Murillo)

1998. Christmas. Multicoloured.
2500 6p. Type **1026** 65 35
2501 12p. "The Virgin's descent to reward San Ildefonso's writings" (detail, El Greco) . . . . 1·25 65

1027 Grand Hotel, Paso del Molino

1998. 250th Anniv of Founding of Paso del Molino, Montevideo.
2502 **1027** 6p. multicoloured . . . 65 35

1028 Alberto Candeau reading Proclamation

1998. 15th Anniv of 27 November Democracy Demonstrations.
2503 **1028** 6p. brown and black . . 65 35

1029 Statuette

1998. Morosoli Cultural Awards.
2504 **1029** 6p. multicoloured . . . 65 35

1030 Children

1998. 50th Anniv of Universal Declaration of Human Rights.
2505 **1030** 6p. black, blue and red 65 35

1031 Stylized Athlete and Emblem

1998. 75th Anniv of Uruguayan Olympic Committee.
2506 **1031** 6p. multicoloured . . . 65 35

1032 Juan Lopez (football manager)

1998. Sports Personalities. Multicoloured.
2507 6p. Type **1032** 65 35
2508 6p. Hector Scarone (footballer) 65 35
2509 6p. Leandro Gomez Harley (basketball player) 65 35
2510 6p. Liberto Corney (boxer) 65 35

1033 Mother with Baby and Dr. Roberto Caldeyro Barcia

1998. Research Doctors. Multicoloured.
2511 6p. Type **1033** (gynaecologist) 65 35
2512 6p. Dr. Jose Verocay and Verocay neurinomes (anatomist, 70th death anniv) 65 35
2513 6p. Dr. Jose L. Duomarco and patient (cardiologist) 65 35

1034 Zola

1999. Centenary of Publication of "I Accuse" (Emile Zola's open letter regarding the Dreyfus case) in *L'Aurore* (newspaper).
2514 **1034** 14p. multicoloured . . 1·40 70

1035 Olive-backed Warbler and Beach

1999. 50th Anniv of Las Canas Resort.
2515 **1035** 7p. multicoloured . . . 75 40

1036 Map showing Borders

1999. 25th Anniv of Treaty of the River Plate (agreement on maritime borders between Uruguay and Argentine Republic).
2516 **1036** 7p. multicoloured . . . 75 40

1037 Luis Ernesto Aroztegui (artist) and "Self-Portrait" (tapestry)

1999. Anniversaries. Multicoloured.
2517 7p. Type **1037** (fifth death anniv) 75 40
2518 7p. Juan Jose Morosoli (writer, birth centenary) and detail of manuscript of "A Definition of Poetry" 75 40
2519 7p. Joaquin Torres Garcia (painter, 50th death anniv) and detail of "Barco Constructivo, America" 75 40

1038 Fawn-breasted Tanager (*Pipraeidea melanonota*) and *Psidium cattleianum* (shrub)

1999. Flora and Fauna. Multicoloured.
2520 7p. Type **1038** 75 40
2521 7p. *Tabebuia ipe* (tree) and Glittering-bellied emerald (*Chlorostilbon aureoventris*) 75 40
2522 7p. Chestnut-backed tanager (*Tangara preciosa*) and *Duranta repens* (shrub) . . 75 40
2523 7p. *Citharexylum montevidense* (tree) and many-coloured rush tyrant (*Tachuris rubigastra*) . . . 75 40

1039 Break de Chasse

1999. Carriages. Multicoloured.
2524 7p. Type **1039** 75 40
2525 7p. Mylord 75 40
2526 7p. Coupe Trois Quarts . . 75 40
2527 7p. Break de Champ 75 40

1040 B. and C. Cespedes, M. Nebel and Parque Central (first ground)

1999. Centenary of Nacional Football Club. Mult.
2528 7p. Type **1040** 75 40
2529 7p. H. Castro, P. Cea, A. Ciocca and club flag 75 40
2530 7p. R. Porta, A. Garcia, S. Gambetta and present ground 75 40

1041 Spacecraft orbiting Earth (Stefani Andrea Furtado)

1999. Year 2000. "Stampin' the Future". Showing second prize winning entries in "Year 2000" children's stamp design competition. Mult.
2531 7p. Type **1041** 75 40
2532 7p. "2000" (with monkey and people in zeros) (Pilar Trujillo) 75 40
2533 7p. Road, lights and houses (Lucia Lavie) 75 40
2534 7p. Futuristic housing and park (Cecilia Chopitea) 75 40

1042 Chebataroff

1999. 90th Birth Anniv of Jorge Chebataroff (teacher).
2535 **1042** 7p. multicoloured . . . 75 40

1043 "The Battle of Estero Bellaco" (Diogenes Hequet)

1999. Military Anniversaries. Multicoloured.
2536 7p. Type **1043** (60th anniv of No. 1 Infantry Brigade) 75 40
2537 7p. "Battle of Monte Caseros" (Carlos Penuti and Alejandro Bernhein) (160th anniv of No. 2 Infantry Battalion) . . . 75 40
2538 7p. "The Battle of Boqueron" (Diogenes Hequet) (170th anniv of No. 1 Infantry Battalion) 75 40

1044 St. Augustine Church

1046 Festival Poster

1999. 150th Anniv of Villa de la Restauracion.
2539 **1044** 7p. multicoloured . . . 75 40

1999. 1st Film Critics' Festival.
2541 **1046** 7p. multicoloured . . . 75 40

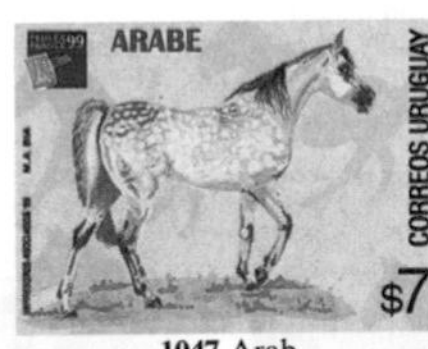

1047 Arab

1999. "Philexfrance 99" International Stamp Exhibition, Paris. Horses. Multicoloured.
2542 7p. Type **1047** 75 40
2543 7p. American quarter horse 75 40
2544 7p. Thoroughbred 75 40
2545 7p. Shetland pony 75 40

1048 Emblem and Title Page of *Marcha*

1999. 60th Anniv of *Marcha* (weekly publication).
2546 **1048** 7p. multicoloured . . . 75 40

1049 Trapeze Bike and Emblem

1999. Inauguration of Permanent Space Science Visitor Centre.
2547 **1049** 7p. multicoloured . . . 75 40

1050 Artigas Base

1999. 15th Anniv of Artigas Antarctic Scientific Base.
2548 **1050** 7p. multicoloured . . . 75 40

1051 University Facade

1999. 150th Anniv of University of the Republic (first Uruguayan university).
2549 **1051** 7p. yellow and black . . 75 40

1052 Emblem

1053 Senaque (medicine man) and Chief Vaimaca-Peru (lancer) (left-hand detail)

1999. 50th Anniv of Regional Office of Science and Technology for Latin America and the Caribbean, Montevideo.
2550 **1052** 7p. multicoloured . . . 75 40

1999. "The Last Charruas" (painting) by Delaunois. Multicoloured.
2551 7p. Type **1053** 75 40
2552 7p. Warrior and wife (right-hand detail) 75 40
Nos. 2551/2 were issued together, se-tenant, forming a composite design of the complete painting.

1055 Emblem

1057 Cocker Spaniel

1056 Piper J-3 Float Plane

1999. 50th Anniv of El Galpon Theatre.
2554 **1055** 7p. multicoloured . . . 75 40

1999. "China 1999" International Stamp Exhibition, Peking. Airplanes. Multicoloured.
2555 7p. Type **1056** 75 40
2556 7p. Short S.25 Sunderland flying boat 75 40

1999. Dogs. Multicoloured.
2557 7p. Type **1057** 75 40
2558 7p. German shepherd . . . 75 40
2559 7p. Dalmatian 75 40
2560 7p. Basset hound 75 40

1058 Mining Bee on *Oxalis* sp.

1999. Insects and Flowers. Multicoloured.
2561 7p. Type **1058** 75 40
2562 7p. *Apanteles* sp. and *Epidendrum paniculosum* 75 40
2563 7p. *Metabolosia univita* and *Baccaris trimera* 75 40
2564 7p. Cantarido and flower . . 75 40

1059 Orlando Aldama (poet and writer)

1060 Open Book

1999. Personalities. Multicoloured.
2565 7p. Type **1059** 75 40
2566 7p. Julio Martinez Oyanguren (guitarist) . . 75 40

1999. Mercosur. The Book. National Heritage Day.
2567 **1060** 7p. multicoloured . . . 75 40

1061 Olympic Poster and Gold Medal

1999. 75th Anniv of Victory of Uruguay Football Team in Olympic Games, Paris, France. Mult.
2568 7p. Type **1061** 75 40
2569 7p. Winning team 75 40
Nos. 2568/9 were issued together, se-tenant, forming a composite design.

1062 Emblem

1999. International Year of the Elderly (1st issue).
2570 **1062** 7p. multicoloured . . . 75 40
See also No. 2576.

1063 "Exuberant Philatelic Gathering" (Mariano Bartasan)

1999. Stamp Day.
2571 **1063** 7p. multicoloured . . . 75 40

1064 Projects and Emblem

1999. 40th Anniv of Inter-American Development Bank.
2572 **1064** 7p. multicoloured . . . 75 40

1065 Weapons in Dustbin

1999. America. A New Millennium without Arms. Multicoloured.
2573 7p. Type **1065** 75 40
2574 14p. Satellites and Earth . . 1·40 70

1066 Cattle pulling Caravan

1999. 50th Anniv of El Ceibo (society for the protection of traditional customs).
2575 **1066** 7p. multicoloured . . . 75 40

1067 Children and Elderly Couple

1999. International Year of the Elderly (2nd issue).
2576 **1067** 7p. multicoloured . . . 75 40

1068 Sunset and Emblem

1999. 3rd International Sports Ministers' and Officials' Conference, Punta del Este.
2577 **1068** 7p. multicoloured . . . 75 40

1070 Emblem

1999. 60th Anniv of Uruguayan Institute of Technical Standards.
2579 **1070** 7p. multicoloured . . . 75 40

1071 Batalla

1072 Front Cover of *Mundo Uruguayo* (magazine), 29 April 1929

1999. 1st Death Anniv of Hugo Batalla (lawyer).
2580 **1071** 7p. multicoloured . . . 75 40

1999. Art and Design in the 1920s.
2581 **1072** 7p. multicoloured . . . 75 40

1073 "1999" and Palacio Salvo, Parliament House, Centenario Stadium's Homage Tower, Engineering Faculty and the University Hospital

1999. Millennium. Multicoloured.
2582 3p.30 Type **1073** 35 20
2583 3p.50 "2000" and Hotel Casino Conrad, airport, Radison Victoria Plaza Hotel, World Trade Centre and Communications Tower 40 20

1074 Cowboy and Indian fighting

1999. 75th Birth Anniv of Celmar Poume (cartoonist).
2584 **1074** 7p. multicoloured . . . 75 40

1075 Christmas Tree and Decorations

1999. Christmas. Multicoloured.
2585 9p. Type **1075** . . . . . . 1·00 50
2586 18p. Carol singers (vert) . . 2·00 1·00

1076 "Bearded Drinker" (Nelson Romero)

1999. 20th Anniv of Juanico Wine Cellar. Winning Designs in "Art and Wine" Competition. Mult.
2587 9p. Type **1076** . . . . . . 1·00 50
2588 9p. "Carport of the Old Wine Cellar" (Nelson Ramos) . . . . 1·00 50

1077 Council Offices

1999. Inauguration of Maldonado Department Council Building.
2589 **1077** 9p. multicoloured . . . 1·00 50

1078 Stylized Sun (Carlos Paez Vilaro)

2000. Contemporary Art.
2590 **1078** 9p. multicoloured . . . 1·00 50

1080 *Cattleya corcovado*

1081 Punta del Este Lighthouse

2000. Orchids. Multicoloured.
2592 4p. Type **1080** 45 25
2593 4p. *Cattleya* sp. hybrid . . . 45 25
2594 5p. *Laelia purpurata* . . . 55 30
2595 5p. *Laelia tenebrosa* 55 30

2000. Lighthouses. Multicoloured.
2596 4p. Type **1081** 45 25
2597 4p. Cabo Polonio 45 25
2598 5p. Flores Island 55 30
2599 5p. Punta Brava 55 30

1082 Quijano

2000. Birth Centenary of Carlos Quijano (journalist).
2600 **1082** 9p. multicoloured . . . 1·00 50

1083 Charlie Chaplin (leading actor)

2000. "LUBRAPEX 2000" Brazilian–Portuguese Stamp Exhibition, San Salvador de Bahia, Brazil. 75th Anniv of *The Gold Rush* (silent film).
2601 **1083** 18p. multicoloured . . 1·50 90

1084 Chapel

2000. 250th Anniv of El Cordon, Montevideo.
2602 **1084** 9p. multicoloured . . . 75 45

1085 Mural (right-hand detail)

1086 Garcia

2000. Indigenous Flora Mural, Luis Koster Stadium, Mercedes City. Multicoloured.
2603 4p. Type **1085** 35 25
2604 5p. Mural (left-hand detail) 40 25
Nos. 2603/4 were issued together, se-tenant, forming a composite design of a portion of the mural.

2000. 144th Birth Anniv of Francisco Garcia y Santos (Director General of Posts and Telegraphs, 1901–17).
2605 **1086** 9p. multicoloured . . . 75 45

1087 Emblem

1088 Emblem

2000. 125th Anniv of Association of Uruguayan Notaries.
2606 **1087** 9p. multicoloured . . . 75 45

2000. International Museums Day.
2607 **1088** 9p. multicoloured . . . 75 45

1089 Skyscrapers (Maria Pia Pereyra)

2000. "Stampin' the Future". Winning Entries in Children's International Painting Competition. Multicoloured.
2608 4p. Type **1089** 35 25
2609 4p. "2000", fish and national colours (Virginia Regueiro) 35 25
2610 5p. People building globe (Helena Perez Acevedo) 40 25
2611 5p. Letters between postman and computer (Blanca Esther Lima) 40 25

1090 Emblem

2000. 90th Anniv of Club Soriano (cultural and sports association).
2612 **1090** 9p. multicoloured . . . 75 45

1091 Antonio Rupenian (founder)

1092 Woman reading

2000. 65th Anniv of Radio Armenia (Armenian community radio service).
2613 **1091** 18p. multicoloured . . 1·50 90

2000. Centenary of The 1900 Generation (Uruguayan writers).
2614 **1092** 9p. multicoloured . . . 75 45

1093 *Echinopsis multiplex*

2000. Cacti. Multicoloured.
2615 4p. Type **1093** 35 25
2616 5p. Thorn ball (*Notocactus ottonis*) 40 25

1094 Team (Olympic Champion, Amsterdam, 1928)

2000. Centenary of Uruguay Football Association. Multicoloured.
2617 4p. Type **1094** 35 25
2618 4p. Stadium (first World Cup Football Champion, Uruguay, 1930) 35 25
2619 5p. Team (Olympic Champion, Paris, 1924) 40 25
2620 5p. Player scoring goal (World Cup Football Champion, Brazil, 1950) 40 25

1095 Georges Bizet (composer) and Scene from *Carmen*

2000. Opera Anniversaries. Multicoloured.
2621 9p. Type **1095** (125th anniv of first performance) . . . 75 45
2622 9p. Giacomo Puccini (composer) and scene from *Tosca* (centenary of first performance) 75 45

1096 Emblem

2000. 20th Anniv of Latin American Association of Integration.
2623 **1096** 18p. multicoloured . . 1·50 90

1097 Vought Sikorsky OS2U Kingfisher (seaplane)

2000. 75th Anniv of Uruguay Naval Aviation.
2624 **1097** 9p. multicoloured . . . 75 45

1098 Fingerprints and Emblem

2000. 120th Anniv of O.R.T. (educational organization).
2625 **1098** 9p. multicoloured . . . 75 45

1099 De La Robla

2000. Luis de la Robla (first Postmaster General in Uruguay) Commemoration.
2626 **1099** 9p. multicoloured . . . 75 45

1100 Rodriguez and Racing Car

2000. 1st Death Anniv of Gonzalo Rodriguez (racing driver). Multicoloured.
2627 9p. Type **1100** 75 45
2628 9p. Racing car and Rodriguez with trophy . . 75 45

1101 Map and Artigas

2000. 150th Death Anniv of Jose Artigas.
2629 **1101** 9p. multicoloured . . . 75 45

1102 Common Miner (*Geositta cunicularia*)

2000. "Espana 2000" World Stamp Exhibition, Madrid. Birds. Multicoloured.
2630 4p. Type **1102** 35 25
2631 4p. Freckle-breasted thornbird (*Phacellodomus striaticollis*) 35 25
2632 5p. Long-tailed reed finch (*Donacospiza albifrons*) . . 40 25
2633 5p. Golden-winged cacique (*Cacicus chrysopterus*) . . 40 25

1103 T. Makiguchi, J. Toda and Emblem

2000. 25th Anniv of Soka Gakkai International (Buddhist organization).
2634 **1103** 18p. multicoloured . . 1·50 90

1104 Noughts and Crosses

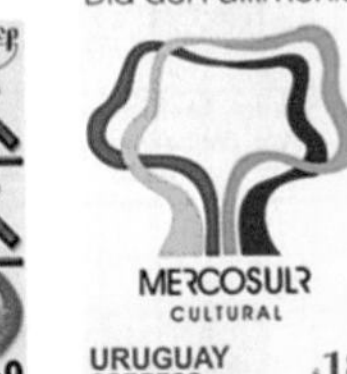

1105 Emblem

2000. America. A.I.D.S. Awareness. Multicoloured.
2635 9p. Type **1104** 75 45
2636 18p. A.I.D.S. ribbon and needle . . . . 1·50 90

2000. Mercosur. Cultural Heritage Day.
2637 **1105** 18p. multicoloured . . 1·50 90

1106 "Dragon"

2000. 105th Birth Anniv of Luis Mazzey (artist).
2638 **1106** 9p. multicoloured . . . 75 45

1107 Firemen on Roof

2000. Firemen. Multicoloured.
2639 9p. Type **1107** 75 45
2640 9p. Firemen attending motor vehicle fire (horiz) 75 45

1108 Prof. Julio Ricaldoni (engineer)

2000. 50th Anniv of and 29th South American Conference on Structural Engineering, Punta Del Este.
2641 **1108** 9p. multicoloured . . . 75 45

1109 *Capitan Miranda*

2000. 70th Anniv *Capitan Miranda* (cadet ship).
2642 **1109** 9p. multicoloured . . . 75 45

1110 Charles V and Map

2000. 500th Birth Anniv of Charles V, Holy Roman Emperor.
2643 **1110** 22p. multicoloured . . 2·00 1·25

1111 Fireworks

2000. Christmas. Multicoloured.
2644 11p. Type **1111** 90 55
2645 22p. Holy Family (crib figures) . . . . 2·00 1·25

1112 Emblem

1114 Little Monkey Frog (*Phyllomedusa iheringii*)

1113 Emblem

2000. 125th Anniv of Sarandi Del Yi, Montevideo.

2646 **1112** 11p. multicoloured . . 90 55

2001. Forest Fire Prevention Campaign.

2647 **1113** 11p. multicoloured . . 90 55

2001. Amphibians and Reptiles. Multicoloured.

2648 11p. Type **1114** 90 55

2649 11p. Black spine-necked swamp turtle (*Acanthochelys spixii*) . . 90 55

2650 11p. Hilaire's side-necked turtle (*Phrynops hilarii*) . . 90 55

2651 11p. Striped snouted treefrog (*Scinax squalirostris*) 90 55

1115 Clubhouse, River and Emblem

2001. Centenary of Paysandu Rowing Club.

2652 **1115** 11p. multicoloured . . 90 55

1116 Map of South America and Emblem

1117 Building Facade

2001. 18th Congress of Latin American Confederation of Organizers of Congresses and Similar Events (COCAL) and 17th Congress of International Convention and Congress Association, Montevideo.

2653 **1116** 11p. multicoloured . . 90 55

2001. Bicentenary of Belen.

2654 **1117** 11p. multicoloured . . 90 55

1118 Crow's Gorge

2001. Natural Sights. Multicoloured. Self-adhesive gum.

2655 2p. Waterfall, Salto del Penitente 20 10

2658 11p. Type **1118** 90 55

2661 20p. Palace Cave (vert) . . 1·60 1·00

2664 100p. Hill of Shells . . . . 8·00 5·00

1119 "David"

2001. 500th Anniv of "David" (sculpture, Michelangelo).

2665 **1119** 22p. black, yellow and red . . . . 2·00 1·25

1120 Musicians and Emblem

2001. 50th Anniv of Uruguayan Society of Performers (S.U.D.E.I.).

2666 **1120** 11p. multicoloured . . 90 55

1121 Figure and Emblem

1122 Emblem

2001. 75th Anniv of Casal Catala (Catalan cultural organization).

2667 **1121** 11p. multicoloured . . 90 55

2001. 85th Anniv of Engineering School, Montevideo.

2668 **1122** 11p. blue 90 55

1123 Talice

2001. 2nd Death Anniv of Rudolfo Talice (biologist).

2669 **1123** 11p. multicoloured . . 1·10 70

1124 Anniversary Emblem

2001. 50th Anniv of Lion's Club, Montevideo.

2670 **1124** 11p. multicoloured . . 1·10 70

1125 Early Telephone and Alexander Graham Bell

2001. 125th Anniv of the Telephone.

2671 **1125** 22p. multicoloured . . 2·25 1·40

1126 Urtutu Pit Viper (*Bothrops alternatus*)

2001. Snakes. Multicoloured.

2672 11p. *Philodyras olfersii* . . . 1·10 70

2673 11p. Type **1126** . . . . . . 1·10 70

1127 "Two Ways" (detail, oil painting)

2001. Death Centenary of Juan Manuel Blanes (artist).

2674 **1127** 11p. multicoloured . . 1·10 70

1128 Dr. Morquio

1129 "*Rheingold*"

2001. Centenary of Appointment of Dr. Luis Morquio as Professor of Paediatrics at Uruguay University.

2675 **1128** 11p. multicoloured . . 1·10 70

2001. 125th Anniv of First Performance of Richard Wagner's *Ring of the Nibelungs*. Scenes from the operas. Multicoloured.

2676 11p. Type **1129** . . . . . . 1·10 70

2677 11p. *Valkyrie* . . . . 1·10 70

2678 11p. *Siegfried* . . . . 1·10 70

2679 11p. *Decline of the Gods* and Wagner . . . . 1·10 70

1130 Emblem

1131 Edison

2001. 50th Anniv of International Organization for Migration.

2680 **1130** 22p. blue and black . . 2·25 1·40

2001. 75th Death Anniv of Thomas Alva Edison (inventor).

2681 **1131** 22p. multicoloured . . 2·25 1·40

1132 Container Ship

2001. Centenary of Montevideo Port.

2682 **1132** 11p. multicoloured . . 1·10 70

1133 New Hampshire

2001. Domestic Chickens. Designs showing pairs of each breed. Multicoloured.

2683 11p. Type **1133** . . . . . . 1·10 70

2684 11p. Buff Orpingtons . . . 1·10 70

2685 11p. Araucanas . . . . . . 1·10 70

2686 11p. Light brown leghorns 1·10 70

1134 Moby Dick and Whalers

2001. 150th Anniv of Publication of *Moby Dick* (novel by Herman Melville).

2687 **1134** 22p. multicoloured . . 2·25 1·40

1135 Flags, Globe and Gonzalez Pecotche

2001. Birth Centenary of Carlos Bernado Gonzalez Pecotche (founder of Logosophy self-development).

2688 **1135** 11p. multicoloured . . 1·10 70

1136 Concorde

2001. 25th Anniv of First Flight of Concorde.

2689 **1136** 22p. multicoloured . . 2·25 1·40

1137 "Louis Philippe"

1139 Bicentenary Emblem

1138 Bee-keepers

2001. Roses. Multicoloured.

2690 11p. Type **1137** . . . . . . 1·10 70

2691 11p. "Souvenir de Mme Leonie Viennot" . . . . 1·10 70

2692 11p. "Kronenbourg" . . . . 1·10 70

2693 11p. "Lady Hillingdon" . . 1·10 70

2001. Bee-keeping. Multicoloured.

2694 12p. Type **1138** . . . . . . 1·25 75

2695 12p. Honey bee on flower 1·25 75

Nos. 2694/5 were issued together, se-tenant, forming a composite design.

2001. Bicentenary of Dolores (village), Soriano Department.

2696 **1139** 12p. multicoloured . . 1·25 75

1140 Girl and Flowers

2001. 80th Anniv of Uruguay–Japan Diplomatic Relations.

2697 **1140** 24p. multicoloured . . 2·40 1·40

1141 Stylized Sun with Face

2001. 75th Anniv of Uruguay Philatelic Club. Multicoloured.

2698 12p. Type **1141** . . . . . . 1·25 75

2699 12p. Square sun . . . . . . 1·25 75

1142 Basilica of the Blessed Sacrament, Colonia Family, Sauce

1144 Altarpiece, Temple of the Sacred

1143 "Experience" (Carlos Amoretti)

2001. America. World Heritage. Multicoloured.
2700 12p. Type **1142** . . . . . . 1·25 75
2701 24p. San Benito Chapel, Colonia . . . . 2·40 1·40

2001. "50 Years in Art" Exhibition by Carlos Amoretti.
2702 **1143** 12p. multicoloured . . 1·25 75

2001. 150th Anniv of Sauce, Canelones.
2703 **1144** 12p. multicoloured . . 1·25 75

1145 "Life and Health" (Mariana Tarigo)

2001. Anti-drugs Campaign. Winning Entry in Stamp Design Competition.
2704 **1145** 12p. multicoloured . . 1·25 75

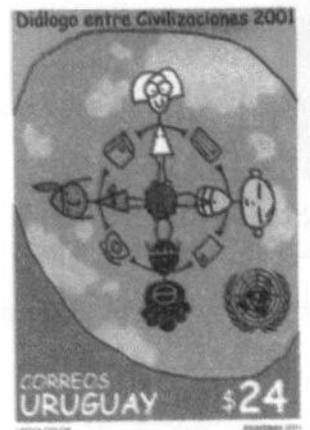

1146 Children encircling Globe

1147 Family flying Kite

2001. United Nations Year of Dialogue among Civilizations.
2705 **1146** 24p. multicoloured . . 2·40 1·40

2001. Honorary Anti-Cancer Campaign Committee.
2706 **1147** 12p. multicoloured . . 1·25 75

1148 Newspapers on Conveyor-belt

1150 Blood Droplet Figure

1149 Emblem, Basket and Ball

2001. 20th Anniv of *Ultimas Noticias* (newspaper).
2707 **1148** 12p. multicoloured . . 1·25 75

2001. 50th Anniv of Sauce Basketball Club.
2708 **1149** 12p. multicoloured . . 1·25 75

2001. Voluntary Blood Donation Day.
2709 **1149** 12p. multicoloured . . 1·25 75

1151 San Martin Portrait overlaid with Grid Pattern

2001. 70th Death Anniv of Juan Zorrilla de San Martin (writer).
2710 **1151** 12p. multicoloured . . 1·25 75

1152 *Oyarvide* (survey ship)

2001.
2711 **1152** 12p. multicoloured . . 1·25 75

1153 Mr. and Mrs. King

2001. Visit to Uruguay of Mr. Richard King (president of Rotary Club International).
2712 **1153** 24p. multicoloured . . 2·40 1·40

1154 Emblems

2001. 110th Anniv of Penarol Athletics Club.
2713 **1154** 12p. multicoloured . . 1·25 75

1155 Sosa

1156 Nasazzi

2001. 75th Birth Anniv of Julio Sosa (singer).
2714 **1155** 12p. black and violet 1·25 75

2001. Birth Cent of Jose Nasazzi (footballer).
2715 **1156** 12p. multicoloured . . 1·25 75

1157 "Adoration of the Shepherds" (Jose Ribera)

1158 Bell Tower

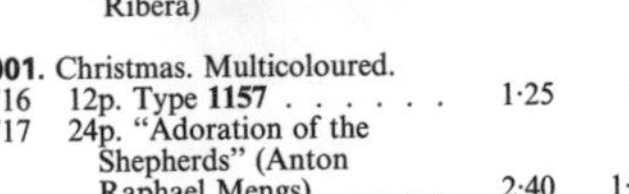

2001. Christmas. Multicoloured.
2716 12p. Type **1157** . . . . . . 1·25 75
2717 24p. "Adoration of the Shepherds" (Anton Raphael Mengs) . . . . 2·40 1·25

2001. Bicentenary of San Carlos Church.
2718 **1158** 12p. multicoloured . . 1·25 75

1159 "Cosmic Monument" (Joaquiin Torres Garcia)

2001. 90th Anniv of National Museum of Visual Arts.
2719 **1159** 12p. multicoloured . . 1·25 75

1160 Building Facade

2001. 90th Anniv of State Insurance Bank.
2720 **1160** 12p. multicoloured . . 1·25 75

1161 *Guettarda uruguensis*

2001. Mercosur.
2721 **1161** 24p. multicoloured . . 2·40 1·40

1162 Josemaria Escriva

2002. Birth Centenary of Josemaria Escriva de Balaguer (founder of Opus Dei religious order). Multicoloured.
2722 12p. Type **1162** . . . . . 1·20 70
2723 12p. Facing front . . . . . 1·20 70
2724 12p. Facing left . . . . . . 1·20 70
2725 12p. With mother and baby 1·20 70

2002. Flowers. As T **1025**. Multicoloured. Self-adhesive gum.
2726 1p. *Oxalis pudica* 10 10
2727 5p. As No. 2726 but with colour changed 50 30
2728 10p. *Aechmea recurvata* . . 1·00 60

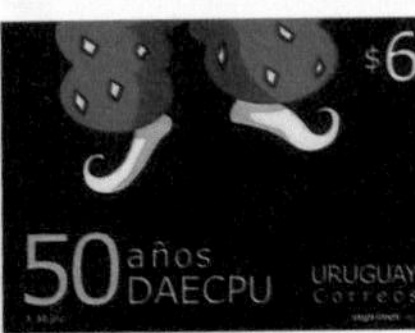

1163 Legs

2002. 50th Anniv of DAECPU (carnival directors).
2742 **1163** 6p. black and blue . . 60 35
2743 – 6p. black and magenta 60 35
2744 – 12p. black . . . . 1·20 70
DESIGNS: Type **1163**; 6p.Cane, legs and top hat; 12p. Legs (different).

1164 Church

2001. 1700th Anniv of Christianity in Armenia.
2745 **1164** 12p. multicoloured . . 1·20 70

1165 Hoof Print

2001. Year of the Horse.
2746 **1165** 24p. blue, black and magenta . . . . . . 2·40 1·40

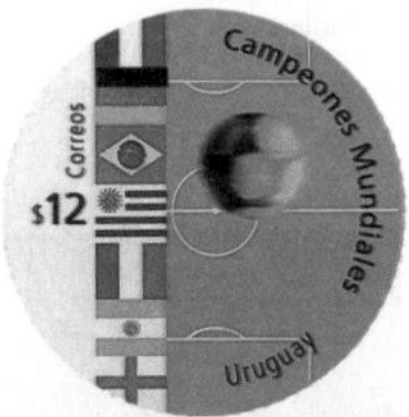

1166 Winners' Flags and Football

2002. World Cup Football Championship, Japan and South Korea. Multicoloured.
2747 12p. Type **1166** . . . . . 1·20 70
2748 12p. Footballer . . . . . . 1·20 70

1167 "N"

2002. Book Day.
2749 **1167** 12p. multicoloured . . 1·20 70

1168 Stylized Children

2002. 75th Anniv of Inter-America Children's Institute.
2750 **1168** 12p. multicoloured . . 1·20 70

1169 Bernabe Rivera and Arms

2002. 165th Anniv of the Foundation of Tacuarembo.
2751 **1169** 12p. multicoloured . . 1·20 70

1170 Lighthouse Building

2002. Bicentenary of Cerro de Montevideo Lighthouse. Multicoloured.
2752 12p. Type **1170** . . . . . 1·20 70
2753 24p. Entrance to lighthouse (vert) . . . . 2·40 1·40

1171 Building Facade

2002. 150th Anniv of Villa Constitucion, Salto Department.
2754 **1171** 12p. multicoloured . . 1·20 70

1172 Jose Leandro Andrade (footballer)

2002. Sportsmen. Multicoloured.

2755	12p. Type **1172**	1·20	70
2756	12p. Cesar Gallardo (fencer, rower and basketball player)	1·20	70
2757	12p. Alvaro Gestido (footballer)	1·20	70
2758	12p. Pedro Petrone (footballer)	1·20	70
2759	12p. Lorenzo Fernandez (footballer)	1·20	70

1173 Figures enclosing Globe

2002. "United We Stand". 175th Anniv of Postal Service. Sheet 100 × 80 mm containing T **1173** and similar horiz designs. Multicoloured.
MS2760 6p. × 3 Type **1172** × 3 . . . 3·50 3·50

1174 Tourism Emblem

2002. Tourism.
2761 **1174** 24p. blue and yellow . . 2·40 1·40

1175 Museum Building and *Erthrina crista-galli*

1176 Man carrying Cane

2002. Centenary of Montevideo Botanical Museum. Multicoloured.

2762	12p. Type **1175**	1·20	70
2763	12p. Oxblood lily (*Rhodophiala bifida*)	1·20	70
2764	12p. Atilio Lombardo (founder) and *Tillandsia arequitae*	1·20	70
2765	12p. *Heteroterys dumetorum*	1·20	70

2002. Centenary of Montevideo Wanderers Football Club.
2766 **1176** 12p. black . . . . . . 1·20 70

1177 Elvis Presley

1178 Agustin Bisio

2002. 25th Death Anniv of Elvis Presley (entertainer).
2767 **1177** 24p. multicoloured . . 2·40 1·40

2002. 50th Death Anniv of Agustin Bisio (writer). Self-adhesive gum.
2768 **1178** 12p. multicoloured . . 1·20 70

1179 Obelisk to the Heroes of 1825

2002. 150th Anniv of Foundation of Artigas City. Self-adhesive.
2769 **1179** 12p. multicoloured . . 1·20 70

1180 Early and Modern Buses

2002. 65th Anniv of CUTSA (society of bus services).
2770 **1180** 12p. multicoloured . . 1·20 70

1181 Sigmund Freud

2002. Latin-American Psychoanalysis Conference, Montevideo.
2771 **1181** 12p. multicoloured . . 1·20 70

1182 Horacio Arredondo and San Miguel Fort

2002. 35th Death Anniv of Horacio Arredondo (historian). National Heritage Day.
2772 **1182** 12p. multicoloured . . 1·20 70

1183 1905 Lieutenant Colonel's Uniform and Barracks Building

2002. Paso del Rey Barrack, Sarandi del Yi.
2773 **1183** 12p. multicoloured . . 1·20 70

1184 Bathers (Patrica Torres and Patricia Molina)

2002. International Year of Ecotourism. Winning Entry in Design a Stamp Competition.
2774 **1184** 12p. multicoloured . . 1·20 70

1185 Post Office Building

2002. 175th Anniv of Uruguay Post Office. Multicoloured.
2775 12p. Type **1185** . . . . . . 1·20 70
MS2776 100 × 90 mm. 12p. Post box. Imperf . . . . 1·20 1·20

1186 Brigadier General Juan Antonio Lavalleja on Horseback (statue) (Juan Manuel Ferrari)

2002. Centenary of Erection of First Equestrian Statue.
2777 **1186** 12p. multicoloured . . 1·20 70

1187 Letters

2002. America. Literacy Campaign. Multicoloured.
2778 12p. Type **1187** . . . . . . 1·20 70
2779 24p. Alphabet soup . . . . 2·20 1·40

1188 Wreath

2002. Christmas.
2780 **1188** 12p. multicoloured . . 1·20 70

1189 Pharmacy Centre Building

2002. 65th Anniv of Pharmacy Centre.
2781 **1189** 12p. multicoloured . . 1·10 70

1190 Wine Bottle

2002. 125th Anniv of Tannat Wine Producers.
2782 **1190** 12p. multicoloured . . 1·20 70

1191 *Maldonado* (hydrographic ship)

2002. 185th Anniv of Uruguay Navy.
2783 **1191** 12p. multicoloured . . 1·20 70

1192 Jigsaw Puzzle Piece and Emblem

2002. 24th Anniv of National Organs and Tissue Bank. National Organ Donation Day.
2784 **1192** 12p. multicoloured . . 1·20 70

1193 Early and Modern Taxis

2002. Centenary of Taxi Service.
2785 **1193** 12p. multicoloured . . 1·20 70

1194 Brigadier General Manuel Oribe

2002. 145th Birth Anniv of Brigadier General Manuel Oribe (politician).
2786 **1194** 12p. multicoloured . . 1·20 70

1195 Guitar Neck wrapped in Black Ribbon

2002. 1st Death Anniv of George Harrison (musician).
2787 **1195** 24p. multicoloured . . 2·20 1·40

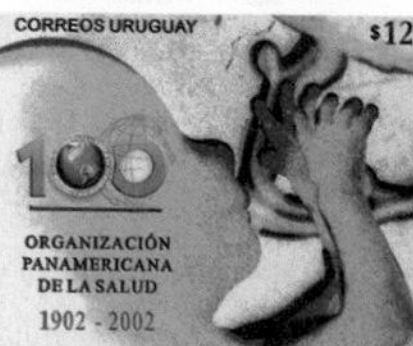
1196 Baby in Womb

2002. Centenary of Pan American Health Organization.
2788 **1196** 12p. multicoloured . . 1·20 70

1197 Emblems, Map and Soldiers

2002. 50th Anniv of Uruguay Army's Participation in United Nations Peace Keeping Force.
2789 **1197** 12p. multicoloured . . 1·20 70

1198 "Costa Azul" (Alfredo Testoni)

2002. Alfredo Testoni (artist).
2790 **1198** 12p. multicoloured . . 1·20 70

1199 Coast and Ship at Night

2002. Mercosur. Tourism. Multicoloured.
2791 12p. Type **1199** . . . . . . 1·20 70
2792 24p. Beach . . . . 2·20 1·40

1200 Village Square and School Building

2002. 130th Anniv of Juanico.
2793 **1200** 12p. multicoloured . . 1·20 70

1201 Ships under Fire

2002. 175th Anniv of Juncal Sea Battle.
2794 **1201** 12p. multicoloured . . 1·20 70

1202 Cavalry Charge

2002. 175th Anniv of Ituzaingo Battle.
2795 **1202** 12p. multicoloured . . 1·20 70

EXPRESS MAIL STAMPS

1921. Overprinted **MENSAJERIAS**.
E389 **120** 2c. orange 50 20

E **126** Caduceus
E **153** Caduceus 

1923.
E415 E **126** 2c. red 30 10
E416 2c. blue 30 10

1928.
E591 E **153** 2c. black on green 15 10
E635a 2c. green 15 10
E636 2c. blue 15 10
E637 2c. pink 15 10
E638 2c. brown 10 10

1957. Surch **$ 0.05.**
E1065 E **153** 5c. on 2c. brown . . 15 10

E **859** Motor Scooter
E **913** 

1994. International Service.
E2170 E **859** 1p. orange and blue 20 15

1996.
E2275 E **913** 8p. yellow and blue 1·25 65

LATE FEE STAMPS

L **175**

1936.
L774 L **175** 3c. green 10 10
L775 5c. violet 15 10
L776 6c. green 15 10
L777 7c. brown 20 10
L778 8c. red 40 25
L779 12c. blue 60 50

NEWSPAPER STAMPS

1922. Optd **PRENSA** (= Printed Matter) or surch also.
N519 **128** 3c. olive (imperf) . . . 40 25
N447 **118** 3c. on 2c. black and lake (perf) 40 35
N403 **120** 3c. on 4c. yellow (perf) 20 30
N448 **118** 6c. on 4c. blue and orange (perf) 40 35
N449 9c. on 5c. brown and blue (perf) 40 35
N520 **128** 9c. on 10c. green (imperf) 45 35
N521 15c. mauve (imperf) . . 60 40

OFFICIAL STAMPS

1880. Optd **OFICIAL**. Perf.
O51 **9** 15c. yellow . . . . 2·00 2·00

1880. Optd **OFICIAL**. Roul.
O48 **10** 1c. brown . . . . 1·10 1·10
O49 **11** 5c. green 45 45
O61 **15** 7c. blue (perf) . . . . . 1·50 1·50
O50 **10** 10c. red 70 70
O52 20c. bistre 95 95
O53 50c. black . . . . 6·25 6·25
O55 1p. blue . . . . 6·25 6·25

1883. Optd **OFICIAL**.
O64 **16** 1c. green . . . . 2·00 2·00
O65 – 2c. red (No. 63) . . . . 3·75 3·00

1883. Optd **OFICIAL**.
O70 **18** 1c. green . . . . 11·50 11·50
O71 2c. red . . . . 3·70 3·75
O72 **20** 5c. blue . . . . 1·10 85
O73 **21** 10c. brown . . . . 2·75 1·40

1884. Optd **FRANCO** in frame.
O74 **18** 1c. green . . . . 13·50 11·50

1884. Optd **OFICIAL**.
O80 **10** 1c. on 10c. (No. 76) . . . 80 80
O81 – 2c. red (No. 77) . . . . . 2·25 2·25
O82 **26** 5c. blue 95 70

1884. Optd **OFICIAL**. Roul.
O 91a **28** 1c. grey . . . . 3·75 2·00
O 91 1c. green 75 45
O 92 **29** 2c. red 45 30
O 93a **28** 5c. blue . . . . 1·25 1·40
O 94 5c. lilac . . . . 1·50 1·25
O 95 **31** 7c. brown . . . . . . 1·10 65
O110 7c. orange . . . . . . 1·10 75
O 96 **32** 10c. brown 60 35
O111 **36** 10c. violet . . . . . . 5·75 3·00
O 97 **33** 20c. mauve . . . . . . 1·10 65
O112 20c. brown . . . . . . 5·75 2·25
O 98 **34** 25c. lilac . . . . 1·10 75
O113 25c. red . . . . 5·75 2·25

1890. Optd **OFICIAL**. Perf.
O124 **38** 1c. green 40 20
O125 **39** 2c. red 40 20
O126 **40** 5c. blue 75 80
O127 **41** 7c. brown 60 60
O128 **42** 10c. green 60 50
O129 **43** 20c. orange 60 50
O130 **44** 25c. brown 60 50
O131 **45** 50c. blue . . . . 2·75 2·75
O132 **46** 1p. violet . . . . 3·00 2·75

1891. Optd **OFICIAL**.
O134 **28** 5c. lilac (No. 133) . . . 75 75

1895. Optd **OFICIAL**.
O164 **38** 1c. blue 85 85
O165 **39** 2c. brown . . . . 1·10 1·10
O166 **40** 5c. red . . . . 1·50 1·50
O167 **45** 50c. purple . . . . . . 3·00 3·00

1895. Optd **OFICIAL**.
O168 **56** 1c. bistre 20 20
O169 **57** 2c. blue 20 20
O170 **58** 5c. red . . . . 5·50 2·25
O171 **59** 7c. green 40 40
O172 **60** 10c. brown 40 40
O173 **61** 20c. black and green . . 2·25 60
O174 **62** 25c. black and brown . . 60 60
O175 **63** 50c. black and blue . . . 55 55
O176 **64** 1p. black and brown . . 2·75 2·75

1897. Nos. 180/2 optd **OFICIAL**.
O194 **67** 1c. black and red 60 60
O195 **68** 5c. black and blue . . . 70 60
O196 – 10c. black and lake . . . 95 75

1897. Optd **OFICIAL**.
O201 **56** 1c. blue 35 30
O202 **57** 2c. purple 60 55
O203 **58** 5c. green . . . . 6·25 2·50
O204 **72** 10c. red . . . . 2·00 1·10
O205 **61** 20c. black and mauve . . 7·00 2·00
O206 **62** 25c. blue and red . . . . 2·25 1·10
O207 **63** 50c. brown and green . . 3·00 1·10
O208 **64** 1p. blue and brown . . . 4·50 3·00

1899. Optd **OFICIAL**.
O226 **39** 2c. orange 50 25
O227 **58** 5c. blue . . . . 5·50 2·25
O228 **72** 10c. purple 95 95
O243 **43** 20c. blue . . . . 3·00 2·25

1901. Optd **OFICIAL**.
O238 **78** 1c. green 20 25
O239 **79** 2c. red 25 25
O240 **80** 5c. blue 25 30
O241 **81** 7c. brown 30 30
O242 **82** 10c. lilac 35 35
O245 **46** 1p. green . . . . 3·75 3·00

1904. Optd **OFICIAL**.
O272 **86** 1c. green 20 15
O262 **87** 2c. orange 20 20
O263 **88** 5c. blue 20 20
O275 **89** 10c. lilac 20 15
O276 **90** 20c. green . . . . 1·10 70
O277 **91** 25c. bistre 75 35

1907. Optd **OFICIAL**.
O273 **96** 5c. blue 20 15
O274 7c. brown 20 15
O278 50c. red 45 40

1910. Optd **OFICIAL 1910**.
O288 **79** 2c. red . . . . 3·75 2·25
O289 **80** 5c. blue . . . . 2·25 2·00
O290 **82** 10c. lilac . . . . 1·10 70
O291 **43** 20c. green . . . . 1·10 70
O292 **44** 25c. brown . . . . 2·00 1·40
O293 **96** 50c. red . . . . 2·50 1·40

O **110**

1911.
O307 O **110** 2c. brown 25 25
O308 5c. blue 25 20
O309 8c. slate 25 20
O310 20c. brown 40 30
O311 23c. red 60 40
O312 50c. orange 75 45
O313 1p. red . . . . 2·00 70

1915. Optd **Oficial**.
O340 **107** 2c. pink 40 45
O341 5c. blue 40 45
O342 8c. blue 40 45
O343 20c. brown 85 35
O344 **108** 23c. blue . . . . 8·00 4·00
O345 50c. orange . . . . . . 13·00 4·00
O346 1p. red . . . . 11·50 4·00

1919. Optd **Oficial**.
O365 **115** 2c. grey and red 60 30
O366 5c. grey and blue . . . 70 25
O367 8c. brown and blue . . 70 25
O368 20c. grey and brown . . 1·40 45
O369 23c. brown and green 1·40 45
O370 50c. blue and brown . . 2·00 95
O371 1p. blue and red . . . . 5·00 1·50

1924. Optd **OFICIAL** in frame. (a) Perf.
O439 **128** 2c. mauve 75 30
O440 5c. blue 75 30
O593 8c. red . . . . 1·75 45
O594 10c. green . . . . . . 2·50 45
O441 12c. blue 45 30
O442 20c. brown 45 45
O443 36c. green . . . . . . 1·75 1·40
O444 50c. orange . . . . . . 3·75 2·75
O445 1p. red . . . . 6·50 5·00
O446 2p. green . . . . 12·00 9·25

(b) Imperf.
O499 **128** 2c. mauve 70 10
O500 5c. blue 70 20
O501 8c. red 70 25
O502 12c. blue . . . . 1·10 25
O503 20c. brown . . . . . . 1·75 45
O504 36c. pink . . . . 3·75 70

PARCEL POST STAMPS

P **123**
P **144** 

1922. (a) Inscr "EXTERIOR".
P391 P **123** 5c. green on buff . . . 20 10
P516 5c. black on yellow . . 30 10
P392 10c. green on blue . . 35 10
P517 10c. black on blue . . 40 10
P393 20c. green on rose . . 1·10 50
P518 20c. black on pink . . 85 15
P394 30c. green on green . . 1·10 20
P395 50c. green on blue . . 2·00 30
P396 1p. green on orange 2·75 70

(b) Inscr "INTERIOR".
P397 P **123** 5c. green on buff . . . 25 10
P512 5c. black on yellow . . 30 10
P398 10c. green on blue . . 25 10
P513 10c. black on blue . . 35 10
P399 20c. green on pink . . 50 25
P514 20c. black on pink . . 45 15
P400 30c. green on green . . 85 25
P515 30c. black on green . . 85 25
P401 50c. green on blue . . 1·10 30
P402 1p. green on orange 3·00 60

1927.
P522 P **144** 1c. blue 10 10
P606 1c. violet 10 10
P523 2c. green 10 10
P524 4c. violet 15 10
P609a 5c. red 15 10
P526 10c. brown 30 10
P527 20c. orange 40 20

P **152**
P **155** 
P **177** Sea and Rail Transport 

1928.
P587 P **152** 5c. black on yellow . . 10 10
P588 10c. black on blue . . 15 10
P589 20c. black on red . . 35 10
P590 30c. black on green . . 55 10

1929. Agricultural Parcels.
P610 P **155** 10c. orange 30 20
P611 15c. blue 30 20
P612 20c. brown 45 30
P613 25c. red 50 35
P614 50c. grey 95 45
P615 75c. violet . . . . . 3·75 3·75
P616 1p. olive . . . . . . 2·75 1·40

1938.
P 971 P **177** 5c. orange 10 35
P 801 10c. red 65 40
P 972 10c. purple . . . . . 1·00 65
P1066 10c. green 30 40
P 973 20c. red 65 55
P1067 20c. blue 55 40
P 974 30c. blue 85 45
P1068 30c. purple 35 40
P1069 50c. green 50 50
P 805 1p. red . . . . . . 4·00 2·75
P 975 1p. blue . . . . . . 3·00 2·50
P1070 1p. green . . . . . 1·40 1·50

P **188**
P **204** University 

1943.
P876 P **188** 1c. red 10 10
P877 2c. green 10 10

1944. Optd **ANO 1943**.
P882 P **155** 10c. orange 20 10
P883 15c. blue 20 20
P884 20c. brown 30 20
P885 25c. red 50 30
P886 50c. grey 70 50
P887 75c. violet . . . . . 1·40 95
P888 1p. olive . . . . . . 1·75 1·40

1945.
P 909 A 1c. green 10 10
P 999 P **204** 1c. red 10 10
P 910 2c. violet 10 10
P1000 A 2c. blue 10 10
P1047 B 5c. grey 35 10
P1045 5c. brown 10 10
P1001 A 10c. turqoise 10 10
P1002 10c. olive 10 10
P1048 C 20c. yellow 10 10
P1049 20c. brown 15 10
P1046 D 1p. blue . . . . . . 4·50 4·50
P1290 1p. brown 10 10
DESIGNS—HORIZ: A, Bank. VERT: B, Customs House; C. Solis Theatre; D. Montevideo Railway Station.

P **211** Customs House
P **212** Mail Coach (Guillermo Rodriguez) 

1946.
P934 P **211** 5c. blue and brown . . 15 10

1946.
P935 P **212** 5p. brown and red . . 7·00 2·25

1946. Armorial type as T **187** obliterated by arrow-head device. (a) Optd **IMPUESTO** and **ENCOMIENDAS**.

P936	1c. mauve	10	10
P937	2c. brown	10	10
P938	5c. blue	10	10

(b) Optd **ENCOMIENDAS** only.

P939	1p. blue	75	20
P940	5p. red	2·50	95

1957. No. P1047 surch **$ 0.30**.

P1064	30c. on 5c. grey	20	10

P **263** National Printing Works

1960.

P1127	P **263** 30c. green	10	10

1965. Surch with caduceus and **$ 5.00 ENCOMIENDAS**.

P1268	**217** 5p. on 84c. orange	30	15

1966. No. 1092 surch with caduceus and **ENCOMIENDAS 1.00 PESO**.

P1289	**254** 1p. on 38c. black	10	10

P **355** Sud Aviation Caravelle and Motor-coach

1969.

P1397	P **355** 10p. black, red & grn	15	10
P1398	– 20p. yellow, blk & bl	30	20

DESIGN: 20p. Side views of Sud Aviation Caravelle and motor-coach.

1971. No. 1121 surch **Encomiendas $ 0.60**.

P1448	**261** 60c. on 1p.+10c. violet and orange	45	30

1971. No. 1380 surch **IMPUESTOS A ENCOMIENDAS $0.60** and diesel locomotive.

P1472	60c. on 6p. black and green	30	25

1972. Nos. 1401/2 surch **$1 IMPUESTO A ENCOMIENDAS** and caduceus.

P1507	**358** 1p. on 6p. black, red and blue	40	40
P1508	– 1p. on 6p. black, red and blue	40	40

P **460** Parcels and Arrows

1974.

P1555	P **460** 75p. multicoloured	15	10

P **461** Mail-van

1974. Old-time Mail Transport.

P1556	P **461** 100p. multicoloured	30	20
P1557	– 150p. multicoloured	1·60	1·90
P1558	– 300p. black, bl & orge	75	50
P1559	– 500p. multicoloured	1·25	70

DESIGNS: 150p. Steam locomotive; 300p. Paddle-steamer; 500p. Monoplane.

POSTAGE DUE STAMPS

D **84**

1902.

D795	D **84** 1c. green	10	10
D405	2c. red	25	15
D796	2c. brown	10	10
D491	3c. brown	35	25
D797	3c. red	10	10
D798	4c. violet	10	10
D799	5c. blue	10	10
D746	5c. red	35	20
D494	6c. brown	40	30
D800	8c. red	15	10
D249	10c. blue	45	35
D409a	10c. green	30	15
D250	20c. orange	85	45

1904. Surch **PROVISORIO UN cent'mo.**

D267	D **84** 1c. on 10c. blue	45	45

UZBEKISTAN Pt. 10

Formerly a constituent republic of the Soviet Union, Uzbekistan became independent in 1991.

1992. 100 kopeks = 1 rouble.
1994. (June) Sum (temporary coupon currency).
1994. (Sept) 100 tyin = 1 sum.

1 Princess Nadira (from portrait by Sh. Khasanov)

2 "Melitaea acreina" (butterfly)

1992. Birth Bicentenary of Princess Nadira (poetess).
1 **1** 20k. multicoloured 10 10

1992. Nature Protection.
2 **2** 1r. multicoloured 15 10

3 National Flag and Kukeldash Mosque, Tashkent

1992. 1st Anniv of Independence.
3 **3** 1r. multicoloured 10 10

4 Kutlug-Murad-inak Mosque, Khiva

1992. Uzbek Architecture.
4 **4** 50k. multicoloured 10 10

5 Mosque, Registan Square, Samarkand

1992. Award of Aga Khan Prize for Architecture to Samarkand.
5 **5** 10r. multicoloured 15 10

6 Copper Water Pot, Kokand, and Sculptured Relief

1992. Uzbek Handicrafts.
6 **6** 50k. multicoloured 10 10

7 Plate-tailed Gecko

ЎЗБЕКИСТОН 15-00
(8)

1993. Animals. Multicoloured.
7 1r. Type **7** 10 10
8 2r. Cobra 10 10
9 2r. Muskrat (vert) 10 10
10 3r. Osprey (vert) 20 20
11 5r. Penduline tit (vert) 25 25
12 10r. Forest dormouse (vert) . . 20 10
13 15r. Desert monitor 30 15
MS14 90 × 60 mm. 20r. Red deer 25 25

1993. Stamps of Russia surch as T **8**.
15 2r. on 1k. brown (No. 5940) 30 10
16 8r. on 4k. red (No. 4672) . . . 40 20
17 15r. on 2k. mauve (No. 4670) 1·50 1·00
18 15r. on 2k. brown (No. 6073) 1·50 1·00
19 15r. on 3k. green (No. 5941) 1·50 1·00
20 15r. on 4k. red (No. 4672) . . 1·50 1·00
21 15r. on 4k. blue (No. 6075) . . 1·50 1·00
22 15r. on 5k. red (No. 6076) . . 1·50 1·00
23 15r. on 6k. blue (No. 4673) . . 1·50 1·00
24 15r. on 7k. blue (No. 6077) . . 1·50 1·00
25 15r. on 10k. brown (No. 6078) 1·50 1·00
26 15r. on 15k. blue (No. 6081) 1·50 1·00
27 20r. on 4k. red (No. 4672) . . 80 40
28 30r. on 3k. red (No. 4671) . . 35 20
29 100r. on 1k. green (No. 4533) 60 30
30 500r. on 1k. green (No. 4533) 1·40 80

9 Arms and Flag

10 "Colchicum kesselringii"

1993.
31 **9** 8r. multicoloured 10 10
32 15r. multicoloured 15 10
33 50r. mult (19 × 27 mm) . . . 40 20
34 100r. multicoloured 80 40

1993. Flowers. Multicoloured.
35 20r. Type **10** 15 10
36 20r. "Dianthus uzbekistanicus" 15 10
37 25r. "Crocus alatavicus" . . . 20 10
38 25r. "Salvia bucharica" . . . 20 10
39 30r. "Tulipa kaufmanniana" 25 15
40 30r. "Tulipa greigii" 25 15
MS41 61 × 90 mm. 50r. Tulip . . 35 35

11 Tournament Emblem

1194. President's Cup Tennis Championships, Tashkent. Sheet 91 × 66 mm.
MS42 **11** 500s. multicoloured . . 30 30

12 Arms

13 Bakhouddin Nakshband Mosque, Bukhara

1994.
43 **12** 75s. red 10 10
See also Nos. 58/60 and 103/7. For a similar design inscr "O'ZBEKISTON" see Nos. 160/5.

1994. 675th Birth Anniv of Sheikh Bakhouddin Nakshband.
44 **13** 100s. multicoloured 15 10

14 Statue of Timur, Tashkent

15 Ulugh Beg Mosque, Samarkand

1994.
45 **14** 20t. multicoloured 10 10

1994. 600th Birth Anniv of Ulugh Beg (central Asian ruler).
46 30t. Type **15** 15 10
47 35t. Ulugh Beg Mosque, Bukhara 20 10
48 40t. Astronomical equipment 25 15
49 45t. Statue, Tashkent 30 15
MS50 70 × 90 mm. 60t. Ulugh Beg 40 40

ЎЗБЕКИСТОН 200 сўм
(16)

ЎЗБЕКИСТОН 2-00
(17)

1995. Stamps of Russia surch. (a) With T **16** in coupon currency.
51 200s. on 2k. brown (No. 6073) 2·10 1·00
52 200s. on 2k. brown (imperf) (No. 6073) 75 35
53 200s. on 4k. blue (No. 6075) 75 35
54 200s. on 5k. blue (No. 5061) 75 35
55 200s. on 15k. blue (No. 6081) 75 35

(b) With T **17** in permanent currency.
56 2s. on 1k. green (No. 4533) . . 75 75
57 2s. on 3k. turquoise (No. 5941) 35 35

1995. As T **12** but value expressed as "1.00" etc.
(a) Size 14 × 22 mm.
58 1s. green 10 10

(b) Size 22 × 33 mm.
59 3s. red 25 15
60 6s. blue 35 20

18 Statue, Tashkent

1995. 50th Anniv of End of Second World War. Sheet 100 × 68 mm.
MS61 **18** 20s. multicoloured . . . 1·40 1·40

19 Markhor

1995. Endangered Species. The Markhor. Mult.
62 6s. Type **19** 35 20
63 10s. Three markhors on rocks 60 30
64 10s. Head 60 30
65 15s. Lying down 90 45

20 "The Fool"

22 Gur Amir Mausoleum, Samarkand

21 Player and Emblem

1995. Folk Tales. Multicoloured.
66 6s. Type **20** 40 40
67 10s. "The Golden Melon" . . 65 35
68 10s. Man and white stork on nest ("Are you Stupid?") . . 65 35
69 10s. Woman and monster bird ("Thousand Plaits") 35 35
70 15s. "Story of the Parrot" . . 95 50

1995. 2nd President's Cup Tennis Championships.
71 **21** 10s. multicoloured 65 35

1995. Architecture of the Silk Road (1st series). Multicoloured.
72 6s. Type **22** 30 15
73 10s. Mausoleum, Shakhrisabz 50 30
74 10s. Mosque, Bukhara 50 30
75 15s. Kaltaminor Minaret, Khiva 75 45
MS76 91 × 71 mm. 20s. Camel, Kaltaminor Minaret and map of Silk Road . . . . 1·25 1·25
See also No. 155/**MS**159.

23 Emblem

1995. 1st Anniv of Membership of Univeral postal Union. Sheet 91 × 71 mm.
MS77 **23** 20s. yellow, blue and deep blue . . . . 1·40 1·40

24 "Karanasa abramovi"

1995. Butterflies and Moths. Multicoloured.
78 6s. Type **24** 40 20
79 10s. "Colias romanovi" . . . 70 35
80 10s. "Parnassius delphius" . . 70 35
81 10s. "Chasara staudingeri" . . 70 35
82 10s. "Colias wiskotti" 70 35
83 10s. "Neohipparchia fatua" . . 70 35
84 15s. "Parnassius tianschanicus" . . . . . . 1·10 55
MS85 90 × 70 mm. 20s. "Colias christophi" . . . . 1·60 1·60

25 Lisunov Li-2 Airliner

1995. Aircraft. Multicoloured.
86 6s. Type **25** 40 20
87 10s. Kamov Ka-22 helicopter 70 35
88 10s. Antonov An-8 transport 70 35
89 10s. Antonov An-12 transport 70 35
90 10s. Antonov An-22 Anteus jet transport 70 35
91 10s. Ilyushin Il-76 jet transport 70 35
92 15s. Ilyushin Il-114 . . . . . 1·10 55
MS93 91 × 71 mm. 20s. As No. 92 (51 × 36 mm) . . . . 1·60 1·60

26 "Madjnun and Laila"

27 Bactrian Camel

1995. 540th Birth Anniv of Kemal ad-Din Behsad (Persian miniaturist).
94 **26** 15s. multicoloured . . . . . 1·00 1·00

1995. Tashkent Zoo. Multicoloured.
95 6s. Type **27** 40 20
96 10s. Brown bear 70 35
97 10s. Cinereous vulture . . . 70 35
98 10s. Rhesus macaque 70 35
99 10s. Dalmatian pelican . . . 70 35
100 10s. Zebra 70 35
101 15s. African elephant . . . . 1·10 55
MS102 91 × 70 mm. 20s. Makhor 1·75 1·75

1995. As T **12**. Value expressed as "2 SUM" etc.
(a) Size 14 × 22½ mm.
103 **12** 2s. green 15 10
104 6s. green 25 15

(b) Size 20 × 32 mm.
105 **12** 3s. mauve 20 10
106 6s. mauve 40 20
107 15s. blue . . . . 1·00 90

28 Argali

1996. Mammals. Multicoloured.
108 10s. Type **28** 55 25
109 15s. Argali ("Ovis ammon cycloceros") 85 30
110 15s. Argali ("Ovis ammon severtzov") 85 30
111 15s. Argali ("Ovis ammon karelini") 85 30
112 15s. Red deer ("Cervus elaphas") 85 30
113 15s. Siberian ibex ("Capra sibirica") 85 30
114 20s. Saiga ("Saiga tatarica") 1·10 35
MS115 90 × 70 mm. 25s. Goitred gazelle . . . . 1·50 1·50

29 Pike Asp

1996. "Save the Aral Sea". Sheet 128 × 108 mm containing T **29** and similar horiz designs. Multicoloured.
MS116 15s. Caracal; 15s. Aral trout; 20s. Striped hyena; 20s. Kaufmann's shovelnose; 25s. Type **29** . . . . . . 3·25 3·25

30 Football

1996. Olympic Games, Atlanta, U.S.A. Mult.
117 6s. Type **30** 25 10
118 10s. Show jumping 40 10
119 15s. Boxing 70 25
120 20s. Cycling 85 30

31 Timur

32 State Arms and Flag

1996. 660th Anniv of Timur (Tamerlane) Sheet 70 × 90 mm. (a) Wrongly dated "1336—1401".
MS121 **31** 20s. multicoloured . . 3·50 3·50
(b) Correctly dated "1336—1405"
MS122 **31** 20s. multicoloured . . 1·60 1·60

1996. 5th Anniv of Independence. Sheet 90 × 90 mm.
MS123 **32** 20s. multicoloured . . 1·00 1·00

33 Trophy

34 Zhuzhaev

1996. 3rd President's Cup Tennis Championships.
124 **33** 12s. green and grey 65 25

1996. Birth Centenary of Faizulla Zhuzhaev (politician).
125 **34** 15s. black and green . . . 70 25

35 Fitrat

36 Spacecraft

1996. 110th Birth Anniv of Abdurauf Fitrat (writer).
126 **35** 15s. black and brown . . . 70 25

1997. Fantasy Spacecraft. Multicoloured.
127 9s. Type **36** 40 15
128 15s. Spacecraft landing on planet 70 25
129 15s. Spacecraft with external "wings" and "probes" . . 70 25
130 15s. Spacecraft and sun's rays (horiz) 70 25
131 15s. Spacecraft passing sun (horiz) 70 25
132 15s. Spacecraft passing Saturn's rings (horiz) . . . 70 25
133 25s. Two cosmonauts in spacecraft . . . . . . 1·10 35
MS134 90 × 70 mm. 30s. Two spacecraft (39 × 49 mm) . . . 2·00 2·00

37 Bird of Paradise

1997. Folk Tales. Multicoloured.
135 15s. Type **37** 70 25
136 15s. Jinn 70 25
137 20s. Queen looking in mirror 90 30
138 20s. Man riding on monkey 90 30
139 25s. Eagle and deer . . . . 1·10 30
140 25s. Monster and horse . . . 1·10 30
141 30s. Two men kneeling before throne . . . . . . 1·40 45
MS142 70 × 90 mm. 35s. Horse rider 2·25 2·25

38 Leopard

39 Cho'lpon

1997. The Leopard. Multicoloured.
143 9s. Type **38** 50 20
144 15s. Leopard yawning . . . 80 30
145 15s. Leopard stretching . . . 80 30
146 25s. Leopard on prowl . . . 1·25 45
MS147 90 × 70 mm. 30s. Head of leopard (29 × 39 mm) . . . . . 2·00 2·00

1997. Birth Centenary of Abdulhamid Sulaymon Cho'lpon.
148 **39** 6s. black and mauve . . . 15 10

40 Trophy

1997. 4th President's Cup Tennis Championships. Each green and blue.
149 6s. Type **40** 30 15
150 6s. Woman player 30 15
151 6s. Camel and ball 30 15

41 Tico

1997. Uz-Daewoo Automobile Works. Mult.
152 9s. Type **41** 60 20
153 12s. Damas 80 30
154 15s. Nexia . . . . . . 1·00 35

42 Ismail Samani Mausoleum, Bukhara

43 Astronomical Instruments

1997. Architecture of the Silk Road (2nd series). Multicoloured.
155 15s. Type **42** 70 25
156 15s. Citadel, Bukhara (horiz) 70 25
157 15s. Minaret, Khiva 70 25
158 15s. Gateway, Khiva (horiz) 70 25
MS159 Two sheets, each 90 × 70 mm. (a) 30s. Mosque, Bukhara (29 × 39 mm); (b) 30s. Mosque, Khiva (39 × 29 mm) 4·00 4·00

1998. As T **12** (value expressed as "2-00" etc.) but inscr "O'ZBEKISTON".
160 2s. green 10 10
161 3s. pink 10 10
162 6s. green 20 10
163 12s. green 40 15
164 15s. pink 50 15
165 45s. blue . . . . . . 1·60 50
For 6s. with face value inscr "6 SO'M" see No. 181.

1998. Ahmad al-Farg'ony (astronomer).
166 **43** 15s. ultramarine, green and blue 50 20

44 Students honouring Imam al-Buchari (miniature)

45 Festival Emblem

1998. Mohammed Ibn Ismail al–Buchari, 810–870 (scholar).
167 **44** 15s. multicoloured 50 20

1998. "Sharq Teronalari" International Music Festival, Samarkand.
168 **45** 15s. multicoloured 50 20

46 Player

47 Berdaq (statue), Nukus

1998. 5th President's Cup International Tennis Championship.
169 **46** 15s. brown, blue and black 40 15

1998. 170th Birth Anniv of Berdaq (poet).
170 **47** 15s. brown and blue . . . 40 15

48 Miniature by Kamoliddin Behzod

50 Steam Locomotive (1897–1917)

49 Mother and Baby

1998.
171 **48** 15s. green and red 40 15

1998. Alpomish (folktale). Multicoloured.
172 8s. Type **49** 20 10
173 10s. Rainbow and mountains 25 10
174 15s. Men sitting around fire 35 10
175 15s. Old man and soldier . . 35 10
176 18s. Horsemen 40 15
177 18s. Archers 40 15
178 20s. Blacksmith 45 15
179 20s. Man wrestling lion . . . 45 15
180 25s. Man and woman 55 20
Nos. 172/80 were issued together, se-tenant, forming a composite design.

1999. As No. 162 but value expressed as "6 SO'M".
181 **12** 6s. green 15 10

1999. Locomotives. Multicoloured.
182 18s. Type **50** 20 10
183 18s. Steam locomotive (1931–1935) 20 10
184 28s. Steam locomotive . . . 30 10
185 36s. Steam locomotive . . . 35 15
186 56s. Steam locomotive . . . 60 20
187 56s. VL-22 electric locomotive 60 20
188 69s. TEP-60 electric passenger locomotive 80 30

51 Horse

52 Woman

1999. Horses. Multicoloured.
189 18s. Type **51** 15 10
190 28s. White horse (horiz) . . . 25 10
191 36s. Man on horseback (horiz) 30 10
192 69s. Jockey on racehorse (horiz) 70 25
MS193 90 × 70 mm. 75s. Horse's head (horiz) 80 80

1999. Badal Qorachi (folktale). Multicoloured.
194 18s. Type **52** 15 10
195 18s. Two horsemen 15 10
196 28s. Horseman 25 10
197 36s. Moon behind demon . . 30 10
198 56s. Man fighting demon . . 55 20
199 56s. Witch with cat 55 20
200 69s. Man and woman 70 25

53 Steppenrunner

1999. Reptiles. Multicoloured.
202 18s. Type **53** 15 10
203 18s. Orsinis' viper ("Vipera ursinii") 15 10
204 28s. Toad-headed agama . . 25 10
205 36s. Halys viper 30 10
206 56s. Steppe agama ("Trapelus sanguinolentus") (vert) . . 55 20
207 56s. Schneider's skink ("Eumeces schneideri") . . 55 20
208 69s. Levantine viper 70 25
MS209 70 × 90 mm. 75s. Two lizards 80 80

54 Emblem and City

55 Ogahiy (poet)

1999. 125th Anniv of Universal Postal Union.
210 **54** 45s. black and green . . . 60 20

1999. Ogahiy Commemoration.
211 **55** 30s. red and green 40 15

VANUATU Pt. 1

The New Hebrides became the Republic of Vanuatu on 30 July 1980.

1980. 100 centimes = 1 franc (Vanuatu).
1981. Vatus.

99 Island of Erromango and Kauri Pine

1980. As Nos. 242/54 of New Hebrides but inscr "VANUATU" and without royal and republican cyphers. (a) Inscr in English.
287E 5f. Type **99** 15 25
288E 10f. Territory map and copra making 15 25
289E 15f. Espiritu Santo and cattle 20 30
290E 20f. Efate and Vila P.O. . . 20 40
291E 25f. Malakula and headdresses 25 40
292E 30f. Aoba, Maewo and pigs' tusks 35 55
293E 35f. Pentecost and land diver 40 60

294E 40f. Tanna and John Frum cross 40 70
295E 50f. Shepherd Is. and outrigger canoe 45 80
296E 70f. Banks Is. and custom dancers . . . . 50 1·75
297E 100f. Ambrym and idols . . 50 80
298E 200f. Aneityum and baskets 60 1·40
299E 500f. Torres Is. and archer fisherman . . . . 75 3·00

(b) Inscr in French.
287F 5f. Type **99** 35 15
288F 10f. Territory map and copra making 40 15
289F 15f. Espiritu Santo and cattle 45 25
290F 20f. Efate and Vila P.O. . . 50 30
291F 25f. Malakula and headdresses 55 40
292F 30f. Aoba, Maewo and pigs' tusks 55 55
293F 35f. Pentecost and land diver 60 60
294F 40f. Tanna and John Frum cross 75 60
295F 50f. Shepherd Is. and outrigger canoe 80 80
296F 70f. Banks Is. and custom dancers . . . . 1·00 1·50
297F 100f. Ambrym and idols . . 1·25 1·10
298F 200f. Aneityum and baskets 1·50 1·75
299F 500f. Torres Is. and archer fisherman . . . . 1·75 3·50

100 Rotary International

1980. 75th Anniv of Rotary International. Multicoloured. (a) Inscr in English.
300E 10f. Type **100** 10 10
301E 40f. Rotary emblem (vert) 30 30

(b) Inscr in French.
300F 10f. Type **100** 15 15
301F 40f. Rotary emblem (vert) 45 45

101 Kiwanis Emblem and Globe

102 "The Virgin and Child enthroned with Saints and Angels" (Umkreis Michael Pacher)

1980. Kiwanis International (service club), New Zealand District Convention, Port Vila. (a) Inscr in English.
302E **101** 10f. gold, blue and brown 10 20
303E – 40f. green and blue . . . 30 80

(b) Inscr in French.
302F **101** 10f. gold, blue and brown 40 65
303F – 40f. green and blue . . . 85 1·10
DESIGN: 40f. Kiwanis and Convention emblems.

1980. Christmas. Details from Paintings. Mult.
304 10f. Type **102** 10 10
305 15f. "The Virgin and Child with Saints, Angels and Donors" (Hans Memling) 10 10
306 30f. "The Rest on the Flight to Egypt" (Adriaen van der Werff) 20 20

103 Blue-faced Parrot Finch

104 Tribesman with Portrait of Prince Philip

1981. Birds (1st series). Multicoloured.
307 10f. Type **103** 35 25
308 20f. Emerald dove 40 45
309 30f. Golden whistler 45 80
310 40f. Silver-shouldered fruit dove . . . . 50 1·00
See also Nos. 327/30.

1981. 60th Birthday of Prince Philip, Duke of Edinburgh. Multicoloured.
311 15v. Type **104** 10 15
312 25v. Prince Philip in casual dress 15 20
313 35v. Queen and Prince Philip with Princess Anne and Master Peter Phillips . . . 15 25
314 45v. Prince Philip in ceremonial dress 20 35

105 Prince Charles with his Dog, Harvey

106 National Flag and Map of Vanuatu

1981. Royal Wedding. Multicoloured.
315 15v. Wedding bouquet from Vanuatu 10 10
316 45v. Type **105** 20 15
317 75v. Prince Charles and Lady Diana Spencer 35 45

1981. 1st Anniv of Independence.
318 **106** 15v. multicoloured . . . 15 15
319 – 25v. multicoloured . . . 15 15
320 – 45v. yellow and brown . . 20 20
321 – 75v. multicoloured . . . 35 70
DESIGNS—HORIZ: 25v. Vanuatu emblem; 45v. Vanuatu national anthem. VERT: 75v. Vanuatu coat of arms.

107 Three Shepherds

1981. Christmas. Children's Paintings. Mult.
322 15v. Type **107** 10 10
323 25v. Vanuatu girl with lamb (vert) 15 15
324 35v. Angel as butterfly . . . 15 20
325 45v. Boy carrying torch and gifts (vert) 25 30
MS326 133 × 94 mm. Nos. 322/5 80 1·25

108 New Caledonian Myiagra Flycatchers

109 "Flickingeria comata"

1982. Birds (2nd series). Multicoloured.
327 15v. Type **108** 30 20
328 20v. Rainbow lorys 40 30
329 25v. Buff-bellied flycatchers 45 35
330 45v. Collared grey fantails . . 50 65

1982. Orchids. Multicoloured.
331 1v. Type **109** 10 50
332 2v. "Calanthe triplicata" . . 10 50
333 10v. "Dendrobium sladei" . . 15 30
334 15v. "Dendrobium mohlianum" 20 20
335 20v. "Dendrobium macrophyllum" 25 30
336 25v. "Dendrobium purpureum" 30 35
337 30v. "Robiquetia mimus" . . 35 40
338 35v. "Dendrobium mooreanum" (horiz) . . . 50 50
339 45v. "Spathoglottis plicata" (horiz) 55 70
340 50v. "Dendrobium seemannii" (horiz) 60 80
341 75v. "Dendrobium conanthum" (horiz) . . . 1·00 1·50
342 100v. "Dendrobium macranthum" . . . . . . 1·25 1·50
343 200v. "Coelogyne lamellata" 1·50 2·75
344 500v. "Bulbophyllum longiscapum" . . . . . . 2·00 6·50

110 Scouts round Campfire

1982. 75th Anniv of Boy Scout Movement. Multicoloured.
345 15v. Type **110** 25 20
346 20v. First aid 30 20
347 25v. Constructing tower . . . 30 30
348 45v. Constructing raft . . . 40 50
349 57v. Scout saluting 50 90

111 Baby Jesus

1982. Christmas. Nativity Scenes. Mult.
350 15v. Type **111** 30 35
351 25v. Mary and Joseph . . . 50 45
352 35v. Shepherds (vert) . . . . 60 1·00
353 45v. Kings bearing gifts (vert) 65 1·40
MS354 132 × 92 mm. As Nos. 350/3 but without yellow borders . . 1·50 2·25

112 "Euploea sylvester"

1983. Butterflies. Multicoloured.
355 15v. Type **112** 50 65
356 15v. "Hypolimnas octocula" 50 65
357 20v. "Papilio canopus" . . . 60 80
358 20v. "Polyura sacco" 60 80
359 25v. "Luthrodes cleotas" . . 60 80
360 25v. "Danaus pumila" . . . 60 80

113 President Afi George Sokomanu

1983. Commonwealth Day. Multicoloured.
361 15v. Type **113** 15 10
362 20v. Fisherman and liner "Oriana" 20 15
363 25v. Herdsman and cattle . . 25 15
364 75v. World map showing position of Vanuatu with Commonwealth and Vanuatu flags 50 70

114 Map of Northern Vanuatu

115 Montgolfier Balloon of De Rozier and D'Arlandes, 1783

1983. Economic Zone. Sheet 120 × 120 mm, containing T **114** and similar vert designs. Multicoloured.
MS365 25v. × 6 Yellow-finned tuna; Type **114**; Map of Matthew Island; Map of Hunter Island; Cornet grouper; Skipjack tuna 2·75 2·75

1983. Bicentenary of Manned Flight. Mult.
366 15v. Type **115** 15 15
367 20v. J. A. C. Charles hydrogen balloon (first use of hydrogen, 1783) 20 25
368 25v. Blanchard and Jeffries crossing English Channel, 1785 . . . . 20 30
369 35v. Giffard's steam-powered dirigible airship, 1852 (horiz) 30 40
370 40v. "La France" (airship of Renard and Krebs), 1884 (horiz) 35 45
371 45v. "Graf Zeppelin" (first aerial circumnavigation, 1929) (horiz) 40 55

116 Mail at Bauerfield Airport

1983. World Communications Year. Mult.
372 15v. Type **116** 20 25
373 20v. Switchboard operator . . 30 35
374 25v. Telex operator 35 40
375 45v. Satellite earth station . . 65 70
MS376 138 × 95 mm. Nos. 372/5 2·00 2·75

117 "Cymatoderma elegans var. lamellatum"

118 Port Vila

1984. Fungi. Multicoloured.
377 15v. Type **117** 50 45
378 25v. "Lignosus rhinocerus" 60 85
379 35v. "Stereum ostrea" (horiz) 80 1·25
380 45v. "Ganoderma boninense" 1·00 1·90

1984. 250th Anniv of "Lloyd's List" (newspaper). Multicoloured.
381 15v. Type **118** 20 25
382 20v. "Induna" (container ship) 30 35
383 25v. Air Vanuatu Boeing 737 aircraft 35 40
384 45v. "Brahman Express" (container ship) 65 70

1984. Universal Postal Union Congress, Hamburg. As No. 371 but inscr "UPU CONGRESS HAMBURG" and U.P.U. logo.
385 45v. multicoloured 80 80

119 Charolais

1984. Cattle. Multicoloured.
386 15v. Type **119** 15 20
387 25v. Charolais-afrikander . . 20 30
388 45v. Friesian 40 55
389 75v. Charolais-brahman . . . 60 1·00

120 "Makambo"

1984. "Ausipex" International Stamp Exn, Melbourne. Inter-island Freighters. Multicoloured.
390 25v. Type **120** 60 50
391 45v. "Rockton" 80 90
392 100v. "Waroonga" . . . . . 1·25 3·50
MS393 140 × 70 mm. Nos. 390/2 4·00 5·50

121 Father Christmas in Children's Ward

1984. Christmas. Multicoloured.
394 25v. Type **121** 45 40
395 45v. Nativity play 80 70
396 75v. Father Christmas distributing presents . . . 1·40 1·25

1985. No. 331 surch.
397 5v. on 1v. Type **109** 65 50

123 Ambrym Island Ceremonial Dance

124 Peregrine Falcon diving

1985. Traditional Costumes. Multicoloured.
398 20v. Type **123** 35 35
399 25v. Pentecost Island marriage ceremony 40 40

400 45v. Women's grade ceremony, South West Malakula 75 70
401 75v. Ceremonial dance, South West Malakula . . . . . 1·10 1·25

1985. Birth Bicentenary of John J. Audubon (ornithologist). Peregrine Falcon. Mult.
402 20v. Type **124** 60 35
403 35v. Peregrine falcon in flight 75 50
404 45v. Peregrine falcon perched on branch 90 80
405 100v. "Peregrine Falcon" (John J. Audubon) . . . . 1·60 1·75

125 The Queen Mother with the Queen on her 80th Birthday

1985. Life and Times of Queen Elizabeth the Queen Mother. Multicoloured.
406 5v. Duke and Duchess of York on wedding day, 1923 . . . . 30 1·00
407 20v. Type **125** 70 45
408 35v. At Ancona, Italy 90 70
409 55v. With Prince Henry at his christening (from photo by Lord Snowdon) . . . . . 1·10 1·00
MS410 91 × 73 mm. 100v. At Royal Opera House, Covent Garden 1·75 1·50

126 "Mala" (patrol boat)

1985. 5th Anniv of Independence and "Expo '85" World Fair, Japan. Multicoloured.
411 35v. Type **126** 45 50
412 45v. Japanese fishing fleet . . 55 70
413 55v. Vanuatu Mobile Force Band 60 85
414 100v. Prime Minister Fr. Walter H. Lini . . . . . . 65 1·75
MS415 116 × 102 mm. Nos. 411/14 2·50 4·25

127 "Youth Activities" (Alain Lagaliu)

1985. Int Youth Year. Children's Paintings. Mult.
416 20v. Type **127** 55 35
417 30v. "Village" (Peter Obed) 65 45
418 50v. "Beach and 'PEACE' Slogan" (Mary Estelle) . . 1·10 75
419 100v. "Youth Activities" (different) (Abel Merani) 1·75 1·50

128 Map of Vanuatu with National and U.N. Flags

1985. 4th Anniv of United Nations Membership.
420 **128** 45v. multicoloured . . . 1·25 70

129 Elizabeth's Nudibranch

130 Scuba Diving

1985. Marine Life (1st series). Sea Slugs. Multicoloured.
421 20v. Type **129** 25 25
422 35v. Tessellated nudibranch (horiz) 35 40
423 55v. "Chromodoris kuniei" (horiz) 60 80

424 100v. "Notodoris minor" . . 1·00 1·75
See also Nos. 442/5 and 519/22.

1986. Tourism. Multicoloured.
425 30v. Type **130** 60 40
426 35v. Yasur volcano, Tanna 75 45
427 55v. Land diving, Pentecost Island 75 70
428 100v. Windsurfing . . . . . 90 1·50

1986. 60th Birthday of Queen Elizabeth II. As T **145a** of St. Helena. Multicoloured.
429 20v. With Prince Charles and Princess Anne, 1951 . . . 15 30
430 35v. Prince William's Christening, 1982 . . . . 20 45
431 45v. In New Hebrides, 1974 25 60
432 55v. On board Royal Yacht "Britannia", Mexico, 1974 30 70
433 100v. At Crown Agents Head Office, London, 1983 . . . 40 1·25

131 Liner S.S. "President Coolidge" leaving San Francisco

1986. "Ameripex '86" International Stamp Exhibition, Chicago. Sinking of S.S. "President Coolidge". Multicoloured.
434 45v. Type **131** . . . . 1·10 60
435 55v. S.S. "President Coolidge" as troopship, 1942 . . . . 1·10 70
436 135v. Map of Espiritu Santo showing site of sinking, 1942 . . . . 2·25 1·75
MS437 80 × 105 mm. Nos. 434/6 4·25 3·00

132 Halley's Comet and Vanuatu Statue

1986. Appearance of Halley's Comet. Mult.
438 30v. Type **132** 90 50
439 45v. Family watching Comet 1·25 1·00
440 55v. Comet passing Earth . . 1·40 1·25
441 100v. Edmond Halley . . . . 2·00 3·25

133 Daisy Coral

1986. Marine Life (2nd series). Corals. Mult.
442 20v. Type **133** 65 40
443 45v. Organ pipe coral . . . . 1·00 75
444 55v. Sea fan . . . . 1·25 1·10
445 135v. Soft coral . . . . . . 2·50 3·50

134 Children of Different Races

1986. Christmas. Int Peace Year. Mult.
446 30v. Type **134** . . . . 1·00 50
447 45v. Church and boy praying 1·40 85
448 55v. U.N. discussion and Headquarters Building, New York . . . . 1·60 1·40
449 135v. People of different races at work . . . . . . 3·00 5·00

135 Datsun "240Z" (1969)

1987. Motor Vehicles. Multicoloured.
450 20v. Type **135** 30 30
451 45v. Ford "Model A" (1927) 60 60
452 55v. Unic lorry (1924–5) . . 70 70
453 135v. Citroen "DS19" (1975) 1·60 2·25

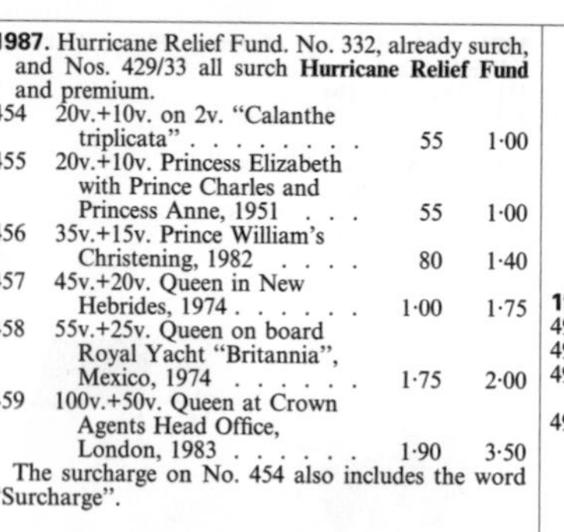

1987. Hurricane Relief Fund. No. 332, already surch, and Nos. 429/33 all surch **Hurricane Relief Fund** and premium.
454 20v.+10v. on 2v. "Calanthe triplicata" . . . . 55 1·00
455 20v.+10v. Princess Elizabeth with Prince Charles and Princess Anne, 1951 . . . 55 1·00
456 35v.+15v. Prince William's Christening, 1982 . . . . 80 1·40
457 45v.+20v. Queen in New Hebrides, 1974 . . . . . . 1·00 1·75
458 55v.+25v. Queen on board Royal Yacht "Britannia", Mexico, 1974 . . . . . . 1·75 2·00
459 100v.+50v. Queen at Crown Agents Head Office, London, 1983 . . . . . . 1·90 3·50
The surcharge on No. 454 also includes the word "Surcharge".

137 Young Coconut Plants

1987. 25th Anniv of I.R.H.O. Coconut Research Station. Multicoloured.
460 35v. Type **137** 40 45
461 45v. Coconut flower and fronds 50 60
462 100v. Coconuts . . . . . . 85 1·40
463 135v. Research station . . . 1·10 2·00
The inscriptions on Nos. 462/3 are in French.

138 Spotted Hawkfish

1987. Fishes. Multicoloured.
464 1v. Type **138** 10 10
465 5v. Moorish idol 15 10
466 10v. Black-saddled pufferfish 15 10
467 15v. Dusky anemonefish . . 20 20
468 20v. Striped surgeonfish . . . 30 25
469 30v. Six-barred wrasse . . . 40 35
470 35v. Yellow-striped anthias ("Purple queenfish") . . . 45 40
471 40v. Squirrelfish 50 45
472 45v. Clown triggerfish . . . 60 55
473 50v. Dragon wrasse 65 65
474 55v. Regal angelfish 70 70
475 65v. Lionfish 80 80
476 100v. Freckled hawkfish . . . 1·25 1·40
477 300v. Undulate triggerfish . . 3·00 4·00
478 500v. Saddled butterflyfish . . 4·00 6·00

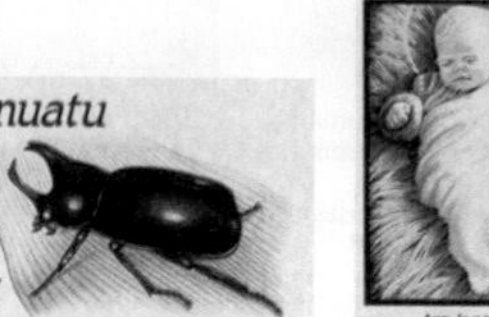

139 "Xylotrupes gideon" (beetle)

140 "Away in a Manger"

1987. Insects. Multicoloured.
479 45v. Type **139** 55 60
480 55v. "Phyllodes imperialis" (moth) 65 70
481 65v. "Cyphogastra sp." (beetle) 75 85
482 100v. "Othreis fullonia" (moth) . . . . 1·10 1·75

1987. Christmas. Christmas Carols. Mult.
483 20v. Type **140** 60 30
484 45v. "Once in Royal David's City" 95 65
485 55v. "While Shepherds watched their Flocks" . . 1·10 90
486 65v. "We Three Kings of Orient Are" . . . . 1·25 1·00

1987. Royal Ruby Wedding. Nos. 429/33 optd **40TH WEDDING ANNIVERSARY**.
487 20v. Princess Elizabeth with Prince Charles and Princess Anne, 1951 . . . . 30 30
488 35v. Prince William's Christening, 1982 . . . . 45 45
489 45v. Queen Elizabeth II in New Hebrides, 1974 . . . . 60 60
490 55v. On board Royal Yacht "Britannia", Mexico, 1974 70 70
491 100v. At Crown Agents Head Office, London, 1983 . . . 1·25 1·25

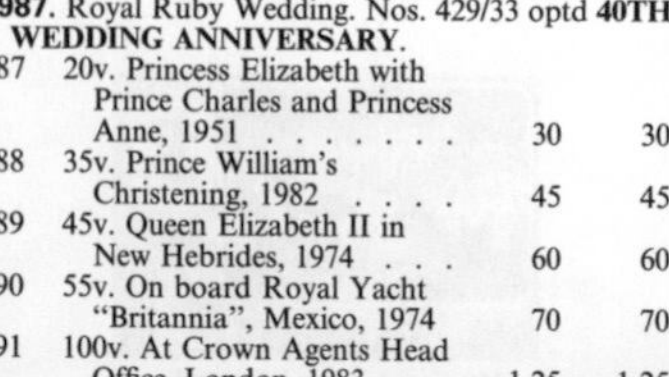

141 Dugong Cow and Calf

1988. Endangered Species. Dugong. Multicoloured.
492 5v. Type **141** 90 35
493 10v. Dugong underwater . . 1·40 35
494 20v. Two dugongs surfacing to breathe . . . . 1·90 1·00
495 45v. Four dugongs swimming 3·25 2·50

142 "Tambo"

1988. Bicentenary of Australian Settlement. Freighters. Multicoloured.
496 20v. Type **142** 20 25
497 45v. "Induna" 50 55
498 55v. "Morinda" 60 65
499 65v. "Marsina" 70 75

143 Captain James Cook

144 Boxer in training

1988. "Sydpex '88" National Stamp Exhibition, Sydney.
500 **143** 45v. black and red . . . 1·00 1·00

1988. "Expo '88" World Fair, Brisbane. Sheet 100 × 80 mm, containing designs as Nos. 427/8, but with addition of Australian Bicentenary symbol and imprint date. Multicoloured.
MS501 55v. Land diving, Pentecost Island; 100v. Windsurfing . . . 3·00 3·25

1988. Olympic Games, Seoul. Multicoloured.
502 20v. Type **144** 20 25
503 45v. Athletics 50 55
504 55v. Signing Olympic agreement 60 65
505 65v. Soccer 70 75
MS506 54 × 66 mm. 150v. Tennis 3·00 2·40

1988. 300th Anniv of Lloyd's of London. As T **152a** of St. Helena. Multicoloured.
507 20v. Interior of new Lloyd's Building, 1988 . . . . . . 30 25
508 55v. "Shirrabank" (freighter) (horiz) . . . . 1·25 65
509 65v. "Adela" (ferry) (horiz) 1·40 75
510 145v. "General Slocum" (excursion paddle-steamer) on fire, New York, 1904 2·25 2·50

145 Agricultural Crops

1988. F.A.O. Multicoloured.
511 45v. Type **145** 40 55
512 55v. Fisherman with catch (vert) 45 65
513 65v. Livestock on smallholding (vert) 50 75
514 120v. Market women with produce . . . . 60 1·40

146 Virgin and Child ("Silent Night")

1988. Christmas. Carols. Multicoloured.
515 20v. Type **146** 25 25
516 45v. Angels ("Angels from the Realms of Glory") . . 45 55
517 65v. Shepherd boy with lamb ("O Come all ye Faithful") 55 75
518 155v. Baby ("In that Poor Stable how Charming Jesus Lies") . . . . 1·50 1·90

147 "Periclimenes brevicarpalis"

1989. Marine Life (3rd series). Shrimps. Mult.
519 20v. Type **147** 50 25
520 45v. "Lysmata grabhami" . . 80 55
521 65v. "Rhynchocinetes sp." . . 95 75
522 150v. "Stenopus hispidus" . . 2·25 2·50

148 Consolidated Catalina Flying Boat

1989. Economic and Social Commission for Asia and the Pacific. Aircraft.
523 **148** 20v. black and blue . . . 85 30
524 – 45v. black and green . . . 1·25 65
525 – 55v. black and yellow . . 1·50 80
526 – 200v. black and red . . . 4·25 3·00
DESIGNS: 45v. Douglas DC-3; 55v. Embraer EMB-110 Bandeirante; 200v. Boeing 737-300.

149 Porte de Versailles Hall No. 1

1989. "Philexfrance '89" International Stamp Exhibition, Paris. Multicoloured.
527 100v. Type **149** . . . . . . 2·25 1·50
528 100v. Eiffel Tower . . . . . . 2·25 1·50
MS529 115 × 101 mm. 100v. black, grey and scarlet (Revolt of French troops, Nancy, 1790 (42 × 28 mm)) 1·40 1·50
Nos. 527/8 were printed together, se-tenant, forming a composite design.

1989. 20th Anniv of First Manned Landing on Moon. As T **50a** of St. Kitts. Multicoloured.
530 45v. Command module seen from lunar module . . . . 1·50 80
531 55v. Crew of "Apollo 17" (30 × 30 mm) . . . . . . 1·50 90
532 65v. "Apollo 17" emblem (30 × 30 mm) . . . . . . 1·60 1·00
533 120v. Launch of "Apollo 17" 2·75 3·50
MS534 99 × 82 mm. 100v. Recovery of "Apollo 11" . . . . 1·75 1·75

1989. "Melbourne Stampshow '89". No. 332 surch **100** and Stampshow emblem.
535 100v. on 2v. "Calanthe triplicata" . . . . 3·50 4·25

151 New Hebrides 1978 "Concorde" 30f. (French inscr) Stamp

1989. "World Stamp Expo '89" International Stamp Exhibition, Washington. Multicoloured.
536 65v. Type **151** . . . . 3·50 2·50
MS537 105 × 100 mm. 65v. New Hebrides 1978 Concorde 10f. (English inscr) stamp; 100v. White House, Washington . . . . . 8·50 8·50

152 "Alocasia macrorrhiza"

153 Kava (national plant)

1990. Flora. Multicoloured.
538 45v. Type **152** 60 55
539 55v. "Acacia spirorbis" . . . 70 70
540 65v. "Metrosideros collina" 80 80
541 145v. "Hoya australis" . . . 1·75 2·50

1990. "Stamp World London 90" International Stamp Exhibition. Multicoloured.
542 45v. Type **153** 80 55
543 65v. Luganville Post Office 1·00 95
544 100v. Embraer EMB-110 Bandeirante mail plane and sailing packet . . . . . . 1·90 2·00
545 200v. Penny Black and Vanuatu 1980 10f. definitive . . . . 3·00 3·75
MS546 110 × 70 mm. 150v. New Hebrides 1974 New Post Office tê-bêe pair with first day postmark . . . . 6·50 6·50

154 National Council of Women Logo

1990. 10th Anniv of Independence.
547 **154** 25v. black and blue . . . 55 40
548 – 50v. multicoloured . . . 85 80
549 – 55v. purple, black and buff 90 80
550 – 65v. multicoloured . . . 1·50 90
551 – 80v. multicoloured . . . 1·50 1·40
MS552 109 × 82 mm. 150v. multicoloured . . . . 5·00 6·50
DESIGNS: 50v. President Frederick Kalomuana Timakata; 55v. Preamble to the Constitution; 65v. Vanuaaku Pati party flag; 80v. Reserve Bank of Vanuatu; 150v. Prime Minister Fr. Walter Lini taking oath.
No. **MS**552 also commemorates the South Pacific Forum, Port Vila, 1990.

155 General De Gaulle at Bayeux, 1944

1990. Birth Centenary of General Charles de Gaulle (French statesman). Multicoloured.
553 20v. Type **155** . . . . 3·25 4·50
554 25v. Generals De Lattre de Tassigny, De Gaulle, Devers and Patch in Alsace, 1945 . . . . 3·25 4·50
555 30v. De Gaulle as President of the French Republic . . 90 1·00
556 45v. De Gaulle at Biggin Hill, 1942 . . . . 95 1·10
557 55v. Roosevelt, De Gaulle and Churchill, Casablanca, 1943 . . . . 1·00 1·10
558 65v. General De Gaulle and Liberation of Paris, 1944 1·10 1·25

156 Angel facing Right

157 "Parthenos sylvia"

1990. Christmas. Multicoloured.
559 25v. Type **156** 45 65
560 50v. Shepherds . . . . 70 1·00
561 65v. Nativity . . . . 80 1·10
562 70v. Three Kings . . . . . . 85 1·25
563 80v. Angel facing left . . . . 85 1·40
Nos. 559/63 were printed together, se-tenant, forming a composite design.

1991. Butterflies. Multicoloured.
564 25v. Type **157** 55 30
565 55v. "Euploea leucostictus" 95 60
566 80v. "Lampides boeticus" . . 1·40 1·25
567 150v. "Danaus plexippus" . . 2·25 3·25

158 Dance Troupe from South-west Malakula

160 White-collared Kingfisher

1991. 2nd National Art Festival, Luganville. Multicoloured.
568 25v. Type **158** 35 30
569 65v. Women weavers and baskets 85 85
570 80v. Woodcarver and carved animals, masks, dish and ceremonial figures . . . . 1·10 1·25
571 150v. Musicians playing bamboo flute, youtatau and pan pipes . . . . . . 1·90 2·50

1991. Nos. 332/4 and 337 surch.
572 20v. on 2v. "Calanthe triplicata" 50 50
573 60v. on 10v. "Dendrobium sladei" . . . . 1·25 1·60
574 70v. on 15v. "Dendrobium mohlianum" . . . . 1·40 1·75
575 80v. on 30v. "Robiquetia mimus" . . . . 1·40 1·75
See also No. 622.

1991. 65th Birthday of Queen Elizabeth II and 70th Birthday of Prince Philip. As T **165a** of St. Helena. Multicoloured.
576 65v. Queen Elizabeth II . . . 1·00 1·25
577 70v. Prince Philip . . . . . 1·00 1·25

1991. "Phila Nippon '91" International Stamp Exhibition, Tokyo. Birds. Multicoloured.
578 50v. Type **160** 65 70
579 55v. Palm lorikeet ("Green Palm Lorikeet") 70 75
580 80v. Scarlet robin . . . . . 95 1·10
581 100v. Pacific swallow . . . . 1·10 1·75
MS582 75 × 56 mm. 150v. Reef heron . . . . 2·25 3·00

161 Group of Islanders

1991. World AIDS Day. Multicoloured.
583 25v. Type **161** 55 30
584 65v. Caring for AIDS victim 1·00 85
585 80v. AIDS shark . . . . . . 1·25 1·50
586 150v. Children's playground 2·25 3·00

1992. 40th Anniv of Queen Elizabeth II's Accession. As T **168a** of St. Helena. Mult.
587 20v. Reserve Bank of Vanuatu Building, Port Vila 30 30
588 25v. Port Vila 40 30
589 60v. Mural, Parliament House 85 75
590 65v. Three portraits of Queen Elizabeth 90 80
591 70v. Queen Elizabeth II . . . 95 1·50

162 Grumman F4F Wildcat

1992. 50th Anniv of Outbreak of the Pacific War (1st issue). Multicoloured.
592 50v. Type **162** . . . . 2·25 1·25
593 55v. Douglas SBD-3 Dauntless . . . . 2·25 1·25
594 65v. Consolidated PBY-5A Catalina . . . . 2·50 1·50
595 80v. U.S.S. "Hornet" (aircraft carrier) . . . . . 3·25 3·25
MS596 94 × 62 mm. 200v. Vought-Sikorsky OS-2-3 Kingfisher over Port Vila . . . . 8·50 8·50
See also Nos. 623/7.

163 Meteorological Station, Port Vila

165 Breast-feeding

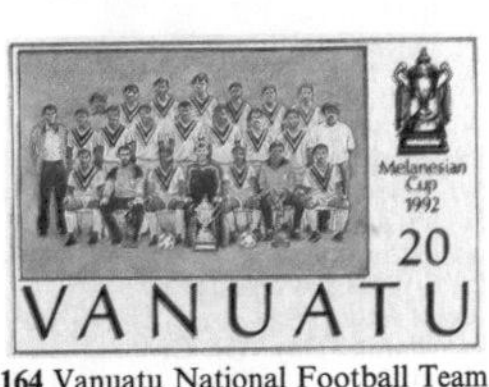

164 Vanuatu National Football Team

1992. 10th Anniv of Vanuatu's Membership of World Meteorological Organization. Mult.
597 25v. Type **163** 40 30
598 60v. Satellite picture of tropical cyclone 80 80
599 80v. Weather chart of Pacific showing cyclone . . . . . 1·00 1·25
600 105v. Radio Vanuatu broadcasting cyclone warning . . . . 1·25 1·75

1992. Vanuatu's Participation in Melanesian Football Cup and Olympic Games, Barcelona. Multicoloured.
601 20v. Type **164** 65 40
602 65v. Melanesian Cup Final, 1990 . . . . 1·50 1·25
603 70v. Baptiste Firiam (800 m) 1·75 1·50
604 80v. Mary Estelle Kapalu (400, 400 hurdles, and 800 m) . . . . 1·90 2·00

1992. World Food Day. Each brown and green.
605 20v. Type **165** 30 25
606 70v. Central Hospital, Port Vila 95 90
607 80v. Children eating . . . . 1·10 1·00
608 150v. Nutritious food . . . . 1·75 2·50

166 Leatherback Turtle

167 "Hibiscus rosa-sinensis" "Agnes Goult"

1992. Turtles. Multicoloured.
609 55v. Type **166** . . . . 1·25 1·10
610 65v. Loggerhead turtle laying eggs . . . . 1·40 1·25
611 70v. Hawksbill turtle swimming . . . . 1·60 1·40
612 80v. Green turtle under water 2·25 2·00
MS613 81 × 96 mm. 200v. Green turtle hatching on beach . . . 3·75 4·00

1993. Hibiscus Flowers (1st series). Multicoloured.
614 25v. Type **167** 30 30
615 55v. "Hibiscus tiliaceus" . . 70 70
616 80v. "Hibiscus rosa-sinensis linnaeus" . . . . 95 1·00
617 150v. "Hibiscus rosa-sinensis" "Rose of China" . . . . . 1·60 2·50
See also Nos. 682/5 and 736/9.

1993. 14th World Orchid Conference, Glasgow. Nos. 339 and 341/3 surch **WORLD ORCHID CONFERENCE 1993** and value.
618 40v. on 45v. "Spathoglottis plicata" (horiz) 50 50
619 55v. on 75v. "Dendrobium conanthum" (horiz) . . . 70 75
620 65v. on 100v. "Dendrobium macranthum" 75 80
621 150v. on 200v. "Coelogyne lamellata" . . . . 1·60 4·25

1993. No. 338 surch **20**.
622 20v. on 35v. "Dendrobium mooreanum" . . . . . . 5·00 70

1993. 50th Anniv of Outbreak of the Pacific War (2nd issue). As T **162**. Multicoloured.
623 20v. Grumman F6F Hellcat 1·75 80
624 55v. Lockheed P-38F Lightning . . . . 2·75 1·75
625 65v. Grumman TBF Avenger 2·75 1·75
626 80v. U.S.S. "Essex" (aircraft carrier) . . . . 3·00 3·00
MS627 82 × 58 mm. 200v. Douglas C-47 Skytrain . . . . 8·50 8·50

170 Port Vila and Iririki Island

1993. Local Scenery. Multicoloured.
628 5v. Type **170** 20 50
629 10v. Yachts and Iririki Island 30 30
630 15v. Court House, Port Vila 40 40
631 20v. Two girls, Pentecost Island 40 40
632 25v. Women dancers, Tanna Island 45 30
633 30v. Market, Port Vila . . . 50 35
634 45v. Man in canoe, Erakor Island (vert) 60 45
635 50v. Coconut trees, Champagne Beach 60 50
636 55v. Coconut trees, North Efate Islands 70 55
637 60v. Underwater shoal of fishes, Banks Group . . . 75 60
638 70v. Sea fan, Tongoa Island (vert) . . . . 1·00 90
639 75v. Santo Island . . . . . 1·00 95
640 80v. Sunset, Port Vila harbour (vert) . . . . . . 1·25 1·00
641 100v. Mele Waterfall (vert) 2·25 1·50
642 300v. Yasur Volcano, Tanna Island (vert) . . . . . . 4·00 5·50
643 500v. Aerial view of Erakor Island . . . . 5·50 8·00
For miniature sheet containing Nos. 629, 636/7 and 639 see **MS**673.

171 Commercial Trochus

1993. Shells (1st series). Multicoloured.
644 55v. Type **171** . . . . 1·10 85
645 65v. Camp pitar venus . . . 1·25 95
646 80v. Tapestry turban . . . . 1·60 1·75
647 150v. Trapezium horse conch 2·75 3·75
See also Nos. 665/8 and 692/5.

172 "St. Joseph the Carpenter" (detail) (De la Tour)

1993. Christmas. Bicentenary of the Louvre, Paris. Religious Paintings by Georges de la Tour. Multicoloured.
648 25v. Type **172** 45 30
649 55v. "Holy Child" (detail) . . 80 65
650 80v. "Adoration of the Shepherds" (detail) . . . . 1·00 1·00
651 150v. "Adoration of the Shepherds" (different detail) . . . . 1·75 2·50

1993. South Pacific Mini Games, Port Vila. Nos. 602, 604, 631 and 633 surch **SOUTH PACIFIC MINI GAMES PORT VILA DECEMBER 1993** and value.
652 15v. on 20v. Two girls, Pentecost Island 30 30
653 25v. on 30v. Market, Port Vila 45 40
654 55v. on 65v. Melanesian Cup Final, 1990 . . . . 85 75
655 70v. on 80v. Mary Estelle Kapalu (400, 400 hurdles and 800 m) . . . . 95 1·50

174 Charity Horse Race and Kiwanis Emblem

175 Silhouetted Family

1994. "Hong Kong '94" International Stamp Exhibition. Charitable Organizations. Mult.
656 25v. Type **174** 50 30
657 60v. Twin Otter airplane and Lions Club emblem (horiz) 80 75
658 75v. Mosquito and Rotary International emblem . . . 90 1·00
659 150v. Blood donor service ambulance and Red Cross emblem (horiz) . . . . . 1·60 2·50
MS660 126 × 96 mm. 200v. Charity emblems (horiz) . . . . 2·00 3·00

1994. International Year of the Family.
661 **175** 25v. brown and violet . . 35 30
662 60v. green and red . . . 70 75
663 90v. brown and green . . 1·00 1·10
664 150v. violet and brown . . 1·60 2·25

1994. Shells (2nd series). As T **171**. Multicoloured.
665 60v. Eyed cowrie . . . . . . 2·25 1·00
666 70v. Marble cone . . . . . 2·25 1·25
667 85v. Chiragra spider conch 2·50 2·25
668 155v. Adusta murex . . . . 3·75 6·00

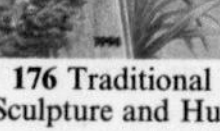
176 Traditional Sculpture and Hut

178 Consolidated PBY-5 Catalina Flying Boat

177 Pink Anemonefish

1994. Tourism. Multicoloured.
669 25v. Type **176** 70 80
670 75v. Outrigger canoe and inflatable dinghy . . . . . 1·40 1·50
671 90v. Yachts, airliner and parrot . . . . 1·75 1·90
672 200v. Helicopter and local woman with fruit . . . . 2·75 3·00
Nos. 669/72 were printed together, se-tenant, forming a composite design.

1994. "Philakorea '94" International Stamp Exhibition. Sheet 130 × 68 mm, containing Nos. 629, 636/7 and 639. Multicoloured.
MS673 10v. Yachts and Iririki Island; 55v. Coconut trees, North Efate Islands; 60v. Underwater shoal of fishes, Banks Group; 75v. Santo Island . . . . 3·25 4·00

1994. Anemonefish. Multicoloured.
674 55v. Type **177** . . . . 2·25 80
675 70v. Yellow-tailed anemonefish . . . . 2·50 1·25
676 80v. Fire anemonefish . . . 2·75 2·00
677 140v. Orange-finned anemonefish . . . . 4·75 6·50
MS678 80 × 60 mm. No. 677 . . 3·75 4·50
No. **MS**678 shows the "Philakorea '94" International stamp Exhibition logo on the sheet margin.

1994. 50th Anniv of I.C.A.O. Multicoloured.
679 25v. Type **178** 65 45
680 60v. Douglas DC-3 . . . . . 1·10 90
681 75v. De Havilland D.H.A.3 Drover . . . . 1·25 1·40
682 90v. Boeing 737 on runway 1·50 2·00

179 "Hibiscus rosa-sinensis" "The Path"

1995. Hibiscus Flowers (2nd issue). Multicoloured.
683 25v. Type **179** 60 45
684 60v. "Hibiscus rosa-sinensis" "Old Frankie" . . . . . . 1·10 1·00
685 90v. "Hibiscus sinensis" "Fijian White" . . . . . . 1·60 1·75
686 200v. "Hibiscus rosa-sinensis" "Surfrider" . . . . 3·25 4·50

180 "Emoia nigromarginata"

1995. Lizards. Multicoloured.
687 25v. Type **180** 75 45
688 55v. "Nactus multicarinatus" 1·40 1·00
689 70v. "Lepidodactylus" . . . 1·50 1·50
690 80v. "Emoia caeruleocauda" 1·60 1·60
691 140v. "Emoia sanfordi" . . . 2·50 3·75

1995. Shells (3rd series). As T **171**. Multicoloured.
692 25v. "Epitonium scalare" . . 60 50
693 55v. "Strombus latissimus" 1·25 1·25
694 90v. "Conus bullatus" . . . 1·75 1·75
695 200v. "Pterynotus pinnatus" 3·50 4·50

181 "Tanna Girls" (A. Toni)

1995. 15th Anniv of Independence. Multicoloured.
696 25v. Type **181** 45 40
697 55v. "Black Coral Dancers" (sculpture, E. Watt) (vert) 90 90
698 75v. Erromango tapestry by Juliet Peta (vert) . . . . 1·25 1·25
699 90v. "Parade Day" (H. Di-Donna) . . . . 1·40 1·75
700 140v. "Banks Dancers" (J. John) . . . . 2·00 3·00
MS701 100 × 75 mm. No. 699 . . 3·50 5·00
No. **MS**701 also includes the "Singapore '95" International Stamp Exhibition logo on the sheet margin.

182 Children with Doves and Flags

183 Rambaramp (effigy), Malakula

1995. 50th Anniv of United Nations.
702 **182** 60v. multicoloured . . . 1·25 1·00

1995. 50th Anniv of End of Second World War in the Pacific. As T **162** showing aircraft. Mult.
703 60v. Curtiss SB2C Helldiver 2·75 1·75
704 70v. Supermarine Spitfire Mk VIII . . . . 2·75 1·90
705 75v. Chance Vought F4U-1A Corsair . . . . 2·75 2·00
706 80v. Lockheed PV-1 Ventura 2·75 2·00
MS707 94 × 68 mm. 140v. Japanese delegation at signing of Unconditional Surrender, Tokyo Bay . . . . 4·00 4·50
No. **MS**707 also includes the "Singapore '95" International Stamp Exhibition logo on the sheet margin.

1995. Vanuatu Culture (1st series). Opening of New National Museum. Artefacts. Multicoloured.
708 25v. Type **183** 35 30
709 60v. Pot from Wusi, Espiritu Santo 75 75
710 75v. Slit gong from Mele, Efate . . . . 90 1·10
711 90v. Tapa cloth, Erromango 1·25 1·75
See also Nos. 772/6.

184 Boy throwing Cast Net

1996. Fishing. Multicoloured.
712 55v. Type **184** 85 65
713 75v. Fishing canoes . . . . . 1·10 90
714 80v. "Etelis" (fishing boat) and deep water fish (vert) 1·25 1·10
715 140v. Game fisherman catching sailfish (vert) . . . 2·50 3·50

185 "Pteropus anetianus"

1996. Endangered Species. Flying Foxes. Mult.
716 25v. Type **185** 40 55
717 25v. "Notopteris macdonaldi" upside down eating fruit (horiz) 40 55
718 25v. "Pteropus anetianus" hanging on branch 40 55
719 25v. "Notopteris macdonaldi" on branch (horiz) 40 55

1996. "CHINA '96" 9th Asian International Stamp Exhibition, Peking.
MS720 75 × 85 mm. No. 711 . . 1·75 2·00
MS721 75 × 85 mm. 90v. "Pteropus tonganus" (flying fox); 140v. "Pteropus tonganus" (different) 5·00 5·50

186 Immunization Programme

1996. 50th Anniv of UNICEF. Multicoloured.
722 55v. Type **186** . . . . 1·50 1·00
723 60v. Breast-feeding programme . . . . 1·50 1·00

187 Airliner and Radio Waves

1996. Centenary of Radio. Multicoloured.
724 60v. Type **187** . . . . 90 1·25
725 75v. Radio Vanuatu broadcaster . . . . 1·10 1·40
726 80v. Guglielmo Marconi . . 1·25 1·50
727 90v. Cruise liner and radio waves . . . . 1·40 1·60
Nos. 724/7 were issued together, se-tenant, forming a composite aerial view of Port Vila.

188 Marie Kapalu, Tawai Keiruan, Baptiste Firiam and Tava Kalo

1996. Centenary of Modern Olympics Games. Multicoloured.
728 25v. Type **188** 35 30
729 70v. Athletes training . . . 95 95
730 75v. Athletes from 1950s . . 1·00 1·00
731 200v. Athletes in 1896 . . . 2·75 4·00

189 Children in Front of Presbyterian Church and Roman Catholic Cathedral

1996. Christmas. Religious Buildings. Mult.
732 25v. Type **189** 45 30
733 60v. Children and Church of Christ 90 80
734 75v. Children and Seventh Day Adventist and Apostolic churches . . . . 95 1·00
735 90v. Children and Anglican church . . . . 1·25 1·60

190 "Hibiscus rosa-sinensis" "Lady Cilento"

1996. Hibiscus Flowers (3rd issue). Multicoloured.
736 25v. Type **190** 40 30
737 60v. "Hibiscus rosa-sinensis" "Kinchen's Yellow" . . . 90 70
738 90v. "Hibiscus rosa-sinensis" "D. J. O'Brien" . . . . . 1·25 1·25
739 200v. "Hibiscus rosa-sinensis" "Cuban Variety" . . . . . 3·00 4·25
For miniature sheet containing Nos. 736 and 739 see No. **MS**745.

191 Coral Garden

1997. Diving. Multicoloured.
740 70v. Type **191** 90 80
741 75v. Carving on the "President Coolidge" . . . 95 85
742 90v. "Boris" (Giant grouper) 1·25 1·25
743 140v. Wreck of the "President Coolidge" . . . 2·25 3·75
MS744 124 × 75 mm. Nos. 740/3 7·00 7·50
For further miniature sheet containing Nos. 741 and 743 see No. **MS**750.

1997. "HONG KONG '97" International Stamp Exhibition. Sheet 100 × 85 mm, containing Nos. 736 and 739. Multicoloured.
MS745 25v. Type **190**; 200v. "Hibiscus rosasinensis" "Cuban Variety" . . . . 4·50 5·00

192 View from Cockpit

1997. 10th Anniv of Air Vanuatu. Multicoloured.

746 25v. Type **192** 55 40
747 60v. Boeing 737-400 airliner being serviced, Bauerfield International Airport, Port Vila (81 × 31 mm) . . . . 1·00 75
748 90v. Air stewardess serving drinks . . . . 1·50 1·40
749 200v. Passengers disembarking . . . . . . 2·50 4·00

1997. "Pacific '97" International Philatelic Exhibition, San Francisco. Sheet 100 × 86 mm, containing Nos. 741 and 743. Multicoloured.

MS750 75v. Carving on the "President Coolidge"; 140v. Wreck of the "President Coolidge" 3·75 4·50

193 Sharp-tailed Sandpiper

1997. Birds (1st series). Coastal Birds. Mult.

751 25v. Type **193** 45 40
752 55v. Greater crested tern ("Crested Tern") 80 70
753 60v. Little pied cormorant . . 85 75
754 75v. Brown booby . . . . . 1·00 1·00
755 80v. Reef heron (vert) . . . 1·10 1·25
756 90v. Red-tailed tropic bird (vert) . . . . 1·25 1·50

See also Nos. 804/7 and 848/52.

194 Thomas Edison and Light Bulb

1997. 150th Birth Anniv of Thomas Edison (inventor). Multicoloured.

757 60v. Type **194** . . . . 1·50 1·50
758 70v. Hydro-electric dam, Espiritu Santo . . . . . . 1·50 1·50
759 200v. Port Vila at dusk (80 × 29 mm) . . . . . . 3·00 4·00

195 Yellow-faced Angelfish

1997. Angelfish. Multicoloured.

760 25v. Type **195** 40 30
761 55v. Flame angelfish 85 70
762 60v. Lemonpeel angelfish . . 90 80
763 70v. Emperor angelfish . . . 1·10 1·00
764 140v. Multi-barred angelfish 2·25 3·00

1998. No. 638 surch **5**.

765 5v. on 70v. Sea fan, Tongoa Island (vert) . . . . 2·00 2·00

197 Fale, Espiritu Santo

1998. Local Architecture. Multicoloured.

766 30v. Type **197** 35 35
767 65v. National Cultural Centre 80 80
768 80v. University of South Pacific 95 95
769 200v. Chiefs' Nakamal . . . 1·90 3·00

1998. Diana, Princess of Wales Commemoration. As T **62a** of Tokelau. Multicoloured.

770 95v. Wearing black jacket, 1997 . . . . 1·00 1·10
MS771 145 × 70 mm. 75v. Wearing green jacket, 1987; 85v. Wearing cream jacket and hat, 1991; 95v. No. 769; 145v. Wearing red dress, 1992 (sold at 400v. + 50v. charity premium) . . . . 3·75 5·00

198 Nalawan Headdresses from South West Bay, Malakula

1998. Vanuatu Culture (2nd series). Masks. Mult.

772 30v. Type **198** 50 35
773 65v. Rom mask from North Ambrym 75 65
774 75v. Tamate mask from Gaua Island 85 85
775 85v. Banglulu headdress from Uripiv Island, north-east Malakula . . . . 95 1·00
776 95v. Chubwan masks from Vao Island, Malakula, and from Pentecost . . . . . . 1·10 1·40

199 "Danaus plexippus"

1998. Butterflies. Self-adhesive. Multicoloured.

777 30v. Type **199** 50 35
778 60v. "Hypolimnas bolina" . . 75 60
779 65v. "Eurema hecabe" 80 65
780 75v. "Nymphalidae" sp. . . . 95 75
781 95v. "Precis villida" . . . . 1·10 1·25
782 205v. "Tirumala hamata" . . 2·00 3·00
MS783 105 × 79 mm. No. 782 . . 2·25 2·75

No. MS783 also commemorates "SINGPEX '98" International Stamp Exhibition, Singapore.

200 Yasur, Tanna

1998. Volcanoes in Vanuatu. Multicoloured.

784 30v. Type **200** 45 40
785 60v. Marum and Benbow, Ambrym 65 60
786 75v. Mount Garet, Gaua . . 85 85
787 80v. Lopevi 90 90
788 145v. Lake Manaro Voui, Ambae . . . . 1·40 2·50

1998. Nos. 631, 634, 636/42 surch.

789 1v. on 100v. Mele Waterfall (vert) . . . . 70 1·25
790 2v. on 45v. Man in canoe, Erakor Island (vert) . . . 2·00 2·50
791 2v. on 55v. Coconut trees, North Efate Islands . . . 70 1·25
792 3v. on 60v. Underwater shoal of fishes, Banks Group . . . . 70 1·25
793 3v. on 75v. Santo Island . . 2·50 2·50
794 4v. on 45v. Man in canoe, Erakor Island (vert) . . . 1·75 2·50
795 5v. on 70v. Sea fan, Tongoa Island (vert) . . . . . . 8·50 8·50
796a 34v. on 20v. Two girls, Pentecost Island . . . . 1·75 2·00
796b 67v. on 300v. Yasur Volcano, Tanna Island (vert) . . . . 2·50 2·75
797 73v. on 80v. Sunset, Port Vila harbour (vert) . . . 1·75 2·00

Nos. 789/97 were produced as a result of the addition of VAT at 13% to postal rates from 14 September 1998.

204 De Quiros and "San Pedro y Paulo"

1999. Early Explorers. Multicoloured.

798 34v. Type **204** 80 50
799 73v. De Bougainville and "La Boudeuse" . . . . 1·25 1·00
800 84v. Cook and H.M.S. "Resolution" . . . . . . 1·40 1·40
801 90v. La Perouse and "L'Astrolabe" . . . . . . 1·60 1·60
802 96v. Dumont d'Urville and "L'Astrolabe" . . . . . . 1·75 2·25

No. 802 is inscribed "1788" in error.

1999. "Australia '99" World Stamp Exhibition, Melbourne. Multicoloured.

MS803 95 × 82 mm. Nos. 800/2 2·50 2·75

205 Chestnut-bellied Kingfisher ("Vanuatu Kingfisher")

206 Banks Islands Dancers

1999. Birds (2nd series). Bush and Lowland Birds. Multicoloured.

804 34v. Type **205** 70 50
805 67v. Golden-bronze cuckoo ("Shining Cuckoo") . . . 1·00 90
806 73v. Peregrine falcon . . . . 1·10 1·10
807 107v. Rainbow lorikeet . . . 1·60 2·25
MS808 111 × 95 mm. No. 807 (sold at 214v.) . . . . 2·75 3·25

No. MS808 has the frame, series inscription and artist's signature shown in gold die-stamping on sheet margins.

1999. "PhilexFrance '99" International Stamp Exhibition, Paris. Multicoloured.

MS809 105 × 82 mm. Nos. 799 and 801/2 . . . . 3·50 4·00

1999. Vanuatu Dances. Multicoloured.

810 1v. Type **206** 10 30
811 2v. Small Nambas, Lamap-Malakula 10 30
812 3v. Small Nambas, Malakula 10 30
813 5v. Smol Bag Theatre 10 30
814 35v. Snake Dance, Banks Island (horiz) 35 40
815 100v. Toka Dance, Tanna (horiz) . . . . 95 1·00
816 107v. South West Bay, Malakula . . . . 1·50 1·50
817 200v. Big Nambas, Malakula 2·50 2·75
818 300v. Rom Dance, Ambrym (horiz) . . . . 2·75 3·00
819 500v. Pentecost Island . . . 6·50 7·00
820 1000v. Brasive Dance, Futuna (horiz) . . . . . . 9·50 9·75

1999. "China '99" International Stamp Exhibition, Beijing. Sheet as No. MS808, but 100 × 80 mm, without gold die-stamped features, with "China '99" logo added to the margin in carmine.

MS822 107v. No. 807 . . . . . 1·25 1·50

207 "Pterois antennata"

1999. Lionfish. Multicoloured.

823 34v. Type **207** 60 40
824 84v. Head of "Pterois antennata" . . . . 1·25 1·10
825 90v. "Pterois volitans" . . . 1·40 1·40
826 96v. Head of "Pterois volitans" . . . . 1·50 2·00

208 Clown Triggerfish

1999. New Millennium. Sheet 165 × 75 mm, containing T **208** and similar multicoloured designs.

MS827 165 × 75 mm. 34v. Type **208**; 68v. Young girl and Pentecost Island land diver (vert); 84v. Statue and pig's tusk (vert); 90c. Vanuatu kingfisher; 96v. Tanna islander blowing Triton shell and Yasur volcano . . . . 4·00 5·00

2000. "The Stamp Show 2000" International Stamp Exhibition, London. Queen Elizabeth the Queen Mother's 100th Birthday. Sheet 105 × 70 mm, containing vert designs as T **274** of Tonga. Multicoloured.

MS828 100v. Queen Elizabeth the Queen Mother holding bouquet; 107v. Lady Elizabeth Bowes-Lyon as young girl . . . . 3·75 4·00

209 Launch of "Intelsat" Satellite

2000. "EXPO 2000" World Stamp Exhibition, Anaheim, U.S.A. Satellite Communications. Multicoloured. Self-adhesive.

829 10v. Type **209** 30 30
830 34v. Port Villa Ground Station 60 40
831 100v. "Intelsat" satellite in orbit over Vanuatu . . . . 1·40 1·40
832 225v. Tam Tam drum and Intelsat satellite . . . . . 2·50 3·50
MS833 122 × 97 mm. Nos. 830 and 832 . . . . 2·75 3·25

210 Abstract Painting (Sero Kuautonga)

2000. 20th Anniv of Independence. Local Art. Mult.

834 34v. Type **210** 70 40
835 67v. Tapa cloth art (Moses Pita) . . . . 1·00 70
836 73v. Tapestry (Juliet Pita) . . 1·10 90
837 84v. Carving (Emmanuel Watt) . . . . 1·10 1·40
838 90v. "Tree of Peace" (watercolour) (Joseph John) . . . . 1·40 1·75

211 Running

2000. Olympic Games, Sydney. Each including the Olympic Torch. Multicoloured.

839 56v. Type **211** 75 75
840 67v. Weightlifting 85 85
841 90v. High-jumping . . . . . 1·10 1·10
842 96v. Boxing . . . . 1·25 1·50

212 Common Dolphin

2000. Dolphins. Multicoloured.

843 34v. Type **212** 70 50
844 73v. Spotted dolphin . . . . 1·10 90
845 84v. Spinner dolphin . . . . 1·25 1·25
846 107v. Bottlenose dolphin . . 1·50 1·75
MS847 Circular, 100 mm diameter. Nos. 845/6 . . . . 2·75 3·25

No. MS847 includes the "HONG KONG 2001" Stamp Exhibition logo on the sheet margin.

213 Cardinal Honeyeater

214 Vanilla

2001. Birds (3rd series). Highland Birds. Mult.

848	35v. Type **213**	80	45
849	60v. Yellow-fronted white-eye ("Vanuatu White-eye")	1·10	65
850	90v. Mountain starling ("Santo Mountain Starling")	1·50	1·40
851	100v. Red-headed parrotf inch ("Royal Parrot finch")	1·60	1·90
852	110v. White-billed honeyeater ("Vanuatu Mountain Honeyeater")	1·60	2·00

In addition to being available in separate sheets Nos. 848/52 were also printed together, se-tenant, with the backgrounds forming a composite design.

2001. Food Exports. Multicoloured.

853	35v. Type **214**	60	40
854	75v. Cacao	95	80
855	90v. Coffee	1·25	1·25
856	110v. Copra	1·40	1·75

215 Sperm Whales

2001. Whales. Joint Issue with New Caledonia. Multicoloured.

857	60v. Type **215**	85	85
858	80v. Humpback whales (vert)	1·00	1·00
859	90v. Blue whales	1·25	1·25
MS860	220 × 90 mm. Nos. 857/9	3·00	3·50

No. **MS**860 is in the shape of a pair of Humpback whales.

216 Lyre-shaped Sand Drawing

2001. Sand Drawings. Multicoloured.

861	60v. Type **216**	75	60
862	90v. Interwoven scroll design	1·25	1·00
863	110v. Drawing of turtle	1·40	1·50
864	135v. Drawing of fish	1·60	2·00

217 Vanuatan, Yasur Volcano and Pentecost Island Land Diver

2002. U.N. Year of Eco Tourism. Multicoloured.

865	35v. Type **217**	60	40
866	60v. Making kava and dancers	75	60
867	75v. Siri Falls and birds (vert)	1·50	1·25
868	110v. Tourist kayaks and scuba diving (vert)	1·75	1·90
869	135v. Tourist village	2·00	2·50
MS870	170 × 76 mm. Nos. 865/9	6·00	7·00

218 Horse pulling Plough

2002. Local Horses. Multicoloured.

871	35v. Type **218**	65	40
872	60v. Cattle round-up	85	65
873	75v. Horse racing	1·00	1·00
874	80v. Pony trekking on beach	1·10	1·10
875	200v. Wild horse from Tanna	2·75	3·25

219 Children's Football

2002. Vanuatu Football Federation. Multicoloured.

877	35v. Type **219**	65	40
878	80v. Under 17's football	1·10	80
879	110v. Women's football	1·60	1·75
880	135v. International football	1·90	2·25

220 Young Girl holding Breadfruit Plant

2002. Year of Reforestation. Multicoloured. Self-adhesive.

881	35v. Type **220**	65	40
882	60v. Man and boy planting seedling (*Endospermum medullosum*)	1·00	60
883	90v. Man hollowing out canoe	1·40	1·40
884	110v. Woman and boy eating fruit	1·75	2·00

2002. "Philakorea 2002" International Stamp Exhibition, Seoul. Multicoloured.

MS885	115 × 90 mm. No. 875	2·75	3·25

221 Adult Dugong with Calf

2002. Dugong. Multicoloured.

886	35v. Type **221**	65	40
887	75v. Adult and calf swimming	1·00	85
888	80v. Adult Dugong	1·10	95
889	135v. Dugong feeding	1·75	2·00
MS890	133 × 112 mm. Nos. 888/9	4·00	4·25

222 *Dendrobium gouldii*

2002. Orchids. Multicoloured.

891	35v. Type **222**	65	40
892	60v. *Dendrobium polysema*	85	60
893	90v. *Dendrobium spectabile*	1·25	1·40
894	110v. *Flickingeria comata*	1·60	1·90

223 Limousin Cattle

2003. "Year Blong Buluk". Beef Production in Vanuatu. Multicoloured.

895	35v. Type **223**	65	40
896	80v. Charolais cattle	1·10	80
897	110v. Simmental cattle	1·50	1·60
898	135v. Red Brahman cattle	1·75	2·00

224 Land Diver on Platform

2003. Pentecost Island Land Diving. Multicoloured.

899	35v. Type **224**	60	40
900	80v. Islander making dive	1·10	80
901	110v. Diving tower and dancers	1·60	1·60
902	200v. Land diver jumping from tower (33 × 89 mm)	2·75	3·25
MS903	90 × 110 mm. No. 902	2·75	3·25

225 Snorkeller and Butterflyfish

2003. Snorkelling. Multicoloured.

904	35v. Type **225**	50	40
905	80v. Snorkeller over coral (vert)	90	80
906	90v. Two snorkellers over coral (vert)	1·00	85
907	110v. Snorkellers underwater and at surface	1·25	1·40
908	135v. Snorkeller and fish of three species	1·50	1·90
MS909	175 × 80 mm. Nos. 904/8		

226 Planting Natanggura Palm

227 Diver taking Letter to Underwater Post Office

2003. Natanggura Palm. Multicoloured.

910	35v. Type **226**	50	40
911	80v. Thatching roof with leaves	90	80
912	90v. Carving seeds	1·00	85
913	135v. Carved fish and seahorse	1·50	1·90

2003. Underwater Post Office, Hideaway Island (1st series).

914 **227**	90v. multicoloured	1·25	1·25

See also Nos. 923/**MS**927.

228 *Hippocampus kuda*

2003. Seahorses. Multicoloured.

915	60v. Type **228**	65	60
916	90v. *Hippocampus histrix*	90	85
917	200v. *Hippocampus bargibanti*	2·25	2·50
MS918	105 × 70 mm. No. 917	2·25	2·50

229 *Daphnis hypothous*

2003. Moths. Multicoloured.

919	35v. Type **229**	50	40
920	90v. *Hippotion celerio*	90	85
921	110v. *Euchromia creusa*	1·25	1·40
922	135v. *Eudocima salaminia*	1·50	1·90

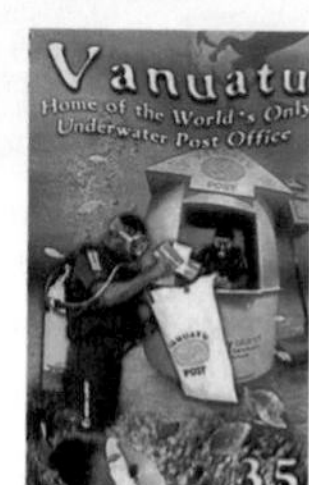

230 Diver collecting Mail

2004. Underwater Post Office, Hideaway Island (2nd series). Multicoloured.

923	35v. Type **230**	35	40
924	80v. Diver putting letter in underwater postbox	75	80
925	110v. Diver above reef, diver at Underwater Post Office and postbox	1·00	1·10
926	220v. Underwater Post Office and diver at postbox	2·00	2·00
MS927	92 × 71 mm. 220v. No. 926	2·00	2·00

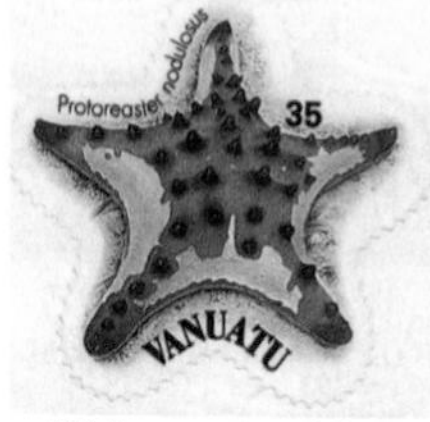

231 *Protoreaster nodulosus*

2004. Starfish. Multicoloured. Self-adhesive.

928	35v. Type **231**	35	40
929	60v. *Linckia laevigata*	55	60
930	90v. *Fromia monilis*	85	90
931	250v. *Echinaster callosus*	2·40	2·50

232 Red-tailed Tropic Birds

2004. Red-tailed Tropic Birds. Multicoloured.

932	35v. Type **232**	35	40
933	50v. Bird feeding chick (vert)	45	50
934	75v. Chick and adult bird flying (vert)	70	75
935	135v. Bird in flight	1·20	1·30
936	200v. Adult feeding juvenile bird	1·90	2·00
MS937	175 × 80 mm. Nos. 932/6	4·50	4·75

233 Two Yachts and Trimaran

2004. 25th Anniv of the Musket Cove—Port Vila Yacht Race. Multicoloured.

938	35v. Type **233**	35	40
939	80v. Sailing with spinnakers raised (vert)	75	80
940	90v. Sailors at helm and yachts racing alongside	80	85
941	200v. Racing along the coast	1·90	2·00
MS942	100 × 70 mm. 200v. As No. 941	1·90	2·00

Stamps of a similar design were issued by Fiji.

234 Red and Black Anemonefish

2004. Tropical Marine Life. Sheet 187 × 140 mm containing T **234** and similar horiz designs. Multicoloured. Self-adhesive.

MS943	35v. × 12, Type **234**; Longfin bannerfish; Goldman's sweetlips; Green turtle; Clark's anemonefish; Harlequin sweetlips; Yellowtail coris; Emperor angelfish; Hairy red hermit crab; Spotfin lionfish; Yellow-lipped sea krait; Clam	4·25	4·50

No. **MS**943 was issued together, se-tenant, forming a composite design.

VATHY — Pt. 6

A town on the island of Samos, where there was a French Post Office which closed in 1914.

25 centimes = 1 piastre.

1893. Stamps of France optd **Vathy** or surch also.

82	10	5c. green	4·50	9·00
84		10c. black and lilac	10·00	16·00
86		15c. blue	7·50	6·25
87		1pi. on 25c. black on pink	5·75	7·50
88		2pi. on 50c. pink	22·00	27·00
89		4pi. on 1f. green	24·00	10·50
90		8pi. on 2f. brown on blue	65·00	65·00
91		20pi. on 5f. mauve	90·00	80·00

VATICAN CITY — Pt. 8

A small area in Rome under the independent sovereignty of the Pope since 1929.

1929. 100 centesimi = 1 lira.
2002. 100 cents = 1 euro.

1 Papal Tiara and St. Peter's Keys

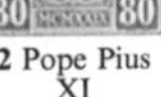

2 Pope Pius XI

4

1929.

1	1	5c. brown on pink	20	25
2		10c. green on green	30	35
3		20c. violet on lilac	75	55
4		25c. blue on blue	90	55
5		30c. black on yellow	1·10	70
6		50c. black on orange	1·60	70
7		75c. red on grey	2·20	1·30
8	2	80c. red	1·60	40
9		1l.25 blue	2·50	95
10		2l. brown	5·00	1·90
11		2l.50 red	4·25	2·75
12		5l. green	5·00	9·75
13		10l. black	11·00	14·50

1931. Surch **C. 25** and bars.

14	1	25c. on 30c. black on yellow	2·75	1·20

1933. "Holy Year" (1933–1934).

15	4	25c.+10c. green	6·75	4·75
16		75c.+15c. red	14·00	15·00
17		80c.+20c. brown	36·00	22·00
18		1l.25+25c. blue	10·50	16·00

The 80c. and 1l.25 have inscriptions and frame differently arranged.

6 Arms of Pope Pius XI

9 Pope Pius XI

1933.

19	6	5c. red	10	10
20	–	10c. black and brown	10	10
21	–	12½c. black and green	10	10
22	–	20c. black and orange	10	10
23	–	25c. black and green	10	10
24	–	30c. brown and black	10	10
25	–	50c. brown and purple	10	10
26	–	75c. brown and red	10	10
27	–	80c. brown and pink	10	10
28	9	1l. black and violet	4·25	2·75
29		1l.25 black and blue	15·00	5·50
30		2l. black and brown	36·00	22·00
31		2l.75 black and purple	44·00	45·00
32	–	5l. green and brown	20	30
33	–	10l. green and blue	20	35
34	–	20l. green and black	35	45

DESIGNS—As Type **6**: 10c. to 25c. Wing of Vatican Palace; 30c. to 80c. Vatican Gardens and Dome of St. Peter's. As Type **9**: 5l. to 20l. St. Peter's Basilica.

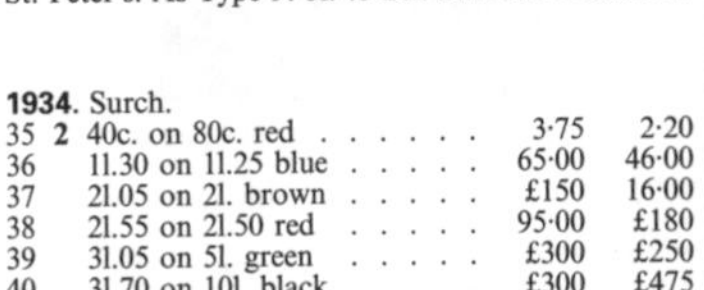

1934. Surch.

35	2	40c. on 80c. red	3·75	2·20
36		1l.30 on 1l.25 blue	65·00	46·00
37		2l.05 on 2l. brown	£150	16·00
38		2l.55 on 2l.50 red	95·00	£180
39		3l.05 on 5l. green	£300	£250
40		3l.70 on 10l. black	£300	£475

13 Tribonian presenting Pandects to Justinian

15 Doves and Bell

1935. International Juridical Congress, Rome. Frescoes by Raphael.

41	13	5c. orange	1·80	1·40
42		10c. violet	1·80	1·40
43		25c. green	6·25	4·75
44	–	75c. red	42·00	21·00
45	–	80c. brown	30·00	18·00
46	–	1l.25 blue	34·00	10·50

DESIGN: 75c. to 1l.25, Pope Julius II (wrongly inscribed as representing Pope Gregory IX).

1936. Catholic Press Exhibition, Rome.

47	15	5c. green	1·10	1·00
48	–	10c. black	1·10	1·00
49	–	25c. green	26·00	6·25
50	15	50c. purple	1·00	1·00
51	–	75c. red	26·00	24·00
52	–	80c. brown	1·40	2·10
53	–	1l.25 blue	1·25	2·10
54	–	5l. brown	1·25	5·75

DESIGNS: 10, 75c. Church and Bible; 25, 80c. St. John Bosco; 1l.25, 5l. St. Francis of Sales.

16 Statue of St. Peter

17 Ascension of Elijah

1938. Air.

55	16	25c. brown	10	10
56	–	50c. green	10	10
57	17	75c. red	20	30
58	–	80c. blue	20	45
59	16	1l. violet	35	55
60	–	2l. blue	75	90
61	17	5l. black	1·80	2·00
62	–	10l. purple	1·80	2·00

DESIGNS: 50c., 2l. Dove with olive branch and St. Peter's Square; 80c., 10l. Transportation of the Holy House.

18 Crypt of Basilica of St. Cecilia

20 Coronation

1938. International Christian Archaeological Congress. Inscr "CONGRESSVS INTERNAT. ARCHAEOLOGIAE CHRIST".

63	18	5c. brown	20	25
64		10c. red	20	25
65		25c. green	30	30
66	–	75c. red	7·25	6·25
67	–	80c. violet	22·00	19·00
68	–	1l.25 blue	29·00	24·00

DESIGN: 75, 80c. and 1l.25, Basilica of Saints Nereus and Achilles in the Catacombs of Domitilla.

1939. Death of Pope Pius XI. Optd **SEDE VACANTE MCMXXXIX**.

69	1	5c. brown on pink	31·00	7·25
70		10c. green on green	35	25
71		20c. violet on lilac	35	25
72		25c. blue on blue	3·75	3·50
73		30c. black on yellow	75	20
74		50c. black on orange	75	25
75		75c. red on grey	75	25

1939. Coronation of Pope Pius XII.

76	20	25c. green	1·30	35
77		75c. red	30	50
78		80c. violet	3·75	2·75
79		1l.25 blue	30	50

21 Arms of Pope Pius XII

22 Pope Pius XII

1940. 1st Anniv of Coronation of Pope Pius XII.

80	21	5c. red	10	10
99		5c. grey	10	10
100		30c. brown	10	10
101		50c. green	10	10
81	22	1l. black and violet	20	10
102	–	1l. black and brown	15	10
82	–	1l.25 black and blue	20	10
103	–	1l.50 black and red	15	10
83	22	2l. black and brown	75	1·10
104	–	2l.50 black and blue	15	15
84	–	2l.75 black and purple	1·30	2·20
105	22	5l. black and lilac	20	25
106		20l. black and green	35	40

DESIGN: 1l. (No. 102), 1l.25, 1l.50, 2l.50, and 2l.75, as Type **22** but with portrait of Pope facing left.

23

24 Consecration of Archbishop Pacelli

1942. Prisoners of War Relief Fund (1st series). Inscr "MCMXLII".

85	23	25c. green	10	20
86		80c. brown	10	20
87		1l.25 blue	10	20

See also Nos. 92/4 and 107/9.

1943. Pope's Episcopal Silver Jubilee.

88	24	25c. turquoise and green	10	10
89		80c. chocolate and brown	10	20
90		1l.25 blue and ultramarine	10	20
91		5l. blue and black	15	35

1944. Prisoners of War Relief Fund (2nd series). Inscr "MCMXLIII".

92	23	25c. green	10	10
93		80c. brown	10	10
94		1l.25 blue	10	15

25 Raphael

27 St. Ignatius of Loyola

1944. 4th Centenary of Pontifical Academy of the Virtuosi of the Pantheon.

95	25	25c. olive and green	20	20
96	–	80c. violet and lilac	30	35
97	–	1l.25 blue and violet	30	30
98	–	10l. bistre and yellow	55	1·80

PORTRAITS: 80c. Antonio da Sangallo (architect); 1l.25, Carlo Maratti (painter) (after Francesco Maratta); 10l. Antonio Canova (sculptor, self-portrait).

1945. Prisoners of War Relief Fund (3rd series). Inscr "MCMXLIV".

107	23	1l. green	10	15
108		3l. red	10	15
109		5l. blue	10	15

1946. Surch in figures between bars.

110	21	20c. on 5c. grey	10	10
111		25c. on 30c. brown	10	10
112		1l. on 50c. green	10	10
113	–	1l.50 on 1l. black and brown (No. 102)	10	10
114	–	3l. on 1l.50 black and red (No. 103)	30	10
115	–	5l. on 2l.50 black and blue (No. 104)	45	25
116	22	10l. on 5l. black and lilac	1·60	65
117		30l. on 20l. black and green	4·25	2·20

1946. 400th Anniv of Inauguration of Council of Trent.

118	–	5c. brown and bistre	25	25
119	–	25c. brown and violet	25	25
120	–	50c. sepia and brown	25	25
121	27	75c. brown and black	25	25
122	–	1l. brown and purple	25	25
123	–	1l.50 brown and red	25	25
124	–	2l. brown and green	25	25
125	–	2l.50 brown and blue	25	25
126	–	3l. brown and red	25	25
127	–	4l. brown and bistre	25	25
128	–	5l. brown and blue	25	25
129	–	10l. brown and red	25	25

DESIGNS: 5c. Trent Cathedral; 25c. St. Angela Merici; 50c. St. Anthony Maria Zaccaria; 1l. St. Cajetan of Thiene; 1l.50, St. John Fisher, Bishop of Rochester; 2l. Cristoforo Madrussi, Bishop of Trent; 2l.50, Reginald Pole, Archbishop of Canterbury; 3l. Marcello Cervini; 4l. Giovanni Maria Del Monte; 5l. Emperor Charles V; 10l. Pope Paul III Farnese.

28 Dove with Olive Branch over St. Peter's Forecourt

29 Barn Swallows circling Spire of St. Peter's Basilica

1947. Air.

130	28	1l. red	10	10
131	–	4l. brown	10	10
132	28	5l. blue	10	10
133	29	15l. violet	1·30	1·10
134	–	25l. green	4·50	2·40
135	29	50l. black	6·50	4·25
136		100l. orange	31·00	8·00

DESIGN—As Type **28**: 4l., 25l. Transportation of the Holy House.

30 "Raphael accompanying Tobias" (after Botticelli)

1948. Air.

137	30	250l. black	36·00	7·25
138		500l. blue	£550	£350

31 St. Agnes's Basilica

32 Pope Pius XII

1949.

139	31	1l. brown	10	10
140	–	3l. violet	10	10
141	–	5l. orange	10	10
142	–	8l. green	15	15
143	–	13l. green	3·25	3·25
144	–	16l. grey	30	30
145	–	25l. red	6·50	85
146	–	35l. mauve	36·00	16·00
147	–	40l. blue	30	20
148	32	100l. black	4·00	4·00

DESIGNS (Basilicas)—VERT: 3l. St. Clement; 5l. St. Praxedes; 8l. St. Mary in Cosmedin. HORIZ: 13l. Holy Cross; 16l. St. Sebastian; 25l. St. Laurence's; 35l. St. Paul's; 40l. Sta. Maria Maggiore.

33 Angels over Globe

1949. Air. 75th Anniv of U.P.U.

149	33	300l. blue	27·00	11·00
150		1000l. green	£130	90·00

34 "I Will Give You the Keys of the Kingdom"

35 Guards Marching

1949. "Holy Year".

151	34	5l. brown and light brown	10	10
152	–	6l. brown and black	10	10
153	–	8l. green and blue	90	50
154	–	10l. blue and green	30	10
155	34	20l. brown and green	1·50	35
156	–	25l. blue and brown	75	35
157	–	30l. purple and green	1·80	1·10
158	–	60l. red and brown	1·20	1·10

DESIGNS: 6, 25l. Four Basilicas; 8, 30l. Pope Boniface VIII; 10, 60l. Pope Pius XII opening the Holy Door.

1950. Centenary of Papal Guard.

No.	Type	Description	Mint	Used
159	35	25l. brown	5·75	4·00
160		35l. green	3·25	4·00
161		55l. brown	1·80	4·00

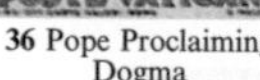

36 Pope Proclaiming Dogma

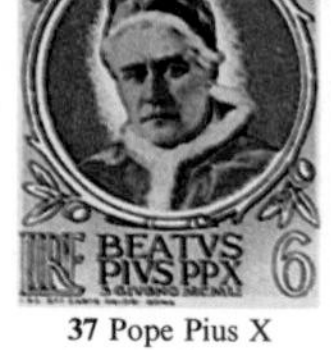

37 Pope Pius X

1951. Proclamation of Dogma of the Assumption.

No.	Type	Description	Mint	Used
162	36	25l. purple	10·00	90
163	–	55l. blue	4·25	13·50

DESIGN: 55l. Angels over St. Peter's.

1951. Beatification of Pope Pius X.

No.	Type	Description	Mint	Used
164	37	6l. gold and violet	10	15
165		10l. gold and green	15	15
166	–	60l. gold and blue	7·25	7·25
167	–	115l. gold and brown	22·00	22·00

DESIGN: 60, 115l. Pope looking left.

38 Final Session of Council (fresco)

1951. 1500th Anniv of Council of Chalcedon.

No.	Type	Description	Mint	Used
168	38	5l. grey	35	35
169	–	25l. red	3·00	2·40
170	38	35l. red	5·75	4·50
171	–	60l. blue	18·00	14·50
172	38	100l. brown	55·00	36·00

DESIGN: 25, 60l. "Pope Leo I meeting Attila" (Raphael).

39 Gratian

41 Mail Coach and First Stamp

1951. Air. 800th Anniv of Decree of Gratian.

No.	Type	Description	Mint	Used
173	39	300l. purple	£300	£200
174		500l. blue	36·00	18·00

1952. No. 143 surch **L. 12** and bars.

No.	Type	Description	Mint	Used
175		12l. on 13l. green	1·60	95

1952. Centenary of First Papal States' Stamp.

No.	Type	Description	Mint	Used
176	41	50l. black & blue on cream	4·25	4·25
MS176a		112×121 mm. No. 176 (block of four)	£170	£170

42 St. Maria Goretti

43 St. Peter and Inscription

1953. 50th Anniv of Martyrdom of St. Maria Goretti.

No.	Type	Description	Mint	Used
177	42	15l. violet and brown	4·25	2·50
178		25l. brown and red	3·00	2·20

1953. St. Peter's Basilica. Medallions in black.

No.	Type	Description	Mint	Used
179	43	3l. red	10	10
180	–	5l. grey	10	10
181	–	10l. green	10	10
182	–	12l. brown	10	10
183	–	20l. violet	20	10
184	–	25l. brown	10	10
185	–	35l. red	10	10
186	–	45l. brown	20	20
187	–	60l. blue	10	10
188	–	65l. red	30	20
189	–	100l. purple	10	10

DESIGNS: 5l. Pius XII and Roman sepulchre; 10l. St. Peter's tomb; 12l. St. Sylvester I and Constantine's basilica (previous building); 20l. Julius II and Bramante's design; 25l. Paul III and apse; 35l. Sixtus V and cupola; 45l. Paul V and facade; 60l. Urban VIII and baldaquin; 65l. Alexander VII and colonnade; 100l. Pius VI and sacristy.

44 Dome of St. Peter's

45 St. Clare of Assisi (after Giotto)

1953. Air.

No.	Type	Description	Mint	Used
190	44	500l. brown & deep brown	24·00	8·25
190a		500l. green and turquoise	7·25	3·75
191		1000l. blue and deep blue	65·00	15·00
191a		1000l. red and lake	75	75

1953. 700th Death Anniv of St. Clare (founder of Poor Clares Order).

No.	Type	Description	Mint	Used
192	45	25l. dp brown, brown & bl	1·80	1·80
193		35l. brown, lt brown & red	18·00	16·00

46 "St. Bernard" (after Lippi)

47 Lombard's Episcopal Seal

1953. 800th Death Anniv of St. Bernard of Clairvaux.

No.	Type	Description	Mint	Used
194	46	20l. purple and green	75	75
195		60l. green and blue	7·25	6·50

1953. 800th Anniv of "Libri Sententiarum" (theological treatise by Peter Lombard, Bishop of Paris).

No.	Type	Description	Mint	Used
196	47	100l. yellow, blue and red	44·00	33·00

48 Pope Pius XI and Vatican City

1954. 25th Anniv of Lateran Treaty.

No.	Type	Description	Mint	Used
197	48	25l. red, brown and blue	1·10	90
198		60l. blue, grey and brown	3·25	3·00

49 Pope Pius XII

1954. Marian Year and Centenary of Dogma of the Immaculate Conception.

No.	Type	Description	Mint	Used
199	–	3l. violet	10	10
200	49	4l. red	10	10
201	–	6l. red	10	10
202	49	12l. green	1·10	90
203	–	20l. brown	90	90
204	49	35l. blue	1·80	1·60

DESIGN: 3, 6, 20l. Pope Pius IX facing right with different inscr and dates "1854–1954".

50 St. Pius X

1954. Canonization of Pope Pius X.

No.	Type	Description	Mint	Used
205	50	10l. yellow, red and brown	20	20
206		25l. yellow, red and violet	2·75	2·00
207		35l. yellow, red and black	4·25	3·75

51 Basilica of St. Francis of Assisi

1954. Bicentenary of Elevaion of Basilica of St. Francis of Assisi to Papal Chapel.

No.	Type	Description	Mint	Used
208	51	20l. black and cream	1·80	1·10
209		35l. brown and cream	1·50	1·80

52 "St. Augustine" (after Botticelli)

1954. 1600th Birth Anniv of St. Augustine.

No.	Type	Description	Mint	Used
210	52	35l. green	90	75
211		50l. brown	1·60	1·50

53 Madonna of Ostra Brama, Vilna

1954. Termination of Marian Year.

No.	Type	Description	Mint	Used
212	53	20l. multicoloured	1·30	90
213		35l. multicoloured	9·75	8·25
214		60l. multicoloured	16·00	14·50

54 St. Boniface and Fulda Cathedral

55 "Pope Sixtus II and St. Lawrence" (fresco, Niccolina Chapel)

1955. 1200th Anniv of Martyrdom of St. Boniface.

No.	Type	Description	Mint	Used
215	54	10l. green	10	10
216		35l. violet	55	45
217		60l. green	85	75

1955. 500th Death Anniv of Fra Giovanni da Fiesole, "Fra Angelico" (painter).

No.	Type	Description	Mint	Used
218	55	50l. red and blue	4·25	2·75
219		100l. blue and flesh	3·00	2·75

56 Pope Nicholas V

57 St. Bartholomew

1955. 5th Death Centenary of Pope Nicholas V.

No.	Type	Description	Mint	Used
220	56	20l. brown and blue	30	20
221		35l. brown and pink	35	30
222		60l. brown and green	65	65

1955. 900th Death Anniv of St. Bartholomew the Young.

No.	Type	Description	Mint	Used
223	57	10l. black and brown	10	10
224		25l. black and red	45	35
225		100l. black and green	2·20	1·70

58 "Annunciation" (Melozzo da Forli)

59 Corporal of the Guard

1956. Air.

No.	Type	Description	Mint	Used
226	58	5l. black	10	10
227	A	10l. green	10	10
228	B	15l. orange	30	30
229	58	25l. red	10	10
230	A	35l. red	3·00	3·00
231	B	50l. brown	10	10
232	58	60l. blue	55	55
233	A	100l. brown	10	10
234	B	300l. violet	65	65

PAINTINGS: A, "Annunciation" (P. Cavallini); B, "Annunciation" (Leonardo da Vinci).

1956. 450th Anniv of Swiss Guard.

No.	Type	Description	Mint	Used
235	–	4l. red	15	10
236	59	6l. orange	15	10
237	–	10l. blue	15	10
238	–	35l. brown	55	55
239	59	50l. violet	75	75
240	–	60l. green	85	85

DESIGNS: 4, 35l. Captain Roust; 10, 60l. Two drummers.

60 St. Rita

61 St. Ignatius presenting Jesuit Constitution to Pope Paul III

1956. 5th Death Centenary of St. Rita at Cascia.

No.	Type	Description	Mint	Used
241	60	10l. grey	10	10
242		25l. brown	55	55
243		35l. blue	40	40

1956. 4th Death Centenary of St. Ignatius of Loyola.

No.	Type	Description	Mint	Used
244	61	35l. brown	55	55
245		60l. grey	90	90

62 St. John of Capistrano

63 Madonna and Child

1956. 5th Death Centenary of St. John of Capistrano.

No.	Type	Description	Mint	Used
246	62	25l. green and black	2·00	2·00
247		35l. brown and purple	75	75

1956. "Black Madonna" of Czestochowa Commemoration.

No.	Type	Description	Mint	Used
248	63	35l. black and blue	35	35
249		60l. blue and green	45	45
250		100l. purple and brown	65	60

64 St. Domenico Savio

65 Cardinal D. Capranica (founder) and Capranica College

1957. Death Centenary of St. Domenico Savio.

No.	Type	Description	Mint	Used
251	64	4l. brown	10	10
252	–	6l. red	10	10
253	64	25l. green	20	20
254	–	60l. blue	1·20	85

DESIGN: 6, 60l. St. Domenico Savio and St. John Bosco.

1957. 5th Centenary of Capranica College.

No.	Type	Description	Mint	Used
255	65	5l. red	10	10
256	–	10l. brown	10	10
257	65	35l. grey	10	10
258	–	100l. blue	65	65

DESIGNS: 10, 100l. Pope Pius XII and plaque.

66 Pontifical Academy of Science

1957. 20th Anniv of the Pontifical Academy of Science.

No.	Type	Description	Mint	Used
259	66	35l. green and blue	55	45
260		60l. blue and brown	55	55

67 Mariazell Basilica

1957. 8th Centenary of Mariazell Basilica.

261	**67**	5l. green	10	10
262	–	15l. black	10	10
263	**67**	60l. blue	85	85
264	–	100l. violet	1·00	1·00

DESIGN: 15, 100l. Statue of the Virgin of Mariazell within Sanctuary.

68 Apparition of the Virgin Mary

1958. Centenary of Apparition of the Virgin Mary at Lourdes.

265	**68**	5l. blue	10	10
266	–	10l. green	10	10
267	–	15l. brown	10	10
268	**68**	25l. red	10	10
269	–	35l. brown	10	10
270	–	100l. violet	10	10

DESIGNS: 10, 35l. Invalid at Lourdes; 15, 100l. St. Bernadette.

69 "Civitas Dei" ("City of God" at Exhibition)

70 Pope Clement XIII (from sculpture by A. Canova)

1958. Brussels International Exhibition.

271	–	35l. purple	30	30
272	**69**	60l. red	65	65
273		100l. violet	1·60	1·50
274	–	300l. blue	1·10	1·30
MS274a		91 × 149 mm. Nos. 271/4	20·00	20·00

DESIGN: 35, 300l. Pope Pius XII.

1958. Birth Bicentenary of Antonio Canova (sculptor).

275	**70**	5l. brown	10	10
276	–	10l. red	10	10
277	–	35l. green	30	20
278	–	100l. blue	90	90

SCULPTURES: 10l. Pope Clement XIV; 35l. Pope Pius VI; 100l. Pope Pius VII.

71 St. Peter's Keys

1958. "Vacant See".

279	**71**	15l. brown on yellow	1·40	75
280		25l. brown	10	10
281		60l. brown on lilac	10	10

72 Pope John XXIII

1959. Coronation of Pope John XXIII. Inscr "IV-XI MCMLVIII".

282	**72**	25l. multicoloured	10	10
283	–	35l. multicoloured	10	10
284	**72**	60l. multicoloured	10	10
285	–	100l. multicoloured	10	10

DESIGN: 35, 100l. Arms of Pope John XXIII.

73 St. Lawrence

74 Pope Pius XI

1959. 1700th Death Annivs (15 to 100l. in 1958) of Martyrs under Valerian.

286	**73**	15l. brown, yellow and red	10	10
287	–	25l. brown, yellow and lilac	10	10
288	–	50l. multicoloured	10	15
289	–	60l. brown, yellow & green	10	15
290	–	100l. brown, yellow & pur	10	15
291	–	300l. sepia and brown	35	35

PORTRAITS: 25l. Pope Sixtus II; 50l. St. Agapitus; 60l. St. Filisissimus; 100l. St. Cyprian; 300l. St. Fructuosus.

1959. 30th Anniv of Lateran Treaty.

292	**74**	30l. brown	10	10
293		100l. blue	20	20

75 Radio Mast

76 Obelisk and St. John Lateran Basilica

1959. 2nd Anniv of St. Maria di Galeria Radio Station Vatican City.

294	**75**	25l. pink, yellow and black	10	10
295		60l. yellow, red and blue	15	25

1959. Air. Roman Obelisks.

296	**76**	5l. violet	10	10
297	–	10l. green	10	10
298	–	15l. brown	10	10
299	–	25l. green	10	10
300	–	35l. blue	10	10
301	**76**	50l. green	10	10
302	–	60l. red	10	10
303	–	100l. blue	15	10
304	–	200l. brown	20	15
305	–	500l. brown	35	35

DESIGNS: 10, 60l. Obelisk and Church of Sta. Maria Maggiore; 15, 100l. Vatican Obelisk and Apostolic Palace; 25, 200l. Obelisk and Churches of St. Mary in Montesanto and St. Mary of the Miracles, Piazza del Popolo; 35, 500l. Sallustian Obelisk and Trinita dei Monti Church.

77 St. Casimir, Vilna Palace and Cathedral

1959. 500th Birth Anniv of St. Casimir (patron saint of Lithuania).

306	**77**	50l. brown	10	10
307		100l. green	20	20

78 "Christ Adored by the Magi" (after Raphael)

1959. Christmas.

308	**78**	15l. black	10	10
309		25l. red	10	10
310		60l. blue	20	25

79 "St. Antoninus" (after Dupre)

80 Transept of St. John Lateran Basilica

1960. 500th Death Anniv of St. Antoninus of Florence.

311	**79**	15l. blue	10	10
312	–	25l. green	10	10
313	**79**	60l. brown	30	25
314	–	110l. purple	45	45

DESIGN: 25, 110l. "St. Antoninus preaching sermon" (after Portigiani).

1960. Roman Diocesan Synod.

315	**80**	15l. brown	10	10
316		60l. black	15	20

81 "The Flight into Egypt" (after Beato Angelico)

82 Cardinal Sarto (Pius X) leaving Venice for Conclave in Rome

1960. World Refugee Year.

317	**81**	5l. green	10	10
318	–	10l. brown	10	10
319	–	25l. red	20	15
320	**81**	60l. violet	30	30
321	–	100l. blue	1·10	95
322	–	300l. green	1·00	85

DESIGNS: 10, 100l. "St. Peter giving Alms" (Masaccio); 25, 300l. "Madonna of Mercy" (Piero della Francesca).

1960. 1st Anniv of Transfer of Relics of Pope Pius X from Rome to Venice.

323	**82**	15l. brown	20	25
324	–	35l. red	75	65
325	–	60l. green	1·40	1·20

DESIGNS: 35l. Pope John XXIII kneeling before relics of Pope Pius X; 60l. Relics in procession across St. Mark's Square, Venice.

83 "Feeding the Hungry"

1960. "Corporal Works of Mercy". Della Robbia paintings. Centres in brown.

326	**83**	5l. brown	10	10
327	–	10l. green	10	10
328	–	15l. black	10	10
329	–	20l. red	10	10
330	–	30l. violet	10	10
331	–	35l. brown	10	10
332	–	40l. orange	10	10
333	–	70l. stone	10	10

DESIGNS: 10l. "Giving drinks to the thirsty"; 15l. "Clothing the naked"; 20l. "Sheltering the homeless"; 30l. "Visiting the sick"; 35l. "Visiting the imprisoned"; 40l. "Burying the dead"; 70l. Pope John XXIII between "Faith" and "Charity".

84 "The Nativity" after Gerard Honthorst (Gherardo delle Notte)

1960. Christmas.

334	**84**	10l. black and green	10	10
335		15l. deep brown and brown	10	10
336		70l. blue and turqoise	10	15

85 St. Vincent de Paul

1960. Death Tercentenaries of St. Vincent de Paul and St. Louise de Marillac.

337	**85**	40l. violet	20	15
338	–	70l. black	20	20
339	–	100l. brown	40	35

DESIGNS: 70l. St. Louise de Marillac; 100l. St. Vincent giving child to care of St. Louise.

86 St. Meinrad

87 "Pope Leo I meeting Attila" (Algardi)

1961. 11th Death Centenary of St. Meinrad.

340	**86**	30l. black	35	35
341	–	40l. lilac	75	65
342	–	100l. brown	1·50	1·30

DESIGNS—VERT: 40l. The "Black Madonna", Einsiedeln Abbey. HORIZ: 100l. Einsiedeln Abbey, Switzerland.

1961. 15th Death Centenary of Pope Leo I.

343	**87**	15l. red	10	15
344		70l. green	55	50
345		300l. brown	1·50	1·20

88 Route of St. Paul's Journey to Rome

1961. 1900th Anniv of St. Paul's Arrival in Rome.

346	**88**	10l. green	10	10
347	–	15l. black and brown	10	10
348	–	20l. black and red	20	10
349	**88**	30l. blue	30	25
350	–	75l. black and brown	35	30
351	–	200l. black and blue	1·30	1·00

DESIGNS: 15, 75l. St. Paul's arrival in Rome (after sculpture by Maraini); 20, 200l. Basilica of St. Paul-outside-the-Walls, Rome.

89 "L'Osservatore Romano", 1861 and 1961

1961. Centenary of "L'Osservatore Romano" (Vatican newspaper).

352	**89**	40l. black and brown	20	25
353	–	70l. black and blue	55	50
354	–	250l. black and yellow	1·70	1·30

DESIGNS: 70l. "L'Osservatore Romano" offices; 250l. Printing machine.

90 St. Patrick (ancient sculpture)

1961. 15th Death Centenary of St. Patrick.

355	**90**	10l. green and buff	10	10
356	–	15l. brown and blue	10	10
357	**90**	40l. green and yellow	10	10
358	–	150l. brown and blue	40	35

DESIGN: 15, 150l. St. Patrick's Sanctuary, Lough Derg.

91 Arms of Roncalli Family

92 "The Nativity"

1961. Pope John XXIII's 80th Birthday.

359	**91**	10l. brown and black	10	10
360	–	25l. green and brown	10	10
361	–	30l. violet and blue	10	10
362	–	40l. blue and violet	10	10
363	–	70l. brown and grey	10	15
364	–	115l. black and brown	20	25

DESIGNS: 25l. Church of St. Mary, Sotto il Monte; 30l. Church of St. Mary, Monte Santo; 40l. Church of Saints Ambrose and Charles, Rome; 70l. St. Peter's Chair, Vatican Basilica; 115l. Pope John XXIII.

1961. Christmas. Centres multicoloured.
365 **92** 15l. green 10 10
366 40l. black 10 10
367 70l. purple 15 20

93 "Annunciation" (after F. Valle)

94 "Land Reclamation" Medal of 1588

1962. Air.
368 **93** 1000l. brown . . . . . . 1·10 95
369 1500l. blue . . . . 1·60 1·50

1962. Malaria Eradication.
370 **94** 15l. violet 10 10
371 – 40l. red 10 10
372 **94** 70l. brown 10 10
373 – 300l. green 30 30
DESIGN: 40, 300l. Map of Pontine Marshes reclamation project (at time of Pope Pius VI).

95 "The Good Shepherd" (statue, Lateran Museum)

96 St. Catherine (after Il Sodoma (Bazzi))

1962. Religious Vocations.
374 **95** 10l. black and violet . . . 10 10
375 – 15l. brown and blue . . . 10 10
376 **95** 70l. black and green . . . 20 20
377 – 115l. brown and red . . . 1·30 1·10
378 **95** 200l. black and brown . . 1·30 1·10
DESIGN: 15, 115l. Wheatfield ready for harvest.

1962. 5th Centenary of St. Catherine of Siena's Canonization.
379 **96** 15l. brown 10 10
380 60l. violet 20 25
381 100l. blue 30 30

97 Paulina M. Jaricot

99 "Faith" (after Raphael)

98 St. Peter and St. Paul (from graffito on child's tomb)

1962. Death Centenary of Paulina M. Jaricot (founder of Society for the Propagation of the Faith). Multicoloured centres.
382 **97** 10l. lilac 10 10
383 50l. green 20 20
384 150l. grey 25 30

1962. 6th International Christian Archaeology Congress, Ravenna.
385 **98** 20l. brown and violet . . . 10 10
386 – 40l. green and brown . . . 10 10
387 **98** 70l. brown and turquoise 10 10
388 – 100l. green and red 10 10
DESIGN: 40, 100l. "The Passion" (from bas relief on tomb in Domitilla cemetery, near Rome).

1962. Ecumenical Council.
389 **99** 5l. brown and blue 10 10
390 – 10l. brown and green . . . 10 10
391 – 15l. brown and red 10 10
392 – 25l. grey and red 10 10
393 – 30l. black and mauve . . . 10 10
394 – 40l. brown and red . . . 10 10
395 – 60l. brown and green . . . 10 10
396 – 115l. red 10 10
DESIGNS—Divine Virtues: 10l. "Hope"; 15l. "Charity" (both after Raphael); 25l. Arms of Pope John XXIII and symbols of Evangelists (frontispiece of "Humanae Salutis" by Arrigo Bravi); 30l. Central Nave, St. Peter's (council venue); 40l. Pope John XXIII; 60l. "St. Peter" (bronze in Vatican Basilica); 115l. The Holy Ghost in form of dove.

100 "The Nativity"

1962. Christmas. Centres multicoloured.
397 **100** 10l. grey 10 10
398 15l. drab 10 10
399 90l. green 10 10

101 "Miracle of the Loaves and Fishes" (after Murillo)

102 Pope John XXIII

1963. Freedom from Hunger.
400 **101** 15l. sepia and brown . . 10 10
401 – 40l. green and red 10 10
402 **101** 100l. brown and blue . . 10 10
403 – 200l. green and turquoise 20 15
DESIGN: 40, 200l. "Miracle of the Fishes" (after Raphael).

1963. Award of Balzan Peace Prize to Pope John XXIII.
404 **102** 15l. brown 10 10
405 160l. black 15 20

103 St. Peter's Keys

104 Pope Paul VI

1963. "Vacant See".
406 **103** 10l. brown 10 10
407 40l. brown on yellow . . 10 10
408 100l. brown on violet . . 10 10

1963. Coronation of Pope Paul VI.
409 **104** 15l. black 10 10
410 – 40l. red 10 10
411 **104** 115l. brown 15 15
412 – 200l. grey 15 20
DESIGN: 40, 200l. Arms of Pope Paul VI.

105 "The Nativity" (African terracotta statuette)

106 St. Cyril

1963. Christmas.
413 **105** 10l. brown and light brown 10 10
414 40l. brown and blue . . . 10 10
415 100l. brown and green . . 10 10

1963. 1100th Anniv of Conversion of Slavs by Saints Cyril and Methodius.
416 **106** 30l. purple 10 10
417 – 70l. brown 10 10
418 – 150l. purple 10 15
DESIGNS: 70l. Map of Moravia; 150l. St. Methodius.

107 Pope Paul VI

108 St. Peter, Pharaoh's Tomb, Wadi-es-Sebua

1964. Pope Paul's Visit to the Holy Land.
419 **107** 15l. black 10 10
420 – 25l. red 10 10
421 – 70l. sepia 10 10
422 – 160l. blue 10 10
DESIGNS: 25l. Church of the Nativity, Bethlehem; 70l. Church of the Holy Sepulchre, Jerusalem; 160l. Well of the Virgin Mary, Nazareth.

1964. Nubian Monuments Preservation.
423 **108** 10l. brown and blue . . . 10 10
424 – 20l. multicoloured 10 10
425 **108** 70l. brown and light brown 10 10
426 – 200l. multicoloured . . . 10 10
DESIGN: 20, 200l. Philae Temple.

109 Pope Paul VI

110 Michelangelo

1964. Vatican City's Participation in New York World's Fair.
427 **109** 15l. blue 10 10
428 – 50l. brown 10 10
429 **109** 100l. blue 10 10
430 – 250l. brown 10 15
DESIGNS: 50l. Michelangelo's "Pieta"; 250l. Detail of Madonna's head from "Pieta".

1964. 400th Death Anniv of Michelangelo. Paintings in the Sistine Chapel.
431 **110** 10l. black 10 10
432 – 25l. purple 10 10
433 – 30l. green 10 10
434 – 40l. violet 10 10
435 – 150l. green 10 10
PAINTINGS: 25l. Prophet Isaiah; 30l. Delphic Sibyl; 40l. Prophet Jeremiah; 150l. Prophet Joel.

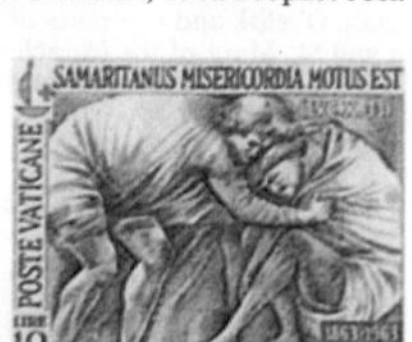

111 "The Good Samaritan" (after Emilio Greco)

1964. Red Cross Centenary (1963). Cross in red.
436 **111** 10l. brown 10 10
437 30l. blue 10 10
438 300l. brown 20 20

112 "Christmas Scene" (after Kimiko Koseki)

114 Pope Paul at prayer

113 Cues's Birthplace

1964. Christmas.
439 **112** 10l. multicoloured 10 10
440 15l. multicoloured 10 10
441 135l. multicoloured . . . 10 10

1964. 500th Death Anniv of Nicholas Cues (Cardinal Cusanus).
442 **113** 40l. green 10 10
443 – 200l. red 10 15
DESIGN: 200l. Cardinal Cusanus's sepulchre, St. Peter's (relief by A. Bregno).

1964. Pope Paul's Visit to India.
444 **114** 15l. purple 10 10
445 – 25l. green 10 10
446 – 60l. brown 10 10
447 – 200l. purple 10 15
DESIGN—HORIZ: 25l. Public altar, "The Oval", Bombay; 60l. "Gateway to India", Bombay. VERT: 200l. Pope Paul walking across map of India.

115 Sts. Mbaga Tuzinde, Carolus Lwanga and Kizito

116 Dante (after Raphael)

1965. Ugandan Martyrs.
448 – 15l. turquoise 10 10
449 **115** 20l. brown 10 10
450 – 30l. blue 10 10
451 – 75l. black 10 10
452 – 100l. red 10 10
453 – 160l. violet 10 10
DESIGNS: 15l. St. Joseph Mukasa and six other martyrs; 30l. Sts. Matthias Mulumba, Noe Mawagalli and Lucas Banabakintu; 75l. Sts. Gonzaga Gonza, Athanasius Bazzekuketta, Pontianus Ngondwe and Bruno Serunkuma; 100l. Sts. Anatolius Kiriggwajjo, Andreas Kaggwa and Adulphus Mukasa; 160l. Sts. Mukasa Kiriwananvu and Gyavira.

1965. 700th Anniv of Dante's Birth.
454 **116** 10l. brown and light brown 10 10
455 – 40l. brown and red . . . 10 10
456 – 70l. brown and green . . 10 10
457 – 200l. brown and blue . . 10 15
DESIGNS—After drawings by Botticelli: 40l. "Inferno"; 70l. "Purgatory"; 200l. "Paradise".

117 St. Benedict (after Perugino)

118 Pope Paul

1965. Declaration of St. Benedict as Patron Saint of Europe.
458 **117** 40l. brown 10 10
459 – 300l. green 20 20
DESIGN: 300l. Montecassino Abbey.

1965. Pope Paul's Visit to the U.N., New York.
460 **118** 20l. brown 10 10
461 – 30l. blue 10 10
462 – 150l. green 10 10
463 **118** 300l. purple 20 20
DESIGN: 30, 150l. U.N.O. Headquarters, New York.

119 "The Nativity" (Peruvian setting)

120 Pope Paul

1965. Christmas.
464 **119** 20l. red 10 10
465 40l. brown 10 10
466 200l. green 10 15

1966.
467 **120** 5l. brown 10 10
468 – 10l. violet 10 10
469 – 15l. brown 10 10
470 – 20l. green 10 10
471 – 30l. brown 10 10
472 – 40l. turquoise 10 10
473 – 55l. blue 10 10
474 – 75l. purple 10 10
475 – 90l. mauve 10 10
476 – 130l. green 10 10
DESIGNS (SCULPTURES): 10l. "Music"; 15l. "Science"; 20l. "Painting"; 30l. "Sculpture"; 40l. "Building"; 55l. "Carpentry"; 75l. "Agriculture"; 90l. "Metallurgy"; 130l. "Learning".

121 Queen Dabrowka and King Mieszko I

1966. Poland's Christian Millennium.

477 **121** 15l. black 10 10
478 – 25l. violet 10 10
479 – 40l. red 10 10
480 – 50l. red 10 10
481 – 150l. grey 10 10
482 – 220l. brown 10 15

DESIGNS: 25l. St. Adalbert (Wojciech) and Wroclaw and Gniezno Cathedrals; 40l. St. Stanislas, Skalka Cathedral and Wawel Royal Palace, Cracow; 50l. Queen Jadwiga (Hedwig); Ostra Brama Gate with Mater Misericordiae, Wilno, and Jagellon University Library, Cracow; 150l. "Black Madonna", Jasna Gora Monastery (Czestochowa) and St. John's Cathedral, Warsaw; 220l. Pope Paul VI greeting Poles.

122 Pope John XXIII and St. Peter's, Rome

1966. 4th Anniv of Opening of Ecumenical Council.

483 **122** 10l. black and red 10 10
484 – 15l. green and brown . . 10 10
485 – 55l. mauve and brown . . 10 10
486 – 90l. black and green . . . 10 10
487 – 100l. yellow and green . . 10 10
488 – 130l. sepia and brown . . 10 10

DESIGNS: 15l. Book of Prayer, St. Peter's; 55l. Mass; 90l. Pope Paul with Patriarch Athenagoras; 100l. Episcopal ring; 130l. Pope Paul at closing ceremony (12.10.65).

123 "The Nativity" (after sculpture by Scorzelli)

124 Jetliner over St. Peter's

1966. Christmas.

489 **123** 20l. purple 10 10
490 55l. green 10 10
491 225l. brown 10 15

1967. Air.

492 **124** 20l. violet 10 10
493 – 40l. lilac and pink 10 10
494 – 90l. blue and grey 10 10
495 **124** 100l. black and red . . . 10 10
496 – 200l. lilac and grey . . . 10 15
497 – 500l. brown & light brown 35 30

DESIGNS: 40, 200l. Radio mast and St. Gabriel's statue; 90, 500l. Aerial view of St. Peter's.

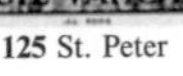

125 St. Peter

126 "The Three Shepherd Children" (sculpture)

1967. 1900th Anniv of Martyrdom of Saints Peter and Paul. Multicoloured.

498 15l. Type **125** 10 10
499 20l. St. Paul 10 10
500 55l. The two Saints 10 10
501 90l. Bernini's baldachin, St. Peter's 10 10
502 220l. Arnolfo di Cambio's tabernacle, St. Paul's Basilica 15 15

1967. 50th Anniv of Fatima Apparitions. Multicoloured.

503 30l. Type **126** 10 10
504 50l. Basilica of Fatima . . . 10 10
505 200l. Pope Paul VI praying before Virgin's statue at Fatima 20 20

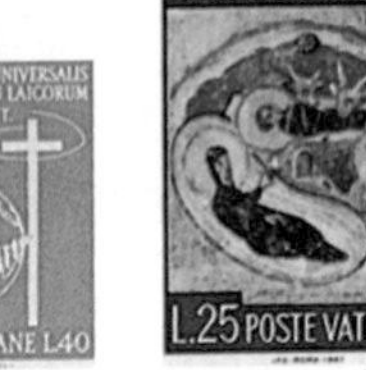

127 Congress Emblem

128 "The Nativity" (Byzantine carving)

1967. 3rd World Apostolic Laity Congress, Rome.

506 **127** 40l. red 15 15
507 130l. blue 15 15

1967. Christmas.

508 **128** 25l. multicoloured 10 10
509 55l. multicoloured 10 10
510 180l. multicoloured . . . 10 15

129 "Angel Gabriel" (detail from "The Annunciation" by Fra Angelico)

130 Pope Paul VI

1968. Air.

511 **129** 1000l. red on cream . . . 85 65
512 1500l. black on cream . . 1·20 1·00

1968. Pope Paul's Visit to Colombia.

513 **130** 25l. brown and black . . 10 10
514 – 55l. brown, grey and black 10 10
515 – 220l. brown, blue & black 10 15

DESIGNS: 55l. Monstrance (Raphael's "Disputa"); 220l. Map of South America.

131 "The Holy Child of Prague"

132 "The Resurrection" (Fra Angelico)

1968. Christmas.

516 **131** 20l. purple and red . . . 10 10
517 50l. violet and lilac . . . 10 10
518 250l. blue and light blue 20 20

1969. Easter.

519 **132** 20l. red and buff 10 10
520 90l. green and buff . . . 10 10
521 180l. blue and buff . . . 10 10

133 Colonnade

134 Pope with Young Africans

1969. Europa.

522 **133** 50l. brown and grey . . . 10 10
523 90l. brown and red . . . 15 15
524 130l. brown and green . . 15 20

1969. Pope Paul's Visit to Uganda.

525 **134** 25l. brown and ochre . . 10 10
526 – 55l. brown and red . . . 10 10
527 – 250l. multicoloured . . . 10 15

DESIGNS: 55l. Pope with African bishops; 250l. Map of Africa and olive branch.

135 Pope Pius IX

136 "Expo 70" Emblem

1969. Centenary of St. Peter's Circle Society.

528 **135** 30l. brown 10 10
529 – 50l. grey 10 10
530 – 220l. purple 10 15

DESIGNS: 50l. Monogram of Society; 220l. Pope Paul VI.

1970. "Expo 70" World's Fair, Osaka. Mult.

531 25l. Type **136** 10 10
532 40l. Osaka Castle 10 10
533 55l. "Madonna and Child" (Domoto) 10 10
534 90l. Vatican pavilion 10 10
535 110l. Mt. Fuji 10 10

137 Commemorative Medal of Pius IX

1970. Centenary of 1st Vatican Council.

536 **137** 20l. brown and orange . . 10 10
537 – 50l. multicoloured 10 10
538 – 180l. purple and red . . . 10 15

DESIGNS: 50l. Arms of Pius IX; 180l. Council souvenir medal.

138 "Christ" (Simone Martini)

1970. 50th Anniv of Pope Paul's Ordination as Priest. Multicoloured.

539 15l. Type **138** 10 10
540 25l. "Christ" (R. v. d. Weyden) 10 10
541 50l. "Christ" (Durer) 10 10
542 90l. "Christ" (El Greco) . . . 10 10
543 180l. Pope Paul VI 10 10

139 "Adam" (Michelangelo)

140 Pope Paul VI

1970. 25th Anniv of United Nations.

544 20l. Type **139** 10 10
545 90l. "Eve" (Michelangelo) . . 10 10
546 220l. Olive branch 10 15

1970. Pope Paul's Visit to Asia and Oceania. Multicoloured.

547 25l. Type **140** 10 10
548 55l. "Holy Child of Cebu" (Philippines) 10 10
549 100l. "Madonna and Child", Darwin Cathedral (G. Hamori) 10 10
550 130l. Manila Cathedral . . . 10 10
551 220l. Sydney Cathedral . . . 10 15

141 "Angel with Lectern"

142 "Madonna and Child" (F. Gnissi)

1971. Racial Equality Year. Multicoloured.

552 20l. Type **141** 10 10
553 40l. "Christ Crucified, and Doves" 10 10
554 50l. Type **141** 10 10
555 130l. As 40l. 10 10

1971. Easter. Religious Paintings. Multicoloured.

556 25l. Type **142** 10 10
557 40l. "Madonna and Child" ("Sassetta", S. di Giovanni) 10 10
558 55l. "Madonna and Child" (C. Crivelli) 10 10
559 90l. "Madonna and Child" (C. Maratta) 10 10
560 180l. "The Holy Family" (G. Ceracchini) 10 15

143 "St. Dominic Guzman" (Sienese School)

1971. 800th Birth Anniv of St. Dominic Guzman (founder of Preaching Friars Order). Mult.

561 25l. Type **143** 10 10
562 55l. Portrait by Fra Angelico 10 10
563 90l. Portrait by Titian . . . 10 10
564 180l. Portrait by El Greco . . 10 15

144 "St. Matthew"

1971. Air.

565 **144** 200l. black and green . . 20 20
566 – 300l. black and brown . . 30 25
567 – 500l. black and pink . . . 55 45
568 – 1000l. black and mauve 65 55

DESIGNS—"The Four Evangelists" (ceiling frescoes by Fra Angelico in the Niccolina Chapel, Vatican City): 300l. "St. Mark"; 500l. "St. Luke"; 1000l. "St. John".

145 "St. Stephen" (from chasuble, Szekesfehervar Church, Hungary)

146 Bramante's Design for Cupola, St. Peter's

1971. Millennium of St. Stephen, King of Hungary.

569 **145** 50l. multicoloured 10 10
570 – 180l. black and yellow . . 10 15

DESIGN: 180l. "Madonna, Patroness of Hungary", (sculpture, circa 1511).

1972. Bramante Celebrations.

571 **146** 25l. black and yellow . . 10 10
572 – 90l. black and yellow . . 10 10
573 – 130l. black and yellow . . 15 15

DESIGNS: 90l. Donato Bramante (architect) from medal; 130l. Spiral staircase, Innocent VIII's Belvedere, Vatican.

147 "St. Mark at Sea" (mosaic)

1972. UNESCO "Save Venice" Campaign. Multicoloured.

574 25l. Type **147** 20 20
575 50l. Venice (top left-hand section) 15 20
576 50l. Venice (top right-hand section) 15 20
577 50l. Venice (bottom left-hand section) 15 20
578 50l. Venice (bottom right-hand section) 15 20
579 180l. St. Mark's Basilica . . 90 70
MS580 113 × 161 mm. Nos. 574/9 1·75 1·75

Nos. 575/8 are smaller 39 × 28 mm and were issued together, se-tenant, forming a composite design of a 1581 fresco showing a panoramic map of Venice.

148 Gospel of St. Mark (from codex "Biblia dell'Aracoeli")

1972. International Book Year. Illuminated Manuscripts. Multicoloured.
581 30l. Type **148** 10 10
582 50l. Gospel of St. Luke ("Biblia dell'Aracoeli") 10 10
583 90l. 2nd Epistle of St. John (Bologna codex) 10 10
584 100l. Revelation of St. John (Bologna codex) 10 10
585 130l. Epistle of St. Paul to the Romans (Italian codex) 15 15

149 Luigi Orione (founder of "Caritas")

1972. Birth Centenaries. Multicoloured.
586 50l. Type **149** 10 10
587 180l. Lorenzo Perosi (composer) 10 15

150 Cardinal Bassarione (Roselli fresco, Sistine Chapel)
151 Congress Emblem

1972. 500th Death Anniv of Cardinal Bassarione.
588 – 40l. green 10 10
589 **150** 90l. red 10 10
590 – 130l. black 15 15
DESIGNS: 40l. "Reading of Bull of Union" (relief); 130l. Arms of Cardinal Bassarione.

1973. Int Eucharistic Congress. Melbourne. Mult.
591 25l. Type **151** 10 10
592 75l. Michelangelo's "Pieta" 10 10
593 300l. Melbourne Cathedral 20 20

152 St. Theresa's Birthplace
153 Torun (birthplace)

1973. Birth Centenary of St. Theresa of Lisieux.
594 **152** 25l. black and red 10 10
595 – 55l. black and yellow 10 10
596 – 220l. black and blue 20 15
DESIGNS: 55l. St. Theresa; 220l. Basilica of Lisieux.

1973. 500th Birth Anniv of Copernicus.
597 **153** 20l. green 10 10
598 – 50l. brown 10 10
599 **153** 100l. purple 15 15
600 – 130l. blue 15 20
DESIGN: 50, 130l. Copernicus.

154 "St. Wenceslas"

1973. Millenary of Prague Diocese. Mult.
601 20l. Type **154** 10 10
602 90l. Arms of Prague Diocese 10 10
603 150l. Tower of Prague Cathedral 20 15
604 220l. "St. Adalbert" 20 20

155 Church of St. Hripsime
156 "Angel" (porch of St. Mark's, Venice)

1973. 800th Death Anniv of St. Narsete Shnorali (Armenian patriarch).
605 **155** 25l. brown and ochre 10 10
606 – 90l. black and lilac 10 10
607 – 180l. purple and green 15 20
DESIGNS: 90l. Armenian "khatchkar" (stone stele) inscribed "Victory"; 180l. St. Narsete Shnorali.

1974. Air.
608 **156** 2500l. multicoloured 2·00 1·50

157 "And there was Light"
159 Pupils

158 Noah's Ark and Dove

1974. International Book Year (1973). "The Bible". Biblical Texts. Multicoloured.
609 15l. Type **157** 10 10
610 25l. "Noah entrusts himself to God" (horiz) 10 10
611 50l. "The Annunciation" 10 10
612 90l. "The Nativity" 10 10
613 180l. "The Lord feeds His People" (horiz) 15 20

1974. Centenary of U.P.U. Mosaics. Multicoloured.
614 50l. Type **158** 10 10
615 90l. Sheep in landscape 20 20

1974. 700th Death Anniv of St. Thomas Aquinas (founder of Fra Angelico School). "The School of St. Thomas" (painting, St. Mark's Convent, Florence). Each brown and gold.
616 50l. Type **159** 10 10
617 90l. St. Thomas and pupils (24 × 40 mm) 15 15
618 220l. Pupils (different) 20 15
Nos. 616/18 were issued together, se-tenant, forming a composite design.

160 "Civita" (medieval quarter), Bagnoregio
161 Christus Victor

1974. 700th Death Anniv of St. Bonaventura of Bagnoregio. Wood-carvings. Multicoloured.
619 40l. Type **160** 10 10
620 90l. "Tree of Life" (13th-century motif) 10 10
621 220l. "St. Bonaventura (B. Gozzoli) 15 20

1974. Holy Year (1975). Multicoloured.
622 10l. Type **161** 10 10
623 25l. Christ 10 10
624 30l. Christ (different) 10 10
625 40l. Cross and dove 10 10
626 50l. Christ enthroned 10 10
627 55l. St. Peter 10 10
628 90l. St. Paul 10 10
629 100l. St. Peter 10 10
630 130l. St. Paul 10 10
631 220l. Arms of Pope Paul VI 15 20
632 250l. Pope Paul VI giving blessing 15 20

162 Fountain, St. Peter's Square

1975. European Architectural Heritage Year. Fountains.
633 **162** 20l. black and brown 10 10
634 – 40l. black and lilac 10 10
635 – 50l. black and pink 10 10
636 – 90l. black and green 10 10
637 – 100l. black and green 10 10
638 – 200l. black and blue 20 15
FOUNTAINS: 40l. Piazza St. Martha; 50l. Del Forno; 90l. Belvedere courtyard; 100l. Academy of Sciences; 200l. Galley fountain.

163 "Pentecost" (El Greco)

1975. Pentecost.
639 **163** 300l. orange and red 25 25

164 "Miracle of Loaves and Fishes" (gilt glass)

1975. 9th International Christian Archaeological Congress. 4th-century Art. Multicoloured.
640 30l. Type **164** 20 10
641 150l. Christ (painting) 20 10
642 200l. Raising of Lazarus (gilt glass) 20 20

165 Pope Sixtus IV investing Bartolomeo Sacchi as First Librarian (fresco)

1975. 500th Anniv of Apostolic Library.
643 **165** 70l. red and violet 10 10
644 – 100l. green and light green 10 10
645 – 250l. red and blue 20 20
DESIGNS—VERT: 100l. Pope Sixtus IV (codex). HORIZ: 250l. Pope Sixtus IV visiting library (fresco).

166 Passionists' House, Argentario

1975. Death Bicentenary of St. Paul of the Cross (founder of Passionist religious order). Mult.
646 50l. Type **166** 10 10
647 150l. "St. Paul" (D. della Porta) (26 × 31 mm) 15 15
648 300l. Basilica of Saints John and Paul 20 20

167 Detail from Painting
168 "The Last Judgement" (detail)

1975. International Women's Year. Painting by Fra Angelico. Multicoloured.
649 100l. Type **167** 20 15
650 200l. Detail from painting (different) 20 20

1976. Air.
651 **168** 500l. brown and blue 90 75
652 – 1000l. brown and blue 1·00 75
653 – 2500l. brown and blue 1·40 1·00
DESIGNS: 1000l., 2500l. Different motifs from Michelangelo's "The Last Judgement".

169 "Madonna in Glory with the Child Jesus and Six Saints" (detail)

1976. 400th Death Anniv of Titian. Details from "The Madonna in Glory with the Child Jesus and Six Saints".
654 **169** 100l. red 20 20
655 – 300l. red 25 25

170 Eucharist Ear of Wheat and Globe
171 "Transfiguration" (detail)

1976. 41st Int Eucharist Congress, Philadelphia.
656 **170** 150l. multicoloured 20 15
657 – 200l. gold and blue 20 20
658 – 400l. gold and green 35 30
DESIGNS: 200l. Eucharist within protective hands; 400l. Adoration of the Eucharist.

1976. Details of Raphael's "Transfiguration". Multicoloured.
659 30l. Type **171** ("Moses") 10 10
660 40l. "Christ Transfigured" 10 10
661 50l. "Prophet Elijah" 10 10
662 100l. "Two Apostles" 10 10
663 150l. "The Relatives" 15 10
664 200l. "Landscape" 20 20

172 St. John's Tower and Fountain

1976. Architecture.
665 **172** 50l. brown and lilac 10 10
666 – 100l. sepia and brown 10 10
667 – 120l. black and green 10 10
668 – 180l. black and grey 20 15
669 – 250l. brown and stone 20 20
670 – 300l. purple 20 20
DESIGNS: 100l. Fountain of the Sacrament; 120l. Fountain at entrance to Gardens; 180l. Cupola of St. Peter's and Sacristy Basilica; 250l. Borgia Tower, Sistine Chapel and Via della Fondamenta; 300l. Apostolic Palace, Courtyard of St. Damasius.

173 "Canticles of Brother Sun" (detail)

1977. 750th Death Anniv of St. Francis of Assisi. Details from "Canticles of Brother Sun" by D. Cambellotti. Multicoloured.
671 50l. Type **173** ("The Lord's Creatures") 10 10
672 70l. "Brother Sun" 10 10
673 100l. "Sister Moon and Stars" 10 10
674 130l. "Sister Water" 10 15
675 170l. "Praise in Infirmities and Tribulations" 15 15
676 200l. "Praise for Bodily Death" 20 15

174 Detail from Fresco
175 "Death of the Virgin"

1977. 600th Anniv of Return of Pope Gregory from Avignon. Fresco by G. Vasari. Multicoloured.
677 170l. Type **174** 20 20
678 350l. Detail from fresco (different) 35 25

1977. Festival of Assumption. Miniatures from Apostolic Library. Multicoloured.
679 200l. Type **175** 20 20
680 400l. "Assumption of Virgin into Heaven" 35 30

176 "God of the Nile"

1977. Classical Sculpture in Vatican Museums (1st series). Statues. Multicoloured.
681 50l. Type **176** 10 10
682 120l. "Pericles" 10 10
683 130l. "Husband and Wife with joined Hands" . . . 15 15
684 150l. "Belvedere Apollo" . . 15 15
685 170l. "Laocoon" 15 20
686 350l. "Belvedere Torso" . . . 20 25
See also Nos. 687/92.

177 "Creation of the Human Race"

1977. Classical Sculpture in Vatican Museums (2nd series). Paleo-Christian Sarcophagi Carvings. Multicoloured.
687 50l. Type **177** 10 10
688 70l. "Three Youths in the Fiery Furnace" 10 10
689 100l. "Adoration of the Magi" 10 10
690 130l. "Christ raising Lazarus from the Dead" 15 15
691 200l. "The Good Shepherd" 20 20
692 400l. "Resurrection" 30 30

178 "Madonna with the Parrot" (detail)

180 Arms of Pope Pius IX

179 "The Face of Christ"

1977. 400th Birth Anniv of Rubens.
693 **178** 350l. multicoloured . . . 30 30

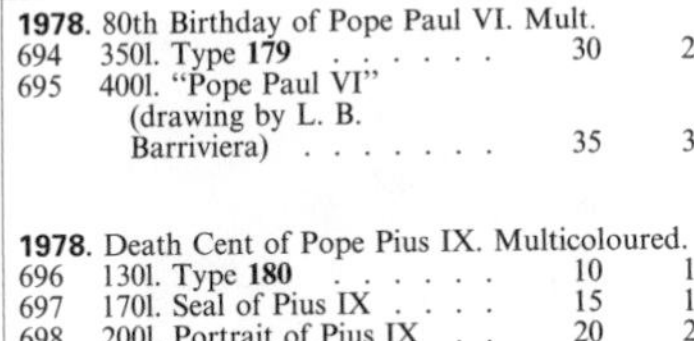

1978. 80th Birthday of Pope Paul VI. Mult.
694 350l. Type **179** 30 25
695 400l. "Pope Paul VI" (drawing by L. B. Barriviera) 35 30

1978. Death Cent of Pope Pius IX. Multicoloured.
696 130l. Type **180** 10 10
697 170l. Seal of Pius IX 15 15
698 200l. Portrait of Pius IX . . 20 20

181 Microwave Antenna and Radio Vatican Emblem

182 St. Peter's Keys

1978. Air. 10th World Telecommunications Day.
699 **181** 1000l. multicoloured . . . 85 65
700 2000l. multicoloured . . . 1·70 1·40
701 3000l. multicoloured . . . 2·50 1·90

1978. "Vacant See".
702 **182** 120l. blue and violet . . . 20 15
703 150l. pink and violet . . . 20 15
704 250l. yellow and violet . . 20 20

183 St. Peter's Keys

184 Pope John Paul I on Throne

1978. "Vacant See".
705 **183** 120l. yellow, blue & black 20 15
706 200l. yellow, red and black 20 15
707 250l. multicoloured . . . 20 20

1978. Pope John Paul I Commem. Mult.
708 70l. Type **184** 10 10
709 120l. The Pope smiling . . . 15 15
710 250l. The Pope in Vatican Gardens 20 20
711 350l. The Pope giving blessing (horiz) 20 20

185 Arms of Pope John Paul II
186 The Martyrdom (14th-century Latin codex)

1979. Inauguration of Pontificate of Pope John Paul II. Multicoloured.
712 170l. Type **185** 20 15
713 250l. The Pope giving his blessing 20 20
714 400l. "Christ handing the keys to St. Peter" (relief, A. Buonvicino) 35 30

1979. 900th Death Anniv of St. Stanislaus. Multicoloured.
715 120l. Type **186** 20 15
716 150l. St. Stanislaus appears to the people (14th century Latin codex) 20 15
717 250l. Gold reliquary 20 20
718 500l. Cracow Cathedral . . . 40 35

187 Meteorograph

1979. Death Centenary of Angelo Secchi (astronomer). Multicoloured.
719 180l. Type **187** 20 15
720 220l. Spectroscope 20 20
721 300l. Telescope 25 25

188 St. Basil and Vignette "Handing Monastic Laws to a Hermit"

189 Aerial View of Vatican City

1979. 1600th Death Anniv of St. Basil the Great. Multicoloured.
722 150l. Type **188** 20 15
723 520l. St. Basil and vignette "Caring for the Sick" . . . 40 35

1979. 50th Anniv of Vatican City State.
724 **189** 50l. brown, black and pink 10 10
725 – 70l. multicoloured 10 10
726 – 120l. multicoloured . . . 10 10
727 – 150l. multicoloured . . . 10 10
728 – 170l. multicoloured . . . 20 15
729 – 250l. multicoloured . . . 20 20
730 – 450l. multicoloured . . . 35 40
DESIGNS—POPES AND ARMS: 70l. Pius XI; 120l. Pius XII; 150l. John XXIII; 170l. Paul VI; 250l. John Paul I; 450l. John Paul II.

190 Child in Swaddling Clothes (relief, Foundling Hospital, Florence)

1979. International Year of the Child. Sculptures by Della Robbia.
731 **190** 50l. multicoloured 15 15
732 – 120l. multicoloured . . . 20 15
733 – 200l. multicoloured . . . 20 20
734 – 350l. multicoloured . . . 25 30
DESIGNS: 120l. to 350l. Similar sculptures.

191 Abbot Desiderius offering Codices to St. Benedict

1980. 1500th Birth Anniv of St. Benedict of Nursia (founder of Benedictine Order). Multicoloured.
735 80l. Type **191** 10 10
736 100l. St. Benedict composing rules of the Order . . . 10 10
737 150l. Page of St. Benedict's Rules 15 15
738 220l. Death of St. Benedict 20 15
739 450l. Montecassino Abbey (after Paul Bril) 35 35

192 Hands reaching out to Pope and Arms of Santo Domingo

1980. Air. Pope John Paul II's Journeys (1st series). Different coats of arms.
740 **192** 200l. multicoloured . . . 20 15
741 – 300l. multicoloured . . . 30 20
742 – 500l. violet, red and black 45 35
743 – 1000l. multicoloured . . . 90 70
744 – 1500l. multicoloured . . . 1·40 95
745 – 2000l. red, blue and black 1·80 1·50
746 – 3000l. black, red and blue 2·75 2·10
COATS OF ARMS: 300l. Mexico; 500l. Poland; 1000l. Ireland; 1500l. United States; 2000l. United Nations; 3000l. Pope John Paul II, Archbishop Dimitrios and arms of Turkey.
See also Nos. 768/78, 814/25, 862/9, 886/93, 912/16, 940/4, 963/6, 992/6, 1019/22, 1049/51, 1076/80, 1113/14, 1136/41, 1174/9, 1206/11, 1236/40, 1284/8 and 1312/16.

193 Bernini (self-portrait) and Medallion showing Baldacchino, St. Peter's

1980. 300th Death Anniv of Gian Lorenzo Bernini (artist and architect). Multicoloured.
747 80l. Type **193** 10 10
748 170l. Bernini and medallion showing his plan for St. Peter's 20 15
749 250l. Bernini, medallion of bronze chair and group "Doctors of the Church", St. Peter's 20 20
750 350l. Bernini and medallion of Apostolic Palace stairway 30 30

194 St. Albertus on Mission of Peace

1980. 700th Death Anniv of St. Albertus Magnus. Multicoloured.
751 300l. Type **194** 25 25
752 400l. St. Albertus as Bishop 35 30

195 Communion of the Saints

1980. Feast of All Saints. Multicoloured.
753 250l. Type **195** 20 20
754 500l. Christ and saints . . . 40 40

196 Marconi, Pope Pius XI and Radio Emblem

1981. 50th Anniv of Vatican Radio. Mult.
755 100l. Type **196** 10 10
756 150l. Microphone 15 15
757 200l. Antenna of Santa Maria di Galeria Radio Centre and statue of Archangel Gabriel 20 20
758 600l. Pope John Paul II . . . 45 40

197 Virgil and his Writing-desk

1981. Death Bimillenary of Virgil (Roman poet). Multicoloured.
759 350l. Type **197** 35 40
760 600l. As Type **197** but inscr "P. VERGILI MARONIS AENEIDOS LIBRI" . . . 55 55

198 Congress Emblem and Apparition of Virgin to St. Bernadette

1981. 42nd International Eucharistic Congress, Lourdes. Multicoloured.
761 80l. Congress emblem 10 10
762 150l. Type **198** 15 15

763 200l. Emblem and pilgrims going to Lourdes 20 20
764 500l. Emblem and Bishop with faithful venerating Virgin 45 40

199 Jan van Ruusbroec writing Treatise

201 Arms of John Paul II

200 Turin Shroud and I.Y.D.P. Emblem

1981. 600th Death Anniv of Jan van Ruusbroec (Flemish mystic). Multicoloured.
765 200l. Type **199** 20 20
766 300l. Ruusbroec 25 30

1981. International Year of Disabled Persons.
767 **200** 600l. multicoloured . . . 45 45

1981. Pope John Paul II's Journeys (2nd series). Multicoloured.
768 50l. Type **201** 10 10
769 100l. Crucifix and map of Africa 10 10
770 120l. Hands holding crucifix 15 15
771 150l. Pope performing baptism 15 15
772 200l. Pope embracing African bishop 20 20
773 250l. Pope blessing sick man 25 25
774 300l. Notre-Dame Cathedral, Paris 30 25
775 400l. Pope addressing UNESCO, Paris 35 35
776 600l. "Christ of the Andes", Rio de Janeiro 55 50
777 700l. Cologne Cathedral . . 65 60
778 900l. Pope giving blessing . . 85 75

202 Agnes handing Church to Grand Master of the Crosiers of the Red Star

203 "Pueri Cantores" (left panel)

1982. 700th Death Anniv of Blessed Agnes of Prague. Multicoloured.
779 700l. Type **202** 65 55
780 900l. Agnes receiving letter from St. Clare 80 70

1982. 500th Death Anniv of Luca della Robbia (sculptor).
781 **203** 1000l. green and blue . . 90 75
782 – 1000l. multicoloured . . . 90 75
783 – 1000l. green and blue . . 90 75
DESIGNS—As T **203**: No. 783, "Pueri Cantores" (right panel). 44 × 36 mm: No. 782, "Virgin Mary in Prayer".

204 Virgin Mary and St. Joseph clothe St. Theresa

205 Examining Globe

1982. 400th Death Anniv of St. Theresa of Avila.
784 **204** 200l. orange, grey and red 20 15
785 – 600l. grey, orange and blue 55 45
786 – 1000l. grey, orange and mauve 90 75
DESIGNS: 600l. Ecstasy of St. Theresa; 1000l. St. Theresa writing "The Interior Castle".

1982. 400th Anniv of Gregorian Calendar. Details from Pope Gregory XIII's tomb.
787 **205** 200l. green 20 15
788 – 300l. black 30 25
789 – 700l. mauve 65 60
MS790 159 × 109 mm. Nos. 787/9 2·00 1·75
DESIGNS: 300l. Presenting proposals to Pope Gregory XIII; 700l. Kneeling figures.

206 "Nativity" (Veit Stoss)

1982. Christmas.
791 **206** 300l. stone, brown & gold 30 25
792 – 450l. lilac, purple and silver 35 35
DESIGN: 450l. "Nativity with Pope John Paul II" (Enrico Manfrini).

207 Crucifixion

208 Greek Vase

1983. Holy Year. Multicoloured.
793 300l. Type **207** 30 25
794 350l. Christ the Redeemer . . 35 25
795 400l. Pope bringing message of redemption to world . . 40 30
796 2000l. Dove of the Holy Spirit passing through Holy Door . . . . 1·80 1·50

1983. "The Vatican Collections: The Papacy and Art—U.S.A. 1983" Exhibition (1st issue). 125 × 170 mm containing T **208** and similar vert designs. Multicoloured.
MS797 100l. Type **208**, 200l. Italiante vase; 250l. Terracotta female bust; 300l. Bust of Emperor Marcus Aurelius; 350l. Bird (fresco fragment); 400l. Sacred vestment of Pope Clement VIII 2·50 2·30
See also Nos. **MS**802 and **MS**803.

209 "Theology"

1983. 500th Birth Anniv of Raphael (artist).
798 **209** 50l. blue and ultramarine 10 10
799 – 400l. purple and mauve 35 35
800 – 500l. brown and chestnut 50 40
801 – 1200l. green and turquoise 1·10 95
DESIGNS—Allegories on the Segnatura Room ceiling: 400l. "Poetry"; 500l. "Justice"; 1200l. "Philosophy".

1983. "The Vatican Collections: The Papacy and Art—U.S.A. 1983" Exhibition (2nd issue). Sheet 124 × 171 mm containing vert designs as T **208**. Multicoloured.
MS802 100l. Etruscan terracotta horse's head; 200l. Greek relief of horseman; 300l. Etruscan head of man; 400l. Head of Apollo Belvedere;500l. Fresco of Moses; 1000l. "Madonna and Child" (Bernardo Daddi) . . . . . . 2·50 2·50

1983. "The Vatican Collections: The Papacy and Art—U.S.A. 1983" Exhibition (3rd issue). Sheet 124 × 171 mm containing vert designs as T **208**. Multicoloured.
MS803 150l. Oedipus and Sphinx (Greek cup); 200l. Votive statue of child (Etruscan bronze); 350l. Statue of Emperor Augustus; 400l. Statue of Good Shepherd; 500l. "St. Nicholas saving ship" (Gentile Fabriano);1200l. "The Holy Face" (Georges Rouault) 3·00 3·00

210 "Moses explaining the Law to the People" (Luca Signorelli)

1983. Air. World Communications Year. Multicoloured.
804 2000l. Type **210** . . . . . . 1·80 1·30
805 5000l. "St. Paul preaching in Athens" (Raphael) . . . . 4·00 3·25

211 Mendel and Hybrid Experiment

212 St. Casimir and Vilna Cathedral and Castle

1984. Death Centenary of Gregor Johan Mendel (geneticist).
806 **211** 450l. multicoloured . . . 55 50
807 1500l. multicoloured . . . 1·50 1·20

1984. 500th Death Anniv of St. Casimir (patron saint of Lithuania).
808 **212** 550l. multicoloured . . . 55 50
809 1200l. multicoloured . . . 1·30 1·10

213 Pontifical Academy of Sciences

1984. Cultural and Scientific Institutions.
810 **213** 150l. yellow and brown 20 20
811 – 450l. multicoloured . . . 50 40
812 – 550l. yellow and violet . . 60 50
813 – 1500l. yellow and blue . . 1·50 1·20
DESIGNS: 450l. Seals and document from Vatican Secret Archives; 550l. Entrance to Vatican Apostolic Library; 1500l. Vatican Observatory, Castelgandolfo.

214 Pope in Karachi

1984. Pope John Paul II's Journeys (3rd series). Multicoloured.
814 50l. Type **214** 10 10
815 100l. Pope and image of Our Lady of Penafrancia, Philippines 10 10
816 150l. Pope with crucifix (Guam) 15 15
817 250l. Pope and Tokyo Cathedral 35 30
818 300l. Pope at Anchorage, Alaska 20 20
819 400l. Crucifix, crowd and map of Africa 30 25
820 450l. Pope and image of Our Lady of Fatima (Portugal) 35 25
821 550l. Pope, Archbishop of Westminster and Canterbury Cathedral . . . 90 65
822 1000l. Pope and image of Our Lady of Lujan (Argentina) . . . . 1·60 1·10
823 1500l. Pope, Lake Leman and Geneva . . . . 2·40 1·70
824 2500l. Pope and Mount Titano (San Marino) . . . 4·00 2·75
825 4000l. Pope and Santiago de Compostela Cathedral (Spain) . . . . 6·25 4·50

215 Damascus and Sepulchre of Sts. Marcellinus and Peter

1984. 1600th Death Anniv of Pope St. Damasus. Multicoloured.
826 200l. Type **215** 20 20
827 500l. Damasus and epigraph from St. Januarius's tomb 55 55
828 2000l. Damasus and basilica ruins . . . . 1·80 1·70

216 More (after Holbein) and Map

1985. 450th Death Anniv of Saint Thomas More. Multicoloured.
829 250l. Type **216** 30 30
830 400l. St. Thomas More and title page of "Utopia" . . 45 45
831 2000l. St. Thomas More and title page of "Life of Thomas More" by Domenico Regi . . . . . 2·00 1·80

217 St. Methodius holding Religious Paintings

1985. 1100th Death Anniv of Saint Methodius. Multicoloured.
832 500l. Type**217** 55 50
833 600l. Saints Cyril and Methodius with Pope Clement I's body 75 65
834 1700l. Saints Benedict, Cyril and Methodius . . . . . 1·60 1·50

218 Cross on Map of Africa

219 Eagle (from Door, St. Paul's Basilica, Rome)

1985. 43rd International Eucharistic Congress, Nairobi. Multicoloured.
835 100l. Type **218** 20 15
836 400l. Assembly of bishops . . 45 40
837 600l. Chalice 70 50
838 2300l. Family gazing at cross 2·75 2·10

1985. 900th Death Anniv of Pope Gregory VII. Multicoloured.
839 150l. Type **219** 20 20
840 450l. Pope Gregory VII . . . 55 50
841 2500l. Pope Gregory's former sarcophagus (horiz) . . . . 3·00 2·40

220 Mosaic Map of Italy and Symbol of Holy See

1985. Ratification of Modification of 1929 Lateran Concordat.
842 **220** 400l. multicoloured . . . 45 40

221 Carriage

222 "Nation shall not Lift up Sword against Nation. . ."

1985. "Italia '85" Int Stamp Exn, Rome.
843 **221** 450l. red and blue 35 40
844 – 1500l. blue and mauve . . 1·20 1·10
MS845 161 × 108 mm. Nos. 843/4 2·75 2·50
DESIGN: 1500l. Carriage (different).

1986. International Peace Year. Multicoloured.
846 50l. Type **222** 10 10
847 350l. Messenger's feet ("How beautiful ... are the feet ...") 40 35
848 450l. Profiles and olive branch ("Blessed are the peace-makers ...") 60 50
849 650l. Dove and sun ("Glory to God in the highest ...") 75 65
850 2000l. Pope's hand releasing dove over rainbow ("Peace is a value with no frontiers ...") . . . . 2·20 1·60

223/228 Vatican City (½-size illustration)

1986. World Heritage. Vatican City. Mult.
851 **223** 550l. multicoloured . . . 80 70
852 **224** 550l. multicoloured . . . 80 70
853 **225** 550l. multicoloured . . . 80 70
854 **226** 550l. multicoloured . . . 80 70
855 **227** 550l. multicoloured . . . 80 70
856 **228** 550l. multicoloured . . . 80 70
Nos. 851/6 were printed together, se-tenant, forming the composite design illustrated.

229 St. Camillus saving Invalid from Flood (after Pierre Subleyras)

1986. Centenary of Proclamation of St. Camillus de Lellis and St. John of God as Patron Saints of Hospitals and the Sick.
857 **229** 700l. green, violet and red 85 70
858 – 700l. blue, green and red 85 70
859 – 2000l. multicoloured . . . 2·40 2·10
DESIGNS: No. 858, St. John supporting the sick (after Gomez Moreno); 859, Emblems of Ministers of the Sick and Brothers Hospitallers, and Pope John Paul II talking to patient.

230 "The Philosophers"

1986. 50th Anniv of Pontifical Academy of Sciences. Details from fresco "School of Athens" by Raphael. Multicoloured.
860 1500l. Type **230** . . . . . . 1·80 1·50
861 2500l. "The Scientists" . . . 2·75 2·30

231 Pope and Young People (Central America)

232 "St. Augustine reading St. Paul's Epistles" (fresco, Benozzo Gozzoli)

1986. Air. Pope John Paul II's Journeys (4th series). Multicoloured.
862 350l. Type **231** 40 35
863 450l. Pope in prayer, Warsaw Cathedral and Our Lady of Czestochowa (Poland) . . 55 50
864 700l. Pope kneeling and crowd at Lourdes (France) 85 65
865 1000l. Sanctuary of Mariazell and St. Stephen's Cathedral, Vienna (Austria) 1·20 90
866 1500l. Pope and representatives of nations visited (Alaska, Asia and Pacific Islands) . . . . . . 1·60 1·30
867 2000l. Image of St. Nicholas of Flue, Basilica of Einsiedeln and Pope (Switzerland) . . . . . . 2·20 1·50
868 2500l. Crosses, Notre Dame Cathedral, Quebec, and Pope (Canada) . . . . . . 2·75 1·90
869 5000l. Pope, bishop and young people with cross (Spain, Dominican Republic and Puerto Rico) 5·50 3·75

1987. 1600th Anniv of Conversion and Baptism of St. Augustine. Multicoloured.
870 300l. Type **232** 35 35
871 400l. "Baptism of St. Augustine" (Bartolomeo di Gentile) 45 45
872 500l. "Ecstasy of St. Augustine" (fresco, Benozzo Gozzoli) 55 50
873 2200l. "Dispute of the Sacrament" (detail of fresco, Raphael) . . . . . 2·30 1·90

233 Statue of Christ, Lithuanian Chapel, Vatican Crypt

234 Chapter of Riga Church Seal

1987. 600th Anniv of Conversion to Christianity of Lithuania. Multicoloured.
874 200l. Type **233** 30 20
875 700l. Statue of Virgin Mary with body of Christ and two angels 85 75
876 3000l. Lithuanian shrine . . 3·25 2·75

1987. 800th Anniv of Conversion to Christianity of Latvia. Multicoloured.
877 700l. Type **234** 90 70
878 2400l. Basilica of the Assumption, Aglona . . . 3·50 2·75

235 Judge

236 Stamp Room and 1929 5c. Stamp

1987. "Olymphilex '87" Olympic Stamps Exhibition, Rome. Figures from Caracalla Baths floor mosaic. Multicoloured.
879 400l. Type **235** 45 40
880 500l. Runner 65 50
881 600l. Discus-thrower 75 50
882 2000l. Athlete . . . . 2·20 1·60
MS883 151 × 100 mm. As Nos. 879/82 but with Greek key borders . . . . 4·75 4·75

1987. Inauguration of Philatelic and Numismatic Museum. Multicoloured.
884 400l. Type **236** 45 40
885 3500l. Coin room and reverse of 1000l. 1986 coin . . . . 3·50 3·00

1987. Pope John Paul II's Journeys (5th series). As T **231**. Multicoloured.
886 50l. Youths, Pope and Machu Picchu (Venezuela, Ecuador, Peru, Trinidad and Tobago) 20 15
887 250l. Antwerp Cathedral, smoke stacks and Pope (Netherlands, Luxembourg and Belgium) 55 45
888 400l. People, buildings and Pope (Togo, Ivory Coast, Cameroun, Central African Republic, Zaire, Kenya and Morocco) 90 70
889 500l. Pope holding Cross and youths (Liechtenstein) . . . 1·10 85
890 600l. Pope, Indians and Delhi Mosque (India) . . . . . 1·30 1·00
891 700l. Pope, people, ceramic and Bogota Cathedral (Colombia and St. Lucia) 1·50 1·10
892 2500l. Pope, Cure d'Ars and Lyon Cathedral (France) 5·50 4·25
893 4000l. Hands releasing dove and symbols of countries visited (Bangladesh, Singapore, Fiji, New Zealand, Australia and Seychelles) . . . . 9·00 7·00

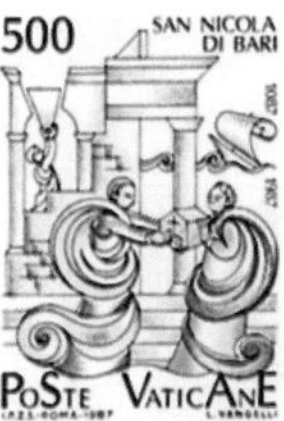

237 Arrival of Relics

238 Children and Sister of Institute of the Daughters of Mary Help of Christians

1987. 900th Anniv of Transfer of St. Nicholas's Relics from Myra to Bari. Multicoloured.
894 500l. Type **237** 75 80
895 700l. St. Nicholas giving purses of gold to save from dishonour the three daughters of a poor man 1·10 1·10
896 3000l. St. Nicholas saving a ship . . . . 7·75 6·00

1988. Death Centenary of St. John Bosco (founder of Salesian Brothers). Multicoloured.
897 500l. Type **238** 55 50
898 1000l. Bosco and children . . 90 90
899 2000l. Children and Salesian lay brother . . . . 1·80 1·90
Nos. 897/9 were printed together, se-tenant, forming a composite design.

239 The Annunciation

240 Prince Vladimir the Great (15th-century icon)

1988. Marian Year. Multicoloured.
900 50l. Type **239** 10 10
901 300l. Nativity 30 25
902 500l. Pentecost 45 40
903 750l. The Assumption . . . 65 55
904 1000l. Mother of the Church 90 75
905 2400l. Refuge of Sinners . . 2·00 1·80

1988. Millenary of Conversion to Christianity of Rus of Kiev. Multicoloured.
906 450l. Type **240** 45 40
907 650l. St. Sophia's Cathedral, Kiev 65 60
908 2500l. "Mother of God in Prayer" (mosaic, St. Sophia's Cathedral) . . 2·20 2·00

241 "Marriage at Cana" (detail)

242 Angel with Olive Branch

1988. 400th Death Anniv of Paolo Veronese (painter).
909 **241** 550l. blue and red 75 55
910 – 650l. multicoloured . . . 90 75
911 – 3000l. red and brown . . 2·40 2·00
DESIGNS—HORIZ: 650l. "Self-portrait". VERT: 3000l. "Marriage at Cana" (different detail).

1988. Air. Pope John Paul II's Journeys (6th series). As T **231**. Multicoloured.
912 450l. Hands releasing dove, St. Peter's, Rome, Santiago Cathedral and Sanctuary of Our Lady, Lujan (Uruguay, Chile and Argentina) 55 50
913 650l. Pope in act of blessing, Speyer Cathedral and youths (German Federal Republic) 85 70
914 1000l. Hands releasing dove, Gdansk altar and intertwined flowers and thorns (Poland) . . . . . 1·00 90
915 2500l. Skyscrapers and Pope blessing youths (U.S.A.) . . 2·75 2·20
916 5000l. Hands releasing dove, tepee at Fort Simpson and American Indians (Canada) 5·00 4·50

1988. Christmas. Multicoloured.
917 50l. Type **242** 10 10
918 400l. Angel holding olive branch in both hands . . . 35 30
919 500l. Angel with olive branch (flying from right) 55 45
920 550l. Shepherds 60 50
921 850l. Nativity 85 70
922 1500l. Wise Men . . . . . . 1·30 1·10
MS923 120 × 140 mm. As Nos. 917/22 but with gold backgrounds . . . . 4·75 4·75

243 Head of Apis

244 The Annunciation

1989. 150th Anniv of Gregorian Egyptian Museum. Sheet 140 × 100 mm containing T **243** and similar vert designs. Multicoloured.
MS924 400l. Type **243**; 650l. Double-headed statue of Isis and Apis; 750l. Headless statue of physician Ugiahorresne, 2400l. Phoraoh Mentuhotep . . . . 4·75 4·75

1989. 600th Anniv of Feast of Visitation of Virgin Mary. Illuminated Initials. Multicoloured.
925 550l. Type **244** 65 55
926 750l. Virgin Mary and St. Elizabeth 75 65
927 2500l. Virgin Mary and St. Elizabeth with Jesus and John the Baptist as babies . . . . 2·30 2·00

245 Purple-naped Lory ("Parrot")

246 Broken Bread (Congress emblem)

1989. Birds featured in "Histoire Naturelle des Oiseaux" by Eleazar Albin. Multicoloured.
928 100l. Type **245** 20 15
929 150l. Green woodpecker . . . 20 20
930 200l. Goldcrest ("Crested wren") and winter ("Common") wren 20 20
931 350l. River kingfisher 30 30
932 500l. Common cardinal ("Red Groas Beak of Virginia") 45 45
933 700l. Northern bullfinch ("Bullfinch") 65 60
934 1500l. Northern lapwing ("Lapwing Plover") . . . 1·40 1·30
935 3000l. Green-winged ("French") teal . . . . . 3·00 2·75

1989. 44th International Eucharistic Congress, Seoul.
936 **246** 550l. red and green . . . 55 45
937 – 850l. multicoloured . . . 85 70
938 – 1000l. multicoloured . . . 1·00 85
939 – 2500l. green, pink and violet . . . . 2·40 2·00
DESIGNS: 850l. Cross; 1000l. Cross and fishes; 2500l. Small cross on wafer.

247 Pope's Arms, Map of South America and Pope

1989. Pope John Paul II's Journeys (7th series). Multicoloured.
940 50l. Type **247** 20 15
941 550l. Austria 55 50
942 800l. Southern Africa . . . . 1·00 75
943 1000l. France . . . . 1·20 1·00
944 4000l. Italy . . . . 4·25 3·50

248 Basilica of the Assumption, Baltimore

249 Vision of Ursulines on Mystical Stair

1989. Bicentenary of 1st Catholic Diocese in U.S.A. Each agate and brown.
945 450l. Type **248** 55 50
946 1350l. John Carroll (first Archbishop of Baltimore) 1·60 1·30
947 2400l. Cathedral of Mary Our Queen, Baltimore (after Martin Barry) . . . 2·50 2·10

1990. 450th Death Anniv of St. Angela Merici (founder of Company of St. Ursula). Mult.
948 700l. Type **249** 85 70
949 800l. St. Angela teaching Ursulines . . . . 1·00 85
950 2800l. Ursulines . . . . . . 3·75 2·75

250 Ordination and Arrival in Frisia

251 Abraham

1990. 1300th Anniv of Beginning of St. Willibrord's Missions. Multicoloured.
951 300l. Type **250** 30 30
952 700l. St. Willibrord in Antwerp, creation as bishop by Pope Sergius I and gift of part of Echternach by Abbess of Euren 75 65
953 3000l. Gift of Echternach by King Pepin and St. Willibrord's death . . . 3·00 2·50

1990. 40th Anniv of Caritas Internationalis. Details of mosaic from Basilica of Sta. Maria Maggiore, Rome. Multicoloured.
954 450l. Type **251** 55 50
955 650l. Three visitors 90 70
956 800l. Sarah making bread . . 1·10 95
957 2000l. Visitors seated at Abraham's table . . . . . 2·50 2·20
MS958 100 × 135 mm. As Nos. 954/7 but without gold frame . . . . 6·00 6·00

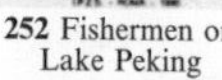

252 Fishermen on Lake Peking

253 Pope and African Landscape

1990. 300th Anniv of Peking–Nanking Diocese. Details of two enamelled bronze vases given by Peking Apostolic Delegate to Pope Pius IX. Multicoloured.
959 500l. Type **252** 45 45
960 750l. Church of the Immaculate Conception (first Peking church, 1650) 65 60
961 1500l. Lake Peking . . . . . 1·50 1·30
962 2000l. Church of the Redeemer, Peking, 1703 . . 1·80 1·60

1990. Air. Pope John Paul II's Journeys (8th series). Multicoloured.
963 500l. Type **253** 45 45
964 1000l. Northern European landscape (Scandinavia) . . 65 65
965 3000l. Cathedral (Santiago de Compostela, Spain) . . . . 1·50 1·50
966 5000l. Oriental landscape (Korea, Indonesia and Mauritius) . . . . 1·80 1·80

254 Choir of Angels

1990. Christmas. Details of painting by Sebastiano Mainardi. Multicoloured.
967 50l. Type **254** 20 20
968 200l. St. Joseph 20 20
969 650l. Holy Child 75 75
970 750l. Virgin Mary 90 90
971 2500l. "Nativity" (complete picture) (vert) . . . . . . 2·75 2·75

255 "Eleazar" (left half)

1991. Restoration of Sistine Chapel. Details of Lunettes of the Ancestors of Christ by Michelangelo. Multicoloured.
972 50l. Type **255** 20 20
973 100l. "Eleazar" (right half) 20 20
974 150l. "Jacob" (left half) . . . 20 20
975 250l. "Jacob" (right half) . . 20 20
976 350l. "Josiah" (left half) . . 30 30
977 400l. "Josiah" (right half) . . 35 35
978 500l. "Asa" (left half) 45 45
979 650l. "Asa" (right half) . . . 60 60
980 800l. "Zerubbabel" (left half) 75 75
981 1000l. "Zerubbabel" (right half) 90 90
982 2000l. "Azor" (left half) . . . 1·80 1·80
983 3000l. "Azor" (right half) . . 2·75 2·75

256 Title Page and Pope Leo XIII's Arms

1991. Centenary of "Rerum Novarum" (encyclical on workers' rights).
984 **256** 600l. blue and green . . . 55 55
985 – 750l. green and brown . . 75 75
986 – 3500l. purple and black 3·50 3·00
DESIGNS: 750l. Allegory of Church, workers and employers (from Leo XIII's 15th Anniv medal, 1892); 3500l. Profile of Pope Leo XIII (from same medal).

257 Astrograph (astronomical camera)

258 "Apparition of Virgin Mary" (Biagio Puccini)

1991. Centenary of Vatican Observatory. Mult.
987 750l. Type **257** 65 60
988 1000l. Castelgandolfo observatory (horiz) . . . . 1·00 95
989 3000l. Vatican Observatory telescope, Mount Graham, Tucson, U.S.A. . . . . . 3·00 2·50

1991. 600th Anniv of Canonization of St. Bridget (founder of Order of the Holy Saviour). Multicoloured.
990 1500l. Type **258** . . . . . . 1·40 1·20
991 2000l. "Revelation of Christ" (Biagio Puccini) . . . . . 1·90 1·60

259 Cathedral of the Immaculate Conception, Ouagadougou

260 Colonnade of St. Peter's Cathedral, Rome

1991. Pope John Paul II's Journeys (9th series). Multicoloured.
992 200l. Type **259** (Cape Verde, Guinea-Bissau, Mali, Burkina Faso and Chad) 20 20
993 550l. St. Vitus's Cathedral, Prague (Czechoslovakia) 55 55
994 750l. Basilica of Our Lady of Guadaloupe (Mexico and Curacao) 75 75
995 1500l. Ta'Pinu Sanctuary, Gozo (Malta) . . . . . . 1·60 1·60
996 3500l. Cathedral of Christ the King, Giteca (Tanzania, Burundi, Rwanda and Ivory Coast) . . . . 4·25 4·25

1991. Synod of Bishops' Special Assembly for Europe. Each black and brown.
997 300l. Type **260** 30 30
998 500l. St. Peter's Cathedral and square 45 45
999 4000l. Apostolic Palace and colonnade . . . . 4·00 4·00
Nos. 997/9 were issued together, se-tenant, forming a composite design.

261 Christopher Columbus

262 "Our Lady of Childbirth"

1992. 500th Anniv of Discovery of America by Columbus. Multicoloured.
1000 500l. Type **261** 45 45
1001 600l. St. Pedro Claver . . . 55 55
1002 850l. "Virgin of the Catholic Kings" 75 70
1003 1000l. Bortolome de las Casas . . . . 1·00 90
1004 2000l. Junipero Serra . . . 2·00 1·80
MS1005 138 × 95 mm. 1500l. Details of nautical chart from atlas of Battista Agnese . . . . 6·00 6·00

1992. 500th Death Anniv of Piero della Francesca (painter). Multicoloured.
1006 300l. Type **262** 30 30
1007 750l. "Our Lady of Childbirth" (detail) . . . 75 75
1008 1000l. "The Resurrection" 1·00 1·00
1009 3000l. "The Resurrection" (detail) . . . . 3·00 3·00

263 St. Giuseppe comforting the Sick

264 Maize

1992. 150th Death Anniv of St. Giuseppe Benedetto Cottolengo. Multicoloured.
1010 650l. Type **263** 65 65
1011 850l. St. Giuseppe holding Piccolo Casa della Divina Provvidenza (infirmary), Turin . . . . 1·00 1·00

1992. Plants of the New World. Illustrations from the 18th-century "Phytanthoza Iconographia". Multicoloured.
1012 850l. Type **264** 80 80
1013 850l. Tomatoes ("Solanum pomiferum") 80 75
1014 850l. Cactus ("Opuntia") . . 80 80
1015 850l. Cacao ("Cacaos, Cacavifera") 80 80
1016 850l. Peppers ("Solanum tuberosum") 80 75
1017 850l. Pineapple ("Ananas sagitae") 80 75

265 Our Lady of Guadalupe, Crucifix and Mitres

266 Pope, Dove and Map of Europe

1992. 4th Latin American Episcopal Conference, Santo Domingo.
1018 **265** 700l. gold, emerald and green 85 85

1992. Air. Pope John Paul II's Journeys (10th series). Multicoloured.
1019 500l. Type **266** (Portugal) 45 45
1020 1000l. Map of Europe highlighting Poland . . . 1·00 90
1021 4000l. Our Lady of Czestochowa and map highlighting Poland and Hungary . . . . 3·75 3·25
1022 6000l. Map of South America highlighting Brazil . . . . 6·50 5·00

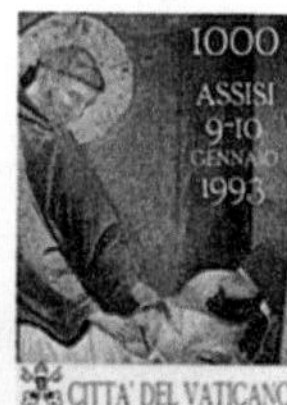

267 "The Annunciation"

268 "St. Francis healing the Man from Ilerda" (fresco by Giotto in Upper Church, Assisi)

1992. Christmas. Mosaics in Church of Sta.Maria Maggiore, Rome. Multicoloured.
1023 600l. Type **267** 75 75
1024 700l. "Nativity" 85 85
1025 1000l. "Adoration of the Kings" . . . . 1·20 1·20
1026 1500l. "Presentation in the Temple" . . . . 1·60 1·60

1993. "Peace in Europe" Prayer Meeting, Assisi.
1027 **268** 1000l. multicoloured . . 1·40 1·40

269 Dome of St. Peter's Cathedral

270 "The Sacrifice of Isaac"

1993. Architectural Treasures of Rome and the Vatican. Multicoloured.
1028 200l. Type **269** 20 20
1029 300l. St. John Lateran's Basilica 20 20
1030 350l. Basilica of Sta. Maria Maggiore 30 30
1031 500l. St. Paul's Basilica . . 45 45
1032 600l. Apostolic Palace, Vatican 55 55
1033 700l. Apostolic Palace, Lateran 65 65
1034 850l. Papal Palace, Castelgandolfo 75 75
1035 1000l. Chancery Palace . . 90 90
1036 2000l. Palace of Propagation of the Faith . . . . . . 1·60 1·60
1037 3000l. San Calisto Palace . . 2·50 2·50

1993. Ascension Day. Multicoloured.
1038 200l. Type **270** 20 20
1039 750l. Jesus handing New Law to St. Peter 90 90
1040 3000l. Christ watching servant washing Pilate's hands . . . . 3·25 3·25
Nos. 1038/40 were issued together, se-tenant, forming a composite design of the bas-relief "Traditio Legis" from 4th-century sarcophagus.

271 Cross and Grape Vines

273 St. John, Cross, Carp and Moldava River

272 "Crucifixion" (Felice Casorati)

1993. 45th Int Eucharistic Congress, Seville. Mult.
1041 500l. Type **271** 45 45
1042 700l. Cross and hands offering broken bread . . 65 65
1043 1500l. Hands holding chalice 1·40 1·40
1044 2500l. Cross, banner and ears of wheat . . . . . . 2·30 2·30

1993. Europa. Contemporary Art. Multicoloured.
1045 750l. Type **272** 65 75
1046 850l. "Rouen Cathedral" (Maurice Utrillo) 85 85

1993. 600th Death Anniv of St. John of Nepomuk (patron saint of Bohemia). Multicoloured.
1047 1000l. Type **273** 90 90
1048 2000l. Charles Bridge, Prague . . . . 1·80 1·80

274 Pope praying

1993. Pope John Paul II's Journeys (11th series). Multicoloured.
1049 600l. Type **274** (Senegal, Gambia and Guinea) . . 55 55
1050 1000l. Pope with Pastoral Staff (Angola and St. Thomas and Prince Islands) . . . . 1·10 1·10
1051 5000l. Pope with hands clasped in prayer (Dominican Republic) . . 5·00 5·00

275 "Madonna of Solothurn" (detail)

1993. 450th Death Anniv of Hans Holbein the Younger (artist). Multicoloured.
1052 700l. Type **275** 75 75
1053 1000l. "Madonna of Solothurn" . . . . . . 1·10 1·10
1054 1500l. "Self-portrait" . . . 1·60 1·60

276 "Creation of the Planets" (left detail)
277 Crosier and Dome

1994. Completion of Restoration of Sistine Chapel. Multicoloured.
1055 350l. Type **276** 40 40
1056 350l. God creating planets (right detail) 40 40
1057 500l. Adam (left detail, "The Creation of Adam") . . . 60 60
1058 500l. God (right detail) . . 60 60
1059 1000l. Adam and Eve taking forbidden fruit (left detail, "The Original Sin") . . . 1·20 1·20
1060 1000l. Angel casting out Adam and Eve from the Garden (right detail) . . . 1·20 1·20
1061 2000l. People climbing from swollen river (left detail, "The Flood") . . . . . . 2·40 2·40
1062 2000l. Floodwaters surrounding temporary shelter (right detail) . . . 2·40 2·40
MS1063 80 × 110 mm. 4000l. Christ and Virgin Mary (detail, "The Last Judgement") . . . . . . 5·00 5·00

Stamps of the same value were issued together, se-tenant, each pair forming a composite design.

1994. Special Assembly for Africa of Synod of Bishops. Multicoloured.
1064 850l. Type **277** 75 75
1065 1000l. Crucifix, dome of St. Peter's and African scene (horiz) 90 90

278 God creating Man and Woman

280 Bishop Euphrasius and Archdeacon Claudius

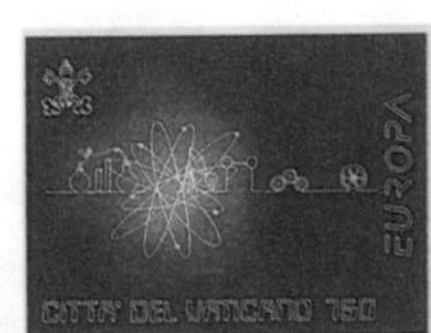

279 Timeline of Knowledge from Wheel to Atom

1994. Int Year of the Family. Mult.
1066 400l. Type **278** 35 35
1067 750l. Family 65 65
1068 1000l. Parents teaching son 85 85
1069 2000l. Youth helping elderly couple . . . . 1·80 1·80

1994. Europa. Discoveries. Multicoloured.
1070 750l. Type **279** 75 75
1071 850l. Galileo, solar system and scientific apparatus 90 90

1994. 13th International Congress on Christian Archaeology, Split and Porec, Croatia. Mosaics from Euphrasian Basilica, Porec. Multicoloured.
1072 700l. Type **280** 55 55
1073 1500l. Madonna and Child with two angels . . . . . 1·30 1·30
1074 3000l. Jesus Christ between Apostles St. Peter and St. Paul . . . . 2·75 2·75

281 Route Map, Mongolian Village and Giovanni da Montecorvino

1994. 700th Anniv of Evangelization of China.
1075 **281** 1000l. multicoloured . . 90 90

282 Houses, Mahdi's Mausoleum, Omdurman, and St. Mary's Basilica, Lodonga (Benin, Uganda and Sudan)

1994. Pope John Paul II's Journeys (12th series).
1076 **282** 600l. brown, green & red 55 55
1077 – 700l. violet, brown & grn 65 65
1078 – 1000l. brown, blue & vio 90 90
1079 – 2000l. black, blue and red . . . . 1·80 1·80
1080 – 3000l. blue, violet & brn 2·75 2·75

DESIGNS: 700l. St. Mary's Church, Apollonia, Mosque and statue of Skanderbeg, Tirana (Albania); 1000l. Church of the Saint, Huelva Region, and The Giralda, Real Maestranza and Golden Tower, Seville (Spain); 2000l. Skyscrapers and St. Thomas's Theological Seminary, Denver, "El Castillo" (pyramid), Kulkulkan, Jamaican girl and Mexican boy (Jamaica, Mexico and United States); 3000l. Tallin, "Hymn to Liberty" (monument), Riga, and Tower, Cathedral Square, Vilnius (Lithuania, Latvia and Estonia).

283 Holy Family

1994. Christmas. Details of "Nativity" by Tintoretto. Multicoloured.
1081 700l. Type **283** 75 75
1082 1000l. Upper half of painting (45 × 28 mm) . . 1·30 1·30
1083 1000l. Lower half of painting (45 × 28 mm) . . 1·30 1·30

Nos. 1082/3 were issued together, se-tenant, forming a composite design of the complete painting.

284 Angel with Chalice (Melozzo da Forli) (St. Mark's)
286 Fountain of the Triton (Bernini), Vatican Gardens

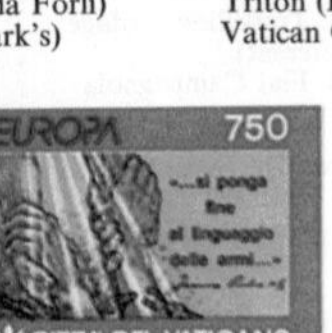

285 Hands and Broken Chains

1995. 700th Anniv of Shrine of the Holy House, Loreto. Details from the vaults of sacristies. Multicoloured.
1084 600l. Type **284** 50 50
1085 700l. Angel with lamb (Melozzo) (Sacristy of St. Mark) 55 55
1086 1500l. Angel with lute (Luca Signorelli) (St. John's) . . 1·20 1·20
1087 2500l. Angel (Signorelli) (St. John's) . . . . 2·40 2·40
MS1088 75 × 110 mm. 3000l. Madonna and Child (detail of "Translation of the Holy House" (marble relief) (35 × 35 mm) . . 3·25 3·25

1995. Europa. Peace and Freedom. Multicoloured.
1089 750l. Type **285** 65 70
1090 850l. Globe, olive wreath, dove and handclasp . . . 85 85

1995. European Nature Conservation Year. Multicoloured.
1091 200l. Type **286** 20 20
1092 300l. Avenue of roses, Castelgandolfo 30 30
1093 400l. Statue of Apollo, Vatican Gardens 35 35
1094 550l. Ruins of Domitian's Villa, Castelgandolfo . . . 45 45
1095 750l. Box elder, Vatican Gardens 65 65
1096 1500l. Belvedere Gardens, Castelgandolfo . . . . . 1·40 1·40
1097 2000l. Eagle fountain, Vatican Gardens . . . . 1·80 1·80
1098 3000l. Avenue of cypresses, Castelgandolfo . . . . . 2·50 2·50

287 Guglielmo Marconi and Transmitter

1995. One Hundred Years of Radio. Multicoloured.
1099 850l. Type **287** 90 90
1100 1000l. Archangel Gabriel, Pope John Paul II with microphone and Vatican broadcasting station . . . 1·10 1·10

288 St. Antony of Padua (statue by Donatello)

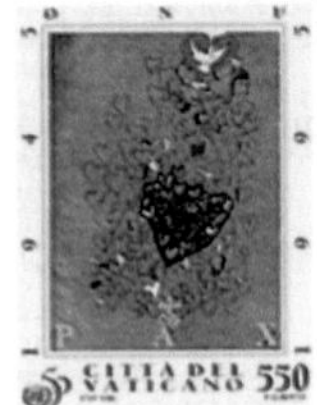

289 Dove and Hearts

1995. Saints' Anniversaries.
1101 **288** 500l. brown and green 45 45
1102 – 750l. green and violet . . 65 65
1103 – 3000l. blue and purple 2·75 2·75

DESIGNS: 500l. Type **288** (800th birth anniv); 750l. St. John of God (founder of Order of Hospitallers, 500th birth anniv) (sculpture, Filippo Valle); 3000l. St. Philip Neri (founder of Friars of the Oratory, 400th death anniv) (sculpture, Giovanni Battista Maini).

1995. 50th Anniv of U.N.O. Multicoloured.
1104 550l. Type **289** 45 45
1105 750l. Human faces 65 65
1106 850l. Doves 75 75
1107 1250l. Symbolic lymph system . . . . 1·10 1·10
1108 2000l. People gazing at "explosion" of flowers . . 1·80 1·80

290 "The Annunciation" (Johannes of Ienzenstein)

291 Pope, Statue of Virgin Mary and Zagreb Cathedral

1995. Holy Year 2000 (1st issue). Illustrations from illuminated manuscripts in Vatican Apostolic Library. Multicoloured.
1109 400l. Type **290** 35 35
1110 850l. "Nativity" (from King Matthias I Corvinus's breviary) 75 75
1111 1250l. "Flight into Egypt" (from Book of Hours) . . 1·10 1·10
1112 2000l. "Jesus among the Teachers" (Pietro Lombardo) . . . . 2·20 2·20

See also Nos. 1132/5, 1167/70, 1197/1200, 1231/4, 1242/9 and 1265/8.

1995. Pope John Paul II's Journeys (13th series). Multicoloured.
1113 1000l. Type **291** (Croatia) 90 90
1114 2000l. Pope, Genoa Lantern, Orvieto Cathedral and Valley of the Temples, Agrigento (Italy) . . . . 1·80 1·80

292 Marco Polo receiving Golden Book from the Great Khan

1996. 700th Anniv of Marco Polo's Return from China. Multicoloured.
1115 350l. Type **292** 30 30
1116 850l. The Great Khan giving alms to poor, Cambaluc 60 60
1117 1250l. Marco Polo delivering Pope Gregory X's letter to the Great Khan 90 90
1118 2500l. Marco Polo in Persia listening to Nativity story 2·20 2·20
MS1119 138 × 100 mm. 2000l. black (Marco Polo) (vert) . . . . . 1·90 1·90

293 Angel with Crosses

294 Gianna Molla (surgeon)

1996. Anniversaries. Multicoloured.
1120 1250l. Type **293** (400th Anniv of Union of Brest-Litovsk) 90 90
1121 2000l. Latin and Byzantine mitres and Tree of Life (350th Anniv of Union of Uzhorod) . . . . 1·60 1·60

1996. Europa. Famous Women.
1122 **294** 750l. blue 65 75
1123 – 850l. brown 75 80
DESIGN: 850l. Edith Stein (Carmelite nun).

295 "Sun and Steel" **297** "Baptism of Jesus"

296 Wawel Cathedral

1996. Cent of Modern Olympic Games. Mult.
1124 1250l. Type **295** . . . . . 1·80 1·80
1125 1250l. "Solar Plexus" . . . 1·80 1·80
1126 1250l. Hand and golden beams . . . . 1·80 1·80
1127 1250l. "Speculum Aevi" (athlete and shadow) . . 1·80 1·80
1128 1250l. Hercules . . . . . . 1·80 1·80

1996. 50th Anniv of Ordination of Karol Wojtyla (Pope John Paul II) at Wawel Cathedral, Crakow, Poland. Multicoloured.
1129 500l. Type **296** 75 75
1130 750l. Pope John Paul II . . 1·10 1·10
1131 1250l. St. John Lateran's Basilica in Rome (seat of Bishop of Eternal City) 1·80 1·80

1996. Holy Year 2000 (2nd issue). Illustrations from 13th-century illuminated New Testament in Vatican Apostolic Library. Multicoloured.
1132 550l. Type **297** 40 40
1133 850l. "Temptation in the Desert" 60 60
1134 1500l. "Cure of a Leper" . . 1·10 1·10
1135 2500l. "Jesus the Teacher" . 2·30 2·30

298 Philippines, Papua New Guinea, Australia and Sri Lanka

1996. Pope John Paul II's Journeys (14th series).
1136 **298** 250l. blue and black . . 20 20
1137 – 500l. green and black . . 35 35
1138 – 750l. green and black . . 55 55
1139 – 1000l. brown and black 75 75
1140 – 2000l. grey and black . . 1·80 1·80
1141 – 5000l. pink and black . . 4·25 4·25
DESIGNS: 500l. Czech Republic and Poland; 750l. Belgium; 1000l. Slovakia; 2000l. Cameroun, South Africa and Kenya; 5000l. United States of America and United Nations Headquarters.

299 "Nativity" (Murillo)

1996. Christmas.
1142 **299** 750l. multicoloured . . . 75 65

300 Pope St. Celestine V **302** Halberdier

301 Travelling Carriage

1996. Saints' Anniversaries. Multicoloured.
1143 1250l. Type **300** (700th death) 60 60
1144 1250l. St. Alfonso Maria de' Liguori (founder of Redemptorists Order) (300th birth) 70 70

1997. Papal Transport. Multicoloured.
1145 50l. Type **301** 10 10
1146 100l. Graham Paige motor car 10 10
1147 300l. Ceremonial berlin (carriage) 20 20
1148 500l. Citroen Lictoria VI motor car 35 35
1149 750l. Grand ceremonial berlin 55 55
1150 850l. Mercedes Benz motor car 60 60
1151 1000l. Semi-ceremonial berlin 85 85
1152 1250l. Mercedes Benz 300 SEL motor car . . . . . 1·10 1·10
1153 2000l. Travelling carriage (different) . . . . . . 1·60 1·60
1154 4000l. Fiat Campagnola . . 3·75 3·75

1997. Europa. The Swiss Guard. Multicoloured.
1155 750l. Type **302** 55 55
1156 850l. Swordsman 60 60

303 Aristotle describing the Species ("De Historia Animalium" by Aristotle)

1997. "Looking at The Classics" Exhibition. Illustrations from manuscripts of the Classics. Multicoloured.
1157 500l. Type **303** 35 35
1158 750l. Bacchus riding dragon ("Metamorphoses" by Ovid) 65 65
1159 1250l. General reviewing his soldiers ("Iliad" by Homer) . . . . 1·00 1·00
1160 2000l. Horsemen leaving Canne ("Ab Urbe Condita" by Livy) . . . . 1·60 1·60
MS1161 100 × 135 mm. 1000l. Male and female masks; 1000l. Two female masks; 1000l. Two male masks (Comedies by Terence) 2·10 2·10

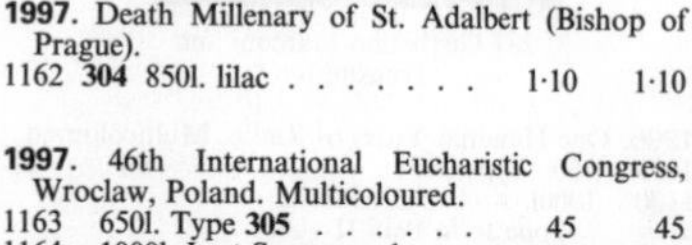

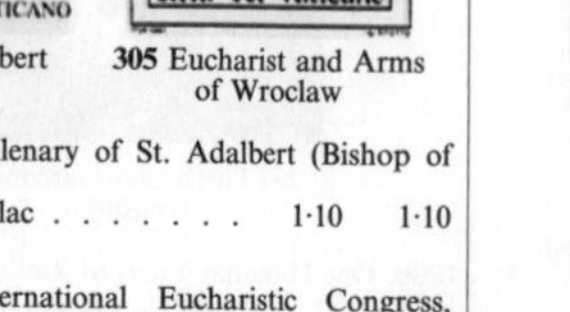

304 St. Adalbert **305** Eucharist and Arms of Wroclaw

1997. Death Millenary of St. Adalbert (Bishop of Prague).
1162 **304** 850l. lilac . . . . 1·10 1·10

1997. 46th International Eucharistic Congress, Wroclaw, Poland. Multicoloured.
1163 650l. Type **305** 45 45
1164 1000l. Last Supper and Congress emblem 80 80
1165 1250l. Wroclaw Cathedral and the Holy Dove . . . 90 90
1166 2500l. Cross, doves and hands around globe . . . 2·20 2·20

306 Jesus healing Paralysed Man **307** St. Ambrose and Ambrosiana Basilica

1997. Holy Year 2000 (3rd issue). Illustrations from 14th-century illuminated New Testament in Vatican Apostolic Library. Multicoloured.
1167 400l. Type **306** 30 30
1168 800l. Calming the tempest 65 65
1169 1300l. Feeding the five thousand . . . . 1·60 1·60
1170 3600l. Peter acclaiming Christ as the Messiah . . 4·00 4·00

1997. 1600th Death Anniv of St. Ambrose, Bishop of Milan.
1171 **307** 800l. multicoloured . . . 1·10 1·10

308 Pope Paul VI **309** Guatemala Pyramid and Amerindian Boy

1997. Birth Centenary of Pope Paul VI.
1172 **308** 900l. multicoloured . . . 65 65

1997. Aid for Earthquake Victims. As No. **MS**958 but additionally inscr "PRO TERREMOTATI 1997" in the margin.
MS1173 100 × 135 mm. As No. **MS**958 (sold at 8000l.) . . . . 15·00 16·00
No. **MS**1173 was issued in an illustrated folder.

1997. Pope John Paul II's Journeys (15th series). Multicoloured.
1174 400l. Type **309** (Guatemala, Nicaragua, El Salvador, Venezuela) 30 30
1175 900l. St. Francis de Paul and St. Olive's Cathedral and Mosque (Tunisia) . . 65 65
1176 1000l. St. Nicholas's Cathedral, Ljubljana, and Blessed Lady's monument, Maribor (Slovenia) . . . 75 75
1177 1300l. Paderborn Cathedral and Brandenburg Gate, Berlin (Germany) 95 95
1178 2000l. St. Martin's Abbey, Pannonhalma, and St. Stephen's crown (Hungary) . . . . 1·80 1·80
1179 4000l. Reims Cathedral, baptism of Clovis and St. Martin of Tours (France) . . . . 3·75 3·75

310 "Madonna of the Belt" (detail of altarpiece, Gozzoli)

1997. Christmas. 500th Death Anniv of Benozzo Gozzoli (artist).
1180 **310** 800l. multicoloured . . . 3·75 3·75

311 Pope Boniface VIII (1300) **312** St. Peter

1998. Popes and their Holy Years (1st series). Multicoloured.
1181 200l. Type **311** 20 20
1182 400l. Clement VI (1350) . . 30 30
1183 500l. Boniface IX (1390 and 1400) 35 35
1184 700l. Martinus V (1423) . . 50 50
1185 800l. Nicholas V (1450) . . 75 75
1186 900l. Sistus IV (1475) . . . 90 90
1187 1300l. Alexander VI (1500) 1·30 1·30
1188 3000l. Clement VII (1525) 4·00 4·00
See also Nos. 1213/20 and 1255/63.

1998. Europa. National Festival. The Feast of St. Peter and St. Paul. Multicoloured.
1189 800l. Type **312** 65 80
1190 900l. St. Paul 80 85
The designs are details from the Stefaneschi Triptych by Giotto.

313 Angel **315** Turin Shroud

314 Entry into Jerusalem

1998. Musical Angels from "The Ascension" by Melozzo da Forli in the Basilica of the Apostles, Rome. Multicoloured.
1191 450l. Type **313** 35 35
1192 650l. Angel playing lute . . 45 45
1193 800l. Angel playing drum 60 60
1194 1000l. Angel playing viol . . 90 90
1195 1300l. Angel playing violin 1·20 1·20
1196 2000l. Angel with tamborine 2·00 2·00

1998. Holy Year 2000 (4th issue). Illustrations from the illuminated New Testament in Vatican Apostolic Library. Multicoloured.
1197 500l. Type **314** 35 35
1198 800l. Washing of the Apostles' feet 60 60
1199 1500l. The Last Supper . . 1·00 1·00
1200 3000l. The Crucifixion . . . 2·75 2·75

1998. Exhibition of the Holy Shroud, Turin Cathedral.
1201 **315** 900l. white, brown and green 75 75
1202 – 2500l. black, pink and green . . . . 2·20 2·20
DESIGN: 2500l. Turin Cathedral.

316 Pope John Paul II and his Message

1998. "Italia 98" International Stamp Exhibition, Milan (1st issue). Stamp Day.
1203 **316** 800l. multicoloured . . . 1·10 1·10
See also No. 1204.

317 "The Good Shepherd"

1998. "Italia 90" International Stamp Exhibition, Milan (2nd issue). Art Day. T **317** and similar designs showing sculptures from sarcophagi. Multicoloured.
1204 900l. Type **317** 75 75
MS1205 106 × 130 mm. 600l. Peter's Denial; 900l. Praying woman; 1000l. Christ with the Cross and two Apostles . . . . 3·00 3·00

318 Pope and War Refugees
319 "Nativity" (Giulio Clovio)

1998. Pope John Paul II's Journeys (16th series). Multicoloured.
1206 300l. Type **318** (Bosnia and Herzegovina) 20 20
1207 600l. Kneeling in front of statue of Jesus (Czech Republic) 45 45
1208 800l. With girls (Lebanon) 60 60
1209 900l. Welcome by garlanded girls (Poland) 65 65
1210 1300l. With young people (France) 95 95
1211 5000l. With children (Brazil) 3·75 3·75

1998. Christmas.
1212 **319** 800l. multicoloured . . . 65 65

1999. Popes and their Holy Years (2nd series). As T **311**. Multicoloured.
1213 300l. Julius III (1550) . . . 35 35
1214 600l. Gregory XIII (1575) 55 55
1215 800l. Clement VIII (1600) 75 75
1216 900l. Urban VIII (1625) . . 90 90
1217 1000l. Innocent X (1650) . . 1·10 1·10
1218 1300l. Clement X (1675) . . 1·30 1·30
1219 1500l. Innocent XII (1700) 1·60 1·60
1220 2000l. Benedict XIII (1725) 2·50 2·50

320 Rose "John Paul II"

1999. Europa. Parks and Gardens. Multicoloured.
1221 800l. Type **320** 60 60
1222 900l. Water lilies (Fountain of the Frogs, Vatican Gardens) 65 65

321 Father Pio

1999. Beatification of Father Pio da Pietrelcina (Capuchin friar who bore the stigmata). Multicoloured.
1223 800l. Type **321** 60 60
MS1224 86 × 115 mm. 300l. Monastery Church, San Giovanni Rotondo (29 × 39 mm); 600l. San Giovanni Rotondo new church (29 × 39 mm); 900l. Type **321** (59 × 39 mm) . . . . 1·30 1·30

322 Bethlehem

1999. Sacred Places in the Holy Land. Illustrations from "The Holy Land" by I. Messmer. Multicoloured.
1225 200l. Type **322** 20 20
1226 500l. Nazareth 35 35
1227 800l. Lake Tiberius 60 60
1228 900l. Jerusalem 65 65
1229 1300l. Mount Tabor 95 95
MS1230 110 × 86 mm. 1000l. × 4, composite design of map of the Holy Land (from 17th-century Geographia Blaviana) (each 50 × 38 mm) . . . . 2·75 2·75

323 Deposition from the Cross

1999. Holy Year 2000 (5th issue). Illustrations from illuminated New Testament in Vatican Apostolic Library. Multicoloured.
1231 400l. Type **323** 30 30
1232 700l. The Resurrection . . . 50 50
1233 1300l. Pentecost 95 95
1234 3000l. The Last Judgement 2·20 2·20

324 Refugees

1999. Kosovo Relief Fund.
1235 **324** 3600l. black . . . . . . 2·50 2·50

325 Visit to Cuba
326 Hot Air Balloons, Jigsaw Puzzle of Europe and Magnifying Glass

1999. Pope John Paul II's Journeys (17th series). Multicoloured.
1236 600l. Type **325** 45 45
1237 800l. Stole over hands and staff (Nigeria) 55 55
1238 900l. Dove, cathedral and disabled people (Austria) 75 75
1239 1300l. With crucifix and statue (Croatia) . . . . . 1·10 1·10
1240 2000l. Quirinal Palace, Rome (Italy) . . . . . . 2·00 2·00

1999. 50th Anniv of Council of Europe.
1241 **326** 1200l. multicoloured . . 60 60

327 "The Cherubim at the Doors of Paradise" and "The Banishment from the Garden of Eden"

1999. Holy Year 2000 (6th issue). Opening of Holy Door, St. Peter's Basilica. Door panels. Mult.
1242 200l. Type **327** 20 20
1243 300l. "The Annunciation" and "Angel" 20 20
1244 400l. "Baptism of Christ" and "Straying Sheep" . . 30 30
1245 500l. "The Merciful Father" and "Curing Paralysed Man" 35 35
1246 600l. "The Penitent Woman" and "The Obligation to Forgive" . . 45 45
1247 800l. "Peter's Denial" and "A Thief in Paradise" . . 65 65
1248 1000l. "Jesus appears to Thomas" and "Jesus appears to the Eleven" . . 90 90
1249 1200l. "Jesus appears to Saul" and "Opening of the Holy Door" . . . 1·10 1·10
MS1250 106 × 142 mm. As Nos. 1242/9 . . . . 4·50 4·50

328 St. Joseph (detail)

1999. Christmas. "St. Joseph, the Virgin Mary and the Holy Child" (Giovanni di Petro). Multicoloured.
1251 500l. Type **328** 35 35
1252 800l. Holy Child (detail) . . 55 55
1253 900l. Virgin Mary (detail) 90 90
1254 1200l. Complete painting . . 1·10 1·10

2000. Popes and their Holy Years (3rd series). As T **311**. Multicoloured.
1255 300l. Benedict XIV (1750) 30 30
1256 400l. Pius VI (1775) 35 35
1257 500l. Leo XII (1825) 45 45
1258 600l. Pius IX (1875) 55 55
1259 700l. Leo XIII (1900) . . . 65 65
1260 800l. Pius XI (1925) 75 75
1261 1200l. Pius XII (1950) . . . 1·10 1·10
1262 1500l. Paul VI (1975) . . . 1·30 1·30
1263 2000l. John Paul II (2000) 2·00 2·00
MS1264 137 × 103 mm. 2000l. John Paul II resting face on hand . . 1·50 1·50

329 St. Peter's Basilica

2000. Holy Year 2000 (7th issue). Multicoloured.
1265 800l. Type **329** 55 55
1266 1000l. St. John Lateran Basilica 75 75
1267 1200l. St. Mary Major Basilica 90 90
1268 2000l. St. Paul-outside-the-Walls Basilica . . . . . . 1·50 1·50

330 Embroidered Altar Frontal, Holar Cathedral

2000. Millenary of Christianity in Iceland.
1269 **330** 1500l. multicoloured . . 1·10 1·10

331 "Building Europe"
332 Pope John Paul II

2000. Europa.
1270 **331** 1200l. multicoloured . . 90 90

2000. 80th Birthday of Pope John Paul II.
1271 **332** 800l. lilac 55 55
1272 – 1200l. blue 90 90
1273 – 2000l. green . . . . . . 1·50 1·50
DESIGNS: 1200l. Black Madonna of Czestochowa; 2000l. Pastoral Staff.

333 "The Calling of St. Peter and St. Andrew" (Domenico Ghirlandaio)

2000. Restoration of the Sistine Chapel (1st series). Multicoloured.
1274 500l. Type **333** 35 35
1275 1000l. "The Trials of Moses" (Sandro Botticelli) 75 75

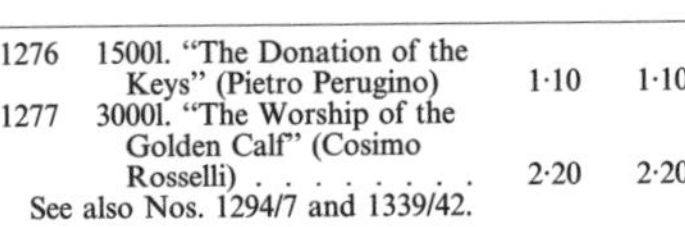
1276 1500l. "The Donation of the Keys" (Pietro Perugino) 1·10 1·10
1277 3000l. "The Worship of the Golden Calf" (Cosimo Rosselli) . . . . 2·20 2·20
See also Nos. 1294/7 and 1339/42.

334 Congress Emblem
335 Pope John Paul II and Youths' Faces

2000. 47th International Eucharistic Congress, Rome.
1278 **334** 1200l. multicoloured . . 1·10 1·10

2000. 15th World Youth Day, Rome. Multicoloured.
(a) Ordinary gum.
1279 800l. Type **335** 55 55
1280 1000l. Girl waving flag . . . 65 65
1281 1200l. Youths' cheering . . 70 90
1282 2000l. Youth waving flag . . 1·20 1·20

(b) Self-adhesive.
1283 1000l. As No. 1280 . . . . 75 75

336 Pope and Children
337 Pope John XXIII

2000. Pope John Paul II's Journeys (18th series). Multicoloured.
1284 1000l. Type **336** (Mexico and United States of America) 75 75
1285 1000l. Pope praying, building and children waving (Rumania) 75 75
1286 1000l. Holding Pastoral Staff (Poland) 75 75
1287 1000l. Pope and Bishop Anton Martin Slomsek (Slovenia) 75 75
1288 1000l. Pope, churches and crowd (India and Georgia) 75 75

2000. Beatification of Pope John XXIII.
1289 **337** 1200l. multicoloured . . 90 90

338 Nativity (fresco)

2000. Christmas. Designs showing Fresco by Giotto from St. Francis Basilica. Multicoloured.
1290 800l. Type **338** 55 55
1291 1200l. Baby Jesus (detail) . . 90 90
1292 1500l. Mary (detail) . . . . 1·10 1·10
1293 2000l. Joseph (detail) . . . 1·50 1·50

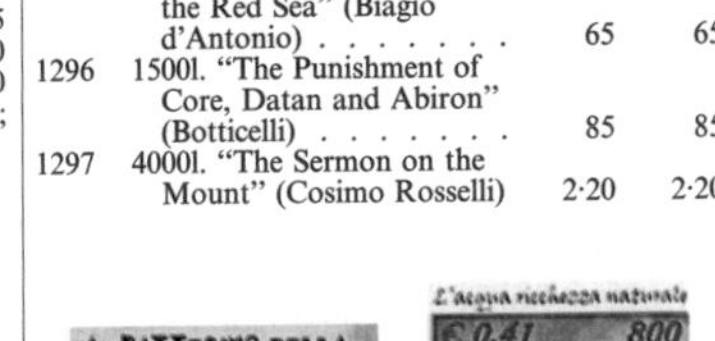
2001. Restoration of the Sistine Chapel (2nd series). As T **333**. Multicoloured.
1294 800l. "The Baptism of Christ" (Pietro Perugino) 45 45
1295 1200l. "The Passage through the Red Sea" (Biagio d'Antonio) 65 65
1296 1500l. "The Punishment of Core, Datan and Abiron" (Botticelli) 85 85
1297 4000l. "The Sermon on the Mount" (Cosimo Rosselli) 2·20 2·20

339 Freedom of St. Gregory
340 Hands holding Water and Globe

2001. 1700th Anniv of the Adoption of Christianity in Armenia. Multicoloured.
1298 1200l. Type **339** 65 65
1299 1500l. St. Gregory making Agatangel write 85 85
1300 2000l. St. Gregory and King Tirade meet Emperor Constantine and Pope Sylvester I . . . . 1·10 1·10

2001. Europa. Water Resources. Multicoloured.
1301 800l. Type **340** 45 45
1302 1200l. Hand and catching rain water 65 65

341 Verdi and Score of *Nabucco*

2001. Death Centenary of Giuseppe Verdi (composer). Multicoloured.
1303 800l. Type **341** 45 45
1304 1500l. Verdi and character from *Aida* 85 85
1305 2000l. Verdi and scene from *Otello* . . . . 1·10 1·10

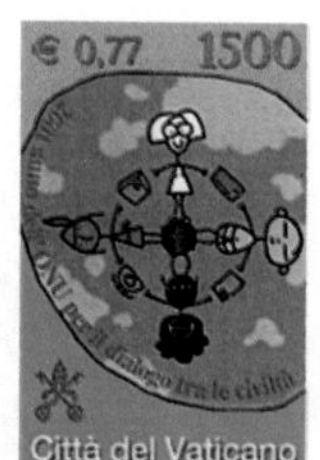

342 Children encircling Globe

2001. U.N. Year of Dialogue between Civilizations.
1306 **342** 1500l. multicoloured . . 85 85

343 Couple feeding Poor Man

2001. Cancellation of Foreign Debt of Poor Countries. Showing illustrations from "Works of Corporal Mercy" (15th-century panels by Carlo di Camerino). Multicoloured.
1307 200l. Type **343** 20 20
1308 400l. Giving alms 20 20
1309 800l. Giving clothing . . . 45 45
1310 1000l. Women caring for sick man 55 55
1311 1500l. Man visiting prisoner 85 85

344 Mount Sinai, Monastery of Holy Catherine and Pope

2001. Pope John Paul II's Journeys (19th series). The Holy Land. Multicoloured.
1312 500l. Type **344** 30 30
1313 800l. Pope before Crucifix, Mount Nebo 45 45
1314 1200l. Pope celebrating Mass 65 65
1315 1500l. Pope at prayer Holy Sepulchre 85 85
1316 5000l. Pope praying at Shrine of Fatima . . . . 2·75 2·75
MS1317 85 × 115 mm. 3000l. Pope at Western Wall, Jerusalem (35 × 27 mm) . . . . 2·10 2·10

345 "The Annunciation"

2001. Christmas. Designs showing scenes from "Life of Christ" (enamel, Egino G. Weinert). Multicoloured.
1318 800l. Type **345** 45 45
1319 1200l. "The Nativity" . . . 65 65
1320 1500l. "Adoration of the Magi" 85 85

346 Fibula, 675–650 B.C.

2001. Etruscan Museum Exhibits. Multicoloured.
1321 800l. Type **346** 35 35
1322 1200l. 6th-century earrings 55 55
1323 1500l. Embossed Greek stud, 425–400 B.C 70 70
1324 2000l. 3rd-century Greek head of Medusa 90 90

347 Emblem

2001. 80th Anniv of Guiseppe Toniolo Institute for Higher Studies and the Catholic University of the Sacred Heart.
1325 **347** 1200l. blue and red . . . 65 65

348 Our Lady of Women in Labour (14th-century fresco) **349** Pope Clement XI

2002. Our Lady in the Vatican Basilica. Multicoloured.
1326 8c. Type **348** 15 15
1327 15c. Our Lady with people praying (mosaic) 20 20
1328 23c. Our Lady at the Tomb of Pius XII (15th-century fresco) 30 30
1329 31c. Our Lady of the Fever (13th-century) 45 45
1330 41c. Our Lady of the Slap 60 60
1331 52c. Mary Immaculate (mosaic) 75 75
1332 62c. Our Lady of Christians 90 90
1333 77c. The Virgin of the Deesis . . . . 1·10 1·10
1334 €1.03 L'Addolorata (painting, Lippo Memmi) 1·40 1·40
1335 €1.55 Presentation of Mary at the Temple (mosaic) . . 2·20 2·20

2002. 300th Anniv of Pontifical Ecclesiastical Academy, Rome.
1336 **349** 77c. purple . . . . . . 1·10 1·10
1337 – 77c. green (46 × 33 mm) 1·10 1·10
1338 – 77c. purple . . . . . . 1·10 1·10
DESIGNS: No. 1337 Facade of Piazza della Minerva Institute, Rome; 1338 Pope John Paul II.

2002. Restoration of the Sistine Chapel (3rd series). As T **333**. Multicoloured.
1339 26c. "The Temptation of Christ" (Botticelli) 35 35
1340 41c. "The Last Supper" (Cosimo Rosselli) 60 60
1341 77c. "Moses' Journey into Egypt" (Pietro Perugino) 1·10 1·10
1342 €1.55 "The Last Days of Moses" (Luca Signorelli) 2·20 2·20

350 Regina Viarum (Appian Way) and 1852 Papal States Stamp

2002. Centenary of Pontifical Stamps.
1343 **350** 41c. deep brown, purple and brown 60 60
1344 – 52c. multicoloured . . . 75 75
1345 – €1.03 blue, indigo and green . . . . 1·40 1·40
MS1346 €1.55 brown, buff and purple . . . . 2·30 2·30
DESIGNS: No. 1344, Cassian Way and 1868 80ch. Papal States stamp; 1345, Porta Angelica, Vatican and 1929 Vatican City State 10ch. stamp. 30 × 30 mm (circular)—MS1346, Courtyard, Palazzo Madama, Rome.

351 "Christ and the Circus" (Aldo Carpi)

2002. Europa. Circus. Multicoloured.
1347 41c. Type **351** 60 60
1348 62c. Christ with clown (detail of "Christ and the Circus") 90 90

352 Crucifix, St. Dominic Church, Arezzo

2002. 700th Death Anniv of Cenni di Pepo (Cimabue) (artist). Showing the Crucifix and details thereof. Multicoloured.
1349 41c. Type **352** 60 60
1350 62c. Jesus 90 90
1351 77c. Mary . . . . 1·10 1·10
1352 €1.03 John the Baptist . . 1·40 1·40

353 Pope Leo IX and Wall Inscription

2002. Birth Millenary of Pope Leo IX. Multicoloured.
1353 41c. Type **353** 60 60
1354 62c. Arrival in Rome as pilgrim and coronation as Pope 90 90
1355 €1.29 Leo IX in chains . . 1·90 1·90

354 "The Nativity" (15th-century painting in style of Di Baldese) (⅔-size illustration)

2002. Christmas.
1356 **354** 41c. multicoloured . . . 60 60
A stamp of a similar design was issued by New Zealand.

355 Pope John Paul II (Malta)

2002. Journeys of Pope John Paul II in 2001. Multicoloured.
1357 41c. Type **355** 60 60
1358 62c. Praying (Ukraine) . . . 90 90
1359 €1.55 Wearing mitre (Kazakhstan) . . . . . . 2·20 2·20

356 Pope John Paul II on Balcony of St. Peter's Basilica, 1978

2003. 25th Anniv of the Pontificate of Pope John Paul II (1st issue). Multicoloured.
1360 41c. Type **356** 60 60
1361 41c. Celebrating mass, Victory Square, Warsaw, 1979 . . . . 60 60
1362 41c. Addressing young people, Parc des Princes Stadium, Paris, 1980 . . . 60 60
1363 41c. Assassination attempt, St. Peter Square, 1981 . . . 60 60
1364 41c. Giving homily surrounded by flowers, Portugal, 1982 . . . . . 60 60
1365 41c. Kneeling in front of Holy Doors, start of Holy Year of Redemption, 1983
1366 41c. Meeting Sandro Pertini, President of Italy, 1984 60 60
1367 41c. International Youth Day, Rome, 1985 . . . . 60 60
1368 41c. First visit of Pope to Synagogue, 1986 . . . . 60 60
1369 41c. Inaugurating Year of Mary, 1987 . . . . . . 60 60
1370 41c. Visiting European Parliament, Strasbourg, 1988 . . . . 60 60
1371 41c. Meeting President Mikhail Gorbachev, Soviet Union, 1989 . . . 60 60
1372 41c. Visiting lepers in Guinea-Bissau, 1990 . . . 60 60
1373 41c. Addressing Bishop's Synod, 1991 . . . . . . 60 60
1374 41c. Pronouncing the Catechism, 1992 . . . . 60 60
1375 41c. Enthroned, Assissi, 1993 . . . . 60 60
1376 41c. Celebrating Mass in the Sistine Chapel, 1994 . . 60 60
1377 41c. Addressing the United Nations, 1995 . . . . . 60 60
1378 41c. Walking through the Brandenburg Gate with Chancellor Helmut Kohl, 1996 . . . . 60 60
1379 41c. Celebrating Mass in Sarajevo, 1997 . . . . . 60 60
1380 41c. With Fidel Castro, Cuba, 1998 . . . . . . 60 60
1381 41c. Opening door, Christmas, 1999 . . . . . 60 60
1382 41c. With young people, World Youth Day, Rome, 2000 . . . . 60 60
1383 41c. Closing door of St. Peter's Basilica, 2001 60 60
1384 41c. Visiting the Italian Parliament, 2002 . . . . 60 60
Stamps of the same design were issued by Poland.

357 Pope John Paul II

358 Dove (Holy Year 1975)

2003. 25th Anniv of the Pontificate of Pope John Paul II (2nd issue). Self-adhesive.
1385 **357** €2.58 silver . . . . . . 2·60 2·60
A stamp of the same design was issued by Poland.

2003. Europa. Poster Art. Multicoloured.
1386 41c. Type **358** 60 60
1387 62c. St. Cyril and St. Methodius 90 90

359 St. Sixtus ordaining St. Lawrence

2003. Paintings from the Niccolina Chapel by Friar Giovanni da Fiesole (Beato Angelico). Multicoloured.
1388 41c. Type **359** 60 60
1389 62c. St. Stephen preaching 90 90
1390 77c. St. Lawrence on trial 1·10 1·10
1391 €1.03 Stoning of St. Stephen . . . . 1·40 1·40

360 St. George slaying Dragon

362 Mother Teresa

361 Dragon

2003. 1700th Anniv of Death of St. George.
1392 **360** 62c. multicoloured . . . 90 90

2003. Animal Paintings from the Vatican Basilica. Multicoloured.
1393 21c. Type **361** 30 30
1394 31c. Camel 40 40
1395 77c. Horse . . . . 1·10 1·10
1396 €1.03 Leopard . . . . . . 1·40 1·40

2003. Beatification of Mother Teresa (humanitarian worker).
1397 **362** 41c. multicoloured . . . 60 60

363 "Blessed are the Pure in Heart"

2003. Artists' Anniversaries. Multicoloured.
1398 41c. Type **363** (death centenary) 60 60
1399 62c. "The Pieta" (Vincent van Gogh) (150th birth anniv) 90 90

364 Josemaria Escriva

2003. Birth Centenary (2002) of Josemaria Escriva De Balaguer (founder of Opus Dei (religious organization)).
1400 **364** 41c. multicoloured . . . 55 55

365 The Nativity

2003. Christmas. 25th Death Anniv of Pope Paul VI (**MS**1402).
1401 **365** 41c. multicoloured . . . 55 55
MS1402 106 × 83 mm. **365** 41c. multicoloured 55 55

366 Orthodox Priests and Pope John Paul II (Bulgaria and Azerbaijan)

2003. Journeys of Pope John Paul II in 2002. Multicoloured.
1403 62c. Type **366** 80 80
1404 77c. Pope John Paul II and World Youth Day emblem (Canada, Guatemala and Mexico City) . . . . 1·00 1·00
1405 €2.55 With raised hand (Poland) . . . . 3·50 3·50

EXPRESS LETTER STAMPS

E 3

1929.
E14 E **3** 2l. red . . . . 20·00 14·50
E15 2l.50 blue . . . . 16·00 18·00

E **12** Vatican City

1933.
E 35 E **12** 2l. brown and red . . . 35 35
E 36 2l.50 brown and blue 35 65
E107 3l.50 blue and red . . 45 55
E108 5l. green and blue . . . 75 1·00

1945. Surch in figures over bars.
E118 E **12** 6l. on 3l.50 blue & red 5·50 2·75
E119 12l. on 5l. green & blue 5·50 2·75

E **28** Matthew Giberti, Bishop of Verona

1946. 400th Anniv of Council of Trent.
E130 E **28** 6l. brown and green . . 20 20
E131 – 12l. sepia and brown 20 20
DESIGN: 12l. Cardinal Gaspare Contarini, Bishop of Belluno.

1949. As Nos. 139/48 (Basilicas), but inscr "ESPRESSO".
E149 40l. grey . . . . 14·50 4·50
E150 80l. brown . . . . 50·00 28·00
DESIGNS—HORIZ: 40l. St. Peter's; 80l. St. John's.

1953. Designs as Nos. 179/89, but inscr "ESPRESSO".
E190 50l. brown and turquoise 20 20
E191 85l. brown and orange . . 35 25
DESIGNS: 50l. St. Peter and tomb; 85l. Pius XII and sepulchre.

1960. Designs as Nos. 326/33 (Works of Mercy), but inscr "ESPRESSO". Centres in brown.
E334 75l. red 10 10
E335 100l. blue 10 10
DESIGN: 75, 100l. Arms of Pope John XXIII between "Justice" and "Hope".

1966. Designs as Nos. 467/76, but inscr "ESPRESSO".
E477 – 150l. brown 10 10
E478 **120** 180l. brown 15 15
DESIGN: 150l. Arms of Pope Paul VI.

PARCEL POST STAMPS

1931. Optd **PER PACCHI**.
P15 **1** 5c. brown on pink 20 55
P16 10c. green on green 20 55
P17 20c. violet on lilac . . . . 1·60 2·50
P18 25c. blue on blue . . . . . 7·25 5·75
P19 30c. black on yellow . . . . 8·00 5·75
P20 50c. black on orange . . . 12·50 5·75
P21 75c. red on grey . . . . . 1·50 5·75
P22 **2** 80c. red . . . . 1·10 5·75
P23 1l.25 blue . . . . 1·50 5·75
P24 2l. brown . . . . 1·10 5·75
P25 2l.50 red . . . . 2·00 5·75
P26 5l. green . . . . 2·20 5·75
P27 10l. black . . . . 1·80 5·75

PARCEL POST EXPRESS STAMPS

1931. Optd **PER PACCHI**.
PE15 E **3** 2l. red . . . . 1·50 5·75
PE16 2l.50 blue . . . . 1·50 5·75

POSTAGE DUE STAMPS

1931. Optd **SEGNATASSE** and cross or surch also.
D15 **1** 5c. brown on pink 20 55
D16 10c. green on green 20 55
D17 20c. violet on lilac . . . . 1·50 1·80
D18 40c. on 30c. black on yell 2·50 4·25
D19 **2** 60c. on 2l. brown . . . . . 33·00 26·00
D20 1l.10 on 2l.50 red . . . . . 6·50 18·00

D **26**

D **49** State Arms

1945. Coloured network shown in brackets.
D107 D **26** 5c. black (yellow) . . 10 10
D108 20c. black (violet) . . 10 10
D109 80c. black (red) . . . 10 10
D110 1l. black (green) . . . 10 10
D111 2l. black (blue) 10 10
D112 5l. black (grey) 15 15

1954. Coloured network shown in brackets.
D199 D **49** 4l. black (red) 10 10
D200 6l. black (green) . . . 15 15
D201 10l. black (yellow) . . 10 10
D202 20l. black (blue) . . . 30 30
D203 50l. black (brown) . . 10 10
D204 70l. black (brown) . . 10 10

D **130**

1968.
D513 D **130** 10l. black on grey . . 10 10
D514 20l. black on blue . . 10 10
D515 50l. black on pink . . 10 10
D516 60l. black on green 10 10
D517 100l. black on buff 10 10
D518 180l. black on mauve 10 10

VEGLIA Pt. 8

During the period of D'Annunzio's Italian Regency of Carnaro (Fiume), separate issues were made for the island of Veglia (now Krk).

100 centesimi = 1 lira.

1920. Nos. 148 etc of Fiume optd **VEGLIA**.
1B 5c. green . . . . 4·50 5·25
2B 10c. red . . . . 10·50 11·50
3B 20c. bistre . . . . 24·00 18·00
4B 25c. blue . . . . 14·50 18·00
5 50 on 20c. bistre . . . . . . 26·00 18·00
6 55 on 5c. green . . . . 26·00 18·00

EXPRESS LETTER STAMPS

1920. Nos. E163/4 of Fiume optd **VEGLIA**.
E7 30c. on 20c. bistre . . . . . 95·00 35·00
E8 50 on 5c. green . . . . 95·00 35·00

VENDA Pt. 1

The Republic of Venda was established on 13 September 1979, being constructed from tribal areas formerly part of the Republic of South Africa. This independence did not receive international political recognition, but the stamps were accepted as valid on international mail.

Venda was reincorporated into South Africa on 27 April 1994.

100 cents = 1 rand.

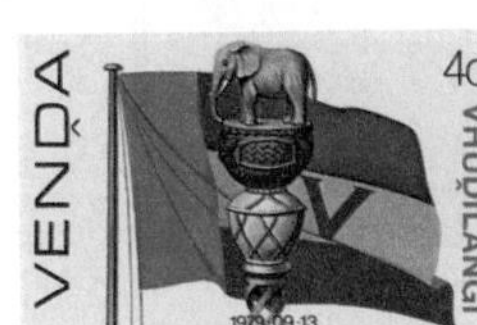

1 Flag and Mace

1979. Independence. Multicoloured.
1 4c. Type **1** 25 25
2 15c. Government Buildings, Thohoyandou 30 60
3 20c. Chief Minister P. R. Mphephu 40 70
4 25c. Coat of arms . . . . . . 60 1·10

2 "Tecomaria capensis"

3 Man drinking Beer

1979. Flowers. Multicoloured.
5 1c. Type **2** 10 10
6a 2c. "Catophractes alexandri" 20 15
7 3c. "Tricliceras longipedunculatum" . . . 30 10
8 4c. "Dissotis princeps" . . . 30 10
9a 5c. "Gerbera jamesonii" . . 30 10
10 6c. "Hibiscus mastersianus" 15 10
11 7c. "Nymphaea caerulea" . . 20 10
12a 8c. "Crinum lugardiae" . . . 30 15
13 9c. "Xerophyta retinervis" . . 20 15
14a 10c. "Hypoxis angustifolia" 40 15
14b 11c. "Combretum microphyllum" 55 15
14c 12c. "Clivia caulescens" . . . 30 15
15 15c. "Pycnostachys urticifolia" 30 15
16 20c. "Zantedeschia jucunda" 75 15
17a 25c. "Leonotis mollis" . . . 50 40
18 30c. "Littonia modesta" . . 40 30
19 50c. "Protea caffra" 40 40
20 1r. "Adenium multiflorum" 75 85
21 2r. "Strelitzia caudata" . . . 1·25 2·00

1980. Wood Carving. Multicoloured.
22 5c. Type **3** 15 15
23 10c. Frying mealies in gourd 25 25
24 15c. King Nebuchadnezzar (horiz) 40 40
25 20c. Python squeezing woman to death (horiz) 50 60

4 Tea Plants in Nursery

1980. Tea Cultivation. Multicoloured.
26 5c. Type **4** 15 10
27 10c. Tea pluckers 20 20
28 15c. Withering in the factory 35 35
29 20c. Cut, twist, curl unit . . . 40 45

5 Young Banana Plants

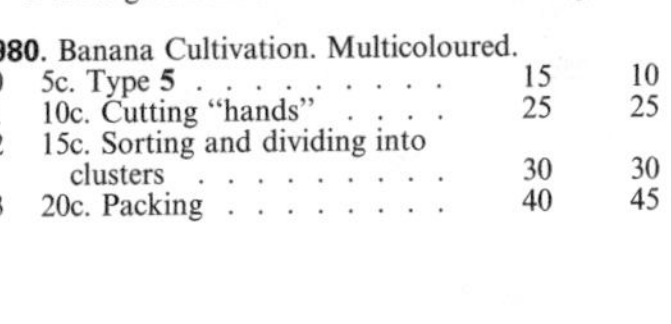

6 "Precis tugela"

1980. Banana Cultivation. Multicoloured.
30 5c. Type **5** 15 10
31 10c. Cutting "hands" 25 25
32 15c. Sorting and dividing into clusters 30 30
33 20c. Packing 40 45

1980. Butterflies. Multicoloured.
34 5c. Type **6** 20 15
35 10c. "Charaxes bohemani" . . 30 40
36 15c. "Catacroptera cloanthe" 40 55
37 20c. "Papilio dardanus" . . . 50 70

7 Collared Sunbird

1981. Sunbirds. Multicoloured.
38 5c. Type **7** 20 15
39 15c. Mariqua sunbird 30 40
40 20c. Southern white-bellied sunbird 35 45
41 25c. Scarlet-chested sunbird . . 35 55

8 Nwandei Dam

1981. Lakes and Waterfalls. Multicoloured.
42 5c. Type **8** 15 10
43 15c. Mahovhohovho Falls . . 30 30
44 20c. Phiphidi Falls 35 35
45 25c. Lake Fundudzi 35 40

9 "Cynorkis kassnerana"

10 Mbila

1981. Orchids. Multicoloured.
46 5c. Type **9** 15 10
47 15c. "Eulophia fridericii" . . . 30 35
48 20c. "Bonatea densiflora" . . 35 45
49 25c. "Mystacidium braybonae" 35 55
MS50 96 × 120 mm. Nos. 46/9 . . 1·25 1·40

1981. Musical Instruments.
51 **10** 5c. orange and black . . . 10 10
52 – 15c. orange and black . . . 25 25
53 – 20c. brown and black . . . 30 35
54 – 25c. brown and black . . . 30 35
DESIGNS: 15c. Phalaphala; 20c. Tshizambi; 25c. Ngoma.

11 Gathering Sisal

1982. Sisal Cultivation. Multicoloured.
55 5c. Type **11** 10 10
56 10c. Drying 20 20
57 20c. Grading 30 35
58 25c. Baling 30 40

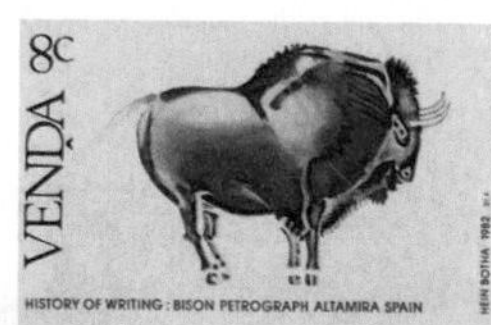
12 Bison Petrograph, Altamira, Spain

1982. History of Writing (1st series). Mult.
59 8c. Type **12** 15 10
60 15c. Petroglyph, Eastern California 30 30
61 20c. Pictograph script (Sumerian tablet) 40 40
62 25c. Bushman burial stone, Humansdorp 45 45
No. 59 is inscr "AHAMIRA" in error.
See also Nos. 75/8, 87/90, 107/10, 139/42, 171/4 and 203/6.

13 "Euphorbia ingens"

1982. Indigenous Trees (1st series). Multicoloured.
63 8c. Type **13** 15 10
64 15c. "Pterocarpus angolensis" 25 30
65 20c. "Ficus ingens" 30 40
66 25c. "Andansonia digitata" . . 40 55
See also Nos. 79/82, 95/8 and 227/30.

14 "Rana angolensis"

1982. Frogs. Multicoloured.
67 8c. Type **14** 15 10
68 15c. "Chiromantis xerampelina" 25 30
69 20c. "Leptopelis sp" 30 40
70 25c. "Ptychadena anchietae" 40 55

15 European Bee Eater

1983. Migratory Birds (1st series). Multicoloured.
71 8c. Type **15** 25 15
72 20c. Tawny eagle ("Steppe Eagle") 50 65
73 25c. Violet starling ("Plum-coloured Starling") 60 75
74 40c. Abdim's stork ("White-bellied Stork") . . . . . . 90 1·50
See also Nos. 91/4.

1983. History of Writing (2nd series). As T **12**. Multicoloured.
75 10c. Indus Valley script . . . 15 10
76 20c. Sumerian cuneiform . . . 20 25
77 25c. Egyptian hieroglyphics . . 25 30
78 40c. Chinese handscroll . . . 50 70

1983. Indigenous Trees (2nd series). As T **13**. Multicoloured.
79 10c. "Gardenia spatulifolia" 15 10
80 20c. "Hyphaene natalensis" . . 25 30
81 25c. "Albizia adianthifolia" . . 30 40
82 40c. "Sesamothamnus lugardii" 40 60

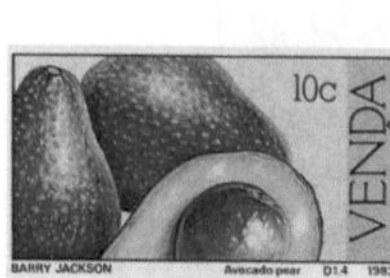
16 Avocado

17 African Paradise Flycatcher ("Paradise Flycatcher")

1983. Subtropical Fruit. Multicoloured.
83 10c. Type **16** 15 10
84 20c. Mango 25 30
85 25c. Papaya 30 40
86 40c. Litchi 40 60

1983. History of Writing (3rd series). As T **12**. Multicoloured.
87 10c. Evolution of cuneiform sign 15 10
88 20c. Evolution of Chinese character 25 30
89 25c. Development of Cretan hieroglyphics 30 40
90 40c. Development of Egyptian hieroglyphics 40 60

1984. Migratory Birds (2nd series). Multicoloured.
91 11c. White stork 30 20
92 20c. Type **17** 50 50
93 25c. Black kite ("Yellow-billed kite") 60 60
94 30c. Wood sandpiper 70 85

1984. Indigenous Trees (3rd series). As T **13**. Mult.
95 11c. "Afzelia quanzensis" . . 15 10
96 20c. "Peltophorum africanum" 25 30
97 25c. "Gyrocarpus americanus" 30 40
98 30c. "Acacia sieberana" . . . 40 55

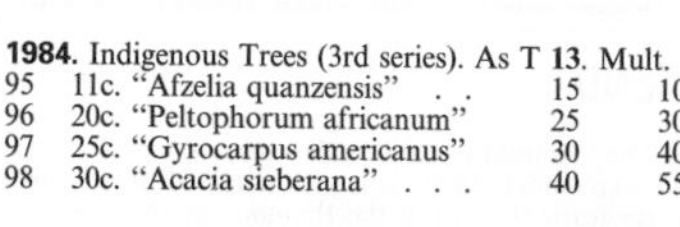

18 Dzata Ruins, Nzhelele Valley

19 White-browed Robin Chat

1984. 5th Anniv of Independence. Multicoloured.
99 11c. Type **18** 15 10
100 25c. Traditional hut 25 30
101 30c. Sub-economical house 30 35
102 45c. Modern home 45 65

1985. Songbirds. Multicoloured.
103 11c. Type **19** (inscr "Heuglin's Robin") 25 20
104 25c. Black-collared barbet . . 35 40
105 30c. African black-headed oriole ("Black-headed Oriole") 40 50
106 50c. Kurrichane thrush . . . 60 80

1985. History of Writing (4th series). As T **12**. Multicoloured.
107 11c. Southern Arabic characters 15 10
108 25c. Phoenician characters . . 25 30
109 30c. Aramaic characters . . . 30 40
110 50c. Canaanite characters . . 50 75

20 Transvaal Red Milkwood

21 "Pellaea dura"

1985. Food from the Veld (1st series). Multicoloured.
111 12c. Type **20** 15 10
112 25c. Buffalo thorn 25 30
113 30c. Wild water melon . . . 30 35
114 50c. Brown ivory 40 60
See also Nos. 163/6.

1985. Ferns. Multicoloured.
115 12c. Type **21** 15 10
116 25c. "Actiniopteris radiata" 25 25
117 30c. "Adiantum hispidulum" 30 35
118 50c. "Polypodium polypodioides" 40 65

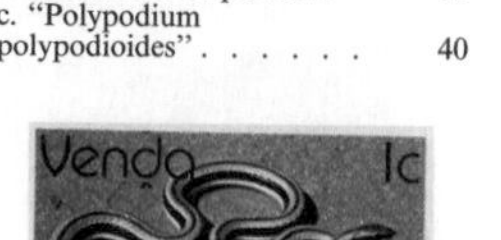
22 Three-lined Grass Snake

1986. Reptiles. Multicoloured.
119 1c. Type **22** 10 10
120 2c. Mole snake 10 10
121 3c. Ornate scrub lizard . . . 10 10
122 4c. Puff adder 10 10
123 5c. Three-lined skink . . . 10 10
124 6c. Egyptian cobra 15 10
125 7c. Blue-tailed kopje skink 15 10
126 8c. Spotted bush snake . . 20 20
127 9c. Yellow-throated plated lizard 20 20
128 10c. Northern lined shovelsnout 20 20
129 14c. Transvaal flat lizard . . 1·25 20
130 15c. Soutpansberg lizard . . 30 20
131 16c. Iguana water leguan . . 60 20
132 18c. Black mamba 75 20
133 20c. Transvaal flat gecko . . 30 20
133b 21c. Flap-necked chameleon 75 20
134 25c. Longtailed garter snake 40 30
135 30c. Tigroid thick-toed gecko 40 35
136 50c. Cape file snake 40 50
137 1r. Soutpansberg girdled lizard . . . . 55 1·00
138 2r. African python . . . . 70 2·00

23 Etruscan Dish

1986. History of Writing (5th series). Multicoloured.
139 14c. Type **23** 15 10
140 20c. Greek inscription, A.D. 70 . . . . 30 30
141 25c. Roman inscription . . . 40 40
142 30c. Cyrllic inscription (Byzantine mosaic) 55 60

24 Planting Pine Seedlings

1986. Forestry. Multicoloured.
143 14c. Type **24** 20 15
144 20c. Mule hauling logs . . . 30 30
145 25c. Off-loading logs at sawmill 40 40
146 30c. Using timber in construction 55 60

25 Maxwell, 1910

1986. FIVA International Veteran Car Rally. Multicoloured.
147 14c. Type **25** 20 15
148 20c. Bentley 4½ litre, 1929 . . 30 30
149 25c. Plymouth Coupe, 1933 40 40
150 30c. Mercedes Benz 220, 1958 55 60

26 Comb Duck

1987. Waterfowl. Multicoloured.
151 14c. Type **26** . . . . 1·00 40
152 20c. White-faced whistling duck . . . . 1·10 70
153 25c. Spur-winged goose (horiz) . . . . 1·25 90
154 30c. Egyptian goose (horiz) 1·40 1·25

27 "Iron Master"

28 Tigerfish

1987. Wood Sculptures by Meshack Matamela Raphalalani. Multicoloured.
155 16c. Type **27** 15 15
156 20c. "Distant Drums" . . . 25 25
157 25c. "Sunrise" 30 30
158 30c. "Obedience" 40 40

1987. Freshwater Fishes. Multicoloured.
159 16c. Type **28** 25 20
160 20c. Barred minnow 35 35
161 25c. Mozambique mouthbrooder 45 45
162 30c. Sharp-toothed catfish . . 55 60

29 Cross-berry

30 Picking Berries

1987. Food from the Veld (2nd series). Multicoloured.
163 16c. Type **29** 20 15
164 30c. Wild date palm 30 30
165 40c. Tree fuchsia 40 40
166 50c. Wild cucumber 50 55

1988. Coffee Industry. Multicoloured.
167 16c. Type **30** 20 20
168 30c. Weighing bags of berries 30 30
169 40c. Drying beans in sun . . 35 35
170 50c. Roasting graded beans 45 45

31 "Universal Love" in Chinese

1988. History of Writing (6th series).
171 **31** 16c. stone, black and red 20 20
172 – 30c. stone, black and red 25 35
173 – 40c. stone, black and red 35 45
174 – 50c. black and gold 45 60
DESIGNS: 30c. "Picture of a lion on a stone" in Devanagari (Indian script); 40c. "Information" in Russian; 50c. "Peace be upon you" in Thuluth (Arabic script).

32 College

1988. 5th Anniv of Shayandima Nurses' Training College. Multicoloured.
175 16c. Type **32** 20 15
176 30c. Students using microscope 30 35
177 40c. Anatomy class 35 40
178 50c. Clinical training 40 50

33 "Fetching Water"

1988. Watercolours by Kenneth Thabo. Mult.
179 16c. Type **33** 20 15
180 30c. "Grinding Maize" . . . 30 35
181 40c. "Offering Food" 35 40
182 50c. "Kindling the Fire" . . 40 50

34 Ndongwana (clay bowls)

1989. Traditional Kitchenware. Multicoloured.
183 16c. Type **34** 15 20
184 30c. Ndilo (wooden porridge bowls) 25 30
185 40c. Mufaro (basket with lid) 30 40
186 50c. Muthatha (dish woven from ilala palm) 40 45

35 Domba 36 Southern Ground Hornbill

1989. Traditional Dances. Multicoloured.
187 18c. Type **35** 15 20
188 30c. Tshinzerere 25 30
189 40c. Malende 30 40
190 50c. Malombo 40 45

1989. Endangered Birds. Multicoloured.
191 18c. Type **36** 80 30
192 30c. Lappet-faced vulture . . 1·10 70
193 40c. Bateleur . . . . 1·40 90
194 50c. Martial eagle . . . . . 1·60 1·25

37 Pres. Gota F. N. Ravele 38 Lion

1989. 10th Anniv of Independence. Multicoloured.
195 18c. Type **37** 20 20
196 30c. Presidential offices . . . 30 30
197 40c. President's residence . . 40 40
198 50c. Thohoyandou Sports Stadium 45 45

1990. Nwanedi National Park. Multicoloured.
199 18c. Type **38** 40 25
200 30c. Common zebra 70 55
201 40c. Cheetah 75 65
202 50c. White rhinoceros . . . . 1·50 1·25

39 Calligraphy 40 "Aloe globuligemma"

1990. History of Writing (7th series).
203 **39** 21c. black and grey 20 15
204 – 30c. black and brown . . . 40 40
205 – 40c. black and green . . . 50 50
206 – 50c. deep blue, blue & black 60 65

DESIGNS: 30c. Part of score for Beethoven's "Moonlight Sonata"; 40c. Characters from personal computer; 50c. Television picture of message transmitted into outer space from Arecibo 1000 radio telescope.

1990. Aloes. Multicoloured.
207 21c. Type **40** 30 25
208 35c. "Aloe aculeata" 50 50
209 40c. "Aloe lutescens" 60 70
210 50c. "Aloe angelica" 70 90

41 "Pseudacraea boisduvalii"

42 Cape Puff-back Flycatchers

1990. Butterflies. Multicoloured.
211 21c. Type **41** 70 40
212 35c. "Papilio nireus" . . . . 1·00 75
213 40c. "Charaxes jasius" . . . 1·10 1·00
214 50c. "Aeropetes tulbaghia" 1·25 1·25

1991. Birds. Paintings by Claude Finch-Davies. Multicoloured.
215 21c. Type **42** 50 40
216 35c. Red-capped robin chat 75 80
217 40c. Collared sunbirds . . . 85 1·00
218 50c. Yellow-streaked greenbul 1·10 1·40

43 Paper made from Pulp

44 Venda Sun Hotel Complex, Thohoyandou

1991. Inventions (1st series). Multicoloured.
219 25c. Type **43** 55 35
220 40c. Magnetic compass . . . 1·00 75
221 50c. Abacus . . . . 1·10 1·00
222 60c. Gunpowder . . . . . . 1·75 1·25
See also Nos. 239/42 and 260/3.

1991. Tourism. Multicoloured.
223 25c. Type **44** 55 35
224 40c. Mphephu resort 85 75
225 50c. Sagole Spa 95 95
226 60c. Luphephe-Nwanedi resort . . . . 1·00 1·25

1991. Indigenous Trees (4th series). As T **13**. Multicoloured.
227 27c. Fever tree 60 35
228 45c. Transvaal beech . . . . 1·00 75
229 65c. Transvaal wild banana 1·10 1·10
230 85c. Sausage tree . . . . . . 1·40 1·50

45 Setting the Web

1992. Clothing Factory. Multicoloured.
231 27c. Type **45** 45 25
232 45c. Knitting 60 55
233 65c. Making up garment . . 90 1·00
234 85c. Inspection of finished product . . . . 1·25 1·50

46 "Apis mellifera"

1992. Bees. Multicoloured.
235 35c. Type **46** 70 40
236 70c. "Anthidium cordiforme" 1·10 90
237 90c. "Megachile frontalis" . . 1·50 1·25
238 1r.05 "Xylocopa caffia" . . . 1·60 1·40

47 Egyptian Plough

1992. Inventions (2nd series). Multicoloured.
239 35c. Type **47** 60 40
240 70c. Early wheel, Mesopotamia . . . . . . 1·00 90
241 90c. Making bricks, Egypt . . 1·40 1·25
242 1r.05 Early Egyptian sailing ship . . . . 1·50 1·40

48 Nile Crocodile

1992. Crocodile Farming. Multicoloured.
243 35c. Type **48** 75 40
244 70c. Egg laying . . . . . . 1·25 90
245 90c. Eggs hatching . . . . . 1·50 1·40
246 1r.05 Mother carrying young 1·60 1·60

49 Burmese

1993. Domestic Cats. Multicoloured.
247 45c. Type **49** . . . . 1·00 45
248 65c. Tabby . . . . 1·40 1·00
249 85c. Siamese . . . . 1·60 1·40
250 1r.05 Persian . . . . 1·75 1·75

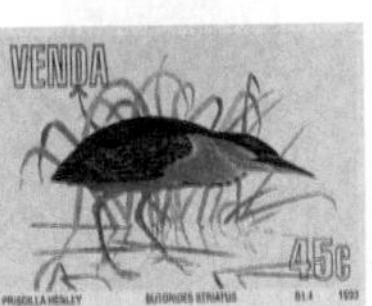
50 Green-backed Heron

51 Punching-out Sole Lining

1993. Herons. Multicoloured.
251 45c. Type **50** 80 50
252 65c. Black-crowned night heron . . . . 1·10 95
253 85c. Purple heron . . . . . 1·40 1·40
254 1r.05 Black-headed heron . . 1·60 1·90
MS255 86 × 132 mm. Nos. 251/4 4·50 4·75

1993. Shoe Factory. Multicoloured.
256 45c. Type **51** 30 25
257 65c. Shaping heel 55 60
258 85c. Joining the upper to inner sole 75 85
259 1r.05 Forming sole . . . . . 90 1·25

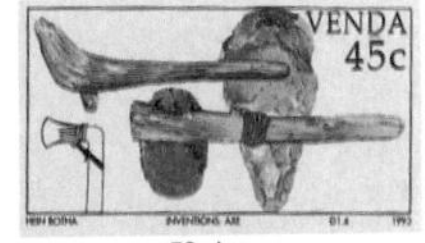
52 Axes

1993. Inventions (3rd series). Multicoloured.
260 45c. Type **52** 30 35
261 65c. Armour 55 65
262 85c. Arches 75 85
263 1r.05 Pont du Gard aqueduct 85 1·25

53 Cocker Spaniel

1994. Dogs. Multicoloured.
264 45c. Type **53** 90 50
265 65c. Maltese . . . . 1·25 1·00
266 85c. Scottish terrier . . . . . 1·50 1·50
267 1r.05 Miniature schnauzer . . 1·90 2·00

54 Savanna Monkey

1994. Monkeys. Multicoloured.
268 45c. Type **54** 75 55
269 65c. Lesser bushbaby . . . . 1·00 1·00
270 85c. Diademed monkey . . . 1·25 1·50
271 1r.05 Thick-tailed bushbaby 1·50 2·00
MS272 119 × 70 mm. Nos. 268/71 4·00 4·50

55 Red-shouldered Glossy Starlings

1994. Starlings. Multicoloured.
273 45c. Type **55** . . . . 1·00 65
274 70c. Violet starlings . . . . 1·50 1·50
275 95c. African red-winged starlings . . . . 1·75 1·90
276 1r.15 Wattled starlings . . . 2·00 2·25

VENEZIA GIULIA AND ISTRIA Pt. 3

Formerly part of Italy. Stamps issued during Allied occupation, 1945–47. The Peace Treaty of 1947 established the Free Territory of Trieste (q.v.) and gave the rest of the territory to Yugoslavia.

For stamps of Austria overprinted Venezia Giulia see AUSTRIAN TERRITORIES ACQUIRED BY ITALY in Volume 1.

100 centesimi = 1 lira.

A. YUGOSLAV OCCUPATION PROVISIONAL ISSUES

Issue for Trieste.

1945. Stamps of Italian Social Republic 1944, surch **1.V.1945 TRIESTE TRST**, five-pointed star and value.
4 – 20c.+1l. on 5c. brn (No. 106) 15 40
5 **13** +1l. on 25c. green 15 40
6 – +1l. on 30c. brown (No. 110) 15 40
7 – +1l. on 50c. violet (No. 111) 15 40
8 – +1l. on 1l. violet (No. 113) 15 40
9 – +2l. on 1l.25 blue (No. 114) 15 40
2 **12** 2+2l. on 25c. green 15 40
10 – +2l. on 3l. green (No. 115) 15 40
11 – 5+5l. on 1l. violet (No. 113) 15 40
12 – 10+10l. on 30c. brn (No. 110) . . . . 1·70 2·75
13 – 20+20l. on 5c. brn (No. 106) 5·00 7·25

Issue for Istria.

In 1945 various stamps of Italy were overprinted "ISTRA" and further surcharged for use in Istria and Pola but they were not issued. However, four of these were further surcharged and issued later.

1945. Stamps of Italy (No. 14) or Italian Social Republic (others) surch **ISTRA** with new value and bars obliterating old surch.
14 **99** 4l. on 2l. on 1l. (No. 249) violet 60 80
15 – 6l. on 1,50l. on 75c. (No. 112) red . . . . . 3·75 5·25
16 – 10l. on 0,10l. on 5c. (No. 106) brown . . . . 21·00 16·00
17 **103** 20l. on 1l. on 50c. (No. 247) violet . . . . 4·00 6·00

Issue for Fiume.

1945. Stamps of Italian Social Republic 1944, surch **3-V-1945 FIUME RIJEKA**, five-pointed star over rising sun and new value.
18 **12** 2l. on 25c. green 15 40
20 – 4l. on 1l. violet (No. 113) 15 40
21 – 5l. on 10c. brn (No. 107) 15 40
22 – 6l. on 10c. brn (No. 107) 20 40
23 **13** 10l. on 25c. green 15 40
24 – 16l. on 75c. red (No. 112) 7·00 8·25
25 E **16** 20l. on 1l.25c. green . . . 1·90 2·50

B. ALLIED MILITARY GOVERNMENT

1945. Stamps of Italy optd **A.M.G. V.G.** in two lines.

(a) Imperial Series.
26 – 10c. brown (No. 241) . . . 10 45
27 – 10c. brown (No. 633) . . . 10 50
28 **99** 20c. red (No. 243) . . . . 15 1·60
29 20c. red (No. 640) 15 75
31 – 60c. red (No. 636) 15 85
32 **103** 60c. green (No. 641) . . . 15 25
33 **99** 1l. violet (No. 637) 20 15
34 – 2l. red (No. 638) 30 15
35 **98** 5l. red (No. 645) 70 25
36 – 10l. violet (No. 646) . . . 80 40
37 **99** 20l. green (No. 257) . . . 1·70 3·25

(b) Stamps of 1945–48.
38 – 25c. blue (No. 649) 15 55
39 – 2l. brown (No. 656) . . . 55 40
40 – 3l. red (No. 657) 40 30
41 – 4l. red (No. 658) 55 30
42 **195** 6l. violet (No. 660) . . . . 1·30 1·70
43 – 20l. purple (No. 665) . . . 36·00 2·75
44 **196** 25l. green (No. 666) . . . 4·50 5·75
45 50l. purple (No. 668) . . . 5·00 8·75
46 **197** 100l. red (No. 669) . . . . 19·00 29·00

1945. Air stamps of Italy, optd as above.
47 **110** 50c. brown (No. 271) . . . 15 30
48 **198** 1l. grey (No. 670) . . . . 40 3·25
49 – 2l. blue (No. 671) . . . . 40 1·40
50 – 5l. green (No. 673) . . . . 2·00 1·60
51 **198** 10l. red (No. 674) . . . . 2·00 1·60
52 – 25l. blue (No. 675) . . . . 2·50 2·00
53 – 25l. brown (No. 676) . . . 20·00 22·00
54 **198** 50l. green (No. 677) . . . 4·25 5·50

EXPRESS LETTER STAMPS

1946. Express Letter Stamps of Italy optd **A.M.G. V.G.** in two lines.
E55 – 10l. blue (No. E680) . . 3·00 1·90
E56 E **200** 30l. violet (No. E683) 7·25 11·50

C. YUGOSLAV MILITARY GOVERNMENT

6 Grapes

7 Roman Amphitheatre, Pula, and Istrian Fishing Vessel

8 Blue-finned Tuna

1945. Inscr "ISTRA SLOVENSKO PRIMORJE – ISTRIA LITTORALE SLOVENO".
74 **6** 0.25l. green 25 35
58 – 0.50l. brown 40 40
59 – 1l. red 40 40
76 – 1l. green 50 60
77 – 1.50l. green 25 35
78 – 2l. green 25 35
100 – 3l. red . . . . 4·00 3·25
62 **7** 4l. blue 35 35
79 4l. red 25 35
80 – 5l. black 25 35
101 **7** 6l. blue . . . . 6·00 6·00
81 – 10l. brown . . . . 90 1·00
65 **8** 20l. purple . . . . 8·50 10·50
82 20l. blue . . . . 3·50 4·25
83 – 30l. mauve . . . . 3·50 5·75
DESIGNS—As Type **6**: 0.50l. Donkey and view; 1l. Rebuilding damaged homes; 1.50l. Olive branch; 2, 3l. Duino Castle near Trieste. As Type **7**: 5l. Birthplace of Vladimir Gortan, Piran; 10l. Ploughing. As Type **8**: 30l. Viaduct over River Solkan.

1946. Nos. 82 and 66 surch.
96 **8** 1 on 20l. blue . . . . 1·40 1·50
97 – 2 on 30l. mauve . . . . . . 1·40 1·50

1947. As Nos. 514 and O540 of Yugoslavia with colours changed, surch **VOJNA UPRAVA JUGOSLAVENSKE ARMIJE** and new value.
102 1l. on 9d. pink 40 50
103 1.50l. on 0.50d. blue 40 50
104 2l. on 9d. pink 40 50
105 3l. on 0.50d. blue 40 50
106 5l. on 9d. pink 50 60
107 6l. on 0.50d. blue 35 45
108 10l. on 9d. pink 50 60
109 15l. on 0.50d. blue 70 80
110 35l. on 9d. pink 70 80
111 50l. on 0.50d. blue . . . . . 90 1·00

POSTAGE DUE STAMPS

1945. Stamps of 1945 surch **PORTO** and value in **Lit**.
D72 **8** 0.50 on 20l. purple . . . . 1·30 1·60
D67 **6** 1l. on 0.25l. green . . . . 10·50 3·50
D73 – 2l. on 30l. mauve . . . . 2·50 3·25
D68 – 4l. on 0.50l. brown . . . . 1·40 1·30
D69 – 8l. on 0.50l. brown . . . . 1·40 1·30
D70 – 10l. on 0.50l. brown . . . 9·25 3·25
D71 – 20l. on 0.50l. brown . . . 10·50 8·00

1946. Stamps of 1945 surch **PORTO** and value expressed in **Lira**.
D90 **6** 1l. on 0.25l. green 60 50
D84 – 1l. on 1l. green (No. 76) . . 40 50
D91 **6** 2l. on 0.25l. green 95 70
D85 – 2l. on 1l. green (No. 76) . . 40 60
D92 **6** 4l. on 0.25l. green 60 50
D86 – 4l. on 1l. green (No. 76) . . 60 80
D93 **8** 10l. on 20l. blue . . . . . 5·00 4·00
D87 – 10l. on 30l. mauve (No. 66) 5·75 4·00
D94 **8** 20l. on 20l. blue . . . . . 11·00 9·25
D88 – 20l. on 30l. mauve (No. 66) 11·00 9·25
D95 **8** 30l. on 20l. blue . . . . . 11·00 9·25
D89 – 30l. on 30l. mauve (No. 66) 11·00 9·75

1947. No. D528 of Yugoslavia with colour changed and surch **Vojna Uprava Jugoslavenske Armije** and value.
D112 1l. on 1d. green . . . . . 95 1·00
D113 2l. on 1d. green 35 40
D114 6l. on 1d. green 35 40
D115 10l. on 1d. green 75 80
D116 30l. on 1d. green 75 80

VENEZUELA Pt. 20

A republic in the N. of S. America, independent since 1811.

1859. 100 centavos = 8 reales = 1 peso.
1879. 100 centesimos = 1 venezolano.
1880. 100 centimos = 1 bolivar.

1 2 3

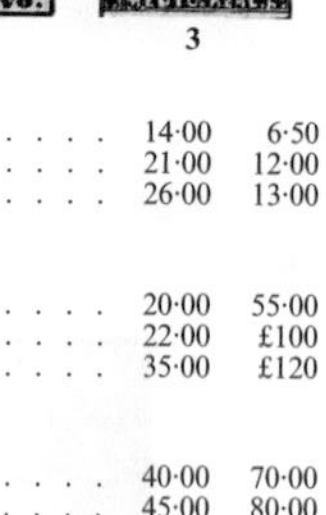

1859. Imperf.
7 **1** ½r. orange . . . . 14·00 6·50
8 1r. blue . . . . 21·00 12·00
9 2r. red . . . . 26·00 13·00

1862. Imperf.
13 **2** ½c. green . . . . 20·00 55·00
14 ½c. lilac . . . . 22·00 £100
15 1c. brown . . . . 35·00 £120

1863. Imperf.
16 **3** ½c. red . . . . 40·00 70·00
17a 1c. grey . . . . 45·00 80·00
21 ½r. yellow . . . . 5·25 2·10
19 1r. blue . . . . 15·00 6·50
20 2r. green . . . . 23·00 18·00

4

5 Bolivar

1866. Imperf.
22 **4** ½c. green £160 £225
23 1c. green £160 £180
24 ½r. red . . . . 6·75 2·00
26 1r. red . . . . 32·00 10·00
27a 2r. yellow . . . . £120 60·00

1871. Optd with inscription in very small letters. Imperf.
58 **5** 1c. yellow 90 30
59d 2c. yellow . . . . 1·25 35
60 3c. yellow . . . . 2·25 70
61 4c. yellow . . . . 2·40 40
62b 5c. yellow . . . . 2·40 40
63b 1r. red . . . . 2·00 30
64a 2r. red . . . . 3·75 75
65a 3r. red . . . . 4·50 75
66a 5r. red . . . . 4·25 85
52a 7r. red . . . . 5·75 2·00
53a 9r. green . . . . 12·50 3·50
54 15r. green . . . . 26·00 7·25
68 20r. green . . . . 60·00 11·00
56 30r. green . . . . £300 95·00
70 50r. green £800 £200

1873. Optd with inscription in very small letters. Imperf.
74a **4** 1c. lilac . . . . 6·50 13·50
75a 2c. green . . . . 32·00 38·00
76a ½r. pink . . . . 22·00 3·00
77a 1r. red . . . . 29·00 7·75
78a 2r. yellow . . . . 95·00 42·00

7 Bolivar

8 Bolivar

1879. New Currency. Optd with inscription in small letters. Imperf.
83 **7** 1c. yellow . . . . 2·25 15
84 5c. yellow . . . . 3·00 30
85 10c. blue . . . . 4·25 40
86 30c. blue . . . . 5·50 1·00
87 50c. blue . . . . 6·50 1·00
88 90c. blue . . . . 27·00 5·50
89 1v. red . . . . 55·00 12·00
90 3v. red . . . . £100 25·00
91 5v. red . . . . £170 60·00

1880. New Currency. Without opt. Perf.
92 **7** 5c. yellow . . . . 1·00 15
93 10c. yellow . . . . 1·60 15
94 25c. yellow . . . . 1·50 20
95 50c. yellow . . . . 3·00 25
96 1b. blue . . . . 7·75 60
97 2b. blue . . . . 12·00 70
98 5b. blue . . . . 28·00 1·25
99 10b. red . . . . £140 45·00
100 20b. red £750 £170
101 25b. red £3500 £425

1880.
107 **8** 5c. blue . . . . 9·75 4·00
108 10c. red . . . . 15·00 7·50
109 25c. yellow . . . . 9·75 4·00
110 50c. brown . . . . 55·00 23·00
106 1b. green . . . . 85·00 32·00

9 Bolivar

10 Bolivar

1882. Various frames. Perf or roul.
111 **9** 5c. green 10 10
112 10c. brown 10 10
113 25c. orange 10 10
114 50c. blue 15 10
115 1b. red 20 10
116 3b. violet 20 10
117 10b. brown 65 50
118 20b. purple 80 55

1882. Various frames. Perf or roul.
119 **10** 5c. blue 50 10
120 10c. brown 50 10
121 25c. brown 90 20
122 50c. green . . . . 2·00 50
123 1b. violet . . . . 3·00 1·25

1892. Surch **RESOLUCION DE 10 DE OCTUBRE DE 1892** and value in circle.
134 **9** 25c. on 5c. green . . . . . 7·00 4·00
138 **10** 25c. on 5c. blue . . . . . 29·00 29·00
135 **9** 25c. on 10c. brown . . . . 7·00 4·00
139 **10** 25c. on 10c. brown . . . 12·50 10·50
136 **9** 1b. on 25c. orange . . . . 8·00 5·00
140 **10** 1b. on 25c. brown . . . . 12·50 10·50
137 **9** 1b. on 50c. blue . . . . . 12·00 5·00
141 **10** 1b. on 50c. green . . . . 13·50 12·50

1893. Optd with coat of arms and diagonal shading.
142 **9** 5c. green 10 10
150 **10** 5c. blue 20 10
143 **9** 10c. brown 10 10
151 **10** 10c. brown 55 65
144 **9** 25c. orange 10 10
152 **10** 25c. brown 35 25
145 **9** 50c. blue 10 10
153 **10** 50c. green 50 20
146 **9** 1b. red 55 20
154 **10** 1b. violet . . . . 1·75 50
147 **9** 3b. violet 50 35
148 10b. brown . . . . 1·90 1·25
149 20b. purple . . . . 1·75 1·25

13 Bolivar

14 Bolivar

1893. Schools Tax stamps.
155 **13** 5c. grey 10 10
156 10c. green 10 10
157 25c. blue 10 10
158 50c. orange 10 10
159 1b. purple 30 10
160 3b. red 45 20
161 10b. violet 55 60
162 20b. brown . . . . 2·25 1·50
See also Nos. 227/35.

1893.
163 **14** 5c. brown 90 10
164 10c. blue . . . . 3·50 65
165 25c. mauve . . . . 16·00 20
166 50c. purple . . . . 3·50 20
167 1b. green . . . . 3·75 65

15 Landing of Columbus

1893. Columbian Exposition, Chicago, and 400th Anniv of Discovery of America by Columbus.
168 **15** 25c. purple . . . . 12·00 65

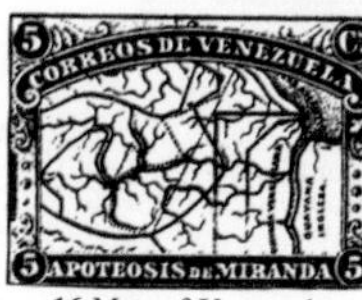
16 Map of Venezuela

18 Bolivar

1896. 80th Death Anniv of Gen. Miranda.
169 **16** 5c. green . . . . 3·25 2·10
170 10c. blue . . . . 3·25 2·10
171 25c. yellow . . . . 3·75 4·25
172 50c. red . . . . 38·00 18·00
173 1b. mauve . . . . 35·00 18·00

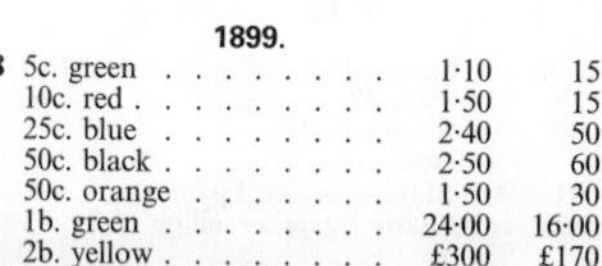

1899.
179 **18** 5c. green . . . . 1·10 15
180 10c. red . . . . 1·50 15
181 25c. blue . . . . 2·40 50
182 50c. black . . . . 2·50 60
183 50c. orange . . . . 1·50 30
184 1b. green . . . . 24·00 16·00
185 2b. yellow £300 £170

(21) "R.T.M." = Ramon Tellos Mendoza, Minister of Interior

(23)

1900. Stamps of 1893 optd with T **21**.
191 **13** 5c. grey 10 10
192 10c. green 10 10
193 25c. blue 10 10
194 50c. orange 10 10
195 1b. purple 20 10
196 3b. red 30 10
197 10b. violet 65 40
198 20b. brown . . . . 4·25 4·25

1900. Stamps of 1899 optd with T **21**.
199 **18** 5c. green 80 30
200 10c. red 80 35
201 25c. blue . . . . 5·50 60
202 50c. black . . . . 2·75 50
203 1b. green . . . . 1·25 40
204 2b. yellow . . . . 2·25 1·25

1900. Stamps of 1893 optd **1900**. Colours changed.
206 **13** 5c. orange 10 10
207 10c. blue 10 10
208 25c. purple 10 10
209 50c. green 60 10
210 1b. black . . . . 4·75 55
211 3b. brown . . . . 1·25 60
212 10b. red . . . . 5·00 1·40
213 20b. violet . . . . 10·00 2·75

1900. Stamps of 1899 optd **1900**.
214 **18** 5c. green £200 £200
215 10c. red £200 £200
216 25c. blue £275 £120
217 50c. orange . . . . 16·00 85
218 1b. black . . . . 1·10 60

1900. Stamps of 1899 optd with T **23**.
219 **18** 5c. green . . . . 5·00 50
220 10c. red . . . . 4·50 55
221 25c. blue . . . . 5·00 50

1901. Re-issue of T **13** in new colours.
227 **13** 5c. orange 10 10
228 10c. red 10 10
229 10c. blue 10 10
231 50c. green 15 15
232 1b. black . . . . 4·50 1·10
233 3b. brown 20 10
234 10b. red 35 25
235 20b. violet 80 50

1902. Stamp of 1901 optd **1901**.
236 **13** 1b. black 45 30

1904. No. 231 surch **CORREOS Vale B 0,05 1904**.
310 **13** 5c. on 50c. green 40 55

38 General Sucre

39 Bolivar

1904.
311 **38** 5c. green 40 15
312 10c. red 25 15
313 15c. violet 45 30
314 25c. blue . . . . 3·25 30
315 50c. red 45 40
316 1b. red 50 40

1904.
317 **39** 5c. green 10 10
318 10c. grey 10 10
319 25c. red 10 10
320 50c. yellow 10 10
321 1b. red . . . . 1·40 25
322 3b. blue 35 15
323 10b. violet 45 25
324 20b. red 75 35

41 President Castro

42 Liberty

1905. 6th Anniv of General Castro's Revolt.
330 **41** 5c. red . . . . 2·50 2·40
331a 10c. blue . . . . 3·75 3·00
332a 25c. yellow . . . . 1·40 1·25

1910. Independence Centenary.
333 **42** 25c. blue . . . . 9·50 45

43 F. de Miranda

44

1911. Portraits as T **43**.
340 **43** 5c. green 25 15
341 10c. red 35 10
342 – 15c. grey (Urdaneta) . . . 3·75 20
343 – 25c. blue (Urdaneta) . . . 2·00 25
344 – 50c. violet (Bolivar) . . . 2·50 25
339 – 1b. orange (Bolivar) . . . 2·50 1·00

1911. Portraits as T **44**.
345 – 5c. blue (Vargas) 10 10
346 – 10c. yellow (Avila) 10 10
347 – 25c. grey (Sanz) 10 10
348 **44** 50c. red (Blanco) 10 10
349 – 1b. green (Bello) 10 10
350 – 2b. brown (Sanabria) . . . 55 35
351 – 3b. violet (Paez) 55 25
352 – 10b. purple (Sucre) . . . . 1·10 50
353 – 20b. blue (Bolivar) . . . . 1·10 70

46 Bolivar

47 Bolivar

1914.
359 **46** 5c. green . . . . 22·00 25
360 10c. red . . . . 20·00 40
361 25c. blue . . . . 3·75 20

1915. Various Frames.
362a **47** 5c. green . . . . 2·75 25
379 5c. brown 55 10
570 7½c. green . . . . 1·10 35
571 10c. red . . . . 2·50 30
380 10c. green 20 10
381 15c. olive . . . . 1·60 50
382 15c. brown 30 10
383 25c. blue . . . . 1·60 10
384 25c. red 20 10
368 40c. green . . . . 16·00 6·25
385 40c. blue 55 20
369 50c. violet . . . . . . 4·25 40
386 50c. blue 55 20
371 75c. turquoise . . . . . 40·00 12·50
387 1b. black 55 25
388 3b. orange . . . . 1·40 75
389 5b. violet . . . . 15·00 7·50
See also Nos. 414/5.

48 Bolivar and Sucre

1924. Centenary of Battle of Ayacucho.
390 **48** 25c. blue . . . . 2·25 35

1926. Fiscal stamps surch **CORREOS VALE 1926** and value.
392 0,05b. on 1b. olive 40 35
393 0,25b. on 5c. brown 40 40
DESIGNS: No. 392, Portrait of Sucre; No. 393, Numeral.

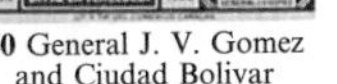
50 General J. V. Gomez and Ciudad Bolivar

51 Biplane and Venezuela

1928. 25th Anniv of Capture of Ciudad Bolivar and Peace in Venezuela.
394 **50** 10c. green . . . . 1·40 55

1930. Air.
395 **51** 5c. brown 15 10
575 5c. green 30 10
396 10c. yellow 15 10
576 10c. orange 60 15
577 12½c. purple 80 50
397 15c. grey 15 10
578 15c. blue 70 15
398 25c. violet 15 10
579 25c. brown . . . . 1·40 20
399 40c. green 15 10
581 70c. red . . . . 21·00 7·00
400 75c. red 45 15
401 1b. blue 55 15
402 1b.20 green 75 35
403 1b.70 blue 95 40
404 1b.90 green . . . . . . 1·00 50
405 2b.10 blue . . . . 1·50 40
406 2b.30 red . . . . 1·50 50
407 2b.50 blue . . . . 1·75 50
408 3b.70 green . . . . 1·75 75
409 10b. purple . . . . 3·50 1·50
410 20b. green . . . . 7·50 4·00
See also Nos. 426/49.

52 Simon Bolivar

1930. Death Centenary of Bolivar.
411 **52** 5c. yellow 85 40
412 10c. blue 85 30
413 25c. red 85 30

53

1932. Stamps of 1915 on paper printed with pattern as T **53**.
414 **47** 5c. violet 40 10
415 7½c. green 75 40
416 10c. green 50 10
417 15c. yellow . . . . 1·00 25
418 22½c. red . . . . 2·25 35
419 25c. red 85 10
420 37½c. blue . . . . 3·00 1·25
421 40c. blue . . . . 3·00 30
422 50c. olive . . . . 3·00 40
423 1b. blue . . . . 4·00 45
424 3b. brown . . . . 24·00 10·50
425 5b. brown . . . . 35·00 13·50

1932. Air. Air stamps as 1930 on paper printed with pattern as T **53**.
426 **51** 5c. brown 40 10
427 10c. yellow 40 10
428 15c. grey 40 10
429 25c. blue 55 10
430 40c. green 50 10
431 70c. red 65 10
432 75c. orange 70 25
433 1b. slate 85 10
434 1b.20 green . . . . 1·50 60
435 1b.70 brown . . . . 3·25 40
436 1b.80 blue . . . . 1·90 30
437 1b.90 green . . . . 4·00 2·50
438 1b.95 blue . . . . 4·25 2·10
439 2b. brown . . . . 3·50 1·75
440 2b.10 blue . . . . 6·50 4·25
441 2b.30 red . . . . 3·00 1·60
442 2b.50 blue . . . . 4·50 1·00
443 3b. violet . . . . 4·50 75
444 3b.70 green . . . . 5·00 4·25
445 4b. orange . . . . 4·50 1·00
446 5b. black . . . . 7·00 2·25
447 8b. red . . . . 12·50 3·50
448 10b. violet . . . . 24·00 7·00
449 20b. green . . . . 50·00 19·00

54 Arms of Bolivar

1933. 150th Birth Anniv of Bolivar.
450 **54** 25c. red . . . . 2·25 1·25

1934. Surch **1933** and figures of value and old value blocked out.
451 **47** 7½ on 10c. green (380) . . 55 30
453 22½ on 25c. red (384) . . . 1·40 60
452 22½ on 25c. red (419) . . . 1·25 1·00
454 37½ on 40c. blue (385) . . 1·50 60

1937. Air. Air stamps of 1932 surch **1937 VALE POR** and new value.
455 **51** 5c. on 1b.70 brown . . . . 12·00 6·00
456 10c. on 3b.70 green . . . . 12·00 6·00
457 15c. on 4b. orange . . . . 5·75 3·00
458 25c. on 5b. black . . . . 5·75 3·00
459 1b. on 8b. red . . . . . 4·75 4·00
460 2b. on 2b.10 blue . . . . 32·00 22·00

1937. Surch **1937 VALE POR** and value.
461 **47** 25c. on 40c. (No. 421) . . 5·25 80

59 Nurse and Child

60 Ploughing

61 "Flight"

64 Caribbean Coast

1937. (a) Postage.
463 **59** 5c. violet 60 25
464 – 10c. green . . . . 1·10 25
465 – 15c. brown . . . . 1·00 35
466 **59** 25c. red . . . . 1·10 40
467 – 50c. green . . . . 6·00 3·25
468 **60** 3b. red . . . . 10·00 6·00
469 **59** 5b. brown . . . . 19·00 12·00
DESIGNS—VERT: 10c. Sailing barges on Orinoco; 15c. Women gathering cocoa-beans. HORIZ: 50c. Rounding up cattle.

(b) Air.
470 **61** 5c. brown 35 35
471 – 10c. orange 20 10
472 – 15c. black 40 35
473 **64** 25c. violet 50 35
474 – 40c. green 95 40
475 **61** 70c. red 95 35
476 – 75c. bistre . . . . 1·90 65
477 **61** 1b. grey . . . . 1·25 45
478 – 1b.20 green . . . . 4·50 1·90
479 **61** 1b.80 blue . . . . 2·50 1·25
480 – 1b.95 blue . . . . 7·50 4·00
481 **64** 2b. brown . . . . 2·75 1·75
482 2b.50 blue . . . . 10·00 6·50
483 – 3b. lilac . . . . 4·75 3·00
484 **64** 3b.70 red . . . . 10·00 8·00
485 – 10b. purple . . . . 17·00 10·00
486 **61** 20b. black . . . . 22·00 14·00
DESIGNS—HORIZ: 10, 40c., 1b.20, 3b. Puerto Cabello; 15, 75c., 1b.95, 10b. Caracas.

65 "Venezuela" welcoming La Guaira

67 Bolivar

1937. Acquisition of La Guaira Harbour.
487 **65** 25c. blue (postage) . . . . 1·40 55
488 – 70c. green (air) . . . . . 3·00 80
489 – 1b.80 blue . . . . 5·50 1·50
DESIGN: 70c., 1b.80, Statue of Bolivar and La Guaira Harbour.

1937. Red Cross Fund.
490 **67** 5c. green 75 50

1937. Stamps of 1937 optd **RESELLADO 1937-1938**.
491 **59** 5c. violet (postage) . . . . 3·75 1·60
492 – 10c. green . . . . 1·40 65
493 **59** 25c. red . . . . 1·25 55
494 **60** 3b. red . . . . £140 60·00
495 – 10c. orange (air) . . . . . 1·25 55
496 **64** 25c. violet . . . . 2·00 75
497 – 40c. green . . . . 2·00 1·10
498 **61** 70c. red . . . . 1·60 75
499 1b. grey . . . . 2·50 1·10
500 – 1b.20 green . . . . 32·00 16·00
501 **61** 1b.80 blue . . . . 5·00 85
502 – 1b.95 blue . . . . 7·50 3·75
503 **64** 2b. brown . . . . 60·00 23·00
504 2b.50 blue . . . . 65·00 21·00
505 – 3b. lilac . . . . 32·00 8·50
506 – 10b. purple . . . . 80·00 42·00
507 **61** 20b. black . . . . 90·00 40·00

69 Gathering Coffee Beans

72 La Guaira

1938. (a) Postage. As T **69**.
508 **69** 5c. green 40 15
509 A 10c. red 40 15
510 B 15c. violet . . . . 1·10 25
544 15c. green 55 30
511 A 25c. blue 40 15
546 37½c. blue . . . . 1·90 55
513 B 40c. sepia . . . . 15·00 4·25
547 40c. black . . . . 12·00 4·25
514 **69** 50c. olive . . . . 18·00 4·50
548 50c. violet . . . . 7·00 55
515 A 1b. brown . . . . 8·25 5·25
516 **69** 3b. orange . . . . 65·00 28·00
517 B 5b. black . . . . 10·00 4·50
750 5b. orange . . . . 35·00 18·00
751 5b. brown . . . . 10·50 4·00
DESIGNS: A, Bolivar; B, G.P.O., Caracas.

(b) Air. As T **72**.
550 **72** 5c. green 20 10
551 C 10c. red 20 10
552 **72** 12½c. violet 35 30
520 D 15c. violet . . . . 2·50 75
553 15c. blue 60 10
521 **72** 25c. blue . . . . 2·50 75
554 25c. brown 25 10
555 D 30c. violet . . . . 1·75 20
522 C 40c. violet . . . . 2·75 1·10
556 40c. brown . . . . 2·00 20
557 **72** 45c. green 95 20
558 C 50c. blue . . . . 1·00 10
523 D 70c. red 60 40
524 **72** 75c. brown . . . . 6·00 1·50
559 75c. green . . . . 1·25 25
560 D 90c. red 90 20
525 C 1b. green . . . . 5·50 1·75
561 1b. violet . . . . 1·10 20
526 D 1b.20 orange . . . . . . 16·00 5·00
562 1b.20 green . . . . 1·40 60
527 **72** 1b.80 blue . . . . 1·40 60
528 C 1b.90 black . . . . 4·00 2·10
529 D 1b.95 blue . . . . 3·25 1·90
530 **72** 2b. green . . . . 32·00 11·50
563 2b. red . . . . 1·50 75
531 C 2b.50 brown . . . . 32·00 13·00
564 2b.50 orange . . . . 10·50 2·50
565 D 3b. green . . . . 4·00 1·50
533 **72** 3b.70 black . . . . 6·00 3·50
566 D 5b. red . . . . 6·75 1·60
771 5b. green . . . . 5·50 2·10
534 C 10b. purple . . . . 22·00 2·50
773 10b. yellow . . . . 7·50 2·75
535 D 20b. orange . . . . 70·00 26·00
DESIGNS: C, National Pantheon; D, Oil Wells.

1938. Surch **VALE Bs. 0,40 1938**.
536 **59** 40c. on 5b. brown . . . . 7·50 2·75

1938. Air. Postage stamps surch **1938 VALE** and value in words.
537 **61** 5c. on 1b.80 blue 70 50
538 **64** 10c. on 2b.50 blue . . . . 2·10 60
539 15c. on 2b. brown . . . . 1·00 60
540 – 25c. on 40c. green (No. 474) . . . . 1·10 70
541 **64** 40c. on 3b.70 red . . . . 2·50 1·60

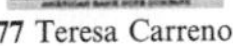
77 Teresa Carreno

78 Allegory of Labour and Statue of Bolivar

1938. Repatriation of Ashes of Teresa Carreno (concert pianist).
567 **77** 25c. blue . . . . 3·25 55

1938. Labour Day.
568 **78** 25c. blue . . . . 3·75 55

80 Monument at Carabobo

81 Monument at Carabobo

82 Gen. J. I. Paz Castillo

1938. Air. Independence Issue.
583 – 20c. brown 50 35
584 **80** 30c. violet 60 35
585 **81** 45c. blue 85 25
586 – 50c. blue 70 25
587 **81** 70c. red . . . . 15·00 8·00

588 80 90c. orange . . . . 1·25 60
589 81 1b.35 black . . . . 1·60 75
590 – 1b.40 slate . . . . 6·25 1·75
591 80 2b.25 green . . . . 3·25 1·50
DESIGN: 20, 50c., 1b.40, Airplane over Sucre Monument.

1939. 80th Anniv of Venezuelan Posts.
592 82 10c. red . . . . 1·75 55

83 View of Ojeda
84 Dr. Cristobal Mendoza

1939. Founding of Ojeda.
593 83 25c. blue . . . . 6·00 40

1939. Centenary of Death of Dr. Mendoza.
594 84 5c. green 25 30
595 10c. red 25 30
596 15c. violet . . . . 1·00 40
597 25c. blue 90 30
598 37½c. blue . . . . 12·00 5·25
599 50c. olive . . . . 12·00 3·75
600 1b. brown . . . . 5·75 3·00

85 Diego B. Urbaneja
86 Bolivar and Carabobo Monument

1940. Independence Issue.
601 85 5c. green (postage) 50 15
602 7½c. green 40 25
603 15c. olive 55 25
604 37½c. blue . . . . 1·10 40
605 40c. blue 90 30
745 40c. mauve 55 25
746 40c. orange 55 25
606 50c. violet . . . . 4·25 1·10
607 1b. brown . . . . 2·00 55
748 1b. blue . . . . 1·25 25
608 3b. red . . . . 6·50 2·25
749 3b. grey . . . . 2·10 55
609 86 15c. blue (air) 50 15
610 20c. olive 45 10
611 25c. brown . . . . 1·90 35
612 40c. brown . . . . 1·50 15
613 1b. lilac . . . . 3·50 25
614 2b. red . . . . 6·50 60

87 Foundation of Greater Colombia

1940. Air. 50th Anniv of Pan-American Union.
615 87 15c. brown . . . . 1·00 55

88 Battle of Carabobo
89 "The Crossing of the Andes" (after Salas)

1940. 150th Birth Anniv of Gen. Paez.
616 88 25c. blue . . . . 4·00 55

1940. Death Centenary of Gen. Santander.
617 89 25c. blue . . . . 4·00 55

90 Monument and Urn
91 Statue of Bolivar at Caracas

1940. 110th Anniv of Death of Simon Bolivar. (a) Postage.
738 90 5c. green 10 10
739 5c. blue 15 10
619 – 10c. pink 30 10
620 – 15c. green 40 15
741 – 15c. red 30 10
621 – 20c. blue 70 10
622 – 25c. blue 40 10
742 – 25c. violet 25 10
623 – 30c. mauve . . . . 1·25 25
743 – 30c. black . . . . 1·00 35
744 – 30c. purple 50 15
624 – 37½c. blue . . . . 2·10 70
625 – 50c. violet . . . . 1·50 50
747 – 50c. green 55 25
DESIGNS—VERT: 15c. Bolivar's baptism; 25c. Simon Bolivar on horseback. HORIZ: 10c. Bolivar's bed; 20c. House where Bolivar was born; 30c. Courtyard and Bolivar's baptismal font; 37½c. Courtyard of house where Bolivar was born; 50c. "Rebellion of 1812".

(b) Air.
626 91 5c. green 10 10
752 5c. orange 10 10
627 10c. red 10 10
753 10c. green 10 10
628 12½c. violet 45 35
754 12½c. brown 25 45
629 15c. blue 25 10
755 15c. grey 15 10
630 20c. brown 35 10
756 20c. violet 20 10
631 25c. brown 25 10
757 25c. green 15 10
632 30c. violet 25 10
758 30c. blue 20 10
633 40c. brown 35 10
759 40c. green 35 10
634 45c. green 50 15
760 45c. red 30 15
635 50c. blue 50 10
761 50c. claret 30 15
636 70c. pink . . . . 1·40 35
762 70c. red 55 30
637 75c. olive . . . . 4·25 1·00
763 75c. orange . . . . 3·50 2·00
764 75c. violet 30 15
638 90c. orange 65 35
765 90c. black 45 40
639 1b. mauve 35 10
766 1b. blue 35 20
640 1b.20 green . . . . 1·75 60
767 1b.20 brown 65 45
641 1b.35 black . . . . 7·00 3·00
642 2b. red . . . . 1·40 20
643 3b. black . . . . 2·50 65
768 3b. brown . . . . 11·50 2·75
769 3b. blue . . . . 1·40 35
644 4b. black . . . . 2·00 35
645 5b. brown . . . . 12·00 5·25

1941. No. 622 surch **HABILITADO 1941 VALE BS. 0.20.**
646 20c. on 25c. blue 40 15

1941. Optd **HABILITADO 1940.**
647 59 5c. violet . . . . 1·50 50
648 – 10c. green (No. 464) . . . 1·25 35

94 Bolivar's Funeral

95 Condor

1941. Centenary of Arrival of Bolivar's Ashes at Caracas and Liberator's Monument Fund.
649 94 20c.+5c. blue (postage) . . 4·50 35
650 95 15c.+10c. brown (air) . . . 1·10 45
651 30c.+5c. violet . . . . . . 1·10 60

96 Symbolical of Industry
97 Caracas Cathedral
100 National and Red Cross Flags

1942. National Industrial Exhibition.
652 96 10c. red 60 25

1943.
653 97 10c. red 40 15
740 10c. orange 10 10

1943. Surch **Habilitado Vale Bs. 0.20.**
654 59 20c. on 25c. red . . . . . 22·00 19·00
655 65 20c. on 25c. blue . . . . . 55·00 42·00
656 77 20c. on 25c. blue . . . . . 14·50 11·00
657 78 20c. on 25c. blue . . . . . 14·50 11·00

1943. Optd **Resellado 1943.**
658 59 5c. violet . . . . 10·50 5·75
659 – 10c. green (No. 464) . . . 5·00 3·50
660 – 50c. green (No. 467) . . . 6·00 2·75
661 60 3b. red . . . . 32·00 11·50

1943. Air. Optd **Resellado 1943.**
662 – 10c. orange (No. 471) . . . 1·25 80
663 64 25c. violet . . . . 1·25 1·00
664 – 40c. green (No. 474) . . . 1·40 1·00
665 61 70c. red . . . . 1·50 1·00
666 – 70c. green (No. 488) . . . 1·50 1·00
667 – 75c. bistre (No. 476) . . . 1·75 1·10
668 61 1b. grey . . . . 1·90 1·25
669 – 1b.20 green (No. 478) . . . 2·50 1·40
670 61 1b.80 blue . . . . 2·25 1·40
671 – 1b.80 blue (No. 489) . . . 3·00 1·50
672 – 1b.95 blue (No. 480) . . . 3·75 2·00
673 64 2b. brown . . . . 3·75 2·75
674 2b.50 blue . . . . 4·00 2·75
675 – 3b. lilac (No. 483) . . . . 5·50 3·25
676 64 3b.70 red . . . . 55·00 45·00
677 – 10b. purple (No. 485) . . . 21·00 14·50
678 61 20b. black . . . . 35·00 28·00

1944. Air. 80th Anniv of Int Red Cross and 37th Anniv of Adherence of Venezuela.
680 100 5c. green 10 10
681 10c. mauve 15 10
682 20c. blue 15 10
683 30c. blue 35 10
684 40c. brown 50 15
685 45c. green 90 35
686 90c. orange 85 30
687 1b. black . . . . 1·25 25

101 Baseball Players
103 Charles Howarth

1944. Air. 7th World Amateur Baseball Championship Games, Caracas. Optd **AEREO.**
688 101 5c. brown 35 25
689 10c. green 40 25
690 20c. blue 50 35
691 30c. red 40 50
692 45c. purple . . . . 1·50 45
693 90c. orange . . . . 2·40 90
694 1b. grey . . . . 2·50 90
695 1b.20 green . . . . 8·00 5·25
696 1b.80 yellow . . . . 10·50 7·50

1944. Air. No. 590 surch **Habilitado 1944 VALE Bs. 0.30.**
697 30c. on 1b.40c. slate 35 35

1944. Air. Cent of Rochdale Co-operative Society.
698 103 5c. black 25 15
699 10c. violet 25 15
700 20c. brown 50 30
701 30c. green 60 60
702 1b.20 brown . . . . 1·90 1·75
703 1b.80 blue . . . . 3·50 2·50
704 3b.70 red . . . . 4·75 4·00

104 Antonio Jose de Sucre
105 Antonio Jose de Sucre and Douglas DC-4

1945. 150th Anniv of Birth of Gen. Sucre.
705 104 5c. yellow (postage) . . . 75 35
706 10c. blue . . . . 1·25 70
707 20c. red . . . . 1·50 70
708 105 5c. orange (air) 20 15
709 10c. purple 25 20
710 20c. black 35 25
711 30c. green 55 40
712 40c. olive 55 35
713 45c. brown 70 35
714 90c. brown . . . . 1·25 45
715 1b. mauve 90 35
716 1b.20 black . . . . 2·50 2·25
717 2b. yellow . . . . 3·75 1·50

106 Andres Bello
107 Gen. Rafael Urdaneta

1946. 80th Death Anniv of A. Bello (educationalist).
718 106 20c. blue (postage) . . . 85 35
719 30c. green (air) 70 30

1946. Death Centenary of Gen. R. Urdaneta.
720 107 20c. blue (postage) . . . 85 35
721 30c. green (air) 70 30

108 Allegory of Republic
110 Western Hemisphere and Anti-tuberculosis Inst, Maracaibo

1946. 1st Anniv of Revolution.
722 108 20c. blue (postage) . . . 80 35
723 – 15c. blue (air) 20 30
724 – 20c. bistre 25 30
725 – 30c. violet 30 25
726 – 1b. red . . . . 3·00 1·50
Nos. 723/6 are as Type **108**, but vert.

1947. 12th Pan-American Health Conf, Caracas.
727 110 20c. yellow & bl (postage) 50 35
728 – 15c. yellow and blue (air) 35 25
729 – 20c. yellow and brown . . 35 40
730 – 30c. yellow and violet . . 35 25
731 – 1b. yellow and red . . . 4·25 2·10
Nos. 728/31 are as Type **110** but vert.

1947. Surch **J. R. G. CORREOS Vale Bs.0.15 1946.**
732 85 15c. on 1b. brown 80 35

1947. Air. Surch **J. R. G. AEREO Vale Bs.**, new value, and **1946.**
733 47 10c. on 22½c. red (No. 418) 20 10
734 – 15c. on 25c. blue (No. 622) 45 15
735 91 20c. on 50c. blue 40 25
736 85 70c. on 1b. brown 50 35
737 – 20b. on 20b. orange (No. 535) . . . . 23·00 12·00

1947. Nos. 743 and 624 surch **CORREOS Vale Bs.**, new value, and **1947**. (a) Postage.
776 5c. on 30c. black 25 10
777 5c. on 37½c. blue 30 10

(b) Air. No. 621 with **AEREO** instead of **CORREOS.**
778 5c. on 20c. blue 40 10
779 10c. on 20c. blue 40 10

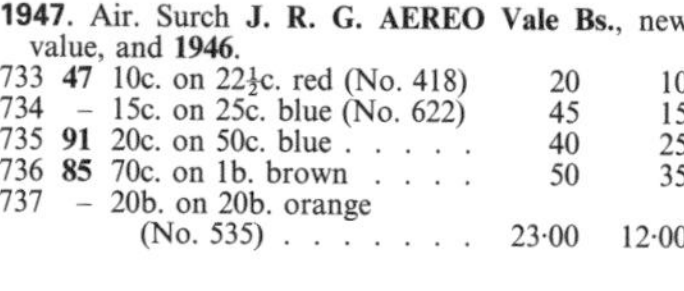

116 Freighter "Republica de Venezuela" and Ship's Wheel
117 Freighter "Republica de Venezuela" and Ship's Wheel

1948. 1st Anniv of Greater Colombia Merchant Marine. Frame size 37½ × 22½ mm or 22½ × 37½ mm. Inscr "AMERICAN BANK NOTE COMPANY" at foot.
780 116 5c. blue (postage) 20 10
781 7½c. red 70 35
782 10c. red 55 10
783 15c. grey 75 15
784 20c. sepia 40 10
785 25c. violet 75 20
786 30c. yellow . . . . 5·75 1·90
787 37½c. brown . . . . 2·50 1·40
788 40c. olive . . . . 3·75 1·75
789 50c. mauve 85 25
790 1b. green . . . . 2·50 50
791 117 5c. brown (air) 10 10
792 10c. green 10 10
793 15c. buff 15 10
794 20c. purple 20 10
795 25c. grey 25 10
796 30c. olive 35 15
797 45c. blue 60 25
798 50c. black 80 35
799 70c. orange . . . . 2·10 35
800 75c. blue . . . . 3·75 45
801 90c. red . . . . 2·10 1·00
802 1b. violet . . . . 2·50 70
803 2b. slate . . . . 2·75 1·00
804 3b. green . . . . 11·00 3·25
805 4b. blue . . . . 5·50 3·25
806 5b. red . . . . 21·00 5·50
For stamps as T **116/17** in larger size and inscribed "COURVOISIER S.A." at foot, see Nos. 1012/7.

118 Arms of Venezuela

1948. New Constitution Promulgation.
807 118 5c. blue . . . . 1·40 55
808 10c. red . . . . 1·75 60

120 Santos Michelena

121 Santos Michelena and Silhouette of Douglas DC-3

1949. 110th Anniv of 1st International Postal Convention, Bogota.

810 120 5c. blue (postage) 25 15
811 10c. red 50 15
812 20c. sepia 1·50 35
813 1b. green 4·25 1·60

814 121 5c. brown (air) 40 15
815 10c. grey 50 15
816 15c. orange 60 15
817 25c. green 1·10 30
818 30c. purple 1·10 30
819 1b. violet 6·25 1·25

122 Columbus, Indian, "Santa Maria" and Map

123 Columbus, Indian, "Santa Maria" and Map

1949. 450th Anniv of Columbus's Discovery of America.

820 122 5c. blue (postage) 1·25 15
821 10c. red 5·00 85
822 20c. sepia 7·00 1·25
823 1b. green 14·50 4·50

824 123 5c. brown (air) 1·25 10
825 10c. grey 1·40 25
826 15c. orange 2·00 30
827 25c. green 3·75 90
828 30c. mauve 5·00 1·25
829 1b. violet 20·00 3·75

124 Hand, Bird, Airplane and Globe

125 Francisco de Miranda

126 Declaration of Independence

1950. Air. 75th Anniv of U.P.U.

830 124 5c. lake 20 10
831 10c. green 10 10
832 15c. brown 20 10
833 25c. grey 50 40
834 30c. olive 65 20
835 50c. black 25 25
836 60c. blue 1·40 60
837 90c. red 1·75 70
838 1b. violet 2·00 60

1950. Birth Bicentenary of Miranda.

839 125 5c. blue (postage) 25 10
840 10c. green 30 10
841 20c. brown 95 25
842 1b. red 4·50 1·50

843 126 5c. red (air) 35 15
844 10c. brown 35 15
845 15c. violet 30 35
846 30c. blue 90 25
847 1b. green 3·75 1·75

127 Tabebuia (National Tree)

128 Map and Statistics

1950. Air. Protection of Flora. Centres in yellow.

848 127 5c. brown 60 20
849 10c. green 50 10
850 15c. mauve 60 15
851 25c. green 4·00 1·60
852 30c. orange 4·50 2·25
853 50c. grey 2·50 60
854 60c. blue 4·00 1·00
855 90c. red 7·50 2·10
856 1b. violet 9·00 2·50

1950. Census of the Americas.

857 128 5c. blue (postage) 20 10
858 10c. grey 20 10
859 15c. sepia 30 10
860 25c. green 50 15
861 30c. red 60 25
862 50c. violet 1·00 25
863 1b. brown 2·75 1·10

864 5c. grey (air) 15 10
865 10c. green 10 10
866 15c. olive 30 15
867 25c. black 50 25
868 30c. orange 60 20
869 50c. brown 50 25
870 60c. blue 50 35
871 90c. red 1·50 60
872 1b. violet 2·50 1·75

129 Alonso de Ojeda

131

1950. 450th Anniv of Discovery of Lake Maracaibo.

873 129 5c. blue (postage) 25 15
874 10c. red 35 15
875 15c. grey 40 20
876 20c. blue 1·40 40
877 1b. green 5·75 2·10

878 5c. brown (air) 25 10
879 10c. red 35 15
880 15c. sepia 45 20
881 25c. purple 45 40
882 30c. orange 1·25 35
883 1b. green 5·00 1·90

1951. Surch **RESELLADO** and new value.

884 116 5c. on 7½c. red 40 15
885 10c. on 37½c. brown 40 15

1951. Telegraph stamps surch as in T **131**.

886 5c. on 5c. brown 15 10
887 10c. on 10c. green 35 10
888 20c. on 1b. black 40 15
889 25c. on 25c. red 55 30
890 30c. on 2b. olive 1·00 55

132 Arms of Caracas and View

133 Statue of Bolivar, New York

1951. Arms issue. Federal District of Caracas.

891 132 5c. green (postage) 50 10
892 10c. red 65 10
893 15c. brown 1·50 25
894 20c. blue 2·75 25
895 25c. brown 3·75 55
896 30c. blue 3·25 60
897 35c. violet 32·00 18·00

898 5c. turquoise (air) 65 15
899 7½c. green 2·50 60
900 10c. red 25 25
901 15c. brown 5·50 40
902 20c. blue 4·00 40
903 30c. blue 6·75 85
904 45c. purple 4·00 55
905 60c. green 13·00 1·00
906 90c. red 7·75 4·25

See also Nos. 922/37, 938/53, 954/69, 970/85, 991/1006, 1018/33, 1034/49, 1050/65, 1066/81, 1082/97, 1098/113, 1137/52, 1153/68, 1169/84, 1185/1200, 1201/16, 1217/32, 1258/73, 1274/89, 1290/1305, 1306/21, 1322/37, and 1338/53.

1951. Transfer of Statue of Bolivar to Central Park, New York.

907 133 5c. green (postage) 35 10
908 10c. red 35 25
909 20c. blue 60 25
910 30c. grey 70 40
911 40c. green 95 40
912 50c. brown 2·00 45
913 1b. black 6·25 2·50

914 5c. violet (air) 65 15
915 10c. green 25 15
916 20c. grey 25 15
917 25c. olive 40 20
918 30c. red 60 25
919 40c. brown 60 25
920 50c. slate 1·75 45
921 70c. orange 3·00 1·75

134 Arms of Venezuela and Bolivar Statue

138 Isabella the Catholic

1951. Arms issue. National Arms of Venezuela.

922 134 5c. green (postage) 25 10
923 10c. red 35 10
924 15c. brown 2·75 35
925 20c. blue 2·75 45
926 25c. brown 4·25 70
927 30c. blue 4·25 70
928 35c. violet 24·00 13·50

929 5c. turquoise (air) 25 10
930 7½c. green 1·00 55
931 10c. red 35 15
932 15c. brown 2·75 55
933 20c. blue 3·75 40
934 30c. blue 6·25 90
935 45c. purple 2·75 35
936 60c. green 13·50 2·25
937 90c. red 8·50 5·00

1951. Arms issue. State of Tachira. As T **132** showing Arms of Tachira and agricultural products.

938 5c. green (postage) 25 10
939 10c. red 30 25
940 15c. brown 60 20
941 20c. blue 1·90 35
942 50c. orange £110 13·00
943 1b. green 1·90 55
944 5b. purple 4·75 2·10

945 5c. turquoise (air) 15 15
946 10c. red 50 10
947 15c. brown 1·00 40
948 30c. blue 13·50 1·25
949 60c. green 10·50 1·25
950 1b.20 lake 10·50 6·25
951 3b. green 2·75 1·10
952 5b. purple 5·75 2·40
953 10b. violet 8·50 4·75

1951. Arms issue. State of Zulia. As T **132** showing Arms of Zulia and Oil Well.

954 5c. green (postage) 25 10
955 10c. red 25 10
956 15c. brown 90 25
957 20c. blue 1·10 35
958 50c. orange 7·00 3·75
959 1b. green 2·50 55
960 5b. purple 5·00 2·50

961 5c. turquoise (air) 55 15
962 10c. red 15 10
963 15c. brown 60 35
964 30c. blue 4·00 1·40
965 60c. green 2·25 35
966 1b.20 lake 9·75 6·00
967 3b. green 2·50 90
968 5b. purple 4·00 2·25
969 10b. violet 7·25 4·50

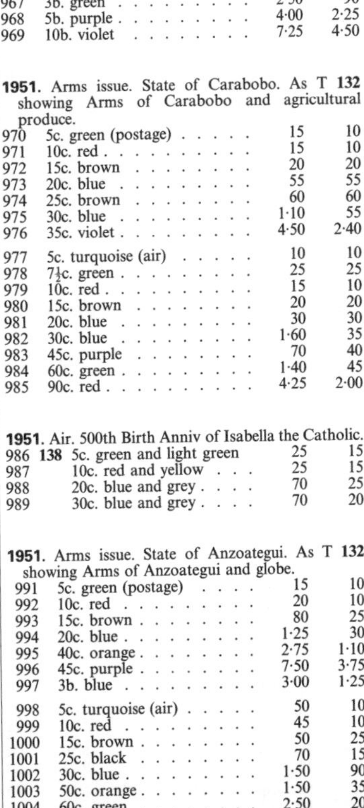

1951. Arms issue. State of Carabobo. As T **132** showing Arms of Carabobo and agricultural produce.

970 5c. green (postage) 15 10
971 10c. red 15 10
972 15c. brown 20 20
973 20c. blue 55 55
974 25c. brown 60 60
975 30c. blue 1·10 55
976 35c. violet 4·50 2·40

977 5c. turquoise (air) 10 10
978 7½c. green 25 25
979 10c. red 15 10
980 15c. brown 20 20
981 20c. blue 30 30
982 30c. blue 1·60 35
983 45c. purple 70 40
984 60c. green 1·40 45
985 90c. red 4·25 2·00

1951. Air. 500th Birth Anniv of Isabella the Catholic.

986 138 5c. green and light green 25 15
987 10c. red and yellow 25 15
988 20c. blue and grey 70 25
989 30c. blue and grey 70 20

1951. Arms issue. State of Anzoategui. As T **132** showing Arms of Anzoategui and globe.

991 5c. green (postage) 15 10
992 10c. red 20 10
993 15c. brown 80 25
994 20c. blue 1·25 30
995 40c. orange 2·75 1·10
996 45c. purple 7·50 3·75
997 3b. blue 3·00 1·25

998 5c. turquoise (air) 50 10
999 10c. red 45 10
1000 15c. brown 50 25
1001 25c. black 70 15
1002 30c. blue 1·50 90
1003 50c. orange 1·50 35
1004 60c. green 2·50 20
1005 1b. violet 3·00 90
1006 2b. violet 5·50 2·10

140 National Stadium

147 Juan de Villegas

1951. Air. 3rd Bolivarian Games, Caracas.

1007 140 5c. green 85 50
1008 10c. red 95 50
1009 20c. brown 1·10 60
1010 30c. blue 1·25 70

1951. As Nos. 780/806 but frame size 38 × 23½ mm or 23½ × 38 mm. Inscr "COURVOISIER S.A." at foot.

1012 116 5c. green (postage) 85 15
1013 10c. red 1·40 15
1014 15c. slate 4·75 15

1015 117 5c. brown (air) 1·10 15
1016 10c. brown 1·75 15
1017 15c. olive 2·40 15

1952. Arms issue. State of Aragua. As T **132** showing Arms of Aragua and Stylized Farm.

1018 5c. green (postage) 20 10
1019 10c. red 15 10
1020 15c. brown 60 10
1021 20c. blue 55 30
1022 25c. brown 1·25 40
1023 30c. blue 1·25 35
1024 35c. violet 7·00 3·75

1025 5c. turquoise (air) 60 15
1026 7½c. green 25 85
1027 10c. red 15 10
1028 15c. brown 1·40 65
1029 20c. blue 75 65
1030 30c. blue 2·40 25
1031 45c. purple 1·90 65
1032 60c. green 3·75 60
1033 90c. red 20·00 9·50

1952. Arms issue. State of Bolivar. As T **132** showing Arms of Bolivar and Iron Foundry.

1034 5c. green (postage) 15 10
1035 10c. red 25 10
1036 15c. brown 25 20
1037 20c. blue 80 30
1038 40c. orange 3·00 95
1039 45c. purple 7·75 5·00
1040 3b. blue 3·50 2·25

1041 5c. turquoise (air) 4·50 25
1042 10c. red 15 10
1043 15c. brown 55 15
1044 25c. black 50 10
1045 30c. blue 2·50 1·10
1046 50c. red 1·60 35
1047 60c. green 3·50 45
1048 1b. violet 2·50 35
1049 2b. violet 5·50 2·10

1952. Arms issue. State of Lara. As T **132** showing Arms of Lara and Sisal Industry.

1050 5c. green (postage) 50 10
1051 10c. red 50 10
1052 15c. brown 45 30
1053 20c. blue 90 35
1054 25c. brown 1·10 45
1055 30c. blue 1·75 35
1056 35c. violet 7·50 3·50

1057 5c. turquoise (air) 40 15
1058 7½c. green 25 25
1059 10c. red 15 10
1060 15c. brown 80 20
1061 20c. blue 1·25 30
1062 30c. blue 2·75 35
1063 45c. purple 1·25 30
1064 60c. green 2·75 55
1065 90c. red 17·00 10·50

1952. Arms issue. State of Miranda. As T **132** showing Arms of Miranda and Agricultural Products.

1066 5c. green (postage) 20 10
1067 10c. red 25 10
1068 15c. brown 35 20
1069 20c. blue 65 30
1070 25c. brown 85 40
1071 30c. blue 1·40 55
1072 35c. violet 8·50 4·75

1073 5c. turquoise (air) 60 10
1074 7½c. green 70 25
1075 10c. red 15 10
1076 15c. brown 60 30
1077 20c. blue 85 40
1078 30c. blue 1·40 35
1079 45c. purple 1·10 30
1080 60c. green 3·00 45
1081 90c. red 15·00 7·75

1952. Arms issue. State of Sucre. As T **132** showing Arms of Sucre, Palms and Seascape.

1082 5c. green (postage) 45 10
1083 10c. red 45 10
1084 15c. brown 75 20
1085 20c. blue 75 15
1086 40c. orange 3·00 55
1087 45c. purple 10·00 5·00
1088 3b. blue 2·40 1·40

1089 5c. turquoise (air) 45 15
1090 10c. red 45 10
1091 15c. brown 50 20
1092 25c. black 9·50 25
1093 30c. blue 3·25 70

1094 50c. red 1·40 35
1095 60c. green 2·00 55
1096 1b. violet 2·50 40
1097 2b. violet 5·50 2·25

1952. Arms issue. State of Trujillo. As T **132** showing Arms of Trujillo and Stylised Coffee Plant.
1098 5c. green (postage) 15 10
1099 10c. red 25 10
1100 15c. brown 1·10 25
1101 20c. blue 1·10 35
1102 50c. orange 6·75 3·50
1103 1b. green 1·60 45
1104 5b. purple 4·00 2·10
1105 5c. turquoise (air) 7·00 30
1106 10c. red 15 10
1107 15c. brown 1·75 15
1108 30c. blue 8·00 1·25
1109 60c. green 6·00 1·10
1110 1b.20 lake 5·75 3·00
1111 3b. green 2·75 1·10
1112 5b. purple 5·75 2·40
1113 10b. violet 9·50 5·00

1952. 4th Centenary of Barquisimeto.
1114 **147** 5c. green (postage) 35 10
1115 10c. red 35 10
1116 20c. slate 80 35
1117 40c. orange 3·50 1·75
1118 50c. brown 2·00 90
1119 1b. violet 3·50 1·25
1120 5c. turquoise (air) 55 10
1121 10c. red 15 10
1122 20c. blue 25 10
1123 25c. black 60 25
1124 30c. blue 75 20
1125 40c. orange 4·00 1·50
1126 50c. bronze 1·25 35
1127 1b. purple 5·25 1·90

148 Our Lady of Coromoto

157 G.P.O., Caracas

1952. 300th Anniv of Apparition of Our Lady of Coromoto.
1128 **148** 1b. red (17×26½ mm) 6·25 1·00
1129 1b. red (26½×41 mm) 4·25 1·00
1130 1b. red (36×65 mm) 2·50 80

1952. National Objective Exn. Telegraph stamps as T **131** surch **Correos Exposicion Objetiva Nacional 1948 - 1952** and new value.
1131 5c. on 25c. red 35 10
1132 10c. on 1b. black 35 10

1952. Telegraph stamps as T **131** surch **CORREOS HABILITADO 1952** and new value.
1133 20c. on 25c. red 45 15
1134 30c. on 2b. olive 2·10 1·00
1135 40c. on 1b. black 85 50
1136 50c. on 3b. orange 2·75 1·25

1953. Arms issue. State of Merida. As T **132** showing Arms of Merida and Church.
1137 5c. green (postage) 15 10
1138 10c. red 15 10
1139 15c. brown 20 25
1140 20c. blue 95 25
1141 50c. orange 4·25 1·40
1142 1b. green 1·10 45
1143 5b. purple 4·25 1·90
1144 5c. turquoise (air) 20 15
1145 10c. red 20 10
1146 15c. brown 60 15
1147 30c. blue 5·25 90
1148 60c. green 2·40 60
1149 1b.20 lake 4·25 2·25
1150 3b. green 2·40 90
1151 5b. purple 5·25 2·25
1152 10b. violet 7·25 4·25

1953. Arms issue. State of Monagas. As T **132** showing Arms of Monagas and Horses.
1153 5c. green (postage) 15 10
1154 10c. red 20 10
1155 15c. brown 25 25
1156 20c. blue 35 35
1157 40c. orange 2·40 60
1158 45c. purple 7·50 3·50
1159 3b. blue 3·00 1·90
1160 5c. turquoise (air) 20 15
1161 10c. red 15 10
1162 15c. brown 65 20
1163 25c. black 50 15
1164 30c. blue 4·50 1·00
1165 50c. red 1·75 35
1166 60c. green 1·90 35
1167 1b. violet 3·00 70
1168 2b. violet 4·00 2·00

1953. Arms issue. State of Portuguesa. As T **132** showing Arms of Portuguesa and Woodland.
1169 5c. green (postage) 15 10
1170 10c. red 15 10
1171 15c. brown 20 20
1172 20c. blue 80 20
1173 50c. orange 4·00 2·25
1174 1b. green 1·10 25
1175 5b. purple 4·75 2·40
1176 5c. turquoise (air) 1·40 40
1177 10c. red 60 10
1178 15c. brown 65 25
1179 30c. blue 4·75 1·60
1180 60c. green 3·25 40
1181 1b.20 lake 8·25 4·00
1182 3b. green 2·50 1·10
1183 5b. purple 4·75 2·10
1184 10b. violet 7·25 5·00

1953. Arms issue. Federal Territory of Delta Amacuro. As T **132** showing Arms of Delta Amacuro and map.
1185 5c. green (postage) 15 10
1186 10c. red 20 10
1187 15c. brown 25 15
1188 20c. blue 40 25
1189 40c. orange 1·90 85
1190 45c. purple 8·50 4·25
1191 3b. blue 2·00 1·25
1192 5c. turquoise (air) 25 10
1193 10c. red 15 10
1194 15c. brown 35 25
1195 25c. black 80 40
1196 30c. blue 3·00 80
1197 50c. red 1·25 40
1198 60c. green 2·25 40
1199 1b. violet 3·00 90
1200 2b. violet 4·50 3·00

1953. Arms issue. State of Falcon. As T **132** showing Arms of Falcon and Stylised Oil Refinery.
1201 5c. green (postage) 15 10
1202 10c. red 20 10
1203 15c. brown 60 15
1204 20c. blue 60 20
1205 50c. orange 2·75 1·10
1206 1b. green 1·60 65
1207 5b. purple 5·25 2·00
1208 5c. turquoise (air) 65 30
1209 10c. red 15 10
1210 15c. brown 60 25
1211 30c. blue 5·25 1·10
1212 60c. green 3·50 1·10
1213 1b.20 lake 4·75 3·50
1214 3b. green 4·75 2·25
1215 5b. purple 8·00 4·25
1216 10b. violet 8·00 4·75

1953. Arms issue. State of Guarico. As T **132** showing Arms of Guarico and Factory.
1217 5c. green (postage) 15 10
1218 10c. red 15 10
1219 15c. brown 30 25
1220 20c. blue 60 30
1221 40c. orange 2·50 1·10
1222 45c. purple 6·25 2·50
1223 3b. blue 2·75 1·00
1224 5c. turquoise (air) 25 10
1225 10c. red 60 10
1226 15c. brown 60 20
1227 25c. black 90 25
1228 30c. blue 3·50 1·10
1229 50c. red 1·60 75
1230 60c. green 1·90 80
1231 1b. violet 3·25 80
1232 2b. violet 5·25 2·25

1953. Inscr "EE. UU. DE VENEZUELA".
1233 **157** 5c. green (postage) 15 10
1234 7½c. green 30 20
1235 10c. red 35 10
1236 15c. black 30 10
1237 20c. blue 40 15
1238 25c. mauve 30 10
1239 30c. blue 2·00 25
1240 35c. mauve 70 25
1241 40c. orange 1·25 35
1242 45c. violet 2·00 55
1243 50c. orange 1·25 35
1244 5c. orange (air) 10 10
1245 7½c. green 20 20
1246 15c. purple 15 10
1247 20c. slate 20 10
1248 25c. sepia 30 10
1249 30c. brown 1·75 85
1250 40c. red 30 15
1251 45c. purple 30 15
1252 50c. red 45 10
1253 60c. red 1·75 1·00
1254 70c. myrtle 90 45
1255 75c. blue 3·75 65
1256 90c. brown 75 35
1257 1b. violet 75 35
See also Nos. 1365/82.

1953. Arms issue. State of Cojedes. As T **132** showing Arms of Cojedes and Cattle.
1258 5c. green (postage) 10 10
1259 10c. red 25 10
1260 15c. brown 25 10
1261 20c. blue 30 15
1262 25c. brown 1·25 35
1263 30c. blue 1·75 35
1264 35c. violet 2·40 90
1265 5c. turquoise (air) 3·00 45
1266 7½c. green 80 50
1267 10c. red 20 10
1268 15c. brown 35 15
1269 20c. blue 40 20
1270 30c. blue 3·50 40
1271 45c. purple 1·40 35
1272 60c. green 3·00 35
1273 90c. red 4·00 1·50

1954. Arms issue. Federal Territory of Amazonas. As T **132** showing Arms of Amazonas and Orchid.
1274 5c. green (postage) 40 10
1275 10c. red 40 10
1276 15c. brown 1·25 20
1277 20c. blue 3·50 40
1278 40c. orange 4·25 1·25
1279 45c. purple 6·50 3·00
1280 3b. blue 9·25 3·50
1281 5c. turquoise (air) 1·10 10
1282 10c. red 65 10
1283 15c. brown 1·10 25
1284 25c. black 2·40 25
1285 30c. blue 5·75 35
1286 50c. red 5·00 60
1287 60c. green 5·75 60
1288 1b. violet 22·00 2·50
1289 2b. violet 9·50 3·25

1954. Arms issue. State of Apure. As T **132** showing Arms of Apure, Horse and Bird.
1290 5c. green (postage) 15 10
1291 10c. red 15 10
1292 15c. brown 25 20
1293 20c. blue 2·25 25
1294 50c. orange 2·50 1·90
1295 1b. green 85 55
1296 5b. purple 5·50 2·50
1297 5c. turquoise (air) 60 15
1298 10c. red 15 10
1299 15c. brown 60 20
1300 30c. blue 2·75 95
1301 60c. green 2·75 35
1302 1b.20 lake 4·25 2·25
1303 3b. green 2·75 95
1304 5b. purple 5·25 2·00
1305 10b. violet 7·50 4·25

1954. Arms issue. State of Barinas. As T **132** showing Arms of Barinas, Cow and Horse.
1306 5c. green (postage) 15 10
1307 10c. red 15 10
1308 15c. brown 20 20
1309 20c. blue 2·40 35
1310 50c. orange 2·50 1·25
1311 1b. green 80 35
1312 5b. purple 6·00 2·40
1313 5c. turquoise (air) 60 15
1314 10c. red 15 10
1315 15c. brown 95 25
1316 30c. blue 3·25 1·10
1317 60c. green 3·25 40
1318 1b.20 lake 4·75 2·00
1319 3b. green 3·00 1·10
1320 5b. purple 4·75 1·25
1321 10b. violet 7·00 4·00

1954. Arms issue. State of Nueva Esparta. As T **132** showing Arms of Nueva Esparta and Fishes.
1322 5c. green (postage) 15 10
1323 10c. red 15 10
1324 15c. brown 35 25
1325 20c. blue 65 15
1326 40c. orange 2·75 70
1327 45c. purple 6·50 3·25
1328 3b. blue 3·00 1·75
1329 5c. turquoise (air) 30 15
1330 10c. red 20 10
1331 15c. brown 80 20
1332 25c. black 1·40 35
1333 30c. blue 2·75 40
1334 50c. red 2·75 40
1335 60c. green 2·75 40
1336 1b. violet 3·75 85
1337 2b. violet 5·25 2·25

1954. Arms issue. State of Yaracuy. As T **132** showing Arms of Yaracuy and Tropical Foliage.
1338 5c. green (postage) 30 10
1339 10c. red 15 10
1340 15c. brown 25 20
1341 20c. blue 35 30
1342 25c. brown 80 40
1343 30c. blue 90 30
1344 35c. violet 2·25 90
1345 5c. turquoise (air) 35 20
1346 7½c. green 7·00 7·00
1347 10c. red 20 10
1348 15c. brown 80 15
1349 20c. blue 1·10 15
1350 30c. blue 2·40 40
1351 45c. purple 1·40 40
1352 60c. green 1·40 40
1353 90c. red 4·25 2·40

164 Simon Rodriguez

165 Bolivar and 1824 Edict

1954. Air. Death Cent of Rodriguez (Bolivar's tutor).
1354 **164** 5c. turquoise 35 10
1355 10c. red 50 10
1356 20c. blue 35 10
1357 45c. purple 55 35
1358 65c. green 2·40 85

1954. Air. 10th Pan-American Conf, Caracas.
1359 **165** 15c. black and brown 15 10
1360 25c. brown and grey 45 15
1361 40c. brown and orange 35 15
1362 65c. black and blue 1·25 45
1363 80c. brown and red 1·00 35
1364 1b. violet and mauve 2·00 30

1954. As T **157** but inscr "REPUBLICA DE VENEZUELA".
1365 5c. green (postage) 15 10
1366 10c. red 15 10
1367 15c. black 30 10
1368 20c. blue 35 10
1369 30c. blue 55 50
1370 35c. mauve 55 20
1371 40c. orange 1·10 30
1372 45c. violet 1·25 40
1373 5c. yellow (air) 15 10
1374 10c. bistre 15 10
1375 15c. purple 20 10
1376 20c. slate 35 10
1377 30c. brown 35 10
1378 40c. red 60 30
1379 45c. purple 60 40
1380 70c. green 2·00 70
1381 75c. blue 1·25 40
1382 90c. brown 55 30

166

167

1955. 400th Anniv of Valencia Del Rey.
1383 **166** 5c. green (postage) 25 10
1384 20c. blue 50 10
1385 25c. brown 55 10
1386 50c. orange 1·25 35
1387 5c. turquoise (air) 10 10
1388 10c. red 15 10
1389 20c. blue 25 10
1390 25c. black 25 10
1391 40c. violet 35 35
1392 50c. red 35 35
1393 60c. olive 1·00 35

1955. 1st Postal Convention, Caracas.
1394 **167** 5c. green (postage) 25 10
1395 20c. blue 1·10 10
1396 25c. lake 95 10
1397 50c. orange 1·25 10
1398 5c. yellow (air) 15 10
1399 15c. brown 35 10
1400 25c. black 35 10
1401 40c. red 35 20
1402 50c. orange 35 25
1403 60c. red 1·10 50

168 O'Leary College, Barinas

1956. Air. Public Works.
1404 **168** 5c. yellow 15 10
1405 10c. sepia 15 10
1406 15c. brown 20 10
1407 A 20c. blue 20 10
1408 25c. black 50 10
1409 30c. brown 50 15
1410 B 40c. red 55 20
1411 45c. brown 20 15
1412 50c. orange 60 15
1413 C 60c. olive 60 25
1414 65c. blue 1·00 35
1415 **168** 70c. green 1·00 25
1416 C 75c. blue 1·10 30
1417 A 80c. red 1·25 35
1418 B 1b. purple 75 20
1419 C 2b. red 1·50 85
DESIGNS—HORIZ: A, University Hospital, Caracas; B, Caracas–La Guaira Highway; C, Simon Bolivar Centre.

169

170

1956. 1st American Book Festival, Caracas.
1420 **169** 5c. turq & grn (postage) 10 10
1421 10c. purple and red 10 10
1422 20c. blue and ultramarine 25 10
1423 25c. grey and green 35 15
1424 30c. blue and light blue 35 15
1425 40c. sepia and brown 50 25
1426 50c. brown and red 55 35
1427 1b. slate and violet 85 40
1428 **170** 5c. brown and orange (air) 10 10
1429 10c. sepia and brown 15 10
1430 20c. blue and turquoise 15 10
1431 25c. slate and violet 35 10
1432 40c. purple and red 50 15
1433 45c. brown and chocolate 35 15
1434 60c. grey and olive 1·00 35

171 Tamanaco Hotel, Caracas 172 Simon Bolivar

1957. Tamanaco Hotel, Caracas Commem.
1435 171 5c. green (postage) . . . 10 10
1436 10c. red 10 10
1437 15c. black 65 10
1438 20c. blue 25 10
1439 25c. purple 25 10
1440 30c. blue 70 35
1441 35c. lilac 25 15
1442 40c. orange 35 25
1443 45c. purple 70 35
1444 50c. yellow 95 25
1445 1b. myrtle . . . . 1·25 35

1446 5c. yellow (air) 10 10
1447 10c. brown 10 10
1448 15c. brown 15 10
1449 20c. slate 55 10
1450 25c. brown 50 10
1451 30c. blue 15 20
1452 40c. red 45 15
1453 45c. brown 50 15
1454 50c. orange 50 20
1455 60c. green 75 25
1456 65c. orange . . . . . . 2·10 85
1457 70c. black . . . . 1·10 30
1458 75c. turquoise . . . . . 1·25 35
1459 1b. purple . . . . 1·25 35
1460 2b. black . . . . 2·25 45

1957. 150th Anniv of Oath of Monte Sacro and 125th Anniv of Death of Bolivar.
1461 172 5c. green (postage) . . . 10 10
1462 10c. red 15 10
1463 20c. blue 50 15
1464 25c. red 50 15
1465 30c. blue 70 15
1466 40c. orange . . . . . . 1·00 25
1467 50c. yellow . . . . . . 1·40 40

1468 5c. orange (air) 15 10
1469 10c. brown 20 10
1470 20c. blue 70 20
1471 25c. purple 75 25
1472 40c. red 70 20
1473 45c. purple 80 35
1474 65c. brown . . . . . . 1·25 35

173 G.P.O., Caracas 174 Arms of Santiago de Merida

1958.
1475 173 5c. green (postage) . . . 10 10
1476 10c. red 10 10
1477 15c. grey 10 10
1478 20c. blue 20 10
1479 25c. yellow 20 10
1480 30c. grey 25 10
1481 35c. purple 30 10
1482 40c. red 50 15
1483 45c. violet . . . . 1·25 70
1484 50c. yellow 45 15
1485 1b. olive 60 50

1486 5c. yellow (air) 10 10
1487 10c. brown 10 10
1488 15c. brown 10 10
1489 20c. blue 10 10
1490 25c. grey 20 10
1491 30c. blue 20 10
1492 35c. olive 30 10
1493 40c. green 30 10
1494 50c. red 30 10
1495 55c. olive 70 20
1496 60c. mauve 15 20
1497 65c. red 20 20
1498 70c. green 80 25
1499 75c. brown . . . . 1·10 20
1500 80c. brown . . . . 1·10 35
1501 85c. red . . . . 1·40 50
1502 90c. violet 30 35
1503 95c. purple . . . . . . 1·25 50
1504 1b. mauve 35 35
1505 1b.20 brown . . . . . . 5·75 3·50

1958. 400th Anniv of Santiago de Merida de los Caballeros.
1506 174 5c. green (postage) . . . 10 10
1507 10c. red 10 10
1508 15c. grey 10 10
1509 20c. blue 20 10
1510 25c. purple 35 10
1511 30c. violet 35 15
1512 35c. violet 65 15
1513 40c. orange 75 35
1514 45c. purple 25 15
1515 50c. yellow 70 35
1516 1b. grey . . . . 1·90 70

1517 5c. ochre (air) 10 10
1518 10c. brown 10 10
1519 15c. brown 15 10
1520 20c. blue 15 10
1521 25c. olive 40 15
1522 30c. blue 35 10
1523 40c. red 75 15
1524 45c. purple 75 20

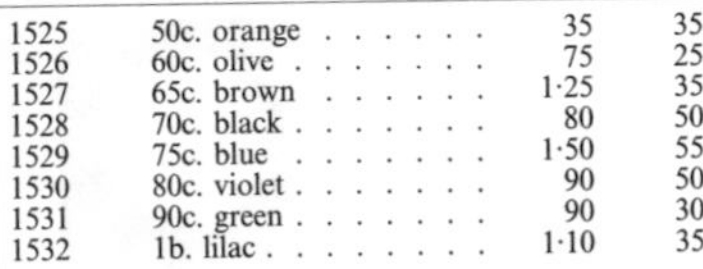

1525 50c. orange 35 35
1526 60c. olive 75 25
1527 65c. brown . . . . . . 1·25 35
1528 70c. black 80 50
1529 75c. blue . . . . 1·50 55
1530 80c. violet 90 50
1531 90c. green 90 30
1532 1b. lilac . . . . 1·10 35

175 G.P.O., Caracas 176 Arms of Trujillo and Bolivar Monument

1958.
1533 175 5c. green (postage) . . . 35 10
1534 10c. red 50 10
1535 15c. black 40 10

1536 5c. yellow (air) 35 10
1537 10c. brown 50 10
1538 15c. brown 40 10

1958. 400th Anniv of Trujillo.
1539 176 5c. green (postage) . . . 10 10
1540 10c. red 10 10
1541 15c. grey 10 10
1542 20c. blue 15 10
1543 25c. mauve 35 10
1544 30c. blue 50 15
1545 35c. lilac 55 25
1546 45c. purple 65 35
1547 50c. yellow 65 25
1548 1b. olive . . . . 1·40 55

1549 5c. buff (air) 10 10
1550 10c. brown 10 10
1551 15c. brown 25 10
1552 20c. blue 30 15
1553 25c. grey 65 20
1554 30c. blue 65 20
1555 40c. green 25 25
1556 50c. orange 25 30
1557 60c. mauve 60 40
1558 65c. red . . . . 1·60 55
1559 1b. violet . . . . 1·10 25

177 Caracas Stadium 178 "Eternal Flame"

1959. 8th Central American and Caribbean Games.
1560 177 5c. green (postage) . . . 25 10
1561 10c. mauve 25 10
1562 20c. blue 60 35
1563 30c. blue 80 40
1564 50c. lilac . . . . 1·40 35

1565 178 5c. yellow (air) 15 10
1566 10c. brown 35 15
1567 15c. orange 40 20
1568 30c. slate 65 40
1569 50c. green 95 50

179 Venezuelan ½ Real Stamp of 1859, Gen. J. I. Paz Castillo and Postman 180 Alexander von Humboldt

1959. Cent of First Venezuelan Postage Stamps.
1570 179 25c. ochre (postage) . . 25 15
1571 – 50c. blue 45 35
1572 – 1b. red . . . . 1·90 70

1573 179 25c. ochre (air) 25 15
1574 – 50c. blue 35 35
1575 – 1b. red . . . . 1·50 70
DESIGNS: 50c. (2), 1 real stamp of 1859, Don Jacinto Gutierrez and postman on mule; 1b. (2), 2 reales stamp of 1859, Don Miguel Herrera, steam mail train and Douglas DC-6 airliner.

1960. Death Centenary of Von Humboldt (naturalist).
1576 180 5c. olive & grn (postage) 35 10
1577 30c. violet and blue . . . 85 20
1578 40c. brown and orange 1·25 50

1579 5c. brown and bistre (air) 35 10
1580 20c. turquoise and blue 85 20
1581 40c. bronze and olive . . 1·40 50

181 Bolivar Peak, Merida

1960. Tourist issue.
1582 181 5c. green and emerald (postage) . . . . . . 1·10 85
1583 – 15c. grey and purple . . 3·25 2·25
1584 – 35c. purple and light purple . . . . 2·75 1·90

1585 181 30c. blue and deep blue (air) . . . . 2·50 1·60
1586 – 50c. brown and orange 2·50 1·60
1587 – 65c. brown and orange 2·50 1·60
DESIGNS: 15, 50c. Caroni Falls, Bolivar; 35, 65c. Cuacharo Caves, Monagas.

182 National Pantheon, Caracas 183 A. Eloy Blanco

1960. Pantheon in olive.
1588 182 5c. green (postage) . . . 10 10
1589 20c. blue 50 15
1590 25c. olive 70 20
1591 30c. grey 85 25
1592 40c. brown . . . . 1·50 50
1593 45c. violet . . . . 1·50 50

1594 5c. bistre (air) 10 10
1595 10c. brown 25 10
1596 15c. brown 35 10
1597 20c. blue 75 15
1598 25c. grey . . . . 1·60 35
1599 30c. violet . . . . 1·75 55
1600 40c. green 75 15
1601 45c. violet . . . . 1·10 20
1602 60c. mauve . . . . . . 1·10 40
1603 65c. red . . . . 1·10 40
1604 70c. grey . . . . 1·25 35
1605 75c. blue . . . . 2·75 60
1606 80c. blue . . . . 2·25 50
1607 1b.20 yellow . . . . . . 2·75 70

1960. 5th Death Anniv of Blanco (poet). Portrait in black.
1608 183 5c. green (postage) . . . 15 10
1609 30c. grey 35 15
1610 50c. yellow 60 30

1611 20c. blue (air) 35 15
1612 75c. turquoise . . . . . 1·25 40
1613 90c. violet . . . . 1·40 40

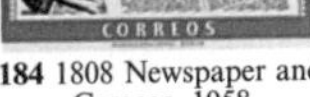

184 1808 Newspaper and Caracas, 1958 185 A. Codazzi

1960. 150th Anniv of "Gazeta de Caracas". Centres in black.
1614 184 10c. red (postage) . . . 35 15
1615 20c. blue 45 20
1616 35c. violet . . . . 1·10 70

1617 5c. yellow (air) . . . . . 1·90 65
1618 15c. brown . . . . 1·25 35
1619 65c. orange . . . . . . 1·50 60

1960. Death Centenary of Codazzi (geographer).
1620 185 5c. deep green and light green (postage) . . . 10 10
1621 15c. black and grey . . . 70 15
1622 20c. blue and light blue 65 15
1623 45c. purple and lilac . . 70 30

1624 5c. brown and orange (air) 10 10
1625 10c. sepia and brown . . 15 10
1626 25c. black and grey . . . 60 10
1627 30c. deep blue and blue 70 15
1628 50c. brown and light brown . . . . 1·10 30
1629 70c. black and brown . . 2·10 45

186 Declaration of Independence

1960. 150th Anniv of Independence. Centres multicoloured.
1630 186 5c. green (postage) . . . 50 10
1631 20c. blue . . . . 1·00 30
1632 30c. blue . . . . 1·00 40

1633 50c. orange (air) 80 30
1634 75c. turquoise . . . . . 1·00 35
1635 90c. violet . . . . 1·25 40

187 Drilling for Oil 188 L. Caceres de Arismendi

1960. Oil Industry.
1636 187 5c. myrtle and turquoise (postage) . . . . . . 1·40 70
1637 10c. brown and red . . . 70 25
1638 15c. mauve and purple 85 30

1639 – 30c. indigo and blue (air) 50 20
1640 – 40c. olive and green . . 85 35
1641 – 50c. brown and orange 1·00 40
DESIGN: Nos. 1639/41, Oil refinery.

1960. 94th Death Anniv of Luisa Caceres de Arismendi. Centres multicoloured.
1642 188 20c. blue (postage) . . . 1·00 30
1643 25c. yellow 85 30
1644 30c. blue . . . . 1·10 40

1645 5c. bistre (air) 80 30
1646 10c. brown . . . . 1·00 45
1647 60c. red . . . . 1·90 55

189 Gen. J. A. Anzoategui 190 Gen. A. J. de Sucre

1960. 140th Death Anniv of Gen. Anzoategui.
1648 189 5c. olive & grn (postage) 20 10
1649 15c. purple and brown 65 10
1650 20c. deep blue and blue 70 15

1651 25c. brown and grey (air) 65 20
1652 40c. olive and yellow . . 65 40
1653 45c. purple and mauve 85 30

1960. 130th Death Anniv of Gen. A. J. de Sucre.
1654 190 10c. mult (postage) . . . 35 15
1655 15c. multicoloured . . . 40 20
1656 20c. multicoloured . . . 60 30

1657 25c. multicoloured (air) 60 30
1658 30c. multicoloured . . . 1·10 40
1659 50c. multicoloured . . . 1·60 60

191 Skyscraper 192 "Population and Farming"

1961. National Census. Skyscraper in orange.
1660 191 5c. green 10 10
1661 10c. red 10 10
1662 15c. grey 10 10
1663 20c. blue 15 10
1664 25c. brown 25 15
1665 30c. blue 25 10
1666 35c. purple 35 15
1667 40c. brown 50 25
1668 45c. violet 70 35
1669 50c. yellow 50 20

1961. Air. 9th Population Census and 3rd Farming Census. Animal's head and inscr in black.
1670 192 5c. yellow 10 10
1671 10c. brown 10 10
1672 15c. orange 10 10
1673 20c. blue 15 10
1674 25c. grey 20 10
1675 30c. blue 25 10
1676 40c. green 35 15
1677 45c. violet 35 20
1678 50c. orange 40 25
1679 60c. mauve 50 25
1680 65c. red 70 35
1681 70c. grey . . . . 1·00 50
1682 75c. turquoise 55 40
1683 80c. violet 85 35
1684 90c. violet . . . . 1·25 70

193 R. M. Baralt

195 Arms of San Cristobal

1961. Death Centenary of R. M. Baralt (writer).

No.	Type	Description	Unused	Used
1685	193	5c. turq & grn (postage)	10	10
1686		15c. brown and grey	25	10
1687		35c. violet and mauve	65	15
1688		25c. sepia and grey (air)	70	30
1689		30c. violet and blue	80	35
1690		40c. bronze and green	90	35

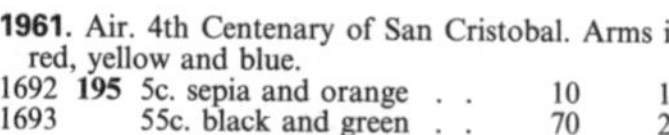

1961. Air. 4th Centenary of San Cristobal. Arms in red, yellow and blue.

No.	Type	Description	Unused	Used
1692	195	5c. sepia and orange	10	10
1693		55c. black and green	70	25

196 Yellow-crowned Amazon

1961. Birds. Multicoloured.

No.	Description	Unused	Used
1694	30c. Type **196** (postage)	1·25	50
1695	40c. Snowy egret	1·75	50
1696	50c. Scarlet ibis	4·00	1·00
1697	5c. Troupial (air)	2·75	1·50
1698	10c. Guianan cock of the rock	1·25	70
1699	15c. Tropical mockingbird	1·75	80

197 J. J. Aguerrevere (first College President)

1961. Engineering College Centenary.

No.	Type	Description	Unused	Used
1700	197	25c. blue	15	10

198 Battle Scene

1961. 140th Anniv of Battle of Carabobo. Centres multicoloured.

No.	Type	Description	Unused	Used
1702	198	5c. green (postage)	10	10
1703		40c. brown	70	30
1704	–	50c. blue (air)	70	15
1705	–	1b.05 orange	1·10	60
1706	–	1b.50 mauve	1·60	60
1707	–	1b.90 violet	1·90	85
1708	–	2b. sepia	2·10	85
1709	–	3b. blue	2·75	1·00

DESIGN: 50c. to 3b. Cavalry charge.

199 Cardinal's Arms

200 Archbishop Blanco

1962. Air. Elevation to Cardinal of Jose Humberto Quintero.

No.	Type	Description	Unused	Used
1710	199	5c. mauve	10	10

1962. Air. 4th Anniv of Archbishop Blanco's Pastoral Letter.

No.	Type	Description	Unused	Used
1712	200	75c. mauve	70	30

201 "Oncidium papilio Lindl"

1962. Orchids. Multicoloured.

No.	Description	Unused	Used
1713	5c. Type **201** (postage)	10	10
1714	10c. "Caularthron bilamellatum (Rchb. f.) R.E. Schultes"	15	10
1715	20c. "Stanhopea Wardii Lodd. ex Lindl"	40	10
1716	25c. "Catasetum pileatum Rchb f."	35	10
1717	30c. "Masdevallia tovarensis Rchb f."	40	15
1718	35c. "Epidendrum Stamfordianum Batem" (horiz)	45	25
1719	50c. "Epidendrum atropurpureum Willd"	80	35
1720	3b. "Oncidium falcipetalum Lindl."	4·25	1·60
1721	5c. "Oncidium volvox Rchb f." (air)	10	10
1722	20c. "Cycnoches chlorochilon Kl."	20	10
1723	25c. "Cattleya Gaskelliana Rchb f.var. alba"	55	15
1724	30c. "Epidendrum difforme Jacq." (horiz)	45	15
1725	40c. "Catasetum callosum Lindl" (horiz)	55	20
1726	50c. "Oncidium bicolor Lindl"	65	30
1727	1b. "Brassavola nodosa Lindl" (horiz)	90	25
1728	1b.05 "Epidendrum lividum Lindl"	2·75	1·10
1729	1b.50 "Schomburgkia undulata Lindl"	3·00	1·25
1730	2b. "Oncidium zebrinum Rchb f."	3·50	1·75

202 Signing of Independence

1962. 150th Anniv of Declaration of Independence. Multicoloured centres; frame colours given.

No.	Type	Description	Unused	Used
1731	202	5c. green (postage)	15	10
1732		20c. blue	35	15
1733		25c. orange	55	30
1734		55c. green (air)	45	20
1735		1b.05 mauve	1·75	60
1736		1b.50 violet	1·50	55

1962. Air. Bicentenary of Upata. Surch **BICENTENARIO DE UPATA 1762 - 1962 RESELLADO AEREO VALOR Bs 2,00.**

No.	Type	Description	Unused	Used
1739	173	2b. on 1b. olive	1·60	75

204 Putting the Shot

1962. 1st National Games, Caracas, 1961.

No.	Type	Description	Unused	Used
1740	204	5c. green (postage)	10	10
1741	–	10c. mauve	15	10
1742	–	25c. blue	30	15
1744	–	40c. grey (air)	40	25
1745	–	75c. brown	60	35
1746	–	85c. red	1·75	55

SPORTS: 10c. Football; 25c. Swimming; 40c. Cycling; 75c. Baseball; 85c. Gymnastics.

Each value is arranged in blocks of 4 within the sheet, with the top corners of each stamp converging to the centre of the block.

205 Vermilion Cardinal

206 Campaign Emblem and Map

1962. Birds. Multicoloured.

No.	Description	Unused	Used
1748	5c. Type **205** (postage)	10	10
1749	10c. Great kiskadee	30	10
1750	20c. Glossy-black thrush	60	15
1751	25c. Collared trogons	70	25
1752	30c. Swallow tanager	1·00	30
1753	40c. Long-tailed sylph	1·25	50
1754	3b. Black-necked stilts	8·00	5·50
1755	5c. American kestrel (air)	30	10
1756	20c. Red-billed whistling duck (horiz)	60	10
1757	25c. Amazon kingfisher	70	25
1758	30c. Rufous-vented chachalaca	90	30
1759	50c. Oriole blackbird	1·40	55
1760	55c. Common pauraque	2·75	80
1761	2b.30 Red-crowned woodpecker	8·50	4·25
1762	2b.50 Lined quail dove	8·50	3·75

1962. Malaria Eradication.

No.	Type	Description	Unused	Used
1763	206	50c. brn & blk (postage)	40	20
1764	–	30c. green and black (air)	35	20

DESIGN: As T **206** but size 26 × 36 mm.

207 Collared Peccary

208 Fisherman

1963. Venezuelan Wild Life. Multicoloured.

No.	Description	Unused	Used
1766	5c. White-tailed deer (postage)	10	10
1767	10c. Type **207**	10	10
1768	35c. Widow monkey	25	10
1769	50c. Giant otter	70	25
1770	1b. Puma	2·50	1·40
1771	3b. Capybara	5·00	2·50
1772	5c. Spectacled bear (vert) (air)	20	10
1773	40c. Paca	85	25
1774	50c. Pale-throated sloth	1·10	35
1775	55c. Giant anteater	1·40	40
1776	1b.50 Brazilian tapir	4·00	1·60
1777	2b. Jaguar	6·25	2·10

1963. Freedom from Hunger.

No.	Type	Description	Unused	Used
1778	208	25c. bl on pink (postage)	30	15
1779	–	40c. red on green (air)	50	25
1780	–	75c. sepia on yellow	30	40

DESIGNS: 40c. Farmer with lambs; 75c. Harvester.

209 Bocono Cathedral

211 Flag

210 St. Peter's Basilica, Vatican City

1963. 400th Anniv of Bocono.

No.	Type	Description	Unused	Used
1781	209	50c. mult on buff (postage)	45	20
1782	–	1b. mult on buff (air)	1·25	40

DESIGNS: 1b. Bocono Arms.

1963. Ecumenical Council, Vatican City.

No.	Type	Description	Unused	Used
1783	210	35c. brown & bl (postage)	35	15
1784		45c. brown and green	35	20
1785	–	80c. multicoloured (air)	1·10	35
1786	–	90c. multicoloured	1·10	40

DESIGN: 80, 90c. Arms of Vatican City and Venezuela.

1963. National Flag and Arms Centenary. Mult.

No.	Description	Unused	Used
1787	30c. Type **211** (postage)	20	15
1788	70c. Venezuela Arms (vert) (air)	85	50

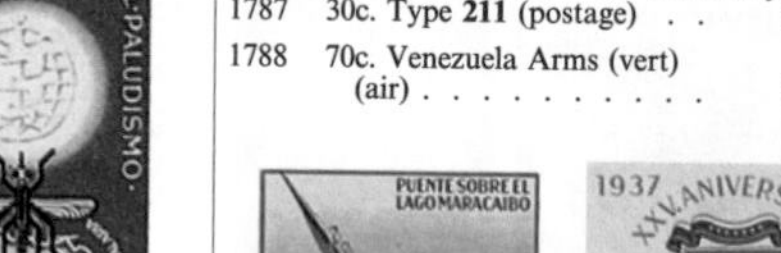

212 Maracaibo Bridge

213 Arms, Map and Guardsman

1963. Opening of Higher Bridge, Lake Maracaibo.

No.	Type	Description	Unused	Used
1789	212	30c. brown & bl (postage)	75	10
1790		35c. brown and green	90	20
1791		80c. brown and green	1·60	40
1792	–	90c. ochre, brown and green (air)	1·40	50
1793	–	95c. ochre, brown & blue	1·40	55
1794	–	1b. ochre, brown and blue	95	50

DESIGN—HORIZ: 90c. to 1b. Aerial view of bridge and mainland.

1963. 25th Anniv of National Guard.

No.	Type	Description	Unused	Used
1795	213	50c. green, red and blue on cream (postage)	40	20
1796		1b. blue and red on cream (air)	1·60	70

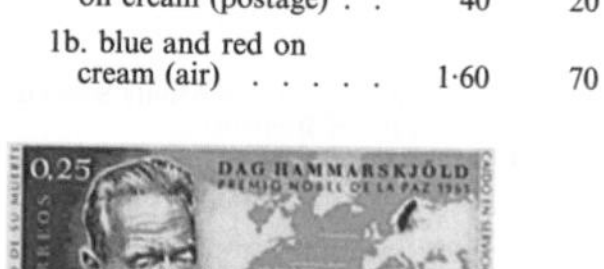

214 Dag Hammarskjold and Atlantic Map

1963. 1st Death Anniv (1962) of Dag Hammarskjold (U.N. Secretary-General, 1953–61).

No.	Type	Description	Unused	Used
1797	214	25c. indigo & bl (postage)	20	15
1798		55c. green and turquoise	75	35
1799		80c. blue and deep blue (air)	75	45
1800		90c. violet and blue	1·00	60

215 Dr. L. Razetti (medallion)

216 Dr. F. A. Risquez (Venezuelan Red Cross President, 1922–23)

1963. Birth Centenary (1962) of Dr. Luis Razetti (founder of University School of Medicine and of Vargas Hospital).

No.	Type	Description	Unused	Used
1802	215	35c. brown, ochre and blue (postage)	35	20
1803		45c. brown, ochre & mve	50	20
1804	–	95c. blue and mauve (air)	90	60
1805	–	1b.05 sepia and green	1·25	70

DESIGN: 95c., 1b.05, Portrait of Dr. Razetti.

1963. Red Cross Centenary. Multicoloured.

No.	Description	Unused	Used
1806	15c. Type **216** (postage)	15	10
1807	20c. Dr. Carlos J. Bello (President of Venezuelan Red Cross, 1928–31)	20	10
1808	40c. Sir Vincent K. Barrington (first President of Venezuelan Red Cross) (air)	40	35
1809	75c. Nurse and child	70	50

All designs show centenary emblem.

217 Labourer

218 Pedro Gual

1964. Centenary of Venezuelan Ministry of Works and National Industries Exhibition, Caracas. Multicoloured.

No.	Description	Unused	Used
1810	5c. Type **217** (postage)	10	10
1811	10c. Petrol industry	20	10
1812	15c. Building construction	25	10
1813	30c. Road and rail transport	80	45
1814	40c. Agricultural machine	60	25

1815 5c. Loading ship (air) . . . 10 10
1816 10c. Tractor and maize . . 10 10
1817 15c. Type **217** 15 10
1818 20c. Petrol industry 20 10
1819 50c. Building construction 60 30

1964. Death Cent (1962) of Pedro Gual (statesman).
1820 **218** 40c. olive (postage) . . . 40 20
1821 50c. brown 45 25
1822 75c. turquoise (air) . . . 60 25
1823 1b. mauve 70 30

219 Dr. C. Arvelo

1964. Death Cent (1962) of Carlos Arvelo (physician).
1824 **219** 1b. black and blue . . . 1·40 40

220 Blast Furnace

1964. Inaug of Orinoco Steel Works. Mult.
1825 20c. Type **220** (postage) . . 25 10
1826 50c. Type **220** 50 20
1827 80c. Cauldron and map (air) 85 35
1828 1b. As 80c. . . . . 1·40 40
The 80c. and 1b. are vert.

221 Arms of Ciudad Bolivar

222 R. Gallegos

1964. Air. Bicentenary of Ciudad Bolivar.
1829 **221** 1b. multicoloured . . . 1·10 70

1964. 80th Birth Anniv of Romulo Gallegos (novelist).
1830 **222** 5c. green and yellow (postage) 10 10
1831 10c. blue and light blue 15 10
1832 15c. purple and mauve 25 15
1833 – 30c. brown & yellow (air) 30 15
1834 – 40c. purple and pink . . 40 20
1835 – 50c. brown and orange 55 30
DESIGN: Nos. 1833/5, Gallegos and book.

223 Angel Falls (Bolivar State)

1964. Tourist Publicity. Inscr "Conozca a Venezuela Primera" ("See Venezuela First"). Multicoloured.
1836 5c. Type **223** 10 10
1837 10c. Tropical landscape (Sucre) 15 10
1838 15c. Rocks, San Juan (Guarico) 20 10
1839 30c. Fishermen casting nets (Anzoategui) 40 15
1840 40c. Mountaineering (Merida) 85 15

224 Eleanor Roosevelt

1964. Air. 15th Anniv (1963) of Declaration of Human Rights.
1841 **224** 1b. orange and violet . . 1·10 40

1965. Various stamps surch **RESELLADO VALOR** and new value. (a) Postage.
1842 5c. on 1b. (No. 1485) . . . 50 10
1843 10c. on 45c. (1668) 15 10
1844 15c. on 55c. (1798) 15 10
1845 20c. on 3b. (1754) 25 20
1846 25c. on 45c. (1623) 20 15
1847 25c. on 3b. (1720) 25 15
1848 25c. on 1b. (1770) 35 15
1849 25c. on 3b. (1771) 20 15
1850 30c. on 1b. (1516) 25 15
1851 40c. on 1b. (1824) 70 20
1852 60c. on 80c. (1791) 85 35

(b) Air.
1853 5c. on 55c. (1495) 10 10
1854 5c. on 70c. (1498) 10 10
1855 5c. on 80c. (1500) 15 10
1856 5c. on 85c. (1501) 10 10
1857 5c. on 90c. (1502) 10 10
1858 5c. on 95c. (1503) 10 10
1859 5c. on 1b. (1796) 50 35
1860 10c. on 3b. (804) 15 10
1861 10c. on 4b. (805) 70 35
1862 10c. on 70c. (1681) 35 15
1863 10c. on 90c. (1684) 25 10
1864 10c. on 1b.05 (1705) 50 25
1865 10c. on 1b.90 (1707) 25 15
1866 10c. on 2b. (1708) 35 15
1867 10c. on 3b. (1709) 35 15
1868 10c. on 80c. (1785) 15 10
1869 10c. on 90c. (1786) 15 10
1870 15c. on 3b. (769) 35 15
1871 15c. on 90c. (1613) 25 10
1872 15c. on 80c. (1799) 25 10
1873 15c. on 90c. (1800) 25 10
1874 15c. on 1b. (1829) 35 15
1875 20c. on 2b. (1460) 40 15
1876 20c. on 55c. (1693) 30 10
1877 20c. on 55c. (1760) 90 30
1878 20c. on 2b.30 (1761) 55 30
1879 20c. on 2b.50 (1762) 90 30
1880 20c. on 70c. (1788) 50 35
1881 25c. on 70c. (1629) 55 30
1882 25c. on 1b.05 (1728) 35 15
1883 25c. on 1b.50 (1729) 35 15
1884 25c. on 2b. (1730) 50 25
1885 25c. on 1b.50 (1776) 50 15
1886 25c. on 2b. (1777) 50 25
1887 25c. on 95c. (1804) 45 25
1888 25c. on 1b.05 (1805) 50 25
1889 30c. on 1b. (1782) 70 35
1890 40c. on 1b.05 (1736) 50 25
1891 50c. on 65c. (1603) 25 15
1892 50c. on 1b.20 (1607) 70 35
1893 50c. on 1b. (1841) 35 15
1894 60c. on 90c. (1792) 70 25
1895 60c. on 95c. (1793) 75 35
1896 75c. on 85c. (1746) 75 40

(c) Revenue stamps additionally optd **CORREOS**.
1897 5c. on 5c. green 10 10
1898 5c. on 20c. brown 10 10
1899 10c. on 10c. bistre 10 10
1900 15c. on 40c. green 10 10
1901 20c. on 3b. blue 35 15
1902 25c. on 5b. blue 70 35
1903 25c. on 5b. blue 35 15
1904 60c. on 3b. blue 60 40

226 Pres. Kennedy and Alliance Emblem

227 Federation Emblem

1965. "Alliance for Progress".
1905 **226** 20c. black (postage) . . 35 15
1906 40c. violet 50 20
1907 60c. turquoise (air) . . . 70 30
1908 80c. brown 85 35

1965. Air. 20th Anniv of Venezuelan Medical Federation.
1909 **227** 65c. red and black . . . 1·00 45

228 Venezuelan Pavilion

229 Andres Bello

1965. Air. New York World's Fair.
1910 **228** 1b. multicoloured . . . 90 35

1965. Air. Death Cent of Andres Bello (poet).
1911 **229** 80c. brown and orange 1·00 60

230 Restrepo's Map, 1827

1965. Guyana Claim. Multicoloured.
1912 5c. Codazzi's map, 1840 (vert) (postage) 10 10
1913 15c. Type **230** 30 10
1914 40c. L. de Surville's map, 1778 . . . . 55 15
1915 25c. Cruz Cano's map, 1775 (air) 40 15
1916 40c. (50c.) Map stamp of 1896 (vert) 55 15
1917 75c. Foreign Relations Ministry map 75 35

231 I.T.U. Emblem, Satellite, and Aerials of 1865 and 1965

1965. Air. I.T.U. Centenary.
1919 **231** 75c. black and green . . 70 30

232 Bolivar and Part of Letter

233 Children on "Magic Carpet" and "Three Kings"

1965. Air. 150th Anniv of Bolivar's Letter from Jamaica.
1920 **232** 75c. black and blue . . . 60 30

1965. Air. Children's (Christmas) Festival.
1921 **233** 70c. blue and yellow . . 1·10 55

234 Father F. Toro

1965. Air. Death Cent of Father Fermin Toro.
1922 **234** 1b. black and orange . . 85 30

235 Sir Winston Churchill

1965. Air. Churchill Commemoration.
1923 **235** 1b. black and lilac . . . 90 40

236 I.C.Y. Emblem

237 Emblem and Map

1965. Air. International Co-operation Year.
1924 **236** 85c. violet and gold . . 1·00 40

1965. Air. 75th Anniv of Organization of American States.
1925 **237** 50c. gold, black and blue 85 35

238 "Eurytides protesilaus"

239 Farms of 1936 and 1966

1966. Butterflies. Multicoloured.
1926 20c. Type **238** (postage) . . 40 15
1927 30c. "Morpho peleides" . . 55 20
1928 50c. "Papilio zagreus" . . . 80 30
1929 65c. "Anaea marthesia" (air) 1·00 40
1930 85c. "Anaea clytemnestra" 1·60 55
1931 1b. "Caligo atreus" . . . . 2·10 60

1966. Air. 30th Anniv of Ministry of Agriculture and Husbandry.
1932 **239** 55c. black, green & yellow 85 25

240 19th-century Sailing Packet crossing Atlantic

1966. Bicentenary of Maritime Mail.
1933 **240** 60c. black, blue & brown 2·00 50

241 Sebucan Dance

1966. "Popular Dances". Multicoloured.
1934 5c. Type **241** (postage) . . . 10 10
1935 10c. Candlemas 20 10
1936 15c. Chichamaya 30 10
1937 20c. Carite 40 15
1938 25c. "Round Drum" 60 25
1939 35c. Devil Dance, Feast of Corpus Christi 65 35
1940 40c. Tamunanque (air) . . . 75 35
1941 50c. Parranda de San Pedro 90 40
1942 60c. Las Turas 60 25
1943 70c. Joropo . . . . 1·10 55
1944 80c. Chimbanguele . . . . 1·40 35
1945 90c. "The Shepherds" . . . 1·60 50

242 Title Page

1966. Air. 150th Death Anniv (1964) of Jose Lamas (composer).
1946 **242** 55c. black, bistre & green 60 30
1947 95c. black, bistre & mve 85 40

243 A. Michelena (self-portrait)

244 Lincoln

1966. Birth Centenary (1963) of Arturo Michelena (painter). Multicoloured.
1948 95c. sepia and cream (Type **243**) (postage) . . . 1·25 35
1949 1b. "Pentesilea" (battle scene) . . . . 1·10 35
1950 1b.05 "La Vara Rota" ("The Red Cloak") . . . 1·25 35
1951 95c. "Escena de Circo" ("Circus Scene") (air) . . 1·25 35
1952 1b. "Miranda in La Carraca" . . . . 1·10 35
1953 1b.05 "Carlota Corday" . . 1·25 35
Nos. 1949/53 are horiz.

1966. Air. Death Cent (1965) of Abraham Lincoln.
1954 **244** 1b. black and drab . . . 70 55

245 Construction Worker

1966. 2nd O.E.A. Labour Ministers Conference.
1955 **245** 10c. black and yellow . . 10 10
1956 20c. black and turquoise 20 10

1957 – 30c. violet and blue . . . 15 15
1958 – 35c. olive and yellow . . 25 15
1959 – 50c. purple and pink . . 40 20
1960 – 65c. purple and red . . . 60 30
DESIGNS: 30, 65c. Labour Monument; 35c. Machinist; 50c. Car assembly line.

246 Dr. Hernandez

1966. Air. Birth Centenary (1964) of Dr. Jose Hernandez (physician).
1961 **246** 1b. deep blue and blue 1·25 45

247 Dr. M. Dagnino (founder) and Hospital

1966. Air. Centenary of Chiquinquira Hospital, Maracaibo.
1962 **247** 1b. deep green and green 1·00 40

248 Oscar

249 R. Arevalo Gonzalez

1966. Fishes. Multicoloured.
1963 15c. Type **248** (postage) . . 20 10
1964 25c. Peacock cichlid 40 20
1965 45c. Orinoco piranha . . . 1·25 35
1966 75c. Spotted headstander (vert) (air) . . . . 1·60 70
1967 90c. Sword-tailed characin 1·60 70
1968 1b. Ramirez's dwarf cichlid 1·60 70

1966. Air. Birth Centenary of Rafael Arevalo Gonzalez.
1969 **249** 75c. black and yellow . . 90 35

250 Simon Bolivar, 1816 (after anonymous artist)

251 "Justice"

1966. Air. Bolivar Commemoration.
1970 **250** 5c. multicoloured 10 10
1971 10c. multicoloured . . . 10 10
1972 20c. multicoloured . . . 10 10
1973 – 25c. multicoloured . . . 15 10
1974 – 30c. multicoloured . . . 20 10
1975 – 35c. multicoloured . . . 15 10
1976 – 40c. multicoloured . . . 30 15
1977 – 50c. multicoloured . . . 30 15
1978 – 60c. multicoloured . . . 30 15
1979 – 80c. multicoloured . . . 85 30
1980 – 1b.20 multicoloured . . 1·25 60
1981 – 4b. multicoloured . . . 4·00 1·90
BOLIVAR PORTRAITS: 25, 30, 35c. After paintings by Jose Gil de Castro, 1825; 40, 50, 60c. Anonymous artist, 1825; 80c., 1b.20., 4b. Anonymous artist, c. 1829.

1966. Air. 50th Anniv of Political and Social Sciences Academy.
1982 **251** 50c. purple and lilac . . 85 25

252 Nativity

253 Globe and Communications Emblems

1966. Christmas.
1983 **252** 65c. black and violet . . 80 25

1966. 30th Anniv of Venezuelan Communications Ministry.
1984 **253** 45c. multicoloured . . . 65 20

254 Angostura Bridge

1967. Air. Opening of Angostura Bridge, Orinoco River.
1985 **254** 40c. multicoloured . . . 35 20

255 Ruben Dario (poet)

256 University Building and Arms

1967. Birth Centenary of Ruben Dario.
1986 **255** 70c. indigo and blue . . 85 35

1967. 75th Anniv of Zulia University.
1987 **256** 80c. black, red and gold 85 35

257 Venzuelan Pavilion

1967. Air. World Fair, Montreal.
1988 **257** 1b. multicoloured . . . 85 30

258 Cacique Guaicaipuro (statue)

259 Francisco Esteban Gomez

1967. Air. 400th Anniv of Caracas. Multicoloured.
1989 10c. Palace of the Academies (horiz) 10 10
1990 15c. Type **258** 10 10
1991 45c. Capt. F. Fajardo . . . 35 15
1992 50c. St. Teresa's Church . . 35 15
1993 55c. Diego de Losada (founder) 45 20
1994 60c. Constellations over Caracas (horiz) 50 25
1995 65c. Arms of Caracas . . . 55 30
1996 70c. Federal Legislative Building (horiz) 55 25
1997 75c. University City (horiz) 70 30
1998 85c. El Pulpo road junction (horiz) 70 35
1999 90c. Map of Caracas (horiz) 75 35
2000 1b. Plaza Mayor, Caracas c. 1800 (horiz) . . 85 45
2001 2b. Avenida Libertador (horiz) . . . . 2·00 65

1967. Air. 150th Anniv of Battle of Matasiete.
2003 **259** 90c. multicoloured . . . 70 35

260 J. V. Gonzalez

261 Child with Toy Windmill

1967. Air. Death Centenary of Juan Gonzalez (journalist).
2016 **260** 80c. black and yellow . . 80 30

1967. Air. Children's Festival.
2017 **261** 45c. multicoloured . . . 40 20
2018 75c. multicoloured . . . 60 25
2019 90c. multicoloured . . . 70 35

262 "The Madonna of the Rosary" (Lochner)

263 Dr. J. M. Nunez Ponte (educator)

1967. Air. Christmas.
2020 **262** 1b. multicoloured . . . 1·25 40

1968. Air. 3rd Death Anniv of Dr. Jose Manuel Nunez Ponte.
2021 **263** 65c. multicoloured . . . 60 25

264 General Miranda and Printing Press

1968. Air. 150th Death Anniv of General Francisco de Miranda. Multicoloured.
2022 20c. Type **264** 20 10
2023 35c. Portrait and Houses of Parliament, London . . . 35 15
2024 45c. Portrait and Arc de Triomphe, Paris 55 30
2025 70c. Portrait (vert) 90 25
2026 80c. Bust and Venezuelan flags (vert) . . . . 1·10 45

265 Title Page and Printing Press

266 "Spodoptera frugiperda"

1968. 150th Anniv of Newspaper "Correo del Orinoco".
2027 **265** 1b.50 multicoloured . . 1·25 50

1968. Insects. Multicoloured.
2028 20c. Type **266** (postage) . . 50 20
2029 75c. "Anthonomus grandis" 85 30
2030 90c. "Manduca sexta" . . . 1·10 40
2031 5c. "Atta sextens" (air) . . 15 10
2032 15c. "Aeneolamia varia" . . 35 15
2033 20c. "Systena sp." 50 20
The 20 (air), 75 and 90c. are horiz.

267 Keys

268 Pistol-shooting

1968. Air. 30th Anniv of Office of Controller-General.
2034 **267** 95c. multicoloured . . . 90 30

1968. Air. Olympic Games, Mexico. Mult.
2035 5c. Type **268** 10 10
2036 15c. Running (horiz) 25 10
2037 30c. Fencing (horiz) 60 20
2038 75c. Boxing (horiz) . . . . 1·10 35
2039 5b. Sailing . . . . 5·25 1·40

269 Guayana Sub-station

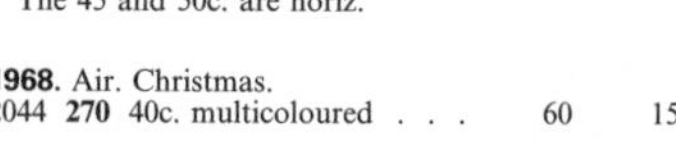
270 "The Holy Family" (F. J. de Lerma)

1968. Rural Electrification. Multicoloured.
2040 15c. Type **269** 15 10
2041 45c. Encantado Dam . . . 40 20
2042 50c. Macagua Dam 55 20
2043 80c. Guri Dam . . . . . . 1·10 40
The 45 and 50c. are horiz.

1968. Air. Christmas.
2044 **270** 40c. multicoloured . . . 60 15

271 House and Savings Bank

272 Children and Star

1968. National Savings System.
2045 **271** 45c. multicoloured . . . 55 20

1968. Air. Children's Festival.
2046 **272** 80c. orange and violet 80 25

273 Planting a Tree

1968. Conservation of Natural Resources. Multicoloured designs each incorporating central motif as in T **273**.
2047 15c. Type **273** (postage) . . 10 10
2048 20c. Plantation 15 10
2049 30c. Waterfall 30 15
2050 45c. Logs 35 15
2051 55c. Cultivated land 70 35
2052 75c. Palambra (fish) 80 25
2053 15c. Marbled wood quails (air) 35 30
2054 20c. Scarlet ibis, jabiru, great blue heron and red-billed whistling duck . . . 35 30
2055 30c. Wood-carving 25 10
2056 90c. Brown trout . . . . . 1·00 35
2057 95c. Mountain highway . . 1·25 55
2058 1b. Red-eyed vireo and shiny-headed cowbird (young) . . . . 1·60 50
The 15c. (both), 20c. (air), 30c. (both) and 55c. are vert, the remainder are horiz.

274 Colorada Beach, Sucre

1969. Tourism. Multicoloured.
2059 15c. Type **274** (postage) . . 15 10
2060 45c. San Francisco de Yare Church, Miranda 50 15
2061 90c. Houses on stilts, Zulia 75 55
2062 15c. Desert landscape, Falcon (air) 20 10
2063 30c. Humboldt Hotel, Caracas 25 15
2064 40c. Mountain cable-car, Merida 45 25

275 Bolivar addressing Congress

1969. 150th Anniv of Angostura Congress.
2066 **275** 45c. multicoloured . . . 65 20

276 Dr. Martin Luther King

278 "On the Balcony" (C. Rojas)

277 "Tabebuia pentaphylla"

1969. 1st Death Anniv of Martin Luther King (American Civil Rights leader).
2067 **276** 1b. multicoloured 80 25

1969. Nature Conservation. Trees. Multicoloured.
2068 50c. Type **277** (postage) 50 20
2069 65c. "Erythrina poeppigiana" 70 30
2070 90c. "Platymiscium sp." 1·25 50
2071 5c. "Cassia grandis" (air) 10 10
2072 20c. "Triplaris caracasana" 25 10
2073 25c. "Samanea saman" 35 15

1969. Paintings by Cristobal Rojas. Multicoloured.
2074 25c. Type **278** 20 15
2075 35c. "The Pheasant" 35 20
2076 45c. "The Christening" 55 30
2077 50c. "The Empty Place" 70 35
2078 60c. "The Tavern" 1·10 40
2079 1b. "The Arm" (27 × 55 mm) 1·50 70
Nos. 2075/8 are horiz.

279 I.L.O. Emblem

1969. 50th Anniv of I.L.O.
2080 **279** 2b.50 black and brown 2·10 1·10

280 Charter and Arms of Guayana

1969. Industrial Development. Multicoloured.
2081 45c. Type **280** 45 20
2082 1b. SIDOR steel-works 90 30

281 Arcade, Casa del Balcon

282 "Alexander von Humboldt" (J. Stieler)

1969. 400th Anniv of Carora. Multicoloured.
2083 20c. Type **281** 15 10
2084 25c. Ruins of La Pastora Church 25 15
2085 55c. Chapel of the Cross 90 30
2086 65c. Museum and library building 1·10 35

1969. Air. Birth Bicent of Alexander von Humboldt (German naturalist).
2087 **282** 50c. multicoloured 50 20

283 A. Alfinger, A. Pacheco and P. Maldonado (founders)

1969. Air. 400th Anniv of Maracaibo. Mult.
2088 20c. Type **283** 20 15
2089 25c. Map of Maracaibo, 1562 25 15
2090 40c. City coat-of-arms 30 20
2091 70c. University Hospital 60 35
2092 75c. Cacique Mara Monument 70 40
2093 1b. Baralt Plaza 80 50
Nos. 2089/92 are vert.

284 "Bolivar's Wedding" (T. Salas)

1969. "Bolivar in Spain".
2094 **284** 10c. multicoloured 10 10
2095 – 15c. black and red 20 10
2096 – 35c. multicoloured 35 15
DESIGNS—VERT: 15c. "Bolivar as a Student" (artist unknown); 35c. Bolivar's statue, Madrid.

285 Astronauts and Moon Landing

1969. Air. 1st Man on the Moon.
2098 **285** 90c. multicoloured 1·25 45

286 "Virgin of the Rosary" (17th-cent Venetian School)

1969. Air. Christmas. Multicoloured.
2100 75c. Type **286** 85 25
2101 80c. "The Holy Family" (Landaeta School, Caracas, 18th cent) 90 30

287 "Children and Birds"

1969. Children's Day. Multicoloured.
2102 5c. Type **287** 10 10
2103 45c. "Children's Camp" 55 30

288 Map of Greater Colombia

1969. 150th Anniv of Greater Colombia Federation.
2104 **288** 45c. multicoloured 50 20

289 San Antonio Church, Clarines

1970. Architecture of the Colonial Era. Mult.
2105 10c. Type **289** 10 10
2106 30c. Church of the Conception, Caroni 25 15
2107 40c. San Miguel Church, Burbusay 50 25
2108 45c. San Antonio Church, Maturin 70 35
2109 75c. San Nicolas Church, Moruy 85 40
2110 1b. Coro Cathedral 1·25 50

290 Seven Hills of Valera

291 "Simon Bolivar" (M. N. Bate)

1970. 150th Anniv of Valera.
2112 **290** 95c. multicoloured 65 30

1970. Air. Portraits of Bolivar. Stamps in brown on buff; inscriptions in green; colours of country name and value given below.
2113 **291** 15c. brown 15 10
2114 45c. blue 35 15
2115 55c. orange 50 25
2116 – 65c. brown 50 25
2117 – 70c. blue 55 35
2118 – 75c. orange 45 40
2119 – 85c. brown 90 45
2120 – 90c. blue 95 25
2121 – 95c. orange 1·10 25
2122 – 1b. brown 1·10 25
2123 – 1b.50 blue 1·25 55
2124 – 2b. orange 2·75 90
PORTRAITS BY: 65, 70, 75c. F. Roulin; 85, 90, 95c. J. M. Espinoza (1828); 1, 1b.50, 2b. J. M. Espinoza (1830).

292 Gen. A. Guzman Blanco and Dr. M. J. Sanabria

1970. Air. Centenary of Free Compulsory Education in Venezuela.
2125 **292** 75c. black, green & brown 75 30

293 Map of Venezuela

1970. States of Venezuela. Maps and Arms of the various States. Multicoloured.
2126 5c. Federal District (postage) 10 10
2127 15c. Monagas 15 10
2128 20c. Nueva Esparta 20 10
2129 25c. Portuguesa (vert) 25 10
2130 45c. Sucre 35 15
2131 55c. Tachira (vert) 20 20
2132 65c. Trujillo 30 25
2133 75c. Yaracuy 45 35
2134 85c. Zulia (vert) 85 35
2135 90c. Amazonas Federal Territory (vert) 1·25 40
2136 1b. Federal Island Dependencies 1·40 45
2137 5c. Type **293** (air) 10 10
2138 15c. Apure 20 10
2139 20c. Aragua 25 10
2140 20c. Anzoategui 25 10
2141 25c. Barinas 25 10
2142 25c. Bolivar 25 10
2143 45c. Carabobo 55 20
2144 55c. Cojedes (vert) 60 25
2145 65c. Falcon 65 25
2146 75c. Guarico 60 30
2147 85c. Lara 95 35
2148 90c. Merida (vert) 95 40
2149 1b. Miranda 95 50
2150 2b. Delta Amacuro Federal Territory 2·00 80

294 "Monochaetum humboldtianum"

295 "The Battle of Boyaca" (M. Tovar y Tovar)

1970. Flowers of Venezuela. Multicoloured.
2151 20c. Type **294** (postage) 30 10
2152 25c. "Symbolanthus vasculosus" 60 15
2153 45c. "Cavendishia splendens" 80 35
2154 1b. "Befaria glauca" 1·10 50
2155 20c. "Epidendrum secundum (air) 25 10
2156 25c. "Oyedaea verbesinoides" 35 15
2157 45c. "Heliconia villosa" 80 35
2158 1b. "Macleania nitida" 1·10 50

1970. 150th Anniv (1969) of Battle of Boyaca.
2159 **295** 30c. multicoloured 35 15

296 Archiepiscopal Cross

297 "Caracciolo Parra Olmedo" (T. Salas)

1970. Religious Art. Multicoloured.
2160 35c. Type **296** 35 15
2161 40c. "Our Lady of the Valley" 45 25
2162 60c. "Our Lady of Belen de San Mateo" 90 35
2163 90c. "The Virgin of Chiquinquira" 1·10 50
2164 1b. "Our Lady of Socorro de Valencia" 1·40 55

1970. Air. 150th Birth Anniv of Caracciola Parra Olmedo (lawyer).
2166 **297** 20c. multicoloured 25 10

298 National Flags and Exhibition Emblem

299 "Guardian Angel" (J. P. Lopez)

1970. "EXFILCA 70" Philatelic Exhibition, Caracas. Multicoloured.
2167 20c. Type **298** 20 10
2168 25c. 1871 1c. stamp and emblem (horiz) 30 15
2169 70c. 1930 2b.50 air stamp and emblem 50 30

1970. Christmas.
2171 **299** 45c. multicoloured 60 15

300 Caudron G-3 Biplane and Dassault Mirage III

1970. 50th Anniv of Venezuelan Air Force.
2172 **300** 5c. multicoloured 20 10

301 People in Question Mark

1971. National Census.
2173 **301** 30c. black, green and red (postage) 60 30
2174 – 70c. multicoloured (air) 95 45
DESIGN: 70c. National flag and "pin-men".

302 Battle Scene

1971. 150th Anniv of Battle of Carabobo.
2175 **302** 2b. multicoloured . . . 1·40 80

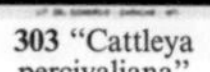

303 "Cattleya percivaliana"
304 Adoration of the Child

1971. Air. Venezuelan Orchids. Multicoloured.
2176 20c. Type **303** 25 15
2177 25c. "Cattleya gaskelliana" (horiz) 30 20
2178 75c. "Cattleya mossiae" . . 85 40
2179 90c. "Cattleya violacea o superba" (horiz) 90 35
2180 1b. "Cattleya lawrenceana" (horiz) . . . . 1·10 40

1971. Christmas. Multicoloured.
2181 25c. Type **304** 25 15
2182 25c. Madonna and Child . . 25 15

305 Dr. Luis D. Beauperthuy
306 Constitution and Government Building

1971. Death Centenary of Luis P. Beauperthuy (scientist).
2183 **305** 1b. multicoloured . . . 70 30

1971. Air. 10th Anniv of 1961 Constitution.
2184 **306** 90c. multicoloured . . . 1·10 35

307 Heart-shaped Globe
308 Arms of Venezuela and National Flags

1972. World Heart Month.
2185 **307** 1b. black, red and blue 85 40

1972. "Venezuela in the Americas". Mult.
2186 3b. Type **308** . . . . . . 2·40 85
2187 4b. Venezuelan flag . . . . 2·75 1·40
2188 5b. National anthem . . . . 3·25 1·90
2189 10b. "Araguaney" (national tree) . . . . 6·75 2·75
2190 15b. Map of the Americas 10·50 3·75

309 Tower Blocks

1972. Central Park Housing Project. Mult.
2191 30c. Type **309** 25 15
2192 30c. View from ground level 25 15
2193 30c. Aerial view 25 15

310 Mahatma Gandhi

1972. Birth Centenary (1969) of Mahatma Gandhi.
2194 **310** 60c. multicoloured . . . 75 35

311 Children making Music
313 Planetary System

312 Head of "Drymarchon corais"

1972. Christmas. Multicoloured.
2195 30c. Type **311** 25 15
2196 30c. Children roller-skating 25 15
Nos. 2195/6 were issued together, se-tenant, forming a composite design.

1972. Snakes. Multicoloured.
2197 10c. Type **312** 10 10
2198 15c. "Spilotes pullatus" . . 15 10
2199 25c. "Bothrops venezuelensis" 40 15
2200 30c. "Micrurus dumerili carinicaudus" 50 20
2201 60c. "Crotalus vegrandis" 50 35
2202 1b. Boa constrictor 75 50

1973. 500th Birth Anniv of Copernicus (astronomer). Multicoloured.
2203 5c. Type **313** 10 10
2204 10c. Copernicus 20 10
2205 15c. Book "De Revolutionibus Orbium Coelestium" 25 10

314 The Sun
315 Part of Solar System (left-hand)

1973. 10th Anniv of Humboldt Planetarium. Multicoloured. (a) As Type **314**.
2206 5c. Type **314** 10 10
2207 5c. Earth 10 10
2208 20c. Mars 35 10
2209 20c. Saturn 25 10
2210 30c. Asteroids 30 15
2211 40c. Neptune 35 20
2212 50c. Venus 75 35
2213 60c. Jupiter 85 40
2214 75c. Uranus . . . . 1·00 50
2215 90c. Pluto . . . . 1·25 40
2216 90c. Moon . . . . 1·40 70
2217 1b. Mercury . . . . 1·60 60

(b) As Type **315**.
2218 10c. Type **315** 30 10
2219 15c. Solar System (centre) 40 10
2220 15c. Solar System (right-hand) 40 10
Nos. 2218/20 form a composite design of the Solar System.

316 O.A.S. Emblem and Map

1973. 25th Anniv of Organization of American States.
2221 **316** 60c. multicoloured . . . 50 20

317 General Paez in Uniform
319 Bishop Ramos de Lora

318 Admiral Padilla, Gen. Montilla and Gen. Manrique

1973. Death Centenary of General Jose A. Paez.
2222 **317** 10c. multicoloured . . . 10 10
2223 – 30c. gold, black and red 25 15
2224 – 50c. black, ultramarine and blue 50 25
2225 – 1b. multicoloured . . . 75 50
2226 – 2b. multicoloured . . . 1·25 75
DESIGNS—VERT: 30c. Paez and horse (old engraving); 50c. Gen. Paez in civilian dress; 1b. Street of the Lancers, Puerto Cabello. HORIZ: 2b. "The Charge at Centauro".

1973. 150th Anniv of Naval Battle of Maracaibo. Multicoloured.
2227 50c. Type **318** 40 20
2228 1b. "Battle of Maracaibo" (M. F. Rincon) 90 40
2229 2b. Plan of opposing fleets 1·40 60

1973. 250th Birth Anniv (1972) of Bishop Ramos de Lora.
2230 **319** 75c. gold and brown . . 45 20

320 Ship, Jet Airliner and Map
322 General Paez Dam

321 Waterfall and Map

1973. Margarita Island Free Zone.
2231 **320** 5c. multicoloured 15 10

1973. Completion of Golden Highway. Mult.
2232 5c. Type **321** 10 10
2233 10c. Map and scarlet macaw 25 25
2234 20c. Map and Santa Elena Church, Uairen 25 10
2235 50c. Map and ancient mountain sanctuary . . . 65 25
2236 60c. As 50c. 65 25
2237 90c. Map and Santa Teresita church, Cabanayen . . . 85 35
2238 1b. Map and flags of Venezuela and Brazil . . 90 40

1973. Completion of General Paez Dam, Merida.
2239 **322** 30c. multicoloured . . . 30 10

323 Child on Slide

1973. Children's Festival. Multicoloured.
2240 10c. Type **323** 25 15
2241 10c. Fairy tale animals . . . 25 15
2242 10c. "Paginas Para Imaginar" (children's book) 25 15
2243 10c. Holidaymakers leaving airliner 25 15

324 King on White Horse
326 Vase and Lace ("Handicrafts")

325 Regional Map

1973. Christmas. Multicoloured.
2244 30c. Type **324** 25 10
2245 30c. Two Kings 25 10

1973. Regional Development.
2246 **325** 25c. multicoloured . . . 30 10

1973. Venezuelan Industrial Development Commission. Multicoloured.
2247 15c. Type **326** 15 10
2248 35c. Industrial estate ("Construction") 35 10
2249 45c. Cogwheels and chimney ("Small and medium industries") 50 20

327 Map and Revellers

1974. 10th Anniv of Carupano Carnival.
2250 **327** 5c. multicoloured 10 10

328 Congress Emblem

1974. 9th Venezuelan Engineering Congress, Maracaibo.
2251 **328** 50c. multicoloured . . . 50 15

329 "Law of the Sea" Emblem

1974. 3rd Law of the Sea Conference, Caracas. Multicoloured.
2252 15c. Type **329** 10 10
2253 35c. Great barracuda in seaweed 35 10
2254 75c. Sea-bed scene 70 25
2255 80c. Underwater grotto . . 75 35

330 Pupil and New School

1974. "Pay Your Taxes" Campaign.
2256 **330** 5c. multicoloured 10 10
2257 10c. multicoloured . . . 10 10
2258 15c. multicoloured . . . 10 10
2259 20c. multicoloured . . . 10 10
2260 A 25c. multicoloured . . . 15 10
2261 30c. multicoloured . . . 40 20
2262 35c. multicoloured . . . 20 10
2263 40c. multicoloured . . . 35 15
2264 B 45c. multicoloured . . . 35 15
2265 50c. multicoloured . . . 35 15
2266 55c. multicoloured . . . 55 30
2267 60c. multicoloured . . . 45 20
2268 C 65c. multicoloured . . . 1·00 50
2269 70c. multicoloured . . . 50 20
2270 75c. multicoloured . . . 50 25
2271 80c. multicoloured . . . 50 25
2272 D 85c. multicoloured . . . 50 25
2273 90c. multicoloured . . . 70 25
2274 95c. multicoloured . . . 1·00 70
2275 1b. multicoloured . . . 70 35
DESIGNS: A, Suburban housing project; B, City centre motorway; C, Sports stadium; D, Surgical team in operating theatre.

331 "Bolivar at Junin" (A. H. Tovar)

1974. 150th Anniv of Battle of Junin.
2276 **331** 2b. multicoloured . . . 1·60 70

332 World Map

1974. Centenary of U.P.U. Multicoloured.
2277 45c. Type **332** 35 15
2278 50c. Mounted courier, sailing packet, modern liner and jet airliner . . . 40 20

333 Rufino Blanco-Fombona and Books

1974. Birth Centenary of Rufino Blanco-Fombona (writer).
2279 **333** 10c. multicoloured . . . 10 10
2280 – 30c. multicoloured . . . 20 10
2281 – 45c. multicoloured . . . 30 15
2282 – 90c. multicoloured . . . 50 25
DESIGNS: Nos. 2280/2, Portraits of Rufino Blanco-Fombona against a background of books similar to Type **333**.

334 Children on Paper Dart

1974. Children's Festival.
2283 **334** 70c. multicoloured . . . 40 20

335 Marshal Sucre **336** "Shepherd"

1974. 150th Anniv of Battle of Ayacucho. Multicoloured.
2284 30c. Type **335** 20 10
2285 50c. South American flags on globe 30 25
2286 1b. Map showing battle sites 55 35
2287 2b. "Battle of Ayacucho" (43½ × 22 mm) . . . . . 1·25 70

1974. Christmas. Details from "The Adoration of the Shepherds" (J. B. Mayno). Multicoloured.
2288 30c. Type **336** 25 15
2289 30c. "Holy Family" 25 15
Nos. 2288/9 were issued together se-tenant, forming a composite design.

337 Road Construction, 1905, and El Ciempies Junction, 1972

1974. Centenary of Ministry of Public Works. Multicoloured.
2290 5c. Type **337** 10 10
2291 20c. J. Munoz Tebar (first Minister of Public Works) 25 10
2292 25c. Bridges on Caracas–La Guaira Road, 1912 and 1953 . . . . 30 10
2293 40c. Views of Caracas, 1874 and 1974 . . . . 30 15
2294 70c. Tucacas Railway Station, 1911, and projected Caracas underground railway terminal . . . . 2·25 55
2295 80c. Anatomical Institute, 1911, and Social Security Hospital, 1969 . . . . . 85 30
2296 85c. Quininari River bridge, 1904, and Orinoco River bridge, 1967 . . . . . . 1·00 35
2297 1b. As 20c. . . . . 1·40 50

338 Women in Profile **340** The Nativity

339 Emblem and "Tents"

1975. International Women's Year.
2298 **338** 90c. multicoloured . . . 50 30

1975. 14th World Scout Jamboree.
2299 **339** 20c. multicoloured . . . 15 10
2300 80c. multicoloured . . . 55 25

1975. Christmas. Multicoloured.
2301 30c. Type **340** 20 10
2302 30c. "The Shepherds" . . . 20 10
Nos. 2301/2 were issued se-tenant, forming a composite design.

341 Red Cross Nurse **342** Altar

1975. Venezuelan Red Cross.
2303 **341** 30c.+15c. mult 35 20
2304 50c.+25c. mult 50 30

1976. Centenary of National Pantheon.
2305 **342** 30c. grey and blue . . . 15 10
2306 – 1b.05 brown and red . . 50 25
DESIGN: 1b.05, Pantheon building.

343 Coloured Panels

1976. 150th Anniv of Bolivian Independence (1975).
2307 **343** 60c. multicoloured . . . 25 15

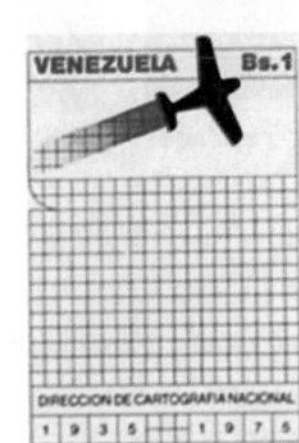

344 "Charting from Aircraft"

1976. 40th Anniv of National Cartographic Institute (1975).
2308 **344** 1b. black and blue . . . 50 20

345 Signature of General Jose Felix Ribas

1976. Birth Bicentenary of General Jose Ribas. Multicoloured.
2309 **345** 40c. green and red . . . 25 10
2310 – 55c. multicoloured . . . 35 15
DESIGN—HORIZ: (40 × 30 mm): 55c. General Jose Felix Ribas.

346 "Musicians of Chacao School" (A. Barrios)

1976. Birth Bicentenary (1975) of Jose Angel Lamas (composer).
2311 **346** 75c. multicoloured . . . 45 25
2312 – 1b.25 red, grey and buff 65 35
DESIGN—40 × 28 mm: 1b.25, Lamas' colophon.

347 "Bolivar" (J. M. Espinoza) **348** Maze symbolizing Opportunity

1976.
2313 **347** 5c. turquoise 10 10
2314 10c. red 10 10
2315 15c. brown 10 10
2316 20c. black 10 10
2317 25c. orange 10 10
2613 25c. red 10 10
2318 30c. blue 10 10
2319 45c. lilac 15 10
2320 50c. orange 20 10
2614 50c. blue 10 10
2321 65c. blue 25 10
2615 75c. mauve 10 10
2322 1b. red 35 15
2616 1b. orange 10 10
2323 2b. grey 70 35
2617 2b. yellow 15 10
2324 3b. blue . . . . 1·10 50
2618 3b. green 10 10
2325 4b. orange . . . . . . 1·25 45
2619 4b. brown 15 10
2620 5b. red 15 10
2327 10b. lilac . . . . 3·00 1·10
2621 10b. yellow 40 15
2328 15b. blue . . . . 4·50 1·60
2622 15b. purple 70 15
2329 20b. red . . . . 6·00 2·25
2623 20b. blue . . . . 1·10 40
2329a 25b. blue . . . . 6·25 2·25
2623a 25b. bistre . . . . . . 1·25 60
2329b 30b. blue . . . . 7·00 2·75
2623b 30b. lilac . . . . 1·75 75
2329c 50b. purple . . . . . . 12·00 4·50
2623c 50b. red . . . . 2·75 1·25
Nos. 2323/9 are larger, 27 × 33 mm.

1976. 250th Anniv of Central University.
2330 **348** 30c. multicoloured . . . 15 10
2331 – 50c. black, orange & yell 25 15
2332 – 90c. yellow and black . . 50 30
DESIGNS: 50c. University building; 90c. Faculty symbols.

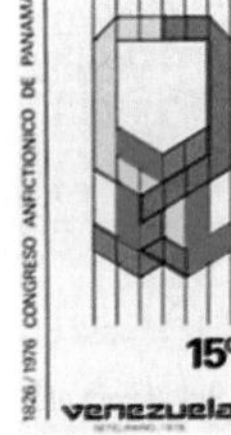

349 C. A. Fernadez de Leoni (founder) **350** "Unity" Emblem

1976. Children's Foundation. Multicoloured.
2333 30c.+15c. Type **349** 25 20
2334 50c.+25c. Children in "home" (31 × 44 mm) . . 45 30

1976. 150th Anniv of Panama Amphictyonic Congress.
2335 **350** 15c. multicoloured . . . 10 10
2336 – 45c. multicoloured . . . 25 10
2337 – 1b.25 multicoloured . . . 55 30
DESIGN: 45c., 1b.25, As Type **275**, but with different "Unity" emblems.

351 George Washington

1976. Bicentenary of American Revolution.
2338 **351** 1b. black and brown . . 55 35
2339 – 1b. black and green . . 55 55
2340 – 1b. black and purple . . 55 35
2341 – 1b. black and blue . . . 55 35
2342 – 1b. black and brown . . 55 35
DESIGNS: No. 2339, Thomas Jefferson; No. 2340, Abraham Lincoln; No. 2341, Franklin D. Roosevelt; No. 2342, John F. Kennedy.

352 Valve in Oil Pipeline **353** "The Nativity" (B. Rivas)

1976. Oil Nationalization.
2343 **352** 10c. multicoloured . . . 10 10
2344 – 30c. multicoloured . . . 15 10
2345 – 35c. multicoloured . . . 20 10
2346 – 40c. multicoloured . . . 20 10
2347 – 55c. multicoloured . . . 30 15
2348 – 90c. multicoloured . . . 55 25
DESIGNS: 30c. to 90c. Various computer drawings of valves and pipelines.

1976. Christmas.
2349 **353** 30c. multicoloured . . . 25 10

354 Patient **355** Declaration Emblem

1976. Anti-tuberculosis Society Fund.
2350 **354** 10c.+5c. multicoloured 15 15
2351 30c.+10c. multicoloured 20 20

1976. 10th Anniv of Bogota Declaration.
2352 **355** 60c. black and yellow . . 30 15

356 Arms of Barinas

1977. 400th Anniv of Barinas.
2353 **356** 50c. multicoloured . . . 30 15

357 "Christ Crucified"

1977. 400th Anniv (1976) of La Grita.
2354 **357** 30c. multicoloured . . . 15 10

358 Coro Settlement

1977. 450th Anniv of Coro.
2355 **358** 1b. multicoloured . . . 35 15

359 I.P.C.T.T. Emblem and Stylized Dove

1977. 9th Inter-American Postal and Telecommunications Staff Congress, Caracas.
2356 **359** 85c. multicoloured . . . 35 15

360 Cable Links to Domestic Equipment

361 "VENEZUELA" and Value as Rolled Steel

1977. Inauguration of "Columbus" Submarine Cable.
2357 **360** 95c. grey, blue and green 60 15

1977. 1st Anniv of Nationalization and Exploitation of Steel.
2358 **361** 30c. black and yellow . . 15 10
2359 – 50c. black and orange 25 10
2360 – 80c. black and grey . . . 35 15
2361 – 1b.05 black and red . . 40 20
2362 – 1b.25 black and yellow 45 20
2363 – 1b.50 black and grey . . 65 25
DESIGNS: 50c. to 1b.50, Similar to Type **361** but each differently arranged.

362 J. P. Duarte

363 "The Holy Family"

1977. Death Cent (1976) of Juan Pablo Duarte.
2364 **362** 75c. black and mauve . . 30 15

1977. Christmas.
2365 **363** 30c. multicoloured . . . 15 10

364 O.P.E.C. Emblem

1977. 50th O.P.E.C. Conference, Caracas.
2366 **364** 1b.05 black and blue . . 50 15

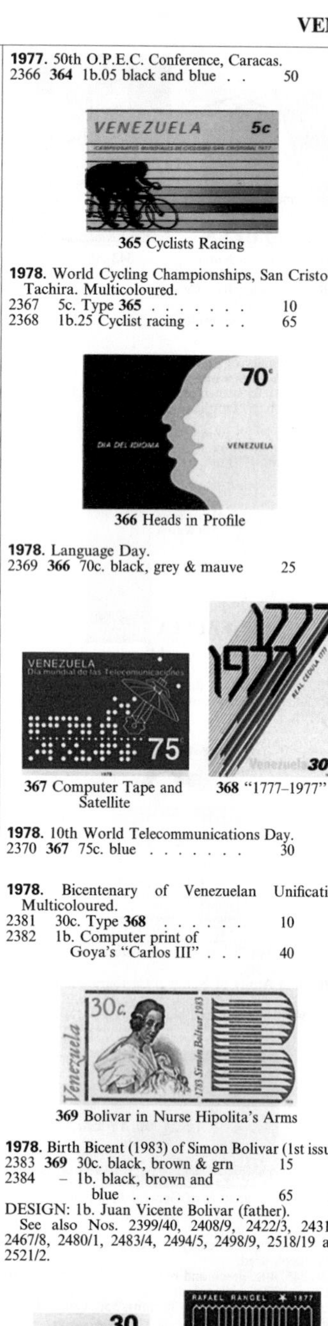

365 Cyclists Racing

1978. World Cycling Championships, San Cristobal, Tachira. Multicoloured.
2367 5c. Type **365** 10 10
2368 1b.25 Cyclist racing 65 20

366 Heads in Profile

1978. Language Day.
2369 **366** 70c. black, grey & mauve 25 15

367 Computer Tape and Satellite

368 "1777–1977"

1978. 10th World Telecommunications Day.
2370 **367** 75c. blue 30 20

1978. Bicentenary of Venezuelan Unification. Multicoloured.
2381 30c. Type **368** 10 10
2382 1b. Computer print of Goya's "Carlos III" . . . 40 15

369 Bolivar in Nurse Hipolita's Arms

1978. Birth Bicent (1983) of Simon Bolivar (1st issue).
2383 **369** 30c. black, brown & grn 15 10
2384 – 1b. black, brown and blue 65 25
DESIGN: 1b. Juan Vicente Bolivar (father).
See also Nos. 2399/40, 2408/9, 2422/3, 2431/2, 2467/8, 2480/1, 2483/4, 2494/5, 2498/9, 2518/19 and 2521/2.

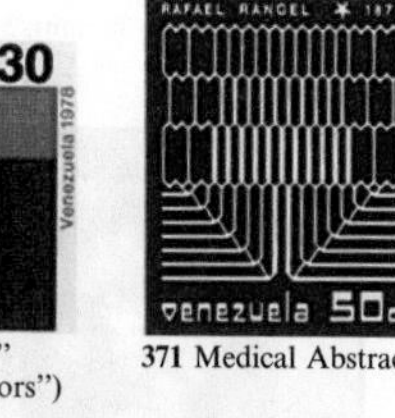

370 "T" ("Trabajadors")

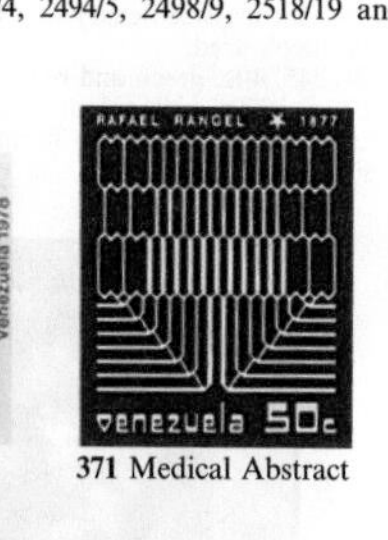

371 Medical Abstract

1978. Workers' Day.
2385 **370** 30c. red and black . . . 10 10
2386 – 30c. blue and black . . . 10 10
2387 – 30c. yellow, blue & black 10 10
2388 – 30c. red, blue and black 10 10
2389 – 30c. red and black . . . 10 10
2390 – 95c. black and red . . . 30 15
2391 – 95c. grey and blue . . . 30 15
2392 – 95c. black and red . . . 30 15
2393 – 95c. blue and black . . . 30 15
2394 – 95c. multicoloured . . . 30 15
DESIGNS: Nos. 2386/94 based on the letter "T", also inscribed "CTV".

1978. Birth Centenary (1977) of Rafael Rangel (physician and scientist).
2395 **371** 50c. brown 40 20

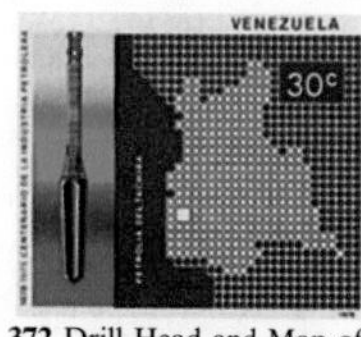

372 Drill Head and Map of Tachira Oilfield

1978. Centenary of Venezuelan Oil Industry. Multicoloured.
2396 30c. Type **372** 15 10
2397 1b.05 Letter "P" as pipeline 50 20

373 Christmas Star

1978. Christmas.
2398 **373** 30c. multicoloured . . . 15 10

1978. Birth Bicentenary (1983) of Simon Bolivar (2nd issue). As T **369**.
2399 30c. black, brown and purple 10 10
2400 1b. black, grey and red . . 30 15
DESIGNS: 30c. Bolivar at 25 (after M. N. Bate); 1b. Simon Rodriguez (Bolivar's tutor).

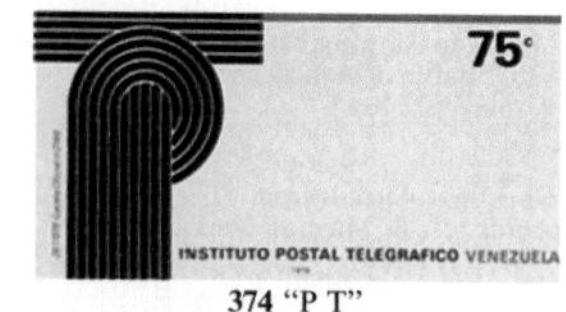

374 "P T"

1979. Creation of Postal and Telegraph Institute.
2402 **374** 75c. blk & red on cream 25 15

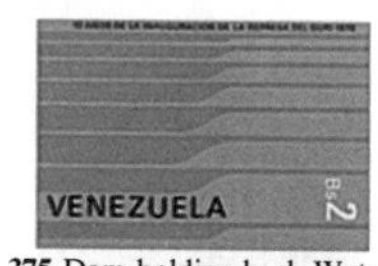

375 Dam holding back Water

1979. 10th Anniv of Guri Dam.
2403 **375** 2b. silver, grey and black 70 30

376 "General San Martin" (E. J. Maury)

1979. Birth Bicentenary of General Jose de San Martin. Multicoloured.
2404 40c. Type **376** 15 10
2405 60c. Portrait by Mercedes San Martin 25 10
2406 70c. San Martin Monument, Guayaquil 30 15
2407 75c. San Martin's signature 35 20

1979. Birth Bicentenary (1983) of Simon Bolivar (3rd series). As T **369**.
2408 30c. black, violet and red . . 10 10
2409 1b. black, orange and red 30 15
DESIGNS: 30c. Alexandre Sabes Petion (President of Haiti); 1b. Bolivar's signature.

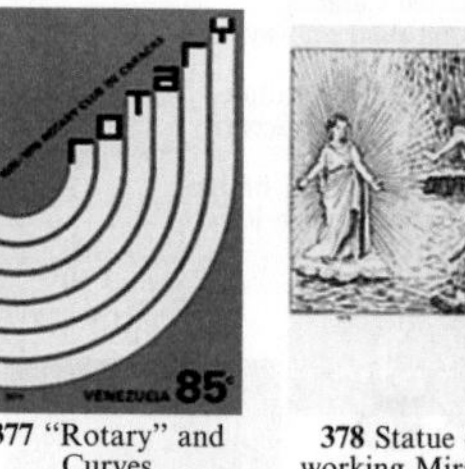

377 "Rotary" and Curves

378 Statue of Virgin working Miracles, 1654

1979. 50th Anniv of Rotary Club of Caracas.
2411 **377** 85c. black and gold . . . 25 15

1979. 25th Anniv of Canonization of Virgin of Coromoto.
2412 **378** 55c. black and red . . . 20 10

379 Miranda, London Residence and Arms

1979. Acquisition by Venezuela of Francisco de Miranda's House in London.
2413 **379** 50c. multicoloured . . . 20 10

380 O'Leary and Maps

1979. 125th Death Anniv of Daniel O'Leary (publisher of Bolivar's memoirs).
2414 **380** 30c. multicoloured . . . 10 10

381 Boy with Nest

382 Candle

1979. International Year of the Child.
2415 **381** 70c. black and blue . . . 25 15
2416 – 80c. multicoloured . . . 30 15
DESIGN: 80c. Boys playing in sea.

1979. Christmas.
2417 **382** 30c. multicoloured . . . 10 10

383 Caudron G-3 Biplane

1979. "Exfilve 79" National Stamp Exhibition and 59th Anniv of Air Force. Multicoloured.
2418 75c. Type **383** 35 20
2419 75c. Stearman Kaydett biplane 35 20
2420 75c. Bell Iroquois helicopter 35 20
2421 75c. Dassault Mirage IIIC jet fighter 35 20

1979. Birth Bicentenary (1983) of Simon Bolivar (4th series). As T **369**.
2422 30c. black, red and turquoise 10 10
2423 1b. black, blue and red . . 30 15
DESIGNS: 30c. Bolivar; 1b. Slave.

384 Emblem and World Map

1979. Introduction of New Emblem for Postal and Telegraph Institute.
2425 **384** 75c. multicoloured . . . 25 15

385 Queen Victoria and Hill

1980. Death Centenary of Sir Rowland Hill (1979).
2426 **385** 55c. multicoloured . . . 20 10

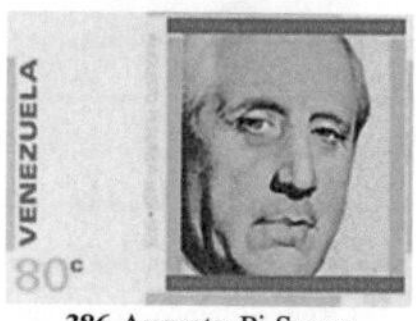

386 Augusto Pi Suner

1980. Birth Centenary (1979) of Dr. Augusto Pi Suner (physiologist).
2427 **386** 80c. multicoloured . . . 30 15

387 "Cotyledon hispanica"

388 Lovera (self-portrait)

1980. 250th Birth Anniv of Pedro Loefling (Swedish botanist).
2428 **387** 50c. multicoloured . . . 20 10

1980. Birth Bicentenary (1978) of Juan Lovera (artist).
2429 **388** 60c. blue and red 20 10
2430 75c. violet and orange 25 15

1980. Birth Bicentenary (1983) of Simon Bolivar (5th issue). As T **369**.
2431 30c. black, green and purple 10 10
2432 1b. black, dp brown & brown 30 15
DESIGNS: 30c. Signing document; 1b. Congress House, Angostura.

389 "Self-portrait with Children" (detail)
390 Bernardo O'Higgins

1980. 25th Death Anniv (1979) of Armando Reveron (artist). Multicoloured.
2434 50c. Type **389** 20 10
2435 65c. "Self-portrait" (26×41 mm) 35 20

1980. 204th Birth Anniv of Bernardo O'Higgins.
2436 **390** 85c. black, red and blue 50 25

391 Frigate "Mariscal Sucre"

1980. Venezuelan Navy. Multicoloured.
2437 1b.50 Type **391** . . . . . 1·25 50
2438 1b.50 Submarine "Picua" 1·25 50
2439 1b.50 Naval School . . . . 1·25 50
2440 1b.50 Cadet barque "Simon Bolivar" (33×52 mm) . . 1·25 50

392 Figures supporting O.P.E.C. Emblem

1980. 20th Anniv of Organization of Petroleum Exporting Countries. Multicoloured.
2441 1b.50 Type **392** 50 25
2442 1b.50 O.P.E.C. emblem and globe 50 25

393 "The Death of Bolivar" (Antonio Herrera Toro)

1980. 150th Death Anniv of Simon Bolivar.
2443 **393** 2b. multicoloured . . . 70 30

394 Antonio Jose de Sucre

395 "The Adoration of the Shepherds" (Rubens)

1980. 150th Death Anniv of Marshal Antonio Jose de Sucre.
2444 **394** 2b. multicoloured . . . 70 30

1980. Christmas.
2445 **395** 1b. multicoloured . . . 20 10

396 Helen Keller's Initials in Braille and Print

1981. Birth Centenary (1980) of Helen Keller.
2446 **396** 1b.50 grey, orange & blk 40 15

397 Gateway, San Felipe

398 Jean Baptiste de la Salle (founder)

1981. 250th Anniv of San Felipe.
2447 **397** 3b. blue, grey and red 95 35

1981. 300th Anniv (1980) of Brothers of Christian Schools.
2448 **398** 1b.25 silver, red & black 30 15

399 Municipal Theatre

1981. Centenary of Caracas Municipal Theatre.
2449 **399** 1b.25 pink, black & lilac 30 15

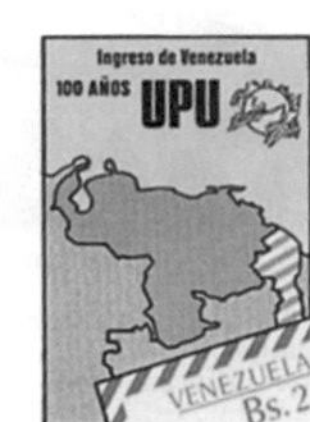

400 U.P.U. Emblem, Map of Venezuela and Envelope

1981. Centenary of Admission to Universal Postal Union.
2450 **400** 2b. multicoloured . . . 75 20

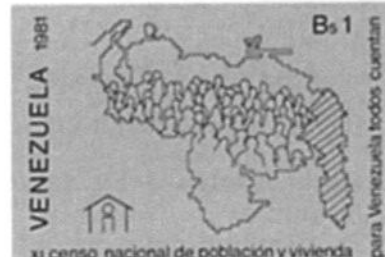

401 People on Map

1981. 11th National Population and Housing Census.
2451 **401** 1b. lilac, violet, and black 30 15

402 Games Emblem

404 Musicians

403 "Penny-farthing" Bicycle

1981. 9th Bolivarian Games, Barquisimeto.
2452 **402** 95c. multicoloured . . . 30 15

1981. Transport History (1st series). Mult.
2453 1b. Type **403** 35 20
2454 1b.05 Steam locomotive, 1926 . . . . 1·10 50
2455 1b.25 Buick car, 1937 . . . 40 25
2456 1b.50 Horse-drawn cab . . 50 25
See also Nos. 2490/3 and 2514/7.

1981. Christmas.
2457 **404** 1b. multicoloured . . . 25 10

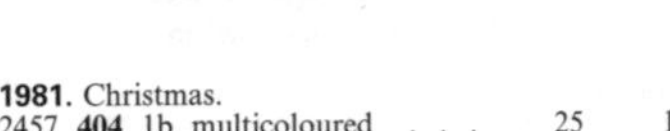

405 Mt. Autana

407 "Landscape"

406 Calligraphic Script and Arms

1982. 50th Anniv of Venezuelan Natural Sciences Society. Multicoloured.
2458 1b. Type **405** 30 20
2459 1b.50 Sarisarinama 50 20
2460 2b. Guacharo Cave 80 35

1982. 20th Anniv of Constitution.
2461 **406** 1b.85 gold and black . . 70 25

1982. 20th Anniv of Agricultural Reform.
2462 **407** 3b. multicoloured . . . 1·00 40

408 Jules Verne

410 Rose

409 Bars of National Anthem

1982. Jules Verne (writer) Commemoration.
2463 **408** 1b. deep blue and blue 30 15

1982. Centenary of National Anthem (1981).
2464 **409** 1b. multicoloured . . . 30 15

1982. 1300th Anniv of Bulgarian State.
2465 **410** 65c. multicoloured . . . 20 10

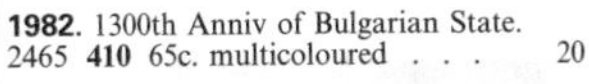

411 Flags

412 Cecilio Acosta

1982. 6th National Plan.
2466 **411** 2b. multicoloured . . . 70 15

1982. Birth Bicentenary (1983) of Simon Bolivar (6th issue). As T **369**.
2467 30c. black, brown and orange 10 10
2468 1b. black, brown and green 50 15
DESIGNS: 30c. Col. Rondon; 1b. General Anzoategui.

1982. Death Centenary (1981) of Cecilio Acosta (statesman).
2469 **412** 3b. black, blue and violet 85 25

413 "Fourcroya humboldtiana"

1982. Flora and Fauna. Multicoloured.
2471 1b.05 Type **413** 35 15
2472 2b.55 Turtle ("Podocnemis expansa") . . . . 1·10 30
2473 2b.75 "Oyedaea verbesinoides" . . . . . 1·25 35
2474 3b. Oilbird . . . . 2·25 35

414 Andres Bello and Initials

1982. Birth Bicentenary of Andres Bello (1981).
2475 **414** 1b.05 light blue, blue and black 50 15
2476 2b.55 yellow, violet and black 70 30
2477 2b.75 blue, deep blue and black 80 35
2478 3b. olive, deep olive and black 85 40

415 "Nativity"

416 Bermudez

1982. Christmas.
2479 **415** 1b. multicoloured . . . 20 10

1982. Birth Bicentenary (1983) of Simon Bolivar (7th issue). As T **369**.
2480 30c. black, grey and red . . 10 10
2481 1b. black, grey and red . . 50 15
DESIGNS: 30c. Carabobo Monument; 1b. Gen. Jose Antonio Paez.

1982. Birth Bicentenary (1983) of Simon Bolivar (8th issue). As T **369**.
2483 30c. black, blue and deep blue 10 10
2484 1b. black, violet and red . . 50 15
DESIGNS: 30c. Commemorative plaque to the meeting at Guayaquil; 1b. Bolivar and San Martin (detail of monument).

1982. Birth Bicentenary of General Jose Francisco Bermudez (statesman).
2486 **416** 3b. multicoloured . . . 85 30

417 Briceno

1982. Birth Bicentenary of Antonio Nicolas Briceno (liberation hero).
2487 **417** 3b. multicoloured . . . 85 30

418 Rejoicing Crowd and Flag

1983. 25th Anniv of 1958 Reforms.
2488 **418** 3b. multicoloured . . . 85 30

419 Police Badge

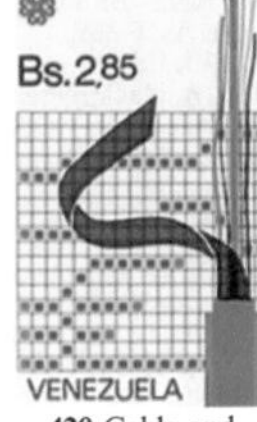

420 Cable and Computer Circuitboard

1983. 25th Anniv of Judicial Police Technical Department.
2489 **419** 4b. red and green . . . 1·00 30

1983. Transport History (2nd series). As T **403**. Multicoloured.
2490 75c. Lincoln touring car, 1923 . . . . 20 10
2491 80c. Steam locomotive No. 129, 1889 . . . . . 1·25 75
2492 85c. Willys truck, 1927 . . . 50 10
2493 95c. Cleveland motorcycle, 1920 . . . . 50 10

1983. Birth Bicentenary of Simon Bolivar (9th issue). As T **369**.
2494 30c. black, red and blue . . 10 10
2495 1b. black, gold and blue . . 50 15
DESIGNS: 30c. Gen. Antonio Sucre; 1b. Sword hilt.

1983. World Communications Year.
2497 **420** 2b.85 multicoloured . . 75 30

1983. Birth Bicentenary of Simon Bolivar (10th issue). As T **369**.
2498 30c. multicoloured 10 10
2499 1b. black, yellow and blue . . 50 15
DESIGNS: 30c. Flags; 1b. "Ascent of Potosi".

421 Map of the Americas

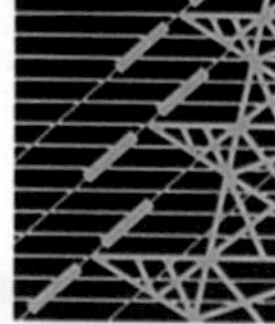

422 Power Pylon

1983. 9th Pan-American Games, Caracas. Multicoloured.
2501 2b. Type **421** 45 20
2502 2b. Swimming 45 20
2503 2b.70 Cycling 60 30
2504 2b.70 Fencing 60 30
2505 2b.85 Weightlifting 75 40
2506 2b.85 Running 75 40

1983. 25th Anniv of State Electricity Authority.
2508 **422** 3b. blue, silver and red 70 30

423 Nativity

1983. Christmas.
2509 **423** 1b. multicoloured . . . 35 10

424 Erecting a Tent

1983. 75th Anniv (1982) of Scout Movement. Multicoloured.
2510 2b.25 Type **424** 60 15
2511 2b.55 Nature watch 60 15
2512 2b.75 Mountaineering . . . 65 15
2513 3b. Camp at night 65 15

1983. Transport History (3rd series). Caracas Underground Railway. As T **403**. Multicoloured.
2514 55c. black, orange and silver 40 20
2515 75c. black, yellow and silver 60 30
2516 95c. black, green and silver 75 30
2517 2b. black, blue and silver . . 1·75 60
DESIGNS: 55c. Central computer building; 75c. Maintenance bay; 95c. Train on elevated section; 2b. Train at Cano Amarillo station.

1984. Birth Bicentenary of Simon Bolivar (11th issue). As T **369**.
2518 30c. black, red and brown 10 10
2519 1b. black, green and blue . . 35 10
DESIGNS: 30c. Open volume of "Opere de Raimondo Montecuccoli"; 1b. Dr. Jose Maria Vargas (President, 1835–36).

1984. Birth Bicentenary of Simon Bolivar (12th issue). As T **369**.
2521 30c. black, red and lilac . . 10 10
2522 1b. black, green and orange 35 10
DESIGNS: 30c. Pedro Gual (President, 1859 and 1861); 1b. Jose Faustino Sanchez Carrion.

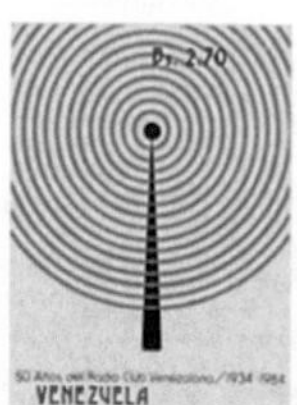

425 Radio Mast and Waves

426 Doves and Hands covering Eyes

1984. 50th Anniv of Venezuela Radio Club.
2524 **425** 2b.70 multicoloured . . 60 15

1984. "Intelligentsia for Peace". Multicoloured.
2525 1b. Type **426** 10 10
2526 2b.70 Profile head 55 15
2527 2b.85 Profile head, flower and hexagonal nut . . . 60 15

427 Romulo Gallegos

1984. Birth Centenary of Romulo Gallegos (writer and President, 1948). Multicoloured.
2528 **427** 1b.70 multicoloured . . 25 15
2529 – 1b.70 multicoloured . . 25 15
2530 – 1b.70 green, grey and black 25 15
2531 – 1b.70 deep green, green and black 25 15
DESIGNS: Nos. 2529/31, Different portraits of Gallegos.

428 Emblem and Digital Eight

1984. 18th Pan-American Union of Engineering Associations Convention.
2532 **428** 2b.55 buff and blue . . . 60 15

429 "Nativity" (Maria Candelaria de Ramirez)

1984. Christmas.
2533 **429** 1b. multicoloured . . . 10 10

430 Pope and "Virgin of Coromoto"

1985. Visit of Pope John Paul II (1st issue).
2534 **430** 1b. multicoloured . . . 20 10
See also Nos. 2628/33.

431 Cross, Hand holding Candle and Agricultural Scene

1985. Bicentenary of Valle de la Pascua City.
2535 **431** 1b.50 multicoloured . . 45 10

432 St. Vincent de Paul

434 "Divine Shepherdess"

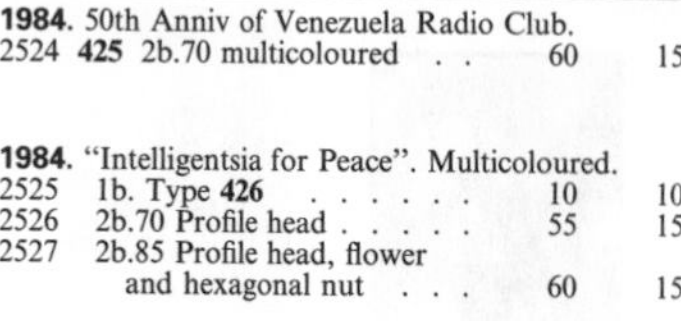

433 Text and "SELA"

1985. Centenary of Venezuelan Society of St. Vincent de Paul.
2536 **432** 1b. brown, yellow and red 15 10

1985. 10th Anniv of Latin American Economic System.
2537 **433** 4b. black and red . . . 70 35

1985. 2000th Birth Anniv of Virgin Mary. Multicoloured.
2538 1b. Type **434** 20 15
2539 1b. "Virgin of Chiquinquira" 20 15
2540 1b. "Virgin of Coromoto" 20 15
2541 1b. "Virgin of the Valley" 20 15
2542 1b. "Virgin of Perpetual Succour" 20 15
2543 1b. "Virgin of Peace" . . . 20 15
2544 1b. "Virgin of the Immaculate Conception" 20 15
2545 1b. "Virgin of Solitude" . . 20 15
2546 1b. "Virgin of Consolation" 20 15
2547 1b. "Virgin of the Snow" 20 15

435 Map and Emblem

1985. 25th Anniv of Organization of Petroleum Exporting Countries.
2548 **435** 6b. black, blue and light blue 95 35

436 Dr Briceno-Iragorry

1985. 27th Death Anniv of Dr. Mario Briceno-Iragorry (politician).
2549 **436** 1b.25 silver and red . . 15 10

437 Museum

1985. 10th Anniv (1983) of Museum of Modern Art, Caracas.
2550 **437** 3b. multicoloured . . . 35 20

438 Emblem and Dove as Hand

1985. 40th Anniv of U.N.O.
2551 **438** 10b. blue and red . . . 1·40 60

439 Rainbow and Emblem

1985. International Youth Year.
2552 **439** 1b.50 multicoloured . . 20 10

440 Shepherds and Camels

1985. Christmas. Multicoloured.
2553 2b. Type **440** 25 10
2554 2b. Holy Family and the Three Kings 25 10
Nos. 2553/4 were printed together, se-tenant, forming a composite design of the Nativity.

441 Petroleos de Venezuela Emblem

1985. 10th Anniv of National Petrochemical Industry.
2555 **441** 1b. blue and black . . . 15 10
2556 – 1b. multicoloured . . . 15 10
2557 – 2b. multicoloured . . . 25 15
2558 – 2b. multicoloured . . . 25 15
2559 – 3b. multicoloured . . . 35 20
2560 – 3b. multicoloured . . . 1·25 40
2561 – 4b. multicoloured . . . 50 25
2562 – 4b. multicoloured . . . 50 25
2563 – 5b. multicoloured . . . 60 30
2564 – 5b. multicoloured . . . 60 30
DESIGNS: No. 2556, Refinery and Isla S.A. emblem; 2557, Bariven oil terminal; 2558, Pequiven storage tank; 2559, Corpoven drilling site; 2560, Support vessel, oil rig and Maraven emblem; 2561, Meneven refinery; 2562, Intervep scientist; 2563, "Nodding Donkey"; 2564, Lagoven refinery.

442 Five Reales Silver Coin, 1873

443 Drago

1985. Coins with Portrait of Simon Bolivar. Multicoloured.
2565 2b. Type **442** 25 15
2566 2b.70 Five bolivares gold coin, 1886 . . . . . . 30 15
2567 3b. Birth bicentenary gold proof coin, 1983 . . . . 35 20

1985. 125th Birth Anniv (1984) of Dr. Luis Maria Drago (Argentine politician).
2568 **443** 2b.70 black, orge & red 30 15

444 Guayana City

1985. 25th Anniv of Guayana Development Corporation. Multicoloured.
2569 2b. Type **444** 25 15
2570 3b. Orinoco steel mill . . . 35 20
2571 5b. Raul Leoni-Guri dam 60 35

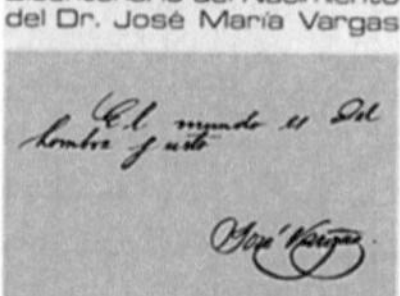

445 Signature

1985. Birth Bicentenary of Dr. Jose Maria Vargas (President, 1835–36). Multicoloured.
2572 3b. Type **445** 30 15
2573 3b. "Vargas" (Martin Tovar y Tovar) (vert) 30 15
2574 3b. Statue at Palace of Academies (vert) 30 15
2575 3b. "Exfilbo '86" National Stamp Exhibition emblem and flags 30 15

2576 3b. Facade of Vargas Hospital, Caracas 30 15
2577 3b. Title page of Vargas's "Manual and Compendium of Surgery" (vert) 30 15
2578 3b. "Vargas" (Alirio Palacios) (vert) 30 15
2579 3b. "Gesneria vargasii" (flower) 30 15
2580 3b. Portraits of Vargas and Bolivar on Sixth Venezuelan Congress of Medical Sciences medal 30 15
2581 3b. "Vargas" (anonymous) (vert) 30 15

446 Francisco Miranda

1986. Bicentenary (1981) of Francisco Miranda's Work for Latin American Liberation.
2583 **446** 1b.05 multicoloured . . 10 10

447 Children painting Wall

1986. Foundation for Educational Buildings and Equipment. Multicoloured.
2584 3b. Type **447** 50 15
2585 5b. Boys at woodwork class 70 15

448 Lorries and Processing Plant

1986. 45th Anniv of Venezuelan Dairy Industry Corporation. Multicoloured.
2586 2b.55 Type **448** 20 15
2587 2b.70 Map and milk containers 50 15
2588 3b.70 Processing plant Machiques, Edo Zulia (horiz) 60 15

449 Emblem

1986. 25th Anniv of VIASA (airline). Mult.
2589 3b. Type **449** 35 20
2590 3b. Douglas DC-8 in flight 35 20
2591 3b. Douglas DC-8 on ground 35 20
2592 3b. Boeing 747 flying out to sea 35 20
2593 3b. Tail fins of Douglas DC-10s 35 20
2594 3b.25 Hemispheres 35 20
2595 3b.25 Douglas DC-10 flying through cloud 35 20
2596 3b.25 Douglas DC-8 and DC-10 on ground 35 20
2507 3b.25 Douglas DC-9 flying over mountains 35 20
2598 3b.25 Manned flight deck 35 20

450 Giant Armadillo

1986. Flora and Fauna. Dated "1983". Mult.
2599 70c. Type **450** 10 10
2600 85c. "Espeletia angustifolia" 10 10
2601 2b.70 Orinoco crocodile . . 45 10
2602 3b. Mountain rose 45 10

451 Romulo Betancourt

452 Library Entrance

1986. 5th Death Anniv of Romulo Betancourt (President, 1959–64). Each black, deep brown and brown.
2603 2b. Type **451** 20 10
2604 2b.70 Betancourt in armchair 20 10
2605 2b.70 Betancourt and inscription 20 10
2606 2b.70 Betancourt wearing sash 20 10
2607 2b.70 Betancourt working 20 10
2608 3b. As No. 2606 . . . . . 25 15
2609 3b. As No. 2607 . . . . . 25 15
2610 3b. As No. 2605 . . . . . 25 15
2611 3b. Type **451** 25 15
2612 3b. As No. 2604 . . . . . 25 15

1986. 40th Anniv of Re-opening of Zulia University. Each grey, black and blue.
2624 2b.70 Type **452** 20 10
2625 2b.70 University building . . 20 10

453 Map and Droplets

1986. 11th Venezuelan Engineers, Architects and Affiliated Professions Congress.
2626 **453** 1b.40 blue, black & yell 25 15
2627 1b.55 multicoloured . . 25 15

454 Pope and Andes

1986. Visit of Pope John Paul II (1985) (2nd issue). Multicoloured.
2628 1b. Type **454** 10 10
2629 1b. Pope and Maracaibo bridge 15 10
2630 3b. Pope kissing ground . . 25 15
2631 3b. Pope and "Virgin of Coromoto" 25 15
2632 4b. Pope holding crucifix, Caracas 60 15
2633 5b.25 Pope and waterfall . . 80 20

455 "United Families" (Vianny Hernandez)

1986. 20th Anniv of Childrens' Paintings. Multicoloured.
2634 2b.55 Type **455** 20 10
2635 2b.55 "Love and Peace" (Yuraima L. Jimenez) . . 20 10
2636 2b.55 "Woodland Animals" (Maria Valentina Arias) 20 10
2637 2b.55 "Noah's Ark" (Andreina Acero) 20 10
2638 2b.55 "House on Hillside" (Yenelsa) 20 10
2639 2b.70 "Flowers on Table" (Yenny Jimenez) 20 10
2640 2b.70 "Peace Lover" (Ramon Briceno) 20 10
2641 2b.70 "Children for World Peace" (Blanca Yesenia Hernandez) 20 10
2642 2b.70 "Lighthouse and Cable Railway" (Julio V. Hernandez) 20 10
2643 2b.70 "Flowers of a Thousand Colours" (with butterfly) (Maryolin Rodriguez Ortega) 20 10

456 Three Kings

1986. Christmas. Crib figures modelled by Eliecer Alvarez. Multicoloured.
2644 2b. Type **456** 15 10
2645 2b. Nativity 15 10
Nos. 2644/5 were printed together, se-tenant, forming a composite design.

457 Treating Accident Victim

1986. 17th Anniv of Caracas City Police. Multicoloured.
2646 2b.70 Type **457** 20 10
2647 2b.70 On duty at sporting event 20 10
2648 2b.70 Computer identification bar code . . 20 10
2649 2b.70 Cadets on parade . . 20 10
2650 2b.70 Motor cycle police . . 20 10

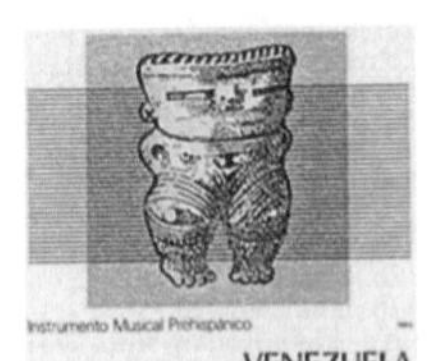

458 Prehispanic Musical Instrument

1987. Native Art. Multicoloured.
2651 2b. Type **458** 15 10
2652 2b. Woven fabric 15 10
2653 3b. Prehispanic ceramic bottle 25 15
2654 3b. Basket design 25 15

459 Robert Koch (discoverer) and Bacillus Symbol

1987. Centenary (1982) of Discovery of Tubercle Bacillus.
2655 **459** 2b.55 multicoloured . . 20 10

460 "Entry of Jesus into Jerusalem" (Antonio Herrera Toro)

1987. Holy Week. Multicoloured.
2656 2b. Type **460** 15 10
2657 2b. "Christ at the Pillar" (statue, Jose Francisco Rodriguez) 15 10
2658 2b. "Jesus of Nazareth" (wood carving, School of Seville) 15 10
2659 2b. "Descent from the Cross" (Jose Rivadefrecha, El Campeche) 15 10
2660 2b. "Virgin of Solitude" (sculpture) 15 10
2661 2b.25 "The Last Supper" (Arturo Michelena) . . . 15 10
2662 2b.25 "Ecce Homo" (sculpture) 15 10
2663 2b.25 "The Crucifixion" (sculpture, Gregorio de Leon Quintana) 15 10
2664 2b.25 "Holy Sepulchre" (sculpture, Sebastian de Ochoa Montes) 15 10
2665 2b.25 "The Resurrection" (attr. Peter Paul Rubens) 15 10

461 "Bolivar and Bello"(Marisol Escobar)

1987. World Neurochemical Congress. Mult.
2666 3b. Type **461** 25 15
2667 4b.25 Retinal cells 30 15

462 Barquisimeto Hilton Hotel

1987. Tourism Development. Multicoloured.
2668 6b. Type **462** 60 15
2669 6b. Lake Hotel Intercontinental, Maracaibo 60 15
2670 6b. Macuto Sheraton Hotel, Caraballeda 60 15
2671 6b. Melia Caribe Hotel, Caraballeda 60 15
2672 6b. Melia Hotel, Puerto la Cruz 70 20
2673 6b.50 Pool, Barquisimeto Hilton Hotel 60 15
2674 6b.50 Lake Hotel Intercontinental, Maracaibo, at night . . . 60 15
2675 6b.50 Macuto Sheraton Hotel, Caraballeda, and marina 70 20
2676 6b.50 Melia Caribe Hotel, Caraballeda (different) . . 60 15
2677 6b.50 Melia Hotel, Puerto la Cruz (different) 70 20

463 Amazon Federal Terrritory Map and Ship's Bow

1987. 35th Anniv of National Canals Institute. Multicoloured.
2678 2b. Type **463** 10 10
2679 4b.25 Map of River Orinoco and buoy 25 15

464 Music School, Caracas

1987. Birth Centenary of Vicente Emilio Sojo (composer). Each deep brown and brown.
2680 2b. Type **464** 15 10
2681 4b. Conducting choir . . . 25 15
2682 5b. Score of "Hymn to Bolivar" 30 15
2683 6b. Standing beside blackboard 40 20
2684 7b. Sojo and signature . . . 50 25

465 "Simon Bolivar, Academician" (Roca Rey)

1987. 20th Anniv of Simon Bolivar University. Multicoloured.
2685 2b. Type **465** 10 10
2686 3b. "Solar Delta" (sculpture, Alejandro Otero) 15 10
2687 4b. Rector's residence . . . 20 10
2688 5b. Laser beam 25 15
2689 6b. Owl sculpture 30 15

466 Motor Vehicles

1987. 10th Anniv of Ministry of Transport and Communications. Multicoloured.

No.	Description		
2690	2b. Type **466**	10	10
2691	2b. Bulk carrier and crane	40	15
2692	2b. Local electric train	30	15
2693	2b. Envelopes and telegraph key	10	10
2694	2b. Transmission masts and globe	10	10
2695	2b.25 Motorway interchange system	10	10
2696	2b.25 Boeing 737 airliner	35	20
2697	2b.25 Mainline diesel train	35	20
2698	2b.25 Dish aerial	10	10
2699	2b.25 Globe and communications satellite	10	10

Nos. 2690/9 were printed together, se-tenant, each horizontal pair forming a composite design.

467 Administration Building, Caracas

1987. 70th Anniv of Venezuelan Navigation Company. Multicoloured.

No.	Description		
2700	2b. Type **467**	10	10
2701	2b. Containers being loaded	10	10
2702	3b. Company emblem on ship's funnel	15	10
2703	3b. Ship's engine-room	15	10
2704	4b. "Zulia" (freighter) at sea	75	20
2705	4b. "Guarico" (freighter) off Venezuelan coast	75	20
2706	5b. "Cerro Bolivar" (bulk carrier)	75	20
2707	5b. Ship's bridge	25	15
2708	6b. Map	30	15
2709	6b. Containers being loaded onto Ro-Ro ferry	30	15

468 Air-sea Rescue

1987. 50th Anniv of National Guard. Mult.

No.	Description		
2710	2b. Type **468**	50	20
2711	2b. Traffic patrol	10	10
2712	2b. Guard on horseback	10	10
2713	2b. Guard with children	10	10
2714	2b. Armed guard on industrial site	10	10
2715	4b. As No. 2714	20	10
2716	4b. As No. 2713	20	10
2717	4b. As No. 2712	20	10
2718	4b. As No. 2711	20	10
2719	4b. Type **468**	80	30

469 "Departure from Puerto Palos" (detail, Jacobo Borges)

1987. 500th Anniv (1992) of Discovery of America by Columbus. Multicoloured.

No.	Description		
2720	2b. Type **469**	10	10
2721	7b. "Discovery of America" (Tito Salas)	55	15
2722	11b.50 "Fr. de las Casas, Protector of the Indians" (detail, Tito Salas)	85	25
2723	12b. "Trade in Venezuela during the Time of the Conquest" (detail, Tito Salas)	1·40	70
2724	12b.50 "Rout of Guaicaipuro" (Jacobo Borges)	90	25

470 "Annunciation" (Juan Pedro Lopez)

1987. Christmas. Multicoloured.

No.	Description		
2725	2b. Type **470**	10	10
2726	3b. "Nativity" (Jose Francisco Rodriguez)	15	10
2727	5b.50 "Adoration of the Kings" (anon)	30	15
2728	6b. "Flight into Egypt" (Juan Pedro Lopez)	30	15

471 Steel Plant Building

1987. 25th Anniv of Steel Production by National SIDOR Mills.

No.	Description		
2729 **471**	2b. multicoloured	10	10
2730 –	2b. multicoloured	10	10
2731 –	6b. multicoloured	30	15
2732 –	6b. multicoloured	30	15
2733 –	7b. multicoloured	30	15
2734 –	7b. multicoloured	30	15
2735 –	11b.50 multicoloured	75	25
2736 –	11b.50 multicoloured	75	25
2737 –	12b. black	80	25
2738 –	12b. multicoloured	80	25

DESIGNS: No. 2730, Rolling strip; 2731, Walkways and towers of plant; 2732, Drawing steel bars; 2733, Walkway, towers and buildings; 2734, Slab mill; 2735, Building and towers; 2736, Steel bar production; 2737, Company emblem; 2738, Anniversary emblem.

Nos. 2729/38 were printed together, se-tenant, Nos. 2729, 2731, 2733 and 2735 forming a composite design of the SIDOR steel plant.

472 Flags

1987. 1st Meeting of Eight Latin-American Presidents of Contadora and Lima Groups, Acapulco.

No.	Description		
2739 **472**	6b. multicoloured	30	15

473 Plastics

1987. 10th Anniv of Petro-Chemical Company of Venezuela. Multicoloured.

No.	Description		
2740	2b. Type **473**	10	10
2741	6b. Formulae (oil refining)	30	15
2742	7b. Leaves (fertilizers)	30	15
2743	11b.50 Pipes (installations)	1·00	25
2744	12b. Expansion	1·10	25

474 St. John Bosco and People on Map

1987. Birth Centenary of St. John Bosco (founder of Salesian Brothers). Multicoloured.

No.	Description		
2745	2b. Type **474**	10	10
2746	3b. National Temple, Caracas	15	10
2747	4b. Vocational training	15	10
2748	5b. Church of Maria Auxiliadora	45	10
2749	6b. Missionary work	50	15

475 Emblem

1988. 29th Governors' Meeting of Inter-American Development Bank.

No.	Description		
2750 **475**	11b.50 multicoloured	60	30

476 Bank Branch

1988. 30th Anniv of Banco Republica. Mult.

No.	Description		
2751	2b. Type **476**	10	10
2752	2b. Pottery (small business finance)	10	10
2753	2b. Factory and security guards (industrial finance)	10	10
2754	2b. Laboratory workers (technology finance)	10	10
2755	2b. Quay-side scene (exports and imports)	10	10
2756	6b. Farm workers (agricultural finance)	35	15
2757	6b. Fishing boat (fisheries finance)	45	15
2758	6b. Milk production (livestock development)	35	15
2759	6b. Building site (construction finance)	35	15
2760	6b. Tourist bus (tourism development)	35	15

477 "Mother and Children" and Emblems

1988. Rotary International Anti-polio Campaign Victory Day.

No.	Description		
2761 **477**	11b.50 multicoloured	90	35

478 Carlos Eduardo Frias (publicist)

1989. 50th Anniv of Publicity Industry. Mult.

No.	Description		
2762	4b. Three profiles of Frias	30	15
2763	10b. Type **478**	60	30

479 Smelter

1988. 10th Anniv of Venalum (aluminium company).

No.	Description		
2764 **479**	2b. multicoloured	10	10
2765 –	6b. black	30	15
2766 –	7b. multicoloured	55	15
2767 –	11b.50 multicoloured	90	35
2768 –	12b. multicoloured	90	35

DESIGNS: 6b. Plan of electrolytic cell; 7b. Aluminium pipes; 11b.50, Loading ship with aluminium for export; 12b. Workers playing football.

480 Red Siskins

1988. Endangered Birds. Multicoloured.

No.	Description		
2769	2b. Type **480**	25	15
2770	6b. Scarlet ibis	80	35
2771	11b.50 Harpy eagle	1·50	55
2772	12b. Greater flamingoes	1·75	60
2773	12b.50 Helmeted curassow	2·00	65

481 Bolivar in Dress Uniform, 1828

1988. Army Day. Multicoloured.

No.	Description		
2774	2b. Type **481**	10	10
2775	2b. Lieutenant in ceremonial uniform, 1988	10	10
2776	6b. Gen. Jose Antonio Paez in dress uniform, 1821	30	15
2777	6b. Major-General in No. 1 dress, 1988	30	15
2778	7b. Major-General, 1820	55	15
2779	7b. Line infantryman, 1820	55	15
2780	11b.50 Brigadier-General, 1820	85	30
2781	11b.50 Garrison infantryman, 1820	85	30
2782	12b. Artilleryman, 1836	85	30
2783	12b. Light cavalryman, 1820	85	30

482 Urdaneta (after Salas)

1988. Birth Bicentenary of General Rafael Urdaneta. Multicoloured.

No.	Description		
2784	2b. Sword and scabbard	10	10
2785	4b.75 "Wedding of the General" (Tito Salas)	20	10
2786	6b. Type **482**	30	15
2787	7b. "Siege of Valencia" (Tito Salas)	60	15
2788	12b. "Retreat from San Carlos" (Tito Salas)	90	35

483 Marino (after Martin Tovar y Tovar)

1988. Birth Bicentenary of General Santiago Marino.

No.	Description		
2789 **483**	4b.75 multicoloured	20	10

484 Games Emblem

1988. Olympic Games, Seoul.

No.	Description		
2790 **484**	12b. multicoloured	85	30

485 "Virgin of Copacabana" (Bolivia)

1988. Marian Year. Multicoloured.

No.	Description		
2791	4b.75 Type **485**	25	15
2792	4b.75 "Virgin of Chiquinquira" (Colombia)	25	15
2793	4b.75 "Virgin of Coromoto" (Venezuela)	25	15
2794	4b.75 "Virgin of the Cloud" (Ecuador)	25	15
2795	4b.75 "Virgin of Antigua" (Panama)	25	15
2796	6b. "Virgin of Evangelisation" (Peru)	30	15

2797 6b. "Virgin of Lujan" (Argentina) 30 15
2798 6b. "Virgin of Altagracia" (Dominican Republic) . . 30 15
2799 6b. "Virgin of Aparecida" (Brazil) 30 15
2800 6b. "Virgin of Guadelupe" (Mexico) 30 15

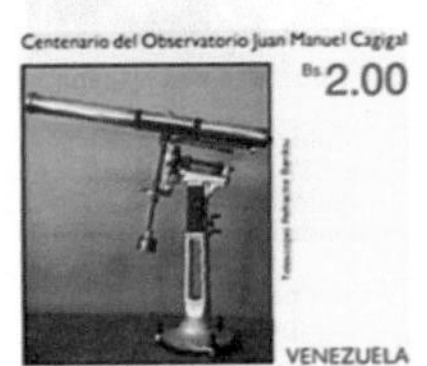

486 Bardou Refracting Telescope

1988. Centenary of Juan Manuel Cagigal Observatory. Multicoloured.
2801 2b. Type **486** 20 10
2802 4b.75 Universal "AUZ-27" theodolite 25 15
2803 6b. Bust of Cagigal 30 15
2804 11b.50 Boulton Cupola and night sky over Caracas in September 85 30
2805 12b. Satellite photographing Hurricane Allen 90 35

487 Keys

488 Commemorative Medal

1988. 50th Anniv of Controller-General's Office.
2806 **487** 10b. multicoloured . . . 45 25

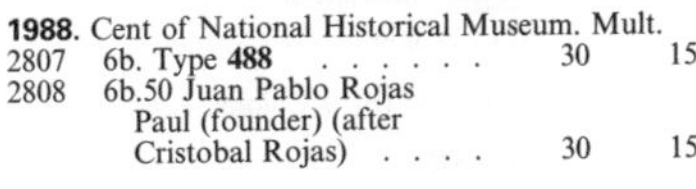

1988. Cent of National Historical Museum. Mult.
2807 6b. Type **488** 30 15
2808 6b.50 Juan Pablo Rojas Paul (founder) (after Cristobal Rojas) 30 15

489 First Headquarters

1988. Centenary of Electricity Industry. Mult.
2809 2b. Type **489** 10 10
2810 4b.75 "Electrical Plant, 1888" (Jaime Carrillo) . . 20 15
2811 10b. Plaza Bolivar, 1888 . . 70 25
2812 11b.50 Baralt Theatre, 1888 90 30
2813 12b.50 Ramon Laguna Central Thermo-electricity Station 90 30

490 "Nativity" (Tito Salas, left-hand detail)

1988. Christmas. Multicoloured.
2814 4b. Type **490** 20 10
2815 6b. "Christ Child" (anonymous) 30 15
2816 15b. "Nativity" (Salas, right-hand detail) . . . . 1·00 35
Nos. 2814 and 2816 form a composite design.

491 "Bolivar and Ricardo" (John de Pool)

1989. "The Liberator at Curacao". Multicoloured.
2817 10b. Type **491** 60 15
2818 10b. "The Octagon" (John de Pool) 60 15
2819 11b. "Doctor Mordechay Ricardo" 75 20
Nos. 2817/19 were printed together, se-tenant, Nos. 2817/18 forming a composite design.

492 Cardinal Quintero (Archbishop of Caracas, 1960–80)

1989. 25th Anniv of Convention with Holy See. Multicoloured.
2820 4b. Type **492** 15 10
2821 4b. Dr. Raul Leoni (President, 1964–69) . . . 15 10
2822 12b. Arms of Luciano Storero (Papal Nuncio) 70 20
2823 12b. Arms of Cardinal Lebrun (Archbishop of Caracas) 70 20
2824 16b. Pope Paul VI 90 25

493 "Cacao Harvest" (Tito Salas)

1989. Centenary of Bank of Venezuela. Mult.
2825 4b. Type **493** 15 10
2826 4b. "Teaching Sowing Time of Coffee" (Tito Salas) . . 15 10
2827 4b. Head Office, Caracas . . 15 10
2828 4b. Archive of the Liberator, Caracas 15 10
2829 4b. Tree-planting programme 15 10
2830 4b. Family planting tree . . 15 10
2831 8b. Left-hand side of 50b. banknote 25 15
2832 8b. Right-hand side of 50b. banknote 25 15
2833 8b. Portrait of Bolivar on left-hand side of 500b. banknote 25 15
2834 8b. Right-hand side of 500b. banknote 25 15
Nos. 2825/34 were printed together, se-tenant, Nos. 2831/2 and 2833/4 forming composite designs.

494 Dish

1989. America. Pre-Columbian Artefacts. Mult.
2835 6b. Type **494** 20 10
2836 24b. Figure . . . . 2·00 1·00

495 Shepherds and Sheep

1989. Christmas. Multicoloured.
2837 5b. As Type **495** but inscr at top 10 10
2838 5b. Type **495** 10 10
2839 6b. Angel and shepherds (inscr at top) 15 10
2840 6b. As No. 2839 but inscr at bottom 15 10
2841 6b. Nativity (inscr at top) 15 10
2842 6b. As No. 2841 but inscr at bottom 15 10
2843 12b. Shepherds (inscr at top) 70 15
2844 12b. As No. 2843 but inscr at bottom 70 15
2845 15b. Adoration of the Magi (inscr at top) 85 15
2846 15b. As No. 2845 but inscr at bottom 85 45

Nos. 2837/46 were printed together, each horizontal strip forming a composite design.

496 Araguaney Tree and State Arms

1990. 20th Anniv of Bank of Venezuela Foundation. Multicoloured.
2847 10b. Type **496** 20 10
2848 10b. Silk-cotton tree and Federal District arms . . 20 10
2849 10b. "Myrospermum frutescens" and Anzoategui State arms . . 20 10
2850 10b. "Pithecellobium saman" and Aragua State arms 20 10
2851 10b. West Indian cedar and Barinas State arms . . . 20 10
2852 10b. "Dipteryx punctata" and Bolivar State arms . . 20 10
2853 10b. Pink trumpet tree and Cojedes State arms . . . 20 10
2854 10b. "Prosopis juliflora" and Falcon State arms 20 10
2855 10b. "Copernicia tectorum" and Guarico State arms 20 10
2856 10b. Mountain immortelle and Merida State arms . . 20 10
2857 10b. "Brawnea leucantha" and Miranda State arms 20 10
2858 10b. "Mauritia flexuosa" and Monagas State arms 20 10
2859 10b. Mahogany and Portuguesa State arms . . 20 10
2860 10b. "Platymiscium diadelphum" and Sucre State arms 20 10
2861 10b. "Prumnopitys montana de Laub" and Tachira State arms 20 10
2862 10b. "Roystonea venezuelana" and Yaracuy State arms . . . 20 10
2863 10b. Coconut palm and Zulia State arms 20 10
2864 10b. "Hevea benthamiana" and Amazonas Federal Territory arms 20 10
2865 40b. "Licania pyrofolia" and Apure State arms . . 1·60 85
2866 40b. "Malpighia glabra" and Lara State arms . . . 1·60 85
2867 40b. "Erythrina fusca" and Trujillo State arms . . . 1·60 85
2868 50b. "Sterculia apetala" and Carabobo State arms . . 2·10 1·00
2869 50b. "Lignum vitae" and Nueva Esparta State arms 2·10 1·00
2870 50b. Mangrove and Amacuro Federal Territory arms . . . . . 2·10 1·00

497 Dr. Francisco Ochoa (founder)

1990. Centenary of Zulia University.
2871 **497** 10b. black and blue . . 20 10
2872 – 10b. black and blue . . 20 10
2873 – 15b. multicoloured . . . 60 15
2874 – 15b. multicoloured . . . 60 15
2875 – 20b. multicoloured . . . 85 25
DESIGNS: No. 2872, Dr. Jesus E. Lossada (Rector, 1946–47); 2873, Research into acid soils; 2874, Petroleum research; 2875, Transplant surgery.

498 Santa Capilla, 1943

1990. 50th Anniv of Central Bank. Multicoloured.
2876 10b. Type **498** 20 10
2877 10b. Headquarters, 1967 . . 20 10
2878 10b. Left half of 1940 500b. note 20 10
2879 10b. Right half of 1940 500b. note 20 10
2880 10b. "Sun of Peru" decoration, 1825 . . . . 20 10
2881 10b. Medals 20 10
2882 15b. Peruvian sword, 1825 60 15
2883 15b. Cross, Bucaramanga, 1830 . . . . 60 15
2884 40b. Medallion of George Washington, 1826 . . . . 1·60 85
2885 50b. Gen. O'Leary (enamel portrait) . . . . 2·10 1·00
Nos. 2876/85 were printed together, se-tenant, Nos. 2878/9 forming a composite design.

500 "St. Joseph and the Child" (Juan Pedro Lopez)

1990. Christmas. Multicoloured.
2887 10b. Type **500** 20 10
2888 10b. "Nativity" (Juan Pedro Lopez) 20 10
2889 10b. "Return from Egypt" (Matheo Moreno) 20 10
2890 20b. "Holy Family" (anon) 85 25
2891 20b. "Nativity" (Juan Pedro Lopez) (different) 85 25

501 Lake House, Maracaibo

1990. America. The Natural World. Mult.
2892 10b. Type **501** 20 10
2893 40b. East Venezuelan shore 1·90 80

502 Globe and "30"

1990. 30th Anniv of O.P.E.C. Multicoloured.
2894 10b. Type **502** 20 10
2895 10b. O.P.E.C. emblem . . . 20 10
2896 20b. Anniversary emblem 85 25
2897 30b. O.P.E.C. emblem and dates . . . . 1·25 60
2898 40b. Members' flags around O.P.E.C. emblem . . . . 1·60 85

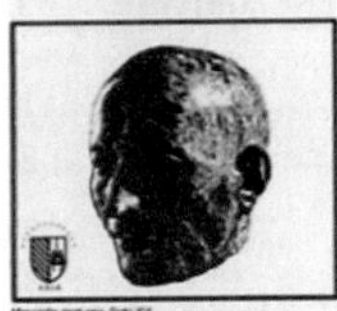

503 Death Mask

1991. 500th Birth Anniv of St. Ignatius de Loyola (founder of Society of Jesus). Multicoloured.
2899 12b. Type **503** 25 15
2900 12b. St. Ignatius de Loyola College, Caracas 25 15
2901 40b. Silver statue of Loyola by Francisco de Vergara 1·90 75
2902 50b. "Our Lady of Montserrat" (wooden statue) . . . . 2·40 95

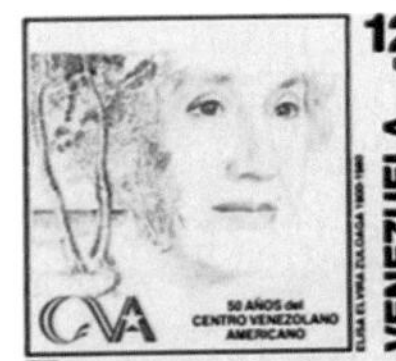

504 Elisa Elvira Zuloaga (painter and engraver)

1991. 50th Anniv of American–Venezuelan Cultural Centre. Designs showing Centre directors.
2903 **504** 12b. green and black . . 25 15
2904 – 12b. violet and black . . 25 15
2905 – 12b. red and black . . . 25 15
2906 – 40b. blue and black . . 1·90 80
2907 – 50b. brown and black . . 2·40 80

DESIGNS: No. 2904, Gloria Stolk (writer); 2905, Caroline Lloyd (composer); 2906, Jules Waldman (linguist and journalist); 2907, William Coles (entrepreneur).

505 "Acineta alticola"

1991. Orchids. Multicoloured.
2908 12b. Type **505** 50 15
2909 12b. "Brassavola nodosa" 50 15
2910 12b. "Brachionidium brevicaudatum" 50 15
2911 12b. "Bifrenaria maguirei" 50 15
2912 12b. "Odontoglossum spectatissimum" 50 15
2913 12b. "Catasetum macrocarpum" 50 15
2914 40b. "Mendocella jorisiana" 1·25 65
2915 40b. "Cochleanthes discolor" 1·25 65
2916 50b. "Maxillaria splendens" 1·50 75
2917 50b. "Pleurothallis dunstervillei" 1·50 75

506 Voters at Ballot Box

1991. 50th Anniv of Democratic Action Party.
2919 **506** 12b. multicoloured 25 15
2920 – 12b. multicoloured 25 15
2921 – 12b. multicoloured 25 15
2922 – 12b. black and blue 25 10
DESIGNS: No. 2920, Agrarian reform; 2921, Education; 2922, Nationalization of petroleum industry.

507 Rodrigues Suarez and Terepaima Chieftain

1991. America. Voyages of Discovery. Showing paintings by Pedro Centeno. Multicoloured.
2923 12b. Type **507** 25 15
2924 40b. Paramaconi chieftain and Garcia Gonzalez 1·50 80

508 Family in House

1991. 25th Anniv of Children's Foundation. Multicoloured.
2925 12b. Type **508** 45 10
2926 12b. Children's playground 45 10
2927 12b. Fairground 45 10
2928 12b. Mother and daughter 45 10
2929 12b. Boy in hospital 45 10
2930 12b. Children and tree 45 10
2931 40b. Girls at home 1·40 65
2932 40b. Children in classroom 1·40 65
2933 50b. Children acting in play 1·60 75
2934 50b. Children playing ring-a-ring of roses 1·60 75

509 "Stable" (Barbaro Rivas)

1991. Christmas. Multicoloured.
2935 10b. Type **509** 15 10
2936 12b. "Nativity" (Elsa Morales) 45 10
2937 20b. "Nativity" (model, Glenda Mendoza) 60 15
2938 25b. "Shepherds watching flock (Maritza Marin) 85 45
2939 30b. "Nativity" (Antonia Azuaje) 1·00 55

1991. Nos. 2613/15 surch **RESELLADO** and value.
2940 **347** 5b. on 25c. red 10 10
2941 5b. on 75c. mauve 10 10
2942 10b. on 25c. red 15 10
2943 10b. on 75c. mauve 15 10
2944 12b. on 50c. blue 20 10
2945 12b. on 75c. mauve 20 10
2946 20b. on 50c. blue 65 15
2947 20b. on 75c. mauve 65 35
2948 40b. on 50c. blue 1·75 65
2949 40b. on 75c. mauve 1·75 65
2950 50b. on 50c. blue 1·90 85
2951 50b. on 75c. mauve 1·90 85

512 Columbus's Arms

1991. 500th Anniv (1992) of Discovery of America by Columbus.
2953 **512** 12b. multicoloured 45 10
2954 – 12b. black, blue & orange 60 20
2955 – 12b. multicoloured 45 10
2956 – 40b. black, brown & orge 1·10 35
2957 – 50b. black and orange 1·60 40
DESIGNS: No. 2954, "Santa Maria"; 2955, Juan de la Cosa's map; 2956, Sighting land; 2957, Columbus before King Ferdinand and Queen Isabella the Catholic.

513 Anniversary Emblem

1992. "Expo 92" World's Fair, Seville. 500th Anniv of Discovery of America by Columbus.
2958 **513** 12b. black, red and blue 45 10
2959 – 12b. multicoloured 45 10
2960 – 12b. multicoloured 45 10
2961 – 12b. multicoloured 45 10
2962 – 12b. multicoloured 50 20
2963 – 12b. multicoloured 45 10
2964 – 40b. multicoloured 1·25 60
2965 – 40b. multicoloured 1·25 60
2966 – 50b. multicoloured 1·60 65
2967 – 50b. black and brown 1·60 65
DESIGNS: No. 2959, Venezuelan pavilion at "Expo 92"; 2960, Landmarks and map of southern Spain; 2961, Columbus; 2962, "Encounters"; 2963, "0x500 America"; 2964, "Imago-Mundi"; 2965, "The Grand Voyage"; 2966, "Golden Beach"; 2967, Idols.

514 Red-footed Tortoise

1992. Tortoises. Multicoloured.
2969 12b. Type **514** 45 10
2970 12b. "Red-footed tortoise ("Geochelone carbonaria") (different) 45 10
2971 12b. South American river turtle ("Podocnemis expansa") (on land) 45 10
2972 12b. South American river turtle (swimming) 45 10

515 Native Hut

1992. Electricity Distribution in the South.
2973 **515** 12b. multicoloured 20 10
2974 – 12b. black and blue 20 10
2975 – 12b. multicoloured 20 10
2976 – 40b. multicoloured 90 35
2977 – 50b. multicoloured 1·10 40
DESIGNS: No. 2974, Pylons; 2975, Horses galloping through water; 2976, Engineers working on pylon; 2977, Traditional baskets beside lake.

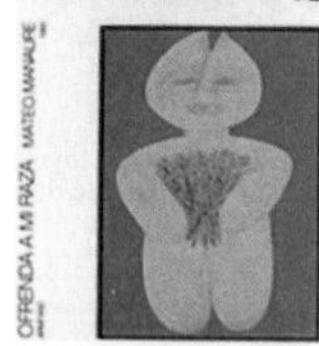

516 Figure holding Sheaf of Wheat

1992. "Offering to My Race" (Mateo Manaure). Designs showing various "mother" figures. Multicoloured.
2978 12b. Type **516** 20 10
2979 12b. Orange figure 20 10
2980 12b. Yellow figure 20 10
2981 12b. Pink figure 20 10
2982 40b. Brown figure 1·00 35
2983 40b. Purple and orange figures 1·00 35
2984 50b. Three-quarter length figure 1·25 65
2985 50b. Head and shoulders 1·25 65

517 Catechism in Venezuela, 1975

518 "And on the Third Voyage" (Elio Caldera)

1992. Beatification of Josemaria Escriva (founder of Opus Dei).
2986 **517** 18b. multicoloured 50 10
2987 – 18b. multicoloured 50 10
2988 – 18b. multicoloired 50 10
2989 – 18b. black and yellow 50 10
2990 – 18b. multicoloured 50 10
2991 – 18b. Multicoloured 50 10
2992 – 60b. multicoloured 1·60 65
2993 – 60b. multicoloured 1·60 65
2994 – 75b. multicoloured 1·90 75
2995 – 75b. multicoloured 1·90 75
DESIGNS: No. 2987, Celebrating mass; 2988, Jose Escriva and Dolores Albas (parents); 2989, Text and autograph; 2990, With statuette of Madonna and Child; 2991, Commemorative medal; 2992, With Pope Paul VI, 1964; 2993, Writing at desk; Portrait; 2995, Portrait in St. Peter's Square, 17 May 1992.

1992. America. 500th Anniv of Discovery of America by Columbus. Multicoloured.
2996 18b. Type **518** 45 10
2997 60b. "Descontextura" (Juan Pablo Nascimiento) 1·25 60

519 "Adoration of the Shepherds"

520 Simon Bolivar

1992. Christmas. Paintings by Lucio Rivas. Multicoloured.
2998 18b. Type **519** 45 10
2999 75b. "Adoration of the Magi" 1·40 75

1993. Portraits and Monuments.
3001 **520** 1b. silver 10 10
3002 2b. blue 10 10
3005 – 5b. red 10 10
3006 – 10b. purple 10 10
3007 – 20b. green 25 15
3008 – 25b. orange 25 15
3009 – 35b. green 35 20
3010 – 40b. blue 40 20
3011 – 50b. orange 1·10 55
3012 – 50b. mauve 50 25
3013 – 100b. brown 2·25 1·10
3014 – 100b. blue 95 50
3015 – 200b. orange 1·90 95
DESIGNS: 5b. National Pantheon, Caracas; 10b. War of Independence Memorial, Carabobo; 20b. General Jose Antonio de Paez (President, 1830–35, 1837–43 and 1861–63); 25b. Luisa Caceres de Arismendi; 35b. General Ezespiel Zamora (politician); 40b. Cristobal Mendoza (jurist and provincial governor); 50b. (3011) National Library; 50b. (3012) Jose Felix, Ribas (independence fighter); 100b. (3013), 200. Bolivar (different); 100b. (3014) General Manuel Piar.

521 "Cattleya percivaliana"

1993. Orchids. Multicoloured.
3016 20b. Type **521** 25 15
3017 20b. "Anguloa ruckeri" 25 15
3018 20b. "Chondrorhyncha flaveola" 25 15
3019 20b. "Stenia pallida" 25 15
3020 20b. "Zygosepalum lindeniae" 25 15
3021 20b. "Maxillaria triloris" 25 15
3022 80b. "Stanhopea wardii" 1·50 70
3023 80b. "Oncidium papilio" 1·50 70
3024 100b. "Oncidium hastilabium" 1·75 80
3025 100b. "Sobralia cattleya" 1·75 80

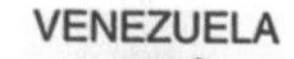

522 Woman

524 Smoker and Non-Smoker

523 Locomotive "Tucacas"

1993. 150th Anniv of Tovar Colony, Aragua State. Multicoloured.
3027 24b. Type **522** 30 15
3028 24b. Children 30 15
3029 24b. Catholic church 30 15
3030 24b. St. Martin of Tours (patron saint) 30 15
3031 24b. Vegetables and fruit 30 15
3032 24b. School 30 15
3033 80b. House of Augustin Codazzi (founder) 1·40 70
3034 80b. House of Alexander Benitz 1·40 70
3035 100b. Breidenbach mill 1·60 80
3036 100b. Procession of Jokili (carnival group) 1·60 80

1993. 19th Pan-American Railways Congress. Multicoloured.
3037 24b. Type **523** 60 15
3038 24b. Locomotive "Halcon" heading "El Encanto" on Las Mostazas bridge 60 15
3039 24b. Locomotive "Maracaibo" 60 15
3040 24b. Tender and carriages in Palo Grande station 60 15
3041 24b. Fiat diesel railcar, 1957 60 15
3042 24b. GP-9-L diesel locomotive, 1957 60 15
3043 80b. GP-15-L diesel locomotive, 1982 1·60 80
3044 80b. Underground train, Caracas 1·60 80
3045 100b. Electric multiple unit set (left half) 2·00 1·00
3046 100b. Electric multiple unit set (right half) 2·00 1·00
Nos. 3037/46 were issued together, se-tenant, Nos. 3039/40 and 3043/4 forming composite designs.

1993. World No Smoking Day. Each black, blue and red.
3047 24b. Type **524** 55 15
3048 80b. No smoking sign 1·25 70

525 Yellow-shouldered Amazon

526 Yanomami Boys

1993. America. Endangered Animals. Mult.
3049 24b. Type **525** 50 50
3050 80b. Scarlet macaw 2·25 2·25

1993. Amerindians (1st series). Multicoloured.
3051 1b. Type **526** 10 10
3052 1b. Yanomami woman preparing casabe 10 10
3053 40b. Panare children in Katyayinto ceremony . . 50 25
3054 40b. Taurepan man paddling canoe 50 25
3055 40b. Piaroa mother holding child 50 25
3056 40b. Panare man playing nose flute 50 25
3057 40b. Taurepan woman weaving 50 25
3058 40b. Masked Piaroa dancers in Warime ceremony . . . 50 25
3059 100b. Hoti man with blowpipe . . . . 1·25 65
3060 100b. Hoti woman carrying child and fruit . . . . . 1·25 65
See also Nos. 3170/9, 3266/75, 3392/3401 and 3568/77.

527 Joseph

1993. Christmas. (a) Each cream, brown and black
3062 24b. Type **527** 30 15
3063 24b. Madonna and Child . . 30 15
3064 24b. Shepherd girl, wise man and sheep 30 15
3065 80b. Wise man and shepherd girl . . . . . . 1·10 55
3066 100b. Wise man and shepherd girl . . . . . . 1·25 65
(b) Each cream, purple and black
3067 24b. Type **527** 30 15
3068 24b. As No. 3063 . . . . . 30 15
3069 24b. As No. 3064 . . . . . 30 15
3070 80b. As No. 3065 . . . . . 1·10 55
3071 100b. As No. 3066 . . . . 1·25 65
Nos. 3062/71 were issued together, se-tenant, each horizontal strip forming a composite design of the Nativity.

528 "Chrysocycnis schlimii"

1994. Orchids. Multicoloured.
3072 35b. Type **528** 60 20
3073 35b. "Galeandra minax" . . 60 20
3074 35b. "Oncidium falcipetalum" 60 20
3075 35b. "Oncidium lanceanum" 60 20
3076 40b. "Sobralia violacea" . . 65 20
3077 40b. "Sobralia infundibuligera" 65 20
3078 80b. "Mendoncella burkei" 1·10 40
3079 80b. "Phragmipedium caudatum" . . . . 1·10 40
3080 100b. "Phragmipedium kaieteurum" . . . . . . 1·40 50
3081 200b. "Stanhopea grandiflora" . . . . . . 2·75 1·25

529 Federation Emblem

1994. 50th Anniv of Federation of Chambers of Industry and Commerce.
3083 – 35b. blue, gold and black 25 15
3084 – 35b. black and brown . . 25 15
3085 **529** 35b. blue and black . . 25 15
3086 80b. blue and black . . 90 30
3087 – 80b. black, brown and blue 90 30
3088 – 80b. blue, gold and black 90 30
DESIGNS: Nos. 3083, 3088, "50" on text; 3084, 3087, Luis Gonzalo Marturet (first Federation President).

530 State Arms

1994. Judicial Service.
3089 **530** 100b. multicoloured . . 1·10 40

531 "Nativity" (School of Jose Lorenzo de Alvarado)

1994. Christmas. Multicoloured.
3090 35b. Type **531** 25 15
3091 35b. "Nativity" 25 15
3092 35b. "Nativity" (School of Jose Lorenzo de Alvarado) 25 15
3093 35b. Holy Family (inscr "Adoracion de los Pastores") 25 15
3094 35b. "Nativity" (School of Tocuyo) 25 15
3095 80b. As No. 3094 . . . . . 90 30
3096 80b. Type **531** 90 30
3097 80b. As No. 3091 . . . . . 90 30
3098 80b. As No. 3092 . . . . . 90 30
3099 80b. As No. 3093 but inscr "El Nacimiento" 90 30

532 Sucre (anonymous portrait)

1995. Birth Bicentenary of Antonio Jose de Sucre (President of Bolivia, 1825–29). Multicoloured.
3100 25b. Type **532** 20 10
3101 25b. Mariana Carcelen y Larrea, Marquesa de Solanda (Sucre's wife) (after Juan Pinto Ortiz) 20 10
3102 35b. Equestrian statue of Sucre (Turini Verana), Cumana 25 15
3103 35b. Base of statue 25 15
3104 40b. "Battle of Pichincha" (top detail) (Victor Mideros Almeida) 30 15
3105 40b. "Battle of Pichincha" (bottom detail) 30 15
3106 80b. "Battle of Ayacucho" (left detail) (Antonio Herrera Toro) 90 30
3107 80b. "Battle of Ayacucho" (right detail) 90 30
3108 100b. "Capitulation of Ayacucho" (left detail) (Daniel Hernandez) . . . 1·10 40
3109 100b. "Capitulation of Ayacucho" (right detail) 1·10 40
Nos. 3100/9 were issued together, se-tenant, the 35, 40, 80 and 100b. values forming four composite designs.

533 Short S.7 Skyvan Mail Plane

1995. America (1994). Postal Transport. Mult.
3111 35b. Mobile post office . . 25 15
3112 80b. Type **533** . . . . . . 1·10 55

534 St. John Bosco (founder) and Boy with Salesian

1995. Centenary of Salesian Brothers in Venezuela. Multicoloured.
3113 35b. Type **534** 25 15
3114 35b. Boy sitting in street and Virgin and Child . . 25 15
3115 35b. Men working machinery 25 15
3116 35b. Youths working on radio 25 15
3117 35b. Boys playing baseball 25 15
3118 35b. Youths playing basketball 25 15
3119 80b. Men planting saplings 90 30
3120 80b. Youth and boxes of produce 90 30
3121 100b. Salesian and Amerindian boys . . . . 1·10 40
3122 100b. Amerindian youth . . 1·10 40

535 Laboratory Technicians

1995. 50th Anniv of Christian Brothers' La Colina School, Caracas. Multicoloured.
3123 35b. As T **535** but country inscr at right 25 15
3124 35b. Young people camping (country inscr at left) . . 25 15
3125 35b. Youths playing football (country inscr at right) . . 25 15
3126 35b. Type **535** 25 15
3127 35b. As No. 3124 but country inscr at right . . 25 15
3128 35b. As No. 3125 but country inscr at left . . . 25 15
3129 80b. School building (country inscr at left) . . 90 30
3130 80b. As No. 3129 but country inscr at right . . 90 30
3131 100b. Jean Baptiste de la Salle (founder of Order) (country inscr at right) . . 1·10 40
3132 100b. As No. 3131 but country inscr at left . . . 1·10 40

536 "Maxillaria guareimensis"

1995. Orchids. Multicoloured.
3133 35b. Type **536** 50 15
3134 35b. "Paphinia lindeniana" 50 15
3135 35b. "Coryanthes biflora" 50 15
3136 35b. "Catasetum pileatum" 50 15
3137 35b. "Mormodes convolutum" 50 15
3138 35b. "Huntleya lucida" . . 50 15
3139 50b. "Catasetum longifolium" 70 20
3140 50b. "Anguloa clowesii" . . 70 20
3141 80b. "Maxillaria histrionica" 1·00 55
3142 80b. "Sobralia ruckeri" . . 1·00 55

537 Anniversary Emblem

1995. 25th Anniv of Andean Pact (international co-operation group).
3144 **537** 80b. multicoloured . . . 60 30

538 People of Different Races

1995. 50th Anniv of U.N.O. Multicoloured.
3145 50b. Type **538** 40 20
3146 50b. U.N. flag 40 20
Nos. 3145/6 were issued together, se-tenant, forming a composite design.

539 Mother Maria

1995. Beatification of Mother Maria de San Jose. Multicoloured.
3147 35b. Type **539** 50 15
3148 35b. Pope John Paul II . . 50 15
3149 35b. Handing out books to girls 50 15
3150 35b. Embroidering 50 15
3151 35b. Statue of Virgin Mary and altar 50 15
3152 35b. Mother Maria in prayer before altar . . . 50 15
3153 80b. Mother Maria and three nuns in hospital ward 85 30
3154 80b. Nun beside hospital beds 85 30
3155 100b. Nuns with poor children . . . . 1·25 65
3156 100b. Nun giving alms to beggar . . . . 1·25 65
Nos. 3147/56 were issued together, se-tenant, each horizontal pair forming a composite design.

540 Monagas

1995. Birth Bicentenary of Jose Gregorio Monagas (anti-slavery campaigner and President 1851–55). Multicoloured.
3157 50b. Type **540** 40 20
3158 50b. Freed slaves 40 20
Nos. 3157/8 were issued together, se-tenant, forming a composite design.

541 Chirino

1995. Bicentenary of Jose Chirino's Insurrection. Multicoloured.
3159 50b. Type **541** 40 20
3160 50b. Insurrectionists 40 20
Nos. 3159/60 were issued together, se-tenant, forming a composite design.

542 Red Cross Workers and Child

1995. Centenary of Venezuelan Red Cross. Multicoloured.
3161 35b. Type **542** 25 15
3162 35b. Volunteers carrying injured man on stretcher 25 15
3163 35b. Operating theatre . . . 25 15
3164 80b. Carlos J. Bello Hospital 90 30
3165 100b. Red Cross flag . . . 1·25 65

543 River

1995. America. Environmental Protection. Mult.
(a) With thin frame line over face value.
3166 35b. Type **543** 25 15
3167 80b. Hillside 90 30
(b) Without thin frame line over face value.
3168 35b. Type **543** 25 15
3169 80b. As No. 3167 . . . . . 1·00 30

544 Ye'kuana Chief

1995. Amerindians (2nd series). Multicoloured.
3170 25b. Type **544** 20 10
3171 25b. Ye'kuana woman making manioc cake . . . 20 10
3172 35b. Guahibo musicians . . 25 15
3173 35b. Guahibo shaman treating boy 25 15
3174 50b. Uruak fisherman . . . 70 30
3175 50b. Uruak woman cooking 40 20
3176 80b. Warao woman making thread 90 30
3177 80b. Warao couple transporting belongings in sailing canoe 90 30
3178 100b. Bari men hunting . . 1·00 40
3179 100b. Bari man making fire 1·00 40

545 Ricardo Zuloaga (pioneer)

1995. Centenary of Electricity in Caracas. Mult.

3181 35b. Type **545** 25 15
3182 35b. El Encantado Plant 25 15
3183 35b. Caracas sub-station 25 15
3184 35b. Electric tram 25 15
3185 35b. Streetlamps outside Congress building 25 15
3186 35b. Streetlamps, Plaza Bolivar 25 15
3187 80b. Engineer repairing streetlamp 90 30
3188 80b. Avila Cross 90 30
3189 100b. Teresa Carreno Cultural Centre 1·00 40
3190 100b. Ricardo Zuloaga power station 1·00 40

546 The Annunciation

1995. Christmas. Multicoloured.

3191 35b. Type **546** 15 15
3192 35b. Mary and Joseph turned away from the inn 25 15
3193 35b. Archangel Gabriel visits shepherds 25 15
3194 35b. Three wise men bearing gifts 25 15
3195 40b. Family gathering 30 15
3196 40b. Children on rollerskates 30 15
3197 40b. Women and girl preparing food 30 15
3198 40b. Woman and children preparing food 30 15
3199 100b. Mary and Joseph holding Child Jesus 1·10 40
3200 100b. Box of toys 1·10 40

Nos. 3191/3200 were issued together, se-tenant, Nos. 3195/6 and 3197/8 forming composite designs.

547 Arms

1995. 450th Anniv of El Tocuyo. Multicoloured.

3201 35b. Type **547** 25 15
3202 35b. Cutting sugar cane 25 15
3203 35b. Church of Our Lady of the Immaculate Conception 25 15
3204 35b. "Our Lady of the Immaculate Conception" (statue) 25 15
3205 35b. Ruins of Santo Domingo Temple 25 15
3206 35b. Cultural centre 25 15
3207 80b. Natural vegetation 90 30
3208 80b. Cactus 90 30
3209 100b. Sword dance 1·00 40
3210 100b. Man playing guitar 1·00 40

Nos. 3201/10 were issued together, se-tenant, Nos. 3209/10 forming a composite design.

548 Oil Tanker

1995. 20th Anniv of PDVSA National Fossil Fuels Association. Multicoloured.

3211 35b. Type **548** 25 15
3212 35b. Orimulsion storage tanks 25 15
3213 35b. Coal 25 15
3214 35b. Lorry carrying sacks 25 15
3215 35b. Petrol station 25 15
3216 35b. Gas storage cylinders 25 15
3217 80b. Drilling for oil 90 30
3218 80b. Refinery 90 30
3219 100b. Emblems ("Lagoven" at top) 1·00 40
3220 100b. Emblems ("bitor" at top) 1·00 40

549 Pope John Paul II with Children

1996. Papal Visit. Multicoloured.

3221 25b. Type **549** 20 10
3222 25b. Pope with young couple 20 10
3223 40b. Pope with family 30 15
3224 40b. Pope with elderly man 30 15
3225 50b. Pope with mother and son 35 20
3226 50b. Pope with patient 35 20
3227 60b. Pope with prisoner 70 25
3228 60b. Pope with workman 70 25
3229 100b. Pope giving speech to workers 1·00 40
3230 100b. Pope with priest and nuns 1·00 40

550 "Epidendrum fimbriatum"

1996. Orchids. Multicoloured.

3232 60b. Type **550** 45 25
3233 60b. "Myoxanthus reymondii" 45 25
3234 60b. "Catasetum pileatum" 45 25
3235 60b. "Ponthieva maculata" 45 25
3236 60b. "Maxillaria triloris" 45 25
3237 60b. "Scaphosepalum breve" 45 25
3238 60b. "Cleistes rosea" 45 25
3239 60b. "Maxillaria sophronitis" 45 25
3240 60b. "Catasetum discolor" 45 25
3241 60b. "Oncidium ampliatum" 45 25

551 National Olympic Committee Emblem

1996. Olympic Games, Atlanta. Multicoloured.

3243 130b. Type **551** 95 50
3244 130b. Swimming 95 50
3245 130b. Boxing 95 50
3246 130b. Cycling 95 50
3247 130b. Medal winners on podium 95 50

552 Emblem

1996. 25th Anniv of Liberator Simon Bolivar International Airport, Maiquetia, as Autonomous Company. Multicoloured.

3248 80b. Type **552** 60 30
3249 80b. Flight paths into airport 60 30
3250 80b. La Guaira Aerodrome, 1929 60 30
3251 80b. Maiquetia Airport, 1944 60 30
3252 80b. Liberator Simon Bolivar Airport, 1972 60 30
3253 80b. Airport interior by Carlos Cruz Diez 60 30
3254 80b. Control tower and airport police 60 30
3255 80b. Fire tender 60 30
3256 80b. Airplanes at terminal building 60 30
3257 80b. Boeing 747 airliner and terminal buildings 60 30

Nos. 3248/57 were issued together, se-tenant, Nos. 3256/7 forming a composite design.

553 Woman

1996. America. Traditional Costume. Multicoloured.

3258 60b. Type **553** 15 10
3259 130b. Man 35 20

554 As Child in Trujillo, 1913

1996. Birth Centenary (1997) of Dr. Mario Briceno-Iragorry (politician). Designs showing different periods of his life. Multicoloured.

3260 80b. Type **554** 20 10
3261 80b. Student at Merida University, 1919 20 10
3262 80b. Politician making speech, 1944 20 10
3263 80b. Writer, 1947 20 10
3264 80b. Historian of Caracas, 1952 20 10

555 Emblem

1996. 70th Anniv of Rotary International in Caracas.

3265 **555** 50b. multicoloured 15 10

556 Man planting Yucca

1996. Amerindians (3rd series). Multicoloured.

3266 80b. Type **556** 20 10
3267 80b. Child gathering fruits 20 10
3268 80b. Women harvesting reed-mace 20 10
3269 80b. Youth gathering bananas 20 10
3270 80b. Mother carrying child 20 10
3271 100b. Guajiros indians 25 15
3272 100b. Man carrying bundle 25 15
3273 100b. Man fishing with bow and arrow 25 15
3274 100b. Couple grinding maize 25 15
3275 100b. Weaver 25 15

558 Dr. Hernandez as a Boy

1996. 132nd Birth Anniv of Dr. Jose Hernandez (physician). Designs representing different aspects of his life. Multicoloured.

3278 60b. Type **558** 15 10
3279 60b. Student 15 10
3280 60b. Kneeling in prayer and statue of the Madonna 15 10
3281 60b. Dining and distributing food to the needy 15 10
3282 60b. Research scientist examining test-tube 15 10
3283 60b. University professor teaching students 15 10
3284 60b. Administering to patient 15 10
3285 60b. Meeting room of Academy of Numbers 15 10
3286 60b. Portrait and statue of Hernandez and Vargas hospital 15 10
3287 60b. Dr. Jose Gregorio Hernandez hospital and statue 15 10

559 Child and Nativity figures

1996. Christmas. Multicoloured.

3289 60b. Type **559** 15 10
3290 60b. Guitar players and percussionist 15 10
3291 60b. Crowing cockerel and musicians 15 10
3292 60b. Traditional dancers 15 10
3293 60b. Drummers, maracas player and guitarist 15 10
3294 80b. Woman and girl exchanging traditional food 20 10
3295 80b. Family meal 20 10
3296 80b. Child in hammock and gifts 20 10
3297 80b. Couple with child 20 10
3298 80b. Mother kissing baby's foot 20 10

560 As Boy

561 Simon Bolivar (after Jose Maria Espinoza)

1997. Birth Centenary of Andres Eloy Blanco (writer and politician). Multicoloured.

3299 100b. Type **560** 25 10
3300 100b. Councillor for Caracas 25 10
3301 100b. With family 25 10
3302 100b. With two men 25 10
3303 100b. Politician 25 10
3304 100b. President of Constitutional Assembly 25 10
3305 100b. Poet and Juan Bimba (character from poem) 25 10
3306 100b. Chancellor of the Republic and Lincoln Memorial 25 10
3307 100b. Eloy Blanco and "Santa Maria" ("Canto a Espana") 25 10
3308 100b. "Pinto" and "Nina" and Don Quixote ("Canto a Espana") 25 10

Nos. 3299/3308 were issued together, se-tenant, Nos. 3307/8 forming a composite design.

1997.

3311 **561** 15b. green 10 10
3312 20b. orange 10 10
3313 40b. brown 10 10
3314 50b. red 15 10
3315 70b. purple 15 10
3316 90b. blue 20 10
3317 200b. blue 45 25
3318 300b. green 70 35
3319 400b. grey 95 50
3320 500b. drab 1·25 65
3321 600b. brown 1·40 70
3322 800b. brown 1·90 95
3323 900b. blue 2·40 1·10
3324 1000b. copper 2·75 1·25
3325 2000b. green 5·25 2·40

562 "Scuticaria steelei"

1997. Orchids. Multicoloured.

3330 165b. "Phragmipedium lindleyanum" 45 25
3331 165b. "Zygosepalum labiosum" 45 25
3332 165b. "Acacallis cyanea" 45 25
3333 165b. "Maxillaria camaridii" 45 25
3334 165b. Type **562** 45 25
3335 165b. "Aspasia variegata" 45 25
3336 165b. "Comparettia falcata" 45 25
3337 165b. "Scaphyglottis stellata" 45 25
3338 165b. "Maxillaria rufescens" 45 25
3339 165b. "Vanilla pompona" 45 25

563 Espana and Meeting of Conspirators

1997. Bicentenary of Independence Movement of Manuel Gual and Jose Maria Espana. Multicoloured.
3341 165b. Type **563** 40 20
3342 165b. Soldiers escorting Espana to his execution 40 20
3343 165b. Gual, conspirators and soldiers with bayonets 40 20
3344 165b. Gual in exile on Trinidad 40 20
3345 165b. Flag 40 20
Nos. 3341/5 were issued together, se-tenant, each horiz pair forming a composite design.

564 "The People boil"

1997. 30th Anniv of Tlatelolco Treaty (Latin American and Caribbean treaty banning nuclear weapons). Paintings by Alirio Rodriguez from his "Hiroshima" sequence. Multicoloured.
3346 140b. Type **564** 35 20
3347 140b. "An empty Epicentre where Once even a Whisper Sounded" (white and black disc) 35 20
3348 140b. "Darkness like the high Horizon" (red disc on black panel) 35 20
3349 140b. "My God! In the Shell, Emptiness" (red and black "shelves") . . . 35 20
3350 140b. "Devil. Perverse geometry" (yellow atomic model) 35 20
3351 140b. "At the Heart of the Area the Bareness of the Disaster" (four blue discs) 35 20
3352 140b. "Without Thought, only Grief in living Flesh" figure within atomic model) 35 20
3353 140b. "Thus in order to Reveal" (red panel) . . . 35 20
3354 140b. "Calvary of multiple Symbiosis" (drab atomic model) 35 20
3355 140b. "Released Energy which attempts to Silence the Scream" (screaming head with legs) 35 20
Distinguishing parts of the design are given in brackets to aid identification.

565 Rabbit watching Jaguar

1997. Children's Stories (1st series). "Uncle Jaguar and Uncle Rabbit". Multicoloured.
3356 55b. Type **565** 10 10
3357 55b. Rabbit listening to conversation between Jaguar and Anteater . . . 10 10
3358 55b. Jaguar catching Turtle 10 10
3359 55b. Rabbit going to help Turtle 10 10
3360 55b. Rabbit freeing Anteater from net 10 10
3361 55b. Anteater telling Jaguar that his vegetables have been stolen 10 10
3362 55b. Anteater and Rabbit looking at wasps' nest in tree 10 10
3363 55b. Rabbit releasing Turtle from Jaguar's bag and replacing him with wasps' nest 10 10
3364 55b. Jaguar returning from fruitless pursuit 10 10
3365 55b. Jaguar opening bag and being stung by wasps 10 10
A number and the relevant portion of the story is printed on the back of each stamp over the gum.
See also Nos. 3537/46.

566 Dog growling at Postman

1997. America. The Postman. Multicoloured.
3367 110b. Type **566** 25 15
3368 280b. Postman's moped punctured in rain 65 35

567 Signature of Juan Xavier Misares de Solorzano (first owner)

1997. Bicentenary of Quinta de Anauco (historic house). Multicoloured.
3369 110b. Type **567** 25 15
3370 110b. Principal facade . . . 25 15
3371 110b. Entrance passage . . 25 15
3372 110b. Inner courtyard . . . 25 15
3373 110b. Passageway to kitchen 25 15
3374 110b. Kitchen 25 15
3375 110b. Living quarters . . . 25 15
3376 110b. Coach house with fountain 25 15
3377 110b. Cart in stable 25 15
3378 110b. Water trough and stable 25 15

568 Jarwaharlal Nehru (first Prime Minister)

1997. 50th Anniv of Independence of India. Multicoloured.
3379 165b. Type **568** 40 20
3380 165b. Congress building, New Delhi 40 20
3381 165b. Ritual cleansing in River Ganges 40 20
3382 165b. Actress and film cameraman 40 20
3383 165b. "INSAT-1B" meteorological satellite orbiting Earth 40 20
3384 200b. Sardar Patel (politician) and flag . . . 45 25
3385 200b. Mahatma Gandhi . . 45 25
3386 200b. Rabindranath Tagore (poet and philosopher) . . 45 25
3387 200b. Musician playing traditional instrument . . 45 25
3388 200b. Woman at computer 45 25
Nos. 3379/88 were issued together, se-tenant, forming a composite design.

569 Von Stephan (after Anton Weber)

1997. Death Centenary of Heinrich von Stephan (founder of U.P.U.). Multicoloured.
3390 110b. Type **569** 25 15
3391 280b. U.P.U. monument, Berne 65 35

570 Ye'Kuana Basket

1997. Amerindians (4th series). Basketwork. Multicoloured.
3392 140b. Type **570** 35 20
3393 140b. Ye'Kuana basket with handle 35 20
3394 140b. Ye'Kuana lidded jar with bird decoration . . . 35 20
3395 140b. Panare round dish . . . 35 20
3396 140b. Pemon baby carrier 35 20
3397 140b. Yanomani basket with strap 35 20
3398 140b. Ye'Kuana lidded jar 35 20
3399 140b. Ye'Kuana dish . . . 35 20
3400 140b. Panare oval dish . . . 35 20
3401 140b. Warao fluted basket 35 20

571 The Annunciation

1997. Christmas. Multicoloured.
3403 110b. Type **571** 25 15
3404 110b. Mary visits St. Isabel 25 15
3405 110b. Mary and Joseph arrive at Bethlehem . . . 25 15
3406 110b. The Nativity 25 15
3407 110b. Angel and shepherds 25 15
3408 110b. Adoration of the Shepherds 25 15
3409 110b. Wise Men following star 25 15
3410 110b. Wise Men offer gifts 25 15
3411 110b. Presentation in the Temple 25 15
3412 110b. Flight into Egypt . . 25 15

572 Workers and Scales of Justice (social justice)

1997. 7th Summit of Latin American Heads of State, Isla de Margarita. Multicoloured.
3413 165b. Type **572** 40 20
3414 165b. Voting box (open elections) 40 20
3415 165b. Summit emblem . . . 40 20
3416 165b. Broadcaster (true information) 40 20
3417 165b. Constitution and people (human rights) . . 40 20
3418 200b. As No. 3417 . . . . 45 25
3419 200b. As No. 3416 . . . . 45 25
3420 200b. As No. 3415 . . . . 45 25
3421 200b. As No. 3414 . . . . 45 25
3422 200b. As No. 3413 . . . . 45 25

573 Monastery Church, Puerta de Agua

1997. Centenary of Diocese of Zulia. Mult.
3423 110b. Type **573** 25 15
3424 110b. St. Anne's Church . . 25 15
3425 110b. Reliquary of the Virgin of the Rosary, Chiquinquira 25 15
3426 110b. Basilica of St. John of God, Chiquinquira . . . 25 15
3427 110b. Santo Cristo de Aranza church 25 15
3428 110b. Maracaibo cathedral 25 15
3429 110b. Machiques cathedral 25 15
3430 110b. Arms of Archbishop Ovidio Perez Morales . . 25 15
3431 110b. Cabimas cathedral . . 25 15
3432 110b. Cathedral of El Vigia and San Carlos del Zulia 25 15

574 Jubilee Emblem

1998. "40 Years of Democracy". Multicoloured.
3433 110b. Type **574** 25 15
3434 110b. People voting 25 15
3435 110b. Child studying globe 25 15
3436 110b. Underground train . . 25 15
3437 110b. Man making speech (freedom of expression) 25 15
3438 110b. Senate and Constitution 25 15
3439 110b. Orchestra 25 15
3440 110b. Children and Scales of Justice 25 15
3441 110b. Brown bear and El Avila National Park (protection of environment) 25 15
3442 110b. Adult education . . . 25 15

575 Fishermen

577 Helmeted Curassow

576 "Oncidium orthostates"

1998. 500th Anniv of Discovery of Margarita Island. Multicoloured.
3443 100b. Type **575** 25 20
3444 100b. Petronila Mata (freedom fighter) 25 20
3445 100b. Yellow-shouldered amazon 25 20
3446 200b. Angel Rock 45 25
3447 200b. Simon Bolivar 45 25
3448 200b. Pearl diver 45 25
3449 200b. General Santiago Marino 45 25
3450 200b. General Juan Bautista Arismendi 45 25
3451 265b. Christopher Columbus 60 30
3452 265b. "Our Lady the Virgin of the Valley" and church 60 30
Nos. 3443/52 were issued together, se-tenant, Nos. 3446 with 3451 and Nos. 3448/52 forming composite designs.

1998. Orchids. Multicoloured.
3454 185b. Type **576** 40 20
3455 185b. "Epidendrum praetervisum" 40 20
3456 185b. "Odontoglossum schilleranum" 40 20
3457 185b. "Bletia lansbergii" . . 40 20
3458 185b. "Caularthron bicornutum" 40 20
3459 185b. "Darwiniera bergoldii" 40 20
3460 185b. "Houlletia tigrina" . . 40 20
3461 185b. "Pleurothallis acuminata" 40 20
3462 185b. "Elleanthus lupulinus" 40 20
3463 185b. "Epidendrum ferrugineum" 40 20

1998. 60th Anniv of Henri Pittier National Park. Multicoloured.
3465 140b. Type **577** 30 15
3466 140b. Swallow tanager ("Tersina virdis") 30 15
3467 150b. Ornate hawk eagle ("Spizaetus ornatus") . . 30 15
3468 150b. Leaf frog ("Phyllomedusa trinitatis") 30 15
3469 200b. Lilac-tailed parrotlet ("Touit collaris") 45 25
3470 200b. Collared trogon ("Trogon collaris") . . . 45 25
3471 200b. Emperor ("Morpho peleides") 45 25
3472 200b. Longhorn beetle ("Acrocinus longimanus") 45 25
3473 350b. Green jay ("Cyanocorax yncas") . . 75 40
3474 350b. Hercules beetle ("Dynastes hercules") . . 75 40

578 Gumersindo Torres Millet (first Comptroller)

1998. 60th Anniv of Office of Comptroller General. Black, red and blue (Nos. 3477, 3479) or multicoloured (others).
3475 140b. Type **578** 30 15
3476 140b. Luis Antonio Pieri Yepez (comptroller, 1958–69) 30 15
3477 140b. Congress building . . 30 15
3478 140b. Flag 30 15
3479 200b. Banknotes and coins 45 25

3480 200b. Numbers 45 25
3481 350b. Newspapers 75 40
3482 350b. Scales of Justice . . . 75 40
3483 350b. Code of Ethics . . . 75 40
3484 350b. Emblem of Seventh Assembly of Latin American and Caribbean Organization of Higher Fiscal Bodies 75 40

579 Anniversary Emblem

1998. 50th Anniv of Organization of American States. Multicoloured.
3486 140b. Type **579** 25 15
3487 140b. Institutional emblem 25 15
3488 150b. Soldier uncovering landmine 30 15
3489 150b. Official with prisoner (Defence of Human Rights) 30 15
3490 200b. Simon Bolivar 40 20
3491 200b. Scroll commemorating 50th anniv of American Declaration of Human Rights 40 20
3492 200b. Map of the Americas on road sign 40 20
3493 200b. Three rock climbers (anti-drugs co-operation) 40 20
3494 350b. Members' flags including Brazil and U.S.A. forming double helix 70 35
3495 350b. Members' flags including Jamaica and Venezuela forming a double helix 70 35
Nos. 3486/7, 3492/3 and 3494/5 were issued together, se-tenant, forming composite designs.

580 Brown Booby, Turtle and Crab

1998. "Expo '98" World's Fair, Lisbon. Mult.
3496 140b. Type **580** 25 15
3497 140b. Fishermen in boat . . 25 15
3498 150b. Shells, baby turtle and jellyfish 30 15
3499 150b. Yellow-finned tuna and snapper 30 15
3500 200b. Great barracuda and underwater vegetation (value at top) 40 20
3501 200b. Octopus, fishes and underwater vegetation (value at foot) 40 20
3502 200b. Horse rider 40 20
3503 200b. Cattle in water and common squirrel-monkey 40 20
3504 350b. Great egret and scarlet ibis 70 35
3505 350b. Red howler (monkey), waterfall and plants . . . 70 35
Nos. 3496/3505 were issued together, se-tenant, forming a composite design.

581 Athletics

1998. 18th Central American and Caribbean Games, Maracaibo. Multicoloured.
3506 150b. Type **581** 30 15
3507 150b. Ten-pin bowling . . . 30 15
3508 150b. Cycling 30 15
3509 150b. Gymnastics 30 15
3510 150b. Swimming 30 15
3511 200b. Basketball 40 20
3512 200b. Boxing 40 20
3513 200b. Fencing 40 20
3514 200b. Weightlifting 40 20
3515 200b. Tennis 40 20

582 Anthropomorphic Vessel

1998. 500th Anniv of Discovery of Venezuela. Multicoloured.
3516 140b. Type **582** 25 15
3517 140b. "Catholic Royal Couple" (wood carving, Manuel Cabrera) 25 15
3518 150b. Three women of different races 30 15
3519 150b. Mixed-race people . . 30 15
3520 200b. Lake houses on stilts 40 20
3521 200b. Modern city 40 20
3522 200b. Juan de la Cosa and 1499 map 40 20
3523 200b. Detail of 1599 map by Jodocus Hondius 40 20
3524 350b. Christopher Columbus 70 35
3525 350b. Alonso de Ojeda . . . 70 35

583 Columbus, Vespucci and Galleon

1998. 500th Anniversaries of Christopher Columbus's Discovery of America and Amerigo Vespucci's Exploration of Venezuela.
3526 **583** 400b. multicoloured . . 80 40

584 River Casiquiare, Amazon Basin

1998. 20th Anniv of Amazon Co-operation Treaty. Multicoloured.
3527 200b. Type **584** 40 20
3528 200b. River Casiquiare, Amazon Basin (right-hand detail) 40 20
3529 200b. Berries of "Bactris gasipaes" 40 20
3530 200b. "Neblinaria celiae" (plant) 40 20
3531 200b. Cardinal tetra ("Paracheidon axelrodi") 40 20
3532 200b. Yellow-banded poison-arrow frogs ("Dendrobates leucomelas") 40 20
3533 200b. Nocturnal curassows ("Nocthocrax urumatum") 40 20
3534 200b. Bush dogs ("Speothos venaticus") 40 20
3535 200b. Cocuy Stone 40 20
3536 200b. Neblina Ridge 40 20
Nos. 3527/8 were issued together, se-tenant, forming a composite design.

585 Martinez Cockroach cleaning

1998. Children's Stories (2nd series). "Martinez Cockroach and Perez Rat" from "Uncle Jaguar and Uncle Rabbit" by Antonio Arraiz. Mult.
3537 130b. Type **585** 25 15
3538 130b. Doctor Ass writing on pad 25 15
3539 130b. Parakeet in dress . . 25 15
3540 130b. Photographer and reporter 25 15
3541 130b. Piojo (cat) 25 15
3542 130b. Martinez Cockroach and pig 25 15
3543 130b. Chivo (goat) 25 15
3544 130b. Martinez Cockroach and Perez Rat gazing at moon 25 15
3545 130b. Perez Rat sniffing cauldron in which he later drowned 25 15
3546 130b. Guinea-hen and Misia Rata reviving Martinez Cockroach 25 15
A number and the relevant portion of the story is printed on the back of each stamp over the gum.

586 Ram's-horn Blower

1998. 50th Anniv of State of Israel. Multicoloured.
3548 140b. Type **586** 25 25
3549 140b. Book Museum . . . 25 25
3550 200b. King David 40 20
3551 200b. Knesset building, Jerusalem 40 20
3552 200b. Dr. Theodor Herzl (founder of World Zionist Movement) 40 20
3553 200b. David Ben Gurion (first Israeli Prime Minister) 40 20
3554 350b. Moses holding Ten Commandments 70 35
3555 350b. Man at Wailing Wall 70 35
3556 350b. Menorah 70 35
3557 350b. Torah 70 35

587 Handing Letter over Post Office Counter

1998. 125th Anniv of Universal Postal Union. Multicoloured.
3558 100b. Type **587** 20 10
3559 100b. Checking barcode on envelope 20 10
3560 100b. Computer operators using e-mail 20 10
3561 100b. Woman holding computer disc 20 10
3562 100b. Arrows and binary code, offices and factory 20 10
3563 300b. As Type **587** but design reversed 60 30
3564 300b. As No. 3559 but design reversed 60 30
3565 300b. As No. 3560 but design reversed 60 30
3566 300b. As No. 3561 but design reversed 60 30
3567 300b. As No. 3562 but design reversed 60 30

588 Caruao

1998. Amerindians (5th series). Paintings of Indian Chiefs by Primi Manteiga. Multicoloured.
3568 420b. Type **588** 80 40
3569 420b. Manaure 80 40
3570 420b. Guacamayo 80 40
3571 420b. Tapiaracay 80 40
3572 420b. Mamacuri 80 40
3573 420b. Maniacuare 80 40
3574 420b. Mara 80 40
3575 420b. Chacao 80 40
3576 420b. Tamanaco 80 40
3577 420b. Tiuna 80 40

589 Father Francisco de Cordoba and Juan Garces

1998. 500th Anniv of First Christian Missions to Venezuela. Multicoloured.
3579 100b. Type **589** 20 10
3580 100b. Father Matias Ruiz Blanco 20 10
3581 100b. Father Vicente de Requejada 20 10
3582 100b. Jose Gumilla 20 10
3583 100b. Antonio Gonzalez de Acuna 20 10
3584 300b. Father Pedro de Cordoba 60 30
3585 300b. Father Francisco de Pamplona 60 30
3586 300b. Father Bartolome Diaz 60 30
3587 300b. Felipe Salvador Gilij 60 30
3588 300b. Mariano Marti . . . 60 30

590 Opening Parade

1998. 30th Anniv of First Special Olympics. Mult.
3590 180b. Type **590** 35 20
3591 180b. Two people hugging 35 20
3592 180b. Football 35 20
3593 180b. Medal winner 35 20
3594 180b. Gymnastics 35 20
3595 420b. Swimming 80 40
3596 420b. Athletes and officials walking on track 80 40
3597 420b. Volleyball 80 40
3598 420b. Cheering medal winners 80 40
3599 420b. Baseball 80 40

591 Girl with Sparkler

1998. Christmas. Multicoloured.
3600 180b. Type **591** 35 20
3601 180b. Boy with figurine and paintbrush 35 20
3602 180b. Girl with kite 35 20
3603 180b. Boy with toy windmill 35 20
3604 180b. Girls with tambourine and drum 35 20
3605 420b. Boy in go-cart 80 40
3606 420b. Girl with yo-yo and rag doll 80 40
3607 420b. Boy with bell 80 40
3608 420b. Girl in hat with spinning toy 80 40
3609 420b. Boy on skateboard . . 80 40

592 Teresa de la Parra (writer)

1998. America. Famous Women. Multicoloured.
3610 180b. Type **592** 35 20
3611 420b. Teresa Carreno (pianist) 80 40

593 Amazonian Umbrellabird

1998. 100 Years of Venezuela–United States Solidarity. Each showing a portrait of William Phelps (ornithologist and entrepreneur). Mult.
3612 200b. Type **593** 40 20
3613 200b. Crimson topaz ("Topaza pella") 40 20
3614 200b. Great antpitta ("Grallaria excelsa") . . . 40 20
3615 200b. Ruby-throated hummingbird ("Chrysolampis mosquitus") 40 20
3616 200b. Yellow-bellied tanager ("Tangara xanthogastra") 40 20
3617 300b. Radio microphone (founder of Broadcasting Caracas) 60 30
3618 300b. Phelps Peak 60 30
3619 300b. Baseball in glove . . . 60 30
3620 300b. Phelps Library, San Antonio de Maturin . . . 60 30
3621 300b. Cash register 60 30

594 Jauregui

597 Angel appearing to Wise Men

595 Worker and Old Lady

1999. Monseigneur Jesus Manuel Jauregui Moreno. Multicoloured.

3622	500b. Type **594**	80	50
3623	500b. Crucifix	80	50
3624	500b. Church of Our Lady of the Angels, La Grita	80	50
3625	500b. Our Lady of the Angels (statue)	80	50
3626	500b. Jauregui in Cardinal's robes	80	50

1999. Centenary of Consecration of Church of the Blessed Sacrament, Caracas. Multicoloured.

3627	250b. Type **595**	40	25
3628	250b. Priest	40	25
3629	250b. Reliquary	40	25
3630	250b. Boy and girl	40	25
3631	250b. Family	40	25
3632	250b. Doctor	40	25
3633	250b. Woman with flower in hair	40	25
3634	250b. Angels beside base of reliquary	40	25
3635	250b. Soldier	40	35
3636	250b. Boy with spear	40	25

1999. Christmas. Multicoloured.

3639	300b. Type **597**	50	30
3640	300b. Wise men on camels	50	30
3641	300b. Wise men presenting gifts	50	30
3642	300b. Flight into Egypt	50	30
3643	300b. Roman soldier chasing Mary and Baby Jesus	50	30
3644	500b. Mary and Joseph	50	30
3645	500b. Mary and Archangel Gabriel	50	30
3646	500b. Women talking	50	30
3647	500b. Joseph with Mary on donkey	50	30
3648	500b. Mary, Baby Jesus and old man	50	30

599 Angel Falls

2000. Organization of Petroleum Exporting Countries Conference, Caracas. Multicoloured.

3650	300b. Type **599**	50	30
3651	300b. View over Forest	50	30
3652	300b. Waterfall	50	30
3653	300b. Aerial view of swamp	50	30
3654	300b. Auyantipuy Peak from Rio Carrao	50	30
3655	400b. Lake Maracaibo	50	30
3656	400b. Humboldt Peak	50	30
3657	400b. Aerial view of swamp	50	30
3658	400b. Rio Morichal swamp	50	30
3659	400b. Auyantepuy Peak	50	30
3660	550b. Emblem of "Riyadh, Cultural Capital of Arab World, 2000", Saudi Arabia	50	30
3661	550b. "Mohammed Racim" (painting, detail), Algeria	50	30
3662	550b. Dubai, United Arab Emirates	50	30
3663	550b. Greater bird of paradise, Indonesia	50	30
3664	550b. Figure from relief depicting Assyrian War, Iraq	50	30
3665	550b. Procession, Tehran, Iran	50	30
3666	550b. National emblem, Kuwait	50	30
3667	550b. "The Great Artificial River" project emblem, Libya	50	30
3668	550b. Bronze mask, Nigeria	50	30
3669	550b. Al-Zubarah Fort, Qatar	50	30

600 Cherub and "Gloria"

2000. Christmas. Multicoloured.

3670	300b. Type **600**	30	15
3671	300b. Cherub and "a"	30	15
3672	300b. Cherub and "en los"	30	15
3673	300b. Cherub and "Tielos"	30	15
3674	300b. Shepherd carrying lamb	30	15
3675	300b. Woman carrying jug	30	15
3676	550b. Joseph	50	30
3677	550b. Mary	50	30
3678	650b. Cherub and "Dios"	65	35
3679	650b. Baby Jesus	65	35

Nos. 3670/9 were issued together, se-tenant, with the whole forming a composite design.

601 Finger over Rifle End

2000. America. Millennium without Arms. Multicoloured.

3680	300b. Type **601**	30	15
3681	650b. Seated man holding lyre	65	35

602 School Buildings, Caracas

2001. Educational Building and Endowment Foundation. Multicoloured.

3682	300b. Type **602**	40	20
3683	300b. Las Salinas, Vargas	40	20
3684	300b. Las Matas "Education for All" centre, Portuguesa	40	20
3685	400b. Santo Domingo school, Merida	55	30
3686	400b. Miguel Flores school, Yaracuy	55	30

603 *Galeottia jorisiana*

2001. Orchids. Two sheets. Multicoloured.
MS3687 (a) 136 × 210 mm. 200b. × 2, Type **603**; *Lycaste longipetala*; 300b. × 2, *Coryanthes albertinae*; *Hexisea bidentata*; 400b. × 2, *Lycaste macrophylla*; *Masdevallia maculate*; 550b. × 4, *Ada aurantiaca*; *Kefersteinia graminea*; *Sobralia liliastrum*; Gongora maculata (b) 146 × 120 mm. 650b. *Masdevallia tovarensis*. Set of 2 sheets . . . 5·25 5·25

604 Josemaria Escriva

2001. Birth Centenary of Josemaria Escriva de Balaguer (founder of Opus Dei (religious organization)). Sheet 192 × 115 mm containing T **604** and similar vert designs. Multicoloured.
MS3688 300b. × 6, Type **604**; Bells, Opus Dei foundation, Madrid; Infant Jesus; With men from five continents; Commemorative plaque, Caracas Cathedral; Crowds, St. Peter's Square, Vatican; 550b. × 4, With women from many nations; Receiving honorary doctorate, Navarra University; With children, Venezuela; Josemaria Escriva (different) . . . 5·25 5·25

605 Thomas Ferriar

2001. 180th Anniv of Battle of Carabobo. Sheet 252 × 126 mm containing T **605** and similar vert designs showing paintings. Multicoloured.
MS3689 400b. × 5, Type **605** (battalion commander); "Bolivar in Buenavista" (Martin Tovar y Tovar); Letter (detail) (Simon Bolivar (leading general, War of Independence)); Commemorative column; Pedro Camejo (cavalry lieutenant, War of Independence); 600b. × 5, "Jose Antonio Paez" (post-Independence president) (Martin Tovar y Tovar); "General Santiago Marino" (Martin Tovar y Tovar); "Simon Bolivar" (M. Eberstein); "Manuel Cedeno" (Tito Salas); "Ambrosio Plaza" (Tito Salas) . . . 6·75 6·75

606 Angel and Holy Family

2001. Christmas. Sheet 133 × 210 mm containing T **606** and similar horiz designs. Multicoloured.
MS3690 200b. Type **606**; 200b. Family and angel playing guitar; 220b. Family and angel playing lute; 220b. Family and angel playing trumpet; 280b. Family and angel playing violin; 280b. Family and angel playing harp; 400b. Family and angel playing bagpipes; 400b. Family and angel playing panpipes; 500b. Family and angel playing drum; 500b. Family and angel playing bowed instrument . . . 4·50 4·50

607 South Cardinal Buoy, Acueducto de Margarita

2002. 160th Anniv of Maritime Signalling. Sheet 210 × 120 mm containing T **607** and similar vert designs showing buoys (300b.) or lighthouses (others). Multicoloured.
MS3691 300b. × 2, Type **607**; North Cardinal buoy; 450b. × 4, Lighthouses, Punta Brava; Punta Macolla; Los Roques; Redonda Island; 500b. × 4, Punta Faagoza; Punta Ballena; Punta Tigre; Recalada de Guiria . . . 5·50 5·50

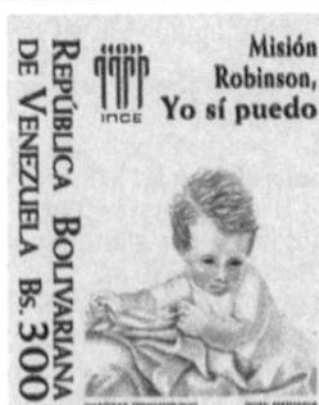

609 Toddler

2003. Mission Robinson (educational initiative). Sheet 97 × 228 mm containing T **609** and similar vert designs. Multicoloured.
MS3693 300b. × 4, Type **609**; Boy reading; Simon Bolivar and torch; Simon "Robinson" Rodriguez (Bolivar's teacher); 400b. × 2, Rodriguez and Eiffel Tower, Paris; Bolivar and flag; 500b. × 4, Bolivar and Rodriguez reading; Rodriguez seated and Bolivar standing; Rodriguez and reading class; Natives reading . . . 5·50 5·50

610 Cattle

2003. 4th Anniv of FONDAFA (Agricultural, fisheries and forestry fund). Sheet 135 × 210 mm containing T **610** and similar horiz designs. Multicoloured.
MS3694 300b. × 6, Type **610**; Ploughing with cattle; Tractors; Farmer holding beet; Maize; FONDAFA boats; 400b. × 2, Corn cob; Farmer driving tractor; 500b. × 2, Cacao pods; Cacao beans . . . 5·00 5·00

611 Sucre

2003. 28th Anniv of FONDUR (National urban development fund). Sheet 136 × 210 mm containing T **611** and similar horiz designs showing urban areas. Multicoloured.
MS3695 300b. × 6, Type **611**; Trujillo; Carabobo; Miranda; Barinas; Portuguesa; 400b. × 2, Tachira; Vargas; 500b. × 2, Emblem; Lara . . . 5·00 5·00

612 Uruguay Avenue, Lara

2003. 12th Anniv of FONTUR (National urban transportation fund). Sheet 135 × 210 mm containing T **612** and similar horiz designs. Multicoloured.
MS3696 300b. × 3, Type **612**; Parama highway, Merida; Gumana Avenue, Sucre; 400b. × 3, Santa Lucia—Jocoa highway, Barinas; Francisco Fajardo freeway, Caracas; Students; 500b. × 4, El Paraiso tunnel, Caracas; Vivex monitoring station; Trucks financed by FONTUR; Cruz Paredes Avenue, Barinas . . . 6·00 6·00

613 Native Children

2003. 12th Anniv of CONATEL (National telecommunications commission). Sheet 210×135 mm containing T **613** and similar vert designs. Multicoloured.
MS3697 300b. ×4, Type **613**; Children, hammock and dogs; Mountains; Caracas city; 400b. ×2, Child holding bow standing in boat; Beach; 500b. ×2, Children firing arrows; Angel Falls; 600b. ×2, Children making baskets; Sand and palms 5·75 5·75
No. **MS**3697 has a brief description of each stamp printed in the margin.

614 Women, Rainbow, Flag and Sun

2004. 42nd Anniv of FUNDCOMUN (Community and municipal reconstruction development fund). Sheet 135×209 mm containing T **614** and similar horiz designs. Multicoloured.
MS3698 300b. ×3, Type **614** (Miranda); House and kites (Trujillo); Mountains, house and couple (Merida); 400b. ×3, Sun, sand and buildings (Falcon); House, boy, beach ball and fish (Vargas); Yachts, rainbow and church (Esparta); 500b. ×4, Houses, rainbow, woman and children (Caracas); Children in playground (Caracas); Maracas, moon and houses (Barinas); Temple, children, sun and houses (Lara) 6·00 6·00

615 Houses and People in Doorway

2004. Mission Barrio Adentro (health initiative). Two sheets containing T **615** and similar vert designs. Multicoloured.
MS3699 (a) 210×134 mm. 300b. ×2, Type **615**; Smiling woman and street scene; 500b. ×4, Men pushing barrows and woman holding child; Family and children; Boys playing baseball and boat; Fence, people and man wearing cap; 750b. Man and sand dunes; 1500b. ×2, Man holding guitar and cattle; Mountain and girl; 1700b. Aboriginals and river (b) 205×120 mm. 1000b. Men pushing barrows. Set of 2 sheets 12·00 12·00

EXPRESS LETTER STAMPS

E **119**

E **194**

1949.
E809 E **119** 30c. lake 30 25

1961.
E1691 E **194** 30c. orange 50 25

OFFICIAL STAMPS

O **17**

1898.
O174 O **17** 5c. black and green 30 50
O175 10c. black and red 85 90
O176 25c. black and blue 1·10 1·25
O177 50c. black and yellow 1·90 1·90
O178 1b. black and mauve 2·10 1·75

1899. Surch **1899** and new value.
O187 O **17** 5c. on 50c. blk & yell 3·75 2·75
O188 5c. on 1b. blk & mve 14·00 13·00
O189 25c. on 50c. blk & yell 14·00 13·00
O190 25c. on 1b. blk & mve 9·50 9·00

1900. Optd **1900** in upper corners.
O222 O **17** 5c. black and green 35 35
O223 10c. black and red 45 45
O224 25c. black and blue 45 45
O225 50c. black and yellow 50 50
O226 1b. black and mauve 55 55

O **40** With Stars

O **45** Without Stars

1904.
O325 O **40** 5c. black and green 25 25
O326 10c. black and red 50 50
O327 25c. black and blue 50 50
O328 50c. black and red 2·40 1·90
O329 1b. black and lake 1·25 90

1912.
O354 O **45** 5c. black and green 15 25
O355 10c. black and red 15 25
O356 25c. black and blue 15 25
O357 50c. black and violet 20 35
O358 1b. black and yellow 40 35

REGISTRATION STAMPS

R **19** Bolivar

1899.
R186 R **19** 25c. brown 2·50 1·60

1899. Optd with T **21**.
R205 R **19** 25c. brown 1·75 1·25

VICTORIA Pt. 1

The south-eastern state of the Australian Commonwealth, whose stamps it now uses.

12 pence = 1 shilling;
20 shillings = 1 pound.

1 Queen Victoria ("half length")

2 Queen on Throne

1850. Imperf.
28 **1** 1d. red to brown £450 38·00
10 2d. lilac to grey £1000 £160
17 2d. brown £700 £130
31a 3d. blue £425 38·00

1852. Imperf.
21 **2** 2d. brown to lilac £160 24·00

3

4

1854. Imperf.
25 **3** 1s. blue £700 23·00

1854. Imperf.
32a **4** 6d. orange £180 18·00
35 2s. green on yellow £1400 £150

7 Queen on Throne

8 Emblems in Corners

1856. Imperf.
40 **7** 1d. green £150 23·00

1857. Imperf.
41 **8** 1d. green £100 15·00
45 2d. lilac £225 11·00
43 4d. red £160 7·50

1857. Rouletted.
72 **8** 1d. green £275 25·00
69 2d. lilac £120 8·50
48 **1** 3d. blue — £190
71c **8** 4d. red £120 3·50
53a **4** 6d. orange — 38·00
54 **3** 1s. blue — 90·00
56 **4** 2s. green on yellow £4000 £400

1858. Rouletted.
73 **7** 6d. blue £170 14·00

1859. Perf.
98 **8** 1d. green 70·00 4·50
100 2d. grey £110 5·50
101b 2d. lilac £110 11·00
78 **1** 3d. blue £750 £110
87 4d. red £120 7·50
102 **4** 6d. black £170 42·00
81 **3** 1s. blue £140 15·00
82 **4** 2s. green on yellow £275 35·00
129b 2s. blue on green £150 4·75

9

12

1860. Perf.
90 **9** 3d. blue £130 7·00
91 3d. purple £120 25·00
92a 4d. red 85·00 4·00
93 6d. orange £3750 £250
94 6d. black £120 5·50

1861.
104a **12** 1d. green 65·00 6·00

13 **14**

15 **16**

17

18

1862.
107 **13** 6d. black 80·00 5·00

1863.
131d **14** 1d. green 60·00 3·00
132b 2d. lilac 50·00 3·25
118 **15** 3d. lilac £130 27·00
378 3d. orange 15·00 2·50
135d **14** 4d. pink 70·00 3·00
136c **16** 6d. blue 30·00 2·00
380 6d. green 9·00 7·00
112 **14** 8d. orange £350 55·00
146 8d. brown on pink 75·00 8·00
119 **16** 10d. grey £500 £110
123c 10d. brown on pink 65·00 2·75
124 **17** 1s. blue on blue 65·00 2·75
139 **18** 5s. blue on yellow £1800 £300
148 5s. blue and red £180 13·00
383 5s. red and blue 48·00 42·00
For designs additionally inscribed "POSTAGE" see Nos. 399 etc.

20

1870.
169a **20** 2d. lilac 60·00 1·00

1871. Surch in figures and words.
174 **14** ½d. on 1d. green 50·00 13·00
171 **16** 9d. on 10d. brown on pink £325 10·00

22

23

24

25

26

27

1873.
176b **22** ½d. red 11·00 1·00
195 ½d. red on pink 35·00 22·00
376 ½d. green 2·00 1·50
177b **23** 1d. green 26·00 1·50
196 1d. green on yellow 90·00 15·00
197 1d. green on grey £130 55·00
179 **24** 2d. mauve 35·00 65
198 2d. mauve on lilac — £700
199 2d. mauve on green £170 21·00
200 2d. mauve on brown £160 21·00
172a **25** 9d. brown on pink 70·00 14·00
319 9d. green 27·00 9·00
366 9d. red 18·00 1·75
180 **26** 1s. blue on blue 65·00 3·50
381 1s. yellow 50·00 38·00
190 **27** 2s. blue on green £120 18·00
382 2s. blue on pink 42·00 24·00
For designs additionally inscribed "POSTAGE" see Nos. 399 etc.

1876. Surch **8d.. 8d.. EIGHTPENCE.**
191 **25** 8d. on 9d. brown on pink £190 16·00

30

31

1880. Frame differs in 4d.
209b **30** 1d. green 23·00 1·50
202d **31** 2d. brown 24·00 60
377 2d. mauve 8·00 1·50
213 4d. red 55·00 8·50
379 4d. yellow 25·00 15·00
For designs additionally inscribed "POSTAGE" see Nos. 416 etc.

34

35

36

37

1884. Inscr "STAMP STATUTE". Frames differ.
220 – 1d. green 45·00 35·00
221 **34** 3d. mauve £600 £325

222	–	4d. pink	£500	£250
223a	–	6d. blue	60·00	20·00
224	–	1s. blue on blue	70·00	23·00
225	**35**	2s. blue on green	£110	70·00
232	**36**	2s.6d. yellow	£300	£130
227	–	5s. blue on yellow	£300	75·00
228	–	10s. brown on pink	£900	£225
229	–	£1 violet on yellow	£650	£170
230	**37**	£5 black and green	£3750	£850

DESIGNS—As T **34/36**: 1d., 6d., 1s., 5s. to £1, Uncrowned portrait of Queen Victoria in centre; 4d. Obverse and reverse of fourpenny coin.

1884. No. 220 surch **½d HALF**.

234	½d. on 1d. green	60·00	60·00

39

40

44

52

56

58

61

1884. Inscr "STAMP DUTY". Frames differ.

253	**39**	1d. green	55·00	23·00
254	**40**	1d. bistre	18·00	3·75
255	–	6d. blue	70·00	11·00
256	–	1s. blue on blue	80·00	5·50
257	–	1s. blue on yellow	95·00	24·00
267	–	1s.6d. red to pink	£140	26·00
258c	**44**	2s. blue on green	£140	27·00
259	–	3s. purple on blue	£350	32·00
345	–	3s. drab	55·00	18·00
371	–	3s. green	£130	23·00
269	–	4s. red to orange	80·00	15·00
260	–	5s. purple on yellow	55·00	6·00
347	–	5s. red	80·00	13·00
348	–	6s. green	85·00	23·00
240	–	10s. brown on pink	£450	85·00
349	–	10s. green	£150	18·00
241	–	15s. mauve	£1200	£200
350	–	15s. brown	£425	55·00
262b	–	£1 orange	£350	55·00
274	**52**	£1 5s. pink	£1200	95·00
275	–	£1 10s. green	£850	85·00
245	–	35s. violet	£5500	
276a	–	£2 blue	£800	80·00
247	**44**	45s. lilac	£2500	£190
248	**56**	£5 red	£3000	£450
249	**58**	£6 blue on pink	—	£700
250		£7 violet on blue	—	£700
251	–	£8 red on yellow	—	£850
252	–	£9 green on green	—	£850
279	**61**	£10 mauve	£2750	£120

DESIGNS—As T **39/52**: 6d. to 1s.6d., 4s. to £1, £1 10s., £2, Various arms; 35s. "V R STAMP DUTY". As T **56/8**: £8, Crown; £9, Arms.

62

1884.

351	**62**	£25 green	—	£150
352		£50 mauve	—	£200
291		£100 red	—	£325

63

1884.

292a	**63**	2s.6d. yellow	80·00	11·00

64

65

66

67

68

1884. Inscr "STAMP DUTY".

296	**64**	½d. red	9·00	1·00
297	**65**	1d. green	13·00	1·25
298	**66**	2d. mauve	12·00	30
361	**65**	3d. buff	7·00	2·25
362		3d. green	22·00	10·00
300	**67**	4d. mauve	50·00	3·00
301a	**65**	6d. blue	45·00	2·10
293	**68**	8d. red on pink	27·00	6·50
294	**66**	1s. blue on yellow	80·00	8·50
303	**68**	2s. green on green	30·00	5·00
304a		2s. green on white	18·00	10·00

1885. Optd **STAMP DUTY**.

308	**15**	3d. orange	60·00	25·00
309	**31**	4d. red	55·00	38·00
306	**26**	1s. blue on blue	95·00	20·00
307	**27**	2s. blue on green	95·00	18·00

70

71

72

73

74

75

76

77

78

79

80

81

1886. Inscr "STAMP DUTY".

310	**70**	½d. grey	21·00	5·00
330		½d. red	4·00	70
356		½d. green	4·75	40
312	**71**	1d. green	9·00	65
329	**72**	1d. brown on pink	6·00	2·50
332		1d. brown	6·00	10
357a		1d. red	4·50	10
358		1d. green	6·00	4·00
333	**81**	1½d. green	3·00	3·50
355		1½d. red on yellow	3·00	1·75
314d	**73**	2d. purple	4·50	20
315b	**74**	2½d. red on yellow	13·00	70
335		2½d. blue	8·50	7·00
363	**75**	4d. red	8·50	2·25
317a	**76**	5d. brown	8·00	2·00
365	**77**	6d. blue	10·00	2·00
341	**78**	1s. red	15·00	2·00
322	**79**	1s.6d. blue	£140	70·00
323a		1s.6d. orange	19·00	7·00
324	**80**	£5 blue and purple	£2000	90·00
325		£6 yellow and blue	£2250	£120
326		£7 red and black	£2500	£130
327		£8 mauve and orange	£2750	£160
328		£9 green and red	£3000	£170

For designs additionally inscribed "POSTAGE" see Nos. 416 etc.

83

84

1897. Hospital Charity Fund.

353	**83**	1d. (1s.) blue	18·00	18·00
354	**84**	2½d. (2s.6d.) brown	85·00	70·00

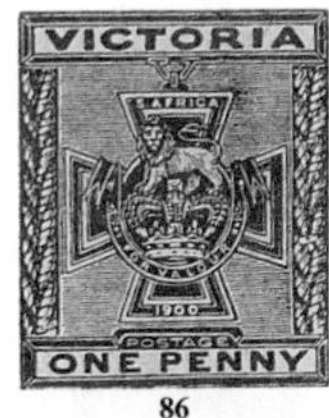

86

87

1900. Empire Patriotic Fund.

374	**86**	1d. (1s.) brown	75·00	45·00
375	**87**	2d. (2s.) green	£150	£150

93

101

1901. As previous types but inscr "POSTAGE" instead of "STAMP DUTY" or with "POSTAGE" added to design, and new designs.

416	**22**	½d. green	2·50	30
417a	**30**	1d. red	1·25	10
386b	**81**	1½d. brown on yellow	2·10	55
418a	**31**	2d. mauve	6·00	25
419	**74**	2½d. blue	3·00	40
389a	**93**	3d. brown	7·50	55
390	**31**	4d. yellow	5·50	65
391a	**76**	5d. brown	9·50	40
392	**16**	6d. green	12·00	90
424d	**25**	9d. red	9·50	1·25
425	**26**	1s. orange	8·00	2·00
395	**27**	2s. blue on pink	22·00	2·00
398	**18**	5s. red and blue	60·00	16·00
399	**101**	£1 pink	£250	£120
400	–	£2 blue	£500	£300

DESIGN: £2, as Type **101** but different frame.

1912. Surch **ONE PENNY**.

456	**31**	1d. on 2d. mauve (No. 387)	70	50

POSTAGE DUE STAMPS

D 1

1890.

D 1a	**D 1**	½d. blue and red	2·75	3·75
D 2		1d. blue and red	6·00	1·40
D 3		2d. blue and red	10·00	1·75
D 4		4d. blue and red	14·00	2·25
D 5		5d. blue and red	13·00	2·00
D 6		6d. blue and red	14·00	3·25
D 7		10d. blue and red	75·00	48·00
D 8		1s. blue and red	48·00	7·00
D 9		2s. blue and red	£110	50·00
D10		5s. blue and red	£160	90·00

1895.

D11a	**D 1**	½d. red and green	3·75	1·75
D12		1d. red and green	4·50	1·50
D13		2d. red and green	9·00	1·75
D14		4d. red and green	9·50	1·50
D15a		5d. red and green	11·00	7·50
D25		6d. red and green	9·50	4·25
D17		10d. red and green	22·00	10·00
D18		1s. red and green	16·00	3·25
D19		2s. red and green	60·00	20·00
D20		5s. red and green	£100	40·00

REGISTRATION STAMP

6

1854. Imperf.

34	**6**	1s. red and blue	£1300	£140

1857. Roul.

55	**6**	1s. red and blue	£5000	£250

TOO LATE STAMP

1855. As T **6** but inscr "TOO LATE". Imperf.

33	6d. lilac and green	£1000	£170

VICTORIA LAND Pt. 1

Stamps issued in connection with Capt. Scott's Antarctic Expedition.

12 pence = 1 shilling.

1911. Scott Expedition. Stamps of New Zealand optd **VICTORIA LAND**.

A2	**51**	½d. green	£550	£650
A3	**53**	1d. red	45·00	85·00

VIETNAM Pt. 21

A. DEMOCRATIC REPUBLIC

The Democratic Republic was proclaimed by the Viet Minh Nationalists on 2 September 1945 and recognised by France on 6 March 1946 as a free state within the Indo-China Federation. It consisted of Tongking, Annam and Cochin-China.

1945. 100 cents = 1 piastre.
1945. 100 xu = 10 hao = 1 dong.

Stamps of Indo-China overprinted.

VIET-NAM
DAN-CHU CONG-HOA
DOC-LAP
TU-DO HANH-PHUC
BUU-CHINH III
(1)

("DAN-CHU CONG-HOA" = Democratic Republic; "DOC-LAP TU-DO HANH-PHUC = Independence, Freedom, Happiness; "BUU-CHINH" = Postage.)

1945. Independence. Variously optd as T **1** (all with **DOC-LAP TU-DO HANH-PHUC** in opt).

1	**53**	1c. brown	1·50	1·50
2	–	2c. mauve (No. 315)	1·50	1·50
3	–	3c. brown (Courbet)	1·50	1·50
4	–	4c. brown (No. 316)	1·50	1·50
5	–	5c. sepia (De Genouilly)	1·50	1·50
6	–	6c. red (No. 304)	1·50	1·50
7	–	6c. red (No. 305)	2·75	2·75
8	–	10c. green (No. 307)	2·30	2·30
9	–	10c. green (No. 322)	3·75	11·50
10	–	20c. red (No. 309)	3·75	11·50
11	**64**	40c. blue	3·75	11·50

12 – $1 green (No. 311) . . . . 7·50 19·00
Nos. 3 and 5 were not issued without opt and are as Nos. 304 and 305 of Indo-China respectively.

1945. Variously optd. (a) **VIET-NAM DAN-CHU CONG-HOA.**
13 **69** 10c. purple and yellow . . . 6·00 7·50
14 – 15c. purple (No. 292) . . . 2·30 3·00
15 – 30c. brown (No. 294) . . . 2·30 2·30
16 **69** 50c. red . . . . 15·00 19·00
17 – $1 green (No. 295) . . . . 2·30 3·75

(b) **VIET-NAM DAN-CHU CONG-HOA BUU-CHINH.**
18 **53** 3c. brown . . . . 2·30 2·30
19 – 4c. yellow (No. 317) . . . . 2·30 2·30
20 **53** 6c. red . . . . 2·30 2·30
21 10c. green . . . . 3·75 3·75
22 – 10c. green (No. 320) . . . . 3·75 4·50
23 – 20c. red (Pavie) . . . . . 2·30 2·30
24 **53** 40c. blue 40 40
25 40c. grey . . . . 7·50 7·50
No. 23 was not issued without opt and is as No. 320 of Indo-China.

VIET-NAM
3$00 DAN-CHU
CONG-HOA

CUU-DOI
(2 "CUU-DOI" = Famine Relief)

1945. Famine Relief. Surch as T **2**.
26 **70** "2$00" on 15c.+60c. purple 19·00 19·00
27 "3$00" on 40c.+$1.10c. blue 19·00 19·00

1945. War Wounded. Surch as T **2** but with **Binh-si Bi-nan** (= Fund for War Wounded).
28 **70** "5$00" on 15c.+60c. purple 30·00 30·00

1945. Surch in new currency and variously optd as before (except Nos. 43/7). (a) **VIET-NAM DAN-CHU CONG-HOA BUU-CHINH.**
29 **64** 30x. on 1c. brown . . . . . 2·30 2·75
30 – 30x. on 15c. purple (Garnier) . . . . 1·50 2·30
31 **67** 50x. on 1c. brown . . . . . 3·00 3·75
32 – 60x. on 1c. brown (No. 313) 3·75 3·75
33 – 1d. on 5c. brown (No. 303) 6·00 6·00
34 – 1d.60x. on 10c. green (No. 319) . . . . 2·30 3·00
35 **64** 3d. on 15c. purple . . . . . 3·00 4·50
36 **67** 3d. on 15c. purple . . . . . 4·50 5·25
37 – 4d. on 1c. brown (No. 302) 3·00 4·50
38 – 5d. on 1c. brown (No. 301) 4·50 5·25

(b) **VIET-NAM DAN-CHU CONG-HOA.**
39 – 1d. on 5c. purple (No. 318) 2·30 3·00
40 **49** 2d. on 3c. brown . . . . . 34·00 34·00
41 – 2d. on 10c. green (No. 321) 3·00 3·75
42 **49** 4d. on 6c. red . . . . . . 34·00 34·00

(c) Surch only.
43 **56** 50x. on 1c. brown . . . . . 3·75 4·50
44 2d. on 6c. red . . . . . . 23·00 23·00
45 **48** 5d. on 1c. orange . . . . . 34·00 34·00
46 10d. on 6c. violet . . . . . 38·00 38·00
47 15d. on 25c. blue . . . . . 38·00 38·00
No. 30 was not issued without opt and is as No. 301 of Indo-China.

OVERPRINT. Nos. 48/55 are all optd **VIET-NAM DAN-CHU CONG-HOA** with varying additional words as noted in headings.

1945. National Defence (**Quoc-Phong**).
48 **49** "+5d." on 3c. brown . . . 6·00 7·50
49 "+10d." on 6c. red . . . . 6·00 9·00

1946. People's Livelihood. (**DAN SINH**).
50 **57** "30xu.+3d." on 6c. red . . 1·50 2·30
51 **55** "30xu.+3d." on 6c. red . . 1·90 2·30

1946. Campaign against Illiteracy (**Chong nan mu chu**).
52 **59** "+4dong" on 6c. red . . . 7·50 7·50

1946. New Life Movement (**Doi song moi**).
53 **66** "+4dong" on 6c. red . . . 3·75 4·50

1946. Child Welfare (**Bao-Anh**).
54 – "+2dong" on 6c. red (No. 290) . . . . 3·75 5·25

1946. War Wounded (**Binh si bi nan**).
55 – "+3dong" on 20c. red (No. 293) . . . . 6·75 6·75

Definitive issues.

3 Ho Chi Minh

1946.
56 **3** 1h. green 75 75
57 3h. red 75 75
58 9h. yellow 75 75

1946. National Defence.
59 **3** 4+6h. blue . . . . 1·90 3·75
60 6+9h. brown . . . . 1·90 3·75
The Viet-Minh Government was at war with the French from 19 December 1946 until July 1954, and the stamps issued by the Democratic Republic in this period are listed as North Vietnam Nos. N1/13, NO1/9 and ND1/4.

B. INDEPENDENT STATE

On 14 June 1949, Vietnam, comprising Tongking, Annam and Cochin-China, became an independent state within the French Union under Emperor Bao-Dai. Until the 1951 issue Indo-Chinese stamps continued in use.

By the Geneva Declaration of 21 July 1954, Vietnam was partitioned near the 17th Parallel, and all authority of Bao-Dai's Government north of that line ended. Later issues are therefore those of SOUTH VIETNAM and NORTH VIETNAM.

100 cents = 1 piastre.

4 Bongour Falls, Dalat

1951.
61 **4** 10c. bronze 40 15
62 – 20c. purple . . . . 1·10 15
63 – 30c. blue . . . . 1·10 30
64 – 50c. red . . . . 2·10 15
65 **4** 60c. sepia . . . . 1·10 15
66 – 1p. brown . . . . 1·10 15
67 – 1p.20 brown . . . . 7·50 1·90
68 – 2p. violet . . . . 2·10 15
69 – 3p. blue . . . . 7·50 15
70 **4** 5p. green . . . . 5·75 30
71 – 10p. red . . . . 13·50 40
72 – 15p. brown . . . . 45·00 2·30
73 – 30p. green . . . . £110 2·75
DESIGNS—HORIZ: 20c., 2p., 10p. Imperial Palace, Hue; 30c., 15p. Small Lake, Hanoi; 50c., 1p. Temple of Remembrance, Saigon. VERT: 1p.20, 3p., 30p. Emperor Bao Dai.

9

1952. Air.
74 **9** 3p.30 green and lake 85 60
75 4p. yellow and brown . . . . 1·10 40
76 5p.10 pink and blue . . . . 1·10 85
77 – 6p.30 red and yellow (symbolic of airlines) . . . 1·20 1·00

10 Empress Nam Phuong

11 Globe and Lightning

1952.
78 **10** 30c. brown, yellow & purple 1·10 30
79 50c. brown, yellow and blue 1·50 45
80 1p.50 brown, yellow & olive 3·50 30

1952. 1st Anniv of Admission of Vietnam into I.T.U.
81 **11** 1p. blue . . . . 6·00 1·10

12 Dragon

1952. Air. Day of Wandering Souls.
82 **12** 40c. red . . . . 1·50 30
83 70c. green . . . . 1·90 40
84 80c. blue . . . . 1·90 40
85 90c. brown . . . . 1·90 40
86 – 3p.70 purple . . . . 4·25 60
DESIGN—VERT: 3p.70, Fish dragon.

13 U.P.U. Monument, Berne, and Coastline

1952. 1st Anniv of Admission of Vietnam into U.P.U.
87 **13** 5p. brown . . . . 3·50 1·50

1952. Red Cross. T **10** surch with red cross and **+50c.**
88 **10** 1p.50+50c. brn, yell & bl . . 7·50 2·75

15 Emperor Bao Dai and Gateway

1952. 40th Birthday of Emperor.
89 **15** 1p.50 purple . . . . 3·75 1·10

16 Sabres and Flag

17 Crown Prince Bao Long

1952. Wounded Soldiers' Relief Fund.
90 **16** 3p.30+1p.70 lake . . . . . 2·75 2·30

1959.
91 **17** 40c. turquoise 40 40
92 70c. lake 40 40
93 80c. sepia 40 40
94 – 90c. green . . . . 1·10 1·10
95 – 20p. red . . . . 1·50 1·50
96 – 50p. violet . . . . 5·25 5·25
97 **17** 100p. blue . . . . 7·50 7·50
PORTRAIT: 90c. to 50p. Crown Prince in uniform.

POSTAGE DUE STAMPS

D 10 Dragon

1952.
D78 **D 10** 10c. green and red . . . 75 75
D79 20c. yellow and green . . 75 75
D80 30c. orange and violet . . 75 75
D81 40c. pink and green . . 75 75
D82 50c. grey and lake . . . 75 75
D83 1p. silver and blue . . . 1·50 1·50

C. SOUTH VIETNAM

100 cents = 1 piastre.
INDEPENDENT STATE
(Within the French Union)

1 Turtle

1955. 1st Anniv of Govt of Ngo Dinh Diem.
S1 **1** 30c. purple . . . . 1·20 85
S2 50c. green . . . . 5·75 3·25
S3 1p.50 blue . . . . 3·25 1·20

2 Phoenix

1955. Air.
S4 **2** 4p. mauve and violet . . . . 2·30 2·30

3 Refugees

1955. 1st Anniv of Arrival of Refugees from North Vietnam.
S 5 **3** 70c. red . . . . 2·00 1·20
S 6 80c. purple . . . . 5·00 2·75
S 7 10p. blue . . . . 9·00 5·25
S 8 20p. brown, orange & violet 18·00 6·75
S 9 35p. sepia, yellow and blue 36·00 28·00
S10 100p. purple, orange & green . . . . 85·00 45·00
No. S9 is inscribed "CHIEN-DICH-HUYNE-DE" in margin at foot.
See also No. S26.

REPUBLIC
(from 26th October, 1955)

4 G.P.O., Saigon

5 Pres. Ngo Dinh Diem

1956. 5th Anniv of Entry of Vietnam into U.P.U.
S11 **4** 60c. green . . . . 2·75 1·20
S12 90c. violet . . . . 5·25 2·00
S13 3p. brown . . . . 9·75 2·75

1956.
S14 **5** 20c. brown 40 40
S15 30c. purple 85 40
S16 50c. red 40 40
S17 1p. violet 85 40
S18 1p.50 violet . . . . 1·60 40
S19 3p. sepia . . . . 1·60 40
S20 4p. blue . . . . 2·30 85
S21 5p. brown . . . . 3·25 85
S22 10p. blue . . . . 4·25 1·20
S23 20p. black . . . . 9·75 2·00
S24 35p. green . . . . 27·00 5·00
S25 100p. brown . . . . 55·00 25

1956. No. S9 with bottom marginal inscription obliterated by bar.
S26 **3** 35p. sepia, yellow and blue 20·00 14·50

1956. Optd **Cong-thu Buu-dien** (= "Government Postal Building").
S27 **4** 60c. green . . . . 3·25 1·60
S28 90c. violet . . . . 5·00 1·60
S29 3p. brown . . . . 7·25 2·40

7 Bamboo

8 Refugee Children

1956. 1st Anniv of Republic.
S30 **7** 50c. red 75 75
S31 1p.50 purple 75 75
S32 2p. green . . . . 1·50 1·50
S33 4p. blue . . . . 3·00 3·00

1956. United Nations "Operation Brotherhood".
S34 **8** 1p. mauve 85 40
S35 2p. turquoise . . . . 1·60 85
S36 6p. violet . . . . 2·40 85
S37 35p. blue . . . . 17·00 7·25

9 Hunters on Elephants

10 Ship's Cargo being offloaded at Saigon

1957. 3rd Anniv of Govt of Ngo Dinh Diem.
S38 **9** 20c. purple and green . . . 85 40
S39 30c. red and bistre . . . . 1·20 40
S40 – 90c. sepia and green . . . 1·60 85
S41 – 2p. blue and green . . . . 2·75 85
S42 – 3p. brown and violet . . . 3·50 1·60
DESIGN—VERT: 90c. to 3p. Mountain hut.

1957. 9th Colombo Plan Conference, Saigon.
S43 **10** 20c. purple 75 75
S44 40c. olive 75 75
S45 50c. red 75 75
S46 2p. blue 75 75
S47 3p. green . . . . 1·50 1·50

11 Torch and Constitution

12 Youth felling Tree

1957. Inauguration of National Assembly.
S48 **11** 50c. salmon, green & black 40 40
S49 80c. purple, blue and black 85 40
S50 1p. red, green and black 85 40
S51 4p. brown, myrtle and black . . . . 1·60 85

S52 5p. olive, turquoise & black 2·00 85
S53 10p. brown, blue and black 3·25 2·00

1958. Better Living Standards.
S54 **12** 50c. green 85 40
S55 1p. violet 1·20 85
S56 2p. blue 1·60 85
S57 10p. red 3·50 1·60

13 Young Girl with Chinese Lantern **14**

1958. Children's Festival.
S58 **13** 30c. lemon 40 40
S59 50c. red 40 40
S60 2p. red 85 85
S61 3p. green 1·60 85
S62 4p. olive 2·00 85

1958. United Nations Day.
S63 **14** 1p. light brown 85 40
S64 2p. turquoise 1·20 85
S65 4p. red 1·60 85
S66 5p. purple 2·40 1·20

15 UNESCO Emblem and Building **16** U.N. Emblem and "Torch of Freedom"

1958. Inauguration of UNESCO Headquarters Building, Paris.
S67 **15** 50c. blue 75 40
S68 2p. red 75 85
S69 3p. purple 1·50 85
S70 6p. violet 2·30 1·20

1958. 10th Anniv of Declaration of Human Rights.
S71 **16** 50c. blue 85 40
S72 1p. lake 1·20 85
S73 2p. green 1·60 85
S74 6p. purple 2·40 1·20

17 Phu-Cam Cathedral **18** Saigon Museum

1958.
S75 **17** 10c. slate 85 40
S76 – 30c. green 1·20 85
S77 **18** 40c. green 85 40
S78 – 50c. green 85 40
S79 – 2p. blue 1·20 85
S80 – 4p. lilac 1·60 85
S81 **18** 5p. red 2·00 85
S82 **17** 6p. brown 2·00 85
DESIGNS—HORIZ: 30c., 4p. Thien Mu Pagoda; 50c., 2p. Palace of Independence, Saigon.

19 Trung Sisters (national heroines) on Elephants

1959. Trung Sisters Commemoration.
S83 **19** 50c. multicoloured 2·75 2·00
S84 2p. multicoloured 5·00 2·40
S85 3p. multicoloured 7·25 3·50
S86 6p. multicoloured 11·50 5·25

20 **21** Diesel Train

1959. Agricultural Reform.
S87 **20** 70c. purple 40 40
S88 2p. green and blue 85 40
S89 3p. olive 1·20 40
S90 6p. red and deep red 2·40 1·20

1959. Re-opening of Trans-Vietnam Railway. Centres in green.
S91 **21** 1p. violet 1·30 40
S92 2p. grey 2·50 85
S93 3p. blue 2·50 1·20
S94 4p. lake 5·00 1·20

22 Tilling the Land **25** Scout climbing Mountain

1959. 4th Anniv of Republic.
S95 **22** 1p. brown, green and blue 1·20 40
S96 2p. violet, green and orange 1·20 85
S97 4p. indigo, blue and bistre 2·40 1·20
S98 5p. brown, olive and light brown 3·25 1·60

1959. 1st National Scout Jamboree, Trang Bom.
S 99 **25** 3p. green 1·50 30
S100 4p. mauve 1·90 45
S101 8p. mauve and purple 3·50 1·10
S102 20p. dp turquoise & turq 9·75 2·40

26 "Family Code"

1960. 1st Anniv of Family Code.
S103 **26** 20c. green 75 75
S104 30c. blue 75 75
S105 2p. red and orange 1·50 1·50
S106 6p. violet and red 1·50 1·50

27 Refugee Family in Flight **28** Henri Dunant

1960. World Refugee Year.
S107 **27** 50c. mauve 1·20 40
S108 3p. green 1·20 85
S109 4p. red 2·40 1·20
S110 5p. violet 3·25 1·60

1960. Red Cross Day. Cross in red.
S111 **28** 1p. blue 1·60 85
S112 3p. green 2·00 85
S113 4p. red 2·75 1·20
S114 6p. mauve 3·50 2·00

29 Co-operative Farm

1960. Establishment of Co-operative Rice Farming.
S115 **29** 50c. blue 85 40
S116 1p. green 85 40
S117 3p. orange 1·60 85
S118 7p. mauve 2·75 1·20

30 X-ray Camera and Patient **31** Flag and Map

1960. National T.B. Relief Campaign Day.
S119 **30** 3p.+50c. green and red 2·00 2·00

1960. 5th Anniv of Republic. Flag and map in red and yellow.
S120 **31** 50c. turquoise 75 75
S121 1p. blue 75 75
S122 3p. violet 1·50 1·50
S123 7p. green 2·30 2·30

32 Woman with Rice

1960. F.A.O. Regional Conference, Saigon.
S124 **32** 2p. turquoise and green 1·50 1·50
S125 4p. ultramarine and blue 2·30 2·30

33 Crane carrying Letter

1960. Air.
S126 **33** 1p. green 3·75 1·50
S127 4p. blue and turquoise 5·25 2·30
S128 5p. violet and brown 6·75 3·00
S129 10p. mauve 10·50 4·50

34 Farm Tractor **35** Child and Plant

1961. Agricultural Development and Pres. Diem's 60th Birthday.
S130 **34** 50c. brown 85 40
S131 70c. mauve 85 40
S132 80c. red 85 85
S133 10p. mauve 2·75 1·20

1961. Child Welfare.
S134 **35** 70c. blue 85 40
S135 80c. blue 85 40
S136 4p. bistre 1·20 85
S137 7p. green and turquoise 2·40 1·20

36 Pres. Ngo Dinh Diem **37** Young People and Torch

1961. 2nd Term of President.
S138 **36** 50c. blue 85 40
S139 1p. red 1·20 85
S140 2p. purple 1·60 85
S141 4p. violet 2·40 85

1961. Sports and Youth.
S142 **37** 50c. red 40 40
S143 70c. mauve 85 40
S144 80c. mauve and red 1·20 85
S145 8p. purple and red 2·75 1·20

38 Bridge over Mekong

1961. Inaug of Saigon–Bien Hoa Motor Highway.
S146 **38** 50c. green 85 40
S147 1p. brown 85 40
S148 2p. blue 1·20 85
S149 5p. purple 2·00 85

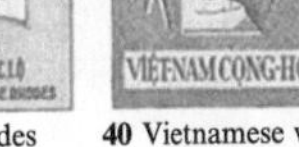

39 Alexander of Rhodes **40** Vietnamese with Torch

1961. Death Tercent of Alexander of Rhodes.
S150 **39** 50c. red 40 40
S151 1p. purple 85 40
S152 3p. bistre 1·20 85
S153 6p. green 2·00 85

1961. Youth Moral Rearmament.
S154 **40** 50c. red 85 40
S155 1p. green 85 40
S156 3p. red 1·20 85
S157 8p. brown and purple 2·00 85

41 Gateway of Van Mieu Temple, Hanoi **42** Tractor and Cottages

1961. 15th Anniv of UNESCO.
S158 **41** 1p. green 75 75
S159 2p. red 75 75
S160 5p. olive 1·50 1·50

1961. Rural Reform.
S161 **42** 50c. green 75 75
S162 1p. lake and blue 75 75
S163 2p. brown and green 75 75
S164 10p. turquoise 3·00 3·00

43 Attack on Mosquito **44** Postal Cheque Building, Saigon

1962. Malaria Eradication.
S165 **43** 50c. mauve 85 40
S166 1p. orange 85 40
S167 2p. green 1·20 85
S168 6p. blue 2·40 85

1962. Inauguration of Postal Cheques Service.
S169 **44** 70c. green 75 75
S170 80c. brown 75 75
S171 4p. purple 75 75
S172 7p. red 2·30 2·30

45 St. Mary of La Vang **46** Armed Guards and Fortified Village

1962. St. Mary of La Vang Commemoration.
S173 **45** 50c. red and violet 85 40
S174 1p. blue and brown 85 40
S175 2p. lake and brown 1·20 40
S176 8p. blue and turquoise 3·25 1·20

1962. Strategic Villages.
S177 **46** 50c. red 40 40
S178 1p. bronze 85 40
S179 1p.50 purple 1·20 40
S180 7p. blue 2·00 1·20

47 Gougah Waterfalls, Dalat **48** Trung Sisters Monument

1963. Pres. Ngo Dinh Diem's 62nd Birthday and Spring Festival.
S181 **47** 60c. red 85 45
S182 1p. blue 1·20 45

1963. Women's Day.
S183 **48** 50c. green 85 40
S184 1p. red 85 40
S185 3p. purple 1·20 85
S186 8p. blue 2·00 1·20

49 Harvester

1963. Freedom from Hunger.
S187 **49** 50c. red 85 40
S188 1p. red 85 40
S189 3p. purple . . . . 1·20 85
S190 5p. violet . . . . 2·00 1·20

50 Sword and Fortress **51** Soldier and Emblem

1963. Communal Defence and 9th Anniv of Inaug of Pres. Diem.
S191 **50** 30c. bistre 40 40
S192 50c. mauve 85 40
S193 3p. green . . . . 1·60 85
S194 8p. red . . . . 2·40 1·20

1963. Republican Combatants.
S195 **51** 50c. red 75 75
S196 1p. green 75 75
S197 4p. violet 75 75
S198 5p. orange . . . . 2·30 2·30

52 Centenary Emblem and Globe **53** Scales of Justice and Book

1963. Red Cross Centenary. Cross in red.
S199 **52** 50c. blue 75 40
S200 1p. red . . . . 1·10 75
S201 3p. orange . . . . 1·50 75
S202 6p. brown . . . . 2·50 1·50

1963. 15th Anniv of Declaration of Human Rights.
S203 **53** 70c. orange 75 75
S204 1p. mauve 75 75
S205 3p. green 75 75
S206 8p. ochre . . . . 2·30 2·30

54 Danhim Hydro-electric Station

1964. Inauguration of Danhim Hydro-electric Station.
S207 **54** 40c. red 75 75
S208 1p. brown 75 75
S209 3p. violet 75 75
S210 8p. green . . . . 2·30 2·30

55 Atomic Reactor

1964. Peaceful Uses of Atomic Energy.
S211 **55** 80c. olive 75 40
S212 1p.50 brown 75 40
S213 3p. brown . . . . 1·50 75
S214 7p. blue . . . . 2·20 1·10

56 "Meteorology" **57** "Unification"

1964. World Meteorological Day.
S215 **56** 50c. ochre 75 75
S216 1p. red 75 75
S217 1p.50 lake 75 75
S218 10p. green . . . . 2·30 2·30

1964. 10th Anniv of Partition of Vietnam.
S219 **57** 30c. blue and green . . . 75 75
S220 50c. blue, red and yellow 75 75
S221 1p.50 indigo, blue & orange 75 75

58 Hatien Beach

1964.
S222 **58** 20c. blue 75 40
S223 3p. green . . . . 1·10 40

59 "Support of the People"

1964. 1st Anniv of Revolution of 1 November 1963.
S224 **59** 50c. blue and purple . . . 75 75
S225 – 80c. brown and lilac . . . 75 75
S226 – 3p. brown and blue . . . 2·30 2·30
DESIGNS—HORIZ: 80c. Soldier breaking chain. VERT: 3p. Allegory of Revolution.

60 Temple and Monument, Botanic Gardens, Saigon

1964. Monuments and Views.
S227 **60** 50c. brown, green and blue . . . . 1·10 55
S228 – 1p. slate and bistre . . . 1·10 55
S229 – 1p.50 green and drab . . 1·70 1·10
S230 – 3p. red, green and violet 3·50 1·10
DESIGNS: 1p. Tomb of Minh Mang, Hue; 1p.50, Phan Thiet waterfront; 3p. General Le Van Duyet Temple, Gia Dinh.
For 1p. in smaller size, see No. S352.

61 Face of Bronze Drum

1965. Hung Vuong (legendary founder of Vietnam, 2000 B.C.).
S231 **61** 3p. orange and lake . . . 5·75 2·30
S232 100p. violet and purple 49·00 23·00

62 Dharmachakra and "Fire of Clemency" **63** I.T.U. Emblem and Symbols

1965. Buddhism.
S233 **62** 50c. red 75 40
S234 – 1p.50 orange, blue and deep blue 75 40
S235 – 3p. deep brown, sepia and brown . . . . 1·10 75
DESIGNS—HORIZ: 1p.50, Dharmachakra, lotus and globe. VERT: 3p. Dharmachakra and flag.

1965. I.T.U. Centenary.
S236 **63** 1p. red and bistre 75 75
S237 3p. red, mauve and brown 1·10 75

64 "World Solidarity" **65** Ixora

1965. International Co-operation Year.
S238 **64** 50c. blue and brown . . . 75 40
S239 1p. sepia and brown . . . 75 40
S240 1p.50 red and grey . . . 1·10 40

1965. Mid-Autumn Festival.
S241 **65** 70c. red, green & dp green . . . . 1·10 40
S242 – 80c. purple, green & mve 1·10 75
S243 – 1p. yellow, blue and deep blue . . . . 2·20 75
S244 – 1p.50 green and olive . . 2·50 75
S245 – 3p. orange and green . . 4·25 1·10
FLOWERS—VERT: 80c. Orchid; 1p. Chrysanthemum; 3p. "Ochna harmandii". HORIZ: 1p.50, Nenuphar.

66 Student and University Building

1965. Re-opening of Vietnam University.
S246 **66** 50c. brown 75 75
S247 1p. green 75 75
S248 3p. red 75 75
S249 7p. violet . . . . 1·50 1·50

67 Young Farmers

1965. 10th Anniv of "4-T" Rural Youth Clubs.
S250 **67** 3p. red and green . . . . 1·50 75
S251 – 4p. violet, blue and purple 1·50 75
DESIGN: 4p. Young farmer and club banner.

68 Basketball **69** Aerial Mast and Equipment

1965. 3rd S.E. Asia Peninsular Games, Kuala Lumpur (Malaysia).
S252 **68** 50c. bistre, brown and red 1·10 40
S253 – 1p. red and brown . . . 1·50 75
S254 – 1p.50 green . . . . . . 2·20 75
S255 – 10p. lake and purple . . . 6·50 1·90
DESIGNS: 1p. Throwing the javelin; 1p.50, "Physical Culture" (gymnasts and Olympic Games' symbols); 10p. Pole-vaulting.

1966. 1st Anniv of Saigon Microwave Station.
S256 **69** 3p. sepia, blue and brown 75 40
S257 – 4p. purple, red and green 1·10 75
DESIGN: 4p. Aerial mast, telephone dial and map.

70 Hook and Hemispheres **71** Help for Refugees

1966. "Free World's Aid to Vietnam".
S258 **70** 3p. red and grey 75 40
S259 4p. violet and brown . . 75 40
S260 6p. blue and green . . . 1·10 75

1966. Refugee Aid.
S261 **71** 3p. olive, mauve & brown 75 40
S262 7p. violet, brown & mauve . . . . 1·10 75

72 Paper "Soldiers"

1966. Wandering Souls' Festival.
S263 **72** 50c. bistre, brown and red 75 40
S264 – 1p.50 red, green & brown 1·10 40
S265 – 3p. vermilion, crim & red 1·50 75
S266 – 5p. brown, ochre and deep brown . . . . . 2·20 75
DESIGNS: 1p.50, Obeisance; 3p. Pool of candles; 5p. Votive offering.

73 "Violinist"

1966. Ancient Musical Instruments.
S267 **73** 1p. deep brown, mauve and brown 75 40
S268 – 3p. violet and purple . . 75 40
S269 – 4p. brown and red . . . 1·10 75
S270 – 7p. deep blue and blue . . 2·50 1·10
DESIGNS: 3p. "Harpist"; 4p. Small band; 7p. "Flautists".
For 3p. in smaller size, see No. S302.

74 W.H.O. Building

1966. Inaug of W.H.O. Headquarters, Geneva.
S271 **74** 50c. purple, violet and red 75 40
S272 – 1p.50 black, blue and lake 75 40
S273 – 8p. blue, sepia & turquoise . . . . 1·10 75
DESIGNS—VERT: 1p.50, W.H.O. Building and flag; 8p. U.N. flag and W.H.O. Building.

75 Spade in Hand, and Soldiers

1966. 3rd Anniv of Overthrow of Diem Government.
S274 **75** 80c. brown and bistre . . 40 40
S275 – 1p.50 purple, red & yell 75 40
S276 – 3p. green, brown & chest 75 75
S277 – 4p. lake, black and purple 2·20 1·10
DESIGNS—HORIZ: 1p.50, Agricultural workers, soldier and flag. VERT: 3p. Soldier, tractor and labourers; 4p. Soldier and horseman.

76 UNESCO Emblem and Tree **77** Cashew Apples

1966. 20th Anniv of UNESCO.
S278 **76** 1p. brown and lake . . . 75 40
S279 – 3p. brown, turquoise & blue 75 75
S280 – 7p. blue, turquoise and red . . . . 1·90 75
DESIGNS—VERT: 3p. Globe and laurel sprigs. HORIZ: 7p. Pagoda.

1967. Exotic Fruits.
S281 **77** 50c. red, green and blue 1·10 40
S282 – 1p.50 orange, green & brown . . . . 1·50 40
S283 – 3p. brown, green & choc 1·90 75
S284 – 20p. olive, green and lake 5·00 2·20
FRUITS—HORIZ: 1p.50, Bitter "cucumbers"; 3p. Cinnamon apples; 20p. Areca-nuts.

78 Phan Boi Chau

1967. Vietnamese Patriots.
S285 **78** 1p. purple, brown and red 75 75
S286 – 20p. black, violet & green 3·00 3·00
DESIGN: 20p. Phan Chau-Trinh (portrait and making speech).

79 Horse-cab

1967. Life of the People.
S287 – 50c. ultramarine, blue & green 75 75
S288 – 1p. violet, green & myrtle 75 75
S289 **79** 3p. lake and red 75 75
S290 – 8p. violet and red . . . . 1·50 1·50
DESIGNS: 50c. Itinerant merchant; 1p. Market-place; 8p. Pastoral activities.

80 Pottery-making

1967. Arts and Crafts. Multicoloured.
S291 50c. Type **80** 40 40
S292 1p.50 Wicker basket and vase 75 40
S293 3p. Weavers and potters . . 1·90 1·10
S294 35p. Baskets and pottery . . 5·25 2·50
The 3p. is a horiz design.

81 Wedding Procession

1967. Vietnamese Wedding.
S295 **81** 3p. red, violet and purple 1·50 75

82 "Culture"

1967. Foundation of Vietnamese Cultural Institute.
S296 **82** 10p. multicoloured . . . 1·90 75

83 "Freedom and Justice"

1967. Democratic Elections. Multicoloured.
S297 4p. Type **83** . . . . 1·10 75
S298 5p. Vietnamese and hands casting votes . . . . 1·50 75
S299 30p. Two Vietnamese with Constitution and flaming torch . . . . 1·90 1·90

84 Lions Emblem and Pagoda

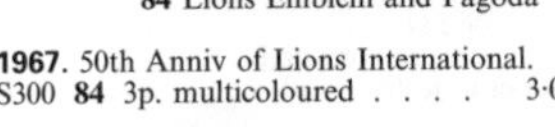
1967. 50th Anniv of Lions International.
S300 **84** 3p. multicoloured . . . . 3·00 1·10

85 Class on Globe

1967. World Literacy Day (8 Sept).
S301 **85** 3p. multicoloured . . . . 1·10 40

1967. Mobile Post Office Inaug. As No. S268 but smaller, size 23 × 17 mm.
S302 3p. violet and purple . . . 45·00 38·00

87 Tractor

1968. Rural Development. Multicoloured.
S303 1p. Type **87** 75 40
S304 9p. Bulldozer . . . . 1·10 75
S305 10p. Workers with wheel-barrow and tractor . . . 1·50 75
S306 20p. Building construction 3·25 1·10

88 W.H.O. Emblem

1968. 20th Anniv of W.H.O.
S307 **88** 10p. yellow, black & green . . . . 1·50 75

89 Flags of Allied Nations

1968. Thanks for International Aid. Mult.
S308 1p. Handclasp, flags and soldiers 40 40
S309 1p.50 S.E.A.T.O. emblem and flags 75 75
S310 3p. Handclasp and flags . . 1·50 1·10
S311 50p. Type **89** . . . . 5·00 2·75

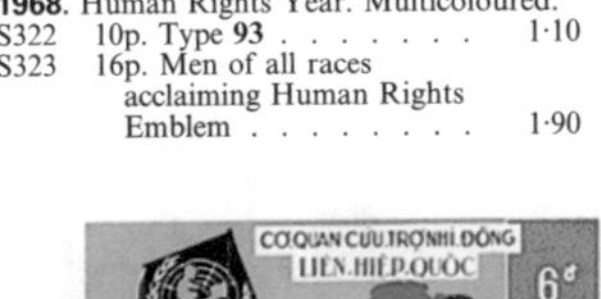
92 Farmers, Farm, Factory and Transport

93 Human Rights Emblem

1968. Development of Private Ownership. Mult.
S318 80c. Type **92** 75 75
S319 2p. Motor vehicles and labourers 75 75
S320 10p. Tractor and tri-car . . 75 75
S321 30p. Motor vehicles and labourers . . . . 4·50 4·50

1968. Human Rights Year. Multicoloured.
S322 10p. Type **93** . . . . 1·10 40
S323 16p. Men of all races acclaiming Human Rights Emblem . . . . 1·90 75

94 Children with UNICEF "Kite"

1968. UNICEF Day. Multicoloured.
S324 6p. Type **94** . . . . 1·50 75
S325 16p. Mother and child . . . 2·75 75

95 Diesel Train, Map and Mechanical Loader

97 Peasant Woman

1968. Re-opening of Trans-Vietnam Railway. Mult.
S326 1p.50 Type **95** 75 40
S327 3p. Type **95** . . . . 1·10 75
S328 9p. Diesel train and permanent-way workers 2·30 1·10
S329 20p. As No. S328 . . . . . 5·25 2·75

1969. Vietnamese Women.
S331 **97** 50c. violet, ochre and blue 75 75
S332 – 1p. brown and green . . 75 75
S333 – 3p. black, blue and sepia 75 75
S334 – 20p. multicoloured . . . 2·30 2·30
DESIGNS—VERT: 1p. Tradeswoman; 20p. "Ladies of fashion". HORIZ: 3p. Nurse.

98 Soldier and Militiaman

1969. "Open-arms" National Unity Campaign. Mult.
S335 2p. Type **98** 75 75
S336 50p. Family welcoming soldier . . . . 3·75 3·75

99 Vietnamese and Scales of Justice

1969. 1st Anniv of New Constitution. Mult.
S337 1p. Type **99** 75 75
S338 20p. Voters at polling station . . . . 2·30 2·30

100 Mobile Post Office Van in Street

1969. Vietnamese Mobile Post Offices System. Multicoloured.
S339 1p. Type **100** 75 75
S340 3p. Clerk serving customers 75 75
S341 4p. Child with letter, and mobile post office 75 75
S342 20p. Queue at mobile post office, and postmark . . . 2·30 2·30

101 Djarai Woman

1969. 2nd Anniv of Ethnic Minorities Statute. Multicoloured.
S343 1p. Type **101** . . . . 1·50 75
S344 6p. Mnong-gar woman . . 3·75 1·10
S345 50p. Bahnar man . . . . . 15·00 5·75

102 "Civilians to Soldiers"

1969. General Mobilization.
S346 **102** 1p.50 multicoloured . . 40 40
S347 – 3p. multicoloured . . . 75 40
S348 – 5p. brown, red and yellow . . . . 1·10 75
S349 – 10p. multicoloured . . . 1·50 75
DESIGNS: 3p. Bayonet practice; 5p. Recruits arriving at depot; 10p. Happy conscripts.

103 I.L.O. Emblem and Globe

104 Imperial Palace, Hue

1969. 50th Anniv of I.L.O.
S350 **103** 6p. black, grey and green 75 40
S351 20p. black, grey and red 1·90 75

1970. Reconstruction of Hue.
S352 **104** 1p. blue and brown . . 32·00 32·00

105 Asian Golden Weaver and Baya Weaver

1970. Birds of Vietnam. Multicoloured.
S353 2p. Type **105** . . . . 3·50 1·50
S354 6p. Chestnut mannikin . . . 3·50 1·50
S355 7p. Great Indian hornbill 5·25 2·30
S356 30p. Eurasian tree sparrow 14·50 4·50

106 Ruined House and Family

1970. Aid for Victims of Communist Tet Offensive. Multicoloured.
S357 10p. Type **106** 75 75
S358 20p. Refugee family, and First Aid . . . . 2·30 2·30

107 Man, Woman and Priest in Traditional Costume

1970. Vietnamese Traditional Costumes. Mult.
S359 1p. Type **107** 75 40
S360 2p. Seated woman (horiz) 75 40
S361 3p. Three women with carved lion (horiz) . . . 1·50 75
S362 100p. Man and woman (horiz) . . . . 9·75 5·25

108 Builders and Pagoda

1970. Reconstruction of Hue. Multicoloured.
S363 6p. Type **108** . . . . 1·50 75
S364 20p. Mixing cement . . . . 2·75 1·10

109 Ploughing Paddyfield

1970. "Land to the Tiller". Agrarian Reform Law.
S365 **109** 6p. black, green & brown . . . . 1·50 75

110 Scaffolding and New Building

1970. Reconstruction after Tet Offensive. Mult.

S366	8p. Type **110**	75	75
S367	16p. Construction workers	2·30	2·30

111 A.P.Y. Symbol

1970. Asian Productivity Year.

S368	**111** 10p. multicoloured	1·50	75

112 Nguyen Dinh Chieu and Poems

113 I.E.Y. Emblem

1970. Nguyen Dinh Chieu (poet) Commem.

S369	**112** 6p. brown, red and violet	75	75
S370	10p. brown, red & green	1·90	75

1970. International Education Year.

S371	**113** 10p. black, yellow & brown	1·50	75

114 Senate House

115 Two Dancers

1970. 9th Council Meeting and 6th General Assembly of Asian Interparliamentary Union, Saigon. Multicoloured.

S372	6p. Type **114**	75	75
S373	10p. House of Representatives	1·10	75

1971. Vietnamese Traditional Dances.

S374	**115** 2p. multicoloured	1·10	40
S375	– 6p. brown, blue & green	1·50	75
S376	– 7p. red, blue and brown	2·30	75
S377	– 10p. multicoloured	2·75	1·10

DESIGNS—HORIZ: 6p. Drum dance; 7p. Drum dancers in various positions. VERT: 10p. Flower dance.

116 Paddyfield, Peasants and Agrarian Law

1971. 1st Anniv of "Land to the Tiller" Agrarian Reform Law. Multicoloured.

S378	2p. Type **116** (dated "26.3.1971")	1·10	75
S378a	2p. Type **116** (dated "26.3.1970")		
S379	3p. Tractor and Law	1·10	75
S380	16p. Peasants ringing Law	1·50	75

117 Postal Courier

119 Hog-deer

118 Armed Forces on Map of Vietnam

1971. History of Vietnam Postal Service. Mult.

S381	2p. Type **117**	1·10	75
S382	6p. Mounted courier with banner	2·75	1·10

1971. Armed Forces Day.

S383	**118** 3p. multicoloured	1·10	1·10
S384	40p. multicoloured	1·90	75

1971. Vietnamese Fauna. Multicoloured.

S385	9p. Type **119**	1·90	75
S386	30p. Tiger	4·50	2·30

120 Rice Harvesters

1971. "The Rice Harvest".

S387	**120** 1p. multicoloured	75	75
S388	– 30p. lilac, black and red	3·00	3·00
S389	– 40p. brown, yellow & blue	3·00	3·00

DESIGNS: 30p. Threshing and winnowing rice; 40p. Harvesters in paddyfield.

121 New H.Q. Building

1971. New U.P.U. Headquarters Building, Berne.

S390	**121** 20p. multicoloured	2·75	1·10

122 Percoid fish

123 "Local Delivery"

1971. Vietnam Fishes. Multicoloured.

S391	2p. Type **122**	75	40
S392	10p. Striped scat (horiz)	3·00	75
S393	100p. Freshwater angelfish (horiz)	21·00	10·50

1971. Development of Rural Post System. Mult.

S394	5p. Type **123**	1·10	75
S395	10p. Symbolic crane	3·00	3·00
S396	20p. Cycle postman delivering letter	2·30	75

124 Fishermen in Boat, and Modern Trawler

1972. Vietnamese Fishing Industry. Multicoloured.

S397	4p. Type **124**	1·10	75
S398	7p. Fishermen hauling net	1·10	75
S399	50p. Trawl net	6·00	3·00

125 Emperor Quang Trung

126 Community Workers

1972. Emperor Quang Trung (victor of Dong Da) Commemoration.

S400	**125** 6p. multicoloured	75	75
S401	20p. multicoloured	2·30	2·30

1972. Community Development Projects.

S403	**126** 3p. multicoloured	75	40
S404	8p. multicoloured	1·10	40

127 Harvesting Rice

1972. Farmers' Day. Multicoloured.

S405	1p. Type **127**	75	40
S406	10p. Sowing rice	1·10	75

128 Boeing 727 over Dalat

1972. 20th Anniv of Viet-Nam Airlines. Mult.

S407	10p. Type **128**	1·10	75
S408	10p. Boeing 727 over Ha Tien	1·10	75
S409	10p. Boeing 727 over Hue	1·10	75
S410	10p. Boeing 727 over Saigon	1·10	75
S411	25p. Type **128**	2·30	2·30
S412	25p. As No. S408	2·30	2·30
S413	25p. As No. S409	2·30	2·30
S414	25p. As No. S410	2·30	2·30

129 Vietnamese Scholar

130 Sentry

1972. Vietnamese Scholars. Multicoloured.

S415	5p. Type **129**	75	75
S416	20p. Scholar with pupils	1·50	1·50
S417	50p. Scholar with scroll	4·50	4·50

1972. Civilian Self-defence Force. Multicoloured.

S418	2p. Type **130**	75	40
S419	6p. Young volunteer and badge (horiz)	1·10	1·10
S420	20p. Volunteers at rifle practice	1·50	1·10

131 Hands supporting Savings Bank

1972. Treasury Bonds Savings Scheme.

S421	**131** 10p. multicoloured	75	75
S422	25p. multicoloured	1·50	1·50

132 Three Guards with Horse

133 Wounded Soldier

1972. Traditional Vietnamese Frontier Guards. Mult.

S423	10p. Type **132**	75	75
S424	30p. Pikeman (vert)	2·30	2·30
S425	40p. Guards on parade	3·75	3·75

1972. Vietnamese War Veterans. Multicoloured.

S426	9p. Type **133**	75	75
S427	16p. Soldier on crutches	75	75
S428	100p. Veterans' memorial	9·00	9·00

134 Soldiers on Tank, and Memorial

1972. Victory at Binh Long. Mulicoloured.

S429	5p. Type **134**	75	40
S430	10p. Soldiers on map of An Loc (vert)	1·10	40

135 "Books for Everyone"

136 "200,000th Returnees"

1972. International Book Year. Multicoloured.

S431	2p. Type **135**	75	75
S432	4p. Book Year emblems encircling globe	75	75
S433	5p. Emblem, books and globe	75	75

1973. 200,000th Returnees under "Open Arms" National Unity Campaign.

S434	**136** 10p. multicoloured	1·50	75

137 Soldiers raising Flag

138 Satellite and Globe

1973. Victory at Quang Tri. Multicoloured.

S435	3p. Type **137**	75	40
S436	10p. Map and defenders	1·10	75

1973. World Meteorological Day.

S437	**138** 1p. multicoloured	1·10	75

139 Programme Emblem and Farm-workers

1973. Five-Year Agricultural Development Programme. Multicoloured.

S438	2p. Type **139**	40	40
S439	5p. Ploughing in paddy-field	75	40
S439a	10p. As T **149** but dated "26-03-1973" (34 × 54 mm)	£130	

140 Emblem and H.Q. Paris

1973. 50th Anniv of International Criminal Police Organization (Interpol). Multicoloured.

S440	1p. Type **140**	75	75
S441	2p. "INTERPOL 1923 1973"	75	75
S442	25p. Emblem and view of headquarters (different)	2·30	2·30

141 I.T.U. Emblem

142 Lamp in Hand

1973. World Telecommunications Day.

S443	**141** 1p. multicoloured	75	40
S444	– 2p. black and blue	75	40
S445	– 3p. multicoloured	1·10	40

DESIGNS: 2p. Globe; 3p. I.T.U. emblem in frame.

1973. National Development.

S446	**142** 8p. multicoloured	75	75
S447	– 10p. blue, black & brown	1·10	75
S448	– 15p. multicoloured	1·50	75

DESIGNS: 10p. "Agriculture, Industry and Fisheries"; 15p. Workers on power pylon.

143 Water Buffaloes

1973. "Year of the Buffalo". Multicoloured.

S449	5p. Type **143**	1·90	75
S450	10p. Water buffalo	2·75	75

144 Flame Emblem and "Races of the World"

1973. 25th Anniv of Declaration of Human Rights. Multicoloured.

S451	15p. Type **144**	1·50	75
S452	100p. Flame emblem and scales of justice (vert)	3·00	1·10

145 Emblem within "25"

1973. 25th Anniv of W.H.O.
S453 **145** 8p. multicoloured . . . 1·10 75
S454 – 15p. blue, red and brown 2·75 1·10
DESIGN: 15p. W.H.O. emblem and inscription.

146 Sampan crossing River

1974. Vietnamese Sampan Women. Multicoloured.
S455 5p. Type **146** . . . . 1·50 1·10
S456 10p. Sampan and passengers 2·30 1·10

147 Flags and Soldiers of Allies

1974. Allies Day. Multicoloured.
S457 8p. Type **147** 75 75
S458 15p. Soldiers and flags . . . 1·50 75
S459 15p. Allied Nations Monument . . . . 1·50 75
S460 60p. Raising South Vietnamese flag, and map (vert) . . . . 3·00 1·50

148 Trung Sisters on Elephant

1974. Trung Sisters' Festival.
S461 **148** 8p. green, yellow & black . . . . 1·10 75
S462 15p. red, yellow and black . . . . 1·50 75
S463 80p. blue, pink and black . . . . 3·00 1·10

149 Pres. Thieu holding Agrarian Reform Law

1974. Farmers' Day. Multicoloured.
S464 10p. Type **149** 75 75
S465 20p. Farm-workers (32 × 22 mm) 75 75
S466 70p. Girl harvesting rice (22 × 32 mm) . . . . . . 95·00 £110

150 King Hung Vuong

1974. King Hung Vuong (first Vietnamese monarch) Commemoration. Multicoloured.
S467 20p. Type **150** . . . . . . 1·10 75
S468 100p. Banner inscribed "Hung Vuong, National Founder" . . . . 4·50 1·90

151 National Library

152 Allied Nations Memorial, Saigon

1974. New National Library Building. Mult.
S469 10p. Type **151** 75 75
S470 15p. Library and Phoenix bas-relief . . . . 1·10 75

1974. Surch.
S470a **142** 10p. on 8p. mult . . .
S470b **145** 10p. on 8p. mult . . .
S470c **120** 25p. on 1p. mult . . .
S470d **140** 25p. on 1p. mult . . .
S470e **138** 25p. on 1p. mult . . .
S470f **141** 25p. on 1p. mult . . .
S470g – 25p. on 7p. red, blue and brown (No. S376) . . . .
S470h **147** 25p. on 8p. mult . . .
S470i – 25p. on 16p. mult (No. S427) . . . .
S470j – 25p. on 16p. mult (No. S380) . . . .

1974. International Aid Day. Multicoloured.
S471 10p. Type **152** 75 75
S472 20p. Flags on crane (horiz) 75 75
S473 60p. Crate on hoist . . . . 2·30 2·30

153 "Tourist Attractions"

1974. Tourism. Multicoloured.
S474 5p. Type **153** . . . . 1·10 75
S475 10p. Xom Bong Bridge Nhatrang . . . . 1·10 75
S476 15p. Thien Mu Pagoda, Hue (vert) . . . . 1·50 75

154 "Rhynchostylis gigantea"

1974. Orchids. Multicoloured.
S477 10p. Type **154** . . . . . . 1·90 1·50
S478 20p. "Cypripedium callosum" (vert) . . . . 1·90 1·50
S479 200p. "Dendrobium nobile" 17·00 12·00

155 "International Exchange of Mail"

157 Conference Emblem

156 Hien Lam Pavilion, Hue

1974. Centenary of U.P.U. Multicoloured.
S480 20p. Type **155** . . . . . . 1·90 75
S481 30p. "U.P.U. letter" and Hemispheres . . . . . . 3·00 75
S482 300p. U.P.U. emblem and Vietnamese girl (vert) . . 9·50 4·25

1975. Historical Sites. Multicoloured.
S483 25p. Type **156** . . . . . . 1·10 1·10
S484 30p. Throne Room, Imperial Palace, Hue . . 1·50 1·50
S485 60p. Tu Duc's Pavilion, Hue 1·90 1·90

1975. International Conference on Children and National Development, Saigon. Multicoloured.
S486 20p. Type **157** . . . . . . 1·10 1·10
S487 70p. Vietnamese family (32 × 22 mm) . . . . . . 1·50 1·50

158 Unicorn Dance

1975. Vietnamese New Year Festival. Mult.
S488 20p. Type **158** . . . . . . 1·50 1·10
S489 30p. Letting-off fire-crackers (vert) . . . . 1·90 1·10
S490 100p. New Year greeting custom (vert) . . . . . . 4·25 3·00

159 Military Mandarin ("San Hau" play)

1975. "Hat Bo" Vietnamese Traditional Theatre. Multicoloured.
S491 25p. Type **159** . . . . . . 1·50 75
S492 40p. Two characters from "Tam Ha Nam Duong" (vert) . . . . 2·30 2·30
S493 100p. Heroine "Luu Kim Giai Gia Tho Chau" (vert) . . . . 7·50 3·75

160 Produce for Export and Map

1975. Farmers' Day. Multicoloured.
S494 10p. Type **160** 75 75
S495 50p. Ancient and modern irrigation . . . . . . 2·30 2·30

MILITARY FRANK STAMPS

MF 29 Soldier and Barracks

1961. No value indicated. Roul.
SMF115 **MF 29** (–) yellow, brown, green and black . . . . . 49·00 38·00
SMF116 (–) yellow, brown and green . . . 49·00 38·00

POSTAGE DUE STAMPS

D 1 Dragon

1955.
SD 1 **D 1** 2p. yellow and mauve 1·10 1·10
SD 2 3p. turquoise and violet 1·50 1·50
SD 3 5p. yellow and violet 2·30 2·30
SD 4 10p. red and green . . 2·75 2·75
SD14 – 20p. green and red . . 7·50 1·10
SD15 – 30p. yellow and green 11·50 1·50
SD16 – 50p. yellow and brown 24·00 2·30
SD17 – 100p. yellow and violet 38·00 2·75
The 20p. to 100p. are inscribed "BUU-CHINH" instead of "TIMBRE TAXE".

D 90 Butterfly

D 91 Butterflies

1968.
SD312 **D 90** 50c. multicoloured 1·50 1·50
SD313 1p. multicoloured . . 1·50 1·50
SD314 2p. multicoloured . . 1·90 1·90
SD315 **D 91** 3p. multicoloured . . 6·00 6·00
SD316 5p. multicoloured . . 12·00 12·00
SD317 10p. multicoloured 15·00 15·00

1974. Surch.
SD470k **D 91** 5p. on 3p. mult . . 15·00
SD470l **D 90** 10p. on 50c. mult 15·00
SD470m 40p. on 1p. mult 15·00
SD470n 60p. on 2p. mult 15·00

D. NATIONAL FRONT FOR THE LIBERATION OF SOUTH VIETNAM

The National Front for the Liberation of South Vietnam was formed by the Communists, known as the Vietcong, in December 1960. With the support of troops from North Vietnam the Vietcong gradually gained control of more and more territory within South Vietnam until the surrender of the last South Vietnamese Republican forces in May 1975 enabled them to take control of the entire country. The following stamps were used in those areas controlled by the National Liberation Front.

1963. 100 xu = 1 dong.

The value of the N.L.F. dong fluctuated considerably and was not on parity with the North Vietnamese currency.

1 Vietcong Flag

1963. 3rd Anniv of National Liberation Front.
NLF1 **1** 20x. multicoloured (English inscr) . . . . 3·75 3·75
NLF2 20x. multicoloured (French inscr) . . . . 3·75 3·75
NLF3 20x. multicoloured (Spanish inscr) . . . . 3·75 3·75

2 Attack on Village

1963. 3rd Anniv of Revolutionary Struggle in South Vietnam. Multicoloured.
NLF4 10x. Type **2** . . . . 7·50 7·50
NLF5 10x. Attack on U.S. helicopter . . . . 7·50 7·50

3 Demonstrators with Banner

1964. 4th Anniv of National Liberation Front.
NLF6 10x. Type **3** . . . . . . 3·75 3·75
NLF7 20x. multicoloured . . . . 3·75 3·75
NLF8 30x. green and blue . . . 3·75 3·75
DESIGNS: 20x. Harvesting rice; 30x. Sinking of U.S.S. "Card" (destroyer).

4 Attack on Bien Hoa Airfield

1965. 5th Anniv of National Liberation Front.
NLF 9 **4** 10x. multicoloured . . . 3·75 3·75
NLF10 – 20x. black, grey and red 3·75 3·75
NLF11 – 40x. multicoloured . . . 4·50 4·50
DESIGNS: 20x. Nguyen Van Troi facing firing squad; 40x. Vietcong flags.

5 Vietcong Soldiers on U.S. Tanks

6 "Guerrilla"

1967. 7th Anniv of National Liberation Front. Mult.
NLF12 20x. Type **5** . . . . . . 3·75 3·75
NLF13 20x. Vietcong guerrillas (horiz) . . . . 3·75 3·75
NLF14 30x. Crowd with banners 3·75 3·75

1968. "The Struggle For Freedom". Paintings. Mult.
NLF15 10x. Type **6** . . . . 3·75 3·75
NLF16 20x. "Jungle Patrol" (horiz) . . . . 3·75 3·75
NLF17 30x. "Woman Soldier" 3·75 3·75
NLF18 40x. "Towards the Future" (horiz) . . . . 3·75 3·75

7 Casting Votes

1968. 8th Anniv of National Liberation Front. Mult.
NLF19 20x. Type **7** . . . . . . 3·75 3·75
NLF20 20x. Bazooka crew and burning airplane . . . 3·75 3·75
NLF21 30x. Vietcong flag and crowd (French inscr) 3·75 3·75
NLF22 30x. Vietcong flag and crowd (English inscr) 3·75 3·75

8 Lenin and Vietcong Flag

1970. Birth Centenary of Lenin.
NLF23 **8** 20x. multicoloured . . . 3·75 3·75
NLF24 30x. multicoloured . . . 3·75 3·75
NLF25 50x. multicoloured . . . 4·50 4·50
NLF26 2d. multicoloured . . . 5·75 5·75

9 Ho Chi Minh watering Kainito Plant

10 Vietcong "Lightning Flash"

1970. 80th Birth Anniv of Ho Chi Minh.
NLF27 **9** 20x. multicoloured . . . 3·75 3·75
NLF28 30x. multicoloured . . . 3·75 3·75
NLF29 50x. multicoloured . . . 4·50 4·50
NLF30 2d. multicoloured . . . 5·75 5·75

1970. 10th Anniv of National Liberation Front.
NLF31 **10** 20x. multicoloured . . 40 40
NLF32 30x. multicoloured . . 75 75
NLF33 50x. multicoloured . . 1·10 1·10
NLF34 3d. multicoloured . . . 3·75 3·75

11 Home Guards defending Village

1971. 10th Anniv of People's Liberation Armed Forces. Multicoloured.
NLF35 20x. Type **11** . . . . . . 3·75 3·75
NLF36 30x. Surrender of U.S. tank . . . . 3·75 3·75
NLF37 50x. Agricultural workers 4·50 4·50
NLF38 1d. Vietcong ambush . . 5·75 5·75

12 Children in School

13 Harvesting Rice

14 Ho Chi Minh with Vietcong Soldiers

1971. 2nd Anniv of Provisional Government. Life in Liberated Areas. Multicoloured.
NLF39 20x. Type **12** 75 75
NLF40 30x. Women sewing Vietcong flag . . . . 1·50 1·50
NLF41 40x. Fortifying village . . 2·30 2·30
NLF42 50x. Medical clinic . . . 3·00 3·00
NLF43 1d. Harvesting . . . . . 4·50 4·50

1974. 5th Anniv of Provisional Government. Mult.
NLF44 10d. Type **13** . . . . . . 1·90 1·90
NLF45 10d. Demonstrators with banner . . . . 1·90 1·90
NLF46 10d. Schoolchildren . . . 1·90 1·90
NLF47 10d. Women home guards 1·90 1·90
NLF48 10d. Vietcong conference delegate . . . . 1·90 1·90
NLF49 10d. Soldiers and tanks 1·90 1·90
NLF50 10d. Type **14** 75 75
NLF51 20d. Type **14** . . . . . . 1·10 1·10
For other values as Type **14**, see Nos. NLF57/60.

15 Ho Chi Minh watering Kainito Plant

1975. 85th Birth Anniv of Ho Chi Minh (1st issue).
NLF52 **15** 5d. multicoloured . . 40 40
NLF53 10d. multicoloured . . 75 75
NLF54 30d. mult (mve frame) 3·75 3·75
NLF54a 30d. mult (grn frame) 3·75 3·75

1975. 15th Anniv of National Front for Liberation of South Vietnam. As T **14** but 35½ × 26 mm.
NLF55 **14** 15d. black and green 75 75
NLF56 30d. black and red . . 1·50 1·50
NLF57 60d. black and blue . . 2·30 2·30
NLF58 300d. black and yellow 7·50 7·50

1975. 85th Birth Anniv of Ho Chi Minh (2nd issue). As T **284** of North Vietnam, but inscr "MIEN NAM VIET NAM".
NLF59 30d. multicoloured . . . 1·10 1·10
NLF60 60d. multicoloured . . . 2·30 2·30

1976. Various stamps surch in South Vietnamese currency.
NLF61 – 10p. on 1d. multicoloured (No. NLF38) . . . . . .
NLF62 – 20p. on 6x. yellow and red (No. NLF75) . .
NLF63 – 20p. on 20x. multicoloured (No. NLF27) . . . . . .
NLF64 – 20p. on 40x. multicoloured (No. NLF11) . . . . . .
NLF65 **9** 20p. on 2d. multicoloured (No. NLF30) . . . . . .
NLF66 **15** 20p. on 5d. multicoloured (No. NLF52) . . . . . .
NLF67 **14** 20p. on 10d. multicoloured (No. NLF50) . . . . . .
NLF68 **15** 20p. on 10d. multicoloured (No. NLF53) . . . . . .
NLF69 20p. on 30d. multicoloured (No. NLF54) . . . . . .
NLF70 20p. on 30d. mult (No. NLF54a) . . . . .

17 "Cocos nucifera"

1976. Fruits. Multicoloured.
NLF71 20d. Type **17** . . . . . . 2·30 2·30
NLF72 30d. "Garcinia mangostana" . . . . . 3·75 3·75
NLF73 60d. "Nargifera indica" 7·25 7·25

1976. First Elections to Unified National Assembly. As Nos. N858/60 of North Vietnam, but inscr "MIEN NAM VIET NAM".
NLF74 6x. red and blue (as No. N858) 40 40
NLF75 6x. yellow and red (as No. N859) 40 40
NLF76 12x. red and green (as No. N860) . . . . 1·10 75

18 Flag of Provisional Revolutionary Government

1976. 1st Anniv of Liberation of South Vietnam.
NLF77 **18** 30d. multicoloured . . 1·30 1·10

1976. 1st Session of Unified National Assembly. As Nos. N861/2 of North Vietnam, but inscr "MIEN NAM VIET NAM".
NLF78 6x. brown, red and yellow 40 40
NLF79 12x. turquoise, red & yell 1·10 75

The unified National Assembly proclaimed the reunification of Vietnam on 2 July 1976 and the united country was then known as the Socialist Republic of Vietnam.

E. NORTH VIETNAM

(Vietnam Democratic Republic)

Issues before April 1954 were made in Tongking and Central Annam, in areas under Viet Minh control. From 21 July 1954 French troops withdrew from north of the 17th Parallel and the Ho Chi Minh Government assumed complete control.

1946. 100 cents = 1 dong.
1959. 100 xu = 1 dong.

GUM. All stamps were issued without gum unless otherwise stated.

I. TONGKING

1946. No. 190 of Indo-China optd **V VIET-NAM N DAN-CHU CONG-HOA BUU CHINH.**
N1 25c. blue . . . . 75·00 90·00

2 Ho Chi Minh

5 Blacksmith

3 Ho Chi Minh and Vietnam Map

1948.
N2a **2** 2d. brown . . . . 15·00 £150
N3a 5d. red . . . . 15·00 £150

1951. Imperf or perf.
N4 **3** 100d. green . . . . 23·00 23·00
N5 100d. brown . . . . 23·00 23·00
N6 200d. red . . . . 23·00 23·00

1953. Production Campaign.
N11 **5** 100d. violet . . . . 6·00 3·00
N12 500d. brown . . . . 9·00 4·50

7 Malenkov, Ho Chi Minh, Mao Tse-tung and Flags

1954. Friendship Month.
N13 **7** 100d. red . . . . 15·00 15·00

II. CENTRAL ANNAM

NA 1 Ho Chi Minh

1950. Imperf. (a) Figures of value in white.
NA1 **NA 1** 1d. violet . . . .
NA2 1d. green . . . .
NA3 5d. green . . . .
NA4 15d. brown . . . .

(b) Figures coloured.
NA7 **NA 1** 300d. blue £350 £350
NA8 500d. red £750 £750

1952. Surch in figures. Imperf. (a) Figures in white.
NA5 **NA 1** 30d. on 5d. green . . £250 £200
NA6 60d. on 1d. violet . . £275 £250
NA8a 90d. on 3d. red . . .

(b) Figures coloured.
NA8b **NA 1** 5d. on 10d. mauve
NA8c 100d. on 300d. blue

III. GENERAL ISSUES

8 Malenkov, Ho Chi Minh and Mao Tse-tung

1954.
N14 **8** 50d. brown and red . . . . 21·00 21·00
N15 100d. red and yellow . . . 23·00 23·00

9 Battlefield

1954. Dien Bien Phu Victory. Imperf or perf.
N16a **9** 10d. bistre and red . . . 15·00 15·00
N17a 50d. ochre and red . . . 15·00 5·50
N18d 150d. blue and brown . . 15·00 7·50
See also No. NO24.

1954. (a) Handstamped **10 dNH**.
N19 **3** 10d. on 100d. green . . . . 19·00 19·00
N20 10d. on 100d. brown . . . 19·00 19·00
N21 20d. on 200d. red . . . . . 19·00 19·00

(b) Handstamped **10d.**
N22 **3** 10d. on 100d. green . . . . 20·00 20·00
N25 10d. on 100d. brown . . . 20·00 20·00
N28 20d. on 200d. red . . . . . 45·00 55·00
See also Nos. N46/9.

12 Lake of the Returned Sword, Hanoi

1954. Proclamation of Hanoi as Capital.
N30 **12** 10d. blue . . . . 4·50 90
N31 50d. green . . . . 4·50 75
N32 150d. red . . . . 7·50 75

13 Distribution of Title Deeds

1955. Land Reform.
N33 **13** 5d. green . . . . 7·25 3·75
N34 10d. grey . . . . 7·25 3·75
N35 20d. orange . . . . 11·50 3·75
N36 50d. mauve . . . . 24·00 3·75
N37 100d. brown . . . . . . 38·00 3·75

14 Crowd welcoming Steam Train

1956. Hanoi–China Railway Re-opening.
N38 **14** 100d. blue . . . . 19·00 3·75
N39 200d. turquoise . . . . . 19·00 3·75
N40 300d. violet . . . . 38·00 3·75
N41 500d. brown . . . . . . 45·00 3·75

15 Parade, Ba Dinh Square, Hanoi

1956. Return of Govt to Hanoi.
N42 **15** 1000d. violet . . . . . . 45·00 7·50
N43 1500d. blue . . . . 60·00 7·50
N44 2000d. turquoise . . . . . 60·00 7·50
N45 3000d. turquoise . . . . . 75·00 7·50

1956. Surch **10 d** in frame.
N46 **3** 10d. on 100d. green . . . . 23·00 23·00
N48 10d. on 100d. brown . . . 23·00 23·00
N49 20d. on 200d. red . . . . . 15·00 15·00

17 Tran Dang Ninh

1956. 1st Death Anniv of Tran Dang Ninh (patriot).

N50	17	5d. green	4·25	1·90
N51		10d. red	4·25	1·90
N52		20d. brown	5·25	2·75
N53		100d. blue	6·00	3·50

18 Mac Thi Buoi

1956. 5th Death Anniv of Mac Thi Buoi (guerilla heroine).

N54	18	1000d. red	41·00	15·00
N55		2000d. brown	85·00	23·00
N56		4000d. green	£170	34·00
N57		5000d. blue	£200	55·00

19 Bai Thuong Dam

1956. Reconstruction of Bai Thuong Dam.

N58	19	100d. violet and brown	7·50	6·00
N59		200d. red and black	9·75	6·00
N60a		300d. red and lake	10·50	10·50

1956. Surch **50 DONG**.

N61	2	50d. on 5d. red	60·00	75·00

21 Cotton Mill

1957. 1st Anniv of Opening of Nam Dinh Mill.

N62	21	100d. brown and red	5·75	5·75
N63		200d. grey and blue	6·50	6·50
N64		300d. light green and green	8·25	8·25

22 Pres. Ho Chi Minh

23 Arms of Republic

1957. President's 67th Birthday.

N65	22	20d. green	3·00	1·10
N66		60d. bistre	3·00	1·10
N67		100d. blue	4·50	1·90
N68		300d. brown	7·50	3·50

1957. 12th Anniv of Democratic Republic.

N69	23	20d. green	2·30	1·50
N70		100d. red	5·25	3·75

24 Congress Emblem

1957. 4th World T.U. Congress, Leipzig.

N71	24	300d. purple	7·50	5·25

See also Nos. NO69/72.

25 Presidents Voroshilov and Ho Chi Minh

1957. 40th Anniv of Russian Revolution.

N72	25	100d. red	7·50	6·00
N73		500d. brown	11·50	9·00
N74		1000d. orange	19·00	15·00

26 Open-air Class

27 Girl Gymnast

1958. Education Campaign.

N75	26	50d. blue	4·50	60
N76		150d. red	7·50	60
N77		1000d. brown	18·00	60

1958. Physical Education.

N78	27	150d. brown and blue	11·50	1·10
N79		500d. brown and rose	19·00	1·10

28

29 Congress Emblem

1958. Labour Day.

N80	28	50d. yellow and red	3·75	55
N81		150d. red and yellow	6·00	55

1958. 4th International Congress of Democratic Women, Vienna.

N82	29	150d. blue	7·50	75

30 Cup, Basket and Lace

31 Hanoi–Saigon Railway Reconstruction

1958. Arts and Crafts Fair, Hanoi.

N83	30	150d. sepia and turquoise	3·00	40
N84		2000d. black and lilac	19·00	1·50

1958. Re-unification of Vietnam Propaganda.

N85	31	50d. blue	1·90	40
N86		150d. brown	2·75	40

32 Revolution in Hanoi

1958. 13th Anniv of Vietnamese Revolution.

N87	32	150d. red	2·30	55
N88		500d. blue	3·75	55

33 Woman Potter

1958. Handicrafts Exhibition.

N89	33	150d. lake and red	2·30	75
N90		1000d. brown and ochre	5·25	75

34 Vo Thi Sau and Crowd

35 Tran Hung Dao

1958. 13th Anniv of South Vietnam Resistance Movement.

N91	34	50d. green and buff	3·00	40
N92		150d. red and orange	4·50	40

1958. 658th Death Anniv of Tran Hung Dao.

N93	35	150d. grey and blue	2·30	40

36 Hanoi Factories

37 Harvesting Rice

1958. Hanoi Mechanical Engineering Plant.

N94	36	150d. sepia	2·75	40

1958. Mutual Aid Teams.

N95	37	150d. lake	2·30	1·30
N96		500d. brown	5·25	1·30

38 Temple of Jade, Hanoi

39 Furniture-makers

1958.

N 97	38	150d. green	2·30	1·90
N 98	–	150d. blue	2·30	60
N 99	–	350d. brown	3·75	1·20
N100	38	2000d. green	17·00	1·90

DESIGNS—HORIZ: 150d. blue; 350d. Bay of Halong.

1958. Furniture Co-operatives.

N101	39	150d. blue	2·75	60

40 Cam Pha Coal Mines

41 The Trung Sisters

1959.

N102	40	150d. blue	5·75	40

1959. Trung Sisters Commemoration.

N103	41	5x. red and yellow	2·30	60
N104		8x. deep brown and brown	4·50	60

42 Mother and Child

1959. 10th Anniv of World Peace Movement.

N105	42	12x. violet	1·10	60

43 Xuan Quan Dam

1959. Bac Hung Hai Irrigation Project.

N106	43	6x. yellow, green & violet	1·50	40
N107		12x. ochre, blue and grey	4·50	40

44 Victims in Phu Loi Concentration Camp

45 Radio Mast

1959. The Phu Loi Massacre on 1 December 1958.

N108	44	12x. salmon, olive & black	1·50	40
N109		20x. ochre, grey and black	3·75	40

1959. Me Tri Radio Station.

N110	45	3x. green and orange	1·50	40
N111		12x. sepia and blue	2·30	70

46 Hien Luong Railway Bridge

1959. Vietnam Day.

N112	46	12x. red and black	2·30	75

47 Rifle-shooting

1959. Sports.

N113	47	1x. deep blue and blue	1·10	40
N114	–	6x. olive and red	1·90	40
N115	–	12x. red and rose	3·00	40

DESIGNS: 6x. Swimming; 12x. Wrestling.

48 Balloons

49 Coconuts

1959. 10th Anniv of Chinese People's Republic.

N116	48	12x. red, yellow and green	3·75	75

1959. Fruits. Multicoloured.

N117	3x. Type 49	75	40
N118	12x. Bananas	1·90	40
N119	30x. Pineapple	3·50	40

50 Convair CV 340

1959. Air.

N120	50	20x. black and blue	7·50	1·90

51 Soldiers

1959. 15th Anniv of N. Vietnam People's Army.

N121	51	12x. yellow, brown & blue	2·30	40

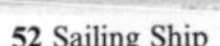

52 Sailing Ship

53 Girl in "E-De" Costume

1959. 30th Anniv of N. Vietnam Workers' Party.

N122	52	2x. multicoloured	1·10	40
N123		12x. multicoloured	3·00	40

1960. National Costumes.

N124	53	2x. red, blue and purple	1·10	55
N125	–	10x. blue, orange & green	1·50	55
N126	–	12x. blue and brown	2·30	55
N127	–	12x. blue and buff	2·30	55

COSTUMES: No. N125, "Meo"; N126, "Thai"; N127, "Tay".

54 Women of Vietnam

1960. National Census.
N128 **54** 1x. green 25 40
N129 – 12x. brown and red . . . 2·75 75
DESIGN: 12x. Workers and factories.

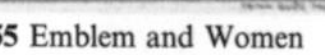

55 Emblem and Women 56 Hung Vuong Temple

1960. 50th Anniv of International Women's Day.
N130 **55** 12x. multicoloured . . . 1·50 75

1960. Hung Vuong Anniversary Day.
N131 **56** 12x. green and buff . . . 3·75 1·50
N132 4d. brown and blue . . . 38·00 21·00

57 Lenin 58 Ballot Box

1960. 90th Birth Anniv of Lenin.
N133 **57** 5x. red and blue . . . . 1·10 40
N134 12x. blue and buff . . . 3·50 75
MSN134a 50 × 77 mm. **57** 5x. blue and brown. Imperf . . . . . . 60·00 60·00

1960. 2nd Election of Parliamentary Deputies.
N135 **58** 12x. multicoloured . . . 1·50 45

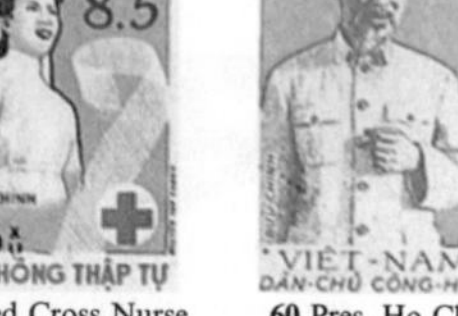

59 Red Cross Nurse 60 Pres. Ho Chi Minh

1960. International Red Cross Commemoration.
N136 **59** 8x. blue, red and bistre 1·50 40
N137 12x. green, red and grey 2·30 40

1960. President Ho Chi Minh's 70th Birthday.
N138 **60** 4x. lilac and green . . . 1·50 40
N139 12x. purple and rose . . 2·30 40
N140 – 12x. multicoloured . . . 2·30 40
MSN140a Two sheets, 60 × 85 mm and 58 × 78 mm. 10x. brown and ochre (as N139) and 10x. multicoloured (as N140). Imperf 19·00 19·00
DESIGN—24½ × 39 mm: No. N140, Ho Chi Minh and children.

61 "New Constitution"

1960. Opening of 2nd National Assembly.
N141 **61** 12x. sepia and ochre . . 2·30 1·10

62 Pres. Ho Chi Minh at Microphone

1960. 15th Anniv of Vietnam Democratic Republic.
N142 **62** 4x. multicoloured . . . . 2·30 40
N143 12x. multicoloured . . . 3·50 40
N144 – 12x. deep blue and blue 3·50 40
N145 – 12x. green and yellow . 3·50 40
N146 – 12x. blue and brown . . 3·50 40
DESIGNS: No. N144, Ploughing; N145, Electricity Works, Vietri; N146, Classroom.

63 Workers and Flags

1960. 3rd Vietnam Workers' Party Congress.
N147 **63** 1x. multicoloured . . . . 2·30 40
N148 12x. multicoloured . . . 2·75 40

64 Handclasp of Three Races

1960. 15th Anniv of W.F.T.U.
N149 **64** 12x. black and red . . . 4·50 40

65 Dragon

1960. 950th Anniv of Hanoi.
N150 **65** 8x. yellow, brown & turquoise . . . . . . 2·30 40
N151 12x. yellow, brown & blue . . . . 3·75 40
MSN151a 98 × 67 mm. No. N151. Imperf . . . . 11·50 11·50

66 Exhibition Entrance

1960. "Fifteen Years of Republic" Exhibition.
N152 **66** 2x. grey and red . . . . 1·10 40
N153 12x. green and red . . . 1·90 40

67 Badge, Dove and Flag

1960. 15th Anniv of World Federation of Democratic Youth.
N154 **67** 12x. multicoloured . . . 2·75 40

68 Emblem of Vietnamese Trade Unions 69 Woman, Globe and Dove

1961. 2nd National Congress of Trade Unions.
N155 **68** 12x. red, blue and yellow 1·90 40

1961. 3rd National Congress of Women.
N156 **69** 6x. green and blue . . . 2·75 60
N157 12x. green and salmon 2·75 90

IMPERF STAMPS. Many issues from here onwards also exist imperf.

70 Sambar 71 Ly Tu Trong (revolutionary)

1961. Vietnamese Fauna.
N158 **70** 12x. buff, black and olive 3·00 90
N159 – 20x. multicoloured . . . 4·50 90
N160 – 50x. grey, black and green . . . . 6·75 90
N161 – 1d. black, grey and green 9·00 90
DESIGNS: 20x. Sun bear; 50x. Indian elephant; 1d. Crested gibbon.

1961. 3rd Congress of Vietnam Labour Youth Union.
N162 **71** 2x. olive and blue . . . 90 45
N163 12x. olive and salmon . . 1·90 45

72 Bugler and Drummer 73 Disabled Soldier learning to use Crutches

1961. 20th Anniv of Vietnam Youth Pioneers.
N164 **72** 1x. multicoloured . . . . 1·10 45
N165 12x. multicoloured . . . 2·75 45

1961. 101st Anniv of Proposal for Int Red Cross.
N166 **73** 6x. multicoloured . . . . 2·30 45
N167 12x. multicoloured . . . 3·75 45

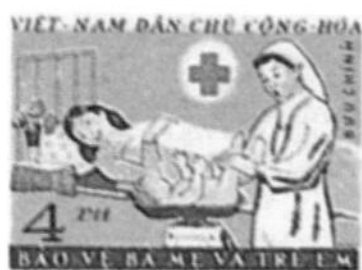

74 Nurse weighing Baby

1961. International Children's Day.
N168 **74** 4x. green, black and red 1·50 35
N169 12x. yellow, black and red . . . . 3·00 35

75 Major Yuri Gagarin

1961. World's First Manned Space Flight.
N170 **75** 6x. red and violet . . . . 9·00 1·10
N171 12x. red and green . . . 9·00 1·10

76 77 Women

1961. Vietnam Reunification Campaign.
N172 **76** 12x. multicoloured . . . 75 50
N173 2d. multicoloured . . . . 6·75 60

1961. Tripling of Hanoi, Hue and Saigon.
N174 **77** 12x. multicoloured . . . 3·00 50
N175 3d. brown, myrtle and green . . . . 12·00 8·00

78 Mother and Child 79 Prospecting Team

1961. National Savings Campaign.
N176 **78** 3x. multicoloured . . . . 1·10 40
N177 12x. multicoloured . . . 1·90 40

1961. Geological Research.
N178 **79** 2x. green, blue and purple . . . . 1·10 40
N179 12x. brown, black & turquoise . . . . . . 1·90 40

80 Thien Mu Tower, Hue 81 Workers and Rocket

1961. Ancient Towers.
N180 **80** 6x. brown and chestnut 1·10 60
N181 – 10x. olive and buff . . . 1·90 85
N182 – 12x. olive and green . . 2·30 1·00
N183 – 12x. brown and blue . . 2·30 1·00
TOWERS: No. N181, Pen Brush, Bac Ninh; N182, Binh Son, Vinh Phuc; N183, Cham, Phan Rang.

1961. 22nd Communist Party Congress, Moscow.
N184 **81** 12x. red and black . . . 2·75 40

82 Major Titov and Rocket

1961. 2nd Manned Space Flight.
N185 **82** 6x. multicoloured . . . . 2·30 40
N186 12x. multicoloured . . . 3·75 40

83 Freighter at Haiphong

1961. Haiphong Port Commemoration.
N187 **83** 5x. grey, green and myrtle . . . . 2·30 40
N188 12x. brown, light brown and sepia . . . . . . 5·25 40

84 Cymbalist 85 Congress Emblem

1961. 3rd Writers and Artists Congress. Mult.
N189 12x. Type **84** . . . . 1·50 45
N190 12x. Flautist . . . . 1·50 45
N191 30x. Fan dancer . . . . . 3·75 45
N192 50x. Guitarist . . . . . . 5·25 45
MSN192a 136 × 102 mm. Nos. N189/92 in strip of four . . . 45·00 45·00

1961. 5th W.F.T.U. Congress, Moscow.
N193 **85** 12x. mauve and drab . . 1·10 45

86 Resistance Fighters

1961. 15th Anniv of National Resistance.
N194 **86** 4x. multicoloured 55 25
N195 12x. multicoloured . . . 1·00 40

87 "Pigs"

1962. New Year.
N196 **87** 6x. multicoloured . . . . 3·00 60
N197 – 12x. multicoloured . . . 3·00 90
DESIGN: 12x. "Poultry".

88 Watering Tree

89 Tea Plant

1962. Tree-planting Festival.
N198 **88** 12x. multicoloured . . . 1·90 40
N199 40x. multicoloured . . . 3·50 40

1962. Multicoloured.
N200 2x. Type **89** . . . . 1·10 60
N201 6x. Aniseed . . . . 1·10 60
N202 12x. Coffee . . . . 4·25 60
N203 12x. Castor-oil . . . . . . 4·25 60
N204 30x. Lacquer-tree . . . . . 7·50 60

90 Gong Dance

91 Hibiscus

1962. Folk-dancing. Multicoloured.
N205 12x. Type **90** . . . . 2·30 55
N206 12x. Bamboo dance . . . . 2·30 55
N207 30x. Hat dance . . . . . . 3·75 55
N208 50x. Parasol dance . . . . 6·75 55
MSN208a 67 × 91 mm. **90** 30x. 15·00 15·00

1962. Flowers. Multicoloured.
N209 12x. Type **91** . . . . 2·30 75
N210 12x. Frangipani . . . . . 2·30 75
N211 20x. Chrysanthemum . . . 3·00 75
N212 30x. Lotus . . . . 4·50 75
N213 50x. Ipomoea . . . . 7·50 75
MSN213a 64 × 87 mm. No. N212 11·50 11·50

92 Kim Lien Flats, Hanoi

93 Workers and Rose

1962. 1st Five-Year Plan (1st issue).
N214 **92** 1x. blue, black and grey 40 25
N215 – 3x. multicoloured 90 40
N216 – 8x. violet, black and stone . . . . 1·40 60
DESIGNS: 3x. State agricultural farm; 8x. Institute of Hydraulic and Electro-Dynamic Studies.
See also Nos. N245/8, N251/2, N270/1 and N294/6.

1962. 3rd National "Heroes of Labour" Congress.
N217 **93** 12x. orange, olive and red . . . . 2·30 55

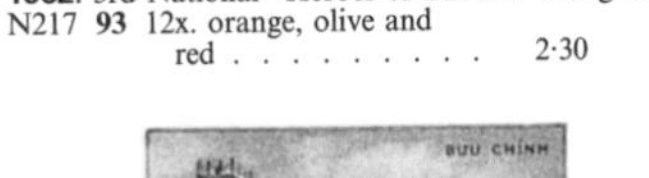

94 Dai Lai Lake

1962.
N218 **94** 12x. turquoise and brown 1·90 1·40

95 "Plough of Perfection"

1962.
N219 **95** 6x. black and turquoise 1·10 45

96 Titov greeting Children

1962. Visit of Major Titov.
N220 **96** 12x. sepia and blue . . . 40 25
N221 – 20x. sepia and salmon . . 90 40
N222 – 30x. sepia and green . . 1·40 60
DESIGNS: 20x. Pres. Ho Chi Minh pinning medal on Titov; 30x. Titov in space-suit.

97 Mosquito and Red Cross

1962. Malaria Eradication.
N223 **97** 8x. red, black and blue 1·30 55
N224 12x. red, black and violet 1·70 55
N225 20x. red, black and purple . . . . 2·75 55

98 Factory and Soldiers

99 Ban Gioc Falls

1962. 8th Anniv of Geneva Vietnamese Agreements.
N226 **98** 12x. multicoloured . . . 2·30 40

1962. Vietnamese Scenery.
N227 – 12x. purple and blue . . 1·50 45
N228 **99** 12x. sepia and turquoise 1·50 45
DESIGN—HORIZ: (32½ × 23 mm): No. N227, Ba Be Lake.

99a Weightlifting

1962. Int Military Sports Festival of Socialist States, Prague.
N228a **99a** 12x. multicoloured . . 75·00 £110

100 Quang Trung

101 Groundnuts

1962. National Heroes.
N229 **100** 3x. yellow, brown & grey 75 30
N230 – 3x. orange, blk & ochre 75 30
N231 **100** 12x. yellow, green & grey . . . . 1·90 40
N232 – 12x. orange, blk & grey 1·90 40
PORTRAIT: Nos. N230, N232, Nguyen Trai.

1962. Multicoloured.
N233 1x. Type **101** 40 30
N234 4x. Haricot beans 70 30
N235 6x. Sweet potatoes 90 45
N236 12x. Maize . . . . 2·10 1·00
N237 30x. Manioc . . . . 5·00 2·40

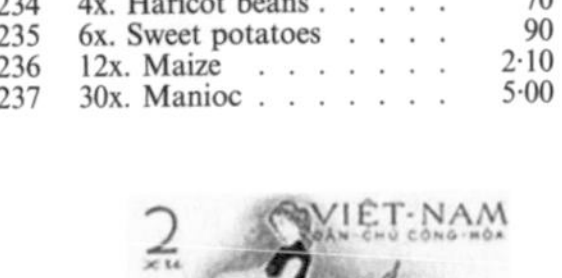

102 Girl feeding Poultry

1962. Farm Stock-breeding.
N238 **102** 2x. red, grey and blue 45 40
N239 – 12x. ochre, turquoise and blue . . . . . 1·50 45
N240 – 12x. brown, green and deep green . . . . . 1·50 45
N241 – 12x. buff, mauve and sepia . . . . 1·50 45
DESIGNS: No. N239, Woman tending pigs; N240, Herdgirl with oxen; N241, Boy feeding buffalo.

103 Popovich in "Vostok 4"

1962. First "Team" Manned Space Flights.
N242 **103** 12x. multicoloured . . . 1·10 40
N243 – 20x. ochre, blue & black 1·50 40
N244 – 30x. red, blue and black 2·30 40
DESIGNS—HORIZ: 20x. Nikolaev in "Vostok 3". VERT: 30x. "Vostoks 3 and 4".

104 Teacher and Students

1962. 1st Five-Year Plan (2nd issue). Higher Education and Land Cultivation.
N245 **104** 12x. black and yellow 90 45
N246 – 12x. black, brown & buff . . . . 2·30 45
DESIGN: No. N246, Tree felling.

105 Guerrilla Fighter

106 Hoang Hoa Tham

1963. 1st Five-Year Plan (3rd issue). National Defence.
N247 **105** 5x. green and grey . . . 90 25
N248 12x. brown and buff . . 1·40 25

1963. 50th Death Anniv of Hoang Hoa Tham (freedom fighter).
N249 **106** 6x. myrtle and blue . . 90 40
N250 12x. black and brown 1·40 55

107 Workers in Field

108 Karl Marx

1963. 1st Five-Year Plan (4th issue). Agricultural and Chemical Manufacture.
N251 **107** 12x. multicoloured . . . 1·10 40
N252 – 12x. red, mauve and black 75 40
DESIGN: No. N252, Lam Thao Fertilizer Factory.

1963. 80th Death Anniv of Karl Marx.
N253 **108** 3x. black and green . . 60 30
N254 12x. black and drab on pink . . . . 1·70 40

109 Castro and Vietnamese Soldiers

111 Nurse tending Child

110 Doves and Labour Emblem

1963. Vietnamese–Cuban Friendship.
N255 **109** 12x. multicoloured . . . 1·50 55

1963. Labour Day.
N256 **110** 12x. orange, black & bl 1·50 45

1963. Red Cross Centenary.
N257 **111** 12x. red, black and blue 1·50 40
N258 – 12x. red, grey & turq . . 1·50 40
N259 – 20x. red, grey and yellow . . . . 2·30 40
DESIGNS: No. N258, Child and syringe inscr "BCG". 25 × 42 mm: 20x. Centenary emblem.

112 "Mars 1" Interplanetary Station

1963. Launching of Soviet Rocket "Mars 1". Mult.
N260 6x. Type **112** 75 40
N261 12x. Type **112** . . . . . . 1·10 40
N262 12x. "Mars 1" in space (vert) . . . . 1·50 40
N263 20x. "Mars 1" in space (vert) . . . . 2·30 40

113 Common Carp

1963. Fishing Industry. Multicoloured.
N264 12x. Type **113** . . . . . . 3·75 40
N265 12x. Fishes and trawler . . 3·75 40

114 Pres. Ho Chi Minh embracing Prof. Nguyen Van Hien of South Vietnam

1963. Campaign for Reunification of Vietnam.
N266 **114** 12x. black, blue & turq 1·50 40

115 Globe and "Vostoks 3 and 4"

1963. 1st Anniv of "Team" Manned Space Flights.
N267 **115** 12x. black, brown & yellow 75 40
N268 – 20x. black, blue & green 1·50 40
N269 – 30x. black, violet & blue 3·00 40
DESIGNS: 20x. Nikolaev and "eagle" motif; 30x. Popovich and "phoenix" motif.

116 Viet Tri Insecticide Factory

1963. 1st Five-Year Plan (5th issue).
N270 **116** 3x. buff, brown and blue 60 25
N271 – 12x. pink, brown and bistre . . . . 1·70 40
DESIGN: 12x. Viet Tri chemical factory.

117 Black Carp

1963. Freshwater Fish Culture. Multicoloured.
N272 12x. Type **117** . . . . . . 1·50 60
N273 12x. Common carp ("Cyprinus carpio") . . . 1·50 60
N274 12x. Silver carp ("Hypophthalmichthys molitrix) . . . . 1·50 60
N275 20x. Asiatic snakehead . . 3·75 60
N276 30x. Mozambique mouth-brooder . . . . 4·50 60

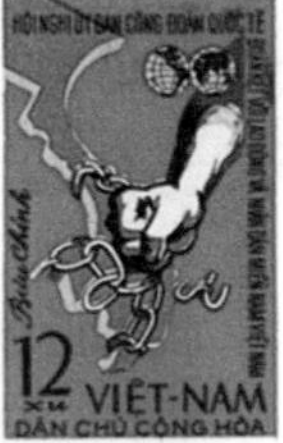

118 Chinese Francolin **119** Broken Chain and Map

1963. Birds. Multicoloured.

No.	Type	Description	Mint	Used
N277		12x. Type **118**	2·30	60
N278		12x. Chinese jungle mynah	2·30	60
N279		12x. White-throated kingfisher	2·30	60
N280		20x. Siamese fireback pheasant (horiz)	4·50	60
N281		30x. Eastern reef heron	6·75	60
N282		40x. Slaty-headed parakeet	9·00	60
MSN282a		64 × 93 mm. 50x. (as 30x.)	70·00	70·00

1963. W.F.T.U. Assembly, Hanoi.

No.	Type	Description	Mint	Used
N283	**119**	12x. multicoloured	1·50	40

120 Football **121** "Rauwolfia verticillata"

1963. "GANEFO" Athletic Games, Jakarta.

No.	Type	Description	Mint	Used
N284	**120**	12x. black, grey & ochre	75	40
N285	–	12x. black, grey & orange	75	40
N286	–	12x. black, grey and blue	75	40
N287	–	30x. black, grey & mag	1·50	40

DESIGNS—VERT: No. N285, Volleyball. HORIZ: No. N286, Swimming; N287, High-jumping.

1963. Medicinal Plants. Multicoloured.

No.	Type	Description	Mint	Used
N288		6x. Type **121**	75	40
N289		12x. "Chenopodium ambrosioides"	90	40
N290		12x. "Sophora japonica"	90	40
N291		12x. "Fibraurea tinctoria"	90	40
N292		20x. "Momordica cochinchinensis"	2·30	40

122 "Solidarity" **123** Pylon

1963. 3rd Anniv of South Vietnam National Liberation Front.

No.	Type	Description	Mint	Used
N293	**122**	12x. black, brn & ochre	60	40

1964. 1st Five-Year Plan (6th issue).

No.	Type	Description	Mint	Used
N294	–	6x. black, red and purple	45	40
N295	–	12x. multicoloured	1·10	60
N296	**123**	12x. black, grey & orange	1·10	60

DESIGNS—HORIZ: (40 × 22½ mm): 6x. Tapping cast-iron; No. N295, Thai Ngyuen Iron and Steel Works.

124 Sun, Globe and Dragon

1964. International Quiet Sun Years.

No.	Type	Description	Mint	Used
N297	**124**	12x. orange, black & green	1·10	40
N298		50x. drab, black & pur	85	40

125 Twin Space Flights

1964. Space Flights of Bykovsky and Tereshkova. Multicoloured.

No.	Type	Description	Mint	Used
N299		12x. Type **125**	1·10	40
N300		12x. Bykovsky and "Vostok 5"	1·10	40
N301		30x. Tereshkova and "Vostok 6"	3·00	40

126 "Hibiscus mutabilis" **127** Rural Costume

1964. Flowers. Multicoloured.

No.	Type	Description	Mint	Used
N302		12x. Type **126**	90	40
N303		12x. "Persica vulgaris"	90	40
N304		12x. "Saraca dives"	90	40
N305		12x. "Passiflora hispida"	90	40
N306		20x. "Michelia champaca"	2·75	40
N307		30x. "Camellia amplexicaulis"	4·50	40

1964. National Costumes. Multicoloured.

No.	Type	Description	Mint	Used
N308		6x. Type **127**	75	40
N309		12x. "Ceremonial"	1·50	40
N310		12x. "Everyday"	1·50	40

128 Artillery **130** Spotted Deer

129 Ham Rong Railway Bridge

1964. 10th Anniv of Battle of Dien Bien Phu.

No.	Type	Description	Mint	Used
N311	**128**	3x. black and red	75	40
N312	–	6x. black and blue	90	40
N313	–	12x. black and yellow	1·50	40
N314	–	12x. black and purple	1·90	40

DESIGNS: 6x. Machine-gun post; No. N313, Bomb-disposal; N314, Dien Bien Phu and tractor.

1964. Inaug of Reconstructed Ham Rong Bridge.

No.	Type	Description	Mint	Used
N315	**129**	12x. multicoloured	1·90	40

1964. Wild Animals. Multicoloured.

No.	Type	Description	Mint	Used
N316		12x. Type **130**	90	40
N317		12x. Malayan tapir (horiz)	90	40
N318		12x. Tiger	90	40
N319		20x. Water buffalo (horiz)	2·30	40
N320		30x. Sumatran rhinoceros (horiz)	3·50	40
N321		40x. Banteng (horiz)	4·50	40

131 Women Fighters, Map, Industrial Scene and Watch-towers

1964. 10th Anniv of Geneva Agreements on Vietnam.

No.	Type	Description	Mint	Used
N322	**131**	12x. multicoloured	1·10	40
N323	–	12x. multicoloured	1·10	40

DESIGN—VERT: (23 × 45 mm): No. N323, Map of Vietnam, T.U. emblem and flag, inscr ("NHAN DAN MIEN NAM") etc.

132 Nhu Quynh Pumping Station

1964. Irrigation for Agriculture.

No.	Type	Description	Mint	Used
N324	**132**	12x. slate and black	1·50	40

133 Populace Greeting Soldiers

1964. 10th Anniv of Liberation of Hanoi. Mult.

No.	Type	Description	Mint	Used
N325		6x. Type **133**	1·10	40
N326		12x. Building construction	1·90	40

134 Naval Longboat

1964. "National Defence" Games.

No.	Type	Description	Mint	Used
N327	**134**	5x. black, grey and blue	75	45
N328	–	12x. black, grey & yellow	1·50	60
N329	–	12x. black, brown & blue	1·50	60
N330	–	12x. multicoloured	1·50	60

DESIGNS—HORIZ: No. N328, Pistol-shooting. VERT: No. N329, Gliding; N330, Parachuting.

135 "Guarcinia mangostana"

1964. Tropical Fruits. Multicoloured.

No.	Type	Description	Mint	Used
N331		12x. Type **135**	90	40
N332		12x. "Mangifera indica"	90	40
N333		12x. "Nephelium litchi"	90	40
N334		20x. "Anona squamosa"	2·30	40
N335		50x. "Citrus medica"	5·00	40

136 Conference Building

1964. World Solidarity Conf, Hanoi. Mult.

No.	Type	Description	Mint	Used
N336		12x. Type **136**	1·10	40
N337		12x. Soldier greeting workers	1·10	40
N338		12x. Clenched fist, ships and Boeing B-52 Stratofortress	1·10	40

137 Soldiers with Standard

1964. 20th Anniv of Vietnamese People's Army. Multicoloured.

No.	Type	Description	Mint	Used
N339		12x. Type **137**	1·10	40
N340		12x. Coastguards	1·10	40
N341		12x. Frontier guards (vert)	1·10	40

138 Cuban Revolutionaries **139** Le Hong Phong

140 Party Flag

1965. 6th Anniv of Cuban Republic.

No.	Type	Description	Mint	Used
N342	**138**	12x. black, red and blue	1·50	40
N343	–	12x. multicoloured	1·50	1·50

DESIGN: No. N343, Flags of Cuba and North Vietnam.

1965. 35th Anniv of Vietnamese Workers' Party.

(a) As T **139**. Portraits and inscr purple-brown; background colours given.

No.	Type	Description	Mint	Used
N344	**139**	6x. grey	40	40
N345	–	6x. bistre	40	40
N346	–	6x. drab	40	40
N347	–	6x. brown	40	40
N348	–	6x. lilac	40	40

DESIGNS: No. N345, Tran Phu; N346, Hoang Van Thu; N347, Hgo Gia Tu; N348, Nguyen van Cu (Party leaders).

(b) As T **140**.

No.	Type	Description	Mint	Used
N349	**140**	12x. yellow, red and mauve	1·10	75
N350	–	12x. mauve, yellow and red	1·10	75

DESIGN: No. N350, Foundryman and guerilla fighter.

141 Women tending Maize **142** Steam Locomotive and Nguyen Van Troi (patriot)

1965. Populating Mountain Settlements.

No.	Type	Description	Mint	Used
N351	**141**	2x. multicoloured	25	40
N352		3x. multicoloured	75	40
N353	–	12x. indigo, orange and blue	90	40

DESIGN: 12x. Young girls going to school.

1965. Transport Ministers' Congress, Hanoi.

No.	Type	Description	Mint	Used
N354	**142**	12x. blue and red	1·90	40
N355	–	30x. black and green	3·50	40

DESIGN: 30x. As Type **142** but position of locomotive, portrait and value transposed.

143 Cosmonauts Komarov, Feoktistov, Yegorov, and "Voskhod I"

1965. Three-manned Space Flight.

No.	Type	Description	Mint	Used
N356	**143**	20x. violet, green & blue	1·50	40
N357	–	1d. violet, red & mauve	5·25	40

DESIGN: 1d. "Voskhod I" and cosmonauts.

144 Lenin with Red Guards **145** Pres. Ho Chi Minh

1965. Lenin's 95th Birth Anniv.

No.	Type	Description	Mint	Used
N358	**144**	8x. purple and buff	1·10	40
N359		12x. purple and grey	1·10	40

1965. Pres. Ho Chi Minh's 75th Birthday.

No.	Type	Description	Mint	Used
N360	**145**	6x. violet, yellow & green	75	40
N361		12x. violet, yellow & buff	1·10	40

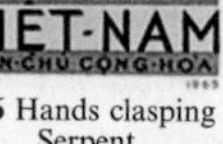

146 Hands clasping Serpent **147** Two Soldiers advancing

1965. 10th Anniv of Afro-Asian Conf, Bandung.
N362 **146** 12x. multicoloured . . . 1·50 40

1965. Trade Union Conference, Hanoi.
N363 **147** 12x. blue and purple . . 1·10 40
N364 – 12x. multicoloured . . . 1·10 40
N365 – 12x. red, black and green . . . . . . 1·10 40
DESIGNS—HORIZ: No. N364, Sea battle; N365, "Peoples of the World" on Globe, and soldiers.

148 Yellow-throated Marten

1965. Fauna Protection. Multicoloured.
N366 12x. Type **148** . . . . . . 1·10 40
N367 12x. Owston's palm civet 1·10 40
N368 12x. Chinese pangolin . . . 1·10 40
N369 12x. Francois' monkey (vert) . . . . 1·10 40
N370 20x. Red giant flying squirrel . . . . 3·00 40
N371 50x. Lesser slow loris (vert) 5·25 40

149 Marx and Lenin **150** Nguyen Van Troi (patriot)

1965. Postal Ministers Congress, Peking.
N372 **149** 12x. multicoloured . . . 2·75 40

1965. Nguyen Van Troi Commemoration.
N373 **150** 12x. sepia, brown & green 75 40
N374 50x. sepia, brn & ochre 1·50 40
N375 4d. sepia and red . . . 4·50 40

151 "Rhynchocoris humeralis"

1965. Noxious Insects. Multicoloured.
N376 12x. Type **151** . . . . . . 1·10 40
N377 12x. "Tessaratoma papillosa" . . . . . . 1·10 40
N378 12x. "Poeciliocoris latus" 1·10 40
N379 12x. "Tosena melanoptera" 1·10 40
N380 20x. "Cicada sp." . . . . 2·75 40
N381 30x. "Fulgora candelaria" 3·50 40
Nos. N379/81 are vert, 20½ × 38 mm.

152 Revolutionaries

1965. 20th Anniv of August Revolution.
N382 **152** 6x. brown, black & blue 75 40
N383 12x. black and red . . . 1·50 40

153 Prawn

1965. Marine Life. Multicoloured.
N384 12x. Type **153** . . . . . . 1·50 40
N385 12x. Shrimp . . . . 1·50 40
N386 12x. Swimming crab . . . 1·50 40
N387 12x. Serrate swimming crab 1·50 40
N388 20x. Spiny lobster . . . . 3·00 40
N389 50x. Fiddler crab . . . . . 6·00 40

154 Air Battle **155** Foundryman ("Heavy Industries")

1965. "500th U.S. Aircraft Brought Down over North Vietnam".
N390 **154** 12x. green and lilac . . 4·25 2·75

1965. 20th Anniv of Republic and Completion of 1st Five-Year Plan.
N391 **155** 12x. black and orange 90 55
N392 – 12x. black and green . . 90 55
N393 – 12x. black and purple 90 55
DESIGNS: No. N392, Irrigation, pylon and power station ("Hydro-electric Power"); N393, Nurse examining child ("Social Medicine").
See also Nos. N417/19.

156 Drummer and Peasants

1965. 35th Anniv of Movement of Nghe An and Ha Tinh Soviet Peasants.
N394 **156** 10x. multicoloured . . . 1·10 40
N395 12x. multicoloured . . . 1·20 40

157 Girls and Flags

1965. 16th Anniv of Friendship between China and Vietnam. Multicoloured.
N396 12x. Type **157** . . . . . . 3·75 75
N397 12x. Vietnamese and Chinese girls with flags (vert) . . . . 3·75 75

158 Tsiolkovsky and "Sputnik 1"

1965. Space Flight of "Voskhod 2".
N398 **158** 12x. blue and purple . . 75 40
N399 – 12x. ochre and blue . . 75 40
N400 – 50x. blue and green . . 2·30 1·10
N401 – 50x. blue and turquoise 2·30 1·10
DESIGNS: No. N399, Leonov, Belyaev and "Voskhod 2"; N400, Gagarin; N401, Leonov in space.

159 Red Lacewing

1965. Butterflies. Multicoloured.
N402 12x. Type **159** . . . . . . 1·90 40
N403 12x. Leopard lacewing . . 1·90 40
N404 12x. Blue triangle . . . . . 1·90 40
N405 12x. Indian purple emperor 1·90 40
N406 20x. Paris peacock . . . . 3·75 40
N407 30x. Common rose . . . . 5·25 40

160 Norman R. Morrison and Demonstrators **161** Birthplace of Nguyen Du (poet)

1965. Homage to Norman R. Morrison (American Quaker who immolated himself).
N408 **160** 12x. black and red . . . 2·30 40

1965. Nguyen Du Commem. Multicoloured.
N409 12x. Type **161** 75 40
N410 12x. Nguyen Du Museum 75 40
N411 20x. "Kieu" (volume of poems) . . . . 1·10 40
N412 1d. Scene from "Kieu" . . 1·90 40

162 Pres. Ho Chi Minh

163 Rice-field and Insecticide-sprayer ("Agriculture")

1965. Engels' 145th Birth Anniv. Multicoloured.
N413 12x. Type **162** 75 40
N414 12x. Marx 75 40
N415 12x. Lenin 75 40
N416 50x. Engels . . . . 2·30 40

1965. Completion of 1st Five-Year Plan (2nd issue).
N417 **163** 12x. orange and green 90 30
N418 – 12x. blue and red . . . 90 30
N419 – 12x. orange and blue . . 90 30
DESIGNS: No. N418, Factory-worker ("Light Industries"); N419, Children at play and students ("Social Education").

164 Soldier and Demonstrators

1965. 5th Anniv of South Vietnam National Liberation Front.
N420 **164** 12x. violet and lilac . . 1·90 40

165 Casting Votes

1966. 20th Anniv of 1st Vietnamese General Elections.
N421 **165** 12x. black and red . . . 1·90 55

166 "Dendrobium moschatum" **167** Child on Rocking-horse

1966. Orchids. Multicoloured.
N422 12x. Type **166** . . . . . . 1·10 40
N423 12x. "Vanda teres" . . . . 1·10 40
N424 12x. "Dendrobium crystallinum" . . . . . 1·10 40
N425 12x. "Dendrobium nobile" 1·10 40
N426 20x. "Vandopsis gigantea" 1·90 40
N427 30x. "Dendrobium" . . . . 2·75 40

1966. New Year.
N428 **167** 12x. multicoloured . . . 1·90 40

168 "Physignathus cocincinus"

1966. Protection of Nature—Reptiles. Multicoloured.
N429 12x. Type **168** . . . . . . 1·10 40
N430 12x. "Trionyx sinensis" . . 1·10 40
N431 12x. Gecko (inscr "GEKKO GECKO") . . 1·10 40
N432 12x. "Testudo elongata" . . 1·10 40
N433 20x. "Varanus salvator" . . 1·50 40
N434 40x. "Eretmochelys imbricata" . . . . 3·00 40

169 Wrestling **170** Ly Tu Trong (revolutionary), Badge and Banner

1966. National Games.
N435 **169** 12x. multicoloured . . . 1·30 40
N436 – 12x. multicoloured . . . 1·30 40
N437 – 12x. multicoloured . . . 1·30 40
GAMES: No. N436, Archery (with crossbow); N437, "Fencing".

1966. 35th Anniv of Labour Youth Union.
N438 **170** 12x. multicoloured . . . 1·50 55

171 Republic Thunderchief in Flames

1966. "1,000th U.S. Aircraft Brought Down over North Vietnam".
N439 **171** 12x. multicoloured . . . 5·25 3·75

172 Worker and Rifle **174** Children and Banners

173 Battle Scene on Con Co Island

1966. Labour Day.
N440 **172** 6x. black, red and salmon . . . . 1·50 40

1966. Defence of Con Co ("Steel Island").
N441 **173** 12x. multicoloured . . . 1·50 40

1966. 25th Anniv of Vietnam Youth Pioneers.
N442 **174** 12x. black and red . . . 1·50 40

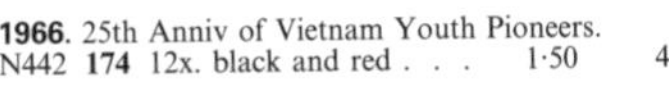

175 View of Dien An (Yenan) **176** "Luna 9" in Space

1966. 45th Anniv of Chinese Communist Party. Multicoloured.
N443 3x. Type **175** . . . . 1·50 40
N444 12x. Ho Chi Minh and Mao Tse-tung . . . . . 1·50 40

1966. "Luna 9" Space Flight. Multicoloured. Inscr "MAT TRANG 9".
N445 12x. Type **176** . . . . . . 1·50 75
N446 50x. "Luna 9" on Moon 3·75 75

177 Airplane in Flames

1966. "1,500th U.S. Aircraft Brought Down over North Vietnam".
N447 **177** 12x. multicoloured . . . 7·50 2·75
N448 12x. mult (optd **NGAY 14.10.1966**) . . . . . 11·50 2·75

178 Liberation Fighter

1966. Victories of Liberation Army. Inscr "1965–1966".
N449 **178** 1x. purple . . . . . . 1·30 55
N450 12x. multicoloured . . . 1·30 55
N451 – 12x. multicoloured . . . 1·30 55
DESIGN: No. N451, Soldier escorting prisoners-of-war.
See also No. 646.

179 Women from different Regions, and Child

1966. 20th Anniv of Vietnamese Women's Union.
N452 **179** 12x. black and salmon 75 40

180 Moluccan Pittas

1966. Birds. Multicoloured.
N453 12x. Type **180** 90 40
N454 12x. Black-naped orioles . . 90 40
N455 12x. River kingfisher . . . 90 40
N456 12x. Long-tailed broadbill 90 40
N457 20x. Hoopoe . . . . 1·70 40
N458 30x. Maroon orioles . . . 2·50 45
Nos. N454/5 and N457 are vert.

181 Football

1966. Ganefo Games. Multicoloured.
N459 12x. Type **181** . . . . . . 1·10 40
N460 12x. Rifle-shooting . . . . 1·10 40
N461 30x. Swimming . . . . . . 1·50 40
N462 30x. Running . . . . . . 1·50 40

182 Harvesting Rice

1967. Agricultural Production.
N463 **182** 12x. multicoloured . . . 1·10 40

183 Ho Chi Minh Text and Fighters

1967. Ho Chi Minh's Appeal.
N464 **183** 12x. purple and red . . 90 40
N465 – 12x. purple and red . . 1·10 40
DESIGN: No. N465, Ho-Chi-Minh text and marchers with banners.
See also Nos. 519/22.

184 Bamboo ("Arundinaria rolleana")

1967. Bamboo. Multicoloured.
N466 12x. Type **184** 90 40
N467 12x. "Arundinaria racemosa" 90 40
N468 12x. "Bambusa bingami" 90 40
N469 12x. "Bambusa arundinaceu" 90 40
N470 30x. "Bambusa nutans" . . 1·70 40
N471 50x. "Dendrocalamus patellaris" . . . . 2·30 40

185 Dhole

1967. Wild Animals. Multicoloured.
N472 12x. Type **185** 75 40
N473 12x. Binturong 75 40
N474 12x. Hog-badger 75 40
N475 20x. Large Indian civet . . 1·50 40
N476 40x. Bear macaque . . . . 2·30 40
N477 50x. Clouded leopard . . . 3·00 40

186 Captured Pilot
187 Rocket Launching and Agricultural Scene

1967. "2,000th U.S. Aircraft Brought Down over North Vietnam".
N478 **186** 6x. black and red on pink . . . . 2·75 1·50
N479 12x. black & red on grn 2·75 1·50

1967. Launching of First Chinese Rocket. Mult.
N480 12x. Type **187** . . . . . . 1·90 90
N481 30x. Rocket launching, and Gate of Heavenly Peace, Peking . . . . 3·00 1·50

188 Belted Bearded Grunt

1967. Vietnamese Fishes. Multicoloured.
N482 12x. Type **188** 75 40
N483 12x. Japanese mackerel ("Scomberomorus niphonius") 75 40
N484 12x. Thread-finned lizardfish ("Saurida filamentosa") 75 40
N485 20x. Adjutant emperor . . 1·50 40
N486 30x. Black pomfret . . . . 2·30 40
N487 50x. Blood snapper . . . . 3·00 40

189 Lenin and Revolutionary Soldiers

1967. 50th Anniv of October Revolution. Mult.
N488 6x. Type **189** 45 40
N489 12x. Lenin and revolutionaries 85 40
N490 12x. Lenin, Marx and Vietnamese soldiers . . . 85 40
N491 20x. Cruiser "Aurora" . . 1·20 40

190 Air Battle

1967. "2,500th U.S. Aircraft Brought Down over North Vietnam".
N492 **190** 12x. black, red and green . . . . 3·25 95
N493 – 12x. black, red and blue 3·25 95
DESIGN—VERT: No. N493, Boeing B-52 Stratofortress falling in flames.

191 Atomic Symbol and Gate of Heavenly Peace, Peking

1967. 1st Chinese "H"-Bomb Test. Multicoloured.
N494 12x. Type **191** . . . . . . 1·50 75
N495 20x. Chinese lantern, atomic symbol & dove (30 × 35 mm) . . . . . . 2·30 75

192 Factory Anti-aircraft Unit

1967. Anti-aircraft Defences. Multicoloured.
N496 12x. Type **192** 45 40
N497 12x. Rifle-fire from trenches 45 40
N498 12x. Seaborne gun-crew . . 45 40
N499 12x. Militiawoman with captured U.S. pilot . . . 45 40
N500 20x. Air battle 90 40
N501 30x. Military anti-aircraft post . . . . 1·80 40

193 Chickens

1968. Domestic Fowl. Multicoloured designs showing cocks and hens.
N502 12x. Type **193** 60 40
N503 12x. Inscr "Ga ri" 60 40
N504 12x. Inscr "Ga trong thien ri" 60 40
N505 12x. Inscr "Ga den chanchi" 60 40
N506 20x. Junglefowl . . . . . 1·10 40
N507 30x. Hen . . . . 1·50 40
N508 40x. Hen and chicks . . . 2·30 40
N509 50x. Two hens . . . . . . 2·75 40

194 Gorky

1968. Birth Centenary of Maxim Gorky.
N510 **194** 12x. black and brown 1·10 40

195 Burning Village

1968. Victories of 1966–67.
N511 **195** 12x. brown and red . . 60 60
N512 – 12x. brown and red . . 60 60
N513 – 12x. brown and red . . 60 60
N514 – 12x. brown and red . . 60 60
N515 – 12x. black and violet . . 60 60
N516 – 12x. black and violet . . 60 60
N517 – 12x. black and violet . . 60 60
N518 – 12x. black and violet . . 60 60
DESIGNS: No. N512, Firing mortars; N513, Attacking tanks with rocket-gun; N514, Sniping; N515, Attacking gun-site; N516, Escorting prisoners; N517, Interrogating refugees; N518, Civilians demonstrating.

197 Ho Chi Minh Text and Fighters
198 Hong boch Rose

1968. Intensification of Production.
N519 **197** 6x. blue on yellow . . . 75 25
N520 12x. blue . . . . 1·10 25
N521 12x. purple . . . . . . 1·10 25
N522 12x. red . . . . 1·10 25

1968. Roses. Multicoloured.
N523 12x. Type **198** 75 40
N524 12x. Hong canh sap 75 40
N525 12x. Hong leo 75 40
N526 20x. Hong vang . . . . . 1·50 40
N527 30x. Hong nhung . . . . . 2·30 35
N528 40x. Hong canh tim . . . . 3·00 40

199 Ho Chi Minh and Flag
200 Karl Marx

1968. Ho Chi Minh's New Year Message.
N529 **199** 12x. brown and violet 1·50 45

1968. 150th Birth Anniv of Karl Marx.
N530 **200** 12x. black and green . . 1·50 40

201 Anti-aircraft Machine-gun Crew

1968. "3,000th U.S. Aircraft Brought Down over North Vietnam". Multicoloured.
N531 12x. Type **201** . . . . . . 1·50 1·10
N532 12x. Women manning anti-aircraft gun . . . . . . 1·50 1·10
N533 40x. Aerial dogfight . . . . 3·75 1·10
N534 40x. Anti-aircraft missile . . 3·75 1·10

202 Rattan-cane Work

1968. Arts and Crafts. Multicoloured.
N535 6x. Type **202** 40 40
N536 12x. Bamboo work 45 40
N537 12x. Pottery 45 40
N538 20x. Ivory carving 75 40
N539 30x. Lacquer work . . . . 1·10 40
N540 40x. Silverware . . . . . . 1·50 40

203 Quarter-staff Contest

1968. Traditional Sports. Multicoloured.

N541	12x. Type **203**	60	40
N542	12x. Dagger fighting	60	40
N543	12x. Duel with sabres	60	40
N544	30x. Unarmed combat	1·50	40
N545	40x. Scimitar fighting	2·00	40
N546	50x. Sword and buckler	2·30	40

205 Temple, Khue

1968. Vietnamese Architecture. Multicoloured.

N548	12x. Type **205**	45	40
N549	12x. Bell tower, Keo Pagoda	45	40
N550	20x. Bridge, Bonze Pagoda (horiz)	60	40
N551	30x. Mot Cot Pagoda, Hanoi	75	40
N552	40x. Gateway, Ninh Phuc Pagoda (horiz)	1·20	40
N553	50x. Tay Phuong Pagoda (horiz)	1·50	40

206 Vietnamese Militia

1968. Cuban–North Vietnamese Friendship. Mult. With gum.

N554	12x. Type **206**	75	60
N555	12x. Cuban revolutionary (vert)	75	60
N556	20x. "Revolutionary Solidarity" (vert)	1·10	75

207 "Ploughman with Rifle"

1968. "The War Effort". Paintings. With gum.

N557	**207** 12x. black, blue & yellow	40	30
N558	– 12x. multicoloured	40	30
N559	– 30x. brown, blue and turquoise	90	75
N560	– 40x. multicoloured	1·40	1·10

DESIGNS—HORIZ: No. N558, "Defending the Mines"; N559, "Repairing Railway Track"; N560, "Crashed Aircraft".

208 Nam Ngai shooting down Aircraft

1969. Lunar New Year. Victories of the National Liberation Front. Multicoloured.

N561	12x. Type **208**	40	40
N562	12x. Tay Nguyen throwing grenade	40	40
N563	12x. Gun crews, Tri Thien	40	40
N564	40x. Insurgents, Tay Ninh	1·10	40
N565	50x. Home Guards	4·50	40

209 Loading Timber Lorries

1969. North Vietnamese Timber Industry. Mult.

N566	6x. Type **209**	45	40
N567	12x. Log raft on river	85	40
N568	12x. Tug towing "log train"	85	40
N569	12x. Elephant hauling logs	85	40
N570	12x. Insecticide spraying	85	40
N571	20x. Buffalo hauling log	1·10	40
N572	30x. Logs on overhead cable	1·90	40

210 "Young Guerrilla" (Co Tan Long Chau)

1969. "South Vietnam—Land and People". Paintings. Multicoloured.

N573	12x. Type **210**	45	40
N574	12x. "Scout on Patrol" (Co Tan Long Chau)	45	40
N575	20x. "Woman Guerrilla" (Le Van Chuong) (vert)	75	40
N576	30x. "Halt at a Relay Station" (Co Tan Long Chau)	1·00	40
N577	40x. "After a Skirmish" (Co Tan Long Chau)	1·50	40
N578	50x. "Liberated Hamlet" (Huynh Phuong Dong)	2·30	40

211 Woman Soldier, Ben Tre

1969. Victories in Tet Offensive (1968).

N579	**211** 8x. black, green and pink	60	45
N580	12x. black, emer & green	60	45
N581	– 12x. multicoloured	60	45
N582	– 12x. multicoloured	60	45
N583	– 12x. multicoloured	60	45

DESIGNS—VERT: No. N581, Urban guerilla and attack on U.S. Embassy, Saigon; N582, Two soldiers with flag, Hue; N583, Mortar crew, Khe Sanh.

212 Soldier with Flame-thrower

1969. 15th Anniv of Liberation of Hanoi.

N584	**212** 12x. black and red	1·50	40
N585	– 12x. multicoloured	1·50	40

DESIGN: No. N585, Children with construction toy.

213 Grapefruit

214 Tribunal Emblem and Falling Airplane

1969. Fruits. Multicoloured.

N586	12x. Type **213**	30	10
N587	12x. Pawpaw	30	10
N588	20x. Tangerines	40	25
N589	30x. Oranges	60	40
N590	40x. Lychees	1·10	60
N591	50x. Persimmons	1·90	1·10

See also Nos. N617/21 and N633/6.

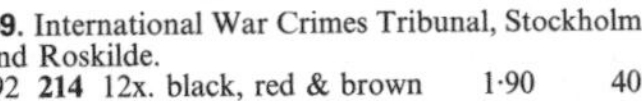

1969. International War Crimes Tribunal, Stockholm and Roskilde.

N592	**214** 12x. black, red & brown	1·90	40

215 Ho Chi Minh in 1924

1970. 40th Anniv of Vietnamese Workers' Party. Multicoloured.

N593	12x. Type **215**	75	60
N594	12x. Ho Chi Minh in 1969	75	60
N595	12x. Le Hong Phong	75	60
N596	12x. Tran Phu	75	60
N597	12x. Nguyne Van Cu	75	60

Nos. N595/7 are smaller, size 40 × 24 mm.

216 Playtime in Nursery School

1970. Children's Activities. Multicoloured.

N598	12x. Type **216**	50	40
N599	12x. Playing with toys	30	40
N600	20x. Watering plants	55	40
N601	20x. Pasturing buffalo	55	40
N602	30x. Feeding chickens	60	40
N603	40x. Making music	75	40
N604	50x. Flying model airplane	1·10	40
N605	60x. Going to school	1·50	40

217 Lenin and Red Flag

1970. Birth Centenary of Lenin.

N606	**217** 12x. multicoloured	40	40
N607	– 1d. purple, red & yellow	3·00	40

DESIGN: 1d. Portrait of Lenin.

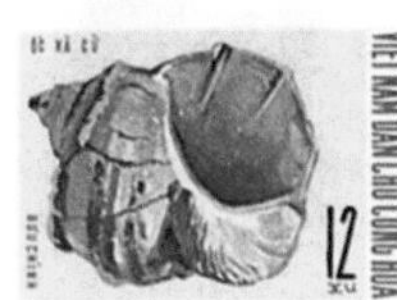

218 Great Green Turban

1970. Sea-shells. Multicoloured.

N608	12x. Type **218**	75	40
N609	12x. Indian volute	75	40
N610	20x. Tiger cowrie	1·10	40
N611	1d. Trumpet triton	2·75	40

219 Ho Chi Minh in 1930

1970. Ho Chi Minh's 80th Birth Anniv.

N612	**219** 12x. black, brn & flesh	40	40
N613	– 12x. black, blue & green	40	40
N614	– 2d. black, ochre & yell	3·00	40

MSN615 Two sheets 134 × 93 mm, each containing Nos. N612/14.(a) Background in pale orange(b) Background in mauve. Imperf 5·25 5·25

PORTRAITS: No. N613, In 1945 with microphone; N614, In 1969.

220 Vietcong Flag

1970. 1st Anniv of National Liberation Front Provisional Government in South Vietnam.

N616	**220** 12x. multicoloured	1·10	40

221 Water-melon

222 Power Linesman

1970. Fruits. Multicoloured.

N617	12x. Type **221**	40	40
N618	12x. Pumpkin	40	40
N619	20x. Cucumber	60	40
N620	50x. Courgette	1·10	40
N621	1d. Charantais melon	2·30	40

1970. North Vietnamese Industries.

N622	**222** 12x. blue and red	55	40
N623	– 12x. red, yellow and blue	55	40
N624	– 12x. black, orange & blue	55	40
N625	– 12x. yellow, purple & green	55	40

DESIGNS—VERT: No. N623, Hands winding thread on bobbin ("Textiles"); N624, Stoker and power station ("Electric Power"); N625, Workers and lorry ("More coal for the Fatherland").

223 Peasant Girl with Pigs

225 Chuoi Tieu Bananas

224 Ho Chi Minh proclaiming Republic, 1945

1970. North Vietnamese Agriculture.

N626	**223** 12x. multicoloured	1·50	40

1970. 25th Anniv of Democratic Republic of Vietnam.

N627	**224** 12x. black, brown & red	30	40
N628	– 12x. deep brown, brown and green	30	40
N629	– 12x. brown, grey and red	30	40
N630	– 12x. deep brown, brown and green	30	40
N631	– 20x. brown, red & bistre	55	40
N632	– 1d. brown, drab and chestnut	1·90	40

DESIGNS: No. N628, Vo Thi Sau facing firing-squad; N629, Nguyen Van Troi and captors; N630, Phan Dinh Giot attacking pill-box; N631, Nguyen Viet Xuan encouraging troops; N632, Nguyen Van Be attacking tank.

1970. Bananas. Multicoloured.

N633	12x. Type **225**	40	40
N634	12x. Chuoi Tay	40	40
N635	50x. Chuoi Ngu	90	40
N636	1d. Chuoi Mat	1·40	40

226 Flags, and Bayonets in Helmet

1970. Indo-Chinese People's Summit Conference.

N637	**226** 12x. multicoloured	1·50	40

227 Engels and Signature

1970. 150th Birth Anniv of Friedrich Engels.

N638	**227** 12x. black, brown & red	75	40
N639	1d. black, brown & grn	1·50	40

228 "Akistrodon ciatus"

1970. Snakes. Multicoloured.
N640 12x. Type **228** 60 40
N641 20x. "Calliophis macclellandii" 90 40
N642 50x. "Bungarus faciatus" 1·10 40
N643 1d. "Trimeresurus gramineus" . . . . . . 1·90 40

229 Mother and Child with Flag

1970. 10th Anniv of National Front for Liberation of South Vietnam. Multicoloured.
N644 6x. Type **229** 75 40
N645 12x. Vietcong flag and torch (horiz) . . . . . . 1·50 40

1971. Victories of Liberation Army. As No. N449, but value and colours changed.
N646 **178** 2x. black and orange . . 1·50 40

232 Satellite in Earth Orbit

1971. 1st Anniv of Launching of Chinese Satellite.
N649 **232** 12x. multicoloured . . . 75 40
N650 50x. multicoloured . . . 1·10 40

234 Ho Chi Minh Medal

1971. 81st Birth Anniv of Pres. Ho Chi Minh.
N652 **234** 1x. multicoloured . . . 30 25
N653 3x. multicoloured . . . 35 30
N654 10x. multicoloured . . . 55 45
N655 12x. multicoloured . . . 60 55
MSN656 90 × 130 mm. **234** 12x. multicoloured (53 × 52 mm). Imperf . . . . 4·50 4·50

235 Emperor Quang Trung liberating Hanoi

1971. Bicentenary of Tay Son Rising.
N657 **235** 6x. multicoloured . . . 75 40
N658 12x. multicoloured . . . 1·50 40

236 Karl Marx and Music of the "Internationale"

1971. Centenary of Paris Commune.
N659 **236** 12x. black, red and pink 90 40

237 Hai Thuong Lan Ong

1971. 250th Birth Anniv of Hai Thuong Lan Ong (physician).
N660 **237** 12x. black, green & brn 75 40
N661 50x. multicoloured . . . 1·10 40

238 "Kapimala"

1971. Folk Sculptures in Tay Phuong Pagoda. Multicoloured.
N662 12x. Type **238** 45 40
N663 12x. "Sangkayasheta" . . . 45 40
N664 12x. "Vasumitri" 45 40
N665 12x. "Dhikaca" 45 40
N666 30x. "Bouddha Nandi" . . 1·10 40
N667 40x. "Rahulata" . . . . . 1·10 40
N668 50x. "Sangha Nandi" . . . 1·90 40
N669 1d. "Cakyamuni" . . . . . 2·40 40

239 Ho Chi Minh, Banner and Young Workers

1971. 40th Anniv of Ho Chi Minh Working Youth Union.
N670 **239** 12x. multicoloured . . . 90 40

240 "Luna 16" on Moon **241** "Luna 17" landing on Moon

1971. Moon Flight of "Luna 16".
N671 – 12x. multicoloured . . . 75 40
N672 – 12x. multicoloured . . . 75 40
N673 **240** 1d. brown, blue & turq 2·30 40
DESIGNS: No. N671, Flight to Moon; N672, Return to Earth. Nos.
N671/2 were issued together horizontally, se-tenant, each pair forming a composite design.

1971. Moon Flight of "Luna 17".
N674 **241** 12x. red, blue and green 75 40
N675 – 12x. pink, green & myrtle 75 40
N676 – 1d. pink, brown & green 2·30 40
DESIGNS—HORIZ: No. N675, "Luna 17" on Moon; N676, "Lunokhod 1" crossing Moon crevasse.

243 "White Tiger"

1971. "The Five Tigers" (folk-art paintings). Mult.
N679 12x. Type **243** 40 40
N680 12x. "Yellow Tiger" . . . 40 40
N681 12x. "Red Tiger" 40 40
N682 40x. "Green Tiger" . . . . 1·50 40
N683 50x. "Grey Tiger" . . . . 1·90 40
N684 1d. "Five Tigers" . . . . . 2·75 40
MS685 90 × 120 mm. 1d. As No. N684 but size 47 × 63 mm. Imperf 9·00 9·00

244 Flags and Gate of Heavenly Peace, Peking **245** Mongolian Emblem

1971. 50th Anniv of Chinese Communist Party.
N686 **244** 12x. multicoloured . . . 75 40

1971. 50th Anniv of Mongolian People's Republic.
N687 **245** 12x. multicoloured . . . 75 40

246 Drum Procession

1972. Dong Ho Folk Engravings.
N688 **246** 12x. pink, brown & blk 75 75
N689 – 12x. pink and black . . 75 75
N690 – 12x. multicoloured . . . 75 75
N691 – 12x. multicoloured . . . 75 75
N692 – 40x. multicoloured . . . 1·90 75
N693 – 50x. multicoloured . . . 2·75 75
DESIGNS—HORIZ: No. N689, "Traditional Wrestling"; N692, "Wedding of Mice"; N693, "The Toads' School". VERT: No. N690, "Jealous Attack"; N691, "Gathering Coconuts".

247 Workers

1972. 3rd Vietnamese Trade Unions Congress.
N694 **247** 1x. black and blue . . . 75 40
N695 – 12x. black and orange 75 40
DESIGN: 12x. As Type **247**, but design reversed.

248 Planting Rice

1972. 25th Anniv of National Resistance.
N696 **248** 12x. multicoloured . . . 55 40
N697 – 12x. multicoloured . . . 55 40
N698 – 12x. multicoloured . . . 55 40
N699 – 12x. turq, red & pink 55 40
DESIGNS: No. N697, Munitions worker; N698, Soldier with flame-thrower; N699, Text of Ho Chi Minh's Appeal.

249 Ho Chi Minh's Birthplace

1972. 82nd Birth Anniv of Ho Chi Minh.
N700 **249** 12x. black, drab & ochre . . . . 1·10 40
N701 – 12x. black, green & pink 1·10 40
DESIGN: No. N701, Ho Chi Minh's house, Hanoi.

250 Captured Pilot and Falling Airplane **251** Georgi Dimitrov

1972. "3,500th U.S. Aircraft Brought Down over North Vietnam".
N702 **250** 12x. green and red . . . 1·90 1·10
N703 12x. black and red . . . 1·90 1·10
No. N703 has the inscription amended to record the actual date on which the 3,500th aircraft was brought down: 20.4.1972.

1972. 90th Birth Anniv of Georgi Dimitrov (Bulgarian statesman).
N704 **251** 12x. brown and green 1·00 40
N705 – 12x. black and pink . . 1·00 40
DESIGN: No. N705, Dimitrov at Leipzig Court, 1933.

252 Falcated Teal **253** Anti-aircraft Gunner

1972. Vietnamese Birds. Multicoloured.
N706 12x. Type **252** 55 40
N707 12x. Red-wattled lapwing 55 40
N708 30x. Cattle egret 90 40
N709 40x. Water cock . . . . . 1·30 40
N710 50x. Purple swamphen . . 1·90 40
N711 1d. Greater adjutant stork 4·25 40

1972. "4,000th U.S. Aircraft Brought Down over North Vietnam".
N712 **253** 12x. black, mauve and pink . . . . 2·30 75
N713 – 12x. green, black and red . . . . 2·30 75
DESIGN: No. N713, Anti-aircraft gunner with shell.

254 Umbrella Dance

1972. Tay Nguyen Folk Dances. Multicoloured.
N714 12x. Type **254** 40 30
N715 12x. Drum dance 40 30
N716 12x. Shield dance 40 30
N717 20x. Horse dance 60 40
N718 30x. Ka-Dong dance . . . 75 40
N719 40x. Grinding-rice dance . . 90 40
N720 50x. Gong dance . . . . . 1·50 40
N721 1d. Cham Rong dance . . 2·75 40

255 "Soyuz 11" Spacecraft and "Salyut" Space Laboratory

1972. Space Flight of "Soyuz 11".
N722 **255** 12x. blue and lilac . . . 75 40
N723 – 1d. brown and flesh . . 1·90 40
DESIGN: 1d. "Soyuz 11" astronauts.

256 Dhole

1973. Wild Animals (1st series). Multicoloured.
N724 12x. Type **256** 55 40
N725 30x. Leopard 90 40
N726 50x. Leopard cat . . . . . 1·90 40
N727 1d. European otter . . . . 2·75 40
See also Nos. N736/9.

257 Copernicus and Globe

1973. 500th Birth Anniv of Copernicus (astronomer).
N728 **257** 12x. black, red & brown 75 60
N729 – 12x. black, red & brown 75 60
N730 – 30x. black and brown 1·10 75
DESIGNS—HORIZ: No. N729, Copernicus and sun. VERT: 30x. Copernicus and facsimile signature.

258 "Drummers"

1973. Engravings from Ngoc Lu Bronze Drums. Each yellow and green.
N731 12x. Type **258** 60 40
N732 12x. "Pounding rice" . . . 60 40
N733 12x. "Folk-dancing" . . . 60 40
N734 12x. "War canoe" 60 40
N735 12x. "Birds and beasts" . . 60 40

259 Lesser Malay Chevrotain

260 Striated Canegrass Warblers

1973. Wild Animals (2nd series). Multicoloured.
N736 12x. Type **259** 40 40
N737 30x. Mainland serow . . . 75 40
N738 50x. Wild boar . . . . . . 1·10 40
N739 1d. Siberian musk deer . . 1·50 40

1973. Birds useful to Agriculture. Multicoloured.
N740 12x. Type **260** 40 40
N741 12x. Red-whiskered bulbuls 40 40
N742 20x. Magpie robin 40 40
N743 40x. White-browed fantails 1·10 40
N744 50x. Great tits . . . . . . 1·50 40
N745 1d. Japanese white-eyes . . 1·90 40

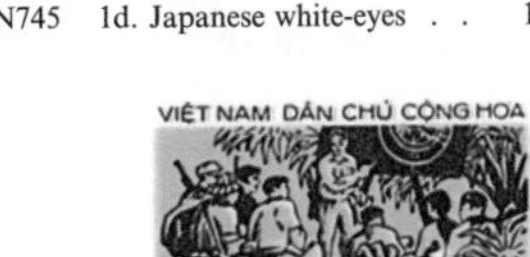

262 "Ready to Learn"

1973. "Three Readies" Youth Movement.
N748 **262** 12x. brown and green 55 40
N749 – 12x. violet and blue . . 55 40
N750 – 12x. green and mauve 55 40
DESIGNS: No. N749, Soldiers on the march ("Ready to Fight"); N750, Road construction ("Ready to Work").

263 Flags of North Vietnam and North Korea

1973. 25th Anniv of People's Republic of Korea.
N751 **263** 12x. multicoloured . . . 75 40

264 Dogfight over Hanoi

1973. Victory over U.S. Air Force.
N752 **264** 12x. multicoloured . . . 75 45
N753 – 12x. multicoloured . . . 75 45
N754 – 12x. multicoloured . . . 75 45
N755 – 1d. black and red . . . 3·00 45
DESIGNS: No. N753, Boeing B-52 Stratofortress exploding over Haiphong; N754, Anti-aircraft gun; N755, Aircraft wreckage in China Sea.

266 Elephant hauling Logs

267 Dahlia

1974. Vietnamese Elephants. Multicoloured.
N758 12x. Type **266** 40 40
N759 12x. War elephant 35 40
N760 40x. Elephant rolling logs 1·10 40
N761 50x. Circus elephant . . . 1·10 40
N762 1d. Elephant carrying war supplies . . . . 2·30 40

1974. Flowers.
N763 **267** 12x. red, lake and green 60 40
N764 – 12x. red, lake and green 60 40
N765 – 12x. yellow, green & blue 60 40
N766 – 12x. multicoloured . . . 90 40
N767 – 12x. multicoloured . . . 90 40
FLOWERS: No. N764, Rose; N765, Chrysanthemum; N766, Bach Mi; N767, Dai Doa.

268 Soldier planting Flag

269 Armed Worker and Peasant

1974. 20th Anniv of Victory at Dien Bien Phu.
N768 12x. Type **268** 90 40
N769 12x. Victory badge 90 40

1974. "Three Responsibilities" Women's Movement.
N770 **269** 12x. blue and pink . . . 90 40
N771 – 12x. blue and pink . . . 90 40
DESIGN: No. N771, Woman operating loom.

270 Cuc Nau Chrysanthemum

271 "Corchorus capsularis"

1974. Vietnamese Chrysanthemums. Mult.
N772 12x. Type **270** 40 25
N773 12x. Cuc Vang 40 25
N774 20x. Cuc Ngoc Khong Tuoc 45 25
N775 30x. Cuc Trang 60 30
N776 40x. Kim Cuc 75 45
N777 50x. Cuc Hong Mi 90 55
N778 60x. Cuc Gam . . . . . . 1·10 60
N779 1d. Cuc Tim . . . . 1·50 1·10

1974. Textile Plants.
N780 **271** 12x. brown, green and olive 40 10
N781 – 12x. brown, grn & pink 40 10
N782 – 30x. brown, green & yellow 75 25
DESIGNS: No. N781, "Cyperus tojet jormis"; N782, "Morus alba".

272 Nike Statue, Warsaw

1974. 30th Anniv of People's Republic of Poland.
N783 **272** 1x. purple, pink and red 40 30
N784 2x. red, pink and red . . 40 30
N785 3x. brown, pink and red 40 30
N786 12x. light red, pink & red 75 60

273 Flags of China and Vietnam

1974. 25th Anniv of People's Republic of China.
N787 **273** 12x. multicoloured . . . 75 40

274 Handclasp with Vietnamese and East German Flags

1974. 25th Anniv of German Democratic Republic.
N788 **274** 12x. multicoloured . . . 75 40

275 Woman Bricklayer

276 Pres. Allende with Chilean Flag

1974. 20th Anniv of Liberation of Hanoi. Mult.
N789 12x. Type **275** 75 40
N790 12x. Soldier with child . . 75 40

1974. 1st Death Annivs of Salvador Allende (President of Chile) and Pablo Neruda (Chilean poet).
N791 **276** 12x. blue and red . . . 75 40
N792 – 12x. blue (Pablo Neruda) 75 40

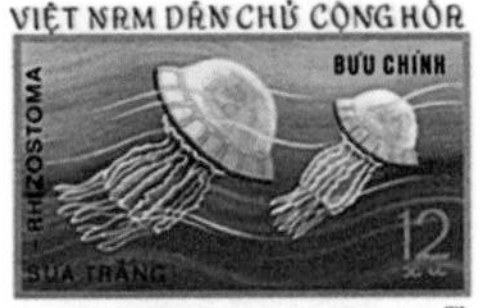

277 "Rhizostoma"

1974. Marine Life. Multicoloured.
N793 12x. Type **277** 40 10
N794 12x. "Loligo" 40 10
N795 30x. Variously coloured abalone 75 25
N796 40x. Japanese pearl oyster 90 25
N797 50x. Common cuttlefish . . 1·40 25
N798 1d. "Palinurus japonicus" 1·90 1·00

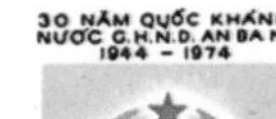

278 Flags of Algeria and Vietnam

279 Albanian Emblem

1974. 20th Anniv of Algerian War of Liberation.
N799 **278** 12x. multicoloured . . . 75 40

1974. 30th Anniv of People's Republic of Albania. Multicoloured.
N800 12x. Type **279** 75 40
N801 12x. Girls from Albania and North Vietnam . . . 75 40

280 Signing of Paris Agreement

1975. 2nd Anniv of Paris Agreement on Vietnam.
N802 **280** 12x. black, green & emerald 20 10
N803 – 12x. black, blue and grey 20 10
DESIGN: No. N803, International Conference in session.

281 Tran Phu

1975. 45th Anniv of Vietnamese Workers' Party.
N804 **281** 12x. brown, red and pink 25 25
N805 – 12x. brown, red and pink 25 25
N806 – 12x. brown, red and pink 25 25
N807 – 12x. brown, red and pink 25 25
N808 – 60x. brown, chestnut and pink 90 45
PORTRAITS—HORIZ: No. N805, Nguyen Van Cu; N806, Le Hong Phong; N807, Ngo Gia Tu. VERT: No. N808, Ho Chi Minh in 1924.

282 "Costus speciosus"

1975. Medicinal Plants. Multicoloured.
N809 12x. Type **282** 40 40
N810 12x. "Rosa laevigata" . . . 40 40
N811 12x. "Curcuma zedoaria" 40 40
N812 30x. "Erythrina indica" . . 60 40
N813 40x. "Lilium brownii" . . . 75 40
N814 50x. "Hibiscus sagittifolius" 90 40
N815 60x. "Papaver somniferum" 90 40
N816 1d. "Belamcanda chinensis" 2·30 40

283 "Achras sapota"

1975. Fruits. Multicoloured.
N817 12x. Type **283** 40 40
N818 12x. "Persica vulgaris" . . 40 40
N819 20x. "Eugenia jambos" . . 40 40
N820 30x. "Chrysophyllum cainito" 40 40
N821 40x. "Lucuma mamosa" . . 75 40
N822 50x. "Prunica granitum" 75 40
N823 60x. "Durio ziberthinus" 1·10 40
N824 1d. "Prunus salicina" . . . 1·90 40

284 Ho Chi Minh

285 Ho Chi Minh proclaiming Independence, 1945

1975. 85th Birth Anniv of Ho Chi Minh.
N825 **284** 12x. multicoloured . . . 75 40
N826 60x. multicoloured . . . 1·50 75

1975. 30th Anniv of Democratic Republic of Vietnam. Multicoloured.
N827 12x. Type **285** 55 40
N828 12x. Democratic Republic emblem 55 40
N829 12x. Democratic Republic flag 55 40
MSN829 130 × 100 mm. 20x. Type **285** (45 × 30 mm). Imperf 11·50 11·50

286 "Dermochelys coriacea"

287 Arms of Hungary

1975. Reptiles. Multicoloured.
N831 12x. Type **286** 40 40
N832 12x. "Physignathus cocincinus" 40 40
N833 20x. "Hydrophis brookii" 60 40
N834 30x. "Platysternum megacephalum" 75 40
N835 40x. "Leiolepis belliana" . . 90 40
N836 50x. "Python molurus" . . 1·00 40
N837 60x. "Naja hannah" . . . 1·20 40
N838 1d. "Draco maculatus" . . 1·50 40

1975. 30th Anniv of Liberation of Hungary.
N839 **287** 12x. multicoloured . . . 75 40

288 "Pathysa antiphates"

1976. Butterflies. Multicoloured.
N840 12x. Type **288** 40 40
N841 12x. "Danaus plexippus" 40 40
N842 20x. "Gynautocera papilionaria" 75 40
N843 30x. "Maenas salaminia" 85 40
N844 40x. "Papilio machaon" . . 90 40
N845 50x. "Ixias pyrene" . . . . 1·00 40
N846 60x. "Eusemia vetula" . . 1·20 40
N847 1d. "Eriboea sp." . . . . . 1·50 40

289 Hoang Thao Orchid

1976. Lunar New Year.
N848 **289** 6x. yellow, green & blue 1·50 75
N849 12x. yellow, green & red 1·50 75

290 Masked Palm Civet

1976. Wild Animals. Multicoloured.
N850 12x. Type **290** 55 10
N851 12x. Belly-banded squirrel 55 10
N852 20x. Rhesus macaque . . 55 10
N853 30x. Chinese porcupine . . 75 10
N854 40x. Racoon-dog 75 25
N855 50x. Asiatic black bear . . 75 30
N856 60x. Leopard 90 45
N857 1d. Malayan flying lemur 1·40 60

291 Voters and Map

1976. 1st Elections Unified National Assembly.
N858 **291** 6x. red and sepia . . . 60 40
N859 – 6x. yellow and red . . . 60 40
N860 **291** 12x. red and blue . . . 1·50 40
DESIGN:—35 × 24 mm: No. N859, Map and ballot box.
See also Nos. NLF64/6 of National Front for the Liberation of South Vietnam.

292 Map and Text

1976. 1st Session of Unified National Assembly.
N861 **292** 6x. purple, red & yellow 40 40
N862 12x. turquoise, red & yellow 75 40
N863 – 12x. bistre, red & yellow 75 40
DESIGN—VERT (27 × 42 mm): No. N863, Vietnam map and design from Ngoc Lu Drum. No. N862 shows different text from Type **292**.
See also Nos. NLF68/9 of National Front for the Liberation of South Vietnam.

293 "Dendrobium devonianum"

1976. Orchids. Multicoloured.
N864 12x. Type **293** 45 10
N865 12x. "Habenaria rhodocheila" 45 10
N866 20x. "Dendrobium tortile" 60 10
N867 30x. "Doritis pulcherima" 60 10
N868 40x. "Dendrobium farmeri" 75 10
N869 50x. "Dendrobium aggregatum" 90 25
N870 60x. "Eria pannae" . . . . 1·10 40
N871 1d. "Paphiopedilum concolor" . . . . 1·90 50

FRANK STAMPS

F 29

F 42 Invalids in Rice-field

1958. No value indicated.
NF82 F **29** (–) red, yellow and green . . . . 11·50 4·50
Issued to war-disabled persons for private correspondence.

1959. No value indicated.
NF105 F **42** (–) brown . . . . . 3·75 1·10
NF106 (–) olive and blue . . 5·75 1·70
Issued to invalids in agriculture for private correspondence.

F **230** Invalid's Badge

1971. No value indicated.
NF647 F **230** (–) brown and red 1·10 1·10
Issued to disabled ex-servicemen for private correspondence.

F **233** Disabled Soldier with Baby

F **261** "Returning Home"

1971. No value indicated.
NF651 F **233** (–) brn, red & yell 1·10 1·10

1973.
NF746 F **261** 12x. black and red 40 40
NF747 – 12x. black and blue 40 40
DESIGN—22 × 33 mm: No. NF747, Disabled soldier with drill.
Issued to disabled veterans for private correspondence.

MILITARY FRANK STAMPS

MF **46** Soldier and Steam Train

1959. No value indicated.
NMF112 MF **46** (–) black & green 3·75 1·50

MF **68** Mounted Frontier Guard

MF **118** Military Medal and Invalid's Badge

1961. No value indicated.
NMF154 MF **68** (–) mult . . . . 13·00 7·50

1963.
NMF277 MF **118** 12x. mult . . . 3·75 3·75
For use on disabled soldiers' mail.

MF **133** Soldier and Army Badge

MF **150** Soldier in Action

1964. No value indicated.
NMF325 MF **133** (–) green, black and orge . . 3·75 3·75

1965. No value indicated.
NMF373 MF **150** (–) black and red . . . . . 3·75 3·75
NMF374 (–) black & green . . . . 3·75 3·75

MF **177** Soldiers and Weapons

1966. No value indicated.
NMF447 MF **177** (–) violet & black . . . . 7·50 7·50

MF **189** "Star" Badge of People's Army

MF **204** Soldiers attacking

1967. No value indicated.
NMF488 MF **189** (–) mult . . . . 1·10 1·10

1968. No value indicated.
NMF519 (–) brown and green . . 11·00 11·00
No. NMF519 is similar in design to No. NMF447, but shows more modern equipment and is dated "1967".

1968. No value indicated.
NMF547 MF **204** (–) lilac . . . . 1·20 1·20

1969. Type MF 177, but undated. No value indicated.
NMF579 MF **177** (–) brown & green . . . . 15·00

MF **231** Nguyen Van Be attacking Tank

1971. No value indicated.
NMF648 MF **231** (–) blk, red & drab . . . . 1·10 1·10

MF **242** Nguyen Viet Yuan and Anti-aircraft Gun

1971. No value indicated.
NMF677 MF **242** (–) black, pink and buff . . 75 75
NMF678 (–) brown & green 75 75

MF **265** Soldier with Bayonet advancing

1974. No value indicated.
NMF756 MF **265** (–) black, yellow & blue 40 40
NMF757 – (–) black, red and brown 40 40
NMF758 MF **265** (–) black, flesh and red . . . 75 75
DESIGN: No. NMF757, Soldier with sub-machine gun, and tanks. No. NMF757 is 40 × 24 mm; No. NMF758 31 × 21 mm.

OFFICIAL STAMPS

The values on Official stamps issued 1952 to 1954 are in kilogrammes of rice, the basis of the State's economy.

A. Tongking.

O **6** Rice-harvester

1953. Production and Economy Campaign.
NO17 O **6** 0.600k. red . . . . . . 9·50 1·90
NO18 1.000k. brown . . . . 9·50 3·75
NO19 2.000k. orange . . . . 7·50 11·50
NO20 5.000k. slate . . . . . 11·50 15·00

B. Central Annam.

NAO **3** "Family Left Behind"

1952. Issue for Central Annam. Imperf.
NAO 9 NAO **3** 0.050k. red . . . £180
NAO10 0.300k. red . . . £190
NAO11 0.300k. violet . . £190
NAO12 0.600k. green . . £190
NAO13 0.600k. blue . . . £375
NAO14 1000k. green . . . £375

1954. No. NA5 surch **TEMSU VU 0.k300 THOC.**
NAO15 NA **1** 0.300k. on 30d. on 5d. green £375 £275

1954. Nos. 56/7 of Vietnam Democratic Republic surch in **Kg.** No. NAO17 also optd **LKV** at top and **THOC** below value.
NAO16 **3** 0kg05 on 1h. green . . £190
NAO17 0kg050 on 3h. red . . . £190

1954. Surch **TEMSU VU** and new value. (a) On unsurcharged stamps with coloured (NAO20) or white (others) figures.
NAO20 NA **1** 0,750k. on 10d. mauve . . . . .
NAO21 0,800k. on 1d. violet . . . . .
NAO22 0,900k. on 5d. green . . . . .

(b) On stamps with coloured figures, previously surcharged.
NAO23 NA 1 0,030k. on 3d. on 35d. purple . . .
NAO24 0,050k. on 35d. on 300d. blue . . .
NAO25 0,350k. on 70d. on 100d. grey . . .

C. General issues.

1954. Dien-Bien-Phu Victory. As T **9** but value in "KILO". Imperf.
NO24 0.600k. ochre and sepia . . 13·50 7·50

1955. Surch **0 k, 100 THOC.**
NO33 **2** 0.100k. on 2d. brown . . £170 £130
NO34 0.100k. on 5d. red £170 £130

1955. Land Reform. As T **13** but inscr "SU VU".
NO38 40d. blue . . . . 10·50 5·75
NO39 80d. red . . . . 15·00 6·50

O **17** Cu Chinh Lan (Tank Destroyer)

1956. Cu Chinh Lan Commemoration.
NO50 O **17** 20d. green & turquoise . . . . . 3·50 3·50
NO51 80d. mauve and red 3·75 3·75
NO52 100d. sepia and drab 4·50 4·50
NO53 500d. blue & light blue . . . . 13·00 13·00
NO54 1000d. brown & orge 30·00 30·00
NO55 2000d. purple & green 45·00 45·00
NO56 3000d. lake and lilac 85·00 85·00

1957. 4th World T.U. Conference, Leipzig. As T **24** but inscr "SU VU".
NO69 20d. green . . . . 2·30 2·30
NO70 40d. blue . . . . 3·00 3·00
NO71 80d. lake . . . . 3·75 3·75
NO72 100d. brown . . . . . . 7·50 7·50

O **26** Mot Cot Pagoda, Hanoi

O **30** Lathe

1957.
NO75 O **26** 150d. brown and green . . . . . . 7·50 3·50
NO76 150d. black and yellow . . . . . . 8·25 3·50

1958. Arts and Crafts Fair, Hanoi.
NO83 O **30** 150d. black and pink 2·75 2·00
NO84 200d. blue and orange 3·50 2·75

O **31** Congress Symbol

1958. 1st World Congress of Young Workers, Prague.
NO85 O **31** 150d. red and green 2·75 1·40

O **34** Soldier, Factory and Crops

1958. Military Service.
NO91 O **34** 50d. blue and purple 2·00 70
NO92 150d. brown and green . . . . . . 2·75 90
NO93 200d. red and yellow 4·25 1·10

O **40** Footballer and Hanoi Stadium

1958. Opening of New Hanoi Stadium.
NO102 O **40** 10d. lilac and blue 75 30
NO103 20d. olive and salmon . . . . . 1·20 55
NO104 80d. brown and ochre . . . . . . 2·00 55
NO105 150d. brown & turq 3·50 1·10

O **97** Armed Forces on Boat

O **100** Woman with Rice-planter

1962. Miltiary Service.
NO223 O **97** 12x. multicoloured 5·00 1·90

1962. Rural Service.
NO229 O **100** 3x. red 55 55
NO230 6x. turquoise . . . 75 75
NO231 12x. olive . . . . . 1·00 1·00

O **176** Postman delivering Letter

1966. Rural Service.
NO445 O **176** 3x. purple, bistre and lilac 45 45
NO446 – 6x. purple, bistre and turquoise . . 60 60
DESIGN: 6x. As Type O **176** but design reversed.

POSTAGE DUE STAMPS

1952. Handstamped **TT** in diamond frame.
ND33 **3** 100d. green . . . . . . 55·00 45·00
ND34 100d. brown . . . . . . 55·00 45·00
ND35 **5** 100d. violet . . . . . . 55·00 49·00
ND36 **3** 200d. red . . . . 55·00 49·00

D **13** Letter Scales

D **39**

1955.
ND40 D **13** 50d. brown and lemon . . . . . . 12·00 9·00

1958.
ND101 D **39** 10d. red and violet 85 75
ND102 20d. green & orange 1·70 1·10
ND103 100d. red and slate 3·50 3·00
ND104 300d. red and olive 5·25 3·75

F. SOCIALIST REPUBLIC OF VIETNAM

Following elections in April 1976 a National Assembly representing the whole of Vietnam met in Hanoi on 24 June 1976 and on 2 July proclaimed the reunification of the country as the Socialist Republic of Vietnam, with Hanoi as capital.

100 xu = 1 dong.

18 Red Cross and Vietnam Map on Globe

1976. 30th Anniv of Vietnamese Red Cross.
99 **18** 12x. red, blue and green . . 1·90 40

20 Emperor Snapper

1976. Marine Fishes. Multicoloured.
102 12x. Type **20** 40 40
103 12x. Black-striped dottyback 40 40
104 20x. Tigerperch 45 40
105 30x. Two-striped anemonefish 55 40
106 40x. Stripe-tailed damselfish 60 40
107 50x. Pennant coralfish . . . 70 40
108 60x. Large-mouthed anemonefish 75 40
109 1d. Sail-finned snapper . . . 90 40

22 Party Flag and Map

1976. 4th Congress of Vietnam Workers' Party (1st issue). Flag in yellow and red, background colours given below.
111 **22** 2x. blue 45 40
112 3x. purple 45 40
113 5x. green 45 40
114 10x. green 45 40
115 12x. green 45 40
116 20x. green 45 40

23 Workers and Flag

24 Ho Chi Minh and Map of Vietnam

1976. 4th Congress of Vietnam Workers' Party (2nd issue).
117 **23** 12x. black, red and yellow 75 40
118 – 12x. red, orange and black 75 40
DESIGN: No. 118, Industry and agriculture.

1976. "Unification of Vietnam".
119 **24** 6x. multicoloured 90 40
120 12x. multicoloured 90 40

25 Soldiers seizing Buon Me Thuot

1976. Liberation of South Vietnam. Mult.
121 2x. Type **25** 40 40
122 3x. Soldiers on Son Tra peninsula, Da Nang . . . 40 40
123 6x. Soldiers attacking Presidential Palace, Saigon 40 40
124 50x. Type **25** 40 40
125 1d. As 3x. 75 40
126 2d. As 6x. . . . . 1·90 40

1976. As Nos. N848/9 but inscr "VIET NAM 1976" at foot and background colours changed.
126a **289** 6x. yellow, green & orange . . . . . . 1·90 1·10
126b 12x. yellow, light green and green . . . . . 1·90 1·10

26 "Crocothemis servilia" (Ho)

1977. Dragonflies. Multicoloured.
127 12x. Type **26** 40 10
128 12x. "Ictinogomphus clavatus" (Bao) 40 10
129 20x. "Rhinocypha fenestrella" 40 10
130 30x. "Neurothemis tullia" . . 40 10
131 40x. "Neurobavis chinensis" 75 10
132 50x. "Neurothemis fulvia" . . 90 10
133 60x. "Rhyothemis variegata" 90 20
134 1d. "Rhyothemis fuliginosa" 1·20 40

27 Great Indian Hornbill and Emblem of Protection

28 Thang Long Tower and Bronze Drum

1977. Rare Birds. Multicoloured.
135 12x. Type **27** 40 10
136 12x. Tickell's hornbill . . . 40 10
137 20x. Long-crested hornbill . . 45 10
138 30x. Wreathed hornbill . . . 55 10
139 40x. Indian pied hornbill . . 90 20
140 50x. Black hornbill 90 20
141 60x. Great Indian hornbill . . 1·20 40
142 1d. Rufous-necked hornbill 1·40 55

1977. 1st Anniv of National Assembly General Election.
143 **28** 4x. multicoloured 40 40
144 – 5x. multicoloured 45 40
145 – 12x. bistre, black and green 75 40
146 – 50x. multicoloured . . . . 1·50 75
DESIGNS: 5x. Map of Vietnam and drum; 12x. Lotus flower and drum; 50x. Vietnamese flag and drum.

29 "Anoplophora bowringii"

1977. Beetles. Multicoloured.
147 12x. Type **29** 40 10
148 12x. "Anoplophora horsfieldi" 40 10
149 20x. "Aphrodisium griffithi" 45 10
150 30x. Musk beetle 55 10
151 40x. "Calloplophora tonkinea" 60 15
152 50x. "Thysia wallacei" . . . 75 15
153 60x. "Aristobia approximator" 80 25
154 1d. "Batocera rubus" . . . . 1·40 55

30 "Thevetia peruviana"

1977. Wild Flowers. Multicoloured.
155 12x. Type **30** 25 10
156 12x. "Broussonetia papyrifera" 25 10
157 20x. "Aleurites montana" . . 40 10
158 30x. "Cerbera manghes" . . 40 10
159 40x. "Cassia multijuga" . . . 45 15
160 50x. "Cassia nodosa" 60 15
161 60x. "Hibiscus schizopetalus" 75 20
162 1d. "Lagerstroesnia speciosa" 1·10 55

31 Pink Dahlias (Hoa Dong Tien)

32 Children drawing Map of Vietnam

1977. Cultivated Flowers (1st series). Mult.
163 6x. Type **31** 75 15
164 6x. Orange cactus dahlias (Bong tien kep) 75 15
165 12x. Type **31** 75 15
166 12x. As No. 164 . . . . . . 75 15
See also Nos. 192/5.

1977. Unification of Vietnam.
167 **32** 4x. multicoloured 40 40
168 5x. multicoloured 40 40
169 10x. multicoloured 75 40
170 12x. multicoloured 75 40
171 30x. multicoloured . . . . 1·10 40

33 Goldfish (Dong Nai Hoa)

1977. Veil-tailed Goldfish. Multicoloured.
172 12x. Type **33** 25 10
173 12x. Hoa nhung 25 10
174 20x. Tau xanh 40 10
175 30x. Mat rong 40 10
176 40x. Cam trang 55 15
177 50x. Ngu sac 60 25
178 60x. Dong nai 75 25
179 1d. Thap cam . . . . 1·50 45

34 Ho Chi Minh and Lenin Banner

35 Southern Grackle

1977. 60th Anniv of Russian Revolution. Mult.
180 12x. Type **34** (blue background) 40 40
181 12x. Type **34** (bistre background) 40 40
182 50x. Mother holding child with flag 40 40
183 1d. Workers, banner, Moscow Kremlin and battleship "Aurora" . . . 1·10 40

1978. Songbirds. Multicoloured.
184 12x. Type **35** 15 10
185 20x. Spotted-neck dove . . . 25 10
186 20x. Melodious laughing thrush 25 10
187 30x. Black-headed shrike . . 40 10
188 40x. Crimson-winged laughing thrush 60 15
189 50x. Black-throated laughing thrush 75 15
190 60x. Chinese jungle mynah 1·10 25
191 1d. Yersin's laughing thrush 1·90 55

1978. Cultivated Flowers (2nd series). As T **31**. Multicoloured.
192 5x. Sunflower 90 15
193 6x. Marguerites 90 15
194 10x. As 5x. 90 15
195 12x. As 6x. 90 15

36 Vietnamese Children

37 Throwing the Discus

1978. International Children's Day.
196 **36** 12x. multicoloured . . . . 1·10 40

1978. Athletics. Multicoloured.
197 12x. Type **37** 25 10
198 12x. Long jumping 25 10
199 20x. Hurdling 30 10
200 30x. Throwing the hammer 40 10
201 40x. Putting the shot 45 15
202 50x. Throwing the javelin . . 55 15
203 60x. Sprinting 75 25
204 1d. High jumping 90 55

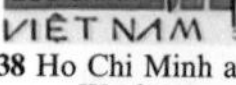
38 Ho Chi Minh and Workers

39 Ho Chi Minh

1978. 4th Vietnamese Trade Union Congress. Multicoloured.
205 10x. Trade Union Emblem 15 10
206 10x. Type **38** 25 10

1978. 88th Birth Anniv of Ho Chi Minh. Mult.
207 10x. Type **39** 75 40
208 12x. Ho Chi Minh Monument (38 × 22 mm) 75 40

40 Young Pioneers' Cultural House, Hanoi

1978. International Children's Day.
209 **40** 10x. black, flesh and red 90 40

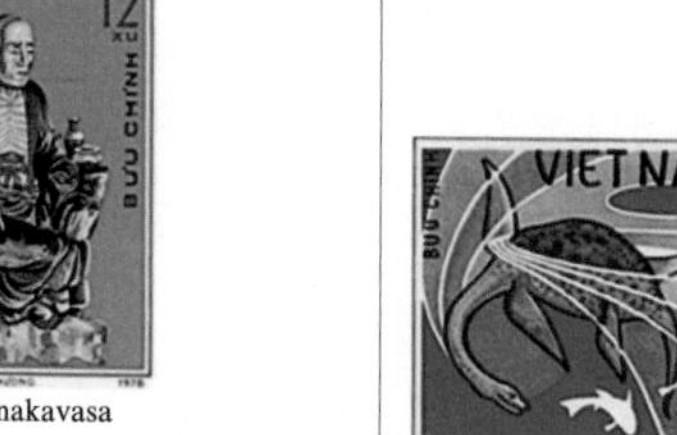
41 Sanakavasa

1978. Sculptures from Tay Phuong Pagoda. Mult.
210 12x. Type **41** 40 10
211 12x. Parsva 40 10
212 12x. Punyasas 40 10
213 20x. Kumarata 40 10
214 20x. Nagarjuna 40 10
215 30x. Yayata 40 10
216 40x. Cadiep 75 15
217 50x. Ananda 75 25
218 60x. Buddhamitra . . . . . 1·10 25
219 1d. Asvaghosa . . . . 1·90 25

42 Cuban Flag

43 Worker, Peasant, Soldier and Intellectual

1978. 25th Anniv of Cuban Revolution.
220 **42** 6x. red, black and blue . . 90 35
221 12x. red, black and blue . . 1·00 35

1978. 33rd Anniv of Proclamation of Vietnam Democratic Republic.
222 **43** 6x. red, yellow and mauve 60 40
223 – 6x. turquoise, green & blue 60 40
224 **43** 12x. red, yellow and mauve 90 40
225 – 12x. red and pink 90 75
DESIGN: Nos. 223 and 225, Industrial complex and tractor on field.

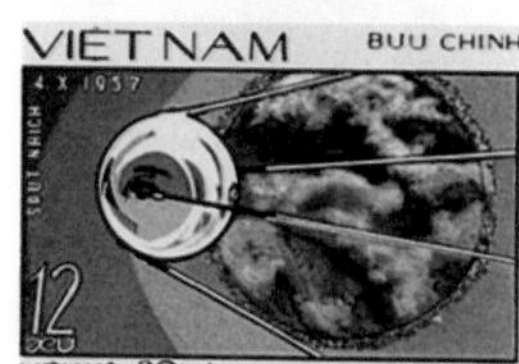
44 "Sputnik"

1978. 20 Years of Russian Space Exploration. Multicoloured.
226 12x. Type **44** 30 10
227 12x. "Venus 1" 30 10
228 30x. Space capsules docking 40 10
229 40x. "Molniya 1" satellite . . 60 15
230 60x. "Soyuz" 75 25
231 2d. A. Gubarev and G. Grechko . . . . 1·50 70

45 Printed Circuit

47 Chrysanthemum "Cuc Tim"

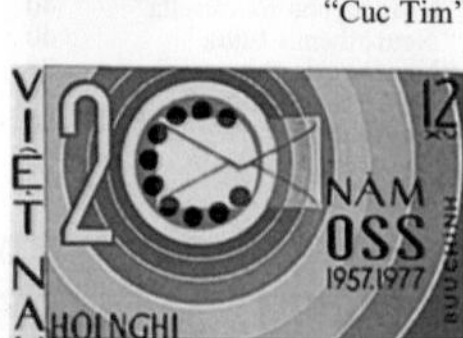
46 Telephone Dial and Letter

1978. World Telecommunications Day.
232 **45** 12x. orange and brown . . 90 40
233 – 12x. brown and orange . . 90 40
DESIGN: No. 233, I.T.U. emblem.

1978. 20th Congress of Socialist Countries' Postal Ministers.
234 **46** 12x. multicoloured . . . . 1·10 40

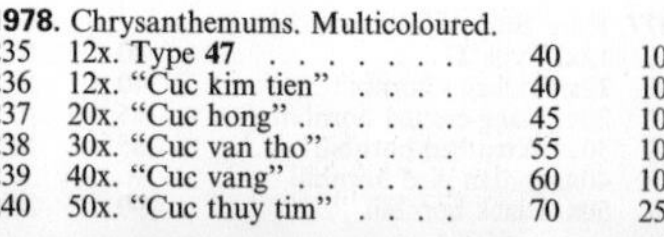

1978. Chrysanthemums. Multicoloured.
235 12x. Type **47** 40 10
236 12x. "Cuc kim tien" 40 10
237 20x. "Cuc hong" 45 10
238 30x. "Cuc van tho" 55 10
239 40x. "Cuc vang" 60 10
240 50x. "Cuc thuy tim" 70 25
241 60x. "Cuc vang mo" 75 25
242 1d. "Cuc nau do" . . . . . 1·40 45

48 Plesiosaurus

49 Cuban and Vietnamese Flags and Militiawomen

1979. Prehistoric Animals. Multicoloured.
243 12x. Type **48** 45 10
244 12x. Brontosaurus 45 10
245 20x. Iguanodon 60 10
246 30x. Tyrannosaurus 75 10
247 40x. Stegosaurus 90 10
248 50x. Mozasaurus . . . . . . 1·10 15
249 60x. Triceratop . . . . . . 1·40 25
250 1d. Pteranodon . . . . . . 1·90 40

1979. 20th Anniv of Socialist Republic of Cuba.
251 **49** 12x. multicoloured . . . . 1·10 40

50 Battle Plan

51 Einstein

1979. 190th Anniv of Quang Trung's Victory over the Thanh.
252 **50** 12x. green, red and blue . . 90 40
253 – 12x. multicoloured 90 40
DESIGN: No. 253, Quang Trung.

1979. Birth Cent of Albert Einstein (physicist).
254 **51** 12x. black, brown and blue 75 15
255 – 60x. multicoloured . . . 1·50 40
DESIGN: 60x. Equation, sun and planets.

52 Ram

53 Emblem

1979. Domestic Animals. Multicoloured.
256 10x. Type **52** 30 10
257 12x. Ox 30 10
258 20x. Ewe and lamb 40 10
259 30x. White buffalo (vert) . . 40 10
260 40x. Cow 40 10
261 50x. Goat 75 15
262 60x. Buffalo and calf 75 25
263 1d. Young goat (vert) 90 40

1979. Five Year Plan.
264 **53** 6x. mauve and light mauve 75 40
265 – 6x. green and buff 75 40
266 – 6x. green and purple . . . 75 40
267 – 6x. orange and green . . . 75 40
268 – 6x. blue and yellow 75 40
269 **53** 12x. red and pink 75 40
270 – 12x. brown and pink . . . 75 40
271 – 12x. green and yellow . . . 75 40
272 – 12x. blue and brown . . . 75 40
273 – 12x. purple and blue . . . 75 40
DESIGNS: Nos. 265, 270, Worker; 266, 271, Peasant and tractor; 267, 272, Soldier; 268, 273, Intellectual.

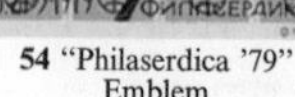
54 "Philaserdica '79" Emblem

55 Ho Chi Minh and Children

1979. "Philaserdica '79" International Stamp Exhibition, Sofia, Bulgaria.
274 **54** 12x. blue, brown & orange 90 40
275 30x. blue, brown and pink 90 40

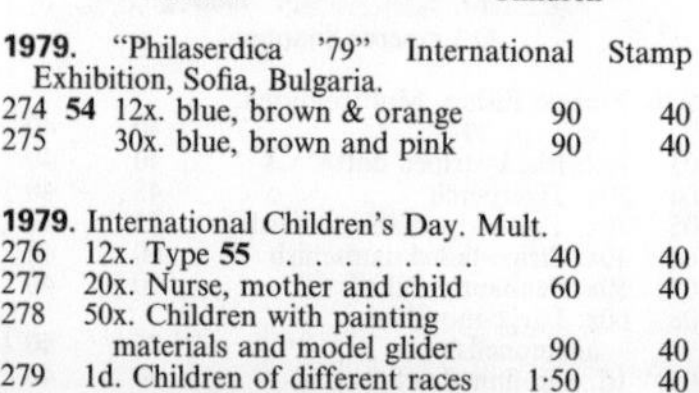

1979. International Children's Day. Mult.
276 12x. Type **55** 40 40
277 20x. Nurse, mother and child 60 40
278 50x. Children with painting materials and model glider 90 40
279 1d. Children of different races 1·50 40

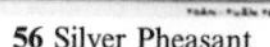
56 Silver Pheasant

58 Cat (Meo Muop)

57 "Dendrobium heterocacpum"

1979. Ornamental Birds. Multicoloured.
280 12x. Siamese fireback pheasant ("Lophura diardi") (horiz) 40 15
281 12x. Temminck's tragopan ("Tragopan temminckii") (horiz) 40 15
282 20x. Common pheasant (horiz) 40 15
283 30x. Edwards's pheasant (horiz) 40 15
284 40x. Type **56** 40 15
285 50x. Germain's peacock-pheasant 75 25
286 60x. Great argus pheasant . . 75 25
287 1d. Green peafowl . . . . . 1·50 45

1979. Orchids. Multicoloured.
288 12x. Type **57** 40 15
289 12x. "Cymbidium hybridum" 40 15
290 20x. "Rhynchostylis gigantea" 40 15
291 30x. "Dendrobium nobile" 40 15
292 40x. "Aerides falcatum" . . . 40 15
293 50x. "Paphiopedilum callosum" 75 25
294 60x. "Vanda teres" 75 25
295 1d. "Dendrobium phalaenopsis" . . . . . . 1·50 45

1979. Cats. Multicoloured.
296 12x. Type **58** 30 40
297 12x. Meo Tam The (horiz) 30 40
298 20x. Meo Khoang 30 40
299 30x. Meo Dom Van (horiz) 30 40
300 40x. Meo Muop Dom . . . 30 40
301 50x. Meo Vang 60 40
302 60x. Meo Xiem (horiz) . . . 90 40
303 1d. Meo Van Am (horiz) . . 1·40 40

60 Citizens greeting Soldiers

1979. 35th Anniv of Vietnam People's Army.
306 **60** 12x. brown and green . . . 40 40
307 – 12x. brown and green . . . 40 40
DESIGN: No. 307, Soldiers in action.

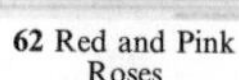
62 Red and Pink Roses

63 "Nelumbium nuciferum"

1980. Roses. Multicoloured.
311 1x. Type **62** 75 40
312 2x. Single pink rose 75 40
313 12x. Type **62** 75 40
314 12x. As No. 312 . . . . . . 75 40

1980. Water Flowers. Multicoloured.
315 12x. Type **63** 40 10
316 12x. "Nymphala stellata" . . 40 10
317 20x. "Ipomola reptans" . . . 45 10
318 30x. "Nymphoides indicum" 45 10
319 40x. "Jussiala repens" . . . 45 10
320 50x. "Eichhornia crassipes" 85 25
321 60x. "Monochoria voginalis" 90 25
322 1d. "Nelumbo nucifera" . . . 1·50 30

64 Peasants with Banner and Implements as Weapons

1980. 50th Anniv of Vietnamese Communist Party. Multicoloured.

323 12x. Type **64** 40 40
324 12x. Ho Chi Minh proclaiming independence 40 40
325 20x. Soldiers with flag at Dien Bien Phu 40 40
326 20x. Map of Vietnam and soldiers and tanks storming Palace (Unification of Vietnam) 40 40
327 2d. Ho Chi Minh, soldier and workers and industrial and agricultural scene . . . . . 1·90 40

65 Lenin

1980. 110th Birth Anniv of Lenin.

328 **65** 6x. flesh and green 40 40
329 12x. flesh and purple . . . 40 40
330 1d. flesh and blue . . . . 1·10 1·10

66 Running

67 Ho Chi Minh in 1924

1980. Olympic Games, Moscow. Multicoloured.

331 12x. Type **66** 40 10
332 12x. Hurdles 40 10
333 20x. Basketball 40 10
334 30x. Football 40 10
335 40x. Wrestling 40 10
336 50x. Gymnastics (horiz) . . . 75 15
337 60x. Swimming (horiz) . . . 75 25
338 1d. Sailing (horiz) . . . . . 1·50 40

1980. President Ho Chi Minh's 90th Birthday.

339 12x. Type **67** 45 40
340 40x. Ho Chi Minh as President . . . . 1·10 75

68 Children dancing around Globe

69 Soviet and Vietnamese Cosmonauts

1980. International Children's Day.

341 **68** 5x. multicoloured 75 40

1980. Soviet–Vietnamese Space Flight. Mult.

342 12x. Type **69** 40 10
343 12x. Launch of rocket . . . 40 10
344 20x. "Soyuz 37" 40 10
345 40x. "Soyuz–Salyut" space complex 75 10
346 1d. "Soyuz" re-entering Earth's atmosphere . . . . 1·50 25
347 2d. Parachute landing . . . . 3·25 55
MS348 111 × 91 mm. 3d. Cosmonauts and "Soyuz—Salyut" 4·50 4·50

70 Whale Shark

1980. Fishes. Multicoloured.

349 12x. Type **70** 30 15
350 12x. Tiger shark 30 15
351 20x. Bearded shark 40 15
352 30x. Zebra horn shark . . . 40 15
353 40x. Coachwhip stingray . . 55 25
354 50x. Wide sawfish 55 25
355 60x. Scalloped hammerhead 75 25
356 1d. Tobij-ei eagle ray . . . . 1·50 40

71 Ho Chi Minh telephoning

72 Pink Rose (Hong Bach)

1980. Posts and Telecommunications Day. Mult.

357 12x. Ho Chi Minh reading newspaper "Nhan Dan" 45 40
358 12x. Type **71** 55 40
359 50x. Kim Dong, "the heroic postman", carrying magpie robin in cage 75 40
360 1d. Dish aerial . . . . 1·50 40

1980. Flowers.

361 **72** 12x. pink and green . . . 75 40
362 – 12x. red and green 75 40
363 – 12x. mauve and green . . . 75 40

DESIGNS—As Type **72**: No. 362, Red roses (Hong nhung). 15 × 20 mm: No. 363, Camellia.

73 Telephone Switchboard Operator

74 Ho Chi Minh

1980. National Telecommunications Day.

364 12x. Type **73** 90 40
365 12x. Diesel train and railway route map 90 40

1980. 35th Anniv of Democratic Republic of Vietnam. Multicoloured.

366 12x. Type **74** 40 40
367 12x. Arms of Vietnam (29 × 40 mm) 40 40
368 40x. Pac Bo cave (29 × 40 mm) 75 40
369 1d. Source of Lenine (40 × 29 mm) . . . . . . 1·90 40

75 Vietnamese Arms

76 Nguyen Trai

1980. National Emblems.

370 **75** 6x. multicoloured . . . . 1·10 40
371 – 12x. yellow, red and black 1·10 40
372 – 12x. black, orange & yellow . . . . 1·10 40

DESIGNS—VERT: No. 372, National Anthem. HORIZ: No. 371, National flag.

1980. 600th Birth Anniv of Nguyen Trai (national hero).

373 **76** 12x. yellow and black . . . 40 40
374 – 50x. black and blue . . . 1·50 40
375 – 1d. black and brown . . . 2·30 40

DESIGNS—HORIZ: 50x. Three books by Nguyen Trai. VERT: 1d. Ho Chi Minh reading commemorative stele in Con Son Pagoda.

77 Ho Chi Minh with Women

78 "Biguoniaceae venusta"

1980. 50th Anniv of Vietnamese Women's Union.

376 **77** 12x. green, blue and lilac 60 40
377 – 12x. blue and lilac 60 40

DESIGN: No. 377, Group of women.

1980. Flowers. Multicoloured.

378 12x. Type **78** 40 10
379 12x. "Ipomoea pulchella" . . 40 10
380 20x. "Petunia hybrida" . . . 45 10
381 30x. "Trapaeolum majus" . . 45 10
382 40x. "Thunbergia grandiflora" 55 10
383 50x. "Anlamanda cathartica" 75 15
384 60x. "Campsis radicans" . . 85 25
385 1d. "Bougainvillaea spectabilis" . . . . 1·50 40

79 Blue Discus

1981. Ornamental Fishes. Multicoloured.

386 12x. Type **79** 40 40
387 12x. Siamese fighting fish . . 40 40
388 20x. Platy 45 40
389 30x. Guppy 45 40
390 40x. Tiger barb 55 40
391 50x. Freshwater angelfish . . 75 40
392 60x. Swordtail 85 40
393 1d. Pearl gourami . . . . . 1·50 40

80 Rocket, Flowers and Flag

82 Green Imperial Pigeon

81 Bear Macaque

1981. 26th U.S.S.R. Communist Party Congress. Multicoloured.

394 20x. Type **80** 40 40
395 50x. Young citizens with flag 1·50 40

1981. Animals of Cue Phuong Forest. Mult.

396 12x. Type **81** 40 15
397 12x. Crested gibbons 40 15
398 20x. Asiatic black bears . . . 45 15
399 30x. Dhole 55 15
400 40x. Wild boar 75 15
401 50x. Sambars 85 25
402 60x. Leopard 90 25
403 1d. Tiger . . . . 1·50 40

1981. Turtle Doves. Multicoloured.

404 12x. Type **82** 30 40
405 12x. Japanese green pigeon (horiz) 30 40
406 20x. Red-collared dove . . . 30 40
407 30x. Bar-tailed cuckoo dove 30 40
408 40x. Mountain imperial pigeon 45 40
409 50x. Pin-tailed green pigeon (horiz) 55 40
410 60x. Emerald dove (horiz) . . 85 40
411 1d. Yellow-vented pin-tailed green pigeon (horiz) . . . 1·50 40

83 Yellow-backed Sunbird

85 "Elaeagnus latifolia"

1981. Nectar-sucking Birds. Multicoloured.

412 20x. Type **83** 30 15
413 20x. Ruby-cheeked sunbird 30 15
414 30x. Black-throated sunbird 30 15
415 40x. Mrs. Gould's sunbird . . 30 15
416 50x. Macklot's sunbird . . . 60 25
417 50x. Blue-naped sunbird . . 60 25
418 60x. Van Hasselt's sunbird 85 25
419 1d. Green-tailed sunbird . . 1·30 40

1981. Fruits. Multicoloured.

422 20x. Type **85** 30 10
423 20x. "Fortunella japonica" 30 10
424 30x. "Nephelium lappaceum" 40 10
425 40x. "Averrhoa bilimbi" . . 40 10
426 50x. "Ziziphus mauritiana" 55 15
427 50x. Strawberries ("Fragaria vesca") 55 15
428 60x. "Bouea oppositifolia" 60 25
429 1d. "Syzygium aqueum" . . 1·10 40

86 Girl with Rice Sheaf

87 Ho Chi Minh planting Tree

1981. World Food Day.

430 **86** 30x. green 45 40
431 50x. green 60 40
432 – 2d. orange . . . . 2·00 40

DESIGN: 2d. F.A.O. emblem and rice.

1981. Tree Planting Festival.

433 **87** 30x. orange and blue . . . 70 25
434 – 30x. pink and blue 70 25

DESIGN: No. 434, Family planting tree.

88 European Bison

1981. Animals. Multicoloured.

435 30x. Type **88** 40 10
436 30x. Orang-utan 40 10
437 40x. Hippopotamus 45 15
438 40x. Red kangaroo 45 15
439 50x. Giraffe 60 15
440 50x. Javan rhinoceros 60 15
441 60x. Common zebra 75 25
442 1d. Lion 90 45

89 Congress Emblem

1982. 10th World Trade Unions Congress, Havana, Cuba.

443 **89** 50x. multicoloured 75 40
444 5d. multicoloured . . . . 3·00 40

90 Ho Chi Minh and Party Flag

1982. 5th Vietnamese Communist Party Congress (1st issue). Multicoloured.

445 30x. Type **90** 75 40
446 30x. Hammer, sickle and rose 75 40

See also Nos. 455/6.

91 "Thyreus decorus" (carpenter bee)

1982. Bees and Wasps. Multicoloured.
447 20x. Type **91** 40 10
448 20x. "Vespa affinis" (wasp) 40 10
449 30x. "Eumenes esuriens" (mason wasp) 40 10
450 40x. "Polistes 45 15
451 50x. "Sphex sp." (wasp) . . . 60 25
452 50x. "Chlorion lobatum" (wasp) 60 25
453 60x. "Xylocopa sp." (carpenter bee) 85 25
454 1d. Honey bee 90 45

92 Electricity Worker and Pylon

1982. 5th Vietnamese Communist Party Congress (2nd issue).
455 **92** 30x. stone, black and mauve 75 40
456 – 50x. multicoloured . . . . 1·10 40
DESIGN: 50x. Women harvesting rice.

93 Football

1982. Football Training Movement.
457 **93** 30x. multicoloured 30 10
458 – 30x. multicoloured (Two players) 30 10
459 – 40x. multicoloured 40 10
460 – 40x. multicoloured (diag striped background) . . 40 15
461 – 50x. multicoloured (vert striped background) . . 55 15
462 – 50x. multicoloured (horiz striped background) . . 55 15
463 – 60x. multicoloured 60 25
464 – 1d. multicoloured . . . . 1·10 40
DESIGNS: Nos. 458/64, Various football scenes.

94 Militiawoman

1982.
465 **94** 30x. multicoloured . . . . 1·10 75
See also Nos. MF466/7.

95 Arms of Bulgaria

1982. 1300th Anniv of Bulgarian State.
468 **95** 30x. pink and red 45 40
469 50x. stone and red 90 40
470 2d. orange and red . . . . 2·40 40

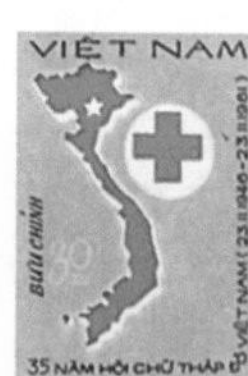
96 Map of Vietnam and Red Cross

97 Georgi Dimitrov

1982. 35th Anniv of Vietnamese Red Cross.
471 **96** 30x. red, blue and black . . 55 40
472 – 1d. red, green and black 1·90 40
DESIGN: 1d. Red Cross.

1982. Birth Centenary of Georgi Dimitrov (Bulgarian statesman).
473 **97** 30x. orange and black . . 40 40
474 3d. brown and black . . . 3·50 40

98 Rejoicing Women

99 Common Kestrel

1982. 5th National Women's Congress. Mult.
475 12x. Type **98** 75 40
476 12x. Congress emblem and three women 75 40

1982. Birds of Prey. Multicoloured.
477 30x. Type **99** 40 10
478 30x. Pied falconet 40 10
479 40x. Black baza 45 10
480 50x. Black kite 60 15
481 50x. Lesser fishing eagle . . . 60 15
482 60x. White-rumped pygmy falcon (horiz) 75 15
483 1d. Black-shouldered kite (horiz) . . . . 1·50 55
484 1d. Short-toed eagle . . . . 1·50 55

100 Red Dahlia

101 Dribble

1982. Dahlias. Multicoloured.
485 30x. Type **100** 40 10
486 30x. Orange dahlia 40 10
487 40x. Rose dahlia 45 10
488 50x. Red decorative dahlia 60 15
489 50x. Yellow dahlia 60 15
490 60x. Red single dahlia . . . 75 25
491 1d. White dahlia . . . . . . 1·10 55
492 1d. Pink dahlia . . . . . . 1·10 55

1982. World Cup Football Championship, Spain. Multicoloured.
493 50x. Type **101** 60 40
494 50x. Tackle 60 40
495 50x. Passing ball 60 40
496 1d. Heading ball 90 40
497 1d. Goalkeeper saving ball 90 40
498 2d. Shooting . . . . 2·40 40

102 Cuban Flag

104 Rabindranath Tagore

103 Ho Chi Minh and Children planting Tree

1982. 20th Anniv of Cuban Victory at Giron.
499 **102** 30x. multicoloured . . . 1·10 40

1982. World Environment Day.
500 **103** 30x. green and black . . . 75 40
501 – 30x. green and black . . . 75 40
DESIGN: No. 501, U.N. environment emblem and plants.

1982. 120th Birth Anniv (1981) of Rabindranath Tagore (Indian poet).
502 **104** 30x. orange, brown and black . . . . 1·10 40

105 "Sycanus falleni" (soldier bug)

106 Lenin and Cruiser "Aurora"

1982. Harmful Insects. Multicoloured.
503 30x. Type **105** 30 10
504 30x. "Catacanthus incarnatus" (shieldbug) . . 30 10
505 40x. "Nezara viridula" (shield-bug) 30 10
506 50x. "Helcomeria spinosa" (squashbug) 45 15
507 50c. "Lohita grandis" (fire bug) 45 15
508 60x. "Chrysocoris stolli" (shieldbug) 55 25
509 1d. "Tiarodes ostentans" (soldier bug) . . . . . . 1·10 55
510 1d. "Pterygamia grayi" (squashbug) . . . . 1·10 55

1982. 65th Anniv of Russian Revolution.
511 **106** 30x. red and black . . . 75 40
512 – 30x. red and black . . . 75 40
DESIGN: No. 512, Russian man and woman, Lenin and space station.

108 Swimming

1982. 9th South East Asian Games, New Delhi.
514 **108** 30x. blue and lilac 75 40
515 – 30x. blue and mauve . . . 75 40
516 – 1d. orange and blue . . . 1·10 40
517 – 2d. green and brown . . . 1·50 40
DESIGNS: 30x. (No. 515) Table tennis; 1d. Wrestling; 2d. Rifle shooting.

109 Gray's Crested Flounder

1982. Fishes. Soles. Multicoloured.
518 30x. Type **109** 40 10
519 30x. Chinese flounder 40 10
520 40x. Queensland halibut ("Psettodes erumei") . . . 45 10
521 40x. Zebra sole ("Zebrias zebra") 45 10
522 50x. Peacock sole ("Pardachirus pavoninus") 60 15
523 50x. Spotted tonguesole ("Cynoglossus puncticeps") 60 15
524 60x. Oriental sole 75 30
525 1d. Iijima lefteye flounder . . 90 45

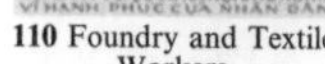
110 Foundry and Textile Workers

112 Sampan

111 Lenin on Map

1982. "All for the Socialist Fatherland, All for Happiness of the People".
526 **110** 30x. light blue and blue 60 40
527 – 30x. brown and yellow . . 55 40
528 – 1d. brown and green . . . 1·10 40
529 – 2d. pink and purple . . . 2·30 40
DESIGNS: 30x. Women holding sheaf of wheat and basket of grain; 1d. Soldiers; 2d. Nurse with children holding books.

1982. 60th Anniv of U.S.S.R.
530 **111** 30x. multicolouired . . . 1·90 40

1983. Boats. Multicoloured.
531 30x. Type **112** 40 10
532 50x. Junk with striped sails 45 10
533 1d. Houseboats 55 15
534 3d. Junk 90 25
535 5d. Sampan with patched sails . . . . 1·50 40
536 10d. Sampan (horiz) . . . . 2·30 1·00

113 Type 231-300

1983. Steam Railway Locomotives. Multicoloured.
537 30x. Type **113** 25 10
538 50x. Type 230-000 . . . . . 40 10
539 1d. Type 140-601 . . . . . 45 15
540 2d. Type 241-000 . . . . . 75 30
541 3d. Type 141-500 . . . . . 1·10 30
542 5d. Type 150-000 . . . . . 1·50 55
543 8d. Type 40-300 . . . . . . 2·00 85

114 Montgolfier Balloon, 1783

1983. Bicentenary of Manned Flight. Mult.
544 30x. Type **114** 25 10
545 50x. Charles's hydrogen balloon, 1783 . . . . . . 40 10
546 1d. Parseval Sigsfeld kite-type observation balloon, 1898 45 15
547 2d. Eugene Godard's balloon "L'Aigle", 1864 . . . . 90 25
548 3d. Blanchard and Jeffries' balloon, 1785 . . . . . 1·10 25
549 5d. Nadar's balloon "Le Geant", 1863 . . . . . . 1·50 40
550 8d. Balloon . . . . 2·30 60
MS551 70 × 80 mm. 10d. Montgolfier balloon (different) (31 × 31 mm) . . . . 4·50 1·50

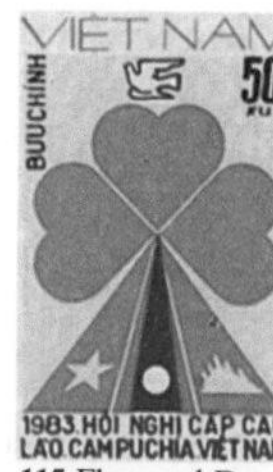
115 Flags and Dove

1983. Laos–Kampuchea–Vietnam Summit Conf.
552 **115** 50x. red, yellow and blue 40 40
553 5d. red, blue and yellow 2·30 40

116 Robert Koch

1983. Centenary of Discovery of Tubercle Bacillus.
554 **116** 5d. black, blue and red 2·30 75

117 "Teratolepis fasciata"

1983. Reptiles. Multicoloured.
555 30x. Type **117** 25 40
556 30x. Jackson's chameleon . . 25 40
557 50x. Spiny-tailed agamid . . 40 40
558 80x. "Heloderma suspectum" 45 40
559 1d. "Chamaeleo meileri" . . 55 40
560 2d. "Amphibolurus barbatus" 1·10 40
561 5d. "Chlamydosaurus kingi" 1·50 40
562 10d. "Phrynosoma coronatum" . . . . 2·75 40

118 A. Gubarev and V. Remek

1983. Cosmonauts. Multicoloured.
563 30x. Type **118** 40 10
564 50x. P. Klimuk and Miroslaw Hermaszewski 40 10
565 50x. V. Bykovsky and Sigmund Jahn 40 10
566 1d. Nikolai Rukavishnikov and Georgi Ivanov 40 10
567 1d. Bertalan Farkas and V. Kubasov 40 10
568 2d. V. Gorbatko and Pham Tuan 75 25
569 2d. Arnaldo Tamayo Mendez and I. Romanenko 75 25
570 5d. V. Dzhanibekov and Gurragcha . . . . 1·50 40
571 8d. L. Popov and D. Prunariu . . . . 1·90 60
MS572 80 × 80 mm. 10d. Yuri Gagarin (first man in space) (36 × 28 mm) . . . . 3·75 1·50

119 "Madonna of the Chair"

121 Burmese King and Rook

1983. 500th Birth Anniv of Raphael (artist). Mult.
573 30x. Type **119** 25 10
574 50x. "Madonna of the Grand Duke" 40 10
575 1d. "Sistine Madonna" . . . 55 10
576 2d. "The Marriage of Mary" 90 25
577 3d. "The Beautiful Gardener" 1·10 30
578 5d. "Woman with Veil" . . . 1·50 45
579 8d. "Self-portrait" . . . . . 1·90 70
MS580 93 × 71 mm. 10d. Close-up of "Self-portrait" . . . . 5·00 1·50

1983. Chess Pieces. Multicoloured.
582 30x. Type **121** 25 10
583 50x. 18th-century Delhi king (elephant) 30 10
584 1d. Lewis knight and bishop 45 10
585 2d. 8th/9th-century Arabian king (elephant) 75 25
586 3d. 12th-century European knight . . . . 1·10 30
587 5d. 16th-century Russian rook (sailing boat) . . . . 1·50 45
588 8d. European Chinese-puzzle bishop and rook (fool and elephant) . . . . 1·90 70
MS589 77 × 79 mm. 10d. Abstract king and queen (28 × 36 mm) 6·00 1·50

122 Coach and Horse

1983. "Tembal '83" International Stamp Exhibition, Basel. Sheet 90 × 70 mm.
MS590 **122** 10d. multicoloured 4·50 1·50

123 Long Jumping

124 Toco Toucan

1983. Olympic Games, Los Angeles (1984). Mult.
591 30x. Type **123** 40 10
592 50x. Running 40 15
593 1d. Javelin throwing 40 10
594 2d. High jumping (horiz) . . 75 25
595 3d. Hurdling (horiz) . . . . 1·10 30
596 5d. Putting the shot . . . . 1·50 45
597 8d. Pole vaulting . . . . . . 1·90 70
MS598 82 × 71 mm. 10d. Throwing the discus (31 × 39 mm) . . . . 5·25 1·50

1983. "Brasiliana '83" International Stamp Exhibition, Rio de Janeiro. Sheet 69 × 95 mm.
MS599 **124** 10d. multicoloured 4·50 1·50

125 Common Grass Yellow

128 Karl Marx

127 Steam Car

1983. Butterflies. Multicoloured.
600 30x. Type **125** 40 40
601 30x. Green dragontail ("Leptocircus meges") . . 40 40
602 40x. "Nyctalemon patroclus" 45 40
603 40x. Tailed jay ("Zetides agamemnon") 45 40
604 50x. Peacock ("Precis almana") 75 40
605 50x. "Papilio chaon" 75 40
606 60x. Tufted jungle king . . . 90 40
607 1d. Leaf buttefly . . . . . . 1·40 40

1983. "Bangkok 1983" International Stamp Exhibition. Sheet 102 × 67 mm.
MS616 **127** 10d. multicoloured 7·50 1·50

1983. Death Centenary of Karl Marx.
617 **128** 50x. black and red . . . 75 40
618 10d. black and purple . . 3·00 75

129 Postman

1983. World Communications Year. Mult.
619 50x. Type **129** 25 25
620 2d. Mail sorting office . . . 75 40
621 8d. Telephonists . . . . . . 1·70 40
622 10d. Wireless operator and dish aerial . . . . 2·30 55
MS623 77 × 64 mm. 10d. Telephone, air mail envelope, dish aerial, truck and boat . . . . 3·00 1·50

130 Running, Stadium and Sports Pictograms

1983. National Youth Sports Festival.
624 **130** 30x. blue and turquoise 40 40
625 1d. brown and orange . . 1·50 40

131 Oyster Fungus ("Pleurotus ostreatus")

1983. Fungi. Multicoloured.
626 50x. Type **131** 40 40
627 50x. Common ink cap ("Coprinus atramentarius") 40 40
628 50x. Golden mushroom ("Flammulina velutipes") 40 40
629 50x. Chanterelle ("Cantharellus cibarius") 40 40
630 1d. Chinese mushroom . . . 75 40
631 2d. Red-staining mushroom 1·10 40
632 5d. Common morel . . . . . 2·30 40
633 10d. Caesar's mushroom . . 3·75 40

132 Child with Fish

1983. World Food Day. Multicoloured.
634 50x. Type **132** 40 40
635 4d. Family . . . . 1·50 40

133 Envelope with I.T.U. Emblem

1983. World Telecommunications Year.
636 **133** 50x.+10x. blue, green & red . . . . 1·10 40
637 – 50x.+10x. red, buff and brown . . . . 1·10 40
DESIGN: No. 637, W.C.Y. emblem and dish aerial.

134 Building Dam

1983. 5th Anniv of U.S.S.R.–Vietnam Co-operation Treaty.
638 – 20x. green and yellow . . 1·50 1·50
639 – 50x. chestnut and brown 2·30 1·50
640 **134** 4d. grey and black . . . 7·50 1·50
641 20d. pink and brown . . 26·00 1·50
DESIGNS: 20x. Building Cultural Palace; 50x. Building road/rail bridge.

135 Girl with Flowers

1983. 5th Trade Unions Congress.
642 **135** 50x. blue, orange and black 40 40
643 – 2d. black, blue and brown 75 40
644 – 30d. black, blue and pink 4·50 75
DESIGNS: 2, 30d. Worker and industrial complex.

136 Grey Herons

137 Conference Emblem and Hands

1983. Birds. Multicoloured.
645 50x. Type **136** 40 40
646 50x. Painted storks ("Ibis leucocephalus") 40 40
647 50x. Black storks ("Ciconia nigra") 40 40
648 50x. Purple herons ("Ardea purpurea") 40 40
649 1d. Common cranes 55 40
650 2d. Black-faced spoonbills . . 75 40
651 5d. Black-crowned night herons . . . . 1·90 40
652 10d. Asian open-bill storks 2·75 40

1983. World Peace Conference, Prague.
653 – 50x. blue, red and yellow 15 15
654 **137** 3d. green, red and yellow 1·10 40
655 5d. lilac, red and yellow 2·30 60
656 20d. blue, red and yellow 4·50 75
DESIGN: 50x. Conference emblem and women.

138 Biathlon

140 Orchid Tree

139 Marbled Cat

1984. Winter Olympic Games, Sarajevo. Mult.
657 50x. Type **138** 40 10
658 50x. Cross-country skiing . . 40 10
659 1d. Speed skating 45 10
660 2d. Bobsleighing 75 25
661 3d. Ice hockey (horiz) . . . . 1·10 30
662 5d. Ski jumping (horiz) . . . 1·50 45
663 6d. Slalom (horiz) . . . . . 1·90 70
MS664 72 × 88 mm. 20d. Ice skating (39 × 31 mm) . . . . 3·75 1·50

1984. Protected Animals. Multicoloured.
665 50x. Type **139** 25 10
666 50x. Leopard 25 10
667 50x. Tiger 25 10
668 1d. Common gibbon 45 15
669 1d. Slow loris 45 15
670 2d. Indian elephant . . . . . 1·30 25
671 2d. Gaur . . . . 1·30 25

1984. Flowers. Multicoloured.
672 50x. Type **140** 40 10
673 50x. "Caesalpinia pulcherrima" 40 10
674 1d. Golden shower 40 10
675 2d. Flamboyant 75 15
676 3d. "Artabotrys uncinatus" 1·10 45
677 5d. "Corchorus olitorius" . . 1·50 70
678 8d. "Bauhinia grandiflora" 1·90 90
MS679 70 × 106 mm. 10d. As No. 675 but with inscriptions rearranged . . . . 3·75 1·50

141 "Brasse cattleya"

144 White Storks

143 Flyingfish

1984. Orchids. Multicoloured.
680 50x. Type **141** 25 10
681 50x. "Cymbidium sp." . . . 25 10
682 1d. "Cattleya dianx" var. "alba" 40 10
683 2d. "Cymbidium sp." (different) 75 25
684 3d. "Cymbidium hybridum" 1·10 30
685 5d. Phoenix-winged orchids 1·50 45
686 8d. Yellow queen orchids . . 1·90 70

1984. Nos. 362 and 373 surch **50xu.**
687 – 50x. on 12x. red and green 1·50 40
688 **76** 50x. on 12x. yellow and black . . . . 1·50 40

1984. Deep Sea Fishes. Multicoloured.
688a 30x. Type **143** 15 15
688b 30x. Long-horned cowfish 15 15
688c 50x. Porcupinefish 40 40
688d 80x. Copper-banded butterflyfish 45 40
688e 1d. Bearded anglerfish . . . 45 40
688f 2d. Plane-tailed lionfish . . 75 40
688g 5d. Oceanic sunfish . . . . 1·50 45
688h 10d. Lionfish . . . . 2·30 75

1984. "Espana 84" International Stamp Exhibition, Madrid. Sheet 81 × 80 mm.
MS689 **144** 10d. multicoloured 4·50 1·50

146 Ho Chi Minh discussing Battle Plan

1984. 30th Anniv of Battle of Dien Bien Phu. Multicoloured.

691 50x. Type **146** 30 10
692 50x. Vietnamese soldiers and truck 30 10
693 1d. Students carrying provisions 45 10
694 2d. Pulling field gun up hill 60 25
695 3d. Anti-aircraft gun and crashed airplane 75 30
696 5d. Fighting against tanks 1·20 45
697 8d. Vietnamese soldiers with flag on bunker 1·70 70
MS698 99 × 110 mm. 10d. Type **146** (36 × 26 mm) 3·75 1·50

147 Junkers Ju 52/3m

1984. Universal Postal Union, Congress, Hamburg and 50th Anniv of First South Atlantic Air Service. Sheet 68 × 60 mm.

MS699 **147** 10d. multicoloured 4·25 1·50

148 Three-spotted Gourami

1984. Fishes. Multicoloured.

700 50x. Type **148** 15 10
701 50x. Zebra danio 15 10
702 1d. Paradise fish 40 15
703 2d. Black widow tetra 60 30
704 3d. Serpa tetra 75 45
705 5d. Red-tailed black shark 1·10 75
706 8d. Siamese fightingfish 1·90 1·30

149 Nguyen Duc Canh

1984. 55th Anniv of Vietnamese Trade Union Movement.

707 **149** 50x. red and black 15 15
708 – 50x. red and black 15 15
709 – 1d. multicoloured 45 15
710 – 2d. multicoloured 75 30
711 – 3d. multicoloured 1·10 45
712 – 5d. multicoloured 1·50 90
MS713 99 × 98 mm. 2d. multicoloured. Imperf 7·50 7·50

DESIGNS—VERT: No. 708, Founder's house. HORIZ: No. 709, Workers presenting demands to employer; 710, **MS**713, Ho Chi Minh with workers; 711, Factory; 712, Workers, procession and doves.

150 Hon Dua

1984. Coastal Scenes. Multicoloured.

714 50x. Type **150** 30 10
715 50x. Hang Con Gai 30 10
716 50x. Hang Bo Nau 30 10
717 50x. Nui Yen Ngua 30 10
718 1d. Hon Ga Choi 45 15
719 1d. Hon Coc 45 15
720 2d. Hon Dinh Huong 60 25
721 3d. Hon Su Tu 75 30
722 5d. Hon Am 1·20 55
723 8d. Nui Bai Tho 1·50 85

151 Styracosaurus

1984. Prehistoric Animals. Multicoloured.

724 50x. Type **151** 55 40
725 50x. Diplodocus 55 40
726 1d. Rhamphorhynchus 85 40
727 1d. Corythosaurus 85 40
728 2d. Seymouria 1·10 40
729 3d. Allosaurus 1·50 40
730 5d. Dimetrodon 2·30 40
731 8d. Brachiosaurus 3·75 40

153 Dove and Flags

155 Students and Cultural and Industrial Motifs

154 Koala

1984. Laos–Kampuchea–Vietnam Co-operation.

733 **153** 50x. red, blue and yellow 15 15
734 10d. red, blue and yellow 3·50 60

1984. Ausipex 84 International Stamp Exhibition, Melbourne.

MS735 **154** 10d. multicoloured 7·50 1·50

1984. 5th Anniv of Kampuchea–Vietnam Friendship Treaty. Multicoloured.

736 50x. Type **155** 15 15
737 3d. Type **155** 1·10 60
738 50d. Kampuchean and Vietnamese dancers 6·50 75

156 Bridge

1984. 30th Anniv of Liberation of Hanoi.

739 **156** 50x. green and yellow 60 40
740 – 1d. brown and red 1·10 40
741 – 2d. brown and mauve 1·70 40

DESIGNS: 1d. Gateway; 2d. Ho Chi Minh mausoleum.

157 Vis-a-vis

160 "Madonna and Child with St. John"

159 "Lenin" (V. A. Serov)

1984. Motor Cars. Multicoloured.

743 50x. Type **157** 25 15
744 50x. Two-seater 25 15
745 1d. Tonneau 40 15
746 2d. Double phaeton 60 30
747 3d. Landaulet 75 45
748 5d. Torpedo 90 60
749 6d. Town coupe 1·40 70

1984. 60th Death Anniv of Lenin. Multicoloured.

751 50x. Type **159** 30 15
752 1d. Painting by A. Plotnov of Lenin at meeting 45 15
753 3d. Painting by K. V. Filatov of Lenin at factory 90 45
754 5d. Painting by V. A. Serov of Lenin with three comrades 1·40 70

1984. 450th Death Anniv of Correggio (artist). "Madonna and Child" Paintings. Multicoloured.

755 50x. Type **160** 15 15
756 50x. Bolognini Madonna 15 15
757 1d. Campori Madonna 30 15
758 2d. "Virgin adoring the Child" 60 30
759 3d. "Madonna della Cesta" 75 45
760 5d. "Madonna della Scodella" 1·10 60
761 6d. "Madonna and Child with Angels" 1·50 70
MS762 59 × 73 mm. 10d. "Madonna and Child with St. Catherine" (31 × 39 mm) 4·50 1·90

161 "Keep the Peace" (Le Quoc Loc)

1984. UNICEF. Multicoloured.

763 30x. Type **161** 15 15
764 50x. "Sunday" (Nguyen Tien Chung) 15 15
765 1d. "Baby of the Mining Region" (Tran Van Can) 30 15
766 3d. "Little Thuy" (Tran Van Can) (vert) 75 30
767 5d. "Children at Play" (Nguyen Phan Chanh) 1·10 70
768 10d. "After Guard Duty" (Nguyen Phan Chanh) (vert) 2·30 1·20

162 Mounted Frontier Guards

163 Water Buffalo

1984. 25th Anniv of Frontier Forces.

769 **162** 50x. black, blue and brown 15 15
770 30d. black, green & turq 8·25 1·70

1984.

771 **163** 20x. brown 10 10
772 – 30x. red 10 10
773 – 50x. green 15 10
774 – 50x. red 15 10
775 – 50x. mauve 15 10
776 – 50x. brown 15 10
777 – 1d. violet 40 15
778 – 1d. orange 40 15
779 – 1d. blue 40 15
780 – 1d. blue 40 15
781 – 2d. brown 85 40
782 – 2d. orange 85 40
783 – 2d. red 85 40
784 – 5d. mauve 2·30 55
785 – 10d. green 3·75 1·10

DESIGNS: No. 772, Marbled cat; 773, Siamese fighting fish; 774, Cabbage rose; 775, Hibiscus; 776, Lesser panda; 777, "Chrysanthemum sinense"; 778, Tiger; 779, Water lily; 780, Eastern white pelican; 781, Slow loris; 782, Dahlia; 783, Crab-eating macaque; 784, Tokay gecko; 785, Great Indian hornbill.

165 Ho Chi Minh and Troops

1984. 40th Anniv of Vietnamese People's Army. Multicoloured.

787 50x. Type **165** 25 15
788 50x. Oath-taking ceremony 25 15
789 1d. Soldier with flag and Boeing B-52 Stratofortress bomber on fire 40 15
790 2d. Civilians building gun emplacement 60 25
791 5d. Soldiers and tank breaking through gates 85 40
792 5d. Soldier instructing civilians 1·10 85
793 8d. Map and soldiers 1·50 1·10
MS794 78 × 58 mm. 10d. Flag and Vietnamese soldiers, sailor and airman 3·00 1·50

166 Boy on Buffalo

167 "Echinocereus knippelianus"

1985. New Year. Year of the Buffalo.

795 **166** 3d. purple and pink 90 40
796 5d. brown and orange 1·40 40

1985. Flowering Cacti. Multicoloured.

797 50x. Type **167** 25 25
798 50x. "Lemaireocereus thurberi" 25 25
799 1d. "Notocactus haselbergii" 45 40
800 2d. "Parodia chrysacanthion" 75 40
801 3d. "Pelecyphora pseudopectinata" 1·10 40
802 5d. "Rebutia frebrighii" 1·50 40
803 8d. "Lobivia aurea" 1·80 55

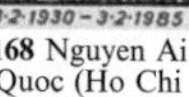

168 Nguyen Ai Quoc (Ho Chi Minh)

169 Soldiers with Weapons

1985. 55th Anniv of Vietnam Communist Party.

804 **168** 2d. grey and red 75 40

1985. 10th Anniv of Reunification of South Vietnam. Multicoloured.

805 1d. Type **169** 40 40
806 2d. Soldiers and tank 75 40
807 4d. Soldier and oil rig 1·10 40
808 5d. Map, flag and girls 1·50 40
MS809 65 × 90 mm. 10d. As No. 806 3·00 1·70

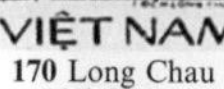

170 Long Chau Lighthouse

172 Soviet Memorial, Berlin-Treptow

171 Ho Chi Minh and Soldiers

1985. 30th Anniv of Liberation of Haiphong.

810 **170** 2d. multicoloured 60 40
811 – 5d. multicoloured 1·30 40
MS812 110 × 75 mm. 10d. brown and green 2·75 1·50

DESIGN—HORIZ: 5d. An Duong bridge. VERT: 10d. To Hieu (Communist Party official in Haiphong).

1985. 95th Birth Anniv of Ho Chi Minh (President). Multicoloured.

813 1d. Type **171** 40 15
814 2d. Ho Chi Minh reading in cave at Viet Bac 60 30
815 4d. Portrait (vert) 90 60
816 5d. Ho Chi Minh writing in garden of Presidential Palace 1·10 85
MS817 74 × 99 mm. 10d. As No. 815 but smaller (28 × 35 mm) 3·00 1·30

1985. 40th Anniv of Victory in Europe Day. Multi.

818 1d. Type **172** 40 15
819 2d. Soldier and fist breaking swastika 60 25

820 4d. Hand releasing dove and eagle falling . . . 1·30 55
821 5d. Girl releasing doves . . . 1·50 70
MS822 115 × 78 mm. 10d. Type **172** 3·00 1·50

173 Globe and People carrying Flags

1985. 12th World Youth and Students' Festival, Moscow. Multicoloured.
823 2d. Type **173** 75 40
824 2d. Workers, pylons and dish aerial 75 40
825 4d. Coastguards and lighthouse . . . . 1·10 40
826 5d. Youths and balloons . . 1·50 40
MS827 82 × 100 mm. 10d. Main motif of Type **173** and plan of Moscow Kremlin (39 × 32 mm) 2·75 1·30

174 Daimler, 1885

1985. Centenary of Motor Cycle. Multicoloured.
828 1d. Type **174** (wrongly inscr "1895") 30 15
829 1d. Three-wheeled vehicle, France, 1898 . . . . . . 30 15
830 2d. Harley Davidson, U.S.A., 1913 . . . . 45 40
831 2d. Cleveland, U.S.A., 1918 45 40
832 3d. Simplex, U.S.A., 1935 . . 75 40
833 4d. Minarelli, Italy, 1984 . . 90 40
834 6d. Honda, Japan, 1984 . . . 1·40 75
MS835 82 × 48 mm. 10d. Honda, Japan, 1984 (31 × 39 mm) . . . 3·00 1·30

175 King Penguin

1985. "Argentina '85". International Stamp Exhibition, Buenos Aires. Multicoloured.
836 1d. Type **175** 45 15
837 1d. Patagonian cavy 45 15
838 2d. Capybara (horiz) 60 25
839 2d. Leopard (horiz) 60 25
840 3d. Lesser rhea . . . . . . 1·10 40
841 4d. Giant armadillo (horiz) 1·50 45
842 6d. Andean condor (horiz) 2·30 90
MS843 97 × 80 mm. 10d. Llama (39 × 31 mm) . . . . 3·75 1·50

176 "Holothuria monacaria"

1985. Marine Life. Multicoloured.
844 3d. Type **176** 10 40
845 3d. "Stichopus chloronotus" 10 40
846 3d. "Luidia maculata" . . . 10 40
847 3d. "Nadoa tuberculata" . . 10 40
848 4d. "Astropyga radiata" . . 1·10 40
849 4d. "Linckia laevigata" . . . 1·10 40
850 4d. "Astropecten scoparius" 1·10 40

177 Flag and Sickle "40"

178 Globe, Transport and People around Postman

1985. 40th Anniv of Socialist Republic. Mult.
851 2d. Type **177** 45 45
852 3d. Doves around globe as heart above handclasp . . 60 45
853 5d. Banner . . . . 1·10 45
854 10d. Ho Chi Minh, flag and laurel branch . . . . . . 1·70 45
MS855 70 × 100 mm. 10d. Similar to Type **177** (25 × 35 mm) . . . . 3·00 1·30

1985. 40th Anniv of Postal and Telecommunications Service. Multicoloured.
856 2d. Type **178** 55 25
857 2d. Telephonist and telegraph operator 55 25
858 4d. Wartime deliveries and postwoman Nguyen Thi Nghia 75 45
859 5d. Dish aerial 90 45

179 Profile of Ho Chi Minh and Policeman

1985. 40th Anniv of People's Police.
860 **179** 10d. red and black . . . 3·50 40

180 Gymnasts

1985. 1st National Sports and Gymnastics Games. Multicoloured.
862 5d. Type **180** . . . . 1·10 40
863 10d. Badminton player, gymnast, athlete and swimmer . . . . 2·75 40

181 Locomotive "Beuth", 1843

1985. 150th Anniv of German Railways. Multi.
864 1d. Type **181** 40 15
865 1d. German tank locomotive, 1900 . . . . 40 15
866 2d. Locomotive "Saxonia", 1836, Saxony 60 25
867 2d. German passenger locomotive 60 25
868 3d. Prussian steam locomotive No. 2024, 1910 85 45
869 4d. Prussian tank locomotive, 1920 . . . . 1·20 45
870 6d. Bavarian State steam locomotive No. 659, 1890 1·50 85
MS871 80 × 53 mm. 10d. Stephenson locomotive "Adler", 1985 (31 × 39 mm) . . . . 3·75 1·50

182 Off-shore Rig, Derrick and Helicopter

1985. 30th Anniv of Geological Service.
872 **182** 1d. blue and purple . . . 85 40
873 – 1d. green and brown . . . 85 40
DESIGN: No. 873, Airplane over coastline.

183 Alfa Romeo, 1922

1985. "Italia'85" International Stamp Exhibition, Rome. Motor Cars. Multicoloured.
874 1d. Type **183** 30 15
875 1d. Bianchi "Berlina", 1932 30 15
876 2d. Isotta Fraschini, 1928 . . 45 25
877 2d. Bugatti, 1930 . . . . . . 45 25
878 3d. Itala, 1912 . . . . 75 30
879 4d. Lancia "Augusta", 1934 90 45
880 6d. Fiat, 1927 . . . . 1·50 85
MS881 76 × 60 mm. 10d. Fiat (1927) (different) (39 × 31 mm) . . . . 3·00 1·30

184 Sei Whale

1985. Marine Mammals. Multicoloured.
882 1d. Type **184** 30 15
883 1d. Blue whale 30 15
884 2d. Killer whale 45 25
885 2d. Common dolphin 45 25
886 3d. Humpback whale 75 30
887 4d. Fin whale 90 45
888 6d. Black right whale . . . . 1·50 85

185 Goalkeeper attempting to save Ball

1985. World Cup Football Championship, Mexico (1986) (1st issue). Multicoloured.
889 1d. Type **185** 25 15
890 1d. Scoring goal 25 15
891 2d. Goalkeeper diving for ball 45 25
892 2d. Goalkeeper holding ball (vert) 45 25
893 3d. Goalkeeper preparing to catch ball (vert) 75 30
894 4d. Punching ball away (vert) 90 40
895 6d. Goalkeeper catching ball (vert) . . . . 1·50 40
MS896 92 × 67 mm. 10d. Goalmouth scene (39 × 31 mm) . . . . . 3·00 1·30
See also Nos. 920/**MS**927.

186 Laotian Girl and Dove

1985. 10th Anniv of Laos People's Democratic Republic. Multicoloured.
897 1d. Type **186** 60 60
898 1d. Laotian girl and arms . . 60 60

187 Decorated Drum

1985. Traditional Musical Instruments. Mult.
899 1d. Type **187** 30 40
900 1d. Xylophone 30 40
901 2d. Double-ended drum . . . 45 40
902 2d. Flutes 45 40
903 3d. Single-stringed instrument 75 40
904 4d. Four-stringed instrument 90 40
905 6d. Double-stringed bowed instrument . . . . 1·50 40

188 Agriculture

189 Hands, Emblem and Dove

1985. 40th Anniv of Independence.
906 10d. Type **188** . . . . 3·75 1·50
907 10d. Industry . . . . 3·75 1·50
908 20d. Health care . . . . . . 7·50 3·75
909 30d. Education . . . . . . 11·50 4·50

1986. 40th Anniv of U.N.O.
910 **189** 1d. multicoloured 70 45

190 Ho Chi Minh, Map, Line of Voters and Ballot Box

191 Isaac Newton

1986. 40th Anniv of First Assembly Elections.
911 **190** 50x. mauve and black . . 40 40
912 1d. orange and black . . 75 75

1986. Appearance of Halley's Comet.
913 2d. Type **191** 40 40
914 2d. Edmond Halley 40 40
915 3d. Launch of "Vega" space probe and flags 75 40
916 5d. Comet and planet . . . . 1·50 40

192 Map of U.S.S.R. and Kremlin Buildings

193 Plan of Battle of Chi Lang

1986. 27th Communist Party Congress, Moscow. Multicoloured.
917 50x. Type **192** 40 40
918 1d. Lenin on flag and transport, industrial and scientific motifs 75 40

1986. 600th Birth Anniv (1985) of Le Loi (founder of Le Dynasty).
919 **193** 1d. multicolourerd 75 40

194 Footballer

1986. World Cup Football Championship, Mexico (2nd issue). Multicoloured.
920 1d. Type **194** 25 15
921 1d. Two players 25 15
922 2d. Player heading ball . . . 45 15
923 3d. Player tackling 75 40
924 3d. Two players chasing ball 75 40
925 5d. Footballer (different) . . 1·10 60
926 5d. Two players (different) 1·10 60
MS927 113 × 52 mm. 10d. Goalkeeper (39 × 31 mm) . . . 3·00 1·30

195 Konstantin Tsiolkovski and "Sputnik 1"

1986. 25th Anniv of 1st Man in Space. Mult.
928 1d. Type **195** 25 15
929 1d. Rocket on launch vehicle, Baikanur cosmodrome . . 25 15
930 2d. Yuri Gagarin and "Vostok 1" 45 15
931 3d. Valentina Tereshkova and "Vostok VI" on launch vehicle (vert) 75 40
932 3d. Cosmonaut Leonov and cosmonaut on space walk 75 40
933 5d. "Soyuz"–"Apollo" link and crews . . . . 1·10 60
934 5d. "Salyut"–"Soyuz" link and two cosmonauts . . . 1·10 60
MS935 60 × 81 mm. 10d. Cosmonauts (31 × 39 mm) . . 3·00 1·30

196 Thalmann and Flag

1986. Birth Centenary of Ernst Thalmann (German Communist leader).
936 **196** 2d. red and black 90 40

197 Flag, Hammer and Globe in Sickle

1986. Centenary of May Day.
937 **197** 1d. red and blue 30 15
938 5d. red and brown 1·20 25

198 Hawker Hart

1986. "Expo '86" World's Fair, Vancouver. Historic Aircraft. Multicoloured.
939 1d. Type **198** 25 10
940 1d. Curtiss JN-4 "Jenny" 25 10
941 2d. PZL P-23 Karas 45 15
942 3d. Yakovlev Yak-11 75 30
943 3d. Fokker Dr-1 triplane 75 30
944 5d. Boeing P12, 1920 1·10 55
945 5d. Nieuport-Delage 29C1, 1929 1·10 55

199 Ho Chi Minh and People working on Barriers

1986. 40th Anniv of Committee for Protection of Flood Barriers.
946 **199** 1d. pink and brown 60 45

200 Black and White Cat

1986. Cats. Multicoloured.
947 1d. Type **200** 25 15
948 1d. Grey and white cat 25 15
949 2d. White cat 45 15
950 3d. Brown-faced cat 75 40
951 3d. Beige cat 75 40
952 5d. Black-faced cat (vert) 1·10 60
953 5d. Beige and cream cat 1·10 60

201 Thai Den House

1986. Traditional Architecture. Multicoloured.
954 1d. Type **201** 25 15
955 1d. Nung house 25 15
956 2d. Thai Trang house 45 25
957 3d. Tay house 75 40
958 3d. H'mong house 75 40
959 5d. Dao house 1·10 70
960 5d. Tay Nguyen house (vert) 1·10 70
MS961 100 × 70 mm. 10d. As No. 960 1·10 65

202 European Bee Eater **203** Plymouth Rock Cock

1986. "Stockholmia 86" International Stamp Exhibition. Birds. Multicoloured.
962 1d. Type **202** 25 15
963 1d. Green magpie 25 15
964 2d. Red-winged shrike babbler 45 15
965 3d. White-crested laughing thrush 75 40
966 3d. Long-tailed broadbill (horiz) 75 40
967 5d. Pied wagtail 1·10 60
968 5d. Azure-winged magpie (horiz) 1·10 60
MS969 95 × 65 mm. 10d. White-rumped shamas (31 × 39 mm) 3·75 1·30

1986. Domestic Fowl. Multicoloured.
970 1d. Type **203** 25 40
971 1d. Common turkey 25 40
972 2d. Rhode Island red cock 45 40
973 2d. White Plymouth rock cock 45 40
974 3d. Rhode Island (inscr "Islan") red hen 75 40
975 3d. White leghorn cock 75 40
976 3d. Rhode Island red cock (different) 75 40
977 5d. Barred Plymouth rock cock 1·10 40

204 Emblem

1986. 11th World Federation of Trades Unions Congress, Berlin.
978 **204** 1d. blue and red 70 40

206 Woman-shaped Sword Handle

1986. Historic Bronzes Excavated at Mt. Do. Mult.
980 1d. Type **206** 25 40
981 1d. Seated figure with man on back 25 40
982 2d. Saddle pommel (horiz) 45 40
983 3d. Shoe-shaped hoe (horiz) 75 40
984 3d. Bowl (horiz) 75 40
985 5d. Vase (horiz) 1·10 40
986 5d. Pot with lid (horiz) 1·10 40
MS987 107 × 88 mm. 10d. As No. 981 3·00 1·30

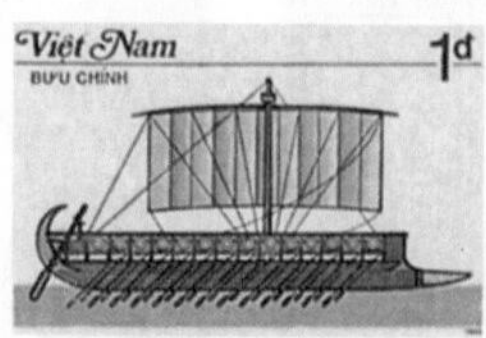

207 Greek Bireme

1986. Sailing Ships. Multicoloured.
988 1d. Type **207** 25 10
989 1d. Viking longship 25 10
990 2d. Medieval kogge (36 × 46 mm) 45 15
991 3d. Greek cargo galley 75 30
992 3d. Phoenician war galley with ram 75 30
993 5d. Ancient Mediterranean cargo ship 1·10 55
994 5d. Roman trireme 1·10 55

208 Hands cupping Red Cross in Flower

1986. 40th Anniv of Vietnamese Red Cross.
995 **208** 3d. mauve and blue 75 40

209 "Catopsilia scylla"

1986. Butterflies. Multicoloured.
996 1d. Type **209** 25 10
997 1d. "Euploea midamus" 25 10
998 2d. Orange albatross 45 15
999 3d. Common mormon ("Papilio polytes") 75 30
1000 3d. African monarch ("Danaus chrysippus") 75 30
1001 5d. Tawny rajah ("Charaxes polyxena") 1·10 55
1002 5d. Magpie crow ("Euploea diocletiana") 1·10 55

210 Red Flag and Symbols of Industry and Agriculture

1986. 6th Vietnamese Communist Party Congress. Multicoloured.
1003 1d. Type **210** 45 40
1004 2d. Red flag and weapons 90 40
1005 4d. Red flag and Ho Chi Minh 1·50 40
1006 5d. Red flag and symbols of peace 1·70 40
MS1007 73 × 110 mm. 10d. Type **210**. Imperf 3·00 1·30

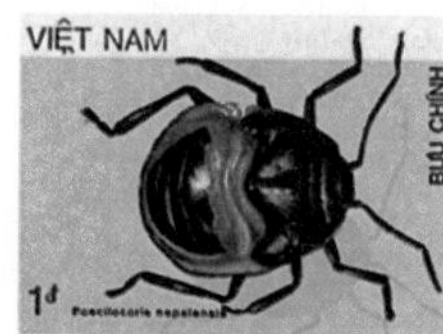

211 "Poecilocoris nepalensis" (shieldbug)

1986. Insects. Multicoloured.
1008 1d. Type **211** 25 25
1009 1d. "Bombus americanorum" (bee) 25 25
1010 2d. "Romalea microptera" (grasshopper) 45 40
1011 3d. "Chalcocoris rutilans" (shieldbug) 75 40
1012 3d. "Chrysocoris sellatus" (shieldbug) 75 40
1013 5d. "Crocisa crucifera" (wasp) 1·10 40
1014 5d. "Paranthrene palmi" (moth) 1·10 55
MS1015 78 × 78 mm. 10d. "Anabrus simplex" (31 × 39 mm) 3·00 1·30

212 Dove and Emblem **213** "Ficus glomerata"

1986. International Peace Year.
1016 **212** 1d. green and black 45 40
1017 3d. pink and black 1·10 40

1986. Bonsai. Multicoloured.
1018 1d. Type **213** 25 40
1019 1d. "Ficus benjamina" 25 40
1020 2d. "Ulmus tonkinensis" 45 40
1021 3d. "Persica vulgaris" 75 40
1022 3d. "Strebius asper" 75 40
1023 5d. "Podocarpus macrophyllus" 1·10 40
1024 5d. "Pinus khasya" 1·10 40
MS1025 86 × 66 mm. 10d. "Serissa foetida" (41 × 29 mm) 3·00 1·30

214 Basket

1986. Basketry and Wickerwork. Multicoloured.
1026 1d. Type **214** 25 40
1027 1d. Tall basket with lid and handles 25 40
1028 2d. Stool 45 40
1029 3d. Handbag 75 40
1030 3d. Dish 75 40
1031 5d. Tall basket for carrying on back 1·10 40
1032 5d. Square basket with star-shaped foot 1·10 40
MS1033 107 × 90 mm. 10d. Tall basket 3·00 1·30

215 Soldiers and Women **216** "Fokienia hodginsii"

1986. 40th Anniv of National Resistance.
1034 **215** 2d. brown and green 90 40

1986. Fruits of Conifers. Multicoloured.
1035 1d. Type **216** 25 40
1036 1d. "Amentotaxus yunnanensis" 25 40
1037 2d. "Pinus kwangtungensis" 45 40
1038 3d. "Cupressus torulosa" 75 40
1039 3d. "Taxus chinensis" 75 40
1040 5d. "Tsuga yunnanensis" 1·10 40
1041 5d. "Ducampopinus krempfii" 1·10 40
MS1042 67 × 85 mm. 10d. "Abies nukiangensis" 3·00 1·30

217 Mother and Calf

1986. Elephants.
1043 1d. Type **217** 25 10
1044 1d. Two elephants 25 10
1045 3d. Elephant (vert) 75 25
1046 3d. Elephant feeding 75 25
1047 5d. Working elephant (vert) 1·10 45
1048 5d. Elephants by water (68 × 27 mm) 1·10 45

218 Girl watering Tree **219** My Chan

1987. New Year. Year of the Cat.
1049 **218** 3d. brown and mauve 70 45

1987. "Son Tinh-Thuy Tinh" (folktale). Mult.
1050 3d. Type **219** 75 40
1051 3d. Mountain Genius bearing gift and leading horse 75 40
1052 3d. Elephants carrying materials for flood barrier 75 40
1053 3d. Men working through the night against flood sent by Water Genius 75 40
1054 3d. Men felling trees 75 40

1055 3d. Pounding rice in preparation for festival after storms 75 40
1056 3d. Canoes bringing fruit and grain 75 40
1057 3d. Canoe 75 35

Nos. 1050/7 were issued together, se-tenant, forming a composite design.

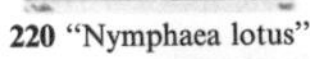
220 "Nymphaea lotus"

222 Temple, Da Nang

221 Crowd attacking Building (August 1945 Revolution)

1987. Water Lilies. Multicoloured.

1058 5d. Type **220** 15 15
1059 10d. "Nymphaea nouchali" 30 15
1060 10d. "Nymphaea pubescens" 45 15
1061 20d. "Nymphaea rubra" . . 60 25
1062 20d. "Nymphaea gigantea" 75 30
1063 30d. "Nymphaea laydekeri" 85 40
1064 50d. "Nymphaea capensis" 1·10 55

1987. 8th National Assembly. Multicoloured.

1065 10d. Type **221** 75 40
1066 20d. Proclamation of Democratic Republic (September 1945) . . . . 1·10 40
1067 30d. Fall of Dien Bien Phu (May 1954) . . . . 1·50 40
1068 50d. Tank entering Saigon (April 1975) . . . . . . 1·90 40

1987. Cham Culture. Multicoloured.

1069 3d. Type **222** 25 15
1070 10d. Temple, Phu Khanh . . 45 25
1071 15d. Temple, Da Nang (different) 75 25
1072 20d. Figure of dancer, Nghia Binh 90 40
1073 25d. Bust, Da Nang . . . . 1·10 40
1074 30d. Woman playing flute (statuette), Nghia Binh . . 1·20 55
1075 40d. Figure of dancer on capital, Da Nang . . . . 1·50 70
MS1076 80 × 100 mm. 50d. As No. 1074 . . . . 3·00 1·30

223 Hanoi

1987. Tourism. Multicoloured.

1077 5d. Type **223** 15 25
1078 10d. Hai Phong 30 40
1079 15d. Thien Mu Pagoda, Hue 45 40
1080 20d. Da Nang 60 40
1081 25d. Nha Trang 75 40
1082 30d. Waterfall, Da Lat . . . 85 40
1083 40d. Ho Chi Minh City . . 1·10 45
MS1084 87 × 105 mm. 50d. Quang Ninh . . . . 3·00 1·20

224 Cactus

226 Man from Bana

225 People on Globe

1987. Cacti.

1085 **224** 5d. multicoloured . . . 15 15
1086 – 10d. multicoloured . . . 30 15
1087 – 15d. multicoloured . . . 45 15
1088 – 20d. multicoloured . . . 60 25
1089 – 25d. multicoloured . . . 75 30
1090 – 30d. multicoloured . . . 85 40
1091 – 40d. multicoloured . . . 1·10 55
MS1092 60 × 72 mm. 50d. multicoloured (31 × 39 mm) . . 3·00 1·20

DESIGNS: 10d. to 50d. Various flowering cacti.

1987. Day of Five Billion Inhabitants of Earth.

1093 **225** 5d. mauve and blue . . 70 45

1987. Costumes. Multicoloured.

1094 5d. Type **226** 25 15
1095 20d. Woman from Bana . . 75 40
1096 20d. Woman from Gia Rai 75 40
1097 30d. Man from Gia Rai . . 1·10 40
1098 30d. Man from Ede . . . . 1·10 40
1099 40d. Woman from Ede . . . 1·50 70

227 Silhouettes of Soldiers and Disabled Soldier

228 Rose

1987. 40th Anniv of Association of Disabled Soldiers.

1100 **227** 5d. red and violet . . . 60 40

1987. Roses. Multicoloured.

1101 5d. Type **228** 15 25
1102 10d. Red hybrid tea 30 40
1103 15d. Pink hybrid tea 45 40
1104 20d. Species rose 60 40
1105 25d. Species rose (different) 75 40
1106 30d. Floribunda 85 40
1107 40d. "Rosa odorata" . . . 1·10 45
MS1108 65 × 85 mm. 50d. Roses (28 × 36 mm) . . . . 3·00 1·20

229 Postwoman and Mail Transport

1987. 40th Anniv of Postal Trade Union.

1109 **229** 5d. black and pink . . . 60 40
1110 – 30d. black and green . . 90 75

DESIGN: 30d. Linesman, dish aerial and telephonist.

230 Siamese Fighting Fish

1987. Fishes. Multicoloured.

1111 5d. Type **230** 15 15
1112 10d. Red-tailed black shark 30 15
1113 15d. Tiger barb 45 15
1114 20d. Pearl danio 60 25
1115 25d. Rosy barb 75 30
1116 30d. Rasbora 85 45
1117 40d. Silver loach . . . . . 1·10 55

231 I.Y.S.H. Emblem

1987. International Year of Shelter for the Homeless.

1118 **231** 5d. black and blue . . . 60 40

233 Crested Gibbons

235 Industrial and Agricultural Symbols

234 "Three Musicians"

1987. Monkeys. Multicoloured.

1120 5d. Type **233** 75 40
1121 5d. Variegated langurs . . . 75 40
1122 15d. Crested gibbon (different) . . . . 1·50 40
1123 40d. Variegated langur (different) . . . . 3·00 40

1987. Paintings by Picasso. Multicoloured.

1124 3d. Type **234** 15 15
1125 20d. Horse-drawn wagon . . 60 25
1126 20d. Winged horse on shore 60 25
1127 30d. "Child with Dove" (vert) 90 30
1128 30d. "Gertrude Stein" (vert) 90 30
1129 40d. "Guernica" (44 × 27 mm) . . . . . . 1·50 55
MS1130 75 × 100 mm. 50d. "Artist's Son as Harlequin" (39 × 31 mm) 3·75 1·50

1987. 70th Anniv of Russian Revolution. Mult.

1131 5d. Type **235** 25 40
1132 20d. Soviet Memorial, Berlin-Treptow, cruiser "Aurora" and Lenin . . . 45 40
1133 30d. "70" and symbols of progress 85 40
1134 50d. Ho Chi Minh and scenes of Vietnamese history . . . . 1·50 40
MS1135 90 × 90 mm. 65d. As No. 1133 . . . . 3·00 1·20

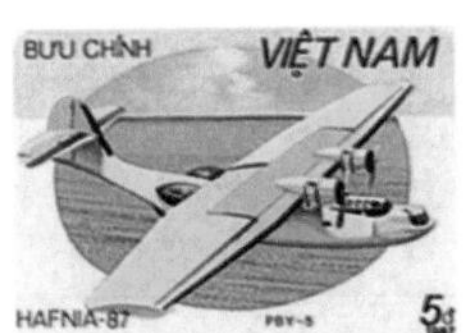

236 Consolidated PBY-5 Catalina Flying Boat

1987. "Hafnia 87" International Stamp Exhibition, Copenhagen. Flying Boats. Multicoloured.

1136 5d. Type **236** 15 15
1137 10d. Liore et Olivier LeO 246 . . . . 30 15
1138 15d. Dornier Do-18 . . . . 45 15
1139 20d. Short Sunderland . . . 60 25
1140 25d. Flying boat, 1923 . . . 75 30
1141 30d. Chetverikov ARK-3 . . 85 40
1142 40d. Cant Z.509 . . . . . 1·10 55
MS1143 87 × 54 mm. 50d. Flying boat . . . . 2·75 1·20

237 Epanouis

1987. Corals. Multicoloured.

1144 5d. Type 237 . . . . 25 25
1145 10d. Acropora 45 40
1146 15d. Rhizopsammia 70 40
1147 20d. Acropora (different) . . 90 40
1148 25d. Alcyone . . . . 1·10 40
1149 30d. Corollum . . . . . . 1·40 40
1150 40d. Cristatella . . . . . . 1·80 45

238 Doves as Clasped Hands forming Heart

1987. 5th Anniv of Vietnam–Czechoslovak Friendship Treaty. Each blue, yellow and red.

1151 10d. Type **238** 75 40
1152 50d. Pagoda on One Pillar (Hanoi), flags and buildings of Prague . . . 1·90 40

239 Symbols of Industry and Agriculture

1987. Soviet–Vietnam Friendship Treaty.

1153 **239** 5d. pink, black and orange 40 40
1154 – 50d. pink, brown and orange . . . . 1·90 40

DESIGN: 50d. Buildings of Moscow Kremlin and Hanoi.

240 Coloured Circles

1987. Peace.

1155 **240** 10d. multicoloured . . . 90 40

241 Saddle-back Fungus

243 Wrecked Boeing B-52 Stratofortress Bomber and Girl watering Flowers

242 Dove on Open Hands

1987. Fungi. Multicoloured.

1156 5d. Type **241** 15 15
1157 10d. Trumpet agaric 30 25
1158 15d. "Tricholoma terreum" 45 25
1159 20d. Golden russula 60 25
1160 25d. Spindle shank 75 25
1161 30d. "Cortinarius violaceus" 85 40
1162 40d. Bronze boletus . . . . 1·10 55

1987. 30th Anniv of Africa–Asia Co-operation Committee.

1163 **242** 10d. blue, black & yellow 40 40
1164 – 30d. black, brown and yellow . . . . 1·10 40

DESIGN—VERT: 30d. Hands and map.

1987. 15th Anniv of U.S. Air Bombardment of Vietnam.

1165 **243** 10d. black and yellow . . 40 40
1166 – 30d. black and orange 1·10 40

DESIGN: 30d. Young Pioneers and weapons.

244 Woman carrying Bales of Cloth

246 Anniversary Emblem and Dove

245 Junk, Man blowing Horn and Map

1987. 6th Party Congress Decisions.

1167 **244** 5d. green and brown . . 40 40
1168 – 20d. orange and brown 60 40
1169 – 30d. violet and blue . . 90 40

DESIGNS: 20d. Tractor driver; 30d. Loading crate on freighter.

1988. Paracel and Spratley Islands.
1170 **245** 10d. black, pink and red . . . 40 15
1171 – 100d. light brown, black and brown . . . . . 2·75 75
DESIGN: 100d. Maps showing Paracel Islands.

1988. 125th Anniv of International Red Cross.
1172 **246** 10d. red, black and blue . . . 1·00 40

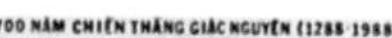

247 Fleet

1988. 700th Anniv of Battle of Bach Dang River.
1173 **247** 80d. black, red and pink . . 75 25
1174 – 200d. multicoloured . . 2·75 55
DESIGN: 200d. Battle scene.

248 Oil Rig

249 Blue and Yellow Macaw

1988. Oil Industry.
1175 **248** 1000d. black, blue and red . . . . 7·50 1·90

1988. Parrots. Multicoloured.
1176 10d. Type **249** 30 40
1177 10d. Slaty-headed parakeet . . 30 40
1178 20d. Red-winged parrot ("Aprosmictus erythropterus") 60 40
1179 20d. Green-winged macaw ("Ara chloroptera") . . . 60 60
1180 30d. Moustached parakeet ("Psittacula alexandri") . . 85 40
1181 30d. Military macaw ("Ara militaris") 85 40
1182 50d. Vernal hanging parrot . 1·10 40
MS1183 65 × 85 mm. 80d. Scarlet macaw . . . . 3·50 1·30

250 Map

251 Child and Syringe

1988. 33rd Council for Mutual Economic Aid Meeting and 10th Anniv of Vietnam's Membership.
1184 **250** 200d. multicoloured . . 1·50 55
1185 – 300d. blue and bistre . . 2·30 75
DESIGN: 300d. COMECON headquarters building, Moscow.

1988. Child Vaccination Campaign.
1186 **251** 60d. orange, black & blue 90 75

252 Emblem and Building

1988. 30th Anniv of "Peace and Socialism" (magazine).
1187 **252** 20d. multicoloured . . . 75 40

253 Ton Duc Thang

254 Emblem

1988. Birth Centenary of Pres. Ton Duc Thang.
1188 **253** 150d. multicoloured . . 1·10 40

1988. 6th Trade Unions Congress. Multicoloured.
1189 50d. Type **254** 60 40
1190 100d. "VI" and couple . . . 90 40

255 Pointed-scaled Pit Viper

1988. Snakes. Multicoloured.
1191 10d. Type **255** 40 15
1192 10d. Pope's pit viper ("Trimeresurus popeorum") 40 15
1193 20d. Banded krait ("Bungarus fasciatus") . . 60 25
1194 20d. Malayan krait ("Bungarus candidus") . . 60 25
1195 30d. Coral snake ("Calliophis maclellandi") 70 30
1196 30d. Striped beaked snake ("Ancistridon acutus") . . 70 30
1197 50d. King cobra (vert) . . . 90 45

256 Family (Trieu Khac Tien)

1988. Children's Drawings. Multicoloured.
1198 10d. Type **256** 30 25
1199 10d. Couple and house (Phuong Ti) 30 25
1200 20d. Fishermen (Lam Hoang Thang) 60 40
1201 20d. Children flying kite (Nguyen Xuan Anh) . . . 60 40
1202 30d. Couple (Hong Hanh) (vert) 85 40
1203 30d. Animals and girl playing guitar (Quynh May) 85 40
1204 50d. Woman holding dove (Ta Phuong Tra) (vert) . . 1·10 55
MS1205 100 × 80 mm. 80d. Couple with child (Hong Hanh) (vert) 3·00 1·30

257 Tri An

1988. U.S.S.R.–Vietnam Co-operation. Hydro-electric Power Stations.
1206 **257** 2000d. black, orge & red 3·75 2·30
1207 – 3000d. black, bistre and red . . . . 5·25 3·00
DESIGN: 3000d. Hoa Binh.

258 Kamov Ka-26

1988. Helicopters. Multicoloured.
1208 10d. Type **258** 30 15
1209 10d. Boeing-Vertol 234 Commercial Chinook . . 30 15
1210 20d. MBB-Bolkow Bo 105 55 25
1211 20d. Mil Mi-10K 55 25
1212 30d. Kawasaki-Hughes 369HS 60 30
1213 30d. Bell JetRanger 60 30
1214 50d. Mil Mi-8 . . . . . . 75 45
MS1215 87 × 86 mm. 80d. Sud Aviation SA 330 Puma (39 × 31 mm) . . . . 2·75 1·30

259 Gaur

260 Flower and Banners

1988. Mammals. Multicoloured.
1216 10d. Type **259** 25 15
1217 10d. Banteng 25 15
1218 20d. Malayan tapir ("Tapirus indicus") . . . 60 25
1219 20d. Hog deer ("Axis porcinus") 60 25
1220 30d. Mainland serow ("Capricornis sumatraensis") 75 40
1221 30d. Wild boar ("Sus scrofa") 75 40
1222 50d. Water buffalo . . . . 1·10 55
MS1223 82 × 62 mm. 80d. Javan rhinoceros . . . . 3·00 1·30

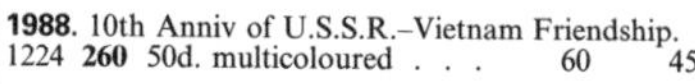
1988. 10th Anniv of U.S.S.R.–Vietnam Friendship.
1224 **260** 50d. multicoloured . . . 60 45

261 Indian Star Tortoise ("Testudo elegans")

262 Skaters

1988. Turtles and Tortoises.
1225 10d. Type **261** 40 25
1226 10d. Three-banded box turtle ("Cuora trifasciata") 40 25
1227 20d. Big-headed turtle ("Platysternon megacephalum") 55 30
1228 20d. Hawksbill turtle ("Eretmochelys imbricata") 55 30
1229 30d. Indian Ocean green turtle ("Chelonia mydas") 60 40
1230 30d. Leatherback turtle ("Dermochelys coriacea") 60 40
1231 50d. Loggerhead turtle ("Caretta caretta") . . . 75 45
MS1232 80 × 98 mm. 80d. Loggerhead turtle (different) 2·75 1·20

1988. Ice Skating. Multicoloured.
1233 **262** 10d. multicoloured . . . 25 10
1234 – 10d. multicoloured . . . 25 10
1235 – 20d. multicoloured . . . 45 15
1236 – 20d. multicoloured (horiz) 45 15
1237 – 30d. multicoloured . . . 60 30
1238 – 30d. multicoloured (horiz) 60 30
1239 – 50d. multicoloured (horiz) 75 45
MS1240 100 × 65 mm. 80d. multicoloured (39 × 31 mm) . . 3·00 1·20
DESIGNS: 1234/**MS**1240, Different skating scenes.

263 Bowden "Spacelander"

1988. Bicycles. Multicoloured.
1241 10d. Type **263** 30 15
1242 10d. Rabasa Derbi with red tyres 30 15
1243 20d. Huffy 55 25
1244 20d. Rabasa Derbi with black tyres 55 25
1245 30d. VMX-PL 60 30
1246 30d. Premier 60 30
1247 50d. Columbia RX5 . . . . 75 45

264 Fidel Castro

265 Cosmonauts on Spacecraft Wing

1988. 30th Anniv of Cuban Revolution. Mult.
1248 100d. Type **264** 30 10
1249 300d. National flags and Cuban and Vietnamese workers 85 35

1988. Cosmonauts Day. Multicoloured.
1250 10d. Type **265** 15 10
1251 10d. Spacecraft moving across surface of planet 15 10
1252 20d. Space rocket heading for planet 45 15
1253 20d. Spacecraft and cosmonauts on planet with Earth in sky 45 15
1254 30d. Spacecraft hovering over surface 75 30
1255 30d. "Soyuz"–"Salyut" complex 75 30
1256 50d. Space "bubble" and rocket . . . . 1·10 45
MS1257 65 × 75 mm. 80d. Spacecraft (31 × 39 mm) . . . . 3·00 1·20

266 Soldier Cone

1988. Sea Shells. Multicoloured.
1258 10d. Type **266** 25 25
1259 10d. Silver conch ("Strombus lentiginosus") 25 25
1260 20d. Common frog shell ("Bursa rana") 45 40
1261 20d. Tapestry turban ("Turbo petholatus") . . 45 40
1262 30d. Red-mouth olive ("Oliva erythrostoma") 75 40
1263 30d. Chambered nautilus ("Nautilus") 75 40
1264 50d. Episcopal mitre . . . . 1·10 55
MS1265 90 × 65 mm. 80d. "Tonna tessellate" . . . . 3·00 1·30
The inscriptions on Nos. 1261 and 1263 have been transposed.

267 Class VL85 Diesel Locomotive, Russia

1988. Railway Locomotives. Multicoloured.
1266 20d. Type **267** 45 25
1267 20d. LRC high speed diesel, Canada 45 25
1268 20d. Monorail train, Japan 45 25
1269 20d. KiHA 80 diesel railcar, Japan 45 25
1270 30d. Class DR 1A diesel-electric, Russia 75 30
1271 30d. Class RC 1 electric, Sweden 75 30
1272 50d. Class TE-136 diesel-electric, Russia . . . . . 1·10 75
MS 1273 102 × 71 mm. 80d. "Z6400", France (36 × 26 mm) 3·00 1·20

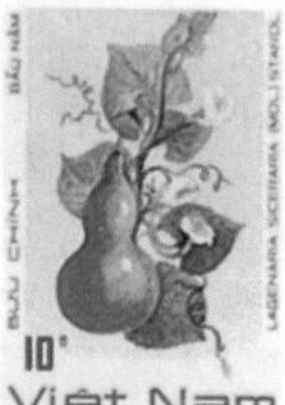
268 Gourd

1988. Fruits. Multicoloured.
1274 10d. Type **268** 25 40
1275 10d. "Momordica charantia" 25 40
1276 20d. Pumpkin ("Cucurbita moschata") 60 40
1277 20d. Eggplant ("Solanum melongena") 60 40
1278 30d. "Benincasa hispida" . . 75 40
1279 30d. Luffa gourd 75 40
1280 50d. Tomatoes . . . . . . 1·10 40

269 Soldiers and Field Workers

1989. 10th Anniv of People's Republic of Kampuchea. Multicoloured.
1281 100d. Type **269** 45 40
1282 500d. Crowd greeting soldier and mother with child . . 1·80 75

270 Junk from Quang Nam

1989. Regional Fishing Junks. Multicoloured.
1283 10d. Type **270** 40 30
1284 10d. Quang Tri 40 30
1285 20d. Thua Thien 55 30
1286 20d. Da Nang 55 30
1287 30d. Quang Tri (different) . . 60 30
1288 30d. Da Nang (different) . . 60 30
1289 50d. Hue 75 30

271 Caribbean Buckeye ("Junonia evarete")

1989. "India-89" International Stamp Exhibition, New Delhi (1st issue). Butterflies. Multicoloured.
1290 50d. Type **271** 30 40
1291 50d. "Anaea echemus" . . . 30 40
1292 50d. Great southern white ("Ascia monuste") . . . 30 40
1293 100d. Red-splashed sulphur ("Phoebis avellaneda") . . 45 40
1294 100d. Jamaican orange ("Eurema proterpia") . . 45 40
1295 200d. "Papilio palamedes" 90 40
1296 300d. Monarch ("Danaus plexippus") . . . . 1·10 40
MS1297 87 × 77 mm. 400d. "Parides gundlachiamus" (39 × 31 mm) 2·75 1·20
See also Nos. 1298/1301.

272 Flag and T-e-l-ecommunications

274 Emblems on Banner

273 Festival

1989. "India-89" International Stamp Exhibition, New Delhi (2nd issue).
1298 **272** 100d. multicoloured . . 40 30
1299 – 100d. multicoloured . . 40 30
1300 – 300d. multicoloured . . 85 30
1301 – 600d. brown, orge & green . . . . 1·80 60
DESIGNS: 100d. (No. 1299), Oil and electricity industries; 300d. Government Secretariat and Asokan capital; 600d. Jawaharlal Nehru (Indian statesman, birth centenary).

1989. Bicentenary of Battle of Dongda.
1302 **273** 100d. violet and green 40 25
1303 – 1000d. mauve and pink 2·30 1·30
DESIGN: 1000d. Battle scene.

1989. Centenary of Interparliamentary Union.
1304 **274** 100d. multicoloured . . 45 30
1305 – 200d. gold, ultramarine and blue . . . . 1·10 30
DESIGN: 200d. "100" on banner.

275 Dachshunds

1989. Dogs. Multicoloured.
1306 50d. Type **275** 30 10
1307 50d. Basset hounds 30 10
1308 50d. Setter (vert) 30 10
1309 100d. Hunting dog (vert) . . 45 25
1310 100d. Basset hounds (66 × 25 mm) 45 25
1311 200d. Hound (vert) 90 40
1312 300d. Basset hound puppy 90 60

276 Footballers

277 Jug

1989. World Cup Football Championship, Italy (1st issue). Multicoloured.
1313 50d. Type **276** 30 10
1314 50d. Striker and goalkeeper 30 10
1315 50d. Goalkeeper 30 10
1316 100d. Player No. 5 tackling 45 25
1317 100d. Tackling (vert) . . . 45 25
1318 200d. Player No. 3 (vert) . . 90 40
1319 300d. Players heading ball (vert) . . . . 1·10 60
MS1320 62 × 92 mm. 400d. Player (31 × 39 mm) . . . . 3·00 1·20
See also Nos. 1382/MS1389 and 1482/9.

1989. Pottery. Multicoloured.
1321 50d. Type **277** 30 15
1322 100d. Bowl with geometric pattern 45 25
1323 100d. Round pot with flower decoration 45 25
1324 200d. Tall pot with animal decoration 90 40
1325 300d. Vase . . . . 1·10 55

278 Baby Thanh Giong with Mother

1989. Legend of Thanh Giong. Multicoloured.
1326 50d. Type **278** 30 15
1327 100d. Thanh Giong with King's messenger 45 25
1328 100d. Thanh Giong at head of army 45 25
1329 200d. Thanh Giong beating out flames 90 40
1330 300d. Thanh Giong riding to heaven . . . . 1·10 55

279 "Fuchsia fulgens"

280 Bird carrying Envelope above Dish Aerial

1989. Flowers. Multicoloured.
1331 50d. Type **279** 30 10
1332 50d. Bird-of-paradise flower ("Strelitzia reginae") . . . 30 10
1333 100d. Glory lily ("Gloriosa superba") 45 25
1334 100d. Orange day lily ("Hemerocallis fulva") . . 45 25
1335 200d. "Paphiopedilum siamense" 90 40
1336 300d. "Iris sp." . . . . . . 1·10 60
On Nos. 1332 and 1335 the inscriptions have been transposed.

1989. Communications.
1337 **280** 100d. brown 60 25

281 Birds

283 Man and Ox

282 "Return from Varennes"

1989. Bicentenary of French Revolution and "Philexfrance 89" International Stamp Exhibition, Paris. (a) As T **281**. Multicoloured.
1338 100d. Type **281** 30 25
1339 500d. "Liberty guiding the People" (detail, Eugene Delacroix) . . . . 1·20 55

(b) As T **282**.
1340 50d. Type **282** 30 15
1341 50d. "Revolutionary Court" 30 15
1342 50d. "Oath of the Tennis Court" (Jacques-Louis David) (vert) 30 15
1343 100d. "Assassination of Marat" (David) (vert) . . 45 25
1344 100d. "Storming the Bastille" (vert) 45 25
1345 200d. Two children (Pierre-Paul Prud'hon) (vert) . . 90 40
1346 300d. "Slave Trade" (Jean-Leon Gerome) . . . . . 1·40 85
MS1347 105 × 105 mm. 400d. "Liberty guiding the People" (Eugene Delacroix) (32 × 43 mm) 2·75 1·30

1989. Rice Cultivation. Multicoloured.
1348 50d. Type **283** 30 15
1349 100d. Ploughing with ox . . 45 25
1350 100d. Flooding fields . . . 45 25
1351 200d. Fertilizing 90 40
1352 300d. Harvesting crop . . . 1·10 55

284 Appaloosa

1989. Horses. Multicoloured.
1353 50d. Type **284** 30 10
1354 50d. Tennessee walking horse 30 10
1355 50d. Tersky 30 10
1356 100d. Kladruber 45 25
1357 100d. Welsh cob 45 25
1358 200d. Pinto 90 40
1359 300d. Pony and bridle (68 × 27 mm) . . . . . . 1·10 60

285 Brandenburg Gate, Flag and Emblem

1989. 40th Anniv of German Democratic Republic.
1360 **285** 200d. yellow, black and mauve 75 40

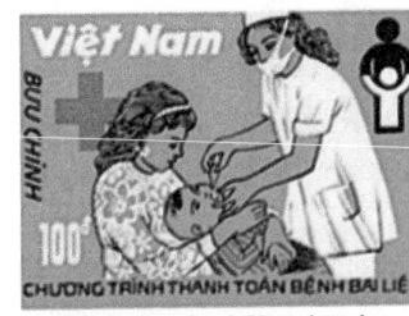

286 Polio Oral Vaccination

1989. Immunization Campaign.
1361 **286** 100d. brown, black & red 40 30
1362 – 100d. pink, black & green 40 30
1363 – 100d. green, black and red 40 30
DESIGNS: No. 1362, Vaccinating pregnant woman; 1363, Health clinic.

287 Horse

1989. Paintings of Horses by Hsu Pei-Hung. Mult.
1364 100d. Type **287** 15 15
1365 200d. Two horses galloping 25 15
1366 300d. Three horses grazing 40 15
1367 500d. Horse galloping (horiz) 55 15
1368 800d. Galloping horse . . . 90 25
1369 1000d. Two horses under tree . . . . 1·20 30
1370 1500d. Galloping horse (different) . . . . 1·50 40
MS1371 117 × 72 mm. 2000d. Horses (43 × 32 mm) . . . . 4·50 1·30

288 "Nina", "Pinta" and "Santa Maria" and Mochica Ceramic Figure ($\frac{2}{3}$-size illustration)

1989. 500th Anniv (1992) of Discovery of America by Columbus (1st issue). Multicoloured.
1372 50d. Type **288** 25 25
1373 100d. Columbus and King Ferdinand the Catholic and Peruvian ceramic bottle 55 55
1374 100d. Columbus's arrival at Rabida and Mexican decorated vessel 55 55
1375 100d. Columbus offering gifts (18th-century engraving) and human-shaped jug 55 55
1376 200d. Early map and Peruvian ceramic . . . . 1·00 1·00
1377 200d. Portrait and arms of Columbus and Nazca ceramic . . . . 1·00 1·00
1378 300d. Chart by Toscanelli and Chimu vessel . . . . 1·10 1·10
MS1379 85 × 69 mm. 500d. Teotihuacana lidded vessel (36 × 30 mm) . . . . 2·75 2·75
See also Nos. 1545/MS1552 and 1664/MS1699.

289 Storming of Presidential Palace, Saigon, and Ho Chi Minh

1990. 60th Anniv of Vietnamese Communist Party. Multicoloured.
1380 100d. Type **289** 45 40
1381 500d. Industry, workers, hammer and sickle and flag . . . . 1·80 75

290 Players

1990. World Cup Football Championship, Italy (2nd issue). Multicoloured.
1382 100d. Type **290** 10 10
1383 200d. Argentina player with possession 10 10
1384 300d. Netherlands and Scotland players 15 15
1385 500d. Soviet Union player tackling 30 15
1386 1000d. Scotland and West Germany player 60 25
1387 2000d. Soviet Union player losing possession 90 40
1388 3000d. Goalkeeper . . . . 1·40 45
MS1389 90 × 67 mm. 3500d. Boy with ball behind goal net (30 × 37 mm) . . . . 2·30 1·20

291 Hybrids of Mallard and Local Species

1990. Ducks. Multicoloured.

1390 100d. Type **291** 10 15
1391 300d. European mallard . . 15 15
1392 500d. Mallards 30 15
1393 1000d. Red-billed pintails 60 25
1394 2000d. White duck preening 1·10 40
1395 3000d. African yellow-bills 1·50 45

292 Mack Truck and Trailer

1990. Trucks. Multicoloured.

1396 100d. Type **292** 15 15
1397 200d. Volvo "F89" tipper 15 15
1398 300d. Tatra "915 S1" tipper 25 15
1399 500d. Hino "KZ30000" lorry 25 15
1400 1000d. Italia Iveco 45 25
1401 2000d. Leyland-Daf "Super Comet" tipper 90 40
1402 3000d. Kamaz "53212" lorry . . . . 1·40 40

293 8th/9th-century Viking Longship

1990. Sailing Ships. Multicoloured.

1403 100d. Type **293** 10 10
1404 500d. 15th-century caravel 30 30
1405 1000d. 15th-century carrack (vert) 60 60
1406 1000d. 14th/15th-century carrack 60 60
1407 1000d. 17th-century frigate 60 60
1408 2000d. 16th-century galleons and pinnace (vert) . . . . 1·20 1·20
1409 3000d. 16th-century galleon 1·50 1·50
MS1410 60 × 53 mm. 4200d. Ancient Egyptian Nile galley (43 × 32 mm) 2·75 2·75

294 Bubble-eyed Goldfish

1990. Goldfish. Multicoloured.

1411 100d. Type **294** 15 15
1412 300d. Calico veil-tailed . . . 15 15
1413 500d. Red-capped 30 15
1414 1000d. Veil-tailed (vert) . . 55 25
1415 2000d. Celestial (vert) . . . 1·10 40
1416 3000d. Comet (vert) . . . . 1·50 45

295 Gate of Noble Mankind

1990. Hue Temples. Multicoloured.

1417 100d. Type **295** 40 15
1418 100d. Lotus pool at tomb of Emperor Tu Duc 40 15
1419 200d. Southern Gate 60 25
1420 300d. Thien Pagoda . . . . 90 1·00
MS1421 97 × 68 mm. 400d. Great Stairway, Khai-Dinh burial place 1·90 1·10

296 "Antonia Zarate" (Francisco de Goya)

1990. "Stamp World London 90" International Stamp Exhibition. Multicoloured.

1422 100d. Type **296** 10 10
1423 200d. "Girl with Paper Fan" (Auguste Renoir) 10 10
1424 300d. "Janet Grizel" (John Russell) 15 15
1425 500d. "Love unfasten's Beauty's Girdle" (Joshua Reynolds) 30 15
1426 1000d. "Portrait of a Lady" (George Romney) (wrongly inscr "Omney") 60 25
1427 2000d. "Mme. Ginoux" (Vincent van Gogh) . . . 1·10 40
1428 3000d. "Lady in Green" (Thomas Gainsborough) 1·50 45
MS1429 90 × 70 mm. 3500d. "Girl sitting in a Wheat Field" (Vincent van Gogh) (26 × 38 mm) . . . 3·00 1·20

297 Henry Giffard's Steam-powered Dirigible Airship

1990. "Helvetia 90" International Stamp Exhibition, Geneva. Airships. Mult. With or without gum.

1430 100d. Type **297** 10 10
1431 200d. Lebaudy-Juillot airship No. 1 "La Jaune" 10 10
1432 300d. "Graf Zeppelin' . . . 15 15
1433 500d. R-101 . . . . 30 30
1434 1000d. "Osoaviakhim" . . . 60 60
1435 2000d. Tissandier Brothers' airship . . . . 1·20 1·20
1436 3000d. U.S. Navy "N" Class airship . . . . 1·80 1·80
MS1437 77 × 104 mm. 3500d. Zodiac (35 × 28 mm) . . . . 2·10 2·10

No. 1431 is wrongly inscr "Lebandy".

298 Silver Tabby and White Cat

1990. Cats. Multicoloured.

1438 100d. Type **298** 10 10
1439 200d. Black cat (vert) . . . 10 10
1440 300d. Black and white cat 25 15
1441 500d. Brown tabby and white (vert) 40 15
1442 1000d. Silver tabby 70 25
1443 2000d. Tortoiseshell and white (vert) 90 40
1444 3000d. Tortoiseshell tabby and white (vert) . . . . . 1·10 45
MS1445 67 × 95 mm. 3500d. Silver tabby (43 × 32 mm) . . . . . 2·75 1·10

299 Ho Chi Minh, 1923

300 King Charles Spaniel

1990. Birth Centenary of Ho Chi Minh. Mult.

1446 100d. Type **299** 10 10
1447 300d. Ho Chi Minh, 1945 15 15
1448 500d. Dove, hand holding rifle, and Ho Chi Minh 30 30
1449 1000d. Ho Chi Minh conducting 60 60
1450 2000d. Ho Chi Minh embracing child 90 90
1451 3000d. Globe and Ho Chi Minh . . . . 1·10 1·10
MS1452 86 × 94 mm. 3500d. Ho Chi Minh and star (29 × 42 mm) . . 2·10 2·10

1990. "New Zealand 90" International Stamp Exhibition, Auckland. Dogs. Multicoloured.

1453 100d. Type **300** 10 10
1454 200d. Spaniel 10 10
1455 300d. Saluki 25 15
1456 500d. Dachshund 40 15
1457 1000d. Dalmatian 70 25
1458 2000d. Highland terrier . . 90 40
1459 3000d. Boxer . . . . 1·10 45
MS1460 85 × 85 mm. 3500d. Rough collie and pups (32 × 43 mm) 2·75 1·10

301 Gorgosaurus

1990. Prehistoric Animals. Multicoloured.

1461 100d. Type **301** 10 10
1462 500d. Ceratosaurus 40 15
1463 1000d. Ankylosaurus . . . 65 65
1464 2000d. Ankylosaurus (different) . . . . 1·70 1·70
1465 3000d. Edaphosaurus . . . 2·00 2·00

302 High Jumping

1990. 11th Asian Games, Peking. Multicoloured.

1466 100d. Type **302** 10 10
1467 200d. Basketball 10 10
1468 300d. Table tennis 15 15
1469 500d. Volleyball 30 30
1470 1000d. Gymnastics 60 60
1471 2000d. Tennis . . . . . . 1·20 1·20
1472 3000d. Judo . . . . 1·80 1·80
MS1473 73 × 93 mm. 3500d. Steeplechase (32 × 43 mm) . . 2·10 2·10

1990. Tourism. Nos. 626/33 optd **DULICH'90** and emblem.

1474 50x. Type **131** 15 15
1475 50x. Common ink cap ("Coprinus atramentarius") 15 15
1476 50x. Golden mushroom ("Flammulina velutipes") 15 15
1477 50x. Chanterelle ("Cantharellus cibarius") 15 15
1478 1d. Chinese mushroom . . . 30 30
1479 2d. Red-staining mushroom 90 90
1480 5d. Common morel . . . . 1·50 1·50
1481 10d. Caesar's mushroom . . 3·00 3·00

1990. World Cup Football Championship, Italy (3rd series). Nos. 457/64 optd **ITALIA'90** and ball.

1482 **90** 30x. multicoloured . . . 30 30
1483 – 30x. mult (No. 458) . . . 30 30
1484 – 40x. mult (No. 459) . . . 35 35
1485 – 40x. mult (No. 460) . . . 35 35
1486 – 50x. mult (No. 461) . . . 50 50
1487 – 50x. mult (No. 462) . . . 50 50
1488 – 60x. multicoloured . . . 60 60
1489 – 1d. multicoloured . . . . 1·10 1·10

305 "Pyotr Yemtsov" (container ship)

1990. Ships. Multicoloured.

1490 100d. Type **305** 10 10
1491 300d. Mexican Lines container ship 15 15
1492 500d. Liner 30 30
1493 1000d. "Ben Nevis" (tanker) 60 60
1494 2000d. Roll-on roll-off ferry 1·20 1·20
1495 3000d. Sealink train ferry "Nord Pas de Calais" . . 1·80 1·80

306 Emblem, Globe and Dove

1990. 45th Anniv of Postal Service. Mult.

1496 100d. Type **306** 10 10
1497 1000d. Emblem, dish aerial and globe 60 60

307 Red Flags and Symbols of Construction and Agriculture

308 Thach Sanh collecting Wood

1990. 45th Anniv of Independence. Multicoloured.

1498 100d. Type **307** 10 10
1499 500d. Map, storming of Government Palace (1945), siege of Dien Bien Phu and tank entering Presidential Palace, Saigon (1975) 30 30
1500 1000d. Satellite communications ship, dish aerial and "VI" 45 60
1501 3000d. Hammer and sickle, industrial symbols and couple . . . . 1·80 1·80
MS1502 69 × 105 mm. 3500d. State arms and Ho Chi Minh proclaiming independence (32 × 43 mm) . . . . 2·10 2·10

1990. Legend of Thach Sanh. Multicoloured.

1503 100d. Type **308** 10 10
1504 300d. Ly Thong 15 15
1505 500d. Thach Sanh fighting fire-breathing snake . . . 30 30
1506 1000d. Thach Sanh shooting down bird 60 60
1507 2000d. Thach Sanh in prison 1·20 1·20
1508 3000d. Thach Sanh and wife 1·80 1·80

1990. World Cup Football Championship Results. Nos. 1382/**MS**1389 optd **1. GERMANY 2. ARGENTINA 3. ITALY.**

1509 **290** 100d. multicoloured . . 10 10
1510 – 200d. multicoloured . . 10 10
1511 – 300d. multicoloured . . 15 15
1512 – 500d. multicoloured . . 30 30
1513 – 1000d. multicoloured . . 60 60
1514 – 2000d. multicoloured . . 1·20 1·20
1515 – 3000d. multicoloured . . 1·80 1·80
MS1516 90 × 67 mm. 3500d. multicoloured . . . . 2·75 2·75

1990. Red Cross. Nos. N598/605 optd with red cross and **FOR THE FUTURE GENERATION** in various languages (given in brackets).

1517 12x. multicoloured (Italian) 25 25
1518 12x. multicoloured (Chinese) 25 25
1519 20x. multicoloured (German) 40 40
1520 20x. mult (Vietnamese) . . . 40 40
1521 30x. multicoloured (English) 60 60
1522 40x. multicoloured (Russian) 75 75
1523 50x. multicoloured (French) 90 90
1524 60x. multicoloured (Spanish) 1·10 1·10

311 Soldier

1990. 60th Anniv of Vietnamese Women's Union. Multicoloured.

1525 100d. Type **311** 10 10
1526 500d. Women in various occupations 30 30

312 Emblems

1990. 20th Anniv of Asian–Pacific Postal Training Centre, Bangkok.

1527 **312** 150d. multicoloured . . 40 40

313 Hands holding Forest and City

1990. Preservation of Forests. Multicoloured.
1528 200d. Type **313** 25 10
1529 1000d. Forest fire, "S.O.S." and river 85 25

314 Panther Cap **315** Yachting

1991. Poisonous Fungi. Multicoloured.
1530 200d. Type **314** 10 10
1531 300d. Death cap 25 10
1532 1000d. Destroying angel . . 55 40
1533 1500d. Fly agaric 85 40
1534 2000d. "Russula emetica" . 1·20 40
1535 3000d. Satan's mushroom 1·70 70

1991. Olympic Games, Barcelona (1992). Mult.
1536 200d. Type **315** 10 10
1537 300d. Boxing 25 10
1538 400d. Cycling 25 15
1539 1000d. High jumping . . . 70 25
1540 2000d. Show jumping . . . 1·10 25
1541 3000d. Judo . . . . 1·50 55
1542 3000d. Wrestling (horiz) . . 1·50 55
MS1543 80 × 92 mm. 5000d. Football (43 × 32 mm) . . . . 2·75 1·20
See also Nos. 1679/**MS**1686.

316 Nguyen Binh Khiem

1991. 500th Birth Anniv of Nguyen Binh Khiem (poet).
1544 **316** 200d. black, brown and ochre 40 25

317 "Marisiliana"

318 Woman in Blue Tunic

1991. 500th Anniv (1992) of Discovery of America by Columbus (2nd issue). Multicoloured.
1545 200d. Type **317** 10 10
1546 400d. "Venitien" 25 15
1547 400d. "Cromster" (vert) . . 25 15
1548 2000d. "Pinta" . . . . . . 1·00 25
1549 2000d. "Nina" . . . . . . 1·00 25
1550 3000d. "Howker" (vert) . . 1·40 40
1551 5000d. "Santa Maria" . . . 2·30 70
MS1552 98 × 74 mm. 6500d. Columbus (39 × 27 mm) . . . 2·75 1·20

1991. Golden Heart Charity.
1553 **318** 200d. multicoloured . . 10 10
1554 – 500d. multicoloured . . 15 15
1555 – 1000d. multicoloured . . 55 15
1556 – 5000d. multicoloured . . 2·40 70
DESIGNS: 500d. to 5000d. Traditional women's costumes.

319 Japanese White-naped Crane

1991. Birds. Multicoloured.
1557 200d. Type **319** 15 15
1558 300d. Sarus crane chick (vert) 15 15
1559 400d. Manchurian crane (vert) 30 15
1560 1000d. Sarus cranes (adults) (vert) 45 15
1561 2000d. Black-necked crane (vert) . . . . 1·00 45
1562 3000d. South African crowned cranes (vert) . . 1·70 60
1563 3000d. Great white crane . . 1·70 60

320 Black-finned Reef Shark

1991. Sharks. Multicoloured.
1564 200d. Type **320** 10 10
1565 300d. Grey reef shark . . . 10 10
1566 400d. Leopard shark 25 15
1567 1000d. Great hammerhead 40 15
1568 2000d. White-tipped reef shark 85 40
1569 3000d. Sand tiger . . . . . 1·50 55
1570 3000d. Bull shark . . . . . 1·50 55

321 Lobster

1991. Shellfish. Multicoloured.
1571 200d. Type **321** 10 10
1572 300d. "Alpheus bellulus" . . 10 10
1573 400d. "Periclemenes brevicarpalis" 25 15
1574 1000d. Lobster (different) 40 15
1575 2000d. Lobster (different) 85 40
1576 3000d. Lobster (different) 1·50 55
1577 3000d. "Astacus sp." . . . 1·50 55

322 "Fusee", 1829 **323** Ho Chi Minh, "VII" and Buildings

1991. Early Locomotives. Multicoloured.
1578 400d. Type **322** 15 15
1579 400d. Blenkinsop's rack locomotive (wrongly inscr "Puffing Billy") 15 15
1580 500d. John Stevens rack locomotive, 1825 (horiz) 25 15
1581 1000d. Crampton No 80 locomotive, 1852, France (horiz) 40 25
1582 2000d. "Locomotion", 1825 (horiz) 85 40
1583 3000d. "Saint-Lo", 1843 (horiz) . . . . 1·50 55
1584 3000d. "Coutances", 1855 (horiz) . . . . 1·50 55
MS1585 83 × 62 mm. 5000d. "Atlantic", 1843 (32 × 43 mm) 2·75 1·20

1991. 7th Vietnamese Communist Party Congress. Multicoloured.
1586 200d. Type **323** 25 15
1587 300d. Workers 40 25
1588 400d. Mother and children 55 25

324 Pioneers **326** Yellow-banded Poison-arrow Frog

325 Lada

1991. 50th Anniv of Vietnam Youth Pioneers (200d.) and United Nations Convention on Children's Rights (400d.). Multicoloured.
1589 200d. Type **324** 40 25
1590 400d. Child's face and U.N. emblem 70 40

1991. Rally Cars. Multicoloured.
1591 400d. Type **325** 15 15
1592 400d. Nissan 15 15
1593 500d. Ford Sierra RS Cosworth 25 15
1594 1000d. Suzuki 40 15
1595 2000d. Mazda "323" . . . 85 40
1596 3000d. Peugeot . . . . . . 1·50 55
1597 3000d. Lancia . . . . . . 1·50 55
MS1598 85 × 75 mm. 5000d. Peugeot "405" (43 × 29 mm) . . . . . 3·50 1·20

1991. Frogs. Multicoloured.
1599 200d. Type **326** 15 15
1600 400d. Edible frog 15 15
1601 500d. Golden mantella . . . 30 15
1602 1000d. Dyeing poison-arrow frog 45 15
1603 2000d. Tree frog . . . . . 1·00 45
1604 3000d. Red-eyed tree frog ("Agalychnis calidryas") 1·70 60
1605 3000d. Golden tree frog ("Hyla aurea") . . . . . 1·70 60

327 Ho Chi Minh and Party Emblem **328** Speed Skating

1991. 60th Anniv (1990) of Vietnamese Communist Party.
1606 **327** 100d. red 55 15

1991. Winter Olympic Games, Albertville (1992) (1st issue). Multicoloured.
1607 200d. Type **328** 15 15
1608 300d. Freestyle skiing . . . 15 15
1609 400d. Four-man bobsleighing (horiz) . . . 25 15
1610 1000d. Biathlon (rifle shooting) (horiz) 40 15
1611 2000d. Skiing (horiz) . . . 85 40
1612 3000d. Cross-country skiing 1·50 55
1613 3000d. Ice skating . . . . . 1·50 55
MS1614 93 × 106 mm. 5000d. Ice Hockey (32 × 43 mm) . . . . 2·75 1·20
See also Nos. 1659/63.

329 "Arsinoitherium zitteli"

1991. Prehistoric Animals. Multicoloured.
1615 200d. Type **329** 15 15
1616 500d. "Elephas primigenius" 25 15
1617 1000d. "Baluchitherium" . . 40 25
1618 2000d. "Deinotherium giganteum" . . . . 1·20 40
1619 3000d. "Brontops" . . . . 1·70 55
1620 3000d. "Uintatherium" . . 1·70 55

330 Pawn

1991. Chess. Staunton Pieces.
1621 200d. Type **330** 15 15
1622 300d. Knight 25 15
1623 1000d. Rook 40 25
1624 2000d. Queen . . . . 1·00 55
1625 3000d. Bishop . . . . . . 1·50 55
1626 3000d. King . . . . 1·50 55
MS1627 92 × 70 mm. 5000d. Knight, pawn and king . . . . 2·75 1·20

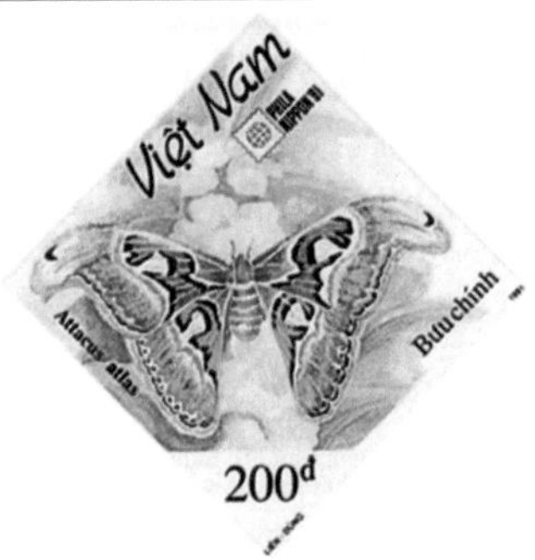

331 Atlas Moth

1991. "Phila Nippon '91" International Stamp Exhibition, Tokyo. Moths and Butterflies. Mult.
1628 200d. Type **331** 15 15
1629 400d. Blue morpho 25 15
1630 500d. Birdwing 25 15
1631 1000d. Red admiral 55 25
1632 1000d. "Papilio demetrius" 55 25
1633 3000d. "Papilio weiskei" . . 1·40 55
1634 5000d. Lesser purple emperor . . . . 2·00 70
MS1635 85 × 87 mm. 5500d. "Heliconius melpomene-aglaope" (43 × 32 mm) . . . . 2·75 1·20

332 Means of Communication

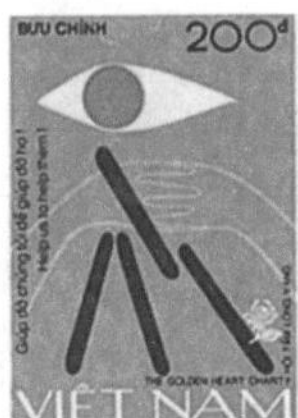

333 Eye and Clasped Hands

1991. 25th Anniv of Post and Telecommunications Research Institute. Multicoloured.
1636 200d. Type **332** 40 25
MS1637 90 × 73 mm. 3500d. Means of communication (different) (43 × 32 mm) . . . . 1·90 1·10

1991. Golden Heart Charity for Disabled People.
1638 **333** 200d. blue, lilac & orange 15 15
1639 – 3000d. violet, blue and turquoise . . . . . . 1·40 55
DESIGN: 3000d. Tennis player in wheelchair.

334 Gymnastics

1992. Olympic Games, Los Angeles (1984). Mult.
1640 50x. Type **334** 15 10
1641 50x. Football (vert) 15 10
1642 1d. Wrestling 30 15
1643 2d. Volleyball (vert) 60 15
1644 3d. Hurdling 75 30
1645 5d. Basketball (vert) 90 55
1646 8d. Weightlifting . . . . . 1·90 85
MS1647 80 × 100 mm. 10d. Running (31 × 39 mm) . . . . 3·75 1·90

1992. "Expo '92" World's Fair, Seville. Nos. 1372/8 optd **SEVILLA'92** and emblem.
1648 **288** 50d. multicoloured . . . 25 15
1649 – 100d. mult (No. 1373) 55 25
1650 – 100d. mult (No. 1374) 55 25
1651 – 100d. mult (No. 1375) 55 25
1652 – 200d. mult (No. 1376) 1·00 40
1653 – 200d. mult (No. 1377) 1·00 40
1654 – 300d. multicoloured . . 1·70 1·00
MS1655 85 × 69 mm. 500d. multicoloured . . . . 3·50 1·40

336 Chu Van An teaching

1992. 700th Death Anniv of Chu Van An.
1656 **336** 200d. multicoloured . . 2·30 2·30

337 Atomic Symbol, Communications, Industry and Agriculture

1992. Resolutions of 7th Communist Party Congress. Multicoloured.
1657 200d. Type **337** 15 15
1658 2000d. Hands clasped and map of Asia . . . . . . 1·80 1·50

338 Biathlon

1992. Winter Olympic Games, Albertville (2nd issue). Multicoloured.
1659 200d. Type **338** 15 15
1660 2000d. Ice hockey 55 15
1661 4000d. Skiing (slalom) . . . 1·00 25
1662 5000d. Ice skating . . . . . 1·20 55
1663 6000d. Skiing (downhill) . . 1·70 70

339 Columbus's Fleet

1992. 500th Anniv of Discovery of America by Columbus (3rd issue). Multicoloured.
1664 400d. Type **339** 15 15
1665 3000d. "Santa Maria" . . . 70 25
1666 4000d. Columbus and flag on land . . . . 1·10 25
1667 6000d. Columbus offering gifts to Amerindians . . . 1·50 55
1668 8000d. Ship returning home 1·80 70
MS1669 102 × 70 mm. 11000d. Columbus before King Ferdinand and Queen Isabella (vert) . . . 3·50 1·20

340 Tupolev Tu-154M

1992. Aircraft. Multicoloured.
1670 400d. Type **340** 15 15
1671 500d. Concorde 15 15
1672 1000d. Airbus Industrie A-320 . . . . 25 15
1673 3000d. Airbus Industrie A340-300 . . . . 30 25
1674 4000d. De Havilland D.H.C.8 Dash Eight-400 90 25
1675 5000d. Boeing 747-200 . . . 1·30 55
1676 6000d. McDonnell Douglas MD-11CF . . . . 1·50 55

341 Weather System and Forecasting Equipment

342 Archery

1992. International Decade for Natural Disaster Reduction. Multicoloured.
1677 400d. Type **341** 15 15
1678 4000d. Man taking flood depth readings . . . . . 1·00 40

1992. Olympic Games, Barcelona (2nd issue). Mult.
1679 400d. Type **342** 15 15
1680 600d. Volleyball 15 15
1681 1000d. Wrestling 25 15
1682 3000d. Fencing 55 25
1683 4000d. Running 90 25
1684 5000d. Weightlifting . . . . 1·10 40
1685 6000d. Hockey . . . . . . 1·50 70
MS1686 94 × 74 mm. 10000d. Basketball (27 × 39 mm) . . . 3·00 1·20

343 Suzuki "500 F"

1992. Racing Motor Cycles. Multicoloured.
1687 400d. Type **343** 15 15
1688 500d. Honda "CBR 600F" 15 15
1689 1000d. Honda "HRC 500F" 25 15
1690 3000d. Kawasaki "250F" (vert) 55 25
1691 4000d. Suzuki "RM 250 F" (vert) 90 25
1692 5000d. Suzuki "500F" . . . 1·10 40
1693 6000d. BMW "1000F" . . . 1·50 70
MS1694 103 × 78 mm. 10000d. Suzuki "RM 250 F" (different) (32 × 42 mm) . . . . 3·00 1·20

344 Shuttle Launch

VIỆT NAM 200d
BƯU CHÍNH

346 Footballer

345 Main Entrance

1992. International Space Year. Multicoloured.
1695 400d. Type **344** 15 15
1696 500d. Launch of space shuttle "Columbia" . . . 15 15
1697 3000d. "Columbia" in space (horiz) 70 25
1698 4000d. Projected shuttle "Hermes" docked at space station (horiz) . . . 90 40
1699 5000d. "Hermes" in space with solar panel (horiz) 1·10 40
1700 6000d. Astronauts repairing Hubble space telescope . . 1·50 70

1992. Centenary of Saigon Post Office. Mulicoloured.
1701 200d. Type **345** 75 25
MS1702 84 × 69 mm. 10000d. Post Office . . . . 2·30 1·20

1992. European Cup Football Championship. Mult.
1703 200d. Type **346** 15 15
1704 2000d. Goalkeeper 40 15
1705 4000d. Two players with ball on ground 85 40
1706 5000d. Two players with ball in air . . . . 1·10 55
1707 6000d. Three players . . . . 1·70 70
MS1708 70 × 93 mm. 9000d. Players (42 × 30 mm) . . . . 3·50 1·20

347 "Portrait of a Girl" (Francisco de Zurbaran)

1992. "Expo '92" World's Fair, Seville. Paintings by Spanish Artists. Multicoloured.
1709 400d. Type **347** 15 15
1710 500d. "Woman with a Jug" (Bartolome Esteban Murillo) 15 15
1711 1000d. "Maria Aptrickaia" (Diego Velazquez) 25 15
1712 3000d. "Holy Family with St. Katharine" (Jose de Ribera) 60 25
1713 4000d. "Madonna and Child with Sts. Agnes and Thekla" (El Greco) . . . 90 40
1714 5000d. "Woman with Jug" (Francisco Goya) . . . . 1·50 40
1715 6000d. "The Naked Maja" (Francisco Goya) (horiz) 1·50 55
MS1716 82 × 85 mm. 10000d. "Three Women" (Pablo Picasso) (43 × 32 mm) . . . . 3·00 1·20

348 Clean Water sustaining Life and Polluted Water

1992. 20th Anniv of United Nations Conference on Environmental Protection. Multicoloured.
1717 200d. Type **348** 15 15
1718 4000d. Graph comparing current world development and environmentally sound development . . . . . . 1·00 40

349 Cu Lao Xanh Lighthouse

350 "Citrus maxima"

1992. "Genova '92" International Thematic Stamp Exhibition. Lighthouses. Multicoloured.
1719 200d. Type **349** 15 15
1720 3000d. Can Gio 55 25
1721 5000d. Vung Tau . . . . . 1·10 40
1722 6000d. Long Chau . . . . 1·70 55

1992. Flowers. Multicoloured.
1723 200d. Type **350** 15 15
1724 2000d. "Nerium indicum" 45 15
1725 4000d. "Ixora coccinea" . . 75 25
1726 5000d. "Cananga oborata" 1·00 25
1727 6000d. "Cassia surattensis" 1·50 55

351 Australian Pied Imperial Pigeons

353 Memorials and "45"

352 Guinea Pig

1992. Pigeons and Doves. Multicoloured.
1728 200d. Type **351** 15 15
1729 2000d. Red-plumed pigeon 45 15
1730 4000d. Feral rock pigeon . . 75 25
1731 5000d. Top-knot pigeon . . 1·10 25
1732 6000d. Laughing doves (horiz) . . . . 1·40 55

1992. Rodents. Multicoloured.
1733 200d. Type **352** 15 15
1734 500d. Guinea pigs 15 15
1735 3000d. Indian crested porcupine 60 25
1736 4000d. Lesser Egyptian gerbil (vert) 90 25
1737 5000d. Red giant flying squirrel (vert) . . . . . . 1·10 55
1738 6000d. Common rabbit (vert) . . . . 1·70 70

1992. 45th Anniv of Disabled Soldiers' Day.
1739 **353** 200d. multicoloured . . 40 25

354 Stylized Sportsmen

1992. 3rd Phu Dong Games.
1740 **354** 200d. blue, ultramarine and light blue 40 25

355 Siamese Fighting Fish

1992. Siamese Fighting Fishes.
1741 **355** 200d. multicoloured . . 15 15
1742 – 500d. multicoloured . . 15 15
1743 – 3000d. multicoloured . . 75 25
1744 – 4000d. multicoloured . . 90 25
1745 – 5000d. multicoloured . . 1·10 55
1746 – 6000d. multicoloured . . 1·50 70
DESIGNS: 500d. to 6000d. Different Siamese fighting fishes.

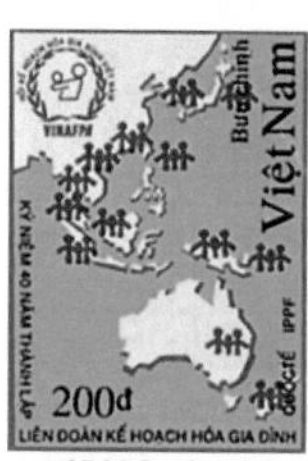

356 Members' Locations on Map

358 Adult protecting Child

357 Trainee Doctors

1992. 40th Anniv of International Planned Parenthood Federation. Multicoloured.
1747 200d. Type **356** 15 15
1748 4000d. Emblem on world map (horiz) . . . . . . 1·00 40

1992. 90th Anniv of Hanoi Medical School. Mult.
1749 200d. Type **357** 15 15
1750 5000d. Alexandre Yersin (bacteriologist) and school 1·10 40

1992. SOS Children's Villages. Multicoloured.
1751 200d. Type **358** 15 15
1752 5000d. Houses and woman with children . . . . . . 1·10 40

359 Kick Boxing

1993. 17th South-East Asian Games, Singapore.
1753 **359** 200d. multicoloured . . 40 25

360 Giant Bee

1993. Bees. Multicoloured.
1754 200d. Type **360** 15 15
1755 800d. "Apis koschevnikovi" 25 15
1756 1000d. "Apis laboriosa" . . 40 15
1757 2000d. "Apis cerana japonica" 55 25
1758 5000d. "Apis cerana cerana" 1·10 55
1759 10000d. Honey bee (vert) . . 2·10 85

361 Tam-Cam returning from the River

362 Rooster with Family

1993. Legend of Tam-Cam. Multicoloured.

1760 200d. Type **361** 15 15
1761 800d. Apparition of old man by goldfish basin 25 15
1762 1000d. Tam-Cam with unsold rice at the market 40 15
1763 3000d. Tam-Cam trying on slipper for Prince 60 25
1764 4000d. Tam-Cam rising from lotus 1·10 55
1765 10000d. The royal couple 2·10 85

1993. New Year. Year of the Cock. Multicoloured.

1766 200d. Type **362** 15 15
1767 5000d. Rooster with family (different) 1·10 40

363 "Atractylodes macrocephala"

364 Communications Equipment

1993. Medicinal Plants. Multicoloured.

1768 200d. Type **363** 15 15
1769 1000d. Rangoon creeper ("Quisqualis indica") 25 15
1770 1000d. Japanese honeysuckle ("Lonicera japonica") 25 15
1771 3000d. "Rehmannia glutinosa" 90 25
1772 12000d. "Gardenia jasminoides" 3·00 85

1993. "Communication in Service of Life". Mult.

1773 200d. Type **364** 10 10
1774 2500d. Fibre-optic cable and map of Hong Kong–Sri Racha submarine cable route 55 25

365 Giant Panda

1993. Mammals. Multicoloured.

1775 200d. Type **365** 10 10
1776 800d. Tiger 25 15
1777 1000d. Indian elephant 25 15
1778 3000d. Indian rhinoceros 75 25
1779 4000d. Family of gibbons 1·10 40
1780 10000d. Clouded leopard 1·80 90
MS1781 79 × 85 mm. 10000d. Kouprey ("Bos sauveli") 2·75 1·20

366 Players, Statue of Liberty and Emblem

1993. World Cup Football Championship, U.S.A. (1994) (1st issue).

1782 **366** 200d. multicoloured 10 10
1783 – 1500d. multicoloured 40 15
1784 – 7000d. multicoloured 1·50 40

DESIGNS: 1500, 7000d. Different match scenes.

See also Nos. 1865/**MS**1871.

367 Wheelbarrow

1993. Traditional Transport. Multicoloured.

1785 200d. Type **367** 10 10
1786 800d. Buffalo cart 25 15
1787 1000d. Rickshaw 25 15
1788 2000d. Rickshaw with passenger 60 15
1789 5000d. Rickshaw (different) 1·20 40
1790 10000d. Horse-drawn carriage 1·80 1·10

368 Pylon and Lightbulb

1993. 500 kV Electricity Lines.

1791 **368** 300d. black, orange and red 25 15
1792 400d. black, blue and orange 40 15

369 "Sunflowers" (Vincent van Gogh)

1993. "Polska'93" International Stamp Exhibition, Poznan. Paintings. Multicoloured.

1793 200d. Type **369** 10 10
1794 1000d. "Young Woman" (Amedeo Modigliani) 25 15
1795 1000d. "Couple in Forest" (Henri Rousseau) 25 15
1796 5000d. "Harlequin with Family" (Pablo Picasso) 1·20 25
1797 10000d. "Female Model" (Henri Matisse) (horiz) 2·40 60
MS1798 85 × 85 mm. 10000d. "Dr. Gachet" (Vincent van Gogh) (27 × 37 mm) 2·75 1·20

370 "Paphiopedilum hirsutissimum"

1993. Centenary of Da Lat. Orchids. Multicoloured.

1799 400d. Type **370** 10 10
1800 1000d. "Paphiopedilum gratrixianum" 25 15
1801 1000d. "Paphiopedilum malipoense" 25 15
1802 12000d. "Paphiopedilum hennisianum" 3·00 1·20

371 Wat Phra Sri Rattana Satsadaram, Thailand

1993. Historic Asian Architecture. Multicoloured.

1803 400d. Type **371** 10 10
1804 800d. Prambanan Temple, Indonesia 15 15
1805 1000d. City Hall, Singapore 25 15
1806 2000d. Angkor Vat, Cambodia (horiz) 45 15
1807 2000d. Ubudiah Mosque, Kuala Kangsar, Malaysia (horiz) 45 15
1808 6000d. That Luang, Laos (horiz) 1·10 40
1809 8000d. Omar Ali Saifuddin Mosque, Brunei (horiz) 1·70 45
MS1810 86 × 116 mm. 10000d. Chua Keo, Thai Binh, Vietnam (31 × 42 mm) 2·75 1·50

372 Industry and Communications

1993. 7th Trade Unions Congress. Multicoloured.

1811 400d. Type **372** 10 10
1812 5000d. Doves, atomic symbol, hammer in hand and flowers 1·10 30

373 "Scylla serrata"

1993. Salt-water Crabs. Multicoloured.

1813 400d. Type **373** 10 10
1814 800d. "Portunus sanguinolentus" 15 15
1815 1000d. "Charybdis bimaculata" 25 15
1816 2000d. "Paralithodes brevipes" 40 15
1817 5000d. "Portunus pelagicus" 1·10 40
1818 10000d. "Lithodes turritus" 1·90 60

374 Stamps and Globe

1993. Stamp Day. Multicoloured.

1819 400d. Type **374** 10 10
1820 5000d. Airmail letter 1·10 30

375 Player

376 Lo Lo Costume

1994. Tennis.

1821 **375** 400d. multicoloured 10 10
1822 – 1000d. multicoloured (male player) 30 15
1823 – 1000d. multicoloured (female player) 30 15
1824 – 12000d. multicoloured 2·40 90

DESIGNS: Nos. 1822/4, Different players.

1993. "Bangkok 1993" International Stamp Exhibition.

1825 400d. Type **376** 10 10
1826 800d. Thai costume 15 15
1827 1000d. Dao Do costume 25 15
1828 2000d. H'mong costume 40 15
1829 5000d. Kho Mu costume 1·10 40
1830 10000d. Kinh costume 1·50 75
MS1831 78 × 108 mm. 10000d. Precious stones (42 × 31 mm) 2·75 1·20

377 Dog with Puppies

1994. New Year. Year of the Dog. Multicoloured.

1832 400d. Type **377** 10 10
1833 6000d. Dog 1·50 40

378 Peach

380 Hoi Lim

379 Anatoly Karpov

1994. Flowers of the Four Seasons. Multicoloured.

1834 400d. Type **378** (spring) 40 15
1835 400d. "Chrysanthemum morifolium" (autumn) 40 15
1836 400d. "Rosa chinensis" (winter) 40 15
1837 15000d. "Delonix regia" (summer) 3·50 1·10

1994. Chess. Multicoloured.

1838 400d. Type **379** 10 10
1839 1000d. Gary Kasparov 25 15
1840 2000d. Robert Fischer 55 25
1841 4000d. Emanuel Lasker 1·10 25
1842 10000d. Jose Raul Capablanca 2·00 75
MS1843 85 × 90 mm. 10000d. Chess piece (vert) 2·75 1·20

No. 1840 is wrongly inscribed "Robers".

1994. "Hong Kong '94" Stamp Exhibition. Traditional Festivals. Multicoloured.

1844 400d. Type **380** 10 10
1845 800d. Cham 25 10
1846 1000d. Tay Nguyen 40 10
1847 12000d. Nam Bo 2·75 90

381 Loi Nhuoc

382 Red Gladioli

1994. Operatic Masks. Multicoloured.

1848 400d. Type **381** 10 10
1849 500d. Dao Tax Xuan 10 10
1850 2000d. Ta Ngoc Lan 40 15
1851 3000d. Ly Khac Minh 70 25
1852 4000d. Ta On Dinh 90 25
1853 7000d. Khuong Linh Ta 1·70 75

1994. Gladioli. Multicoloured.

1854 400d. Type **382** 10 10
1855 2000d. Salmon gladioli 40 15
1856 5000d. White gladioli 1·10 25
1857 8000d. Magenta gladioli 1·70 70

383 Painting by Utamaro Kitagawa

1994. Paintings by Japanese Artists. Multicoloured.

1858 400d. Type **383** (wrongly inscr "Kigatawa") 10 10
1859 500d. Harunobu Suzuki 10 10
1860 1000d. Hokusai Katsushika 25 15
1861 2000d. Hiroshige 45 15
1862 3000d. Hokusai Katsushika (different) 60 25
1863 4000d. Utamaro Kitagawa (different) 75 25
1864 9000d. Choki Eishosai 2·00 75

384 Footballers

386 Pioneers reading Newspaper

385 Hauling Piece of Equipment

1994. World Cup Football Championship, U.S.A. (2nd issue). Multicoloured.

1865	400d. Type **384**	10	10
1866	600d. Running with ball	10	10
1867	1000d. Heading ball	25	15
1868	2000d. Goalkeeper	40	15
1869	3000d. Two players chasing ball	75	30
1870	11000d. Tackling	2·75	90
MS1871	102 × 77 mm. 10000d. Play at goalmouth (31 × 42 mm)	2·75	1·20

1994. 40th Anniv of Victory at Dien Bien Phu.

1872 **385**	400d. brown, cinnamon and black	15	10
1873 –	3000d. ultramarine, blue and black	75	40

DESIGN: 3000d. Entertaining the troops.

1994. 40th Anniv of "Young Pioneer" (newspaper).

1874 **386**	400d. red and black	40	15

387 Estuarine Crocodile

1994. Reptiles. Multicoloured.

1875	400d. Type **387**	10	10
1876	600d. Mississippi alligator	10	10
1877	2000d. Nile crocodile	40	15
1878	3000d. Chinese alligator	55	25
1879	4000d. Paraguay caiman	90	40
1880	9000d. Australian crocodile	2·00	75
MS1881	100 × 67 mm. 10000d. Spectacled caiman (42 × 31 mm)	2·75	1·20

388 Alexandre Yersin

389 Pierre de Coubertin (founder)

1994. Centenary of Discovery of Plague Bacillus.

1882 **388**	400d. multicoloured	55	15

1994. Cent of International Olympic Committee. Multicoloured.

1883	400d. Anniversary and National Committee emblems and sports pictograms	75	40
1884	6000d. Type **389**	1·50	55

390 "Cicindela aurulenta"

1994. Beetles. Multicoloured.

1885	400d. Type **390**	15	15
1886	1000d. "Harmonia octomaculata"	25	15
1887	6000d. "Cicindela tennipes"	1·10	40
1888	7000d. "Collyris sp."	1·50	55

391 Anniversary Emblem

1994. 120th Anniv of U.P.U. Multicoloured.

1889	400d. Type **391**	10	40
1890	5000d. Envelopes forming world map	1·10	45
MS1891	100 × 80 mm. 10000d. UPU emblem (29 × 41 mm)	2·75	60

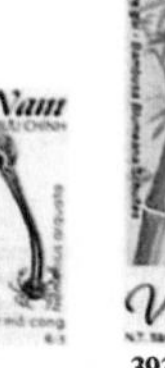

392 Curlew

393 "Bambusa blumeana"

1994. "Philakorea 1994" International Stamp Exhibition, Seoul. Sea Birds. Multicoloured.

1892	400d. Type **392**	10	10
1893	600d. Wilson's storm petrel	10	10
1894	1000d. Great frigate bird	25	15
1895	2000d. Cape gannet	40	15
1896	3000d. Tufted puffins	75	30
1897	11000d. Band-tailed gulls	2·75	75
MS1898	78 × 65 mm. 10000d. Grey-rumped swiftlet (38 × 31 mm)	2·75	1·20

1994. "Singpex '94" Stamp Exhibition, Singapore. Bamboos. Multicoloured.

1899	400d. Type **393**	10	10
1900	1000d. "Phyllostachys aurea"	25	15
1901	2000d. "Bambusa vulgaris"	45	15
1902	4000d. "Tetragonocalamus quadrangularis"	75	25
1903	10000d. "Bambusa venticosa"	2·75	90

394 Log Bridge with Handrail

1994. Rudimentary Bridges. Multicoloured.

1904	400d. Type **394**	10	10
1905	900d. Interwoven bridge	30	30
1906	8000d. Log bridge on stilts	1·50	55

395 Girl in Wheelchair and Boy playing

1994. "For Our Children's Future". Multicoloured.

1907	400d.+100d. Type **395**	10	10
1908	2000d. Children dancing around emblem (vert)	55	30

396 Electric Tramcar No. 1

1994. Trams. Multicoloured.

1909	400d. Type **396**	10	10
1910	900d. Paris double-deck battery-powered tram	10	10
1911	8000d. Philadelphia U.S. Mail electric tram	85	25

397 Civilians greeting Soldiers

1994. 40th Anniv of Liberation of Hanoi. Mult.

1912	400d. Type **397**	10	10
1913	2000d. Workers and students and symbols of development	55	30

398 Airplane in Air

1994. 50th Anniv of I.C.A.O. Multicoloured.

1914	400d. Type **398**	15	10
1915	3000d. Airplane on ground	75	30

399 Parade

1994. 50th Anniv of Vietnamese People's Army. Multicoloured.

1916	400d. Type **399**	10	10
1917	1000d. Plan of attacks on Saigon	25	15
1918	2000d. Veteran recounting the past to young girl	40	25
1919	4000d. Naval anti-aircraft gun crew	90	30

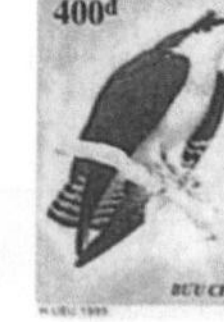

400 Sow with Piglets

401 Osprey ("Pandion haliaetus")

1995. New Year. Year of the Pig. Multicoloured.

1920	400d. Type **400**	15	10
1921	8000d. Pig	1·70	55

1995. Birds.

1922 **401**	400d. blue	10	10
1923 –	400d. green	10	10
1924 –	400d. purple	10	10
1925 –	400d. orange	10	10
1926 –	5000d. red	1·00	45

DESIGNS—HORIZ: No. 1923, Sociable weaver ("Philetarius socius"); 1924, Sharpbill ("Oxyruncus cristatus"); 1925, Golden plover ("Pluvialis apricaria"). VERT: No. 1926, Red-legged seriema ("Cariama cristata").

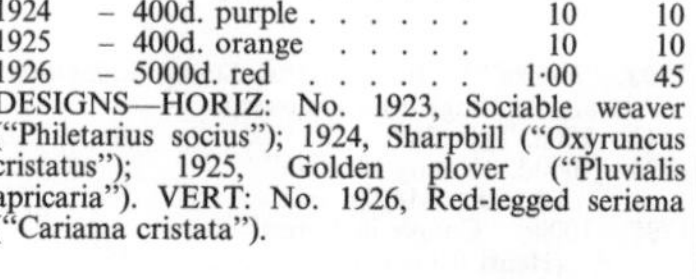

402 Girls with Bicycle

403 Statue and Building

1995. Women's Costumes. Multicoloured.

1927	400d. Type **402**	10	10
1928	3000d. Girl with sheaf of flowers	55	25
1929	5000d. Girl with traditional hat	1·10	45

1995. "Vietstampex '95" Stamp Exhibition. F.I.A.P. Executive Committee Meeting.

1930 **403**	5500d. multicoloured	1·20	55

404 Brown Fish Owl

1995. Owls. Multicoloured.

1931	400d. Type **404**	10	10
1932	1000d. Tawny owl	25	15
1933	2000d. Great grey owl	40	15
1934	5000d. Spotted wood owl	90	40
1935	10000d. White-faced scops owl	1·70	75
MS1936	64 × 81 mm. 12500d. Barn owl (31 × 42 mm)	2·75	1·10

405 Grey Angelfish

1995. Fishes. Multicoloured.

1937	400d. Type **405**	10	10
1938	1000d. Rectangle triggerfish	25	15
1939	2000d. Regal angelfish	40	15
1940	4000d. Queen angelfish	60	25
1941	5000d. Queen triggerfish	1·00	30
1942	9000d. Clown triggerfish	1·50	60

406 Throwing the Hammer

407 Lenin

1995. Olympic Games, Atlanta (1996) (1st issue). Multicoloured.

1943	400d. Type **406**	10	10
1944	3000d. Cycling	55	25
1945	4000d. Running	60	30
1946	10000d. Pole vaulting	1·90	75
MS1947	59 × 100 mm. 12500d. Handball	2·75	1·10

See also Nos. 2063/5.

1995. 125th Birth Anniv of Lenin.

1948 **407**	400d. black and red	25	15

408 Adult and Young

1995. The Malayan Tapir. Multicoloured. (a) With World Wildlife Fund emblem.

1949	400d. Type **408**	30	40
1950	1000d. Standing	40	40
1951	2000d. Walking	45	40
1952	4000d. Calling	75	40

Nos. 1949/52 were issued together, se-tenant, forming a composite design.

(b) Without W.W.F. emblem.

1953	4000d. Standing by trees	60	40
1954	4000d. Eating	60	40
1955	5000d. Swimming	70	40
1956	6000d. In water	85	40

Nos. 1953/6 were issued together, se-tenant, forming a composite design.

409 Dove and "50"

1995. 50th Anniv of End of Second World War in Europe.

1957 **409**	400d. multicoloured	25	15

410 Montgolfier's Hot Air Balloon, 1783

411 Parachutist

1995. "Finlandia 95" International Stamp Exhibition, Helsinki. Balloons. Multicoloured.

1958	500d. Type **410**	10	10
1959	1000d. Jacques Charles and Marie-Noel Robert's balloon (first untethered flight by manned hydrogen balloon)	15	15
1960	2000d. Jean-Pierre Blanchard's oared balloon	40	15

1961 3000d. Jean-Francois Pilatre de Rozier and Jules Romain's balloon over English Channel, 1785 . . 55 15
1962 4000d. Free balloon 60 25
1963 5000d. Captive balloon over Red Square, Moscow, 1890 . . . . 75 25
1964 7000d. Auguste Piccard's balloon "F.N.R.S.", 1931 1·30 55

1995. Parachuting. Multicoloured.
1965 400d. Type **411** 15 10
1966 2000d. Two parachutists . . 40 15
1967 3000d. Landing 60 25
1968 4000d. Gathering in the parachute . . . . 1·50 70
Nos. 1965/8 were issued together, se-tenant, forming a composite design.

412 "Rhododendron fleuryi"

1995. Rhododendrons. Multicoloured.
1969 400d. Type **412** 10 10
1970 1000d. "Rhododendron sulphoreum" 25 15
1971 2000d. "Rhododendron sinofalconeri" 40 15
1972 3000d. "Rhododendron lyi" 55 25
1973 5000d. "Rhododendron ovatum" 90 30
1974 9000d. "Rhododendron tanastylum" . . . . . . 1·70 60

413 Tan and Lang pay Court to Lu's Daughter

1995. "Betel and Areca Nut" (fable). Multicoloured.
1975 400d. Type **413** 10 10
1976 1000d. Girl chooses Tan . . 25 15
1977 3000d. Lang changes into rock 55 25
1978 10000d. Girl changes into betel pepper plant and Tan into areca nut palm 1·70 55
Nos. 1975/8 were issued together, se-tenant, forming a composite design.

414 Statue of Mother and Child

415 Flags around Emblem

1995. 65th Anniv of Women's Union (400d.) and World Conference on Women, Peking (3000d.). Multicoloured.
1979 400d. Type **414** 15 10
1980 3000d. Globe and women of different races (horiz) . . 55 30

1995. Admission of Vietnam to Association of South East Asian Nations.
1981 **415** 400d. multicoloured . . 30 15

416 Ho Chi Minh, Dove and Crowd

1995. Anniversaries. Multicoloured.
1982 400d. Type **416** (65th anniv of Communist Party of Indo-China) 10 10
1983 400d. Ho Chi Minh embracing child (105th birth anniv) 10 10
1984 1000d. Civic building, road bridge, power lines and oil derrick (40th anniv of evacuation of French troops from North Vietnam) 15 15
1985 1000d. Ho Chi Minh saluting and building flying flags (20th anniv of end of Vietnam war) . . . 15 15
1986 2000d. Soldiers and flag (50th anniv of National Liberation Army) 40 25
1987 2000d. Radio mast, dish aerial, motor cycle couriers and mail van (50th anniv of postal and telecommunications services) 40 25

417 Bust of Hill and Penny Black

1995. Birth Bicentenary of Sir Rowland Hill (instigator of postage stamp).
1988 **417** 4000d. multicoloured . . 75 25

418 Torch Carriers and Sports Pictograms

1995. National Sports Festival.
1989 **418** 400d. blue, red and lilac 25 15

419 "Paphiopedilum druryi"

1995. "Singapore'95" International Stamp Exhibition. Orchids. Multicoloured.
1990 400d. Type **419** 10 10
1991 2000d. "Dendrobium ochraceum" 40 15
1992 3000d. "Vanda sp." 55 15
1993 4000d. "Cattleya sp." 60 25
1994 5000d. "Paphiopedilum hirsutissimum" 90 25
1995 6000d. "Christenosia vietnamica" . . . . . . 1·30 55
MS1996 65 × 90 mm. 12500d. "Angraecum sesquipedale" (31 × 42 mm) . . . . 2·75 1·10

420 Palace, Hue

1995. Asian Cityscapes. Multicoloured.
1997 400d. Type **420** 10 10
1998 3000d. Park, Doanh Chau 55 25
1999 4000d. Temple, Macao . . . 60 25
2000 5000d. Kowloon, Hong Kong 90 25
2001 6000d. Pagoda, Dai Loan 1·00 40

421 Dove and Anniversary Emblem

1995. 50th Anniv of U.N.O.
2002 **421** 2000d. multicoloured . . 40 15

422 Woman with Vase of Flowers (To Ngoc Van)

1995. Paintings. Multicoloured.
2003 400d. Type **422** 15 15
2004 2000d. Woman washing hair (Tran Van Can) 40 40
2005 6000d. Woman and vase of flowers (To Ngoc Van) . . 1·00 1·00
2006 8000d. Two women resting (Tran Van Can) . . . . . 1·40 1·40

423 Map and Eclipse

1995. Total Eclipse of the Sun.
2007 **423** 400d. multicoloured . . 30 30

424 Rats carrying Canopy and on Horseback

1996. New Year. Year of the Rat. Multicoloured.
2008 400d. Type **424** 15 15
2009 8000d. Rats in and carrying sedan chair . . . . 1·20 1·20
MS2010 110 × 75 mm. 13000d. Rat carrying placard (31 × 42 mm) 1·90 1·90

425 Apricot

1996. Flowers.
2011 **425** 400d. brown 10 10
2012 – 400d. purple 10 10
2013 – 400d. red 10 10
2014 – 400d. blue 10 10
2015 – 5000d. red 75 75
DESIGNS—HORIZ: No. 2012, Chrysanthemums; 2013, Orchid; 2014, Orchids (different). VERT: No. 2015, Asters.

426 Communist Symbols and Ho Chi Minh

1996. 8th Vietnamese Communist Party Congress. Multicoloured.
2016 400d. Type **426** 10 10
2017 3000d. Symbols of communications, industry, Communism and agriculture within outline of dove 55 55

427 Thanh Tru Tai

429 White-throated Kingfisher

428 Tsintaosaurus

1996. Statues in Tay Phuong Pagoda, Thach That. Multicoloured.
2018 400d. Type **427** 10 10
2019 600d. Tich Doc Than . . . 10 10
2020 1000d. Hoang Tuy Cau . . 15 15
2021 2000d. Bach Tinh Thuy . . 30 30
2022 3000d. Xich Thanh Hoa . . 45 45
2023 5000d. Dinh Tru Tai . . . 70 70
2024 6000d. Tu Hien Than . . . 85 85
2025 8000d. Dai Than Luc . . . 1·20 1·20

1996. Prehistoric Animals. Multicoloured.
2026 400d. Type **428** 10 10
2027 1000d. Archaeopteryx . . . 15 15
2028 2000d. Psittacosaurus . . . 30 30
2029 3000d. Hypsilophodon . . . 55 55
2030 13000d. Parasaurolophus . . 2·00 2·00

1996. Kingfishers. Multicoloured.
2031 400d. Type **429** 10 10
2032 1000d. Belted kingfisher . . 15 15
2033 2000d. River kingfisher . . 30 30
2034 4000d. Ruddy kingfisher . . 60 60
2035 12000d. Lesser pied kingfisher . . . . 1·90 1·90

430 Temple of Literature, Hanoi

431 Dan Ty Ba

1996. Asian Temples. Multicoloured.
2036 400d. Type **430** 10 10
2037 2000d. Wat Mahathtat, Sukhothai, Thailand . . . 30 30
2038 3000d. Lingaraja Temple, Bhubaeshwar, India . . . 45 45
2039 4000d. Kinkakuju Temple, Kyoto, Japan 70 70
2040 10000d. Borobudur Temple, Java, Indonesia . . . . . 1·50 15

1996. "China '96" Ninth Asian International Stamp Exhibition, Peking. Stringed Musical Instruments. Multicoloured.
2041 400d. Type **431** 10 10
2042 3000d. Dan nhi 45 45
2043 4000d. Dan day 60 60
2044 9000d. Dan tranh . . . . . 1·30 1·30

432 Ho Chi Minh

1996. 50th Anniv of Vietnamese Red Cross.
2045 **432** 3000d. multicoloured . . 60 60

433 Children of Different Races

434 Tiger Beetle

1996. 50th Anniv of UNICEF. Multicoloured.
2046 400d. Type **433** 15 15
2047 7000d. Water droplets containing symbols and globe "plant" . . . . . . 1·20 1·20

1996. Beetles. Multicoloured.
2048 400d. Type **434** 10 10
2049 500d. "Calodema wallacei" 10 10
2050 1000d. Blister beetle 15 15
2051 4000d. "Chrysochroa buqueti" 60 60
2052 5000d. "Ophioniea nigrofasciata" 85 85
2053 12000d. Ground beetle . . . 1·70 1·70

435 Emblem in Hand

1996. 50th Natural Disaster Reduction Day.
2054 **435** 400d. multicoloured . . 25 25

436 Goalkeeper

1996. European Football Championship, England. Multicoloured.
2055 400d. Type **436** 15 15
2056 8000d. Player . . . . 1·40 1·40
Nos. 2055/6 were issued together, se-tenant, forming a composite design.

437 Airbus Industrie A320

1996. Aircraft. Multicoloured.
2057 400d. Type **437** 10 10
2058 1000d. Antonov An-72 . . . 15 15
2059 2000d. McDonnell Douglas MD-11F 30 30
2060 6000d. RJ-85 . . . . 1·00 1·00
2061 10000d. Boeing 747-400F . . 1·50 1·50
MS2062 86 × 50 mm. 13000d. Space shuttle riding on Boeing 747 (42 × 31 mm) . . . . 2·00 2·00

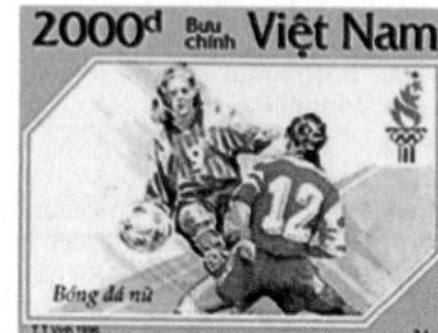

438 Women's Football

1996. Olympic Games, Atlanta, U.S.A. (2nd issue). Multicoloured.
2063 2000d. Type **438** 40 30
2064 4000d. Yachting 75 60
2065 5000d. Hockey . . . . . . 1·00 1·00

439 1946 1h. Stamp

1996. Stamp Day. 50th Anniv of First Unoverprinted Vietnamese Stamp.
2066 **439** 400d. multicoloured . . 25 25

440 Orange Peel Fungus **441** Pupils at Main Gate

1996. Fungi. Multicoloured.
2067 400d. Type **440** 10 10
2068 500d. "Morchella conica" . . 15 15
2069 1000d. "Anthurus archeri" . 30 30
2070 4000d. Chicken mushroom . 60 60
2071 5000d. "Filoboletus manipularis" 75 75
2072 12000d. "Tremiscus helvelloides" . . . . . . 1·90 1·90

1996. Centenary of Hue School. Multicoloured.
2073 400d. Type **441** 15 15
2074 3000d. Main building . . . 45 45

442 Woman and Vase of Lotus Flowers

1996. Paintings by Nguyen Sang. Multicoloured.
2075 400d. Type **442** 15 15
2076 8000d. Soldiers at Dien Bien Phu . . . . 1·20 1·20

443 Variegated Langurs

1996. "Taipeh '96" International Stamp Exhibition, Taiwan. Endangered Animals. Mult.
2077 400d. Type **443** 15 15
2078 2000d. Tigers 40 40
2079 4000d. Javan rhinoceroses 60 60
2080 10000d. South African crowned cranes . . . . . 1·50 1·50

444 Tree of Children's Heads

1996. Campaign for Use of Iodized Salt.
2081 **444** 400d. multicoloured . . 30 30

445 Armed Combatants, National Flag and Quote from Ho Chi Minh

1996. 50th Anniv of Formation of National Front for the Liberation of South Vietnam.
2082 **445** 400d. multicoloured . . 30 30

446 Rambutan

1997. Fruits.
2083 **446** 400d. red and black . . 15 15
2084 – 400d. brown and black 15 15
2085 – 400d. green and black 15 15
2086 – 400d. violet and black 15 15
2087 – 400d. purple and black 15 15
DESIGNS: No. 2084, Durian; 2085, Avocado; 2086, Mangostela; 2087, Queen-of-the-night.

447 Ox and Calf

1997. New Year. Year of the Ox. Multicoloured.
2088 400d. Type **447** 15 15
2089 8000d. Ox . . . . 1·40 1·40

448 Flags and Symbols of Development

1997. 8th Vietnamese Communist Party Congress.
2090 **448** 400d. multicoloured . . 30 30

449 Red-capped Goldfish **450** Snake Design

1997. The Goldfish. Multicoloured.
2091 400d. Type **449** 10 10
2092 1000d. Black and red and long-tailed red goldfishes 15 15
2093 5000d. Goldfish with gaping mouth 75 75
2094 7000d. Black and yellow goldfishes . . . . 1·10 1·10
2095 8000d. Red goldfish with black tail and fins . . . . 1·30 1·30
MS2096 110 × 80 mm. 14000d. Two red-capped goldfinches (42 × 31 mm) . . . . 2·30 2·30

1997. Ly Dynasty Sculptures. Multicoloured.
2097 400d. Type **450** 10 10
2098 1000d. Terracotta dragon's head 15 15
2099 3000d. Musicians in rectangular panel (horiz) 55 55
2100 5000d. Lion base (horiz) . . 1·00 1·00
2101 10000d. Vessel with dragon design (horiz) . . . . . . 1·70 1·70

451 Pagoda in Lake, Ha Tay

1997. Landscapes. Multicoloured.
2102 400d. Type **451** 10 10
2103 5000d. Bamboo suspension bridge, Lai Chau 85 85
2104 7000d. Mist-wreathed trees behind village, Lao Cai 1·10 1·10

452 Red Lily **453** Huynh Thuc Khang

1997. The Lily. Multicoloured.
2105 400d. Type **452** 10 10
2106 1000d. White lily 15 15
2107 5000d. Pink and white lily 85 85
2108 10000d. Red and cream lily 1·70 1·70

1997. 50th Death Anniv of Huynh Thuc Khang.
2109 **453** 400d. multicoloured . . 30 30

454 Tennis

1997. Sports for Disabled People. Multicoloured.
2110 1000d. Type **454** 15 15
2111 6000d. Rifle shooting . . . 1·00 1·00

455 Owton's Palm Civet

1997. Cat Ba National Park. Multicoloured.
2112 400d. Type **455** 10 10
2113 3000d. European otter . . . 45 45
2114 4000d. Palla's squirrel . . . 70 70
2115 10000d. Leopard cat . . . . 1·70 1·70

456 Golden Gate Bridge, San Francisco

1997. "Pacific '97" International Stamp Exhibition, San Francisco. Suspension Bridges. Multicoloured.
2116 400d. Type **456** 10 10
2117 5000d. Raippaluoto Bridge, Finland 85 85
2118 10000d. Seto Great road and rail bridge, Japan . . 1·70 1·70

457 Women and Girl **458** Umbrella protecting Children

1997. 8th Vietnamese Women's Union Congress.
2119 **457** 400d. multicoloured . . 30 30

1997. Children's Rights. Multicoloured.
2120 400d. Type **458** (United Nations Convention on Rights of the Child) . . . 10 10
2121 5000d. Mother breast-feeding ("Breastmilk is Best") 85 85

459 Chua Lang, Hanoi, Vietnam

1997. Asian Temples. Multicoloured.
2122 400d. Type **459** 10 10
2123 1000d. Persepolis, Iran . . . 15 15
2124 3000d. Statue, Denion, Iraq 45 45
2125 5000d. Kyaiktiyo Pagoda, Myanmar 85 85
2126 10000d. Sleeping Buddha, Polonnaruwa, Sri Lanka 1·70 1·70

460 San Chay **461** Ringing Bell

1997. Women's Costumes. Multicoloured.
2127 400d. Type **460** 10 10
2128 2000d. Daco 30 30
2129 5000d. Phu La 85 85
2130 10000d. Kho Me . . . . . 1·70 1·70

1997. Anti-AIDS Campaign.
2131 **461** 400d. multicoloured . . 30 30

462 War Memorial, Cu Chi

1997. 50th Anniv of War Disabled Day.
2132 **462** 400d. multicoloured . . 30 30

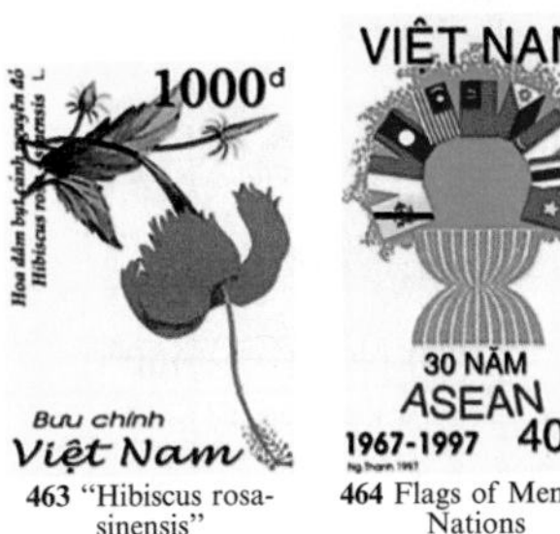

463 "Hibiscus rosa-sinensis" **464** Flags of Member Nations

1997. Flowers. Multicoloured.
2133 1000d. Type **463** 15 15
2134 3000d. "Hibiscus schizopetalus" 45 45
2135 5000d. "Hibiscus syriacus" (pink) 90 90
2136 9000d. "Hibiscus syriacus" (yellow) . . . . 1·50 1·50

1997. 30th Anniv of Association of South East Asian Nations.
2137 **464** 400d. multicoloured . . 30 30

465 Statue and Women using Modern Technology **466** Seahorses

1997. 50th Anniv of Vietnamese Post and Telecommunications Union.
2138 **465** 400d. multicoloured . . 30 30

1997. Seahorses. Multicoloured.
2139 400d. Type **466** 10 10
2140 1000d. Seahorses 15 15
2141 3000d. Common seahorse 45 45
2142 5000d. "Hippocampus kelloggi" 85 85
2143 6000d. "Hippocampus japonicus" . . . . 1·10 1·10
2144 7000d. Short-snouted seahorse . . . . 1·20 1·20

467 Globe and Emblem

1997. 7th Francophone Summit, Hanoi.
2145 **467** 5000d. multicoloured . . 1·70 1·70

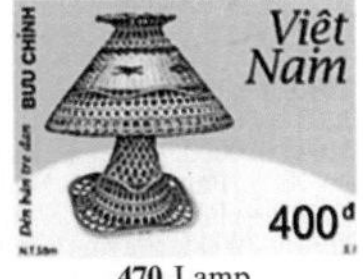

468 Table Tennis Player **470** Lamp

469 Elliot's Pheasant

1997. 19th South East Asian Games, Djakarta.
2146 **468** 5000d. multicoloured . . 90 90

1997. Pheasants. Multicoloured.
2147 400d. Type **469** 10 10
2148 3000d. Siamese fireback pheasant 45 45
2149 5000d. Common pheasant 85 85
2150 6000d. Lady Amherst's pheasant . . . . 1·10 1·10
2151 8000d. Germain's peacock-pheasant . . . . 1·40 1·40
MS2152 80 × 87 mm. 14000d. Imperial pheasants (42 × 30 mm) 2·30 2·30

1998. Wickerwork.
2153 **470** 400d. brown, black and green 10 10
2154 – 400d. black, red and blue 10 10
2155 – 400d. stone, black and blue 10 10
2156 – 400d. lilac, brown and black 10 10
2157 – 2000d. grey, pink and black 60 60
DESIGNS: No. 2154, Dish and bowl; 2155, Swan-shaped basket; 2156, Deer-shaped basket; 2157, Basket with handle.

471 Mother Tiger with Cubs

1998. New Year. Year of the Tiger. Multicoloured.
2158 400d. Type **471** 10 10
2159 8000d. Tiger . . . . 1·20 1·20

472 Flag, Helmet and Rifle **474** Karl Marx and Friedrich Engels (authors)

473 Ca Na Beach, Ninh Thuan Province

1998. 30th Anniv of Tet Offensive.
2160 **472** 400d. multicoloured . . 30 30

1998. Central Vietnam Landscapes. Multicoloured.
2161 400d. Type **473** 10 10
2162 400d. Phong Nha Cave, Quang Binh Province . . 10 10
2163 10000d. Hoi An Town, Quang Nam Province . . 1·50 1·50

1998. 150th Anniv of "Communist Manifesto".
2164 **474** 400d. multicoloured . . 30 30

475 "Limonia acidissima"

1998. Bonsai Trees. Multicoloured.
2165 400d. Type **475** 10 10
2166 400d. "Deeringia polysperma" 10 10
2167 400d. "Pinus merkusii" (vert) 10 10
2168 4000d. "Barringtonia acutangula" (vert) 60 60
2169 6000d. India rubber-tree (vert) 90 90
2170 10000d. "Wrightia religiosa" (vert) . . . . 1·50 1·50
MS2171 75 × 99 mm. 14000d. Desert rose ("Adenium obesum") . . 2·00 2·00

476 Thi Kinh is falsely accused of killing Husband

1998. "Quan Am Thi Kinh" (opera). Multicoloured.
2172 400d. Type **476** 10 10
2173 1000d. Thi Kinh as Buddhist novice and Thi Mau (with fan) 15 15
2174 2000d. Thi Mau and servant with basket on head . . . 30 30
2175 4000d. Me Dop (village chief) and Thi Mau . . . 60 60
2176 6000d. Me Dop, Thi Mau and Thi Kinh 90 90
2177 9000d. Thi Kinh with Thi Mau's baby begging for alms . . . . 1·40 1·40

477 Pres. Ho Chi Minh and Nha Rong Wharf

1998. 300th Anniv of Ho Chi Minh City (formerly Saigon). Multicoloured.
2178 400d. Type **477** 10 10
2179 5000d. "Uncle Ho with Children" (sculpture, Diep Minh Chau) 85 85
MS2180 110 × 102 mm. 14000d. Statue of Nguyen Huu Canh (founder of Saigon) . . . . . 2·30 2·30

478 Western Honey Buzzard

1998. Birds. Multicoloured.
2181 400d. Type **478** 10 10
2182 400d. Northern goshawk ("Accipter gentilis") . . . 10 10
2183 400d. Ornate hawk eagle ("Spizaetus ornatus") . . 10 10
2184 3000d. Common buzzard . . 45 45
2185 5000d. Pied harrier 75 75
2186 12000d. White-tailed sea eagle . . . . 1·70 1·70

479 "Paphiopedilum appletonianum"

1998. Orchids. Multicoloured.
2187 400d. Type **479** 10 10
2188 6000d. "Paphiopedilum helenae" . . . . 1·10 1·10

480 Children going to School (Nguyen Tram)

1998. Vietnamese Children's Fund. Winning Paintings in UNICEF Contest. Multicoloured.
2189 400d. Type **480** 10 10
2190 5000d. Children playing in park (Vu Thi Tuyet) . . . 85 85

481 Players competing for Ball

1998. World Cup Football Championship, France. Multicoloured.
2191 400d. Type **481** 10 10
2192 5000d. Players chasing ball 75 75
2193 7000d. Tackle . . . . . . 1·10 1·10

482 Dragon, Boi Khe Pagoda

1998. Sculptures from Tran Dynasty. Mult.
2194 400d. Type **482** 10 10
2195 400d. Birds with human heads, Thai Lac Pagoda 10 10
2196 1000d. Dragons' heads, ship's planks and waves (throne back), Thay Pagoda 15 15
2197 8000d. Fairy offering flower, Hang Pagoda . . . . . . 1·30 1·30
2198 9000d. Kneeling figure, Thai Lac Pagoda . . . . . . 1·40 1·40

483 Wushu

1998. 13th Asian Games, Bangkok.
2199 **483** 2000d. multicoloured . . 55 55

484 Underwater Scene

1998. International Year of the Ocean.
2200 **484** 400d. multicoloured . . 30 30

485 Alexander Graham Bell's Telephone, 1876

1998. Stamp Day. 35th Anniv of Posts and Telecommunications Department.
2201 **485** 400d. multicoloured . . 30 30

486 Ton Duc Thang

488 "Dragonfly and Lotus"

487 "Antheraea helferi"

1998. 110th Birth Anniv of Ton Duc Thang (President 1969–80).
2202 **486** 400d. multicoloured . . 30 30

1998. Moths. Multicoloured.
2203 400d. Type **487** 10 10
2204 400d. Atlas moth ("Attacus atlas") 10 10
2205 4000d. Tailed comet moth (vert) 75 75
2206 10000d. "Argema maenas" (vert) . . . . 1·70 1·70

1998. 135th Birth Anniv of Qi Baishi (painter). Multicoloured.
2207 400d. Type **488** 10 10
2208 1000d. "Chickens and Chrysanthemum" 15 15
2209 2000d. "Shrimps" 30 30
2210 4000d. "School of Crabs" 60 60
2211 6000d. "Ducks and Lotus" 90 90
2212 9000d. "Shrimps" (different) 1·40 1·40

489 Milan Cathedral and Statue

1998. "Italia 98" International Stamp Exhibition, Milan. Sheet 100 × 62 mm.
MS2213 **489** 16000d. multicoloured 2·75 2·40

490 King Le Loi on Boat

1998. Legend of Restored Sword Lake, Hanoi. Multicoloured.
2214 400d. Type **490** 30 30
2215 400d. Jade Hill Temple and Huc Sunrise bridge . . . 30 30

491 King Le Thang Tong (statue)

1998. 500th Death Anniv (1997) of King Le Thang Tong.
2216 **491** 400d. multicoloured . . 30 30

492 Emblem and Couple

1998. 8th Trade Unions Congress.
2217 **492** 400d. multicoloured . . 30 30

493 King Quang Trung (statue) and Quy Nhon Port

1998. Centenary of Quy Nhon as Binh Dinh Provincial Capital.
2218 **493** 400d. multicoloured . . 30 30

494 Duong Quang Ham (first Vietnamese headmaster) and School

1998. 90th Anniv of Buoi Chu Van An Secondary School, Hanoi. Multicoloured.
2219 400d. Type **494** 10 10
2220 5000d. Ho Chi Minh and students 85 85

495 Doves around Emblem

1998. 6th Association of South East Asian Nations Summit, Hanoi.
2221 **495** 1000d. multicoloured . . 40 40

496 Industrial Symbols, Revolutionary Memorial, Havana and Cuban Flag forming "40"

1998. 40th Anniv (1999) of Cuban Revolution.
2222 **496** 400d. multicoloured . . 30 30

497 Spring

498 Cat going to Tet Flower Market

1999. Four Seasons Paintings (1st series). Mult.
2223 400d. Type **497** 10 10
2224 1000d. Summer 15 15
2225 3000d. Autumn 40 40
2226 12000d. Winter . . . . . . 1·70 1·70
See also Nos. 2391/3.

1999. New Year. Year of the Cat. Multicoloured.
2227 400d. Type **498** 10 10
2228 8000d. Cats fighting . . . . 1·30 1·30
MS2229 100 × 73 mm. 13000d. Kittens (31 × 42 mm) . . . . . . 2·00 2·00

499 Eagle Kite

1999. Kites. Multicoloured.
2230 400d. Type **499** 10 10
2231 5000d. Kite with bamboo flute 75 75
2232 7000d. Peacock . . . . . . 1·10 1·10

500 Ha Long Bay Net Boat

1999. "Australia '99" World Stamp Exhibition, Melbourne. Local Craft. Multicoloured.
2233 400d. Type **500** 10 10
2234 400d. Cua Lo bamboo junk 10 10
2235 7000d. Nha Trang bamboo junk . . . . 1·00 1·00
2236 9000d. Ne Cape junk . . . 1·20 1·20

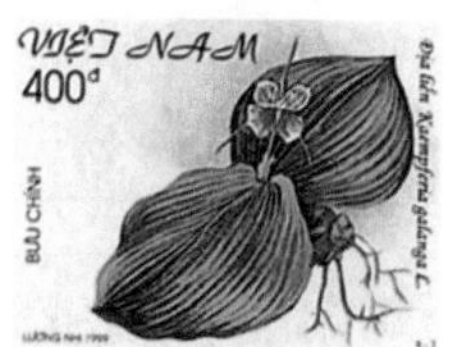

501 *Kaempferia galanga*

1999. Medicinal Herbs. Multicoloured.
2237 400d. Type **501** 10 10
2238 400d. *Tacca chantrieri* Andree (vert) 10 10
2239 400d. *Alpinia galanga* Willd (vert) 10 10
2240 6000d. *Typhonium trilobatum* Schott (vert) 85 85
2241 13000d. *Asarum maximum* Hemsl (vert) . . . . . . 1·80 1·80

502 Syringe, Fields, City and Family

1999. International Day Against Drugs.
2242 **502** 400d. multicoloured . . 30 30

503 Van Trong Mask

1999. Tuong Stage Masks. Multicoloured.
2243 400d. Type **503** 10 10
2244 1000d. Hoang Phi Ho . . . 15 15
2245 2000d. Chau Thuong . . . 30 30
2246 5000d. Tiet Cuong 70 70
2247 6000d. Mao At 85 85
2248 10000d. Tran Long . . . . 1·40 1·40

504 *Octopus gibertianus*

1999. "iBRA 99" International Stamp Exhibition, Nuremberg, Germany. Octopuses. Multicoloured.
2249 400d. Type **504** 10 10
2250 400d. *Philonexis catenulata* 10 10
2251 4000d. *Paroctopus yendoi* . . 60 60
2252 12000d. Common octopus 1·80 1·80

505 Cape, Ca Mau Province

1999. Southern Vietnam Landscapes. Mult.
2253 400d. Type **505** 10 10
2254 400d. Father and Son Islet, Kien Giang Province . . 10 10
2255 12000d. Vinh Hung Tower, Bac Lieu Province . . . . 1·80 1·90

506 Emblem, Map and Satellite

1999. 20th Anniv of Asia-Pacific Telecommunity.
2256 **506** 400d. multicoloured . . 1·50 1·50

507 Greater flame-backed Woodpecker

508 Large Hand and Child cowering

1999. Woodpeckers. Multicoloured.
2257 400d. Type **507** 10 10
2258 1000d. Speckled piculet . . 15 15
2259 3000d. Red-collared woodpecker 45 45
2260 13000d. Bay woodpecker . . 2·00 2·00

1999. Vietnamese Children's Fund.
2261 **508** 400d. lilac, green and black 10 10
2262 – 5000d. blue, grey and black 75 75
DESIGN: 5000d. Young man carrying buildings.

509 Northern Government Office, Hanoi

1999. Architecture. Multicoloured.
2263 400d. Type **509** 10 10
2264 400d. History Museum, Ho Chi Minh City 10 10
2265 12000d. Duc Ba Cathedral (vert) . . . . 1·90 1·90
MS2266 96 × 94 mm. 15000d. Big Theatre, Hanoi (42 × 31 mm) 2·40 2·40

510 Da Rang Bridge and Nhan Mountains

1999. Phu Yen Province.
2267 **510** 400d. multicoloured . . 40 40

511 Man fighting Tiger, Chay Communal House, Ha Nam Province

1999. Le Dynasty Sculptures. Multicoloured.
2268 1000d. Type **511** 25 25
2269 1000d. Phoenix, But Thap Pagoda, Bac Ninh Province 25 25
2270 3000d. Playing chess, Ngoc Canh Communal House, Vinh Phuc Province (vert) 70 70

2271 7000d. Oster, Quang Phuc Communal House, Ha Tay Province (vert) 1·70 1·70
2272 9000d. Stone dragon, Kinh Thien Temple, Hanoi 2·10 2·10

512 Globe and Family

1999. Birth of World's Six Billionth Inhabitant.
2273 **512** 400d. multicoloured 25 25

513 Van Tho Hill, Di Hoa Park, Peking

1999. Chinese Landscapes. Multicoloured.
2274 400d. Type **513** 10 10
2275 2000d. Hoang Mountain, An Huy 30 30
2276 3000d. Bong Lai Cap, Dong Hill 45 45
2277 10000d. Di Hoa Park, Peking 1·40 1·40
MS2278 93 × 88 mm. 14000d. Great Wall, China 2·10 2·10

514 Racing Boats, North Vietnam

1999. Traditional Boat Racing Festivals. Mult.
2279 400d. Type **514** 10 10
2280 2000d. Three boats, Central Vietnam 30 30
2281 10000d. Two boats, South Vietnam 1·40 1·40

515 Buffaloes fighting

1999. Buffalo Festival. Multicoloured.
2282 400d. Type **515** 10 10
2283 5000d. Buffalo No. 2 goring fallen animal 70 70

516 Traditional Velvet Dress

518 Van Sieu and The Tower of the Pen Brush, Ba Dinh

517 Ngo Quyen (statue) and Battle of Bach Dang, 938

1999. Women's Costumes. Multicoloured.
2284 400d. Type **516** 10 10
2285 400d. Magenta brocade dress 10 10
2286 12000d. Green dress 1·70 1·70

1999. 1100th (1998) Birth Anniv of Ngo Quyen (ruler).
2287 **517** 400d. multicoloured 30 30

1999. Birth Bicentenary of Nguyen Van Sieu (scholar).
2288 **518** 400d. multicoloured 30 30

519 Tran Xan Soan

1999. 150th Birth Anniv of Tran Xuan Soan (revolutionary).
2289 **519** 400d. multicoloured 30 30

520 Fisherwoman, Farmer and Woman carrying Child

1999. United Nations Development Programme. Fight Against Poverty. Multicoloured.
2290 400d. Type **520** 10 10
2291 8000d. Buildings and villagers' meeting 1·10 1·10

521 Hammer and Sickle above Workers (forming of Vietnamese Communist Party, 1930)

2000. The Twentieth Century. Multicoloured.
2292 400d. Type **521** 10 10
2293 400d. Pres. Ho Chi Minh making Independence speech (formation of Democratic Republic, 1945) 10 10
2294 1000d. Flag, tank and people celebrating (liberation of South Vietnam, 1975) 15 15
2295 1000d. Symbols of agriculture and industry (Communist Party's ten year renovation plan) 15 15
2296 8000d. Symbols of industry and communications (industrialization) 1·10 1·10
2297 12000d. Emblems (integration into international community) 1·70 1·70
MS2298 194 × 124 mm. Nos. 2292/7 3·50 3·50

522 Dragon

2000. New Year. Year of the Dragon. Mult.
2299 400d. Type **522** 10 10
2300 8000d. Dragon and One Pillar Pagoda, Hanoi 1·40 1·40

523 Globe and UNESCO "City for Peace" Prize (Hanoi, 1999)

2000. International Year of Culture and Peace.
2301 **523** 400d. multicoloured 30 30

524 Pres. Ho Chi Minh (founder)

2000. 70th Anniv of Communist Party. Mult.
2302 400d. Type **524** 15 15
2303 400d. Tran Phu (first General Secretary, 1930–31) 15 15
2304 400d. Le Hong Phong (General Secretary, 1935–36) 15 15
2305 400d. Ha Huy Tap (General Secretary, 1936–38) 15 15
2306 400d. Nguyen Van Cu (General Secretary, 1938–41) 15 15
2307 400d. Truong Chinh (General Secretary, 1941–56 and 1986) 15 15
2308 400d. Le Duan (General Secretary, 1960–86) 15 15
2309 400d. Nguyen Van Linh (General Secretary, 1986–91) 15 15

525 Cocks fighting (Double Cock's Kick)

2000. Cock Fighting. Showing cocks fighting. Multicoloured.
2310 400d. Type **525** 10 10
2311 400d. "Long vu da dao" posture 10 10
2312 7000d. "Song long phuing hoang" posture 1·30 1·30
2313 9000d. "Nhan o giap chien" posture 1·60 1·60

526 Fringed Palanquin

2000. "Bangkok 2000" International Stamp Exhibition. Processional Litters. Multicoloured.
2314 400d. Type **526** 10 10
2315 7000d. Throne-shaped litter 1·30 1·30
2316 8000d. Palanquin with pagoda-style roof 1·40 14·50
MS2317 95 × 65 mm. 15000d. Palanquin being carried 2·75 2·75

527 Marriage of Lac Long Quan and Au Co

529 Sao La

528 Iveco Magirus Fire Engine, Germany

2000. Legend of Lac Long Quan and Au Co. Mult.
2318 400d. Type **527** 10 10
2319 400d. Au Co surrounded by sons 10 10
2320 500d. Au Co and children riding elephants 10 10
2321 3000d. Lac Long Quan and sons by the sea 55 55
2322 4000d. Eldest son Hung Vuong 70 70
2323 11000d. Vietnamese ethnic groups 2·00 2·00

2000. Fire Engines. Sheet 104 × 89 mm. containing T **528** and similar horiz designs. Multicoloured.
MS2324 400d. Type **528**; 1000d. Hino, Japan; 5000d. ZIL 130E, Russia; 12000d. FPS.32 Camiva, France 3·00 3·00

2000. Endangered Species. Sao La. Multicoloured.
2325 400d. Type **529** 10 10
2326 400d. Juvenile in grass 10 10
2327 5000d. Beside lake 85 85
2328 10000d. Head of adult 1·70 1·70

530 Ho Chi Minh and Birthplace

532 Young Girl waving Flag

531 Buffon Teu

2000. 110th Birth Anniv of President Ho Chi Minh.
2329 **530** 400d. multicoloured 30 30

2000. "World Stamp Expo 2000", Anaheim, California. Water Puppetry. Showing traditional puppets. Multicoloured.
2330 400d. Type **531** 10 10
2331 400d. Fairy and phoenix 10 10
2332 400d. Ploughman 10 10
2333 3000d. Peasant woman 45 45
2334 9000d. Drummer 1·40 1·40
2335 11000d. Fisherman 1·80 1·80

2000. 50th Anniv of Youth Volunteers.
2336 **532** 400d. multicoloured 25 25

533 Swimmers and Emblem

2000. 5th National Youth Sports Festival, Dong Thap.
2337 **533** 400d. multicoloured 25 25

534 Coral Hind

2000. Coral Reef Fishes. Multicoloured.
2338 400d. Type **534** 10 10
2339 400d. Emperor angelfish (*Pomacanthus imperator*) 10 10
2340 400d. Honeycomb grouper (*Epinephelus merra*) 10 10
2341 4000d. Moorish idol (*Zanclus cornutus*) (vert) 40 40
2342 6000d. Saddle butterflyfish (vert) 90 90
2343 12000d. Pennant coralfish (vert) 1·90 1·90
MS2344 74 × 99 mm. 15000d. Racoon butterflyfish 2·30 2·30

535 Postal Workers and Means of Communications

2000. 55th Anniv of Vietnam Posts and Telecommunications Service.
2345 **535** 400d. multicoloured 30 30

536 Ho Chi Minh with Policemen

2000. 55th Anniv of National Police Force. Mult.
2346 400d. Type **536** 10 10
2347 2000d. Police personnel (vert) 40 40

537 Statue of Nguyen Tri Phuong, Da Nang

2000. Birth Bicentenary of Nguyen Tri Phuong (provincial Governor).
2348 **537** 400d. multicoloured . . 30 30

538 Children and Emblem

2000. 10th Anniv of United Nations Convention on Children's Rights. Multicoloured.
2349 400d. Type **538** 10 10
2350 5000d. Children's faces around emblem (vert) . . 90 90

539 Running

2000. Olympic Games, Sydney. Multicoloured.
2351 400d. Type **539** 10 10
2352 6000d. Shooting 90 90
2353 7000d. Taekwondo (vert) . . 1·10 1·10

540 Tran Hung Dao Monument, An Phu

2000. 700th Death Anniv of General Tran Hung Dao.
2354 **540** 400d. multicoloured . . 30 30

541 Silver-eared Mesia

2000. Birds. Multicoloured.
2355 400d. Type **541** 10 10
2356 400d. Eliott's pitta (*Pitta ellioti*) 10 10
2357 400d. Coral-billed scimitar babbler (*Pomatorhinus ferruginosus*) (inscr "Pomatorinus") 10 10
2358 5000d. Greater racquet-tailed drongo (vert) . . . 90 90
2359 7000d. Sultan tit (vert) . . . 1·10 1·10
2360 10000d. Spot-necked tree babbler (vert) . . . . 1·50 1·50
MS2361 106 × 81 mm. 15000d. Blue-backed fairy bluebird (42 × 31 mm) . . . . 2·30 2·30

542 North Vietnam 1976 12x. Stamp, Magnifying Glass and Emblem

2000. 40th Anniv of Vietnamese Philatelic Association.
2362 **542** 400d. multicoloured . . 30 30

543 Pigs feeding and Agricultural Workers

2000. 70th Anniv of Vietnamese Farmers' Association.
2363 **543** 400d. multicoloured . . 30 30

544 Dien Huu Pagoda and King Ly Thai To

2000. 990th Anniv of Hanoi. Multicoloured.
2364 400d. Type **544** 10 10
2365 3000d. Van Mieu-Quoc Tu Giam (Confucian temple) and university 55 55
2366 10000d. Hanoi city scene . . 1·50 1·50
MS2367 97 × 90 mm. 15000d. Women releasing doves (42 × 31 mm) . . . . 2·30 2·30

545 Harlequin Bat (*Scotomanes ornatus*)

2000. Bats. Multicoloured.
2368 400d. Type **545** 10 10
2369 400d. *Pteropus lylei* 10 10
2370 2000d. *Rhinolophus paradoxolophus* 30 30
2371 6000d. Cave fruit bat (*Eonycteris spelaea*) . . . 90 90
2372 11000d. Short-nosed fruit bat (*Cynopterus sphinx*) 1·70 1·70

546 "70" and Dove

2000. 70th Anniv of Vietnamese Women's Union.
2373 **546** 400d. multicoloured . . 30 30

547 Workers

2000. 6th National "Heroes of Labour" Congress. Multicoloured.
2374 400d. Type **547** 10 10
2375 3000d. Flower and industrial symbols (vert) 60 60

548 *Oxyspora* sp.

2000. Cornflowers. Multicoloured.
2376 400d. Type **548** 10 10
2377 5000d. *Melastoma villosa* . . 1·00 1·00

549 Ho Chi Minh and Crowd

551 Banners and Satellite

550 Hon Khoai Island and Statue

2000. 70th Anniv of Vietnam Fatherland Front.
2378 **549** 400d. multicoloured . . 30 30

2000. 60th Anniv of Hon Khoai Uprising.
2379 **550** 400d. multicoloured . . 30 30

2001. New Millennium.
2380 **551** 400d. multicoloured . . 30 30

552 Snake

2001. New Year. Year of the Snake. Multicoloured.
2381 400d. Type **552** 10 10
2382 8000d. Green snake . . . . 1·40 1·40

553 Archerfish (*Toxotes macrolepis*)

2001. "HONG KONG 2001" International Stamp Exhibition. Freshwater Fish. Multicoloured.
2383 400d. Type **553** 10 10
2384 800d. Carp (*Cosmochilus harmandi*) (wrongly inscr "Cosmocheilus") 15 15
2385 2000d. Indian short-finned eel (*Anguilla bicolor pacifica*) 40 40
2386 3000d. *Chitala ornata* . . . 55 55
2387 7000d. Indo-Pacific tarpon (*Megalops cyprinoides*) . . 90 90
2388 8000d. Esok (*Probarbus jullieni*) . . . . 1·10 1·10

554 Alfred Nobel (founder)

555 Spring

2001. Centenary of Nobel Prizes.
2389 **554** 400d. blue, yellow and black 30 30

2001. Four Seasons Paintings (2nd series). Mult.
2390 400d. Type **555** 10 10
2391 800d. Summer 15 15
2392 4000d. Autumn 60 60
2393 10000d. Winter . . . . . . 1·50 1·50

556 *Rubus cochinchinensis*

2001. Forest Fruits. Multicoloured.
2394 400d. Type **556** 10 10
2395 400d. *Rhizophora mucronata* 10 10
2396 400d. *Podocarpus neriifolius* 10 10
2397 400d. *Magnolia pumila* . . . 10 10
2398 15000d. *Taxus chinensis* . . 2·00 2·00

557 Co Tien Mountains, Ha Giang Province

2001. Northern Vietnam Landscapes. Mult.
2399 400d. Type **557** 10 10
2400 400d. Dong Pagoda, Yen Tu, Quang Ninh Province 10 10
2401 10000d. King Dinh Temple, Ninh Binh Province . . . 1·50 1·50

558 Medals and Mastheads on "50"

2001. 50th Anniv of *Nhan Dan* (Communist Party newspaper).
2402 **558** 400d. multicoloured . . 30 30

559 Starlight Ruby

2001. Rubies. Design showing named rubies before and after cutting. Multicoloured.
2403 400d. Type **559** 10 10
2404 6000d. Vietnam Star 90 90

560 Youths and Emblem

2001. 70th Anniv of Ho Chi Minh Youth Union.
2405 **560** 400d. multicoloured . . 30 30

561 David's Tree Partridge (*Arborophila davidi*)

2001. Animals in Cat Tien National Park. Mult.
2406 400d. Type **561** 10 10
2407 800d. Jungle queen butterfly (*Stichophthalma uemurai*) 15 15
2408 3000d. Vietnamese Javan rhino (*Rhinoceros sondaicus annamiticus*) . . 60 60
2409 5000d. Siamese crocodile (*Crocodylus siamensis*) . . 1·10 1·10

562 Ho Chi Minh, Flag and Map of Vietnam

2001. 9th Vietnamese Communist Party Congress. Multicoloured.
2410 400d. Type **562** 10 10
2411 3000d. Hammer, sickle and Ngoc Lu drum head (vert) 45 45

563 Veiled Stinkhorn (*Phallus indusiatus*)

2001. Fungi. Multicoloured.
2412 400d. Type **563** 10 10
2413 400d. *Aseroe arachnoidea* . . 10 10
2414 400d. *Phallus tenuis* 10 10
2415 2000d. *Phallus impudicus* . . 30 30
2416 5000d. *Phallus rugulosus* . . 75 75
2417 6000d. *Simblum periphragmoides* 90 90
2418 7000d. *Mutinus bambusinus* 1·10 1·10
MS2419 86 × 86 mm. 13000d. *Pseudocolus schellenbergiae* (42 × 31 mm) . . . . 2·30 2·30

564 Ho Chi Minh, Girl and Flowers

2001. 60th Anniv of Vietnam Youth Pioneers.
2420 **564** 400d. multicoloured . . 30 30

565 Ho Chi Minh, Crowd and Flag

2001. 60th Anniv of Vietnam Independence League.
2421 **565** 400d. multicoloured . . 30 30

566 Cigarette and Flower
567 Children wearing Protective Clothing

2001. World No-Smoking Day.
2422 **566** 800d. multicoloured . . 45 45

2001. United Nations Children's Fund (400d.) and United Nations General Assembly Special Session on Children (5000d.). Multicoloured.
2423 400d. Type **567** 10 10
2424 5000d. Children of different races and emblem 90 90

568 Locomotive D18E

2001. Diesel Locomotives. Multicoloured.
2425 400d. Type **568** 10 10
2426 400d. Locomotive D4H . . . 10 10
2427 800d. Locomotive D11H in station 15 15
2428 2000d. Locomotive D5H . . 40 40
2429 6000d. Locomotive D9E . . 1·10 1·10
2430 7000d. Locomotive D12E 1·30 1·30
MS2431 96 × 66 mm. 13000d. Locomotive D11H on lakeside track (42 × 31 mm) . . . . . . 2·30 2·30

569 *Vanda* sp.

2001. Orchids. Multicoloured.
2432 800d. Type **569** 15 15
2433 800d. *Dendrobium lowianum* 15 15
2434 800d. *Phajus wallachii* . . . 15 15
2435 800d. *Habenaria medioflexa* 15 15
2436 800d. *Arundina graminifolia* (vert) 15 15
2437 12000d. *Calanthe clavata* (vert) . . . . 1·90 1·90

570 Golden Birdwing (*Troides aeacus*)

2001. "PHILA NIPPON '01" International Stamp Exhibition, Tokyo. Butterflies. Multicoloured.
2438 800d. Type **570** 15 15
2439 800d. Peacock (*Inachis io*) 15 15
2440 800d. *Ancyluris formosissima* 15 15
2441 5000d. Red glider (*Cymothoe sangaris*) (wrongly inscr "sanguris") 55 55
2442 7000d. *Taenaris selene* . . . 90 90
2443 10000d. Raja Brooke's birdwing (*Trogonoptera brookiana*) . . . . 1·50 1·50
MS2444 94 × 69 mm. 13000d. *Atrophaneura horishanus* (31 × 42 mm) . . . . 2·30 2·30

571 Footballer

2001. World Cup Football Championship, Japan and South Korea. Multicoloured.
2445 800d. Type **571** 15 15
2446 3000d. Footballer and map including Americas . . . 60 60
Nos. 2445/6 were issued together, se-tenant, forming a composite design.

572 Ho Gao

2001. Traditional Musical Instruments. Mult.
2447 800d. Type **572** 15 15
2448 800d. Kenh (pan-pipes) . . 15 15
2449 800d. Dan Tu (stringed instrument) (vert) 15 15
2450 2000d. Dan T'rung (vert) . . 30 30
2451 6000d. Trong Kinang (drum) (vert) 75 75
2452 9000d. Tinh Tau (stringed instrument) (vert) . . . . 1·40 1·40

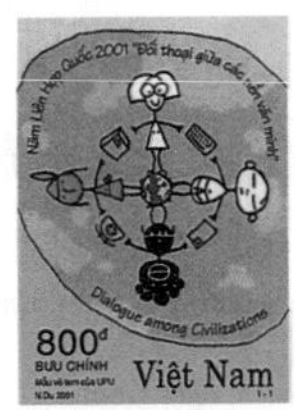
573 Children encircling Globe

2001. United Nations Year of Dialogue among Civilizations.
2453 **573** 800d. multicoloured . . 40 40

574 Tran Huy Lieu and Books

2001. Birth Centenary of Tran Huy Lieu (writer and revolutionary).
2454 **574** 800d. multicoloured . . 40 40

575 Nam Cao and Titles of his Works

2001. 50th Death Anniv of Nam Cao (Tran Huu Tri) (writer).
2455 **575** 800d. multicoloured . . 40 40

576 Leaves around Globe

2001. Environment Protection. Multicoloured.
2456 800d. Type **576** 15 15
2457 3000d. Globe in tree with nesting peace dove . . . 60 60

577 "To He" Horse

2002. New Year. Year of the Horse. Multicoloured.
2458 800d. Type **577** 15 15
2459 8000d. Horse with parasol 90 90
MS2460 76 × 66 mm. 14000d. Flying horse (42 × 31 mm) . . . . . 2·30 2·30

578 Giap Tuong Nam

2002. Tuong (classical opera) Costumes. Costumes. Multicoloured.
2461 1000d. Type **578** 15 15
2462 1000d. Giap Tuong Nu . . 15 15
2463 2000d. Giap Tuong Phan Dien 30 30
2464 3000d. Long Chan 45 45
2465 5000d. Giap Tuong Phien 75 75
2466 9000d. Lung Xiem Quan Giap . . . . 1·20 1·20

579 Vo Thi Sau

2002. 50th Death Anniv of Vo Thi Sau (resistance fighter).
2467 **579** 1000d. multicoloured . . 40 40

580 Symbols of Industry and Communications
581 *Echinocereus lbatus*

2002. 9th Communist Party Congress Resolutions. Multicoloured.
2468 800d. Type **580** 15 15
2469 3000d. Thang Long Citadel gate, flag and people . . . 45 45

2002. Cacti. Multicoloured.
2470 1000d. Type **581** 15 15
2471 1000d. *Echinocereus delaetii* 15 15
2472 1000d. *Cylindropuntia bigelowii* 15 15
2473 5000d. *Echinocereus triglochidatus* 60 60
2474 10000d. *Epiphyllum truncatum* . . . . 1·20 1·20

582 Emblem and Woman's Face

2002. 9th National Women's Congress.
2475 **582** 800d. multicoloured . . 40 40

583 Hugo and "Liberty Guiding the People" (painting, Eugene Delacroix)

2002. Birth Bicentenary of Victor Hugo (writer).
2476 **583** 1000d. multicoloured . . 40 40

584 Black-crowned Barwing (*Actinodura sodangorum*)

2002. Birds. Multicoloured.
2477 600d. Type **584** 10 10
2478 800d. Golden-winged laughing thrush (*Garrulax ngoclinhensis*) 15 15
2479 800d. Long-billed scimitar babbler (*Pomatorhinus hypoleucos*) 15 15
2480 800d. Greater necklaced laughing thrush (*Garrulax pectoralis*) 15 15
2481 5000d. Red-tailed minla (*Minla ignotincta*) 75 75
2482 8000d. Blue-winged minla (*Minla cynouroptera*) . . . 1·10 1·10

585 Ganh Son Coast, Binh Thuan Province

2002. Central Vietnam Landscapes. Multicoloured.
2483 800d. Type **585** 15 15
2484 800d. Tung Estuary, Quang Tri Province 15 15
2485 10000d. Sa Huynh Harbour, Quang Ngai Province . . 1·40 1·40

586 Golden-headed Langur (*Trachypithecus poliocephalus*)

587 Bui Thi Xuan riding Elephant

2002. Primates. Multicoloured.
2486 600d. Type **586** 10 10
2487 800d. Delacour's langur (*Trachypithecus delacouri*) 10 10
2488 1000d. Tonkin snub-nosed monkey (*Rhinopithecus avunculus*) 15 15
2489 2000d. Grey-shanked douc langur (*Pygathrix cinerea*) 30 30
2490 4000d. Black crested gibbon (*Nomascus concolor*) . . . 45 45
2491 5000d. Ha Tinh langur (*Trachypithecus laotum hatinhensis*) 60 60
2492 7000d. Phayre's langur (*Trachypithecus phayrei*) 90 90
2493 9000d. Red-shanked douc langur (*Pygathrix nemaeus nemaeus*) . . . . 1·20 1·20
MS2494 179 × 141 mm. Nos. 2486/93 plus label . . . . 3·75 3·75

2002. Death Bicentenary of Commander-in-Chief Bui Thi Xuan.
2495 **587** 1000d. multicoloured . . 40 40

588 Footballer

589 Yellow Slipper Orchid (*Paphiopedilum concolor*)

2002. World Cup Football Championship, Japan and South Korea. Sheet 112 × 100 mm containing T **588** and similar vert designs. Multicoloured.
MS2496 1000d. Type **588**; 2000d. Two players; 5000d. Player with ball; 7000d. Goalkeeper . . . 2·30 2·30

2002. Flowers of Ha Long Bay. Multicoloured.
2497 600d. Type **589** 10 10
2498 800d. Velvet-pod tree (*Sterculia lanceolata*) . . . 15 15
2499 1000d. Ha Long schefflera (*Schefflera alongensis*) . . 15 15
2500 2000d. Sea hibiscus (*Hibiscus tiliaceus*) 30 30
2501 3000d. White butterfly tree (*Mussaenda glabra*) . . . 45 45
2502 5000d. Puff-fruit tree (*Boniodendron parviflorum*) 75 75
2503 9000d. Fragrant bauhinia (*Bauhinia ornate*) . . . . 1·10 1·10

590 Chau Van Liem

2002. Birth Centenary of Chau Van Liem (revolutionary).
2504 **590** 800d. multicoloured . . 40 40

591 Winged Envelopes and Globe

2002. Stamp Day. 25th Anniv of Vietnam Stamp Company.
2505 **591** 800d. multicoloured . . 40 40

592 Victory Statue, People and Nup (revolutionary)

2002. Tay Nguyen (Western highlands).
2506 **592** 800d. multicoloured . . 40 40

593 Asian Giant Soft-shelled Turtle (*Pelochelys bibroni*)

2002. Soft-shelled Turtles. Showing soft-shelled turtles. Multicoloured.
2507 800d. Type **593** 15 15
2508 2000d. Chinese turtle (*Pelodiscus sinensis*) . . . 30 30
2509 5000d. Wattle-necked turtle (*Palea steindachneri*) . . . 60 60
2510 9000d. Black-rayed turtle (*Trionyx cartilaginous*) . . 1·20 1·20
MS2511 173 × 100 mm. Nos. 2507/10, each × 2 . . . . 4·50 4·50

594 Khue Van Pavilion, Vietnam and That Luang, Laos

2002. 25th Anniv of Friendship and Co-operation Treaty. 40th Anniv of Vietnam–Laos Diplomatic Relations.
2512 **594** 800d. multicoloured . . 40 40

595 Beech 200 Super King Air

2002. Civilian Aircraft. Multicoloured.
2513 800d. Type **595** 15 15
2514 2000d. Fokker 70 twin-engine jet airliner 30 30
2515 3000d. ATR72-202 twin-turboprop engine aircraft 45 45
2516 8000d. Boeing 767-300 ER 1·10 1·10
MS2517 90 × 60 mm. 14000d. Beech 200 Super King Air (different) 2·10 2·10

596 Ong Sao Lantern

2002. Mid-Autumn Festival Lanterns. Multicoloured.
2518 800d. Type **596** 15 15
2519 800d. Ong Su lantern . . . 15 15
2520 2000d. Con Tho Om Trang lantern 30 30
2521 7000d. Chinese lantern . . . 90 90

597 Statue, Computer Operators and Satellite

2002. 55th Anniv of Posts and Telecommunication Worker's Trade Union.
2522 **597** 800d. multicoloured . . 40 40

598 Long Bien Bridge

2002. Bridges. Multicoloured.
2523 800d. Type **598** 15 15
2524 800d. Song Han bridge . . 15 15
2525 2000d. Truong Tien bridge 30 30
2526 10000d. My Thuan bridge 1·40 1·40

599 Open Book and Flowers

2002. 72nd Anniv of Ideology and Culture Commission.
2527 **599** 800d. multicoloured . . 30 30

600 Ho Hac Di (first principal) and College Building

2002. Centenary of Hanoi Medical University.
2528 **600** 800d. multicoloured . . 30 30

601 Teacher and Pupil

603 One Pillar Pagoda, Hanoi

602 Goat

2002. 20th Anniv of Teachers' Day.
2529 **601** 800d. multicoloured . . 30 30

2002. New Year. Year of the Goat. Multicoloured.
2530 800d. Type **602** 15 15
2531 8000d. Goat (different) . . . 1·10 1·10

2002. 10th Anniv of Vietnam–North Korea Diplomatic Relations. Multicoloured.
2532 800d. Type **603** 30 30
2533 800d. Dabotap Pagoda, Bulguksa Temple, North Korea 30 30

FRANK STAMPS

F 19 Invalid's Badge

F 158 Children and Disabled Teacher

1976. For use by disabled veterans. Dated "27.7.75". No value indicated.
F100 **F 19** (–) red and blue . . . 75 75
F101 – (–) green, light green and brown 75 75
DESIGN: No. F101, Disabled veteran in factory.

1984. Disabled and Invalids. No value indicated.
F750 **F 158** (–) brown and ochre 60 45

1985. No value indicated. As T **179**.
F861 (–) red and black (Policeman and militia members) 55 55

MILITARY FRANK STAMPS

MF 21 Soldier and Map of Vietnam

1976. No value indicated.
MF110 **MF 21** (–) black and red 75 75

MF 59 Pilot

1979. 35th Anniv of Vietnam People's Army. No value indicated.
MF304 **MF 59** (–) purple and pink . . . . . 1·10 1·10
MF305 – (–) purple and pink . . . . . 1·10 1·10
DESIGN: No. MF305, Badge of People's Army.

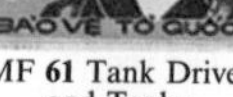

MF 61 Tank Driver and Tanks

MF 84 Ho Chi Minh in Naval Uniform

1979. No value indicated.
MF308 **MF 61** (–) black and mauve . . . . . 1·10 40
MF309 – (–) violet and green . . . . . 1·10 40
MF310 – (–) black and red 1·10 40
DESIGNS: No. MF309, Sailor and ship; MF310, Pilot and jet fighters.

1981. No value indicated.
MF420 **MF 84** (–) pink and blue 75 75
MF421 – (–) multicoloured 75 75
DESIGN—13 × 17 mm: No. MF421, Factory militiawoman.

1982. Multicoloured. No value indicated.
MF466 (–) Soldier and militiawoman 75 75
MF467 (–) Type **94** 75 75

MF 107 Disabled Soldier

1982. 35th Anniv of Disabled Soldiers' Day. No value indicated.
MF513 **MF 107** (–) mauve and green 55 40

MF 120 Militia

1983. No value indicated.
MF581 **MF 120** (–) multicoloured 75 75

MF 145 Star and Soldiers on Bunker

MF 152 Coastal Militia

1984. 30th Anniv of Battle of Dien Bien Phu. No value indicated.
MF690 MF **145** (-) yellow, orange & brn 60 45

1984. No value indicated.
MF732 MF **152** (-) brown, orange & yellow . . . 75 45

MF **164** Soldiers and Emblem

MF **205** Soldier and Woman holding Sheaf of Rice

1984. No value indicated.
MF786 MF **164** (-) orange, red and black . . . 55 45

1986.
MF979 MF **205** 1d. brown and black 70 70

MF **232** Armed Forces Personnel and Flag

1987.
MF1119 MF **232** 5d. red & brown 90 90

WADHWAN Pt. 1

A state of Kathiawar, India. Now uses Indian stamps.

4 pice = 1 anna.

1

1888.
5 **1** ½pice black . . . . 8·00 9·00

WALLIS AND FUTUNA ISLANDS Pt. 6

A group of French islands in the Pacific Ocean north-east of Fiji. Attached to New Caledonia for administrative purposes in 1888. In 1961 they became a French Overseas Territory.

100 centimes = 1 franc.

1920. Stamps of New Caledonia optd **ILES WALLIS et FUTUNA.**
1 **15** 1c. black on green . . . . . 15 2·25
2 2c. brown . . . . 15 2·40
3 4c. blue on orange . . . . 20 2·40
4 5c. green . . . . 65 2·60
18 5c. blue . . . . 50 2·40
5 10c. red . . . . 90 2·60
19 10c. green . . . . 90 2·40
6 15c. lilac . . . . 1·50 3·00
7 **16** 20c. brown . . . . 65 3·25
8 25c. blue on green . . . . . 2·00 3·25
21 25c. red on yellow . . . . . 1·90 3·00
9 30c. brown on orange . . . 2·50 3·50
22 30c. red . . . . 1·50 3·00
24 30c. green . . . . 65 4·00
10 35c. black on yellow . . . . 1·40 3·25
11 40c. red on green . . . . . 1·50 3·25
12 45c. purple . . . . 1·40 3·25
13 50c. red on orange . . . . 2·25 3·00
25 50c. blue . . . . 90 3·25
26 50c. grey . . . . 2·25 3·75
27 65c. blue . . . . 4·25 5·50
14 75c. green . . . . 2·25 4·25
15 **17** 1f. blue on green . . . . . 3·50 5·25
28 1f.10 brown . . . . 1·10 4·50
16 2f. red on blue . . . . . . 6·50 8·00
17 5f. black on orange . . . . 11·00 13·50

1922. As last surch.
29 **15** 0,01 on 15c. lilac . . . . . 50 2·50
30 0,02 on 15c. lilac . . . . . 55 2·50
31 0,04 on 15c. lilac . . . . . 50 2·50
32 0,05 on 15c. lilac . . . . . 75 2·50
33 **17** 25c. on 2f. red on blue . . . 1·50 3·25
34 25c. on 5f. black on orange 1·50 3·25
35 **16** 65 on 40c. red on green . . 2·25 3·25
36 85 on 75c. green . . . . . 2·00 3·25
37 90 on 75c. red . . . . . . 1·10 3·75
38 **17** 1f.25 on 1fr. blue . . . . . 2·50 3·00
39 1f.50 on 1fr. blue on blue 3·75 4·50
40 3f. on 5f. mauve . . . . . 7·00 8·75
41 10f. on 5f. green on mauve 23·00 32·00
42 20f. on 5f. red on yellow . . 32·00 45·00

1930. Stamps of New Caledonia, some with colours changed, optd **ILES WALLIS et FUTUNA.**
43 **22** 1c. blue and purple . . . . 20 2·75
44 2c. green and brown . . . . 15 2·75
45 3c. blue and red . . . . . 35 2·50
46 4c. green and red . . . . . 20 2·75
47 5c. brown and blue . . . . 25 2·50
48 10c. brown and lilac . . . . 40 3·00
49 15c. blue and brown . . . . 45 3·00
50 20c. brown and red . . . . 45 3·00
51 25c. brown and green . . . 2·25 3·25
52 **23** 30c. turquoise and green . . 70 3·25
53 35c. green and deep green 2·00 3·25
54 40c. green and red . . . . 45 3·00
55 45c. red and blue . . . . . 2·50 3·25
56 45c. green and turquoise . . 1·90 3·25
57 50c. brown and mauve . . . 90 3·00
58 55c. red and blue . . . . . 1·75 4·25
59 60c. red and blue . . . . . 75 3·25
60 65c. blue and brown . . . . 2·25 3·50
61 70c. brown and mauve . . . 2·25 3·25
62 75c. drab and blue . . . . 3·00 4·00
63 80c. green and purple . . . 2·50 3·25
64 85c. brown and green . . . 1·75 5·00
65 90c. carmine and red . . . 1·40 4·00
66 90c. red and brown . . . . 2·25 3·25
67 **24** 1f. red and drab . . . . . 4·50 5·00
68 1f. carmine and red . . . . 3·00 3·25
69 1f. green and red . . . . . 90 3·00
70 1f.10 brown and green . . . 30·00 35·00
71 1f.25 green and brown . . . 2·50 4·25
72 1f.25 carmine and red . . . 2·50 3·25
73 1f.40 red and blue . . . . . 2·25 3·25
74 1f.50 blue and ultramarine 2·25 3·25
75 1f.60 brown and green . . . 2·75 3·25
76 1f.75 red and blue . . . . . 14·00 14·00
77 1f.75 blue . . . . 3·25 4·00
78 2f. brown and orange . . . 1·75 3·00
79 2f.25 blue and ultramarine 2·75 3·25
80 2f.50 brown . . . . 2·50 3·25
81 3f. brown and purple . . . 1·60 3·50
82 5f. brown and blue . . . . 2·75 3·50
83 10f. brown & mauve on pink . . . . 1·00 4·50
84 20f. brown and red on yellow . . . . 1·25 5·75

1931. "Colonial Exhibition" key-types.
85 E 40c. green and black . . . . 4·75 7·75
86 F 50c. mauve and black . . . 4·75 7·75
87 G 90c. red and black . . . . . 4·50 7·75
88 H 1f.50 blue and black . . . . 5·50 7·75

1939. New York World's Fair. As T **41** of St. Pierre et Miquelon.
89 1f.25 red . . . . 2·25 4·00
90 2f.25 blue . . . . 2·25 4·00

1939. 150th Anniv of French Revolution. As T **42** of St. Pierre et Miquelon.
91 45c.+25c. green and black . . 11·00 19·00
92 70c.+30c. brown and black . . 9·00 19·00
93 90c.+35c. orange and black . . 13·50 19·00
94 1f.25c.+1f. red and black . . 11·00 19·00
95 2f.25c.+2f. blue and black . . 11·00 19·00

1941. Adherence to General de Gaulle. Stamps of 1930 optd **France Libre.**
96 **22** 1c. blue and purple . . . 1·00 3·25
97 2c. green and brown . . . 1·25 3·25
97a 3c. blue and red £100 £100
98 4c. green and orange . . 75 3·25
99 5c. brown and blue . . . 1·25 3·25
100 10c. brown and lilac . . . 65 3·25
101 15c. blue and brown . . . 2·50 3·25
102 20c. brown and red . . . 3·25 4·25
103 25c. brown and green . . 3·25 4·25
104 **23** 30c. green . . . . 2·75 4·25
105 35c. green . . . . 2·00 3·25
106 40c. green and red . . . . 3·00 4·25
107 45c. red and blue . . . . 3·75 4·25
107a 45c. green and turquoise . £100 £100
108 50c. brown and mauve . . 1·75 3·25
109 55c. red and blue . . . . 2·00 3·25
109a 60c. red and blue £100 £100
110 65c. blue and brown . . . 1·50 3·75
111 70c. brown and mauve . . 1·90 3·75
112 75c. drab and blue . . . 3·00 4·75
113 80c. green and purple . . 1·75 3·75
114 85c. brown and green . . 2·50 4·75
115 90c. carmine and red . . 2·50 3·75
116 **24** 1f. carmine and red . . . 2·75 4·75
117 1f.25 green and brown . . 2·75 4·75
118 1f.50 blue and deep blue 2·50 3·75
119 1f.75 blue . . . . 1·90 3·75
120 2f. brown and orange . . 2·75 5·00
121 2f.50 brown £150 £150
122 3f. brown and purple . . 2·25 4·25
123 5f. brown and blue . . . 8·00 8·00
124 10f. brown and mauve on pink . . . . 40·00 65·00
125 20f. brown & red on yell 55·00 £100

5 Native Ivory Head

1944. Free French Administration.
126 **5** 5c. brown . . . . 15 2·75
127 10c. blue . . . . 15 2·75
128 25c. green . . . . 15 2·75
129 30c. orange . . . . 15 2·75
130 40c. green . . . . 40 2·75
131 80c. purple . . . . 30 3·00
132 1f. purple . . . . 70 2·75
133 1f.50 red . . . . 80 2·75
134 2f. black . . . . 60 2·75
135 2f.50 blue . . . . 1·40 3·00
136 4f. violet . . . . 75 3·00
137 5f. yellow . . . . 80 3·00
138 10f. brown . . . . 1·60 3·50
139 20f. green . . . . 2·50 4·00

1944. Mutual Aid and Red Cross Funds. As T **49** of St. Pierre et Miquelon.
140 5f.+20f. orange . . . . . . 1·40 3·75

1945. Surch.
141 **5** 50c. on 5c. brown . . . . . 85 3·00
142 60c. on 5c. brown . . . . . 70 3·25
143 70c. on 5c. brown . . . . . 65 3·25
144 1f.20 on 5c. brown . . . . 65 3·00
145 2f.40 on 35c. green . . . . 85 3·00
146 3f. on 25c. green . . . . . 90 3·25
147 4f.50 on 25c. green . . . . 1·50 4·00
148 15f. on 2f.50 blue . . . . . 1·75 4·00

1946. Air. Victory. As T **52** of St. Pierre et Miquelon.
149 8f. violet . . . . 25 3·25

1946. Air. From Chad to the Rhine. As T **53** of St. Pierre et Miquelon.
150 5f. violet . . . . 2·00 3·75
151 10f. green . . . . 2·25 3·75
152 15f. brown . . . . 2·25 3·75
153 20f. blue . . . . 2·25 4·25
154 25f. orange . . . . 1·75 4·50
155 50f. red . . . . 5·75 11·00

1949. Air. 75th Anniv of Universal Postal Union. As T **58** of St. Pierre et Miquelon.
156 10f. multicoloured . . . . . 3·75 12·50

1949. Air. Nos. 325/6 of New Caledonia, with colours changed, optd **WALLIS ET FUTUNA.**
157 **37** 50f. red and yellow . . . . 6·25 12·00
158 – 100f. brown and yellow . . 9·50 18·00

1952. Centenary of Military Medal. As T **60** of St. Pierre et Miquelon.
159 2f. turquoise, yellow and green . . . . 3·50 4·75

1954. Air. 10th Anniv of Liberation. As T **61** of St. Pierre et Miquelon.
160 3f. brown and deep brown 5·75 11·00

7 Making Tapa (cloth)

8 Father Chanel

1955. (a) Postage, as T **7**.
161 – 3f. purple, mauve and lilac 75 3·25
162 **7** 5f. chocolate, brown & grn 3·00 3·50
163 – 7f. brown and turquoise . . 3·50 4·00
164 – 9f. deep purple, purple and blue . . . . 1·25 4·50
165 – 17f. multicoloured . . . . . 4·50 4·75
166 – 19f. green and red . . . . . 5·00 5·25

(b) Air, as T **8**.
167 **8** 14f. blue, green and indigo 1·60 4·25
168 – 21f. green, brown and blue 7·00 6·75
168a – 27f. green, blue and brown 5·75 3·75
169 – 33f. brown, blue & turq . . 12·00 12·50
DESIGNS—HORIZ: 9f. Wallisian and island view; 7f. Preparing kava; 17f. Dancers; 21f. View of Mata-Utu, Queen Amelia and Mgr. Bataillon; 27f. Wharf, Mata-Utu; 33f. Map of Wallis and Futuna Islands and "Stella Matutina" (full-rigged ship). VERT: 19f. Paddle dance.

1958. Tropical Flora. As T **67** of St. Pierre et Miquelon.
170 5f. multicoloured . . . . . . 3·00 5·00
DESIGN—HORIZ: 5f. "Montrouziera".

1958. 10th Anniv of Declaration of Human Rights. As T **66** of St. Pierre et Miquelon.
171 17f. blue and ultramarine . . 2·25 8·75

8a Map of Pacific and Palms

1962. 5th South Pacific Conference, Pago Pago.
172 **8a** 16f. multicoloured . . . . 3·75 4·00

9 Trumpet Triton

10 Throwing the Javelin

1962. Marine Fauna.
173 **9** 25c. brown and green (postage) . . . . 65 2·25
174 – 1f. red and green . . . . . 1·25 2·25
175 – 2f. brown and blue . . . . 1·50 2·75
176 – 4f. brown and blue . . . . 2·00 2·25
177 – 10f. multicoloured . . . . . 5·00 6·25
178 – 20f. brown and blue . . . . 10·00 10·00

179 – 50f. brown, blue & pur (air) 6·75 8·50
180 – 100f. black, green & purple 17·00 20·00
DESIGNS—As T **9**: 1f. Episcopal mitre; 2f. Bull-mouth helmet; 4f. Venus comb murex; 10f. Red-mouth olive; 20f. Tiger cowrie. 26½ × 48 mm: 50f. Ventral harp. 48 × 26½ mm: 100f. Fishing underwater for commercial trochus shells.

1962. Air. 1st Trans-Atlantic TV Satellite Link. As T **71** of St. Pierre et Miquelon.
181 12f. blue, purple and violet 1·60 4·50

1963. Red Cross Centenary. As T **75** of St. Pierre et Miquelon.
182 12f. red, grey and purple . . 3·00 3·25

1963. 15th Anniv of Declaration of Human Rights. As T **76** of St. Pierre et Miquelon.
183 29f. ochre and red . . . . . 7·25 8·00

1964. "PHILATEC 1964" Int Stamp Exn, Paris. As T **77** of St. Pierre et Miquelon.
184 9f. red, green and deep green 2·25 3·50

1964. Air. Olympic Games. Tokyo.
185 **10** 31f. purple, red and green 13·00 18·00

11 Inter-island Ferry "Reine Amelia"

1965.
186 **11** 11f. multicoloured . . . . 7·00 7·25

1965. Air. Centenary of I.T.U. As T **80** of St. Pierre et Miquelon.
187 50f. brown, purple and red 15·00 22·00

1966. Air. Launching of 1st French Satellite. As T **82** of St. Pierre et Miquelon.
188 7f. red, claret and vermilion 4·25 5·00
189 10f. red, claret and vermilion 5·25 6·25

1966. Air. Launching of Satellite "D1". As T **82** of St. Pierre et Miquelon.
190 10f. red, lake and green . . . 2·50 4·50

12 W.H.O. Building

1966. Air. Inauguration of W.H.O. Headquarters, Geneva.
191 **12** 30f. red, yellow and blue 3·50 5·50

13 Art Students

1966. Air. 20th Anniv of UNESCO.
192 **13** 50f. brown, green & orange 4·75 6·25

14 Athlete and Decorative Pattern

1966. Air. South Pacific Games, Noumea.
193 **14** 32f. multicoloured . . . . 4·25 4·50
194 – 38f. green and mauve . . . 6·00 6·25
DESIGN: 38f. Woman with ball, and decorative pattern.

15 Samuel Wallis's Frigate H.M.S. "Dolphin" at Uvea

1967. Air. Bicentenary of Discovery of Wallis Island.
195 **15** 12f. multicoloured . . . . 8·25 6·25

1968. 20th Anniv of W.H.O. As T **90** of St. Pierre et Miquelon.
196 17f. purple, orange and green 4·75 6·25

1968. Human Rights Year. As T **92** of St. Pierre et Miquelon.
197 19f. brown, mauve and purple . . . . 3·25 4·50

1969. Air. 1st Flight of Concorde. As T **94** of St. Pierre et Miquelon.
198 20f. black and purple . . . . 13·50 11·00

16 Gathering Coconuts

1969. Scenes of Everyday Life. Multicoloured.
199 1f. Launching outrigger canoe (35 × 22 mm) (postage) . . 2·50 2·50
200 20f. Type **16** (air) . . . . . 3·25 2·75
201 32f. Horse-riding . . . . . . 5·00 3·25
202 38f. Wood-carving . . . . . 4·50 3·75
203 50f. Fishing . . . . 8·50 6·25
204 100f. Marketing fruit . . . . 12·50 9·75

1969. 50th Anniv of Int Labour Organization. As T **100** of St. Pierre et Miquelon.
205 9f. blue, brown and salmon 3·00 3·75

1970. Inauguration of New U.P.U. Headquarters Building, Berne As T **101** of St. Pierre et Miquelon.
206 21f. brown, blue and purple 4·50 4·50

1971. Surch.
207 12f. on 19f. (No. 166) (postage) . . . . 2·75 2·75
208 21f. on 33f. (No. 169) (air) 5·50 5·00

18 Weightlifting

20 Pacific Island Dwelling

19 Commission Headquarters, Noumea

1971. 4th South Pacific Games, Papeete, Tahiti.
209 **18** 24f. brown, blue and green (postage) . . . . . . 4·75 4·25
210 – 36f. blue, olive and red . . 6·00 5·00
211 – 48f. brown, green and lilac (air) . . . . 6·00 2·25
212 – 54f. red, purple and blue 6·50 6·25
DESIGNS—As T **18**: 36f. Basketball. 47 × 27 mm: 48f. Pole-vaulting; 54f. Archery.

1971. 1st Death Anniv of General Charles de Gaulle. As T **110** of St. Pierre et Miquelon.
213 30f. black and blue . . . . . 8·75 5·00
214 70f. black and blue . . . . . 16·00 10·50

1972. Air. 25th Anniv of South Pacific Commission.
215 **19** 44f. multicoloured . . . . 7·00 5·00

1972. Air. South Pacific Arts Festival, Fiji.
216 **20** 60f. violet, green and red 8·75 6·25

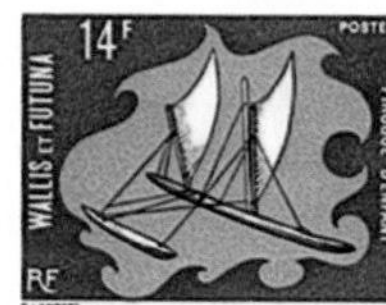

21 Model Pirogue

1972. Sailing Pirogues. Multicoloured.
217 14f. Type **21** (postage) . . . 6·75 4·25
218 16f. Children with model pirogues . . . . 6·50 4·25
219 18f. Racing pirogue . . . . 7·50 6·25
220 200f. Pirogue race (47 × 27 mm) (air) . . . . 13·00 8·00

22 La Perouse and "La Boussole"

1973. Air. Explorers of the Pacific.
221 **22** 22f. brown, grey and red 4·25 3·50
222 – 28f. green, red and blue . . 5·25 4·50
223 – 40f. brown, blue & lt blue 8·50 6·50
224 – 72f. brown, blue and violet 13·00 8·50
DESIGNS: 28f. Samuel Wallis and H.M.S. "Dolphin"; 40f. Dumont d'Urville and "L'Astrolabe"; 72f. Bougainville and "La Boudeuse".

23 General De Gaulle

1973. Air. 3rd Death Anniv of General Charles de Gaulle.
225 **23** 107f. purple and brown . . 15·00 11·00

24 "Plumeria rubra"

1973. Air. Flora of Wallis Islands. Multicoloured.
226 12f. Type **24** . . . . 2·75 2·50
227 17f. "Hibiscus tiliaceus" . . . 2·75 2·50
228 19f. "Phaeomeria magnifica" 3·00 3·75
229 21f. "Hibiscus rosa sinensis" 3·00 3·00
230 23f. "Allamanda cathartica" 3·50 3·50
231 27f. "Barringtonia asiatica" 3·50 4·00
232 39f. Bouquet in vase . . . . 8·75 6·25

25 Rhinoceros Beetle

1974. Insects Multicoloured.
233 15f. Type **25** . . . . 3·00 2·50
234 25f. "Cosmopolites sordidus" (weevil) . . . . 3·50 3·00
235 35f. Tropical fruit-piercer . . 4·50 3·25
236 45f. "Pantala flavescens" (darter) . . . . 7·50 5·00

26 "Flower Hand" holding Letter

1974. Air. Centenary of Universal Postal Union.
237 **26** 51f. purple, brown & green 6·75 5·00

27 "Holy Family" (Kamalielf-Filimoehala)

1974. Air. Christmas.
238 **27** 150f. multicoloured . . . . 11·00 10·00

28 Tapa Pattern

1975. Air. Tapa Mats. Each brown, gold and yellow.
239 3f. Type **28** . . . . 1·90 2·25
240 24f. "Villagers" . . . . . . 2·25 2·75
241 36f. "Fishes" . . . . 4·00 3·50
242 80f. "Fishes and Dancers" . . 8·00 7·25

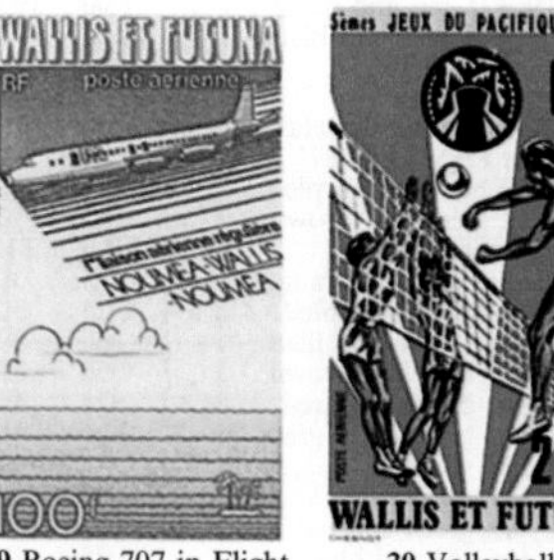

29 Boeing 707 in Flight 30 Volleyball

1975. Air. 1st Regular Air Service to New Caledonia.
243 **29** 100f. multicoloured . . . . 8·25 7·25

1975. Air. 5th South Pacific Games, Guam. Mult.
244 26f. Type **30** . . . . . . 2·25 2·50
245 44f. Football . . . . 2·50 3·00
246 56f. Throwing the javelin . . 3·25 4·00
247 105f. Skin diving . . . . . . 6·00 8·00

1976. Pres. Pompidou Commemoration. As T **131** of St. Pierre et Miquelon.
248 50f. grey and blue . . . . . 5·25 4·50

31 Lalolalo Lake, Wallis

1976. Landscapes. Multicoloured.
249 10f. Type **31** (postage) . . . 2·00 2·00
250 29f. Vasavasa, Futuna (air) 3·00 2·75
251 41f. Sigave Bay, Futuna . . . 4·00 3·25
252 68f. Gahi Bay, Wallis . . . . 5·75 4·50

32 Concorde

1976. Air. 1st Commercial Flight of Concorde.
253 **32** 250f. multicoloured . . . . 30·00 20·00

33 Washington and Battle of Yorktown

1976. Bicentenary of American Revolution.
254 **33** 19f. green, blue and red . . 2·50 2·50
255 – 47f. purple, red and blue 11·75 5·75
DESIGN: 47f. Lafayette and Battle of Virginia Capes.

34 Throwing the Hammer

1976. Air. Olympic Games, Montreal.
256 **34** 31f. purple, blue and red 3·25 3·25
257 – 39f. mauve, red and purple 4·75 3·75
DESIGN: 39f. High-diving.

35 Admiral Cone

1976. Sea Shells. Multicoloured.
258 20f. Type **35** . . . . 3·00 3·00
259 23f. Banded cowrie . . . . . 3·00 3·00
260 43f. Tapestry turban . . . . 5·25 4·50
261 61f. Papal mitre . . . . . . 7·75 7·25

36 Father Chanel and Sanctuary Church, Poi

1977. Father Chanel Memorial. Multicoloured.
262 22f. Type **36** . . . . . . 2·50 2·50
263 32f. Father Chanel and map 3·25 2·75

36a De Gaulle Memorial

1977. 5th Anniv of General de Gaulle Memorial.
264 **36a** 100f. multicoloured . . . 8·00 8·00

37 Tanoa (bowl), Lali (mortar trough) and Ipu (coconut shell)

1977. Handicrafts. Multicoloured.
265 12f. Type **37** . . . . 2·25 2·00
266 25f. Wallis and Futuna kumetes (bowls) and tuluma (box) . . . . . . 2·75 2·25
267 33f. Milamila (comb), ike (club) and tutua (model outrigger) . . . . 3·00 2·50
268 45f. Kolo (Futuna clubs) . . 3·25 3·00
269 69f. Kailao (Wallis and Futuna lances) . . . . . . 4·75 3·75

1977. Air. 1st Commercial Flight of Concorde, Paris–New York. Optd **PARIS NEW-YORK 22.11.77 ler VOL COMMERCIAL.**
270 **32** 250f. multicoloured . . . . 20·00 18·00

39 Post Office, Mata-Utu

1977. Building and Monuments. Multicoloured.
271 27f. Type **39** . . . . 2·75 2·50
272 50f. Sia Hospital, Mata-Utu 2·75 3·00
273 57f. Government Buildings, Mata-Utu . . . . 3·00 4·25
274 63f. St Joseph's Church, Sigave . . . . 4·25 4·25
275 120f. Royal Palace, Mata-Utu 5·25 5·50

1977. Bicentenary of Captain Cook's Discovery of Hawaii. Nos. 254/5 optd **JAMES COOK Bicentenaire de la decouverte des Iles Hawaii 1778–1978.**
276 **33** 19f. green, blue and red . . 3·75 3·25
277 – 47f. purple, red and blue 7·25 5·00

41 Clown Triggerfish

1977. Air. Fishes. Multicoloured.
278 26f. Type **41** . . . . 2·50 2·25
279 35f. Barrier Reef anemonefish 2·75 3·50
280 49f. Emperor angelfish . . . 3·50 3·50
281 51f. Moorish idol . . . . . 4·50 3·75

42 Map of Futuna and Alofi

1978. Maps of Wallis and Futuna Islands.
282 **42** 300f. turquoise, blue and ultramarine . . . . . . 19·00 17·00
283 – 500f. brown, blue and ultramarine . . . . . . 25·00 23·00
DESIGN—VERT: 500f. Map of Wallis Island.

43 Father Bataillon and Churches

1978. Air. Arrival of 1st French Missionaries. Mult.
284 60f. Type **43** . . . . 3·00 3·25
285 72f. Monsgr. Pompallier and map . . . . 3·50 3·75

44 I.T.U. Emblem and Antennae

1978. Air. World Telecommunications Day.
286 **44** 66f. multicoloured . . . . 2·75 3·25

45 "Triomphant" (destroyer)

1978. Free French Pacific Naval Force, 1940–44. Multicoloured.
287 150f. Type **45** . . . . 12·00 9·00
288 200f. "Cap des Palmes" and "Chevreuil" (patrol boats) 10·50 11·50
289 280f. "Savorgnan de Brazza" (destroyer) . . . . 14·50 18·00

46 "Solanum seaforthianum"

1978. Tropical Flowers. Multicoloured.
290 16f. Type **46** . . . . . . 1·90 2·00
291 24f. "Cassia alata" . . . . . 2·00 2·25
292 29f. "Gloriosa superba" . . . 2·50 2·50
293 36f. "Hymenocallis littoralis" 3·00 2·75

47 Reef Heron

1978. Ocean Birds. Multicoloured.
294 17f. Type **47** . . . . 1·40 1·75
295 18f. Red-footed booby . . . 1·40 1·75
296 28f. Brown booby . . . . . 1·75 2·25
297 35f. White tern . . . . . . 2·25 2·50

48 Costumed Carpet-sellers

1978. Costumes and Traditions. Multicoloured.
298 53f. Type **48** . . . . 3·00 2·75
299 55f. "Festival of God" procession . . . . 2·75 3·25
300 59f. Guards of honour . . . 3·25 3·25

49 Nativity Scene

1978. Air. Christmas.
301 **49** 160f. multicoloured . . . . 6·25 6·25

50 Human Rights Emblem

1978. 30th Anniv of Declaration of Human Rights.
302 **50** 44f. multicoloured . . . . 2·75 2·75
303 56f. multicoloured . . . . 2·75 3·25

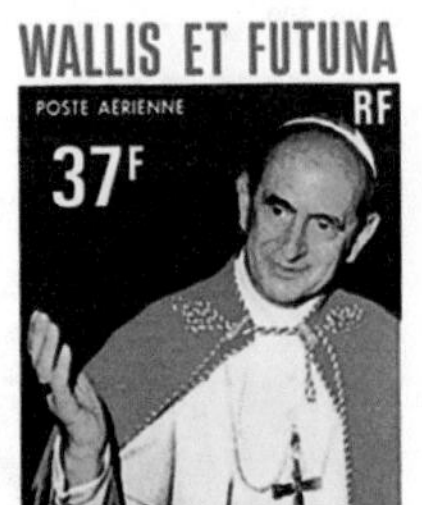
51 Pope Paul VI

1979. Air. Popes. Multicoloured.
304 37f. Type **51** . . . . 2·00 2·75
305 41f. Pope John-Paul I . . . . 2·00 3·00
306 105f. St. Peter's, Rome, and Popes Paul VI and John-Paul I (horiz) . . . . . . 4·75 4·50

52 Britten Norman Islander

1979. Air. Inter-Island Communications (1st series). Multicoloured.
307 46f. Type **52** . . . . 3·00 2·50
308 68f. Freighter "Moana II" . . 1·75 3·00
309 80f. Hihifo Airport . . . . . 4·25 3·25
See also Nos. 349/51.

53 Fishing Boat

1979. Tagging Skipjack Tuna. Multicoloured.
310 10f. Type **53** . . . . 1·60 2·00
311 30f. Weighing skipjack tuna 2·50 2·25
312 34f. Young skipjack tuna . . 2·50 2·50
313 38f. Tagging skipjack tuna 2·25 2·50
314 40f. Angling for skipjack tuna . . . . 2·50 2·75
315 48f. Skipjack tuna . . . . . 3·00 3·25
MS316 174 × 100 mm. Nos. 310/5 plus 3 labels . . . . 14·50 16·00

54 Boy with Model Outrigger Canoe

1979. International Year of the Child. Mult.
317 52f. Type **54** . . . . 2·75 2·75
318 58f. Girl on horseback . . . 3·25 2·75

55 "Bombax ellipticum"

1979. Flowering and Fruiting Trees. Mult.
319 50f. Type **55** . . . . 2·00 2·50
320 64f. "Callophyllum inophyllum" . . . . 2·50 2·75
321 76f. "Pandanus odoratissimus" . . . . . . 3·25 3·50

56 French 1876 5c. Stamp and "Eole" Meteorological Satellite

1979. Air. Death Centenary of Sir Rowland Hill.
322 **56** 5f. multicoloured . . . . . 50 2·00
323 – 70f. multicoloured . . . . 2·50 2·75
324 – 90f. black and red . . . . 2·50 3·25
325 – 100f. brown, yellow & blue 2·75 3·75
DESIGNS—VERT: 70f. Hibiscus and Wallis and Futuna 1920 1f. stamp. HORIZ: 90f. Sir Rowland Hill and Great Britain Penny Black; 100f. "Birds" (Kano School) and Japan 1872 ½s. stamp.

57 Normal and Distorted Landscapes

1979. Anti-alcoholism Campaign.
326 **57** 22f. multicoloured . . . . 1·75 2·50

58 Heads looking at Cross of Lorraine

1979. Air. 39th Anniv of 18 June Appeal by General de Gaulle.
327 **58** 33f. red, blue and grey . . 2·75 2·75

59 "Crinum moorei"

1979. Flowers (1st series). Multicoloured.
328 20f. Type **59** . . . . 1·10 2·00
329 42f. Passion flower . . . . . 2·00 2·50
330 62f. "Canna indica" . . . . 2·25 3·00
See also Nos. 392/4.

60 Map of Islands and French Arms

1979. Air. Presidential Visit.
331 **60** 47f. multicoloured . . . . 3·00 2·75

61 Cook and Death Scene, Hawaii

1979. Air. Death Bicentenary of Captain Cook.
332 **61** 130f. grey, blue and brown 6·50 5·00

62 Swimmers

1979. 6th South Pacific Games, Fiji.
333 **62** 31f. olive, red and green 3·00 2·50
334 – 39f. brown, turquoise & green 3·50 2·75
DESIGN: 39f. High-jumper.

63 Garlands

1979. Necklaces. Multicoloured.
335 110f. Type **63** 3·75 3·75
336 140f. Coral necklaces 5·25 4·50

64 Satellite and Dish Aerial

1979. Air. 3rd World Telecommunications Exhibition, Geneva.
337 **64** 120f. multicoloured 3·75 4·50

65 Detail of Painting by Mme. Sutita

1979. Works of Local Artists. Multicoloured.
338 27f. Painting by Mme Sutita (detail) (different) 2·25 2·50
339 65f. Painting by M. A. Pilioko (detail) (vert) 3·00 3·00
340 78f. Type **65** 3·75 3·50

66 Squilla

1979. South Pacific Fauna. Multicoloured.
341 15f. Type **66** 1·50 2·00
342 23f. Spanish dancer 1·60 2·25
343 25f. Cat's-tongue thorny oyster 2·00 2·25
344 43f. Sea fan 2·25 2·25
345 45f. Starfish 2·00 2·50
346 63f. Fluted giant clam 3·00 3·50

67 "Virgin of the Crescent Moon" (detail, Durer)

1979. Air. Christmas.
347 **67** 180f. black and red 9·00 7·25
See also No. 554.

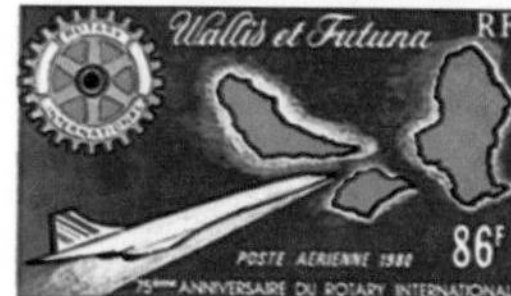

68 Concorde, Map and Rotary Emblem

1980. Air. 75th Anniv of Rotary International.
348 **68** 86f. multicoloured 5·25 4·50

1980. Inter-Island Communications (2nd series). As Nos. 307/9.
349 1f. Type **52** 90 1·00
350 3f. As No. 308 50 1·00
351 5f. As No. 309 1·00 1·00

69 Radio Station

71 Rochambeau and Soldiers

70 "Jesus laid in the Tomb" (Maurice Denis)

1980. 1st Anniv of Radio Station FR3.
352 **69** 47f. multicoloured 2·75 2·25

1980. Easter.
353 **70** 25f. multicoloured 1·90 1·75

1980. Air. Bicentenary of Rochambeau's Landing at Newport, Rhode Island.
354 **71** 102f. sepia, blue and brown 6·25 5·00

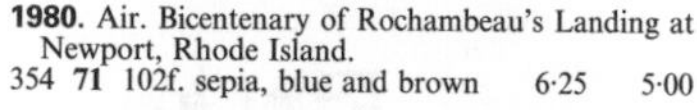

72 Flags and Island

1980. Air. National Day.
355 **72** 71f. multicoloured 3·00 2·25

73 Mozambique Emperor

1980. Fishes. Multicoloured.
356 23f. Type **73** 1·40 1·40
357 27f. Crimson jobfish 1·60 1·60
358 32f. Ruby snapper 2·00 2·00
359 51f. Golden hind 2·75 2·50
360 59f. Rusty jobfish 4·00 3·75

74 Mermoz and "Arc en Ciel"

1980. Air. 50th Anniv of 1st South Atlantic Airmail Flight.
361 **74** 122f. blue, deep blue & red 6·25 4·50

1980. "Sydpex 80" International Stamp Exhibition, Sydney. No. 315 surch **50F SYDPEX 80 29 Septembre**.
362 50f. on 48f. multicoloured 3·50 2·25

76 Fleming and Penicillin Slide

1980. Air. 25th Death Anniv of Alexander Fleming (discoverer of penicillin).
363 **76** 101f. blue, brown and red 4·50 3·25

77 Charles de Gaulle

1980. Air. 10th Death Anniv of Charles de Gaulle (French statesman).
364 **77** 200f. green and brown 9·75 7·25

78 "The Virgin, Child and St. Catherine" (Lorenzo Lotto)

1980. Air. Christmas.
365 **78** 150f. multicoloured 6·00 4·50

79 Alan Shepard and "Freedom 7"

1981. Air. 20th Anniv of First Men in Space. Multicoloured.
366 37f. Type **79** 1·75 1·75
367 44f. Yuri Gagarin and "Vostok 1" 2·50 2·00

80 Ribbons and I.T.U. and W.H.O. Emblems forming Caduceus and Satellite

1981. World Telecommunications Day.
368 **80** 49f. multicoloured 2·50 2·00

81 Curie and Laboratory Equipment

1981. 75th Death Anniv of Pierre Curie (physicist and discoverer of radium).
369 **81** 56f. multicoloured 2·50 2·25

82 Coral 84 Section of Globe

83 Doctor inoculating Child

1981. Undersea Fauna. Multicoloured.
370 28f. Type **82** 1·25 1·60
371 30f. Blue-green algae 1·25 1·60
372 31f. "Ceratium vultur" (dinoflagellate) 1·50 1·75
373 35f. Tomato anemonefish 1·50 1·75
374 40f. Textile cone 1·75 2·00
375 55f. Feather-star (echinoderm) 2·00 2·25

1981. 60th Anniv of 1st B.C.G. Anti-tuberculosis Inoculation.
376 **83** 27f. multicoloured 1·75 1·50

1981. International Year of Disabled Persons.
377 **84** 42f. multicoloured 2·50 1·90

85 Edison and Phonograph

1981. 50th Death Anniv of Thomas Edison (inventor).
378 **85** 59f. black, blue and red 2·75 2·25

1981. No. 341 surch **5F**.
379 5f. on 15f. multicoloured 1·10 1·10

87 Battle Scene

1981. Bicentenary of Battle of Virginia Capes.
380 – 66f. purple, blue and slate 2·75 2·25
381 **87** 74f. green, violet and light green 3·50 2·25
DESIGN: 66f. Admiral Francois de Grasse and battle scene.

88 "Vase of Flowers" (Cezanne)

1981. Air. 75th Death Anniv of Paul Cezanne and Birth Centenary of Pablo Picasso (artists).
382 53f. Type **88** 2·75 2·25
383 135f. "Harlequin leaning" (Picasso) 6·25 4·00

89 Football

1981. Air. World Cup Football Championship, Spain (1982).
384 **89** 120f. brown, black & green 4·50 3·75
385 120f. brown, mauve and green 4·50 3·75

90 Patrol Boat "La Dieppoise"

1981. Surveillance of 200-mile Zone. Mult.
386 60f. Type **90** 2·00 2·25
387 85f. Frigate "Protet" 2·75 3·00

91 Crib

1981. Air. Christmas.
388 **91** 180f. multicoloured 7·00 5·00

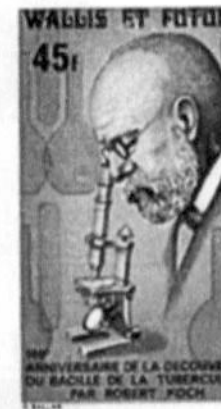

92 "Pilioko Aloi" (tapestry) **93** Dr. R. Koch at Microscope

1982. Air.
389 **92** 100f. multicoloured 4·00 3·25

1982. Centenary of Discovery of Tubercle Bacillus.
390 **93** 45f. multicoloured 2·25 2·00

94 "Fishing Boats at Collioure"

1982. Air. Death Cent of Georges Braque (painter).
391 **94** 300f. multicoloured 11·00 8·25

1982. Flowers (2nd series). Multicoloured.
392 1f. As Type **59** 75 1·00
393 2f. As No. 329 1·00 1·00
394 3f. As No. 330 1·00 1·00

95 1930 Stamp

1982. "Philexfrance" International Stamp Exhibition, Paris.
395 **95** 140f. violet, blue and red 4·25 3·25

96 "Acanthe phippium"

1982. Orchids. Multicoloured.
396 34f. Type **96** 1·40 1·60
397 68f. "Acanthe phippium" (different) 2·50 2·50
398 70f. "Spathoglottis pacifica" 3·00 2·50
399 83f. "Mussaenda raiateensis" 3·75 3·25

97 Lord Baden-Powell

1982. 125th Birth Anniv of Lord Baden-Powell (founder of Boy Scout Movement).
400 **97** 80f. multicoloured 3·50 2·50

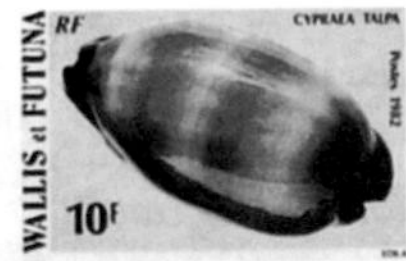

98 Mole Cowrie

1982. Sea Shells (1st series). Multicoloured.
401 10f. Type **98** 95 1·00
402 15f. Pacific deer cowrie 1·10 1·00
403 25f. Eyed cowrie 1·25 1·25
404 27f. Closely-related carnelian cowrie 1·40 1·10
405 40f. All-red map cowrie 1·75 1·60
406 50f. Tiger cowrie 2·25 2·00
See also Nos. 428/33, 440/5, 459/64, 481/6 and 510/15.

99 Santos-Dumont, Airship "Ballon No. 14" and Biplane "14 bis"

1982. Air. 50th Death Anniv of Alberto Santos-Dumont (aviation pioneer).
407 **99** 95f. brown, green and blue 4·00 2·75

1982. Air. World Cup Football Championship Result. No. 384 optd **ITALIE VAINQUEUR 1982.**
408 **89** 120f. brown, black and green 4·50 3·75

101 Beach

1982. Air. Overseas Week.
409 **101** 105f. multicoloured 3·50 3·25

102 Coral

1982. Marine Life. Multicoloured.
410 32f. Type **102** 1·75 1·40
411 35f. Starfish 1·90 1·40
412 46f. Spanish dancer 2·25 1·90
413 63f. Cat's-tongue thorny oyster 3·00 2·25

103 Hands reaching towards Eye

1982. Air. Blind Day.
414 **103** 130f. blue, scarlet and red 4·00 3·75

104 St. Theresa of Avila

1982. 400th Death Anniv of St. Theresa of Avila.
415 **104** 31f. brown, green and deep brown 1·75 1·60
See also No. 447.

105 "Adoration of the Virgin" (Correggio)

1982. Air. Christmas.
416 **105** 170f. multicoloured 5·75 4·50

106 Wallis Meeting House

1983.
417 **106** 19f. multicoloured 1·00 1·75

107 Eiffel and Eiffel Tower under Construction

1983. 60th Death Anniv of Gustave Eiffel (engineer).
418 **107** 97f. purple, red and green 3·50 3·00

108 Windsurfing **110** Vincenzo Lunardi's Balloon, 1784

109 Island Scene and U.P.U. Emblem

1983. Air.
419 **108** 270f. multicoloured 9·75 6·00

1983. Air. World U.P.U. Day.
420 **109** 100f. multicoloured 4·00 2·75

1983. Air. Bicentenary of Manned Flight.
421 **110** 205f. multicoloured 7·50 5·00

111 "Cat"

1983. Air. 15th Death Anniv of Foujita (painter).
422 **111** 102f. multicoloured 3·75 2·75

112 Thai Goddess **113** Javelin-thrower

1983. "Bangkok 1983" International Stamp Exn.
423 **112** 92f. red, black and blue 3·00 2·25

1983. Air. Olympic Games, Los Angeles (1984) (1st issue).
424 **113** 250f. brown, green & yellow 8·00 6·50
See also No. 438.

114 Nobel

1983. Air. 150th Birth Anniv of Alfred Nobel (inventor of dynamite and founder of Nobel Prizes).
425 **114** 150f. red and green 5·25 3·75

115 Satellite, Dish Aerial and W.C.Y. Emblem **117** Tulip Cone

116 Niepce and Early Photograph

1983. World Communications Year.
426 **115** 20f. multicoloured 1·10 1·25

1983. Air. Death Centenary of Nicephore Niepce (pioneer of photography).
427 **116** 75f. purple and green 3·25 2·25

1983. Sea Shells (2nd series). Multicoloured.
428 10f. Type **117** 65 1·00
429 17f. Captain cone 75 1·10
430 21f. Virgin cone 75 1·10
431 39f. Calf cone 1·10 1·10
432 52f. Marble cone 1·40 1·90
433 65f. Leopard cone 2·00 2·25

118 "Triumph of Galatea"

1983. Air. 500th Birth Anniv of Raphael (artist).
434 **118** 167f. multicoloured . . . 5·75 4·50

119 Pandanus Tree

1983. Air.
435 **119** 137f. multicoloured . . . 4·75 3·25

120 "Madonna and Pope Sixtus" (Raphael)

1983. Air. Christmas.
436 **120** 200f. multicoloured . . . 7·00 5·00

121 Frigate "Commandant Bory"

1984. Air.
437 **121** 67f. multicoloured . . . . 2·75 2·25

122 Weightlifting

1984. Air. Olympic Games, Los Angeles (2nd issue).
438 **122** 85f. multicoloured . . . . 3·50 2·75

123 Frangipani

1984. Air.
439 **123** 130f. multicoloured . . . 4·50 3·25

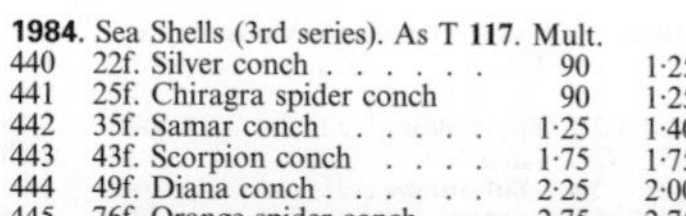

1984. Sea Shells (3rd series). As T **117**. Mult.
440 22f. Silver conch . . . . . . 90 1·25
441 25f. Chiragra spider conch 90 1·25
442 35f. Samar conch . . . . . 1·25 1·40
443 43f. Scorpion conch . . . . 1·75 1·75
444 49f. Diana conch . . . . . . 2·25 2·00
445 76f. Orange spider conch . . 2·75 2·75

124 "Deposition of Christ" (Alele Chapel)

1984. Air. Easter.
446 **124** 190f. multicoloured . . . 6·00 4·50

1984. "Espana 84" International Stamp Exhibition, Madrid. As T **104** but with "Espana 84" emblem.
447 70f. sepia, green and brown 2·50 2·25

125 Diderot and Title Page of Encyclopedia

1984. Death Bicentenary of Denis Diderot (encyclopedist).
448 **125** 100f. brown and blue . . 3·50 2·75

126 Killer Whale

1984. Nature Protection.
449 **126** 90f. multicoloured . . . . 3·75 2·25

127 Painting

1984. Air. 95th Birth Anniv of Jean Cocteau (artist).
450 **127** 150f. multicoloured . . . 4·75 4·00

128 Tiki

129 "Alice"

1984. Air. Soane Hoatau Sculpture.
451 **128** 175f. multicoloured . . . 6·00 4·50

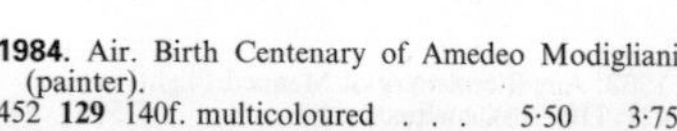

1984. Air. Birth Centenary of Amedeo Modigliani (painter).
452 **129** 140f. multicoloured . . . 5·50 3·75

130 "Pilioko Aloi" (tapestry)

1984. Air. "Ausipex 84" International Stamp Exhibition, Melbourne.
453 **130** 180f. multicoloured . . . 6·25 4·00

131 "Local Dances" (Jean Michon)

1984. Air.
454 **131** 110f. multicoloured . . . 4·50 3·25

132 Altar, Mount Lulu Chapel

1984. Air.
455 **132** 52f. multicoloured . . . . 2·25 1·90

133 Islanders wearing Leis

1985. 4th Pacific Arts Festival.
456 **133** 160f. multicoloured . . . 5·25 4·00

134 Common Spider Conch and Virgin and Child

1984. Air. Christmas.
457 **134** 260f. multicoloured . . . 9·00 5·00

135 Lapita Pottery

136 Victor Hugo

1985. Archaeological Expedition, 1983.
458 **135** 53f. multicoloured . . . . 2·25 1·60

1985. Sea Shells (4th series). As T **117**. Mult.
459 2f. Chambered nautilus . . . 35 80
460 3f. Adusta murex 35 80
461 41f. Vibex bonnet . . . . . 1·25 1·40
462 47f. Flag cone . . . . 1·75 1·75
463 56f. True harp . . . . 1·75 1·90
464 71f. Ramose murex . . . . . 2·50 2·25

1985. Death Centenary of Victor Hugo (writer).
465 **136** 89f. deep blue, blue and red . . . . 3·50 2·50

137 "Pilioko Aloi" (tapestry)

1985. Air.
466 **137** 500f. multicoloured . . . 14·50 10·00

138 Flying Fox

1985.
467 **138** 38f. multicoloured . . . . 2·00 1·60

139 Children

1985. International Youth Year.
468 **139** 64f. multicoloured . . . . 2·50 1·90

140 "The Post Office"

1985. Air. 30th Death Anniv of Maurice Utrillo (artist).
469 **140** 200f. multicoloured . . . 6·25 4·00

141 Hands and U.N. Emblem

1985. 40th Anniv of U.N.O.
470 **141** 49f. green, blue and red 2·25 1·75

142 Sailing Canoe

1985. Air.
471 **142** 350f. multicoloured . . . 10·50 6·00

143 Ronsard, Organist and Muse of Poetry

1985. 400th Death Anniv of Pierre de Ronsard (poet).
472 **143** 170f. brown, deep brown and blue . . . . 6·25 4·00

144 Landing Ship "Jacques Cartier"

145 "Portrait of Young Woman" (Patrice Nielly)

1985. Air.
473 **144** 51f. deep blue, blue and turquoise . . . . 1·75 1·75

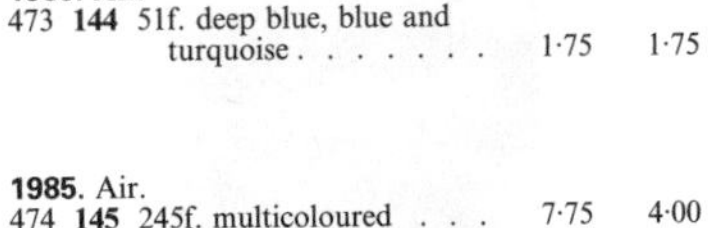

1985. Air.
474 **145** 245f. multicoloured . . . 7·75 4·00

146 Schweitzer, African Boy and Cathedral Organ

1985. 20th Death Anniv of Dr. Albert Schweitzer (missionary).
475 **146** 50f. black, purple & brown . . . . 2·25 1·75

147 "Virgin and Child" (Jean Michon)

1985. Air. Christmas.
476 **147** 330f. multicoloured . . . 10·50 7·25

148 Bread-fruit

1986. Food and Agriculture Organization.
477 **148** 39f. multicoloured . . . . 1·90 1·60

149 Flamboyant Flower

1986.
478 **149** 38f. multicoloured . . . . 1·75 1·60

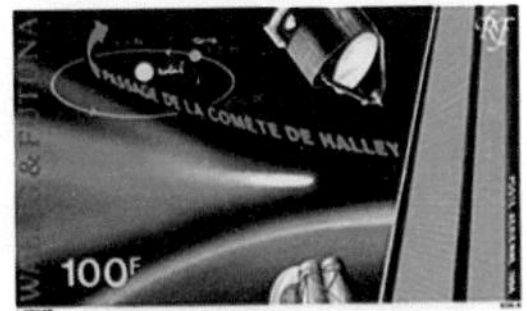

150 Comet and "Giotto" Space Probe

1986. Air. Appearance of Halley's Comet.
479 **150** 100f. multicoloured . . . 3·25 2·75

151 Vianney praying

1986. Air. Birth Bicentenary of Cure d'Ars.
480 **151** 200f. light brown, brown and black . . . . . . 6·50 4·50

1986. Sea Shells (5th series). As T **117**. Mult.
481 4f. Giant spider conch . . . 55 1·00
482 5f. Trumpet triton . . . . . 35 1·00
483 10f. Red-mouth olive . . . . 60 1·00
484 18f. Common distorsio . . . 75 1·10
485 25f. Episcopal mitre . . . . 1·10 1·25
486 107f. Distant cone . . . . . 3·00 2·75

152 Players and Boy with Football

1986. World Cup Football Championship, Mexico.
487 **152** 95f. multicoloured . . . . 3·25 2·50

153 Willem Schouten and "Eendracht"

1986. 370th Anniv of Discovery of Horn Islands. Each purple, green and blue.
488 8f. Type **153** . . . . 1·10 1·00
489 9f. Jacob le Maire and "Hoorn" . . . . 1·10 1·00
490 155f. Map of Futuna and Alofi Islands . . . . 5·50 4·50

154 Watt and Steam Engine

1986. 250th Birth Anniv of James Watt (inventor).
491 **154** 74f. red and black . . . . 3·25 3·25

155 Queen Amelia

1986. Air. Centenary of Request for Protectorate and 25th Anniv of French Overseas Territory Status. Each purple, red and blue.
492 90f. Type **155** . . . . 3·25 3·25
493 137f. Law of 1961 bestowing Overseas Territory status 4·50 4·50

156 Patrol Boat "La Lorientaise"

1986. Naval Ships.
494 **156** 6f. red, purple and blue 1·00 1·00
495 – 7f. violet, orange and red 1·00 1·00
496 – 120f. turquoise, red & blue . . . . 4·00 3·00
DESIGNS: 7f. Frigate "Commandant Blaison"; 120f. Frigate "Balny".

157 Oleander

1986.
497 **157** 97f. multicoloured . . . . 3·50 2·75

158 U.P.U. Emblem and Dove carrying Envelope

1986. Air. World Post Day.
498 **158** 270f. multicoloured . . . 8·75 6·50

159 New York, Statue and Paris

1986. Air. Centenary of Statue of Liberty.
499 **159** 205f. multicoloured . . . 6·50 4·50

160 "Virgin and Child" (Botticelli)

1986. Christmas.
500 **160** 250f. multicoloured . . . 7·25 5·50

161 "Papilio montrouzieri"

162 Father Chanel and Basilica

1987. Butterflies. Multicoloured.
501 2f. Type **161** . . . . 95 1·10
502 42f. Caper white . . . . . 1·60 1·40
503 46f. "Delias ellipsis" . . . . 1·75 1·60
504 50f. "Danaus pumila" . . . 1·90 1·75
505 52f. "Lutbrodes cleotas" . . 1·90 1·75
506 59f. Meadow argus . . . . . 2·50 2·00

1987. Air. 1st Anniv of Poi Basilica.
507 **162** 230f. multicoloured . . . 7·75 4·50

163 "Telstar", Globe and Pleumeur-Bodou

1987. Air. World Communications Day. 25th Anniv of Launch of "Telstar" Communications Satellite.
508 **163** 200f. blue, black and red 6·25 3·75

164 Wrestlers

1987. World Wrestling Championships, Clermont-Ferrand.
509 **164** 97f. multicoloured . . . . 3·50 2·50

1987. Sea Shells (6th series). As T **117**. Mult.
510 3f. Common hairy triton . . 35 1·00
511 4f. Textile cone . . . . . . 35 1·00
512 28f. Humpback cowrie . . . 95 1·25
513 44f. Giant frog shell . . . . 1·40 1·60
514 48f. Turtle cowrie . . . . . 1·50 1·75
515 78f. Bull-mouth helmet . . . 2·25 2·25

165 Piccard, Stratosphere Balloon "F.N.R.S." and Bathyscaphe

167 Bust of Girl

1987. Air. 25th Death Anniv of Auguste Piccard (physicist).
516 **165** 135f. deep blue, blue and green . . . . 4·50 3·00

1987. "Olymphilex 87" Olympic Stamps Exhibition, Rome. No 509 optd **OLYMPHILEX '87 ROME** and Olympic rings.
517 **164** 97f. multicoloured . . . . 3·50 2·50

1987. 70th Death Anniv of Auguste Rodin (sculptor).
518 **167** 150f. purple . . . . . . 5·00 3·25
See also No. 557.

168 Letters between Globes and Postbird

1987. World Post Day.
519 **168** 116f. blue, deep blue and yellow . . . . 4·00 2·75

169 Pacific Black Duck

1987. Birds. Multicoloured.
520 6f. Type **169** 30 85
521 19f. Pacific golden plover . . 50 95
522 47f. Friendly quail dove . . . 1·40 1·25
523 56f. Ruddy turnstone . . . . 1·60 1·50
524 64f. Buff-banded rail . . . . 1·75 1·50
525 68f. Bar-tailed godwit . . . . 2·25 1·75

170 Mgr. Bataillon, French Frigate and Islands

1987. Air. 150th Anniv of Arrival of First Missionaries.
526 **170** 260f. turquoise, blue and brown . . . . 8·50 5·50

171 Nativity Scene

1987. Air. Christmas.
527 **171** 300f. multicoloured . . . 9·75 6·50

172 Carco and Parisian Scenes

1988. 30th Death Anniv of Francis Carco (writer).
528 **172** 40f. multicoloured . . . . 1·90 1·40

173 Morane Saulnier Type I and Garros

1988. Air. 70th Death Anniv of Roland Garros (aviator).
529 **173** 600f. deep blue, brown and blue . . . . 18·00 12·50

174 La Perouse, "L'Astrolabe" and "La Boussole"

1988. Bicentenary of Disappearance of La Perouse's Expedition.
530 **174** 70f. green, blue and brown . . . . 2·75 2·00

175 "Self-portrait wearing Lace Jabot"

1988. Air. Death Bicentenary of Maurice Quentin de la Tour (painter).
531 **175** 500f. multicoloured . . . 16·00 11·00

176 Arrows and Dish Aerial

1988. Air. World Telecommunications Day.
532 **176** 100f. multicoloured . . . 3·00 2·50

177 Map and Bishop with Crosier

1988. Air. South Pacific Episcopal Conference.
533 **177** 90f. multicoloured . . . . 2·75 2·25

178 Nurse, Child and Anniversary Emblem

1988. 125th Anniv of International Red Cross.
534 **178** 30f. black, green and red 1·25 1·40

179 Throwing the Javelin

1988. Olympic Games, Seoul. Each brown, red and blue.
535 11f. Type **179** . . . . 1·25 1·10
536 20f. Volleyball . . . . 1·25 1·25
537 60f. Windsurfing . . . . . . 2·50 2·25
538 80f. Sailing . . . . 3·00 2·75

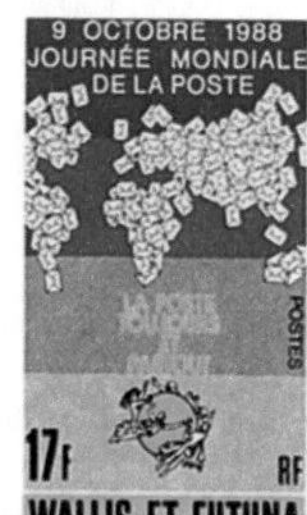

180 Envelopes forming Map

1988. World Post Day.
539 **180** 17f. yellow, blue and black . . . . 1·25 1·10

181 Becquerel

1988. Birth Bicent of Antoine Cesar Becquerel (physicist).
540 **181** 18f. black and blue . . . 1·25 1·10

182 Nativity Scene

1988. Air. Christmas.
541 **182** 400f. multicoloured . . . 12·00 8·25

183 "Amiral Charner" (frigate)

1989. International Maritime Organization.
542 **183** 26f. multicoloured . . . . 1·40 1·40

184 Renior and Scene from "The Great Illusion"

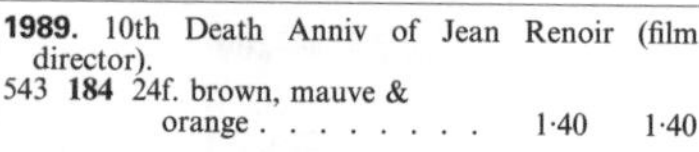
1989. 10th Death Anniv of Jean Renoir (film director).
543 **184** 24f. brown, mauve & orange . . . . 1·40 1·40

185 Royal Throne (Aselo Kulimoetoke) 186 Map

1989. Air.
544 **185** 700f. multicoloured . . . 21·00 13·00

1989. Futuna Hydro-electric Power Station.
545 **186** 25f. multicoloured . . . . 1·40 1·25

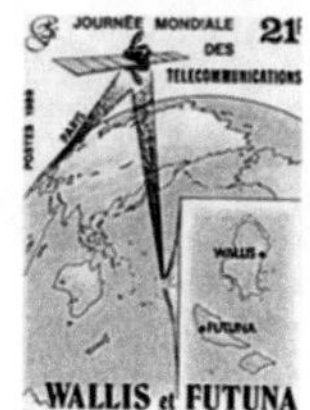

188 Satellite above Earth

1989. International Telecommunications Day.
546 **188** 21f. multicoloured . . . . 1·00 1·25

189 Mural (H. Tailhade)

1989.
547 **189** 22f. multicoloured . . . . 1·40 1·25

190 Globe and Emblem

1989. "Philexfrance '89" International Stamp Exhibition, Paris (548) and Bicentenary of Declaration of Rights of Man and South Pacific Youth Meeting (549). Multicoloured.
548 29f. Type **190** (postage) . . . 1·40 1·25
549 900f. Sportsmen (air) . . . . 24·00 10·50
MS550 200 × 90 mm. Nos. 548/9 (sold at 1000f.) . . . . 29·00 32·00

191 Cyclists

1989. World Cycling Championships, France.
551 **191** 10f. black, brown & green 1·25 1·00

192 Envelopes around Globe of Flags

1989. World Post Day.
552 **192** 27f. multicoloured . . . . 1·40 1·25

193 Landscape

1989.
553 **193** 23f. multicoloured . . . . 1·75 1·60

1989. Air. Christmas. As No. 347 but date, value and colour changed.
554 **67** 800f. mauve . . . . 23·00 16·00

194 "Star of Bethlehem"

1990.
555 **194** 44f. multicoloured . . . . 1·90 1·60

195 Tortoise Fossil

1990.
556 **195** 48f. multicoloured . . . . 1·75 1·60

1990. 150th Birth Anniv of Auguste Rodin (sculptor). As No. 518 but value and colour changed.
557 **167** 200f. blue . . . . 6·50 4·00

197 Footballers

1990. World Cup Football Championship, Italy.
558 **197** 59f. multicoloured . . . . 2·25 1·90

198 Orchids

1990. Mothers' Day.
559 **198** 78f. multicoloured . . . . 3·00 2·25

199 "Avion III", Airbus Industrie A310 and Clement Ader

1990. Air. Cent of First Heavier-than-Air Flight and 1st Anniv of Wallis–Tahiti Air Link.
560 **199** 56f. brown, mauve and red . . . . 1·75 1·75

200 Red-tailed Tropic Bird

1990. Multicoloured.
561 300f. Type **200** . . . . . . 7·50 5·50
562 600f. South Pacific islet . . . 20·00 12·50

201 "Moana II" (inter-island freighter)

1990. Ships.
563 **201** 40f. brown, green and blue . . . . 2·00 1·60
564 – 50f. brown, blue and green . . . . 2·25 1·90
DESIGN: 50f. "Moana III" (container ship) at jetty.

202 Traditional Dwellings

1990.
565 **202** 28f. multicoloured . . . . 1·50 1·25

203 Doves and Globe

1990. Stamp Day.
566 **203** 97f. multicoloured . . . . 3·50 2·75

204 Outrigger Canoe

1990.
567 **204** 46f. multicoloured . . . . 2·25 1·75

205 De Gaulle

1990. Air. Birth Centenary of Charles de Gaulle (French statesman).
568 **205** 1000f. multicoloured . . . 26·00 19·00

206 Palm Trees

1990. "Best Wishes".
569 **206** 100f. multicoloured . . . 3·50 2·75

207 Patrol Boat "La Glorieuse"

1991.
570 **207** 52f. blue, green and red 3·00 2·00
See also No. 578.

208 Warrior

1991. Tradition.
571 7f. Breadfruit gatherer . . . 90 1·00
572 54f. Taro planter . . . . . . 2·00 1·60
573 62f. Spear fisherman . . . . 2·25 1·75
574 72f. Type **208** . . . . 2·25 1·75
575 90f. Kailao dancer . . . . . 3·00 1·90
MS576 185 × 104 mm. Nos. 571/5 (sold at 300f.) . . . . 9·75 10·00

209 Aspects of Health Care

1991. 20th Anniv of Medecins sans Frontieres (medical charity).
577 **209** 55f. multicoloured . . . . 2·25 1·75

1991. Patrol Boat "La Moqueuse". As T **207**.
578 42f. black, blue and red . . . 2·50 1·75

210 Chanel and Reliquary

1991. Air. 150th Death Anniv of Father Chanel (missionary).
579 **210** 235f. multicoloured . . . 7·50 5·00

211 Players through the Ages (½-size illustration)

1991. Air. Centenary of French Open Tennis Championships.
580 **211** 250f. black, orange & green . . . . 8·50 5·00

212 Map and Microlight

1991. Microlight Aircraft Flying in Wallis and Futuna.
581 **212** 85f. multicoloured . . . . 3·25 2·25

213 "Portrait of Jean"

1991. 150th Birth Anniv of Pierre Auguste Renior (painter). Perf or imperf (self-adhesive).
582 **213** 400f. multicoloured . . . 11·50 7·25

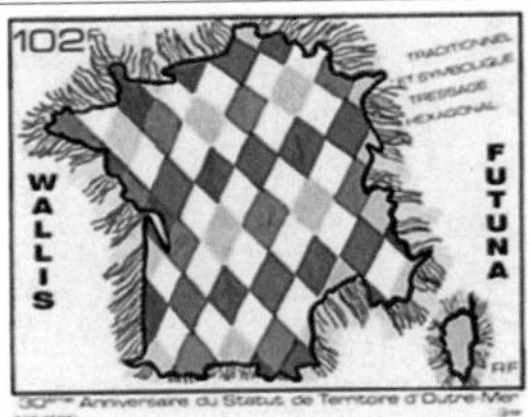
214 Map

1991. 30th Anniv of French Overseas Territory Status.
584 **214** 102f. multicoloured . . . 3·00 2·25

215 Islanders in Festive Dress and Angel

1991. Feast of the Assumption.
585 **215** 30f. multicoloured . . . . 1·60 1·25

216 Mozart and Scene from "The Marriage of Figaro"

1991. Air. Death Bicentenary of Wolfgang Amadeus Mozart (composer).
586 **216** 500f. blue, lilac and red 14·00 8·25

217 Imprisoned Figure

1991. 30th Anniv of Amnesty International.
587 **217** 140f. yellow, violet & blue 4·75 2·75

218 House and Generator

1991. 50th Anniv of Central Economic Co-operation Bank.
588 **218** 10f. multicoloured . . . . 1·00 1·00

219 "Allamanda cathartica"

1991. Flowers. Multicoloured.
589 1f. Type **219** . . . . 90 1·00
590 4f. "Hibiscus rosa sinensis" (vert) . . . . 1·00 1·00
591 80f. Water lily . . . . 2·75 2·00

220 Santa Claus on Beach

1991. Christmas.
592 **220** 60f. multicoloured . . . . 2·25 1·60

221 Ski Jumping

1992. Winter Olympic Games, Albertville.
593 **221** 150f. multicoloured . . . 5·00 3·00

222 Map, Plants and Dassault Breguet Mystere Falcon 20

1992. "Escadrille 9S" Maritime Surveillance Service.
594 **222** 48f. multicoloured . . . . 2·00 1·40

223 Canadian 1938 $1 and Wallis and Futuna 1920 2f. Stamps (½-size illustration)

1992. "Canada 92" International Youth Philatelic Exhibition, Montreal.
595 **223** 35f. black, red and violet 1·40 1·25

224 Throwing the Javelin

1992. Olympic Games, Barcelona.
596 **224** 106f. indigo, blue & green 3·00 2·25

225 Spanish 1975 4p. Stamp and Wallis Post Office

1992. "Granada 92" International Stamp Exhibition.
597 **225** 100f. black, blue & purple 2·75 2·00

226 Columbus's Fleet, Pavilion and Seville

1992. "Expo 92" World's Fair, Seville.
598 **226** 200f. green, blue & orange 5·00 4·00

227 Saddle Butterflyfish

1992. Butterfly and Angel Fishes. Multicoloured.
599 21f. Type **227** . . . . 1·10 1·10
600 22f. Thread-finned butterflyfish . . . . 1·25 1·10
601 23f. Masked bannerfish . . . 1·25 1·10
602 24f. Regal angelfish . . . . . 1·25 1·10
603 25f. Conspicuous angelfish . . 1·25 1·10
604 26f. Teardrop butterflyfish . . 1·25 1·25

228 Columbus and Map

1992. Air. "World Columbian Stamp Expo 92", Chicago.
605 **228** 100f. multicoloured . . . 2·50 1·90
See also No. 612.

229 Three Spearmen

1992. Wallis Islands. Multicoloured.
606 70f. Type **229** . . . . 2·00 1·60
607 70f. Two spearmen and palm trees . . . . 2·00 1·60
608 70f. Pirogues . . . . 2·00 1·60
609 70f. Two fishermen and palm trees . . . . 2·00 1·60
610 70f. Three fishermen and palm trees . . . . 2·00 1·60
MS611 210 × 92 mm. Nos. 606/10 (sold at 450f.) . . . . 10·00 10·50
Nos. 606/10 were issued together, se-tenant, forming a composite design.

1992. Air. "Genova '92" International Thematic Stamp Exhibition. As T **228** but with different Exhibition emblem.
612 800f. multicoloured . . . . . 16·00 11·00

230 Victorious Marianne

1992. Air. Bicentenary of Year One of First French Republic.
613 **230** 350f. black, blue and red 8·00 5·00

231 "La Garonne" (supply vessel)

1992.
614 **231** 20f. multicoloured . . . . 1·25 1·00

232 "L'Idylle d'Ixelles"

1992. 75th Death Anniv of Auguste Rodin (sculptor).
615 **232** 300f. black and mauve . . 6·75 4·25

233 "Mirabilis jalapa"

1992.
616 **233** 200f. multicoloured . . . 4·00 3·00

234 Dassault Breguet Gardian, Frigate and Native Canoes

1993. French Naval Forces in the Pacific.
617 **234** 130f. multicoloured . . . 3·00 2·50

235 Abstract (J. E. Korda)

1993. School Art.
618 **235** 56f. multicoloured . . . . 3·00 2·25
See also Nos. 635/6.

236 Buff-banded Rail

1993. Birds. Multicoloured.
619 50f. Type **236** . . . . 1·50 1·40
620 60f. Purple swamphen . . . 1·60 1·50
621 110f. Grey's fruit dove . . . 2·75 2·00

237 Building Facade

1993. Air. Bicentenary of the Louvre, Paris.
622 **237** 315f. ultramarine, red and blue . . . . 7·25 4·50

238 Copernicus and Planetary Model

1993. Air. "Polska 93" International Stamp Exhibition, Poznan. 450th Death Anniv of Nicolas Copernicus (astronomer).
623 **238** 600f. red, brown and crimson . . . . 13·50 8·75

239 Hibiscus

1993. Mothers' Day. Multicoloured.
624 95f. Type **239** . . . . 2·50 1·90
625 120f. Bouquet of stephanotis 2·75 2·25

240 Sail-finned Tang

1993. Fishes. Multicoloured.
626 27f. Spotted rabbitfish . . . 70 1·00
627 35f. Type **240** . . . . 1·40 1·25
628 45f. Palette surgeonfish . . . 1·60 1·40
629 53f. Fox-faced rabbitfish . . 1·90 1·60

241 D'Entrecasteaux and Flagship

1993. Death Bicentenary of Bruni d'Entrecasteaux (explorer).
630 **241** 170f. red, blue and black 4·00 2·75

242 Symbols of Taiwan

1993. "Taipei '93" International Stamp Exhibition.
631 **242** 435f. multicoloured . . . 7·50 6·00

243 Tepa Church, Wallis Island

1993. Churches. Multicoloured.
632 30f. Type **243** 60 50
633 30f. Vilamalia Church, Futuna Island 60 50

244 "La Marseillaise"

1993. Air. Bicentenary of Year Two of First French Republic.
634 **244** 400f. red, blue and black 7·50 5·50

1993. School Art. As T **235**.
635 28f. blue, black and grey . . 60 40
636 52f. multicoloured . . . . . 1·00 60
DESIGNS—HORIZ: 28f. Palm trees (T. Tuhimutu). VERT: 52f. People (M. Hakula).

245 Nativity

1993. Christmas.
637 **245** 80f. multicoloured . . . . 1·60 1·00

246 "Wallis Landscape" (P. Legris)

1994. Air.
638 **246** 400f. multicoloured . . . 7·00 5·50

247 Landscape and Emblem

1994. Air. "Hong Kong '94" International Stamp Exhibition.
639 **247** 700f. multicoloured . . . 13·00 10·50

248 Emblem

1994. Traditional Crafts Show, Wallis and Futuna.
640 **248** 80f. multicoloured . . . . 1·60 1·10

249 Manning the Barricades

1994. 50th Anniv of Liberation of Paris.
641 **249** 110f. black, red and blue 2·40 1·50

250 Pacific Islands on Globe

1994. Air. South Pacific Geographical Days.
642 **250** 85f. multicoloured . . . . 1·60 1·40

251 Earth Station

1994. Satellite Communications.
643 **251** 10f. multicoloured 30 30

252 Goalkeeper saving Ball

1994. World Cup Football Championship, U.S.A.
644 **252** 105f. multicoloured . . . 2·00 1·00

253 Uvean Princesses, 1903

1994.
645 **253** 90f. black, red and blue 1·75 1·25

254 Seaplane

1994. Microlight Aircraft.
646 **254** 5f. multicoloured 10 10

255 Four Suits

1994. Bridge.
647 **255** 40f. multicoloured 80 50

256 Dahlia

257 Trees and Coconuts

1994. Air. 1st European Stamp Salon, Flower Gardens, Paris.
648 **256** 300f. multicoloured . . . 5·50 3·50

1994. The Coconut.
649 **257** 36f. multicoloured 70 50

258 Saint-Exupery and Aircraft

1994. Air. 50th Death Anniv of Antoine de Saint-Exupery (author and pilot).
650 **258** 800f. olive, green and blue 14·50 9·50

259 Blue-crowned Lories

1994. Parrots of Futuna.
651 **259** 62f. multicoloured . . . . 1·60 1·10

260 Lodge Emblem and Symbols of Freemasonry

1994. Centenary of Grand Lodge of France.
652 **260** 250f. brown, turquoise and blue . . . . 4·50 3·50

261 Polynesian Baby

1994. Air. Christmas.
653 **261** 150f. multicoloured . . . 3·00 1·90

262 Preparing Traditional Meal (after P. Legris)

1995.
654 **262** 80f. multicoloured . . . . 1·60 90

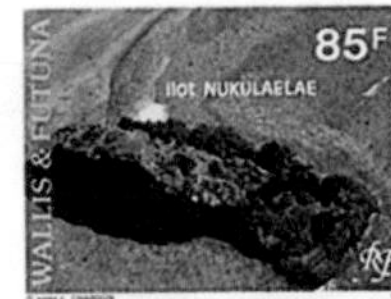

263 Nukulaelae

1995. Aerial Views of Lagoon Islets. Mult.
655 85f. Type **263** . . . . 1·60 80
656 90f. Nukufetau (vert) . . . . 1·75 90
657 100f. Nukufotu and Nukuloa 1·90 1·50

264 Pasteur

1995. Air. Death Cent of Louis Pasteur (chemist).
658 **264** 350f. multicoloured . . . 6·25 3·50

265 Outrigger Canoes (emblem of district)

266 Emblem

1995. Mua District.
659 **265** 35f. multicoloured 70 40

1995. University of the Pacific Teacher Training Institute.
660 **266** 115f. multicoloured . . . 2·00 1·50

267 Coconuts

1995. Air.
661 **267** 200f. multicoloured . . . 4·00 2·25

268 U.N. Helmet and Blitzed and Rebuilt Cities (½-size illustration)

1995. 50th Anniv of Signing of U.N. Charter.
662 **268** 55f. multicoloured . . . . 1·00 60

269 Young People

1995. Air. 10th Anniv of International Youth Year.
663 **269** 450f. multicoloured . . . 8·25 4·50

270 Javelin Thrower

1995. 10th South Pacific Games, Tahiti.
664 **270** 70f. multicoloured . . . . 1·40 90

271 City Skyline

1995. Air. "Singapore'95" Int Stamp Exn.
665 **271** 500f. multicoloured . . . 8·00 5·50

272 Lumiere Brothers and Film (½-size illustration)

1995. Air. Centenary of Motion Pictures.
666 **272** 600f. multicoloured . . . 9·50 5·50

273 Breadfruit

1995. Shrubs. Multicoloured.
667 20f. Type **273** 50 40
668 60f. Tarot . . . . 1·25 65
669 65f. Kava . . . . 1·40 80
See also Nos. 675/6.

274 De Gaulle

1995. Air. 25th Death Anniv of Charles de Gaulle (French statesman).
670 **274** 315f. black, red and blue 5·50 4·00

275 Human Activities

276 Three Generations

1995. Tapa (bark of paper-mulberry tree) Designs. Multicoloured.
671 25f. Type **275** 50 40
672 26f. Marine life (horiz) . . . 50 40

1995. Island Mothers.
673 **276** 80f. multicoloured . . . . 1·50 90

277 Golf Course

1995. Golfing on Wallis.
674 **277** 95f. multicoloured . . . . 1·75 1·25

1996. Tuberous Plants. As T **273**. Multicoloured.
675 28f. Taro ("Mahoaa") . . . 70 50
676 52f. Yam ("Ufi") . . . . . . 1·00 60

278 Pirogue

1996. Air. World Polynesian Pirogue Championships, Noumea.
677 **278** 240f. multicoloured . . . 4·00 3·00

279 Emblems

280 "Cananga odorata"

1996. Air. Sisia College, Futuna.
678 **279** 235f. multicoloured . . . 4·00 3·00

1996. Flowers. Multicoloured.
679 27f. Type **280** 50 40
680 45f. Hibiscus 80 50

281 Trees reflected in Water

1996. Swamplands.
681 **281** 53f. multicoloured 90 70

282 Chessmen and Board

1996. Chess in Wallis and Futuna.
682 **282** 110f. multicoloured . . . 1·90 1·50

283 Guglielmo Marconi (inventor) and Radio Equipment

1996. Air. Centenary of Radio-telegraphy.
683 **283** 550f. brown, blue and orange . . . . 8·50 6·50

284 Stadium and Sportsmen

1996. Air. Centenary of Modern Olympic Games.
684 **284** 1000f. blue . . . . 17·00 13·00

285 Caladium

1996. Flowers. Multicoloured.
685 30f. Type **285** 60 40
686 48f. Caladium (different) . . 80 50

286 Woman with Stamps in Hair

1996. Air. 50th Autumn Stamp Fair.
687 **286** 175f. multicoloured . . . 3·00 2·25

287 Map and Perroton

1996. Francoise Perroton (first woman missionary to Wallis) Commemoration.
688 **287** 50f. multicoloured 90 70

288 Distressed Woman with Children and Drunken Man

1996. Air. Campaign against Alcohol Abuse.
689 **288** 260f. multicoloured . . . 4·00 3·00

289 Children and Emblem

1996. 50th Anniv of UNICEF.
690 **289** 25f. multicoloured 50 40

290 Emblem

1997. 50th Anniv of South Pacific Commission.
691 **290** 7f. multicoloured 10 10

291 King Lavelua of Uvea (Wallis)

1997. Royal Standards.
692 **291** 56f. red, black and blue 85 40
693 – 60f. multicoloured 90 40
694 – 70f. multicoloured . . . . 1·00 45
DESIGNS: 60f. King Tuiagaifo of Alo (Futuna); 70f. King Tuisigave of Sigave (Futuna).

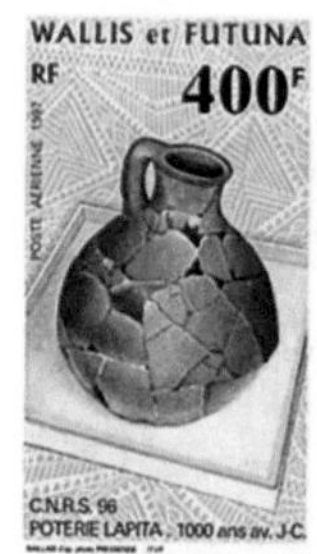

292 Lapita Pot (1000 B.C.)
293 Kava Brewer

1997. Air. National Centre for Scientific Research.
695 **292** 400f. multicoloured . . . 5·50 4·00

1997.
696 **293** 170f. multicoloured . . . 3·00 2·00

294 Story-telling

1997. Scenes of Island Life. Multicoloured.
697 10f. Type **294** 10 10
698 36f. Hand-weaving mat (vert) 60 50
699 40f. Feasting 70 50

295 Turtle on Beach

1997. The Green Turtle. Multicoloured.
700 62f. Type **295** . . . . 1·00 70
701 80f. Turtle swimming . . . . 1·40 90

296 Airplane approaching Airport

1997. Air. Inauguration of Hihifo Airport.
702 **296** 130f. multicoloured . . . 1·75 1·50

297 Treble Clef, Dancers, Theatre Masks and Fireworks over Papal Palace

1997. 50th Anniv of Avignon Festival.
703 **297** 160f. multicoloured . . . 2·00 1·60

298 Medals and Shot Putter
299 Sunset over Lagoon (after Rebecca Hoatau)

1997. "Handisport" Sporting Event, Berlin.
704 **298** 35f. multicoloured 50 40

1997. Air.
705 **299** 300f. multicoloured . . . 4·00 3·00

300 Club Emblem (½-size illustration)

1997. Uvea Karate Club, Wallis.
706 **300** 24f. multicoloured 40 30

301 Stamps on Globe

1997. Air. 4th Stamp World Cup and 51st Autumn stamp Show. Multicoloured.
707 350f. Type **301** . . . . . . 4·50 3·50
MS708 150 × 85 mm. 100f. Two views of Earth encircled by stamps. Imperf . . . . 12·00 12·00

302 Notre Dame Cathedral, Tanks and Leclerc

1997. Air. 50th Death Anniv of Marshal Leclerc.
709 **302** 800f. multicoloured . . . 10·00 8·00

303 Couple

1997. Anti-AIDS Campaign.
710 **303** 5f. multicoloured 10 10

304 Daudet, Windmill, Foxgloves and Goat

1997. Air. Death Centenary of Alphonse Daudet (writer).
711 **304** 710f. multicoloured . . . 8·50 7·00

305 Nativity

1997. Christmas.
712 **305** 85f. multicoloured . . . . 1·25 90

306 "Preparation of Umu" (Christiane Pierret)

1998.
713 **306** 800f. multicoloured . . . 9·75 6·25

307 "Vanda T.M.A."

1998. Orchids. Multicoloured.
714 70f. Type **307** 90 60
715 85f. "Cattleya Bow Bells" (horiz) . . . . 1·25 70
716 90f. "Arachnis" . . . . . . 1·25 70
717 105f. "Cattleya" (horiz) . . . 1·50 85

308 Modern Technology

1998. Telecom 2000.
718 **308** 7f. multicoloured 10 10

309 Alofi Beach

1998. Air.
719 **309** 315f. multicoloured . . . 4·00 3·00

310 Fisherman casting Net

1998. Lagoon Fishing. Multicoloured.
720 50f. Type **310** 60 40
721 52f. Fisherman with catch . . 60 40

311 Footballers

1998. World Cup Football Championship, France.
722 **311** 80f. multicoloured 95 60

312 Darter

1998. Insects. Multicoloured.
723 36f. Type **312** 40 25
724 40f. Cicada 45 30

313 Coral

1998. Corals.
725 **313** 4f. multicoloured 10 10
726 – 5f. multicoloured 10 10
727 – 10f. multicoloured 10 10
728 – 15f. multicoloured 15 10
DESIGNS: 5f. to 15f. Different corals.

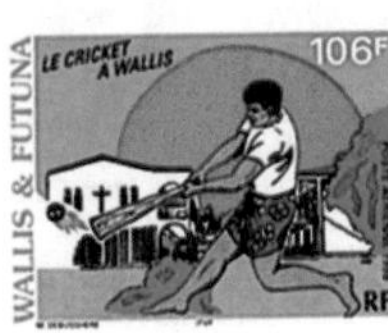

314 Cricketer

1998. Air. Cricket.
729 **314** 106f. multicoloured . . . 1·25 75

315 Gauguin and View of Island

1998. Air. 150th Birth Anniv of Paul Gauguin (artist).
730 **315** 700f. multicoloured . . . 8·00 5·00

316 Coral, Sail Canoe and Fishes

1998. 52nd Autumn Stamp Show, Paris.
731 **316** 175f. multicoloured . . . 2·00 1·75

317 "The Garden of Happiness"

1998. Air.
732 **317** 460f. multicoloured . . . 5·25 3·25

318 Jigsaw Pieces

1998. World Anti-AIDS Day.
733 **318** 62f. multicoloured 70 40

319 Polynesian Dancer

321 Precious Wentletrap

320 Carrying Kava

1998. Air.
734 **319** 250f. multicoloured . . . 2·75 1·75

1999. Air.
735 **320** 600f. multicoloured . . . 7·00 4·25

1999. Air. Shells. Multicoloured.
736 95f. Type **321** . . . . 1·10 65
737 100f. Horned helmet . . . . 1·10 65
738 110f. Trumpet triton (horiz) 1·25 75
739 115f. Common spider conch (horiz) . . . . 1·25 75

322 Rock Formation

1999. Islet of Nuku Taakimoa.
740 **322** 130f. multicoloured . . . 1·50 90

323 "Finemui" (½-size illustration)

1999. Air.
741 **323** 900f. multicoloured . . . 10·50 6·25

324 Marine Life

1999. Marine Life. Sheet 170 × 86 mm containing T **324** and similar square designs. Multicoloured.
MS742 20f. Type **324**; 855f. Flying fish and diver . . . . 10·00 6·00

325 Little Egrets

1999. Air. Birds of Nuku Fotu. Multicoloured.
743 10f. Type **325** 10 10
744 20f. Audubon's shearwaters 25 15
745 26f. Ascension frigate bird ("Christmas Island Frigate Birds") 30 20
746 54f. Red-tailed tropic bird . . 60 35

326 Emblem and Hibiscus

1999. "Philexfrance 99" International Stamp Exhibition, Paris.
747 **326** 200f. multicoloured . . . 2·00 1·25

327 Senate and Marianne

1999. Bicentenary of French Senate.
748 **327** 125f. blue and red . . . . 1·40 85

328 Assembly Building

1999. Territorial Assembly.
749 **328** 17f. multicoloured 20 10

329 Pandanus Tree

1999.
750 **329** 25f. multicoloured 30 20

330 Carving Pirogue

1999.
751 **330** 55f. multicoloured 60 35

331 "Wind Song" (modern tourist ship)

1999. Air.
752 **331** 325f. blue, green & ultramarine . . . . . . 3·75 2·25

332 1931 50c. International Colonial Exhibition Stamp

1999. 150th Anniv of First French Postage Stamp.
753 **332** 65f. multicoloured 75 45

333 Sunrise over Lagoon

1999. Air.
754 **333** 500f. multicoloured . . . 5·75 3·50

334 Firework and Globe

2000. New Millennium.
755 **334** 350f. multicoloured . . . 4·00 2·40

335 Mata'Utu Cathedral

2000.
756 **335** 300f. multicoloured . . . 3·50 2·10

336 *La Glorieuse* (patrol boat)

2000.
757 **336** 155f. black, blue and green . . . . 1·75 1·25

337 Makape

2000. 2nd Death Anniv of Sosefo Papilio Makape (President of General Council, 1962–77).
758 **337** 115f. red and blue . . . . 1·25 85

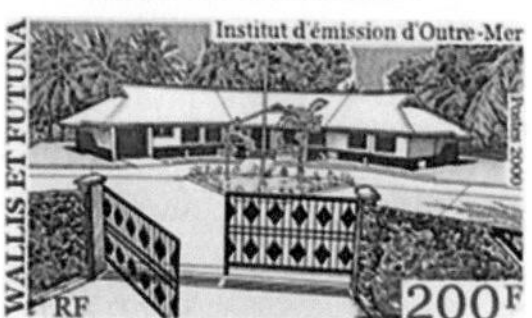

338 Institute Building

2000. French Overseas Monetary Institute.
759 **338** 200f. multicoloured . . . 2·00 1·25

339 Crops

2000.
760 **339** 275f. multicoloured . . . 2·75 1·75

340 Airport and Aircraft

2000. Air. 30th Anniv of Air Transport on Futuna Island.
761 **340** 350f. multicoloured . . . 4·00 2·40

341 Man throwing Spear

2000. Olympic Games, Sydney. Traditional Sports of Wallis and Futuna. Multicoloured.
762 85f. Type **341** . . . . 1·00 60
763 85f. Racing outrigger canoes 1·00 60
764 85f. Kayak racing . . . . . 1·00 60
765 85f. Volleyball . . . . 1·00 60

342 Tattooed Profiles

2000. 8th Pacific Arts Festival, Kanaky, New Caledonia.
766 **342** 330f. multicoloured . . . 3·75 2·25

343 Dolphin (fish)

2000. Fishes. Multicoloured.
767 115f. Type **343** . . . . . . 1·25 85
768 115f. Blue-finned trevally (*Caranx melampygus*) (inscr "melanpygus") . . . . . . 1·25 85
769 115f. Yellow-finned tuna (*Thunnus albacares*) . . . . 1·25 85

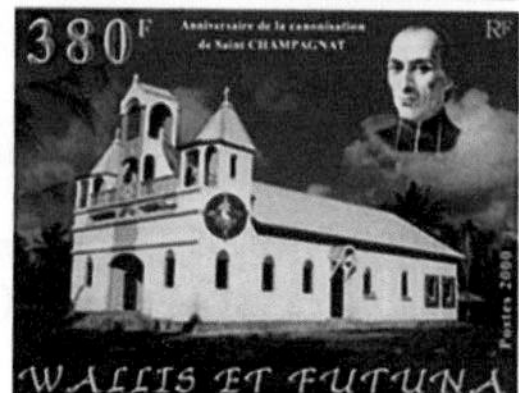

344 Champagnat

2000. Holy Year 2000. First Anniversary of Canonization of Marcellin Champagnat (educationalist and founder of Marist Order).
770 **344** 380f. multicoloured . . . 4·25 2·50

345 Talietumu

2000. Archaeology.
771 **345** 205f. multicoloured . . . 2·00 1·25

346 Mother and Child

2000. Christmas.
772 **346** 225f. multicoloured . . . 2·25 1·40

347 *Jacques Cartier* (landing ship)

2001.
773 **347** 225f. black, blue and green . . . . 2·25 1·40

348 Bottle and Cans

2001. Campaign against Alcoholism.
774 **348** 75f. multicoloured 85 50

349 Design including Shells

2001. Tapas (bark of paper-mulberry tree). Mult.
775 90f. Type **349** . . . . 1·10 65
776 90f. Design including leaves, diamonds and triangles . . 1·10 65
777 90f. Scenes of island life . . . 1·10 65
778 90f. Design including overlapping ovals . . . . 1·10 65

350 Mixed Flowers (M. Uhilamoafa)

2001. Children's Flower Paintings. Multicoloured.
779 50f. Type **350** 55 30
780 55f. Stem of flowers 60 35
781 95f. Vase of red and yellow flowers . . . . 1·10 65
782 100f. Pink orchid . . . . . . 1·10 65

351 Man with Arm Raised

2001. 40th Anniv of French Overseas Territory Status.
783 **351** 165f. multicoloured . . . 1·60 1·40

352 Apple Canelle (T. Taika)

2001. Children's Fruit Paintings. Multicoloured.
784 65f. Type **352** 60 50
785 65f. Breadfruit (E. Mougatoga) 60 50
786 65f. Pineapple (E. Hamaivao) 60 50
787 65f. Mango (I. Mougatoga) 60 50

353 Emblem

2001. 1st Anniv of Installation of Delegate of Mediator of the Republic.
788 **353** 800f. multicoloured . . . 7·75 6·25

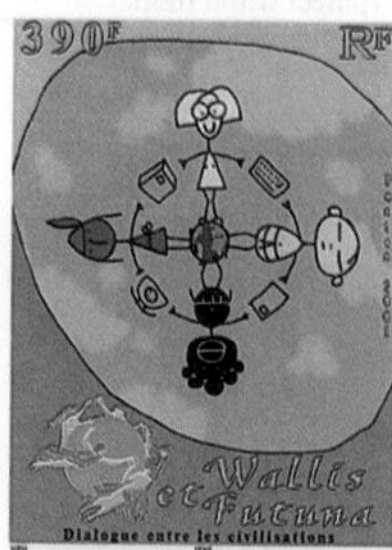

354 Children encircling Globe

2001. United Nations Year of Dialogue among Civilizations.
789 **354** 390f. multicoloured . . . 3·75 3·00

355 Pacific Pigeon (*Ducula pacifica*)

2001. 55th Autumn Stamp Show. Birds. Mult.
790 150f. Type **355** (inscr "Dacula") . . . . 1·40 1·25
791 150f. Blue-crowned lory (*Vini australis*) . . . . 1·40 1·25
792 150f. Barn owl (*Tyto alba*) 1·40 1·25

356 Grave

2001. Grave of Fakavelikele (first king of Wallis and Futuna).
793 **356** 325f. multicoloured . . . 3·25 2·75

357 Building

2002. Inauguration of Finemui College, Teesi (French college).
794 **357** 115f. multicoloured . . . 1·40 1·10

358 Queen Aloisia

2002. International Women's Day.
795 **358** 800f. brown . . . . . . 9·50 7·50

359 Arms

360 Emblem

2002. Monseigneur Pompallier (first bishop of Western Oceanie).
796 **359** 500f. buff, green and red 6·00 4·75

2002. Fire Service of Uvea Island.
797 **360** 85f. multicoloured . . . . 1·00 80

361 Stylized Footballer

2002. World Cup Football Championship, Japan and South Korea.
798 **361** 65f. multicoloured 40 30

362 Tree, Bird, Turtle and Sea

2002. World Environment Day.

799	**362**	330f. multicoloured . . .	4·00	3·25

363 House with Veranda

2002. Traditional Thatched Houses (fale). Houses. Multicoloured.

800	50f. Type **363**	60	50
801	50f. Without walls (vert) . .	60	50
802	55f. With window shutters . .	65	55
803	55f. Amongst tall trees (vert)	65	55

364 Jacob Lemaire

2002. Discovery of Futuna.

804	125f. Type **364** (joint finder)	1·50	1·25
805	125f. Futuna and Aloti islands	1·50	1·25
806	125f. William Schouten (joint finder)	1·50	1·25
MS807	175 × 100 mm (oval). Nos. 804/6	4·50	4·50

365 Utua Bay

2002. Landscapes. Multicoloured.

807	95f. Type **365**	1·10	90
808	100f. Liku Bay	1·25	1·00
809	105f. Kingfisher and Vele Point	1·25	1·00
810	135f. Aka Aka Bay	1·60	1·25

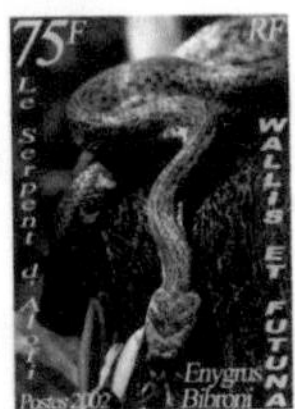

366 *Enygrus bibroni* (snake)

2002.

811	**366**	75f. multicoloured	90	70

367 Fu Manchu Lion Fish (*Dendrochirus biocellatus*)

2002. 56th Autumn Stamp Show. Fish. Mult.

812	110f. Type **367**	1·25	1·00
813	110f. Spikefin goby (*Discordipina griessingeri*)	1·25	1·00
814	110f. Spotfin frogfish (*Antennarius nummifer*) (inscr "Antennacius") . . .	1·25	1·00
815	110f. Dragon wrasse (*Novaculichthys taeniourus*)	1·25	1·00

368 Yacht, Sea Cliffs and Beach

2002. Christmas.

816	**368**	140f. multicoloured . . .	1·60	1·25

369 Avro Type 683 Lancaster WU 21 and Insignia of Escadrille 9S

2003. 40th Anniv of Last Flight of Escadrille 9S Lancaster WU 21 (26 January 1963).

817	**369**	135f. multicoloured . . .	1·60	1·25

370 Sailing Canoe Enclosed in Heart-shape

2003. St. Valentine's Day.

818	**370**	85f. multicoloured	1·00	85

371 Euro Coin

2003. 1st Anniv of Introduction of Euro.

819	**371**	125f. multicoloured . . .	1·50	1·10

POSTAGE DUE STAMPS

1920. Postage Due Stamps of New Caledonia optd **ILES WALLIS et FUTUNA.**

D18	D **18**	5c. blue	40	3·25
D19		10c. brown on buff . .	40	3·25
D20		15c. green	1·25	3·25
D21		20c. black on yellow . .	80	3·50
D22		30c. red	50	3·50
D23		50c. blue on cream . .	2·00	4·00
D24		60c. green on blue . .	1·75	4·25
D25		1f. green on cream . .	2·50	4·75

1927. As Postage Due stamp of New Caledonia, but colour changed, surch.

D43	D **18**	2f. on 1f. mauve . . .	5·75	17·00
D44		3f. on 1f. brown . . .	7·25	18·00

1930. Postage Due stamps of New Caledonia optd **ILES WALLIS et FUTUNA.**

D85	D **25**	2c. brown and blue . .	20	2·75
D86		4c. green and red . . .	15	3·00
D87		5c. blue and red	20	3·00
D88		10c. blue and purple . .	15	3·00
D89		15c. red and green . . .	20	3·00
D90		20c. brown and purple	25	3·00
D91		25c. blue and brown . .	90	3·00
D92		30c. brown and green	1·00	3·50
D93		50c. red and brown . .	1·25	3·00
D94		60c. red and mauve . .	1·75	4·25
D95		1f. green and blue . . .	2·00	3·75
D96		2f. brown and red . . .	2·00	3·75
D97		3f. brown and mauve	2·00	3·75

1943. Nos. D85/97 optd **FRANCE LIBRE.**

D126	D **25**	2c. brown and blue . .	11·50	60·00
D127		4c. green and red . . .	11·50	60·00
D128		5c. blue and red . . .	10·50	60·00
D129		10c. blue and purple	10·50	60·00
D130		15c. red and green . .	25·00	60·00
D131		20c. brown and purple	10·50	60·00
D132		25c. blue and brown	10·50	60·00
D133		30c. brown and green	10·50	60·00
D134		50c. red and brown . .	10·00	60·00
D135		60c. red and mauve . .	10·00	60·00
D136		1f. green and blue . .	16·00	65·00
D137		2f. brown and red . .	10·00	65·00
D138		3f. brown and mauve	10·00	65·00

D **10** Moorish Idol

1963. Fishes.

D182	D **10**	1f. black, yellow & bl	2·00	2·25
D183	–	3f. red, green and blue	2·25	2·75
D184	–	5f. orange, black & bl	3·00	3·25

DESIGNS—HORIZ: 3f. Moon wrasse; 5f. Orange clownfish.

WENDEN — Pt. 10

Formerly part of W. Russia but later became part of Latvia. Issued stamps for use within the district until 1903.

100 kopeks = 1 rouble.

2

3

1863. Inscr "Briefmarke des WENDEN-schen Kreises". Imperf.
1 **2** 2k. black and red £200 £250

1863. Inscr "Packenmarke des WENDEN-schen Kreises". Imperf.
2 **3** 4k. black and green £150 £250

6

7

8

1863. Imperf.
6 **6** 2k. green and red . . . . . . 20·00 24·00

1864. As T **6**, but with horse in central oval. Imperf.
5 2k. green and red . . . . . . 60·00 £140

1871. Imperf.
7 **7** 2k. green and red . . . . . . 20·00 25·00

1872. Perf.
8 **8** 2k. red and green . . . . . . 25·00 30·00

9 Arms of Wenden

10 Arms of Wenden

1875.
9 **9** 2k. green and red . . . . . . 6·00 8·50

1878.
10 **10** 2k. green and red . . . . . 6·00 12·00
11 2k. red, brown and green . . 6·00 12·00
13 2k. green, black and red . . 4·00 10·00

11 Castle of Wenden

1901.
14 **11** 2k. brown and green . . . . 5·00 12·00
15 2k. red and green . . . . 5·00 12·00
16 2k. purple and green . . . . 5·00 12·00

WEST IRIAN — Pt. 21

The following stamps superseded Nos. 1/19 of West New Guinea, after the former Dutch territory became part of Indonesia. From 1971 Indonesian stamps have been used.

100 cents or sen = 1 rupiah.

1963. Stamps of Indonesia optd **IRIAN BARAT** or surch also.
1 – 1s. on 70s. red (No. 724) 10 30
2 – 2s. on 90s. green (No. 727) 10 30
3 – 5s. grey (No. 830) 10 30
4 – 6s. on 20s. bistre (No. 833) 10 30
5 – 7s. on 50s. blue (No. 835) 10 30
6 – 10s. brown (No. 831) . . . 10 30
7 – 15s. purple (No. 832) . . . 10 30
8 **134** 25s. green 15 30
9 – 30s. on 75s. red (No. 836) 15 50
10 – 40s. on 1r.15 red (No. 837) 25 55
11 **99** 1r. mauve . . . . 65 1·00
12 2r. green . . . . 1·20 1·80
13 3r. blue . . . . 2·00 3·00
14 5r. brown . . . . 3·50 6·00

1a Indonesia, from Atjeh to Merauke

1963. Acquisition of West Irian.
21 **1a** 12s. orange, red and black 10 25
22 17s. orange, red and black 10 30
23 – 20s. blue, green and purple 25 50
24 – 50s. blue, green and purple 25 80
25 – 60s. brown, yellow and green 55 90
26 – 75s. brown, yellow and green . . . . 70 1·60
DESIGNS: 20, 50s. Parachutist; 60, 75s. Greater bird of paradise.

2 "Maniltoa gemmipara"

4 Mother and Child Figurine

3 Map of Indonesia

1968. Flora and Fauna.
27 **2** 5s. purple and green 55 95
28 – 15s. violet and green . . . . 80 1·60
29 – 30s. green and orange . . . . 1·10 2·50
30 – 40s. violet and yellow . . . . 1·60 3·00
31 – 50s. black and purple . . . . 2·40 3·75
32 – 75s. black and blue . . . . 3·00 4·75
33 – 1r. black and brown . . . . 3·50 7·25
34 – 3r. black and green . . . . 6·50 9·75
35 – 5r. multicoloured . . . . . . 1·50 4·00
36 – 10r. multicoloured . . . . . . 1·80 6·75
DESIGNS: 15s. "Dendrobium lancifolium"; 30s. "Gardenia gjellerupii"; 40s. "Maniltoa gemmipara" (blossom); 50s. Common phalanger; 75s. One-wattled cassowary; 1r. Common forest wallaby; 3r. Blue crowned pigeons; 5r. Black-capped lory; 10r. Greater bird of paradise.

1968. West Irian People's Pledge of 9 May 1964.
43 **3** 10s. gold and blue . . . . . 2·75 1·50
44 25s. gold and red . . . . . 4·75 2·50

1970. West Irian Woodcarvings. Multicoloured.
45 5s. Type **4** 30 55
46 6s. Carved shield 30 55
47 7s. Man and serpents . . . . 55 2·40
48 10s. Drum . . . . 55 2·40
49 25s. Seated warrior 55 55
50 30s. "Female" drum 65 80
51 50s. Bamboo vessel 70 80
52 75s. Seated man and tree . . . 80 95
53 1r. Decorated shield . . . . . 90 1·20
54 2r. Seated figure . . . . . . 1·00 1·40
Nos. 45/54 are inscr "I.B." ("Irian Barat").

POSTAGE DUE STAMPS

1963. Postage Due Stamps as Type D **100** of Indonesia optd **IRIAN BARAT**.
D15 1s. slate 10 40
D16 5s. olive 10 50
D17 10s. turquoise 15 50
D18 25s. slate 25 90
D19 40s. orange . . . . 40 1·40
D20 100s. brown . . . . 1·00 2·50

1968. As Type D **100** of Indonesia, but with coloured network background incorporating "1968", optd **IRIAN BARAT.**
D37 1s. blue and green 15 55
D38 5s. green and pink 15 65
D39 10s. red and grey 15 65
D40 25s. green and yellow . . . 25 1·00
D41 40s. purple and green . . . 50 1·60
D42 100s. red and olive . . . . . 1·10 3·25

WEST NEW GUINEA — Pt. 4

U.N. Administration of former Netherlands New Guinea from 1 October 1962 to 30 April 1963, when it became known as West Irian and became part of Indonesia.

100 cents = 1 gulden.

1962. "United Nations Temporary Executive Authority". Stamps of Netherlands New Guinea optd **UNTEA.**
1 **5** 1c. yellow and red 50 65
21 – 2c. orange 50 60
3 **5** 5c. yellow and brown 75 65
4 – 7c. purple, bl & brn (No. 60) 80 1·00
5 – 10c. brown and blue (No. 27) 75 60
6 – 12c. pur, bl & grn (No. 61) 1·00 1·25
7 – 15c. brown & yell (No. 28) 1·00 1·25
8 – 17c. pur, bl & blk (No. 62) 1·00 1·00
9 – 20c. brown & green (No. 29) 1·00 1·00
10 **6** 25c. red 85 90
11 30c. blue . . . . 95 1·00
12 40c. orange . . . . 95 1·00
13 45c. green . . . . 2·00 1·90
14 55c. turquoise . . . . 1·50 3·25
34 80c. grey . . . . 10·00 12·00
35 85c. brown . . . . 4·50 5·00
36 1g. purple . . . . 4·50 4·50
37 – 2g. brown (No. 20) . . . . . 11·00 12·50
19 – 5g. green (No. 21) . . . . . 8·50 9·00

For later issues see **WEST IRIAN**.

WEST UKRAINE — Pt. 10

Before the 1914/18 War this district, known as E. Galicia was part of Austria. It achieved temporary independence after the war when stamps were issued. In June 1919 it became part of Poland but was transferred to the Ukraine in 1945.

100 heller = 1 krone.

(5)

1919. Stamps of Austria 1916 optd with T **5**.
70 **49** 3h. violet 30
71 5h. green 30
72 6h. orange 30
73 10h. red 30
74 12h. blue 30
75 **60** 15h. red 30
76 20h. green 30
77 25h. blue 30
78 30h. violet 30
79 **51** 40h. olive 40
80 50h. green 40
81 60h. blue 40
82 80h. brown 50
83 90h. purple 50
84 1k. red on yellow 55
85 **52** 2k. blue 65
86 3k. red 90
87 4k. green . . . . 5·00
88 10k. violet . . . . 6·50

For other issues, which were mainly of a local character, see Part 10 (Russia) of the standard catalogue.

WESTERN AUSTRALIA — Pt. 1

The western state of the Australian Commonwealth, whose stamps it now uses.

12 pence = 1 shilling;
20 shillings = 1 pound.

1

2

3

1854. Imperf or roul.
1 **1** 1d. black £900 £200
25 2d. orange . . . . 80·00 75·00
3 **2** 4d. blue £300 £180
26 **1** 4d. blue £250 £1600
28 6d. green £1500 £400
4c **3** 1s. brown £400 £300

5

7

1857. Imperf or roul.
15 **5** 2d. brown on red £2500 £550
18 6d. bronze to black £3750 £550

1861. Perf.
103 **1** 1d. red . . . . 18·00 3·25
76 1d. yellow . . . . 24·00 1·50
41 2d. blue . . . . 80·00 24·00
77 2d. yellow . . . . 27·00 1·50
104 2d. grey . . . . 48·00 1·25
56 4d. red . . . . 75·00 4·75
105 4d. brown . . . . 75·00 21·00
42 6d. brown . . . . £275 50·00
79 6d. lilac . . . . 90·00 3·00
61 1s. green . . . . £120 12·00

1871.
87 **7** 3d. brown . . . . 8·50 2·25

1874. Surch **ONE PENNY**.
67 **1** 1d. on 2d. yellow . . . . . £400 55·00

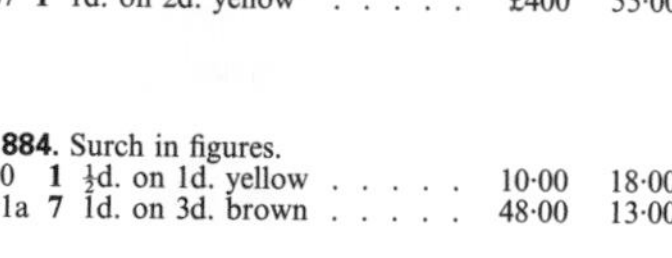

1884. Surch in figures.
90 **1** ½d. on 1d. yellow . . . . . 10·00 18·00
91a **7** 1d. on 3d. brown . . . . . 48·00 13·00

12

13

14

15

1885.
94 **12** ½d. green . . . . 4·00 70
112 **13** 1d. red . . . . 5·50 10
96a **14** 2d. grey . . . . 25·00 1·25
113 2d. yellow . . . . 15·00 1·75
97a 2½d. blue . . . . 11·00 1·50
98 4d. brown . . . . 10·00 1·25
99 5d. yellow . . . . 9·00 3·25
100 **15** 6d. violet . . . . 15·00 1·25
102 1s. green . . . . 18·00 4·25

1893. Surch in words.
110a **7** ½d. on 3d. brown . . . . 6·00 24·00
107 1d. on 3d. brown . . . . 12·00 3·50

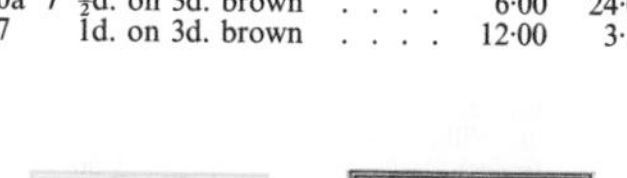

23 19

24

21 28 29 30

31

32

1901.
140 **23** 2d. yellow . . . . 6·50 1·75
114 **19** 2½d. blue . . . . 9·00 75
142b **24** 4d. brown . . . . 10·00 2·75
143 **15** 5d. olive . . . . 16·00 8·50
168 **19** 6d. violet . . . . 12·00 9·00
121 **12** 8d. green . . . . 18·00 2·50
145 **24** 9d. orange . . . . 25·00 4·50
123 **19** 10d. red . . . . 30·00 7·50
116 **21** 1s. green . . . . 27·00 3·50
124b **28** 2s. red on yellow . . . . 42·00 9·00
125 **29** 2s.6d. blue on red . . . . 42·00 8·00
126 **30** 5s. green . . . . 70·00 24·00
127 **31** 10s. mauve . . . . £160 75·00
128 **32** £1 orange £325 £170

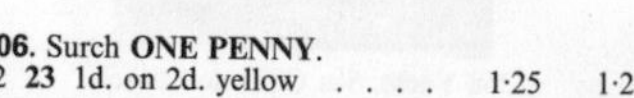

1906. Surch **ONE PENNY**.
172 **23** 1d. on 2d. yellow . . . . 1·25 1·25

WURTTEMBERG Pt. 7

Formerly an independent kingdom, Wurttemberg became part of the German Empire in 1902.

1851. 60 kreuzer = 1 gulden.
1875. 100 pfennige = 1 mark.

1

2

1851. Imperf.
1 **1** 1k. black on buff £1100 £100
3 3k. black on yellow £300 6·50
5 6k. black on green £1500 38·00
7 9k. black on pink £5000 38·00
9 18k. black on lilac £1500 £650

1857. Imperf.
10 **2** 1k. brown £600 75·00
24 3k. orange £300 8·50
15 6k. green £600 60·00
17 9k. red £1000 60·00
19 18k. blue £2750 £1200
85 70k. violet £1900 £4250

1859. Perf.
45 **2** 1k. brown £325 £300
40 3k. yellow 70·00 30·00
41 6k. green £275 70·00
42 9k. red £800 £170
43 9k. purple £950 £250
44 18k. blue £1700 £1300

1863. Perf or roul.
60 **2** 1k. green 43·00 8·00
63 3k. pink 43·00 2·75
54 6k. blue £170 55·00
66 7k. blue £1000 £150
57 9k. brown £275 55·00
59 18k. orange £1200 £400

3

4

1869. Roul or perf (1k.); perf (others).
72 **3** 1k. green 30·00 2·50
74 2k. orange £190 £140
77 3k. pink 15·00 1·30
78 7k. blue 65·00 17·00
80 9k. bistre 85·00 43·00
82 14k. yellow 85·00 47·00

1875. New Currency.
123 **4** 2pf. grey 2·10 1·10
89 3pf. green 19·00 1·90
124 3pf. brown 85 65
91 5pf. mauve 8·50 85
127 5pf. green 1·70 65
93 10pf. red 1·30 85
95 20pf. blue 1·30 1·10
97 25pf. brown £120 10·50
130 25pf. orange 3·00 1·30
151 30pf. black and orange 3·50 4·75
152 40pf. black and red 4·25 6·00
99 50pf. grey £700 43·00
101 50pf. green 65·00 6·00
132 50pf. brown 3·00 1·10
102 2m. yellow £800 £275
103 2m. red on orange £2000 £150
121 2m. black and orange 8·50 10·00
122 5m. black and blue 47·00 £190

For issues of 1947–49 see Germany (French Zone).

MUNICIPAL SERVICE STAMPS

M 5

1875.
M147 **M 5** 2pf. grey 2·10 1·90
M169 2½pf. grey 70 35
M170 3pf. brown 85 35
M104 5pf. mauve 38·00 2·75
M171 5pf. green 85 35
M172 7½pf. orange 70 35
M173 10pf. red 85 35
M261 10pf. orange 45 35
M174 15pf. brown 1·70 35
M262 15pf. violet 45 35
M176 20pf. blue 1·70 35
M263 20pf. green 45 35
M177 25pf. orange 85 35
M178 25pf. black and brown 1·10 35
M179 35pf. brown 1·70 1·00
M264 40pf. red 45 35
M265 50pf. purple 95 35
M266 60pf. green 1·30 35
M267 1m.25 green 95 35
M268 2m. grey 95 35
M269 3m. brown 95 35

1906. Centenary of Establishment of Kingdom. Optd **1806–1906** under crown.
M153 **M 5** 2pf. grey 43·00 15·00
M154 3pf. brown 15·00 13·00
M155 5pf. green 4·75 5·50
M156 10pf. pink 4·75 5·00
M157 25pf. orange 55·00 14·00

1916. Surch **25 Pf.**
M199 **M 5** 25pf. on 25pf. orange 3·50 85

M 9

M 14

1916. Jubilee of King Wilhelm II.
M202 **M 9** 2½pf. grey 2·10 1·70
M203 7½pf. red 2·10 1·70
M204 10pf. red 2·10 1·70
M205 15pf. bistre 2·10 1·70
M206 20pf. blue 2·10 1·70
M207 25pf. grey 4·25 1·70
M208 50pf. brown 8·50 1·70

1919. Surch **2.**
M219 **M 5** 2 on 2½pf. grey 85 75

1919. Optd **Volksstaat Wurttemberg.**
M222 **M 5** 2½pf. grey 45 85
M223 3pf. brown 13·00 85
M224 5pf. green 45 85
M225 7½pf. orange 85 85
M226 10pf. pink 45 85
M227 15pf. purple 45 85
M228 20pf. blue 45 85
M229 25pf. black and brown 45 85
M230 35pf. brown 5·00 85
M231 50pf. purple 6·00 85

1920.
M245 **M 14** 10pf. purple 3·00 1·70
M246 15pf. brown 3·00 1·70
M247 20pf. blue 2·50 1·70
M248 30pf. green 2·50 1·70
M249 50pf. yellow 2·50 1·70
M250 75pf. bistre 5·00 2·00

1922. Surch in Marks.
M270 **M 5** 5m. on 10pf. orange 45 45
M271 10m. on 15pf. violet 45 45
M272 12m. on 40pf. red 45 45
M273 20m. on 10pf. orange 45 45
M274 25m. on 20pf. green 45 45
M275 40m. on 20pf. green 45 45
M276 50m. on 60pf. green 45 45
M277 60m. on 1m.25 green 45 45
M278 100m. on 40pf. red 45 45
M279 200m. on 2m. grey 45 45
M280 300m. on 50pf. purple 45 45
M281 400m. on 3m. brown 60 45
M282 1000m. on 60pf. green 60 50
M283 2000m. on 1m.25 grn 60 50

1923. Surch with new value (T = Tausend (thousand); M = Million; Md = Milliard).
M284 **M 5** 5T. on 10pf. orange 60 50
M285 20T. on 40pf. red 50 50
M286 50T. on 15pf. violet 2·50 50
M287 75T. on 2m. grey 6·50 50
M288 100T. on 20pf. green 50 50
M289 250T. on 3m. brown 50 50
M290 1M. on 60pf. green 4·25 50
M291 2M. on 50pf. purple 60 50
M292 5M. on 1m.25 green 1·10 50
M293 4Md. on 50pf. purple 17·00 50
M294 10Md. on 3m. brown 10·50 50

1923. Surch in figures only, representing gold pfennige.
M295 **M 5** 3pf. on 25pf. orange 85 35
M296 5pf. on 25pf. orange 85 35
M297 10pf. on 25pf. orange 85 35
M298 20pf. on 25pf. orange 85 35
M299 50pf. on 25pf. orange 1·90 35

OFFICIAL STAMPS

O 5

O 10 King Wilhelm II

1881.
O181 **O 5** 2pf. grey 50 35
O182 2½pf. grey 65 35
O108 3pf. green 24·00 4·75
O183 3pf. brown 50 25
O112 5pf. mauve 6·50 2·50
O184 5pf. green 50 35
O185 7½pf. orange 65 35
O186 10pf. pink 50 25
O187 15pf. brown 65 35
O188 15pf. purple 2·10 45
O189 20pf. blue 50 25
O117 25pf. brown 38·00 8·00
O191 25pf. orange 50 25
O192 25pf. black and brown 1·10 45
O193 30pf. black and orange 50 25
O194 35pf. brown 2·50 3·50
O195 40pf. black and red 50 25
O119 50pf. green 8·50 11·50
O141 50pf. brown £250 £1600
O196 50pf. purple 50 25
O120 1m. yellow 80·00 £225
O197 1m. violet 2·50 35
O198 1m. black and grey 4·75 85

1906. Centenary of Establishment of Kingdom. Optd **1806–1906** under crown.
O158 **O 5** 2pf. grey 30·00 26·00
O159 3pf. brown 6·00 45
O160 5pf. green 5·00 45
O161 10pf. pink 5·00 45
O162 20pf. blue 5·00 45
O163 25pf. orange 13·00 13·50
O164 30pf. black and orange 13·00 13·50
O165 40pf. black and red 38·00 16·00
O166 50pf. purple 38·00 16·00
O167 1m. violet 70·00 16·00

1916. Surch.
O200 **O 5** 25pf. on 25pf. orange 3·00 1·10
O201 50pf. on 50pf. purple 3·00 85

1916. Jubilee of King Wilhelm II.
O209 **O 10** 2½pf. grey 1·90 70
O210 7½pf. red 1·90 70
O211 10pf. red 1·90 70
O212 15pf. bistre 1·90 70
O213 20pf. blue 1·90 70
O214 25pf. grey 3·75 75
O215 30pf. green 3·75 75
O216 40pf. purple 6·00 75
O217 50pf. brown 6·50 75
O218 1m. mauve 6·50 75

1919. Surch in figures only.
O220 **O 5** 2 on 2½pf. grey 3·25 1·70
O221 75 on 3pf. brown (O183) 2·50 1·30

1919. Optd **Volksstaat Wurttemberg.**
O232 **O 5** 2½pf. grey 1·30 45
O233 3pf. brown 17·00 85
O234 5pf. green 85 45
O235 7½pf. orange 1·00 45
O236 10pf. pink 85 45
O237 15pf. purple 85 45
O238 20pf. blue 1·00 45
O239 25pf. black and brown 1·00 45
O240 30pf. black and orange 1·60 45
O241 35pf. brown 1·30 45
O242 40pf. black and red 1·10 45
O243 50pf. purple 1·70 70
O244 1m. black and green 1·90 85

O 16 Ulm

1920.
O251 – 10pf. purple 60 1·20
O252 **O 16** 15pf. brown 60 1·20
O253 – 20pf. blue 60 1·20
O254 – 30pf. green 60 1·20
O255 – 50pf. yellow 60 1·20
O256 **O 16** 75pf. bistre 60 1·20
O257 – 1m. red 60 1·20
O258 – 1m.25 violet 60 1·20
O259 – 2m.50 blue 3·75 1·20
O260 – 3m. green 5·00 1·20
VIEWS: 10, 50pf., 2m.50, 3m. Stuttgart; 20pf., 1m. Tubingen; 30pf., 1m.25, Ellwangen.

YEMEN Pt. 19

A Republic in S.W. Arabia, ruled as a kingdom and imamate until 1962. From 1962 stamps were issued concurrently by the Republican Government and the Royalists. The latter are listed after the Republican issues.

In 1990 the Yemen Arab Republic and Yemen People's Democratic Republic united (see YEMEN REPUBLIC (combined)).

1926. 40 bogaches = 1 imadi.
1964. 40 bogaches = 1 rial.
1975. 100 fils = 1 riyal.

KINGDOM

1 (2½b.)

1926. Imperf or perf.
1 **1** 2½b. black on white 60·00 60·00
2 2½b. black on orange 60·00 60·00
3 5b. black on white 60·00 60·00

2

3

1930.
10 **2** ½b. yellow 40 30
11 1b. green 40 30
5 2b. green 1·00 60
12 2b. brown 60 55
13 3b. lilac 75 60
14 4b. red 1·20 90
15 5b. grey 1·40 1·00
16 **3** 6b. blue 1·90 1·40
17 8b. purple 2·30 1·50
18 10b. brown 3·00 1·90
19 20b. green 9·25 7·75
9 1i. blue and brown 27·00 15·00
20 1i. green and purple 23·00 15·00

4 Flags of Saudi Arabia, Yemen and Iraq

7

(6)

8

1939. 2nd Anniv of Arab Alliance.
21 **4** 4b. blue and red 1·40 90
22 6b. ultramarine and blue 1·70 1·20
23 10b. blue and brown 2·30 1·90
24 14b. blue and green 3·75 3·75
25 20b. blue and green 5·50 4·50
26 1i. blue and purple 11·50 11·00

1939. Surch with T **6**.
27 **2** 4b. on ½b. yellow 15·00 15·00
65 4b. on 1b. green 2·75 1·20
66 4b. on 2b. brown 17·00 8·50
67 4b. on 3b. lilac 2·75 1·50
68 4b. on 5b. grey 2·75 1·50

1940.
28 **7** ½b. blue and orange 55 40
29 1b. red and green 55 40
30 2b. violet and bistre 60 40
31 3b. blue and mauve 60 40
32 4b. green and red 60 40
33 5b. bistre and green 75 45
34 **8** 6b. orange and blue 90 45
35 8b. blue and purple 1·20 75
36 10b. green and orange 1·40 90
37 14b. violet and green 1·70 1·20
38 18b. black and green 2·30 1·90
39 20b. purple and green 3·50 2·75
40 1i. red, green and purple 8·50 5·50

The 5b. (for which there had originally been no postal use) was released in 1957 to serve as 4b., without surcharge.

9

10

1942.
41 **9** 1b. green and orange 45 25
42 2b. green and orange 75 40
43 4b. green and orange 90 40
44 6b. blue and orange 1·30 45
45 8b. blue and orange 1·80 75
46 10b. blue and orange 2·40 90
47 12b. blue and orange 1·70 1·70
48 20b. blue and orange 3·50 3·50

Although inscribed "TAXE A PERCEVOIR" these stamps were only used for ordinary postage purposes as there was no postage due system in Yemen.

1945. Surch with T **6**.
49a **7** 4b. on ½b. blue and orange 3·75 1·50
50 4b. on 1b. red and green 3·75 3·75
51a 4b. on 2b. violet and bistre 3·75 3·75
52a 4b. on 3b. blue and mauve 3·75 3·75
53 4b. on 5b. bistre and green 3·75 1·50

1949. Inauguration of Yemeni Hospital.
54 **10** 4b. black and green 1·70 1·40
55 6b. pink and green 3·00 2·50
56 10b. blue and green 3·75 3·00
57 14b. olive and green 7·00 5·50

11 Coffee Plant

12 Douglas DC-4 Airliner over Sana'a

1947.
58 **11** ½b. brown (postage) 40 30
59 1b. purple 75 60
60 2b. violet 1·50 1·20
61 – 4b. red 2·30 1·50
62 – 5b. blue 2·75 1·90
62a **11** 6b. green 3·75 2·30
63 **12** 10b. blue (air) 7·75 3·75
64 20b. green 11·50 7·75
DESIGN—VERT: 4b., 5b. Palace, Sana'a.
The 5b. was put on sale in 1957 to serve as 4b., without surcharge.

1949. Surch as T **6** (size varies).
68a **11** 4b. on ½b. brown 3·75 3·75
69a 4b. on 1b. purple 3·00 3·75
70b 4b. on 2b. blue 6·25 4·50

13 View of Sana'a Parade Ground

15 Palace of the Rock, Wadi Dhahr

14 Flag and View of Sana'a and Hodeida

1951. (a) Postage.
71 **13** 1b. brown 45 25
72 2b. brown 90 45
73 3b. mauve 1·20 75
74 – 5b. red and blue 1·90 1·20
75 – 6b. red and purple 2·20 1·40
76 – 8b. green and blue 2·30 1·50
77 – 10b. purple 2·75 1·90
78 – 14b. green 3·50 2·75
79 – 20b. red 5·00 3·75
80 – 1i. violet 11·50 7·75
DESIGNS—HORIZ: 5b. Yemeni flag; 10b. Mosque, Sana'a; 14b. Walled city of Sana'a; 20b., 1i. Taiz and citadel. VERT: 6b. Eagle and Yemeni flag; 8b. Coffee plant.

(b) Air. With airplane.
81 6b. blue 1·50 1·20
82 8b. brown 1·90 1·50
83 10b. green 2·30 1·90
84 12b. blue 2·75 2·30
85 16b. purple 3·50 2·75
86 20b. orange 4·25 3·00
87 1i. red 11·00 6·25
DESIGNS—HORIZ: 6b., 8b. Sana'a; 10b. Trees; 16b. Taiz Palace. VERT: 12b. Palace of the Rock, Wadi Dhahr; 20b. Crowd of people; 1i. Land-scape.
The 5b. postage stamp was released in 1956 to serve as 4b. without surcharge and it was again put on sale as 8b. in 1957. The 6b. and 8b. air stamps were released in 1957 to serve as ordinary postage stamps.

1952. 4th Anniv of Accession of King Ahmed. Flag in red. Perf or imperf.
88 **14** 1i. black and lake (postage) 15·00 11·50
89 1i. blue and brown (air) 15·00 11·50

1952. 4th Anniv of Victory. As T **14** but inscr "COMMEMORATION OF VICTORY". Flag in red. Perf or imperf.
90 30b. green and red (postage) 11·50 9·25
91 30b. blue and green (air) 11·50 9·25

1952. Surch as T **6**.
91a **13** 4b. on 1b. brown 7·75 6·25
92 4b. on 2b. brown 7·75 6·25
93 4b. on 3b. mauve 11·50 9·25

1952. Sky in blue. Perf or imperf.
94 **15** 12b. green & brn (postage) 7·75 6·25
95 – 20b. brown and red 11·00 9·25
96 **15** 12b. brown and green (air) 9·25 7·75
97 – 20b. brown and blue 9·25 7·75
DESIGN: 20b. (2), Walls of Ibb.

1953. Surch as T **6**.
98 **9** 4b. on 1b. green and orange 11·50 9·25
99 4b. on 2b. green and orange 11·50 9·25

16

16a Bab al-Yemen Gate, Sana'a

1953.
100 **16** 4b. orange (postage) 1·50 1·20
101 6b. blue 2·30 1·50
102 8b. green 3·00 1·90
103 10b. red (air) 3·75 2·30
104 12b. blue 4·50 3·00
105 20b. brown 7·75 3·75

1956. Unissued official stamps issued for ordinary postal use without surch.
105a **16a** 1b. brown 1·20 4·50
105b 5b. blue 1·40 3·75
105c 10b. blue 1·70 3·75
The 1 and 5b. were each sold for use as 4b. and the 10b. as 10b. for inland registered post.

1957. Arab Postal Union. As T **96a** of Syria but inscr "YEMEN" at top and inscriptions in English.
106 4b. brown 2·30 1·50
107 6b. green 2·75 1·90
108 16b. violet 5·00 4·25

1959. 1st Anniv of Proclamation of United Arab States (U.A.R. and Yemen). As T **139a** of Syria.
109 1b. black and red (postage) 40 30
110 2b. black and green 55 40
111 4b. red and green 75 60
112 6b. black and orange (air) 1·20 75
113 10b. black and red 1·90 1·50
114 16b. red and violet 3·00 2·30

1959. Arab Telecommunications Union. As T **138a** of Syria.
115 4b. red 1·90 1·20

1959. Inauguration of Automatic Telephone, Sana'a. Optd **AUTOMATIC TELEPHONE INAUGURATION SANAA MARCH 1959** in English and Arabic.
116 **3** 6b. blue 1·20 90
117 8b. red 1·50 1·20
118 10b. brown 2·20 1·90
119 20b. green 4·50 3·00
120 1i. green and red 6·25 4·50

1960. Air. Optd with Douglas DC-4 airliner and **AIR MAIL 1959** in English and Arabic.
121 **3** 6b. blue 1·90 1·50
122 10b. brown 3·00 2·30

1960. Inaug of Arab League Centre, Cairo. As T **154a** of Syria but with different arms.
123 4b. black and green 1·00 1·00

IMPERF STAMPS. From this point many issues also exist imperf. This applies also to Republican and Royalist issues.

1960. World Refugee Year. As T **155a** of Syria.
124 4b. brown 1·20 1·20
125 6b. green 2·00 2·00
MS125a 103 × 85 mm. Nos. 124/5 in new colours. Imperf 46·00 46·00

19 Olympic Torch

1960. Olympic Games, Rome.
126 **19** 2b. red and black 60 60
127 4b. yellow and black 90 90
128 6b. orange and black 1·30 1·30
129 8b. green and brown 2·30 2·30
130 20b. orange and violet 5·50 5·50
MS130a 100 × 60 mm. No. 127. Imperf 90·00 90·00

20 U.N. Emblem

1961. 15th Anniv of U.N.O.
131 **20** 1b. violet 40 30
132 2b. green 45 40
133 3b. blue 55 45
134 4b. blue 60 55
135 6b. purple 75 60
136 14b. red 1·20 90
137 20b. brown 1·90 1·50
MS137a 100 × 60 mm. No. 134. Imperf 23·00 27·00

21 Hodeida Port and Freighter

1961. Inauguration of Hodeida Port.
138 **21** 4b. multicoloured 90 75
139 6b. multicoloured 1·50 1·20
140 16b. multicoloured 3·00 3·00
MS140a 160 × 130 mm. Nos. 138/40. Imperf 16·00 7·50

22 Alabaster Death-mask

23 Imam's Palace, Sana'a

1961. Statues of Marib.
141 1b. black and orange (postage) 40 25
142 2b. black and violet 60 30
143 4b. black and brown 85 40
144 8b. black and mauve 1·00 60
145 10b. black and yellow 1·70 75
146 12b. black and blue 2·00 90
147 20b. black and grey 2·50 1·50
148 1i. black and green 5·00 1·90
149 6b. black and green (air) 1·00 45
150 16b. black and blue 2·75 1·40
DESIGNS: 1b. Type **22**; 2b. Horned head (8th-century B.C. frieze, Temple of the Moon God); 4b. Bronze head of Himyaritic emperor of 1st or 2nd century; 6b. "Throne of Bilqis" (8th-century B.C. limestone columns, Moon God Temple); 8b. Bronze figure of Himyaritic Emperor Dhamar Ali, 2nd or 3rd century; 10b. Alabaster statuette of 2nd or 3rd-century child; 12b. Entrance to Moon God Temple; 16b. Control tower and spillway, Marib dam; 20b. 1st-century alabaster relief of boy with dagger riding legendary monster, Moon God Temple; 1i. 1st-century alabaster relief of woman with grapes, Moon God Temple.

1961. Yemeni Buildings.
151 4b. black, grn & turq (postage) 40 40
152 8b. black, green and mauve 60 60
153 10b. black, green and orange 75 75
154 6b. black, green and blue (air) 90 90
155 16b. black, green and pink 1·50 1·50
DESIGNS—VERT: 4b. Type **23**; 10b. Palace of the Rock, Wadi Dhahr; 16b. Palace of the Rock (different view). HORIZ: 6b. Bab al-Yemen Gate, Sana'a; 8b. Imam's Palace, Sana'a (different view).

24 Hodeida–Sana'a Highway

1961. Inaug of Hodeida–Sana'a Highway.
156 **24** 4b. multicoloured 85 60
157 6b. multicoloured 1·00 1·00
158 10b. multicoloured 1·70 1·20
MS158a 160 × 130 mm. Nos. 156/8. Imperf 7·75 7·75

25 Nubian Temple

1962. UNESCO. Campaign for Preservation of Nubian Monuments.
159 **25** 4b. brown 3·75 3·00
160 6b. green 7·00 3·75
MS160a 111 × 90 mm. Nos. 159/60. Imperf 14·00 14·00

1962. Arab League Week. As T **178** of Syria.
161 4b. green 75 60
162 6b. blue 90 75
MS162a 95 × 80 mm. Nos. 161/2. Imperf 3·75 3·75

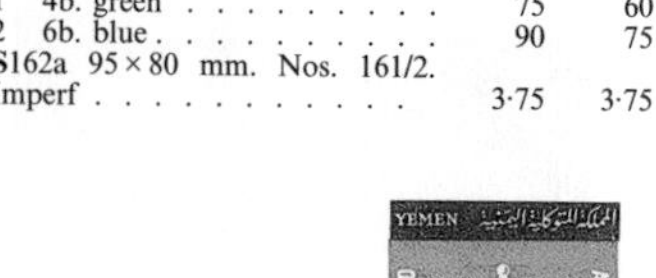

26 Nurse weighing Child

26a Campaign Emblem

1962. Maternity and Child Centre. Multicoloured.
163 2b. Putting child to bed 70 55
164 4b. Type **26** 90 70
165 6b. Taking child's temperature 1·20 85
166 10b. Weighing baby 1·90 1·20

1962. Malaria Eradication.
167 **26a** 4b. orange and black 75 75
168 – 6b. green and brown 1·20 1·20
MS168a 95 × 80 mm. Nos. 167/8. Imperf 15·00 15·00
DESIGN: 6b. As T **26a** but with laurel and inscription around emblem.

1962. 17th Anniv of U.N.O. Nos. 131/7 optd **1945-1962** in English and Arabic with bars over old dates.
169 **20** 1b. violet 1·50 1·50
170 2b. green 1·50 1·50
171 3b. blue 1·50 1·50
172 4b. blue 1·50 1·50
173 6b. purple 1·50 1·50
174 14b. red 1·50 1·50
175 20b. brown 1·50 1·50

REPUBLIC

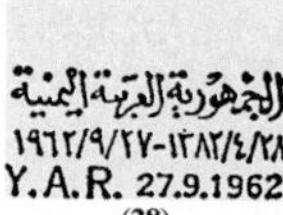

(28)

1963. Various issues optd as T **28**. (a) Nos. 141/50.
176 1b. black and orange (postage) 15 15
177 2b. black and violet 25 25
178 4b. black and brown 50 50
179 8b. black and mauve 85 85
180 10b. black and yellow 1·30 1·30
181 12b. black and blue 1·70 1·70
182 20b. black and grey 2·50 2·50
183 1i. black and green 7·00 7·00
184 6b. black and turquoise (air) 70 70
185 16b. black and blue 2·30 2·30

(b) Nos. 151/5.
186 4b. black, grn & turq (postage) 70 70
187 8b. black, green and mauve 1·30 1·30
188 10b. black, green and orange 2·20 2·20
189 6b. black, green and blue (air) 1·00 1·00
190 16b. black, green and pink 3·50 3·50

(c) Nos. 163/6.
191 2b. multicoloured 50 50
192 4b. multicoloured 70 70
193 6b. multicoloured 85 85
194 10b. multicoloured 2·20 2·20

29 "Torch of Freedom"

1963. "Proclamation of Republic".
195 – 4b. brown & mauve (postage) 70 70
196 – 6b. red and blue 1·00 1·00
197 – 8b. black and purple (air) 1·70 1·70
198 **29** 10b. red and violet 2·50 2·50
199 – 16b. red and green 3·50 3·50
MS199a Two sheets each 165 × 140 mm. Nos. 195/6 and 199 in new colours. Imperf 19·00 19·00
DESIGNS—VERT: 4b. Soldier with flag; 6b. Tank and flag; 8b. Bayonet and torch. HORIZ: 16b. Flag and torch.

29a Cow and Emblem

1963. Freedom from Hunger.
200 **29a** 4b. brown and red . . . 1·00 85
201 – 6b. yellow and violet . . 1·10 1·00
MS201a 110 × 120 mm. Nos. 200/1. Imperf . . . . 17·00 17·00
DESIGN: 6b. Corn-cob and ear of wheat.

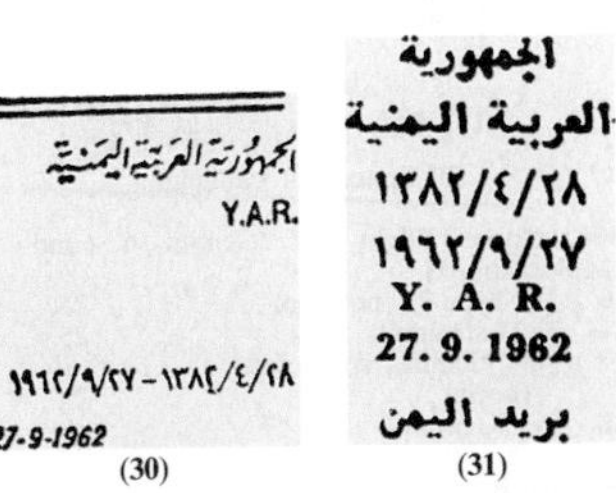
(30) (31)

1963. Various issues optd. (a) With T **30**. On Nos. 161/2.
202 4b. green . . . . 8·75 8·75
203 6b. blue . . . . 8·75 8·75

(b) With T **31**.
207 **2** 5b. grey . . . . 1·70 1·70
204 **3** 6b. blue . . . . 2·20 2·20
208 8b. purple . . . . 2·50 2·50
205 10b. brown . . . . 3·00 3·00
210 20b. green . . . . 3·50 3·50
206 1i. blue and brown . . . . 8·75 8·75
211 1i. green and purple . . . . 6·50 6·50

(c) As T **31** but with lowest line of inscription at top.
212 **10** 6b. pink and green . . . . 2·20 2·20
213 10b. blue and green . . . 3·00 3·00
214 14b. olive and green . . . 8·75 8·75

(d) As T **31** but with lowest line of inscription omitted and bar at top. On Nos. 167/8.
215 4b. orange and black . . . . 2·40 2·40
216 6b. green and brown . . . . 3·00 3·00

(32)

(e) With T **32**. (i) On Nos. 139/40.
217 **21** 6b. multicoloured . . . . 2·20 2·20
218 16b. multicoloured . . . . 3·00 3·00
MS218a Sheet No. **MS**140a optd on each stamp . . . . 17·00 17·00

(ii) On Nos. 157/8.
219 **24** 6b. multicoloured . . . . 2·20 2·20
220 10b. multicoloured . . . . 3·00 3·00

(f) As T **32** but with only one bar over old inscription. (i) Nos. 126/8.
221 **19** 2b. red and black . . . . 6·00 6·00
222 4b. yellow and black . . . . 6·00 6·00
223 6b. orange and black . . . 6·00 6·00

(ii) Nos. 159/60.
224 **25** 4b. brown . . . . 7·00 7·00
225 6b. green . . . . 10·50 10·50

(34) **35** Flag and Laurel Sprig

(g) Air. With T **34**.
226 **4** 6b. ultramarine and blue . . 1·70 1·70
227 10b. blue and brown . . . . 2·20 2·20
228 14b. blue and green . . . . 2·50 2·50
229 20b. blue and green . . . . 3·50 3·50
230 1i. blue and purple . . . . 7·50 7·50

1963. 1st Anniv of Revolution.
231 – 2b. red, green and black 45 35
232 – 4b. red, black and green 70 50
233 **35** 6b. red, black and green 1·10 85
MS233a 150 × 90 mm. Nos. 231/3. Imperf . . . . 15·00 15·00
DESIGNS—HORIZ: 4b. Flag, torch and broken chain. VERT: 2b. Flag, torch and candle.

36 Hands reaching for Centenary Emblem

38 Globe and Scales of Justice

37

1963. Red Cross Centenary. Crescent red; inscription black.
234 **36** ¼b. blue 50 50
235 ⅓b. brown 50 50
236 ½b. grey 70 70
237 – 4b. lilac 85 85
238 – 8b. stone . . . . 1·70 1·70
239 – 20b. green . . . . 4·25 4·25
MS239a 100 × 75 mm. Nos. 237/8. Imperf . . . . 13·00 13·00
DESIGN: 4b. to 20b. Centenary emblem.

1963. Air. "Honouring Astronauts". T **37** and similar designs showing rockets, etc.
240 **37** ¼b. multicoloured . . . . 1·00 85
241 – ⅓b. multicoloured . . . . . 1·00 85
242 – ½b. multicoloured . . . . 1·00 85
243 – 4b. multicoloured . . . . 2·20 1·70
244 – 20b. multicoloured . . . . 7·75 7·00
MS244a 90 × 100 mm. No. 244. Imperf . . . . 10·50 10·50

1963. 15th Anniv of Declaration of Human Rights.
245 – 4b. black, orange and lilac 70 70
246 **38** 6b. black, green & turquoise . . . . 1·60 1·60
MS246a 78 × 93 mm. Nos. 245/6. Imperf . . . . 13·00 13·00
DESIGN: 4b. As Type **38** but differently arranged.

39 Darts

40 Factory, Bobbins and Cloth

1964. Olympic Games, Tokyo (1st issue).
247 ¼b. green, brown and orange (postage) 15 15
248 ⅓b. brown, blue and violet . . 15 15
249 ½b. brown, blue and mauve 15 15
250 1b. brown, green and blue . . 70 45
251 1½b. red, brown and grey . . 85 45
252 4b. brown, black and blue (air) 10 60
253 20b. blue, deep blue and brown . . . . 25 2·20
254 1r. red, brown and green . . 80 6·00
MS254a Two sheets each 90 × 70 mm. Nos. 252 and 253. Imperf . . . . 14·00 14·00
DESIGNS—HORIZ: ¼b. Type **39**; ⅓ b. Table tennis; 4b. Horse-racing; 20b. Pole vaulting. VERT: ½b. Running; 1b. Volleyball; 1½b. Football; 1r. Basketball. All designs include the Olympic "Rings" symbol.
See also Nos. 272/**MS**280a.

1964. Inauguration of Bagel Spinning and Weaving Factory.
255 – 2b. blue & yellow (postage) 35 15
256 – 4b. blue and yellow 50 35
257 **40** 6b. brown and blue 70 45
258 – 16b. orange, blue and grey (air) . . . . 1·90 1·70
MS258a 76 × 61 mm. No. 258. Imperf . . . . 5·25 5·25
DESIGNS—VERT: 2b. Factory, bobbins and cloth (different); 4b. Loom. HORIZ: 16b. Factory and lengths of cloth.

1964. Air. President Kennedy Memorial Issue. Nos. 240/2 optd **JOHN F. KENNEDY 1917 1963** in English and Arabic and with portrait and laurel.
259 **37** ¼b. multicoloured . . . . 1·70 1·70
260 – ⅓b. multicoloured . . . . . 1·70 1·70
261 – ½b. multicoloured . . . . 1·70 1·70
MS261a Sheet No. **MS**244a optd 50·00 50·00

42 Boeing 707 on Runway

1964. Inauguration of Hodeida Airport.
262 **42** 4b. yellow and blue 50 45
263 – 6b. green and blue 70 60
264 – 10b. blue, yellow & dp blue 95 70
MS264a 72 × 62 mm. No. 264. Imperf . . . . 4·25 4·25
DESIGNS: 6b. Control tower and Boeing 707 on runway; 10b. Control tower, Boeing 707 and ship.

43 New York, Boeing 707 and Sana'a

1964. New York World's Fair.
265 **43** ¼b. brn, bl & grn (postage) 35 15
266 – ⅓b. black, red and green . . 50 15
267 – ½b. green, red and blue . . 70 35
268 **43** 1b. indigo, blue and green 85 45
269 – 4b. blue, red and green . . 1·60 1·00
270 – 16b. brown, red & blue (air) . . . . 3·50 2·30
271 **43** 20b. purple, blue and green 4·25 3·00
MS271a 100 × 70 mm. No. 271. Imperf . . . . 7·00 7·00
DESIGNS: ⅓b., 4b. Flag, Empire State Building, New York, and Mosque, Sana'a; ½b., 16b. Statue of Liberty, New York, liner and Harbour, Hodeida.

44 Globe and Flags **45** Scout hoisting Flag

1964. Olympic Games, Tokyo (2nd issue). Multicoloured.
272 ¼b. Type **44** (postage) 15 15
273 ⅓b. Olympic Torch 25 15
274 ½b. Discus-thrower 35 25
275 1b. Yemeni flag 45 25
276 1½b. Swimming (horiz) . . . 50 25
277 4b. Swimming (horiz) (air) . . 85 45
278 6b. Olympic Torch . . . . . 1·30 50
279 12b. Type **44** . . . . 2·50 85
280 20b. Discus-thrower . . . . 4·25 1·70
MS280a 70 × 90 mm. No. 280. Imperf . . . . 7·00 7·00

1964. Yemeni Scouts. Multicoloured.
281 ¼b. Type **45** (postage) 15 15
282 ⅓b. Scout badge and scouts guarding camp 15 15
283 ½b. Bugler 15 15
284 1b. As No. 282 . . . . . . 35 25
285 1½b. Scouts by camp-fire . . 50 35
286 4b. Type **45** (air) 60 35
287 6b. As No. 282 . . . . . . 70 45
288 16b. Bugler . . . . 1·20 85
289 20b. Scouts by camp-fire . . 2·30 1·70
MS289a Two sheets each 70 × 90 mm. Nos. 288/9. Perf or imperf . . . . 10·50 10·50

46 Hamadryas Baboons

1964. Animals.
290 **46** ¼b. brown & lilac (postage) 15 15
291 – ⅓b. brown and blue 15 15
292 – ½b. brown and orange . . . 25 15
293 – 1b. brown and blue 35 25
294 – 1½b. brown and blue 50 25
295 – 4b. red and green (air) . . 85 45
296 – 12b. brown and buff . . . 2·20 1·30
297 – 20b. brown and blue . . . 4·25 1·70
ANIMALS: ⅓b. Arab horses; ½, 12b. Bullock; 1, 20b. Lion and lioness; 1½, 4b. Mountain gazelles.

47 Gentian

49 A.P.U. Emblem

48 Boeing 707 and Hawker Siddeley Comet 4 Airliners over Mountains

1964. Flowers. Multicoloured.
298 ¼b. Type **47** (postage) 15 15
299 ⅓b. Lily 15 15
300 ½b. Poinsettia 25 15
301 1b. Rose 45 25
302 1½b. Viburnum 60 35
303 4b. Rose (air) 85 45
304 12b. Poinsettia . . . . 2·20 85
305 20b. Viburnum . . . . . . 4·25 2·20

1964. Inauguration of Sana'a Int Airport.
306 **48** 1b. brown & blue (postage) 45 45
307 – 2b. brown and blue 45 45
308 – 4b. brown and blue 45 45
309 **48** 8b. brown and blue 85 85
310 – 6b. brown and blue (air) 85 85
MS310a 120 × 70 mm. Nos. 308 and 310. Imperf . . . . 5·25 5·25
DESIGNS: 2b., 4b. Boeing 707 and Vickers Viscount 800 airliners over runway; 6b. Hawker Siddeley Comet 4 airliners in flight and on ground.

1964. 10th Anniv of Arab Postal Union's Permanent Office, Cairo.
311 **49** 4b. black, red and orange (postage) 95 80
312 6b. black, green and turquoise (air) . . . . . 1·20 95
MS312a 77 × 97 mm. No. 312. Imperf . . . . 3·50 3·50

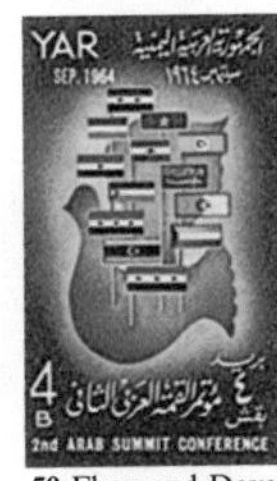
50 Flags and Dove

51 Flaming Torch

1964. 2nd Arab Summit Conference.
313 **50** 4b. green 95 80
314 – 6b. brown . . . . 1·20 95
MS314a 80 × 130 mm. No. 313/14. Imperf . . . . 3·50 3·50
DESIGN: 6b. Arms within conference emblem and map.

1964. 2nd Anniv of Revolution.
315 **51** 2b. brown and blue 45 35
316 – 4b. green and yellow . . . 85 60
317 – 6b. pink, red and green . . 85 60
MS317a 102 × 80 mm. No. 317. Imperf . . . . 3·50 3·50
DESIGNS: 4b. Yemeni soldier; 6b. Candles on map.

52 Western Reef Heron ("Reef Heron") and Little Egret

52a Dagger on Deir Yassin, Palestine

1965. Birds. Multicoloured.
318 ¼b. Type **52** (postage) 35 15
319 ⅓b. Arabian chukar (inscr "Arabian red-legged partridge") 45 15
320 ½b. Desert eagle owl ("Eagle Owl") (vert) 45 15
321 1b. Hammerkop 70 25
322 1½b. Yemeni linnets 85 45
323 4b. Hoopoes . . . . 1·70 85
324 6b. Violet starlings (air) . . . 2·10 1·00
325 8b. Waldrapp (inscr "Bald ibis") (vert) . . . . 2·50 1·30
326 12b. Arabian woodpecker (vert) . . . . 3·50 1·70
327 20b. Bateleur (vert) . . . . 6·00 2·50

328 1r. Yellow-bellied ("Bruce's") green pigeon . . . . 12·00 4·25
MS328a 76 × 60 mm. 20b. in design of 1½b. Imperf . . . . 31·00 22·00

1965. Deir Yassin Massacre.
329 **52a** 4b. purple and blue (postage) 95 50
330 6b. red and orange (air) 1·20 70

53 I.T.U. Emblem and Symbols

1965. I.T.U. Centenary.
331 – 4b. red and blue 85 60
332 **53** 6b. green and red . . . . 1·00 70
MS332a 106 × 67 mm. No. 332 5·25 4·25
DESIGN—VERT: 4b. As Type **53** but rearranged.

53a Lamp and Burning Library

1965. Burning of Algiers Library.
333 **53a** 4b. green, red and black (postage) 85 60
334 6b. blue, red and deep red (air) . . . . 1·00 70
MS334a 75 × 65 mm. No. 334 . . 3·00 2·20

54 Tractor and Agricultural Produce

1965. 3rd Anniv of Revolution.
335 **54** 4b. blue and yellow 85 60
336 – 6b. blue and yellow . . . . 1·00 70
MS336a 81 × 72 mm. No. 336. Imperf . . . . 3·50 3·00
DESIGN: 6b. Tractor and landscape.

55 I.C.Y. and U.N. Emblems

57 Belyaev and Rocket

56 Pres. Kennedy, Map and Rocket-launching

1965. International Co-operation Year.
337 **55** 4b. green and orange . . . 95 70
338 – 6b. brown and blue . . . . 1·30 80
MS338a 71 × 80 mm. No. 338. Imperf . . . . 4·25 3·50
DESIGN: 6b. U.N. Headquarters and General Assembly Building, New York.

1965. Pres. Kennedy Commem. Designs each include portrait of Pres. Kennedy. Multicoloured.
339 ¼b. Type **56** (postage) 35 15
340 ¼b. Rocket gantries 35 15
341 ¼b. Rocket 35 15
342 ⅓b. Type **56** 35 15
343 ½b. Rocket 35 15
344 4b. Capsule and U.S. flag . . 95 80
345 8b. Capsule in ocean (air) . . 2·10 1·60
346 12b. Rocket gantries . . . . 4·00 2·50
MS346a Two sheets each 90 × 80 mm. Nos. 344 and 345. Imperf . . . . 13·00 13·00

1965. Space Achievements. Multicoloured.
347 ¼b. Type **57** (postage) 15 10
348 ¼b. Leonov and rocket . . . 15 10
349 ¼b. Scott and capsule 15 10
350 ⅓b. Carpenter and rocket gantry 15 10
351 ½b. Scott and capsule 15 10
352 4b. Leonov and rocket (air) 1·20 85
353 8b. Type **57** . . . . 2·30 1·70
354 16b. Carpenter and rocket gantry . . . . 4·25 3·50
MS355 90 × 80 mm. 16b. black, cobalt and blue (Scott and Carpenter, and astronaut filming in space). Imperf . . . . . . 13·00 10·50

1966. Anti T.B. Campaign. Nos. 200/1 optd **Tuberculous Campaign 1965** in English and Arabic.
356 4b. brown and red . . . . . 1·30 85
357 6b. yellow and violet . . . . 2·20 1·30
MS358 110 × 120 mm. No. 356/7. Imperf . . . . 13·00 13·00

59 Torch Signalling

1966. Telecommunications.
359 **59** ¼b. black and red (postage) 25 15
360 – ¼b. black and blue 25 15
361 – ¼b. black and brown . . . 25 15
362 – ⅓b. black and red 25 15
363 – ½b. black and blue 25 15
364 – 4b. black and green (air) 80 45
365 – 6b. black and brown . . . 1·20 85
366 – 20b. black and blue . . . 4·00 3·50
MS367 90 × 70 mm. No. 366. Imperf 8·75 4·25
DESIGNS: No. 360, Morse telegraphy; 361, Early telephone; 362, Wireless telegraphy; 363, Television; 364, Radar; 365, Telex; 366, "Early Bird" Satellite.

1966. Prevention of Cruelty to Animals. Nos. 318/20 optd **Prevention of Cruelty to Animals** in English and Arabic.
368 **52** ¼b. multicoloured 70 45
369 – ½b. multicoloured 60 50
370 – ¾b. multicoloured . . . . 1·70 80
MS370a 76 × 60 mm. 20b. multicoloured. Imperf . . . . 9·50 7·00

1966. 3rd Arab Summit Conference Nos. 313/14 optd **3rd. Arab Summit Conference 1965** in English and Arabic.
371 **50** 4b. green 85 60
372 – 6b. brown . . . . 1·00 70
MS373 Sheet No. MS314a optd on each stamp . . . . 5·25 5·25

62 Pres. Kennedy and Globe

1966. "Builders of World Peace". (a) Postage. Size 39 × 28½ mm.
374 **62** ¼b. brown 15 15
375 – ¼b. green 15 15
376 – ¼b. blue 15 15
377 – ⅓b. brown 25 15
378 – ½b. purple 25 15
379 **62** 4b. purple 85 45
MS380 90 × 70 mm. 4b. purple (portraits only as in Nos. 374/6). Imperf . . . . 4·25 3·50

(b) Air. Size 51 × 38 mm.
381 – 6b. brown and green . . . . 1·00 70
382 – 10b. brown and blue . . . . 1·40 85
383 – 12b. brown and mauve . . . 1·70 1·30
MS384 90 × 70 mm. 8b. brown and blue (portraits only as in Nos. 381/3). Imperf . . . . . 8·75 7·00
PORTRAITS: Nos. 375, 377, Dag Hammarskjold; 376, 378, Nehru; 381, Mohammed Abdul Chalek Hassuna; 382, U. Thant; 383, Pope Paul VI.

63 Red Junglefowl

1986. Animals and Insects. Multicoloured. (a) Postage.
385 ¼b. Type **63** 25 15
386 ¼b. Brown hare 25 15
387 ¼b. Pony 25 15
388 ⅓b. Cat 25 15
389 ½b. Sheep and lamb 25 15
390 4b. Dromedary . . . . 1·10 85

(b) Air. Butterflies.
391 6b. Red admiral . . . . 3·50 1·30
392 8b. Swallowtail . . . . 4·25 1·50
393 10b. Garden tiger moth . . . 5·25 1·70
394 16b. Mocker swallowtail . . 7·75 2·50
MS395 90 × 70 mm. 22b. multicoloured (Farmyard scene). Imperf . . . . 5·75 4·25

1966. Space Flight of "Luna 9". Nos. 347/54 optd **LUNA IX 3 February 1966** in English and Arabic and spacecraft.
396 **57** ¼b. multicoloured (postage) 25 15
397 – ¼b. multicoloured 25 15
398 – ¼b. multicoloured 25 15
399 – ⅓b. multicoloured 25 15
400 – ½b. multicoloured 25 15
401 – 4b. multicoloured (air) . . 50 35
402 **57** 8b. multicoloured . . . . 1·20 85
403 – 16b. multicoloured . . . . 1·70 1·40
MS404 90 × 80 mm. 16b. (No.MS355 optd) . . . . . . 10·50 10·50

65 Jules Rimet Cup

66 Traffic Signals

1966. World Cup Football Championships, England.
405 **65** ¼b. multicoloured (postage) 15 15
406 – ¼b. multicoloured 15 15
407 – ¼b. multicoloured 15 15
408 – ⅓b. multicoloured 15 15
409 – ½b. multicoloured 15 15
410 – 4b. multicoloured (air) . . 70 60
411 – 5b. multicoloured . . . . 1·20 1·00
412 – 20b. multicoloured . . . . 2·50 2·30
MS413 70 × 90 mm. No. 412. Imperf . . . . 7·75 5·25
DESIGNS: No. 406/11, Footballers in play (all different); 412, World Cup emblem.

1966. Traffic Day.
414 **66** 4b. red, emerald and green 85 60
415 6b. red, emerald and green 1·00 70
MS416 84 × 75 mm. No. 415. Imperf 4·75 4·25

1966. Space Flight of "Surveyor 1". Nos. 347/51 surch with spacecraft, **SURVEYOR 1 2 June 1966** and new value in English and Arabic.
417 **57** 1b. on ¼b. multicoloured 85 70
418 – 1b. on ¼b. multicoloured 85 70
419 – 1b. on ¼b. multicoloured 85 70
420 – 3b. on ⅓b. multicoloured 1·30 95
421 – 4b. on ½b. multicoloured 2·20 1·70

68 Yemeni Flag

1966. 4th Anniv of Revolution.
422 **68** 2b. black, red and green 35 25
423 – 4b. multicoloured 70 45
424 – 6b. multicoloured . . . . 1·10 60
MS424a 82 × 102 mm. Nos. 423/4. Imperf . . . . 4·25 3·50
DESIGNS—VERT (25 × 42 mm): 4b. Automatic weapon; 6b. "Agriculture and Industry".

1966. "World Fair, Sana'a, 1965". Nos. 265/71 optd **1965 SANA'A** in English and Arabic.
425 **43** ¼b. brn, bl & grn (postage) 25 15
426 – ⅓b. black, red and green . . 25 15
427 – ½b. green, red and blue . . 25 15
428 **43** 1b. indigo, blue and green 45 25
429 – 4b. blue, red and green . . 1·00 85
430 – 16b. brown, red & blue (air) . . . . 3·50 3·25
431 **43** 20b. purple, blue and green 4·75 4·00
MS432 100 × 70 mm. No. 431. Imperf . . . . 10·50 8·75

70 Galen, Helianthus and W.H.O. Building

1966. Inauguration of W.H.O. Headquarters, Geneva. Designs incorporating W.H.O. Building. Mult.
433 ¼b. Type **70** (postage) 35 25
434 ¼b. Hippocrates and ipomoeas 35 25
435 ¼b. Ibn Sina (Avicenna) and peonies 35 25
436 4b. Type **70** (air) 85 45
437 8b. As No. 434 . . . . . . 1·70 85
438 16b. As No. 435 . . . . . . 3·50 2·30
MS439 130 × 100 mm. No. 438. Imperf . . . . 10·50 7·00

71 Spacecraft Launching

1966. Space Flight of "Gemini 6" and "7". Multicoloured.
440 ¼b. Type **71** (postage) 25 15
441 ¼b. Astronauts 25 15
442 ¼b. "Gemini" spacecraft (horiz) 25 15
443 ⅓b. "Gemini 6" and "7" (horiz) 25 15
444 ½b. Recovery operations at sea 25 15
445 2b. As ⅓b. 50 35
446 8b. As ½b. (air) . . . . . . 1·50 1·20
447 12b. "Gemini 6" and "7" link (horiz) . . . . 1·20 1·50
MS448 105 × 78 mm. No. 447. Imperf . . . . 10·50 7·00

1966. Space Flight of "Gemini 9". Nos. 440/7 optd **GEMINI IX CERNAN - STAFFORD JUNE 3-1966** in English and Arabic.
449 **71** ¼b. multicoloured (postage) 25 15
450 – ¼b. multicoloured 25 15
451 – ¼b. multicoloured 25 15
452 – ⅓b. multicoloured 25 15
453 – ½b. multicoloured 25 15
454 – 2b. multicoloured 50 35
455 – 8b. multicoloured (air) . . 1·90 1·40
456 – 12b. multicoloured . . . . 2·50 1·70
MS457 105 × 78 mm. No. 456. Imperf . . . . 10·50 7·00

73 Figs

1967. Fruits. Multicoloured.
458 ¼b. Type **73** (postage) 15 10
459 ¼b. Quinces 15 10
460 ¼b. Grapes 15 10
461 ⅓b. Dates 15 10
462 ½b. Apricots 15 10
463 2b. Quinces 45 15
464 4b. Oranges 85 45
465 6b. Bananas (air) . . . . . . 1·30 60
466 8b. Type **73** . . . . 1·70 85
467 10b. Grapes . . . . 2·20 1·00

1967. Arab League Day. As No. 908 of Egypt.
471 4b. brown and violet 70 60
472 6b. brown and violet . . . . 1·50 1·10
473 8b. brown and violet . . . . 2·10 1·70
474 20b. brown and green . . . . 3·00 2·10
475 40b. black and green . . . . 7·50 6·00

73a Women in Factory

1967. Labour Day.
475a **73a** 2b. blue and violet . . . 60 50
475b 4b. green and red . . . . 1·10 1·00
475c 6b. purple and green . . 1·70 1·30
475d 8b. green and blue . . . 2·20 1·30
MS475e 78 × 70 mm. **73a** 10b. emerald and vermilion . . . . 10·50 10·50

74 Ploughing and Sunset

1967.
476 **74** 1b. multicoloured 15 10
477 2b. multicoloured 25 15
478 4b. multicoloured 45 25
479 6b. multicoloured 70 45

480 8b. multicoloured . . . . 1·00 70
481 10b. multicoloured . . . . 1·30 95
482 12b. multicoloured . . . . 1·70 1·30
483 16b. multicoloured . . . . 2·20 1·70
484 20b. multicoloured . . . . 3·00 2·20
485 40b. multicoloured . . . . 6·50 2·50

75 Pres. Al-Salal and Soldiers

1968. 6th Anniv of Revolution. Multicoloured.
486 2b. Type **75** 35 35
487 4b. Yemen Arab Republic flag 70 70
488 6b. Pres. Abdullah al-Salal (vert) . . . . 1·00 1·00
MS489 80 × 98 mm. No. 488. Imperf 3·25 3·25

76 Map of Yemen and Dove

1969. 7th Anniv of Revolution. Multicoloured.
490 2b. Type **76** 25 25
491 4b. Government building (horiz) 50 50
492 6b. Yemeni workers (horiz) 1·10 1·10
MS493 80 × 100 mm. No. 492. Imperf . . . . 8·75 8·75

77 "Lenin addressing Crowd"

1970. Air. Birth Centenary of Lenin. Mult.
494 6b. Type **77** . . . . . . 1·70 1·30
495 10b. "Lenin with Arab Delegates" . . . . . . 3·50 2·20

78 Arab League Flag, Arms and Map

1970. 25th Anniv of Arab League.
496 **78** 5b. purple, green and orange 45 45
497 7b. brown, green and blue 95 95
498 16b. blue, green and olive 2·30 2·30
MS499 84 × 76 mm. No. 498 . . 4·00 4·00

1971. Various 1968 issues listed in Appendix surch.
499a 40b. on 10b. black, red and green on gold foil (Yemen Red Crescent issue) . . . 7·50 7·50
499b 60b. on 15b. multicoloured on gold foil (Olympics—Chariot Racing issue) . . 9·50 9·50
499c 80b. on 10b. multicoloured on gold foil (Int Human Rights and U Thant issue) . . . . 13·00 13·00

79 Yemeni Castle

1971. 8th Anniv (1970) of Revolution. Mult.
500 5b. Type **79** (postage) 85 85
501 7b. Yemeni workers and soldier (air) . . . . 1·30 1·30
502 16b. Clasped hands, flag and torch . . . . 1·70 1·70
MS503 100 × 78 mm. No. 502 . . 6·00 6·00

1971. Air. Proclamation of first Permanent Constitution. No. 502 optd **PROCLAMATION OF THE INSTITUTION 1/11/1390 H. 28/12/1970 C.** in English and Arabic.
504 16b. multicoloured . . . . . 8·75 8·75

81 U.N. Emblems and Globe

1971. 25th Anniv (1970) of U.N.O.
505 **81** 5b. purple, green and olive 70 50
506 7b. indigo, green and blue 1·10 85
MS507 83 × 73 mm. **81** 16b. chocolate, emerald and salmon. Imperf . . . . 2·50 1·70

82 View of Sana'a

1972. 9th Anniv (1971) of Revolution.
508 7b. Type **82** . . . . 1·30 1·30
509 18b. Military parade . . . . 2·20 2·20
510 24b. Mosque, Sana'a . . . . 3·50 3·50
MS511 97 × 77 mm. No. 510. Imperf 4·25 4·25

83 A.P.U. Emblem and Flags

1972. 25th Anniv (1971) of Founding of Arab Postal Union at Sofar Conference.
512 **83** 3b. multicoloured 45 45
513 7b. multicoloured 85 85
514 10b. multicoloured . . . . 1·70 1·70
MS515 77 × 97 mm. **83** 16b. multicoloured . . . . 2·50 2·50

84 Arms and Flags

85 Skeleton and Emblem

1972. 10th Anniv of Revolution.
516 **84** 7b. multicoloured (postage) 1·10 1·10
517 10b. multicoloured . . . . 1·70 1·70
518 21b. multicoloured (air) . . 4·75 4·75

1972. 25th Anniv of W.H.O.
519 **85** 2b. multicoloured 45 35
520 21b. multicoloured . . . . 3·00 2·30
521 37b. multicoloured . . . . 5·75 4·75

86 Dome of the Rock, Jerusalem

1973. 2nd Anniv of Burning of Al-Aqsa Mosque, Jerusalem.
522 **86** 7b. multicoloured (postage) 1·30 85
523 18b. multicoloured . . . . 3·00 2·20
524 24b. multicoloured (air) . . 4·25 3·50
MS525 83 × 73 mm. No. 524. Imperf 4·25 4·25

87 Arab Child with Book

1973. 25th Anniv (1971) of UNICEF.
526 **87** 7b. multicoloured (postage) 1·00 70
527 10b. multicoloured . . . . 1·90 1·30
528 18b. multicoloured (air) . . 2·30 1·90
MS529 83 × 73 mm. No. 528. Imperf 4·00 3·00

88 Modern Office Building

1973. Air. 11th Anniv of Revolution.
530 **88** 7b. red and green 60 45
531 – 10b. orange and green . . . 80 70
532 – 18b. violet and green . . . 1·90 1·50
DESIGNS: 10b. Factory; 18b. Flats.

89 U.P.U. Emblem

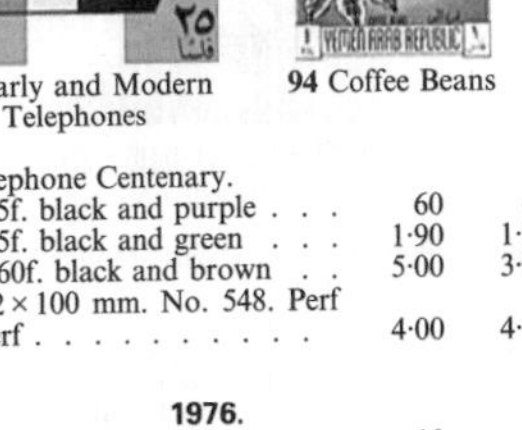

90 Yemeni Town and Emblem

1974. Centenary of U.P.U.
533 **89** 10b. red, black and blue 60 45
534 30b. red, black and green 1·50 1·30
535 40b. red, black and stone 4·00 1·70

1975. 10th Anniv of F.A.O. World Food Programme.
536 **90** 10b. multicoloured 70 35
537 30b. multicoloured . . . . 2·20 1·70
538 63b. multicoloured . . . . 4·25 3·50

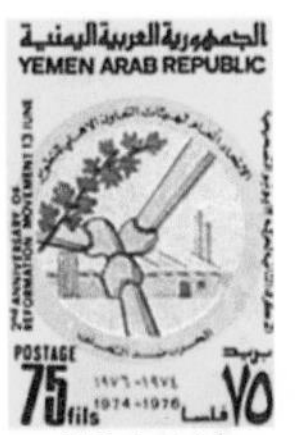

91 Janad Mosque

1975. 12th Anniv (1974) of Revolution. Mult.
539 25f. Type **91** 85 60
540 75f. Althawra Hospital . . . 2·75 2·20

1975. Various stamps surch.
541 **84** 75f. on 7b. mult (postage) 3·25 3·25
542 **86** 75f. on 7b. multicoloured 3·25 3·25
542b **85** 75f. on 21b. mult . . . . 3·25 3·25
542c **89** 160f. on 40b. red, black and stone . . . . . . 6·50 6·50
543 **86** 278f. on 7b. mult . . . . 10·50 10·50
544 **87** 75f. on 18b. mult (air) . . 3·25 3·25
544a **84** 75f. on 21b. mult . . . . 3·50 3·50
545 **88** 90f. on 7b. red and green 7·00 3·50
546 – 120f. on 18b. violet and green (No. 532) . . . . 5·25 5·25

93 Early and Modern Telephones

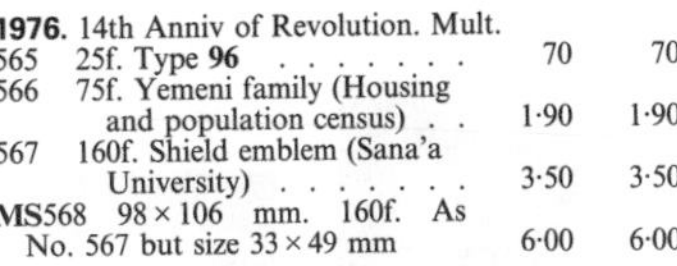

94 Coffee Beans

1976. Telephone Centenary.
547 **93** 25f. black and purple . . . 60 60
548 75f. black and green . . . 1·90 1·90
549 160f. black and brown . . 5·00 3·00
MS550 92 × 100 mm. No. 548. Perf or imperf . . . . 4·00 4·00

1976.
551 **94** 1f. multicoloured 10 85
552 3f. multicoloured 10 85
553 5f. multicoloured 10 85
554 10f. multicoloured 15 15
555 25f. multicoloured 35 35
556 50f. multicoloured 85 85
557 75f. multicoloured . . . . 1·60 1·10
558 1r. multicoloured . . . . . 2·20 1·60
559 1r.50 multicoloured . . . . 4·00 3·00
560 2r. multicoloured . . . . . 6·00 4·00
561 5r. multicoloured . . . . . 14·00 9·50
Nos. 558/61 are larger, 22 × 30 mm.

95 Industrial Scaffolding

96 Emblem of National Institute of Public Administration

1976. 2nd Anniv of Reformation Movement. Multicoloured.
562 75f. Type **95** . . . . 1·90 1·90
563 135f. Hand holding pick . . 3·00 3·00
MS564 99 × 105 mm. 135f. As No. 563 but size 32 × 47 mm 5·25 5·25

1976. 14th Anniv of Revolution. Mult.
565 25f. Type **96** 70 70
566 75f. Yemeni family (Housing and population census) . . 1·90 1·90
567 160f. Shield emblem (Sana'a University) . . . . 3·50 3·50
MS568 98 × 106 mm. 160f. As No. 567 but size 33 × 49 mm 6·00 6·00

97 President Ibrahim M. al-Hamdi

1977. 1st Anniv of Assassination of Pres. Ibrahim al-Hamdi.
569 **97** 25f. green and black . . . 45 45
570 75f. brown and black . . . 1·50 1·30
571 160f. blue and black . . . 3·00 2·20
MS572 82 × 85 mm. 160f. No. 571 6·00 5·25

98 Sa'ada and Sana'a

1978. 15th Anniv (1977) of Revolution. Mult.
573 25f. Type **98** 50 45
574 75f. Television and transmitter . . . . 1·40 95
575 160f. Type **98** . . . . . . 3·00 2·30
MS576 101 × 75 mm. No. 575 . . 6·00 5·25

99 A.P.U. Emblem

100 Dish Aerial

1978. 25th Anniv of Arab Postal Union.
577 **99** 25f. multicoloured . . . . 1·00 85
578 60f. multicoloured . . . . 2·50 1·90
MS579 73 × 78 mm. No. 578 . . 6·00 5·25

1978. 3rd Anniv of Correction Movement. Multicoloured.
580 25f. Type **100** 50 35
581 75f. Operating a computer . . 1·40 80
MS582 82 × 95 mm. No. 581 . . 4·75 4·25

101 View of Sana'a

1979. 30th Anniv (1977) of I.C.A.O.
583 **101** 75f. multicoloured . . . . 2·20 1·10
584 135f. multicoloured . . . 3·50 1·90
MS585 80 × 70 mm. No. 584 . . 6·00 5·25

102 Koran on Map of World

1979. The Arabs.
586 **102** 25f. multicoloured 70 45
587 75f. multicoloured . . . . 1·70 1·10
MS588 99 × 75 mm. No. 587 . . 4·25 4·00

103 Viewers and Video-screen
104 Dome of the Rock, Jerusalem

1980. World Telecommunications Day (1979). Multicoloured.
589 75f. Type **103** . . . . 2·10 1·10
590 135f. As No. 589 (horiz) . . 3·25 1·90
MS591 67 × 75 mm. No. 590 . . 6·00 5·25

1980. Palestinian Welfare.
592 **104** 5f. multicoloured 50 10
593 10f. multicoloured 70 15

105 Girl and Chaffinch

1980. Int Year of the Child (1979). Mult.
594 25f. Type **105** (postage) . . . 2·00 45
595 50f. Girl and great tit . . . . 2·50 95
596 75f. Child and butterfly . . . 2·75 1·50
597 80f. Girl and northern bullfinch (air) . . . . . . 3·75 1·50
598 100f. Child and butterfly . . 3·75 1·50
599 150f. Child and butterfly . . 5·25 2·20
Each stamp shows a different variety of bird or butterfly.

106 Scoring a Goal (Austria v. Spain)

1980. World Cup Football Championship, Argentina (1978). Multicoloured.
601 25f. Type **106** (postage) . . . 70 70
602 30f. Tunisia v. Mexico . . . 80 70
603 35f. Netherlands v. Iran . . . 1·00 70
604 50f. Brazil v. Sweden . . . . 1·50 1·00
605 60f. Peru v. Scotland (air) . . 1·90 1·00
606 75f. Italy v. France . . . . . 2·50 1·30
607 80f. Argentina v. Hungary . . 2·75 1·50
608 100f. West Germany v. Poland . . . . 4·25 2·20

107 Scout Fishing

1980. World Scout Jamboree. Multicoloured.
610 25f. Type **107** (postage) . . . 70 35
611 35f. Scouts and Concorde Supersonic airliner . . . . 1·60 60
612 40f. Parade and scout on horseback . . . . 1·40 60
613 50f. Scouts with telescope . . 1·70 80
614 60f. Parade and cyclist (air) 2·30 95
615 75f. Poppy and fencer . . . 2·75 1·30
616 120f. Scouts catching butterflies . . . . 4·25 1·70

108 Match Scene and Flag of Poland

1980. World Cup Football Championship Quarter Finalists. Match Scenes and Flags. Multicoloured.
617 25f. Type **108** (postage) . . . 70 35
618 30f. Peru 85 45
619 35f. Brazil 95 50
620 50f. Austria . . . . 1·40 95
621 60f. Italy (air) . . . . 1·50 95
622 75f. Netherlands . . . . . . 2·20 1·10
623 80f. West Germany . . . . . 2·40 1·30
624 100f. Argentina (winners) . . 3·00 1·70

109 Kaaba, Mecca

1980. Pilgrimage to Mecca. Multicoloured.
625 25f. Type **109** 15 15
626 75f. Type **109** 50 35
627 160f. Pilgrims around the Kaaba . . . . 1·00 60
MS628 89 × 76 mm. No. 627 . . 4·25 4·25

110 Government Buildings, Sana'a

1980. 18th Anniv of Revolution. Multicoloured.
629 25f. Arm and cogwheel encircling flower and factories (vert) 25 15
630 75f. Type **110** 85 70
MS631 88 × 77 mm. 100f. Emblem (as No. 629) and Government buildings . . . . 2·50 2·20

111 Al-Rawdha Mosque

1980. 1400th Anniv of Hegira. Multicoloured.
632 25f. Type **111** 35 15
633 75f. Al-Aqsa Mosque . . . . 1·20 70
634 100f. Al-Nabawi Mosque . . 3·00 1·30
635 160f. Al-Haram Mosque . . 3·75 2·50
MS636 139 × 75 mm. 160f. Al-Nabawi, Al-Haram and Al-Aqsa Mosques (110 × 47 mm) . . . 6·50 6·00

112 Figure clothed in Palestinian Flag

1980. Int Day of Solidarity with Palestinian People.
637 **112** 25f. multicoloured 25 15
638 75f. multicoloured 85 60

113 Al-Aamiriya Mosque

1981. 9th Arab Archaeological Conf. Mult.
639 75f. Type **113** . . . . 1·00 50
640 125f. Al-Hadi Mosque . . . 1·40 70
MS641 82 × 117 mm. Nos. 639/40 2·50 2·20

114 Tower and Ramparts

1981. World Tourism Conf, Manila. Mult.
642 25f. Type **114** 15 15
643 75f. Mosque and houses . . 60 35
644 100f. Columns (horiz) 70 45
645 135f. Bridge 85 50
646 160f. View of Sana'a (horiz) 1·30 70
MS647 88 × 79 mm. No. 646 . . 4·25 4·00

115 Hill and U.P.U. Emblem

1981. Sir Roland Hill Commemoration. Mult.
648 25f. Type **115** (postage) . . . 1·30 60
649 30f. U.P.U. and A.P.U. emblems and Y.A.R. 4b. stamp of 1963 . . . . . . 1·50 85
650 50f. Hill, magnifying glass and stamps . . . . 2·20 1·30
651 75f. Hill and jet airliner circling globe (air) . . . . 3·50 2·20
652 100f. Hill, album and hand holding stamp with tweezers . . . . 4·75 2·50
653 150f. Air letter, jet airliner and Y.A.R. 160f. stamp of 1976 . . . . 8·75 4·00

1981. Nos. 551/5 surch.
654 **94** 125f. on 1f. multicoloured 2·30 1·20
655 150f. on 3f. multicoloured 2·50 1·50
656 325f. on 5f. multicoloured 6·00 3·50
657 350f. on 10f. multicoloured 7·00 3·75
658 375f. on 25f. multicoloured 7·50 4·25

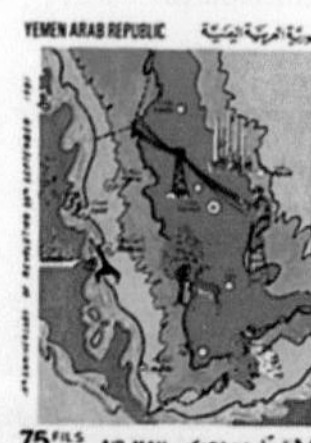

117 Map of Yemen

1982. Air. 19th Anniv (1981) of Revolution. Multicoloured.
659 75f. Type **117** . . . . 1·00 50
660 125f. Yemenis looking towards map within sun . . 1·60 85
661 325f. Sun, fist, dove with flags for wings and industrial scene . . . . . 4·75 3·00
662 400f. Air display . . . . . . 6·00 3·75
MS663 95 × 120 mm. No. 661 . . 12·00 11·50

118 Al-Hasan ibn Ahmed al-Hamadani

1982. Air. Birth Millenary of Al-Hasan ibn Ahmed al-Hamadani (philosopher).
664 **118** 125f. multicoloured . . . 1·70 95
665 325f. multicoloured . . . 4·25 2·30
MS666 111 × 90 mm. 375f. multicoloured . . . . 14·00 13·00
DESIGN—VERT: Portrait as in centre of T **118**.

119 Common Rabbits

1982. World Food Day. Multicoloured.
667 25f. Type **119** . . . . 1·40 60
668 50f. Cock and hens . . . . . 2·75 1·30
669 60f. Common turkeys . . . . 3·25 1·60
670 75f. Sheep . . . . 4·00 1·90
671 100f. Cow and calf . . . . . 5·25 2·30
672 125f. Red deer . . . . 5·75 2·75
MS673 Two sheets, each 138 × 118 mm. (a) 100f. Aubergines; 100f. Tomatoes; 100f. Beetroot and runner beans; 100f. Carrots and cauliflower. (b) 125f. Birds in garden; 125f. Pelicans by lake; 125f. Fish in basket by shore; 125f. Swans on lake . . . . . 30·00 30·00

120 Gymnast

1982. Air. Olympic Games, Moscow (1980). Multicoloured.
674 25f. Type **120** . . . . 1·40 60
675 50f. Pole vault . . . . 2·50 1·00
676 60f. Throwing the javelin . . 3·25 1·30
677 75f. Runner . . . . 4·00 1·60
678 100f. Basketball . . . . . . 5·25 2·30
679 125f. Football . . . . 5·75 2·75
MS680 Two sheets, each 139 × 118 mm. (a) 100f. Boxing; 100f. Wrestling; 100f. Canoeing; 100f. Swimming. (b) 125f. Weightlifting; 125f. Discus throwing; 125f. Long jumping; 125f. Fencing . . . . 19·00 19·00

121 Otto Lilienthal's Monoplane Glider and Satellite

1982. Air. Progress in Air Transport. Multicoloured.
681 25f. Type **121** . . . . 1·50 50
682 50f. Alberto Santos-Dumonts biplane "14 bis" . . . . . 2·20 80
683 60f. Biplane and satellite . . 2·75 85
684 75f. Early airplane and satellite . . . . 3·25 1·00
685 100f. De Havilland D.H.60G Gipsy Moth biplane and satellite . . . . 3·75 1·60

686 125f. Fokker F.VIIa/3m airplane and satellite . . . 5·25 2·20
MS687 Two sheets, each 138 × 117 mm. (a) 100f. Airplane and cylinder satellite; 100f. Early glider; 100f. Airship; 100f. Airplane and round satellite. (b) 125f. Airplane; 125f. Concorde and satellite with four "arms"; 125f. Concorde; 125f. Helicopter 19·00 19·00

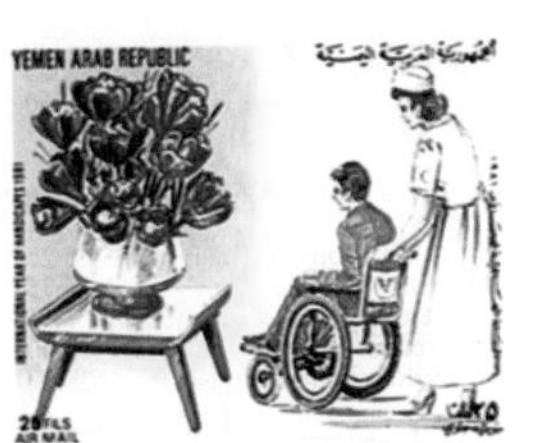

122 Crocuses and Nurse pushing Wheelchair

1982. Air. International Year of Disabled Persons (1981). Multicoloured.
688 25f. Type **122** . . . . 1·50 50
689 50f. Bowl of roses and nurse pushing wheelchair . . . . 1·70 95
690 60f. Bowl of pasque flowers and nurse pushing wheelchair . . . . 2·20 1·30
691 75f. Mixed flower arrangement and nurse pushing wheelchair . . . . 3·75 1·90
692 100f. Bowl of lilies and nurse pushing wheelchair . . . . 4·75 2·50
693 125f. Bowl of gladioli and nurse pushing wheelchair 5·75 2·75
MS694 Two sheets, each 139 × 117 mm. (a) 100f. IYDP emblem and carnation; 100f. IYDP emblem on globe; 100f. IYDP, World Health Organization and United Nations emblems and Yemeni flags; 100f. Nurse pushing trolley of presents. (b) 125f. Nurse and globe pierced with flags; 125f. UN and WHO emblems and lily; 125f. Wheelchair user and IYDP emblem; 125f. Nurse pushing trolley of presents . . . . . . 35·00 35·00

123 Aerials and Satellite circling Globe

1982. Air. Telecommunications Progress. Mult.
695 25f. Modern radio communications 70 45
696 50f. Type **123** . . . . 1·00 50
697 60f. Radio masts, watch and dish aerials . . . . 1·30 85
698 75f. Dish aerials and landscape . . . . 1·60 1·00
699 100f. Dish aerials, satellites and morse transmitter . . 1·90 1·30
700 125f. Aerials, jet airliner and globe . . . . 2·50 1·90
MS701 Two sheets, each 139 × 120 mm. (a) 100f. Dish aerials and satellite orbit; 100f. Cameraman, satellite orbit and television screen; 100f. Satellite orbit and telex operator; 100f. Urban building, telephone and satellite orbit. (b) 125f. Dish aerials, satellite and ship; 125f. Switchboard and dish aerials; 125f. Dish aerials and modes of transport; 125f. Radar operator and dish aerials . . . . 19·00 19·00

124 Oranges, "TB" and Cross of Lorraine

1982. Air. Centenary of Discovery of Tubercle Bacillus. Multicoloured.
702 25f. Type **124** 80 35
703 50f. Blossom, pears, cross of Lorraine and Robert Koch 1·20 50
704 60f. Pomegranates, flowers and cross of Lorraine . . . 1·50 70
705 75f. Roses, grapes and bacillus . . . . 1·70 95
706 100f. Cherries, blossom and microscope . . . . 2·30 1·10
707 125f. Lemons, cross of Lorraine and microscope 3·00 1·60
MS708 Two sheets, each 139 × 119 mm. (a) 100f. Strawberries and Robert Koch with microscope; 100f. Plums and Robert Koch with microscope; 100f. Apples and Robert Koch with microscope; 100f. Apricots and Robert Koch with microscope. (b) 125f. Roses, cross of Lorraine and Robert Koch; 125f. Dandelions, cross of Lorraine and Robert Koch; 125f. Blossom, cross of Lorraine and Robert Koch; 125f. Mimosa, cross of Lorraine and Robert Koch 26·00 26·00

125 Tackling

1982. Air. World Cup Football Championship, Spain. Multicoloured.
709 25f. Type **125** 60 25
710 50f. Marking the opposition 95 35
711 60f. Players with ball . . . . 1·40 60
712 75f. Scoring a goal . . . . . 1·60 80
713 100f. Dribbling . . . . . . 1·90 1·00
714 125f. Intercepting the ball . . 2·30 1·30
MS715 Two sheets, each 139 × 118 mm. (a) 75f. Marking the opposition; 75f. Players with goalkeeper; 75f. Dribbling; 75f. Tackling. (b) 75f. Tackling; 75f. Preparing to score; 75f. Intercepting the ball; 75f. Scoring a goal . . . . 17·00 17·00

126 Map, Boy with Flag, Tents and Dome of the Rock

1982. Air. Palestinian Children's Day. Multicoloured.
716 75f. Type **126** . . . . 1·90 95
717 125f. As Type **126** but girl with flag . . . . 3·00 1·90
718 325f. As Type **126** but boy and girl . . . . 7·00 3·75
MS719 120 × 90 mm. No. 718 . . 10·50 6·00

127 Map under Grid and Airplane

1982. Air. 30th Anniv of Arab Postal Union. Multicoloured.
720 75f. Type **127** . . . . 1·30 70
721 125f. Map under grid and ship . . . . 2·20 1·00
722 325f. Map under grid and emblem . . . . 5·75 2·30
MS723 120 × 90 mm. No. 722 . . 11·50 4·25

128 Passengers and Airliners

1983. 20th Anniv of Yemen Airways.
724 **128** 75f. multicoloured . . . . 1·50 85
725 125f. multicoloured . . . . 2·50 1·40
726 325f. multicoloured . . . 5·75 3·00

129 Man with Donkey and Foal

1983. Traditional Costumes. Multicoloured.
727 50f. Type **129** (postage) . . . 2·50 1·40
728 50f. Woman in embroidered veil carrying jug on head 2·50 1·40
729 50f. Shepherds in country . . 2·50 1·40
730 50f. Man walking through city and shepherds . . . . 2·50 1·40
731 75f. Women at well (horiz) (air) . . . . 4·00 2·20
732 75f. Woman sitting by shore (horiz) . . . . 4·00 2·20
733 75f. Man ploughing with camel (horiz) . . . . . . 4·00 2·20
734 75f. Man reading (horiz) . . . 4·00 2·20
MS735 Two sheets, each 119 × 93 mm. (a) 200f. Woman wearing silver jewellery (perf); 200f. Three-quarter length portrait of man (imperf) . . . . 21·00 21·00

130 Map of Yemen

1983. 20th Anniv (1982) of Revolution. Mult.
736 100f. Houses, airliner, telephone and dish aerial 1·90 1·00
737 150f. Literacy campaign emblem . . . . 2·50 1·60
738 325f. Tree and houses . . . . 6·00 3·50
739 400f. Type **130** . . . . . . 8·75 4·25

131 Emblem, Satellite, Dish Aerial and Telephone on Flag

1983. World Communications Year.
741 **131** 150f. multicoloured . . . 3·00 1·70
742 325f. multicoloured . . . 6·50 4·00
MS743 120 × 80 mm. No. 742 . . 11·50 6·50

132 Man at Window and Men planting Tree

1984. 21st Anniv (1983) of Revolution. Mult.
744 100f. Type **132** . . . . 2·50 1·20
745 150f. Fist and bust . . . . . 2·75 1·70
746 325f. Sun, tank and open gates . . . . 6·00 3·25
MS747 120 × 90 mm. No. 746 . . 12·00 6·50

133 Woman in Bombed Street

134 Profiles and Clasped Hands as Doves

1984. "Israeli Aggression against Lebanon".
748 **133** 150f. multicoloured . . . 2·50 1·30
749 325f. multicoloured . . . 7·00 4·00
MS750 90 × 120 mm. As No. 749 but larger. Imperf . . . . 12·00 7·50

1985. International Anti-apartheid Year (1978).
751 **134** 150f. multicoloured . . . 2·50 1·30
752 325f. multicoloured . . . 6·00 3·50
MS753 79 × 120 mm. No. 752 . . 12·00 6·00

135 Winged Figure and Globe

1985. 40th Anniv of I.C.A.O.
754 **135** 25f. multicoloured 45 15
755 50f. multicoloured 85 35
756 150f. multicoloured . . . 2·20 1·00
757 325f. multicoloured . . . 5·25 2·30
MS758 120 × 90 mm. No. 757 . . 12·00 6·00

136 Monument of Unknown Soldier

1985. 22nd Anniv (1984) of Revolution. Mult.
759 50f. Type **136** . . . . 1·10 50
760 150f. Reconstruction of Marem Dam . . . . . . 3·25 1·90
761 325f. Althawrah Sports Stadium . . . . 6·50 3·75
MS762 120 × 90 mm. No. 761 . . 12·00 6·00

137 Wrestling

1985. Air. Olympic Games, Los Angeles (1984). Multicoloured.
763 20f. Type **137** 45 25
764 30f. Boxing 50 35
765 40f. Running 70 50
766 60f. Hurdling 85 70
767 150f. Pole vaulting . . . . . 1·90 1·20
768 325f. Throwing the javelin . . 4·25 2·50
MS769 Two sheets, each 140 × 130 mm. (a) 75f. Gymnastics; 75f. Weightlifting; 75f. Putting the shot; 75f. Throwing the discus. (b) 75f. Diving; 75f. Swimming; 75f. Rowing; 75f. Canoeing . . . . 30·00 30·00

138 Emblem and Satellite over Globe

1986. 1st Anniv of "Arabsat" Communications Satellite.
770 **138** 150f. multicoloured . . . 3·50 1·70
771 325f. multicoloured . . . 7·00 3·50
MS772 120 × 90 mm. No. 771 . . 9·50 5·75

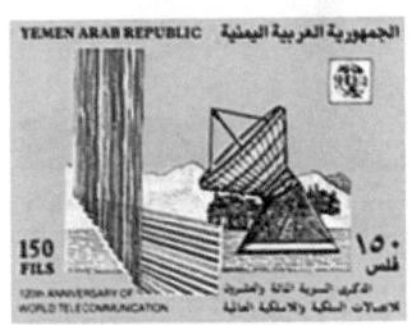

139 Dish Aerial and Cables

1986. 120th Anniv of World Telecommunications.
773 **139** 150f. multicoloured . . . 3·50 1·70
774 325f. multicoloured . . . 7·00 3·50
MS775 120 × 90 mm. No. 774 . . 8·25 5·75

140 Emblem

1986. 2nd Anniv of General People's Conference.
776 **140** 150f. multicoloured . . . 3·00 1·70
777 325f. multicoloured . . . 5·75 3·50
MS778 120 × 90 mm. No. 777 . . 7·00 5·75

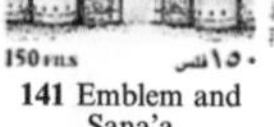

141 Emblem and Sana'a 142 Emblem and Dove

1986. 15th Islamic Foreign Ministers Conference, Sana'a (1984).
779 **141** 150f. multicoloured . . . 3·00 1·70
780 325f. multicoloured . . . 5·75 3·50
MS781 90 × 120 mm. No. 783 . . 7·00 5·75

1986. 40th Anniv of U.N.O.
782 **142** 150f. multicoloured . . . 3·00 1·70
783 325f. multicoloured . . . 5·75 3·50
MS784 90 × 120 mm. No. 783 . . 7·00 5·75

143 Members' Flags, Map and Emblem

1986. 39th Anniv (1984) of Arab League.
785 **143** 150f. multicoloured . . . 3·00 1·70
786 325f. multicoloured . . . 5·75 3·50

144 Anniversary Emblem

1987. 25th Anniv of Revolution.
787 **144** 100f. multicoloured . . . 1·00 35
788 150f. multicoloured . . . 1·50 80
789 425f. multicoloured . . . 4·25 2·75
790 450f. multicoloured . . . 4·75 2·75
MS791 90 × 70 mm. No. 789 . . 4·75 4·25

145 Dove, Emblems and Open Hands

1987. International Youth Year (1985).
792 **145** 150f. multicoloured . . . 3·00 1·30
793 425f. multicoloured . . . 5·75 3·00
MS794 90 × 70 mm. No. 793 . . 4·75 4·25

146 Burning Oil

1987. 3rd Anniv of Discovery of Oil in Yemen Arab Republic. Multicoloured.
795 150f. Type **146** . . . . . . 3·00 1·30
796 425f. Oil derrick and refinery 5·75 3·00
MS797 90 × 70 mm. 425f. No. 796 7·00 5·25

147 Numbers and Emblem

1987. General Population and Housing Census (1986).
798 **147** 150f. multicoloured . . . 3·00 1·30
799 425f. multicoloured . . . 5·75 4·00
MS800 90 × 70 mm. No. 799 . . 7·00 5·25

148 Footballers and Pique (mascot) 149 Skin Diving

1988. World Cup Football Championship, Mexico (1986). Multicoloured.
801 100f. Type **148** . . . . . . 1·30 60
802 150f. Goalkeeper saving ball 2·20 1·10
803 425f. Players and Pique (horiz) . . . . 5·25 2·50
MS804 90 × 70 mm. No. 803 . . 8·75 5·25

1988. 17th Scout Conference, Sana'a. Scout Activities. Multicoloured.
805 25f. Type **149** 35 15
806 30f. Table tennis 50 15
807 40f. Tennis 60 25
808 50f. Game with flag 80 35
809 60f. Volleyball 95 45
810 100f. Tug-of-war . . . . . . 1·60 70
811 150f. Basketball . . . . . . 2·20 1·00
812 425f. Archery . . . . 6·00 3·25
MS813 90 × 70 mm. 425f. Scout, emblem and salute (horiz) . . 7·00 5·25

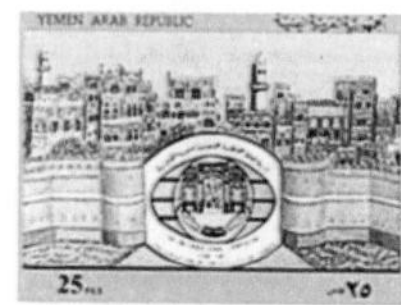

150 Old City

1988. Int Campaign for Preservation of Old Sana'a.
814 **150** 25f. multicoloured 35 15
815 50f. multicoloured 70 35
816 100f. multicoloured . . . 1·50 70
817 150f. multicoloured . . . 2·20 1·00
818 425f. multicoloured . . . 6·00 3·00
MS819 90 × 70 mm. No. 818 . . 6·50 5·25

151 Horseman

1988. 800th Anniv (1987) of Battle of Hattin.
820 **151** 150f. multicoloured . . . 2·50 1·70
821 425f. multicoloured . . . 9·50 4·25
MS822 90 × 70 mm. No. 821 . . 12·00 8·75

152 Building, Dish Aerial, Telephone and Emblem

1988. Arab Telecommunications Day (1987).
823 **152** 100f. multicoloured . . . 1·70 80
824 150f. multicoloured . . . 2·75 1·40
825 425f. multicoloured . . . 7·75 3·75
MS826 90 × 70 mm. No. 825 . . 10·50 8·75

153 Torch and Symbols of Development

1989. 26th Anniv (1988) of Revolution. Mult.
827 300f. Type **153** . . . . . . 1·70 70
828 375f. Type **153** . . . . . . 2·50 95
829 850f. Flag, Koran and symbols of agriculture and industry (vert) . . . . . . 5·25 1·90
830 900f. As No. 829 . . . . . . 5·25 2·20

154 Old and New Cities and Crowd

1989. 25th Anniv of 14th October Revolution. Multicoloured.
831 300f. Type **154** . . . . . . 1·70 70
832 375f. Type **154** . . . . . . 5·25 95
833 850f. City street and crowd (vert) . . . . 5·25 1·90
834 900f. As No. 833 (vert) . . . 5·25 2·20

155 Sports

1989. Olympic Games, Seoul (1988). Mult.
835 300f. Type **155** . . . . . . 1·90 70
836 375f. Football . . . . 2·50 95
837 850f. Football and judo (vert) 6·00 1·90
838 900f. Emblem and torch bearer . . . . 6·00 1·90
MS839 90 × 70 mm. As No. 836 but 37 × 27 mm . . . . 14·00 9·50

156 Flag, Couple and Fist

1989. Palestinian "Intifida" Movement. Multicoloured.
840 300f. Type **156** . . . . . . 1·70 70
841 375f. Soldier raising flag (vert) . . . . 2·50 95
842 850f. Dome of the Rock, youths and burning tyres 5·25 1·90
843 900f. Crowd of youths (vert) 5·25 2·20
MS844 70 × 90 mm. As No. 841 but 31 × 40 mm . . . . 14·00 9·50

157 Emblem

1990. 1st Anniv of Arab Co-operation Council.
845 **157** 300f. multicoloured . . . 1·70 70
846 375f. multicoloured . . . 2·50 95
847 850f. multicoloured . . . 5·25 1·90
848 900f. multicoloured . . . 5·25 2·20
MS849 90 × 70 mm. As No. 846 but 36 × 27 mm . . . . 14·00 9·50

158 Loading Tanker

1990. 1st Shipment of Oil. Multicoloured.
850 300f. Type **158** . . . . . . 1·70 70
851 375f. Type **158** . . . . . . 2·50 95
852 850f. Pipeline around globe and tanker . . . . 5·25 1·90
853 900f. As No. 852 . . . . . . 5·25 2·20
MS854 90 × 67 mm. No. 851 . . 14·00 9·50

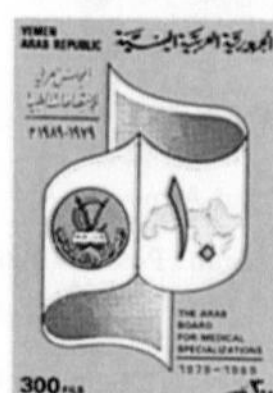

159 Emblem 160 Woman feeding Baby

1990. 10th Anniv (1989) of Arab Board for Medical Specializations.
855 **159** 300f. multicoloured . . . 1·40 70
856 375f. multicoloured . . . 1·70 85
857 850f. multicoloured . . . 3·75 1·70
858 900f. multicoloured . . . 4·00 1·90
MS859 70 × 90 mm. No. 856 . . 4·25 2·20

1990. Immunization Campaign. Multicoloured.
860 300f. Type **160** . . . . . . 1·70 70
861 375f. Type **160** . . . . . . 2·50 95
862 850f. Nurse weighing baby (horiz) . . . . 5·25 1·90
863 900f. As No. 862 . . . . . . 5·25 2·20
MS864 70 × 90 mm. As No. 861 but 26 × 37 mm . . . . 14·00 9·50

For further issues see **YEMEN REPUBLIC (combined)**.

POSTAGE DUE STAMPS

1964. Designs as Nos. 291, 295/6 (Animals), but inscr "POSTAGE DUE".
D298 4b. brown and green . . . 2·50 85
D299 12b. brown and orange . . 5·25 2·50
D300 20b. black and violet . . . 9·50 3·50
DESIGNS: 4b. Mountain gazelles; 12b. Bullock; 20b. Arab horses.

1964. Designs as Nos. 303/5, but inscr "POSTAGE DUE". Multicoloured.
D306 4b. Roses . . . . 2·50 85
D307 12b. Poinsettia . . . . . . 5·25 1·70
D308 20b. Viburnum . . . . . . 9·50 3·75

1966. Nos. 324/8 optd **POSTAGE DUE** in English and Arabic.
D371 6b. multicoloured . . . . . 5·25 3·50
D372 8b. multicoloured . . . . . 5·75 4·25
D373 12b. multicoloured . . . . 7·75 5·25
D374 20b. multicoloured . . . . 13·00 9·50
D375 1r. multicoloured . . . . . 28·00 19·00

1966. Designs as Nos. 410/12 (Football), but inscr "POSTAGE DUE".
D414 4b. multicoloured . . . . . 2·50 1·30
D415 5b. multicoloured . . . . . 4·25 3·00
D416 20b. multicoloured . . . . 8·75 6·00

1967. Designs as Nos. 465/7, but inscr "POSTAGE DUE" instead of "AIR MAIL". Multicoloured.
D468 – 6b. Bananas . . . . . . 1·70 85
D469 **73** 8b. Figs . . . . 3·50 1·70
D470 – 10b. Grapes . . . . . . 5·25 2·50

ROYALIST CIVIL WAR ISSUES

Fighting continued between the Royalists and Republicans until 1970. In 1970 Saudi Arabia recognised the Republican government as the rulers of Yemen, and the royalist position crumbled.

1962. Various issues optd. (i) Optd **FREE YEMEN FIGHTS FOR GOD, IMAM, COUNTRY** in English and Arabic.
R1 **19** 2b. red and black . . . . . 4·25 2·20
R3 4b. yellow and black . . . 4·25 2·20

(ii) Optd **FREE YEMEN FIGHTS FOR GOD, IMAM & COUNTRY** in English and Arabic. (a) Nos. 156/8.
R5 **24** 4b. multicoloured . . . . . 8·75 7·00
R6 6b. multicoloured . . . . . 8·75 7·00
R7 10b. multicoloured . . . . 10·50 8·75

(b) Nos. 159/60.
R8 **25** 4b. brown . . . . 31·00 26·00
R9 6b. green . . . . 31·00 26·00

(c) Nos. 161/2.
R10 4b. green . . . . 8·75 7·00
R11 6b. blue . . . . 8·75 7·00

(d) Nos. 167/8.
R12 4b. orange and black . . . . 3·50 3·50
R13 6b. green and brown . . . . 5·25 5·25

(e) Nos. 126/30.
R14 **19** 2b. red and black . . . .
R15 4b. yellow and black . . .
R16 6b. orange and black . . .
R17 8b. green and brown . . .
R18 20b. orange and violet
Set of 5 . . . . £130 £100

(f) Nos. 169/75.
R19 **20** 1b. violet . . . . 3·50 3·00
R20 2b. green . . . . 3·50 3·00
R21 3b. blue . . . . 7·00 5·25
R22 4b. blue . . . . 8·75 7·75
R23 6b. purple . . . . 14·00 11·50
R24 14b. red . . . . 17·00 15·00
R25 20b. brown . . . . 24·00 23·00

R 6 Five Ears of Wheat

1963. Air. Freedom from Hunger.
R26 **R 6** 4b. red, green and stone 1·70 1·70
R27 6b. red, green and blue 2·50 2·50

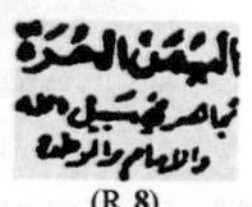

(R 7) (R 8)

1963. Captured Y.A.R. stamps variously optd. (a) No. 195 optd with Type **R 7**.
R28 4b. brown and mauve . . . 75·00 70·00

(b) No. 196 optd with Type **R 7** plus first line of Arabic inscr repeated at foot.
R29 6b. red and blue . . . . . . 75·00 70·00

(c) No. 196 optd with Types **R 7** and **R 8**.
R30 6b. red and blue . . . . . . 85·00 80·00

1963. Surch in figures with stars over old value, for use on circulars.
R31 R **6** 1b. on 4b. red, green and stone . . . . 3·25 3·50
R32 2b. on 6b. red, green and blue . . . . 3·25 3·50

R **10** Red Cross Field Post

1963. Red Cross Cent. Flags in red; inscr in black.
R33 R **10** ⅛b. violet (postage) . . . 85 70
R34 ¼b. mauve 85 70
R35 ½b. brown 85 70
R36 4b. green . . . . 1·30 1·20
R37 6b. blue (air) . . . . . 2·20 1·90
MSR37a 110 × 80 mm. Nos. R36/7. Imperf . . . . 16·00 16·00

R **11**

1963. Consular Fee stamp optd **YEMEN** in English and "POSTAGE 1383" (Moslem Year) in Arabic with bar over old inscr, as in Type R **11**.
R38 R **11** 10b. black and red . . £850 £850

R **12** Troops in Action

1964. Air. "The Patriotic War". Flags and emblem in red.
R39 R **12** ½b. green . . . . 1·00 85
R40 1b. black . . . . 1·00 85
R41 2b. purple . . . . . . 1·10 1·00
R42 4b. green . . . . 1·10 1·00
R43 6b. blue . . . . 2·30 1·40
MSR43a 112 × 90 mm. R **12** 24b. blue (57 × 37 mm). Imperf . . 17·00 13·00

1964. Air. Surch **AIR MAIL**, red cross, **1963–64 HONOURING BRITISH RED CROSS SURGICAL TEAM** and value and Arabic equivalent.
R44 R **12** 10b. on 4b. green . . . 7·00 6·00
R45 18b. on ½b. green . . . 10·50 9·50

1964. Air. Surch **AIR MAIL** and value in English and Arabic and airplane motif.
R46 R **10** 10b. on ⅛b. violet . . . 4·25 3·50
R47 18b. on ¼b. mauve . . . 7·00 6·00
R48 28b. on ½b. brown . . . 11·50 10·50

1964. Air. Surch **4 REVALUED** in English and Arabic with dotted frameline around stamp.
R49 R **12** 4b. on ½b. green . . . . 10·50 8·75
R50 4b. on 1b. black . . . . 10·50 8·75
R51 4b. on 2b. purple . . . 10·50 8·75

R **16** Olympic Flame and "Rings"

1964. Olympic Games, Tokyo.
R52 R **16** 2b. blue (postage) . . . 1·70 85
R53 4b. violet . . . . 3·00 2·50
R54 6b. brown (air) . . . . 4·00 3·50
MSR54a 102 × 80 mm. R **16** 4b. ultramarine (38 × 38 mm). Imperf 17·00 13·00

R **17** Rocket

1964. Astronauts.
R55 R **17** 2b. orange, violet and black (postage) . . . 2·50 2·50
R56 4b. brown, blue and black . . . . 3·50 3·50
R57 6b. yellow & black (air) 4·25 4·25
MSR57a 89 × 63 mm. R **17** 6b. blue and sepia (48 × 38 mm). Imperf 16·00 16·00

R **18** (½-size illustration)

1964. Consular Fee stamps optd across a pair as in Type R **18**.
R58 R **18** 10b. (5b.+5b.) purple £1100 £1100

Owing to a shortage of 10b. postage stamps, 5b. Consular Fee stamps were optd across pairs with **YEMEN** in English and "POSTAGE 1383" (Moslem Year) in Arabic, in frame, together with the Ministry of Communications' Royal Arms seal and a bar over old inscription at foot.

1965. Air. British Yemen Relief Committee. Nos. R 46/8 additionally optd **HONOURING BRITISH YEMEN RELIEF COMMITTEE 1963 1965** in English and Arabic.
R59 R **10** 10b. on ⅛b. violet . . . 4·25 4·25
R60 18b. on ¼b. mauve . . . 8·75 8·75
R61 28b. on ½b. brown . . . 10·50 10·50

R **20** Seif-al-Islam Ali

1965. Prince Seif-al-Islam Ali Commemoration.
R62 R **20** 4b. grey and red . . . 8·75 8·75

R **21** Kennedy as Young Man

1965. Pres. Kennedy Commemoration.
R63 R **21** ⅛b. black, mauve and gold (postage) 60 60
R64 – ¼b. violet, turq & gold 70 70
R65 – ½b. brown, blue and gold 85 85
R66 – 4b. brown, yell & gold 2·50 2·50
R67 – 6b. black, green and gold (air) . . . . . . 4·00 4·00
MSR67a 134 × 102 mm. 4b. multicoloured (Kennedy with family). Imperf . . . . 23·00 23·00
DESIGNS (Kennedy): ¼b. As naval officer; ½b. Sailing with Mrs. Kennedy; 4b. In rocking-chair; 6b. Full face portrait.

1965. Churchill Commemoration (1st issue). No. R62, with colours changed, optd **IN MEMORY OF SIR WINSTON CHURCHILL 1874-1965** in English and Arabic.
R68 R **20** 4b. blue and red . . . 13·00 13·00

R **23** Satellite and Emblems

1965. I.T.U. Centenary.
R69 R **23** 2b. yellow, violet and black (postage) . . . 3·00 3·00
R70 4b. red, blue and black 4·00 4·00
R71 6b. green, violet and black (air) . . . . . 5·75 5·75
MSR71a 90 × 65 mm. No. R70. Imperf . . . . 16·00 16·00

R **24** Hammerkop

1965. Birds. Multicoloured.
R72 ⅛b. Type R **24** (postage) . . 1·30 15
R73 ¼b. Yemeni linnet . . . . . 1·60 15
R74 ½b. Hoopoe . . . . 2·20 15
R75 4b. Arabian woodpecker . . 3·75 1·00
R76 6b. Violet starling (air) . . . 8·75 1·60
MSR76a 89 × 65 mm. No. R75. Imperf . . . . 26·00 26·00

R **25** Sir Winston Churchill and St. Paul's Cathedral

1965. Churchill Commem (2nd issue). Mult.
R77 ⅛b. Type R **25** 35 15
R78 ¼b. Churchill and Houses of Parliament 35 15
R79 ½b. Full-face portrait 45 15
R80 1b. Type R **25** . . . . . . 1·00 35
R81 2b. Churchill and Houses of Parliament . . . . 1·70 45
R82 4b. Full-face portrait . . . . 3·00 85
MSR82a 109 × 85 mm. 4b. red, blue and gold (Churchill seated and flags). Imperf . . . . 13·00 13·00

R **26** Iman Al-Badr

1965.
R83 R **26** 1b. black & bl (postage) 50 45
R83a 1½b. black and green 22·00 44·00
R84 – 2b. red and green . . . 1·30 85
R85 R **26** 4b. black and purple 1·70 1·30
R86 – 6b. red and violet (air) 2·30 1·70
R87 – 18b. red and brown . . 6·50 3·00
R88 – 24b. red and blue . . 10·50 4·25
DESIGNS—VERT: 2b., 18b. Royal arms. HORIZ: 6b., 24b. Flag.

1965. Space Flight of "Mariner 4". Nos. R55/7 optd **MARINER 4** in English and Arabic.
R89 R **17** 2b. orange, violet and black (postage) . . . 3·50 3·50
R90 4b. brown, blue & black 7·00 7·00
R91 6b. yellow & black (air) 10·50 10·50
MSR91a Sheet No. **MS**R57a optd as Nos. R89/91 . . . . 22·00 22·00

R **28** I.C.Y. Emblem, King Faisal of Saudi Arabia and Iman Al-Badr

1965. International Co-operation Year.
R92 R **28** 2b. blue and brown (postage) . . . . . 1·30 1·30
R93 4b. red and green . . . 2·20 2·20
R94 6b. brown and blue (air) 3·00 3·00
MSR94a 101 × 76 mm. No. R93 in new colours. Imperf . . . . . 10·50 8·50

1965. Space Flight of "Gemini 5". Nos. R69/71 optd **'GEMINI-V' GORDON COOPER & CHARLES CONRAD AUGUST 21-29, 1965** and space capsule.
R95 R **23** 2b. yellow, violet and black (postage) . . . 3·50 3·50
R96 4b. red, blue and black 7·00 7·00
R97 6b. green, violet and black (air) . . . . . 11·50 11·50
MSR98 Sheet No. **MS**R71a optd as Nos. R95/7 . . . . 65·00 £130

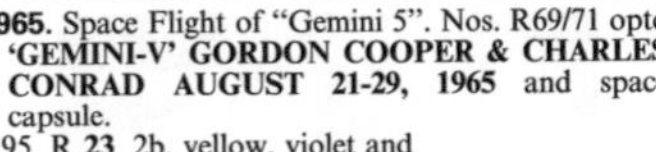

R **30** Black Persian

1965. Cats. Multicoloured.
R 99 ⅛b. Type R **30** 45 35
R100 ¼b. Tortoiseshell 45 35
R101 ½b. Sealpoint Siamese . . . 70 60
R102 1b. Silver tabby Persian . . 1·10 75
R103 2b. Cream Persian . . . . 2·20 1·20
R104 4b. Red tabby . . . . . . 4·00 3·00
MSR105 120 × 90 mm. 4b. multicoloured incorporating designs of Nos. R99/104. Imperf 16·00 16·00
Nos R102/4 are vert.

R **31** Red Saxifrage

1965. Flowers. Multicoloured.
R106 ⅛b. Verbena (vert) 35 10
R107 ¼b. Dianthus (vert) 45 15
R108 ½b. Dahlia (vert) 50 25
R109 1b. Nasturtium . . . . . . 1·00 50
R110 2b. Type R **31** . . . . . . 2·20 70
R111 4b. Wild rose . . . . . . 4·25 85
MSR112 102 × 76 mm. No. R111. Imperf . . . . 19·00 19·00

R **32** Flag and Globe

1965. Pope Paul's Visit to U.N. Organization.
R113 R **32** 2b. red, black and green . . . . 2·20 1·70
R114 4b. red, black and violet . . . . 3·50 3·00
R115 6b. red, black and blue 4·00 3·50
MSR116 177 × 127 mm. Nos. R113/15. Imperf . . . . 13·00 13·00

R **33** Moon Landing

1965. Space Achievements. Multicoloured.
(a) Postage. (i) Size as Type R **33**.
R117 ⅛b. Type R **33** 35 15
R118 ¼b. Astronauts on Moon 45 15
R119 ½b. Pres. Kennedy and Cape Kennedy (vert) . . . 50 15
(ii) Size 48 × 28 mm.
R120 4b. Belyaev and Leonov in space . . . . 3·50 70
(b) Air. Size 48 × 28 mm.
R121 6b. White and Mcdivitt in space . . . . 5·75 1·00
MSR122 114 × 84 mm. 4b. multicoloured incorporating designs of Nos. R119/21. Imperf 22·00 22·00

R 34 Football and Gold Medal

1965. Winners of Olympic Games, Tokyo (1964). Each design showing a sport with a gold medal. Multicoloured.
R123 ⅛b. Type R **34** (postage) . . 35 15
R124 ¼b. Running 45 15
R125 ½b. Throwing the discus . . 50 15
R126 2b. Judo . . . . 2·20 35
R127 4b. Wrestling . . . . 3·00 70

R128 6b. Horse-jumping (air) . . 4·00 1·00
MSR129 101 × 77 mm. 4b. multicoloured (design adapted from No. R128). Imperf . . . 12·00 12·00

R 35 Arms

1966. Air. Size varies. Imperf.
R130 R **35** 10b. red on white . . .
R131 10b. violet on white . .
R132 10b. red on yellow . .
R133 10b. violet on orange
R134 10b. violet on mauve
These handstamps were also applied directly to envelopes and aerogrammes.

R 36 Nehru

1966. Builders of World Peace (1st series). Portraits in gold and black; inscr in black.
R136 R **36** ⅛b. green 35 15
R137 – ¼b. brown 35 15
R138 – ½b. grey 35 15
R139 – 1b. blue . . . . . . 1·60 60
R140 – 4b. green . . . . . . 2·50 1·00
MSR141 120 × 100 mm. 4b. black, gold and grey (incorporating portraits of Nos. R136/40). Imperf 13·00 13·00
DESIGNS: ¼b. Dag Hammarskjold; ½b. Pope John XXIII; 1b. Sir Winston Churchill; 4b. Pres. Kennedy.
See also Nos. R146/51.

1966. Nos. R63/5 and R67 surch with new values in English and Arabic.
R142 R **21** 4b. on ⅛b. black, mauve and gold (postage) 85 85
R143 – 8b. on ¼b. violet, turquoise and gold 1·70 1·70
R144 – 10b. on ½b. brown, blue and gold . . . 2·50 2·50

R145 – 1r. on 6b. black, green and gold (air) . . . 7·75 7·75

1966. Builders of World Peace (2nd series). As Type R **36**. Portraits in black and gold; inscr in black.
R146 ⅛b. yellow 15 10
R147 ¼b. pink 15 10
R148 ½b. mauve 15 15
R149 1b. blue . . . . 1·30 50
R150 1b. green . . . . 1·30 50
R151 4b. green . . . . 3·50 1·30
MSR152 120 × 100 mm. 4b. black, gold and buff (incorporating portraits of Nos. R146/9 and R151). Imperf . . . . 10·50 10·50
PORTRAITS: ⅛b. Pres. Lubke; ¼b. Pres. De Gaulle; ½b. Pope Paul VI; 1b. (R149) Pres. Johnson; 1b. (R150) King Faisal of Saudi Arabia; 4b. U Thant.

1966. Newspaper Stamps. Optd **PERIODICALS** in English and Arabic in frame. (a) Similar to Nos. R26/7, but imperf.
R153 R **6** 4b. red, green and stone 17·00 22·00
R154 6b. red, green and blue 17·00 22·00

(b) Unissued 1963 Red Cross Centenary issue (Nos. R26/7 surch).
R155 R **6** 1b. on 4b. red, green and stone . . . . . 22·00 26·00
R156 2b. on 6b. red, green and blue . . . . . 35·00 39·00

Miniature Sheet. Unissued 1963 Red Cross issue No. **MS**27a optd as Nos. R154/4, but larger 36 × 15 mm in Arabic only on 4b. and in English only on 6b.
MSR157 107 × 80 mm. Imperf . . 60·00 85·00
The overprint on **MS**R157 reads "**RED GRESCENT**" instead of "**RED CRESCENT**" and for this reason it was not issued originally in 1963.

(R 39)

1966. Air. Olympic Games Preparation, Mexico (1968). Nos. R123/5 in new colours and **MS**R129 surch as Type R **39**.
R158 12b. on ⅛b. multicoloured 5·25 7·50
R159 28b. on ¼b. multicoloured 7·75 7·75
R160 34b. on ½b. multicoloured 8·75 8·75
MSR161 101 × 77 mm. No. **MS**R129 optd as Type R **39** but without surch or "AIR MAIL" etc . . 22·00 22·00

R 40 Yemeni Cannon

1966. Shaharah Fortress. Frame and stars in red.
R162 R **40** ½b. bistre (postage) . . 45 45
R163 – 1b. grey 85 85
R164 – 1½b. blue . . . . 1·30 1·30
R165 – 2b. brown . . . . 1·70 1·70
R166 – 4b. green . . . . 2·20 2·20

R167 – 6b. violet (air) . . . . 2·50 2·50
R168 – 10b. black . . . . 4·00 4·00
MSR169 114 × 88 mm. 10b. green. Imperf . . . . 10·50 10·50
DESIGNS—VERT: 1b. Bombed Mosque; 2b. Victory Gate; 4b. Yemeni cannon (different); 10b. Bombed houses. HORIZ: 1½b. Shaharah Fortress; 6b. Yemeni cannon (different); 10b. (**MS**R169), Type R**40**.

1966. Nos. R33/5 surch **4B REVALUED** in English and Arabic within border of stars. Flags red; inscr in black.
R170 R **10** 4b. on ⅛b. violet . . . 85·00 85·00
R171 4b. on ¼b. mauve . . . 85·00 85·00
R172 4b. on ½b. brown . . . 85·00 85·00

R 42 President Kennedy

1967. 3rd Anniv of Pres. Kennedy's Death and Inauguration of Arlington Grave.
R173 R **42** 12b. multicoloured . . 1·30 45
R174 28b. multicoloured . . 3·00 70
R175 34b. multicoloured . . 4·25 1·00
MSR176 115 × 77 mm. 24b. multicoloured (Arlington Grave and scrolls). Imperf . . . . . 6·50 6·50

1967. England's Victory in World Cup Football Championship (1966). Nos. R123/8 optd **WORLD CHAMPIONSHIP-CUP ENGLAND 1966** in English and Arabic, **ENGLAND WINNER** in English only and World Cup emblem.
R177 R **34** ⅛b. mult (postage) . . 50 50
R178 – ¼b. multicoloured . . . 35 35
R179 – ½b. multicoloured . . . 50 50
R180 – 2b. multicoloured . . . 1·70 1·70
R181 – 4b. multicoloured . . . 3·00 3·00

R182 – 6b. multicoloured (air) 4·25 4·25

1967. Surch **4B REVALUED** in English and Arabic within border of stars. (a) Nos. R123/5.
R183 R **34** 4b. on ⅛b. mult . . . .
R184 – 4b. on ¼b. mult . . .
R185 – 4b. on ½b. mult . . .

(b) Nos. R177/9.
R186 R **34** 4b. on ⅛b. mult . . . .
R187 – 4b. on ¼b. mult . . .
R188 – 4b. on ½b. mult . . .

R 44 Bazooka

1967. Freedom Fighters. Designs showing Freedom Fighters with various weapons. Multicoloured.
R189 4b. Type R **44** . . . . . . 1·30 45
R190 4b. Fighter in fez with rifle 1·30 45
R191 4b. Bare-headed man with rifle . . . . 1·30 45
R192 4b. Fighters holding bazooka and round . . . 1·30 45
R193 4b. Anti-aircraft gun . . . 1·30 45
R194 4b. Heavy machine-gun . . 1·30 45
R195 4b. Light machine-gun . . 1·30 45
R196 4b. Fighter with bazooka on mount and rifle . . . 1·30 45
MSR197 114 × 77 mm. No. R196 (sold at 10b.) . . . . 6·50 4·25

R 45 Rembrandt—Self-portrait

1967. "AMPHILEX" Stamp Exhibition, Amsterdam. Rembrandt Paintings. Multicoloured. (a) Borders in gold.
R198 2b. "An Elderly Man as St. Paul" 25 15
R199 4b. Type R **45** 35 15
R200 6b. "Portrait of Jacob Trip" 50 15
R201 10b. "An Old Man in an Armchair" 70 35
R202 12b. Self-portrait (different) 1·00 45
R203 20b. "A Woman Bathing" 1·60 45
MSR204 177 × 150 mm. Nos. R198/203 . . . . 7·75 3·00

(b) Borders in silver.
R205 2b. As No. R198 . . . . . 35 15
R206 4b. Type R **45** 50 15
R207 6b. As No. R200 . . . . . 70 15
R208 10b. As No. R201 . . . . 85 35
R209 12b. As No. R202 . . . . 1·60 45
R210 20b. As No. R203 . . . . 2·50 45
MSR211 177 × 150 mm. Nos. R205/10 . . . . 7·75 3·00

1967. Pres. Kennedy's 50th Birth Anniv. Nos. R173/5 optd **50th. ann. 29 MAY** in English only.
R212 R **42** 12b. multicoloured . . 1·30 45
R213 28b. multicoloured . . 3·00 70
R214 34b. multicoloured . . 4·25 1·00
MSR215 115 × 77 mm. 24b. multicoloured. Imperf . . . . 6·50 6·50

R 47 Triggerfish

1967. Red Sea Fish. Multicoloured.
R216 ⅛b. Type R **47** (postage) . . 80 35
R217 ¼b. Striped rudderfish . . . 80 35
R218 ½b. Hooded butterflyfish . . 80 35
R219 1b. Spotted coral grouper 95 35
R220 4b. Lionfish . . . . 1·10 35
R221 6b. Brown anemonefish . . 1·50 35
R222 10b. Violet-hued berycid . . 2·40 35

R224 12b. As No. R222 (air) . . 85 10
R225 14b. Cuckoo wrasse . . . . 1·00 10
R226 16b. Japanese bonyhead . . 1·20 15
R227 18b. As No. R221 . . . . 1·40 25
R228 24b. As No. R220 . . . . 1·60 35
R229 34b. As No. R219 . . . . 1·90 50
MSR223 147 × 109 mm. 10b. Butterflyfish . . . . 5·75 4·25
Nos. R216/22 are Type R **47**; Nos. R224/9 are larger, size 58 × 42 mm.

R 48 "The Gipsy Girl" (Frans Hals)

1967. Air. Famous Paintings. Multicoloured.
R230 8b. Type R **48** 45 15
R231 10b. "The Zouave" (Van Gogh) 60 15
R232 12b. Self-portrait (Rubens) 80 25
R233 14b. "Boys Eating Melon" (Murilio) 95 25
R234 16b. "The Knight's Dream" (Raphael) . . . . 1·20 25
R235 20b. "St. George and the Dragon" (Ucello) (horiz) 1·30 35

1967. "For Poison Gas Victims". Surch **FOR POISON GAS VICTIMS** and surcharge in English and Arabic, with skull and crossbones within frame.
R236 R **40** ½b.+1b. (No. R162) (postage) . . . . .
R237 – 1b.+1b. (R163) . . . .
R238 – 1½b.+1b. (R164) . . .
R239 – 2b.+1b. (R84) . . . .
R240 – 2b.+1b. (R126) . . . .
R241 – 2b.+1b. (R165) . . . .
R242 R **20** 4b.+2b. (R62) . . . .
R243 – 4b.+2b. (R66) . . . .
R244 R **20** 4b.+2b. (R68) . . . .
R245 R **26** 4b.+2b. (R85) . . . .
R246 R **34** 4b.+2b. (R93) . . . .
R247 – 4b.+2b. (R127) . . . .
R248 – 4b.+2b. (R166) . . . .

R249 – 6b.+3b. (R86) (air) . .
R250 – 6b.+3b. (R128) . . . .
R251 – 6b.+3b. (R167) . . . .
R252 R **35** 10b.+5b. (R130) . . .
R253 – 10b.+5b. (R168) . . .
R254 R **32** 12b.+6b. (R158) . . .
R255 – 18b.+9b. (R87) . . . .
R256 R **12** 24b.+12b. red and blue (imperf, size 57 × 36 mm) . . . .
R257 – 24b.+12b. (R88) . . .
R258 – 28b.+14b. (R159) . . .
R259 – 34b.+17b. (R160) . . .
MSR260 24b.+12b. (**MS**R43a) 31·00 31·00
The amount of surcharge was 50 per cent of the face value of each stamp (except Nos. R236/8 where the surcharge was 1b. each). Some higher values have two handstamps, which, when added together, make up the 50 per cent.

1967. Jordan Relief Fund. Surch **JORDAN RELIEF FUND** and value in English and Arabic with Crown. (a) No. R66 (Kennedy).
R261 – 4b.+2b. brown, yellow and gold . . . . 7·00 7·00

(b) Nos. R75/6 (Birds).
R262 – 4b.+2b. mult (postage) . . 3·50 3·50

R263 – 6b.+3b. mult (air) . . . . 5·25 5·25
MSR264 4b.+2b. . . . . 8·75 8·75

(c) Nos. R92/4 (I.C.Y.).
R265 R **34** 2b.+1b. blue and brown (postage) . . 85 85
R266 4b.+2b. red and green 1·30 1·30

R267 6b.+3b. brown and blue (air) . . . . . 1·70 1·70
MSR268 4b.+2b. . . . . 8·75 8·75

(d) Nos. R102/4 (Cats).
R269 – 1b.+1b. multicoloured . . 1·30 1·30
R270 – 2b.+1b. multicoloured . . 1·70 1·70
R271 – 4b.+2b. multicoloured . . 3·00 3·00
MSR272 4b.+2b. . . . . 8·75 8·75

(e) R109/11 (Flowers).
R273 – 1b.+1b. multicoloured 1·30 1·30
R274 R **30** 2b.+1b. multicoloured 1·70 1·70
R275 – 4b.+2b. multicoloured 2·20 2·20
MSR276 4b.+2b. 10·50 10·50

(f) Nos. R136/40 (Builders of World Peace).
R277 R **36** ⅛b.+1b. gold, black and green 85 85
R278 – ¼b.+1b. gold, black and brown . . . . 1·30 1·30
R279 – ½b.+1b. gold, black and grey . . . . 1·30 1·30
R280 – 1b.+1b. gold, black and blue . . . . 1·30 1·30
R281 – 4b.+2b. gold, black and green . . . . 2·50 2·50
MSR282 4b.+2b. 35·00

(g) Nos. R146/51 (Builders of World Peace).
R283 – ⅛b.+1b. gold, black and yellow 85 85
R284 – ¼b.+1b. gold, black and pink 85 85
R285 – ½b.+1b. gold, black and mauve 85 85
R286 – 1b.+1b. gold, black and blue . . . . 1·70 1·70
R287 – 1b.+1b. gold, black and green 85 85

R288 –	4b.+2b. gold, black and green	4·25	4·25
MSR289	4b.+2b.	17·00	17·00

R 51 "The Pharmacy"

1967. Air. Paintings. Multicoloured. (a) Asiatic Paintings.

R290	⅛b. "Mountains and Forests" (Wang Hwei)	15	15
R291	¼b. "Tiger" (Sim Sajoug)	15	15
R292	½b. "Mountain Views" (Tong K'itch'ang)	25	20
R293	¾b. "Rama Lakshama and Shiva" (Indian 16th century)	25	20
R294	1b. "Ladies" (T. Kiyomitsu)	35	25
	(b) Arab Paintings.		
R295	1½b. "Bayad plays the Oud and sings"	45	35
R296	2b. Type R **51**	50	45
R297	3b. "Dioscorides and a Student"	60	50
R298	4b. "The Scribe"	85	70
R299	6b. "Abu Zayd asks to be taken over by boat"	1·30	80
MSR300	90 × 72 mm. No. R299. Imperf	5·25	5·25

The ⅛, 1½, 2 and 6b. are horiz and the remainder vert.

R 52 Bugler

1967. World Scout Jamboree, Idaho. Mult.

R301	¼b. Type R **52** (postage)	10	10
R302	½b. Campfire	10	10
R303	4b. Type R **52**	50	10
R304	6b. As ½b.	85	25
R305	⅛b. Scout badge and Yemeni flag (air)	15	10
R306	10b. As ⅛b.	1·30	45
R307	20b. Scout and satellite	2·50	70
MSR308	72 × 99 mm. No. R307 but larger. Imperf	5·25	5·25

1967. Jordan Refugees Relief Fund. Surch **JORDAN REFUGEES RELIEF FUND** and value in English and Arabic, and Refugee Emblem. (a) Nos. R52/4 (Olympic Games).

R309	R **16**	2b.+2b. bl (postage)	85	85
R310		4b.+4b. violet	1·70	1·70
R311		6d.+6d. brown (air)	2·50	2·50
MSR312		4b.+2b.	10·50	10·50
		(b) Nos. R55/7 (Astronauts).		
R313	R **17**	2b.+2b. brown, violet and black (postage)	85	85
R314		4b.+4b. brown, blue and black	1·70	1·70
R315		6b.+6b. yellow and black (air)	2·50	2·50
MSR316		6b.+6b.	10·50	10·50
		(c) Nos. R63/7 (Kennedy).		
R317	R **21**	⅛b.+⅛b. black, mauve and gold (postage)	15	15
R318	–	¼b.+¼b. violet, turquoise and gold	35	35
R319	–	½b.+½b. brown, blue and gold	70	70
R320	–	4b.+4b. brown, yellow and gold	3·50	3·50
R321	–	6b.+6b. black, green and gold (air)	6·00	6·00
MSR322		4b.+4b.	13·00	
		(d) No. R68 (Churchill opt).		
R323	R **20**	4b.+4b. blue and red	13·00	13·00
		(e) R69/71 (I.T.U.).		
R324	R **23**	2b.+2b. yellow, violet and black (postage)	85	1·90
R325		4b.+4b. red, blue and black	1·70	3·50
R326		6b.+6b. green, violet and black (air)	2·50	7·50
MSR327		4b.+4b.	26·00	26·00
		(f) R77/82 (Churchill).		
R328	R **25**	⅛b.+⅛b. multicoloured	10	10
R329	–	¼b.+¼b. multicoloured	35	35
R330	–	½b.+½b. multicoloured	50	50
R331	R **25**	1b.+1b. multicoloured	85	85
R332	–	2b.+2b. multicoloured	1·70	1·70
R333	–	4b.+4b. multicoloured	3·00	3·00
MSR334		4b.+4b.	13·00	13·00

R 54 Vaquero

1967. Olympic Games, Mexico (1968). Multicoloured.

R335	⅛b. Type R **54** (postage)	10	10
R336	¼b. Fishermen on Lake Patzcuaro	10	10
R337	½b. Football (vert)	10	10
R338	4b. Avenida de la Reforma, Mexico City	45	15
R339	8b. Fine Arts Theatre, Mexico City	70	25
R340	12b. Mayan ruins (air)	85	35
R341	16b. Type R **54**	1·30	45
R342	20b. As ¼b.	1·70	50
MSR343	97 × 70 mm. 16b. As Type R **54**, but larger and without flag. Imperf	7·00	7·00

R 55 Battle Scene

1967. Moorish Art in Spain. Multicoloured.

R344	2b. Moor slaying knight (horiz) (postage)	15	10
R345	4b. Arab kings of Granada (horiz)	35	10
R346	6b. Diagram of chess game (from King Alfonso X's "Book of Chess, Dice and Tablings") (horiz)	50	10
R347	10b. Type R **55**	85	10
R348	12b. Moors with prisoners	1·00	10
R349	20b. Meeting of Moor and Christian (air)	1·40	15
R350	22b. Bullfight	1·70	25
R351	24b. Lute players	1·90	45
MSR352	106 × 80 mm. 28b. black, red and light blue (interior of Alhambra, Granada and treasures). Imperf	5·25	2·20

APPENDIX

The following stamps have either been issued in excess of postal needs or have not been available to the public in reasonable quantities at face value. Such stamps may later be given full listing if there is evidence of regular postal use.

REPUBLIC

1967.

5th Anniv of Revolution Nos. 476/81 optd in Arabic 1, 2, 4, 6, 8, 10b.

Paintings by Flemish Masters. Postage ¼, ⅓, ½b.; Air 3, 6b.

Paintings by Florentine Masters. Postage ¼, ⅓, ½b.; Air 3, 6b.

Paintings by Spanish Masters. Postage ¼, ⅓, ½b.; Air 3, 6b.

Winter Olympic Games, Grenoble (1968) (1st issue). Embossed on gold foil. Air 5, 10, 15, 50b.

Winter Olympic Games, Grenoble (1968) (2nd issue). Sports ¼, ⅓, ½, 3, 6b.

Chancellor Adenauer Commemoration (1st issue). Embossed on gold foil. Air 50b.

1968.

Yemen Red Crescent. Embossed on gold foil. Air 5, 10, 15, 50b.

Paintings by Gauguin. Postage ¼, ¼, ⅓, ⅓, ½, ½b.; Air 3, 3, 6, 6b.

Paintings by Van Gogh. Postage ¼, ¼, ⅓, ⅓, ½, ½b.; Air 3, 3, 6, 6b.

Paintings by Rubens. Postage ¼, ¼, ⅓, ⅓, ½, ½b.; Air 3, 3, 6, 6b.

Provisionals. Various 1930/31 values optd "Y.A.R." and date in English and Arabic. ½, 1, 1, 2, 2, 3, 4, 4, 5, 6, 6, 10, 10, 20b., 1, 1i.

Gold Medal Winners. Winter Olympic Games, Grenoble (1st issue). 1967 Winter Olympic Games (1st issue) optd with names of various winners. Air 50b. × 4.

1st Death Anniv of Vladimir Komarov (Russian cosmonaut). Air 5, 10, 15, 50b.

International Human Rights Year and U Thant Commemoration. Embossed on gold foil. Air 5, 10, 15, 50b.

Chancellor Adenauer Commemoration (2nd issue). Air 5, 10, 15b.

Refugee Relief. Adenauer (2nd issue) optd in Arabic only. Air 5, 10, 15, 50b.

Olympic Games, Mexico (1st issue). Chariot-racing. Embossed on gold foil. Air 5, 10, 15, 50b.

Paintings of Horses. Postage ¼, ⅓, ½b.; Air 3, 6b.

Paintings by Raphael. Postage ¼, ⅓, ½b.; Air 3, 6b.

Paintings by Rembrandt. Postage ¼, ⅓, ½b.; Air 3, 6b.

Dr. Martin Luther King Commemoration (1st issue). Human Rights issue optd. Air 50b.

Gold Medal Winners. Winter Olympic Games, Grenoble (2nd issue). Postage ¼, ⅓, ½, 2b.; Air 3, 4b.

Olympic Games, Mexico (2nd issue). Greek and Mexican Folklore. Postage ¼, ⅓, ½, 2b.; Air 3, 4b.

Gold Medal Winners, Olympic Games, Mexico (1st issue). Mexico Olympics (1st issue) optd with names of various winners. Air 50b. × 4.

Gold Medal Winners Olympic Games, Mexico (2nd issue). Postage ¼, ⅓, ½, 2b.; Air 3, 4b.

Dr. Martin Luther King Commemoration (2nd issue). Embossed on gold foil. 16b.

Emblems of Winter Olympic Games. Postage ¼, ⅓, ½, 2b.; Air 3, 4b.

Emblems of Olympic Games. Postage ¼, ⅓, ½, 2b.; Air 3, 4b.

Dag Hammarskjold and Kennedy Brothers Commemoration. ½, 2, 6, 14b.

Dr. Christian Barnard's Heart Transplant Operations. ¼, ¾, 8, 10b.

Dr. Martin Luther King Commemoration (3rd issue). 1, 4, 12, 16b.

John and Robert Kennedy Commemoration. Embossed on gold foil. 10b.

1969.

Paintings from the Louvre, Paris. Postage ¼, ⅓, ½, 2b.; Air 3, 4b.

1st Death Anniv of Yurstet Gagarin (Russian cosmonaut). Optd on 1968 Komarov issue. Air 50b.

Paintings from the Uffizi Gallery, Florence. Postage ¼, ⅓, ½, 2b.; Air 3, 4b.

Paintings from the Prado, Madrid. Postage ¼, ⅓, ½, 2b.; Air 3b, 4b.

Birth Bicentenary of Napoleon (1st issue). Embossed on gold foil. Air 4b.

Space Exploration (1st series). Inscr "DISCOVERIES OF UNIVERSE". Postage ¼, ¼, ⅓, ⅓b.; Air 3, 6, 10b.

Space Exploration (2nd series). Inscr "FLIGHTS TO THE PLANETS". Postage ¼, ¼, ⅓, ⅓ b.; Air 2, 4, 22b.

First Man on the Moon. Embossed on gold foil. Air 10b.

50th Anniv of International Labour Organization. Postage 1, 2, 3, 4b.; Air 6, 8, 10b.

Space Exploration (3rd series). Inscr "MAN IN SPACE". Postage ¼, ¼, ⅓, ⅓b.; Air 3, 6, 10b.

Birth Bicentenary of Napoleon (2nd issue). Postage ¼, ⅓, ½, ¾b.; Air 4, 8, 10b.

Space Exploration (4th series). "Apollo" Moon Flights. Postage ¼, ¼, ⅓, ⅓b.; Air 2, 4, 22b.

Winter Olympic Games, Sapporo (1972) Preparation. Optd on 1967 Grenoble Winter Olympics issue. Air 50b.

Olympic Games, Munich (1972) Preparation. Optd on 1968 Mexico Olympics issue. Air 50b.

Paintings from the National Gallery, Washington. Postage ¼, ⅓, ½, 2b.; Air 3, 4b.

Paintings from the National Gallery, London. Postage ¼, ⅓, ½, 2b.; Air 3, 4b.

French Monarchs and Statesmen. Postage 1¾, 2, 2¼, 2½b.; Air 3½, 5, 6b.

1970.

Tutankhamun Exhibition, Paris. Postage ¼, ⅓, ½, 2b.; Air 3, 4b.

Siamese Sculptures. Postage ¼, ⅓, ½, 2b.; Air 3, 4b.

"EXPO 70" World Fair, Osaka, Japan (1st issue). Japanese Paintings. Postage ¼, ⅓, ½, 2b.; Air 3, 4b.

EXPO 70" World Fair, Osaka, Japan (2nd issue). Japanese Puppets. Postage ¼, ⅓, ½, 2b.; Air 3, 4b.

World Cup Football Championship, Mexico (1st issue). Views and Maps. Postage 1¾, 2, 2¼, 2½b.; Air 3½, 5, 6, 7, 8b.

World Cup Football Championship, Mexico (2nd issue). Jules Rimet. Embossed on gold foil. Air 10b.

"United Europe". Postage 1⅓, 1¾, 2¼, 2½, 5b.; Air 7, 8, 10b.

25th Anniv of Victory in Second World War. Gen. de Gaulle. Embossed on gold foil. Air 6b.

Moon Mission of "Apollo 12". Postage 1, 1¼, 1⅓, 1½b.; Air 4, 4½, 7b.

World Cup Football Championship, Mexico (3rd issue). Teams. Postage ¼, ⅓, ½, ¾b.; Air 4, 4½b.

World Cup Football Championship, Mexico (4th issue). Beckenbauer and Pele. Embossed on gold foil. Air 10b.

World Cup Football Championship, Mexico (5th issue). Footballers and Mexican Antiquities. Postage 1, 1¼, 1⅓, 1½b.; Air 3, 10b.

Interplanetary Space Travel. Postage 1¾, 2, 2¼, 2½b.; Air 5, 8, 10, 22b.

Inaug of New U.P.U. Headquarters Building, Berne. Postage ⅓, 1¼, 1½, 2b.; Air 3½, 4½, 6b.

"Philympia 70" Stamp Exhibition, London. Postage ¼, ½, 1, 3b.; Air 4b.

8th Anniv of Revolution. Flowers. ¼b. × 5.

Olympic Games, Munich (1972) (1st issue). Buildings. Postage 1, 1¾, 2½, 3, 3½b.; Air 8, 10b.

Olympic Games, Munich (2nd issue). Statue. Embossed on gold foil. Air 6b.

25th Anniv of United Nations. Human Rights Year issue of 1968 optd. Air 50b.

Winter Olympic Games, Sapporo (1st issue). Buildings and Emblem. Postage 1½, 2½, 4½, 5, 7b.; Air 8, 10b.

Winter Olympic Games, Sapporo (2nd issue). Snow Sculpture. Embossed on gold foil. Air 40b.

General Charles de Gaulle Commemoration. 1970 25th Anniv of Victory issue optd. Air 6b.

German Gold Medal Winners in Olympic Games. Postage ¼, ¼, ⅓, ⅓b. Air 6b.

1971.

Pres. Gamal Nasser of Egypt Commemoration. Postage ¼b. × 4, ½b. × 2; Air 1, 2, 5, 7, 10, 16b.

International Sporting Events. Postage ¼, ⅓, ½, 2b.; Air 3, 4b.

Olympic Games, Munich (3rd issue). Theatre Productions. Postage ½, 1¼, 1¾, 2¼, 4½b.; Air 5, 6b.

Moon Mission of "Apollo 14" 1969 Moon Landing issue optd. Air 10b.

Olympic Games, Munich (4th issue). Paintings from the Pinakothek. Postage ¼, ⅓, ¾, 1½, 2b.; Air 4, 7b.

Chinese Paintings. Postage ¼, ⅓, ½, 2b.; Air 3, 4b.

Winter Olympic Games, Sapporo (3rd issue). Winter Sports and Japanese Works of Art. Postage ¼, ½, 1, 1⅓, 2b.; Air 3, 4b.

Winter Olympic Games, Sapporo (4th issue). Japanese Skier. Embossed on gold foil. Air 8b.

Launching of Soviet "Salyut" Space Station. Interplanetary issue of 1970 optd. Air 22b.

Olympic Games, Munich (5th issue). Sports and Sculptures. Postage ⅛, 1, 1⅓, 1¾, 2¼b.; Air 4½, 7, 10b.

Olympic Games, Munich (6th issue). Gold Medals. Embossed on gold foil. Air 8b.

Exploration of Outer Space. Postage ¼, ⅓, ½, ¾b.; Air 3, 3½, 6b.

Birth Bicentenary of Beethoven. Postage ¼ × 4, ½b. × 2; Air 1, 2, 5, 7, 10b.

Indian Paintings. Postage ¼, ⅓, ½, 2b.; Air 3, 4b.

Olympic Games, Munich (7th issue). Sailing Events at Kiel. Postage ¼, ½, 1¼, 2, 3b.; Air 4b.

Winter Olympic Games, Sapporo (5th issue). Sports. Postage ⅓, ¾, 1¼, 1¾, 2¼b.; Air 3½, 6b.

Winter Olympic Games, Sapporo (6th issue). Slalom Skier. Embossed on gold foil. Air 10b.

Persian Miniatures. Postage ¼, ⅓, ½, 2b.; Air 3, 4b.

Olympic Games, Munich (8th issue). Sports. Postage 1½, 2½, 3½, 5b.; Air 6, 8b.

Olympic Games, Munich (9th issue). Discus-thrower. Embossed on gold foil. Air 10b.

Italian Gold Medal Winners in Olympic Games. Postage ¼b. × 2, ⅓b. × 2; Air 22b.

1972.

French Gold Medal Winners in Olympic Games. Postage 2, 3b.; Air 4, 10b.

Works of Art. Postage 1, 1¼, 1⅓, 1½b.; Air 3, 4½, 7b.

ROYALIST ISSUES

1967.

Visit of Queen of Sheba to Solomon. ⅛, ¼, ½, 4, 6, 20, 24b.

Arab Horses. ⅛, ¼, ½, 4, 10b.

1968.

Winter Olympic Games, Grenoble (1st issue). Nos. R216/29 optd. Postage ⅛, ¼, ½, 1, 4, 6, 10b.; Air 12, 14, 16, 24, 34b.

Butterflies. Air 16, 20, 40b.

Postage Due. Butterflies and Horse. 4, 16, 20b.

Winter Olympic Games, Grenoble (2nd issue). Sports. Postage 1, 2, 3, 4, 6b.; Air 10, 12, 18, 24, 28b.

Gold Medal Winners, Grenoble Winter Olympics. Winter Olympic Games, Grenoble (2nd issue) optd with names of various medal winners. Postage 1, 2, 3, 4, 6b.; Air 10, 12, 18, 24, 28b.

20th Anniv of UNESCO. ½, 1, 1½, 2, 3, 4, 6, 10b.

Mothers' Day. Paintings. Postage 2, 4, 6b.; Air 24, 28, 34b.

Olympic Games, Mexico (1st issue). Sports. Postage 1, 2, 3, 4, 6b.; Air 10, 12, 18, 24, 28b.

UNESCO. "Save Florence" Campaign. Paintings. Postage 2, 4, 6b.; Air 10, 12, 18b.

UNESCO. "Save Venice" Campaign. Paintings. ½, 1, 1½, 24b.; Air 28, 34b.

Olympic Games, Mexico (2nd issue). Athletes and Flags. 4b. × 11.

Winter Olympic Games since 1924. Competitors and Flags. Postage. 1, 2, 3, 4, 6b.; Air 10, 12, 18, 24, 28b.

International Human Rights Year. 2b. × 4, 4b. × 4, 6b. × 4.

Paintings by European and American Artists. Postage 1, 2, 3, 4, 6, 10b.; Air 12, 18, 24, 28b.

Coronation of Shah of Iran. Postage 1, 2, 3, 4b.; Air 24, 28b.

International Philately. Postage 1, 2, 3, 4, 6b.; Air 10, 12, 18, 24, 28b.

World Racial Peace. Postage 4, 6, 18b.; Air 10b.

Children's Day. Paintings. Postage 1, 2, 3, 4b.; Air 6, 10, 12, 18, 24, 28b.

Gold Medal Winners, Mexico Olympic Games (1st issue). Mexico Olympics (1st issue) optd with names of various medal winners. Postage 1, 2, 3, 4, 6b.; Air 10, 12, 18, 24, 28b.

Gold Medal Winners, Mexico Olympics (2nd issue). Athletes and Medals. Air 12, 18, 24, 28, 34b.

Gold Medal Winners, Mexico Olympics (3rd issue). Embossed on gold foil. 28b.

"EFIMEX 68" Stamp Exhibition, Mexico City. Air 12, 18, 24, 28, 34b.

1969.

Motor-racing Drivers. Postage 1, 2, 3, 4, 6b.; Air 10, 12, 18, 24, 28b.

Space Flight of "Apollo 7". 4, 8, 12, 24, 28b.

Space Flight of "Apollo 8" (1st issue). 4, 6, 10, 18, 34b.

Space Flight of "Apollo 8" (2nd issue). Embossed on gold foil. 28b.

5th Anniv of Imam's Meeting with Pope Paul VI at Jerusalem (1st issue). Scenes from Pope's Visit. ¼, ½, ¾, 1, 1½, 2, 3, 4, 5, 6b.

5th Anniv of Imam's Meeting with Pope Paul VI at Jerusalem (2nd issue). Paintings of the Life of Christ. Postage 1, 2, 3, 4, 5, 6, 7, 8, 9, 10b.; Air 11, 12, 13, 14, 15, 16, 17, 18, 19, 20, 21, 22, 23, 24, 25, 26, 27, 28, 29, 30b.

5th Anniv of Imam's Meeting with Pope Paul VI at Jerusalem (3rd issue). Abraham's Tomb, Hebron. 4b.

Paintings by Rembrandt (1st series). Postage 1, 2, 4b.; Air 6, 12b., 1i.

Paintings by Rembrandt (2nd series). Embossed on gold foil. 20b.

Paintings by European Artists. Postage ½, 1½, 3, 5b.; Air 10, 18, 24, 28, 34b.

"Apollo" Moon Programme. Postage 1, 2, 3, 4, 5b.; Air 6, 7, 8, 9, 10, 11, 12, 13, 14, 15b.

Moon Flight of "Apollo 10". Postage 2, 4, 6b.; Air 8, 10, 12, 18, 24, 28, 34b.

Olympic Games, Munich (1972). Athletes and Olympic Rings. Postage 1, 2, 4, 5, 6b.; Air 10, 12, 18, 24, 34b.

World Wildlife Conservation. Postage ½b. × 2 1b. × 2, 2b. × 2, 4b. × 2, 6b. × 2; Air 8b. × 2, 10b. × 2, 18b. × 2.

First Man on the Moon (1st issue). Air 6, 10, 12, 18b.

First Man on the Moon (2nd issue). Air 6, 10, 12, 18, 24b.

First Man on the Moon (3rd issue). Embossed on gold foil. 24b. × 2.

First Man on the Moon (4th issue). Embossed on gold foil. 28b.

First Man on the Moon (5th issue). Air 10, 12 18, 24b.

Palestine Holy Places. Postage 4b. × 4, 6b. × 10; Air 12b. × 8.

Famous Men. Postage 4b. × 4, 6b. × 10; Air 12b. × 2.

History of Space Exploration. Air 6b. × 27.

Olympic Sports. Postage 1, 2, 4, 5, 6b.; Air 10, 12, 18, 24, 34b.

World Cup Football Championship, Mexico. Air 12b. × 8.

Christmas. Ikons. Postage ½, 1, 1½, 2, 4, 5, 6b.; Air 10, 12, 18, 24, 28, 34b.

Burning of Al-Aqsa Mosque, Jerusalem. Postage 4b.+2b., 6b.+3b.; Air 10b.+5b.

1970.

Brazil's Victory in World Cup Football Championship, Mexico. 1969 World Cup issue optd. Air 12b. × 3.

Dogs. Postage 2, 4, 6b.; Air 8, 12b.

Paintings of Horses. Postage 2, 4, 6b.; Air 8, 12b.

We close the Appendix with stamps believed to have been issued prior to July 1970, when first Saudi Arabia and then the United Kingdom recognised the Republican government in Yemen.

YEMEN PEOPLE'S DEMOCRATIC REPUBLIC — Pt. 19

The former People's Republic of Southern Yemen was known by the above title from 30 November 1970.

In 1990 it united with Yemen Arab Republic (see YEMEN REPUBLIC (combined)).

1000 fils = 1 dinar.

22 Temple of Isis, Philae, Egypt

1971. Preservation of Philae Temples Campaign.

65	**22**	5f. multicoloured	15	15
66		35f. multicoloured	60	40
67		65f. multicoloured	1·50	1·00

23 Symbols of Constitution

1971. Introduction of First Constitution.

68	**23**	10f. multicoloured	15	15
69		15f. multicoloured	30	25
70		35f. multicoloured	60	45
71		50f. multicoloured	85	70

24 Heads of Three Races and Flame

1971. Racial Equality Year.

72	**24**	20f. multicoloured	25	25
73		35f. multicoloured	55	55
74		75f. multicoloured	1·20	90

25 Map, Flag and Products

26 Hand holding Sub-machine Gun, and Map

1971.

75	**25**	5f. multicoloured	10	10
76		10f. multicoloured	10	10
77		15f. multicoloured	15	10
78		20f. multicoloured	15	15
79		25f. multicoloured	25	15
80		35f. multicoloured	30	15
81		40f. multicoloured	45	15
82		50f. multicoloured	60	45
82a		60f. multicoloured	1·30	55
83		65f. multicoloured	85	55
84		80f. multicoloured	1·00	75
84a		90f. multicoloured	1·40	60
84b	–	110f. multicoloured	1·90	85
85	–	125f. multicoloured	1·50	1·40
86	–	250f. multicoloured	2·75	1·90
87	–	500f. multicoloured	5·75	3·75
88	–	1d. multicoloured	13·00	7·75

DESIGN—42 × 25 mm: Nos. 84b/8, "Dam-al-Khawain" tree, Socotra.

1971. 6th Anniv of Revolutionary Activity in Arabian Gulf Area. Multicoloured.

89		15f. Type **26**	25	15
90		45f. Girl guerrilla and emblem (horiz)	60	55
91		50f. Guerrilla on the march	1·10	70

27 Hands supporting Cogwheel

29 Gamal Nasser

28 Eagle and Flags

1971. 2nd Anniv of "Corrective Move" in Revolutionary Government. Multicoloured.

92		15f. Type **27**	15	15
93		25f. Torch and revolutionary emblems	55	45
94		65f. Salt-works and windmill	1·20	70

1971. 9th Anniv of 26 September Revolution. Multicoloured.

95		10f. Type **28**	25	15
96		40f. Flag on "United Jemen"	70	55

1971. 1st Death Anniv of Gamal Nasser (Egyptian statesman).

97	**29**	65f. multicoloured	1·20	60

30 "Children of the World"

31 Domestic Pigeons

1971. 25th Anniv of UNICEF.

98	**30**	15f. black, red and orange	15	15
99		40f. black, purple and blue	45	40
100		50f. black, red and green	60	55

1971. Birds.

101	**31**	5f. black, purple and blue	25	15
102	–	40f. multicoloured	1·20	60
103	–	65f. black, red and green	2·75	1·00
104	–	100f. multicoloured	4·50	1·80

DESIGNS: 40f. Arabian chukar (inscr "Partridge"); 65f. Helmeted guineafowl and Arabian chukar (inscr "Partridge"); 100f. Black kite (inscr "Glede").

32 Dhow-building

1972. Dhow-building in Aden. Multicoloured.

105		25f. Type **32**	70	40
106		80f. Dhow at sea (vert)	2·00	1·50

33 Singer with Oud (lute), and Band

1972. Folk Dances. Multicoloured.

107		10f. Type **33**	10	10
108		25f. Yemeni girls dancing	30	25
109		40f. Dancing teams	75	45
110		80f. Festival dance	1·50	90

34 Palestinian Guerrilla and Barbed-wire

1972. Palestine Day.

111	**34**	5f. multicoloured	15	10
112		20f. multicoloured	45	25
113		65f. multicoloured	1·50	1·10

35 Police Colour Party

1972. Police Day. Multicoloured.

114		25f. Type **35**	55	15
115		80f. Girls of People's Militia on parade	1·90	1·20
MS116		122 × 74 mm. Nos. 114/15 (sold at 150f.)	7·75	7·75

36 Start of Cycle Race

1972. Arab Youth Week. Multicoloured.

117		10f. Type **36**	40	10
118		15f. Girls on parade	55	15
119		40f. Guides and scouts	1·00	55
120		80f. Acrobatic team (vert)	1·50	1·10

37 Turtle

1972. Marine Life. Multicoloured.

121		15f. Type **37**	70	30
122		40f. Sailfish	90	60
123		65f. Narrow-barred Spanish mackerel and John Dory	1·40	1·00
124		125f. Lobster	2·75	1·90

38 Book Year Emblem

1972. International Book Year.

125	**38**	40f. multicoloured	60	55
126		65f. multicoloured	1·10	75

39 Farmworkers and Field

1972. Agriculture Day.

127	**39**	10f. multicoloured	15	10
128		25f. multicoloured	60	40
129		40f. multicoloured	1·20	70

40 Soldiers advancing

1972. 5th Anniv of Independence. Multicoloured.

130		5f. Type **40**	15	10
131		20f. Soldier and town	45	30
132		65f. Vignettes of Yemeni life (vert)	1·10	75
MS133		134 × 142 mm. Nos. 130/2 (sold at 125f.)	3·50	3·00

41 Population Graph

1973. Population Census.

134	**41**	25f. emerald, red and green	45	25
135		40f. lt blue, mauve and blue	75	55

42 W.H.O. Emblem within "25"

43 Taweela Tanks, Aden

1973. 25th Anniv of W.H.O. Multicoloured.
136 5f. Type **42** 10 10
137 25f. W.H.O. emblem on globe (horiz) 40 25
138 125f. "25" and W.H.O. emblem (horiz) . . . . . . 1·70 1·50

1973. Tourism. Multicoloured.
139 20f. Type **43** 30 15
140 25f. Shibam Town (horiz) . . 45 30
141 40f. Elephant Bay, Aden (horiz) . . . . 1·00 60
142 100f. Al-Mohdar Mosque, Tarim (horiz) . . . . . . 1·70 1·20

44 Modern Apartments and Slum Clearance

1973. Nationalization of Buildings (1972). Mult.
143 20f. Type **44** 40 15
144 80f. Street scene (vert) . . . 1·40 1·00

45 Women's Corps on Parade

1973. People's Army. Multicoloured.
145 10f. Type **45** 15 10
146 20f. Soldiers marching . . . 30 15
147 40f. Naval contingent 90 60
148 80f. Column of tanks . . . . 1·50 1·10

46 Quayside Crane

1973. 10th Anniv of World Food Programme. Multicoloured.
149 20f. Type **46** 30 15
150 80f. Granary workers . . . . 1·40 90

47 "U.P.U. Letter"

1974. Centenary of U.P.U. Multicoloured.
151 5f. Type **47** 10 10
152 20f. "100" formed of people and U.P.U. emblems . . . 40 25
153 40f. U.P.U. emblem and Yemeni flag (vert) 60 45
154 125f. Map of People's Republic (vert) . . . . . . 1·20 1·10

48 Irrigation Canal

1974. Agricultural Progress. Multicoloured.
155 10f. Type **48** 15 15
156 20f. Bulldozers clearing land 40 15
157 100f. Tractors with harrows 1·20 90

49 Lathe Operator

50

1975. Industrial Progress. Multicoloured.
158 10f. Type **49** 15 10
159 40f. Workers in clothing factory 60 45
160 80f. Women textile workers (horiz) . . . . 1·20 85

1975. Women's Costumes.
161 **50** 5f. brown and black . . . 10 10
162 – 10f. violet and black . . . 15 10
163 – 15f. green and black . . . 25 15
164 – 25f. purple and black . . . 45 40
165 – 40f. blue and black 70 60
166 – 50f. brown and black . . . 1·20 1·20
DESIGNS: Nos. 162/6 show different costumes.

51 Women in Factory

1975. International Women's Year.
167 **51** 40f. black and brown . . . 60 40
168 50f. black and green . . . 75 55

52

53 Lunar Launch

1976. Yemeni Football.
169 **52** 5f. multicoloured 10 10
170 – 40f. multicoloured 60 45
171 – 80f. multicoloured . . . . 1·20 1·00
DESIGNS: Nos. 170/1 show footballers in different positions.

1976. Russian Space Exploration. Multicoloured.
172 10f. Type **53** 10 10
173 15f. V. A. Shatalov (cosmonaut) 25 15
174 40f. Luna vehicle (horiz) . . 90 55
175 65f. Valentina Tereshkova and rocket . . . . 1·40 75

54 Members of Presidential Council

1977. 1st Anniv of Unification Congress. Multicoloured.
176 25f. Type **54** 30 25
177 35f. Text of document . . . 55 45
178 65f. Girls of People's Militia 75 70
179 95f. Aerial view of textile factory . . . . 1·00 90

55 Traffic Policeman and Woman Trainee

1977. Traffic Change to Right.
180 **55** 25f. black and red 40 25
181 60f. black and yellow . . . 90 75
182 75f. black and green . . . 1·40 1·20
183 110f. black and blue . . . 2·30 1·50

56 A.P.U. Emblem within Flags of Member States

1977. 25th Anniv of Arab Postal Union.
184 **56** 20f. multicoloured 30 15
185 60f. multicoloured 70 55
186 70f. multicoloured 90 75
187 90f. multicoloured . . . . 1·10 85

57 Festive Volute

58 Dove of Peace and Flag

1977. Cowries. Multicoloured.
188 60f. Type **57** 90 40
189 90f. Pringle's marginella (horiz) . . . . 1·40 60
190 110f. Clay cone (horiz) . . . 1·70 90
191 180f. Broderip's cowrie (horiz) . . . . 3·00 1·70

1977. 10th Anniv of Independence. Multicoloured.
192 5f. Type **58** 10 10
193 20f. Man with broken manacle 25 10
194 90f. Oil pipeline 45 45
195 110f. "Pillar of Freedom" . . 90 55

59 Dome of the Rock, Jerusalem

1978. Palestinian Welfare.
196 **59** 5f. multicoloured 60 30
For smaller design with value at top right, see No. 264.

60 Almarfaa (drum)

1978. Musical Instruments. Multicoloured.
197 35f. Type **60** 30 15
198 60f. Almizmar (pipes) 70 30
199 90f. Alqnboos (fiddle) . . . 1·20 45
200 110f. Simsimiya (lyre) . . . . 1·50 60

61 Almotl (armbands)

1978. Silver Ornaments. Multicoloured.
201 10f. Type **61** 10 10
202 15f. Aloodhad (ring) 25 15
203 20f. Al Hizam (necklace) . . 30 25
204 60f. Alhoogaalah (bangle) . . 60 30
205 90f. Al Muk-Hala (perfume flask) 90 45
206 110f. Al Janbiya (dagger) . . 1·20 60

62 Palm Tree Emblem

63 "V" for Vanguard and Cogwheel

1978. 11th World Youth Festival, Cuba. Mult.
207 5f. Type **62** 10 10
208 60f. Global emblem 55 30
209 90f. Flower emblem 75 45
210 110f. Girl, youth and emblems . . . . 1·10 70

1978. 1st Conference of Vanguard Party.
211 **63** 5f. multicoloured 10 10
212 20f. multicoloured 15 10
213 60f. multicoloured 30 25
214 180f. multicoloured . . . . 1·20 75

64 Calligraphic Emblem, Symbols of Peace and Freedom

1978. 15th Anniv of 14 October Revolution. Mult.
215 10f. Type **64** 10 10
216 35f. Emblems of growth (vert) 25 15
217 60f. Candle and figure "15" (vert) 45 25
218 110f. Revolutionaries and figure "15" (vert) 60 45

65 Map of Yemen, Child with Olive-branch and Dove

66 "Agricultural Progress"

1979. International Year of the Child.
219 **65** 15f. multicoloured 15 10
220 20f. multicoloured 25 10
221 60f. multicoloured 45 25
222 90f. multicoloured 85 55

1979. 10th Anniv of "Corrective Move" in Revolutionary Government. Multicoloured.
223 20f. Type **66** 10 10
224 35f. "Industrial Progress" . . 25 15
225 60f. Students 45 25
226 90f. Woman with star and doves 60 45

67 Sir Rowland Hill and Yemeni Costume Stamp of 1970

1979. Death Cent of Sir Rowland Hill. Mult.
227 90f. Type **67** 55 40
228 110f. Yemeni camel stamp of 1970 . . . . 60 55
MS229 125 × 90 mm. 250f. Aden dhow stamp of 1937 . . . . . 1·90 1·70

68 World Map, Koran and Symbols of Arab Achievements

1979. The Arabs.
230 **68** 60f. multicoloured 60 60

69 Emblem of Yemeni Socialist Party

70 "Cassia adenensis"

1979. 1st Anniv of Yemeni Socialist Party.
231 **69** 60f. multicoloured 60 40

1979. Flowers (1st series). Multicoloured.
232 20f. Type **70** 15 10
233 90f. "Nerium oleander" . . . 60 55
234 110f. "Calligonum comosum" 1·20 60
235 180f. "Adenium obesum" . . 1·70 90
See also Nos. 265/8.

71 Ayatollah Khomeini and Crowd

73 Woman Basket-making

72 "Dido"

1980. 1st Anniv of Iranian Revolution.
236 **71** 60f. multicoloured . . . . 1·00 85

1980. Screw Steamers. Multicoloured.
237 110f. Type **72** 90 70
238 180f. "Anglia" . . . . 1·40 1·20
239 250f. "India" . . . . 1·80 1·50

1980. "London 1980". Handicrafts. Mult.
240 60f. Type **73** 40 25
241 90f. Making a hubble-bubble pipe 60 40
242 110f. Man at loom 90 60
243 250f. Boy making clay pot . . 1·50 1·20

74 Skink

1980. Reptiles. Multicoloured.
244 20f. Type **74** 30 15
245 35f. Mole viper 45 30
246 110f. Gecko . . . . 1·30 55
247 180f. Cobra . . . . 2·20 90

75 Misha the Bear (Olympic Mascot)

77 Lenin

76 Farming

1980. Olympic Games, Moscow.
248 **75** 110f. multicoloured 90 45

1980. 10th Anniv of Peasants' Uprising. Multicoloured.
249 50f. Type **76** 40 15
250 90f. Peasants 60 40
251 110f. Corn sickle and fist . . 90 45

1980. 110th Birth Anniv of Lenin.
252 **77** 35f. multicoloured 45 25

78 Douglas DC-3

1981. Democratic Yemen Airlines. Multicoloured.
253 60f. Type **78** 70 45
254 90f. Boeing 707 . . . . . . 1·40 75
255 250f. De Havilland D.H.C.7 Dash Seven . . . . 3·00 1·80

79 Map, Dish Aerial and Satellite

80 "Conocarpus lancifolius"

1981. Ras Boradli Satellite Station.
256 **79** 60f. multicoloured 75 45

1981. Trees. Multicoloured.
257 90f. Type **80** 85 40
258 180f. "Ficus vasta" . . . . . 1·70 90
259 250f. "Maerua crassifolia" . . 2·50 1·40

81 Council Building, Citizens and Flag

1981. 10th Anniv of Supreme People's Council.
260 **81** 180f. multicoloured . . . . 1·40 1·00

82 Sand Fox

1981. Wildlife Conservation. Multicoloured.
261 50f. Type **82** 60 30
262 90f. Leopard . . . . 1·20 90
263 250f. Ibex . . . . 2·75 2·00

1981. Palestinian Welfare. As T **59**, but smaller, 25 × 27 mm, and value at top right.
264 5f. multicoloured 40 15

1981. Flowers (2nd series). As T **70**. Mult.
265 50f. "Tephrosia apollinea" 55 30
266 90f. "Citrullus colocynthis" 1·00 55
267 110f. "Aloe squarrosa" . . . 1·50 55
268 250f. "Lawsonia inermis" . . 3·00 1·70

83 Blind People Basket-weaving and Typing

1982. International Year of Disabled Persons.
269 **83** 50f. multicoloured 40 25
270 100f. multicoloured 90 55
271 150f. multicoloured . . . . 1·40 75

84 Microscope Slides and Lungs

1982. Centenary of Discovery of Tubercle Bacillus.
272 **84** 50f. black, orange and red 90 40

85 A.P.U. Emblem and Map within Heart

1982. 30th Anniv of Arab Postal Union.
273 **85** 100f. red, black and blue 1·20 60

86 Footballers

1982. World Cup Football Championship, Spain. Multicoloured.
274 50f. Type **86** 60 40
275 100f. Match scene . . . . . 1·20 60
276 150f. Players and shield . . . 1·90 1·20
277 200f. Player and flags . . . . 2·50 1·40
MS278 114 × 94 mm. Nos. 274/7 6·25 3·75

87 Emblems and Flags of Russia and Yemen

1982. 60th Anniv of U.S.S.R.
279 **87** 50f. multicoloured 60 40

1982. World Cup Football Championship Result. Nos. 274/7 optd **WORLD CUP WINNERS 1982 1st ITALY 2nd W-GERMANY 3rd POLAND 4th FRANCE** and player holding trophy.
280 50f. Type **86** 60 40
281 100f. Match scene . . . . . 1·20 60
282 150f. Players and shield . . . 1·90 1·20
283 200f. Player and flags . . . . 2·50 1·40
MS284 114 × 94 mm. Nos. 280/3 6·25 3·75

89 Yasser Arafat

1983. Palestinian Solidarity. Multicoloured.
285 50f. Type **89** 85 60
286 100f. Yasser Arafat and Dome of the Rock . . . . 1·90 75
MS287 100 × 80 mm. No. 286. Imperf . . . . 2·75 2·30

1983. "Tembal 83" Stamp Exhibition, Basel. No. 248 optd **TEMBAL 83 MAY 21st-29th, 1983** and emblem.
288 **75** 110f. multicoloured . . . . 4·25 1·70

91 Man with Letter, Postal Barge and Postman

1983. World Communications Year.
289 **91** 50f. black and blue 60 45
290 – 100f. black and red . . . . 1·30 70
291 – 150f. black, green and olive 2·00 1·00
292 – 200f. multicoloured . . . . 2·50 1·10
MS293 120 × 91 mm. 150f. multicoloured . . . . 2·75 2·30
DESIGNS: 100f. Postman, stage coach and morse code equipment; 150f. Motor coach and telephones; 150f. (**MS**293), Amalgam of motifs from Nos. 289/92; 200f. Transmitter, airplane, satellite, television, envelope and dish aerial.

92 "The Poor Family"

1983. 10th Death Anniv of Picasso (artist). Multicoloured.
294 50f. Type **92** 75 30
295 100f. "Woman with Crow" 1·20 60
MS296 Two sheets. (a) 130 × 75 mm. 50f. "Le Gourmet"; 100f. "Woman with Child on Beach"; 150f. "Sitting Beggar"; (b) 120 × 91 mm. 150f. "The Solar Family" (49 × 39 mm) . . . . 17·00 17·00

93 Show Jumping

1983. Olympic Games, Los Angeles (1st issue). Equestrian Events. Multicoloured.
297 25f. Type **93** 90 30
298 50f. Show jumping (different) 1·30 60
299 100f. Horse crossing water (Three-day event) . . . . 2·00 1·20
MS300 Two sheets. (a) 130 × 75 mm. 20f. Head of bay (*vert*), 40f. Head of grey (*vert*), 60f. Bay (*vert*), 80f. Arabian (*vert*); (b) 121 × 150 mm. 200f. Show jumping (*vert*) . . . 20·00 20·00
See also Nos. 316/**MS**319.

94 Class P8 Steam Locomotive, 1905, Prussia

1983. Railway Locomotives. Multicoloured.
301 25f. Type **94** . . . . 1·20 45
302 50f. Class 880 steam locomotive, 1915, Italy . . 2·20 90
303 100f. Class Gt2 steam locomotive, 1923, Bavaria 3·50 1·70
MS304 Two sheets. (a) 118 × 121 mm. 40f. Class D51 steam locomotive, 1936, 60f. Series 45 locomotive, 1937, 100f. Class Pt47 locomotive, 1948; (b) 92 × 94 mm. 200f. Class P36 locomotive, 1950 . . . . . . 34·00 31·00

95 Liner "Europa"

1983. Ships. Multicoloured.
305 50f. Type **95** . . . . 1·20 60
306 100f. Liner "World Discoverer" . . . . 2·30 1·30
MS307 Two sheets. (a) 174 × 130 mm. 20f. "Kruzenshtern" (Russian cadet barque), 40f. "Grossherzogin Elisabeth" (German cadet schooner), 60f. "Sedov" (Russian cadet barque), 80f. "Dar Pomorza" (Polish cadet full-rigged ship); (b) 120 × 91 mm. 200f. "Gorch Fock" (German cadet barque) . . . . 28·00 25·00

96 "20" and Hand holding Sheaf of Corn

1983. 20th Anniv of Revolution. Multicoloured.
308 50f. Type **96** 85 45
309 100f. Flag, man with gun and "XX" . . . . 1·80 85

97 Pierre Testu-Brissy's Balloon, 1798

1983. Bicentenary of Manned Flight. Mult.
310 50f. Type **97** 75 40
311 100f. Unmanned Montgolfier balloon, 1783 . . . . . . 1·50 75
MS312 Two sheets. (a) 130×175 mm. 20f. Vincenzo Lunardi's balloon (1785), 40f. Charles's hydrogen balloon (1783), 60f. John Wise's balloon *Atlantic* (1859), 80f. Blanchard and Jefferies balloon (1785); (b) 90×120 mm. 200f. Eugene Godard's quintuple acrobatic balloon (1850) . . . . 25·00 21·00

98 Skiing

1983. Winter Olympic Games, Sarajevo. Multicoloured.
313 50f. Type **98** 75 40
314 100f. Bobsleigh . . . . . . 1·50 75
MS315 Two sheets. (a) 130×175 mm. 40f. Ski jumping, 60f. Figure skating (pairs), 100f. No. 314; (b) 90×120 mm. 200f. Ice hockey . . . . 18·00 15·00

99 Fencing

1984. Olympic Games, Los Angeles (2nd issue). Multicoloured.
316 25f. Type **99** 40 15
317 50f. Fencing (different) . . . 75 40
318 100f. Fencing (different) . . . 1·20 60
MS319 Two sheets. (a) 130×175 mm. 20f. Gymnastics, 40f. Water polo, 80f. Show jumping, 60f. Wrestling; (b) 120×90 mm. 200f. Show jumping (different) . . . . 18·00 15·00

100 "Soyuz 10"–"Salyut 1" Link-up, 1971

1984. Space. Multicoloured.
320 15f. Type **100** 15 10
321 20f. "Apollo 8" and Moon, 1968 . . . . 25 15
322 50f. "Apollo 11" and first man on Moon, 1969 . . . 60 40
323 100f. "Soyuz"–"Apollo" link-up, 1975 . . . . 1·20 90
MS324 118×88 mm. 200f. "Columbia" (space shuttle) returning to Earth's atmosphere 5·50 4·50

1984. Nos. 83 and 84b surch.
325 **25** 50f. on 65f. multicoloured 85 55
326 – 100f. on 110f. mult . . . . 1·80 85

102 Starry Triggerfish

105 Victory Parade, Red Square

104 Women writing

1984. Fishes. Multicoloured.
327 10f. Type **102** 10 10
328 15f. Golden trevally 10 10
329 20f. Saddled grunt 15 10
330 35f. Diagonal butterflyfish . . 25 15
331 35f. Emperor angelfish . . . 30 15
332 50f. Indian mackerel 45 25
333 100f. Kawakawa 90 30
334 150f. Pennant coralfish . . . 1·50 75
335 200f. Yellow-banded angelfish 2·00 90
336 250f. Plane-tailed lionfish . . 2·75 1·50
337 400f. Long-spined seabream 4·25 2·00
338 500f. Coachwhip stingray . . 5·50 2·75
339 1d. Brown-spotted grouper 11·50 6·50
340 2d. Long-finned drepane . . 25·00 12·50

1984. Olympic Winners, Sarajevo. No. 314 optd **WINNERS B.Lehmann–B. Musiol (DDR)**.
341 100f. multicoloured . . . . . 6·50 5·75
MS342 130×175 mm. 40f. As No. 341 60f. "WINNERS J. Torvill–C. Dean (GB)"; 100f. "WINNERS W. Hoppe–D. Schauerhammer (DDR) . . . 14·00 11·50

1985. National Literacy Campaign. Mult.
343 50f. Type **104** . . . . 1·20 60
344 100f. Pen held in manacled fist . . . . 2·50 1·00

1985. 40th Anniv of End of Second World War.
345 **105** 100f. multicoloured . . . 1·40 60

106 Flag within Emblem

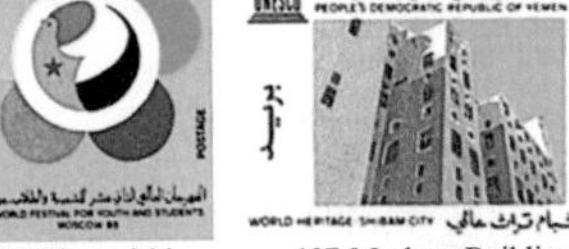
107 Modern Buildings

1985. 12th World Youth and Students' Festival, Moscow. Multicoloured.
346 50f. Type **106** . . . . 1·30 60
347 100f. Hand holding emblem as placard . . . . 2·50 1·10

1985. UNESCO World Heritage Site. Shibam City. Multicoloured.
348 50f. Type **107** 75 45
349 50f. View of city 75 45
350 100f. Screen . . . . 1·50 1·10
351 100f. Gate (vert) . . . . . . 1·50 1·10

108 Industrial Symbols

109 Mother feeding Child

1985. 3rd Yemeni Socialist Party General Congress. Multicoloured.
352 25f. Type **108** 60 40
353 50f. Crane loading ship . . . 1·10 55
354 100f. Combine harvesters . . 2·00 90

1985. UNICEF Child Survival Campaign. Multicoloured.
355 50f. Type **109** 75 60
356 50f. Immunization 75 60
357 100f. Breastfeeding . . . . . 1·50 1·10
358 100f. Oral rehydration therapy . . . . 1·50 1·10

110 Wheat and Al-Mohdar Mosque, Tarim

111 Lenin addressing Crowd in Red Square

1986. World Food Day. 40th Anniv (1985) of F.A.O. Multicoloured.
359 20f. Type **110** 75 25
360 180f. Palm trees . . . . . . 3·00 1·50

1986. 27th Russian Communist Party Congress. Multicoloured.
361 **111** 75f. multicoloured . . . . 1·50 60
362 250f. multicoloured . . . 3·00 1·70

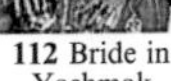
112 Bride in Yashmak

113 Ali Ahmed N. Antar

1986. Brides and Bridegrooms of Yemen. Mult.
363 50f. Type **112** 70 45
364 50f. Bride with striped shawl 70 45
365 50f. Bride with long dressed hair 70 45
366 100f. Bridegroom in modern jacket with knife . . . . . 1·40 1·10
367 100f. Bridegroom in traditional clothes with gun 1·40 1·10
368 100f. Bride in modern dress 1·40 1·10

1986. "Party and Homeland Martyrs". Mult.
369 75f. Type **113** 90 60
370 75f. Saleh Musleh Kasim . . 90 60
371 75f. Ali Shayaa Hadi 90 60
372 75f. Abdul Fattah Ismail . . 90 60

114 Immunizing Pregnant Woman against Tetanus

1987. UNICEF Immunization Campaign. Multicoloured.
373 20f. Type **114** 30 15
374 75f. Immunizing baby . . . 90 55
375 140f. Nurse giving oral poliomyelitis vaccine to baby . . . . 1·70 85
376 150f. Pregnant woman and children carrying syringes 1·80 1·00

115 Party Emblem and Worker

116 Lenin and Soldier

1987. Yemeni Socialist Party General Conference.
377 **115** 75f. multicoloured 90 40
378 150f. multicoloured . . . 1·80 85

1987. 70th Anniv of Russian October Revolution.
379 **116** 250f. multicoloured . . . 3·50 1·90

117 Steps to King's Court

1987. Shabwa Remains. Multicoloured.
380 25f. Type **117** 40 25
381 75f. Royal Palace 90 45
382 140f. Winged lion, King's Court (vert) . . . . 1·70 90
383 150f. Inscribed bronze plaque (vert) . . . . 2·00 1·10

118 Students and College Buildings

1987. 20th Anniv of Independence. Mult.
384 25f. Type **118** 30 15
385 75f. Family and housing . . 85 40
386 140f. Workers, oil derrick and power station . . . . 1·70 75
387 150f. Party headquarters and members . . . . 1·80 85

119 Tank and Liberty Monument, Sana'a

1988. 25th Anniv (1987) of 26th September Revolution in Yemen.
388 **119** 75f. multicoloured 90 40

120 Tap, Boy and Rainbow (safe water)

121 Weightlifting

1988. World Health Day. 40th Anniv of W.H.O. Multicoloured.
389 40f. Type **120** 30 25
390 75f. Child with globe as head breaking cigarette (No Smoking day) 85 30
391 140f. Nurse immunizing baby (immunization campaign) 1·50 60
392 250f. Red Crescent worker instructing group (Health for all) . . . . 2·30 1·20

1988. Olympic Games, Seoul. Multicoloured.
393 40f. Type **121** 40 25
394 75f. Running 85 40
395 140f. Boxing . . . . 1·70 90
396 150f. Football . . . . 1·10 1·20

122 Crowd and Flag

123 Yellow-bellied Green Pigeon

1988. 25th Anniv of 14 October Revolution.
397 **122** 25f. black and red 30 15
398 – 75f. multicoloured 85 30
399 – 300f. multicoloured . . . 3·50 1·50
DESIGNS—HORIZ: 75f. Radfan mountains and revolutionary. VERT: 300f. Anniversary emblem.

1988. Birds. Multicoloured.
400 40f. Type **123** 45 25
401 50f. Lilac-breasted roller (vert) 70 45
402 75f. Hoopoe (vert) . . . . . 1·20 70
403 250f. Houbara bustard . . . 3·00 1·70

124 Incense Burner

125 Shipping entering Old Harbour

1988. Traditional Crafts. Multicoloured.
404 25f. Type **124** 25 25
405 70f. Mashjub (rack used when impregnating dresses with incense) 85 40

406 150f. Cosmetic basket made of palm fibre with cowrie shell decoration . . . . . 1·50 90
407 250f. Woman making palm fibre basket . . . . 2·75 1·50

1988. Centenary of Port of Aden. Mult.
408 75f. Type **125** . . . . 1·20 45
409 300f. Section of new harbour project . . . . 3·50 1·80

126 Old City

1988. International Campaign for Preservation of Old Sana'a. Multicoloured.
410 75f. Type **126** 75 55
411 250f. City (different) . . . . 3·00 1·30

127 Sand Cat Kitten

1989. Endangered Animals. Multicoloured.
412 20f. Type **127** . . . . 1·20 15
413 25f. Adult sand cat . . . . . 1·20 25
414 50f. Fennec fox cub . . . . 2·30 40
415 75f. Adult fennec fox . . . . 3·00 60

128 Symbols of War in Star

129 Ismail

1989. 20th Anniv of "Corrective Move" in Revolutionary Government. Multicoloured.
416 25f. Type **128** 30 15
417 35f. Industrial symbols in hook 40 15
418 40f. Agricultural symbols . . 45 25

1989. 50th Birth Anniv of Adbul Fattah Ismail (founder of People's Socialist Party).
419 **129** 75f. multicoloured 55 45
420 150f. multicoloured . . . 1·20 1·10

130 "Children at Play" (Abeer Anwer)

131 Sana'a and Fighters

1989. 15th Anniv of Ali Anter Pioneer Organization. Multicoloured.
421 10f. Type **130** 10 10
422 25f. Girl pioneer 25 15
423 75f. Pioneers parading at Khormaksar (horiz) . . . 70 45

1989. 22nd Anniv of Siege of Sana'a.
424 **131** 150f. multicoloured . . . 1·70 85

132 Taj Mahal and Nehru

133 Coffee Plant

1989. Birth Centenary of Jawaharal Nehru (Indian statesman).
425 **132** 250f. black and brown . . 2·50 1·20

1989. Centenary of Interparliamentary Union.
426 **133** 300f. multicoloured . . . 3·50 1·90

134 Seera Rock, Aden, Birds and Arc de Triomphe, Paris

1989. Bicentenary of French Revolution.
427 **134** 250f. multicoloured . . . 3·00 1·90

135 U.S.A. v Belgium (Uruguay, 1930)

1990. World Cup Football Championship, Italy. Matches from previous championships. Mult.
428 5f. Type **135** 10 10
429 10f. Switzerland v Netherlands (Italy, 1934) 10 10
430 20f. Italy v France (France, 1938) 10 10
431 35f. Sweden v Spain (Brazil, 1950) 25 25
432 50f. West Germany v Austria (Switzerland, 1954) 30 30
433 60f. Brazil v England (Sweden, 1958) 40 40
434 500f. U.S.S.R. v Uruguay (Chile, 1962) . . . . . . 3·50 75
MS435 90 × 61 mm. 340f. Footballers . . . . 2·75 1·50

YEMEN REPUBLIC (combined)

Pt. 19

A draft joint constitution was ratified by the parliaments of Yemen Arab Republic and the Yemen People's Democratic Republic on 21 May 1990 and the unification of the two countries was declared the following day.

The currencies of both the previous republics have legal validity throughout Yemen.

100 fils = 1 rial (North Yemen).
1000 fils = 1 dinar (South Yemen).

1 Scouts supporting Globe

1990. 60th Anniv of Arab Scout Movement. Multicoloured.
1 300f. Type **1** . . . . 1·50 75
2 375f. Type **1** . . . . 1·70 90
3 850f. Oil derrick, scouts with flag, anniversary emblem and tower . . . . 3·75 1·80
4 900f. As No. 3 . . . . 4·25 2·00
MS5 90 × 70 mm. As No. 2 but 37 × 27 mm . . . . 6·75 3·75

Nos. 1/**MS**5 are inscribed "YEMEN ARAB REPUBLIC".

2 Pintail

3 City Rooftops

1990. Ducks. Multicoloured.
6 10f. Type **2** 10 10
7 20f. European wigeon 10 10
8 25f. Ruddy shelduck 20 10
9 40f. Gadwall 25 20
10 75f. Common shelduck . . . 45 35
11 150f. Common shoveler pair 1·10 45
12 600f. Green-winged teal . . . 4·25 1·00
MS13 89 × 67 mm. 460f. Pintail flying . . . . 9·00 2·30

1990. 40th Anniv of U.N. Development Programme.
14 **3** 150f. multicoloured . . . . . 1·20 90

4 "Dirphia multicolor"

1990. Moths and Butterflies. Multicoloured.
15 5f. Type **4** 10 10
16 20f. "Automeris io" 10 10
17 25f. Swallowtail 20 10
18 40f. Bhutan glory 25 20
19 55f. Silver king shoemaker . . 35 25
20 75f. Tiger moth 45 35
21 700f. "Attacus edwardsii" (moth) . . . . 5·00 1·30
MS22 65 × 90 mm. 460f. Oleander hawk moth (vert) . . . . . . 9·00 2·30

5 Protembolotherium

1990. Prehistoric Animals. Multicoloured.
23 5f. Type **5** 10 10
24 10f. Diatryma 10 10
25 35f. Mammoth (horiz) 20 20
26 40f. Edaphosaurus (horiz) . . 20 20
27 55f. Dimorphodon (horiz) . . 35 25
28 75f. Phororhacos (horiz) . . . 45 35
29 700f. Ichthyosaurus (wrongly inscr "Ichtyosaurus") . . . 5·50 1·40
MS30 62 × 90 mm. 460f. Tyrannosaurus rex. Imperf . . 5·00 2·30

6 Abyssinian Kitten

7 "Boletus aestivalis"

1990. Cats. Multicoloured.
31 5f. Type **6** 10 10
32 15f. Blue longhair 10 10
33 35f. Siamese 20 20
34 55f. Burmese 35 25
35 60f. Sealpoint colourpoint . . 35 25
36 150f. Red British shorthair . . 1·10 45
37 600f. Leopard cat . . . . . . 4·25 90
MS38 70 × 90 mm. 460f. Black-smoke longhair kitten. Imperf 9·00 2·30

1991. Fungi. Multicoloured.
39 50f. Type **7** 35 20
40 60f. Butter mushroom 45 25
41 80f. Beefsteak morel 65 35
42 100f. Brown birch bolete . . . 80 45
43 130f. Fly agaric . . . . 1·10 55
44 200f. Flaky-stemmed witches' mushroom . . . . 1·80 65
45 300f. Red cap . . . . 2·50 75
MS46 70 × 90 mm. 460f. Verdigris agaric. Imperf . . . . 4·50 2·30

8 State Arms

9 Shaking Hands

1991. 1st Anniv of Yemen Republic. Mult.
47 300f. Type **8** 80 35
48 375f. Type **8** . . . . 1·00 55
49 850f. Hand holding flag, map and sun . . . . 2·40 75
50 900f. As No. 49 . . . . 2·40 90
MS51 90 × 70 mm. As No. 48 but 36 × 27 mm . . . . 2·30 1·40

1991. Signing of Unity Agreement (in November 1989) Commemoration. Multicoloured.
52 225f. Type **9** 55 25
53 300f. Hand holding flag over map 90 45
54 375f. As No. 53 . . . . 1·20 65
55 650f. Type **9** . . . . 1·80 80
56 850f. As No. 53 . . . . 2·40 1·10
MS57 70 × 90 mm. As No. 54 but 27 × 36 mm . . . . 2·30 1·40

10 Cigarettes and Skull on Globe

1991. World Anti-smoking Day. Multicoloured.
58 225f. Type **10** 55 25
59 300f. Skull smoking and man 90 45
60 375f. As No. 59 . . . . 1·30 55
61 650f. Type **10** . . . . 2·00 90
62 850f. As No. 59 . . . . 2·50 1·10
MS63 90 × 70 mm. As No. 60 but 36 × 26 mm . . . . 2·75 1·40

11 Emblem

1991. 45th Anniv of U.N.O.
64 **11** 5r. multicoloured . . . . . 1·80 75
65 8r. multicoloured . . . . . 2·30 1·10
66 10r. multicoloured . . . . . 3·25 1·40
67 12r. multicoloured . . . . . 3·75 2·30
MS68 90 × 70 mm. **11** 6r. multicoloured (37 × 27 mm) . . 2·30 1·50

1993. Various stamps surch. (a) Stamps of Yemen Arab Republic. (i) Postage.
69 **94** 5r. on 75f. multicoloured 3·25 3·25
70 **144** 8r. on 425f. multicoloured 3·75 3·75
71 **150** 8r. on 425f. multicoloured 3·75 3·75
72 – 10r. on 900f. mult (No. 830) . . . . 4·00 4·00
73 – 10r. on 900f. mult (No. 834) . . . . 4·00 4·00
74 – 10r. on 900f. mult (No. 838) . . . . 4·00 4·00
75 – 10r. on 900f. mult (No. 843) . . . . 4·00 4·00
76 **157** 10r. on 900f. multicoloured 4·00 4·00
77 – 10r. on 900f. mult (No. 853) . . . . 4·00 4·00
78 **159** 10r. on 900f. multicoloured 4·00 4·00
79 – 10r. on 900f. mult (No. 863) . . . . 4·00 4·00
80 – 12r. on 850f. mult (No. 829) . . . . 5·50 5·50
81 – 12r. on 850f. mult (No. 833) . . . . 5·50 5·50
82 – 12r. on 850f. mult (No. 837) . . . . 5·50 5·50
83 – 12r. on 850f. mult (No. 842) . . . . 5·50 5·50
84 **157** 12r. on 850f. multicoloured 5·50 5·50
85 – 12r. on 850f. mult (No. 852) . . . . 5·50 5·50
86 **159** 12r. on 850f. multicoloured 5·50 5·50

(ii) Air. Additionally optd **AIR MAIL** (except for No. 87).
87 **118** 3r. on 125f. multicoloured 1·80 1·80
88 – 3r. on 125f. mult (No. 672) . . . . . . 1·80 1·80
89 – 3r. on 125f. mult (No. 679) . . . . . . 1·80 1·80
90 – 3r. on 125f. mult (No. 686) . . . . . . 1·80 1·80
91 – 3r. on 125f. mult (No. 700) . . . . . . 1·80 1·80
92 – 3r. on 125f. mult (No. 707) . . . . . . 1·80 1·80
93 – 5r. on 75f. mult (No. 670) 75 30
94 – 5r. on 75f. mult (No. 677) 75 30
95 – 5r. on 75f. mult (No. 684) 75 30
96 – 5r. on 75f. mult (No. 691) 75 30
97 – 5r. on 75f. mult (No. 698) 75 30
98 – 5r. on 75f. mult (No. 705) 75 30
99 **145** 8r. on 425f. multicoloured 4·00 4·00
100 – 8r. on 425f. mult (No. 796) . . . . . . 4·00 4·00
101 **147** 8r. on 425f. multicoloured 4·00 4·00
102 – 8r. on 425f. mult (No. 803) . . . . . . 4·00 4·00
103 – 8r. on 425f. mult (No. 812) . . . . . . 4·00 4·00
104 **151** 8r. on 425f. multicoloured 4·00 4·00
105 **152** 8r. on 425f. multicoloured 4·00 4·00
106 – 12r. on 850f. mult (No. 862) . . . . . . 7·25 7·25

(b) Stamps of Yemen Republic (combined).
107 – 10r. on 900f. mult (No. 4) 4·50 4·50
108 – 10r. on 900f. mult (No. 50) 4·50 4·50
109 – 12r. on 850f. mult (No. 3) 1·80 75
110 – 12r. on 850f. mult (No. 49) 1·80 75
111 – 12r. on 850f. mult (No. 56) 1·80 75
112 – 12r. on 850f. mult (No. 62) 1·80 75
113 – 50r. on 150f. mult (No. 11) 23·00 13·50
114 **3** 50r. on 150f. multicoloured 23·00 13·50
115 **10** 50r. on 225f. multicoloured
116 **8** 50r. on 375f. multicoloured 23·00 13·50
117 – 50r. on 375f. mult (No. 54) 23·00 13·50
118 – 50r. on 375f. mult (No. 60) 23·00 13·50
119 **8** 100r. on 300f. mult . . . . 41·00 23·00
120 – 100r. on 300f. mult (No. 53) . . . . . .
121 – 100r. on 300f. mult (No. 59) . . . . . .

(c) Stamps of Yemen People's Democratic Republic. (i) In Western and Arabic figures.
122 – 8r. on 110f. mult (No. 84b) . . . . . . 3·25 2·00
123 – 8r. on 110f. mult (No. 200) . . . . . . 3·25 2·00
124 – 8r. on 110f. mult (No. 206) . . . . . . 3·25 2·00
125 – 8r. on 110f. mult (No. 218) . . . . . . 3·25 2·00
126 – 8r. on 110f. mult (No. 234) . . . . . . 3·25 2·00
127 **72** 8r. on 110f. multicoloured 3·25 2·00
128 – 8r. on 110f. mult (No. 246) . . . . . . 3·25 2·00
129 – 8r. on 110f. mult (No. 267) . . . . . . 3·25 2·00
130 – 50r. on 500f. mult (No. 434) . . . . . .

131 **133** 100r. on 300f. mult . . . 41·00 23·00
132 – 100r. on 2d. mult (No. 340) . . . . . . 41·00 23·00
133 **25** 200r. on 5f. multicoloured 80·00 45·00
134 **135** 200r. on 5f. multicoloured
135 **127** 200r. on 20f. multicoloured . . . . . 80·00 45·00
136 – 200r. on 20f. mult (No. 430) . . . . . .
137 – 200r. on 75f. mult (No. 423) . . . . . . 80·00 45·00
138 **132** 200r. on 250f. black & brn . . . . 80·00 45·00

(ii) Surch **R.** and Arabic figures.

139 **100** 200r. on 15f. multicoloured . . . . . 80·00 45·00
140 – 200r. on 15f. mult (No. 328) . . . . . . 80·00 45·00
141 – 200r. on 20f. mult (No. 321) . . . . . . 80·00 45·00
142 – 200r. on 20f. mult (No. 329) . . . . . . 80·00 45·00

15 Sana'a

16 Player dribbling Ball

1994. 4th Anniv of Yemen Republic.
143 – 3r. multicoloured 75 35
144 – 5r. multicoloured . . . . . 1·40 65
145 **15** 8r. multicoloured . . . . . 2·00 1·00
146 – 20r. multicoloured . . . . 5·00 2·50
MS147 70 × 60 mm. 20r. multicoloured . . . . 5·00 2·30
DESIGNS: Nos.143/4, 146, **MS**147. Different views of the principal building Type **15**.

1994. World Cup Football Championship, U.S.A. Multicoloured.
148 2r. Type **16** 55 25
149 6r. Dribbling (different) . . . 1·50 75
150 10r. Goalkeeper catching ball (horiz) . . . . 2·40 1·20
151 12r. Player heading ball . . . 3·00 1·50
MS152 70 × 60 mm. 12r. Tackling (horiz) . . . . 3·25 2·30

17 Arabian Leopard

18 Hand holding Seedling

1995. World Environmental Protection Day. Multicoloured.
153 15r. Type **17** . . . . 1·50 90
154 20r. Caracal lynx . . . . . . 1·60 1·00
155 30r. Helmeted guineafowl (horiz) . . . . 2·40 1·30
MS156 70 × 60 mm. 50r. Partridge (horiz) . . . . 4·50 3·25

1995. 50th Anniv of F.A.O. Multicoloured.
157 10r. Type **18** 80 55
158 25r. Hand holding seeds . . 1·80 1·00
159 30r. Hand holding fish . . . 2·40 1·20
MS160 70 × 60 mm. 50r. Hand holding plant . . . . 4·00 2·75

19 Old Sana'a

20 Kashmim

1995. 50th Anniv of U.N.O. Multicoloured.
161 10r. Type **19** 80 55
162 20r. Different viewpoint of scene on 10r . . . . 1·80 1·00
163 25r. Rampart walk (horiz) . . 2·40 1·20
MS164 70 × 60 mm. 50r. Aden reservoir (horiz) . . . . 4·00 2·75

1995. Naseem Hamed Kashmim (boxer). Mult.
165 10r. Kashmim with Lonsdale Belt 80 45
166 20r. Type **20** . . . . 1·60 75
167 25r. Scene from boxing match (horiz) . . . . 2·00 90
168 30r. Kashmim raising arm in triumph . . . . 2·40 1·10
MS169 70 × 60 mm. 50r. Scene from boxing match (different) (horiz) 4·00 2·75

21 Shanghai

1996. "China '96" International Stamp Exhibition, Peking. Sheet 100 × 140 mm.
MS170 **21** 80r. multicoloured . . 6·00 3·75

22 Wrestling

23 Popular Heritage Museum, Seiyoan

1996. Olympic Games, Atlanta, U.S.A. Mult.
171 20r. Type **22** 80 45
172 50r. High jumping (horiz) . . 2·20 1·40
173 60r. Running . . . . 2·50 1·60
174 70r. Gymnastics . . . . . . 3·00 2·00
175 100r. Judo . . . . 4·25 2·30
MS176 70 × 60 mm. 150r. Throwing the javelin . . . . 8·25 4·50

1996. Heritage Sites. Multicoloured.
177 10r. Type **23** 25 10
178 15r. Rock Palace, Wadi Dhahr (vert) 45 20
179 20r. Old Sana'a city 65 25
180 30r. Al-Mohdhar minaret, Tarim (vert) . . . . 1·00 35
181 40r. As 15r. . . . . 1·20 55
182 50r. As 30r. . . . . 1·50 75
183 60r. As 15r. . . . . 2·00 90
184 70r. As 10r. . . . . 2·40 1·10
185 100r. As 20r. . . . . 3·25 1·40
186 150r. As 30r. . . . . 4·50 1·80
187 200r. As 20r. . . . . 6·25 2·30
188 250r. As 10r. . . . . 8·25 2·75
189 300r. As 30r. . . . . 11·00 3·25
190 500r. As 15r. . . . . 16·00 4·50

24 Barn Owl

1996. Birds. Multicoloured.
191 20r. Type **24** 75 45
192 50r. Philby's rock partridge 1·80 90
193 60r. Lammergeier . . . . . 2·40 1·10
194 70r. Arabian chukar . . . . 2·50 1·60
195 100r. Houbara bustard . . . 3·50 2·30
MS196 60 × 70 mm. 150r. Little bittern (vert) . . . . 6·75 4·00
See also Nos. 220/**MS**225.

25 "Parodia maasii"

26 Girls reading

1996. Multicoloured. (a) Rare Plants.
197 20r. Type **25** 75 45
198 50r. "Notocatus cristata" . . 1·60 90
199 60r. "Adenium obesum socotranum" . . . . . . 2·00 1·10
200 70r. Dragon's blood tree . . 2·40 1·60
201 100r. "Mammillaria erythrosperma" . . . . . 3·25 2·30
MS202 70 × 60 mm. 150r. "Parodia maasii" (different) . . . . . . 6·00 4·00

(b) Fishes.

203 20r. Moorish idol 65 45
204 50r. Hump-headed wrasse . . 1·30 90
205 60r. Purple tang . . . . . . 2·00 1·10
206 70r. Emperor angelfish . . . 2·40 1·60
207 100r. Yellow-faced angelfish 3·25 2·30
MS208 60 × 70 mm. 150r. As No. 204 . . . . 6·75 4·00

1996. 50th Anniv of UNICEF. Multicoloured.
209 20r. Type **26** 80 45
210 50r. Girls playing . . . . . 1·60 90
211 60r. Mother and child . . . 2·00 1·10
212 70r. Mother with three children . . . . 2·40 1·60
MS213 70 × 60 mm. 150r. Girl making jewellery (horiz) . . . 6·25 4·00

27 Players chasing Ball

1998. World Cup Football Championship, France. Multicoloured.
214 10r. Type **27** 45 25
215 15r. Heading ball 75 35
216 35r. Tackle . . . . 1·50 75
217 65r. Tackle (different) . . . . 2·50 1·30
218 75r. Kicking high ball . . . 3·00 1·50
MS219 200 × 100 mm. Nos. 214/18 8·25 4·50

28 Arabian Bustard

1998. Birds. Multicoloured.
220 10r. Type **28** 55 25
221 15r. Egyptian vulture 75 35
222 35r. Abyssinian roller . . . . 1·50 75
223 65r. Violet starling . . . . . 2·50 1·30
224 75r. Dark chanting goshawk 3·00 1·50
MS225 200 × 100 mm. Nos. 220/4 8·25 4·50

29 Upraised Hands and Anniversary Emblem

1998. 50th Anniv of Universal Declaration of Human Rights. Multicoloured.
226 15r. Type **29** 75 45
227 35r. Handshakes . . . . . . 1·50 80
228 100r. Outspread hands reaching to emblem . . . 3·75 1·80
MS229 205 × 105 mm. Nos. 226/8 6·00 3·50

30 Dhows and Emblem

2000. 1st General Conference of Yemeni Immigrants, Sana'a. Multicoloured.
230 60r. Type **30** . . . . 1·70 90
231 90r. Wadi Dhahr and emblem 2·50 1·80
MS232 97 × 69 mm. Nos. 230/1 4·25 3·25

31 Emblem

32 *Euphorbia abdalkuri*

2000. 10th Anniv of Unification. National Day.
233 **31** 30r. multicoloured 80 65
234 50r. multicoloured . . . . 1·50 1·00
235 70r. multicoloured . . . . 2·00 1·50
MS236 69 × 109 mm. **31** 150r. multicoloured . . . . 4·50 3·25

2000. Plants of Socotra Archipelago. Multicoloured.
237 30r. Type **32** 80 55
238 70r. *Dendrosicyos socotranus* 2·00 1·30
239 80r. *Caralluma socotrana* . . 2·40 1·60
240 120r. *Dracaena cinnabari* . . 3·50 2·00
MS241 97 × 69 mm. "Exacum affine" . . . . 9·00 6·25

33 Emblem

34 Mohammed Al Durra

2000. Olympic Games, Sydney. Showing sports pictograms. Multicoloured.
242 50r. Type **33** . . . . 1·60 1·10
243 70r. Running . . . . 2·20 1·30
244 80r. Hurdling . . . . 2·40 1·50
245 100r. Rifle shooting . . . . 3·00 1·60
MS246 69 × 109 mm. 300r. Tennis 9·00 6·25

2002. Intifada. Multicoloured.
247 30r. Type **34** 55 55
248 60r. Eiman Hajjo . . . . . . 1·10 1·10
MS249 112 × 78 mm. 90r. Mosque. Imperf . . . . 1·60 1·60

35 Scout leading Elderly Man across Road

2002. 75th Anniv of Yemen Boy Scouts. Multicoloured.
250 30r. Type **35** 55 55
251 60r. Planting . . . . 1·10 1·10
252 70r. In rowing boat . . . . 1·30 1·30
MS253 77 × 112 mm. 160r. Saluting (20 × 30 mm) . . . . 3·00 3·00

36 Player and Football

37 Stone Idols (3000 BC)

2002. World Cup Football Championship, Japan and South Korea. Multicoloured.
254 30r. Type **36** 55 55
255 70r. Two players (horiz) . . . 1·30 1·30
256 100r. Player running . . . . 1·80 1·80
257 120r. Player preparing to kick ball . . . . 2·20 2·20
MS258 116 × 16 mm. Circular:— 160r. × 2 Leg and ball (33 × 33 mm)ampionship trophy (33 × 33 mm) . . . . 6·00 6·00

2002. Antiquities. (1st series). Multicoloured.
259 30r. Type **37** 55 55
260 70r. Ma'adi Karib (statue, 800 BC) . . . . 1·30 1·30
261 100r. Horned griffin (plaque, 300 AD) . . . . 1·80 1·80
262 120r. Awsan Yasduq Eil (statue, 100 BC) . . . . . 2·20 2·20
MS263 111 × 78 mm. 320r. Stele with bull's head (100 BC). Imperf 6·00 6·00
See also Nos. 272/**MS**275.

38 Abdullah Al Baradony

39 Anniversary Emblem

2002. Poets. Multicoloured.
264 30r. Type **38** 55 55
265 30r. Hussein Al-Muhdhar wearing turban 55 55
266 60r. Abdullah Al Baradony facing left . . . . 1·10 1·10
267 60r. Hussein Al-Muhdhar wearing fez . . . . 1·10 1·10
MS268 112 × 78 mm. 70c. × 2 Hussein Al-Muhdhar (20 × 30 mm); Abdullah Al Baradony (20 × 30 mm) . . . . 2·75 2·75

2002. 40th Anniv of Revolution.
269 **39** 30r. multicoloured 55 55
270 60r. multicoloured . . . . 1·10 1·10
MS271 111 × 77 mm. 90r. emblem. Imperf . . . . 1·60 1·60

40 Two Players and Ball

2003. Yemen Under 17 Qualifying Team FIFA World Championship Final 2003. Showing two players with football.
272 30r. Type **40** 20 15
273 50r. Player wearing white . . 30 20
274 70r. Player wearing red . . . 40 25
275 100r. Player wearing green and white 55 35
MS276 109 × 75 mm. 250r. Team members. Imperf . . . . . . 1·40 85

41 Stone Statue **42** Woman wearing Striped Headdress

2003. Antiquities (2nd series). Multicoloured.
277 20r. Type **41** 15 10
278 40r. Carved pillar 25 15
279 50r. Bearded man (statue) . . 30 20
280 150r. Man wearing kilt (plaque) 85 50
MS281 111 × 76 mm. 260r. Musician (plaque) (horiz) . . . . 1·50 90

2003. Traditional Women's Costumes. Multicoloured.
282 30r. Type **42** 20 15
283 60r. Wearing striped dress with bodice 35 20
284 70r. Older woman wearing hat 40 25
285 100r. Wearing transparent face covering 55 35
286 150r. Wearing black and white dress 85 50
MS287 111 × 76 mm. Wearing turban (horiz) . . . . 2·30 1·40

43 Girl on Globe **44** Old City, Sana'a

2003. Winning Designs in Children's Painting Competition. Multicoloured.
288 20r. Type **43** 15 10
289 30r. Dove above ruins . . . 20 15
290 40r. Dove carrying children 25 15
291 50r. Houses, road, children and tree (horiz) 30 20
292 60r. Trees, animals and river (horiz) 35 20
293 70r. Park and houses (horiz) 40 25

2003. Sana'a, Arab City of Culture, 2004. Multicoloured.
294 30r. Type **44** 20 15
295 50r. al-Aqil minaret 30 20
296 70r. Five-storied building . . 40 25
297 100r. Street market 55 35
298 150r. al-Milh souk 85 50
MS299 111 × 76 mm. 400r. Buildings with takhrim windows (horiz) 2·25 1·40

YUGOSLAVIA Pt. 3

The kingdom of the Serbs, Croats and Slovenes, in S.E. Europe, established after the 1914–18 war and comprising Serbia, Montenegro, Bosnia, Herzegovina and parts of pre-war Hungary.

From 1945 it was a Federal Republic comprising six republics. In 1991 four of these republics seceded, from when the Federation consisted of the Republics of Montenegro and Serbia and the two autonomous provinces of Kosovo and Vojvodina.

A. KINGDOM OF THE SERBS, CROATS AND SLOVENES

I. ISSUES FOR BOSNIA AND HERZEGOVINA

100 heller = 1 kruna.

1918. 1910 commem stamps of Bosnia (with date labels) optd **DRZAVA S.H.S. 1918 1918 Bosna i Hercegovina** or the same in Cyrillic characters or surch also.
1 3h. olive (No. 345) . . . . . 60 1·50
2 5h. green 30 45
3 10h. red 25 35
4 20h. sepia 25 35
5 25h. blue 25 35
6 30h. green 25 50
7 40h. orange 25 35
8 45h. red 25 35
9 50h. purple 50 50
10 60h. on 50h. purple 25 40
11 80h. on 6h. brown 25 40
12 90h. on 35h. green 25 40
13 2k. green 40 60
14 3k. on 3h. olive . . . . . . 75 1·75
15 4k. on 1k. lake . . . . . . 2·50 3·50
16 10k. on 2h. violet . . . . . 4·00 4·50

1918. Newspaper Express stamps of Bosnia. 5h. optd as last and **HELERA** and 2h. the same but in Cyrillic.
17 N **35** 2h. red . . . . 4·00 5·00
18 5h. green . . . . 2·00 2·50
These were issued for use as ordinary postage stamps.

1918. Bosnian War Invalids Fund stamps optd **DRAVA S.H.S. Bosna Hercegovina** or the same in Cyrillic characters.
19 **31** 5h. (+2h.) green £150 £160
20 – 10h. (+2h.) red . . . . . . 95·00 £140
21 – 10h. (+2h.) blue . . . . . . 70 4·50
22 **31** 15h. (+2h.) brown . . . . . 1·75 4·00

6a

КРАЉЕВСТВО

(7)

1918. Newspaper stamps of Bosnia of 1913 (as T **6a**) surch. Imperf.
50 **6a** 2 on 6h. mauve £100 £175
51 2 on 10h. red . . . . 50·00 75·00
52 2 on 20h. green . . . . . . 6·00 12·00
23 3 on 2h. blue 20 40
24 5 on 6h. mauve 20 40
Most of these were used for ordinary postage purposes.

1919. Perf.
25 **6a** 2h. blue 20 25
26 6h. mauve . . . . 50 1·00
27 10h. red 25 25
28 20h. green 20 25
The above were issued for use as ordinary postage stamps.
These stamps imperforate were issued as Newspaper stamps for Bosnia q.v.

1919. Types of Bosnia optd with T **7** or similar type with wording **KRALJEVSTVO S.H.S.**, or surch also.
29 **25** 3h. lake 20 75
30 5h. green 20 30
31 10 on 6h. black 20 20
32 **26** 20 on 35h. green 20 20
33 **25** 25h. blue 20 20
34 30h. red 30 45
35 **26** 45h. brown 30 45
36 **33** 45 on 80h. brown 20 20
37 **26** 50h. blue . . . . 45·00 60·00
38 50h. on 72h. blue 20 20
39 60h. purple 20 40
40 **33** 80h. brown 20 40
41 90h. purple 25 40
42 – 2k. green (No. 200) . . . 30 50
43 **26** 3k. red on green 35 75
44 **34** 4k. red on green . . . . . 1·50 2·00
45 **26** 5k. lilac on grey . . . . . 1·50 2·25
46 **34** 10k. violet on grey . . . . 2·50 3·00

1919. War Victims' Fund. Stamps of Bosnia of 1906 surch **KRALJEVSTVO Srba. Hrvata i Slovenaca** or same in Cyrillic characters and new value.
47 – 10x.+10x. on 40h. orange (No. 196) . . . . 1·25 2·25
48 – 20x.+10x. on 20h. sepia (No. 192) . . . . 65 1·50
49 **5** 45x.+15x. on 1k. lake . . . . 4·00 6·00

II. ISSUES FOR CROATIA

100 filir (heller) = 1 kruna (krone).

The provisional issues on Hungarian stamps were sold in Yugoslavia "heller" and "krone" currency, but as this is not expressed on the stamps (except for Nos. 69/73) we have retained the Hungarian descriptions to facilitate reference to the original stamps.

1918. Various issues of Hungary optd **HRVATSKA SHS** and bar or wheel. "Turul" issue of 1900.
53 **7** 6f. olive . . . . 75 1·50
54 50f. lake on blue . . . . . 1·00 1·75

"Harvesters" and "Parliament" issues of 1916.
55 **18** 2f. brown 30 30
56 3f. red 30 30
57 5f. green 30 30
58 6f. green 30 30
59 10f. red . . . . 6·50 6·50
60 15f. violet (No. 244) . . . . 50·00 70·00
61 15f. violet (No. 251) 30 30
62 20f. brown 30 30
63 25f. blue 30 40
64 35f. brown 30 30
65 40f. green 30 50
66 **19** 50f. purple 30 30
67 75f. blue 30 30
68 80f. green 30 45
69 1k. red 30 30
70 2k. brown 30 30
71 3k. grey and violet 30 45
72 5k. light brown and brown 2·00 2·50
73 10k. mauve and brown . . . 10·00 12·50
The kroner values are overprinted **KRUNA** or **KRUNE** also.

"Charles" and "Zita" issue of 1918.
74 **27** 10f. red 30 40
75 20f. brown 30 40
76 25f. blue 30 65
77 **28** 40f. olive 30 40

1918. Stamps of Hungary optd **HRVATSKA SHS ZF ZA NAROD VIJECE.** War Charity issue of 1916.
78 **20** 10+2f. red 35 45
79 – 15+2f. violet 10 35
80 **22** 40+2f. lake 10 35

Coronation issue of 1916.
81 **23** 10f. mauve . . . . 50·00 70·00
82 – 15f. red . . . . 50·00 70·00

20 "Freedom of Croatia"

1918. Freeing of the Yugoslavs.
83 **20** 10h. red . . . . 2·25 2·75
84 20h. violet . . . . 2·50 3·75
85 25h. blue . . . . 4·25 6·50
86 45h. grey . . . . 40·00 45·00

21 Angel of Peace **22** Sailor with Standard and Falcon **23** Falcon ("Liberty")

1919.
87 **21** 2h. brown 10 35
88 3h. mauve 10 40
89 5h. green 10 10
90 **22** 10h. red 10 10
91 20h. brown 10 10
92 25h. blue 10 10
93 45h. olive 15 15
94 **23** 1k. red 20 20
95 – 3k. purple 65 85
96 – 5k. brown . . . . 1·00 75
DESIGN: 3, 5k. as Type **5** but light background behind falcon.

III. ISSUES FOR SLOVENIA

1919. 100 vinar (heller) = 1 kruna (krone).
1920. 100 paras = 1 dinar.

25 Chainbreaker **26** Chainbreaker

27 "Yugoslavia" with Three Falcons **28** Angel of Peace

29 King Petar I

1919. Perf or rouletted.
97a **25** 3v. violet 15 10
107 5v. green 10 10
108 10v. red 15 10
100 15v. blue 15 10
101 **26** 20v. brown 50 15
102 25v. blue 30 10
103 30v. pink 30 10
111 30v. red 35 15
104a 40v. yellow 35 10
122 **27** 50v. green 25 10
135 60v. violet 60 30
136 **28** 1k. red 45 25
120 2k. blue 50 20
126 **29** 5k. red 50 20
139 10k. blue . . . . 2·75 75
105 15k. green . . . . 7·00 10·00
106 20k. purple . . . . 1·50 2·25

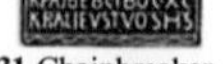

31 Chainbreaker **32** "Yugoslavia" with Three Falcons

34 King Petar I

1920. Perf (2d. to 10d.) or roul.
150 **31** 5p. olive 15 10
151 10p. green 10 10
152 15p. brown 10 10
153 20p. red 35 30
154 25p. brown 35 10
155 **32** 40p. violet 10 15
156 45p. yellow 10 15
157 50p. blue 10 10
158 60p. brown 10 10
159 **34** 1d. brown 10 10
160 – 2d. black 10 10
161 **34** 4d. slate 15 15
162 – 6d. olive 10 50
163 – 10d. brown 30 60
The 2, 6 and 10d. are as Type **34** but larger.

1920. Carinthian Plebiscite. Newspaper stamps of Yugoslavia of 1919 surch **1920 KGCA** and new value. Imperf.
163a N **30** 5p. on 4v. grey 10 25
163b 15p. on 4v. grey . . . 10 25
163c 25p. on 4v. grey . . . 10 50
163d 45p. on 2v. grey . . . 15 1·00
163e 50p. on 2v. grey . . . 10 1·10
163f 2d. on 2v. grey . . . . 1·00 5·00
These stamps were sold at three times face value on aid of the Plebiscite Propaganda Fund.

IV. ISSUES FOR THE WHOLE KINGDOM

100 paras = 1 dinar.

35 King Alexander when Prince **37** Kosovo Maiden, 1389

1921. Inscr "KRALJEVSTVO" at foot.
164 **35** 2p. brown 10 10
165 5p. green 10 10
166 10p. red 10 10
167 15p. purple 10 10
168 20p. black 10 10
169 25p. blue 10 10
170 50p. olive 10 10
171 60p. red 20 10
172 75p. violet 10 10
173 – 1d. orange 15 10
174 – 2d. olive 30 10
175 – 4d. green 50 10
176 – 5d. red . . . . 1·75 10
177 – 10d. brown . . . . 5·00 30
DESIGN: 1d. to 10d. as Type **35**, but portrait of King Petar I.

1921. Disabled Soldiers' Fund.
178 **37** 10+10p. red 10 10
179 – 15+15p. brown 10 10
180 – 25+25p. blue 10 15
DESIGN: 15p. Wounded soldier typifying retreat through Albania, 1915; 25p. Symbol of national unity.

1922. Nos. 178/180 surch.
181 1d. on 10p. red 10 10
183 1d. on 15p. brown 10 10
182 1d. on 25p. blue 10 10
184 3d. on 15p. brown 25 10
186 8d. on 15p. brown . . . . . 1·00 20
187 20d. on 15p. brown . . . . 7·50 65
188 30d. on 15p. brown . . . . 10·00 1·50

1923. As T **35**, but inscr "KRALJEVINA" at foot.
189 **35** 1d. brown 90 10
190 5d. red 35 10

191		8d. purple	7·00	25
192		20d. green	18·00	75
193		30d. orange	50·00	2·25

1924. Nos. 171 and 191 surch.

195	35	20p. on 60p. red	25	10
196		5d. on 8d. purple	8·50	50

44 King Alexander 46 King Alexander

1924.

197	44	20p. black	10	10
198		50p. brown	10	10
199		1d. red	10	10
200		2d. green	30	10
201		3d. blue	30	10
202		5d. brown	1·25	10
203	–	10d. violet	10·00	10
204	–	15d. green	8·00	20
205	–	20d. orange	8·00	15
206	–	30d. green	4·00	1·00

The 10d. to 30d. have the head in a square panel.

1925. Surch.

207	44	25p. on 3d. blue	10	10
208		50p. on 3d. blue	10	10

1926.

209	46	25p. green	10	10
210		50p. brown	10	10
211		1d. red	15	10
212		2d. black	15	10
213		3d. blue	30	10
214		4d. red	50	10
215		5d. violet	75	10
216		8d. brown	2·75	10
217		10d. green	1·50	10
218		15d. brown	10·00	10
219		20d. violet	12·50	20
220		30d. orange	90·00	40

1926. Danube Flood Fund. Surch.

221	46	25p.+0.25 green	10	10
222		50p.+0.50 brown	10	10
223		1d.+0.50 red	10	10
224		2d.+0.50 black	20	10
225		3d.+0.50 blue	20	10
226		4d.+0.50 red	25	10
227		5d.+0.50 violet	40	10
228		8d.+0.50 brown	85	30
229		10d.+1.00 green	1·75	10
230		15d.+1.00 brown	5·00	60
231		20d.+1.00 violet	7·00	50
232		30d.+1.00 orange	20·00	2·50

1928. Nos. 223/32 optd **XXXX** over previous surch.

233	46	1d. red	15	15
234		2d. black	50	15
235		3d. blue	90	30
236		4d. red	2·10	40
237		5d. violet	1·75	15
238		8d. brown	6·00	70
239		10d. green	12·00	15
240		15d. brown	55·00	2·00
241		20d. violet	30·00	2·00
242		30d. orange	75·00	8·50

B. KINGDOM OF YUGOSLAVIA

100 paras = 1 dinar.

49 Duvno Cathedral

1929. Millenary of Croatian Kingdom (1925).

243	49	50p.+50p. olive	15	15
244	–	1d.+50p. red	50	30
245	–	3d.+1d. blue	1·25	85

DESIGNS—As Type **49**: 3d. King Tomislav. Horiz (34 × 23 mm): Kings Tomislav and Alexander I.

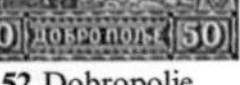
52 Dobropolje 53 Serbian War Memorial, Paris

1931. Serbian War Memorial (Paris) Fund.

246	52	50p.+50p. green	10	10
247	53	1d.+50p. red	10	10
248	–	3d.+1d. blue	15	15

DESIGN—As Type **52**: 3d. Kajmakcalan.

55 King Alexander 57 Rowing "four" on Lake Bled

1931.

249	55	25p. black	10	10
250		50p. green	10	10
262		75p. green	25	10
251		1d. red	15	10
263		1d.50 red	60	10
263b		1d.75 red	1·10	25
252		3d. blue	1·00	10
263c		3d.50 blue	1·50	25
253		4d. orange	2·50	10
254		5d. violet	2·50	10
255		10d. olive	9·00	10
256		15d. brown	8·50	10
257		20d. purple	17·00	10
258		30d. red	9·00	45

1931. Optd **KRALJEVINA JUGOSLAVIJA** and also in Cyrillic characters.

259	49	50p.+50p. olive	10	10
260	–	1d.+50p. red	10	10
261	–	3d.+1d. blue	30	50

1932. European Rowing Championship. Inscr ending "EUROPE 1932".

264	–	75p.+50p. green	40	90
265	57	1d.+½d. red	40	90
266	–	1½d.+½d. red	75	1·10
267	–	3d.+1d. blue	1·40	2·00
268	–	4d.+1d. blue and orange	6·00	13·50
269	–	5d.+1d. lilac and violet	6·00	10·00

DESIGNS—HORIZ: 75p. Single sculler on Danube at Smederevo; 1½d. Rowing "eight" on Danube at Belgrade; 3d. Rowing "pair" at Split harbour. VERT: 4d. Rowing "pair" on river and Zagreb Cathedral; 5d. Prince Peter.

1933. 11th International PEN Club Congress, Dubrovnik. As T **55** with additional value and "XI. int. kongres Pen-Klubova u Dubrovniku 1933" inscr below in Roman or Cyrillic characters.

270	55	50p.+25p. black	3·75	8·50
271		75p.+25p. green	3·75	8·50
272		1d.50+50p. red	3·75	8·50
273		3d.+1d. blue	3·75	8·50
274		4d.+1d. green	3·75	8·50
275		5d.+1d. yellow	3·75	8·50

60 Crown Prince Petar in "Sokol" Uniform

62

1933. "Sokol" Meeting, Ljubjana.

276	60	75p.+25p. green	20	25
277		1½d.+½d. red	20	25

1933. Optd **JUGOSLAVIJA** in Roman and Cyrillic characters. (a) Postage.

278	46	25p. green	10	10
279		50p. brown	10	10
280		1d. red	30	10
281		2d. black	50	15
282		3d. blue	1·75	10
283		4d. red	1·00	10
284		5d. violet	1·75	10
285		8d. brown	3·50	1·25
286		10d. olive	9·00	15
287		15d. brown	10·00	1·50
288		20d. violet	19·00	75
289		30d. orange	16·00	75

(b) Charity stamps. Nos. 221/3.

290	46	25p.+0.25 green	40	15
291		50p.+0.50 brown	40	10
292		1d.+0.50 red	1·25	40

1933. Obligatory Tax. Red Cross.

293	62	50p. red and blue	15	20

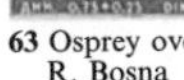
63 Osprey over R. Bosna

64 Athlete and Falcon (from sculpture by Krsinic)

1934. 20th Anniv of "Sokol" Games, Sarajevo.

294	63	75p.+25p. green	5·75	5·75
295		1d.50+50p. red	8·00	8·00
296		1d.75+25p. brown	17·00	17·00

1934. 60th Anniv of Croat "Sokol" Games, Zagreb.

297	64	75p.+25p. green	2·00	2·75
298		1d.50+50p. red	2·50	4·50
299		1d.75+25p. brown	7·50	10·00

65 Dubrovnik

69 Mostar Bridge

1934. Air.

300	65	50p. purple	10	15
301	–	1d. green	20	15
302	–	2d. red	35	35
303	–	3d. blue	1·10	40
304	69	10d. orange	2·50	3·00

DESIGNS: 1d. Lake of Bled; 2d. Waterfall at Jajce; 3d. Oplenac.

1934. King Alexander Mourning issue. With black margins.

305	55	25p. black (postage)	10	10
306		50p. green	10	10
307		75p. green	10	10
308		1d. red	10	10
309		1d.50 red	10	10
310		1d.75 red	10	10
311		3d. blue	10	10
312		3d.50 blue	20	10
313		4d. orange	20	10
314		5d. violet	40	10
315		10d. olive	1·25	10
316		15d. brown	2·75	20
317		20d. purple	5·00	20
318		30d. red	3·50	40
319	–	3d. blue (No. 303) (air)	3·75	3·50

70 King Petar II

71 King Alexander

1935.

320	70	25p. black	10	10
321		50p. orange	10	10
322		75p. green	15	10
323		1d. brown	15	10
324		1d.50 red	15	10
325		1d.75 red	25	10
325a		2d. red	15	10
326		3d. orange	15	10
327		3d.50 blue	35	10
328		4d. green	90	10
329		4d. blue	30	10
330		10d. violet	75	10
331		15d. brown	90	10
332		20d. blue	3·50	25
333		30d. pink	1·75	25

1935. 1st Anniv of King Alexander's Assassination.

334	71	75p. green	20	35
335		1d.50 red	20	35
336		1d.75 brown	25	75
337		3d.50 blue	1·25	2·00
338		7d.50 red	1·00	1·75

72

73 Queen Marie

1935. Winter Relief Fund.

339	72	1d.50+1d. brown	1·00	1·00
340		3d.50+1d.50 blue	1·50	2·50

1936. Child Welfare.

341	73	75p.+25p. green	25	35
342		1d.50+50p. red	25	35
343		1d.75+75p. brown	1·00	1·10
344		3d.50+1d. blue	1·50	2·00

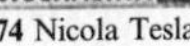
74 Nicola Tesla

75 Prince Paul

1936. 80th Birthday of Dr. Tesla (physicist).

345	74	75p. brown and green	15	20
346		1d.75 grey and blue	15	25

1936. Red Cross Fund.

347	75	75p.+50p. green	10	25
348		1d.50+50p. red	10	25

76 Dr. Vladan Djordjevic (founder)

77 Princess Tomislav and Andrej

1936. Obligatory Tax. Jubilee of Serbian Red Cross.

349	76	50p. brown	20	25

1937. Child Welfare. T **77** and similar horiz portrait.

350	–	25p.+25p. brown	15	25
351	–	75p.+75p. orange	30	40
352	77	1d.50+1d. orange	35	50
353		2d.+1d. mauve	50	1·00

78 Oplenac

79 Macedonian Costume

1937. Little Entente.

354	78	3d. green	85	50
355		4d. blue	85	1·00

1937. 1st Yugoslav Philatelic Exhibition, Belgrade (ZEFIB). Sheet 109 × 150 mm, comprising T **79** and similar designs showing girls in national costumes.

MS356 1d. green (T **79**); 1d.50 purple (Bosnia); 2d. scarlet (Slovenia); 4d. blue (Croatia) Sold at the Exhibition P.O. at 15d. . . . . 3·00 7·00

80 St. Naum Convent, Lake Ohrid

83 Arms of Yugoslavia, Greece, Rumania and Turkey

1937. Air.

360	80	50p. brown	10	10
361	–	1d. green	15	10
362	–	2d. blue	20	15
363	–	2d.50 red	30	15
364	80	5d. violet	30	25
365a	–	10d. red	55	25
366	–	20d. green	85	85
367	–	30d. blue	1·10	1·50

DESIGNS—VERT: 1, 10d. Rab (Arbe) Harbour. HORIZ: 2, 20d. Sarajevo; 2d.50, 30d. Laibach (Ljubljana).

1937. Balkan Entente.

368	83	3d. green	70	35
369		4d. blue	1·00	85

84

85

1938. Child Welfare.

370	84	50p.+50p. brown	10	15
371	85	1d.+1d. green	20	35
372	84	1d.50+1d.50 red	45	85
373	85	2d.+2d. mauve	1·00	1·75

86 Searchlight Display and Parachute Tower

87 Entrance to Demir Kapija Cliff

1938. Int Aeronautical Exhibition, Belgrade, and Yugoslav Air Club Fund.

374	86	1d.+50p. green	35	75
375		1d.50+1d. red	50	1·00
376		2d.+1d. mauve	1·50	2·00
377		3d.+1d. blue	2·00	3·50

1938. Railway Employees' Hospital Fund.

378	87	1d.+1d. green	40	45
379	–	1d.50+1d.50 red	1·10	95
380	–	2d.+2d. mauve	2·00	2·10
381	–	3d.+3d. blue	2·40	2·40

DESIGNS—HORIZ: 1d.50, Demir Kapija Hospital. VERT: 2d. Runner carrying torch; 3d. King Alexander.

90 Hurdling

1938. 9th Balkan Games.
382 – 50p.+50p. orange . . . . 75 1·00
383 **90** 1d.+1d. green . . . . . . 1·50 2·10
384 – 1d.50+1d.50 mauve . . . . 2·00 2·75
385 – 2d.+2d. blue . . . . 2·75 3·50
DESIGNS—HORIZ: 1d.50, Pole vaulting. VERT: 50p. Breasting the tape; 2d. Putting the shot.

91 Maiden of Kosovo (after P. Jovanovic)

1938. Obligatory Tax. Red Cross.
386 **91** 50p. multicoloured 20 25
386a 50p. red and blue 25 35

1938. Child Welfare. Optd **SALVATE PARVULOS**.
387 **84** 50p.+50p. brown 30 50
388 **85** 1d.+1d. green 30 65
389 **84** 1d.50+1d.50 red . . . . . 60 1·00
390 **85** 2d.+2d. mauve . . . . . . 1·25 2·00

93 Mail Carrier

1939. Postal Centenary and Railway Benevolent Association Fund.
391 – 50p.+50p. orange and brown 25 50
392 **93** 1d.+1d. green and black . . 25 50
393 – 1d.50+1d.50 red . . . . . 2·75 1·25
394 – 2d.+2d. purple and violet . 1·25 2·50
395 – 4d.+4d. blue and light blue . 2·25 4·50
DESIGNS: 50p. Mounted postmen; 1d.50, Steam mail train; 2d. Mail coach; 4d. Lockheed 10 Electra mail plane.

94 Meal-time 95 Milos Obilic

1939. Child Welfare.
396 **94** 1d.+1d. green 40 85
397 – 1d.50+1d.50 red & brown . 2·00 3·00
398 – 2d.+2d. mauve & brown . . 1·25 2·50
399 – 4d.+4d. light blue & blue . 1·50 3·50
DESIGNS—HORIZ: 2d. Young carpenter. VERT: 1d.50, Children playing on sands; 4d. Children whispering.

1939. 550th Anniv of Battle of Kosovo.
400 – 1d.+1d. green and olive . . 1·25 1·50
401 **95** 1d.50+1d.50 red and carmine . . . . 1·25 1·50
DESIGN: 1d. Prince Lazar.

96 Motor Cycle and Sidecar 97 Cadet Barquentine "Jadran"

1939. 1st International Motor Races, Belgrade.
402 **96** 50p.+50p. orange and brown 50 75
403 – 1d.+1d. green and black . 90 1·25
404 – 1d.50+1d.50 carmine and red . . . . 1·40 2·00
405 – 2d.+2d. blue and indigo . . 2·25 3·00
DESIGNS—HORIZ: 1, 2d. Racing cars. VERT: 1d.50, Motor cycle.

1939. King Petar's Birthday and Adriatic Guard Fund.
406 **97** 50p.+50p. red . . . . . . 1·10 1·00
407 – 1d.+50p. green . . . . . . 1·25 1·00
408 – 1d.50+1d. red . . . . . . 1·60 1·75
409 – 2d.+1d.50 blue . . . . . . 2·75 2·25
DESIGNS: 1d. Liner "King Alexander"; 1d.50, Freighter "Triglav"; 2d. Destroyer "Dubrovnik".

98 Unknown Warrior's Tomb, Avala 99 King Petar II

1939. 5th Death Anniv of King Alexander. War Invalids' Fund.
410 **98** 1d.+50p. green . . . . . . 85 1·25
411 1d.50+1d. red . . . . . . 85 1·25
412 2d.+1d.50 purple . . . . . 1·25 1·75
413 3d.+2d. blue . . . . 2·00 3·00

1939.
414 **99** 25p. black 10 10
415 50p. orange 10 10
416 1d. green 10 10
417 1d.50 red 10 10
418 2d. pink 10 10
419 3d. brown 15 10
420 4d. blue 15 10
420a 5d. blue 15 15
420b 5d.50 violet 45 10
421 6d. blue 85 10
422 8d. brown 85 10
423 12d. violet . . . . . . 1·50 10
424 16d. purple . . . . . . 2·00 25
425 20d. blue . . . . . . 2·00 25
426 30d. pink . . . . . . 4·25 50

100 Postman delivering Letters 101 Arrival of Thorval

1940. Belgrade Postal Employees' Fund. Inscr "ZA DOM P.T.T. ZVAN. I SLUŽ".
427 **100** 50p.+50p. orange & brn 50 85
428 – 1d.+1d. green and black 50 85
429 – 1d.50+1d.50 red & brown 90 1·75
430 – 2d.+2d. mauve & purple 6·25 4·00
431 – 4d.+4d. blue and grey . 3·50 5·00
DESIGNS—VERT: 1d. Postman collecting letters; 4d. Telegraph linesman. HORIZ: 1d.50, Mail-van; 2d. Loading mail train.

1940. Zagreb Postal Employees' Fund. Inscr "ZA DOM P.T.T. CINOV U ZAGREBU".
432 **101** 50p.+50p. orange & brown 30 35
433 – 1d.+1d. green 30 35
434 – 1d.50+1d.50 red 45 50
435 – 2d.+2d. red . . . . . . 1·00 1·50
436 – 4d.+2d. blue . . . . . . 1·25 1·50
DESIGNS—25½ × 35½ mm: 1d. King Tomislav enthroned; 1d.50, Death of Matija Gubec. 37 × 27 mm: 2d. Radic Brothers. 34 × 25 mm: 4d. Divisional map of Yugoslavia.

102 Winter Games

1940. Child Welfare. Inscr "ZA NASU DECU".
437 **102** 50p.+50p. orange and red 15 35
438 – 1d.+1d. green and olive 15 35
439 **102** 1d.50+1d.50 red and brown 50 75
440 – 2d.+2d. mauve and violet 1·00 1·25
DESIGN—VERT: 1, 2d. Children at seaside (Summer Games).

103 Arms of Yugoslavia, Greece, Rumania and Turkey 104 Zagreb Cathedral and Junkers Ju 86

1940. Balkan Entente. Inscr "JUGOSLAVIJA" alternately at top in Cyrillic (A) or Roman (B) thoughout the sheet. A.
441A **103** 3d. blue 70 40
442A 4d. blue 70 40

B.
441B **103** 3d. blue 70 40
442B 4d. blue 70 40

1940. Air.
443 **104** 40d. green . . . . 1·75 1·75
444 – 50d. blue . . . . 2·00 3·00
DESIGN: 50d. Suspension Bridge at Belgrade and Fokker F.VIIa/3m.

105 Obod, Scene of early Press, 1493 109 Kamenita Gate, Zagreb

107 St. Peter's Cemetery, Ljubljana

1940. 500th Anniv of Invention of Printing Press by Johannes Gutenberg.
445 **105** 5d.50 deep green and green . . . . 1·50 2·75

1940. Anti-T.B. Fund. Nos. 364/7 surch.
446 **80** 50p.+50p. on 5d. violet . . 15 15
447 – 1d.+1d. on 10d. red . . . 20 40
448 – 1d.50+1d.50 on 20d. green 90 1·25
449 – 2d.+2d. on 30d. blue . . . 1·25 2·00

1941. Ljubljana War Veterans' Fund.
450 **107** 50p.+50p. green 20 25
451 – 1d.+1d. red 20 25
452 – 1d.50+1d.50 green 50 85
453 – 2d.+2d. lilac and blue . . 85 1·25
DESIGNS—HORIZ: 2d. War Memorial, Brezje. VERT: 1d. National costumes; 1d.50, Memorial Chapel, Kajmakcalan.

1941. Philatelic Exhibitions. (a) 2nd Croatian Philatelic Exhibition, Zagreb.
454 **109** 1d.50+1d.50 brown . . . 60 1·25
455 – 4d.+3d. black . . . . . . 60 1·25

(b) 1st Philatelic Exhibition, Slav Brod.
456 **109** 1d.50+1d.50 black . . . . 9·00 15·00
457 – 4d.+3d. brown . . . . . 9·00 15·00
DESIGN: 4d. (2) Old Cathedral, Zagreb.

NOTE. From 1941 until 1945 Yugoslavia ceased to exist as a stamp-issuing entity, except for the following series, Nos 468/81, which were issued by the exiled government for the use of the Yugoslav Merchant Navy working with the Allies.

110 King Petar II 112 V. Vodnik (poet)

1943. 2nd Anniv of Overthrow of Regency and King Petar's Assumption of Power.
468 **110** 2d. blue 10 50
469 3d. grey 10 50
470 5d. red . . . . 15 1·00
471 10d. black . . . . 20 1·50

1943. Red Cross Fund. Surch **CRVENI KRST+ 12.50.**
472 **110** 2d.+12d.50 blue . . . . . 50 2·50
473 3d.+12d.50 grey . . . . . 50 2·50
474 5d.+12d.50 red . . . . . 50 2·50
475 10d.+12d.50 black . . . . 50 2·50

1943. 25th Anniv of Formation of Yugoslavia.
476 **112** 1d. black and red 10
477 – 2d. black and green . . . 15
478 – 3d. blue and blue 15
479 – 4d. brown and violet . . . 40
480 – 5d. brown and purple . . 40
481 – 10d. deep brown and brown . . . . 1·25
MS481a 127 × 185 mm. Nos. 476/81 28·00
DESIGNS: 2d. Petar Njegos (poet); 3d. Ljudevit Gaj (writer); 4d. Vuk Karadzic (poet); 5d. Bishop Josip Strosmajer (politician); 10d. Djordje Petrovic (Karageorge).

C. DEMOCRATIC FEDERATION OF YUGOSLAVIA
I. REGIONAL ISSUES
Bosnia and Herzegovina

Currency: Croatian Kunas.

1945. Mostar Issue. Stamps of Croatia surch **Demokratska Federativna Jugoslavija** and value. (a) Pictorial Stamps of 1941–43.
R 1 10k. on 25b. red 50 50
R 2 10k. on 50b. green 20 20
R 3 10k. on 2k. red 35 35
R 4 10k. on 3k.50 brown 75 75
R 5 40k. on 1k. green 20 20
R 6 50k. on 4k. blue . . . . . 4·50 4·50
R 7 50k. on 5k. blue . . . . . . 18·00 18·00
R 8 50k. on 6k. green . . . . . 4·50 4·50
R 9 50k. on 7k. red . . . . . . 60·00 60·00
R10 50k. on 8k. brown . . . . . 75·00 75·00
R11 50k. on 10k. violet 60 60

(b) Famous Croats issue of 1943.
R12 30k. on 1k. blue 35 35
R13 30k. on 12k.50 purple . . . 20 20

(c) Boskovic issue of 1943.
R14 **28** 30k. on 3k.50 blue . . . . 1·50 1·50
R15 30k. on 12k.50 purple . . 75 75

(d) War Victims Charity Tax stamps of 1944.
R16 **34** 20k. on 1k. green 15 15
R17 **35** 20k. on 2k. red 25 25
R18 20k. on 5k. green 25 25
R19 20k. on 10k. blue 25 25
R20 20k. on 20k. brown . . . 70 70

Croatia

Currency: Kunas.

DEMOKRATSKA FEDERATIVNA

20
KUNA

(R 2)

1945. Split issue. Stamps of Croatia 1941–43 surch as Type R **2**.
R21 10k. on 25b. red 15 15
R22 10k. on 50b. green 15 15
R23 10k. on 75b. green 15 15
R24 10k. on 1k. green 15 15
R25 20k. on 2k. red 15 15
R26 20k. on 3k. brown 15 15
R27 20k. on 3k.50 brown 15 15
R28 20k. on 4k. blue 15 15
R29 20k. on 5k. blue 30 30
R30 20k. on 6k. green . . . . . 9·00 9·00
R31 30k. on 7k. red 15 15
R32 30k. on 8k. brown . . . . . 12·00 12·00
R33 30k. on 10k. violet 15 15
R34 30k. on 12k.50 black 15 15
R35 40k. on 20k. brown 15 15
R36 40k. on 30k. brown 20 20
R37 50k. on 50k. green 15 15

1945. Zagreb issue. Stamps of Croatia, 1941–43, surch **DEMOKRATISKA FEDERATIVNA JUGOSLAVIJA**, value and star.
R38 20k. on 5k. blue 25 25
R39 40k. on 1k. green 25 25
R40 60k. on 3k.50 brown 25 25
R41 80k. on 2k. red 25 25
R42 160k. on 50b. green 25 25
R43 200k. on 12k.50 black . . . 25 25
R44 400k. on 25b. red 25 25

Montenegro

Currency: Italian Lire.

Демократска
Федеративна
Југославија

(R 4)

1945. Cetinje issue. Stamps of Italian Occupation surch with Type R **4**. (a) National Poem Issue of 1943.
R50 1l. on 10c. green 75 90
R51 2l. on 25c. green 50 60
R52 3l. on 50c. mauve 50 60
R53 5l. on 1l.25 blue 50 60
R54 10l. on 15c. brown . . . . . 90 1·25
R55 15l. on 20c. orange . . . . . 90 1·25
R56 20l. on 2l. green . . . . . . 90 1·25

(b) Air stamps of 1943, for use as ordinary postage stamps.
R57 3l. on 50c. brown . . . . . 4·00 4·50
R58 6l. on 1l. blue . . . . . . 4·00 4·50
R59 10l. on 2l. red . . . . . . 4·00 4·50
R60 20l. on 5l. green . . . . . 4·00 4·50

Serbia

Currency: Hungarian Filler.

1944. Senta issue. Various stamps of Hungary optd with a large star, **8.X.1944** and "Yugoslavia" in Cyrillic characters.
R63 1f. grey . . . . 5·50 4·50
R64 2f. red . . . . 5·50 4·50
R65 3f. blue . . . . 5·50 4·50
R66 4f. brown . . . . 5·50 4·50
R67 5f. red . . . . 5·50 4·50
R68 8f. green . . . . 5·50 4·50
R69 10f. brown . . . . 90·00 90·00
R70 20f. brown . . . . 80·00 80·00
R71 24f. purple . . . . 8·00 8·00
R72 30f. red . . . . 90·00 90·00

Slovenia

Currencies: Italian (Ljubljana).
German (Maribor).
Hungarian (Murska Sobota).

(R 5)

1945. Ljubljana issue. Pictorial stamps of German Occupation, 1945, optd as Type R **5**.
R74 5c. brown 30 30
R75 10c. orange 30 30
R76 20c. brown 30 30
R77 25c. green 30 30
R78 50c. violet 30 30
R79 75c. red 50 50
R80 1l. green 30 50
R81 1l.25 blue 30 30
R82 1l.50 green 30 30
R83 2l. blue 30 30
R84 2l.50 brown 30 30
R85 3l. mauve 35 35
R86 5l. brown 50 60
R87 10l. green 35 45
R88 20l. blue . . . . 4·00 4·00
R89 30l. red . . . . 18·00 18·00

1945. Maribor issue. Hitler stamps of Germany, 1941–44, optd **SLOVENIJA 9.5. 1945 JUGOSLAVIJA** and star.
R 90 **173** 1pf. grey . . . . . . 5·00 5·00
R 91 3pf. brown 50 50
R 92 4pf. grey . . . . . . 4·00 4·00
R 93 5pf. green . . . . . . 3·00 3·00
R 94 6pf. violet 50 50
R 95 8pf. red 75 75
R 96 10pf. brown (No. 775) 3·00 3·00
R 97 12pf. red (No. 776) . . 35 35
R 98 15pf. brown . . . . . 6·00 6·00
R 99 20pf. blue . . . . . 3·50 3·50
R100 24pf. brown . . . . . 3·75 3·75
R101 25pf. blue . . . . . 10·00 10·00
R102 30pf. green 75 75
R103 40pf. mauve 75 75
R104 **225** 42pf. green 60 60
R105 **173** 50pf. green . . . . . 3·00 3·00
R106 60pf. brown 75 75
R107 80pf. blue . . . . . 1·75 1·75

1945. Murska Sobota issue. Various stamps of Hungary optd as Nos. R90/107.
R108 1f. grey . . . . 6·00 6·00
R109 4f. brown 50 50
R110 5f. red . . . . 6·00 6·00
R111 10f. brown 50 50
R112 18f. black 50 50
R113 20f. brown 50 50
R114 30f. red 50 50
R115 30f. red 50 50
R116 50f. blue . . . . 10·00 10·00
R117 70f. brown . . . . 10·00 10·00
R118 80f. brown . . . . 50·00 50·00
R119 1p. green . . . . 6·00 6·00

II. GENERAL ISSUES

100 paras = 1 dinar.

(113)

1944. Monasteries. Stamps of German Occupation of Serbia, 1942, surch as T **113**.
482 – 3d.+2d. pink (No. 64) . . . 10 20
485 – 4d.+21d. blue (No. 65) . . . 10 20
483 – 7d.+3d. green (No. 66) . . . 10 20

114 Marshal Tito **115** Chapel at Prohor Pcinjski

1945.
491 **114** 25p. green 20 15
492 50p. green 20 10
493 1d. red . . . . 3·00 40
494 2d. red 20 10
495 4d. blue 40 10
487 5d. green 10 10
496 6d. violet 50 10
497 9d. brown . . . . 1·00 20
488 10d. red 10 10
498 20d. yellow . . . . 4·50 1·40
489 25d. violet 15 15
490 30d. blue 25 15

1945. 1st Anniv of Anti-Fascist Chamber of Deputies, Macedonia.
499 **115** 2d. red 70 25

116 Partisans

1945. Red Cross Fund.
500 **116** 1d.+4d. blue 90 80
501 – 2d.+6d. red 90 80
DESIGN—VERT: 2d.+6d. Child's head.

119 Partisans

120 Marshal Tito

1945. Partisans.
502 **119** 50p. brown 10 10
503 1d. green 15 10
504 – 1d.50 brown 15 10
505 **120** 2d. red 15 10
506 – 2d.50 red 45 10
507 – 3d. brown . . . . 1·25 10
508 – 3d. red 45 10
509 **120** 4d. blue 25 10
510 – 5d. green . . . . 1·25 10
511 – 5d. blue . . . . 1·40 10
512 – 6d. black 45 10
513 – 8d. orange . . . . 1·25 10
514 – 9d. purple 40 10
515 – 12d. blue 80 10
516 **119** 16d. blue 80 10
517 – 20d. red . . . . 1·75 20
DESIGNS—As Type **119**: 1d.50, 12, 20d. Riflemen. VERT: 3, 5d. Town of Jajce inscr "29-XI-1943". HORIZ: 2d.50, 6, 8, 9d. Girl with flag.

122 Russian and Yugoslav Flags

1945. 1st Anniv of Liberation of Belgrade.
518 **122** 2d.+5d. multicoloured . . 70 40

124 "Industry and Agriculture"

126

1945. Meeting of the Constituent Assembly. Inscr in Cyrillic at top and Roman characters at foot (A) or vice-versa (B).
519 **124** 2d. red (A) . . . . . . 3·75 3·75
519b 2d. red (B) . . . . . . 3·75 3·75
520 4d. blue (A) . . . . . . 3·75 3·75
520b 4d. blue (B) . . . . . . 3·75 3·75
521 6d. green (A) . . . . . . 3·75 3·75
521b 6d. green (B) . . . . . . 3·75 3·75
522 9d. red (A) . . . . . . 3·75 3·75
522b 9d. red (B) . . . . . . 3·75 3·75
523 16d. blue (A) . . . . . . 3·75 3·75
523b 16d. blue (B) . . . . . . 3·75 3·75
524 20d. brown (A) . . . . . . 3·75 3·75
524b 20d. brown (B) . . . . . . 3·75 3·75
MS524c 150 × 110 mm. Nos. 522 and 524 (A) . . . . 22·00 22·00
MS524d Nos. 522b and 524b (B) 22·00 22·00

D. FEDERAL PEOPLE'S REPUBLIC

100 paras = 1 dinar.

1946. Type of 1945 (Girl with flag), surch.
525 2d.50 on 6d. red 60 10
526 8d. on 9d. orange . . . . . 1·00 10

1946. 1st Anniv of Victory over Fascism. Star in red.
527 **126** 1d.50 yellow 35 40
528 2d.50 red 80 60
529 5d. blue . . . . . . 1·40 1·25

127 Symbolic of Communications

128 Railway Construction

1946. Postal Congress.
530 **127** 1d.50+1d. green . . . . . 4·25 3·50
531 2d.50+1d.50 red . . . . 4·25 3·50
532 5d.+2d. blue . . . . . 4·25 3·50
533 8d.+3d.50 brown . . . . 4·25 3·50

1946. Volunteer Workers' Railway Reconstruction Fund.
534 **128** 50p.+50p. brown, blue and red . . . . 3·50 2·00
535 1d.50+1d. green, blue and red . . . . 3·50 1·75
536 2d.50+2d. lilac, blue and red . . . . 3·50 1·75
537 5d.+3d. grey, blue & red 3·50 2·25

129 Svetozar Markovic

130 Theatre in Sofia

1946. Birth Centenary of S. Markovic (socialist writer).
538 **129** 1d.50 green 75 40
539 2d.50 purple 75 45

1948. Slav Congress.
540 **130** ½d. brown and buff . . . 10 10
541 – 1d. green and light green 15 10
542 – 1½d. red and pink 20 15
543 – 2½d. orange and buff . . 25 15
544 – 5d. blue and light blue . . 1·25 60
DESIGNS—HORIZ: 1d. Charles Bridge and Hradcany, Prague. VERT: 1½d. Sigismund Monument, Warsaw; 2½d. Victory Monument, Belgrade; 5d. Kremlin Tower, Moscow.

131 Roofless Houses

132 Ilyushin Il-4 DB-3 Bomber over Kalimegdan Terrace, Belgrade

1947. Obligatory Tax. Red Cross.
545 **131** 50p. brown 15 10

1947. Air. Inscr in Cyrillic at top and Roman characters at foot (A) or vice versa (B).
546 **132** 50p. green and brown (A) 15 15
546b 50p. green and brown (B) 15 15
547 – 1d. green and red (A) . . 25 20
547b – 1d. green and red (B) . . 25 20
548 **132** 2d. blue and black (A) 40 25
548b 2d. blue and black (B) 40 25
549 – 5d. drab and green (A) 45 30
549b – 5d. drab and green (B) 45 30
550 – 10d. brown and sepia (A) 55 40
550b – 10d. brown and sepia (B) 55 40
551 **132** 20d. green and blue (A) 1·00 65
551b 20d. green and blue (B) 1·00 65
DESIGN: 1, 5, 20d. Ilyushin Il-4 DB-3 over Dubrovnik.

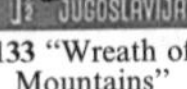
133 "Wreath of Mountains"

134 Petar Njegos (author)

1947. Centenary of Publication of "Wreath of Mountains".
552 **133** 1½d. black and green . . 15 10
553 **134** 2d.50 red and buff . . 20 15
554 **133** 5d. black and blue . . . 35 20

135 Girl Athlete, Star and Flags **137** Gymnast

1947. Federal Sports Meeting.
555 – 1d.50 brown 15 10
556 **135** 2d.50 red 20 15
557 – 4d. blue 50 40
DESIGNS—VERT: 1d.50, Physical training groups. HORIZ: 4d. Parade of athletes.

1947. Balkan Games.
558 **137** 1d.50+0.50 green 15 10
559 2d.50+0.50 red 30 20
560 4d.+0.50 blue 40 35

138 Star and Map of Julian Province

139 Railway Construction

1947. Annexation of Julian Province to Yugoslavia.
561 **138** 2d.50 red and blue . . . 15 10
562 5d. brown and green . . . 15 10

1947. Juvenile Labour Organizations' Relief Fund.
563 **139** 1d.+0.50 orange 30 15
564 1d.50+1d. green 35 25
565 2d.50+1d.50 red 60 30
566 5d.+2d. blue . . . . . . 1·25 70

140 Music Book and Fiddle

141 Vuk Karadzic (poet)

1947. Centenary of Serbian Literature.
567 **140** 1d.50 green 10 10
568 **141** 2d.50 red 15 15
569 **140** 5d. blue 20 20

142 "B.C.G. Vaccine defeating Tuberculosis"

143 "Illness and Recovery"

144 "Fight against Tuberculosis"

145 Map of Yugoslavia and Symbols of Industry and Agriculture

1948. Anti-T.B. Fund.
570 **142** 1d.50+1d. green and red 10 10
571 **143** 2d.50+2d. green and red 15 15
572 **144** 5d.+3d. blue and red . . 25 20

1948. International Fair, Zagreb.
573 **145** 1d.50 green, blue and red 10 10
574 2d.50 purple, blue and red 10 10
575 5d. indigo, blue and red 15 10

146 Flag-bearers

147 Djura Danicic

1948. 5th Yugoslav Communist Party Congress, Belgrade.
576 **146** 2d. green and deep green 20 15
577b 3d. purple and red . . . 20 15
578a 10d. ultramarine and blue 45 45

1948. 80th Anniv of Yugoslav Academy.
579 **147** 1d.50+0.50 green 15 15
580 – 2d.50+1d. red 25 15
581 – 4d.+2d. blue 35 30
PORTRAITS: 2d.50, Franjo Racki; 4d. Bishop Josip Strosmajer (inscr "Strossmayer").

148 "Krajina" (former royal yacht) passing under Danube Railway Bridge

1948. Danube Conference.
582 148 2d. green 2·40 2·40
583 3d. red 3·50 3·50
584 5d. blue 4·50 4·50
585 10d. brown 8·50 8·50

149 Lovrenz Kosir
150 Kosir and his Birthplace

1948. 80th Death Anniv of Kosir ("idealogical creator of first postage stamp").
586 149 3d. purple (postage) 15 10
587 5d. blue 15 15
588 10d. orange 20 10
589 12d. green 35 25
590 150 15d. mauve (air) 90 45

151 Putting the Shot
152
153 Arms of Montenegro

1948. Projected Balkan Games.
591 151 2d.+1d. green 20 15
592 – 3d.+1d. red 30 20
593 – 5d.+2d. blue 50 40
DESIGNS: 3d. Girl hurdler; 5d. Pole vaulting.

1948. Obligatory Tax. Red Cross.
594 152 50p. red and blue 20 15

1948. 5th Anniv of Republic.
595 – 3d. blue (Serbia) 35 25
596 – 3d. red (Croatia) 35 25
597 – 3d. orange (Slovenia) 35 25
598 – 3d. green (Bosnia and Herzegovina) 35 25
599 – 3d. mauve (Macedonia) 35 25
600 153 3d. black 35 25
601 – 10d. red (Yugoslavia) 2·00 2·00
No. 601 is larger, 24½ × 34½ mm.

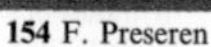
154 F. Preseren

155 Ski-jump, Planica

1949. Death Centenary of Franc Preseren (author).
602 154 3d. blue 20 15
603 5d. orange 25 20
604 10d. sepia 1·50 35

1949. Ski Jumping Competition, Planica.
605 155 3d. red 50 30
606 – 12d. blue (Ski jumper) 1·25 65

156 Soldiers

158 Globe, Letters and Forms of Transport

1949. 5th Anniv of Liberation of Macedonia.
(a) Postage
607 156 3d. red 50 40
608 – 5d. blue 1·25 65
608a – 12d. brown 2·50 2·50
DESIGNS: 5d. Industrial and agricultural workers; 12d. Arms and flags of Yugoslavia and Macedonia.

(b) Air. Optd with Lisunov Li-2 airplane and **AVIONSKA POSTA**.
609 156 3d. red 2·50 2·50
610 – 5d. blue (No. 608) 2·50 2·50
610a – 12d. brown (No. 608a) 2·50 2·50

1949. 75th Anniv of U.P.U.
611 158 3d. red 2·75 2·75
612 – 5d. blue 40 40
613 158 12d. brown 45 45
DESIGN—HORIZ: 5d. Airplane, train and mail coach.

1949. Surch with bold figures and bars.
614 O 130 3d. on 8d. brown 50 10
615 3d. on 12d. violet 60 10

160 Nurse and Child

1949. Obligatory Tax. Red Cross.
616 160 50p. brown and red 20 15

ФНР ЈУГОСЛАВИЈА
≡ D3
FNR JUGOSLAVIJA
(161)

F
N
R
D10
≡
JUGOSLAVIJA
(162)

1949. Surch with T 161 or 162.
617 – 3d. on 8d. yellow (No. 513) 65 10
618 – 10d. on 20d. red (No. 517) 85 10

FNR JUGOSLAVIJA
(163)

Ф Н Р

F N R
(164)

F
N
R
JUGOSLAVIJA
(165)

1949. Optd with T 163 on 2d., 164 on 3d. and 5d., or 165 on others.
619 119 50p. olive 10 10
620 1d. green 10 10
621 1d. orange 30 10
622 120 2d. red 15 10
623 2d. green 30 10
624 – 3d. red (No. 508) 15 10
625 – 3d. pink 30 10
626 – 5d. blue (No. 511) 40 20
627 – 5d. blue 1·10 10
628 – 12d. violet (No. 515) 35 10
629 119 16d. blue 1·25 40
630 20d. red 85 15

166 Class 151 Steam Locomotive, 1885

1949. Centenary of National Railways.
631 166 2d. green 1·50 35
632 – 3d. red 1·50 35
633 – 5d. blue 5·75 65
633a – 10d. orange 27·00 8·50
As No. 633a but colour, sheet 49 × 70 mm. Perf and Imperf.
MS633b 10d. purple £100 45·00
DESIGNS: 3d. Class 389 steam locomotive, 1930; 5d. Diesel locomotive, 1937, France; 10d. Electric train on bridge over River Vintgar.

167 Surveying

1950. Completion of Belgrade–Zagreb Road.
634 167 2d. green 40 15
635 – 3d. purple 25 15
636 – 5d. blue 1·00 70
DESIGNS: 3d. Map, road and car; 5d.Youth, road and flag.

168 Marshal Tito

169 Child Eating

1950. May Day.
637 168 3d. red 2·00 1·00
638 5d. blue 2·00 1·00
639 10d. brown 32·00 18·00
640 12d. black 2·00 2·00

1950. Child Welfare.
641 169 3d. red 35 10

170 Launching Model Glider

171 Chessboard and Bishop

1950. 3rd Aeronautical Meeting.
642 170 2d. green 80 90
643 – 3d. red 85 90
644 – 5d. violet 2·10 50
645 – 10d. brown 2·25 1·50
646 – 20d. blue 15·00 15·00
DESIGNS—VERT: 3d. Glider in flight; 5d. Parachutists landing; 10d. Woman pilot; 20d. Glider on water.

1950. 9th Chess Olympiad, Dubrovnik.
647 171 2d. brown 80 40
648 – 3d. bistre, brown and drab 80 30
649 – 5d. blue, yellow and green 1·50 50
650 – 10d. yellow, purple and blue 2·40 1·25
651 – 20d. yellow and blue 30·00 20·00
DESIGNS—VERT: 3d. Rook and flags; 5d. Globe and chessboard showing 1924 Capablanca v. Lasker game; 10d. Chequered globe, map and players; 20d. Knights and flags.

172 Girl Harvester

173 Steam Locomotive and Map

1950.
652 – 50p. brown 10 10
653 – 1d. green 15 10
705 – 1d. grey 20 10
654 172 2d. orange 15 10
706 2d. red 40 10
655 – 3d. red 20 10
656 – 5d. blue 65 10
719 – 5d. orange 4·50 10
657 – 7d. grey 75 10
720 – 8d. blue 4·00 15
658 – 10d. brown 75 10
721 – 10d. green 7·00 10
659 – 12d. brown 3·75 10
723 – 15d. red 19·00 10
660 – 16d. blue 2·25 30
723a – 17d. purple 4·50 10
661 – 20d. olive 2·25 35
710 – 20d. purple 3·50 10
711a 172 25d. bistre 13·00 10
662 – 30d. brown 5·00 55
712 – 30d. blue 1·90 10
713 – 35d. brown 2·50 10
662a – 50d. violet 45·00 20·00
714 – 50d. green 3·25 10
715 – 75d. violet 3·00 10
716 – 100d. sepia 6·75 15
DESIGNS—VERT: 50, 100d. Metallurgy; 1d. Electrical supply engineer; 3, 35d. Man and woman with wheelbarrow; 5d. Fishing; 7, 8d. Mining; 10d. Apple-picking; 12, 75d. Lumbering; 14, 15, 16d. Picking sunflowers; 17, 20d. Woman and farm animals; 30d. Girl printer; 50d. Dockers unloading cargo.

1950. Zagreb Exhibition.
663 173 3d. red 1·60 50

174 Girl in National Costume

175 Galleon

1950. Obligatory Tax. Red Cross.
664 174 50p. green and red 20 15

1950. Navy Day.
665 175 2d. purple 25 15
666 – 3d. brown 25 10
667 – 5d. green 1·75 20
668 – 10d. blue 65 15
669 – 12d. grey 1·60 50
670 – 20d. red 3·75 2·00
DESIGNS: 3d. Partisan patrol boat; 5d. Freighter discharging cargo; 10d. "Zagreb" (freighter) and globe; 12d. Yachts; 20d. Sailor, gun and "Golesnica" (torpedo boat).

176 Patriots of 1941

177 Franc Stane-Rozman

1951. 10th Anniv of Revolt against Pact with Axis.
671 176 3d. lake and red 2·25 1·40

1951. 10th Anniv of Partisan Rising in Slovenia.
672 177 3d. brown 50 25
673 – 5d. blue (Boy courier) 75 35

178 Children Painting

1951. International Children's Day.
674 178 3d. red 70 25

179 "Iron Gates", Danube

181 Zivorad Jovanovic

1951. Air.
675 179 1d. orange 15 10
676 – 2d. green 25 10
677 – 3d. red 25 10
677a – 5d. brown 30 10
678 – 6d. blue 4·50 4·00
679 – 10d. brown 50 10
680 – 20d. grey 75 10
681 – 30d. red 2·50 10
682 – 50d. violet 3·75 10
683 – 100d. grey 60·00 5·00
683a – 100d. green 1·40 15
683b – 200d. red 1·75 25
683c – 500d. blue 7·00 1·25
DESIGNS: (all show airplane)—As T 179: 2, 5d. Plitvice Cascades; 3, 100d. (green) Gozd-Martuljak (mountain village); 6, 200d. Old Bridge, Mostar; 10d. Ohrid; 20d. Kotor Bay; 30d. Dubrovnik; 50d. Bled. 40 × 27 mm: 100d. (grey), 500d. Belgrade.

1951. Air. Zagreb Philatelic Exhibition. No. 678 in new colour optd **ZEFIZ 1951**.
684 6d. green 90 70
As No 683, but colour changed, sheet 70 × 70 mm. Imperf.
MS684a 100d. brown £140 £110

1951. 10th Anniv of Serbian Insurrection.
685 181 3d. brown 60 40
686 – 5d. blue 1·25 65
DESIGN—HORIZ: 5d. Armed insurgents.

183 Mt. Kopaonik

184 Sava Kovacevic

1951. Air. International Mountaineering Assn Meeting, Bled. Inscr "UIAA-1951".
687 183 3d. mauve 3·50 3·25
688 – 5d. blue 3·50 3·25
689 – 20d. green 90·00 60·00
DESIGNS: 5d. Mt. Triglav, Slovenia; 20d. Mt. Kalnik, Croatia.

1951. 10th Anniv of Montenegrin Insurrection.
690 184 3d. red 75 55
691 – 5d. blue 1·50 85
DESIGN—HORIZ: 5d. Partisan and mountains.

185 Marko Oreskovic (statue)

186 Simo Solaja

1951. 10th Anniv of Croatian Insurrection.
692 185 3d. red 75 35
693 – 5d. green 1·25 65

DESIGN: 5d. "Transport of a Wounded Man" (sculpture, A. Augustincic).

1951. 10th Anniv of Insurrection of Bosnia and Herzegovina.
694 **186** 3d. red 90 40
695 – 5d. blue 1·25 65
DESIGN—VERT: 5d. Group of insurgents.

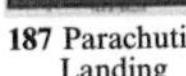

187 Parachutists Landing
189 Primoz Trubar (writer)

1951. Air. 1st World Parachute Jumping Championship, Bled.
696 **187** 6d. lake 5·00 2·00

As No. 682 in new colour optd **I SVETSKO TAKMICENJE PADOBRANACA 1951**.
697 50d. blue 80·00 45·00

1951. Cultural Anniversaries.
698 **189** 10d. black 40 25
699 – 12d. red 40 25
700 – 20d. lilac 4·00 3·25
DESIGNS: 12d. Marko Marulic (Croatian writer, 500th birth anniv (1950)); 20d. Tsar Stepan Dusan (600th anniv (1949) of "Tsar Dusan's Book of Laws").

190 National Products
191 Hoisting the Flag

1951. Zagreb International Fair.
701 **190** 3p. yellow, red and blue 1·10 35

1951. Obligatory Tax. Red Cross.
702 **191** 50p. blue and red 20 15

192 Mirce Acev
193 P. P. Njegos

1951. 10th Anniv of Macedonian Insurrection.
703 **192** 3d. mauve 60 50
704 – 5d. violet 1·25 75
DESIGN—HORIZ: 5d. War Victims' Monument, Skopje.

1951. Death Centenary of Petar Njegos (poet).
724 **193** 15d. purple 1·50 55

194 Soldier and Badge
195 Marshal Tito

1951. Army Day.
725 **194** 15d. red (postage) 45 10
726 **195** 150d. blue (air) 12·50 6·25

196 Marshal Tito
197 Marshal Tito

1952. Marshal Tito's 60th Birthday.
727 **196** 15d. brown 1·00 1·00
728 **197** 28d. lake 1·75 1·75
729 – 50d. green 35·00 25·00
DESIGN—As T **196**: 50d. Statue of Marshal Tito.

198
199 Gymnastics

1952. Children's Week.
730 **198** 15d. red 7·50 1·25

1952. 15th Olympic Games, Helsinki. Inscr "XV OLIMPIJADA 1952".
731 **199** 5d. brown on buff 60 25
732 – 10d. brown on yellow 90 25
733 – 15d. blue on pink 90 30
734 – 28d. brown on flesh 2·50 90
735 – 50d. green on cream 6·50 3·00
736 – 100d. brown on mauve 50·00 20·00
DESIGNS: 10d. Running; 15d. Swimming; 28d. Boxing; 50d. Basketball; 100d. Football.

200 "Fishing Boat" (from relief by Krsinic)
200a Belgrade (16th century)

1952. Navy Day. Views. Inscr "1952".
737 – 15d. purple 1·75 60
738 **200** 28d. brown 3·25 90
739 – 50d. black 23·00 19·00
DESIGNS: 15d. Split, Dalmatia; 50d. Sveti Stefan, Montenegro.

1952. Philatelic Exhibition, Belgrade.
739a **200a** 15d. purple 8·00 8·00
No. 739a was only sold at the Exhibition at 35d. (20d. entrance fee).

201
202 Workers in Procession (from fresco by Slavko Pengov)

1952. Obligatory Tax. Red Cross.
740 **201** 50p. red, grey and black 30 10

1952. 6th Yugoslavia Communist Party Congress.
741 **202** 15d. brown 1·50 1·10
742 15d. turquoise 1·50 1·10
743 15d. brown 1·50 1·10
744 15d. blue 1·50 1·10

203 Nikola Tesla
204 Fresco, Sopocani Monastery

1953. 10th Death Anniv of Tesla (inventor).
745 **203** 15d. lake 80 15
746 30d. blue 4·00 40

1953. United Nations Commemoration.
747 **204** 15d. green 1·25 35
748 – 30d. blue 2·10 35
749 – 50d. lake 17·00 3·00
DESIGNS—VERT: 30d. Fresco, St. Panteleimon Church, Nerezim, Skopje; 50d. Fresco, St. Dimitri Church, Pec.

205

1953. Adriatic Car and Motor Cycle Rally.
750 **205** 15d. mauve and orange 30 15
751 – 30d. deep blue and blue 85 20
752 – 50d. brown and yellow 1·75 20
753 – 70d. green and emerald 6·00 1·60
DESIGNS—HORIZ: 30d. Motor cyclist and coastline; 50d. Racing car and flags; 70d. Saloon car descending mountain roadway.

206 Marshal Tito
207

1953. Marshal Tito Commemoration.
754 **206** 50d. violet 9·00 2·00

1953. 38th Esperanto Congress, Zagreb.
755 **207** 15d. green & black (postage) 3·25 1·75
756 300d. green and blue (air) £250 £225

208 "Insurrection" (Borko Lazevski)
209

1953. 50th Anniv of Macedonian Insurrection.
757 **208** 15d. purple 80 75
758 – 30d. green 2·75 2·00
DESIGN: 30d. Nikola Karev (revolutionary).

1953. 10th Anniv of Liberation of Istria and Slovene Coast.
759 **209** 15d. green 12·50 1·75

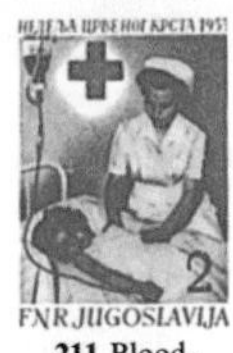

210 B. Radicevic
211 Blood-transfusion

1953. Death Centenary of Branko Radicevic (poet).
760 **210** 15d. purple 6·00 1·25

1953. Obligatory Tax. Red Cross.
761 **211** 2d. red and purple 35 25

212 Jajce
213 European Souslik

1953. 10th Anniv of 1st Republican Legislative Assembly.
762 **212** 15d. green 1·25 40
763 – 30d. red 1·50 95
764 – 50d. sepia 10·00 8·75
DESIGNS: 30d. Assembly Building; 50d. Marshal Tito addressing assembly.

1954. Animals.
765 **213** 2d. grey, buff and green 20 10
766 – 5d. brown, buff and green 35 15
767 – 10d. brown and black 60 25
768 – 15d. brown and blue 80 30
769 – 17d. brown and purple 1·40 30
770 – 25d. yellow, blue and violet 2·40 40
771 – 30d. brown and blue 2·40 40
772 – 35d. black and brown 6·00 90
773 – 50d. brown and green 16·00 1·75
774 – 65d. black and red 22·00 12·00
775 – 70d. brown and green 19·00 10·50
776 – 100d. black and blue 60·00 30·00
DESIGNS—HORIZ: 5d. Lynx; 10d. Red deer; 15d. Brown bear; 17d. Chamois; 25d. Eastern white pelican. VERT: 30d. Lammergeier; 35d. "Procerus gigas" (ground beetle); 50d. "Callimenius pancici" (cricket); 65d. Black Dalmatian lizard; 70d. Blind cave-dwelling salamander; 100d. Brown trout.

214 Ljubljana (17th century)

1954. Philatelic Exhibition, Ljubljana.
777 **214** 15d. brown, green & black 13·50 10·00

No. 777 was only sold at the Exhibition at 35d. (20d. entrance fee).

215 Cannon, 1804

1954. 150th Anniv of Serbian Insurrection. Mult.
778 15d. Serbian flag 1·25 40
779 30d. Type **215** 2·00 75
780 50d. Seal of insurgents' council 3·75 1·50
781 70d. Karageorge 40·00 12·00

215a
216

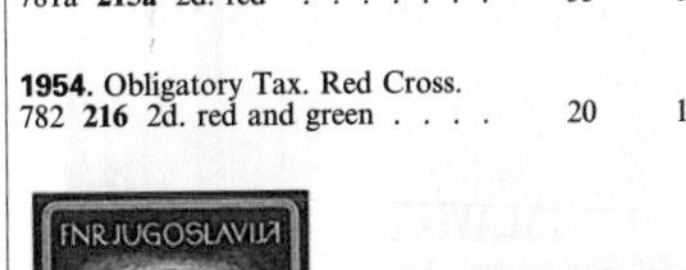

1954. Children's Week.
781a **215a** 2d. red 35 60

1954. Obligatory Tax. Red Cross.
782 **216** 2d. red and green 20 10

217 Vatroslav Lisinski (composer)
218 "A Midsummer Night's Dream" (Shakespeare)

1954. Cultural Anniversaries.
783 **217** 15d. green 3·00 45
784 – 30d. brown 2·25 1·00
785 – 50d. purple 2·50 1·60
786 – 70d. blue 5·00 3·00
787 – 100d. violet 22·00 18·00
PORTRAITS: 15d. Type **217** (death centenary); 30d. Andrija Kacic-Miosic (writer, 250th birth anniv); 50d. Jury Vega (mathematician, birth bicentenary); 70d. Jovan Jovanovic-Zmaj (poet, 50th death anniv); 100d. Filip Visnjic (poet and musician, 120th death anniv).
See also Nos. 975/80.

1955. Dubrovnik Festival.
788 – 15d. lake 80 35
789 **218** 30d. blue 3·00 1·10
DESIGN—VERT: 15d. Scene from "Robinja" by Hanibal Lucic.

219
220

1955. 1st Int Exn of Engraving, Ljubljana.
790 **219** 15d. brown and green on stone 2·50 75

1955. 2nd World Congress of the Deaf and Dumb.
791 **220** 15d. red 1·50 40

221 Hops
222 Laughing Girl

1955. Floral Designs.
792 **221** 5d. green and brown 15 10
793 – 10d. purple, green and buff 15 10
794 – 15d. multicoloured 20 10
795 – 17d. buff, green and lake 30 15
796 – 25d. yellow, green and blue 40 15
797 – 30d. multicoloured 70 45
798 – 50d. red, green and brown 3·75 1·50
799 – 70d. orange, green and brown 5·00 2·50
800 – 100d. multicoloured 25·00 15·00

FLOWERS: 10d. Tobacco; 15d. Opium poppy; 17d. Small-leaved lime; 25d. False chamomile; 30d. Sage; 50d. Dog rose; 70d. Great yellow gentian; 100d. Yellow pheasant's-eye.

1955. Obligatory Tax. Children's Week.
801 **222** 2d. red and cream 25 15

223 Peace Monument, U.N. Building, New York (A. Augustincic)

224 Red Cross Nurse

1955. 10th Anniv of United Nations.
802 **223** 30d. black and blue . . . 1·25 55

1955. Obligatory Tax. Red Cross.
803 **224** 2d. black, grey and red 25 15

225 Woman and Dove

226 St. Donat's Church, Zadar

1955. 10th Anniv of Republic.
804 **225** 15d. violet 40 20

1956. Yugoslav Art.
805 **226** 5d. grey 45 10
806 – 10d. green 45 10
807 – 15d. brown 50 10
808 – 20d. brown 50 15
809 – 25d. sepia 65 15
810 – 30d. purple 65 20
811 – 35d. green . . . . 1·25 35
812 – 40d. brown . . . . 2·25 45
813 – 50d. brown . . . . 5·50 35
814 – 70d. green . . . . 12·00 8·25
815 – 100d. purple . . . . . . 32·00 19·00
816 – 200d. blue . . . . 55·00 22·00
DESIGNS—VERT: 10d. Bas-relief of Croat King, Diocletian Palace, Split; 15d. Church portal, Studenica, Serbia; 20d. Master Radovan's portal, Trogir Cathedral; 25d. Fresco, Sopocani, Serbia; 30d. Monument, Radimije, Herzegovina; 50d. Detail from Bozidarevic Triptych, Dubrovnik; 70d. Carved figure, Belec Church, Croatia; 100d. Self-portrait of Rikard Jakopic; 200d. Peace Monument by A. Augustinic, New York. HORIZ: 35d. Heads from Cathedral cornice, Sibenik, Dalmatia; 40d. Frieze, Kotor Cathedral, Montenegro.

227 Zagreb through the Centuries

228 Houses ruined by Avalanche

1956. Yugoslav Int Philatelic Exn, Zagreb.
817 **227** 15d. deep brown, brown and black (postage) . . 30 15
818 30d. blue, red and black (air) . . . . . . 1·50 55

1956. Obligatory Tax. Red Cross.
819 **228** 2d. sepia, brown and red 30 20

229 "Technical Education"

230 Induction Motor

1956. Air. 10th Anniv of Technical Education.
820 **229** 30d. black and red . . . 1·25 90

1956. Birth Centenary of Nikola Tesla (inventor).
821 **230** 10d. olive 15 10
822 – 15d. brown 40 10
823 – 30d. blue 70 15
824 – 50d. purple . . . . 2·25 1·00
DESIGNS: 15d. Transformer; 30d. "Telekomanda" (invention); 50d. Portrait of Tesla.

231 Short-snouted Seahorse

232

1956. Adriatic Sea Creatures.
825 **231** 10d. brown, purple & green 15 10
826 – 15d. black, pink and blue 15 10
827 – 20d. multicoloured . . . 20 10
828 – 25d. multicoloured . . . 35 10
829 – 30d. multicoloured . . . 45 10
830 – 35d. mauve, yellow & blue 90 15
831 – 50d. red, yellow and blue 3·50 85
832 – 70d. multicoloured . . . 5·00 1·40
833 – 100d. multicoloured . . . 16·00 3·75
DESIGNS: 15d. Common paper nautilus; 20d. Rock lobster; 25d. Rainbow wrasse; 30d. Painted comber; 35d. Striped red mullet; 50d. Red scorpionfish; 70d. Cuckoo wrasse; 100d. John Dory.

1956. Obligatory Tax. Children's Week.
834 **232** 2d. green 30 20

233 Running

234

1956. Olympic Games. Figures, values and country name in ochre.
835 **233** 10d. red 10 10
836 – 15d. blue (Canoeing) . . 10 10
837 – 20d. blue (Skiing) 20 10
838 – 30d. green (Swimming) . . 30 10
839 – 35d. sepia (Football) . . . 45 10
840 – 50d. green (Water polo) 1·25 15
841 – 70d. purple (Table tennis) 4·00 1·40
842 – 100d. red (Shooting) . . . 7·00 2·75

1957. Obligatory Tax. Red Cross.
843 **234** 2d. red, black and blue 25 15

235 Common Centaury

236 Factory in Worker's Hand

1957. Flowers. Multicoloured.
844 10d. Type **235** 10 10
845 15d. Deadly nightshade . . . 15 10
846 20d. Saffron crocus 20 10
847 25d. Marsh mallow 20 10
848 30d. Common valerian . . . 25 15
849 35d. Woolly foxglove 30 15
850 50d. Male fern . . . . 2·25 40
851 70d. Green-winged orchid . . 4·00 75
852 100d. Pyrethrum . . . . . . 16·00 7·50

1957. 1st Congress of Workers' Councils, Belgrade.
853 **236** 15d. lake 40 10
854 30d. blue 85 25

237 Gymnastics

1957. 2nd Gymnastics Festival, Zagreb. Vert designs as T **237**.
855 **237** 10d. olive and black . . . 25 10
856 – 15d. brown and black . . 25 10
857 – 30d. blue and black . . . 65 10
858 – 50d. brown and black . . 2·00 1·50

239 Musician and Dancers of Slovenia

240 Children

1957. Yugoslav Costumes (1st series).
860 – 10d. multicoloured . . . 15 10
861 – 15d. multicoloured . . . 25 10
862 – 30d. multicoloured . . . 25 10
863 – 50d. green, brown and buff 90 20
864 – 70d. black, brown and buff . . . . 1·00 35
865 **239** 100d. multicoloured . . . 5·50 2·50
DESIGNS—HORIZ: 10d. Montenegrin musician, man and woman; 15d. Macedonian dancers; 30d. Croatian shepherdess and shepherd boys. VERT: 50d. Serbian peasants; 70d. Bosnian villagers.
See also Nos. 1020/5.

1957. Obligatory Tax. Children's Week.
866 **240** 2d. slate and red 25 15

241 Revolutionaries

242 Simon Gregorcic (poet)

1957. 40th Anniv of Russian Revolution.
867 **241** 15d. red and ochre . . . 40 20

1957. Cultural Anniversaries.
868 **242** 15d. sepia 30 10
869 – 30d. blue 40 10
870 – 50d. brown 90 10
871 – 70d. violet . . . . 8·50 2·25
872 – 100d. green . . . . 14·00 13·00
PORTRAITS: 15d. Type **242** (50th death anniv (1956)); 30d. Anton Linhart (dramatist, birth bicentary (1956)); 50d. Oton Kucera (physicist, birth centenary); 70d. Stevan Mokranjac (composer, birth centenary (1956)); 100d. Jovan Popovic (writer, death centenary (1956)).

244

245 Fresco of Sopocani Monastery

1958. 7th Yugoslav Communist Party Congress.
877 **244** 15d. purple 20 10

1958. Obligatory Tax. Red Cross.
878 **245** 2d. multicoloured 30 20

246 Mallard

247 Pigeon

1958. Yugoslav Game Birds. Birds in natural colours. Background colours given below.
879 **246** 10d. brown 15 15
880 – 15d. mauve 20 15
881 – 20d. blue 40 15
882 – 25d. green 65 15
883 – 30d. turquoise 80 20
884 – 35d. bistre 90 20
885 – 50d. purple . . . . 4·25 1·25
886 – 70d. blue . . . . 7·75 3·00
887 – 100d. brown . . . . . . 17·00 8·00
DESIGNS—HORIZ: 15d. Western capercaillie; 20d. Common pheasant; 35d. Water rail; 70d. Eurasian woodcock. VERT: 25d. Black coot; 30d. Water rail; 50d. Rock partridge; 100d. Common crane.

1958. Opening of Postal Museum, Belgrade.
888 **247** 15d. black 30 10

248 Battle Flag

249 Pomet (hero of Drzic's comedy "Dundo Maroje") and Ancient Fountain at Dubrovnik

1958. 15th Anniv of Battle of Sutjeska River.
889 **248** 15d. lake 25 15

1958. 450th Birth Anniv of Marin Drzic (writer).
890 **249** 15d. brown and black . . 25 10

243 Steel Plant, Sisak

250 Children at Play

1958.
891 – 2d. green 10 10
892 – 5d. red 15 10
983 – 5d. orange 30 10
893 – 8d. purple 20 10
984 – 8d. violet 25 10
894 **243** 10d. green 30 10
985 10d. brown 25 10
896 – 15d. red 45 10
986 – 15d. green 35 10
898 – 17d. purple 65 10
899 – 20d. red 50 10
987 – 20d. blue 40 10
987a – 20d. green 40 10
900 – 25d. grey 50 10
988 – 25d. red 30 10
901 – 30d. blue 25 10
989 – 30d. brown . . . . . . 4·00 10
989a – 30d. red 70 10
902 – 35d. red 25 10
903 – 40d. red 30 10
904 – 40d. blue . . . . 1·40 10
990 – 40d. purple 25 10
905 – 50d. blue 30 10
991 – 50d. blue 70 10
906 – 55d. red . . . . 2·00 10
992 – 65d. green 25 10
907 – 70d. red . . . . 1·75 10
908 – 80d. red . . . . 8·50 10
909 – 100d. green . . . . . . 6·00 10
993 – 100d. green . . . . . . 2·50 10
994 – 150d. red 90 15
910 – 200d. brown . . . . . 2·50 30
995 – 200d. blue 60 10
996 – 300d. green . . . . . . 2·25 30
911 – 500d. blue . . . . . . 5·00 30
997 – 500d. violet . . . . . 1·50 10
998 – 1000d. brown . . . . . 2·25 10
999 – 2000d. purple . . . . . 5·25 30
DESIGNS—VERT: 2, 100d. (993) Oil derricks, Nafta; 5d. Shipbuilding; 8, 17d. Timber industry, cable railway; 15 (896), 20d. Jablanica Dam; 15 (986), 25d. (900) Ljubljana–Zagreb motor road; 25d. (988) Cable industry; 30d. "Litostroj" turbine factory, Ljubljana; 35, 40d. (990) Coke plant, Lukavac; 50d. (991) Iron foundry, Zenica; 65d. Furnace, Sovojno. HORIZ: 40 (903/4), 150d. Hotel Titograd; 50 (905), 55, 200d. (995) Skopje; 70, 80, 300d. Sarajevo railway station and obelisk; 100 (909), 500d. (997) Bridge, Ljubljana; 200 (910), 1000d. Theatre, Zagreb; 500 (911), 2000d. Parliament House, Belgrade.
See also Nos. 1194/1204.

1958. Obligatory Tax. Children's Week.
912 **250** 2d. black, olive and yellow 20 10

251 Ship with Oceanographic Equipment

252 "Human Rights"

1958. International Geophysical Year.
913 **251** 15d. purple (postage) . . 55 15
914 – 300d. blue (air) . . . . . 7·50 2·25
DESIGN: 300d. Moon and Earth with orbital tracks of artificial satellites.

1958. 10th Anniv of Declaration of Human Rights.
915 **252** 30d. green 65 45

253 Old City, Dubrovnik　**254** Communist Party Emblem and Red Flags

1959. Tourist Publicity (1st series). Views.
916 **253** 10d. yellow and red . . . 10 10
917 – 10d. blue and green . . . 10 10
918 – 15d. violet and blue . . . 10 10
919 – 15d. green and blue . . . 10 10
920 – 20d. green and brown . . 15 10
921 – 20d. green and blue . . . 15 10
922 – 30d. violet and orange . . 1·25 10
923 – 30d. green and blue . . . 1·25 10
924 – 70d. black and blue . . . 4·25 1·50
DESIGNS: No. 917, Bled; 918, Postojna grottoes; 919, Ohrid; 920, Plitvice Lakes; 921, Opatija; 922, Split; 923, Sveti Stefan; 924, Belgrade.
See also Nos. 1033/41, 1080/5 and 1165/70.

1959. 40th Anniv of Yugoslav Communist Party.
925 **254** 20d. multicoloured . . . 15 10

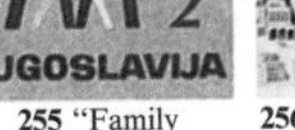

255 "Family Assistance"　**256** Dubrovnik (15th century

1959. Obligatory Tax. Red Cross.
926 **255** 2d. blue and red 25 20

1959. Philatelic Exhibition, Dubrovnik ("JUFIZ IV").
927 **256** 20d. myrtle, green and blue 75 65

257 Dutch Lavender　**258** Tug-of-War

1959. Medicinal Plants.
928 **257** 10d. violet, green and blue 10 10
929 – 15d. multicoloured . . . 10 10
930 – 20d. multicoloured . . . 10 10
931 **257** 25d. lilac, green and olive 20 10
932 – 30d. green, blue and pink 30 15
933 – 35d. blue, green and brown 60 20
934 – 50d. yellow, green & brn 2·40 50
935 – 70d. multicoloured . . . 3·50 1·00
936 – 100d. grey, green & brown . . . . 6·00 2·75
FLOWERS: 15d. Alder blackthorn; 20d. Scopolia; 25d. Monkshood; 30d. Bilberry; 35d. Common juniper; 50d. Cowslip; 70d. Pomegranate; 100d. Thorn-apple.

1959. "Partisan" Physical Culture Festival, Belgrade.
937 **258** 10d. black and ochre . . 10 10
938 – 15d. blue and sepia . . . 10 10
939 – 20d. violet and brown . . 10 10
940 – 35d. purple and grey . . 15 10
941 – 40d. violet and grey . . . 25 10
942 – 55d. green and brown . . 40 10
943 – 80d. olive and slate . . . 90 50
944 – 100d. violet and ochre . . 2·75 90
DESIGNS—HORIZ: 15d. High jumping and running; 20d. Gymnastics; 35d. Female exercises with hoops; 40d. Sailors' exercises; 55d. Handball and basketball; 80d. Swimming and diving. VERT: 100d. "Partisan" Association insignia.

259 Fair Emblem　**260**

1959. Zagreb International Fair.
945 **259** 20d. black and blue . . . 45 15

1959. Obligatory Tax. Children's Week.
946 **260** 2d. slate and yellow . . . 25 15

261 Athletes　**262** "Reconstruction" (sculpture by L. Dolinar)

1960. Olympic Games.
947 **261** 15d. yellow, buff and violet 10 10
948 – 20d. drab, lavender & blue 10 10
949 – 30d. blue, stone & ultram 15 10
950 – 35d. grey, brown & purple 15 10
951 – 40d. drab, green and bronze 20 10
952 – 55d. blue, drab and green 35 10
953 – 80d. ochre, grey and red 50 25
954 – 100d. ochre, drab and violet 60 30
DESIGNS: 20d. Swimming; 30d. Skiing; 35d. Graeco-Roman wrestling; 40d. Cycling; 55d. Yachting; 80d. Equestrian; 100d. Fencing.
Nos. 948, 950, 952 and 954 are inscr in Cyrillic characters.

1960. Obligatory Tax. Red Cross.
955 **262** 2d. blue and red 25 15

1960. Yugoslav Forest Mammals. As T **213**. Animals in natural colours. Background colours given.
956 15d. blue (West European hedgehog) 10 10
957 20d. olive (Eurasian red squirrel) 15 10
958 25d. turquoise (Pine marten) 15 10
959 30d. olive (Brown hare) . . . 20 10
960 35d. brown (Red fox) 25 10
961 40d. lake (Eurasian badger) 30 10
962 55d. blue (Wolf) 45 20
963 80d. violet (Roe deer) 70 20
964 100d. red (Wild boar) . . . . 1·25 90

263 Lenin　**264** Accelerator

1960. 90th Birth Anniv of Lenin.
965 **263** 20d. grey and green . . . 15 10

1960. Nuclear Energy Exhibition, Belgrade.
966 **264** 15d. green 10 10
967 – 20d. red 10 10
968 – 40d. blue 20 15
DESIGNS: 20d. Neutron generator; 40d. Nuclear reactor.

265 Young Girl　**266** Serbian National Theatre. Novi Sad (Centenary)

1960. Obligatory Tax. Children's Week.
969 **265** 2d. red 20 15

1960. Anniversaries.
970 **266** 15d. black 10 10
971 – 20d. sepia 10 10
972 – 40d. blue 10 10
973 – 55d. purple 15 10
974 – 80d. green 15 10
DESIGNS: 20d. Detail of "Illyrian Renaissance", V. Bukovac (cent of Croat National Theatre, Zagreb); 40d. Edvard Rusijan and Bleriot XI airplane (50th anniv of 1st flight in Yugoslavia); 55d. Symbolic hand holding fruit (15th anniv of Republic); 80d. Symbol of nuclear energy (15th anniv of U.N.O.).

1960. Portraits as T **217**.
975 15d. green 10 10
976 20d. brown 10 10
977 40d. brown 10 10
978 55d. red 10 10
979 80d. blue 20 10
980 100d. blue 40 15
PORTRAITS: 15d. Ivan Cankar (writer); 20d. Silvije Kranjcevic (poet); 40d. Paja Jovanovic (painter); 55d. Djura Jaksic (writer); 80d. Mihajlo Pupin (physicist); 100d. Rudjer Boskovic (astronomer).

268 "Blood Transfusion"　**269** "Atomic Energy"

1961. Obligatory Tax. Red Cross. Perf or imperf.
981 **268** 2d. multicoloured 25 15

1961. Int Nuclear Electronic Conference, Belgrade.
982 **269** 25d. multicoloured . . . 15 10

1961. Medicinal Plants. As T **257**. Multicoloured.
1000 10d. Yellow foxglove . . . 10 10
1001 15d. Marjoram 10 10
1002 20d. Hyssop 15 10
1003 25d. Hawthorn 15 10
1004 40d. Hollyhock 15 10
1005 50d. Soapwort 25 10
1006 60d. Clary 35 15
1007 80d. Blackthorn 70 15
1008 100d. Pot marigold . . . . 1·40 60
See also Nos. 1074/9.

271 Stevan Filipovic (statue by V. Bakic)　**273** St. Clement (14th-century wood-carving)

272

1961. 20th Anniv of Yugoslav Insurrection. Inscriptions in gold.
1009 **271** 15d. brown and red . . 10 10
1010 – 20d. yellow and sepia . . 10 10
1011 – 25d. green and turquoise 10 10
1012 – 60d. violet and blue . . 15 10
1013 – 100d. indigo and blue . . 30 20
MS1013a 64 × 82 mm. 500d. indigo, blue and gold. Imperf £150 £150
DESIGNS: 20d. Insurrection Monument, Bosansko Grahovo (relief by S. Stojanivic); 25d. Executed Inhabitants Monument, Kagujevac (by A. Grzetic); 60d. Nova Gradisks Victory Monument (A. Augustincic); 100, 500d, Marshal Tito (Revolution Monument, Titovo Uzice, (statue by F. Krsinic).

1961. Non-Aligned Countries Conf, Belgrade.
1014 **272** 25d. sepia (postage) . . 10 10
1015 – 50d. green 20 10
MS1015a 72 × 65 mm. 1000d. purple (T **272**). Imperf . . . . 12·00 12·00

1016 **272** 250d. purple (air) . . . 75 50
1017 – 500d. blue . . . . 2·25 1·25
DESIGN: 50, 500d. National Assembly Building, Belgrade.

1961. 12th International Congress of Byzantine Studies, Ohrid.
1018 **273** 25d. sepia and olive . . 25 15

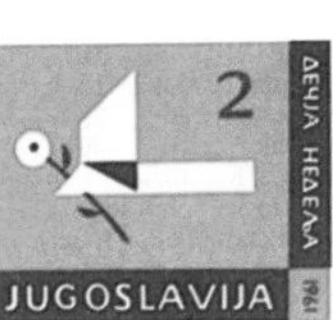

274 Bird with Flower in Beak　**275** Luka Vukalovic (revolutionary leader)

1961. Obligatory Tax. Children's Week.
1019 **274** 2d. orange and violet . . 15 10

1961. Yugoslav Costumes (2nd series). As T **239**. Inscr "1941–1961".
1020 15d. multicoloured 15 10
1021 25d. black, red and brown 15 10
1022 30d. sepia, red and brown 25 10
1023 50d. multicoloured 35 10
1024 65d. multicoloured 45 15
1025 100d. multicoloured . . . . 1·60 60
DESIGNS—HORIZ: Costumes of: 15d. Serbia; 25d. Montenegro; 30d. Bosnia and Herzegovina; 50d. Macedonia; 65d. Croatia; 100d. Slovenia.

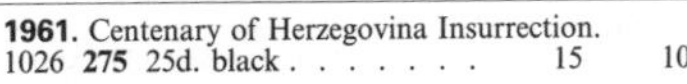

1961. Centenary of Herzegovina Insurrection.
1026 **275** 25d. black 15 10

276 Hands holding Flower and Rifle　**277** Dimitur and Konstantin Miladinov

1961. 20th Anniv of Yugoslav Partisan Army.
1027 **276** 25d. blue and red . . . 20 10

1961. Centenary of Publication of Macedonian National Songs by Miladinov Brothers.
1028 **277** 25d. purple and buff . . 20 10

278 "Mother's Play" (after P. Krsinic)　**279** Mosquito

1962. 15th Anniv of UNICEF.
1029 **278** 50d. black on drab . . . 15 10

1962. Malaria Eradication.
1030 **279** 50d. black on blue . . . 15 10

280 Goddess Isis (from Temple at Kalabscha)　**281** Bandages and Symbols

1962. 15th Anniv of UNESCO. Save Nubian Monuments.
1031 **280** 25d. green on stone . . . 10 10
1032 – 50d. brown on drab . . 20 10
DESIGN: 50d. Rameses II (from temple, Abu Simbel).

1962. Tourist Publicity (2nd series). Views as T **253**. Inscr "1941–1961".
1033 15d. brown and blue 15 10
1034 15d. bistre and turquoise . . 15 10
1035 25d. brown and blue 15 10
1036 25d. blue and light blue . . . 15 10
1037 30d. blue and brown 25 10
1038 30d. blue and purple 40 10
1039 50d. turquoise and bistre . . 1·00 10
1040 50d. blue and bistre . . . . 1·00 10
1041 100d. grey and green . . . 4·00 70
VIEWS: No. 1033, Portoroz; 1034, Jajce; 1035, Zadar; 1036, Popova Sapka; 1037, Hvar; 1038, Kotor Bay; 1039, Djerdap; 1040, Rab; 1041, Zagreb.

1962. Obligatory Tax. Red Cross.
1042 **281** 5d. red, brown and grey 15 10

282 Marshal Tito (after sculpture by A. Augustincic)　**283** Pole Vaulting

1962. Marshal Tito's 70th Birthday.
1043 **282** 25d. green 10 10
1044 – 50d. brown 20 10
1045 **282** 100d. blue 65 20
1046 – 200d. green and brown 1·50 75
MS1046a 76 × 104 mm. Nos. 1043/6. Imperf (sold at 400d.) . . . . 20·00 18·00
DESIGNS: 50, 200d. As T **282** but profile view of bust.

1962. Amphibians and Reptiles. As T **213**.
1047 15d. brown, red and green 15 10
1048 20d. black, yellow and violet 15 10
1049 25d. multicoloured 15 10
1050 30d. brown, green and blue 15 10
1051 50d. brown, yellow and red 20 10
1052 65d. black, stone and green 25 10
1053 100d. green, brown and black 40 25
1054 150d. red, black and brown 1·00 50
1055 200d. black, drab and red 2·25 1·25

DESIGNS: 15d. Crested newt; 20d. Spotted salamander; 25d. Yellow-bellied toad; 30d. Marsh frog; 50d. European pond turtle, 100d. Green lizard; 200d. Adder.

1962. 7th European Athletic Championships, Belgrade. Sportsmen in black.
1056 **283** 15d. blue 10 10
1057 – 25d. purple 10 10
1058 – 30d. green 10 10
1059 – 50d. red 10 10
1060 – 65d. blue 15 10
1061 – 100d. turquoise 25 10
1062 – 150d. orange 35 20
1063 – 200d. brown 65 40
MS1063a 57 × 71 mm. 600d. black and violet. Imperf . . . . . . 2·75 2·75
DESIGNS—HORIZ: 25d. Throwing the discus; 50d. Throwing the javelin; 100d. Start of sprint; 200d. High jumping. VERT: 30d. Running; 65d. Putting the shot; 150d. Hurdling; 600d. Army Stadium, Belgrade.

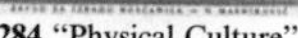

284 "Physical Culture" **285** "Bathing the Newborn Child" (Decani Monastery)

1962. Children's Week.
1064 **284** 25d. black and red . . . 15 10

1962. Yugoslav Art. Multicoloured.
1065 25d. Situla of Vace (detail from bronze vessel) (horiz) 10 10
1066 30d. Golden Mask of Trebiniste (5th-cent burial mask) (horiz) 10 10
1067 50d. The God Kairos (Trogir Monastery) . . . 15 10
1068 65d. Pigeons of Nerezi (detail from series of frescoes, "The Visitation", Nerezi Church, Skopje) 25 20
1069 100d. Type **285** 40 30
1070 150d. Icon of Ohrid (detail from 14th-cent icon, "The Annunciation") (horiz) . . 90 70
See also Nos. 1098/1103.

286 Ear of Wheat and Parched Earth **287** Andrija Mohorovicic (meteorologist)

1963. Freedom from Hunger.
1071 **286** 50d. purple on stone . . 20 10

1963. World Meteorological Day.
1072 **287** 50d. blue on grey . . . 20 10

288 Centenary Emblem **289** Partisans in File

1963. Obligatory Tax. Red Cross Centenary and Red Cross Week.
1073 **288** 5d. red, grey and ochre 20 10

1963. Medicinal Plants.
1074 15d. black, green & lt green 15 10
1075 25d. multicoloured 15 10
1076 30d. multicoloured 15 10
1077 50d. multicoloured 20 10
1078 65d. multicoloured 40 15
1079 100d. drab, green and black 1·40 60
FLOWERS: 15d. Lily of the valley; 25d. Iris; 30d. Bistort; 50d. Henbane; 65d. Perforate St. John's wort; 100d. Caraway.

1963. Tourist Publicity (3rd series). Views as T **253**. Inscr "1963". Multicoloured.
1080 15d. Pula 10 10
1081 25d. Vrnjacka Banja 10 10
1082 30d. Crikvenica 10 10
1083 50d. Korcula 20 10
1084 65d. Durmitor 20 15
1085 100d. Ljubljana . . . . . . 1·50 40

1963. 20th Anniv of Battle of Sutjeska River.
1086 **289** 15d. green and drab . . 10 10
1087 – 25d. green 10 10
1088 – 50d. violet and brown 20 10

DESIGNS—VERT: 25d. Sutjeska Gorge. HORIZ: 50d. Partisans in battle.
See also No. 1125.

290 Gymnast on "Horse" **291** "Mother"

1963. 5th European Cup Gymnastic Championships.
1089 **290** 25d. green and black . . 10 10
1090 – 50d. blue and black . . 10 10
1091 – 100d. brown and black 40 35
DESIGNS—Gymnast: 50d. on parallel bars; 100d. exercising with rings.

1963. Sculptures by Ivan Mestrovic.
1092 **291** 25d. bistre on brown . . 10 10
1093 – 50d. olive on green . . . 15 10
1094 – 65d. green on blue . . . 50 30
1095 – 100d. black on grey . . 65 50
SCULPTURES: 50d. "Reminiscence" (nude female figure); 65d. "Kraljevic Marko" (head); 100d. "Indian on horseback".

292 Children with Toys **293** Soldier and Emblem

1963. Children's Week.
1096 **292** 25d. multicoloured . . . 25 10

1963. 20th Anniv of Yugoslav Democratic Federation.
1097 **293** 25d. red, green and drab 15 10

1963. Yugoslav Art. As T **285**. Inscr "1963". Multicoloured.
1098 25d. "Man", relief on Radimlje tombstone (13th–15th century) . . . 10 10
1099 30d. Detail of relief on door of Split Cathedral (Andrija Buvina) (13th century) (horiz) 10 10
1100 50d. Detail of fresco in Beram Church (15th cent) (horiz) 15 10
1101 65d. Archangel Michael from plaque in Dominican Monastery, Dubrovnik (15th cent) 20 15
1102 100d. Figure of man on Baroque fountain, by Francesco Robba, Ljubljana (18th cent) . . 25 15
1103 150d. Archbishop Eufraise, detail of mosaic in Porec Basilica (6th cent) 70 70

294 Dositej Obradovic (writer) **295** Parachute

1963. Cultural Celebrities.
1104 **294** 25d. black on buff . . . 10 10
1105 – 30d. black on blue . . . 10 10
1106 – 50d. black on cream . . 15 10
1107 – 65d. black on lilac . . 25 20
1108 – 100d. black on pink . . 40 35
PORTRAITS: 30d. Vuk Karadzic (language reformer); 50d. Franc Miklosic (philologist); 65d. Ljudevit Gaj (writer); 100d. Petar Njegos (poet).
See also Nos. 1174/9.

1964. Obligatory Tax. Red Cross Week and 20th Anniv of Yugoslav Red Cross.
1109 **295** 5d. red, purple and blue 15 10

296 Peacock **297** Fireman saving Child

1964. Butterflies. Multicoloured.
1110 25d. Type **296** 10 10
1111 30d. Camberwell beauty . . 10 10
1112 40d. Oleander hawk moth 10 10
1113 50d. Apollo 15 10
1114 150d. Viennese emperor moth 45 35
1115 200d. Swallowtail 65 50

1964. Centenary of Voluntary Fire Brigade.
1116 **297** 25d. sepia and red . . . 20 10

298 Running **299** "Reconstruction"

1964. Olympic Games, Tokyo.
1117 **298** 25d. yellow, black & grey 10 10
1118 – 30d. violet, black and grey 10 10
1119 – 40d. green, black and grey 10 10
1120 – 50d. multicoloured . . . 10 10
1121 – 150d. multicoloured . . 20 15
1122 – 200d. blue, black and grey 30 25
DESIGNS: 30d. Boxing; 40d. Rowing; 50d. Basketball; 150d. Football; 200d. Water polo.

1964. 1st Anniv of Skopje Earthquake.
1123 **299** 25d. brown 15 10
1124 – 50d. blue 20 10
DESIGN: 50d. "International Aid" (U.N. flag over town).

1964. 20th Anniv of Occupation of Vis Island. As T **289** but inscr "VIS 1944–1964" at foot.
1125 25d. red and grey 15 10

300 Costumes of Kosovo-Metohija (Serbia) **301** Friedrich Engels

1964. Yugoslav Costumes (3rd series). As T **300**. Multicoloured.
1126 25d. Type **300** 10 10
1127 30d. Slovenia 10 10
1128 40d. Bosnia and Herzegovina 10 10
1129 50d. Hrvatska (Croatia) . . 10 10
1130 150d. Macedonia 40 25
1131 200d. Crna Gora (Montenegro) 65 40

1964. Centenary of "First International".
1132 **301** 25d. black on cream . . 10 10
1133 – 50d. black on lilac . . . 15 10
DESIGN: 50d. Karl Marx.

302 Children on Scooter **303** "Victor" (after Ivan Mestrovic)

1964. Children's Week.
1134 **302** 25d. green, black and red 20 10

1964. 20th Anniv of Liberation of Belgrade.
1135 **303** 25d. black and green on pink 15 10

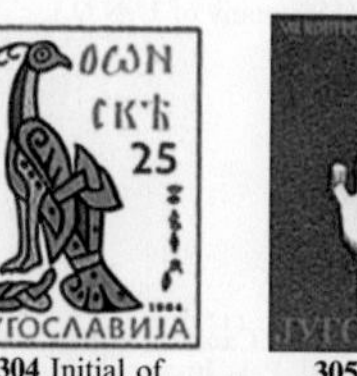

304 Initial of Hilander's Gospel (13th cent) **305** "Hand of Equality"

1964. Yugoslav Art. Inscr "1964". Multicoloured.
1136 25d. Type **304** 10 10
1137 30d. Initial of Miroslav's gospel (12th cent) 10 10
1138 40d. Detail from Cetinje octateuch (15th cent) . . 10 10
1139 50d. Miniature from Trogir's gospel (13th cent) 10 10
1140 150d. Miniature from Hrvoe's missal (15th cent) 20 10
1141 200d. Miniature from Herman Priory, Bistrica (14th cent) (horiz) 40 30

1964. 8th Yugoslav Communist League Congress. Multicoloured.
1142 25d. Type **305** 10 10
1143 50d. Dove and factory ("Peace and Socialism") 10 10
1144 100d. Industrial plant ("Socialism") 20 15

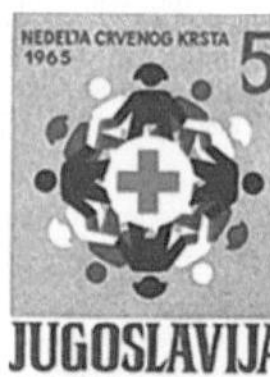

306 Player **307** Children around Red Cross

1965. World Table Tennis Championships, Ljubljana.
1145 **306** 50d. multicoloured . . . 15 10
1146 – 150d. multicoloured . . 25 20
DESIGN: 150d. As Type **306** but design arranged in reverse.

1965. Obligatory Tax. Red Cross Week.
1147 **307** 5d. red and brown . . . 15 10

308 Titograd **309** Young Partisan (after D. Andrejevic-Kun)

1965. 20th Anniv of Liberation. Yugoslav Capitals.
1148 **308** 25d. purple 10 10
1149 – 30d. brown 10 10
1150 – 40d. violet 10 10
1151 – 50d. green 10 10
1152 – 150d. violet 15 30
1153 – 200d. blue 35 55
CAPITALS: 30d. Skopje; 40d. Sarajevo; 50d. Ljubljana; 150d. Zagreb; 200d. Belgrade.

1965. "Twenty Years of Freedom" Pioneer Games.
1154 **309** 25d. black & brown on buff 15 10

310 T.V. Tower, Avala (Belgrade) **311** Yarrow

1965. Centenary of I.T.U.
1155 **310** 50d. blue 15 10

1965. Inauguration of Djerdap Hydro-electric Project. As Nos. 3271/2 of Rumania.
1156 – 25d. (30b.) green and grey 10 10
1157 – 50d. (55b.) red and grey . . 25 10
MS1157a 103 × 80 mm. 80b., 1l.20, 100,150d. multicoloured (sold at 500d. or 4l.) . . . . 2·75 2·75
DESIGN: 25d. Djerdap Gorge; 50d. Djerdap Dam.
Nos. 1156/7 were issued simultaneously in Rumania.

1965. Medicinal Plants. Multicoloured.
1158 25d. Type **311** 10 10
1159 30d. Rosemary 10 10
1160 40d. Elecampane 10 10
1161 50d. Deadly nightshade . . 10 10
1162 150d. Peppermint 15 10
1163 200d. Rusty foxglove . . . 70 40

312 I.C.Y. Emblem

313 Sibenik

1965. International Co-operation Year.
1164 **312** 50d. violet, indigo and blue 15 10

1965. Tourist Publicity (4th series). Multicoloured.
1165 25d. Rogaska Slatina . . . 10 10
1166 30d. Type **313** 10 10
1167 40d. Prespa Lake 10 10
1168 50d. Prizren 10 10
1169 150d. Skadar Lake 25 10
1170 200d. Sarajevo 40 40

314 Cat

316 Marshal Tito

1965. Children's Week.
1171 **314** 30d. lake and yellow . . 35 10

1965. Nos. 984 and 988 surch.
1172 5d. on 8d. violet 40 10
1173 50d. on 25d. red 40 10

1965. Cultural Celebrities. Portraits as T **294**.
1174 30d. red on pink 10 10
1175 50d. slate on blue 10 10
1176 60d. sepia on brown 10 10
1177 85d. indigo on blue 15 10
1178 200d. olive on olive 15 15
1179 500d. mauve on purple . . . 35 30
PORTRAITS: 30d. Branislav Nusic (author and dramatist); 50d. Antun Matos (poet); 60d. Ivan Mazuranic (author); 85d. Fran Levstik (writer); 200d. Josif Pancic (botanist); 500d. Dimitrije Tucovic (politician).

Currency revalued. 100 paras = 1 dinar = 100 old dinars.

1966.
1180 **316** 20p. green 25 10
1181 30p. red 45 10

317 Long Jumping (Balkan Games, Sarajevo)

318 "T", 15th-cent Psalter

1966. Sports Events.
1182 **317** 30p. red 10 10
1183 – 50p. violet 10 10
1184 – 1d. green 10 10
1185 – 3d. brown 20 15
1186 – 5d. blue 45 35
DESIGNS AND EVENTS: 50p. Ice hockey and 3d. Ice hockey sticks and puck (World Ice Hockey Championships, Jesenice, Ljubljana and Zagreb); 1d. Rowing and 5d. Oars (World Rowing Championships, Bled).

1966. Yugoslav Art. Manuscript initials. Mult.
1187 30p. Type **318** 10 10
1188 50p. "V", 14th-cent Divos gospel 10 10
1189 60p. "R", 12th-cent Libri moralium of Gregory I 10 10
1190 85p. "P", 12th-cent Miroslav gospel 10 10
1191 2d. "B", 13th-cent Radomir gospel 20 10
1192 5d. "F", 11th-cent passional 40 30

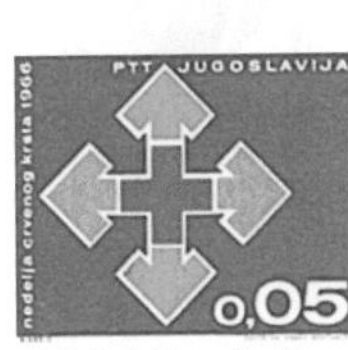
319 Red Cross Emblem

320 Beam Aerial on Globe

1966. Obligatory Tax. Red Cross Week.
1193 **319** 5p. multicoloured . . . 15 10

1966. As Nos. 983, etc, but values expressed "0.05" etc, colours changed and new values.
1194 5p. orange 10 10
1195 10p. brown 10 10
1196 15p. blue 55 10
1197 20p. green 25 10
1198 30p. red 60 10
1199 40p. purple 25 10
1200 50p. blue 25 10
1201 60p. brown 30 10
1202 65p. green 30 10
1203 85p. purple 35 10
1204 1d. olive 65 10
NEW VALUES: 60p. as No. 988, 85p. as No. 984.

1966. International Amateur Radio Union Regional Conference, Opatija.
1205 **320** 85p. blue 15 10

321 Stag Beetle

322 Serbian 1 para Stamp of 1866

1966. Insects. Multicoloured.
1206 30p. Type **321** 10 10
1207 50p. Rose chafer 10 10
1208 60p. "Meloe violaceus" (oil beetle) 10 10
1209 85p. Seven-spotted ladybird 15 10
1210 2d. Alpine longhorn beetle 25 15
1211 5d. Great diving beetle . . . 55 25

1966. Serbian Stamp Centenary.
1212 **322** 30p. green, lake & brown 10 10
1213 – 50p. lake, bistre and ochre 10 10
1214 – 60p. orange and green 10 10
1215 – 85p. red and blue . . . 15 15
1216 – 2d. blue, deep green & green 45 25
MS1217 62½ × 73½ mm. 10d. multicoloured. Imperf . . . . 1·50 1·60
DESIGNS—(Serbian Stamps of 1866): 50p.—2p.; 60p.—10p.; 85p.—20p.; 2d.—40p.; 10d. —1p.

323 Rebels on Shield

324 Josip Strossmayer and Racki (founders)

1966. 25th Anniv of Yugoslav Insurrection.
1218 **323** 20p. brown, gold & green 10 10
1219 30p. mauve, gold & buff 10 10
1220 85p. blue, gold and stone 10 10
1221 2d. violet, gold and blue 15 15

1966. Centenary of Yugoslav Academy, Zagreb.
1222 **324** 30p. black, stone and drab 15 10

325 Old Bridge, Mostar

325a Medieval View of Sibenik

1966. 400th Anniv of Old Bridge, Mostar.
1223 **325** 30p. purple 70 10

1966. 900th Anniv of Sibenik.
1224 **325a** 30p. purple 30 10

326 "The Girl in Pigtails"

327 UNESCO Emblem

1966. Children's Week.
1225 **326** 30p. multicoloured . . . 50 10

1966. 20th Anniv of UNESCO.
1226 **327** 85p. blue 20 10

328 Stylized Winter Landscape

329 Dinar of Durad I Balsic

1966. Christmas.
1227 **328** 15p. yellow and blue . . 10 10
1228 – 20p. yellow and violet 10 10
1229 – 30p. yellow and green . . 10 10
DESIGNS: 20p. Father Christmas; 30p. Stylized Christmas tree.
See also Nos. 1236/8.

1966. Yugoslav Art. Designs showing different coins.
1230 **329** 30p. multicoloured . . . 10 10
1231 – 50p. multicoloured . . . 10 10
1232 – 60p. multicoloured . . . 10 10
1233 – 85p. multicoloured . . . 10 10
1234 – 2d. multicoloured . . . 20 10
1235 – 5d. multicoloured . . . 50 25
MEDIEVAL COINS (Dinars of): 50p. King Stefan Tomasevic; 60p. Djurad Brankovic; 85p. Ljubljana; 2d. Split; 5d. Emperor Stefan Dusan.

1966. New Year. As Nos. 1227/9 but colours changed.
1236 15p. gold, blue and indigo 15 15
1237 20p. gold, red and pink . . 15 15
1238 30p. gold, myrtle and green 15 15

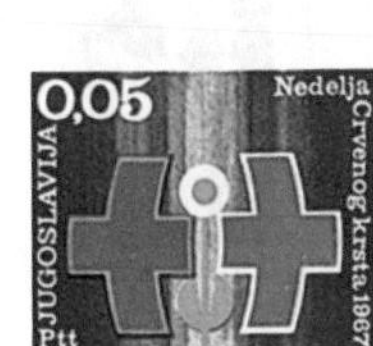
330 Flower between Red Crosses

331 Arnica

1967. Obligatory Tax. Red Cross Week.
1239 **330** 5p. red, green and blue 15 10

1967. Medicinal Plants. Multicoloured.
1240 30p. Type **331** 10 10
1241 50p. Common flax 10 10
1242 85p. Oleander 10 10
1243 1d.20 Gentian 15 10
1244 3d. Laurel 30 10
1245 5d. African rue 65 40

332 President Tito

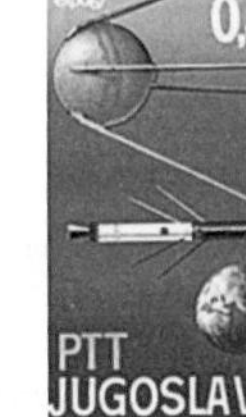
333 "Sputnik I" and "Explorer I"

1967. Pres. Tito's 75th Birthday. (a) Size 20 × 27 mm.
1246 **332** 5p. orange 10 10
1247 10p. brown 10 10
1248 15p. violet 10 10
1249 20p. green 10 10
1260 20p. blue . . . . . . 1·50 10
1261 25p. purple 15 10
1250 30p. red 10 10
1263 30p. myrtle 30 10
1251 40p. black 10 10
1252 50p. turquoise 10 10
1266a 50p. red 30 10
1253 60p. lilac 15 10
1268 70p. sepia 40 10
1269 75p. green 50 10
1270 80p. brown . . . . . . 2·25 10
1270a 80p. red 45 10
1254 85p. blue 20 10
1272 90p. brown 35 10
1273 1d. red 25 10
1274 1d.20 blue 75 10
1274a 1d.20 green 70 10
1275 1d.25 blue 55 10
1276 1d.50 green 50 10

(b) Size 20 × 30 mm.
1277 **332** 2d. sepia . . . . . . 1·50 10
1278 2d.50 green . . . . . . 1·50 10
1279 5d. purple . . . . . . 1·25 20
1280 10d. purple . . . . . . 3·00 35
1281 20d. green . . . . . . 2·75 40

1967. World Fair, Montreal. Space Achievements. Multicoloured.
1282 30p. Type **333** 10 10
1283 50p. "Tiros", "Telstar" and "Molyna" 10 10
1284 85p. "Luna 9" and lunar orbiter 10 10
1285 1d.20 "Mariner 4" and "Venus 3" 15 10

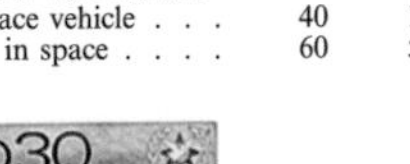
1286 3d. "Vostok I" and Gemini-Agena space vehicle . . . 40 15
1287 5d. Leonov in space 60 50

334 St. Tripun's Church, Kotor

1967. International Tourist Year.
1288 **334** 30p. green and blue . . 10 10
1289 – 50p. violet and brown 10 10
1290 – 85p. purple and blue . . 10 10
1291 – 1d.20 brown and purple 15 10
1292 – 3d. olive and brown . . 25 10
1293 – 5d. brown and olive . . 50 45
DESIGNS: 50p. Town Hall, Maribor; 85p. Trogir Cathedral; 1d.20, Fortress gate, Nis; 3d. Bridge, Visegrad; 5d. Ancient bath, Skopje.

335 Northern Bobwhite

336 Congress Emblem

1967. International Hunting and Fishing Exhibition and Fair, Novi Sad. Multicoloured.
1294 30p. Type **335** 15 15
1295 50p. Northern pike 15 10
1296 1d.20 Red deer 25 10
1297 5d. Peregrine falcon 65 50

1967. Int Astronautical Federation Congress, Belgrade.
1298 **336** 85p. gold, light blue and blue 15 10

337 Old Theatre Building

338 "Winter Landscape" (A. Becirovic)

1967. Centenary of Slovene National Theatre, Ljubljana.
1299 **337** 30p. brown and green . . 15 10

1967. Children's Week.
1300 **338** 30p. multicoloured . . . 50 10

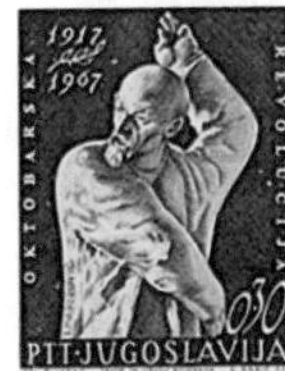
339 "Lenin" (from bust by Ivan Mestrovic)

340 Four-leaved Clover

1967. 50th Anniv of October Revolution.
1301 **339** 30p. violet 10 10
1302 85p. brown 15 10
MS1303 58 × 77 mm. **339** 10d. lake. Imperf . . . . 5·50 4·00

1967. New Year. Inscr "1968".
1304 **340** 20p. gold, blue and green 10 10
1305 – 30p. gold, violet and yellow 10 10
1306 – 50p. gold, red and lilac 10 10
DESIGNS: 30p. Sweep with ladder; 50p. Horseshoe and flower.
See also Nos. 1347/9.

341 "The Young Sultana" (Vlaho Bukovac)

1967. Yugoslav Paintings. Multicoloured.
1307 85p. "The Watchtower" (Djura Jaksic) (vert) . . . 10 10
1308 1d. Type **341** 15 10
1309 2d. "At Home" (Josip Petkovsek) 20 15
1310 3d. "The Cock-fight" (Paja Jovanovic) 30 25
1311 5d. "Summer" (Ivana Kobilca) (vert) 50 40
See also Nos. 1337/41, 1399/1404. 1438/43, 1495/1500, 1535/40, 1570/5, 1616/19, 1750/5 and 1793/8.

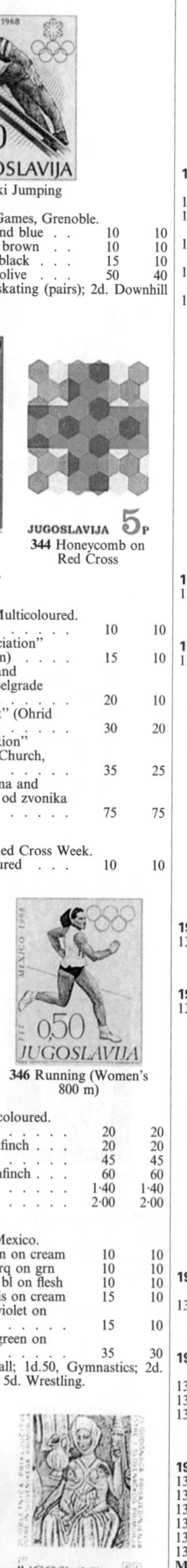
342 Ski Jumping

1968. Winter Olympic Games, Grenoble.
1312 **342** 50p. purple and blue . . 10 10
1313 – 1d. olive and brown . . 10 10
1314 – 2d. lake and black . . . 15 10
1315 – 5d. blue and olive . . . 50 40
DESIGNS: 1d. Figure skating (pairs); 2d. Downhill skiing; 5d. Ice hockey.

343 "The Madonna and Child" (St. George's Church, Prizren)

344 Honeycomb on Red Cross

1968. Medieval Icons. Multicoloured.
1316 50p. Type **343** 10 10
1317 1d. "The Annunciation" (Ohrid Museum) 15 10
1318 1d.50 "St. Sava and St. Simeon" (Belgrade Museum) 20 10
1319 2d. "The Descent" (Ohrid Museum) 30 20
1320 3d. "The Crucifixion" (St. Clement's Church, Ohrid) 35 25
1321 5d. "The Madonna and Child" (Gospe od zvonika Church, Split) 75 75

1968. Obligatory Tax. Red Cross Week.
1322 **344** 5p. multicoloured . . . 10 10

345 Northern Bullfinch

346 Running (Women's 800 m)

1968. Song Birds. Multicoloured.
1323 50p. Type **345** 20 20
1324 1d. Eurasian goldfinch . . . 20 20
1325 1d.50 Chaffinch 45 45
1326 2d. Western greenfinch . . . 60 60
1327 3d. Red crossbill . . . . . 1·40 1·40
1328 5d. Hawfinch . . . . 2·00 2·00

1968. Olympic Games, Mexico.
1329 **346** 50p. pur & brn on cream 10 10
1330 – 1d. olive & turq on grn 10 10
1331 – 1d.50 sepia & bl on flesh 10 10
1332 – 2d. green & bis on cream 15 10
1333 – 3d. indigo & violet on blue 15 10
1334 – 5d. purple & green on mauve 35 30
DESIGNS: 1d. Basketball; 1d.50, Gymnastics; 2d. Sculling; 3d. Water polo; 5d. Wrestling.

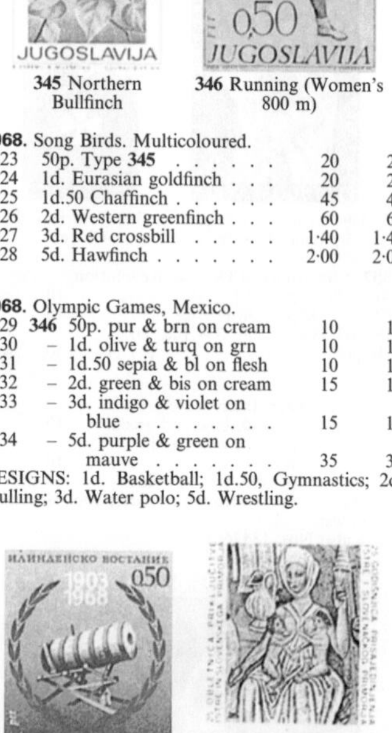
347 Rebel Cannon

348 "Mother and Children" (fresco in Hrastovlje Church, Slovenia)

1968. 65th Anniv of Ilinden Uprising.
1335 **347** 50p. brown and gold . . 15 10

1968. 25th Anniv of Partisan Occupation of Istria and Slovenian Littoral.
1336 **348** 50p. multicoloured . . . 15 10

349 "Lake of Klansko" (Marko Pernhart)

1968. Yugoslav Paintings. 19th-cent Landscapes. Multicoloured.
1337 1d. Type **349** 10 10
1338 1d.50 "Bavarian Landscape" (Milan Popovic) 15 10
1339 2d. "Gateway, Zadar" (Ferdo Quiquerez) 25 10
1340 3d. "Triglav from Bohinj" (Anton Karinger) 35 20
1341 5d. "Studenica Monastery" (Djordje Krstic) 85 90

350 A. Santic

351 "Promenade" (Marina Cudov)

1968. Birth Centenary of Aleksa Santic (poet).
1342 **350** 50p. blue 10 10

1968. Children's Week.
1343 **351** 50p. multicoloured . . . 20 10

352 Karl Marx (after sculpture by N. Mitric)

353 Aztec Emblem and Olympic Rings

1968. 150th Birth Anniv of Karl Marx.
1344 **352** 50p. red 15 10

1968. Obligatory Tax. Olympic Games Fund.
1345 **353** 10p. multicoloured . . . 10 10

354 Old Theatre and View of Kalemegdan

355 Hassan Brkic

1968. Centenary of Serbian National Theatre, Belgrade.
1346 **354** 50p. brown and green . . 15 10

1968. New Year. Designs as Nos. 1304/6 but colours changed and inscr "1969".
1347 20p. gold, blue and lilac . . 10 10
1348 30p. gold, violet and green 10 10
1349 50p. gold, red and yellow 10 10

1968. Yugoslav National Heroes.
1350 **355** 50p. violet 10 10
1351 – 75p. black 15 10
1352 – 1d.25 brown 15 10
1353 – 2d. blue 20 10
1354 – 2d.50 green 25 15
1355 – 5d. lake 60 60
MS1356 Two sheets each 156 × 108 mm. (a) 2 × Nos. 1350/2 (b) 2 × 1353/5 Pair . . . . . . 25·00 20·00
PORTRAITS: 75p. Ivan Milutinovic; 1d.25, Rade Koncar; 2d. Kuzman Josifovski; 2d.50, Tone Tomsic; 5d. Mosa Pijade.

356 "Family" (sculpture by J. Soldatovic) and Human Rights Emblem

357 I.L.O. Emblem

1968. Human Rights Year.
1357 **356** 1d.25 blue 15 10

1969. 50th Anniv of I.L.O.
1358 **357** 1d.25 black and red . . 15 10

358 Dove on Hammer and Sickle Emblem

359 "St. Nikita" (Manasija Monastery)

1969. 50th Anniv of Yugoslav Communist Party.
1359 **358** 50p. red and black . . . 10 10
1360 – 75p. black and ochre . . 10 10
1361 – 1d.25 black and red . . 15 10
MS1362 118 × 140 mm. Nos. 1359 (4), 1360 (2), 1361 (2) and 10d. chocolate . . . . 6·50 6·50
DESIGNS: 75p. "Tito" and star (wall graffiti); 1d.25 Five-pointed crystal formation; 10d. President Tito.

1969. Medieval Frescoes in Yugoslav Monasteries. Multicoloured.
1363 50p. Type **359** 10 10
1364 75p. "Jesus and the Apostles" (Sopocani) . . 10 10
1365 1d.25 "The Crucifixion" (Studenica) 10 10
1366 2d. "Cana Wedding Feast" (Kalenic) 20 10
1367 3d. "Angel guarding Tomb" (Mileseva) 30 10
1368 5d. "Mourning over Christ" (Nerezi) 90 75

360 Roman Memorial and View of Ptuj

1969. 1900th Anniv of Ptuj (Poetovio) (Slovene town).
1369 **360** 50p. brown 10 10

361 Vasil Glavinov

362 Globe between Hands

1969. Birth Centenary of Vasil Glavinov (Macedonian revolutionary).
1370 **361** 50p. purple and brown 10 10

1969. Obligatory Tax. Red Cross Week.
1371 **362** 20p. black, red and deep red 10 10

363 Thin-leafed Peony

365 Games' Emblem

364 "Eber" (V. Ivankovic)

1969. Flowers. Multicoloured.
1372 50p. Type **363** 10 10
1373 75p. Coltsfoot 10 10
1374 1d.25 Primrose 15 10
1375 2d. Hellebore 25 10
1376 2d.50 Sweet violet 30 10
1377 5d. Pasque flower 75 75

1969. Dubrovnik Summer Festival. Sailing Ships. Multicoloured.
1378 50p. Type **364** 15 10
1379 1d.25 "Tare in Storm" (Franasovic) 20 10
1380 1d.50 "Brigantine Sela" (Ivankovic) 30 10
1381 2d.50 "16th-century Dubrovnik Galleon" . . . 35 20
1382 3d.25 "Frigate Madre Mimbelli" (A. Roux) . . 65 25
1383 5d. "Shipwreck" (16th-century icon) . . . 1·50 1·25

1969. 9th World Deaf and Dumb Games, Belgrade.
1384 **365** 1d.25 lilac and red . . . 20 10

366 Bosnian Mountain Horse

1969. 50th Anniv of Veterinary Faculty, Zagreb. Multicoloured.
1385 75p. Type **366** 10 10
1386 1d.25 Lipizzaner horse . . . 15 10
1387 3d.25 Ljutomer trotter . . . 30 10
1388 5d. Yugoslav half-breed . . 75 65

367 Children and Chicks

368 Arms of Belgrade

1969. Children's Week.
1389 **367** 50p. multicoloured . . . 15 10

1969. 25th Anniv of Yugoslav Liberation. Arms of Regional Capitals. Multicoloured.
1390 50p. Type **368** 15 10
1391 50p. Skopje 15 10
1392 50p. Titograd (Podgorica) 15 10
1393 50p. Sarajevo 15 10
1394 50p. Zagreb 15 10
1395 50p. Ljubljana 15 10
MS1396 89 × 106 mm. Nos. 1390/5 and 12d. gold, red and black (Yugoslav Arms) with two stamp-size labels. Size of individual designs reduced to $21\frac{1}{2} \times 27\frac{1}{2}$ mm. 11·00 10·00

369 Dr. Josip Smodlaka

370 Torch, Globe and Olympic Rings

1969. Birth Centenary of Dr. Josip Smodlaka (politician).
1397 **369** 50p. blue 10 10

1969. Obligatory Tax. Olympic Games Fund.
1398 **370** 10p. multicoloured . . . 10 10

371 "Gipsy Girl" (Nikola Martinoski)

1969. Yugoslav Nude Paintings. Multicoloured.
1399 50p. Type **371** 15 10
1400 1d.25 "Girl in Red Armchair" (Sava Sumanovic) 20 10
1401 1d.50 "Girl Brushing Hair" (Marin Tartaglia) 25 10
1402 2d.50 "Olympia" (Miroslav Kraljevic) (horiz) 40 20
1403 3d.25 "The Bather" (Jovan Bijelic) 70 40
1404 5d. "Woman on a Couch" (Matej Sternen) (horiz) . . 1·50 1·50

372 University Building

1969. 50th Anniv of Ljubljana University.
1405 **372** 50p. green 10 10

373 University Seal

374 Colonnade

1969. 300th Anniv of Zagreb University.
1406 **373** 50p. gold, purple and blue 15 10

1969. Europa.
1407 **374** 1d.25 brown, light brown and green . . . . . . 2·50 2·50
1408 3d.25 blue, grey & purple . . . . 7·50 7·50

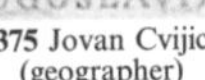
375 Jovan Cvijic (geographer)

376 "Punishment of Dirka" (4th-cent mosaic)

1970. Famous Yugoslavs.
1409 **375** 50p. purple 10 10
1410 – 1d.25 black 10 10
1411 – 1d.50 purple 15 10
1412 – 2d.50 olive 15 15
1413 – 3d.25 brown 25 15
1414 – 5d. blue 30 40
CELEBRITIES: 1d.25, Dr. Andrija Stampar (hygienist); 1d.50, Joakim Krcovski (author); 2d.50, Marko Miljanov (soldier); 3d.25, Vasa Pelagic (socialist revolutionary); 5d. Oton Zupancic (poet).

1970. Mosaics. Multicoloured.
1415 50p. Type **376** 10 10
1416 1d.25 "Cerberus" (5th-cent) (horiz) 10 10
1417 1d.50 "Angel of Annunciation" (6th-cent) 15 10
1418 2d.50 "Hunters" (4th-cent) 25 10
1419 3d.25 "Bull beside Cherries" (5th-cent) (horiz) 35 15
1420 5d. "Virgin and Child Enthroned" (6th-cent) . . 90 90

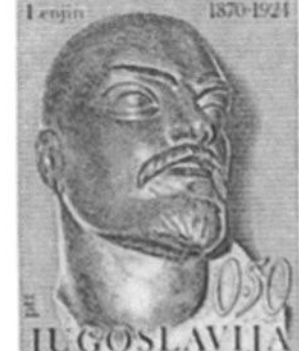
377 Lenin (after sculpture by S. Stojanovic)

378 Trying for Goal

1970. Birth Centenary of Lenin.
1421 **377** 50p. lake 10 10
1422 – 1d.25 blue 15 10
DESIGN: 1d.25, As Type **377**, but showing left side of Lenin's bust.

1970. 6th World Basketball Championships.
1423 **378** 1d.25 red 15 10

379 Red Cross Trefoil

1970. Obligatory Tax. Red Cross Week.
1424 **379** 20p. multicoloured . . . 10 10

380 "Flaming Sun"

1970. Europa.
1425 **380** 1d.25 deep blue, turquoise and blue . . 15 10
1426 3d.25 brown, vio & pur 35 35

381 Istrian Short-haired Hound

382 Olympic Flag

1970. Yugoslav Dogs. Multicoloured.
1427 50p. Type **381** 10 10
1428 1d.25 Yugoslav tricolour hound 15 10
1429 1d.50 Istrian hard-haired hound 15 10
1430 2d.50 Balkan hound 25 15
1431 3d.25 Dalmatian 40 20
1432 5d. Shara mountain dog . . 1·25 75

1970. Obligatory Tax. Olympic Games Fund.
1433 **382** 10p. multicoloured . . . 10 10

383 Telegraph Key

384 "Bird in Meadow" (Lidija Dobronjovska)

1970. Centenary of Montenegro Telegraph Service.
1434 **383** 50p. gold, black & brown 10 10

1970. Children's Week.
1435 **384** 50p. multicoloured . . . 15 10

385 "Gymnast"

388 Rusty-leaved Alpenrose

386 "Hand Holding Dove" (Makoto)

1970. 17th World Gymnastics Championships, Ljubljana.
1436 **385** 1d.25 blue and purple . . 15 10

1970. 25th Anniv of United Nations.
1437 **386** 1d.25 multicoloured . . 15 10

1970. Yugoslav Paintings. Baroque Period. Designs as T **341** but vert. Multicoloured.
1438 50p. "The Ascension" (Teodor Kracun) 10 10
1439 75p. "Abraham's Sacrifice" (Federiko Benkovic) . . . 10 10
1440 1d.25 "The Holy Family" (Francisek Jelovsek) . . . 15 10
1441 2d.50 "Jacob's Dream" (Hristofor Zefarovic) . . 20 15
1442 3d.25 "Christ's Baptism" (Serbian village artist) . . 30 15
1443 5d.75 "Coronation of the Virgin" (Tripo Kokolja) 65 75

1970. Nature Conservation Year. Multicoloured.
1444 1d.25 Type **388** . . . . . 1·00 1·00
1445 3d.25 Lammergeier . . . . 8·25 8·25

389 Frano Supilo

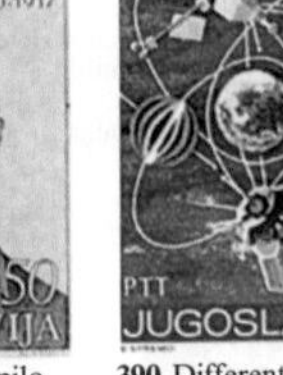
390 Different Nations' Satellites ("International Co-operation")

1971. Birth Cent of Frano Supilo (politician).
1446 **389** 50p. brown and buff . . 10 10

1971. Space Exploration. Multicoloured.
1447 50p. Type **390** 10 10
1448 75p. Telecommunications satellite 15 10
1449 1d.25 Unmanned Moon flights 20 10
1450 2d.50 Exploration of Mars and Venus (horiz) . . . 30 15
1451 3d.25 Space-station (horiz) 45 30
1452 5d.75 Astronauts on the Moon (horiz) . . . . . . 1·50 1·25

391 "Proclamation of the Commune" (A. Daudenarde, after A. Lamy)

1971. Centenary of Paris Commune.
1453 **391** 1d.25 brown and orange 15 10

392 Red Cross Ribbon

1971. Obligatory Tax. Red Cross Week.
1454 **392** 20p. multicoloured . . . 10 10

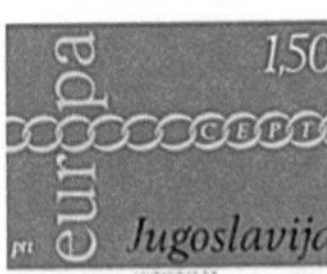
393 Europa Chain

1971. Europa.
1455 **393** 1d.50 multicoloured . . 15 15
1456 4d. pink, purple & mauve 60 55

394 Congress Emblem (A. Pajvancic)

1971. 20th Anniv of Yugoslav "Self-Managers" Movement.
1457 **394** 50p. red, black and gold 15 10
1458 – 1d.25 red, black and gold 60 60
DESIGN: 1d.25, "Self-Managers" emblem (designed by M. Miodragovic).

395 Common Mallow

396 Olympic "Spiral" and Rings

1971. Flowers. Multicoloured.
1459 50p. Type **395** 10 10
1460 1d.50 Buckthorn 10 10
1461 2d. White water-lily 20 10
1462 2d.50 Common poppy . . . 40 10
1463 4d. Chicory 50 15
1464 6d. Chinese lantern 90 70

1971. Obligatory Tax. Olympic Games Fund.
1465 **396** 10p. black, purple & blue 10 10

397 Krk, Dalmatia

398 "Prince Lazar Hrebeljanovic" (from fresco, Lazarica Church)

1971. Tourism.
1641 – 5p. orange 10 10
1642 – 10p. brown 10 10
1468 – 20p. lilac 15 10
1644 – 25p. red 20 10
1469 **397** 30p. green 55 10
1645 30p. olive 15 10
1646 – 35p. red 15 10
1647 – 40p. olive 15 10
1473 – 50p. red . . . . . . 1·00 15
1474 – 50p. green 20 10
1650 – 60p. purple 15 10
1476 – 75p. green 50 10
1652 – 75p. purple 20 10
1477 – 80p. red . . . . . . 1·10 10
1478 – 1d. red . . . . . . 2·25 30
1656 – 1d. lilac 15 10
1657 – 1d. green 15 10
1479 – 1d.20 green . . . . . . 1·40 30
1480 – 1d.25 blue 65 15
1481 – 1d.50 blue 30 10
1660 – 1d.50 red 20 10
1482 – 2d. turquoise 60 10
1661 – 2d.10 green 25 10
1483 – 2d.50 violet 60 15
1662a – 2d.50 red 20 10
1663 – 2d.50 blue 20 10
1664a – 3d. grey 10 10
1665 – 3d.20 blue 45 10
1666 – 3d.40 green 20 10
1667 – 3d.50 red 20 10
1668a – 4d. red 10 10
1669 – 4d.90 blue 35 10
1670 – 5d. green 15 10
1671 – 5d.60 olive 25 10
1672 – 6d. brown 15 10
1673a – 6d.10 green 20 10
1674 – 8d. grey 30 10
1675a – 8d.80 grey 25 10
1676 – 10d. purple 20 10
1677 – 16d.50 blue 25 10
1678 – 26d. blue 30 10
1679 – 38d. mauve 50 10
1680 – 70d. blue 50 25

DESIGNS: 5p. Krusevo, Macedonia; 10p. Gradacac; 20p., 75p. Bohinj, Slovenia; 25p. Budva; 35p. Omis, Dalmatia; 40p. Pec; 50p. (1473/4), Krusevac, Serbia; 60p. Logarska valley; 75p. (1652), Rijeka; 80p. Piran; 1d. (1478), Bitola, Macedonia; 1d. (1656/7), 16d.50, Ohrid; 1d.20, 4d. Pocitelj; 1d.25, 1d.50 (1481), 8d.80, Herceg Novi; 1d.50 (1660), Bihac; 2d. Novi Sad; 2d.10, 6d.10, Hvar; 2d.50 (1483), Rijeka Crnojevica, Montenegro; 2d.50 (1662a/3), Kragujevac; 3d., 3d.20, Skofja Loka; 3d.40, Vranje; 3d.50, Vrsac; 4d.90, Perast; 5d. Osijek; 5d.60, Travnik; 6d. Kikinda; 8d. Dubrovnik; 10d. Sarajevo; 26d. Korcula; 38d. Maribor; 70d. Zagreb.

1971. 600th Anniv of City of Krusevac.
1487 **398** 50p. multicoloured . . . 10 10

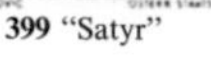

399 "Satyr" **400** "Children in Balloon"

1971. Bronze Archaeological Discoveries. Mult.
1488 50p. Head of Emperor Constantine 10 10
1489 1d.50 "Boy with Fish" (statuette) 10 10
1490 2d. "Hercules" (statuette) 15 10
1491 2d.50 Type **399** 25 10
1492 4d. "Goddess Aphrodite" (head) 35 15
1493 6d. "Citizen of Emona" (statue) 60 60

1971. Children's Week and 25th Anniv of UNICEF.
1494 **400** 50p. multicoloured . . . 30 10

1971. Yugoslav Portraits. As T **371**. Multicoloured.
1495 50p. "Girl in Serbian Dress" (Katarina Ivanovic) . . . 10 10
1496 1d.50 "Ivanisevic the Merchant" (Anastas Bocaric) 10 10
1497 2d. "Anne Kresic" (Vjekoslav Karas) 15 10
1498 2d.50 "Pavla Jagodica" (Konstantin Danil) . . . 20 10
1499 4d. "Louise Pasjakova" (Mihael Stroj) 30 15
1500 6d. "Old Man at Ljubljana" (Matevz Langus) 90 75

402 "Postal Codes" **403** Dame Gruev

1971. Introduction of Postal Codes.
1501 **402** 450p. multicoloured . . 10 10

1971. Birth Cent of Dame Gruev (Macedonian revolutionary).
1502 **403** 50p. blue 15 15

404 Speed Skating

1972. Winter Olympic Games, Sapporo, Japan. Multicoloured.
1503 1d.25 Type **404** 60 45
1504 6d. Skiing . . . . 2·00 1·75

405 First Page of Statute **406** Ski-jump, Planica

1972. 700th Anniv of Dubrovnik Law Statutes.
1505 **405** 1d.25 multicoloured . . 15 10

1972. 1st World Ski-jumping Championships, Planica.
1506 **406** 1d.25 multicoloured . . 20 10

407 Water-polo **408** Red Cross and Hemispheres

1972. Olympic Games, Munich. Multicoloured.
1507 50p. Type **407** 10 10
1508 1d.25 Basketball 10 10
1509 2d.50 Swimming 15 10
1510 3d.25 Boxing 20 10
1511 5d. Running 30 15
1512 6d.50 Sailing 60 55

1972. Obligatory Tax. Red Cross Week.
1513 **408** 20p. multicoloured . . . 15 10

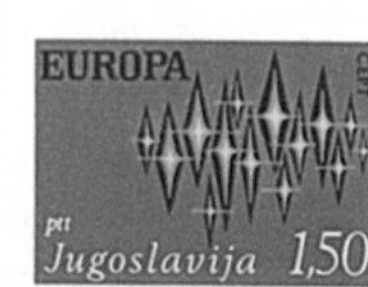

409 "Communications" **410** Wallcreeper

1972. Europa.
1514 **409** 1d.50 multicoloured . . 25 20
1515 5d. multicoloured . . . 90 90

1972. Birds. Multicoloured.
1516 50p. Type **410** 10 10
1517 1d.25 Little bustard 10 10
1518 2d.50 Red-billed chough . . 20 20
1519 3d.25 White spoonbill . . . 45 35
1520 5d. Eagle owl . . . . . . 1·10 45
1521 6d.50 Rock ptarmigan . . . 2·75 1·75

411 President Tito **412** Communications Tower, Olympic Rings and 1972 Games' Emblem

1972. President Tito's 80th Birthday.
1522 **411** 50d. brown and buff . . 15 10
1523 1d.25 blue and grey . . 45 20
MS1524 61 × 76 mm. **411** 10d. brown and drab. Imperf . . . . . . 2·50 2·00

1972. Obligatory Tax. Olympic Games Fund.
1525 **412** 10p. multicoloured . . . 10 10

413 Locomotive No. 1 "King of Serbia", 1882

1972. 50th Anniv of International Railway Union. Multicoloured.
1526 1d.50 Type **413** 30 10
1527 5d. Electric locomotive No. 441.013, 1967 . . . . 1·00 40

414 Glider in Flight **415** Pawn

1972. 13th World Gliding Championships, Vrsac.
1528 **414** 2d. black, blue and gold 20 15

1972. 20th Chess Olympiad, Skopje.
1529 **415** 1d.50 brown, vio & pur 30 10
1530 – 6d. black, blue & dp blue 80 75
DESIGN: 6d. Chessboard, king and queen.

416 "Child on Horse" (B. Zlatec) **417** G. Delcev

1972. Children's Week.
1531 **416** 80p. multicoloured . . . 15 10

1972. Birth Cent of Goce Delcev (Macedonian revolutionary).
1532 **417** 80p. black and green . . 15 10

418 Father Martic (sculpture, Ivan Mestrovic)

1972. 150th Birth Anniv of Father Grge Martic (politician).
1533 **418** 80p. black, green and red 10 10

419 National Library

1972. 140th Anniv of and Re-opening of National Library, Belgrade.
1534 **419** 50p. brown 10 10

420 "Fruit Dish and Broken Majolica Vase" (Milos Tenkovic)

1972. Yugoslav Art. Still Life. Multicoloured.
1535 50p. Type **420** 10 10
1536 1d.25 "Mandoline and Book" (Jozef Petkovsec) (vert) 10 10
1537 2d.50 "Basket with Grapes" (Katarina Jovanovic) . . 20 10
1538 3d.25 "Water-melon" (Konstantin Danil) . . . 35 15
1539 5d. "In a Stable" (Nikola Masic) (vert) 45 20
1540 6d.50 "Scrap-books" (Celestin Medovic) . . . 70 65

421 Battle of Stubica

1973. 500th Anniv of Slovenian Peasant Risings and 400th Anniv of Croatian–Slovenian Rebellion. Multicoloured.
1541 2d. Type **421** 20 10
1542 6d. Battle of Krsko 75 60

422 R. Domanovic

1973. Birth Centenary of Radoje Domanovic (Serbian satirist).
1543 **422** 80p. brown and drab . . 25 10

423 Skofja Loka

1973. Millenary of Skofja Loka.
1544 **423** 80p. brown and buff . . 20 10

424 "Novi Sad" (Petar Demetrovic)

1973. Old Engravings of Yugoslav Towns. Each black and gold.
1545 50p. Type **424** 10 10
1546 1d.25 "Zagreb" (Josef Szeman) 10 10
1547 2d.50 "Kotor" (Pierre Montier) 15 10
1548 3d.25 "Belgrade" (Mancini) 15 10
1549 5d. "Split" (Louis Cassas) 30 15
1550 6d.50 "Kranj" (Matthaus Merian) 50 40

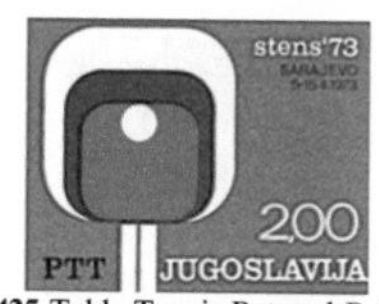

425 Table Tennis Bat and Ball

1973. 32nd World Table Tennis Championships, Sarajevo.
1551 **425** 2d. multicoloured . . . 30 10

426 Red Cross Emblem **427** Europa "Posthorn"

1973. Obligatory Tax. Red Cross Week.
1552 **426** 20p. multicoloured . . . 10 10

1973. Europa.
1553 **427** 2d. lilac, green and blue 15 10
1554 5d.50 pink, green & purple . . . . 1·40 1·25

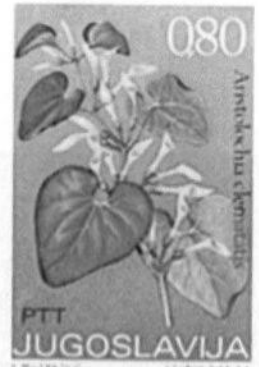

428 Birthwort **429** Globe and Olympic Rings

1973. Medicinal Plants. Multicoloured.
1555 80p. Type **428** 10 10
1556 2d. Globe thistle 20 10
1557 3d. Olive 30 10
1558 4d. "Corydalis cava" . . . 45 15
1559 5d. Mistletoe 65 20
1560 6d. Comfrey . . . . 1·40 1·25

1973. Obligatory Tax. Olympic Games Fund.
1561 **429** 10p. multicoloured . . . 10 10

430 A. Jansa and Bee **431** Aquatic Symbol

1973. Death Bicent of Anton Jansa (apiculturist).
1562 **430** 80p. black 15 10

1973. 1st World Aquatic Championships, Belgrade.
1563 **431** 2d. multicoloured . . . 20 10

432 "Children on Boat" (Ivan Vukovic)

433 Posthorn

1973. Children's Week.
1564 **432** 80p. multicoloured . . . 25 10

1973.

1565	**433**	30p. brown	15	10
1565a		50p. blue	15	10
1566		80p. red	15	10
1566a		1d. green	15	10
1567		1d.20 red	20	10
1567a		1d.50 red	20	10

434 Dalmatinac (after sculpture by Ivan Mestrovic)
435 "Self-portrait"

1973. 500th Death Anniv of Juraj Dalmatinac (sculptor and architect).
1568 **434** 80p. green and grey . . 15 10

1973. Birth Cent of Nadezda Petrovic (painter).
1569 **435** 2d. multicoloured . . . 20 15

436 "The Plaster Head" (Marko Celebonovic)

1973. Yugoslav Art. Interiors. Multicoloured.

1570	80p. Type **436**	10	10
1571	2d. "St. Duja Church" (Emanuel Vidovic) . . .	10	10
1572	3d. "Slovenian Housewife" (Marino Tartaglia) . . .	10	10
1573	4d. "Dedicated to Karas" (Miljenko Stancic)	15	15
1574	5d. "My Studio" (Milan Konjovic)	25	15
1575	6d. "Tavern in Stara Loka" (France Slana)	40	60

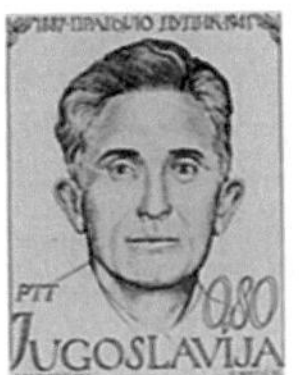

437 Dragojlo Dudic

438 "M" for "Metrication"

1973. National Heroes. (a) Each black.

1576	80p. Type **437**	10	10
1577	80p. Strahil Pindzur	10	10
1578	80p. Boris Kidric	10	10
1579	80p. Radoje Dakic	10	10

(b) Each red.

1580	2d. Josip Mazar-Sosa . . .	15	15
1581	2d. Zarko Zrenjanin	15	15
1582	2d. Emin Duraku	15	15
1583	2d. Ivan Lola Ribar	15	15

1974. Centenary of Introduction of Metric System in Yugoslavia.
1584 **438** 80p. multicoloured . . . 10 10

439 Skater

440 Satjeska Monument

1974. European Figure Skating Championships, Zagreb.
1585 **439** 2d. multicoloured . . . 40 20

1974. Monuments.

1586	–	3d. green	60	10
1587	–	4d.50 brown	90	10
1588	–	5d. violet	90	10
1589	**440**	10d. green	1·10	20
1590	–	20d. purple	1·40	20
1828	–	50d. blue	1·50	40

DESIGNS—VERT: 3d. Ljubljana; 4d.50, Kozara; 5d. Belcista. HORIZ: 20d. Podgaric; 50d. Kragujevac.

441 Mailcoach

1974. Centenary of Universal Postal Union.

1592	**441**	80p. black, yellow and buff	10	10
1593	–	2d. black, red and rose	10	10
1594	–	8d. black, blue and pale blue	40	45

DESIGNS: 2d. U.P.U. H.Q. Building; 8d. Boeing 707 jetliner.

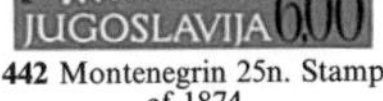

442 Montenegrin 25n. Stamp of 1874

443 President Tito

1974. Montenegro Stamp Centenary.

1595	–	80p. bistre, gold and green	15	10
1596	**442**	6d. purple, gold and claret	35	35

DESIGN: 80p. Montenegrin 2n. stamp of 1874.

1974.

1597	**443**	50p. green	10	10
1598		80p. red	15	10
1599		1d.20 green	20	10
1600		2d. blue	25	10

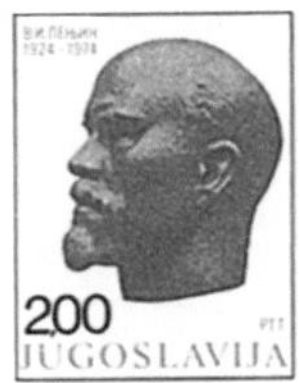

444 Lenin

445 Red Cross Emblems

1974. 50th Death Anniv of Lenin.
1601 **444** 2d. black and silver . . . 15 10

1974. Obligatory Tax. Red Cross Week.
1602 **445** 20p. multicoloured . . . 10 10

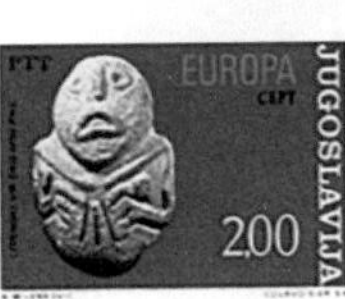

446 "Dwarf" (Lepenski settlement, c. 4950 B.C.)

447 Great Tit

1974. Europa. Sculptures. Multicoloured.

1603	2d. Type **446**	15	15
1604	6d. "Widow and Child" (Ivan Mestrovic)	1·00	1·00

1974. Youth Day. Multicoloured.

1605	80p. Type **447**	85	10
1606	2d. Roses	50	15
1607	6d. Cabbage white (butterfly)	2·00	1·10

448 Congress Poster

449 Olympic Rings and Stadium

1974. 10th Yugoslav League of Communists' Congress, Belgrade.

1608	**448**	80p. multicoloured . . .	10	10
1609		2d. multicoloured . . .	15	10
1610		6d. multicoloured . . .	35	30

1974. Obligatory Tax. Olympic Games Fund.
1611 **449** 10p. multicoloured . . . 10 10

450 Dish Aerial, Ivanjica

451 World Cup

1974. Inauguration of Satellite Communications Station, Ivanjica.

1612	**450**	80p. blue	20	10
1613	–	6d. lilac	90	60

DESIGN: 6d. "Intelstat 4" in orbit.

1974. World Cup Football Championship, West Germany.
1614 **451** 4d.50 multicoloured . . 70 50

452 Edelweiss and Klek Mountain

1974. Centenary of Croatian Mountaineers' Society.
1615 **452** 2d. multicoloured . . . 15 10

453 "Children's Dance" (Jano Knjazovic)

1974. Paintings. Multicoloured.

1616	80p. Type **453**	10	10
1617	2d. "Crucified Rooster" (Ivan Generalic) (vert) . .	10	10
1618	5d. "Laundresses" (Ivan Lackovic) (vert)	25	15
1619	8d. "Dance" (Janko Brasic)	85	75

454 "Rooster and Flower" (Kaca Milinojsin)

1974. Children's Week and 6th "Joy of Europe" Meeting, Belgrade. Children's Paintings. Mult.

1620	1d.20 Type **454**	10	10
1621	3d.20 "Girl and Boy" (Eva Medrzecka) (vert)	15	10
1622	5d. "Cat and Kitten" (Jelena Anastasijevic) . .	50	25

455 Interior of Library

1974. Bicent of National and University Library.
1623 **455** 1d.20 black 15 10

456 "White Peonies" (Petar Dobrovic)

458 Dove and Map of Europe

457 Title Page of Volume I

1974. Floral Paintings. Multicoloured.

1624	80p. Type **456**	10	10
1625	2d. "Carnations" (Vilko Gecan)	10	10
1626	3d. "Flowers" (Milan Konjovic)	10	10
1627	4d. "White Vase" (Sava Sumanovic)	20	15
1628	5d. "Branching Larkspurs" (Stane Kregar)	35	15
1629	8d. "Roses" (Petar Lubarda)	50	45

1975. 150th Anniv of "Matica Srpska" Annals.
1630 **457** 1d.20 black, olive and green 10 10

1975. 2nd European Security and Co-operation Conference, Belgrade.

1631	**458**	3d.20 multicoloured . .	20	10
1632		8d. multicoloured . . .	90	65

459 Gold-plated Bronze Ear-ring (14th–15th century), Alisici, Bosnia

460 "Svetozar Markovic" (sculpture by S. Bodnarov)

1975. Archaeological Discoveries. Multicoloured.

1633	1d.20 Type **459**	10	10
1634	2d.10 Silver bracelet (19th-century), Kosovo . .	10	10
1635	3d.20 Gold-plated silver buckle (18th-century), Bitola	15	10
1636	5d. Gold-plated ring (14th-century), Novi Sad	20	10
1637	6d. Silver necklace (17th-century), Kosovo . .	30	15
1638	8d. Gold-plated bronze bracelet (18th-century), Bitola	50	50

1975. Death Centenary of Svetozar Markovic (writer and statesman).
1639 **460** 1d.20 blue 10 10

461 "Fettered" (sculpture by F. Krsinic)

1975. International Women's Year.
1640 **461** 3d.20 brown and gold 15 15

462 Red Cross and Hands

1975. Obligatory Tax. Red Cross Week.
1681 **462** 20p. multicoloured . . . 10 10

463 "Still Life with Eggs" (Mosa Pijade)

1975. Europa. Paintings. Multicoloured.

1682	3d.20 Type **463**	15	15
1683	8d. "The Three Graces" (Ivan Radovic)	60	60

464 "Liberation Monument" (Dzamonja) **465** Garland Flower

1975. 30th Anniv of Liberation.
1684 **464** 3d.20 multicoloured . . 15 10

1975. National Youth Day. Flowers. Mult.
1685 1d.20 Type **465** 10 10
1686 2d.10 Touch-me-not balsam 10 10
1687 3d.20 Rose-mallow 10 10
1688 5d. Dusty cranesbill 15 10
1689 6d. Crocus 20 15
1690 8d. Rosebay willowherb . . 50 40

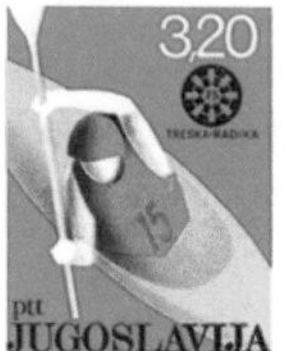

466 Games Emblem **467** Canoeing

1975. Obligatory Tax. Olympic Games Fund.
1691 **466** 10p. multicoloured . . . 10 10

1975. World Canoeing Championships, Macedonia.
1692 **467** 3d.20 multicoloured . . 20 10

468 "Herzegovinian Insurgents in Ambush"

1975. Cent of Bosnian-Herzegovinian Uprising.
1693 **468** 1d.20 multicoloured . . 15 10

469 "Skopje Earthquake" **470** Stjepan Mitrov Ljubisa

1975. Obligatory Tax. Solidarity Week.
1694 **469** 30p. black, grey and blue 35 35
See also Nos. 1885 and 1933.

1975. Writers.
1695 **470** 1d.20 black and red . . 10 10
1696 – 2d.10 black and green 10 10
1697 – 3d.20 black and bistre 10 10
1698 – 5d. black and orange . . 15 10
1699 – 6d. black and green . . 15 10
1700 – 8d. black and blue . . 25 25
PORTRAITS: 2d.10, Ivan Prijatelj; 3d.20, Jakov Ignjatovic; 5d. Dragojla Jarnevic; 6d. Svetozar Corivic; 8d. Ivana Brlic-Mazuranic.

471 "Young Lion" (A. Savic)

1975. Children's Week and 7th "Joy of Europa" Meeting, Belgrade. Children's Paintings. Mult.
1701 3d.20 Type **471** 15 10
1702 6d. "Baby in Pram" 75 40

472 Peace Dove within "EUROPA"

1975. European Security and Co-operation Conference, Helsinki.
1703 **472** 3d.20 multicoloured . . 10 10
1704 8d. multicoloured . . . 40 25

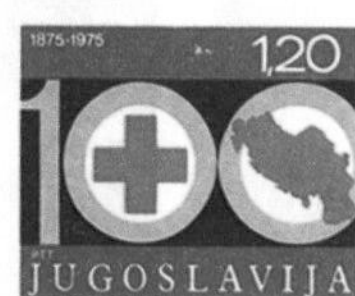

473 Red Cross and Map within "100"

1975. Centenary of Red Cross. Multicoloured.
1705 1d.20 Type **473** 15 10
1706 8d. Red Cross and people 50 25

474 "Folk Kitchen" (Djordje Andrejevic-Kun)

1975. Republic Day. Paintings. Multicoloured.
1707 1d.20 Type **474** 10 10
1708 2d.10 "On the Doorstep" (Vinko Grdan) 10 10
1709 3d.20 "The Drunken Coach-load" (Marijan Detoni) (horiz) 10 10
1710 5d. "Lunch" (Tone Kralj) (horiz) 15 10
1711 6d. "Waterwheel" (Lazar Licenoski) 25 15
1712 8d. "Justice" (Krsto Hegedusic) 45 40

475 Diocletian's Palace, Split (3rd-century)

1975. European Architectural Heritage Year.
1713 **475** 1d.20 brown 10 10
1714 – 3d.20 black 10 10
1715 – 8d. blue 40 40
DESIGNS—VERT: 3d.20, House in Ohrid (19th century). HORIZ: 8d. Gracanica Monastery, Kosovo (14th century).

476 Ski Jumping

1976. Winter Olympic Games, Innsbruck.
1716 **476** 3d.20 blue 15 10
1717 – 8d. lake 55 50
DESIGN: 8d. Figure skating.

477 Red Flag

1976. Centenary of "Red Flag" Insurrection (workers' demonstration), Kragujevac.
1718 **477** 1d.20 multicoloured . . 15 10

478 Svetozar Miletic

1976. 150th Birth Anniv of Svetozar Miletic (politician).
1719 **478** 1d.20 green and grey . . 15 10

479 Bora Stankovic

1976. Birth Cent of Bora Stankovic (writer).
1720 **479** 1d.20 red, brown and yellow 15 10

480 "King Matthias" (sculpture, J. Pogorelec)

1976. Europa. Handicrafts. Multicoloured.
1721 3d.20 Type **480** 10 10
1722 8d. Base of beaker 40 40

481 Ivan Cankar

1976. Birth Centenary of Ivan Cankar (Slovenian writer).
1723 **481** 1d.20 purple, brown and pink 10 10

482 Stylized Figure

1976. Obligatory Tax. Red Cross Week.
1724 **482** 20p. multicoloured . . . 60 60

483 Electric Train crossing Viaduct **485** Vladimir Nazor

484 Emperor Dragonfly

1976. Inauguration of Belgrade–Bar Railway.
1725 **483** 3d.20 brown 35 15
1726 – 8d. blue 90 45
DESIGN: 8d. Electric train crossing bridge.

1976. Youth Day. Freshwater Fauna. Multicoloured.
1727 1d.20 Type **484** 10 10
1728 2d.10 River snail 10 10
1729 3d.20 Rudd 15 10
1730 5d. Common frog 30 10
1731 6d. Ferruginous duck . . . 15 15
1732 8d. Muskrat 60 60

1976. Birth Centenary of Vladimir Nazor (writer).
1733 **485** 1d.20 blue and lilac . . . 15 15

486 "Battle of Vucji Dol" (from "Eagle" journal of 1876)

1976. Centenary of Montenegrin Liberation Wars.
1734 **486** 1d.20 brown, yellow and gold 15 15

487 Jug, Aleksandrovac, Serbia

1976. Ancient Pottery. Multicoloured.
1735 1d.20 Type **487** 10 10
1736 2d.10 Pitcher, Ptuj, Slovenia 10 10
1737 3d.20 Coffee-pot, Visnjica, Sarajevo 15 10
1738 5d. Pitcher, Backi Breg, Vojvodina 15 15
1739 6d. Goblet, Vranestica, Macedonia 20 15
1740 8d. Jug, Prizren, Kosovo . . 50 35

488 Nikola Tesla Monument and Niagara Falls

1976. 120th Birth Anniv of Nikola Tesla (scientist).
1741 **488** 5d. blue and green . . . 25 10

489 Long Jumping

1976. Olympic Games, Montreal.
1742 **489** 1d.20 purple 10 10
1743 – 3d.20 green 15 10
1744 – 5d. brown 25 10
1745 – 8d. blue 50 35
DESIGNS: 3d.20, Handball; 5d. Shooting; 8d. Rowing.

490 Stadium and Olympic Rings **492** "Navy Day" (Nikola Mitar)

491 Globe

1976. Obligatory Tax. Olympic Games Fund.
1746 **490** 10p. blue 10 10

1976. 5th Non-aligned Nations' Summit Conf, Colombo.
1747 **491** 4d.90 multicoloured . . 20 10

1976. Children's Week and 8th "Joy of Europe" Meeting, Belgrade. Children's Paintings. Mult.
1748 4d.90 Type **492** 15 10
1749 8d. "Children's Trains" (Wiggo Gulbrandsen) . . 50 40

493 "Battle of Montenegrins" (Djura Jaksic) **495** Nenadovic (after Uros Knezevic)

1976. Paintings. Historical Events. Mult.
1750 1d.20 Type **493** 10 10
1751 2d.10 "Nikola Subic Zrinjski at Siget" (Oton Ivekovic) 15 10
1752 3d.20 "Herzegovinian Fugitives" (Uros Predic) (horiz) 15 10
1753 5d. "The Razlovic Uprising" (Borko Lazeski) (horiz) 20 15

1754 6d. "Enthronement of the Slovenian Duke, Gospovsetsko Field" (Anton Gojmir Kos) (horiz) 35 20
1755 8d. "Breach of the Solun Front" (Veljko Stanojevic) (horiz) 50 45

1976. No. 1203 surch.
1756 1d. on 85p. purple 15 10

1977. Birth Bicentenary of Prota Mateja Nenadovic (soldier and diplomat).
1757 **495** 4d.90 multicoloured . . 20 25

496 Rajko Zinzifov **497** Phlox

1977. Death Centenary of Rajko Zinzifov (writer).
1758 **496** 1d.50 brown and sepia 10 10

1977. Flowers. Multicoloured.
1759 1d.50 Type **497** 10 10
1760 3d.40 Tiger lily 15 10
1761 4d.90 Bleeding heart 20 10
1762 6d. Zinnia 25 15
1763 8d. French marigold 30 15
1764 10d. Geranium 55 50

498 Institute Building **499** Alojz Kraigher

1977. 150th Anniv of Croatian Music Institute.
1765 **498** 4d.90 brown and black 20 10

1977. Birth Centenary of Alojz Kraigher (author).
1766 **499** 1d.50 brown and black 10 10

500 "Kotor Bay" (Milo Milunovic)

1977. Europa. Landscapes. Multicoloured.
1767 4d.90 Type **500** 15 10
1768 10d. "Zagorje in November" (Ljubo Babic) 40 40

501 Figure and Emblems

1977. Obligatory Tax. Red Cross Week.
1769 **501** 20p. red and brown . . 1·75 70
1770 50p. red and green . . . 50 20
1771 1d. red and blue 25 10

502 "President Tito" (Omer Mujadzic)

503 Alpine Scene

1977. 85th Birthday of President Tito.
1772 **502** 1d.50 brown, olive and gold 10 10
1773 4d.90 brown, pink and gold 20 15
1774 8d. brown, olive and gold 50 45

1977. International Environment Protection Day. Multicoloured.
1775 4d.90 Type **503** 20 10
1776 10d. Plitvice waterfall and red-breasted flycatcher . . 50 50

504 Petar Kocic

1977. Birth Centenary of Petar Kocic (writer).
1777 **504** 1d.50 mauve and green 10 10

505 Dove and Map of Europe

1977. European Security and Co-operation Conf, Belgrade.
1778 **505** 4d.90 multicoloured . . 30 15
1779 10d. multicoloured . . . 1·50 1·50

506 Tree

507 "Bather" (Mrak Franci)

1977. Obligatory Tax. Anti-tuberculosis Week.
1780 **506** 50p. multicoloured . . . 3·00 3·00
1781 1d. multicoloured . . . 40 20

1977. Children's Week and 9th "Joy of Europe" Meeting, Belgrade. Children's Paintings. Mult.
1782 4d.90 Type **507** 15 10
1783 10d. "One Fruit into Pail — the other into Mouth" (Tanja Ilinskaja) 50 40

508 Congress Building, Belgrade

509 Exhibition Emblem

1977. European Security and Co-operation Conf, Belgrade.
1784 **508** 4d.90 grey, blue and gold 25 15
1785 10d. red, rose and gold 1·50 1·50

1977. "Balkanphila 6" Stamp Exhibition, Belgrade.
1786 **509** 4d.90 multicoloured . . 15 10

510 Double Flute

1977. Musical Instruments in Ethnographical Museum, Belgrade.
1787 **510** 1d.50 brown and yellow 10 10
1788 – 3d.40 brown and green 10 10
1789 – 4d.90 yellow and brown 15 10
1790 – 6d. brown and blue . . . 20 15
1791 – 8d. brown and orange 35 20
1792 – 10d. brown and green . . 50 45
DESIGN: 3d.40, Tambura (string instrument; 4d.90, Gusle (string instrument); 6d. Lijerica (string insrtument); 8d. Bagpipe; 10d. Pan's flute.

511 Ivan Vavpotic

1977. Self-portraits. Multicoloured.
1793 1d.50 Type **511** 10 10
1794 3d.40 Mihailo Vukotic . . . 15 10
1795 4d.90 Kosta Hakman . . . 20 10
1796 6d. Miroslav Kraljevic . . . 25 15
1797 8d. Nikola Martinovski . . 35 20
1798 10d. Milena Paviovic-Barili 60 65

512 Globe and Olympic Rings

1977. Obligatory Tax. Olympic Games Fund.
1799 **512** 10p. yellow, turq & bl 10 10

513 "Ceremony of Testaccio" (miniature from Officum Virginis)

514 Pre-stamp Letter (Bavaniste-Kubin)

1978. 400th Death Anniv of Julije Klovic (Croat miniaturist). Multicoloured.
1800 4d.90 Type **513** 15 10
1801 10d. "Portrait of Klovic" (El Greco) 40 30

1978. Post Office Museum Exhibits. Mult.
1802 1d.50 Type **514** 10 10
1803 3d.40 19th-century mail box 10 10
1804 4d.90 Ericsson induction table telephone 15 10
1805 10d. Morse's first electro-magnetic telegraph set . . 30 30

515 Battle of Pirot

1978. Centenary of Serbo-Turkish War.
1806 **515** 1d.50 multicoloured . . 1·10 45

516 S-49A Trainer, 1949

1978. Aeronautical Day.
1807 **516** 1d.50 pink, brown and orange 10 10
1808 – 3d.40 blue, black and slate 15 10
1809 – 4d.90 black and brown 25 10
1810 – 10d. yellow, brown & grn 60 50
DESIGNS: 3d.40, SOKO Gabeb 3 jet trainer; 4d.90, UTVA 75 elementary trainer; 10d. Jurom Orao jet fighter.

517 Golubac

518 Boxing Glove on Glove

1978. Europa. Multicoloured.
1811 4d.90 Type **517** 20 15
1812 10d. St. Naum Monastery 1·00 1·00

1978. 2nd World Amateur Boxing Championship, Belgrade.
1813 **518** 4d.90 brown, blue and deep blue 20 10

519 Symbols of Red Crescent, Red Cross and Red Lion

520 Honey Bee

1978. Obligatory Tax. Red Cross Week. No. 1814 surch.
1814 **519** 20p. on 1d. blue and red 30 10
1815 1d. blue and red 10 10

1978. Bees. Multicoloured.
1816 1d.50 Type **520** 10 10
1817 3d.40 "Halictus scabiosae" (mining bee) 25 10
1818 4d.90 Blue carptenter bee 40 15
1819 10d. Buff-tailed bumble bee 90 70

521 Filip Filipovic and Radovan Dragovic

1978. Birth Centenaries of F. Filipovic and R. Dragovic (socialist movement leaders).
1820 **521** 1d.50 green and red . . 10 10

522 President Tito (poster)

524 Conference Emblem over Belgrade

1978. 11th Communist League Congress. Mult.
1821 2d. Type **522** 10 10
1822 4d.90 Hammer and sickle (poster) 25 10
MS1823 70 × 93 mm. 15d. As No. 1821. Imperf . . . . . . 2·75 2·50

1978. Various stamps surch.
1829 – 35p. on 10p. brown (No. 1642) 15 10
1830 **332** 60p. on 85p. blue (No. 1271) 15 10
1831 **443** 80p. on 1d.20 green (No. 1599) 15 10
1832 – 2d. on 1d. green (No. 1657) 15 10
1833 – 3d.40 on 2d.10 green (No. 1662) 20 10

1978. Conference of Foreign Ministers of Non-aligned Countries.
1834 **524** 4d.90 blue and light blue 15 10

525 Championship Emblem

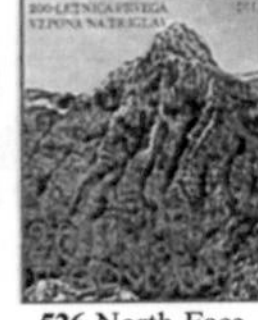

526 North Face, Mount Triglav

1978. 14th Kayak and Canoe "Still Water" World Championships, Belgrade.
1835 **525** 4d.90 black, blue and light blue 20 10

1978. Bicent of First Ascent of Mount Triglav.
1836 **526** 2d. multicoloured . . . 15 10

527 Hand holding Flame

528 Black Lake, Durmitor

1978. Obligatory Tax. Anti-tuberculosis Week.
1837 **527** 1d. multicoloured . . . 20 10

1978. Protection of the Environment. Multicoloured.
1838 4d.90 Type **528** 15 10
1839 10d. River Tara 50 40

529 Olympic Rings on Map of World

1978. Obligatory Tax. Olympic Games Fund.
1840 **529** 30p. multicoloured . . . 10 10

530 Star Map

1978. 29th International Astronautical Federation Congress, Dubrovnik.
1841 **530** 4d.90 multicoloured . . 20 10

531 "People in Forest" (Ivana Balen)

1978. Children's Week and 10th "Joy of Europe" Meeting, Belgrade. Multicoloured.
1842 4d.90 Type **531** 20 10
1843 10d. "Family round a Pond" (Vincent Christel) 50 40

532 Seal

1978. Centenary of Kresna Uprising.
1844 **532** 2d. black, brown and gold 15 10

533 Old College Building

1978. Bicentenary of Teachers' Training College, Sombor.
1845 **533** 2d. brown, yellow & gold 15 10

534 Red Cross

1978. Centenary of Croatian Red Cross.
1846 **534** 2d. red, blue and black 15 10

535 Metallic Sculpture "XXII" (Dusan Dzamonja)

1978. Modern Sculpture.
1847 **535** 2d. black, brown & silver 10 10
1848 – 3d.40 blue, grey and silver 15 10
1849 – 4d.90 olive, brown and silver 15 10
1850 – 10d. brown, buff and silver 40 45
DESIGNS—VERT: 3d.40, "Circulation in Space I" (Vojin Bakic); 4d.90, "Tectonic Octopod" (Olga Jevric). HORIZ: 10d. "The Tree of Life" (Drago Trsar).

536 "Crossing the Neretva" (Ismet Mujezinovic) **537** "People from the Seine" (Marijan Detoni)

1978. 35th Anniv of Battle of Neretva.
1851 **536** 2d. multicoloured . . . 15 10

1978. Republic Day. Graphic Art.
1852 **537** 2d. black, stone and gold 10 10
1853 – 3d.40 black, grey and gold 10 10
1854 – 4d.90 black, yellow and gold 15 10
1855 – 6d. black, flesh and gold 20 15
1856 – 10d. black, flesh and gold 35 40
DESIGNS—3d.40, "Labourers" (Maksim Sedej); 4d.90, "Felling of Trees" (Daniel Ozmo); 6d. "At a Meal" (Pivo Karamatijevic); 10d. "They are not afraid, even at a most loathsome crime" (Djordje Andrejevic Kun).

538 Eurasian Red Squirrel **539** Masthead

1978. New Year. Multicoloured.
1857 1d.50 Type **538** 15 10
1858 1d.50 Larch 15 10
1859 2d. Red deer 15 10
1860 2d. Sycamore 15 10
1861 3d.40 Rock partridge (pink background) 85 15
1861a 3d.40 Rock partridge (green background) . . . 85 25
1862 3d.40 Alder (pink background) 25 10
1862a 3d.40 Alder (green background) 40 15
1863 4d.90 Western capercaillie (green background) . . . 95 15
1863a 4d.90 Western capercaillie (yellow background) . . 95 25
1864 4d.90 Oak (green background) 30 10
1864a 4d.90 Oak (yellow background) 55 25

1979. 75th Anniv of "Politika" Newspaper.
1865 **539** 2d. black and gold . . . 15 10

540 Flags **541** Games Mascot

1979. 10th Anniv of Self-Managers' Meeting.
1866 **540** 2d. multicoloured . . . 15 10

1979. Obligatory Tax. Mediterranean Games Fund.
1867 **541** 1d. blue and deep blue 15 10
See also No. 1886.

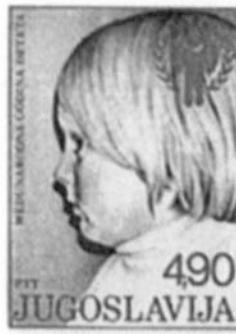

542 Child **543** Sabre, Mace and Enamluk (box holding Koranic texts)

1979. International Year of the Child.
1868 **542** 4d.90 blue and gold . . 40 30

1979. Ancient Weapons from Ethnographic Museum, Belgrade. Multicoloured.
1869 2d. Type **543** 10 10
1870 3d.40 Pistol and ammunition stick 10 10
1871 4d.90 Carbine and powder-horn 20 10
1872 10d. Rifle and cartridge-pouch 50 45

544 Hammer and Sickle on Star **545** University

1979. 60th Anniv of Yugoslav Communist Party and League for Communist Youth.
1873 **544** 2d. multicoloured . . . 10 10
1874 4d.90 multicoloured . . 15 15

1979. 30th Anniv of Cyril and Methodius University, Skopje.
1875 **545** 2d. brown, buff and pink 10 10

546 "Panorama of Belgrade" (Carl Goebel)

1979. Europa. Multicoloured.
1876 4d.90 Type **546** 15 15
1877 10d. Postilion and view of Ljubljana (after Jan van der Heyden) 40 40

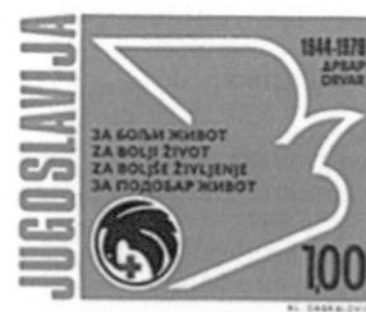
547 Stylized Bird

1979. Obligatory Tax. Red Cross Week.
1878 **547** 1d. turquoise, blue & red 15 10

548 Alpine Sow-thistle **549** Milutin Milankovic (after Paja Jovanovic)

1979. Alpine Flowers. Multicoloured.
1879 2d. Type **548** 10 10
1880 3d.40 "Anemone narcissiflora" 10 10
1881 4d.90 Milk-vetch 25 15
1882 10d. Alpine clover 50 40

1979. Birth Centenary of Milutin Milankovic (scientist).
1883 **549** 4d.90 multicoloured . . 20 10

550 Kosta Abrasevic **551** Rowing Crew

1979. Birth Centenary of Kosta Abrasevic (poet).
1884 **550** 2d. grey, pink and black 10 10

1979. Obligatory Tax. Solidarity Week. As T **469** but inscribed "1.-7.VI".
1885 30p. black, grey and blue . . 45 25
See also Nos. 1933 and 2218/19.

1979. Obligatory Tax. Mediterranean Games Fund. As No. 1867 but colour changed.
1886 **541** 1d. blue and deep blue 10 10

1979. 9th World Rowing Championships. Bled.
1887 **551** 4d.90 multicoloured . . 30 10

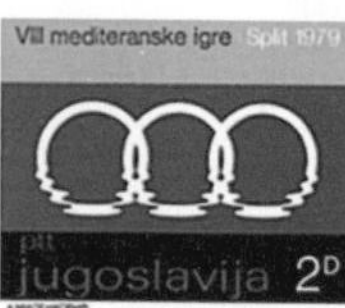

552 Games Emblem **553** Girl playing Hopscotch

1979. 8th Mediterranean Games. Multicoloured.
1888 2d. Type **552** 10 10
1889 4d.90 Mascot and emblem 15 10
1890 10d. Map and flags of participating countries . . 30 25

1979. Obligatory Tax. Anti-tuberculosis Week.
1891 **553** 1d. multicoloured . . . 20 15

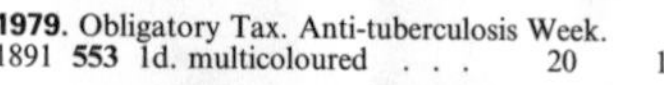

554 Arms of Zagreb, 1499

1979. 450th Anniv of Zagreb Postal Service.
1892 **554** 2d. grey and red 15 10

555 Lake Palic

1979. Environmental Protection. Multicoloured.
1893 4d.90 Type **555** 15 10
1894 10d. Lake in Prokletije range 45 30

556 Emblems

1979. Meeting of International Bank for Reconstruction and Development and of International Monetary Fund.
1895 **556** 4d.90 multicoloured . . 15 10
1896 10d. multicoloured . . . 40 30

557 Street in Winter (Mirjana Markovic)

1979. 11th "Joy of Europe" Meeting, Belgrade. Children's Paintings. Multicoloured.
1897 4d.90 Type **557** 15 10
1898 10d. House and garden (Jacques An) 50 45

558 Milhailo Pupin **559** Olympic Rings

1979. 125th Birth Anniv of Milhailo Pupin (scientist).
1899 **558** 4d.90 brown, light blue and blue 20 10

1979. Obligatory Tax. Olympic Games Fund.
1900 **559** 30p. red and blue . . . 15 10
MS1900 60 × 83 mm. 30d. brown, gold and silver. Imperf . . . . 1·25 1·25
DESIGN: 30d. Lenin Monument and Star of Order.

560 Marko Cepenkov **561** Pristina University

1979. 150th Anniv of Marko Cepenkov (author and folklorist).
1901 **560** 2d. brown, green and olive 15 10

1979. 10th Anniv of Pristina University.
1902 **561** 2d. multicoloured . . . 15 10

562 Lion on Column (Trogir Cathedral)

563 Sarajevo University

1979. Romanesque Sculpture. Multicoloured.
1903 2d. Type **562** 10 10
1904 3d.40 Apostle (detail of choir stall, Split Cathedral) 15 10
1905 4d.90 Window (Church of the Ascension, Decani) . . 20 10
1906 6d. Detail of Buvina door (Split Cathedral) 30 20
1907 10d. Virgin and Child (West door, Church of the Virgin, Studenica) 40 40

1979. 30th Anniv of Sarajevo University.
1908 **563** 2d. black, brown and grey 15 10

564 Djakovic and Hecimovic

1979. 50th Death Anniv of Djuro Djakovic and Nikola Hecimovic (leaders of socialist movement).
1909 **564** 2d. multicoloured . . . 15 10

565 Paddle-steamer "Srbija"

1979. Danube Conference. Multicoloured.
1910 4d.90 Paddle-steamer "Deligrad" 80 50
1911 10d. Type **565** . . . . . . 1·60 1·00

566 Milton Manaki

567 Edvard Kardelj

1980. Birth Centenary of Milton Manaki (first Balkan film maker).
1912 **566** 2d. purple, yellow and brown 15 10

1980. 70th Birth Anniv of Edvard Kardelj (revolutionary).
1913 **567** 2d. multicoloured . . . 15 10

1980. Renaming of Ploce as Kardeljevo. No. 1913 optd **PLOCE-1980-KARDELJEVO**.
1914 **567** 2d. multicoloured . . . 15 10

569 Speed Skating

1980. Winter Olympic Games, Lake Placid. Mult.
1915 4d.90 Type **569** 25 15
1916 10d. Skiing . . . . 1·25 90

570 Belgrade University

1980. 75th Anniv of Belgrade University.
1917 **570** 2d. multicoloured . . . 15 10

571 Fencing

1980. Olympic Games, Moscow. Multicoloured.
1918 2d. Type **571** 10 10
1919 3d.40 Cycling 15 10
1920 4d.90 Hockey 20 10
1921 10d. Archery 40 40

572 President Tito (relief by Antun Augustincic)

1980. Europa. Multicoloured.
1922 4d.90 Type **572** 25 25
1923 13d. Portrait of Tito by Djordje Prudnikov . . . 1·25 1·25

573 Pres. Tito

1980. Death of President Tito. Portraits by Bozidar Jakac.
1924 **573** 2d.50 purple 15 10
1925 – 4d.90 black . . . . . . 85 1·00
DESIGN: 4d.90, Different portrait of President Tito.

574 Sculpture of S. Kovacevic

1980. Obligatory Tax. Red Cross Week.
1926 **574** 1d. multicoloured . . . 25 15

575 Sava Kovacevic

1980. 75th Birth Anniv of Sava Kovacevic (partisan).
1927 **575** 2d. brown, orange & yell 15 10

576 Estafette and Letter from Youth of Belgrade, 1945

1980. 35th Anniv of Tito's 1st Estafette (youth celebration of Tito's birthday).
1928 **576** 2d. multicoloured . . . 15 10

577 Flying Gurnard

578 Decius Trajan (249–51)

1980. Adriatic Sea Fauna, Multicoloured.
1929 2d. Type **577** 15 10
1930 3d.40 Turtle 25 15
1931 4d.90 Little tern 25 25
1932 10d. Common dolphin . . . 45 40

1980. Obligatory Tax. Solidarity Week. As No. 1885.
1933 **469** 1d. black, grey and blue 50 30

1980. Roman Emperors on Coins. Multicoloured.
1934 2d. Type **578** 10 10
1935 3d.40 Aurelian (270–75) . . 15 10
1936 4d.90 Probus (276–82) . . . 25 10
1937 10d. Diocletian (284–305) 45 40

1980. Nos. 1660 and 1652 surch.
1938 2d.50 on 1d.50 red 20 10
1939 5d. on 75p. purple 50 10
See also Nos. 1992/3.

580 Lipica Horses

581 Tito

1980. 400th Anniv of Lipica Stud Farm.
1940 **580** 2d.50 black 20 10

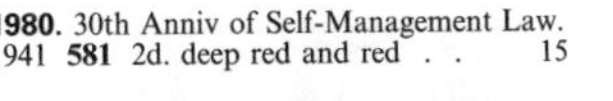

1980. 30th Anniv of Self-Management Law.
1941 **581** 2d. deep red and red . . 15 10

582 Novi Sad University

1980. 20th Anniv Novi Sad University.
1942 **582** 2d.50 green 15 10

583 Mljet

1980. Protection of the Environment. National Parks. Multicoloured.
1943 4d.90 Type **583** 25 10
1944 13d. Galicica, Ohrid 65 50

584 Pyrrhotine

585 Lake

1980. Crystals. Multicoloured.
1945 2d.50 Type **584** 10 10
1946 3d.40 Dolomite 15 10
1947 4d.90 Sphalerite 25 15
1948 13d. Wulfenite 50 40

1980. Obligatory Tax. Anti-tuberculosis Week.
1949 **585** 1d. multicoloured . . . 15 10

586 Kotor

1980. 21st Session of UNESCO General Conference, Belgrade.
1950 **586** 4d.90 blue, gold, and deep blue 20 10

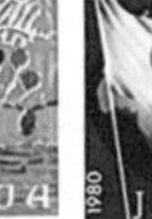

587 "Children with Balloons" (Gabrijela Radojevic)

588 Olympic Flag and Globe

1980. 12th "Joy of Europe" Meeting, Belgrade. Children's Drawings. Multicoloured.
1951 4d.90 Type **587** 15 10
1952 13d. "Face" (Renata Pisarcikova) 50 40

1980. Obligatory Tax. Olympic Games Fund.
1953 **588** 50p. multicoloured . . . 15 10

589 Dove and Madrid

1980. European Security and Co-operation Conference, Madrid.
1954 **589** 4d.90 green and deep green 20 15
1955 13d. bistre and brown 40 40

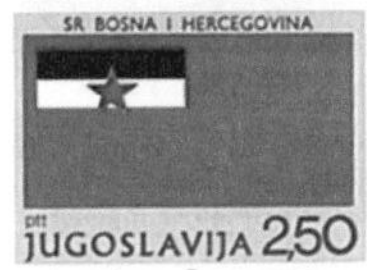

590 Flag of Bosnia and Herzegovina Socialist Republic

1980. Flags of Yugoslav Socialist Republics and of Federal Republic.
1956 **590** 2d.50 multicoloured . . 10 10
1957 – 2d.50 multicoloured . . 10 10
1958 – 2d.50 multicoloured . . 10 10
1959 – 2d.50 multicoloured . . 10 10
1960 – 2d.50 multicoloured . . 10 10
1961 – 2d.50 red, gold and grey 10 10
1962 – 2d.50 multicoloured . . 10 10
1963 – 2d.50 multicoloured . . 10 10
DESIGNS: No. 1957, Montenegro; 1958, Croatia; 1959, Yugoslavia (inscr in Roman alphabet); 1960, Yugoslavia (inscr in Cyrillic alphabet); 1961, Macedonia; 1962, Slovenia; 1963, Serbia.

591 "Complaint" (Milos Vuskovic)

593 Ivan Ribar

592 Sports Complex, Novi Sad

1980. Paintings. Multicoloured.
1964 2d.50 "Woman in a Straw Hat" (Stojan Aralica) (horiz) 10 10
1965 3d.40 "Atelier No. 1" (Gabrijel Stupica) (horiz) 10 10
1966 4d.90 "To the Glory of Sutjeska Fighters" (detail Ismet Mujezinovic) (horiz) 15 10
1967 8d. "Serenity" (Marino Tartaglia) 20 10
1968 13d. Type **591** 40 35

1980. Obligatory Tax. World Table Tennis Championships, Novi Sad.
1969 **592** 1d. green, yellow and blue 15 10

1981. Birth Centenary of Ivan Ribar (politician).
1970 **593** 2d.50 black and red . . 15 10

594 "Cementusa" Hand Bomb

1981. Partisan Arms in Belgrade Military Museum.
1971 **594** 3d.50 black and red . . 10 10
1972 – 5d.60 black and green 15 10
1973 – 8d. black and brown . . 20 10
1974 – 13d. black and purple . . 35 30
DESIGNS: 5d.60, "Partizanka" rifle; 8d. Cannon; 13d. Tank.

595 Virgin of Eleousa Monastery

1981. 900th Anniv of Virgin of Eleousa Monastery, Veljusa, Macedonia.
1975 **595** 3d.50 grey, brown and blue 15 10

596 Table Tennis

1981. "SPENS '81" World Table Tennis Championships, Novi Sad.
1976 **596** 8d. multicoloured . . . 30 15

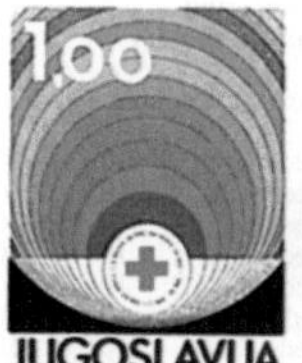

597 "Lamp"

598 "Herzegovinian Wedding" (detail)

1981. Obligatory Tax. Red Cross Week.
1977 **597** 1d. multicoloured . . . 10 10

1981. Europa. Paintings by Nikola Arsenovic. Multicoloured.
1978 8d. Type **598** 25 10
1979 13d. "Witnesses at a Wedding" 50 30

599 Tucovic and Dimitrije Tucovic Square

600 Tito (after Milivoje Unkovic)

1981. Birth Centenary of Dimitrije Tucovic (socialist leader).
1980 **599** 3d.50 blue and red . . . 15 10

1981. 89th Birth Anniv of Tito.
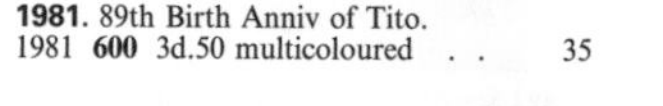
1981 **600** 3d.50 multicoloured . . 35 20

601 Sunflower

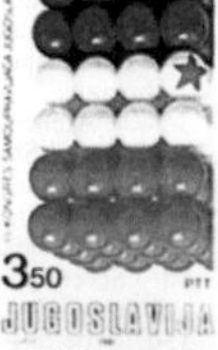

602 Congress Emblem

1981. Cultivated Plants. Multicoloured.
1982 3d.50 Type **601** 10 10
1983 5d.60 Hop 15 10
1984 8d. Corn 25 15
1985 13d. Wheat 50 35

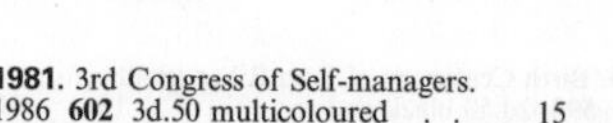
1981. 3rd Congress of Self-managers.
1986 **602** 3d.50 multicoloured . . 15 10

603 Djordje Petrov

604 Star

1981. 60th Death Anniv of Djordje Petrov (politician).
1987 **603** 3d.50 yellow and red . . 15 10

1981. 40th Anniv of Yugoslav Insurrection.
1988 **604** 3d.50 yellow and red . . 15 10
1989 8d. orange and red . . . 25 15
MS1990 60 × 83 mm. 30d. brown, gold and silver. Imperf . . . . 1·25 1·25
DESIGN: 30d. Lenin Monument and Star of Order.

605 Apple and Target

1981. Obligatory Tax. "Spet 81" European Shooting Championships, Titograd.
1991 **605** 1d. blue, red and orange 3·00 3·00

1981. Nos. 1666 and 1669 surch.
1992 3d.50 on 3d.40 green . . . 20 10
1993 5d. on 4d.90 blue 25 10

606 Varazdin (18th-century illustration)

1981. 800th Anniv of Varazdin.
1994 **606** 3d.50 yellow and blue . . 15 10

607 Parliament Building, Belgrade

608 "Flower"

1981. 20th Anniv of 1st Non-aligned Countries Conference, Belgrade.
1995 **607** 8d. blue and red 25 10

1981. Obligatory Tax. Anti-tuberculosis Week.
1996 **608** 1d. red, yellow and blue 15 10

609 Printing Press and Serbian Newspaper

1981. 150th Anniv of First Serbian Printing House.
1997 **609** 3d.50 pink and blue . . 15 10

610 Fran Levstik

1981. 150th Birth Anniv of Fran Levstik (writer).
1998 **610** 3d.50 grey and red . . . 15 10

611 "Village Scene" (Saso Arsovski)

1981. 13th "Joy of Europe" Meeting, Belgrade. Children's Drawings. Multicoloured.
1999 8d. Type **611** 15 10
2000 13d. "Skiers" (Aino Jokinen) 45 40

612 Tug "Karlovac" pushing Barges

1981. 125th Anniv of European Danube Commission. Multicoloured.
2001 8d. Type **612** 55 25
2002 13d. Paddle-steamer towed by steam railway locomotive on Sip Canal 1·50 70

613 Postal Savings Bank Emblem

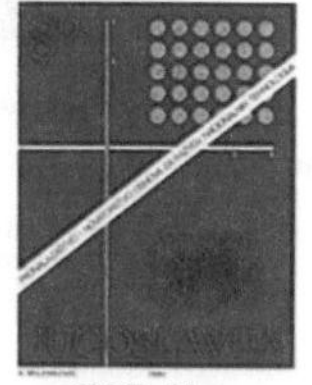

614 Emblem

1981. 60th Anniv of Postal Savings Bank.
2003 **613** 3d.50 red and yellow . . 15 10

1982. World Intellectual Property Organization Conference.
2004 **614** 8d. red and gold 25 15

615 Forsythia and Rugovo Ravine

1981. Protection of Nature. Multicoloured.
2005 8d. Type **615** 25 10
2006 13d. Lynx and Prokletije . . 60 40

616 August Senoa

617 "Still Life with Fish" (Jovan Bijelic)

1981. Death Centenary of August Senoa (writer).
2007 **616** 3d.50 purple and brown 15 10

1981. Paintings of Animals. Multicoloured.
2008 3d.50 Type **617** 10 10
2009 5d.60 "Raven" (Milo Milunovic) 15 10
2010 8d. "Bird on Blue Background" (Marko Celebonovic) 15 10
2011 10d. "Horses" (Peter Lubarda) 40 15
2012 13d. "Sheep" (Nikola Masic) 40 35

618 Mosa Pijade (politician)

1982. 40th Anniv of Foca Regulations.
2013 **618** 3d.50 blue and mauve 15 10

619 Mastheads

620 Cetinje

1982. 60th Anniv of "Borba" (newspaper).
2014 **619** 3d.50 black and red . . 15 10

1982. 500th Anniv of City of Cetinje.
2015 **620** 3d.50 brown and black 15 10

621 Visin's Ship "Splendido"

1982. Europa. Multicoloured.
2016 8d. Capt. Ivo Visin (first Yugoslav to sail round world) and naval chart . . 25 15
2017 15d. Type **621** 80 25

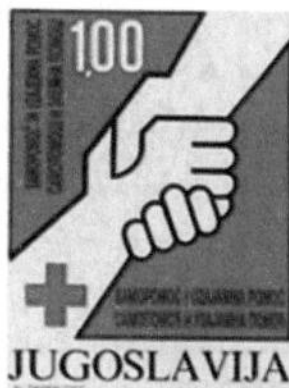

622 Clasped Hands

624 House Sparrow (male)

623 Ball placed for Kick-off

1982. Obligatory Tax. Red Cross Week.
2018 **622** 1d. black and red . . . 15 10

1982. World Cup Football Championship, Spain. Sheet 97 × 84 mm containing T **623** and similar horiz designs. Multicoloured.
MS2019 3d.50 Type **623**; 5d.60, Ball placed for corner kick; 8d. Ball in top of net; 15d. Player carrying ball under arm . . . . 1·25 1·25

1982. Multicoloured.
2020 3d.50 Type **624** 30 30
2021 5d.60 House sparrow (female) 35 35
2022 8d. Spanish sparrow (female) 50 50
2023 15d. Eurasian tree sparrow (male) . . . . 1·50 1·50

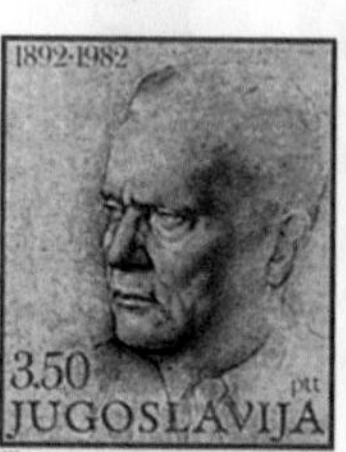

625 Tito (after Dragan Dosen)

627 Jaksic (self-portrait)

626 Poster (Dobrilo Nikolic)

1982. 90th Birth Anniv of Tito.
2024 **625** 3d.50 multicoloured . . 15 10

1982. 12th Communist League Congress, Belgrade.
2025 **626** 3d.50 brown, orge & red 15 10
2026 8d. light grey, grey and red 25 15
MS2027 70 × 95 mm. **626** 10d. orange and scarlet; 20d. grey, olive and scarlet . . . . 1·00 1·00

1982. 150th Birth Anniv of Dura Jaksic (writer and painter).
2028 **627** 3d.50 multicoloured . . 15 10

628 Kayaks

629 Ivan Zajc

1982. Sports Championships.
2029 **628** 8d. light blue and blue 25 15
2030 – 8d. light green and green 25 15
2031 – 8d. pink and red 25 15
DESIGNS AND EVENTS: No. 2029, Type **628** (17th World Kayak and Canoe Still Water Championships, Belgrade); 2030, Weightlifting(36th World Weightlifting Championships, Ljubljana); 2031, Gymnastics (6th World Gymnastics Cup, Zagreb).

1982. 150th Birth Anniv of Ivan Zajc (composer).
2032 **629** 4d. orange and brown 15 10

630 Breguet 19 and Potez 25 Biplanes

1982. 40th Anniv of Air Force, Anti-aircraft Defence and Navy.
2033 **630** 4d. black and blue . . . 20 10
2034 – 6d.10 multicoloured . . 30 10
2035 – 8d.80 black and green 50 15
2036 – 15d. multicoloured . . . 90 30
DESIGNS: 6d.10, SOKO G-4 Super Galeb jet trainer; 8d.80, National Liberation Army armed tug; 15d. "Rade Koncar" (missile gunboat).

631 Tara National Park and Pine Cones

1982. Nature Protection. Multicoloured.
2037 8d.80 Type **631** 25 15
2038 15d. Kornati National Park and Mediterranean monk seal 50 40

632 Dr. Robert Koch

1982. Obligatory Tax. Anti-tuberculosis Week.
2039 **632** 1d. orange, black and red 10 10

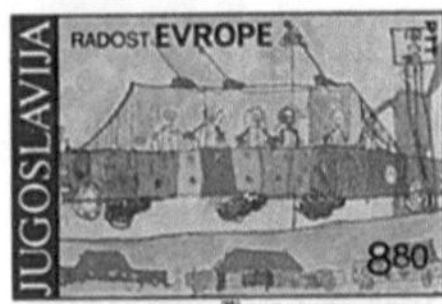

633 "Traffic" (Tibo Bozo)

1982. 14th "Joy of Europe" Meeting, Belgrade. Children's Drawings. Multicoloured.
2040 8d.80 Type **633** 15 15
2041 15d. "In the Bath" (Heiko Jakel) 40 35

634 Small Onofrio Fountain, Dubrovnik

1982. 16th World Federation of Travel Agents' Associations Congress, Dubrovnik.
2042 **634** 8d.80 multicoloured . . 20 15

635 Herceg Novi (from old engraving)

1982. 600th Anniv of Herceg Novi.
2043 **635** 4d. multicoloured . . . 60 25

636 Bridge, Miljacka

1982. Winter Olympic Games, Sarajevo. Each black, light blue and blue.
2044 4d. Type **636** 30 15
2045 6d.10 Mosque tower and cable cars, Sarajevo . . . 35 25
2046 8d.80 Evangelical Church, Sarajevo 45 30
2047 15d. Old Street, Sarajevo . . 85 70

637 Bihac

1982. 40th Anniv of Avnoj-a (anti-fascist council) Session, Bihac.
2048 **637** 4d. brown and orange 15 10

638 "Prophet on Golden Background" (Joze Ciuha)

639 Predic (self-portrait)

1982. Modern Art. Multicoloured.
2049 4d. Type **638** 10 10
2050 6d.10 "Journey to the West" (Andrej Jemec) 10 10
2051 8d.80 "Black Comb with Red Band" (Riko Debenjak) 15 15
2052 10d. "Manuscript" (Janez Bernik) (horiz) 20 20
2053 15d. "Display Case" (Adriana Maraz) (horiz) 40 35

1982. 125th Birth Anniv of Uros Predic (painter).
2054 **639** 4d. orange and brown 15 10

641 Pioneer Badge

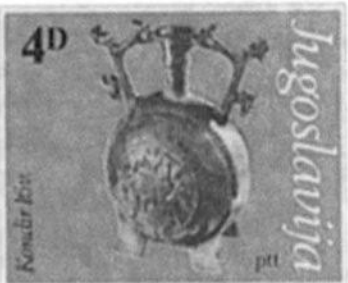

644 Lead Pitcher (16th century)

1982. 40th Anniv of Pioneer League.
2056 **641** 4d. brown, silver and red 15 10

1983. Nos. 1663 and 1667 surch.
2057 30p. on 2d.50 blue 25 10
2055a 50p. on 2d.50 blue 10 10
2058 60p. on 2d.50 blue 40 10
2059a 1d. on 3d.50 red 10 10
2060 2d. on 2d.50 red 10 10

1983. Museum Exhibits.
2061 **644** 4d. black, bistre and silver 10 10
2062 – 6d.10 black, brown and silver 15 10
2063 – 8d.80 gold, purple and grey 20 15
2064 – 15d. gold, purple and grey 40 25
DESIGNS: 6d.10, Silver-plated tin jar (18th century); 8d.80, Silver-gilt dish (16th century); 15d. Bronze mortar (15th century).

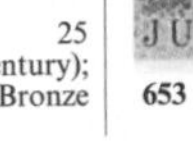

645 Jalovec Mountain Peak and Edelweiss

646 Ericsson Wall Telephone and War Ministry, Belgrade

1983. 90th Anniv of Slovenian Mountaineering Society.
2065 **645** 4d. blue, light blue and deep blue 15 10

1983. Centenary of Telephone in Serbia.
2066 **646** 3d. brown and blue . . . 15 10

647 I.M.O. Emblem and Freighters

1983. 25th Anniv of International Maritime Organization.
2067 **647** 8d.80 multicoloured . . 35 15

648 Field Mushroom

1983. Edible Mushrooms. Multicoloured.
2068 4d. Type **648** 20 10
2069 6d.10 Common morel . . . 30 10
2070 8d.80 Cep 50 15
2071 15d. Chanterelle . . . . . 1·25 55

649 Series 401 Steam Locomotive

650 Monument, Landovica

1983. 110th Anniv of Rijeka Railway.
2072 **649** 4d. grey and red 30 10
2073 – 23d.70 on 8d.80 grey and red 80 15
DESIGN: 23d.70, Series 442 electric locomotive. No. 2073 was only issued surcharged.

1983. 40th Death Anniv of Boro Vukmirivic and Ramiz Sadiku (revolutionaries).
2074 **650** 4d. grey and violet . . . 15 10

651 Nobel Prize Medal and Manuscript of "Travnik Chronicle" by Andric

1983. Europa. Multicoloured.
2075 8d.80 Type **651** 20 15
2076 20d. Ivo Andric (author and Nobel Prize winner) and bridge over the Drina . . 50 40

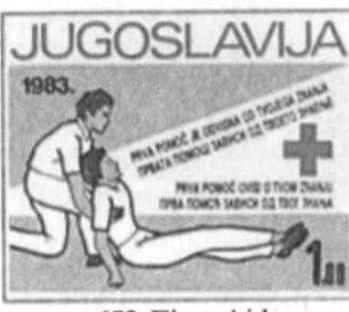

652 First Aid

1983. Obligatory Tax. Red Cross Week.
2077 **652** 1d. deep brown, brown and red 15 10
2078 2d. deep brown, brown and red 15 10

653 Combine Harvester

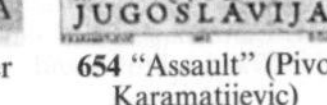

654 "Assault" (Pivo Karamatijevic)

1983. 50th International Agriculture Fair, Novi Sad.
2079 **653** 4d. green and purple . . 15 10

1983. 40th Anniv of Battle of Sutjeska.
2080 **654** 3d. pink and brown . . 15 10

655 Tito (after Bozidar Jakac) and Parliament Building

656 Delahaye Postbus, 1903

1983. 30th Anniv of Tito's Election to Presidency.
2081 **655** 4d. brown and green . . 10 10

1983. 80th Anniv of Postbus Service in Montenegro.
2082 **656** 4d. black and brown . . 10 10
2083 – 16d.50 black and brown 40 25
DESIGN: 16d.50, Road used by first postbus.

657 Statue by V. Bakic, Valjevo

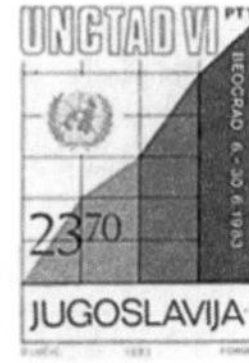

658 Graph

1983. Monuments.
2084 **657** 100d. orange and blue 2·00 40
2085 – 200d. orange and green 1·90 75
DESIGN—HORIZ: 200d. Triumphal Arch, Titograd.

1983. 6th U.N. Conference for Trade and Development Session, Belgrade.
2086 **658** 23d.70 multicoloured . . 60 30

659 Pazin (after engraving by Valvasor)

660 Skopje

1983. Millenary of Pazin.
2087 **659** 4d. brown and green . . 15 10

1983. 20th Anniv of Skopje Earthquake.
2088 **660** 23d.70 red 40 30

661 "The Victor"

663 Apple

662 Gentian and Kupaonik National Park

1983. Birth Cent of Ivan Mestrovic (sculptor).
2089 **661** 6d. deep brown, brown and blue 15 10

1983. Nature Protection. Multicoloured.
2090 16d.50 Type **662** 40 25
2091 23d.70 Chamois and Sutjeska National Park 50 30

1983. Obligatory Tax. Anti-tuberculosis Week.
2092 **663** 1d. red, black & turquoise 10 10
2093 2d. red, black & turquoise 15 10

664 "Newly Weds" (Vesna Paunkovic)

665 School and Seal

1983. 15th "Joy of Europe" Meeting, Belgrade. Children's Drawings.
2094 **664** 16d.50 yellow, black and red 20 15
2095 – 23d.70 multicoloured . . 40 20
DESIGN: 23d.70, "Andres and his Mother" (Marta Lopez-Ibor).

1983. 150th Anniv of Kragujevac Grammar School.
2096 **665** 5d. brown and blue . . . 15 10

666 Monument by Antun Augustincic

667 Skier and Games Emblem

1983. Centenary of Timocka Buna Uprising.
2097 **666** 5d. blue and purple . . . 15 10

1983. Obligatory Tax. Winter Olympic Games, Sarajevo.
2098 **667** 2d. blue and deep blue 15 10

668 Zmaj and "Neven" Periodical

1983. 150th Birth Anniv of Jovan Jovanovic Zmaj (poet and editor).
2099 **668** 5d. red and green . . . 10 10

669 Ski Jump, Malo Polje, Mt. Igman

1983. Winter Olympic Games, Sarajevo (1st issue).
2100 **669** 4d. black, green & brown 10 10
2101 – 4d. dp blue, blue & brown 10 10
2102 – 16d.50 lilac, deep brown and brown 35 20
2103 – 16d.50 green, blue & brn 35 20
2104 – 23d.70 deep brown, green and brown . . . 45 30
2105 – 23d.70 black, green and brown 45 30
MS2106 60 × 74 mm. 50d. ultramarine and magenta. Imperf 1·60 1·60
DESIGNS: No. 2101, Women's slalom run, Mt. Jahorina, 2102, Bob-sleigh and luge run, Mt. Trebevic; 2103, Men's alpine downhill ski run. Mt. Bjelasnice; 2104, Olympic Hall (for ice hockey and figure skating), Zetra; 2105 Speed skating rink, Zetra. 26 × 33 mm 50d. Games emblem.

670 "The Peasant Wedding" (Brueghel the Younger)

671 Jajce

1983. Paintings. Multicoloured.
2107 4d. Type **670** 10 10
2108 16d.50 "Susanna and the Elders" (Master of "The Prodigal Son") 25 15
2109 16d.50 "The Allegory of Wisdom and Strength" (Paolo Veronese) 25 15
2110 23d.70 "The Virgin Mary from Salamanca" (Robert Campin) 40 30
2111 23d.70 "St. Anne with the Madonna and Jesus" (Albrecht Durer) 40 30

1983. 40th Anniv of 2nd Avnoj-a (anti-fascist council) Session, Jajce.
2112 **671** 5d. red and blue 15 10
MS2113 59 × 74 mm. 30d. red, grey and gold (Tito). Imperf 75 75

672 Drawing by Hasukic Sabina

673 Koco Racin

1983. World Communications Year.
2114 **672** 23d.70 multicoloured . . 40 25

1983. 75th Birth Anniv of Koco Racin (writer).
2115 **673** 5d. blue and brown . . . 15 10

674 First Issue of "Politika"

1984. 80th Anniv of "Politika" (daily newspaper).
2116 **674** 5d. black and red . . . 15 10

675 Veljko Petrovic

677 Marija Bursac

676 Giant Slalom

1984. Birth Centenary of Veljko Petrovic (writer).
2117 **675** 5d. brown, orange and grey 15 10

1984. Winter Olympic Games, Sarajevo (2nd issue).
2118 **676** 4d. multicoloured . . . 10 10
2119 – 4d. multicoloured . . . 10 10
2120 – 5d. multicoloured . . . 15 10
2121 – 5d. multicoloured . . . 15 10
2122 – 16d.50 multicoloured . . 30 20
2123 – 16d.50 multicoloured . . 30 20
2124 – 23d.70 multicoloured . . 50 30
2125 – 23d.70 multicoloured . . 50 30
MS2126 Two sheets, each 60 × 74 mm. Imperf (a) 50d. blue, magenta and silver; (b) 100d. magenta, gold and blue . . . . 3·25 3·25
DESIGNS: No. 2119, Biathlon; 2120, slalom; 2121, Bobsleigh; 2122, Speed skating; 2123, Ice hockey; 2124, Ski jumping; 2125, Downhill skiing. 26 × 33 mm—50d. Olympic flame; 100d. Flame and map of Yugoslavia.

1984. Women's Day. National Heroines. Each grey, blue and black.
2127 5d. Type **677** 15 10
2128 5d. Jelena Cetkovic 15 10
2129 5d. Nada Dimic 15 10
2130 5d. Elpida Karamandi . . . 15 10
2131 5d. Toncka Cec Olga . . . 15 10
2132 5d. Spasenija Babovic Cana 15 10
2133 5d. Jovanka Radivojevic Kica 15 10
2134 5d. Sonja Marinkovic . . . 15 10

678 Bond and Banknote

1984. 40th Anniv of Slovenian Monetary Institute.
2135 **678** 5d. blue and red 15 10

679 Belgrade Central Station and Steam Mail Train, 1884

1984. Centenary of Serbian Railway.
2136 **679** 5d. brown and deep brown 10 10

680 Jure Franko and Silver Medal

682 Globe as Jigsaw Pieces

681 Bridge

1984. 1st Yugoslav Winter Olympics Medal.
2137 **680** 23d.70 multicoloured . . 45 25

1984. Europa. 25th Anniv of European Post and Telecommunications Conference.
2138 **681** 23d.70 multicoloured . . 35 20
2139 50d. multicoloured . . . 75 40

1984. Obligatory Tax. Red Cross Week.
2140 **682** 1d. multicoloured . . . 10 10
2141 2d. multicoloured . . . 15 10
2142 4d. multicoloured . . . 30 10
2143 5d. multicoloured . . . 35 25

683 Basketball

1984. Olympic Games, Los Angeles. Multicoloured.
2144 5d. Type **683** 15 10
2145 16d.50 Diving 30 20
2146 23d.70 Equestrian 40 30
2147 50d. Running 80 50

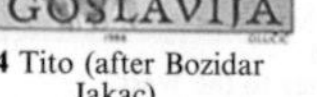

684 Tito (after Bozidar Jakac)

685 "Skopje Earthquake"

1984. 40th Anniv of Failure of German Attack on National Liberation Movement's Headquarters at Drvar.
2148 **684** 5d. brown and light brown 15 10

1984. Obligatory Tax. Solidarity Week. Self-adhesive. Imperf.
2149 **685** 1d.50 blue and red . . . 60 35

686 Mt. Biokovo Natural Park and "Centaurea gloriosa"

1984. Nature Protection. Multicoloured.
2150 26d. Type **686** 30 25
2151 40d. Pekel Cave and "Anophthalmus schmidti" (Longhorn beetle) 60 35

687 Great Black-backed Gull

1984. Birds. Multicoloured.
2152 4d. Type **687** 15 10
2153 5d. Black-headed gull . . . 20 10
2154 16d.50 Herring gull 50 20
2155 40d. Common tern . . . . 1·40 50

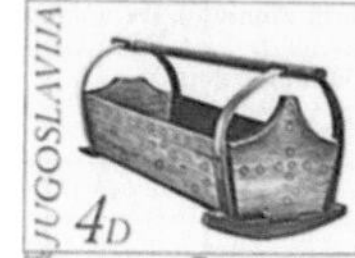

688 Cradle from Bihac, Bosnia and Herzegovina

1984. Museum Exhibits. Cradles.
2156 **688** 4d. green 10 10
2157 – 5d. purple and red . . . 10 10
2158 – 26d. light brown and brown 35 25
2159 – 40d. ochre and orange . . 60 40
DESIGNS: Cradles from—5d. Montenegro; 26d. Macedonia; 40d. Rasina, Serbia.

689 Red Cross and Leaves

691 "National Costume" (Erika Sarcevic)

690 Olive Trees, Mirovica

1984. Obligatory Tax. Anti-tuberculosis Week.
2160 **689** 1d. multicoloured . . . 10 10
2161 2d. multicoloured . . . 10 10
2162 2d.50 multicoloured . . 15 10
2163 4d. multicoloured . . . 20 15
2164 5d. multicoloured . . . 25 15

1984.
2165 **690** 5d. multicoloured . . . 15 10

1984. 16th "Joy of Europe" Meeting, Belgrade. Children's Paintings. Multicoloured.
2166 26d. Type **691** 35 20
2167 40d. "Girl pushing bear in buggy" (Eva Gug) . . . 60 40

692 Virovitica (17th-century engraving)

1984. 750th Anniv of Virovitica.
2168 **692** 5d. orange and black . . 15 10

693 Map and Radio Waves

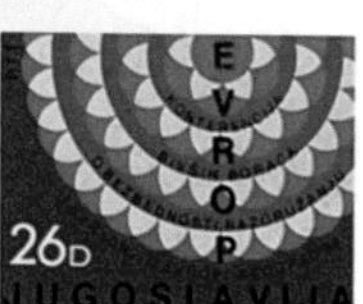

694 "Flower"

1984. 80th Anniv of Radio-Telegraphic Service in Montenegro.
2169 **693** 6d. blue and green . . . 15 10

1984. Veterans' Conference on Security, Disarmament and Co-operation in Europe, Belgrade.
2170 **694** 26d. pink, black and violet . . . . 1·00 1·00
2171 40d. green, black and blue . . . . 1·00 1·00

695 City Arms and "40"

696 Milojevic and Music Score

1984. 40th Anniv of Liberation of Belgrade.
2172 **695** 6d. red, silver and blue 15 10

1984. Birth Centenary of Miloje Milojevic (composer).
2173 **696** 6d. lilac and green . . . 15 10

697 Issues of 1944 and 1984

1984. 40th Anniv of "Nova Makedoniya" (newspaper).
2174 **697** 6d. blue and red 15 10

698 Boxing

1984. Yugoslav Olympic Games Medal Winners. Each blue and red.
2175 26d. Type **698** 30 20
2176 26d. Wrestling 30 20
2177 26d. Canoeing 30 20
2178 26d. Handball 30 20
2179 26d. Football 30 20
2180 26d. Basketball 30 20
2181 26d. Water polo 30 20
2182 26d. Rowing 30 20

699 "Madame Tatichek" (Ferdinand Waldmuller)

1984. Paintings. Multicoloured.
2183 6d. Type **699** 15 10
2184 26d. "The Bathers" (Pierre-Auguste Renoir) 35 20
2185 26d. "At the Window" (Henri Matisse) 35 20
2186 38d. "The Tahitians" (Paul Gauguin) (horiz) . . . 40 25
2187 40d. "The Ballerinas" (Edgar Degas) (horiz) . . 60 40

1984. Nos. 1675a, 1668a and 2088 surch.
2188a 2d. on 8d.80 grey 15 10
2189 6d. on 4d. red 15 10
2190 20d. on 23d.70 red 25 10

701 "Aturia aturi" (cephalopod)

1985. Museum Exhibits. Fossils.
2191 **701** 5d. purple and blue . . . 10 10
2192 – 6d. brown and light brown 10 10
2193 – 33d. brown and yellow 45 25
2194 – 60d. brown and orange 75 45
DESIGNS: 6d. "Pachyophis woodwardi" (snake); 33d. Hoefer's butterflyfish; 60d. Skull of Neanderthal man.

702 Hopovo Church **703** Three Herons in Flight

1985. 40th Anniv of Organized Protection of Yugoslav Cultural Monuments.
2195 **702** 6d. red, yellow and green 20 10

1985. 50th Anniv of Planica Ski-jump.
2196 **703** 6d. multicoloured . . . 90 30

704 Lammergeier and Douglas DC-10 Jetliner over Mountains **705** Osprey

1985. Air. Multicoloured.
2197 500d. Type **704** . . . . . 1·75 65
2199 1000d. Red-rumped swallow and airplane at airport . . 2·50 1·25

1985. Nature Protection. Birds. Multicoloured.
2202 42d. Type **705** . . . . . . 1·75 75
2203 60d. Hoopoe . . . . 2·40 1·25

706 Three Herons in Flight **707** "St. Methodius" (detail "Seven Slav Saints", St. Naum's Church Ohrid)

1985. Obligatory Tax. 50th Anniv of Planica Ski-jump.
2204 **706** 2d. blue and green . . . 10 10

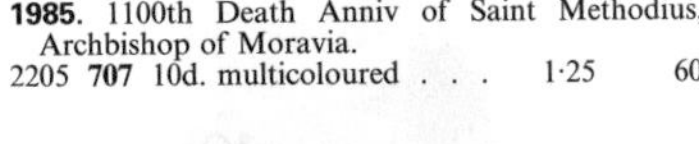
1985. 1100th Death Anniv of Saint Methodius, Archbishop of Moravia.
2205 **707** 10d. multicoloured . . . 1·25 60

708 Handshake

1985. 10th Anniv of Osimo Agreements between Yugoslavia and Italy.
2206 **708** 6d. blue and deep blue 15 10

709 Flute, Darabukka and Josip Slavenski (composer)

1985. Europa. Multicoloured.
2207 60d. Type **709** 60 60
2208 80d. Score of "Balkanophonia" (Slavenski) 60 60

710 Red Cross and Faces **711** Vujic (after Dimitrije Auramovic)

1985. Obligatory Tax. Red Cross Week.
2209 **710** 1d. violet and red . . . 10 10
2210 2d. violet and red . . . 10 10
2211 3d. violet and red . . . 10 10
2212 4d. violet and red . . . 15 10

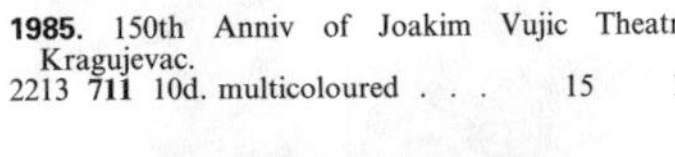
1985. 150th Anniv of Joakim Vujic Theatre, Kragujevac.
2213 **711** 10d. multicoloured . . . 15 10

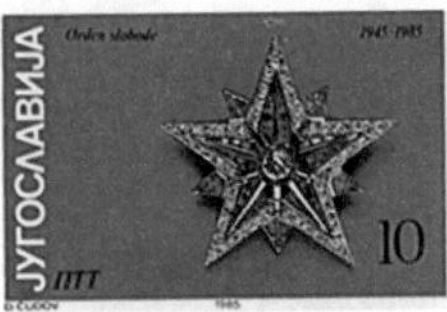

712 Order of Liberty

1985. 40th Anniv of V.E. (Victory in Europe) Day. Multicoloured.
2214 10d. Type **712** 15 10
2215 10d. Order of National Liberation 15 10

713 Franjo Kluz and Rudi Cajavec (pilots) and Potez 25 Biplane **714** Tito (after Bozidar Jakac)

1985. Air Force Day.
2216 **713** 10d. blue, purple & brown 30 10

1985. 93rd Birth Anniv of Tito.
2217 **714** 10d. multicoloured . . . 40 10

715 Red Cross and "Skopje Earthquake" **716** Villa, Map of Islands and Arms

1985. Obligatory Tax. Solidarity Week. (a) As Nos. 1885 and 1933.
2218 2d.50 black, grey and blue 35 25
2219 3d. black, grey and blue . . 40 25

(b) Type **715**.
2220 **715** 3d. blue and red . . . . 1·50 1·25
See also Nos. 23215/16, 2460, 2532, 2636 and 2716.

1985. Centenary of Tourism in Cres-Losinj Region.
2221 **716** 10d. multicoloured . . . 15 10

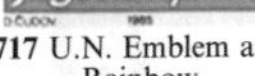

717 U.N. Emblem and Rainbow **718** Regatta Emblem

1985. 40th Anniv of U.N.O.
2222 **717** 70d. multicoloured . . . 50 35

1985. 30th Anniv of International European Danubian Regatta.
2223 **718** 70d. multicoloured . . . 45 35
MS2224 95 × 79 mm. 100d. silver, blue and deep blue (regatta course) (34 × 28 mm) . . . . 1·25 1·25

719 Aerial View of Yacht **720** Model Airplane

1985. Nautical Tourism. Multicoloured.
2225 8d. Type **719** 10 10
2226 10d. Windsurfing 15 10
2227 50d. Yacht in sunset 60 35
2228 70d. Yacht by coastline . . 80 50

1985. World Free Flight Aeromodels Championships, Livno.
2229 **720** 70d. multicoloured . . . 80 35

721 Emblem and Text **722** Boy with Football

1985. Obligatory Tax. 20th European Shooting Championships, Osijek.
2230 **721** 3d. blue 10 10

1985. Obligatory Tax. Anti-tuberculosis Week.
2231 **722** 2d. black, orange and red 10 10
2232 3d. black, orange and red 10 10
2233 4d. black, orange and red 15 10
2234 5d. black, orange and red 20 10

723 "Corallina officinalis" and Seahorses

1985. Marine Flora. Multicoloured.
2235 8d. Type **723** 10 10
2236 10d. "Desmarestia viridis" 10 10
2237 50d. Bladder wrack seaweed 45 25
2238 70d. "Padina pavonia" . . . 1·00 75

724 Federation Emblem

1985. 73rd International Stomatologists Federation Congress, Belgrade.
2239 **724** 70d. multicoloured . . . 45 35

725 Selling Vegetables from Cart (Branka Lukic)

1985. 17th "Joy of Europe" Meeting, Belgrade. Children's Paintings. Multicoloured.
2240 50d. Type **725** 40 20
2241 70d. "Children playing" (Suzanne Straathof) . . . 1·10 1·10

726 Detail of Theatre Facade

1985. 125th Anniv of Croatian National Theatre, Zagreb.
2242 **726** 10d. multicoloured . . . 15 10

727 Miladin Popovic **728** State Arms

1985. 75th Birth Anniv and 40th Death Anniv of Miladin Popovic (Communist Party worker).
2243 **727** 10d. brown and orange 15 10

1985. 40th Anniv of Federal Republic.
2244 **728** 10d. multicoloured . . . 15 10
MS2245 62 × 75 mm. **728** 100d. multicoloured (15 × 25 mm). Imperf . . . . 1·10 1·10

729 "Royal Procession" (Iromie Wijewardena)

1985. Paintings. Multicoloured.
2246 8d. Type **729** 10 10
2247 10d. "Return from Hunting" (Mama Cangare) 15 10
2248 50d. "Drum of Coca" (Agnes Ovando Sanz de Franck) 40 20
2249 50d. "The Cock" (Mariano Rodriguez) (vert) 40 20
2250 70d. "Three Women" (Quamrul Hassan) (vert) 90 80

1985. Nos. 1641, 1644, 1646, 1671, 1672 and 1677/9 surch.
2251 1d. on 25p. red 60 10
2252 2d. on 5p. orange 35 10
2253 3d. on 35p. red 15 10
2254 4d. on 5d.60 olive 65 40
2255 8d. on 6d. brown 15 10
2256 20d. on 26d. blue 15 10
2257 50d. on 16d.50 blue 60 15
2258 70d. on 38d. mauve 90 20

731 Zagreb Exhibition Hall

1986.
2259 **731** 100d. violet and yellow 60 30

732 Patrol Car

1986. 40th Anniv of Yugoslav Automobile Association. Multicoloured.
2260 10d. Type **732** 10 10
2261 70d. Red Cross helicopter 1·25 75

733 Wildlife on River Bank

734 Church of the Virgin

1986. Nature Protection. River Tara. Mult.
2262 100d. Type **733** 40 40
2263 150d. Bridge over river . . . 90 90

1986. 800th Anniv of Studenica Monastery.
2264 **734** 10d. red, green and blue 60 30

735 Postman on Motor Cycle

736 Player and Ball in Goal

1986. Postal Services.
2265a **735** 20d. purple 15 10
2266a – 30d. brown 20 10
2267 – 40d. red 15 10
2268 – 50d. violet 25 10
2269 – 60d. green 15 10
2270 – 93d. blue 15 10
2271 – 100d. purple 30 10
2272 – 106d. red 15 10
2272a – 106d. brown 15 10
2273 – 120d. green 15 10
2274 – 140d. red 15 10
2275 – 170d. green 15 15
2276 – 200d. blue . . . . . . 1·25 30
2277 – 220d. brown 15 15
2278 – 300d. red 20 15
2279 – 500d. blue and orange 40 30
2279a – 500d. blue and yellow 30 20
2280 **735** 800d. blue 15 15
2281 – 1000d. violet and green 40 20
2282 – 2000d. green and orange 25 20
2283 – 5000d. blue and red . . 90 50
2284a – 10000d. violet & orange 30 15
2285a – 20000d. brown and green . . . . 1·00 50

DESIGNS—As T **735**. HORIZ: 40d. Forklift truck; 50, 20000d. Electric train; 200d. Freighter. VERT: 30, 10000d. Postman giving letters to man; 60d. Posting letters; 93d. Envelope and leaflet; 106d. (2272), Woman working at computer and woman filling envelopes; 106 (2272a), 140d. Woman working at computer; 120d. Woman with Valentine card; 170, 300d. Flower and post box; 220d. Mail coach and cover; 500d. (both) Postal sorter; 1000d. Woman using public telephone; 2000d. Telephone card, tokens and handset; 5000d. Posthorn, globe and bird with stamp. 20 × 18 mm: 100d. Postman and van.
See also Nos. 2587/98.

1986. World Cup Football Championship, Mexico. Multicoloured.
2286 70d. Type **736** 60 60
2287 150d. Players and ball in goal 60 60

737 St. Clement and Model of Ohrid (fresco, Church of St. Spas)

1986. 1100th Anniv of Arrival of St. Clement of Ohrid in Macedonia.
2288 **737** 10d. multicoloured . . . 1·00 60

1986. No. 1674 surch.
2289 5d. on 8d. grey 10 10

739 Human Brain as Nuclear Cloud

740 Judo

1986. Europa. Multicoloured.
2290 100d. Type **739** 50 30
2291 200d. Injured deer on road 90 50

1988. European Men's Judo Championships, Belgrade.
2292 **740** 70d. brown, pink and blue 45 30

741 Graph and Blood Drop within Heart

742 Costume of Slovenia

1986. Obligatory Tax. Red Cross Week.
2293 **741** 2d. black, blue and red 10 10
2294 3d. black, blue and red 10 10
2295 4d. black, blue and red 10 10
2296 5d. black, blue and red 15 15
2297 11d. black, blue and red 15 15
2298 20d. black, blue and red 40 30

1986. Yugoslav Costumes. Multicoloured.
2299 50d. Type **742** 30 20
2300 50d. Vojvodina (woman with red apron) 30 20
2301 50d. Croatia (man in embroidered trousers) . . 30 20
2302 50d. Macedonia (woman hand spinning) 30 20
2303 50d. Serbia (woman in bolero) 30 20
2304 50d. Montenegro (man with rifle) 30 20
2305 50d. Kosovo (woman carrying basket) 30 20
2306 50d. Bosnia and Herzegovina (man carrying bag on back) . . 30 20

743 Yachts

744 Tito (after Safet Zec)

1986. "Flying Dutchman" Class European Sailing Championships, Moscenicka Draga. Mult.
2307 50d. Type **743** 60 15
2308 80d. Yachts (different) . . . 85 25
MS2309 66 × 85 mm. 100d. Yachts (different). Imperf . . . . . . 1·25 1·25

1986. 94th Birth Anniv of Tito.
2310 **744** 10d. multicoloured . . . 15 10

745 Peacock Moth

746 "Skopje Earthquake"

1986. Butterflies and Moths. Multicoloured.
2311 10d. Type **745** 10 10
2312 20d. Peacock 15 10
2313 50d. Apollo 40 30
2314 100d. Purple emperor . . . 90 70

1986. Obligatory Tax. Solidarity Week. (a) As No. 2200.
2315 **715** 10d. blue and red . . . 70 50

(b) As Type **715** but inscr "Solidarity Week" in four languages.
2316 10d. blue and red 70 50

(c) Type **746**.
2317 **746** 10d. lilac and red . . . 70 50

747 Bosancica Manuscript

1986. Museum Exhibits. Ancient Manuscripts. Multicoloured.
2319 10d. Type **747** 10 10
2320 20d. Leontije's Gospel . . . 10 10
2321 50d. Astrological writing, Mesopotamia 30 25
2322 100d. Hagada (ritual book), Spain 60 50

748 Congress Poster (Branislav Dobanovacki)

1986. 13th Communist League Conference, Belgrade.
2323 **748** 10d. black and red . . . 10 10
2324 – 20d. black and red . . . 10 10
MS2325 60 × 75 mm. 100d. black and vermilion. Imperf 55 65
DESIGN: 20, 100d. Showing parts of Congress advertising poster.

749 Trubar and Title Page of "Abecedari"

1986. 400th Death Anniv of Primoz Trubar (founder of Slovenian literary language and religious reformer).
2326 **749** 20d. multicoloured . . . 45 25

750 Emblem

751 Dancers

1986. 125th Anniv of Serbian National Theatre, Novi Sad.
2327 **750** 40d. multicoloured . . . 20 10

1986. Rugovo Dance.
2328 **751** 40d. multicoloured . . . 20 10

753 Crosses forming Earth and Sky

1986. Obligatory Tax. Anti-tuberculosis Week.
2330 **753** 2d. multicoloured . . . 10 10
2331 5d. multicoloured . . . 10 10
2332 6d. multicoloured . . . 10 10
2333 7d. multicoloured . . . 15 10
2334 8d. multicoloured . . . 15 10
2335 10d. multicoloured . . . 15 10
2336 11d. multicoloured . . . 20 15
2337 14d. multicoloured . . . 20 15
2338 20d. multicoloured . . . 20 15

754 Volleyball

755 "Bird and Child running on Globe" (Tanja Faletic)

1986. "Universiade '87" University Games, Zagreb. Zagi (games mascot). Multicoloured.
2339 30d. Type **754** 10 10
2340 40d. Canoeing 15 10
2341 100d. Gymnastics 40 30
2342 150d. Fencing 75 50

1986. 18th "Joy of Europe" Meeting, Belgrade. Children's Paintings. Multicoloured.
2343 100d. Type **755** 40 25
2344 150d. "City of the Future" (Johanna Kraus) 60 35

756 Diagram of Rotary Selector and Bled

1986. 50th Anniv of Automatic Telephone Exchange Network.
2345 **756** 40d. multicoloured . . . 15 10

757 Criminal in Stocking Mask

758 Brigade Member addressing Crowd (after Djordje Andrejevic-Kun)

1986. 55th Interpol General Assembly Session, Belgrade.
2346 **757** 150d. multicoloured . . 50 25

1986. 50th Anniv of Formation of International Brigades in Spain.
2347 **758** 40d. brown, gold and orange 15 10

759 Academy

1986. Centenary of Serbian Academy of Arts and Sciences.
2348 **759** 40d. multicoloured . . . 15 10

760 People riding on Doves (Branislav Barnak)

1986. International Peace Year.
2349 **760** 150d. multicoloured . . 65 35

761 "Portrait" (Bernard Buffet)

1986. Paintings in Museum of Contemporary Arts, Skopje. Multicoloured.
2350 30d. "Still Life" (Frantisek Muzika) 10 10
2351 40d. "Disturbance" (detail, Rafael Canogar)(horiz) . . 15 10
2352 100d. Type **761** 40 25
2353 100d. "IOL" (Victor Vasarely) 40 25
2354 150d. "Woman's Head" (Pablo Picasso) 60 35

762 European Otter

1987. Protected Animals. Multicoloured.
2355 30d. Type **762** 10 10
2356 40d. Argali 15 10
2357 100d. Red deer 40 30
2358 150d. Brown bear 75 60

763 Boskovic, Brera Observatory and Solar Eclipse

1987. Death Bicentenary of Ruder Boskovic (astronomer).
2359 **763** 150d. multicoloured . . 50 35

764 Mountains, Woodlands and Animal Feeder

766 Mateja Svet

765 Potez 29-4 Biplane

1987. Nature Protection. Triglav National Park. Multicoloured.
2360 150d. Type **764** 50 50
2361 400d. Mountains, woodland and glacial lake . . . . . 1·60 1·60

1987. 60th Anniv of Civil Aviation in Yugoslavia. Multicoloured.
2362 150d. Type **765** 75 40
2363 400d. Douglas DC-10 jetliner . . . . 1·75 1·00

1987. Yugoslav Medals at World Alpine Skiing Championships, Crans Montana.
2364 **766** 200d. multicoloured . . 60 50

767 Kole Nedelkovski

1987. 75th Birth Anniv of Kole Nedelkovski (poet and revolutionary).
2365 **767** 40d. multicoloured . . . 15 10

768 Gusle and Battle Flags of Vucji Do and Grahovo

1987. 125th Anniv of Liberation Wars of Montenegro.
2366 **768** 40d. multicoloured . . . 15 10

769 "Founding the Party at Cebine, 1937" (Anton Gojmir Kos)

1987. 50th Anniv of Slovenian Communist Party.
2367 **769** 40d. multicoloured . . . 15 10

770 Tito Bridge (Ilija Stojadinovic)

771 Children of Different Races in Flower

1987. Europa. Architecture. Multicoloured.
2368 200d. Type **770** 65 65
2369 400d. Bridges over River Ljubljanica (Joze Plecnik) 1·75 1·00

1987. Obligatory Tax. Red Cross Week.

2370	**771**	2d. multicoloured . . .	25	20
2371		4d. multicoloured . . .	25	20
2372		5d. multicoloured . . .	25	20
2373		6d. multicoloured . . .	25	20
2374		7d. multicoloured . . .	25	20
2375		8d. multicoloured . . .	25	20
2376		10d. multicoloured . . .	25	20
2377		11d. multicoloured . . .	25	20
2378		12d. multicoloured . . .	25	20
2379		14d. multicoloured . . .	25	20
2380		17d. multicoloured . . .	25	20
2381		20d. multicoloured . . .	25	20

772 Almonds

773 Tito (after Mosa Pijade)

1987. Fruit. Multicoloured.
2382 60d. Type **772** 10 10
2383 150d. Pear 20 15
2384 200d. Apple 55 45
2385 400d. Plum . . . . 1·10 90

1987. 95th Birth Anniv of Josip Broz Tito.
2386 **773** 60d. multicoloured . . . 15 10

774 "Skopje Earthquake"

776 Mail Coach in Zrenjanin

775 Bust of Karadzic (Petar Ubavkic), Trsic (birthplace) and Vienna

1987. Obligatory Tax. Solidarity Week.
2387 **774** 30d. multicoloured . . . 40 25

1987. Birth Bicentenary of Vuk Stefanovic Karadzic (linguist and historian). Multicoloured.
2388 60d. Type **775** 15 10
2389 200d. Serbian alphabet and Karadzic (portrait by Uros Knezevic) 35 25

1987. 250th Anniv of Postal Services in Zrenjanin.
2390 **776** 60d. multicoloured . . . 15 10

777 Emblem and Mascot

778 Hurdling

1987. Obligatory Tax. "Universiade '87" University Games, Zagreb.
2391 **777** 20d. blue and green . . 30 20

1987. "Universiade '87" University Games, Zagreb. Multicoloured.
2392 60d. Type **778** 15 10
2393 150d. Basketball 25 20
2394 200d. Gymnastics 30 25
2395 400d. Swimming . . . . . 1·10 85

779 Canadair CL-215 Amphibian spraying Forest Fire

780 Monument, Anindol Park

1987. Fire Fighting. Multicoloured.
2396 60d. Type **779** 25 25
2397 200d. Fire-fighting tug . . . 25 15

1987. 50th Anniv of Croatian Communist Party.
2398 **780** 60d. multicoloured . . . 15 10

781 School and Foundation Document

782 Crosses and Children's Head

1987. 150th Anniv of Sabac High School.
2399 **781** 80d. brown, orange and blue 15 10

1987. Obligatory Tax. Anti-tuberculosis Week.

2400	**782**	2d. multicoloured . . .	10	10
2401		4d. multicoloured . . .	10	10
2402		6d. multicoloured . . .	10	10
2403		8d. multicoloured . . .	10	10
2404		10d. multicoloured . . .	10	10
2405		12d. multicoloured . . .	10	10
2406		14d. multicoloured . . .	10	10
2407		20d. multicoloured . . .	10	10
2408		25d. multicoloured . . .	10	10
2409		40d. multicoloured . . .	10	10

783 Emblem, Map and Flowers

1987. "Balkanphila XI" Balkans Stamp Exhibition, Novi Sad. Multicoloured.
2410 250d. Type **783** 30 30
MS2411 60 × 75 mm. 400d. Novi Sad behind Petrovaradin Fortress (22 × 32 mm). Imperf 80 80

1987. No. 2269 surch **80**.
2412 80d. on 60d. green 10 10

785 "Children playing amongst Trees" (Bedic Aranka)

786 SPRAM Emblem

1987. 19th "Joy of Europe" Meeting. Mult.
2413 250d. Type **785** 45 45
2414 400d. "Child and scarecrow in orchard" (Ingeborg Schaffer) 75 75

1987. Obligatory Tax. Model Airplane Championships, Belgrade.
2415 **786** 20d. blue 10 10

787 Arslanagica Bridge, Trebinje

1987. Bridges. Multicoloured.
2416 80d. Type **787** 10 10
2417 250d. Terzija Bridge, Djakovica 20 15

788 Tug in Canal

1987. 600th Anniv of Titov Vrbas.
2418 **788** 80d. multicoloured . . . 15 10

789 Eclipse, First Telescope and Old Observatory Building

1987. Cent of Astronomical and Meteorological Observatory, Belgrade.
2419 **789** 80d. multicoloured . . . 15 10

790 "St. Luke the Evangelist" (Raphael)

1987. Paintings in Mimara Museum, Zagreb. Multicoloured.
2420 80d. Type **790** 15 10
2421 200d. "Infanta Maria Theresa" (Diego Velazquez) 25 15

2422 250d. "Nicolaus Rubens" (Peter Paul Rubens) . . . 25 15
2423 400d. "Louise Laure Sennegon" (Camille Corot) 75 60

791 Bull Fighting (Grmec)

1987. Museum Exhibits. Folk Games. Mult.
2424 80d. Type **791** 15 10
2425 200d. Sword used in Ljuvicevo Horse Games 25 15
2426 250d. Crown worn at Moresca Games (Korcula) 25 15
2427 400d. Sinj Iron Ring 75 60

792 Codex and Novi Vinodol

1988. 700th Anniv of Vinodol Law Codex.
2428 **792** 100d. multicoloured . . 15 10

793 Skier **794** Cub

1988. 25th Anniv of Golden Fox Skiing Competition, Maribor.
2429 **793** 350d. multicoloured . . 35 15

1988. Protected Wildlife. The Brown Bear. Mult.
2430 70d. Type **794** 15 10
2431 80d. Bears among branches 15 10
2432 200d. Adult bear 35 15
2433 350d. Adult stalking prey 60 30

795 Skier **797** Basketball

796 Map of Europe

1988. Winter Olympic Games, Calgary. Multicoloured.
2434 350d. Type **795** 35 25
2435 1200d. Ice hockey . . . . . 1·10 85

1988. Balkan Countries' Foreign Affairs Ministers Meeting, Belgrade. Sheet 69 × 75 mm.
MS2436 **796** 1500d. multicoloured 1·50 1·50

1988. Olympic Games, Seoul. Multicoloured.
2437 106d. Type **797** 15 10
2438 450d. High jumping . . . 55 40
2439 500d. Gymnastics 60 50
2440 1200d. Boxing . . . . . . 1·50 1·25
MS2441 62 × 77 mm. 1500d. Korean landscape. Imperf . . . . . . 1·75 1·75

798 White Carnations **799** "INTELSAT V-A", Globe and Dish Aerials, Ivanjica

1988. Obligatory Tax. Anti-cancer Campaign. Multicoloured.
2442 4d. Type **798** 10 10
2443 8d. Red flowers 10 10
2444 12d. Red roses 10 10

1988. Europa. Transport and Communications. Multicoloured.
2445 450d. Type **799** 30 20
2446 1200d. Woman using mobile telephone and methods of transport . . . . 1·10 60

800 Anniversary Emblem **801** Great Top Shell

1988. Obligatory Tax. 125th Anniv of Red Cross.
2447 **800** 4d. blue, red and grey 20 15
2448 8d. blue, red and grey 20 15
2449 10d. blue, red and grey 20 15
2450 12d. blue, red and grey 20 15
2451 20d. blue, red and grey 20 15
2452 30d. blue, red and grey 20 15
2453 50d. blue, red and grey 20 15

1988. Molluscs. Multicoloured.
2454 106d. Type **801** 10 10
2455 550d. St. James's scallop . . 55 45
2456 600d. Giant tun 60 50
2457 1000d. "Argonauta cygnus" (wrongly inscr "argo") . . 1·00 85

802 Tito **803** "Skopje Earthquake"

1988. 60th Anniv of Trial of Josip Broz Tito.
2458 **802** 106d. brown and black 10 10

1988. Obligatory Tax. Solidarity Week. (a) Type **803**.
2459 **803** 50d. grey, brown and red 35 20

(b) As No. 2220 but value changed.
2460 **715** 50d. blue and red . . . 35 20

(c) No. 2387 surch **50** and emblem.
2461 **774** 50d. on 30d. mult . . . 35 20

805 First Lyceum Building **806** Krleza

1988. 150th Anniv of Belgrade University.
2462 **805** 106d. multicoloured . . 15 10

1988. Obligatory Tax. Culture Fund. 95th Birth Anniv of Miroslav Krleza (writer).
2463 **806** 30d. brown and orange 15 10

1988. Nos. 2270 and 2272a surch.
2464 120d. on 93d. blue 15 10
2465 140d. on 106d. brown . . . 15 10

808 "Phelypaea boissieri" **809** Globe and Flags

1988. Nature Protection Macedonian Plants. Multicoloured.
2466 600d. Type **808** 45 45
2467 1000d. "Campanula formanekiana" 75 75

1988. Centenary of Esperanto (invented language).
2468 **809** 600d. blue and green . . 50 40

810 Shipping on the Danube **811** Globe as Ball in Basket

1988. 40th Anniv of Danube Conference. Multicoloured.
2469 1000d. Type **810** 45 35
MS2470 84 × 68 mm. 2000d. Map of Danube. Imperf . . . . 1·40 1·40

1988. 13th European Junior Basketball Championships, Tito Vrbas and Srbobran.
2471 **811** 600d. multicoloured . . 30 25

812 Horse Racing

1988. 125th Anniv of Belgrade Horse Races. Multicoloured.
2472 140d. Type **812** 15 10
2473 600d. Show jumping 35 30
2474 1000d. Trotting race 50 45

813 Douglas DC-10 Jetliner and Globe

1988. Air.
2475 **813** 2000d. multicoloured . . 90 30

814 Museum and Bosnian Bellflower **815** Flame and Hand

1988. Centenary of Bosnia amd Herzegovina Museum, Sarajevo.
2476 **814** 140d. multicoloured . . 10 10

1988. Obligatory Tax. Anti-tuberculosis Week. (a) Type **815**.
2477 **815** 4d. multicoloured . . . 15 15
2478 8d. multicoloured . . . 15 15
2479 12d. multicoloured . . . 15 15
2480 20d. multicoloured . . . 15 15
2481 50d. multicoloured . . . 15 15
2482 70d. multicoloured . . . 15 15

(b) No. 2039 surch **1988 12**.
2483 **632** 12d. on 1d. orange, black and red . . . . 3·25 3·25

817 Arm and Crab's Claw (anti-cancer) **818** "Daughter of the Artist" (Peter Ranosovic)

1988. Health Campaigns. Multicoloured.
2484 140d. Type **817** 15 10
2485 1000d. Screaming mouth in splash of blood (anti-AIDS) 45 40

1988. 20th "Joy of Europe" Meeting. Mult.
2486 1000d. Type **818** 55 50
2487 1100d. "Girl wuth Straw Hat" (Pierre-Auguste Renoir) 65 60

819 1701 Arms and Present Emblem

1988. 50th Anniv of Slovenian Academy of Arts and Sciences.
2488 **819** 200d. multicoloured . . 15 10

820 Galicnik Wedding

1988. Museum Exhibits. Traditional Crafts and Customs. Multicoloured.
2489 200d. Type **820** 15 10
2490 1000d. Weapons from Bay of Kotor 40 25
2491 1000d. Vojvodina embroidery (horiz) . . . 40 25
2492 1100d. Masks from Ptuj (horiz) 60 40

821 Title Page of "Gorski Vijenac" and Petar II (after J. Boss)

1988. 175th Birth Anniv of Prince-Bishop Petar II of Montenegro. Multicoloured.
2493 200d. Type **821** 15 10
2494 1000d. Njegos Mausoleum, Lovcen and Petar II in bishop's robes (after Josip Tominc) 45 30

822 "Girl with Lyre"

1988. Greek Terracotta Figures from Josip Broz Tito Memorial Centre Collection. Multicoloured.
2495 200d. Type **822** 15 10
2496 1000d. "Girl on a stone" . . 40 25
2497 1000d. "Eros and Psyche" . . 40 25
2498 1100d. "Girl by Stele" . . . 60 40

823 Krsmanovic House, Belgrade

1988. 70th Anniv of Yugoslavian State.
2499 **823** 200d. multicoloured . . 10 10

1988. Nos. 2273/4 surch.
2500 170d. on 120d. green . . . 15 10
2501 220d. on 140d. red . . . 15 10

825 Pistol shooting

1988. Yugoslavian Medals at Olympic Games. Multicoloured.
2502 500d. Type **825** (2 gold, 1 bronze) 15 10
2503 500d. Handball (bronze) . . 15 10
2504 500d. Table tennis (silver and bronze) 15 10
2505 500d. Wrestling (silver) . . . 15 10
2506 500d. Rowing (bronze) . . . 15 10
2507 500d. Basketball (2 silver) 15 10
2508 500d. Water polo (gold) . . 15 10
2509 500d. Boxing (bronze) . . . 15 10

826 Gundulic and Dubrovnik

1989. 400th Birth Anniv of Ivan Gundulic (poet).
2510 **826** 220d. multicoloured . . 10 10

827 Mallards **827a** Emblem

1989. Wild Ducks. Multicoloured.
2511 300d. Type **827** 20 20
2512 2100d. Green-winged teal . . 1·10 1·10
2513 2200d. Pintail . . . . 1·25 1·25
2514 2200d. Common shoveler 1·25 1·25

1989. Obligatory Tax. Anti-cancer Week. (a) Type **827a**.
2514a **827a** 110d. multicoloured 25 10
(b) Inscr "YUGOSLAVIJA MAKEDONIJA". Surch **1989** and value.
2514b – 110d. on 20d. black, red and gold 25 10
DESIGN: No. 2514b, Sword emblem with blade doubling as Aesculapius rod enclosing crab against background of "flower".

828 Valvasor and Wagensperg Castle

1989. 300th Anniv of Publishing of "The Glory of the Duchy of Kranjska" by Johann Weickhard Valvasor.
2515 **828** 300d. multicoloured . . 15 10

829 "Bulbocodium vernum"

1989. Flowers. Multicoloured.
2516 300d. Type **829** 10 10
2517 2100d. White water-lily . . 70 35
2518 2200d. "Fritillaria degeniana" (vert) 75 40
2519 3000d. "Orchis simia" (vert) 1·00 60

830 Envelopes and Dish Aerial

1989. Air.
2520 **830** 10000d. blue, mauve and yellow . . . . 1·50 90
2521 – 20000d. orange, violet and red . . . . 1·40 1·25
DESIGN: 20000d. Europe on globe and satellite.

1989. No. 1657 surch **100**.
2522 100d. on 1d. green 15 10

832 Competitor

1989. 6th World Air Gun Championships, Sarajevo.
2523 **832** 3000d. multicoloured . . 50 40

833 Girl looking through Magic Cube **834** Anniversary Emblem

1989. Europa. Children's Games and Toys. Multicoloured.
2524 3000d. Type **833** 75 60
2525 6000d. Boy playing with marbles and paper boats 1·50 1·10

1989. Obligatory Tax. 125th Anniv (1988) of International Red Cross.
2526 **834** 20d. blue, silver and red 15 15
2527 80d. blue, silver and red 15 15
2528 150d. blue, silver and red 15 15
2529 160d. blue, silver and red 15 15

835 Josip Broz Tito **836** "Skopje Earthquake"

1989. 70th Anniv of Yugoslavian Communist Party.
2530 **835** 300d. multicoloured . . 15 10

1989. Obligatory Tax. Solidarity Week. (a) Perf.
2531 **836** 250d. silver and red . . 60 35
(b) Rouletted.
2532 **715** 400d. blue and red . . . 80 55

837 Pole Vaulting **838** Racers

1989. 15th European Trophy Athletic Clubs Championship, Belgrade.
2533 **837** 4000d. multicoloured . . 40 25

1989. Motor Cycle Grand Prix, Rijeka. Mult.
2534 500d. Type **838** 20 15
2535 4000d. Racers (different) . . 45 30
MS2536 85 × 65 mm. 6000d. Race participants numbers 18 and 6 (53 × 34 mm) . . . . 1·25 1·25

839 Ancient Greek Galleys

1989. Sailing Ships. Multicoloured.
2537 1000d. Type **839** 55 25
2538 1000d. Roman warships . . 55 25
2539 1000d. 13th-century Crusader nefs 55 25
2540 1000d. 16th-century Dubrovnik navas 55 25
2541 1000d. 17th-century French warships 55 25
2542 1000d. 18th-century ships of the line 55 25
MS2543 115 × 85 mm. 3000d. Engraving of Dubrovnik (74 × 32 mm) 80 80

840 Flags of Netherlands, Italy, U.S.S.R. and Spain and Ball

1989. 26th European Men's Basketball Championship, Zagreb. Multicoloured.
2544 2000d. Type **840** (Group A) 15 15
2545 2000d. Flags of France, Yugoslavia, Greece and Bulgaria and ball (Group B) 15 15

841 "Battle of Kosovo" (lithograph, Adam Stefanovic)

1989. 600th Anniv of Battle of Kosovo.
2546 **841** 500d. multicoloured . . 15 10

842 Danilovgrad

1989. Centenary of First Reading Room at Danilovgrad.
2547 **842** 500d. multicoloured . . 15 10

1989. No. 2277 surch **700**.
2548 700d. on 220d. brown . . . 15 10

1989. Nos. 2266 and 2275 surch.
2549 400d. on 30d. brown . . . 25 15
2550 700d. on 170d. green . . . 25 15

845 Stone Tablet, Detail of Charter and Mule Train **846** Emblem

1989. 800th Anniv of Kulin Ban Charter (granting free trade to Dubrovnik).
2551 **845** 500d. multicoloured . . 15 10

1989. Obligatory Tax. Construction of Youth House.
2552 **846** 400d. blue and red . . . 15 10

847 Rowers of Bled Lake **848** Houses of Parliament, London

1989. World Rowing Championship, Bled.
2553 **847** 10000d. multicoloured 50 40

1989. Centenary of Interparliamentary Union.
2554 10000d. Type **848** 40 30
2555 10000d. Notre Dame Cathedral, Paris 40 30

849 Belgrade and Cairo

1989. 9th Heads of Non-aligned Countries Conference, Belgrade. Previous Host Cities. Multicoloured.
2556 10000d. Type **849** 50 40
2557 10000d. Lusaka and Algiers 50 40
2558 10000d. Colombo and Havana 50 40
2559 10000d. New Delhi and Harare 50 40
MS2560 64 × 85 mm. 20000d. View of Belgrade and maps showing member states in 1961 and 1989 1·25 1·25

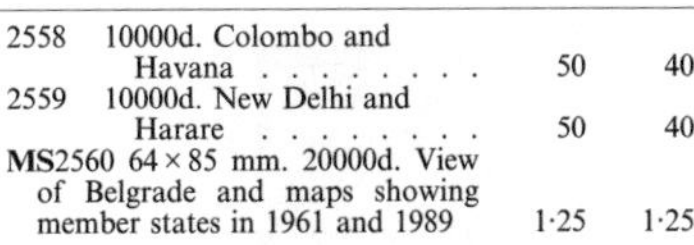

850 Jazinac Lake, Brezovica, and "Paeonia officinalis" **851** Crosses as Basket of Flowers

1989. Nature Protection. Kosovo. Multicoloured.
2561 8000d. Type **850** 40 25
2562 10000d. Mirusa Canyon and "Paeonia corallina" . . . 60 45

1989. Obligatory Tax. Anti-tuberculosis Week.
2563 **851** 20d. red and black . . . 15 10
2564 200d. red and black . . 15 10
2565 250d. red and black . . 15 10
2566 400d. red and black . . 15 10
2567 650d. red and black . . 15 10

852 "Child with Lamb" (Jovan Popovic) **853** Men Fighting

1989. 21st "Joy of Europe" Meeting. Mult.
2568 10000d. Type **852** 50 30
2569 10000d. "Girl feeding Dog" (Aelbert Cuyp) 50 30

1989. 300th Anniv of Karpos Insurrection.
2570 **853** 1200d. multicoloured . . 15 10

854 Cancelled 100d. Stamp, Quill and Seal

1989. Stamp Day.
2571 **854** 1200d. multicoloured . . 15 10

855 Packsaddle Maker

1989. Museum Exhibits. Traditional Crafts. Multicoloured.
2572 1200d. Type **855** 10 10
2573 14000d. Cooper 45 35
2574 15000d. Wine maker 50 40
2575 30000d. Weaver 95 80

856 Aerospatiale/Aeritalia ATR 42 Airliner, Arrows and Map **856a** Emblem

1989. Air.
2576 **856** 50000d. blue and orange 1·60 80

1989. Obligatory Tax. 29th Chess Olympiad, Novi Sad.
2577 **856a** 600d. black and blue 25 10
See also No. 2660.

857 "Apostle Matthias"

1989. Frescoes by Iohannes de Kastua from Holy Trinity Church, Hrastovlje, Slovenia. Multicoloured.
2578 2100d. Type **857** 10 10
2579 21000d. "St. Barbara" . . . 45 40
2580 30000d. "Creation of the Universe, the Fourth Day" (horiz) 75 65
2581 50000d. "Creation of the Universe, the Fifth Day" (horiz) . . . . 1·10 1·00

858 Barn Swallow, Envelope and Flower

1989.
2582 **858** 100000d. green & orange 15 15

1989. No. 1680 surch **700**.
2583 700d. on 70d. blue 25 15

860 Colour Spectrum entering Star

1990. 14th Extraordinary Congress of League of Communists of Yugoslavia, Belgrade.
2584 **860** 10000d. multicoloured 30 15
2585 – 50000d. multicoloured 40 35
MS2586 66 × 86 mm. 100000d. red, ultramarine and silver. Imperf 1·25 1·25
DESIGNS—HORIZ: 50000d. Hammer and sickle on computer screen. VERT: 100000d. Congress poster (Ivan Dorogi).

1990. Postal Services. As T **735** but in revised currency.
2587 10p. violet and green . . . 10 10
2588 20p. red and yellow 25 10
2589 30p. green and orange . . . 15 10
2590 40p. green and purple . . . 15 10
2591 50p. green and violet . . . 25 10
2592 60p. mauve and red 25 10
2593 1d. blue and purple 15 15
2594 2d. blue and red 30 15
2595 3d. blue and red 40 25
2596 5d. ultramarine and blue . . 70 40
2597 10d. blue and red . . . . . 4·75 4·75
2598 20d. red and orange 35 25
DESIGNS—VERT: 10p. Man posting letters; 20p. Postal sorter; 30p. Postman giving letters to man; 40p., 20d. Woman telephoning; 50p. Posthorn, globe and bird; 60p. Telephone card, tokens and handset; 3d. Post-box; 5d. Airplane, letters and map; 10d. Barn swallow, flower and envelope. HORIZ: 1d. Electric train; 2d. Freighter.

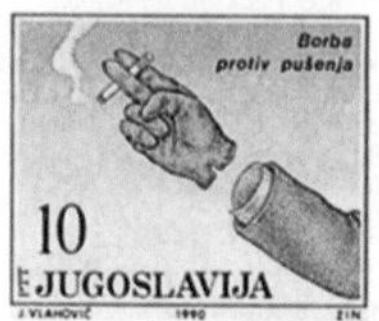

861 Gloved Hand holding Lighted Cigarette

1990. Anti-smoking Campaign.
2605 **861** 10d. multicoloured . . . 1·00 85

862 Northern Pike

862a Pink Flowers

1990. Endangered Fishes. Multicoloured.
2606 1d. Type **862** 25 15
2607 5d. Wels 65 30
2608 10d. Burbot . . . . 1·25 90
2609 15d. Eurasian perch . . . . 1·75 1·40

1990. Obligatory Tax. Anti-cancer Week.
2610 30p. Type **862a** 25 10
2611 30p. Yellow flowers 25 10

863 Zabljak Fortress, Printed Page from 1494 and Arms

1990. 500th Anniv of Enthronement of Djuradj Crnojevic of Montenegro.
2612 **863** 50p. multicoloured . . . 45 35

864 Telegraphist and V.D.U. Screen

1990. 125th Anniv of I.T.U.
2613 **864** 6d.50 multicoloured . . 70 60

865 Footballers

866 Skopje Posts and Telecommunications Centre

1990. World Cup Football Championship, Italy.
2614 – 6d.50 multicoloured . . 1·00 60
2615 **865** 10d. multicoloured . . . 1·40 1·00
DESIGN: 6d.50, Footballers (different).

1990. Europa. Post Office Buildings. Mult.
2616 6d.50 Type **866** . . . . . 1·00 75
2617 10d. Belgrade Telephone Exchange . . . . 1·40 1·10

867 Chicago Water Tower and Carnation

868 Record, Notes and Pen

1990. Centenary of Labour Day.
2618 **867** 6d.50 multicoloured . . 75 50

1990. Eurovision Song Contest, Zagreb. Mult.
2619 6d.50 Type **868** 75 50
2620 10d. Conductor and score of "Te Deum" by Marc-Antoine Charpentier (theme tune of contest) . . 1·40 1·00

869 Cross and Leaves

870 Large Yellow Flowers

1990. Obligatory Tax. (a) Red Cross Week.
2621 **869** 10p. red and green . . . 15 10
2622 20p. red and green . . . 15 10
2623 30p. red and green . . . 15 10
(b) 45th Anniv of Macedonian Red Cross. Flower Paintings by Zivko Popovski. Multicoloured.
2624 20p. Type **870** 15 10
2625 20p. Arrangement of small yellow flowers 15 10
2626 20p. Anniversary emblem 15 10
See also Nos. 2633/4.

871 Server

873 Tito (bronze, Antun Augustincic)

1990. Yugoslav Open Tennis Championship, Umag. Multicoloured.
2627 6d.50 Type **871** 75 60
2628 10d. Receiver . . . . 1·50 1·10

1990. No. 2282 surch **0,50**.
2629 **735** 50p. on 800d. blue . . . 20 10

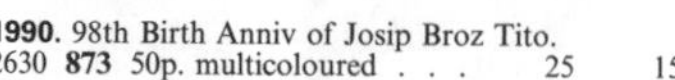
1990. 98th Birth Anniv of Josip Broz Tito.
2630 **873** 50p. multicoloured . . . 25 15

874 "Tartar Post Riders" (Carl Goebel)

1990. 150th Anniv of Public Postal Service in Serbia.
2631 **874** 50p. multicoloured . . . 60 40

875 "Skopje Earthquake"

876 "Skopje Earthquake"

1990. Obligatory Tax. Solidarity Week.
2632 **875** 20p. brown, silver and red 70 35
2633 – 20p. multicoloured . . . 15 10
2634 – 20p. multicoloured . . . 15 10
2635 **876** 20p. blue and red . . . 45 45
2636 **715** 30p. blue and red . . . 40 25
DESIGNS—As T **875**: No. 2633, Mauve flowers; 2634, Red and yellow flowers.
See also No. 2711.

877 Fantail

879 Newspaper Offices, Museum and Mastheads

878 Idrija Town

1990. Pigeons. Multicoloured.
2637 50p. Type **877** 15 10
2638 5d. Serbian high flier . . . 75 55
2639 6d.50 Carrier pigeon (vert) 1·25 85
2640 10d. Pouter (vert) . . . . . 1·75 1·25

1990. 500th Anniversaries of Idrija Town (2641) and Mercury Mine (2642). Multicoloured.
2641 50p. Type **878** 15 10
2642 6d.50 Mine 85 50

1990. 50th Anniv of "Vjesnik" (newspaper).
2643 **879** 60p. multicoloured . . . 30 20

1990. Nos. 2588/9 surch.
2644 50p. on 20p. red and yellow 25 15
2645 1d. on 30p. green and orange 20 15

881 Runners leaving Blocks

881a Emblem

1990. European Athletics Championships, Split. Multicoloured.
2646 1d. Type **881** 45 30
2647 6d.50 Runners' feet 80 70
MS2648 85 × 65 mm. 10d. Runners and their reflections (52 × 34 mm) 1·50 1·50

1990. Obligatory Tax. European Athletics Championships, Split.
2649 **881a** 50p. blue and red . . . 25 10

882 Nurse and Sun

883 Flowers in Vase and Birds

1990. Obligatory Tax. Anti-tuberculosis Week.
2650 **882** 20p. yellow, blue and red 15 10
2651 25p. yellow, blue and red 15 10
2652 50p. yellow, blue and red 15 10
2653 **883** 50p. brown, red and grey 15 10

884 "Pec Patriachate" (Dimitrije Cudov)

1990. 300th Anniv of Great Migration of Serbs. Multicoloured.
2654 1d. Type **884** 15 10
2655 6d.50 "Migration of Serbs" (Paja Jovanovic) 85 70

1990. No. 2590 surch **2**.
2656 2d. on 40p. green and purple 45 15

887 "Little Sisters" (Ivana Kobilca)

888 Chess Pieces

1990. 22nd "Joy of Europe" Meeting. Mult.
2658 6d.50 Type **887** 75 60
2659 10d. "Willem III of Orange as a child" (Adriaen Hanneman) (vert) . . . . 1·50 1·10

1990. Obligatory Tax. 29th Chess Olympiad, Novi Sad. As No. 2577 but value in reformed currency.
2660 **856a** 1d. black and blue . . 25 10

1990. 29th Chess Olympiad, Novi Sad. Mult.
2661 1d. Type **888** 15 10
2662 5d. Rook, bishop, knight and chessboard 75 50
2663 6d.50 Knights, queen, king, pawn and chessboard . . 1·00 75
2664 10d. Chess pieces and symbols . . . . 2·00 1·75
MS2665 84 × 97 mm. As Nos. 2661/4 but with emblem in gold (instead of silver). Imperf . . . . . . 4·50 4·50

888a Dubrovnik

889 "St. Vlaho and Ragusa" (detail of triptych, Nikola Bozidarevic) and Penny Black

1990. Obligatory Tax. European Judo Championships, Dubrovnik.
2666 **888a** 1d. violet and blue . . 25 10

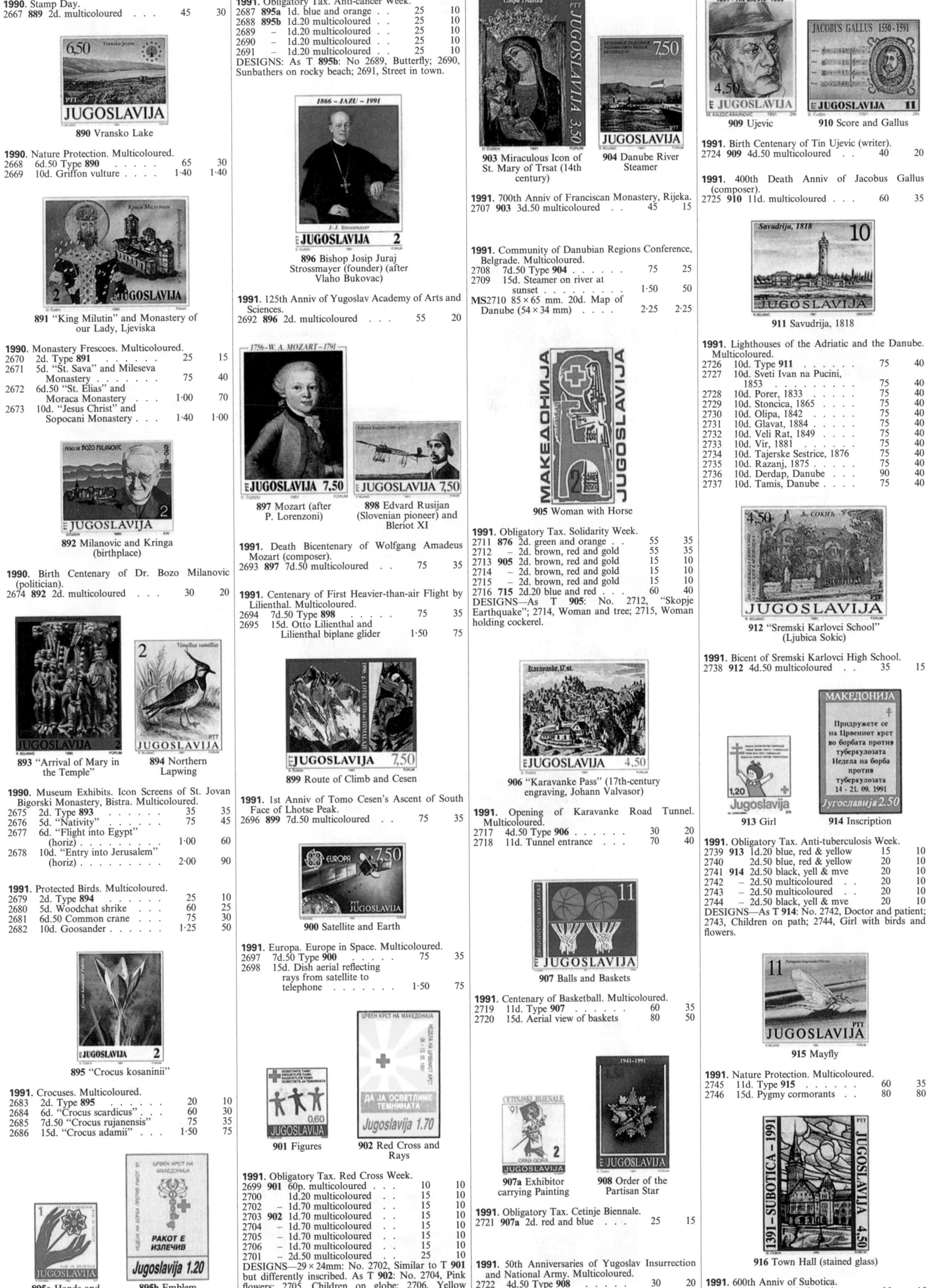

1990. Stamp Day.
2667 **889** 2d. multicoloured . . . 45 30

890 Vransko Lake

1990. Nature Protection. Multicoloured.
2668 6d.50 Type **890** 65 30
2669 10d. Griffon vulture . . . . 1·40 1·40

891 "King Milutin" and Monastery of our Lady, Ljeviska

1990. Monastery Frescoes. Multicoloured.
2670 2d. Type **891** 25 15
2671 5d. "St. Sava" and Mileseva Monastery 75 40
2672 6d.50 "St. Elias" and Moraca Monastery . . . 1·00 70
2673 10d. "Jesus Christ" and Sopocani Monastery . . . 1·40 1·00

892 Milanovic and Kringa (birthplace)

1990. Birth Centenary of Dr. Bozo Milanovic (politician).
2674 **892** 2d. multicoloured . . . 30 20

893 "Arrival of Mary in the Temple"

894 Northern Lapwing

1990. Museum Exhibits. Icon Screens of St. Jovan Bigorski Monastery, Bistra. Multicoloured.
2675 2d. Type **893** 35 35
2676 5d. "Nativity" 75 45
2677 6d. "Flight into Egypt" (horiz) . . . . 1·00 60
2678 10d. "Entry into Jerusalem" (horiz) . . . . 2·00 90

1991. Protected Birds. Multicoloured.
2679 2d. Type **894** 25 10
2680 5d. Woodchat shrike . . . 60 25
2681 6d.50 Common crane . . . 75 30
2682 10d. Goosander . . . . . . 1·25 50

895 "Crocus kosaninii"

1991. Crocuses. Multicoloured.
2683 2d. Type **895** 20 10
2684 6d. "Crocus scardicus" . . . 60 30
2685 7d.50 "Crocus rujanensis" 75 35
2686 15d. "Crocus adamii" . . . 1·50 75

895a Hands and Flower

895b Emblem

1991. Obligatory Tax. Anti-cancer Week.
2687 **895a** 1d. blue and orange . . 25 10
2688 **895b** 1d.20 multicoloured . . 25 10
2689 – 1d.20 multicoloured . . 25 10
2690 – 1d.20 multicoloured . . 25 10
2691 – 1d.20 multicoloured . . 25 10
DESIGNS: As T **895b**: No 2689, Butterfly; 2690, Sunbathers on rocky beach; 2691, Street in town.

896 Bishop Josip Juraj Strossmayer (founder) (after Vlaho Bukovac)

1991. 125th Anniv of Yugoslav Academy of Arts and Sciences.
2692 **896** 2d. multicoloured . . . 55 20

897 Mozart (after P. Lorenzoni)

898 Edvard Rusijan (Slovenian pioneer) and Bleriot XI

1991. Death Bicentenary of Wolfgang Amadeus Mozart (composer).
2693 **897** 7d.50 multicoloured . . 75 35

1991. Centenary of First Heavier-than-air Flight by Lilienthal. Multicoloured.
2694 7d.50 Type **898** 75 35
2695 15d. Otto Lilienthal and Lilienthal biplane glider 1·50 75

899 Route of Climb and Cesen

1991. 1st Anniv of Tomo Cesen's Ascent of South Face of Lhotse Peak.
2696 **899** 7d.50 multicoloured . . 75 35

900 Satellite and Earth

1991. Europa. Europe in Space. Multicoloured.
2697 7d.50 Type **900** 75 35
2698 15d. Dish aerial reflecting rays from satellite to telephone . . . . 1·50 75

901 Figures

902 Red Cross and Rays

1991. Obligatory Tax. Red Cross Week.
2699 **901** 60p. multicoloured . . . 10 10
2700 1d.20 multicoloured . . 15 10
2702 – 1d.70 multicoloured . . 15 10
2703 **902** 1d.70 multicoloured . . 15 10
2704 – 1d.70 multicoloured . . 15 10
2705 – 1d.70 multicoloured . . 15 10
2706 – 1d.70 multicoloured . . 15 10
2701 – 2d.50 multicoloured . . 25 10
DESIGNS—29 × 24mm: No. 2702, Similar to T **901** but differently inscribed. As T **902**: No. 2704, Pink flowers; 2705, Children on globe; 2706, Yellow flowers.

903 Miraculous Icon of St. Mary of Trsat (14th century)

904 Danube River Steamer

1991. 700th Anniv of Franciscan Monastery, Rijeka.
2707 **903** 3d.50 multicoloured . . 45 15

1991. Community of Danubian Regions Conference, Belgrade. Multicoloured.
2708 7d.50 Type **904** 75 25
2709 15d. Steamer on river at sunset . . . . 1·50 50
MS2710 85 × 65 mm. 20d. Map of Danube (54 × 34 mm) . . . . 2·25 2·25

905 Woman with Horse

1991. Obligatory Tax. Solidarity Week.
2711 **876** 2d. green and orange . . 55 35
2712 – 2d. brown, red and gold 55 35
2713 **905** 2d. brown, red and gold 15 10
2714 – 2d. brown, red and gold 15 10
2715 – 2d. brown, red and gold 15 10
2716 **715** 2d.20 blue and red . . . 60 40
DESIGNS—As T **905**: No. 2712, "Skopje Earthquake"; 2714, Woman and tree; 2715, Woman holding cockerel.

906 "Karavanke Pass" (17th-century engraving, Johann Valvasor)

1991. Opening of Karavanke Road Tunnel. Multicoloured.
2717 4d.50 Type **906** 30 20
2718 11d. Tunnel entrance . . . 70 40

907 Balls and Baskets

1991. Centenary of Basketball. Multicoloured.
2719 11d. Type **907** 60 35
2720 15d. Aerial view of baskets 80 50

907a Exhibitor carrying Painting

908 Order of the Partisan Star

1991. Obligatory Tax. Cetinje Biennale.
2721 **907a** 2d. red and blue . . . 25 15

1991. 50th Anniversaries of Yugoslav Insurrection and National Army. Multicoloured.
2722 4d.50 Type **908** 30 20
2723 11d. Order for Bravery . . . 70 40

909 Ujevic

910 Score and Gallus

1991. Birth Centenary of Tin Ujevic (writer).
2724 **909** 4d.50 multicoloured . . 40 20

1991. 400th Death Anniv of Jacobus Gallus (composer).
2725 **910** 11d. multicoloured . . . 60 35

911 Savudrija, 1818

1991. Lighthouses of the Adriatic and the Danube. Multicoloured.
2726 10d. Type **911** 75 40
2727 10d. Sveti Ivan na Pucini, 1853 . . . . 75 40
2728 10d. Porer, 1833 . . . . . 75 40
2729 10d. Stoncica, 1865 . . . . 75 40
2730 10d. Olipa, 1842 . . . . . 75 40
2731 10d. Glavat, 1884 . . . . . 75 40
2732 10d. Veli Rat, 1849 . . . . 75 40
2733 10d. Vir, 1881 . . . . . . 75 40
2734 10d. Tajerske Sestrice, 1876 75 40
2735 10d. Razanj, 1875 . . . . . 75 40
2736 10d. Derdap, Danube . . . 90 40
2737 10d. Tamis, Danube 75 40

912 "Sremski Karlovci School" (Ljubica Sokic)

1991. Bicent of Sremski Karlovci High School.
2738 **912** 4d.50 multicoloured . . 35 15

913 Girl

914 Inscription

1991. Obligatory Tax. Anti-tuberculosis Week.
2739 **913** 1d.20 blue, red & yellow 15 10
2740 2d.50 blue, red & yellow 20 10
2741 **914** 2d.50 black, yell & mve 20 10
2742 – 2d.50 multicoloured . . 20 10
2743 – 2d.50 multicoloured . . 20 10
2744 – 2d.50 black, yell & mve 20 10
DESIGNS—As T **914**: No. 2742, Doctor and patient; 2743, Children on path; 2744, Girl with birds and flowers.

915 Mayfly

1991. Nature Protection. Multicoloured.
2745 11d. Type **915** 60 35
2746 15d. Pygmy cormorants . . 80 80

916 Town Hall (stained glass)

1991. 600th Anniv of Subotica.
2747 **916** 4d.50 multicoloured . . 35 15

917 Honey Bees and Congress Emblem

918 "Little Dubravka" (Jovan Bijelic)

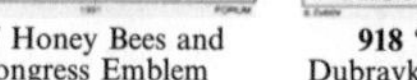

1991. "Apimondia" 33rd International Bee Keeping Congress, Split.

2748 **917** 11d. multicoloured . . . 70 40

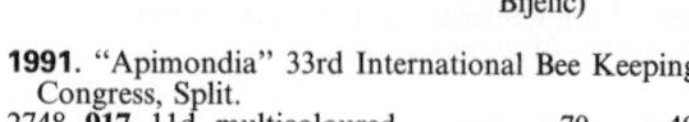

1991. 23rd "Joy of Europe" Meeting. Mult.

2749 5d. Type **918** 30 15
2750 30d. "Little Girl with a Cat" (Mary Cassatt) . . . . . 1·75 1·00

919 Statue of Prince Michael Obrenovic and Serbian 1866 1p. Newspaper Stamp

919a Protecting Refugee

1991. Stamp Day.

2751 **919** 4d.50 multicoloured . . 35 15

1991. Obligatory Tax. Serbian Refugee Fund.

2752 **919a** 2d. mauve and blue . . 25 15

920 Battle of Vucji. Flag and Medal for Military Valour

1991. Cetinje Museum Exhibits, Montenegrin Flags and Medals. Multicoloured.

2753 20d. Type **920** 25 15
2754 30d. Battle of Grahovo flag and medal 60 45
2755 40d. State flag and Medal for bravery . . . . . . 1·00 75
2756 50d. Court flag and Petrovic dynasty commemorative medal . . . . 1·50 1·00

921 Angel carrying Sun (Andrija Raicevic) (17th century)

923 Delcev

1991. Illustrations from Ancient Manuscripts. Multicoloured.

2757 20d. Type **921** 25 15
2758 30d. "April" (Celnica Gospel) (14th century) . . 60 45
2759 40d. "Annunciation" (Trogir Evangeliarum) (13th century) . . . . 1·00 75
2760 50d. Mary Magdalene in initial V (Miroslav Gospel) (12th century) . . 1·50 1·00

1991. Nos. 2592 and 2587 surch.

2761 5d. on 60p. mauve and red 30 15
2762 10d. on 10p. violet and green 80 40

1992. 120th Birth Anniv of Goce Delcev (Macedonian revolutionary).

2763 **923** 5d. multicoloured . . . 90 75

924 Trophies and Club Emblem

925 Luge

1992. Victories of Red Star Club, Belgrade, in European and World Football Championships.

2764 **924** 17d. multicoloured . . . 2·50 2·00

1992. Winter Olympic Games, Albertville, France. Multicoloured.

2765 80d. Type **925** . . . . . . 1·25 75
2766 100d. Acrobatic skiing . . . 1·75 1·50

926 European Hare

927 "Mary feeding Jesus" (fresco, Pec Patriarchate)

1992. Protected Animals. Multicoloured.

2767 50d. Type **926** 30 20
2768 60d. Siberian flying squirrels 70 50
2769 80d. Forest dormouse . . . 1·50 1·25
2770 100d. Common hamsters . . 2·00 1·75

1992. United Nations Children's Fund Breastfeeding Campaign.

2771 **927** 80d. multicoloured . . . 1·25 1·00

928 Skier

1992. Centenary of Skiing in Montenegro.

2772 **928** 8d. multicoloured . . . 1·75 1·00

929 Fountain, Belgrade

930 "Titanic"

1992.

2773 **929** 50d. violet and lilac . . 45 30
2774 – 100d. deep green and green . . . . 5·00 3·00

DESIGN: 100d. Fisherman Fountain, Kalemegdan Fortress, Belgrade.

See also Nos. 2825/32 and 2889/90.

1992. 80th Anniv of Sinking of Liner "Titanic".

2783 **930** 150d. multicoloured . . 2·50 1·00

931 La Barqueta Bridge and Seville (engraving)

1992. "Expo '92" World's Fair, Seville.

2784 **931** 150d. multicoloured . . 1·50 1·00

932 Christopher Columbus

1992. Europa. 500th Anniv of Discovery of America by Columbus. Multicoloured.

2785 300d. Type **932** . . . . . 1·75 1·25
2786 500d. Columbus's fleet . . . 2·75 2·00
MS2787 85 × 65 mm. 1200d. "Lisbon Harbour" (engraving) (52 × 34 mm) . . . . 8·00 8·00

934 Water Polo

935 Players' Legs

1992. Olympic Games, Barcelona. Multicoloured.

2791 500d. Type **934** 90 70
2792 500d. Shooting 90 70
2793 500d. Tennis 90 70
2794 500d. Handball 90 70

1992. European Football Championship, Sweden. Multicoloured.

2795 1000d. Type **935** . . . . . 1·50 1·25
2796 1000d. Players . . . . . . 1·50 1·25

936 Red Tabby

1992. Domestic Cats. Multicoloured.

2797 1000d. Type **936** . . . . . 1·10 75
2798 1000d. White Persian . . . 1·10 75
2799 1000d. Blue and white British shorthair . . . . 1·10 75
2800 1000d. Red-point colourpoint longhair . . . 1·10 75

937 Class 162, 1880

1992. Steam Railway Locomotives. Multicoloured.

2801 1000d. Type **937** . . . . . 1·50 1·50
2802 1000d. Class 151, 1885 . . . 1·50 1·50
2803 1000d. Class 73, 1913 . . . 1·50 1·50
2804 1000d. Class 83, 1929 . . . 1·50 1·50
2805 1000d. Class 16 locomotive "Sava", 1936 . . . . . . 1·50 1·50
2806 1000d. Prince Nicholas's steam railcar, 1909 . . . 1·50 1·50

Currency reform.
10 (old) dinars = 1 (new) dinar.

1992. Various stamps surch.

2807 2d. on 30p. green and orange (No. 2589) 40 20
2808 5d. on 20p. red and yellow (No. 2588) 40 20
2809 5d. on 40p. green and purple (No. 2590) 40 20
2810 10d. on 50p. green and violet (No. 2591) 40 20
2811 10d. on 5d. ultramarine and blue (No. 2596) 40 20
2812 20d. on 1d. blue and purple (No. 2593) . . . . 1·00 50
2813 20d. on 5d. blue, green and yellow (as No. 2596) . . . 40 20
2814 50d. on 2d. blue and red (No. 2594) 40 30
2815 100d. on 3d. blue and red (No. 2595) 50 25

No. 2813 was not issued without surcharge.

939 Fischer (champion, 1972–75)

941 "Ballerina" (Edgar Degas)

940 Old Telephone and Buildings in Novi Sad, Subotica and Zrenjanin

1992. Unofficial Chess Re-match between Former World Champions Robert Fischer and Boris Spassky. Multicoloured.

2816 500d. Type **939** . . . . . 1·60 1·25
2817 500d. Spassky (1969–72) . . 1·60 1·25

1992. Centenary of Telephone Service in Vojvodina.

2818 **940** 10d. multicoloured . . . 50 35

1992. 24th "Joy of Europe" Meeting. Paintings. Multicoloured.

2819 500d. Type **941** . . . . . 1·40 1·00
2820 500d. Youth (V. Knezevic) 1·40 1·00

942 Montenegro 1874 25n. Stamp and Musician

1992. Stamp Day.

2821 **942** 50d. multicoloured . . . 60 40

943 Western Capercaillie, Durmitor Mountains

944 Book and Emblem

1992. Nature Protection. Multicoloured.

2822 500d. Type **943** . . . . . 2·50 2·00
2823 500d. Eastern white pelican ("Pelecanus onocrotalus"), Skadar Sea . . . . 2·50 2·00

1992. Centenary of Serbian Literary Association.

2824 **944** 100d. multicoloured . . 60 40

1992. As T **929**.

2825 5d. brown and green 30 15
2826 50d. blue and azure 20 10
2827 100d. lilac and pink 20 10
2828 300d. brown and chestnut 40 10
2829 500d. green and flesh . . . 40 10
2830 3000d. orange 20 20
2831 5000d. purple and yellow . . 40 10
2832 500000d. violet and blue . . 50 25

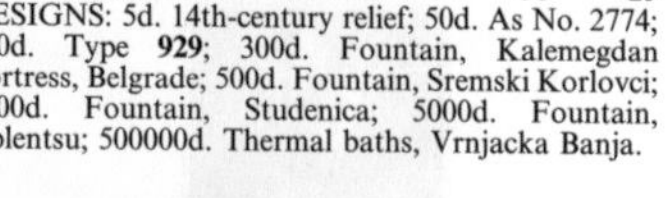

DESIGNS: 5d. 14th-century relief; 50d. As No. 2774; 100d. Type **929**; 300d. Fountain, Kalemegdan Fortress, Belgrade; 500d. Fountain, Sremski Korlovci; 3000d. Fountain, Studenica; 5000d. Fountain, Oplentsu; 500000d. Thermal baths, Vrnjacka Banja.

945 Brvnara Summer Pasture Hut, Zlatibor

946 Sun over Able-bodied and Disabled People

1992. Museum Exhibits. Traditional Houses. Multicoloured.

2833 500d. Type **945** 95 85
2834 500d. House, Morava . . . 95 85
2835 500d. House, Metokhija . . 95 85
2836 500d. Farmhouse, Vojvodina 95 85

1992. Obligatory Tax. Disabled Persons' Week.

2837 **946** 13d. yellow and blue . . 15 10

947 St. Simeon Nemanja with Model of Church of the Blessed Virgin, Studenica (mosaic, Oplenac)

1992. Mosaics and Icons. Multicoloured.
2838 500d. Type **947** 95 85
2839 500d. Prince Lazarevic with model of Ravanica Monastery (mosaic),Oplenac) 95 85
2840 500d. St. Petka (icon) and St. Petka's Church, Belgrade (horiz) 95 85
2841 500d. St. Vasilii Ostronoski (icon) and Monastery, Montenegro (horiz) . . . 95 85

948 Bleriot XI (monoplane)

949 Detail of Fresco, Sirmium

1992. 80th Anniv of Aviation in Yugoslavia.
2842 **948** 500d. multicoloured . . 1·00 1·00

1993. 1700th Anniv of Formation of the Tetrarchy (Diocletian's reform of government of Roman Empire).
2843 **949** 1500d. multicoloured . . 90 75

950 Museum and Medal

1993. Centenary of Cetinje State Museum.
2844 **950** 2500d. multicoloured . . 90 75

1993. Obligatory Tax. Anti-cancer Week. No. 2687 surch **1500 d.**
2844a **895a** 1500d. on 1d. blue and orange 90 75

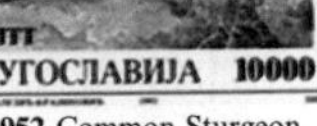

952 Common Sturgeon

953 Charter and 1868 10p. Coin

1993. Marine Animals. Multicoloured.
2845 10000d. Type **952** 90 75
2846 10000d. Red scorpionfish . . 90 75
2847 10000d. Swordfish 90 75
2848 10000d. Bottle-nosed dolphin 90 75

1993. 125th Anniv of Reintroduction of Serbian Coins (2849) and 120th Anniv of the Dinar (2850). Multicoloured.
2849 10000d. Type **953** . . . . 1·00 85
2850 10000d. 5d. banknote and 1879 5d. coin . . . . . . 1·00 85

954 Milos Crnjanski (writer)

955 Girl holding Flowers, and Bird (M. Markovski)

1993. Anniversaries. Multicoloured.
2851 40000d. Type **954** (birth centenary) . . . . 1·25 1·00
2852 40000d. Nikola Tesla (physicist, 50th death anniv) . . . . 1·25 1·00
2853 40000d. Mihailo Petrovic (mathematician, 50th death anniv) . . . . . . 1·25 1·00
2854 40000d. Aleksa Santic (poet, 125th birth anniv) . . . . 1·25 1·00

1993. Children for Peace. Multicoloured.
2855 50000d. Type **955** . . . . 1·50 1·75
2856 50000d. Birds flying above children (J. Rugovac) . . 2·00 1·75

956 Illuminated Letter from Miroslav Gospel

957 "Nude with Mirror" (M. Milunovic)

1993. No value expressed.
2857 **956** A (3000d.) red (18 × 22 mm) 15 10
See also No. 3100.

1993. Europa. Contemporary Art. Multicoloured.
2858 95000d. Type **957** . . . . 2·00 1·75
2859 95000d. "Composition" (Milena Barili) . . . . . 2·00 1·75

958

959 Map of Europe and Envelopes

1993. Obligatory Tax. Red Cross Week.
2860 **958** 350d. black and red . . 20 10
2861 1000d. black and red . . 40 15
No. 2860 was for use in Montenegro and No. 2861 for Serbia.

1993.
2862 **959** 50000d. silver and blue 35 15
2863 – 100000d. blue and red 65 30
DESIGN: 100000d. Airplane.

961 Sutorina

1993. Fortresses. Multicoloured.
2865 900000d. Type **961** 75 75
2866 900000d. Kalemegdan, Belgrade 75 75
2867 900000d. Medun 75 75
2868 900000d. Petrovaradin . . . 75 75
2869 900000d. Bar 75 75
2870 900000d. Golubac 75 75

962 Marguerites and Roses

1993. Flower Arrangements. Multicoloured.
2871 1000000d. Type **962** . . . 80 70
2872 1000000d. Roses and gerbera 80 70
2873 1000000d. Roses and lilies 80 70
2874 1000000d. Rose, carnations and stephanotis 80 70

963 Generating Plant, Street Lamp and Town

1993. Centenary of Electrification of Serbia.
2875 **963** 2500000d. mult 60 45

964 Jays

1993. Nature Protection. Fruska Highlands. Mult.
2876 300,000,000d. Type **964** . . 1·75 1·50
2877 300,000,000d. Golden oriole 1·75 1·50

Currency reform.
1000000 (old) dinars = 1 (new) dinar.

1993. Various stamps surch.
2878 10d. on 100000d. blue and red (No. 2863) 30 15
2879 50d. on 5d. brown and green (No. 2825) 30 15
2880 100d. on 5000d. purple and yellow (No. 2831) 30 15
2881 500d. on 50d. blue and azure (No. 2826) 30 15
2882 1000d. on 3000d. orange (No. 2830) 30 15
2883 10000d. on 300d. brown and chestnut (No. 2828) . . . 30 15
2884 50000d. stone, brown and green (No. 2825) 30 15

966 River Freighters

1993. The Danube, "River of Co-operation". Multicoloured.
2885 15000d. Type **966** . . . . 1·75 1·50
2886 15000d. Passenger ferry . . 1·75 1·50
MS2887 87 × 57 mm. 20000d. Course of River Danube on map (34 × 29 mm) . . . . 3·00 3·00

967 Jagodina Cancellation and Market

968 "Boy with Cat" (Sava Sumanovic)

1993. Stamp Day. 150th Anniv of Jagodina Postal Service.
2888 **967** 12000d. multicoloured 1·00 75

1993. Thermal Baths. As T **929**.
2889 10000d. blue and violet . . 30 15
2890 100000d. brown and red . . 30 15
DESIGNS: 10000d. As No. 2832; 100000d. Bukovicka Banja.

1993. 25th "Joy of Europe" Meeting. Multicoloured.
2891 2000000d. Type **968** . . . 1·40 1·25
2892 2000000d. "Circus Rider" (Georges Rouault) . . . . 1·40 1·25

969 "Madonna and Child" (from Bogorodica Ljeviska)

970 Summer Pasture Hut, Savardak

1993. Icons. Multicoloured.
2893 400,000,000d. Type **969** . . 1·10 95
2894 400,000,000d. "Christ entering Jerusalem" (from Oplenac) . . . . 1·10 95
2895 400,000,000d. "Birth of Christ" (from Studenica) 1·10 95
2896 400,000,000d. "The Annunciation" (from Mileseva) . . . . 1·10 95

Currency reform.
1,000,000,000 (old) dinars = 1 (new) dinar.

1993. Museum Exhibits. Traditional Buildings. Multicoloured.
2897 50d. Type **970** . . . . . . 1·10 95
2898 50d. "Crmnicka" house, Bar 1·10 95
2899 50d. Watchtower, Chardak (vert) . . . . 1·10 95
2900 50d. Coast house, Primorsten (vert) . . . . 1·10 95

971 Illuminated Page

972 Egyptian Vultures

1994. 500th Anniv of Printing of "Oktoukh" (book). Multicoloured.
2901 1000d. Type **971** 70 60
2902 1000d. Illustration of church and saints 70 60

Currency reform.
13,000,000 (old) dinars = 1 new dinar.

1994. Birds. Multicoloured.
2903 80p. Type **972** . . . . . . 1·60 1·10
2904 80p. Saker falcons ("Falco cherrug") . . . . 1·60 1·10
2905 80p. Long-legged buzzards ("Buteo rufinus") . . . . 1·60 1·10
2906 80p. Lesser kestrels ("Falco naumanni") . . . . . . 1·60 1·10

973 Mimosa

974 Illumination from Miroslav Gospel and Museum

1994. International Mimosa Festival, Herceg Novi.
2907 **973** 80p. multicoloured . . . 1·00 75

1994. 150th Anniv of National Museum (2908) and 125th Anniv of National Theatre (2909), Belgrade. Multicoloured.
2908 80p. Type **974** . . . . . . 1·00 75
2909 80p. Prince Milos Obrenovic and theatre . . . . 1·00 75

975 Speed Skating

976 Caudron C-61 and Route Map

1994. Winter Olympic Games, Lillehammer, Norway. Multicoloured.
2910 60p. Type **975** . . . . . . 1·00 75
2911 60p. Olympic rings and flame . . . . 1·00 75
2912 60p. Skiing . . . . 1·00 75

1994. Europa. 71st Anniv of First Paris–Belgrade–Bucharest–Istanbul Regular Night Flight. Multicoloured.
2913 60p. Type **976** . . . . . . 1·50 1·10
2914 1d.80 Caudron C-61, Belgrade and route map 2·50 1·75

977 Balloons

1994. Obligatory Tax. Red Cross Week.
2915 **977** 10p. red, black and blue 35 15

978 "The Burning of St. Sava"

1994. 400th Anniv of Burning of St. Sava's Relics.
2916 **978** 60p. multicoloured . . . 1·40 1·00

979 Jubilant Players

980 Basset Hound

1994. World Cup Football Championship, U.S.A. Multicoloured.
2917 60p. Type **979** . . . . . . 1·25 90
2918 1d. Goalkeeper and players on ground . . . . 1·75 1·10

1994. Dogs. Multicoloured.
2919 60p. Type **980** . . . . . . 1·10 80
2920 60p. Maltese terrier . . . . 1·10 80
2921 60p. Welsh terrier . . . . . 1·10 80
2922 1d. Husky . . . . 1·10 80

1994. Nos. 2888/9 surch.
2923 10p. on 100000d. brn & red 30 15
2924 50p. on 10000d. blue & violet 60 30

982 Bell and Globe

983 River Valley

1994. Assembly of Eastern Orthodox Nations.
2925 **982** 60p. multicoloured . . . 95 70

1994. Protection of Environment in Montenegro.
2926 **983** 50p. multicoloured . . . 95 70

984 Moraca

985 St. Arsenius and Sremski

1994. Churches.
2927 **984** 1p. violet and bistre . . 10 10
2928 – 5p. blue and orange . . 10 10
2929 – 10p. green and red . . . 10 10
2930 – 20p. purple and lilac . . 10 10
2931 – 20p. black and red . . . 75 10
2932 – 50p. purple and violet 15 10
2933 – 1d. red and blue 35 10
2935 – 5d. violet and blue . . . 1·60 75
2936 – 10d. red and orange . . 3·25 2·00
2938 – 20d. turquoise and blue 6·50 3·50
DESIGNS: 5p. Gracanica; 10p. Ostrog Monastery; 20p. (2930/1) Lazarica; 50p. Studenica; 1d. Sopocani; 5d. Ljeviska; 10d. Zica Monastery; 20d. Decani Monastery.

1994. Bicentenary of St. Arsenius Seminary, Sremski Karlovci.
2940 **985** 50p. multicoloured . . . 1·00 75

986 Syringe

1994. Obligatory Tax. Anti-tuberculosis Week.
2941 **986** 10p. black, yellow and red 30 15

987 River Bojana

988 Painting by U. Knezevic

1994. Nature Protection. Multicoloured.
2942 1d. Type **987** . . . . . . 1·50 1·10
2943 1d.50 Lake Biograd . . . . 2·00 1·50

1994. 26th "Joy of Europe" Meeting.
2944 **988** 1d. multicoloured . . . 1·50 1·10

989 "Revenge" (English galleon)

990 Aerospatiale ATR 42 Mail Plane, Mail Coach and Letter

1994. Ships in Bottles. Multicoloured.
2945 50p. Type **989** 75 75
2946 50p. 17th-century yacht . . 75 75
2947 50p. "Santa Maria" (Columbus's flagship) . . 75 75
2948 50p. 15th-century nau . . . 75 75
2949 50p. "Mayflower" (Pilgrim Fathers' ship) 75 75
2950 50p. 14th-century caravel . . 75 75

1994. Stamp Day.
2951 **990** 50p. multicoloured . . . 1·10 80

991 Tombstone

992 "Madonna and Child" (T. Cesljar)

1994. Museum Exhibits. Illustrated Tombstones. Multicoloured.
2952 50p. Type **991** 85 60
2953 50p. Double stone and railing 85 60
2954 50p. Two stones 85 60
2955 50p. Cemetery 85 60

1994. Paintings. Multicoloured.
2956 60p. Type **992** 90 65
2957 60p. "Adoration of the Three Wise Men" (N. Neshkovic) 90 65
2958 60p. "The Annunciation" (D. Bacevic) 90 65
2959 60p. "St. John baptizing Christ" (T. Kracun) . . . 90 65

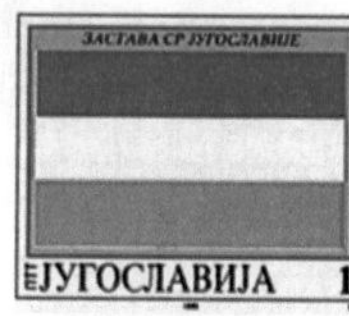
993 National Flag

1995. Multicoloured.
2960 1d. Type **993** . . . . . . 1·10 80
2961 1d. National arms . . . . . 1·10 80

994 Wilhelm Steinitz (1886–94)

1995. Chess (1st series). Chessmen or World Champions. Multicoloured.
2962 60p. Type **994** 90 65
2963 60p. Pieces 90 65
2964 60p. Emanuel Lasker (1894–1921) 90 65
2965 60p. Black knight 90 65
2966 60p. Pawns, king and knight 90 65
2967 60p. Jose Raul Capablanca (1921–27) 90 65
2968 60p. Rook, bishop, queen and pawns 90 65
2969 60p. Aleksandr Alekhine (1927–35 and 1937–46) . . 90 65
See also Nos. 2988/95 and 3021/9.

995 Emblem

1995. 50th Anniv of Red Star Sports Club, Belgrade.
2970 **995** 60p. red, blue and gold 1·25 90

996 Fire Salamander

997 Sportsman and Emblem

1995. Amphibians. Multicoloured.
2971 60p. Type **996** 90 65
2972 60p. Alpine newt ("Triturus alpestris") 90 65
2973 60p. Stream frog ("Rana graeca") 90 65
2974 60p. Eastern spadefoot ("Pelobates syriacus balcanicus") 90 65

1995. 75th Anniv of Radnicki Sports Club, Belgrade.
2975 **997** 60p. multicoloured . . . 1·00 75

998 Lammergeier over Mountainside

999 Globes

1995. Europa. Peace and Freedom. Multicoloured.
2976 60p. Type **998** . . . . . . 1·40 1·00
2977 1d.90 Child with tricycle and elderly couple on park bench (horiz) . . . . . . 2·00 1·50

1995. Obligatory Tax. Red Cross Week.
2978 **999** 10p. yellow, blue and red 30 15

1000 Dove with Black Bird in Beak

1001 Station Concourse and Train

1995. 50th Anniv of End of Second World War.
2979 **1000** 60p. multicoloured . . 1·25 90

1995. Opening of Vukov Monument Underground Railway Station, Belgrade.
2980 **1001** 60p. multicoloured . . 1·10 80

1002 Leaves and Flowers

1995. The Whitlow-grass. Multicoloured.
2981 60p. Type **1002** 85 60
2982 60p. Clumps of leaves and flowers 85 60
2983 60p. Plant growing on mountainside 85 60
2984 60p. Plant and tree branch 85 60

1003 Shore Lark, Rtanj

1995. Nature Protection. Multicoloured.
2985 60p. Type **1003** . . . . . 1·50 1·10
2986 1d.90 Blasius's horseshoe bat, Lazareva Reka Canyon . . . . 2·00 1·50

1004 "Slovakian Village Gathering" (Zuzka Medvedova)

1995.
2987 **1004** 60p. multicoloured . . 1·00 75

1995. Chess (2nd series). Chessmen or World Champions. As T **994**. Multicoloured.
2988 60p. Max Euwe (1935–37) 80 60
2989 60p. Pawn and chessboard and pieces 80 60
2990 60p. Mikhail Botvinnik (1948–57, 1958–60 and 1961–63) 80 60
2991 60p. Queen and chessboard and pieces 80 60
2992 60p. Board and white bishop and knight 80 60
2993 60p. Vasily Smyslov (1957–58) 80 60
2994 60p. Rook, knight, queen and board 80 60
2995 60p. Mikhail Tal (1960–61) 80 60

1005 Wilhelm Rontgen (discoverer of X-rays)

1006 Player on Globe

1995. Obligatory Tax. Anti-tuberculosis Week.
2996 **1005** 10p. red and blue . . . 15 15

1995. Centenary of Volleyball.
2997 **1006** 90p. multicoloured . . 1·00 75

1007 Church

1008 Coronation of King Petar II

1995. 800th Anniv of St. Luke's Church, Kotor.
2998 **1007** 80p. multicoloured . . 1·00 75

1995. Centenary of Motion Pictures. Each brown and orange.
2999 1d.10 Type **1008** . . . . . 1·00 75
3000 2d.20 Auguste and Louis Lumiere (cine camera pioneers) . . . . 2·00 1·50

1009 Club Emblem

1010 "Flower Seller" (Milos Tenkovic)

1995. 50th Anniv of Partizan Army Sports Club.
3001 **1009** 80p. multicoloured . . 1·00 75

1995. 27th "Joy of Europe" Meeting. Multicoloured.
3002 1d.10 Type **1010** . . . . . 1·00 75
3003 2d.20 "Child at Table" (Pierre Bonnard) . . . . 2·00 1·50

1011 Golden Gate Bridge, San Francisco

1012 Post Office, Seal and Letter

1995. 50th Anniv of U.N.O.
3004 **1011** 1d.10 multicoloured . . 90 65
San Francisco was where the Charter was signed.

1995. Stamp Day.
3005 **1012** 1d.10 multicoloured . . 90 65

1013 Montenegro 1898 10n. and Serbia 1866 40p. Stamps

1995. "Jufia VIII" National Stamp Exhibition, Budva. Sheet 71 × 95 mm.
MS3006 **1013** 2d.50 multicoloured 1·90 1·90

1014 Saric No. 1

1015 "Birth of Christ" (D. Milojevic)

1995. Museum Exhibits. Aircraft. Multicoloured.
3007 1d.10 Type **1014** 60 45
3008 1d.10 Douglas DC-3 . . . . 60 45
3009 2d.20 Fizir FN biplane . . . 1·10 80
3010 2d.20 Sud Aviation Caravelle jetliner . . . . 1·10 80

1995. Paintings. Multicoloured.
3011 1d.10 Type **1015** 60 45
3012 1d.10 "Flight into Egypt" (Z. Halupova) (horiz) . . 60 45
3013 2d.20 "Sunday" (M. Rasic) 1·10 80
3014 2d.20 "Traditional Christmas Festival" (J. Brasic) (horiz) . . . . 1·10 80

1016 Battle Scene

1017 Painting

1996. 70th Anniv of Battle of Mojkovac.
3015 **1016** 1d.10 multicoloured . . 60 45

1996. Birth Centenary of Save Sumanovic (painter).
3016 **1017** 1d.10 multicoloured . . 60 45

1018 "Pyrgomorphela serbica"

1996. Protected Insects. Multicoloured.
3017 1d.10 Type **1018** 60 45
3018 1d.10 Red wood ant ("Formica rufa") 60 45
3019 2d.20 Searcher ("Calosoma sycophanta") . . . . . . 1·10 80
3020 2d.20 Owl-fly ("Ascalaphus macaronius") . . . . . . 1·10 80

1996. Chess (3rd series). Chessmen and Timepieces or World Champions. As T **994**. Multicoloured.
3021 1d.50 Tigran Vartanovich Petrosyan (1963–69) . . . 55 40
3022 1d.50 Queen, knight and portable sundial 55 40
3023 1d.50 Boris Vasilevich Spassky (1969–72) 55 40
3024 1d.50 Competition clock, chessboard and pieces . . 55 40
3025 1d.50 Garry Kimovich Kasparov (1985–93) . . . 55 40
3026 1d.50 Chessboard, pieces and hourglass 55 40
3027 1d.50 Robert Fischer (1972–75) 55 40
3028 1d.50 Chess pieces, clocks and chessboard 55 40
3029 1d.50 Anatoly Yevgenievich Karpov (1975–85 and 1993–) 55 40

1019 Discus Throwers

1996. Centenary of Modern Olympic Games. Multicoloured.
3030 1d.50 Type **1019** 60 45
3031 2d.50 Ancient Greek and modern athletes . . . . . 1·10 1·10

1020 Athletics

1996. Olympic Games, Atlanta. Multicoloured.
3032 1d.50 Type **1020** 70 50
3033 1d.50 Basketball 70 50
3034 1d.50 Handball 70 50
3035 1d.50 Shooting 70 50
3036 1d.50 Volleyball 70 50
3037 1d.50 Water polo 70 50
MS3038 107 × 60 mm. 5d. Tara (house from "Gone with the Wind") . . . . 2·00 2·00

1021 Postman, Railway Mail Van and Arms of Royal Serbian Post

1022 Isidora Sekulic

1996. Stamp Day.
3039 **1021** 1d.50 multicoloured . . 65 45

1996. Europa. Famous Women Writers. Mult.
3040 2d.50 Type **1022** . . . . . 1·10 80
3041 5d. Desanka Maksimovic . . 2·25 1·60

1023 Dr. Vladan Djordjevic (founder)

1024 Child and Cross

1996. 120th Anniv of Serbian Red Cross.
3042 **1023** 1d.50 multicoloured . . 50 35

1996. Obligatory Tax. Red Cross Week.
3043 **1024** 15p. blue, brown and red 10 10

1025 Columns, Caryatid and Diagrams of Proportion

1026 White Spoonbill

1996. 150th Anniv of Architecture Education in Serbia.
3044 **1025** 1d.50 light blue, deep blue and blue 50 35

1996. Nature Protection. Multicoloured.
3045 2d.50 Type **1026** 80 60
3046 5d. Glossy ibis . . . . . . 1·60 1·25

1027 Prince Petar I Petrovic (Battle of Martinici)

1996. Battle Bicentenaries. Multicoloured.
3047 1d.50 Type **1027** 50 35
3048 2d.50 "Prince's Guard" (Theodore Valerio) (Battle of Kruse) (vert) 80 60

1028 Waiting for the Off

1996. Ljubicevo Race Meeting. Multicoloured.
3049 1d.50 Type **1028** 50 35
3050 2d.50 Horses racing 80 60

1029 Palm Cockatoo

1030 Landscape on Leaf

1996. 60th Anniv of Belgrade Zoo. Multicoloured.
3051 1d.50 Type **1029** 50 35
3052 1d.50 Common zebra . . . 50 35
3053 2d.50 Maroon-breasted crowned pigeon . . . . . 1·00 75
3054 2d.50 Tiger . . . . 1·00 75

1996. Obligatory Tax. Anti-tuberculosis Week.
3055 **1030** 20p. multicoloured . . 10 10

1031 Fantasy Scene

1996. 28th "Joy of Europe" Meeting. Multicoloured.
3056 1d.50 Type **1031** 50 35
3057 2d.50 Toucan . . . . 1·00 75

1032 Basketball (silver)

1033 Coins, Banknotes and Credit Card

1996. Olympic Games Medal Winners. Mult.
3058 2d.50 Type **1032** 80 60
3059 2d.50 Small-bore rifle shooting (gold) 80 60
3060 2d.50 Air-rifle shooting (bronze) 80 60
3061 2d.50 Volleyball (bronze) . . 80 60

1996. 75th Anniv of Post Office Savings Bank.
3062 **1033** 1d.50 multicoloured . . 45 30

1034 Footballer

1035 Mother and Child (statuette)

1996. Centenary of Football in Serbia.
3063 **1034** 1d.50 multicoloured . . 45 30

1996. Museum Exhibits. Archaeological Finds. Multicoloured.
3064 1d.50 Type **1035** 45 30
3065 1d.50 Tombstone depicting Genius, god of autumn (Komani, nr. Pljevlja) . . 45 30
3066 2d.50 Marble head of woman (from Podgorica) 70 50
3067 2d.50 Statuette of red-headed goddess 70 50

1036 "The Annunciation" (Nikola Neskovic)

1037 Putnik in Dress Uniform

1996. Icons from Serbian Orthodox Church Museum, Belgrade. Multicoloured.
3068 1d.50 Type **1036** 45 30
3069 1d.50 "Madonna and Child" 45 30
3070 2d.50 "Nativity" 70 50
3071 2d.50 "Entry of Christ into Jerusalem" (Stanoje Popovic) 70 50

1997. 150th Birth Anniv of Radomir Putnik (army Commander in Chief).
3072 **1037** 1d.50 multicoloured . . 35 25

1038 Film Frames

1039 Great Spotted Woodpecker

1997. 25th International Film Festival, Belgrade.
3073 **1038** 1d.50 multicoloured . . 35 25

1997. Nature Protection. Woodland Birds. Multicoloured.
3074 1d.50 Type **1039** 35 25
3075 1d.50 Crested tit ("Parus cristatus") 35 25
3076 2d.50 Spotted nutcracker ("Nucifraga caryocatactes") 60 45
3077 2d.50 European robin ("Erithacus rubecula") . . 60 45

1040 Christ and King Dragutin holding Model of Church (fresco)

1041 St. Petar

1997. 700th Anniv of St. Ahilije's Church, Arilje.
3078 **1040** 1d.50 multicoloured . . 35 25

1997. 250th Birth Anniv of Prince-Bishop Petar I of Montenegro (St. Petar of Cetinje).
3079 **1041** 1d.50 multicoloured . . 35 25

1042 Belgrade and Emblem

1043 Ambulance, 1876, and Association Building

1997. 10th Belgrade Marathon.
3080 **1042** 2d.50 multicoloured . . 60 45

1997. 125th Anniv of Serbian Medical Association.
3081 **1043** 2d.50 multicoloured . . 60 45

1044 Loading Air Mail at Night

1997. Stamp Day.
3082 **1044** 2d.50 multicoloured . . 50 30

1045 "1997" and Cross **1046** Belgrade

1997. Obligatory Tax. Red Cross Week.
3083 **1045** 20p. red and blue . . . 10 10

1997. Tennis Championships in Yugoslavia. Design showing player and Town Arms. Multicoloured.
3084 2d.50 Type **1046** 50 30
3085 2d.50 Budva 50 30
3086 2d.50 Novi Sad 50 30

1047 Bas Celik shackled before King

1997. Europa. Myths and Legends. Multicoloured.
3087 2d.50 Type **1047** 50 30
3088 6d. Prince on horseback fighting chained Bas Celik 1·25 75

1048 "Cerambyx cerdo" (longhorn beetle)

1997. Nature Protection. Multicoloured.
3089 2d.50 Type **1048** 50 30
3090 6d. Pedunculate oak . . . . 1·25 75

1049 Prince Bishop Peter Njegos, Village and Printing Press **1050** Binicki

1997. 150th Anniv of Publication of "Gorski Vijenc".
3091 **1049** 2d.50 multicoloured . . 50 30

1997. 125th Birth Anniv of Stanislav Binicki (composer).
3092 **1050** 2d.50 multicoloured . . 50 30

1051 "Pelargonium grandiflorum" **1053** Dr. Milutin Rankovic

1052 Statue by Dragomir Arambasic before Cvijeta Zuzoric Art Gallery (venue)

1997. Flowers. Multicoloured.
3093 1d.50 Type **1051** 30 20
3094 1d.50 "Hydrangea x macrophylla" 30 20
3095 2d.50 African violet ("Saintpaulia ionantha") 50 30
3096 2d.50 "Oncidium varicosum" 50 30

1997. "Jufiz IX" National Stamp Exhibition, Belgrade. Sheet 96 × 75 mm.
MS3097 **1052** 5d. multicoloured 60 60

1997. Obligatory Tax. Anti-tuberculosis Week.
3098 **1053** 20p. brown, ochre and red 10 10

1054 Society Emblem **1055** Collage (Milan Ugrisic)

1997. Centenary of Serbian Chemical Association.
3099 **1054** 2d.50 multicoloured . . 30 20

1997. No value expressed. As No. 2857 but 18 × 20 mm.
3100 **956** A red 10 10

1997. 29th "Joy of Europe" Meeting. Multicoloured.
3101 2d.50 Type **1055** 25 15
3102 5d. Collage (Stanislava Antic) 55 35

1056 "May Assembly, Sremski Karlovci, 1848" (Pavle Simic)

1997. 150th Anniv of Matica Srpska Art Gallery.
3103 **1056** 2d.50 multicoloured . . 25 15

1057 Helmet from Srem (4th century) **1058** "Christ Pantocrator"

1997. Archaeological Finds in Vojvodina Museum. Multicoloured.
3104 1d.50 Type **1057** 15 10
3105 1d.50 Two-headed terracotta figure from Srem 15 10
3106 2d.50 Teracotta figure from Backa 25 15
3107 2d.50 "Madonna and Child" (relief from Srem, 12th century) 25 15

1997. Icons from Chelandari Serbian Monastery, Mount Athos. Multicoloured.
3108 1d.50 Type **1058** 15 10
3109 1d.50 "Madonna and Child" 15 10
3110 2d.50 "Madonna and Child" (different) 25 15
3111 2d.50 "Three-handed Madonna with Child" . . 25 15

1059 Savina **1060** Ice Skater

1998. Monasteries in Montenegro. Multicoloured.
3112 1d.50 Type **1059** 15 10
3113 2d.50 Donji Brceli 25 15

1998. Winter Olympic Games, Nagano, Japan. Multicoloured.
3114 2d.50 Type **1060** 25 15
3115 6d. Skier 65 40

1061 Mare and Foal

1998. Horses. Multicoloured.
3116 1d.50 Type **1061** 15 10
3117 1d.50 Stallion 15 10
3118 2d.50 Head of grey 25 15
3119 2d.50 Racehorse 25 15

1062 Women and Flowers

1998. International Women's Day.
3120 **1062** 2d.50 multicoloured . . 25 15

1063 Glider and Emblems

1998. 50th Anniv of Yugoslav Aeronautics Association.
3121 **1063** 2d.50 multicoloured . . 25 15

1064 "The Adornment of the Bride" (Paja Jovanovic)

1998. Europa. National Festivals. Multicoloured.
3122 6d. Type **1064** 65 40
3123 9d. "The Prince-Bishop celebrates Victory" (Pero Pocek) . . . . 1·00 60

1065 Metropolitan Mihailo Jovanovic **1066** Player evading Tackle

1998. Obligatory Tax. Red Cross Week.
3124 **1065** 20p. multicoloured . . 10 10

1998. World Cup Football Championship, France. Multicoloured.
3125 6d. Type **1066** 65 40
3126 9d. Goalkeeper and players 1·00 60

1067 Map of Europe

1998. 50th Anniv of Danube Commission. Sheet 88 × 65 mm.
MS3127 **1067** 9d. multicoloured 1·00 1·00

1068 "Hieracium blecicii" **1069** Djura Jaksic (poet and painter)

1998. Nature Protection. Multicoloured.
3128 6d. Type **1068** 65 40
3129 9d. Oceanic sunfish . . . . 1·00 60

1998. Anniversaries. Each brown, black and ochre.
3130 1d.50 Type **1069** (120th death anniv) 15 10
3131 1d.50 Nadezda Petrovic (painter, 125th birth anniv) 15 10
3132 1d.50 Radoje Domanovic (satirist, 125th birth anniv) 15 10
3133 1d.50 Vasilije Mokranjac (composer, 75th birth anniv) 15 10
3134 1d.50 Sreten Stojanovic (sculptor, birth centenary) 15 10
3135 1d.50 Milan Konjovic (painter, birth centenary) 15 10
3136 1d.50 Desanka Maksimovic (writer, birth centenary) 15 10
3137 1d.50 Ivan Tabakovic (painter, birth centenary) 15 10

1070 Trophy

1998. Victory of Yugoslavia in World Basketball Championship, Athens. Sheet 80 × 98 mm.
MS3138 **1070** 10d. multicoloured 1·10 1·10

1071 Pine Marten **1072** Machine-gunners

1998. 50th Anniv of Serbian Nature Protection Institute. Multicoloured.
3139 2d. Type **1071** 20 15
3140 2d. Demoiselle crane ("Anthropoides virgo") 20 15
3141 5d. Lynx ("Lynx lynx") . . 55 35
3142 5d. Red crossbill ("Loxia curvirostra") 55 35

1998. 80th Anniv of Thessalonica Front.
3143 **1072** 5d. grey and brown . . 55 35
3144 – 5d. brown and sepia . . 55 35
DESIGN: No. 3144, Field gun.

1073 "50 Years" on Stamp **1074** "Sea Life" (Bojan Dakic)

1998. Stamp Day. 50th Anniv of Serbian Philatelic Society.
3145 **1073** 6d. blue 65 40

1998. 30th "Joy of Europe" Meeting. Multicoloured.
3146 6d. Type **1074** 65 40
3147 9d. "Sea Life" (collage by Ana Rockov) . . . . . . 1·00 60

1075 Steam Locomotive, 1847

1998. Locomotives. Multicoloured.
3148 2d.50 Type **1075** 30 20
3149 2d.50 Steam locomotive, 1900 . . . . 30 20
3150 2d.50 Steam locomotive, 1920 . . . . 30 20
3151 2d.50 Steam locomotive, 1930 . . . . 30 20
3152 2d.50 Diesel locomotive "Kennedy" 30 20
3153 2d.50 High speed train, 1990 30 20

1076 *Pjerino* (brig), 1883

1998. Museum Exhibits. Ship Paintings by Vasilije Ivankovic. Multicoloured.

3154	2d. Type **1076**	20	15
3155	2d. *Vera Cruz* (steamer), 1873	20	15
3156	5d. *Vizin-Florio* (full-rigged ship)	60	40
3157	5d. *Draghetto* (barque), 1865	60	40

1077 Hilandar Monastery

1998. 800th Anniv of Hilandar Monastery. Paintings by Milutin Dedic. Multicoloured.

3158	2d. Type **1077**	20	15
3159	2d. Monastery facade	20	15
3160	5d. Hills behind Monastery buildings	60	40
3161	5d. Aerial view of Monastery	60	40

1078 Flags around Envelope on Map

1998. South-East European Postal Ministers Congress.

3162 **1078** 5d. multicoloured . . . 60 40

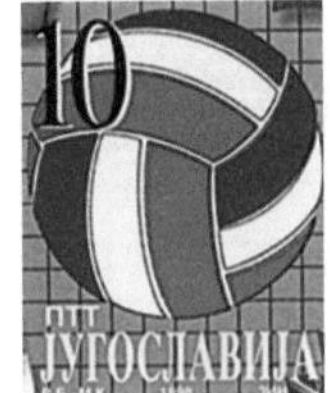

1079 Volleyball

1998. Yugoslavia. Silver Medal Winners in World Volleyball Championship, Japan. Sheet 70 × 78 mm.

MS3163 **1079** 10d. multicoloured 1·10 1·10

1080 Postal Messenger arriving in Belgrade

1081 Visoki Decani Monastery

1998. 75th Anniv of Post and Telecommunications Museum.

3164	**1080**	5d. brown and green	60	40
3165		5d. red and brown	60	40

1999. Serbian Monasteries. Paintings by Milutin Dedic. Multicoloured.

3166	2d. Type **1081**	20	15
3167	5d. Gracanica Monastery	60	40

1082 Woolly Pig

1999. Animals. Multicoloured.

3168	2d. Type **1082**	20	15
3169	2d. Cattle	20	15
3170	6d. Balkan goat	70	45
3171	6d. Hungarian sheep	70	45

1083 Scouts making Campfire and Emblem

1084 Emblem, Goddess Justitia and Globe

1999. Scouts.

3172 **1083** 6d. multicoloured . . . 70 45

1999. 70th Anniv of Bar Association.

3173 **1084** 6d. brown and buff . . 70 45

1085 Target

1086 Emblem and Player

1999. No value expressed.

3174	**1085**	A black	10	10
3175	–	A black and red	10	10

DESIGN: No. 3175, Target with heart at centre.

1999. World Table Tennis Championships, Belgrade. Multicoloured.

3176	6d. Type **1086**	70	40
3177	6d. Player facing left	70	40

1087 Kopaonik National Park

1088 Red Cross Volunteers

1999. Europa. Parks and Gardens. Multicoloured.

3178	6d. Type **1087**	70	40
3179	15d. Lovcen National Park	1·75	1·10

1999. Obligatory Tax Red Cross Week.

3180 **1088** 1d. multicoloured . . . 15 10

1089 Emblem, Cobweb and Spade

1090 Destroying Angel (*Amanita virosa*)

1999. Nature Protection. Multicoloured.

3181	6d. Type **1089**	70	40
3182	15d. Thumb squeezing water droplet from Earth	1·75	1·10

1999. Fungi. Multicoloured.

3183	6d. Type **1090**	70	40
3184	6d. False blusher (*Amanita pantherina*)	70	40
3185	6d. Clustered woodlover (*Hypholoma fasciculare*)	70	40
3186	6d. *Ramaria pallida*	70	40

1091 Stjepan Mitrov Ljubisa (author)

1092 Thistle

1999. Personalities. Each brown, yellow and black.

3187	2d. Type **1091**	25	15
3188	2d. Marko Miljanov (author)	25	15
3189	2d. Pero Pocek (painter)	25	15
3190	2d. Risto Stijovic (sculptor)	25	15
3191	2d. Milo Milunovic (painter)	25	15
3192	2d. Petar Lubarda (painter)	25	15
3193	2d. Vuko Radovic (painter)	25	15
3194	2d. Mihailo Lalic (author)	25	15

1999. Obligatory Tax. Anti-tuberculosis Week.

3195 **1092** 1d. multicoloured . . . 15 10

1093 World Map and Emblem

1999. 125th Anniv of Universal Postal Union. Multicoloured.

3196	6d. Type **1093**	70	40
3197	12d. Envelopes encircling globe	1·40	85

1094 Lion (Luka Minic)

1095 Chopin and Music Score

1999. 31st "Joy in Europe" Meeting. Winning Designs in Children's Painting Competition. Multicoloured.

3198	6d. Type **1094**	70	40
3199	15d. Girl with doll (Andreas Kaparis) (vert)	1·75	1·10

1999. 150th Death Anniv of Frederic Chopin (composer).

3200 **1095** 10d. multicoloured . . 1·25 75

1096 Mastheads

1999. Stamp Day. 50th Anniv of *Philatelist* (magazine).

3201 **1096** 10d. multicoloured . . 1·25 75

1097 Murino Bridge

1999. Bombed Bridges. Multicoloured.

3202	2d. Type **1097**	25	15
3203	2d. Varadinski Most	25	15
3204	2d. Ostruznica	25	15
3205	6d. Bistrica	70	40
3206	6d. Grdelica	70	40
3207	6d. Zezeljev Most	70	40

1098 Fragments of Roman Altars, Sremska Mitrovica and Jupiter (statue), Sabac

1999. Year 2000. Multicoloured.

3208	6d. Type **1098**	70	40
3209	6d. Mosaic depicting Emperor Trajan with army leaders, Sirmium, lamp and lead mirror	70	40
3210	6d. Mosaic of Dionysus and painting of Belgrade	70	40
3211	6d. Haghia Sophia, mosaic and bust of Emperor Constantin	70	40
3212	6d. Gold artefacts, pot and lamp	70	40
3213	6d. St. Peter's Church and title page of *Temnic*	70	40

MS3214 138 × 88 mm. 15d. Birth and crucifixion of Christ, ships and scenes of everyday life (105 × 54 mm) . . . 1·60 1·60

1099 Fireman dousing Flames

1999. Bombed Buildings. Multicoloured.

3215	2d. Type **1099**	25	15
3216	2d. Oil refinery	25	15
3217	2d. Dish aerials	25	15
3218	6d. Hospital	70	40
3219	6d. Radio and television station	70	40
3220	6d. Television tower, Mt. Avala	70	40

1100 Saints

1999. 500th Anniv of Poganovo Monastery Frescoes. Multicoloured.

3221	6d. Type **1100**	70	40
3222	6d. Four saints with long beards	70	40
3223	6d. Four saints, one holding a scroll and one an open book	70	40
3224	6d. Four saints, three holding scrolls and one with a stick	70	40

1101 Couple washing for Gold

1999. Museum Exhibits. Gold Washing on the River Pek. Multicoloured.

3225	6d. Type **1101**	70	40
3226	6d. Man and two youths panning for gold	70	40
3227	6d. Women digging gravel panning for gold	70	40
3228	6d. Man holding spade and pan with two boys	70	40

1102 Krushedol Monastery

2000. Monasteries. Multicoloured.

3229	10d. Type **1102**	1·25	75
3230	10d. Rakovac Monastery	1·25	75

1103 Building and Emblem

2000. 50th Anniv of National Archives.

3231 **1103** 10d. lilac and blue . . . 1·25 75

1104 Large Tortoiseshell (*Nymphalis polychloros*)

2000. Butterflies. Multicoloured.

3232	10d. Type **1104**	1·25	75
3233	10d. Southern festoon (*Parnalius polyxena*)	1·25	75
3234	10d. Poplar admiral (*Limenitis populi*)	1·25	75
3235	10d. Marbled white (*Melanargia galathea*)	1·25	75

1105 Grey Partridges (*Perdix perdix*)

2000. Endangered Species. Partridges. Mult.
3236 10d. Type **1105** . . . . . . 1·25 75
3237 10d. Grey partridge (different) . . . . 1·25 75
3238 10d. Rock partridge (*Alectoris graeca*) on nest 1·25 75
3239 10d. Two rock partridges . . 1·25 75

1106 General Staff Building, Belgrade

2000. Bombed Buildings.
3240 **1106** 10d. blue . . . . 1·25 75
3241 – 20d. brown . . . . 2·25 1·40
DESIGN: No. 3241, Air Force and Air Defence Command, Zemun.

1107 Exhibition Medal (P90)

1108 Tree and World Map

2000. "Jufiz X" National Stamp Exhibition, Belgrade. Sheet 68 × 75 mm.
MS3242 **1107** 15d. multicoloured 1·60 1·60

2000. Environment Protection. Multicoloured.
3243 30d. Type **1108** . . . . . . 3·50 2·25
3244 30d. Barn swallows in nest 3·50 2·25

1109 "2000" and View of Bethlehem

1110 Players chasing Ball

2000. Europa. Multicoloured.
3245 30d. Type **1109** . . . . . . 3·50 2·25
3246 30d. "2000" and astronaut on Moon . . . . 3·50 2·25

2000. European Football Championship, Belgium and The Netherlands. Multicoloured.
3247 30d. Type **1110** . . . . . . 3·50 2·25
3248 30d. Players heading ball . . 3·50 2·25

1111 Post Office Building, Post Van, Post Box, Letter, Envelope and Quill

2000. 160th Anniv of Postal Service in Serbia.
3249 **1111** 10d. multicoloured . . 1·25 75

1112 Map of Australia and Kangaroo

2000. Olympic Games, Sydney. Showing map of Australia and animal or bird. Multicoloured.
3250 6d. Type **1112** 25 10
3251 12d. Emu 35 15
3252 24d. Koala . . . . 1·00 60
3253 30d. Cockatoo . . . . . . 1·10 65

1113 Airship LZ-127 "Graf Zeppelin" (1928) and Cover

2000. Stamp Day. Centenary of First Zeppelin Flight.
3254 **1113** 10d. multicoloured . . 30 15

1114 Goats

2000. 32nd "Joy in Europe" Meeting. Winning Designs in Children's Painting Competition. Multicoloured.
3255 30d. Type **1114** . . . . . . 1·10 65
3256 40d. Storks (vert) . . . . . 1·40 95

1115 Hand holding Pen

2000. UNESCO. World Teachers' Day.
3257 **1115** 10d. multicoloured . . 30 15

1116 Bee on Flower

2000. 13th Apislavia (Slavonic bee-keeping association) Congress.
3256 **1116** 10d. multicoloured . . 30 15

1117 Water Polo (bronze)

2000. Yugoslav Medals at Olympic Games. Multicoloured.
3259 20d. Type **1117** 50 30
3260 20d. Air pistol (silver) . . . 50 30
MS3261 70 × 83 mm. 30d. Volleyball (gold) (34 × 46 mm) . . . . . 1·10 1·10

1118 Sailing Ships

2000. New Millennium. Multicoloured.
3262 12d. Type **1118** 35 15
3263 12d. Parchment production 35 15
3264 12d. Man and instruments (first accurate maps and optical instruments) . . . 35 15
3265 12d. G. and R. Stephenson's *Rocket* (1829) and *Clermont* (first commercial paddle-steamer) 35 15
3266 12d. Nikola Tesla (Yugoslav scientist), telegraph and telephone 35 15
3267 12d. Futuristic settlement, astronaut and satellite . . 35 15
MS3268 138 × 86 mm. 40d. Horses on river bank, ship in full sail and ice-bound ship (104 × 54 mm) 1·40 1·40

1119 Christ bathing (fresco, Monastery, Pec)

1120 Waistcoat (Jagodina)

2000. No value expressed.
3269 **1119** A multicoloured . . . 10 10

2000. Museum Exhibits. 19th-century Serbian Costumes. Multicoloured.
3270 6d. Type **1120** 25 10
3271 12d. Dress (Metohija) . . . 35 15
3272 24d. Blouse (Pec) . . . . . 1·00 60
3273 30d. Waistcoat (Kupres) . . 1·40 95

1121 Mary and Jesus (icon, Piva Monastery)

2000. Art. Icons and Frescoes of Montenegro. Multicoloured.
3274 6d. Type **1121** 25 10
3275 12d. Nativity (fresco, Holy Cross Church) 35 15
3276 24d. St. Luke painting an icon (fresco, Moraca Monastery) . . . . 1·00 60
3277 30d. Mary and Jesus, St. John and St. Stephen (fresco, Mary of the Ascension Church, Moraca) . . . . 1·40 95

1122 Map of Europe and Emblem

2000. Yugoslavia's Resumption of Membership of the Organization for Security and Co-operation in Europe (3278) and the United Nations (3279). Multicoloured.
3278 6d. Type **1122** 25 10
3279 12d. Emblem (vert) 35 15

1123 Vatoped Monastery

2001. Monasteries on Mount Athos. Multicoloured.
3280 10d. Type **1123** 30 15
3281 27d. Esfigmen monastery . . 1·25 75

1124 Association Building

2001. 175th Anniv of "Matice Srpske" (Serbian literary association).
3282 **1124** 15d. multicoloured . . 40 25

1125 Lions

1126 Vera Mencikova

2001. 50th Anniv of Zoo Palic, Subotica. Endangered Species. Multicoloured.
3283 6d. Type **1125** (*Panthera leo*) (inscr "Felis leo") 25 10
3284 12d. Polar bear and cub (*Ursus maritimus*) 35 15
3285 24d. Japanese macaques (*Macaca fuscata*) . . . . 1·00 65
3286 30d. Humboldt penguins (*Spheniscus humboldti*) . . 1·40 95

2001. Women World Chess Champions. Multicoloured.
3287 10d. Type **1126** 30 15
3288 10d. Lyudmila Vladimirovna Rudenko 30 15
3289 10d. Elizaveta Ivanova Bykova 30 15
3290 10d. Olga Nikelaevna Rubtsova 30 15
3291 10d. Nona Terentievna Gaprindashvili 30 15
3292 10d. Maia Grigorevna Chiburdanidze 30 15
3293 10d. Zsusza Polgar 30 15
3294 10d. Jun Xie 30 15

1127 Stevan Stojanovic Mokranjac (portrait, Uros Predic)

1128 Rose-of-Sharon (*Hibiscus syriacus*)

2001. Personalities. Multicoloured.
3295 50d. Type **1127** (composer) 2·10 1·25
3296 100d. Nikola Tesla (inventor) . . . . 4·25 2·50

2001. Flora. Multicoloured.
3297 6d. Type **1128** 25 10
3298 12d. Oleander (*Nerium oleander*) 35 15
3299 24d. Chilean bellflower (*Lapageria rosea*) . . . . 1·00 60
3300 30d. Rowan (*Sorbus aucuparia*) . . . . 1·10 65

1129 River Vratna, Eastern Serbia

2001. Europa. Water Resources. Multicoloured.
3301 30d. Type **1129** . . . . . . 1·10 65
3302 45d. Jerme Gorge, Dimitrovgrad . . . . . . 1·60 95

1130 Mountains, Emblem and Climbers

2001. Centenary of Serbian Mountaineering Association.
3303 **1130** 15d. multicoloured . . 40 25

1131 Lake Ludasko and Heron

2001. Nature Protection. Lakes. Multicoloured.
3304 30d. Type **1131** . . . . . . 1·10 65
3305 45d. Lake and stork in flight, Carska Bara Special Nature Reserve . . . 1·60 95

1132 Illuminated Letter

2001. No value expressed.
3306 **1132** E multicoloured 15 10

1133 Players and Ball (½-size illustration)

2001. European Water Polo Champions. Sheet 86 × 67 mm.
MS3307 **1133** 30d. multicoloured 1·10 1·10

1134 Seated Figure

2001. 50th Anniv of Serbian Stamps. "SRBIJAFILA 12" National Stamp Exhibition. Sheet 97 × 85 mm.
MS3308 **1134** 30d. multicoloured 1·10 1·10

1135 Sun and Emblems

1136 Hands holding Bridge

2001. Energy Conservation. Solar Power.
3309 **1135** 15d. multicoloured . . 40 25

2001. Danube Commission. Cleaning the Danube. Multicoloured.
3310 30d. Type **1136** . . . . . . 1·10 65
3311 45d. Hand, clock and ship 1·60 95

1137 "The Child" (Marko Celbonovic)

1138 Ball and Outstretched Arms

2001. 33rd "Joy in Europe" Meeting. Children's Day. Paintings. Multicoloured.
3312 30d. Type **1137** . . . . . . 1·10 65
3313 45d. "Girl in Orchard" (Beta Vukanovic) . . . . 1·60 95

2001. Yugoslavia, European Basketball (No. 3314) and Volleyball (3315) Champions. Multicoloured.
3314 30d. Type **1138** . . . . . . 1·10 65
3315 30d. Players, ball and net 1·10 65

1139 Stamps and Society Emblem

2001. Stamp Day. 75th Anniv of Federation Internationale de Philatelie (the International Philatelic Federation or FIP).
3316 **1139** 15d. multicoloured . . 40 25

1140 Antimonite

2001. Museum Exhibits. Minerals. Multicoloured.
3317 7d. Type **1140** 20 10
3318 14d. Calcite 40 25
3319 26d.20 Quartz 70 35
3320 28d.70 Calcite and Galenite 85 55
Nos. 3317/20 were issued together, se-tenant, forming a composite design of a cave within the sheet.

1141 School Building

2001. Centenary of Tanasije Pejanovic Secondary School, Pljevlja.
3321 **1141** 15d. multicoloured . . 40 25

1142 Telephone Box and Man using "Candlestick" Telephone

2001. Centenary of First Serbian Telephone Box.
3322 **1142** 15d. multicoloured . . 40 25

1143 The Nativity (14th-century fresco)

2001. Christmas. Showing paintings of the Nativity. Multicoloured.
3323 7d. Type **1143** . . . . . .
3324 14d. Nativity, Lesnovo Monastery 40 25
3325 26d.20 Nativity (different) 70 35
3326 28d.70 Nativity, Sveta Trojica 85 55

1144 Players

2002. Junior World Ice Hockey Championship, Czech Republic.
3327 **1144** 14d. multicoloured . . 40 20

1145 Skier

2002. Winter Olympic Games, Salt Lake City. Multicoloured.
3328 28d.70 Type **1145** 85 55
3329 50d. Bobsleigh (vert) . . . . 1·50 75

1146 Jovan Karamata

1147 Stonechat (*Saxicola torquata*)

2002. Birth Centenary of Jovan Karamata (mathematician).
3330 **1146** 14d. multicoloured . . 40 20

2002. Songbirds. Multicoloured.
3331 7d. Type **1147** 20 10
3332 14d. Whinchat (*Saxicola rubetra*) 40 20
3333 26d.20 Blue tit (*Parus caeruleus*) 80 40
3334 28d.70 Song thrush (*Turdus philomelos*) 85 55

1148 Crucified Christ (1208)

1149 Woman wearing Blouse and Skirt with Sash (Bunjevac)

2002. Easter. Multicoloured.
3335 7d. Type **1148** 20 10
3336 14d. Christ surrounded by angels (1300) 40 20
3337 26d.20 Resurrection (1540) 80 40
3338 28d.70 Churches and acorn (painting) (1980) 85 55

2002. National Costumes. Multicoloured.
3339 7d. Type **1149** 20 10
3340 28d.70 Woman wearing dress and bonnet carrying scarf (Bunjevac) 85 55

1150 Zarko Tomic-Sremac

2002. Zarko Tomic-Sremac (folk hero) Commemoration.
3341 **1150** 14d. multicoloured . . 40 20

1151 Roach (*Rutilus rutilus*)

2002. Fish. Multicoloured.
3342 7d. Type **1151** 20 10
3343 14d. Sterlet (*Acipenser ruthenus*) 40 20
3344 26d.20 Beluga (*Huso huso*) 80 40
3345 28d.70 Zander (*Stizostedion lucioperca*) 85 55

1152 Trapeze Artistes

2002. Europa. Circus. Multicoloured.
3346 28d.70 Type **1152** 85 55
3347 50d. Tigers . . . . 1·50 75
MS3348 85 × 74 mm. 45d. Circus ring (47 × 35 mm) . . . . . . 1·70 1·70

1153 Potez 29 Bi-plane

2002. 75th Anniv of Civil Aviation. Multicoloured.
3349 7d. Type **1153** 20 10
3350 28d.70 Boeing 737 . . . . . 85 55

1154 Valley, Tara National Park

2002. Nature Protection. National Parks. Multicoloured.
3351 28d.70 Type **1154** 85 55
3352 50d. Flower and hills, Golija 1·50 75

1155 Windmill, Melenci

1156 City Museum, Niksic

2002. Mills. Multicoloured.
3353 7d. Type **1155** 20 10
3354 28d.70 Watermill, Ljuberadja 85 55

2002. 125th Anniv of Liberation of Niksic.
3355 **1156** 14d. multicoloured . . 40 20

1157 Hand and Globe

2002. Yugoslavia—World Basketball Champions, Indianapolis (2002). Sheet 84 × 73 mm.
MS3356 **1157** 30d. multicoloured 90 90

1158 Buildings, Belgrade

2002. Jufiz XI, Yugoslav Philatelic Exhibition, Belgrade. Sheet 84 × 65 mm.
MS3357 **1158** 30d. multicoloured 90 90

1159 Houseboat (Jana Misurovic)

1160 John the Baptist and Monastery

2002. 34th "Joy in Europe" Meeting. Children's Day. Multicoloured.
3358 28d.70 Type **1159** 85 55
3359 50d. Bird (Manja Pavicevic) 1·50 75

2002. 750th Anniv of Maraca Monastery.
3360 **1160** 16d. multicoloured . . 50 25

2002. No. 2928 surch **0,50.**
3361 50p. on 5p. blue and orange 10 10

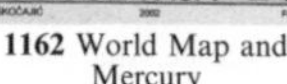

1162 World Map and Mercury — **1163** Man's Costume, Kusadak

2002. Stamp Day. 50th Anniv of ifsda (International Federation of Stamp Dealers Association).
3362 **1162** 16d. multicoloured . . 50 25

2002. Museum Exhibits. Serbian Folk Costumes. Multicoloured.
3363 16d. Type **1163** 50 25
3364 24d. Woman's costume, Komodraz 70 35
3365 26d.20 Man's costume, Novo Selo 80 40
3366 28d.70 Woman and child, Kumodraz 85 55

2002. No. 2889 surch **10**.
3367 10d. on 10000d. blue and violet 30 15

1165 The Nativity, 1546

2002. Christmas. Art. Multicoloured.
3368 12d. Type **1165** 35 20
3369 16d. Nativity, 1618 . . . . 50 25
3370 26d.20 Nativity (15th-century) 80 40
3371 28d.70 Nativity (Sandro Botticelli) 85 55

2002. No. 2927 surch **12**.
3372 12d. on 1p. violet and bistre 35 20

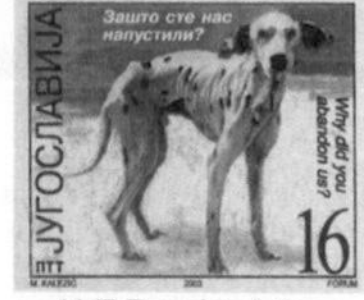

1167 Emaciated Dog

2003. Prevention of Abandoned Dogs Campaign. Multicoloured.
3373 16d. Type **1167** 50 25
3374 24d. Caged dog 70 35
3375 26d.20 Two dogs 80 40
3376 28d.70 Puppy 85 55

On 4 February 2003 Yugoslavia became Serbia & Montenegro. See Serbia & Montenegro for subsequent issues.

EXPRESS LETTER STAMP

CROATIA

1918. Express Letter stamp of Hungary optd **HRVATSKA SHS ZURNO**.
E84 **E 18** 2f. olive and red 10 30

NEWSPAPER STAMPS
CROATIA

1918. Newspaper stamp of Hungary optd **HRVATSKA SHS**.
N83 **N 9** 2f. orange 10 30

SLOVENIA

N 25

1919. Imperf.
N97 **N 25** 2h. yellow . . . . . . 10 1·00

N 30 Cherub with Newspapers

1919. Imperf.
N150 **N 30** 2v. grey 10 15
N155 2v. blue 10 10
N151 4v. grey 15 35
N156 4v. blue 10 15
N152 6v. grey . . . . 3·00 3·75
N157 6v. blue . . . . 4·00 5·00
N153 10v. grey 10 20
N158 10v. blue 10 10
N154 30v. grey 10 35

(N 35) (N 36)

1920. Surch as Type N **35** (2 to 6p.) or Type N **36** (10p. and 30p.).
N164 **N 30** 2p. on 2v. grey . . . 30 85
N169 2p. on 2v. blue . . . 10 30
N165 4p. on 2v. grey . . . 30 85
N170 4p. on 2v. blue . . . 10 30
N166 6p. on 2v. grey . . . 40 85
N171 6p. on 2v. blue . . . 10 30
N167 10p. on 2v. grey . . . 45 1·00
N172 10p. on 2v. blue . . . 15 50
N168 30p. on 2v. grey . . . 45 1·00
N173 30p. on 2v. blue . . . 20 70

OBLIGATORY TAX STAMPS
SERBIA

The following obligatory tax stamps were for use in Serbia only. Except for the Children's Week issues they are all inscribed "SRBIJA".

S 1 Child — **S 2** Children

1990. Children's Week.
S1 **S 1** 30p. red 10 10

1991. Children's Week.
S2 **S 2** 3d. blue 25 10

S 3 Hands and Flower — **S 4** Mother and Child

1992. Anti-cancer Week.
S3 **S 3** 3d. violet and orange . . . 25 10

1993. Anti-cancer Week. No. S3 surch **1500**.
S4 **S 3** 1500d. on 3d. violet and orange 90 75

1993. Serbian Refugee Fund.
S5 **S 4** 42d. green and yellow . . . 20 10
S6 75d. blue and light blue . . 30 15
S7 150d. violet and lilac . . . 40 20

S 5 Hands and Flower — **S 6**

1994. Anti-cancer Week.
S8 **S 5** 12p. violet 25 10
See also No. S11.

1994.
S9 **S 6** 6p. purple 15 10

S 7 Museum

1994. 150th Anniv of National Museum, Belgrade.
S10 **S 7** 5p. blue 15 10

1995. Anti-cancer Week.
S11 **S 5** 6p. mauve 15 10

OFFICIAL STAMPS

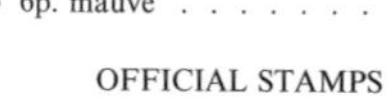

O 130

1946.
O540 **O 130** 50p. orange 15 10
O541 1d. green 15 10
O542 1d.50 olive 30 10
O543 2d.50 red 30 10
O544 4d. brown 65 10
O545 5d. blue 85 10
O546 8d. brown . . . . . 1·25 15
O547 12d. violet . . . . . 1·60 30

POSTAGE DUE STAMPS
BOSNIA AND HERZEGOVINA

ДРЖАВА С.Х.С.
БОСНА И
ХЕРЦЕГОВИНА

хелера

(D 5)

КРАЉЕВСТВО
СРБА. ХРВАТА
И СЛОВЕНАЦА

ПОРТО

5 X

(D 13)

1918. Postage Due Stamps of Bosnia optd as Type **D 5** or **DRZAVA S.H.S. BOSNA I HERCEGOVINA HELERA.**
D19 **D 35** 2h. red 10 10
D20 4h. red 40 40
D21 5h. red 10 10
D22 6h. red 75 50
D23 10h. red 10 10
D24 15h. red . . . . 5·00 6·00
D25 20h. red 10 10
D26 25h. red 50 50
D27 30h. red 50 50
D28 40h. red 25 25
D29 50h. red . . . . 1·00 1·00
D30 1k. blue 50 50
D31 3k. blue 40 40

1919. "Eagle" type of Bosnia surch as Type **D 13** or **KRALJEVSTVO SRBA, HRVATA I SLOVENACA PORTO** and value.
D50 **2** 2h. on 35h. blue and black 50 75
D51 5h. on 45h. blue and black 75 1·00
D52 10h. on 10h. red 10 10
D53 15h. on 40h. orange and black 50 60
D54 20h. on 5h. green 10 10
D55 25h. on 20h. pink and black 35 45
D56 30h. on 30h. bistre and black 35 45
D57 1k. on 50h. purple 15 50
D58 3k. on 25h. blue 35 50

КРАЉЕВСТВО
СРБА, ХРВАТА
И СЛОВЕНАЦА
40

40 хелера 40

(D 14)

1919. Postage Due stamps of Bosnia with surch or optd as Type **D 14** or **KRALJEVSTVO SRBA, HRVATA SLOVENACA,** and value.
D59 **D 4** 40h. on 6h. black, red and yellow 10 10
D60 50h. on 8h. black, red and yellow 10 10
D61 200h. black, red & green 6·00 5·00
D62 4k. on 7h. black, red and yellow 40 50

CROATIA

1919. Postage Due stamps of Hungary, with figures in red (except 50f. in black), optd **HRVATSKA SHS.**
D85 **D 9** 1f. green (No. D190) . . 25·00 35·00
D86 2f. green . . . . 1·25 1·25
D87 10f. green 90 90
D88 12f. green . . . . 70·00 90·00
D89 15f. green 65 65
D90 20f. green 65 65
D91 30f. green . . . . 1·75 1·75
D92 50f. green (No. D177) . . 28·00 35·00

SLOVENIA

D 30

1919.
D150 **D 30** 5v. red 10 10
D151 10v. red 10 10
D152 20v. red 10 10
D153 50v. red 10 10
D154 1k. blue 30 30
D155 5k. blue 60 30
D156 10k. blue . . . . . . 1·10 75

(D 35) (D 36)

1920. Stamps of 1919 issue surch as Types **D 35** or **D 36.**
D164 **25** 5p. on 15v. blue 10 10
D165 10p. on 15v. blue 60 60
D166 20p. on 15v. blue 15 10
D167 50p. on 15v. blue 10 10
D168 **26** 1d. on 30v. pink (or red) 15 15
D169 3d. on 30v. pink (or red) 30 15
D170 8d. on 30v. pink (or red) 85 65

GENERAL ISSUES

D 39 King Alexander I when Prince — **D 40**

1921.
D182 **D 39** 10 on 5p. green . . . 15 10
D183 30 on 5p. green . . . 25 10

1921.
D184 **D 40** 10p. red 10 10
D185 30p. green 15 10
D197 50p. violet 10 10
D198 1d. brown 15 10
D188 2d. blue 25 10
D200 5d. orange . . . . . 1·50 10
D190 10d. brown . . . . . 6·00 10
D191 25d. pink . . . . . . 30·00 1·25
D192 50d. green . . . . . . 25·00 1·50
There are two issues in this type, differing in the lettering, etc.

1928. Surcharged **10.**
D233 **D 40** 10 on 25d. pink . . . 3·00 25
D234 10 on 50d. green . . . 3·00 25

D 56 — (D 62)

1931.
D259 **D 56** 50p. violet 10 10
D260 1d. red 10 10
D261 2d. blue 10 10
D262 5d. orange 10 10
D263 10d. brown 20 15

1933. Optd with Type **D 62.**
D293a **D 40** 50p. violet 15 10
D294a 1d. brown 15 10
D295a 2d. blue 30 10
D296b 5d. orange 75 10
D297a 10d. brown . . . . . 3·50 10

1933. Red Cross. As T **62** but inscr "PORTO" in Latin and Cyrillic characters.
D298 **62** 50p. red and green . . . 40 10

DEMOCRATIC FEDERATION OF YUGOSLAVIA
(a) REGIONAL ISSUES
CROATIA

1945. Zagreb issue. Croatian Postage Due stamps of 1942 surch **DEMOKRATSKA FEDERATIVNA JUGOSLAVIJA,** value and star.
RD45 **D 15** 40k. on 50b. brown and blue 25 25
RD46 60k. on 1k. brown and blue 25 25
RD47 80k. on 2k. brown and blue 25 25
RD48 100k. on 5k. brown and blue 25 25
RD49 200k. on 6k. brown and blue 25 25

MONTENEGRO

1945. Cetinje issue. National Poem issue of Italian Occupation surch as Type R **4**, with "PORTO" in addition.
RD61 10l. on 5c. violet £225 £250
RD62 20l. on 5l. red on buff . . 75·00 70·00

SERBIA

1944. Senta issue. No. D684 of Hungary optd with a large star, **8.X.1944** and "Yugoslavia" in Cyrillic characters and surch in addition.
RD73 D **115** 10(f.) on 2f. brown 40·00 40·00

(b) GENERAL ISSUES

D 114 **D 115** **D 126**

1944. Postage Due stamps of Serbia optd in Cyrillic characters, as Type D **114**.
D487 10d. red 30 50
D488 20d. blue 30 50

1945. (a) Value in black.
D489 D **115** 2d. brown 10 10
D490 3d. violet 10 10
D491 5d. green 10 10
D492 7d. brown 10 10
D493 10d. lilac 15 10
D494 20d. blue 20 10
D495 30d. green 35 15
D496 40d. red 40 20

(b) Value in colour.
D497 D **115** 1d. green 10 10
D498 1d.50 blue 10 10
D499 2d. red 15 10
D500 3d. brown 30 10
D501 4d. violet 40 20

1946.
D 527 D **126** 50p. orange 10 10
D 528 1d. orange 10 10
D 724 1d. brown 40 10
D 529 2d. blue 15 10
D 725 2d. green 40 10
D 530 3d. green 20 10
D 531 5d. violet 20 10
D 726 5d. blue 60 10
D 532 7d. red 75 15
D 533 10d. pink . . . . . 1·25 25
D 727 10d. red . . . . . . 2·50 10
D 534 20d. lake . . . . . 1·75 50
D1030 20d. violet . . . . . 2·50 10
D1031 30d. orange . . . . 5·50 20
D1032 50d. blue . . . . . 27·00 80
D1033 100d. purple . . . . 13·00 1·00

1947. Red Cross. As No. 545, but with "PORTO" added. Colour changed.
D546 **131** 50p. green and red . . . 30 10

1948. Red Cross. As No. 594, but inscr "PORTO".
D595 **152** 50p. red and green . . . 25 10

1949. Red Cross. As T **160** but inscr "PORTO".
D617 **160** 50p. purple and red . . 40 10

ФНРЈУГОСЛАВИЈА

FNR JUGOSLAVIJA

(D **168**) **D 175** Map

1950. Optd with Type D **168**.
D637 D **115** 1d.50 blue 10 10
D638 3d. brown 10 10
D639 4d. violet 20 15

1950. Red Cross.
D665 D **175** 50p. brown and red 30 10

1951. Red Cross. Inscr "PORTO".
D703 **191** 50p. green and red . . . 30 10

D 202 **D 251** Child with Toy

1952. Red Cross.
D741 D **202** 50p. red and grey . . 40 10

1953. Red Cross. Inscr "PORTO".
D762 **211** 2d. red and brown . . . 50 15

1954. Red Cross. Inscr "PORTO".
D783 **216** 2d. red and lilac 45 15

1955. Children's Week. Inscr "PORTO".
D802 **222** 2d. green and light green 40 15

1955. Red Cross. Inscr "PORTO".
D804 **224** 2d. brown, choc & red 40 20

1956. Red Cross. Inscr "PORTO".
D820 **228** 2d. green, turq & red 40 15

1956. Children's Week. Inscr "PORTO".
D835 **232** 2d. chocolate & lt brn 40 15

1957. Red Cross. Inscr "PORTO".
D844 **234** 2d. red, black and grey 40 15

1957. Children's Week. Inscr "PORTO".
D867 **240** 2d. brown and blue . . 40 15

1958. Red Cross. Inscr "PORTO".
D879 **245** 2d. multicoloured . . . 70 25

1958. Children's Week.
D913 D **251** 2d. black and blue 50 15

1959. Red Cross. Inscr "PORTO".
D927 **255** 2d. orange and red . . 30 15

1959. Children's Week. As T **260**. Inscr "PORTO".
D947 2d. purple and yellow . . . 35 15
DESIGN: Tree, cockerel and ears of wheat.

1960. Red Cross. Inscr "PORTO".
D956 **262** 2d. purple and red . . . 30 15

1960. Children's Week. As T **265**. Inscr "PORTO".
D970 2d. blue (Young boy) . . . 30 15

1961. Red Cross. Inscr "PORTO". Perf or imperf.
D982 **268** 2d. multicoloured . . . 35 15

1961. Children's Week. Inscr "PORTO".
D1020 **274** 2d. green and sepia . . 30 15

1962. Red Cross. Inscr "PORTO".
D1043 **281** 5d. red, brown and blue 30 15

1963. Red Cross Cent. and Week. Inscr "PORTO".
D1074 **288** 5d. red, purple & orge 35 15

REGISTERED LETTER STAMPS

R 960 Hands holding Envelope

1993. No value expressed.
R2864 R **960** R (11000d.) blue . . 55 15

YUNNANFU Pt. 17

Yunnanfu (formerly Yunnansen), the chief city of the Chinese province of Yunnan, had an Indo-Chinese Post Office from 1900 to 1922.

1901. 100 centimes = 1 franc.
1918. 100 cents = 1 piastre.

Stamps of Indo-China surcharged.

1903. "Tablet" key-type surch with value in Chinese and **YUNNANSEN.**
1 D 1c. black and red on blue . . 7·25 7·75
2 2c. brown and blue on buff 7·00 7·25
3 4c. brown and blue on grey 5·75 7·50
4 5c. green and red . . . . 5·50 6·50
5 10c. red and blue . . . . 5·00 6·50
6 15c. grey and red . . . . 6·50 6·50
7 20c. red and blue on green 6·50 8·25
8 25c. blue and red . . . . 6·00 8·00
9 30c. brown and blue on drab 9·25 8·50
10 40c. red and blue on yellow 70·00 50·00
11 50c. red and blue on pink £275 £275
12 50c. brown and red on blue £160 £160
13 75c. brown and red on orange . . . . . . 60·00 55·00
14 1f. green and red . . . . 55·00 60·00
15 5f. mauve and blue on lilac £100 £110

1906. Surch **Yunnan-Fou** and value in Chinese.
16 **8** 1c. green . . . . 2·75 3·50
17 2c. purple on yellow . . . 3·00 4·00
18 4c. mauve on blue . . . . 3·25 3·75
19 5c. green . . . . 3·75 4·00
20 10c. pink . . . . 3·50 4·50
21 15c. brown on blue . . . 8·00 8·75
22 20c. red on green . . . . 4·75 5·25
23 25c. blue . . . . 5·25 5·50
24 30c. brown on cream . . . 5·00 5·25
25 35c. black on yellow . . . 9·00 9·25
26 40c. black on grey . . . . 6·25 6·50
27 50c. brown on cream . . . 7·25 10·50
28 D 75c. brown on orange . . 50·00 55·00
29 **8** 1f. green . . . . 21·00 30·00
30 2f. brown on yellow . . . . 21·00 30·00
31 D 5f. mauve on lilac . . . . . 70·00 85·00
32 **8** 10f. red on green . . . . . 80·00 90·00

1908. Native types surch **YUNNANFOU** and value in Chinese.
33 **10** 1c. black and brown . . . . 1·25 70
34 2c. black and brown . . . . 1·60 1·40
35 4c. black and blue . . . . . 1·75 1·75
36 5c. black and green . . . . 1·75 1·60
37 10c. black and red . . . . 2·00 1·00
38 15c. black and violet . . . . 4·25 4·00
39 **11** 20c. black and violet . . . . 5·00 5·25
40 25c. black and blue . . . . 5·00 5·25
41 30c. black and brown . . . 6·75 7·00
42 35c. black and green . . . . 6·50 7·00
43 40c. black and brown . . . 9·00 10·50
44 50c. black and red . . . . 8·00 10·50
45 **12** 75c. black and orange . . . 9·25 10·00
46 1f. black and red . . . . . 14·50 15·00
47 2f. black and green . . . . 24·00 30·00
48 5f. black and blue . . . . 55·00 60·00
49 10f. black and violet . . . . 95·00 £110

1919. As last, surch in addition with value in figures and words.
50 **10** ⅖c. on 1c. black and brown 1·10 70
51 ⅘c. on 2c. black and brown 1·25 2·00
52 1⅗c. on 4c. black and blue 1·25 3·25
53 2c. on 5c. black and green 1·75 1·40
54 4c. on 10c. black and red 2·50 90
55 6c. on 15c. black and violet 2·00 1·40
56 **11** 8c. on 20c. black and violet 3·00 3·25
57 10c. on 25c. black and blue 3·75 3·75
58 12c. on 30c. black & brown 3·50 3·50
59 14c. on 35c. black and green 4·75 4·75
60 16c. on 40c. black & brown 4·75 4·25
61 20c. on 50c. black and red 3·50 3·25
62 **12** 30c. on 75c. black & orange 4·50 5·25
63 40c. on 1f. black and red . . 5·75 6·00
64 80c. on 2f. black and green 7·75 8·25
65 2p. on 5f. black and blue . . 35·00 42·00
66 4p. on 10f. black and violet 20·00 18·00

ZAIRE Pt. 14

In 1971 the Congo Republic (Kinshasa), formerly Belgian Congo, changed its name to Zaire.

100 sengi = 1 (li)kuta; 100 (ma)kuta = 1 zaire.

176 Nurse tending Child

177 Pres. Mobutu, Memorial and Emblem

1971. 25th Anniv of UNICEF. Multicoloured.
788 4k. Type **176** 30 20
789 14k. Zaire Republic on map of Africa 85 55
790 17k. Child in African village 1·10 90

1972. 5th Anniv of Revolution.
791 **177** 4k. multicoloured . . . . 3·25 2·75
792 14k. multicoloured . . . 3·25 2·75
793 22k. multicoloured . . . 4·50 3·25

177a Arms

177b Pres. Mobutu

1972.
794 **177a** 10s. orange and black . . 10 10
795 40s. blue and black . . . 10 10
796 50s. yellow and black . . 10 10
797 **177b** 1k. multicoloured . . . 10 10
798 2k. multicoloured . . . 10 10
799 3k. multicoloured . . . 10 10
800 4k. multicoloured . . . 10 10
801 5k. multicoloured . . . 15 10
802 6k. multicoloured . . . 15 10
803 8k. multicoloured . . . 20 15
804 9k. multicoloured . . . 30 15
805 10k. multicoloured . . . 35 15
806 14k. multicoloured . . . 45 20
807 17k. multicoloured . . . 50 35
808 20k. multicoloured . . . 65 40
809 50k. multicoloured . . . 1·75 85
810 100k. multicoloured . . . 3·50 2·00

178 Inga Dam

1973. Inga Dam. Completion of 1st Stage.
811 **178** 0.04z. multicoloured . . . 10 10
812 0.14z. multicoloured . . . 45 35
813 0.18z. multicoloured . . . 80 45

1973. As T **177b**, but face values in Zaires.
814 0.01z. multicoloured 10 10
815 0.02z. multicoloured 10 10
816 0.03z. multicoloured 10 10
817 0.04z. multicoloured 10 10
818 0.10z. multicoloured 45 20
819 0.14z. multicoloured 80 35

179 Africa on World Map

1973. 3rd International Fair, Kinshasa.
820 **179** 0.04z. multicoloured . . . 15 10
821 0.07z. multicoloured . . . 30 15
822 0.18z. multicoloured . . . 80 45

180 Emblem on Hand

1973. 50th Anniv of Criminal Police Organization (Interpol).
823 **180** 0.06z. multicoloured . . . 35 20
824 0.14z. multicoloured . . . 80 35

181 Leopard with Football on Globe

1974. World Cup Football Championship, Munich.
825 **181** 1k. multicoloured 10 10
826 2k. multicoloured 10 10
827 3k. multicoloured 15 10
828 4k. multicoloured 20 10
829 5k. multicoloured 30 10
830 14k. multicoloured . . . 1·40 55

182 Muhamed Ali and George Foreman

185 Waterfall

1974. World Heavyweight Boxing Title Fight, Kinshasa.
831 **182** 1k. multicoloured 10 10
832 4k. multicoloured 15 10
833 6k. multicoloured 20 10
834 14k. multicoloured . . . 55 30
835 20k. multicoloured . . . 90 40

1975. World Heavyweight Boxing Title Fight, Kinshasa. As T **182** optd with amended date **25-9-74.**
836 **182** 0.01z. multicoloured . . . 10 10
837 0.04z. multicoloured . . . 10 10
838 0.06z. multicoloured . . . 20 10
839 0.14z. multicoloured . . . 45 15
840 0.20z. multicoloured . . . 80 30

Nos. 836/40 differ from Type **182** by having the face values expressed as decimals of the zaire. Both dates are in fact incorrect as the fight was held on 30 October 1974.

1975. 12th General Assembly of International Union for Conservation of National Resources, Kinshasa.
858 **185** 1k. multicoloured 15 15
859 2k. multicoloured 15 15
860 3k. multicoloured 30 15
861 4k. multicoloured 45 15
862 5k. multicoloured 60 15

186 Okapis

1975. 50th Anniv of Virunga National Park.
863 **186** 1k. multicoloured 20 20
864 2k. multicoloured 40 20
865 3k. multicoloured 65 20
866 4k. multicoloured 85 20
867 5k. multicoloured 1·10 20

187 Woman Judge with Barristers

1975. International Women's Year.
868 **187** 1k. multicoloured 10 10
869 2k. multicoloured 10 10
870 4k. multicoloured 20 10
871 14k. multicoloured 65 20

188 Sozacom Building

189 Pende Statuette

1976. 10th Anniv of "New Regime". Mult.
872 1k. Type **188** 10 10
873 2k. Siderna Maluku Industrial Complex (horiz) 10 10
874 3k. Flour mill, Matadi 10 10
875 4k. Women parachutists (horiz) 20 10
876 8k. Pres. Mobutu with Mao Tse-Tung 35 10
877 10k. Soldiers clearing vegetation along the Salongo (horiz) 45 20
878 14k. Pres. Mobutu addressing U.N. General Assembly, 4 October 1973 (horiz) 65 30
879 15k. Rejoicing crowd (horiz) 80 20

1977. Masks and Statuettes. Multicoloured.
880 2z. Type **189** 10 10
881 4z. Type **189** 10 10
882 5z. Tshokwe mask 10 10
883 7z. As 5k. 15 10
884 10z. Suku mask 20 10
885 14z. As 10k. 35 15
886 15z. Kongo statuette 40 15
887 18z. As 15k. 45 30
888 20z. Kuba mask 65 35
889 25z. As 20k. 80 45

190 U.P.U. Emblem on Map

192 Freshwater Butterflyfish

1977. Centenary of Universal Postal Union.
890 **190** 1k. multicoloured 10 10
891 4k. multicoloured 20 10
892 7k. multicoloured 50 35
893 50k. multicoloured 4·25 2·25

1977. Various stamps of Congo (Kinshasa) and Zaire, surch **REPUBLIQUE DU ZAIRE** or with new value only (No. 904).
894 **158** 1k. on 10s. red and black 10 10
895 **152** 2k. on 9.6k. black on red 10 10
896 **158** 5k. on 30s. green & black 10 10
897 **173** 10k. on 10s. mult 40 10
898 **158** 10k. on 15s. blue & black 15 10
899 – 20k. on 9.6k. mult (No. 673) 40 10
900 **167** 25k. on 10s. mult 75 20
901 **174** 30k. on 12s. mult 75 20
902 **159** 40k. on 9.6k. mult 1·10 30
903 **168** 48k. on 10s. mult 1·25 35
904 **158** 100k. on 40s. blue & black 2·75 60

1978. Fishes. Multicoloured.
905 30s. Type **192** 10 15
906 70s. Striped killifish 10 15
907 5k. Banded ctenopoma 15 15
908 8k. Electric catfish 25 15
909 10k. Jewel cichlid 45 20
910 30k. Isidor's elephantfish 70 60
911 40k. Blotched upsidedown catfish 1·10 65
912 48k. Golden Julie 1·40 80
913 100k. Brien's notho 3·50 1·75

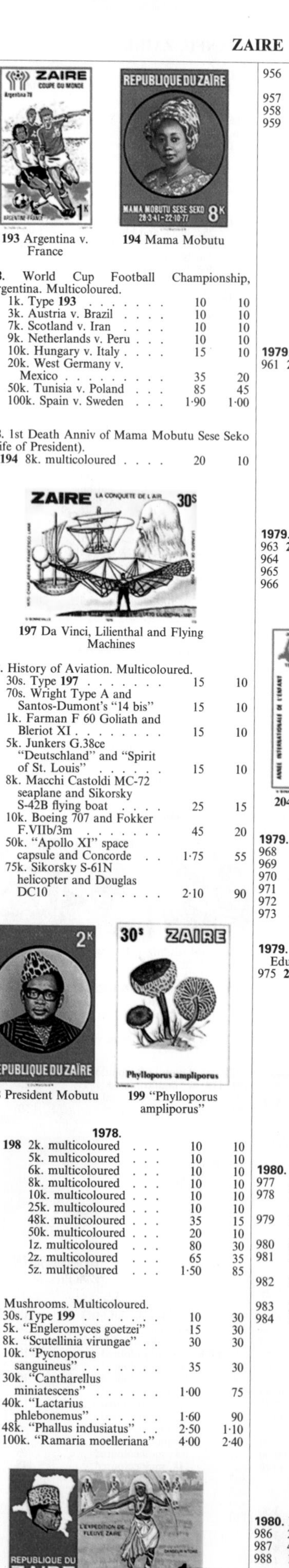

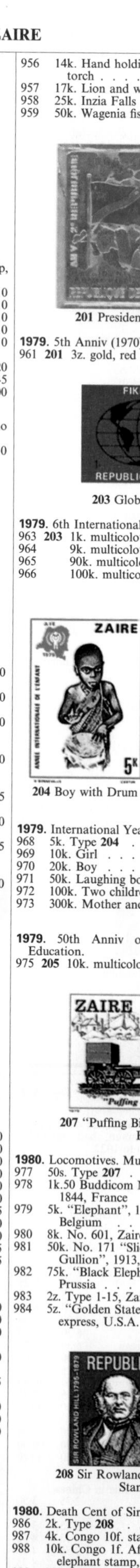

193 Argentina v. France

194 Mama Mobutu

1978. World Cup Football Championship, Argentina. Multicoloured.
915 1k. Type **193** 10 10
916 3k. Austria v. Brazil 10 10
917 7k. Scotland v. Iran 10 10
918 9k. Netherlands v. Peru 10 10
919 10k. Hungary v. Italy 15 10
920 20k. West Germany v. Mexico 35 20
921 50k. Tunisia v. Poland 85 45
922 100k. Spain v. Sweden 1·90 1·00

1978. 1st Death Anniv of Mama Mobutu Sese Seko (wife of President).
924 **194** 8k. multicoloured 20 10

197 Da Vinci, Lilienthal and Flying Machines

1978. History of Aviation. Multicoloured.
927 30s. Type **197** 15 10
928 70s. Wright Type A and Santos-Dumont's "14 bis" 15 10
929 1k. Farman F 60 Goliath and Bleriot XI 15 10
930 5k. Junkers G.38ce "Deutschland" and "Spirit of St. Louis" 15 10
931 8k. Macchi Castoldi MC-72 seaplane and Sikorsky S-42B flying boat 25 15
932 10k. Boeing 707 and Fokker F.VIIb/3m 45 20
933 50k. "Apollo XI" space capsule and Concorde 1·75 55
934 75k. Sikorsky S-61N helicopter and Douglas DC10 2·10 90

198 President Mobutu

199 "Phylloporus ampliporus"

1978.
936 **198** 2k. multicoloured 10 10
937 5k. multicoloured 10 10
938 6k. multicoloured 10 10
939 8k. multicoloured 10 10
940 10k. multicoloured 10 10
941 25k. multicoloured 10 10
942 48k. multicoloured 35 15
942a 50k. multicoloured 20 10
943 1z. multicoloured 80 30
943a 2z. multicoloured 65 35
943b 5z. multicoloured 1·50 85

1979. Mushrooms. Multicoloured.
944 30s. Type **199** 10 30
945 5k. "Engleromyces goetzei" 15 30
946 8k. "Scutellinia virungae" 30 30
947 10k. "Pycnoporus sanguineus" 35 30
948 30k. "Cantharellus miniatescens" 1·00 75
949 40k. "Lactarius phlebonemus" 1·60 90
950 48k. "Phallus indusiatus" 2·50 1·10
951 100k. "Ramaria moelleriana" 4·00 2·40

200 Ntore Dancer

1979. Zaire River Expedition. Multicoloured.
952 1k. Type **200** 10 10
953 3k. Regal sunbird 1·50 25
954 4k. African elephant 10 10
955 10k. Diamond, cotton boll and tobacco 10 10
956 14k. Hand holding flaming torch 15 10
957 17k. Lion and water lily 20 15
958 25k. Inzia Falls 30 15
959 50k. Wagenia fisherman 55 35

201 President Mobutu and Flag

1979. 5th Anniv (1970) of 2nd Republic.
961 **201** 3z. gold, red and blue 26·00

203 Globe and Drummer

1979. 6th International Fair, Kinshasa.
963 **203** 1k. multicoloured 10 10
964 9k. multicoloured 10 10
965 90k. multicoloured 65 30
966 100k. multicoloured 80 35

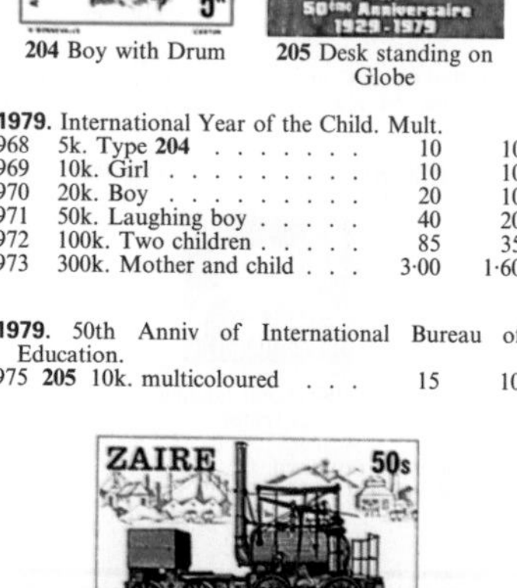

204 Boy with Drum

205 Desk standing on Globe

1979. International Year of the Child. Mult.
968 5k. Type **204** 10 10
969 10k. Girl 10 10
970 20k. Boy 20 10
971 50k. Laughing boy 40 20
972 100k. Two children 85 35
973 300k. Mother and child 3·00 1·60

1979. 50th Anniv of International Bureau of Education.
975 **205** 10k. multicoloured 15 10

207 "Puffing Billy", 1813–14, Great Britain

1980. Locomotives. Multicoloured.
977 50s. Type **207** 10 10
978 1k.50 Buddicom No. 33, 1844, France 10 10
979 5k. "Elephant", 1835, Belgium 10 10
980 8k. No. 601, Zaire 10 10
981 50k. No. 171 "Slieve Gullion", 1913, Ireland 70 70
982 75k. "Black Elephant", Prussia 1·00 1·00
983 2z. Type 1-15, Zaire 2·75 2·75
984 5z. "Golden State Limited" express, U.S.A. 7·00 7·00

208 Sir Rowland Hill and Congo 5f. Stamp, 1886

1980. Death Cent of Sir Rowland Hill. Mult.
986 2k. Type **208** 10 10
987 4k. Congo 10f. stamp, 1887 10 10
988 10k. Congo 1f. African elephant stamp, 1884 10 10
989 20k. Belgian Congo overprinted 3f.50 stamp, 1909 15 10
990 40k. Belgian Congo 10f. African Elephant stamp, 1925 20 10
991 150k. Belgian Congo 1f.50+1f.50 Chimpanzees stamp, 1939 85 40
992 200k. Belgian Congo 1f.75 Leopard stamp, 1942 1·25 60
993 250k. Belgian Congo 2f.50 Railway stamp, 1948 3·00 2·50

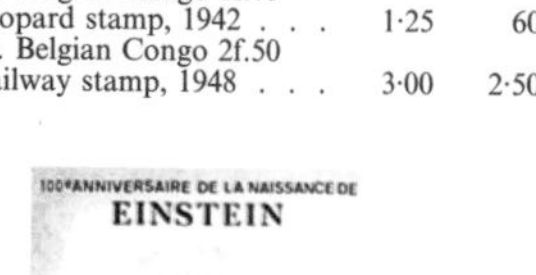

209 Einstein

1980. Birth Cent of Albert Einstein (physicist).
995 **209** 40s. brown, black & mve 10 10
996 2k. brown, black & green 10 10
997 4k. brown, black & yell 10 10
998 15k. brown, black & blue 15 10
999 50k. brown, black and red 35 20
1000 300k. brown, blk & lilac 2·00 1·00

210 Booth Memorial Medical Centre, Flushing, New York

1980. Centenary of Salvation Army in the United States. Multicoloured.
1002 50s. Type **210** 10 10
1003 4k.50 Arrival of Railton in America 10 10
1004 10k. Mobile dispensary, Musina, Zaire 10 10
1005 20k. General Evangeline Booth and salvationist holding child (vert) 10 10
1006 40k. Army band 20 15
1007 75k. Mobile clinic in bush, Zaire 45 20
1008 1z.50 Canteen serving firefighters 90 40
1009 2z. American unit marching with flags (vert) 1·40 55

212 Musical Instrument

1980. 75th Anniv of Rotary International. Mult.
1013 50k. Drawing of mother and child (Kamba) 30 15
1014 100k. Type **212** 55 30
1015 500k. Statuette (Liyolo) (vert) 2·00 1·40

213 Red-tailed butterflyfish

1980. Tropical Fishes Multicoloured.
1017 1k. Type **213** 10 10
1018 5k. Sail-finned tang 10 10
1019 10k. Yellow-faced angelfish 10 10
1020 20k. Blue-ringed angelfish 20 10
1021 50k. Flame angelfish 45 20
1022 150k. Harlequin filefish 1·25 55
1023 200k. Black triggerfish 1·75 90
1024 250k. Picasso triggerfish 2·25 1·10

214 Belgium 40c. Congo Independence Stamp, 1960 and "Phibelza"

1980. "Phibelza" Belgian–Zaire Stamp Exhibition, Kinshasa. Multicoloured.

1026	1z. Type **214**	40	30
1027	1z. Congo 20f. Independence stamp, 1960	40	30
1028	2z. Belgium 10f.+5f. Zoo stamp, 1968	80	20
1029	2z. Congo 40c. Birds stamp, 1963	85	40
1030	3z. Belgium 10f.+5f. Brussels stamp, 1971	1·25	85
1031	3z. Zaire 22k. stamp, 1972	1·25	85
1032	4z. Belgium 25f.+10f. stamp, 1980	1·60	1·10
1033	4z. Congo 24f. stamp, 1966	1·60	1·10

Nos. 1026/33 exist in two versions with the exhibition logo either at the right or the left of the design. Prices are the same for either version.

1980. 20th Anniv of Independence. Various stamps optd **20e Anniversaire - Independance - 1960-1980.**

1034	**207**	50s. "Puffing Billy"	25	25
1035	–	1k.50 Buddicom locomotive No. 33 (No. 978)	40	40
1036	–	10k. Boeing 707 and Fokker F.VIIb/3m (No. 932)	50	50
1037	–	50k. "Slieve Gullion" (No. 981)	60	60
1038	–	75k. Sikorsky S-61N helicopter and Douglas DC-10 (No. 934)	70	70
1039	**203**	100k. Globe and drummer	45	25
1040	–	1z. on 5z. on 100k. Two children (No. 972)	45	25
1041	–	250k. Rowland Hill and railway stamp of 1948 (No. 993)	3·50	3·50
1042	–	5z. on 100k. Two children (No. 972)	2·75	1·25

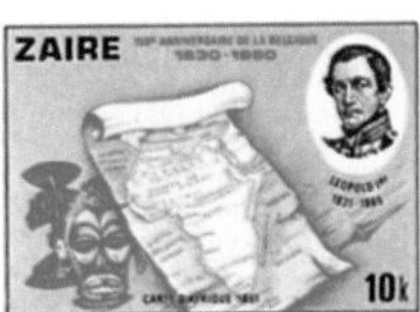

216 Leopold I and 1851 Map of Africa

1980. 150th Anniv of Belgian Independence.

1043	**216**	10k. green and blue	10	10
1044	–	75k. brown and blue	45	20
1045	–	100k. violet and blue	45	20
1046	–	145k. blue and deep blue	1·60	50
1047	–	270k. red and blue	1·60	85

DESIGNS: 75k. Leopold II and Stanley's expedition; 100k. Albert I and colonial troops of 1914–18 war; 145k. Leopold III and African animals; 270k. Baudouin I and visit to Zaire of King Baudouin and Queen Fabiola.

217 Angels appearing to Shepherds

1980. Christmas. Multicoloured.

1048	10k. Type **217**	10	10
1049	75k. Flight into Egypt	35	20
1050	80k. Three Kings	45	20
1051	145k. In the stable	80	45

218 Girl dancing to Cello

1981. Norman Rockwell Paintings. Multicoloured.

1053	10k. Type **218**	10	10
1054	20k. Couple with saluting boy scout	10	10
1055	50k. Sorter reading mail	20	10
1056	80k. Cupid whispering in youth's ear	35	15
1057	100k. Signing Declaration of Independence	50	20
1058	125k. Boy looking through telescope held by sailor	80	25
1059	175k. Boy in armchair playing trumpet	1·10	55
1060	200k. Weakling exercising with dumb bells	1·10	50

219 Pope John-Paul II and Pres. Mobutu **220** Footballers

1981. Papal Visit. Multicoloured.

1061	5k. Pope kneeling at shrine (horiz)	10	10
1062	10k. Pres. Mobutu greeting Pope (horiz)	10	10
1063	50k. Type **219**	20	10
1064	100k. Pope talking to child (horiz)	65	35
1065	500k. Pope leading prayers	2·75	1·25
1066	800k. Pope making speech (horiz)	4·00	2·00

1981. World Cup Football Championship, Spain (1982).

1067	**220**	2k. multicoloured	10	10
1068	–	10k. multicoloured	10	10
1069	–	25k. multicoloured	10	10
1070	–	90k. multicoloured	35	15
1071	–	2z. multicoloured	65	35
1072	–	3z. multicoloured	1·25	55
1073	–	6z. multicoloured	2·40	1·10
1074	–	8z. multicoloured	3·25	1·60

DESIGN: Nos. 1068/74, Similar football scenes.

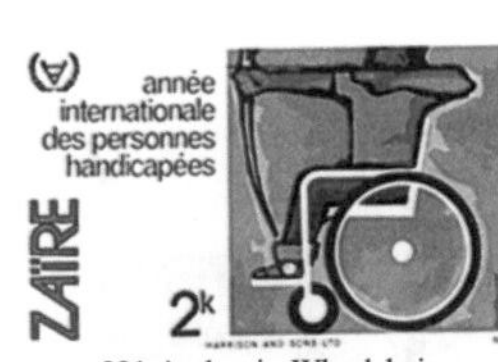

221 Archer in Wheelchair

1981. International Year of Disabled People. Multicoloured.

1076	2k. Type **221**	10	10
1077	5k. Ear and sound wave	10	10
1078	10k. One-legged person with crutch	10	10
1079	18k. Glasses, Braille and white cane	10	10
1080	50k. Crippled legs	20	10
1081	150k. Sign language	45	20
1082	500k. Hand and model showing joints	1·60	90
1083	800k. Dove shedding feathers	2·50	1·60

222 Children performing Carols **224** Red Cross Helicopters

1981. Christmas. Multicoloured.

1084	25k. Type **222**	10	10
1085	1z. Boy lighting candle	35	15
1086	1z.50 Boy praying	45	20
1087	3z. Girl with presents	95	45
1088	5z. Children admiring baby	1·75	85

1982. Telecommunications and Health. Mult.

1091	1k. Type **224**	10	10
1092	25k. Doctor and telephone	10	10
1093	90k. Antenna and map	20	15
1094	1z. Patient	35	15
1095	1z.70 Teleprinter	45	20
1096	3z. Nurse and television	90	35
1097	4z.50 Tape recorder	1·60	85
1098	5z. Babies and walkie-talkie	1·75	85

225 U.P.U. Emblem

1982. 20th Anniv (1981) of African Postal Union.

1099	**225**	1z. green and gold	45	20

226 El Salvador v. Hungary

1982. World Cup Football Championship, Spain. Multicoloured.

1100	2k. Type **226**	10	10
1101	8k. Cameroun v. Peru	10	10
1102	25k. Brazil v. Russia	10	10
1103	50k. Kuwait v. Czechoslovakia	10	10
1104	90k. Yugoslavia v. Northern Ireland	30	15
1105	1z. Austria v. Chile	35	15
1106	1z.45 France v. England	45	15
1107	1z.70 West Germany v. Algeria	55	35
1108	3z. Spain v. Honduras	1·00	50
1109	3z.50 Belgium v. Argentina	1·10	60
1110	5z. Scotland v. New Zealand	1·60	85
1111	6z. Italy v. Poland	2·00	95

228 Hands reaching towards Zaire

1982. Ninth French and African Heads of State Conference, Kinshasa.

1113	**228**	75k. multicoloured	20	10
1114		90k. multicoloured	30	15
1115		1z. multicoloured	35	15
1116		1z.50 multicoloured	45	20
1117		3z. multicoloured	95	50
1118		5z. multicoloured	1·60	85
1119		8z. multicoloured	2·50	1·10

229 Lions

1982. Virunga National Park. Multicoloured.

1120	1z. Type **229**	40	25
1121	1z.70 African buffalo	65	50
1122	3z.50 African elephant	1·25	90
1123	6z.50 Topi	2·25	1·40
1124	8z. Hippopotamus	3·25	1·90
1125	10z. Savanna monkey	4·50	2·25
1126	10z. Leopard	4·50	2·25

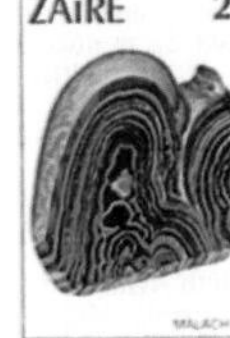

230 Scout Camp **233** Malachite

231 Red-billed Quelea

1982. 75th Anniv of Boy Scout Movement. Multicoloured.

1127	90k. Type **230**	30	15
1128	1z.70 Camp-fire	55	25
1129	3z. Scout	95	45
1130	5z. Scout carrying injured person	1·75	85
1131	8z. Scout signalling with flags	2·75	1·10

1982. Birds. Multicoloured.

1133	25k. Type **231**	10	10
1134	50k. African pygmy kingfisher	15	10
1135	90k. Green turaco	35	15
1136	1z.50 Three-banded plover	45	25
1137	1z.70 Temminck's courser	55	30
1138	2z. Bennett's woodpecker	65	45
1139	3z. Little grebe	80	60
1140	3z.50 Lizard buzzard (vert)	1·00	80
1141	5z. African black crake	2·00	90
1142	8z. White-headed vulture (vert)	3·25	1·75

1983. Minerals. Multicoloured.

1144	2k. Type **233**	10	10
1145	45k. Quartz (horiz)	20	10
1146	75k. Gold (horiz)	35	10
1147	1z. Uranium and pitchblende (horiz)	45	15
1148	1z.50 Bournonite	55	30
1149	3z. Cassiterite (horiz)	1·10	50
1150	6z. Dioptase	2·25	95
1151	8z. Cuprite	3·25	1·40

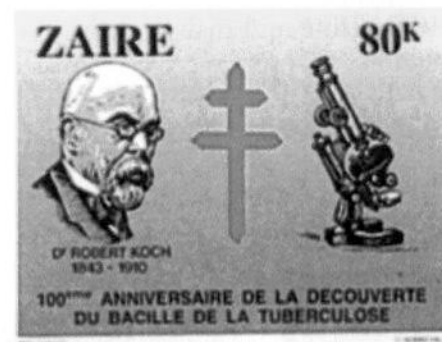

234 Dr. Koch and Microscope

1983. Centenary (1982) of Discovery of Tubercle Bacillus.

1153	**234**	80k. multicoloured	20	15
1154		1z.20 multicoloured	35	20
1155		3z.60 multicoloured	1·10	55
1156		9z.60 multicoloured	2·75	1·40

235 "Zaire Diplomat" (Lufwa Mawidi)

1983. Kinshasa Monuments. Multicoloured.

1157	50k. Type **235**	15	10
1158	1z. "Echo of Zaire" (Lufwa Mawidi) (horiz)	25	15
1159	1z.50 "Messengers" (Liyolo Limbe Mpuanga)	40	20
1160	3z. "Shield of Revolution" (Liyolo Limbe Mpuanga)	85	20
1161	5z. "Weeping Woman" (Wuma Mbambila) (horiz)	1·40	85
1162	10z. "The Militant" (Liyolo Limbe Mpuanaga)	2·50	1·25

236 Satellite over Globe

1983. I.T.U. Delegates' Conference, Nairobi. Multicoloured.

1163	2k. Type **236**	10	10
1164	4k. Dish aerial	10	10
1165	25k. Dish aerial (different)	10	10
1166	1z.20 Satellite and microwave antenna	45	15
1167	2z.05 Satellite	65	30
1168	3z.60 Satellite and microwave antenna (different)	1·10	45
1169	6z. Map of Zaire	1·60	70
1170	8z. Satellite (different)	2·40	1·40

238 Giant Eland

1984. Garamba National Park. Multicoloured.

1172	10k. Type **238**	10	10
1173	15k. Tawny eagles	1·00	30
1174	3z. Servals	25	10
1175	10z. White rhinoceros	90	35
1176	15z. Lions	1·10	55
1177	37z.50 Warthogs	3·00	1·10
1178	40z. Kori bustards	5·75	2·00
1179	40z. South African crowned cranes and game lodge	5·75	2·00

239 Visual Display Unit and Ferry

1984. World Communications Year. Multicoloured.
1180 10k. Type **239** 10 10
1181 15k. Communications satellite 10 10
1182 8z.50 Radio telephone . . . 1·50 75
1183 10z. Satellite and aerial . . 55 35
1184 15z. Video camera 95 80
1185 37z.50 Satellite and dish antenna . . . . 2·75 1·25
1186 80z. Switchboard operator 5·50 2·75

240 "Hypericum revolutum" **241** Basketball

1984. Flowers. Multicoloured.
1187 10k. Type **240** 10 15
1188 15k. "Borreria dibrachiata" 10 15
1189 3z. "Disa erubescens" . . . 15 15
1190 8z.50 "Scaevola plumieri" 40 50
1191 10z. "Clerodendron thompsonii" 60 50
1192 15z. "Thumbergia erecta" 85 95
1193 37z.50 "Impatiens niamniamensis" . . . . . 2·10 2·25
1194 100z. "Canarina eminii" . . 6·00 4·75

1984. Olympic Games, Los Angeles. Multicoloured.
1195 2z. Type **241** 15 10
1196 3z. Equestrian 20 10
1197 10z. Running 70 35
1198 15z. Long jump . . . . . . 1·10 55
1199 20z. Football . . . . 1·60 80

242 Montgolfier Balloon, 1783 **243** Okapi feeding

1984. Bicentenary of Manned Flight. Mult.
1201 10k. Type **242** 10 10
1202 15k. Charles's hydrogen balloon, 1783 . . . . . . 10 10
1203 3z. Montgolfier balloon "Le Gustave", 1784 . . . . . 15 10
1204 5z. Santos-Dumont's airship "Ballon No. 3", 1899 . . 30 15
1205 10z. Piccard's stratosphere balloon "F.N.R.S.", 1931 70 40
1206 15z. Airship "Hindenburg" 1·10 60
1207 37z.50 Balloon "Double Eagle II", 1978 . . . . . 2·50 1·40
1208 80z. Hot-air balloons . . . 6·00 3·00

1984. Wildlife Protection. Okapi. Multicoloured.
1209 2z. Type **243** 40 50
1210 3z. Okapi resting 85 50
1211 8z. Okapi and foal . . . . 1·75 2·00
1212 10z. Okapi crossing stream 2·40 2·00

1985. 50th Anniv of SABENA Brussels–Kinshasa Air Service. Nos. 927/34 surch **SABENA/1935-1985** and new value.
1214 2z.50 on 30s. multicoloured 15 10
1215 5z. on 5k. multicoloured . . 40 20
1216 6z. on 70s. multicoloured . . 45 30
1217 7z.50 on 1k. multicoloured 55 35
1218 8z.50 on 1k. multicoloured 65 40
1219 10z. on 8k. multicoloured 80 45
1220 12z.50 on 75k. multicoloured 90 60
1221 30z. on 50k. multicoloured 2·25 1·25

245 Swimming

1985. "Olymphilex '85" Olympic Stamps Exhibition, Lausanne. Multicoloured.
1223 1z. Type **245** 10 10
1224 2z. Football (vert) 15 10
1225 3z. Boxing 20 10
1226 4z. Basketball (vert) 30 15
1227 5z. Show jumping 35 20
1228 10z. Volleyball (vert) 70 45
1229 15z. Running . . . . 1·00 65
1230 30z. Cycling (vert) . . . . . 2·25 1·25

1985. 2nd Papal Visit. Nos. 1061/5 surch **AOUT 1985**.
1231 2z. on 5k. multicoloured . . 15 10
1232 3z. on 10k. multicoloured 20 15
1233 5z.50 multicoloured 45 20
1234 10z. on 100k. multicoloured 90 50
1235 15z. on 500k. multicoloured 1·40 65
1236 40z. on 800k. multicoloured 3·00 1·40

247 Great Egrets

1985. Birth Bicentenary of John J. Audubon (ornithologist). Multicoloured.
1238 5z. Type **247** 60 30
1239 10z. Black scoter . . . . . 1·25 60
1240 15z. Black-crowned night heron . . . . 2·10 95
1241 25z. Surf scoter . . . . . . 4·25 2·00

248 National Flag and "25" on Flag **249** U.N. and Zaire Flags

1985. 25th Anniv of Independence.
1242 **248** 5z. multicoloured 20 10
1243 10z. multicoloured . . . 45 20
1244 15z. multicoloured . . . 65 35
1245 20z. multicoloured . . . 90 40

1985. 40th Anniv of U.N.O. and 25th Anniv of Zaire Membership. Multicoloured.
1247 10z. Type **249** 45 30
1248 50z. U.N. building and emblem . . . . 2·25 1·10

1985. International Youth Year. Nos. 1127/31 optd **1985** and I.Y.Y. emblem and surch also.
1249 3z. on 3z. multicoloured . . 10 10
1250 5z. on 5z. multicoloured . . 20 10
1251 7z. on 90k. multicoloured 35 15
1252 10z. on 90k. multicoloured 45 15
1253 15z. on 1z.70 multicoloured 55 25
1254 20z. on 8z. multicoloured . . 1·10 45
1255 50z. on 90k. multicoloured 2·75 1·00

252 "Kokolo" (pusher tug)

1985. 50th Anniv of National Transport Office.
1258 7z. Type **252** 50 20
1259 10z. Early steam locomotive 75 40
1260 15z. "Luebo" (pusher tug) 75 35
1261 50z. Modern diesel locomotive . . . . 2·25 1·10

253 Pope John Paul II

1985. Beatification of Sister Anuarite Nengapeta. Multicoloured.
1262 10z. Type **253** 45 20
1263 15z. Sister Anuarite 65 35
1264 25z. Pope and Sister Anuarite (horiz) . . . . . 1·10 55

254 Map and 1886 25c. Stamp

1988. Centenary of 1st Congo Free State Stamp.
1266 **254** 25z. blue, grey and deep blue . . . . 1·10 55

255 Congo Free State 1898 10f. stamp

1988. "Cenzapost" Stamp Centenary Exhibition. Multicoloured.
1267 7z. Type **255** 30 10
1268 15z. Belgian Congo 1939 1f.25+1f.25 stamp 55 30
1269 20z. Belgian Congo 1942 50f. stamp (vert) 65 30
1270 25z. Zaire 1982 8k. stamp 80 35
1271 40z. Zaire 1984 37z.50 stamp (vert) . . . . . . 1·40 65

256 African Egg Eater

1987. Reptiles. Multicoloured.
1273 2z. Type **256** 15 20
1274 5z. Rainbow lizard 15 20
1275 10z. Royal python 25 20
1276 15z. Cape chameleon . . . 60 30
1277 25z. Green mamba . . . . 1·00 60
1278 50z. Black-necked cobra . . 1·60 1·10

257 "Virgin and Child with Angels" (from Cortone triptych)

1987. Christmas. Paintings by Fr. Angelico. Mult.
1279 50z. Type **257** 65 35
1280 100z. "St. Catherine and St. Peter adoring the Child" . . . . 1·40 65
1281 120z. "Virgin and Child of the Angels and Four Saints" (detail, Fiesole Retable) . . . . 1·60 80
1282 180z. "Virgin and Child and Six Saints" (detail, Annalena Retable) . . . 2·50 1·10

1990. Various stamps surch.
1283 – 20z. on 20k. mult (No. 920) 15 20
1284 **236** 40z. on 2k. mult 30 55
1285 – 40z. on 4k. mult (1164) 30 55
1286 **218** 40z. on 10k. mult . . . 30 55
1287 **231** 40z. on 25k. mult . . . 30 55
1288 – 40z. on 25k. mult (1165) 30 40
1289 – 40z. on 50k. mult (1055) 30 55
1290 – 40z. on 50k. mult (1134) 30 35
1291 **235** 40z. on 50k. mult . . . 30 55
1292 **228** 40z. on 75k. mult . . . 30 55
1293 – 40z. on 80k. mult (1056) 30 40
1294 – 40z. on 90k. mult (1093) 30 55
1295 **228** 40z. on 90k. mult . . . 30 35
1296 – 40z. on 90k. mult (1135) 30 40
1297 **236** 80z. on 2k. mult 55 60
1298 – 80z. on 4k. mult (1164) 60 65
1299 **218** 80z. on 10k. mult . . . 60 65
1300 **231** 80z. on 25k. mult . . . 55 60
1301 – 80z. on 25k. mult (1165) 55 70
1302 – 80z. on 50k. mult (1134) 60 65
1303 **235** 80z. on 50k. mult . . . 55 60
1304 **228** 80z. on 75k. mult . . . 55 60
1305 – 80z. on 80k. mult (1056) 55 45
1306 – 80z. on 90k. mult (1093) 55 60
1307 **228** 80z. on 90k. mult . . . 60 65
1308 – 80z. on 90k. mult (1135) 55 70
1309 **209** 100z. on 40s. brown, black and mauve . . . 70 80
1311 **220** 100z. on 2k. mult . . . 70 80
1312 **221** 100z. on 2k. mult . . . 70 80
1313 **226** 100z. on 2k. mult . . . 70 80
1314 **209** 100z. on 4k. brown, black and yellow . . . 70 65
1315 – 100z. on 5k. mult (930) 70 80
1316 – 100z. on 5k. mult (1061) 70 80
1317 – 100z. on 5k. mult (1077) 70 65
1318 – 100z. on 8k. mult (908) 95 55
1319 – 100z. on 8k. mult (931) 70 65
1320 – 100z. on 8k. mult (946) 70 80
1322 – 100z. on 10k. mult (947) 70 65
1323 – 100z. on 10k. mult (969) 70 80
1324 – 100z. on 10k. mult (1036) 65 70
1325 **217** 100z. on 10k. mult . . . 65 70
1326 – 100z. on 10k. mult (1062) 70 65
1327 – 100z. on 10k. mult (1068) 70 65
1328 **209** 100z. on 15k. brown, black and blue 65 70
1329 – 100z. on 18k. mult (1079) 65 70
1330 – 100z. on 20k. mult (970) 70 65
1331 – 100z. on 20k. mult (1020) 95 80
1332 **177** 100z. on 22k. mult . . . 70 80
1333 – 100z. on 25k. mult (1069) 65 70
1335 – 100z. on 48k. mult (912) 70 65
1336 – 100z. on 48k. mult (950) 65 70
1337 – 100z. on 50k. mult (1013) 70 80
1338 – 100z. on 50k. mult (1080) 85 90
1339 – 100z. on 50k. mult (1103) 65 70
1340 – 100z. on 75k. mult (1038) 70 80
1341 – 100z. on 75k. mult (1049) 70 80
1342 **203** 100z. on 90k. mult . . . 70 80
1343 – 100z. on 80k. mult (1050) 70 70
1344 **234** 100z. on 80k. mult . . . 70 80
1345 – 100z. on 90k. mult (1070) 85 90
1346 – 100z. on 90k. mult (1104) 70 65
1348 **233** 300z. on 2k. mult . . . 2·25 3·00
1349 – 300z. on 8k. mult (980) 3·25 5·50
1350 **216** 300z. on 10k. green & bl 2·25 3·00
1351 – 300z. on 14k. mult (789) 2·25 3·00
1352 **159** 300z. on 17k. mult (807) 2·25 3·00
1353 – 300z. on 20k. mult (989) 2·25 3·00
1354 – 300z. on 45k. mult (1145) . . . . 2·25 2·00
1355 – 300z. on 75k. brown and blue (1044) . . . . . 2·25 2·00
1356 – 300z. on 75k. mult (1146) . . . . 2·10 2·50
1357 **198** 500z. on 8k. mult . . . 4·75 5·50
1358 500z. on 10k. mult . . . 3·75 3·50
1359 500z. on 25k. mult . . . 4·00 5·00
1360 500z. on 48k. mult . . . 4·00 3·50

259 "Sida" forming Owl's Face

1990. Anti-AIDS Campaign. Multicoloured.
1361 30z. Type **259** 50 20
1362 40z. Skeleton firing arrow through "SIDA" 60 35
1363 80z. Leopard . . . . 1·10 80

260 Administration Building

1990. 50th Anniv of Regideso (development organization). Multicoloured.
1365 40z. Type **260** 55 35
1366 50z. Modern factory 65 45
1367 75z. Old water treatment plant . . . . 1·00 65
1368 120z. Communal water tap 1·40 80

261 Maps of France and Zaire and Birds

1990. Bicentenary of French Revolution. Mult.
1369 40z. Type **261** 55 35
1370 50z. Article 1 of Declaration of Rights of Man and the Citizen within outline of person 65 45
1371 100z. Crowd . . . . 1·25 65
1372 120z. Globe . . . . 1·40 80

262 Stairs of Venus, Mount Hoyo

1990. Tourist Sites. Multicoloured.
1373 40z. Type **262** 45 20
1374 60z. Scenic road to village 65 35
1375 100z. Lake Kivu . . . . . 1·25 55
1376 120z. Niyara Gongo volcano 1·60 25

1991. Various stamps surch.
1379 – 1000z. on 100k. mult (1064) 25 25
1380 – 1000z. on 1z. mult (1105) 25 25
1381 **214** 1000z. on 1z. mult (1026) 25 25
1383 – 1000z. on 1z. mult (1027) 25 25
1385 – 2000z. on 100k. violet and blue (1045) . . . 50 50
1386 – 2000z. on 1z. mult (1147) 50 50
1387 **228** 2500z. on 1z. mult . . . 65 65
1388 **225** 3000z. on 1z. green and gold 75 75
1389 – 4000z. on 1z. mult (1158) 1·00 1·00
1390 – 5000z. on 1z. mult (1158) 1·25 1·25
1391 **228** 10000z. on 1z. mult . . . 2·50 2·50
1392 **225** 15000z. on 1z. green and gold . . . . 3·75 3·75

Nos. 1381 and 1383 exist in two versions with the exhibition logo either at the right or left of the design.

1992. Various stamps surch.
1393 – 50,000z. on 125k. multicoloured (1058) 55 70
1394 – 100,000z. on 1z.20 multicoloured (1166) 55 70
1395 **234** 150,000z. on 1z.20 multicoloured 55 70
1396 – 200,000z. on 145k. blue and indigo (1046) . . 80 70
1397 **234** 250,000z. on 1z.20 multicoloured . . . . 1·10 1·00
1398 – 300,000z. on 1z.20 multicoloured (1166) 1·40 1·40
1399 **234** 500,000z. on 1z.20 multicoloured . . . . 1·90 1·75

1993. Various stamps surch. (a) Nos. 944/51.
1400 **199** 500,000z. on 30s. multicoloured 30 50
1401 – 500,000z. on 5k. multicoloured 30 50
1402 – 750,000z. on 8k. multicoloured 45 50
1403 – 750,000z. on 10k. multicoloured 45 50
1404 – 1,000,000z. on 30k. multicoloured 60 70
1405 – 1,000,000z. on 40k. multicoloured 60 70
1406 – 5,000,000z. on 48k. multicoloured . . . . 3·00 2·75
1407 – 10,000,000z. on 100k. multicoloured . . . . 5·75 5·25

(b) Nos. 1262/4.
1408 **253** 3,000,000z. on 10z. multicoloured . . . . 1·25 1·50
1409 – 5,000,000z. on 15z. multicoloured . . . . 2·50 2·50
1410 – 10,000,000z. on 25z. multicoloured . . . . 5·00 4·75

BOGUS SURCHARGES. Surcharges with commemorative inscriptions on Nos. 1365/8 for the inauguration of a pumping station and on Nos. 1373/6 for the sixth anniversary of the National Tourism Office are bogus.

Currency reform.

1 (new) zaire = 3000000 (old) zaire.

268 Eland and Calf

1993. 50th Anniv of Garamba National Park. Multicoloured.
1412 30k. Type **268** 30 30
1413 50k. African elephants . . . 30 30
1414 1z.50 Giant elands 60 30
1415 3z.50 Two white rhinoceros 90 75
1416 5z. Bongo . . . . 1·75 1·40

1993. Various stamps surch. (a) Nos. 1201/8.
1417 **242** 30k. on 10k. mult . . . 30 35
1418 – 50k. on 15k. mult . . . 65 65
1419 – 1z.50 on 3z. mult . . . . 1·25 1·25
1420 – 2z.50 on 5z. mult . . . . 1·75 1·75
1421 – 3z.50 on 10z. mult . . . 2·40 2·40
1422 – 5z. on 15z. mult . . . . 3·50 3·50
1423 – 7z.50 on 37z.50 mult . . 4·75 4·75
1424 – 10z. on 80z. mult . . . . 6·75 6·75

(b) Nos. 1043/7.
1425 **216** 30k. on 10k. green and blue 40 15
1426 – 50k. on 75k. brown and blue 60 20
1427 – 1z.50 on 100k. violet and blue . . . . 1·90 60
1428 – 3k.50 on 145k. blue and deep blue . . . . . . 2·75 90
1429 – 5z. on 270k. red and blue . . . . 3·00 1·00

(c) Nos. 1238/41.
1430 **247** 50k. on 5z. mult 60 80
1431 – 1z.50 on 10z. mult . . . 1·90 2·40
1432 – 3z.50 on 15z. mult . . . 2·75 3·50
1433 – 5z. on 25z. mult . . . . 3·00 4·00

1994. Various stamps surch.
1434 – 20z. on 3z. mult (No. 1139) 10 15
1435 – 40z. on 270k. red and blue (No. 1047) . . . 10 15
1436 – 50z. on 3z. mult (No. 1174) 15 15
1437 – 75z. on 3z. mult (No. 1196) 20 15
1438 – 100z. on 2z.05 mult (No. 1167) 35 30
1439 – 150z. on 1z.70 mult (No. 1121) 40 35
1440 – 200z. on 50k. mult (No. 1413) 50 40
1441 – 250z. on 1z.50 mult (No. 1136) 55 60
1442 **234** 300z. on 3z.60 mult . . . 65 65
1443 – 500z. on 3z.60 mult (No. 1168) 90 90

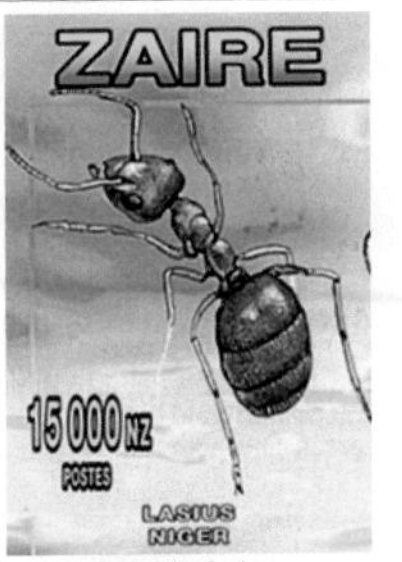

272 Black Ant

271 Show Jumping

1996. Olympic Games, Atlanta, U.S.A. Mult.
1444 1000z. Type **271** 10 10
1445 12500z. Boxing 65 40
1446 25000z. Table tennis . . . 1·25 75
1447 35000z. Basketball (vert) . . 1·75 1·10
1448 50000z. Tennis . . . . . . 2·50 1·50

1996. Various stamps. Surch.
1449 – 100z. on 3z.50 mult (No. 1109) 10 15
1450 **234** 500z. on 3z.60 mult . . . 10 15
1451 – 1000z. on 2z.05 mult (No. 1167) 20 20
1452 – 2500z. on 1z.50 multicoloured (No. 1136) 35 35
1453 – 5000z. on 3z.60 multicoloured (No. 1168) 75 75
1454 – 6000z. on 1z.50 multicoloured (No. 1136) 80 80
1455 **234** 15000z. on 3z.60 multicoloured . . . . 1·10 1·10
1456 – 25000z. on 3z.60 multicoloured (No. 1168) . . . . . 1·40 1·50

1996. Fauna, Flora and Minerals. Multicoloured.
1457 15000z. Type **272** . . . . . 1·25 1·25
1458 15000z. Calopterygides . . . 1·25 1·25
1459 15000z. Green lynx spider (Peucetia) . . . . . . 1·25 1·25
1460 15000z. Sphecides . . . . . 1·25 1·25
1461 20000z. Scutellosaurus . . . 1·40 1·40
1462 20000z. Compsognathus . . 1·40 1·40
1463 20000z. Dryosaurus . . . . 1·40 1·40
1464 20000z. Velociraptor . . . 1·40 1·40
1465 25000z. Panda eating (face value at left) . . . . . 2·40 2·40
1466 25000z. Panda eating (face value at right) . . . . 2·40 2·40
1467 25000z. Sitting . . . . . . 2·40 2·40
1468 25000z. Walking . . . . . 2·40 2·40
1469 25000z. *Eulophia streptopetala* . . . . . . 1·60 1·60
1470 25000z. *Oeceoclades saundersiana* . . . . . . 1·60 1·60
1471 25000z. *Eulophia gracilis* . . 1·60 1·60
1472 25000z. *Bulbophyllum falcatum* . . . . 1·60 1·60
1473 35000z. *Termitomyces aurantiacus* . . . . . . 2·10 2·10
1474 35000z. *Tricholoma lobayensis* . . . . 2·10 2·10
1475 35000z. *Lepiota esculenta* 2·10 2·10
1476 35000z. *Phlebopus sudanicus* 2·10 2·10
1477 40000z. Uraninite . . . . . 1·75 1·75
1478 40000z. Malachite . . . . . 1·75 1·75
1479 40000z. Ruby . . . . 1·75 1·75
1480 40000z. Diamond . . . . . 1·75 1·75
1481 50000z. Congo serpent eagle 3·00 3·00
1482 50000z. Crowned eagle ("Aigle Couronne") . . . 3·00 3·00
1483 50000z. Dark chanting goshawk (*Melierax metabates*) . . . . 3·00 3·00
1484 50000z. African long-tailed hawk (*Urotriorchis macrourus*) . . . . . . 3·00 3·00
1485 70000z. Red glider (*Cymthoe sangaris*) . . . . 3·50 3·50
1486 70000z. Purple-tip (*Colotis zoe*) . . . . 3·50 3·50
1487 70000z. Physcaeneura leda 3·50 3·50
1488 70000z. Green-veined charaxes (*Charaxes candiope*) . . . . 3·50 3·50
1489 100000z. Diamond . . . . 5·75 5·75
1490 100000z. Dioptase . . . . . 5·75 5·75
1491 100000z. Cuprite . . . . . 5·75 5·75
1492 100000z. Chrysocolle . . . 5·75 5·75

Nos. 1457/60 (insects), 1461/4 (dinosaurs), 1465/8 (pandas), 1469/72 (orchids), 1473/6 (fungi), 1477/80, 1489/92 (minerals), 1481/4 (birds) and 1485/8 (butterflies) respectively were issued together, se-tenant, with the backgrounds forming a composite design.

OFFICIAL STAMPS

1975. Optd **SP**.
O841 **172** 10s. orange and black 10 10
O842 40s. blue and black . . 10 10
O843 50s. yellow and black 10 10
O844 **177b** 1k. multicoloured . . . 10 10
O845 2k. multicoloured . . . 10 10
O846 3k. multicoloured . . . 10 10
O847 4k. multicoloured . . . 15 10
O848 5k. multicoloured . . . 20 10
O849 6k. multicoloured . . . 20 10
O850 8k. multicoloured . . . 35 15
O851 9k. multicoloured . . . 35 20
O852 10k. multicoloured . . 45 20
O853 14k. multicoloured . . 55 25
O854 17k. multicoloured . . 80 45
O855 20k. multicoloured . . 1·00 50
O856 50k. multicoloured . . 2·50 1·00
O857 100k. multicoloured . . 6·75 2·75

For later issues see **CONGO DEMOCRATIC REPUBLIC**.

ZAMBEZIA Pt. 9

Formerly administered by the Zambezia Co. This district of Portuguese E. Africa was later known as Quelimane and is now part of Mozambique.

1000 reis = 1 milreis.

1894. "Figures" key-type inscr "ZAMBEZIA".
1 R 5r. orange 30 25
2 10r. mauve 50 45
3 15r. brown 95 70
4 20r. lilac 95 70
12 25r. green . . . . 1·70 1·20
13 50r. blue . . . . 1·70 1·20
14 75r. pink . . . . 4·00 3·50
15 80r. green . . . . 3·25 2·50
8 100r. brown on buff . . . . 2·40 1·90
16 150r. red on pink . . . . . 4·00 3·00
17 200r. blue on blue . . . . . 4·00 3·00
18 300r. blue on brown . . . . 6·00 4·50

1898. "King Carlos" key-type inscr "ZAMBEZIA". Name and value in red (500r.) or black (others).
20 S $2\frac{1}{2}$r. grey 40 35
21 5r. red 40 35
22 10r. green 65 35
23 15r. brown . . . . 1·10 80
55 15r. green . . . . 1·20 1·00
24 20r. lilac . . . . 1·10 80
25 25r. green . . . . 1·10 80
56 25r. red 95 65
26 50r. blue . . . . 1·10 80
57 50r. brown . . . . 2·10 1·90
58 65r. blue . . . . 6·50 5·25
27 75r. pink . . . . 7·75 4·25
59 75r. purple . . . . 2·75 1·90
28 80r. mauve . . . . 4·50 2·50
29 100r. blue on blue . . . . . 1·70 1·40
60 115r. brown on pink . . . . 7·25 4·75
61 130r. brown on yellow . . . 7·25 4·75
30 150r. brown on yellow . . . 5·00 2·75
31 200r. purple on pink . . . . 5·25 2·75
32 300r. blue on pink . . . . . 5·50 2·75
62 400r. blue on cream . . . . 9·75 7·00
33 500r. black on blue . . . . . 9·50 5·25
34 700r. mauve on yellow . . . 12·00 6·50

1902. Surch.
63 S 50r. on 65r. blue . . . . . 4·75 2·50
35 R 65r. on 10r. mauve . . . . 7·25 5·50
36 65r. on 15r. brown . . . . . 7·25 5·50
37 65r. on 20r. lilac . . . . . . 7·25 5·50
38 65r. on 300r. blue on brown 7·25 5·50
40 115r. on 5r. orange . . . . 7·25 5·50
41 115r. on 25r. green . . . . 7·25 5·50
42 115r. on 80r. green . . . . 7·25 5·50
46 V 130r. on $2\frac{1}{2}$r. brown . . . . 7·25 5·50
43 R 130r. on 75r. pink . . . . . 5·75 3·75
45 130r. on 150r. red on pink 4·25 4·00
47 400r. on 50r. blue . . . . . 1·70 1·50
49 400r. on 100r. brown on buff 1·70 1·50
50 400r. on 200r. blue on blue 1·50 1·50

1902. 1898 issue optd **PROVISORIO**.
51 S 15r. brown . . . . 1·60 1·00
52 25r. green . . . . 1·60 1·00
53 50r. blue . . . . 1·60 1·00
54 75r. pink . . . . 4·50 2·40

1911. 1898 issue optd **REPUBLICA**.
64 S $2\frac{1}{2}$r. grey 30 20
65 5r. red 30 20
66 10r. green 30 25
67 15r. green 30 25
68 20r. lilac 45 30
69 25r. red . . . . 1·20 75
108 25r. green . . . . 9·25 7·50
70 50r. brown 30 30
71 75r. purple 95 65
72 100r. blue on blue 95 65
73 115r. brown on pink 95 65
74 130r. brown on yellow . . . 95 65
75 200r. purple on pink 95 65
76 400r. blue on cream . . . . 1·70 85
77 500r. black on blue . . . . 1·70 85
78 700r. mauve on yellow . . . 1·70 1·30

1914. Provisionals of 1902 optd **REPUBLICA**.
94 S 50r. blue (No. 53) 60 45
95 50r. on 65r. blue . . . . . 2·40 1·50
81 75r. pink (No. 54) . . . . . 1·20 90
96 R 115r. on 5r. orange 55 45
97 115r. on 25r. green 55 45
98 115r. on 80r. green 55 45
99 V 130r. on $2\frac{1}{2}$r. brown 55 45
100 R 130r. on 75r. pink 55 45
102 130r. on 150r. red on pink 60 45
90 400r. on 50r. blue . . . . . 1·70 1·40
92 400r. on 100r. brn on buff . 2·00 1·50
93 400r. on 200r. blue on blue 2·00 1·50

NEWSPAPER STAMP

1893. "Newspaper" key-type inscr "ZAMBEZIA".
N1 V $2\frac{1}{2}$r. brown 40 35

ZAMBIA Pt. 1

Formerly Northern Rhodesia, attained independence on 24 October 1964 and changed its name to Zambia.

1964. 12 pence = 1 shilling;
20 shillings = 1 pound.
1968. 100 ngwee = 1 kwacha.

11 Pres. Kaunda and Victoria Falls

1964. Independence.
91 **11** 3d. sepia, green and blue . . 10 10
92 – 6d. violet and yellow . . . 15 20
93 – 1s.3d. multicoloured . . . 20 25

DESIGNS—HORIZ: 6d. College of Further Education, Lusaka. VERT: 1s.3d. Barotse dancer.

14 Maize – Farmer and Silo

22 Tobacco Worker

1964.

94 **14** ½d. red, black and green . . . 10 1·50
95 – 1d. brown, black and blue . . . 10 10
96 – 2d. red, brown and orange . . . 10 10
97 – 3d. black and red 10 10
98 – 4d. black, brown and orange 15 10
99 – 6d. orange, brown and turquoise 15 10
100 – 9d. red, black and blue . . 15 10
101 – 1s. black, bistre and blue . . 15 10
102 **22** 1s.3d. multicoloured . . . 20 10
103 – 2s. multicoloured 25 30
104 – 2s.6d. black and yellow . . 60 35
105 – 5s. black, yellow and green 1·00 75
106 – 10s. black and orange . . . 3·50 3·75
107 – £1 multicoloured . . . . . 2·00 5·50

DESIGNS—VERT (as Type **14**): 1d. Health – radiographer; 2d. Chinyau dancer; 3d. Cotton-picking. (As Type **22**): 2s. Tonga basket-making; £1 Makishi dancer. HORIZ (as Type **14**): 4d. Angoni bull. (As Type **22**): 6d. Communications, old and new; 9d. Zambezi sawmills and redwood flower; 1s. Fishing at Mpulungu; 2s.6d. Luangwa Game Reserve; 5s. Education – student; 10s. Copper mining.

28 I.T.U. Emblem and Symbols

1965. Centenary of I.T.U.
108 **28** 6d. violet and gold 15 10
109 2s.6d. grey and gold . . . 85 1·50

29 I.C.Y. Emblem

1965. International Co-operation Year.
110 **29** 3d. turquoise and gold . . 15 10
111 1s.3d. blue and gold . . . 35 45

30 State House, Lusaka

35 University Building

34 W.H.O. Building and U.N. Flag

1965. 1st Anniv of Independence. Mult.
112 3d. Type **30** 10 10
113 6d. Fireworks, Independence Stadium 10 10
114 1s.3d. Clematopsis (vert) . . 15 10
115 2s.6d. "Tithonia diversifolia" (vert) . . . . 30 1·25

1966. Inaug of W.H.O. Headquarters, Geneva.
116 **34** 3d. brown, gold and blue 20 10
117 1s.3d. violet, gold and blue 80 95

1966. Opening of Zambia University.
118 **35** 3d. green and bronze . . . 10 10
119 1s.3d. violet and bronze . . 20 10

36 National Assembly Building

1967. Inaug of National Assembly Building.
120 **36** 3d. black and gold 10 10
121 6d. green and gold 10 10

37 Airport Scene

1967. Opening of Lusaka International Airport.
122 **37** 6d. blue and bronze . . . 15 10
123 2s.6d. brown and bronze 60 1·00

38 Youth Service Badge

43 Lusaka Cathedral

1967. National Development.
124 **38** 4d. black, red and gold . . 10 10
125 – 6d. black, gold and blue 10 10
126 – 9d. black, blue and silver 15 50
127 – 1s. multicoloured 50 10
128 – 1s.6d. multicoloured . . . 70 2·25

DESIGNS—HORIZ: 6d. "Co-operative Farming"; 1s.6d. Road link with Tanzania. VERT: 9d. "Communications"; 1s. Coalfields.

1968. Decimal Currency.
129 **43** 1n. multicoloured 10 10
130 – 2n. multicoloured 10 10
131 – 3n. multicoloured 10 10
132 – 5n. brown and bronze . . 10 10
133 – 8n. multicoloured 15 10
134 – 10n. multicoloured 25 10
135 – 15n. multicoloured . . . . 2·75 10
136 – 20n. multicoloured . . . . 4·50 10
137 – 25n. multicoloured 25 10
138 – 50n. brown, orange and bronze 30 15
139 – 1k. blue and bronze . . . 4·50 20
140 – 2k. black and bronze . . . 2·25 1·25

DESIGNS—VERT (as Type **43**): 2n. Baobab tree; 5n. National Museum, Livingstone; 8n. Vimbuza dancer; 10n. Tobacco picking. (26 × 32 mm): 20n. South African crowned cranes; 25n. Angoni warrior; 50n. Chokwe dancer. HORIZ (as Type **43**): 3n. Zambia Airways Vickers VC-10 jetliner. (32 × 26 mm): 15n. "Imbrasia zambesina" (moth); 1k. Kafue Railway Bridge; 2k. Eland.

55 Ndola on Outline of Zambia

1968. Trade Fair, Ndola.
141 **55** 15n. green and gold . . . 10 10

56 Human Rights Emblem and Heads

1968. Human Rights Year.
142 **56** 3n. blue, violet and gold 10 10

57 W.H.O. Emblem

1968. 20th Anniv of World Health Organization.
143 **57** 10n. gold and violet . . . 10 10

58 Group of Children

1968. 22nd Anniv of UNICEF.
144 **58** 25n. black, gold and blue 15 70

59 Copper Miner

61 Zambia outlined on Map of Africa

1969. 50th Anniv of Int Labour Organization.
145 **59** 3n. copper and violet . . . 25 10
146 – 25n. yellow, copper & brown . . . . 1·00 1·00

DESIGN—HORIZ: 25n. Poling a furnace.

1969. International African Tourist Year. Mult.
147 5n. Type **61** 10 10
148 10n. Waterbuck (horiz) . . . 15 10
149 15n. Kasaba Bay golden perch (horiz) 35 40
150 25n. Carmine bee eater . . . 1·00 1·75

65 Satellite "Nimbus 3" orbiting the Earth

66 Woman collecting Water from Well

1970. World Meteorological Day.
151 **65** 15n. multicoloured 20 50

1970. Preventive Medicine.
152 **66** 3n. multicoloured 15 10
153 – 15n. multicoloured 30 30
154 – 25n. blue, red and sepia . . 65 70

DESIGNS: 15n. Child on scales; 25n. Child being immunized.

67 "Masks" (mural by Gabriel Ellison)

1970. Conference of Non-Aligned Nations.
155 **67** 15n. multicoloured 30 30

68 Ceremonial Axe

1970. Traditional Crafts. Multicoloured.
156 3n. Type **68** 10 10
157 5n. Clay smoking-pipe bowl 10 10
158 15n. Makishi mask 25 30
159 25n. Kuomboka Ceremony 40 1·00
MS160 133 × 83 mm. Nos. 156/9. Imperf . . . . 6·00 13·00

SIZES—HORIZ: 5n. as T **68**; 25n. 72 × 19 mm. VERT: 15n. 30 × 47 mm.

69 Dag Hammarskjold and U.N. General Assembly

1971. 10th Death Anniv of Dag Hammarskjold. Multicoloured.
161 4n. Type **69** 10 10
162 10n. Tail of aircraft 15 10
163 15n. Dove of Peace 15 25
164 25n. Memorial tablet . . . . 30 1·50

70 Red-breasted Tilapia

1971. Fish. Multicoloured.
165 4n. Type **70** 30 10
166 10n. Long-finned tilapia ("Green-headed bream") 50 40
167 15n. Tigerfish . . . . 60 2·50

71 North African Crested Porcupine

1972. Conservation Year (1st issue). Mult.
168 4n. Cheetah (horiz) 15 25
169 10n. Lechwe (horiz) 20 60
170 15n. Type **71** 25 85
171 25n. African elephant . . . . 1·25 3·00

Nos. 168/9 are size 58 × 21 mm.

1972. Conservation Year (2nd issue). As T **71**. Multicoloured.
172 4n. Soil conservation 15 20
173 10n. Forestry 15 30
174 15n. Water 20 80
175 25n. Maize . . . . 45 1·60

Nos. 174/5 are size 58 × 21 mm.

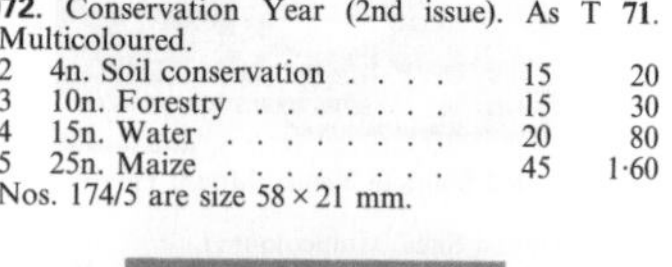

72 Giraffe and Common Zebra

1972. National Parks. Sheet 114 × 140 mm, containing T **72** and similar vert designs. Multicoloured.
MS176 10n. (× 4) Type **72**; Black rhinoceros; hippopotamus and common panther, lion . . . . 6·50 12·00

Each design includes part of a map showing Zambian National Parks, the four forming a composite design.

73 Zambian Flowers

1972. Conservation Year (3rd issue). Mult.
177 4n. Type **73** 30 30
178 10n. "Papilio demodocus" (butterfly) 80 80
179 15n. "Apis mellifera" (bees) 85 1·40
180 25n. "Nomadacris septemfasciata" (locusts) 1·25 2·25

74 Mary and Joseph

1972. Christmas. Multicoloured.
181 4n. Type **74** 10 10
182 9n. Mary, Joseph and Jesus 10 10

183 15n. Mary, Jesus and the shepherds 10 10
184 25n. The Three Wise Men . . 20 40

75 Oudenodon and Rubidgea

1973. Zambian Prehistoric Animals. Mult.
185 4n. Type **75** 85 85
186 9n. Broken Hill Man 90 90
187 10n. Zambiasaurus . . . . . 1·00 1·50
188 15n. "Luangwa drysdalli" . . 1·10 2·00
189 25n. Glossopteris . . . . . . 1·25 3·00
Nos. 186/9 are smaller, 38 × 21 mm.

76 "Dr. Livingstone, I Presume"

1973. Death Cent of Dr. Livingstone. Mult.
190 3n. Type **76** 15 15
191 4n. Scripture lesson 15 15
192 9n. Victoria Falls 30 40
193 10n. Scattering slavers . . . 20 45
194 15n. Healing the sick . . . . 30 1·60
195 25n. Burial place of Livingstone's heart . . . . 30 2·75

77 Parliamentary Mace

1973. 3rd Commonwealth Conference of Speakers and Presiding Officers, Lusaka.
196 **77** 9n. multicoloured 35 55
197 15n. multicoloured . . . . 40 1·10
198 25n. multicoloured . . . . 50 1·50

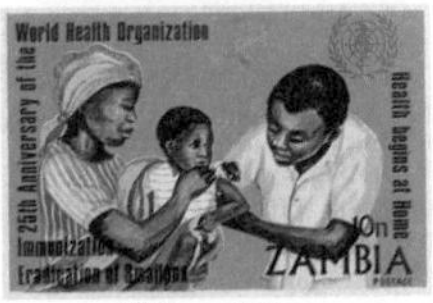

78 Inoculation

1973. 25th Anniv of W.H.O. Multicoloured.
199 4n. Mother washing baby (vert) . . . . 40·00 23·00
200 9n. Nurse weighing baby (vert) . . . . 45 2·25
201 10n. Type **78** . . . . 50 3·00
202 15n. Child eating meal . . . 90 5·00

79 U.N.I.P. Flag

80 President Kaunda at Mulungushi

1974. 1st Anniv of Second Republic. Mult.
203 4n. Type **79** . . . . 7·00 7·00
204 9n. Freedom House . . . . 30 1·50
205 10n. Army band . . . . . . 30 2·00
206 15n. "Celebrations" (dancers) 50 3·25
207 25n. Presidential chair . . . 75 5·00

1974. 50th Birthday of President Kaunda. Multicoloured.
208 4n. Type **80** 40 40
209 9n. President's former residence 20 20
210 15n. President holding Independence flame . . . . 50 1·25

81 Nakambala Sugar Estate

1974. 10th Anniv of Independence. Mult.
211 3n. Type **81** 15 10
212 4n. Local market 15 10
213 9n. Kapiri glass factory . . . 20 10
214 10n. Kafue hydro-electric scheme 25 10
215 15n. Kafue Railway Bridge 50 95
216 25n. Non-aligned Conference, Lusaka, 1970 . . . . . . 60 1·25
MS217 141 × 105 mm. 15n. (× 4) Academic Education; Teacher Training College; Technical Education; Zambia University 5·00 8·50

82 Mobile Post-van

1974. Centenary of U.P.U. Multicoloured.
218 4n. Type **82** 20 15
219 9n. Hawker Siddeley H.S.748 airplane on tarmac 30 30
220 10n. Chipata Post Office . . 30 40
221 15n. Modern training centre 45 1·75

83 Dish Aerial

1974. Opening of Mwembeshi Earth Station. Multicoloured.
222 4n. Type **83** 25 20
223 9n. View at dawn 35 30
224 15n. View at dusk 40 70
225 25n. Aerial view . . . . . . 50 1·50

84 Black Rhinoceros and Calf

86 Map of Namibia

85 Independence Monument

1975. Multicoloured.
226 1n. Type **84** . . . . 75 1·00
227 2n. Helmeted guineafowl . . 75 1·00
228 3n. National Dancing Troupe 15 1·00
229 4n. African fish eagle . . . . 1·00 10
230 5n. Knife-edge Bridge . . . . 1·00 1·00
231 8n. Sitatunga (antelope) . . . 1·00 75
232 9n. African elephant, Kasaba Bay . . . . 1·25 70
233 10n. Temminck's ground pangolin 20 10
234 15n. Type **85** 30 10
235 20n. Harvesting groundnuts 85 1·25
236 25n. Tobacco growing . . . 1·25 50
237 50n. Flying Doctor service . . 3·25 2·50
238 1k. Lady Ross's turaco . . . 4·50 1·75
239 2k. Village scene . . . . . . 3·00 6·00
Nos. 234/9 are as Type **85**.

1975. Namibia Day.
240 **86** 4n. green and yellow . . . 15 20
241 9n. blue and green 20 30
242 15n. orange and yellow . . 30 75
243 25n. red and orange . . . 45 1·50

87 Erection of Sprinkler Irrigation

1975. Silver Jubilee of International Commission on Irrigation and Drainage. Multicoloured.
244 4n. Type **87** 15 15
245 9n. Sprinkler irrigation . . . 30 40
246 15n. Furrow irrigation . . . 65 1·50

88 Mutondo

1976. World Forestry Day. Multicoloured.
247 3n. Type **88** 15 10
248 4n. Mukunyu 15 10
249 9n. Mukusi 25 25
250 10n. Mopane 25 25
251 15n. Musuku . . . . 45 1·40
252 25n. Mukwa . . . . 55 2·00

89 Passenger Train

1976. Opening of Tanzania–Zambia Railway. Multicoloured.
253 4n. Type **89** 30 30
254 9n. Copper exports 45 55
255 15n. Machinery imports . . . 70 95
256 25n. Goods train . . . . . . 1·10 1·75
MS257 140 × 106 mm. 10n. Clearing bush; 15n. Laying track; 20n. Railway workers; 25n. Completed track . . . . 3·00 4·00

90 Kayowe Dance

1977. 2nd World Black and African Festival of Arts and Culture, Nigeria. Multicoloured.
258 4n. Type **90** 15 10
259 9n. Lilombola dance 15 15
260 15n. Initiation ceremony . . 30 40
261 25n. Munkhwele dance . . . 55 1·00

91 Grimwood's Longclaw

1977. Birds of Zambia. Multicoloured.
262 4n. Type **91** 40 10
263 9n. Shelley's sunbird 55 60
264 10n. Black-cheeked lovebird 55 60
265 15n. Locust finch . . . . . 1·25 2·00
266 20n. White-chested tinkerbird 1·40 2·25
267 25n. Chaplin's barbet . . . . 1·50 2·75

92 Girls with Building Blocks

1977. Decade for Action to Combat Racism and Racial Discrimination. Multicoloured.
268 4n. Type **92** 15 10
269 9n. Women dancing 20 20
270 15n. Girls with dove . . . . 30 1·00

93 Angels and Shepherds

1977. Christmas. Multicoloured.
271 4n. Type **93** 10 10
272 9n. The Holy Family 10 10
273 10n. The Magi 10 15
274 15n. Jesus presented to Simeon . . . . 20 1·00

94 African Elephant and Road Check

1978. Anti-poaching Campaign. Multicoloured.
275 8n. Type **94** 45 20
276 18n. Lechwe and canoe patrol 30 65
277 28n. Warthog and Bell 206 JetRanger helicopter . . . 75 1·10
278 32n. Cheetah and game guard patrol . . . . 75 1·50

1979. Various stamps surch.
279 – 8n. on 9n. multicoloured (No. 232) 70 10
280 – 10n. on 3n. multicoloured (No. 228) 10 10
281 – 18n. on 25n. mult (No. 236) 15 15
282 **85** 28n. on 15n. mult 20 25

96 Kayowe Dance

1979. Commonwealth Summit Conference, Lusaka. Multicoloured.
283 18n. Type **96** 15 25
284 32n. Kutambala dance . . . 20 40
285 42n. Chitwansombo drummers 20 60
286 58n. Lilombola dance 25 80

97 "Kalulu and the Tug of War"

1979. International Year of the Child. Mult.
287 18n. Type **97** 20 30
288 32n. "Why the Zebra has no Horns" 25 55
289 42n. "How the Tortoise got his Shell" 30 85
290 58n. "Kalulu and the Lion" 40 1·00
MS291 90 × 120 mm. Nos. 287/91 1·50 2·75

98 Children of Different Races holding Anti-Apartheid Emblem

1979. International Anti-Apartheid Year. Mult.
292 18n. Type **98** 15 25
293 32n. Children with toy car . . 25 40
294 42n. Young children with butterfly 35 70
295 58n. Children with microscope . . . . 50 1·00

99 Sir Rowland Hill and 2s. Definitive Stamp of 1964

1979. Death Cent of Sir Rowland Hill. Mult.
296 18n. Type **99** 15 25
297 32n. Sir Rowland Hill and mailman 20 55
298 42n. Sir Rowland Hill and Northern Rhodesia 1963 ½d. definitive stamp 20 70
299 58n. Sir Rowland Hill and mail-carrying oxwaggon . . 20 1·10
MS300 112 × 89 mm. Nos. 296/9 1·00 2·50

1980. "London 1980" International Stamp Exhibition. Nos. 296/9 optd **LONDON 1980**.
301 **99** 18n. multicoloured 25 40
302 – 32n. multicoloured 30 60
303 – 42n. multicoloured 40 75
304 – 58n. multicoloured 60 90
MS305 112 × 89 mm. Nos. 301/4 2·50 3·75

101 Rotary Anniversary Emblem

1980. 75th Anniv of Rotary International.
306 **101** 8n. multicoloured 10 10
307 32n. multicoloured . . . 30 40
308 42n. multicoloured . . . 35 50
309 58n. multicoloured . . . 45 80
MS310 115 × 89 mm. Nos. 306/9 1·50 2·25

102 Running

1980. Olympic Games, Moscow. Multicoloured.
311 18n. Type **102** 20 25
312 32n. Boxing 30 45
313 42n. Football 40 80
314 58n. Swimming . . . . . . 50 1·25
MS315 142 × 144 mm. Nos. 311/14 2·50 3·25

103 "Euphaedra zaddachi"

1980. Butterflies. Multicoloured.
316 18n. Type **103** 15 15
317 32n. "Aphnaeus questiauxi" . . 25 40
318 42n. "Abantis zambesiaca" . . 40 90
319 58n. "Spindasis modesta" . . 60 1·75
MS320 114 × 86 mm. Nos. 316/19 4·25 4·25

104 Zambia Coat of Arms

105 Nativity and St. Francis of Assisi (stained glass window, Ndola Church)

1980. 26th Commonwealth Parliamentary Association Conference, Lusaka.
321 **104** 18n. multicoloured . . . 15 25
322 32n. multicoloured . . . 25 45
323 42n. multicoloured . . . 30 75
324 58n. multicoloured . . . 40 1·50

1980. 50th Anniv of Catholic Church on the Copperbelt.
325 **105** 8n. multicoloured 10 10
326 28n. multicoloured . . . 30 70
327 32n. multicoloured . . . 30 70
328 42n. multicoloured . . . 45 1·10

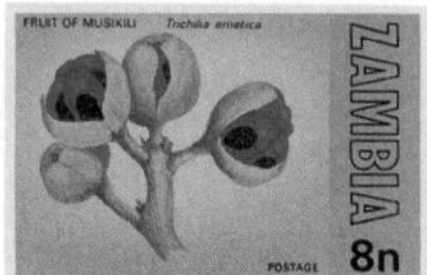

106 Musikili

1981. World Forestry Day. Seedpods. Mult.
329 8n. Type **106** 10 10
330 18n. Mupapa 20 45
331 28n. Mulunguti 25 90
332 32n. Mulama . . . . 25 1·40

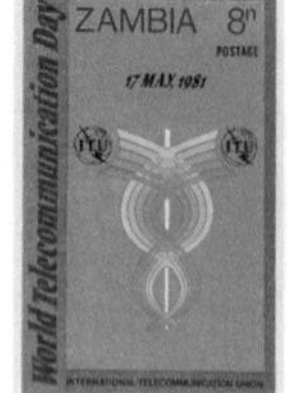

107 I.T.U. Emblem

108 Mask Maker

1981. World Telecommunications and Health Day. Multicoloured.
333 8n. Type **107** 20 10
334 18n. W.H.O. emblems . . . 25 35
335 28n. Type **107** 30 70
336 32n. As 18n. 35 85

1981. Native Crafts. Multicoloured.
337 1n. Type **108** 10 10
338 2n. Blacksmith 10 10
339 5n. Pottery making 10 10
340 8n. Straw-basket fishing . . . 10 10
341 10n. Thatching 10 10
342 12n. Mushroom picking . . . 3·00 1·75
343 18n. Millet grinding on stone 30 10
344 28n. Royal Barge paddler . . 75 10
345 30n. Makishi tightrope dancer 50 10
346 35n. Tonga Ila granary and house 55 10
347 42n. Cattle herding . . . . . 55 1·75
348 50n. Traditional healer (38 × 26 mm) 75 10
349 75n. Women carrying water (38 × 26 mm) 55 60
350 1k. Pounding maize (38 × 26 mm) 55 60
351 2k. Pipe smoking, Gwembe Valley belle (38 × 26 mm) 55 60

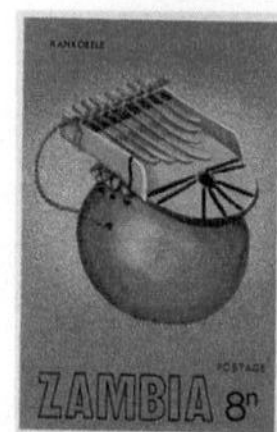

109 Kankobele

110 Banded Ironstone

1981. Traditional Musical Instruments. Mult.
356 8n. Type **109** 20 10
357 18n. Inshingili 25 55
358 28n. Ilimba . . . . 30 1·50
359 32n. Bango . . . . 35 1·75

1982. Minerals (1st series). Multicoloured.
360 8n. Type **110** . . . . 1·00 10
361 18n. Cobaltocalcite . . . . 2·00 80
362 28n. Amazonite . . . . . . 2·75 2·25
363 32n. Tourmaline . . . . . . 3·00 2·75
364 42n. Uranium ore . . . . . 3·25 4·00
See also Nos. 370/4.

111 Zambian Scouts

1982. 75th Anniv of Boy Scout Movement. Multicoloured.
365 8n. Type **111** 20 10
366 18n. Lord Baden-Powell and Victoria Falls 60 40
367 28n. African buffalo and Zambian scout patrol pennant 60 50
368 1k. African fish eagle and Zambian conservation badge . . . . 1·40 4·50
MS369 105 × 78 mm. Nos. 365/8 2·50 5·00

1982. Minerals (2nd series). As T **110**. Mult.
370 8n. Bornite 95 10
371 18n. Chalcopyrite . . . . . 2·25 90
372 28n. Malachite . . . . 2·75 3·00
373 32n. Azurite . . . . 2·75 3·00
374 42n. Vanadinite . . . . . . 3·25 4·25

112 Drilling Rig, 1926

1983. Early Steam Engines. Multicoloured.
375 8n. Type **112** 45 10
376 18n. Fowler road locomotive, 1900 . . . . 55 70
377 28n. Borsig ploughing engine, 1925 . . . . 1·00 2·25
378 32n. Rhodesian Railways 7th Class steam locomotive, 1900 . . . . 1·25 2·50

113 Cotton Picking

1983. Commonwealth Day. Multicoloured.
379 12n. Type **113** 20 10
380 18n. Mining 40 30
381 28n. Ritual pot and traditional dances 30 50
382 1k. Violet-crested turaco and Victoria Falls . . . . . . 2·75 5·50

114 "Eulophia cucullata"

115 Giraffe

1983. Wild Flowers. Multicoloured.
383 12n. Type **114** 20 10
384 28n. "Kigelia africana" . . . 25 40
385 35n. "Protea gaguedi" . . . 30 80
386 50n. "Leonotis nepetifolia" . . 50 2·25
MS387 141 × 71 mm. Nos. 383/6 1·00 3·50

1983. Wildlife of Zambia. Multicoloured.
388 12n. Type **115** 70 10
389 28n. Blue wildebeest 75 70
390 35n. Lechwe 80 90
391 1k. Yellow-backed duiker . . 1·25 4·25

116 Tigerfish

1983. Fishes of Zambia. Multicoloured.
392 12n. Type **116** 35 15
393 28n. Silver catfish 50 70
394 35n. Large-spotted squeaker 60 1·75
395 38n. Red-breasted tilapia . . 60 1·75

117 The Annunciation

1983. Christmas. Multicoloured.
396 12n. Type **117** 15 10
397 28n. The Shepherds 30 40
398 35n. Three Kings . . . . . . 40 1·25
399 38n. Flight into Egypt . . . 45 1·75

118 Boeing 737

1984. Air Transport. Multicoloured.
400 12n. Type **118** 25 10
401 28n. De Havilland D.H.C.2 Beaver 45 40
402 35n. Short S-45A Solent 3 flying boat 55 70
403 1k. De Havilland D.H.66 Hercules "City of Basra" 1·00 3·00

119 Receiving Flowers

1984. 60th Birthday of President Kaunda. Mult.
404 12n. Type **119** 20 10
405 28n. Swearing-in ceremony (vert) 25 40
406 60n. Planting cherry tree . . 50 2·25
407 1k. Opening of 5th National Assembly (vert) . . . . . 65 3·25

120 Football

1984. Olympic Games, Los Angeles. Multicoloured.
408 12n. Type **120** 25 10
409 28n. Running 30 50
410 35n. Hurdling 40 80
411 60n. Boxing . . . . 45 1·75

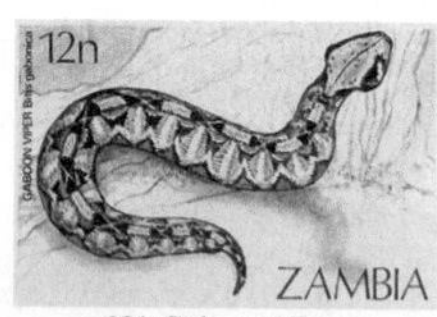

121 Gaboon Viper

1984. Reptiles. Multicoloured.
412 12n. Type **121** 20 10
413 28n. Chameleon 40 50
414 35n. Nile crocodile 50 70
415 1k. Blue-headed agama . . . 1·00 2·75
MS416 120 × 101 mm. Nos. 412/15 2·00 4·00

122 Pres. Kaunda and Mulungushi Rock

1984. 26th Anniv of United National Independence Party and 20th Anniv of Independence (1st issue). Multicoloured.
417 12n. Type **122** 20 10
418 28n. Freedom Statue 30 50
419 1k. Pres. Kaunda and agricultural produce ("Lima Programme") . . . 75 3·00

123 "Amanita flammeola"

1984. Fungi. Multicoloured.
420 12n. Type **123** . . . . . . 1·10 30
421 28n. "Amanita zambiana" . . . 1·25 1·25
422 32n. "Termitomyces letestui" 1·25 2·25
423 75n. "Cantharellus miniatescens" . . . . . . 1·75 4·50

1985. No. 237 surch **K5**.
424 5k. on 50n. Flying Doctor service . . . . 1·75 3·25

125 Chacma Baboon

1985. Zambian Primates. Multicoloured.
425 12n. Type **125** 55 10
426 20n. Diademed monkey . . . 75 40
427 45n. Diademed monkey (different) . . . . 1·25 1·25
428 1k. Savanna monkey . . . . 2·00 4·50

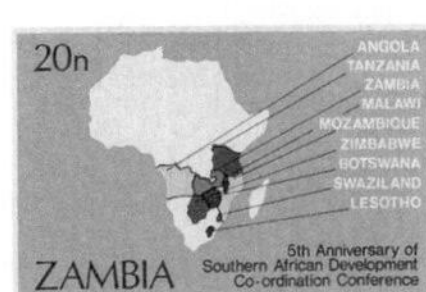

126 Map showing S.A.D.C.C. Member States

1985. 5th Anniv of Southern African Development Co-ordination Conference.
429 **126** 20n. multicoloured . . . 75 15
430 – 45n. black, blue and light blue . . . . 1·75 1·10
431 – 1k. multicoloured . . . . 2·00 3·75
DESIGNS: 45n. Mining; 1k. Flags of member states and Mulungushi Hall.

127 The Queen Mother in 1980

130 Boy in Maize Field

129 Postman and Lusaka Post Office, 1958

1985. Life and Times of Queen Elizabeth the Queen Mother.
432 **127** 25n. multicoloured . . . 10 10
433 – 45n. blue and gold . . . 10 15
434 – 55n. blue and gold . . . 15 25
435 – 5k. multicoloured . . . . 1·25 2·75
DESIGNS—VERT: 45n. The Queen Mother at Clarence House, 1963. HORIZ: 55n. With the Queen and Princess Margaret, 1980; 5k. At Prince Henry's Christening, 1984.

1985. Nos. 340 and 342 surch.
436 20n. on 12n. Mushroom picking . . . . 2·75 1·00
437 25n. on 8n. Straw-basket fishing . . . . 1·00 65

1985. 26th Anniv of United National Independence Party (No. 438) and 20th Anniv of Independence (others) (2nd issue). As Nos. 417/19 but larger, 55 × 34 mm. On gold foil.
438 5k. As Type **122** . . . . . 70 2·00
439 5k. Freedom Statue . . . . 70 2·00
440 5k. Pres. Kaunda and agricultural produce ("Lima Programme") . . . 70 2·00

1985. 10th Anniv of Posts and Telecommunication Corporation. Multicoloured.
441 20n. Type **129** 55 10
442 45n. Postman and Livingstone Post Office, 1950 . . . . 85 25
443 55n. Postman and Kalomo Post Office, 1902 . . . . . 1·00 70
444 5k. Africa Trans-Continental Telegraph Line under construction, 1900 . . . . 2·50 6·00

1985. 40th Anniv of United Nations Organization.
445 **130** 20n. multicoloured . . . 25 10
446 – 45n. black, blue and brown 40 20
447 – 1k. multicoloured . . . . 75 2·00
448 – 2k. multicoloured . . . . 1·10 3·00
DESIGNS: 45n. Logo and "40"; 1k. President Kaunda addressing U.N. General Assembly, 1970; 2k. Signing of U.N. Charter, San Francisco, 1945.

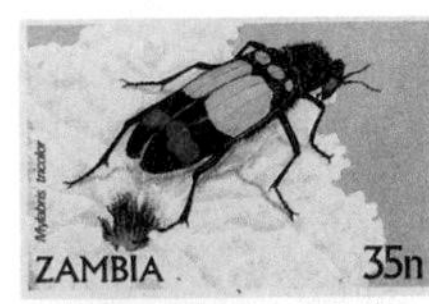

131 "Mylabris tricolor"

1986. Beetles. Multicoloured.
449 35n. Type **131** 15 10
450 1k. "Phasgonocnema melanianthe" 20 20
451 1k.70 "Amaurodes passerinii" 30 50
452 5k. "Ranzania petersiana" . . 85 2·00

1986. 60th Birthday of Queen Elizabeth II. As T **145a** of St. Helena. Multicoloured.
453 35n. Princess Elizabeth at Flower Ball, Savoy Hotel, 1951 . . . . 10 10
454 1k.25 With Prince Andrew, Lusaka Airport, 1979 . . . 15 20
455 1k.70 With President Kaunda 15 25
456 1k.95 In Luxembourg, 1976 15 30
457 5k. At Crown Agents Head Office, London, 1983 . . . 25 85

1986. Royal Wedding. As T **146a** of St. Helena. Multicoloured.
458 1k.70 Prince Andrew and Miss Sarah Ferguson . . . 30 35
459 5k. Prince Andrew in Zambia, 1979 . . . . . . 80 1·40

132 Goalkeeper saving Goal

1986. World Cup Football Championship, Mexico. Multicoloured.
460 35n. Type **132** 85 15
461 1k.25 Player kicking ball . . 2·00 1·40
462 1k.70 Two players competing for ball . . . . 2·25 1·90
463 5k. Player scoring goal . . . 3·25 6·00

133 Sculpture of Edmond Halley by Henry Pegram

1986. Appearance of Halley's Comet.
464 **133** 1k.25 multicoloured . . . 1·00 55
465 – 1k.70 multicoloured . . . 1·25 85
466 – 2k. multicoloured . . . . 1·75 1·75
467 – 5k. blue and black . . . 3·50 6·50
DESIGNS: 1k.70, "Giotto" spacecraft approaching nucleus of Comet; 2k. Studying Halley's Comet in 1682 and 1986; 5k. Part of Halley's chart of southern sky.

134 The Nativity

1986. Christmas. Children's Paintings. Mult.
468 35n. Type **134** 40 10
469 1k.25 Visit of the Three Kings . . . . 1·50 75
470 1k.60 The Holy Family with Shepherd and King . . . . 1·75 1·50
471 5k. Angel and Christmas tree 3·75 7·00

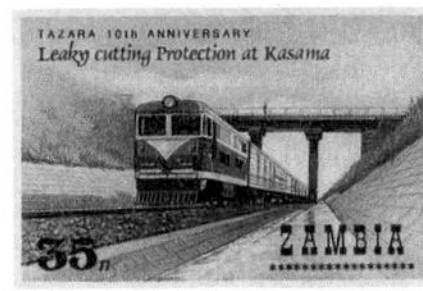

135 Diesel Train in Kasama Cutting

1986. 10th Anniv of Tanzania–Zambia Railway. Multicoloured.
472 35n. Type **135** 25 10
473 1k.25 Passenger train leaving Tunnel No. 21 . . . . . . 35 50
474 1k.70 Train between Tunnels Nos. 6 and 7 . . . . . . 35 70
475 5k. Trains near Mpika Station . . . . 70 3·00

136 President Kaunda and Graduate

1987. 20th Anniv of University of Zambia. Multicoloured.
476 35n. Type **136** 25 10
477 1k.25 University badge (vert) 55 60
478 1k.60 University statue . . . 60 1·00
479 5k. President Kaunda laying foundation stone (vert) . . 2·00 6·50

137 Arms of Kitwe

138 African Chestnut-headed Crake

1987. Arms of Zambian Towns. Mult.
480 35n. Type **137** 10 10
481 1k.25 Ndola 15 10
482 1k.70 Lusaka 20 25
483 20k. Livingstone . . . . . . 3·00 6·00

1987. Birds (1st series). Multicoloured.
484 5n. Cloud-scraping cisticola 10 10
485 10n. White-winged starling 10 10
486a 20n. on 1n. Yellow swamp warbler 20 20
487 25n. Type **138** . . . . . . 2·50 1·00
488 30n. Miombo pied barbet 20 10
489 35n. Black and rufous swallow . . . . 2·50 2·25
490 40n. Wattled crane 20 10
491 50n. Slaty egret 20 10
492 75n. on 2n. Olive-flanked robin chat . . . . 30 1·40
493 1k. Bradfield's hornbill . . . 2·50 40
494 1k.25 Boulton's puff-back flycatcher ("Margaret's Batis") . . . . 2·50 3·00
495 1k.60 Anchieta's sunbird . . 2·50 1·50
496 1k.65 on 30n. Miombo pied barbet . . . . 30 1·75
497 1k.70 Boehm's bee eater . . 2·50 3·00
498 1k.95 Perrin's bush shrike 2·50 2·25
499 2k. Whale-headed stork ("Shoebill") 35 35
500 5k. Taita falcon . . . . . . 3·00 80
501 10k. on 50n. Slaty egret . . 1·10 2·50
502 20k. on 2k. Whale-headed stork . . . . 1·25 3·75
Nos. 491, 493/5 and 497/502 are larger, size 24 × 39 mm.
No. 502 is surcharged "K20". For No. 499 surcharged "K20.00" see No. 594.
See also Nos. 587/95 and 625/38.

139 Look-out Tree, Livingstone

1987. Tourism. Multicoloured.
503 35n. Type **139** 30 15
504 1k.25 Rafting on Zambezi . . 30 25
505 1k.70 Tourists photographing lions, Luangwa Valley . . 1·75 90
506 10k. Eastern white pelicans ("White Pelican") . . . . 7·00 9·00

1987. Various stamps surch. (a) Nos. 432/5.
507 **127** 3k. on 25n. mult 90 90
508 – 6k. on 45n. blue and gold 1·75 1·75
509 – 10k. on 55n. blue and gold . . . . 2·25 2·25
510 – 20k. on 5k. mult . . . . 4·50 6·00

(b) Nos. 453/7.
511 3k. on 35n. Princess Elizabeth at Flower Ball, Savoy Hotel, 1951 . . . . 55 65
512 4k. on 1k.25 With Prince Andrew, Lusaka Airport, 1979 . . . . 65 75
513 6k. on 1k.70 With President Kaunda . . . . 1·00 1·25
514 10k. on 1k.95 In Luxembourg, 1976 . . . . 1·60 2·00
515 20k. on 5k. At Crown Agents Head Office, London, 1983 4·00 4·50

(c) Nos. 460/3.
516 3k. on 35n. Type **132** . . . 90 75
517 6k. on 1k.25 Player kicking ball . . . . 1·75 1·50
518 10k. on 1k.70 Two players competing for ball . . . . 2·25 2·25
519 20k. on 5k. Player scoring goal . . . . 4·25 6·00

(d) Nos. 464/7.
520 **133** 3k. on 1k.25 mult . . . . 1·75 1·00
521 – 6k. on 1k.70 mult . . . . 2·50 2·00
522 – 10k. on 2k. mult . . . . 3·75 4·00
523 – 20k. on 5k. blue and black . . . . 7·00 8·50

141 De Havilland D.H.C.2 Beaver

1987. 20th Anniv of Zambia Airways. Aircraft. Multicoloured.
524 35n. Type **141** 85 10
525 1k.70 Douglas DC-10 . . . . 2·00 70
526 5k. Douglas DC-3 . . . . . 4·25 3·75
527 10k. Boeing 707 . . . . . . 6·50 8·00

142 Friesian/Holstein Cow

1987. 40th Anniv of F.A.O. Multicoloured.
528 35n. Type **142** 10 10
529 1k.25 Simmental bull 20 25
530 1k.70 Sussex bull 20 30
531 20k. Brahman bull . . . . . 1·00 3·00

143 Mpoloto Ne Mikobango

144 Black Lechwe at Waterhole

1987. People of Zambia. Multicoloured.
532 35n. Type **143** 10 10
533 1k.25 Zintaka 20 25
534 1k.70 Mufuluhi 25 30
535 10k. Ntebwe . . . . 75 1·50
536 20k. Kubangwa Aa Mbulunga . . . . 1·25 3·00

1987. Black Lechwe. Multicoloured.
537 50n. Type **144** 65 10
538 2k. Black lechwe resting by pool (horiz) . . . . 1·75 40
539 2k.50 Running through water (horiz) . . . . 1·75 80
540 10k. Watching for danger . . 4·50 6·00
MS541 Two sheets, each 105 × 74 mm. (a) 20k. Caracal (predator). (b) 20k. Cheetah (predator) Set of 2 sheets . . . 13·00 11·00

145 Cassava Roots

1988. International Fund for Agricultural Development. Multicoloured.
542 50n. Type **145** 15 10
543 2k.50 Fishing 70 50
544 2k.85 Farmer and cattle . . . 75 55
545 10k. Picking coffee beans . . 1·50 2·50

146 Breast-feeding

147 Asbestos Cement

1988. UNICEF Child Survival Campaign. Multicoloured.
546 50n. Type **146** 20 10
547 2k. Growth monitoring . . . 50 30
548 2k.85 Immunization 60 70
549 10k. Oral rehydration . . . . 1·25 3·25

1988. Preferential Trade Area Fair. Mult.
550 50n. Type **147** 10 10
551 2k.35 Textiles 20 30
552 2k.50 Tea 20 40
553 10k. Poultry . . . . 75 2·75

148 Emergency Food Distribution

1988. 125th Anniv of Int Red Cross. Mult.
554 50n. Type **148** 20 10
555 2k.50 Giving first aid 50 60
556 2k.85 Practising bandaging 55 75
557 10k. Henri Dunant (founder) 1·75 3·50

149 Aardvark

1988. Endangered Species of Zambia. Mult.
558 50n. Type **149** 25 10
559 2k. Temminck's ground pangolin 50 40
560 2k.85 Hunting dog 60 75
561 20k. Black rhinoceros and calf . . . . 6·00 7·00

150 Boxing

1988. Olympic Games, Seoul. Multicoloured.
562 50n. Type **150** 15 10
563 2k. Athletics 35 40
564 2k.50 Hurdling 40 70
565 20k. Football . . . . 3·75 6·50
MS566 Two sheets, each 97×72 mm. (a) 30k. Tennis. (b) 30k. Karate Set of 2 sheets . . 8·00 11·00

151 Red Toad

1989. Frogs and Toads. Multicoloured.
567 50n. Type **151** 15 10
568 2k.50 Puddle frog 50 50
569 2k.85 Marbled reed frog . . 55 75
570 10k. Young reed frogs . . . 1·60 3·25

152 Common Slit-faced Bat

1989. Bats. Multicoloured.
571 50n. Type **152** 15 10
572 2k.50 Little free-tailed bat . . 45 55
573 2k.85 Hildebrandt's horseshoe bat 55 75
574 10k. Peters' epauletted fruit bat . . . . 1·50 3·25

153 Pope John Paul II and Map of Zambia

156 "Parinari curatellifolia"

1989. Visit of Pope John Paul II. Designs each with inset portrait. Multicoloured.
575 50n. Type **153** 75 20
576 6k.85 Peace dove with olive branch . . . . 2·75 2·75
577 7k.85 Papal arms . . . . . 3·00 3·25
578 10k. Victoria Falls . . . . . 4·50 4·50

1989. Various stamp surch. (a) On Nos. 339, 341/3, 345/6, 349 and 351.
579 1k.20 on 35n. Tonga Ila granary and house 20 15
580 3k.75 on 5n. Pottery making 30 20
581 8k.11 on 10n. Thatching . . 50 50
582 9k. on 30n. Makishi tightrope dancer 50 50
583 10k. on 75n. Women carrying water (38×26 mm) 50 50
584 18k.50 on 2k. Pipe-smoking Gwembe Valley belle (38×26 mm) . . . . . . 1·00 1·75
585 19k.50 on 12n. Mushroom picking . . . . 3·00 3·00
586 20k.50 on 18n. Millet grinding on stone . . . . 1·25 2·25

(b) On Nos. 484, 489, 493/5 and 497/500.
587 70n. on 35n. Black and rufous swallow . . . . . . 1·00 15
588 3k. on 5n. Cloud-scraping cisticola . . . . 1·00 30
589 8k. on 1k.25 Boulton's puff-back flycatcher . . . . . . 1·25 60
590 9k.90 on 1k.70 Boehm's bee eater . . . . 1·25 80
591 10k.40 on 1k.60 Anchieta's sunbird . . . . 1·25 90
592 12k.50 on 1k. Bradfield's hornbill . . . . 1·25 1·25
593 15k. on 1k.95 Perrin's bush strike . . . . 1·25 2·00
594 20k. on 2k. Whale-headed stork . . . . 1·75 2·50
595 20k.35 on 5k. Taita falcon . . 1·75 2·50
No. 594 shows the surcharge as "K20.00". The previously listed 20k. on 2k., No. 499, is surcharged "K20" only.

1989. Edible Fruits. Multicoloured.
596 50n. Type **156** 15 10
597 6k.50 "Uapaca kirkiana" . . 1·25 1·50
598 6k.85 Wild fig . . . . 1·25 2·00
599 10k. Bottle palm . . . . . . 2·25 3·25

157 "Lamarckiana sp."

1989. Grasshoppers. Multicoloured.
600 70n. Type **157** 20 10
601 10k.40 "Dictyophorus sp." 1·50 1·75
602 12k.50 "Cymatomera sp." . . 1·75 2·50
603 15k. "Phymateus iris" . . . 2·25 4·00

158 Fireball

160 Footballer and Ball

159 Postvan, Postman on Bicycle and Main Post Office, Lusaka

1989. Christmas. Flowers. Multicoloured.
604 70n. Type **158** 15 10
605 10k.40 Flame lily . . . . . . 1·00 1·25
606 12k.50 Foxglove lily . . . . 1·40 1·75
607 20k. Vlei lily . . . . 2·40 4·00

1990. "Stamp World London 90" International Stamp Exhibition. Multicoloured.
608 1k.20 Type **159** 30 10
609 19k.50 Zambia 1980 18n. butterflies stamp . . . . . 2·75 2·75
610 20k.50 Rhodesia and Nyasaland 1962 9d. and Northern Rhodesia 1925 ½d. stamps . . . . 2·75 2·75
611 50k. 1840 Penny Black and Maltese Cross cancellation 5·00 7·00

1990. World Cup Football Championship, Italy.
612 **160** 1k.20 multicoloured . . . 10 10
613 – 18k.50 multicoloured . . 2·00 2·50
614 – 19k.50 multicoloured . . 2·00 2·50
615 – 20k.50 multicoloured . . 2·00 2·50
MS616 100×73 mm. 50k. multicoloured . . . . 9·00 9·50
DESIGNS: 18k.50 to 50k, Different football scenes.

161 Road Tanker

1990. 10th Anniv of Southern African Development Co-ordination Conference. Each showing map of Southern Africa. Multicoloured.
617 1k.20 Type **161** 30 10
618 19k.50 Telecommunications 2·00 2·25
619 20k.50 "Regional Co-operation" . . . . 2·00 2·25
620 50k. Transporting coal by cable . . . . 7·00 8·00

162 Irrigation

1990. 26th Anniv of Independence. Mult.
621 1k.20 Type **162** 10 10
622 19k.50 Shoe factory . . . . 1·10 1·40
623 20k.50 Mwembeshi II satellite earth station . . . . 1·25 1·60
624 50k. "Mother and Child" (statue) . . . . 2·50 4·25

1990. Birds (2nd series). As T **138**. Mult.
625 10n. Livingstone's flycatcher 65 50
626 15n. Bar-winged weaver . . . 65 50
627 30n. Purple-throated cuckoo shrike 85 50
628 50n. Retz's red-billed helmet shrike 85 50
629 50n. As 10n. . . . . 1·40 70
630 1k. As 15n. . . . . 1·40 50
631 1k.20 Bronze-naped pigeon ("Western Bronze-naped Pigeon") . . . . 1·25 20
632 2k. As 30n. . . . . 1·40 70
633 3k. As 50n. . . . . 1·40 70
634 5k. As 1k.20 . . . . 1·75 70
635 15k. Corn crake 50 40
636 20k. Dickinson's kestrel . . . 2·25 1·50
637 20k.50 As 20k. . . . . 70 1·00
638 50k. Denham's bustard . . . 50 1·25
Nos. 635/8 are larger, size 23×39 mm.

163 The Bird and the Snake

166 Woman cooking

164 Genet

1991. Int Literacy Year. Folklore. Mult.
639 1k.20 Type **163** 30 10
640 18k.50 Kalulu and the Leopard . . . . 2·75 3·00
641 19k.50 The Mouse and the Lion . . . . 2·75 3·00
642 20k.50 Kalulu and the Hippopotamus . . . . . . 2·75 3·00

1991. Small Carnivores. Multicoloured.
643 1k.20 Type **164** 30 10
644 18k.50 Civet . . . . 2·75 3·25
645 19k.50 Serval . . . . 2·75 3·25
646 20k.50 African wild cat . . . 2·75 3·25

1991. Nos. 441/4 surch **K2**.
647 2k. on 20n. Type **129** . . . . 8·00 5·50
648 2k. on 45n. Postman and Livingstone Post Office, 1950 . . . . 8·00 5·50
649 2k. on 55n. Postman and Kalomo Post Office, 1902 8·00 5·50
650 2k. on 5k. African Trans-Continental Telegraph Line under construction, 1900 8·00 5·50

1991. Soya Promotion Campaign. Mult.
651 1k. Type **166** 10 10
652 2k. Soya bean and field . . . 10 10
653 5k. Mother feeding child . . 20 15
654 20k. Healthy and malnourished children . . 1·25 1·75
655 50k. President Kaunda holding child . . . . . . 2·25 3·25

1991. Various stamps surch **K2**.
656 **130** 2k. on 20n. mult . . . . 32·00 5·00
657 **127** 2k. on 25n. mult . . . . 80·00 5·00
658 – 2k. on 28n. mult (No. 344) . . . . . . 32·00 5·00
659 – 2k. on 28n. mult (No. 393) . . . . . . 42·00 5·00
660 – 2k. on 28n. mult (No. 401) . . . . . . — 5·00
661 – 2k. on 28n. mult (No. 418) . . . . . . — 5·00
662 – 2k. on 32n. mult (No. 422) . . . . . . 26·00 5·00
663 – 2k. on 35n. mult (No. 453) . . . . . . — 5·00
664 **134** 2k. on 35n. mult . . . . 70·00 5·00
665 **137** 2k. on 35n. mult . . . . 42·00 5·00
666 – 2k. on 45n. mult (No. 427) . . . . . . 42·00 5·00
667 – 2k. on 45n. black, blue and light blue (No. 430) 55·00 5·00
668 – 2k. on 45n. blue and gold (No. 433) . . . . . . 80·00 5·00
669 – 2k. on 45n. black, blue and brown (No. 446) 42·00 5·00
670 – 2k. on 1k.60 mult (No. 470) . . . . . . 70·00 5·00
671 – 2k. on 1k.70 mult (No. 451) . . . . . . 42·00 5·00
672 – 2k. on 1k.70 mult (No. 482) . . . . . . — 5·00
673 – 2k. on 5k. mult (No. 435) 15·00 5·00
674 – 2k. on 5k. mult (No. 452) 15·00 5·00
675 – 2k. on 6k.50 mult (No. 597) . . . . . . 42·00 5·00
676 – 2k. on 6k.85 mult (No. 576) . . . . . . 55·00 5·00
677 – 2k. on 6k.85 mult (No. 598) . . . . . . 15·00 5·00
678 – 2k. on 7k.85 mult (No. 577) . . . . . . 80·00 5·00

167 Chilubula Church near Kasama

169 "Disa hamatopetala"

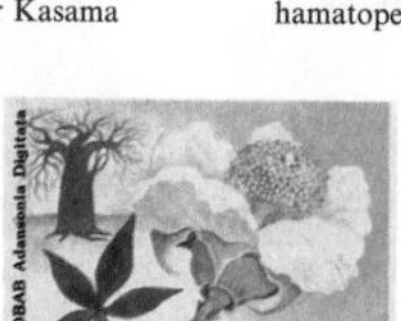

168 "Adansonia digitata"

1991. 500th Birth Anniv of St. Ignatius Loyola. Multicoloured.
679 1k. Type **167** 10 10
680 2k. Chikuni Church near Monze 15 15
681 20k. Bishop Joseph du Pont 2·25 2·50
682 50k. Saint Ignatius Loyola 4·00 5·50

1991. Flowering Trees. Multicoloured.
683 1k. Type **168** 20 10
684 2k. "Dichrostachys cinerea" 30 15
685 10k. "Stereospermum kunthianum" . . . . . . 1·75 1·40
686 30k. "Azana garckeana" . . 3·25 4·25
No. 685 is inscribed "Sterospermum" in error.

1992. 40th Anniv of Queen Elizabeth II's Accession. As T **168a** of St. Helena. Mult.
687 4k. Queen's House 10 10
688 32k. Traditional village . . . 1·00 70
689 35k. Fisherman hauling nets 1·00 90
690 38k. Three portraits of Queen Elizabeth . . . . 1·25 1·25
691 50k. Queen Elizabeth II . . . 1·60 2·75

1992. Orchids. Multicoloured.
692 1k. Type **169** 50 15
693 2k. "Eulophia paivaeana" . . 50 20
694 5k. "Eulophia quartiniana" 85 40
695 20k. "Aerangis verdickii" . . 3·50 5·00

170 Kasinja Mask

1992. Tribal Masks. Multicoloured.
696 1k. Type **170** 15 10
697 2k. Chizaluke 20 10
698 10k. Mwanapweu 80 65
699 30k. Maliya . . . . 2·25 3·50

171 Bushbuck

1992. Antelopes. Multicoloured.
700 4k. Type **171** 10 30
701 40k. Eland 80 50
702 45k. Roan antelope 80 50
703 100k. Sable antelope . . . . 1·60 3·75

172 De Havilland D.H.66 Hercules "City of Basra"
174 Hurdling

173 Wise Men with Gifts

1992. 60th Anniv of Airmail Service. Mult.
704 4k. Type 172 . . . . 50 40
705 40k. Vickers Super VC-10 . . 2·00 85
706 45k. Short S.45A Solent 3 flying boat "Severn" . . . 2·00 85
707 100k. Douglas DC-10 . . . . 3·50 5·50

1992. Christmas. Multicoloured.
708 10k. Type 173 . . . . . . 20 10
709 80k. Nativity . . . . 1·75 1·90
710 90k. Angelic choir . . . . . 1·90 2·25
711 100k. Angel and shepherds 1·90 2·50
MS712 209 × 57 mm. Nos. 708/11 10·00 11·00

1992. Olympic Games, Barcelona. Mult.
713 10k. Type 174 . . . . . . 20 10
714 40k. Boxing 60 40
715 80k. Judo . . . . 1·25 2·00
716 100k. Cycling . . . . 3·25 3·50

175 Nkundalila Falls

1993. Waterfalls. Multicoloured.
717 50k. Type 175 . . . . . . 40 10
718 200k. Chishimba Falls . . . 1·25 1·25
719 250k. Chipoma Falls . . . . 1·40 1·60
720 300k. Lumangwe Falls . . . 1·50 1·90

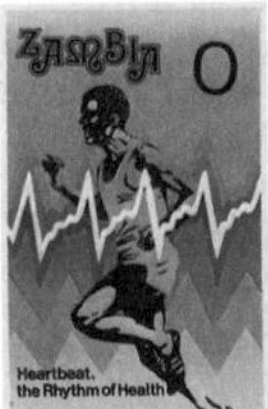

176 Athlete and Cardiograph

1993. Heartbeat Campaign. Multicoloured.
721 (O) Type 176 . . . . 75 55
722 (P) Heart and cardiograph 75 55
These stamps were initially sold at 50k. (No. 721) for ordinary post and 80k. (No. 722) for priority mail. These face values were increased to reflect postage rate increases.

177 Bronze Sunbird
178 Tiger Snake

1994. Sunbirds. Multicoloured. (a) Face values as T 177.
723 20k. Type 177 . . . . . . 40 65
724 50k. Violet-backed sunbird 50 50
725 100k. Scarlet-chested sunbird 70 10
726 150k. Bannerman's sunbird 80 10
727 200k. Oustalet's white-bellied sunbird 80 10
728 250k. Anchieta's sunbird ("Red and blue sunbird") 80 20
729 300k. Olive sunbird 90 40
730 350k. Green-headed sunbird 90 40
731 400k. Red-tufted malachite sunbird 90 50
732 500k. Variable sunbird . . . 90 50
733 800k. Coppery sunbird . . . 1·25 1·40
734 1000k. Southern orange-tufted sunbird ("Orange-tufted Sunbird") . . . . . 1·40 1·60
735 1500k. Amethyst sunbird ("Black Sunbird") . . . . 1·50 2·25
736 2000k. Green-throated sunbird . . . . 1·75 2·50

(b) Face values shown as capital letters.
737 (O) Mariqua sunbird ("Marico Sunbird") . . . 1·00 55
738 (P) Eastern double-collared sunbird . . . . 1·00 55
Nos. 737/8 were initially sold at 50k. for ordinary post (No. 737) and 80k. for priority mail (No. 738). These rates were increased to 100k. for ordinary post and 150k. for priority mail on 20th June 1994. On 1 March 1995 the difference between the two rates was abolished and both "O" and "P" stamps were sold at 500k. This was reduced to 400k. each on 1 April 1995, but the rate reverted to 500k. on 8 February 1996.

1994. Snakes. Multicoloured.
739 50k. Type 178 . . . . . . 40 10
740 200k. Egyptian cobra . . . . 1·25 60
741 300k. African python . . . . 1·50 1·25
742 500k. Green mamba . . . . 1·90 2·50

179 Women working on Road

1995. 75th Anniv of I.L.O. Multicoloured.
743 100k. Type 179 . . . . . . 50 20
744 450k. Women making cement blocks . . . . 1·75 2·00

180 Angel playing Kalimba and Flowers

1995. Christmas (1994). Multicoloured.
745 100k. Type 180 . . . . . . 35 10
746 300k. Angel at prayer and animals 80 60
747 450k. Angel with flute and birds . . . . 1·10 1·25
748 500k. Angel with drum and Baobab trees . . . . . . 1·25 1·50

181 Anniversary Emblem, Rainbow and Map
182 David Livingstone (missionary) and Memorial

1995. 50th Anniv of United Nations.
749 181 700k. multicoloured . . . 2·00 2·75

1995. Monuments. Multicoloured.
750 100k. Type 182 . . . . . . 25 10
751 300k. Mbereshi Mission . . . 70 60
752 450k. Von Lettow-Vorbeck Monument . . . . 1·10 1·40
753 500k. Niamkolo Church . . 1·25 1·50

183 Saddle-bill Stork

1996. Endangered Species. Birds. Multicoloured.
754 200k. Type 183 . . . . . . 40 20
755 300k. Black-cheeked lovebird 55 35
756 500k. Pair of black-cheeked lovebirds 75 85
757 900k. Saddle-bill stork and chicks . . . . 1·00 1·60
MS758 120 × 90 mm. Nos. 754/7 55·00 55·00

1996. Christmas. Nos. 709/10 surch.
759 (O) on 90k. Angelic choir . . 25 15
760 900k. on 80k. Nativity . . . 1·00 1·10
No. 759 was sold at 500k., which was the minimum local postage rate for ordinary post.

185 "Precis octavia sesamus"
187 Verreaux's Eagle Owl

1997. Butterflies and Moths. Multicoloured.
761 300k. Type 185 . . . . . . 50 20
762 500k. "Argema mimosae" . . 80 35
763 700k. "Imbrasia dione" . . . 1·10 1·00
764 900k. "Papilio ophidicephalus cotterell" . . . . 1·40 1·60
MS765 85 × 120 mm. As Nos. 761/4, but each with face value of 900k. 4·50 5·00

1997. Nos. 688/90 surch.
766 (O) on 32k. Traditional village . . . . 1·50 55
767 500k. on 35k. Fishermen hauling nets . . . . 1·50 70
768 900k. on 38k. Three portraits of Queen Elizabeth . . . . 3·00 3·25
No. 766 was sold at 500k. which was the minimum local postage rate for ordinary post.

1997. Owls of Zambia. Multicoloured.
769 300k. Type 187 . . . . . . 75 30
770 500k. Pel's fishing owl . . . 1·25 55
771 700k. Barn owl . . . . . . 1·50 1·50
772 900k. Spotted eagle owl . . . 1·75 2·00
MS773 128 × 85 mm. As Nos. 769/72, but each with face value of 900k. . . . . 5·50 6·00

188 Gandhi as Law Student, London, 1888
190 Traveller and Dog ("Luchele nganga")

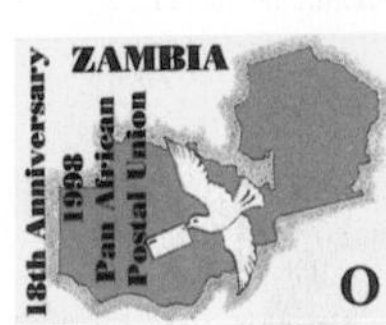

189 Dove and Map of Zambia

1998. 50th Death Anniv of Mahatma Gandhi. Multicoloured.
774 250k. Type 188 . . . . . . 75 55
775 (O) Gandhi at Red Fort, Delhi . . . . 1·25 1·25
776 500k. Gandhi with Nehru, 1946 (horiz) . . . . 1·25 1·25
777 900k. Gandhi at prayer . . . 1·75 2·00
MS778 70 × 100 mm. 2000k. At Second Round Table Conference, London, 1931 . . . . 3·50 3·75
No. 775 was sold at 500k. which was the minimum local postage rate for ordinary post.

1998. 18th Anniv of Pan African Postal Union.
779 189 (O) multicoloured . . . . 1·00 55
780 – 500k multicoloured . . . 1·00 55
781 – 900k. black, red and orange . . . . 1·50 1·75
DESIGNS: 500k. Lechwe at Kafue Flats; 900k. Dove with "18th" note in beak.
No. 779 was sold at 500k. which was the minimum local postage rate for ordinary post.

1998. Christmas. Traditional Stories. Mult.
782 300k. Type 190 . . . . . . 75 30
783 500k. Man feeding crocodile ("Kasuli") . . . . 1·00 70
MS784 111 × 70 mm. 2000k. Type 190; 2000k. As 500k. . . 4·00 4·50

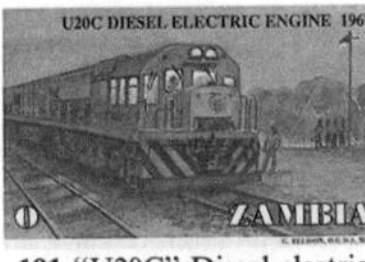

191 "U20C" Diesel-electric Locomotive, 1967

1999. Trains. Multicoloured.
785 (O) Type 191 . . . . 40 30
786 800k. Beyer-Garratt Class 15A No. 401 steam locomotive, 1950 . . . . . 1·00 1·00
787 800k. Class 7 No. 70 steam locomotive, 1900 . . . . . 1·00 1·00
788 900k. Class 20 No. 708 steam locomotive, 1954 . . . . . 1·10 1·10
789 900 k . H.P. diesel-electric railcar, 1966 . . . . 1·10 1·10
MS790 112 × 85 mm. 1000k. Class 7 No. 955 steam locomotive, 1892 1·40 1·60

1999. No. 743 surch K500.
791 500k. on 100k. Type 179 . . 2·50 1·25

193 Conference Emblem and Dam

1999. 11th International Conference on AIDS and STDs in Africa, Lusaka. Multicoloured.
792 500k. Type 193 . . . . . . 1·00 50
793 900k. Conference emblem and Victoria Falls . . . . 1·40 1·60

194 Blacksmith Plover

1999. Water Birds. Multicoloured.
794 50k. Type 194 . . . . . . 10 10
795 100k. Sacred ibis 10 10
796 200k. Purple swamphen ("Purple Gallinule") . . . 10 10
797 250k. Purple heron 10 10
798 300k. Glossy ibis 10 10
799 400k. Marabou stork 10 15
800 450k. African spoonbill . . . 10 15
801 500k. Peters's finfoot ("African Finfoot") . . . 10 15
802 (O) Comb duck ("Knob-billed Duck") 10 15
803 600k. African darter 15 20
804 700k. African skimmer . . . 1·00 35
805 800k. Spur-winged goose . . 20 25
806 900k. Hammerkop 20 25
807 1000k. Eastern white pelican 1·25 1·00
808 1500k. Black-winged stilt . . 1·75 1·75
809 2000k. Black-crowned night heron 45 50
No. 802 was sold at 500k. which was the minimum local postage rate for ordinary post.
No. 794 is inscribed "Sarkidiomis melamotos" and No. 805 "Plectroterus gambensis", both in error.

2000. No. 750 surch K700.
813 700k. on 100k. Type 182 . . 2·50 1·50

2000. Nos. 774 and 776 surch K1,200.
814 1200k. on 250k. Type 188 2·75 2·00
815 1500k. on 500k. Gandhi with Nehru, 1946 (horiz) . . . 2·75 2·75
No. 775 was re-issued with Nos. 814/15 and sold at 700k.

197 Map of Africa showing COMESA Member States

2000. Common Market for Eastern and Southern Africa (COMESA). Multicoloured.
816 600k. Type 197 . . . . . . 30 20
817 700k. Truck crossing free trade border 35 35
818 1000k. Exchange of money and sale of goods at border 45 60

198 "Creation in Clay"

2000. African Legends of Creation. Multicoloured.
819 600k. Type **198** 30 15
820 1000k. "The Chameleon and the Lizard" 45 50
821 1400k. "Why the Stones do not Die" 70 85
MS822 128 × 125 mm. As Nos. 819/21, but with brown borders, each × 3 . . . . . . 4·00 4·50
MS823 90 × 70 mm. 3500k. "The Rooster in the Sky" . . . . .

199 Feeding Refugee Children

2001. 50th Anniv of United Nations High Commissioner for Refugees. Multicoloured.
824 700k. Type **199** 45 25
825 1500k. Refugees fleeing from conflict . . . . 80 1·00

200 African Buffalo

2001. Animals of Africa. Multicoloured.
826 500k. Type **200** 30 15
827 1000k. Cheetah (vert) 50 40
828 2000k. African elephant . . . 1·25 1·25
829 3200k. Ruffed lemur (vert) 1·50 1·75
MS830 145 × 78 mm. 2000k. Cheetah; 2000k. Three adult and one young Impala; 2000k. Four adult impala; 2000k. Warthog; 2000k. Two lionesses; 2000k. Four lionesses . . . . 4·50 5·00
MS831 74 × 165 mm. 2000k. Crimson-breasted shrike; 2000k. European bee eater ("Common Bee Eater"); 2000k. Blue monkey; 2000k. Chimpanzee; 2000k. Lesser bushbaby; 2000k. Small-spotted genet (all vert) . . . . 4·50 5·00
MS832 145 × 78 mm. 2000k. Defussa waterbuck; 2000k. Crowned crane; 2000k. Hartebeest; 2000k. Pygmy hippopotamus; 2000k. White rhinoceros; 2000k. Giant forest hog . . . . 4·50 5·00
MS833 Three sheets, each 85 × 62 mm. (a) 6000k. African elephant. (b) 6000k. Grevy's zebra. (c) 6000k. Black rhinoceros Set of 3 sheets . . . . 5·50 6·00

201 Woman watching Eclipse

2001. Solar Eclipse of 21 June 2001. Multicoloured.
834 1000k. Type **201** 50 30
835 1500k. Stylized bird 70 70
836 1700k. Chameleon on branch 80 90
837 1800k. Hand holding spear and elephant 80 90
838 2200k. Man with spear watching eclipse . . . . . 1·00 1·25

202 "Sanjo Kantaro II and Ichikawa Monnosuke I, 1720s" (Okumura Masanobu)

203 President Chiluba receiving Master's Degree, Warwick University

2001. "Philanippon '01" International Stamp Exhibition, Tokyo. Japanese Art. Multicoloured (except No. 841).
839 500k. Type **202** 30 20
840 500k. "Nakamura Senya as Toknatsu" (Torii Kiyomasu I) 30 20
841 1000k. "Standing Figure of a Woman" (Torii Kiyomasu I) (black, green and brown) 55 60
842 1000k. "Sanjo Kantaro and Ichikawa Monosuke, c. 1730" (Masanobu) 55 60
843 1500k. "Ono no Komachii?" (Masanobu) 80 90
844 1800k. "Dog bringing a Love Letter" (Shigenaga) . . . . 90 1·10
MS845 140 × 94 mm. 3200k. "Nakamura Kumetaro I" (Shunsho); 3200k. "Actor in Female Role" (Kiyomasu I); 3200k. "Segawa Kikunojo leaning on Sugoroku Board" (Kiyomasu I); 3200k. "Ichikawa Gennosuke as a Wakashu" (Kiyomasu I) 4·50 5·00
MS846 140 × 94 mm. 3200k. "Nakamura Matsue as a Cat Woman" (Shunsho); 3200k. "Sanjo Kantaro with Branch of Bamboo" (Kiyomasu I); 3200k. "Yamashika Kinsaku I as Peddler" (Torii Kiyomasu I); 3200k. "Portrait of an Actor" (Shunsho) . . . . 4·50 5·00
MS847 Two sheets. (a) 6000k. "Akashi of the Tamaya" (Hishikawa Ryukoku). (b) 6000k. "Events of Year in the Floating World" (Moroshige) (horiz) Set of 2 sheets . . . . 4·25 4·75

2001. Frederick Chiluba (President of Zambia, 1991–2002). Multicoloured.
848 1000k. Type **203** 50 30
849 1500k. President Chiluba signing affidavit for second term of office, 1996 . . . . 70 70
850 1700k. President after PHI Housing Empowerment of the people (horiz) . . . . 80 1·00
MS851 73 × 98 mm. 6000k. President receiving Master's Degree . . . 3·00 3·50

204 Children playing

2001. SOS Children's Villages (Kinderdorf International).
852 **204** 2500k. multicoloured . . 1·00 1·25

205 Princess Victoria as Young Girl

206 Princess Elizabeth as Baby

2001. Death Centenary of Queen Victoria. T **205** and similar vert designs. Multicoloured.
MS853 2000k. Type **205**; 2000k. Queen Victoria as widow; 2000k. With baby daughter; 2000k. With Prince Albert; 2000k. After being crowned Empress of India, 1876; 2000k. Princess Victoria as teenager . . . . 2·75 3·00
MS854 93 × 126 mm. 7000k. Young Queen Victoria . . . . 1·60 1·90

2001. 25th Death Anniv of Mao Tse-tung (Chinese leader). As T **102** of St. Kitts. Multicoloured.
MS855 177 × 183 mm. 3200k. As student, 1918; 3200k. Mao in 1945; 3200k. As guerrilla leader, 1937 . . . . 2·75 3·00
MS856 132 × 128 mm. 4000k. Writing . . . . 1·00 1·25

2001. 75th Death Anniv of Claude-Oscar Monet (French artist). As T **103** of St. Kitts. Multicoloured.
MS857 136 × 177 mm. 1500k. "The Promenade at Argenteuil"; 1500k. "View of the Argenteuil Plain from the Sannois Hills"; 1500k. "The Seine at Argenteuil"; 1500k. "The Basin at Argenteuil" . . 2·00 2·25
MS858 137 × 110 mm. 6000k. "Rouen Cathedral, Portal, Overcast Weather" (vert) . . . 2·00 2·25

2001. 75th Birthday of Queen Elizabeth II. Multicoloured.
MS859 157 × 175 mm. 4000k. Type **206**; 4000k. Princess Elizabeth as schoolgirl; 4000k. As young girl in garden; 4000k. In Women's Army Auxilliary Unit uniform, c. 1942 . . . . 3·50 3·75
MS860 79 × 109 mm. 8000k. Queen Elizabeth II as young woman (42 × 56 mm) . . . . 1·90 2·00

2001. Death Centenary of Giuseppe Verdi (Italian composer). As T **105** of St. Kitts showing scenes from *Falstaff* (opera). Multicoloured.
MS861 160 × 180 mm. 4000k. Benjamin Luxon as Falstaff (in white shirt); 4000k. Benjamin Luxon as Falstaff (in red and gold); 4000k. Paul Plishka as Falstaff; 4000k. Anne Collin as Mistress Quickly . . . . 5·00 5·00
MS862 79 × 109 mm. 8000k. 19th-century poster for Falstaff 2·50 2·50

207 HMS *Tabard*, 1946

2001. Centenary of Royal Navy Submarine Service. Submarines. Multicoloured.
MS863 2000k. Type **207**; 2000k. HMS *Opossum*, 1963; 2000k. HMS *Unicorn*, 1992; 2000k. HMS *Churchill*, 1968; 2000k. HMS *Victorious*, 1992; 2000k. HMS *Triumph*, 1982 . . . . 4·50 5·00
MS864 101 × 78 mm. 6000k. Lieut-Commander Wanklyn (VC) and crew of HMS *Upholder*, 1941 (vert) . . . . 2·40 2·75

208 LZ-1, 1900

2001. Zeppelins. Multicoloured.
MS865 145 × 132 mm. 2000k. Type **208**; 2000k. Parseval PL25, 1915; 2000k. LZ-3, 1906; 2000k. Baldwin, 1908; 2000k. LZ-129 *Hindenburg*, 1936; 2000k. *Norge*, 1926 . . . . 4·50 5·00

2002. "United We Stand". Support for Victims of 11 September 2001 Terrorist Attacks. As T **445** of St. Vincent. Multicoloured.
866 3200k. U.S. flag around Statue of Liberty and Zambian flag . . . . . . 1·00 1·25

209 Norman Borlaug (USA, 1970)

211 Ferenc Puskas (Hungary)

210 Horse-taming Figurines, Tang Dynasty

2002. Centenary of Nobel Prizes. Multicoloured.
MS867 146 × 210 mm. 2000k. Type **209**; 2000k. Lester B. Pearson (Canada, 1957); 2000k. International Red Cross (1944); 2000k. Anwar Sadat (Egypt, 1978); 2000k. Georges Pire (Belgium, 1958); 2000k. Linus Pauling (USA, 1962) . . . . . 4·00 4·50
MS868 146 × 210 mm. 2000k. Seamus Heaney (Ireland, 1995); 2000k. Toni Morrison (USA, 1993); 2000k. Gunter Grass (Germany, 1999); 2000k. Wislawa Szymborska (Poland, 1996); 2000k. Dario Fo (Italy, 1997); 2000k. Jose Saramango (Portugal, 1998) . . . . 4·00 4·50
MS869 146 × 210 mm. 2000k. Isaac Bashevis Singer (USA, 1978); 2000k. Gao Xingjian (China, 2000); 2000k. Claude Simon (France, 1985); 2000k. Naguib Mahfouz (Egypt, 1988); 2000k. Camilo Jose Cela (Spain, 1989); 2000k. Czeslaw Milosz (USA, 1980) . . . . 4·00 4·50
MS870 Three sheets, each 106 × 128 mm. (a) 6000k. George Marshall (Peace, USA, 1953). (b) 6000k. Gerard Debreu (Economics, USA, 1983). (c) 6000k. Robert Fogel (Economics, USA, 1993) Set of 3 sheets . . 5·00 5·50
No. **MS**868 shows recipients of Nobel Peace Prizes and Nos. **MS**869/70 Literature Prize winners.

2002. Chinese New Year ("Year of the Horse"). Sheet 108 × 76 mm.
MS871 **210** 5000k. multicoloured 1·40 1·60

2002. World Cup Football Championship, Japan and Korea (2002). Multicoloured.
MS872 142 × 164 mm. 2000k. Type **211**; 2000k. Official poster of 1962 World Cup, Chile; 2000k. Spanish player; 2000k. England player; 2000k. Player and Jeonju World Cup Stadium, Korea (57 × 42 mm) . . . . 2·00 2·50
MS873 142 × 164 mm. 2000k. Official poster of 1954 World Cup, Switzerland; 2000k. Stanley Matthews (England); 2000k. Scotland player; 2000k. Belgian player; 2000k. Player and Daejeon World Cup Stadium, Korea (57 × 42 mm) . . . . 3·00 3·50
MS874 Two sheets, each 70 × 100 mm. (a) 8000k. Bryan Robson (England) scoring goal against France, 1982 (42 × 57 mm). (b) 8000k. Salenko (Russia) scoring goal against Cameroon, 1994 (57 × 42 mm) Set of 2 sheets . . . . 4·50 5·00

2002. Nos. 724, 739, 743 and 745 surch.
875 250k. on 50k. Type **178** . . . 20 10
876 300k. on 50k. Violet-backed Sunbird 20 10
877 500k. on 100k. Type **179** . . 30 10
878 1000k. on 100k. Type **180** . . 55 30

2002. Golden Jubilee. As T **110** of St. Kitts. Multicoloured.
MS879 132 × 100 mm. 3200k. Queen Elizabeth II disembarking from plane; 3200k. Wearing pink blouse; 3200k. With Prince Edward; 3200k. Wearing tiara 4·00 4·50
MS880 76 × 108 mm. 7500k. With Duke of Edinburgh in library 2·50 2·75

2002. Winter Olympic Games, Salt Lake City. As T **111** of St. Kitts. Multicoloured.
881 1000k. Ice hockey 60 45
882 3200k. Cross-country skier 1·50 1·75

2002. 20th World Scout Jamboree, Thailand. As T **116** of St. Kitts. Multicoloured.
MS883 153 × 115 mm. 3200k. Troop hiking; 3200k. Knot tying; 3200k. Archery; 3200k. Fire-making 4·00 4·50
MS884 58 × 76 mm. 8000k. Scout by campfire (vert) . . . . 2·75 3·00

2002. International Year of Mountains. As T **115** of St. Kitts. Multicoloured.
MS885 151 × 109 mm. 1500k. Mount Whitney, USA; 1500k. Aconcagua, Argentina/Chile border; 1500k. Mönch, Switzerland; 1500k. Mount Ararat, Turkey . . . . . . 2·50 2·75
MS886 74 × 56 mm. 9000k. Mount Everest, Nepal/China border 3·50 3·75

213 White-fronted Bee Eater

2002. Birds of Zambia. Multicoloured. (a) Size 35 × 28 mm.
887 700k. Type **213** 15 20
888 1200k. Blue-cheeked bee eater 60 35
889 1400k. Boehm's bee eater . . 30 35
890 1500k. Little bee eater . . . 70 40

(b) Size 25 × 21 mm.

891		1000k. Type **213**	25	30
892		1200k. Little bee eater	25	30
893		1500k. Blue-cheeked bee eater	35	40
894		1800k. Boehm's bee eater	40	45

214 Camelsfoot (*Bauhinia galpinii*)

2002. Flowers, Butterflies and Mushrooms of Zambia. Multicoloured.

MS895	120 × 120 mm. 2500k. Type **214**; 2500k. Christmas bells (*Sandersonia aurantiaca*); 2500k. Impala lily (*Adenium obesum*); 2500k. Everlasting (*Helichrysum ecklonis*); 2500k. *Anomatheca grandiflora*; 2500k. Soldier Lily (*Cyrtanthus obliquus*)	4·00	4·50
MS896	120 × 120 mm. 2500k. False monarch (*Mimicraea marshalli*); 2500k. Golden piper (*Eurytera dryope*); 2500k. Blue pansy (*Junonia orithya*); 2500k. Christmas treeacraea (*Acraea anemosa*); 2500k. Grass yellow (*Eurema brigitta*); 2500k. Gold-spotted sylph (*Metisella metis*)	4·00	4·50
MS897	120 × 120 mm. 2500k. Copper trumpet (*Clitocybe olearia*); 2500k. King bolete (*Boletus edulis*); 2500k. Death cap (*Amanita phalloides*); 2500k. Fly agaric (*Amanita muscaria*); 2500k. Chantarelle (*Cantharellus cibarius*); 2500k. Deadly fiber cap (*Inocybe erubescens*)	4·00	4·50
MS898	Three sheets, each 100 × 70 mm. (a) 8000k. Arum lily (*Zantedeschia aethiopica*). (b) 8000k. African monarch (*Danaus chrysippus*). (c) 8000k. Stump brittle-head (*Psathyrella piluliformis*) Set of 3 sheets	7·00	7·50

215 Queen Elizabeth II

216 Prince William

2003. 50th Anniv of Coronation. Multicoloured.

MS899	156 × 93 mm. 5000k. Type **215**; 5000k. Wearing tiara and smiling; 5000k. Wearing fuchsia hat and outfit	3·00	3·25
MS900	76 × 106 mm. 10000k. Wearing floral hat and outfit	2·50	2·60

2003. 21st Birthday of Prince William. Multicoloured.

MS901	157 × 104 mm. 5000k. Type **216**; 5000k. As young boy; 5000k. Wearing yellow polo neck shirt	3·00	3·25
MS902	68 × 98 mm. 10000k. Wearing cream round neck jumper and laughing	2·50	2·60

POSTAGE DUE STAMPS

D 3

1964.

D11	D 3	1d. orange	30	2·50
D12		2d. blue	35	2·50
D13		3d. lake	45	1·75
D14		4d. blue	45	2·25
D15		6d. purple	45	2·25
D16		1s. green	55	4·25

APPENDIX

The following stamps have either been issued in excess of postal needs, or have not been made available to the public in reasonable quantities at face value.

1984.

Olympic Games, Los Angeles. 90n. × 5, each embossed on gold foil.

1987.

Classic Cars 1k.50 × 25, each embossed on gold foil.

The following issues are reported by the Zambia Postal Services Corporation as being available from Philatelic Counters only.

1997.

Disney's Chinese New Year. 250, 400, 500k. × 7, 600, 750, 1000k.

Endangered Species. 500k. × 6, 1000k. × 6

Trains of the World. 200, 300, 500k. × 7, 900, 1000, 1500k.

Golden Wedding of Queen Elizabeth II and Prince Philip. 500k. × 6.

50th Death Anniv of Paul P. Harris (founder of Rotary International). 1000k.

"Pacific '97" International Stamp Exhibition, San Francisco. Death Centenary of Heinrich von Stephan (founder of the U.P.U.). 1000k. × 3.

Christmas. Religious Paintings. 50k. × 2, 100k. × 2, 500, 1000k.

1998.

Diana, Princess of Wales Commemoration. 500k. × 6, 700k. × 6.

Flowers. 500k. × 13.

Chinese New Year ("Year of the Tiger"). 700k. × 4.

Indian landmarks. 900k. × 3.

Indian art. 700k. × 4.

World Cup Football Championship, France. 450k. × 8, 500k. × 16.

Muhamed Ali. 500k. × 6.

Parrots, Lories and Cockatoos. 500k. × 6, 1000k. × 6.

Mushrooms. 250k. × 2, 450k. × 2, 500k. × 2, 900k. × 14, 1000k. × 2.

Cars. 300k., 500, 900k. × 13, 1000k.

1999.

Lunar New Year ("Year of the Rabbit"). 700k. × 4.

Orchids. 100k. × 2, 500k. × 2, 900k. × 18, 1000k. × 2.

China '99 International Stamp Exhibition, Beijing. Hang Daqian Paintings. 500k. × 10.

"Queen Elizabeth the Queen Mother's Century". 2000k. × 4.

Prehistoric Animals. 50, 100, 500, 900k. × 19, 1000, 1800k.

Fauna and Flora. 50, 100, 500k. × 5, 700k. × 36, 900k., 1000, 1800k.

250th Birth Anniv of Johann von Goethe (German writer). 2000k. × 3.

Royal Wedding. 500k., 900k., 1000k.

"iBra '99" International Stamp Exhibition, Nuremberg. 1000, 3200k.

Cats and Dogs. 50, 100k. × 2, 500k. × 2, 900k. × 2, 1000k. × 25.

Princess Diana Photomosaic. 1000k. × 8.

New Millennium. Events of Second Half of 20th Century. 500k. × 18.

2000.

"The Stamp Show 2000" International Stamp Exhibition, London. Orchids. 1500k. × 22.

Popes of the Millennium. 1500k. × 12.

Birds of the World. 400, 500, 600, 700, 800, 100k. × 10, 1200k. × 9, 1400k. × 9, 1500k. × 25, 2000, 3000k.

ZANZIBAR

Pt. 1

A Br. Protectorate consisting of several islands off the coast of Tanganyika, E. Africa. Independent in 1963 and a republic within the Br. Commonwealth in 1964. The "United Republic of Tanganyika and Zanzibar" was proclaimed in July 1964, and the country was later renamed Tanzania. Separate issues for Zanzibar ceased on 1 January 1968 and Tanzania stamps became valid for the whole country.

1895. 16 annas = 1 rupee.
1908. 100 cents = 1 rupee.
1936. 100 cents = 1 shilling.

1895. Stamps of India (Queen Victoria) optd **Zanzibar**.

3	23	½a. turquoise	4·00	3·75
4		1a. purple	4·25	3·75
5		1¼a. brown	4·75	3·50
6	–	2a. blue	5·00	4·75
8	–	2½a. green	8·00	5·00
10	–	3a. orange	12·00	10·00
12	–	4a. green (No. 96)	12·00	14·00
13	–	6a. brown (No. 80)	19·00	11·00
15	–	8a. mauve	17·00	23·00
16	–	12a. purple on red	17·00	10·00
17	–	1r. grey	80·00	75·00
18	37	1r. green and red	17·00	25·00
19	38	2r. red and orange	55·00	80·00
20		3r. brown and green	50·00	60·00
21		5r. blue and violet	60·00	80·00

1895. Nos. 4/6 surch **2½**.

23	23	2½ on 1a. purple	£150	£100
22		2½ on 1¼a. brown	50·00	40·00
26	–	2½ on 2a. blue	50·00	30·00

1896. Stamps of British East Africa (Queen Victoria) optd **Zanzibar**.

41	11	½a. green	30·00	17·00
42		1a. red	26·00	16·00
43		2½a. blue	75·00	45·00
44		4½a. yellow	45·00	50·00
45		5a. brown	50·00	32·00
46		7½a. mauve	38·00	50·00

13 Sultan Seyyid Hamed-bin-Thwain

19 Sultan Seyyid Hamoud-bin-Mahommed bin Said

1896. The Rupee values are larger.

178	13	½a. green and red	1·50	35
179		1a. blue and red	2·25	55
159		2a. brown and red	2·75	75
181		2½a. blue and red	2·75	30
182		3a. grey and red	5·50	60
183		4a. green and red	3·25	1·00
184		4½a. orange and red	7·50	1·00
166		5a. brown and red	4·25	2·50
167		7½a. mauve and red	3·50	2·75
187		8a. olive and red	12·00	2·25
169	–	1r. blue and red	14·00	9·00
171	–	2r. green and red	24·00	9·50
172	–	3r. purple and red	24·00	9·50
173	–	4r. lake and red	19·00	13·00
174	–	5r. brown and red	25·00	13·00

1896. Surch **2½**.

175	13	2½ on 4a. green and red	60·00	40·00

1899. The Rupee values are larger.

188	19	½a. green and red	2·00	60
189		1a. blue and red	4·50	20
190		1a. red	2·00	20
191		2a. brown and red	2·50	50
192		2½a. blue and red	2·25	60
193		3a. grey and red	3·00	2·25
194		4a. green and red	3·25	1·50
195		4½a. orange and red	12·00	4·00
196		4½a. black and red	14·00	12·00
197		5a. brown and red	3·00	1·25
198		7½a. mauve and red	3·25	3·75
199		8a. olive and red	3·25	4·50
200	–	1r. blue and red	18·00	15·00
201	–	2r. green and red	18·00	18·00
202	–	3r. purple and red	30·00	35·00
203	–	4r. lake and red	48·00	55·00
204	–	5r. brown and red	55·00	65·00

1904. Surch in words.

205	19	1 on 4½a. orange and red	4·00	5·00
206		1 on 4½a. black and red	4·50	18·00
207		2 on 4a. green and red	14·00	18·00
208		2½ on 7½a. mauve and red	13·00	20·00
209		2½ on 8a. olive and red	17·00	30·00

23 Monogram of Sultan Seyyid Ali bin Hamoud bin Naherud

1904. The Rupee values are larger.

210	23	½a. green	1·75	90
211		1a. red	1·75	10
212		2a. brown	1·75	45
213		2½a. blue	2·50	35
214		3a. grey	2·50	2·25
215		4a. green	2·25	1·60
216		4½a. black	3·00	2·50
217		5a. brown	3·75	1·25
218		7½a. mauve	4·50	7·00
219		8a. olive	3·75	2·75
220	–	1r. blue and red	22·00	12·00
221	–	2r. green and red	25·00	38·00
222	–	3r. violet and red	40·00	75·00
223	–	4r. deep red and red	48·00	90·00
224	–	5r. brown and red	48·00	95·00

25

27 Sultan Ali bin Hamoud

26

28 View of Port

1908.

225	25	1c. grey	2·25	30
226		3c. green	5·50	10
227		6c. red	9·50	10
228		10c. brown	2·75	2·00
229a		12c. violet	12·00	1·25
230	26	15c. blue	12·00	40
231		25c. brown	3·50	1·00
232		50c. green	6·00	4·50
233		75c. black	11·00	12·00
234	27	1r. green	25·00	12·00
235		2r. violet	18·00	14·00
236		3r. bistre	25·00	48·00
237		4r. red	48·00	75·00
238		5r. blue	40·00	55·00
239	28	10r. green and brown	£140	£250
240		20r. black and green	£300	£475
241		30r. black and brown	£350	£650
242		40r. black and orange	£475	
243		50r. black and mauve	£425	
244		100r. black and blue	£650	
245		200r. brown and black	£1100	

29 Sultan Kalif bin Harub

30 Sailing Canoe

31 Dhow

1913.

246	29	1c. grey	40	20
247		3c. green	50	20
278		3c. yellow	30	10
279		4c. green	50	60
280		6c. red	30	50
281		6c. purple on blue	35	10
264		8c. purple on yellow	75	3·75
249		10c. brown	1·10	2·00
265		10c. green on yellow	75	30
283		12c. violet	40	30
284		12c. red	40	40
251		15c. blue	1·25	30
286		20c. blue	1·00	30
252		25c. brown	1·00	1·00
288		50c. green	1·25	3·75
254		75c. black	2·00	3·00
270	30	1r. green	4·00	3·50
291		2r. violet	3·25	9·00
292		3r. bistre	4·25	7·50
293		4r. red	12·00	35·00
259		5r. blue	35·00	38·00
260	31	10r. green and brown	£120	£200
260b		20r. black and green	£170	£375
260c		30r. black and brown	£180	£450
260d		40r. black and orange	£375	£650
260e		50r. black and purple	£350	£650
260f		100r. black and blue	£425	
260g		200r. brown and black	£700	

32 Sultan Kalif bin Harub

33 Sultan Kalif bin Harub

1926.

299	32	1c. brown	50	10
300		3c. orange	20	15
301		4c. green	20	30
302		6c. violet	20	10
303		8c. grey	1·00	4·50
304		10c. olive	1·00	40
305		12c. red	1·50	10
306		20c. blue	50	30
307		25c. purple on yellow	4·25	2·50
308		50c. red	2·00	35
309		75c. sepia	18·00	23·00

1936.

310	33	5c. green	10	10
311		10c. black	10	10
312		15c. red	10	1·25
313		20c. orange	10	10
314		25c. purple on yellow	10	10
315		30c. blue	10	10
316		40c. brown	15	10
317		50c. red	30	10
318	30	1s. green	50	10
319		2s. violet	1·00	1·75
320		5s. red	13·00	6·00
321		7s.50c. blue	24·00	26·00
322	31	10s. green and brown	26·00	22·00

In Type **33** the letters of the word "CENTS" are without serifs. In Type **32** they have serifs.

36 Sultan Kalif bin Harub

37 "Sham Alam" (Sultan's dhow)

1936. Silver Jubilee of Sultan.
323 **36** 10c. black and olive . . . 2·25 30
324 20c. black and purple . . . 4·50 1·00
325 30c. black and blue . . . . 10·00 35
326 50c. black and orange . . 10·00 4·00

1944. Bicentenary of Al Busaid Dynasty.
327 **37** 10c. blue . . . . 85 2·75
328 20c. red . . . . 85 3·25
329 50c. green 85 30
330 1s. purple 85 65

1946. Victory. Optd **VICTORY ISSUE 8TH JUNE 1946.**
331 **33** 10c. black 20 50
332 30c. blue 20 50

1948. Silver Wedding. As T **33b/c** of St. Helena.
333 20c. orange . . . . 30 1·50
334 10s. brown . . . . 19·00 29·00

1949. 75th Anniv of U.P.U. As T **33d/g** of St. Helena.
335 20c. orange . . . . 30 3·00
336 30c. blue . . . . 1·75 1·00
337 50c. mauve . . . . 1·00 2·50
338 1s. green . . . . 1·00 4·50

39 Sultan Kalif bin Harub

40 Seyyid Khalifa Schools, Beit-el-Ras

1952.
339 **39** 5c. black 10 10
340 10c. orange 10 10
341 15c. green . . . . 65 2·00
342 20c. red 50 70
343 25c. purple . . . . 1·00 10
344 30c. green . . . . 1·00 10
345 35c. blue . . . . 65 3·25
346 40c. brown . . . . 65 1·25
347 50c. violet . . . . 2·25 10
348 **40** 1s. green and brown . . . 60 10
349 2s. blue and purple . . . . 2·25 2·50
350 5s. black and red . . . . . 2·25 3·75
351 7s.50 black and green . . . 19·00 23·00
352 10s. red and black . . . . 10·00 12·00

41 Sultan Kalif bin Harub

42 Cloves

43 "Ummoja Wema" (dhow)

47 Dimbani Mosque

1954. 75th Birthday of Sultan.
353 **41** 15c. green 10 10
354 20c. red 10 10
355 30c. blue 10 10
356 50c. purple 20 10
357 1s.25 red 20 75

1957.
358 **42** 5c. orange and green . . . 10 40
359 10c. green and red 10 10
360 **43** 15c. green and sepia . . . 20 2·75
361 – 20c. blue 10 10
362 – 25c. brown and black . . . 10 1·25
363 **43** 30c. red and black . . . . 15 1·25
364 – 35c. slate and green . . . 15 20
365 – 40c. brown and black . . . 15 10
366 – 50c. blue and myrtle . . . 15 30
367 **47** 1s. red and black 20 30
368 **43** 1s.25 slate and red . . . . 3·50 20
369 **47** 2s. orange and green . . . 3·50 2·25
370 – 5s. blue . . . . 5·00 2·00
371 – 7s.50 green . . . . 8·00 4·00
372 – 10s. red . . . . 9·00 6·00
DESIGNS—HORIZ (as Type **47**): 20c. Sultan's Barge; 25, 35, 50c. Map of East African coast. VERT (as Type **47**): 40c. Minaret Mosque. (As Type **43**) 5, 7s.50c., 10s. Kibweni Palace.

49 Sultan Seyyid Sir Abdulla bin Khalifa

50 "Protein Foods"

1961. As 1957 issue but with portrait of Sultan Sir Abdulla as in T **49**.
373 5c. orange and green . . . . 10 1·00
374 10c. green and red 10 10
375 15c. green and sepia . . . . 75 2·75
376 20c. blue 30 30
377 25c. brown and black 60 75
378 30c. red and black . . . . . 2·75 1·25
379 35c. slate and green . . . . 2·50 3·50
380 40c. brown and black 30 20
381 50c. blue and myrtle . . . . 1·25 10
382 1s. red and black . . . . . . 40 1·00
383 1s.25 slate and red . . . . . 2·50 3·50
384 2s. orange and green . . . . 70 3·25
385 5s. blue . . . . 3·25 7·50
386 7s.50 green . . . . 3·00 15·00
387 10s. red . . . . 3·00 9·00
388 20s. sepia (Kibweni Palace) 17·00 28·00

1963. Freedom from Hunger.
389 **50** 1s.30 sepia . . . . 1·25 75

51 Zanzibar Clove

58 Axe, Spear and Dagger

1963. Independence. Inscr "UHURU 1963". Multicoloured.
390 30c. Type **51** 10 30
391 50c. "To Prosperity" (Zanzibar doorway) . . . 10 30
392 1s.30 "Religious Tolerance" (mosques and churches) . . 15 4·00
393 2s.50 "Towards the Light" (Mangapwani Cave) . . . 20 4·75
No. 392 is horiz.

1964. Optd **JAMHURI 1964**. (a) Nos. 373/88.
414 5c. orange and green 10 10
415 10c. green and red 10 10
416 15c. green and sepia 10 10
417 20c. blue 10 10
418 25c. brown and black 10 10
419 30c. red and black 10 10
420 35c. slate and green 10 10
421 40c. brown and black 10 10
422 50c. blue and myrtle 10 10
423 1s. red and black 10 10
424 1s.25 slate and red . . . . . 1·50 20
425 2s. orange and green 50 20
426 5s. blue 50 35
407 7s.50 green . . . . 2·00 1·75
408 10s. red . . . . 2·00 1·75
429 20s. sepia . . . . 2·25 8·00

(b) Nos. 390/3.
430 30c. multicoloured 10 10
431 50c. multicoloured 10 10
432 1s.30 multicoloured 10 10
433 2s.50 multicoloured 15 30
The opt is in two lines on Nos. 421, 423, 425/429, 430, 431, 433.

NOTE. For the set inscribed "UNITED REPUBLIC OF TANGANYIKA & ZANZIBAR" see Nos. 124/7 of Tanganyika.

1964. Multicoloured.
434 5c. Type **58** 20 10
435 10c. Bow and arrow breaking chains 30 10
436 15c. Type **58** 30 10
437 20c. As 10c. 50 10
438 25c. Zanzibari with rifle . . . 50 10
439 30c. Zanzibari breaking manacles 30 10
440 40c. As 25c. 50 10
441 50c. As 30c. 30 10
442 1s. Zanzibari, flag and sun 30 10
443 1s.30 Hands breaking chains (horiz) 30 70
444 2s. Hand waving flag (horiz) 30 30
445 5s. Map of Zanzibar and Pemba on flag (horiz) . . . 55 2·50
446 10s. Flag on map . . . . . 3·25 3·50
447 20s. National flag (horiz) . . 3·25 18·00

68 Soldier and Maps

1965. 1st Anniv of Revolution.
448 **68** 20c. light green and green 10 10
449 – 30c. brown and orange . . 10 10
450 **68** 1s.30 blue and deep blue 10 10
451 – 2s.50 violet and red 10 15
DESIGN—VERT: 30c., 2s.50, Building construction.

70 Planting Rice

1965. Agricultural Development.
452 **70** 20c. sepia and blue . . . . 10 1·00
453 – 30c. sepia and mauve . . . 10 1·00
454 – 1s.30 sepia and orange . . 20 2·00
455 **70** 2s.50 sepia and green . . . 30 3·75
DESIGN: 30 c, 1s.30, Hands holding rice.

72 Freighter, Tractor, Factory and Open Book and Torch

74 Tree-felling

1966. 2nd Anniv of Revolution. Mult.
456 20c. Type **72** 20 20
457 50c. Soldier 15 20
458 1s.30 Type **72** 15 20
459 2s.50 As 50c. . . . . 25 1·00

1966.
460 **74** 5c. purple and olive . . . 70 80
461 – 10c. purple and green . . . 70 80
462 – 15c. purple and blue . . . 70 80
463 – 20c. blue and orange . . . 40 20
464 – 25c. purple and yellow . . 40 30
465 – 30c. purple and yellow . . 70 20
466 – 40c. brown and red 80 20
467 – 50c. green and yellow . . . 80 20
468 – 1s. purple and blue 80 20
469 – 1s.30 purple and turquoise 80 2·25
470 – 2s. purple and green . . . 80 30
471 – 5s. red and blue . . . . . 1·25 4·25
472 – 10s. red and yellow . . . . 2·25 16·00
473 **74** 20s. brown and mauve . . 4·25 25·00
DESIGNS—HORIZ: 10c., 1s. Clove cultivation; 15c., 40c. Chair-making; 20c., 5s. Lumumba College; 25c., 1s.30, Agriculture; 30c., 2s. Agricultural workers. VERT: 50c., 10s. Zanzibar street.

81 "Education"

1966. Introduction of Free Education.
474 **81** 50c. black, blue and orange 10 1·00
475 1s.30 black, blue and green 15 1·75
476 2s.50 black, blue and pink 40 4·50

82 A.S.P. Flag

1967. 10th Anniv of Afro-Shirazi Party.
477 **82** 30c. multicoloured . . . . 10 1·00
478 – 50c. multicoloured . . . . 10 1·00
479 – 1s.30 multicoloured . . . . 10 2·00
480 **82** 2s.50 multicoloured . . . . 30 3·25
DESIGN—VERT: 50c., 1s.30, Vice-President M. A. Karume of Tanzania, flag and crowd.

84 Voluntary Workers

1967. Voluntary Workers Brigade.
481 **84** 1s.30 multicoloured . . . . 15 2·25
482 2s.50 multicoloured . . . . 40 5·50

POSTAGE DUE STAMPS

Insufficiently prepaid. Postage due. 9 cents.

D 1

1930. Roul or roul × imperf.
D 1 **D 1** 1c. black on orange . . 11·00 £110
D18 2c. black on orange . . 15·00 29·00
D 3 3c. black on orange . . 5·00 45·00
D19 3c. black on red . . . 3·00 48·00
D21 6c. black on yellow . . . 3·00 32·00
D 5 9c. black on orange . . 2·75 23·00
D 6 12c. black on orange . . £9500 £8500
D 7 12c. black on green . . . £1400 £600
D22 12c. black on blue . . . 4·00 26·00
D 8 15c. black on orange . . 2·75 25·00
D 9 18c. black on orange . . 4·25 42·00
D11 20c. black on orange . . 4·00 60·00
D12 21c. black on orange . . 3·50 35·00
D13 25c. black on purple . . £2750 £1300
D14 25c. black on orange . . £11000 £11000
D23 25c. black on red . . . 9·00 75·00
D24 25c. black on lilac . . . 15·00 50·00
D15 31c. black on orange . . 9·50 80·00
D16 50c. black on orange . . 21·00 £170
D17 75c. black on orange . . 65·00 £350

D 3

1936.
D25 **D 3** 5c. violet . . . . 4·75 9·00
D26 10c. red . . . . 4·00 2·75
D27 20c. green . . . . . . 2·25 4·50
D28a 30c. brown . . . . . . 35 13·00
D29a 40c. blue . . . . 75 32·00
D30a 1s. grey . . . . 1·00 21·00

ZIL ELWANNYEN SESEL Pt. 1

Beginning in June 1980 stamps were issued for use in Zil Elwannyen Sesel (Seychelles Outer Islands), including Aldabra, Coetivy, Farquhar and the Amirante Islands.

100 cents = 1 rupee.

A. Inscr "ZIL ELOIGNE SESEL"

1980. As Nos. 404/19 of Seychelles but inscr "ZIL ELOIGNE SESEL".
1 – 5c. multicoloured 15 75
2 – 10c. multicoloured 15 75
3 – 15c. multicoloured 15 75
4 – 20c. multicoloured 20 75
5 – 25c. multicoloured . . . . 1·00 75
6 **103** 40c. multicoloured 30 75
7 – 50c. multicoloured 30 60
8 – 75c. multicoloured 35 60
9 – 1r. multicoloured . . . . . 1·25 1·00
10 – 1r.10 multicoloured . . . . 40 1·00
11 – 1r.25 multicoloured . . . . 1·50 70
12 – 1r.50 multicoloured 45 70
13 – 5r. multicoloured . . . . . 70 1·00
14 – 10r. multicoloured . . . . 80 1·50
15 – 15r. multicoloured . . . . 80 3·00
16 – 20r. multicoloured . . . . 80 3·25

2 "Cinq Juin"

1980. Establishment of Travelling Post Office. Multicoloured.
17 1r.50 Type **2** 20 20
18 2r.10 Hand-stamping covers 25 25
19 5r. Map of Zil Eloigne Sesel 40 40

3 Yellow-finned Tuna

1980. Marine Life. Multicoloured.
20 1r.50 Type **3** 15 20
21 2r.10 Blue marlin 20 35
22 5r. Sperm whale 50 70

1981. Royal Wedding. As T **14a/b** of St. Kitts. Multicoloured.
23 40c. "Royal Escape" 10 10
24 40c. Prince Charles and Lady Diana Spencer 40 55
25 5r. "Victoria and Albert" . . 35 40
31 5r. As No. 24 . . . . 1·00 1·75
27 10r. "Britannia" 60 85
28 10r. As No. 24 . . . . 1·50 3·25
MS29 120 × 109 mm. 7r.50 As No. 24 . . . . 1·40 1·75

4 Wright's Skink

1981. Wildlife. (1st series). Multicoloured.

32	1r.40 Type **4**	15	15
33	2r.25 Tree frog	20	20
34	5r. Robber crab	40	40

See also Nos. 45/7.

5 "Cinq Juin" ("Communications")

1982. Island Development. Ships.

35	**5**	1r.75 black and orange	35	30
36	–	2r.10 black and blue	40	45
37	–	5r. black and red	50	60

DESIGNS: 2r.10, "Junon" (fisheries protection); 5r. "Diamond M. Dragon" (drilling ship).

B. Inscr "ZIL ELWAGNE SESEL"

6 "Paulette"

1982. Local Mail Vessels. Multicoloured.

38	40c. Type **6**	35	45
39	1r.75 "Janette"	40	80
40	2r.75 "Lady Esme"	50	95
41	3r.50 "Cinq Juin"	50	1·00

7 Birds flying over Island

1982. Aldabra, World Heritage Site. Mult.

42	40c. Type **7**	30	15
43	2r.75 Map of the atoll	45	35
44	7r. Giant tortoises	50	75

8 Red Land Crab

1983. Wildlife (2nd series). Multicoloured.

45	1r.75 Type **8**	35	40
46	2r.75 Black terrapin	45	55
47	7r. Madagascar green gecko	90	1·25

9 Map of Poivre Island and Ile du Sud

1983. Island Maps. Multicoloured.

48	40c. Type **9**	20	40
49	1r.50 Ile des Roches	40	55
50	2r.75 Astove Island	50	80
51	7r. Coetivy Island	80	1·60
MS52	93 × 129 mm. Nos. 48/51	1·75	3·00

10 Aldabra Warbler

1983. Birds. Multicoloured.

53	5c. Type **10**	40	60
54	10c. Zebra dove ("Barred Ground Dove")	1·00	60
55	15c. Indian nightjar	30	40
56	20c. Madagascar cisticola ("Malagasy Grass Warbler")	30	40
57	25c. Madagascar white-eye	60	60
58	40c. Mascarene fody	30	40
59	50c. White-throated rail	5·00	60
60	75c. Black bulbul	40	60
61	2r. Western reef heron ("Dimorphic little egret")	2·00	1·25
62	2r.10 Souimanga sunbird	50	1·00
63	2r.50 Madagascar turtle dove	1·00	65
64	2r.75 Sacred ibis	70	75
65	3r.50 Black coucal (vert)	1·00	1·10
66	7r. Seychelles kestrel (vert)	3·00	1·90
67	15r. Comoro blue pigeon (vert)	3·00	5·00
68	20r. Greater flamingo (vert)	3·50	5·50

See also Nos. 165 etc. (1985).

11 Windsurfing

1983. Tourism. Multicoloured.

69	50c. Type **11**	10	10
70	2r. Hotel	25	25
71	3r. View of beach	30	35
72	10r. Islands at sunset	75	1·75

1983. Nos. 23/8 surch.

73	30c. on 40c. "Royal Escape"	25	25
74	30c. on 40c. Prince Charles and Lady Diana Spencer	50	60
75	2r. on 5r. "Victoria and Albert II"	70	70
76	2r. on 5r. As No. 74	1·25	1·75
77	3r. on 10r. "Britannia"	85	85
78	3r. on 10r. As No. 74	1·60	2·50

12 Map of Aldabra and Commemorative Postmark

1984. Re-opening of Aldabra Post Office. Multicoloured.

79	50c. Type **12**	15	30
80	2r.75 White-throated rail	60	1·10
81	3r. Giant tortoise	60	1·25
82	10r. Red-footed booby	2·25	3·50

13 Fishing from Launch

1984. Game Fishing. Multicoloured.

83	50c. Type **13**	15	30
84	2r. Hooked fish (vert)	45	75
85	3r. Weighing catch (vert)	60	1·00
86	10r. Fishing from boat (different)	2·00	3·00

14 Giant Hermit Crab

1984. Crabs. Multicoloured.

87	50c. Type **14**	25	40
88	2r. Fiddler crabs	55	1·10
89	3r. Sand crab	65	1·50
90	10r. Spotted pebble crab	1·40	4·25

15 Constellation of "Orion"

1984. The Night Sky. Multicoloured.

91	50c. Type **15**	25	15
92	2r. "Cygnus"	50	55
93	3r. "Virgo"	60	80
94	10r. "Scorpio"	1·40	2·25

C. Inscr "ZIL ELWANNYEN SESEL"

16 "Lenzites elegans"

17 The Queen Mother attending Royal Opera House, Covent Garden

1985. Fungi. Multicoloured.

95	50c. Type **16**	60	85
96	2r. "Xylaria telfairei"	1·50	2·00
97	3r. "Lentinus sajor-caju"	1·50	2·00
98	10r. "Hexagonia tenuis"	2·75	3·50

1985. As Nos. 53/4, 57 and 61 but inscr "Zil Elwannyen Sesel".

165	5c. Type **10**	2·50	2·25
166	10c. Zebra dove ("Barred Ground Dove")	2·50	2·25
103	25c. Madagascar white eye	2·00	1·50
105	50c. White-throated rail	3·00	1·60
226	2r. Western reef heron ("Diomorphic Little Egret")	3·50	3·75

1985. Life and Times of Queen Elizabeth the Queen Mother. Multicoloured.

115	1r. The Queen Mother, 1936 (from photo by Dorothy Wilding)	20	25
116	2r. With Princess Anne at Ascot, 1974	35	50
117	3r. Type **17**	45	70
118	5r. With Prince Henry at his christening (from photo by Lord Snowdon)	60	1·25
MS119	91 × 73 mm. 10r. In a launch, Venice, 1985	1·50	2·75

18 Giant Tortoise

1985. Giant Tortoises of Aldabra (1st series). Multicoloured.

120	50c. Type **18**	3·25	1·25
121	75c. Giant tortoises at stream	3·50	1·40
122	1r. Giant tortoises on grassland	3·75	1·60
123	2r. Giant tortoise (side view)	4·75	2·25
MS124	70 × 60 mm. 10r. Two tortoises	15·00	15·00

For stamps as Nos. 120/3 but without circular inscription around W.W.F. emblem see Nos. 153/6.

19 Phoenician Trading Ship (600 B.C.)

1985. Famous Visitors. Multicoloured.

125	50c. Type **19**	80	80
126	2r. Sir Hugh Scott and H.M.S. "Sealark", 1908	1·50	2·00
127	10r. Vasco da Gama and "Sao Gabriel", 1502	2·50	4·50

1986. 60th Birthday of Queen Elizabeth II. As T **145a** of St. Helena. Multicoloured.

128	75c. Princess Elizabeth at Chester, 1951	15	25
129	1r. Queen and Duke of Edinburgh at Falklands Service, St. Paul's Cathedral, 1985	15	25
130	1r.50 At Order of St. Michael and St. George service, St. Paul's Cathedral, 1968	25	40
131	3r.75 In Mexico, 1975	40	90
132	5r. At Crown Agents Head Office, London, 1983	45	1·25

1986. Royal Wedding. As T **146a** of St. Helena. Multicoloured.

133	3r. Prince Andrew and Miss Sarah Ferguson on Buckingham Palace balcony	45	75
134	7r. Prince Andrew in naval uniform	65	1·75

20 "Acropora palifera" and "Tubastraea coccinea"

21 "Hibiscus tiliaceus"

1986. Coral Formations. Multicoloured.

135	2r. Type **20**	1·75	1·75
136	2r. "Echinopora lamellosa" and "Favia pallida"	1·75	1·75
137	2r. "Sarcophyton sp." and "Porites lutea"	1·75	1·75
138	2r. "Goniopora sp." and "Goniastrea retiformis"	1·75	1·75
139	2r. "Tubipora musica" and "Fungia fungites"	1·75	1·75

Nos. 135/9 were printed together, se-tenant, forming a composite design.

1986. Flora. Multicoloured.

140	50c. Type **21**	35	30
141	2r. "Crinum angustum"	1·60	1·50
142	3r. "Phaius tetragonus"	2·25	2·00
143	10r. "Rothmannia annae"	3·75	4·00

22 Teardrop Butterflyfish and Lined Butterflyfish

23 Coconut

1987. Coral Reef Fishes. Multicoloured.

144	2r. Type **22**	1·10	1·40
145	2r. Knifejaw	1·10	1·40
146	2r. Narrow-banded batfish	1·10	1·40
147	2r. Ringed-sergeant	1·10	1·40
148	2r. Lined butterflyfish and Meyer's butterflyfish	1·10	1·40

Nos. 144/8 were printed together, se-tenant, forming a composite design.

1987. Trees. Multicoloured.

149	1r. Type **23**	80	85
150	2r. Mangrove	1·40	1·75
151	3r. Pandanus palm	2·00	2·50
152	5r. Indian almond	3·00	3·75

1987. Giant Tortoises of Aldabra (2nd series). Designs as Nos. 120/3 but without circular inscr around W.W.F. emblem. Multicoloured.

153	50c. As Type **18**	2·25	1·75
154	75c. Giant tortoises at pool	2·75	2·50
155	1r. Giant tortoises on grassland	3·75	3·50
156	2r. Giant tortoise (side view)	4·75	4·50

1987. Royal Ruby Wedding. Nos. 128/32 optd **40TH WEDDING ANNIVERSARY.**

157	75c. Princess Elizabeth at Chester, 1951	20	20
158	1r. Queen and Duke of Edinburgh at Falklands Service, St. Paul's Cathedral, 1985	25	25
159	1r.50 At Order of St. Michael and St. George service, St. Paul's Cathedral, 1968	35	40
160	3r.75 In Mexico, 1975	50	90
161	5r. At Crown Agents Head Office, London, 1983	60	1·25

24 "Vallee de Mai" (Christine Harter)

1987. Tourism. Multicoloured.
162 3r. Type **24** . . . . 3·00 3·00
163 3r. Ferns . . . . 3·00 3·00
164 3r. Bamboo . . . . 3·00 3·00
Nos. 162/4 were printed together, se-tenant, forming a composite picture.

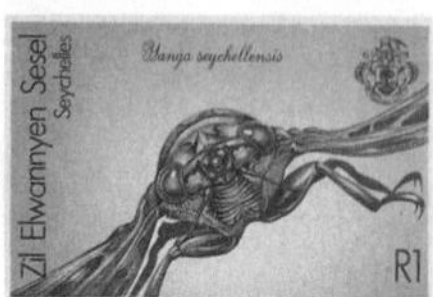

25 "Yanga seychellensis" (beetle)

1988. Insects. Multicoloured.
180 1r. Type **25** . . . . 1·00 1·00
181 2r. "Belenois aldabraensis" (butterfly) . . . . 1·75 1·60
182 3r. "Polyspilota seychelliana" (mantid) . . . . 2·00 2·25
183 5r. "Polposipus herculeanus" (beetle) . . . . 2·50 3·00

26 Olympic Rings

1988. Olympic Games, Seoul. Sheet 99 × 73 mm.
MS184 **26** 10r. multicoloured . . 4·00 2·75

1988. 300th Anniv of Lloyd's of London. As T **152a** of St. Helena. Multicoloured.
185 1r. Modern Lloyd's Building, London 70 65
186 2r. "Retriever" (cable ship) (horiz) . . . . 1·50 1·10
187 3r. "Chantel" (fishing boat) (horiz) . . . . 2·00 1·50
188 5r. Wreck of "Torrey Canyon" (tanker), Cornwall, 1967 . . . . . 2·75 1·75

27 "Father Christmas landing with Presents" (Jean-Claude Boniface)

1988. Christmas. Children's Paintings. Mult.
189 1r. Type **27** 35 40
190 2r. "Church" (Francois Barra) (vert) 60 80
191 3r. "Father Christmas flying on Bird" (Wizy Ernesta) (vert) . . . . 85 1·25
192 5r. "Father Christmas in Sleigh over Island" (Federic Lang) . . . . . . 1·40 2·00

1989. 20th Anniv of First Manned Landing on Moon. As T **50a** of St. Kitts. Multicoloured.
193 1r. Firing Room, Launch Control Centre . . . . . 1·75 1·50
194 2r. Crews of "Apollo–Soyuz" mission (30 × 30 mm) . . . 2·25 2·25
195 3r. "Apollo–Soyuz" emblem (30 × 30 mm) . . . . . . 2·50 3·00
196 5r. "Apollo" and "Soyuz" docking in space . . . . . 3·50 4·50
MS197 82 × 100 mm. 10r. Recovery of "Apollo 11" . . . . 11·00 12·00

28 Dumb Cane

1989. Poisonous Plants (1st series). Mult.
198 1r. Type **28** . . . . 2·50 1·75
199 2r. Star of Bethlehem . . . . 3·00 2·75
200 3r. Indian liquorice . . . . . 3·25 3·25
201 5r. Black nightshade . . . . 4·25 4·75
See also Nos. 214/17.

29 Tec-Tec Broth

1989. Creole Cooking. Multicoloured.
202 1r. Type **29** . . . . 1·50 1·50
203 2r. Pilaff a la Seychelloise . . 2·00 2·25
204 3r. Mullet grilled in banana leaves . . . . 2·25 2·50
205 5r. Daube . . . . 3·25 3·75
MS206 125 × 80 mm. Nos. 202/5 11·00 12·00

30 1980 Marine Life 5r. Stamp

1990. "Stamp World London 90" International Stamp Exhibition. Showing stamps. Mult.
207 1r. Type **30** . . . . 2·25 1·75
208 2r. 1980 5r. definitive . . . . 2·75 2·50
209 3r. 1983 2r.75 definitive . . . 3·00 3·00
210 5r. 1981 Wildlife 5r. . . . . 4·00 4·50
MS211 124 × 84 mm. Nos. 207/10 10·00 12·00

1990. 90th Birthday of Queen Elizabeth the Queen Mother. As T **116a** of St. Helena.
212 2r. multicoloured . . . . . . 2·00 2·50
213 10r. black and brown . . . . 3·75 5·50
DESIGNS—21 × 36 mm: 2r. Duchess of York with baby Princess Elizabeth, 1926. 29 × 37 mm: 10r. King George VI and Queen Elizabeth visiting bombed district, London, 1940.

1990. Poisonous Plants (2nd series). As T **28**. Multicoloured.
214 1r. Ordeal plant . . . . . . 1·75 1·75
215 2r. Thorn apple . . . . . . 2·25 2·50
216 3r. Strychnine tree . . . . . 2·50 2·75
217 5r. Bwa zasmen . . . . . . 3·50 4·00

1991. 65th Birthday of Queen Elizabeth II and 70th Birthday of Prince Philip. As T **165a** of St. Helena. Multicoloured.
234 4r. Queen Elizabeth II . . . 1·75 2·25
235 4r. Prince Philip . . . . . . 1·75 2·25

31 "St. Abbs" (full-rigged ship), 1860

1991. Shipwrecks. Multicoloured.
236 1r.50 Type **31** . . . . 2·50 2·00
237 3r. "Norden" (barque), 1862 3·00 2·50
238 3r.50 "Clan Mackay" (freighter), 1894 . . . . . 3·25 2·75
239 10r. "Glenlyon" (freighter), 1905 . . . . 7·00 7·50

1992. 40th Anniv of Queen Elizabeth II's Accession. As T **168a** of St. Helena. Mult.
240 1r. Beach 75 75
241 1r.50 Aerial view of Desroches . . . . 1·10 1·25
242 3r. Tree-covered coastline . . 1·50 1·75
243 3r.50 Three portraits of Queen Elizabeth II . . . . 1·60 1·90
244 5r. Queen Elizabeth II . . . 1·75 2·25

32 "Lomatopyllum aldabrense" (plant)

1992. 10th Anniv of Aldabra as a World Heritage Site. Multicoloured.
245 1r.50 Type **32** . . . . . . 1·75 1·75
246 3r. White-throated rail . . . 5·00 3·50
247 3r.50 Robber crab . . . . . 2·75 3·50
248 10r. Aldabra drongo . . . . 9·50 11·00

ZIMBABWE Pt. 1

Rhodesia became independent on 18 April 1980 and was renamed Zimbabwe.

100 cents = 1 dollar.

113 Morganite

114 Rotary Anniversary Emblem

1980. As Nos. 555/69 of Rhodesia and new value inscr "ZIMBABWE".
576 1c. Type **113** 10 30
577 3c. Amethyst 15 30
578 4c. Garnet 15 10
579 5c. Citrine 15 10
580 7c. Blue topaz 15 10
581 9c. White rhinoceros 15 10
582 11c. Lion 15 15
583 13c. Warthog 15 15
584 15c. Giraffe 15 20
585 17c. Common zebra 15 20
586 21c. Odzani Falls 15 25
587 25c. Goba Falls 15 30
588 30c. Inyangombi Falls . . . 15 50
588a 40c. Bundi Falls . . . . . 3·50 4·50
589 $1 Bridal Veil Falls . . . . 20 1·50
590 $2 Victoria Falls . . . . . 35 3·00

1980. 75th Anniv of Rotary International.
591 **114** 4c. multicoloured 10 10
592 13c. multicoloured 15 20
593 21c. multicoloured 20 35
594 25c. multicoloured 20 60
MS595 140 × 84 mm. Nos. 591/4 75 1·60

115 Olympic Rings

1980. Olympic Games, Moscow.
596 **115** 17c. multicoloured 30 40

116 Gatooma Post Office, 1912

1980. 75th Anniv of Post Office Savings Bank.
597 **116** 5c. black and brown . . . 10 10
598 – 7c. black and orange . . 10 10
599 – 9c. black and yellow . . . 10 10
600 – 17c. black and white . . . 25 25
MS601 125 × 84 mm. Nos. 597/600 55 1·25
DESIGNS: 7c. Salisbury Post Office, 1912; 9c. Umtali Post Office, 1901; 17c. Bulawayo Post Office, 1895.

117 Stylized Blind Person

118 Msasa

1981. Int Year of Disabled Persons. Mult.
602 5c. Type **117** 10 10
603 7c. Deaf person 10 10
604 11c. Person with one leg . . 15 10
605 17c. Person with one arm . . 20 25

1981. National Tree Day. Multicoloured.
606 5c. Type **118** 10 10
607 7c. Mopane 10 10
608 21c. Flat-crowned acacia . . 20 25
609 30c. Pod mahogany 25 45

119 Painting from Gwamgwadza Cave, Mtoko Area

1982. Rock Paintings. Multicoloured.
610 9c. Type **119** 25 15
611 11c. Epworth Mission, near Harare 30 15
612 17c. Diana's Vow, near Harare 30 20
613 21c. Gwamgwadza Cave, Mtoko Area (different) . . 45 25
614 25c. Mucheka Cave, Msana Communal Land 50 75
615 30c. Chinzwini Shelter, Chiredzi Area 50 90

120 Scout Emblem

1982. 75th Anniv of Boy Scout Movement. Multicoloured.
616 9c. Type **120** 15 10
617 11c. Scouts around campfire 15 10
618 21c. Scouts map-reading . . 20 35
619 30c. Lord Baden-Powell . . . 25 65

121 Dr. Robert Koch

122 "Wing Woman" (Henry Mudzengerere)

1982. Centenary of Dr. Robert Koch's Discovery of Tubercle Bacillus.
620 **121** 11c. orange, black and grey 40 10
621 – 30c. multicoloured . . . . 60 1·50
DESIGN: 30c. Man looking through microscope.

1983. Commonwealth Day. Sculptures. Mult.
622 9c. Type **122** 10 10
623 11c. "Telling Secrets" (Joseph Ndandarika) (horiz) . . . 10 10
624 30c. "Hornbill Man" (John Takawira) (horiz) 15 15
625 $1 "The Child" (Nicholas Mukomberanwa) . . . . . 40 1·25

123 Traditional Ploughing Team (moving right)

1983. World Ploughing Contest. Mult.
626 21c. Type **123** 15 25
627 21c. Traditional ploughing team (moving left) 15 25
628 30c. Tractor ploughing . . . 20 35
629 30c. Modern plough 20 35
The two designs of each value were issued in horizontal se-tenant pairs, forming composite designs.

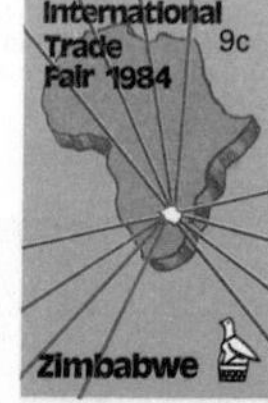

124 Postman on Cycle

125 Map of Africa showing Zimbabwe

1983. World Communications Year. Mult.
630 9c. Type **124** 20 10
631 11c. Aircraft controller directing airliner 20 10
632 15c. Switchboard operator . . 20 20
633 17c. Printing works 20 20
634 21c. Road transport (horiz) 35 40
635 30c. Rail transport (horiz) . . 45 1·00

1984. Zimbabwe Int Trade Fair, 1984. Mult.
636 9c. Type **125** 10 10
637 11c. Globe 15 10
638 30c. Zimbabwe flag and Trade Fair logo 45 50

126 Cycling

1984. Olympic Games, Los Angeles. Children's Pictures. Multicoloured.
639 11c. Type **126** 30 15
640 21c. Swimming 25 20
641 30c. Running 35 55
642 40c. Hurdling . . . . 40 1·10

127 Liberation Heroes

1984. Heroes' Day. Multicoloured.
643 9c. Type **127** 20 10
644 11c. Symbolic tower and flame (vert) 20 10
645 17c. Bronze sculpture (vert) 30 30
646 30c. Section of bronze mural 40 70
DESIGNS: 9c. to 30c. Various aspects of Heroes' Acre.

128 African Fish Eagle ("Fish Eagle")

1984. Birds of Prey. Multicoloured.
647 9c. Type **128** 40 20
648 11c. Long-crested eagle . . . 40 20
649 13c. Bateleur 50 30
650 17c. Verreaux's eagle ("Black Eagle") 60 30
651 21c. Martial eagle 70 60
652 30c. African hawk eagle . . . 1·00 1·25

129 9th Class Locomotive No. 86

1985. "Zimbabwe Steam Safaris". Railway Locomotives. Multicoloured.
653 9c. Type **129** 40 15
654 11c. 12th Class locomotive No. 190 . . . . 40 15
655 17c. 15th Class Beyer-Garratt locomotive No. 424 "Isilwane" 55 20
656 30c. 20th Class Garratt locomotive No. 726 "Gwaai" . . . . 1·00 1·25

130 "Intelsat V" Telecommunications Satellite

131 Tobacco

1985. Earth Satellite Station. Mazowe. Mult.
657 26c. Type **130** 50 40
658 57c. Earth Satellite Station, Mazowe (65 × 25 mm) . . 1·25 3·50

1985. National Infrastructure. Multicoloured.
659 1c. Type **131** 10 10
660 3c. Maize 10 10
661 4c. Cotton 15 10
662 5c. Tea 30 10
663 10c. Cattle 30 10
664 11c. Birchenough Bridge . . 75 10
665 12c. Ore stamp mill . . . . 1·25 10
666 13c. Gold pouring . . . . . 2·25 15
667 15c. Dragline coal mining . . 1·75 15
668 17c. Uncut amethyst . . . . 2·25 1·25
669 18c. Electric locomotive . . . 2·25 2·50
670 20c. Kariba Dam . . . . . 1·50 30
671 23c. Elephants at water hole 4·00 45
672 25c. Sunset over Zambezi . . 65 30
673 26c. Baobab tree 65 20
674 30c. Ruins of Great Zimbabwe 75 70
675 35c. Traditional dancing . . 60 30
676 45c. Village women crushing maize 75 40
677 57c. Woodcarving 75 70
678 $1 Playing Mbira (musical instrument) . . . . 1·25 90
679 $2 Mule-drawn Scotch cart 2·00 3·00
680 $5 Zimbabwe coat-of-arms 2·25 4·50

132 Chief Mutapa Gatsi Rusere and 17th-century Seal

1985. 50th Anniv of National Archives. Multicoloured.
681 12c. Type **132** 20 15
682 18c. Chief Lobengula, seal and 1888 Treaty 25 40
683 26c. Exhibition gallery . . . 35 45
684 35c. National Archives building 45 75

133 Computer Operator

1985. U.N. Decade for Women. Mult.
685 10c. Type **133** 30 10
686 17c. Nurse giving injection 50 40
687 26c. Woman student . . . . 1·00 2·00

134 Harare Conference Centre

1986. Harare Int Conference Centre. Mult.
688 26c. Type **134** 40 20
689 35c. Interior of conference hall 70 90

135 Grain Storage Silo

1986. 6th Anniv of Southern African Development Co-ordination Conference. Multicoloured.
690 12c. Type **135** 55 20
691 18c. Rhinoceros and hawk at sunset . . . . 2·50 1·50
692 26c. Map showing S.A.D.C.C. member states and Boeing 737 . . . . . 2·50 2·00
693 35c. Map and national flags of S.A.D.C.C. members . . 2·75 2·25

136 "Bunaeopsis jacksoni"

1986. Moths of Zimbabwe. Multicoloured.
694 12c. Type **136** 65 20
695 18c. "Deilephila nerii" . . . 1·00 80
696 26c. "Bunaeopsis zaddachi" 1·25 1·10
697 35c. "Heniocha apollonia" 1·50 4·00

137 Victoria Falls

1986. 8th Non-Aligned Summit Conference. Multicoloured.
698 26c. Type **137** . . . . 1·75 30
699 $1 Ruins of Great Zimbabwe (62 × 24 mm) . . . . . . 2·75 5·00

138 Sopwith Motorcycle (1921)

1986. Centenary of Motoring. Multicoloured.
700 10c. Type **138** 40 10
701 12c. Gladiator motor car (1902) 40 20
702 17c. Douglas motorcycle (1920) 50 20
703 26c. Ford "Model A" (1930) 60 30
704 35c. Schacht motor car (1909) 80 1·25
705 40c. Benz three-wheeled car (1886) . . . . 1·25 1·75

139 Growth Monitoring

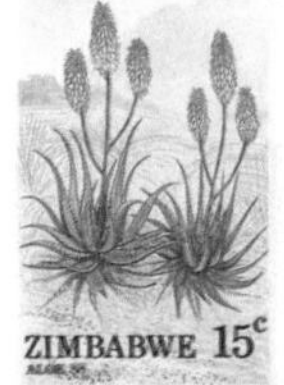
140 African Barred Owlet ("Barred Owl")

1987. Child Survival Campaign. Mult.
706 12c. Type **139** . . . . 1·50 1·75
707 12c. Breast-feeding . . . . . 1·50 1·75
708 12c. Oral rehydration therapy 1·50 1·75
709 12c. Immunization . . . . . 1·50 1·75

1987. Owls (1st series). Multicoloured.
710 12c. Type **140** . . . . 2·50 40
711 18c. Pearl-spotted owlet ("Pearl Spotted Owl") . . 3·00 1·00
712 26c. White-faced scops owl ("White Faced Owl") . . . 3·50 1·00
713 35c. African scops owl ("Scops Owl") . . . . . . 4·75 3·00
See also Nos. 850/3 and 988/91.

141 Brownie, Guide and Ranger saluting ("Commitment")

1987. 75th Anniv of Girl Guides Association of Zimbabwe. Multicoloured.
714 15c. Type **141** 55 15
715 23c. Guides preparing meal over campfire ("Adventure") 75 30
716 35c. Guide teaching villagers to read ("Service") 85 45
717 $1 Handshake and globe ("International Friendship") . . . . 2·00 3·00

142 Common Grey Duiker

144 "Cockerel" (Arthur Azevedo)

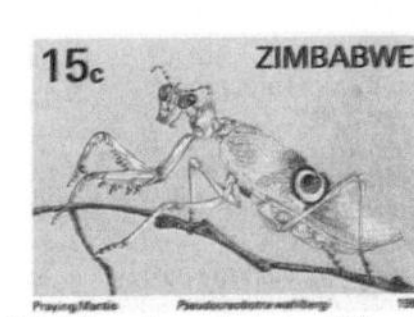

143 "Pseudocreobotra wahlberghi" (mantid)

1987. Duikers of Africa Survey. Mult.
718 15c. Type **142** 70 15
719 23c. Zebra duiker 80 25
720 25c. Yellow-backed duiker . . 80 90
721 30c. Blue duiker . . . . . . 95 1·10
722 35c. Jentink's duiker . . . . 95 1·25
723 38c. Red duiker . . . . . . 1·00 1·75

1988. Insects. Multicoloured.
724 15c. Type **143** 70 15
725 23c. "Dicranorrhia derbyana" (beetle) 85 30
726 35c. "Dictyophorus spumans" (grasshopper) . . . . . . 1·10 85
727 45c. "Chalcocoris rutilus" (bug) . . . . 1·40 2·00

1988. 30th Anniv of National Gallery of Zimbabwe. Designs showing painting (38c.) or sculptures (others). Multicoloured.
728 15c. Type **144** 20 10
729 23c. "Man into Hippo" (Bernard Matemera) . . . 30 20
730 30c. "Spirit Python" (Henry Munyaradzi) 35 30
731 35c. "Spirit Bird carrying People" (Thomas Mukarobgwa) (horiz) . . . 35 30
732 38c. "The Song of the Herd Boy" (George Nene) (horiz) 35 40
733 45c. "War Victim" (Joseph Muzondo) (horiz) 40 50

145 "Aloe cameronii var. bondana"
146 White-faced Whistling Duck ("White-faced Duck")

1988. Aloes. Multicoloured.
734 15c. Type **145** 20 10
735 23c. "Orbeopsis caudata" . . 35 20
736 25c. "Euphorbia wildii" . . . 35 35
737 30c. "Euphorbia fortissima" 40 45
738 35c. "Aloe aculeata" 40 55
739 38c. "Huernia zebrina" . . . 45 70

1988. Wild Ducks and Geese of Zimbabwe. Multicoloured.
740 15c. Type **146** 75 20
741 23c. African pygmy goose ("Pygmy Goose") 85 20
742 30c. Hottentot teal 95 85
743 35c. Comb duck ("Knob-billed duck") . . . . . . 1·10 1·00
744 38c. White-backed duck . . . 1·10 1·25
745 45c. Maccoa duck . . . . . 1·60 2·25

147 O'Shaughnessy's Banded Gecko

1989. Geckos. Multicoloured.
746 15c. Type **147** 80 15
747 23c. Tiger rock gecko 95 40
748 35c. Tasman's gecko . . . . 1·50 1·25
749 45c. Bibron's gecko . . . . . 1·75 2·00

148 Spotted Leaved Arum-Lily

1989. Wild Flowers (1st series). Multicoloured.
750 15c. Type **148** 50 10
751 23c. Grassland vlei-lily . . . 60 25
752 30c. Manica protea 65 40
753 35c. Flame lily 75 40
754 38c. Poppy hibiscus 80 55
755 45c. Blue sesbania 90 65
See also Nos. 1093/99.

149 Red-breasted Tilapia

1989. Fishes (1st series). Multicoloured.
756 15c. Type **149** 60 15
757 25c. Chessa 80 25
758 30c. Eastern bottlenose . . . 90 70
759 35c. Vundu 90 70
760 38c. Large-mouthed black bass . . . . 1·00 1·00
761 45c. Lesser tigerfish . . . . . 1·40 1·75
See also Nos. 864/9.

150 Black Rhinoceros

1989. Endangered Species. Multicoloured.

No.	Description	Unused	Used
762	15c. Type **150**	1·25	40
763	23c. Cheetah	1·25	45
764	30c. Wild dog	1·40	90
765	35c. Pangolin	1·40	1·25
766	38c. Brown hyena	1·50	2·00
767	45c. Roan antelope	1·60	2·25

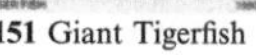

151 Giant Tigerfish **152** Headrest

153 Bicycles

1990. Multicoloured. (a) Wildlife. As T **151**.

No.	Description	Unused	Used
768	1c. Type **151**	30	20
769	2c. Helmeted guineafowl	75	20
770	3c. Scrub hare	20	20
771	4c. Temminck's ground pangolin	40	20
772	5c. Greater kudu	40	20
773	9c. Black rhinoceros	1·75	30

(b) Cultural Artifacts. As T **152**.

No.	Description	Unused	Used
774	15c. Type **152**	20	20
775	20c. Hand axe and adze	20	20
776	23c. Gourd and water pot	20	20
777	25c. Snuff container	20	20
778	26c. Winnowing tray and basket	50	30
779	30c. Grinding stone	30	30

(c) Transport. As T **153**.

No.	Description	Unused	Used
780	33c. Type **153**	1·00	30
781	35c. Buses	1·75	40
782	38c. Diesel train	1·75	40
783	45c. Mail motorcycle and trailer	1·50	40
784	$1 Air Zimbabwe Boeing 737 airliner	2·00	90
785	$2 Lorry	1·50	1·60

154 Pres. Mugabe and Joshua Nkomo at Signing of Unity Accord, 1987

1990. 10th Anniv of Independence. Mult.

No.	Description	Unused	Used
786	15c. Type **154**	40	10
787	23c. Conference Centre, Harare	45	20
788	30c. Children in class	50	40
789	35c. Intelsat aerial, Mazowe Earth Satellite Station	60	70
790	38c. National Sports Stadium	60	80
791	45c. Maize field	90	1·40

155 Runhare House, 1986

1990. Cent of the City of Harare. Mult.

No.	Description	Unused	Used
792	15c. Type **155**	30	10
793	23c. Market Hall, 1894	50	20
794	30c. Charter House, 1959	55	35
795	35c. Supreme Court, 1927	60	80
796	38c. Standard Chartered Bank, 1911	60	90
797	45c. The Town House, 1933	80	1·40

156 Speaker's Mace **157** Small-spotted Genet

1990. 36th Commonwealth Parliamentary Conference, Harare. Multicoloured.

No.	Description	Unused	Used
798	35c. Type **156**	50	25
799	$1 Speaker's chair	1·25	2·00

1991. Small Mammals. Multicoloured.

No.	Description	Unused	Used
800	15c. Type **157**	80	20
801	23c. Red squirrel	85	30
802	35c. Night-ape	1·25	1·25
803	45c. Bat-eared fox	1·75	2·25

158 Hosho (rattles) **159** Snot-apple

1991. Traditional Musical Instruments. Mult.

No.	Description	Unused	Used
804	15c. Type **158**	45	10
805	23c. Mbira (thumb piano)	50	15
806	30c. Ngororombe (pan pipes)	55	40
807	35c. Chipendani (mouth bow)	65	70
808	38c. Marimba (xylophone)	65	80
809	45c. Ngoma (drum)	75	1·10

1991. Wild Fruits (1st series). Multicoloured.

No.	Description	Unused	Used
810	20c. Type **159**	50	10
811	39c. Marula	50	30
812	51c. Mobola plum	60	80
813	60c. Water berry	70	85
814	65c. Northern dwaba berry	75	85
815	77c. Mahobohobo	85	1·10

See also Nos. 1038/43.

160 Bridal Veil Falls **162** "Amanita zambiana"

161 Lion

1991. Commonwealth Heads of Government Meeting, Harare. Multicoloured.

No.	Description	Unused	Used
816	20c. Type **160**	75	15
817	39c. Meeting logo	65	35
818	51c. Chinhoyi Caves	1·25	75
819	60c. Kariba Dam	1·25	1·00
820	65c. Victoria Falls	1·50	1·25
821	77c. Balancing rocks	1·75	1·50

1992. Wildlife Conservation. Big Cats. Mult.

No.	Description	Unused	Used
822	20c. Type **161**	70	15
823	39c. Leopard	1·10	40
824	60c. Cheetah	1·50	1·75
825	77c. Serval	1·90	2·00

1992. Edible Mushrooms. Multicoloured.

No.	Description	Unused	Used
826	20c. Type **162**	50	20
827	39c. "Boletus edulis"	70	40
828	51c. "Termitomyces sp."	75	75
829	60c. "Cantharellus densifolius"	90	1·00
830	65c. "Cantharellus longisporus"	1·00	1·25
831	77c. "Cantharellus cibarius"	1·25	1·50

163 Garden Bulbul ("Blackeyed Bulbul") **164** "Charaxes jasius"

1992. Birds. Multicoloured.

No.	Description	Unused	Used
832	25c. Type **163**	80	15
833	59c. Fiscal shrike	1·10	45
834	77c. Forktailed drongo	1·25	80
835	90c. Cardinal woodpecker	1·40	95
836	98c. Southern yellow-billed hornbill ("Yellowbilled Hornbill")	1·40	95
837	$1.16 Crested francolin	1·50	1·40

1992. Butterflies. Multicoloured.

No.	Description	Unused	Used
838	25c. Type **164**	1·10	20
839	59c. "Eronia leda"	1·75	75
840	77c. "Princeps ophidicephalus"	1·90	1·25
841	90c. "Junonia oenone"	2·50	1·75
842	98c. "Danaus chrysippus"	2·50	1·90
843	$1.16 "Junonia octavia"	2·75	2·25

165 Uranium

1993. Minerals. Multicoloured.

No.	Description	Unused	Used
844	25c. Type **165**	1·60	20
845	59c. Chrome	2·25	55
846	77c. Copper	2·75	1·00
847	90c. Coal	3·00	1·50
848	98c. Gold	3·00	1·75
849	$1.16 Emerald	3·25	2·25

1993. Owls (2nd series). As T **140**. Mult.

No.	Description	Unused	Used
850	25c. African wood owl ("Wood Owl")	2·50	50
851	59c. Pel's fishing owl	3·50	1·10
852	90c. Spotted eagle owl	4·50	4·50
853	$1.16 Verreaux's eagle owl ("Giant Eagle Owl")	5·00	6·50

166 Hadyana (relish pot) **167** "Polystachya dendrobiflora"

1993. Household Pottery. Multicoloured.

No.	Description	Unused	Used
854	25c. Type **166**	65	10
855	59c. Chirongo (water jar)	80	30
856	77c. Mbiya (relish bowl)	90	60
857	90c. Pfuko (water jar)	1·00	85
858	98c. Tsaya (cooking pot)	1·10	85
859	$1.16 Gate (beer pot)	1·25	1·00

1993. Orchids. Multicoloured.

No.	Description	Unused	Used
860	35c. Type **167**	1·25	20
861	$1 "Diaphananthe subsimplex"	2·25	75
862	$1.50 "Ansellia gigantea"	3·00	1·90
863	$1.95 "Vanilla polyepis"	3·25	2·50

1994. Fishes (2nd series). As T **149**. Mult.

No.	Description	Unused	Used
864	35c. Manyame labeo ("Hunyani salmon")	50	10
865	$1 Sharp-toothed catfish ("Barbel")	80	30
866	$1.30 Rainbow trout	90	65
867	$1.50 African mottled eel	95	70
868	$1.65 Common carp	1·00	85
869	$1.95 Nembwe ("Robustus bream")	1·10	1·00

168 City Hall, 1940

1994. Centenary of Bulawayo. Multicoloured.

No.	Description	Unused	Used
870	35c. Type **168**	15	10
871	80c. Cresta Churchill Hotel, 1974	30	20
872	$1.15 High Court, 1938	40	40
873	$1.75 Douslin House, 1902	50	70
874	$1.95 Goldfields Building, 1895	60	90
875	$2.30 Parkade Centre, 1975	85	1·25

169 Strelitzia **170** The Annunciation

1994. Export Flowers. Multicoloured.

No.	Description	Unused	Used
876	35c. Type **169**	35	10
877	80c. Protea	65	25
878	$1.15 Phlox	80	60
879	$1.75 Chrysanthemum	90	1·40
880	$1.95 Ullum	1·10	1·90
881	$2.30 Rose	1·40	2·50

1994. Christmas. Multicoloured.

No.	Description	Unused	Used
882	35c. Type **170**	30	10
883	80c. Journey to Bethlehem	55	15
884	$1.15 The Nativity	70	40
885	$1.75 Shepherds	1·00	1·50
886	$1.95 Wise Men	1·10	1·90
887	$2.30 Mary and Jesus	2·50	2·50

171 Harvesting Maize **173** Football

172 Spider-hunting Wasp

1995. Zimbabwe Culture. Multicoloured.

No.	Description	Unused	Used
888	1c. Type **171**	10	40
889	2c. Loading sugar cane	10	40
890	3c. Sunflowers	10	40
891	4c. Sorghum	10	40
892	5c. Miners	40	30
893	10c. Drilling for gold	70	30
894	20c. Opencast coal mining, Wankie	80	30
895	30c. Chrome smelting, Kwekwe	85	30
896	40c. Opencast iron extraction, Redcliff	85	20
896a	45c. Underground mining team	1·00	20
897	50c. Gold smelting	75	20
898	70c. Bogie Clock Tower, Gweru	20	20
899	80c. Masvingo Watchtower	20	20
900	$1 Hanging Tree, Harare	20	25
901	$2 Cecil House, Harare	20	40
902	$5 The Toposcope, Harare	35	75
903	$10 Paper House, Kwekwe	60	1·25

1995. Insects. Multicoloured.

No.	Description	Unused	Used
904	35c. Type **172**	50	10
905	$1.15 European dragonfly	1·25	55
906	$1.75 Foxy charaxes (butterfly)	2·00	2·50
907	$2.30 Antlion	2·50	3·25

1995. 6th All-Africa Games, Harare. Each showing sport within map of Africa. Multicoloured.

No.	Description	Unused	Used
908	35c. Type **173**	35	10
909	80c. Running	45	20
910	$1.15 Boxing	50	30
911	$1.75 Swimming	75	1·00
912	$1.95 Hockey	3·25	2·75
913	$2.30 Volleyball	1·60	3·00

174 Weighing Baby (Health) **175** Fernandoa Tree

1995. 50th Anniv of United Nations. Multicoloured.

No.	Description	Unused	Used
914	35c. Type **174**	15	10
915	$1.15 Women at pump (Environment)	30	35
916	$1.75 Workers on lorry (Food distribution)	50	80
917	$2.30 Teacher and children (Education)	60	1·60

1996. Indigenous Flowering Trees. Multicoloured.
918 45c. Type **175** 30 10
919 $1 Round leaf mukwa . . . 50 20
920 $1.50 Luckybean ree 70 60
921 $2.20 Winter cassia . . . . . 85 1·00
922 $2.50 Sausage tree . . . . . 90 1·40
923 $3 Sweet thorn . . . . . . 1·00 1·75

176 Mazvikadei Dam

1996. Dams of Zimbabwe. Multicoloured.
924 45c. Type **176** 15 10
925 $1.50 Mutirikwi Dam 45 40
926 $2.20 Ncema Dam 65 90
927 $3 Odzani Dam . . . . . . 75 1·40

177 Matusadonha National Park at Sunset

1996. Scenic Views. Multicoloured.
928 45c. Type **177** 15 10
929 $1.50 Juliasdale rocky outcrop 45 40
930 $2.20 Honde Valley . . . . 75 1·00
931 $3 Finger Rocks at Morgenster Mission . . . 85 1·60

178 Carved Frog

1996. Animal Wood Carvings. Multicoloured.
932 45c. Type **178** 15 10
933 $1.50 Tortoise 30 20
934 $1.70 Kudu 35 40
935 $2.20 Chimpanzee 50 80
936 $2.50 Porcupine 55 90
937 $3 Rhinoceros . . . . 60 1·10

179 Mashona Cow

1997. Cattle Breeds. Multicoloured.
938 45c. Type **179** 35 10
939 $1.50 Tuli cow 65 25
940 $2.20 Nkoni bull . . . . . . 85 1·00
941 $3 Brahman bull . . . . . . 1·25 1·75

180 Cycad

1997. 10th Meeting of Convention on International Trade in Endangered Species Members, Harare. Multicoloured.
942 45c. Type **180** 10 10
943 $1.50 Peregrine falcon . . . 80 55
944 $1.70 Temminck's ground pangolin 30 60
945 $2.20 Black rhinoceros . . . 1·00 1·25
946 $2.50 African elephant . . . 1·00 1·25
947 $3 Python . . . . 70 1·40

181 Wood Carving

1997. Rural Life. Multicoloured.
948 65c. Type **181** 15 10
949 $1 Winnowing 15 10
950 $2.40 Dancing 25 35
951 $2.50 Ploughing 25 35
952 $3.10 Stamping cereals . . . 30 50
953 $4.20 Fetching water 45 70

182 Passenger Coach No. 1826

1997. Centenary of Zimbabwe Railways. Mult.
954 65c. Type **182** 20 15
955 $1 Class 12 steam locomotive No. 257 . . . . 20 15
956 $2.40 Class 16A steam locomotive No. 605 . . . 25 35
957 $2.50 Class EL 1 electric locomotive No. 4107 . . . 25 35
958 $3.10 Steam locomotive No. 7 "Jack Tar" 30 50
959 $4.20 Class DE 2 diesel-electric locomotive No. 1211 . . . . 40 70

183 Aardwolf

1998. Lesser Known Animals of Zimbabwe. Multicoloured.
960 65c. Type **183** 20 10
961 $2.40 Large grey mongoose 25 30
962 $3.10 Clawless otter 30 55
963 $4.20 Antbear 35 80

184 Honeybee on Flower

186 Variable Sunbird ("Yellow-bellied Sunbird")

185 Fossil Fish

1998. Bees and Bee-keeping. Multicoloured.
964 $1.20 Type **184** 20 10
965 $4.10 Queen, worker and drone 25 35
966 $4.70 Queen and retinue . . 25 35
967 $5.60 Rural bee-keeper . . . 30 40
968 $7.40 Commercial bee-keepers 40 70
969 $9.90 Products of the hive . . 55 90

1998. Fossils. Multicoloured.
970 $1.20 Type **185** 80 10
971 $5.60 Allosaurus footprints 1·10 70
972 $7.40 Left foot of Massospondylus . . . . . 1·25 1·10
973 $9.90 Fossil wood . . . . . 1·50 1·75

1998. Birds. Multicoloured.
974 $1.20 Type **186** 50 15
975 $4.10 Lesser blue-eared glossy starling ("Lesser Blue-eared Starling") 70 35
976 $4.70 Grey-headed kingfisher ("Grey-hooded Kingfisher") 70 45
977 $5.60 Miombo grey tit . . . 75 75
978 $7.40 Chirinda apalis . . . . 85 1·00
979 $9.90 Swynnerton's robin . . 95 1·40

187 Philatelic Counter

188 Serval

1999. 125th Anniv of U.P.U. Multicoloured.
980 $1.20 Type **187** 20 10
981 $5.60 Postman delivering letters 55 25
982 $7.40 19th-century runner, motorcycle and truck . . . 1·50 70
983 $9.90 Harare Central Sorting Office 60 80

1999. Cats. Multicoloured.
984 $1.20 Type **188** 30 10
985 $5.60 Cheetah 65 45
986 $7.40 Caracal 80 90
987 $9.90 Leopard . . . . 1·25 1·60

1999. Owls (3rd series). As T **140**. Multicoloured.
988 $1.20 Cape eagle owl 75 25
989 $5.60 Grass owl . . . . . . 1·25 60
990 $7.40 Barn owl . . . . . . 1·50 1·50
991 $9.90 African marsh owl ("Marsh Owl") . . . . . 1·60 1·75

189 Canoe Safari

190 Family Reunion

1999. Tourism in Zimbabwe. Multicoloured.
992 $2 Type **189** 15 15
993 $6.70 Rock climbing 40 40
994 $7.70 Flying microlight . . . 45 50
995 $9.10 White water rafting . . 60 70
996 $12.00 Mountain scenery . . 70 95
997 $16.00 Game watching . . . 1·00 1·50
No. 997 is inscribed "Game Veiwing" in error.

1999. Christmas. Multicoloured.
998 $2 Type **190** 15 10
999 $6.70 Elephants around Christmas tree 25 25
1000 $7.70 Children and dog with balloons 25 25
1001 $9.10 Flame Lily 30 35
1002 $12 Madonna and Child . . 45 65
1003 $16 The Nativity 55 85

191 Nyala

192 Basketball

2000. Fauna, Industry and Development. Mult.
1004 1c. Type **191** 10 20
1005 10c. Building development 10 20
1006 30c. Timber yard 10 20
1007 50c. Tobacco auction . . . 10 20
1008 70c. Central Sorting Office, Harare 10 30
1009 80c. Harare New International Airport . . 50 30
1010 $1 Westgate shopping complex 10 20
1011 $2 Nile Crocodile 50 30
1012 $3 Pungwe river water project 20 30
1013 $4 Zebra 50 30
1014 $5 Mining 65 35
1015 $7 National University of Science and Technology 20 35
1016 $10 Ostrich . . . . 1·00 40
1017 $15 Brown-necked parrot ("Cape Parrot") . . . . 1·00 60
1018 $20 Leather products . . . 60 80
1019 $30 Lilac-breasted roller 1·50 1·00
1020 $50 Victoria Falls . . . . 1·60 1·60
1021 $100 Mukorsi Dam, Tokwe River . . . . . 2·25 3·00
1021a (–) Bateleur 10 10
1021b $500 Goliath heron 10 10
1021c $1000 White rhinoceros . . 10 10
1021d $5000 Cheetah 40 45
No. 1021a is inscribed "Standard postage" and was intially sold at $100.

2000. Sporting Activities. Multicoloured.
1022 $2 Type **192** 15 10
1023 $6.70 Tennis 40 35
1024 $7.70 Netball 40 45
1025 $9.10 Weightlifting 40 50
1026 $12 Taekwondo 55 65
1027 $16 Diving 65 75

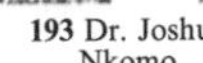
193 Dr. Joshua Nkomo

194 Nurse with Baby and Ministry of Health Logo

2000. 1st Death Anniv of Dr. Joshua Nkomo (nationalist leader). Multicoloured.
1028 $2 Type **193** 15 10
1029 $9.10 Nkomo in traditional costume 40 50
1030 $12 Type **193** 55 65
1031 $16 As $9.10 . . . . 65 75

2000. Health Promotion Campaign. Multicoloured.
1032 $2 Type **194** 15 10
1033 $6.70 Boy with football and anti-tuberculosis emblem 30 30
1034 $7.70 Couple with baby and "New Start" logo 35 30
1035 $9.10 Health technician on motorcycle and Riders for Health badge 60 50
1036 $12 Ribbon emblem on map and Ministry of Health logo 65 70
1037 $16 Fisherman and Rotary International emblem . . 70 80

195 Masawu Fruit

2000. Wild Fruits (2nd series). Multicoloured.
1038 $2 Type **195** 15 10
1039 $6.70 Spiny monkey orange 30 30
1040 $7.70 Bird plum 30 35
1041 $9.10 Shakama plum . . . 40 45
1042 $12 Wild medlar 60 65
1043 $16 Wild custard apple . . 65 75

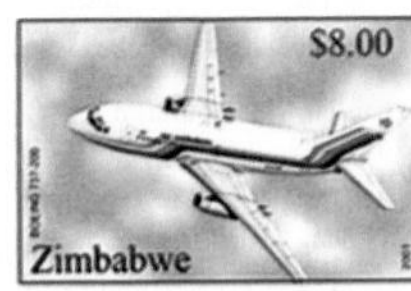

196 Boeing 737-200

2001. Aircraft. Multicoloured.
1044 $8 Type **196** 40 25
1045 $12 BAe Hawk MK 60 . . 55 40
1046 $14 Hawker Hunter FGA-9 60 60
1047 $16 Cessna/Reims F-337 . . 70 75
1048 $21 Aerospatiale Alouette III helicopter 85 95
1049 $28 Boeing 767-200ER . . . 1·10 1·40

197 Prominences (solar gas outbursts) during Total Solar Eclipse

198 "The Hare who rode Horseback"

2001. Total Solar Eclipse, 21 June 2001. Multicoloured.
1050 $8 Type **197** 45 25
1051 $21 Path of eclipse over Southern Africa . . . . . 95 1·10
1052 $28 Phases of total solar eclipse (62 × 22 mm) . . . 1·10 1·40

2001. African Folk Tales. Multicoloured..
1053 $8 Type **198** 35 25
1054 $12 "The Hippo who lost his Hair" 45 35
1055 $13 "The Lion who was saved by a Mouse" . . . 45 40
1056 $16 "The Bush Fowl who wakes the Sun" 60 50
1057 $21 "The Chameleon who came too Late" 85 90
1058 $28 "The Tortoise who collected Wisdom" . . . 1·10 1·40
MS1059 126 × 105 mm. Nos. 1053/8 3·50 3·50

199 Entrance, Heroes Acre Memorial, Harare

200 "Three Faces" (N. Mguni) (national winner)

2001. 21st Anniv of Independence. Heroes Acre Memorial, Harare. Multicoloured.
1060 $8 Type **199** 40 25
1061 $16 Statue of Unknown Soldier 60 45
1062 $21 Obelisk . . . . 80 1·00
1063 $28 Aerial view . . . . . . 1·10 1·40

2001. U.N. Dialogue Among Civilizations. Mult.
1064 $8 Type **200** 35 25
1065 $21 "Children encircling globe" (Urska Golob) (international winner) . . 90 1·25

201 *Charaxes bohemani*(butterfly)

2001. Butterflies (2nd series). Multicoloured.

1066	$12 Type **201**	50	35
1067	$20 *Vanessa cardui*	75	70
1068	$25 *Precis oenone cebrene*	80	80
1069	$30 *Euphaedra neophron*	95	1·10
1070	$35 *Iolaus silas* (female)	1·10	1·25
1071	$45 *Acrea aglanice*	1·40	1·75
MS1072	140 × 95 mm. Nos. 1066/71	5·00	6·00

202 Knitting and Crotchet Work

2002. Local Crafts. Multicoloured.

1073	$12 Type **202**	45	35
1074	$20 Art and design	60	55
1075	$25 Baskets	70	70
1076	$30 Pottery	80	90
1077	$35 Woodcarving	90	1·10
1078	$45 Sculpture	1·25	1·40

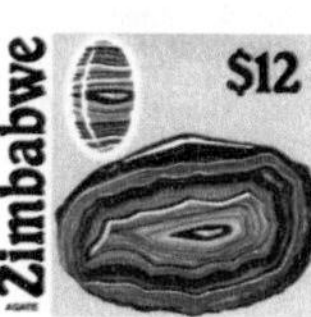

203 Agate

2002. Gemstones. Multicoloured.

1079	$12 Type **203**	45	35
1080	$25 Aquamarine	75	75
1081	$35 Diamond	95	1·10
1082	$45 Emerald	1·40	1·60

204 "Two Girls arm-in-arm" (Tazivei Makwavarara)

2002. 5th Anniv of Childline in Zimbabwe. Multicoloured.

1083	$12 Type **204**	45	35
1084	$25 "Girl using telephone" (Ashley Elkington)	75	75
1085	$35 "Teddy bear" (Goldine Hobbs)	95	1·10
1086	$45 "Hand holding telephone" (Admire Kacheche)	1·40	1·60

205 Sally Mugabe

2002. 10th Death Anniv of Sally Mugabe (wife of President). Multicoloured.

1087	$20 Type **205**	70	55
1088	$50 Mrs. Mugabe in black and white dress	1·50	1·60
1089	$70 Type **205**	1·90	2·00
1090	$90 As $50	2·50	2·75

206 "Mail Runner and Local Post Office" (Agreement Ngwenya)

2002. "Technology Today" School Design Competition Winners. Multicoloured.

1091	$20 Type **206**	75	55
1092	$70 "Mail runner and Airliner" (Kudzai Chikomo)	2·25	2·50

207 *Dissotis princeps*

2002. Wild Flowers (2nd series). Multicoloured.

1093	$20 Type **207**	65	55
1094	$35 *Leonotis nepetifolia*	90	80
1095	$40 *Hibiscus vitifolius*	1·10	1·10
1096	$50 *Boophane disticha*	1·40	1·40
1097	$70 *Pycnostachys urticifolia*	1·75	2·00
1098	$90 *Gloriosa superba*	2·50	3·00
MS1099	120 × 105 mm. Nos. 1093/8	8·00	8·50

208 Society Logo

209 Logo

2003. 50th Anniv of History Society of Zimbabwe. Multicoloured.

1100	$30 Type **208**	15	10
1101	$80 Books and scroll (Historical Evidence)	35	20
1102	$110 Oral traditions	45	45
1103	$140 Old buildings	50	55

2003. Harare International Festival of the Arts. Multicoloured.

1104	$30 Type **209**	15	10
1105	$80 Green logo and pink daisy	30	20
1106	$110 Eye logo and three pink daisies	35	45
1107	$140 Pink logo with pink and orange daisies	40	55

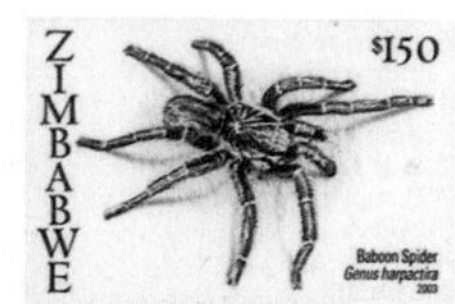

210 Baboon Spider (*Genus harpactira*)

2003. Spiders of Zimbabwe. Multicoloured.

1108	$150 Type **210**	15	10
1109	$200 Rain spider (*Genus palystes*)	15	10
1110	$600 Black button (Widow) spider (*Latrodectus renivulvatus*)	20	15
1111	$900 Wolf spider (*Lycosidae*)	25	25
1112	$1250 Violin spider (*Loxoscelidae*)	30	40
1113	$1600 Wall spider (*Selenopidae*)	40	50
MS1114	159 × 98 mm. Nos. 1108/13	65	70

211 Woman Graduate with Briefcase and Hoe (Tamuka Makuluni)

212 Wild Verbena

2003. Empowerment of Women. Winning entries from national stamp design competition. Multicoloured.

1115	$300 Type **211**	15	10
1116	$2100 Woman graduate with friend (Chloe Edwards)	50	50

2003. Endangered Medicinal Herbs of Zimbabwe. Multicoloured.

1117	$200 Type **212**	10	10
1118	$500 Pimpernel	10	10
1119	$1000 African arrowroot	15	10
1120	$3000 Bird pepper	25	25
1121	$4200 Wild garlic	35	40
1122	$5400 Cleome	50	60
MS1123	116 × 116 mm. Nos. 1117/22	1·20	1·30

213 Environment Africa Emblem

2004. Environment Africa.

1115 **213**	$500 green	10	10
1116 –	$3000 multicoloured	40	30
1117 –	$4200 blue, cobalt and black	50	50
1118 –	$5400 black, yellow and emerald	60	70

DESIGNS: $3000 Sondela emblem; $4200 Water Africa emblem; $5400 Tree Africa emblem.

POSTAGE DUE STAMPS

D 4 Zimbabwe Bird (soapstone sculpture)

D 5

1980.

D23 **D 4**	1c. green	20	1·25
D24	2c. blue	20	1·25
D25	5c. violet	25	1·25
D26	6c. yellow	30	2·00
D27	10c. red	40	2·50

1985.

D28 **D 5**	1c. orange	30	1·00
D29	2c. mauve	30	1·00
D30	6c. green	65	1·25
D31	10c. brown	70	1·25
D32	13c. blue	70	1·25

1990. No. D27 surch **25**.

D33 **D 4**	25c. on 10c. red	4·50	4·50

D 7

D 8 Bird Carving

1995.

D34 **D 7**	1c. yellow	10	60
D35	2c. orange	10	60
D36	5c. mauve	10	60
D37	10c. blue	10	60
D38	25c. violet	15	60
D39	40c. green	25	70
D40	60c. orange	35	80
D41	$1 brown	45	1·00

2000.

D42 **D 8**	1c. black and green	10	20
D43	10c. black and blue	10	20
D44	50c. black and brown	10	20
D45	$1 black and red	15	20
D46	$2 black and yellow	20	30
D47	$5 black and mauve	40	50
D48	$10 black and red	70	1·00

ZULULAND Pt. 1

A territory of south-eastern Africa, annexed by Great Britain in 1887, and incorporated in Natal in 1897.

12 pence = 1 shilling;
20 shillings = 1 pound.

1888. Stamps of Gt. Britain (Queen Victoria) optd **ZULULAND.**

1 **71**	½d. red	3·50	2·50
2 **57**	1d. lilac	25·00	3·75
3 **73**	2d. green and red	15·00	26·00
4 **74**	2½d. purple on blue	23·00	20·00
5 **75**	3d. purple on yellow	25·00	22·00
6 **76**	4d. green and brown	42·00	55·00
7 **78**	5d. purple and blue	90·00	£120
8 **79**	6d. purple on red	13·00	17·00
9 **80**	9d. purple and blue	90·00	90·00
10 **82**	1s. green	£110	£130
11 –	5s. red (No. 181)	£500	£600

1888. Natal stamps optd **ZULULAND.**

13 **23**	½d. green	23·00	38·00
16 –	6d. lilac (No. 103)	55·00	55·00

3

1894.

20 **3**	½d. mauve and green	3·25	4·25
21	1d. mauve and red	5·00	2·00
22	2½d. mauve and blue	14·00	8·50
23	3d. mauve and brown	8·00	3·00
24	6d. mauve and black	20·00	20·00
25	1s. green	38·00	38·00
26	2s.6d. green and black	75·00	85·00
27	4s. green and red	£110	£150
28	£1 purple on red	£450	£550
29	£5 purple and black on red	£4500	£1500

INDEX

Stanley Gibbons would have loved the Internet...

Stanley Gibbons built the most famous name in stamps from scratch by starting with a desk in his father's chemists and a small scale mail order business based in Plymouth.

Even in those inauspicious circumstances, Gibbons was able to build a highly successful business, which eventually grew too big for the chemist shop and even Plymouth. Just imagine if he had the Internet as a tool of his trade as well...

- over 50,000 stamps available to buy
- a philatelic reference point at your fingertips
- all Stanley Gibbons products and other leading brands available
- accessible at any time, from anywhere
- philatelic news as it breaks
- archives of images and articles
- live auctions
- value your collection

150 years of progress and invention allow us to bring you so that you can find anything you want in the world of philately from the comfort of your own home.

www.stanleygibbons.com

Keep an eye on stanleygibbons.com...

We will be presenting an official site to mark our 150th Anniversary during 2006

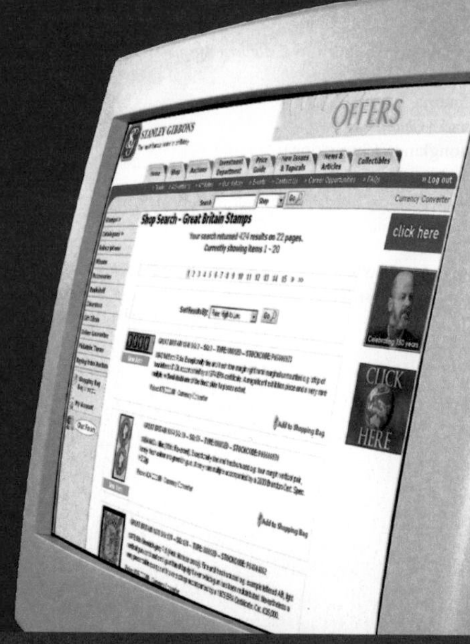

www.stanleygibbons.com

Publications

> “*My business was always carried on by correspondence.*”
>
> *E. S. Gibbons, The Monthly Journal 1893*

Stamp collecting made as easy as 1, 2, 3...

1 ✆ **Ring us on 0800 611622 (Freephone UK only) or +44 1425 472 363**

2 ✉ **Mail to Stanley Gibbons Publications,**
7 Parkside,
Christchurch Road,
Ringwood,
Hampshire
BH24 3SH

3 **Email us at sales@stanleygibbons.co.uk**

Stanley Gibbons Product Guide 2005

Order Hotline 0800 611 622
International +44 1425 472 363
www.stanleygibbons.com

www.stanleygibbons.com